D1483445

Best Books for Children

seventh edition

Best Books for Children

John T. Gillespie

Preschool Through Grade 6

LIBRARIES
UNLIMITED

A Member of the Greenwood Publishing Group

Westport, Connecticut • London

Library of Congress Cataloging-in-Publication Data

Gillespie, John Thomas, 1928–
  Best books for children / John T. Gillespie.—7th ed.
      p.   cm.
    Includes bibliographical references and indexes.
    ISBN 0–313–32068–3 (alk. paper)
    1. Children—Books and reading—United States.   2. Children's
  literature—Bibliography.   3. Best books—United States.   I. Title.
  Z1037.G48   2002
  011.62—dc21   2001037971

British Library Cataloguing in Publication Data is available.

Library of Congress Catalog Card Number: 2001037971
ISBN: 0–313–32068–3

First published in 2002

Libraries Unlimited, 88 Post Road West, Westport, Ct 06881
A Member of the Greenwood Publishing Group, Inc.
www.lu.com

Printed in the United States of America

The paper used in this book complies with the
Permanent Paper Standard issued by the National
Information Standards Organization (Z39.48-1984).

10 9 8 7 6 5 4 3 2

Dedication

To Jack and Paul for their friendship,
encouragement, and understanding.

Contents

Major Subjects Arranged Alphabetically   xv

Preface   xvii

Literature

Books for Younger Readers	**3**
Alphabet, Concept, and Counting Books	3
Alphabet Books	3
Concept Books	10
GENERAL	10
COLORS	15
PERCEPTION	16
SIZE AND SHAPE	17
Counting and Number Books	19
Bedtime Books and Nursery Rhymes	31
Bedtime Books	31
Nursery Rhymes	40
Stories Without Words	44
Picture Books	46
Imaginative Stories	46
FANTASIES	46
IMAGINARY ANIMALS	82
Realistic Stories	135
ADVENTURE STORIES	135
COMMUNITY AND EVERYDAY LIFE	139
FAMILY STORIES	163
FRIENDSHIP STORIES	185
HUMOROUS STORIES	190
NATURE AND SCIENCE	204
OTHER TIMES, OTHER PLACES	213
PERSONAL PROBLEMS	229

REAL AND ALMOST REAL ANIMALS	239
SCHOOL STORIES	255
TRANSPORTATION AND MACHINES	259
Stories About Holidays and Holy Days	262
GENERAL AND MISCELLANEOUS	262
BIRTHDAYS	264
CHRISTMAS	268
EASTER	279
HALLOWEEN	279
JEWISH HOLY DAYS	283
THANKSGIVING	287
VALENTINE'S DAY	288
Books for Beginning Readers	289
Fiction for Older Readers	**316**
Adventure and Mystery	316
Animal Stories	336
Ethnic Groups	344
Family Stories	347
Fantasy and the Supernatural	354
Friendship Stories	387
Growing into Maturity	394
Family Problems	394
Personal Problems	401
Physical and Emotional Problems	416
Historical Fiction and Foreign Lands	419
General and Miscellaneous	419
Prehistory	420
Africa	420
Asia	421
Europe	423
Great Britain and Ireland	426
Latin America	429
United States	429

NATIVE AMERICANS	429
COLONIAL PERIOD	432
THE REVOLUTION	433
THE YOUNG NATION, 1789–1861	435
PIONEERS AND WESTWARD EXPANSION	440
THE CIVIL WAR	446
RECONSTRUCTION TO WORLD WAR II, 1865–1941	448
World War II and After	455
Holidays and Holy Days	458
Humorous Stories	461
School Stories	474
Science Fiction	479
Short Stories and Anthologies	484
Sports Stories	485

Fairy Tales	**491**

Folklore	**499**
General	499
Africa	505
Asia	509
General and Miscellaneous	509
China	510
India	512
Japan	513
Southeast Asia	515
Australia and the Pacific Islands	515
Europe	516
General and Miscellaneous	516
France	516
Germany	517
Great Britain and Ireland	520
Greece and Italy	525
Russia	527
Scandinavia	528
Spain and Portugal	529
Jewish Folklore	530
Middle East	532
North America	533
Inuit	533
Native Americans	533
United States	539
South and Central America	542
Mexico and Other Central American Lands	542
Puerto Rico and Other Caribbean Islands	544
South America	545

Mythology	**546**
General and Miscellaneous	546
Classical	547
Scandinavian	550

Poetry	**551**
General	551
African American Poetry	562
Animals	563
Haiku	566
Holidays	566
Humorous Poetry	567
Native Americans	571
Nature and the Seasons	571
Sports	574

Plays	**576**
General	576
Shakespeare	578

Biography

Adventurers and Explorers	**581**
Collective	581
Individual	582

Artists, Composers, Entertainers, and Writers	**588**
Collective	588
Artists	590
Composers	597
Entertainers	599
Writers	608

Contemporary and Historical Americans	**617**
Collective	617
African Americans	621
Hispanic Americans	628
Historical Figures and Important Contemporary Americans	629
Native Americans	637
Presidents	639
First Ladies and Other Women	645

Scientists, Inventors, and Naturalists	**651**
Collective	651
Individual	652

Sports Figures	**661**
Collective	661
Automobile Racing	664
Baseball	664
Basketball	669
Boxing	673
Figure Skating	673
Football	674
Tennis	677

Track and Field 678
Miscellaneous Sports 679

World Figures 682
Collective 682
Individual 683

The Arts and Language

Art and Architecture 695
General and Miscellaneous 695
Africa 698
The Ancient World 698
Native American Arts and Crafts 699
Middle Ages and the Renaissance 699
United States 699

Communication 701
General and Miscellaneous 701
Codes and Ciphers 701
Flags 701
Language and Languages 702
Reading, Speaking, and Writing 702
Books, Printing, Libraries, and Schools 702
Signs and Symbols 703
Words and Grammar 704
Writing and Speaking 706

Music 710
General 710
Ballads and Folk Songs 711
Holidays 714
Musical Instruments 715
National Anthems and Patriotic Songs 715
Singing Games and Songs 716

Performing Arts 718
Circuses, Fairs, and Parades 718
Dance 718
Marionettes and Puppets 720
Motion Pictures, Radio, and Television 720
Theater and Play Production 721

History and Geography

History and Geography in General 725
Miscellaneous 725
Maps and Globes 727

Paleontology and Dinosaurs 728

Anthropology and Prehistoric Life 735

Archaeology 737

World History 739
General 739
Ancient History 741
General and Miscellaneous 741
Egypt and Mesopotamia 742
Greece 746
Rome 748
Middle Ages 750
Renaissance 752
World War I 753
World War II 753

Geographical Regions 759
Africa 759
General 759
Central and Eastern Africa 760
Northern Africa 762
Southern Africa 762
Western Africa 764
Asia 766
General 766
China 767
India 769
Japan 770
Other Asian Lands 771
Australia and the Pacific Islands 775
Europe 777
General and Miscellaneous 777
Central and Eastern Europe 777
France 779
Germany 780
Great Britain and Ireland 781
Greece and Italy 782
Low Countries 784
Russia and the Former Soviet States 784
Scandinavia, Iceland, Greenland, and Finland 786
Spain and Portugal 787
The Middle East 788
General 788
Egypt 789
Israel 790
Other Middle Eastern Lands 791
North and South America (Excluding the United States) 792
North and South America 792
Canada 792

Mexico	794
Other Central American Lands	797
Puerto Rico and Other Caribbean Islands	799
South America	800
Polar Regions	804
United States	806
General	806
General History and Geography	807
Historical Periods	810
NATIVE AMERICANS	810
DISCOVERY AND EXPLORATION	818
COLONIAL PERIOD	820
REVOLUTIONARY PERIOD	825
THE YOUNG NATION, 1789–1861	827
PIONEER LIFE AND WESTWARD EXPANSION	830
THE CIVIL WAR	836
RECONSTRUCTION TO THE KOREAN WAR, 1865–1950	839
THE 1950S TO THE PRESENT	842
Regions	844
MIDWEST	844
MOUNTAIN STATES	847
NORTHEAST	849
PACIFIC STATES	855
SOUTH	859
SOUTHWEST	862

Social Institutions and Issues

Business and Economics	**867**
General	867
Consumerism	868
Money-Making Ideas and Budgeting	868
Retail Stores and Other Workplaces	869
Ecology and Environment	**870**
General	870
Cities	871
Garbage and Waste Recycling	871
Pollution	872
Population	873
Government and Politics	**874**
Courts and the Law	874
United Nations and International Affairs	874
United States	875
Civil Rights	875
Constitution	876
Crime and Criminals	877
Elections and Political Parties	878
Federal Government and Agencies	879
State Government and Agencies	880
Municipal Government and Agencies	880
Social Problems and Solutions	880
Religion and Holidays	**883**
General and Miscellaneous	883
Bible Stories	887
Holidays and Holy Days	891
General and Miscellaneous	891
Christmas	895
Easter	896
Halloween	897
Jewish Holy Days and Celebrations	897
Thanksgiving	900
Valentine's Day	900
Prayers	901
Social Groups	**903**
Ethnic Groups	903

Personal Development

Behavior	**909**
General	909
Etiquette	911
Family Relationships	911
Personal Problems and Relationships	914
Careers	**917**
General and Miscellaneous	917
Arts and Entertainment	919
Engineering, Technology, and Trades	919
Health and Medicine	920
Police and Fire Fighters	921
Science	922
Transportation	922
Veterinarians	923
Health and the Human Body	**924**
Aging and Death	924
Alcohol, Drugs, and Smoking	924
Bionics and Transplants	926
Disabilities, Physical and Mental	926
Disease and Illness	928
Doctors and Medicine	932
Genetics	933
Hospitals	933
The Human Body	934
General	934
Circulatory System	936
Digestive and Excretory Systems	936
Nervous System	937

Respiratory System	938
Senses	938
Skeletal-Muscular System	940
Skin and Hair	941
Teeth	941
Hygiene, Physical Fitness, and Nutrition	941
Safety and Accidents	943
Sleep and Dreams	943

Sex Education and Reproduction	**944**
Babies	944
Reproduction	944
Sex Education and Puberty	945

Physical and Applied Sciences

General Science	**949**
Miscellaneous	949
Experiments and Projects	950

Astronomy	**955**
General	955
Earth	958
Moon	958
Planets	959
Solar System	961
Stars	963
Sun and the Seasons	964

Biological Sciences	**966**
General	966
Animal Life	967
General	967
Amphibians and Reptiles	971
GENERAL AND MISCELLANEOUS	971
ALLIGATORS AND CROCODILES	972
FROGS AND TOADS	973
LIZARDS	974
SNAKES	975
TURTLES AND TORTOISES	976
Animal Behavior and Anatomy	977
GENERAL	977
BABIES	981
CAMOUFLAGE	982
COMMUNICATION	982
DEFENSES	982
HIBERNATION	983
HOMES	983
REPRODUCTION	983
Animal Species	984
GENERAL AND MISCELLANEOUS	984

APE FAMILY	987
BATS	989
BEARS	990
BIG CATS	991
COYOTES, FOXES, AND WOLVES	993
DEER FAMILY	995
ELEPHANTS	996
GIRAFFES	996
MARSUPIALS	996
PANDAS	997
RODENTS	997
Birds	998
GENERAL AND MISCELLANEOUS	998
BEHAVIOR	1003
DUCKS, GEESE, AND SWANS	1003
EAGLES, HAWKS, AND OTHER BIRDS OF PREY	1004
GULLS AND OTHER SEA BIRDS	1005
OWLS	1006
PENGUINS	1006
Conservation of Endangered Species	1007
Insects and Arachnids	1009
GENERAL AND MISCELLANEOUS	1009
ANTS	1013
BEES AND WASPS	1014
BEETLES	1014
CATERPILLARS, BUTTERFLIES, AND MOTHS	1015
SPIDERS AND SCORPIONS	1016
Land Invertebrates	1018
Marine and Freshwater Life	1019
GENERAL AND MISCELLANEOUS	1019
CORALS AND JELLYFISH	1020
CRUSTACEANS	1021
DOLPHINS AND PORPOISES	1022
FISH	1022
MOLLUSKS, SPONGES, AND STARFISH	1024
OCTOPUS	1024
SEA MAMMALS	1024
SHARKS	1025
SHELLS	1026
WHALES	1026
Microscopes and Microbiology	1028
Oceanography	1029
GENERAL	1029
COMMERCIAL FISHING	1030
CURRENTS, TIDES, AND WAVES	1030
SEASHORES AND TIDAL POOLS	1031
UNDERWATER EXPLORATION	1032
Pets	1032
GENERAL AND MISCELLANEOUS	1032
CATS	1034

Contents

DOGS	1035
FISH	1037
HORSES AND PONIES	1037
Zoos and Marine Aquariums	1039
Botany	1039
General and Miscellaneous	1039
Flowers	1040
Foods and Farming	1040
GENERAL	1040
FARMS, RANCHES, AND FARM ANIMALS	1040
FOODS	1042
FRUITS	1045
NUTRITION	1046
VEGETABLES	1046
Fungi	1047
Leaves and Trees	1047
Plants	1049
Seeds	1051

Chemistry	**1052**

Geology and Geography	**1054**
Earth and Geology	1054
Earthquakes and Volcanoes	1056
Icebergs and Glaciers	1057
Physical Geography	1057
General and Miscellaneous	1057
Deserts	1059
Forests and Rain Forests	1061
Mountains	1064
Ponds, Rivers, and Lakes	1065
Prairies and Grasslands	1066
Rocks, Minerals, and Soil	1067

Mathematics	**1069**
General	1069
Geometry	1070
Mathematical Puzzles	1071
Numbers and Number Systems	1072
Time, Clocks, and Calendars	1072
Weights and Measures	1073

Meteorology	**1074**
General	1074
Air	1074
Storms	1075
Water	1077
Weather	1078

Physics	**1082**
General	1082

Energy and Motion	1083
General	1083
Coal, Gas, and Oil	1084
Nuclear Energy	1084
Solar Energy	1085
Heat and Fire	1085
Light and Color	1085
Magnetism and Electricity	1086
Optical Illusions	1088
Simple Machines	1088
Sound	1089

Space Exploration	**1091**

Technology, Engineering, and Industry	**1096**
General and Miscellaneous Industries and Inventions	1096
Aeronautics and Airplanes	1098
Building and Construction	1100
General	1100
Houses	1103
Clothing, Textiles, and Jewelry	1103
Computers and Automation	1104
Electronics	1107
Machinery	1107
Metals	1108
Telegraph, Telephone, and Telecommunications	1108
Television, Motion Pictures, Radio, and Recording	1109
Transportation	1109
General	1109
Automobiles and Trucks	1110
Railroads	1112
Ships, Boats, and Lighthouses	1113
Weapons, Submarines, and the Armed Forces	1114

Recreation

Crafts	**1119**
General and Miscellaneous	1119
American Historical Crafts	1124
Clay and Other Modeling Crafts	1125
Costume and Jewelry Making	1126
Drawing and Painting	1127
Masks and Mask Making	1129
Paper Crafts	1129
Printmaking	1131
Sewing and Needle Crafts	1131
Toys and Dolls	1131
Woodworking	1132

Hobbies   **1133**

General and Miscellaneous   1133

Cooking   1133

Gardening   1138

Magic   1138

Model Making   1139

Photography and Filmmaking   1139

Stamp, Coin, and Other Types of Collecting   1140

Jokes, Puzzles, Riddles, Word Games   **1141**

Jokes and Riddles   1141

Puzzles   1143

Word Games   1144

Mysteries, Monsters, Curiosities, and Trivia   **1145**

Sports and Games   **1150**

General and Miscellaneous   1150

Automobile Racing   1156

Baseball   1156

Basketball   1158

Bicycles   1159

Camping and Backpacking   1160

Chess   1160

Fishing   1161

Football   1161

Gymnastics   1162

Horsemanship   1162

Ice Hockey   1162

Ice Skating   1163

Indoor Games   1164

Motor Bikes and Motorcycles   1164

Olympic Games   1164

Running and Jogging   1165

Sailing and Boating   1165

Self-Defense   1166

Skateboarding   1166

Snowboarding   1166

Soccer   1167

Surfing   1168

Swimming and Diving   1168

Tennis   1168

Track and Field   1168

Author/Illustrator Index   **1169**

Title Index   **1401**

Subject/Grade Level Index   **1527**

Major Subjects Arranged Alphabetically

Adventurers and Explorers 581
ENTRIES 12056–12156

Africa 759
ENTRIES 14899–15050

Animal Life 967
ENTRIES 18601–20031

Anthropology and Prehistoric Life 735
ENTRIES 14488–14518

Archaeology 737
ENTRIES 14519–14542

Art and Architecture 695
ENTRIES 13870–13964

Artists, Composers, Entertainers
and Writers 588
ENTRIES 12157–12632

Asia 766
ENTRIES 15051–15221

Astronomy 955
ENTRIES 18375–18575

Australia and the Pacific Islands 775
ENTRIES 15222–15256

Behavior 909
ENTRIES 17601–17737

Biological Sciences 966
ENTRIES 18576–20274

Books for Younger Readers 3
ENTRIES 1–6726

Botany 1039
ENTRIES 20032–20274

Business and Economics 867
ENTRIES 16918–16951

Careers 917
ENTRIES 17738–17856

Chemistry 1052
ENTRIES 20275–20292

Communication 701
ENTRIES 13965–14118

Contemporary and Historical
Americans 617
ENTRIES 12633–13200

Crafts 1119
ENTRIES 21410–21664

Ecology and Environment 870
ENTRIES 16952–17010

Europe 777
ENTRIES 15257–15485

Fairy Tales 491
ENTRIES 10375–10527

Fiction for Older Readers 316
ENTRIES 6727–10374

Folklore 499
ENTRIES 10528–11445

Geographical Regions 759
ENTRIES 14899–16917

Geology and Geography   1054
ENTRIES 20293–20576

Government and Politics   874
ENTRIES 17011–17160

Health and the Human Body   924
ENTRIES 17857–18227

History and Geography   725
ENTRIES 14326–16917

Hobbies   1133
ENTRIES 21665–21811

Jokes, Puzzles, Riddles, Word
Games   1141
ENTRIES 21812–21887

Mathematics   1069
ENTRIES 20577–20659

Meteorology   1074
ENTRIES 20660–20797

Middle East   788
ENTRIES 15486–15561

Music   710
ENTRIES 14119–14262

Mysteries, Monsters, Curiosities,
and Trivia   1145
ENTRIES 21888–21964

Mythology   546
ENTRIES 11446–11520

North and South America
(excluding the United States)   792
ENTRIES 15562–15791

Paleontology and Dinosaurs   728
ENTRIES 14373–14487

Performing Arts   718
ENTRIES 14263–14325

Physical and Applied Sciences   949
ENTRIES 18271–21409

Physics   1082
ENTRIES 20798–20944

Plays   576
ENTRIES 12009–12055

Poetry   551
ENTRIES 11521–12008

Polar Regions   804
ENTRIES 15792–15848

Recreation   1119
ENTRIES 21410–22319

Religion and Holidays   883
ENTRIES 17161–17537

Science   949
ENTRIES 18271–21409

Scientists, Inventors, and Naturalists   651
ENTRIES 13201–13359

Sex Education and Reproduction   944
ENTRIES 18228–18270

Social Groups   903
ENTRIES 17538–17600

Space Exploration   1091
ENTRIES 20945–21020

Sports and Games   1150
ENTRIES 21965–22319

Sports Figures   661
ENTRIES 13360–13722

Technology, Engineering,
and Industry   1096
ENTRIES 21021–21409

United States   806
ENTRIES 15849–16917

World Figures   682
ENTRIES 13723–13869

World History   739
ENTRIES 14543–14898

Preface

This is the seventh edition of *Best Books for Children*. The primary aim of this work, as with the earlier editions, is to provide a list of books recommended to satisfy both a child's recreational reading needs and the demands of a typical school curriculum. These recommendations are gathered from a number of sources, which are discussed on the following pages. For greatest depth, coverage has been limited to the age group including preschool children through readers in the sixth grade. Books that could be used with advanced sixth-graders but are best suited to readers in grades seven through ten are listed in the companion volume *Best Books for Young Teen Readers* (Bowker, 2000). It is suggested that this title be used to enrich collections for gifted fifth- and sixth-grade readers.

Of the 23,429 titles in this seventh edition of *Best Books for Children*, 22,319 are individually numbered entries. The remaining 1,110 titles—those cited within the annotations—are additional recommended titles by the main entry author. These related titles are listed with the publication date; internal titles that have separate entries are listed without publication date. In some cases where there are a large number of titles in a series, additional entries have been used. Also, some series are so extensive that, due to space limitations, only representative titles are included. More than one third of the 22,319 numbered entries are new to this edition.

For most titles, at least two recommendations were required from the sources consulted for a title to be considered for listing. However, in some cases, a single recommendation could also make a title a candidate for inclusion. This was particularly true of nonfiction books in a series. The reviewing policies of many journals do not allow for the inclusion of all titles in a series. Some give little or no coverage to series books, while others review only representative titles or list titles without reviews. Where only a single recommendation was available, the reviewing history of the series was taken into consideration and, in most cases, books in the series were examined and evaluated by the editor from copies supplied by the publisher. In these cases, such criteria as availability, currency, accuracy, usefulness, and relevance were applied.

Several sources were used to compile this annotated bibliography. At the outset there was a thorough perusal and evaluation of the entries in the sixth (1998) edition of *Best Books for Children*. All out-of-print titles were dropped, as well as those that were considered no longer timely or suitable. The other sources consulted were numerous and varied. The major tools were current reviewing periodicals, especially those issues from April 1998 (where coverage of the sixth edition ceased) through March 2001. The main periodicals consulted were *Booklist, Bulletin of the Center for Children's Books, Horn Book, Horn Book Guide,* and *School Library Journal.*

It is hoped that this bibliography will be used in four different ways: (1) as a tool to evaluate the adequacy of existing collections; (2) as a book-selection instrument for beginning and expanding collections; (3) as an aid for giving reading guidance to children; and (4) as a base for the preparation of bibliographies and reading lists. To increase the book's usefulness, particularly in the two latter areas, the chosen titles are arranged under broad interest areas or, as in the case of nonfiction works, by curriculum-oriented subjects rather than by the Dewey Decimal Classification System. For example, a book on religious practices in colonial America might be cataloged under religion, but in this book it would be included with other books on "United States–Colonial Period." In this way, analogous titles that otherwise would be in separate sections are brought together and can be seen in relation to other books on the same broad topic.

For this seventh edition, a thorough review of each broad subject area and its subdivisions was made—new ones added, others dropped, and many rearranged, often to provide easier alphabetical access. It is hoped that these changes will reflect current reading needs and will aid the usability of this bibliography. In this regard, some arbitrary decisions had to be made; for example, books of mathematical puzzles are placed in the Mathematics section. In general, the titles that appear in the section Books for Younger Readers are those usually read to children or used in assisted-reading situations. The one exception in this section is the listing of "Books for Beginning Readers." This area contains books of fiction easy enough to be read by beginning readers; nonfiction beginning readers are integrated into the appropriate subject areas with mention in the annotation that the work is suitable for beginning readers. Interactive books, such as books containing tabs, pop-ups, or flaps, are integrated into appropriate sections but their annotations mention the nature of their format.

The "Imaginative Stories" section in the Picture Books area is divided into two categories: Fantasies and Imaginary Animals. The first contains both books that depict humans, usually children, in fanciful, unrealistic situations (many bordering on the supernatural) and books that include (as characters) such mythological beasts as dragons and unicorns. The Imaginary Animals category includes stories about anthropomorphized beasts in which ordinary animals engage in human activities (such as pigs going to school) and display human motivations and behavior.

Simple chapter books and similar nonfiction titles that bridge the reading abilities and interests of children in the upper primary grades and early middle grades are integrated into the appropriate sections for older readers and their annotations indicate that they are easily read.

In the Fiction for Older Readers areas, only general anthologies of short stories are included under "Short Stories and Anthologies." Collections of short stories on a single topic, such as sports stories, are found under that specific topic. In the fiction section labeled "Ethnic Groups," only those novels in which ethnicity is the central theme are included. Other novels that simply include members of minority groups are integrated into other more appropriate topical areas. Similarly, in the nonfiction Biography section under "African Americans," "Hispanic Americans," and "Native Americans," only those individuals who have been associated primarily with race-related activities are included. For example, a biography of Martin Luther King, Jr., would be found under "African Americans" but a life story of golfer Tiger Woods would be under sports biographies. Also in the nonfiction area, general books of science projects and experiments are found under "General Science—Experiments and Projects," but books of activities related to a specific area of science are included in that area.

Some types of books have been omitted from this bibliography. These include reference books such as dictionaries and encyclopedias, professional books (for example, other bibliographies), and such mass-market series as the Nancy Drew and Hardy Boys books, although individual libraries might wish to purchase them.

Special features that have been retained in this edition include a listing of "Major Subjects Arranged Alphabetically." This special list provides both the range of entry numbers and page numbers for the largest subject areas covered in the volume. Other features also continued are the International Standard Book Number (ISBN) for both hardcover and paperback editions, nonfiction series titles, and Dewey Decimal numbers for nonfiction titles. Also included are review citations for all books published and reviewed from 1985 through March 2001. These review citations will give librarians sources from which to obtain more detailed information about each of the books listed. The five sources are:

Booklist (BL)
Bulletin of the Center for Children's Books (BCCB)
Horn Book (HB)
Horn Book Guide (HBG)
School Library Journal (SLJ)

The citing of only one review does not necessarily mean that the book received only a single recommendation; it might easily also have been listed in one or more of the other bibliographies consulted. Books without review citations or Dewey numbers are pre-1985 imprints and reprints of older recommended books recently brought back into print (the original publication date is indicated within the annotation if it was readily available). An asterisk following a review citation denotes an outstanding recommendation from that source.

Entry Information

As in previous editions, titles in the main section of the book are assigned an entry number. The entry contains the following information where applicable: (1) author or editor; (2) title; (3) suitable grade levels; (4) adapter or translator; (5) indication of illustrations or illustrator's name (usually only for picture books); (6) series title for nonfiction books; (7) date of publication; (8) publisher and price of hardbound edition (LB=library binding); (9) ISBN of hardbound edition; (10) paperback (paper) publisher (if no publisher is listed, it is the same as the hardbound edition) and price; (11) ISBN of paperback edition; (12) annotation; (13) review citations; (14) Dewey Decimal number. Bibliographic information and prices were verified in *Books in Print 2001*, as well as many publishers' catalogs.

Indexes

Best Books for Children includes three indexes: author/illustrator, book title, and subject/grade level. *Best Books for Children* has grown with each new edition, and for this new edition we have introduced some changes in the indexes that are intended to keep the book to one volume and eliminate some overlaps without sacrificing valuable information. Authors and illustrators—who so often are the same individuals in books for young children—now appear in a single Author/Illustrator Index. In this index, authors and illustrators are listed alphabetically by last name, followed by book titles and entry numbers; fiction titles are indicated by (F). In the Title Index, both main entry titles and internal titles cited within the annotation are included, all with entry numbers and (F) notations. Subtitles are no longer included.

The Subject/Grade Level Index includes thousands of subject headings. Within each subject, entries are listed according to grade-level suitabilities. For example, under the subject Humorous Stories there may be numerous entry numbers given first for Primary (P) readers; then for the Primary-Intermediate (PI) group; for the Intermediate (I) group; for the Intermediate-Junior High (IJ) readers; and finally for all readers, covering grades from preschool through grade 8 (All). This will enable the professional to select the most appropriate titles for use. Biographical entries are listed in this index by the last name of the subject of the biography. The following codes are used to give approximate grade level:

P (Primary) preschool through grade 3

PI (Primary-Intermediate) grades 2 through 4

I (Intermediate) grades 4 through 6

IJ (Intermediate-Junior High) grades 5 through 8 (or in a few cases some higher grades)

All (All readers) preschool through grade 8 (or higher)

Specific, more exact grade-level suitabilities are given (parenthetically) for each book in its main text entry.

To facilitate quick reference, all listings in all indexes refer the user to entry number, not page number.

Many people were involved in the preparation of this bibliography. I am especially grateful to my wonderful editor Catherine Barr and to our computer genius Julie Miller. Thank you for not only your tremendous work, but also your encouragement and understanding. Also, a special thanks to Nancy Bucenec who helped me through so many earlier editions.

John Gillespie

Literature

Books for Younger Readers

Alphabet, Concept, and Counting Books

Alphabet Books

1 Alda, Arlene. *Arlene Alda's ABC* (PS–K). Illus. 1993, Tricycle Pr. $12.95 (1-883672-01-5). 32pp. Objects turn into letters in this unusual alphabet book. (Rev: BL 1/1/94)

2 Anglund, Joan Walsh. *In a Pumpkin Shell* (PS–2). Illus. by author. 1977, Harcourt paper $6.00 (0-15-644425-9). 32pp. A Mother Goose ABC book.

3 Anno, Mitsumasa. *Anno's Alphabet: An Adventure in Imagination* (PS–2). Illus. by author. 1992, HarperCollins paper $22.95 (0-06-443315-3). 64pp. A most unusual and distinctive alphabet book that shows the letters as pieces of rough-grained wood and, on the opposite pages, objects beginning with that letter. An excellent introduction to art as well.

4 Aylesworth, Jim. *The Folks in the Valley: A Pennsylvania Dutch ABC* (PS–2). Illus. by Stefano Vitale. 1994, HarperCollins paper $5.95 (0-064-43363-3). 32pp. Celebrating the way of life for a Pennsylvania Dutch family, from the alarm clock to the Z sound of sleep. (Rev: BL 5/1/92*; HB 1–2/92; SLJ 5/92)

5 Aylesworth, Jim. *Old Black Fly* (PS–2). Illus. by Stephen Gammell. 1992, Holt $16.95 (0-8050-1401-2). 32pp. A fun alphabet book that describes the 26 awful things Old Black Fly did one day. (Rev: BCCB 7–8/92; BL 2/15/92*; HB 5–6/92; SLJ 4/92*)

6 Azarian, Mary. *A Gardener's Alphabet* (K–2). Illus. by author. 2000, Houghton $16.00 (0-618-03380-7). Stunning black woodcuts hand-tinted with watercolors are featured in this handsome alphabet book that uses words associated with gardens and gardening. (Rev: BCCB 9/00; BL 4/15/00; HBG 10/00; SLJ 6/00)

7 Baker, Alan. *Black and White Rabbit's ABC* (PS–K). Illus. 1994, Kingfisher $9.95 (1-85697-951-2). 24pp. A simple ABC book about a rabbit and his antics. (Rev: BL 7/94)

8 Balian, Lorna. *Humbug Potion: An A-B-Cipher* (1–2). Illus. 1993, Humbug $12.95 (0-687-37102-3). 32pp. Each letter is given a number (one to 26) in this unusual alphabet book.

9 Barron, Rex. *Fed Up! A Feast of Frazzled Foods* (K–3). Illus. 2000, Putnam $15.99 (0-399-23450-0). 32pp. Moody foods from Anxious Apples to Zen Zucchini are the subjects in this humorous alphabet book. (Rev: BL 11/1/00; HB 1–2/01; HBG 3/01; SLJ 10/00)

10 Beaton, Clare. *Zoe and Her Zebra* (PS). Illus. 1999, Barefoot $14.95 (1-902283-75-9). 32pp. A clever alphabet book in which children named for each letter of the alphabet (e.g., Alice, Ben) are chased by animals similarly arranged (e.g., alligator, bear). (Rev: BL 10/15/99; SLJ 12/99)

11 Berg, Cami. *D Is for Dolphin* (PS–3). Illus. by Janet Biondi. 1991, Windom $18.95 (1-879244-01-2). 56pp. In this alphabet book, every letter stands for a word associated with dolphins. (Rev: BCCB 6/91; BL 9/15/91; SLJ 7/91)

12 Bond, Michael. *Paddington Bear and the Busy Bee Carnival* (PS–1). Illus. by R. W. Alley. 1998, HarperCollins $12.95 (0-06-027765-3). 40pp. A pleasant picture book in which Paddington Bear enters a contest by listing all the things he sees that begin with the letter *B*. (Rev: BL 5/15/98; HBG 10/98; SLJ 8/98)

13 Boynton, Sandra. *A Is for Angry: An Animal and Adjective Alphabet* (PS–K). Illus. 1987, Workman paper $6.95 (0-89480-507-X). 48pp. Adjectives are the focus of this alphabet book.

14 Bragg, Ruth G. *Alphabet Out Loud* (1–2). Illus. 1992, Picture Book paper $14.95 (0-88708-172-X). An unusual book in which the letters of the alphabet are used to introduce various activities. (Rev: SLJ 4/92)

15 Bruce, Lisa. *Oliver's Alphabets* (1–2). Illus. by Debi Gliori. 1993, Bradbury $13.95 (0-02-735996-4). The alphabet is introduced using everyday people and events in young Oliver's life, like his family, friends, and home. (Rev: SLJ 12/93)

16 Bullard, Lisa. *Not Enough Beds!* (PS–K). Illus. by Joni Oeltjenbruns. 1999, Lerner $15.95 (1-57505-356-X). 32pp. In this alphabet book, family members must find unusual sleeping arrangements when they all arrive for Christmas. (Rev: BL 9/15/99; HBG 3/00; SLJ 10/99)

17 Bunting, Jane. *My First ABC* (PS–1). Illus. 1993, DK $16.95 (1-56458-403-8). 32pp. In this alphabet book, children play with objects starting with each letter of the alphabet. (Rev: BL 12/15/93; SLJ 5/94)

18 Cahoon, Heather. *Word Play ABC* (1–3). Illus. by author. 1999, Walker LB $16.85 (0-8027-8684-7). 32pp. Each letter of the alphabet is accompanied by a pun or play on words; for example, for C, there is a picture of a crocodile in a pot and the word *crockpot*. (Rev: BCCB 7–8/99; BL 7/99; HBG 10/99; SLJ 4/99)

19 Carlson, Nancy. *ABC I Like Me!* (PS–1). Illus. 1997, Viking $14.99 (0-670-87458-2). 32pp. A little pig and his friends take a trip through the alphabet. (Rev: BL 4/1/97; SLJ 6/97)

20 Chandra, Deborah. *A Is for Amos* (PS–2). Illus. by Keiko Narahashi. 1999, Farrar $16.00 (0-374-30001-1). 32pp. In this alphabet book, a young girl rides around the family farm on her rocking horse. (Rev: BCCB 2/99; BL 3/15/99; HB 3–4/99; HBG 10/99; SLJ 3/99)

21 Chaplin, Susan Gibbons. *I Can Sign My ABCs* (K–3). Illus. by Laura McCaul. 1986, Gallaudet Univ. $9.95 (0-930323-19-X). 56pp. The ABCs of sign language, with color illustrations. (Rev: BL 2/15/87)

22 Chin-Lee, Cynthia. *A Is for Asia* (K–4). Illus. by Yumi Heo. 1997, Orchard LB $17.99 (0-531-33011-7). 32pp. A variety of topics, from geography to holidays, are covered in this unique alphabet book. (Rev: BCCB 5/97; BL 3/1/97; SLJ 4/97)

23 Chin-Lee, Cynthia, and Terri de la Pena. *A Is for the Americas* (2–4). Illus. by Enrique O. Sanchez. 1999, Orchard LB $16.99 (0-531-33194-6). 32pp. An alphabet book for older children that uses geographical and historical names — most of them associated with Hispanic and Native American culture. (Rev: BL 9/1/99; HBG 3/00; SLJ 10/99) [970]

24 Chwast, Seymour. *The Alphabet Parade* (K–3). Illus. by author. 1991, Smithmark $3.98 (0-831-70005-X). In this wordless book, the letters of the alphabet join a parade filled with other fascinating paraders. (Rev: SLJ 10/91)

25 Cleary, Beverly. *The Hullabaloo ABC* (PS–K). Illus. by Ted Rand. 1998, Morrow LB $15.93 (0-688-15183-3). 40pp. A rhyming alphabet — mostly farm related — in which each letter stands for a sound (e.g., G is for Grunt). (Rev: BL 4/1/98; HBG 10/98; SLJ 7/98)

26 Cohen, Izhar. *A B C Discovery! An Alphabet Book of Picture Puzzles* (PS–2). Illus. 1998, Dial $17.99 (0-8037-2321-0). 58pp. An alphabet featuring letters and lists of items on one page to find in the pictures that are on the opposite page. (Rev: BL 1/1–15/99; HBG 3/99; SLJ 12/98) [411]

27 Crosbie, Michael J. *Arches to Zigzags: An Architecture ABC* (PS–3). Illus. by Kit Rosenthal and Steve Rosenthal. 2000, Abrams $18.95 (0-8109-4218-6). 32pp. In rhyme and illustrated with color photos from around America, this book uses architectural elements to introduce the alphabet (e.g., B is for balcony). (Rev: BCCB 12/00; BL 2/1/01; SLJ 12/00) [721]

28 Crowther, Robert. *My Pop-up Surprise ABC* (PS–K). Illus. by author. 1997, Orchard $16.95 (0-531-30038-2). A simple alphabet book that uses large, easily manipulated flaps and pull tabs. (Rev: SLJ 8/97)

29 Darling, Kathy. *ABC Cats* (K–3). Illus. by Tara Darling. 1998, Walker LB $16.85 (0-8027-8667-7). 32pp. Full-color photos of cats illustrate this charming alphabet book. (Rev: BL 11/1/98; HBG 10/99; SLJ 11/98)

30 Darling, Kathy. *Amazon ABC* (PS–1). Illus. by Tara Darling. 1996, Lothrop LB $15.93 (0-688-13779-2). 32pp. In a series of striking photographs, the alphabet is introduced through animals of the Amazon rain forest. (Rev: BL 3/1/96; SLJ 5/96)

31 Demarest, Chris L. *The Cowboy ABC* (PS). Illus. 1999, DK $15.95 (0-7894-2509-2). Readers are taken on a cattle drive while learning their ABCs with entries such as "L is for Lariat." (Rev: BL 4/15/99; HBG 10/99; SLJ 4/99) [978]

32 Demarest, Chris L. *Firefighters A to Z* (PS–K). Illus. 2000, Simon & Schuster $16.95 (0-689-83798-4). 40pp. Beginning with "A is for Alarm," this is a large-format alphabet book showing fire fighters, their equipment, and their activities. (Rev: BL 7/00; HB 7–8/00; HBG 3/01; SLJ 12/00)

33 Dragonwagon, Crescent. *Alligator Arrived with Apples: A Potluck Alphabet Feast* (PS–2). Illus. by Jose Aruego and Ariane Dewey. 1987, Macmillan $15.95 (0-02-733090-7); paper $5.99 (0-689-71613-3). 40pp. An alliterative alphabet story about the menu and guests of an unusual Thanksgiving feast. (Rev: BL 9/15/87; SLJ 11/87)

34 Edens, Cooper, et al. *An ABC of Fashionable Animals* (PS–K). Illus. 1989, Simon & Schuster $12.95 (0-88138-122-5). 56pp. Costumed animals team up with the alphabet to amuse young readers. (Rev: BL 7/89)

35 Edwards, Pamela Duncan. *The Wacky Wedding: A Book of Alphabet Antics* (PS–2). Illus. by Henry Cole. 1999, Hyperion LB $15.49 (0-7868-2248-1). 32pp. An ant wedding fraught with problems is the humorous setting for this wacky alphabet book. (Rev: BL 5/1/99; HBG 10/99; SLJ 6/99)

36 Edwards, Richard. *Amazing Animal Alphabet* (PS–1). Illus. 1999, Orchard $14.95 (0-531-30123-0). Arranged in alphabetical order, different animals are found hiding under flaps in this interactive book. (Rev: BL 12/15/99; SLJ 6/99)

37 Ehlert, Lois. *Eating the Alphabet: Fruits and Vegetables from A to Z* (PS–1). Illus. by author. 1989, Harcourt $16.00 (0-15-224435-2); paper $5.95 (0-15-201036-X). 32pp. An eye-catching alphabet book. (Rev: BL 3/15/89; HB 5–6/89; SLJ 6/89)

38 Eichenberg, Fritz. *Ape in a Cape: An Alphabet of Odd Animals* (PS–1). Illus. by author. 1952, Harcourt $17.00 (0-15-203722-5); paper $7.00 (0-15-607830-9). 32pp. Each letter of the alphabet is represented by a full-page color picture of an animal with a brief nonsense rhyme explaining it.

39 Ernst, Lisa Campbell. *The Letters Are Lost!* (PS–1). Illus. 1996, Viking $15.99 (0-670-86336-X). 32pp. Alphabet blocks find homes that match their letters (e.g., *A* is an airplane) in this imaginative alphabet book. (Rev: BL 1/1–15/96; HB 3–4/96)

40 Fisher, Leonard Everett. *The ABC Exhibit* (PS–1). Illus. 1991, Macmillan $15.95 (0-02-735251-X). 32pp. An unusual picture book that teaches the alphabet through full-color paintings. (Rev: BCCB 7–8/91; BL 3/15/91; SLJ 5/91)

41 Geisert, Arthur. *Pigs from A to Z* (1–4). Illus. by author. 1986, Houghton $17.95 (0-395-38509-1). 64pp. Complicated etchings hide letters, and it will take somewhat older-than-usual alphabet book readers to figure them out. (Rev: BL 11/15/86; HB 1–2/87; SLJ 12/86)

42 Gerstein, Mordicai. *The Absolutely Awful Alphabet* (1–3). Illus. 1999, Harcourt $15.00 (0-15-201494-2). 32pp. Using alliterative texts, each letter of the alphabet is introduced by a hideous monster. (Rev: BL 4/1/99; HBG 10/99; SLJ 5/99) [428.1]

43 Girnis, Meg. *A B C for You and Me* (PS–2). Illus. by Shirley Leamon Green. 2000, Albert Whitman $14.95 (0-8075-0101-8). 32pp. Using photographs of children with Down syndrome, this alphabet book celebrates the beauty of all kinds of children. (Rev: BL 7/00; HB 5–6/00; HBG 10/00; SLJ 4/00)

44 Golding, Kim. *Alphababies* (PS). Illus. 1998, DK $9.95 (0-7894-2529-7). 26pp. A colorful, imaginative alphabet book that combines computer graphics and pictures of babies. (Rev: BL 11/1/98; HBG 3/99; SLJ 12/98)

45 Grassby, Donna. *A Seaside Alphabet* (1–3). Illus. by Susan Tooke. 2000, Tundra $19.95 (0-88776-516-5). Picture puzzles and nautical scenes featuring the seaside introduce the alphabet. (Rev: HBG 10/00; SLJ 6/00)

46 Hague, Kathleen. *Alphabears: An ABC Book* (PS–K). Illus. by Michael Hague. 1984, Holt paper $5.95 (0-8050-1637-6). 32pp. Twenty-six lovable bears are introduced, one for each letter.

47 Hansen, Biruta A. *Parading with Piglets: A Playful ABC Pop-up* (PS–1). Illus. 1996, National Geographic $16.95 (0-7922-2711-5). 14pp. Animals move when tabs are pulled in this alphabet book. (Rev: BL 12/15/96)

48 Harness, Cheryl. *Midnight in the Cemetery: A Spooky Search-and-Find Alphabet Book* (2–4). 1999, Simon & Schuster $16.00 (0-689-80873-9). 32pp. For older primary-grade readers, this book of alphabetically arranged objects uncovers scary and macabre beings and creatures drifting around the tombstones in a cemetery. (Rev: BL 11/15/99; HBG 3/00; SLJ 11/99)

49 Harrison, Ted. *A Northern Alphabet: A Is for Arctic* (K–2). Illus. by author. 1989, Tundra paper $7.95 (0-88776-233-6). 32pp. Scenes, people, and objects associated with the far north are used in this alphabet book. A reissue.

50 Heidelbach, Nikolaus. *Where the Girls Are* (2–4). Trans. from German by A. W. Millyard. Illus. by author. 1994, Annick paper $8.95 (1-55037-974-7). In this imaginative alphabet book, 26 girls engage in unusual activities. (Rev: SLJ 12/94)

51 Heller, Nicholas. *Ogres! Ogres! Ogres! A Feasting Frenzy from A to Z* (K–4). Illus. by Joseph A. Smith. 1999, Greenwillow $16.00 (0-688-16986-4). 32pp. An offbeat alphabet book in which monsters from Abednego through Zuleika satisfy some weird food fetishes. (Rev: BL 10/15/99; HBG 3/00; SLJ 10/99)

52 Helman, Andrea. *O Is for Orca: A Pacific Northwest Alphabet Book* (K–2). Photos by Art Wolfe. 1995, Sasquatch $14.95 (1-57061-038-X). Stunning color photos are used in this alphabet book to present some of the animals, people, plants, and geographical features of the Pacific Northwest. (Rev: SLJ 2/96)

53 Hepworth, Cathi. *ANTics! An Alphabetical Anthology* (K–2). Illus. by author. 1992, Putnam LB $16.99 (0-399-21862-9). 32pp. This inventive picture book for older children features the names of people and concepts that contain the word "ant." (Rev: BL 5/15/92*; SLJ 7/92*)

54 Hoban, Tana. *26 Letters and 99 Cents* (PS–1). Illus. by author. 1987, Greenwillow $15.93 (0-688-06362-4). 32pp. An ABC and counting book combined by turning the book upside down. (Rev: BCCB 4/87; BL 3/1/87; SLJ 4/87)

55 Hobbie, Holly. *Toot and Puddle: Puddle's ABC* (PS–1). Illus. 2000, Little, Brown $14.95 (0-316-36593-9). 48pp. To teach Otto the turtle the alphabet, little pig Puddle paints 26 clever pictures that illustrate the letters. (Rev: BCCB 12/00; BL 9/15/00; HBG 3/01; SLJ 11/00)

56 Horenstein, Henry. *A Is for . . .? A Photographer's Alphabet of Animals* (PS–3). Photos by author. 1999, Harcourt $16.00 (0-15-201582-5). An alphabet puzzle that shows a close-up photo of a part of an animal for each letter; the answers are in the back. (Rev: BCCB 11/99; HBG 3/00; SLJ 10/99) [591]

57 Howland, Naomi. *ABCDrive! A Car Trip Alphabet* (PS–1). Illus. 1994, Clarion $15.00 (0-395-66414-4). 32pp. An alphabet book that uses names of vehicles and terms connected with traveling. (Rev: BCCB 6/94; BL 4/15/94; SLJ 6/94)

58 Hughes, Langston. *The Sweet and Sour Animal Book* (PS–1). Illus. 1994, Oxford $17.95 (0-19-509185-X). 48pp. This alphabet book by the distinguished poet uses illustrations by children from the Harlem School of the Arts. (Rev: BCCB 1/95; BL 10/15/94; SLJ 2/95)

59 Hughes, Shirley. *Alfie's ABC* (PS–1). Illus. 1998, Lothrop $16.00 (0-688-16126-X). 32pp. An alphabet book that uses children's favorite things (e.g., "S is for seaside, swimming, and sand castles") to introduce each letter. (Rev: BL 8/98*; HBG 3/99; SLJ 9/98)

60 Hunt, Jonathan. *Bestiary: An Illuminated Alphabet of Medieval Beasts* (2–5). Illus. 1998, Simon & Schuster $17.00 (0-689-81246-9). 48pp. This handsome alphabet book displays 26 mythical beasts from around the world, beginning with the two-headed Amphisbaena and ending with Ziphius, a sea monster. (Rev: BL 9/1/98; HBG 3/99; SLJ 9/98) [398.24]

61 Isadora, Rachael. *ABC Pop!* (PS–2). Illus. 1999, Viking $15.99 (0-670-88329-8). 32pp. With a bow to the art of Roy Lichtenstein, this book presents the alphabet using pop art illustrations. (Rev: BCCB 6/99; BL 7/99; HB 5–6/99; HBG 10/99; SLJ 6/99)

62 Isadora, Rachael. *City Seen from A to Z* (PS–2). Illus. by Rachel Isadora. 1983, Greenwillow $15.93 (0-688-01803-3). 32pp. Everyday objects in the city are the theme of this alphabet book.

63 Jahn-Clough, Lisa. *ABC Yummy* (PS–2). Illus. 1997, Houghton $5.95 (0-395-84542-4). 32pp. A tiny picture book that uses fruits and vegetables on a trip through the alphabet. (Rev: BL 4/1/97; SLJ 6/97)

64 Jernigan, Gisela. *Agave Blooms Just Once* (2–4). Illus. by E. Wesley Jernigan. 1989, Harbinger paper $10.95 (0-943173-44-2). An alphabet book introducing the flora and fauna of the Sonoran Desert in rhyming verse. (Rev: BL 3/1/90)

65 Johnson, Jean. *Firefighters A to Z* (PS–1). Illus. 1985, Walker LB $11.85 (0-8027-6590-4). 39pp. An alphabet book organized around the workings of a fire-fighting unit. Others in this series are: *Librarians A to Z* (1989); *Police Officers A to Z* (1986); *Postal Workers A to Z* (1987); *Teachers A to Z* (1987). (Rev: BL 3/1/86)

66 Johnson, Odette, and Bruce Johnson. *Apples, Alligators and Also Alphabets* (PS–K). Illus. 1992, Stoddart paper $3.95 (0-19-540906-X). 32pp. An inventive alphabet book with whimsical words and actions. (Rev: BL 4/15/91; SLJ 6/91)

67 Joyce, Susan. *ABC Animal Riddles* (K–3). Illus. by Doug DuBosque. 1998, Peel $13.95 (0-939217-51-1). 32pp. For each letter of the alphabet, there is a mystery animal whose identity can be determined from an accompanying rhyming riddle. (Rev: BL 7/99; HBG 10/99; SLJ 4/99) [818]

68 Joyce, Susan. *ABC Nature Riddles* (K–3). Illus. by Doug DuBosque. Series: ABC Riddles. 2000, Peel $13.95 (0-939217-53-8). An appealing book with an imaginative rhyming text and color drawings that presents a nature riddle for each letter of the alphabet. (Rev: HBG 3/01; SLJ 10/00)

69 Joyce, Susan. *Alphabet Riddles* (K–3). Illus. by Doug DuBosque. 1998, Peel $13.95 (0-939217-50-3). A rhyming riddle book with clues that include the first and last letters and characteristics of the answer. (Rev: BL 7/98; HBG 10/98; SLJ 6/98)

70 Kalman, Bobbie. *Christmas Long Ago from A to Z* (K–2). Series: AlphaBasiCs. 1999, Crabtree LB $14.97 (0-86505-385-5); paper $7.16 (0-86505-415-0). 31pp. An alphabet book that uses the symbols and activities associated with Christmas as a source for the letters. (Rev: SLJ 10/99)

71 Kaye, Buddy, et al. *A You're Adorable* (PS–1). Illus. by Martha Alexander. 1994, Candlewick $9.95 (1-56402-237-4). 32pp. A charming alphabet book that uses the words of a song that was popular more than 50 years ago. (Rev: BL 7/94)

72 Kellogg, Steven. *Aster Aardvark's Alphabet Adventures* (PS–3). Illus. 1987, Morrow paper $4.95 (0-688-11571-3). 40pp. The alphabet is interpreted through 26 vignettes, one to three pages long. (Rev: BL 9/1/87; HB 11–12/87; SLJ 12/87)

73 King-Smith, Dick. *Dick King-Smith's Alphabeasts* (PS–K). Illus. by Quentin Blake. 1992, Macmillan $14.95 (0-02-750720-3). 64pp. Mirth-provoking verses celebrate the animal kingdom. (Rev: BCCB 12/92; BL 9/15/92; SLJ 12/92)

74 Kirk, David. *Miss Spider's ABC* (PS–3). Illus. 1998, Scholastic $16.95 (0-590-28279-4). 32pp. An ABC book in which a number of creatures, mainly bugs, prepare a surprise party for Miss Spider. (Rev: BL 12/1/98; HBG 3/99; SLJ 12/98)

75 Kitamura, Satoshi. *From Acorn to Zoo and Everything in Between in Alphabetical Order* (PS–1). Illus. 1992, Farrar $15.00 (0-374-32470-0). 32pp. A number of objects starting with the same letter are pictured on each page of this attractive British alphabet book. (Rev: BL 7/92; HB 5–6/92*; SLJ 7/92)

76 Layne, Steven L. *Thomas's Sheep and the Great Geography Test* (1–3). Illus. by Perry Board. 1998, Pelican $14.95 (1-56554-274-6). In this alphabet book, Thomas sends four imaginary sheep on a worldwide trip, which involves a variety of activities such as acting in Australia and kayaking in Kenya. (Rev: HBG 10/98; SLJ 9/98)

77 Lear, Edward. *An Edward Lear Alphabet* (1–2). Illus. by Vladimir Radunsky. 1999, HarperCollins LB $14.89 (0-06-028114-6). 32pp. Introduces the nonsense alphabet of Edward Lear accompanied by droll illustrations. (Rev: BL 4/1/99; HBG 10/99; SLJ 6/99) [821]

78 Lester, Alison. *Alice and Aldo* (K–3). Illus. 1998, Houghton $15.00 (0-395-87092-5). 32pp. Young Alice and her stuffed donkey, Aldo, present the alphabet through a series of everyday activities. (Rev: BL 3/1/98; HB 7–8/98; HBG 10/98; SLJ 8/98)

79 Lester, Mike. *A Is for Salad* (1–4). Illus. 2000, Putnam $9.99 (0-399-23388-1). 40pp. For children who already know their letters, this is a hilarious alphabet book that claims, for example, that L is for hair dryer and D is for remote control. (Rev: BCCB 7–8/00; BL 6/1–15/00*; HB 3–4/00; HBG 10/00; SLJ 4/00)

80 Lindbergh, Reeve. *The Awful Aardvarks Go to School* (PS–2). Illus. by Tracey Campbell Pearson. 1997, Viking $15.99 (0-670-85920-6). 32pp. In this hilarious alphabet book, three aardvarks create chaos when they invade a classroom. (Rev: BL 10/15/97*; HBG 3/98; SLJ 12/97)

81 Livingston, Myra Cohn. *B Is for Baby: An Alphabet of Verses* (PS–K). Photos by Steel Stillman. 1996, Simon & Schuster $15.00 (0-689-80950-6).

This alphabet book celebrates babyhood in a series of simple, catchy rhymes. (Rev: SLJ 9/96)

82 Lobel, Anita. *Away from Home* (PS–3). Illus. 1994, Greenwillow $15.89 (0-688-10355-3). 32pp. Each letter of the alphabet depicts a boy in a different place, e.g., Adam arrives in Amsterdam. (Rev: BCCB 9/94; BL 8/94; SLJ 10/94)

83 Lobel, Arnold. *On Market Street* (PS–1). Illus. by Anita Lobel. 1981, Greenwillow $16.89 (0-688-84309-3); Morrow paper $6.95 (0-688-08745-0). 40pp. A merry alphabet book with objects from apples to zippers.

84 Lyne, Alice. *A My Name Is . . .* (PS–2). Illus. by Lynne W. Cravath. 1997, Whispering Coyote $14.95 (1-879085-40-2); paper $5.95 (1-879085-41-0). Introduces the alphabet through pictures of animals and humans. (Rev: SLJ 5/97)

85 MacDonald, Suse. *Alphabatics* (PS–1). Illus. by author. 1986, Macmillan $17.95 (0-02-761520-0). 64pp. An alphabet book that forms a letter into part of the picture illustrating the sound of the letter, such as "m" as part of a mustache. (Rev: BL 12/15/86; SLJ 12/86)

86 McDonnell, Flora. *Flora McDonnell's ABC* (PS–K). Illus. 1997, Candlewick $16.99 (0-7636-0118-7). 32pp. A witty, delightful introduction to the alphabet using animals and fish engaging in zany activities. (Rev: BCCB 7–8/97; BL 4/15/97)

87 McLean, Dirk. *Play Mas! A Carnival ABC* (1–4). Illus. by Ras Stone. 2000, Tundra $16.95 (0-88776-486-X). This Caribbean alphabet book contains fascinating facts about Carnival. (Rev: HBG 10/00; SLJ 12/00)

88 Marshall, Janet. *Look Once, Look Twice* (K–2). Illus. 1995, Ticknor $14.00 (0-395-71644-6). 64pp. A clever alphabet book that uses interesting patterns to introduce letters and words that begin with them. (Rev: BCCB 4/95; BL 2/1/95; HB 5–6/95; SLJ 4/95)

89 Martin, Bill, Jr., and John Archambault. *Chicka Chicka Boom Boom* (PS–2). Illus. by Lois Ehlert. 1989, Simon & Schuster $15.00 (0-671-67949-X). 32pp. The letters of the alphabet enjoy a series of adventures. (Rev: BL 10/15/89*; HB 1–2/90*; SLJ 11/89)

90 Martin, Mary Jane. *From Anne to Zach* (PS–K). Illus. by Michael Grejniec. 1996, Boyds Mills $15.95 (1-56397-573-4). This ABC book introduces the alphabet by using a lot of first names, both common and obscure. (Rev: SLJ 12/96)

91 Mathers, Petra. *A Cake for Herbie* (PS–2). Illus. 2000, Simon & Schuster $15.00 (0-689-83017-3). 32pp. Herbie the duck decides to enter a poetry contest by making up poems about food, one for each letter of the alphabet. (Rev: BL 5/1/00*; HB 5–6/00; HBG 10/00; SLJ 6/00)

92 Maurer, Donna. *Annie, Bea, and Chi Chi Dolores: A School Day Alphabet* (PS–4). Illus. by Denys Cazet. 1993, Orchard LB $16.99 (0-531-08617-8). A day in a kindergarten supplies the letters to introduce an alphabet. (Rev: BL 2/13/93; HB 7–8/93; SLJ 5/93)

93 Mayers, Florence Cassen. *ABC: The Alef-Bet Book* (K–4). Illus. 1989, Abrams $12.95 (0-8109-1885-4). Each letter of the Hebrew alphabet is illustrated by an object from the Israel Museum in Jerusalem. (Rev: SLJ 11/89)

94 Mayers, Florence Cassen. *ABC: The Museum of Modern Art, New York* (PS–4). Illus. 1986, Abrams $12.95 (0-8109-1849-8). 32pp. Introducing children to the alphabet and fine art. (Rev: BL 2/15/87)

95 Mayers, Florence Cassen. *Baseball ABC* (1–3). Illus. 1994, Abrams $12.95 (0-8109-1938-9). An unusual alphabet book that uses baseball terminology, equipment, teams, and players to introduce the ABCs. (Rev: SLJ 12/94)

96 Mayers, Florence Cassen. *A Russian ABC: Featuring Masterpieces from the Hermitage* (K–4). Illus. 1992, Abrams $12.95 (0-8109-1919-2). 36pp. An ABC series featuring art reproductions from the museum's collection. (Rev: BL 11/1/92; SLJ 2/93)

97 Merriam, Eve. *Where Is Everybody? An Animal Alphabet* (PS–3). Illus. by Diane De Groat. 1992, Simon & Schuster paper $14.95 (0-671-64964-7). 40pp. An alphabet book with many, many details in each picture. (Rev: BL 6/15/89; HB 7–8/89)

98 Metaxas, Eric. *The Birthday ABC* (K–3). Illus. by Tim Raglin. 1995, Simon & Schuster $15.00 (0-671-88306-2). 32pp. Animals in proper 18th century attire illustrate the letters of the alphabet. (Rev: BL 8/95; SLJ 6/95)

99 Micklethwait, Lucy, ed. *I Spy: An Alphabet in Art* (K–2). Illus. 1992, Greenwillow $19.00 (0-688-11679-5). 64pp. Young readers are asked to find objects in full-page reproductions of paintings. (Rev: BCCB 2/93; BL 11/1/92; HB 1–2/93; SLJ 10/92)

100 Miller, Jane. *Farm Alphabet Book* (PS–K). Illus. 1987, Scholastic paper $2.99 (0-590-31991-4). 32pp. Photographs of farm life make an unusual ABC book.

101 Miranda, Anne. *Pignic: An Alphabet Book in Rhyme* (PS–2). Illus. by Rosekrans Hoffman. 1996, Boyds Mills $14.95 (1-56397-558-0). 32pp. A pig picnic is used as a locale for introducing the 26 letters through objects and activities. (Rev: BL 3/1/96; SLJ 5/96)

102 Modesitt, Jeanne. *The Story of Z* (K–2). Illus. by Lonni S. Johnson. 1990, Picture Book paper $14.95 (0-88708-105-3). 28pp. Z becomes tired of being last and decides to leave the alphabet. (Rev: BL 6/1/90; SLJ 1/91)

103 Moncure, Jane Belk. *My "a" Sound Box* (K–1). Illus. by Colin King. Series: New Sound Box Library. 2000, Child's World LB $21.36 (1-56766-767-8). 30pp. Many words beginning with the letter "a" are found and put in the "a" sound box. Others in this series are *My "c" Sound Box,"* and *My "d" Sound Box* (both 2000). (Rev: SLJ 3/01)

104 Most, Bernard. *A B C T-Rex* (PS–K). Illus. 2000, Harcourt $13.00 (0-15-202007-1). 32pp. A comical ABC book in which a suburban dinosaur eats his way through the alphabet. (Rev: BL 4/1/00; HBG 10/00; SLJ 4/00)

105 *My Big Alphabet Book* (PS–K). Series: Big Tab Board Books. 1999, DK $9.95 (0-7894-4681-2). An oversized board book that uses photos, drawings, and tabs to introduce the letters of the alphabet. (Rev: SLJ 2/00)

106 Onyefulu, Ifeoma. *A Is for Africa* (K–3). Illus. 1993, Dutton $15.99 (0-525-65147-0). 32pp. A series of photos of people, places, and things in Nigeria introduce the alphabet. (Rev: BL 8/93)

107 Owens, Mary Beth. *A Caribou Alphabet* (PS–1). Illus. by author. 1988, Farrar paper $4.95 (0-374-41043-7). 40pp. An alphabet book featuring caribous. (Rev: BL 9/1/88; HB 11–12/88; SLJ 10/88)

108 Oxenbury, Helen. *Helen Oxenbury's ABC of Things* (PS–K). Illus. by author. 1993, Simon & Schuster paper $3.95 (0-689-71761-X). 56pp. Groups of unlikely animals and objects are pictured together in this imaginative and humorous alphabet book.

109 Pallotta, Jerry. *The Frog Alphabet Book . . . and Other Awesome Amphibians* (PS–1). Illus. by Ralph Masiello. 1990, Charlesbridge $16.95 (0-88106-463-7); paper $6.95 (0-88106-462-9). 32pp. This alphabet book introduces amphibians and gives salient facts about different varieties. (Rev: BL 9/1/90)

110 Paul, Ann W. *Eight Hands Round: A Patchwork Alphabet* (1–4). Illus. by Jeanette Winter. 1991, HarperCollins LB $15.89 (0-06-024704-5). 32pp. An alphabet book that shows how the art of patchwork grew and why. (Rev: BCCB 7–8/91; BL 6/1/91; SLJ 7/91)

111 Paul, Anne Whitford. *Everything to Spend the Night: From A to Z* (PS–K). Illus. by Maggie Smith. 1999, DK $15.95 (0-7894-2511-4). In this alphabet book, a little girl packs several items such as apples, bunny, chalk, etc., for her overnight stay with her grandfather, but she forgets her pajamas. (Rev: BL 4/1/99; HB 3–4/99; HBG 10/99; SLJ 6/99)

112 Pelham, David. *A Is for Animals: An Animal ABC* (PS–K). 1991, Simon & Schuster $16.95 (0-671-72495-9). Animals pop out of squares in this alphabet book. (Rev: BL 9/15/91)

113 Pelletier, David. *The Graphic Alphabet* (PS–2). Illus. 1996, Orchard $17.95 (0-531-36001-6). 32pp. Letters of the alphabet are pictured in various imaginative positions. (Rev: BCCB 12/96; BL 11/1/96; HB 11–12/96; SLJ 11/96)

114 Pomeroy, Diana. *Wildflower ABC: An Alphabet of Potato Prints* (PS–2). Illus. 1997, Harcourt $16.00 (0-15-201041-6). 40pp. Wildflowers including the columbine and dandelion are pictured in potato prints in this alphabet book. (Rev: BL 2/15/97; SLJ 11/97)

115 Pratt, Kristin J. *A Swim Through the Sea* (PS–3). Illus. by author. 1994, Dawn $16.95 (1-883220-03-3); paper $7.95 (1-883220-04-1). An alphabet book in which Seamore the seahorse introduces a number of creatures from the deep. (Rev: SLJ 8/94)

116 Pratt, Kristin J. *A Walk in the Rainforest* (2–4). Illus. by author. 1992, Dawn $16.95 (1-878265-99-7); paper $7.95 (1-878265-53-9). 33pp. In this book written and illustrated by a high school student, plants and animals found in the rain forest are used to introduce the alphabet. (Rev: SLJ 7/92)

117 Press, Judy. *Alphabet Art: With A to Z Animal Art and Fingerplays* (PS–K). Illus. by Sue Dennen. Series: Little Hands Books. 1998, Williamson paper $12.95 (1-885593-14-7). 134pp. For teachers and parents, this book explains how to teach the alphabet using crafts, games, poems, and fingerplays. (Rev: SLJ 3/98)

118 Rey, H. A. *Curious George Learns the Alphabet* (K–2). Illus. by author. 1963, Houghton $14.95 (0-395-16031-6); paper $5.95 (0-395-13718-7). 72pp. George makes learning the alphabet a wonderful and amusing game.

119 Rose, Deborah L. *Into the A, B, Sea* (PS–3). Illus. by Steve Jenkins. 2000, Scholastic $15.95 (0-439-09696-0). 40pp. From anemones to zooplankton, this alphabet book cleverly explores all sorts of sea life. (Rev: BCCB 12/00; BL 9/15/00; SLJ 10/00) [591.77]

120 Rosen, Michael. *Michael Rosen's ABC* (PS–1). Illus. by Bee Willey. 1997, Millbrook LB $25.90 (1-56294-138-0). 64pp. Strange characters and happenings in the woods are used in this whimsical ABC book. (Rev: BL 6/1–15/97; SLJ 3/97)

121 Rosenberg, Liz. *A Big and a Little Alphabet* (PS–1). Illus. by Vera Rosenberry. 1997, Orchard LB $16.99 (0-531-33050-8). 32pp. An ABC book that uses big and small animals to show the differences between upper and lowercase. (Rev: BL 11/1/97; HBG 3/98; SLJ 10/97)

122 Rotner, Shelley. *Action Alphabet* (PS–2). Illus. 1996, Simon & Schuster $16.00 (0-689-80086-X). 32pp. An alphabet book that uses as its focus a variety of outdoor activities. (Rev: BCCB 6/96; BL 8/96; SLJ 1/97)

123 Ruschak, Lynette. *Annie Ate Apples* (PS–K). Illus. by Bonnie Matthews. 1998, DK $14.95 (0-7894-2478-9). Tabs and pop-ups are used in this alphabet book featuring 52 children (a girl and a boy for each letter of the alphabet). (Rev: BL 1/1–15/99; HBG 10/98)

124 Ryden, Hope. *ABC of Crawlers and Flyers* (2–4). Illus. 1996, Clarion $14.95 (0-395-72808-8). 32pp. Each letter of the alphabet introduces a different insect. (Rev: BL 9/15/96; SLJ 10/96)

125 Sabuda, Robert. *A B C Disney* (PS–K). Illus. 1998, Disney $21.95 (0-7868-3132-4). An alphabet book that uses flaps to reveal familiar Disney characters. (Rev: BCCB 12/98; BL 1/1–15/99; HBG 3/99)

126 Sandved, Kjell B. *The Butterfly Alphabet* (K–3). Illus. 1996, Scholastic $16.95 (0-590-48003-0). 72pp. In double-page spreads, the alphabet is introduced with breathtaking close-ups of wing patterns of butterflies and moths. (Rev: BL 3/15/96; SLJ 5/96)

127 Schnur, Steven. *Spring: An Alphabet Acrostic* (2–5). Illus. by Leslie Evans. 1999, Clarion $15.00 (0-395-82269-6). 32pp. Various aspects of spring are covered in this illustrated alphabet book that also uses acrostics. (Rev: BL 4/1/99; HBG 10/99; SLJ 4/99) [793.73]

128 Schnur, Steven. *Summer: An Alphabet Acrostic* (2–5). Illus. 2001, Clarion $15.00 (0-618-02372-0). 32pp. An alphabet book of poems about summer in which the first letter of each line of the poem combines in acrostic fashion to spell the name of the object described. (Rev: BL 3/15/01)

129 Seeley, Laura L. *The Book of Shadowboxes: A Story of the ABC's* (PS–3). Illus. 1990, Peachtree $16.95 (0-934601-65-8). Using objects in shadowboxes as illustrations, the letters of the alphabet are introduced. (Rev: SLJ 4/91)

130 Seuss, Dr. *Dr. Seuss' ABC* (K–2). Illus. by author. 1963, Random $11.99 (0-394-90030-8). 72pp. A master author creates a strikingly popular alphabet book.

131 Shaw, Eve. *Grandmother's Alphabet* (PS–K). Illus. by author. 1996, Pfeifer-Hamilton paper $14.95 (1-57025-127-4). An alphabet book that describes a number of activities and professions that grandmothers can be involved in. (Rev: SLJ 5/97)

132 Shepard, Ernest H. *Winnie-the-Pooh's ABC: Inspired by A. A. Milne* (PS–K). Illus. 1995, Dutton $9.99 (0-525-45365-2). 32pp. An alphabet book that uses illustrations that first appeared in the Pooh books. (Rev: BL 1/15/95)

133 Sierra, Judy. *There's a Zoo in Room 22* (PS–2). Illus. by Barney Saltzberg. 2000, Harcourt $16.00 (0-15-202033-0). 40pp. Miss Darling introduces an animal alphabet to her students including such pets as Claude the Cat, Katy Katydid, and Vincent Vulture. (Rev: BCCB 10/00; BL 8/00; HBG 3/01; SLJ 10/00)

134 Sloat, Teri. *Patty's Pumpkin Patch* (PS–2). Illus. 1999, Putnam $15.99 (0-399-23010-6). 32pp. From seed to pumpkin stand, this alphabet book presents the stages in the growth of a pumpkin and discusses all the creatures that visit the plant while it is growing. (Rev: BCCB 10/99; BL 9/1/99; HBG 3/00; SLJ 10/99)

135 Staake, Bob. *My Little ABC Book* (PS–K). Illus. by author. 1998, Simon & Schuster paper $6.99 (0-689-81659-6). The letters of the alphabet are presented in this board book that uses bright colors and pleasant graphics. (Rev: HBG 10/98; SLJ 3/98)

136 Tapahonso, Luci, and Eleanor Schick. *Navajo ABC: A Dine Alphabet Book* (PS–3). Illus. by Eleanor Schick. 1995, Simon & Schuster $16.00 (0-689-80316-8). 24pp. Various objects and words associated with the Navajo people are used to introduce their alphabet and the English alphabet. (Rev: BL 12/15/95; SLJ 12/95)

137 *The Timbertoes ABC Alphabet Book* (PS–1). Illus. 1997, Boyds Mills $7.95 (1-56397-604-8). 32pp. The Timbertoes, a family of wooden figures, introduce the letters of the alphabet. (Rev: BL 3/1/97; SLJ 7/97)

138 Tobias, Tobi, ed. *A World of Words: An ABC of Quotations* (PS–3). Illus. by Peter Malone. 1998, Lothrop LB $15.93 (0-688-12130-6). 40pp. Poems and brief quotations are arranged alphabetically under such subjects as Animal, Book, Yard, and Zoo. (Rev: BL 10/1/98; HBG 3/99; SLJ 9/98) [811]

139 Tryon, Leslie. *Albert's Alphabet* (PS–1). Illus. by author. 1991, Macmillan $16.00 (0-689-31642-9). 40pp. Out of a variety of materials, a school carpenter creates an alphabet for the playground. (Rev: BL 4/15/91; SLJ 7/91)

140 Turner, Priscilla. *The War Between the Vowels and the Consonants* (K–3). Illus. by Whitney Turner. 1996, Farrar $16.00 (0-374-38236-0). 30pp. Rivalry between vowels and consonants is used as a lively introduction to letters. (Rev: BL 12/1/96; SLJ 10/96)

141 Viorst, Judith. *The Alphabet from Z to A: With Much Confusion on the Way* (1–3). Illus. by Richard Hull. 1994, Atheneum LB $15.00 (0-689-31768-9). 32pp. The alphabet is presented backward in amusing verses. (Rev: BL 3/1/94; SLJ 4/94)

142 Voake, Charlotte. *Alphabet Adventure* (PS). Illus. by author. 2000, Jonathan Cape $19.95 (0-22-403596-7). A girl and boy board an airplane and fly past objects and living things representing letters of the alphabet from A for airplane to Z for zebras. (Rev: SLJ 7/00)

143 Walton, Rick. *So Many Bunnies: A Bedtime ABC and Counting Book* (PS). Illus. by Paige Miglio. 1998, Lothrop LB $15.89 (0-688-13657-5). A combination ABC and counting book that is also a bedtime book because it tells how Mother Rabbit tucked her 26 babies in for the night. (Rev: HBG 10/98; SLJ 3/98)

144 Watson, Clyde. *Applebet: An ABC* (PS–2). Illus. by Wendy Watson. 1982, Farrar paper $5.95 (0-374-40427-5). 32pp. An alphabet book in which apples and a country fair provide the links from letter to letter.

145 Wells, Ruth. *A to Zen: A Book of Japanese Culture* (2–4). Illus. by Yoshi. 1992, Picture Book $17.00 (0-88708-175-4). 32pp. An alphabet-book format introduces young readers to Japanese culture and life. (Rev: BCCB 12/92; BL 1/15/93; SLJ 4/93)

146 Wethered, Peggy, and Ken Edgett. *Touchdown Mars! An ABC Adventure* (K–3). Illus. by Michael Chesworth. 2000, Putnam $15.99 (0-399-23214-1). 40pp. In this alphabet picture book, nine children and a cat take off for a mission to Mars. (Rev: BCCB 6/00; BL 5/15/00; HBG 10/00; SLJ 10/00)

147 Willard, Nancy. *An Alphabet of Angels* (PS–3). Illus. 1994, Scholastic $16.95 (0-590-48480-X). 64pp. Using the alphabet as a framework, the artist creates and photographs pieces of sculpture that depict various angels. (Rev: BCCB 10/94; BL 9/15/94; SLJ 10/94)

148 Williams, Laura Ellen. *A B C Kids* (PS). Illus. 2000, Putnam $15.99 (0-399-23370-9). 32pp. Using real children as models, this alphabet book illustrates common objects (A is for apple, U for underwear). (Rev: BCCB 10/00; BL 7/00; HBG 10/00; SLJ 6/00)

149 Wilner, Isabel. *B Is for Bethlehem: A Christmas Alphabet* (K–3). Illus. by Elisa Kleven. 1990, Dutton $14.99 (0-525-44622-2). 32pp. A Christmas story alphabet book. (Rev: BL 9/15/90*)

150 Wojtowycz, David. *Animal ABC* (K–1). Illus. by author. 2000, David & Charles $14.95 (1-86233-

107-3). A host of animals from an athletic aardvark to a zig-zag zebra introduce the alphabet. (Rev: SLJ 9/00)

151 Yorinks, Arthur. *The Alphabet Atlas* (1–4). Illus. by Adrienne Yorinks and Jeanyee Wong. 1999, Winslow $19.95 (0-890817-14-7). This alphabet book features countries of the world and, on each page, an illustration using different textiles in the shape of the country. (Rev: SLJ 7/99)

Concept Books

GENERAL

152 Aliki. *Feelings* (K–2). Illus. 1984, Greenwillow $15.93 (0-688-03832-8); Morrow paper $4.95 (0-688-06518-X). 32pp. An introduction to various emotions.

153 *Baby's First Words* (PS). Illus. by Lars Wik. 1985, Random $3.99 (0-394-86945-1). 28pp. Photos of everyday objects known by toddlers and babies. (Rev: BL 6/15/85)

154 Baker, Alan. *Brown Rabbit's Day* (PS–K). Illus. by author. Series: Little Rabbit Books. 1995, Kingfisher $9.95 (1-85697-584-3). In this concept book, Brown Rabbit invites friends over for a party where they have an opportunity to identify colors, count, and tell time. (Rev: SLJ 3/96)

155 Baker, Alan. *Gray Rabbit's Odd One Out* (PS–K). Illus. by author. Series: Little Rabbit Books. 1995, Kingfisher $8.95 (1-85697-585-1). Object identification and the use of various colors to build objects are covered in this concept book. (Rev: SLJ 3/96)

156 Baker, Alan. *Little Rabbits' First Time Book* (PS–K). Illus. 1999, Kingfisher $10.95 (0-7534-5220-0). 16pp. The activities of three bunnies throughout a day illustrate the passage of hours, which can be traced by using the movable hands on a clock. (Rev: BL 12/1/99; SLJ 2/00)

157 Barner, Bob. *Which Way to the Revolution? A Book About Maps* (1–3). Illus. by author. 1998, Holiday $16.95 (0-8234-1352-7). In this concept book about maps, a little mouse informs Paul Revere that the British are coming. Together, they travel from Boston to Lexington, using a map to plot their journey. (Rev: HBG 10/98; SLJ 5/98)

158 Beaton, Clare. *How Big Is a Pig?* (PS–K). Illus. 2000, Barefoot $14.99 (1-84148-077-0). 32pp. Double-page spreads are used in this amusing book that illustrates opposites in animals — fast and slow dogs and quiet and jumpy frogs. (Rev: BL 10/1/00; HBG 3/01; SLJ 12/00)

159 Berenstain, Stan, and Jan Berenstain. *Inside, Outside, Upside Down* (PS–1). Illus. by authors. 1968, Random LB $11.99 (0-394-91142-3). A bear has a brief trip that explains various concepts.

160 Bernhard, Durga. *Earth, Sky, Wet, Dry: A Book of Nature Opposites* (PS–2). Illus. 2000, Orchard LB $17.99 (0-531-33213-6). 40pp. Opposites are introduced using scenes from nature that demonstrate, for example, the difference between light and dark. (Rev: BL 2/1/00; HBG 10/00; SLJ 3/00)

161 Blackstone, Stella. *Baby High, Baby Low* (PS). Illus. by Denise Fraifield and Fernando Azevedo. 1998, Holiday $14.95 (0-8234-1345-4). 32pp. The author introduces the concept of opposites — such as high and low — using illustrations of activities involving babies of many races and their parents. (Rev: BL 12/1/98; HBG 3/99; SLJ 10/98)

162 Blackstone, Stella. *Can You See the Red Balloon?* (PS–K). Illus. by Debbie Harter. 1998, Orchard $14.95 (0-531-30077-3). A concept book that teaches color and shape identification through a series of double-page spreads filled with cartoon animals and objects. (Rev: HBG 10/99; SLJ 12/98)

163 Blackstone, Stella. *You and Me* (PS–1). Illus. by Giovanni Manna. 2000, Barefoot $15.99 (1-84148-263-3). 32pp. The author explores the concept of opposites using a boy and a girl on double-page spreads engaging in different activities. (Rev: BL 12/1/00; HBG 3/01; SLJ 12/00)

164 Blos, Joan W. *Hello, Shoes!* (PS). Illus. by Ann Boyajian. 1999, Simon & Schuster $13.00 (0-689-81441-0). 32pp. A picture book showing the love between a youngster and his grandfather while also teaching counting and colors. (Rev: BL 10/15/99; HBG 10/99; SLJ 7/99)

165 Bond, Michael. *Paddington's Opposites* (PS–2). Illus. by John Lobban. Series: Paddington. 1991, Viking $11.99 (0-670-84105-6). 32pp. The concept of opposites is introduced by Paddington by using common experiences and objects. (Rev: BL 12/15/91)

166 Bown, Deni. *Happy Times* (PS). Illus. Series: Snapshot. 1995, DK $3.95 (0-7894-0229-7). 10pp. Children learn about the concept of time through a series of colorful illustrations. Also use *Color Fun* (1995). (Rev: BL 1/1–15/96; SLJ 7/96)

167 Buehner, Caralyn. *I Did It, I'm Sorry* (K–4). Illus. by Mark Buehner. 1998, Dial LB $15.89 (0-8037-2011-4). 32pp. This picture book uses animal characters to explore cheating, littering, using bad language, and accepting responsibility, and then offers readers multiple-choice quizzes of possible actions. (Rev: BCCB 6/98; BL 4/15/98; SLJ 6/98)

168 Carle, Eric. *From Head to Toe* (PS). Illus. 1997, HarperCollins LB $16.89 (0-06-023516-0). 32pp. Children make the same movements as animals in this concept book illustrated with lively collages. (Rev: BCCB 6/97; BL 4/15/97; SLJ 4/97) [613.7]

169 Carrier, Lark. *Do Not Touch* (1–3). Illus. by author. 1991, Picture Book paper $15.95 (0-88708-061-8). 28pp. A picture book with the concept of words within words. (Rev: BL 4/1/89)

170 Carter, David A. *More Bugs in Boxes* (PS–3). Illus. 1990, Simon & Schuster $13.95 (0-671-69577-0). A board book that explores the world of shapes and colors. (Rev: SLJ 8/90)

171 Cendrars, Blaise. *Shadow* (K–3). Trans. and illus. by Marcia Brown. 1982, Macmillan $17.00 (0-684-17226-7). 40pp. This Caldecott winner (1983) explores the mysterious world of shadows.

172 Charles, N. N. *What Am I? Looking Through Shapes at Apples and Grapes* (PS–K). Illus. by Leo Dillon and Diane Dillon. 1994, Scholastic $16.95 (0-590-47891-5). 36pp. Geometric shapes are used creatively to illustrate a number of clever riddles in this interactive book. (Rev: BL 11/15/94; SLJ 1/95)

173 Chesanow, Neil. *Where Do I Live?* (K–3). Illus. by Ann Iosa. 1995, Barron's paper $6.95 (0-8120-9241-4). 48pp. The concept of belonging is explored, from a room of one's own to being a part of the solar system. (Rev: BL 2/1/96) [910]

174 Crews, Nina. *A High, Low, Near, Far, Loud, Quiet Story* (PS). Illus. 1999, Greenwillow LB $15.93 (0-688-16795-0). 24pp. The activities of a sister and younger brother are used to introduce a number of opposites. (Rev: BL 9/15/99; HBG 3/00; SLJ 12/99)

175 Crozon, Alain. *I Can Fly!* (PS–3). Illus. by author. Series: A Who Am I/What Am I Book. 1999, Chronicle $7.95 (0-8118-2407-1). This book contains pictures of 21 objects that can fly, such as a boomerang, a dandelion seed, and a superhero. For things on wheels use *I Can Roll* (1999). (Rev: SLJ 11/99)

176 Dale, Elizabeth. *How Long?* (PS–K). Illus. by Alan Marks. 1998, Orchard $14.95 (0-531-30101-X). 32pp. When a mouse mother postpones paying attention to her daughter for a minute or more, the little mouse wonders how long a minute is. (Rev: BL 10/1/98; HBG 3/99; SLJ 10/98)

177 Dodd, Emma. *Dog's Colorful Day* (PS–K). Illus. 2001, Dutton $14.99 (0-525-46528-6). 32pp. A color and counting book that shows how a dog gains a number of unwanted spots on its coat including some chocolate, a grass stain, and a splat of red jam. (Rev: BL 2/15/01; SLJ 3/01)

178 Emberley, Rebecca. *My Opposites/Mis Opuestos* (PS). 2000, Little, Brown $5.95 (0-316-23345-5). 20pp. A concept board book that introduces opposites in English and Spanish. (Rev: BCCB 12/00*; HBG 3/01; SLJ 9/00)

179 Falwell, Cathryn. *Word Wizard* (K–3). Illus. 1998, Clarion $15.00 (0-395-85580-2). 32pp. In this picture book, Anna discovers the world of anagrams while eating a bowl of alphabet cereal, then she embarks on a series of adventures in which, for example, she turns an ocean into a canoe. (Rev: BL 5/15/98; HBG 10/98)

180 Fleming, Denise. *The Everything Book* (PS). Illus. 2000, Holt $18.95 (0-8050-6292-0). 64pp. This book offers all sorts of information on topics ranging from the seasons and days of the week to parts of the body plus poems, songs, and games. (Rev: BCCB 10/00; BL 7/00; HBG 3/01; SLJ 10/00)

181 Ford, Miela. *What Color Was the Sky Today?* (PS–1). Illus. by Sally Noll. 1997, Greenwillow LB $14.93 (0-688-14559-0). 24pp. Using fewer than 100 words, this book introduces the concepts of colors, counting, time, and the weather. (Rev: BL 5/1/97; SLJ 3/97)

182 Fowler, Allan. *North, South, East, and West* (1–2). Illus. Series: Rookie Readers. 1993, Children's Book Pr. LB $18.50 (0-516-06011-2); Children's paper $4.95 (0-516-46011-0). 32pp. This is an introduction to the concept of directions for beginning readers in an attractive small format

using many color photographs. (Rev: BL 9/1/93) [526]

183 Gibbons, Gail. *Playgrounds* (PS–1). Illus. by author. 1985, Holiday LB $16.95 (0-8234-0553-2). 32pp. A concept book that shows young readers playground scenes that are familiar. (Rev: BCCB 6/85; BL 5/15/85; SLJ 5/85)

184 Goley, Elaine P. *Learn the Value of Trust* (PS–2). Illus. by Debbie Crocker. 1987, Rourke LB $15.94 (0-86592-378-7). 32pp. A simple text with examples drawn from a child's experiences. Others in this series are: *Learn the Value of Understanding Others* and *Learn the Value of Patience* (both 1988). (Rev: BL 6/15/88)

185 Goor, Ron, and Nancy Goor. *Shadows: Here, There, and Everywhere* (PS–3). Illus. by authors. 1981, HarperCollins LB $15.89 (0-690-04133-0). 48pp. A simple book that explains what shadows are and how to make them.

186 Got, Yves. *Sweet Dreams, Sam* (PS). Illus. 2000, Chronicle $8.95 (0-8118-2985-5). This interactive book uses different textures to explore the sense of touch, such as simulating the crinkly skin of an elephant. (Rev: BL 12/1/00)

187 Grejniec, Michael. *Good Morning, Good Night* (PS). Illus. 1997, North-South paper $6.95 (1-55858-704-7). 28pp. A concept book with basic vocabulary that demonstrates opposites. (Rev: BL 3/15/93; SLJ 8/93)

188 Grunwald, Lisa. *Now Soon Later* (PS). Illus. by Jane Johnson. 1996, Greenwillow $15.00 (0-688-13946-9). 24pp. Concepts involving time — like "now," "soon," and "later" — are explained through a girl's day-long activities. (Rev: BCCB 10/96; BL 7/96; SLJ 9/96)

189 Haring, Keith. *Big* (PS–K). Illus. by author. 1998, Hyperion $6.95 (0-7868-0390-8). This concept board book uses synonyms for *big*, while identifying different colors and various articles of clothing. (Rev: HBG 10/98; SLJ 7/98)

190 Harper, Dan. *Telling Time with Big Mama Cat* (PS–2). Illus. by Barry Moser and Cara Moser. 1998, Harcourt $15.00 (0-15-201738-0). 28pp. Using a foldout clock with movable hands, young readers can trace the daily activities of Big Mama Cat while they learn to tell time. (Rev: BCCB 11/98; BL 8/98*; HBG 3/99; SLJ 12/98)

191 Harris, Pamela. *Hot, Cold, Shy, Bold* (PS–K). Illus. 1998, Kids Can $10.95 (1-55074-153-5). 32pp. A successful book of opposites that uses a rhyming text and color photos. (Rev: BL 3/15/98; HBG 10/98) [428.1]

192 Harris, Trudy. *Pattern Fish* (PS–1). Illus. by Anne Canevari Green. 2000, Millbrook LB $20.90 (0-7613-1712-0). This attractive concept book explores the world of patterns. (Rev: BCCB 9/00; SLJ 12/00)

193 Hartman, Gail. *As the Crow Flies: A First Book of Maps* (PS–1). Illus. by Harvey Stevenson. 1993, Aladdin paper $5.99 (0-689-71762-8). 32pp. The concept of maps is introduced by using the environments of different animals. (Rev: BL 3/1/91; HB 5–6/91; SLJ 3/91)

194 Heide, Florence Parry, et al. *It's About Time!* (PS–1). Illus. by Cathryn Falwell. 1999, Clarion $15.00 (0-395-86612-X). 32pp. Fourteen easy-to-read poems that deal with the concept of time. (Rev: BCCB 4/99; BL 3/15/99; HBG 10/99; SLJ 5/99) [811]

195 Hill, Eric. *Spot's Big Book of Colors, Shapes and Numbers* (PS–K). Illus. 1994, Putnam $10.95 (0-399-22679-6). 26pp. The dog Spot guides youngsters in this introduction to colors, shapes, and numbers. (Rev: BL 6/1–15/94)

196 Hindley, Judy. *Ten Bright Eyes* (PS–1). Illus. by Alison Bartlett. 1998, Peachtree $14.95 (1-56145-173-8). As a mother bird roams the countryside looking for food for her young, the reader is introduced to numbers, shapes, and patterns as well as some related activities. (Rev: HBG 10/98; SLJ 11/98)

197 Hoban, Tana. *Black on White* (PS). Illus. 1993, Greenwillow $5.95 (0-688-11918-2). The photographs show black objects on a white background. A companion book is: *White on Black* (1993). (Rev: HB 7–8/93; SLJ 8/93)

198 Hoban, Tana. *Exactly the Opposite* (PS–1). Illus. 1990, Greenwillow $15.89 (0-688-08862-7). 32pp. A concept book that challenges children to think on more than one level. (Rev: BCCB 10/90; BL 9/1/90; HB 11–12/90*; SLJ 10/90)

199 Hoban, Tana. *What Is That?* (PS). Illus. 1994, Greenwillow paper $5.95 (0-688-12920-X). 12pp. Using silhouettes, a number of common animals are pictured in this board book. Also use *Who Are They?* (1994). (Rev: BL 12/1/94; HB 11–12/94; SLJ 11/94)

200 Hoberman, Mary Ann. *A House Is a House for Me* (K–2). Illus. by Betty Fraser. 1978, Puffin paper $5.99 (0-14-050394-3). 48pp. This picture book explores the idea that various objects can serve as houses.

201 Inkpen, Mick. *Kipper's Book of Opposites* (PS). Illus. by author. 1999, Harcourt $4.95 (0-15-202297-X). A simple concept book that explains opposites and gives a number of examples. (Rev: SLJ 10/99)

202 Jay, Alison. *Picture This . . .* (PS–K). Illus. 2000, Dutton $15.99 (0-525-46380-1). 40pp. Using spectacular illustrations, this word book features a common word per page. (Rev: BCCB 6/00; BL 5/15/00*; HBG 10/00; SLJ 6/00)

203 Jenkins, Sandra. *Flip-Flap* (PS). Illus. 1995, DK $14.95 (0-7894-0121-5). 24pp. By lifting flaps and turning wheels, one explores concepts like colors, numbers, and shapes. (Rev: BL 2/1/96) [910]

204 Krauss, Ruth. *A Hole Is to Dig* (PS). Illus. by Maurice Sendak. 1952, HarperCollins $15.95 (0-06-023405-9); paper $5.95 (0-06-443205-X). 48pp. Child-perceived definitions, such as "the world is so you have something to stand on," complemented by whimsical drawings.

205 Leopold, Niki Clark. *Once I Was . . .* (PS–2). Illus. by Woodleigh Hubbard. 1999, Putnam $15.99 (0-399-23105-6). 32pp. Through a series of short, illustrated rhymes, the processes of growing up and of change are explained. (Rev: BCCB 2/99; BL 2/15/99; HB 5–6/99; HBG 10/99; SLJ 4/99)

206 Llewellyn, Claire. *My First Book of Time* (PS–2). Illus. 1992, DK $14.95 (1-879431-78-5). 32pp. An oversize book with enticing photos and drawings provides an excellent introduction to the concept of time. (Rev: BCCB 7–8/92; BL 5/1/92; HB 7–8/92; SLJ 8/92) [529.7]

207 Lobel, Anita. *One Lighthouse, One Moon* (PS–2). Illus. 2000, Greenwillow LB $15.89 (0-688-15540-5). 40pp. This concept book introduces the days of the week, seasons, colors, and counting in three charming stories. (Rev: BCCB 7–8/00; BL 4/1/00; HB 7–8/00; HBG 10/00; SLJ 5/00)

208 Lynn, Sara. *Clothes* (PS). Illus. by author. 1986, Macmillan paper $2.95 (0-689-71095-X). 14pp. A baby's board book that focuses on familiar clothes. (Rev: BL 1/1/87; SLJ 3/87)

209 Maccarone, Grace. *Monster Math School Time* (K–2). Illus. by Margaret A. Hartelius. Series: Hello Math Reader. 1997, Scholastic $3.99 (0-590-30859-9). A beginning reader that teaches how to tell time through the antics of 12 monsters and their daily activities. (Rev: SLJ 1/98)

210 Manning, Linda. *Dinosaur Days* (PS–1). Illus. by Vlasta Van Kampen. 1994, Troll $12.95 (0-8167-3315-5). 32pp. Days of the week are introduced by seven dinosaurs, each of which causes a household emergency. (Rev: BL 7/94; SLJ 8/94)

211 Marzollo, Jean. *I Spy School Days: A Book of Picture Riddles* (PS–2). Illus. by Walter Wick. Series: I Spy. 1995, Scholastic $12.95 (0-590-48135-5). 38pp. Riddles and puzzles using photographs are featured, each related to school activities. (Rev: BL 12/1/95; SLJ 10/95)

212 Matthias, Catherine. *Over-Under* (PS–1). Illus. by Gene Sharp. 1984, Children's paper $4.95 (0-516-42048-8). 32pp. Spatial concepts are explained in an easy-to-read format.

213 Miller, Margaret. *Can You Guess?* (PS–K). Illus. 1993, Greenwillow $14.93 (0-688-11181-5). 40pp. Concepts about everyday objects are explored in this book of questions and answers. (Rev: BCCB 10/93; BL 12/1/93; HB 11–12/93; SLJ 1/94)

214 Modesitt, Jeanne. *Sometimes I Feel Like a Mouse: A Book About Feelings* (PS–1). Illus. by Robin Spowart. 1996, Scholastic paper $4.99 (0-590-44836-6). 32pp. Various emotions, like happy and proud, are pictured through poses of familar animals. (Rev: BL 10/1/92; SLJ 5/93)

215 Morris, Ann. *Play* (PS–3). Illus. 1998, Lothrop $15.00 (0-688-14551-3). 32pp. A concept book that shows children from different countries engaged in various play activities common to their cultures. (Rev: BL 5/15/98) [790.1]

216 Morris, Ann. *Teamwork* (PS–2). Illus. 1999, Lothrop LB $15.93 (0-688-16995-3). 32pp. The concept of teamwork is explored in a series of pictures depicting such activities as preschoolers playing soccer, Vietnam villagers harvesting rice, and dogs pulling a sled. (Rev: BL 12/1/99; HBG 3/00; SLJ 10/99) [302.3]

217 Morris, Ann. *Work* (PS–3). Illus. 1998, Lothrop $15.00 (0-688-14866-2). 32pp. Examples of activities from countries including Mexico, Israel, Egypt, Kenya, and Togo are used to explain the concept of work as it is performed around the world. (Rev: BL 5/15/98; HBG 10/98) [306.3]

218 Most, Bernard. *A Pair of Protoceratops* (PS–1). Illus. 1998, Harcourt $11.00 (0-15-201443-8). 36pp. The concept of the collective noun *pair* is introduced in alliterative prose describing dinosaurs in playful moods. (Rev: BL 4/15/98; HBG 10/98)

219 Most, Bernard. *A Trio of Triceratops* (PS–1). Illus. 1998, Harcourt $11.00 (0-15-201448-9). 36pp. Fun-loving dinosaurs demonstrate the concept of the collective noun *trio* in this delightful picture book. (Rev: BL 4/15/98; HBG 10/98)

220 Murphy, Chuck. *Chuck Murphy's Black Cat White Cat: A Pop-Up Book of Opposites* (K–2). Illus. 1998, Simon $12.95 (0-689-81415-1). An interactive book that can be manipulated to produce opposites such as a black cat that turns into a white cat. (Rev: BL 1/1–15/99)

221 Murphy, Mary. *If . . .* (PS–K). Illus. by author. 2000, Houghton paper $4.95 (0-618-03399-8). In this flap book, a little penguin demonstrates cause and effect (e.g., if you plant a seed/a tree can grow). The concept of choice is explored in the companion volume *You Choose* (2000). (Rev: SLJ 6/00)

222 Murphy, Mary. *Some Things Change* (PS). Illus. 2001, Houghton $9.95 (0-618-00334-7). 32pp. The concept of change is explored in this book about a young penguin, his teddy bear, and experiences they share — like a sunny day that becomes cloudy. (Rev: BL 3/15/01; SLJ 3/01)

223 Murphy, Stuart J. *Beep Beep, Vroom Vroom!* (PS–K). Illus. by Chris L. Demarest. Series: Math-Start. 2000, HarperCollins LB $15.89 (0-06-028017-4); paper $4.95 (0-06-446728-7). 32pp. In this book about pattern recognition, little Molly plays with her brother's toy cars of different colors. (Rev: BL 5/1/00; HBG 10/00; SLJ 5/00)

224 Murphy, Stuart J. *The Best Vacation Ever* (PS–3). Illus. by Nadine Bernard Westcott. 1997, HarperCollins LB $15.89 (0-06-026767-4); paper $4.95 (0-06-446706-6). 40pp. The concepts of collecting and analyzing data and making charts are introduced as a girl helps her family decide on a vacation spot. (Rev: BL 2/1/97; SLJ 3/97)

225 Murphy, Stuart J. *Game Time!* (2–3). Illus. by Cynthia Jabar. 2000, HarperCollins LB $15.89 (0-06-028025-5); paper $4.95 (0-06-446732-5). 33pp. The concept of measuring time — including weeks, days, hours, and seconds — is explored in this exciting tale of the Huskies, a girls' soccer team, and their big game. (Rev: HBG 3/01; SLJ 1/01)

226 Murphy, Stuart J. *Give Me Half!* (PS–3). Illus. by G. Brian Karas. 1996, HarperCollins LB $15.89 (0-06-025874-8). 40pp. A boy and his sister learn how to share when they find they have only one pizza and a single can of juice. (Rev: BCCB 5/96; BL 5/1/96; SLJ 6/96)

227 Murphy, Stuart J. *The Greatest Gymnast of All* (PS–K). Illus. by Cynthia Jabar. Series: MathStart. 1998, HarperCollins LB $14.89 (0-06-027609-6); paper $4.95 (0-06-446718-X). 40pp. Using Zoe's gymnastics routine as a framework, the rhyming text introduces opposites, such as inside and outside, on and off, and high and low. (Rev: BL 12/1/98; HBG 3/99; SLJ 12/98) [516]

228 Murphy, Stuart J. *Probably Pistachio* (1–3). Illus. by Marsha Winborn. Series: MathStart. 2001, HarperCollins LB $15.89 (0-06-028029-8); paper $4.95 (0-06-446734-1). 40pp. Throughout his day, Stuart makes predictions based on sound reasoning in this entertaining concept book about probability. (Rev: BL 2/15/01; SLJ 3/01) [519.2]

229 Murphy, Stuart J. *Rabbit's Pajama Party* (PS–K). Illus. by Frank Remkiewicz. Series: Math-Start. 1999, HarperCollins LB $15.89 (0-06-027617-7); paper $4.95 (0-06-446722-8). 40pp. Rabbit and friends enjoy a number of events in this concept book, which explains terms in sequencing such as *about, then,* and *when.* (Rev: BL 12/1/99; HBG 3/00; SLJ 9/99) [515]

230 Murphy, Stuart J. *Super Sand Castle Saturday* (1–3). Illus. by Julia Gorton. Series: MathStart. 1999, HarperCollins LB $15.89 (0-06-027613-4). The concept of measurement is introduced by three friends trying to determine who built the tallest sand castle with the longest moat and the longest wall. (Rev: HBG 10/99; SLJ 7/99)

231 *Opposites* (PS–1). Illus. by Sue Hendra. Series: Flip and Find. 1999, Candlewick $7.99 (0-7636-0894-7). Readers are asked to find the correct opposite of such words as big, slow, fat, rough, loud, and black, which are hidden under the flaps on the pages. (Rev: SLJ 12/99)

232 Patilla, Peter. *Fun with Patterns* (PS–1). Illus. by Brigitte McDonald. Series: Fun With. 1998, Millbrook LB $22.40 (0-7613-0960-8). 32pp. This clever learning game asks readers to match different objects with similar geometric patterns. (Rev: BL 3/15/99; HBG 10/99; SLJ 3/99) [510]

233 Patilla, Peter. *Patterns* (2–4). Illus. Series: Math Links. 1999, Heinemann LB $19.95 (1-57572-967-9). 32pp. Different patterns are introduced in this concept book that uses double-page spreads and is arranged by order of difficulty. (Rev: BL 2/1/00; SLJ 12/99) [510]

234 Paul, Ann W. *Hello Toes! Hello Feet!* (PS). Illus. by Nadine Bernard Westcott. 1998, DK $15.95 (0-7894-2481-9). An interactive picture book in which a girl introduces her hands and feet and describes all of the things they do. (Rev: BL 3/1/98; HBG 10/98; SLJ 3/98)

235 Penner, Lucille R. *Where's That Bone?* (PS–2). Illus. by Lynn Adams. Series: Math Matters. 2000, Kane paper $4.95 (1-57565-097-5). 32pp. A dog forgets where he has buried his bones so Jill draws him a map in this concept book about distance and maps. (Rev: SLJ 2/01)

236 Potter, Keith R., and Ken Fulk. *Shake, Rattle and Roll: An Action-Packed Verb Book* (PS–K). Illus. by Keith R. Potter and Jana Leo. Series: Doodlezoo. 1999, Chronicle $6.95 (0-8118-2178-1). A colorful board book that uses animal photos and computer-generated "doodle" animals to introduce such action verbs as *climb, eat,* and *dig.* Also use in this series *Those That Float, Those That Don't* (1999). (Rev: SLJ 10/99)

237 Potter, Keith R., and Ken Fulk. *This and That: A Book of Opposites* (PS–K). Illus. by Keith R. Potter and Jana Leo. 1999, Chronicle $6.95 (0-8118-2179-X). Animal photos and graphic images are used to teach common opposites in this simple board book. (Rev: SLJ 10/99)

238 Priddy, Roger. *Baby's Book of Nature* (PS). Illus. 1995, DK $9.95 (0-7894-0003-0). 21pp. Photographs are used to introduce various concepts in nature, such as color, shapes, and patterns. (Rev: BL 6/1–15/95) [508]

239 Rose, Emma. *Pumpkin Faces: A Glowing Book You Can Read in the Dark!* (PS–K). Illus. by Judith Moffatt. 1997, Scholastic $6.95 (0-590-13454-X). A simple concept book that uses the faces of Halloween jack-o'-lanterns to express a variety of emotions. (Rev: SLJ 11/97)

240 Scarry, Richard. *Richard Scarry's Lowly Worm Word Book* (PS). Illus. by author. 1981, Random $3.99 (0-394-84728-8). 28pp. A tiny book showing familiar objects belonging to Lowly Worm.

241 Schwartz, David M. *If You Hopped Like a Frog* (K–4). Illus. by James Warhola. 1999, Scholastic $15.95 (0-590-09857-8). 32pp. This picture book discusses the concepts of ratio and proportion, using animal facts to explore topics such as relative strength. (Rev: BCCB 12/99; BL 11/15/99; HBG 3/00; SLJ 11/99) [513.2]

242 Sendak, Maurice. *The Nutshell Library* (PS–3). Illus. by author. 1962, HarperCollins $15.95 (0-06-025500-5). Miniature volumes include an alphabet book, *Alligators All Around,* and a counting book, *One Was Johnny* (both 1962).

243 Serfozo, Mary. *What's What? A Guessing Game* (PS–K). Illus. by Keiko Narahashi. 1996, Simon & Schuster paper $15.00 (0-689-80653-1). 32pp. A concept book that explores various physical properties and their opposites, like soft and hard. (Rev: BCCB 10/96; BL 10/1/96I; SLJ 10/96*)

244 Shields, Carol D. *Day by Day a Week Goes Round* (PS–K). Illus. by True Kelley. 1998, Dutton $7.99 (0-525-45457-8). 20pp. Double-page spreads illustrate the days of the week through the activities they are associated with. (Rev: BL 12/15/98; HBG 3/99; SLJ 12/98)

245 Shields, Carol D. *Month by Month a Year Goes Round* (PS–K). Illus. by True Kelley. 1998, Dutton $7.99 (0-525-45458-6). 24pp. Seasonal activities are portrayed, and the passing of a year is explained, using two-page spreads, each devoted to two consecutive months. (Rev: BL 12/1/98; HBG 3/99; SLJ 12/98)

246 Simon, Francesca. *Calling All Toddlers* (PS–K). Illus. by Susan Winter. 1999, Orchard $15.95 (0-531-30120-6). 33pp. In 16 verses, children are introduced to colors, shapes, movement, humor, and play. (Rev: BCCB 2/99; BL 4/15/99; HBG 10/99; SLJ 6/99)

247 Siomades, Lorianne. *Kangaroo and Cricket* (PS–1). Illus. by author. 1999, Boyds Mills $10.95 (1-56397-780-X). Two different animals on every page reveal how they are similar; for example, both dogs and squirrels bury things. (Rev: HBG 3/00; SLJ 12/99)

248 Slate, Joseph. *Miss Bindergarten Celebrates the 100th Day of Kindergarten* (PS–1). Illus. by Ashley Wolff. 1998, Dutton $15.99 (0-525-46000-4). 32pp. Superteacher Miss Bindergarten asks her students to bring 100 things to class to celebrate the 100th day of kindergarten in this combination alphabet and counting book. (Rev: BL 10/15/98; HBG 3/99; SLJ 9/98)

249 Swinburne, Stephen R. *What's Opposite?* (PS–1). Illus. 2000, Boyds Mills $15.95 (1-56397-881-4). 32pp. Using handsome photographs, this book explores the world of common opposites. (Rev: BL 9/1/00; HBG 3/01; SLJ 10/00)

250 Szekeres, Cyndy. *I Love My Busy Book* (PS–1). Illus. 1997, Scholastic $12.95 (0-590-69195-3). 48pp. Concepts like colors, manners, and parts of the body are introduced in double-page spreads. (Rev: BCCB 3/97; BL 2/1/97; SLJ 4/97)

251 Thomas, Shelley M. *Somewhere Today: A Book of Peace* (PS–3). Illus. by Eric Futran. 1998, Whitman $14.95 (0-8075-7545-3). 24pp. A book in which children and their activities illustrate the concepts of peaceful living, sharing, helping, and joining together. (Rev: BL 4/1/98; HBG 10/98; SLJ 8/98)

252 Thompson, Margot. *Make a Change Opposites* (PS–2). Illus. 2000, Millbrook $8.95 (0-7613-1043-6). This pull-the-tab book illustrates opposites through the actions of various animals. (Rev: BL 12/1/00)

253 Tomczyk, Mary. *Shapes, Sizes and More Surprises!* (PS–1). Illus. by Loretta Braren. Series: Little Hands Early Learning Books. 1996, Williamson paper $12.95 (0-913589-95-0). 141pp. An activity book for youngsters filled with stories, puzzles, counting exercises, and games. (Rev: SLJ 10/96)

254 Van Fleet, Matthew. *One Yellow Lion* (PS). Illus. by author. 1992, Dial $9.99 (0-8037-1099-2). This book, with foldout pages and plenty of drawings of animals, presents the concepts of color and counting. (Rev: SLJ 9/92)

255 Walters, Virginia. *Are We There Yet, Daddy?* (PS–3). Illus. by S. D. Schindler. 1999, Viking $15.99 (0-670-87402-7). 32pp. Math and map skills are taught painlessly in this story about a boy, his father, and their dog on a car trip to Grandma's home 100 miles away. (Rev: BCCB 12/99; BL 9/15/99; HBG 3/00; SLJ 10/99)

256 Wildsmith, Brian. *What the Moon Saw* (PS–1). Illus. by author. 1978, Oxford paper $11.95 (0-19-272157-7). 32pp. The Sun shows the Moon many things that involve such basic concepts as numbers and weight.

257 Wilson-Max, Ken. *Wake Up, Sleep Tight* (PS–K). Illus. 1998, Scholastic $11.95 (0-590-76779-8). 16pp. Two simple board books in one — one about morning activities and the other about going to bed

— are unified by a cutout clock with movable hands. Readers can change the clock to the hours mentioned in each rhyme. (Rev: BL 11/1/98)

258 Wood, Douglas. *Making the World* (PS–2). Illus. by Yoshi Miyazaki and Hibiki Miyazaki. 1998, Simon & Schuster $16.00 (0-689-81358-9). 40pp. The concepts of change and of cause and effect are explored in this easy-to-read book that presents delicate watercolors and lyrical but simple prose. (Rev: BL 7/98; HBG 3/99; SLJ 8/98)

259 Ziefert, Harriet. *A Dozen Dozens* (PS–3). Illus. by Chris L. Demarest. Series: Math Easy-to-Read. 1998, Viking paper $3.99 (0-14-038819-2). The concept of dozens and half-dozens is explored in this happy picture-book easy reader. (Rev: HBG 10/98; SLJ 2/98)

COLORS

260 Baker, Alan. *White Rabbit's Color Book* (PS–K). Illus. 1994, Kingfisher $7.95 (1-85697-953-9). 24pp. A rabbit falls into different pots of paint in this book that identifies many colors. (Rev: BL 7/94)

261 Bown, Deni. *Color Fun* (PS). Illus. Series: Snapshot. 1995, DK $3.95 (0-7894-0230-0). 12pp. Colors are revealed by pulling tabs that open double-page spreads filled with objects of a particular color. (Rev: BL 1/1–15/96; SLJ 7/96) [701.85]

262 Bryant-Mole, Karen. *Blue* (PS–1). Illus. Series: Images. 1996, Silver Pr. LB $10.95 (0-382-39590-5); paper $4.95 (0-382-39626-X). 24pp. A concept book that focuses on a single color and a variety of objects. Also use *Texture* (1996). (Rev: SLJ 1/97)

263 Carle, Eric. *Hello, Red Fox* (K–3). Illus. 1998, Simon & Schuster $16.00 (0-689-81775-4). 32pp. The author invites readers to experience a simple story by employing the phenomenon whereby staring at a color and then at a blank white page reveals a complementary color as if by magic. (Rev: BCCB 7–8/98; BL 4/1/98; HBG 10/98; SLJ 7/98)

264 Deeter, Catherine. *Seymour Bleu* (K–4). Illus. by author. 1998, Simon & Schuster $16.00 (0-689-80137-8). While artist Seymour Bleu is looking for an inspiration, the reader is introduced to a multitude of colors and bits of information about famous artists and paintings. (Rev: HBG 3/99; SLJ 12/98)

265 Dodds, Dayle Ann. *The Color Box* (PS–1). Illus. by Giles Laroche. 1992, Little, Brown $14.95 (0-316-18820-4). 32pp. Alexander, a young monkey, opens doors and discovers a variety of colors. (Rev: BCCB 3/92; BL 5/1/92; SLJ 6/92)

266 Ehlert, Lois. *Color Farm* (PS–K). Illus. 1990, HarperCollins LB $15.89 (0-397-32441-3). 40pp. Various animals are pictured by using a number of different shapes and colors. (Rev: BL 11/15/90; HB 1–2/91; SLJ 11/90)

267 Ehlert, Lois. *Color Zoo* (PS–2). Illus. by author. 1989, HarperCollins LB $16.89 (0-397-32260-7). 32pp. How basic shapes can be combined to make familiar objects. (Rev: BL 5/15/89; SLJ 4/89)

268 Emberley, Rebecca. *My Colors/Mis Colores* (PS). 2000, Little, Brown $5.95 (0-316-23347-1). 20pp. A board book in English and Spanish introduces the basic colors. (Rev: BCCB 12/00*; HBG 3/01; SLJ 9/00)

269 Faulkner, Keith. *My Colors: Let's Learn About Colors* (PS). Illus. by Jonathan Lambert. 1995, Simon & Schuster $7.95 (0-671-89829-9). 22pp. In a series of double-page spreads, white pages are filled with colored objects when tabs are pulled in this book that introduces ten colors. (Rev: BL 6/1–15/95)

270 Godwin, Laura. *Little White Dog* (1–2). Illus. by Dan Yaccarino. 1998, Hyperion LB $15.49 (0-7868-2256-2). 32pp. Pattern-recognition skills are encouraged in this book in which various animals seem to disappear when placed on a field the same color as they are. (Rev: BCCB 7–8/98; BL 5/15/98; SLJ 6/98)

271 Goldsen, Louise. *Colors* (K–2). Illus. by P. M. Valet and Sylvaine Perols. 1991, Scholastic paper $12.95 (0-590-45236-3). Through the use of clear acetate sheets, various colors are introduced and identified. (Rev: SLJ 5/92) [535.5]

272 Hill, Eric. *Spot Looks at Colors* (PS). Illus. by author. 1986, Putnam $3.99 (0-399-21349-X). 14pp. Spot, the puppy, lures young readers into this basic concept board book. (Rev: BL 10/15/86; SLJ 10/86)

273 Hoban, Tana. *Colors Everywhere* (PS–K). Illus. 1995, Greenwillow $15.93 (0-688-12763-0). 32pp. A wordless picture book that identifies the colors found in each of the photographs used. (Rev: BCCB 3/95; BL 5/1/95; HB 7–8/95; SLJ 7/95)

274 Hoban, Tana. *Is It Red? Is It Yellow? Is It Blue?* (PS). Illus. 1978, Greenwillow $16.00 (0-688-84171-6); Morrow paper $4.95 (0-688-07034-5). 32pp. Without words, this picture book explains the concept of color.

275 Hoban, Tana. *Of Colors and Things* (PS–1). Illus. by author. 1989, Greenwillow $15.93 (0-688-07535-5). 24pp. Colors explained in picture-book style. (Rev: BCCB 3/89; BL 4/1/89; SLJ 4/89)

276 Hoban, Tana. *Red, Blue, Yellow Shoe* (PS). Illus. by author. 1986, Greenwillow paper $5.95 (0-688-06563-5). 12pp. A very simple introduction to color in a board book. (Rev: BCCB 1/87; BL 10/15/86; HB 11–12/86)

277 Hughes, Shirley. *Colors* (PS). Illus. by author. 1986, Lothrop paper $4.95 (0-688-04206-6). 24pp. Rhymes help to explain the concept of color. (Rev: BL 12/15/86; HB 1–2/87; SLJ 12/86)

278 Inkpen, Mick. *Kipper's Book of Colors* (PS). Illus. by author. 1999, Harcourt $4.95 (0-15-202285-6). This concept book about different colors features a lovable pup as a guide. (Rev: SLJ 10/99)

279 Jonas, Ann. *Color Dance* (PS–K). Illus. 1989, Greenwillow $15.93 (0-688-05991-0). 32pp. Dancers wave colored scarves and introduce various colors. (Rev: BL 8/89; SLJ 12/89)

280 Leuck, Laura. *Teeny, Tiny Mouse: A Book About Colors* (PS–1). Illus. by Pat Schories. 1998, BridgeWater $15.95 (0-8167-4547-1). A teeny, tiny mouse and her teeny, tiny child introduce the reader to colors as they list objects in their dollhouse. (Rev: HBG 10/98; SLJ 5/98)

281 Lionni, Leo. *Little Blue and Little Yellow* (PS–1). Illus. by author. 1959, Astor-Honor $13.00 (0-8392-3018-4). All the characters are blobs of color; an ingenious story intended to give the young child an awareness of color.

282 MacKinnon, Debbie. *Eye Spy Colors* (PS–K). Illus. by Anthea Sieveking. 1998, Charlesbridge $8.95 (0-88106-334-7). 24pp. Colors are introduced through a series of double-page spreads and peepholes. (Rev: BL 1/1–15/99; HBG 3/99)

283 Martin, Bill, Jr. *Brown Bear, Brown Bear, What Do You See?* (PS–1). Illus. by Eric Carle. 1992, Holt $15.95 (0-8050-1744-5). 32pp. This brightly illustrated easy-reader book first appeared in 1967 and is a fine introduction to colors. (Rev: BL 3/1/92; SLJ 5/92)

284 Miller, Margaret. *I Love Colors* (PS–1). Illus. Series: Look Baby! 1999, Simon & Schuster $4.99 (0-689-82356-8). 14pp. In this board book about colors, babies are shown wearing different-colored headgear. (Rev: BL 8/99; SLJ 8/99)

285 Murphy, Chuck. *Color Surprises* (PS–1). Illus. 1997, Simon & Schuster paper $13.95 (0-689-81504-2). Introduces colors using flaps of the same color as the animal underneath. (Rev: BL 12/15/97)

286 Pienkowski, Jan. *Colors* (K–1). Illus. by author. 1989, Simon & Schuster $3.50 (0-671-68134-6). 14pp. Ten objects are used as examples of colors.

287 Rockwell, Anne. *Mr. Panda's Painting* (PS–K). Illus. 1993, Macmillan LB $14.95 (0-02-777451-1). 32pp. Mr. Panda, a painter, brings a variety of colors back with him when he goes shopping in a paint store. (Rev: BL 11/1/93)

288 Serfozo, Mary. *Who Said Red?* (PS–K). Illus. by Narahashi Keiko. 1988, Macmillan paper $5.99 (0-689-71592-7). 32pp. A little boy is looking for his lost kite in this picture book about colors. (Rev: BL 9/1/88; SLJ 1/89)

289 Seuss, Dr. *My Many Colored Days* (PS). Illus. by Steve Johnson and Lou Fancher. 1996, Knopf LB $17.99 (0-679-97597-7). 32pp. Various moods are linked with colors in this rhyming picture book. (Rev: BL 11/1/96; SLJ 12/96)

290 Sharratt, Nick. *The Green Queen* (PS). Illus. by author. 1992, Candlewick $5.95 (1-56402-093-2). A green queen introduces the readers to colors in objects around her. (Rev: SLJ 11/92)

291 Siomades, Lorianne. *My Box of Color* (PS–1). Illus. by author. 1998, Boyds Mills $8.95 (1-56397-711-7). This book helps children explore their perceptions of color by presenting common objects in unusual colors and asking, for instance, whether a blue sun would be just as warm. (Rev: HBG 3/99; SLJ 11/98)

292 Westray, Kathleen. *A Color Sampler* (2–5). Illus. 1993, Ticknor $14.95 (0-395-65940-X). 32pp. This book uses objects found in classic quilts to illustrate and introduce various colors. (Rev: BL 7/93) [535.6]

293 Winograd, Deborah. *My Color Is Panda* (PS). Illus. by author. 1993, Simon & Schuster $13.00 (0-671-79152-4). 20pp. A panda introduces his world and a number of colors. (Rev: BL 8/93)

294 Yamaka, Sara. *The Gift of Driscoll Lipscomb* (1–3). Illus. by Joung Un Kim. 1995, Simon & Schuster paper $15.00 (0-02-793599-X). 32pp. Through gifts from an artist neighbor, a young girl learns the nature and value of colors. (Rev: BL 6/1–15/95; SLJ 8/95)

295 Yates, Irene. *All About Color* (PS–1). Illus. by Jill Newton. Series: All About. 1997, Benchmark LB $21.36 (0-7614-0514-3). 32pp. Each of the double-page spreads introduces a color, poses questions, and describes a simple activity or craft. (Rev: HBG 3/98; SLJ 4/98)

296 Yee, Patrick. *Rosie Rabbit's Colors* (PS). Illus. 1998, Simon & Schuster $3.99 (0-689-81842-4). 16pp. This is one of four small, square, very simple board books that introduce concepts. The others are *Rosie Rabbit's Shapes, Rosie Rabbit's Numbers* and *Rosie Rabbit's Opposites* (all 1998). (Rev: BL 2/1/98; SLJ 2/98)

PERCEPTION

297 Aruego, Jose, and Ariane Dewey. *We Hide, You Seek* (PS). Illus. by authors. 1979, Greenwillow $15.89 (0-688-84201-1); Morrow paper $4.95 (0-688-07815-X). 32pp. An almost wordless picture book in which a rhinoceros sets out to find his friends who are playing hide-and-seek with him.

298 Ashbe, Jeanne. *What's Inside* (PS). Illus. by author. Series: Curious Nell. 2000, Kane/Miller $9.95 (0-916291-97-9). This flap book explores the inside of things, such as a suitcase and a TV set — and examines three different stages of an unborn baby's development. (Rev: BCCB 6/00; HB 5–6/00; HBG 10/00; SLJ 5/00)

299 Axworthy, Anni. *Guess What I Am* (PS–1). Illus. Series: Peephole Books. 1998, Candlewick $7.99 (0-7636-0625-1). 28pp. One two-page spread offers clues concerning the identity of a particular animal and a peephole that reveals part of the animal. The following spread gives the full picture as well as some information. (Rev: BL 11/15/98; HBG 3/99; SLJ 4/99)

300 Axworthy, Anni. *Guess What I'll Be* (PS–1). Illus. Series: Peephole Books. 1998, Candlewick $7.99 (0-7636-0626-X). 28pp. After showing a young animal in an early stage of its development (e.g., a tadpole, chick, or caterpillar), readers are asked what it will be when it grows up. (Rev: BL 11/15/98; HBG 3/99; SLJ 4/99)

301 Ayres, Pam. *Guess What?* (PS–K). Illus. by Julie Lacome. 1994, Candlewick $3.99 (1-56402-346-X). 32pp. Readers guess objects in answer to rhymed questions. (Rev: BL 6/1/88; SLJ 7/88)

302 Baylor, Byrd. *The Other Way to Listen* (K–3). Illus. by Peter Parnall. 1978, Macmillan $16.95 (0-684-16017-X). 32pp. An old man teaches a young boy how to listen.

303 Becker, Bonny. *Tickly Prickly* (PS). Illus. by Shari Halpern. 1999, HarperFestival $9.95 (0-694-

01239-4). 24pp. Using paper cutouts as illustrations, this book explores the sense of touch by describing how various objects and animals feel. (Rev: BL 7/99; HBG 10/99; SLJ 8/99)

304 Burns, Kate. *Jump Like a Frog!* (PS–K). Illus. 1999, David & Charles $6.95 (1-899607-35-8). 12pp. Five picture puzzles are found in this flap book, which asks young readers to find hidden animals. Also use *Snap like a Crocodile*. (Rev: BL 9/15/99; SLJ 10/99)

305 Carrier, Lark. *There Was a Hill . . .* (PS–1). Illus. by author. 1991, Picture Book paper $15.95 (0-907234-70-4). 40pp. An attractive picture book with a guessing game woven into the irresistible pages. (Rev: BL 9/15/85; SLJ 10/85)

306 Ellwand, David. *Alfred's Camera* (K–2). Illus. 1998, Dutton $15.99 (0-525-45978-2). 32pp. This is an amusing puzzle book with a simple plot line and a series of photo collages that contain hidden items. (Rev: BL 11/1/98; HBG 3/99; SLJ 2/99)

307 Hoban, Tana. *I Read Signs* (PS–2). Illus. by author. 1983, Greenwillow LB $17.93 (0-688-02318-5); Morrow paper $4.95 (0-688-07331-X). 32pp. An introduction to some common signs and their meaning. Also use: *I Read Symbols* (1983).

308 Hoban, Tana. *Is It Rough? Is It Smooth? Is It Shiny?* (PS). Illus. by author. 1984, Greenwillow $17.95 (0-688-03823-9). 32pp. Textures are explored in a series of photographs.

309 Hoban, Tana. *Look Again!* (PS–2). Illus. by author. 1971, Macmillan $15.00 (0-02-744050-8). 40pp. A concept book in which photographs of objects appear in part, as a whole, and then as a part within a composition.

310 Maclay, Elise. *The Forest Has Eyes* (PS–2). Illus. by Bev Doolittle. 1998, Greenwich Workshop $16.95 (0-86713-055-5). 32pp. Each of these nature paintings has a subject camouflaged within it (e.g., a snow pattern on a mountain is actually an eagle). (Rev: BL 10/15/98; SLJ 11/98) [970]

311 McMillan, Bruce. *Mouse View: What the Class Pet Saw* (PS–3). Illus. 1993, Holiday LB $16.95 (0-8234-1008-0). 32pp. Familiar classroom sights are shown from a mouse's point of view. (Rev: BL 3/15/93*; SLJ 4/93)

312 Marshall, Janet. *Banana Moon* (PS–3). Illus. 1998, Greenwillow $12.95 (0-688-15768-8). 32pp. A picture book about perception in which objects are first viewed through a small circle on a black page. When readers turn the page and the whole picture is revealed, the shape becomes a different object. (Rev: BCCB 3/98; BL 5/15/98; HBG 10/98; SLJ 7/98)

313 Shaw, Charles. *It Looked Like Spilt Milk* (K–2). Illus. by author. 1947, HarperCollins LB $14.89 (0-06-025565-X); paper $5.95 (0-06-443159-2). 30pp. White material appears on each page, but its identity is not revealed until the end. Originally published in 1947.

314 Steiner, Joan. *Look-Alikes* (PS–3). Illus. 1998, Little, Brown $12.95 (0-316-81255-0). 32pp. Everyday objects like buttons, crackers, pencils, and bottles are used to make 11 dioramas of places — among them a railroad station, a general store, and a fancy hotel — in Look-Alike City. (Rev: BCCB 9/98; BL 10/15/98; HB 9–10/98; HBG 3/99; SLJ 9/98) [793.7]

315 Turner, Ann. *Angel Hide and Seek* (K–2). Illus. by Lois Ehlert. 1998, HarperCollins LB $14.89 (0-06-027086-1). 40pp. Winged angels peek out of paper collages, giving readers an opportunity to stretch their imaginations and find hidden patterns in the pictures. (Rev: BCCB 7–8/98; BL 5/15/98; HBG 10/98; SLJ 9/98)

316 West, Colin. *One Day in the Jungle* (PS–K). Illus. 1995, Candlewick $9.95 (1-56402-646-9). 24pp. The sounds made by various jungle animals get louder and louder as a sneezing fit progresses from a tiny butterfly to a huge elephant. (Rev: BL 1/1–15/96; SLJ 2/96)

317 Wood, A. J. *Hidden Pictures* (2–4). Illus. 1996, Millbrook LB $23.90 (1-56294-369-3). 40pp. A number of animals are hidden in a series of pictures that depict various habitats. (Rev: BL 4/15/96; SLJ 5/96) [591]

318 Yates, Irene. *All About Pattern* (PS–1). Illus. by Jill Newton. Series: All About. 1997, Benchmark LB $21.36 (0-7614-0517-8). 32pp. Teaches pattern perception via double-page spreads containing interactive questions and answers and simple activities or crafts. (Rev: HBG 3/98; SLJ 4/98)

SIZE AND SHAPE

319 Adler, David A. *Shape Up! Fun with Triangles and Other Polygons* (2–5). Illus. by Nancy Tobin. 1998, Holiday $15.95 (0-8234-1346-2). An introduction to shapes and angles, using household items such as pretzels, bread, and pencil and paper. (Rev: BCCB 9/98; HBG 10/98; SLJ 9/98)

320 Baker, Alan. *Brown Rabbit's Shape Book* (PS–K). Illus. 1994, Kingfisher $8.95 (1-85697-950-4). 24pp. A rabbit explores different shapes when he finds an assortment of balloons that he blows up. (Rev: BL 7/94)

321 Baranski, Joan Sullivan. *Round Is a Pancake* (PS–1). Illus. by Yu-Mei Han. 2001, Dutton $14.99 (0-525-46173-6). 32pp. Using an opulent medieval setting, this picture-book fantasy introduces various shapes to young readers, with a concentration on circles. (Rev: BL 2/1/01; SLJ 2/01)

322 Blackstone, Stella. *Bear in a Square* (PS–K). Illus. by Debbie Harter. 1998, Bearfoot $13.95 (1-901223-58-2). 32pp. This book is both an introduction to shapes and a counting book. (Rev: BL 10/1/98; SLJ 10/98)

323 Cohen, Caron L. *Where's the Fly?* (PS–3). Illus. by Nancy Barnet. 1996, Greenwillow $15.00 (0-688-14044-0). 32pp. Color pictures are used to explore the concepts of relative size and distance using, for example, closeups. (Rev: BCCB 4/96; BL 3/1/96; HB 7–8/96; SLJ 5/96)

324 Dotlich, Rebecca. *What Is a Triangle?* (PS). Illus. by Maria Ferrari. Series: Growing Tree. 2000, HarperFestival $9.95 (0-694-01392-7). 24pp. This simple reader introduces youngsters to a variety of objects — an ice cream cone and a slice of pizza, for example — that are shaped like triangles. (Rev: BL 12/15/00; HBG 3/01; SLJ 11/00) [516]

325 Dotlich, Rebecca. *What Is Round?* (PS). Illus. by Maria Ferrari. Series: Harper Growing Tree. 1999, HarperFestival $9.95 (0-694-01208-4). 24pp. The concept of roundness is explored in this picture book, which shows many objects that are round and others that are not. (Rev: BL 7/99; HBG 10/99; SLJ 4/99)

326 Dotlich, Rebecca. *What Is Square?* (PS). Photos by Maria Ferrari. Series: Harper Growing Tree. 1999, HarperFestival $9.95 (0-694-01207-6). All kinds of square objects are presented in this interactive concept book. (Rev: HBG 10/99; SLJ 8/99)

327 Emberley, Rebecca. *My Shapes/Mis Formas* (PS). 2000, Little, Brown $5.95 (0-316-23355-2). 20pp. Different shapes are introduced in English and Spanish in this board book. (Rev: BCCB 12/00*; HBG 3/01; SLJ 9/00)

328 Falwell, Cathryn. *Shape Space* (PS–2). Illus. 1992, Houghton $14.95 (0-395-61305-1). 32pp. A cut-paper girl plays and builds with colorful cut-paper shapes. (Rev: BL 10/15/92; HB 1–2/93; SLJ 10/92)

329 Florian, Douglas. *A Pig Is Big* (PS–K). Illus. 2000, Greenwillow $15.95 (0-688-17125-7). 24pp. Using animals as subjects, this book explores the concept of comparative size. (Rev: BCCB 12/00*; BL 9/15/00; HB 11–12/00; HBG 3/01; SLJ 10/00)

330 Fosberg, John. *Cookie Shapes* (PS). Illus. by author. 1997, Simon & Schuster $4.99 (0-689-81288-4). A board book that uses cookies to introduce ten different shapes. Also use *Ice Cream Colors* (1997). (Rev: SLJ 12/97)

331 Greene, Rhonda Gowler. *When a Line Bends . . . A Shape Begins* (PS–2). Illus. by James Kaczman. 1997, Houghton $16.00 (0-395-78606-1). In this concept book, ten different shapes — including a circle, square, triangle, diamond, and heart — are introduced. (Rev: HBG 3/98; SLJ 10/97)

332 Henkes, Kevin. *The Biggest Boy* (PS). Illus. by Nancy Tafuri. 1995, Greenwillow $14.93 (0-688-12830-0). 32pp. The concept of size is explored in this story of a youngster who dreams of being the biggest boy in the world. (Rev: BL 3/1/95; HB 5–6/95; SLJ 4/95)

333 Henkes, Kevin. *Circle Dogs* (PS–K). Illus. by Dan Yaccarino. 1998, Greenwillow LB $14.93 (0-688-15447-6). 32pp. Everyday circular shapes are explored in this picture book about a toddler and his two pet "circle" dachshunds. (Rev: BCCB 11/98; BL 9/15/98; HBG 3/99; SLJ 9/98)

334 Hoban, Tana. *Circles, Triangles, and Squares* (PS–2). Illus. by author. 1974, Macmillan LB $15.00 (0-02-744830-4). 32pp. A series of five photographs show the three most familiar geometric forms.

335 Hoban, Tana. *Cubes, Cones, Cylinders, and Spheres* (PS–K). Illus. 2000, Greenwillow LB $15.89 (0-688-15326-7). 24pp. Delightful pictures introduce different shapes in everyday objects. (Rev: BCCB 12/00; BL 10/15/00; HBG 3/01; SLJ 10/00) [513]

336 Hoban, Tana. *Is It Larger? Is It Smaller?* (PS–1). Illus. by author. 1997, Morrow paper $4.95 (0-688-15287-2). 32pp. Effective photographs and design illustrate the concepts of large and small, without words. (Rev: BCCB 4/85; BL 3/15/85; SLJ 4/85)

337 Hoban, Tana. *Over, Under and Through and Other Spacial Concepts* (K–2). Illus. by author. 1973, Macmillan LB $17.00 (0-02-744820-7). 32pp. Spacial concepts are conveyed through brief text and photographs.

338 Hoban, Tana. *Shapes, Shapes, Shapes* (PS–1). Illus. by author. 1986, Greenwillow $15.89 (0-688-05833-7). 32pp. Eleven shapes are sought in the color photos. (Rev: BCCB 4/86; BL 3/1/86; HB 5–6/86)

339 Hoban, Tana. *So Many Circles, So Many Squares* (PS–1). Illus. 1998, Greenwillow $15.00 (0-688-15165-5). 32pp. In this wordless concept book, the author explores different things that are round or square. (Rev: BL 3/1/98; HB 7–8/98; HBG 10/98; SLJ 3/98) [516]

340 Hutchins, Pat. *Shrinking Mouse* (PS–K). Illus. 1997, Greenwillow $14.93 (0-688-13962-0). 32pp. A clever exploration of space and perspective using woodland animals and birds. (Rev: BL 2/15/97; SLJ 4/97*)

341 Jenkins, Steve. *Big and Little* (PS–2). Illus. 1996, Houghton $14.95 (0-395-72664-6). 32pp. The concept of size is explored in this book that contrasts various animals. (Rev: BL 10/1/96; SLJ 10/96*)

342 Kalan, Robert. *Blue Sea* (K–3). Illus. by Donald Crews. 1979, Morrow paper $5.95 (0-688-11509-8). 24pp. Big fish and little fish in the sea convey the idea of size.

343 MacDonald, Suse. *Sea Shapes* (PS–K). Illus. 1994, Harcourt $13.95 (0-15-200027-5); paper $6.00 (0-15-201700-3). 32pp. Sea creatures and attractive collages are used to introduce a number of shapes. (Rev: BL 9/1/94; HB 11–12/94; SLJ 11/94)

344 MacKinnon, Debbie. *Eye Spy Shapes: A Peephole Book* (PS). Photos by Anthea Sieveking. 2000, Charlesbridge $8.95 (0-88106-135-2). In this interactive book, various shapes are introduced through a peephole guessing game. (Rev: SLJ 9/00)

345 Murphy, Chuck. *Bow Wow: A Pop-Up Book of Shapes* (PS–3). Illus. 1999, Simon $12.95 (0-689-82265-0). Each page features a particular shape, and when the shape is opened it reveals a pop-up surprise. (Rev: BCCB 9/99; BL 12/15/99)

346 Murphy, Stuart J. *The Best Bug Parade* (PS–1). Illus. by Holly Keller. Series: MathStart. 1996, HarperCollins LB $15.89 (0-06-025872-1); paper $4.95 (0-06-446700-7). 33pp. A parade of bugs is used to introduce the concept of size. (Rev: BCCB 5/96; SLJ 6/96)

347 Murphy, Stuart J. *Circus Shapes* (PS). Illus. by Edward Miller. Series: MathStart. 1998, HarperCollins LB $15.89 (0-06-027437-9). 40pp. Objects associated with the circus are pictured in this concept book that introduces various shapes. (Rev: BL 3/1/98; HBG 10/98; SLJ 4/98)

348 Murphy, Stuart J. *Let's Fly a Kite* (PS–3). Illus. by Brian Floca. 2000, HarperCollins LB $15.89 (0-06-028035-2); paper $4.95 (0-06-446737-6). 40pp. Geometry and symmetry in everyday life are the concepts explored in this picture book about two quarreling siblings. (Rev: BL 9/15/00; HBG 3/01; SLJ 11/00)

349 Myller, Rolf. *How Big Is a Foot?* (K–2). Illus. by author. 1991, Dell paper $3.99 (0-440-40495-9). The problem of relative sizes, humorously and imaginatively described.

350 Nathan, Cheryl, and Lisa McCourt. *The Long and Short of It* (K–2). Illus. by Cheryl Nathan. 1998, BridgeWater $15.95 (0-8167-4545-5). This book not only explores the concept of size but also introduces different animals to make valid comparisons. (Rev: HBG 10/98; SLJ 5/98)

351 Onyefulu, Ifeoma. *A Triangle for Adaora: An African Book of Shapes* (PS–3). Illus. 2000, Dutton $16.99 (0-525-46382-8). 32pp. A little girl, Adaora, goes through her African village identifying different shapes. (Rev: BCCB 11/00; BL 3/1/01; HBG 3/01; SLJ 12/00)

352 Patilla, Peter. *Fun with Shapes* (PS–1). Series: Fun With. 1998, Millbrook LB $22.40 (0-7613-0958-6). 32pp. Using a series of games and puzzles and colorful drawings, this book introduces a variety of shapes. (Rev: BL 3/15/99; HBG 10/99; SLJ 3/99)

353 Patilla, Peter. *Fun with Sizes* (PS–1). Series: Fun With. 1998, Millbrook LB $22.40 (0-7613-0959-4). 32pp. Concepts involving sizes (e.g., big and little) are introduced, using a series of activities, games, and puzzles. (Rev: BL 3/15/99; HBG 10/99)

354 Patilla, Peter. *Measuring* (2–4). Illus. Series: Math Links. 1999, Heinemann LB $19.95 (1-57572-965-2). 32pp. A clear, attractive presentation of concepts involved in measuring that uses a series of double-page spreads. (Rev: BL 2/1/00) [530.8]

355 Rotner, Shelley, and Richard Olivo. *Close, Closer, Closest* (PS–1). Illus. 1997, Simon & Schuster $15.00 (0-689-80762-7). 40pp. This concept book explores perspective and scale in a series of pictures that show objects at different distances. (Rev: BCCB 4/97; BL 4/1/97; HB 5–6/97; SLJ 7/97) [152.14]

356 Salzmann, Mary Elizabeth. *Circles* (PS–1). Series: What Shape Is It? 2000, ABDO LB $12.95 (1-57765-163-4). 24pp. A slim book that introduces circles and various objects that are circular in shape. Also use *Rectangles, Stars, Triangles* (all 2000). (Rev: HBG 10/00; SLJ 7/00)

357 Schlein, Miriam. *Round and Square* (PS–2). Illus. by Linda Bronson. 1999, Mondo $15.95 (1-57255-719-2). 32pp. With a rhyming text, this colorful picture book introduces the concepts of round and square. (Rev: BL 1/1–15/00)

358 *Shapes Galore* (PS). Illus. Series: Snapshot. 1995, DK $3.95 (0-7894-0231-9). 12pp. Preschoolers learn about shapes like triangles and circles through everyday objects, such as sailboats and a sandwich. (Rev: BL 1/1–15/96; SLJ 7/96) [561.15]

359 Steiner, Joan. *Look-Alikes Jr.* (K–4). Illus. by Thomas Lindley. 1999, Little, Brown $12.95 (0-316-81307-9). 32pp. Scenes are constructed from various foods in this imaginative book that shows different ways of seeing. (Rev: BCCB 10/99; BL 12/1/99; HB 9–10/99; HBG 3/00; SLJ 9/99) [793.73]

360 Swinburne, Stephen R. *Lots and Lots of Zebra Stripes: Patterns in Nature* (PS–2). Illus. 1998, Boyds Mills $15.95 (1-56397-707-9). 32pp. Using wonderful photos, this book explores repeating patterns of lines and shapes and shows how they can be found in a number of objects great and small. (Rev: BL 9/15/98; HBG 3/99; SLJ 12/98) [778.9]

361 Thompson, Margot. *Make a Change Shapes* (PS–2). Illus. 2000, Millbrook $8.95 (0-7613-1044-4). Different shapes are introduced in this interactive book that uses tabs and pop-ups. (Rev: BL 12/1/00)

362 Thong, Roseanne. *Round Is a Mooncake* (PS–1). Illus. by Grace Lin. 2000, Chronicle $13.95 (0-8118-2676-7). 40pp. An Asian American girl looks at shapes she sees in her neighborhood in this book that explores circles, squares, and rectangles. (Rev: BL 12/1/00; HBG 3/01; SLJ 8/00)

363 Wegman, William. *Triangle, Square, Circle* (PS–K). Illus. 1995, Hyperion $6.95 (0-7868-0104-2). 16pp. Shapes are introduced in a series of photographs involving dogs. (Rev: BCCB 7–8/95; BL 5/15/95; SLJ 8/95)

364 Wells, Robert E. *Is a Blue Whale the Biggest Thing There Is?* (PS–3). Illus. 1993, Albert Whitman LB $13.95 (0-8075-3655-5); paper $6.95 (0-8075-3656-3). 32pp. The concept of size is explored, first by comparing an elephant to the huge blue whale and ending with our galaxy being compared to the universe. (Rev: BCCB 11/93; BL 12/15/93; SLJ 1/94)

365 Wells, Robert E. *What's Smaller Than a Pygmy Shrew?* (1–4). Illus. 1995, Albert Whitman LB $13.95 (0-8075-8837-7); paper $6.95 (0-8075-8838-5). 32pp. The concept of smallness is explored using examples from nature. (Rev: BL 8/95; SLJ 5/95)

Counting and Number Books

366 Adler, David A. *How Tall How Short How Far Away* (K–3). Illus. by Nancy Tobin. 1999, Holiday $15.95 (0-8234-1375-6). Methods of measurement such as length, height, and distance are introduced in this attractive concept book. (Rev: BCCB 9/99; BL 4/1/99; HB 3–4/99; HBG 10/99; SLJ 4/99) [530.8]

367 Alda, Arlene. *Arlene Alda's 1 2 3* (PS–2). Illus. 1998, Tricycle Pr. $12.95 (1-883672-71-6). 24pp. Photographs of shapes that look like numbers, such as a 3 found in the curl of a banana peel, illustrate the numbers 1 to 10 and back again. (Rev: BL 11/1/98; HB 11–12/98; HBG 3/99; SLJ 12/98)

368 Anderson, Lena. *Tea for Ten* (PS). Trans. from Swedish by Elisabeth Kallick Dyssegaard. Illus. by author. 2000, R&S $14.00 (91-29-64557-3). This rhyming counting book features a number of delightful animals including Hedgehog, Duck,

Teddy, Frog, Pig, and Elephant. (Rev: HBG 10/00; SLJ 5/00)

369 Anno, Mitsumasa. *Anno's Counting Book: An Adventure in Imagination* (PS–K). Illus. by author. 1977, HarperCollins LB $16.89 (0-690-01288-8); paper $6.95 (0-06-443123-1). 32pp. An appealing book on numbers in which the same landscapes are used throughout; houses, birds, trees, and people are added as the seasons progress.

370 Anno, Mitsumasa. *Anno's Magic Seeds* (K–3). Illus. 1995, Putnam $19.99 (0-399-22538-2). 42pp. An arithmetic allegory about the beginnings of agriculture that involves magic seeds given to Jack by a wizard. (Rev: BCCB 4/95; BL 4/1/95*; HB 9–10/95; SLJ 9/95)

371 Appelt, Kathi. *Bat Jamboree* (PS–2). Illus. by Melissa Sweet. 1996, Morrow $15.93 (0-688-13883-7). A delightful counting book that focuses on the annual Bat Jamboree staged by some enterprising bats. (Rev: SLJ 9/96)

372 Appelt, Kathi. *Bats on Parade* (K–3). Illus. by Melissa Sweet. 1999, Morrow LB $15.93 (0-688-15666-5). 32pp. Basic multiplication is introduced in this story about a bat parade told with rhymes and peppy illustrations. (Rev: BL 4/1/99; HBG 10/99; SLJ 6/99)

373 Appelt, Kathi. *Toddler Two-Step* (PS). Illus. by Ward Schumaker. 2000, HarperFestival $9.95 (0-694-01244-0). A simple counting book that uses pictures of toddlers to count to ten and back again. (Rev: HBG 10/00; SLJ 7/00)

374 Aylesworth, Jim. *One Crow: A Counting Rhyme* (PS–K). Illus. by Ruth Young. 1990, HarperCollins paper $5.95 (0-06-443242-4). 32pp. Farm life introduces numbers. (Rev: BL 6/15/88; SLJ 12/88)

375 Baker, Keith. *Big Fat Hen* (PS–1). Illus. 1994, Harcourt $15.00 (0-15-292869-3). 32pp. A counting book that uses the rhyme "One, two, buckle my shoe" as a basis. (Rev: BL 4/1/94; SLJ 4/94)

376 Baker, Keith. *Quack and Count* (PS–1). Illus. 1999, Harcourt $14.00 (0-15-292858-8). 24pp. This book shows how to have fun with the number seven while counting ducks in various combinations to reach that number. (Rev: BL 10/15/99; HBG 3/00; SLJ 11/99)

377 Bang, Molly. *Ten, Nine, Eight* (PS–1). Illus. by author. 1983, Greenwillow $15.89 (0-688-00907-7); Morrow paper $5.95 (0-688-10480-0). 24pp. A counting-down book (from ten to one) involving an African American child going to bed. (Rev: BL 11/15/98)

378 Barrett, Judith. *I Knew Two Who Said Moo* (PS–1). Illus. by Daniel Moreton. 2000, Simon & Schuster $16.00 (0-689-82104-2). 32pp. Numbers from one to ten are introduced on double-page spreads with witty animal-oriented illustrations that entertain as well as instruct. (Rev: BCCB 7–8/00; BL 2/1/01; SLJ 10/00)

379 Bassede, Francine. *George's Store at the Shore* (PS). Illus. 1998, Orchard paper $14.95 (0-531-30083-8). 32pp. In this delightful counting book, George the duck and Mary the cat go to the beach. (Rev: BL 2/15/98; HBG 10/98; SLJ 4/98)

380 Beaton, Clare. *One Moose, Twenty Mice* (PS–1). Illus. 1999, Barefoot $14.95 (1-902283-37-6). 32pp. A counting book containing different animals from one to 20, but posing the question "Where's the cat?" (Rev: BCCB 7–8/99; BL 5/15/99; SLJ 6/99)

381 Behrman, Carol H. *The Ding Dong Clock* (PS–K). Illus. by Hideko Takahashi. 1999, Holt $12.95 (0-8050-5804-4). In this counting book the grandfather clock marks the hours from 1:00 A.M. to 1:00 P.M. in a house where all sorts of activities are taking place. (Rev: HBG 10/99; SLJ 6/99)

382 Bender, Robert. *The A to Z Beastly Jamboree* (PS–2). Illus. by author. 1996, Lodestar $15.99 (0-525-67520-5). An animal ABC that can also serve as a counting book because the number of animals changes with each letter. (Rev: SLJ 7/96)

383 Bennett, David. *One Cow Moo Moo!* (PS–2). Illus. by Andy Cooke. 1990, Holt $16.95 (0-8050-1416-0). In this cumulative story about farm animals and their sounds, counting skills are presented. (Rev: SLJ 12/90)

384 Blackstone, Stella. *Grandma Went to Market: A Round-the-World Counting Rhyme* (PS–2). Illus. by Bernard Lodge. 1996, Houghton $13.95 (0-395-74045-2). 32pp. In this counting rhyme, Grandma goes on a global shopping spree. (Rev: BL 2/1/96; SLJ 4/96)

385 Bond, Michael. *Paddington's 1, 2, 3* (PS–2). Illus. by John Lobban. Series: Paddington. 1991, Viking $11.99 (0-670-84103-X). 32pp. The beloved bear introduces very young children to the world of counting. (Rev: BL 12/15/91; SLJ 2/92)

386 Bowen, Betsy. *Gathering: A Northwoods Counting Book* (K–4). Illus. by author. 1999, Houghton $16.00 (0-395-98133-6); paper $5.95 (0-395-98134-4). This counting book shows preparations taken in the North for a long, hard winter, starting in the spring with planting a garden. (Rev: HBG 3/00; SLJ 9/99)

387 Bown, Deni. *Let's Count* (PS). Illus. Series: Snapshot. 1995, DK $3.95 (0-7894-0232-7). 12pp. Using photos of favorite animals, food, and toys, children learn to count from one to ten. Also use *Shapes Galore* (1995). (Rev: BL 1/1–15/96; SLJ 7/96) [513.2]

388 Brooks, Alan. *Frogs Jump: A Counting Book* (PS–1). Illus. by Steven Kellogg. 1996, Scholastic $15.95 (0-590-45528-1). 48pp. Madcap animals introduce basic numbers through unusual activities. (Rev: BL 10/15/96; SLJ 10/96)

389 Brooks, Bruce. *NBA by the Numbers* (K–3). Illus. 1997, Scholastic $10.95 (0-590-97578-1). 32pp. This book uses basketball terms to introduce the numbers 1–10, 20, 30, 40, and 50. (Rev: BL 3/1/97)

390 Brown, Paula. *Moon Jump: A Cowntdown* (PS–1). Illus. 1996, Puffin paper $4.99 (0-140-54454-2). 32pp. A group of cows enter a contest to see which one can jump over the moon; also can be used as a counting book. (Rev: BCCB 3/93; BL 1/1/93)

391 Brusca, Maria C., and Tona Wilson. *Three Friends: A Counting Book/Tres Amigos: Un Cuento* *para Contar* (PS–2). Illus. by Maria C. Brusca. 1995, Holt $15.95 (0-8050-3707-1). 32pp. Learning to count from one to ten in Spanish and English through watching the actions of a cowboy, a cowgirl, and a horse. (Rev: BL 11/15/95; SLJ 12/95)

392 Burns, Marilyn. *How Many Feet? How Many Tails? A Book of Math Riddles* (1–2). Illus. by Lynn Adams. 1996, Scholastic paper $3.99 (0-590-67360-2). 32pp. During a walk with Grandpa, a child learns about numbers in this easy-to-read book. (Rev: BL 2/1/97)

393 Burton, Katherine. *One Gray Mouse* (PS). Illus. by Kim Fernandes. 1997, Kids Can $9.95 (1-55074-225-6). 24pp. Different numbers of animals are presented in this pleasant picture book that teaches the concepts of counting and colors. (Rev: BL 11/15/97; SLJ 12/97) [513.2]

394 Butler, John. *While You Were Sleeping* (PS). Illus. 1999, Peachtree $15.95 (1-56145-211-4). 32pp. In this simple counting book a mother describes events that occurred while her child was asleep — such as the two mice that made a nest and the three bears that played chase. (Rev: BL 12/1/99; HBG 3/00; SLJ 12/99)

395 Cabrera, Jane. *Over in the Meadow* (PS). Illus. 2000, Holiday $16.95 (0-8234-1490-6). 32pp. Readers learn numbers while naming animals and copying their actions in this fresh new treatment of the traditional counting song. (Rev: BCCB 5/00; BL 2/1/00; HBG 10/00; SLJ 4/00) [513.2]

396 Carle, Eric. *1, 2, 3 to the Zoo* (PS–K). Illus. by author. 1968, Putnam $16.99 (0-399-61172-X); paper $7.95 (0-399-21970-6). 34pp. A counting book illustrated with pictures of animals in a zoo train. Originally published in 1968.

397 Carle, Eric. *Roosters Off to See the World* (PS–K). Illus. by author. 1991, Picture Book $16.95 (0-88708-042-1). 28pp. In this counting book originally published in 1972, a rooster gathers together a group of animals to explore the world. Addition and subtraction are also introduced.

398 Carlstrom, Nancy White. *Let's Count It Out, Jesse Bear* (PS–1). Illus. by Bruce Degen. 1996, Simon & Schuster paper $15.00 (0-689-80478-4). 28pp. In rhyming couplets, the numbers one to 20 are introduced. (Rev: BCCB 9/96; BL 9/15/96; SLJ 9/96)

399 Cato, Sheila. *Addition* (1–4). Illus. by Sami Sweeten. Series: A Question of Math Book. 1999, Carolrhoda LB $18.95 (1-57505-320-9). 32pp. Using cartoon characters and one addition problem per double-page spread, this book demonstrates the basic processes of addition. Also use *Subtraction* and *Counting and Numbers* (both 1999). (Rev: HBG 3/00; SLJ 11/99)

400 Cato, Sheila. *Division* (1–4). Illus. by Sami Sweeten. Series: A Question of Math Book. 1999, Carolrhoda LB $18.95 (1-57505-319-5). 32pp. Using a series of problems followed by clear answers and explanations, the principles of division are covered. Also use *Multiplication* (1999). (Rev: HBG 3/00; SLJ 11/99)

401 Chandra, Deborah. *Miss Mabel's Table* (PS–2). Illus. by Max Grover. 1994, Harcourt $14.95 (0-15-276712-6). 32pp. A counting book about Miss Mabel, her restaurant, and the food she serves. (Rev: BCCB 4/94; BL 3/15/94; SLJ 6/94)

402 Charles, Faustin. *A Caribbean Counting Book* (K–3). Illus. by Roberta Arenson. 1996, Houghton $13.95 (0-395-77944-8). 32pp. Using Caribbean settings, this colorful counting book uses 12 rhymes from nine islands. (Rev: BCCB 5/96; BL 4/15/96; SLJ 6/96)

403 Cheng, Andrea. *Grandfather Counts* (PS–3). Illus. by Ange Zhang. 2000, Lee & Low $15.95 (1-58430-010-8). 32pp. In this unusual counting book, Helen, a little Chinese-American girl, and her grandfather count the cars on a passing train in both English and Chinese. (Rev: BL 12/15/00; HBG 3/01; SLJ 11/00)

404 Chorao, Kay. *Number One Number Fun* (PS–1). Illus. 1995, Holiday LB $15.95 (0-8234-1142-7). 32pp. Simple arithmetic is highlighted through a series of clever rhymes involving addition and subtraction. (Rev: BCCB 2/95; BL 2/15/95; SLJ 3/95)

405 Christelow, Eileen, reteller. *Five Little Monkeys Jumping on the Bed* (PS–K). Illus. by Eileen Christelow. 1989, Ticknor $15.00 (0-89919-769-8); paper $5.95 (0-395-55701-1). An exuberant rendition of the favorite nursery rhyme. (Rev: BL 6/1/89)

406 Christelow, Eileen. *Five Little Monkeys Sitting in a Tree* (PS–K). Illus. 1991, Houghton $15.00 (0-395-54434-3). 32pp. The numbers one through five are taught through the antics of five little monkeys. A sequel is: *Don't Wake Up Mama!* (1992). (Rev: BL 5/15/91; SLJ 8/91)

407 Cleveland, David. *The April Rabbits* (PS–1). Illus. by Nurit Karlin. 1986, Scholastic paper $4.99 (0-590-42369-X). 32pp. The days of the month and a group of rabbits are used in this counting book. Reissue of a 1978 edition.

408 Coats, Laura J. *Ten Little Animals* (PS–1). Illus. 1990, Macmillan LB $14.00 (0-02-719054-4). 32pp. A young boy's bedtime is disturbed by his ten rollicking stuffed animals. (Rev: BL 4/15/90; HB 3–4/90; SLJ 9/90)

409 Coats, Lucy. *One Smiling Sister* (PS). Illus. by Emily Bolam. Series: Toddler Storybook. 2000, DK paper $5.95 (0-7894-5622-2). 24pp. In this short, simple story, the numbers one to ten are introduced through a preschooler's day at home and in day care. (Rev: SLJ 10/00)

410 Coleman, Michael. *One, Two, Three, Oops!* (PS–K). Illus. by Gwyneth Williamson. 1999, Little Tiger $14.95 (1-888444-45-2). 32pp. When Mr. Rabbit begins to count his children, he has to work out which ones have been counted and which haven't. (Rev: BL 1/1–15/99; HBG 10/99; SLJ 3/99)

411 *Counting Book* (PS–1). Illus. by Dave King. 1998, DK $12.95 (0-7894-3448-2). 30pp. This counting book employs a very large format and bright photographs of groups of familiar objects to illustrate numbers one to 20, then it counts by tens to 100, ending with a view of 1,000 objects. (Rev: BL 11/1/98; HBG 3/99)

412 Coxe, Molly. *6 Sticks* (PS–1). Illus. by author. Series: Early Step into Reading + Math. 1999, Random LB $11.99 (0-679-98689-8); paper $3.99 (0-679-88689-3). 31pp. Using six popsicle sticks, two young mice create different number combinations in this easy math book. (Rev: HBG 10/99; SLJ 8/99)

413 Crews, Donald. *Ten Black Dots* (PS–K). Illus. by author. 1986, Greenwillow $15.89 (0-688-06068-4). 32pp. Dots form an integral part of this counting book, originally published in 1968, such as "five dots make buttons on a coat." (Rev: BL 3/1/86; SLJ 5/86)

414 Crowther, Robert. *My Pop-Up Surprise 123* (PS–K). Illus. by author. 1997, Orchard $16.95 (0-531-30039-0). A simple counting book using easily manipulated flaps and pull tabs. (Rev: SLJ 8/97)

415 Cuyler, Margery. *100th Day Worries* (K–2). Illus. by Arthur Howard. 2000, Simon & Schuster $16.00 (0-689-82979-5). 32pp. In this counting book, first-grader Jessica is asked to bring 100 objects to celebrate the 100th day of school. (Rev: BCCB 2/00; BL 11/1/99; HBG 10/00; SLJ 1/00)

416 De Regniers, Beatrice S. *So Many Cats!* (PS–1). Illus. by Ellen Weiss. 1985, Houghton paper $6.95 (0-89919-700-0). 32pp. One by one, new cats arrive at the narrator's house, until there are 12. (Rev: BL 1/1/86; HB 11–12/85; SLJ 1/86)

417 deRubertis, Barbara. *A Collection for Kate* (1–2). Illus. by Gioia Fiammenghi. Series: Math Matters. 1999, Kane paper $4.95 (1-57565-089-4). 32pp. In this easy reader, Kate adds up her classmates' collections for a "collection week" at school and discovers that, when she combines her own small collections, she isn't far behind them after all. (Rev: BL 12/1/99; SLJ 1/00)

418 deRubertis, Barbara. *Count on Pablo* (1–2). Illus. by Rebecca Thornburgh. Series: Math Matters. 1999, Kane paper $4.95 (1-57565-090-8). 32pp. In this easy reader, a boy helps his grandmother gather, count, group, and package vegetables for market. (Rev: BL 12/1/99; SLJ 1/00)

419 deRubertis, Barbara. *Lulu's Lemonade* (1–3). Illus. by Paige Billin-Frye. Series: Math Matters. 2000, Kane paper $4.95 (1-57565-093-2). 32pp. In this easy-reader, Mattie and Martin learn measurements like teaspoons, cups, pints, etc., as they prepare a gallon of lemonade. (Rev: SLJ 6/00)

420 Dodd, Lynley. *Sniff-Snuff-Snap!* (K–2). Illus. by author. Series: Gold Star First Reader. 2000, Gareth Stevens LB $15.95 (0-8368-2677-9). 31pp. A beginning reader about a bossy warthog that is also a counting book. (Rev: SLJ 3/01)

421 Dodds, Dayle Ann. *The Great Divide: A Mathematical Marathon* (1–4). Illus. by Tracy Mitchell. 1999, Candlewick $15.99 (0-7636-0442-9). Using 80 contestants in a race, this book explores the principle of division as many of the participants are gradually eliminated. (Rev: HBG 3/00; SLJ 11/99)

422 Dorros, Arthur. *Ten Go Tango* (PS–1). Illus. by Emily Arnold McCully. 2000, HarperCollins LB $15.89 (0-06-027691-6). 40pp. Assorted animals dance across the pages in this zany counting book that also teaches the basic steps for ten different dances. (Rev: BL 4/15/00; HBG 10/00; SLJ 5/00)

423 Duke, Kate. *One Guinea Pig Is Not Enough* (PS–1). Illus. 1998, Dutton $15.99 (0-525-45918-9). 48pp. A group of guinea pigs enjoy different zany activities in this counting book, which also introduces addition. (Rev: BCCB 3/98; BL 2/1/98; HBG 10/98; SLJ 3/98)

424 Duke, Kate. *Twenty Is Too Many* (PS–2). Illus. 2000, Dutton $15.99 (0-525-42026-6). 48pp. The concept of subtraction is painlessly introduced using a shipload of 20 guinea pigs. (Rev: BL 7/00; HBG 3/01; SLJ 8/00)

425 Dunbar, Joyce. *Ten Little Mice* (PS–1). Illus. by Maria Majewska. 1990, Harcourt $15.00 (0-15-200601-X). 24pp. Ten frolicking mice depart, one by one, to their cozy nest. (Rev: BL 4/15/90)

426 Edens, Cooper. *How Many Bears?* (1–3). Illus. by Marjett Schille. 1994, Atheneum $14.95 (0-689-31923-1). A clever math problem is solved by studying the answer to the question "How many bears does it take to run the bakery in Little Animal Town?" (Rev: SLJ 12/94)

427 Edwards, Pamela Duncan. *Roar! A Noisy Counting Book* (PS–2). Illus. by Henry Cole. 2000, HarperCollins LB $15.89 (0-06-028385-8). 32pp. A boisterous counting book involving animals, a jungle habitat, and lots of lions roaring. (Rev: BL 8/00; HBG 10/00; SLJ 6/00)

428 Ehlert, Lois. *Fish Eyes: A Book You Can Count On* (PS–K). Illus. 1990, Harcourt $14.95 (0-15-228050-2). 32pp. Compelling color and design introduce this counting book. (Rev: BL 3/1/90*; SLJ 5/90)

429 Emberley, Rebecca. *My Numbers/Mis Numeros* (PS). 2000, Little, Brown $5.95 (0-316-23350-1). 20pp. This counting board book introduces the numbers in both English and Spanish. (Rev: BCCB 12/00*; HBG 3/01; SLJ 9/00)

430 Enderle, Judith R., and Stephanie G. Tessler. *Where Are You, Little Zack?* (PS–1). Illus. by Brian Floca. 1997, Houghton $14.95 (0-395-73092-9). A counting book that involves four duck brothers and their adventures in New York City. (Rev: SLJ 4/97)

431 Ernst, Lisa Campbell. *Up to Ten and Down Again* (PS–K). Illus. by author. 1995, Morrow paper $4.95 (0-688-14391-1). 32pp. Beginning with "one duck is swimming," this simple counting book teaches numbers and tells a story. (Rev: BCCB 3/86; BL 3/1/86; SLJ 8/86)

432 Evans, Lezlie. *Can You Count Ten Toes? Count to 10 in 10 Different Languages* (PS–3). Illus. by Denis Roche. 1999, Houghton $15.00 (0-395-90499-4). 32pp. Using double-page spreads, children from several countries count different objects from one to ten in their native language. (Rev: BL 3/15/99; HBG 10/99; SLJ 6/99) [513.2]

433 Falwell, Cathryn. *Feast for 10* (PS–K). Illus. 1993, Houghton $15.00 (0-395-62037-6). 32pp. Using the common experience of shopping and preparing dinner, this book, which features an African American family, teaches youngsters the numbers from one to ten. (Rev: BCCB 6/93; BL 6/1–15/93; SLJ 6/93)

434 Flather, Lisa. *Ten Silly Dogs: A Countdown Story* (PS–K). Illus. 1999, Orchard $15.95 (0-531-30192-3). 32pp. Counting down from ten to one, this tale presents a number of dogs in various shapes and colors that one by one disappear from the action. (Rev: BL 9/15/99; HBG 3/00; SLJ 11/99)

435 Fleming, Denise. *Count!* (PS–K). Illus. by author. 1992, Holt $16.95 (0-8050-1595-7). Brightly colored animals and birds are used to introduce basic numbers. (Rev: SLJ 3/92)

436 French, Vivian. *One Ballerina Two* (PS–K). Illus. by Jan Ormerod. 1991, Lothrop $13.95 (0-688-10333-2). 32pp. The focus is on ballet in this simple counting book. (Rev: BCCB 12/91; BL 12/1/91; SLJ 12/91)

437 Freymann, Saxton, and Joost Elffers. *One Lonely Sea Horse* (PS–2). Illus. 2000, Scholastic $15.99 (0-439-11014-9). 32pp. Using various fruits and vegetables, photographs create a sea world of underwater creatures in this innovative counting book. (Rev: BCCB 7–8/00; BL 5/1/00; HBG 3/01; SLJ 7/00)

438 Friedman, Aileen. *The King's Commissioners* (K–2). Illus. by Susan Guevara. 1995, Scholastic $14.95 (0-590-48989-5). 40pp. In this sophisticated counting book, a king decides to take an inventory of his employees. (Rev: BCCB 2/95; BL 2/15/95; SLJ 3/95)

439 Fuchshuber, Annegert. *Two Peas in a Pod* (PS–1). Illus. 1998, Millbrook LB $20.40 (0-7613-0410-X); paper $14.95 (0-7613-0339-1). 32pp. Multiple births in the animal kingdom (e.g., Mother Mole has four children; Mama Owl has five) are used to introduce numbers in this unique counting book. (Rev: BL 7/98; HBG 10/98)

440 Galdone, Paul. *Over in the Meadow: An Old Nursery Counting Rhyme* (PS–K). Illus. by author. 1989, Simon & Schuster paper $5.95 (0-671-67837-X). The old nursery rhyme in a full-color picture book featuring ten animal families. (Rev: BL 12/15/86; SLJ 2/87)

441 Garne, S. T. *One White Sail: A Caribbean Counting Book* (PS–1). Illus. by Lisa Etre. 1992, Simon & Schuster $14.00 (0-671-75579-X). 32pp. A counting book that uses the colors and objects of the Caribbean to illustrate numbers. (Rev: BL 5/15/92; HB 9–10/92; SLJ 5/92)

442 Geisert, Arthur. *Pigs from 1 to 10* (PS–2). Illus. by author. 1991, Houghton $16.00 (0-395-58519-8). 32pp. In a series of hidden-picture illustrations, pigs search for a lost place and uncover the numbers zero to ten. (Rev: BL 11/1/92; HB 9–10/92*)

443 Giganti, Paul. *Each Orange Had Eight Slices* (PS–3). Illus. by Donald Crews. 1992, Greenwillow $15.89 (0-688-10429-0). This well-designed book challenges young readers to think analytically about what it portrays. (Rev: BCCB 4/92; BL 3/15/92; SLJ 3/92) [513.5]

444 Giganti, Paul. *How Many Snails?* (PS–K). Illus. by Donald Crews. 1988, Greenwillow $15.93 (0-688-06370-5). 24pp. A counting book that focuses on visual discrimination as well as numbers. (Rev: BL 8/88; SLJ 3/89)

445 Glass, Julie. *Counting Sheep* (1). Illus. by Mike Wohnoutka. Series: Step into Reading + Math. 2000, Random LB $11.99 (0-375-90619-3); paper $3.99 (0-375-80619-9). 32pp. In this easy-to-read counting book, a young boy starts counting sheep to get to sleep. The sheep are soon joined by kangaroos, monkeys, and bees. (Rev: BL 12/1/00)

446 Glass, Julie. *A Dollar for Penny* (1–2). Illus. by Joy Allen. Series: Step into Reading. 2000, Random LB $11.99 (0-679-98973-0); paper $3.99 (0-679-88973-6). 32pp. For beginning readers, this counting book tells how a little girl sells lemonade and, in one day, makes 100 cents or one dollar. (Rev: BL 7/00; HBG 10/00)

447 Golding, Kim. *Counting Kids* (PS–K). Illus. 2000, DK $9.95 (0-7894-2678-1). 32pp. Computer-enhanced photographs of children are used to introduce both counting from one to ten and number sets. (Rev: BL 7/00; HBG 10/00; SLJ 6/00)

448 Grossman, Bill. *My Little Sister Ate One Hare* (K–3). Illus. by Kevin Hawkes. 1996, Crown LB $18.99 (0-517-59601-6). A counting book with outrageous illustrations about swallowing a variety of slimy creatures. (Rev: BCCB 1/97; SLJ 12/96*)

449 Grossman, Virginia. *Ten Little Rabbits* (PS–1). Illus. by Sylvia Long. 1991, Chronicle $13.95 (0-87701-552-X). 32pp. This counting book of rabbits dressed as Indians introduces the cultures of various American tribes. (Rev: BL 4/1/91; SLJ 6/91)

450 Grover, Max. *Amazing and Incredible Counting Stories: A Number of Tall Tales* (K–3). Illus. 1995, Harcourt $14.00 (0-15-200090-9). 32pp. These 27 delightful stories feature numbers and the counting concept. (Rev: BL 2/15/96; SLJ 12/95)

451 Gustafson, Scott. *Scott Gustafson's Animal Orchestra: A Counting Book* (K–3). Illus. 1995, Greenwich Workshop $14.95 (0-86713-030-X). 32pp. An assembly of animals in tuxedo splendor. (Rev: BL 1/15/89; SLJ 2/89)

452 Guy, Ginger F. *¡Fiesta!* (PS–2). Illus. by René King Moreno. 1996, Greenwillow $15.00 (0-688-14331-8). Numbers are introduced in English and Spanish in this book about collecting articles to celebrate a Mexican fiesta. (Rev: SLJ 9/96)

453 Hague, Kathleen. *Ten Little Bears* (PS–K). Illus. by Michael Hague. 1999, Morrow LB $15.93 (0-688-16732-2). 24pp. In this counting book, ten little bears go out to play, but one by one they become separated. (Rev: BL 5/15/99; HBG 10/99)

454 Halls, Kelly M. *I Bought a Baby Chicken* (PS–1). Illus. by Karen Stormer Brooks. 2000, Boyds Mills $14.95 (1-56397-800-8). 32pp. In this comical counting book, a young girl and her family go out to buy some baby chickens. (Rev: BL 4/1/00; HBG 10/00; SLJ 7/00)

455 Halsey, Megan. *Circus 1-2-3* (PS–K). Illus. 2000, HarperCollins LB $14.89 (0-688-17105-2). 24pp. Two cute mice hide out in every picture in this counting book that introduces numbers from one to ten and is set in a circus. (Rev: BL 11/15/00; SLJ 11/00)

456 Halsey, Megan. *3 Pandas Planting* (PS–2). Illus. 1994, Macmillan paper $14.95 (0-02-742035-3). 32pp. A reverse counting book that shows all sorts of endangered species helping to save the earth — for example, condors collecting litter. (Rev: BL 5/15/94; SLJ 6/94)

457 Hamm, Diane J. *How Many Feet in the Bed?* (PS–2). Illus. by Kate S. Palmer. 1991, Simon & Schuster paper $14.00 (0-671-72638-2). 32pp. As more people hop into the family bed, there are more feet to count. (Rev: BL 7/91; SLJ 10/91)

458 Haring, Keith. *Ten* (PS–K). Illus. by author. 1998, Hyperion $6.95 (0-7868-0391-6). This counting board book offers numbers in four languages — French, English, Spanish, and German. (Rev: HBG 10/98; SLJ 7/98)

459 Harris, Trudy. *100 Days of School* (PS–K). Illus. by Beth Griffis Johnson. 1999, Millbrook LB $21.90 (0-7613-1271-4). 32pp. Various combinations of familiar objects are used to reach the number 100 in this innovative counting book. (Rev: BL 11/15/99; HBG 3/00; SLJ 11/99)

460 Harshman, Marc. *Only One* (PS–3). Illus. by Barbara Garrison. 1993, Dutton $15.99 (0-525-65116-0). 32pp. This counting book shows that a collective noun consists of several parts, for example, nine players make a baseball team. (Rev: BL 5/15/93)

461 Heinst, Marie. *My First Number Book* (PS–3). Illus. 1992, DK $16.95 (1-879431-73-4). 48pp. A bright, absorbing introduction to mathematics. (Rev: BL 6/15/92; SLJ 6/92) [513.2]

462 Helman, Andrea. *1, 2, 3 Moose: A Pacific Northwest Counting Book* (PS–2). Illus. by Art Wolfe. 1996, Sasquatch $15.95 (1-57061-078-9). 32pp. A one-to-20 counting book that employs the flora and fauna of the Pacific Northwest. (Rev: BL 11/1/96; SLJ 1/97) [428.1]

463 Hendra, Sue. *Numbers* (PS–K). Illus. Series: Flip and Find. 1999, Candlewick $7.99 (0-7636-0893-9). 24pp. Using flaps and illustrations of animals, this entertaining, interactive counting book identifies various numbers. (Rev: BL 11/15/99; SLJ 12/99) [921]

464 Hill, Eric. *Spot Counts from 1 to 10* (PS–1). Illus. by author. Series: Little Spot Board Books. 1989, Putnam $3.95 (0-399-21672-3). In this simple counting board book, Spot the dog counts many different barnyard animals. (Rev: SLJ 8/89)

465 Hoban, Tana. *Count and See* (PS–K). Illus. 1972, Macmillan LB $17.00 (0-02-744800-2). 40pp. Beginning with numbers one to 15, then going to 100; clear photographs of familiar objects are easily recognized and fun to count.

466 Hoban, Tana. *Let's Count* (PS–1). Illus. 1999, Greenwillow $16.00 (0-688-16008-5). 40pp. Amazing photos are used in this counting book to highlight objects from one to 15, then by tens to 50, and finally to 100. (Rev: BL 9/15/99; HBG 3/00; SLJ 9/99) [513.2]

467 Hoban, Tana. *More, Fewer, Less* (PS–2). Illus. 1998, Greenwillow LB $14.93 (0-688-15694-0). 32pp. Photographs explore groups of different objects and how those objects can be grouped and regrouped according to different characteristics. (Rev: BL 10/15/98; HBG 3/99; SLJ 11/98) [511.3]

468 Hoban, Tana. *1, 2, 3* (PS). Illus. by author. 1985, Greenwillow paper $4.95 (0-688-02579-X). 12pp. Starting with one birthday cake, photos present objects in a baby's world. (Rev: BCCB 3/85; BL 3/15/85; SLJ 9/85)

469 Holland, Cheri. *Maccabee Jamboree: A Hanukkah Countdown* (PS). Illus. by Rosalyn Schanzer. 1998, Kar-Ben paper $4.95 (1-58013-019-4). Eight Maccabees play different Hanukkah games as one by one they disappear in this counting book. (Rev: SLJ 10/98)

470 Huck, Charlotte. *A Creepy Countdown* (PS–2). Illus. by Joseph A. Smith. 1998, Greenwillow LB $14.93 (0-688-15461-1). 24pp. This counting book uses Halloween figures and situations to present the numbers one to ten and back again. (Rev: BCCB 10/98; BL 9/1/98; HBG 3/99; SLJ 9/98)

471 Hughes, Shirley. *Alfie's 1-2-3* (PS). Illus. 2000, Lothrop $15.95 (0-688-17705-0). 32pp. Playful activities of a preschooler's day form the framework of this simple counting book. (Rev: BL 4/15/00; HBG 10/00; SLJ 5/00)

472 Hulme, Joy N. *Sea Squares* (K–3). Illus. by Carol Schwartz. 1993, Hyperion paper $5.95 (1-56282-520-8). 32pp. Children can visualize multiplication in this picture book with an underwater theme. (Rev: BL 12/1/91; SLJ 1/92) [513.5]

473 Hutchins, Pat. *One Hunter* (PS–2). Illus. by author. 1982, Morrow paper $4.95 (0-688-06522-8). 24pp. A counting book with a hunter and hidden African animals.

474 Hutchins, Pat. *Ten Red Apples* (PS–2). Illus. 2000, Greenwillow $23.95 (0-688-16797-7). 32pp. A charming counting book about a farmer and his apple crop. (Rev: BL 5/1/00; HBG 10/00; SLJ 5/00)

475 Inkpen, Mick. *Kipper's Book of Numbers* (PS). Illus. by author. 1999, Harcourt $4.95 (0-15-202286-4). A simple concept book in which youngsters are taught to count frogs, snails, and hedgehogs. (Rev: SLJ 10/99)

476 Isadora, Rachael. *1 2 3 Pop!* (PS–2). Illus. 2000, Viking $15.99 (0-670-88859-1). 32pp. Using a Pop Art style, this counting book features monkeys, gargoyles, superheroes, and so forth. (Rev: BCCB 6/00; BL 5/1/00; HB 5–6/00; HBG 10/00; SLJ 6/00) [513.2]

477 Jahn-Clough, Lisa. *1 2 3 Yippie* (PS). Illus. 1998, Houghton $5.95 (0-395-87003-8). 32pp. A small, square counting book that deals with two children who have a party for different numbers of animals. (Rev: BL 3/15/98; HBG 10/98; SLJ 7/98)

478 Jennings, Linda. *Nine Naughty Kittens* (PS–1). Illus. by Caroline Jayne Church. 1999, Little Tiger $14.95 (1-888444-62-2). A flap book that is also a counting book about kittens. (Rev: BCCB 1/00; HBG 3/00; SLJ 2/00)

479 Johnson, Stephen T. *City by Numbers* (2–5). Illus. 1998, Viking $15.99 (0-670-87251-2). 32pp. Through cityscapes found in New York City, the numbers one to 21 are introduced effectively. (Rev:

BCCB 4/99; BL 2/15/99; HBG 3/99; SLJ 2/99) [513.2]

480 Jonas, Ann. *Splash!* (PS–1). Illus. 1995, Greenwillow $14.89 (0-688-11052-5). 24pp. Principles of addition and subtraction are shown by counting the animal life in and around a backyard pond. (Rev: BCCB 6/95; BL 6/1–15/95; HB 9–10/95; SLJ 6/95)

481 Keats, Ezra Jack. *One Red Sun: A Counting Book* (PS). Illus. 1999, Viking $5.99 (0-670-88478-2). 14pp. A very effective board book that teaches the numbers through everyday objects such as stoplights and birds. (Rev: BL 7/99; HBG 10/99; SLJ 8/99)

482 Kellogg, Steven. *Give the Dog a Bone* (K–3). Illus. 2000, North-South LB $15.88 (1-58717-002-7). 40pp. A riotous counting book that involves a grand total of 250 dogs (and one chicken). (Rev: BL 12/1/00; HBG 3/01; SLJ 11/00)

483 Kharms, Daniil. *First, Second* (PS–3). Trans. by Richard Pevear. Illus. by Marc Rosenthal. 1996, Farrar $16.00 (0-374-32339-9). 32pp. The concepts of "first" through "tenth" are introduced in this rollicking cumulative story. (Rev: BCCB 2/96; BL 4/15/96; HB 9–10/96; SLJ 4/96)

484 Kitamura, Satoshi. *When Sheep Cannot Sleep: The Counting Book* (PS–1). Illus. by author. 1986, Farrar paper $5.95 (0-374-48359-0). 32pp. Woolly the sheep can't sleep so he takes a walk — chasing one butterfly, watching two ladybugs, and so on. (Rev: BL 10/1/86; HB 11–12/86; SLJ 12/86)

485 Kneen, Maggie. *When You're Not Looking: A Storytime Counting Book* (PS–2). Illus. by author. 1996, Simon & Schuster paper $15.00 (0-689-80026-6). Ten double-page spreads invite children to make up their own stories and find a number of objects hidden in the pictures in this unusual counting book. (Rev: SLJ 12/96)

486 Koller, Jackie F. *One Monkey Too Many* (PS–2). Illus. by Lynn Munsinger. 1999, Harcourt $16.00 (0-15-200006-2). 32pp. A raucous counting book — from one to six — about monkeys who cram themselves into places they shouldn't. (Rev: BCCB 5/99; BL 4/15/99; HB 3–4/99; HBG 10/99; SLJ 5/99)

487 Kuskin, Karla. *James and the Rain* (PS–1). Illus. by Reg Cartwright. 1995, Simon & Schuster $15.00 (0-671-88808-0). 32pp. During his outing on a rainy day, James meets a variety of animals in this amusing counting book. (Rev: BL 6/1–15/95; SLJ 7/95)

488 Kusugak, Michael A. *My Arctic 1, 2, 3* (K–3). Illus. by Vladyana Krykorka. 1996, Annick $16.95 (1-55037-505-9); paper $6.95 (1-55037-504-0). Using Arctic animals as a focus, this counting book presents the numbers one through ten, 20, 100, and a million in both English and the Inuit language. (Rev: SLJ 5/97)

489 Lee, Huy Voun. *1, 2, 3, Go!* (PS–1). Illus. 2001, Holt $16.00 (0-8050-6205-X). 32pp. This introduction to Chinese numbers gives the Chinese characters for one to ten and for the words used to illustrate each number. (Rev: BL 2/1/01) [495.1]

490 Leedy, Loreen. *Fraction Action* (K–2). Illus. 1994, Holiday LB $16.95 (0-8234-1109-5). 32pp.

How to divide various objects and the meaning of fractions are explored in this simple, colorful arithmetic book. (Rev: BCCB 3/94; BL 3/15/94) [513.2]

491 Leedy, Loreen. *Subtraction Action* (1–3). Illus. 2000, Holiday $16.95 (0-8234-1454-X). 32pp. In seven short chapters, Miss Prime and her class learn how to do subtraction. (Rev: BL 9/15/00; HBG 3/01; SLJ 9/00)

492 Le Sieg, Theo. *Wacky Wednesday* (PS–1). Illus. by George Booth. 1974, Random $11.99 (0-394-92912-8). 48pp. In this counting book, every page has a number of things out of place.

493 Lesser, Carolyn. *Spots: Counting Creatures from Sky to Sea* (PS–1). Illus. by Laura Regan. 1999, Harcourt $16.00 (0-15-200666-4). 32pp. Spotted creatures such as jaguars, butterflies, and squids are used to introduce numbers from one to ten. (Rev: BCCB 5/99; BL 3/15/99; HBG 10/99; SLJ 4/99) [513.2]

494 Leuck, Laura. *My Baby Brother Has Ten Tiny Toes* (PS–K). Illus. by Clara Vulliamy. 1997, Albert Whitman LB $14.95 (0-8075-5310-7). 24pp. A charming counting book that uses characteristics of a baby as its focus. (Rev: BL 4/15/97; SLJ 3/97)

495 Lionel. *Peekaboo Babies* (PS–K). Illus. 1997, Orchard $12.95 (0-531-30016-1). 12pp. A counting book that uses tabs and flaps to find baby animals. (Rev: BL 12/15/97)

496 Lodge, Jo. *Busy Farm: A Counting Book with Pull-Out Tabs* (PS). Illus. 1999, Dial $9.99 (0-8037-2416-0). Using 3-D illustrations and a guessing game about farm animals, this book also serves as a simple counting book. (Rev: BL 12/15/99)

497 Long, Lynette. *Dealing with Addition* (1–3). 1998, Charlesbridge LB $15.95 (0-88106-269-3); paper $6.95 (0-88106-270-7). Playing cards are used to teach addition in this entertaining book. (Rev: HBG 10/98; SLJ 9/98)

498 Loomis, Christine. *One Cow Coughs: A Counting Book for the Sick and Miserable* (PS–K). Illus. by Pat Dypold. 1994, Ticknor $14.95 (0-395-67899-4). 32pp. A counting book that uses sick animals and the treatments they receive as its subjects. (Rev: BL 10/15/94; SLJ 10/94)

499 Lyon, George E. *Counting on the Woods* (PS–4). Illus. by Ann W. Olson. 1998, DK $15.95 (0-7894-2480-0). This gem of a counting book can also be used as a science book because of its brilliant color photos of animals. (Rev: BL 3/1/98*; HBG 10/98; SLJ 4/98) [513.2]

500 Maccarone, Grace. *Monster Math Picnic* (1). Illus. by Margaret A. Hartelius. Series: Hello Math Reader. 1998, Scholastic paper $3.50 (0-590-37127-4). 24pp. Using ten monsters as subjects, this simple math book explores the various combinations of numbers that add up to ten. (Rev: BL 5/1/98; SLJ 7/98)

501 Maccarone, Grace. *Monster Money* (PS–1). Illus. by Margaret A. Hartelius. Series: Hello Reader! 1998, Scholastic paper $3.50 (0-590-12007-7). In this math concept book, several monsters learn how to count money when they go to a pet store to a buy a pet. (Rev: SLJ 2/99)

502 McCourt, Lisa. *The Rain Forest Counts!* (PS–1). Illus. by Cheryl Nathan. 1997, Troll $15.95 (0-8167-4388-6). 32pp. This rhyming counting book features the animals and plants of the rain forest. (Rev: BL 12/15/97; HBG 3/98; SLJ 11/97)

503 MacDonald, Elizabeth. *Mike's Kite* (PS–K). Illus. by Robert Kendall. 1993, Harcourt paper $11.40 (0-15-300320-0). 32pp. In this counting book, Mike and a number of bystanders get carried away on the tail of a kite. (Rev: BL 7/90; SLJ 9/90)

504 MacDonald, Suse. *Look Whooo's Counting* (PS–1). Illus. 2000, Scholastic $14.95 (0-590-68320-9). 32pp. While flying through the air and looking down on different groups of animals, little Owl learns to count from one to ten. (Rev: BL 10/15/00; HBG 3/01; SLJ 12/00)

505 McGrath, Barbara Barbieri. *The Baseball Counting Book* (PS–1). Illus. by Brian Shaw. 1999, Charlesbridge $15.95 (0-88106-332-0); paper $6.95 (0-88106-333-9). 32pp. Two Little League teams compete while the reader learns numbers from zero to 20. (Rev: BL 2/15/99; HBG 10/99; SLJ 3/99) [513.2]

506 McGrath, Barbara Barbieri. *The Cheerios Counting Book* (PS). Illus. by Rob Bolster and Frank Mazzola. 1998, Scholastic $10.95 (0-590-00321-6). 32pp. Using round cereal bits as objects to count, this book explains the numbers one to ten and then groups of ten up to 100. (Rev: BL 10/1/98; HBG 3/99; SLJ 9/98)

507 McMillan, Bruce. *Eating Fractions* (PS–2). Illus. 1991, Scholastic $15.95 (0-590-43770-4). 32pp. Challenging fractions at the beginning level. (Rev: BCCB 9/91; BL 8/91; SLJ 9/91*) [513.2]

508 McMillan, Bruce. *Jelly Beans for Sale* (PS–2). Illus. 1996, Scholastic $15.95 (0-590-86584-6). 32pp. Counting and basic math concepts are illustrated in this book about selling candies. (Rev: BCCB 10/96; BL 9/1/96; SLJ 10/96) [332.4]

509 McMillan, Bruce. *One, Two, One Pair!* (PS). Illus. 1996, Scholastic paper $4.95 (0-590-46082-X). 32pp. The concept of pairs is explored with sharp color images. (Rev: BCCB 2/91; BL 1/15/91; SLJ 2/91) [515.5]

510 Marzollo, Jean. *Ten Cats Have Hats: A Counting Book* (PS–K). Illus. by David McPhail. 1994, Scholastic $6.95 (0-590-20656-7). A counting book that uses intriguing pictures containing unusual details to present numbers one to ten. (Rev: SLJ 11/94)

511 Masurel, Claire. *Ten Dogs in the Window* (PS–K). Illus. by Pamela Paparone. 1997, North-South LB $15.88 (1-55858-755-1). 32pp. This amusing counting book starts with ten and goes to one by using the sale of dogs in a pet store as a framework. (Rev: BL 11/15/97; HBG 3/98; SLJ 12/97)

512 Melville, Kirsty. *Splash! A Penguin Counting Book* (PS–1). Illus. by Jonathan Chester. 2001, Tricycle Pr. paper $5.95 (1-58246-042-6). 32pp. A slight story teaches counting from one to ten using charming penguins. (Rev: BL 1/1–15/01)

513 Merriam, Eve. *Ten Rosy Roses* (PS–1). Illus. by Julia Gorton. 1999, HarperCollins LB $14.89 (0-06-027888-9). 32pp. In this counting rhyme from ten down to one, children pick roses to make a bouquet for their teacher. (Rev: BCCB 4/99; BL 6/1–15/99; HBG 10/99; SLJ 6/99)

514 Michelson, Richard. *Ten Times Better* (PS–1). Illus. by Leonard Baskin. 2000, Marshall Cavendish $17.95 (0-7614-5070-X). 40pp. In this counting book, various animals brag about the number of appendages they have; for example, the squid is proud of his ten tentacles. (Rev: BCCB 1/01; BL 10/1/00; HBG 3/01; SLJ 10/00)

515 Miller, Jane. *Farm Counting Book* (PS–1). Illus. by author. 1992, Simon & Schuster LB $5.95 (0-671-66552-9). 24pp. A counting book using photographs of farm animals.

516 Min, Laura. *Mrs. Sato's Hens* (1–2). Illus. by Benrei Huang. 1994, Scott Foresman $2.95 (0-673-36193-4). 8pp. In an easy-to-read counting book, every morning Mrs. Sato counts the eggs that her hens are laying. (Rev: BL 1/1/95)

517 Miranda, Anne. *Monster Math* (K–2). Illus. by Polly Powell. 1999, Harcourt $16.00 (0-15-201835-2). Introducing numbers that range from one to 50, this counting book tells of groups of monsters attending and leaving a birthday party. (Rev: HBG 3/00; SLJ 10/99)

518 Miranda, Anne. *Vroom, Chugga, Vroom-Vroom* (PS–1). Illus. by David Murphy. 1998, Turtle $15.95 (1-890515-07-8). 30pp. A number book in which race cars numbered one to 20 battle it out on the action-filled racetrack. (Rev: BL 5/1/98; HBG 10/98; SLJ 7/98)

519 Moore, Elaine. *Roly-Poly Puppies: A Counting Book* (PS–K). Illus. by Jacqueline Rogers. 1996, Scholastic $6.95 (0-590-46665-8). 32pp. The numbers one to ten are introduced through the antics of ten roly-poly puppies. (Rev: BL 9/15/96; SLJ 12/96)

520 Mora, Pat. *Uno, Dos, Tres: One, Two, Three* (PS–2). Illus. by Barbara Lavallee. 1996, Clarion $15.00 (0-395-67294-5). 43pp. The numbers one to ten are introduced in English and Spanish. (Rev: BL 6/1–15/96; HB 5–6/96; SLJ 4/96)

521 Morozumi, Atsuko. *One Gorilla: A Counting Book* (PS–K). Illus. 1990, Farrar $15.00 (0-374-35644-0). 26pp. This counting book contains different animals, always accompanied by one gorilla. (Rev: BL 11/1/90; SLJ 1/91)

522 Mullins, Patricia. *One Horse Waiting for Me* (PS–1). Illus. 1998, Simon & Schuster paper $16.00 (0-689-81381-3). 32pp. All kinds of horses, even those from fantasies, appear in this handsome counting book. (Rev: BCCB 3/98; BL 3/1/98*; HBG 10/98; SLJ 5/98)

523 Murphy, Stuart J. *Animals on Board* (1–2). Illus. by R. W. Alley. Series: MathStart. 1998, HarperCollins $14.95 (0-06-027442-5). 40pp. Five simple addition problems are presented in this arithmetic book involving a girl watching a series of trucks carrying different animals. (Rev: BL 11/1/98; HBG 3/99; SLJ 1/99)

524 Murphy, Stuart J. *Divide and Ride* (PS–3). Illus. by George Ulrich. Series: MathStart. 1997, Harper-Collins LB $15.89 (0-06-026777-1). 40pp. Concepts of division are illustrated by problems posed when 11 friends visit various carnival attractions. (Rev: BL 2/1/97; SLJ 3/97) [513.2]

525 Murphy, Stuart J. *Every Buddy Counts* (PS–3). Illus. by Fiona Dunbar. Series: MathStart. 1997, HarperCollins LB $15.89 (0-06-026773-9). 40pp. A simple counting book in which a girl counts up the number of friends she has. (Rev: BL 2/1/97; SLJ 3/97)

526 Murphy, Stuart J. *A Fair Bear Share* (1–2). Illus. by John Speirs. Series: MathStart. 1998, HarperCollins LB $15.89 (0-06-027439-5). Bear cubs count out the food they have gathered into groups of ten in this simple math book. (Rev: BL 3/1/98; HBG 10/98; SLJ 5/98)

527 Murphy, Stuart J. *Henry the Fourth* (1–3). Illus. by Scott Nash. Series: MathStart. 1999, Harper-Collins LB $15.89 (0-06-027611-8). 40pp. Ordinal numbers are introduced in this story of four performing dogs. (Rev: BL 4/15/99; HBG 10/99; SLJ 1/99) [513]

528 Murphy, Stuart J. *Jump, Kangaroo, Jump!* (1–3). Illus. by Kevin O'Malley. Series: MathStart. 1999, HarperCollins LB $15.89 (0-06-027615-0). 40pp. This book about 12 campers introduces simple division to young mathematicians. (Rev: BL 4/15/99; HBG 10/99; SLJ 2/99) [513.2]

529 Murphy, Stuart J. *Missing Mittens* (PS–2). Illus. by G. Brian Karas. Series: MathStart. 2001, Harper-Collins LB $15.89 (0-06-028027-1); paper $4.95 (0-06-446733-3). 40pp. Farmer Bill and all of his farmyard animals are missing mittens in this entertaining math book that explains the concept of odd and even and includes several follow-up activities. (Rev: BL 2/15/01; SLJ 3/01) [513]

530 Murphy, Stuart J. *Monster Musical Chairs* (PS–K). Illus. by Scott Nash. Series: MathStart. 2000, HarperCollins LB $15.89 (0-06-028021-2); paper $4.95 (0-06-446730-9). 40pp. Bouncy rhymes and lovable monsters are used to present the basics of subtraction in this easily read book. (Rev: BL 10/15/00; HBG 3/01; SLJ 1/01)

531 Murphy, Stuart J. *The Penny Pot* (1–3). Illus. by Lynne W. Cravath. Series: MathStart. 1998, Harper-Collins LB $14.89 (0-06-027607-X). 40pp. While Jessie tries different coin combinations to get enough money to have her face painted at the school fair, the reader learns about counting money and addition. (Rev: BL 12/15/98; HBG 3/99; SLJ 12/98) [513.2]

532 Murphy, Stuart J. *Spunky Monkeys on Parade* (1–3). Illus. by Lynne W. Cravath. Series: Math-Start. 1999, HarperCollins LB $15.89 (0-06-028015-8); paper $4.95 (0-06-446727-9). 40pp. A Monkey Day parade is used to present groups of animals in ones, twos, threes, etc. (Rev: BL 12/1/99; HBG 3/00; SLJ 12/99)

533 *My Big Counting Book* (PS–K). Series: Big Tab Board Books. 1999, DK $9.95 (0-7894-4682-0). Flaps are used with photos and drawings of different numbers of babies to introduce numerals 1 to 10, 15, and 20. (Rev: SLJ 2/00)

534 *My First Look at Numbers* (PS). Illus. Series: My First Look At. 1990, Random $9.00 (0-679-80533-8). This basic numbers book uses familiar objects to illustrate numbers from one to ten, 20, and 100. (Rev: SLJ 12/90) [513.2]

535 Nagel, Karen. *The Lunch Line* (2–4). Illus. by Jerry Zimmerman. 1996, Scholastic $3.99 (0-590-60246-2). 32pp. Kim has lost her lunch and must buy one in this simple book on calculation. (Rev: BL 2/1/97)

536 Naylor, Phyllis Reynolds. *Ducks Disappearing* (PS–K). Illus. by Tony Maddox. 1997, Simon & Schuster $13.00 (0-689-31902-9). 30pp. A young child solves the mystery of missing ducklings in this counting book. (Rev: BCCB 2/97; BL 2/1/97; SLJ 3/97)

537 Neuschwander, Cindy. *Amanda Bean's Amazing Dream: A Mathematical Story* (1–3). Illus. by Liza Woodruff. 1998, Scholastic $16.95 (0-590-30012-1). 40pp. Amanda enjoys counting everything and finally discovers the joy of multiplication. (Rev: BL 9/15/98; HBG 3/99; SLJ 9/98)

538 Nikola-Lisa, W. *One Hole in the Road* (PS–2). Illus. by Dan Yaccarino. 1996, Holt $15.95 (0-8050-4285-7). 24pp. Events caused by a pothole are used to introduce numbers in this clever counting book. (Rev: BL 10/1/96; SLJ 10/96)

539 Nikola-Lisa, W. *1, 2, 3 Thanksgiving!* (PS–1). Illus. by Robin Kramer. 1991, Whitman LB $14.95 (0-8075-6109-6). 32pp. Each page adds something new to the traditional feast. (Rev: BL 9/1/91)

540 Ochiltree, Dianne. *Cats Add Up! Math Activities by Marilyn Burns* (1–2). Illus. by Marcy Dunn-Ramsey. 1998, Scholastic paper $3.99 (0-590-12005-0). 40pp. In this easy-to-read counting book, a little girl starts with one cat and soon has ten. (Rev: BL 3/15/99)

541 Ochs, Carol P. *When I'm Alone* (PS–3). Illus. by Vicki Jo Redenbaugh. 1993, Carolrhoda LB $18.95 (0-87614-752-X). 32pp. In this counting book, various animals upset a girl's attempts to keep her part of the house tidy. (Rev: BL 2/1/93; SLJ 6/93)

542 O'Keefe, Susan Heyboer. *One Hungry Monster: A Counting Book in Rhyme* (PS–K). Illus. by Lynn Munsinger. 2001, Little, Brown $5.95 (0-316-60804-1). 16pp. A little boy tries to keep ten hungry monsters out of trouble. (Rev: BL 3/1/01)

543 Olyff, Clotilde. *1 2 3 . . .* (PS–K). Illus. by author. 1994, Ticknor $13.95 (0-395-70736-6). A pop-up book that introduces numbers from one to the zero in ten, each in a different, attractive typeface. (Rev: SLJ 11/94)

544 *1 to 10 and Back Again: A Getty Museum Counting Book* (K–2). Photos by Jack Ross. Illus. by Nancy Ogami. 1999, Getty Museum $16.95 (0-89236-525-0). This counting book, which features French phases, cleverly uses the numbers one to ten as the furniture and items found in the Getty Museum are counted. (Rev: HBG 3/00; SLJ 7/99)

545 *One, Two, Skip a Few! First Number Rhymes* (PS–1). Illus. by Roberta Arenson. 1998, Barefoot

$15.95 (1-901223-99-X). 32pp. Using different folk rhymes — like "one potato, two potato" — this energetic book covers numbers, counting, subtraction, and even some multiplication. (Rev: BL 12/1/98; SLJ 9/98) [398.8]

546 Orgel, Doris. *Two Crows Counting* (PS–1). Illus. by Judith Moffatt. 1995, Byron Preiss paper $4.50 (0-553-37573-3). 32pp. Two crows fly over a landscape and count from one to ten and back again in this easily read book. (Rev: BL 10/1/95; SLJ 2/96)

547 Ormerod, Jan. *Joe Can Count* (PS–3). Illus. 1993, Mulberry paper $3.95 (0-688-04588-X). 24pp. An African American toddler uses animals to count to ten. A reissue.

548 Packard, Edward. *Big Numbers* (1–4). Illus. by Sal Murdocca. 2000, Millbrook LB $22.40 (0-7613-1570-5). 32pp. This oversize book also deals with oversize numbers from one to ten to 100, 1,000, and then on to a million, billion, trillion, etc. (Rev: BCCB 3/00; BL 3/15/00; HBG 10/00; SLJ 4/00)

549 Pallotta, Jerry. *Underwater Counting: Even Numbers* (1–3). Illus. by David Biedrzycki. 2001, Charlesbridge $16.95 (0-88106-952-3); paper $6.95 (0-88106-800-4). 32pp. A variety of underwater creatures are introduced in this counting book that gives even numbers from zero to 50. (Rev: BL 3/1/01)

550 Parker, Vic. *Bearobics: A Hip-Hop Counting Story* (PS–3). Illus. by Emily Bolam. 1997, Viking $14.99 (0-670-87034-X). 32pp. A bear turns on his boom box in the forest and brings out a variety of dancing animals in this counting book. (Rev: BL 2/15/97; SLJ 2/97*)

551 Patilla, Peter. *Fun with Numbers* (PS–1). Illus. by Brigitte McDonald. Series: Fun With. 1998, Millbrook LB $22.40 (0-7613-0957-8). 32pp. Clever picture puzzles enliven this book, which introduces the numbers one to ten. (Rev: BL 3/15/99; HBG 10/99; SLJ 3/99) [513.2]

552 Peek, Merle. *Roll Over! A Counting Song* (PS). Illus. by author. 1991, Houghton paper $5.95 (0-395-58105-2). 32pp. A counting book from ten to one about animals in a bed.

553 Penner, Lucille R. *Lights Out!* (1–3). Illus. by Jerry Smath. Series: Math Matters. 2000, Kane paper $4.95 (1-57565-092-4). 32pp. The concept of subtraction is explored in this story about a girl who watches as the 32 lights outside her apartment go out. (Rev: SLJ 6/00)

554 Piers, Helen. *Is There Room on the Bus?* (PS–1). Illus. by Hannah Giffard. 1996, Simon & Schuster $14.00 (0-689-80610-8). 32pp. In this cumulative counting story, Sam picks up various numbers of animals as he travels around the world in his bus. (Rev: BL 5/1/96; SLJ 7/96)

555 Pinczes, Elinor J. *Arctic Fives Arrive* (K–2). Illus. by Holly Berry. 1996, Houghton $14.95 (0-395-73577-7). 32pp. Counting by fives is introduced in this book about animals on an ice floe. (Rev: BL 9/15/96; SLJ 11/96)

556 Pinczes, Elinor J. *Inchworm and a Half* (PS–3). Illus. by Randall Enos. 2001, Houghton $15.00 (0-

395-82849-X). 32pp. The concept of fractions is explored in this amusing book about different-sized inchworms and the objects they measure. (Rev: BCCB 3/01; BL 3/15/01)

557 Pinczes, Elinor J. *One Hundred Hungry Ants* (K–3). Illus. by Bonnie Mackain. 1993, Houghton $16.00 (0-395-63116-5). 32pp. Ants group and regroup on their march to a picnic site. (Rev: BL 3/1/93; SLJ 8/93)

558 Pinczes, Elinor J. *A Remainder of One* (PS–2). Illus. by Bonnie Mackain. 1995, Houghton $15.00 (0-395-69455-8). 32pp. An arithmetic book that uses a parade of beetles before the queen as a focal point. (Rev: BL 3/1/95*; SLJ 5/95)

559 Pittman, Helena Clare. *Sunrise* (PS). Illus. by Michael Rex. 1998, Harcourt $12.00 (0-15-201684-8). 32pp. A counting book that progresses from one to ten using pictures with phrases that rhyme with *sunrise,* such as "baby cries" and "laundry dries." (Rev: BL 12/1/98; HBG 3/99; SLJ 10/98)

560 Pomerantz, Charlotte. *One Duck, Another Duck* (PS). Illus. by Jose Aruego and Ariane Dewey. 1984, Greenwillow $15.89 (0-688-03745-3). 24pp. Danny tries to count ducks but has problems.

561 Pomeroy, Diana. *One Potato: A Counting Book of Potato Prints* (PS–2). Illus. 1996, Harcourt $16.00 (0-15-200300-2). 32pp. A counting book from one to 100 using imaginative potato prints, with additional information on how to create your own prints. (Rev: BL 4/1/96; HB 7–8/96; SLJ 6/96) [513.2]

562 Potter, Keith R. *Count Us In: A 1 to 10 Book* (PS–K). Illus. by Keith R. Potter and Jana Leo. Series: Doodlezoo. 1999, Chronicle $6.95 (0-8118-2064-5). Animal photos and cartoon creatures are used to introduce numbers from one to ten. (Rev: SLJ 10/99)

563 Raffi. *Five Little Ducks* (PS–1). Illus. by Jose Aruego and Ariane Dewey. 1988, Crown paper $5.99 (0-517-58360-7). 32pp. Mother Duck and her ducklings waddle "over the hills and far away" in this addition to the Songs to Read series. (Rev: BL 6/1/89; HB 5–6/89)

564 Rankin, Laura. *The Handmade Counting Book* (PS–2). Illus. by author. 1998, Dial LB $15.89 (0-8037-2311-3). This counting book teaches children to count to 100 and displays the American Sign Language equivalents for these numbers. (Rev: HB 11–12/98; HBG 3/99; SLJ 11/98)

565 Rathmann, Peggy. *10 Minutes till Bedtime* (K–2). Illus. 1998, Putnam $16.99 (0-399-23103-X). 46pp. A very active counting book involving a ten-minute countdown to bed for a little boy and ten mischievous hamsters numbered one through ten. (Rev: BCCB 12/98; BL 10/15/98; HB 9–10/98; HBG 3/99; SLJ 9/98)

566 Roche, Denis. *Only One Ollie* (PS). Illus. 1997, Houghton $4.95 (0-395-81123-6). 14pp. Ollie, a little dog, counts objects in his house from one to ten in this charming board book. (Rev: BCCB 6/97; BL 4/15/97; SLJ 8/97)

567 Rocklin, Joanne. *The Case of the Shrunken Allowance* (1–3). Illus. by Cornelius Van Wright and Ying-Hwa Hu. Series: Hello Reader! 1999, Scholastic paper $3.99 (0-590-12006-9). The concept of money denominations and making change are introduced in a light plot about P. B.'s shrinking savings. (Rev: SLJ 3/99)

568 Rocklin, Joanne. *One Hungry Cat* (1–2). Illus. by Rowan Barnes-Murphy. Series: Hello Math Reader. 1997, Scholastic paper $3.99 (0-590-93972-6). A slapstick easy reader that introduces simple arithmetic by using cookies that a hungry cat enjoys eating. (Rev: BL 5/1/97; SLJ 7/97)

569 Root, Phyllis. *One Duck Stuck* (PS–1). Illus. by Jane Chapman. 1998, Candlewick $15.99 (0-7636-0334-1). 40pp. In this counting book that uses alliterative rhymes, different animals try to free a duck that gets stuck in the muck. (Rev: BL 4/1/98; HBG 10/98; SLJ 6/98)

570 Roth, Carol. *Ten Dirty Pigs, Ten Clean Pigs: An Upside-Down, Turn-Around Bathtime Counting Book* (K–2). Illus. by Pamela Paparone. 1999, North-South LB $15.88 (0-7358-1090-7). 32pp. By turning the book over, young readers can have two stories that feature pigs and counting from one to ten. (Rev: BCCB 11/99; BL 12/1/99; HBG 3/00; SLJ 11/99)

571 Roth, Susan L. *Night-Time Numbers: A Scary Counting Book* (PS–1). Illus. by author. Series: A Barefoot Beginner Book. 1999, Barefoot $15.95 (1-84148-001-0). Monsters and an angel are used to introduce the numbers one to ten in his book illustrated with collages. (Rev: SLJ 10/99)

572 Ryan, Pam M. *One Hundred Is a Family* (PS–3). Illus. by Benrei Huang. 1994, Hyperion LB $14.49 (1-56282-673-5). 32pp. Different kinds of families are highlighted in this counting book that goes from one to ten and then by tens to 100. (Rev: BL 11/1/94; SLJ 10/94)

573 Samton, Sheila W. *Moon to Sun: An Adding Book* (PS–1). Illus. 1991, Boyds Mills $9.95 (1-878093-13-4). Moon and clouds and other sky objects introduce adding. Also use: *On the River: An Adding Book* (1991). (Rev: SLJ 1/92)

574 Saul, Carol P. *Barn Cat* (PS–K). Illus. by Mary Azarian. 1998, Little, Brown $15.95 (0-316-76113-3). 32pp. In this counting book, Barn Cat sees all sorts of insects and animals, such as one green grasshopper and two brown crickets, before he discovers what he really wants — a saucer of milk. (Rev: BCCB 11/98; BL 9/15/98; HBG 3/99; SLJ 11/98)

575 Schlein, Miriam. *More Than One* (PS–3). Illus. by Donald Crews. 1996, Greenwillow $14.93 (0-688-14103-X). 24pp. Using the concept of "one" as a framework, other numbers and groups of numbers are introduced. (Rev: BCCB 1/97; BL 11/1/96; SLJ 12/96) [513]

576 Schlein, Miriam. *What the Dinosaurs Saw* (1–2). Illus. by Carol Schwartz. Series: Hello Reader! 1998, Scholastic paper $3.50 (0-590-37128-2). 32pp. Using a counting-book format, this easy reader introduces some of the plants and animals that have lived on Earth since the days of the dinosaurs. (Rev: BL 5/1/98) [560]

577 Schnur, Steven. *Night Lights* (PS–1). Illus. by Stacey Schuett. 2000, Farrar $16.00 (0-374-35522-3). 32pp. A counting book that goes well beyond ten in a story about Melinda who counts a number of objects in her room and outside before she goes to bed. (Rev: BCCB 6/00; BL 5/1/00; HBG 10/00; SLJ 7/00)

578 Schumaker, Ward. *In My Garden* (PS–1). Illus. 2000, Chronicle $13.95 (0-8118-2689-9). 32pp. A lively counting book that uses garden tools, plants, and outdoor creatures as props. (Rev: BL 7/00; HBG 10/00; SLJ 5/00)

579 Sendak, Maurice. *Seven Little Monsters* (K–2). Illus. by author. 1977, HarperCollins LB $14.89 (0-06-025478-5). 16pp. A counting book involving monsters that townspeople try to eliminate.

580 Serfozo, Mary. *Who Wants One?* (PS–1). Illus. by Keiko Narahashi. 1989, Macmillan paper $15.00 (0-689-50474-8). 32pp. A young girl dressed as a magician brings forth many objects that introduce the numbers from one to ten. (Rev: BL 11/1/89; SLJ 12/89)

581 Simon, Charnan. *One Happy Classroom* (1–2). Illus. by Rebecca M. Thornburgh. 1997, Children's LB $18.00 (0-516-20318-5). 32pp. An easy-to-read counting book that takes place in a classroom and involves counting from one to ten and back. (Rev: BL 5/1/97)

582 Sis, Peter. *Waving: A Counting Book* (PS–1). Illus. 1988, Greenwillow LB $12.88 (0-688-07160-0). 24pp. A story chain of people waving provides the fun in this counting book. (Rev: BL 3/15/88; HB 5–6/88)

583 Slater, Teddy. *Stay in Line* (1–2). Illus. 1996, Scholastic paper $3.99 (0-590-22713-0). 32pp. Children on a field trip learn various numerical ways of lining up. (Rev: BL 8/96)

584 Smith, Maggie. *Counting Our Way to Maine* (PS–2). Illus. 1995, Orchard LB $16.99 (0-531-08734-4). 32pp. Numbers from one to 20 are introduced by using a family's summer trip to Maine. (Rev: BCCB 3/95; BL 4/1/95; SLJ 5/95*)

585 Staake, Bob. *My Little 123 Book* (PS–K). Illus. by author. 1998, Simon & Schuster paper $6.99 (0-689-81660-X). A board book that uses bright colors and pleasant graphics to present numbers from one to 20. (Rev: HBG 10/98; SLJ 3/98)

586 Stoeke, Janet Morgan. *Five Little Kitty Cats* (PS). Illus. 1998, Dutton $5.99 (0-525-45739-9). 18pp. A simple board book that teaches counting from one to five through the antics of five kittens who play together until one by one they separate. (Rev: BL 12/1/98; SLJ 12/98)

587 Stoeke, Janet Morgan. *One Little Puppy Dog* (PS). Illus. 1998, Dutton $5.99 (0-525-45740-2). 18pp. Puppy Dog and his three siblings are frightened by bees and run home to Mama in this simple board book that teaches counting from one to five. (Rev: BL 12/1/98; SLJ 12/98)

588 Sturges, Philemon. *Ten Flashing Fireflies* (PS–1). Illus. by Anna Vojtech. 1995, North-South LB $15.88 (1-55858-421-8). 32pp. Ten fireflies are captured by two youngsters in this counting book that also introduces subtraction. (Rev: BCCB 7–8/95; BL 6/1–15/95; SLJ 8/95*)

589 Swinburne, Stephen R. *Water for One, Water for Everyone: A Counting Book of African Animals* (PS–2). Illus. by Melinda Levine. 1998, Millbrook LB $21.40 (0-7613-0269-7); paper $6.95 (0-7613-0347-2). Animals, from one tortoise to ten elephants, come to an African watering hole in this simple counting book, which also gives the numbers in Swahili. (Rev: HBG 10/98; SLJ 6/98)

590 Swinburne, Stephen R. *What's a Pair? What's a Dozen?* (PS–1). Illus. 2000, Boyds Mills $15.95 (1-56397-827-X). 32pp. This advanced mathematical concept book introduces words and phrases such as even and odd, first and second, uni- and bi-, and baker's dozen. (Rev: BL 3/15/00; HBG 10/00; SLJ 4/00) [510]

591 Szekeres, Cyndy. *I Can Count 100 Bunnies: And So Can You!* (PS–1). Illus. 1999, Scholastic $12.95 (0-590-38361-2). 48pp. Wilbur counts 99 bunnies who come to welcome number 100 — Wilbur's new baby sister. (Rev: BL 1/1–15/99; HBG 10/99; SLJ 2/99)

592 Szekeres, Cyndy. *Learn to Count, Funny Bunnies* (PS). Illus. by author. 2000, Scholastic $6.99 (0-439-14994-0). In this board book, youngsters will learn to count to ten as the relatives of Wilbur Bunny arrive for his birthday party. (Rev: SLJ 5/00)

593 Tafuri, Nancy. *Who's Counting?* (PS). Illus. by author. 1986, Greenwillow LB $15.93 (0-688-06131-1). 24pp. Each double-page spread is devoted to a number from one to ten. (Rev: BL 3/1/86; HB 5–6/86; SLJ 4/86)

594 Thorne-Thomsen, Kathleen, and Paul Rocheleau. *The Shaker's Dozen* (PS–2). Illus. 1999, Chronicle $15.95 (0-8118-2299-0). 32pp. Full-color photographs of artifacts are used to illustrate this book, which is part counting book and part introduction to Shaker life and culture. (Rev: BCCB 12/99; BL 10/15/99; HBG 3/00; SLJ 11/99) [289]

595 Tildes, Phyllis L. *Counting on Calico* (PS–K). Illus. 1995, Charlesbridge paper $6.95 (0-88106-862-4). 32pp. The features of a calico cat are used to introduce basic numbers, ending with 20 wet paw prints. (Rev: BL 6/1–15/95)

596 *The Timbertoes 123 Counting Book* (PS–1). Illus. 1997, Boyds Mills $7.95 (1-56397-627-7). 32pp. Basic numbers are introduced by the Timbertoes, a family of wooden figures, when they visit an apple orchard. (Rev: BL 3/1/97; SLJ 7/97)

597 *Toddler Two* (PS). Illus. by Winnie Cheon. 2000, Lee & Low $6.95 (1-58430-015-9). The concept of two is explored in this interactive board book with flaps and pop-ups. (Rev: SLJ 1/01)

598 Toft, Kim Michelle, and Allan Sheather. *One Less Fish* (K–3). Illus. 1998, Charlesbridge $15.95 (0-88106-322-3); paper $6.95 (0-88106-323-1). 32pp. Counting down from 12 to one, this book shows the perils fish face, including such threats as offshore oil drilling. (Rev: BL 7/98; HBG 10/98) [513.2]

599 Trinca, Rod, and Kerry Argent. *One Woolly Wombat* (PS–2). Illus. by Kerry Argent. 1985, Kane/Miller paper $6.95 (0-916291-10-3). 32pp. A charming 1-to-14 counting book featuring Australian animals. (Rev: BL 7/85; HB 7–8/85; SLJ 9/85)

600 Van Laan, Nancy. *A Tree for Me* (PS–1). Illus. by Sheila W. Samton. 2000, Knopf LB $17.99 (0-679-99384-3). 32pp. In this counting book, a child and a dog look for a tree to climb but find that they are inhabited by various numbers of animals. (Rev: BL 2/1/00; SLJ 3/00)

601 Wadsworth, Ginger. *One Tiger Growls: A Counting Book of Animal Sounds* (PS–3). Illus. by James M. Needham. 1999, Charlesbridge LB $15.95 (0-88106-273-1); paper $6.95 (0-88106-274-X). 32pp. Using several double-page spreads, numbers are introduced by different animal sounds. (Rev: BL 2/1/99; HBG 10/99; SLJ 4/99) [513.2]

602 Walsh, Ellen S. *Mouse Count* (PS–K). Illus. 1991, Harcourt $13.00 (0-15-256023-8). 32pp. In this counting book, ten little mice fall asleep unaware that a hungry snake is nearby. (Rev: BL 2/15/91; HB 5–6/91; SLJ 5/91*)

603 Walton, Rick. *How Many How Many How Many* (PS–1). Illus. by Cynthia Jabar. 1993, Candlewick $14.95 (1-56402-062-2). A variety of items are used in this effective counting book that covers the numbers one through 12. (Rev: SLJ 2/94)

604 Walton, Rick. *One More Bunny: Adding from One to Ten* (PS–1). Illus. by Paige Miglio. 2000, Lothrop LB $15.89 (0-688-16848-5). 24pp. Readers participate in this counting book as they are asked to find bunnies in illustrations and add them up. (Rev: BL 4/15/00; HBG 10/00; SLJ 7/00)

605 Watson, Amy, et al. *The Folk Art Counting Book* (PS–2). Illus. 1992, Abrams $12.95 (0-8109-3306-3). 40pp. Collections from the Rockefeller Folk Art Center in Williamsburg, Virginia, invite the younger reader to count to 20. (Rev: BL 6/15/92; SLJ 8/92) [745]

606 Wells, Robert. *Can You Count to a Googol?* (PS–1). Illus. 2000, Albert Whitman $14.95 (0-8075-1060-2); paper $6.95 (0-8075-1061-0). 32pp. This counting book starts with one and moves to ten, 100, 1,000 until reaching a googol, the number one followed by 100 zeros. (Rev: BL 3/1/00; HBG 10/00; SLJ 5/00)

607 Wells, Rosemary. *Emily's First 100 Days of School* (PS–2). Illus. 2000, Hyperion LB $14.90 (0-7868-2443-3). 64pp. A large-format counting book that also involves a school story as bunnies, cats, pigs, and other animals go about a series of imaginative activities. (Rev: BCCB 7–8/00; BL 5/15/00; HB 3–4/00; HBG 10/00; SLJ 5/00)

608 Williams, Rozanne Lanczak. *The Coin Counting Book* (PS–3). Illus. 2001, Charlesbridge $16.95 (0-88106-325-8); paper $6.95 (0-88106-326-6). 32pp. This counting book uses coins to show how five pennies make a nickel and so on until the reader discovers the various combinations that make a dollar. (Rev: BL 3/1/01)

609 Williams, Sue. *Let's Go Visiting* (PS–K). Illus. by Julie Vivas. 1998, Harcourt $15.00 (0-15-201823-9). 32pp. In this counting and color-identification book, a young child and his dog visit barnyard friends — one brown foal, two red calves, etc. (Rev: BL 11/1/98; HBG 3/99; SLJ 12/98)

610 Wilson, Anna. *Over in the Grasslands* (PS–1). Illus. by Alison Bartlett. 2000, Little, Brown $14.95 (0-316-93910-2). 32pp. Using the African grasslands as a setting, animal mothers and their babies introduce numbers one to ten. (Rev: BL 10/1/00; HBG 3/01; SLJ 11/00)

611 Winter, Jeanette. *Josefina* (PS–3). Illus. 1996, Harcourt $15.00 (0-15-201091-2). 36pp. An original counting book that features the Mexican woman Josefina and her amazing collection of clay figures. (Rev: BCCB 10/96; BL 10/15/96*; SLJ 10/96)

612 Wojtowycz, David. *Animal Antics from 1 to 10* (PS). Illus. 2000, Holiday $16.95 (0-8234-1552-X). 26pp. When readers visit Hotel 1 2 3, they are introduced to the numbers one to ten and some very unusual beasts like two tangoing toucans. (Rev: BL 10/15/00; HBG 3/01; SLJ 10/00)

613 Wood, Jakki. *Moo Moo, Brown Cow* (PS–1). Illus. by Rog Bonner. 1992, Harcourt $14.00 (0-15-200533-1). 28pp. In this large-sized counting book, a kitten asks farm animals about their young. (Rev: BL 6/15/92; SLJ 8/92)

614 Yektai, Niki. *Bears at the Beach: Counting 10 to 20* (PS–1). Illus. 1996, Millbrook LB $21.90 (0-7613-0047-3). 32pp. A wordless counting book that covers numbers from ten to 20. (Rev: BL 7/96; SLJ 6/96)

615 Zabar, Abbie. *55 Friends* (PS–3). Illus. by author. 1994, Hyperion $13.95 (0-7868-0021-6). In a fanciful text, animals from one to ten are introduced and then combined in various ways to reach 55. (Rev: SLJ 11/94)

Bedtime Books and Nursery Rhymes

Bedtime Books

616 Ahlberg, Allan. *Mockingbird* (PS). Illus. by Paul Howard. 1998, Candlewick $16.99 (0-7636-0439-9). 40pp. Throughout the day, a baby receives gifts that don't work, including a mockingbird that doesn't sing. (Rev: BCCB 10/98; BL 9/15/98*; HBG 3/99; SLJ 10/98) [782.4]

617 Alexander, Martha. *You're a Genius, Blackboard Bear* (PS–K). Illus. 1995, Candlewick $12.95 (1-56402-238-2). 32pp. Anthony and Blackboard Bear build a rocket ship but decide it is better to remain at home. (Rev: BCCB 6/96; BL 5/1/95; SLJ 6/95)

618 *All the Pretty Little Horses: A Traditional Lullaby* (PS–K). Illus. by Linda Saport. 1999, Clarion $14.00 (0-395-93097-9). 32pp. In this version of the classic lullaby, pictures from a bygone era depict an African American woman rocking her baby on a porch in the rural South. (Rev: BL 11/1/99; HBG 3/00; SLJ 12/99) [782.4]

619 Anholt, Catherine, and Laurence Anholt. *The Twins, Two by Two* (PS–K). Illus. 1992, Candlewick $13.95 (1-56402-041-X). 32pp. Twins Min-

nie and Max learn how to go to bed, from the story of Noah's ark. (Rev: BL 2/1/92)

620 Appelt, Kathi. *Bayou Lullaby* (PS–1). Illus. by Neil Waldman. 1995, Morrow LB $15.93 (0-688-12857-2). 40pp. A Cajun bedtime tale of a land ruled over by the king of the bullfrogs. (Rev: BL 3/15/95; SLJ 4/95*)

621 Appelt, Kathi. *Cowboy Dreams* (PS–1). Illus. by Barry Root. 1999, HarperCollins $14.95 (0-06-027763-7). 32pp. In this bedtime book, the author takes tired young cowboys from their palominos and gently guides them to their beds. (Rev: BL 1/1–15/99; HBG 10/99; SLJ 2/99)

622 Appelt, Kathi. *I See the Moon* (PS–K). Illus. by Debra R. Jenkins. 1997, Eerdmans $15.00 (0-8028-5118-5). 24pp. A bedtime book about a little girl all alone on the sea in a tiny boat. (Rev: BCCB 5/97; BL 3/15/97)

623 Apperley, Dawn. *Nighty-Night* (PS). Illus. by author. Series: A Baby Bunny Board Book. 1999, Little, Brown $5.95 (0-316-60427-5). This board book pictures such activities as evening games, stories, drinking milk, and hugs and kisses before bed. Also use *Wakey-wakey* (1999) by the same author. (Rev: SLJ 5/99)

624 Apple, Margot. *Brave Martha* (PS–K). Illus. 1999, Houghton $15.00 (0-395-59422-7). 32pp. Without her cat Sophie to check her bedroom at night for monsters, Martha has to do it herself and not nearly as well. (Rev: BL 9/15/99; HBG 3/00; SLJ 9/99)

625 Arnold, Tedd. *Five Ugly Monsters* (PS–K). Illus. 1995, Scholastic $6.95 (0-590-22226-0). 24pp. Several groups of monsters interrupt a little boy's plans to go to sleep. (Rev: BCCB 10/95; BL 11/15/95; SLJ 12/95)

626 Arnold, Tedd. *Huggly Takes a Bath* (PS). Illus. 1999, Scholastic $15.95 (0-590-91820-6). 32pp. A naive little monster comes out from under the bed at night and, while exploring the bathroom, enjoys such delightful discoveries as bubble bath. (Rev: BL 2/1/99; HBG 10/99; SLJ 4/99)

627 Asch, Frank. *Barnyard Lullaby* (PS–2). Illus. 1998, Simon & Schuster $15.00 (0-689-81363-5). 40pp. At first, it is only a mother hen who is singing a lullaby, but soon all the other animals and the farmer's wife join in. (Rev: BCCB 3/98; BL 1/1–15/98*; HBG 10/98; SLJ 2/98)

628 Asch, Frank. *Good Night, Baby Bear* (PS). Illus. 1998, Harcourt $14.00 (0-15-200836-5). 32pp. Mother Bear has a hard time getting Baby Bear to bed down for the winter, particularly when he asks for the moon. (Rev: BL 7/98; HBG 3/99; SLJ 9/98)

629 Aylesworth, Jim. *The Good-Night Kiss* (PS–1). Illus. by Walter L. Krudop. 1993, Atheneum $14.95 (0-689-31515-5). 32pp. Various animals view one another, but the last to be seen is a child getting a good-night kiss. (Rev: BL 9/1/93; SLJ 12/93)

630 Aylesworth, Jim. *Teddy Bear Tears* (PS–1). Illus. by Jo Ellen McAllister-Stammen. 1997, Simon & Schuster $16.00 (0-689-31776-X). 32pp. When the lights go out at bedtime, a young boy tells his four teddy bears that they must not be scared. (Rev: BL 4/1/97; SLJ 6/97)

631 Ballard, Robin. *Tonight and Tomorrow* (PS–K). Illus. 2000, Greenwillow $15.95 (0-688-16790-X). 24pp. As he goes to bed, a young boy imagines all the wonderful activities that are in store for him the next day. (Rev: BCCB 5/00; BL 4/15/00; HBG 10/00; SLJ 6/00)

632 Ballard, Robin. *When We Get Home* (PS–1). Illus. 1999, Greenwillow $16.00 (0-688-16168-5). 24pp. As a young girl drives home with her mother at night, she thinks of the comforting bedtime rituals that await her. (Rev: BL 4/1/99; HBG 10/99; SLJ 6/99)

633 Banks, Kate. *And If the Moon Could Talk* (PS–2). Illus. by Georg Hallensleben. 1998, Farrar $15.00 (0-374-30299-5). 32pp. At bedtime, a little girl's actions are duplicated in the outside world by a number of different animals. (Rev: BCCB 4/98; BL 2/15/98; HB 3–4/98*; HBG 10/98; SLJ 2/98*)

634 Banks, Kate. *The Night Worker* (PS–2). Illus. by Georg Hallensleben. 2000, Farrar $16.00 (0-374-35520-7). 40pp. Alex follows his Papa, a construction worker on the night shift, and helps him all night long until morning when he comes home to bed. (Rev: BCCB 7–8/00; BL 8/00*; HBG 3/01; SLJ 8/00)

635 Bauer, Marion Dane. *Sleep, Little One, Sleep* (PS–K). Illus. by JoEllen M. Stammen. 1999, Simon & Schuster $16.00 (0-689-82250-2). 32pp. A father describes to his daughter what falling asleep means by using examples from the animal kingdom such as a spider, puppy, mouse, and bird. (Rev: BL 8/99; HBG 3/00; SLJ 9/99)

636 Beck, Ian. *Home Before Dark* (PS–K). Illus. 2001, Scholastic $15.95 (0-439-17522-4). 32pp. A stuffed bear falls out of Lily's stroller in a park, but manages to find his way back home just in time to accompany Lily to bed. (Rev: BL 3/1/01; SLJ 3/01)

637 Blos, Joan W. *Bedtime!* (PS–1). Illus. by Stephen Lambert. 1998, Simon & Schuster $12.00 (0-689-81031-8). 32pp. A young child sends each of his stuffed animals to bed before he decides it is time to join them. (Rev: BCCB 4/98; BL 5/15/98; HBG 10/98; SLJ 7/98)

638 Brown, Margaret Wise. *Goodnight Moon* (PS). Illus. by Clement Hurd. 1947, HarperCollins LB $14.89 (0-06-020706-X); paper $5.95 (0-06-443017-0). 32pp. A soothing go-to-sleep story. A pop-up book version is *The Goodnight Moon Room: A Pop-Up Book* (1985).

639 Brown, Margaret Wise. *The Sleepy Men* (PS–K). Illus. by Robert Rayevsky. 1996, Hyperion LB $15.49 (0-7868-2126-4). 32pp. A bedtime story about a big sleepy man who tells a little sleepy man a bedtime story. (Rev: BCCB 1/97; BL 10/1/96; SLJ 12/96)

640 Buchholz, Quint. *Sleep Well, Little Bear* (K–3). Trans. by Peter F. Neumeyer. Illus. 1994, Farrar $15.00 (0-374-37026-5). 33pp. At night, a toy bear thinks about the day just past and about the mysterious night outside. (Rev: BL 12/1/94; SLJ 12/94)

641 Bunting, Eve. *No Nap* (PS–1). Illus. by Susan Meddaugh. 1989, Houghton $15.95 (0-89919-813-9). 28pp. Whenever bedtime is suggested, Susie says, "No nap." (Rev: BCCB 10/89; BL 9/15/89; HB 1–2/90; SLJ 10/89)

642 *The Candlewick Book of Bedtime Stories* (PS–2). Illus. 1995, Candlewick $19.99 (1-56402-652-3). 96pp. Nineteen well-known picture books suitable for bedtime reading are reprinted, many with abridged illustrations. (Rev: BL 11/15/95; SLJ 12/95)

643 Carlstrom, Nancy White. *Swim the Silver Sea, Joshie Otter* (PS–K). Illus. by Ken Kuroi. 1997, Putnam paper $6.99 (0-698-11447-7). 40pp. At bedtime, a baby otter swims back to his mother and the love she gives him. (Rev: BL 4/1/93; SLJ 5/93)

644 Carlstrom, Nancy White. *Where Does the Night Hide?* (PS–1). Illus. by Thomas B. Allen and Laura Allen. 1990, Macmillan LB $13.95 (0-02-717390-9). 32pp. A mother and daughter search in many places to find where the night hides during the day. (Rev: BL 10/15/90; SLJ 2/91)

645 Cazet, Denys. *Night Lights: 24 Poems to Sleep On* (PS–2). Illus. by author. 1997, Orchard LB $16.99 (0-531-33010-9). There are 24 bedtime rhymes in this nighttime collection; some are lullabies, others are amusing poems about animals at night. (Rev: SLJ 5/97)

646 Charlip, Remy. *Sleepytime Rhyme* (PS). Illus. 1999, Greenwillow $16.00 (0-688-16271-1). 24pp. In this bedtime book, a mother plays with her child while telling him (or her) all the body parts she loves. (Rev: BCCB 10/99; BL 11/15/99; HBG 3/00; SLJ 9/99)

647 Chislett, Gail. *Whump* (PS–1). Illus. by Vladyana Krykorka. 1992, Firefly paper $0.99 (1-55037-253-X). A little boy has trouble adjusting to his big new bed. (Rev: SLJ 3/90)

648 Chorao, Kay. *The Baby's Bedtime Book* (PS–K). Illus. by author. 1984, Dutton $16.99 (0-525-44149-2). 64pp. Twenty-seven verses suitable for bedtime reading.

649 Christiana, David. *Drawer in a Drawer* (K–3). Illus. 1990, Farrar $13.95 (0-374-31874-3). 32pp. A first picture book of a surreal world with quick-changing patterns. (Rev: BL 7/90; SLJ 10/90)

650 Cleary, Beverly. *Petey's Bedtime Story* (K–3). Illus. by David Small. 1993, Morrow LB $14.89 (0-688-10661-7). 32pp. Petey prolongs his bedtime rituals until his parents fall asleep from exhaustion. (Rev: BL 9/1/93; SLJ 2/94)

651 Conrad, Pam. *Animal Lullabies* (K–3). Illus. by Richard Cowdrey. 1997, HarperCollins LB $14.89 (0-06-024719-3). 32pp. Each of the different animals sings a lullaby that brings out one of their characteristics. (Rev: BL 9/1/97; HBG 3/98; SLJ 1/98)

652 Cooper, Susan. *Matthew's Dragon* (K–2). Illus. by Joseph A. Smith. 1991, Macmillan $14.95 (0-689-50512-4). After a bedtime story involving dragons, Matthew is visited by a friendly one. (Rev: SLJ 10/91)

653 Corentin, Philippe. *Papa!* (PS–1). Illus. by author. 1997, Chronicle $13.95 (0-8118-1640-0). At night, a little boy and a monster child frighten each other and are comforted by their respective parents. (Rev: SLJ 9/97)

654 Cowell, Cressida. *What Shall We Do with the Boo-Hoo Baby?* (PS–1). Illus. by Ingrid Godon. 2000, Scholastic $15.95 (0-439-15311-5). 32pp. Animals try different tactics to hush a crying baby and become so tired that they nap, which causes the baby to smile. (Rev: BCCB 2/01; BL 1/1–15/01; HBG 3/01; SLJ 3/01)

655 Cuneo, Mary L. *Mail for Husher Town* (PS–2). Illus. by Pamela Paparone. 2000, Greenwillow $15.95 (0-688-16525-7). 24pp. Julia, her cat, and three stuffed animals enjoy playing on the girl's green bedspread just before going to sleep. (Rev: BL 7/00; HBG 10/00; SLJ 6/00)

656 Dale, Penny. *Ten Play Hide-and-Seek* (PS). Illus. by author. 1998, Candlewick $15.99 (0-7636-0654-5). At bedtime, a child's stuffed animals play a game of hide-and-seek with him. (Rev: HBG 3/99; SLJ 1/99)

657 Davis, Karen. *Star Light, Star Bright* (PS–1). Illus. 1993, Simon & Schuster $15.00 (0-671-79455-8). 24pp. Louisa searches throughout her house and in the sky for a special star on which she can wish. (Rev: BL 6/1–15/93)

658 Davis, Kate. *I Hate to Go to Bed!* (PS–2). Illus. 1999, Harcourt $14.00 (0-15-201920-0). 36pp. A young girl tries all sorts of tricks to avoid going to sleep. (Rev: BL 10/15/99; HBG 3/00; SLJ 3/00)

659 Day, Alexandra. *Boswell Wide Awake* (PS). Illus. by author. 1999, Farrar $15.00 (0-374-39973-5). An almost wordless book about a young bear who wanders around his house and garden before going to sleep. (Rev: HBG 3/00; SLJ 12/99)

660 Doherty, Berlie. *The Midnight Man* (K–3). Illus. by Ian Andrew. 1998, Candlewick $15.99 (0-7636-0700-2). 32pp. Harry and Mister Dog follow the midnight man as he scatters stars and, after they fall asleep, are brought home by the moon. (Rev: BL 2/15/99; HBG 3/99; SLJ 11/98)

661 Dotlich, Rebecca. *Sweet Dreams of the Wild: Poems for Bedtime* (PS–K). Illus. by Katharine Dodge. 1996, Boyds Mills $15.95 (1-56397-180-1). 32pp. A delightful picture book that explores in poetry and illustrations the many places animals sleep. (Rev: BL 1/1–15/96; SLJ 3/96) [811.54]

662 Downing, Julie, comp. *Lullaby and Good Night: Songs for Sweet Dreams* (PS). Illus. by Julie Downing. 1999, Simon & Schuster $15.00 (0-689-81085-7). A collection of 14 lullabies illustrated with beautifully detailed watercolors. (Rev: HBG 3/00; SLJ 12/99)

663 Dragonwagon, Crescent. *Half a Moon and One Whole Star* (PS–1). Illus. by Jerry Pinkney. 1990, Simon & Schuster paper $5.99 (0-689-71415-7). 32pp. Susan is falling asleep as the sights and sounds of the night surround her. (Rev: BCCB 5/86; BL 3/15/86; SLJ 4/86)

664 *Dreamtime: A Book of Lullabies* (PS–1). Ed. by Belinda Hollyer. Illus. by Robin Bell Cornfield.

1999, Viking $16.99 (0-670-88363-8). 48pp. Combining traditional chants and songs with the work of modern poets, this book presents bedtime lullabies illustrated with gentle watercolor and pen drawings. (Rev: BCCB 1/99; BL 1/1–15/99; HB 3–4/99; HBG 10/99; SLJ 4/99) [782.4215]

665 Dunbar, Joyce. *Tell Me Something Happy Before I Go to Sleep* (PS). Illus. by Debi Gliori. 1998, Harcourt $16.00 (0-15-201795-X). A young bunny has trouble getting to sleep until she begins thinking of all the nice things that will happen to her the next day. (Rev: HBG 3/99; SLJ 11/98)

666 Dunbar, Joyce. *The Very Small* (PS–1). Illus. by Debi Gliori. 2000, Harcourt $16.00 (0-15-202346-1). 26pp. Giant Baby Bear finds a little creature in the woods and cares for him until the tiny thing is reunited with his parents, who tuck him into bed with his own teddy bear. (Rev: BL 12/15/00; HBG 3/01; SLJ 11/00)

667 Dyer, Jane. *Animal Crackers: A Delectable Collection of Pictures, Poems, and Lullabies for the Very Young* (PS). Illus. 1996, Little, Brown $17.95 (0-316-19766-1). 64pp. An immensely appealing collection of lullabies, poems, and nursery rhymes accompanied by muted illustrations. (Rev: BCCB 3/96; BL 4/15/96; SLJ 5/96)

668 Eduar, Gilles. *Dream Journey* (PS–K). Illus. by author. 1999, Orchard $15.95 (0-531-30202-4). While a little boy sleeps on his back, a camel travels through oceans, jungles, mountains, cities, and storms. (Rev: HBG 3/00; SLJ 12/99)

669 Eilenberg, Max. *Cowboy Kid* (PS–2). Illus. by Sue Heap. 2000, Candlewick $15.99 (0-7636-1058-5). 32pp. At bedtime, a little boy makes sure his stuffed toys also get a goodnight hug and kiss. (Rev: BCCB 9/00; BL 10/15/00; HBG 3/01; SLJ 7/00)

670 Emberley, Ed. *Go Away, Big Green Monster!* (PS–1). Illus. 1993, Little, Brown $15.95 (0-316-23653-5). 32pp. This toy book deals with a child's nighttime fears in a lighthearted way that will be both a joy and a comfort to young people. (Rev: BCCB 3/93; BL 4/15/93*; HB 7–8/93)

671 Engel, Diana. *Circle Song* (PS–1). Illus. 1999, Marshall Cavendish $15.95 (0-7614-5040-8). 32pp. A brief bedtime rhyme that evokes circles, including the moon. (Rev: BL 4/1/99; HBG 10/99; SLJ 6/99)

672 Faulkner, Keith. *The Scared Little Bear: A Not-Too-Scary Pop-up Book* (PS–2). Illus. by Jonathan Lambert. 2000, Scholastic $9.95 (0-531-30267-9). A pop-up book in which a young bear discovers that the scary sounds he hears in the night are only his father snoring. (Rev: SLJ 2/01)

673 Fernandes, Eugenie. *Baby Dreams* (PS). Illus. by author. 1999, Stoddart $13.95 (0-7737-3139-3). An imaginative view of the images a sleeping baby might experience — being in a land of sleeping infants or being cradled on a rabbit's back. (Rev: SLJ 1/00)

674 Field, Eugene. *Wynken, Blynken, and Nod: A Poem* (PS–K). Illus. by Johanna Westerman. 1995, North-South LB $15.88 (1-55858-423-4). 24pp. New illustrations enhance this edition of the classic bedtime poem. (Rev: BL 11/1/95; SLJ 11/95) [811]

675 *Fishing for a Dream: Ocean Lullabies and Night Dreams* (PS–2). Ed. by Kate Kiesler. Illus. 1999, Clarion $16.00 (0-395-94149-0). 32pp. A collection of lullabies that focus on the nighttime sea and the images it evokes. (Rev: BL 12/15/99; HBG 3/00; SLJ 12/99) [782.4215]

676 Fox, Mem. *A Bedtime Story* (PS–2). Illus. by Elivia Savadier. 1996, Mondo $13.95 (1-57255-136-4). Polly and Bed Rabbit look forward to a bedtime story from their parents. (Rev: SLJ 12/96)

677 Fox, Mem. *Sleepy Bears* (PS–2). Illus. by Kerry Argent. 1999, Harcourt $16.00 (0-15-202016-0). 32pp. Mama Bear sings a different lullaby to each of her six cubs as they settle in for a winter's sleep. (Rev: BL 11/15/99; HBG 3/00; SLJ 10/99)

678 Fox, Mem. *Time for Bed* (PS). Illus. by Jane Dyer. 1993, Harcourt $16.00 (0-15-288183-2). 32pp. Various animals put their babies to sleep in this quiet bedtime book. (Rev: BCCB 10/93; BL 10/1/93; SLJ 10/93)

679 French, Vivian. *A Song for Little Toad* (PS–1). Illus. by Barbara Firth. 1995, Candlewick $14.99 (1-56402-614-0). Every animal thinks that Mother Toad's croaking lullaby is ugly except Little Toad. (Rev: HB 11–12/95; SLJ 9/95)

680 Garelick, May. *Look at the Moon* (K–3). Illus. by Barbara Garrison. 1996, Mondo $14.95 (1-57255-142-9). 30pp. A young girl wonders if animals experience the same thrill of seeing moonlight as she does. (Rev: BL 11/15/96; SLJ 1/97)

681 George, Lindsay Barrett. *My Bunny and Me* (PS–2). Illus. 2001, Greenwillow LB $15.89 (0-688-16075-1). 32pp. A boy draws a bunny that comes to life and the two play together until the boy goes to bed and the bunny hops off into a field. (Rev: BL 1/1–15/01)

682 Gerber, Carole. *Firefly Night* (PS–3). Illus. by Marty Husted. 2000, Charlesbridge $16.95 (1-58089-051-2); paper $6.95 (1-58089-066-0). 32pp. Based on some lines from Longfellow's *Hiawatha*, this is the gentle story of a young Chippewa girl who is guided home at night by a firefly. (Rev: BL 11/1/00; HBG 3/01; SLJ 1/01)

683 Gerber, Carole. *Hush! A Gaelic Lullaby* (PS–2). Illus. by Marty Husted. 1997, Whispering Coyote $16.95 (1-879085-57-7). In this lullaby, an Irish family puts baby to bed while taking precautions against a storm that is approaching their farm. (Rev: HB 1–2, 3–4, 5-6/97; HBG 3/98; SLJ 1/98)

684 Gerstein, Mordicai. *Bedtime, Everybody!* (PS–2). Illus. 1996, Hyperion $13.49 (0-7868-2138-8). 32pp. Daisy has difficulty getting her many stuffed animals to go to bed. (Rev: BL 6/1–15/96; SLJ 6/96)

685 Ginsburg, Mirra, adapt. *The Sun's Asleep Behind the Hill* (PS–1). Illus. by Paul O. Zelinsky. 1982, Greenwillow LB $15.93 (0-688-00825-9). 32pp. At the end of the day all life prepares for rest.

686 Giuliano, Katie, and Michael Giuliano. *All the Way to God* (PS–1). Illus. by Giuliano Children. Series: Family Storytime Book. 1999, Golden Bks. $9.95 (0-307-10223-8). At bedtime a father and his daughter try to express how much they love one another. (Rev: HBG 10/99; SLJ 7/99)

687 Godwin, Laura. *Barnyard Prayers* (2–4). Illus. by Brian Selznick. 2000, Hyperion LB $15.49 (0-7868-2302-X). 32pp. A child's toy animals join him for bedtime prayers. (Rev: BCCB 5/00; BL 5/1/00; HB 3–4/00; HBG 10/00; SLJ 3/00) [811]

688 Goodman, Joan E. *Bernard's Nap* (PS–1). Illus. by Dominic Catalano. 1999, Boyds Mills $14.95 (1-56397-728-1). 32pp. While trying to get Bernard, a baby elephant, to take his nap, the rest of his family nod off, but not Bernard — until he eventually gives in. (Rev: BL 3/15/99; HBG 10/99; SLJ 4/99)

689 Graff, Nancy P. *In the Hush of the Evening* (PS–2). Illus. by G. Brian Karas. 1998, HarperCollins $14.95 (0-06-022099-6). 32pp. In this bedtime book, a mother tells her child about all the sounds of the evening. (Rev: BL 3/15/98; HBG 10/98; SLJ 8/98)

690 Greenstein, Elaine. *Dreaming: A Countdown to Sleep* (PS–1). Illus. 2000, Scholastic $15.95 (0-439-06302-7). 32pp. With a text that involves counting down from ten to one, this picture book evokes a dreamy atmosphere before sleep comes. (Rev: BCCB 5/00; BL 2/1/00; HBG 3/01; SLJ 6/00)

691 Griffin, Sandra U. *Earth Circles* (PS–3). Illus. by author. 1989, Walker LB $13.85 (0-8027-6845-8). The circle of life from birth to death, including the need to sleep at the end of each day, is introduced as it appears in nature. (Rev: SLJ 11/89)

692 Hagen, Jeff. *Hiawatha Passing* (K–3). Illus. by Kenneth Shue. 1995, Holt $15.95 (0-8050-1832-8). 32pp. A boy listens to the sounds of a train in the night before he falls asleep. (Rev: BL 11/15/95; SLJ 1/96)

693 Hamm, Diane J. *Rockabye Farm* (PS). Illus. by Rick Brown. 1992, Simon & Schuster paper $15.00 (0-671-74773-8). One by one, a farmer rocks the farm animals to sleep, including his own baby. (Rev: SLJ 7/92)

694 Harley, Bill. *Nothing Happened* (K–2). Illus. by Ann Miya. 1995, Tricycle Pr. $14.95 (1-883672-09-0). 32pp. Jack is determined to stay awake so he can share in all the exciting things he believes happen to his family when he is asleep. (Rev: BL 4/15/95; SLJ 6/95)

695 Harrison, Troon. *The Dream Collector* (PS–3). Illus. by Alan Daniel and Lea Daniel. 1999, Kids Can $15.95 (1-55074-437-2). 32pp. When the dream collector can't collect all the creatures left over from people's dreams because of a broken truck, little Zachary gives him a hand. (Rev: BL 3/1/99; HBG 10/99; SLJ 7/99)

696 Harshman, Marc. *All the Way to Morning* (PS–3). Illus. by Felipe Davalos. 1999, Marshall Cavendish $15.95 (0-7614-5042-4). 32pp. On a camping trip, a father tells his son what children in other countries such as Israel, Japan, and Kenya hear as they go to sleep at night. (Rev: BL 9/15/99; HBG 3/00; SLJ 11/99)

697 Hazelaar, Cor. *Zoo Dreams* (PS–1). Illus. by author. 1997, Farrar $14.00 (0-374-39730-9). Simple text and muted watercolors show how zoo animals sleep. (Rev: HB 3–4/97; SLJ 3/97)

698 Hazen, Barbara S. *Where Do Bears Sleep?* (PS). Illus. by Mary Morgan Van Royen. 1998, Harper-Festival $9.95 (0-694-01037-5). A gentle bedtime book that illustrates where a variety of animals spend their nights. (Rev: HBG 10/98; SLJ 6/98)

699 Hendry, Diana. *The Very Noisy Night* (PS–2). Illus. by Jane Chapman. 1999, Dutton $15.99 (0-525-46261-9). 36pp. Little Mouse can't sleep and wants to crawl into Big Mouse's bed but is rebuffed because his paws are too cold. (Rev: BL 12/1/99; HBG 3/00; SLJ 11/99)

700 Hest, Amy. *Mabel Dancing* (PS–1). Illus. by Christine Davenier. 2000, Candlewick $15.99 (0-7636-0746-0). Before going to sleep, Mabel creeps downstairs to join her parents as they dance at their party. (Rev: BCCB 9/00; HBG 10/00; SLJ 6/00)

701 Hillert, Margaret. *The Sky Is Not So Far Away: Night Poems for Children* (PS–1). Illus. by Thomas Werner. 1996, Boyds Mills $15.95 (1-56397-223-9). 32pp. A simple poetry book that contains poems on night themes, such as dreams and bedtime rituals. (Rev: BCCB 11/96; SLJ 9/96) [811]

702 Hines, Anna Grossnickle. *My Own Big Bed* (PS–K). Illus. by Mary Watson. 1998, Greenwillow $15.00 (0-688-15599-5). 24pp. At bedtime, a young girl enjoys her new, roomy bed, where Mommy and Daddy can sit next to her. (Rev: BL 10/15/98; HBG 3/99; SLJ 4/99)

703 Ho, Minfong. *Hush! A Thai Lullaby* (PS–3). Illus. by Holly Meade. 1996, Orchard LB $16.99 (0-531-08850-2). 32pp. In this lullaby, a mother quiets the animals, one by one, so that her baby can sleep. (Rev: BCCB 4/96; BL 4/15/96; HB 11–12/96; SLJ 3/96)

704 Hoellwarth, Cathryn C. *The Underbed* (PS–K). Illus. by Sibyl G. Grieg. 1990, Good Bks. $12.95 (0-934672-79-2). 24pp. Mother helps Tucker get rid of the monster he believes is under the bed. (Rev: BL 3/1/91; SLJ 7/91)

705 Hood, Thomas. *Before I Go to Sleep* (K–2). Illus. by Maryjane Begin. 1999, Morrow $16.00 (0-688-12424-0). In this 19th-century poem, a boy who is going to bed imagines what he would be doing if he were various animals such as a giraffe or mountain goat. (Rev: HBG 10/99; SLJ 6/99)

706 Hort, Lenny. *How Many Stars in the Sky?* (PS–1). Illus. by James E. Ransome. 1991, Morrow LB $15.93 (0-688-10104-6). 32pp. A boy and his father go out into the night to count the stars in the sky. (Rev: BCCB 6/91; BL 5/1/91; SLJ 5/91)

707 Howe, James. *There's a Monster Under My Bed* (PS–1). Illus. by David S. Rose. 1986, Macmillan $16.00 (0-689-31178-8); paper $5.99 (0-689-71409-2). 32pp. A child is sure there are monsters under his bed, only to find that the noises come from little brother Alex, who sees monsters of his own. (Rev: BL 5/1/86; HB 7–8/86; SLJ 5/86)

708 *Hush, Little Baby: A Traditional Lullaby* (PS). Illus. by Shari Halpern. 1997, North-South LB $15.88 (1-55858-808-6). 22pp. This lullaby is illus-

trated with fresh pictures that resemble parts of a quilt. (Rev: BL 10/15/97; HBG 3/98; SLJ 1/98)

709 Ingman, Bruce. *A Night on the Tiles* (PS–3). Illus. 1999, Houghton $15.00 (0-395-93655-1). 32pp. A ginger cat explains to Martha, who is about to go to sleep, all the things he does during the night, including going to a movie, attending night school, and going to a barbershop for a whisker trim. (Rev: BL 4/1/99; HBG 10/99; SLJ 3/99)

710 James, Betsy. *The Dream Stair* (K–3). Illus. by Richard J. Watson. 1990, HarperCollins $13.95 (0-06-022787-7). 32pp. After Grandmother tucks her into bed, a little girl dreams of wandering "past clouds, past angels." (Rev: BL 3/1/90; SLJ 7/90)

711 Jewell, Nancy. *Five Little Kittens* (PS). Illus. by Elizabeth Sayles. 1999, Clarion $9.95 (0-395-77517-5). 32pp. Five little kittens go through their daily routines and then contentedly fall asleep at the end of the day. (Rev: BL 8/99; HBG 3/00; SLJ 8/99)

712 Jewell, Nancy. *Sailor Song* (PS–1). Illus. by Stefano Vitale. 1999, Clarion $13.00 (0-395-82511-3). A lovely lullaby sung by a mother to her child that tells of a sailor's journey across sea and land to reach his snug house and waiting family. (Rev: HB 7–8/99; HBG 10/99; SLJ 5/99)

713 Jordan, Sandra. *Down on Casey's Farm* (PS–K). Illus. by author. 1996, Orchard LB $16.99 (0-531-08853-7). A bedtime book that introduces a number of farm animals through the fantasies of a young boy. (Rev: SLJ 10/96)

714 Kalman, Maira. *Hey Willy, See the Pyramids* (K–2). Illus. by author. 1988, Viking $16.99 (0-670-82163-2). 40pp. Sister Lulu tells a young boy an offbeat story about a woman and three cross-eyed dogs. (Rev: BL 2/1/89; SLJ 9/88)

715 Katz, Karen. *Counting Kisses* (PS). Illus. 2001, Simon & Schuster $14.00 (0-689-83470-5). 32pp. Every family member showers a baby with kisses until the young child peacefully drops off to sleep. (Rev: BCCB 2/01; BL 2/1/01; SLJ 2/01)

716 Kellogg, Steven. *A-hunting We Will Go!* (PS–K). Illus. 1998, Morrow LB $15.93 (0-688-14945-6). 40pp. Two youngsters who are not ready for bed engage in pre-bedtime activities in the company of some of their animal friends. (Rev: BL 8/98; HBG 3/99; SLJ 11/98) [782.4216]

717 Kirk, Daniel. *Hush, Little Alien* (PS–K). Illus. 1999, Hyperion LB $13.49 (0-7868-2469-7). 24pp. This lullaby uses the folk song "Hush Little Baby" for a variation on space aliens, shooting stars, rocket ships, and astronauts. (Rev: BL 11/15/99; HBG 3/00; SLJ 12/99)

718 Knutson, Kimberley. *Bed Bouncers* (PS–K). Illus. 1995, Simon & Schuster paper $14.00 (0-02-750871-4). 32pp. A brother and sister bounce from their beds into space in this bedtime story. (Rev: BL 5/15/95; SLJ 8/95)

719 Koller, Jackie F. *No Such Thing* (K–3). Illus. by Betsy Lewin. 1997, Boyds Mills $14.95 (1-56397-490-8). 32pp. A monster and her son under the bed are undergoing the same comforting bedtime rituals as a real mother and son. (Rev: BCCB 3/97; BL 4/1/97; SLJ 6/97)

720 Koralek, Jenny. *Night Ride to Nanna's* (PS–3). Illus. by Mandy Sutcliffe. 2000, Candlewick $15.99 (0-7636-1192-1). 32pp. A gentle family story about the nighttime ride that Amy and her family take to her grandmother's home where she is put to bed. (Rev: BL 12/1/00; HBG 3/01; SLJ 12/00)

721 Lansky, Bruce. *Sweet Dreams: Bedtime Poems, Songs and Lullabies* (PS). Illus. by Vicki Wehrman. 1996, Meadowbrook Pr. $15.00 (0-671-57046-3). 32pp. A collection of original poems and traditional songs and rhymes about going to bed and to sleep. (Rev: SLJ 10/96)

722 Lesser, Carolyn. *The Goodnight Circle* (PS–2). Illus. by Lorinda Bryan Cauley. 1984, Harcourt $14.95 (0-15-232158-6); paper $7.00 (0-15-232159-4). 30pp. What animals do between night and morning.

723 Leuck, Laura. *Sun Is Falling, Night Is Calling* (PS). Illus. by Ora Eitan. 1994, Simon & Schuster paper $15.00 (0-671-86940-X). 32pp. A loving bunny soothes her child to sleep in this quiet bedtime book. (Rev: BCCB 6/94; BL 6/1–15/94)

724 Lindgren, Astrid. *I Don't Want to Go to Bed* (PS–1). Trans. by Barbara Lucas. Illus. by Ilon Wikland. 1988, Farrar $12.95 (91-29-59066-3). 32pp. Five-year-old Larry won't go to bed until Aunt Lottie gives him a pair of magic glasses. (Rev: BL 12/1/88; SLJ 4/89)

725 Loh, Morag. *Tucking Mommy In* (PS–1). Illus. by Donna Rawlins. 1988, Orchard paper $5.95 (0-531-07025-5). 40pp. Mommy falls asleep and the children tuck her in. (Rev: BCCB 9/88; BL 10/1/88; SLJ 10/88)

726 London, Jonathan. *Froggy Goes to Bed* (PS–K). Illus. by Frank Remkiewicz. 2000, Viking $15.99 (0-670-88860-5). 32pp. The nighttime rituals become so prolonged that Froggy's mother falls asleep before he does. (Rev: BL 3/1/00; HBG 10/00; SLJ 6/00)

727 London, Jonathan. *Snuggle Wuggle* (PS). Illus. by Michael Rex. 2000, Harcourt $13.00 (0-15-202159-0). 32pp. After showing how a number of different animals hug one another, this book ends with a mother and child hugging at bedtime. (Rev: BCCB 4/00; BL 3/15/00; HBG 10/00; SLJ 5/00)

728 London, Jonathan. *What Do You Love?* (PS–K). Illus. by Karen L. Schmidt. 2000, Harcourt $14.00 (0-15-201919-7). 32pp. A sweet story about a young dog who accompanies his mother through a day of happy activities including, just before bed, a moonlit walk. (Rev: BL 1/1–15/01; HBG 3/01; SLJ 12/00)

729 Long, Sylvia. *Hush Little Baby* (PS–1). Illus. 1997, Chronicle $12.95 (0-8118-1416-5). 32pp. This song, a tender lullaby, focuses on the relationship between a mother and her baby bunny. (Rev: BL 6/1–15/97)

730 *Lullabies: An Illustrated Songbook* (PS–1). Illus. 1997, Harcourt $23.00 (0-15-201728-3). 96pp. Thirty-seven lullabies with simple piano accompaniment and guitar chords, as well as background

information on each song. (Rev: BL 12/15/97; HBG 3/98; SLJ 1/98) [782]

731 Lum, Kate. *What! Cried Granny: An Almost Bedtime Story* (PS–K). Illus. by Adrian Johnson. 1999, Dial $14.99 (0-8037-2382-2). 32pp. While visiting his grandmother, Patrick puts her to work constructing a bed, knitting a blanket, making a pillow, etc., so he can go to bed properly. (Rev: BCCB 3/99; BL 5/1/99; HB 3–4/99; HBG 10/99; SLJ 3/99)

732 McBratney, Sam. *Guess How Much I Love You* (PS–K). Illus. by Anita Jeram. 1995, Candlewick $15.99 (1-56402-473-3). 32pp. In this bedtime book, a young rabbit tries to tell his father how much he loves him. (Rev: BL 3/15/95*; HB 7–8/95; SLJ 5/95)

733 McCain, Becky Ray. *Grandmother's Dreamcatcher* (K–2). Illus. by Stacey Schuett. 1998, Whitman $15.95 (0-8075-3031-X). 32pp. A young Chippewa boy goes to live with his grandmother, who cures him of having bad dreams by placing a dreamcatcher above his bed. (Rev: BL 10/1/98; HBG 3/99; SLJ 12/98)

734 McCourt, Lisa. *I Love You, Stinky Face* (PS–K). Illus. by Cyd Moore. 1997, Troll $15.95 (0-8167-4392-4). 32pp. In this tender bedtime story, a young girl tests the limits of her mother's love with a series of questions like "Would you love me if I were a big scary ape?" (Rev: BL 10/15/97*; HBG 3/98; SLJ 10/97)

735 MacDonald, Margaret Read. *Tuck-Me-In Tales: Bedtime Stories from Around the World* (PS–1). Illus. by Yvonne Davis. 1996, August House $19.95 (0-87483-461-9). 64pp. Five traditional bedtime stories from around the world are lavishly illustrated. (Rev: BL 10/1/96; SLJ 11/96) [398.2]

736 McDonald, Megan. *My House Has Stars* (PS–3). Illus. by Peter Catalanotto. 1996, Orchard LB $16.99 (0-531-08879-0). 32pp. Eight children from around the world tell about their homes in the evening and at night. (Rev: BCCB 11/96; BL 11/1/96; SLJ 10/96)

737 McKellar, Shona, ed. *A Child's Book of Lullabies* (1–4). Illus. by Mary Cassatt. 1997, DK $14.95 (0-7894-1507-0). 32pp. Using 13 reproductions of Mary Cassatt's paintings, several traditional lullabies are introduced. (Rev: BL 6/1–15/97)

738 McMullan, Kate. *If You Were My Bunny* (PS–K). Illus. by David McPhail. 1996, Scholastic $7.95 (0-590-52749-5). 32pp. A bedtime book with lullabies sung by different loving animal mothers to their attentive offspring. (Rev: BL 5/1/96; HB 7–8/96)

739 McMullan, Kate. *Papa's Song* (PS–1). Illus. by Jim McMullan. 2000, Farrar $15.00 (0-374-35732-3). 32pp. Baby Bear has trouble going to sleep until Papa Bear takes him by boat onto a river where the rocking lulls him to sleep. (Rev: BL 2/15/00; HB 3–4/00; HBG 10/00; SLJ 5/00)

740 Mallat, Kathy. *Seven Stars More!* (PS). Illus. by author. 1998, Walker $14.95 (0-8027-8675-8). A counting book that is also a bedtime book about a little girl who counts objects to put herself to sleep. (Rev: HBG 3/99; SLJ 11/98)

741 Marshall, James. *What's the Matter with Carruthers? A Bedtime Story* (K–3). Illus. by author. 1972, Houghton $18.00 (0-395-13895-7). 32pp. Carruthers, a very large bear, gets grumpy because it's time for his sleep.

742 Massie, Diane Redfield. *The Baby Beebee Bird* (PS–2). Illus. by Steven Kellogg. 2000, Harper-Collins LB $15.89 (0-06-028084-0). 32pp. In this bedtime book, the animals in the zoo can't sleep at night because of the shrill cries of a newcomer, the nocturnal beebee bird. (Rev: BL 12/15/00; SLJ 9/00)

743 Melmed, Laura K. *I Love You As Much . . .* (PS–K). Illus. by Henri Sorensen. 1993, Lothrop LB $15.89 (0-688-11719-8). 24pp. In a series of double-page spreads, various animal mothers tell their offspring how much they love them in this attractive bedtime book. (Rev: BL 9/1/93; SLJ 3/94)

744 Melmed, Laura K. *Jumbo's Lullaby* (PS). Illus. by Henri Sorensen. 1999, Lothrop LB $15.93 (0-688-16996-1). 24pp. Mama Elephant tries to get her young child to sleep by describing how other animals go to bed. (Rev: BL 10/1/99; HBG 3/00; SLJ 9/99)

745 Miller, Virginia. *Go to Bed!* (PS). Illus. 2000, Candlewick $5.99 (0-7636-1267-7). 24pp. In this board book, big bear George has to be firm to get little bear Ba to go to bed. (Rev: BL 11/15/00; HBG 3/01)

746 Miller, Virginia. *I Love You Just the Way You Are* (PS). Illus. by author. 1998, Candlewick $15.99 (0-7636-0664-2). Ba, a young bear cub, has a bad day, but his adult friend George has patience, tells him he loves him anyway, and sends him happily off to bed. (Rev: HBG 3/99; SLJ 12/98)

747 Miranda, Anne. *Night Songs* (PS–K). Illus. 1993, Macmillan LB $13.95 (0-02-767250-6). 32pp. This lullaby describes the rising of the moon in words and pictures. (Rev: BL 4/1/93; SLJ 6/93)

748 Morris, Winifred. *What If the Shark Wears Tennis Shoes?* (PS). Illus. by Betsy Lewin. 1990, Macmillan $12.95 (0-689-31587-2). 32pp. A mother patiently answers her son's farfetched questions about being left alone at night. (Rev: BL 12/15/90; SLJ 10/90)

749 Morrissey, Dean. *Ship of Dreams* (K–3). Illus. by author. 1994, Millpond: Abrams $17.95 (0-8109-3848-0). In this bedtime book, Joey takes off in his red wagon on a flight to see if the sandman really exists. (Rev: SLJ 12/94)

750 Murray, Dennis. *The Stars Are Waiting* (PS–K). Illus. by Jacqueline Rogers. 1998, Marshall Cavendish $15.95 (0-7614-5024-6). 32pp. In this bedtime book, nighttime beckons all the animals of the forest to go to sleep and finally does the same to three young children in a neighboring farmhouse. (Rev: BL 8/98; HBG 10/98; SLJ 6/98)

751 Narahashi, Keiko. *Is That Josie?* (PS–1). Illus. 1994, Macmillan paper $14.95 (0-689-50606-6). 32pp. A young girl pretends to be a number of different animals before allowing her mother to hug her at bedtime. (Rev: BCCB 10/94; BL 11/1/94; SLJ 11/94*)

752 Newfield, Marcia. *Where Did You Put Your Sleep?* (PS–1). Illus. by Andrea Da Rif. 1983, Macmillan LB $13.95 (0-689-50286-9). 32pp. A little girl who can't go to sleep plays a game with her father.

753 Nye, Naomi S. *Benito's Dream Bottle* (PS–3). Illus. by Yu Cha Pak. 1995, Simon & Schuster $15.00 (0-02-768467-9). 32pp. A young boy tries to find out what dreams are and where they come from. (Rev: BL 5/1/95; SLJ 6/95)

754 Nye, Naomi S. *Lullaby Raft* (PS–1). Illus. by Vivienne Flesher. 1997, Simon & Schuster $16.00 (0-689-80521-7). 32pp. A fantasy world is introduced to a youngster by his mother through the words of her lullaby. (Rev: BL 11/1/97; HBG 3/98; SLJ 9/97)

755 O'Keefe, Susan Heyboer. *Good Night, God Bless* (PS–K). Illus. by Hideko Takahashi. 1999, Holt $15.95 (0-8050-6008-1). 32pp. A prayerful bedtime book in which a young boy, his family, some animals, and the whole town seek God's blessing. (Rev: BL 10/1/99; HBG 3/00; SLJ 10/99)

756 Ongman, Gudrun. *The Sleep Ponies* (PS–1). Illus. 2000, MindCastle $16.95 (0-9677204-0-0). 32pp. Dreaming children are able to ride sleep ponies and travel through wonderful landscapes in this soothing picture book. (Rev: BL 12/15/00)

757 Ormerod, Jan. *Midnight Pillow Fight* (PS–1). Illus. 1993, Candlewick $14.95 (1-56402-169-6). 32pp. At bedtime, Polly and her pillow engage in a fight with other cushions. (Rev: BL 1/15/93; SLJ 5/93)

758 Osofsky, Audrey. *Dreamcatcher* (PS–3). Illus. by Ed Young. 1992, Orchard LB $16.99 (0-531-08588-0). 32pp. An Ojibwa baby watches everyday events in his family's life and later sleeps peacefully. (Rev: BCCB 7–8/92; BL 2/15/92; SLJ 4/92)

759 Pank, Rachel. *Sonia and Barnie and the Noise in the Night* (PS–K). Illus. 1991, Scholastic paper $13.95 (0-590-44657-6). 32pp. Her cowardly cat may hide up in a tree, but brave and bossy Sonia takes on the "monster" who frightened them. (Rev: BL 6/1/91; SLJ 12/91)

760 Pedersen, Judy. *When Night Time Comes Near* (PS–1). Illus. by author. 2000, Viking $15.99 (0-670-88259-3). This bedtime book shows all the activities that occur in a neighborhood as night approaches, like bringing in the flags. (Rev: HBG 10/00; SLJ 2/00)

761 Plenkowski, Jan. *Good Night: A Pop-Up Lullaby* (PS). 1999, Candlewick $14.99 (0-7636-0763-0). Using pop-ups, this book describes all the different reasons why a little bear can't get to sleep. (Rev: BL 12/15/99; HBG 3/00; SLJ 12/99)

762 Plourde, Lynn. *Wild Child* (PS–3). Illus. by Greg Couch. 1999, Simon & Schuster $16.00 (0-689-81552-2). Mother Earth has a difficult time getting her child Autumn to go to sleep, but she does so just in time to welcome a new child, Winter. (Rev: HBG 3/00; SLJ 12/99)

763 Price, Hope Lynne. *These Hands* (PS–1). Illus. by Bryan Collier. 1999, Hyperion LB $15.49 (0-7868-2320-8). A picture book that follows the activities of a little girl from waking until saying her prayers by her bed at night. (Rev: HBG 3/00; SLJ 12/99)

764 Raschka, Chris. *Can't Sleep* (PS–1). Illus. 1995, Orchard LB $15.99 (0-531-08779-4). 32pp. A young dog with insomnia takes comfort in having the moon watch over him until he goes to sleep. (Rev: BCCB 10/95; BL 9/15/95; SLJ 9/95*)

765 Raya-Norman, Faye. *Wolf Songs* (PS–2). Illus. by Richard Ziehler-Martin. 1999, Portunus $15.95 (1-886440-04-2). In this bedtime fantasy, young Matthew is led on a night walk by a silver wolf and is accompanied by a full moon, northern lights, and stars. (Rev: SLJ 2/00)

766 Roberts, Bethany. *Gramps and the Fire Dragon* (PS–3). Illus. by Melissa Iwai. 2000, Clarion $15.00 (0-395-69849-9). 32pp. Not ready for bed, a boy and his grandfather dream of wild adventures as they conjure up pictures from the fireplace flames and, at last, doze off. (Rev: BL 1/1–15/01; HBG 3/01; SLJ 11/00)

767 Rock, Lois. *I Wish Tonight* (PS–2). Illus. by Anne Wilson. 2000, Good Bks. $16.00 (1-56148-315-X). In bed at night, a young boy wishes on a star and travels into a world of make-believe. (Rev: SLJ 12/00)

768 Roth, Carol. *Little Bunny's Sleepless Night* (PS–K). Illus. by Valeri Gorbachev. 1999, North-South LB $15.88 (0-7358-1070-2). 32pp. Little Bunny is lonely at night, so he tries sleeping with other animals. Each proves unsatisfactory (e.g., Bear snores), and so he returns home happily to his own bed. (Rev: BL 6/1–15/99; HBG 10/99; SLJ 7/99)

769 Rydell, Katy. *Wind Says Good Night* (PS–1). Illus. by David Jorgensen. 1994, Houghton $16.00 (0-395-60474-5). 42pp. This cumulative bedtime story tells how all the animals and birds cooperate so a little girl can go to sleep. (Rev: BCCB 5/94; BL 4/1/94; SLJ 4/94*)

770 Rylant, Cynthia. *Bear Day* (PS–K). Illus. by Jennifer Selby. 1998, Harcourt $12.00 (0-15-201090-4). 28pp. This jaunty picture book follows a little bear through a typical day of dressing in the morning, caring for his pets, walking in the forest, and then preparing for bed. (Rev: BL 10/15/98; HBG 3/99; SLJ 1/99)

771 Rylant, Cynthia. *Night in the Country* (PS–1). Illus. by Mary Szilagyi. 1986, Macmillan LB $14.95 (0-02-777210-1); paper $5.99 (0-689-71473-4). 32pp. A description of the sounds of night in the country that makes the dark seem not at all frightening. (Rev: BCCB 9/86; BL 3/15/86; SLJ 5/86)

772 Rymill, Linda R. *Good Knight* (PS–2). Illus. by G. Brian Karas. 1998, Holt $15.95 (0-8050-4129-X). The bedtime rituals of a young boy, ending with a story from his mother. (Rev: BCCB 4/98; HBG 10/98; SLJ 3/98)

773 Sanroman, Susana. *Señora Regañona* (PS–3). Illus. by Domi. 1998, Douglas & McIntyre $14.95 (0-88899-320-X). 32pp. A child conquers her fear of the dark, which she calls "Señora Regañona," when she flies into the sky one night and makes a friend of the Señora. (Rev: BL 8/98; HBG 10/98; SLJ 9/98)

774 Schaefer, Carole L. *Down in the Woods at Sleepytime* (PS). Illus. by Vanessa Cabban. 2000, Candlewick $15.99 (0-7636-0843-2). 32pp. None of the animals in the woods is ready to go to bed, but when Grandma Owl shouts that it is story time everyone settles down. (Rev: BL 11/15/00; SLJ 11/00)

775 Schlein, Miriam. *Sleep Safe, Little Whale: A Lullaby* (PS–K). Illus. by Peter Sis. 1997, Greenwillow $14.95 (0-688-14757-7). 24pp. This soothing lullaby describes a number of baby animals that are in safe places when they go to sleep. (Rev: BL 11/15/97; HBG 3/98)

776 Schotter, Roni. *Bunny's Night Out* (PS–1). Illus. by Margot Apple. 1989, Little, Brown $13.95 (0-316-77465-0). A bunny sneaks out at night and experiences adventures before coming home to his welcome bed. (Rev: SLJ 7/89)

777 Siegen-Smith, Nikki, comp. *A Pocketful of Stars: Poems About the Night* (K–3). Illus. by Emma Shaw-Smith. 1999, Barefoot $16.95 (1-902283-84-8). 40pp. An anthology of 21 short poems about the night and sleep by such poets as Walter de la Mare, Ogden Nash, and Ann Bonner. (Rev: SLJ 1/00) [811]

778 Southwell, Jandelyn. *The Little Country Town* (PS–1). Illus. by Kay Chorao. 2001, Holt $16.00 (0-8050-5711-0). 32pp. At night, the people in a town enjoy the sights and sounds of the countryside and the natural world that surrounds them at bedtime. (Rev: BL 1/1–15/01; SLJ 1/01)

779 Spetter, Jung-Hee. *Lily and Trooper's Spring* (PS). Illus. 1999, Front Street $8.95 (1-886910-36-7). 32pp. Lily and her dog, Trooper, have a series of misadventures while attempting a quiet picnic in the country, and both of them need baths before bedtime. (Rev: BL 5/1/99; SLJ 7/99)

780 Spetter, Jung-Hee. *Lily and Trooper's Summer* (PS–K). Illus. 1999, Front Street $8.95 (1-886910-37-5). 32pp. Lily and her dog, Trooper, spend a wonderful day outdoors and then are so tired that they fall asleep on top of the covers. (Rev: BL 5/15/99; SLJ 7/99)

781 Spinelli, Eileen. *Naptime, Laptime* (PS). Illus. by Melissa Sweet. 1995, Scholastic $6.95 (0-590-48510-5). 24pp. A child wonders where various animals sleep and then decides it's best on grandmother's lap. (Rev: BCCB 2/96; BL 12/1/95; SLJ 2/96)

782 Spinelli, Eileen. *Night Shift Daddy* (PS–2). Illus. by Melissa Iwai. 2000, Hyperion LB $15.49 (0-7868-2424-7). 32pp. After putting his daughter to bed Daddy goes to his night job, and when he returns in the morning the bedtime roles are reversed. (Rev: BCCB 6/00; BL 8/00; HBG 10/00; SLJ 10/00)

783 Spohn, Kate. *The Mermaids' Lullaby* (PS–K). Illus. 1998, Random LB $18.99 (0-679-99175-1). 32pp. In this peaceful bedtime book, an underwater community, including mermaid babies, prepares for bedtime. (Rev: BL 7/98)

784 Spooner, Michael. *A Moon in Your Lunch Box* (K–3). Illus. by Ib Ohlsson. 1995, Holt paper $7.95 (0-8050-3545-1). 67pp. This is a collection of original poems about the moon, night, and changes they produce. (Rev: BCCB 7–8/93; BL 6/1–15/93; SLJ 6/93) [811]

785 Stevenson, Harvey. *Big, Scary Wolf* (PS–1). Illus. 1997, Clarion $14.00 (0-395-74213-7). 32pp. At bedtime, a father reassures his daughter that there isn't a wolf hiding in her room. (Rev: BL 9/1/97; HBG 3/98; SLJ 8/97)

786 Stevenson, James. *What's Under My Bed?* (1–3). Illus. by author. 1983, Greenwillow LB $15.93 (0-688-02327-4); Morrow paper $4.95 (0-688-09350-7). 32pp. A grandfather helps reduce his grandchildren's fears. A sequel is: *Worse Than Willy!* (1984).

787 Stoddard, Sandol. *Turtle Time: A Bedtime Story* (PS–3). Illus. by Lynn Munsinger. 1995, Houghton $13.95 (0-395-56754-8). 32pp. A bedtime story about a little girl and her pet turtle. (Rev: BL 4/1/95; SLJ 4/95)

788 Storm, Theodor. *Little Hobbin* (PS–1). Trans. by Anthea Bell. Illus. by Lisbeth Zwerger. 1995, North-South LB $15.88 (1-55858-461-7). 18pp. In this soothing bedtime lullaby, Little Hobbin takes a journey in his bed at night. (Rev: BL 2/1/96; SLJ 1/96)

789 Sutherland, Marc. *The Waiting Place* (PS–3). Illus. by author. 1998, Abrams $14.95 (0-8109-3994-0). 24pp. A bedroom becomes populated with a variety of objects and beings that enter through an open window in this unusual book about going to bed. (Rev: HBG 3/99; SLJ 3/99)

790 Swain, Ruth Freeman. *Bedtime!* (PS–3). Illus. by Cat B. Smith. 1999, Holiday $15.95 (0-8234-1444-2). This history of beds highlights simple mats, dorm bunks, hammocks, Pullman sleepers, Murphy beds, and so on. (Rev: BL 9/15/99; HBG 3/00; SLJ 11/99) [392.3]

791 Szekeres, Cyndy. *The Deep Blue Sky Twinkles with Stars* (PS–K). Illus. 1998, Scholastic $12.95 (0-590-69198-8). 40pp. This bedtime book shows five young rabbits getting ready for bed and a story from Dad. (Rev: BL 2/15/98; HBG 10/98; SLJ 3/98)

792 Tafuri, Nancy. *I Love You, Little One* (PS–1). Illus. 1998, Scholastic $15.95 (0-590-92159-2). 32pp. In this bedtime story, different animal mothers try to tell their children how much they love them. (Rev: BL 2/1/98; HBG 10/98; SLJ 3/98)

793 Thomas, Joyce C. *Hush Songs: African American Lullabies* (PS). Illus. by Brenda Joysmith. 2000, Hyperion $15.99 (0-7868-0562-5). 48pp. A collection of ten African American lullabies with the words and full musical scores. (Rev: BL 12/15/00) [782.4]

794 Trapani, Iza. *Shoo Fly!* (PS–1). Illus. by author. 2000, Charlesbridge LB $15.95 (1-58089-052-0). This adaptation of a perky song concerns a little mouse and pesky fly and how they are both tucked in at night. (Rev: SLJ 1/01)

795 *Twilight Verses, Moonlight Rhymes* (PS). Ed. by Mary Joslin. Illus. by Liz Pichon. 1999, Augsburg $16.95 (0-8066-3885-0). 60pp. An anthology of nighttime rhymes that includes lullabies, nursery rhymes, and some prayers. (Rev: BL 12/15/99; HBG 3/00; SLJ 3/00) [821.008]

796 Tyers, Jenny. *When It Is Night, When It Is Day* (PS–2). Illus. 1996, Houghton $14.95 (0-395-71546-6). 32pp. The behavior of various animals at night is explored in this charming bedtime book. (Rev: BL 3/1/96; SLJ 4/96)

797 Vulliamy, Clara. *Good Night, Baby* (PS). Illus. by author. 1996, Candlewick $4.99 (1-56402-817-8). A board book featuring a blond, blue-eyed baby being put to bed. Also use *Wide Awake!* (1996). (Rev: SLJ 6/96)

798 Waddell, Martin. *Can't You Sleep, Little Bear?* (PS). Illus. by Barbara Firth. 1992, Candlewick $15.99 (1-56402-007-X). 32pp. Even lanterns don't comfort Little Bear, who is scared of the dark, until Father Bear offers the comfort of his arms. (Rev: BCCB 4/92; BL 3/1/92*; SLJ 1/92*)

799 Waddell, Martin. *Night Night, Cuddly Bear* (PS–K). Illus. by Penny Dale. 2000, Candlewick $15.99 (0-7636-1195-6). 32pp. Every night Joe and his family must search for the boy's teddy bear before he can get to sleep. (Rev: BL 11/15/00; HBG 3/01; SLJ 11/00)

800 Waddell, Martin. *Who Do You Love?* (PS). Illus. by Camilla Ashforth. 1999, Candlewick $12.99 (0-7636-0586-7). 32pp. At bedtime, kitten Molly tells her mother about all the people she loves, saving her mother for the last. (Rev: BL 6/1–15/99; HBG 10/99; SLJ 6/99)

801 Wahl, Jan. *Humphrey's Bear* (PS–1). Illus. by William Joyce. 1987, Holt paper $5.95 (0-8050-1169-2). 32pp. Father thinks Humphrey is too old to sleep with a toy bear, but he doesn't know of their great adventures. (Rev: BCCB 6/87; BL 5/15/87; SLJ 8/87)

802 Wallace, Nancy E. *Rabbit's Bedtime* (PS). Illus. by author. 1999, Houghton $9.95 (0-395-98266-9). Before a youngster goes to sleep, he and his mother recall all the loving things they did together during the day. (Rev: HBG 3/00; SLJ 11/99)

803 Walsh, Melanie. *Hide and Sleep* (PS). Illus. 1999, DK $9.95 (0-7894-4820-3). 21pp. Poppy, who always wears a crown, hides in many place in the house, but eventually she finds the perfect spot — her bed. (Rev: BL 12/15/99; HBG 3/00; SLJ 1/00)

804 Walton, Rick. *My Two Hands, My Two Feet* (PS–1). Illus. by Julia Gorton. 2000, Putnam $14.99 (0-399-23338-5). 32pp. Half of this picture book celebrates all the things hands can do; flip the book over and the same treatment is given to feet, with the two meeting in the middle at bedtime. (Rev: BL 10/1/00; SLJ 11/00)

805 Warnick, Elsa. *Bedtime* (PS–K). Illus. 1998, Harcourt $10.00 (0-15-201471-3). 28pp. This warmly illustrated picture book introduces all the small rituals associated with going to bed, such as using the potty and brushing one's teeth. (Rev: BL 8/98; HBG 3/99; SLJ 9/98)

806 Welch, Willy. *Grumpy Bunnies* (PS–1). Illus. by Tammie Lyon. 2000, Charlesbridge $16.95 (1-58089-053-9); paper $6.95 (1-58089-060-1). 32pp. The day improves as it goes along for three little rabbits who go to bed looking forward to tomorrow. (Rev: HBG 10/00; SLJ 5/00)

807 Wellington, Monica. *Bunny's First Snowflake* (PS). Illus. 2000, Dutton $7.99 (0-525-46464-6). 16pp. As winter approaches, different animals prepare for the cold and, in the end, go to bed for the night. (Rev: BL 10/15/00; SLJ 10/00)

808 Wells, Rosemary. *Goodnight Max* (PS). Illus. by author. 2000, Viking $9.99 (0-670-88707-2). In this board book that contains touch-and-feel surprises Max the rabbit has to change his pajamas three times before he can get to sleep. (Rev: SLJ 4/00)

809 Wells, Rosemary. *Max's Bedtime* (PS). Illus. by author. Series: Max and Ruby Board Books. 1998, Dial $5.99 (0-8037-2267-2). In this board book, a little bunny prepares for bed. (Rev: HBG 10/98; SLJ 7/98)

810 Whitman, Candace. *The Night Is Like an Animal* (PS–1). Illus. 1995, Farrar $13.00 (0-374-35521-5). 32pp. Night, a little furry animal, goes to sleep close to a little child's dreams. (Rev: BCCB 10/95; BL 11/15/95; SLJ 11/95)

811 Winthrop, Elizabeth. *Asleep in a Heap* (PS–1). Illus. by Mary Morgan. 1993, Holiday LB $15.95 (0-8234-0992-9). 32pp. Julia is much too busy to go to bed, but her antics send the rest of the family to sleep. (Rev: BL 11/15/93; SLJ 1/94)

812 Winthrop, Elizabeth. *Maggie and the Monster* (PS–K). Illus. by Tomie dePaola. 1987, Holiday LB $15.95 (0-8234-0639-3); paper $5.95 (0-8234-0698-9). 32pp. Every single night a small girl monster comes into Maggie's room. (Rev: BL 4/1/87; SLJ 5/87)

813 Wong, Janet S. *Grump* (PS). Illus. by John Wallace. 2001, Simon & Schuster $16.00 (0-689-83485-3). 32pp. Mommy is so tired taking care of baby that, at nap time, she is the one to go to sleep. (Rev: BCCB 2/01; BL 2/15/01; SLJ 3/01)

814 Wood, Douglas. *Northwoods Cradle Song: From a Menominee Lullaby* (PS–K). Illus. by Lisa Desimini. 1996, Simon & Schuster paper $15.00 (0-689-80503-9). An American Indian song in which animals, including a mother and child, fall asleep at night, while around them the nocturnal world awakens. (Rev: HB 5–6/96; SLJ 5/96)

815 Yaccarino, Dan. *Good Night, Mr. Night* (PS–3). Illus. 1997, Harcourt $15.00 (0-15-201319-9). 40pp. A gentle bedtime story in which Mr. Night enters a boy's bedroom to close his eyes. (Rev: BL 11/1/97; HBG 3/98; SLJ 10/97)

816 Yolen, Jane. *How Do Dinosaurs Say Goodnight?* (PS–1). Illus. by Mark Teague. 2000, Scholastic $15.95 (0-590-31681-8). 40pp. A bedtime book that features all sorts of baby dinosaurs behaving like human children at bedtime. (Rev: BCCB 6/00; BL 4/1/00*; HBG 10/00; SLJ 6/00)

817 Yolen, Jane, ed. *Sleep Rhymes Around the World* (PS–4). Illus. 1994, Boyds Mills $16.95 (1-56397-243-3). 40pp. Twenty-one lullabies from as far away as Iran and Uganda are included in this handsome anthology that includes the text in English and the original language. (Rev: BL 2/1/94; SLJ 3/94) [808.81]

818 Zerner, Amy, and Jessie S. Zerner. *The Dream Quilt* (K–4). Illus. 1995, Tuttle $19.95 (0-8048-1999-8). 96pp. Alex has dreams of adventure when he wraps himself up in his great-great-grandfather's quilt at bedtime. (Rev: BL 8/95; SLJ 6/95)

819 Ziefert, Harriet. *Clara Ann Cookie, Go to Bed!* (PS–3). Illus. by Emily Bolam. 2000, Houghton $15.00 (0-395-97381-3). 32pp. Clara Ann, who has been resisting her mother's efforts to put her to bed, gets the same treatment when her teddy bear refuses to accompany her when she finally gives in. (Rev: BL 9/1/00; HBG 3/01; SLJ 10/00)

820 Ziefert, Harriet. *Moonride* (PS–K). Illus. by Seymour Chwast. 2000, Houghton $15.00 (0-618-00229-4). 32pp. A little boy accepts a ride from the moon and attends a night baseball game before he returns to his bed and sleep. (Rev: BL 3/15/00; HBG 10/00; SLJ 12/00)

821 Zolotow, Charlotte. *Sleepy Book* (PS–1). Illus. by Ilse Plume. 1988, HarperCollins LB $14.89 (0-06-026968-5). 32pp. Spare text tells how various birds, insects, and animals sleep. (Rev: BL 5/15/88; SLJ 12/88)

Nursery Rhymes

822 Anholt, Catherine, et al. *The Candlewick Book of First Rhymes* (PS–K). Illus. 1996, Candlewick $17.99 (0-7636-0015-6). 64pp. A selection of well-known rhymes taken from prestigious, previously published collections. (Rev: BL 11/15/96; SLJ 1/97) [811]

823 Aylesworth, Jim. *The Completed Hickory Dickory Dock* (PS–K). Illus. by Eileen Christelow. 1994, Aladdin paper $5.99 (0-689-71862-4). 32pp. The "whole" story of what happened when the clock struck. (Rev: BL 10/1/90; SLJ 2/91) [811]

824 Beaton, Clare, comp. *Mother Goose Remembers* (PS). Illus. by Clare Beaton. 2000, Barefoot $16.99 (1-84148-073-8). 64pp. A highly appealing collection of 46 Mother Goose rhymes with pictures made of felt and other fabrics. (Rev: HBG 3/01; SLJ 9/00)

825 Beil, Karen M. *A Cake All for Me!* (PS–2). Illus. by Paul Meisel. 1998, Holiday $16.95 (0-8234-1368-3). Using a nursery rhyme format, this is the story of Piggy who makes a cake and shares it with others. (Rev: HBG 3/99; SLJ 9/98)

826 Benjamin, Floella. *Skip Across the Ocean: Nursery Rhymes from Around the World* (PS–K). Illus. by Sheila Moxley. 1995, Orchard $15.95 (0-531-09455-3). 48pp. Thirty-two nursery rhymes from around the world, including several lullabies. (Rev: BL 10/1/95; SLJ 11/95)

827 Bornstein, Harry, and Karen L. Saulnier. *Nursery Rhymes from Mother Goose Told in Signed English* (K–2). Illus. by Patricia Peters and Linda C. Tom. 1993, Gallaudet Univ. $14.95 (0-930323-99-8). 41pp. Fourteen rhymes with signing symbols for the deaf. (Rev: SLJ 6/93) [398.8]

828 Boyle, Alison. *Twinkle, Twinkle, Little Star* (PS). Illus. 2000, David & Charles $10.95 (1-86233-111-1). In this interactive book using the familiar rhyme, a little star enters a house looking for a bear. (Rev: BL 12/1/00)

829 Brown, Marc. *Play Rhymes* (PS–1). Illus. 1993, Puffin paper $5.99 (0-140-54936-6). 32pp. There is humor, warmth, and coziness in these play rhymes. Also use: *Hand Rhymes* (1985). (Rev: BL 12/1/87; HB 11–12/87; SLJ 10/87) [398.8]

830 Brown, Ruth. *Ladybug, Ladybug* (PS–1). Illus. by author. 1992, Puffin paper $5.99 (0-14-054543-3). 32pp. An extended version of the Mother Goose rhyme. (Rev: BL 11/1/88) [398.8]

831 *A Child's Treasury of Nursery Rhymes* (PS–K). Ed. by Kady MacDonald Denton. Illus. 1998, Kingfisher $17.95 (0-7534-5109-3). 96pp. An excellent collection of rhymes that includes old favorites plus tongue twisters, riddles, and limericks, all illustrated with joyous watercolors. (Rev: BCCB 1/99; BL 11/1/98; HBG 3/99; SLJ 11/98)

832 Chorao, Kay. *Knock at the Door and Other Baby Action Rhymes* (PS). Illus. 1999, Dutton $15.99 (0-525-45969-3). 32pp. A joyous collection of nursery rhymes, such as "This Little Piggy," reproduced with charming illustrations featuring all sorts of animals. (Rev: BL 7/99; HBG 3/00; SLJ 10/99) [398.8]

833 Cousins, Lucy. *Humpty Dumpty and Other Nursery Rhymes* (PS). Illus. 1996, Dutton paper $6.99 (0-525-45675-9). 14pp. This board book contains 11 well-known nursery rhymes. (Rev: BL 9/15/96; SLJ 1/97)

834 Cousins, Lucy. *Jack and Jill and Other Nursery Rhymes* (PS). Illus. 1996, Dutton paper $6.99 (0-525-45676-7). 14pp. Eleven popular nursery rhymes are contained in this attractive board book. (Rev: BL 9/15/96; SLJ 1/97)

835 Cousins, Lucy. *The Lucy Cousins Book of Nursery Rhymes* (PS–1). Illus. 1999, Dutton $17.99 (0-525-46133-7). 64pp. The author has chosen and illustrated 64 well-known nursery rhymes in this delightful collection. (Rev: BL 4/1/99; HBG 10/99) [398.8]

836 Cummings, Pat. *My Aunt Came Back* (PS). Illus. by author. Series: Harper Growing Tree. 1998, HarperFestival $5.95 (0-694-01059-6). In this board book, featuring seven different rhymes, a little girl receives presents from her globe-trotting aunt. (Rev: HBG 10/98; SLJ 10/98)

837 Dabcovich, Lydia. *The Keys to My Kingdom: A Poem in Three Languages* (PS–2). Illus. 1992, Smithmark $3.98 (0-831-73052-8). 32pp. A girl and her dog travel to Grandma's from city to country in this trilingual — English, French, Spanish — retelling of the nursery rhyme. (Rev: BL 4/1/92; SLJ 4/92) [398.8]

838 dePaola, Tomie. *The Comic Adventures of Old Mother Hubbard and Her Dog* (PS–3). Illus. by author. 1981, Harcourt $13.95 (0-15-219541-6); paper $7.00 (0-15-219542-4). 32pp. A handsome version of the classic nursery rhyme. [398.8]

839 Edens, Cooper, sel. *The Glorious Mother Goose* (PS–3). 1998, Simon & Schuster $18.00 (0-689-82050-X). 88pp. Using old-fashioned illustrations by such masters as Randolph Caldecott and Kate Greenaway, this book presents 42 popular nursery rhymes, each illustrated by two artists. (Rev: HBG 3/99; SLJ 1/99)

840 Emerson, Sally, comp. *Nursery Rhyme Songbook with Easy Music to Play for Piano and Guitar* (PS–K). Illus. by Colin Maclean and Moira Maclean. 1995, Kingfisher paper $11.95 (1-85697-635-1). 72pp. A collection of nursery rhymes accompanied by easy-to-play scoring for piano and guitar. (Rev: SLJ 3/93) [784]

841 Emerson, Sally, ed. *The Nursery Treasury: A Collection of Baby Games, Rhymes, and Lullabies* (PS). Illus. by Moira Maclean and Colin Maclean. 1988, Doubleday $24.95 (0-385-24650-1). 128pp. All sorts of songs and rhymes for young children. (Rev: BL 11/1/88; SLJ 1/89) [398.8]

842 *Five Little Ducks: An Old Rhyme* (PS–K). Illus. by Pamela Paparone. 1995, North-South LB $15.88 (1-55858-474-9). 30pp. Though they wander into the woods during the day, the five little ducks always return home to their mother at night. (Rev: BL 12/15/95)

843 Foreman, Michael. *Michael Foreman's Mother Goose* (PS–K). Illus. by author. 1991, Harcourt $22.00 (0-15-255820-9). 160pp. A rewarding visual tour of nursery rhymes. (Rev: BL 9/15/91; SLJ 10/91*) [398.8]

844 Galdone, Paul. *Three Little Kittens* (2–4). Illus. by author. 1986, Houghton $15.00 (0-89919-426-5); paper $5.95 (0-89919-796-5). 32pp. A lively reworking of the old nursery rhyme. (Rev: BL 10/1/86; SLJ 12/86) [398.8]

845 Hale, Sarah Josepha. *Mary Had a Little Lamb* (PS–1). Illus. by Salley Mavor. 1995, Orchard LB $16.99 (0-531-08725-5). 32pp. An effective version of the famous rhyme using collages for illustrations. (Rev: BCCB 5/95; BL 5/15/95; HB 3–4/95, 7–8/95, 11–12/95; SLJ 6/95*) [811]

846 Hallworth, Grace, ed. *Down by the River: Afro-Caribbean Rhymes, Games, and Songs for Children* (PS–1). Illus. by Caroline Binch. 1996, Scholastic $16.95 (0-590-69320-4). 40pp. More than 20 playground rhymes from the Caribbean are included in this joyful book illustrated with watercolors. (Rev: BCCB 1/97; BL 10/15/96; SLJ 12/96) [811]

847 Hawkins, Colin, and Jacqui Hawkins. *Hey Diddle Diddle* (PS). Illus. by authors. 1992, Candlewick $6.95 (1-56402-014-2). This board book contains five attractively illustrated rhymes. Five more are found in: *Humpty Dumpty* (1992). (Rev: SLJ 5/92) [398.8]

848 Hayes, Sarah. *This Is the Bear* (PS). Illus. by Helen Craig. 1993, HarperCollins LB $11.89 (0-397-32171-6); Candlewick paper $2.50 (0-06-443103-7). 32pp. Written in "House That Jack Built" style, the story of the bear named Fred who is taken to the local dump and awaits rescue. A reissue. A sequel is *This Is the Bear and the Picnic Lunch* (1989). (Rev: BL 4/1/86; SLJ 9/86) [398.8]

849 *Hey Diddle Diddle* (PS–K). Illus. by Marilyn Janovitz. 1992, Hyperion LB $7.49 (1-56282-169-5). This book is illustrated with watercolors that humorously reproduce the old nursery rhyme. (Rev: SLJ 8/92) [398.8]

850 Hopkins, Lee Bennett. *Animals from Mother Goose* (PS–2). Illus. by Kathryn Hewitt. 1989, Harcourt $6.95 (0-15-200406-8). 28pp. In this puzzle book, questions about animals in Mother Goose rhymes are answered by lifting page flaps. A companion volume is *People from Mother Goose: A Question Book* (1989). (Rev: BL 11/1/89; SLJ 1/90) [398.8]

851 *If All the Seas Were One Sea* (PS–1). Illus. by Janina Domanska. 1987, Macmillan LB $16.95 (0-02-732540-7). 32pp. First published in 1971, this nursery rhyme is given new dimensions by swirling illustrations. A 1972 Caldecott Honor Book. [398.8]

852 Ivimey, John W. *The Complete Story of the Three Blind Mice* (PS–K). Illus. by Paul Galdone. 1987, Houghton $13.95 (0-89919-481-8). 32pp. A collection of antique British stories in this illustrator's last book. (Rev: BL 11/1/87)

853 Johnson, David A. *Old Mother Hubbard: A Nursery Rhyme* (PS–1). Illus. 1998, Simon & Schuster $16.00 (0-689-81485-2). 32pp. An expansion of the old nursery rhyme in which the poor housekeeper visits a number of local tradespeople to satisfy every need of her clever, contrary dog. (Rev: BL 4/15/98; HB 3–4/98; HBG 10/98) [398.8]

854 Kirk, Daniel. *Humpty Dumpty* (PS–2). Illus. 2000, Putnam $15.99 (0-399-23332-6). 32pp. A new look at the Humpty Dumpty rhyme in which young King Moe, a puzzle freak, is able to put Humpty back together again. (Rev: BL 5/15/00; HBG 10/00; SLJ 6/00)

855 *Little Robin Redbreast: A Mother Goose Rhyme* (PS–1). Illus. by Shari Halpern. 1994, North-South LB $14.88 (1-55858-248-7). 32pp. The old nursery rhyme is given new life in this large-print edition with illustrations of collages with acrylics. (Rev: BL 3/15/94; SLJ 7/94)

856 Lobel, Arnold. *Whiskers and Rhymes* (PS–3). Illus. by author. 1985, Morrow paper $4.95 (0-688-08291-2). 48pp. Original nursery rhymes featuring cats in old-fashioned costumes. (Rev: BCCB 10/85; BL 9/15/85; SLJ 10/85) [398.8]

857 Lodge, Bernard. *There Was an Old Woman Who Lived in a Glove* (PS–K). Illus. 1992, Whispering Coyote LB $14.95 (1-879085-55-0). 25pp. A round, white-haired lady and her dove set out to see the world in this takeoff on the classic rhyme. (Rev: BL 10/15/92; SLJ 2/92) [398.8]

858 McKellar, Shona, comp. *Playtime Rhymes* (PS). Illus. by Priscilla Lamont. 1998, DK $12.95 (0-7894-2861-X). 29pp. A collection of nursery rhymes for the very young, including some old favorites, with small photos that illustrate appropriate actions for each rhyme. (Rev: BL 4/1/98; HBG 10/98; SLJ 6/98) [398.8]

859 Manson, Christopher. *The Tree in the Wood* (K–4). Illus. 1993, North-South LB $14.88 (1-55858-193-6). 28pp. This book illustrated by wood-cuts is an adaptation of the nursery song "The Green Grass Grew All Around." (Rev: BL 3/1/93; SLJ 5/93) [398.8]

860 Marks, Alan, ed. *Over the Hills and Far Away: A Book of Nursery Rhymes* (PS–1). Illus. 1994, North-South $19.95 (1-55858-285-1). 97pp. Sixty of the most popular Mother Goose rhymes are contained in this well-designed volume. (Rev: BL 9/1/94*; SLJ 10/94) [398.8]

861 Marks, Alan. *Ring-a-Ring O'Roses and Ding, Dong Bell* (PS–K). Illus. by author. 1991, Picture Book $19.95 (0-88708-187-8). 96pp. A delightful collection of 76 familiar nursery rhymes with watercolor and ink illustrations. (Rev: BL 3/1/92; HB 5–6/92; SLJ 3/92) [398.8]

862 Marshall, James. *James Marshall's Mother Goose* (PS–1). Illus. by author. 1979, Farrar paper $6.95 (0-374-43723-8). 40pp. An ebullient, breezy treatment of traditional material. [398.8]

863 Martin, Bill, Jr. *"Fire! Fire!" Said Mrs. McGuire* (PS–K). Illus. by Richard Egielski. 1996, Harcourt $15.00 (0-15-227562-2). 32pp. With humorous illustrations, the traditional nursery rhyme is given a modern touch. (Rev: BCCB 4/96; BL 3/15/96; SLJ 6/96) [398.8]

864 Martin, David. *Five Little Piggies* (PS–K). Illus. by Susan Meddaugh. 1998, Candlewick $16.99 (1-56402-918-2). 40pp. A slapstick variation on the old finger rhyme with each of the little piggies demanding attention from loving Momma Piggy. (Rev: BCCB 5/98; BL 6/1–15/98*; HB 3–4/98; HBG 10/98; SLJ 6/98)

865 Melling, David. *Over the Moon! Best Loved Nursery Rhymes* (PS–K). Illus. 2000, Dutton $14.99 (0-525-46498-0). An interactive book that uses movable parts of pages to illustrate favorite nursery rhymes. (Rev: BL 12/1/00)

866 Mother Goose. *Gregory Griggs and Other Nursery Rhyme People* (PS–1). Illus. by Arnold Lobel. 1987, Macmillan paper $3.95 (0-688-07042-6). Out-of-the-ordinary nursery rhymes are included in this refreshingly different collection. Reissue of 1978 edition. [398.8]

867 Mother Goose. *Mother Goose* (PS–2). Illus. by Brian Wildsmith. 1982, Oxford paper $11.95 (0-19-272180-1). 80pp. Original artistic conceptions of the old rhymes with wonderful action in brilliantly colored animal and human figures. [398.8]

868 Mother Goose. *Mother Goose: A Canadian Sampler* (PS–1). 1996, Groundwood $18.95 (0-88899-213-0). 63pp. Using illustrations from 29 of Canada's prominent picture book illustrators, this is a fine edition of Mother Goose rhymes. (Rev: SLJ 5/96)

869 Mother Goose. *Mother Goose: A Collection of Classic Nursery Rhymes* (PS–K). Illus. by Michael Hague. 1984, Holt $18.95 (0-8050-0214-6). 80pp. Forty-five nursery rhymes delicately illustrated. [398.8]

870 Mother Goose. *Mother Goose: A Sampler* (PS–K). Illus. 1996, Douglas & McIntyre $18.95 (0-88899-260-2). 64pp. Twenty-eight modern Canadian artists illustrate favorite rhymes from Mother Goose. (Rev: BL 6/1–15/96)

871 Mother Goose. *Real Mother Goose* (PS–3). Illus. by Blanche Fisher Wright. 1991, Checkerboard $12.95 (1-56288-041-1). 128pp. A reprint of the golden anniversary edition with introduction by May Hill Arbuthnot. [398.8]

872 Mother Goose. *The Real Mother Goose Clock Book* (PS–1). Illus. by Blanche Fisher Wright. n.d., Checkerboard $6.95 (1-56288-095-0). 22pp. Time-related rhymes and a clock with movable hands help children associate the clock with daily routines. [398.8]

873 Mother Goose. *Tomie dePaola's Mother Goose* (PS–1). Illus. by Tomie dePaola. 1985, Putnam $24.95 (0-399-21258-2). 127pp. Large format and lavish illustrations accompany these old favorites. (Rev: BCCB 11/85; BL 9/1/85; HB 1–2/86) [398.8]

874 *My First Action Rhymes* (PS). Illus. by Lynne W. Cravath. Series: Growing Tree. 2000, Harper-Festival $9.95 (0-694-01418-4). 24pp. A collection of ten playful action rhymes that often point out parts of the body. (Rev: BL 10/15/00; SLJ 11/00) [811]

875 *My First Nursery Rhymes* (PS). Illus. by Bruce Whatley. Series: Growing Tree. 1999, HarperFestival $9.95 (0-694-01205-X). 24pp. A joyous collection of ten favorite rhymes, including "Little Bo-Peep" and "Humpty Dumpty." (Rev: BL 2/1/99; HBG 10/99; SLJ 4/99) [398.8]

876 O'Brien, John. *The Farmer in the Dell* (PS–1). Illus. 2000, Boyds Mills $14.95 (1-56397-775-3). 40pp. Hilarious illustrations give new life to this favorite rhyme. (Rev: BL 11/1/00; HBG 3/01; SLJ 9/00) [782.42]

877 *Old Mother Hubbard and Her Wonderful Dog* (PS–K). Illus. by James Marshall. 1991, Farrar $13.95 (0-374-35621-1). 32pp. While Mother Hubbard tries to get some food for her dog, he is busy dancing a jig or playing a flute. (Rev: BL 6/15/91; HB 7–8/91; SLJ 8/91*) [398.8]

878 Opie, Iona, ed. *Here Comes Mother Goose* (PS). Illus. by Rosemary Wells. 1999, Candlewick $21.99 (0-7636-0683-9). 107pp. More than 50 well-known nursery rhymes are given fresh interpretations through clever new illustrations. (Rev: BCCB 12/99; BL 10/1/99*; HB 11–12/99; HBG 3/00; SLJ 10/99) [398.8]

879 Opie, Iona. *Humpty Dumpty and Other Rhymes* (PS–K). Illus. by Rosemary Wells. 1997, Candlewick $6.99 (0-7636-0353-8). 16pp. A board book version of popular Mother Goose rhymes featuring all sorts of animals. Also use *Little Boy Blue and Other Rhymes Pussycat, Pussycat and Other Rhymes* and *Wee Willie Winkie and Other Rhymes* (all 1997). (Rev: BL 3/1/98; HBG 3/98; SLJ 12/97)

880 Opie, Iona, ed. *My Very First Mother Goose* (PS). Illus. by Rosemary Wells. 1996, Candlewick $21.99 (1-56402-620-5). 108pp. A basic collection of 60 standard rhymes illustrated with imagination and charm. (Rev: BCCB 12/96; BL 9/1/96; HB 11–12/96; SLJ 10/96*) [398.8]

881 Ormerod, Jan. *Jan Ormerod's To Baby with Love* (PS). Illus. 1994, Lothrop $16.00 (0-688-12558-1). 40pp. Five catchy nursery rhymes that are attractively illustrated. (Rev: BL 8/94; SLJ 10/94)

882 Patz, Nancy, reteller. *Moses Supposes His Toses Are Roses: And Seven Other Silly Old Rhymes* (K–3). Illus. by Nancy Patz. 1983, Harcourt paper $6.00 (0-15-255691-5). 32pp. Eight wonderful nonsense rhymes are well illustrated. [398.8]

883 Penney, Ian. *Ian Penney's Book of Nursery Rhymes* (PS–K). Illus. 1994, Abrams $14.95 (0-8109-3733-6). 40pp. Using pictures based on scenes from English formal gardens, this book presents 14 Mother Goose rhymes in lavish settings. (Rev: BL 11/15/94; SLJ 3/95)

884 Petersham, Maud, and Miska Petersham. *The Rooster Crows: A Book of American Rhymes and Jingles* (K–2). Illus. by authors. 1969, Macmillan LB $17.00 (0-02-773100-6). 64pp. Rope skipping, counting, and other game rhymes form the bulk of this jaunty collection. A reissue of the 1946 Caldecott Medal winner. [398.8]

885 Prelutsky, Jack. *Beneath a Blue Umbrella* (PS–2). Illus. by Garth Williams. 1990, Greenwillow $15.95 (0-688-06429-9). 64pp. A miscellany of 28 gaily illustrated rhymes by Mother Goose; good read-aloud material. (Rev: BCCB 3/90; HB 3–4/90; SLJ 6/90) [398.8]

886 Roffey, Maureen, and Bernard Lodge. *The Grand Old Duke of York* (PS–2). Illus. 1993, Whispering Coyote $13.95 (1-879085-79-8). 32pp. A book of familiar rhymes with added verses. (Rev: BL 3/15/93) [398.8]

887 Sabuda, Robert. *Movable Mother Goose* (PS–1). 1999, Simon & Schuster $19.95 (0-689-81192-6). Pop-ups and flaps are used to illustrate this collection of favorite Mother Goose rhymes. (Rev: BL 12/15/99; HBG 3/00; SLJ 2/00)

888 Scott, Steve. *Teddy Bear, Teddy Bear* (PS). Illus. Series: Growing Tree. 1998, HarperFestival $9.95 (0-694-01162-2). 24pp. A version of the familiar nursery rhyme nicely illustrated with bright paper collages. (Rev: BL 7/98; HBG 10/98; SLJ 8/98)

889 Sendak, Maurice. *Hector Protector, and As I Went over the Water* (K–1). Illus. by author. 1965, HarperCollins paper $7.95 (0-06-443237-8). 64pp. Two brief Mother Goose rhymes expanded with many drawings that make them both humorous and appealing. [398.8]

890 Sewall, Marcia. *Animal Song* (PS–K). Illus. by author. 1988, Little, Brown $14.95 (0-316-78191-6). 128pp. An old chanting rhyme using animal names. (Rev: BL 3/15/88; SLJ 6–7/88) [398.8]

891 Siomades, Lorianne. *Three Little Kittens* (PS–1). Illus. 2000, Boyds Mills $9.95 (1-56397-845-8). 32pp. The classic nursery rhyme is given a bright, mischievous treatment that involves both the kittens and some thieving mice. (Rev: BL 2/15/00; HBG 10/00; SLJ 4/00)

892 Still, James. *An Appalachian Mother Goose* (K–3). Illus. by Paul Johnson. 1998, Univ. Pr. of Kentucky $25.00 (0-8131-2070-5). 64pp. Familiar nursery rhymes are given an Appalachian flavor in these short poems by Kentucky's former poet laureate. (Rev: BL 3/1/99) [398.8]

893 Sutherland, Zena, ed. *The Orchard Book of Nursery Rhymes* (PS–1). Illus. by Faith Jaques. 1990, Orchard $22.95 (0-531-05903-0). 88pp. A collection of 72 familiar and lesser-known rhymes. (Rev: BCCB 10/90; BL 9/1/90; HB 1–2/91; SLJ 9/90*) [398.8]

894 *Sylvia Long's Mother Goose* (PS–K). Illus. by Sylvia Long. 1999, Chronicle $19.95 (0-8118-2088-2). 109pp. Animals, reptiles, and insects replace humans in the delightful illustrations featured in this Mother Goose anthology. (Rev: BCCB 12/99; BL 11/15/99; HBG 3/00; SLJ 12/99*) [398.8]

895 *The Three Little Pigs* (PS). Illus. by Terri Super. 1984, Putnam $3.95 (0-448-10214-5). 18pp. A favorite nursery rhyme retold in traditional fashion with color illustrations and sturdy binding. [398.8]

896 Trapani, Iza, reteller. *Mary Had a Little Lamb* (PS–1). Illus. by Iza Trapani. 1998, Whispering Coyote $15.95 (1-58089-009-1). An expanded version of the nursery rhyme in which the little lamb has misadventures in a farmyard. (Rev: HBG 3/99; SLJ 11/98)

897 Unobagha, Uzo. *Off to the Sweet Shores of Africa* (PS). Illus. by Julia Cairns. 2000, Chronicle $16.95 (0-8118-2378-4). 56pp. Playful verses about African subjects are contained in this collection that seems inspired by Mother Goose. (Rev: BL 11/1/00; HBG 3/01; SLJ 10/00) [811]

898 Ward, Jennifer, and T. J. Marsh. *Somewhere in the Ocean* (PS–1). Illus. by Kenneth J. Spengler. 2000, Northland $15.95 (0-87358-748-0). 32pp. The nursery rhyme "Over in the Meadow" is changed so the setting is now the ocean and the animals are all sea creatures. (Rev: BL 4/1/00; HBG 10/00; SLJ 7/00)

899 Wells, Rosemary. *The Bear Went Over the Mountain* (PS). Illus. Series: Bunny Reads Back. 1998, Scholastic $4.99 (0-590-02910-X). 16pp. A board book that presents the familiar nursery rhyme with pictures showing a little bear leaving his mother, going over the mountain, and returning with a gift of flowers for her. (Rev: BL 12/15/98; HBG 3/99; SLJ 2/99)

900 Wells, Rosemary. *The Itsy-Bitsy Spider* (PS). Illus. Series: Bunny Reads Back. 1998, Scholastic $4.99 (0-590-02911-8). 16pp. The familiar nursery rhyme about a tiny spider climbing a waterspout is presented in a clever format in this board book. (Rev: BL 12/15/98; HBG 3/99; SLJ 2/99)

901 Winters, Jeanette. *The House That Jack Built* (PS–2). Illus. 2000, Dial $13.99 (0-8037-2524-8). 32pp. The old folk rhyme is retold in the form of a rebus puzzle with clever illustrations. (Rev: BCCB 7–8/00; BL 5/15/00; HBG 10/00; SLJ 5/00) [398.8]

902 Wood, Jakki. *Fiddle-i-fee* (PS–1). Illus. 1994, Bradbury paper $14.95 (0-02-793396-2). 32pp. A lively version of the nursery rhyme that begins "I had a cat; and the cat pleased me." (Rev: BL 6/1–15/94)

903 Yolen, Jane, ed. *The Lap-Time Song and Play Book* (PS). Illus. by Margot Tomes. 1989, Harcourt $15.95 (0-15-243588-3). 32pp. A collection of 16 nursery games and songs with a history for each and simple piano arrangements. (Rev: BL 10/1/89; HB 11–12/89; SLJ 10/89) [782.42]

904 Yolen, Jane, and Adam Stemple. *Jane Yolen's Mother Goose Songbook* (PS–2). Illus. by Rosekrans Hoffman. 1992, Boyds Mills LB $16.95 (1-878093-52-5). 96pp. This Mother Goose collection, with brief folklore and history notes for each rhyme, is attractive to older children. (Rev: BL 12/15/92; HB 3–4/93) [398.8]

905 Ziefert, Harriet, ed. *Mother Goose Math* (PS–1). Illus. by Emily Bolam. 1997, Viking $14.99 (0-670-87569-4). 32pp. This charming picture book contains nursery rhymes that deal with numbers, like "One, two, buckle my shoe." (Rev: BCCB 7–8/97; BL 6/1–15/97; HBG 3/98; SLJ 2/98)

Stories Without Words

906 Aruego, Jose. *Look What I Can Do!* (K–2). Illus. by author. 1971, Macmillan paper $5.99 (0-689-71205-7). 32pp. Almost wordless picture book about the antics that result when one caribou challenges another.

907 Bang, Molly. *The Grey Lady and the Strawberry Snatcher* (PS–1). Illus. by author. 1984, Macmillan $16.00 (0-02-708140-0). 48pp. The snatcher tries to get the strawberries from the Grey Lady.

908 Banyai, Istvan. *Zoom* (1–3). Illus. 1995, Viking $14.99 (0-670-85804-8). 64pp. A clever picture book that begins with small objects and zooms to larger perspectives. (Rev: BCCB 2/95; BL 2/1/95; SLJ 3/95)

909 Blake, Quentin. *Clown* (PS–1). Illus. 1996, Holt $15.95 (0-8050-4399-3). 32pp. A wordless book in which a discarded toy clown has amazing adventures alone in a big city. (Rev: BL 4/15/96; HB 7–8/96; SLJ 5/96)

910 Blue, Rose. *Good Yontif: A Picture Book of the Jewish Year* (K–2). Illus. by Lynne Feldman. 1997, Millbrook $16.95 (0-7613-0142-9). A wordless book that shows how a family observes such Jewish holy days as Rosh Hashanah, Yom Kippur, Purim, Passover, and Shabbat. (Rev: SLJ 3/97)

911 Briggs, Raymond. *The Snowman* (K–3). Illus. by author. 1978, Random $17.00 (0-394-83973-0); paper $7.99 (0-394-88466-3). 32pp. A small boy has adventures with the snowman he has made.

912 Carle, Eric. *Do You Want to Be My Friend?* (PS–K). Illus. by author. 1971, HarperCollins LB $15.89 (0-690-01137-7); paper $6.95 (0-06-443127-4). 32pp. The end of an animal's tail appears on each page, and the child must guess the animal before turning the page to see the rest of it.

913 Crews, Donald. *Truck* (1–3). Illus. by author. 1980, Greenwillow $15.89 (0-688-84244-5); Morrow paper $4.95 (0-688-10481-9). 32pp. This picture book traces a truck trip from loading dock to its San Francisco destination.

914 Cristini, Ermanno, and Luigi Puricelli. *In My Garden* (PS–2). Illus. by authors. 1991, Picture Book paper $12.95 (0-907234-05-4). 28pp. A journey across a garden where a variety of plants, animals, and insects live.

915 Day, Alexandra. *Carl's Masquerade* (PS–1). Illus. 1992, Farrar $12.95 (0-374-31094-7). 32pp. Carl, the rottweiler baby-sitter, takes his young charge and follows its parents to a masquerade ball. (Rev: BCCB 12/92; BL 2/1/93; SLJ 11/92)

916 dePaola, Tomie. *The Hunter and the Animals: A Wordless Picture Book* (K–3). Illus. by author. 1981, Holiday LB $16.95 (0-8234-0397-1); paper $6.95 (0-8234-0428-5). 32pp. A hunter lost in the forest is helped by the animals.

917 Geisert, Arthur. *Oink Oink* (PS–2). Illus. 1993, Houghton $14.95 (0-395-64048-2). 32pp. This saga of eight piglets on an adventure uses only the word *oink*. (Rev: BL 3/1/93; HB 5–6/93; SLJ 6/93)

918 Goodale, Rebecca. *Island Dog* (PS–1). Illus. by author. 1999, Two Dog $17.95 (1-891090-03-8). In this wordless picture book, a dog spends a playful day on an island in Maine. (Rev: SLJ 1/00)

919 Goodall, John S. *Creepy Castle* (PS–K). Illus. by author. 1992, Smithmark $4.98 (0-831-74679-3). 60pp. Depicted in a medieval setting, this concerns the adventures of two mice who get locked in a castle, are rescued, and foil the villain.

920 Goodall, John S. *Paddy Under Water* (PS–1). Illus. by author. 1991, Harcourt $12.95 (0-689-50297-4). 32pp. A cleverly designed book without words that tells of the aquatic adventures of a young pig. A reissue.

921 Goodall, John S. *The Story of a Main Street* (K–3). Illus. by author. 1987, Macmillan $14.95 (0-689-50436-5). 60pp. The history of "main street" in a town is chronicled without words. (Rev: BL 12/1/87; SLJ 9/87)

922 Hutchins, Pat. *Changes, Changes* (PS–1). Illus. by author. 1971, Macmillan LB $16.00 (0-02-745870-9). 32pp. A wooden doll couple rearrange a set of building blocks to suit different situations.

923 Jenkins, Steve. *Looking Down* (PS–2). Illus. 1995, Houghton $14.95 (0-395-72665-4). 32pp. A wordless picture book that starts with a view of earth from space and ends with a close-up of a ladybug. (Rev: BL 8/95; HB 11–12/95; SLJ 9/95)

924 McCully, Emily Arnold. *Four Hungry Kittens* (PS–K). Illus. 2001, Dial $15.99 (0-8037-2505-1). 32pp. An engaging story about four hungry kittens on a farm who await their mother while she is out hunting for food. (Rev: BL 1/1–15/01; SLJ 3/01)

925 McCully, Emily Arnold. *Picnic* (PS–2). Illus. by author. 1984, HarperCollins LB $16.89 (0-06-024100-4). 32pp. An eventful picnic for the mouse family.

926 McCully, Emily Arnold. *School* (PS–1). Illus. by author. 1987, HarperCollins LB $15.89 (0-06-024133-0); paper $5.95 (0-06-443233-5). 32pp. The littlest mouse decides to follow her siblings to school to see what it's like. (Rev: BL 9/1/87; SLJ 10/87)

927 Mariotti, Mario. *Hands Off!* (PS–3). Illus. 1990, Kane/Miller $10.95 (0-916291-29-4). This wordless picture book depicts a soccer game in action. (Rev: SLJ 1/91)

928 Mariotti, Mario. *Hanimations* (PS–3). Illus. 1989, Kane/Miller $10.95 (0-916291-22-7). In this wordless book, hands are transformed into all kinds of familiar animals and birds. (Rev: SLJ 1/90)

929 Martin, Rafe. *Will's Mammoth* (K–2). Illus. by Stephen Gammell. 1989, Putnam $16.99 (0-399-21627-8). 32pp. A boy named Will travels back in time to when mammoths and saber-toothed tigers roamed the earth. (Rev: BCCB 11/89; BL 9/15/89; HB 3–4/90*; SLJ 10/89*)

930 Oxenbury, Helen. *Dressing* (PS). Illus. by author. 1981, Simon & Schuster $4.95 (0-671-42113-1). 14pp. For one- and two-year olds, a wordless book that shows common objects. Also part of this series is *Working* (1981).

931 Peddle, Daniel. *Snow Day* (PS–1). Illus. 2000, Doubleday $12.95 (0-385-32693-9). 24pp. A wordless book about the creation of a snowman, his moment of glory, and his disappearance in the morning sun. (Rev: BL 2/15/00; HBG 10/00; SLJ 3/00)

932 Sis, Peter. *Dinosaur!* (PS–K). Illus. 2000, Greenwillow $14.95 (0-688-17049-8). 24pp. In this wordless book, the bath a boy takes with his toy dinosaur is suddenly transformed into a prehistoric scene where many dinosaurs are roaming in their native habitat. (Rev: BCCB 6/00; BL 3/15/00; HB 7–8/00; HBG 10/00; SLJ 6/00)

933 Sis, Peter. *Ship Ahoy!* (PS–K). Illus. 1999, Greenwillow $14.95 (0-688-16644-X). 24pp. A wordless picture book about a boy who takes imaginary voyages on a variety of different ships. (Rev: BCCB 11/99; BL 9/1/99; HB 9–10/99; HBG 3/00; SLJ 9/99)

934 Tafuri, Nancy. *Early Morning in the Barn* (PS). Illus. by author. 1983, Greenwillow LB $16.93 (0-688-02329-0). 24pp. Only the sounds of farm animals are heard in the pages of this book.

935 Tafuri, Nancy. *Junglewalk* (PS–K). Illus. by author. 1988, Greenwillow LB $15.93 (0-688-07183-X). 32pp. A bedtime story sends a young boy off to dreamland and adventures with a majestic tiger. (Rev: BL 3/1/88; HB 3–4/88)

936 Van Allsburg, Chris. *The Mysteries of Harris Burdick* (1–8). Illus. by author. 1984, Houghton $17.95 (0-395-35393-9). 32pp. A group of pictures are presented and youngsters are asked to supply the stories.

937 Ward, Lynd. *The Silver Pony: A Story in Pictures* (2–4). Illus. by author. 1973, Houghton $18.00 (0-395-14753-0); paper $6.95 (0-395-64377-5). Handsome pictures grace this story about a farm boy's imaginative adventures on a magnificent winged horse.

938 Weitzman, Jacqueline Preiss. *You Can't Take a Balloon into The Metropolitan Museum* (K–3). Illus. by Robin P. Glasser. 1998, Dial $16.99 (0-8037-2301-6). 35pp. In this wordless picture book, a guard tends a balloon for a girl who is visiting the

Metropolitan Museum of Art. When it gets loose, he chases it around Central Park and into the Plaza Hotel. (Rev: BL 11/15/98*; HB 11–12/98; HBG 3/99; SLJ 12/98)

939 Wiesner, David. *Free Fall* (PS–K). Illus. by author. 1988, Lothrop LB $17.89 (0-688-05584-2); paper $6.95 (0-688-10990-X). 32pp. An atlas falls from a boy's lap as he sleeps and opens his imagination to exotic places. (Rev: BCCB 5/88; BL 6/1/88; SLJ 6–7/88)

940 Wilson, April. *Magpie Magic: A Tale of Colorful Mischief* (PS–3). Illus. 1999, Dial $14.99 (0-8037-2354-7). 40pp. In this wordless book, a little boy draws simple pictures that come to life. (Rev: BL 4/15/99; HB 3–4/99; HBG 10/99; SLJ 4/99)

Picture Books

Imaginative Stories

FANTASIES

941 Ada, Alma F. *Dear Peter Rabbit* (PS–1). Illus. by Leslie Tryon. 1994, Atheneum LB $16.00 (0-689-31850-2). 48pp. A number of fairy tale characters like Goldilocks and Peter Rabbit write letters to each other in this clever picture book. (Rev: BCCB 4/94; BL 5/1/94; SLJ 7/94*)

942 Ada, Alma F. *Jordi's Star* (PS–3). Illus. by Susan Gaber. 1996, Putnam $15.95 (0-399-22832-2). 32pp. A shepherd befriends a star whose reflection he sees every night in a pool. (Rev: BCCB 12/96; BL 12/1/96*; SLJ 12/96)

943 Ada, Alma F. *Yours Truly, Goldilocks* (PS–2). Illus. by Leslie Tryon. 1998, Simon & Schuster $16.00 (0-689-81608-1). 40pp. In this sequel to *Dear Peter Rabbit,* the letter-writing format continues with a series of letters exchanged by fairy-tale characters as they plan a housewarming party for the Three Little Pigs. (Rev: BL 5/1/98; HBG 10/98; SLJ 7/98)

944 Adinolfi, JoAnn. *The Egyptian Polar Bear* (PS–1). Illus. 1994, Houghton $14.95 (0-395-68074-3). 32pp. A lost polar bear finds himself in Egypt and a friend of the young pharaoh. (Rev: BL 11/1/94; SLJ 1/95)

945 Agee, Jon. *The Incredible Painting of Felix Clousseau* (PS–3). Illus. by author. 1988, Farrar paper $4.95 (0-374-43582-0). 32pp. A very laid-back artist is oblivious to the havoc his paintings cause. (Rev: BCCB 11/88; BL 11/1/88; HB 1–2/89)

946 Ahlberg, Allan. *The Snail House* (K–3). Illus. by Gillian Tyler. 2001, Candlewick $13.99 (0-7636-0711-8). Grandma tells a story to her grandchildren about three youngsters who shrink in size until they can live in a snail house. (Rev: SLJ 3/01)

947 Alborough, Jez. *My Friend Bear* (PS–1). Illus. 1998, Candlewick $16.99 (0-7636-0583-2). 32pp. Eddie hides a bear's toy teddy bear but gives it back to him when the two become fast friends. (Rev: BL 1/1–15/99; HBG 3/99; SLJ 12/98)

948 Alborough, Jez. *Watch Out! Big Bro's Coming!* (PS–K). Illus. 1997, Candlewick $16.99 (0-7636-0130-6). 24pp. A little mouse warns the other animals that Big Bro is coming and all of them wonder what the fuss is about. (Rev: BL 9/1/97; SLJ 8/97)

949 Alexander, Martha. *And My Mean Old Mother Will Be Sorry, Blackboard Bear* (PS–1). Illus. 2000, Candlewick $10.99 (0-7636-0668-5). 40pp. This is a large-format version of the charming picture book originally issued in 1969. (Rev: BL 11/15/00)

950 Allen, Judy. *Whale* (K–3). Illus. by Tudor Humphries. 1993, Candlewick $15.95 (1-56402-160-2). 32pp. As Anya and her parents are in a boat, they witness a whale and her calf being saved by the ghosts of dead whales. (Rev: BCCB 5/93; BL 7/93)

951 Alper, Ann Fitzpatrick. *Harry McNairy, Tooth Fairy* (PS–3). Illus. by Bridget S. Taylor. 1998, Albert Whitman $15.95 (0-8075-3166-9). 32pp. Dapper Harry McNairy, the local tooth fairy, faces a problem when Michael doesn't want to give up his tooth. (Rev: BL 11/1/98; HBG 3/99; SLJ 9/98)

952 Anderson, Bob. *Obo* (K–3). Illus. by author. 1999, Hampton Roads $16.00 (1-57174-123-2). 45pp. A young monkey who is enchanted with the song of a pretty little bird sets out to find the bird's home, which is known as Paradise. (Rev: SLJ 8/99)

953 Anholt, Catherine, and Laurence Anholt. *Bear and Baby* (PS). Illus. 1993, Candlewick $5.95 (1-56402-235-8). 24pp. For the very young, this is the story of a child and her big protective teddy bear. Also use *Toddlers* (1993). (Rev: BL 11/1/93; SLJ 1/94)

954 Anholt, Catherine, and Laurence Anholt. *Come Back, Jack!* (PS–3). Illus. 1994, Candlewick $12.95 (1-56402-313-3). 32pp. A little girl follows her brother into a book, where they meet characters from four nursery rhymes. (Rev: BCCB 3/94; BL 6/1–15/94; SLJ 7/94)

955 Anholt, Laurence. *Summerhouse* (PS–3). Illus. by Lynne Russell. 1999, DK $14.95 (0-7894-4377-5). In this fantasy, Ella goes into the summerhouse one wintry day and finds everything transformed into a summer landscape. (Rev: BL 2/15/99; HBG 10/99; SLJ 5/99)

956 Appelt, Kathi. *Elephants Aloft* (1–3). Illus. by Keith Baker. 1993, Harcourt $13.95 (0-15-225384-X). 40pp. In this language book, various prepositions are introduced during a flight to Africa by two elephants in a hot-air balloon. (Rev: BL 12/15/93; SLJ 1/94)

957 Argueta, Manlio. *Magic Dogs of the Volcanoes: Los Perros Mágicos de los Volcanoes* (K–3). Illus. by Elly Simmons. 1990, Children's Book Pr. $14.95 (0-89239-064-6). 30pp. From El Salvador, this dual-language book tells the story of the magical dogs that live at the foot of volcanoes. (Rev: SLJ 2/91)

958 Armour, Peter. *Stop That Pickle!* (K–3). Illus. by Andrew Shachat. 1993, Houghton $16.00 (0-395-66375-X). 32pp. The last pickle in the jar flees the deli and is pursued by a number of food items in this comic gem. (Rev: BL 1/1/94; SLJ 2/94)

959 Armstrong, Jennifer. *The Snowball* (K–1). Illus. by Jean Pidgeon. 1996, Random paper $3.99 (0-679-86444-X). 32pp. A snowball gathers up children as it rolls down a hill. (Rev: BL 2/1/97)

960 Arnold, Tedd. *No Jumping on the Bed!* (PS–3). Illus. by author. 1987, Dial $13.89 (0-8037-0039-3). 32pp. Walter jumps so high and hard on his bed that he goes right through to the apartment below, and so on down . . . Also use: *Ollie Forgot* (1988). (Rev: BL 10/15/87; SLJ 10/87)

961 Arnold, Tim. *The Winter Mittens* (2–4). Illus. 1988, Macmillan LB $13.95 (0-689-50449-7). 32pp. Addie uses the magic mittens she finds to make it snow. (Rev: BCCB 12/88; BL 12/15/88; HB 11–12/88)

962 Auch, Mary Jane. *The Easter Egg Farm* (PS–2). Illus. 1992, Holiday LB $16.95 (0-8234-0917-1). 32pp. Humor and chaos infect a chicken ranch where the owner wears dangling earrings and trendy clothes and Pauline the hen lays "ugly" eggs. (Rev: BL 3/1/92*; SLJ 4/92)

963 Auch, Mary Jane. *Monster Brother* (PS–2). Illus. 1994, Holiday LB $15.95 (0-8234-1095-1). 32pp. Rodney is visited by a monster every night, but his brother, Sidney, has a unique solution. (Rev: BCCB 11/94; BL 11/15/94; SLJ 11/94)

964 Aylesworth, Jim. *The Full Belly Bowl* (K–3). Illus. by Wendy A. Halperin. 1999, Simon & Schuster $16.00 (0-689-81033-4). 40pp. In this handsomely illustrated tale, an old man who is always hungry is given a magical food bowl by a tiny creature he has saved from being eaten by a fox. (Rev: BCCB 12/99; BL 11/1/99*; HBG 3/00; SLJ 10/99)

965 Aylesworth, Jim. *My Sister's Rusty Bike* (K–3). Illus. by Richard Hull. 1996, Simon & Schuster $16.00 (0-689-31798-0). 32pp. A fantasy in which a boy meets unusual creatures as he travels American byways. (Rev: BL 11/15/96; SLJ 10/96)

966 Aylesworth, Jim. *The Tale of Tricky Fox* (PS–2). Illus. by Barbara McClintock. 2001, Scholastic $15.95 (0-439-09543-3). 32pp. Tricky Fox, who thinks he has caught a pig for dinner, is outwitted by an old woman who puts a ferocious bulldog in the fox's sack instead. (Rev: BCCB 3/01; BL 2/1/01; SLJ 3/01)

967 Babbitt, Natalie. *Bub; or, The Very Best Thing* (PS–1). Illus. 1994, HarperCollins $15.95 (0-06-205044-3). 32pp. A king and queen discover that the best way to raise their young prince is with plenty of love. (Rev: BCCB 6/94; BL 2/15/94; HB 5–6/94; SLJ 4/94)

968 *Baby Bear's Treasury: 25 Stories for the Very, Very Young* (PS). Illus. 1995, Candlewick $19.99 (1-56402-655-8). 64pp. A fine collection of previously published stories and rhymes by famous authors and artists. (Rev: BL 12/15/95)

969 Bailey, Debbie. *Let's Pretend* (PS). Photos by Susan Huszar. Series: Talk-About-Books. 1999, Annick $5.95 (1-55037-558-X). In the color photos in this board book, children play by taking the roles of parents, doctors, cooks, monsters, firemen, and princesses. (Rev: SLJ 9/99)

970 Baker, Keith. *The Dove's Letter* (1–4). Illus. by author. 1993, Harcourt paper $5.95 (0-15-224134-5). 32pp. A dove finds an obviously lost letter and attempts to deliver it to the proper person. (Rev: BL 5/1/88; SLJ 7/88)

971 Baker, Keith. *The Magic Fan* (PS–2). Illus. 1989, Harcourt $14.95 (0-15-250750-7). 32pp. Village people don't like Yoshi's magic bridge until it saves them from a tidal wave. (Rev: BCCB 2/90; BL 11/1/89; HB 1–2/90; SLJ 10/89*)

972 Balian, Lorna. *Humbug Witch* (1–3). Illus. by author. 1992, Humbug LB $14.95 (1-881772-24-1). 32pp. A little witch doesn't seem to get the hang of witchcraft.

973 Balian, Lorna. *Leprechauns Never Lie* (K–3). Illus. by author. 1994, Humbug LB $14.95 (1-881-77207-1). 32pp. Lazy Ninny Nanny is outwitted by a clever leprechaun.

974 Balian, Lorna. *Wilbur's Space Machine* (PS–1). Illus. 1990, Holiday LB $19.95 (0-8234-0836-1). 32pp. Violet and Wilbur build a space machine to escape the world's pollution and an unwelcome guest, Googie. (Rev: BL 10/15/90; SLJ 2/91)

975 Bang, Molly. *Delphine* (PS–1). Illus. by author. 1988, Morrow $12.95 (0-688-05636-9). 32pp. Delphine takes a wild ride down the mountain to the post office where Gram's gift awaits her. (Rev: BCCB 10/88; HB 9–10/88; SLJ 9/88)

976 Bang, Molly. *The Paper Crane* (PS–1). 1985, Greenwillow paper $5.95 (0-688-07333-6). 32pp. A paper crane left by a thankful stranger leads to good fortune for a restaurant owner down on his luck. (Rev: BCCB 3/86; BL 1/15/86; HB 1–2/86)

977 Banks, Kate. *Alphabet Soup* (K–2). Illus. by Peter Sis. 1994, Knopf paper $5.99 (0-679-86723-6). 32pp. Instead of eating his alphabet soup, a little boy daydreams. (Rev: BL 11/1/88; SLJ 1/89)

978 Bannerman, Helen. *The Story of Little Babaji* (PS–1). Illus. by Fred Marcellino. 1996, HarperCollins LB $14.89 (0-06-205065-6). 72pp. An excellent version of *Little Black Sambo,* now set in India and without racial slurs. (Rev: BL 9/1/96*; HB 9–10/96; SLJ 10/96)

979 Barasch, Lynne. *Old Friends* (2–3). Illus. by author. 1998, Farrar $16.00 (0-374-35611-4). Reincarnation is the theme of this book about a girl who, after the death of her friend, finds a dog that seems to speak to her as her friend did. (Rev: HBG 10/98; SLJ 4/98)

980 Barrett, Judith. *Cloudy with a Chance of Meatballs* (K–3). Illus. by Ron Barrett. 1978, Macmillan $16.00 (0-689-30647-4); paper $5.99 (0-689-70749-5). 32pp. In the land of ChewandSwallow, food falls from the skies.

981 Barrett, Judith. *Pickles to Pittsburgh: The Sequel to Cloudy with a Chance of Meatballs* (K–2). Illus. by Ron Barrett. 1997, Simon & Schuster $16.00 (0-689-80104-1). The people of the town of Chewandswallow take all their excess food and distribute it around the world — for example, eggplants to Ecuador and pickles to Pittsburgh. (Rev: HBG 3/98; SLJ 11/97)

982 Barrett, Judith. *Things That Are Most in the World* (PS–1). Illus. by John Nickle. 1998, Simon & Schuster $16.00 (0-689-81333-3). 32pp. Picturing such superlatives as "The wiggliest thing in the world is a snake ice-skating," this book of nonsense brings delightful imaginary situations to a young audience. (Rev: BCCB 7–8/98; BL 9/15/98; HBG 10/98; SLJ 6/98)

983 Barwin, Gary. *The Magic Mustache* (K–3). Illus. by Stephane Jorisch. 1999, Annick LB $17.95 (1-55037-607-1); paper $6.95 (1-55037-606-3). In this fantasy, a nose who lives with his parents, two eyes, goes to market to trade a pair of eyeglasses for food. (Rev: SLJ 3/00)

984 Base, Graeme. *The Sign of the Seahorse: A Tale of Greed and High Adventure in Two Acts* (1–3). Illus. 1992, Abrams $19.95 (0-8109-3825-1). 48pp. A fable about undersea life that brings a lesson about the dangers of pollution. (Rev: BL 11/15/92; SLJ 11/92)

985 Bateman, Teresa. *Leprechaun Gold* (PS–K). Illus. by Rosanne Litzinger. 1998, Holiday $15.95 (0-8234-1344-6). 32pp. After Donald O'Dell refuses a gift of gold for saving a leprechaun's life, the little one devises a scheme to reward him. (Rev: BL 8/98; HB 7–8/98; HBG 10/98; SLJ 6/98)

986 Bateson-Hill, Margaret. *Lao Lao of Dragon Mountain* (K–3). Illus. by Francesca Pelizzoli. 1998, Larousse $14.95 (1-84089-035-5). 32pp. The story of Lao Lao and her beautiful cutouts is told in English and Chinese. (Rev: BCCB 1/97; BL 12/15/96; SLJ 1/97)

987 Batman, Teresa. *Harp O' Gold* (PS–2). Illus. by Jill Weber. 2001, Holiday $16.95 (0-8234-1523-6). 32pp. When Irish minstrel Tom trades his old harp for a new bright gold one owned by a leprechaun, he knows he has made a good exchange but still longs for his old harp. (Rev: BL 3/1/01)

988 Battle-Lavert, Gwendolyn. *The Shaking Bag* (K–4). Illus. by Aminah Brenda and Lynn Robinson. 2000, Albert Whitman $15.95 (0-8075-7328-0). 32pp. After Annie Mae feeds Raven Reed, the stranger responds by shaking a magic bag that spills out all sorts of presents. (Rev: BCCB 4/00; BL 4/1/00; HB 7–8/00; HBG 10/00; SLJ 4/00)

989 Baum, L. Frank. *The Wizard of Oz* (K–3). Illus. by Lisbeth Zwerger. 1996, North-South $19.95 (1-55858-638-5). 103pp. A Viennese artist reworks this classic tale with unusual, refreshing illustrations and an abridged text. (Rev: BL 10/15/96; SLJ 11/96*)

990 Beck, Andrea. *Elliot's Bath* (PS–1). Illus. 2001, Kids Can $12.95 (1-55074-802-5). 32pp. Elliot, a toy mouse, and Socks, a rag monkey, are looking forward to performing in the evening's talent show, but when they fall into a bathroom sink they become so soggy they are afraid they won't be able to perform. (Rev: BL 3/15/01)

991 Beck, Andrea. *Elliot's Emergency* (PS–2). Illus. 1998, Kids Can $12.95 (1-55074-441-0). 32pp. Elliot Moose, a stuffed toy, panics when he snags his fur on a nail. His friend Beaverton sews him up good as new. (Rev: BL 11/15/98; HBG 3/99; SLJ 12/98)

992 Beck, Ian. *Emily and the Golden Acorn* (K–2). Illus. 1992, Simon & Schuster paper $14.00 (0-671-75979-5). Emily's favorite oak tree is transformed into a sailing ship. (Rev: SLJ 11/92)

993 Beeke, Jemma, and Tiphanie Beeke. *The Brand New Creature* (PS–2). 1998, Sterling $14.95 (1-899607-66-8). 32pp. When a young girl sets out to find a crocodile, she realizes that she doesn't know what a crocodile looks like, so she must ask the identity of a number of animals she meets. (Rev: BL 1/1–15/99; SLJ 6/99)

994 *Benjamin's First Book* (PS). Illus. 1997, Sterling $5.95 (0-8069-0389-9). 26pp. A board book that features photos of a delightful teddy bear named Benjamin. Also use *Benjamin's Toys* and *Shopping with Benjamin* (both 1997). (Rev: BL 2/1/98)

995 Berger, Barbara Helen. *Angels on a Pin* (K–3). Illus. 2000, Putnam $16.99 (0-399-23247-8). 40pp. This book presents an unusual visual experience in the notion of whole cities existing on the head of pins. (Rev: BL 2/1/00; HBG 10/00; SLJ 2/00)

996 Berger, Barbara Helen. *The Jewel Heart* (PS–3). Illus. 1994, Putnam $15.95 (0-399-22681-8). 28pp. The clown doll Gemino loses his jewel heart in the woods, and the ballerina Pavelle tries to help him. (Rev: BL 9/1/94; SLJ 10/94)

997 Berger, Barbara Helen. *A Lot of Otters* (PS). Illus. by author. 1997, Philomel $16.99 (0-399-22910-8). At night, a toddler climbs into a cardboard box with his book and sails off into waters filled with fun-loving otters. (Rev: HBG 3/98; SLJ 9/97*)

998 Berkeley, Laura. *The Seeds of Peace* (K–3). Illus. by Alison Dexter. 1999, Barefoot LB $15.95 (1-84148-007-X). An old hermit tries to show an unhappy, wealthy merchant how he can plant the seeds of peace within himself. (Rev: SLJ 1/00)

999 Berkeley, Laura. *The Spirit of the Maasai Man* (K–3). Illus. 2000, Barefoot $16.95 (1-902283-74-0). 32pp. When animals in a zoo hear the song of the Maasai Man they remember their natural homes. (Rev: BL 3/15/00; SLJ 7/00)

1000 Birchmore, Daniel A. *The White Curtain* (PS–2). Illus. by Gail Lucas. 1997, Cucumber Island Storytellers $15.95 (1-887813-09-8). Gusts of wind blow a white curtain outdoors, where it can enjoy exploring the world. (Rev: SLJ 2/98)

1001 Blake, Robert J. *Spray* (1–4). Illus. 1996, Putnam $15.95 (0-399-22770-9). 32pp. When Justin gets lost in his boat, the ghost of the mariner Joshua Slocum brings him to safety. (Rev: BL 6/1–15/96; SLJ 6/96)

1002 Bliss, Corinne D. *The Littlest Matryoshka* (PS–2). Illus. by Kathryn Brown. 1999, Hyperion LB $16.49 (0-7868-2125-6). 32pp. Six sister dolls in a Russian matryoshka set of nesting dolls travel to an American toy shop where the smallest gets lost but is miraculously reunited with her sisters. (Rev: BCCB 1/00; BL 9/15/99*; HBG 3/00; SLJ 12/99)

1003 Bloom, Becky. *Mice Make Trouble* (K–2). Illus. by Pascal Biet. 2000, Orchard LB $16.99 (0-531-33253-5). 32pp. When he uses his sister's magical pencils, everything that Henry draws comes to life, including six mischievous mice. (Rev: BL 4/1/00; HBG 10/00; SLJ 3/00)

1004 Boesky, Amy. *Planet Was* (K–3). Illus. by Nadine Bernard Westcott. 1990, Little, Brown $14.95 (0-316-10084-6). 32pp. Young Prince Hierre introduces change into the life of Planet Was. (Rev: BL 12/1/90; SLJ 1/91)

1005 Bontemps, Arna, and Langston Hughes. *The Pasteboard Bandit* (K–3). Illus. by Peggy Turley. 1997, Oxford $16.95 (0-19-511476-0). 96pp. A fantasy written in the 1930s about the friendship between a Mexican boy and an American boy and of their pasteboard carnival toy. (Rev: BL 1/1–15/98; HB 11–12/97; HBG 3/98; SLJ 1/98)

1006 Bornstein, Ruth. *The Dancing Man* (K–4). Illus. 1998, Clarion $15.00 (0-395-83429-5). 32pp. In this tale set in a poor village near the Baltic Sea, a boy finds a pair of magical shoes and spends his life dancing in them to produce happiness and joy for others. (Rev: BL 4/15/98; HBG 10/98; SLJ 6/98)

1007 Bowden, Joan. *Why the Tides Ebb and Flow* (1–3). Illus. by Marc Brown. 1979, Houghton paper $7.95 (0-395-54952-3). 48pp. In her search for a hut, Old Woman causes the tides.

1008 Boyd, Lizi. *Willy and the Cardboard Boxes* (PS). Illus. 1999, NAL paper $3.95 (0-140-54342-2). 32pp. In his father's office, a small boy imagines all sorts of adventures when he plays with large cardboard boxes. (Rev: BL 6/15/91; SLJ 8/91)

1009 Breathed, Berkeley. *Edwurd Fudwupper Fibbed Big: Explained by Fannie Fudwupper* (K–3). Illus. by author. 2000, Little, Brown $15.95 (0-316-10675-5). A boy's constant fibbing gets him into serious trouble particularly when it causes the arrival of an angry monster from space. (Rev: HBG 3/01; SLJ 11/00)

1010 Brett, Jan. *Trouble with Trolls* (PS–3). Illus. 1992, Putnam $16.99 (0-399-22336-3). 32pp. In this Scandinavian-type tale, Treva has trouble with trolls when they try to steal her dog Tuffi. (Rev: BCCB 12/92; BL 9/1/92*; SLJ 9/92)

1011 Briggs, Raymond. *The Bear* (PS–3). Illus. 1994, Random LB $20.99 (0-679-96944-6). 36pp. Tilly is befriended by a white bear that creeps into her bedroom when she is asleep. (Rev: BCCB 3/95; BL 2/1/95; SLJ 2/95)

1012 Briggs, Raymond. *Jim and the Beanstalk* (PS–2). Illus. by author. 1997, Putnam paper $5.99 (0-698-11577-5). 40pp. A humorous, fast-moving sequel to the well-known tale.

1013 Brooks, Nigel, and Abigail Horner. *Country Mouse Cottage: How We Lived a Hundred Years Ago* (PS–2). Illus. 2000, Walker $15.95 (0-8027-8752-5). 32pp. In England circa 1900, Edward Country Mouse takes the reader on a tour of his rural house including the kitchen, laundry room, bed, bathroom, and even the schoolroom. (Rev: BCCB 12/00; BL 3/1/01; HBG 3/01; SLJ 12/00)

1014 Brown, Jeff. *Flat Stanley* (1–3). Illus. by Tomi Ungerer. 1964, HarperCollins LB $15.89 (0-06-020681-0). 64pp. A falling bulletin board flattens Stanley so he is only one-half-inch thick.

1015 Brown, Jeff. *Invisible Stanley* (2–3). Illus. by Steve Bjorkman. 1996, HarperTrophy paper $4.25 (0-06-442029-9). 81pp. When Stanley suddenly becomes invisible, he performs many humanitarian acts, including foiling a bank robbery. (Rev: SLJ 12/96)

1016 Brown, Marc. *Witches Four* (PS–1). Illus. by author. 1980, Parents LB $5.95 (0-8193-1014-X). 48pp. Four witches lose their magic hats, which are found by four homeless cats.

1017 Brown, Margaret Wise. *The Little Scarecrow Boy* (PS–K). Illus. by David Diaz. 1998, Harper-Collins LB $15.89 (0-06-026290-7). 40pp. When his father tells him to wait until he is older before going into the field to scare crows, the little scarecrow disobeys and ventures out — with unexpected results. (Rev: BL 9/1/98; HB 11–12/98; HBG 3/99; SLJ 11/98)

1018 Brown, Ruth. *Mad Summer Night's Dream* (K–2). Illus. 1999, Dutton $15.99 (0-525-46010-1). 32pp. A sleeping child and her teddy venture into a dreamworld where there are singing flowers and fluorescent birds. (Rev: BL 6/1–15/99; HBG 10/99; SLJ 7/99)

1019 Browne, Anthony. *My Dad* (PS–3). Illus. 2001, Farrar $16.00 (0-374-35101-5). 32pp. A little boy imagines all the things his dad could do if he wanted — walk on a tightrope or sing in the opera, for example. (Rev: BL 3/1/01)

1020 Brumbeau, Jeff. *The Quiltmaker's Gift* (K–3). Illus. by Gail de Marcken. 1999, Pfeifer-Hamilton $17.95 (1-57025-199-1). 48pp. A greedy king learns a lesson about giving when he demands that a woman who crafts quilts for the poor make one for him. (Rev: BL 1/1–15/00; SLJ 2/00)

1021 Buffett, Jimmy, and Savannah Buffett. *The Jolly Mon* (2–5). Illus. by Lambert Davis. 1988, Harcourt $16.00 (0-15-240530-5). 32pp. The story of Jolly Mon in the Caribbean whose musical voice gains him a magical guitar. (Rev: BCCB 6/88; BL 4/1/88; SLJ 7/88)

1022 Buffett, Jimmy, and Savannah Buffett. *Trouble Dolls* (K–3). Illus. by Lambert Davis. 1991, Harcourt $16.00 (0-15-290790-4). 32pp. Four tiny dolls come alive to help a young girl search for her missing father. (Rev: BL 3/15/91; SLJ 6/91)

1023 Bunting, Eve. *Ducky* (PS–2). Illus. by David Wisniewski. 1997, Clarion $15.00 (0-395-75185-3). 32pp. A yellow plastic duck has many adventures when he is washed overboard from an ocean liner. (Rev: BL 8/97; HB 11–12/97; HBG 3/98; SLJ 9/97)

1024 Bunting, Eve. *The Man Who Could Call Down Owls* (K–3). Illus. by Charles Mikolaycak. 1984, Macmillan LB $16.00 (0-02-715380-0). 32pp. A fantasy about a man who could communicate with owls.

1025 Bunting, Eve. *Night of the Gargoyles* (PS–3). Illus. by David Wiesner. 1994, Clarion $14.95 (0-395-66553-1). 28pp. A horror story in which gargoyles come alive at night. (Rev: BCCB 11/94; BL 10/1/94; SLJ 10/94*)

1026 Bunting, Eve. *Riding the Tiger* (2–4). Illus. by David Frampton. 2001, Clarion $16.00 (0-395-79731-4). 32pp. In this picture-book fantasy about the abuse of power, a young boy realizes how frightening he can become when he rides through town on the back of a ferocious tiger. (Rev: BL 3/1/01*; SLJ 3/01)

1027 Burleigh, Robert. *It's Funny Where Ben's Train Takes Him* (K–3). Illus. by Joanna Yardley. 1999, Orchard LB $16.99 (0-531-33106-7). 32pp. A fantasy in which a young boy enters the world of the toys he has in his bedroom. (Rev: BL 2/1/99; HBG 10/99; SLJ 4/99)

1028 Burningham, John. *Whaddayamean* (K–3). Illus. 1999, Crown $18.95 (0-517-80066-7). 32pp. God, along with two children, visits the earth and is unhappy with the killing, pollution, and quarreling that He sees. (Rev: BL 9/1/99; HBG 3/00; SLJ 7/99)

1029 Burns, Marilyn. *The Greedy Triangle* (K–3). Illus. by Gordon Silveria. 1995, Scholastic $15.95 (0-590-48991-7). 40pp. A little triangle is tired of his shape and becomes a quadrilateral. (Rev: BCCB 3/95; BL 2/1/95; SLJ 3/95)

1030 Bursik, Rose. *Amelia's Fantastic Flight* (PS–3). Illus. 1994, Holt paper $6.95 (0-8050-3386-6). 32pp. Amelia flies from country to country in the plane she has built, returning home in time for dinner. (Rev: BL 3/1/92)

1031 Butterworth, Nick. *The Rescue Party* (PS–1). Illus. by author. 1993, Little, Brown $14.95 (0-316-11923-7). A park keeper enjoys playing with his animal buddies until a young rabbit falls down a well. (Rev: SLJ 2/94)

1032 Cabban, Vanessa. *Bertie and Small and the Brave Sea Journey* (PS). Illus. 1999, Candlewick $12.99 (0-7636-0878-5). 24pp. Bertie, a toddler who turns a cardboard box into a ship, takes his stuffed rabbit, named Small, and his pet dog on a sea voyage. Also use *Bertie and Small and the Fast Bike Ride* (1999). (Rev: BL 12/1/99; HBG 3/00; SLJ 10/99)

1033 Camp, Lindsay. *Why?* (PS–3). Illus. by Tony Ross. 1999, Putnam $15.99 (0-399-23396-2). 32pp. Lily's constant questioning finally pays off when she dissuades a corps of invading aliens from causing harm to our planet. (Rev: BCCB 9/99; BL 7/99; HBG 10/99; SLJ 7/99)

1034 Campbell, Ann-Jeanette. *Dora's Box* (1–3). Illus. by Fabian Negrin. 1998, Knopf LB $18.99 (0-679-97642-6). 32pp. Granted three wishes by a witch, a couple asks for a child they can protect from evil and who will be loved by all. They get their wishes, but in an unexpected way. (Rev: BL 8/98; HBG 3/99; SLJ 9/98)

1035 Carle, Eric. *Draw Me a Star* (PS–2). Illus. 1992, Putnam $16.99 (0-399-21877-7). 36pp. The story of creation is told through the artist's drawings of various objects. (Rev: BCCB 12/92; BL 9/15/92; SLJ 10/92)

1036 Carle, Eric. *Little Cloud* (PS–K). Illus. 1996, Putnam $15.95 (0-399-23034-3). 32pp. A little cloud transforms itself into a variety of shapes and finally produces rain. (Rev: BL 4/1/96; HB 5–6/96; SLJ 5/96)

1037 Carle, Eric. *Papa, Please Get the Moon for Me* (PS–K). Illus. by author. 1986, Picture Book $19.00 (0-88708-026-X). 32pp. A little girl's father gets a high ladder to climb to the moon, but has to admit

it's too large to bring home. (Rev: BL 6/1/86; SLJ 8/86)

1038 Carlstrom, Nancy White. *The Way to Wyatt's House* (PS–K). Illus. by Mary Morgan. 2000, Walker LB $16.85 (0-8027-8742-8). 32pp. Two quiet children have a loud and lovely time visiting with friend Wyatt and all the animals on his farm. (Rev: BL 9/1/00; HBG 3/01; SLJ 10/00)

1039 Carmack, Lisa Jobe. *Philippe in Monet's Garden* (PS–1). Illus. by Lisa Canney Chesaux. 1998, Museum of Fine Arts, Boston $10.95 (0-87846-456-5). 24pp. A frog escapes to Monet's Giverny garden where he gives the artist some tips and inspiration. (Rev: BL 1/1–15/99; HBG 3/99)

1040 Carmichael, Clay. *Used-Up Bear* (PS–K). Illus. 1998, North-South $13.95 (1-55858-901-5). 46pp. A little white teddy bear is afraid that he has become too old and shabby to remain Clara's favorite toy. (Rev: BL 8/98; HBG 10/98; SLJ 8/98)

1041 Carr, Jan. *Big Truck and Little Truck* (PS–3). Illus. by Ivan Bates. 2000, Scholastic $15.95 (0-439-07177-1). 32pp. On Farley's farm, Little Truck remembers everything Big Truck has taught him and is able to save himself after sliding into a ditch. (Rev: BL 11/15/00; HBG 3/01; SLJ 11/00)

1042 Carrick, Carol. *Melanie* (K–3). Illus. by Alisher Dianov. 1996, Clarion $14.95 (0-395-66555-8). 32pp. Blind Melanie sets out to find her grandfather, who has disappeared in the Dark Forest. (Rev: BCCB 11/96; BL 9/15/96; SLJ 11/96)

1043 Carrick, Carol. *Patrick's Dinosaurs on the Internet* (1–2). Illus. by David Milgrim. 1999, Clarion $16.00 (0-395-50949-1). 32pp. A dinosaur appears on young Patrick's computer screen and then whisks the boy off to a distant planet where the dinosaurs now live. (Rev: BL 12/1/99; HBG 3/00; SLJ 9/99)

1044 Carter, Anne. *Tall in the Saddle* (K–2). Illus. by David McPhail. 1999, Orca $14.95 (1-55143-154-8). 32pp. As a boy walks down a modern city street, everything becomes transformed into a scene from the Wild West. (Rev: BL 9/1/99; HBG 3/00; SLJ 9/99)

1045 Cecil, Laura. *Noah and the Space Ark* (K–3). Illus. by Emma C. Clark. 1998, Carolrhoda $14.95 (1-57505-255-5). 32pp. When the earth becomes too polluted to sustain life, Noah and his family build a spaceship to find a safe new home for Earth's creatures. (Rev: BL 8/98; HBG 10/98; SLJ 7/98)

1046 Cecil, Laura, ed. *A Thousand Yards of Sea: A Collection of Sea Stories and Poems* (PS–3). Illus. by Emma C. Clark. 1993, Greenwillow $18.00 (0-688-11437-7). 80pp. A delightful collection of poems and stories that explore various aspects of the sea and its inhabitants. (Rev: BL 4/15/93)

1047 Chall, Marsha Wilson. *Rupa Raises the Sun* (PS–3). Illus. by Rosanne Litzinger. 1998, DK $15.95 (0-7894-2496-7). 32pp. Rupa feels she deserves a vacation after faithful service in raising the sun each morning. (Rev: BL 9/1/98; HBG 3/99; SLJ 11/98)

1048 Chambers, Catherine. *The Elephants' Ears* (PS–1). Illus. by Caroline Mockford. 2000, Barefoot

$15.95 (1-84148-052-5). 32pp. A story about brother and sister elephants that explains why the ears of the elephants are different in India and in Africa. (Rev: BL 4/1/00; SLJ 4/00)

1049 Charles, Veronika M. *Stretch, Swallow and Stare* (K–4). Illus. by Veronika Martenova Charles. 1999, Stoddart $16.95 (0-7737-3098-2). A young boy finds his sister with the help of three female companions, each of whom possesses an unusual power. (Rev: SLJ 1/00)

1050 Charlip, Remy, and Burton Supree. *Mother Mother I Feel Sick Send for the Doctor Quick Quick Quick* (PS–K). Illus. 2001, Tricycle Pr. $15.95 (1-58246-043-4). 48pp. A boy who complains of being sick is operated on and objects including a teapot and a bicycle are removed from his stomach. (Rev: BL 3/1/01)

1051 Charlton, Nancy Lee. *Derek's Dog Days* (PS–1). Illus. by Chris L. Demarest. 1996, Harcourt $14.00 (0-15-223219-2). Derek wants to be a dog and acts like one until he goes to school and finds out it's better to be a boy. (Rev: SLJ 7/96)

1052 Cherry, Lynne. *The Dragon and the Unicorn* (2–4). Illus. 1995, Harcourt $16.00 (0-15-224193-0). 40pp. The importance of conservation is shown in this medieval fantasy in which a dragon and a unicorn see their sacred forest destroyed by King Orlando and his men. (Rev: BL 1/1–15/96; SLJ 2/96)

1053 Child, Lauren. *Beware of the Storybook Wolves* (PS–2). Illus. 2001, Scholastic $15.95 (0-439-20500-X). 32pp. Two hungry wolves appear in a boy's bedroom but, by quick thinking, he is able to thwart their plan to eat him. (Rev: BL 2/1/01*)

1054 Christiana, David. *The First Snow* (PS–3). Illus. 1996, Scholastic $15.95 (0-590-22855-2). 32pp. Aunt Arctica persuades Mother Nature to let Winter come into her kingdom. (Rev: BL 2/1/97; SLJ 2/97)

1055 Christiana, David. *A Tooth Fairy's Tale* (K–2). Illus. 1994, Farrar $16.00 (0-374-37677-8). 32pp. The tooth fairy wants to get possession of a beautiful blue stone owned by a giant. (Rev: BL 5/1/94; SLJ 7/94)

1056 Chwast, Seymour. *Traffic Jam* (PS–2). Illus. 1999, Houghton $15.00 (0-395-97495-X). 32pp. Officer Grumm stops traffic to allow a cat and her kitten to cross the street, and the resultant traffic jam can be seen in a series of pull-out pages. (Rev: BL 9/15/99; HBG 3/00; SLJ 11/99)

1057 Cibula, Matt. *What's Up With You, Taquandra Fu?* (K–2). Illus. by Brian Strassburg. 1997, Zino $16.95 (1-55933-212-3). Taquandra Fu is an oddball, but when she tries to become conventional she prefers her old, erratic self. (Rev: SLJ 4/98)

1058 Clark, Emma C. *Catch That Hat!* (K–2). Illus. 1990, Little, Brown $12.95 (0-316-14496-7). 28pp. A rhymed story about the adventures of a runaway hat. (Rev: BL 5/15/90*; SLJ 8/90)

1059 Clark, Emma C. *I Love You, Blue Kangaroo!* (PS–2). Illus. 1999, Doubleday $15.95 (0-385-32638-6). 32pp. When Lily loses interest in her Blue Kangaroo, it switches its loyalties to Lily's younger brother. (Rev: BL 1/1–15/99; HBG 10/99; SLJ 3/99)

1060 Clark, Emma C. *Where Are You, Blue Kangaroo?* (PS–2). Illus. 2001, Doubleday $15.95 (0-385-32797-8). 32pp. Blue Kangaroo is so afraid that absent-minded Lily will lose him at the beach that he hides so he won't have to go. (Rev: BCCB 3/01; BL 1/1–15/01)

1061 Clement, Rod. *Just Another Ordinary Day* (K–3). Illus. by author. 1997, HarperCollins LB $15.89 (0-06-027667-3). A clever picture book from Australia in which ordinary daily occurrences are pictured in very extraordinary ways with outlandish characters. (Rev: BCCB 9–8/97; SLJ 6/97*)

1062 Coffelt, Nancy. *Dogs in Space* (PS–2). Illus. 1993, Harcourt $14.95 (0-15-200440-8). 32pp. High-flying dogs visit one planet after another. (Rev: BL 2/15/93; SLJ 4/93)

1063 Coffelt, Nancy. *Tom's Fish* (PS–2). Illus. 1994, Harcourt $13.95 (0-15-200587-0). 32pp. Tom can't understand why his pet goldfish, Jessie, swims upside down. (Rev: BL 3/15/94; HB 9–10/93; SLJ 5/94)

1064 Cohen, Caron L. *Crookjaw* (1–3). Illus. by Linda Bronson. 1997, Holt $15.95 (0-8050-5300-X). When her husband is swallowed by a giant whale named Crookjaw, Smilinda decides to save him by using a silver harpoon in this comic fantasy. (Rev: HBG 3/98; SLJ 9/97)

1065 Cohen, Miriam. *Down in the Subway* (PS–3). Illus. by Melanie Hope Greenberg. 1998, DK $16.95 (0-7894-2510-6). 32pp. On a hot, stuffy subway car, Oscar is amazed when the Island Lady pulls from her bag such wonders as a cool island breeze and the green Caribbean Sea. (Rev: BCCB 10/98; BL 11/15/98; HBG 3/99; SLJ 12/98)

1066 Cole, Babette. *The Trouble with Mom* (K–2). Illus. by author. 1997, Putnam paper $5.95 (0-698-11593-7). 32pp. In this humorous fantasy, a boy has a witch for a mother. Originally published in 1984.

1067 Cole, Brock. *Alpha and the Dirty Baby* (K–2). Illus. 1995, Farrar paper $5.95 (0-374-40357-0). 32pp. When Mama and Papa have a spat, the imp behind the couch changes the entire family. (Rev: BCCB 12/91; BL 10/1/91*; SLJ 11/91*)

1068 Cole, Brock. *The Winter Wren* (K–2). Illus. by author. 1984, Farrar $15.00 (0-374-38454-1); paper $4.95 (0-374-48408-2). 32pp. Simon and Meg go out looking for spring.

1069 Cole, Joanna. *Golly Gump Swallowed a Fly* (PS–3). Illus. by Bari Weissman. 1982, Parents $5.95 (0-8193-1069-7). 48pp. A new version of "The Old Woman Who Swallowed a Fly" story.

1070 Compton, Kenn, and Joanne Compton. *Granny Greenteeth and the Noise in the Night* (PS–2). Illus. by Kenn Compton. 1993, Holiday LB $14.95 (0-8234-1051-X). In this humorous cumulative tale, Granny Greenteeth tries to get help to discover what is making the noise that comes from under her bed. (Rev: SLJ 3/94)

1071 Conover, Chris. *The Lion's Share* (PS–3). Illus. 2000, Farrar $16.00 (0-374-39974-3). 40pp. When young Prince Leo visits King Otto of a rival kingdom he discovers that Otto's greatest treasure is his book-filled palace and the ability to read. (Rev: BL 3/15/00; HBG 10/00; SLJ 5/00)

1072 Conrad, Pam. *The Tub Grandfather* (PS–1). Illus. by Richard Egielski. 1993, HarperCollins LB $14.89 (0-06-022896-2). 32pp. Little wooden figures find a missing grandfather when their ball rolls under a radiator. (Rev: BL 10/15/93; SLJ 3/94*)

1073 Conrad, Pam. *The Tub People* (PS–2). Illus. by Richard Egielski. 1989, HarperCollins $15.00 (0-060-21340-X); paper $6.95 (0-06-443306-4). 32pp. In this fantasy, wooden figures who enjoy playing in the tub are swept down the drain. (Rev: BCCB 11/89; BL 8/89; HB 11–12/89*; SLJ 12/89)

1074 Cooke, Trish. *Mr. Pam Pam and the Hullabazoo* (PS–2). Illus. by Patrice Aggs. 1994, Candlewick $14.95 (1-56402-411-3). Mr. Pam Pam amuses a young boy and his mother with his fantastic story about seeing the Hullabazoo, a creature with yellow hands, a green mustache, and red-and-black dots on his face. (Rev: BCCB 11/94; SLJ 11/94)

1075 Coombs, Patricia. *Dorrie and the Haunted Schoolhouse* (PS–1). Illus. 1992, Houghton $15.00 (0-395-60116-9). 32pp. When their teacher is missing, little witch Dorrie and her friends try to teach themselves. (Rev: BL 9/1/92; SLJ 2/93)

1076 Coristine, Philip. *Serena and the Wild Doll* (K–3). Illus. by Julia Gukova. 2000, Annick LB $19.95 (1-55037-649-7); paper $6.95 (1-55037-648-9). 32pp. Serena, a proper doll who lives in an attic, is joined by a wild doll in a tattered dress and a fox, and the three venture out to see the city. (Rev: BL 2/15/01; HBG 3/01; SLJ 11/00)

1077 Cornette. *Purple Coyote* (PS–2). Illus. by Rochette. 1999, Doubleday $12.95 (0-385-32664-5). Jim, who meets a dancing purple coyote on a hill near his house, decides to find out why he dances and why he is purple. (Rev: HBG 10/99; SLJ 8/99)

1078 Cottringer, Anne. *Ella and the Naughty Lion* (PS–1). Illus. by Russell Ayto. 1996, Houghton $14.95 (0-395-79753-5). 32pp. Ella saves her baby brother when their pet lion becomes too playful. (Rev: BCCB 10/96; BL 9/1/96; SLJ 12/96)

1079 Cousins, Lucy. *Katy Cat and Beaky Boo* (PS). Illus. by author. 1996, Candlewick $14.99 (1-56402-884-4). 24pp. A flap book in which Katy Cat and puffin friend Beaky Boo discuss different characteristics of animals. (Rev: SLJ 1/97)

1080 Cowan, Catherine. *My Friend the Piano* (K–3). Illus. by Kevin Hawkes. 1998, Lothrop $16.00 (0-688-13239-1). 32pp. A young girl's piano likes her improvising and refuses to play anything else. When her parents object, she and the piano escape to the sea. (Rev: BL 9/1/98; HBG 3/99; SLJ 2/99)

1081 Cowan, Catherine, trans. and adapt. *My Life with the Wave: Based on the Story by Octavio Paz* (K–3). Illus. by Mark Buehner. 1997, Lothrop LB $15.89 (0-688-12661-8). At the seashore, a boy captures a wave and takes it home, with unfortunate results. (Rev: HB 9–10/97; HBG 3/98; SLJ 8/97*)

1082 Cowen-Fletcher, Jane. *Baby Angels* (PS). Illus. 1996, Candlewick $15.99 (1-56402-666-3). 24pp. Baby angels protect a toddler when the baby begins exploring its immediate surroundings. (Rev: BL 3/1/96; SLJ 5/96)

1083 Cowley, Joy. *Singing Down the Rain* (K–2). Illus. by Jan S. Gilchrist. 1997, HarperCollins LB $14.00 (0-06-027603-7). 32pp. Fantasy and reality blend in this story about a young girl, a drought, and a tiny woman who is a "rain singer." (Rev: BL 11/15/97; SLJ 10/97)

1084 Cox, Judy. *The West Texas Chili Monster* (1–4). Illus. by John O'Brien. 1998, BridgeWater $15.95 (0-8167-4546-3). Attracted to a chili cook-off, a creature from outer space samples a lot of different chilies but chooses Mama's as the best. (Rev: HBG 10/98; SLJ 6/98)

1085 Coy, John. *Vroomaloom: Zoom* (PS–K). Illus. by Joe Cepeda. 2000, Crown $15.95 (0-517-80009-8). 24pp. Because little Carmela can't sleep, her father takes her on a wild joyride that involves driving through farmlands, cities, swamps, seashores, and many other areas. (Rev: BCCB 1/01; BL 12/1/00; HBG 3/01; SLJ 10/00)

1086 Creech, Sharon. *Fishing in the Air* (K–3). Illus. by Chris Raschka. 2000, HarperCollins LB $15.89 (0-06-028112-X). 32pp. A highly imaginative fantasy in which objects seen by a boy and his father on a fishing trip change into images inspired by Chagall and Picasso. (Rev: BL 11/1/00; HBG 3/01; SLJ 9/00)

1087 Crews, Nina. *I'll Catch the Moon* (PS–K). Illus. by author. 1996, Greenwillow $14.89 (0-688-14135-8). A mood piece in which a young boy fantasizes about climbing to the moon and circling the earth. (Rev: BCCB 5/96; HB 5–6/96; SLJ 5/96)

1088 Crews, Nina. *You Are Here* (PS–3). Illus. 1998, Greenwillow $16.00 (0-688-15753-X). 32pp. Using computer-enhanced photographs, this picture book shows how the imagination of two young African American girls transforms their house into a magical fantasy land. (Rev: BL 10/15/98*; HBG 3/99; SLJ 12/98)

1089 Cummings, Pat. *Carousel* (K–2). Illus. 1994, Bradbury $14.95 (0-02-725512-3). 32pp. When Alex breaks the carousel given to her on her birthday, she dreams that the animals on the carousel come to life and take her on a ride in the night sky. (Rev: BL 7/94; SLJ 8/94)

1090 Cuneo, Diane. *Mary Louise Loses Her Manners* (PS–3). Illus. by Jack E. Davis. 1999, Doubleday $15.95 (0-385-32538-X). Because she is acting very rudely, Mary Louise is told she has lost her manners, and so she sets out to find them. (Rev: BCCB 5/99; BL 11/1/99; HBG 3/00; SLJ 9/99)

1091 Curtis, Jamie Lee. *Where Do Balloons Go? An Uplifting Mystery* (K–2). Illus. by Laura Cornell. 2000, HarperCollins LB $16.89 (0-06-027981-8). A child wonders what happens to balloons when they are set free. Do they, for example, get married or tango with airplanes? (Rev: HBG 3/01; SLJ 12/00)

1092 Cuyler, Margery. *The Biggest, Best Snowman* (PS–2). Illus. by Will Hillenbrand. 1998, Scholastic

$15.95 (0-590-13922-3). 32pp. Little Nell is always left out of family activities because she is told she is too small, but her animal friends give her the confidence to build the biggest snowman ever. (Rev: BCCB 12/98; BL 12/15/98; HBG 3/99; SLJ 4/99)

1093 Cyrus, Kurt. *Slow Train to Oxmox* (PS–1). Illus. 1998, Farrar $16.00 (0-374-37047-8). 32pp. A whimsical story about Edwin Blink and his unusual journey when he misses the Oxmox Express and must take instead a slow train filled with passengers that include horses, goats, and a rooster. (Rev: BL 8/98; HBG 3/99)

1094 Czernecki, Stefan. *Zorah's Magic Carpet* (K–3). Illus. by author. 1996, Hyperion LB $15.49 (0-7868-2066-7). In this tale set in Morocco, a young woman weaves a magic carpet that takes her to exotic places that she later weaves into other carpets. (Rev: HB 7–8/96; SLJ 4/96)

1095 Dahl, Roald. *The Minpins* (PS–3). Illus. by Patrick Benson. 1991, Viking $17.00 (0-670-84168-4). 48pp. Little Billy encounters a monster when he disobeys orders and goes into the Forest of Sin. (Rev: BCCB 11/91; BL 10/15/91; HB 1–2/92; SLJ 11/91)

1096 Dale, Penny. *Wake Up, Mr. B.!* (PS–1). Illus. by author. 1992, Candlewick $14.95 (1-56402-104-1). Annie goes on a fantasy trip with the family dog, Mr. B. (Rev: SLJ 10/92)

1097 Daly, Niki. *Mama, Papa, and Baby Joe* (PS–K). Illus. 1999, Puffin paper $4.99 (0-140-54969-2). 32pp. A most unusual family goes out on a weird shopping trip. (Rev: BL 9/15/91; SLJ 10/91)

1098 Daniels, Teri. *G-Rex* (K–2). Illus. by Tracey Campbell Pearson. 2000, Orchard LB $17.99 (0-531-33243-8). A boy turns himself into a dinosaur so he can get more attention at home. (Rev: HBG 3/01; SLJ 10/00)

1099 Darling, Christina. *Mirror* (PS–2). Illus. by Alexandra Day. 1997, Farrar $16.00 (0-374-34720-4). 32pp. A fifth-grader tells about the magical mirror that hung in her bedroom when she was only 7. (Rev: BL 3/1/97; SLJ 3/97)

1100 Darrow, Sharon. *Old Thunder and Miss Raney* (K–2). Illus. by Kathryn Brown. 2000, DK $15.95 (0-7894-2619-6). 32pp. In this light-hearted tall tale, Miss Raney at last wins a prize at the state fair, but not for her biscuits as expected. (Rev: BCCB 11/00; BL 11/1/00; HB 9–10/00; HBG 3/01; SLJ 10/00)

1101 David, Lawrence. *Beetle Boy* (K–3). Illus. by Delphine Durand. 1999, Doubleday $15.95 (0-385-32549-5). Gregory Sampson wakes up one morning to find that he has been turned into a beetle. (Rev: BCCB 2/99; HBG 10/99; SLJ 3/99)

1102 Davol, Marguerite W. *How Snake Got His Hiss* (PS–3). Illus. by Mercedes McDonald. 1996, Orchard LB $15.99 (0-531-08768-9). 32pp. Not only does this tale tell how a snake got its hiss but also how the hyena got its spots and the lion its mane. (Rev: BCCB 4/96; BL 4/15/96; SLJ 3/96)

1103 Davol, Marguerite W. *The Loudest, Fastest, Best Drummer in Kansas* (PS–2). Illus. by Cat B. Smith. 2000, Orchard LB $16.99 (0-531-33191-1). 32pp. In this tall tale, Maggie proves that the loud

noises she makes on her drums can have beneficial results. (Rev: BL 3/15/00; HBG 10/00; SLJ 5/00)

1104 Davol, Marguerite W. *The Paper Dragon* (PS–3). Illus. by Robert Sabuda. 1997, Simon & Schuster $18.00 (0-689-31992-4). 60pp. This story set in China tells how Mi Fei accomplishes his task of putting a destructive dragon to sleep. (Rev: BL 10/15/97*; HBG 3/98; SLJ 11/97)

1105 Day, Alexandra. *Carl Makes a Scrapbook* (PS–4). Illus. 1994, Farrar $12.95 (0-374-31129-3). 32pp. Madeleine, with the help of her dog Carl, combine pages of her mother's photo album with those from Carl's scrapbook about dogs. (Rev: BCCB 11/94; BL 11/15/94; SLJ 11/94)

1106 Day, Alexandra, and Cooper Edens. *Darby, the Special-Order Pup* (PS–2). Illus. by Alexandra Day. 2000, Dial $15.99 (0-8037-2496-9). 32pp. Darby, an English bull terrier pup, is an incorrigible chewer who, in time, uses this trait to save his master's family. (Rev: BL 11/1/00; HBG 3/01; SLJ 10/00)

1107 Deedy, Carmen A. *The Library Dragon* (K–2). Illus. by Michael P. White. 1994, Peachtree $16.95 (1-56145-091-X). The new librarian is a real fire-breathing dragon who in time learns to trust children with her books. (Rev: BCCB 2/95; SLJ 12/94)

1108 Dematons, Charlotte. *Looking for Cinderella* (PS–3). Illus. 1996, Front Street $15.95 (1-886910-13-8). 32pp. In an old windmill, Hilda encounters many fairy tale characters, including Hansel and Gretel and Tom Thumb. (Rev: BCCB 10/96; BL 9/15/96; SLJ 1/97)

1109 Demi. *Liang and the Magic Paintbrush* (2–4). Illus. by author. 1980, Holt paper $5.95 (0-8050-0801-2). 32pp. A boy in old China finds that everything he dreams comes to life.

1110 Denton, Kady M. *Would They Love a Lion?* (PS–K). Illus. 1995, Kingfisher $16.95 (1-85697-546-0). 32pp. A young child who is anxious to be noticed imagines herself as various animals. (Rev: BCCB 7–8/95; BL 8/95; SLJ 7/95)

1111 dePaola, Tomie. *Big Anthony: His Story* (PS–3). Illus. 1998, Putnam $16.99 (0-399-23189-7). 32pp. Klutzy Big Anthony goes out on his own to earn his fortune and finds himself at the door of the Italian witch Strega Nona. (Rev: BL 11/15/98; HBG 3/99; SLJ 11/98)

1112 dePaola, Tomie. *Bill and Pete* (K–2). Illus. by author. 1996, Putnam paper $5.99 (0-698-11400-0). 32pp. Pete is a toothbrush (alias a bird) who helps young Bill in a series of world misadventures.

1113 dePaola, Tomie. *Jamie O'Rourke and the Pooka* (PS–3). Illus. 2000, Putnam $16.99 (0-399-23457-5). 32pp. A humorous original folktale about the laziest man in Ireland and the strange donkey-like beast, the pooka, that helps clean his house. (Rev: BL 1/1–15/00; HBG 10/00; SLJ 3/00)

1114 dePaola, Tomie. *Sing, Pierrot, Sing: A Picture Book in Mime* (PS–2). Illus. by author. 1983, Harcourt paper $3.95 (0-15-274989-6). 32pp. A group of children comfort Pierrot at his loss of Columbine.

1115 dePaola, Tomie. *Strega Nona Meets Her Match* (K–2). Illus. 1993, Putnam $15.95 (0-399-22421-1). 34pp. Strega Amelia comes to town and takes away business from the town's other witch, Strega Nona. (Rev: BCCB 12/93; BL 11/1/93; HB 11–12/93)

1116 dePaola, Tomie. *Strega Nona Takes a Vacation* (K–3). Illus. 2000, Putnam $16.99 (0-399-23562-0). 32pp. While Strega Nona is away on vacation, Big Anthony uses too many bath crystals and creates enough soapsuds to flow into town. (Rev: BL 10/15/00; HBG 3/01; SLJ 10/00)

1117 dePaola, Tomie. *The Unicorn and the Moon* (PS–3). Illus. 1994, Silver Burdett LB $18.95 (0-382-24658-6). 32pp. When the moon becomes trapped between two mountains, a unicorn tries to rescue it. (Rev: BL 1/1/95)

1118 Desimini, Lisa. *Moon Soup* (PS–3). Illus. 1993, Hyperion LB $15.49 (1-56282-464-3). 32pp. An unusual man concocts a brew he calls moon soup and flies to the moon to eat it. (Rev: BL 11/1/93; SLJ 1/94)

1119 Desimini, Lisa. *Sun and Moon: A Giant Love Story* (PS–3). Illus. 1999, Scholastic $16.95 (0-590-18720-1). 40pp. An enchanting fable about the growing love between a girl and a boy whose heads are literally in the clouds. (Rev: BCCB 1/99; BL 1/1–15/99; HBG 10/99; SLJ 3/99)

1120 Devlin, Wende, and Harry Devlin. *Old Black Witch!* (K–3). Illus. by Harry Devlin. 1992, Macmillan $13.95 (0-02-729185-5). 32pp. When Nicky and his mother buy an old house, they find a witch living in the chimney. (Rev: BL 11/15/92)

1121 Dewan, Ted. *Crispin: The Pig Who Had It All* (PS–2). Illus. 2000, Doubleday $15.95 (0-385-32540-1). 32pp. Two children teach a spoiled rich little pig named Crispin to appreciate the simple things in life in this bright, imaginative picture book. (Rev: BCCB 12/00; BL 11/15/00*; HBG 3/01)

1122 Dewan, Ted. *The Sorcerer's Apprentice* (K–2). Illus. 1998, Doubleday $15.95 (0-385-32537-1). 32pp. A variation on "The Sorcerer's Apprentice" in which an inventor creates a robot to clean up his workshop. (Rev: BCCB 7–8/98; BL 2/1/98; HB 3–4/97; HBG 10/98; SLJ 2/98)

1123 Dickens, Charles. *The Child's Story* (2–4). Illus. by Harvey Chan. 2000, Simon & Schuster $17.00 (0-689-83482-9). 32pp. In this fantasy, a traveler meets a series of people, starting with a child and ending with an old man, who outline for him the stages of life. (Rev: BL 12/1/00; HBG 3/01; SLJ 10/00)

1124 Dillon, Jana. *Jeb Scarecrow's Pumpkin Patch* (PS–2). Illus. 1992, Houghton $16.00 (0-395-57578-8). 32pp. Tension builds between Jeb Scarecrow and the crows as he guards the family's pumpkin patch. (Rev: BL 10/1/92*; SLJ 9/92)

1125 Dillon, Jana. *Lucky O'Leprechaun Comes to America* (PS–1). Illus. by author. 2000, Pelican $14.95 (1-56554-816-7). A fantasy in which Lucky O'Leprechaun gets caught in the luggage of three Irish immigrant girls and is forced to travel with them to America. (Rev: SLJ 1/01)

1126 Diterlizzi, Tony. *Jimmy Zangwow's Out-of-This-World Moon Pie Adventure* (K–2). Illus. by author. 2000, Simon & Schuster $16.00 (0-689-82215-4). When Jimmy's mother refuses to give him a Moon Pie, the young boy travels to the moon to get his own. (Rev: BCCB 5/00; HBG 10/00; SLJ 4/00)

1127 Dollinger, Renate. *The Rabbi Who Flew: A Grandma Hanne Sheyne Story* (K–3). Illus. 2000, Booksmythe $18.00 (0-945585-20-9). 48pp. When a rabbi gains the power to fly, his friends realize that he has holes in his shoes and devise a plan to mend them. (Rev: BL 2/1/01)

1128 Donnelly, Liza. *Dinosaur Beach* (PS–2). Illus. by author. 1991, Scholastic paper $2.50 (0-685-43744-2). A boy and his dog spend a lovely day playing with the dinosaurs at a beach. (Rev: SLJ 7/89)

1129 Donnelly, Liza. *Dinosaur Garden* (PS–3). Illus. 1991, Scholastic paper $3.25 (0-590-43172-2). 32pp. Rex's seedlings sprout into a tropical jungle that is soon home to plant-eating dinosaurs. (Rev: BL 4/15/90; SLJ 3/90)

1130 Dorros, Arthur. *Abuela* (K–2). Illus. by Elisa Kleven. 1991, Dutton $16.99 (0-525-44750-4). 40pp. Rosalba and her grandmother fly over New York City in her imagination. (Rev: BCCB 9/92; BL 10/15/91*; HB 11–12/91*; SLJ 10/91)

1131 Dorros, Arthur. *The Fungus that Ate My School* (1–4). Illus. by David Catrow. 2000, Scholastic $15.95 (0-590-47704-8). 32pp. A science experiment goes awry and a fungus takes over a school in this psychedelic fantasy. (Rev: BCCB 7–8/00; BL 6/1–15/00; HB 3–4/00; HBG 10/00; SLJ 4/00)

1132 Doyle, Charlotte. *You Can't Catch Me* (PS–1). Illus. by Rosanne Litzinger. 1998, HarperFestival $9.95 (0-694-01038-3). In a hide-and-seek series of pictures, various animals are playfully caught by their pursuers in the same way that a little girl is captured by her mother in a loving embrace. (Rev: HBG 10/98; SLJ 7/98)

1133 Dragonwagon, Crescent. *Brass Button* (K–3). Illus. by Susan Paradise. 1997, Simon & Schuster $16.00 (0-689-80582-9). 40pp. Mrs. Morrison loses a button from her new red coat, and it falls into several different hands before she gets it back. (Rev: BL 6/1–15/97; SLJ 6/97)

1134 Drawson, Blair. *Flying Dimitri* (K–3). Illus. 1997, Orchard $14.95 (0-531-30037-4). 40pp. A fantasy in which a young boy flies to Mars to save a princess but is happy to get home, where his father tucks him into bed. (Rev: BL 12/15/97; HBG 3/98; SLJ 4/98)

1135 Drawson, Blair. *Mary Margaret's Tree* (K–3). Illus. 1996, Orchard LB $16.99 (0-531-08871-5). 32pp. In this fantasy, Mary Margaret views the change of seasons from atop a tree that she has planted. (Rev: BL 10/1/96; SLJ 10/96)

1136 Drescher, Henrik. *The Boy Who Ate Around* (K–3). Illus. 1994, Hyperion LB $15.49 (0-7868-2011-X). 40pp. When young Mo objects to the family dinner fare, he turns into a ravenous warthog that eats everything in sight. (Rev: BL 11/1/94; SLJ 10/94)

1137 Drescher, Henrik. *Simon's Book* (PS–1). Illus. by author. 1983, Lothrop paper $5.95 (0-688-10484-3). 32pp. A frightening monster chases Simon through the pages of his drawing pad.

1138 Drummond, Allan. *The Willow Pattern Story* (2–4). Illus. 1992, North-South $14.95 (1-558-58171-5); paper $5.95 (1-558-58413-7). 28pp. The author spins a tale from the story depicted on willow pattern china. (Rev: BL 10/15/92; SLJ 12/92)

1139 Drury, Tim. *When I'm Big* (K–2). Illus. by Nila Aye. 1999, Orchard $15.95 (0-531-30189-3). Confined to their home because of rain, a young brother and sister think of all the things they will do when they grow up. (Rev: HBG 3/00; SLJ 12/99)

1140 Dunbar, Joyce. *The Sand Children* (PS–2). Illus. by Mark Edwards. 1999, Crocodile $15.95 (1-56656-309-7). A boy and his father build a sand giant and, that night, the boy sees the giant come to life and fashion a set of sand children. (Rev: HBG 10/99; SLJ 7/99)

1141 Duncan, Lois. *The Longest Hair in the World* (K–2). Illus. by Jon McIntosh. 1999, Doubleday $15.95 (0-385-32113-9). Emily gets her wish of having the longest hair in the world but finds this has its disadvantages, like not being able to fit into the family car. (Rev: HBG 3/00; SLJ 12/99)

1142 Dunn, Carolyn. *A Pie Went By* (PS–3). Illus. by Christopher Santoro. 2000, HarperCollins LB $14.89 (0-06-028808-6). King Bing, who is off to court a queen, attracts a number of animals who follow him when they see the lovely cherry pie he carries on his head. (Rev: HBG 10/00; SLJ 6/00)

1143 Dunrea, Olivier. *The Trow-Wife's Treasure* (K–3). Illus. 1998, Farrar $16.00 (0-374-37792-8). 32pp. In this fantasy set in Scotland, a kindly farmer sets out to find the lost child of a troll-like woman who has supernatural powers. (Rev: BCCB 6/98; BL 4/15/98; HB 7–8/98; HBG 10/98; SLJ 4/98)

1144 Duquennoy, Jacques. *The Ghosts' Trip to Loch Ness* (PS–2). Illus. by author. 1996, Harcourt $11.00 (0-15-201440-3). A quartet of ghosts travels to Scotland for a glimpse of the Loch Ness monster in this amusing fantasy. (Rev: BCCB 10/96; SLJ 10/96)

1145 Dwyer, Mindy. *Aurora: A Tale of the Northern Lights* (K–2). Illus. by author. 1997, Alaska Northwest $15.95 (0-88240-494-6). A fantasy that traces the origins of the aurora borealis through the story of a young girl's search for a place filled with darkness. (Rev: HBG 3/98; SLJ 2/98)

1146 Eaton, Deborah, and Susan Halter. *No One Told the Aardvark* (PS–2). Illus. by Jim Spence. 1997, Charlesbridge paper $6.95 (0-88106-871-3). In this humorous story, a young boy thinks of all the advantages there would be if he were different animals. (Rev: SLJ 6/97)

1147 Egan, Tim. *Distant Feathers* (K–3). Illus. 1998, Houghton $15.00 (0-395-85808-9). 32pp. A giant bird taps on Sedrick Van Pelt's window and asks for bread in this humorous picture book. (Rev: BL 3/15/98; HBG 10/98; SLJ 5/98)

1148 Egielski, Richard. *Buz* (PS–2). Illus. 1995, HarperCollins LB $15.89 (0-06-023567-5). 32pp. A bug that is eaten accidently by a boy finally finds an escape route via the boy's ear. (Rev: BCCB 10/95; BL 8/95; SLJ 9/95)

1149 Egielski, Richard. *Three Magic Balls* (PS–2). Illus. 2000, HarperCollins $15.95 (0-06-026032-7). 40pp. Young Rudy tries out his skills with three magical rubber balls but can't control the results. (Rev: BCCB 9/00; BL 9/1/00; HBG 3/01; SLJ 9/00)

1150 Elgar, Susan. *The Brothers Gruesome* (K–3). Illus. by Drahos Zak. 2000, Houghton $15.00 (0-618-00515-3). 32pp. Three horrible-looking brothers do all sorts of horrible things until they meet a monster a little more horrible than they are. (Rev: BCCB 4/00; BL 5/15/00; HBG 10/00; SLJ 4/00)

1151 Emberley, Rebecca. *My Mother's Secret Life* (PS–3). Illus. 1998, Little, Brown $15.95 (0-316-23496-6). 32pp. When a young girl's mother goes upstairs to take a rest, the girl wonders if her mother isn't really living a double life as a housewife and also a circus star. (Rev: BCCB 6/98; BL 4/15/98; HBG 10/98; SLJ 4/98)

1152 Enderle, Judith R., and Stephanie G. Tessler. *Upstairs* (K–2). Illus. by Kate S. Palmer. 1998, Boyds Mills $14.95 (1-56397-466-5). An entertaining book about a boy who discovers that his new upstairs neighbors have several farm animals as pets. (Rev: HBG 3/99; SLJ 11/98)

1153 Enright, Elizabeth. *Tatsinda* (K–4). Illus. by Katie T. Treherne. 1991, Harcourt $16.95 (0-15-284280-2). 64pp. A golden-haired girl is carried off by an ogre. (Rev: SLJ 7/91)

1154 Esterl, Arnica. *Okino and the Whales* (K–3). Illus. by Marek Zawadzki. 1995, Harcourt $16.00 (0-15-200377-0). 32pp. A mother tells her son the story of how his great-great-grandmother rescued her daughter from the underwater kingdom of Iwa. (Rev: BL 10/15/95; SLJ 1/96)

1155 Evans, Dilys, ed. *Monster Soup and Other Spooky Poems* (PS–1). Illus. by Jacqueline Rogers. 1992, Scholastic $14.95 (0-590-45208-8). 40pp. Watercolor paintings illustrate 16 poems that monster fans are sure to love. (Rev: BL 8/92; SLJ 10/92) [811]

1156 Eyles, Heather. *Well, I Never!* (K–2). Illus. by Terry Ross. 1990, Overlook $11.95 (0-87951-383-7). Polly complains to her mother that there are monsters in her room — and she's right. (Rev: BCCB 3/90; SLJ 3/90)

1157 Farjeon, Eleanor. *Elsie Piddock Skips in Her Sleep* (K–3). Illus. by Charlotte Voake. 2000, Candlewick $16.99 (0-7636-0790-8). 48pp. Elsie Piddock uses her magic skipping rope to foil the plans of a developer who wants to build houses on Mount Cabum, the town's favorite spot for skipping. (Rev: BL 11/1/00; SLJ 10/00)

1158 Fernandes, Eugenie. *Sleepy Little Mouse* (PS–K). Illus. by Kim Fernandes. 2000, Kids Can $12.95 (1-55074-701-0). 24pp. When Little Mouse cries at nap time, she produces so many tears that her bed floats down a river and into the sea where she is found by sea creatures. (Rev: BL 10/1/00; HBG 3/01)

1159 Fisher, Leonard Everett. *Sailboat Lost* (PS–2). Illus. 1991, Macmillan $15.95 (0-02-735351-6). 32pp. A toy sailboat has adventures during the time it is adrift at sea. (Rev: BL 9/1/91)

1160 Fleischman, Paul. *Weslandia* (K–3). Illus. by Kevin Hawkes. 1999, Candlewick $15.99 (0-7636-0006-7). 40pp. In this offbeat fantasy, unconventional Wesley cultivates magical seeds that serve as the basis of a new civilization. (Rev: BCCB 7–8/99; BL 7/99*; HB 3–4/99; HBG 10/99; SLJ 6/99)

1161 Florian, Douglas. *Monster Motel* (PS–1). Illus. 1993, Harcourt $13.95 (0-15-255320-7). Many of the 13 poems that are presented deal with monsters who live in a motel. (Rev: SLJ 6/93)

1162 Foreman, Michael. *Jack's Fantastic Voyage* (K–3). Illus. 1992, Harcourt $14.95 (0-15-239496-6). 32pp. Jack doubts that his grandfather really had the adventures he claims until one night the two experience together an equally amazing voyage. (Rev: BL 11/15/92; SLJ 11/92)

1163 Fowler, Susi G. *Circle of Thanks* (PS–2). Illus. by Peter Catalanotto. 1998, Scholastic $15.95 (0-590-10066-1). 32pp. When a woman rescues an otter pup in the tundra, the act sets off a chain of events that end with her son being saved and returned to her with the help of an arctic fox. (Rev: BL 9/15/98; HBG 3/99; SLJ 12/98)

1164 Fox, Mem. *Feathers and Fools* (1–4). Illus. by Nicholas Wilton. 1996, Harcourt $16.00 (0-15-200473-4). An antiwar allegory about the rivalry between peacocks and swans. (Rev: SLJ 7/96)

1165 Fox, Mem. *The Straight Line Wonder* (K–4). Illus. by Marc Rosenthal. 1997, Mondo $14.95 (1-57255-206-9). 24pp. Three straight lines are dear friends until one of them wants to change its shape. (Rev: BL 10/15/97; HBG 3/98; SLJ 1/98)

1166 Frascino, Edward. *Nanny Noony and the Magic Spell* (PS–3). Illus. by author. 1988, Pippin $15.95 (0-945912-00-5). 32pp. How the spell on the farm is undone. (Rev: BL 11/15/88; SLJ 1/89)

1167 Freeman, Don. *A Rainbow of My Own* (K–3). Illus. by author. 1966, Puffin paper $5.99 (0-14-050328-5). 32pp. A boy's search for a rainbow ends in his own home.

1168 French, Vivian. *Once upon a Time* (PS–K). Illus. by John Prater. 1993, Candlewick $14.99 (1-56402-177-7). 32pp. In this story in verse, a family moves into a country house in a neighborhood where all sorts of nursery rhyme characters live. (Rev: BCCB 4/93; BL 5/1/93)

1169 Frieden, Sarajo. *The Care and Feeding of Fish* (K–3). Illus. 1996, Houghton $15.95 (0-395-71251-3). 32pp. Loulou's pet fish grows to the size of a human and shares many adventures with her. (Rev: BCCB 10/96; BL 11/15/96; SLJ 10/96)

1170 Friend, Catherine. *My Head Is Full of Colors* (PS–3). Illus. by Kiki. 1994, Hyperion $14.95 (1-56282-360-4). 32pp. Maria finds she has amazing hair that each day contains a different set of objects. (Rev: BL 3/15/94; SLJ 6/94)

1171 Frissen. *Yann and the Whale* (K–3). Illus. by Hanze. Series: Cranky Nell Books. 1997, Kane/Miller $13.95 (0-916291-71-5). When Yann is

saved from drowning by a whale, he vows never to hunt these creatures again. (Rev: SLJ 6/97)

1172 Gackenbach, Dick. *Barker's Crime* (PS–2). Illus. 1996, Harcourt $15.00 (0-15-200628-1). 32pp. Greedy Mr. Gobble takes Barker the dog to court for inhaling the aroma of the miser's meals. (Rev: BL 3/1/96; SLJ 7/96)

1173 Gackenbach, Dick. *Harry and the Terrible Whatzit* (PS–2). Illus. by author. 1979, Houghton $15.00 (0-395-28795-2); paper $6.95 (0-89919-223-8). 32pp. Harry follows his mother into the dark cellar to confront the terrible two-headed Whatzit.

1174 Galchutt, David. *There Was Magic Inside* (1–3). Illus. 1993, Simon & Schuster paper $14.00 (0-671-75978-7). In this tale set in an Asian land, Toshi accidentally awakens a dangerous sea monster. (Rev: SLJ 8/93)

1175 Galdone, Paul. *The Magic Porridge Pot* (K–3). Illus. by author. 1976, Houghton $16.00 (0-395-28805-3). 32pp. The familiar tale of the magic pot that produces porridge but runs amuck when the words that stop it are forgotten.

1176 Gammell, Stephen. *Is That You, Winter?* (PS–2). Illus. 1997, Harcourt $16.00 (0-15-201415-2). 32pp. Old Man Winter discovers for whom he is busy making snow. (Rev: BL 9/1/97; HBG 3/98; SLJ 10/97)

1177 Gammell, Stephen. *Twigboy* (PS–K). 2000, Harcourt $16.00 (0-15-202137-X). 32pp. After a rock saves Twigboy from attacking bugs, it is his turn to be the rescuer when the rock falls into a swamp. (Rev: BCCB 5/00; BL 4/15/00; HBG 10/00; SLJ 5/00)

1178 Gauch, Patricia L. *Poppy's Puppet* (K–3). Illus. by David Christiana. 1999, Holt $16.95 (0-8050-5291-7). 32pp. A magical tale about a toy maker who makes a ballerina marionette out of a piece of wood that was intended to become a tightrope walker. (Rev: BL 9/15/99; HBG 3/00; SLJ 10/99)

1179 Gay, Marie-Louise. *On My Island* (PS–1). Illus. 2001, Groundwood $16.95 (0-88899-396-X). 32pp. In this fantasy set on an island, a young boy who shares his home with a variety of animals claims nothing ever happens, but the opposite is true. (Rev: BL 3/15/01)

1180 Geeslin, Campbell. *How Nanita Learned to Make Flan* (PS–3). Illus. by Petra Mathers. 1999, Simon & Schuster $16.00 (0-689-81546-8). 32pp. An original fairy tale about a little Mexican girl whose new shoes take her to a grand house where she is put to work and learns to make the best dessert flan. (Rev: BCCB 11/99; BL 12/1/99; HBG 3/00; SLJ 12/99)

1181 Geisert, Arthur. *The Etcher's Studio* (PS–2). Illus. 1997, Houghton $15.95 (0-395-79754-3). 32pp. After describing the etching process, a young boy imagines that he is in his grandfather's pictures. (Rev: BCCB 6/97; BL 4/1/97; HB 5–6/97; SLJ 4/97)

1182 Geras, Adele. *From Lullaby to Lullaby* (PS–1). Illus. by Kathryn Brown. 1997, Simon & Schuster $16.00 (0-689-80568-3). 40pp. Each of the objects depicted in a blanket that a mother is knitting for her daughter comes to life and expresses its wishes. (Rev: BL 4/15/97; SLJ 7/97)

1183 Gershator, David, and Phillis Gershator. *Palampam Day* (PS–2). Illus. by Enrique O. Sanchez. 1997, Marshall Cavendish $15.95 (0-7614-5002-5). 32pp. Set in the West Indies, this story tells about a boy who is suddenly having conversations with all sorts of objects, like a coconut, a dog, and a bowl of bananas. (Rev: BL 8/97; HBG 3/98; SLJ 9/97)

1184 Gerstein, Mordicai. *Behind the Couch* (2–3). Illus. by author. 1996, Hyperion paper $3.95 (0-7868-1139-0). 57pp. In this fantasy, a young boy discovers a whole new world after his stuffed toy falls behind the couch. (Rev: BCCB 9/96; SLJ 7/96)

1185 Gerstein, Mordicai. *Stop Those Pants!* (K–3). Illus. 1998, Harcourt $14.00 (0-15-201495-0). 32pp. When his jeans decide to hide and his socks begin hopping around the room one morning, Murray has trouble getting dressed. (Rev: BL 7/98; HBG 10/98; SLJ 6/98)

1186 Getz, David. *Floating Home* (1–3). Illus. by Michael Rex. 1997, Holt $15.95 (0-8050-4497-3). 32pp. When teacher wants Maxine to see her home in a new way, she becomes an astronaut to see it from space. (Rev: BCCB 5/97; BL 5/1/97; SLJ 5/97)

1187 Giblin, James Cross. *The Dwarf, the Giant, and the Unicorn: A Tale of King Arthur* (2–4). Illus. by Claire Ewart. 1996, Clarion $15.95 (0-395-60520-2). 44pp. When King Arthur's ship is stranded on an island, he encounters three unusual creatures. (Rev: BL 12/1/96; SLJ 10/96)

1188 Gill, Janet. *Basket Weaver and Catches Many Mice* (K–2). Illus. by Yangsook Choi. 1999, Knopf LB $18.99 (0-679-98922-6). 32pp. A cat named Catches Many Mice helps his master, Basket Weaver, make a prize-winning cradle for the empress's baby. (Rev: BL 6/1–15/99; HBG 10/99; SLJ 7/99)

1189 Gillerlain, Gayle, reteller. *The Reverend Thomas's False Teeth* (K–3). Illus. by Dena Schutzer. 1995, BridgeWater $14.95 (0-8167-3303-1). When the Reverend Thomas's false teeth fall into deep water, Gracie thinks of an ingenious way to retrieve them. (Rev: SLJ 12/95)

1190 Gilliland, Judith Heide. *Not in the House, Newton!* (PS–3). Illus. by Elizabeth Sayles. 1995, Clarion $15.00 (0-395-61195-4). 32pp. When Newton draws objects using his magical red crayon, they jump off the pages. (Rev: BL 12/15/95; SLJ 1/96)

1191 Gillmor, Don. *Yuck, a Love Story* (K–4). Illus. by Marie-Louise Gay. 2000, Stoddart $14.95 (0-7737-3218-7). Austin Grouper develops a crush on the girl next door and, to prove his love, lassos the moon as a gift. (Rev: SLJ 11/00)

1192 Gilman, Phoebe. *The Gypsy Princess* (PS–3). Illus. 1997, Scholastic $15.95 (0-590-86543-9). 32pp. Cinnamon tires of being a princess and longs for the gypsy life. (Rev: BCCB 3/97; BL 2/1/97; SLJ 3/97)

1193 Ginsburg, Mirra. *Where Does the Sun Go at Night?* (PS–1). Illus. by Jose Aruego and Ariane Dewey. 1980, Morrow paper $4.95 (0-688-07041-8). 32pp. A question-and-answer format is used in this adaptation of an Armenian song.

1194 Givens, Terryl. *Dragon Scales and Willow Leaves* (PS–1). Illus. by Andrew Portwood. 1997, Putnam $12.95 (0-399-22619-2). 32pp. In this fantasy, two children on a walk in the woods imagine different experiences. The boy sees adventure and the girl finds beauty. (Rev: BL 10/15/97; HBG 3/98; SLJ 12/97)

1195 Glassman, Peter. *My Working Mom* (K–3). Illus. by Tedd Arnold. 1994, Morrow $15.93 (0-688-12260-4). This working mom is different from others because she is a practicing witch. (Rev: BCCB 5/94; SLJ 8/94)

1196 Goble, Paul. *Dream Wolf* (K–2). Illus. by author. 1990, Macmillan LB $14.95 (0-02-736585-9). 32pp. A friendly wolf leads two lost Plains Indian children home. (Rev: BL 2/15/90)

1197 Goennel, Heidi. *I Pretend* (PS). Illus. 1995, Morrow LB $15.93 (0-688-13593-5). 32pp. A child imagines wonderful adventures out of commonplace events. (Rev: BL 4/1/95; SLJ 6/95)

1198 Gogol, Nikolai. *Sorotchintzy Fair* (1–4). Trans. by Daniel Reynolds. Illus. by Gennady Spirin. 1991, Godine $16.95 (0-87923-879-8). 24pp. Based on a Gogol story, this is a tale about a young girl who falls in love with a stranger she meets at a county fair. (Rev: BCCB 6/92; BL 5/15/91; HB 9–10/91; SLJ 8/91)

1199 Gold, Bernice. *My Four Lions* (PS–K). Illus. by Joanne Stanbridge. 1999, Annick LB $17.95 (1-55037-603-9); paper $6.95 (1-55037-602-0). A young boy lets himself into a lonely apartment after school and plays with his four imaginary friends, paper lions, until his mother gets home. (Rev: SLJ 3/00)

1200 Goldin, David. *Go-Go-Go!* (PS–3). Illus. 2000, Abrams $16.95 (0-8109-4141-4). 32pp. Maurice hopes to win the great bicycle race on his bike, Red Lightning, but he is slowed down when he picks up passengers including an elephant, a monkey, and a musician. (Rev: BL 12/1/00; HBG 3/01; SLJ 9/00)

1201 Gollub, Matthew. *Ten Oni Drummers* (K–4). Illus. by Kazuko Stone. 2000, Lee & Low $15.95 (1-58430-011-6). Ten Japanese oni, or goblins, come to a boy's house and scare away his spooky dreams in this fantasy that also introduces Japanese numbers from one to ten. (Rev: HBG 3/01; SLJ 1/01)

1202 Gordon, Amy. *Midnight Magic* (2–4). Illus. by Judy Clifford. 1995, BridgeWater $12.95 (0-8167-3660-X). 63pp. When colorful Uncle Harry comes to baby-sit for his two young nephews, so many strange things happen that the boys think he uses magic. (Rev: SLJ 12/95)

1203 Graham, Bob. *Max* (PS–2). Illus. 2000, Candlewick $15.99 (0-7636-1138-7). 32pp. Born of superhero parents, Max has inherited all the family traditions as well as a superhero suit, but he still doesn't know how to fly. (Rev: BCCB 1/01; BL 11/1/00; HBG 3/01; SLJ 9/00)

1204 Graves, Keith. *Frank Was a Monster Who Wanted to Dance* (PS–2). Illus. 1999, Chronicle $12.95 (0-8118-2169-2). 26pp. Frank, a monster, dances so strenuously at a theater that his head becomes undone and he loses his brains. (Rev: BCCB 6/99; BL 7/99; HBG 3/00; SLJ 7/99)

1205 Graves, Keith. *Pet Boy* (1–3). Illus. 2001, Chronicle $12.95 (0-8118-2672-4). 32pp. Like the many pets he owns, Stanley is confined and told to perform tricks when he is captured by an extraterrestrial hunter and sold to an alien boy. (Rev: BL 3/15/01)

1206 Gray, Libba M. *Is There Room on the Feather Bed?* (PS–1). Illus. by Nadine Bernard Westcott. 1997, Orchard $16.95 (0-531-30013-7). 32pp. On a rainy night, animals ask to be allowed to share the comfortable feather bed of a farm couple. (Rev: BL 3/1/97; SLJ 4/97)

1207 Greenspun, Adele Aron. *Bunny and Me* (PS). Illus. 2000, Scholastic $9.95 (0-439-14700-X). 40pp. A baby and bunny enjoy playing together; when the bunny goes away, the baby is heartbroken until he reappears. (Rev: BL 3/15/00; HBG 10/00; SLJ 4/00)

1208 Greenstein, Elaine. *Mrs. Rose's Garden* (PS–2). Illus. 1996, Simon & Schuster paper $15.00 (0-689-80215-3). 32pp. When Mr. and Mrs. Rose produce enormous vegetables from a super fertilizer, complications arise. (Rev: BCCB 6/96; BL 6/1–15/96; SLJ 6/96)

1209 Gruelle, Johnny. *How Raggedy Ann Got Her Candy Heart* (PS–1). Illus. by Jan Palmer. 1998, Simon & Schuster $15.00 (0-689-81119-5). 32pp. A friendly housepainter helps Raggedy Ann after she falls into a can of paint. The painter's wife sews her up with a candy heart inside. (Rev: BL 7/98; HBG 3/99)

1210 Gruelle, Johnny. *Raggedy Ann and Andy and the Camel with the Wrinkled Knees* (PS–1). Illus. by Jan Palmer. 1998, Simon & Schuster $15.00 (0-689-81120-9). 32pp. Raggedy Ann and Andy encounter a camel, an old horse, and some pirates while they look for Babette, a doll friend. (Rev: BL 7/98; HBG 3/99)

1211 Gruelle, Johnny. *Raggedy Ann Stories* (PS–3). Illus. 1993, Macmillan LB $16.00 (0-02-737585-4). 96pp. This story features the lovable rag doll. A reissue. Also use: *Raggedy Andy Stories* (1993).

1212 Guenther, James. *Turnagain Ptarmigan! Where Did You Go?* (PS–2). Illus. by Shannon Cartwright. 2000, Sasquatch $15.95 (1-57061-271-4). 32pp. The state bird of Alaska is introduced in this sweet book about a girl who plays hide-and-seek with a ptarmigan, the bird that changes color with the seasons. (Rev: BL 2/15/01; SLJ 12/00)

1213 Guthrie, Donna. *The Witch Who Lives Down the Hall* (PS–2). Illus. by Amy Schwartz. 1985, Harcourt $12.95 (0-15-298610-3). 32pp. A young boy thinks his new high-rise neighbor is a witch, and proves it when the two of them fly above the city on her magic carpet. (Rev: BCCB 1/86; BL 9/15/85; SLJ 10/85)

1214 Guy, Ginger F. *Black Crow, Black Crow* (PS–2). Illus. by Nancy Winslow Parker. 1991, Greenwillow $13.95 (0-688-08956-9). 24pp. A little girl imagines that crows lead the same kind of life she does. (Rev: BL 4/15/91; HB 3–4/91; SLJ 6/91)

1215 Haas, Irene. *The Maggie B* (K–2). Illus. by author. 1975, Macmillan $39.95 (0-689-50021-1); Simon & Schuster paper $6.99 (0-689-81507-7). 32pp. Beautiful watercolors enhance this story of a little girl and her adventures on an imaginary ship named for her — the Maggie B.

1216 Haas, Irene. *A Summertime Song* (PS–3). Illus. 1997, Simon & Schuster paper $16.00 (0-689-50549-3). 32pp. A frog presents a little girl with a magic paper hat that shrinks her so she is able to attend a birthday party with little animals like a mouse and an inchworm. (Rev: BL 5/15/97; HB 5–6/97; SLJ 6/97)

1217 Hafner, Marylin. *Molly and Emmett's Camping Adventure* (PS–1). Illus. 2000, McGraw Hill $12.95 (1-57768-894-5). 32pp. When the rain comes after Molly and her cat have prepared for an outdoor camping adventure, they move indoors and have their picnic under the kitchen table. (Rev: BL 12/1/00; HBG 3/01; SLJ 3/01)

1218 Hamanaka, Sheila. *I Look Like a Girl* (PS–2). Illus. 1999, Morrow $16.00 (0-688-14625-2). 32pp. This poem is about the power of imagination as it depicts young girls who can be creatively seen as other objects and beings. (Rev: BCCB 11/99; BL 10/1/99; HBG 3/00; SLJ 6/00)

1219 Harder, Dan. *Colliding with Chris* (K–3). Illus. by Kevin O'Malley. 1998, Hyperion LB $15.89 (0-7868-2098-5). Chris loses control of his new bike and careens through town and country, gathering passengers during his madcap adventure. (Rev: BCCB 6/98; HBG 3/99; SLJ 6/98)

1220 Harley, Bill. *Sarah's Story* (K–2). Illus. by Eve Aldridge. 1996, Tricycle Pr. $15.95 (1-883672-20-1). Sarah has some amazing adventures when she visits an ant colony. (Rev: BCCB 3/97; SLJ 1/97)

1221 Harper, Piers. *If You Love a Bear* (PS). Illus. by author. 1998, Candlewick $9.99 (0-7636-0371-6). A bear and a boy go through their daily routine, having breakfast, taking a bath, and describing their likes and dislikes. (Rev: HBG 10/98; SLJ 9/98)

1222 Harrison, David L. *The Animals' Song* (PS–K). Illus. by Chris L. Demarest. 1997, Boyds Mills $14.95 (1-56397-144-5). 32pp. When a little girl and boy play their flute and drum, all the animals join in. (Rev: BCCB 6/97; BL 4/1/97; SLJ 3/97)

1223 Harrison, Joanna. *When Mom Turned into a Monster* (PS–3). Illus. 1996, Carolrhoda $15.95 (1-57505-013-7). 32pp. Her pesky and interfering children cause Mom to gradually turn into a monster. (Rev: BL 11/15/96)

1224 Harrison, Troon. *Don't Dig So Deep, Nicholas!* (PS–1). Illus. by Gary Clement. 1997, Firefly $17.95 (1-895688-51-5); paper $6.95 (1-895688-60-4). 32pp. Nicholas digs such a big hole in the sand that he reaches Australia, and soon the beach is covered with kangaroos, dingos, wombats, koalas, and other creatures from Down Under. (Rev: SLJ 10/97)

1225 Harrison, Troon. *The Floating Orchard* (1–3). Illus. by Miranda Jones. 2000, Tundra $16.95 (0-88776-439-8). 32pp. A woman named Damson chops down her plum tree, the Orchard Queen, to make a mast for her boat and escape flooding. But when she reaches land, her tears cause the tree to sprout once again. (Rev: BL 11/1/00; HBG 3/01)

1226 Harter, Debbie. *Walking Through the Jungle* (PS–1). Illus. by author. 1997, Orchard $14.95 (0-531-30035-8). A humorous fantasy in which a young girl encounters a number of fierce creatures on her walk through the jungle. (Rev: HBG 3/98; SLJ 10/97)

1227 Hartman, Gail. *As the Roadrunner Runs: A First Book of Maps* (PS–1). Illus. by Cathy Bobak. 1994, Bradbury paper $14.95 (0-02-743092-8). 32pp. The separate worlds of different animals of the U.S. Southwest are described and then brought together into one large map that shows the combined region. A companion to *As the Crow Flies* (1991). (Rev: BCCB 1/95; BL 11/15/94; SLJ 1/95)

1228 Hawkins, Colin, and Jacqui Hawkins. *Come for a Ride on the Ghost Train* (PS–1). Illus. by authors. 1993, Candlewick $12.95 (1-56402-236-6). Ugly monsters take the reader on trips to such scary places as a graveyard, a dark crypt, and a haunted chapel. (Rev: SLJ 2/94)

1229 Hayes, Sarah. *Lucy Anna and the Finders* (K–2). Illus. 2000, Candlewick $15.99 (0-7636-1200-6). 32pp. Lucy Anna is convinced that the striped, forest green creatures known as the Finders have taken her red pony, so she sets out into the woods to find him. (Rev: BCCB 12/00; BL 12/15/00; HBG 3/01; SLJ 12/00)

1230 Heckman, Philip. *Waking Upside Down* (1–4). Illus. by Dwight Been. 1996, Simon & Schuster $16.00 (0-689-31930-4). 32pp. A boy discovers that he can walk on the ceiling. (Rev: BCCB 5/96; BL 7/96; SLJ 7/96)

1231 Heidbreder, Robert. *I Wished for a Unicorn* (PS–3). Illus. by Kady M. Denton. 2000, Kids Can $14.95 (1-55074-543-3). 32pp. A young girl's dog is transformed into a unicorn and together they travel into a magic land. (Rev: BCCB 5/00; BL 4/15/00; HBG 10/00; SLJ 8/00)

1232 Heller, Nicholas. *Peas* (PS–1). Illus. 1993, Greenwillow $13.93 (0-688-12407-0). 24pp. Lewis dreams about the peas that he has refused to eat at dinner and how they get their revenge. (Rev: BL 9/15/93)

1233 Hendrick, Mary J. *If Anything Ever Goes Wrong at the Zoo* (PS–2). Illus. by Jane Dyer. 1993, Harcourt $15.00 (0-15-238007-8). 32pp. When the zoo floods, Leslie and her mother make room in their home and yard for the animals. (Rev: BL 6/1–15/93; SLJ 7/93*)

1234 Henkes, Kevin. *Oh!* (PS). Illus. by Laura Dronzek. 1999, Greenwillow LB $14.93 (0-688-17054-4). 24pp. A delightful picture book that depicts how children and a variety of animals react to a fresh fall of snow. (Rev: BCCB 10/99; BL 10/1/99*; HBG 3/00; SLJ 10/99)

1235 Henterly, Jamichael. *Good Night, Garden Gnome* (PS–1). Illus. by author. 2001, Dial $15.99 (0-8037-2531-0). In this fantasy, a garden ornament comes to life and returns a lost stuffed animal to its owner. (Rev: SLJ 3/01)

1236 Hiatt, Fred. *If I Were Queen of the World* (PS–2). Illus. by Mark Graham. 1997, Simon & Schuster paper $16.00 (0-689-80700-7). 32pp. A little girl thinks of all the benefits she could enjoy if she were queen of the whole wide world. (Rev: BCCB 6/97; BL 5/1/97; SLJ 5/97)

1237 Hickox, Rebecca. *Per and the Dala Horse* (PS–3). Illus. by Yvonne Gilbert. 1995, Doubleday $15.95 (0-385-32075-2). 32pp. With the help of his magic wooden horse, Per, the youngest in his family, is able to retrieve the Communion cup from the trolls. (Rev: BL 11/15/95; SLJ 1/96)

1238 Highet, Alistair. *The Yellow Train* (K–3). Illus. by Francois Roca. 2000, Creative Co. $17.95 (1-56846-128-3). 40pp. Theo and Grandpa travel back in time and embark on a magical journey through unspoiled landscapes as they ride the Yellow Train with Grandpa at the controls. (Rev: BL 12/15/00; HBG 3/01; SLJ 12/00)

1239 Hill, Susan. *Beware Beware* (K–2). Illus. by Angela Barrett. 1993, Candlewick $14.95 (1-56402-245-5). 32pp. A girl thinks she sees all sorts of scary beasts when she explores the woods in the evening in this picture book set in Victorian England. (Rev: BCCB 12/93; BL 11/15/93; SLJ 2/94)

1240 Hippely, Hilary H. *Adventure on Klickitat Island* (PS–2). Illus. by Barbara Upton. 1998, Dutton $15.99 (0-525-45293-1). A boy and his stuffed animal venture out into the stormy night to help crying woodland creatures get shelter from the rain. (Rev: HBG 10/98; SLJ 7/98)

1241 Hoban, Russell. *The Sea-Thing Child* (1–4). Illus. by Patrick Benson. 1999, Candlewick $15.99 (0-7636-0847-5). A "sea-thing child" is washed ashore and after trying to make friends with several creatures of the sea, flies away to find new places to discover. (Rev: HBG 3/00; SLJ 12/99)

1242 Hobbs, Will. *Beardream* (1–4). Illus. by Jill Kastner. 1997, Simon & Schuster $16.00 (0-689-31973-8). 32pp. When a great bear fails to reappear in the spring, a boy climbs into the mountains to look for it. (Rev: BL 4/15/97; SLJ 4/97)

1243 Hoberman, Mary Ann. *And to Think That We Thought That We'd Never Be Friends* (PS–K). Illus. by Kevin Hawkes. 1999, Crown LB $17.99 (0-517-80070-5). 40pp. A cumulative tale about how squabbles can be turned into outbursts of friendship and result in a friendship parade. (Rev: BL 12/15/99; HBG 3/00; SLJ 12/99)

1244 Hoberman, Mary Ann. *It's Simple, Said Simon* (PS–3). Illus. by Meilo So. 2001, Knopf LB $17.99 (0-375-91201-0). Simon has a busy summer day when he encounters a series of animals including a tiger with an appetite for small boys. (Rev: BCCB 3/01; SLJ 3/01)

1245 Hoberman, Mary Ann. *Miss Mary Mack* (PS). Illus. by Nadine Bernard Westcott. 2001, Little, Brown $5.95 (0-316-36642-0). 24pp. This bouncy board book presents a clapping rhyme that features Miss Mary Mack and her pet elephant. (Rev: BL 2/15/01)

1246 Hoberman, Mary Ann. *The Two Sillies* (PS–2). Illus. by Lynne W. Cravath. 2000, Harcourt $16.00 (0-15-202221-X). 32pp. Silly Lilly gets a new cat and, when she sees mice in the barn, she knows exactly how to put the cat to work. (Rev: BL 12/1/00; HB 11–12/00; HBG 3/01; SLJ 12/00)

1247 Hodges, Margaret. *Molly Limbo* (PS–2). Illus. by Elizabeth Miles. 1996, Simon & Schuster $16.00 (0-689-80581-0). 32pp. Mr. Means saves money for rent by living in a haunted house. (Rev: BCCB 10/96; BL 9/15/96; HB 11–12/96; SLJ 9/96)

1248 Hoffman, Alice. *Horsefly* (K–3). Illus. by Steve Johnson and Lou Fancher. 2000, Hyperion $15.99 (0-7868-0367-3). 48pp. Jewel cures her fear of horses when she cares for a foal and, as an added bonus, learns that her pet can fly. (Rev: BL 12/1/00; HBG 3/01; SLJ 10/00)

1249 Hol, Coby. *The Birth of the Moon* (PS–K). Illus. 2000, North-South LB $13.88 (0-7358-1250-0). 32pp. An original story about the sun helping animals at night by creating the moon. (Rev: BL 6/1–15/00; HBG 10/00; SLJ 5/00)

1250 Horn, Sandra Ann. *The Dandelion Wish* (PS–K). Illus. by Jason Crockcroft. 2000, DK $15.95 (0-7894-6326-1). 32pp. When they blow all the seeds off a dandelion with one breath, Sam and Jo get their wish: a carnival comes to their quiet meadow. (Rev: BL 8/00; HBG 3/01; SLJ 12/00)

1251 Howe, James. *There's a Dragon in My Sleeping Bag* (PS–2). Illus. by David S. Rose. 1994, Atheneum $15.00 (0-689-31873-1). 40pp. Alex invents imaginary playmates but decides that being with his brother is best. (Rev: BL 12/15/94; SLJ 3/95)

1252 Hubbard, Patricia. *My Crayons Talk* (PS–1). Illus. by G. Brian Karas. 1996, Holt $15.95 (0-8050-3529-X). 32pp. Crayons in a box unite to produce a series of colorful pictures. (Rev: BCCB 5/96; BL 4/1/96; SLJ 5/96)

1253 Hughes, Shirley. *Stories by Firelight* (K–3). Illus. 1993, Lothrop $16.00 (0-688-04568-5). 64pp. This collection of stories, many of which are fantasies, explore wintry themes and are linked by poems. (Rev: BL 12/1/93; SLJ 1/94)

1254 Hughes, Ted. *How the Whale Became and Other Stories* (PS–3). Illus. by Jackie Morris. 2000, Orchard $25.00 (0-531-30303-9). 96pp. From the great English poet, this is a collection of creation fables explaining how individual creatures, such as the whale, owl, and cat, came to be. (Rev: BCCB 12/00; BL 12/1/00*; SLJ 11/00)

1255 Hutchins, Hazel. *It's Raining, Yancy and Bear* (PS). Illus. by Ruth Ohi. 1998, Annick $15.95 (1-55037-529-6); paper $5.95 (1-55037-528-8). Yancy, a young boy, and his stuffed friend, Bear, change places, visit a museum with Grandfather, and later plant a garden. (Rev: SLJ 1/99)

1256 Hutchins, Hazel. *Two So Small* (K–2). Illus. by Ruth Ohi. 2000, Annick $19.95 (1-55037-651-9); paper $7.95 (1-55037-650-0). 32pp. A boy and his

goat wander into the land of the giants while walking to Grandmother's house, and there help a baby giant whose parents reward them by showing them the correct way to Grandmother's. (Rev: BL 11/15/00; SLJ 10/00)

1257 Hutchins, Pat. *Silly Billy!* (K–3). Illus. 1992, Greenwillow LB $14.93 (0-688-10818-0). 32pp. Hazel, a monster child, has trouble with her pesky young brother, Billy. (Rev: BL 1/1/93; SLJ 9/92)

1258 Hutchins, Pat. *The Very Worst Monster* (K–2). Illus. by author. 1985, Greenwillow $16.88 (0-688-04011-X); paper $4.95 (0-688-07816-8). 32pp. A monster family has a new addition, and Hazel is not happy with her baby brother. (Rev: BCCB 4/85; HB 5–6/87; SLJ 5/85)

1259 Huth, Holly. *Twilight* (PS–3). Illus. by David McPhail. 2000, Atheneum $16.00 (0-689-81975-7). 32pp. In New York City, a little girl who believes she is in charge of twilight flies into the sky to get all the elements, including the stars, ready for the change from day to night. (Rev: BL 11/1/00; HBG 3/01; SLJ 11/00)

1260 Huth, Holly Young. *Darkfright* (K–3). Illus. by Jenny Stow. 1996, Simon & Schuster $16.00 (0-689-80188-2). 32pp. A wounded star helps a Caribbean woman conquer her fear of the dark. (Rev: BCCB 1/97; BL 11/1/96; SLJ 1/97)

1261 Ichikawa, Satomi. *The First Bear in Africa!* (PS–3). Illus. 2001, Putnam $14.99 (0-399-23485-3). 32pp. A tourist drops her teddy bear while visiting an African village, but Meto, a small boy, returns it with the help of some jungle animals. (Rev: BCCB 3/01; BL 2/15/01)

1262 Inkpen, Mick. *Nothing* (PS–K). Illus. 1998, Orchard $14.95 (0-531-30076-5). 32pp. A stuffed toy that is left behind when a family moves finds a new home with the help of a cat. (Rev: BCCB 3/98; BL 3/15/98; HBG 10/98; SLJ 6/98)

1263 Ishinabe, Fusako. *Spring Snowman* (PS–1). Illus. 1991, Garrett LB $14.60 (0-944483-83-6). 32pp. Animals in the forest find that when spring comes their snowman disappears. (Rev: BL 5/1/91)

1264 Jackson, Jean. *Big Lips and Hairy Arms* (PS–3). Illus. by Vera Rosenberry. 1998, DK $15.95 (0-7894-2521-1). 32pp. Two monsters who are enjoying an evening together receive mysterious phone calls warning that a being with big lips and hairy arms is getting closer and closer. (Rev: BL 12/15/98; HBG 3/99; SLJ 10/98)

1265 Jackson, Jean. *Mrs. Piccolo's Easy Chair* (PS–1). Illus. by Diane Greenseid. 1999, DK $15.95 (0-7894-2580-7). The behavior of Mrs. Piccolo's easy chair is getting unbearable, particularly when it burps and sends the old lady flying. (Rev: BCCB 11/99; HBG 3/00; SLJ 9/99)

1266 Jackson, Shelley. *The Old Woman and the Wave* (PS–4). 1998, DK $15.95 (0-7894-2484-3). 32pp. An old woman who lives in constant fear of a greenish-blue wave that hovers over her house gradually realizes that the wave loves her and gives her special gifts. (Rev: BCCB 3/98; BL 5/15/98*; HBG 10/98; SLJ 3/98*)

1267 Jacobson, Jennifer Richard. *A Net of Stars* (PS–3). Illus. by Greg Shed. 1998, Dial LB $15.89 (0-8037-2088-2). 32pp. Etta learns to conquer her fear of heights by taking a trip to the stars on a Ferris wheel. (Rev: BL 6/1–15/98; HBG 10/98; SLJ 8/98)

1268 James, J. Alison. *Eucalyptus Wings* (PS–3). Illus. by Demi. 1995, Simon & Schuster $16.00 (0-689-31886-3). 40pp. Through the use of magical powers, Kiria and her friend Mica are able to fly like the eucalyptus leaves that float from the trees. (Rev: BL 1/1–15/96; SLJ 3/96)

1269 James, Simon. *Sally and the Limpet* (PS–1). Illus. 1991, Macmillan $13.95 (0-689-50528-0). At the beach, Sally finds a shell that attaches itself to her. (Rev: HB 3–4/91; SLJ 6/91)

1270 Jaramillo, Raquel. *Ride, Baby, Ride!* (PS). Photos by author. Series: Look Baby! 1998, Simon & Schuster $4.99 (0-689-82027-5). Using computer-enhanced photographs, this board book shows a baby traveling in a variety of ways including a space ship, a race car, and astride a dolphin. (Rev: SLJ 3/99)

1271 Jarrett, Clare. *Catherine and the Lion* (PS–K). Illus. 1997, Carolrhoda $15.95 (1-57505-035-8). 24pp. One day, in her bedroom, Catherine finds a new friend, a lion. (Rev: BL 12/15/96; SLJ 2/97)

1272 Johnson, Lindsay L. *Hurricane Henrietta* (PS–3). Illus. by Wally Neibart. 1998, Dial LB $15.89 (0-8037-1977-9). 32pp. Henrietta's extremely long hair is her pride and joy, but one day she receives an ultimatum: she must cut her untamed mane if she wants to attend Safari Camp. (Rev: BL 7/98; SLJ 9/98)

1273 Johnson, Paul B. *Bearhide and Crow* (K–3). Illus. 2000, Holiday $16.95 (0-8234-1470-1). 32pp. When Amos, a happy-go-lucky farmer, gets cheated by shifty Sam, Crow helps him get even. (Rev: BCCB 5/00; BL 4/1/00; HBG 10/00; SLJ 5/00)

1274 Johnson, Paul B. *The Cow Who Wouldn't Come Down* (K–2). Illus. 1993, Orchard LB $16.99 (0-531-08631-3). 32pp. Miss Rosemary has problems getting her cow back to earth once it learns how to fly. (Rev: BCCB 7–8/93; BL 2/1/93; HB 5–6/93; SLJ 5/93*)

1275 Johnson, Paul B. *A Perfect Pork Stew* (K–2). Illus. 1998, Orchard $15.95 (0-531-30070-6). 32pp. In this original Baba Yaga tale, a witch mistakes some dirt for a pig and makes a stew of it that gives her a tummy ache. (Rev: BL 3/15/98; HBG 10/98; SLJ 4/98)

1276 Johnston, Tony. *Alice Nizzy Nazzy: The Witch of Santa Fe* (PS–1). Illus. by Tomie dePaola. 1995, Putnam $15.99 (0-399-22788-1). 32pp. In a variation on the Baba Yaga stories, Manuela almost becomes the dinner of a witch named Alice Nizzy Nazzy. (Rev: BCCB 5/95; BL 3/15/95; SLJ 4/95)

1277 Jonas, Ann. *The Trek* (PS–1). Illus. by author. 1985, Morrow paper $4.95 (0-688-08742-6). 32pp. A young girl imagines she is trekking through a dangerous jungle on her way to school. (Rev: BCCB 3/86; BL 11/15/85; SLJ 10/85)

1278 Jonell, Lynne. *Mommy Go Away!* (PS). Illus. by Petra Mathers. 1997, Putnam $12.99 (0-399-

23001-7). 25pp. In this role-reversal fantasy, Christopher makes his bossy mother so tiny that he can lecture her as she does him. (Rev: BL 10/15/97; HB 9–10/97; HBG 3/98; SLJ 12/97)

1279 Jones, Joy. *Tambourine Moon* (1–3). Illus. by Terry Widener. 1999, Simon & Schuster $16.00 (0-689-80648-5). A young African American girl is told a tall tale by her grandfather about how he accidentally created the moon in the sky. (Rev: BCCB 12/99; HBG 3/00; SLJ 11/99)

1280 Jorg, Sabine. *Mina and the Bear* (1–4). Trans. by Charise Neugebauer. Illus. by Alexander Reichstein. 1999, North-South LB $15.88 (0-7858-1037-0). Mina's health is endangered because of her intense longing for a teddy bear, so after a bear story from the doctor, she becomes a bear. (Rev: BL 4/1/99)

1281 Joslin, Mary. *The Shore Beyond* (K–3). Illus. by Alison Jay. 2000, Good Bks. $16.00 (1-56148-316-8). 28pp. In this parable about the journey through life, two girls weave willows into boats so they can explore the world beyond their homes. (Rev: BL 12/1/00; SLJ 2/01)

1282 Joslin, Mary. *The Tale of the Heaven Tree* (K–3). Illus. by Meilo So. 1999, Eerdmans $16.00 (0-8028-5190-8). In this story, a small child hears a voice from the Maker to help save Earth by planting trees. (Rev: BL 10/1/99; HBG 3/00; SLJ 3/00)

1283 Joyce, William. *Rolie Polie Olie* (PS–K). Illus. 1999, HarperCollins LB $15.89 (0-06-027164-7). 48pp. A whimsical story about a day in the life of Rolie Polie Olie, a round, robotlike creature, and his family as they perform chores and have fun. (Rev: BCCB 10/99; BL 11/1/99; HBG 3/00; SLJ 10/99)

1284 Kadono, Eiko. *Grandpa's Soup* (1–3). Illus. by Satomi Ichikawa. 1999, Eerdmans $16.00 (0-8028-5195-9). 32pp. Grandpa tries to duplicate the soup that Grandma used to make, and with each new try he attracts more animals to sample his creation. (Rev: BL 12/1/99; HBG 3/00; SLJ 2/00)

1285 Kamish, Daniel, and David Kamish. *The Night the Scary Beasties Popped Out of My Head* (K–3). Illus. by authors. 1998, Random LB $15.99 (0-679-99039-9). When Dan's nightmares come to life, he draws a six-legged dog and a fire truck to chase them. (Rev: HBG 10/99; SLJ 11/98)

1286 Karim, Roberta. *This Is a Hospital, Not a Zoo!* (K–3). Illus. by Sue Truesdell. 1998, Clarion $15.00 (0-395-72070-2). 48pp. When nurses and doctors want to poke or prod young Filbert MacFee, he simply turns himself into a wild animal like a penguin or giraffe. (Rev: BL 3/1/98)

1287 Karlin, Nurit. *The Tooth Witch* (PS–K). Illus. by author. 1985, HarperCollins LB $13.89 (0-397-32120-1). 32pp. The story of Abra Cadabra and how she becomes the first Tooth Fairy. (Rev: BCCB 10/85; BL 6/15/85; SLJ 9/86)

1288 Karlins, Mark. *Salmon Moon* (K–3). Illus. by Hans Poppel. 1993, Simon & Schuster paper $14.00 (0-671-73624-8). 32pp. In this fantasy, Mr. Lutz finds a salmon in a fish store and plots with his friends to return it to the ocean. (Rev: BL 11/1/93)

1289 Keats, Ezra Jack. *Regards to the Man in the Moon* (PS–1). Illus. by author. 1987, Macmillan paper $5.99 (0-689-71160-3). 32pp. Lewis and his friend visit outer space via their imaginations. Originally published in 1981.

1290 Keens-Douglas, Richardo. *The Miss Meow Pageant* (K–3). Illus. by Marie Lafrance. 1998, Annick LB $16.95 (1-55037-537-7); paper $6.95 (1-55037-536-9). Henrietta, a teacher, adopts a stray cat she names Sparrow and decides to enter her pet in "The Miss Meow Pageant." (Rev: SLJ 1/99)

1291 Keller, Laurie. *The Scrambled States of America* (K–3). Illus. 1998, Holt $16.95 (0-8050-5802-8). In this lighthearted introduction to the 50 states, Kansas and Nebraska decide to have a party where the states exchange places, but complications occur when, for example, Minnesota gets a sunburn while Florida is freezing. (Rev: BCCB 10/98; BL 1/1–15/99; HBG 3/99; SLJ 11/98)

1292 Kelley, Marty. *Fall Is Not Easy* (PS–K). Illus. 1998, Zino Pr. $12.95 (1-55933-234-4). 32pp. In the fall of the year, a tree tries out new colors and designs for its leaves, including red-and-white stripes, polka dots, and rainbow faces. (Rev: BL 1/1–15/99)

1293 Kellogg, Steven. *The Missing Mitten Mystery* (PS–1). Illus. 2000, Dial $15.99 (0-8037-2566-3). 32pp. In this reworking of the 1974 title, a little girl sets off with her dog Oscar to find a lost mitten and discovers it is acting as the heart of a snowman. (Rev: BL 10/15/00*; HBG 3/01)

1294 Kellogg, Steven. *Ralph's Secret Weapon* (PS–3). Illus. by author. 1983, Dial paper $3.95 (0-8037-0307-4). 32pp. Ralph's bassoon playing is so bad, his aunt thinks it will charm a bothersome sea monster.

1295 Kelly, Mij. *William and the Night Train* (PS–1). Illus. by Alison Jay. 2001, Farrar $16.00 (0-374-38437-1). 32pp. William and his mother are the only normal-looking people on the train to Tomorrow; the others have tiny heads and huge bodies and the cargo consists of different animals and unusual objects. (Rev: BL 2/15/01*; SLJ 3/01)

1296 Kerins, Tony. *The Brave Ones* (PS). Illus. 1996, Candlewick $9.99 (1-56402-812-7). 24pp. Five courageous toy animals are frightened by Little Clancy, a tiny turtle. (Rev: BL 7/96; SLJ 7/96)

1297 Ketteman, Helen. *Bubba, The Cowboy Prince: A Fractured Texas Tale* (K–3). Illus. by James Warhola. 1997, Scholastic $15.95 (0-590-25506-1). 32pp. A Western version of the Cinderella story in which a cow is the fairy godmother. (Rev: BL 12/1/97; HBG 3/98)

1298 Ketteman, Helen. *Heat Wave* (K–3). Illus. by Scott Goto. 1998, Walker LB $16.85 (0-8027-8645-6). 32pp. In this hilarious fantasy, a heat wave gets stuck on a rural weather vane causing a great upheaval for plants and animals. (Rev: BL 2/1/98; HBG 10/98; SLJ 3/98)

1299 Ketteman, Helen. *Luck with Potatoes* (1–3). Illus. by Brian Floca. 1995, Orchard LB $15.99 (0-531-08773-5). 32pp. A tall tale about a farmer who finds his lost cows in the giant potatoes he has been growing. (Rev: BL 10/1/95; SLJ 10/95)

1300 Kilborne, Sarah S. *Peach and Blue* (K–3). Illus. by Lou Fancher and Steve Johnson. 1994, Knopf $18.00 (0-679-83929-1). 32pp. A tender story about the friendship between Blue, a toad, and a peach, and how Blue helps the peach see the world. (Rev: BCCB 11/94; BL 12/15/94; SLJ 10/94)

1301 Kimmel, Eric A. *Grizz!* (PS–3). Illus. by Andrew Glass. 2000, Farrar $17.00 (0-374-36824-4). 288pp. Cowboy Lucky Doolin makes a pact with the devil that he will gain great wealth if he doesn't bathe, shave, or change his clothes for seven years. (Rev: BL 5/1/00; SLJ 3/00)

1302 Kimmel, Eric A. *Robin Hook, Pirate Hunter!* (PS–3). Illus. by Michael Dooling. 2001, Scholastic $15.95 (0-590-68199-0). 32pp. A teenage superhero dressed like Robin Hood thwarts pirates with the help of other children and some animals. (Rev: BL 1/1–15/01; SLJ 3/01)

1303 Kimmel, Eric A. *The Tale of Ali Baba and the Forty Thieves: A Story from the Arabian Nights* (1–3). Illus. by Will Hillenbrand. 1996, Holiday LB $15.95 (0-8234-1258-X). 30pp. Ali Baba and the story of his amazing treasure trove are covered in colorful prose. (Rev: BCCB 2/97; BL 12/1/96; SLJ 12/96)

1304 Kimmel, Margaret Mary. *Magic in the Mist* (1–3). Illus. by Trina S. Hyman. 1975, Macmillan $15.00 (0-689-50026-2). 32pp. A young Welsh boy and his toad Jeremy find a dragon.

1305 Kinsey-Warnock, Natalie. *The Fiddler of the Northern Lights* (K–3). Illus. by Leslie Bowman. 1996, Dutton $15.99 (0-525-65215-9). 32pp. A fantasy set in the far North about a fiddler whose music makes the northern lights dance. (Rev: BL 11/15/96; SLJ 11/96)

1306 Kinsey-Warnock, Natalie. *On a Starry Night* (PS–1). Illus. by David McPhail. 1994, Orchard LB $16.99 (0-531-08670-4). 32pp. When her father throws her into the stars, a young girl visits the stars before returning to his arms. (Rev: BL 2/1/94; HB 7–8/94; SLJ 5/94)

1307 Kinsey-Warnock, Natalie, and Helen Kinsey. *The Bear That Heard Crying* (K–3). Illus. by Ted Rand. 1993, Dutton $14.99 (0-525-65103-9). 32pp. When Sarah wanders off into the woods, she is cared for by a black bear. (Rev: BL 8/93)

1308 Kipling, Rudyard. *How the Camel Got His Hump* (K–4). Illus. by Tim Raglin. Series: Rabbit Ears Storybook Classics. 1989, Picture Book $19.95 (0-88708-097-9). An effective presentation of the Kipling story that is also available with a cassette read by Jack Nicholson. (Rev: SLJ 2/90)

1309 Kipling, Rudyard. *Rikki-Tikki-Tavi* (1–3). Illus. by Lambert Davis. 1992, Harcourt $18.00 (0-15-267015-7). 44pp. A mongoose overcomes snakes that live in the garden of an English family in India. (Rev: BL 9/15/92)

1310 Kirk, Daniel. *Moondogs* (K–2). Illus. 1999, Putnam $15.99 (0-399-23128-5). 32pp. When Willy's parents decide that he needs a dog, the young boy constructs a spaceship and goes to the moon to get one. (Rev: BL 3/15/99; HB 3–4/99; HBG 10/99; SLJ 3/99)

1311 Kirk, Daniel. *Trash Trucks!* (PS–1). Illus. 1997, Putnam $15.95 (0-399-22927-2). 32pp. Kirk imagines the great trucks with jagged teeth that eat up the mountains of trash collected every day. (Rev: BL 5/15/97)

1312 Kirkpatrick, Karey. *Disney's James and the Giant Peach* (K–3). Illus. by Lane Smith. 1996, Disney LB $16.89 (0-7868-5039-6). 48pp. A simplified retelling of Roald Dahl's work, aimed at the primary grades. (Rev: BCCB 6/96; BL 5/1/96)

1313 Kitamura, Satoshi. *Me and My Cat?* (K–3). Illus. 2000, Farrar $16.00 (0-374-34906-1). 40pp. A wrongfully administered witch's curse results in Nicholas changing bodies with his cat Leonardo. (Rev: BCCB 5/00; BL 3/1/00; HB 3–4/00; HBG 10/00; SLJ 3/00)

1314 Kleven, Elisa. *A Monster in the House* (PS–2). Illus. 1998, Dutton $15.99 (0-525-45973-1). 32pp. A little girl describes the monster who lives in her house to her new neighbor, but the creature the neighbor imagines is very different from the real "monster," the girl's baby brother. (Rev: BL 10/1/98; HBG 3/99; SLJ 1/99)

1315 Kleven, Elisa. *The Paper Princess* (K–2). Illus. 1994, Dutton $15.99 (0-525-45231-1). 32pp. A paper princess created by a little girl flies over the city and learns about life. (Rev: BL 7/94; SLJ 6/94*)

1316 Knutson, Kimberley. *Jungle Jamboree* (PS–1). Illus. 1998, Marshall Cavendish $15.95 (0-7614-5032-7). 32pp. In this rainy day fantasy, a group of children who are confined to the house have an imaginary jungle adventure. (Rev: BL 9/1/98; HBG 3/99; SLJ 11/98)

1317 Komaiko, Leah. *My Perfect Neighborhood* (K–2). Illus. by Barbara Westman. 1990, Harper-Collins $13.95 (0-06-023287-0). 32pp. In jiving rhymes, a young girl surveys her most unusual neighborhood. (Rev: BL 3/1/90; SLJ 8/90)

1318 Korman, Justine. *The Luckiest Leprechaun* (PS–2). Illus. by Denise Brunkus. 2000, Troll LB $15.95 (0-8167-6604-5). 32pp. MacKenzie O'Shamrock, a leprechaun, is convinced that his dog Lucky has stolen his gold and, luckily, is proven wrong. (Rev: BL 3/15/00)

1319 Kraft, Erik. *Chocolatina* (1–4). Illus. by Denise Brunkus. 1998, BridgeWater $15.95 (0-8167-4544-7). A humorous story about a girl who is turned into her favorite food, chocolate, and finds that she prefers to eat it rather than be it. (Rev: HBG 10/98; SLJ 5/98)

1320 Krauss, Ruth. *The Carrot Seed* (K–1). Illus. by Crockett Johnson. 1945, HarperCollins LB $14.89 (0-06-023351-6); paper $5.95 (0-06-443210-6). 24pp. A young boy is convinced that the seeds he plants will grow, in spite of his family's doubts.

1321 Krensky, Stephen. *The Youngest Fairy Godmother Ever* (PS–2). Illus. by Diana C. Bluthenthal. 2000, Simon & Schuster $16.00 (0-689-82011-9). 32pp. Mavis wants to be a fairy godmother but, in spite of her persistence, every time she waves her

wand nothing happens. (Rev: BL 7/00; HBG 10/00; SLJ 6/00)

1322 Kroll, Steven. *The Candy Witch* (PS–1). Illus. by Marylin Hafner. 1979, Scholastic paper $2.50 (0-590-44509-X). 32pp. A family of witches perform good work except for the youngest, who undoes their work.

1323 Kroll, Virginia. *Faraway Drums* (K–3). Illus. by Floyd Cooper. 1998, Little, Brown $14.95 (0-316-50449-1). 32pp. Growing up in a noisy, violent, inner-city neighborhood, a young African American girl gets comfort from remembering stories about her family's African past. (Rev: BL 2/15/98; HBG 10/98; SLJ 5/98)

1324 Kroninger, Stephen. *If I Crossed the Road* (PS–1). Illus. 1997, Simon & Schuster $16.00 (0-689-81190-X). 32pp. In this fantasy, a young boy realizes he is too young to engage in many kinds of activities, but he can certainly dream about them. (Rev: BL 12/15/97; HBG 3/98; SLJ 12/97)

1325 Krudop, Walter Lyon. *The Man Who Caught Fish* (K–3). Illus. 2000, Farrar $16.00 (0-374-34786-7). 32pp. Set in ancient Thailand, this is the story of a greedy king who wants more than his legal share of the fish caught by a master fisherman. (Rev: BL 2/15/00; HB 3–4/00; HBG 10/00; SLJ 4/00)

1326 Krudop, Walter Lyon. *Something Is Growing* (K–3). Illus. 1995, Simon & Schuster $15.00 (0-689-31940-1). 32pp. When Peter plants a tiny seed, he does not realize that the plant will grow out of control. (Rev: BL 6/1–15/95; SLJ 6/95*)

1327 Kuskin, Karla. *The Upstairs Cat* (K–3). Illus. by Howard Fine. 1997, Clarion $15.00 (0-395-70146-5). 32pp. The story of two vicious cats who are obsessed with harming each other becomes a parable about the foolishness and waste of wars. (Rev: BL 11/15/97; HBG 3/98; SLJ 12/97)

1328 Lachner, Dorothea. *Andrew's Angry Words* (K–2). Illus. by The Tjong-Khing. 1995, North-South LB $15.88 (1-55858-436-6). 24pp. Andrew's angry words have a surprising effect on a number of people until a lady offers him some kind words to reverse the situation. (Rev: BL 4/15/95; SLJ 6/95)

1329 Lachner, Dorothea. *Meredith: The Witch Who Wasn't* (K–4). Trans. by J. Alison James. Illus. by Christa Unzner. 1997, North-South LB $15.88 (1-55858-782-9). 32pp. Meredith, a novice who has a mind of her own, is afraid she will not be certified as a witch. (Rev: BL 9/1/97; HBG 3/98; SLJ 11/97)

1330 Lachner, Dorothea. *Meredith's Mixed-up Magic* (K–2). Trans. by J. Alison James. Illus. by Christa Unzner. 2000, North-South $15.95 (0-7358-1190-3). 32pp. When witch Meredith utters the wrong spell, she is visited by a bossy sorcerer who, in a battle of wits, turns her into a pink toad. (Rev: BL 9/15/00; HBG 3/01; SLJ 1/01)

1331 Lacome, Julie. *I'm a Jolly Farmer* (PS–K). Illus. 1994, Candlewick $13.95 (1-56402-318-4). 32pp. A little girl and her dog fantasize about all the things they could be and places that they could go. (Rev: BL 6/1–15/94; SLJ 8/94)

1332 Landalf, Helen. *The Secret Night World of Cats* (PS–1). Illus. by Mark Rimland. 1998, Smith & Kraus $16.95 (1-57525-117-5). 32pp. When Amanda's cat goes missing one night, the little girl ventures into a forest where she encounters many cats and is finally reunited with her own beloved pet. (Rev: BL 9/15/98; HBG 3/99; SLJ 9/98)

1333 Langley, Jonathan. *Missing!* (PS–K). Illus. 2000, Marshall Cavendish $15.95 (0-7614-5078-5). 32pp. Lupin the cat, not realizing that it is school vacation, sets off to meet preschooler Daisy and is disturbed when the child doesn't appear. (Rev: BCCB 11/00; BL 9/1/00; HBG 3/01; SLJ 9/00)

1334 Langston, Laura. *The Fox's Kettle* (K–4). Illus. by Victor Bosson. 1998, Orca $14.95 (1-55143-130-0); paper $6.95 (1-55143-132-7). A fantasy set in old Japan about a beautiful storyteller and the magical kettle given her by a samurai she has helped. (Rev: HBG 3/99; SLJ 3/99)

1335 Larrañaga, Ana Martín. *Woo! The Not-So-Scary Ghost* (PS–K). Illus. 2000, Scholastic $15.95 (0-439-16958-5). 32pp. Woo, a little ghost who wants to scare people, runs away and finds that he is the one who becomes scared. (Rev: BL 12/1/00; HBG 3/01; SLJ 9/00)

1336 Larson, Kirby. *The Magic Kerchief* (PS–3). Illus. by Rosanne Litzinger. 2000, Holiday $15.95 (0-8234-1473-6). 32pp. Griselda, an old grump whose bluntness alienates everyone, dons a magic kerchief that allows her only to say nice things. (Rev: BL 8/00; HB 9–10/00; HBG 3/01; SLJ 10/00)

1337 Lasky, Kathryn. *The Emperor's Old Clothes* (PS–3). Illus. by David Catrow. 1999, Harcourt $16.00 (0-15-200384-3). 32pp. Henry, a farm boy, finds the discarded finery of the emperor and puts it on, only to discover that the farm animals think it is ridiculous, as the emperor found when he donned his "new clothes." (Rev: BCCB 3/99; BL 3/1/99; HBG 10/99; SLJ 5/99)

1338 Lasky, Kathryn. *First Painter* (2–5). Illus. by Rocco Baviera. 2000, DK $16.95 (0-7894-2578-5). In this fantasy, a young girl who is the Dream Catcher of her prehistoric tribe, brings much-needed rain when she creates beautiful cave paintings. (Rev: BCCB 11/00; HBG 3/01; SLJ 10/00)

1339 Lasky, Kathryn. *The Gates of the Wind* (PS–3). Illus. by Janet Stevens. 1995, Harcourt $15.00 (0-15-204264-4). Even though she is living a comfortable life, Gamma Lee decides one day to set out with her donkey to explore the Gates of the Wind. (Rev: SLJ 10/95)

1340 Latimer, Jim. *James Bear and the Goose Gathering* (K–3). Illus. by Betsy Franco-Feeney. 1994, Scribners paper $14.95 (0-684-19526-7). 32pp. A flock of geese are tricked by James Bear into performing in a muddy hollow as, they think, their ancestors once did. A sequel to *James Bear's Pie* (1992). (Rev: BL 3/1/94; SLJ 4/94)

1341 Layton, Neal. *Smile If You're Human* (PS–2). Illus. 1999, Dial $14.99 (0-8037-2381-4). 32pp. An alien family visits an Earth zoo hoping to get a glimpse of a human, but the closest they get is a gorilla. (Rev: BCCB 4/99; BL 4/1/99; HB 3–4/99; HBG 10/99; SLJ 4/99)

1342 Leedahl, Shelley A. *The Bone Talker* (PS–2). Illus. by Bill Slavin. 2000, Red Deer $15.95 (0-88995-214-0). 32pp. To help cheer up elderly Grandmother Bones, a little girl gets her to begin making a quilt that later becomes a patchwork of fields across the Great Plains. (Rev: BL 4/15/00)

1343 Leedy, Loreen. *How Humans Make Friends* (1–4). Illus. 1996, Holiday $15.95 (0-8234-1223-7). 32pp. Zork, an extraterrestrial, learns about human behavior, the nature of friendship, and the importance of sharing. (Rev: BL 4/1/96; SLJ 7/96)

1344 Leedy, Loreen. *The Potato Party and Other Troll Tales* (PS–2). Illus. by author. 1989, Holiday LB $14.95 (0-8234-0761-6). 32pp. A delightful collection of seven original stories about trolls. (Rev: SLJ 12/89)

1345 Le Guin, Ursula K. *A Ride on the Red Mare's Back* (PS–2). Illus. by Julie Downing. 1992, Orchard LB $17.99 (0-531-08591-0). 48pp. This original fairy tale tells how a girl rescues her brother from the trolls. (Rev: BCCB 10/92; BL 6/15/92; HB 3–4/93; SLJ 9/92*)

1346 Lester, Alison. *Isabella's Bed* (PS–1). Illus. 1993, Houghton $14.95 (0-395-65565-X). 32pp. Grandmother tells her two grandchildren a story that results in their being taken on a fantastic ride in a magical bed. (Rev: BL 6/1–15/93; SLJ 6/93)

1347 Lester, Helen. *Pookins Gets Her Way* (PS–1). Illus. by Lynn Munsinger. 1990, Houghton paper $7.95 (0-395-53965-X). 32pp. Pookins gets nasty if she doesn't get her own way, but she learns a lesson in self-indulgence from a gnome. (Rev: BL 4/15/87; SLJ 8/87)

1348 Lester, Helen. *Princess Penelope's Parrot* (PS–1). Illus. by Lynn Munsinger. 1996, Houghton $14.95 (0-395-78320-8). 32pp. A browbeaten parrot gets revenge on a bossy princess. (Rev: BCCB 1/97; BL 9/1/96; HB 11–12/96; SLJ 10/96)

1349 Lester, Helen. *The Wizard, the Fairy and the Magic Chicken* (K–2). Illus. by Lynn Munsinger. 1983, Houghton $16.00 (0-395-33885-9); paper $6.95 (0-395-47945-2). 32pp. Three friends are in competition with their magic tricks.

1350 Lester, Julius. *Albidaro and the Mischievous Dream* (PS–3). Illus. by Jerry Pinkney. 2000, Penguin $16.99 (0-8037-1987-6). 32pp. Children and animals dream of a life in which they can do exactly what they want in this noisy, funny picture book. (Rev: BCCB 1/01; BL 9/15/00; HBG 3/01; SLJ 11/00)

1351 Leuck, Laura. *My Monster Mama Loves Me So* (PS). Illus. by Mark Buehner. 1999, Lothrop LB $15.93 (0-688-16867-1). A slight, humorous tale in which a little monster tells the ways his mother loves him — like attending his beastball games. (Rev: HBG 3/00; SLJ 1/00)

1352 Lewis, J. Patrick. *Isabella Abnormella and the Very, Very Finicky Queen of Trouble* (1–4). Illus. by Kyrsten Brooker. 2000, DK $15.95 (0-7894-2605-6). A humorous story in which the town of Trouble is in trouble because the queen can't find a suitable mattress. (Rev: BCCB 10/00; HBG 3/01; SLJ 10/00)

1353 Lewis, J. Patrick. *Night of the Goat Children* (K–4). Illus. by Alexi Natchev. 1999, Dial $15.99 (0-8037-1870-5). 32pp. Princess Birgitta disguises herself as a hag and enlists the help of the town's children to fool a band of outlaws. (Rev: BL 5/15/99; HBG 10/99; SLJ 3/99)

1354 Linch, Tanya. *My Duck* (PS–3). Illus. 2000, Scholastic $14.95 (0-439-20670-7). 32pp. A little girl creates one drawing after another in an effort to please her teacher but the imaginative characters she has drawn always get in the way. (Rev: BL 2/1/01; HBG 3/01; SLJ 10/00)

1355 Lipson, Michael. *How the Wind Plays* (PS–1). Illus. by Daniel Kirk. 1994, Hyperion LB $15.49 (1-56282-326-4). 32pp. The wind, in the shape of a little boy, travels around the world creating fun and excitement. (Rev: BL 5/1/94; SLJ 5/94)

1356 Lodge, Bernard. *Cloud Cuckoo Land* (K–3). Illus. by author. 1999, Houghton $15.00 (0-395-96318-4). Eleven simple rhymes describe fantasy places such as Ice Cone Island, which melts at noon. (Rev: HBG 3/00; SLJ 1/00)

1357 London, Jonathan. *Let the Lynx Come In* (PS–2). Illus. by Patrick Benson. 1996, Candlewick $15.99 (1-56402-531-4). 32pp. A young boy is taken on a ride to the moon on the back of a lynx. (Rev: BL 9/15/96; SLJ 10/96)

1358 Loomis, Christine. *Astro Bunnies* (PS–K). Illus. by Ora Eitan. 2001, Putnam $15.99 (0-399-23175-7). 32pp. A simple, short story that tells of a bunny's trip into outer space. (Rev: BCCB 2/01; BL 2/15/01; HB 1–2/01; SLJ 2/01)

1359 Loredo, Elizabeth. *Boogie Bones* (K–3). Illus. by Kevin Hawkes. 1997, Putnam $15.95 (0-399-22763-6). 32pp. Boogie Bones, a skeleton, disguises himself as a human to enter a dance contest. (Rev: BL 9/1/97; HBG 3/98; SLJ 9/97)

1360 Low, Alice. *Stories to Tell a Five-Year-Old* (PS–1). Illus. by Heather H. Maione. 1996, Little, Brown paper $8.95 (0-316-53416-1). 150pp. Twenty-one short stories to delight the kindergarten set. (Rev: BL 6/1–15/96)

1361 Lowell, Susan. *The Bootmaker and the Elves* (K–4). Illus. by Tom Curry. 1997, Orchard LB $17.99 (0-531-33044-3). 32pp. The old folktale is given a new setting, the Old West, and a new subject, cowboy boots. (Rev: BL 9/15/97; HB 11–12/97; HBG 3/98; SLJ 11/97)

1362 Luenn, Nancy. *Songs for the Ancient Forest* (K–3). Illus. by Jill Kastner. 1993, Macmillan $14.95 (0-689-31719-0). 32pp. Raven has a dream about the fate of the lovely forests of the Pacific Northwest. (Rev: BL 3/1/93; SLJ 3/93)

1363 Lyon, George E. *The Outside Inn* (K–3). Illus. by Vera Rosenberry. 1991, Orchard paper $6.95 (0-531-07086-7). 32pp. All kinds of creatures seek their food, while in the foreground youngsters prepare a "pretend" meal. (Rev: BL 7/91; SLJ 9/91)

1364 McAllister, Angela. *The Clever Cowboy* (PS–2). Illus. by Katherine Lodge. 1998, DK $15.95 (0-7894-3491-1). 28pp. When Clever Cowboy

enters a pancake-tossing contest, his pancake soars so far into the sky that it puts out the sun. (Rev: BCCB 12/98; BL 10/1/98; HBG 3/99; SLJ 10/98)

1365 McBratney, Sam. *Once There Was a Hoodie* (PS–3). Illus. by Paul Hess. 2001, Putnam $15.99 (0-399-23581-7). 32pp. A strange-looking creature known as a Hoodie has no luck finding friends until another Hoodie happens along. (Rev: BL 3/15/01; SLJ 2/01)

1366 McCloskey, Kevin. *Mrs. Fitz's Flamingos* (PS–2). Illus. 1992, Lothrop LB $13.93 (0-688-10475-4). 32pp. To brighten the view from her windows, Mrs. Fitz places plastic flamingos on her neighbor's roof. (Rev: BL 4/15/92; SLJ 6/92)

1367 McCully, Emily Arnold. *Starring Mirette and Bellini* (K–4). Illus. 1997, Putnam $15.99 (0-399-22636-2). 32pp. In this sequel to *Mirette on the High Wire*, high-wire artist Bellini is saved from a czarist prison by his protégé, Mirette. (Rev: BCCB 7–8/97; BL 4/15/97*; SLJ 5/97)

1368 MacDonald, Elizabeth. *John's Picture* (PS–2). Illus. by David McTaggart. 1999, Dutton paper $3.95 (0-14-054344-9). 32pp. After John draws a picture of a man, it comes to life and begins drawing other objects. (Rev: BL 3/15/91; SLJ 10/91)

1369 McElmurry, Jill. *Mad About Plaid* (K–2). Illus. 2000, HarperCollins LB $14.89 (0-688-16952-X). 32pp. Madison Pratt finds a magical plaid purse that turns everything the same plaid pattern. (Rev: BL 4/1/00; HBG 10/00; SLJ 5/00)

1370 McGee, Marni. *Forest Child* (K–3). Illus. by A. Scott Banfill. 1994, Simon & Schuster $15.00 (0-671-86608-7). A feral girl who has been raised by animal friends is rescued when they is captured by a hunter. (Rev: SLJ 3/95)

1371 McGeorge, Constance W. *Snow Riders* (PS–3). Illus. by Mary Whyte. 1995, Chronicle $13.95 (0-8118-0873-4). 32pp. Snow horses created by a brother and sister come to life and take the children on a magic ride. (Rev: BL 1/1–15/96)

1372 MacGill-Callahan, Sheila. *The Last Snake in Ireland: A Story about St. Patrick* (PS–2). Illus. by Will Hillenbrand. 1999, Holiday $15.95 (0-8234-1425-6). 32pp. The last snake in Ireland eludes St. Patrick and finds himself a resident of Loch Ness. (Rev: BCCB 3/99; BL 3/15/99; HBG 10/99; SLJ 3/99)

1373 Machado, Ana María. *Niña Bonita* (PS–3). Trans. from Spanish by Elena Iribarren. Illus. by Rosana Faría. Series: Cranky Nell Books. 1996, Kane/Miller $9.95 (0-916291-63-4). A rabbit envies the dark skin of a little girl he meets in this story set in a South American coastal town. (Rev: SLJ 12/96)

1374 McMillan, Bruce. *Ghost Doll* (K–1). Illus. by author. 1997, Apple Island paper $10.00 (0-934313-01-6). 32pp. Chrissy changes a ghost doll into the real thing.

1375 McMillan, Bruce. *The Remarkable Riderless Runaway Tricycle* (K–3). Illus. by author. 1985, Apple Island paper $10.00 (0-934313-00-8). 48pp. A tricycle, unwilling to be consigned to the dump, sets out on its own trip. This reissued picture book was first published in 1978 and contains black-and-white photographs.

1376 McMullan, Kate. *Hey, Pipsqueak!* (PS–2). Illus. by Jim McMullan. 1995, HarperCollins $14.95 (0-06-205100-8). In his miniature car, a little boy tries to deliver a present but is stopped by a troll. (Rev: SLJ 11/95)

1377 McNaughton, Colin. *Captain Abdul's Pirate School* (1–4). Illus. 1994, Candlewick $16.99 (1-56402-429-6). 40pp. A pirate crew operates a school in which rewards are given for bad deeds and deplorable manners. (Rev: BCCB 12/94; BL 10/15/94; SLJ 1/95)

1378 McNaughton, Colin. *Who's That Banging on the Ceiling?* (PS–3). Illus. 1994, Candlewick paper $5.99 (1-56402-384-2). 32pp. Tenants in a high rise are disturbed by a noisemaker in the building. (Rev: BL 1/15/93; SLJ 3/93)

1379 McNeil, Florence, and David McPhail. *Sail Away* (PS–2). Illus. by David McPhail. 2000, Orca $15.95 (1-55143-147-5). 32pp. Nautical terms are explained in this picture book about a boy dressed as a pirate who, with his animal friends, sails a pirate ship. (Rev: BCCB 10/00; BL 10/1/00; HBG 3/01; SLJ 12/00)

1380 McPhail, David. *Edward and the Pirates* (PS–3). Illus. 1997, Little, Brown $15.95 (0-316-56344-7). 32pp. The pirates that Edward is reading about come alive and kidnap him. (Rev: BCCB 7–8/97; BL 4/15/97; SLJ 5/97)

1381 McPhail, David. *The Party* (PS–1). Illus. 1990, Little, Brown $14.95 (0-316-56330-7). 32pp. A little boy and his stuffed toys have a party after Dad falls asleep. (Rev: BL 10/1/90; SLJ 11/90)

1382 McPhail, David. *The Puddle* (PS–2). Illus. 1998, Farrar $15.00 (0-374-36148-7). 32pp. A fantasy about a boy who goes out in the rain to sail his boat and encounters various animals that play with him. (Rev: BL 2/1/98; HBG 10/98; SLJ 3/98)

1383 McPhail, David. *Tinker and Tom and the Star Baby* (PS–K). Illus. 1998, Little, Brown $14.95 (0-316-56349-8). 32pp. Tinker and his bear friend Tom repair a spaceship that has fallen in their backyard so that its occupant, an alien baby, can go home to its mother. (Rev: BCCB 7–8/98; BL 4/15/98; HBG 10/98; SLJ 4/98)

1384 Madden, Don. *The Wartville Wizard* (K–3). Illus. by author. 1986, Macmillan paper $5.99 (0-689-71667-2). 32pp. An old man who picks up litter is given the "power over trash" by Mother Nature in this tale about littering. (Rev: BL 11/1/86; SLJ 1/87)

1385 Madinaveitia, Horacio. *Sir Robert's Little Outing* (K–3). Illus. 1992, Wonder Well LB $13.95 (1-879567-01-6); paper $7.95 (1-879567-00-8). 30pp. An oafish knight, Sir Robert, sets out on a quest to win the fair Princess Dorothea. (Rev: BL 1/1/93)

1386 Magnier, Thierry. *Isabelle and the Angel* (PS–3). Illus. by Georg Hallensleben. 2000, Chronicle $14.95 (0-8118-2526-4). 36pp. When the little angel in Isabelle's favorite painting at the art galley comes to life, she gets a magical tour of the museum. (Rev: BL 12/1/00; HBG 3/01; SLJ 12/00)

1387 Mahy, Margaret. *Boom, Baby, Boom, Boom!* (PS–K). Illus. by Patricia MacCarthy. 1997, Viking $15.99 (0-670-87314-4). 32pp. When Mama quietly plays her drum, animals enter the house and share a baby's dinner. (Rev: BL 3/1/97; SLJ 5/97)

1388 Mahy, Margaret. *Simply Delicious!* (K–3). Illus. by Jonathan Allen. 1999, Orchard $15.95 (0-531-30181-8). 32pp. As Mr. Minky bicycles home with a super ice-cream cone for his son, he attracts a number of jungle beasts who follow him for a taste. (Rev: BL 9/1/99; HB 9–10/99; HBG 3/00; SLJ 9/99)

1389 Mahy, Margaret. *Tick Tock Tales: Twelve Stories to Read Around the Clock* (K–3). Illus. by Wendy Smith. 1994, Simon & Schuster paper $16.95 (0-689-50604-X). 92pp. Twelve unusual, imaginative tales from a master storyteller. (Rev: SLJ 4/94*)

1390 Maizlish, Lisa. *The Ring* (PS–1). Illus. 1996, Greenwillow $15.00 (0-688-14217-6). 24pp. A magic ring turns winter to summer and allows a boy to fly over New York City. (Rev: BL 6/1–15/96; HB 7–8/96; SLJ 5/96)

1391 Maloney, Peter, and Felicia Zekauskas. *The Magic Hockey Stick* (K–3). Illus. 1999, Dial $12.99 (0-8037-2476-4). 40pp. When her mother buys Wayne Gretzky's hockey stick at an auction, a young hockey player notices that, although her game improves by using the magic stick, Gretzky's declines. (Rev: BL 12/1/99; HBG 10/00; SLJ 10/99)

1392 Manning, Mick. *Honk! Honk! A Story of Migration* (K–2). Illus. by Brita Granström. 1997, Kingfisher $14.95 (0-7534-5103-4). In this fantasy, a child hitches a ride on a Canada goose and migrates to the North and back. (Rev: HBG 3/98; SLJ 11/97)

1393 Mariconda, Barbara. *Witch Way to the Beach* (1–3). Illus. by Jon McIntosh. Series: First Choice Chapter Book. 1997, Bantam paper $3.99 (0-440-41268-4). 48pp. Constance, a witch, does not expect all the adventures she has when she goes to the beach. (Rev: SLJ 11/97)

1394 Mark, Jan. *Fun with Mrs. Thumb* (PS–2). Illus. by Nicola Bayley. 1993, Candlewick $9.95 (1-56402-247-1). 32pp. Simple rhymes describe how a ginger cat attacks the wooden dollhouse in which Mrs. Thumb, a doll, lives. (Rev: BL 1/1/94; SLJ 3/94)

1395 Markes, Julie. *Good Thing You're Not an Octopus!* (PS–K). Illus. by Maggie Smith. 2001, HarperCollins LB $14.89 (0-06-028466-8). 40pp. In this humorous picture book, simple tasks for a boy, like putting on pants, are juxtaposed with an octopus trying to accomplish them. (Rev: BL 1/1–15/01; SLJ 3/01)

1396 Markoe, Merrill. *The Day My Dogs Became Guys* (K–4). Illus. by Eric Brace. 1999, Viking $15.99 (0-670-85344-5). 32pp. During a solar eclipse, Carey's three dogs turn into people but retain their canine personalities. (Rev: BCCB 3/99; BL 2/15/99; HBG 10/99; SLJ 4/99)

1397 Martin, Jacqueline B. *Higgins Bend Song and Dance* (1–4). Illus. by Brad Sneed. 1997, Houghton

$16.00 (0-395-67583-9). Simon Henry vows to use any method possible to catch Oscar, a wily catfish. (Rev: HBG 3/98; SLJ 9/97)

1398 Marzollo, Jean. *Snow Angel* (PS–2). Illus. by Jacqueline Rogers. 1995, Scholastic $14.95 (0-590-48748-5). In this fantasy, a little girl is taken on a flight by a snow angel on a wintry day. (Rev: SLJ 12/95)

1399 Masini, Beatrice. *A Brave Little Princess* (K–3). Illus. by Octavia Monaco. 2000, Barefoot $15.99 (1-84148-267-6). 32pp. A tiny princess doesn't look her age so she goes out into the world to prove that she is stronger and braver than she looks. (Rev: BL 10/1/00; HBG 3/01; SLJ 2/01)

1400 Mathis, Melissa Bay. *Animal House* (K–3). Illus. by Melissa Mathis Bay. 1999, Simon & Schuster $15.95 (0-689-81594-8). Several children imagine the kind of treehouse that each of a group of stuffed animals would prefer to live in. (Rev: HBG 3/00; SLJ 9/99)

1401 Matje, Martin. *Celeste: A Day in the Park* (PS–1). Illus. 1999, Simon & Schuster $12.00 (0-689-82100-X). 40pp. In a city park, Celeste and her teddy bear, Tim, are accosted by a hungry duck until a kindly policeman intervenes. (Rev: BL 7/99; HBG 10/99; SLJ 8/99)

1402 Mayer, Mercer. *Shibumi and the Kitemaker* (2–4). Illus. 1999, Marshall Cavendish $18.95 (0-7614-5054-8). 48pp. An original folktale about an emperor's daughter who is shocked at the peasants' living conditions in her father's kingdom and wants him to do something about it. (Rev: BL 10/15/99; HBG 10/00; SLJ 9/99)

1403 Mayhew, James. *Katie and the Mona Lisa* (K–3). Illus. 1999, Orchard $15.95 (0-531-30177-X). 32pp. In the company of Mona Lisa, Katie enters several famous Renaissance paintings to regain Mona Lisa's famous smile. (Rev: BCCB 9/99; BL 9/1/99; HBG 3/00; SLJ 12/99)

1404 Mayhew, James. *Katie Meets the Impressionists* (PS–2). Illus. 1999, Orchard $15.95 (0-531-30151-6). 32pp. While visiting an art galley with her Grandma, Katie becomes so involved with the work of the Impressionists that she enters the paintings of Renoir, Monet, and Degas. (Rev: BL 4/1/99; HBG 10/99; SLJ 3/99)

1405 Maynard, Bill. *Incredible Ned* (K–2). Illus. by Frank Remkiewicz. 1997, Putnam $15.95 (0-399-23023-8). Ned has a strange problem: every time he mentions an object or animal, it appears. (Rev: HBG 3/98; SLJ 11/97)

1406 Meddaugh, Susan. *Beast* (K–2). Illus. by author. 1985, Houghton paper $3.95 (0-317-18511-X). 32pp. Anna frightens a timid monster.

1407 Meddaugh, Susan. *Cinderella's Rat* (K–2). Illus. 1997, Houghton $15.00 (0-395-86833-5). 32pp. An amusing picture book that tells what happened to the rat that was turned into Cinderella's coachman. (Rev: BL 10/1/97; HB 9–10/97; HBG 3/98; SLJ 10/97*)

1408 Meddaugh, Susan. *Martha Blah Blah* (PS–2). Illus. 1996, Houghton $14.95 (0-395-79755-1). 32pp. Martha the dog, who talks after eating alpha-bet soup, finds her vocabulary constricted when the soup company reduces the letters in each can. (Rev: BCCB 12/96; BL 9/15/96; HB 11–12/96; SLJ 11/96*)

1409 Medearis, Angela Shelf. *The Ghost of Sifty Sifty Sam* (K–3). Illus. by Jacqueline Rogers. 1997, Scholastic $14.95 (0-590-48290-4). 32pp. A chef named Dan uses his cooking to tame a ghost whose wailings have made a house unfit for living. (Rev: BL 12/1/97; HBG 3/98; SLJ 11/97)

1410 Metaxas, Eric, adapt. *Pinocchio: The Classic Italian Tale* (K–3). Illus. by Brian Ajhar. 1996, Simon & Schuster paper $19.95 (0-689-80230-7). A simple retelling of some of the key episodes from the original story, with handsome illustrations. (Rev: SLJ 8/96)

1411 Meyer, Eleanor Walsh. *The Keeper of Ugly Sounds* (PS–2). Illus. by Vlad Guzner. 1998, Winslow $16.95 (1-890817-02-3). 32pp. A young boy is responsible for stuffing bad noises caused by unpleasant acts into bags and sending them out to sea — a chore that he comes to find disagreeable. (Rev: BL 12/1/98; SLJ 1/99)

1412 Michelson, Richard. *Did You Say Ghosts?* (K–2). Illus. by Leonard Baskin. 1993, Macmillan LB $14.95 (0-02-766915-7). 32pp. Ghosts, monsters, and various supernatural beings scare each other in this cumulaive tale. (Rev: BL 9/1/93)

1413 Milich, Melissa. *Miz Fannie Mae's Fine New Easter Hat* (K–3). Illus. by Yong Chen. 1997, Little, Brown $14.95 (0-316-57159-8). 32pp. Tandy and her father buy a magical hat for Mama's Easter. (Rev: BL 5/15/97; SLJ 6/97)

1414 Mills, Lauren. *Fairy Wings* (PS–3). Illus. by Dennis Nolan. 1995, Little, Brown $16.95 (0-316-57397-3). 32pp. Fia is the only fairy in the land of fairies without gossamer wings. (Rev: BL 11/1/95; SLJ 1/96)

1415 Mills, Lauren. *The Goblin Baby* (K–2). Illus. by author. 1999, Dial $15.99 (0-8037-2172-2). With the help of gnome friends, Amanda tries to get her brother back after he has been stolen by goblins and replaced by a changeling. (Rev: HBG 3/00; SLJ 12/99)

1416 Min, Willemien. *Peter's Patchwork Dream* (PS–K). Illus. 1999, Barefoot $15.95 (1-902283-45-7). 26pp. Peter, who is sick in bed, enters the world of his patchwork quilt and is soon traveling through fields, orchards, and across the sea. (Rev: BL 5/1/99; SLJ 6/99)

1417 Mitchell, Adrian. *Nobody Rides the Unicorn* (1–4). Illus. by Stephen Lambert. 2000, Scholastic $16.95 (0-439-11204-4). 32pp. An evil king tricks a young girl into capturing the unicorn, but when she realizes what has happened she is able to free him. (Rev: BCCB 2/00; BL 4/15/00; HBG 10/00; SLJ 1/01)

1418 Modarressi, Mitra. *Monster Stew* (K–2). Illus. 1998, DK $15.95 (0-7894-2517-3). 32pp. This book contains humorous variations on three famous tales: The Princess and the Pea, Jack and the Beanstalk, and Hansel and Gretel. (Rev: BCCB 9/98; BL 7/98; HBG 3/99; SLJ 9/98)

1419 Modarressi, Mitra. *Yard Sale!* (K–3). Illus. 2000, DK $15.95 (0-7894-2651-X). 32pp. When Mr. Flotsam holds a yard sale to dispose of magical items he has collected, the buyers end up turning the town topsy-turvy. (Rev: BL 3/1/00; HBG 10/00; SLJ 7/00)

1420 Moers, Hermann. *Katie and the Big, Brave Bear* (PS–3). Illus. by Jozef Wilkon. 1995, North-South LB $14.88 (1-55858-398-X). 32pp. Big, Brave Bear comes to life out of a storybook to protect Katie when her mother goes to the supermarket and leaves her alone. (Rev: BL 6/1–15/95; SLJ 8/95)

1421 Morimoto, Junko. *The Two Bullies* (PS–1). Trans. by Isao Morimoto. Illus. 1999, Crown LB $18.99 (0-517-80062-4). 32pp. Two strong men — one from Japan and the other from China — feel they must challenge one another in this story about magic and foolish pride. (Rev: BL 8/99; HB 11–12/99; HBG 3/00; SLJ 8/99)

1422 Morozumi, Atsuko. *My Friend Gorilla* (PS–K). Illus. 1998, Farrar $15.00 (0-374-35458-8). 32pp. When a zoo closes down, a boy adopts a gorilla; but in time his friend must go back to his home in Africa. (Rev: BL 2/1/98; HBG 10/98; SLJ 3/98)

1423 Morris, Bob. *Crispin the Terrible* (PS–3). Illus. by Dasha Ziborova. 2000, Callaway $17.95 (0-935112-44-8). 32pp. Crispin the cat feels unappreciated and dreams how his life would be if he had a new identity, like Crispin the Explorer or Crispin the Country Cat. (Rev: BL 1/1–15/01; SLJ 12/00)

1424 Moss, Miriam. *Jigsaw* (K–3). Illus. by Tony Smith. 1997, Millbrook LB $22.40 (0-7613-0044-9). 32pp. An unusual picture book in which items on a journey become parts of a jigsaw puzzle. (Rev: BL 9/15/97; HBG 3/98; SLJ 12/97)

1425 Munsch, Robert. *Mud Puddle* (PS–2). Illus. by Sami Suomalainen. 1996, Annick LB $16.95 (1-55037-469-9); paper $5.95 (1-55037-468-0). 32pp. Jule Ann is attacked by a mud puddle every time she leaves her house. (Rev: BL 4/1/96)

1426 Murphy, Stuart J. *A Pair of Socks* (PS–1). Illus. by Lois Ehlert. 1996, HarperCollins LB $15.89 (0-06-025880-2). 40pp. A sock sets out to find its lost mate. (Rev: BL 10/1/96; SLJ 12/96)

1427 Mutchnick, Brenda, and Ron Casden. *A Noteworthy Tale* (1–4). Illus. by Ian Penney. 1997, Abrams $17.95 (0-8109-1386-0). A fantasy about two lands, one where music is created and cherished and the other where it is banned. (Rev: HBG 3/98; SLJ 1/98)

1428 Napoli, Donna Jo. *Albert* (K–2). Illus. by Jim LaMarche. 2001, Harcourt $16.00 (0-15-201572-8). 32pp. When Albert, a reclusive man, sticks a hand out of his apartment window, two cardinals build a nest in it and Albert must stay in this position until the birds' eggs hatch. (Rev: BL 3/1/01)

1429 Newman, Leslea. *Cats, Cats, Cats!* (PS–2). Illus. by Erika Oller. 2001, Simon & Schuster $16.00 (0-689-83077-7). 32pp. When Mrs. Brown goes to bed at night, her 60 cats knit, eat, read,

write, perform, and party. (Rev: BCCB 3/01; BL 2/15/01; SLJ 3/01)

1430 Nickle, John. *The Ant Bully* (PS–1). Illus. 1999, Scholastic $14.95 (0-590-39591-2). 32pp. Lucas terrorizes the ants in his backyard until they shrink him and put him on trial. (Rev: BCCB 2/99; BL 2/1/99; HB 1–2/99; HBG 10/99; SLJ 3/99)

1431 Nickle, John. *TV Rex* (K–3). Illus. 2001, Scholastic $15.95 (0-439-12043-8). 40pp. Rex crawls inside the TV set to fix it and soon finds he has become part of a series of different programs including a wrestling show and a soap opera. (Rev: BCCB 3/01; BL 1/1–15/01)

1432 Nightingale, Sandy. *Cider Apples* (K–3). Illus. 1996, Harcourt $15.00 (0-15-201244-3). 32pp. Fairies help a young girl and her grandmother save an ailing apple tree. (Rev: BL 9/1/96; SLJ 11/96)

1433 Nightingale, Sandy. *A Giraffe on the Moon* (PS). Illus. 1992, Harcourt $13.95 (0-15-230950-0). 32pp. A fine visual feast in a picture book that begins "I didn't expect to see . . ." (Rev: BL 2/15/92*; SLJ 3/92)

1434 Nolen, Jerdine. *Big Jabe* (1–4). Illus. by Kadir Nelson. 2000, Lothrop LB $15.89 (0-688-13663-X). 32pp. An original tall tale about a man of unusual strength who could lead slaves to freedom. (Rev: BCCB 9/00; BL 4/1/00; HB 7–8/00; HBG 10/00; SLJ 6/00)

1435 Nolen, Jerdine. *Harvey Potter's Balloon Farm* (K–3). Illus. by Mark Buehner. 1994, Morrow $15.95 (0-688-07887-7). 32pp. In this tall tale, a little girl learns all the secrets of trade when she visits Harvey's balloon farm and discovers how they are grown. (Rev: BL 4/15/94; HB 7–8/94; SLJ 5/94)

1436 Nolen, Jerdine. *Raising Dragons* (PS–2). Illus. by Elise Primavera. 1998, Harcourt $16.00 (0-15-201288-5). 32pp. An African American child raises a dragon named Hank on her parents' farm and teaches him to perform useful chores. Eventually, though, she must take him to a land where he will be with his own kind. (Rev: BCCB 6/98; BL 4/1/98; HB 3–4/98; HBG 10/98; SLJ 4/98)

1437 Nones, Eric Jon. *Angela's Wings* (PS–3). Illus. 1995, Farrar $16.00 (0-374-30331-2). 32pp. Angela tries to hide the fact that she has grown wings until she learns to fly. (Rev: BL 9/15/95; SLJ 10/95)

1438 Novak, Matt. *The Robobots* (PS–3). Illus. 1999, DK $15.95 (0-7894-2566-1). 32pp. A family of robots behaves so strangely that neighbors become angry, until they discover that the strangers possess a unique charm. (Rev: BCCB 5/99; BL 6/1–15/99; HBG 10/99; SLJ 6/99)

1439 O Flatharta, Antoine. *The Prairie Train* (PS–3). Illus. by Eric Rohmann. 1999, Crown LB $18.99 (0-517-70989-9). 40pp. During a young boy's trip from Ireland to California he has dreams that the train on which he is traveling becomes a boat and reunites him with his grandfather. (Rev: BL 12/1/99; HBG 3/00; SLJ 12/99)

1440 O'Brien, John. *Poof!* (PS–2). Illus. by author. 1999, Boyds Mills $14.95 (1-56397-815-6). A sleepy wizard and his wife avoid daily chores by waving their magic wands; "Poof!" they solve each problem. (Rev: HBG 3/00; SLJ 11/99)

1441 Oliviero, Jamie. *Som See and the Magic Elephant* (1–3). Illus. by Jo'Anne Kelly. 1995, Hyperion $14.95 (0-7868-0025-9). 32pp. Before Som See's great aunt dies, she wants to touch a white elephant. With the help of magical powers, Som See is eventually able to grant her wish. (Rev: BL 5/1/95; SLJ 5/95)

1442 Olson, Mary W. *An Alligator Ate My Brother* (PS–2). Illus. by Tammie Lyon. 2000, Boyds Mills $15.95 (1-56397-803-2). 32pp. Paul can't convince his parents that an alligator has just eaten baby brother Jimmy. (Rev: BCCB 12/00; BL 12/1/00; HBG 3/01; SLJ 11/00)

1443 Olson, Mary W. *Nice Try, Tooth Fairy* (PS–1). Illus. by Katherine Tillotson. 2000, Simon & Schuster $15.00 (0-689-82422-X). When a girl asks the Tooth Fairy to return her tooth so she can show it to her grandfather, a mistake is made and a hippo's tooth is brought. (Rev: HBG 10/00; SLJ 11/00)

1444 Oram, Hiawyn. *In the Attic* (PS–K). Illus. by Satoshi Kitamura. 1985, Holt paper $5.95 (0-8050-0780-6). 32pp. A little boy climbs his fire engine ladder into his attic, where he has exciting adventures, even though, as his mother tells him, "we don't have an attic." (Rev: BCCB 3/85; BL 6/15/85; SLJ 10/85)

1445 Oram, Hiawyn. *Princess Chamomile Gets Her Way* (PS–1). Illus. by Susan Varley. 1999, Dutton $15.99 (0-525-46148-5). 32pp. Chamomile, a mouse princess, leaves the castle for an adventure and is kidnapped by Bag-Eyes, the bad cat. (Rev: BL 7/99; HBG 10/99; SLJ 6/99)

1446 Orgel, Doris. *Button Soup* (K–3). Illus. by Pau Estrada. Series: Bank Street Easy-to-Read. 1994, Bantam paper $4.50 (0-553-37341-2). 32pp. A variation on the "Stone Soup" story in which an old woman makes soup using a button and water as the only two ingredients. (Rev: SLJ 2/95)

1447 Ormerod, Jan. *Miss Mouse's Day* (PS–K). Illus. 2001, HarperCollins LB $14.89 (0-688-16334-3). 32pp. A toddler's day from getting up to a goodnight kiss and cuddle is described by her best friend, a doll named Miss Mouse. (Rev: BL 3/15/01*; SLJ 3/01)

1448 Osborne, Mary Pope. *Mummies in the Morning* (1–4). Illus. 1993, Random LB $11.99 (0-679-92424-8); paper $3.99 (0-679-82424-3). 72pp. Jack and Annie time-travel to ancient Egypt to help a queen find a copy of the Book of the Dead. (Rev: BL 4/1/94)

1449 Packard, Mary. *We Are Monsters* (K–1). Illus. by John Magine. 1996, Scholastic $3.99 (0-590-68995-9). 32pp. At nighttime, terrible monsters are afraid that children are hiding under their beds in this book with removable flashcards. (Rev: BL 2/1/97)

1450 Palatini, Margie. *Piggie Pie!* (K–3). Illus. by Howard Fine. 1995, Clarion $15.00 (0-395-71691-8). 32pp. Gritch the Witch is off to Old MacDonald's farm in search of eight plump pigs for her favorite pie. (Rev: BL 9/1/95*; SLJ 11/95*)

1451 Palatini, Margie. *Zak's Lunch* (K–3). Illus. by Howard Fine. 1998, Clarion $15.00 (0-395-81674-2). 32pp. When faced with a simple ham-and-cheese sandwich for lunch, Zak dreams of owning his own restaurant, where he will have delicious, forbidden foods every day. (Rev: HBG 10/98; SLJ 6/98)

1452 Palatini, Margie. *Zoom Broom* (1–3). Illus. by Howard Fine. 1998, Hyperion $14.95 (0-7868-0322-3). 32pp. When Gritch the Witch goes shopping for a new flying broomstick, Foxy tries to sell her a magic carpet and Cinderella's pumpkin coach. (Rev: BL 10/1/98; HBG 3/99; SLJ 10/98)

1453 Palazzo, Tony. *Magic Crayon* (PS–2). Illus. by author. 1967, Lion LB $12.95 (0-87460-089-8). Imaginative fun for very young readers.

1454 Papineau, Lucie. *Gontrand and the Crescent Moon* (K–4). Trans. from French by David Homel. Illus. by Alain Reno. 1999, Dominique & Friends paper $8.95 (1-894363-15-9). Set in prehistoric times, this is the story of how the moon was formed in order to guide a group of lost children home. (Rev: SLJ 2/00)

1455 Paraskevas, Betty. *The Tangerine Bear* (PS–2). Illus. by Michael Paraskevas. 1997, HarperCollins LB $14.00 (0-06-205147-4). 32pp. Toy Tangerine Bear wants to become part of a family, but nobody wants him because his smile was sewn on upside down. (Rev: BL 11/1/97)

1456 Park, Barbara. *Psssst! It's Me . . . the Bogeyman* (1–3). Illus. by Stephen Kroninger. 1998, Simon & Schuster $16.00 (0-689-81667-7). 40pp. The bogeyman (the reader sees only his long red fingernails) describes all the malicious antics he likes to engage in but confesses to an allergy to dirty sweat socks. (Rev: BCCB 9/98; BL 8/98; HBG 3/99; SLJ 9/98)

1457 Parnall, Peter. *Spaces* (1–3). Illus. 1993, Millbrook LB $22.90 (1-56294-336-7). 32pp. A fantastic view of what unusual creatures and thoughts can fill all sorts of spaces. (Rev: BL 12/1/93; SLJ 12/93)

1458 Paschkis, Julie. *Play All Day* (PS–K). Illus. 1998, Little, Brown $14.95 (0-316-69043-0). 32pp. A fantasy in which the everyday experiences of a young child become exciting adventures — for example, a bedtime bath becomes a deep-sea dive. (Rev: BL 5/15/98; HBG 10/98; SLJ 7/98)

1459 Pastuchiv, Olga. *Minas and the Fish* (PS–2). Illus. by author. 1997, Houghton $14.95 (0-395-79756-X). 32pp. Minas will be granted a single wish if he frees a strange sea creature that has been caught by his father and brothers. (Rev: BCCB 5/97; SLJ 5/97)

1460 Paterson, Katherine. *Celia and the Sweet, Sweet Water* (1–4). Illus. by Vladimir Vagin. 1998, Clarion $15.00 (0-395-91324-1). 32pp. On a quest to get some sweet water to help cure her mother's ills, Celia and her talking dog set out to find the village her mother comes from. (Rev: BL 9/1/98; HBG 3/99; SLJ 9/98)

1461 Paterson, Katherine. *The King's Equal* (2–5). Illus. by Vladimir Vagin. 1992, HarperCollins LB $16.89 (0-06-022497-5). 64pp. An arrogant king learns humility when the bride he wants does not want him. (Rev: BCCB 1/93; BL 7/92; SLJ 9/92*)

1462 Paton, Priscilla. *Howard and the Sitter Surprise* (PS–2). Illus. by Paul Meisel. 1996, Houghton $15.95 (0-395-71814-7). Howard is a terror to all the baby-sitters until he meets his match in Sarah the bear. (Rev: SLJ 10/96)

1463 Pawagi, Manjusha. *The Girl Who Hated Books* (K–3). Illus. by Leanne Franson. 1999, Beyond Words $14.95 (1-896764-11-8). 24pp. When non-reader Meena accidentally frees a lot of book characters, such as Humpty Dumpty and Ali Baba, from the pages of their books, she has to read the whole family library to find where they belong. (Rev: BL 11/1/99; SLJ 6/99)

1464 Pearson, Susan. *Well, I Never!* (PS–1). Illus. by James Warhola. 1990, Simon & Schuster paper $15.00 (0-671-69199-6). 24pp. Strange things are happening on the farm, such as pigs learning to fly. (Rev: BL 11/15/90; SLJ 2/91)

1465 Peet, Bill. *Big Bad Bruce* (K–3). Illus. by author. 1982, Houghton $16.00 (0-395-25150-8); paper $7.95 (0-395-32922-1). Bruce encounters a witch and is shrunk to the size of a chipmunk.

1466 Peet, Bill. *The Caboose Who Got Loose* (K–3). Illus. by author. 1980, Houghton $16.00 (0-395-14805-7); paper $7.95 (0-395-28715-4). 48pp. When Katy Caboose is jarred loose from the rest of the train, she gets her wish to be a "cabin in the trees," free from noise and smoke.

1467 Peet, Bill. *Jennifer and Josephine* (1–3). Illus. by author. 1980, Houghton paper $7.95 (0-395-29608-0). Jennifer, an old touring car, and her friend Josephine the cat, are driven through several adventures by a reckless driver.

1468 Pendziwol, Jean, and Martine Gourbault. *No Dragons for Tea: Fire Safety for Kids (and Dragons)* (PS–1). Illus. 1999, Kids Can $14.95 (1-55074-569-7). 32pp. A young girl's pet dragon sneezes, and her experiences with the ensuing blaze teach fire safety to readers. (Rev: BCCB 4/99; BL 2/1/99; HBG 10/99; SLJ 4/99)

1469 Peppe, Rodney. *The Magic Toy Box* (PS). Illus. 1996, Candlewick $15.99 (0-7636-0010-5). 32pp. Toys leave their magical toy box to play with newcomer Pongo, a cross between an elephant and a pig. (Rev: BL 9/15/96; SLJ 11/96)

1470 Perry, Sarah. *If . . .* (K–4). Illus. 1995, Getty Museum $16.95 (0-89236-321-5). 46pp. Using a number of unconventional statements beginning with "if," this imaginative book presents a series of eyecatching, ingenious pictures to illustrate each phrase. (Rev: BCCB 1/96; BL 10/15/95*; SLJ 2/96)

1471 Persun, Morgan Reed. *No Pets Allowed* (PS–2). Illus. by Timothy Banks. 1998, Journey Bks. paper $5.49 (1-57924-077-1). 30pp. Every time Percy speaks the name of an animal, that creature appears, until his apartment is jammed. (Rev: SLJ 2/99)

1472 Peterson, Beth. *Myrna Never Sleeps* (1–3). Illus. by John O'Brien. 1995, Atheneum $13.00 (0-689-31893-6). 51pp. When Myrna can't get to sleep, she imagines herself as a superwoman in all sorts of adventures. (Rev: SLJ 7/95)

1473 Picard, Barbara Leonie. *The Midsummer Bride* (PS–3). Illus. by Alan Marks. 2000, Oxford $16.95 (0-19-279879-0). 32pp. Count Alaric learns that in allowing his mysterious wife her complete freedom he is able to offer — and receive — true love. (Rev: BL 2/1/00; HBG 10/00; SLJ 3/00)

1474 Pilkey, Dav. *God Bless the Gargoyles* (K–3). Illus. 1996, Harcourt $15.00 (0-15-200248-0). 40pp. To comfort the feared and rejected gargoyles, angels take them on flights. (Rev: BL 10/1/96; SLJ 11/96)

1475 Pilkey, Dav. *Ricky Ricotta's Giant Robot* (2–4). Illus. by Martin Ontiveros. 2000, Scholastic $16.95 (0-590-30719-3). 111pp. Ricky Ricotta, a tiny mouse, is a victim of bullying until he becomes friends with a large robot who protects him. (Rev: BCCB 5/00; HBG 10/00; SLJ 4/00)

1476 Pilkey, Dav. *Ricky Ricotta's Giant Robot vs. the Mutant Mosquitoes from Mercury* (1–3). Illus. by Martin Ontiveros. 2000, Scholastic paper $3.99 (0-590-30722-3). 127pp. Ricky the mouse and his robot friend fight extraterrestrial insects and an evil robot. (Rev: SLJ 10/00)

1477 Pilkey, Dav. *When Cats Dream* (PS–3). Illus. 1992, Orchard LB $16.99 (0-531-08597-X). 32pp. Cats' dreams are more fun and more colorful than their reality. (Rev: BCCB 9/92; BL 8/92; HB 3–4/93; SLJ 9/92*)

1478 Pinkney, Brian. *The Adventures of Sparrowboy* (PS–3). Illus. 1997, Simon & Schuster $16.00 (0-689-81071-7). 40pp. A paperboy named Henry discovers that, like the sparrows, he can fly. (Rev: BCCB 6/97; BL 4/1/97; HB 7–8/97; SLJ 4/97)

1479 Pinkney, Brian. *Cosmo and the Robot* (PS–3). Illus. 2000, Greenwillow LB $15.89 (0-688-15941-9). 32pp. Cosmo, who is growing up on Mars, saves his sister from the clutches of a robot that has gone haywire. (Rev: BCCB 5/00; BL 7/00; HB 7–8/00; HBG 10/00; SLJ 6/00)

1480 Pinkwater, Daniel. *The Phantom of the Lunch Wagon* (K–3). Illus. 1992, Macmillan LB $13.95 (0-02-774641-0). 32pp. The lunch wagon that Chris has repaired is haunted by its old ghost, who does not want to leave. (Rev: BCCB 11/92; BL 9/1/92; SLJ 12/92)

1481 Pinkwater, Daniel. *Wempires* (PS–3). Illus. 1991, Macmillan paper $13.95 (0-02-774411-6). 32pp. A boy is obsessed by vampires until he has a visit from three of them. (Rev: BCCB 10/91; BL 8/91; SLJ 11/91)

1482 Pittman, Helena Clare. *The Snowman's Path* (PS–3). Illus. by Raul Colon. 2000, Dial $15.99 (0-8037-2170-6). 32pp. Nathan makes a snow lady to keep his snowman company and, when spring comes, the two move on to the north. (Rev: BL 11/15/00; HBG 3/01; SLJ 10/00)

1483 Plourde, Lynn. *Winter Waits* (K–2). Illus. by Greg Couch. 2001, Simon & Schuster $16.00 (0-689-83268-0). 32pp. Father Time is too busy to play with his son Little Winter, but when the boy shows him how he has covered the world with beautiful snow, Father Time rewards him with a round of play. (Rev: BL 12/15/00; SLJ 1/01)

1484 Polacco, Patricia. *Appelemando's Dreams* (PS–2). Illus. 1991, Putnam $15.95 (0-399-21800-9). 32pp. Appelemando teaches the townspeople that they should never question the importance of dreams. (Rev: BL 10/15/91; SLJ 9/91)

1485 Polacco, Patricia. *Babushka's Doll* (PS–2). Illus. 1990, Simon & Schuster $16.95 (0-671-68343-8). 32pp. Natasha, a pest, learns her lesson when a doll comes alive and begins nagging. (Rev: BCCB 11/90; BL 9/15/90*; HB 1–2/91; SLJ 11/90)

1486 Polacco, Patricia. *Rechenka's Eggs* (K–2). Illus. by author. 1988, Putnam $16.99 (0-399-21501-8). 32pp. Old Babushka saves a wild goose, and when her decorated eggs are broken, the goose repays her kindness by laying her own decorated eggs. (Rev: BCCB 6/88; BL 4/1/88; SLJ 5/88)

1487 Pow, Tom. *Who Is the World For?* (PS–3). Illus. by Robert Ingpen. 2000, Candlewick $15.99 (0-7636-1280-4). 32pp. Different animals describe their own habitats when their children ask "Who is the world for?" but a human father's answer is that the world is for all to share and explore. (Rev: BL 12/15/00; HBG 3/01; SLJ 1/01)

1488 Powers, Daniel. *Jiro's Pearl* (PS–3). Illus. 1997, Candlewick $15.99 (1-56402-631-0). 32pp. A Japanese tale about a foolish young boy who is sent by his ailing grandmother to buy medicine. (Rev: BL 10/1/97; SLJ 7/97)

1489 Poydar, Nancy. *Cool Ali* (PS–1). Illus. 1996, Simon & Schuster paper $13.00 (0-689-80755-4). 26pp. Ali cools her neighborhood by drawing items that suggest moderate temperatures. (Rev: BCCB 10/96; BL 8/96; HB 9–10/96; SLJ 9/96)

1490 Prater, John. *Once upon a Picnic* (PS–2). Illus. 1996, Candlewick $14.99 (1-56402-810-0). 32pp. All kinds of fantastic creatures are having picnics at the same time as a very ordinary family is having its picnic. (Rev: BCCB 4/96; BL 8/96; SLJ 8/96)

1491 Preiss, Byron, ed. *The Best Children's Books in the World: A Treasury of Illustrated Stories* (K–3). Illus. 1996, Abrams $29.95 (0-8109-1246-5). 319pp. A fascinating collection of 15 distinguished picture books published in countries around the world as they originally appeared, with translations when necessary. (Rev: SLJ 12/96)

1492 Preston, Tim. *The Lonely Scarecrow* (K–3). Illus. by Maggie Kneen. 1999, Dutton $14.99 (0-525-46080-2). 32pp. A scarecrow is unhappy that he frightens away animals and birds, but when winter comes, he is transformed into a snowman loved by all creatures. (Rev: BCCB 11/99; BL 10/1/99; HBG 3/00; SLJ 1/00)

1493 Prior, R. W. N. *The Great Monarch Butterfly Chase* (PS–2). Illus. by Beth Glick. 1993, Bradbury $14.95 (0-02-775145-7). In this fantasy based on fact, two boys follow a monarch butterfly on its migration to Mexico. (Rev: SLJ 2/94)

1494 Pyle, Howard. *Bearskin* (1–4). Illus. by Trina S. Hyman. 1997, Morrow $15.93 (0-688-09838-X). 48pp. An abandoned youngster is cared for by a bear and grows up to be a dragon-slaying hero. (Rev: BL 11/1/97*; HB 9–10/97; HBG 3/98; SLJ 8/97*)

1495 Ragz, M. M. *Lost Little Angel* (K–3). Illus. by Jane Manning. 1999, Simon & Schuster $16.00 (0-689-81067-9). 32pp. A child-angel, Nicholas, and his dog, Comet, get lost in heaven and cause a cloud fight in which all the angels joyfully participate. (Rev: BL 9/15/99; HBG 3/00; SLJ 1/00)

1496 Rascal. *Oregon's Journey* (K–3). Illus. by Louis Joos. 1994, Troll $15.95 (0-8167-3305-8). 40pp. A dwarf and a performing bear leave the circus and head west to Oregon and freedom. (Rev: BCCB 6/94; BL 4/15/94*; SLJ 8/94)

1497 Raschka, Chris. *Like Likes Like* (PS–K). Illus. 1999, DK $15.95 (0-7894-2564-5). In a world where couples prevail, a lonely white cat finally finds a friend in a brown cat that is also alone. (Rev: BCCB 4/99; BL 4/1/99*; HBG 10/99; SLJ 3/99)

1498 Rassmus, Jens. *Farmer Enno and His Cow* (1–5). Trans. by Dominic Barth. Illus. by author. 1998, Orchard $14.95 (0-531-30081-1). Farmer Enno denies his obsessive dream to buy a ship and become a sailor until his wise cow gives him some sound advice. (Rev: HBG 10/98; SLJ 4/98)

1499 Ratnett, Michael. *Monster Train* (K–3). Illus. by June Goulding. 2000, Orchard $15.95 (0-531-30293-8). This interactive book uses pop-ups and other devices to illustrate a ride on a monster train with passengers like Frankenstein. (Rev: BL 12/1/00)

1500 Ray, Mary L. *Pumpkins: A Story for a Field* (K–4). Illus. by Barry Root. 1992, Harcourt $15.00 (0-15-252252-2). 32pp. A farmer reaches an agreement with a vacant field and together they grow a bumper crop of pumpkins. (Rev: BL 10/15/92; HB 11–12/92; SLJ 3/93)

1501 Reasoner, Charles. *Who Drives This?* (PS). Illus. by author. Series: Sliding Surprise Books. 1996, Price Stern Sloan paper $9.95 (0-8431-3939-0). A board book that uses sliding panels to reveal animals driving various vehicles. Also use *Who Pretends?* (1996). (Rev: SLJ 8/96)

1502 Reese, Della. *God Inside of Me* (1–3). Illus. by Yvonne Buchanan. 1999, Hyperion LB $16.49 (0-7868-2395-X). Kenisha is annoyed with her little brother and also her talking toys but discovers that God has given them all great gifts. (Rev: BL 5/1/99; SLJ 7/99)

1503 Reiner, Annie. *A Visit to the Art Galaxy* (1–3). Illus. 1990, Simon & Schuster $15.95 (0-671-74957-9). 56pp. Two children and their mother enter the Land of Modern Art and discover new ways of looking at paintings. (Rev: BL 5/15/91)

1504 Reynolds, Adrian. *Pete and Polo's Big School Adventure* (PS–K). Illus. 2000, Orchard $15.95 (0-531-30275-X). 32pp. Pete is certain that all will go well on the first day of school but Polo, his stuffed polar bear, isn't so sure. (Rev: BL 9/1/00; SLJ 12/00)

1505 Richardson, Jean. *The Bear Who Went to the Ballet* (PS–1). Illus. by Susan Winter. 1995, DK $14.95 (0-7894-0318-8). 32pp. A teddy bear discovers she is not suited to becoming a ballerina, so she decides to be a teller of ballet stories instead. (Rev: BL 2/15/96; SLJ 3/96)

1506 Richardson, Judith B. *Old Winter* (PS–1). Illus. by R. W. Alley. 1996, Orchard LB $16.99 (0-531-08883-9). 32pp. Old Winter is so angry at people criticizing his season that he decides to remain in the North although spring is scheduled to arrive. (Rev: BCCB 12/96; BL 10/1/96; SLJ 12/96)

1507 Riddle, Tohby. *The Singing Hat* (K–3). Illus. 2001, Farrar $16.00 (0-374-36934-8). 32pp. When Colin Jenkins falls asleep under a tree, a bird builds a nest in his hat and refuses to move until its baby hatches. (Rev: BL 2/15/01)

1508 Ringgold, Faith. *Bonjour, Lonnie* (1–4). Illus. 1996, Hyperion LB $16.49 (0-7868-2062-4). 32pp. Love Bird takes Lonnie to Paris to explore his family tree. (Rev: BL 10/1/96; SLJ 1/97)

1509 Ringgold, Faith. *Tar Beach* (PS–2). Illus. 1991, Crown LB $18.99 (0-517-58031-4). 32pp. A little girl on the rooftop of her apartment building dreams of soaring over New York City. (Rev: BCCB 3/91; BL 1/1/91; HB 5–6/91*; SLJ 2/91*)

1510 Rix, Jamie. *The Last Chocolate Cookie* (PS–3). Illus. by Arthur Robins. 1998, Candlewick paper $4.99 (0-7636-0411-9). 32pp. An amusing story about a boy named Maurice who offers the last chocolate cookie on the plate to everyone, including a monster on a distant planet who would rather eat Maurice than the cookie. (Rev: BL 6/1–15/98; SLJ 7/98)

1511 Roberts, Bethany. *Monster Manners* (PS–2). Illus. by Andrew Glass. 1996, Clarion $15.00 (0-395-69850-2). 32pp. A rhyming book that explains basic manners with brilliantly colored illustrations and the antics of three often misbehaving monsters. (Rev: SLJ 4/96)

1512 Roberts, David, and Corina Fletcher. *Ghoul School* (K–4). Illus. 2000, Abrams $17.95 (0-8109-4140-6). A pop-up book about a school run by Ms. Vampira where strange things take place, like eating worms for lunch. (Rev: BL 12/1/00)

1513 Robertson, M. P. *The Egg* (K–2). Illus. by author. 2001, Penguin $15.99 (0-8037-2546-9). When the egg that George has cared for hatches and a little dragon emerges, George must assume a motherly role and teach his adopted child how to do dragon things like fly, breath fire, and slay knights. (Rev: BCCB 2/01; SLJ 1/01*)

1514 Robinson, Fay. *Where Did All the Dragons Go?* (PS–3). Illus. by Victor Lee. 1996, Troll $15.95 (0-8167-3808-4). 32pp. All kinds of dragons swirl about in the pages of this unusual picture book. (Rev: BL 12/15/96)

1515 Robinson, Tim. *Tobias, the Quig and the Rumplenut Tree* (PS–4). Illus. by author. 2000, Winslow $16.95 (1-890817-20-1). In this fantasy, Tobias must free the quig, an unusual bird, so the bird can spread seeds of the rumplenut tree. (Rev: HBG 10/00; SLJ 10/00)

1516 Rohmann, Eric. *The Cinder-Eyed Cats* (K–4). Illus. 1997, Crown LB $18.99 (0-517-70897-3). 40pp. A memorable picture book about a trip that a boy takes to a lush tropical island and the fantastic animals and fish that keep him company there. (Rev: BL 11/15/97; SLJ 11/97)

1517 Root, Phyllis. *Aunt Nancy and Old Man Trouble* (K–2). Illus. by David Parkins. 1996, Candlewick $16.99 (1-56402-374-8). 32pp. Aunt Nancy outwits Old Man Trouble by posing a question he can't answer. (Rev: BCCB 3/96; BL 5/1/96; HB 9–10/96; SLJ 5/96)

1518 Root, Phyllis. *Grandmother Winter* (PS–2). Illus. by Beth Krommes. 1999, Houghton $15.00 (0-395-88399-7). 32pp. When Grandmother Winter shakes out her quilt and causes a snowfall, all nature responds to the coming of winter. (Rev: BCCB 10/99; BL 11/15/99; HB 9–10/99; HBG 3/00; SLJ 9/99)

1519 Root, Phyllis. *Kiss the Cow!* (PS–1). Illus. by Will Hillenbrand. 2000, Candlewick $15.99 (0-7636-0298-1). 32pp. When Annalisa tries her Mama's elaborate rituals while milking cow Luella, she can't bring herself to kiss the cow's nose and so the cow feels insulted and refuses to give milk. (Rev: BCCB 1/01; BL 11/15/00; HB 1–2/01; HBG 3/01; SLJ 12/00)

1520 Root, Phyllis. *One Windy Wednesday* (PS–K). Illus. by Helen Craig. 1996, Candlewick $10.99 (0-7636-0054-7). 24pp. A strong wind causes the barnyard animals to change the sounds they make so that the cow begins to oink. (Rev: BL 10/15/96; SLJ 11/96)

1521 Root, Phyllis. *Rosie's Fiddle* (K–3). Illus. by Kevin O'Malley. 1997, Lothrop LB $15.93 (0-688-12853-X). 32pp. Rosie O'Grady is challenged by the devil to engage in a fiddling contest in this somewhat scary picture book. (Rev: BCCB 4/97; BL 4/15/97; SLJ 4/97)

1522 Rosen, Michael. *Mission Ziffoid* (PS–K). Illus. by Arthur Robins. 1999, Candlewick $10.99 (0-7636-0805-X); paper $3.29 (0-7636-0806-8). A small boy is taken in by a family of aliens when he lands on a strange planet. (Rev: BCCB 11/99; HBG 3/00; SLJ 12/99)

1523 Rosen, Michael J. *With a Dog Like That, a Kid Like Me . . .* (PS–2). Illus. by Ted Rand. 2000, Dial $15.99 (0-8037-2059-9). A young boy imagines his dog being transformed into other animals. (Rev: HBG 10/00; SLJ 6/00)

1524 Rosenberg, Liz. *The Carousel* (K–3). Illus. by Jim LaMarche. 1995, Harcourt $16.00 (0-15-200853-5). 32pp. Two girls discover that the horses of the carousel in the park have come alive. (Rev: BCCB 12/95; BL 11/15/95; SLJ 1/96*)

1525 Rosenberg, Liz. *Monster Mama* (PS–3). Illus. by Stephen Gammell. 1993, Putnam $15.95 (0-399-21989-7). 32pp. Patrick turns into a monster to protect his mother when local bullies insult her. (Rev: BCCB 7–8/93; BL 1/15/93*; HB 3–4/93; SLJ 6/93)

1526 Ross, Michael E. *Become a Bird and Fly!* (PS–3). Illus. by Peter Parnall. 1992, Millbrook LB $21.90 (1-56294-074-0). 32pp. A boy wants so much to fly that he imagines he has become a bird. (Rev: BL 1/15/93; SLJ 2/93)

1527 Ross, Tom. *Eggbert: The Slightly Cracked Egg* (PS–3). Illus. by Rex Barron. 1994, Putnam $15.95 (0-399-22416-5). 32pp. When Eggbert the egg gets cracked, he notices that the whole world and the objects in it contain many cracks. (Rev: BL 2/1/94; SLJ 5/94)

1528 Ryder, Joanne. *Bears Out There* (K–2). Illus. by Jo Ellen McAllister-Stammen. 1995, Macmillan $15.00 (0-689-31780-8). 32pp. A boy imagines that bears do the same things that he does during a typical summer day. (Rev: BL 4/15/95; SLJ 5/95)

1529 Ryder, Joanne. *Rainbow Wings* (K–4). Illus. by Victor Lee. 2000, HarperCollins LB $15.98 (0-688-14129-3). 40pp. This fantasy in which children get wings to fly also presents the different kinds of wings found in nature such as those of an owl and a monarch butterfly. (Rev: BL 5/1/00; HBG 10/00; SLJ 5/00)

1530 Ryder, Joanne. *The Snail's Spell* (K–2). Illus. by Lynne Cherry. 1992, Puffin paper $5.99 (0-14-050891-0). 32pp. A little boy knows how a snail feels when he shrinks to that size. Originally published in 1982.

1531 Rylant, Cynthia. *Cat Heaven* (PS–3). Illus. 1997, Scholastic $15.95 (0-590-10054-8). 40pp. A picture book about the activities in cat heaven. (Rev: BL 9/1/97; HBG 3/98; SLJ 10/97)

1532 Rylant, Cynthia. *The Great Gracie Chase: Stop That Dog!* (PS–1). Illus. by Mark Teague. 2001, Scholastic $15.95 (0-590-10041-6). 40pp. Gracie Rose decides to break the rules and take a walk by herself, causing a frantic neighborhood search when she seems to be lost. (Rev: BCCB 3/01; BL 2/15/01)

1533 Rylant, Cynthia. *Little Whistle* (PS–K). Illus. by Tim Bowers. 2001, Harcourt $14.00 (0-15-201087-4). 32pp. Little Whistle, a guinea pig who lives in a toy store, loves the nights when all the toys come to life and he can play with them. (Rev: BL 2/15/01)

1534 Rylant, Cynthia. *Scarecrow* (K–3). Illus. by Lauren Stringer. 1998, Harcourt $16.00 (0-15-201084-X). 40pp. A gentle scarecrow tells about his contented life, how he appreciates nature, and of his many animal friends. (Rev: BCCB 6/98; BL 4/1/98; HBG 10/98; SLJ 4/98)

1535 Sabuda, Robert. *The Blizzard's Robe* (K–3). Illus. 1999, Simon & Schuster $16.00 (0-689-31988-6). 32pp. In return for the kindness of the people, the monster Blizzard gives them the Northern Lights to illuminate the winter darkness. (Rev: BL 11/15/99; HBG 3/00; SLJ 10/99)

1536 Sadler, Marilyn. *Alistair in Outer Space* (PS–2). Illus. by Roger Bollen. 1989, Simon & Schuster paper $15.00 (0-671-66678-9). Nerdy Alistair is carried off by a space ship on his way to the library. (Rev: BL 2/1/85; SLJ 11/89)

1537 Sadler, Marilyn. *Alistair Underwater* (PS–3). Illus. by Roger Bollen. 1990, Simon & Schuster paper $5.95 (0-671-79246-6). 44pp. Alistair, in his own submarine, saves a colony of friendly frogs. (Rev: BL 7/90; SLJ 6/90)

1538 Saltzberg, Barney. *This Is a Great Place for a Hot Dog Stand* (1–3). Illus. 1995, Hyperion LB $15.49 (0-7868-2057-8). 32pp. The hot dog stand that the monster Izzy operates is threatened by the construction of a super shopping mall. (Rev: BL 4/15/95; SLJ 5/95)

1539 Sandburg, Carl. *The Wedding Procession of the Rag Doll and the Broom Handle and Who Was in It* (1–3). Illus. by Harriet Pincus. 1978, Harcourt paper $6.00 (0-15-695487-7). 32pp. Illustrated edition of one of the Rootabaga Stories.

1540 Sanfield, Steve. *The Girl Who Wanted a Song* (K–3). Illus. by Stephen T. Johnson. 1996, Harcourt $16.00 (0-15-200969-8). Through contact with a lost Canada goose, orphaned Marici finds that she has a distinctive song to sing, like the birds and animals around her. (Rev: SLJ 7/97)

1541 San Souci, Robert D. *The Boy and the Ghost* (K–3). Illus. by Brian Pinkney. 1989, Simon & Schuster paper $16.00 (0-671-67176-6). 32pp. While spending a night in a haunted house, a boy encounters a ghost. (Rev: BCCB 12/89; BL 10/1/89)

1542 Santoro, Scott. *Isaac the Ice Cream Truck* (PS–K). Illus. 1999, Holt $15.95 (0-8050-5296-8). 32pp. Isaac, the lowly ice-cream truck, finds he can be useful at a fire by supplying a rewarding treat to the fire fighters. (Rev: BL 7/99; HB 5–6/99; HBG 10/99; SLJ 6/99)

1543 Sasso, Sandy Eisenberg. *God Said Amen* (1–3). Illus. by Avi Katz. 2000, Jewish Lights $16.95 (1-58023-080-6). Two children are able to settle the differences between their two kingdoms so that each kingdom can profit from the strengths of the other. (Rev: SLJ 3/01)

1544 Say, Allen. *River Dream* (1–3). Illus. by author. 1988, Houghton $14.95 (0-395-48294-1); paper $6.95 (0-395-65749-0). 32pp. In a dream, Mark learns you don't need to kill fish to enjoy fishing. (Rev: HB 11–12/88)

1545 Schaap, Martine. *Mop to the Rescue* (PS–K). Illus. by Alex de Wolf. 1999, Front Street $15.95 (0-8126-0167-X). 40pp. Seven short stories for the very young about a lovable sheepdog named Mop. (Rev: BL 5/1/99; HBG 10/99; SLJ 11/99)

1546 Schaap, Martine. *Mop's Backyard Concert* (PS–1). Illus. by Alex de Wolf. Series: Mop and Family. 2000, McGraw-Hill $12.95 (1-57768-892-9). 30pp. Twins Julie and Justin lose their dog Mop in a park only to find him singing in a six-piece band. Also enjoy *Mop's Treasure Hunt*. (Rev: BCCB 1/01; HBG 3/01; SLJ 3/01)

1547 Schaefer, Carole L. *The Squiggle* (PS–1). Illus. by Pierre Morgan. 1996, Crown LB $18.99 (0-517-70048-4). 30pp. In a young Chinese girl's imagination, a piece of red string becomes all sorts of wonderful things. (Rev: BCCB 2/97; BL 12/1/96*; SLJ 12/96*)

1548 Scheidl, Gerda M. *Andy's Wild Animal Adventure* (1–3). Trans. by J. Alison James. Illus. 1997, North-South LB $13.88 (1-55858-798-5). 47pp. Andy draws pictures of a lion, an elephant, and a parrot, and miraculously they come to life. (Rev: BL 11/15/97; HBG 3/98)

1549 Schneider, Howie. *Chewy Louie* (PS–1). Illus. 2000, Rising Moon $15.95 (0-87358-765-0). 32pp. Louie can't stop chewing things, but when he starts on the family car and the house, his family must act to stop him. (Rev: BL 8/00; HBG 10/00; SLJ 11/00)

1550 Schubert, Ingrid, and Dieter Schubert. *Abracadabra* (PS–1). Illus. 1997, Front Street $15.95 (1-886910-17-0). 32pp. Macrobius the Magician delights in causing confusion by having animals exchange body parts. (Rev: BL 7/97)

1551 Schwartz, Roslyn. *The Mole Sisters and the Piece of Moss* (PS–K). Illus. by author. Series: The Mole Sisters. 1999, Annick LB $14.95 (1-55037-583-0); paper $4.95 (1-55037-582-2). The mole sisters find an unhappy piece of moss and take it on an adventure. Also use *The Mole Sisters and the Rainy Day* (1999). (Rev: SLJ 2/00)

1552 Scieszka, Jon. *The Good, the Bad and the Goofy* (2–5). Illus. by Lane Smith. 1992, Viking $14.99 (0-670-84380-6). 70pp. There are many near escapes when Joe, Fred, and Sam are taken back in time to 1868 and the days of the Chisholm Trail. (Rev: SLJ 7/92)

1553 Scruggs, Afi-Odelia. *Jump Rope Magic* (PS–4). Illus. by David Diaz. 2000, Scholastic $16.95 (0-590-69327-1). 40pp. This picture book incorporates a number of jump rope rhymes into the story of friends who love skipping rope in spite of a neighbor who hates to hear the noise. (Rev: BCCB 6/00; BL 2/1/00; HBG 10/00; SLJ 4/00)

1554 Seabrooke, Brenda. *The Swan's Gift* (PS–3). Illus. by Wenhai Ma. 1995, Candlewick $15.95 (1-56402-360-5). 32pp. A starving farmer is rewarded when he refuses to shoot a beautiful swan for food. (Rev: BL 12/15/95)

1555 Seibold, J. Otto, and V. L. Walsh. *Penguin Dreams* (K–3). Illus. 1999, Chronicle $13.95 (0-8118-2558-2). 32pp. A penguin dreams of a fabulous flight he would like to take into outer space and through the ocean depths. (Rev: BL 9/15/99; HBG 3/00; SLJ 1/00)

1556 Sendak, Maurice. *Kenny's Window* (K–3). Illus. by author. 1956, HarperCollins $13.95 (0-06-025494-7); paper $7.95 (0-06-443209-2). 64pp. Kenny remembers a garden he has been dreaming about.

1557 Sendak, Maurice. *Maurice Sendak's Really Rosie* (1–4). Illus. by author. 1975, HarperCollins paper $11.95 (0-06-443138-X). 48pp. A book based on the TV presentation, including seven songs used in the program.

1558 Sendak, Maurice. *Outside Over There* (PS–3). Illus. by author. 1981, HarperCollins paper $8.95 (0-06-443185-1). 40pp. Goblins steal Ira's baby sister and leave another made of ice.

1559 Sendak, Maurice. *Very Far Away* (PS–2). Illus. by author. 1957, HarperCollins LB $16.89 (0-06-025515-3). 56pp. Martin decides to go away after his mother doesn't have time to answer his questions.

1560 Sendak, Maurice. *Where the Wild Things Are* (K–3). Illus. by author. 1988, HarperCollins LB $16.89 (0-06-025493-9); paper $6.95 (0-06-443178-9). 48pp. The few moments' wild reverie of a small unruly boy who has been sent supperless to his room. Caldecott Medal winner, 1964.

1561 Seuss, Dr. *And to Think That I Saw It on Mulberry Street* (K–3). Illus. by author. 1989, Random LB $15.99 (0-394-94494-1). 32pp. A rhyme about what Marco saw on Mulberry Street.

1562 Seuss, Dr. *Bartholomew and the Oobleck* (K–2). Illus. by author. 1949, Random LB $12.99 (0-394-90075-8). What happens when sticky green stuff begins falling instead of snow? Also use: *McElligot's Pool* (1947).

1563 Seuss, Dr. *The Butter Battle Book* (K–2). Illus. by author. 1984, Random LB $14.99 (0-394-96580-9). 48pp. A warning about the nuclear arms race in words and pictures.

1564 Seuss, Dr. *The 500 Hats of Bartholomew Cubbins* (K–2). Illus. by author. 1989, Random $15.99 (0-394-94484-4). 48pp. What happened when Bartholomew couldn't take his hat off before the king.

1565 Seuss, Dr. *On Beyond Zebra!* (K–2). Illus. by author. 1955, Random LB $16.99 (0-394-90084-7). A nonsense alphabet that begins after Z.

1566 Shannon, Margaret. *Elvira* (PS–2). Illus. 1993, Ticknor $13.95 (0-395-66597-3). 32pp. A peace-loving dragon leaves home to live with princesses who will appreciate her kindly ways. (Rev: BL 8/93)

1567 Shaw-MacKinnon, Margaret. *Tiktala* (1–3). Illus. by Laszlo Gal. 1996, Holiday $15.95 (0-8234-1221-0). 32pp. In this fantasy, an Inuit girl gains sufficient knowledge and wisdom to become a soapstone carver. (Rev: BL 7/96; HB 7–8/96; SLJ 5/96)

1568 Sheldon, Dyan. *The Whales' Song* (K–3). Illus. by Gary Blythe. 1991, Dial $16.99 (0-8037-0972-2). 32pp. Grandma tells Lilly of a time when whales practically danced on the water. (Rev: BCCB 5/91; BL 6/1/91*; SLJ 7/91)

1569 Shepard, Aaron. *The Legend of Lightning Larry* (K–3). Illus. by Toni Goffe. 1993, Macmillan $14.95 (0-684-19433-3). 32pp. Evil-Eye McNeevil controls the town until Lightning Larry challenges him. (Rev: BL 3/1/93)

1570 Shields, Carol D. *Colors* (1–3). Illus. by Svjetlan Junakovic. Series: Animagicals. 2000, Handprint $9.95 (1-929766-04-1). 24pp. Poems, riddles, illustrations, and flaps are used imaginatively to present colors. Also use in a similar format: *Music* (2000). (Rev: BL 1/1–15/01; HBG 3/01; SLJ 12/00)

1571 Shields, Carol D. *I Wish My Brother Was a Dog* (PS–3). Illus. by Paul Meisel. 1997, Dutton $14.99 (0-525-45464-0). 32pp. In this fantasy, a boy imagines that his baby brother is a dog that he can control and train. (Rev: BL 6/1–15/97; SLJ 7/97)

1572 Shields, Carol D. *Martian Rock* (PS–3). Illus. by Scott Nash. 1999, Candlewick $15.99 (0-7636-0598-0). 40pp. A hilarious tale about three creatures from Mars and their adventures when they come to Earth. (Rev: BL 1/1–15/00; HBG 3/00; SLJ 1/00)

1573 Shipton, Jonathan. *What If?* (PS–1). Illus. by Barbara Nascimbeni. 1999, Dial $15.99 (0-8037-2390-3). A little boy thinks of journeys he might take such as climbing a giant sunflower into the clouds. (Rev: HBG 3/00; SLJ 8/99)

1574 Shulevitz, Uri. *What Is a Wise Bird Like You Doing in a Silly Tale Like This?* (K–4). Illus. 2000, Farrar $16.00 (0-374-38300-6). 40pp. A delightful picture book that contains three intertwining stories involving an emperor, his twin brother, and a very smart bird named Lou. (Rev: BL 8/00*; HB 9–10/00; HBG 3/01; SLJ 8/00)

1575 Siddals, Mary M. *I'll Play With You* (PS–1). Illus. by David Wisniewski. 2000, Clarion $14.00 (0-395-90373-4). 28pp. Children invite various aspects of the natural world like the sun and clouds to come and play with them. (Rev: BCCB 12/00; BL 10/1/00; HBG 3/01; SLJ 11/00)

1576 Silverman, Erica. *Big Pumpkin* (PS–1). Illus. by S. D. Schindler. 1992, Macmillan $16.00 (0-02-782683-X). 32pp. A witch gets help from several friends, including a ghost, a vampire, and a bat, to pick a huge pumpkin in her garden. (Rev: BL 9/1/92; HB 3–4/93; SLJ 9/92)

1577 Silverman, Erica. *Gittel's Hands* (K–3). Illus. by Deborah N. Lattimore. 1996, Troll $14.95 (0-8167-3798-3). 32pp. A beggar, who is the prophet Elijah in disguise, helps a young girl fashion objects from a silver coin. (Rev: BL 5/15/96; HB 7–8/96; SLJ 6/96)

1578 Silverman, Erica. *On the Morn of Mayfest* (PS–3). Illus. by Marla Frazee. 1998, Simon & Schuster $16.00 (0-689-80674-4). 32pp. A fantasy in which a sleepwalking girl leads a parade of people and animals through town on the morning of Mayfest. (Rev: BL 5/15/98; HBG 10/98; SLJ 6/98)

1579 Simon, Carly. *Midnight Farm* (PS–2). Illus. by David Delamare. 1997, Simon & Schuster paper $16.00 (0-689-81237-X). A nighttime fantasy in which twin brothers play with plants and animals that behave like humans — dancing, playing musical instruments, and having fun. (Rev: HBG 3/98; SLJ 9/97)

1580 Sis, Peter. *Fire Truck* (PS–K). Illus. 1998, Greenwillow $14.95 (0-688-15878-1). 24pp. A young boy becomes so obsessed with fire trucks that he becomes one. Only the lure of pancakes can bring him back to his little-boy body. (Rev: BCCB 1/99; BL 9/15/98; HB 9–10/98; HBG 3/99; SLJ 9/98)

1581 Sis, Peter. *Madlenka* (PS–3). Illus. 2000, Farrar $17.00 (0-374-39969-7). 48pp. When Madlenka finds she has a loose tooth, she wanders through her culturally diverse neighborhood telling everyone about her condition in this, at times surreal, picture book. (Rev: BCCB 10/00; BL 9/1/00; HB 9–10/00; HBG 3/01; SLJ 10/00)

1582 Slangerup, Erik Jon. *Dirt Boy* (PS). Illus. by John Manders. 2000, Albert Whitman $15.95 (0-8075-4424-8). 32pp. Fister enjoys playing in the muck with a giant, but when the giant begins to threaten him, Fister runs home for safety and a welcome bath. (Rev: BCCB 5/00; BL 3/1/00; HBG 10/00; SLJ 4/00)

1583 Sloat, Teri. *Farmer Brown Goes Round and Round* (1–3). Illus. by Nadine Bernard Westcott. 1999, DK $15.95 (0-7894-2512-2). 32pp. After a twister, Farmer Brown's animals have switched identities — cows are oinking, sheep are clucking, and so on. Luckily another twister straightens things out. (Rev: BCCB 4/99; BL 3/1/99; HB 3–4/99; HBG 10/99; SLJ 4/99)

1584 Sloat, Teri. *Farmer Brown Shears His Sheep: A Yarn about Wool* (PS–K). Illus. by Nadine Bernard Westcott. 2000, DK $15.95 (0-7894-2637-4). 24pp. After the sheep have been shorn of their wool, they get so cold that Farmer Brown has to knit each one a sweater. (Rev: BL 10/15/00; HB 9–10/00; HBG 3/01; SLJ 10/00)

1585 Small, David. *Imogene's Antlers* (K–2). Illus. by author. 1985, Crown $16.00 (0-517-55564-6); paper $6.99 (0-517-56242-1). 32pp. Imogene wakes up one morning to find she has antlers, which she takes in stride, although her mother doesn't. (Rev: BCCB 5/85; BL 6/1/85; SLJ 4/85)

1586 Small, David. *Paper John* (PS–2). Illus. by author. 1987, Farrar $15.00 (0-374-35738-2); paper $5.95 (0-374-45725-5). 32pp. Gentle John is kind to an evil man who steals money and escapes in John's magnificent kite. (Rev: BCCB 6/87; BL 6/15/87; SLJ 6–7/87)

1587 Smee, Nicola. *The Tusk Fairy* (PS–K). Illus. by author. 1994, BridgeWater paper $3.95 (0-8167-3312-0). When Lizzie's toy elephant begins to unravel, she places it under her pillow, hoping for a visit from the tusk fairy. (Rev: SLJ 8/94)

1588 Smith, Lane. *The Happy Hocky Family* (K–4). Illus. by author. 1993, Viking $13.99 (0-670-85206-6). 60pp. A parody on basal readers that features the Hocky family and the flat repetitious writing style that satirizes the dull Dick and Jane readers. (Rev: SLJ 9/93*)

1589 Sorel, Edward. *Johnny on the Spot* (K–4). Illus. 1998, Simon & Schuster $16.00 (0-689-81293-0). 32pp. When Johnny's ancient radio starts receiving tomorrow's news, he becomes an overnight sensation. (Rev: BL 8/98; HBG 3/99; SLJ 11/98)

1590 Spalding, Andrea. *Sarah May and the New Red Dress* (K–3). Illus. by Janet Wilson. 1999, Orca $14.95 (1-55143-117-3). A little girl wants a red dress and with the help of the West Wind, she gets her wish. (Rev: BL 2/1/99; HBG 10/99; SLJ 6/99)

1591 Speed, Toby. *Brave Potatoes* (PS–3). Illus. by Barry Root. 2000, Putnam $15.99 (0-399-23158-7). 32pp. When prize potatoes at a country fair sneak out for some midway fun, they don't count on Chef Hackemup who is eyeing them for his kitchen in this very funny tale of some gallant spuds. (Rev: BCCB 6/00*; BL 9/15/00; HB 5–6/00; HBG 10/00; SLJ 7/00)

1592 Steig, William. *Caleb and Kate* (PS–3). Illus. by author. 1977, Farrar paper $5.95 (0-374-41038-0). 32pp. Because he constantly quarrels with his wife, Caleb is transformed into a dog by a witch.

1593 Steig, William. *The Toy Brother* (K–4). Illus. 1996, HarperCollins LB $14.89 (0-06-205079-6). 32pp. In this tale set in the Middle Ages, Yorick accidentally shrinks himself until he becomes his younger brother's favorite toy. (Rev: BCCB 2/96; BL 2/15/96; HB 5–6/96; SLJ 2/96*)

1594 Steig, William. *Wizzil* (K–4). Illus. by Quentin Blake. 2000, Farrar $16.00 (0-374-38466-5). 32pp. A rollicking story about Wizzil the witch and her revenge for almost being killed by farmer DeWitt Frimp. (Rev: BCCB 10/00; BL 10/1/00*; HB 7–8/00; HBG 3/01; SLJ 8/00)

1595 Stevenson, James. *Rolling Rose* (PS). Illus. 1992, Greenwillow LB $15.93 (0-688-10675-7). 24pp. No one pays attention to baby Rose in her rolling walker, so she just rolls out the door for adventure. (Rev: BL 3/1/92*; SLJ 6/92)

1596 Stewart, Sarah. *The Money Tree* (PS). Illus. by David Small. 1991, Farrar $16.00 (0-374-35014-0). 32pp. Miss McGillicuddy's pleasant life is interrupted when a strange tree begins blooming with paper money. (Rev: BCCB 12/91*; BL 10/15/91; HB 1–2/92; SLJ 1/92)

1597 Stewig, John W. *Clever Gretchen* (K–3). Illus. by Patricia Wittmann. 2000, Marshall Cavendish $15.95 (0-7614-5066-1). 32pp. In order to win the bride of his choice, young Hans must promise to obey a goat-footed man after a period of seven years. (Rev: BL 9/15/00; HBG 3/01; SLJ 10/00)

1598 Stewig, John W. *The Moon's Choice* (K–3). Illus. by Jan Palmer. 1993, Simon & Schuster paper $15.00 (0-671-76962-6). A silly girl is rescued from her mean-spirited sisters by the moon in this fantasy. (Rev: SLJ 9/93)

1599 Stone, Phoebe. *When the Wind Bears Go Dancing* (PS–1). Illus. 1997, Little, Brown $15.95 (0-316-81701-5). 32pp. While the wind makes noises outside, a little girl dreams of dancing with five white bears in the midnight sky. (Rev: BL 1/1–15/98; HBG 3/98; SLJ 1/98)

1600 *Stories and Fun for the Very Young* (PS). Illus. 1998, Candlewick $19.99 (0-7636-0575-1). 64pp. This large-size anthology contains some complete picture books and excerpts from others, all by well-known writers like Anthony Browne, Helen Oxenbury, and Rosemary Wells. (Rev: BL 11/1/98; HBG 3/99; SLJ 2/99)

1601 *Stories for Me! A Read-Aloud Treasury for Young Children* (PS–K). Illus. 1998, Candlewick $19.99 (0-7636-0267-1). 96pp. This book contains a sampling of 30 favorite picture books from Britain by such authors as Helen Oxenbury, Martin Waddell, and Shirley Hughes. (Rev: BL 4/15/98; HBG 10/98; SLJ 6/98)

1602 Strete, Craig Kee. *The Lost Boy and the Monster* (PS–3). Illus. by Steve Johnson and Lou Fancher. 1999, Putnam $15.99 (0-399-22922-1). 32pp. A Native American boy in the Southwest befriends a rattlesnake and a scorpion that help him escape a monster who wants to eat his feet. (Rev: BCCB 6/99; BL 7/99; HB 5–6/99; HBG 10/99; SLJ 7/99)

1603 Strom, Maria Diaz. *Rainbow Joe and Me* (1–3). Illus. 1999, Lee & Low $15.95 (1-880000-93-8). 32pp. In this picture book, using African American characters, a blind musician shows painter Eloise how he creates colors through his music. (Rev: BL 11/15/99; HBG 3/00; SLJ 11/99)

1604 Sturges, Philemon. *Crocky Dilly* (1–4). Illus. by Paige Miglio. 1998, Museum of Fine Arts, Boston $14.95 (0-87846-458-1). 32pp. This story tells how, in ancient Egypt, the crocodile became known as the Queen of the Nile. (Rev: BL 4/1/99; SLJ 5/99)

1605 Sun, Chyng Feng. *Cat and Cat-face* (K–3). Illus. by Lesley Liu. 1996, Houghton $14.95 (0-395-72038-9). 32pp. A pansy (known as "Cat-face" in Chinese) and a real cat become friends in spite of their differences. (Rev: BL 3/15/96; SLJ 4/96)

1606 Sweeten, Sami. *Wolf* (K–2). Illus. by author. 1994, Albert Whitman LB $14.95 (0-8075-9160-2). One day, Leon meets a wolf who conveniently eats everything that the boy dislikes. (Rev: SLJ 7/94)

1607 Swope, Sam. *The Krazees* (PS–K). Illus. by Eric Brace. 1997, Farrar $16.00 (0-374-34281-4). 32pp. In this wild romp, Iggie gets the Krazees on wet gray days, and soon the Krazees take over the house. (Rev: BL 11/15/97; HBG 3/98; SLJ 12/97)

1608 Taber, Anthony. *The Boy Who Stopped Time* (K–3). Illus. by author. 1993, Macmillan $13.95 (0-689-50460-8). 32pp. Annoyed that he has to go to bed so early, Julian stops the family clock — and time. (Rev: BL 3/1/93)

1609 Tafuri, Nancy. *What the Sun Sees/What the Moon Sees* (PS–K). Illus. 1997, Greenwillow LB $15.93 (0-688-14494-2). 32pp. Two contrasting stories — one from the sun's point of view and the other from the moon's — are told, beginning from opposite covers of this book. (Rev: BL 11/15/97; HBG 3/98; SLJ 10/97)

1610 Talbott, Hudson. *O'Sullivan Stew: A Tale Cooked Up in Ireland* (K–3). Illus. 1999, Putnam $15.99 (0-399-23162-5). 32pp. In this tall tale set in Ireland, imaginative Kate O'Sullivan tells stories to bargain for her life after being arrested because she tried to free a captured horse. (Rev: BL 2/1/99; HBG 10/99; SLJ 1/99)

1611 Tamar, Erika. *Donnatalee* (K–3). Illus. by Barbara Lambase. 1998, Harcourt $16.00 (0-15-200386-X). 32pp. When young Kate enters the water at the beach, she suddenly becomes a mermaid and is able to swim with the goldfish and ride a sea horse. (Rev: BL 10/15/98; HBG 10/98; SLJ 6/98)

1612 Tavares, Matt. *Zachary's Ball* (K–4). Illus. 2000, Candlewick $15.99 (0-7636-0730-4). 32pp. Young Zachary is magically transported to the pitcher's mound at Boston's Fenway Park, where his next pitch will determine the outcome of an exciting game. (Rev: BCCB 5/00; BL 4/15/00; HBG 10/00; SLJ 8/00)

1613 Taylor, Alastair. *Swollobog* (1–3). Illus. 2001, Houghton $15.00 (0-618-04348-9). 32pp. Swollobog, an ugly dog who eats everything, meets her match when she swallows a helium balloon and takes off. (Rev: BL 3/15/01)

1614 Tazewell, Charles. *The Littlest Angel* (PS–3). Illus. by Paul Micich. 1991, Ideals $16.95 (0-8249-8516-8). 32pp. A young angel in heaven keeps getting into trouble because there is nothing to do. (Rev: BL 9/15/91; SLJ 10/98)

1615 Teague, Mark. *The Lost and Found* (K–2). Illus. 1998, Scholastic $15.95 (0-590-84619-1).

32pp. Mischievous Wendell and Floyd enter an unknown world when they disappear into their school's lost-and-found box. (Rev: BL 7/98; HBG 3/99; SLJ 9/98)

1616 Teague, Mark. *The Secret Shortcut* (PS–3). Illus. 1996, Scholastic $15.95 (0-590-67714-4). 32pp. Pirates, space aliens, and a plague of frogs are only three of the obstacles that prevent Wendell and Floyd from getting to school on time. (Rev: BL 9/15/96; SLJ 11/96)

1617 Thayer, Jane. *Gus Loves His Happy Home* (PS–2). Illus. by Seymour Fleishman. 1989, Shoe String LB $17.50 (0-208-02249-X). With time on his hands, Gus the Friendly Ghost goes for a ride on the tail of a kite. (Rev: BL 2/15/90; SLJ 2/90)

1618 Thiel, Elizabeth. *The Polka Dot Horse* (PS). Illus. by Terry Milne. 1993, Simon & Schuster paper $14.00 (0-671-79419-1). 28pp. A discarded toy sets out to find a new home. (Rev: BL 1/15/93; SLJ 4/93)

1619 Thomas, Frances. *What If?* (PS–2). Illus. by Ross Collins. 1999, Hyperion $15.99 (0-7868-0482-3). 32pp. Little Monster scares itself with fantasies involving giant spiders and falling — until Mom takes over and calms the youngster with pleasant experiences. (Rev: BCCB 9/99; BL 7/99; HBG 3/00)

1620 *Thomas Goes to the Circus* (PS). Illus. by Josie Yee. 2000, Random $2.99 (0-375-80240-1). 6pp. In this board book, Thomas the Tank Engine visits a circus and enjoys its sounds, sights, and smells. Two others titles in this series are *Thomas Takes a Trip* and *Thomas' Busy Day*. (Rev: BL 4/1/00)

1621 Thomassie, Tynia. *Feliciana Meets d'Loup Garou* (1–3). Illus. by Cat B. Smith. 1998, Little, Brown $15.95 (0-316-84133-1). 32pp. Left at home for her misdeeds, Feliciana tiptoes to a nearby swamp where she encounters a hairy werewolf who teaches her how to howl. (Rev: BCCB 6/98; BL 4/15/98; HBG 10/98; SLJ 4/98)

1622 Thompson, Richard. *The Follower* (PS–3). Illus. by Martin Springett. 2000, Fitzhenry & Whiteside $15.95 (1-55041-532-8). 32pp. A picture-book poem about a witch who is being followed by a creature that the reader can detect hidden in the illustrations. (Rev: BL 12/15/00; SLJ 12/00)

1623 Tibo, Gilles. *Simon and the Snowflakes* (PS–1). Illus. 1991, Tundra paper $4.95 (0-88776-274-3). 24pp. Young Simon likes to count snowflakes as they come down. (Rev: BL 12/15/88; SLJ 4/89)

1624 Tompert, Ann. *Grandfather Tang's Story* (K–3). Illus. by Robert Andrew Parker. 1990, Crown LB $17.99 (0-517-57272-9). 32pp. As a Chinese grandfather tells his granddaughter a tale about two foxes, he arranges Chinese puzzles to form the animals' shapes. (Rev: BCCB 4/90; BL 4/15/90; SLJ 5/90)

1625 Trottier, Maxine. *Dreamstones* (K–3). Illus. by Stella East. 2000, Stoddart $14.95 (0-7737-3191-1). 22pp. Fantasy and reality blend in this story about a boy who is spending the winter in the Far North with his father and is helped by a mysterious

stranger when he gets lost. (Rev: BL 7/00; SLJ 8/00)

1626 Tucker, Kathy. *Do Knights Take Naps?* (PS–1). Illus. by Nick Sharratt. 2000, Albert Whitman $15.95 (0-8075-1695-3). 32pp. A humorous rhyming story about knights and their activities, the most important being a nap after lunch. (Rev: BL 3/15/00; HBG 10/00; SLJ 4/00)

1627 Tulloch, Shirley. *Who Made Me?* (PS–1). Illus. by Cathie Felstead. 2000, Augsburg $16.99 (0-8066-4045-6). 32pp. Different jungle animals give different answers to a little black girl who asks "Who made me?" And she discovers that all of them are correct. (Rev: BL 4/15/00; HBG 10/00; SLJ 8/00)

1628 Turner, Ann. *Secrets from the Dollhouse* (PS–3). Illus. by Raul Colon. 2000, HarperCollins LB $15.89 (0-06-024567-0). 32pp. This is the story, told in free verse, of a family that inhabits a doll house and how their lives are controlled by the Girl, Boy, and Cat who play with them. (Rev: BL 1/1–15/00*; HBG 10/00; SLJ 2/00)

1629 Tusa, Tricia. *Maebelle's Suitcase* (PS–1). Illus. by author. 1987, Macmillan paper $5.99 (0-689-71444-0). 32pp. An offbeat picture book concerning a 108-year-old woman who lives in a treehouse. (Rev: BCCB 7–8/87; BL 4/1/87; SLJ 6–7/87)

1630 *The 20th Century Children's Book Treasury: Celebrated Picture Books and Stories to Read Aloud* (PS–3). Ed. by Janet Schulman. Illus. 1998, Knopf $40.00 (0-679-88647-8). 308pp. This anthology (a good introduction to children's literature for parents) condenses in size and shape 44 important picture books by such artists as Maurice Sendak, Wanda Gág, and Shirley Hughes. (Rev: BL 10/15/98; HB 11–12/98; HBG 3/99; SLJ 12/98)

1631 Tzannes, Robin. *Professor Puffendorf's Secret Potions* (K–4). Illus. by Korky Paul. 1992, Checkerboard $16.95 (1-56288-267-8). 36pp. A scientist's secret potions are used in her absence by her lazy assistant, Slag. (Rev: BL 2/1/93)

1632 Udry, Janice May. *The Moon Jumpers* (K–2). Illus. by Maurice Sendak. 1959, HarperCollins $15.00 (0-06-026145-5). 32pp. The pleasure and enjoyment of four children as they dance in the moonlight.

1633 Uhlberg, Myron. *Mad Dog McGraw* (PS–2). Illus. by Lydia Monks. 2000, Putnam $15.99 (0-399-23308-3). 32pp. The young narrator is afraid of Mad Dog McGraw, the meanest dog around, but the boy's cat tames him with kindness. (Rev: BCCB 7–8/00; BL 8/00; HBG 3/01; SLJ 8/00)

1634 Ulmer, Wendy K. *A Campfire for Cowboy Billy* (1–3). Illus. by Kenneth J. Spengler. 1997, Northland LB $15.95 (0-87358-681-6). 32pp. Growing up in a big city, little Billy imagines all the sights around him are really part of the Old West, like making a "curbside food stand," a chuck wagon. (Rev: BL 12/1/97; HBG 3/98; SLJ 1/98)

1635 Ungerer, Tomi. *Tortoni Tremolo: The Cursed Musician* (K–3). Illus. 1998, Roberts Rinehart $16.95 (1-57098-226-0). 32pp. A fantasy about a musician whose musical notes turn into edible nuggets. (Rev: BL 1/1–15/99; HBG 10/99)

1636 U'Ren, Andrea. *Pugdog* (PS–3). Illus. 2001, Farrar $16.00 (0-374-36149-5). 32pp. When Mike discovers that his dog, Pug, is female he begins treating her differently and that makes Pug miserable. (Rev: BL 3/1/01)

1637 Vainio, Pirkko. *The Dream House* (K–3). Trans. by J. Alison James. Illus. by author. 1997, North-South LB $15.88 (1-55858-750-0). The land on which Lucas is building his dream house is so small that he must stack the rooms. (Rev: HBG 3/98; SLJ 1/98)

1638 Van Allsburg, Chris. *Bad Day at Riverbend* (K–3). Illus. 1995, Houghton $17.95 (0-395-67347-X). 32pp. This book, set in the Old West, is about a strange light that freezes everything that it touches. (Rev: BCCB 9/95; BL 10/15/95; SLJ 10/95)

1639 Van Allsburg, Chris. *Ben's Dream* (2–4). Illus. by author. 1982, Houghton $16.95 (0-395-32084-4). 32pp. Ben dreams that he is in a flood and passing the great landmarks of the world.

1640 Van Allsburg, Chris. *Jumanji* (1–4). Illus. by author. 1981, Houghton $17.95 (0-395-30448-2). A board game that two children play brings out a jungle world. Caldecott Medal winner, 1982.

1641 Van Allsburg, Chris. *Just a Dream* (K–3). Illus. 1990, Houghton $17.95 (0-395-53308-2). 48pp. Walter, who doesn't recycle his trash, takes a trip into the future and finds the situation bleak. (Rev: BCCB 11/90; BL 10/15/90; HB 1–2/91; SLJ 12/90)

1642 Van Allsburg, Chris. *The Stranger* (K–2). Illus. by author. 1986, Houghton $18.00 (0-395-42331-7). 32pp. Farmer Bailey hits a man with his car and brings him home. Autumn is unaccountably delayed until the strange man departs. (Rev: BL 10/1/86; HB 11–12/86; SLJ 11/86)

1643 Van Allsburg, Chris. *The Widow's Broom* (K–2). Illus. 1992, Houghton $17.95 (0-395-64051-2). 32pp. In this tale of good and evil, a witch's broom falls from the sky with the witch still on it. (Rev: BCCB 10/92*; BL 9/15/92*; HB 1–2/93; SLJ 11/92*)

1644 Van Allsburg, Chris. *The Wretched Stone* (K–3). Illus. 1991, Houghton $17.95 (0-395-53307-4). 32pp. A magical stone that some sailors find turns them into monkeys. (Rev: BCCB 11/91; BL 10/1/91; HB 1–2/92*; SLJ 11/91)

1645 Van Camp, Richard. *A Man Called Raven* (K–3). Illus. by George Littlechild. 1997, Children's Book Pr. $15.95 (0-89239-144-8). A man appears to two boys who have injured a raven and tells them the story of the terrible consequences that befell a man who did the same thing. (Rev: SLJ 6/97)

1646 Vande Velde, Vivian. *Troll Teacher* (PS–3). Illus. by Mary Jane Auch. 2000, Holiday $16.95 (0-8234-1503-1). 32pp. Elizabeth and her classmates can't convince anyone that their new teacher, Miss Turtledove, is really a mean old troll. (Rev: BL 11/15/00; HBG 3/01; SLJ 10/00)

1647 Van Dusen, Chris. *Down to the Sea with Mr. Magee* (K–4). Illus. 2000, Chronicle $13.95 (0-8118-2499-3). 32pp. Mr. Magee and his little dog, Dee, are shipwrecked by a playful whale and find themselves on top of a huge spruce tree. (Rev: BCCB 5/00; BL 6/1–15/00; HBG 10/00; SLJ 5/00)

1648 Van Leeuwen, Jean. *The Strange Adventures of Blue Dog* (K–2). Illus. by Marco Ventura. 1999, Dial LB $15.99 (0-8037-1878-0). Big Billy is attached to Blue Dog, a toy dog, even when he gets a real dog for a pet. (Rev: HBG 10/99; SLJ 7/99)

1649 Varvasovszky, Laszlo. *Henry in Shadowland* (1–4). Illus. 1990, Godine $17.95 (0-87923-785-6). Henry enters his shadow-box theater world to find the king of Shadowland. (Rev: SLJ 2/91)

1650 Vaughan, Marcia. *Dorobo the Dangerous* (K–2). Illus. by Kazuko Stone. Series: Animal Fair. 1994, Silver Burdett LB $14.95 (0-382-24070-7); paper $4.95 (0-382-24453-2). This fantasy with a Japanese setting tells how a young girl sets out to find the culprit that is stealing her fish. (Rev: SLJ 1/95)

1651 Vaughan, Richard Lee. *Eagle Boy: A Pacific Northwest Native Tale* (PS–3). Illus. by Lee Christiansen. 2000, Sasquatch $16.95 (1-57061-171-8). 32pp. When Eagle Boy is left behind by his people, the eagles with whom he has shared his fishing catch bring him food. (Rev: BL 1/1–15/01; SLJ 12/00)

1652 Vesey, Amanda. *The Princess and the Frog* (K–3). Illus. by author. 1985, Little, Brown $14.95 (0-316-90036-2). 32pp. Unlike the Grimm Brothers' tale, this frog remains a frog even after the princess's kiss. (Rev: BCCB 5/85; HB 3–4/86; SLJ 1/86)

1653 Vigna, Judith. *Boot Weather* (PS–K). Illus. by author. 1989, Whitman LB $14.95 (0-8075-0837-3). 32pp. Kim puts on her boots to play in the snow and imagines all sorts of exciting adventures. (Rev: BCCB 2/89; BL 3/1/89; SLJ 5/89)

1654 Vigna, Judith. *Uncle Alfredo's Zoo* (K–3). Illus. 1994, Albert Whitman LB $14.95 (0-8075-8292-1). 32pp. A miracle restores the collection of stone animals to the front of the house formerly owned by Anna's deceased uncle. (Rev: BL 5/1/94; SLJ 6/94)

1655 Vivian, Bart. *Imagine* (1–3). Illus. 1998, Beyond Words $14.95 (1-885223-72-2). 32pp. This book invites daydreamers to think about what everyday objects could become and what the future might bring — with a little imagination. (Rev: BL 10/1/98; HBG 3/99; SLJ 12/98)

1656 Waber, Bernard. *You're a Little Kid with a Big Heart* (PS–2). Illus. by author. 1980, Houghton $14.95 (0-395-29163-1). A little girl is granted her wish — to be an adult.

1657 Waddell, Martin. *The Hollyhock Wall* (PS–3). Illus. by Salley Mavor. 1999, Candlewick $15.99 (1-56402-902-6). 32pp. Mary's rock garden comes to life and there she meets a new friend, Tom. Later, when she visits her grandmother, she meets the real Tom. (Rev: BCCB 10/99; BL 8/99; HBG 10/99; SLJ 7/99)

1658 Waddell, Martin. *Tom Rabbit* (PS). Illus. by Barbara Firth. 2001, Candlewick $15.99 (0-7636-

1089-5). 32pp. When his owner doesn't come to retrieve him, the little stuffed animal named Tom Rabbit is certain he has been abandoned. (Rev: BL 3/1/01)

1659 Wagerin, Walter. *Probity Jones and the Fear Not Angel* (PS–2). Illus. by Tim Ladwig. 1996, Augsburg $16.99 (0-8066-2992-4). 32pp. When Probity is too sick to appear in a Christmas pageant, an angel takes her to witness what she is missing. (Rev: BL 12/15/96)

1660 Wahl, Jan. *Once When the World Was Green* (1–4). Illus. by Fabricio Vandenbroeck. 1996, Tricycle Pr. $14.95 (1-883672-12-0). 32pp. When a Mayan farmer begins killing the animals around him to clothe himself, eagles respond by stealing his son. (Rev: BL 5/1/96; SLJ 7/96)

1661 Wakefield, Ali. *Those Calculating Crows!* (K–2). Illus. by Christy Hale. 1996, Simon & Schuster paper $16.00 (0-689-80483-0). 28pp. A farmer and his wife are outwitted by crows intent on eating small corn plants. (Rev: BL 11/15/96; SLJ 12/96)

1662 Waldman, Neil. *The Starry Night* (PS–2). Illus. 1999, Boyds Mills $15.95 (1-56397-736-2). 32pp. Bernard takes an artist named Vincent around New York City to find a suitable scene to paint, and in turn, Vincent takes Bernard to the Museum of Modern Art and shows him *Starry Night* before disappearing. Could it have been Vincent van Gogh? (Rev: BCCB 1/00; BL 11/1/99; HBG 3/00; SLJ 10/99)

1663 Wallace, Karen. *Scarlette Beane* (PS–1). Illus. by Jon Berkeley. 2000, Dial $15.99 (0-8037-2475-6). 32pp. Scarlette Beane is such a great gardener that she grows a vegetable palace into which she and her family move. (Rev: BCCB 3/00; BL 1/1–15/00; HBG 10/00; SLJ 3/00)

1664 Walter, Mildred P. *Brother to the Wind* (K–2). Illus. by Leo Dillon and Diane Dillon. 1985, Lothrop LB $15.93 (0-688-03812-3). 32pp. A folklike tale set in Africa about a boy who wants to fly. (Rev: BCCB 3/85; HB 7–8/85; SLJ 5/85)

1665 Walton, Rick. *Noah's Square Dance* (PS–3). Illus. by Thor Wickstrom. 1995, Lothrop $16.00 (0-688-11186-6). 32pp. Noah acts as caller during a square dance involving the animals on his ark. (Rev: BL 9/1/95; SLJ 10/95)

1666 Warner, Sunny. *Madison Finds a Line* (PS–2). Illus. by author. 1999, Houghton $15.00 (0-395-88508-6). 32pp. Madison and her cat, Caspar, follow a piece of rope and enter a fantasy land of wonder and adventure. (Rev: HBG 3/00; SLJ 1/00)

1667 Watts, Irene N. *The Fish Princess* (1–3). Illus. by Steve Mennie. 1996, Tundra $17.95 (0-88776-366-9). A young girl, rescued from the sea by a fisherman, is accused of bringing bad luck to the villagers. (Rev: SLJ 3/97)

1668 Wayland, April Halprin. *To Rabbittown* (PS–1). Illus. by Robin Spowart. 1989, Scholastic paper $3.95 (0-590-44777-7). 32pp. A poem about a girl and her pet rabbit and their journey. (Rev: BL 2/1/89; SLJ 4/89)

1669 Weatherby, Mark A. *My Dinosaur* (PS–1). Illus. 1997, Scholastic paper $15.95 (0-590-97203-0). 32pp. A little girl travels through the night sky with her dinosaur before returning to bed. (Rev: BCCB 5/97; BL 3/1/97; SLJ 3/97)

1670 Weeks, Sarah. *Happy Birthday, Frankie* (K–3). Illus. by Warren Linn. 1999, HarperCollins $14.95 (0-06-027965-6). 40pp. A humorous tale in which a zany professor has problems assembling a monster from a do-it-yourself kit. (Rev: BL 1/1–15/00; HBG 3/00; SLJ 9/99)

1671 Weeks, Sarah. *Mrs. McNosh and the Great Big Squash* (PS–K). Illus. by Nadine Bernard Westcott. 2000, HarperFestival $9.95 (0-694-01202-5). 24pp. Mrs. McNosh's squash plant grows out of control but she finds that she can use the giant squash it produces as a house. (Rev: BL 10/1/00; HBG 3/01; SLJ 12/00)

1672 Weilerstein, Sadie R. *K'tonton's Sukkot Adventure* (PS–3). Illus. by Joe Boddy. 1993, Jewish Publication Soc. $12.95 (0-8276-0502-1). A tiny boy disobeys his father and attends Sukkot services in the synagogue by hiding in a small box. (Rev: SLJ 3/94)

1673 Wellington, Monica. *Night House, Bright House* (PS–1). Illus. 1997, Dutton $11.99 (0-525-45491-8). 24pp. When a cat and mice play at night, household objects come alive and talk to them. (Rev: BL 2/1/97; SLJ 4/97)

1674 Westcott, Nadine Bernard. *The Giant Vegetable Garden* (PS–K). Illus. by author. 1981, Little, Brown $14.95 (0-316-93129-2); paper $4.95 (0-316-93130-6). 32pp. A mayor gets his town's residents to grow large vegetables.

1675 Whelan, Gloria. *The Miracle of Saint Nicholas* (PS–3). Illus. by Judith G. Brown. 1997, Ignatius $14.95 (1-883937-18-3). 32pp. After the end of Communism, a young Russian boy who vows to clean up his local church is helped by a miracle. (Rev: BL 11/1/97; HBG 3/98)

1676 Whybrow, Ian. *Harry and the Snow King* (PS–K). Illus. by Adrian Reynolds. 1999, Sterling $14.95 (1-899607-85-4). 32pp. After his tiny snow king melts, Harry is comforted when there is a fresh fall of snow and the yard is full of snow kings. (Rev: BL 7/99; SLJ 6/99)

1677 Whybrow, Ian. *Sammy and the Dinosaurs* (PS–2). Illus. by Adrian Reynolds. 1999, Orchard $15.95 (0-531-30207-5). A charming fantasy about a young boy's attachment to his toy dinosaurs and how he accidentally lost and recovered them. (Rev: BCCB 9/99; HB 9–10/99; HBG 3/00; SLJ 9/99)

1678 Wiesner, David. *June 29, 1999* (PS–3). Illus. 1992, Houghton $15.95 (0-395-59762-5). 32pp. Holly sends small growing vegetables into space in balloons and reaps a fantastic harvest. (Rev: BCCB 11/92; BL 10/15/92; HB 1–2/93*; SLJ 11/92*)

1679 Wiesner, David. *Sector 7* (K–4). Illus. 1999, Clarion $16.00 (0-395-74656-6). 48pp. In an almost wordless fantasy, a young boy who enjoys drawing is taken to a cloud terminal where clouds are hoping they will be made into new exciting shapes. (Rev:

BCCB 1/00*; BL 9/15/99; HB 9–10/99; HBG 3/00; SLJ 9/99)

1680 Wild, Margaret. *Midnight Babies* (PS–K). Illus. by Ann James. 2001, Clarion $15.00 (0-618-10412-7). 32pp. At night, Baby Brenda slips past sleeping Mom and Dad and heads for the Midnight Cafe where the dancing is about to begin. (Rev: BL 2/15/01*)

1681 Wild, Margaret. *The Pocket Dogs* (PS–K). Illus. by Stephen M. King. 2001, Scholastic $15.95 (0-439-23973-7). 32pp. Little dogs Biff and Buff are carried around in the pockets of their master's coat, but Biff slips through a hole in his pocket and finds he is lost in a huge grocery store. (Rev: BCCB 3/01; BL 2/1/01*)

1682 Willard, Nancy. *Pish, Posh, Said Hieronymus Bosch* (K–3). Illus. by Leo Dillon and Diane Dillon. 1991, Harcourt $22.00 (0-15-262210-1). 32pp. Willard's fanciful poem introduces readers to the strange world of grotesque creatures created by Hieronymus Bosch. (Rev: BCCB 12/91; BL 11/15/91; SLJ 12/91*) [811]

1683 Willard, Nancy. *Shadow Story* (1–3). Illus. by David Diaz. 1999, Harcourt $17.00 (0-15-201638-4). 32pp. Using the power she has to create wonderful shadows, Holly Go Lolly defeats the monster Ooboo. (Rev: BCCB 11/99; BL 11/15/99; HB 11–12/99; HBG 3/00; SLJ 11/99)

1684 Willard, Nancy. *The Sorcerer's Apprentice* (1–4). Illus. by Leo Dillon and Diane Dillon. 1993, Scholastic $16.95 (0-590-47329-8). 32pp. Sylvia, the sorcerer's apprentice, is overcome when she is directed to make clothes for the many creatures found in the magician's house. (Rev: BCCB 1/94; BL 11/1/93; SLJ 1/94)

1685 Willard, Nancy. *The Tale I Told Sasha* (K–3). Illus. by David Christiana. 1999, Little, Brown $15.95 (0-316-94115-8). 32pp. A fantasy in which Sasha and her magical yellow ball enter a dreamlike world controlled by the King of Keys. (Rev: BCCB 7–8/99; BL 6/1–15/99*; HBG 10/99; SLJ 6/99)

1686 Williams, Arlene. *Dragon Soup* (K–3). Illus. by Sally J. Smith. 1996, H.J. Kramer $15.95 (0-915811-63-4). 32pp. Tonlu visits the Cloud Dragons to get help in avoiding an arranged marriage. (Rev: BL 7/96; SLJ 6/96)

1687 Williams, Laura E. *The Long Silk Strand* (PS–3). Illus. by Grayce Bochak. 1995, Boyds Mills $15.95 (1-56397-236-0). 32pp. Using a Japanese setting, this is the story of the bond between a girl and her grandmother that is so strong it conquers death. (Rev: BL 2/1/96)

1688 Williams, Linda. *The Little Old Lady Who Was Not Afraid of Anything* (PS–1). Illus. by Megan Lloyd. 1986, HarperCollins LB $15.89 (0-690-04586-7); paper $5.95 (0-06-443183-5). 32pp. The scary tale of a little old woman who comes upon two big shoes in the forest going CLOMP CLOMP all by themselves. (Rev: BCCB 10/86; BL 10/1/86; SLJ 1/87)

1689 Willis, Jeanne. *The Boy Who Lost His Belly Button* (PS–2). Illus. by Tony Ross. 2000, DK $14.95 (0-7894-6164-1). A boy's search for his missing belly button takes him to a jungle where he finds it on the tummy of a crocodile. (Rev: HBG 10/00; SLJ 5/00)

1690 Wilson, Sarah. *Love and Kisses* (PS). Illus. by Melissa Sweet. 1999, Candlewick $9.99 (1-56402-792-9). A circular story in which a little girl kisses a cat who kisses a cow and so on until the kiss is returned to the little girl via the cat. (Rev: HBG 10/99; SLJ 2/99)

1691 Wilson-Max, Ken. *Max's Starry Night* (PS–1). Illus. 2001, Hyperion $14.99 (0-7868-0553-6). 32pp. Max, a little boy, and his friends — an elephant named Blue and a pig named Little Pink — look at the night sky and wish upon a star. (Rev: BL 1/1–15/01; SLJ 3/01)

1692 Winch, John. *The Old Man Who Loved to Sing* (PS–3). Illus. 1996, Scholastic paper $5.99 (0-590-22641-X). 40pp. The animals in the valley are unhappy when their neighbor, an old man, stops serenading them. (Rev: BL 4/15/96; HB 7–8/96; SLJ 4/96)

1693 Winch, John. *The Old Woman Who Loved to Read* (PS–1). Illus. 1997, Holiday $16.95 (0-8234-1281-4); paper $6.95 (0-8234-1348-9). 32pp. An old woman buys a farmhouse in which to retire and read, but she finds unexpected chores awaiting her. (Rev: BL 3/1/97; SLJ 5/97)

1694 Winthrop, Elizabeth. *A Very Noisy Girl* (PS–K). Illus. by Ellen Weiss. 1991, Holiday LB $14.95 (0-8234-0858-2). When Elizabeth's mother asks her to be quiet, Elizabeth responds by turning herself into a dog. (Rev: SLJ 5/91)

1695 Wisniewski, David. *Tough Cookie* (K–3). Illus. 1999, Lothrop $16.00 (0-688-15337-2). 32pp. A parody on hard-boiled detective novels, this story involves Tough Cookie, his former girlfriend, Pecan Sandy, and Cookie's old partner, Chips, who has been badly hurt by Fingers. (Rev: BL 11/1/99; HBG 3/00; SLJ 9/99)

1696 Wolf, Jake. *And Then What?* (PS–1). Illus. by Marylin Hafner. 1993, Greenwillow LB $13.93 (0-688-10286-7). 32pp. After each of Mother's explanations of the day's activities, Willy exclaims "And then what?" until she runs out of activities. (Rev: BL 12/1/93; SLJ 12/93)

1697 Wolff, Ferida. *Seven Loaves of Bread* (K–4). Illus. by Katie Keller. 1993, Morrow LB $15.93 (0-688-11112-2). 32pp. Rose does a poor job when she takes over the bread-baking chores that Milly has to abandon because of illness. (Rev: BL 9/15/93; SLJ 11/93*)

1698 Wolff, Patricia R. *The Toll-Bridge Troll* (PS–2). Illus. by Kimberly B. Root. 1995, Harcourt $15.00 (0-15-277665-6). 24pp. Trigg outwits a troll who demands a toll for crossing the bridge that leads to Trigg's school. (Rev: BL 4/15/95; HB 9–10/95; SLJ 6/95)

1699 Wood, Audrey. *The Bunyans* (K–3). Illus. by David Shannon. 1996, Scholastic $15.95 (0-590-48089-8). 32pp. Meet the rest of the Bunyan family, including two gigantic children. (Rev: BCCB 1/97; BL 9/15/96; SLJ 12/96*)

1700 Wood, Audrey. *Elbert's Bad Word* (PS–1). Illus. by author. 1988, Harcourt $15.00 (0-15-225320-3). 32pp. A bad word flies into Elbert's mouth, which gets him in trouble, so he goes to the local wizard for help. (Rev: BL 10/1/88; HB 1–2/89; SLJ 10/88)

1701 Wood, Audrey. *The Rude Giants* (PS–3). Illus. 1993, Harcourt $13.95 (0-15-269412-9). 32pp. Clever Gerda convinces two dirty, ugly, rude giants to clean up the castle before they eat everybody. (Rev: BCCB 6/93; BL 3/1/93*; SLJ 5/93)

1702 Wood, Audrey. *Sweet Dream Pie* (PS–2). Illus. by Mark Teague. 1998, Scholastic $15.95 (0-590-96204-3). 32pp. Eating too much of Ma Brindle's delicious pie will give one nightmares, and unfortunately everyone but Ma Brindle overindulges. (Rev: BCCB 3/98; BL 2/15/98; HBG 10/98; SLJ 3/98)

1703 Wood, Audrey. *Tickleoctopus* (PS–1). Illus. by Don Wood. 1994, Harcourt $16.00 (0-15-287000-8). 46pp. A young cave boy discovers a friendly monster who tickles him; and for the first time in human history, a smile is born. (Rev: BCCB 7–8/94; BL 3/1/94; SLJ 5/94)

1704 Wood, Audrey, and Mark Teague. *The Flying Dragon Room* (PS–3). Illus. 1996, Scholastic $14.95 (0-590-48193-2). 32pp. With a set of tools he has been given, young Patrick creates a fantastic home, complete with a friendly dinosaur. (Rev: BL 4/1/96*; SLJ 3/96)

1705 Wood, Audrey, and Don Wood. *Piggies* (PS–K). Illus. by Don Wood. 1991, Harcourt $16.00 (0-15-256341-5). 32pp. Fingers can become piggies in this imaginative book with elaborate artwork. (Rev: BCCB 4/91*; BL 3/1/91*; SLJ 5/91*)

1706 Woodruff, Elvira. *The Wing Shop* (PS–2). Illus. by Stephen Gammell. 1991, Holiday LB $16.95 (0-8234-0825-6). 32pp. In an effort to get back to the street where he once lived, Matthew tries to fly with a variety of wings. (Rev: BCCB 6/91; BL 3/15/91; HB 5–6/91; SLJ 11/91)

1707 Yaccarino, Dan. *Zoom! Zoom! Zoom! I'm Off to the Moon* (PS–K). Illus. 1997, Scholastic $15.95 (0-590-95610-8). 32pp. A little boy boards his red rocket for a trip to the moon and back. (Rev: BL 11/15/97; HB 9–10/97; HBG 3/98; SLJ 12/97)

1708 Yen, Clara. *Why Rat Comes First: A Story of the Chinese Zodiac* (PS–1). Illus. by Hideo C. Yoshida. 1991, Children's Book Pr. $14.95 (0-89239-072-7). 32pp. The story of how the 12 years in the Chinese calendar were named after particular animals. (Rev: BL 9/15/91; SLJ 10/91)

1709 Yep, Laurence. *The City of Dragons* (K–3). Illus. by Jean Tseng and Mou-Sien Tseng. 1995, Scholastic $14.95 (0-590-47865-6). 32pp. A boy's very sad face moves dragons to shed tears of pearls. (Rev: BL 11/15/95; SLJ 11/95)

1710 Yolen, Jane. *Moon Ball* (K–3). Illus. by Greg Couch. 1999, Simon & Schuster $16.00 (0-689-81095-4). 40pp. After a disastrous baseball game, Danny dreams of a celestial game in which he bats against the killer pitcher, the moon. (Rev: BL 5/1/99; HBG 10/99; SLJ 3/99)

1711 Yolen, Jane. *Where Have the Unicorns Gone?* (1–3). Illus. by Ruth Sanderson. 2000, Simon & Schuster $16.95 (0-689-82465-3). 32pp. A lyrical poem and outstanding illustrations explore the mythical world of the unicorn and answer the question in the title. (Rev: BL 11/15/00; HBG 3/01; SLJ 10/00)

1712 Yorinks, Arthur. *Harry and Lulu* (PS–2). Illus. by Martin Matje. 1999, Hyperion LB $16.49 (0-7868-2276-7). 32pp. Lulu gets a stuffed dog, Harry, who comes alive and takes her on an adventurous trip to Paris. (Rev: BCCB 6/99; BL 4/1/99*; HBG 10/99; SLJ 5/99)

1713 Yorinks, Arthur. *Louis the Fish* (PS–2). Illus. by Richard Egielski. 1980, Farrar paper $5.95 (0-374-44598-2). 32pp. The story of an unhappy man who is turned into a fish.

1714 Yorinks, Arthur. *Tomatoes from Mars* (1–4). Illus. by Mort Drucker. 1999, HarperCollins $14.95 (0-06-205070-2). Bedlam reigns in Washington when the sky is suddenly filled with saucers containing tomatoes from Mars. (Rev: HBG 3/00; SLJ 1/00)

1715 York, Sarah Mountbatten-Windsor, Duchess of. *Budgie at Bendick's Point* (PS–1). Illus. by John Richardson. 1989, Simon & Schuster paper $14.00 (0-671-67684-9). 36pp. The story of Budgie, a helicopter, and how he saved two boys caught in a gale. Also use: *Budgie the Little Helicopter* (1989). (Rev: BL 12/1/89)

1716 Young, Ed. *Monkey King* (K–3). Illus. 2001, HarperCollins $16.95 (0-06-027919-2). 40pp. This adaptation of a classic Chinese novel tells how a monkey helps a monk as he travels from China to India in search of holy manuscripts. (Rev: BL 2/1/01; SLJ 2/01)

1717 Zarin, Cynthia. *Wallace Hoskins: The Boy Who Grew Down* (K–3). Illus. by Martin Matje. 1999, DK $16.95 (0-7894-2523-8). 32pp. A gentle fantasy about a boy whose passion for always wearing a fireman's hat causes him to grow down instead of up. (Rev: BL 10/15/99; HBG 3/00; SLJ 9/99)

1718 Zemach, Harve, and Kaethe Zemach. *The Princess and Froggie* (PS–2). Illus. by Margot Zemach. 1992, Farrar paper $4.95 (0-374-46011-6). These brief tales are charmingly presented by the Zemachs and their teenage daughter.

1719 Zemach, Kaethe. *The Character in the Book* (PS–2). Illus. 1998, HarperCollins $14.95 (0-06-205060-5). 32pp. Character, who lives in a book, discovers how he can leave his book and visit a different one. (Rev: BL 2/15/98; HBG 10/98; SLJ 4/98)

1720 Zemach, Margot. *Jake and Honeybunch Go to Heaven* (1–3). Illus. by author. 1982, Farrar paper $4.95 (0-374-43714-9). 40pp. A controversial (because of charges of stereotyping) picture book about an African American workingman and his mule.

1721 Zeman, Ludmila. *The First Red Maple Leaf* (PS–2). Illus. by author. 1997, Tundra $15.95 (0-88776-372-3). An American Indian boy saves his people from the cruel Iceheart with the help of magical goose Branta. (Rev: SLJ 9/97)

IMAGINARY ANIMALS

1722 Ada, Alma F. *Friend Frog* (K–2). Illus. by Lori Lohstoeter. 2000, Harcourt $16.00 (0-15-201522-1). Field Mouse is so in awe of Frog's ability to jump, croak, and swim that he wonders if they can ever be friends. (Rev: HBG 10/00; SLJ 5/00)

1723 Adams, Jean Ekman. *Clarence Goes Out West and Meets a Purple Horse* (K–2). Illus. 2000, Rising Moon $15.95 (0-87358-753-7). 32pp. Smoky, a purple horse, introduces a tenderfoot piglet named Clarence to all the fun of line dancing, card playing, and other cowboy pleasures. (Rev: BL 4/1/00; HBG 10/00; SLJ 6/00)

1724 Agell, Charlotte. *To the Island* (PS–K). Illus. 1998, DK $14.95 (0-7894-2505-X). 32pp. A group of animal friends crowd into a boat and spend a wonderful day having an island picnic. (Rev: BL 11/1/98; HBG 3/99; SLJ 6/99)

1725 Agell, Charlotte. *Up the Mountain* (PS–K). Illus. 2000, DK $14.95 (0-7894-2610-2). 32pp. Cat, Dragon, Chicken, and Rabbit have a wonderful time playing in the rain. (Rev: BL 5/15/00; HBG 10/00; SLJ 5/00)

1726 Aggs, Patrice. *The Visitor* (PS–K). Illus. 1999, Orchard LB $15.99 (0-531-33059-1). 32pp. Never having seen a giraffe, two kittens are not sure they want him as a dinner guest, but after they play on his long neck a friendship begins. (Rev: BL 2/1/99; HBG 10/99; SLJ 4/99)

1727 Ahlberg, Allan. *The Bravest Ever Bear* (PS–2). Illus. by Paul Howard. 2000, Candlewick $15.99 (0-7636-0783-5). 32pp. A bear writes an adventure story involving a dragon, princesses, a troll, and a wolf and, of course, starring himself. (Rev: BCCB 6/00; BL 5/15/00; HB 3–4/00; HBG 10/00; SLJ 6/00)

1728 Ahlberg, Allan. *Monkey Do!* (PS–K). Illus. by Andre Amstutz. 1998, Candlewick $15.99 (0-7636-0466-6). 32pp. A curious little monkey escapes from a zoo and has a series of adventures before he returns to the zoo and his mother. (Rev: BCCB 4/98; BL 4/1/98; HBG 3/99; SLJ 6/98)

1729 Alborough, Jez. *Duck in the Truck* (PS–K). Illus. 2000, HarperCollins $14.95 (0-06-028685-7). 40pp. In this humorous tale, Duck's truck becomes stuck in the muck, and he needs the help of Frog, Sheep, and Goat to become unstuck. (Rev: BL 12/15/99; HBG 10/00)

1730 Alborough, Jez. *Hug* (PS–1). Illus. by author. 2000, Candlewick $14.99 (0-7636-1287-1). Bob, a tiny chimp, longs for a hug like he sees other animals getting and finally his mother appears and satisfies his wish. (Rev: HBG 3/01; SLJ 12/00)

1731 Alborough, Jez. *Where's My Teddy?* (PS–1). Illus. 1992, Candlewick $16.99 (1-56402-048-7). 32pp. Eddie loses his teddy bear and retraces his steps in the forest trying to find him. (Rev: BCCB 9/92*; BL 10/1/92; SLJ 8/92)

1732 Alcantara, Ricardo. *Dog and Cat* (PS–K). Trans. from French by Elizabeth Uhlig. Illus. by Gusti. 1999, Millbrook LB $16.90 (0-7613-1420-2). When a kitten and a puppy join a household on the same day they are at first hostile, but when they become lonely they learn to be friends. (Rev: HBG 10/99; SLJ 8/99)

1733 Alexander, Lloyd. *How the Cat Swallowed Thunder* (K–3). Illus. by Judith Byron Schachner. 2000, Dutton $16.99 (0-525-46449-2). 40pp. A cat is given a list of chores to perform but everything he attempts goes wrong in this humorous picture book. (Rev: BCCB 9/00; BL 7/00; HBG 3/01; SLJ 10/00)

1734 Alexander, Sue. *There's More . . . Much More* (PS–1). Illus. by Patience Brewster. 1987, Harcourt $12.95 (0-15-200605-2). 32pp. A squirrel helps a little girl to fill a flower basket and understand the beauties of the forest. (Rev: BL 11/15/87; SLJ 12/87)

1735 Allard, Harry. *The Cactus Flower Bakery* (PS–1). Illus. by Ned Delaney. 1993, HarperCollins paper $4.95 (0-0644-3297-1). 32pp. A nearsighted armadillo becomes friendly with an unpopular snake. (Rev: BL 5/1/91; SLJ 8/91)

1736 Allen, Jonathan. *Mucky Moose* (PS–2). Illus. 1996, Simon & Schuster paper $5.95 (0-689-80651-5). 32pp. Mucky Moose smells so bad that even a wolf won't hunt him. (Rev: BL 3/1/91; HB 9–10/91; SLJ 8/91)

1737 Amoore, Susannah. *Motley the Cat* (PS–3). Illus. by Mary Fedden. 1998, Viking $14.99 (0-670-87730-1). 32pp. When he meets two little girls during his wanderings, Motley the Cat thinks he has found the perfect home. Motley knows, however, that sometimes things worth having are worth waiting for. (Rev: BL 5/15/98; HBG 10/98; SLJ 7/98)

1738 Anaya, Rudolfo A. *Roadrunner's Dance* (K–3). 2000, Hyperion $15.99 (0-7868-0254-5). 32pp. The bully Snake is defeated when Desert Woman creates Roadrunner, who is able to get the best of Snake through his unique dance. (Rev: BCCB 12/00; BL 12/15/00; HBG 3/01; SLJ 9/00)

1739 Anderson, Peggy Perry. *Out to Lunch* (PS–2). Illus. 1998, Houghton $14.00 (0-395-89826-9). 32pp. Joe, the Frogs' little son, misbehaves at a restaurant. In desperation, they must take their lunch with them and let Joe play elsewhere. (Rev: BL 6/1–15/98; HBG 3/99; SLJ 4/98)

1740 Andreae, Giles. *Cock-a-doodle-doo! Barnyard Hullabaloo* (PS). Illus. by David Wotjowycz. 2000, Little Tiger $14.95 (1-888444-75-4). 32pp. Sing-song verses describe the activities of some farmyard animals and the sounds they make. (Rev: BL 3/15/00; HBG 10/00; SLJ 5/00)

1741 Andreae, Giles. *Love Is a Handful of Honey* (PS–1). Illus. by Vanessa Cabban. 1999, Little Tiger $14.95 (1-888444-58-4). 32pp. The daily activities of a little bear, depicted in gentle watercolors, express the joy of childhood and the wonder of love. (Rev: BL 12/1/99; HBG 3/00; SLJ 11/99)

1742 *The Ants Came Marching* (PS). Illus. by Martin Kelly. 2000, Handprint $4.95 (1-929766-11-4). 6pp. A board book based on the famous song that features a host of marching ants. A similar title is

Five Green and Speckled Frogs (2000). (Rev: SLJ 12/00)

1743 Appelt, Kathi. *Bats Around the Clock* (K–2). Illus. by Melissa Sweet. 2000, HarperCollins LB $15.89 (0-688-16470-6). 32pp. During a 12-hour dance marathon, bats engage in dancing the Shrug, Jitterbug, Twist, and other strenuous jigs. (Rev: BL 5/1/00; HBG 10/00; SLJ 6/00)

1744 Appelt, Kathi. *Oh, My Baby, Little One* (PS–K). Illus. by Jane Dyer. 2000, Harcourt $16.00 (0-15-200041-0). 32pp. When baby bird goes off to school, Mama misses her and begins to worry about her well-being. (Rev: BL 3/1/00; HBG 10/00; SLJ 4/00)

1745 Apperley, Dawn. *Hello Little Chicks* (PS). Illus. by author. 2000, David & Charles $3.95 (1-86233-181-2). This board book uses rhymes and watercolor paintings to describe the activities of little chicks. Also use: *Hello Little Ducks*, *Hello Little Lamb*, and *Hello Little Piglet* (all 2000). (Rev: SLJ 2/01)

1746 Ardalan, Hayde. *Milton* (K–3). Illus. by author. 2000, Chronicle $7.95 (0-8118-2762-3). An amusing tale about a cat named Milton who is very impressed with himself and his attributes. (Rev: HBG 10/00; SLJ 5/00)

1747 Arnold, Katya. *Duck, Duck, Goose?* (PS–1). Illus. 1997, Holiday $15.95 (0-8234-1296-2). 32pp. Goose tries in vain to improve her appearance by swapping body parts with other animals. (Rev: BL 7/97; HB 9–10/97; SLJ 9/97)

1748 Arnold, Katya, reteller. *Me Too! Two Small Stories About Small Animals* (PS). Illus. by Katya Arnold. 2000, Holiday $15.95 (0-8234-1483-3). Two gentle animal stories that are translations from the work of Vladimir Suteev. (Rev: HB 3–4/00; HBG 10/00; SLJ 3/00)

1749 Arnold, Katya. *Meow!* (PS–K). Illus. 1998, Holiday $16.95 (0-8234-1361-6). 32pp. While searching for the animal who says "meow," a puppy encounters a number of different animals, each of whom produces its own distinctive sound. (Rev: BCCB 7–8/98; BL 4/15/98; HBG 10/98; SLJ 5/98)

1750 Arnosky, Jim. *Rabbits and Raindrops* (PS–2). Illus. 1997, Putnam $16.99 (0-399-22635-4). 32pp. Five young rabbits explore the world outside their nest until a rain shower interrupts their journey. (Rev: BCCB 3/97; BL 3/1/97; SLJ 3/97)

1751 Arnosky, Jim. *Rattlesnake Dance* (K–3). Illus. by author. 2000, Putnam $15.99 (0-399-22755-5). In this amusing picture book, cartoon-like rattlesnakes gather for a dance. (Rev: HBG 10/00; SLJ 6/00)

1752 Arrhenius, Peter. *The Penguin Quartet* (K–3). Illus. by Ingela Peterson. 1998, Carolrhoda $14.95 (1-57505-252-0). Four dapper penguins — soon to be dads — find it boring waiting for their eggs to hatch, so they pack them up and go to New York where they become the popular Penguin Quartet. (Rev: HBG 3/99; SLJ 11/98)

1753 Aruego, Jose, and Ariane Dewey. *Rockabye Crocodile* (PS–1). Illus. by authors. 1988, Morrow paper $4.95 (0-688-12333-3). 32pp. A retelling of a Philippine fable concerning two elderly boars, one kind, one mean, and their treatment from a mother crocodile. (Rev: BL 9/15/88; HB 9–10/88; SLJ 12/88)

1754 Asch, Devin, and Frank Asch. *Baby Duck's New Friend* (PS–K). Illus. 2001, Harcourt $15.00 (0-15-202257-0). 32pp. When Baby Duck wanders away to the seashore, he discovers he can fly and get home by himself. (Rev: BL 3/15/01)

1755 Asch, Frank. *Baby Bird's First Nest* (PS–2). Illus. by author. 1999, Harcourt $14.00 (0-15-201726-7). When Baby Bird falls out of her nest, Little Frog helps her back after a series of adventures. (Rev: HBG 10/99; SLJ 6/99)

1756 Asch, Frank. *Bear Shadow* (PS–1). Illus. by author. 1988, Simon & Schuster paper $4.95 (0-671-66866-8). 32pp. Bear has a problem; every time he tries to catch a fish, his shadow scares it away! Also use: *Goodbye House* (1989). (Rev: BL 5/15/85; HB 7–8/85; SLJ 8/85)

1757 Asch, Frank. *Bear's Bargain* (PS–K). Illus. by author. 1989, Simon & Schuster $5.99 (0-671-67838-8). Bear and Little Bird discover that there is more than one way to solve a problem when Bear wants to fly and Little Bird wants to grow big. Also use: *Skyfire* (1988). (Rev: BL 11/1/85; HB 1–2/86)

1758 Asch, Frank. *Happy Birthday, Moon* (PS–1). Illus. by author. 1985, Simon & Schuster paper $5.99 (0-671-66455-7). 32pp. A little bear wants to give the moon a birthday present. Two sequels are: *Mooncake* (1986); *Moongame* (Scholastic 1992).

1759 Asch, Frank. *Just Like Daddy* (PS–1). Illus. by author. 1984, Simon & Schuster paper $5.99 (0-671-66457-3). 32pp. Fatherhood is explained by a bear and his dad in this warm, humorous book. Another Bear story is: *Milk and Cookies* (Parents Magazine Pr. 1982).

1760 Asch, Frank. *Moonbear's Dream* (PS–1). Illus. 1999, Simon & Schuster $15.00 (0-689-82244-8). 32pp. Moonbear and Little Bird think they are dreaming when they see a kangaroo and her baby in their backyard, and they act as though they were in a dream until the zookeeper comes to claim his lost charges. (Rev: BL 9/15/99; HBG 3/00; SLJ 10/99)

1761 Asch, Frank. *Moonbear's Pet* (PS–2). Illus. 1997, Simon & Schuster $15.00 (0-689-80794-5). 32pp. Bear and friend Little Bird find in a pond a pet they name Splash, and in time Splash becomes a frog. (Rev: BCCB 7–8/97; BL 6/1–15/97; SLJ 6/97*)

1762 Asch, Frank. *Moondance* (PS–K). Illus. 1993, Scholastic $12.95 (0-590-45487-0). 32pp. Bear wants to dance with the moon, but doesn't feel worthy of the honor. (Rev: BL 2/15/93; SLJ 6/93)

1763 Asch, Frank. *Sand Cake* (K–2). Illus. by author. 1979, Parents LB $5.95 (0-8193-0986-9). 48pp. On the beach, Papa Bear makes a sand cake.

1764 Asch, Frank, and Vladimir Vagin. *Dear Brother* (K–3). Illus. 1992, Scholastic $13.95 (0-590-43107-2). 32pp. Two mouse brothers read letters from two ancestors that prove how important a brother can be. (Rev: BCCB 2/92; BL 6/15/92; SLJ 4/92)

1765 Asch, Frank, and Vladimir Vagin. *Insects from Outer Space* (PS–2). Illus. by Vladimir Vagin. 1995, Scholastic $14.95 (0-590-45489-7). 32pp. Insects from outer space and their earthling counterparts enjoy each other at the Bug Ball. (Rev: BL 2/1/95; SLJ 4/95)

1766 Ashforth, Camilla. *Calamity* (PS–K). Illus. by author. 1993, Candlewick $15.95 (1-56402-252-8). Calamity, a racing donkey, invites Horatio, a tiny stuffed rabbit, to join him in a race. (Rev: SLJ 4/94)

1767 Ashforth, Camilla. *Monkey Tricks* (PS–1). Illus. by author. 1993, Candlewick $15.95 (1-56402-170-X). 32pp. James the bear and Horatio the bunny are expecting a visit to the nursery from a mischievous monkey. (Rev: BL 1/15/93*; SLJ 5/93)

1768 Atkins, Jeannine. *Robin's Home* (PS–1). Illus. by Candace Whitman. 2001, Farrar $16.00 (0-374-36337-4). 32pp. Little Robin is so happy in the nest that he doesn't want to leave it, but in time he learns to fly and the sky becomes his home. (Rev: BL 3/15/01)

1769 Auch, Mary Jane. *Bantam of the Opera* (K–3). Illus. 1997, Holiday LB $16.95 (0-8234-1312-8). 32pp. Luigi, a bantam rooster with a huge voice, gets his chance at the Cosmopolitan Opera Company. (Rev: BL 10/1/97; HBG 3/98; SLJ 10/97*)

1770 Auch, Mary Jane. *Bird Dogs Can't Fly* (PS–1). Illus. 1993, Holiday LB $15.95 (0-8234-1050-1). 32pp. Blue, a bird dog, nurses an injured goose back to health. (Rev: BL 10/15/93; SLJ 12/93)

1771 Auch, Mary Jane. *Eggs Mark the Spot* (PS–3). Illus. 1996, Holiday $16.95 (0-8234-1242-3). 32pp. A hen copies onto her eggs some portraits painted by famous artists. (Rev: BL 3/15/96; SLJ 5/96)

1772 Auch, Mary Jane. *Hen Lake* (PS–3). Illus. 1995, Holiday LB $16.95 (0-8234-1188-5). 32pp. The hen Poulette stages her own ballet and also gets the best of snooty Mr. Peacock. (Rev: BL 8/95; SLJ 10/95)

1773 Auch, Mary Jane. *Peeping Beauty* (PS–3). Illus. 1993, Holiday LB $16.95 (0-8234-1001-3). 32pp. Poulette the hen decides she wants to be a ballerina. (Rev: BL 3/1/93; SLJ 4/93*)

1774 Austin, Margot. *A Friend for Growl Bear* (PS–2). Adapted by Sharon A. Riley. Illus. by David McPhail. 1999, HarperCollins $14.95 (0-06-027802-1). 32pp. Little Growl Bear gains a number of woodland friends when they realize he is too young to be dangerous. (Rev: BL 5/15/99; HB 3–4/99; HBG 10/99; SLJ 2/99)

1775 Axelrod, Amy. *Pigs in the Pantry: Fun with Math and Cooking* (PS–2). Illus. by Sharon McGinley-Nally. 1997, Simon & Schuster $14.00 (0-689-80665-5). 40pp. The story of Mr. Pig's disastrous cooking spree, with some added math facts about measuring ingredients. (Rev: BCCB 5/97; BL 3/1/97; SLJ 4/97)

1776 Axelrod, Amy. *Pigs on a Blanket* (K–3). Illus. by Sharon McGinley-Nally. 1996, Simon & Schuster paper $14.00 (0-689-80505-5). 32pp. Unforeseen problems cause delays for a pig family that wants to spend a day at the beach. (Rev: BL 5/15/96; SLJ 6/96)

1777 Axelrod, Amy. *Pigs Will Be Pigs* (K–3). Illus. by Sharon McGinley-Nally. 1994, Four Winds paper $14.00 (0-02-765415-X). 40pp. To finance a dinner out, the pig family engages in a money hunt around the house. (Rev: BCCB 2/94; BL 2/15/94; SLJ 5/94*)

1778 Axworthy, Anni. *Along Came Toto* (PS–K). Illus. 1993, Candlewick $12.95 (1-56402-172-6). 32pp. Percy the dog has difficulty adjusting to a kitten that arrives unexpectedly at his home. (Rev: BL 4/1/93; SLJ 4/93)

1779 Aylesworth, Jim. *Aunt Pitty Patty's Piggy* (PS–K). Illus. by Barbara McClintock. 1999, Scholastic $15.95 (0-590-89987-2). 32pp. A delightful cumulative tale involving Aunt Pitty Patty's efforts to get her pig home and the many animals she asks for help. (Rev: BCCB 12/99; BL 9/15/99*; HB 9–10/99; HBG 3/00; SLJ 10/99)

1780 Baker, Keith. *Cat Tricks* (PS–3). Illus. 1997, Harcourt $15.00 (0-15-292857-X). 44pp. An entertaining picture book that shows fictitious cat tricks while presenting a series of picture puzzles. (Rev: BL 12/15/97; HBG 3/98; SLJ 12/97)

1781 Baker, Keith. *Who Is the Beast?* (K–2). Illus. 1990, Harcourt $14.95 (0-15-296057-0). 32pp. A tiger tries to make the other jungle animals less afraid of him. (Rev: BL 9/1/90; HB 11–12/90; SLJ 11/90)

1782 Bancroft, Catherine, and Hannah C. Gruenberg. *Felix's Hat* (K–3). Illus. by Hannah C. Gruenberg. 1993, Macmillan LB $14.95 (0-02-708325-X). 32pp. Felix Frog cannot be consoled when he loses his favorite possession, an orange hat. (Rev: BL 3/15/93; SLJ 7/93)

1783 Bang, Molly. *Goose* (PS–3). Illus. 1996, Scholastic $10.95 (0-590-89005-0). 40pp. After hatching from her egg, Duckling finds a surrogate family with a group of woodchucks. (Rev: BCCB 12/96; BL 9/15/96*; HB 11–12/96; SLJ 11/96*)

1784 Banks, Kate. *The Bird, the Monkey, and the Snake in the Jungle* (K–3). Illus. by Tomek Bogacki. 1999, Farrar $16.00 (0-374-30729-6). 32pp. Pictures are substituted for words in this clever story about three animals looking for a new home after the tree they lived in falls down. (Rev: BL 3/1/99*; HBG 10/99; SLJ 3/99)

1785 Barasch, Lynne. *Rodney's Inside Story* (PS–1). Illus. 1992, Smithmark $3.98 (0-831-76836-3). 32pp. Two small rabbits read about each other in their picture books. (Rev: BCCB 10/92; BL 10/1/92; HB 9–10/92; SLJ 9/92)

1786 Barber, Antonia. *The Mousehole Cat* (K–3). Illus. by Nicola Bayley. 1996, Simon & Schuster paper $5.99 (0-689-80837-2). 40pp. A splendid retelling of a fishing legend set in the Cornish village of Mousehole. (Rev: BL 10/1/90*; HB 11–12/90)

1787 Barbot, Daniel. *A Bicycle for Rosaura* (PS–1). Illus. by Morella Fuenmayor. 1991, Kane/Miller $9.95 (0-916291-34-0). 24pp. A pet store owner is in a quandary when her hen Rosaura asks for a bicycle for her birthday. (Rev: BL 6/1/91; SLJ 10/91)

1788 Barnes, Laura T. *Teeny Tiny Ernest* (PS–K). Illus. by Carol A. Camburn. 2000, Barnesyard $15.95 (0-9674681-1-6). 32pp. Ernest, a miniature donkey, tries different methods to look taller but the other animals tell him that they never noticed that he was small because beauty comes from within. (Rev: BL 11/15/00; SLJ 3/01)

1789 Baron, Alan. *Red Fox and the Baby Bunnies* (PS). Illus. 1997, Candlewick $9.99 (0-7636-0085-7). 24pp. Dan Dog and Tabby Cat rescue some bunnies from Red Fox. (Rev: BCCB 4/97; BL 2/1/97; SLJ 3/97)

1790 Baron, Alan. *The Red Fox Monster* (PS–2). Illus. by author. 1996, Candlewick $9.99 (0-7636-0018-0). Dan Dog and Tabby Cat dress in Red Fox's clothing while he has a swim and frighten the other animals. (Rev: SLJ 11/96)

1791 Barracca, Debra, and Sal Barracca. *Maxi, the Hero* (PS–3). Illus. by Mark Buehner. 1991, Dial $14.99 (0-8037-0939-0). 32pp. Maxi, a dog hero, catches the thief who stole a woman's purse. (Rev: BL 8/91; SLJ 10/91)

1792 Bass, Jules. *Herb, the Vegetarian Dragon* (K–3). Illus. by Debbie Harter. 1999, Barefoot LB $15.95 (1-902283-36-8). Herb, a gentle vegetarian dragon, is wrongfully accused of people-eating and escapes death only with the help of a brave girl. (Rev: SLJ 7/99)

1793 Bassede, Francine. *A Day with the Bellyflops* (PS–2). Illus. by author. 2000, Orchard LB $15.99 (0-531-33242-X). Constant interruptions by her three piglets prevent Mrs. Bellyflop from getting her work done. (Rev: HBG 10/00; SLJ 3/00)

1794 Bassede, Francine. *George Paints His House* (PS–K). Illus. 1999, Orchard LB $15.99 (0-531-33150-4). 32pp. Before deciding on a color to paint his house, George, a duck, and his cat friend Mary spend a day in the country asking for color advice for different animals. (Rev: BL 2/15/99; HBG 10/99; SLJ 6/99)

1795 Bate, Lucy. *Little Rabbit's Loose Tooth* (PS–K). Illus. by Diane De Groat. 1975, Crown paper $6.99 (0-517-55122-5). 32pp. Little Rabbit loses her first tooth and makes the most of it in this beguiling story.

1796 Bates, Ivan. *All By Myself* (PS–1). Illus. 2000, HarperCollins $14.95 (0-06-028585-0). 32pp. Maya, an elephant, tries to be an independent food gatherer but can't reach the juicy leaves the way her mother can. (Rev: BL 4/1/00; HBG 10/00)

1797 Baumgart, Klaus. *Where Are You, Little Green Dragon?* (PS–2). Illus. by author. 1993, Hyperion $12.95 (1-56282-344-2); paper $4.95 (0-7868-1073-4). 32pp. The Little Green Dragon with his friendly fly share many adventures. (Rev: SLJ 8/93)

1798 Beck, Scott. *Pepito the Brave* (PS–1). Illus. by author. 2001, Dutton $12.99 (0-525-46524-3). Other animals teach Pepito, a little red bird, how to hop, swim, run, burrow, and climb before he has the courage to try to fly. (Rev: SLJ 2/01)

1799 Bedard, Michael. *Sitting Ducks* (K–4). Illus. 1998, Putnam $15.99 (0-399-22847-0). 40pp. When a little inhabitant of the Colossal Duck Factory discovers that he and his fellows are being fattened to feed the local alligators, he must sound the alarm and rescue all the ducks. (Rev: BCCB 10/98; BL 12/1/98; HBG 3/99; SLJ 10/98)

1800 Beeke, Jemma. *The Rickety Barn Show* (PS–3). Illus. by Lynne Chapman. 2001, Doubleday $14.95 (0-385-32795-1). 32pp. All the farm animals want a part in the show with the result that on the day of the performance there is no audience, only performers. (Rev: BL 2/1/01)

1801 Bellows, Cathy. *The Grizzly Sisters* (PS–3). Illus. 1991, Macmillan $14.95 (0-02-709032-9). 32pp. Bear cubs decide to go out and scare the tourists; instead, they become frightened. (Rev: BL 12/15/91; SLJ 1/92)

1802 Bengamin, Alan. *Curious Critters: A Pop-Up Menagerie* (PS–1). Illus. by David A. Carter. 1998, Simon $16.95 (0-689-81586-7). Pull a flap and strange new animals like a kangarooster perform in this interactive book. (Rev: BL 1/1–15/99)

1803 Benjamin, A. H. *It Could Have Been Worse* (PS–K). Illus. by Tim Warnes. 1998, Little Tiger $14.95 (1-888444-26-6). 28pp. After suffering a series of accidents, Mouse thinks he is having an unlucky day, but each misadventure has actually saved him from his natural enemies. (Rev: BL 5/15/98; HBG 10/98)

1804 Berenstain, Stan, and Jan Berenstain. *The Berenstain Bears in the Dark* (PS–2). Illus. by authors. 1982, Random paper $3.25 (0-394-85443-8). 32pp. Brother and Sister Bear in one of a very large series of books.

1805 Berkes, Marianne. *Marsh Music* (K–3). Illus. by Robert Noreika. 2000, Millbrook LB $21.90 (0-7613-1850-X). 32pp. From dawn to dusk, the world is alive with the sound of frogs making music in this amusing book about marsh life, nature, and song. (Rev: BL 12/1/00; HBG 3/01; SLJ 12/00)

1806 Berliner, Franz. *Wildebeest* (PS–1). Illus. by Lilian Brogger. 1991, Ideals $13.95 (0-8249-8488-9). 32pp. When a wildebeest changes his nature, he gets a new name — gnu. (Rev: BL 1/15/92)

1807 Best, Cari. *Montezuma's Revenge* (PS–2). Illus. by Diane Palmisciano. 1999, Orchard LB $16.99 (0-531-33198-9). 32pp. To show his owner's family his worth, the dog Montezuma switches places with Wild Bill, a dog from the wrong side of the tracks. (Rev: BL 11/15/99; HBG 3/00; SLJ 11/99)

1808 Bianchi, John. *The Lab Rats of Doctor Eclair* (2–3). Illus. by author. 1997, Firefly paper $6.95 (0-921285-48-5). Three pampered lab rats join Doctor Eclair in his crusade to save animals by building a mechanical lab rat. (Rev: SLJ 8/97)

1809 Bingham, Mindy. *Minou* (1–3). Illus. by Itoko Maeno. 1987, Advocacy $14.95 (0-911655-36-0). 64pp. When Minou loses her home in Paris, a smart cat named Celeste grooms her to become a mouser at Notre Dame. (Rev: BL 9/1/87; SLJ 6–7/87)

1810 Birchall, Mark. *Rabbit's Wooly Sweater* (PS–K). Illus. by author. 2001, Carolrhoda LB $15.95 (1-57505-465-5). When little Rabbit's new sweater is washed, it shrinks to become the perfect size for Mr. Cuddles, the stuffed toy that is Rabbit's best friend. (Rev: SLJ 3/01)

1811 Birney, Betty G. *Tyrannosaurus Tex* (K–3). Illus. by John O'Brien. 1994, Houghton $14.95 (0-395-67648-7). 32pp. Everything is larger than life in this tall tale about a Texan cowboy who is really a dinosaur. (Rev: BL 6/1–15/94; HB 5–6/94; SLJ 5/94)

1812 Bishop, Gavin. *Little Rabbit and the Sea* (PS–2). Illus. by author. 1997, North-South LB $15.88 (1-55858-810-8). Little Rabbit dreams of becoming a sailor and asks his family what the ocean is like. (Rev: HBG 3/98; SLJ 12/97)

1813 Bishop, Gavin. *Stay Awake, Bear!* (PS–1). Illus. by author. 2000, Orchard LB $16.99 (0-531-33249-7). Old Bear and his neighbor decide that hibernation is a waste of time and so decide to stay awake all winter. (Rev: HBG 10/00; SLJ 3/00)

1814 Blackstone, Stella. *Bear About Town* (PS). Illus. by Debbie Harter. 2000, Barefoot $13.95 (1-902283-57-0). A bear walks through town and sees new sights and visits new places each day of the week. (Rev: SLJ 7/00)

1815 Blackstone, Stella. *Bear's Busy Family* (PS–1). Illus. by Debbie Harter. 1999, Barefoot $13.95 (1-902283-90-2). 32pp. This book about members of a young bear's family can be used to introduce the names and relationships in an extended family. (Rev: BL 9/15/99; SLJ 8/99)

1816 Blackwood, Mary. *Derek the Knitting Dinosaur* (PS–2). Illus. by Kerry Argent. 1990, Carolrhoda LB $15.95 (0-87614-400-8); paper $5.95 (0-87614-540-3). 32pp. This dinosaur prefers to knit woolly socks and sweaters rather than terrorize the neighborhood like his uncivilized siblings. (Rev: BL 7/90; SLJ 7/90)

1817 Blood, Charles L., and Martin Link. *The Goat in the Rug* (K–2). Illus. by Nancy Winslow Parker. 1990, Simon & Schuster paper $5.99 (0-689-71418-1). 40pp. How a Navajo rug is made, from the goat Geraldine's point of view.

1818 Bloom, Becky. *Wolf!* (PS–4). Illus. by Pascal Biet. 1999, Orchard LB $16.99 (0-531-33155-5). 32pp. Ignored by other animals because he can't read, a wolf decides to go to school to become literate. (Rev: BL 2/15/99; HBG 10/99; SLJ 5/99)

1819 Bodnar, Judit Z. *Tale of a Tail* (PS–2). Illus. by John Sandford. 1998, Lothrop LB $15.93 (0-688-12175-6). 48pp. When Bear asks to share Fox's catch of fresh fish, Fox suggests he catch his own by hanging his tail in the water as bait. The water freezes, encasing Bear's tail in ice, but Bear thinks of an ingenious solution. (Rev: BCCB 11/98; BL 10/1/98*; HBG 3/99; SLJ 11/98)

1820 Boehm, Arlene. *Jack in Search of Art* (PS–3). Illus. by author. 1998, Roberts Rinehart $16.95 (1-57098-244-9); paper $7.95 (1-57098-234-1). A cheerful bear wanders through a gallery in search of "Art," while the reader is introduced to the important works it contains. (Rev: HBG 3/99; SLJ 2/99)

1821 Boelts, Maribeth. *Big Daddy, Frog Wrestler* (PS–2). Illus. by Benrei Huang. 2000, Albert Whitman $14.95 (0-8075-0717-2). 32pp. Curtis, a frog,

is proud that Big Daddy is a championship wrestler, but when his father leaves to fight in a big tournament his son's pride turns to loneliness. (Rev: BL 3/1/00; HBG 10/00; SLJ 3/00)

1822 Boelts, Maribeth. *Dry Days, Wet Nights* (PS–K). Illus. by Kathy Parkinson. 1994, Albert Whitman LB $14.95 (0-8075-1723-2); paper $5.95 (0-8075-1724-0). 32pp. Little Bunny, who is out of diapers during the day, is upset when he wets the bed at night. (Rev: BCCB 4/94; BL 5/1/94; SLJ 4/94)

1823 Boelts, Maribeth. *Little Bunny's Cool Tool Set* (PS–K). Illus. by Kathy Parkinson. 1997, Albert Whitman LB $14.95 (0-8075-4584-8). 32pp. Little Bunny has trouble sharing when he brings his new tool set to school. (Rev: BL 9/15/97; HBG 3/98; SLJ 10/97)

1824 Boelts, Maribeth. *Little Bunny's Pacifier Plan* (PS–K). Illus. by Kathy Parkinson. 1999, Albert Whitman $14.95 (0-8075-4581-3). 32pp. At his dentist's bidding, Little Bunny gradually stops using his pacifier and eventually gives it to his new baby cousin. (Rev: BL 3/1/99; HBG 10/99; SLJ 4/99)

1825 Bogacki, Tomek. *Cat and Mouse* (PS–K). Illus. by author. 1996, Farrar $14.00 (0-374-31225-7). A small mouse and a kitten play together, unaware of the roles that they should be playing. (Rev: SLJ 9/96)

1826 Bogacki, Tomek. *Cat and Mouse in the Night* (PS–1). Illus. 1998, Farrar $16.00 (0-374-31190-0). 32pp. Cat and Mouse venture out at night, and their initial fear turns to wonder when a ghostly owl shows them the moon and the stars. (Rev: BL 8/98; HBG 3/99; SLJ 9/98)

1827 Bogacki, Tomek. *Cat and Mouse in the Snow* (PS–K). Illus. 1999, Farrar $16.00 (0-374-31192-7). 32pp. Playful friends Cat and Mouse get covered with snow, and their chums mistake them for monsters in this charming story about fun in winter. (Rev: BL 10/1/99; HBG 3/00; SLJ 9/99)

1828 Bogacki, Tomek. *The Story of a Blue Bird* (PS–1). Illus. 1998, Farrar $15.00 (0-374-37197-0). 32pp. The story of a young bird who ventures out of the nest alone and learns to fly before returning to tell his brother and sister of his adventure. (Rev: BL 5/1/98; HBG 10/98)

1829 Bogan, Paulette. *Spike in the City* (PS–2). Illus. by author. 2000, Putnam $12.99 (0-399-23442-X). The adventures of Spike, a black-and-white dog, on his first visit to the city — some unpleasant, like stepping on gum, and others pleasant, like catching a Frisbee in the park. (Rev: HBG 10/00; SLJ 5/00)

1830 Boggs, Cary. *W. D. the Wonder Dog* (PS–1). Illus. by Annora Spence. 1998, Simon & Schuster $16.00 (0-689-81376-7). 32pp. W. D. wonders about everything and poses questions to himself like "Why do the birds sing in the morning?" (Rev: BL 3/1/98; HBG 10/98; SLJ 6/98)

1831 Bond, Felicia. *Poinsettia and Her Family* (PS–3). Illus. by author. 1981, HarperCollins LB $14.89 (0-690-04145-4); paper $4.95 (0-06-443076-6). 32pp. Poinsettia, a pig, resents her large family but misses them when they leave temporarily. Also use: *Poinsettia and the Firefighters* (1984).

1832 Bond, Felicia. *Tumble Bumble* (PS–K). Illus. 1996, Front Street $13.95 (1-886910-15-4). 32pp. A simple rhyme about the adventures of a bug that goes for a walk. (Rev: BL 11/15/96; SLJ 10/96)

1833 Bond, Michael. *Paddington Bear* (PS–2). Illus. by R. W. Alley. 1998, HarperCollins $12.95 (0-06-027854-4). 32pp. A simple version of the first Paddington story in which the bear meets the Brown family in Paddington Station. (Rev: BL 1/1–15/99; HBG 3/99)

1834 Bond, Michael. *Paddington Bear All Day* (PS). Illus. by R. W. Alley. 1998, HarperFestival $5.95 (0-694-00893-1). 14pp. In this board book for the very young, the reader is introduced to Paddington Bear and his daily schedule — from getting up in the morning to going to bed at night. (Rev: BL 4/1/98)

1835 Bond, Michael. *Paddington Bear Goes to Market* (PS). Illus. by R. W. Alley. 1998, HarperFestival $5.95 (0-694-00891-5). 14pp. In this board book about Paddington Bear, our furry hero visits the local market and buys buns from the bakery for himself and a friend. (Rev: BL 4/1/98)

1836 Bonnett-Rampersaud, Louise. *Polly Hopper's Pouch* (PS–1). Illus. by Lina Chesak-Liberace. 2001, Dutton $14.99 (0-525-46525-1). 32pp. Polly Hopper, a curious little kangaroo wearing a straw bonnet, wonders why she has this useless shopping bag on her tummy. (Rev: BL 2/15/01)

1837 Bonning, Tony. *Another Fine Mess* (PS–2). Illus. by Sally Hobson. 1998, Little Tiger $14.95 (1-888444-43-6). 32pp. Fox unloads a mess of trash into Badger's living room, but it eventually ends up back at Fox's front door. (Rev: BL 11/15/98; HBG 3/99; SLJ 2/99)

1838 Bornstein, Ruth. *Little Gorilla* (PS). Illus. by author. 1986, Houghton $15.00 (0-395-28773-1); paper $5.95 (0-89919-421-4). 32pp. Even though Little Gorilla grows into a big gorilla, everyone still loves him.

1839 Bornstein, Ruth. *Rabbit's Good News* (PS–1). Illus. 1995, Clarion $13.95 (0-395-68700-4). 32pp. A curious rabbit hops through a meadow awakening to spring to find the source of a strange sound she hears. (Rev: BL 5/1/95; SLJ 4/95)

1840 Bos, Burny. *Alexander the Great* (PS–2). Illus. by Hans de Beer. 2000, North-South LB $15.88 (0-7358-1344-2). 32pp. Alexander, a mouse, disguises himself in a bear costume to fool the mouse-catching house cat, but when he ventures out for food the cat captures him and mistakenly thinks he is one of her kittens. (Rev: BL 12/15/00; SLJ 12/00)

1841 Bos, Burny. *Leave It to the Molesons!* (2–4). Trans. by J. Alison James. Illus. by Hans de Beer. 1995, North-South LB $13.88 (1-55858-432-3). 46pp. Six episodes in the life of a mole family as told from the son's point of view. A sequel to *Meet the Molesons* (1994). (Rev: BL 3/1/96; SLJ 3/96)

1842 Bosschaert, Greet. *Teenie Bird and How She Learned to Fly* (PS–1). Illus. 2001, Abrams $12.95 (0-8109-3586-4). 32pp. Teenie Bird is afraid of fly-

ing but keeps trying until she is a success. (Rev: BL 3/1/01; SLJ 3/01)

1843 Bourgeois, Paulette. *Franklin and the Thunderstorm* (PS–K). Illus. by Brenda Clark. 1998, Kids Can $10.95 (1-55074-403-8). Unlike his animal friend, Franklin Tortoise is afraid of thunderstorms until the wise old owl tells him what causes them. (Rev: HBG 10/98; SLJ 7/98)

1844 Bourgeois, Paulette. *Franklin Goes to the Hospital* (PS–3). Illus. by Brenda Clark. 2000, Kids Can $10.95 (1-55074-732-0). 32pp. Franklin the turtle's shell is cracked during a soccer game and he must go to the hospital for an operation. (Rev: BL 6/1–15/00; HBG 10/00)

1845 Bourgeois, Paulette. *Franklin's Bad Day* (K–2). Illus. by Brenda Clark. 1997, Scholastic paper $4.50 (0-590-69332-8). Franklin the turtle misses his friend Otter so much that he makes a scrapbook to send to her. (Rev: SLJ 5/97)

1846 Bourgeois, Paulette. *Franklin's Classic Treasury* (PS–K). Illus. by Brenda Clark. 1999, Kids Can $15.95 (1-55074-742-8). 128pp. This book contains four previously published books about Franklin the little turtle. (Rev: BL 12/1/99; HBG 3/00)

1847 Bourgeois, Paulette. *Franklin's Classic Treasury, Volume II* (PS–K). Illus. by Brenda Clark. 2000, Kids Can $15.95 (1-55074-813-0). 128pp. A collection of four delightful stories about Franklin the turtle that were originally published separately. (Rev: BL 5/1/00; HBG 10/00)

1848 Bourgeois, Paulette. *Franklin's Friendship Treasury* (PS–K). Illus. by Brenda Clark. 2000, Kids Can $15.95 (1-55074-872-6). 120pp. This is an anthology of four previously published stories about Franklin the turtle including *Franklin Has a Sleepover* (1996), *Franklin's Bad Day* (1996) and *Franklin's Secret Club* (1998). (Rev: BL 12/15/00; HBG 3/01)

1849 Bourgeois, Paulette, and Sharon Jennings. *Franklin's Class Trip* (PS–1). Illus. by Brenda Clark. 1999, Kids Can $10.95 (1-55074-470-4). 32pp. When his class visits a natural history museum, Franklin the turtle is afraid that there will be live dinosaurs. (Rev: BL 3/1/99; HBG 10/99; SLJ 5/99)

1850 Bradman, Tony. *A Goodnight Kind of Feeling* (PS–1). Illus. by Clive Scruton. 1998, Holiday $15.95 (0-8234-1351-9). 32pp. A young cat spends a wonderful day walking in the park, going on an amusement park ride, and having a bath. (Rev: BL 6/1–15/98; HBG 10/98; SLJ 6/98)

1851 Brandenberg, Franz. *Nice New Neighbors* (K–2). Illus. by Aliki. 1990, Scholastic paper $2.75 (0-590-44117-5). 56pp. A family of mouse children generously include their neighbors, who formerly spurned them, when they decide to give a play — The Three Blind Mice.

1852 Breese, Gillian, and Tony Langham. *The Amazing Adventures of Teddy Tum Tum* (PS–1). Illus. by Patrick Lowry. 1992, Arcade $11.95 (1-55970-185-4). 32pp. A teddy bear tells the other toys in the playroom about his adventures. (Rev: BL 6/15/92; SLJ 11/92)

1853 Brenner, Barbara. *Group Soup* (PS–2). Illus. by Lynn Munsinger. 1999, NAL paper $4.99 (0-140-54093-8). Rhonda and her rabbit siblings decide to make soup. (Rev: SLJ 8/92)

1854 Brett, Jan. *Armadillo Rodeo* (PS–2). Illus. 1995, Putnam $16.99 (0-399-22803-9). 32pp. Near-sighted Bo, an armadillo, has fun when he wanders onto the Curly H Ranch. (Rev: BCCB 10/95; BL 9/15/95; SLJ 10/95)

1855 Brett, Jan. *Berlioz Bear* (K–3). Illus. 1991, Putnam $14.95 (0-399-22248-0). 32pp. Berlioz, a bear, is mystified by a strange buzz coming from his bass fiddle. (Rev: BL 9/15/91; HB 11–12/91; SLJ 10/91*)

1856 Brett, Jan. *Comet's Nine Lives* (PS–3). Illus. 1996, Putnam $16.99 (0-399-22931-0). 30pp. Comet, a white cat, has many adventures on Nantucket Island until finding a permanent home in a lighthouse. (Rev: BL 10/15/96; SLJ 12/96)

1857 Brett, Jan. *Fritz and the Beautiful Horses* (K–3). Illus. by author. 1987, Houghton $16.00 (0-395-30850-X); paper $5.95 (0-395-45356-9). 32pp. Pony Fritz is ostracized by the other horses and leads a lonely life.

1858 Brett, Jan. *The Hat* (PS–3). Illus. 1997, Putnam $16.99 (0-399-23101-3). 32pp. When a red wool stocking is blown onto the head of Hedgie the hedgehog, he maintains that it is his new hat. (Rev: BL 9/1/97*; HBG 3/98; SLJ 9/97)

1859 Brett, Jan. *Hedgie's Surprise* (PS–1). Illus. 2000, Putnam $16.99 (0-399-23477-2). 32pp. Henny wants to have family but a hungry troll named Tomten keeps stealing her eggs until she gets help from Hedgie the hedgehog. (Rev: BCCB 10/00; BL 9/1/00; HBG 3/01; SLJ 9/00)

1860 Brett, Jan. *Town Mouse, Country Mouse* (PS–3). Illus. 1994, Putnam LB $16.99 (0-399-22622-2). 32pp. A town cat and a country owl, both of whom enjoy mice for dinner, decide to change places. (Rev: BL 9/1/94; SLJ 9/94)

1861 Brewster, Patience. *Rabbit Inn* (PS–K). Illus. 1991, Little, Brown $14.95 (0-316-10747-6). Two rabbits run an inn and their guests help to spruce up the place. (Rev: SLJ 7/91)

1862 Bridges, Margaret Park. *Will You Take Care of Me?* (PS–2). Illus. by Melissa Sweet. 1998, Morrow LB $15.93 (0-688-15195-7). 32pp. A mother kangaroo assures her baby that she will always care for him, regardless of the circumstances — even if he turns into a star or a field of flowers. (Rev: BL 8/98; HBG 3/99; SLJ 12/98)

1863 Bridwell, Norman. *Clifford's Good Deeds* (PS–1). Illus. by author. 1985, Scholastic paper $3.25 (0-590-44292-9). 32pp. Clifford is a large shaggy dog whose efforts to be helpful result in comic mishaps. Also use: *Clifford Takes a Trip* (1985); *Clifford's Tricks* (1986); *Clifford the Big Red Dog* (1988); *Clifford the Small Red Puppy* (1990); *Clifford at the Circus* (1985); *Clifford Goes to Hollywood* (1986).

1864 Brimner, Larry. *Cat on Wheels* (PS–3). Illus. by Mary Peterson. 2000, Boyds Mills $15.95 (1-56397-747-8). 32pp. A cat imagines what it would be like to travel through town on an orange skateboard with bright blue wheels. (Rev: BL 12/1/00; HBG 3/01; SLJ 11/00)

1865 Brimner, Larry. *If Dogs Had Wings* (PS–1). Illus. by Chris L. Demarest. 1996, Boyds Mills $14.95 (1-56397-146-1). In a dog's-eye view of the world, this fantasy describes what life would be like if dogs had wings. (Rev: SLJ 12/96)

1866 Brock, Betty. *No Flying in the House* (2–4). Illus. by Wallace Tripp. 1970, HarperCollins paper $4.95 (0-06-440130-8). A small dog seeks shelter for herself and her human friends.

1867 Brodzinsky, Anne Braff. *The Mulberry Bird: An Adoption Story*. Rev. ed. (K–4). Illus. by Diane Stanley. 1996, Perspectives $16.00 (0-944934-15-3). 47pp. The process of adoption is the subject of this book about a little bird whose mother can't care for him and so she allows another bird couple to take her place. (Rev: SLJ 11/96)

1868 Brooks, Erik. *The Practically Perfect Pajamas* (1–3). Illus. 2000, Winslow $16.95 (1-890817-22-8). 32pp. Percy the polar bear is made fun of by his peers because of his red, star-studded pajamas, but he is cold and miserable without them. (Rev: BL 5/15/00; HBG 10/00; SLJ 5/00)

1869 Brown, Ken. *Mucky Pup* (PS–1). Illus. 1997, Dutton $14.99 (0-525-45886-7). 32pp. A puppy gets so dirty that only a pig will play with him. (Rev: BL 12/15/97; HBG 3/98; SLJ 12/97)

1870 Brown, Ken. *Nellie's Knot* (PS–K). Illus. 1993, Macmillan LB $13.95 (0-02-714930-7). 32pp. In order not to forget something, a young elephant ties a knot in her trunk, but then she can't remember why. (Rev: BL 4/15/93)

1871 Brown, Ken. *The Scarecrow's Hat* (PS–1). Illus. 2001, Peachtree $15.95 (1-56145-240-8). 32pp. Through a series of barters and exchanges a resourceful chicken finally gets what she wants, the scarecrow's hat. (Rev: BL 3/15/01)

1872 Brown, Marc. *Arthur Lost and Found* (PS–K). Illus. 1998, Little, Brown $15.95 (0-316-10912-6). 32pp. In a balanced tale of fun and caution, Arthur and his pal Buster get lost on the wrong side of town. (Rev: BL 12/1/98; HBG 3/99; SLJ 1/99)

1873 Brown, Marc. *Arthur Meets the President* (PS–3). Illus. 1991, Little, Brown $15.95 (0-316-11265-8). 32pp. Arthur the aardvark writes a prize-winning essay that takes him to Washington to meet the president. Also use: *Arthur's Pet Business* (1990); *Arthur Babysits* (1992). (Rev: BL 5/1/91; HB 7–8/91; SLJ 7/91)

1874 Brown, Marc. *Arthur Writes a Story* (PS–3). Illus. 1996, Little, Brown $15.95 (0-316-10916-9). 32pp. Arthur's classmates embellish the simple story of how he got his puppy. (Rev: BL 9/15/96; SLJ 9/96)

1875 Brown, Marc. *Arthur's Chicken Pox* (PS–3). Illus. by author. Series: Arthur Adventure. 1994, Little, Brown $15.95 (0-316-11384-0). When Arthur gets chicken pox, nobody can console him about his lost trip to the circus. (Rev: HB 5–6/94; SLJ 6/94*)

1876 Brown, Marc. *Arthur's Computer Disaster* (PS–1). Illus. 1997, Little, Brown $15.95 (0-316-11016-7). 32pp. Arthur disobeys his mother and plays with the computer, with unfortunate results. (Rev: BL 9/15/97; HB 11–12/97; HBG 3/98; SLJ 10/97)

1877 Brown, Marc. *Arthur's Eyes* (K–3). 1979, Little, Brown $15.95 (0-316-11063-9); paper $5.95 (0-316-11069-8). 32pp. Some of aardvark Arthur's problems are solved when he gets glasses, but new problems are created. Two others are: *Arthur Goes to Camp* (1984); *Arthur's Nose* (1986).

1878 Brown, Marc. *Arthur's Family Treasury* (PS–1). Illus. 2000, Little, Brown $18.95 (0-316-12147-9). 96pp. Three previously published books about Arthur the aardvark (*Arthur's Birthday*, *Arthur's Family Vacation*, and *Arthur's Baby*) are included in this entertaining anthology. (Rev: BL 6/1–15/00; HBG 10/00)

1879 Brown, Marc. *Arthur's Family Vacation* (PS–3). Illus. 1993, Little, Brown $15.95 (0-316-11312-3). 30pp. Arthur the aardvark reluctantly goes on a family vacation at the beach, and in spite of problems, he finally enjoys himself. (Rev: BL 5/15/93; HB 5–6/93; SLJ 5/93)

1880 Brown, Marc. *Arthur's First Sleepover* (K–3). Illus. 1994, Little, Brown $15.95 (0-316-11445-6). 32pp. Arthur Aardvark and his friends are fooled into thinking that space aliens have landed. (Rev: BCCB 11/94; BL 10/1/94; SLJ 10/94)

1881 Brown, Marc. *Arthur's Mystery Envelope* (K–3). 1998, Little, Brown $12.95 (0-316-11546-0); paper $3.95 (0-316-11547-9). 56pp. When Arthur the aardvark is given a letter to deliver to his parents by his principal, he is so fearful of its contents that he wonders if he should conveniently lose it. (Rev: HBG 10/98; SLJ 6/98)

1882 Brown, Marc. *Arthur's New Puppy* (PS–1). Illus. 1993, Little, Brown $15.95 (0-316-11355-7). 32pp. Arthur the aardvark teaches his new puppy a few basic manners. (Rev: BL 12/1/93; SLJ 2/94)

1883 Brown, Marc. *Arthur's Teacher Moves In* (PS–1). Illus. 2000, Little, Brown $15.95 (0-316-11979-2). 32pp. After Arthur invites his teacher to stay at his home until his roof is repaired, the aardvark is labeled teacher's pet by the other students. (Rev: BL 11/1/00; HBG 3/01; SLJ 1/01)

1884 Brown, Marc. *Arthur's Teacher Trouble* (1–3). Illus. by author. 1989, Little, Brown $15.95 (0-316-11244-5); paper $5.95 (0-316-11186-4). 32pp. Although Arthur is unhappy about having Mr. Ratburn for his third-grade teacher, he manages to win the spelling match. Also use: *Arthur's Tooth* (1985); *Arthur's Baby* (1990). (Rev: BL 11/1/86; SLJ 1/87)

1885 Brown, Marc. *Arthur's TV Trouble* (PS–2). Illus. 1995, Little, Brown $15.95 (0-316-10919-3). 32pp. Arthur's purchase of a Treat Timer for his puppy, Pal, backfires when the device only frightens his pet. (Rev: BL 11/1/95; SLJ 2/96)

1886 Brown, Marc. *Arthur's Underwear* (PS–1). Illus. 1999, Little, Brown $15.95 (0-316-11012-4).

32pp. Arthur experiences the ultimate embarrassment when his pants rip and reveal his underwear. (Rev: BL 1/1–15/00; HBG 3/00)

1887 Brown, Marc. *D.W. Flips* (PS–K). Illus. by author. 1987, Little, Brown $15.95 (0-316-11239-9). D.W. and her first visit to a gymnastics class. Another story about Arthur's young sister is: *D.W. All Wet* (1988). (Rev: BCCB 6/87; BL 5/1/87; SLJ 6–7/87)

1888 Brown, Marc. *D.W. Rides Again!* (PS–3). Illus. 1993, Little, Brown $15.95 (0-316-11356-5). 32pp. D.W. the aardvark learns how to ride a bike from her older brother, Arthur. (Rev: BL 11/1/93; HB 9–10/93; SLJ 12/93)

1889 Brown, Marc. *D.W.'s Lost Blankie* (PS). Illus. 1998, Little, Brown $13.95 (0-316-10914-2). 24pp. Arthur's little sister, D.W., is inconsolable when she loses her beloved blankie. Luckily, Mom knows where to find it. (Rev: BL 5/15/98; HBG 10/98; SLJ 5/98)

1890 Brown, Marc. *D.W. the Picky Eater* (PS–2). Illus. 1995, Little, Brown $14.95 (0-316-10957-6). 32pp. The little aardvark, D.W., is a picky eater who gradually discovers what she is missing. (Rev: BL 2/1/95; HB 7–8/95; SLJ 3/95*)

1891 Brown, Marc. *D.W. Thinks Big* (PS–3). Illus. 1993, Little, Brown $15.95 (0-316-11305-0). 24pp. An aardvark feels left out at the wedding where his brother is ring bearer and his cousin is the flower girl. (Rev: BL 3/15/93; HB 5–6/93; SLJ 5/93)

1892 Brown, Marc, and Laurie Krasny Brown. *The Bionic Bunny Show* (2–3). Illus. by Marc Brown. 1984, Little, Brown $14.95 (0-316-11120-1); paper $5.95 (0-316-10992-4). 32pp. An ordinary rabbit becomes a super TV star thanks to makeup magic.

1893 Brown, Marc, and Stephen Krensky. *Perfect Pigs: An Introduction to Manners* (K–2). Illus. by authors. 1983, Little, Brown paper $6.95 (0-316-11080-9). 32pp. Pig people show the basics of good manners.

1894 Brown, Margaret Wise. *Bunny's Noisy Book* (PS–K). Illus. by Lisa McCue. 1999, Hyperion LB $15.99 (0-7868-2428-X). An inquisitive bunny explores all the noises he hears in the woodland and around the farm. (Rev: SLJ 2/00)

1895 Brown, Margaret Wise. *The Runaway Bunny* (PS–K). Illus. by Clement Hurd. 1972, Harper-Collins LB $14.89 (0-06-020766-3); paper $5.95 (0-06-443018-9). 40pp. With nine colorful illustrations, this new edition of an old favorite is a charming story of mother bunny's love for her restless youngster, who keeps trying to escape but is always found.

1896 Browne, Anthony. *Piggybook* (K–2). Illus. by author. 1990, Knopf paper $7.99 (0-679-80837-X). 32pp. Mrs. Piggot walks out when her family turns into real pigs and takes her for granted. (Rev: BCCB 10/86; BL 10/1/86; SLJ 10/86)

1897 Browne, Anthony. *Willy the Dreamer* (2–4). Illus. 1998, Candlewick $16.99 (0-7636-0378-3). 32pp. A plotless picture book in which Willy the chimp fantasizes about assuming different identities, among them a sumo wrestler, Elvis Presley, and a ballet dancer. (Rev: BCCB 9/98; BL 4/1/98; HB 5–6/98; HBG 10/98)

1898 Browne, Eileen. *No Problem* (PS–3). Illus. by David Parkins. 1993, Candlewick $14.99 (1-56402-200-5). 36pp. When Mouse receives a construction kit in the mail, all her friends have a try at putting it together. (Rev: BL 6/1–15/93; SLJ 7/93)

1899 Browne, Eileen. *Tick-Tock* (PS–1). Illus. by David Parkins. 1994, Candlewick $14.95 (1-56402-300-1). 32pp. Owl helps young Skip Squirrel repair a cuckoo clock he has broken after disobeying his mother's instructions not to play too hard. (Rev: BL 6/1–15/94; SLJ 8/94)

1900 Bullock, Kathleen. *It Chanced to Rain* (PS–1). Illus. by author. 1992, Simon & Schuster paper $3.95 (0-671-77820-X). The walk of several animal triplets is interrupted by the rain. (Rev: SLJ 8/89)

1901 Bunting, Eve. *Can You Do This, Old Badger?* (PS–2). Illus. by LeUyen Pham. 2000, Harcourt $15.00 (0-15-201654-6). 32pp. A conversation between an old badger and a young badger shows the differences in age and knowledge and how one can learn from the other. (Rev: BL 3/15/00; HBG 10/00; SLJ 3/00)

1902 Bunting, Eve. *Swan in Love* (PS–2). Illus. by JoEllen M. Stammen. 2000, Simon & Schuster $16.00 (0-689-82080-1). 32pp. The lesson that love is never wrong is the theme of this tender story about Swan, who falls in love with a swan boat named Dora. (Rev: BCCB 7–8/00; BL 4/1/00; HBG 10/00; SLJ 6/00)

1903 Burgess, Thornton W. *Old Mother West Wind* (2–3). Illus. by Michael Hague. 1990, Holt $18.95 (0-8050-1005-X). 90pp. This book contains 16 classic animal stories. First published in 1910. (Rev: BL 6/15/90)

1904 Bush, John. *The Fish Who Could Wish* (PS–2). Illus. by Korky Paul. 1991, Kane/Miller $13.95 (0-916291-35-9); paper $6.95 (0-916291-48-0). The adventures of a fish whose wishes always come true. (Rev: SLJ 8/91)

1905 Butterworth, Nick, and Mick Inkpen. *Jasper's Beanstalk* (PS–K). Illus. 1997, Simon & Schuster paper $5.99 (0-689-81540-9). 32pp. Jasper the cat becomes impatient when his bean seed doesn't grow into a beanstalk. (Rev: BL 1/15/93; SLJ 4/93)

1906 Bynum, Janie. *Altoona Baboona* (PS–K). 1999, Harcourt $13.00 (0-15-201860-3). 32pp. In this enjoyable fantasy, Altoona Baboona is bored on her dune-a and searches for adventure in a hot air balloon-a. (Rev: HBG 10/99; SLJ 4/99)

1907 Bynum, Janie. *Otis* (PS–K). Illus. 2000, Harcourt $14.00 (0-15-202153-1). 36pp. Otis, a pig, feels like an outsider because, unlike his family and friends, he doesn't enjoy playing in the mud. In time, he makes friends with a frog who shares his dislike of getting dirty. (Rev: BCCB 5/00; BL 3/15/00; HB 7–8/00; HBG 10/00; SLJ 4/00)

1908 Cabrera, Jane. *Dog's Day* (PS–K). Illus. 2000, Orchard $12.95 (0-531-30262-8). 32pp. Dog has a fine day swinging on the trees with Monkey and playing games with other animal friends but best of all is having fun with his dad. (Rev: BL 2/1/00; HBG 10/00; SLJ 3/00)

1909 Cabrera, Jane. *Panda Big and Panda Small* (PS). Illus. by author. Series: DK Toddler Storybook. 1999, DK $9.95 (0-7894-3485-7). Although Panda Big and Panda Small have different interests and tastes, they still enjoy being friends. (Rev: HBG 10/99; SLJ 5/99)

1910 Cain, Sheridan. *Look Out for the Big Bad Fish!* (PS–K). Illus. by Tanya Linch. 1998, Little Tiger $14.95 (1-888444-27-4). 32pp. Little Tadpole has problems jumping like Mother Frog until he encounters the Big Bad Fish. (Rev: BL 7/98; HBG 10/98; SLJ 7/98)

1911 Cain, Sheridan. *Why So Sad, Brown Rabbit?* (PS–1). Illus. by Jo Kelly. 1998, Dutton $14.99 (0-525-45963-4). 32pp. Brown Rabbit gets the family he longs for when three ducklings hatch and think that he is their mother. (Rev: BL 1/1–15/98; HBG 3/99; SLJ 2/98)

1912 Calhoun, Mary. *Blue-Ribbon Henry* (K–3). Illus. by Erick Ingraham. 1999, Morrow LB $15.93 (0-688-14675-9). 40pp. Henry the Siamese cat is the hero of a county fair when he returns a little lost girl to her family. (Rev: BL 6/1–15/99; HBG 10/99; SLJ 8/99)

1913 Calhoun, Mary. *Cross-Country Cat* (K–2). Illus. by Erick Ingraham. 1979, Morrow paper $5.95 (0-688-06519-8). 40pp. A Siamese cat named Henry sets out on a cross-country skiing adventure.

1914 Calhoun, Mary. *Hot-Air Henry* (PS–4). Illus. by Erick Ingraham. 1981, Morrow paper $5.95 (0-688-04068-3). 40pp. Siamese cat Henry sneaks into the basket of a hot-air balloon.

1915 *The Candlewick Book of Animal Tales* (PS–3). Illus. 1996, Candlewick $19.99 (0-7636-0012-1). 96pp. An excellent collection of 20 animal picture books. (Rev: BL 10/1/96; SLJ 1/97)

1916 *The Candlewick Book of Bear Stories* (PS–1). Illus. 1995, Candlewick $19.99 (1-56402-653-1). 96pp. An appealing anthology that reprints several well-known picture books whose subject is bears, including Jez Alborough's *Where's My Teddy?* (1992). (Rev: BL 11/15/95; SLJ 12/95)

1917 Cannon, Janell. *Crickwing* (1–4). Illus. 2000, Harcourt $16.00 (0-15-201790-9). 48pp. Crickwing, a starving cockroach-artist, joins forces with some plucky leafcutter ants to rout a group of voracious army ants in this gripping story set in a rain forest. (Rev: BL 10/15/00*; HBG 3/01; SLJ 11/00)

1918 Cannon, Janell. *Stellaluna* (PS–3). Illus. 1993, Harcourt $16.00 (0-15-280217-7). 48pp. Stellaluna, a fruit bat, is separated from her mother and raised by birds. (Rev: BL 4/1/93; SLJ 6/93)

1919 Cannon, Janell. *Trupp: A Fuzzhead Tale* (K–2). Illus. 1995, Harcourt $15.00 (0-15-200130-1). 48pp. After a narrow escape in the big city, Trupp, a catlike animal, decides to go back to his cave in the cliffs. (Rev: BCCB 5/95; BL 4/15/95; SLJ 7/95)

1920 Cannon, Janell. *Verdi* (K–3). Illus. 1997, Harcourt $16.00 (0-15-201028-9). 48pp. A baby python named Verdi has fun and adventures when he travels alone in the rain forest. (Rev: BCCB 6/97; BL 4/15/97; SLJ 5/97)

1921 Caple, Kathy. *The Wimp* (PS–3). Illus. 1994, Houghton $14.95 (0-395-63115-7). 32pp. Arnold, a pig, tries to get even with some bullies who have been frightening him and his sister. (Rev: BL 6/1–15/94; SLJ 9/94)

1922 Carle, Eric. *The Grouchy Ladybug* (PS–K). Illus. by author. 1977, HarperCollins $15.00 (0-690-01391-4). 48pp. A grouchy ladybug, who is looking for a fight, challenges every insect and animal she meets regardless of size. Brilliantly illustrated in collage, the pages vary in size with the size of the animal.

1923 Carle, Eric. *The Honeybee and the Robber* (PS–1). Illus. 1995, Putnam $19.99 (0-399-20767-8). 16pp. When tabs are pulled, creatures move in this story of a bear and a bee hive. (Rev: BL 2/1/96)

1924 Carle, Eric. *The Mixed-Up Chameleon* (PS–2). Illus. by author. 1984, HarperCollins LB $15.89 (0-690-04397-X); paper $6.95 (0-06-443162-2). 32pp. A new edition of the story of a chameleon who finally decides to be himself.

1925 Carle, Eric. *The Very Busy Spider* (PS–K). Illus. by author. 1989, Putnam $19.99 (0-399-21166-7). 32pp. A spider spins its web in this striking picture book. Also use the story of a crab that outgrows his shell in: *A House for Hermit Crab* (1991, Picture Book). (Rev: BCCB 5/85; BL 6/1/85; SLJ 5/85)

1926 Carle, Eric. *The Very Clumsy Click Beetle* (PS–1). Illus. 1999, Putnam $21.99 (0-399-23201-X). 32pp. A click beetle learns to use its lifesaving device of clicking to turn over when it is on its back, but only in the nick of time. (Rev: BL 10/1/99; HBG 3/00; SLJ 11/99)

1927 Carle, Eric. *The Very Lonely Firefly* (PS–1). Illus. 1995, Putnam $22.99 (0-399-22774-1). 32pp. A little firefly searches for some of his own kind but is confused by such lights as candles and fireworks. (Rev: BCCB 7–8/95; BL 5/15/95; HB 9–10/95; SLJ 8/95)

1928 Carle, Eric. *The Very Quiet Cricket* (PS–1). Illus. 1990, Putnam $21.99 (0-399-21885-8). 48pp. A newly hatched cricket has a problem getting his wings to chirp. (Rev: BCCB 11/90; BL 10/1/90; HB 1–2/91; SLJ 12/90)

1929 Carlson, Nancy. *Harriet and the Garden* (PS–1). Illus. by author. 1982, Carolrhoda LB $15.95 (0-87614-184-X). 32pp. Harriet, a childlike dog, has several simple adventures. Others in the series are: *Harriet and the Roller Coaster; Harriet and Walt; Harriet's Recital* (all 1982).

1930 Carlson, Nancy. *I Like Me!* (PS–K). Illus. by author. 1988, Puffin paper $5.99 (0-14-050819-8). 32pp. An exuberant book that teaches how to appreciate oneself. (Rev: BL 6/15/88; SLJ 9/88)

1931 Carlson, Nancy. *Loudmouth George and the Cornet* (PS–2). Illus. by author. 1983, Carolrhoda LB $15.95 (0-87614-214-5). 32pp. George, a rabbit, gets dismissed from the school band. Others in the series are: *Loudmouth George and the Big Race; Loudmouth George and the Fishing Trip; Loud-*

mouth George and the New Neighbors; Loudmouth George and the Sixth-Grade Bully* (all 1983).

1932 Carlstrom, Nancy White. *Better Not Get Wet, Jesse Bear* (PS–K). Illus. by Bruce Degen. 1988, Macmillan LB $15.00 (0-02-717280-5). 32pp. Jesse Bear can't seem to stay away from water. Also use: *Jesse Bear, What Will You Wear?* (1986). (Rev: BL 4/15/88; HB 5–6/88)

1933 Carlstrom, Nancy White. *Guess Who's Coming, Jesse Bear* (PS–1). Illus. by Bruce Degen. Series: Jesse Bear. 1998, Simon & Schuster $15.00 (0-689-80702-3). 32pp. Jessie Bear dreads a visit from his bossy cousin, but he finds she is much better than expected. (Rev: BL 2/15/98; HBG 3/99; SLJ 4/98)

1934 Carlstrom, Nancy White. *How Do You Say It Today, Jesse Bear?* (PS–K). Illus. by Bruce Degen. 1992, Macmillan paper $15.00 (0-02-717276-7). 32pp. Throughout the year, Jesse Bear finds many ways to say "I Love You." (Rev: BL 9/15/92; SLJ 9/92)

1935 Carlstrom, Nancy White. *I'm Not Moving, Mama!* (K–2). Illus. by Thor Wickstrom. 1990, Macmillan LB $13.95 (0-02-717286-4). Little Mouse does not want to move his house, but Mama persuades him. (Rev: SLJ 1/91)

1936 Carlstrom, Nancy White. *Raven and River* (PS–3). Illus. by Jon Van Zyle. 1997, Little, Brown $15.95 (0-316-12894-5). 32pp. A picture book set in Alaska in which all the animals, beginning with Raven, notice the changes that spring brings to the river. (Rev: BCCB 6/97; BL 5/15/97; SLJ 4/97*)

1937 Carmichael, Clay. *Bear at the Beach* (1–3). Illus. by author. Series: Easy-to-Read. 1996, North-South LB $13.88 (1-55858-570-2). 45pp. Bear desperately wants a father and sets out to find one. (Rev: SLJ 7/96)

1938 Carr, Jan. *Swine Divine* (PS–1). Illus. by Robert Bender. 1999, Holiday $15.95 (0-8234-1434-5). 32pp. Rosie the pig is honored to be photographed in a bonnet and tutu by Mr. Porkpie, but she would rather be on the farm rolling in the mud and eating her swill. (Rev: BL 3/1/99; HBG 10/99; SLJ 6/99)

1939 Carrick, Carol. *What Happened to Patrick's Dinosaurs?* (K–2). Illus. by Donald Carrick. 1988, Houghton $16.00 (0-89919-406-0); paper $5.95 (0-89919-797-3). Patrick explains to his young brother his theory of how dinosaurs disappeared: they left by spaceship. (Rev: HB 8/86; SLJ 5/86)

1940 Casad, Mary Brooke. *Bluebonnet at the Marshall Train Depot* (2–4). Illus. by Benjamin Vincent. 1999, Pelican $14.95 (1-56554-311-4). Bluebonnet, an armadillo, visits a museum that was once a train depot and learns something about Texas's railroad history. (Rev: SLJ 3/00)

1941 Castle, Caroline. *Gorgeous!* (PS–K). Illus. by Sam Childs. 2000, Crown LB $16.99 (0-517-80084-5). A mother zebra protects and teaches her young Little Zeb how to cope. (Rev: HBG 10/00; SLJ 7/00)

1942 Catalanotto, Peter. *Dylan's Day Out* (PS–2). Illus. 1989, Watts LB $16.99 (0-531-08429-9).

32pp. Dylan, a bored dalmatian, escapes for a day of freedom. (Rev: BL 10/1/89; SLJ 11/89)

1943 Cauley, Lorinda Bryan. *The Trouble with Tyrannosaurus Rex* (PS–2). Illus. by author. 1988, Harcourt paper $7.00 (0-15-290881-1). 32pp. The story of how Duckbill and Ankylosaurus scare away Tyrannosaurus Rex, the terror of the forest. (Rev: BL 4/1/88; SLJ 9/88)

1944 Caumartin, Francois. *Now You See Them, Now You Don't* (PS–2). Trans. from French by David Homel. Illus. by author. 1996, Firefly paper $4.95 (1-55209-007-8). 20pp. Whimsical illustrations show animals trying to disguise themselves in different ways to fool Simon the hunter. (Rev: SLJ 1/97)

1945 Cave, Katherine. *Henry's Song* (PS–K). Illus. by Sue Hendra. 2000, Eerdmans $16.00 (0-8028-5198-3). 26pp. When the other animals objects to the quality of Henry's singing voice, the Maker encourages them to sing together in harmony. (Rev: BL 4/15/00; HBG 10/00; SLJ 9/00)

1946 Cazet, Denys. *A Fish in His Pocket* (PS–2). Illus. by author. 1987, Orchard paper $5.95 (0-531-07021-2). 32pp. Russell the bear causes the death of a fish — accidentally — in this story of who is responsible when an accident ends in death. (Rev: BL 8/87; SLJ 12/87)

1947 Cazet, Denys. *Nothing at All* (PS–1). Illus. 1994, Orchard LB $16.99 (0-531-08672-0). 32pp. A humorous picture book about silly farm animals and a scarecrow that has a mouse in his pants. (Rev: BCCB 7–8/94; BL 3/1/94; SLJ 5/94)

1948 Chadwick, Tim. *Cabbage Moon* (PS–1). Illus. by Piers Harper. 1994, Orchard $15.95 (0-531-06827-7). 32pp. A bunny travels to the moon and finds that it is a big, juicy, green cabbage. (Rev: BL 6/1–15/94; SLJ 4/94)

1949 Chall, Marsha Wilson. *Bonaparte* (PS–2). Illus. by Wendy A. Halperin. 2000, DK $16.95 (0-7894-2617-X). 32pp. Bonaparte discovers that no dogs are allowed in the school that his young master is attending, but every day he tries another hilarious scheme to get in. (Rev: BCCB 1/01; BL 10/15/00; HB 9–10/00; HBG 3/01; SLJ 9/00)

1950 Chapman, Nancy Kapp. *Doggie Dreams* (PS–2). Illus. by Lee Chapman. 2000, Putnam $15.99 (0-399-23443-8). 32pp. This book explores dogs' dreams — for example, flying an airplane and earning big bones. (Rev: BL 4/1/00; HBG 10/00; SLJ 6/00)

1951 Charles, Faustin, and Michael Terry. *The Selfish Crocodile* (PS–2). Illus. 1999, Little Tiger $14.95 (1-888444-56-8). 32pp. A selfish crocodile won't allow any animals in his river until a little mouse helps him and he realizes the value of friendship. (Rev: BL 6/1–15/99)

1952 Cherry, Lynne. *Archie, Follow Me* (PS–3). Illus. 1999, Dutton paper $4.99 (0-140-55492-0). 32pp. A girl and her cat alternate in playing follow-the-leader roles. (Rev: BL 10/1/90; HB 9–10/90; SLJ 11/90)

1953 Cherry, Lynne. *The Armadillo from Amarillo* (K–3). Illus. 1994, Harcourt $16.00 (0-15-200359-

2). 32pp. Sasparillo the armadillo wanders the earth and travels on a space shuttle to find out where he fits into the grand scheme of things. (Rev: BL 3/1/94; SLJ 4/94)

1954 Cherry, Lynne. *Who's Sick Today?* (PS–K). Illus. by author. 1998, Harcourt paper $6.00 (0-152-01886-7). 24pp. Showing such novelties as a "snake with an ache" or a "small red fox with chicken pox." (Rev: BL 5/15/88; HB 5–6/88; SLJ 7/88)

1955 Choi, Yangsook. *New Cat* (PS–1). Illus. 1999, Farrar $16.00 (0-374-35512-6). 32pp. New Cat, Mr. Kim's mouser, saves the tofu factory when a mouse gnaws through some electric wires and starts a fire. (Rev: BCCB 5/99; BL 2/1/99; HB 3–4/99; HBG 10/99; SLJ 3/99)

1956 Chorao, Kay. *The Cats Kids* (PS–K). Illus. 1998, Holiday $16.95 (0-8234-1405-1). 48pp. Three simple tales about three sibling kittens present experiences typical of brothers and sisters everywhere. (Rev: BL 11/1/98; HBG 3/99; SLJ 11/98)

1957 Chorao, Kay. *Pig and Crow* (PS–2). Illus. 2000, Holt $16.95 (0-8050-5863-X). 32pp. Pig gets help for his loneliness from Crow, who tries several ways to rid Pig of the blues. (Rev: BL 7/00*; HB 5–6/00; HBG 10/00; SLJ 6/00)

1958 Christelow, Eileen. *Five Little Monkeys Wash the Car* (PS–1). Illus. 2000, Clarion $15.00 (0-395-92566-5). 33pp. Mama, a monkey, gets help from her five little monkeys when she decides to sell the rickety old family car. (Rev: BL 5/1/00; HBG 10/00; SLJ 5/00)

1959 Christelow, Eileen. *Five Little Monkeys with Nothing to Do* (PS–1). Illus. 1996, Clarion $15.00 (0-395-75830-0). 36pp. Five little monkeys prepare for their Grandma Bessie's visit. (Rev: BCCB 12/96; BL 9/1/96; SLJ 11/96)

1960 Christelow, Eileen. *The Great Pig Escape* (PS–1). Illus. 1994, Clarion $14.95 (0-395-66973-1). 32pp. On their way to be sold at market, some pigs escape and disguise themselves as humans. (Rev: BL 9/15/94; SLJ 11/94)

1961 Christelow, Eileen. *Jerome Camps Out* (PS–3). Illus. 1998, Clarion $16.00 (0-395-75831-9). 32pp. On a camping trip, alligator Jerome gets even with the camp bully, Buster, who has put Jerome's clothes in a tree. (Rev: BL 4/15/98; HBG 10/98; SLJ 6/98)

1962 Christelow, Eileen. *The Robbery at the Diamond Dog Diner* (PS–1). Illus. by author. 1988, Houghton paper $6.95 (0-89919-722-1). 32pp. Some zany goings-on at the Diamond Dog Diner when Glenda Feathers announces that jewel thieves are in town. (Rev: BCCB 10/86; BL 11/1/86; SLJ 2/86)

1963 Clement, Gary. *The Great Poochini* (PS–2). Illus. by author. 1999, Groundwood $15.95 (0-88899-331-5). By day he is Jack, an ordinary dog, but at night he becomes the Great Poochini, the famous canine opera singer whose important role is *Dog Giovanni*. (Rev: SLJ 12/99*)

1964 Clements, Andrew. *Circus Family Dog* (PS–2). Illus. by Sue Truesdell. 2000, Clarion $15.00 (0-395-78648-7). 32pp. When a new, active dog joins the circus, old Grumps must learn a new trick to keep up. (Rev: BCCB 7–8/00; BL 6/1–15/00; HBG 10/00; SLJ 8/00)

1965 Clifford, Eth. *Flatfoot Fox and the Case of the Missing Whoooo* (1–3). Illus. by Brian Lies. 1993, Houghton $13.95 (0-395-65364-9). 46pp. The great detective sets out to find the owl's missing "whoooo." (Rev: BCCB 11/93; BL 12/15/93; SLJ 8/93)

1966 Coffey, Maria. *A Cat in a Kayak* (K–2). Illus. by Eugenie Fernandes. 1998, Annick LB $16.95 (1-55037-509-1); paper $6.95 (1-55037-508-3). Cat Teelo leaves his house in an effort to escape the noisy animals his young master brings there, but he finds that in the long run home is best. (Rev: SLJ 7/98)

1967 Cole, Babette. *Hurrah for Ethelyn* (K–3). Illus. 1991, Little, Brown $14.95 (0-316-15189-0). 32pp. A rat named Ethelyn bests the school bully, Tina Toerat. (Rev: BL 9/1/91; SLJ 3/92)

1968 Collington, Peter. *Clever Cat* (K–3). Illus. by author. 2000, Knopf $15.95 (0-375-80477-3). Tibs is such a clever cat that his owners send him out to find a job so he can become self-sufficient. (Rev: BCCB 10/00; BL 8/00; HB 9–10/00; HBG 3/01; SLJ 8/00*)

1969 Conrad, Pam. *This Mess* (K–3). Illus. by Elizabeth Sayles. 1998, Hyperion LB $15.49 (0-7868-2131-0). 32pp. Three children obey their father's wishes to make the living room look better by making such creative improvements as floating the rocking chair and raising the ceiling to let the sunshine in. (Rev: BL 4/15/98; HBG 10/98; SLJ 4/98)

1970 Cooper, Helen. *Pumpkin Soup* (PS–2). Illus. 1999, Farrar $15.00 (0-374-36164-9). 32pp. Cat, Squirrel, and Duck change duties during the traditional ritual of making pumpkin soup — with confusing results. (Rev: BL 9/1/99; HBG 3/00; SLJ 9/99)

1971 Cooper, Melrose. *Pets!* (PS–3). Illus. by Yumi Heo. 1998, Holt $15.95 (0-8050-3893-0). 32pp. A variety of imaginary animals are presented as possible pets in this rollicking picture book. (Rev: BL 4/15/98; HBG 10/98; SLJ 4/98)

1972 Cooper, Patrick. *Never Trust a Squirrel!* (PS–2). Illus. by Catherine Walters. 1999, Dutton $15.99 (0-525-46009-8). 32pp. When a fox approaches, Stella the squirrel leaves her friend William the guinea pig behind, but fortunately William's mother is there to save him. (Rev: BL 3/15/99; HBG 10/99; SLJ 7/99)

1973 Coursen, Valerie. *Mordant's Wish* (K–3). Illus. 1997, Holt $15.95 (0-8050-4374-8). 32pp. A mole named Mordant wishes for a turtle friend and eventually gets his wish. (Rev: BL 9/1/97; HBG 3/98; SLJ 9/97)

1974 Cousins, Lucy. *Maisy at the Farm* (PS–1). Illus. by author. 1998, Candlewick $12.99 (0-7636-0576-X). In this interactive book with tabs and flaps, a little mouse visits a farm and helps with the chores. (Rev: SLJ 10/98)

1975 Cousins, Lucy. *Maisy Dresses Up* (PS). Illus. 1999, Candlewick $9.99 (0-7636-0885-8); paper $3.29 (0-7636-0909-9). 24pp. Maisy, a little mouse,

decides to go to Tallulah's costume party dressed as a zebra. Also use *Maisy's Bedtime* (1999). (Rev: BL 11/15/99; HBG 3/00; SLJ 9/99)

1976 Cousins, Lucy. *Maisy Drives the Bus* (PS). Illus. by author. 2000, Candlewick $9.99 (0-7636-1083-6); paper $3.29 (0-7636-1085-2). Maisy, a young mouse, proves that she is a responsible driver in this simple picture book. Also use *Maisy Takes a Bath* (2000). (Rev: HBG 10/00; SLJ 6/00)

1977 Cousins, Lucy. *Maisy Goes Swimming* (PS). Illus. 1990, Little, Brown $13.95 (0-316-15834-8). Maisy, a mouse, goes to a swimming pool in this book that contains many flaps and tabs. Also use: *Maisy Goes to Bed* (1990). (Rev: BCCB 10/90*; SLJ 9/90)

1978 Cousins, Lucy. *Maisy Goes to School* (PS–K). Illus. 1992, Candlewick $13.99 (1-56402-085-1). Maisy, a little mouse, enjoys all the various activities when she attends preschool. Also use: *Maisy Goes to the Playground* (1992). (Rev: SLJ 11/92)

1979 Cousins, Lucy. *Maisy Makes Gingerbread* (PS). Illus. 1999, Candlewick $9.99 (0-7636-0887-4); paper $3.29 (0-7636-0910-2). 24pp. Maisy the mouse makes gingerbread cookies shaped like animals, using a recipe that children can follow. Also use *Maisy's Pool* (1999). (Rev: BL 11/15/99; HBG 3/00; SLJ 9/99)

1980 Cousins, Lucy. *Where Are Maisy's Friends?* (PS). Illus. by author. 2000, Candlewick $4.99 (0-7636-1119-0). A flap board book in which the reader is asked to play hide-and-seek with Maisy, a mouse, and her friends by lifting the flaps. Also use: *Where Does Maisy Live?* (2000). (Rev: SLJ 12/00)

1981 Cousins, Lucy. *Za-Za's Baby Brother* (PS). Illus. 1995, Candlewick $16.99 (1-56402-582-9). 32pp. At first, Za-Za, a young zebra, has problems adjusting to her mother's new baby. (Rev: BL 9/1/95; SLJ 10/95)

1982 Cowley, Joy. *The Mouse Bride* (PS–1). Illus. by David Christiana. 1995, Scholastic $13.95 (0-590-47503-7). 32pp. A tiny mouse sets out to find a husband and after many rejections finds the mouse of her dreams. (Rev: BCCB 11/95; BL 1/1–15/96; SLJ 11/95)

1983 Cox, Judy. *Rabbit Pirates: A Tale of the Spinach Main* (PS–3). Illus. by Emily Arnold McCully. 1999, Harcourt $16.00 (0-15-201832-8). 32pp. Two elderly rabbits run a restaurant in Provence, France, where they remember their past experiences together. (Rev: BL 10/15/99; HBG 3/00; SLJ 10/99)

1984 Coxon, Michele. *The Cat Who Lost His Purr* (K–2). Illus. by author. 1996, Puffin paper $4.99 (0-140-55608-7). A tabby cat wakes up one morning to find that his purr has gone. (Rev: SLJ 3/92)

1985 Crebbin, June. *Fly by Night* (PS–3). Illus. by Stephen Lambert. 1993, Candlewick $14.95 (1-56402-149-1). 32pp. A young owl waits impatiently through the day for the nighttime when he can fly. (Rev: BL 3/15/93; SLJ 4/93)

1986 Cresp, Gael. *The Tale of Gilbert Alexander Pig* (PS–2). Illus. 2000, Barefoot $15.95 (1-84148-215-3). 32pp. A clever little pig who realizes that the wolf could be a serious threat reaches an agreement with him so they can help each other. (Rev: BL 3/15/00; SLJ 8/00)

1987 Crimi, Carolyn. *Don't Need Friends* (PS–2). Illus. by Lynn Munsinger. 1999, Doubleday $15.95 (0-385-32643-2). 32pp. A rat, who has sworn never to make friends with anyone, changes his mind when he meets a dog who is as grumpy as he is. (Rev: BCCB 1/00; BL 11/15/99; HB 11–12/99; HBG 3/00; SLJ 1/00)

1988 Crisp, Marty. *Black and White* (PS–K). Illus. by Sherry Neidigh. 2000, Rising Moon $12.95 (0-87358-756-1). 24pp. A series of picture puzzles are presented in this picture book about a black-and-white dog that gets lost on a farm where there are only black-and-white animals. (Rev: BL 6/1–15/00; HBG 3/01; SLJ 8/00)

1989 Cronin, Doreen. *Click, Clack, Moo: Cows That Type* (PS–3). Illus. by Betsy Lewin. 2000, Simon & Schuster $15.00 (0-689-83213-3). 32pp. In this humorous tale, barnyard animals go on strike for better working conditions including electric blankets for cold nights. (Rev: BCCB 9/00; BL 4/1/00; HB 3–4/00; HBG 10/00)

1990 Crume, Marion. *Do You See Mouse?* (PS–2). Illus. by Normand Chartier. 1995, Silver Pr. LB $18.95 (0-382-24683-7); paper $5.95 (0-382-24685-3). Visual clues are used so the reader can enter into the animals' game of hide-and-seek. (Rev: SLJ 7/95)

1991 *Curious George and the Puppies* (PS–K). Illus. 1998, Houghton $12.00 (0-395-91217-2); paper $3.95 (0-395-91215-6). 24pp. This is one of a new series of eight books about the mischievous monkey. Other titles include *Curious George Goes to a Movie, Curious George Makes Pancakes,* and *Curious George's Dream.* (Rev: BL 11/15/98; HBG 3/99)

1992 Currey, Anna. *Tickling Tigers* (PS–K). Illus. 1996, Barron's $12.95 (0-8120-6594-8); paper $5.95 (0-8120-9594-4). 32pp. Hannibal, a little mouse, narrowly escapes capture by several tigers whom he has enraged. (Rev: BL 10/15/96)

1993 Curtiss, A. B. *In the Company of Bears* (K–2). Illus. by Barbara Stone. 1994, Oldcastle LB $18.95 (0-932529-72-0). Humorous illustrations depict polar bears engaging in many human activities. (Rev: SLJ 9/94)

1994 Dahan, Andre. *Squiggle's Tale* (PS–2). Illus. 2000, Chronicle $14.95 (0-8118-2664-3). 32pp. Squiggle, a piglet, writes home describing the peaceful day she has spent at play, but the reader sees all sorts of strange activities taking place in the background. (Rev: BL 4/1/00; HBG 10/00; SLJ 4/00)

1995 Dahl, Roald. *The Enormous Crocodile* (K–3). Illus. by Quentin Blake. 1978, Puffin paper $3.99 (0-140-36556-7). 48pp. Animals band together to save a group of children from becoming a crocodile's lunch.

1996 Daugherty, James. *Andy and the Lion* (1–4). Illus. by author. 1938, Puffin paper $5.99 (0-14-050277-7). 80pp. A popular, modern version of the story of Androcles and the lion.

1997 Davenier, Christine. *Leon and Albertine* (PS–1). Illus. 1998, Orchard $15.95 (0-531-30072-2). 32pp. Leo, a pig, is attracted to Albertine, a chicken who is decidedly not interested. (Rev: BCCB 3/98; BL 2/1/98; HBG 10/98; SLJ 3/98*)

1998 Davis, Katie. *Who Hops?* (PS–1). Illus. 1998, Harcourt $13.00 (0-15-201839-5). 36pp. A nonsense book in which a variety of animals perform impossible feats, such as cows hopping like frogs. (Rev: BL 9/15/98; HBG 3/99; SLJ 9/98)

1999 Davol, Marguerite W. *Batwings and the Curtain of Night* (PS–4). Illus. by Mary GrandPré. 1997, Orchard $15.95 (0-531-30005-6). 32pp. In order to get more light, some nocturnal animals decide to pull back the curtain of night in this creation story. (Rev: BCCB 4/97; BL 4/15/97; SLJ 4/97)

2000 Day, Alexandra. *Carl Goes to Daycare* (PS–2). Illus. 1993, Farrar $12.95 (0-374-31093-9). 32pp. In an emergency, Carl the rottweiler has to take care of youngsters at a day care center. (Rev: BCCB 11/93; BL 12/15/93; SLJ 12/93)

2001 Day, Alexandra. *Carl's Afternoon in the Park* (2–6). Illus. 1991, Farrar $12.95 (0-374-31109-9). 32pp. Carl, a rottweiler, is placed in charge of a puppy and a toddler while Mom goes for tea with a friend in the park. (Rev: BCCB 11/91; BL 10/15/91; SLJ 11/91)

2002 Day, Alexandra. *Carl's Christmas* (PS–K). Illus. 1990, Farrar $12.95 (0-374-31114-5). 32pp. On Christmas Eve, Carl, a big black dog, takes the baby he is caring for out to greet the world. (Rev: BCCB 10/90; BL 11/1/90)

2003 Day, Alexandra. *Follow Carl!* (PS–2). Illus. 1998, Farrar $12.95 (0-374-34380-2). 32pp. Carl, the enterprising rottweiler, and a group of children play follow-the-leader. The children soon find themselves rolling in the grass, fetching sticks, and chasing a squirrel. (Rev: BL 8/98; HBG 3/99)

2004 Day, Alexandra. *Frank and Ernest on the Road* (PS–3). Illus. 1994, Scholastic $14.95 (0-590-45048-4). 48pp. Highway slang is introduced as Frank the bear and Ernest the elephant hit the road in a truck. (Rev: BCCB 3/94; BL 12/15/93*; SLJ 2/94*)

2005 Day, Alexandra. *Frank and Ernest Play Ball* (K–4). Illus. 1990, Scholastic $12.95 (0-590-42548-X). 48pp. The intrepid bear and elephant temporarily manage a baseball team. (Rev: BCCB 6/90; BL 3/1/90; SLJ 2/90)

2006 Day, David. *King of the Woods* (K–2). Illus. by Ken Brown. 1993, Four Winds LB $13.95 (0-02-726361-4). A little wren defeats all the stronger animals in the forest and claims as her own the golden apple she has found. (Rev: SLJ 3/94)

2007 De Beer, Hans. *Bernard Bear's Amazing Adventure* (K–3). Illus. 1994, North-South LB $14.88 (1-55858-295-9). 32pp. Bernard the bear wants to spend the winter in Florida, but instead he must hibernate with some dormice. (Rev: BL 12/15/94; SLJ 7/95)

2008 De Beer, Hans. *Little Polar Bear and the Husky Pup* (PS). Illus. by author. 1999, North-South LB $15.88 (0-7358-1155-5). The little polar bear gets lost on a walk and meets a number of other animals on his way home. (Rev: HBG 3/00; SLJ 3/00)

2009 De Beer, Hans. *Little Polar Bear Finds a Friend* (PS–2). 1990, North-South $13.95 (1-55858-092-1). 32pp. A clever walrus is able to help Lars, a polar bear, escape captors. (Rev: BL 11/15/90; SLJ 2/91)

2010 De Beer, Hans. *Little Polar Bear, Take Me Home!* (PS–2). Illus. 1996, North-South LB $15.88 (1-55858-631-8). 32pp. Sasha, a tiger cub, is helped home by Lars, a little polar bear. (Rev: BL 11/1/96; SLJ 11/96)

2011 De Brunhoff, Jean. *The Story of Babar, the Little Elephant* (PS). Illus. by author. 1937, Random LB $5.99 (0-394-90575-X). A time-tested reading favorite about the little French elephant.

2012 De Brunhoff, Laurent. *Babar and the Succotash Bird* (PS–1). Illus. 2000, Abrams $16.95 (0-8109-5700-0). 32pp. Alexander, Babar the elephant's son, encounters a magical bird that squawks "Succotash" and gives him the power of flight. (Rev: BL 12/1/00; HBG 3/01; SLJ 12/00)

2013 Decesare, Angelo. *Flip's Fantastic Journal* (K–3). Illus. by author. 1999, Dutton $13.99 (0-525-46262-7). A little dog, who is experiencing a day where things go wrong, uses his imagination and writes about it as if it were a fantastic one. (Rev: HBG 3/00; SLJ 10/99)

2014 Degen, Bruce. *Daddy Is a Doodlebug* (PS–1). Illus. 2000, HarperCollins LB $15.89 (0-06-028416-1). 40pp. A little bug and his dad spend a fine day together. (Rev: BL 6/1–15/00; HBG 10/00; SLJ 4/00)

2015 Degen, Bruce. *Jamberry* (PS–1). Illus. by author. 1983, HarperCollins LB $15.89 (0-06-021417-1). 32pp. A boy and a bear collect berries for jam.

2016 Degen, Bruce. *Sailaway Home* (PS–K). Illus. 1996, Scholastic $14.95 (0-590-46443-4). 32pp. A little pig imagines all sorts of adventures that could take place aboard his toy boat. (Rev: BL 8/96; SLJ 3/96)

2017 Delano, Marfe Ferguson. *Kangaroos* (PS–K). Series: Animal Safari. 2000, National Geographic $5.95 (0-7922-7125-4). This small board book introduces toddlers to kangaroos. Also use *Tree Frogs* (2000). (Rev: SLJ 8/00)

2018 Demarest, Chris L. *Honk!* (PS–1). Illus. by author. 1998, Boyds Mills $9.95 (1-56397-221-2). Using flaps, different animals and the sounds they make are revealed in this story about a lost duck. (Rev: HBG 3/99; SLJ 10/98)

2019 Demarest, Chris L. *Zookeeper Sue: A Lift-the-Flap Book* (PS). Illus. by author. 1999, Harcourt $10.95 (0-15-202017-9). In this interactive flap book, a frisky parrot accompanies Zookeeper Sue as she feeds the animals. (Rev: SLJ 8/99)

2020 Denim, Sue. *The Dumb Bunnies* (K–2). Illus. by Dav Pilkey. 1994, Scholastic $13.95 (0-590-47708-0). 32pp. The story of the three dumb bunnies and their hectic misadventures. (Rev: BL 1/15/94; SLJ 3/94)

2021 Denim, Sue. *The Dumb Bunnies Go to the Zoo* (1–3). Illus. by Dav Pilkey. 1997, Scholastic $14.95 (0-590-84735-X). 32pp. The three Dumb Bunnies go to the zoo, where they create havoc. (Rev: BL 4/1/97; SLJ 3/97)

2022 Denim, Sue. *Make Way for Dumb Bunnies* (1–3). Illus. by Dav Pilkey. 1996, Scholastic $12.95 (0-590-58286-0). 32pp. A slapstick tale about the misadventures of an unthinking rabbit family. (Rev: BL 2/1/96; SLJ 3/96)

2023 Denslow, Sharon P. *Big Wolf and Little Wolf* (PS–K). Illus. by Cathie Felstead. 2000, Greenwillow $15.95 (0-688-16174-X). 32pp. Little Wolf is frightened by strange noises coming from the bushes and discovers it is his mother playing a trick on him. (Rev: BCCB 7–8/00; BL 5/1/00; HBG 10/00; SLJ 5/00)

2024 dePaola, Tomie. *Bill and Pete Go Down the Nile* (K–3). Illus. by author. 1987, Putnam $15.95 (0-399-21395-3); paper $5.99 (0-698-11401-9). 32pp. A crocodile and a bird in a delightful romp down the Nile. (Rev: BL 5/1/87; SLJ 9/87)

2025 dePaola, Tomie. *Bill and Pete to the Rescue* (PS–2). Illus. 1998, Putnam $15.99 (0-399-23208-7). 48pp. Pete the Crocodile and his friend Bill, a bird, help save Pete's cousin, little Jane Allison, from the hands of Bad Guy's Big Bad Brother. (Rev: BCCB 7–8/98; BL 5/15/98; SLJ 5/98)

2026 dePaola, Tomie. *Bonjour, Mr. Satie* (1–3). Illus. 1991, Putnam $15.95 (0-399-21782-7). 32pp. Mr. Satie, a cat, tells his niece and nephew about exciting experiences in the art salons of Paris. (Rev: BCCB 3/91; BL 3/1/93)

2027 dePaola, Tomie. *Four Stories for Four Seasons* (2–3). Illus. by author. 1994, Simon & Schuster paper $6.95 (0-671-88633-9). 48pp. Dog, Cat, Frog, and Pig are involved in activities for each season in this reissued picture book. Also use: *Michael Bird Boy* (1987).

2028 dePaola, Tomie. *The Knight and the Dragon* (1–3). Illus. by author. 1998, Putnam $16.99 (0-399-20707-4); paper $5.99 (0-698-11623-2). An inexperienced knight and an inexperienced dragon prepare themselves to do battle.

2029 dePaola, Tomie. *Little Grunt and the Big Egg: A Prehistoric Fairy Tale* (PS–3). Illus. 1990, Holiday LB $16.95 (0-8234-0730-6). 32pp. Little Grunt adopts a pet dinosaur named George. (Rev: BL 4/1/90)

2030 Derby, Sally. *The Mouse Who Owned the Sun* (PS–2). Illus. by Friso Henstra. 1993, Four Winds LB $14.95 (0-02-766965-3). A mouse who believes that he controls the sun sets out to explore the world. (Rev: SLJ 5/94)

2031 Desmoinaux, Christel. *Mrs. Hen's Big Surprise* (PS–1). Illus. 2000, Simon & Schuster $12.95 (0-689-83403-9). 32pp. Lonely Mrs. Hen hatches a giant egg she has found and out pops a lovable baby dinosaur. (Rev: BL 4/1/00; HBG 10/00; SLJ 4/00)

2032 De Vries, Anke. *My Elephant Can Do Almost Anything* (PS–1). Illus. by Ilja Walraven. 1996,

Front Street $14.95 (1-886910-06-5). A boy's imaginary playmate, an elephant, is upset when the boy goes to school. (Rev: BCCB 6/96; HB 7–8/96; SLJ 6/96)

2033 De Vries, Anke. *Piggy's Birthday Dream* (PS). Illus. by Jung-Hee Spetter. 1997, Front Street $14.95 (1-886910-21-9). 32pp. Piggy is so shy that she doesn't tell any of the barnyard animals it's her birthday, but they plan their own surprise for her. (Rev: BL 11/15/97; HBG 3/98; SLJ 11/97)

2034 Dodds, Siobhan. *Grumble-Rumble!* (PS). Illus. by author. Series: Toddler Storybook. 2000, DK paper $5.95 (0-7894-5624-9). 24pp. A very simple story about a hungry kangaroo who gets frightened when his stomach begins to rumble. (Rev: SLJ 10/00)

2035 Donaldson, Julia. *The Gruffalo* (PS–3). Illus. by Axel Scheffler. 1999, Dial $15.99 (0-8037-2386-5). 32pp. A mouse frightens away his animal enemies with tales of a make-believe monster, the gruffalo, but unfortunately for him a real gruffalo appears. (Rev: BL 7/99; HBG 10/99; SLJ 8/99)

2036 Donohue, Dorothy. *Veggie Soup* (PS–3). Illus. 2000, Winslow $15.95 (1-890817-21-X). 40pp. When Miss Bun, a rabbit, decides to create her own veggie soup, each of her friends brings a different ingredient. (Rev: BL 11/15/00; HBG 3/01; SLJ 10/00)

2037 Douzou, Olivier. *The Wolf's Lunch* (PS). Illus. by author. 1997, Chronicle $6.95 (0-8118-1806-3). A board book for older children introduces the components of a wolf's head in modernistic drawings. (Rev: SLJ 4/98)

2038 Dragonwagon, Crescent. *Alligators and Others All Year Long: A Book of Months* (PS–1). Illus. by Jose Aruego and Ariane Dewey. 1993, Macmillan $14.95 (0-02-733091-5). 32pp. For each of the months, a different animal engages in a suitable activity, such as a cat ice skating in January. (Rev: BL 10/15/93; SLJ 1/94)

2039 Dubanevich, Arlene. *Pig William* (PS–1). Illus. by author. 1985, Simon & Schuster LB $14.95 (0-02-733200-4). 32pp. Pig William is such a dawdler that his brothers leave without him for a picnic. (Rev: BCCB 12/85; BL 1/15/86)

2040 Duke, Kate. *Aunt Isabel Tells a Good One* (PS–3). Illus. 1992, Dutton $15.99 (0-525-44835-7). 32pp. In this tale-within-a-tale, Aunt Isabel spins a "good story" for her mouse child niece. (Rev: BL 1/15/92; SLJ 3/92)

2041 Dunbar, Joyce. *Baby Bird* (PS–1). Illus. by Russell Ayto. 1998, Candlewick $15.99 (0-7636-0322-8). 32pp. Several animals encounter Baby Bird after he falls out of his nest; he perseveres and saves himself by learning to fly. (Rev: BL 6/1–15/98; HBG 10/98; SLJ 7/98)

2042 Dunbar, Joyce. *The Bowl of Fruit* (PS–2). Illus. by Helen Craig. Series: Panda and Gander Stories. 1999, Candlewick $9.99 (0-7636-0706-1). A slight story about Gander protecting his share of a bowl of fruit after Panda has eaten more than his allotment. Also use *Gander's Pond, Panda's New Toy,* and *The Secret Friend.* (Rev: BCCB 6/99; HBG 10/99; SLJ 8/99)

2043 Dunbar, Joyce. *Eggday* (PS–K). Illus. by Jane Cabrera. 1999, Holiday $15.95 (0-8234-1510-4). 32pp. Dora the Duck declares that tomorrow is Eggday and that each animal, including the horse and pig, should bring their eggs. (Rev: BL 4/1/99; HB 5–6/99; HBG 10/99; SLJ 7/99)

2044 Dunbar, Joyce. *The Pig Who Wished* (PS–K). Illus. by Selina Young. 1999, DK $9.95 (0-7894-3487-3). 28pp. After a pig swallows a magic acorn, she finds that all her wishes come true. (Rev: BL 4/15/99; HBG 10/99; SLJ 5/99)

2045 Duncan, Lois. *I Walk at Night* (PS–3). Illus. by Steve Johnson and Lou Fancher. 2000, Viking $15.99 (0-670-87513-9). 32pp. Told from a cat's point of view, this story describes the feline's independent life. (Rev: BCCB 2/00; BL 2/1/00; HBG 10/00; SLJ 3/00)

2046 Durant, Alan. *Big Bad Bunny* (PS–2). Illus. by Guy Parker-Rees. 2001, Dutton $15.99 (0-525-46667-3). Set in the old West, this is the story of a rabbit that terrorizes a community until Wise Old Bunny changes him into a solid citizen. (Rev: SLJ 2/01)

2047 Duvoisin, Roger. *Petunia* (K–2). Illus. by author. 1962, Knopf LB $17.99 (0-394-90865-1). Petunia, the silly goose, finds a book and carries it around believing this will make her wise, until her own foolishness proves her wrong.

2048 Edens, Cooper, and Daniel Lane. *The Animal Mall* (PS–2). Illus. by Edward Miller. 2000, Dial $15.99 (0-8037-1984-1). 32pp. A family takes Mom to a shopping mall to choose a birthday gift in this zany story where all the shops are run by animals. (Rev: BL 8/00; HBG 3/01; SLJ 9/00)

2049 Eduar, Gilles. *Jooka Saves the Day* (PS–2). Trans. by Dominic Barth. Illus. 1997, Orchard $15.95 (0-531-30036-6). 40pp. Jooka tries to be like all the crocodiles in the rain forest, but it is impossible because he is really a dragon. (Rev: BL 12/1/97; HB 9–10/97; HBG 3/98; SLJ 9/97)

2050 Edward, Pamela Duncan. *Ed and Fred Flea* (PS–3). Illus. by Henry Cole. 1999, Hyperion LB $15.49 (0-7868-2410-7). 32pp. A greedy flea named Fred feigns illness to trick kind flea Ed into leaving his home so that Fred can have the dog they share for himself. (Rev: BL 9/15/99; HBG 3/00; SLJ 9/99)

2051 Edwards, Pamela Duncan. *Dinorella: A Prehistoric Fairytale* (K–3). Illus. by Henry Cole. 1997, Hyperion LB $16.49 (0-7868-2249-X). 32pp. A raucous, exuberant reworking of the Cinderella story using dinosaurs. (Rev: BL 11/1/97; HBG 3/98; SLJ 11/97)

2052 Edwards, Pamela Duncan. *Four Famished Foxes and Fosdyke* (K–3). Illus. by Henry Cole. 1995, HarperCollins LB $14.89 (0-06-024926-9). 32pp. The letter *F* figures prominently in this story about four foraging foxes. (Rev: BL 9/1/95; SLJ 12/95)

2053 Edwards, Pamela Duncan. *The Grumpy Morning* (PS–1). Illus. by Darcia Labrosse. 1998, Hyperion LB $14.49 (0-7868-2279-1). A variety of farm animals impatiently await their morning meal while the mistress of the farm lies asleep. (Rev: HBG 10/98; SLJ 6/98)

2054 Edwards, Pamela Duncan. *Honk!* (1–3). Illus. by Henry Cole. 1998, Hyperion LB $15.49 (0-7868-2384-4). 32pp. When Mimi the swan is bitten by the ballet bug, her determination leads to a sensational debut at the Paris Opera House. (Rev: BCCB 10/98; BL 9/1/98; HB 11–12/98; HBG 3/99; SLJ 9/98)

2055 Edwards, Pamela Duncan. *Livingstone Mouse* (PS–2). Illus. by Henry Cole. 1996, HarperCollins LB $15.89 (0-06-025870-5). 32pp. A mouse decides that China would be a nice place for him to build his nest. (Rev: BL 10/1/96; SLJ 9/96)

2056 Edwards, Pamela Duncan. *Some Smug Slug* (PS–3). Illus. by Henry Cole. 1996, HarperCollins LB $15.89 (0-06-024792-4). 32pp. Alliterations abound in this saga of a slug and a slippery slope. (Rev: BL 5/1/96; SLJ 6/96*)

2057 Edwards, Pamela Duncan. *The Worrywarts* (K–3). Illus. by Henry Cole. 1999, HarperCollins LB $14.89 (0-06-028149-9). 32pp. In this book that focuses on the letter "W," Wombat, Weasel, and Woodchuck wander in the world. (Rev: BL 1/1–15/00; HBG 3/00; SLJ 11/99)

2058 Edwards, Richard. *Copy Me, Copycub* (PS–K). Illus. by Susan Winter. 1999, HarperCollins $14.95 (0-06-028570-2). 32pp. From spring to winter hibernation, this book tells of a year in the life of a mother bear and the little child she calls Copycub because he repeats everything she does. (Rev: BL 9/1/99; HBG 3/00; SLJ 12/99)

2059 Edwards, Richard. *Moles Can Dance* (PS–K). Illus. by Caroline Anstey. 1994, Candlewick $13.95 (1-56402-353-2). 32pp. A little mole learns to dance by watching a girl twirling to music in a deserted field. (Rev: BL 6/1–15/94; SLJ 9/94)

2060 Edwards, Roland. *Tigers* (PS–K). Illus. by Judith Riches. 1992, Morrow LB $14.93 (0-688-11686-8). 32pp. A child imagines hearing a pride of playful tigers just beyond the bedroom door. (Rev: BL 2/1/93; SLJ 12/92)

2061 Egan, Tim. *Burnt Toast on Davenport Street* (K–2). Illus. 1997, Houghton $14.95 (0-395-79618-0). 32pp. A fly — who has granted Arthur, a dog, three wishes — gets the wishes mixed up in this hilarious fantasy. (Rev: BL 4/15/97; SLJ 5/97*)

2062 Egan, Tim. *Friday Night at Hodges' Cafe* (PS–1). Illus. 1994, Houghton $14.95 (0-395-68076-X). 32pp. Hodges, a cafe frequented by elephants, has a no-tigers policy. (Rev: BL 10/1/94; SLJ 9/94*)

2063 Egan, Tim. *Metropolitan Cow* (PS–2). Illus. 1996, Houghton $15.00 (0-395-73096-1). 32pp. The Gibbonses, an upper-crust cow family, are upset when Webster and his pig family move into their apartment building. (Rev: BL 3/1/96*; HB 7–8/96; SLJ 5/96*)

2064 Egielski, Richard. *Jazper* (PS–2). Illus. 1998, HarperCollins LB $14.89 (0-06-027999-0). 32pp. Jazper and his dad are bugs. When Dad breaks three of his four legs, Jazper gets a job house-sitting for

some moths and becomes a magician. (Rev: BCCB 11/98; BL 9/15/98; HBG 3/99; SLJ 9/98)

2065 Ehlert, Lois. *Mole's Hill* (PS–2). Illus. 1994, Harcourt $15.00 (0-15-255116-6). 32pp. Fox demands that Mole move from her hill, but she is able to outwit him and remain. (Rev: BCCB 4/94; BL 3/15/94; HB 7–8/94; SLJ 5/94)

2066 Ehlert, Lois. *Nuts to You!* (PS–2). Illus. 1993, Harcourt $16.00 (0-15-257647-9). A rural squirrel shows how he gathers food in the big city. (Rev: BL 3/1/93; HB 3–4/93; SLJ 4/93)

2067 Ehlert, Lois. *Top Cat* (PS–1). Illus. 1998, Harcourt $16.00 (0-15-201739-9). 40pp. Top Cat resents the arrival of a new striped kitten in his household, but soon they become friends. (Rev: BL 8/98; HBG 3/99; SLJ 9/98)

2068 Elgar, Rebecca. *Jack: It's a Rainy Day* (PS). Illus. by author. Series: Jack. 1999, Kingfisher $10.95 (0-7534-5208-1). Using flaps and tabs, the reader traces the activities of a puppy on a rainy day when he accidentally drops his beloved teddy in a puddle. Also use *Jack: It's a Sunny Day* (1999). (Rev: SLJ 9/99)

2069 Ellwand, David, and Ruth Ellwand. *Midas Mouse* (PS–2). Photos by David Ellwand. 2000, Lothrop $14.95 (0-688-16745-4). 32pp. Midas Mouse gets his wish and everything he touches turns to gold, but he realizes he has problems when his cheese is inedible. (Rev: BL 10/1/00; HBG 3/01; SLJ 11/00)

2070 Elsdale, Bob. *Mac Side Up* (PS–2). Illus. 2000, Dutton $15.99 (0-525-46467-0). 32pp. Mac the cat, aided by Dusty the ferret, rigs up an elaborate experiment to determine why toast always lands buttered side down. (Rev: BCCB 12/00; BL 12/15/00; HBG 3/01; SLJ 11/00)

2071 Elya, Susan Middleton. *Eight Animals on the Town* (1–3). Illus. by Lee Chapman. 2000, Putnam $15.99 (0-399-23437-3). 32pp. English and Spanish words are mixed in this delightful story about eight animals who head into town for dinner. (Rev: BCCB 1/01; BL 12/1/00; HBG 3/01; SLJ 9/00)

2072 Enderle, Judith R., and Stephanie G. Tessler. *Six Sandy Sheep* (PS–1). Illus. by John O'Brien. 1997, Boyds Mills $14.95 (1-56397-582-3). This alliterative story tells how six sheep spend a day at the beach, where they swim, splash, surf, ski, snorkel, and collect shells. (Rev: SLJ 7/97)

2073 Enderle, Judith R., and Stephanie G. Tessler. *What Would Mama Do?* (K–3). Illus. by Chris L. Demarest. 1995, Boyds Mills $14.95 (1-56397-418-5). 32pp. To outwit a clever Fox, Little Lilly, a goose, decides that she must do what her mama would do. (Rev: BL 10/1/95)

2074 Ernst, Lisa Campbell. *Bubba and Trixie* (PS–2). Illus. 1997, Simon & Schuster paper $16.00 (0-689-81357-0). 32pp. Trixie, a ladybug, teaches a timid caterpillar how to enjoy life. (Rev: BL 8/97; HBG 3/98; SLJ 11/97)

2075 Ernst, Lisa Campbell. *Duke the Dairy Delight Dog* (PS–1). Illus. 1996, Simon & Schuster paper $15.00 (0-689-80750-3). 32pp. Duke, a mangy dog, would like to find a home at the local ice cream parlor. (Rev: BCCB 1/97; BL 9/1/96; SLJ 9/96)

2076 Ernst, Lisa Campbell. *Ginger Jumps* (PS–1). Illus. 1996, Simon & Schuster paper $5.99 (0-689-80652-3). 32pp. Ginger learns simple tricks at the circus but doesn't want to jump through hoops. (Rev: BCCB 6/90; BL 5/15/90*; SLJ 7/90*)

2077 Ernst, Lisa Campbell. *Little Red Riding Hood: A Newfangled Prairie Tale* (K–3). Illus. 1995, Simon & Schuster paper $16.00 (0-689-80145-9). 32pp. The wolf is really after Grandma's recipe for muffins in this update of *Little Red Riding Hood*. (Rev: BCCB 10/95; BL 7/95; SLJ 9/95)

2078 Ernst, Lisa Campbell. *Walter's Tail* (K–2). Illus. 1992, Macmillan paper $14.95 (0-02-733564-X). Walter the dog has a wildly waving tail that always gets him into trouble. (Rev: BCCB 5–6/92; SLJ 4/92*)

2079 Ernst, Lisa Campbell. *When Bluebell Sang* (K–3). Illus. by author. 1989, Macmillan paper $5.99 (0-689-71584-6). 40pp. Bluebell the cow finds that life behind the footlights isn't all it's cracked up to be. (Rev: BL 3/1/89; SLJ 4/89)

2080 Eversole, Robyn. *Red Berry Wool* (PS–2). Illus. by Tim Coffey. 1999, Albert Whitman $15.95 (0-8075-0654-0). 32pp. Lalo, a little lamb, tries to make a sweater out of his own wool with disastrous but humorous results. (Rev: BL 9/1/99; HBG 3/00; SLJ 10/99)

2081 Ezra, Mark. *The Frightened Little Owl* (PS–K). Illus. by Gavin Rowe. 1997, Interlink $14.95 (1-56656-264-3). 32pp. Fearful Little Owl takes her first flight in order to find her mother and discovers that she likes it. (Rev: BL 6/1–15/97; SLJ 7/97)

2082 Ezra, Mark. *The Hungry Otter* (PS–2). Illus. by Gavin Rowe. 1996, Crocodile $14.95 (1-56656-216-3). When Little Otter saves a crow from a fox, the crow, in turn, helps the otter by breaking holes in the ice so that the animal can fish. (Rev: SLJ 4/97)

2083 Fair, David. *The Fabulous Four Skunks* (PS–2). Illus. by Bruce Koscielniak. 1996, Houghton $14.95 (0-395-73572-6). 32pp. Four smelly skunks, members of a band, find it difficult to attract an audience. (Rev: BL 2/1/96; SLJ 4/96)

2084 Falconer, Ian. *Olivia* (PS–K). Illus. 2000, Simon & Schuster $16.00 (0-689-82953-1). 40pp. An outstanding picture book about Olivia, a delightful little pig, who is a bundle of energy and talent. (Rev: BCCB 11/00*; BL 8/00*; HBG 3/01; SLJ 9/00)

2085 Falda, Dominique. *The Treasure Chest* (PS–2). Trans. by Rosemary Lanning. Illus. 1999, North-South LB $15.88 (0-7358-1050-8). 24pp. When Squirrel uncovers a treasure chest, each of the forest animals dreams about its contents. (Rev: BL 6/1–15/99; HBG 10/99)

2086 Faulkner, Keith. *The Long-Nosed Pig* (PS–K). Illus. by Jonathan Lambert. 1998, Dial $12.99 (0-8037-2296-6). An interactive pop-up book about a long-nosed pig that has an accident in which it is flattened. (Rev: BL 12/15/97; HBG 10/98; SLJ 8/98)

2087 Faulkner, Keith. *The Wide-Mouthed Frog* (PS–1). Illus. by Jonathan Lambert. 1996, Dial $12.99 (0-8037-1875-6). 14pp. An interactive book that pictures a variety of animals and their eating habits. (Rev: BL 2/1/96; SLJ 4/96)

2088 Feiffer, Jules. *Bark, George* (PS–3). Illus. 1999, HarperCollins LB $14.89 (0-06-205186-5). 32pp. When puppy George is asked to bark by his mother, he manages to produce a range of animal sounds including a "meow" and a "moo," but never an "arf." (Rev: BCCB 11/99; BL 8/99*; HBG 3/00; SLJ 9/99)

2089 Flack, Marjorie. *Ask Mr. Bear* (PS–1). Illus. by author. 1968, Macmillan $14.00 (0-02-735390-7); paper $5.99 (0-02-043090-6). 32pp. To find a present for his mother's birthday, Danny asks a variety of animals for suggestions, with little success until he meets Mr. Bear.

2090 Fleming, Denise. *Lunch* (PS–K). Illus. 1992, Holt $16.95 (0-8050-1636-8). 30pp. A mouse samples all the goodies on a banquet table and gets fatter and fatter. (Rev: BCCB 12/92; BL 11/1/92; HB 1–2/93; SLJ 12/92*)

2091 Fleming, Denise. *Mama Cat Has Three Kittens* (PS–K). Illus. 1998, Holt $15.95 (0-8050-5745-5). 32pp. Two of Mama Cat's kittens are well behaved, but the third, Boris, just loves to nap. (Rev: BCCB 12/98; BL 11/15/98; HBG 3/99; SLJ 11/98)

2092 Fleming, Denise. *Time to Sleep* (PS–1). Illus. 1997, Holt $16.95 (0-8050-3762-4). 32pp. In this cumulative tale, Bear passes along the information that winter is on the way. (Rev: BL 10/1/97; HBG 3/98; SLJ 11/97)

2093 Ford, Miela. *On My Own* (PS). Photos by author. 1999, Greenwillow $5.95 (0-688-16452-8). A board book illustrated with photographs about a polar bear cub who wants to be able to play on his own. (Rev: SLJ 7/99)

2094 Fox, Christyan, and Diane Fox. *Goodnight PiggyWiggy* (PS). Illus. by authors. 2000, Handprint $12.95 (1-929766-06-8). Using a different flap to explore each career, a pig wonders what he will do when he grows up. (Rev: BL 12/1/00; SLJ 12/00)

2095 Fox, Mem. *Hattie and the Fox* (PS–K). Illus. by Patricia Mullins. 1987, Macmillan $16.00 (0-02-735470-9); paper $5.99 (0-689-71611-7). 32pp. A cumulative tale about a big black hen who spies a fox in the farmyard. (Rev: BL 3/15/87; HB 5–6/87; SLJ 5/87)

2096 Fox, Mem. *Koala Lou* (PS–2). Illus. by Pamela Lofts. 1989, Harcourt $15.00 (0-15-200502-1). 32pp. A young koala named Koala Lou finds that her mother is too busy with her younger children to shower the same affection on her as before. (Rev: BL 11/15/89; HB 11–12/89; SLJ 1/90)

2097 Fox, Mem. *Possum Magic* (K–2). Illus. by Julie Vivas. 1990, Harcourt $15.00 (0-15-200572-2); paper $6.00 (0-15-263224-7). 32pp. Grandmother Opossum makes Hush invisible, and then forgets how she did it in this tale from Down Under. (Rev: BL 12/1/87; SLJ 12/87)

2098 Frascino, Edward. *Nanny Noony and the Dust Queen* (PS–3). Illus. 1990, Pippin LB $15.95 (0-

945912-09-9). 32pp. Nanny Noony must grapple with a powerful sorceress, the Dust Queen. (Rev: BL 6/15/90; SLJ 9/90)

2099 Freeman, Don. *Bearymore* (K–3). Illus. by author. 1979, Puffin paper $4.99 (0-14-050279-3). 40pp. A circus bear must build a new act, but he hibernates instead.

2100 Freeman, Don. *Corduroy* (PS–1). Illus. by author. 1968, Puffin paper $5.99 (0-14-050173-8). 32pp. The amusing story of a toy bear whose one missing button from his green corduroy overalls almost costs him the opportunity of belonging to someone. A sequel is: *A Pocket for Corduroy* (1978).

2101 Freeman, Don. *Dandelion* (K–2). Illus. by author. 1964, Puffin paper $5.99 (0-14-050218-1). 48pp. A vain lion goes to a barber shop before a party and makes himself unrecognizable to his friends.

2102 Freeman, Don. *Gregory's Shadow* (PS–1). Illus. 2000, Viking $15.99 (0-670-89328-5). 32pp. Gregory Groundhog doesn't want to be separated from his shadow nor does he want six more weeks of winter — what a dilemma! (Rev: BL 1/1–15/01; HBG 3/01; SLJ 2/01)

2103 French, Vivian. *Little Tiger Goes Shopping* (PS–1). Illus. by Andy Cooke. 1994, Candlewick paper $3.99 (1-56402-263-3). 24pp. When a group of animals find their local store is closed, they pool their ingredients and bake a cake. (Rev: BL 2/1/94)

2104 French, Vivian. *Red Hen and Sly Fox* (PS–2). Illus. by Sally Hobson. 1995, Simon & Schuster $15.00 (0-689-80010-X). 32pp. Sly Fox tries to make a meal of Red Hen, but justice triumphs. (Rev: BCCB 4/95; BL 5/1/95; HB 7–8/95; SLJ 6/95)

2105 Friedman, Jim. *The Mysterious Misadventures of Foy Rin Jin: A Decidedly Dysfunctional Dragon* (K–3). Illus. by Patti Stren. 1999, HarperCollins LB $15.89 (0-06-028551-6). Because he breathes water instead of fire, an unhappy dragon leaves his conventional colleagues and finds happiness with humans. (Rev: HBG 3/00; SLJ 1/00)

2106 Fries, Claudia. *A Pig Is Moving In!* (PS–2). Illus. 2000, Orchard LB $16.99 (0-531-33307-8). 32pp. A fox, a hen, and a hare are mistaken when they jump to the conclusion that, because their new neighbor is a pig, he will be dirty and messy. (Rev: BL 12/15/00; HBG 3/01; SLJ 9/00)

2107 Froehlich, Margaret W. *That Kookoory!* (1–3). Illus. by Marla Frazee. 1995, Harcourt $15.00 (0-15-277650-8). 40pp. This picture book tells of the confrontation between a prideful rooster and his arch enemy the weasel. (Rev: BCCB 5/95; BL 4/15/95; HB 7–8/95; SLJ 5/95)

2108 Fuchs, Diane M. *A Bear for All Seasons* (PS–1). Illus. by Kathryn Brown. 1995, Holt $14.95 (0-8050-2139-6). 32pp. During his winter sleep, Bear is awakened by Fox, who wants to chat. (Rev: BL 10/1/95; SLJ 12/95)

2109 Gantos, Jack. *Back to School for Rotten Ralph* (PS–3). Illus. by Nicole Rubel. 1998, HarperCollins LB $14.89 (0-06-027532-4). 40pp. When Sarah

starts school, leaving her cat, Rotten Ralph, alone, he decides to wear a disguise and pretend to be her new school friend. (Rev: BL 8/98; HBG 3/99; SLJ 10/98)

2110 Gantos, Jack. *Not So Rotten Ralph* (PS–3). Illus. by Nicole Rubel. 1994, Houghton $15.00 (0-395-62302-2). 32pp. Sweet Sarah loses her patience and sends her cat, Rotten Ralph, to obedience school. (Rev: BL 3/1/94; HB 7–8/94; SLJ 4/94)

2111 Gantos, Jack. *Rotten Ralph* (K–3). Illus. by Nicole Rubel. 1976, Houghton $16.00 (0-395-24276-2); paper $6.95 (0-395-29202-6). 48pp. Ralph is truly a nasty cat — mean and disruptive — until he is reformed under unusual circumstances. A sequel is: *Worse Than Rotten, Ralph* (1982).

2112 Gantos, Jack. *Rotten Ralph's Show and Tell* (PS–2). Illus. by Nicole Rubel. 1989, Houghton $15.00 (0-395-44312-1). 32pp. Rotten Ralph the cat makes a mess of show-and-tell at school. (Rev: BL 10/1/89; HB 11–12/89; SLJ 12/89)

2113 Gantos, Jack. *Wedding Bells for Rotten Ralph* (PS–1). Illus. by Nicole Rubel. 1999, HarperCollins LB $14.89 (0-06-027534-0). 40pp. Ralph the red cat is up to his usual rotten tricks; this time he spoils a wedding at which his owner, Sarah, is a flower girl. (Rev: BL 6/1–15/99; HBG 10/99; SLJ 6/99)

2114 Gantschev, Ivan. *Where Is Mr. Mole?* (PS–1). Adapted by Andrew Clements. Illus. 1990, Picture Book paper $15.95 (0-88708-109-6). 28pp. Mr. Mole disappears and his friends are worried until he reappears — with Mrs. Mole. (Rev: BL 3/15/90; SLJ 7/90)

2115 Gantschev, Ivan. *Where the Moon Lives* (PS–2). Illus. 1998, North-South $18.95 (1-55858-921-X). 32pp. A newly hatched duckling has so many questions about the world that he goes to visit a wise old swan for answers. (Rev: BL 6/1–15/98; HBG 10/98; SLJ 7/98)

2116 Garelli, Cristina. *Farm Friends Clean Up* (PS–K). Illus. by Francesca Chessa. 2000, Crown LB $15.99 (0-517-80082-9). Three short tales in which animals learn personal hygiene; in one story Wolf learns to brush his teeth. (Rev: HBG 3/01; SLJ 10/00)

2117 Garland, Michael. *Icarus Swinebuckle* (K–3). Illus. 2000, Albert Whitman $15.95 (0-8075-3495-1). 32pp. Icarus Swinebuckle, a precocious pig, builds wings that enable him to fly. (Rev: BL 2/15/00; HBG 10/00)

2118 Geisert, Arthur. *Oink* (PS–1). Illus. by author. 1991, Houghton $15.00 (0-395-55329-6). 32pp. The only word in this book is "oink," but the Pig family shows how much meaning can be expressed by a single word. (Rev: BL 6/1/91; HB 7–8/91*; SLJ 6/91)

2119 Gershator, Phillis. *When It Starts to Snow* (K–2). Illus. by Martin Matje. 1998, Holt $15.95 (0-8050-5404-9). 32pp. Various animals and birds express in simple rhymes their reactions to the falling snow. (Rev: BCCB 12/98; BL 11/15/98; HBG 3/99; SLJ 11/98)

2120 Gerstein, Mordicai, and Susan Y. Harris. *Daisy's Garden* (PS–3). Illus. 1995, Hyperion LB

$15.49 (0-7868-2080-2). 32pp. A year in the life of a garden tended by rabbits, mice, groundhogs, goats, and other animals. (Rev: BL 7/95; SLJ 4/95)

2121 Giannini, Enzo. *Zorina Ballerina* (PS–K). Illus. 1993, Simon & Schuster paper $14.00 (0-671-74776-2). 29pp. Zorina wants to dance with the other elephants, but she is too young. (Rev: BL 8/93)

2122 Gibbie, Mike. *Small Brown Dog's Bad Remembering Day* (PS–2). Illus. by Barbara Nascimbeni. 2000, Dutton $15.99 (0-525-46397-6). 32pp. A small brown dog has a bad case of amnesia and can't even remember who he is until his friends help him. (Rev: BL 6/1–15/00; HBG 10/00; SLJ 7/00)

2123 Gill, Madeline. *The Spring Hat* (PS–1). Illus. 1993, Simon & Schuster paper $13.00 (0-671-75666-4). 32pp. When three bunnies accidentally lose their mother's hat, they make a new one out of flowers. (Rev: BL 3/1/93; SLJ 5/93)

2124 Ginsburg, Mirra. *Across the Stream* (PS–2). Illus. by Nancy Tafuri. 1982, Greenwillow $15.93 (0-688-01206-X); Morrow paper $4.95 (0-688-10477-0). 24pp. Mother hen saves her three chicks from the fox.

2125 Ginsburg, Mirra, trans. *The Chick and the Duckling* (PS–K). Adapted from the Russian by V. Suteyev. Illus. by Jose Aruego and Ariane Dewey. 1988, Simon & Schuster paper $4.95 (0-689-71226-X). 32pp. A duck and a chick who hatch at the same time become constant companions.

2126 Gliori, Debi. *Mr. Bear Says, Are You There, Baby Bear? A Lift-the-Flap Book* (PS). Illus. by author. 1999, Orchard $9.95 (0-531-30182-6). Movable flaps are used in this story about Papa Bear's search for his missing child. (Rev: SLJ 1/00)

2127 Gliori, Debi. *Mr. Bear Says Peek-a-Boo* (PS). Illus. 1997, Simon & Schuster $4.99 (0-689-81516-6). 10pp. An interactive board book in which a bear and his baby play together. Also use *Mr. Bear Says I Love You* and *Mr. Bear Says Good Night* (both 1997). (Rev: BL 2/1/98)

2128 Gliori, Debi. *Mr. Bear to the Rescue* (PS–1). Illus. 2000, Orchard $15.95 (0-531-30276-8). 32pp. When bunny Flora is missing, Mr. Bear loads his tools into his carriage and sets off to help. (Rev: BL 11/15/00; SLJ 11/00)

2129 Gliori, Debi. *Mr. Bear's New Baby* (PS). Illus. 1999, Orchard $15.95 (0-531-30152-4). 32pp. Small Bear discovers that the new baby will stop crying if the family cuddles together. (Rev: BL 2/1/99; HBG 10/99; SLJ 3/99)

2130 Gliori, Debi. *Mr. Bear's Vacation* (PS–1). Illus. 2000, Orchard $15.95 (0-531-30255-5). 32pp. Mr. and Mrs. Bear and their two small children go on an accident-filled camping trip. (Rev: BL 5/15/00; HBG 10/00; SLJ 3/00)

2131 Gliori, Debi. *No Matter What* (PS–K). Illus. 1999, Harcourt $16.00 (0-15-202061-6). 32pp. Small, a young fox, tests the love that Large feels for him through a series of questions to determine the extent of this love. (Rev: BL 11/15/99; HBG 3/00; SLJ 11/99)

2132 Goldsmith, Howard. *Sleepy Little Owl* (PS–1). Illus. by Denny Bond. 1997, McGraw-Hill $12.95 (0-07-024543-6). 30pp. Through a series of daytime adventures, a young owl realizes that he is a nocturnal creature. (Rev: SLJ 2/98)

2133 Goldstone, Bruce. *The Beastly Feast* (PS–2). Illus. by Blair Lent. 1998, Holt $15.95 (0-8050-3867-1). 32pp. A delightful rhyming story about animals and the different foods each brings to a banquet. (Rev: BL 6/1–15/98; HBG 3/99; SLJ 6/98)

2134 Gollub, Matthew. *The Jazz Fly* (PS–2). Illus. by Karen Hanke. 2000, Tortuga $17.95 (1-889910-17-1). 32pp. A bouncy book with an accompanying CD about a hip fly, his jazz talk, and his job in a club as a drummer. (Rev: BL 8/00; SLJ 8/00)

2135 Goodall, Jane. *Dr. White* (K–3). Illus. by Julie Litty. 1999, North-South LB $15.88 (0-7358-1064-8). 32pp. Dr. White, a cute dog, makes hospital rounds to visit children. (Rev: BL 5/1/99; HBG 10/99)

2136 Goodman, Joan E. *Bernard's Bath* (PS–K). Illus. by Dominic Catalano. 1996, Boyds Mills $14.95 (1-56397-323-5). 32pp. Baby elephant Bernard resists all efforts to get him to take a bath. (Rev: BL 2/1/96; SLJ 3/96)

2137 Gorbachev, Valeri. *Nicky and the Big, Bad Wolves* (PS–K). Illus. 1998, North-South LB $15.88 (1-55858-918-X). 32pp. Mother rabbit helps dispel young Nicky's fears when he tells her about being chased by 100 wolves in his dreams. (Rev: BL 4/15/98; HBG 10/98)

2138 Gorbachev, Valeri. *Nicky and the Fantastic Birthday Gift* (PS–1). Illus. by author. 2000, North-South LB $15.88 (0-7358-1379-5). As a birthday present for his mother, Nicky the rabbit not only draws a picture as his siblings do, but also makes up an elaborate story to go with it. (Rev: HBG 3/01; SLJ 11/00)

2139 Gorbachev, Valeri. *Peter's Picture* (PS–1). Illus. 2000, North-South LB $15.88 (1-55858-966-X). 32pp. Peter the bear gets too much praise from other adults about his painting of a flower, but his parents know exactly how to please their son and put it in a frame. (Rev: BL 4/15/00; HBG 10/00; SLJ 6/00)

2140 Gorbachev, Valeri. *Where Is the Apple Pie?* (PS–2). Illus. 1999, Putnam $15.99 (0-399-23385-7). 32pp. Robbers steal the pie that Goat has bought, starting a chain of unforeseen events. (Rev: BL 2/15/00; HBG 3/00; SLJ 8/99)

2141 Goss, Linda. *The Frog Who Wanted to Be a Singer* (K–3). Illus. by Cynthia Jabar. 1996, Orchard LB $16.99 (0-531-08745-X). 40pp. Scorned by both frogs and birds because he wants to sing, a young frog astounds everyone with his talent. (Rev: BCCB 4/96; BL 4/15/96*; SLJ 5/96)

2142 Graham, Bob. *Benny: An Adventure Story* (PS–3). Illus. 1999, Candlewick $16.99 (0-7636-0813-0). 32pp. A show business dog, who is rejected by his magician master for being too clever, finds a new identity with a music-loving family. (Rev: BL 9/15/99; HBG 3/00; SLJ 7/99)

2143 Graham, Margaret B. *Be Nice to Spiders* (PS–2). Illus. by author. 1967, HarperCollins LB $15.89 (0-06-022073-2). 32pp. Helen, Billy's pet spider, makes all the animals at the zoo happy when she spins webs and catches flies for them.

2144 Grahame, Kenneth. *Duck Song* (PS). Illus. by Joung Un Kim. Series: Harper Growing Tree. 1998, HarperFestival $5.95 (0-694-01163-0). An attractive board book that uses as its text the Grahame poem from *Wind in the Willows*. (Rev: HBG 10/98; SLJ 10/98)

2145 Gray, Kes. *The Get Well Soon Book* (PS–1). Illus. by Mary McQuillan. 2000, Millbrook LB $21.90 (0-7613-1922-0). 32pp. An entertaining picture book that tells how different animals can have accidents and illnesses — Cynthia centipede sprains 98 ankles playing field hockey and Danny the Dalmatian breaks out in stripes. (Rev: BL 12/15/00; HBG 3/01; SLJ 2/01)

2146 Gray, Libba M. *Small Green Snake* (PS–1). Illus. by Holly Meade. 1994, Orchard LB $16.99 (0-531-08694-1). 32pp. A disobedient garter snake wanders away from home and finds himself a prisoner in a jelly jar. (Rev: BL 9/15/94*; SLJ 9/94)

2147 Greene, Rhonda Gowler. *Barnyard Song* (PS–1). Illus. by Robert Bender. 1997, Simon & Schuster $14.00 (0-689-80758-9). 40pp. A variation of the "Old MacDonald" rhyme in which barnyard animals lose their voices because of bad cases of the flu. (Rev: BL 8/97; HBG 3/98; SLJ 9/97*)

2148 Greene, Stephanie. *Not Just Another Moose* (K–3). Illus. by Andrea Wallace. 2000, Marshall Cavendish $15.95 (0-7614-5061-0). A year in the life of Hildy, a pig, and Moose, who worries his antlers won't grow back in the spring. (Rev: HBG 10/00; SLJ 5/00)

2149 Gretz, Susanna. *Duck Takes Off* (PS–K). Illus. 1991, Macmillan LB $12.95 (0-02-737472-6). 32pp. Duck tries to act like a schoolteacher with the result that she loses her friends. Also use in the same series: *Frog in the Middle* (1991). (Rev: BL 5/1/91; SLJ 5/91)

2150 Gretz, Susanna. *Frog, Duck, and Rabbit* (PS–K). Illus. 1992, Macmillan LB $12.95 (0-02-737327-4). 32pp. Three animal friends have difficulty in completing a crocodile costume for a parade. Also use: *Rabbit Rambles On* (1992). (Rev: BL 2/15/92; SLJ 6/92)

2151 Gretz, Susanna. *Rabbit Food* (PS–K). Illus. 1999, Candlewick $15.99 (0-7636-0731-2). 32pp. John, a young rabbit, refuses to eat his vegetables, and when the family calls in respected Uncle Bunny for help, they discover that he does the same thing. (Rev: BCCB 6/99; BL 5/1/99; HBG 10/99; SLJ 4/99)

2152 Grigg, Carol. *The Singing Snowbear* (PS–K). Illus. by author. 1999, Houghton $15.00 (0-395-94223-3). Snowbear learns the song that the whale sings and the two entertain all the creatures of the Arctic. (Rev: HBG 3/00; SLJ 1/00)

2153 Grindley, Sally. *Silly Goose and Dizzy Duck Play Hide-and-Seek* (PS). Illus. by Adrian Reynolds. Series: DK Toddler Storybook. 1999, DK $9.95 (0-7894-4844-0). In a game of hide-and-seek Dizzy Duck is almost eaten by Clever Fox but is saved by Grizzly Bear. (Rev: HBG 3/00; SLJ 12/99)

2154 Grindley, Sally. *What Are Friends For?* (PS–1). Illus. by Penny Dann. 1998, Kingfisher $14.95 (0-7534-5108-5). 32pp. The friendship between Figgy, a young fox, and Jefferson Bear is threatened when Figgy wants to play and Jefferson doesn't. (Rev: BL 4/15/98; HBG 10/98; SLJ 8/98)

2155 Grindley, Sally. *What Will I Do Without You?* (PS–1). Illus. by Penny Dann. 1999, Kingfisher $15.95 (0-7534-5110-7). 32pp. Figgy, a young fox, is lonely when his friend Jefferson the bear hibernates, but in time he becomes friendly with a squirrel named Hoptail. (Rev: BL 12/1/99; HBG 3/00; SLJ 12/99)

2156 Grindley, Sally. *Why Is the Sky Blue?* (PS–K). Illus. by Susan Varley. 1997, Simon & Schuster paper $16.00 (0-689-81486-0). The impatient, inquisitive Rabbit bombards poor Donkey with dozens of questions. (Rev: SLJ 6/97)

2157 Grossman, Bill. *Tommy at the Grocery Store* (K–2). Illus. by Victoria Chess. 1991, HarperCollins paper $5.95 (0-06-443266-1). 32pp. Tommy, the little pig, is left behind in the grocery store and customers mistake him for a salami among other things. (Rev: BCCB 11/89; BL 9/15/89; HB 9–10/89; SLJ 12/89*)

2158 Guarino, Deborah. *Is Your Mama a Llama?* (PS–K). Illus. by Steven Kellogg. 1989, Scholastic $14.95 (0-590-41387-2). 32pp. A pleasing study of who belongs to whom, as a koala and her baby clutch each other or an opossum ambles off with babies aboard her back. (Rev: BCCB 11/89; BL 10/1/89; SLJ 10/89)

2159 Guest, C. Z. *Tiny Green Thumbs* (PS–1). Illus. by Loretta Krupinski. 2000, Hyperion $15.99 (0-7868-0516-1). Tiny Bun and Little Mouse show how to plant and grow a little garden with directions for cultivating vegetables like carrots, green beans, corn, and cucumbers. (Rev: HBG 10/00; SLJ 3/00)

2160 Gutman, Anne, and Georg Hallensleben. *Gaspard on Vacation* (PS–1). Illus. 2001, Knopf $9.95 (0-375-81115-X). 32pp. Gaspard, a black rabbit, is on vacation with his family in Venice where he causes havoc by racing around the canals in a kayak. (Rev: BL 2/1/01*)

2161 Gutman, Anne, and Georg Hallensleben. *Lisa's Airplane Trip* (PS–1). Illus. 2001, Knopf $9.95 (0-375-81114-1). 32pp. Lisa, a small white rabbit, enjoys the thrill of traveling alone on an airplane for the first time, particularly when she in taken into the cockpit. (Rev: BL 2/1/01)

2162 Gwynne, Fred. *Pondlarker* (PS–3). Illus. 1990, Simon & Schuster paper $14.00 (0-671-70846-5). 32pp. Remembering the fairy tale about the frog prince, a small frog acts like a member of royalty. (Rev: BCCB 11/90; BL 11/15/90; SLJ 11/90)

2163 Hadithi, Mwenye. *Hot Hippo* (PS–3). Illus. by Adrienne Kennaway. 1986, Little, Brown LB $14.95 (0-316-33722-6). A folktale-like story of Hot Hippo, who longed to live in the water, and the

101

god of everything, who wanted him to live on land. (Rev: BL 12/1/86; HB 1–2/87; SLJ 2/87)

2164 Hall, Martin. *Charlie and Tess* (PS–2). Illus. by Catherine Walters. 1996, Little Tiger $14.95 (1-888444-06-1). 28pp. An orphaned lamb that has been raised by a farmer's family later saves his flock on a snowy night. (Rev: BL 4/15/97; SLJ 3/97)

2165 Hall, Nancy Christen. *Mouse at Night* (PS–K). Illus. by Buket Erdogan. 2000, Orchard $14.95 (0-531-30260-1). 32pp. At night in Miss Bumbly's house, a mouse emerges from its hole and engages in all sorts of activities, including preparing breakfast for Miss Bumbly. (Rev: BL 5/1/00; HBG 10/00; SLJ 4/00)

2166 Hallensleben, Georg. *Pauline* (PS–1). Illus. 1999, Farrar $16.00 (0-374-35758-7). 32pp. When baby elephant Rabusus is trapped by hunters, his friend Pauline, a small weasel, sets out to rescue him. (Rev: BCCB 11/99; BL 11/15/99; HBG 3/00; SLJ 9/99)

2167 Hanel, Wolfram. *Little Elephant's Song* (PS–K). Trans. from German by J. Alison James. Illus. by Cristina Kadmon. 2000, North-South LB $15.88 (0-7358-1298-5). A young elephant learns many skills including how to trumpet. (Rev: HBG 10/00; SLJ 7/00)

2168 Hanson, Mary Elizabeth. *Snug* (PS). Illus. by Cheryl M. Taylor. 1998, Simon & Schuster $15.00 (0-689-81164-0). 32pp. Common family interactions like playing and getting into trouble are enacted by a bear cub and his ever-watchful mother. (Rev: BCCB 7–8/98; BL 5/15/98; HBG 10/98; SLJ 4/98)

2169 Harley, Bill. *Sitting Down to Eat* (K–3). Illus. by Kitty Harvill. 1996, August House $15.95 (0-87483-460-0). In this cumulative tale, a boy invites so many animals into his house that it explodes. (Rev: SLJ 1/97)

2170 Harper, Jessica. *I'm Not Going to Chase the Cat Today!* (PS–2). Illus. by Lindsay Harper duPont. 2000, HarperCollins $15.95 (0-688-17636-4). 32pp. Various animals decide that, at least for one day, they are going to mend their ways. (Rev: BL 4/15/00; HBG 10/00; SLJ 5/00)

2171 Harris, Lee. *Never Let Your Cat Make Lunch for You* (K–2). Illus. by Debbie Tilley. 1999, Tricycle Pr. $12.95 (1-883672-80-5). 24pp. Although at times the images produced are somewhat gross (e.g., mouse sandwiches), this is a humorous tale of why cats can't prepare proper meals for humans. (Rev: BL 10/15/99; HBG 3/00; SLJ 12/99)

2172 Harrison, David L. *A Farmer's Garden: Rhymes for Two Voices* (PS–1). Illus. by Arden Johnson-Petrov. 2000, Boyds Mills $15.95 (1-56397-776-1). 32pp. A farmer's dog asks various animals and plants what they like best about the farmer's garden and what they do there. (Rev: BL 9/1/00; SLJ 11/00)

2173 Harrison, David L. *When Cows Come Home* (PS–1). Illus. by Chris L. Demarest. 1994, Boyds Mills $15.95 (1-56397-143-7). 32pp. Cows have

wonderful times dancing and playing games when the farmer isn't looking. (Rev: BL 5/1/94; SLJ 2/94)

2174 Harrison, Joanna. *Dear Bear* (PS–2). Illus. 1994, Carolrhoda LB $16.61 (0-87614-839-9). 32pp. Katie is afraid of the bear that lives under the stairs and writes him a letter about her fear. (Rev: BCCB 1/95; BL 1/1/95; SLJ 2/95*)

2175 Harter, Debbie. *The Animal Boogie* (PS–2). Illus. by author. 2000, Barefoot $14.99 (1-84148-094-0). A rhythmic text adds to the fun of seeing various animals boogie-ing to lively music. (Rev: SLJ 12/00)

2176 Hassett, John, and Ann Hassett. *Charles of the Wild* (PS–K). Illus. 1997, Houghton $14.95 (0-395-78575-8). 32pp. A timid little dog has some tame encounters that he interprets as exciting adventures. (Rev: BL 4/1/97; SLJ 5/97)

2177 Hayes, Sarah. *The Grumpalump* (PS–K). Illus. by Barbara Firth. 1991, Houghton $16.00 (0-89919-871-6). 24pp. Several animals try to rouse the grumpalump, but only the gnu succeeds. (Rev: BCCB 6/91; BL 5/15/91; SLJ 9/91)

2178 Hayes, Sarah. *This Is the Bear and the Bad Little Girl* (PS–K). Illus. by Helen Craig. 1995, Candlewick $12.95 (1-56402-648-5). 32pp. When a bad girl tries to steal a teddy bear from a restaurant, a dog comes to his rescue. (Rev: BL 11/15/95; HB 11–12/95; SLJ 12/95)

2179 Hayes, Sarah. *This Is the Bear and the Scary Night* (PS–K). Illus. by Helen Craig. 1998, Little, Brown paper $5.99 (0-7636-0648-0). 28pp. This is a simple story about a gentle, fearless teddy bear and the scary night he spends alone in a park. (Rev: BL 3/1/92; HB 9–10/92; SLJ 4/92*)

2180 Hayles, Karen, and Charles Fuge. *Whale Is Stuck* (PS–1). Illus. 1993, Simon & Schuster $14.00 (0-671-86587-0). 32pp. When Whale lands on an ice floe, the other friendly sea creatures can't free him. (Rev: BL 9/1/93; SLJ 10/93)

2181 Hayles, Marsha. *Pet of a Pet* (PS–3). Illus. by Scott Nash. 2001, Dial $15.99 (0-8037-2512-4). 32pp. On this unusual farm each of the pets has a pet and they all enjoy each other's friendship. (Rev: BL 3/15/01; SLJ 3/01)

2182 Heal, Gillian. *Grandpa Bear's Fantastic Scarf* (K–3). Illus. 1997, Beyond Words $14.95 (1-885223-41-2). 30pp. A young bear learns about life's meaning through studying the colors in his grandpa's scarf, a visual record of his life. (Rev: BL 4/1/97; SLJ 7/97)

2183 Hearn, Diane D. *Bad Luck Boswell* (K–3). Illus. by author. 1995, Simon & Schuster $15.00 (0-689-80303-6). Boswell the cat brings bad luck with him until he discovers he can neutralize a witch's curses. (Rev: SLJ 11/95)

2184 Heine, Helme. *The Boxer and the Princess* (PS–3). Illus. 1998, Simon & Schuster $16.00 (0-689-82195-6). 32pp. At his dad's bidding, Max, a rhino, becomes so tough that he can slay dragons, but the beautiful princess he saves wants someone who is more gentle. (Rev: BL 10/15/98; HBG 3/99; SLJ 11/98)

2185 Heine, Helme. *Friends* (PS–3). Illus. by author. 1982, Macmillan $16.00 (0-689-50256-7); paper $5.99 (0-689-71083-6). 32pp. A rooster, mouse, and pig share an outing on a bicycle.

2186 Heine, Helme. *Friends Go Adventuring* (PS–2). Illus. 1995, Simon & Schuster paper $16.00 (0-689-80463-6). 32pp. Charlie Rooster, Johnny Mouse, and Fat Percy the pig encounter cutthroat pirates and a cannibal cook in this sequel to *Friends*. (Rev: BCCB 1/96; BL 1/1–15/96; SLJ 2/96*)

2187 Heine, Helme. *The Pearl* (PS–3). Illus. 1985, Macmillan paper $3.95 (0-689-71262-6). 32pp. Beaver dreams that his friends envy the prize pearl he has found. (Rev: BL 5/1/85; HB 7–8/85; SLJ 9/85)

2188 Heine, Helme. *The Pigs' Wedding* (PS–3). Illus. by author. 1986, Macmillan $16.00 (0-689-50409-8); paper $5.99 (0-689-71478-5). 32pp. Curlytail and Porker say "I do." A reissue of a 1979 edition.

2189 Heine, Helme. *Seven Wild Pigs: Eleven Picture Book Fantasies* (K–3). Illus. by author. 1988, Macmillan LB $18.95 (0-689-50439-X). 120pp. Poems, stories, and whimsical tales, mostly about unusual animals. (Rev: BCCB 5/88; BL 4/1/88; SLJ 8/88)

2190 Hellard, Susan. *Baby Lemur* (PS–K). Illus. by author. 1999, Holt $14.95 (0-8050-6142-8). Although he is angry and frightened when his mother puts him on the ground, a young lemur learns his first lesson in independence. (Rev: HBG 3/00; SLJ 1/00)

2191 Heller, Nicholas. *Elwood and the Witch* (PS–1). Illus. by Joseph A. Smith. 2000, Greenwillow LB $16.99 (0-688-16946-5). 32pp. Elwood the pig gets on a witch's broom by mistake and doesn't know how to land it. (Rev: BL 8/00; HBG 3/01; SLJ 9/00)

2192 Hendra, Sue. *Oliver's Wood* (PS–1). Illus. 1996, Candlewick $15.99 (1-56402-932-8). 32pp. Oliver the owl has an unusual adventure when he wakes up while the sun is shining. (Rev: BL 7/96; SLJ 9/96)

2193 Henkes, Kevin. *Chrysanthemum* (PS–1). Illus. 1991, Greenwillow $15.89 (0-688-09700-6). 32pp. Other mouse children make fun of Chrysanthemum's name until her music teacher helps out. (Rev: BCCB 10/92; BL 8/91; HB 9–10/91*; SLJ 9/91*)

2194 Henkes, Kevin. *Julius, the Baby of the World* (PS–3). Illus. 1990, Greenwillow $15.89 (0-688-08944-5). 32pp. Lilly, a girl mouse, has a fit of jealousy when her baby brother gets all the attention in the family. (Rev: BCCB 11/90; BL 11/1/90; HB 1–2/91*; SLJ 10/90*)

2195 Henkes, Kevin. *Owen* (PS). Illus. 1993, Greenwillow $15.89 (0-688-11450-4). 24pp. Owen, a mouse, loves his fuzzy yellow blanket more than anything. (Rev: BL 8/93*)

2196 Henkes, Kevin. *Sheila Rae, the Brave* (PS–1). Illus. by author. 1987, Greenwillow $15.89 (0-688-07156-2); Puffin paper $3.95 (0-14-050835-X). 32pp. Sheila Rae, a mouse, fears nothing until she takes the wrong way home. (Rev: BL 9/1/87; SLJ 9/87)

2197 Henkes, Kevin. *A Weekend with Wendell* (PS–1). Illus. by author. 1986, Greenwillow $15.93 (0-688-06326-8); Morrow paper $5.95 (0-688-14024-6). 32pp. Wendell makes his weekend stay seem like a year to Sophie Mouse, until they have a meeting of the minds. (Rev: BCCB 10/86; BL 9/1/86; SLJ 10/86)

2198 Henkes, Kevin. *Wemberly Worried* (PS–1). Illus. 2000, Greenwillow $15.95 (0-688-17027-7). 32pp. Wemberly, a little mouse girl, is a real worrywart until she makes a new friend at school who makes the world look less scary. (Rev: BCCB 9/00; BL 8/00; HB 9–10/00; HBG 3/01; SLJ 8/00)

2199 Hest, Amy. *Baby Duck and the Bad Eyeglasses* (PS–1). Illus. by Jill Barton. 1996, Candlewick $16.99 (1-56402-680-9). 32pp. Baby Duck dislikes her new eyeglasses until Grandpa shows her how to accept them. (Rev: BCCB 10/96; BL 8/96*; HB 9–10/96; SLJ 10/96*)

2200 Hest, Amy. *In the Rain with Baby Duck* (PS–1). Illus. by Jill Barton. 1995, Candlewick $16.95 (1-56402-532-2). 32pp. Grandpa helps Baby Duck adjust to the rain by supplying a red umbrella and boots. (Rev: BL 10/1/95)

2201 Hest, Amy. *Off to School, Baby Duck!* (PS–1). Illus. by Jill Barton. 1999, Candlewick $16.99 (0-7636-0244-2). 26pp. Baby Duck is unhappy and apprehensive about going to school, but with the help of her grandfather and a nice teacher, she enjoys the experience. (Rev: BL 9/15/99*; HBG 3/00; SLJ 9/99)

2202 Hest, Amy. *You're the Boss, Baby Duck!* (PS–K). Illus. by Jill Barton. Series: Baby Duck. 1997, Candlewick $16.99 (1-56402-667-1). 32pp. Baby Duck is unhappy about getting a baby sister, but Grandpa helps her adjust. (Rev: BL 9/1/97; HBG 3/98; SLJ 10/97)

2203 Hill, Eric. *Spot at Home* (PS). Illus. by author. Series: Little Spot Board Books. 1991, Putnam $3.99 (0-399-21774-6). 14pp. This board book features the everyday adventures of the lovable dog Spot. (Rev: BL 6/15/91)

2204 Hill, Eric. *Spot Goes to a Party* (PS–1). Illus. by author. 1992, Putnam $12.99 (0-399-22409-2). In this lift-the-flap book, Spot the dog dresses as a cowboy to go to a costume party. (Rev: SLJ 9/92)

2205 Hill, Eric. *Spot Goes to the Park* (PS–1). Illus. by author. 1991, Putnam $12.99 (0-399-21833-5). In this book with easily lifted flaps, Spot the dog enjoys a day in the park playing with his friends. (Rev: SLJ 12/91)

2206 Hill, Eric. *Spot Sleeps Over* (PS–K). Illus. by author. 1991, Putnam $12.99 (0-399-21815-7). A lift-the-flap book about Spot the dog and first-time sleeping over. (Rev: SLJ 3/91)

2207 Hill, Eric. *Spot's Baby Sister* (PS). Illus. by author. 1989, Putnam $12.99 (0-399-21640-5). In a lift-the-flap format, this is the story of Spot the dog and his little sister. (Rev: SLJ 11/89)

2208 Hillenbrand, Will. *Down by the Station* (PS–2). Illus. 1999, Harcourt $15.00 (0-15-201804-2). 40pp. Inspired by the song "Down by the Station," this joyful picture book depicts a train that is taking baby animals to a children's zoo. (Rev: BL 10/15/99; HB 11–12/99; HBG 3/00; SLJ 10/99)

2209 Hines-Stephens, Sarah. *Bean Soup* (PS). Illus. by Anna Grossnickle Hines. 2000, Harcourt $4.95 (0-15-202164-7). Bean, a black cat, and Soup, a puppy, play together in this sweet board book. Also use: *Soup Too?* and *Soup's Oops!* (both 2000). (Rev: SLJ 6/00)

2210 Hiskey, Iris. *Hannah the Hippo's No Mud Day* (PS–K). Illus. by Karen L. Schmidt. 1991, Simon & Schuster paper $13.95 (0-671-69194-5). 32pp. Hannah, all dressed up, is warned to stay clean, but then she sees the biggest, muddiest puddle in the world! (Rev: BL 6/1/91; SLJ 10/91)

2211 Hissey, Jane. *Little Bear Lost* (PS–K). Illus. 1994, Sandvick paper $9.99 (1-881445-44-5). 32pp. Just when the picnic is about to begin, Little Bear is missing. (Rev: BL 11/1/89)

2212 Hobbie, Holly. *Toot and Puddle* (PS–1). Illus. by author. 1997, Little, Brown $14.95 (0-316-36552-1). While one globe-trotting pig sees the world, his friend stays at home, enjoying life's simple pleasures. (Rev: HBG 3/98; SLJ 12/97)

2213 Hobbie, Holly. *Toot and Puddle: You Are My Sunshine* (PS–2). Illus. by author. 1999, Little, Brown $14.95 (0-316-36562-9). In this story about friendship, two little piglets, Tulip and Puddle, try to cheer up their friend Toot, who is feeling blue. (Rev: BCCB 9/99; HBG 3/00; SLJ 8/99)

2214 Hobbs, Will. *Howling Hill* (K–3). Illus. by Jill Kastner. 1998, Morrow LB $15.93 (0-688-15430-1). 40pp. Hanni, a wolf cub, gets lost and must rely on a bear to help her home in this survival story. Hanni also learns how to howl like the rest of her family. (Rev: BL 9/1/98; HBG 3/99; SLJ 10/98)

2215 Hoberman, Mary Ann. *One of Each* (PS–2). Illus. by Marjorie Priceman. 1997, Little, Brown $15.95 (0-316-36731-1). 32pp. Oliver Tolliver, a dog, is happy that he has only one of everything, but his friend Peggoty Small, a cat, pursuades him that two is also nice. (Rev: BL 11/1/97*; HBG 3/98; SLJ 9/97*)

2216 Hobson, Sally. *Chicken Little* (PS–K). Illus. 1994, Simon & Schuster $14.00 (0-671-89548-6). 32pp. The traditional story of Chicken Little is accompanied by bright, animated drawings. (Rev: BL 10/15/94; SLJ 11/94)

2217 Hoff, Syd. *Duncan the Dancing Duck* (PS–2). Illus. by author. 1994, Clarion $15.00 (0-395-67400-X). 32pp. Duncan gains international fame as a dancing duck, but is happy to return home where he dances only for his mother. (Rev: SLJ 7/94)

2218 Hooper, Meredith. *Dogs' Night* (K–4). Illus. by Allan Curless and Mark Burgess. 2000, Millbrook LB $21.90 (0-7613-1824-0). 32pp. The dogs in the National Gallery in London leave their paintings once a year for a party, but on this occasion they get mixed up and enter the wrong paintings in this hilarious picture book. (Rev: BL 3/15/00; HBG 10/00; SLJ 7/00)

2219 Hoopes, Lyn Littlefield. *My Own Home* (PS–2). Illus. by Ruth Richardson. 1991, HarperCollins $13.95 (0-06-022570-X). A lost little owl is looking for his home. (Rev: SLJ 6/91)

2220 Horn, Peter. *When I Grow Up . . .* (PS–2). Trans. by Rosemary Lanning. Illus. by Cristina Kadmon. 1999, North-South LB $15.88 (0-7358-1149-0). 24pp. A turtle father and son talk about the future and their feelings for one another in this tender picture book. (Rev: BL 10/15/99; HBG 3/00; SLJ 10/99)

2221 Horse, Harry. *A Friend for Little Bear* (PS–2). Illus. by author. 1996, Candlewick $14.99 (1-56402-876-3). When he is stranded on an island, Little Bear tries to find happiness by collecting things. (Rev: SLJ 9/96)

2222 Howard, Arthur. *Cosmo Zooms* (PS–2). Illus. 1999, Harcourt $15.00 (0-15-201788-7). 32pp. Cosmo, a black-and-white dog, accidentally discovers a hidden talent when he falls asleep on a skateboard and begins a fateful trip through town. (Rev: BL 11/1/99; HBG 3/00; SLJ 9/99)

2223 Howe, Deborah, and James Howe. *Teddy Bear's Scrapbook* (2–3). Illus. by David S. Rose. 1994, Aladdin paper $3.95 (0-689-71812-8). 80pp. A teddy bear describes the pictures in his scrapbook to a little girl.

2224 Howe, James. *Horace and Morris But Mostly Dolores* (PS–2). Illus. by Amy Walrod. 1999, Simon & Schuster $16.00 (0-689-31874-X). 32pp. Three mice — two boys and a girl — decide to join unisex clubs, but in time they leave them for a day of exploring together. (Rev: BCCB 3/99; BL 2/15/99*; HBG 10/99; SLJ 3/99)

2225 Howe, James. *I Wish I Were a Butterfly* (PS–2). Illus. by Ed Young. 1987, Harcourt $17.00 (0-15-200470-X). 28pp. Cricket thinks he's ugly; then a butterfly hears his music and wishes he were a cricket. (Rev: BL 11/1/87; SLJ 11/87)

2226 Hunter, Anne. *Possum and the Peeper* (K–2). Illus. by author. 1998, Houghton $15.00 (0-395-84631-5). Other animals join Possum in his search to find the origin of the peeping sound he hears. (Rev: BL 6/1–15/98; HBG 10/98; SLJ 3/98*)

2227 Hunter, Anne. *Possum's Harvest Moon* (PS–1). Illus. 1996, Houghton $15.00 (0-395-73575-0). 32pp. Possum is so inspired by the autumn that he throws a party for his animal friends. (Rev: BCCB 10/96; BL 9/1/96*; HB 9–10/96; SLJ 8/96*)

2228 Hurd, Thacher. *Art Dog* (PS–3). Illus. 1996, HarperCollins LB $15.89 (0-06-024425-9). 32pp. Arthur, a canine museum guard with artistic abilities, solves the mystery of the missing painting, the *Mona Woofa*. (Rev: BCCB 2/96; BL 1/1–15/96; SLJ 2/96)

2229 Hurd, Thacher. *Mama Don't Allow: Starring Miles and the Swamp Band* (PS–1). Illus. by author. 1984, HarperCollins LB $15.89 (0-06-022690-0); paper $5.95 (0-06-443078-2). 40pp. The Swamp Band finds that the only audience that likes them is the alligator.

2230 Hurd, Thacher. *Mystery on the Docks* (1–3). Illus. by author. 1983, HarperCollins paper $6.95 (0-06-443058-8). 32pp. Ralph, an opera lover, rescues his favorite singer from rat-kidnappers.

2231 Hutchins, Pat. *Good-Night, Owl!* (PS–K). Illus. by author. 1972, Macmillan LB $16.00 (0-02-745900-4). 32pp. Owl is kept awake by animal noises as various animals perch on a branch of his tree; but when darkness falls, owl has his turn and wakes everyone with his screeches.

2232 Hutchins, Pat. *Little Pink Pig* (PS–1). Illus. 1994, Greenwillow $16.00 (0-688-12014-8). 32pp. Little Pig fails to heed his mother's call for bedtime because he is busy chasing a butterfly. (Rev: BL 4/1/94; HB 5–6/94; SLJ 5/94)

2233 Hutchins, Pat. *Rosie's Walk* (K–2). Illus. by author. 1968, Macmillan LB $16.00 (0-02-745850-4); paper $5.99 (0-02-043750-1). 32pp. Rosie the hen miraculously escapes capture by a fox.

2234 Hutchins, Pat. *The Surprise Party* (1–3). Illus. 1986, Macmillan LB $14.95 (0-02-745930-6). 32pp. A message about a party is passed from animal to animal, getting more confused each time. (Rev: BL 10/15/86)

2235 Hutchins, Pat. *What Game Shall We Play?* (PS–K). Illus. 1995, Morrow paper $4.95 (0-688-13573-0). 24pp. Duck and Frog ask several of their animal friends what game they should play. (Rev: BCCB 10/90; BL 10/15/90; HB 11–12/90; SLJ 9/90*)

2236 Ingman, Bruce. *When Martha's Away* (K–3). Illus. 1995, Houghton $14.95 (0-395-72360-4). 32pp. When humans are away, Lionel the cat has a great time talking on the phone, preparing lunch, and being friendly with Gladys, the neighbor's kitty. (Rev: BL 1/1–15/96; SLJ 12/95)

2237 Inkpen, Mick. *The Great Pet Sale* (PS–1). Illus. 1999, Orchard $14.95 (0-531-30130-3). 16pp. At a pet store sale, a rat, priced at only one cent, hopes that a young boy will choose him. (Rev: BL 4/15/99; HBG 10/99; SLJ 7/99)

2238 Inkpen, Mick. *Kipper* (PS–K). Illus. 1992, Talman $15.95 (1-85430-333-3). 32pp. When Kipper the dog cleans his basket and gets rid of his toys, he finds it is impossible to be as comfortable as he was before. (Rev: BL 4/1/92; SLJ 5/92)

2239 Inkpen, Mick. *Kipper's Snowy Day* (PS–K). Illus. by author. 1996, Harcourt $14.00 (0-15-201362-8). Two dogs enjoy a day's activities on a snowy day, including making a giant snow dog. (Rev: SLJ 12/96)

2240 Inkpen, Mick. *Picnic* (PS–K). Illus. by author. Series: Little Kipper. 2001, Harcourt paper $4.95 (0-15-216319-0). Kipper and Tiger, two dogs, encounter problems before settling down to have a happy picnic. The same characters also appear in *Thing!* (2001). (Rev: SLJ 3/01)

2241 Inkpen, Mick. *Wibbly Pig Can Make a Tent* (PS). 2000, Viking paper $5.99 (0-670-89264-5). 16pp. A board book in which an endearing little pig finds he can do a lot of things, like play with bubbles. Three other books about Wibbly Pig are *Wibbly Pig Is Happy!*, *Wibbly Pig Likes Bananas*, and *Wibbly Pig Opens His Presents* (all 2000). (Rev: SLJ 10/00)

2242 Irbinskas, Heather. *How Jackrabbit Got His Very Long Ears* (K–3). Illus. by Kenneth J. Spen-

gler. 1994, Northland LB $15.95 (0-87358-566-6). 32pp. When Jackrabbit fails to follow the instructions of the Great Spirit, he is given big ears so that he can hear better. (Rev: BL 6/1–15/94)

2243 Isherwood, Shirley. *The Band over the Hill* (PS–3). Illus. by Reg Cartwright. 1997, Hutchinson $19.95 (0-09-176753-9). Two bears unearth some old band costumes and decide to join the marching band that they hear in the distance. (Rev: SLJ 1/98)

2244 Jackson, Jean. *Thorndike and Nelson: A Monster Story* (K–2). Illus. by Vera Rosenberry. 1997, DK $15.95 (0-7894-2452-5). 32pp. Dot and Thorndike, appealing but ugly monsters, quarrel and insult each other terribly, but eventually they make up. (Rev: BL 10/1/97; HBG 3/98; SLJ 9/97)

2245 Jacobs, Laurie A. *So Much in Common* (PS–3). Illus. by Valeri Gorbachev. 1994, Boyds Mills $14.95 (1-56397-115-1). Though seemingly direct opposites in tastes and interests, Philomena Midge, a hippo, and Horace Abercrombie, a goat, become fast friends. (Rev: SLJ 12/94)

2246 Jacobson, Jennifer Richard. *Moon Sandwich Mom* (PS–K). Illus. by Benrei Huang. 1999, Albert Whitman $14.95 (0-8075-4071-4). 24pp. When Rafferty Fox's mother is too busy to play with him, he tries other animal mothers but returns home knowing his mother is best. (Rev: BL 7/99; HBG 10/99; SLJ 6/99)

2247 James, Simon. *Dear Mr. Blueberry* (PS–K). Illus. 1991, Macmillan $15.00 (0-689-50529-9). 32pp. Emily writes her teacher about a whale she believes she sees in her swimming pool. (Rev: BL 11/15/91; SLJ 10/91)

2248 Janovitz, Marilyn. *Little Fox* (PS–2). Illus. 1999, North-South LB $15.88 (0-7358-1161-X). 32pp. After Little Fox breaks his mother's chair by playing on it, he discovers that finding a replacement isn't easy. (Rev: BL 12/1/99; HBG 3/00; SLJ 11/99)

2249 Jennings, Linda. *Scramcat* (PS–2). Illus. by Rhian N. James. 1994, Crocodile $13.95 (1-56656-137-X). A stray cat that is shunned by everyone suddenly becomes popular when it foils a robbery. (Rev: SLJ 11/94)

2250 Jennings, Sharon. *Franklin's Neighborhood* (K–1). Illus. by Brenda Clark. 1999, Kids Can $10.95 (1-55074-729-0). 32pp. Franklin, a young turtle, faces a great challenge when he is required to draw a picture of his favorite thing in the entire neighborhood. (Rev: HBG 3/00; SLJ 12/99)

2251 Jeram, Anita. *All Together Now* (PS–K). Illus. by author. 2000, Candlewick $13.99 (0-7636-0846-7). Mommy Rabbit and Bunny are joined by Little Duckling and Miss Mouse to make a very special family. (Rev: HBG 10/00; SLJ 2/00)

2252 Jeram, Anita. *Bill's Belly Button* (PS–1). Illus. 1991, Little, Brown $14.95 (0-316-46114-8). 32pp. Bill, an elephant, becomes alarmed when he discovers he does not have a belly button. (Rev: BL 9/15/91; SLJ 10/91)

2253 Jeram, Anita. *Daisy Dare* (PS–K). Illus. 1997, Candlewick paper $3.29 (1-56402-986-7). 24pp. Daisy Dare, a little mouse, shows great bravery when she tries to take the bell off a cat's collar. Also use *Contrary Mary* (1995). (Rev: BL 11/15/95; SLJ 1/96)

2254 Jeschke, Susan. *Perfect the Pig* (K–2). Illus. by author. 1981, Scholastic paper $6.95 (0-8050-4704-2). 40pp. The adventures of a winged pig named Perfect.

2255 Johansen, K. V. *Pippin Takes a Bath* (PS–1). Illus. by Bernice Lum. 1999, Kids Can $12.95 (1-55074-627-8). 32pp. Pippin the dog refuses to take a bath until he has an encounter with a skunk. (Rev: BL 11/15/99; HBG 3/00; SLJ 11/99)

2256 Johnson, D. B. *Henry Hikes to Fitchburg* (PS–3). Illus. 2000, Houghton $15.00 (0-395-96867-4). 32pp. Henry the bear decides to take a nature walk to Fitchburg while his friend will ride the train in this amusing take-off on Thoreau's attitudes and his New England circle. (Rev: BCCB 7–8/00; BL 4/15/00*; HB 5–6/00; HBG 10/00; SLJ 6/00)

2257 Johnson, Gillian. *My Sister Gracie* (PS–3). Illus. by author. 2000, Tundra $16.95 (0-88776-514-9). Fabio, a dog, wants a thoroughbred brother to play with but his family adopts a female mutt from the pound. (Rev: HBG 3/01; SLJ 12/00)

2258 Johnson, Pamela. *A Mouse's Tale* (K–2). Illus. 1991, Harcourt $11.95 (0-15-256032-7). A small mouse collects bits and pieces of materials and makes a sailing craft. (Rev: SLJ 6/91)

2259 Johnson, Paul B. *The Pig Who Ran a Red Light* (PS–2). Illus. 1999, Orchard LB $16.99 (0-531-33136-9). 32pp. Gertrude the cow, who is being mimicked by George the pig, solves the problem by acting like a pig. (Rev: BL 5/1/99; HBG 10/99; SLJ 3/99)

2260 Johnston, Tony. *The Chizzywink and the Alamagoozlum* (PS–3). Illus. by Robert Bender. 1998, Holiday $16.95 (0-8234-1359-4). 32pp. A humorous tale about several animals trying to prevent a giant mosquito (or chizzywink) from entering their house and eating their maple syrup (the alamagoozlum). (Rev: BL 6/1–15/98; HBG 10/98; SLJ 6/98)

2261 Johnston, Tony. *The Iguana Brothers: A Tale of Two Lizards* (PS–2). Illus. by Mark Teague. 1995, Scholastic $15.95 (0-590-47468-5). 32pp. Dom and Tom, iguana brothers, have many differences but remain best friends. (Rev: BCCB 7–8/95; BL 1/15/95*; SLJ 4/95)

2262 Johnston, Tony. *Slither McCreep and His Brother* (PS–3). Illus. by Victoria Chess. 1996, Harcourt paper $5.00 (0-15-201387-3). 32pp. Two snake brothers, Slither and Joe, fight continually because Joe will not share his possessions. (Rev: BL 3/1/92; SLJ 4/92)

2263 Jones, Carol. *Town Mouse Country Mouse* (K–3). Illus. 1995, Houghton $15.00 (0-395-71129-0). 32pp. An imaginative retelling of the fable using modern urban and rural settings. (Rev: BL 4/15/95; HB 3–4/95; SLJ 6/95)

2264 Jones, Carol. *What's the Time, Mr. Wolf?* (PS–3). Illus. 1999, Houghton $15.00 (0-395-95800-8). 32pp. Mr. Wolf invites a number of his tasty friends to a special dinner, but they are aware

of his hidden purpose in this book that uses flaps to anticipate plot developments. (Rev: BL 9/15/99; HBG 3/00; SLJ 12/99)

2265 Jorgensen, Gail. *Crocodile Beat* (PS). Illus. by Patricia Mullins. 1994, Simon & Schuster paper $5.99 (0-689-71881-0). 32pp. An animal tale told in syncopated couplets, followed by a line of rhythmic animal sounds. (Rev: HB 11–12/89; SLJ 10/89)

2266 Jorgensen, Gail. *Gotcha!* (PS–1). Illus. by Kerry Argent. 1997, Scholastic $15.95 (0-590-96208-6). 32pp. Bertha the bear creates mayhem when she chases a fly that has eyes on her birthday cake. (Rev: BCCB 4/97; BL 2/1/97; SLJ 3/97)

2267 Joyce, William. *Bently and Egg* (PS–3). Illus. 1992, HarperCollins $15.95 (0-06-020385-4); paper $5.95 (0-06-443352-8). Bently, a frog, is asked to egg-sit for his friend the duck. (Rev: BCCB 3/92; BL 1/1/92; HB 3–4/92; SLJ 4/92*)

2268 Joyce, William. *The Leaf Men and the Brave Good Bugs* (PS–3). Illus. 1996, HarperCollins LB $16.89 (0-06-027238-4). 40pp. The good bugs in a garden join to help restore an old woman's sickly rosebush. (Rev: BL 10/1/96; SLJ 10/96)

2269 Judes, Marie-Odile. *Max, the Stubborn Little Wolf* (K–3). Trans. by Joan Robins. Illus. by Martine Bourre. 2001, HarperCollins $14.95 (0-06-029417-5). 32pp. When Max, a young wolf, states that he wants to become a florist, his father, who thinks this is an occupation unsuitable for a macho wolf, tries to change his son's mind. (Rev: BL 2/1/01; SLJ 3/01)

2270 Jungman, Ann. *When the People Are Away* (K–3). Illus. by Linda Birch. 1993, Boyds Mills $12.95 (1-56397-202-6). 24pp. While their masters are away on vacation, two cats enjoy such activities as an all-night Tom and Jerry cartoon fest. (Rev: BL 9/1/93; SLJ 1/94)

2271 Kalan, Robert. *Moving Day* (PS–1). Illus. by Yossi Abolafia. 1996, Greenwillow $14.93 (0-688-13949-3). 32pp. A hermit crab sets out to find a new home. (Rev: BL 6/1–15/96; SLJ 7/96)

2272 Kalman, Maira. *Ooh-La-La (Max in Love)* (PS–4). Illus. 1991, Viking $16.99 (0-670-84163-3). 32pp. Max the dog falls for Crepes Suzette, a dalmatian, in fascinating Paris. (Rev: BL 10/15/91; SLJ 11/91)

2273 Kaminsky, Jef. *Poppy and Ella: Three Stories About Two Friends* (PS–1). Illus. by author. 2000, Hyperion LB $15.49 (0-7868-2447-6). Using cartoons as illustrations, this book describes the exploits of two birds who are friends. (Rev: BCCB 9/00; HBG 10/00; SLJ 7/00)

2274 Kasza, Keiko. *Don't Laugh, Joe!* (PS–1). Illus. 1997, Putnam $15.99 (0-399-23036-X). 32pp. A young opossum has an unusual problem: He can't stop giggling while playing dead. (Rev: BL 8/97; SLJ 6/97)

2275 Kasza, Keiko. *Dorothy and Mikey* (K–3). Illus. 2000, Putnam $12.99 (0-399-23356-3). 32pp. Dorothy and Mikey, two hippopotami, are best friends who sometimes compete with each other in these three humorous stories. (Rev: BCCB 9/00; BL 5/1/00; HB 3–4/00; HBG 10/00; SLJ 5/00)

2276 Kasza, Keiko. *A Mother for Choco* (PS–1). Illus. 1992, Putnam LB $15.99 (0-399-21841-6). 32pp. A little bird sets out to find his mother and is adopted by a kindly bear. (Rev: BCCB 4/92; BL 3/15/92; HB 5–6/92; SLJ 4/92*)

2277 Kasza, Keiko. *The Rat and the Tiger* (PS–3). Illus. 1993, Putnam LB $14.95 (0-399-22404-1). 32pp. Rat feels that he is always being taken advantage of by his friend Tiger. (Rev: BCCB 4/93; BL 1/15/93; HB 5–6/93; SLJ 4/93)

2278 Katz, Avner. *Tortoise Solves a Problem* (K–3). Illus. 1993, HarperCollins LB $12.89 (0-06-020799-X). 32pp. While searching for a new house, the tortoise invents the tortoise shell. (Rev: BL 1/15/93)

2279 Keller, Holly. *Brave Horace* (PS–1). Illus. 1998, Greenwillow $15.00 (0-688-15407-7). 32pp. Horace, a young leopard, builds up his courage to attend a monster-movie party. (Rev: BL 3/1/98; HBG 10/98; SLJ 4/98)

2280 Keller, Holly. *Geraldine and Mrs. Duffy* (PS–K). Illus. 2000, Greenwillow LB $15.89 (0-688-16888-4). 32pp. It takes some doing but new babysitter Mrs. Duffy gradually wins over hostile Geraldine, a little pig, and her brother Willy. (Rev: BL 10/1/00; HBG 3/01; SLJ 8/00)

2281 Keller, Holly. *Geraldine's Big Snow* (PS–K). Illus. by author. 1988, Greenwillow $15.89 (0-688-07514-2). 24pp. Young Geraldine, a pig, eagerly awaits the first snow. (Rev: BL 8/88; HB 11–12/88; SLJ 2/89)

2282 Keller, Holly. *Geraldine's Blanket* (PS–2). Illus. by author. 1988, Morrow paper $4.95 (0-688-07810-9). 32pp. A little pig named Geraldine becomes extremely attached to a blanket her aunt gave her.

2283 Keller, Holly. *That's Mine, Horace* (PS–2). Illus. 2000, Greenwillow LB $15.89 (0-688-17160-5). 24pp. After Horace, a little leopard, finds a toy that belongs to a classmate, he lies and says it is his. Then his conscience makes him suffer. (Rev: BL 8/00; HB 7–8/00; HBG 10/00; SLJ 6/00)

2284 Kellogg, Steven, reteller. *Chicken Little* (1–3). Illus. by Steven Kellogg. 1985, Morrow paper $4.95 (0-688-07045-0). 32pp. A wacky version of the old favorite. (Rev: BCCB 11/85; BL 9/1/85; SLJ 10/85)

2285 Kennedy, X. J. *Elympics* (PS–3). Illus. by Graham Percy. 1999, Putnam $15.99 (0-399-23249-4). 32pp. This large-format book tells how the Olympic Games would be played if all the participants were elephants. (Rev: BCCB 1/00; BL 3/1/00; HBG 3/00; SLJ 9/99)

2286 Kent, Jack. *The Caterpillar and the Polliwog* (K–2). Illus. by author. 1985, Simon & Schuster paper $14.00 (0-671-66280-5). 32pp. The caterpillar and the polliwog become a butterfly and a frog.

2287 Kent, Jack. *Joey* (PS–2). Illus. by author. 1987, Simon & Schuster $11.95 (0-671-66459-X). 32pp. Joey, a young kangaroo, is not allowed out of his mother's pouch, so he invites his friends in.

2288 Kern, Noris. *I Love You with All My Heart* (PS–K). Illus. 1998, Chronicle $14.95 (0-8118-2031-9). 32pp. Several Arctic animals tell a polar bear cub how their mothers love them. (Rev: BL 4/15/98; HBG 10/98; SLJ 8/98)

2289 Kessler, Cristina. *Konte Chameleon Fine, Fine, Fine! A West African Folktale* (PS–2). Illus. by Christian Epanya. 1997, Boyds Mills $14.95 (1-56397-181-X). 32pp. An innocent young chameleon panics when he finds that he can change color. (Rev: BL 10/1/97; HBG 3/98; SLJ 9/97)

2290 Ketteman, Helen. *Armadillo Tattletale* (K–3). Illus. by Keith Graves. 2000, Scholastic $15.95 (0-590-99723-8). 32pp. In this original folktale, Armadillo's ears are cut down to a proper size to stop him from hearing — and passing on — gossip. (Rev: BCCB 11/00; BL 12/15/00; HBG 3/01; SLJ 9/00)

2291 Kettner, Christine. *An Ordinary Cat* (PS–K). Illus. 1991, HarperCollins LB $13.89 (0-06-023173-4). 32pp. Inwardly, William is not the ordinary cat that everyone sees. (Rev: BL 1/1/91; SLJ 12/91)

2292 King, Bob. *Sitting on the Farm* (PS–1). Illus. by Bill Slavin. 1992, Scholastic paper $7.99 (0-590-73979-2). 32pp. In successive verses of a silly song, a young girl calls on animals to remove a bug from her knee. (Rev: BL 2/1/92; SLJ 8/92)

2293 Kirby, David, and Allen Woodman. *The Cows Are Going to Paris* (K–3). Illus. by Chris L. Demarest. 1991, St. Martin's $15.95 (1-878093-11-8). 32pp. A group of cows decide to leave the countryside and travel to Paris. (Rev: BL 12/15/91; SLJ 3/92)

2294 Kirk, David. *Little Miss Spider* (PS–1). Illus. 1999, Scholastic $12.95 (0-439-08389-3). 32pp. After hatching, Little Miss Spider sets out to find her mother and is helped by a kindly green beetle named Betty. (Rev: BL 12/1/99; HBG 3/00; SLJ 11/99)

2295 Kirk, David. *Little Miss Spider at Sunny Patch School* (PS–K). Illus. by author. 2000, Scholastic $12.95 (0-439-08727-9). Miss Spider starts school and soon finds she is failing leaf chewing, flying, and stinging but gains high marks in climbing and spinning. (Rev: HBG 3/01; SLJ 9/00)

2296 Kirk, David. *Miss Spider's New Car* (PS–2). Illus. 1997, Scholastic $16.95 (0-590-30713-4). 32pp. Miss Spider and her husband, Holley, go shopping for a car and become the victims of a nefarious car dealer. (Rev: BL 11/1/97; HBG 3/98; SLJ 1/98)

2297 Kirk, David. *Miss Spider's Tea Party* (PS–3). Illus. 1994, Scholastic $16.95 (0-590-47724-2). 32pp. No one wants to accept Miss Spider's invitation to tea for fear of being eaten. (Rev: BL 1/15/94; SLJ 6/94)

2298 Kirk, David. *Miss Spider's Wedding* (K–4). Illus. 1995, Scholastic $16.95 (0-590-56866-3). 40pp. Miss Spider finds she is very wrong when she thinks handsome Spiderus Reeves is "Mr. Right." A sequel to *Miss Spider's Tea Party* (1993). (Rev: BL 10/1/95; SLJ 10/95)

2299 Kirk, David. *Nova's Ark* (1–3). Illus. 1999, Scholastic $17.95 (0-590-28208-5). 40pp. Young Nova, a robot, travels to a distant moon where he builds robot animals from the wreckage of his space ship. (Rev: BL 2/1/99; HBG 10/99; SLJ 3/99)

2300 Kitamura, Satoshi. *Cat Is Sleepy* (PS). Illus. by author. 1996, Farrar $4.95 (0-374-31223-0). In this board book, a cat can't decide where to sleep. Also use *Dog Is Thirsty, Duck Is Dirty,* and *Squirrel Is Hungry* (all 1996). (Rev: SLJ 8/96)

2301 Kitamura, Satoshi. *Sheep in Wolves' Clothing* (PS–2). Illus. 1996, Farrar $15.00 (0-374-36780-9). 32pp. Three sheep seek their revenge when wolves steal their woolly coats while they are swimming. (Rev: BL 5/1/96; HB 7–8/96; SLJ 8/96*)

2302 Kleven, Elisa. *The Puddle Pail* (PS–2). Illus. 1997, Dutton $15.99 (0-525-45803-4). 32pp. Ernst, a little crocodile, wants to have a collecting hobby, but he doesn't know what to collect. (Rev: BL 6/1–15/97; SLJ 6/97*)

2303 Klinting, Lars. *Bruno the Tailor* (PS–3). Illus. 1996, Holt $14.95 (0-8050-4500-7). 32pp. Using a step-by-step approach, Bruno the beaver makes an apron in a way that can be copied by children. (Rev: BL 10/15/96; SLJ 12/96)

2304 Knowles, Sheena. *Edwina the Emu* (PS–1). Illus. by Rod Clement. 1997, HarperTrophy paper $6.95 (0-06-443483-4). At the zoo, Edwina the emu leaves her husband to tend their eggs while she goes out looking for a job. (Rev: SLJ 9/97)

2305 Koci, Marta. *Sarah's Bear* (PS–1). Illus. by author. 1991, Picture Book paper $14.95 (0-88708-038-3). 28pp. Bear joins Sarah's home on a Greek island, which already includes Cat, Dog, Goat, Goose, Pig, and Crow. (Rev: BL 10/15/87; SLJ 12/87)

2306 Koehler, Phoebe. *Making Room* (PS–1). Illus. 1993, Macmillan LB $14.95 (0-02-750875-7). 48pp. A large dog makes room in his household for a woman, a baby, and a cat. (Rev: BL 3/15/93; SLJ 8/93)

2307 Koide, Tan. *May We Sleep Here Tonight?* (PS–1). Illus. by Yasuko Koide. 2000, Simon & Schuster $12.95 (0-689-83288-5). 32pp. Three gophers get lost, enter a strange new house and, after they are joined by several other lost creatures, they all wonder to whom the house belongs. (Rev: BL 4/1/00; HBG 10/00)

2308 Komoda, Beverly. *The Too Hot Day* (PS–K). Illus. 1991, HarperCollins LB $14.89 (0-06-021612-3). 32pp. Mama and her bunny family try to escape the heat through a variety of activities. (Rev: BL 5/15/91; SLJ 8/91)

2309 Komoda, Beverly. *The Winter Day* (PS–1). Illus. 1991, HarperCollins $13.95 (0-06-023301-X). 32pp. The Hopper children, a group of rabbits, are enjoying the snow until a bully named Spike spoils their fun. (Rev: BL 12/1/91; SLJ 1/92)

2310 Koontz, Robin M. *Chicago and the Cat: The Family Reunion* (1–3). Illus. by author. Series: Little Chapter Books. 1996, Cobblehill $14.99 (0-525-65202-7). When Chicago brings his family to visit, the Cat is not very happy about the arrangements, including having to share his room. (Rev: SLJ 9/96)

2311 Kopper, Lisa. *Daisy Knows Best* (PS–K). Illus. 1999, Dutton $12.99 (0-525-45915-4). 32pp. While

Daisy the dog is busy teaching her three pups proper behavior, she takes on a new pupil, the resident baby. (Rev: BL 1/1–15/99; HBG 10/99; SLJ 4/99)

2312 Kopper, Lisa. *Daisy's Babies* (PS). Illus. 2000, Dutton $12.99 (0-525-46231-7). 32pp. Daisy the dog, her three puppies, and Baby explore the contents of Mommy's purse. (Rev: BL 2/1/00; HBG 10/00; SLJ 4/00)

2313 Koscielniak, Bruce. *Geoffrey Groundhog Predicts the Weather* (PS–1). Illus. 1995, Houghton $15.00 (0-395-70933-4). 32pp. When Geoffrey Groundhog emerges from his hole on Groundhog Day, he finds he is part of a media event. (Rev: BCCB 11/95; BL 10/15/95; SLJ 10/95)

2314 Kovalski, Maryann. *Brenda and Edward* (PS–2). Illus. 1997, Kids Can $14.95 (0-919964-77-X). 32pp. Two dogs who adore each other are separated until, years later, a series of coincidences brings them back together. (Rev: BL 10/15/97; SLJ 9/97)

2315 Kovalski, Maryann. *Omar on Ice* (PS–2). Illus. 1999, Fitzhenry & Whiteside $13.95 (1-55041-507-7). 32pp. Omar, a young bear, learns he can produce beautiful pictures on the ice when he whirls and swirls while skating. (Rev: BL 10/15/99)

2316 Kovalski, Maryann. *Queen Nadine* (K–2). Illus. by author. 1998, Orca $14.95 (1-55143-093-2). When a farmer sells his cows to raise corn, he decides to keep Nadine, the dreamy loner of his herd. (Rev: HBG 3/99; SLJ 12/98)

2317 Kranendonk, Anke. *Just a Minute* (PS–K). Illus. by Jung-Hee Spetter. 1998, Front Street $14.95 (1-886910-29-4). 32pp. Every time Piggy wants attention, mama says "Just a minute," little knowing what mischief her son is up to in the meantime. (Rev: BL 4/15/98; HBG 10/98; SLJ 7/98)

2318 Kraus, Robert. *Big Squeak, Little Squeak* (PS–1). Illus. by Kevin O'Malley. 1996, Orchard LB $16.99 (0-531-08774-3). 32pp. Two little mice outwit Mr. Kit Kat, the owner of the local cheese store, who is intent on capturing them. (Rev: BL 10/15/96; SLJ 10/96)

2319 Kraus, Robert. *Herman the Helper* (PS–K). Illus. by Jose Aruego and Ariane Dewey. 1987, Simon & Schuster paper $6.99 (0-671-66270-8). Herman, a green octopus, helps his many friends with his many arms. A reissued title, as are: *Another Mouse to Feed* and *Milton the Early Riser* (both 1987).

2320 Kraus, Robert. *Leo the Late Bloomer* (PS–K). Illus. by Jose Aruego. 1971, HarperCollins LB $15.89 (0-87807-043-5). 32pp. Leo, a lion, is just a late bloomer, as Mother tells Father, but Father is worried. Finally Leo blooms — he can read, write, and eat neatly. A beguiling, humorous story.

2321 Kraus, Robert. *Mort the Sport* (PS–2). Illus. by John Himmelman. 2000, Orchard LB $16.99 (0-531-33247-0). 32pp. Mort the elephant finds that baseball and violin playing don't mix. (Rev: BL 2/15/00; HBG 10/00; SLJ 4/00)

2322 Kraus, Robert. *Mouse in Love* (PS–2). Illus. by Jose Aruego and Ariane Dewey. 2000, Orchard LB $16.99 (0-531-33297-7). 32pp. Mouse searches high and low for the mouse of his dreams and finds that she lives next door. (Rev: BCCB 11/00; BL 9/15/00; HBG 3/01; SLJ 8/00)

2323 Kraus, Robert. *Whose Mouse Are You?* (PS–1). Illus. by Jose Aruego. 1970, Macmillan paper $5.99 (0-689-71142-5). 32pp. A young mouse is asked eight questions by his family — which should delight young children who are asked similar questions by their families.

2324 Krischanitz, Raoul. *Nobody Likes Me!* (K–2). Trans. by Rosemary Lanning. Illus. 1999, North-South LB $15.88 (0-7358-1055-9). A lonely dog, shunned by other animals, is accepted after he becomes friends with a respected fox. (Rev: BL 4/15/99; HBG 10/99)

2325 Kudrna, C. Imbior. *To Bathe a Boa* (PS). Illus. by author. 1986, Carolrhoda LB $15.95 (0-87614-306-0); paper $5.95 (0-87614-490-3). A little boy hunts high and low for his boa, who doesn't want a bath. (Rev: BL 1/1/87; SLJ 2/87)

2326 Kvasnosky, Laura McGee. *See You Later, Alligator* (PS–K). Illus. 1995, Harcourt $10.00 (0-15-200301-0). 24pp. Popular sayings are used to describe a little alligator's day at school. (Rev: BL 9/15/95; SLJ 11/95)

2327 Kvasnosky, Laura McGee. *Zelda and Ivy* (PS–2). Illus. 1998, Candlewick $15.99 (0-7636-0469-0). 48pp. There are many witty situations in this delightful picture book about two fox sisters and the elder's attempts to dominate her younger sibling. (Rev: BCCB 4/98; BL 4/1/98*; HB 7–8/98; HBG 10/98; SLJ 6/98)

2328 Kvasnosky, Laura McGee. *Zelda and Ivy and the Boy Next Door* (K–3). Illus. 1999, Candlewick $15.99 (0-7636-0672-3). 48pp. Three vignettes that feature the little fox sisters Zelda and Ivy. In one, Eugene moves in next door and immediately develops a crush on Zelda. (Rev: BCCB 6/99; BL 5/1/99; HBG 10/99; SLJ 5/99)

2329 Laden, Nina. *Bad Dog* (K–4). Illus. by author. 2000, Walker $15.95 (0-8027-8747-9); paper $16.85 (0-8027-8748-7). After a series of amusing adventures, Bad Dog finds he is in jail. (Rev: BCCB 10/00; HBG 3/01; SLJ 9/00)

2330 Laden, Nina. *Roberto: The Insect Architect* (2–4). Illus. 2000, Chronicle $15.95 (0-8118-2465-9). 40pp. A termite named Roberto achieves his dream of being an architect by planning and building a shelter for homeless bugs. (Rev: BCCB 12/00; BL 11/15/00; HBG 3/01)

2331 Laden, Nina. *When Pigasso Met Mootisse* (K–2). Illus. 1998, Chronicle $15.95 (0-8118-1121-2). 40pp. Two painters, Pigasso, a pig, and Mootisse, a bull, become rivals in the art world in this takeoff on the Picasso-Matisse feud. (Rev: BL 11/1/98; HBG 3/99; SLJ 11/98)

2332 Lancome, Julie. *Ruthie's Big Old Coat* (K–3). Illus. 2000, Candlewick $13.99 (0-7636-0969-2). 32pp. Ruthie the rabbit hates her new hand-me-down coat that is too big, but after friend Fiona shows her how perfect it really is, Ruthie grows to love it. (Rev: BCCB 6/00; BL 4/1/00; HB 5–6/00; HBG 10/00; SLJ 5/00)

2333 Landstrom, Olof, and Lena Landstrom. *Boo and Baa at Sea* (PS). Illus. 1997, Farrar $7.95 (91-29-63921-2). 26pp. In this simple reading book, Boo and Baa get stuck when they take out a rowboat. Also use *Boo and Baa on a Cleaning Spree* (1997). (Rev: BL 7/97; SLJ 7/97)

2334 Landstrom, Olof, and Lena Landstrom. *Boo and Baa in a Party Mood* (PS). Trans. by Joan Sandin. Illus. 1996, Farrar paper $7.95 (91-29-63918-2). 22pp. In this simple picture book, two young sheep, Boo and Baa, prepare for a friend's birthday party. Also use *Boo and Baa in Windy Weather* (1996). (Rev: BL 11/1/96)

2335 Landstrom, Olof, and Lena Landstrom. *Boo and Baa in the Woods* (PS–K). Illus. 2000, Farrar $7.95 (91-29-64754-1). 28pp. Boo and Baa, two sheep, are disappointed when they can't find berries to pick, but some ants accidentally show them a spot where berries are abundant. Also use *Boo and Baa Get Wet* (2000). (Rev: BL 11/15/00; HBG 3/01; SLJ 9/00)

2336 Langreuter, Jutta. *Little Bear and the Big Fight* (PS–K). Illus. by Vera Sobat. 1998, Millbrook LB $21.40 (0-7613-0403-7); paper $6.95 (0-7613-0375-8). 32pp. Little Bear loses his temper during a fight with his kindergarten friend, but later they reconcile and become friends again. (Rev: BL 4/1/98; HBG 10/98; SLJ 8/98)

2337 Langreuter, Jutta. *Little Bear Brushes His Teeth* (PS–K). Illus. by Vera Sobat. 1997, Millbrook LB $21.40 (0-7613-0190-9); paper $7.95 (0-7613-0230-1). 32pp. Little Bear pretends he is a soldier fighting bacteria when he brushes his teeth. Also use *Little Bear Goes to Kindergarten* (1997). (Rev: BL 2/1/97; SLJ 7/97)

2338 Langreuter, Jutta. *Little Bear Is a Big Brother* (PS–K). Illus. by Vera Sobat. 1998, Millbrook LB $21.40 (0-7613-0404-5); paper $6.95 (0-7613-0376-6). 32pp. At first Little Bear is excited about having a new baby brother, but later he becomes anxious and jealous and must undergo a period of adjustment. (Rev: BL 4/1/98; HBG 10/98)

2339 Lansky, Vicki. *It's Not Your Fault, KoKo Bear: A Read-Together Book for Parents and Young Children During Divorce* (PS–2). Illus. by Jane Prince. 1998, Book Peddlers $10.95 (0-916773-46-9); paper $5.99 (0-916773-47-7). When KoKo Bear's parents divorce, the cub goes through the emotions associated with it: anger, guilt, confusion, and sadness. (Rev: HBG 10/98; SLJ 6/98)

2340 Larios, Julie Hofstrand. *On the Stairs* (PS–1). Illus. by Mary Hofstrand Cornish. 1999, Front Street $15.95 (1-886910-34-0). 32pp. Using rhyming verse, this book portrays two mice and the fun they have naming each of the 12 steps on their stairs. (Rev: BL 12/15/99; HBG 3/00; SLJ 12/99)

2341 Larrañaga, Ana Martín. *The Big Wide-Mouthed Frog* (PS–K). Illus. by author. 1999, Candlewick $10.99 (0-7636-0807-6); paper $3.29 (0-7636-0808-4). A wide-mouthed frog sets out to see the world while asking each animal he meets about its food preference, until he meets a crocodile who likes wide-mouthed frogs. (Rev: BCCB 11/99; HBG 3/00; SLJ 8/99)

2342 Lasky, Kathryn. *Lucille's Snowsuit* (PS–K). Illus. by Marylin Hafner. 2000, Crown $14.95 (0-517-80037-3). 32pp. Lucille the pig has trouble getting into her snowsuit when she wants to go out to play in the snow with her brother and sister. (Rev: BCCB 10/00; BL 9/15/00; HBG 3/01; SLJ 9/00)

2343 Lasky, Kathryn. *Lunch Bunnies* (K–3). Illus. by Marylin Hafner. 1996, Little, Brown $14.95 (0-316-51525-6). 32pp. During school lunchtime, Clyde is afraid that he will drop his tray. (Rev: BL 9/15/96; SLJ 9/96)

2344 Lasky, Kathryn. *Science Fair Bunnies* (K–2). Illus. by Marylin Hafner. 2000, Candlewick $15.99 (0-7636-0729-0). 32pp. Clyde, a bunny, uses a loose tooth as the basis of a show-stealing science fair project. (Rev: BL 7/00; HBG 10/00; SLJ 7/00)

2345 Lass, Bonnie, and Philemon Sturges. *Who Took the Cookies from the Cookie Jar?* (PS–K). Illus. by Ashley Wolff. 2000, Little, Brown $14.95 (0-316-82016-4). 32pp. A little skunk, dressed as a cowboy, becomes a detective and inquires of various animals who stole the cookies from the cookie jar. (Rev: BCCB 12/00; BL 10/15/00; HBG 3/01; SLJ 10/00)

2346 Latimer, Jim. *Going the Moose Way Home* (1–3). Illus. by Donald Carrick. 1988, Macmillan LB $15.00 (0-684-18890-2). 32pp. The adventures of Moose as he encounters others. (Rev: BL 12/1/88; SLJ 11/88)

2347 Latimer, Jim. *Moose and Friends* (K–2). Illus. by Carolyn Ewing. 1993, Scribners $14.95 (0-684-19335-3). Three stories of friendship featuring kindhearted Moose, along with Fox, Skunk, and Barbary the sheep. (Rev: SLJ 9/93)

2348 Leaf, Munro. *The Story of Ferdinand* (K–4). Illus. by Robert Lawson. 1936, Puffin paper $6.99 (0-14-050234-3). 72pp. The classic story of the bull who wants only to sit and smell flowers.

2349 Lebrun, Claude. *Little Brown Bear Does Not Want to Eat* (PS). Illus. by Daniele Bour. Series: Little Brown Bear Books. 1996, Children's LB $12.00 (0-531-07823-2); paper $3.50 (0-531-17823-7). A simple book about a childhood problem and its solution. Also use *Little Brown Bear Is Growing Up* and *Little Brown Bear Wants to Be Read To* (both 1996). (Rev: SLJ 9/96)

2350 Leedy, Loreen. *The Furry News: How to Make a Newspaper* (1–4). Illus. 1990, Holiday LB $16.95 (0-8234-0793-4). 32pp. Big Bear becomes disgusted with his local newspaper and decides to publish his own. (Rev: BCCB 5/90; BL 5/1/90)

2351 Leedy, Loreen. *The Great Trash Bash* (K–2). Illus. 1991, Holiday LB $16.95 (0-8234-0869-8). Mayor Hippo discovers that his town has too much trash. (Rev: SLJ 5/91)

2352 Leedy, Loreen. *The Monster Money Book* (2–4). Illus. 1992, Holiday LB $16.95 (0-8234-0922-8). 32pp. Sarah joins a monster club and learns about various denominations of money. (Rev: BCCB 3/92; BL 3/15/92; SLJ 6/92)

2353 Leedy, Loreen. *Pingo the Plaid Panda* (PS–K). Illus. by author. 1989, Holiday LB $13.95 (0-8234-0727-6). 32pp. A panda whose fur is plaid feels he is not liked because he is different. (Rev: SLJ 7/89)

2354 Leemis, Ralph. *Smart Dog* (K–2). Illus. by Chris L. Demarest. 1993, Boyds Mills $14.95 (1-56397-109-7). An old man expects great things from his dog who really just wants to loaf. (Rev: SLJ 6/93)

2355 L'Engle, Madeleine. *The Other Dog* (PS–1). Illus. by Christine Davenier. 2001, North-South $15.95 (1-58717-040-X). 48pp. An older dog wonders why the family has adopted another dog and why the newcomer seems to be getting special attention. (Rev: BL 3/1/01)

2356 Lerman, Rory S. *Charlie's Checklist* (PS–2). Illus. by Alison Bartlett. 1997, Orchard paper $14.95 (0-531-30001-3). 32pp. When Charlie the puppy places a want ad to find a new home in the city, his young country master is forlorn at the thought of him leaving. (Rev: BCCB 6/97; BL 6/1–15/97; SLJ 5/97)

2357 Leslie, Amanda. *Are Chickens Stripy? A Lift-the-Flap Book* (PS). Illus. by author. 2000, Handprint $4.95 (1-929766-09-2). A flap book that describes the behavior of various animals in an amusing way. Also use *Do Crocodiles Moo?* (2000). (Rev: SLJ 12/00)

2358 Lester, Helen. *Hooway for Wodney Wat* (PS–2). Illus. by Lynn Munsinger. 1999, Houghton $15.00 (0-395-92392-1). 32pp. A humorous story about Wodney Wat and his problems pronouncing the letter *r*. (Rev: BL 5/1/99; HB 7–8/99; HBG 10/99; SLJ 5/99)

2359 Lester, Helen. *Listen, Buddy* (PS–3). Illus. by Lynn Munsinger. 1995, Houghton $15.00 (0-395-72361-2). 32pp. Buddy, a daydreaming rabbit, gets into serious trouble because he can't pay attention. (Rev: BL 10/15/95; SLJ 11/95)

2360 Lester, Helen. *Me First* (PS–3). Illus. by Lynn Munsinger. 1992, Houghton $14.95 (0-395-58706-9). 32pp. Pinkerton the pig is so pushy that he will do anything to be first. (Rev: BL 10/1/92; HB 11–12/92; SLJ 10/92*)

2361 Lester, Helen. *A Porcupine Named Fluffy* (PS–K). Illus. by Lynn Munsinger. 1986, Houghton $16.00 (0-395-36895-2); paper $6.95 (0-395-52018-5). Fluffy's ridiculous name leads to a friendship with a rhino, with another ridiculous name — Hippo. (Rev: BL 4/15/86; SLJ 8/86)

2362 Lester, Helen. *Tacky and the Emperor* (PS–3). Illus. by Lynn Munsinger. 2000, Houghton $15.00 (0-395-98210-4). 32pp. Tacky, a penguin, gets royal treatment when he puts on a fancy suit that is actually the emperor's robes. (Rev: BL 8/00; HBG 3/01; SLJ 11/00)

2363 Lester, Helen. *Tacky in Trouble* (PS–1). Illus. by Lynn Munsinger. 1998, Houghton $15.00 (0-395-86113-6). 32pp. Tacky, a fearless penguin, lands on a tropical isle after an ice-surfing spree and becomes a centerpiece in the kitchen of one of the island's elephants. (Rev: BCCB 5/98; BL 4/1/98; HBG 10/98; SLJ 5/98)

2364 Lester, Helen. *Tacky the Penguin* (PS–3). Illus. by Lynn Munsinger. 1988, Houghton $15.00 (0-395-45536-7); paper $5.95 (0-395-56233-3). 32pp. Most penguins wear black, but Tacky prefers Hawaiian shirts and checkered bow ties. (Rev: BCCB 4/88; BL 4/1/88)

2365 Lester, Helen. *Three Cheers for Tacky* (K–2). Illus. by Lynn Munsinger. 1994, Houghton $14.95 (0-395-66841-7). 32pp. Tacky the Penguin has the spirit but not the skill to function in a cheerleading competition. (Rev: BL 2/15/94; HB 9–10/94; SLJ 5/94)

2366 Lester, Julius. *Ackamarackus: Julius Lester's Sumptuously Silly Fantastically Funny Fables* (PS–3). Illus. by Emilie Chollat. 2001, Scholastic $17.95 (0-590-48913-5). 48pp. Six humorous, inventive tales featuring such animal characters as Bernard the Bee, Adalbert the Alligator, and Ellen the Eagle. (Rev: BCCB 3/01; BL 2/1/01; SLJ 3/01)

2367 Lester, Robin, and Helen Lester. *Wuzzy Takes Off* (PS). Illus. by Miko Imai. 1995, Candlewick $8.95 (1-56402-498-9). 32pp. Wuzzy, a teddy bear, confuses an ordinary playground with being on the moon. (Rev: BL 2/1/96)

2368 Lewin, Betsy. *Chubbo's Pool* (PS–2). Illus. 1996, Clarion $14.95 (0-395-72807-X). 32pp. A hippo learns to behave unselfishly toward other animals. (Rev: BCCB 10/96; BL 8/96; SLJ 9/96)

2369 Lewin, Betsy. *What's the Matter, Habibi?* (PS–1). Illus. 1997, Clarion $15.00 (0-395-85816-X). 32pp. Habibi the camel won't budge when her owner wants her to give rides to some children. (Rev: BL 9/15/97; HBG 3/98; SLJ 9/97)

2370 Lewison, Wendy C. *Shy Vi* (PS–K). Illus. by Stephen J. Smith. 1993, Simon & Schuster paper $14.00 (0-671-76968-5). 28pp. A little mouse named Violet is so shy that she can't speak above a whisper. (Rev: BL 5/1/93; SLJ 7/93)

2371 Lidz, Jane. *Zak: The One-of-a-Kind Dog* (PS–2). Photos by author. 1997, Abrams paper $12.95 (0-8109-3995-9). Zak, a mixed-breed dog, wonders about his ancestors and concludes that whoever they were, he is one of a kind. (Rev: BL 4/15/98; HBG 3/98; SLJ 3/98)

2372 Liersch, Anne. *A House Is Not a Home* (K–3). Illus. by Christa Unzner. 1999, North-South LB $15.88 (0-7358-1157-1). 32pp. Bossy Badger alienates all the other woodland creatures, but when winter comes he is lonely and asks if he can join them in their cozy home. (Rev: BL 11/1/99; HBG 3/00; SLJ 11/99)

2373 Lies, Brian. *Hamlet and the Enormous Chinese Dragon Kite* (K–3). Illus. 1994, Houghton $14.95 (0-395-68391-2). 26pp. Hamlet the pig is carried aloft during his first outing with a new Chinese dragon kite. (Rev: BCCB 10/94; BL 10/15/94; SLJ 8/94)

2374 Lillegard, Dee. *The Big Bug Ball* (PS–K). Illus. by Rex Barron. 1999, Putnam LB $15.99 (0-399-23121-8). A rhyming tale about various insects who stage some jazzy entertainment in a city park. (Rev: HBG 10/99; SLJ 7/99)

2375 Lindbergh, Reeve. *The Awful Aardvarks Shop for School* (PS–2). Illus. by Tracey Campbell Pearson. 2000, Viking $15.99 (0-670-88763-3). 32pp. Those awful aardvarks cause havoc when they invade a shopping mall to buy clothes and supplies for the new school year. (Rev: BL 6/1–15/00; HBG 3/01; SLJ 7/00)

2376 Lindgren, Barbro. *Benny's Had Enough!* (PS–K). Trans. by Elisabeth Kallick Dyssegaard. Illus. by Olof Landstrom. 1999, Farrar $14.00 (91-29-64563-8). 28pp. A little piglet runs away but finds that life outside his comfortable home is difficult. (Rev: BL 10/15/99; HB 11–12/99; HBG 3/00; SLJ 12/99)

2377 Lindgren, Barbro. *Rosa Goes to Daycare* (K–2). Illus. by Eva Eriksson. 2000, Douglas & McIntyre $15.95 (0-88899-391-9). 32pp. Rosa, a dog, is frightened about her first day in doggy day care but adjusts beautifully. (Rev: BL 7/00; HBG 10/00; SLJ 8/00)

2378 Lionni, Leo. *Alexander and the Wind-Up Mouse* (K–2). Illus. by author. 1969, Pantheon paper $5.99 (0-394-82911-5). 32pp. Alexander, a real mouse, envies Willy, a toy, windup mouse, who is loved and cuddled.

2379 Lionni, Leo. *The Biggest House in the World* (PS–2). Illus. by author. 1968, Knopf paper $5.99 (0-394-82740-6). 32pp. A young snail, desiring a larger shell, receives fatherly advice and decides that small accommodations are an asset in regaining his mobility.

2380 Lionni, Leo. *An Extraordinary Egg* (PS–2). Illus. 1994, Knopf $16.00 (0-679-85840-7). 32pp. After a frog helps hatch an egg, she thinks that a chicken emerges, but it is really an alligator. (Rev: BCCB 6/94; BL 6/1–15/94; HB 7–8/94; SLJ 6/94*)

2381 Lionni, Leo. *Fish Is Fish* (K–2). Illus. by author. 1970, Knopf paper $5.99 (0-394-82799-6). 32pp. A fable about a fish who learns from a frog how to be happy just being himself.

2382 Lionni, Leo. *Frederick* (PS–2). Illus. by author. 1967, Knopf LB $18.99 (0-394-91040-0); paper $5.99 (0-394-82614-0). 40pp. A field mouse appears to be ignoring the coming of winter, but actually he is not.

2383 Lionni, Leo. *Inch by Inch* (PS–2). Illus. by author. 1962, Astor-Honor $19.00 (0-8392-3010-9). When the birds demand that he measure the length of a nightingale's song, this clever, captive inchworm inches his way to freedom.

2384 Lionni, Leo. *Matthew's Dream* (K–3). Illus. 1995, Random paper $5.99 (0-679-87318-X). With his imagination, Matthew, a little mouse, can turn his dismal home into something stunning. (Rev: BCCB 3/91; BL 1/1/91; SLJ 4/91*)

2385 Lionni, Leo. *Mr. McMouse* (PS–1). Illus. 1992, Knopf $15.00 (0-679-83890-2). 32pp. Timothy, a city mouse, tries to find his true identity with some field mice. (Rev: BL 10/1/92; SLJ 10/92)

2386 Lionni, Leo. *Swimmy* (PS–1). Illus. by author. 1963, Pantheon LB $18.99 (0-394-91713-8); Knopf paper $5.99 (0-394-82620-5). 40pp. A remarkable little fish instructs the rest of his school in the art of protection — swim in the formation of a gigantic fish! Beautiful, full-color illustrations.

2387 Lionni, Leo. *Tillie and the Wall* (PS–3). Illus. by author. 1989, Knopf paper $5.99 (0-679-81357-8). 32pp. Tillie, of all the mice, wonders what's on the other side of the wall. (Rev: BL 3/15/89; HB 7–8/89; SLJ 4/89)

2388 Lloyd, David. *Polly Molly Woof Woof: A Book About Being Happy* (PS–K). Illus. by Charlotte Hard. 2000, Candlewick $13.99 (0-7636-0755-X). When Molly, a little dog, barks in the park she is joined by other dogs and soon there is a canine chorus. (Rev: BCCB 4/00; HBG 10/00; SLJ 7/00)

2389 Lobel, Arnold. *Fables* (2–4). Illus. by author. 1980, HarperCollins LB $15.89 (0-06-023974-3); paper $6.95 (0-06-443046-4). 48pp. An Americanized Aesop with excellent illustrations. Caldecott Medal winner, 1981.

2390 Lodge, Bernard. *Tanglebird* (PS–1). Illus. 1997, Houghton $14.95 (0-395-84543-2). 32pp. Tanglebird searches for material so that he can make a nest as tidy as those of other birds. (Rev: BL 3/1/97; SLJ 4/97)

2391 London, Jonathan. *Froggy Gets Dressed* (PS–1). Illus. by Frank Remkiewicz. 1992, Viking $15.99 (0-670-84249-4). Froggy gets so exhausted dressing and undressing to play in the snow that he decides to sleep for the winter. (Rev: SLJ 9/92)

2392 London, Jonathan. *Froggy Goes to School* (PS–K). Illus. by Frank Remkiewicz. 1996, Viking $15.99 (0-670-86726-8). 32pp. Froggy is embarrassed to find himself at school in his underwear. (Rev: BL 6/1–15/96; SLJ 8/96)

2393 London, Jonathan. *Froggy Learns to Swim* (PS–1). Illus. by Frank Remkiewicz. 1995, Viking $15.99 (0-670-85551-0). After his mother teaches him to swim and he learns how to use flippers and a snorkel, Froggy doesn't want to leave the water. (Rev: SLJ 1/96)

2394 London, Jonathan. *Froggy Plays Soccer* (PS–1). Illus. by Frank Remkiewicz. 1999, Viking $15.99 (0-670-88257-7). 32pp. Froggy is a failure during the soccer game to win the City Cup until he gets a reminder from Dad and kicks the winning goal. (Rev: BL 3/1/99; HBG 10/99; SLJ 3/99)

2395 London, Jonathan. *Froggy's First Kiss* (PS–2). Illus. by Frank Remkiewicz. 1998, Viking $14.99 (0-670-87064-1). When Frogilina responds to Froggy's advances with a big kiss, the young swain retreats in panic. (Rev: BCCB 4/98; HBG 10/98; SLJ 3/98)

2396 London, Jonathan. *Let's Go, Froggy!* (PS–2). Illus. by Frank Remkiewicz. 1994, Viking $15.99 (0-670-85055-1). Preparations for a picnic so exhaust Froggy and his father that they are too tired to travel and decide to have their picnic on the patio. (Rev: SLJ 5/94)

2397 London, Jonathan. *Liplap's Wish* (PS–3). Illus. by Sylvia Long. 1994, Chronicle $13.95 (0-8118-0505-0). 32pp. Liplap, a bunny, finds comfort in the belief that his dead grandmother has become a star in the sky. (Rev: BL 1/15/95; SLJ 11/94)

2398 London, Jonathan. *What Newt Could Do for Turtle* (PS–1). Illus. by Louise Voce. 1996, Candlewick $16.99 (1-56402-259-5). 40pp. Newt and Turtle, two swamp creatures, become friends. (Rev: BCCB 2/97; BL 12/15/96; SLJ 12/96)

2399 London, Jonathan. *Who Bop?* (PS–1). Illus. by Henry Cole. 2000, HarperCollins LB $14.89 (0-06-027918-4). 32pp. A rhythmic rhyme about jazzy animals and how they love a sock hop. (Rev: BCCB 1/00; BL 1/1–15/00; HBG 10/00; SLJ 2/00)

2400 Loomis, Christine. *Cowboy Bunnies* (PS–2). Illus. by Ora Eitan. 1997, Putnam $15.95 (0-399-22625-7). 32pp. In this easy-to-read book, rabbits engage in all sorts of cowboy activities. (Rev: BL 2/15/98; HB 11–12/97; HBG 3/98; SLJ 9/97*)

2401 Lorenz, Lee. *A Weekend in the City* (PS–2). Illus. 1991, Pippin $15.95 (0-945912-15-3). 32pp. Pig and Duck search for some common ground with friend Moose when they propose a visit to the city for his birthday. (Rev: BCCB 11/91; BL 1/1/92; SLJ 12/91)

2402 Low, Joseph. *Mice Twice* (K–3). Illus. by author. 1986, Macmillan paper $5.99 (0-689-71060-7). 32pp. Cat invites Mouse to dinner but Mouse brings along Dog. Reissue of 1980 publication.

2403 Lowell, Susan. *The Three Little Javelinas* (PS–3). Illus. by Jim Harris. 1992, Northland LB $15.95 (0-87358-542-9). 32pp. This Americanized version of the "Three Little Pigs" features a coyote instead of the wolf. (Rev: BL 1/1/93)

2404 Lund, Jillian. *Two Cool Coyotes* (K–3). Illus. 1999, Dutton $15.99 (0-525-46151-5). 32pp. When coyote Frank's best buddy Angelina moves away, he is lost until he finds a new friend. (Rev: BL 9/15/99; HBG 3/00; SLJ 10/99)

2405 Lyon, David. *The Runaway Duck* (K–3). Illus. by author. 1985, Lothrop paper $4.95 (0-688-07334-4). 32pp. Egbert, a wooden duck, is tied to a car bumper, but when the string breaks his adventure really begins. (Rev: BCCB 5/85; BL 6/15/85; SLJ 5/85)

2406 Macaulay, David. *Why the Chicken Crossed the Road* (K–3). Illus. by author. 1987, Houghton $16.00 (0-395-44241-9); paper $6.95 (0-395-58411-6). 32pp. Readers will enjoy the humor of this chain reaction set off when one chicken crosses the road. (Rev: BCCB 11/87; BL 10/15/87; SLJ 12/87)

2407 McBratney, Sam. *The Caterpillow Fight* (PS–2). Illus. by Jill Barton. 1996, Candlewick $9.99 (1-56402-804-6). 24pp. Playful caterpillars engage in some unusual antics. (Rev: BL 5/15/96; SLJ 7/96)

2408 McBratney, Sam. *The Dark at the Top of the Stairs* (PS–1). Illus. by Ivan Bates. 1996, Candlewick $15.99 (1-56402-640-X). 32pp. Young mice discover that the monster at the top of the stairs is actually a cat. (Rev: BL 2/15/96*; SLJ 3/96)

2409 McBratney, Sam. *Just One!* (PS–1). Illus. by Ivan Bates. 1997, Candlewick paper $3.99 (0-7636-0223-X). 24pp. In this cumulative tale, a young squirrel is so generous that he gives away the lovely stack of berries that he and his friend have gathered. (Rev: BL 10/15/97)

2410 McBratney, Sam. *Just You and Me* (PS–3). Illus. by Ivan Bates. 1998, Candlewick $15.99 (0-7636-0436-4). 32pp. Big Gander Goose searches for shelter from a storm in a place that shy Little Goosey will approve of. (Rev: BCCB 6/98; BL 4/15/98; HBG 3/99; SLJ 6/98)

2411 McCarty, Peter. *Little Bunny on the Move* (PS–K). Illus. 1999, Holt $15.95 (0-8050-4620-8). 32pp. A snow white bunny sets out on a long journey to find a home. (Rev: BCCB 11/99; BL 12/15/99; HBG 3/00; SLJ 12/99*)

2412 McCaughrean, Geraldine. *Unicorns! Unicorns!* (K–2). Illus. by Sophie Windham. 1997, Holiday LB $15.95 (0-8234-1319-5). 32pp. Because they are busy helping other animals, two unicorns fail to get on Noah's ark. (Rev: BL 11/15/97; HBG 3/98; SLJ 10/97)

2413 McCully, Emily Arnold. *First Snow* (PS–K). Illus. by author. 1985, HarperCollins $12.95 (0-06-024128-4). 32pp. The littlest girl mouse is afraid to join her siblings sledding on a steep hill in her first snow. (Rev: BL 9/15/85; HB 9–10/85; SLJ 10/85)

2414 McCully, Emily Arnold. *Monk Camps Out* (PS–1). Illus. 2000, Scholastic $15.95 (0-439-09976-5). 32pp. Mouse parents help their son Monk to set up his tent in the backyard and then wait up during the night wondering if their son will become frightened and lonely and want to come back in. (Rev: BL 5/15/00; HB 3–4/00; HBG 10/00; SLJ 4/00)

2415 McCully, Emily Arnold. *My Real Family* (PS–2). Illus. 1994, Harcourt $14.00 (0-15-277698-2). 32pp. When Sarah, the youngest in a troupe of performing bears, feels that Blanche, a sheep, is getting too much attention, she decides to run away. (Rev: BL 4/1/94; HB 7–8/94; SLJ 6/94*)

2416 McCully, Emily Arnold. *Speak Up, Blanche!* (K–3). Illus. 1991, HarperCollins LB $14.89 (0-06-024228-0). 32pp. The sheep Eva drops granddaughter Blanche off to apprentice at the theatrical bears theater. (Rev: BL 9/1/91*; SLJ 9/91)

2417 MacDonald, Alan. *Beware of the Bears!* (K–3). Illus. by Gwyneth Williamson. 1998, Little Tiger $14.95 (1-888444-28-2). 32pp. After Goldilocks makes a mess of the bears' house, they get even by making a mess in a house they mistakenly believe to be hers. (Rev: BL 5/15/98; HBG 10/98)

2418 MacDonald, Alan. *The Pig in a Wig* (PS–1). Illus. by Paul Hess. 1999, Peachtree $15.95 (1-56145-197-5). Peggoty is made to feel ugly by other farm animals but she accepts her appearance when she sees her adoring pig mother with her little baby. (Rev: HBG 3/00; SLJ 12/99)

2419 MacDonald, Amy. *Little Beaver and the Echo* (PS–1). Illus. by Sarah Fox-Davies. 1990, Putnam $15.95 (0-399-22203-0). 32pp. A lonely little beaver mistakenly believes that his echo is a far-off friend. (Rev: BL 1/1/91; SLJ 3/91)

2420 MacDonald, Amy. *The Spider Who Created the World* (PS–3). Illus. by G. Brian Karas. 1996, Orchard LB $16.99 (0-531-08855-3). 32pp. To find a place to lay her egg, Nobb the spider creates the earth with fire and water in this original creation story. (Rev: BCCB 5/96; BL 4/15/96; HB 9–10/96; SLJ 3/96)

2421 MacDonald, Elizabeth. *Dilly-Dally and the Nine Secrets* (K–3). Illus. by Ken Brown. 2000, Dutton $15.99 (0-525-46006-3). 32pp. Dilly-Dally the duck refuses invitations to leave her nest and go for a swim until all her eggs are hatched, and then the whole family enjoys the water. (Rev: BL 2/1/00; HBG 10/00; SLJ 3/00)

2422 MacDonald, Elizabeth. *The Wolf Is Coming!* (PS–K). Illus. by Ken Brown. 1998, Dutton $15.99 (0-525-45952-9). 32pp. A cumulative story about barnyard animals that look for shelter when they hear that the wolf is coming. (Rev: BL 2/1/98; HBG 3/99; SLJ 3/98)

2423 MacDonald, Margaret Read. *Pickin' Peas* (PS–3). Illus. by Pat Cummings. 1998, HarperCollins LB $14.89 (0-06-027970-2). 32pp. Little Girl uses various tactics to prevent Mr. Rabbit from picking the peas in her garden. (Rev: BL 7/98; HBG 10/98; SLJ 10/98)

2424 MacDonald, Maryann. *Rosie and the Poor Rabbits* (K–2). Illus. by Melissa Sweet. 1994, Atheneum $13.95 (0-689-31832-4). 32pp. When Rosie, a rabbit, is asked to contribute gifts to needy rabbits, she finds it difficult to give up things she loves. (Rev: BCCB 3/94; BL 4/1/94; SLJ 6/94)

2425 MacDonald, Maryann. *Rosie's Baby Tooth* (PS–2). Illus. by Melissa Sweet. 1991, Macmillan LB $12.95 (0-689-31626-7). 32pp. Rosie Rabbit resents losing one of her baby teeth and tells the Tooth Fairy how she feels. (Rev: BL 10/15/91; HB 9–10/91; SLJ 10/91)

2426 McDonald, Megan. *The Night Iguana Left Home* (2–4). Illus. by Ponder Goembel. 1999, DK $15.95 (0-7894-2581-5). 32pp. Iguana, who has taken a dishwashing job in a Key West eatery, is alarmed to discover that the restaurant's speciality is iguana stew. (Rev: BL 11/1/99; HB 9–10/99; HBG 3/00; SLJ 9/99)

2427 MacDonald, Suse. *Elephants on Board* (PS–1). Illus. 1999, Harcourt $15.00 (0-15-200951-5). 32pp. When their truck breaks down, ten elephants try to commandeer another vehicle, with humorous results. (Rev: BL 3/15/99; HBG 10/99; SLJ 6/99)

2428 McDonnell, Flora. *I Love Animals* (PS). Illus. 1994, Candlewick $14.95 (1-56402-387-7). 32pp. In double-page spreads, a host of farm animals gather to greet individually a young girl who visits them. (Rev: BL 10/15/94; SLJ 10/94)

2429 McDonnell, Flora. *Splash!* (PS). Illus. 1999, Candlewick $16.99 (0-7636-0481-X). 32pp. On a hot day, all sorts of jungle animals head for the water where they can splash and cool off. (Rev: BCCB 9/99; BL 7/99; HBG 10/99; SLJ 7/99)

2430 McGeorge, Constance W. *Boomer's Big Surprise* (PS–2). Illus. by Mary Whyte. 1999, Chronicle $14.95 (0-8118-1977-9). 32pp. At first, Boomer the golden retriever is jealous of his new sibling, but Baby and he begin playing together and soon become buddies. (Rev: BL 5/1/99; HBG 10/99; SLJ 6/99)

2431 McGrory, Anik. *Mouton's Impossible Dream* (K–3). Illus. 2000, Harcourt $16.00 (0-15-202195-7). 32pp. Three animals — a sheep, a duck, and a rooster — are rewarded by the queen when they help science by taking a ride in a hot-air balloon. (Rev: BCCB 4/00; BL 6/1–15/00; HB 5–6/00; HBG 10/00; SLJ 4/00)

2432 McGuire, Leslie. *Brush Your Teeth, Please* (PS–K). Illus. by Jean Pidgeon. Series: Joshua Morris Books. 1993, Reader's Digest $10.99 (0-89577-474-7). A pop-up book with movable "toothbrushes" in an animal story designed to get kids to brush their teeth. (Rev: SLJ 9/93)

2433 McGuirk, Leslie. *Tucker Off His Rocker* (PS–K). 2000, Penguin $7.99 (0-525-46398-4). 40pp. A playful West Highland terrier travels the globe on a magic carpet, a skateboard, a taxi, and other forms of transportation in this small-format book. Also use *Tucker Over the Top* (2000). (Rev: HBG 3/01; SLJ 11/00)

2434 McKay, Hilary. *Where's Bear?* (PS–1). Illus. by Alex Ayliffe. 1998, Simon & Schuster $15.00 (0-689-82271-5). 32pp. When Snowtop, a white bear, gets a bath from his mother, his friend Simon doesn't recognize him. (Rev: BCCB 1/99; BL 1/1–15/99; HBG 3/99; SLJ 2/99)

2435 McKee, David. *Elmer Again* (PS–2). Illus. 1992, Lothrop $15.00 (0-688-11596-9). 32pp. Elmer, a multicolored elephant, longs for the day he will turn plain gray. (Rev: BL 11/15/92; SLJ 1/93)

2436 McKee, David. *Elmer and the Kangaroo* (PS–K). Illus. 2000, HarperCollins $14.95 (0-688-17951-7). 32pp. Elmer, a patchwork elephant, helps a kangaroo newly arrived in the forest to gain confidence about his jumping ability. (Rev: BL 5/15/00; HBG 10/00; SLJ 5/00)

2437 McKee, David. *Elmer and the Lost Teddy Bear* (PS–K). Illus. 1999, Lothrop $15.00 (0-688-16912-0). 32pp. Elmer, the patchwork elephant, helps Baby Elephant who is sad because he has lost his teddy bear. (Rev: BL 6/1–15/99; HBG 10/99; SLJ 7/99)

2438 McKee, David. *Elmer and Wilbur* (PS). Illus. 1996, Lothrop $15.00 (0-688-14934-0). 32pp. Elmer, a patchwork elephant, sets out to find his cousin Wilbur. (Rev: BL 11/1/96; SLJ 11/96)

2439 McKee, David. *Elmer in the Snow* (PS–1). Illus. by author. 1995, Lothrop $13.00 (0-688-14596-5). In this picture book, a patchwork elephant takes some other elephants to snow-covered mountains so they will appreciate the meaning of cold. (Rev: SLJ 12/95)

2440 McKee, David. *Elmer Takes Off* (PS–1). Illus. 1998, Lothrop $15.00 (0-688-15785-8). 32pp. With the help of his cousin Wilbur, Elmer the patchwork elephant fools the herd into believing he has been blown away. When it really happens, no one believes he is in trouble. (Rev: BL 5/1/98; HBG 10/98; SLJ 6/98)

2441 McKee, David. *I Can Too!* (PS). Illus. by author. 1997, Lothrop $15.95 (0-688-15547-2). In this pop-up book, an elephant takes a walk in the jungle and confronts a variety of animals with different talents. (Rev: HBG 3/98; SLJ 1/98)

2442 McKee, David. *Zebra's Hiccups* (PS–3). Illus. 1993, Simon & Schuster paper $14.00 (0-671-79440-X). Zebra begins to hiccup so violently that he begins to lose his stripes. (Rev: SLJ 6/93)

2443 McLellan, Stephanie Simpson. *The Chicken Cat* (PS–1). Illus. by Sean Cassidy. 2000, Fitzhenry & Whiteside $14.95 (1-55041-531-X). 40pp. Merlin, a kitten, learns to fly and takes his friend Guinevere, a hen, for a ride. (Rev: BL 7/00; SLJ 12/00)

2444 McLeod, Emilie W. *The Bear's Bicycle* (PS–2). Illus. by David McPhail. 1986, Little, Brown paper $5.95 (0-316-56206-8). 32pp. A small boy and his teddy bear have an exciting bicycle ride as he gives the bear safety lessons. When the bear, grown to grizzly bear proportions, does not follow the safety rules, it suffers the consequences.

2445 McMullan, Kate. *No No, Jo!* (PS–1). Illus. by Jim McMullan. 1998, HarperFestival $9.95 (0-694-00904-0). In this picture book, using flaps to further the action, a little kitten tries to help around the house but instead causes problems. (Rev: HBG 10/98; SLJ 5/98)

2446 McNaughton, Colin. *Boo!* (K–2). Illus. by author. 1996, Harcourt $14.00 (0-15-200834-9). A young pig enjoys frightening others until his father catches him. (Rev: SLJ 9/96)

2447 McNaughton, Colin. *Oomph! A Preston Pig Story* (PS–1). Illus. 2001, Harcourt $15.00 (0-15-216463-4). 24pp. While Preston the pig is at the beach he meets another little pig name Maxine and they become fast friends. (Rev: BL 3/15/01)

2448 McNaughton, Colin. *Oops!* (PS–1). Illus. 1997, Harcourt $14.00 (0-15-201588-4). 32pp. Preston Pig, dressed as Little Red Riding Hood, leads Mr. Wolf on a merry chase. (Rev: BL 10/1/97; HBG 3/98; SLJ 9/97)

2449 McNaughton, Colin. *Preston's Goal!* (PS–3). Illus. 1998, Harcourt $15.00 (0-15-201816-6). 32pp. When he is sent out to get a loaf of bread, Preston Pig takes along his soccer ball for fun, but he is unaware that his every movement is being watched by his nemesis, the wolf. (Rev: BL 8/98; HBG 3/99; SLJ 11/98)

2450 McNaughton, Colin. *Shh! (Don't Tell Mr. Wolf!): A Preston Pig Lift-the-Flap Book* (PS–K). Illus. by author. 2000, Harcourt $9.95 (0-15-202341-0). In this amusing flap book, Preston the pig manages to outwit and outfox the villainous Mr. Wolf. (Rev: HBG 10/00; SLJ 5/00)

2451 McNaughton, Colin. *Suddenly!* (PS–2). Illus. 1995, Harcourt $14.00 (0-15-200308-8). 32pp. Preston the pig is unaware that he is being stalked by a big wolf. (Rev: BCCB 7–8/95; BL 5/15/95; SLJ 6/95*)

2452 McNaughton, Colin. *Yum!* (PS–3). Illus. 1999, Harcourt $15.00 (0-15-202064-0). 32pp. Preston, a pig, tired of being chased by a wicked wolf, acts as a counselor and gets the wolf a respectable job. (Rev: BCCB 11/99; BL 9/1/99; HBG 10/00; SLJ 10/99)

2453 McNulty, Faith. *The Elephant Who Couldn't Forget* (1–3). Illus. by Marc Simont. 1980, Harper-Collins $11.95 (0-06-024145-4). 64pp. A moral lesson about an elephant who was unable to forgive and forget. Reissue of 1980 publication.

2454 McPhail, David. *The Bear's Toothache* (PS–K). Illus. by author. 1972, Little, Brown paper $5.95 (0-316-56325-0). 32pp. A very funny story of a little boy's attempt to help extract a bear's tooth and rid him of his toothache.

2455 McPhail, David. *Drawing Lessons from a Bear* (PS–2). Illus. 2000, Little, Brown $14.95 (0-316-56345-5). 32pp. An old bear reminisces about his life as a cub and how he decided to devote his life to drawing and teaching others the love of drawing. (Rev: BCCB 3/00; BL 2/15/00; HBG 10/00; SLJ 5/00)

2456 McPhail, David. *First Flight* (PS–1). Illus. by author. 1991, Little, Brown paper $5.95 (0-316-56332-3). A young boy and his teddy bear go for an airplane ride and the bear acts up. (Rev: BCCB 7–8/87; BL 6/1/87; SLJ 4/87)

2457 McPhail, David. *The Glerp* (PS–3). Illus. 1994, Silver Burdett LB $18.95 (0-382-24668-3); paper $5.95 (0-382-24670-6). 32pp. The glerp, a snail-like animal that eats everything, meets its match when it tries to swallow an elephant. (Rev: BL 2/1/95; SLJ 4/95)

2458 McPhail, David. *Lost!* (PS–K). Illus. 1990, Little, Brown $14.95 (0-316-56329-3). 32pp. A young boy tries to help a bear get home from the big city. (Rev: BL 4/1/90; HB 5–6/90; SLJ 6/90)

2459 McPhail, David. *Mole Music* (PS–3). Illus. 1999, Holt $15.95 (0-8050-2819-6). 32pp. Mole, who lives underground, attracts a large aboveground audience when he becomes a superb violinist. (Rev: BCCB 5/99; BL 2/15/99; HBG 10/99; SLJ 4/99)

2460 McPhail, David. *Pig Pig Gets a Job* (PS–1). Illus. 1990, Dutton $14.99 (0-525-44619-2). 32pp. Pig Pig thinks of exotic ways to make some money. (Rev: BL 11/15/90; HB 11–12/90)

2461 McPhail, David. *Pigs Ahoy!* (PS–3). Illus. 1995, Dutton $14.99 (0-525-45334-2). 32pp. A very funny picture book about pigs on an ocean cruise. (Rev: BL 10/1/95*; SLJ 12/95)

2462 McPhail, David. *Pigs Aplenty, Pigs Galore!* (PS–3). Illus. 1993, Dutton $15.99 (0-525-45079-3). 32pp. An unsuspecting man is suddenly surrounded by hordes of pigs in various costumes engaged in a variety of activities. (Rev: BL 4/1/93*; SLJ 7/93*)

2463 McPhail, David. *Those Can-Do Pigs* (K–3). Illus. 1996, Dutton $14.99 (0-525-45495-0). 32pp. A group of energetic, overachieving pigs perform everyday tasks. (Rev: BL 6/1–15/96; SLJ 9/96)

2464 McQuade, Jacqueline. *At Preschool with Teddy Bear* (PS). Illus. 1999, Dial $5.99 (0-8037-2394-6). 26pp. In this board book, Teddy Bear spends an eventful first day at his preschool. (Rev: BL 9/1/99)

2465 McQuade, Jacqueline. *At the Petting Zoo with Teddy Bear* (PS). Illus. 1999, Dial $5.99 (0-8037-2395-4). 26pp. In this board book, Teddy has a great day petting all the soft animals at the petting zoo

but, back home, decides that his pet is the softest animal of all. (Rev: BL 9/1/99)

2466 Maitland, Barbara. *The Bear Who Didn't Like Honey* (PS–K). Illus. by Odilon Moraes. 1997, Orchard $14.95 (0-531-09546-0). 32pp. Little Bear hides his fears with a series of excuses but later demonstrates that he has unexpected courage. (Rev: BCCB 5/97; BL 2/15/97; SLJ 5/97)

2467 Mallat, Kathy. *Brave Bear* (PS–K). Illus. 1999, Walker $14.95 (0-8027-8704-5). 24pp. A bear cub helps a baby bluebird that has fallen from its nest, by climbing the tree to put the bird back in its home. (Rev: BL 12/1/99; HB 9–10/99; HBG 3/00; SLJ 9/99)

2468 Mammano, Julie. *Rhinos Who Skateboard* (K–4). Illus. by author. 1999, Chronicle $12.95 (0-8118-2356-3). A batch of happy rhinos enjoy skateboarding as they fly through the air and invent a whole new vocabulary. (Rev: SLJ 8/99)

2469 Mammano, Julie. *Rhinos Who Snowboard* (K–3). Illus. by author. 1997, Chronicle $11.95 (0-8118-1715-6). Snowboarding rhinos introduce the slang connected with the sport. (Rev: SLJ 3/98)

2470 Mammano, Julie. *Rhinos Who Surf* (PS–2). Illus. by author. 1996, Chronicle $12.95 (0-8118-1000-3). A group of rhinos go surfing in this action-packed, humorous picture book. (Rev: SLJ 7/96*)

2471 Mangan, Anne. *The Smallest Bear* (PS–K). Illus. by Joanne Moss. 1998, Crocodile $14.95 (1-56656-266-X). A small bear finds a hive filled with honey, and his paws are just tiny enough to fit inside. (Rev: HBG 10/98; SLJ 7/98)

2472 Marcellino, Fred. *I, Crocodile* (K–3). Illus. 1999, HarperCollins LB $15.89 (0-06-205199-7). 32pp. A crocodile, descended from ancient Egyptian gods — and the toast of Paris during Napoleon's time — is forced to live in that city's sewers. (Rev: BCCB 1/00; BL 10/15/99; HBG 3/00; SLJ 11/99)

2473 Marshall, James. *George and Martha* (PS–1). Illus. by author. 1972, Houghton $16.00 (0-395-16619-5); paper $6.95 (0-395-19972-7). 48pp. The friendship of two hippos leads to some very humorous situations. Also use the sequels: *George and Martha Encore* (1973); *George and Martha Rise and Shine* (1977); *George and Martha One Fine Day* (1982); *George and Martha Back in Town* (1984); *George and Martha Tons of Fun* (1986).

2474 Marshall, James. *George and Martha Round and Round* (K–2). Illus. by author. 1988, Houghton $13.95 (0-395-46763-2); paper $6.95 (0-395-58410-8). 48pp. Five stories about hippos George and Martha. (Rev: BCCB 9/88; BL 9/15/88; SLJ 9/88)

2475 Marshall, James. *Swine Lake* (K–3). Illus. by Maurice Sendak. 1999, HarperCollins LB $15.89 (0-06-205172-5). 40pp. A wolf becomes so engrossed by a performance of *Swine Lake* that he forgets to choose one of the porkers for his next meal. (Rev: BCCB 7–8/99; BL 5/1/99*; HB 7–8/99; HBG 10/99; SLJ 7/99)

2476 Marshall, James. *Yummers!* (PS–K). Illus. by author. 1973, Houghton $16.00 (0-395-14757-3); paper $6.95 (0-395-39590-9). 32pp. Emily Pig is worried about her weight, so she goes for a walk for exercise. Unfortunately, the walk is interrupted for several snacks, and the resulting stomachache, Emily Pig suggests, is due to the exercise, not the food!

2477 Marshall, James. *Yummers Too: The Second Course* (PS–1). Illus. by author. 1990, Houghton paper $6.95 (0-395-53967-6). 32pp. Emily Pig has trouble earning back the money when she eats the profits at Eugene's Popsicle business. (Rev: BL 10/1/86; SLJ 11/86)

2478 Martin, Bill, Jr. *A Beasty Story* (PS–3). Illus. by Steven Kellogg. 1999, Harcourt $16.00 (0-15-201683-X). 40pp. Four mice explore a dark, dark house to find the beast they know lives inside. (Rev: BL 9/15/99; HBG 3/00; SLJ 9/99)

2479 Martin, Bill, Jr. *Chicken Chuck* (PS–2). Illus. by Steven Salerno. 2000, Winslow $16.95 (1-890817-31-7). When Chicken Chuck eats a blue seed, a blue feather sprouts from his forehead and he becomes the hit of the barnyard. (Rev: HBG 10/00; SLJ 6/00)

2480 Martin, Bill, Jr. *The Happy Hippopotami* (PS–K). Illus. by Betsy Everitt. 1991, Harcourt $14.00 (0-15-233380-0). 32pp. A herd of happy hippos descends on a beach and has a grand time. (Rev: BL 5/15/91; SLJ 7/91)

2481 Martin, Bill, Jr., and John Archambault. *Barn Dance!* (PS–2). Illus. by Ted Rand. 1986, Holt $16.95 (0-8050-0089-5); paper $6.95 (0-8050-0799-7). 32pp. The animals are holding a lively barn dance on a full-moon night. (Rev: BL 1/15/87; SLJ 2/87)

2482 Martin, Linda. *When Dinosaurs Go to School* (PS–1). Illus. 1999, Chronicle $13.95 (0-8118-2089-0). 32pp. A series of rhymes follow a pair of young dinosaurs through a typical day at school. (Rev: BL 9/1/99; HBG 3/00; SLJ 7/99)

2483 Massie, Elizabeth, and Barbara Spilman Lawson. *Jambo, Watoto! Hello, Children!* (K–2). Illus. by Marsha Heatwole. 1998, Creative Arts Pr. $15.95 (0-9642712-3-0). Four young cheetahs remember their mother's advice and, when she goes out hunting, they stay put in their hiding place in spite of being tempted to come out by other animals. (Rev: SLJ 1/99)

2484 Mathers, Petra. *Lottie's New Friend* (PS–3). Illus. 1999, Simon & Schuster $15.00 (0-689-82014-3). 32pp. Herbie the duck feels threatened when friend Lottie cultivates a glamorous new arrival, Dodo, but soon the three become friends. (Rev: BL 7/99; HBG 10/99; SLJ 3/99)

2485 Mathews, Judith. *There's Nothing to D-o-o-o!* (PS–2). Illus. by Kurt Cyrus. 1999, Harcourt $16.00 (0-15-201647-3). 32pp. A calf ignores her mother's advice and wanders into a strange field where she is later found by her mother and brought home. (Rev: BL 6/1–15/99; HBG 10/99; SLJ 6/99)

2486 Mayne, William. *Lady Muck* (K–3). Illus. by Jonathan Heale. 1997, Houghton $15.95 (0-395-75281-7). 32pp. Two pigs, Boark and Sowk, go to market to sell precious truffles that Boark has unearthed. (Rev: BCCB 4/97; BL 3/1/97*; SLJ 5/97*)

2487 Mead, Alice. *Billy and Emma* (PS–3). Illus. by Christine Hale. 2000, Farrar $16.00 (0-374-30705-9). 32pp. Billy and Emma are macaws who share a cage at the zoo. When Emma is stolen, Nancy the crow helps Billy rescue her. (Rev: BL 4/1/00; HBG 10/00; SLJ 5/00)

2488 Meade, Holly. *John Willy and Freddy McGee* (PS–1). Illus. 1998, Marshall Cavendish $15.95 (0-7614-5033-5). 32pp. John Willy and Freddy McGee, two guinea pigs, escape from their cage and have fun in the pockets of a pool table until the balls begin dropping on them. (Rev: BCCB 1/99; BL 9/1/98; HB 1–2/99; HBG 3/99; SLJ 9/98)

2489 Meddaugh, Susan. *The Best Place* (PS–2). Illus. 1999, Houghton $15.00 (0-395-97994-3). 32pp. A wolf who has sold his comfortable home to a family of rabbits so he can see the world soon regrets his decision. (Rev: BCCB 12/99; BL 11/1/99; HBG 3/00; SLJ 9/99)

2490 Meddaugh, Susan. *Hog-Eye* (K–2). Illus. 1995, Houghton $14.95 (0-395-74276-5). 32pp. A female pig outwits a fox who has problems reading his recipe for pig soup. (Rev: BCCB 10/95; BL 9/1/95; SLJ 10/95*)

2491 Meddaugh, Susan. *Martha and Skits* (PS–2). Illus. 2000, Houghton $15.00 (0-618-05776-5). 32pp. Martha, the talking dog, has her paws full taking care of a young pup named Skits who loves to catch Frisbees. (Rev: BCCB 11/00; BL 6/1–15/00; HBG 3/01; SLJ 8/00)

2492 Meddaugh, Susan. *Martha Calling* (PS–3). Illus. 1994, Houghton $14.95 (0-395-69825-1). 30pp. Martha, the talking dog, must disguise herself as a human to circumvent the "No Dogs Allowed" rule at the Come-On-Inn. (Rev: BCCB 9/94; BL 10/1/94*; HB 11–12/94; SLJ 11/94*)

2493 Meddaugh, Susan. *Martha Speaks* (PS–3). Illus. 1992, Houghton $15.00 (0-395-63313-3). 32pp. Helen feeds her dog alphabet soup, and suddenly she can talk! (Rev: BCCB 11/92*; BL 9/1/92*; HB 1–2/93*; SLJ 12/92)

2494 Meddaugh, Susan. *Martha Walks the Dog* (PS–3). Illus. 1998, Houghton $15.00 (0-395-90494-3). 32pp. Martha, the talking dog, uses kindness, the ultimate weapon, to tame a mean dog who is her new neighbor. (Rev: BCCB 12/98; BL 9/1/98; HB 11–12/98; HBG 3/99; SLJ 10/98)

2495 Meddaugh, Susan. *Tree of Birds* (PS–1). Illus. 1990, Houghton $16.00 (0-395-53147-0). 32pp. When Harry nurses Sally, an injured bird, back to health, her friends arrive to make sure Harry doesn't keep her as a pet. (Rev: BCCB 3/90; BL 4/1/90; HB 9–10/90; SLJ 4/90)

2496 Meeuwissen, Tony. *Remarkable Animals: 1,000 Amazing Amalgamations* (PS–1). Illus. 1998, Orchard $15.95 (0-531-30066-8). Ten animals, including an alligator and rhinoceros, are divided into three sections, and flipping through the pages creates strange new animals. (Rev: BCCB 5/98; BL 1/1–15/99; HB 7–8/98; HBG 10/98; SLJ 4/98)

2497 Meres, Jonathan. *The Big Bad Rumor* (K–2). Illus. by Jacqueline East. 2000, Orchard $14.95 (0-531-30292-X). The rumor that a big bad wolf is coming gets garbled as the news is passed from one farm animal to another. (Rev: HBG 3/01; SLJ 11/00)

2498 Milgrim, David. *Cows Can't Fly* (PS–1). Illus. 1998, Viking $15.99 (0-670-87475-2). 32pp. When cows see a picture a young boy has drawn that shows them flying, it inspires them to do just that. (Rev: BL 8/98; SLJ 5/98)

2499 Millais, Raoul. *Elijah and Pin-Pin* (PS–2). Illus. by author. 1992, Simon & Schuster paper $14.00 (0-671-75543-9). 40pp. Elijah the mole and Pin-Pin the hedgehog share many adventures in and around a castle. (Rev: SLJ 7/92)

2500 Miller, Edna. *Mousekin's Family* (1–3). Illus. by author. 1972, Prentice Hall LB $9.95 (0-13-604462-X). 32pp. Complications occur when a little white-footed mouse mistakenly believes she has found a relative. Other titles in the series are: *Mousekin's Close Call* (1980); *Mousekin's Fables* (1982).

2501 Miller, Virginia. *Be Gentle!* (PS–1). Illus. 1997, Candlewick $15.99 (0-7636-0251-5). 32pp. Ba Bear is brokenhearted when, after playing too hard with a kitten, his new friend runs away. (Rev: BL 8/97; HBG 3/98; SLJ 10/97)

2502 Miller, Virginia. *Eat Your Dinner!* (PS–1). Illus. 1992, Candlewick $14.95 (1-56402-121-1). 32pp. Stubborn Bartholomew is bribed into eating his dinner by big bear George. (Rev: BL 10/1/92; SLJ 12/92)

2503 Modesitt, Jeanne. *Mama, If You Had a Wish* (PS–K). Illus. by Robin Spowart. 1993, Simon & Schuster paper $16.00 (0-671-75437-8). 30pp. When questioned by her son, a bunny mother says she only wants him to be his natural self. (Rev: BL 7/93; SLJ 8/93)

2504 Molk, Laurel. *Good Job, Oliver!* (PS–K). Illus. 1999, Crown LB $15.99 (0-517-70976-7). 32pp. Little Oliver, a rabbit, perseveres in cultivating his precious strawberry plants, hoping that he will win the annual strawberry contest. (Rev: BL 12/15/98; HBG 10/99; SLJ 4/99)

2505 Monks, Lydia. *The Cat Barked?* (PS–1). Illus. 1999, Dial $13.99 (0-8037-2338-5). 32pp. A big orange cat thinks it wants to become a dog, but a little girl points out all the reasons why a cat's life is better. (Rev: BL 3/1/99*; HBG 10/99; SLJ 4/99)

2506 Monsell, Mary Elise. *Underwear!* (PS–3). Illus. by Lynn Munsinger. 1988, Whitman LB $13.95 (0-8075-8308-1). 24pp. Zachary Zebra and Orfo Orangutan love underwear, and they take grumpy Bismark Buffalo to the World's Greatest Grassland Underwear Fair. (Rev: BL 4/1/88; SLJ 5/88)

2507 Moore, Inga. *Six-Dinner Sid* (PS–3). Illus. 1991, Simon & Schuster paper $15.00 (0-671-73199-8). 32pp. Sid the cat has six homes, but eventually his secret is discovered. (Rev: BCCB 3/91; BL 5/1/91; SLJ 8/91)

2508 Mora, Pat. *Delicious Hullabaloo: Pachanga deliciosa* (PS–1). Illus. by Francisco Mora. 1999, Arte Publico $14.95 (1-55885-246-8). 32pp. In this bilingual book, lizards, armadillos, and other exotic

animals enjoy dancing at a desert dinner party. (Rev: BL 5/1/99; HBG 3/99; SLJ 3/99)

2509 Morgan, Michaela. *Helpful Betty Solves a Mystery* (PS–2). Illus. by Moira Kemp. Series: On My Own. 1994, Carolrhoda LB $18.60 (0-87614-832-1). While traveling through the jungle helping friends, Betty, a hippo, solves the mystery of a missing egg. Also use *Helpful Betty to the Rescue* (1994). (Rev: BCCB 9/94; SLJ 10/94)

2510 Morpurgo, Michael. *Wombat Goes Walkabout* (PS–3). Illus. by Christian Birmingham. 2000, Candlewick $16.99 (0-7636-1168-9). 32pp. The animals that Wombat meets on his walk through the Australian bush are scornful at his lack of talent until he saves them by digging a safe retreat during a forest fire. (Rev: BL 8/00; HBG 10/00; SLJ 5/00)

2511 Morton, Jane, and Ted Dreier. *Moozie's Kind Adventure* (K–2). Illus. by Jane Royse. Series: Moozie Adventures. 1999, Best Friends $14.95 (0-9662268-1-X). Moozie, a gentle cow, saves some ducklings who are endangered by a herd of stampeding cows. (Rev: SLJ 1/00)

2512 Most, Bernard. *Cock-A-Doodle-Moo!* (PS–1). Illus. 1996, Harcourt paper $13.00 (0-15-201252-4). 32pp. When a rooster develops a voice problem, a cow tries to help out. (Rev: BL 9/1/96; SLJ 12/96)

2513 Most, Bernard. *The Cow That Went Oink* (PS–1). Illus. 1990, Harcourt $13.00 (0-15-220195-5). A cow and a pig are ridiculed because they aren't the same as other farm animals. (Rev: HB 7–8/90; SLJ 12/90)

2514 Most, Bernard. *If the Dinosaurs Came Back* (1–3). Illus. by author. 1978, Harcourt $16.00 (0-15-238020-5); paper $6.00 (0-15-238021-3). 32pp. All the things that might happen if dinosaurs came back to the world.

2515 Most, Bernard. *Z-Z-Zoink!* (PS–K). Illus. by author. 1999, Harcourt $13.00 (0-15-292845-6). A pig with a serious snoring problem has difficulty finding a place to sleep. (Rev: HBG 10/99; SLJ 7/99)

2516 Moyer, Marshall M. *Rollo Bones, Canine Hypnotist* (K–4). Illus. 1998, Tricycle Pr. $14.95 (1-883672-65-1). 32pp. Rollo Bones, an amazing dog who can hypnotize people, realizes that he must hypnotize his master to keep him in line. (Rev: BL 6/1–15/98; HBG 10/98; SLJ 7/98)

2517 Mozelle, Shirley. *The Pig Is in the Pantry, the Cat Is on the Shelf* (PS–1). Illus. by Jennifer Plecas. 2000, Clarion $15.00 (0-395-78627-4). 32pp. When farmer McDuffel goes to town leaving the farmhouse door open, the animals take over, singing, cooking, taking baths, and making a big mess. (Rev: BL 8/00; HBG 10/00; SLJ 5/00)

2518 Muller, Robin. *Hickory, Dickory, Dock* (K–2). Illus. by Suzanne Duranceau. 1994, Scholastic $15.95 (0-590-47278-X). 32pp. A cat throws a party with unexpected guests in this book with a rhyme for each hour of the day. (Rev: BL 5/1/94; SLJ 5/94)

2519 Murphy, Mary. *Caterpillar's Wish* (PS). Illus. by author. Series: DK Toddler Storybook. 1999, DK $9.95 (0-7894-2593-9). Caterpillar, who wants to fly with with his friends Bee and Ladybird, gets his wish when he becomes a butterfly. (Rev: HBG 10/99; SLJ 5/99)

2520 Murphy, Mary. *Here Comes the Rain* (PS). Illus. by author. 2000, DK paper $5.95 (0-7894-6368-7). A little kitten who thinks he hates rain finds he actually loves it. (Rev: SLJ 12/00)

2521 Murphy, Mary. *I Am an Artist* (PS). Illus. by author. 2000, Houghton $4.95 (0-618-03401-3). In this appealing board book, a little penguin plays at being a nurse, cowboy, and model. The same penguin is featured in *I Make A Cake* (2000). (Rev: SLJ 6/00)

2522 Murphy, Mary. *I Feel Happy and Sad and Angry and Glad* (PS–K). Illus. 2000, DK $9.95 (0-7894-2680-3). 32pp. A straightforward story in which emotions are explored as two dog friends quarrel and make up. (Rev: BL 3/1/00; HBG 10/00; SLJ 4/00)

2523 Murphy, Mary. *I Like It When . . .* (PS). Illus. 1997, Harcourt $10.95 (0-15-200039-9). 32pp. A small penguin tells her mother of her favorite things that they do together. (Rev: BL 4/1/97; SLJ 5/97)

2524 Murphy, Mary. *Roxie and Bo Together* (PS). Illus. 1999, Candlewick $12.99 (0-7636-0870-X). Pull-out tabs and pop-ups are used to illustrate the activities of two friends, a fox and a rabbit. (Rev: BL 12/15/99; SLJ 9/99)

2525 Myers, Walter Dean. *The Blues of Flats Brown* (K–3). Illus. by Nina Laden. 2000, Holiday $16.95 (0-8234-1480-9). 32pp. Two junkyard dogs, the musical Flats Brown and his friend Caleb, escape their mean owner — who wants to make them fighting dogs — by means of Flats' great blues playing. (Rev: BCCB 2/00; BL 3/1/00*; HBG 10/00; SLJ 3/00)

2526 Neugebauer, Charise. *The Real Winner* (K–2). Illus. by Barbara Nascimbeni. 2000, North-South LB $15.88 (0-7358-1253-5). An overly competitive raccoon named Rocky learns how to relax and love life by following the example of a kind young hippo. (Rev: HBG 10/00; SLJ 7/00)

2527 Newton-John, Olivia, and Brian Seth Hurst. *A Pig Tale* (PS–1). Illus. by Sal Murdocca. 1993, Simon & Schuster paper $14.00 (0-671-78778-0). 28pp. Ziggy, a young pig, is unhappy at all the junk her father has collected and brought to their house. (Rev: BL 9/15/93; SLJ 10/93)

2528 Norac, Carl. *Hello, Sweetie Pie* (PS–K). Illus. by Claude K. Dubois. 2000, Doubleday $10.95 (0-385-32733-1). 32pp. When Lulu, a hamster, tells her classmates her nicknames, they are all jealous because the names are terms of affection like sweetie pie. (Rev: BL 4/1/00; HBG 3/01; SLJ 8/00)

2529 Norac, Carl. *I Love You So Much* (PS–1). Illus. by Claude K. Dubois. 1998, Doubleday $9.95 (0-385-32512-6). Lola the hamster is looking for the proper occasion to tell her famiy that she loves them. (Rev: HBG 10/98; SLJ 2/98)

2530 Novak, Matt. *Jazzbo and Googy* (PS–K). Illus. by author. 2000, Hyperion LB $15.49 (0-7868-2340-2). Googy, a little bear, has problems making

friends until he saves Jazzbo's teddy from a mud puddle. (Rev: BCCB 9/00; HBG 10/00; SLJ 6/00)

2531 Novak, Matt. *Jazzbo Goes to School* (PS–1). Illus. by author. 1999, Hyperion LB $13.49 (0-7868-2339-9). A young bear is apprehensive about starting school, so he and his mother set out to find the school that is just right for him. (Rev: HBG 3/00; SLJ 8/99)

2532 Novak, Matt. *Mouse TV* (PS–3). Illus. 1994, Orchard LB $17.99 (0-531-08706-9). 32pp. When their TV breaks down, a mouse family, all of whom are TV addicts, must find new ways to amuse themselves. (Rev: BCCB 10/94; BL 9/1/94; SLJ 10/94*)

2533 Novak, Matt. *Newt* (PS–2). Illus. by author. Series: I Can Read. 1996, HarperCollins LB $15.89 (0-06-024502-6). 48pp. A sportily dressed salamander has three easy-to-read adventures in this book about discovering friendship. (Rev: BCCB 2/96; SLJ 7/96)

2534 Numeroff, Laura. *The Chicken Sisters* (PS–2). Illus. by Sharleen Collicott. 1997, HarperCollins LB $14.89 (0-06-026680-5). 32pp. The three Chicken Sisters mistakenly believe that they have mastered many of the arts. (Rev: BL 5/1/97*; SLJ 5/97)

2535 Numeroff, Laura. *Chimps Don't Wear Glasses* (PS–1). Illus. by Joe Mathieu. 1995, Simon & Schuster paper $14.00 (0-689-80150-5). 32pp. A humorous rhyme that points out how inept animals can be when they try various activities associated with humans. (Rev: BL 9/1/95; SLJ 11/95)

2536 Numeroff, Laura. *Dogs Don't Wear Sneakers* (PS–K). Illus. by Joe Mathieu. 1993, Simon & Schuster $15.00 (0-671-79525-2). Through a series of zany illustrations, this book shows various examples of feats and accomplishments that are not possible for animals. (Rev: SLJ 1/94)

2537 Numeroff, Laura. *If You Give a Moose a Muffin* (PS–2). Illus. by Felicia Bond. 1991, HarperCollins LB $15.89 (0-06-024406-2). 32pp. This circular tale begins with a moose being lured to a boy's house to receive a muffin. (Rev: BCCB 9/91; BL 7/91; SLJ 12/91*)

2538 Numeroff, Laura. *If You Give a Mouse a Cookie* (PS–K). Illus. by Felicia Bond. 1985, HarperCollins LB $14.89 (0-06-024587-5). 32pp. A little mouse asks for a variety of things until the floor is a clutter of goods. (Rev: BCCB 7/85; BL 6/1/85; SLJ 5/85)

2539 Numeroff, Laura. *If You Give a Pig a Pancake* (PS–1). Illus. by Felicia Bond. 1998, HarperCollins LB $14.89 (0-06-026687-2). 32pp. Giving a pig a pancake leads from one consequence to another until we get back to a new plate of pancakes. (Rev: BCCB 6/98; BL 5/15/98; HBG 10/98; SLJ 7/98)

2540 Numeroff, Laura. *If You Take a Mouse to the Movies* (PS–1). Illus. by Felicia Bond. 2000, HarperCollins LB $15.89 (0-06-027868-4). 40pp. A charming picture book that recounts the many amusing consequences of taking a mouse to a movie. (Rev: BCCB 12/00; BL 12/1/00)

2541 Numeroff, Laura. *What Mommies Do Best/ What Daddies Do Best* (PS–1). Illus. by Lynn Munsinger. 1998, Simon & Schuster $13.00 (0-689-

80577-2). 40pp. In these two stories the reader discovers that both parents do all of the activities pictured — making snowmen, reading stories, watching the sunset — equally well. (Rev: BL 4/1/98; HBG 3/99; SLJ 4/98)

2542 Nygaard, Elizabeth. *Snake Alley Band* (PS–3). Illus. by Betsy Lewin. 1998, Doubleday $15.95 (0-385-32323-9). 32pp. Newly awakened from his winter sleep, Little Snake looks for the rest of the snakes in his Snake Alley Band. When they finally wake up, he adds other animals to the group to make splendid music. (Rev: BCCB 7–8/98; BL 9/1/98; HBG 3/99; SLJ 9/98)

2543 Oakley, Graham. *The Church Mice and the Ring* (PS–3). Illus. 1992, Macmillan $14.95 (0-689-31790-5). 32pp. The church mice help a young girl persuade her parents to let her adopt a dog. (Rev: BCCB 12/92; BL 11/15/92; HB 3–4/93; SLJ 1/93)

2544 Oakley, Graham. *Hetty and Harriet* (K–3). Illus. by author. 1982, Macmillan $13.95 (0-689-30888-4). 32pp. Two chickens, Harriet and her sister Hetty, leave the barnyard to find a better place to live.

2545 Oates, Joyce Carol. *Come Meet Muffin!* (PS–2). Illus. by Mark Graham. 1998, Ecco $18.00 (0-88001-556-X). 32pp. Muffin, a wise young cat, guides two lost fawns back to their mother but has problems finding his way back home. (Rev: BL 8/98; HBG 3/99; SLJ 1/99)

2546 O'Callahan, Jay. *Herman and Marguerite: An Earth Story* (K–3). Illus. by Laura O'Callahan. 1996, Peachtree $15.95 (1-56145-103-7). An earthworm that wants to explore aboveground is almost burned by the sun until a caterpillar rescues it. (Rev: SLJ 7/96)

2547 O'Malley, Kevin. *Bud* (K–3). Illus. 2000, Walker LB $16.85 (0-8027-8719-3). 32pp. When a storm ruins the garden of young Bud, a rhino, his grandfather helps him set things straight. (Rev: BCCB 6/00; BL 4/1/00; HBG 10/00; SLJ 6/00)

2548 O'Malley, Kevin. *Leo Cockroach . . . Toy Tester* (PS–2). Illus. 1999, Walker LB $16.85 (0-8027-8690-1). 32pp. Leo Cockroach feels he is unappreciated as a prize toy tester, so he decides to move on. (Rev: BCCB 6/99; BL 4/15/99; HBG 10/99; SLJ 4/99)

2549 Oppenheim, Joanne. *Rooter Remembers: A Bank Street Book About Values* (PS–2). Illus. by Lynn Munsinger. 1991, Dutton paper $3.99 (0-14-054091-1). A book about farmyard animals that explores the concept of honesty. (Rev: SLJ 6/91)

2550 Oram, Hiawyn. *Badger's Bad Mood* (PS–3). Illus. by Susan Varley. 1998, Scholastic $15.95 (0-590-18920-4). 32pp. In order to get Badger out of his blue funk, his animal friends arrange an awards ceremony to honor him for being a true friend. (Rev: BCCB 5/98; BL 5/15/98; HBG 10/98; SLJ 8/98)

2551 Oram, Hiawyn. *Just Dog* (K–2). Illus. by Lisa Flather. 1998, Chronicle $13.95 (0-8118-2247-8). 32pp. Dog tries various stunts to make his owner change his name, but when he considers some of the names he might be called, he decides to remain just Dog. (Rev: BL 11/1/98; HBG 3/99; SLJ 10/98)

2552 Oram, Hiawyn. *Kiss It Better* (PS). Illus. by Frederic Joos. 2000, Dutton LB $12.99 (0-525-46386-0). 32pp. Little Bear always gets comfort and hugs from his parent Big Bear, and so when Big Bear gets bad news Little Bear is the one who gives the hugs. (Rev: BL 8/00; HBG 10/00; SLJ 8/00)

2553 Oram, Hiawyn. *Princess Chamomile's Garden* (PS–1). Illus. by Susan Varley. 2000, Dutton $15.99 (0-525-46387-9). 32pp. Princess Chamomile, a little mouse, designs a garden to her own liking; the result is presented in a triple-page spread. (Rev: BL 6/1–15/00; HBG 10/00; SLJ 5/00)

2554 Oram, Hiawyn. *The Wrong Overcoat* (PS–1). Illus. by Mark Birchall. 2000, Carolrhoda $15.95 (1-57505-453-1). 32pp. In spite of compliments about the new coat his mother bought him, little Chimp dislikes it and takes it back to the store for a replacement. (Rev: BL 7/00; HBG 10/00; SLJ 6/00)

2555 Ormondroyd, Edward. *Broderick* (PS–3). Illus. by John Larrecq. 1969, Houghton LB $5.75 (0-686-86580-4). 40pp. Broderick, a mouse, loves to chew books, but one night he stops chewing and reads one. The book is on surfing, and it changes his life!

2556 Padt, Maartje. *Shanti* (PS–3). Illus. by Mylo Freeman. 1998, DK $14.95 (0-7894-2520-3). 32pp. Shanti, a young zebra, becomes separated from the herd, but after she gives birth, she realizes she is no longer alone. (Rev: BL 1/1–15/99; HBG 3/99; SLJ 12/98)

2557 Palatini, Margie. *Ding Dong Ding Dong* (PS–3). Illus. by Howard Fine. 1999, Hyperion LB $16.49 (0-7868-2367-4). In this pun-filled adventure, an oversize ape in the Big Apple tries to sell his line of Ape-On Cosmetics. (Rev: BCCB 12/99; HBG 3/00; SLJ 9/99)

2558 Palatini, Margie. *Moosetache* (PS–2). Illus. by Henry Cole. 1997, Hyperion LB $16.49 (0-7868-2246-5). 32pp. A funny story about a moose that tries several ways to tame his uncontrollable mustache. (Rev: BL 4/15/97; SLJ 5/97)

2559 Paraskevas, Betty. *Hoppy and Joe* (K–3). Illus. by Michael Paraskevas. 1999, Simon & Schuster $16.00 (0-689-82199-9). 32pp. While spending a lonely summer at the beach, Joe the dog saves and befriends an injured seagull named Hoppy. (Rev: BL 8/99; HBG 10/99; SLJ 5/99)

2560 Parr, Todd. *The Best Friends Book* (K–2). Illus. by author. 2000, Little, Brown $5.95 (0-316-69201-8). A small book that humorously explains the nature of friendship using funny drawings of humans and animals. Also use the equally funny *Zoo Do's and Don'ts* (2000). (Rev: HBG 10/00; SLJ 8/00)

2561 Partis, Joanne. *Stripe* (PS–1). Illus. 2000, Lerner $14.95 (1-57505-450-7). 32pp. Stripe, a curious little tiger, disobeys his parents and wanders alone into the jungle with near-disastrous results. (Rev: BL 4/15/00; HBG 10/00; SLJ 7/00)

2562 Patz, Nancy. *Sarah Bear and Sweet Sidney* (K–2). Illus. by author. 1989, Macmillan LB $13.95 (0-02-770270-7). Sidney Bear thinks that winter and his time of hibernation are over, but Sarah Bear knows that spring has not yet arrived. (Rev: SLJ 9/89)

2563 Paxton, Tom. *The Jungle Baseball Game* (K–3). Illus. by Karen L. Schmidt. 1999, Morrow LB $15.93 (0-688-13980-9). 40pp. A picture-book version of the song about the baseball game between champion monkeys and bumbling hippos. (Rev: BL 5/1/99; HBG 10/99; SLJ 4/99)

2564 Payne, Emmy. *Katy No-Pocket* (PS–1). Illus. by H. A. Rey. 1973, Houghton $17.00 (0-395-17104-0); paper $5.95 (0-395-13717-9). 32pp. Until Katy finds an apron with pockets, she is very sad, for she has no way to carry her baby.

2565 Peet, Bill. *Cock-a-Doodle Dudley* (PS–3). Illus. 1990, Houghton $16.00 (0-395-55331-8). 48pp. Dudley takes credit for making the sun rise. (Rev: BCCB 10/90; BL 9/15/90; HB 11–12/90; SLJ 11/90)

2566 Peet, Bill. *Cowardly Clyde* (K–2). Illus. by author. 1984, Houghton paper $7.95 (0-395-36171-0). 48pp. A horse named Clyde quivers in fear at the thought of fighting a dragon with his master, Sir Galavant. Other titles by this author and publisher are: *Ant and the Elephant* (1980); *The Luckiest One of All* (1985); *No Such Things* (1985); *Pamela Camel* (1986); *Farewell to Shady Glade* (1991).

2567 Peet, Bill. *Eli* (1–3). Illus. by author. 1984, Houghton paper $8.95 (0-395-36611-9). 48pp. An old lion is saved from hunters by playing dead. Others by Bill Peet and published by Houghton are: *Hubert's Hair-Raising Adventure* (1959); *Ella* (1964); *Chester the Worldly Pig* (1978); *Kermit the Hermit* (1980); *Cyrus the Unsinkable Sea Serpent* (1982).

2568 Peet, Bill. *Encore for Eleanor* (K–3). Illus. by author. 1981, Houghton paper $3.95 (0-317-18520-9). 48pp. Eleanor the elephant must face retirement from her circus job. (Rev: HB 9–10/85)

2569 Peet, Bill. *The Gnats of Knotty Pine* (K–3). Illus. by author. 1984, Houghton $16.00 (0-395-21405-X); paper $7.95 (0-395-36612-7). The tiny gnats help save the animals of Knotty Pine at hunting time.

2570 Peet, Bill. *Whingdingdilly* (2–4). Illus. by author. 1977, Houghton $16.00 (0-395-24729-2); paper $7.95 (0-395-31381-3). Scamp, tired of leading a dog's life, is transformed by a witch. Some others by this author and publisher are: *The Spooky Tail of Prewitt Peacock* (1973); *Merle the High Flying Squirrel* (1974); *Fly, Homer, Fly* (1979); *Randy's Dandy Lions* (1979); *Huge Harold* (1982); *How Droofus the Dragon Lost His Head* (1983); *The Pinkish, Purplish, Bluish Egg* (1984).

2571 Peet, Bill. *Zella, Zack, and Zodiac* (PS–1). Illus. 1986, Houghton $16.00 (0-395-41069-X); paper $7.95 (0-395-52207-2). 32pp. The tale of Zack, an ostrich adopted by Zella the zebra, and Zella's colt Zodiac, whom Zack saves. (Rev: BCCB 6/86; BL 3/16/86; SLJ 5/86)

2572 Peguero, Leone. *Lionel and Amelia* (PS–1). Illus. by Adrian Peguero and Gerard Peguero. 1996, Mondo paper $4.95 (1-57255-197-6). 30pp. The

mice, who want to be friends, copy each other's ways but decide it's best to be natural. (Rev: BL 1/1–15/97)

2573 Peters, Lisa Westberg. *Cold Little Duck, Duck, Duck* (PS–1). Illus. by Sam Williams. 2000, Greenwillow LB $15.89 (0-688-16179-0). 32pp. A duck who finds that her pond is still frozen over imagines all the wonders of spring and, before she knows it, spring arrives. (Rev: BL 5/15/00; HB 7–8/00; HBG 10/00)

2574 Pfister, Marcus. *Dazzle the Dinosaur* (K–2). Illus. 1994, North-South LB $18.88 (1-55858-338-6). 32pp. Two young dinosaurs decide to chase away the giant Dragonsaurus, which has invaded their valley paradise. (Rev: BL 2/1/95; SLJ 1/95)

2575 Pfister, Marcus. *Hopper's Treetop Adventure* (PS–1). Illus. 1997, North-South LB $15.88 (1-55858-681-4). 32pp. Hopper the rabbit meets a squirrel who teaches him to dig for nuts, climb trees, and swing from branch to branch. (Rev: BL 4/1/97; SLJ 3/97)

2576 Pfister, Marcus. *Milo and the Magical Stones* (PS–2). Trans. by Marianne Martens. Illus. 1997, North-South $18.95 (1-55858-682-2). 28pp. A choose-your-own-ending book in which a group of mice on an island discover a nugget of gold. (Rev: BL 10/1/97; HBG 3/98; SLJ 9/97)

2577 Pfister, Marcus. *Milo and the Mysterious Island* (K–3). Trans. by Marianne Martens. Illus. 2000, North-South $18.95 (0-7358-1352-3). 32pp. Milo and his mouse friends sail to an new island and, depending on whether the reader chooses the top or bottom of the split page format, the ending is happy or sad. (Rev: BL 11/15/00; SLJ 3/01)

2578 Pfister, Marcus. *Penguin Pete, Ahoy!* (PS–K). Trans. from German by Rosemary Lanning. Illus. by author. Series: Penguin Pete. 1993, North-South LB $15.88 (1-55858-221-5). Penguin Pete makes a new friend of Horatio, a mouse, and together they explore an abandoned ship. (Rev: SLJ 1/94)

2579 Pfister, Marcus. *The Rainbow Fish* (PS–2). Trans. by J. Alison James. Illus. 1992, North-South LB $18.88 (1-55858-010-7). 28pp. Rainbow Fish feels superior to those plain fish that surround him until he finds that sharing brings happiness. (Rev: BL 1/1/93; SLJ 11/92)

2580 Pfister, Marcus. *Rainbow Fish and the Big Blue Whale* (PS–K). Trans. by J. Alison James. Illus. 1998, North-South LB $18.88 (0-7358-1010-9). 32pp. Rainbow Fish and his friends are afraid that a whale who arrives in their area will eat all the krill and then eat them. (Rev: BL 9/15/98; HBG 3/99; SLJ 9/98)

2581 Pfister, Marcus. *The Rainbow Fish Board Book* (PS). Illus. 1996, North-South $9.95 (1-55858-536-2). 12pp. A board book version of the tale first published in 1993 of the lovely rainbow fish and his quest for friends. (Rev: BL 3/15/96)

2582 Pfister, Marcus. *Rainbow Fish to the Rescue!* (PS–1). Illus. 1995, North-South LB $18.88 (1-55858-487-0). 32pp. When Rainbow Fish and his friends face a shark attack, the group accepts a new striped fish into the circle. This is the sequel to *Rainbow Fish* (1992). (Rev: BL 9/15/95; SLJ 9/95)

2583 Piers, Helen. *Who's in My Bed?* (PS). Illus. by Dave Saunders. 1999, Marshall Cavendish $15.95 (0-7614-5046-7). 21pp. Farm animals displace one another when taking over sleeping places in this picture book that uses flaps to tell its story. (Rev: BCCB 7–8/99; BL 4/15/99; HB 5–6/99; HBG 10/99; SLJ 7/99)

2584 Pilkey, Dav. *Dog Breath: The Horrible Trouble with Hally Tosis* (PS–2). Illus. 1994, Scholastic $14.95 (0-590-47466-9). 32pp. Hally Tosis, a dog with terrible breath, uses his affliction to capture two burglars. (Rev: BL 9/15/94; HB 11–12/94; SLJ 1/95)

2585 Pilkey, Dav. *The Moonglow Roll-o-Rama* (PS–3). Illus. 1995, Orchard LB $16.99 (0-531-08726-3). 32pp. Some animals steal off at night to a magical roller skating rink, which is why they sleep during the day. (Rev: BCCB 3/95; BL 2/1/95; SLJ 3/95)

2586 Pilkey, Dav. *The Silly Gooses* (PS–3). Illus. by author. 1998, Scholastic $8.95 (0-590-94733-8). 39pp. A slapstick story about two silly geese who marry and raise a silly family. (Rev: BCCB 4/98; HBG 10/98; SLJ 2/98)

2587 Pinkwater, Daniel. *Bongo Larry* (1–3). Illus. by Jill Pinkwater. 1998, Marshall Cavendish $14.95 (0-7614-5020-3). 32pp. Groovy Larry the polar bear takes up the bongo drums and lands in jail for playing them in a park after curfew. (Rev: BL 7/98; HBG 10/98; SLJ 5/98)

2588 Pinkwater, Daniel. *Ice Cream Larry* (PS–3). Illus. by Jill Pinkwater. 1999, Marshall Cavendish $15.95 (0-7614-5043-2). 32pp. Larry the polar bear gets into trouble when he gobbles up 250 pounds of ice cream. (Rev: BCCB 6/99; BL 4/1/99; HBG 10/99; SLJ 5/99)

2589 Pinkwater, Daniel. *Young Larry* (K–3). Illus. by Jill Pinkwater. 1997, Marshall Cavendish $14.95 (0-7614-5004-1). 32pp. Larry, a polar bear, gets his first job being a lifeguard. Also use *At the Hotel, Larry* (1997). (Rev: BL 9/1/97; HBG 3/98; SLJ 10/97*)

2590 Pitcher, Caroline. *Are You Spring?* (PS–1). Illus. by Cliff Wright. Series: Share-a-Story. 2000, DK $9.95 (0-7894-6352-4); paper $5.95 (0-7894-5614-1). 32pp. An impatient little bear, who has been told not to leave the cave until spring comes, ventures out to meet this stranger named spring. (Rev: BL 10/15/00; HBG 3/01; SLJ 9/00)

2591 Pitcher, Caroline. *Run with the Wind* (PS–K). Illus. by Jane Chapman. 1998, Little Tiger $14.95 (1-888444-29-0). 32pp. A mare reassures her timid foal and helps him conquer his fears so that, when she must leave him to resume her farm chores, he has gained enough confidence to accept her absence. (Rev: BL 8/98; HBG 3/99; SLJ 9/98)

2592 Policoff, Stephen Phillip. *Cesar's Amazing Journey* (K–3). 1999, Viking $15.99 (0-670-88753-6). This is the humorous story of a tree frog and his friend, a spider, who are uprooted from their Florida

wetlands home and have an amazing visit in the Big Apple. (Rev: HBG 3/00; SLJ 12/99)

2593 Polisar, Barry L. *The Trouble with Ben* (PS–3). Illus. by David Clark. 1992, Rainbow Morning Music $14.95 (0-938663-13-5). 32pp. A young bear annoys his human classmates by indulging in bearlike activities. (Rev: BL 6/1/92; SLJ 7/92)

2594 Pomerantz, Charlotte. *The Mousery* (PS–2). Illus. by Kurt Cyrus. 2000, Harcourt $16.00 (0-15-202304-6). Two miserly mice take in four freezing young mice and find that their lives change for the better. (Rev: HBG 3/01; SLJ 11/00)

2595 Pomerantz, Charlotte. *The Piggy in the Puddle* (PS–K). Illus. by James Marshall. 1974, Macmillan LB $15.00 (0-02-774900-2). 32pp. Amusing story of the antics of a pig family enjoying a mud puddle.

2596 Porter, Sue. *Little Wolf and the Giant* (K–3). Illus. 1990, Simon & Schuster paper $13.95 (0-671-70363-3). Little Wolf, on his way to Granny's, is sure there are monsters in the woods. (Rev: SLJ 10/90)

2597 Potter, Beatrix. *The Complete Adventures of Peter Rabbit* (K–3). Illus. by author. 1982, Puffin paper $7.99 (0-14-050444-3). 96pp. An omnibus of the Peter Rabbit stories.

2598 Potter, Beatrix. *The Tales of Peter Rabbit and Benjamin Bunny* (1–2). Adapted by Sindy McKay. Illus. by author. Series: We Both Read. 1998, Treasure Bay $7.99 (1-891327-01-1). Two texts, one for parents and the other for children, face each other in this version that uses the original illustrations. (Rev: SLJ 3/99)

2599 Prater, John. *Again!* (PS–1). Illus. by author. 2000, Barron's $12.95 (0-7641-5279-3). Grandbear becomes exhausted while playing with Baby Bear, but for his efforts he receives hugs over and over again. (Rev: SLJ 11/00)

2600 Prater, John. *On Top of the World* (PS). Illus. 1998, Mondo $15.95 (1-57255-649-8). Four stuffed animals sneak out one night for some fun on a playground slide. (Rev: BL 2/1/99; HBG 3/99)

2601 Prelutsky, Jack. *The Baby Uggs Are Hatching* (K–4). Illus. by James Stevenson. 1982, Greenwillow LB $15.93 (0-688-00923-9); Morrow paper $3.95 (0-688-09239-X). 32pp. A collection of imaginary animals introduced in catchy verse.

2602 Price, Mathew. *Don't Worry, Alfie* (PS). Illus. by Emma C. Clark. 1999, Orchard $9.95 (0-531-30127-3). In this tab book, a mother assures her bear-cub son, Alfie, that she will protect him. Also use *Where's Alfie?* (1999). (Rev: SLJ 7/99)

2603 Price, Mathew. *Patch Finds a Friend* (PS–K). Illus. by Emma C. Clark. 2000, Orchard $5.95 (0-531-30264-4). A tab book in which Patch, a little spotted puppy, makes friends with a small, gray cat. Also use *Patch and the Rabbits* (2000). (Rev: SLJ 5/00)

2604 Pryor, Bonnie. *Louie and Dan Are Friends* (K–3). Illus. by Elizabeth Miles. 1997, Morrow LB $15.93 (0-688-08561-X). 32pp. Because they are so different, two mouse brothers wonder if they will always remain friends. (Rev: BL 10/1/97; HBG 3/98; SLJ 9/97)

2605 Pryor, Bonnie. *The Porcupine Mouse* (PS–2). Illus. by Maryjane Begin. 1988, Morrow $15.93 (0-688-07154-6). 32pp. Louie and Dan don't heed Mama Mouse's warnings when they go off to find a home of their own. (Rev: BL 3/1/88; SLJ 9/88)

2606 Quackenbush, Robert. *Batbaby* (PS–2). Illus. by author. Series: Little Dipper Books. 1997, Random LB $9.99 (0-679-98541-7). When a gust of wind blows Batbaby into Squirrel's treetop nest, Squirrel tries to accommodate his new guest. (Rev: SLJ 12/97)

2607 Quackenbush, Robert. *Henry's Awful Mistake* (PS–2). Illus. by author. 1981, Parents LB $5.95 (0-8193-1040-9). 48pp. Henry, a duck, tries to rid his horse of an ant. A sequel is: *Henry's Important Date* (1982).

2608 Quackenbush, Robert. *Lost in the Amazon: A Miss Mallard Mystery* (2–4). Illus. 1990, Pippin LB $15.95 (0-945912-11-0). Miss Mallard, the detective duck, is off on another case, this one in Brazil. (Rev: SLJ 1/91)

2609 Radford, Derek. *Harry at the Garage* (PS–2). Illus. 1995, Candlewick $12.99 (1-56402-564-0). 32pp. Harry the Hippo learns what goes on in a garage when he takes his car in to be serviced. (Rev: BL 10/15/95; SLJ 1/96)

2610 Ramirez, Michael Rose. *The Little Ant/La Hormiga Chiquita* (K–2). Illus. by Linda D. Sawaya. 1995, Rizzoli $12.95 (0-8478-1922-1). 31pp. In this bilingual book, an ant looks around for someone to blame when she slips on the snow. (Rev: SLJ 3/96)

2611 Rand, Gloria. *Willie Takes a Hike* (1–3). Illus. by Ted Rand. 1996, Harcourt $15.00 (0-15-200272-3). 32pp. In spite of his elaborate preparations, Willie the mouse gets lost on a hiking trip. (Rev: BL 4/1/96; SLJ 6/96)

2612 Rankin, Joan. *Scaredy Cat* (PS–1). Illus. 1996, Simon & Schuster $16.00 (0-689-80948-4). 30pp. A little kitten conquers his fears and takes on a dog many times his size. (Rev: SLJ 9/15/96; SLJ 11/96)

2613 Rankin, Joan. *Wow! It's Great Being a Duck* (PS–1). Illus. by author. 1998, Simon & Schuster paper $16.00 (0-689-81756-8). A little duck learns her survival skills very quickly when she is confronted by a fox. (Rev: BCCB 5/98; BL 6/1–15/98; HBG 10/98; SLJ 3/98)

2614 Rankin, Joan. *You're Somebody Special, Walliwigs!* (PS–3). Illus. 1999, Simon & Schuster $16.00 (0-689-82230-8). 32pp. Separated from his mother, young parrot Walliwigs is raised by chickens until Professor Beak discovers he is really a member of a rare parrot breed. (Rev: BL 7/99; HBG 10/99; SLJ 8/99)

2615 Raschka, Chris. *Arlene Sardine* (K–2). Illus. by author. 1998, Orchard LB $16.99 (0-531-33111-3). The whimsical story of Arlene's two-year life, from her birth in a fjord to her final resting place in a can. (Rev: BCCB 9/98; HBG 3/99; SLJ 9/98)

2616 Raschka, Chris. *The Blushful Hippopotamus* (PS–K). Illus. by author. 1996, Orchard LB $16.99 (0-531-08882-0). Young Roosevelt Hippopotamus can't control his blushing and is ridiculed by his sister. (Rev: HB 9–10/96; SLJ 9/96)

2617 Rathmann, Peggy. *Good Night, Gorilla* (PS–1). Illus. 1994, Putnam $14.99 (0-399-22445-9). 40pp. After the zookeeper says good night to his animals, a playful gorilla lets them out of their cages. (Rev: BCCB 5/94; BL 7/94; HB 7–8/94; SLJ 7/94)

2618 Reich, Janet. *Gus and the Green Thing* (PS–2). Illus. by author. 1993, Walker LB $9.85 (0-8027-8253-1). A dog named Gus follows a leaf from the bleak city into the countryside and finds a new green world. (Rev: SLJ 10/93)

2619 Reiser, Lynn. *Little Clam* (PS–1). Illus. 1998, Greenwillow LB $14.93 (0-688-15909-5). 32pp. Little Clam shows that he can protect himself when he is attacked first by a seagull, then a sea star, and finally a conch. (Rev: BL 8/98; HB 9–10/98; HBG 3/99; SLJ 11/98)

2620 Reiser, Lynn. *Two Mice in Three Fables* (PS–1). Illus. 1995, Greenwillow LB $14.93 (0-688-13390-8). 32pp. A country mouse introduces an indoor mouse to the wonders of nature. (Rev: BL 3/1/95; SLJ 4/95)

2621 Retan, Walter, ed. *Piggies, Piggies, Piggies: A Treasury of Stories, Songs, and Poems* (K–3). Illus. 1993, Simon & Schuster paper $15.00 (0-671-75244-8). 96pp. An anthology of nursery rhymes, poems, stories, and excerpts from novels, all having pigs as their subject. (Rev: BL 1/15/94; SLJ 1/94)

2622 Rex, Michael. *The Painting Gorilla* (PS–2). Illus. 1997, Holt $15.95 (0-8050-5020-5). 32pp. A gorilla in a zoo becomes a millionaire by selling her paintings, but what should she do with the money? (Rev: BL 12/1/97; HBG 3/98; SLJ 9/97)

2623 Rey, H. A. *Cecily G. and the Nine Monkeys* (K–2). Illus. by author. 1974, Houghton $16.00 (0-395-18430-4); paper $5.95 (0-395-50651-4). 32pp. A lonely giraffe and nine homeless monkeys share some uproarious adventures.

2624 Rey, H. A. *Curious George* (K–4). Illus. by author. 1941, Houghton $14.95 (0-395-15993-8); paper $5.95 (0-395-15023-X). 56pp. A small monkey finds himself in difficulties due to his mischievous curiosity. Also use by the same author: *Curious George Takes a Job* (1947); *Curious George Rides a Bike* (1952); *Curious George Gets a Medal* (1957).

2625 Rey, H. A., and Margaret Rey. *Whiteblack the Penguin Sees the World* (PS–2). Illus. 2000, Houghton $15.00 (0-618-07389-2). 32pp. A well-crafted plot about a penguin who leaves Penguinland for a series of adventures that include hatching two ostrich eggs. (Rev: BL 11/1/00; HBG 3/01; SLJ 11/00)

2626 Rey, Margaret. *Curious George Flies a Kite* (K–2). Illus. by H. A. Rey. 1973, Houghton $15.00 (0-395-16965-8); paper $5.95 (0-395-25937-1). 80pp. More predicaments are encountered by this fun-loving monkey. Also use by the same author: *Curious George Goes to the Hospital* (1973).

2627 Rey, Margaret, and H. A. Rey. *Curious George and the Dump Truck* (PS–K). Illus. 1999, Houghton LB $7.95 (0-395-97844-0); paper $3.95 (0-395-97836-X). 32pp. In this adventure, the young monkey uses the contents of a dump truck to create a little island for his duck friends. Also use: *Curious George at the Parade* and *Curious George Goes Camping.* (Rev: BL 1/1–15/00)

2628 Riddle, Tohby. *The Great Escape from City Zoo* (PS–3). Illus. 1999, Farrar $16.00 (0-374-32776-9). 32pp. A humorous story about four different animals who escape from a zoo and decide to have a high time in town. (Rev: BCCB 9/99; BL 1/1–15/00; HBG 3/00; SLJ 11/99)

2629 Riley, Linnea. *Mouse Mess* (PS–2). Illus. 1997, Scholastic $15.95 (0-590-10048-3). 32pp. While the human family is asleep upstairs, a messy mouse is creating havoc downstairs in a search for food. (Rev: BL 10/1/97; HBG 3/98; SLJ 11/97*)

2630 Roberts, Bethany. *Follow Me!* (PS–1). Illus. by Diane Greenseid. 1998, Clarion $15.00 (0-395-82268-8). 32pp. Octopus Mom and her children journey through the seas to visit Grandma who lives in a sunken pirate ship. (Rev: HBG 3/99; SLJ 12/98)

2631 Roche, Denis. *Brave Georgie Goat: Three Little Stories About Growing Up* (PS). Illus. by author. 1997, Crown $17.99 (0-517-70965-1). Three short stories about a little goat and how he conquers fears and achieves some independence. (Rev: BCCB 3/98; HBG 3/98; SLJ 1/98)

2632 Rockwell, Anne. *Hugo at the Park* (PS–1). Illus. by author. 1990, Macmillan LB $13.95 (0-02-777301-9). Hugo, a pup, disobeys his young master and interrupts other people's activities in the park. (Rev: SLJ 3/90)

2633 Rockwell, Norman. *Willie Was Different* (1–3). Illus. by author. 1994, Berkshire House $16.95 (0-936399-61-9). After achieving world renown as a composer, Willie the wood thrush decides it is best to return to his forest home. (Rev: SLJ 12/94)

2634 Roddie, Shen. *Too Close Friends* (PS–1). Illus. by Sally Anne Lambert. 1998, Dial $14.99 (0-8037-2188-9). 32pp. Two close friends, Hippo and Pig, lose their sense of privacy when one cuts down a tall hedge that separates their properties. (Rev: BCCB 6/98; BL 2/1/98; HBG 10/98; SLJ 3/98)

2635 Root, Phyllis. *Foggy Friday* (PS–3). Illus. by Helen Craig. 2000, Candlewick $10.99 (0-7636-0777-0); paper $3.29 (0-7636-0833-5). 24pp. Bonnie Bumble's faithful morning wake-up call is missing when her rooster misplaces his cock-o-doodle-do. *Meow Monday* (2000) also features Bonnie Bumble. (Rev: BCCB 2/01; BL 11/15/00; SLJ 12/00)

2636 Ross, Tony. *Silly Silly* (PS–K). Illus. by author. 1999, Andersen $19.95 (0-86264-740-1). A silly book about two silly characters, a mouse and a goose, who agree to a contest to see who can tell the silliest story. (Rev: SLJ 2/00)

2637 Rotenberg, Lisa. *Rodeo Pup* (PS–2). Illus. 1998, Firefly LB $14.95 (1-55209-245-3). 32pp. Told by his young owner, this is the story of Rodeo Pup, a feisty dalmatian who becomes so famous he eventually has his own Web site. (Rev: BL 9/15/98; SLJ 11/98)

2638 Roth, Susan L. *Cinnamon's Day Out: A Gerbil Adventure* (PS–1). Illus. 1998, Dial LB $15.89 (0-

8037-2323-7). 32pp. Cinnamon, a gerbil, describes to his friend, Snowball, all the adventures he had during the day he escaped from his cage. (Rev: BCCB 9/98; BL 7/98; SLJ 7/98)

2639 Rowe, John. *Monkey Trouble* (K–2). Illus. by John A. Rowe. 1999, North-South LB $15.88 (0-7358-1034-6). A monkey who never listens is taken on an adventure by the wind and has difficulty finding his way home. (Rev: HBG 3/00; SLJ 10/99)

2640 Rowe, John. *Rabbit Moon* (PS–3). Illus. 1993, Picture Book paper $14.95 (0-88708-246-7). A rabbit mistakes a party decoration for the moon. (Rev: SLJ 6/93)

2641 Rowe, John. *Smudge* (PS–2). Illus. 1997, North-South LB $16.88 (1-55858-789-6). 36pp. Smudge, a rat, tries a number of surrogate animal families but finds his own is best. (Rev: BL 12/1/97; HBG 3/98; SLJ 2/98)

2642 Rowinski, Kate. *Ellie Bear and the Fly-Away Fly* (PS–2). Illus. by Dawn Peterson. 1993, Down East $14.95 (0-89272-335-1). On a fishing trip with her uncle, L. L. Bear, Ellie Bear catches a trout but decides to spare its life. (Rev: SLJ 4/94)

2643 Rudolph, Marguerita. *Grey Neck* (PS–3). Illus. by Leslie Shuman Kranz. 1988, Stemmer $13.95 (0-88045-068-1). 32pp. Grey Neck can't leave for the yearly journey south because of a broken wing. (Rev: BL 6/1/88; SLJ 9/88)

2644 Rush, Christopher. *Venus Peter Saves the Whale* (1–3). Illus. by Mairi Hedderwick. 1992, Pelican $14.95 (0-88289-928-7). 26pp. On an isolated Scottish island, seagulls want a young boy to save a stranded whale. (Rev: BL 6/1/92)

2645 Rylant, Cynthia. *Bunny Bungalow* (PS–K). Illus. by Nancy Hayashi. 1999, Harcourt $13.00 (0-15-201092-0). 32pp. A rabbit family transforms a ramshackle cottage into a lovely home with imagination, work, and love. (Rev: BL 4/15/99; HBG 10/99; SLJ 6/99)

2646 Rylant, Cynthia. *The Cookie-Store Cat* (PS–2). Illus. 1999, Scholastic $15.95 (0-590-54329-6). 40pp. A formerly stray cat is now the supervisor of a cookie factory where he also greets the store's regulars. (Rev: BL 5/15/99; HBG 10/99; SLJ 4/99)

2647 Rylant, Cynthia. *Poppleton Has Fun* (PS–1). Illus. by Mark Teague. 2000, Scholastic $15.95 (0-590-84839-9); paper $3.99 (0-590-84841-0). 56pp. This book in the Poppleton Pig series contains three short stories about sharing. (Rev: BL 11/15/00; HBG 3/01; SLJ 12/00)

2648 Rylant, Cynthia. *Thimbleberry Stories* (PS–2). Illus. by Maggie Kneen. 2000, Harcourt $15.00 (0-15-201081-5). 64pp. A beautifully illustrated book that contains four short stories about Nigel Chipmunk who lives on peaceful Thimbleberry Lane. (Rev: BCCB 9/00; BL 5/1/00; HBG 10/00; SLJ 5/00)

2649 Saller, Carol. *Pug, Slug, and Doug the Thug* (K–2). Illus. by Vicki Jo Redenbaugh. 1994, Carolrhoda LB $19.95 (0-87614-803-8). 32pp. In this Western tale, a young boy captures three outlaws when he accidentally starts a chain of events that prove to be their downfall. (Rev: BL 4/1/94)

2650 Sampson, Michael, and Mary Beth Sampson. *Star of the Circus* (PS–K). Illus. 1997, Holt $14.95 (0-8050-4284-9). 32pp. Each of a group of egocentric animals thinks that he or she is the star of the circus. (Rev: BL 4/1/97; SLJ 3/97)

2651 Sansone, Adele. *The Little Green Goose* (PS–3). Trans. by J. Alison James. Illus. by Alan Marks. 1999, North-South LB $15.88 (0-7358-1072-9). 32pp. Mr. Goose hatches an egg given him by a dog and finds that he is raising a dinosaur. (Rev: BCCB 7–8/99; BL 4/15/99; HBG 10/99; SLJ 9/99)

2652 Santore, Charles. *William the Curious: Knight of the Water Lilies* (K–2). Illus. 1997, Random $18.00 (0-679-88742-3). 32pp. The frog William was happy living in a castle moat until it became filled with junk, thanks to the queen's order that imperfect things were to be thrown out of the castle. (Rev: BL 12/15/97; HBG 3/98; SLJ 2/98)

2653 Sardegna, Jill. *The Roly-Poly Spider* (PS–K). Illus. by Tedd Arnold. 1994, Scholastic $13.95 (0-590-47119-8). 32pp. A fat spider uses age-old devices like flattery to lure insect meals into its web. (Rev: BL 11/15/94; SLJ 1/95)

2654 Saunders, Dave, and Julie Saunders. *Brave Jack* (K–3). Illus. by Dave Saunders. 1993, Macmillan $14.95 (0-02-781073-9). 32pp. In spite of warnings, a rabbit named Jack raids a cabbage patch. (Rev: BL 3/15/93; SLJ 6/93)

2655 Saunders, Dave, and Julie Saunders. *Dibble and Dabble* (PS–1). Illus. by Dave Saunders. 1990, Macmillan $14.95 (0-02-781071-2). Two ducks tell their story of seeing a furry snake, which is really just a cat's tail. (Rev: HB 5–6/90; SLJ 4/90)

2656 Saunders, Dave, and Julie Saunders. *Snowtime* (PS–1). Illus. by Dave Saunders. 1991, Macmillan LB $14.95 (0-02-781075-5). 32pp. Two ducks, Dibble and Dabble, become lost in a blizzard and wander into town. (Rev: BL 9/15/91; SLJ 12/91)

2657 Scamell, Ragnhild. *Three Bags Full* (K–1). Illus. by Sally Hobson. 1993, Orchard $14.95 (0-531-05486-1). 26pp. Millie the sheep gives so much of her wool to her friends that she begins to feel the cold. (Rev: BL 7/93)

2658 Scarry, Richard. *Pie Rats Ahoy!* (K–1). Illus. by author. Series: Step into Reading. 1994, Random LB $11.99 (0-679-94760-4); paper $3.99 (0-679-84760-X). 32pp. Uncle Willy hides inside a model of a crocodile to capture pirates who are frightening the residents of Busytown Bay. (Rev: SLJ 9/94)

2659 Schachner, Judith Byron. *The Grannyman* (PS–3). Illus. 1999, Dutton $15.99 (0-525-46122-1). 32pp. In this fantasy an old cat fondly remembers all his activities as a youngster including stalking wildebeest and playing Bach. (Rev: BCCB 1/00; BL 3/15/00; HBG 3/00; SLJ 11/99)

2660 Schami, Rafik. *Albery and Lila* (PS–2). Trans. by Anthea Bell. Illus. by Els Cools and Oliver Streich. 1999, North-South LB $15.88 (0-7358-1183-0). 32pp. Two outcasts in the farmyard, an old hen named Lila and Albery, a white pig, gain respect after they frighten away a dangerous fox. (Rev: BL 10/1/99; HBG 3/00; SLJ 11/99)

2661 Scheffler, Ursel. *Taking Care of Sister Bear* (PS–1). Illus. by Ulises Wensell. 1999, Doubleday $13.95 (0-385-32660-2). 32pp. Little Bear feels dejected when his mother seems to favor baby sister over him. (Rev: BL 9/1/99; HBG 3/00; SLJ 9/99)

2662 Scheffler, Ursel. *Who Has Time for Little Bear?* (PS–K). Illus. by Ulises Wensell. 1998, Doubleday $13.95 (0-385-32536-3). 32pp. Lonely Little Bear looks for a friend and finally finds one in another lonely little bear. (Rev: BL 1/1–15/99; HBG 3/99; SLJ 1/99)

2663 Schlein, Miriam. *The Way Mothers Are* (PS–1). Illus. by Joe Lasker. 1993, Whitman $14.95 (0-8075-8691-9). 32pp. In this new edition of the 1963 book, the story is still of a mother cat's love for her young son. (Rev: BL 4/1/93)

2664 Schoenherr, John. *Bear* (K–3). Illus. 1991, Putnam $14.95 (0-399-22177-8). 32pp. In an Alaska setting, a young bear sets out to find his missing mother. (Rev: BCCB 4/91; BL 4/1/91; HB 5–6/91; SLJ 5/91)

2665 Schubert, Ingrid, and Dieter Schubert. *Bear's Egg* (PS–2). Illus. 1999, Front Street $15.95 (1-886910-46-4). 32pp. When Bear becomes the owner of some untended goose eggs, he faces such problems as hatching the eggs and teaching the young goslings how to survive. (Rev: BL 10/1/99; HBG 3/00; SLJ 11/99)

2666 Schubert, Ingrid, and Dieter Schubert. *There's a Hole in My Bucket* (PS–2). Illus. 1998, Front Street $15.95 (1-886910-28-6). 32pp. Bear and his friend Hedgehog try to repair a hole in a bucket so that Bear can water his flowers. Fortunately the rain comes and solves their problems. (Rev: BL 5/15/98; HBG 10/98; SLJ 7/98)

2667 Schuurmans, Hilde. *Sidney Won't Swim* (PS–K). Illus. by author. 2001, Charlesbridge LB $15.95 (0-57091-476-1). A young dog doesn't want to take swimming lessons until his friends show him how much fun it can be. (Rev: SLJ 2/01)

2668 Schwartz, Henry. *How I Captured a Dinosaur* (PS–K). Illus. by Amy Schwartz. 1989, Orchard paper $5.95 (0-531-07028-X). 32pp. Liz discovers a dinosaur on a camping trip and takes him home. (Rev: BCCB 2/89; BL 2/1/89; SLJ 4/89)

2669 Schwartz, Roslyn. *The Mole Sisters and the Busy Bees* (PS). 2000, Annick $4.95 (1-55037-663-2); paper $4.95 (1-55037-662-4). 32pp. A small book in which two mole sisters watch bees as they go about their work. Also use *The Mole Sisters and the Wavy Wheat* (2000). (Rev: SLJ 11/00)

2670 Sebastian, John. *J.B.'s Harmonica* (K–3). Illus. by Garth Williams. 1993, Harcourt $13.95 (0-15-240091-5). 32pp. A young bear is so bad at playing the harmonica that the neighbors complain. (Rev: BL 3/15/93; SLJ 4/93)

2671 Seibold, J. Otto, and Vivian Walsh. *Free Lunch* (K–3). Illus. 1996, Viking $16.99 (0-670-86988-0). 40pp. The dog Mr. Lunch finds that the quality of the Elephant Brand Bird Seed Company's product is declining. (Rev: BL 9/1/96; SLJ 11/96)

2672 Seibold, J. Otto, and Vivian Walsh. *Mr. Lunch Takes a Plane Ride* (PS–3). Illus. by J. Otto Seibold.

1993, Viking $16.99 (0-670-84775-5). 40pp. The dog Mr. Lunch has fun opening up everyone's luggage when he is confined to the baggage compartment on an airplane flight. (Rev: BCCB 1/94; BL 9/1/93; SLJ 9/93)

2673 Selby, Jennifer. *The Seed Bunny* (PS–2). Illus. 1997, Harcourt $14.00 (0-15-201397-0). 32pp. A small bunny named Sam tries to get rid of a loose tooth so he can see the Seed Bunny, who takes teeth and leaves carrot seeds. (Rev: BCCB 4/97; BL 6/1–15/97; SLJ 4/97)

2674 Selden, George. *Chester Cricket's Pigeon Ride* (2–4). Illus. by Garth Williams. 1983, Dell paper $3.50 (0-440-41389-3). 80pp. A friendly pigeon gives Chester Cricket a bird's-eye view of Manhattan. A sequel is: *Chester Cricket's New Home* (1983).

2675 Seuss, Dr. *Horton Hears a Who!* (K–3). Illus. by author. 1954, Random LB $16.99 (0-394-90078-2). The children's favorite elephant discovers a whole town of creatures so small that they live on a speck of dust. Other titles by Dr. Seuss: *Horton Hatches the Egg* (1940); *If I Ran the Zoo* (1950); *If I Ran the Circus* (1956); *Yertle the Turtle and Other Stories* (1958).

2676 Seuss, Dr. *Hunches in Bunches* (PS–3). Illus. by author. 1982, Random LB $15.99 (0-394-95502-1). 48pp. A rhyming story about the problems of making up one's mind. Three other titles by Dr. Seuss are: *Thidwick, the Big-Hearted Moose* (1948); *Scrambled Eggs Super!* (1953); *I Had Trouble in Getting to Solla Sollew* (1992).

2677 Shah, Idries. *The Silly Chicken* (K–3). Illus. by Jeff Jackson. 2000, Hoopoe $17.00 (1-883536-19-7). 32pp. An amusing story about a chicken who convinces the inhabitants of a town that the earth is going to swallow them up. (Rev: BL 12/15/00; SLJ 3/01)

2678 Shannon, George. *Frog Legs: A Picture Book of Action Verse* (PS–2). Illus. by Amit Trynan. 2000, Greenwillow $15.00 (0-688-17047-1). 32pp. These 24 short poems portray frogs engaging in all sorts of human-like activities such as tricking and treating. (Rev: BL 3/15/00; HBG 10/00; SLJ 6/00)

2679 Shannon, George. *Heart to Heart* (PS–3). Illus. by Steve Bjorkman. 1995, Houghton $14.00 (0-395-72773-1). 32pp. Squirrel prepares a unique valentine for his friend Mole that celebrates all the good times they have had together. (Rev: BL 11/15/95; SLJ 11/95)

2680 Shannon, George. *Lizard's Home* (K–2). Illus. by Jose Aruego and Ariane Dewey. 1999, Greenwillow LB $15.93 (0-688-16003-4). 32pp. Lizard devises a plan to win back his favorite resting place — a rock that has been taken over by Snake. (Rev: BL 10/1/99; HBG 3/00; SLJ 9/99)

2681 Shannon, Margaret. *Gullible's Troubles* (PS–3). Illus. 1998, Houghton $15.00 (0-395-83933-5). 32pp. A humorous story about an innocent little guinea pig named Gullible who is tricked and teased but wins out in the end. (Rev: BCCB 7–8/98; BL 4/1/98; HB 7–8/98; HBG 10/98; SLJ 5/98)

2682 Sharmat, Marjorie W. *I'm Terrific* (PS–1). Illus. by Kay Chorao. 1977, Holiday LB $15.95 (0-8234-0282-7); paper $5.95 (0-8234-0955-4). 32pp. An amusing story of a bear cub who thinks he is marvelous and insists on telling everyone so.

2683 Sharmat, Marjorie W. *Tiffany Dino Works Out* (PS–3). Illus. by Nate Evans. 1995, Simon & Schuster paper $15.00 (0-689-80309-5). 32pp. Tiffany Dino becomes upset with her weight and decides to do something about it. (Rev: BL 11/15/95; SLJ 12/95)

2684 Sharmat, Mitchell. *Gregory, the Terrible Eater* (PS–3). Illus. by Jose Aruego and Ariane Dewey. 1980, Macmillan $16.00 (0-02-782250-8); Scholastic paper $4.99 (0-590-43350-4). 32pp. Gregory, a young goat, prefers a diet of fruit and vegetables to paper, shoes, and clothing.

2685 Shaw, Nancy. *Sheep Take a Hike* (PS–1). Illus. by Margot Apple. 1994, Houghton $13.95 (0-395-68394-7). 32pp. When they get lost in the woods, a flock of sheep find their way home because of bits of wool left on bushes. (Rev: BL 9/15/94; HB 11–12/94; SLJ 9/94*)

2686 Shields, Carol D. *Saturday Night at the Dinosaur Stomp* (PS–2). Illus. by Scott Nash. 1997, Candlewick $15.99 (1-56402-693-0). A group of friendly dinosaurs prepare for and later participate in a big dance called the Dinosaur Stomp. (Rev: HBG 3/98; SLJ 11/97)

2687 Shih, Bernadette L. *Ling Ling: The Most Beautiful Giant Panda in the World* (K–1). Illus. by Dionysia. 1999, Opal Bks. $16.95 (1-902587-04-9). Ling Ling, a panda, seeks reassurance from other animals that she is the most beautiful panda in the world. (Rev: SLJ 10/99)

2688 Sierra, Judy. *Counting Crocodiles* (PS–1). Illus. by Will Hillenbrand. 1997, Harcourt $16.00 (0-15-200192-1). 40pp. A hungry monkey wants bananas from a neighboring island, but she is afraid that crocodiles will catch her if she tries to swim. (Rev: BL 9/1/97; HBG 3/98; SLJ 10/97)

2689 Sierra, Judy. *Good Night Dinosaurs* (PS–1). Illus. by Victoria Chess. 1996, Clarion $15.00 (0-395-65016-X). 32pp. Stylized drawings of dinosaurs portray them in humorous day-to-day activities, such as snoozing in the mud and sucking on baby bottles. (Rev: BCCB 3/96; BL 1/1–15/96; HB 7–8/96; SLJ 4/96)

2690 Silverman, Erica. *Don't Fidget a Feather!* (PS–1). Illus. by S. D. Schindler. 1994, Macmillan paper $16.00 (0-02-782685-6). 32pp. Duck and Gander engage in contests to see who is the champion of champions. (Rev: BCCB 11/94; BL 11/15/94; SLJ 1/95*)

2691 Silverstein, Shel. *Who Wants a Cheap Rhinoceros?* (K–2). Illus. by author. 1983, Macmillan paper $15.95 (0-02-782690-2). 56pp. All the advantages of owning a rhino.

2692 Simmons, Jane. *Come Along, Daisy!* (PS). Illus. 1998, Little, Brown $12.95 (0-316-79790-1). 32pp. Daisy, a duckling, becomes distracted by the pond life around her, gets lost, and decides not to stray again after her mother finds her. (Rev: BCCB 9/98; BL 6/1–15/98*; HBG 10/98; SLJ 8/98)

2693 Simmons, Jane. *Daisy and the Beastie* (PS–K). Illus. 2000, Little, Brown $12.95 (0-316-79785-5). 32pp. Daisy, a duck, and her little brother wander around the farm looking for the "beasties" that their grandfather talked about and discover they are only kittens. (Rev: BCCB 3/00; BL 3/1/00; HBG 10/00; SLJ 5/00)

2694 Simmons, Jane. *Daisy and the Egg* (PS–K). Illus. 1999, Little, Brown $12.95 (0-316-79747-2). 32pp. Duckling Daisy decides to help out by sitting on an egg and is happy when it hatches and a baby duckling appears. (Rev: BL 2/15/99; HB 5–6/99; HBG 10/99; SLJ 7/99)

2695 Simmons, Jane. *Daisy Says Coo!* (PS). Illus. 2000, Little, Brown $5.95 (0-316-79764-2). 8pp. Daisy the duckling encounters various animals and the sounds they make in this large board book. Also use *Daisy's Day Out.* (Rev: BCCB 4/00; BL 4/15/00; SLJ 6/00)

2696 Simmons, Jane. *Daisy's Favorite Things* (PS). Illus. by author. Series: A First Daisy Book. 1999, Little, Brown $5.95 (0-316-79762-6). An oversize board book that tells of Daisy the duckling's favorite things, like playing with butterflies. Also use: *Go to Sleep, Daisy.* (Rev: BCCB 12/99; HBG 3/00; SLJ 9/99)

2697 Simmons, Jane. *Ebb and Flo and the New Friend* (PS–1). Illus. 1999, Simon & Schuster $14.95 (0-689-82483-1). 32pp. Flo, a little girl, and Ebb, a dog, welcome a goose named Bird as a friend until Ebb finds that Bird is making herself at home in all of his favorite spots. (Rev: BCCB 11/99; BL 12/1/99; HBG 3/00; SLJ 10/99)

2698 Simmons, Steven J. *Percy to the Rescue* (PS–3). Illus. by Kim Howard. 1998, Charlesbridge $15.95 (0-88106-390-8). 32pp. Percy, a blue pigeon who visits the tourist sites in London daily, helps rescue two boys who are trapped on an island in a park lake. (Rev: BL 8/98; HBG 3/99)

2699 Simon, Francesca. *Hugo and the Bully Frogs* (PS–1). Illus. by Caroline Jayne Church. 1999, David & Charles $14.95 (1-86233-093-X). Poor Hugo, a little frog, is intimidated by three big bullies in his pond until he gets help from a duck. (Rev: SLJ 3/00)

2700 Simon, Francesca. *Where Are You?* (PS). Illus. by David Melling. 1998, Peachtree $12.95 (1-56145-179-7). 32pp. Harry, a little dog, follows his interest in food while in a supermarket. When he becomes separated from Grandpa, though, he experiences the fear of being lost. (Rev: BL 12/1/98; HBG 3/99; SLJ 5/99)

2701 Simont, Marc. *The Goose That Almost Got Cooked* (K–2). Illus. 1997, Scholastic $15.95 (0-590-69075-2). 40pp. A Canada goose is happy to leave the flock and join some white geese on a farm until she realizes that in this situation she might become somebody's dinner. (Rev: BL 11/1/97; HBG 3/98; SLJ 8/97*)

2702 Slate, Joseph. *Story Time for Little Porcupine* (PS–3). Illus. by Jacqueline Rogers. 2000, Marshall Cavendish $15.95 (0-7614-5073-4). 32pp. At bedtime Papa and Little Porcupine trade stories similar to folktales, like Papa's story on how a trickster moon got the best of Big Porcupine. (Rev: BL 10/15/00; HBG 3/01; SLJ 10/00)

2703 Slotboom, Wendy. *King Snake* (K–2). Illus. by John Manders. 1997, Houghton $14.95 (0-395-74680-9). Two mice named Henry and Tinkerton fall into the clutches of a talkative garter snake. (Rev: SLJ 5/97)

2704 Smith, Barry. *Grandma Rabbitty's Visit* (PS). Illus. by author. Series: DK Toddler Storybook. 1999, DK $9.95 (0-7894-4839-4). Two rabbit children and their mother wonder what sort of vehicle Grandma Rabbitty will use for her visit. (Rev: HBG 3/00; SLJ 12/99)

2705 Smith, Maggie. *Dear Daisy, Get Well Soon* (PS–K). Illus. 2000, Crown $14.95 (0-517-80072-1). 32pp. Every day for a week a little boy sends animals including zebras and hippos over to his sick neighbor's house to deliver get-well presents. (Rev: BCCB 2/00; BL 7/00; HBG 10/00; SLJ 4/00)

2706 Snape, Juliet, and Charles Snape. *Frog Odyssey* (PS–2). Illus. by authors. 1992, Simon & Schuster paper $14.00 (0-671-74741-X). Some frogs leave their polluted pond to find a new home in the city. (Rev: SLJ 7/92)

2707 Snow, Alan. *The Truth About Cats* (K–4). Illus. 1996, Little, Brown $14.95 (0-316-80282-4). 32pp. With great daring, this book reveals that cats are really aliens from the Planet Nip. A companion to *How Dogs Really Work!* (1993). (Rev: BL 4/15/96; SLJ 3/96)

2708 Soto, Gary. *Chato's Kitchen* (PS–3). Illus. by Susan Guevara. 1995, Putnam $16.99 (0-399-22658-3). 32pp. In his Los Angeles barrio home, the cat Chato extends an invitation to some mice to come to dinner. (Rev: BL 3/1/95; HB 9–10/95; SLJ 7/95*)

2709 Speed, Toby. *Two Cool Cows* (PS–2). Illus. by Barry Root. 1995, Putnam $15.99 (0-399-22647-8). 32pp. Two adventurous cows jump to the moon, where they find many dozens of other cows enjoying themselves. (Rev: BL 6/1–15/95; SLJ 6/95)

2710 Spelman, Cornelia Maude. *When I Feel Angry* (PS–1). Illus. by Nancy Cote. 2000, Albert Whitman $14.95 (0-8075-8888-1). 32pp. A young bunny finds that he can deal in a number of ways with the anger he sometimes feels: by resting, crying, exercising, or asking for help. (Rev: BL 3/15/00; HBG 10/00; SLJ 4/00)

2711 Spinelli, Eileen. *Six Hogs on a Scooter* (PS–1). Illus. by Scott Nash. 2000, Orchard LB $16.99 (0-531-33212-8). 40pp. After a series of mishaps, six hogs arrive at the opera house so late that the performance is over and they must wait until the next day for a ride home. (Rev: BL 3/1/00; HBG 10/00; SLJ 4/00)

2712 Spohn, Kate. *Chick's Daddy* (PS). Illus. by author. 1998, Random $4.99 (0-679-88675-3). This attractive board book shows how a chick and its daddy play hide-and-seek. Also use: *Kitten's Nap,*

Piglet's Bath, and *Puppy's Games.* (Rev: HBG 10/98; SLJ 7/98)

2713 Spohn, Kate. *Dog and Cat Make a Splash* (PS–2). Illus. by author. Series: Viking Easy-to-Read. 1997, Viking $13.99 (0-670-87178-8). 31pp. Four gentle stories about Dog and his best friend, Cat. (Rev: SLJ 6/97)

2714 Stadler, John. *Animal Cafe* (K–2). Illus. by author. 1986, Macmillan paper $3.95 (0-689-71063-1). 32pp. Maxwell wonders who is mysteriously buying from his food store. Reissue of a 1980 edition.

2715 Stadler, John. *Hooray for Snail!* (K–2). Illus. by author. 1984, HarperCollins LB $15.89 (0-690-04413-5); paper $6.95 (0-06-443075-8). 32pp. Snail has a humorous journey around the bases in a baseball game.

2716 Steig, William. *Doctor De Soto* (K–3). Illus. by author. 1982, Farrar $16.00 (0-374-31803-4). A mouse dentist outwits a fox.

2717 Steig, William. *Doctor De Soto Goes to Africa* (PS–2). Illus. 1992, HarperCollins LB $14.89 (0-06-205003-6). 32pp. The mouse dentist, Dr. De Soto, travels to Africa to help an elephant with a rotten tooth. (Rev: BCCB 9/92; BL 7/92; SLJ 8/92)

2718 Steig, William. *Farmer Palmer's Wagon Ride* (K–2). Illus. by author. 1992, Farrar paper $4.95 (0-374-42268-0). Farmer Palmer, a pig, and the hired hand, a donkey, have a disastrous ride home from the market in this engaging nonsensical bit of fun.

2719 Steig, William. *Gorky Rises* (1–3). Illus. by author. 1986, Farrar paper $4.95 (0-374-42784-4). 32pp. A frog named Gorky concocts a formula that sends him on a magical journey.

2720 Steig, William. *Solomon the Rusty Nail* (K–2). Illus. by author. 1985, Farrar paper $6.95 (0-374-46903-2). 32pp. A rabbit's ability to change himself into a rusty nail whenever he wishes leads him to some interesting adventures and keeps him away from the prowling cat. (Rev: BCCB 3/86; BL 1/1/86; SLJ 2/86)

2721 Steig, William. *Sylvester and the Magic Pebble* (K–3). Illus. by author. 1988, Simon & Schuster paper $5.99 (0-671-66269-4). 32pp. A donkey who collects pebbles finds a red stone that will grant wishes — and off Sylvester goes on a series of adventures. Caldecott Medal winner, 1970.

2722 Steig, William. *Tiffky Doofky* (K–2). Illus. by author. 1978, Farrar paper $3.95 (0-374-47748-5). A canine garbage collector awaits a fortune-teller's prophecy to come true.

2723 Stenmark, Victoria. *The Singing Chick* (PS–K). Illus. by Randy Cecil. 1999, Holt $15.95 (0-8050-5255-0). 32pp. A circular tale about small to large animals who eat each other — until they are all spit out by a bear. (Rev: BCCB 2/99; BL 3/15/99; HB 5–6/99; HBG 10/99; SLJ 5/99)

2724 Stevens, Janet, and Susan Stevens Crummel. *Cook-a-Doodle-Doo!* (PS–3). Illus. 1999, Harcourt $17.00 (0-15-201924-3). 48pp. A group of farm animals are happy to help Big Brown Rooster prepare strawberry shortcake in this delightful farce. (Rev: BCCB 7–8/99; BL 4/15/99*; HB 5–6/99; HBG 10/99; SLJ 4/99)

2725 Stevens, Janet, and Susan Stevens Crummel. *My Big Dog* (PS–1). Illus. 1999, Golden Bks. $9.95 (0-307-10220-3). 32pp. When Merl the cat decides to leave after a new puppy is adopted by the family, he discovers that the great wide world isn't for him and returns home. (Rev: BL 1/1–15/99; HBG 10/99; SLJ 1/99)

2726 Stevens, Kathleen. *The Beast in the Bathtub* (PS–1). Illus. by Ray Bowler. 1985, Stevens LB $19.93 (0-91883-115-6). 32pp. Lewis claims he will be eaten if he has to take a bath, and indeed there is a big green creature in the tub, but the two get along just fine. (Rev: BL 12/1/85; SLJ 10/85)

2727 Stevenson, James. *Heat Wave at Mud Flat* (K–2). Illus. 1997, Greenwillow $14.93 (0-688-14206-0). 32pp. During a very hot, dry period, a rainmaker visits Mud Flat and the animal inhabitants react in different ways. (Rev: BL 5/15/97; HB 7–8/97; SLJ 5/97*)

2728 Stevenson, James. *The Most Amazing Dinosaur* (PS–3). Illus. 2000, Greenwillow LB $15.89 (0-688-16433-1). 32pp. When Wilfred, a rat, takes refuge from a snowstorm in a natural history museum, he is given a tour by other resident creatures. (Rev: BL 7/00; HBG 10/00; SLJ 6/00)

2729 Stevenson, James. *Mud Flat Spring* (PS–2). Illus. 1999, Greenwillow LB $14.93 (0-688-15773-4). 40pp. In nine short stories, the various animals of Mud Flat greet the spring. (Rev: BL 5/1/99; HBG 10/99; SLJ 3/99)

2730 Stevenson, James. *The Worst Goes South* (K–3). Illus. 1995, Greenwillow LB $14.93 (0-688-13060-7). 32pp. The "Worst" leaves his home and travels to Florida, where he meets an equally dislikable grouch, his brother. (Rev: BL 9/1/95; SLJ 10/95)

2731 Stewart, Paul. *A Little Bit of Winter* (PS–K). Illus. by Chris Riddell. 1999, HarperCollins $12.95 (0-06-028278-9). 24pp. Before Hedgehog hibernates, he asks Rabbit to save him a bit of winter, and Rabbit obliges by saving a snowball. (Rev: BL 3/1/99; HBG 10/99; SLJ 3/99)

2732 Stickland, Paul, and Henrietta Stickland. *Dinosaur Roar!* (PS–K). Illus. 1994, Dutton $13.99 (0-525-45276-1). 32pp. In this tale about two dinosaurs, several antonyms are introduced. (Rev: BL 10/1/94; SLJ 1/95)

2733 Stimson, Joan. *Big Panda, Little Panda* (PS–1). Illus. by Meg Rutherford. 1994, Barron's paper $4.95 (0-8120-1691-2). 32pp. When a new panda arrives in the panda household, his older brother feels left out. (Rev: BL 5/1/94)

2734 Stoeke, Janet Morgan. *A Friend for Minerva Louise* (PS–1). Illus. 1997, Dutton $14.99 (0-525-45869-7). 24pp. The hen Minerva is certain that her neighbors have a new bunny, but it turns out to be a baby. (Rev: BL 7/97; HBG 3/98; SLJ 11/97*)

2735 Stoeke, Janet Morgan. *Minerva Louise at School* (PS–1). Illus. 1996, Dutton $13.99 (0-525-45494-2). 24pp. A hen mistakes a school for a barn, with amusing results. (Rev: BCCB 9/96; BL 8/96; SLJ 8/96*)

2736 Stoeke, Janet Morgan. *Minerva Louise at the Fair* (PS–1). Illus. 2000, Dutton $14.99 (0-525-46439-5). 24pp. Minerva Louise, a chicken, has a string of hilarious misunderstandings beginning with mistaking fireworks for the stars falling. (Rev: BL 9/1/00; HBG 3/01; SLJ 8/00)

2737 Stojic, Manya. *Rain* (PS–1). Illus. 2000, Crown LB $15.89 (0-517-80086-1). 32pp. All the animals in the hot, dry African savanna sense the coming of a welcome rainstorm. (Rev: BCCB 7–8/00; BL 7/00; SLJ 5/00)

2738 Stone, Kazuko G. *Aligay Saves the Stars* (PS–1). Illus. 1991, Scholastic $13.95 (0-590-44382-8). An alligator is sent into space to retrieve the boomerang he threw too high. (Rev: SLJ 1/92)

2739 Stow, Jenny. *Growing Pains* (PS–2). Illus. by author. 1995, BridgeWater $13.95 (0-8167-3500-X). A young rhinoceros, like the children of other animals he knows, is anxious to mature quickly. (Rev: SLJ 12/95)

2740 Strickland, Paul. *Dinosaur Stomp: A Monster Pop-Up* (PS–K). Illus. 1996, Dutton $15.99 (0-525-45591-4). This pop-up book involves dancing dinosaurs. (Rev: BL 12/15/96; SLJ 2/97)

2741 Summers, Kate. *Milly's Wedding* (K–2). Illus. by Maggie Kneen. 1999, Dutton $15.99 (0-525-46046-2). 32pp. Two little mice meet, fall in love, and prepare for their wedding. (Rev: BL 1/1–15/99; HBG 10/99; SLJ 3/99)

2742 Suteyev, V. *Mushroom in the Rain* (K–2). Trans. by Mirra Ginsburg. Illus. by Jose Aruego and Ariane Dewey. 1987, Macmillan paper $5.99 (0-689-71441-6). 32pp. An ant huddled under a mushroom in the rain makes room for a variety of animals. A reissued 1974 book.

2743 Sweeney, Joan. *Once upon a Lily Pad: Froggy Love in Monet's Garden* (PS–2). Illus. by Kathleen Fain. 1995, Chronicle $9.95 (0-8118-0868-8). 32pp. Two married frogs, Hector and Henrietta, play in Monet's lily pond at Giverny, France, and pose for the artist. (Rev: BL 1/1–15/96; SLJ 2/96)

2744 Sykes, Julie. *Dora's Eggs* (PS). Illus. by Jane Chapman. 1997, Little Tiger $14.95 (1-888444-09-6). Dora the hen is disappointed when none of the animals pay attention to her first eggs; but when they hatch, it is a different matter. (Rev: HBG 3/98; SLJ 12/97)

2745 Sykes, Julie. *I Don't Want to Take a Bath* (PS–1). Illus. by Tim Warnes. 1997, Little Tiger $14.95 (1-888444-20-7). 32pp. Little Tiger avoids taking a bath by running into the jungle to play with friends. (Rev: BL 12/1/97; HBG 3/98)

2746 Sykes, Julie. *Little Tiger's Big Surprise!* (PS–K). Illus. by Tim Warnes. 1999, Little Tiger $14.95 (1-888444-52-5). Little Tiger runs away when he is told he will soon have a little brother or sister but, when he returns, he is delighted with the new baby. (Rev: HBG 3/00; SLJ 2/00)

2747 Sykes, Julie. *Smudge* (PS–K). Illus. by Jane Chapman. 1998, Little Tiger $14.95 (1-888444-44-4). 32pp. When Smudge, a dog, and his friends are

caught in a rainstorm, they try to get into a house for shelter, but their attempts fail — until Smudge gets a winning idea. (Rev: BL 10/15/98; HBG 3/99; SLJ 10/98)

2748 Sykes, Julie. *This and That* (PS). Illus. by Tanya Linch. 1996, Farrar $14.00 (0-374-37492-9). 32pp. Cat borrows objects from her farmyard friends to make a nest for her two newborn kittens. (Rev: BCCB 3/96; BL 5/1/96)

2749 Tafuri, Nancy. *Have You Seen My Duckling?* (PS–2). Illus. by author. 1984, Greenwillow $16.89 (0-688-02798-9); Morrow paper $5.95 (0-688-10994-2). 24pp. Mother Duck asks a number of animals if they have seen her missing duckling.

2750 Tafuri, Nancy. *Silly Little Goose!* (PS). Illus. 2001, Scholastic $15.95 (0-439-06304-3). 32pp. When a silly little goose discovers that every place she wants for her nest is already occupied, she finds a farmer's hat and decides it is the perfect place to lay her eggs. (Rev: BL 2/1/01)

2751 Takao, Yuko. *A Winter Concert* (K–2). Illus. by author. 1997, Millbrook LB $18.40 (0-7613-0301-4). As a mouse listens to a concert, his black-and-white world slowly becomes one of color. (Rev: HBG 3/98; SLJ 1/98)

2752 Tallarico, Tony. *Find Freddie* (K–2). Illus. 1990, Troll LB $10.95 (0-8167-1955-1). In each of the picture puzzles in this book, the reader must find the central character and other objects. Also use: *Hunt for Hector; Look for Lisa;* and *Search for Sam* (all 1990). (Rev: SLJ 12/90)

2753 Talley, Linda. *Thank You, Meiling* (K–3). Illus. by Itoko Maeno. 1999, MarshMedia $16.95 (1-55942-118-5). 30pp. A young duck learns about courtesy and Chinese traditions as she accompanies a boy on his preparations for the Chinese Moon Festival celebration. (Rev: SLJ 3/00)

2754 Taylor, Harriet P. *Secrets of the Stone* (1–3). Illus. 2000, Farrar $16.00 (0-374-36648-9). 32pp. Coyote and Badger stumble upon a cave covered with paintings and wonder if their ancestors left them there for their enjoyment. (Rev: BL 11/15/00; HBG 3/01; SLJ 10/00)

2755 Taylor, Harriet P. *Ulaq and the Northern Lights* (PS–K). Illus. 1998, Farrar $16.00 (0-374-38063-5). 32pp. A little white fox tries to find out why there are northern lights. He travels across the tundra and asks various animals, among them Seal, Wolf, Polar Bear, and Snowy Owl. (Rev: BL 12/1/98; HBG 3/99; SLJ 1/99)

2756 Teague, Mark. *Pigsty* (PS–3). Illus. 1994, Scholastic $14.95 (0-590-45915-5). 32pp. Even messy Wendell, a pig, resents his friends creating chaos in his room. (Rev: BL 9/15/94; SLJ 10/94*)

2757 Testa, Fulvio. *Time to Get Out* (PS–K). Illus. by author. 1993, Tambourine LB $13.93 (0-688-12908-9). A cumulative story about a boy and several animals that join forces to track down a loud noise they hear on a tropical island. (Rev: SLJ 10/93)

2758 Tews, Susan. *Lizard Sees the World* (K–3). Illus. by George Crespo. 1997, Clarion $15.00 (0-395-72662-X). 32pp. Not content to sit around catching flies, Lizard sets out to see the world. (Rev: BL 11/1/97; HBG 3/98; SLJ 9/97)

2759 Thaler, Mike. *What Could a Hippopotamus Be?* (PS–K). Illus. by Robert Grossman. 1990, Simon & Schuster paper $13.95 (0-671-70847-3). 32pp. A young hippo tries a variety of careers, including fireman and sailor, without success. (Rev: BL 9/15/90)

2760 Tharlet, Eve. *Little Pig, Bigger Trouble* (K–2). Illus. 1992, Picture Book paper $14.95 (0-88708-237-8). Pierre and his friend, the pig Henri, share adventures when they deliver a blackberry cake. (Rev: SLJ 8/92)

2761 Tompert, Ann. *The Hungry Black Bag* (PS–1). Illus. by Jacqueline Chwast. 1999, Houghton $15.00 (0-395-89418-2). 32pp. A goat, who robs animals selling their goods in a market, finally gets his comeuppance. (Rev: BL 5/15/99; HBG 10/99; SLJ 5/99)

2762 Tompert, Ann. *Just a Little Bit* (PS–K). Illus. by Lynn Munsinger. 1993, Houghton $16.00 (0-395-51527-0). 32pp. In this cumulative tale, several animals try to help Mouse balance the scales when he tries to seesaw with Elephant. (Rev: BL 11/1/93; HB 9–10/93; SLJ 12/93)

2763 Tompert, Ann. *Nothing Sticks Like a Shadow* (PS–3). Illus. by Lynn Munsinger. 1988, Houghton paper $7.95 (0-395-47950-9). 32pp. Rabbit tries to get rid of his shadow.

2764 Trivizas, Eugene. *The Three Little Wolves and the Big Bad Pig* (K–4). Illus. by Helen Oxenbury. 1993, Macmillan $17.00 (0-689-50569-8). 32pp. In this role-reversal story, three wolves are menaced by a big, bad pig who knocks their house down with a sledgehammer when he huffing and puffing won't do the trick. (Rev: BCCB 9/93; BL 9/1/93; SLJ 12/93*)

2765 Tryon, Leslie. *Albert's Field Trip* (PS–2). Illus. 1993, Atheneum $16.00 (0-689-31821-9). 32pp. Gary the skunk reports for the school paper what happened during the field trip his fellow animals take to an apple farm. (Rev: BCCB 10/93; BL 9/15/93; HB 9–10/93; SLJ 10/93)

2766 Tryon, Leslie. *Albert's Halloween: The Case of the Stolen Pumpkin* (K–3). Illus. 1998, Simon & Schuster $16.00 (0-689-81136-5). 40pp. In this mystery that uses visual clues, Chief Inspector Albert, a duck, and his animal friends solve a puzzler involving 18 missing pumpkins. (Rev: BL 9/1/98; HBG 3/99; SLJ 9/98)

2767 Tryon, Leslie. *Albert's Play* (K–3). Illus. by author. 1992, Macmillan $13.95 (0-689-31525-2). Albert and other animal children put on a production of the Owl and the Pussycat. (Rev: BCCB 3/92; SLJ 5/92)

2768 Turnbull, Ann. *Too Tired* (K–2). Illus. by Emma C. Clark. 1994, Harcourt $13.95 (0-15-200549-8). 32pp. There is a crisis on the ark when Noah discovers that the sloths are too tired to board. (Rev: BL 3/15/94; SLJ 4/94)

2769 Ungerer, Tomi. *Crictor* (PS–2). Illus. by author. 1958, HarperCollins paper $5.95 (0-06-443044-8). 32pp. A boa constrictor becomes the hero of a small French town after he captures a burglar.

2770 Ungerer, Tomi. *Flix* (2–4). Illus. by author. 1998, Roberts Rinehart $16.95 (1-57098-161-2). When Cotza, a cat, gives birth to a dog, she and her husband are startled but raise young Flix to be their pride and joy. (Rev: HBG 3/99; SLJ 9/98)

2771 Vail, Rachel. *Over the Moon* (K–2). Illus. by Scott Nash. 1998, Orchard $15.95 (0-531-30068-4). 32pp. A creative monkey director is adapting the rhyme "Hey Diddle Diddle" for the stage but has problems getting the cow to jump over the moon. (Rev: BL 9/15/98; HBG 3/99; SLJ 9/98)

2772 Vainio, Pirkko. *The Best of Friends* (PS–K). Illus. 2000, North-South LB $15.88 (0-7358-1151-2). 32pp. Although Hare and Bear are very different, they become good friends in this gentle story. (Rev: BL 6/1–15/00; HBG 10/00; SLJ 10/00)

2773 Van Allsburg, Chris. *Two Bad Ants* (1–4). Illus. by author. 1988, Houghton $17.95 (0-395-48668-8). 32pp. The story of two adventuresome ants. (Rev: BCCB 12/88; BL 10/1/88; SLJ 11/88)

2774 Van Laan, Nancy. *Little Fish, Lost* (PS–K). Illus. by Jane Conteh-Morgan. 1998, Simon & Schuster $15.00 (0-689-81331-7). 32pp. A little fish explores life in an African watering hole as he searches for his mother. (Rev: BL 5/1/98; HBG 10/98; SLJ 4/98)

2775 Van Laan, Nancy. *Possum Come a-Knockin'* (PS–2). Illus. by George Booth. 1990, Knopf LB $14.99 (0-394-92206-9). 28pp. In this cumulative story, many humans and animals ignore the possum when he comes knocking at their door. (Rev: BL 4/15/90; HB 7–8/90*; SLJ 7/90)

2776 Van Laan, Nancy. *Tickle Tum!* (PS). Illus. by Bernadette Pons. 2001, Simon & Schuster $14.95 (0-689-83143-9). 32pp. It takes patience, creativity, and lots of energy to get food into the mouth of obstinate Baby Rabbit. (Rev: BL 2/1/01; SLJ 3/01)

2777 Varley, Susan. *Badger's Parting Gifts* (1–4). Illus. by author. 1984, Morrow paper $5.95 (0-688-11518-7). 32pp. After initial grief, the animals retain happy memories of their dead friend, Badger. (Rev: SLJ 1/00)

2778 Vaughan, Marcia. *Snap!* (PS–2). Illus. by Sascha Hutchinson. 1996, Scholastic $14.95 (0-590-60377-9). 32pp. A young kangaroo plays with other Australian animals until a crocodile spoils their fun. (Rev: BL 7/96; SLJ 4/96)

2779 Velthuijs, Max. *Crocodile's Masterpiece* (K–3). Illus. 1992, Farrar $14.00 (0-374-31658-9). 32pp. Though Crocodile gives Elephant only a blank canvas as a painting, Elephant is able to imagine some of the most beautiful pictures ever. (Rev: BL 3/15/92; SLJ 8/92)

2780 Verboven, Agnes. *Ducks Like to Swim* (PS). Illus. by Anne Westerduin. 1997, Orchard $13.95 (0-531-30054-4). 32pp. Mother Duck quacks for rain so that her babies can go swimming. (Rev: BL 9/1/97; HBG 3/98; SLJ 9/97)

2781 Vincent, Gabrielle. *Ernest and Celestine at the Circus* (K–2). Illus. 1989, Greenwillow LB $15.93 (0-688-08685-3). 32pp. The beloved bear and mouse score a hit when they appear at the circus. (Rev: BL 8/89; SLJ 10/89)

2782 Volkmann, Roy. *Curious Kittens* (PS–1). Illus. 2001, Doubleday $9.95 (0-385-32778-1). 32pp. After seeing a goldfish in his bowl, three little kittens decide they want to swim but find it is harder than it looks. (Rev: BL 2/1/01; SLJ 3/01)

2783 Waber, Bernard. *An Anteater Named Arthur* (PS–2). Illus. by author. 1967, Houghton $16.00 (0-395-20336-8); paper $5.95 (0-395-25936-3). 48pp. A mother anteater despairs of her son Arthur, who has problems very much like those of a young boy.

2784 Waber, Bernard. *Bearsie Bear and the Surprise Sleepover Party* (PS–K). Illus. 1997, Houghton $15.00 (0-395-86450-X). 40pp. A number of animals are given shelter for the night; but when the porcupine tries to bed down, everybody leaves. (Rev: BL 10/1/97; HB 9–10/97; HBG 3/98; SLJ 10/97)

2785 Waber, Bernard. *Bernard* (K–3). Illus. by author. 1986, Houghton paper $8.95 (0-395-42648-0). 48pp. When his owners quarrel over his custody, Bernard, a dog, leaves home.

2786 Waber, Bernard. *Funny, Funny Lyle* (PS–1). Illus. by author. 1987, Houghton $16.00 (0-395-43619-2); paper $5.95 (0-395-60287-4). 40pp. Felicity, mother of Lyle the crocodile, is picked up for shoplifting, but finds her true calling as a nurse. (Rev: BL 8/87; SLJ 12/87)

2787 Waber, Bernard. *The House on East 88th Street* (K–2). Illus. by author. 1973, Houghton $14.95 (0-395-18157-7); paper $5.95 (0-395-19970-0). 48pp. Adventures of a pet crocodile (Lyle) who lives with a family in a New York City brownstone. Other books about Lyle by the same author and publisher: *Lyle, Lyle, Crocodile* (1965); *Lyle and the Birthday Party* (1966); *Lyle Finds His Mother* (1974); *Lovable Lyle* (1977).

2788 Waber, Bernard. *Ira Says Goodbye* (K–2). Illus. 1988, Houghton $15.00 (0-395-48315-8); paper $5.95 (0-395-58413-2). 40pp. Ira is sad because his best friend is moving away. (Rev: BCCB 10/88; BL 9/1/88; SLJ 9/88)

2789 Waber, Bernard. *A Lion Named Shirley Williamson* (PS–2). Illus. 1996, Houghton $15.95 (0-395-80979-7). 40pp. The other lions in the zoo are jealous of the special attention given to the lion named Shirley Williamson. (Rev: BL 9/1/96*; SLJ 12/96*)

2790 Waber, Bernard. *Lyle at the Office* (PS–3). Illus. 1994, Houghton $14.95 (0-395-70563-0). 46pp. Lyle becomes very popular when he spends a day helping out in Mr. Primm's office. (Rev: BL 6/1–15/94; SLJ 9/94*)

2791 Waber, Bernard. *The Mouse That Snored* (PS–3). Illus. 2000, Houghton $15.00 (0-395-97518-2). 32pp. A mouse who has a terrible snore moves into a house where everyone hates noise so much they won't even eat celery. (Rev: BL 8/00; HB 11–12/00; HBG 3/01; SLJ 10/00)

2792 Waber, Bernard. *The Snake: A Very Long Love Story* (PS). Illus. by author. 1978, Houghton LB $7.95 (0-685-02310-9). A long trip brings the snake back home again.

2793 Waber, Bernard. *You Look Ridiculous, Said the Rhinoceros to the Hippopotamus* (K–2). Illus. by author. 1973, Houghton $17.95 (0-395-07156-9); paper $5.95 (0-395-28007-9). 32pp. The hippopotamus is discontented with her shape and imagines herself with many of the appendages of neighboring animals.

2794 Waddell, Martin. *Farmer Duck* (PS–1). Illus. by Helen Oxenbury. 1992, Candlewick $15.99 (1-56402-009-6). 40pp. Farmer Duck does all the work while the farmer stays in bed; then the farm animals decide to take over. (Rev: BCCB 6/92; BL 4/1/92*; SLJ 5/92)

2795 Waddell, Martin. *Good Job, Little Bear* (PS). Illus. by Barbara Firth. 1999, Candlewick $15.99 (0-7636-0736-3). 32pp. While on a walk, Little Bear tries some dangerous stunts, but Big Bear is always there to save him. (Rev: BL 8/99; HB 3–4/99; HBG 10/99; SLJ 5/99)

2796 Waddell, Martin. *The Happy Hedgehog Band* (PS–1). Illus. by Jill Barton. 1992, Candlewick $15.99 (1-56402-011-8). 32pp. As a member of the Hedgehog Band, Harry teaches other animals how to make music. (Rev: BL 5/15/92; SLJ 6/92)

2797 Waddell, Martin. *Harriet and the Crocodiles* (1–3). Illus. by Mark Burgess. 1984, Little, Brown $11.95 (0-316-91622-6). Harriet loses her pet crocodile and sets out to find him.

2798 Waddell, Martin. *Let's Go Home, Little Bear* (PS–K). Illus. by Barbara Firth. 1993, Candlewick $15.99 (1-56402-131-9). 32pp. Little Bear is frightened of the noises he hears in the woods, so Big Bear carries him home. (Rev: BL 5/1/93; HB 3–4/93; SLJ 3/93)

2799 Waddell, Martin. *Little Mo* (PS–2). Illus. by Jill Barton. 1993, Candlewick $14.95 (1-56402-211-0). A small polar bear tries sliding on the ice but has problems keeping her balance. (Rev: SLJ 1/94)

2800 Waddell, Martin. *Mimi and the Dream House* (PS–2). Illus. by Leo Hartas. 1998, Candlewick paper $3.99 (0-7636-0387-5). A little mouse named Mimi constructs the house of her dreams. (Rev: BL 4/15/98; SLJ 7/98)

2801 Waddell, Martin. *Mimi and the Picnic* (PS–K). Illus. by Leo Hartas. 1998, Candlewick paper $3.99 (0-7636-0587-5). 32pp. During a family picnic, Hugo, Mimi the mouse's younger brother, falls into the pudding bowl and everyone searches frantically to find him. (Rev: BL 4/15/98)

2802 Waddell, Martin. *Owl Babies* (PS–1). Illus. by Patrick Benson. 1992, Candlewick $15.99 (1-56402-101-7). 32pp. Three small owls, left alone by their mother, wonder if she is coming back. (Rev: BL 12/1/92; HB 3–4/93; SLJ 12/92)

2803 Waddell, Martin. *You and Me, Little Bear* (PS–K). Illus. by Barbara Firth. 1996, Candlewick $15.99 (1-56402-879-8). 32pp. Little Bear doesn't realize how tiring household chores can be when he volunteers to help Big Bear. (Rev: BL 10/1/96; SLJ 11/96)

2804 Waddell, Martin. *Yum, Yum, Yummy* (PS–1). Illus. by John Bendall-Brunello. 1998, Candlewick paper $3.29 (0-7636-0479-8). Three cubs, who are gathering honey for Mummy, are bullied by Guzzley Bear but saved by Mummy. (Rev: HBG 10/98; SLJ 7/98)

2805 Wagner, Jenny. *Motor Bill and the Lovely Caroline* (K–3). Illus. by Ron Brooks. 1995, Ticknor $14.95 (0-395-71547-4). 32pp. Bill, a donkey, is happy when Caroline, a goat, agrees to go riding with him. (Rev: BL 1/15/95; SLJ 4/95)

2806 Wagner, Karen. *Bravo, Mildred and Ed!* (PS–3). Illus. by Janet Pedersen. 2000, Walker $17.85 (0-8027-8734-7); paper $17.85 (0-8027-8735-5). Although mice Mildred and Ed enjoy doing things together, they also learn to be independent in this charming tale. (Rev: HBG 3/01; SLJ 9/00)

2807 Wagner, Karen. *A Friend Like Ed* (PS–1). Illus. by Janet Pedersen. 1998, Walker LB $16.85 (0-8027-8663-4). 32pp. Mouse Mildred is getting tired of her friend Ed's antics, but once she cultivates the friendship of bossy, overbearing Pearl instead, she decides that Ed isn't so bad after all. (Rev: BL 9/15/98; HBG 3/99; SLJ 11/98)

2808 Wahl, Jan. *The Field Mouse and the Dinosaur Named Sue* (PS–2). Illus. by Bob Doucet. 2000, Scholastic $12.95 (0-439-09984-6). 32pp. When paleontologists take the dinosaur bone that was once part of his home to the Field Museum in Chicago, Mouse sets out to find the bone they stole. (Rev: BCCB 9/00; BL 5/15/00; HBG 10/00; SLJ 8/00)

2809 Wahl, Jan. *Three Pandas* (PS–1). Illus. by Naava. 2000, Boyds Mills $15.95 (1-56397-749-4). 32pp. Three little pandas have a series of misadventures when they explore beyond their bamboo forest; so they decide to head back home. (Rev: BL 2/15/00; HBG 10/00; SLJ 5/00)

2810 Waite, Judy. *Mouse, Look Out!* (PS–1). Illus. by Norma Burgin. 1998, Dutton $15.99 (0-525-42031-2). 32pp. A little mouse is enjoying a bright autumn day totally unaware that he is being stalked by a big black cat. (Rev: BCCB 11/98; BL 10/1/98; HBG 3/99; SLJ 12/98)

2811 Wallace, Karen. *City Pig* (PS–3). Illus. by Lydia Monks. 2000, Orchard $15.95 (0-531-30252-0). 32pp. Elegant, sophisticated Dolores, a pig, finds her big-city existence unsatisfying and exchanges it for life with country pigs who enjoy simple things. (Rev: BL 2/15/00; HBG 10/00; SLJ 3/00)

2812 Wallace, Nancy E. *Apples, Apples, Apples* (K–2). Illus. 2000, Winslow $15.95 (1-890817-19-8). 40pp. When a rabbit family goes to an orchard to pick apples, they learn a lot about the fruit, the varieties, and how they grow. (Rev: BL 10/15/00; HBG 3/01; SLJ 9/00)

2813 Wallace, Nancy E. *A Taste of Honey* (PS–2). Illus. 2000, Winslow $16.95 (1-890817-51-1). 32pp. Little bear Lily asks Poppy where honey comes from, and his answers trace the story of honey from the jar back to the bees. (Rev: BL 2/15/01)

2814 Walsh, Ellen S. *For Pete's Sake* (PS–1). Illus. 1998, Harcourt $15.00 (0-15-200324-X). Pete is an alligator who thinks he is a flamingo just like all his feathered friends — until he accidentally meets some other alligators. (Rev: BL 10/15/98; HB 11–12/98; HBG 3/99; SLJ 11/98)

2815 Walsh, Ellen S. *Hop Jump* (PS–1). Illus. 1993, Harcourt $13.95 (0-15-292871-5). 32pp. Most of the other frogs enjoy hopping, but Betsy prefers to dance. (Rev: BL 11/1/93; HB 11–12/93; SLJ 10/93)

2816 Walsh, Ellen S. *Mouse Paint* (PS–K). Illus. 1989, Harcourt $14.00 (0-15-256025-4). 32pp. Three mice paint themselves as camouflage and find they like their new look. (Rev: BL 5/15/89; HB 7–8/89; SLJ 9/89)

2817 Walsh, Ellen S. *Pip's Magic* (PS–3). Illus. 1994, Harcourt $14.00 (0-15-292850-2). 32pp. By traveling through shadowy woods and a black night to visit a wizard for help, Pip, a salamander, cures himself of his fear of the dark. (Rev: BCCB 9/94; BL 10/15/94; SLJ 11/94)

2818 Walsh, Ellen S. *Samantha* (PS–1). Illus. 1996, Harcourt $14.00 (0-15-252264-6). 32pp. Samantha, a mouse, doesn't want to become too dependent on the protection that her fairy godmother gives her. (Rev: BCCB 6/96; BL 2/15/96; SLJ 5/96)

2819 Walsh, Ellen S. *You Silly Goose* (PS–1). Illus. by author. 1992, Harcourt $13.95 (0-15-299865-9). Lulu, a goose, mistakes George, a mouse, for the fox that has been reported in the neighborhood. (Rev: HB 1–2/93; SLJ 10/92)

2820 Walters, Catherine. *Are You There, Baby Bear?* (PS–1). Illus. 1999, Dutton $15.99 (0-525-46161-2). 32pp. Alfie, worried when the family baby fails to arrive, becomes lost in the snow looking for it, but when he gets back to the family cave, he finds that his mother has had twins. (Rev: BL 10/15/99; HBG 3/00; SLJ 12/99)

2821 Walton, Rick. *The Bear Came Over to My House* (PS–1). Illus. by James Warhola. 2001, Putnam $14.99 (0-399-23415-2). 32pp. A rhyming, humorous story that allows the reader to guess what will happen next when a bear pays a visit. (Rev: BL 3/15/01)

2822 Walton, Rick. *Once There Was a Bull . . . (frog)* (K–3). Illus. by Greg Hally. 1995, Gibbs Smith $15.95 (0-87905-652-5). 32pp. This clever story about a bullfrog searching for his lost hop uses the splitting of compound words to create different perceptions. (Rev: BL 12/15/95)

2823 Ward, Nick. *Farmer George and the Fieldmice* (PS–1). Illus. by author. 2000, Pavilion $13.95 (1-86205-203-4). Farmyard animals save Mrs. Fieldmouse's house by alerting Farmer George on the combine harvester just in time. Also use *Farmer George and the Lost Chick* (1999). (Rev: SLJ 2/00)

2824 Waterton, Betty. *A Salmon for Simon* (K–3). Illus. by Ann Blades. 1991, Salem paper $14.95 (0-88899-107-X). 32pp. A small Canadian Indian has a great adventure with a live salmon.

2825 Watson, Wendy. *Tales for a Winter's Eve* (2–3). Illus. by author. 1988, Farrar $13.00 (0-374-37373-6); paper $4.95 (0-374-47419-2). 32pp. Freddie Fox breaks his skis, and family and friends cheer him with stories. (Rev: BCCB 11/88; BL 11/15/88; SLJ 2/89)

2826 Watts, Bernadette. *Happy Birthday, Harvey Hare!* (PS–K). Illus. 1998, North-South $15.95 (1-55858-897-3); paper $15.88 (1-55858-898-1). 32pp. Postman Harvey, a rabbit, thinks no one will come to his birthday party, but he is overjoyed when all his friends attend as a surprise. (Rev: BL 6/1–15/98; HBG 3/99; SLJ 5/98)

2827 Watts, Bernadette. *Harvey Hare: Postman Extraordinaire* (PS–K). Illus. 1997, North-South LB $15.88 (1-55858-688-1). 32pp. Because Harvey Hare is such a devoted mail carrier, his friends give him a present to solve his problems with the weather. (Rev: BL 3/15/97; SLJ 3/97)

2828 Wegman, William. *My Town* (K–4). Illus. 1998, Hyperion $16.95 (0-7868-0410-6). 40pp. Weimaraner Chip discovers that he can use the photos he has taken around town for a school report on community helpers. (Rev: BL 12/1/98; HBG 3/99; SLJ 1/99)

2829 Weigelt, Udo. *The Strongest Mouse in the World* (PS–1). Trans. by J. Alison James. Illus. by Nicolas D'Aujourd'Hui. 1998, North-South LB $15.88 (1-55858-896-5). A mouse named Lissie is so impressed with her strength that she decides to wrestle the most powerful animal in the forest, Albert Bear. (Rev: BCCB 5/98; BL 4/15/98; SLJ 6/98)

2830 Weigelt, Udo. *Who Stole the Gold?* (PS–1). Trans. from German by J. Alison James. Illus. by Julia Gukova. 2000, North-South LB $15.88 (0-7358-1373-6). Someone has stolen Hamster's gold and his friend Hedgehog offers to help find the thief. (Rev: HBG 3/01; SLJ 1/01)

2831 Weiss, Leatie. *My Teacher Sleeps in School* (K–2). Illus. by Ellen Weiss. 1985, Puffin paper $5.99 (0-14-050559-8). 32pp. Because their teacher is always there, two elephant children believe their teacher lives in school.

2832 Wellington, Monica. *Bunny's Rainbow Day* (PS). Illus. 1999, Dutton $7.99 (0-525-46047-0). 16pp. A sturdy board book in which a young bunny delights in everyday events such as hopping through the flowers. (Rev: BL 2/1/99; SLJ 2/99)

2833 Wells, Rosemary. *Bunny Money* (PS–1). Illus. 1997, Dial $14.89 (0-8037-2147-1). 32pp. Before bunnies Max and Ruby can buy a birthday present for Grandma, they spend their money in all sorts of unforeseen ways. (Rev: BL 7/97*; SLJ 7/97*)

2834 Wells, Rosemary. *Max Cleans Up* (PS–3). Illus. 2000, Viking $15.99 (0-670-89218-1). 32pp. Max's idea of cleaning up his room is to stuff everything into the front pocket of his overalls in this story about a delightful rabbit. (Rev: BL 2/1/01; SLJ 12/00)

2835 Wells, Rosemary. *Max's Bath* (PS). Illus. by author. Series: Max and Ruby Board Books. 1998, Dial $5.99 (0-8037-2266-4). In this revised board book, Max the bunny enjoys a bath. Others in this series are *Max's Ride* and *Max's Toys*. (Rev: HBG 10/98; SLJ 7/98)

2836 Wells, Rosemary. *Read to Your Bunny* (PS). Illus. by author. 1998, Scholastic $7.95 (0-590-30284-1). Using a cast of bunnies, the author shows that reading can be fun anywhere. (Rev: BL 5/1/98; HBG 10/98; SLJ 3/98)

2837 Wells, Rosemary. *Timothy Goes to School* (PS–K). Illus. 2000, Viking $15.99 (0-670-89182-7). 40pp. Timothy the raccoon fails to fit in during his first day at school until he meets Violet, another outsider. (Rev: BL 6/1–15/00; HBG 3/01)

2838 Weninger, Brigitte. *The Elf's Hat* (K–3). Trans. by J. Alison James. Illus. by John A. Rowe. 2000, North-South LB $15.88 (0-7358-1255-1). 36pp. When an elf loses his hat in the forest, a lot of small animals use it as a home. (Rev: BL 5/1/00; HBG 10/00; SLJ 7/00)

2839 Weninger, Brigitte. *What Have You Done, Davy?* (PS–2). Trans. by Rosemary Lanning. Illus. by Eve Tharlet. 1996, North-South LB $15.88 (1-55858-582-6). 32pp. Davy, a young rabbit, is having a terrible day and leaves a trail of destruction wherever he goes. (Rev: BL 4/15/96; SLJ 7/96)

2840 Weninger, Brigitte. *What's the Matter, Davy?* (PS–1). Illus. by Eve Tharlet. 1998, North-South LB $15.88 (1-55858-900-7). 32pp. Davy, a little rabbit, is distraught when he loses his pet toy rabbit. (Rev: BCCB 6/98; BL 3/15/98; HBG 10/98; SLJ 8/98)

2841 Weninger, Brigitte. *Where Have You Gone, Davy?* (PS–2). Trans. by Rosemary Lanning. Illus. by Eve Tharlet. 1996, North-South LB $15.88 (1-55858-665-2). 24pp. When bunny Davy is wrongfully accused of breaking a bowl, he decides to run away. (Rev: BL 12/1/96; SLJ 1/97)

2842 Weninger, Brigitte. *Why Are You Fighting, Davy?* (1–3). Trans. by Rosemary Lanning. Illus. by Eve Tharlet. 1999, North-South LB $15.88 (0-7358-1074-5). 32pp. Davy the rabbit quarrels with his best friend and later makes up when he gets tired of being alone. (Rev: BL 11/1/99; HBG 3/00; SLJ 11/99)

2843 Weninger, Brigitte. *Will You Mind the Baby, Davy?* (K–3). Illus. by Eve Tharlet. 1997, North-South LB $15.88 (1-55858-732-2). 32pp. Davy the bunny finds that his baby sister needs a strong older brother to help and protect her. (Rev: BL 5/15/97; SLJ 7/97)

2844 West, Colin. *"Buzz, Buzz, Buzz," Went the Bumblebee* (PS–1). Illus. by author. 1996, Candlewick $9.99 (1-56402-681-7). A simple repetitive story featuring silly animals and a bee that journeys from one setting to another. (Rev: SLJ 4/96)

2845 West, Judy. *Have You Got My Purr?* (PS–K). Illus. by Tim Warnes. 2000, Dutton $15.99 (0-525-46390-9). 32pp. Kitten has lost her purr and questions several farmyard animals about it but each makes its own special sound that is not a purr. (Rev: BL 7/00; HBG 10/00; SLJ 7/00)

2846 Weston, Martha. *Tuck in the Pool* (PS–1). Illus. 1995, Clarion $12.95 (0-395-65479-3). 32pp. Tuck, a little pig, doesn't enjoy being in the water and refuses to get dunked. (Rev: BCCB 11/95; BL 11/15/95; SLJ 2/96)

2847 Whippo, Walt. *Little White Duck* (PS–3). Illus. by Joan Paley. 2000, Little, Brown $13.95 (0-316-03227-1). 32pp. The old song about Little White Duck and other animals enjoying a pond is given a fresh treatment with vibrant collage illustrations. (Rev: BCCB 5/00; BL 2/1/00; HBG 10/00; SLJ 4/00)

2848 White, Carolyn. *The Adventure of Louey and Frank* (PS–1). Illus. by Laura Dronzek. 2001, Greenwillow LB $14.89 (0-688-16605-9). 24pp. Louey, a rabbit, and Frank, a bear, encounter a large object on a boating adventure that turns out to be a whale. (Rev: BCCB 3/01; BL 1/1–15/01; SLJ 3/01)

2849 White, Kathryn. *When They Fight* (PS–K). Illus. by Cliff Wright. 2000, Winslow $14.95 (1-890817-46-5). 32pp. A young badger is terrorized and runs away when his parents quarrel. (Rev: BL 4/15/00; HBG 3/01; SLJ 6/00)

2850 Whittle, Emily. *Sailor Cats* (PS–1). Illus. by Jeri Burdick. 1993, Simon & Schuster $14.00 (0-671-79933-9). 28pp. Two adventurous cats, Ping and Pong, are rescued at sea by friendly dolphins. (Rev: BL 9/1/93; SLJ 3/94)

2851 Whybrow, Ian. *Little Wolf's Book of Badness* (2–4). Illus. by Tony Ross. 1999, Carolrhoda LB $12.95 (1-57505-410-8). 132pp. In this hilarious story, Little Wolf is too well behaved so he is sent to Cunning College to learn how to be bad. (Rev: HBG 3/00; SLJ 11/99)

2852 Whybrow, Ian. *Parcel for Stanley* (PS–2). Illus. by Sally Hobson. 1998, Levinson $14.95 (1-899607-53-6). A simple story in which a rabbit, who has a sorry reputation, shines after he learns a few magic tricks. (Rev: SLJ 3/99)

2853 Wickstrom, Lois. *Oliver: A Story About Adoption* (PS–3). Illus. by Priscilla Marden. 1991, Our Child Pr. $14.95 (0-9611872-5-5). When lizard Oliver receives a reprimand from his adoptive father, he thinks his real parents would behave differently. (Rev: SLJ 2/92)

2854 Wiesmuller, Dieter. *The Adventures of Marco and Polo* (PS–3). Trans. from German by Beate Peter. Illus. by author. 2000, Walker $16.95 (0-8027-8729-0). First Marco Monkey visits Polo Penguin's chilly home, then Polo joins Marco in his tropical habitat, and both realize that each should live where he is most comfortable. (Rev: HBG 3/01; SLJ 7/00)

2855 Wiesner, David. *Tuesday* (PS–2). Illus. 1991, Houghton $17.00 (0-395-55113-7). 32pp. Frogs have a wonderful time on Tuesday. Will the pigs have as great a time one week later? Caldecott Medal winner, 1992. (Rev: BCCB 5/91; BL 5/1/91; SLJ 5/91*)

2856 Wild, Margaret. *Rosie and Tortoise* (PS). Illus. by Ron Brooks. 1999, DK $14.95 (0-7894-2630-7). Rosie, a little hare, is afraid to hold her tiny premature brother, but her father reassures her that Bobby will grow up to be as strong as she is. (Rev: BL 12/1/99; HBG 3/00; SLJ 9/99)

2857 Wild, Margaret. *Tom Goes to Kindergarten* (PS–1). Illus. by David Legge. 2000, Albert Whitman $15.95 (0-8075-8012-0). 32pp. Mr. and Mrs.

Panda overstay their welcome when they accompany their son Tom on his first day in school. (Rev: BL 5/1/00; HBG 10/00; SLJ 4/00)

2858 Wilhelm, Hans. *More Bunny Trouble* (PS–1). Illus. by author. 1989, Scholastic paper $4.99 (0-590-41590-5). 32pp. Ralph is tapped to baby-sit his bunny sister, but he lets her get out of sight and lost. (Rev: BL 3/1/89; SLJ 5/89)

2859 Wilhelm, Hans. *The Royal Raven* (PS–3). Illus. 1996, Scholastic $15.95 (0-590-54337-7). 32pp. A raven named Crawford tries to become special by changing his appearance. (Rev: BL 3/15/96; SLJ 7/96)

2860 Wilhelm, Hans. *Tyrone the Horrible* (PS–2). Illus. by author. 1988, Scholastic paper $4.99 (0-590-41472-0). 32pp. Tyrone the terrible bully dinosaur is making Boland's prehistoric life a misery. (Rev: BL 9/1/88; SLJ 12/88)

2861 Williams, Garth. *Benjamin's Treasure* (PS–1). Illus. by Rosemary Wells and Garth Williams. 2001, HarperCollins LB $15.89 (0-06-028741-1). 32pp. When Benjamin, a rabbit, is shipwrecked on a deserted island, he finds a treasure chest but realizes his greatest treasure is his wife back home. (Rev: BL 2/15/01)

2862 Willis, Jeanne. *What Did I Look Like When I Was a Baby?* (PS–3). Illus. by Tony Ross. 2000, Putnam $15.99 (0-399-23595-7). 32pp. Young animals including a human, a hippo, and a frog are surprised to learn what they looked like as babies in this rollicking picture book. (Rev: BL 12/15/00; HBG 3/01; SLJ 11/00)

2863 Wilson, Sarah. *Good Zap, Little Grog* (PS–2). Illus. by Susan Meddaugh. 1995, Candlewick $16.99 (1-56402-286-2). 32pp. In a strange new world, the reader is introduced to such creatures as the Ooglet, Froozel, and the Glipneep. (Rev: BCCB 12/95; BL 10/15/95; SLJ 1/96)

2864 Wilson-Max, Ken. *Max* (PS). Illus. by author. 1998, Hyperion $12.95 (0-7868-0412-2). A flap book in which an African American boy plays with his two friends, a purple pig and a blue elephant. (Rev: HBG 3/99; SLJ 3/99)

2865 Winthrop, Elizabeth. *Bear and Roly-Poly* (K–3). Illus. by Patience Brewster. 1996, Holiday $15.95 (0-8234-1197-4). 32pp. Nora brings Bear a baby sister in the form of Roly-Poly panda. (Rev: BL 3/1/96; SLJ 5/96)

2866 Winthrop, Elizabeth. *Dumpy La Rue* (PS–1). Illus. by Betsy Lewin. 2001, Holt $15.95 (0-8050-6385-4). 32pp. Piggy Dumpy La Rue won't take no for an answer when his family and other barnyard animals tell him it isn't proper for pigs to dance. (Rev: BL 3/15/01)

2867 Wolf, Jake. *What You Do Is Easy, What I Do Is Hard* (2–3). Illus. by Anna Dewdney. 1996, Greenwillow $15.00 (0-688-13440-8). 24pp. Squirrel thinks his life is tougher than that of other animals, but in time he finds he is wrong. (Rev: BL 12/15/96; SLJ 12/96)

2868 Wood, Audrey. *Jubal's Wish* (PS–3). Illus. by Don Wood. 2000, Scholastic $15.95 (0-439-16964-X). 32pp. Jubal wants his friends to join him on a picnic but they are too busy to attend in this story about friendship. (Rev: BL 12/1/00; HBG 3/01; SLJ 10/00)

2869 Wood, Audrey. *Little Penguin's Tale* (PS–2). Illus. 1989, Harcourt $13.95 (0-15-246475-1). 32pp. Little Penguin's escapades result in his being swallowed by a whale. (Rev: BL 11/15/89)

2870 Wood, Audrey. *Oh My Baby Bear!* (PS–1). Illus. 1990, Harcourt $13.95 (0-15-257698-3). 32pp. Baby Bear gradually learns to take care of himself. (Rev: BL 11/1/90; SLJ 11/90)

2871 Wood, Audrey. *Silly Sally* (PS). Illus. 1992, Harcourt $16.00 (0-15-274428-2). 32pp. This delightful nonsense book tells of Silly Sally and her trip into town walking backwards and upside down. (Rev: BCCB 6/92; BL 3/15/92*; SLJ 4/92)

2872 Wood, Douglas. *Old Turtle* (K–4). Illus. by Cheng-Khee Chee. 1991, Pfeifer $17.95 (0-938586-48-3). 48pp. Wise Old Turtle asks people to save the world by experiencing "God in one another . . . and in the beauty of all the earth." (Rev: BL 8/92; SLJ 6/92)

2873 Wood, Douglas. *What Dads Can't Do* (PS–2). Illus. by Doug Cushman. 2000, Simon & Schuster $14.00 (0-689-82620-6). An amusing picture book in which a baby dinosaur lists all the things that regular people can do but dads can't, like crossing the street without holding hands or reading a book by themselves. (Rev: HBG 10/00; SLJ 5/00)

2874 Wood, Douglas. *What Moms Can't Do* (PS). Illus. by Doug Cushman. 2001, Simon & Schuster $14.00 (0-689-83358-X). A young dinosaur helps his mother with all her chores but there is one thing he can't duplicate and that is her love for him. (Rev: SLJ 3/01)

2875 Wormell, Christopher. *Blue Rabbit and Friends* (K–2). Illus. 2000, Penguin $14.99 (0-8037-2499-3). 32pp. While looking for a new home for himself, Blue Rabbit is able to relocate some of his animal friends into more suitable lodgings. (Rev: BL 1/1–15/00; HBG 10/00; SLJ 2/00)

2876 Wormell, Christopher. *Blue Rabbit and the Runaway Wheel* (PS). Illus. by author. 2001, Penguin $15.99 (0-8037-2508-6). Blue Rabbit has a bicycle accident in which he loses one of the wheels, which then whizzes through the neighborhood knocking down animals and objects. (Rev: SLJ 2/01)

2877 Wormell, Christopher. *Puff-Puff, Chugga-Chugga* (PS–2). Illus. 2001, Simon & Schuster $15.00 (0-689-83986-3). 32pp. A tiny train gets overloaded when it picks up a walrus, a bear, and an elephant. (Rev: BL 2/15/01)

2878 Wormell, Mary. *Hilda Hen's Scary Night* (PS–K). Illus. 1996, Harcourt $14.00 (0-15-200990-6). 32pp. In the morning, Hilda Hen sets out to find the creatures that had frightened her the night before. (Rev: BL 9/15/96; SLJ 10/96)

2879 Wormell, Mary. *Hilda Hen's Search* (PS–1). Illus. 1994, Harcourt $13.95 (0-15-200069-0). 32pp. Hilda Hen wanders the barnyard looking for a suitable place to lay her eggs. (Rev: BL 12/1/94; SLJ 11/94)

2880 Wormell, Mary. *Why Not?* (PS–1). Illus. by author. 2000, Farrar $15.00 (0-374-38422-3). A curious kitten who always answers his mother's "Don'ts" with "Why not?" finally learns the reason why. (Rev: BCCB 3/00; HBG 10/00; SLJ 3/00)

2881 Wright, Betty R. *Pet Detectives* (PS–3). Illus. by Kevin O'Malley. 1999, BridgeWater LB $15.95 (0-8167-4952-3). When a burglar breaks into their home, Kitty, a cat, and Belle, a dog, decide that they must work together to catch him. (Rev: SLJ 5/99)

2882 Yaccarino, Dan. *Deep in the Jungle* (PS–3). Illus. 2000, Simon & Schuster $16.00 (0-689-82235-9). 40pp. When an arrogant lion is duped by a hunter into becoming a circus performer he takes revenge by eating his captor and returning to the jungle. (Rev: BCCB 3/00*; BL 3/1/00; HB 3–4/00; HBG 10/00; SLJ 2/00)

2883 Yang, Belle. *Chili-Chili-Chin-Chin* (PS–K). Illus. 1999, Harcourt $15.00 (0-15-202006-3). 32pp. An animal explains to passers-by, who mistake him for other species, that he is a donkey named Chili-Chili-Chin-Chin — the name given to him by an attentive little boy. (Rev: BL 7/99; HBG 10/99; SLJ 6/99)

2884 Yee, Patrick. *Winter Rabbit* (PS). Illus. by author. 1994, Viking $13.99 (0-670-85353-6). A bear and a squirrel build a huge snow bunny before they begin their winter sleep. (Rev: SLJ 7/94)

2885 Yee, Wong H. *Big Black Bear* (PS–K). Illus. 1993, Houghton $15.00 (0-395-66359-8). 32pp. An ill-mannered young bear who bullies a little girl gets a severe bawling out from his mother. (Rev: BL 11/1/93; SLJ 10/93)

2886 Yee, Wong H. *Hamburger Heaven* (PS–2). Illus. by author. 1999, Houghton $15.00 (0-395-87548-X). When it appears that the diner at which she works might close, Pinky Pig designs a new menu to save her job. (Rev: HBG 10/99; SLJ 5/99)

2887 Yee, Wong H. *Here Come Trainmice!* (PS). 2000, Houghton $4.95 (0-395-98401-7). 14pp. This board book describes the different cars of a train, all of which are populated by expressive mice, and all the parts of a train ride. A companion volume about trucks is *Hooray for Truckmice!* (2000). (Rev: SLJ 11/00)

2888 Yee, Wong H. *Mrs. Brown Went to Town* (PS–2). Illus. 1996, Houghton $14.95 (0-395-75282-5). 32pp. A group of domestic animals move into Mrs. Brown's house when the woman is sent to the hospital. (Rev: BL 4/1/96; SLJ 7/96)

2889 Yee, Wong H. *The Officer's Ball* (PS–2). Illus. 1997, Houghton $14.95 (0-395-81182-1). 32pp. While carrying out his duties as a police officer, Sergeant Hippo practices his newly learned dance steps for the big officers ball. (Rev: BL 3/15/97; SLJ 5/97)

2890 Yolen, Jane. *Off We Go!* (PS–K). Illus. by Laurel Molk. 2000, Little, Brown $12.95 (0-316-90228-4). 32pp. A bouncy picture book about several animals, all of whom are on their way to visit their grandmothers. (Rev: BCCB 3/00; BL 3/15/00; HBG 10/00; SLJ 5/00)

2891 Yolen, Jane. *Picnic with Piggins* (K–3). Illus. by Jane Dyer. 1988, Harcourt paper $7.00 (0-15-261535-0). 32pp. Piggins, the pig butler, solves the mystery of the missing Rexy, one of the children of the house. Also use the first story about the Reynard butler, *Piggins* (1987); and *Piggins and the Royal Wedding* (1989). (Rev: BCCB 5/88; BL 4/1/88; HB 7–8/88)

2892 Yorinks, Arthur. *Hey, Al* (2–4). Illus. 1986, Farrar $17.00 (0-374-33060-3); paper $5.95 (0-374-42985-5). 32pp. Eddie the dog wants to change his life, but when a bird takes him and Al the janitor to a bird-inhabited island, Eddie isn't quite so sure. Caldecott Medal winner, 1987. (Rev: BL 1/1/87; SLJ 3/87)

2893 Young, Ed. *Cat and Rat: The Legend of the Chinese Zodiac* (1–4). Illus. 1995, Holt $15.95 (0-8050-2977-X). 32pp. The story of the 12 signs of the Chinese zodiac and how each animal achieved its place. (Rev: BCCB 11/95; BL 11/1/95*; SLJ 12/95) [133.5]

2894 Zalben, Jane Breskin. *Miss Violet's Shining Day* (PS–1). Illus. 1995, Boyds Mills $14.95 (1-56397-234-4). 26pp. A timid bunny named Miss Violet blooms after she learns to play a trombone. (Rev: BL 8/95; SLJ 4/95)

2895 Zalben, Jane Breskin. *Pearl Plants a Tree* (PS–2). Illus. 1995, Simon & Schuster paper $14.00 (0-689-80034-7). 32pp. A little lamb learns from her grandfather and plants an apple seed that later sprouts. (Rev: BL 11/15/95; SLJ 1/96)

2896 Ziefert, Harriet. *Animal Music* (PS–1). Illus. by Donald Saaf. 1999, Houghton $15.00 (0-395-95294-8). 48pp. Several animal musicians perform in two shows — one a marching band concert and the other a country jamboree. (Rev: BL 10/15/99; HBG 3/00; SLJ 10/99)

2897 Ziefert, Harriet. *Elemenopeo* (PS–3). Illus. by David Saaf. 1998, Houghton $15.00 (0-395-90493-5). 32pp. A whimsical story about a cat named Elemenopeo (L-M-N-O-P-O) and its daily activities, which include painting. (Rev: BL 8/98; HBG 3/99; SLJ 9/98)

2898 Ziefert, Harriet. *Pumpkin Pie* (PS–K). Illus. by Donald Dreifuss. 2000, Houghton $15.00 (0-618-04883-9). 32pp. A troublemaking goat named Pumpkin Pie causes problems because of her bad behavior at a county fair. (Rev: BL 12/1/00; HBG 3/01; SLJ 10/00)

2899 Ziefert, Harriet. *Pushkin Meets the Bundle* (PS–1). Illus. by Donald Saaf. 1998, Simon & Schuster $16.00 (0-689-81413-5). 40pp. The life of the dog Pushkin changes with the arrival of a new baby, also known as "the bundle." (Rev: BCCB 5/98; BL 2/1/98; HBG 10/98; SLJ 6/98)

2900 Ziefert, Harriet. *Pushkin Minds the Bundle* (PS–K). Illus. by Donald Saaf. 2000, Simon & Schuster $16.00 (0-689-83216-8). 32pp. Although dog Pushkin is jealous of the attention awarded to Pierre, the new baby referred to as "the Bundle," it is Pushkin who saves Pierre when he wanders off. (Rev: BCCB 5/00; BL 9/1/00; HBG 10/00; SLJ 7/00)

2901 Ziefert, Harriet. *Wee G* (PS–K). Illus. by Donald Saaf. 1997, Simon & Schuster $15.00 (0-689-81064-3). 32pp. In double-page spreads, this simple picture book tells how a little cat named Wee G. gets lost on the way home. (Rev: BL 4/15/97; SLJ 6/97)

2902 Zolotow, Charlotte. *Mr. Rabbit and the Lovely Present* (PS–3). Illus. by Maurice Sendak. 1977, HarperCollins paper $5.95 (0-06-443020-0). 32pp. A little girl meets Mr. Rabbit, and together they find the perfect birthday gift for her mother.

Realistic Stories

ADVENTURE STORIES

2903 Ackerman, Karen. *Bingleman's Midway* (1–4). Illus. by Barry Moser. 1995, Boyds Mills $14.95 (1-56397-366-9). 32pp. A boy becomes so intrigued with a traveling midway that he decides to run away from home and join it. (Rev: BL 10/15/95; SLJ 12/95)

2904 Ahlberg, Allan. *It Was a Dark and Stormy Night* (K–3). Illus. by Janet Ahlberg. 1994, Viking $13.99 (0-670-85159-0). 32pp. A young captive of robbers escapes in the confusion caused by their acting out a story that he has told them. (Rev: BCCB 7–8/94; BL 5/1/94)

2905 Aller, Susan Bivin. *Emma and the Night Dogs* (K–3). Illus. by Marni Backer. 1997, Albert Whitman LB $14.95 (0-8075-1993-6). 32pp. Emma is able to locate a boy who is lost in the woods. (Rev: BCCB 7–8/97; BL 9/15/97; SLJ 5/97)

2906 Arnold, Marsha Diane. *The Bravest of Us All* (PS–3). Illus. by Brad Sneed. 2000, Dial $15.99 (0-8037-2409-8). 32pp. When a tornado comes, young Ruby Jane helps her older sister to take shelter. (Rev: BCCB 6/00; BL 5/1/00; HBG 10/00; SLJ 5/00)

2907 Axtell, David. *We're Going on a Lion Hunt* (PS–1). Illus. 2000, Holt $15.95 (0-8050-6159-2). 32pp. In this variation on the familiar chant, two African girls go out on a lion hunt. (Rev: BCCB 5/00; BL 2/15/00; HBG 10/00; SLJ 5/00)

2908 Bailey, Linda. *When Addie Was Scared* (1–3). Illus. by Wendy Bailey. 1999, Kids Can $14.95 (1-55074-431-3). 32pp. Though Addie is a fearful, timid child, she summons up great courage to frighten off a hawk when it attacks her grandmother's chickens. (Rev: BL 11/15/99; HBG 3/00; SLJ 11/99)

2909 Beard, Darleen Bailey. *Twister* (PS–3). Illus. by Nancy Carpenter. 1999, Farrar $16.00 (0-374-37977-7). 32pp. While two children hide in a cellar near their trailer home during a tornado, their mother ventures out to help an elderly neighbor. (Rev: BL 2/1/99; HBG 10/99; SLJ 3/99)

2910 Blades, Ann. *Back to the Cabin* (K–3). Illus. 1997, Orca paper $6.95 (1-55143-051-7). 32pp. Activities like swimming and fishing take the place of TV watching when two brothers spend a summer in a cabin by a lake. (Rev: BL 6/1–15/97)

2911 Bodkin, Odds. *The Banshee Train* (1–4). Illus. by Ted Rose. 1995, Clarion $14.95 (0-395-69426-

4). 32pp. Engineer Mercer and his crew engage in a life-or-death race with a ghost train. (Rev: BCCB 4/95; BL 6/1–15/95; SLJ 8/95)

2912 Brillhart, Julie. *When Daddy Took Us Camping* (PS–K). Illus. 1997, Albert Whitman LB $13.95 (0-8075-8879-2). 24pp. Two children learn about the outdoors when they go on a camping trip with their father. (Rev: BL 5/1/97; SLJ 5/97)

2913 Brown, Don. *Alice Ramsey's Grand Adventure* (K–3). Illus. 1997, Houghton $15.00 (0-395-70127-9). 32pp. The story of Alice Ramsey's cross-country automobile trip in 1909. (Rev: BL 9/15/97; HB 11–12/97; HBG 3/98; SLJ 9/97*) [917.3]

2914 Bunting, Eve. *Trouble on the T-Ball Team* (PS–2). Illus. by Irene Trivas. 1997, Clarion $13.95 (0-395-66060-2). 32pp. Members of Linda's T-ball team are mysteriously losing things. (Rev: BCCB 4/97; BL 3/1/97; SLJ 5/97)

2915 Burningham, John. *Mr. Gumpy's Motor Car* (K–3). Illus. by author. 1976, HarperCollins LB $17.89 (0-690-00799-X). 48pp. Mr. Gumpy takes his daughter and an assortment of animals for a ride in the country in his old-fashioned touring car. Companion to: *Mr. Gumpy's Outing* (Holt 1995).

2916 Caines, Jeannette. *Just Us Women* (PS–2). Illus. by Pat Cummings. 1984, HarperCollins paper $5.95 (0-06-443056-1). 32pp. A little African American girl is looking forward to a car ride she is going to take with her aunt.

2917 Caple, Kathy. *Hillary to the Rescue* (PS–3). Illus. 2000, Carolrhoda $14.95 (1-57505-420-5). 32pp. Hillary overdresses for her drama club winter outing but finds that these clothes are useful when she has to seek help after the group's bus breaks down. (Rev: BL 11/15/00; HBG 3/01; SLJ 12/00)

2918 Carrick, Carol. *Left Behind* (PS–2). Illus. by Donald Carrick. 1988, Houghton $16.60 (0-89919-535-0). 32pp. On a class visit to the city aquarium, Christopher gets left behind at the subway stop. (Rev: BCCB 9/88; BL 9/15/88; HB 9–10/88)

2919 Carrick, Carol. *Sleep Out* (K–2). Illus. by Donald Carrick. 1982, Houghton paper $6.95 (0-89919-083-9). 32pp. Christopher has an unsettling experience when he spends his first night outdoors in his sleeping bag. Another title by the same author: *Ben and the Porcupine* (1985).

2920 Carter, David A. *In a Dark, Dark Wood: An Old Tale with a New Twist* (PS–1). 1991, Simon & Schuster $10.95 (0-671-74134-9). 24pp. A pop-up, oversized book with a spooky ghost at the end. (Rev: BCCB 12/92; BL 9/15/91)

2921 Cleary, Beverly. *The Real Hole* (PS–1). Illus. by DyAnne DiSalvo-Ryan. 1986, Morrow paper $4.95 (0-688-14741-0). 32pp. Four-year-old Jimmy digs a big hole and puts it to good use. A reissue of the 1960 edition.

2922 Cowley, Joy. *The Video Shop Sparrow* (2–4). Illus. by Gavin Bishop. 1999, Boyds Mills $15.95 (1-56397-826-1). 32pp. Two youngsters, noticing that a sparrow is trapped in a store that will be closed for two weeks, try to get help in rescuing the bird. (Rev: BL 12/1/99; HBG 3/00; SLJ 12/99)

2923 Crews, Donald. *Sail Away* (PS–3). Illus. 1995, Greenwillow LB $15.93 (0-688-11054-1). 32pp. A family weathers a storm in their sailboat. (Rev: BCCB 4/95; BL 4/1/95; HB 9–10/95; SLJ 5/95*)

2924 Demas, Corinne. *Hurricane!* (K–3). Illus. by Lenice U. Strohmeier. 2000, Marshall Cavendish $15.95 (0-7614-5052-1). 32pp. Inspired by Hurricane Bob of 1991, this picture book tells how a little girl and her family prepare for, experience, and survive a hurricane on Cape Cod. (Rev: BL 3/1/00; HBG 10/00; SLJ 4/00)

2925 Elya, Susan Middleton. *Say Hola to Spanish at the Circus* (PS–4). Illus. by Loretta Lopez. Series: Say Hola to Spanish. 2000, Lee & Low $15.95 (1-880000-92-X). 32pp. Using English and about 70 Spanish words, this brightly illustrated book combines the two languages in an introduction to the fun and excitement of the circus. (Rev: BL 7/00; HBG 10/00; SLJ 7/00)

2926 Enderle, Judith R., and Stephanie G. Tessler. *Nell Nugget and the Cow Caper* (K–2). Illus. by Paul Yalowitz. 1996, Simon & Schuster paper $15.00 (0-689-80502-0). In this humorous Western tale, Nell Nugget sets out to find the culprit who has rustled her favorite cow, Goldie. (Rev: BCCB 5/96; HB 9–10/96; SLJ 7/96)

2927 English, Karen. *Big Wind Coming!* (PS–2). Illus. by Cedric Lucas. 1996, Albert Whitman LB $14.95 (0-8075-0726-1). 32pp. A severe windstorm and its effects on an African American family as seen through the eye of the young daughter. (Rev: BCCB 1/97; BL 10/15/96; SLJ 11/96)

2928 Feiffer, Jules. *I Lost My Bear* (PS–2). Illus. by author. 1998, Morrow LB $15.93 (0-688-15148-5). A young girl plays detective when she discovers that her favorite toy is missing. (Rev: BCCB 6/98; BL 4/1/98; HB 3–4/98*; HBG 10/98; SLJ 3/98)

2929 Fleming, Candace. *When Agnes Caws* (PS–2). Illus. by Giselle Potter. 1999, Simon & Schuster $16.00 (0-689-81471-2). 40pp. A girl noted for her birdcalls is sent to the Himalayas to find the pink-headed duck, little realizing that the villainous Colonel Pittsnap is following her. (Rev: BCCB 2/99; BL 2/15/99; HB 3–4/99; HBG 10/99)

2930 Fox, Mem. *Tough Boris* (PS–3). Illus. by Kathryn Brown. 1994, Harcourt $16.00 (0-15-289612-0). 32pp. Boris is a rough and tough pirate, but when his parrot dies, he cries. (Rev: BL 3/1/94; HB 5–6/94; SLJ 5/94)

2931 Franklin, Kristine L. *The Shepherd Boy* (PS–1). Illus. by Jill Kastner. 1994, Atheneum $14.95 (0-689-31809-X). 40pp. Ben, a young Navajo boy, and his dog search the mesa for a lost sheep. (Rev: BCCB 6/94; BL 7/94; SLJ 6/94)

2932 Gerrard, Roy. *Wagons West!* (K–2). Illus. 1996, Farrar $15.00 (0-374-38249-2). 32pp. A rollicking tall tale about Buckskin Dan, leader of a wagon train headed west in the 1840s. (Rev: BCCB 2/96; BL 3/15/96; SLJ 3/96*)

2933 Gershator, Phillis. *Tiny and Bigman* (K–3). Illus. by Lynne W. Cravath. 1999, Marshall Cavendish $15.95 (0-7614-5044-0). 32pp. On their Caribbean island, Miss Tiny, who is married to Mr.

Bigman, vows that, in spite of an oncoming hurricane, she will remain home to have her baby. (Rev: BCCB 12/99; BL 10/15/99; HBG 3/00; SLJ 11/99)

2934 Gould, Deborah. *Camping in the Temple of the Sun* (PS–2). Illus. by Diane Paterson. 1992, Macmillan $13.95 (0-02-736355-4). 32pp. A family's first camping trip begins poorly, but when the sun comes out, things improve. (Rev: BL 2/15/92; SLJ 6/92)

2935 Graham, Georgia. *The Strongest Man This Side of Cremona* (PS–3). Illus. 1998, Northern Lights $15.95 (0-88995-182-9). 32pp. Young Matthew and his dad seek shelter when a tornado approaches their farm on the Canadian prairie. (Rev: BL 2/1/99; SLJ 5/99)

2936 Gregory, Valiska. *Kate's Giants* (PS–4). Illus. by Virginia Austin. 1995, Candlewick $14.95 (1-56402-299-4); paper $5.99 (0-7636-0151-9). 32pp. Kate believes that there are unfriendly monsters hiding behind the door that leads to the attic. (Rev: BL 10/15/95; SLJ 12/95)

2937 Harrison, Troon. *Lavender Moon* (K–2). Illus. by Eugenie Fernandes. 1997, Annick LB $16.95 (1-55037-455-9); paper $6.95 (1-55037-454-0). Lavender Moon, a cafe owner, changes places with a bus driver and sets out to see the world. (Rev: SLJ 1/98)

2938 Haynes, Max. *Dinosaur Island* (PS–2). Illus. 1991, Lothrop $13.95 (0-688-10329-4). 32pp. Maddy and Bing travel in a land where dinosaurs are hidden in the pictures. (Rev: BL 10/1/91; SLJ 1/92)

2939 Hesse, Karen. *Lester's Dog* (PS–3). Illus. by Nancy Carpenter. 1993, Crown LB $16.99 (0-517-58358-5). 32pp. A boy and his hearing-impaired friend rescue an abandoned kitten. (Rev: BL 11/1/93; SLJ 10/93)

2940 Hindley, Judy. *Into the Jungle* (PS–K). Illus. by Melanie Epps. 1994, Candlewick $14.95 (1-56402-423-7). 32pp. A boy and a girl take a walk through a jungle filled with animal life they can't see. (Rev: BL 8/94; SLJ 10/94)

2941 Hopkinson, Deborah. *Birdie's Lighthouse* (PS–4). Illus. by Kimberly B. Root. 1997, Simon & Schuster $16.00 (0-689-81052-0). 32pp. A lighthouse story set in the 1850s about a girl who keeps the lamps burning when her father falls ill during a storm. (Rev: BL 6/1–15/97; HB 7–8/97; SLJ 6/97)

2942 Jam, Teddy. *The Fishing Summer* (K–3). Illus. by Ange Zhang. 1997, Douglas & McIntyre $12.95 (0-88899-285-8). 32pp. A boy stows away on his uncle's fishing boat and works hard to learn the family trade. (Rev: BL 9/15/97; SLJ 2/98)

2943 Jane, Pamela. *The Big Monkey Mix-up* (1–4). Illus. by Cathy Bobak. 1997, Avon paper $3.99 (0-380-78951-5). 65pp. A simple mystery that revolves around a missing monkey and Benjamin's desire to lose at least one of his baby teeth. (Rev: SLJ 1/98)

2944 Jezek, Alisandra. *Miloli's Orchids* (K–3). Illus. by Yoshi Miyake. 1991, Raintree Steck-Vaughn LB $22.83 (0-8172-2784-9). 31pp. Written by a youngster, this story set in Hawaii tells of a young girl's attempts to save orchids from a volcano. (Rev: SLJ 6/91)

2945 Johnson, Neil. *Fire and Silk: Flying in a Hot Air Balloon* (K–3). Illus. 1991, Little, Brown $15.95 (0-316-46959-9). 32pp. The facts and feel of ballooning in a nonfiction book that reads like an adventure story. (Rev: BCCB 4/91; BL 5/1/91; HB 7–8/91; SLJ 7/91) [797.5]

2946 Johnson, Scott. *I Can't Wait Until I'm Old Enough to Hunt with Dad* (1–3). Illus. by Karen Johnson. 1995, Deer Pond $14.95 (1-887251-56-1). 32pp. A young boy accompanies his father on a bow-and-arrow deer hunt. (Rev: BL 2/1/96)

2947 Keats, Ezra Jack. *Maggie and the Pirate* (1–3). Illus. by author. 1987, Scholastic paper $4.95 (0-590-44852-8). 32pp. Maggie tries to find the kidnapper of her pet cricket. A reissue of the 1979 edition.

2948 Kimmel, Eric A. *Four Dollars and Fifty Cents* (2–4). Illus. by Glen Rounds. 1990, Holiday LB $16.95 (0-8234-0817-5). 32pp. To get out of paying a bad debt, cowboy Shorty Long pretends to be dead. (Rev: BL 9/15/90; HB 1–2/91*; SLJ 11/90)

2949 Kinsey-Warnock, Natalie. *The Summer of Stanley* (PS–3). Illus. by Donald Gates. 1997, Dutton $14.99 (0-525-65177-2). 32pp. Stanley, the family goat, changes from pest to hero when he helps save a boy who has fallen into a river. (Rev: BL 7/97; SLJ 6/97)

2950 Kotzwinkle, William. *The Million-Dollar Bear* (K–2). Illus. by David Catrow. 1995, Knopf LB $17.99 (0-679-95295-0). The first-ever teddy bear, who belongs to two millionaires, is accidentally found by a little boy who takes him home. (Rev: SLJ 1/96)

2951 Lasky, Kathryn. *Marven of the Great North Woods* (K–4). Illus. by Kevin Hawkes. 1997, Harcourt $16.00 (0-15-200104-2). 48pp. During the 1918 flu epidemic, 10-year-old Marven is sent to a logging camp in Minnesota, where he has to assume many adult responsibilities. (Rev: BL 12/15/97; HB 11–12/97; HBG 3/98; SLJ 10/97)

2952 Lewis, Kim. *First Snow* (PS–K). Illus. 1993, Candlewick $14.95 (1-56402-194-7). 32pp. When Sara and her mother go to feed the sheep on the hill, there is a heavy snowfall and they have difficulty getting home. (Rev: BL 9/15/93)

2953 London, Jonathan. *The Waterfall* (K–3). Illus. by Jill Kastner. 1999, Viking $15.99 (0-670-87617-8). 32pp. On a camping trip, two boys and their parents climb to the summit of a beautiful waterfall. (Rev: BL 4/1/99; HBG 10/99; SLJ 4/99)

2954 Luciani, Brigitte. *How Will We Get to the Beach?* (PS–1). Trans. by Rosemary Lanning. Illus. by Eve Tharlet. 2000, North-South LB $14.88 (0-7358-1269-1). 36pp. A guessing game woven into a story about a girl and her attempts to get to the beach using different vehicles. (Rev: BL 5/15/00; HBG 10/00; SLJ 6/00)

2955 Lyon, George E. *One Lucky Girl* (K–3). Illus. by Irene Trivas. 2000, DK $15.95 (0-7894-2613-7). 32pp. Based on a true story, this picture book recreates the terror a family experiences when a tornado strikes the trailer park in which they live. (Rev:

BCCB 3/00; BL 3/1/00; HB 5–6/00; HBG 10/00; SLJ 3/00)

2956 Maguire, Gregory. *Crabby Cratchitt* (PS–3). Illus. by Andrew Glass. 2000, Clarion $15.00 (0-395-60485-0). 32pp. Crabby Cratchitt, who can't stand the clucking of her hen, decides to solve the problem by having a chicken dinner, until she sees the hen's nest filled with eggs. (Rev: BL 9/1/00; HBG 3/01; SLJ 8/00)

2957 Martin, Bill, Jr., and John Archambault. *The Ghost-Eye Tree* (K–3). Illus. by Ted Rand. 1985, Holt $16.95 (0-8050-0208-1); paper $6.95 (0-8050-0947-7). 32pp. A brother and sister are sent to fetch a pail of milk on a spooky night past the Ghost-Eye Tree. (Rev: BL 12/15/85; HB 1–2/86; SLJ 2/86)

2958 Martin, Bill, Jr., and John Archambault. *White Dynamite and Curly Kidd* (1–3). Illus. by Ted Rand. 1986, Holt paper $6.95 (0-8050-1018-1). 48pp. A nervous fan carries on a conversation with a bull rider who is about to break out of the chute on White Dynamite. (Rev: BL 7/86; SLJ 4/86)

2959 Martin, Bill, Jr., and Michael Sampson. *Swish!* (K–3). Illus. by Michael Chesworth. 1997, Holt $15.95 (0-8050-4498-1). 32pp. The excitement and energy of a girl's basketball game are captured in this picture book. (Rev: BL 12/15/97; HBG 3/98; SLJ 11/97)

2960 Morck, Irene. *Tyler's New Boots* (K–3). Illus. by Georgia Graham. 1998, Chronicle $14.95 (0-8118-2248-6); paper $6.95 (0-8118-2143-9). 40pp. Tyler is disappointed that his new boots become worn looking before the cattle drive even starts. But his friend Jessica tells him that's how a cowboy's boots should look. (Rev: BL 12/1/98; HBG 3/99; SLJ 11/98)

2961 Mott, Evelyn Clarke. *Balloon Ride* (K–3). Illus. 1991, Walker LB $14.85 (0-8027-8126-8). Megan takes her first trip in a hot-air balloon in this nonfiction account with photos by the author. (Rev: SLJ 10/91) [797.5]

2962 O'Connor, Jane. *Amy's (Not So) Great Camp-Out* (1–3). Illus. by Laurie S. Long. 1993, Putnam paper $5.99 (0-448-40166-5). 64pp. A superactive girl gets sick when her Brownie troop goes on a camping trip. Also use *Corrie's Secret Pal* (1993). (Rev: BL 1/1/94)

2963 Prater, John. *The Greatest Show on Earth* (PS–1). Illus. 1995, Candlewick $14.95 (1-56402-563-2). 32pp. Harry feels inept compared to other members of his family, each a circus star, but he finally finds his own niche. (Rev: BCCB 10/95; BL 10/15/95; SLJ 10/95)

2964 Rex, Michael. *My Fire Engine* (K–2). Illus. 1999, Holt $15.95 (0-8050-5391-3). 28pp. The young narrator joins a fire-engine crew and participates in answering an alarm that saves a family from a burning house. (Rev: BL 3/15/99; HBG 10/99; SLJ 5/99)

2965 Rockwell, Anne. *I Fly* (PS–2). Illus. by Annette Cable. 1997, Crown LB $17.99 (0-517-59684-9). 32pp. A young boy recounts his first airplane trip without his parents. (Rev: BL 8/97; SLJ 7/97)

2966 Rosen, Michael J. *We're Going on a Bear Hunt* (PS–2). Illus. by Helen Oxenbury. 1989, Macmillan $17.00 (0-689-50476-4). 40pp. The storytelling favorite is re-created with expansive pictures that capture the enthusiasm of the story. (Rev: BCCB 9/89; BL 8/89*; HB 11–12/89*; SLJ 8/89*)

2967 Rylant, Cynthia. *Tulip Sees America* (PS–3). Illus. by Lisa Desimini. 1998, Scholastic $15.95 (0-590-84744-9). 32pp. A young man and his dog travel across the United States and find a place by the sea in Oregon where they want to stay. (Rev: BL 3/15/98; HBG 10/98; SLJ 4/98)

2968 Sampson, Michael. *The Football That Won . . .* (PS–2). Illus. by Ted Rand. Series: Bill Martin Books. 1996, Holt $14.95 (0-8050-3504-4). A cumulative romp that features players and spectators at a Super Bowl game between the Dallas Cowboys and the Kansas City Chiefs. (Rev: SLJ 10/96)

2969 Scott, Ann H. *Cowboy Country* (1–3). Illus. by Ted Lewin. 1993, Clarion $14.95 (0-395-57561-3). 40pp. A hardworking cowhand takes a young boy on an overnight trip to show him what life on the range really is. (Rev: BCCB 11/93; BL 9/1/93; HB 11–12/93; SLJ 9/93*)

2970 Seibert, Patricia. *Mush! Across Alaska in the World's Longest Sled-Dog Race* (2–4). Illus. 1992, Houghton paper $5.70 (0-395-64537-9). 32pp. Focusing on the work dogs of the 1,000-plus-mile Iditarod race from Anchorage to Nome. (Rev: BL 9/15/92; SLJ 11/92) [798.8]

2971 Seymour, Tres. *We Played Marbles* (K–3). Illus. by Dan Andreasen. 1998, Orchard LB $16.99 (0-531-33074-5). 32pp. The Civil War battle that took place at Fort Craig, Kentucky, unfolds as two boys play an innocent game on its site. (Rev: BL 2/15/98; HBG 10/98; SLJ 3/98)

2972 Skolsky, Mindy W. *Hannah and the Whistling Teakettle* (1–3). Illus. by Diane Palmisciano. 2000, DK $15.95 (0-7894-2602-1). 38pp. Hannah's unwanted gift to her grandmother of a whistling teakettle, proves its worth by saving Grandma from robbers. (Rev: BL 3/1/00; HB 5–6/00; HBG 10/00; SLJ 4/00)

2973 Steig, William. *Brave Irene* (K–2). Illus. by author. 1986, Farrar $17.00 (0-374-30947-7). 32pp. The incredible adventures of Irene, who sets out in a snowstorm to deliver the duchess's new dress for the ball. (Rev: BCCB 12/86; BL 11/1/86; HB 11–12/86)

2974 Stevenson, James. *"Could Be Worse!"* (K–3). Illus. by author. 1977, Morrow paper $4.95 (0-688-07035-3). 32pp. Grandpa's response to minor catastrophes is always the same.

2975 Stevenson, James. *Sam the Zamboni Man* (PS–2). Illus. by Harvey Stevenson. 1998, Greenwillow $14.93 (0-688-14485-3). 32pp. Grandfather, who operates the Zamboni that smooths the ice at the hockey stadium, invites young Matt to go to a real hockey game. (Rev: BCCB 4/98; BL 2/1/98; HBG 10/98; SLJ 3/98)

2976 Stutson, Caroline. *Cowpokes* (PS–2). Illus. by Daniel San Souci. 1999, Lothrop $15.00 (0-688-13973-6). 24pp. Takes the reader through an action-packed day spent by high-spirited cartoon cowboys riding, roping, eating, making mistakes, and bedding down at night. (Rev: BL 9/15/99; HBG 3/00; SLJ 9/99)

2977 Sullivan, Silky. *Grandpa Was a Cowboy* (K–3). Illus. by Bert Dodson. 1996, Orchard LB $16.99 (0-531-08861-8). 32pp. A young orphan is intrigued by the tales his grandfather spins about his career as a cowboy. (Rev: BL 4/1/96; SLJ 4/96)

2978 Thomassie, Tynia. *Feliciana Feydra LeRoux: A Cajun Tall Tale* (1–3). Illus. by Cat B. Smith. 1995, Little, Brown $14.95 (0-316-84125-0). 32pp. A young Cajun girl joins the rest of her family in an old-fashioned alligator hunt. (Rev: BCCB 5/95; BL 4/1/95; HB 9–10/95; SLJ 4/95*)

2979 Tomlinson, Theresa. *Little Stowaway* (PS–3). Illus. by Jane Browne. 1998, Random $19.95 (1-85681-691-5). 32pp. A young boy stows away on a British fishing boat as it sails into the North Sea so he can be with his father. (Rev: BL 11/15/98)

2980 Tucker, Kathy. *Do Pirates Take Baths?* (PS–2). Illus. by Nadine Bernard Westcott. 1994, Albert Whitman LB $15.95 (0-8075-1696-1). 32pp. A fanciful, humorous account that purports to be an exposé of how pirates really lived. (Rev: BCCB 10/94; BL 2/15/95; SLJ 1/95)

2981 Van Allsburg, Chris. *The Garden of Abdul Gasazi* (K–3). Illus. by author. 1979, Houghton $17.95 (0-395-27804-X). 32pp. Young Alan wanders into the garden of a retired magician with unexpected results.

2982 Wallace, Ian. *A Winter's Tale* (K–3). Illus. 1997, Douglas & McIntyre $15.95 (0-88899-286-6). 32pp. A gentle outdoor adventure in which Abigail is taken camping by her father and brother to celebrate her ninth birthday. (Rev: BL 10/15/97; SLJ 12/97)

2983 Ward, Lynd. *The Biggest Bear* (K–3). Illus. by author. 1952, Houghton $16.00 (0-395-14806-5); paper $6.95 (0-395-15024-8). 88pp. Johnny wanted a bearskin on his barn so he went looking for the biggest bear. Caldecott Medal winner, 1953.

2984 Wiesner, David. *Hurricane* (1–3). Illus. 1990, Houghton $16.00 (0-395-54382-7). 32pp. Two boys take refuge in their hideout in a tree during a hurricane watch. (Rev: BCCB 11/90; BL 12/15/90; HB 1–2/91; SLJ 10/90*)

2985 Williams, Vera B. *Three Days on a River in a Red Canoe* (K–3). Illus. by author. 1981, Greenwillow $15.89 (0-688-84307-7); Morrow paper $5.95 (0-688-04072-1). 32pp. A little girl describes a canoe trip with her cousins and their mother.

2986 Wolff, Ashley. *Stella and Roy Go Camping* (PS–K). Illus. 1999, Dutton $15.99 (0-525-45864-6). 40pp. On a camping trip with his mother and Stella, his know-it-all sister, Roy gets the best of Stella by seeing a bear. (Rev: BL 7/99; HB 5–6/99; HBG 10/99; SLJ 6/99)

COMMUNITY AND EVERYDAY LIFE

2987 Ackerman, Karen. *This Old House* (PS–2). Illus. by Sylvie Wickstrom. 1992, Macmillan LB $14.95 (0-689-31741-7). 40pp. People move out,

but an owl sleeps in the rafters, rabbits nibble, and mice scamper about. (Rev: BL 10/15/92; SLJ 3/93)

2988 Adams, Barbara J. *The Go-Around Dollar* (2–4). Illus. by Joyce A. Zarins. 1992, Macmillan LB $16.00 (0-02-700031-1). 32pp. The dollar is introduced within the framework of a story and the look of a picture book. (Rev: BCCB 2/92; BL 2/15/92; SLJ 5/92) [332.4]

2989 Adorjan, Carol. *I Can! Can You?* (PS–K). Illus. by Miriam Nerlove. 1990, Whitman LB $13.95 (0-8075-3491-9). 24pp. A little girl tells about the skills she has mastered. (Rev: BL 12/15/90; SLJ 2/91)

2990 Agassi, Martine. *Hands Are Not for Hitting* (PS–1). Illus. by Marieka Heinlen. 2000, Free Spirit paper $10.95 (1-57542-077-5). 35pp. This book preaches the lesson that there are better things for hands to do than hurting other people. (Rev: SLJ 2/01)

2991 Alexander, Martha. *How My Library Grew, by Dinah* (PS–K). Illus. by author. 1983, H.W. Wilson $18.00 (0-8242-0679-7). 32pp. Dinah and her teddy bear watch a library being built across the street.

2992 Aliki. *All By Myself!* (PS–K). Illus. 2000, HarperCollins LB $14.89 (0-06-028930-9). 32pp. A picture book that shows a boy going through a typical day and engaging in such activities as practicing a violin, taking a bath, brushing his teeth, and pulling on socks. (Rev: BL 11/1/00; HB 9–10/00; HBG 3/01; SLJ 9/00)

2993 Aliki. *Hello! Good-bye!* (PS–2). Illus. 1996, Greenwillow $14.89 (0-688-14334-2). 32pp. The many ways of saying "hello" and "good-bye" around the world. (Rev: BCCB 12/96; BL 7/96; SLJ 9/96)

2994 Aliki. *Manners* (K–3). Illus. 1990, Greenwillow $15.89 (0-688-09199-7). 32pp. Cartoon-style characters help make manners accessible to young readers. (Rev: BL 10/1/90; SLJ 11/90*) [395]

2995 Anderson, Janet S. *Sunflower Sal* (PS–2). Illus. by Elizabeth Johns. 1997, Albert Whitman LB $15.95 (0-8075-7662-X). 32pp. A young girl plants sunflowers around her farm so that the rows will look like the stitches in a huge quilt. (Rev: BL 10/1/97; HBG 3/98; SLJ 9/97)

2996 Anholt, Catherine, and Laurence Anholt. *Harry's Home* (PS–1). Illus. 2000, Farrar $16.00 (0-374-32870-6). 32pp. This picture describes the feelings of young Harry who loves living in the city but must prepare for a visit with his grandfather in the country. (Rev: BL 5/1/00; SLJ 4/00)

2997 Anholt, Catherine, and Laurence Anholt. *What I Like* (PS). Illus. 1998, Candlewick paper $5.99 (0-7636-0585-9). 32pp. Six children tell about the things they like and dislike. (Rev: BL 9/1/91; SLJ 12/91)

2998 Antoine, Héloïse. *Curious Kids Go to Preschool: Another Big Book of Words* (PS). Illus. by Ingrid Godon. 1996, Peachtree $13.95 (1-56145-129-0). An introduction to preschool experiences through defining such words as *school bus, backpack,* and *lunch box.* (Rev: SLJ 11/96)

2999 Appelt, Kathi. *Watermelon Day* (PS–3). Illus. by Dale Gottlieb. 1996, Holt $15.95 (0-8050-2304-6). Young Jesse grows impatient waiting for her watermelon to grow sufficiently so that it can be eaten when her pappy declares it is a watermelon day. (Rev: BCCB 1/96; SLJ 6/96)

3000 Armstrong, Jennifer. *Pockets* (K–3). Illus. by Mary GrandPré. 1998, Crown LB $18.99 (0-517-70927-9). 32pp. Although she is told to make only practical clothing, the village tailor rebelliously ornaments the insides of pockets with gloriously embroidered scenes of maritime life. (Rev: BL 8/98; HBG 3/99; SLJ 10/98)

3001 Asbury, Kelly. *Bonnie's Blue House* (PS). Illus. 1997, Holt $7.95 (0-8050-4022-6). 32pp. The color blue is explored in this book about Bonnie, her family, and their home. Two other titles in this series are *Rusty's Red Vacation* and *Yoland's Yellow School* (both 1997). (Rev: BL 3/1/97; SLJ 6/97)

3002 Atkins, Jeannine. *Get Set! Swim!* (K–3). Illus. by Hector Viveros Lee. 1998, Lee & Low $15.95 (1-880000-66-0). 32pp. Jessenia's mother and brother attend her swim meet, and swimming reminds Jessenia of her mother's home in Puerto Rico. (Rev: BL 5/15/98; HBG 10/98; SLJ 5/98)

3003 Baer, Edith. *This Is the Way We Eat Our Lunch: A Book About Children Around the World* (PS–3). Illus. by Steve Bjorkman. 1995, Scholastic $14.95 (0-590-46887-1). 32pp. A visit to lunchtime in nine states, two Canadian provinces, and 11 other countries, with accompanying recipes and food facts. (Rev: BCCB 9/95; BL 9/15/95; SLJ 9/95)

3004 Baer, Gene. *Thump, Thump, Rat-a-Tat-Tat* (PS–K). Illus. by Lois Ehlert. 1991, HarperCollins paper $4.95 (0-064-43265-3). 32pp. Re-creates the sights and sounds of a marching band. (Rev: BCCB 2/90; BL 11/1/89*; HB 9–10/89*; SLJ 1/90)

3005 Baker, Jeannie. *Window* (2–4). Illus. 1991, Greenwillow $16.89 (0-688-08918-6). 24pp. The changes from a rural to an urban setting are traced in the changes seen through a window. (Rev: BCCB 3/91; BL 4/15/91; HB 5–6/91; SLJ 3/91*)

3006 Ballard, Robin. *Good-bye, House* (PS–K). Illus. 1994, Greenwillow $13.93 (0-688-12526-3). 24pp. Before she moves, a little girl says good-bye to each room in her old home. (Rev: BL 3/15/94; HB 7–8/94; SLJ 6/94)

3007 Ballard, Robin. *My Day, Your Day* (PS–K). Illus. 2001, Greenwillow LB $14.89 (0-06-029187-7). 32pp. This book about day care shows a picture of children engaging in various group activities on one page and, facing it, a picture of parents at work doing similar things. (Rev: BL 1/1–15/01)

3008 Bang, Molly. *Yellow Ball* (PS–1). Illus. 1991, Morrow LB $15.93 (0-688-06315-2). 24pp. The yellow ball over the sea on the jacket becomes the focus of a game of catch. (Rev: BCCB 4/91; BL 3/1/91*; SLJ 5/91)

3009 Barber, Barbara E. *Allie's Basketball Dream* (PS–3). Illus. by Darryl Ligasan. 1996, Lee & Low $15.95 (1-880000-38-5). 32pp. When she receives her first basketball, Allie perseveres until she is able to shoot a basket. (Rev: BCCB 2/97; BL 1/1–15/97; SLJ 11/96)

3010 Barber, Barbara E. *Saturday at The New You* (PS–3). Illus. by Anna Rich. 1994, Lee & Low $14.95 (1-880000-06-7). 32pp. Shauna, an African American girl, has fun on Saturdays helping at her mother's beauty shop. (Rev: BCCB 12/94; BL 12/1/94; SLJ 1/95)

3011 Barrett, Mary Brigid. *Leaf Baby* (PS). Illus. by Eve Chwast. 1998, Harcourt $5.95 (0-15-201057-2). 12pp. A board book about autumn activities in which a boy and his grandfather walk in a park, play in the leaves, and watch geese swimming. (Rev: BL 11/1/98)

3012 Barrett, Mary Brigid. *Snow Baby* (PS). Illus. by Eve Chwast. 1998, Harcourt $5.95 (0-15-201054-8). 12pp. Winter is pictured in this board book about a youngster taking a snowy walk with Gram and then making angels in the snow. (Rev: BL 11/1/98)

3013 Barrows, Allison. *The Artist's Friends* (PS–3). Illus. 1998, Carolrhoda LB $14.95 (1-57505-054-4). 32pp. A young girl who wants to become an artist goes with her painter father to visit different artists and discover various kinds of art, such as sculpture and portrait painting. (Rev: BL 8/98; HBG 10/98; SLJ 7/98)

3014 Barton, Byron. *Building a House* (PS–2). Illus. by author. 1981, Greenwillow LB $16.93 (0-688-84291-7); Morrow paper $4.95 (0-688-09356-6). 32pp. The stages of building a house are simply presented.

3015 Bartone, Elisa. *American Too* (PS–3). Illus. by Ted Lewin. 1996, Lothrop LB $15.93 (0-688-13279-0). 40pp. An Italian American girl dresses as the Statue of Liberty for the Festival of San Gennaro in New York City. (Rev: BCCB 12/96; BL 8/96; SLJ 12/96)

3016 Bateson-Hill, Margaret. *Shota and the Star Quilt* (PS–3). Illus. by Christine Fowler. 1998, Zero to Ten $14.95 (1-84089-021-5). 32pp. Shota, a Lakota girl, and her friend Esther persuade their landlord not to tear down their apartment building, by showing him a star quilt that celebrates their apartment home. (Rev: BL 2/1/99; HBG 3/99)

3017 Bauch, Patricia L. *Dance, Tanya* (PS–2). Illus. by Satomi Ichikawa. 1989, Putnam $16.99 (0-399-21521-2). 32pp. Tanya's mother says she's too young for ballet lessons, but Tanya proves her wrong. (Rev: BL 9/1/89; SLJ 10/89)

3018 Bauer, Marion Dane. *Jason's Bears* (PS–1). Illus. by Kevin Hawkes. 2000, Hyperion LB $15.49 (0-7868-2303-8). Jason conquers his fear of bears when he eats a Ginger Bear cookie. (Rev: HBG 10/00; SLJ 5/00)

3019 Baylor, Byrd. *The Best Town in the World* (2–4). Illus. by Ronald Himler. 1983, Macmillan $14.95 (0-684-18035-9); paper $5.99 (0-689-71086-0). A description of life in a small Texas town back when Father was a child.

3020 Bedard, Michael. *The Clay Ladies* (K–4). Illus. by Les Tait. 1999, Tundra $16.95 (0-88776-385-5). 38pp. A young girl frequently visits the studio of two Toronto sculptors, Frances Loring and Florence Wyte, and learns about their work. (Rev: BL 5/1/99; SLJ 11/99)

3021 *Bedtime: First Words, Rhymes and Actions* (PS). 1999, Candlewick $7.99 (0-7636-0932-3). This is a fine compilation of simple stories and rhymes from previously published books. Also use: *Playtime: First Words, Rhymes and Actions* (1999). (Rev: HBG 3/00; SLJ 1/00)

3022 Bennett, William J., ed. *The Children's Book of Virtues* (PS–3). Illus. by Michael Hague. 1995, Simon & Schuster $21.00 (0-684-81353-X). 111pp. Stories, poems, and fables illustrate ten virtues in this collection based on the concepts used in the adult *Book of Virtues*. (Rev: BL 1/1–15/96) [808.8]

3023 Bernhard, Emery. *The Way of the Willow Branch* (PS–2). Illus. by Durga Bernhard. 1996, Harcourt $15.00 (0-15-200844-6). 32pp. A broken willow branch floats downstream and is finally found by a child. (Rev: BL 4/1/96; HB 7–8/96; SLJ 5/96)

3024 Best, Cari. *Last Licks: A Spaldeen Story* (K–2). Illus. by Diane Palmisciano. 1999, DK $15.95 (0-7894-2513-0). 32pp. Tells about Annie and the game she plays with her spaldeen — the pink rubber ball that is used in punchball. (Rev: BL 5/1/99; HBG 10/99; SLJ 5/99)

3025 Best, Cari. *Red Light, Green Light, Mama and Me* (PS–2). Illus. by Niki Daly. 1995, Orchard LB $16.99 (0-531-08752-2). 32pp. Lizzie spends an exciting day with her mother, who is a children's librarian in a big downtown library. (Rev: BCCB 9/95; BL 9/1/95; SLJ 10/95)

3026 Birdseye, Tom. *Airmail to the Moon* (K–2). Illus. by Stephen Gammell. 1988, Holiday LB $15.95 (0-8234-0683-0); paper $6.95 (0-8234-0754-3). 32pp. Motor-mouth Ora Mae vows to "send to the moon" the one who stole her tooth. (Rev: BL 3/15/88; HB 5–6/88; SLJ 5/88)

3027 Blackstone, Stella. *Baby Rock, Baby Roll* (PS–1). Illus. by Denise and Fernando. 1997, Holiday LB $13.95 (0-8234-1311-X). 32pp. Three children from different races bounce through a day's activities. (Rev: BL 9/1/97; HBG 3/98; SLJ 10/97)

3028 Blackstone, Stella. *Making Minestrone* (K–3). Illus. by Nan Brooks. 2000, Barefoot $15.99 (1-84148-211-0). 32pp. A group of multiethnic kids get together under the supervision of a lonely boy to make a fine batch of minestrone soup. (Rev: BL 10/1/00; HBG 3/01; SLJ 10/00)

3029 Blake, Robert J. *Yudonsi: A Tale from the Canyons* (1–3). Illus. 1999, Putnam $15.99 (0-399-23320-2). 32pp. A young graffiti artist creates so much ugliness that nature intervenes with a huge rainstorm, washing away his paint and almost himself. (Rev: BL 9/1/99; HBG 3/00; SLJ 2/00)

3030 Bogart, Jo Ellen. *Jeremiah Learns to Read* (K–3). Illus. by Laura Fernandez. 1999, Orchard $15.95 (0-531-30190-7). 32pp. An elderly farmer named Jeremiah is taught to read by the local teacher and children in a one-room school, and in exchange he shares with them some of his animal lore. (Rev: BL 9/15/99; HBG 3/00; SLJ 10/99)

3031 Borden, Louise. *Albie the Lifeguard* (PS–3). Illus. by Elizabeth Sayles. 1993, Scholastic $14.95 (0-590-44585-5). 32pp. Albie is not a confident swimmer, but in his backyard he fantasizes about being a lifeguard. (Rev: BL 3/15/93; SLJ 6/93)

3032 Bourgeois, Paulette. *Big Sarah's Little Boots* (PS–1). Illus. by Brenda Clark. 1992, Scholastic paper $4.95 (0-590-42623-0). 32pp. Preschooler Sarah can't understand why her favorite yellow boots have shrunk. (Rev: BL 1/1/90; SLJ 11/89)

3033 Bourgeois, Paulette. *Fire Fighters* (PS–2). Illus. by Kim LaFave. Series: In My Neighborhood. 1998, Kids Can $12.95 (1-55074-438-0). 32pp. This book about fire fighters and their duties highlights fires in various settings and the ways fire fighters approach them. (Rev: BL 4/15/98; HBG 10/98; SLJ 6/98) [363.37]

3034 Bourgeois, Paulette. *Garbage Collectors* (PS–2). Illus. by Kim LaFave. Series: In My Neighborhood. 1998, Kids Can $12.95 (1-55074-440-2). 32pp. Using realistic paintings as illustrations, this book describes the duties of garbage collectors and how waste is recycled. (Rev: BL 4/15/98; HBG 10/98; SLJ 6/98) [363.72]

3035 Boynton, Sandra. *Hey! Wake Up!* (PS). Illus. by author. 2000, Workman $6.95 (0-7611-1976-0). A board book about morning activities like yawning, stretching, breakfast, and getting dressed. Also use *Pajama Time!* (2000). (Rev: SLJ 2/01)

3036 Brami, Elisabeth. *First Times* (1–3). Trans. from French by Siobhan McGowan. Illus. by Philippe Bertrand. 2000, Stewart, Tabori & Chang $14.95 (1-58479-019-9). This small book celebrates such firsts in a child's life as the first day of school, the first pet, and the first time on a bicycle without training wheels. (Rev: SLJ 6/00)

3037 Brandenberg, Alexa. *Chop, Simmer, Season* (PS–1). Illus. 1997, Harcourt $14.00 (0-15-200973-6). 32pp. Two restaurant workers cook a meal for their customers in this picture book that shows what goes on in a kitchen. (Rev: BL 4/15/97; SLJ 5/97)

3038 Brandenberg, Alexa. *I Am Me!* (PS). Illus. by author. 1996, Harcourt $12.00 (0-15-200974-4). After toddlers mention a number of careers they are interested in, they engage in activities related to each. (Rev: SLJ 12/96)

3039 Brazelton, T. Berry. *Going to the Doctor* (PS–1). Illus. by Alfred Womack and Sam Ogden. 1996, Addison-Wesley $15.00 (0-201-40694-2). 48pp. Using photographs of real-life situations, visits to a doctor's office are explained. (Rev: BL 11/15/96) [618]

3040 Breeze, Lynn. *Pickle and the Ball* (PS). Illus. by author. Series: Pickle. 1998, Kingfisher $4.95 (0-7534-5148-4). In this board book with simple rhyming verses, Pickle, a baby, plays with a ball. Others in this series are *Pickle and the Blanket*, *Pickle and the Blocks*, and *Pickle and the Box*. (Rev: SLJ 1/99)

3041 Brennan, Linda Crotta. *Flannel Kisses* (PS–2). Illus. by Mari Takabayashi. 1997, Houghton $16.00 (0-395-73681-1). 32pp. All the fun of a snowy day is pictured, from making a snowman and having hot soup for lunch to being tucked in at night between flannel sheets. (Rev: BL 10/15/97; HBG 3/98; SLJ 9/97)

3042 Brennan, Linda Crotta. *Marshmallow Kisses* (PS–1). Illus. by Mari Takabayashi. 2000, Houghton $15.00 (0-395-73872-5). 32pp. Various summer activities — swinging on a porch and playing in the sand — are described in pictures and simple words. (Rev: BL 3/15/00; HBG 10/00; SLJ 3/00)

3043 Brisley, Joyce Lankester. *More Milly-Molly-Mandy* (K–3). Illus. by author. 1999, Kingfisher $12.95 (0-7534-0200-9). 224pp. Twenty likable, mild stories about a little girl growing up in a small English town a few years ago. (Rev: HBG 3/00; SLJ 12/99)

3044 Brisson, Pat. *Kate Heads West* (K–3). Illus. by Rick Brown. 1990, Macmillan LB $14.00 (0-02-714345-7). 40pp. In a series of letters, Kate describes her tour of the American West with her friend Lucy. Also use: *Kate on the Coast* (1992). (Rev: BL 9/1/90; SLJ 11/90)

3045 Brisson, Pat. *The Summer My Father Was Ten* (PS–3). Illus. by Andrea Shine. 1998, Boyds Mills $15.95 (1-56397-435-5). A father tells his daughter while they plant a garden together of the guilt he felt when, as a child, he vandalized a neighbor's garden. (Rev: BCCB 5/98; BL 2/1/98*; HBG 10/98; SLJ 4/98)

3046 Brisson, Pat. *Wanda's Roses* (K–2). Illus. by Maryann Cocca-Leffler. 1994, Boyds Mills $14.95 (1-56397-136-4). When the plant she has been tending fails to bloom, Wanda attaches paper flowers to it. (Rev: SLJ 12/94)

3047 Brown, Laurie Krasny, and Marc Brown. *Dinosaurs Alive and Well! A Guide to Good Health* (PS–3). Illus. 1990, Little, Brown paper $6.95 (0-316-11009-4). 32pp. Using dinosaurs, the basic principles of nutrition and hygiene are covered. Also use *Dinosaurs Travel* (1990). (Rev: BCCB 5/90; BL 5/15/90; HB 5–6/90; SLJ 4/90*) [613]

3048 Brown, Laurie Krasny, and Marc Brown. *Visiting the Art Museum* (K–3). Illus. 1992, Dutton paper $6.99 (0-140-54820-3). 32pp. An introduction to the art museum, sometimes an overpowering place for young children. (Rev: BCCB 10/86; BL 9/15/86; SLJ 10/86)

3049 Brown, Marc, and Stephen Krensky. *Dinosaurs, Beware! A Safety Guide* (PS–2). Illus. by authors. 1984, Little, Brown paper $7.95 (0-316-11219-4). 32pp. Sixty safety tips are illustrated with drawings of dinosaurs.

3050 Brown, Margaret Wise. *Another Important Book* (PS–1). Illus. by Chris Raschka. 1999, Harper-Collins LB $15.89 (0-06-026283-4). 32pp. In a series of rhymes, this book identifies important achievements and developments in the first six years of a child's life. (Rev: BCCB 1/00; BL 10/15/99; HB 9–10/99; HBG 3/00; SLJ 9/99)

3051 Brown, Margaret Wise. *Red Light, Green Light* (PS–K). Illus. by Leonard Weisgard. 1994, Scholastic paper $4.95 (0-590-44559-6). 40pp. This introduction to traffic signs was first published in 1944.

3052 Brown, Ruth. *The Shy Little Angel* (PS–1). Illus. 1998, Dutton $15.99 (0-525-46079-9). 32pp. The little angel who is too shy to come and visit the baby Jesus is really a schoolgirl in a Christmas play who is suffering from stage fright. (Rev: BL 10/1/98; HBG 3/99; SLJ 10/98)

3053 Browne, Anthony. *Voices in the Park* (PS–4). Illus. 1998, DK $15.95 (0-7894-2522-X). 32pp. People in a park — apes in human clothing — meet during different seasons. (Rev: BCCB 10/98; BL 9/15/98; HB 11–12/98; HBG 3/99; SLJ 9/98)

3054 Bruce, Lisa. *Fran's Flower* (PS). Illus. by Rosalind Beardshaw. 2000, HarperCollins $14.95 (0-06-028621-0). A little girl fails in her attempts to get a plant to grow, but when she takes it outdoors, sun and rain work the necessary magic. (Rev: HBG 10/00; SLJ 6/00)

3055 Buck, Nola. *Hey, Little Baby!* (PS–K). Illus. by R. Alley. 1999, HarperFestival $9.95 (0-694-01200-9). 24pp. A preschooler shows her baby brother all the delightful things she can do in a day, while stomping her feet and hopping about. (Rev: BL 2/1/99; HBG 10/99; SLJ 3/99)

3056 Bunting, Eve. *The Day the Whale Came* (K–3). Illus. by Scott Menchin. 1998, Harcourt $16.00 (0-15-201456-X). 32pp. When the train carrying a dead whale — a traveling exhibit — breaks down, the townspeople join together to help bury the animal. Tommy feels that putting the whale to rest is the right thing to. (Rev: BCCB 7–8/98; BL 4/15/98; HBG 10/98; SLJ 6/98)

3057 Bunting, Eve. *I Don't Want to Go to Camp* (PS–K). Illus. by Maryann Cocca-Leffler. 1996, Boyds Mills $14.95 (1-56397-393-6). 32pp. Lin loses her fear of going to camp when she helps her mother prepare to go to mothers' camp and later sees what fun there can be in camping. (Rev: BL 1/1–15/96; SLJ 3/96)

3058 Bunting, Eve. *The Pumpkin Fair* (PS–2). Illus. by Eileen Christelow. 1997, Clarion $15.00 (0-395-70060-4). 32pp. All of the activities and fun of an autumn pumpkin fair are here, including the pumpkin-judging contests. (Rev: BL 11/1/97; HBG 3/98; SLJ 9/97)

3059 Bunting, Eve. *Smoky Night* (K–3). Illus. by David Diaz. 1994, Harcourt $16.00 (0-15-269954-6). 32pp. Two families, one Korean American and the other African American, reach out to one another during the terrible Los Angeles riots. Caldecott Medal winner, 1995. (Rev: BCCB 3/94; BL 3/1/94; HB 5–6/94; SLJ 5/94*)

3060 Burke-Weiner, Kimberly. *The Maybe Garden* (K–3). Illus. by Fredrika Spillman. 1992, Beyond Words paper $7.95 (0-941831-57-4). 32pp. A little girl imagines that she has a magical garden complete with fairies instead of the ordinary one her mother tends. (Rev: BL 9/1/92)

3061 Burleigh, Robert. *Messenger, Messenger* (PS–3). Illus. by Barry Root. 2000, Simon & Schuster $16.00 (0-689-82103-4). 32pp. Presents the daily life of a bike messenger in a big city as he travels from slums to skyscrapers and returns home at night to his apartment and a striped orange cat. (Rev: BCCB 11/00; BL 5/15/00*; HBG 10/00; SLJ 6/00)

3062 Burton, Virginia Lee. *The Little House* (1–3). Illus. by author. 1978, Houghton $14.95 (0-395-18156-9); paper $5.95 (0-395-25938-X). Story of a little house in the country that over the years witnesses change and progress. Caldecott Medal winner, 1943.

3063 Caines, Jeannette. *I Need a Lunch Box* (PS–K). Illus. by Pat Cummings. 1988, HarperCollins LB $16.89 (0-06-020985-2); paper $5.95 (0-06-443341-2). 32pp. Mama says no to a lunch box for a little boy who hasn't yet started school. (Rev: BL 9/15/88; SLJ 12/88)

3064 Caple, Kathy. *The Purse* (PS–1). Illus. by author. 1992, Houghton paper $6.95 (0-395-62981-0). 32pp. Her new purse doesn't "clunk" her hard-earned money the way her Band-Aid box did, decides Katie. (Rev: BL 9/15/86; HB 11–12/86; SLJ 1/87)

3065 Capucilli, Alyssa Satin. *The Potty Book for Boys* (PS). 2000, Barron's $5.95 (0-7641-5232-7). 32pp. The male narrator explains how he receives his own potty, how he sits on it, and how he is rewarded if successful. The same story from a girl's point of view is in *The Potty Book for Girls* (2000). (Rev: SLJ 9/00)

3066 Carlstrom, Nancy White. *The Snow Speaks* (PS–2). Illus. by Jane Dyer. 1992, Little, Brown $15.95 (0-316-12861-9). 32pp. Children enjoy the various aspects of a snowstorm in the country from the first flakes to the coming of the snowplows. (Rev: BL 9/15/92)

3067 Carney, Margaret. *At Grandpa's Sugar Bush* (PS–3). Illus. by Janet Wilson. 1998, Kids Can $15.95 (1-55074-341-4). 32pp. During his spring vacation, a young boy visits his grandparents on their Ontario farm and assists them in making maple syrup. (Rev: BL 4/1/98; HBG 10/98; SLJ 4/98)

3068 Charlip, Remy, and Lillian Moore. *Hooray for Me!* (PS–2). Illus. by Vera B. Williams. 1996, Tricycle Pr. $14.95 (1-883672-43-0). 36pp. A new edition of an old favorite that explores a child's relationships. (Rev: BL 11/15/96)

3069 Chinn, Karen. *Sam and the Lucky Money* (PS–2). Illus. by Cornelius Van Wright and Ying-Hwa Hu. 1995, Lee & Low $15.95 (1-880000-13-X). Sam decides that the money he has received at Chinese New Year would be best used by giving it to a poor stranger. (Rev: SLJ 12/95)

3070 Chorao, Kay. *Little Farm by the Sea* (K–3). Illus. 1998, Holt $15.95 (0-8050-5053-1). 32pp. In this large-format picture book, a group of children watch farm activities throughout the year. (Rev: BCCB 7–8/98; BL 5/15/98; HB 3–4/98; HBG 10/98; SLJ 6/98)

3071 Christiansen, Candace. *The Mitten Tree* (K–3). Illus. by Elaine Greenstein. 1997, Fulcrum $16.95 (1-55591-349-0). 32pp. A lonely old woman endears herself to all when she knits mittens for needy children and places them on a tree to be taken. (Rev: BL 10/15/97; HBG 3/98; SLJ 2/98)

3072 Clary, Margie Willis. *A Sweet, Sweet Basket* (K–4). Illus. by Dennis L. Brown. 1995, Sandlapper $15.95 (0-87844-127-1). 40pp. An older woman explains to her granddaughter how baskets are woven from the sweetgrass that grows in South Carolina. (Rev: BL 9/1/95)

3073 Clements, Andrew. *Workshop* (PS–1). Illus. by David Wisniewski. 1999, Clarion $16.00 (0-395-85579-9). As a young apprentice becomes involved in the creation of a carousel, all of the tools of the woodworker are introduced. (Rev: BCCB 7–8/99; BL 4/15/99*; HBG 10/99; SLJ 5/99) [621.9]

3074 Cocca-Leffler, Maryann. *Bus Route to Boston* (PS–2). Illus. 2000, Boyds Mills $15.95 (1-56397-723-0). 32pp. The author-illustrator recalls the thrill of living outside Boston and taking trips by bus into the big city to shop and see the sights. (Rev: BL 2/1/00; HBG 10/00; SLJ 4/00)

3075 Cole, Henry. *Jack's Garden* (PS–4). Illus. 1995, Greenwillow $16.00 (0-688-13501-3). 24pp. In this cumulative tale, the plants and insects found in Jack's garden are introduced. (Rev: BCCB 5/95; BL 4/1/95; HB 5–6/95; SLJ 5/95)

3076 Cole, Joanna. *My Big Boy Potty Book* (PS). Illus. by Maxie Chambliss. 2000, HarperCollins $5.95 (0-688-17042-0). 32pp. In this reassuring picture book, Michael is told that he will succeed in potty training because practice makes perfect. The female counterpart is *My Big Girl Potty Book* (2000). (Rev: BL 2/1/01; HBG 3/01; SLJ 11/00)

3077 Coleman, Evelyn. *To Be a Drum* (K–3). Illus. by Aminah Robinson. 1998, Albert Whitman LB $16.95 (0-8075-8006-6). 32pp. Daddy Wes tells two children about the history of African Americans and their struggles as revealed in the rhythm of drumbeats. (Rev: BL 2/15/98; HBG 10/98; SLJ 5/98)

3078 Collier, Bryan. *Uptown* (PS–3). Illus. 2000, Holt $15.95 (0-8050-5721-8). 32pp. A young boy points out the sights and delights of Harlem — shopping on 125th Street and going to a jazz club. (Rev: BCCB 11/00; BL 6/1–15/00; HBG 10/00; SLJ 7/00)

3079 Conrad, Donna. *See You Soon Moon* (PS–1). Illus. by Don Carter. 2001, Knopf LB $16.99 (0-375-90656-8). As a boy travels by car with his parents at night to Grandma's house, he notices that the moon is following them. (Rev: SLJ 3/01)

3080 Cooke, Trish. *When I Grow Bigger* (PS–1). Illus. by John Bendall-Brunello. 1994, Candlewick $13.95 (1-56402-430-X). 32pp. A baby looks up to everyone, except when Dad puts him on his shoulders. (Rev: BL 9/1/94; SLJ 9/94)

3081 Cooper, Elisha. *Ballpark* (K–2). Illus. 1998, Greenwillow $15.00 (0-688-15755-6). 40pp. An active day at a ballpark is outlined in this colorful picture book that highlights everyone's participation, from groundskeepers and concession workers to fans and players. (Rev: BCCB 3/98; BL 4/1/98; HB 7–8/98; HBG 10/98)

3082 Cooper, Elisha. *Country Fair* (PS–2). Illus. 1997, Greenwillow $15.00 (0-688-15531-6). 40pp. The activities associated with a country fair are pictured. (Rev: BL 9/15/97; HB 9–10/97; HBG 3/98; SLJ 9/97)

3083 Corey, Dorothy. *You Go Away* (PS). Illus. by Diane Paterson. 1999, Albert Whitman $14.95 (0-8075-9442-3). 32pp. The concept of separation — for example, a parent going to work and coming back — is presented in a series of vignettes. (Rev: BL 9/1/99; HBG 3/00)

3084 Cote, Nancy. *Flip-Flops* (PS–2). Illus. 1998, Albert Whitman $13.95 (0-8075-2504-9). 32pp. Penny has a fine day at the beach, using her single flip-flop beach shoe in several ways and making a new friend in Meggie. (Rev: BL 5/15/98; HBG 10/98; SLJ 7/98)

3085 Cousins, Lucy. *Maisy's Pop-Up Playhouse* (2–5). Illus. 1995, Candlewick $19.99 (1-56402-635-3). 16pp. Pop-ups reveal the contents of Maisy's playhouse. (Rev: BL 2/1/96)

3086 Cox, Judy. *Now We Can Have a Wedding!* (PS–2). Illus. by DyAnne DiSalvo-Ryan. 1998, Holiday LB $15.95 (0-8234-1342-X). 32pp. The narrator goes from apartment to apartment in her building and sees that everyone is making a different national dish to bring to her sister's wedding. (Rev: BL 2/15/98; HBG 10/98; SLJ 3/98)

3087 Crebbin, June. *The Train Ride* (PS–1). Illus. by Stephen Lambert. 1995, Candlewick $14.95 (1-56402-546-2). 32pp. A young girl identifies the objects she sees through the window of her train coach. (Rev: BL 5/15/95; SLJ 10/95)

3088 Crews, Donald. *Carousel* (PS–2). Illus. by author. 1982, Greenwillow $15.93 (0-688-00909-3). 32pp. A ride on a carousel is described in pictures and text.

3089 Crews, Donald. *Night at the Fair* (K–2). Illus. 1998, Greenwillow $14.93 (0-688-11484-9). 24pp. Game booths, food concessions, and the Ferris wheel are only three of the attractions at a country fair that are highlighted in this engaging book. (Rev: BCCB 6/98; BL 3/1/98; HB 5–6/98; HBG 10/98; SLJ 4/98)

3090 Crews, Donald. *Parade* (PS–2). Illus. by author. 1983, Greenwillow LB $15.93 (0-688-01996-X); Morrow paper $4.95 (0-688-06520-1). 32pp. A picture-book celebration of a parade — fire engine and all.

3091 Crews, Donald. *Shortcut* (PS–3). Illus. 1992, Greenwillow $15.93 (0-688-06437-X). 32pp. Seven children follow a railroad track back home as the train gets closer and closer. (Rev: BCCB 10/92*; BL 10/15/92*; HB 1–2/93*; SLJ 11/92)

3092 Crews, Nina. *One Hot Summer Day* (PS–K). Illus. 1995, Greenwillow $14.89 (0-688-13394-0). 24pp. Using collages, the author illustrates the many activities associated with a hot summer's day. (Rev: BCCB 6/95; BL 6/1–15/95; HB 7–8/95; SLJ 6/95)

3093 Crews, Nina. *Snowball* (PS–1). Illus. 1997, Greenwillow $14.89 (0-688-14929-4). 24pp. This is the story of an African American child in a city and how she gets her wish for snow. (Rev: BL 12/1/97; HBG 3/98; SLJ 9/97)

3094 Crimi, Carolyn. *Outside, Inside* (PS–1). Illus. by Linnea A. Riley. 1995, Simon & Schuster $15.00

(0-671-88688-6). 32pp. While the rain is falling outside, Molly spends a comfortable time inside with her pets. (Rev: BCCB 5/95; BL 6/1–15/95; HB 9–10/95; SLJ 5/95)

3095 Crunk, Tony. *Big Mama* (PS–1). Illus. by Margot Apple. 2000, Farrar $16.00 (0-374-30688-5). 32pp. Big Mama, who is bring up her orphaned grandson, opens up her heart to all the kids in town and encourages them to be decent, responsible youngsters. (Rev: BL 2/15/00*; HBG 10/00; SLJ 5/00)

3096 Cuyler, Margery. *From Here to There* (PS–3). Illus. by Yu Cha Pak. 1999, Holt $16.95 (0-8050-3191-X). 32pp. A little girl describes where she lives in an ever-widening address — from town to county to state and so on. (Rev: BL 6/1–15/99; HBG 10/99; SLJ 5/99)

3097 Daly, Niki. *The Boy on the Beach* (PS). Illus. 1999, Simon & Schuster $16.00 (0-689-82175-1). 32pp. A young African boy wanders away from his parents on the beach and is rescued by a blond lifeguard in this simple story that shows South Africa's new integration. (Rev: BCCB 7–8/99; BL 5/15/99; HBG 10/99; SLJ 6/99)

3098 Daniels, Teri. *Just Enough* (PS–K). Illus. by Harley Jessup. 2000, Viking $15.99 (0-670-88873-7). 32pp. A young narrator tells of his feelings and actions on a single day during which he engages in such activities as catching a bug, splashing in the bath, riding a swing, and building a house of blocks. (Rev: BL 12/15/00; HBG 3/01; SLJ 11/00)

3099 Danis, Naomi. *Walk with Me* (PS). Illus. by Jacqueline Rogers. Series: Story Corner. 1995, Scholastic $6.95 (0-590-45855-8). A mother and her preschool daughter combine a pleasant outdoor walk with some nature study. (Rev: SLJ 8/95)

3100 Danneberg, Julie. *First Day Jitters* (K–4). Illus. by Judy Love. 2000, Charlesbridge $16.95 (1-58089-054-7). 32pp. A little girl imagines all the terrible things that could happen to her on her first day of school, but is pleasantly surprised with the real thing. (Rev: BL 3/15/00; HBG 10/00; SLJ 5/00)

3101 Delton, Judy. *My Mom Made Me Go to Camp* (1–3). Illus. by Lisa McCue. 1993, Dell paper $2.99 (0-440-40838-5). 32pp. Archie, who does not want to attend summer camp, gradually changes his mind. (Rev: BL 1/1/91; SLJ 2/91)

3102 Derby, Sally. *My Steps* (PS–1). Illus. by Adjoa J. Burrowes. 1996, Lee & Low $15.95 (1-880000-40-7). 32pp. An African American city child tells what a wonderful playground her front steps can be. (Rev: BL 10/15/96; SLJ 10/96)

3103 Diller, Harriet. *Big Band Sound* (PS–2). Illus. by Andrea Shine. 1996, Boyds Mills $14.95 (1-56397-129-1). 32pp. Everyday sounds and objects are used by Arlis to produce her own music. (Rev: BL 1/1–15/96; SLJ 3/96)

3104 Diller, Harriet. *The Faraway Drawer* (K–3). Illus. by Andrea Shine. 1996, Boyds Mills $14.95 (1-56397-190-9). Each of the sweaters found by a young girl in a drawer sends her thoughts to a different place. (Rev: SLJ 11/96)

3105 DiSalvo-Ryan, DyAnne. *Grandpa's Corner Store* (K–3). Illus. 2000, HarperCollins LB $15.89 (0-688-16717-9). 40pp. When Grandpa decides to sell his grocery store, Lucy devises a plan to get him to change his mind. (Rev: BL 5/1/00; HBG 10/00; SLJ 7/00)

3106 *Do Skyscrapers Touch the Sky? First Questions and Answers About the City* (PS–K). Illus. 1994, Time Life $14.95 (0-7835-0886-7). 48pp. Obvious questions about city life — like "What's under the street?" — are answered in well-illustrated double-page spreads. (Rev: BL 2/1/95) [307.76]

3107 Dodd, Anne W. *Footprints and Shadows* (PS–1). Illus. by Henri Sorensen. 1994, Simon & Schuster paper $4.95 (0-671-89905-8). 36pp. This picture book tries to answer the question of where footprints and shadows go. (Rev: BL 12/1/92; SLJ 12/92)

3108 Dodds, Siobhan. *Ting-a-ling!* (PS). Illus. by author. Series: DK Toddler Storybook. 1999, DK $9.95 (0-7894-4841-6). This simple picture book asks who Tilly is talking to on the telephone. (Rev: HBG 3/00; SLJ 12/99)

3109 Dooley, Norah. *Everybody Bakes Bread* (K–3). Illus. by Peter J. Thornton. 1996, Carolrhoda LB $15.95 (0-87614-864-X). 40pp. On an errand for her mother, Carrie sees her neighbors bake a variety of breads in this sequel to *Everybody Cooks Rice* (1991). (Rev: BL 3/1/96; SLJ 4/96)

3110 Dragonwagon, Crescent. *Home Place* (1–3). Illus. by Jerry Pinkney. 1990, Macmillan $14.95 (0-02-733190-3). 40pp. A family out hiking comes on the remains of someone's home. (Rev: BCCB 12/90; BL 8/90; HB 11–12/90; SLJ 2/91)

3111 Dragonwagon, Crescent. *The Itch Book* (K–3). Illus. by Joseph Mahler. 1990, Macmillan LB $13.95 (0-02-733121-0). 32pp. A rhyming text captures the fidgets of a hot summer day in the Ozarks. (Rev: BL 2/1/90)

3112 Dragonwagon, Crescent. *This Is the Bread I Baked for Ned* (PS–2). Illus. by Isadore Seltzer. 1989, Macmillan paper $14.95 (0-02-733220-9). 32pp. A rhythmic story in which Ned gets a nice surprise. (Rev: BL 11/15/89; SLJ 12/89)

3113 Duncan, Debbie. *When Molly Was in the Hospital: A Book for Brothers and Sisters of Hospitalized Children* (PS–2). Illus. by Nina Ollikainen. Series: MiniMed. 1994, Rayve $12.95 (1-877810-44-4). The experiences of a young girl whose younger sister faces major surgery and the many conflicting emotions she feels. (Rev: SLJ 3/95)

3114 Edwards, Richard. *Fly with the Birds: A Word and Rhyme Book* (PS–K). Illus. by Satoshi Kitamura. 1996, Orchard $12.95 (0-531-09491-X). In this flap book, a child narrates her day, from waking up to bedtime and dreamland. (Rev: SLJ 3/96)

3115 Ehlert, Lois. *Circus* (PS–2). Illus. 1992, HarperCollins $15.95 (0-060-20252-1). 40pp. The razzle-dazzle of the circus is translated into the relative quiet of the picture-book experience. (Rev: BL 1/1/92; HB 3–4/92; SLJ 4/92) [791.3]

3116 Ehlert, Lois. *Growing Vegetable Soup* (PS–K). Illus. by author. 1987, Harcourt $15.00 (0-15-

232575-1); paper $6.00 (0-15-232580-8). 40pp. Father and child plant seeds and sprouts "to grow vegetable soup." Also use: *Planting a Rainbow* (1988). (Rev: BL 3/1/87; SLJ 3/87)

3117 Ehlert, Lois. *Hands* (K–2). Illus. 1997, Harcourt $13.00 (0-15-201506-X). 20pp. This picture book describes what hands can accomplish, their uses, and how they can bring people together. (Rev: BL 11/15/97*; HB 9–10/97; HBG 3/98; SLJ 12/97)

3118 Ehlert, Lois. *Market Day: A Story Told with Folk Art* (PS–2). Illus. 2000, Harcourt $16.00 (0-15-202158-2). 36pp. This picture book depicts a day when the farmers load their trucks with goods and go to the market to buy and sell, and work and play. (Rev: BCCB 7–8/00; BL 5/15/00; HBG 10/00; SLJ 7/00)

3119 Ellis, Sarah. *Next Stop!* (PS–K). Illus. by Ruth Ohi. 2000, Fitzhenry & Whiteside $13.95 (1-55041-539-5). 32pp. Little Claire helps the bus driver by calling out the names of the streets and the special attractions found at each stop. (Rev: BL 12/1/00; SLJ 1/01)

3120 Enderle, Judith R., and Stephanie Jacob Gordon. *Something's Happening on Calabash Street: A Story with Thirteen Recipes* (PS–2). Illus. by Donna Ingemanson. 2000, Chronicle $14.95 (0-8118-2450-0). This picture book shows children and adults preparing for a street festival and gives 13 recipes for the foods they cook. (Rev: HBG 10/00; SLJ 7/00)

3121 Ernst, Lisa Campbell. *Bear's Day* (PS). Illus. by author. 2000, Viking $5.99 (0-670-89115-0). A board book that shows a toddler playing with a teddy bear. The same child plays with a cat in *Cat's Play* (2000). (Rev: BCCB 4/00; BL 10/1/00; SLJ 7/00)

3122 Esbensen, Barbara J. *Jumping Day* (PS–1). Illus. by Maryann Cocca-Leffler. 1999, Boyds Mills $9.95 (1-56397-709-5). 24pp. A delightful look at a girl at play as she skips her way to school. (Rev: HBG 10/99; SLJ 4/99)

3123 Evans, Lezlie. *Snow Dance* (PS–1). Illus. by Cynthia Jabar. 1997, Houghton $16.00 (0-395-77849-2). 32pp. Two bored sisters are successful when they engage in a snow dance because it soon begins to fall. (Rev: BL 10/1/97; HBG 3/98; SLJ 12/97)

3124 Evans, Lezlie. *Sometimes I Feel Like a Storm Cloud* (PS–1). Illus. by Marsha Gray Carrington. 1999, Mondo $15.95 (1-57255-621-8). 32pp. A girl's moods are expressed in a series of similes that capture her feelings. (Rev: BL 12/15/99)

3125 Everitt, Betsy. *Up the Ladder, Down the Slide* (PS). Illus. by author. 1998, Harcourt $12.00 (0-15-292886-3). A joyful look at a group of children who are playing together in the park. (Rev: HBG 10/98; SLJ 5/98)

3126 Fair, Sylvia. *The Bedspread* (K–2). Illus. by author. 1982, Morrow $17.00 (0-688-00877-1). 32pp. Two old ladies decide to embroider their bedspreads.

3127 Falwell, Cathryn. *P. J. and Puppy* (PS). Illus. 1997, Clarion $8.95 (0-395-56918-4). 23pp. A boy and his puppy are toilet trained together. (Rev: BL 2/15/97; SLJ 3/97)

3128 Farrell, John. *It's Just a Game* (K–3). Illus. by John E. Cymerman. 1999, Boyds Mills $15.95 (1-56397-785-0). 32pp. Even though they lose every game but one, and in spite of parents who are over-competitive, a group of kids enjoy playing on their soccer team. (Rev: BL 12/1/99; HBG 3/00; SLJ 11/99)

3129 Field, Rachel. *General Store* (PS–1). Illus. by Nancy Winslow Parker. 1988, Little, Brown $15.95 (0-316-28163-8). 24pp. A poem that extols the charms of the old-fashioned store. Another version has illustrations by Giles Laroche (1988, Little, Brown). (Rev: BCCB 5/88; BL 3/1/88; HB 5–6/88)

3130 Fitzpatrick, Marie-Louise. *Lizzy and Skunk* (K–2). Illus. 2000, DK $14.95 (0-7894-6163-3). 32pp. Lizzy doesn't feel afraid when her hand puppet Skunk is around, but when he disappears she must conquer her fears to save him. (Rev: BCCB 7–8/00; BL 5/1/00; HBG 10/00; SLJ 7/00)

3131 Flanagan, Alice K. *A Busy Day at Mr. Kang's Grocery Store* (1–2). Illus. by Christine Osinski. Series: Our Neighborhood. 1996, Children's LB $19.50 (0-516-20047-X). 32pp. Everyday activities in a neighborhood grocery store are pictured and introduced in a simple text. (Rev: BL 1/1–15/97) [381]

3132 Flanagan, Alice K. *Buying a Pet from Ms. Chavez* (PS–1). Series: Our Neighborhood. 1998, Children's LB $19.50 (0-516-20773-3). 32pp. Using a simple photojournalistic technique, this book introduces a pet store owner, her many duties, and her contributions to the community. (Rev: BL 6/1–15/98; HBG 10/98)

3133 Flanagan, Alice K. *Call Mr. Vasquez, He'll Fix It!* (1–2). Illus. by Christine Osinski. Series: Our Neighborhood. 1996, Children's LB $19.50 (0-516-20045-3). 32pp. The activities of a neighborhood repairman are introduced in simple text and pictures. (Rev: BL 1/1–15/97) [647]

3134 Flanagan, Alice K. *Choosing Eyeglasses with Mrs. Koutris* (PS–1). Series: Our Neighborhood. 1998, Children's LB $19.50 (0-516-20775-X). 32pp. A day in the life of an optician is outlined in this account that is heavily illustrated with color photographs. (Rev: BL 6/1–15/98; HBG 10/98) [612.8]

3135 Flanagan, Alice K. *Coach John and His Soccer Team* (PS–1). Series: Our Neighborhood. 1998, Children's LB $19.50 (0-516-20777-6). 32pp. Using a photojournalistic style, this simple book introduces a sports coach and his activities. (Rev: BL 10/15/98; HBG 3/99)

3136 Flanagan, Alice K. *Here Comes Mr. Eventoff with the Mail!* (PS–1). Series: Our Neighborhood. 1998, Children's LB $19.50 (0-516-20776-8). 32pp. The duties of a mail carrier are shown in this photo-essay that uses a simple text. (Rev: BL 10/15/98; HBG 3/99)

3137 Flanagan, Alice K. *Learning Is Fun with Mrs. Perez* (PS–1). Illus. Series: Our Neighborhood. 1998, Children's LB $19.50 (0-516-20774-1). 32pp.

A brief text and large color photographs introduce youngsters to the work of Mrs. Perez, a Cuban immigrant who teaches a bilingual kindergarten in Chicago. (Rev: BL 6/1–15/98; HBG 10/98) [370.117]

3138 Flanagan, Alice K. *Mr. Santizo's Tasty Treats!* (PS–1). Illus. Series: Our Neighborhood. 1998, Children's LB $19.50 (0-516-20771-7). 32pp. The work of Mr. Santizo, a Hispanic American who is a manager at a Swedish bakery, is described in a short text with many color photographs. (Rev: BL 6/1–15/98; HBG 10/98) [664]

3139 Flanagan, Alice K. *Mr. Yee Fixes Cars* (PS–1). Series: Our Neighborhood. 1998, Children's LB $19.50 (0-516-20772-5). 32pp. A day in the life of an automobile mechanic and his contributions to the community are outlined in this book that is illustrated with many color photographs. (Rev: BL 6/1–15/98; HBG 10/98) [629.28]

3140 Flanagan, Alice K. *Ms. Davison, Our Librarian* (1–2). Illus. by Christine Osinski. Series: Our Neighborhood. 1996, Children's LB $20.00 (0-516-20009-7); paper $6.95 (0-516-26060-X). 32pp. The activities and duties of a librarian are described and pictured. (Rev: BL 1/1–15/97; SLJ 2/97) [021]

3141 Flanagan, Alice K. *Riding the Ferry with Captain Cruz* (1–2). Illus. by Christine Osinski. Series: Our Neighborhood. 1996, Children's LB $19.50 (0-516-20046-1); paper $5.95 (0-516-26059-6). 32pp. In text and pictures, the day-to-day work of a ferry captain is presented. (Rev: BL 1/1–15/97; SLJ 2/97) [386]

3142 Flanagan, Alice K. *Riding the School Bus with Mrs. Kramer* (PS–1). Series: Our Neighborhood. 1998, Children's LB $19.50 (0-516-20779-2). 32pp. The daily routine of a school bus driver is shown in pictures and text. (Rev: BL 10/15/98; HBG 3/99)

3143 Flanagan, Alice K. *A Visit to the Gravesens' Farm* (PS–1). Series: Our Neighborhood. 1998, Children's LB $19.50 (0-516-20778-4). 32pp. Farming and the life of a farm family are explored in a simple text and color photographs. (Rev: BL 10/15/98; HBG 3/99)

3144 Flanagan, Alice K. *The Wilsons, a House-Painting Team* (1–2). Illus. by Christine Osinski. Series: Our Neighborhood. 1996, Children's LB $19.50 (0-516-20216-2); paper $6.95 (0-516-26063-4). 32pp. House painting, its importance, and difficulties encountered are portrayed in basic text with many pictures. (Rev: BL 1/1–15/97) [698]

3145 Fleischman, Sid. *The Scarebird* (PS–2). Illus. by Peter Sis. 1988, Greenwillow $15.89 (0-688-07318-2). 32pp. An old farmer named Lonesome John puts up a headless scarecrow to scare the birds, but then decides to give the scarecrow a head. (Rev: BCCB 9/88; BL 9/15/88; SLJ 9/88)

3146 Fleming, Denise. *Where Once There Was a Wood* (PS–2). Illus. 1996, Holt $16.95 (0-8050-3761-6). 32pp. A piece of land is described as it was before a housing development changed it. (Rev: BCCB 3/96; BL 5/1/96; SLJ 6/96)

3147 Ford, Christine. *Snow!* (PS). Illus. by Candace Whitman. Series: Growing Tree. 1999, HarperFestival $9.95 (0-694-01199-1). 24pp. For the very young, this is a rhyming story about a brother and sister who spend a snowy day outdoors with their dad and pet dog. (Rev: BL 1/1–15/00; HBG 3/00; SLJ 12/99)

3148 Ford, Miela. *My Day in the Garden* (PS–3). Illus. by Anita Lobel. 1999, Greenwillow LB $15.93 (0-688-15542-1). 24pp. Little girls at home on a rainy day use their imaginations and the costumes they find to create an indoor garden. (Rev: BCCB 3/99; BL 5/1/99; HBG 10/99; SLJ 5/99)

3149 Frankel, Alona. *Joshua's Book of Clothes* (PS–2). Illus. by author. Series: Joshua and Prudence. 2000, HarperFestival $6.95 (0-694-01381-1). Joshua's mother tells him about clothing and gives a brief history of apparel beginning with the caveman. Also use *Prudence's Baby-Sitter Book* (2000), in which Prudence is told by her mother about her baby-sitter. (Rev: HBG 3/01; SLJ 1/01)

3150 Franklin, Kristine L. *Iguana Beach* (PS–2). Illus. by Lori Lohstoeter. 1997, Crown LB $18.99 (0-517-70901-5). On a beach in Central America, Little Reina finds a lagoon where she can swim without danger. (Rev: SLJ 8/97)

3151 French, Vivian. *Oh No, Anna!* (PS). Illus. by Alex Ayliffe. 1997, Peachtree $14.95 (1-56145-125-8). A flap book that chronicles a number of minor household accidents that befall Anna. (Rev: HBG 3/98; SLJ 12/97)

3152 Galbraith, Kathryn O. *Look! Snow!* (PS–2). Illus. by Nina S. Montezinos. 1992, Macmillan $13.95 (0-689-50551-5). 32pp. Children enjoy the season's first snowfall, particularly when they have the day off from school. (Rev: BL 11/1/92; SLJ 9/92)

3153 Gardella, Tricia. *Blackberry Booties* (PS–2). Illus. by Glo Coalson. 2000, Orchard LB $16.99 (0-531-33184-9). 32pp. Mikki Jo works hard picking blackberries and then uses bartering techniques to get a pair of booties made for her newborn cousin. (Rev: BCCB 4/00; BL 3/15/00; HBG 10/00; SLJ 5/00)

3154 Gardella, Tricia. *Casey's New Hat* (PS–1). Illus. by Margot Apple. 1997, Houghton $14.95 (0-395-72035-4). 32pp. Casey has trouble finding a new hat that she likes and finally settles for an old one that Grandpa no longer wants. (Rev: BL 4/15/97; SLJ 4/97)

3155 Gardella, Tricia. *Just Like My Dad* (PS–2). Illus. by Margot Apple. 1996, HarperCollins paper $4.95 (0-064-43463-X). 32pp. On a ranch, a young boy dressed like a cowboy accompanies his father through the day's chores. (Rev: BL 5/1/93; HB 7–8/93)

3156 Gardiner, Lindsey. *Here Come Poppy and Max* (PS). Illus. by author. 2000, Little, Brown $12.95 (0-316-60346-5). A little girl and her dog pretend to be different animals like a giraffe and a duck in this engaging picture book. (Rev: HBG 3/01; SLJ 9/00)

3157 Garland, Sherry. *The Summer Sands* (PS–1). Illus. by Robert J. Lee. 1995, Harcourt $15.00 (0-15-282492-8). 32pp. Children and their parents use their old Christmas trees to act as a windbreak to form new sand dunes. (Rev: BL 4/15/95; SLJ 6/95)

3158 Gauch, Patricia L. *Tanya and the Magic Wardrobe* (PS–2). Illus. by Satomi Ichikawa. Series: Tanya. 1997, Putnam $16.95 (0-399-22940-X). 32pp. At a ballet performance of *Coppelia*, Tanya, a young dancer, meets an old woman who shows her costumes that are worn in different ballets. (Rev: BL 11/1/97; HBG 3/98; SLJ 10/97)

3159 Gay, Marie-Louise. *Stella: Star of the Sea* (PS–K). Illus. 1999, Douglas & McIntyre $15.95 (0-88899-337-4). 32pp. While at the seashore, Sam delays taking a plunge into the water by asking his older sister, Stella, a multitude of questions. (Rev: BCCB 5/99; BL 5/15/99; SLJ 8/99)

3160 Gay, Marie-Louise. *Stella, Queen of the Snow* (PS–1). Illus. 2000, Douglas & McIntyre $15.95 (0-88899-404-4). 32pp. Little Sam discovers the wonders of snow when his boisterous big sister takes him out to play in it. (Rev: BCCB 1/01; BL 11/1/00; HBG 3/01; SLJ 10/00)

3161 Geisert, Bonnie. *Desert Town* (K–3). Illus. by Arthur Geisert. 2001, Houghton $16.00 (0-395-95387-1). 32pp. A year in a desert town is traced in this book that allows the readers to explore homes in cutaway views. (Rev: SLJ 3/01)

3162 Geisert, Bonnie. *Mountain Town* (1–3). Illus. by Arthur Geisert. 2000, Houghton $16.00 (0-395-95390-1). 32pp. A series of vignettes portray life in a mountain town during different seasons. (Rev: BL 3/15/00; HBG 10/00; SLJ 4/00)

3163 Geisert, Bonnie. *River Town* (1–3). Illus. by Arthur Geisert. 1999, Houghton $16.00 (0-395-90891-4). 32pp. This picture book depicts a small river town over a year's time, during which the river floods and threatens to destroy the community. (Rev: BCCB 6/99; BL 7/99; HBG 10/99; SLJ 5/99) [307.72]

3164 Geisert, Bonnie, and Arthur Geisert. *Prairie Town* (1–3). Illus. 1998, Houghton $16.00 (0-395-85907-7). 32pp. Brief text and detailed etchings colored with washes cover a year in the life of a small Midwestern town. Specific events and sites are illustrated as well as panoramic views of the entire town. (Rev: BL 4/1/98; HB 5–6/98; HBG 10/98; SLJ 4/98)

3165 Gershator, David, and Phillis Gershator. *Bread Is for Eating* (PS–1). Illus. by Emma Shaw-Smith. 1995, Holt $15.95 (0-8050-3173-1). 32pp. This song with lyrics in both English and Spanish explains how bread is made. (Rev: BL 6/1–15/95; SLJ 8/95)

3166 Gibbons, Gail. *Fire! Fire!* (PS–2). Illus. by author. 1984, HarperCollins LB $15.89 (0-690-04416-X); paper $6.95 (0-06-446058-4). 40pp. The various ways a fire is fought.

3167 Gibbons, Gail. *How a House Is Built* (PS–K). Illus. 1990, Holiday LB $16.95 (0-8234-0841-8). 32pp. A good introduction to the construction of a wood frame house. (Rev: BL 10/15/90; SLJ 10/90) [690]

3168 Gibbons, Gail. *Paper, Paper Everywhere* (PS–2). Illus. by author. 1997, Harcourt paper $5.00 (0-152-01491-8). 32pp. A picture book that shows how useful paper is.

3169 Glaser, Linda. *Compost! Growing Gardens from Your Garbage* (PS–1). Illus. by Anca Hariton. 1996, Millbrook LB $21.90 (1-56294-659-5). 32pp. A little girl explains how her family uses waste material to create a compost heap that eventually produces rich earth for spring planting. (Rev: BL 2/15/96; SLJ 4/96) [635]

3170 Glaser, Linda. *Our Big Home: An Earth Poem* (2–3). Illus. by Elisa Kleven. 2000, Millbrook LB $21.90 (0-7613-1650-7). 32pp. Some of the common joys of life — such as water, dirt, sun, moon, wind, sky, dark, and the fact one is alive — are celebrated with outstanding illustrations. (Rev: BL 5/15/00; HBG 10/00; SLJ 4/00)

3171 Godard, Alex. *Mama, Across the Sea* (K–3). Illus. 2000, Holt $16.95 (0-8050-6161-4). 32pp. A little girl who is living on an island while her mother looks for work across the sea eagerly awaits mail. (Rev: BL 7/00; HBG 10/00; SLJ 6/00)

3172 Godwin, Laura. *The Flower Girl* (PS–3). Illus. by John Wallace. 2000, Hyperion $12.99 (0-7868-0408-4). A description of a wedding from the flower girl's point of view. (Rev: SLJ 2/01)

3173 Gomi, Taro. *Everyone Poops* (PS). Trans. by Amanda M. Stinchecum. Illus. Series: Can You Believe It! 1993, Kane/Miller $11.95 (0-916291-45-6). 28pp. This book shows that all animals poop and that this is a natural part of life. (Rev: BCCB 4/93; BL 5/15/93) [612]

3174 Gomi, Taro. *My Friends* (PS–K). Illus. 1995, Chronicle paper $5.95 (0-811-81237-5). 36pp. A little girl talks about all the things she's learned from her friends, such as jumping from her dog. (Rev: BL 7/90; SLJ 7/90)

3175 Gomi, Taro. *Who Ate It?* (PS–K). Illus. 1991, Millbrook LB $13.90 (1-56294-010-4). In this book from Japan, various items are hidden in pictures. A companion puzzle book is: *Who Hid It?* (1992). (Rev: SLJ 4/92)

3176 Good, Merle, and Dan Boltz. *Dan's Pants: The Adventures of Dan, the Fabric Man* (K–3). Illus. by Cheryl Benner. 2000, Good Bks. $16.00 (1-56148-307-9). Dan and his wife Fran sell fabrics, and over the years Fran sews many patches from different bolts of cloth to mend Dan's pants. (Rev: SLJ 12/00)

3177 Gorton, Julia. *The Terrible Twos* (PS). Illus. by author. 1999, Hyperion $10.99 (0-7868-0268-5). A flap book that tells of twin toddlers and their action-packed day. (Rev: SLJ 5/99)

3178 Gould, Deborah. *Aaron's Shirt* (PS–1). Illus. by Cheryl Harness. 1989, Macmillan LB $13.95 (0-02-736351-1). 32pp. A deceptively simple tale about a boy who outgrows his shirt. (Rev: BCCB 4/89; BL 3/1/89; HB 7–8/89)

3179 Graham, Bob. *The Red Woolen Blanket* (PS–K). Illus. by author. 1996, Candlewick paper $4.99 (1-564-02848-8). 32pp. Julia's bright red blanket stays with her from infancy until she enters school. (Rev: HB 5–6/88)

3180 Graham, Bob. *Rose Meets Mr. Wintergarten* (PS–2). Illus. by author. 1992, Candlewick $14.95 (1-56402-039-8). 32pp. When her ball goes over Mr. Wintergarten's fence, Rose is able to find out what her neighbor is really like. (Rev: BCCB 7–8/92; BL 5/15/92; HB 5–6/92; SLJ 8/92)

3181 Gray, Libba M. *When Uncle Took the Fiddle* (PS–2). Illus. by Lloyd Bloom. 1999, Orchard $15.95 (0-531-30137-0). 32pp. Although it's bedtime, an Appalachian family and their neighbors come to life when Uncle picks up his fiddle and starts to play. (Rev: BCCB 11/99; BL 9/15/99; HBG 3/00; SLJ 11/99)

3182 Greenfield, Eloise. *Big Friend, Little Friend* (PS). Illus. by Jan S. Gilchrist. 1991, Writers & Readers $4.95 (0-86316-204-5). 12pp. This is one of a series of board books about the everyday activities of some African American children. Also use: *Daddy and I; I Make Music;* and *My Doll, Keshia* (all 1991). (Rev: BL 12/15/91; SLJ 12/91)

3183 Greenfield, Eloise. *Water, Water* (PS). Illus. by Jan S. Gilchrist. 1999, HarperFestival $9.95 (0-694-01247-5). 24pp. A young boy experiences the wonder of water by wading, fishing, drinking, and simply watching it. (Rev: BL 8/99; HBG 3/00; SLJ 10/99)

3184 Gregory, Valiska. *Looking for Angels* (PS–2). Illus. by Leslie Baker. 1996, Simon & Schuster paper $17.00 (0-689-80500-4). 32pp. The wonders of everyday phenomena make Sarah realize that angels are everywhere. (Rev: BL 6/1–15/96; SLJ 3/96)

3185 Grejniec, Michael. *What Do You Like?* (K–2). Illus. 1995, North-South paper $6.95 (1-55858-417-X). 32pp. A boy and a girl like the same things, but in different ways. (Rev: BL 8/92; SLJ 1/93)

3186 Grimes, Nikki. *Come Sunday* (PS–3). Illus. by Michael Bryant. 1996, Eerdmans $15.00 (0-8028-5108-8); paper $7.50 (0-8028-5134-7). 32pp. Young Latasha finds that going to church on Sunday is an exciting adventure. (Rev: BCCB 3/97; BL 6/1–15/96*; SLJ 6/97)

3187 Gundersheimer, Karen. *Find Cat, Wear Hat* (PS). Illus. 1995, Scholastic $5.95 (0-590-48061-8). 24pp. A beginner's book in which each page explains in two words the accompanying picture. Similar in scope is the author's *Splish Splash, Bang Crash* (1995). (Rev: BL 1/15/95; SLJ 9/95)

3188 Haas, Jessie. *Hurry!* (PS–2). Illus. by Joseph A. Smith. 2000, Greenwillow $15.95 (0-688-16889-2). 24pp. Nora and her grandparents work hard loading hay onto a horse-drawn wagon just before the rains come. (Rev: BL 5/15/00; HB 7–8/00; HBG 10/00; SLJ 6/00)

3189 Haley, Amanda. *It's a Baby's World* (PS). Illus. 2001, Little, Brown $12.95 (0-316-34596-2). 24pp. An engaging book that describes a typical day in the life of a toddler. (Rev: BL 3/15/01)

3190 Hamanaka, Sheila. *All the Colors of the Earth* (PS–2). Illus. 1994, Morrow $15.89 (0-688-11132-7). 32pp. A collection of paintings that show children of various ethnic backgrounds together having fun. (Rev: BCCB 10/94; BL 9/1/94; HB 11–12/94; SLJ 8/94*)

3191 Hamm, Diane J. *Laney's Lost Momma* (PS–1). Illus. by Sally G. Ward. 1991, Whitman LB $14.95

(0-8075-4340-3). 32pp. Mother and daughter are reunited after Laney loses her mother in a department store. (Rev: BL 1/1/92; SLJ 12/91)

3192 Harrison, Troon. *The Memory Horse* (K–3). Illus. by Eugenie Fernandes. 1999, Tundra $15.95 (0-88776-440-1). A quiet story about a town's attempts to save an old carousel and a grandfather who tries to restore one of the horses named Starflyer. (Rev: HBG 10/00; SLJ 5/00)

3193 Hautzig, David. *At the Supermarket* (PS–2). Illus. 1994, Orchard LB $17.99 (0-531-08682-8). 32pp. An hour-by-hour account that describes in pictures and text what happens during a single day in a modern supermarket. (Rev: BL 3/15/94; SLJ 5/94) [381]

3194 Havill, Juanita. *Jamaica's Find* (PS–1). Illus. by Anne S. O'Brien. 1986, Houghton $16.00 (0-395-39376-0); paper $5.95 (0-395-45357-7). 32pp. Jamaica finds a stuffed dog, which she brings home, but her parents make her return to the park where she found it, and where she also finds its true owner. Also use: *Jamaica Tag-Along* (1989). (Rev: BCCB 5/86; BL 4/1/86; SLJ 8/86)

3195 Hayes, Joe. *A Spoon for Every Bite* (PS–3). Illus. by Rebecca Leer. 1996, Orchard LB $17.99 (0-531-08799-9). 32pp. A poor couple fools a rich neighbor into spending his fortune for spoons. (Rev: BCCB 4/96; BL 3/15/96; SLJ 4/96)

3196 Hayes, Sarah. *Eat Up, Gemma* (PS–1). Illus. by Jan Ormerod. 1988, Lothrop $16.00 (0-688-08149-5). 32pp. Gemma is at the stage where food is mostly a toy. (Rev: BCCB 9/88; BL 9/1/88; HB 11–12/88)

3197 Hayles, Marsha. *Beach Play* (PS). Illus. by Hideko Takahashi. 1998, Holt $14.95 (0-8050-4271-7). In this picture book, children enjoy a day at the beach, romping, sunning, climbing, and playing with beach balls. (Rev: HBG 10/98; SLJ 7/98)

3198 Hazen, Barbara S. *Mommy's Office* (PS–1). Illus. by David Soman. 1992, Macmillan $13.95 (0-689-31601-1). 32pp. Emily spends an interesting day when her mother takes her to the office and shows her how she works. (Rev: BCCB 3/92; BL 3/1/92; SLJ 3/92)

3199 Heap, Sue. *Cowboy Baby* (PS–K). Illus. 1998, Candlewick $15.99 (0-7636-0437-2). 32pp. A slight story set in the Southwest about an imaginative boy who would rather play cowboy than go to bed. (Rev: BCCB 5/98; BL 3/1/98; HBG 10/98; SLJ 5/98)

3200 Hedlund, Carey. *Night Fell at Harry's Farm* (PS–K). Illus. 1997, Greenwillow $15.00 (0-688-14932-4). 24pp. The whole family piles into the car for an adventurous ride to Harry's for dinner. (Rev: BL 6/1–15/97; SLJ 5/97)

3201 Heide, Florence Parry. *Some Things Are Scary* (PS–1). Illus. by Jules Feiffer. 2000, Candlewick $15.99 (0-0736-1222-7). 40pp. This is a book about everyday things that young children might find scary — being hugged by a huge adult or finding out that your best friend's best friend isn't you. (Rev: BL 10/15/00*; SLJ 1/01*)

3202 Henderson, Kathy. *The Little Boat* (PS–1). Illus. by Patrick Benson. 1995, Candlewick $15.95 (1-56402-420-2). 32pp. The boat that a boy has made at his beach washes out to sea and is eventually found by a girl on another beach. (Rev: BL 9/1/95; SLJ 10/95)

3203 Henkes, Kevin. *Clean Enough* (PS–2). Illus. by author. 1982, Greenwillow $14.93 (0-688-00829-1). 24pp. A young boy takes a bath.

3204 Henkes, Kevin. *Good-bye, Curtis* (PS–K). Illus. by Marisabina Russo. 1995, Greenwillow $14.89 (0-688-12828-9). 24pp. After 42 years of service, mailcarrier Curtis makes his last rounds. (Rev: BL 10/15/95; HB 11–12/95; SLJ 10/95)

3205 Heo, Yumi. *One Afternoon* (PS–1). Illus. 1994, Orchard $15.95 (0-531-06845-5). 32pp. A mother and her son discover on a big-city walk that everything from a jackhammer to a cash register makes its own distinctive sound. (Rev: BL 8/94; HB 11–12/94; SLJ 11/94)

3206 Herold, Maggie R. *A Very Important Day* (PS–2). Illus. by Catherine Stock. 1995, Morrow $15.93 (0-688-13066-6). 40pp. Families from various racial backgrounds are excited because it is the day they will become U.S. citizens. (Rev: BL 9/1/95; SLJ 11/95)

3207 Herron, Carolivia. *Nappy Hair* (K–4). Illus. by Joe Cepeda. 1997, Knopf LB $18.99 (0-679-97937-9). 32pp. This picture book about an African American girl also touches on slavery, Africa, and family. (Rev: BCCB 2/97; BL 2/1/97; SLJ 1/97)

3208 Hesse, Karen. *Come On, Rain!* (K–2). Illus. by Jon J. Muth. 1999, Scholastic $15.95 (0-590-33125-6). 32pp. A delightful book about a group of children who enjoy a cloudburst during a sweltering day in the big city. (Rev: BCCB 4/99; BL 2/1/99; HB 7–8/99; HBG 10/99; SLJ 3/99)

3209 Hest, Amy. *The Babies Are Coming!* (PS–1). Illus. by Chloe Cheese. 1997, Crown LB $18.99 (0-517-70944-9). 32pp. On a cold winter evening, parents are preparing to take their children to story hour, and the librarian is also preparing by choosing the perfect book to read to them. (Rev: BL 11/1/97; HBG 3/98; SLJ 1/98)

3210 Hest, Amy. *How to Get Famous in Brooklyn* (K–3). Illus. by Linda D. Sawaya. 1995, Simon & Schuster paper $15.00 (0-689-80293-5). 32pp. A young girl faithfully records her experiences in her Brooklyn neighborhood. (Rev: BL 8/95; SLJ 9/95)

3211 Hest, Amy. *The Purple Coat* (K–2). Illus. by Amy Schwartz. 1992, Macmillan paper $5.99 (0-689-71634-6). 32pp. This year Gabrielle wants a purple coat instead of the navy blue coat she always wears, and Grandpa the tailor comes up with an ingenious solution. (Rev: BL 9/1/86; HB 1–2/87; SLJ 11/86)

3212 High, Linda O. *Barn Savers* (PS–3). Illus. by Ted Lewin. 1999, Boyds Mills $15.95 (1-56397-403-7). 32pp. A boy and his father dismantle a barn to save it from bulldozers and salvage its parts for new uses. (Rev: BL 11/1/99*; HBG 3/00; SLJ 11/99)

3213 High, Linda O. *Beekeepers* (K–2). Illus. by Doug Chayka. 1998, Boyds Mills $14.95 (1-56397-486-X). 32pp. A little girl, under the guidance of her grandfather, engages in the many activities involved in bee-keeping, including gathering the honey. (Rev: BCCB 4/98; BL 5/15/98; HBG 3/99; SLJ 6/98)

3214 Hines, Anna Grossnickle. *What Can You Do in the Rain?* (PS). Illus. by Thea Kliros. 1999, Greenwillow $5.95 (0-688-16077-8). 20pp. A board book that encourages toddlers to experience rain fully. (Rev: BL 6/1–15/99; HBG 10/99; SLJ 6/99)

3215 Hines, Anna Grossnickle. *What Can You Do in the Snow?* (PS). Illus. by Thea Kliros. 1999, Greenwillow $5.95 (0-688-16078-6). This small board book filled with watercolor paintings shows multicultural children building snowmen and engaging in other winter activities. Also use *What Can You Do in the Wind?* (1999). (Rev: HBG 10/99; SLJ 6/99)

3216 Hines, Anna Grossnickle. *What Can You Do in the Sun?* (PS). Illus. by Thea Kliros. 1999, Greenwillow $5.95 (0-688-16080-8). 20pp. Several experiences that are associated with being in the sun are joyfully presented in this board book. A companion book is *What Can You Do in the Wind?* (Rev: BL 6/1–15/99; HBG 10/99; SLJ 6/99)

3217 Hoban, Julia. *Amy Loves the Rain* (PS–K). Illus. by Lillian Hoban. 1989, HarperCollins $9.95 (0-06-022357-X). 24pp. Amy sits in her car seat as they go to pick up Daddy in the rain. Also use: *Amy Loves the Sun* (1988). (Rev: BL 4/15/89; HB 7–8/89)

3218 Hoban, Julia. *Amy Loves the Snow* (PS). Illus. by Lillian Hoban. 1989, HarperCollins $9.95 (0-06-022361-8). 24pp. A simple text that dramatizes the fun youngsters have in the snow. (Rev: BL 10/1/89; SLJ 10/89)

3219 Hofsepian, Sylvia A. *Why Not?* (PS–3). Illus. by Friso Henstra. 1991, Macmillan LB $13.95 (0-02-743980-1). This cumulative tale begins with a lonely man bringing home a cat to keep him company. (Rev: SLJ 12/91)

3220 Hooks, Bell. *Happy to Be Nappy* (PS–K). Illus. by Chris Raschka. 1999, Hyperion LB $15.49 (0-7868-2377-1). 32pp. An exuberant picture book that show all kinds of ways to be happy with nappy hair. (Rev: BCCB 1/00; BL 8/99; HBG 3/00; SLJ 11/99)

3221 Hooper, Meredith. *A Cow, a Bee, a Cookie, and Me* (PS–2). Illus. by Alison Bartlett. 1997, Kingfisher $15.95 (0-7534-5067-4). 32pp. While Ben is helping to make honey cookies, his grandmother tells him about the origin of each of the ingredients. (Rev: BL 6/1–15/97; HBG 3/98)

3222 Houghton, Eric. *The Crooked Apple Tree* (PS–2). Illus. by Caroline Gold. 1999, Barefoot LB $15.95 (1-902283-59-7). A year in the life of a young brother and sister as they play imaginative games around an old apple tree as the seasons change. (Rev: SLJ 7/99)

3223 Howard, Elizabeth F. *The Train to Lulu's* (PS–3). Illus. by Robert Casilla. 1994, Macmillan paper $4.95 (0-689-71797-0). 32pp. The story of the train journey of two little girls. (Rev: BCCB 7–8/88; BL 4/15/88; SLJ 5/88)

3224 Hubbell, Patricia. *Sidewalk Trip* (PS–K). Illus. by Mari Takabayashi. 1999, HarperFestival $9.95 (0-694-01174-6). 24pp. Mother and daughter take a walk in the neighborhood and encounter pigeons, dogs, and an ice-cream truck. (Rev: BL 9/15/99; HBG 10/99; SLJ 7/99)

3225 Hubbell, Patricia. *Wrapping Paper Romp* (PS). Illus. by Jennifer Plecas. 1998, HarperFestival $5.95 (0-694-01098-7). 14pp. An appealing board book about the excitement a toddler feels when he unwraps a present and discovers teddy bears inside. (Rev: BL 12/1/98; SLJ 2/99)

3226 Hudson, Cheryl W., and Bernette G. Ford. *Bright Eyes, Brown Skin* (PS). Illus. by George Ford. 1990, Just Us $12.95 (0-940975-10-6). 24pp. This book features four African American children on a typical day in preschool. (Rev: BL 12/1/90*; SLJ 1/91)

3227 Hughes, Shirley. *Being Together* (PS). Illus. by author. 1997, Candlewick $3.99 (0-7636-0399-6). In this board book, a little girl tells about the activities that she shares with her brother. Also use *Playing* (1997). (Rev: HBG 3/98; SLJ 2/98)

3228 Hughes, Shirley. *Bouncing* (PS). Illus. 1993, Candlewick $12.95 (1-56402-128-9). 24pp. A preschooler shows how she spends the days with a number of bouncing activities. Also use: *Giving* (1993). (Rev: BL 5/1/93; SLJ 6/93)

3229 Hughes, Shirley. *Chatting* (PS). Illus. 1994, Candlewick $13.95 (1-56402-340-0). 24pp. A small girl chats with all sorts of people as well as her pet cat. Also use *Hiding* (1994). (Rev: BL 7/94; HB 9–10/94; SLJ 9/94*)

3230 Hughes, Shirley. *Tales of Trotter Street* (PS–2). Illus. 1997, Candlewick $17.99 (0-7636-0090-3). 64pp. An anthology of four Trotter Street books about people who live on the same street. (Rev: BL 2/1/97)

3231 Hughes, Shirley. *Two Shoes, New Shoes* (PS). Illus. by author. 1986, Lothrop paper $4.95 (0-688-04207-4). 24pp. A rhyming board book about clothes. (Rev: BL 12/15/86; HB 1–2/87; SLJ 12/86)

3232 Humphries, Tudor. *Hiding* (PS–K). Illus. 1997, Orchard $14.95 (0-531-30056-0). 32pp. After she has been scolded by her mother, a little girl goes into hiding until she becomes lonely. (Rev: BL 12/1/97; HBG 3/98; SLJ 3/98)

3233 Hurd, Thacher. *Zoom City* (PS). Illus. by author. 1998, HarperFestival $5.95 (0-694-01057-X). A board book that contains bright, action-filled illustrations of cars zooming around. (Rev: HBG 10/98; SLJ 6/98)

3234 Hurwitz, Johanna. *New Shoes for Silvia* (PS–3). Illus. by Jerry Pinkney. 1993, Morrow $15.93 (0-688-05287-8). 32pp. Silvia finds all sorts of uses for her new shoes until her feet are big enough for her to wear them. (Rev: BCCB 11/93; BL 10/15/93; HB 11–12/93; SLJ 10/93)

3235 Hutchins, Pat. *The Doorbell Rang* (K–2). Illus. by author. 1986, Greenwillow $15.93 (0-688-05252-5); Morrow paper $4.95 (0-688-09234-9).

24pp. Every time the doorbell rings, it means more of Ma's cookies are eaten, which leaves less for Victoria and Sam — until Grandma arrives with a package. (Rev: BCCB 3/86; BL 6/15/86; SLJ 4/86)

3236 Intrater, Roberta G. *Smile!* (PS). Photos by Roberta Grobel Intrater. Series: Babyfaces. 1997, Scholastic $4.95 (0-590-05899-1). In this board book, a toddler responds to a photographer's requests. Also use *Peek-a-Boo!* (1997). (Rev: SLJ 2/98)

3237 Isaacs, Gwynne L. *While You Are Asleep* (PS–2). Illus. by Cathi Hepworth. 1991, Walker LB $13.85 (0-8027-6986-1). 32pp. This picture book describes the intersecting lives of several people who work at night. (Rev: BL 9/1/91; SLJ 8/91)

3238 Isadora, Rachael. *Lili at Ballet* (K–3). Illus. 1993, Putnam LB $16.99 (0-399-22423-8). 32pp. A lovely picture book of a child's dance experiences. (Rev: BCCB 4/93; BL 2/1/93*; HB 5–6/93; SLJ 3/93)

3239 Isadora, Rachael. *Lili on Stage* (PS–3). Illus. 1995, Putnam $16.99 (0-399-22637-0). 32pp. The story of Lili's experiences in a small part on opening night of the ballet *Nutcracker*. (Rev: BL 11/15/95; SLJ 12/95)

3240 Isadora, Rachael. *Listen to the City* (PS–1). Illus. 2000, Putnam $15.99 (0-399-23047-5). 32pp. The sounds heard in a big city are re-created in this picture book that spans a single day. (Rev: BL 6/1–15/00; HB 3–4/00; HBG 10/00; SLJ 5/00)

3241 Isadora, Rachael. *Sophie Skates* (PS–3). Illus. 1999, Putnam $15.99 (0-399-23046-7). 32pp. A picture book about Sophie, age 8, an Asian American girl who takes ice-skating lessons before and after school so that she can enter competitions. (Rev: BL 12/1/99; HBG 3/00; SLJ 11/99)

3242 Jabar, Cynthia. *Bored Blue? Think What You Can Do!* (PS–1). Illus. 1991, Little, Brown $14.95 (0-316-43458-2). 32pp. This book suggests all sorts of activities for bored kids, some of them in the world of fantasy, in rhyming text. (Rev: BL 4/1/91; SLJ 6/91)

3243 Jakob, Donna. *Tiny Toes* (PS–1). Illus. by Mireille Levert. 1995, Hyperion LB $14.49 (0-7868-2009-8). 32pp. Toes engage in a variety of activities, including dancing. (Rev: BL 4/1/95; SLJ 6/95)

3244 James, Betsy. *Flashlight* (PS–2). Illus. by Stacey Schuett. 1997, Knopf LB $18.99 (0-679-97970-0). 32pp. Marie is afraid of the dark until her grandfather gives her a flashlight. (Rev: BL 12/15/97; HBG 3/98; SLJ 1/98*)

3245 Jenness, Aylette. *Come Home with Me: A Multicultural Treasure Hunt* (1–4). Photos by Max Belcher. Illus. by Laura DeSantis. Series: Kids Bridge. 1993, New Pr. $16.95 (1-56584-064-X). 48pp. A treasure hunt that introduces four cultural groups represented in various neighborhoods in Boston. (Rev: SLJ 4/94)

3246 Jennings, Sharon. *Into My Mother's Arms* (PS–K). Illus. by Ruth Ohi. 2000, Fitzhenry & Whiteside $14.95 (1-55041-533-6). 32pp. A mother and her daughter spend a busy day, starting with

breakfast, continuing with activities like going shopping, and finally coming home to bed. (Rev: BL 5/15/00; SLJ 7/00)

3247 Johnson, Angela. *The Leaving Morning* (PS–2). Illus. by David Soman. 1996, Orchard paper $5.95 (0-531-07072-7). 32pp. All the sorrow and anticipation of a move are captured in this picture of a family saying good-bye to their home and friends. (Rev: BL 9/1/92; HB 9–10/92; SLJ 9/92)

3248 Johnson, Angela. *Rain Feet* (PS). Illus. by Rhonda Mitchell. 1994, Orchard $4.95 (0-531-06849-8). 12pp. A little African American boy enjoys splashing through puddles in this board book. Also use *Mama Birds, Baby Birds* (1994). (Rev: BL 12/1/94; HB 9–10/94; SLJ 1/95)

3249 Johnson, Angela. *Shoes Like Miss Alice's* (PS–K). Illus. by Ken Page. 1995, Orchard LB $16.99 (0-531-08664-X). 32pp. Sally resents her baby-sitter Miss Alice until she sees her wide assortment of shoes. (Rev: BL 3/15/95; SLJ 7/95)

3250 Johnson, Dolores. *What Kind of Baby-Sitter Is This?* (PS–2). Illus. 1991, Macmillan LB $15.00 (0-02-747846-7). 32pp. Kevin gets a big surprise when he discovers that his new baby-sitter, an elderly lady, loves baseball as much as he does. (Rev: BCCB 10/91; BL 1/1/91; HB 11–12/91; SLJ 12/91)

3251 Johnson, Paul B. *Farmers' Market* (PS–2). 1997, Orchard LB $16.99 (0-531-33014-1). 32pp. On Saturdays during the summer, Laura and her family sell their produce at the Farmers' Market in Lexington, Kentucky. (Rev: BCCB 4/97; BL 3/15/97; SLJ 6/97)

3252 Johnston, Tony. *The Quilt Story* (PS–2). Illus. by Tomie dePaola. 1996, Putnam paper $5.99 (0-698-11368-3). 32pp. The star of this book is the quilt, which gives fun, warmth, and comfort to two generations. (Rev: BCCB 7/85; BL 8/85; SLJ 9/85)

3253 Jonas, Ann. *Reflections* (PS–2). Illus. by author. 1987, Greenwillow $15.93 (0-688-06141-9). 24pp. A book of seaside scenes told in two sets of pictures — one when the book is held upright; the other when it is held upside down. (Rev: BL 9/15/87; SLJ 10/87)

3254 Jonas, Ann. *When You Were a Baby* (PS–1). Illus. by author. 1982, Greenwillow LB $15.93 (0-688-00864-X). 24pp. Simple text shows an infant's progress.

3255 Jordan, June. *Kimako's Story* (K–3). Illus. by Kay Burford. 1991, Houghton paper $3.95 (0-395-60338-2). 42pp. Seven-year-old Kimako explores her neighborhood.

3256 Kalman, Maira. *Next Stop Grand Central* (K–3). Illus. 1999, Putnam LB $15.99 (0-399-22926-4). 32pp. All the excitement and turmoil of rush hour at Grand Central Station — the busiest railroad station in the world, where half a million people converge every day — is captured in this intriguing picture book. (Rev: BCCB 3/99; BL 12/15/98*; HB 5–6/99; HBG 10/99; SLJ 2/99)

3257 Karas, G. Brian. *The Windy Day* (K–3). Illus. by author. 1998, Simon & Schuster $16.00 (0-689-81449-6). Wind brings excitement, change, and color to a town as it passes through it. (Rev: HB 3–4/98*; HBG 10/98; SLJ 6/98)

3258 Katz, Karen. *The Colors of Us* (PS–1). Illus. 1999, Holt $15.95 (0-8050-5864-8). 32pp. Lena discovers that her friends and neighbors are all delicious shades of brown like the foods she enjoys, including peanut butter and chocolate cupcakes. (Rev: BCCB 12/99; BL 9/15/99; HBG 3/00; SLJ 9/99)

3259 Kesselman, Wendy. *Sand in My Shoes* (PS–3). Illus. by Ronald Himler. 1995, Hyperion LB $15.49 (0-7868-2045-4). 32pp. At the end of summer, a little girl says good-bye to the beach she loves but still retains little remembrances like sand in her shoes. (Rev: BL 6/1–15/95; SLJ 7/95)

3260 Ketteman, Helen. *I Remember Papa* (K–3). Illus. by Greg Shed. 1998, Dial $15.89 (0-8037-1849-7). 32pp. Audie remembers the summer in which he attended a Cincinnati Reds game with his father and the heartache he suffered when he lost the money he had saved to buy a baseball glove. (Rev: BL 3/15/98; HBG 10/98; SLJ 6/98)

3261 Kirk, Daniel. *Bigger* (PS–1). Illus. 1998, Putnam $15.99 (0-399-23127-7). 16pp. A young boy traces his growth from inside the womb to after his birth to his present size and level of development. (Rev: BCCB 6/98; BL 5/1/98; HBG 10/98; SLJ 5/98)

3262 Kirk, Daniel. *Lucky's 24-Hour Garage* (K–3). Illus. 1996, Hyperion LB $15.49 (0-7868-2168-X). 32pp. There are all kinds of different customers who use the services of Lucky's Garage. (Rev: BL 9/1/96; SLJ 9/96)

3263 Knutson, Kimberley. *Beach Babble* (PS–K). Illus. 1998, Marshall Cavendish $15.95 (0-7614-5026-2). 32pp. The sounds of a day at the beach are re-created in this picture book illustrated with collage artwork. (Rev: BL 6/1–15/98; HBG 10/98; SLJ 7/98)

3264 Koller, Jackie F. *Bouncing on the Bed* (PS). Illus. by Anna Grossnickle Hines. 1999, Orchard LB $16.99 (0-531-33138-5). 32pp. A description by a toddler of all the fun things in a typical day, such as bouncing on the bed, sliding down the stairs, and snuggling down at bedtime. (Rev: BL 2/1/99; HBG 10/99; SLJ 4/99)

3265 Konigsburg, E. L. *Amy Elizabeth Explores Bloomingdale's* (PS–2). Illus. 1992, Macmillan $14.95 (0-689-31766-2). 32pp. Amy visits her grandmother in New York City, and they set out to explore the sights. (Rev: BCCB 9/92; BL 9/1/92; SLJ 9/92)

3266 Koski, Mary. *Impatient Pamela Calls 9-1-1* (PS–K). Illus. by Dan Brown. 1998, Trellis LB $15.95 (0-9663281-9-1). 32pp. Impatient Pamela learns a number of skills and puts them to use calling 911 when her neighbor Martin begins choking. (Rev: BL 12/1/98)

3267 Krasilovsky, Phyllis. *The Very Little Boy* (PS–1). Illus. by Karen Gundersheimer. 1992, Scholastic paper $4.95 (0-590-44762-9). In this book that describes development, a young boy

grows physically and is able to accomplish more skills. (Rev: SLJ 12/92)

3268 Kruusval, Catarina. *No Clothes Today!* (PS). Illus. by author. 1995, R&S $6.95 (91-29-63074-6). Stubborn Ellen has trouble deciding what clothes to wear, so she puts them on her pets. Also use *Where's the Ball?* (1995). (Rev: SLJ 3/96)

3269 Kunhardt, Edith. *I'm Going to Be a Police Officer* (PS–2). Illus. 1995, Scholastic paper $3.25 (0-590-25485-5). 32pp. An average day in a small-town police officer's day as seen through the eyes of his two children, who spend time with him at the police station. (Rev: BL 1/1–15/96)

3270 Kuskin, Karla. *The Philharmonic Gets Dressed* (1–4). Illus. by Marc Simont. 1982, HarperCollins $15.95 (0-06-023622-1); paper $5.95 (0-06-443124-X). 48pp. One hundred and five musicians are across town getting ready for a big concert.

3271 Laden, Nina. *Ready, Set, Go!* (PS). Illus. by author. 2000, Chronicle $6.95 (0-8118-2601-5). An interactive book in which cut-out circles reveal activities that are viewed completely when the page is turned. (Rev: SLJ 9/00)

3272 Lamstein, Sarah M. *I Like Your Buttons!* (PS–3). Illus. by Nancy Cote. 1999, Albert Whitman $15.95 (0-8075-3510-9). 32pp. A small compliment produces a string of kindnesses that eventually comes back to the thoughtful young girl who began the chain. (Rev: BCCB 4/99; BL 8/99; HBG 10/99; SLJ 12/99)

3273 Landstrom, Olof, and Lena Landstrom. *Will Goes to the Beach* (PS–K). Illus. 1995, Farrar $13.00 (91-29-62914-4). 32pp. Will spends a memorable day at the beach that includes making his first swimming strokes. (Rev: BL 9/1/95)

3274 Landstrom, Olof, and Lena Landstrom. *Will Goes to the Post Office* (PS–2). Trans. from Swedish by Elisabeth Dyssegaard. Illus. 1994, R&S $13.00 (91-29-62950-0). A simple story about a boy who goes to the post office to pick up a package from his uncle. (Rev: SLJ 12/94)

3275 Lasky, Kathryn. *Sophie and Rose* (PS–3). Illus. by Wendy A. Halperin. 1998, Candlewick $15.99 (0-7636-0459-3). 32pp. Sophie loves her old doll, Rose, so much that even when Rose suffers many accidents and becomes chipped and cracked, Sophie's love continues to grow. (Rev: BL 9/15/98; HBG 3/99; SLJ 1/99)

3276 Leghorn, Lindsay. *Proud of Our Feelings* (PS–2). Illus. by author. 1995, Magination $11.95 (0-945354-68-1). A little girl demonstrates the various emotions that her friends feel, like friendliness, sadness, happiness, silliness, and anger. (Rev: SLJ 4/96)

3277 Lester, Alison. *Celeste Sails to Spain* (PS–2). Illus. 1999, Houghton $15.00 (0-395-97395-3). 32pp. Each of the seven children in this book, including Celeste, enjoys a special adventure, such as visiting a dinosaur in the museum or investigating a pond. (Rev: BL 10/1/99; HBG 3/00; SLJ 10/99)

3278 Lester, Alison. *When Frank Was Four* (PS–2). Illus. 1996, Houghton $15.00 (0-395-74275-7).

32pp. Double-page spreads reveal many activities that a group of Australian children engage in from infancy to school age. A sequel to *Clive Eats Alligators* (1986). (Rev: BL 2/15/96; HB 5–6/96; SLJ 4/96)

3279 Lewis, Kim. *My Friend Harry* (PS–1). Illus. 1995, Candlewick $15.95 (1-56402-617-5). 32pp. James finds he has a great friend in his silent companion, a toy elephant named Harry. (Rev: BL 10/15/95; SLJ 9/95*)

3280 Lewis, Kim. *The Shepherd Boy* (PS–2). Illus. 1990, Macmillan LB $13.95 (0-02-758581-6). 32pp. A young boy who longs to be a shepherd like his father practices on a toy lamb. (Rev: BL 12/1/90; SLJ 12/90)

3281 Lewison, Wendy C. *The Princess and the Potty* (PS). Illus. by Rick Brown. 1994, Simon & Schuster paper $15.00 (0-671-87284-2). 32pp. A young princess gets potty trained because she wants a pair of pantalettes. (Rev: BL 4/15/94; SLJ 4/94)

3282 Lindgren, Barbro. *Sam's Potty* (PS). Illus. by Eva Eriksson. 1986, Morrow paper $6.95 (0-688-06603-8). 32pp. Toddler Sam refuses to use his potty until he tries it with his dog on his lap. Also use: *Sam's Wagon* (1986). (Rev: BL 11/1/86; SLJ 12/86)

3283 Lomas Garza, Carmen. *In My Family/En Mi Familia* (1–4). Illus. 1996, Children's Book Pr. $15.95 (0-89239-138-3). 32pp. In 13 paintings labeled bilingually, the artist portrays his childhood in Kingsville, Texas. (Rev: BL 11/1/96; HB 11–12/96)

3284 London, Jonathan. *The Candystore Man* (K–3). Illus. by Kevin O'Malley. 1998, Lothrop $16.00 (0-688-13241-3). 24pp. A hip candy store owner in Bayonne, New Jersey, takes a young boy on a jazzy tour of the neighborhood and teaches him how to become a part of it. (Rev: BL 11/15/98; HBG 3/99; SLJ 10/98)

3285 Loomis, Christine. *In the Diner* (PS–1). Illus. by Nancy Poydar. 1994, Scholastic $14.95 (0-590-46716-6). 32pp. Lots of action words in short sentences are used to describe the hustle and bustle of a diner. (Rev: BL 4/15/94; SLJ 5/94)

3286 Loomis, Christine. *Rush Hour* (PS–2). Illus. by Mari Takabayashi. 1996, Houghton $15.95 (0-395-69129-X). 32pp. Catchy rhymes and lively illustrations show what working parents do after they leave home in the morning. (Rev: BL 7/96; SLJ 9/96)

3287 Lowery, Linda. *Twist with a Burger, Jitter with a Bug* (PS–2). Illus. by Pat Dypold. 1995, Houghton $14.95 (0-395-67022-5). 32pp. Various kinds of dances are suggested in exuberant, rhythmic verses. (Rev: BL 9/1/95; SLJ 9/95)

3288 Ludy, Mark. *The Grump* (2–4). Illus. by author. 2000, Green Pastures $16.95 (0-9664276-1-0). Lydia, a little deaf girl, is able to reform the village grump through small acts of kindness. (Rev: SLJ 2/01)

3289 Lunn, Janet. *Come to the Fair* (K–2). Illus. by Gilles Pelletier. 1997, Tundra $15.95 (0-88776-409-6). The Martin family prepares for a visit to the county fair and spends an enjoyable day there. (Rev: HBG 3/98; SLJ 2/98)

3290 Lyon, George E. *Come a Tide* (PS–2). Illus. by Stephen Gammell. 1990, Orchard LB $16.99 (0-531-08454-X). 32pp. Grandma knows the tide will rise after a four-day deluge. (Rev: BL 2/1/90*; HB 3–4/90; SLJ 6/90*)

3291 Lyon, George E. *Who Came Down That Road?* (K–3). Illus. by Peter Catalanotto. 1992, Orchard paper $5.95 (0-531-07073-5). 32pp. The story of a road through history. (Rev: BL 9/1/92; SLJ 10/92)

3292 Macaulay, David. *Shortcut* (K–4). Illus. 1995, Houghton $15.95 (0-395-52436-9). 64pp. The lives of six people cross in a series of different stories. The author also uses this method of overlapping storytelling in *Black and White* (1990). (Rev: BCCB 9/95; BL 10/15/95; HB 3–4/95; SLJ 9/95*)

3293 McCarty, Peter. *Baby Steps* (PS–K). Illus. 2000, Holt $16.00 (0-8050-5953-9). 32pp. Using clear pencil illustrations, this book traces the growth of baby Suki from one day old to her first steps at one year old. (Rev: BCCB 10/00; BL 10/1/00; HBG 3/01; SLJ 10/00)

3294 McCully, Emily Arnold. *Hurry!* (K–3). Illus. 2000, Harcourt $16.00 (0-15-201579-5). 32pp. A young boy tries to collect enough money to buy a rare talking animal, the farivox, but in spite of all his hurrying he is too late. The animal and his owner have left town in this parable about animal extinction. (Rev: BCCB 5/00; BL 3/15/00; HB 11–12/00; HBG 3/01; SLJ 4/00)

3295 MacDonald, Amy. *Let's Go* (PS). Illus. by Maureen Roffey. 1994, Candlewick $5.95 (1-56402-202-1). In this simple board book, children from different cultures engage in such activities as riding a rocking horse and playing patty-cake. Also use *Let's Pretend* (1994). (Rev: SLJ 5/94)

3296 McDonald, Megan. *The Potato Man* (K–3). Illus. by Ted Lewin. 1991, Orchard LB $16.99 (0-531-08514-7). 32pp. Grampa recalls the time when his neighborhood was regularly visited by peddlers, including the potato man. (Rev: BCCB 2/91; BL 1/15/91*; HB 5–6/91)

3297 McGeorge, Constance W. *Waltz of the Scarecrows* (PS–3). Illus. by Mary Whyte. 1998, Chronicle $14.95 (0-8118-1727-X). 32pp. Grandma and Grandpa dress their scarecrows — one in a fancy ball gown and the other in an evening coat with top hat — in honor of an incident that occurred in their farming community many years before. (Rev: BL 11/15/98; HBG 3/99; SLJ 12/98)

3298 McGrath, Bob. *Uh Oh! Gotta Go! Potty Tales from Toddlers* (PS). Illus. by Shelley Dieterichs. 1996, Barron's $5.95 (0-8120-6564-6). About 20 children describe different potty experiences in this unusual book that will help in toilet training. (Rev: SLJ 1/97) [613]

3299 McGregor, Merideth. *Cowgirl* (PS–1). Illus. 1992, Walker LB $15.85 (0-8027-8171-3). 32pp. Simple, direct text describes the routines of life on a present-day ranch. (Rev: BCCB 2/93; BL 10/1/92; SLJ 12/92) [636.2]

3300 MacKinnon, Debbie. *My Day* (PS–K). Illus. by Anthea Sieveking. 1999, Little, Brown $7.95 (0-316-64898-1). Everyday activities of children are pictured in this interactive book that uses tabs to show action. (Rev: BL 12/15/99)

3301 McLerran, Alice. *Roxaboxen* (K–3). Illus. by Barbara Cooney. 1991, Lothrop LB $15.93 (0-688-07593-2). 32pp. The story of children in the desert who fashion an imaginary town. (Rev: BCCB 3/91*; BL 2/15/91*; HB 3–4/91; SLJ 2/91*)

3302 McPhail, David. *Farm Morning* (PS–K). Illus. by author. 1985, Harcourt $15.95 (0-15-227299-2); paper $7.00 (0-15-227300-X). 32pp. A little girl and her father do early-morning farm chores. (Rev: BCCB 12/85; BL 11/15/85; HB 11–12/85)

3303 Maestro, Betsy. *Taxi: A Book of City Words* (PS–1). Illus. by Giulio Maestro. 1989, Houghton paper $6.95 (0-395-54811-X). A taxi picks up and drops off people over the city and introduces new words. (Rev: BL 4/15/89; SLJ 4/89)

3304 Mahy, Margaret. *Down the Dragon's Tongue* (PS–3). Illus. by Patricia MacCarthy. 2000, Orchard $15.95 (0-531-30272-5). 32pp. When Mr. Prospero, a very proper gentleman, takes his twin children to a playground, he falls in love with riding the slide known as the Dragon's Tongue. (Rev: BL 7/00; HGB 3/01; SLJ 12/00)

3305 Mahy, Margaret. *A Summery Saturday Morning* (PS–2). Illus. by Selina Young. 1998, Viking $15.99 (0-670-87943-6). 32pp. A breezy story about a group of children and dogs at play, chasing cats and boys on bikes. They are eventually chased themselves by a goose and her seven goslings. (Rev: BL 6/1–15/98; HBG 3/99; SLJ 7/98)

3306 Maitland, Barbara. *Moo in the Morning* (PS–K). Illus. by Andrew Kulman. 2000, Farrar $16.00 (0-374-35038-8). 32pp. Seeking relief from city noises, a mother and child retreat to a farm where the early morning animal sounds again create a cacophony. (Rev: BCCB 7–8/00; BL 2/1/01; HBG 3/01)

3307 Maitland, Barbara. *My Bear and Me* (PS). Illus. by Lisa Flather. 1999, Simon & Schuster $12.95 (0-689-82085-2). A small girl describes all of the activities she shares with her teddy bear in this book for toddlers. (Rev: HBG 3/00; SLJ 11/99)

3308 Mansell, Dom. *My Old Teddy* (PS–K). Illus. 1992, Candlewick $12.95 (1-56402-035-5). 32pp. Even a brand new teddy bear can't replace the old worn-out one that a little girl loves. (Rev: BL 6/1/92; SLJ 7/92)

3309 Manushkin, Fran. *Let's Go Riding in Our Strollers* (2–4). Illus. by Benrei Huang. 1993, Hyperion LB $14.49 (1-56282-391-4). 32pp. In a big city, two children enjoy all the excitement of being taken out for a ride by their mothers in their strollers. (Rev: BL 6/1–15/93)

3310 Martin, Bill, Jr., and John Archambault. *Here Are My Hands* (PS). Illus. by Ted Rand. 1987, Holt $15.95 (0-8050-0328-2). 32pp. Children indicate body parts, such as a boy pointing to a bandaged knee, which is for "falling down." (Rev: BL 7/87; SLJ 6–7/87)

3311 Martin, Bill, Jr., and John Archambault. *Listen to the Rain* (PS–2). Illus. by James Endicott. 1988, Holt $15.95 (0-8050-0682-6). 32pp. A rhyming story about rain with double-page watercolors. (Rev: SLJ 10/88)

3312 Martin, Bill, Jr., and John Archambault. *Up and Down on the Merry-Go-Round* (PS–1). Illus. by Ted Rand. 1988, Holt paper $4.95 (0-8050-1638-4). 32pp. A full-color merry-go-round whirls its delighted passengers in rhyming cadence. (Rev: BL 6/15/88; HB 7–8/88)

3313 Martin, Jacqueline B. *Green Truck Garden Giveaway: A Neighborhood Story and Almanac* (K–3). Illus. by Alec Gillman. 1997, Simon & Schuster paper $16.00 (0-689-80498-9). 32pp. This story about two modern Johnny Appleseeds who plant gardens for people they meet also contains information about plants, how they grow, and their characteristics. (Rev: BL 5/1/97; SLJ 6/97)

3314 Masurel, Claire. *Too Big!* (PS–2). Illus. by Hanako Wakiyama. 1999, Chronicle $13.95 (0-8118-2090-4). 36pp. Charlie's family thinks that the toy stuffed dinosaur he has won is just too big, but Charlie finds that its enormous size can be helpful. (Rev: BCCB 7–8/99; BL 8/99; HBG 10/99; SLJ 6/99)

3315 Mathers, Petra. *Lottie's New Beach Towel* (PS–2). Illus. 1998, Simon & Schuster $15.00 (0-689-81606-5). 32pp. Lottie shows her ingenuity when she puts her new beach towel to a variety of uses, including making an improvised sail and shaping it into a veil for a bride. (Rev: BL 6/1–15/98; HB 5–6/98; HBG 10/98; SLJ 6/98)

3316 Maynard, Bill. *Santa's Time Off* (K–3). Illus. by Tom Browning. 1997, Putnam $15.99 (0-399-23138-2). Lighthearted poems about Santa's activities when he has some time free from his duties. (Rev: HBG 3/98; SLJ 10/97)

3317 Medearis, Angela Shelf. *Bye-Bye, Babies!* (PS). Illus. by Patrice Aggs. 1995, Candlewick $4.95 (1-56402-258-7). 14pp. A group of babies plays peekaboo and learns to wave good-bye. Also use *Eat, Babies, Eat!* (1995). (Rev: BL 10/15/95; SLJ 3/96)

3318 Medearis, Angela Shelf. *Dancing with the Indians* (K–3). Illus. by Samuel Byrd. 1991, Holiday LB $16.95 (0-8234-0893-0). 32pp. A young African American girl and her family attend a pow-wow of the Oklahoma Seminoles. (Rev: BCCB 11/91; BL 12/1/91; SLJ 1/92)

3319 Medearis, Angela Shelf. *Poppa's New Pants* (K–3). Illus. by John Ward. 1995, Holiday LB $15.95 (0-8234-1155-9). 32pp. Shortening father's new pants to fit him causes a minor family crisis. (Rev: BCCB 7–8/95; BL 6/1–15/95; SLJ 6/95)

3320 Merriam, Eve. *The Hole Story* (PS–1). Illus. by Ivan Chermayeff. 1995, Simon & Schuster $16.00 (0-671-88353-4). A delightful picture book that explores the world of holes in verse and pictures that combine collage art with photos. (Rev: SLJ 8/95)

3321 Merriam, Eve. *Low Song* (PS–K). Illus. by Pamela Paparone. 2001, Simon & Schuster $16.00 (0-689-82820-9). 32pp. This poem pays tribute to things that are "nice and low" like falling leaves, puddles, sand, floors, and shells. (Rev: BL 1/1–15/01; SLJ 3/01)

3322 Meyers, Susan. *Everywhere Babies* (PS). Illus. by Marla Frazee. 2001, Harcourt $16.00 (0-15-202226-0). 32pp. A charming representation of the first year of a baby's life with a rhyming text and watercolors showing babies being fed and playing games like peek-a-boo. (Rev: BL 3/1/01)

3323 Miller, Margaret. *Baby Food* (PS). Illus. 2000, Simon & Schuster $5.99 (0-689-83190-0). 14pp. This charming board book is filled with pictures of children eating. Toddlers and babies prepare for different activities in the companion work *Get Ready, Baby* (2000). (Rev: BL 7/00)

3324 Miller, Margaret. *Family Time* (PS). Photos by author. Series: Super Chubby Books. 1996, Simon & Schuster $4.99 (0-689-80051-7). This board book illustrated with photos shows toddlers having fun with a variety of relatives. Also use *At the Shore, Happy Days,* and *My Best Friends* (all 1996). (Rev: SLJ 8/96)

3325 Miller, Margaret. *Me and My Bear* (PS–1). Illus. Series: Look Baby! 1999, Simon & Schuster $4.99 (0-689-82355-X). 14pp. A board book of photographs showing babies holding up different stuffed bears. (Rev: BL 8/99; SLJ 8/99)

3326 Miller, Margaret. *Who Uses This?* (PS–K). Illus. 1990, Greenwillow $15.93 (0-688-08279-3). 40pp. The uses of nine tools, such as the hammer and scissors, are pictured. (Rev: BCCB 3/90; BL 3/1/90; HB 9–10/90; SLJ 5/90) [331.7]

3327 Miller, Virginia. *On Your Potty!* (PS). Illus. 2000, Candlewick $5.99 (0-7636-1268-5). 18pp. At first Ba, a little bear, insists that he doesn't have to use the potty, but soon he changes his mind in this board book. (Rev: BL 11/15/00; HBG 3/01)

3328 Miranda, Anne. *Baby-Sit* (PS). Illus. by Dorothy Stott. 1990, Little, Brown $9.95 (0-316-57454-6). The activities of two children and their baby-sitter are portrayed. (Rev: SLJ 10/90)

3329 Miranda, Anne. *To Market, To Market* (K–2). Illus. by Janet Stevens. 1997, Harcourt $16.00 (0-15-200035-6). 36pp. A wildly funny picture book about market day misunderstandings. (Rev: BL 11/1/97; HB 11–12/97; HBG 3/98; SLJ 1/98)

3330 Mitchell, Lori. *Different Just Like Me* (K–3). Illus. 1999, Charlesbridge LB $15.95 (0-88106-975-2). 32pp. April's experiences during the week, when she meets new people, help her appreciate her much-anticipated weekend visit with her Grammie. (Rev: BL 3/1/99; HBG 10/99; SLJ 3/99)

3331 Mora, Pat. *Tomas and the Library Lady* (PS–3). Illus. by Raul Colon. 1997, Knopf LB $18.99 (0-679-90401-8). 40pp. The story of a migrant boy who finds a special place that welcomes and helps him: the library. (Rev: BL 8/97; HBG 3/98; SLJ 10/97)

3332 Morgan, Mary. *Gentle Rosie* (PS). Illus. by author. 1999, Hyperion $5.99 (0-7868-0474-2). This undersized picture book shows Rosie in a quiet mood smelling a flower and looking at books. Her more active side is shown in the companion volume, *Wild Rosie* (1999). (Rev: HBG 10/99; SLJ 8/99)

3333 Morris, Ann. *Hats, Hats, Hats* (PS–1). Illus. by Ken Heyman. 1989, Morrow paper $6.95 (0-688-12274-4). 32pp. A full-color display of varieties of hats. Also use: *Bread, Bread, Bread* (1989). (Rev: BL 4/15/89; SLJ 5/89)

3334 Morris, Ann. *Houses and Homes* (PS–1). Illus. 1992, Lothrop LB $16.93 (0-688-10169-0). 32pp. A fascinating look at how houses are built around the world. (Rev: BCCB 12/92; BL 10/1/92)

3335 Morton, Christine. *Picnic Farm* (PS–K). Illus. by Sarah Barringer. 1998, Holiday LB $15.95 (0-8234-1332-2). After touring a farm, a little girl and boy have a picnic using some of its produce, like eggs, bread, butter, and fruit. (Rev: HBG 10/98; SLJ 3/98)

3336 Moss, Marissa. *Mel's Diner* (PS–3). Illus. 1994, Troll $13.95 (0-8167-3460-7). 32pp. Mabel, an African American child, loves to hang out at her parents' diner. (Rev: BL 10/1/94; SLJ 12/94)

3337 Munsch, Robert. *Ribbon Rescue* (PS–1). Illus. by Eugenie Fernandes. 1999, Scholastic $11.95 (0-590-89012-3). 32pp. A Mohawk girl named Jillian is so helpful to all the members of a wedding party that they make her the flower girl. (Rev: BL 7/99; HBG 10/99; SLJ 6/99)

3338 Nash, Margaret. *Secret in the Mist* (PS–2). Illus. by Stephen Lambert. 1999, Sterling $14.95 (1-899607-98-6). 32pp. A young boy secretly plants a seed and watches it grow both day and night. Finally, his secret is revealed when a beautiful sunflower appears. (Rev: BL 6/1–15/99; SLJ 9/99)

3339 Neitzel, Shirley. *The Bag I'm Taking to Grandma's* (PS–2). Illus. by Nancy Winslow Parker. 1995, Greenwillow LB $14.93 (0-688-12961-7). 32pp. A cumulative story about all the objects a boy wants to take on his visit to Grandma's house. (Rev: BL 6/1–15/95; HB 5–6/95; SLJ 4/95)

3340 Newcome, Zita. *Toddlerobics* (PS). Illus. 1996, Candlewick $15.99 (1-56402-809-7). 32pp. Several youngsters engage in a variety of exercises when they go to their toddler gym. (Rev: BCCB 2/96; BL 4/1/96; SLJ 3/96)

3341 Newcome, Zita. *Toddlerobics: Animal Fun* (PS). Illus. 1999, Candlewick $15.99 (0-7636-0803-3). 32pp. Eight friends attend an exercise class where they learn the motions of several animals. (Rev: BL 12/1/99; HBG 3/00; SLJ 8/99)

3342 Nikola-Lisa, W. *America: My Land, Your Land, Our Land* (K–3). Illus. 1997, Lee & Low $15.95 (1-880000-37-7). 32pp. A handsome picture book that shows many of the contrasts that are present in the United States. (Rev: BL 9/1/97; SLJ 7/97)

3343 Noble, Sheilagh. *More!* (PS). Illus. 2000, Zero to Ten $9.95 (1-84089-127-0). 24pp. A sweet story about a mother and a daughter enjoying a walk in the park. (Rev: BL 1/1–15/01)

3344 Noonan, Julia. *Bath Day* (PS). Illus. by author. Series: Puppy and Me. 2000, Scholastic $6.99 (0-439-11492-6). A slight story about a little girl who plays in her wading pool with her dog. Also use *Breakfast Time* (2000). (Rev: HBG 10/00; SLJ 8/00)

3345 Nunes, Susan. *The Last Dragon* (PS–3). Illus. by Chris K. Soentpiet. 1995, Clarion $15.00 (0-395-

67020-9). 32pp. A Chinese American boy named Peter gets everyone in Chinatown to help him repair a ten-man dragon he has purchased. (Rev: BL 5/1/95; SLJ 5/95)

3346 O'Book, Irene. *Maybe My Baby* (PS). Photos by Paula Hible. 1998, HarperFestival $5.95 (0-694-00872-9). A simple board book in which babies wear a series of job-related hats to help toddlers identify different careers. (Rev: SLJ 6/98)

3347 O'Connor, Jane. *Sarah's Incredible Idea* (1–3). Illus. by Laurie S. Long. 1993, Putnam paper $4.95 (0-448-40162-2). 64pp. A shy girl gets up the nerve to suggest a service project for her Brownie troop. Also use *Make Up Your Mind, Marsha!* (1993). (Rev: BL 1/1/94)

3348 Ogburn, Jacqueline K. *The Jukebox Man* (1–3). Illus. by James E. Ransome. 1998, Dial LB $15.89 (0-8037-1430-0). Set in the late 1950s, a young girl has a wonderful time accompanying her grandfather on his rounds as he checks his jukeboxes. (Rev: HBG 10/98; SLJ 5/98)

3349 Oppenheim, Shulamith Levey. *I Love You, Bunny Rabbit* (PS–1). Illus. by Cyd Moore. 1995, Boyds Mills $14.95 (1-56397-322-7). 32pp. Even though most of its fur has been pulled out, Micah prefers her stuffed Bunny Rabbit above her other toys. (Rev: BCCB 2/95; BL 1/1/95; SLJ 2/95)

3350 Osborne, Mary Pope. *Rocking Horse Christmas* (PS–3). Illus. by Ned Bittinger. 1997, Scholastic $15.95 (0-590-92955-0). 32pp. A young boy has many adventures on his favorite toy, a wooden rocking horse, but in time he outgrows it. (Rev: BL 10/1/97; HBG 3/98; SLJ 10/97)

3351 Ovenell-Carter, Julie. *Adam's Daycare* (PS). Illus. by Ruth Ohi. 1997, Annick LB $15.95 (1-55037-445-1); paper $5.95 (1-55037-444-3). 32pp. Adam enjoys being dropped off at Ina's day-care home because of the toys, musical instruments, and other children he finds there. (Rev: BL 1/1–15/98; SLJ 1/98)

3352 Oxenbury, Helen. *Tom and Pippo Go Shopping* (PS). Illus. by author. 1989, Macmillan paper $5.95 (0-689-71278-2). 14pp. The toddler and his toy monkey on a new adventure. Also use: *Tom and Pippo in the Garden; Tom and Pippo See the Moon; Tom and Pippo's Day* (all 1989). (Rev: BL 3/15/89; HB 5–6/89)

3353 Oxenbury, Helen. *Tom and Pippo Read a Story* (PS). Illus. by author. 1998, Simon & Schuster paper $4.99 (0-689-81958-7). 14pp. Tom wants daddy to read to his stuffed monkey but has to do it himself. (Rev: BL 1/1/89; HB 1–2/89; HBG 10/98; SLJ 4/89)

3354 Page, Debra. *Orcas Around Me: My Alaskan Summer* (K–3). Illus. by Leslie Bowman. 1997, Albert Whitman LB $15.95 (0-8075-6137-1). 40pp. A boy observes the wildlife of the north Pacific coast while he helps on the salmon boats operated by his parents. (Rev: BL 8/97; HBG 3/98; SLJ 9/97) [639.2]

3355 Pallotta, Jerry. *Going Lobstering* (PS–2). Illus. by Rob Bolster. 1990, Charlesbridge $16.95 (0-88106-475-0); paper $7.95 (0-88106-474-2). 32pp.

A boy and his sister spend a fascinating day on a lobster boat. (Rev: BL 12/1/90)

3356 Parr, Todd. *Do's and Don'ts* (PS–1). Illus. by author. 1999, Little, Brown $5.95 (0-316-69213-1). Round stick figures illustrate good and silly behavior in a book that offers some sound advice to toddlers. Also use *The Okay Book, Things That Make You Feel Good/Things That Make You Feel Bad*, and *This Is My Hair* (all 1999). (Rev: HBG 10/99; SLJ 5/99)

3357 Patrick, Denise Lewis. *The Car Washing Street* (PS–2). Illus. by John Ward. 1993, Morrow LB $13.93 (0-688-11453-9). 32pp. One Saturday morning while neighbors are washing their cars, a friendly water fight breaks out and Matthew and his father join in. (Rev: BL 11/1/93; SLJ 1/94)

3358 Paul, Ann W. *Shadows Are About* (PS–2). Illus. by Mark Graham. 1992, Scholastic paper $13.95 (0-590-44842-0). 32pp. A brother and sister accompanied by their shadows explore the world around them. (Rev: BL 7/92; SLJ 4/92)

3359 Paulsen, Gary. *Worksong* (PS–3). Illus. by Ruth W. Paulsen. 1997, Harcourt $15.00 (0-15-200980-9). 32pp. The world of work from blue-collar laborers to computer professionals is celebrated in a fascinating picture book that depicts many different fields of endeavor. (Rev: BL 5/1/97; SLJ 5/97)

3360 Perez, Amada Irma. *My Very Own Room/ Mi propio cuartito* (1–3). Illus. by Maya Christina Gonzalez. 2000, Children's Book Pr $15.95 (0-89239-164-2). 32pp. A bilingual story about a young Mexican American girl who is looking for a little privacy in her crowded home. (Rev: BCCB 11/00; BL 7/00; HB 11–12/00; HBG 3/01; SLJ 8/00)

3361 Pilkey, Dav. *The Paperboy* (PS–1). Illus. 1996, Orchard LB $15.99 (0-531-08856-1). 32pp. This book reflects the thoughts of a young boy when he makes early-morning rounds on his paper route with his dog. (Rev: BCCB 3/96; BL 3/1/96*; HB 7–8/96; SLJ 3/96*)

3362 Pinkney, Brian. *Max Found Two Sticks* (PS–3). Illus. 1994, Simon & Schuster paper $17.00 (0-671-78776-4). 32pp. A lonely boy sitting on the steps of his house is able to imitate the sounds of the big city. (Rev: BL 4/1/94*; HB 5–6/94; SLJ 7/94)

3363 Pinkney, Sandra L. *Shades of Black: A Celebration of Our Children* (PS–2). Illus. by Myles C. Pinkney. 2000, Scholastic $14.95 (0-439-14892-8). 40pp. This book of beautiful photographs shows children whose skin is of various shades of black and whose eyes and hair also show a diversity. (Rev: BCCB 1/01; BL 11/1/00; HBG 3/01; SLJ 12/00)

3364 Pittman, Helena Clare. *Still-Life Stew* (K–4). Illus. by Victoria Raymond. 1998, Hyperion LB $16.49 (0-7868-2206-6). An imaginative picture book in which a girl grows a variety of vegetables for a still-life painting and also for a delicious vegetable stew. (Rev: HBG 10/98; SLJ 6/98)

3365 Pocock, Rita. *Annabelle and the Big Slide* (PS). Illus. 1989, Harcourt $10.95 (0-15-200407-6). 32pp. Annabelle summons up her courage to climb the ladder and zoom down the playground slide. (Rev: BL 1/1/90; HB 11–12/89; SLJ 12/89)

3366 Polacco, Patricia. *Aunt Chip and the Great Triple Creek Dam Affair* (K–3). Illus. 1996, Putnam $15.95 (0-399-22943-4). 32pp. Because of television, a whole town forgets how to read until Aunt Chip, the town librarian, intervenes. (Rev: BCCB 6/96; BL 4/15/96; SLJ 5/96*)

3367 Pomeranc, Marion Hess. *The American Wei* (PS–3). Illus. by DyAnne DiSalvo-Ryan. 1998, Albert Whitman LB $15.95 (0-8075-0312-6). 32pp. Outside the courthouse where his parents are to be naturalized, a young Chinese American boy loses his tooth and is helped by people from all over the world. (Rev: BCCB 4/98; BL 3/15/98; HBG 10/98; SLJ 5/98)

3368 Porter, Barbara J. *Some Answers Are Loud, Some Answers Are Soft* (K–3). Illus. by Dilleen Marsh. 1999, Shadow Mountain $12.95 (1-57345-557-1). 32pp. A variety of moods are explored in this book that explains why answers to questions are expressed differently. (Rev: BL 3/15/00)

3369 Priceman, Marjorie. *Emeline at the Circus* (PS–3). Illus. 1999, Knopf LB $16.99 (0-679-97685-X). 40pp. A little girl, who is attending the circus with her second-grade class, suddenly becomes involved in the action. (Rev: BCCB 7–8/99; BL 4/1/99*; HBG 10/99; SLJ 5/99)

3370 Priddy, Roger. *Baby's Book of the Body* (PS). Illus. 1996, DK $9.95 (0-7894-0198-3). Color photos of children are used to point out body parts, emotions, sounds, actions, and food. (Rev: SLJ 8/96)

3371 Quinsey, Mary Beth. *Why Does That Man Have Such a Big Nose?* (PS–1). Illus. by Wilson Chan. 1986, Parenting Pr. LB $16.95 (0-943990-25-4); paper $5.95 (0-943990-24-6). 32pp. Explaining some of the physical differences among people and how or why they happen. (Rev: BL 1/1/87; SLJ 12/86)

3372 Ransom, Candice. *The Big Green Pocketbook* (PS–1). Illus. by Felicia Bond. 1993, HarperCollins LB $16.89 (0-06-020849-X). 32pp. At every stop during a day of errands with her mother, a little girl is given something for her empty pocketbook. (Rev: BL 7/93; SLJ 7/93)

3373 Raschka, Chris. *Ring! Yo?* (PS–2). Illus. 2000, DK $15.95 (0-7894-2614-5). 38pp. A boy on the phone reacts in various ways to what he hears during a telephone conversation and the reader must use his imagination to guess what is causing these strange emotional reactions. At the end, the author suggests what the other person might have said. (Rev: BCCB 4/00; BL 3/15/00*; HB 3–4/00; HBG 10/00; SLJ 5/00)

3374 Ray, Mary L. *Pianna* (PS–3). Illus. by Bobbie Henba. 1994, Harcourt $14.95 (0-15-261357-9). 32pp. A New England woman looks back on her long life and realizes how much music and her love of the piano have meant to her. (Rev: BL 3/15/94; SLJ 5/94)

3375 Ray, Mary L. *Red Rubber Boot Day* (PS). Illus. by Lauren Stringer. 2000, Harcourt $16.00 (0-

15-213756-4). 32pp. Told from a child's point of view, this book gives details on the indoor and outdoor activities that are possible on a rainy day. (Rev: BL 3/15/00; HBG 10/00; SLJ 4/00)

3376 Reiser, Lynn. *Tomorrow on Rocky Pond* (PS–1). Illus. 1993, Greenwillow LB $13.93 (0-688-10673-0). 32pp. A young girl who has just arrived at her family's summer home thinks of all the wonderful things she will soon be able to do. (Rev: BL 8/93)

3377 Rice, David L. *Because Brian Hugged His Mother* (PS–3). Illus. by K. Dyble Thompson. 1999, Dawn $16.95 (1-883220-90-4); paper $7.95 (1-883220-89-0). 32pp. The hug that Brian gives his mother produces a string of kindnesses throughout the community. (Rev: BL 8/99; HBG 10/99)

3378 Riddell, Edwina. *100 First Words to Say with Your Baby* (PS). Illus. by author. 1992, Barron's paper $4.95 (0-8120-4888-1). This book illustrates 100 common words that prereaders should become familiar with. (Rev: SLJ 9/92)

3379 Ripley, Catherine. *Why Is Soap So Slippery? And Other Bathtime Stories* (PS–1). Illus. by Scot Ritchie. 1995, Firefly $14.95 (1-895688-34-5); paper $5.95 (1-895688-39-6). Through 12 questions about bathroom objects and activities, the reader learns such things as how hot and cold water come out of the same tap, why we brush our teeth, and what happens when the toilet is flushed. (Rev: SLJ 2/96) [394]

3380 Robbins, Ken. *Make Me a Peanut Butter Sandwich (and a Glass of Milk)* (PS–3). Illus. 1992, Scholastic $14.95 (0-590-43550-7). 32pp. Photos and minimal text tell how a favorite snack for children gets to the table. (Rev: BCCB 10/92; BL 9/1/92) [641]

3381 Roche, Denis. *Ollie All Over* (PS). Illus. 1997, Houghton $4.95 (0-395-81124-4). 14pp. A board book about a dog who finds all sorts of places to hide in the house. (Rev: BCCB 6/97; BL 4/15/97; SLJ 8/97)

3382 Rockwell, Anne. *Ferryboat Ride!* (PS–2). Illus. by Maggie Smith. 1999, Crown LB $18.99 (0-517-70960-0). 32pp. A young narrator describes a ferryboat ride to a summer island, noting the various passengers and parts of the ferry. (Rev: BL 7/99; HBG 10/99; SLJ 6/99)

3383 Rockwell, Anne. *Long Ago Yesterday* (PS–K). Illus. 1999, Greenwillow $16.00 (0-688-14411-X). 24pp. Ten two-page short stories about the everyday life experiences of children. (Rev: BL 11/15/99; HBG 3/00; SLJ 10/99)

3384 Rockwell, Anne. *Pots and Pans* (PS). Illus. by Lizzy Rockwell. 1993, Macmillan LB $13.95 (0-02-777631-X). Two tots identify the various pots and pans found in a kitchen. (Rev: BCCB 3/93; HB 5–6/93; SLJ 7/93)

3385 Rockwell, Anne. *What We Like* (PS–K). Illus. 1992, Macmillan paper $13.95 (0-02-777274-8). 24pp. Simple pleasures for young ones, such as building a sand castle and baking cookies. (Rev: BL 10/15/92; SLJ 2/93) [428.1]

3386 Roddie, Shen. *Toes Are to Tickle* (PS). Illus. by Kady M. Denton. 1997, Tricycle Pr. $13.95 (1-883672-49-X). 24pp. A playful picture book that gives pleasant definitions to common articles, like "A tree is to hide behind." (Rev: BL 6/1–15/97; SLJ 9/97)

3387 Rollings, Susan. *New Shoes, Red Shoes* (PS–K). Illus. 2000, Orchard $15.95 (0-531-30268-7). 32pp. Bouncy rhymes are used in this slight story about the fun of going to pick out a new pair of shoes. (Rev: BL 2/1/00; HBG 10/00; SLJ 5/00)

3388 Roop, Peter, and Connie Roop. *A City Album* (2–3). Illus. Series: Long Ago and Today. 1998, Heinemann LB $13.95 (1-57572-600-9). 24pp. Using old and new photographs, this work compares city life today, when people ride subway trains, buses, cars, and bicycles, with city life a century ago, when people walked or rode horses. (Rev: BL 12/15/98) [307.76]

3389 Roop, Peter, and Connie Roop. *A School Album* (2–3). Illus. 1998, Heinemann LB $13.95 (1-57572-603-3). 24pp. Using double-page spreads and historic and modern photos, schools of 100 years ago are compared to schools today. (Rev: BL 12/15/98) [372.97]

3390 Rosa-Casanova, Sylvia. *Mama Provi and the Pot of Rice* (K–3). Illus. by Robert Roth. 1997, Simon & Schuster $16.00 (0-689-31932-0). 32pp. Mama Provi barters some of her arroz con pollo for a variety of other national dishes in this multicultural story. (Rev: BL 5/15/97; SLJ 7/97)

3391 Rose, Emma. *Ballet Magic: A Pop-up Book* (PS–1). Illus. by Jan Palmer. 1996, Scholastic $12.95 (0-590-26242-4). 12pp. Various ballet positions and movements are shown in this pop-up book. (Rev: BL 12/15/96)

3392 Rosenberry, Vera. *Run, Jump, Whiz, Splash* (PS–2). Illus. by author. 1999, Holiday $15.95 (0-8234-1378-0). A simple but lyrical account of the activities of two children throughout the seasons of a year. (Rev: HBG 3/00; SLJ 9/99)

3393 Rosenberry, Vera. *When Vera Was Sick* (PS–K). Illus. 1998, Holt $15.95 (0-8050-5405-7). 24pp. This book chronicles all the problems of being sick and confined to one's room until the magical day when you're well again. (Rev: BCCB 1/99; BL 11/15/98; HB 9–10/98; HBG 3/99; SLJ 12/98)

3394 Ross, Alice, and Kent Ross. *Jezebel's Spooky Spot* (K–3). Illus. by Ted Rand. 1999, Dutton $15.99 (0-525-45448-9). 32pp. To ease her loneliness after her father goes to war, African American Jezebel finds a quiet spot in the woods that she calls her own. (Rev: BL 2/15/99; HBG 10/99; SLJ 4/99)

3395 Ross, Dave. *A Book of Hugs* (PS–K). Illus. by Laura Rader. 1999, HarperCollins $12.95 (0-06-028147-2). 40pp. This cheerful book covers all kinds of hugs, such as Mommy hugs, bear hugs, and knee hugs. (Rev: BL 3/15/99; HBG 10/99; SLJ 3/99)

3396 Ross, Dave. *A Book of Kisses* (PS–1). Illus. by Laura Rader. 2000, HarperCollins LB $12.89 (0-06-028453-6). 40pp. All sorts of different kisses are pictured and the word for kiss is given in 15 differ-

ent languages. (Rev: BL 2/15/00; HBG 10/00; SLJ 2/00)

3397 Ross, Tony. *Wash Your Hands!* (PS–2). Illus. by author. 2000, Kane/Miller paper $6.95 (1-929132-01-8). A young girl learns that it is important to wash your hands after playing and before eating food if you want to stay healthy and avoid bad germs. (Rev: HBG 3/01; SLJ 3/01)

3398 Rotner, Shelley, and Sheila Kelly. *Feeling Thankful* (PS–2). Illus. 2000, Millbrook LB $20.90 (0-7613-1918-2). 24pp. This simple photo-essay enumerates the many things, such as a family or a pet, for which children can be thankful. (Rev: BL 12/1/00; HBG 3/01; SLJ 12/00) [179]

3399 Rotner, Shelley, and Ken Kreisler. *Citybook* (PS–K). Illus. by Shelley Rotner. 1994, Orchard LB $16.99 (0-531-08687-9). 32pp. Ken explains why he loves visiting the city in this picture book filled with color photos of big-city life and sights. (Rev: BL 2/15/94; HB 5–6/94; SLJ 3/94)

3400 Rotner, Shelley, and Ken Kreisler. *Faces* (PS). Illus. 1994, Macmillan paper $14.95 (0-02-777887-8). 32pp. Multicultural children engage in common activities like smelling, thinking, and making faces in this picture book. (Rev: BL 11/15/94; SLJ 12/94) [153.7]

3401 Rounds, Glen. *Cowboys* (PS–1). Illus. 1991, Holiday LB $16.95 (0-8234-0867-1). 32pp. A day in the life of a cowboy is described in sparse text and shown in complementary illustrations. (Rev: BCCB 4/91; BL 6/1/91; SLJ 5/91)

3402 Russo, Marisabina. *Mama Talks Too Much* (PS–2). Illus. 1999, Greenwillow $16.00 (0-688-16411-0). 32pp. On the way to the supermarket, Celeste is impatient with her mother's stops to chat with friends until Celeste meets Mrs. Castro's new puppy, Jake. (Rev: BCCB 9/99; BL 12/1/99; HBG 3/00; SLJ 9/99)

3403 Rylant, Cynthia. *Appalachia: The Voices of Sleeping Birds* (PS–3). Illus. by Barry Moser. 1991, Harcourt $17.00 (0-15-201605-8). 32pp. A loving book in simple text and art about remembering Appalachia. (Rev: BCCB 6/91; BL 2/1/91*; HB 9–10/91*; SLJ 4/91*) [974]

3404 Rylant, Cynthia. *An Everyday Book* (PS–K). Illus. 1997, Simon & Schuster paper $12.95 (0-689-81255-8). 32pp. A collection of five previously released board books about everyday pets, a garden, children, a town, and a house. (Rev: BL 4/15/97)

3405 Rylant, Cynthia. *Everyday Children* (PS). Illus. by author. Series: Everyday Books. 1993, Bradbury paper $4.95 (0-02-778022-8). The children in this board book engage in simple activities like loving different kinds of pets. Also use *Everyday Garden* (1993). (Rev: SLJ 10/93*)

3406 Rylant, Cynthia. *Everyday House* (PS). Illus. by author. Series: Everyday Books. 1993, Bradbury paper $4.95 (0-02-778024-4). In this board book, it is pointed out that an everyday house contains a door, a porch, flowers, cookies, a dog, and a kitten. Also use *Everyday Pets* and *Everyday Town* (both 1993). (Rev: SLJ 10/93*)

3407 Rylant, Cynthia. *Mr. Griggs' Work* (PS–2). Illus. by Julie Downing. 1989, Orchard paper $6.95 (0-531-07037-9). 32pp. Mr. Griggs, who works at the post office, loves his job. (Rev: BCCB 2/89; BL 2/1/89; HB 3–4/89)

3408 Sabuda, Robert. *Cookie Count: A Tasty Pop-Up* (PS–1). Illus. 1997, Simon & Schuster $19.95 (0-689-81191-8). 12pp. Pop-ups involving food are featured in this book, including an amazing gingerbread house. (Rev: BL 12/15/97; HBG 10/98)

3409 Sathre, Vivian. *On Grandpa's Farm* (PS). Illus. by Anne Hunter. 1997, Houghton $16.00 (0-395-76506-4). A day's activities on a farm end when Grandpa takes his young helper fishing. (Rev: HBG 3/98; SLJ 9/97)

3410 Schotter, Roni. *Captain Bob Sets Sail* (PS–2). Illus. by Joe Cepeda. 2000, Simon & Schuster $16.00 (0-689-82081-X). 32pp. A boy named Captain Bob turns his bath into an exciting affair on the Soapy Seas with his mother acting as the great Sea Hand. (Rev: BCCB 9/00; BL 7/00; HBG 10/00; SLJ 5/00)

3411 Schotter, Roni. *Dreamland* (K–2). Illus. by Kevin Hawkes. 1996, Orchard LB $16.99 (0-531-08858-8). 40pp. Theo's fanciful drawings of strange inventions become real when his uncle creates an amusement park. (Rev: BL 4/1/96; SLJ 4/96*)

3412 Schotter, Roni. *Nothing Ever Happens on 90th Street* (PS–2). Illus. by Kyrsten Brooker. 1997, Orchard LB $17.99 (0-531-08886-3). 32pp. Eva's writing assignment changes how her neighborhood acts and interacts. (Rev: BL 3/1/97; SLJ 3/97*)

3413 Schwartz, Amy. *Some Babies* (PS–K). Illus. 2000, Orchard $15.95 (0-531-30287-3). 32pp. A mother obliges when her child wants to hear about other babies by telling stories about activities like playing on a slide or sitting in strollers. (Rev: BL 12/15/00; HB 9–10/00; HBG 3/01; SLJ 10/00)

3414 Scott, Ann H. *Brave as a Mountain Lion* (K–3). Illus. by Glo Coalson. 1996, Clarion $14.95 (0-395-66760-7). 32pp. Spider, a Shoshone boy, gets help from his family to conquer his fears, but it is from watching a real spider that he gets real help. (Rev: BCCB 2/96; BL 3/15/96; SLJ 4/96)

3415 Scott, Ann H. *Hi* (PS). Illus. by Glo Coalson. 1994, Putnam $15.95 (0-399-21964-1). 32pp. At the post office with her mother, little Margarita greets everyone, but no one pays attention until one of the workers smiles at her. (Rev: BL 5/15/94; HB 7–8/94; SLJ 7/94*)

3416 Scott, C. Anne. *Old Jake's Skirts* (K–3). Illus. by David Slonim. 1998, Northland $15.95 (0-87358-615-8). 36pp. Jake uses the skirts he finds in an abandoned steamer trunk for a variety of uses that change his life; however, when the owners come to claim their trunk, there is only one skirt left. (Rev: BCCB 7–8/98; BL 6/1–15/98; HBG 10/98; SLJ 7/98)

3417 Serfozo, Mary. *Joe Joe* (PS–1). Illus. by Nina S. Montezinos. 1993, Simon & Schuster $15.95 (0-689-50578-7). Using only 16 words, the author describes a boy's outdoor walk and his encounter with a mud puddle. (Rev: SLJ 1/94)

3418 Seuss, Dr. *Oh, the Places You'll Go!* (PS–3). Illus. 1990, Random LB $17.99 (0-679-90527-8). This book of advice for youngsters tells them that in spite of problems, they can succeed. (Rev: BL 1/1/90*; SLJ 3/90)

3419 Seymour, Tres. *The Smash-up Crash-up Derby* (K–2). Illus. by S. D. Schindler. 1995, Orchard LB $16.99 (0-531-08731-X). 32pp. A boy and members of his family enjoy the fall fair, particularly the demolition derby. (Rev: BCCB 3/95; BL 2/1/95; SLJ 3/95)

3420 Shaik, Fatima. *The Jazz of Our Street* (PS–3). Illus. by E. B. Lewis. 1998, Dial LB $15.89 (0-8037-1886-1). 32pp. A young girl, her brother, and many onlookers enjoy the stirring music of a marching band as it parades through the streets of the Tremé neighborhood in New Orleans. (Rev: BL 5/1/98; HBG 10/98; SLJ 9/98)

3421 Sharratt, Nick, and Stephen Tucker. *The Time It Took Tom* (PS–2). Illus. by Nick Sharratt. 2000, Little Tiger $14.95 (1-888444-63-0). It takes three weeks to restore the living room to normal after Tom goes wild with a can of red paint. (Rev: HBG 10/00; SLJ 3/00)

3422 Shea, Pegi Deitz. *I See Me!* (PS). Illus. by Lucia Washburn. Series: Growing Tree. 2000, HarperCollins $7.95 (0-694-01278-5). 16pp. In this board book for the very young, a toddler notices her reflection in a mirror, on the back of a metal spoon, on the television screen, and in her mother's sunglasses. (Rev: BL 5/15/00)

3423 Shelby, Anne. *Homeplace* (PS–2). Illus. by Wendy A. Halperin. 1995, Orchard LB $17.99 (0-531-08732-8). 32pp. A grandmother tells her grandchild about the history of her family and the old homestead. (Rev: BCCB 5/95; BL 2/15/95; SLJ 4/95*)

3424 Shelby, Anne. *The Someday House* (PS–2). Illus. by Rosanne Litzinger. 1996, Orchard LB $16.99 (0-531-08860-X). 32pp. Three children imagine living in a variety of different houses and settings. (Rev: BL 3/1/96; SLJ 4/96)

3425 Shulevitz, Uri. *Snow* (PS). Illus. 1998, Farrar $16.00 (0-374-37092-3). 32pp. A young child is able to see the beauty in a single snowflake whereas the more sophisticated adults cannot. (Rev: BCCB 1/99; BL 10/15/98*; HB 1–2/99; HBG 3/99; SLJ 12/98)

3426 Shulevitz, Uri. *Toddlecreek Post Office* (2–4). Illus. 1990, Farrar $14.95 (0-374-37635-2). 32pp. The inhabitants of a small village are told their post office must close. (Rev: BCCB 1/91; BL 11/15/90; SLJ 1/91)

3427 Siddals, Mary M. *Millions of Snowflakes* (PS). Illus. by Elizabeth Sayles. 1998, Clarion $13.00 (0-395-71531-8). 25pp. Using cool pastel drawings and a spare, rhyming text, this playful story describes all the things one can do in the snow, such as making angels and catching snowflakes. (Rev: BL 11/1/98; HBG 3/99; SLJ 9/98)

3428 Silverman, Erica. *Fixing the Crack of Dawn* (K–2). Illus. by Sandra Speidel. 1994, BridgeWater $13.95 (0-8167-3458-5). When Lisa hears that her mother will be home at the crack of dawn, she goes outdoors hoping to mend the crack. (Rev: SLJ 11/94)

3429 Silverman, Erica. *Follow the Leader* (PS–1). Illus. by G. Brian Karas. 2000, Farrar $15.00 (0-374-32423-9). 32pp. Two brothers, who are supposed to be asleep, think up imaginative games taking turns playing follow the leader. (Rev: BL 10/15/00; HB 9–10/00; HBG 3/01; SLJ 10/00)

3430 Simon, Norma. *Wet World* (PS–2). Illus. by Alexi Natchev. 1995, Candlewick $12.95 (1-56402-190-4). 32pp. A wet, rainy day as experienced by a little girl. (Rev: BCCB 6/95; BL 6/1–15/95; SLJ 8/95)

3431 Siomades, Lorianne. *A Place to Bloom* (PS). Illus. by author. 1997, Boyds Mills $7.95 (1-56397-656-0). A collection of random thoughts about attitudes, likes, dislikes, and emotions, all expressed in catchy rhymes. (Rev: HBG 3/98; SLJ 9/97)

3432 Skorpen, Liesel Moak. *We Were Tired of Living in a House* (PS–1). Illus. by Joe Cepeda. 1999, Putnam $15.99 (0-399-23016-5). 32pp. Three children try living in a series of different shelters, including a tree, cave, and seashore before they happily return home. (Rev: BL 3/15/99; HBG 10/99; SLJ 4/99)

3433 Smith, Charles R., Jr. *Brown Sugar Babies* (PS). Photos by author. 2000, Hyperion $14.99 (0-7868-0622-2). The joys of being an infant are captured in photographs of black children and in simple enchanting rhymes. (Rev: HBG 3/01; SLJ 10/00)

3434 Smith, Cynthia Leitich. *Jingle Dancer* (PS–2). Illus. by Cornelius Van Wright and Ying-Hwa Hu. 2000, Morrow LB $15.89 (0-688-16242-8). 32pp. Jenna, a Native American girl, gathers metal jingles to sew onto her dress so she can make pleasant sounds when she dances in the next powwow. (Rev: BCCB 7–8/00; BL 5/15/00; HBG 10/00; SLJ 7/00)

3435 Soentpiet, Chris K. *Around Town* (PS–2). Illus. 1994, Lothrop LB $15.93 (0-688-04573-1). 32pp. Big-city life is celebrated in this picture book about a young girl and her mother strolling around New York City. (Rev: BL 4/1/94; SLJ 5/94) [307.67]

3436 Soto, Gary. *Snapshots from the Wedding* (K–3). Illus. by Stephanie Garcia. 1997, Putnam $15.99 (0-399-22808-X); paper $5.99 (0-698-11752-2). 32pp. A delightful picture book that chronicles the exciting and tearful moments during a Mexican American wedding. (Rev: BCCB 4/97; BL 2/15/97*; SLJ 5/97)

3437 Spetter, Jung-Hee. *Lily and Trooper's Fall* (PS–K). Illus. 1999, Front Street $8.95 (1-886910-38-3). 32pp. Lily and her fun-loving dog Trooper enjoy such fall activities as jumping in a pile of leaves. Also use *Lily and Trooper's Winter* (1999). (Rev: BL 12/1/99; HBG 3/00; SLJ 10/99)

3438 Spier, Peter. *People* (2–4). Illus. by author. 1980, Doubleday $16.95 (0-385-13181-X); paper $12.95 (0-385-24469-X). 48pp. A view of people's varying life-styles and ways of life.

3439 Steen, Sandra, and Susan Steen. *Car Wash* (PS–1). Illus. by G. Brian Karas. 2001, Putnam $15.99 (0-399-23369-5). 32pp. Two twins and their

dad experience the fun and excitement of going through a car wash. (Rev: BCCB 1/01*; BL 1/1–15/01; SLJ 1/01)

3440 Stevenson, James. *Fun/No Fun* (PS–3). Illus. 1994, Greenwillow $13.93 (0-688-11674-4). 32pp. Various everyday events taken from the author's life as he was growing up are classified as being either fun or no fun in this humorous but perceptive picture book. (Rev: BL 3/15/94; HB 7–8/94; SLJ 8/94) [813]

3441 Stevenson, James. *July* (K–3). Illus. by author. 1990, Greenwillow LB $12.88 (0-688-08823-6). 32pp. The author recalls his childhood and the fun he had going to the beach with his grandparents. (Rev: BL 5/1/90; HB 5–6/90; SLJ 3/90*) [741]

3442 Stevenson, James. *Popcorn* (2–5). Illus. 1998, Greenwillow $15.00 (0-688-15261-9). 64pp. Daily life in a small seaside town is captured in a series of quiet, moving poems illustrated with exquisite watercolors. (Rev: BCCB 4/98; BL 5/1/98*; HB 5–6/98; HBG 10/98; SLJ 5/98)

3443 Stewart, Sarah. *The Library* (K–3). Illus. by David Small. 1995, Farrar $16.00 (0-374-34388-8). 32pp. The life story of a woman who loved reading books so much that eventually a library was named after her. (Rev: BCCB 5/95; BL 3/15/95; HB 7–8/95; SLJ 9/95)

3444 Stock, Catherine. *Island Summer* (K–2). Illus. 1999, Lothrop $16.00 (0-688-12780-0). 32pp. After a cold winter, an island springs back to life when the summer residents arrive, only to become quiet again when they leave in the fall. (Rev: BL 10/15/99; HBG 3/00; SLJ 9/99)

3445 Stoeke, Janet Morgan. *Hide and Seek* (PS–K). Illus. by Janet M. Stoeke. Series: A Minerva Louise Board Book. 1999, Dutton $4.99 (0-525-46189-2). Minerva Louise can't find her friends to play with, but the reader will spot the farm animals hiding around the barn in this board book. Also use *Rainy Day* (1999). (Rev: SLJ 7/99)

3446 Strickland, Michael R. *Haircuts at Sleepy Sam's* (PS–2). Illus. by Keaf Holliday. 1998, Boyds Mills $15.95 (1-56397-562-9). Although two African American brothers have a note from their mother for the barber telling him how to cut their hair, the barber, Sam, gives them the cut they want. (Rev: BL 10/15/98; HBG 3/99; SLJ 11/98)

3447 Stuve-Bodeen, Stephanie. *We'll Paint the Octopus Red* (PS–2). Illus. by Pam DeVito. 1998, Woodbine $14.95 (1-890627-06-2). 28pp. A young girl thinks of all the things that she and her new baby brother can do together. When she is told that he has Down syndrome, she maintains that they still will do those things, though now each activity might take a little longer. (Rev: BL 9/15/98; HBG 3/99; SLJ 12/98)

3448 Suen, Anastasia. *Delivery* (PS–2). Illus. by Wade Zahares. 1999, Viking $15.99 (0-670-88455-3). 32pp. Presents various types of deliveries and delivery vehicles — from grocery stores and floral shops to trucks, taxis, and airplanes. (Rev: BL 9/1/99; HBG 3/00; SLJ 11/99)

3449 Swanson, Susan M. *Letter to the Lake* (1–3). Illus. by Peter Catalanotto. 1998, DK $15.95 (0-7894-2483-5). 32pp. On a cold, wintry day while her mother is waiting for someone to jump-start the family car, Rosie remembers the lovely summer days she spent at the lake. (Rev: BL 4/15/98; HBG 10/98; SLJ 5/98)

3450 Tarpley, Natasha A. *I Love My Hair!* (PS–1). Illus. by E. B. Lewis. 1998, Little, Brown $15.95 (0-316-52275-9). 32pp. A young African American girl has fun creating different styles with her hair. (Rev: BCCB 4/98; BL 2/15/98; HBG 10/98; SLJ 2/98)

3451 Temple, Charles. *Train* (PS–1). Illus. by Larry Johnson. 1996, Houghton $14.95 (0-395-69826-X). 32pp. An African American family experiences the excitement and fun of an overnight train trip. (Rev: BL 3/15/96; SLJ 4/96)

3452 Thomas, Joyce C. *Cherish Me!* (PS–K). Illus. by Nneka Bennett. Series: Harper Growing Tree. 1998, HarperFestival $9.95 (0-694-01097-9). The concept of healthy self-esteem is explored in this poem celebrating the life of an African American child. (Rev: BL 1/1–15/99; HBG 3/99; SLJ 12/98)

3453 Thomas, Joyce C. *You Are My Perfect Baby* (PS). Illus. by Nneka Bennett. Series: Harper Growing Tree. 1999, HarperFestival $5.95 (0-694-01096-0). In this board book, an African American mother and her baby engage in simple activities that show off the wonders of the little one's body, like his twinkling toes. (Rev: SLJ 8/99)

3454 Thompson, Carol. *Baby Days* (PS). Illus. 1991, Macmillan $15.95 (0-02-789235-1). 48pp. Illustrates a number of activities that toddlers can engage in from waking to bedtime. (Rev: BL 12/1/91; SLJ 1/92)

3455 Tobias, Tobi. *Serendipity* (1–4). Illus. by Peter H. Reynolds. 2000, Simon & Schuster $12.00 (0-689-83373-3). The meaning of the word *serendipity* is explored with 16 imaginative examples of situations where the word could apply. (Rev: HBG 3/01; SLJ 11/00)

3456 Torres, Leyla. *Subway Sparrow* (PS–2). Illus. 1993, Farrar $15.00 (0-374-37285-3). 30pp. Four people who are riders in a New York City subway car try to help a sparrow that is trapped inside. (Rev: BL 1/15/94; SLJ 2/94)

3457 Tresselt, Alvin. *Wake Up, City!* (PS–K). Illus. by Carolyn Ewing. 1990, Lothrop LB $13.88 (0-688-08653-5). 32pp. Pictures activities in the city from daybreak until the work day begins. (Rev: BCCB 9/90; BL 5/1/90; SLJ 8/90)

3458 Tresselt, Alvin. *White Snow Bright Snow* (K–3). Illus. by Roger Duvoisin. 1988, Lothrop LB $15.89 (0-688-51161-9); Morrow paper $5.95 (0-688-08294-7). Small-town snowfall is chronicled in this reissued Caldecott Medal winner of 1948.

3459 Tryon, Leslie. *Albert's Ballgame* (PS–1). Illus. 1996, Simon & Schuster $16.00 (0-689-80187-4). 32pp. There's lots of action and fun in this humorous description of a baseball game. (Rev: BL 5/1/96; SLJ 3/96*)

3460 Turner, Nancy Byrd. *When Young Melissa Sweeps* (PS–3). Illus. by Debrah Santini. 1998, Peachtree $15.95 (1-56145-157-6). 30pp. First published in 1927, this poem captures a young girl's joy and enthusiasm as she dances with her broom while cleaning the house. (Rev: BL 5/1/98; HBG 10/98)

3461 Tusa, Tricia. *Bunnies in My Head* (PS–2). Illus. 1998, Univ. of Texas. M.D. Anderson Cancer Center $20.00 (0-9664551-8-5). 32pp. Using a brief story line, this book reproduces the artwork created by children at the Anderson Cancer Center in Houston, Texas. (Rev: BL 2/1/99; SLJ 2/99)

3462 Uff, Caroline. *Lulu's Busy Day* (PS–K). Illus. 2000, Walker $14.95 (0-8027-8716-9). 24pp. A little girl named Lulu engages in such activities as coloring, playing ball, swinging in a park, eating dinner, and going to bed. (Rev: BL 3/1/00; HBG 10/00; SLJ 5/00)

3463 Van Wert, Faye. *Empty Pockets* (PS–1). Illus. by author. 2000, Greene Bark $16.95 (1-88085-161-X). When Stevie's mother discovers a frog in his dresser drawer, she puts a stop to his hobby of bringing home everything he finds. (Rev: SLJ 3/01)

3464 Vizurraga, Susan. *Our Old House* (PS–3). Illus. by Leslie Baker. 1997, Holt $15.95 (0-8050-3911-2). 32pp. While her parents restore an old house, a young girl wonders about the people who used to live in it. (Rev: BL 12/1/97; HBG 3/98; SLJ 10/97)

3465 Voake, Charlotte. *Here Comes the Train* (PS–K). Illus. 1998, Candlewick $15.99 (0-7636-0438-0). 96pp. William, Chloe, and Dad ride their bikes to a footbridge in the countryside where they enthusiastically watch the passage of a train. (Rev: BCCB 12/98; BL 9/1/98; HBG 3/99; SLJ 9/98)

3466 Voetberg, Julie. *I Am a Home Schooler* (2–4). Illus. 1995, Albert Whitman LB $15.95 (0-8075-3441-2); paper $6.95 (0-8075-3442-0). 32pp. Nine-year-old Teigen describes why she is a home schooler and the educational routine she follows. Illustrated with photographs. (Rev: BCCB 12/95; BL 1/1–15/96; SLJ 2/96) [649]

3467 Waddell, Martin. *Mimi's Christmas* (PS–K). Illus. by Leo Hartas. 1997, Candlewick paper $3.99 (0-7636-0413-5). A little mouse is comforted by his sister when he begins to worry that Santa Mouse won't bring him the drum he wants. (Rev: SLJ 10/97)

3468 Waddell, Martin. *Once There Were Giants* (PS–1). Illus. by Penny Dale. 1989, Delacorte $13.95 (0-385-29806-4). 32pp. This book captures a child's view of growing up, where adults seem like giants. (Rev: BL 11/1/89; SLJ 12/89)

3469 Walsh, Melanie. *Ned's Rainbow* (PS). Illus. by author. Series: Toddler Storybook. 2000, DK paper $5.95 (0-7894-5623-0). 24pp. In this very simple story for toddlers, a boy is sorry that he can't touch a rainbow so his mother paints one on the wall for him. (Rev: SLJ 10/00)

3470 Walter, Mildred P. *Ty's One-Man Band* (PS–2). Illus. by Margot Tomes. 1987, Macmillan LB $14.95 (0-02-792300-2). 32pp. Andro produces music from a collection of everyday objects. A reissue of the 1980 edition.

3471 Weidt, Maryann N. *Daddy Played Music for the Cows* (PS–3). Illus. by Henri Sorensen. 1995, Lothrop LB $14.93 (0-688-10058-9). 32pp. Life on a farm is recorded in this story of a girl who grows from baby to school age in this environment. (Rev: BL 10/1/95; SLJ 10/95)

3472 Weiss, Nicki. *The World Turns Round and Round* (PS–2). Illus. by author. 2000, Greenwillow LB $15.89 (0-688-17214-8). A charming book about different items of clothing a school class receives from people in places like Russia, Mexico, Kenya, and India. (Rev: HBG 3/01; SLJ 10/00)

3473 Wells, Rosemary. *Bingo* (PS). Illus. by author. Series: Bunny Reads Back. 1999, Scholastic $4.95 (0-590-02913-4). A variation on this familiar song makes Bingo a female in this enchanting board book. (Rev: SLJ 7/99)

3474 Weninger, Brigitte. *Ragged Bear* (PS–2). Trans. from German by Marianne Martens. Illus. by Alan Marks. 1996, North-South LB $15.88 (1-55858-663-6). After poor Teddy is abused by his owner and left in the park, he is adopted by a more caring child. (Rev: SLJ 12/96)

3475 Wilkes, Angela. *My First Word Board Book* (PS). Illus. 1997, DK $6.95 (0-7894-1514-3). For the very young, this board book identifies and labels common items. (Rev: SLJ 7/97)

3476 Williams, Sherley A. *Working Cotton* (PS–2). Illus. by Carole Byard. 1992, Harcourt $14.95 (0-15-299624-9). 32pp. A migrant child laborer tells of her daylong work in the fields. (Rev: BCCB 10/92; BL 9/1/92*; HB 11–12/93; SLJ 11/92)

3477 Williams, Sue. *I Went Walking* (PS–K). Illus. by Julie Vivas. 1990, Harcourt $13.95 (0-15-200471-8). 32pp. This book involves guessing the identity of animals hidden in pictures during a boy's afternoon walk. (Rev: BCCB 12/92; BL 9/1/90*; HB 11–12/90; SLJ 10/90*)

3478 Williams, Vera B. *Cherries and Cherry Pits* (K–3). Illus. by author. 1986, Greenwillow $16.93 (0-688-05146-4); Morrow paper $5.95 (0-688-10478-9). 40pp. Three tales and pictures from young Bidemmi, a black girl, about giving, loving, and making art. (Rev: BL 10/15/86; HB 9–10/86; SLJ 10/86)

3479 Williams, Vera B., and Jennifer Williams. *Stringbean's Trip to the Shining Sea* (2–4). Illus. by Vera B. Williams. 1988, Greenwillow $15.89 (0-688-07162-7); Scholastic paper $5.99 (0-590-44851-X). 48pp. A journey from Kansas to the West Coast, with Stringbean sending postcards along the way, which make up a kind of photo album. (Rev: BCCB 5/88; BL 3/1/88; SLJ 3/88)

3480 Wilson-Max, Ken. *Dexter Gets Dressed!* (PS). Illus. 1998, Kingfisher $12.95 (0-7534-5145-X). This interactive book teaches youngsters, by hands-on experiences, to zip zippers, button buttons, and tie laces. (Rev: BL 1/1–15/99)

3481 Wilson-Max, Ken. *Flush the Potty* (PS). Illus. by author. 2000, Scholastic $7.95 (0-439-17325-6). An effective interactive board book that makes the noise of a flushing toilet to mark the successful transition from diapers to potty. (Rev: SLJ 2/01)

3482 Winthrop, Elizabeth. *Shoes* (PS–K). Illus. by William Joyce. 1986, HarperCollins LB $16.89 (0-06-026592-2); paper $5.95 (0-06-443171-1). 32pp. Rhyming verse about shoes and feet. (Rev: BL 10/1/86; HB 1–2/87; SLJ 12/86)

3483 Wishinsky, Frieda. *Nothing Scares Us* (PS–2). Illus. by Neal Layton. 2000, Carolrhoda LB $15.95 (1-57505-490-6). Two dear friends who think they are fearless discover that each has a secret, hidden fear. (Rev: BCCB 10/00; HBG 3/01; SLJ 11/00)

3484 Wolff, Ferida. *A Weed Is a Seed* (K–2). Illus. by Janet Pedersen. 1996, Houghton $14.95 (0-395-72291-8). A family discovers that objects can be regarded in two ways, e.g., a breeze can bring refreshment or, to others, a sneeze. (Rev: SLJ 4/96)

3485 Wolff, Ferida. *A Year for Kiko* (PS–1). Illus. by Joung Un Kim. 1997, Houghton $15.00 (0-395-77396-2). 32pp. This picture book shows the everyday activities that a little girl named Kiko engaged in during a year. (Rev: BL 12/15/97; HBG 3/98; SLJ 10/97)

3486 Wong, Janet S. *Buzz* (PS–K). Illus. by Margaret Chodos-Irvine. 2000, Harcourt $15.00 (0-15-201923-5). 32pp. A young child lists all the things in his house that make a buzzing sound, like a bee and his father's electric razor. (Rev: BCCB 7–8/00; BL 7/00; HB 5–6/00; SLJ 5/00)

3487 Wong, Olive. *From My Window* (PS–K). Illus. by Anna Rich. 1995, Silver Pr. LB $15.95 (0-382-24665-9); paper $5.95 (0-382-24667-5). A young boy notices several changes in his neighborhood as snow falls. (Rev: SLJ 9/95)

3488 Wood, Audrey. *The Napping House Wakes Up* (PS–2). Illus. by Don Wood. 1994, Harcourt $17.95 (0-15-200890-X). 20pp. All sorts of actions take place in this interactive version of the popular picture book. (Rev: BL 11/15/94; SLJ 11/94)

3489 Woodruff, Elvira. *Can You Guess Where We're Going?* (PS–3). Illus. by Cynthia Fisher. 1998, Holiday $15.95 (0-8234-1387-X). Gramps gives clues to his grandson as to their destination — a place filled with excitement, adventure, and entertainment — which turns out to be the local library. (Rev: HBG 3/99; SLJ 1/99)

3490 Wyeth, Sharon D. *Something Beautiful* (PS–3). Illus. by Chris K. Soentpiet. 1998, Doubleday $16.95 (0-385-32239-9). 32pp. In spite of the squalor and poverty around her, a small African American girl is able to find some things of beauty in her neighborhood. (Rev: BCCB 12/98; BL 9/15/98; HBG 3/99; SLJ 12/98)

3491 Yashima, Taro. *Umbrella* (PS–1). Illus. by author. 1958, Puffin paper $5.99 (0-14-050240-8). 32pp. A 3-year-old Japanese American girl, born in New York City, longs for a rainy day so she can use her new blue umbrella and red rubber boots.

3492 Yee, Wong H. *Fireman Small* (PS–K). Illus. 1994, Houghton $15.00 (0-395-68987-2). 28pp. Every time Fireman Small tries to sleep, he must respond to another emergency. (Rev: BL 2/1/95; SLJ 12/94)

3493 Yim, Natasha. *Otto's Rainy Day* (PS). Illus. by Pamela R. Levy. 2000, Charlesbridge LB $15.95 (1-57091-400-1). 32pp. While Mom is trying to get work done on her home computer, little Otto craves attention and is constantly getting into trouble. (Rev: BL 6/1–15/00; SLJ 8/00)

3494 Yolen, Jane. *Raising Yoder's Barn* (1–3). Illus. by Bernie Fuchs. 1998, Little, Brown $15.95 (0-316-96887-0). 32pp. A lesson in community living is shown when lightning destroys an Amish family's barn and the neighbors come together to raise a new one. Young Matthew is given the task of carrying the designer's instructions to the builders. (Rev: BCCB 12/98; BL 9/15/98; HBG 3/99; SLJ 10/98)

3495 Zarin, Cynthia. *What Do You See When You Shut Your Eyes?* (PS–K). Illus. by Sarah Durham. 1998, Houghton $15.00 (0-395-76507-2). 32pp. An imaginative book in which children are asked questions such as "What do you see when you're asleep?" (Rev: HBG 3/99; SLJ 9/98)

3496 Ziefert, Harriet. *First Night* (PS–3). Illus. by S. D. Schindler. 1999, Putnam $15.99 (0-399-23120-X). 32pp. A delightful picture book about a town's parade on "first night," and all the different townspeople who participate. (Rev: BL 10/15/99; HBG 3/00; SLJ 12/99)

3497 Zimmerman, Andrea. *Trashy Town* (PS–K). Illus. by Dan Yaccarino. 1999, HarperCollins LB $14.89 (0-06-027140-X). 32pp. A day in the life of a cheerful garbageman who collects trash from all over town and takes it to the town dump. (Rev: BCCB 5/99; BL 8/99; HB 3–4/99; HBG 10/99; SLJ 5/99)

3498 Zolotow, Charlotte. *The Beautiful Christmas Tree* (PS–2). Illus. by Yan Nascimbene. 1999, Houghton $15.00 (0-395-91365-9). 32pp. A man, who has moved into an old brownstone and planted a tree in front of his new home, is not accepted by any of his neighbors except a young boy who, along with him, enjoys watching the tree grow strong and beautiful. (Rev: BL 12/1/99; HBG 3/00; SLJ 10/99)

3499 Zolotow, Charlotte. *I Like to Be Little* (K–3). Illus. by Erik Blegvad. 1987, HarperCollins paper $5.95 (0-06-443248-3). 32pp. The advantages of being small are explored in this 1966 picture book originally titled *I Want to Be Little*.

FAMILY STORIES

3500 Ackerman, Karen. *By the Dawn's Early Light* (PS–2). Illus. by Catherine Stock. 1994, Atheneum $16.00 (0-689-31788-3). 40pp. Because mom works the night shift, grandmother must spend nights with the family's two young children. (Rev: BCCB 5/94; BL 4/1/94; SLJ 6/94)

3501 Ackerman, Karen. *Song and Dance Man* (K–3). Illus. by Stephen Gammell. 1988, Knopf LB $16.99 (0-394-99330-6); paper $6.99 (0-679-81995-9). 32pp. Up in the attic, Grandpa shows three children what it's like to be a song-and-dance man. Caldecott Medal winner, 1989. (Rev: BCCB 11/88; BL 10/1/88; HB 11–12/88)

3502 Addy, Sharon Hart. *A Visit with Great-Grandma* (K–2). Illus. by Lydia Halverson. 1989, Whitman LB $14.95 (0-8075-8497-5). 32pp. A little girl's visit to Great-Grandma celebrates their Czechoslovakian heritage. (Rev: BL 4/15/89; SLJ 6/89)

3503 Adoff, Arnold. *Black Is Brown Is Tan* (K–3). Illus. by Emily Arnold McCully. 1973, Harper-Collins $15.00 (0-060-20083-9). 32pp. A story in rhyme, which needs to be read aloud for greater understanding, depicts the warmth and companionship of an interracial family.

3504 Alexander, Martha. *Where Does the Sky End, Grandpa?* (PS). Illus. by author. 1992, Harcourt $12.95 (0-15-295603-4). In this gentle story, a young girl walks through the pastures with her grandfather. (Rev: SLJ 7/92)

3505 Alexander, Sue. *One More Time, Mama* (PS–2). Illus. by David Soman. 1999, Marshall Cavendish $15.95 (0-7614-5051-3). 32pp. A mother tells her daughter of the long wait she had through three seasons — spring, summer, and fall — until the little girl was born. (Rev: BL 11/15/99; HBG 3/00; SLJ 11/99)

3506 Aliki. *Welcome, Little Baby* (PS–K). Illus. by author. 1987, Greenwillow $16.00 (0-688-06810-3). 24pp. Addressed to the newborn child and celebrating the innocence of the infant. (Rev: BL 3/1/87; SLJ 6–7/87)

3507 Anderson, Lena. *Stina* (K–2). Illus. 1989, Greenwillow $13.88 (0-688-08881-3). 40pp. Grandfather's house by the sea provides a wonderful summer for Stina. (Rev: BL 9/15/89; HB 9–10/89; SLJ 10/89)

3508 Anholt, Catherine, and Laurence Anholt. *Catherine and Laurence Anholt's Big Book of Families* (PS–K). Illus. 1998, Candlewick $16.99 (0-7636-0323-6). 32pp. All kinds of families and various members of the family are celebrated in this oversize book with lots of ink and watercolor illustrations. (Rev: BL 12/15/98; HBG 3/99; SLJ 12/98)

3509 Anholt, Catherine, and Laurence Anholt. *Here Come the Babies* (PS–K). Illus. 1993, Candlewick $13.95 (1-56402-209-9). 32pp. Through pictures and light verse, daily activities of babies are chronicled. (Rev: BL 10/15/93; HB 11–12/93; SLJ 1/94) [305.23]

3510 Anholt, Laurence. *Sophie and the New Baby* (PS–1). Illus. by Catherine Anholt. 2000, Albert Whitman $15.95 (0-8075-7550-X). 32pp. A story that stretches over several seasons about a little girl waiting for a sibling to be born and then adjusting to her baby brother. (Rev: BL 9/15/00; HBG 3/01; SLJ 11/00)

3511 Arnold, Marsha Diane. *The Chicken Salad Club* (PS–2). Illus. by Julie Downing. 1998, Dial LB $15.89 (0-8037-1916-7). 32pp. Nathaniel tries various methods to round up an audience to listen to the stories that his 100-year-old great-grandfather tells about his childhood, courtship, and marriage many years before. (Rev: BL 7/98; HBG 10/98; SLJ 8/98)

3512 Asquith, Ros. *My Do It!* (PS). Illus. by Sam Williams. 2000, DK paper $5.95 (0-7894-5648-6). An enjoyable flap book in which a little boy insists that he do a lot of chores that his mother would ordinarily do. (Rev: SLJ 10/00)

3513 Aylesworth, Jim. *Through the Night* (PS–1). Illus. by Pamela Patrick. 1998, Simon & Schuster $16.00 (0-689-80642-6). 32pp. Set in America about 50 years ago, this picture book depicts a father driving home during a lonely night to be with his waiting wife and children. (Rev: BL 4/1/98; HBG 10/98; SLJ 4/98)

3514 Ballard, Robin. *When I Am a Sister* (PS–K). Illus. 1998, Greenwillow $15.00 (0-688-15397-6). 24pp. Kate wonders if she will still be welcome when she visits her father and stepmother after their new baby arrives. (Rev: BL 3/1/98; HBG 10/98; SLJ 4/98)

3515 Barbour, Karen. *Little Nino's Pizzeria* (PS–2). Illus. by author. 1990, Harcourt paper $6.00 (0-15-246321-6). 32pp. When his father's business turns big, Tony is only in the way. (Rev: BL 9/15/87; SLJ 11/87)

3516 Barnwell, Ysaye M. *No Mirrors in My Nana's House* (PS–3). Illus. by Synthia Saint James. 1998, Harcourt $18.00 (0-15-201825-5). 32pp. The idea that people can find beauty in humble surroundings and can rise above a demeaning environment is presented in this picture book about an African American family. (Rev: BL 9/15/98; HBG 3/99; SLJ 10/98)

3517 Barrett, John M. *Daniel Discovers Daniel* (2–3). Illus. by Joe Servello. 1980, Human Sciences $16.95 (0-87705-423-1). 32pp. Daniel tries to satisfy his father's need for a sports-minded son.

3518 Barrett, Mary Brigid. *Day Care Days* (PS). Illus. by Patti Beling Murphy. 1999, Little, Brown $12.95 (0-316-08456-5). 32pp. After saying goodbye to Mommy and Daddy as they go to work, a youngster spends a happy time in a day-care setting. (Rev: BL 9/1/99; HBG 3/00; SLJ 11/99)

3519 Battle-Lavert, Gwendolyn. *The Music in Derrick's Heart* (PS–3). Illus. by Colin Bootman. 2000, Holiday $16.95 (0-8234-1353-5). 32pp. The power of music is explored in this gentle story about a young African American boy who is learning to play the harmonica by taking lessons from his uncle Booker T. (Rev: BCCB 3/00; BL 2/15/00*; HBG 10/00; SLJ 3/00)

3520 Bauer, Marion Dane. *Grandmother's Song* (PS–2). Illus. by Pamela Rossi. 2000, Simon & Schuster $16.00 (0-689-82272-3). 32pp. When her grandson is born, a grandmother recalls the birth of her own daughter, how she had grown inside her, and how her daughter spent her youth. (Rev: BL 8/00; HBG 3/01; SLJ 10/00)

3521 Baylor, Byrd. *Guess Who My Favorite Person Is* (1–3). Illus. by Robert Andrew Parker. 1992, Simon & Schuster $14.95 (0-684-19514-3). 32pp. A sensitive book that celebrates the joy and happiness in listing favorites. A reissue of the 1977 edition.

3522 Baynton, Martin. *Why Do You Love Me?* (PS–1). Illus. 1990, Greenwillow $15.93 (0-688-09157-1). 32pp. A simple text about a boy asking his father why he loves him. (Rev: BL 4/15/90; SLJ 7/90)

3523 Behrens, June. *Fiesta!* (1–3). Illus. by Scott Taylor. 1978, Children's LB $4.95 (0-516-48815-5). 32pp. The fun of celebrating a Mexican American family holiday — Cinco de Mayo.

3524 Beil, Karen M. *Grandma According to Me* (PS–K). Illus. by Ted Rand. 1994, Dell paper $4.99 (0-440-40995-0). 32pp. What a grandmother thinks are her faults, a loving granddaughter turns into virtues. (Rev: BL 12/1/92; SLJ 2/93)

3525 Bernhard, Emery. *A Ride on Mother's Back: A Day of Baby Carrying Around the World* (K–2). Illus. by Durga Bernhard. 1996, Harcourt $16.00 (0-15-200870-5). 40pp. Various ways of carrying babies reflect cultural differences around the world. (Rev: BL 10/15/96; SLJ 10/96) [392]

3526 Bertrand, Diane Gonzales. *Family, Familia* (1–4). Trans. by Julia Mercedes Castilla. Illus. by Pauline Rodriguez Howard. 1999, Piñata $14.95 (1-55885-269-7). A bilingual book in which Daniel Gonzalez enjoys a Tex-Mex feast when he goes to a family reunion in San Antonio. (Rev: HBG 3/00; SLJ 9/99)

3527 Bertrand, Diane Gonzales. *Sip, Slurp, Soup, Soup/Caldo, Caldo, Caldo* (K–3). Illus. by Alex P. DeLange. 1997, Piñata $14.95 (1-55885-183-6). A simple bilingual book about a family making soup. (Rev: HBG 3/98; SLJ 8/97)

3528 Birdseye, Tom. *A Regular Flood of Mishap* (PS–3). Illus. by Megan Lloyd. 1994, Holiday LB $16.95 (0-8234-1070-6). 32pp. In spite of accidentally causing a number of disasters, Ima Bean finds she is still wanted by her family. (Rev: BL 3/15/94; SLJ 3/94)

3529 Birdseye, Tom. *Waiting for Baby* (PS–K). Illus. by Loreen Leedy. 1991, Holiday LB $14.95 (0-8234-0892-2). 32pp. A young boy eagerly awaits an arrival in the family and later is happy with his baby brother. (Rev: BL 1/1/91; SLJ 11/91)

3530 Bittner, Wolfgang. *Wake Up, Grizzly!* (PS–K). Illus. by Gustavo Rosemffet. 1996, North-South LB $15.88 (1-55858-519-2). 30pp. Like a papa and a baby grizzly bear, Toby and his dad share a snoozy Sunday. (Rev: BL 8/96; SLJ 7/96)

3531 Blake, Robert J. *The Perfect Spot* (PS–3). Illus. 1992, Putnam $16.99 (0-399-22132-8). 32pp. A boy and his father spend a wonderful day together in the woods. (Rev: BL 3/15/92; SLJ 7/92)

3532 Blegvad, Lenore. *Once Upon a Time and Grandma* (PS–3). Illus. by author. 1993, Macmillan $14.95 (0-689-50548-5). 32pp. Grandma shows her grandchildren the house she lived in when she was a girl and tells them of her many memories of growing up there. (Rev: BL 6/1–15/93; SLJ 8/93)

3533 Blos, Joan W. *The Grandpa Days* (PS–1). Illus. by Emily Arnold McCully. 1994, Simon & Schuster paper $3.95 (0-671-88244-9). 32pp. The tender story of a little boy who spends a week with his grandfather. (Rev: BL 11/1/89; SLJ 11/89)

3534 Blume, Judy. *The Pain and the Great One* (PS–1). Illus. by Irene Trivas. 1984, Simon & Schuster $17.00 (0-02-711100-8). 32pp. A brother and sister explain why they don't get along.

3535 Bodecker, N. M. *Hurry, Hurry, Mary Dear* (K–3). Illus. by Erik Blegvad. 1998, Simon & Schuster $16.00 (0-689-81770-3). 32pp. In this charming verse, a demanding husband makes his loving wife work so hard that she finally rebels. (Rev: BL 10/15/98; HBG 3/99; SLJ 12/98)

3536 Bogart, Jo Ellen. *Gifts* (PS–2). Illus. by Barbara Reid. 1996, Scholastic $15.95 (0-590-55260-0). 44pp. A joyful picture book in which a grandmother presents her granddaughter with a variety of imaginative gifts. (Rev: BL 2/1/96; SLJ 3/96*)

3537 Bond, Rebecca. *Bravo, Maurice!* (PS–3). Illus. 2000, Little, Brown $14.95 (0-316-10545-7). 32pp. As young Maurice grows, he gets to know about the many members of his extended family and what they do. (Rev: BL 9/15/00; HBG 3/01; SLJ 12/00)

3538 Bond, Rebecca. *Just Like a Baby* (PS–2). Illus. 1999, Little, Brown $14.95 (0-316-10416-7). 32pp. Everyone in the family contributes to preparing a cradle for the new baby, and the baby responds by sleeping happily in it. (Rev: BCCB 9/99; BL 9/15/99; HBG 3/00; SLJ 9/99)

3539 Boon, Debbie. *My Gran* (PS–K). Illus. by author. 1998, Millbrook LB $19.90 (0-7613-0312-X). A little girl makes a poetic tribute to her French grandmother and to the pleasures of her garden. (Rev: HBG 10/98; SLJ 5/98)

3540 Bosak, Susan V. *Something to Remember Me By* (PS–3). Illus. by Laurie McGaw. 1997, Communication Project $15.95 (1-896232-01-9). 32pp. This touching story about the loving relationship between a girl and her grandmother that lasts until the girl is grown and the old lady dies. (Rev: BL 11/1/97; SLJ 12/97)

3541 Bottner, Barbara. *Nana Hannah's Piano* (PS–3). Illus. by Diana C. Bluthenthal. 1996, Putnam $15.95 (0-399-22656-7). 32pp. Through the guidance of his grandmother, a boy learns that there is more to life than baseball. (Rev: BL 11/15/96; SLJ 12/96)

3542 Bradby, Marie. *The Longest Wait* (PS–3). Illus. by Peter Catalanotto. 1998, Orchard $15.95 (0-531-06871-4). 32pp. Thomas and his mother endure a long wait for the return of Thomas's father, who goes out in a terrible blizzard to deliver the mail. (Rev: BL 12/1/98; HBG 3/99; SLJ 12/98)

3543 Bridges, Margaret Park. *Am I Big or Little?* (PS–2). Illus. by Tracy Dockray. 2000, North-South LB $14.88 (1-58717-020-5). 32pp. A loving relationship between mother and child is shown as they discuss the ways in which the girl is big and the ways in which she is little. (Rev: BL 10/1/00; HBG 3/01; SLJ 9/00)

3544 Bridges, Margaret Park. *If I Were Your Father* (PS–K). Illus. by Kady M. Denton. 1999, Morrow $16.00 (0-688-15192-2). 32pp. A little boy and his father talk about fantastic things they could do together, such as shaving with whipped cream. (Rev: BL 8/99; HBG 10/99; SLJ 5/99)

3545 Bridges, Margaret Park. *If I Were Your Mother* (PS–K). Illus. by Kady M. Denton. 1999, Morrow $16.00 (0-688-15190-6). 32pp. While talking with her mother, a little girl imagines that their roles are reversed. (Rev: BL 8/99; HBG 10/99; SLJ 5/99)

3546 Brillhart, Julie. *When Daddy Came to School* (PS). Illus. 1995, Albert Whitman LB $13.95 (0-8075-8878-4). 32pp. On his third birthday, a little boy is delighted when his father visits his nursery school. (Rev: BL 3/1/95; SLJ 5/95)

3547 Brown, Alan. *Nikki and the Rocking Horse* (PS–2). Illus. by Peter Utton. 1999, HarperCollins paper $9.95 (0-00-664517-8). Nikki's mother can't afford the rocking horse her daughter wants, so she makes one in a woodworking class. (Rev: SLJ 2/00)

3548 Brown, Marc. *D. W., Go to Your Room!* (PS–K). Illus. 1999, Little, Brown $13.95 (0-316-10905-3). 32pp. D.W. is sent to her room for grabbing a toy from her baby sister, but soon after, she is won over by her young sister's smile. (Rev: BL 6/1–15/99; HBG 10/99; SLJ 7/99)

3549 Brown, Ruth. *Cry Baby* (PS–2). Illus. 1997, Dutton $15.99 (0-525-45902-2). 32pp. A girl hates to take her younger sister for a walk because she cries over the slightest misadventure. (Rev: BL 7/97; HBG 3/98; SLJ 2/98)

3550 Buck, Nola. *How a Baby Grows* (PS). Illus. by Pamela Paparone. 1998, HarperFestival $5.95 (0-694-00873-7). This nicely illustrated book depicts the various activities in which babies can participate — seeing, speaking, hearing, and sharing. (Rev: HBG 10/98; SLJ 7/98)

3551 Buckley, Helen E. *Grandfather and I* (PS–1). Illus. by Jan Ormerod. 1994, Lothrop $16.00 (0-688-12533-6). 24pp. A young boy describes the fine times he has with his grandfather walking around the neighborhood. Also use *Grandmother and I* (1994). (Rev: BL 2/15/94; HB 7–8/94; SLJ 4/94*)

3552 Buehner, Caralyn. *Fanny's Dream* (1–4). Illus. by Mark Buehner. 1996, Dial $14.89 (0-8037-1497-1). 40pp. With a few important differences, Fanny relives the Cinderella story. (Rev: BCCB 9/96; BL 3/15/96*; HB 7–8/96, 9–10/96; SLJ 4/96*)

3553 Bunting, Eve. *A Day's Work* (K–3). Illus. by Ronald Himler. 1994, Clarion $15.00 (0-395-67321-6). 32pp. A young Mexican American boy must act as guardian and interpreter for his grandfather, newly arrived from Mexico and looking for work. (Rev: BCCB 10/94; BL 11/1/94; SLJ 1/95)

3554 Bunting, Eve. *Flower Garden* (PS–1). Illus. by Kathryn Hewitt. 1994, Harcourt $16.00 (0-15-228776-0). 32pp. A girl and her father create a window box of flowers as a birthday present for her mother. (Rev: BL 2/15/94*; HB 5–6/94; SLJ 4/94*)

3555 Bunting, Eve. *Jin Woo* (PS–3). Illus. by Chris K. Soentpiet. 2001, Clarion $16.00 (0-395-93872-4). 32pp. David is uncertain about his new little brother who is arriving from Korea, but the child, Jin Woo, soon wins his heart. (Rev: BL 3/15/01)

3556 Bunting, Eve. *The Memory String* (K–3). Illus. by Ted Rand. 2000, Clarion $15.00 (0-395-86146-2). 32pp. Laura begins to accept her stepmother, Jane, after Jane helps Laura search for lost buttons from her collection, each of which is associated with a member of her family. (Rev: BL 8/00; HBG 3/01; SLJ 8/00)

3557 Bunting, Eve. *A Picnic in October* (K–3). Illus. by Nancy Carpenter. 1999, Harcourt $16.00 (0-15-201656-2). 32pp. As usual, Grandma has her birthday party on Ellis Island, so she can relive her arrival in America many years before. (Rev: BL 10/15/99; HBG 3/00; SLJ 10/99)

3558 Bunting, Eve. *Sunshine Home* (K–3). Illus. by Diane De Groat. 1994, Clarion $16.00 (0-395-63309-5). 32pp. Timmie is unhappy when he visits his grandmother in her nursing home for the first time. (Rev: BCCB 4/94; BL 3/15/94; SLJ 4/94)

3559 Bunting, Eve. *The Wall* (K–2). Illus. by Ronald Himler. 1990, Houghton $15.00 (0-395-51588-2). 32pp. A picture book on the subject of the Vietnam Veterans War Memorial. (Rev: BCCB 7–8/92; BL 4/1/90*; HB 7–8/90; SLJ 5/90*)

3560 Bunting, Eve. *The Wednesday Surprise* (PS–2). Illus. by Donald Carrick. 1989, Houghton $16.00 (0-89919-721-3); paper $5.95 (0-395-54776-8). 32pp. Anna is proudest of Grandma's surprise — Grandma has learned to read, and Anna has taught her. (Rev: BCCB 3/89; BL 3/1/89; SLJ 6/89)

3561 Burrowes, Adjoa J. *Grandma's Purple Flowers* (PS–3). Illus. 2000, Lee & Low $15.95 (1-880000-73-3). 32pp. A young African American girl grieves after her beloved grandmother's death but gains acceptance when, in the spring, her grandmother's flowers bloom. (Rev: BL 11/1/00; HBG 3/01; SLJ 12/00)

3562 Butterworth, Nick. *My Dad Is Awesome* (PS–2). Illus. by author. 1992, Candlewick paper $4.99 (1-56402-033-9). This father is accomplished in everything, but he still takes a bath with a rubber duck. (Rev: SLJ 10/92)

3563 Caines, Jeannette. *Abby* (PS–1). Illus. by Steven Kellogg. 1973, HarperCollins paper $5.95 (0-06-443049-9). 32pp. Abby, a little African American girl, is adopted and enjoys hearing about the day she became part of her warm, loving family.

3564 Camp, Lindsay. *The Biggest Bed in the World* (PS–K). Illus. by Jonathan Langley. 2000, HarperCollins $14.95 (0-06-028687-3). 40pp. Although the family loves to sleep together, there are no beds big enough to accommodate them when the family grows and grows. (Rev: BL 5/1/00; HBG 3/01)

3565 Campbell, Louisa. *Phoebe's Fabulous Father* (K–2). Illus. by Bridget S. Taylor. 1996, Harcourt $14.00 (0-15-200996-5). Phoebe has always respected her cello-playing father; but when she finds out how much of his music he has sacrificed for his family, she grows to love him more. (Rev: BCCB 11/96; SLJ 12/96)

3566 Carle, Eric. *My Apron: A Story from My Childhood* (PS–1). Illus. 1994, Putnam $22.95 (0-399-22824-1). 32pp. Eric, a small boy, is given a tiny apron when he helps his Uncle Adam, who is a plasterer. (Rev: BL 12/1/94)

3567 Carlson, Nancy. *It's Going to Be Perfect!* (PS–3). Illus. 1998, Viking $15.99 (0-670-87802-2). 32pp. A mother confides in her daughter the differences between the way she imagined her daughter would progress through early childhood and what

actually happened. (Rev: BL 7/98; HBG 10/98; SLJ 8/98)

3568 Carpenter, Mary Chapin. *Halley Came to Jackson* (K–2). Illus. by Dan Andreasen. 1998, HarperCollins $15.95 (0-06-025400-9). 40pp. This picture book spans a lifetime, beginning with a baby being shown Halley's comet by her father in Jackson, Mississippi, and ending with her as an old woman on the same porch looking at the same sight 80 years later. (Rev: BL 10/15/98; HBG 3/99)

3569 Carrick, Carol. *Valentine* (PS–2). Illus. by Paddy Bouma. 1995, Clarion $15.00 (0-395-66554-X). 29pp. In spite of a loving grandmother, Heather misses her mother when she goes to work. (Rev: BL 4/1/95; SLJ 5/95)

3570 Carter, Alden R. *Big Brother Dustin* (PS–2). Illus. by Dan Young and Carol Carter. 1997, Albert Whitman LB $14.95 (0-8075-0715-6). 32pp. A young boy searches for the best name for the baby sister who is expected shortly. (Rev: BL 8/97; HB 5–6/97; SLJ 6/97)

3571 Carter, Donna Renee. *Music in the Family* (K–2). Illus. by Cortrell J. Harris. 1995, Lindsey $15.95 (1-885242-01-8). 30pp. Oliver is crushed when the family tells him that he doesn't play his saxophone well enough to join them in an international music competition. (Rev: SLJ 2/96)

3572 Carter, Dorothy. *Wilhe'mina Miles After the Stork Night* (PS–2). Illus. by Harvey Stevenson. 1999, Farrar $16.00 (0-374-33551-6). 32pp. While her father is up North working, Wilhe'mina is given the responsibility of fetching the midwife when her mother's time comes. (Rev: BL 2/15/99; HB 3–4/99; HBG 10/99; SLJ 6/99)

3573 Caseley, Judith. *Mama Coming and Going* (PS–1). Illus. 1994, Greenwillow $14.00 (0-688-11441-5). 32pp. A child realizes how busy her mother is after the arrival of a new baby. (Rev: BL 3/1/94; HB 5–6/94; SLJ 5/94)

3574 Catalanotto, Peter. *Dad and Me* (PS–2). Illus. 1999, DK $16.95 (0-7894-2584-X). Tommy and his dad usually play astronauts together, but one day when the father is in a bad mood, he rejects his son and later regrets his action. (Rev: BL 9/1/99; HBG 3/00; SLJ 1/00)

3575 Catalanotto, Peter. *The Painter* (PS–2). Illus. by author. Series: Richard Jackson Books. 1995, Orchard LB $16.99 (0-531-08765-4). A joyous picture book that celebrates a loving relationship between a girl and her artist-father. (Rev: SLJ 9/95*)

3576 Cazet, Denys. *Dancing* (PS–1). Illus. 1995, Orchard LB $16.99 (0-531-08766-2). 32pp. The crying of his baby brother drives Alex out of the house onto the porch, where he is comforted by his father. (Rev: BL 9/15/95; SLJ 9/95)

3577 Chaconas, Dori. *On a Wintry Morning* (PS–K). Illus. by Stephen Johnson. 2000, Viking $15.99 (0-670-89245-9). 32pp. A father and his little girl engage in winter activities like making angels and sledding, and finally buy a beagle puppy for a family pet. (Rev: BL 9/15/00; HBG 3/01; SLJ 11/00)

3578 Chall, Marsha Wilson. *Sugarbush Spring* (PS–1). Illus. by Jim Daly. 2000, Lothrop LB $15.93 (0-688-14908-1). A little girl in Minnesota tells about the annual collection of sap from the family sugar bush and how the sap is turned into syrup. (Rev: HBG 10/00; SLJ 3/00)

3579 Chocolate, Deborah M. *On the Day I Was Born* (PS–2). Illus. by Melodye Rosales. 1995, Scholastic $12.95 (0-590-47609-2). 32pp. An African American family greets a new baby in the home with welcoming rituals that go back to tribal Africa. (Rev: BL 12/15/95; SLJ 1/96)

3580 Chocolate, Deborah M. *The Piano Man* (K–3). Illus. by Eric Velasquez. 1998, Walker $15.95 (0-8027-8646-4). 32pp. An African American girl recalls the importance of the piano in the life of her grandfather, who played in silent-movie theaters, medicine shows, and vaudeville. (Rev: BL 2/15/98; HB 3–4/98; HBG 10/98; SLJ 2/98)

3581 Choi, Sook N. *Halmoni and the Picnic* (K–3). Illus. by Karen M. Dugan. 1993, Houghton $14.95 (0-395-61626-3). 24pp. A grandmother newly arrived from Korea has difficulty adjusting to New York City. (Rev: BL 8/93)

3582 Cohen, Barbara. *Molly's Pilgrim*. Rev. ed. (1–4). Illus. by Daniel Duffy. 1998, Lothrop $15.00 (0-688-16279-7); paper $3.99 (0-688-16280-0). 32pp. The mother of a Russian immigrant girl makes her child a pilgrim doll modeled on herself, a modern-day pilgrim. (Rev: BL 11/15/98; HBG 3/99)

3583 Cole, Joanna. *I'm a Big Brother* (PS–1). Illus. by Maxie Chambliss. 1997, Morrow $5.95 (0-688-14507-8). 32pp. Babies and their activities and needs are introduced in terms a big brother can understand. A companion volume that covers the same material is *I'm a Big Sister* (1997). (Rev: BL 3/1/97; SLJ 4/97)

3584 Collins, Pat L. *Waiting for Baby Joe* (PS–2). Illus. by Joan W. Dunn. 1990, Whitman LB $13.95 (0-8075-8625-0). 28pp. When his baby brother is born prematurely, Joey is disappointed that the baby requires everyone's constant attention. (Rev: BCCB 11/90; BL 11/1/90; HB 11–12/90; SLJ 12/90)

3585 Cook, Jean Thor. *Room for a Stepdaddy* (PS–K). Illus. by Martine Gourbault. 1995, Albert Whitman LB $14.95 (0-8075-7106-7). At first, Bill rejects his new stepfather in favor of his real father; but in time, he realizes that he has enough love for both of them. (Rev: SLJ 1/96)

3586 Cooke, Trish. *The Grandad Tree* (1–3). Illus. by Sharon Wilson. 2000, Candlewick $15.99 (0-7636-0815-7). 32pp. The seasons in nature are compared to human life in this touching story about the last year of a beloved grandfather's life. (Rev: BL 6/1–15/00*; HBG 10/00; SLJ 6/00)

3587 Cooney, Barbara. *Island Boy* (2–4). Illus. by author. 1988, Puffin paper $5.99 (0-14-050756-6). 40pp. The life of Matthias Tibbetts of Tibbetts Island, Maine, who sails the world and returns home to raise his own family. (Rev: BCCB 10/88; BL 10/1/88; SLJ 10/88)

3588 Cooper, Melrose. *Gettin' Through Thursday* (1–3). Illus. by Nneka Bennett. 1998, Lee & Low $15.95 (1-880000-67-9). In this sweet story of a single-parent African American family, Mama is proud that her third-grade son makes the honor roll, but the family is too poor to have a celebration. (Rev: HBG 10/99; SLJ 1/99)

3589 Corey, Dorothy. *Will There Be a Lap for Me?* (PS–1). Illus. by Nancy Poydar. 1992, Whitman LB $13.95 (0-8075-9109-2). 24pp. When her mother's lap becomes smaller because she is expecting a baby, Lyle misses her favorite place to sit and be loved. (Rev: BL 3/1/92; SLJ 6/92)

3590 Coville, Bruce. *The Lapsnatcher* (PS–2). Illus. by Marissa Moss. 1997, Troll $15.95 (0-8167-4233-2). 32pp. The thing that a boy dislikes most about the family's new baby is that it takes up all the room on his mother's lap. (Rev: BL 6/1–15/97; SLJ 7/97)

3591 Cowell, Cressida. *Don't Do That, Kitty Kilroy!* (PS–K). Illus. by author. 2000, Orchard $15.95 (0-531-30209-1). Kitty's mother agrees to let her rambunctious daughter do her own thing for a day, with predictable results. (Rev: HBG 10/00; SLJ 3/00)

3592 Cowen-Fletcher, Jane. *Mama Zooms* (PS–1). Illus. 1994, Scholastic $19.95 (0-590-72848-2); paper $4.99 (0-590-45775-6). 32pp. Mama's "zooming machine" turns out to be her wheelchair. (Rev: BL 4/15/93; SLJ 5/93)

3593 Coy, John. *Night Driving* (PS–3). Illus. by Peter McCarty. 1996, Holt $14.95 (0-8050-2931-1). 28pp. A young boy takes his first long nighttime car ride with his father. (Rev: BCCB 12/96; BL 9/1/96; HB 9–10/96; SLJ 10/96)

3594 Crews, Donald. *Bigmama's* (PS–2). Illus. 1991, Greenwillow $15.89 (0-688-09951-3). 32pp. A family's annual summer trip to grandparents' house in the country is a celebration of childhood memories. (Rev: BCCB 11/91*; BL 11/15/91*; HB 9–10/91; SLJ 10/91) [921]

3595 Cummings, Pat. *Angel Baby* (PS–2). Illus. 2000, Lothrop LB $15.89 (0-688-14822-0). 24pp. Amanda Lynn, who has to take care of her baby brother, knows he isn't the angel baby everyone thinks he is. (Rev: BCCB 7–8/00; BL 6/1–15/00; HBG 10/00; SLJ 6/00)

3596 Curtis, Jamie Lee. *Tell Me Again About the Night I Was Born* (PS–1). Illus. by Laura Cornell. 1996, HarperCollins LB $15.89 (0-06-024529-8). 40pp. A young girl gleefully fills in all the details about what happened on the night she was born. (Rev: BCCB 1/97; BL 10/15/96; SLJ 10/96*)

3597 Cutler, Jane. *Darcy and Gran Don't Like Babies* (PS–1). Illus. by Susannah Ryan. 1993, Scholastic $14.95 (0-590-44587-1). 32pp. Darcy dislikes babies, particularly her new baby sister, and finds comfort with her grandmother. (Rev: BCCB 10/93; BL 12/1/93; HB 11–12/93; SLJ 11/93*)

3598 Dale, Penny. *Big Brother, Little Brother* (PS). Illus. 1997, Candlewick $15.99 (0-7636-0146-2). 32pp. A series of episodes show the strong bond between two young brothers. (Rev: BL 9/15/97; HBG 3/98; SLJ 11/97)

3599 Daly, Niki. *Papa Lucky's Shadow* (PS–3). Illus. 1992, Macmillan $16.00 (0-689-50541-8). 32pp. Sugar is thrilled when her grandfather, a real Mr. Bojangles, decides to put on his tap shoes once more. (Rev: BL 9/15/92*; SLJ 10/92)

3600 D'Antonio, Nancy. *Our Baby from China: An Adoption Story* (PS–2). Illus. 1997, Albert Whitman LB $13.95 (0-8075-6162-2). 24pp. The story of a couple's journey to China, where they adopt a little girl, and their trip home with the baby. (Rev: BL 3/1/97; SLJ 6/97)

3601 Darling, Benjamin. *Valerie and the Silver Pear* (K–3). Illus. by Daniel Lane. 1992, Macmillan paper $14.95 (0-02-726100-X). 32pp. Valerie and her grandfather search for the silver pear and find something more enduring in their relationship. (Rev: BL 9/1/92*; SLJ 9/92)

3602 Davol, Marguerite W. *Black, White, Just Right!* (PS–1). Illus. by Irene Trivas. 1993, Albert Whitman LB $14.95 (0-8075-0785-7). 32pp. A child with mixed-race parentage enjoys the many differences she sees in her parents, not only their color. (Rev: BL 11/1/93)

3603 Deedy, Carmen A. *Agatha's Feather Bed: Not Just Another Wild Goose Story* (PS–2). Illus. by Laura L. Seeley. 1991, Peachtree $14.95 (1-56145-008-1). 32pp. Agatha is ashamed when she learns that six geese are featherless so she could have a featherbed. (Rev: BL 6/1/91; SLJ 9/91)

3604 DeGross, Monalisa. *Granddaddy's Street Songs* (K–4). Illus. by Floyd Cooper. 1999, Hyperion LB $15.49 (0-7868-2132-9). 32pp. In this African American family story, a grandfather tells his young grandson about the days when he was an "arabber" — a street vendor selling produce in Baltimore. (Rev: BL 6/1–15/99; HBG 10/99; SLJ 7/99)

3605 Demas, Corinne. *Nina's Waltz* (K–3). Illus. by Deborah Lanino. 2000, Orchard LB $17.99 (0-531-33281-0). When wasp stings prevent Nina's father from playing the fiddle in a competition, she steps in to take his place. (Rev: HBG 3/01; SLJ 11/00)

3606 dePaola, Tomie. *The Baby Sister* (PS–1). Illus. 1996, Putnam $16.99 (0-399-22908-6). 32pp. When Tommy's mother has a baby, his grandmother comes to stay. (Rev: BL 3/15/96; HB 5–6/96; SLJ 5/96)

3607 dePaola, Tomie. *Tom* (K–2). Illus. 1993, Putnam LB $15.95 (0-399-22417-3). 32pp. A picture book about the special relationship between the author/artist and his grandfather. (Rev: BCCB 5/93; BL 1/15/93*; HB 7–8/93*; SLJ 4/93)

3608 dePaola, Tomie. *Watch Out for the Chicken Feet in Your Soup* (K–2). Illus. by author. 1974, Simon & Schuster $12.95 (0-685-35587-X); paper $5.95 (0-685-35588-8). 32pp. Joey is a little embarrassed to take his friend Eugene to his old-fashioned Italian grandmother's for a visit, but in spite of her strange foreign ways, both boys pronounce the visit a great success.

3609 Dodd, Anne W. *The Story of the Sea Glass* (K–2). Illus. by Mary Beth Owens. 1999, Down East $15.95 (0-89272-416-1). 32pp. A young girl and her grandmother revisit the seaside house where

Nana used to live, and this visit inspires memories of past events. (Rev: BL 2/1/00; HBG 3/00; SLJ 3/00)

3610 Dunbar, James. *When I Was Young: One Family Remembers 300 Years of History* (PS–2). Illus. by Martin Remphry. 1999, Carolrhoda LB $15.95 (1-57505-359-4). Josh hears about his family and traces its history back to the 1600s with glimpses of 7-year-old children through the ages. (Rev: HBG 3/00; SLJ 9/99)

3611 Duncan, Alice Faye. *Willie Jerome* (PS–3). Illus. by Tyrone Geter. 1995, Simon & Schuster paper $15.00 (0-02-733208-X). 32pp. No one appreciates Willie's horn playing except his younger sister in this story that captures an inner-city environment. (Rev: BL 6/1–15/95; SLJ 6/95)

3612 Dupasquier, Philippe. *A Sunday with Grandpa* (PS–2). Illus. by author. 1999, Andersen $19.95 (0-86264-791-6). A sunny picture book from England about a young girl who visits her loving grandfather in the countryside. (Rev: SLJ 7/99)

3613 Dwyer, Mindy. *Quilt of Dreams* (1–3). Illus. 2000, Graphic Arts Center $15.95 (0-88240-522-5); paper $8.95 (0-88240-521-7). 32pp. Katy wants to finish the quilt that her grandmother began before her death. (Rev: BL 3/15/01; SLJ 1/01)

3614 Eisenberg, Phyllis R. *You're My Nikki* (PS–1). Illus. by Jill Kastner. 1995, Puffin paper $5.99 (0-140-55463-7). 32pp. Nikki is afraid that her single-parent mother will forget her when she starts her new job. (Rev: BCCB 5/92; BL 5/1/92; SLJ 5/92)

3615 Engel, Diana. *Fishing* (K–2). Illus. 1993, Smithmark $4.98 (0-765-10068-1). 32pp. When her family moves north, more than anything else Loretta misses fishing with her grandfather. (Rev: BL 6/1–15/93; SLJ 6/93)

3616 English, Karen. *Speak English for Us, Marisol!* (PS–3). Illus. by Enrique O. Sanchez. 2000, Albert Whitman $14.95 (0-8075-7554-2). 32pp. Marisol, a young Latin American girl, often acts as a translator to help various members of her family. (Rev: BL 9/15/00; HBG 3/01; SLJ 9/00)

3617 Ericsson, Jennifer A. *The Most Beautiful Kid in the World* (PS–1). Illus. by Susan Meddaugh. 1996, Morrow LB $15.93 (0-688-13942-6). 32pp. Mom's ideas about what Annie should wear to Grandma's birthday party are different from those of her daughter. (Rev: BCCB 10/96; BL 9/15/96; SLJ 10/96)

3618 Evans, Lezlie. *If I Were the Wind* (PS–1). Illus. by Victoria Lisi. 1997, Ideals $14.95 (1-57102-096-9). 32pp. A mother says that even if she is changed by enchantment into other objects she will still protect and love her young daughter. (Rev: BL 8/97; SLJ 6/97)

3619 Falwell, Cathryn. *We Have a Baby* (PS). Illus. 1993, Clarion $15.00 (0-395-62038-4). 32pp. A picture book that shows how a toddler accepts and enjoys having a new baby in the house. (Rev: BCCB 6/96; BL 11/15/93; SLJ 10/93)

3620 Farber, Norma. *Without Wings, Mother, How Can I Fly?* (PS–1). Illus. by Keiko Narahashi. 1998, Holt $15.95 (0-8050-3380-7). 32pp. A mother reassures her child that in this modern world a child can do anything that an animal can. (Rev: BL 3/15/98; HBG 10/98; SLJ 5/98)

3621 Farmer, Patti. *What's He Doing Now?* (PS–2). Illus. by Janet Wilson. 1998, Firefly $15.95 (1-55209-220-8); paper $5.95 (1-55209-218-6). 29pp. Lewis spends several anxious months waiting for his new sibling to be born, and when it finally happens, he welcomes a new sister into the family. (Rev: SLJ 7/98)

3622 Fazio, Brenda Lena. *Grandfather's Story* (PS–3). Illus. 1996, Sasquatch $15.95 (1-57061-028-2). 32pp. In a Japanese setting, this story tells how a grandfather teaches his young grandson about life. (Rev: BL 11/15/96; SLJ 3/97)

3623 Fearnley, Jan. *A Special Something* (PS–K). Illus. 2000, Hyperion $15.99 (0-7868-0589-7). 32pp. A little girl wonders what is inside her mother's big tummy and is surprised when a baby joins the family. (Rev: BCCB 9/00; BL 7/00; HBG 10/00; SLJ 8/00)

3624 Fellows, Rebecca Nevers. *A Lei for Tutu* (1–3). Illus. by Linda Finch. 1998, Albert Whitman $14.95 (0-8075-4426-4). 32pp. Though hospitalized and weak, Tutu and her granddaughter, Nahoa, work hard to produce a special lei for Honolulu's Lei Day Festival. (Rev: BL 9/1/98; HBG 10/99; SLJ 10/98)

3625 Fisher, Iris L. *Katie-Bo: An Adoption Story* (PS–3). Illus. by Miriam Schaer. 1988, Adama $12.95 (0-915361-91-4). The story of Katie-Bo, who is coming from Korea to join her new family, told through the eyes of a young boy. (Rev: BL 5/15/88; SLJ 8/88)

3626 Fleischman, Paul. *Lost! A Story in String* (1–4). Illus. by C. B. Mordan. 2000, Holt $15.95 (0-8050-5583-5). 30pp. When the electricity goes off during a storm, Grandmother entertains her little granddaughter with an adventure story. (Rev: BCCB 10/00; BL 7/00; HBG 10/00; SLJ 6/00)

3627 Fletcher, Ralph. *Grandpa Never Lies* (PS–2). Illus. by Harvey Stevenson. 2000, Clarion $15.00 (0-395-79770-5). 32pp. A little girl has a special relationship with her grandparents and when her grandmother dies, the little girl and Grandpa mourn together. (Rev: BL 12/15/00; HBG 3/01; SLJ 11/00)

3628 Fowler, Susi G. *Beautiful* (PS–2). Illus. by Jim Fowler. 1998, Greenwillow $15.00 (0-688-15111-6). 32pp. Uncle George, who is dying from an incurable illness, teaches his young nephew the joys of gardening and how to nurture the lives of plants. (Rev: BL 4/1/98; HBG 10/98; SLJ 6/98)

3629 Fox, Mem. *Sophie* (K–3). Illus. by Aminah Robinson. 1994, Harcourt $13.95 (0-15-277160-3). 32pp. The story of the love shared by a girl and her grandfather from her birth to his death. (Rev: BCCB 11/94; BL 10/1/94; SLJ 11/94)

3630 Fox, Mem. *Whoever You Are* (K–3). Illus. by Leslie Staub. 1997, Harcourt $16.00 (0-15-200787-3). 32pp. A reassuring book for children that tells them that regardless of their situations, there are toher like them all over the world. (Rev: BL 10/1/97; HBG 3/98; SLJ 10/97)

3631 French, Vivian. *Oliver's Fruit Salad* (PS–2). Illus. by Alison Bartlett. 1998, Orchard $14.95 (0-531-30087-0). 32pp. Oliver remembers how he helped his grandfather pick fruit in his garden, and this helps him enjoy the fruit salad he prepares with his mother and grandparents. (Rev: BCCB 10/98; BL 10/15/98; HBG 3/99; SLJ 9/98)

3632 French, Vivian. *Tiger and the New Baby* (PS). Illus. by Rebecca Elgar. 1999, Kingfisher $8.95 (0-7534-5198-0). 24pp. Tiger doesn't want to accept his new baby brother until Grandpa intervenes. (Rev: BL 5/1/99; HBG 10/99; SLJ 7/99)

3633 French, Vivian. *Tiger and the Temper Tantrum* (PS). Illus. by Rebecca Elgar. 1999, Kingfisher $8.95 (0-7534-5197-2). 24pp. Tiger has a temper tantrum and his mother has a difficult time quieting him. (Rev: BL 5/1/99; HBG 10/99; SLJ 7/99)

3634 French, Vivian, and Alex Ayliffe. *Not Again, Anna!* (PS). Illus. 1998, Sterling $14.95 (1-899607-96-X). 24pp. In this book with foldout pages, Little Anna learns to care for her stuffed bunny in the same way her mother cares for her. (Rev: BL 1/1–15/99; SLJ 3/99)

3635 Friedman, Ina R. *How My Parents Learned to Eat* (2–4). Illus. by Allen Say. 1987, Houghton $15.00 (0-395-35379-3); paper $5.95 (0-395-44235-4). 32pp. John, an American, and Aiko, a Japanese girl, learn each other's eating habits.

3636 Friend, David. *Baseball, Football, Daddy and Me* (K–3). Illus. 1992, Puffin paper $4.50 (0-140-50914-3). 32pp. This slice-of-life account centers around a father and son and sports events. (Rev: BL 2/15/90; SLJ 5/90)

3637 Fruisen, Catherine Myler. *My Mother's Pearls* (PS–3). Illus. 2000, Cedco $12.95 (0-7683-2177-8). 32pp. A little girl tells about the six generations of women in her family who have worn the family heirloom string of pearls. (Rev: BL 8/00; HBG 3/01)

3638 Gackenbach, Dick. *With Love from Gran* (PS–2). Illus. 1990, Houghton paper $6.95 (0-395-54775-X). 32pp. A grandmother takes a trip around the world and sends her grandson gifts. (Rev: BL 10/1/89; SLJ 11/89)

3639 Galbraith, Kathryn O. *Laura Charlotte* (K–2). Illus. by Floyd Cooper. 1990, Putnam $15.95 (0-399-21613-8). Mama tells Laura the story of Charlotte, the stuffed elephant that is part of both their lives. (Rev: SLJ 4/90)

3640 Galindo, Mary Sue. *Icy Watermelon / Sandia fria* (PS–3). Illus. by Pauline Rodriguez Howard. 2000, Arte Publico $14.95 (1-55885-306-5). 32pp. In this bilingual English and Spanish book, three Latino children share stories and jokes with their parents and grandparents on a porch where they are eating watermelon. (Rev: BL 12/15/00; SLJ 1/01)

3641 Garland, Sherry. *My Father's Boat* (K–4). Illus. by Ted Rand. 1998, Scholastic $15.95 (0-590-47867-2). A family story in which a Vietnamese American fisherman and his son head out to sea on their shrimp boat, and the man, remembering his childhood, hopes one day to take his son to meet his grandfather in Vietnam. (Rev: BCCB 9/98; HBG 10/98; SLJ 7/98)

3642 Garrett, Ann. *Keeper of the Swamp* (2–4). Illus. by Karen Chandler. 1999, Turtle $16.95 (1-890515-12-4). A poignant story about a young boy who makes a special trip with his dying grandfather to a swamp to feed an alligator that the grandfather had saved from poachers. (Rev: HBG 3/00; SLJ 7/99)

3643 Gauch, Patricia L. *Christina Katerina and the Great Bear Train* (K–2). Illus. by Elise Primavera. 1990, Putnam $14.95 (0-399-21623-5). Christina decides to travel to the hospital by herself to visit her new sibling. (Rev: SLJ 11/90)

3644 Gelsanliter, Wendy, and Frank Christian. *Dancin' in the Kitchen* (PS–3). Illus. by Marjorie Priceman. 1998, Putnam $15.99 (0-399-23035-1). 32pp. While preparing dinner, a family that includes grandparents, parents, and four children dance to music from the radio in this glowing picture book. (Rev: BCCB 11/98; BL 10/15/98*; HBG 3/99; SLJ 10/98)

3645 Gentieu, Penny. *Baby! Talk!* (PS). Illus. 1999, Crown $13.00 (0-517-80028-4). 24pp. A charming book that shows babies in different poses and activities. (Rev: BL 4/15/99; HBG 10/99; SLJ 6/99)

3646 Gentieu, Penny. *Wow! Babies!* (PS). Photos by author. 1997, Crown $12.00 (0-517-70963-5). Using plenty of photos, this book shows different kinds of babies and their activities. (Rev: SLJ 10/97)

3647 Gewing, Lisa. *Mama, Daddy, Baby and Me* (PS). Illus. by Donna Larimer. 1989, Spirit $14.95 (0-944296-04-1). 32pp. In simple rhymes, a youngster responds to a new baby in the house. (Rev: BL 12/1/89; SLJ 12/89)

3648 Gilchrist, Jan Spivey. *Indigo and Moonlight Gold* (K–3). Illus. 1993, Black Butterfly $13.95 (0-86316-210-X). 32pp. A tender moment between a mother and child is described in moving prose and beautiful oil paintings. (Rev: BCCB 2/94; BL 3/1/94; SLJ 5/94)

3649 Gillard, Denise. *Music from the Sky* (PS–1). Illus. by Stephen Taylor. 2001, Douglas & McIntyre $15.95 (0-88899-311-0). 32pp. A music-loving young African American girl spends time with her grandpa, who makes her a flute so she can make her own music. (Rev: BL 2/15/01)

3650 Girard, Linda Walvoord. *Adoption Is for Always* (K–3). Illus. by Judith Friedman. 1991, Whitman LB $13.95 (0-8075-0185-9); paper $5.95 (0-8075-0187-5). 32pp. Celia is old enough to understand what adoption really means, and she isn't sure that she likes it. (Rev: BL 2/15/87; SLJ 4/87)

3651 Gliori, Debi. *New Big House* (PS–1). Illus. 1992, Candlewick $13.95 (1-56402-036-3). 32pp. As the clutter mounts, a family finds that their house is just too small for them. (Rev: BCCB 4/92; BL 5/15/92; SLJ 8/93)

3652 Godfrey, Jan. *Sam's New Baby* (PS–1). Illus. by Jane Coulson. 1998, Abingdon $12.95 (0-687-09570-0). 24pp. Sam discovers that everyone's fin-gerprints are different. After his baby sister is born, he examines her fingers through a magnifying glass and realizes that she, too, is a unique being. (Rev: BL 9/15/98)

3653 Good, Merle. *Reuben and the Blizzard* (K–3). Illus. by P. Buckley Moss. 1995, Good Bks. $14.95 (1-56148-184-X). 32pp. Young Reuben and his Amish family weather a blizzard and help a neighbor get to the hospital. (Rev: BL 1/1–15/96; SLJ 4/96)

3654 Good, Merle. *Reuben and the Quilt* (PS–3). Illus. by P. Buckley Moss. 1999, Good Bks. $16.00 (1-56148-234-X). 32pp. To help with a neighbor's medical bills, an Amish family sews a quilt, but when it is stolen before the auction, they create an unusual plan for its recovery. (Rev: BL 6/1–15/99; SLJ 6/99)

3655 Gove, Doris. *My Mother Talks to Trees* (K–3). Illus. by Marilynn H. Mallory. 1999, Peachtree $14.95 (1-56145-166-5). 32pp. At first, a little girl finds walking with her mother an embarrassing experience because her mother talks to the trees, but eventually the girl changes her mind and begins talking to a sapling in her yard. (Rev: BL 5/1/99; HBG 10/99; SLJ 7/99)

3656 Graham, Bob. *Spirit of Hope* (PS–3). Illus. 1996, Mondo $14.95 (1-57255-202-6). 30pp. The Fairweathers face a crisis when they are told to vacate their home. (Rev: BL 12/1/96; SLJ 3/97)

3657 Grambling, Lois G. *Daddy Will Be There* (PS–K). Illus. by Walter Gaffney-Kessell. 1998, Greenwillow $15.00 (0-688-14983-9). 24pp. Even though a little girl engages in many different activities, like playing with her friends, she is happy with the assurance that sooner or later she will be reunited with her father. (Rev: BL 5/15/98; HBG 10/98; SLJ 6/98)

3658 Gray, Libba M. *Dear Willie Rudd* (K–3). Illus. by Peter M. Fiore. 1993, Simon & Schuster paper $14.00 (0-671-79774-3). 28pp. Miss Elizabeth wishes she could make amends to the African American housekeeper who took care of her 50 years before. (Rev: BCCB 11/93; BL 9/1/93; SLJ 12/93)

3659 Gray, Libba M. *My Mama Had a Dancing Heart* (PS–3). Illus. by Raul Colon. 1995, Orchard LB $16.99 (0-531-08770-0). 32pp. Evocative pictures are used to illustrate a series of imaginative experiences shared by a mother and daughter in each of the seasons. (Rev: BL 9/15/95*; SLJ 9/95*)

3660 Greenfield, Eloise. *First Pink Light* (PS–1). Illus. by Jan S. Gilchrist. 1991, Writers & Readers $13.95 (0-86316-207-X). A young African American boy waits in a rocking chair to greet his father, who has been away for a year. (Rev: BL 12/15/91; SLJ 1/92)

3661 Greenfield, Eloise. *Grandmama's Joy* (2–5). Illus. by Carole Byard. 1980, Putnam $16.99 (0-399-21064-4). 32pp. The story of Rhondy and the grandmother who has raised her.

3662 Greenfield, Eloise. *Grandpa's Face* (K–3). Illus. by Floyd Cooper. 1988, Philomel $16.99 (0-399-21525-5); Putnam paper $6.99 (0-698-11381-

0). 32pp. Tamika worries about her grandfather's reactions. (Rev: BL 11/15/88; HB 3–4/89; SLJ 11/88)

3663 Greenfield, Eloise. *She Come Bringing Me That Little Baby Girl* (K–2). Illus. by John Steptoe. 1990, HarperCollins paper $6.95 (0-06-443296-3). 32pp. Kevin resents all the attention the new baby is getting; most of all he resents the fact that she is a girl.

3664 Greenfield, Eloise. *William and the Good Old Days* (K–3). Illus. by Jan S. Gilchrist. 1993, Harper-Collins LB $15.89 (0-06-021094-X). 32pp. Young William is upset that his Grandma is now ill and someone else owns her diner, where everyone felt at home. (Rev: BL 9/15/93)

3665 Griffith, Helen V. *Georgia Music* (1–3). Illus. by James Stevenson. 1986, Greenwillow $16.00 (0-688-06071-4); Morrow paper $6.95 (0-688-09931-9). 24pp. A quiet summer spent by a little girl at her grandfather's cabin in Georgia. A sequel is: *Grandaddy's Place* (1987). (Rev: BCCB 12/86; BL 10/1/86; SLJ 10/86)

3666 Grindley, Sally. *A Flag for Grandma* (PS–1). Illus. by Jason Cockcroft. 1998, DK $15.95 (0-7894-3490-3). 28pp. A little boy spends a fine day at the beach with Grandma, and later, at home, the two watch the stars before falling asleep. (Rev: BL 10/1/98; HBG 3/99; SLJ 2/99)

3667 Guettier, Benedicte. *The Father Who Had 10 Children* (PS). Illus. by author. 1999, Dial $15.99 (0-8037-2446-2). A father with ten children builds a boat that will take him away on a much-needed vacation, but after he leaves he realizes that something is missing. (Rev: HB 5–6/99; HBG 10/99; SLJ 6/99)

3668 Guthrie, Donna. *Grandpa Doesn't Know It's Me: A Family Adjusts to Alzheimer's Disease* (K–3). Illus. by Katy K. Arnsteen. 1986, Human Sciences paper $10.95 (0-89885-308-7). The story of Lizzie, who adores her grandfather, and the tragedy of her grandfather's Alzheimer's disease. (Rev: BCCB 7–8/86; BL 8/86)

3669 Hanrahan, Brendan. *My Sisters Love My Clothes* (PS–2). Illus. by Lise Stork. 1992, Perry Heights Pr. $12.95 (0-9630181-0-8). 32pp. Young Louie has a smart wardrobe, but his sisters keep borrowing his clothes. (Rev: BCCB 4/92; BL 9/1/92)

3670 Harris, Robie H. *Happy Birth Day!* (PS–2). Illus. by Michael Emberley. 1996, Candlewick $16.99 (1-56402-424-5). 32pp. A baby's first day after birth is caught in text, narrated by the young parents, and paintings. (Rev: BL 5/1/96*; SLJ 12/96*)

3671 Harris, Robie H. *Hi New Baby!* (PS–3). Illus. by Michael Emberley. 2000, Candlewick $16.99 (0-7636-0539-5). 32pp. Narrated by the father, this is the tender story of a young girl's first meeting with her new baby brother. (Rev: BL 10/1/00; HBG 3/01; SLJ 11/00)

3672 Haskins, Francine. *I Remember "121"* (PS–3). Illus. 1991, Children's Book Pr. $14.95 (0-89239-100-6). 32pp. This is an autobiographical sketch of the artist growing up in an African American neighborhood in Washington, D.C. (Rev: BL 12/15/91; SLJ 3/92) [973]

3673 Hassett, John, and Ann Hassett. *We Got My Brother at the Zoo* (PS). Illus. by authors. 1993, Houghton $14.95 (0-395-62429-0). 32pp. Mary Margaret resents having a new brother and remembers the good old days before he came. (Rev: SLJ 12/93)

3674 Haughton, Emma. *Rainy Day* (PS–2). Illus. by Angelo Rinaldi. 2000, Lerner $15.95 (1-57505-452-3). 32pp. Because of rain, a father and his son engage in activities that involve using the boy's new rubber boots rather than going to the fair. (Rev: BL 5/1/00; HBG 8/00; SLJ 8/00)

3675 Hausherr, Rosmarie. *Celebrating Families* (PS–2). Illus. 1997, Scholastic $16.95 (0-590-48937-2). 32pp. Different kinds of families are pictured in this photo-essay. (Rev: BL 3/1/97; SLJ 3/97)

3676 Havill, Juanita. *Treasure Map* (PS–2). Illus. by Elivia Savadier. 1992, Houghton $15.00 (0-395-57817-5). 32pp. Alicia hears the story of how her great-grandmother left Mexico and came to the United States. (Rev: BL 3/1/92; SLJ 6/92)

3677 Hawxhurst, Joan C. *Bubbe and Gram: My Two Grandmothers* (PS–3). Illus. by Jane K. Bynum. 1996, Dovetail $12.95 (0-9651284-2-3). 32pp. From his two grandmothers — one Jewish, the other Christian — a young girl learns about and accepts two ways of worship. (Rev: BL 1/1–15/97)

3678 Haynes, Max. *Grandma's Gone to Live in the Stars* (PS–2). Illus. 2000, Albert Whitman $15.95 (0-8075-3026-3). 32pp. In this simple luminous book about death, Grandma, who is dying, hovers over the things and people she loves, including her sleeping family, to say goodbye. (Rev: BL 12/1/00*; HBG 3/01; SLJ 12/00)

3679 Haynes, Max. *Ticklemonster and Me* (PS–2). 1999, Doubleday $12.95 (0-385-32582-7). 32pp. Two stories are told at the same time: in the first, a mother is reading to her son; the second is the story she is reading about a young bear who is attacked by the ticklemonster. (Rev: HBG 10/99; SLJ 4/99)

3680 Hazen, Barbara S. *Even If I Did Something Awful?* (K–2). Illus. by Nancy Kincade. 1992, Macmillan LB $13.95 (0-689-30843-4); paper $4.99 (0-689-71600-1). 32pp. Mother still loves you, even when you are bad.

3681 Hazen, Barbara S. *If It Weren't for Benjamin (I'd Always Get to Lick the Icing Spoon)* (PS–2). Illus. by Laura Hartman. 1979, Human Sciences paper $10.95 (0-89885-172-6). 32pp. A younger sibling recounts the reasons for his sense of injustice.

3682 Hearne, Betsy. *Seven Brave Women* (K–3). Illus. by Bethanne Andersen. 1997, Greenwillow $14.89 (0-688-14503-5). 24pp. The narrator introduces seven creative, courageous women in her family who made their quiet but important marks on history, from the Revolutionary War to the present. (Rev: BL 6/1–15/97; HB 9–10/97; HBG 3/98; SLJ 9/97)

3683 Heide, Florence Parry, and Roxanne H. Pierce. *Tio Armando* (1–3). Illus. by Ann Grifalconi. 1998, Lothrop LB $14.93 (0-688-12108-X). The last year in the life of a child's great-uncle is affectionately described in text, in watercolor, and in pencil illustrations. (Rev: HBG 10/98; SLJ 5/98)

3684 Helldorfer, M. C. *Silver Rain Brown* (PS–3). Illus. by Teresa Flavin. 1999, Houghton $15.00 (0-395-73093-7). 32pp. After a scorching dry spell, a young boy and his pregnant mother are overjoyed when rain and the new baby arrive at the same time. (Rev: BL 2/15/99; HBG 10/99; SLJ 5/99)

3685 Henderickson, Karen. *Baby and I Can Play and Fun with Toddlers* (PS–K). Illus. by Marina Megale. 1990, Parenting Pr. LB $17.95 (0-943990-57-2); paper $7.95 (0-943990-56-4). 56pp. This book tells preschoolers how to play safely with young babies. (Rev: BL 9/1/90) [649.64]

3686 Henderson, Kathy. *The Baby Dances* (PS). Illus. by Tony Kerins. 1999, Candlewick $15.99 (0-7636-0374-0). 32pp. The first actions and movements of a baby — from birth to walking and dancing — are conveyed in gentle artwork and sensitive prose. (Rev: BL 7/99*; HBG 10/99; SLJ 7/99)

3687 Henderson, Kathy. *Newborn* (PS–1). Illus. by Caroline Binch. 1999, Dial $15.99 (0-8037-2434-9). 32pp. This book illustrates a baby's awakening to sensations such as a blanket's feel, a daddy's rocking, and a mommy's tender touch. (Rev: BL 5/1/99; HBG 10/99; SLJ 6/99)

3688 Henkes, Kevin. *Shhhh* (PS–1). Illus. 1989, Greenwillow $15.89 (0-688-07986-5). 24pp. A little girl wakes up the whole household with her horn. (Rev: BL 8/89; SLJ 1/90)

3689 Heo, Yumi. *Father's Rubber Shoes* (PS–3). Illus. 1995, Orchard LB $16.99 (0-531-08723-9). 32pp. Yungsu's father tells his lonely son why the family has moved to the United States. (Rev: BL 9/15/95; HB 11–12/95; SLJ 11/95)

3690 Heo, Yumi. *One Sunday Morning* (PS–1). Illus. 1999, Orchard LB $16.99 (0-531-33156-3). 32pp. Minho dreams that he and his father spend a day in the park experiencing its sights and sounds. (Rev: BCCB 5/99; BL 4/1/99; HB 3–4/99; HBG 10/99; SLJ 4/99)

3691 Hesse, Karen. *Poppy's Chair* (K–3). Illus. by Kay Life. 1993, Macmillan LB $14.95 (0-02-743705-1). 32pp. Leah learns from her grandmother how to accept her grandfather's death. (Rev: BL 3/15/93; SLJ 7/93)

3692 Hest, Amy. *The Crack-of-Dawn Walkers* (PS–2). Illus. by Amy Schwartz. 1984, Simon & Schuster LB $13.95 (0-02-743710-8). 32pp. Sadie and her grandfather have lovely walks alone every other Sunday. A reissue of the 1984 edition.

3693 Hest, Amy. *Jamaica Louise James* (PS–3). Illus. by Sheila W. Samton. 1996, Candlewick $15.99 (1-56402-348-6). 32pp. Through her drawings, Jamaica Louise tries to make her Granny's life happier. (Rev: BCCB 9/96; BL 9/1/96; HB 9–10/96; SLJ 12/96)

3694 Hest, Amy. *The Mommy Exchange* (PS–2). Illus. by DyAnne DiSalvo-Ryan. 1988, Macmillan LB $13.95 (0-02-743650-0); paper $3.95 (0-689-71450-5). 32pp. Jason and Jessica, each fed up with home life, decide to trade moms and learn to appreciate their own. (Rev: BL 5/1/88; SLJ 10/88)

3695 Hest, Amy. *Rosie's Fishing Trip* (PS–2). Illus. by Paul Howard. 1994, Candlewick $13.95 (1-56402-296-X). 32pp. While they wait for the fish to bite on their fishing excursion, Rosie's grandfather composes a poem. (Rev: BL 10/15/94; SLJ 2/95)

3696 Hiatt, Fred. *Baby Talk* (PS–1). Illus. by Mark Graham. 1999, Simon & Schuster $14.00 (0-689-82146-8). 32pp. Joey ignores his baby brother until he realizes that he is the only one who can understand his baby talk. (Rev: BL 7/99; HBG 10/99; SLJ 8/99)

3697 Hickman, Martha W. *Robert Lives with His Grandparents* (1–3). Illus. by Tim Hinton. 1995, Albert Whitman LB $14.95 (0-8075-7084-2). 32pp. Robert, who lives with his grandparents, is embarrassed at the thought that his grandmother will be coming to school on parents' day. (Rev: BL 2/1/96; SLJ 1/96)

3698 Himmelman, John. *Wanted: Perfect Parents* (K–2). Illus. 1993, BridgeWater $13.95 (0-8167-3028-8). 32pp. Gregory realizes that perfect parents are those who can tuck him in lovingly at night. (Rev: BL 10/15/93; SLJ 8/93)

3699 Hines, Anna Grossnickle. *Daddy Makes the Best Spaghetti* (PS–K). Illus. by author. 1986, Houghton paper $5.95 (0-89919-794-9). The story of the warm relationship between a father and son as they spend time together doing things at home. (Rev: BL 3/1/86; HB 9–10/86; SLJ 5/86)

3700 Hines, Anna Grossnickle. *Even If I Spill My Milk?* (PS–1). Illus. by author. 1994, Clarion $13.95 (0-395-65010-0). 32pp. Jamie tries every delaying tactic possible to prevent his parents' leaving him with a baby-sitter. (Rev: SLJ 6/94)

3701 Hines, Anna Grossnickle. *Grandma Gets Grumpy* (PS–K). Illus. by author. 1988, Houghton paper $6.95 (0-395-52595-0). 32pp. When Lassen's four cousins show up, her normally "cool" Grandma actually gets annoyed. (Rev: BCCB 6/88; BL 5/1/88; HB 7–8/88)

3702 Hines, Anna Grossnickle. *When We Married Gary* (PS–1). Illus. 1996, Greenwillow $15.00 (0-688-14276-1). 28pp. Two young sisters adjust to Gary, their new stepfather, when their mother remarries. (Rev: BL 3/1/96; HB 7–8/96; SLJ 5/96)

3703 Holman, Sandy Lynne. *Grandpa, Is Everything Black Bad?* (PS–3). Illus. by Lela Kometiani. 1998, Culture C.O.-O.P. $18.95 (0-9644655-0-7). 32pp. A child named Montsho thinks that black is often associated with things that are bad, but his beloved grandfather assures him that black is beautiful. (Rev: BL 1/1–15/99; SLJ 12/98)

3704 Hooks, William H. *The Mighty Santa Fe* (K–3). Illus. by Angela T. Thomas. 1993, Macmillan LB $14.95 (0-02-744432-5). 32pp. William is overjoyed to find that his grandmother shares his enthusiasm for model trains. (Rev: BL 11/15/93)

3705 Houston, Gloria. *My Great-Aunt Arizona* (K–4). Illus. by Susan C. Lamb. 1992, Harper-

Collins LB $15.89 (0-06-022607-2). 32pp. The story of the author's great-aunt, who was born in the Appalachians and lived there until the age of 93. (Rev: BCCB 4/92; BL 1/1/92; SLJ 3/92) [371.1]

3706 Howard, Elizabeth F. *Aunt Flossie's Hats (and Crab Cakes Later)* (PS–3). Illus. by James E. Ransome. 1991, Houghton $16.00 (0-395-54682-6). 32pp. Susan and Sarah visit Great-great Aunt Flossie to hear her tell stories about her hats. (Rev: BL 3/15/91*; HB 9–10/91; SLJ 5/91)

3707 Howard, Elizabeth F. *What's in Aunt Mary's Room?* (PS–2). Illus. by Cedric Lucas. 1996, Clarion $14.95 (0-395-69845-6). 32pp. Aunt Flossie explains the importance in the life of this African American family of the book stored in Aunt Mary's room, the family Bible. A sequel to *Aunt Flossie's Hats (and Crab Cakes Later)* (1991). (Rev: BL 2/15/96; SLJ 5/96)

3708 Howard, Elizabeth F. *When Will Sarah Come?* (PS–K). Illus. by Nina Crews. 1999, Greenwillow LB $15.93 (0-688-16181-2). 24pp. On Sarah's first day at school, younger brother Jonathan waits impatiently for her return. (Rev: BCCB 10/99; BL 10/15/99; HBG 3/00; SLJ 9/99)

3709 Hughes, Shirley. *Abel's Moon* (PS–3). Illus. 1999, DK $15.95 (0-7894-4601-4). 32pp. Although they miss their father when he goes away periodically to work, the family of Abel Grable enjoy the freedom his absence brings. (Rev: BCCB 11/99; BL 12/1/99; HBG 3/00; SLJ 9/99)

3710 Hughes, Shirley. *The Big Alfie and Annie Rose Storybook* (2–3). Illus. by author. 1989, Lothrop $18.00 (0-688-07672-6). 64pp. Stories, poems, and eye-catching artwork featuring Alfie and his little sister. (Rev: BCCB 4/89; BL 3/15/89; HB 5–6/89)

3711 Hughes, Shirley. *The Big Alfie Out of Doors Storybook* (PS–2). Illus. 1992, Lothrop $17.00 (0-688-11428-8). 64pp. Four-year-old Alfie has four happy experiences with different members of his family. (Rev: BCCB 10/92*; BL 10/15/92; HB 1–2/93; SLJ 10/92)

3712 Hurd, Edith Thacher. *I Dance in My Red Pajamas* (PS–1). Illus. by Emily Arnold McCully. 1982, HarperCollins LB $15.89 (0-06-022700-1). 32pp. A little girl stays overnight at her grandparents' house.

3713 Hutchins, Pat. *Titch* (K–3). Illus. by author. 1971, Macmillan paper $5.99 (0-689-71688-5). 32pp. Titch, the youngest in the family, enjoys a moment of triumph. A sequel is: *You'll Soon Grow into Them, Titch* (1983, Greenwillow).

3714 Igus, Toyomi. *Two Mrs. Gibsons* (K–3). Illus. by Daryl Wells. 1996, Children's Book Pr. $14.95 (0-89239-135-9). 32pp. The two Mrs. Gibsons in a young girl's life are her mother and her grandmother. (Rev: BCCB 5/96; BL 5/15/96; SLJ 10/96)

3715 Igus, Toyomi. *When I Was Little* (K–3). Illus. by Higgins Bond. 1992, Just Us $14.95 (0-940975-32-7). 32pp. Noel finds it hard to believe there was no television and other things he takes for granted when his African American grandfather was growing up. (Rev: BL 3/1/93)

3716 Isadora, Rachael. *Lili Backstage* (PS–3). Illus. 1997, Putnam $15.95 (0-399-23025-4). 32pp. Lili explores backstage life when she visits her grandfather, who plays the French horn in a theater orchestra. (Rev: BL 3/15/97; HB 7–8/97; SLJ 6/97)

3717 Jacobs, Kate. *A Sister's Wish* (K–2). Illus. by Nancy Carpenter. 1996, Hyperion LB $15.49 (0-7868-2112-4). A little girl longs to have a sister of her own but later realizes that being a good sister to her brothers is nice, too. (Rev: SLJ 7/96)

3718 Jam, Teddy. *The Year of Fire* (PS–3). Illus. by Ian Wallace. 1993, Macmillan paper $14.95 (0-689-50566-3). 48pp. A grandfather recalls a terrible fire that destroyed the maple grove where he and his granddaughter are now sugaring. (Rev: BCCB 7–8/93; BL 3/15/93; SLJ 5/93)

3719 James, Betsy. *Tadpoles* (PS–2). Illus. 1999, Dutton $14.99 (0-525-46197-3). 32pp. Molly, who has been caring for some frog's eggs, notices the parallels between their development and that of her baby brother Davey. (Rev: BCCB 10/99; BL 7/99; HBG 3/00; SLJ 8/99)

3720 Jenkins, Emily. *Five Creatures* (PS–K). Illus. by Tomek Bogacki. 2001, Farrar $16.00 (0-374-32341-0). 32pp. Child-like drawings are used in this book that describes the everyday activities of a family and their two cats in an entertaining format that is also an exercise in reasoning. (Rev: BCCB 2/01; BL 3/15/01*)

3721 Jennings, Sharon. *The Bye-Bye Pie* (1–3). Illus. by Ruth Ohi. 1999, Fitzhenry & Whiteside $13.95 (1-55041-405-4). 32pp. Chocolate pies are on the menu as two brothers, Alfie and Joey, make preparations for a surprise party for Grandma. (Rev: BL 11/15/99)

3722 Johnson, Angela. *The Aunt in Our House* (PS–3). Illus. by David Soman. 1996, Orchard LB $16.99 (0-531-08852-9). 32pp. An aunt brings new life and interesting talents during a visit to her brother's biracial family. (Rev: BL 3/1/96; SLJ 4/96)

3723 Johnson, Angela. *Do Like Kyla* (PS–1). Illus. by James E. Ransome. 1990, Orchard $15.95 (0-531-05852-2); paper $6.95 (0-531-07040-9). 32pp. The younger of two sisters imitates the older sibling all day long. (Rev: BL 2/15/90; SLJ 4/90)

3724 Johnson, Angela. *Down the Winding Road* (PS–2). Illus. by Shane W. Evans. 2000, DK $15.95 (0-7894-2596-3). 32pp. The Old Ones are seven elderly aunts and uncles who raised Daddy and every year during summer vacation the family goes down a winding road to visit them. (Rev: BCCB 3/00; BL 2/15/00; HBG 10/00; SLJ 5/00)

3725 Johnson, Angela. *One of Three* (PS–K). Illus. by David Soman. 1991, Orchard $15.95 (0-531-05955-3); paper $5.95 (0-531-07061-1). 32pp. A young African American girl remembers the good times growing up with two older sisters. (Rev: BL 7/91; SLJ 10/91)

3726 Johnson, Angela. *Tell Me a Story, Mama* (PS–1). Illus. by David Soman. 1989, Orchard paper $6.95 (0-531-07032-8). 32pp. An African American mother and daughter reminisce about childhood. (Rev: BCCB 2/89; BL 4/1/89; SLJ 3/89)

3727 Johnson, Angela. *The Wedding* (K–2). Illus. by David Soman. 1999, Orchard LB $17.99 (0-531-33139-3). Through the eyes of young Daisy, the reader experiences all the excitement of the preparations for her sister's wedding. (Rev: BCCB 3/99; HBG 10/99; SLJ 3/99)

3728 Johnson, Angela. *When I Am Old with You* (PS–2). Illus. by David Soman. 1990, Orchard LB $16.99 (0-531-08484-1); paper $6.95 (0-531-07035-2). 32pp. A young African American boy daydreams of all the things he and his grandfather can do when the youngster grows older. (Rev: BL 9/1/90; SLJ 9/90*)

3729 Johnson, Dinah. *Sunday Week* (PS–3). Illus. by Tyrone Geter. 1999, Holt $15.95 (0-8050-4911-8). 32pp. The days of the week are explored through the activities of an African American family, climaxing on Sunday when faith, family, and food take over. (Rev: BCCB 6/99; BL 2/15/99; HB 3–4/99; HBG 10/99; SLJ 6/99)

3730 Johnson, Dolores. *Grandma's Hands* (1–3). Illus. by author. 1998, Marshall Cavendish $15.95 (0-7614-5025-4). Initially unhappy at having to live with his grandmother on her farm, a young African American boy grows to love her and her home. (Rev: HBG 10/98; SLJ 5/98)

3731 Johnson, Dolores. *What Will Mommy Do When I'm at School?* (PS–1). Illus. 1990, Macmillan LB $15.00 (0-02-747845-9). 32pp. About to start school, a young girl worries about how her mother will cope. (Rev: BL 12/1/90; SLJ 1/91)

3732 Johnson, Dolores. *Your Dad Was Just Like You* (K–3). Illus. 1993, Macmillan $13.95 (0-02-747838-6). 32pp. Peter understands his father better when his grandfather tells him about his dad's childhood. (Rev: BL 3/1/93; SLJ 8/93)

3733 Johnston, Tony. *Fishing Sunday* (PS–4). Illus. by Barry Root. 1996, Morrow $16.00 (0-688-13458-0). 32pp. A young boy is embarrassed by his grandfather's eccentric behavior during a fishing expedition. (Rev: BL 5/15/96; SLJ 6/96)

3734 Johnston, Tony. *Uncle Rain Cloud* (PS–3). Illus. by Fabricio Vandenbroeck. 2001, Charlesbridge $15.95 (0-88106-371-1). 32pp. A touching picture about Carlos' cranky Uncle Tomas who becomes animated and happy only when telling stories about his homeland, Mexico, and its culture. (Rev: BL 2/15/01*)

3735 Jolin, Dominique. *It's Not Fair!* (PS–3). Illus. by author. 1996, Crossing Pr. $14.95 (0-89594-780-3). A patient father listens as his daughter complains that her friends have more than she does and then reminds her that she has him. (Rev: SLJ 8/96)

3736 Jonell, Lynne. *Let's Play Rough!* (PS–1). Illus. by Ted Rand. 2000, Putnam $13.99 (0-399-23039-4). 32pp. An episodic picture book that depicts the different games that a little boy plays with his dad. (Rev: BL 2/1/00; HBG 10/00; SLJ 3/00)

3737 Jonell, Lynne. *Mom Pie* (PS–2). Illus. by Petra Mathers. 2001, Putnam $12.99 (0-399-23422-5). 32pp. While Mom is busy preparing for company, Christopher and his young brother amuse themselves. (Rev: BL 3/15/01; HB 1–2/01)

3738 Joosse, Barbara M. *I Love You the Purplest* (PS–1). Illus. by Mary Whyte. 1996, Chronicle $15.95 (0-8118-0718-5). 32pp. Two young brothers compete for the attention of their mother, who demonstrates that she loves them equally. (Rev: BL 10/15/96; SLJ 5/97)

3739 Joosse, Barbara M. *Mama, Do You Love Me?* (PS–2). Illus. by Barbara Lavallee. 1991, Chronicle $14.95 (0-87701-759-X). An Eskimo girl asks her mother if she will still be loved even when she is naughty. (Rev: BCCB 12/91; HB 11–12/91; SLJ 11/91)

3740 Joosse, Barbara M. *The Morning Chair* (K–3). Illus. by Marcia Sewall. 1995, Clarion $14.95 (0-395-62337-5). 32pp. The story of a young Dutch boy whose family emigrates to New York City in the 1950s. (Rev: BCCB 6/95; BL 6/1–15/95; HB 5–6/95; SLJ 6/95)

3741 Joslin, Mary. *The Goodbye Boat* (PS–2). Illus. by Claire St Louis Little. 1999, Eerdmans $15.00 (0-8028-5186-X). 28pp. As a metaphor for death, a grandmother leaves her family behind and goes on a long sea journey. (Rev: BL 5/1/99; HBG 10/99; SLJ 6/99)

3742 Jukes, Mavis. *Like Jake and Me* (2–3). Illus. by Lloyd Bloom. 1987, Knopf paper $7.99 (0-394-89263-1). 32pp. Alex and his stepfather explore the meaning of fear.

3743 Kaplan, Howard. *Waiting to Sing* (K–4). Illus. by Herve Blondon. 2000, DK $15.95 (0-7894-2615-3). 32pp. After his mother dies, her young son and his father are comforted when they listen to her favorite music, "Fur Elise." (Rev: BCCB 3/00; BL 3/15/00*; HBG 10/00; SLJ 3/00)

3744 Kaplan, John. *Mom and Me* (PS–1). Illus. 1996, Scholastic $10.95 (0-590-47294-1). 32pp. In photographs and text, three children talk about their mothers and what these maternal bonds mean to them. (Rev: BL 3/1/96; SLJ 4/96) [306]

3745 Katz, Karen. *Over the Moon: An Adoption Tale* (PS–1). Illus. 1997, Holt $16.95 (0-8050-5013-2). 32pp. A husband and wife prepare for the baby they are going to adopt. (Rev: BL 9/1/97; HBG 3/98; SLJ 9/97)

3746 Kaye, Marilyn. *The Real Tooth Fairy* (PS–3). Illus. by Helen Cogancherry. 1990, Harcourt $14.00 (0-15-265780-0). 21pp. Elsie is convinced that her mother is really the tooth fairy. (Rev: BCCB 10/92; BL 9/15/90; SLJ 10/90)

3747 Keller, Holly. *Harry and Tuck* (K–1). Illus. 1993, Greenwillow LB $13.93 (0-688-11463-6). 24pp. Only at school do twins gain sufficient independence to exist separately. (Rev: BL 7/93; HB 7–8/93; SLJ 7/93)

3748 Kellogg, Steven. *Can I Keep Him?* (K–2). Illus. by author. 1971, Dial $15.99 (0-8037-0988-9); Puffin paper $5.99 (0-14-054867-X). 32pp. Arnold, an incorrigible animal lover, constantly distresses his mother with a wide assortment of pets — real, imaginary, and human.

3749 Ketteman, Helen. *Mama's Way* (1–3). Illus. by Mary Whyte. 2001, Dial $15.99 (0-8037-2413-6). 32pp. Wynona despairs of getting a new dress for her sixth-grade graduation, but mama works a miracle and transforms a hand-me-down. (Rev: BCCB 3/01; BL 2/15/01; SLJ 3/01)

3750 Kirk, Daniel. *Snow Family* (PS–3). Illus. 2000, Hyperion $14.99 (0-7868-0304-5). 32pp. When Jacob realizes that the snow children have no parents, he creates a snow mother and father to make a snow family. (Rev: BL 9/1/00*; HBG 3/01; SLJ 9/00)

3751 Koehler, Phoebe. *The Day We Met You* (PS–2). Illus. 1990, Macmillan LB $15.00 (0-02-750901-X). 48pp. This book celebrates the great joy of welcoming an adopted baby into the household. (Rev: BL 5/15/90; SLJ 8/90)

3752 Komaiko, Leah. *Just My Dad and Me* (K–3). Illus. by Jeffrey Greene. Series: Laura Geringer Books. 1995, HarperCollins LB $15.89 (0-06-024574-3). A young girl's dream of spending a day alone with her father is dashed when a carload of relatives arrives. (Rev: SLJ 7/95*)

3753 Kraus, Robert. *Little Louie the Baby Bloomer* (PS–2). Illus. by Jose Aruego. 1998, HarperCollins LB $15.89 (0-06-026294-X). 32pp. Leo is worried about his younger brother, who can't do anything right. (Rev: BL 3/15/98; HBG 10/98; SLJ 7/98)

3754 Krauss, Ruth. *You're Just What I Need* (PS). Illus. by Julia Noonan. 1998, HarperCollins $14.95 (0-06-027514-6). 32pp. A sentimental picture book in which a mother wonders what the strange bundle could be under the blankets in her bed, knowing, of course, that it is her young child playing a game of hide-and-seek. (Rev: BL 7/98; HBG 10/98; SLJ 7/98)

3755 Kroll, Virginia. *Beginnings: How Families Come to Be* (PS–3). Illus. by Stacey Schuett. 1994, Albert Whitman LB $14.95 (0-8075-0602-8). 34pp. Six children — some adopted, others not — discuss with their parents and other family members where they came from. (Rev: BL 3/15/94; SLJ 6/94)

3756 Kroll, Virginia. *Butterfly Boy* (PS–3). Illus. by Gerardo Suzan. 1997, Boyds Mills $15.95 (1-56397-371-5). 32pp. Even though his grandfather can no longer talk, Emilio is certain that he is enjoying himself when they watch the butterflies together. (Rev: BL 11/1/97; SLJ 6/97)

3757 Kroll, Virginia. *She Is Born: A Celebration of Daughters* (K–3). Illus. by John Rowe. 2000, Beyond Words $15.95 (1-885223-94-3). 32pp. This happy book introduces a baby girl into the world with examples of how she will be lovingly treated. (Rev: BL 7/00; HBG 10/00)

3758 Kuklin, Susan. *How My Family Lives in America* (PS–3). Illus. 1992, Macmillan $15.00 (0-02-751239-8). 40pp. Three children — an African American, a Hispanic American, and a Chinese American — talk about their families and their pride in their ancestors. (Rev: BCCB 4/92; BL 3/1/92; SLJ 3/92) [305.8]

3759 Kurtis-Kleinman, Eileen. *When Aunt Lena Did the Rhumba* (PS–3). Illus. by Diane Greenseid. 1997, Hyperion LB $15.49 (0-7868-2067-5). 32pp. When theater-loving Aunt Lena is ill in bed, Sophie

and other relatives put on a show for her. (Rev: BL 5/15/97; SLJ 6/97)

3760 Kurtz, Jane. *Faraway Home* (PS–3). Illus. by E. B. Lewis. 2000, Harcourt $16.00 (0-15-200036-4). 32pp. In this moving family story, a young African American girl has to adjust to the fact that her father must return home to Ethiopia to care for his sick mother. (Rev: BCCB 5/00; BL 2/15/00*; HBG 10/00; SLJ 4/00)

3761 Kuskin, Karla. *I Am Me* (PS–2). Illus. by Dyanna Wolcott. 2000, Simon & Schuster $14.00 (0-689-81473-9). 32pp. Although a young girl realizes that she resembles other members of her family (she has her mother's green eyes, for example), she is, nevertheless, a distinct individual. (Rev: BL 6/1–15/00; HBG 10/00; SLJ 7/00)

3762 Lakin, Patricia. *Dad and Me in the Morning* (K–3). Illus. by Robert G. Steele. 1994, Albert Whitman LB $14.95 (0-8075-1419-5). 32pp. A deaf boy and his father communicate their feelings to each other as they watch a sunrise. (Rev: BL 4/1/94; SLJ 6/94)

3763 Laminack, Lester L. *The Sunsets of Miss Olivia Wiggins* (K–4). Illus. by Constance R. Bergum. 1998, Peachtree $15.95 (1-56145-139-8). 32pp. Although it appears that Miss Olivia Wiggins, an Alzheimer's disease sufferer, does recognize her daughter and great-grandson when they visit her at a nursing home, inwardly she is recalling pleasant times from the past. (Rev: BL 5/1/98; HBG 10/98; SLJ 7/98)

3764 Larose, Linda. *Jessica Takes Charge* (PS–2). Illus. by Leanne Franson. 1999, Annick LB $15.95 (1-55037-563-6); paper $5.95 (1-55037-562-8). Jessica is frightened at night by what she thinks is a monster growling, but she discovers it's her father snoring. (Rev: SLJ 9/99)

3765 Lasky, Kathryn, and Maxwell B. Knight. *A Baby for Max* (PS–2). Illus. by Christopher G. Knight. 1987, Macmillan paper $4.95 (0-689-71118-2). A book about a new addition to the family; illustrated with photographs.

3766 Lawrence, Michael. *Baby Loves Hugs and Kisses* (PS). Illus. by Adrian Reynolds. Series: DK Toddler Storybook. 2000, DK paper $5.95 (0-7894-5649-4). A simple story about a baby who learns to exchange affectionate hugs and kisses with members of the family. (Rev: SLJ 12/00)

3767 Leedy, Loreen. *Who's Who in My Family?* (PS–1). Illus. 1995, Holiday LB $16.95 (0-8234-1151-6). 32pp. Family relationships and the words used to describe them are the subject of this book on all kinds of families. (Rev: BCCB 3/95; BL 3/1/95; SLJ 4/95)

3768 Legge, David. *Bamboozled* (PS–3). Illus. 1995, Scholastic $14.95 (0-590-47989-X). 32pp. A surreal presentation of a girl's visit to her grandfather's house. (Rev: BCCB 3/95; BL 1/15/95; HB 11–12/95; SLJ 3/95*)

3769 Leighton, Audrey O. *A Window of Time* (K–3). Illus. by Rhonda Kyrias. 1995, NADIA $15.95 (0-9636335-1-1). 32pp. Shawn is troubled by his grandfather's frequent loss of memory and mental confusion. (Rev: BL 2/1/96)

3770 Lemieux, Margo. *The Fiddle Ribbon* (1–3). Illus. by Francis Livingston. 1996, Silver Burdett LB $22.00 (0-382-39096-2); paper $5.95 (0-382-39098-9). Jennie learns to play the fiddle and brother Jimmy enjoys folk dancing during the summer they spend on their grandparent's farm. (Rev: SLJ 9/96)

3771 Levy, Janice. *Abuelito Eats with His Fingers* (1–3). Illus. by Layne Johnson. 1999, Eakin $14.95 (1-57168-177-9). Tina is ashamed of her crude, peasantlike grandfather, but one day she discovers they share a love of art. (Rev: HBG 3/00; SLJ 9/99)

3772 Lewis, Cynthia C. *Dilly's Big Sister Diary* (2–4). Illus. by Cynthia Copeland Lewis. 1998, Millbrook LB $19.90 (0-7613-0414-2). Eight-year-old Dilly is given a diary by her parents to chronicle the development of her new younger brother, Matthew. (Rev: HBG 3/99; SLJ 2/99)

3773 Lewis, Rob. *Hide-and-Seek with Grandpa* (1–3). Illus. by author. 1997, Mondo paper $4.50 (1-57255-226-3). 48pp. Young Finley is always surprised at his Grandpa Bear's vim and vigor. Also use *Grandpa Comes to Stay* (1997). (Rev: SLJ 8/97)

3774 Limmer, Milly J. *Where Do Little Girls Grow?* (PS–3). Illus. by Rosekrans Hoffman. 1993, Whitman LB $15.95 (0-8075-8924-1). 32pp. A little girl and her mother explore this age-old question, first with imagination, then with the truth, which seems just as magical as all of the other imagined possibilities. (Rev: BL 6/1–15/93; SLJ 8/93)

3775 Lin, Grace. *The Ugly Vegetables* (K–2). Illus. 1999, Charlesbridge LB $15.95 (0-88106-336-3). 32pp. A Chinese American girl is disappointed in the dullness of her family garden compared with the lovely flowers she sees in other gardens — until harvest time when her mother makes a delicious soup from all the unusual Chinese vegetables. (Rev: BL 9/15/99; HB 9–10/99; HBG 3/00; SLJ 9/99)

3776 London, Jonathan. *A Koala for Katie* (PS–3). Illus. by Cynthia Jabar. 1993, Albert Whitman LB $13.95 (0-8075-4209-1). 32pp. Katie's adoptive parents use a trip to the zoo to explain how in nature substitute parents are often found to take care of orphans. (Rev: BL 11/15/93; SLJ 10/93)

3777 Long, Earlene. *Gone Fishing* (PS–2). Illus. by Richard Brown. 1987, Houghton paper $5.95 (0-395-44236-2). 32pp. A loving story of a boy's fishing trip with his father.

3778 Long, Melinda. *When Papa Snores* (PS–2). Illus. by Holly Meade. 2000, Simon & Schuster $16.00 (0-689-81943-9). 32pp. A little girl feels comfortable and secure when she hears snores from different members of her family. (Rev: BL 2/1/01; HB 9–10/00; HBG 3/01; SLJ 10/00)

3779 Look, Lenore. *Love as Strong as Ginger* (K–4). Illus. by Stephen T. Johnson. 1999, Simon & Schuster $15.00 (0-689-81248-5). 40pp. A young Chinese American girl goes to visit a cannery in the Seattle area where her grandmother, a recent immigrant, has to work backbreaking hours to earn a living. (Rev: BL 10/15/99*; HB 5–6/99; HBG 10/99; SLJ 7/99)

3780 Loomis, Christine. *Across America, I Love You* (K–2). Illus. by Kate Kiesler. 2000, Hyperion LB $16.49 (0-7868-2314-3). Different landscapes and different seasons are used to illustrate the lasting relationship between mother and daughter. (Rev: HBG 3/01; SLJ 7/00)

3781 Lyon, George E. *Five Live Bongos* (PS–1). Illus. by Jacqueline Rogers. 1994, Scholastic $15.95 (0-590-46654-2). 40pp. Five brothers and sisters make so much noise indoors that they are banished to the garage. (Rev: BL 10/15/94; SLJ 10/94)

3782 McCloskey, Robert. *One Morning in Maine* (1–3). Illus. by author. 1952, Puffin paper $5.99 (0-14-050174-6). An exciting day, the loss of Sal's first tooth, is realistically recaptured by this fine storyteller and in the large, extraordinary blue-pencil drawings of Penobscot Bay. Also use: *Blueberries for Sal* (1948).

3783 McCormick, Wendy. *Daddy, Will You Miss Me?* (K–3). Illus. by Jennifer Eachus. 1999, Simon & Schuster $16.00 (0-689-81898-X). A gentle picture book about how a boy misses his father who is in Africa for a month and how he imagines his father's sunny activities while he is at home playing in the winter snow. (Rev: HBG 10/99; SLJ 6/99)

3784 McCormick, Wendy. *The Night You Were Born* (PS–2). Illus. by Sophy Williams. 2000, Peachtree $15.95 (1-56145-225-4). 32pp. While waiting for news of the arrival of a sibling, Jamie listens to a story about the night he was born. (Rev: BL 1/1–15/01; HBG 3/01; SLJ 12/00)

3785 McCourt, Lisa. *I Miss You, Stinky Face* (PS–K). Illus. by Cyd Moore. 1999, Troll $15.95 (0-8167-5647-3). 32pp. A youngster's anxiety about his mother getting home causes a series of "what ifs," such as "What if the airplane forgets to fly?" (Rev: BL 4/15/99; SLJ 5/99)

3786 McCutcheon, John. *Happy Adoption Day!* (PS–2). Illus. by Julie Paschkis. 1996, Little, Brown $15.95 (0-316-55455-3). 32pp. In simple rhymes, the story of an American family's adoption of an Asian child is told. (Rev: BL 12/1/96; SLJ 11/96) [782.42]

3787 McElligott, Matthew. *The Truth About Cousin Ernie's Head* (PS–2). Illus. 1996, Simon & Schuster paper $15.00 (0-689-80179-3). 32pp. Ernie is able to settle a family squabble when he shows an old home movie. (Rev: BL 12/1/96; SLJ 11/96)

3788 McFarlane, Sheryl. *Waiting for the Whales* (PS–3). Illus. by Ron Lightburn. 1991, Orca paper $6.95 (0-920501-96-6). 32pp. On his lonely island an old man and his granddaughter await the sighting of the summer whales. (Rev: BL 5/15/93; SLJ 6/93)

3789 MacLachlan, Patricia. *Mama One, Mama Two* (1–3). Illus. by Ruth Bornstein. 1982, HarperCollins LB $15.89 (0-06-024082-2). 32pp. Maudie is told why she has two mothers in this gentle story of a foster home.

3790 MacLachlan, Patricia. *The Sick Day* (PS–1). Illus. by Jane Dyer. 2001, Doubleday $12.95 (0-385-32150-3). 32pp. Emily's father takes care of her when she gets sick but the next day, when he catches the bug, it's Emily's turn to play nurse. (Rev: BL 2/15/01)

3791 MacLachlan, Patricia. *Through Grandpa's Eyes* (1–3). Illus. by Deborah Kogan Ray. 1980, HarperCollins LB $15.89 (0-06-024043-1); paper $5.95 (0-06-443041-3). 48pp. John's blind grandfather shares with him the special way he sees and moves in the world.

3792 McMillan, Bruce. *Grandfather's Trolley* (K–4). Illus. 1995, Candlewick $15.95 (1-56402-633-7). 32pp. A photo-essay about a small girl who rides the trolley car that her grandfather operates. Two other photo-illustrated books by the author are *Eating Fractions* (Scholastic, 1991) and *Going on a Whale Watch* (Scholastic, 1992). (Rev: BCCB 12/95; BL 10/15/95; SLJ 12/95)

3793 McMillan, Bruce. *Step by Step* (PS). Illus. by author. 1990, Apple Island LB $15.00 (0-688-07234-8). 28pp. Photos trace Evan from four months until he becomes a fast walker at 14 months. (Rev: BL 9/1/87; HB 11–12/87; SLJ 9/87)

3794 McPhail, David. *Sisters* (PS–1). Illus. by author. 1984, Harcourt $14.00 (0-15-275319-2); paper $5.00 (0-15-275320-6). 32pp. Two loving sisters compare their similarities and differences.

3795 Mahy, Margaret. *A Busy Day for a Good Grandmother* (PS–3). Illus. by Margaret Chamberlain. 1993, Macmillan $14.95 (0-689-50595-7). 32pp. Mrs. Oberon is an unconventional grandmother who rides skateboards and fights vultures and alligators. (Rev: BL 10/15/93; SLJ 9/93)

3796 Manning, Mick, and Brita Granström. *Supermom* (PS–K). Illus. 2001, Albert Whitman $15.95 (0-8075-7666-2). 32pp. Using both humans and animals as subjects, this book explores the many tasks that mothers perform. (Rev: BL 3/15/01)

3797 Manson, Ainslie. *Ballerinas Don't Wear Glasses* (PS–3). Illus. by Dean Griffiths. 2000, Orca $15.95 (1-55143-158-0). 32pp. In this warm family story, older brother Ben must help his little sister Alison prepare for her dance recital. (Rev: BL 12/1/00; HBG 3/01; SLJ 8/00)

3798 Mario, Heidi Stetson. *I'd Rather Have an Iguana* (PS–1). Illus. 1999, Charlesbridge $14.95 (0-88106-357-6). 32pp. Big sister doesn't want to have a baby brother, but one day when they are alone, she changes her mind. (Rev: BL 1/1–15/99; HBG 10/99; SLJ 4/99)

3799 Markel, Michelle. *Gracias, Rosa* (K–3). Illus. by Diane Paterson. 1995, Albert Whitman LB $14.95 (0-8075-3024-7). 32pp. Kate learns about Guatemala and the sadness of leaving a daughter behind from the family's new baby-sitter, Rosa. (Rev: BL 6/1–15/95; SLJ 5/95)

3800 Martin, C. L. G. *Three Brave Women* (K–2). Illus. by Peter Elwell. 1991, Macmillan $16.00 (0-02-762445-5). 32pp. Caitlin finds she is afraid of spiders, and her grandmother tells her of her private fears. (Rev: BL 5/1/91; SLJ 5/91)

3801 Maslac, Evelyn Hughes. *Finding a Job for Daddy* (PS–3). Illus. by Kay Life. 1996, Albert Whitman LB $13.95 (0-8075-2437-9). 32pp. Laura

tries to cheer up her father, who is out of work. (Rev: BL 4/1/96)

3802 Matze, Claire Sidhom. *The Stars in My Geddoh's Sky* (PS–3). Illus. by Bill Farnsworth. 1999, Albert Whitman $14.95 (0-8075-5332-8). An Arab grandfather (geddoh) from Palestine comes to the U.S. to visit the family of his grandson, Alex. (Rev: BL 5/15/99; HBG 10/99; SLJ 5/99)

3803 May, Kathy L. *Molasses Man* (PS–3). Illus. by Felicia Marshall. 2000, Holiday $16.95 (0-8234-1438-8). 32pp. Seen through the eyes of a young African American boy, this is the story of how his family makes molasses under the supervision of Grandpa, the Molasses Man. (Rev: BL 10/1/00; HBG 3/01; SLJ 10/00)

3804 Mennen, Ingrid. *One Round Moon and a Star for Me* (PS–1). Illus. by Niki Daly. 1994, Orchard LB $16.99 (0-531-08654-2). 32pp. In this tale that takes place in Lesotho, a young boy needs reassurance when a new baby arrives in the family. (Rev: BCCB 4/94; BL 2/15/94; SLJ 9/94)

3805 Michaels, William. *Clare and Her Shadow* (PS–1). Illus. by author. 1991, Shoe String LB $16.50 (0-208-02301-1). While on a walk with her grandmother, Clare discovers her shadow. (Rev: SLJ 2/92)

3806 Millen, C. M. *The Low-Down Laundry Line Blues* (PS–3). Illus. by Christine Davenier. 1999, Houghton $15.00 (0-395-87497-1). 32pp. A little girl is cheered up when her younger sister uses their laundry line as a skipping rope. (Rev: BL 4/15/99; HB 3–4/99; HBG 10/99; SLJ 5/99)

3807 Miller, Margaret. *Baby Faces* (PS). Illus. 1998, Simon & Schuster $4.99 (0-689-81911-0). 14pp. A board book in which babies' faces are used to illustrate different moods and attitudes. (Rev: BL 7/98; HBG 10/98; SLJ 7/98)

3808 Miller, Margaret. *What's on My Head?* (PS). Illus. 1998, Simon & Schuster $4.99 (0-689-81912-9). 14pp. In this board book, babies wear such unusual headgear as a firefighter's hat, beanbag animals, and a rubber duck. (Rev: BL 7/98; HBG 10/98; SLJ 7/98)

3809 Miller, William. *A House by the River* (K–2). Illus. by Cornelius Van Wright. 1997, Lee & Low $15.95 (1-880000-48-2). 32pp. Belinda is afraid that her house will get flooded if heavy rains come, but her mother tells her about how the house has been a safe haven through the years. (Rev: BL 5/15/97; HB 7–8/97; SLJ 7/97)

3810 Miller, William. *Zora Hurston and the Chinaberry Tree* (PS–3). Illus. by Cornelius Van Wright and Ying-Hwa Hu. 1994, Lee & Low $15.95 (1-880000-14-8); paper $6.95 (1-880000-33-4). 32pp. A picture book that explores the trauma experienced by the author Zora Hurston when her beloved mother died when the girl was only nine. (Rev: BL 10/15/94; SLJ 12/94) [813]

3811 Mitchell, Rhonda. *The Talking Cloth* (PS–2). Illus. 1997, Orchard LB $16.99 (0-531-33004-4). 32pp. When Amber drapes her aunt's cloth from Ghana around herself, she pretends she is an Ashanti princess. (Rev: BCCB 6/97; BL 2/15/97; SLJ 7/97)

3812 Molnar-Fenton, Stephan. *An Mei's Strange and Wondrous Journey* (K–3). Illus. by Vivienne Flesher. 1998, DK $15.95 (0-7894-2477-0). 32pp. An Mei, a Chinese baby left by her mother at an orphanage, describes her experiences when she is adopted by a Caucasian mother and father. (Rev: BL 4/15/98; HBG 10/98; SLJ 4/98)

3813 Monk, Isabell. *Family* (PS–2). Illus. by Janice L. Porter. 2001, Carolrhoda $15.95 (1-57505-485-X). 32pp. Celebrates the fun and food of an African American family reunion (complete with recipes). (Rev: BL 2/15/01)

3814 Monk, Isabell. *Hope* (K–3). Illus. by Janice L. Porter. 1999, Carolrhoda LB $15.95 (1-57505-230-X). 32pp. Hope's great aunt Poogee tells the little girl that she should be proud of her biracial background and that her white father and African American mother represent two important cultures. (Rev: HBG 10/99; SLJ 6/99)

3815 Mora, Pat. *Pablo's Tree* (PS–3). Illus. by Cecily Lang. 1994, Macmillan paper $16.00 (0-02-767401-0). 32pp. Ever since his daughter adopted young Pablo, grandfather decorates a tree on the anniversary of the boy's arrival. (Rev: BCCB 9/94; BL 11/1/94; HB 11–12/94)

3816 Morris, Ann. *The Baby Book* (PS). Illus. Series: World's Family. 1995, Silver Burdett $13.95 (0-382-24698-5); paper $5.95 (0-382-24700-0). 32pp. Full-color photographs show infants from around the world, with ethnic backgrounds explained at the back of the book. (Rev: BL 2/15/96) [305.23]

3817 Morris, Ann. *The Daddy Book* (PS). Illus. Series: The World's Family. 1995, Silver Burdett $13.95 (0-382-24695-0); paper $5.95 (0-382-24697-7). 32pp. In this photograph album, all kinds of daddies engage in everyday activities, like going fishing and telling stories. (Rev: BL 2/15/96; SLJ 5/96) [306]

3818 Morris, Ann. *Loving* (PS–2). Illus. by Ken Heyman. 1990, Lothrop LB $15.93 (0-688-06341-1). 32pp. Clear photos focus on children, their families, and their pets. Also use: *On the Go* (1990). (Rev: BL 1/1/91; SLJ 1/91) [306.7]

3819 Morris, Ann. *The Mommy Book* (PS). Illus. Series: The World's Family. 1995, Silver Burdett LB $22.00 (0-382-24693-4); paper $5.95 (0-382-24694-2). 32pp. Photographs from around the world depict mothers and children in a variety of shared experiences. (Rev: BL 2/15/96; SLJ 5/96) [306]

3820 Muldoon, Kathleen M. *Princess Pooh* (K–4). Illus. by Linda Shute. 1989, Whitman LB $14.95 (0-8075-6627-6). A young girl is jealous of her wheelchair-bound older sister because of the attention she receives. (Rev: SLJ 11/89)

3821 Naylor, Phyllis Reynolds. *Sweet Strawberries* (PS–3). Illus. by Rosalind Charney Kaye. 1999, Atheneum $16.00 (0-689-81338-4). A long-married, middle-aged couple quarrel because the wife wants some strawberries and the husband thinks they are too expensive. (Rev: BCCB 3/99; BL 4/1/99; HBG 10/99; SLJ 5/99)

3822 Newman, Leslea. *Remember That* (PS–3). Illus. by Karen Ritz. 1996, Clarion $14.95 (0-395-66156-0). 32pp. A Jewish child recalls her grandmother Bubbe and the many joyful experiences they have shared. (Rev: BL 2/1/96; SLJ 3/96)

3823 Nodar, Carmen Santiago. *Abuelita's Paradise* (K–2). Illus. by Diane Paterson. 1992, Whitman LB $14.95 (0-8075-0129-8). 32pp. Marita remembers the stories that her grandmother, now dead, told her about growing up in Puerto Rico. (Rev: BL 9/15/92; SLJ 9/92)

3824 Nolen, Jerdine. *In My Momma's Kitchen* (PS–3). Illus. by Colin Bootman. 1999, Lothrop LB $15.93 (0-688-12761-4). 32pp. A loving portrait of an African American family whose activities often center around Mamma's kitchen. (Rev: BCCB 6/99; BL 2/15/99; HBG 10/99; SLJ 5/99)

3825 Numeroff, Laura. *What Grandmas Do Best/ What Grandpas Do Best* (PS–K). Illus. by Lynn Munsinger. 2000, Simon & Schuster $14.00 (0-689-80552-7). 40pp. This is an upside-down book that if read one way shows children happy with their grandmothers and, when turned over, shows similar scenes with grandfathers. (Rev: BL 11/15/00; HBG 3/01; SLJ 10/00)

3826 O'Callahan, Jay. *Orange Cheeks* (PS–2). Illus. by Patricia Raine. 1993, Peachtree $15.95 (1-56145-073-1). 40pp. A young boy tries not to create trouble when he visits his grandmother. (Rev: BL 7/93)

3827 Older, Effin. *My Two Grandmothers* (PS–1). Illus. by Nancy Hayashi. 2000, Harcourt $16.00 (0-15-200785-7). 32pp. Lily loves her two very different grandmothers and spends Hanukkah with Bubbe Silver in her big city apartment and Christmas with Grammy Lane on her farm. (Rev: BL 10/15/00; HBG 3/01; SLJ 10/00)

3828 Ormerod, Jan. *Who's Whose?* (K–3). Illus. 1998, Lothrop LB $15.93 (0-688-14679-1). 32pp. A delightful, breezy account of the members of three families, their activities, and how they help one another. (Rev: BL 3/15/98; HBG 10/98; SLJ 4/98)

3829 Ostrow, Vivian. *My Brother Is from Outer Space: The Book of Proof* (K–3). Illus. by Eric Brace. 1996, Albert Whitman LB $14.95 (0-8075-5325-5). 32pp. Alex is convinced that his young brother is really an alien from outer space. (Rev: BCCB 5/96; BL 4/1/96; SLJ 6/96)

3830 Ovenell-Carter, Julie. *The Butterflies' Promise* (K–3). Illus. by Kitty Macaulay. 1999, Annick LB $15.95 (1-55037-567-9); paper $5.95 (1-55037-566-0). When Milly's grandfather goes to a nursing home, the little girl thinks of a way to bring his beloved garden to him. (Rev: HBG 10/99; SLJ 10/99)

3831 Pak, Soyung. *Dear Juno* (PS–2). Illus. by Susan Kathleen Hartung. 1999, Viking $15.99 (0-670-88252-6). 32pp. Although he can't read Korean, Juno is able to piece together clues about the contents of the letter he has received from his grandmother in Seoul. (Rev: BCCB 1/00; BL 11/15/99; HBG 3/00; SLJ 12/99)

3832 Paradis, Susan. *My Daddy* (PS–1). Illus. 1998, Front Street $15.95 (1-886910-30-8). 32pp. A wonderful picture book about a boy's admiration for his father, who can perform such wonders as riding a two-wheeled bike and finding his way home from work alone. (Rev: BL 7/98*; HBG 10/98; SLJ 1/99)

3833 Patrick, Denise Lewis. *Red Dancing Shoes* (PS–2). Illus. by James E. Ransome. 1993, Morrow $15.89 (0-688-10393-6). Grandma gives her young granddaughter a new pair of dancing shoes. (Rev: BL 3/1/93; SLJ 3/93)

3834 Paxton, Tom. *The Marvelous Toy* (PS–K). Illus. by Elizabeth Sayles. 1996, Morrow $15.93 (0-688-13880-2). This song tells of a boy's pleasure at receiving an unusual gift from his father and, much later, the happiness he gets passing it on to his son. (Rev: SLJ 8/96)

3835 Pegram, Laura. *Daughter's Day Blues* (PS–3). Illus. by Cornelius Van Wright and Ying-Hwa. 2000, Dial $15.99 (0-8037-1557-9). 32pp. Phyllis Mae's mother and grandmother prepare a party to celebrate the first Daughter's Day, a tribute to Phyllis Mae. (Rev: BL 2/15/00; HBG 10/00; SLJ 4/00)

3836 Pellegrini, Nina. *Families Are Different* (PS–3). Illus. 1991, Holiday LB $16.95 (0-8234-0887-6). 32pp. Two adopted Korean girls gradually adjust to their new American family. (Rev: BL 12/15/91; SLJ 10/91)

3837 Petersen, P. J. *Some Days, Other Days* (K–2). Illus. by Diane De Groat. 1994, Scribners paper $14.95 (0-684-19595-X). Jimmy is afraid that he is going to have one of his bad days until mother starts it off well with a big hug. (Rev: SLJ 12/94)

3838 Pittman, Helena Clare. *Uncle Phil's Diner* (PS–2). Illus. 1998, Carolrhoda $14.95 (1-57505-083-8). 32pp. As Ruthie and her father trudge through the snow to get to Uncle Phil's diner for pancakes, they remember all the fun they had the previous summer. (Rev: BL 1/1–15/99; HBG 3/99)

3839 Polacco, Patricia. *The Keeping Quilt* (PS–2). Illus. by author. 1988, Simon & Schuster $16.00 (0-671-64963-9). 32pp. The quilt serves as a link between generations of a family. (Rev: BL 12/1/88; SLJ 10/88)

3840 Polacco, Patricia. *My Ol' Man* (1–3). Illus. 1995, Putnam $16.99 (0-399-22822-5). 32pp. Two youngsters enjoy the stories that their traveling-salesman father tells when he comes home. (Rev: BL 4/1/95; SLJ 5/95)

3841 Polacco, Patricia. *My Rotten Redheaded Older Brother* (K–3). Illus. 1994, Simon & Schuster $16.00 (0-671-72751-6). 30pp. A young girl engages in a fierce rivalry with her brother in spite of an underlying love. (Rev: BL 9/15/94; SLJ 10/94*)

3842 Polacco, Patricia. *Thunder Cake* (PS–3). Illus. 1990, Putnam $15.95 (0-399-22231-6). 32pp. A grandmother helps her young granddaughter conquer her fears of electrical storms by eating Thunder Cake. (Rev: BCCB 3/90; BL 2/15/90*; HB 3–4/90; SLJ 3/90*)

3843 Pomerantz, Charlotte. *The Chalk Doll* (PS–1). Illus. by Frane Lessac. 1989, HarperCollins paper $6.95 (0-06-443333-1). 32pp. Rose is sick, and

Mother tells her stories of her Jamaican girlhood. (Rev: BL 5/15/89; HB 7–8/89)

3844 Porter-Gaylord, Laurel. *I Love My Daddy Because . . .* (PS–K). Illus. by Ashley Wolff. 1991, Dutton $7.99 (0-525-44624-9). 24pp. Reasons for loving one's father are illustrated through both human and animal examples. A companion volume is *I Love My Mommy Because . . .* (Rev: BCCB 2/91; BL 4/15/91; SLJ 1/92)

3845 Prigger, Mary Skillings. *Aunt Minnie McGranahan* (PS–2). Illus. by Betsy Lewin. 1999, Clarion $15.00 (0-395-82270-X). 32pp. Minnie McGranahan accepts nine orphaned nieces and nephews into her household, and although she regulates their schedules, there is always time for fun. (Rev: BCCB 5/99; BL 5/1/99; HBG 10/99; SLJ 5/99)

3846 Pryor, Bonnie. *The Dream Jar* (K–4). Illus. by Mark Graham. 1996, Morrow LB $15.93 (0-688-13062-3). 32pp. In turn-of-the-century New York City, a young immigrant girl helps her family by teaching them English. (Rev: BL 3/1/96; HB 7–8/96; SLJ 3/96)

3847 Quinlan, Patricia. *My Dad Takes Care of Me* (PS–2). Illus. by Vlasta Van Kampen. 1987, Firefly LB $15.95 (0-920303-79-X); paper $4.95 (0-920303-76-5). 24pp. Although a little boy loves his father, he just can't get used to Dad's being home while Mother works. (Rev: BL 7/87; SLJ 9/87)

3848 Rabe, Berniece. *Where's Chimpy?* (PS–2). Illus. by Diane Schmidt. 1988, Whitman LB $14.95 (0-8075-8928-4); paper $6.95 (0-8075-8927-6). 32pp. A little girl with Down's syndrome asks for Chimpy, her missing toy monkey, before she can go to sleep. (Rev: BCCB 10/88; BL 9/1/88; SLJ 12/88)

3849 Rahaman, Vashanti. *Read for Me, Mama* (PS–1). Illus. 1997, Boyds Mills $14.95 (1-56397-313-8). 32pp. An African American boy hopes that his mother, a hotel maid, will have time to read a story to him. (Rev: BCCB 3/97; BL 2/15/97; SLJ 4/97)

3850 Rand, Gloria. *The Cabin Key* (K–3). Illus. by Ted Rand. 1994, Harcourt $15.00 (0-15-213884-6). 32pp. A young girl tells about the wonderful things she loves about the family's log cabin in the mountains. (Rev: BCCB 10/94; BL 11/1/94; SLJ 11/94)

3851 Ransom, Candice. *We're Growing Together* (PS–1). Illus. by Virginia Wright-Frierson. 1993, Bradbury LB $14.95 (0-02-775666-1). 32pp. Two young sisters face problems when they adjust to their new home in the country with a stepfather. (Rev: BL 10/1/93)

3852 Regan, Dian C. *Daddies* (PS). Illus. by Mary Morgan. 1996, Scholastic $5.95 (0-590-47973-3). 32pp. Children engage in a variety of activities with their fathers. (Rev: BL 6/1–15/96; SLJ 7/96)

3853 Reid, Barbara. *The Party* (PS–3). Illus. 1999, Scholastic $15.95 (0-590-97801-2). 32pp. The narrator and her young sister are wary of going to a family gathering, but when the games start, so does the fun. (Rev: BL 5/1/99; HBG 10/99; SLJ 5/99)

3854 Reid, Margarette S. *The Button Box* (K–3). Illus. by Sarah Chamberlain. 1990, Dutton $14.99 (0-525-44590-0). 24pp. A boy imagines interesting stories behind the different buttons in his grandmother's button box. (Rev: BCCB 3/90; BL 4/15/90; SLJ 9/90)

3855 Reiser, Lynn. *Cherry Pies and Lullabies* (PS–1). Illus. 1998, Greenwillow $16.00 (0-688-13391-6). 40pp. A girl shows how four generations in her family have given and received love while continuing treasured family traditions. (Rev: BL 3/1/98; HB 5–6/98; HBG 10/98; SLJ 9/98)

3856 Richardson, Jean. *Thomas's Sitter* (PS–1). Illus. by Dawn Holmes. 1991, Macmillan LB $13.95 (0-02-776146-0). 32pp. Thomas discourages all applicants for his family's baby-sitter job until Dan, a young poet, appears. (Rev: BL 7/91; SLJ 9/91)

3857 Rockwell, Anne. *Pumpkin Day, Pumpkin Night* (PS–1). Illus. by Megan Halsey. 1999, Walker LB $16.85 (0-8027-8697-9). 32pp. A young boy and his mother carve a pumpkin face, bake pies, and toast pumpkin seeds in this engaging picture book. (Rev: BL 9/1/99; HBG 3/00; SLJ 10/99)

3858 Rockwell, Lizzy. *Hello Baby!* (PS–K). Illus. 1999, Crown $15.00 (0-517-80011-X). 32pp. A preschooler prepares for his new sibling and learns how the baby is growing inside his mother. (Rev: BL 3/15/99; HBG 10/99; SLJ 6/99)

3859 Roe, Eileen. *Con Mi Hermano/With My Brother* (PS–K). Illus. by Robert Casilla. 1991, Macmillan LB $14.00 (0-02-777373-6). A bilingual book about the good times a boy spends with his older brother. (Rev: SLJ 4/91)

3860 Rogers, Emma, and Paul Rogers. *Our House* (K–2). Illus. by Priscilla Lamont. 1993, Candlewick $14.95 (1-56402-134-3). 40pp. This picture book tells of four incidents that occurred in the same house over a period of 200 years. (Rev: BL 4/1/93; SLJ 8/93)

3861 Root, Phyllis. *What Baby Wants* (PS–K). Illus. by Jill Barton. 1998, Candlewick $15.99 (0-7636-0207-8). 40pp. Of all the family members, it is Little Brother who knows what Baby really wants in this picture book for the very young. (Rev: BCCB 1/99; BL 9/15/98; HBG 3/99; SLJ 9/98)

3862 Rosenberg, Liz. *The Silence in the Mountains* (1–3). Illus. by Chris K. Soentpiet. 1999, Orchard LB $16.99 (0-531-33084-2). 32pp. Iskander and his family must leave their war-torn country and find peace in America. (Rev: BL 2/1/99; HBG 10/99; SLJ 7/99)

3863 Ross, Lillian. *Buba Leah and Her Paper Children* (1–4). Illus. by Mary Morgan. 1991, Jewish Publication Soc. $17.95 (0-8276-0375-4). 32pp. The "paper children" to which Great-Aunt Buba Leah refers turn out to be her real children, who sailed to America to build a better life. (Rev: BL 1/1/92; SLJ 1/92)

3864 Russo, Marisabina. *The Big Brown Box* (PS–1). Illus. 2000, Greenwillow $15.95 (0-688-17096-X). 32pp. Sam uses a big brown box to imagine all sorts of objects and when his younger brother gets a smaller brown box the two pretend the boxes are space ships. (Rev: BL 5/1/00; HBG 10/00; SLJ 5/00)

3865 Russo, Marisabina. *Grandpa Abe* (PS–3). Illus. 1996, Greenwillow LB $14.93 (0-688-14098-X). 32pp. Sarah adjusts to the death of her beloved grandfather-by-marriage. (Rev: BL 5/15/96; HB 5–6/96; SLJ 7/96)

3866 Russo, Marisabina. *Hannah's Baby Sister* (K–3). Illus. by author. 1998, Greenwillow LB $14.93 (0-688-15832-3). 32pp. Hannah is disappointed when her mother has another boy, but when she holds him, she changes her mind. (Rev: HBG 3/99; SLJ 9/98)

3867 Russo, Marisabina. *A Visit to Oma* (PS–2). Illus. 1991, Greenwillow LB $13.88 (0-688-09624-7). 32pp. Celeste visits her great-grandmother, who does not speak English. (Rev: BL 4/15/91; HB 3–4/91; SLJ 7/91)

3868 Ryder, Joanne. *My Father's Hands* (PS–3). Illus. by Mark Graham. 1994, Morrow LB $15.93 (0-688-09190-3). 32pp. A little girl watches her father work the soil with his hands and is fascinated by the many tiny animals he finds in the garden. (Rev: BL 10/1/94; SLJ 9/94)

3869 Rylant, Cynthia. *The Relatives Came* (K–2). Illus. by Stephen Gammell. 1985, Macmillan LB $16.00 (0-02-777220-9). 32pp. Details abound in this telling of the day the relatives came — in an old station wagon — hugs, fun, and laughter. (Rev: BCCB 12/85; BL 10/15/85; SLJ 10/85)

3870 Saenz, Benjamin Alire. *A Gift from PapaDiego* (K–4). Illus. by Geronimo Garcia. 1998, Cinco Puntos paper $10.95 (0-938317-33-4). 40pp. Little Diego wants a Superman suit so he can fly to Mexico to visit with his beloved grandfather. When that fails, his disappointment is lessened by the news that his grandfather is coming to visit. (Rev: BL 5/1/98; HB 7–8/98)

3871 Saint James, Synthia. *Sunday* (PS–1). Illus. 1996, Albert Whitman LB $15.95 (0-8075-7658-1). 30pp. Two African American sisters and their parents spend a quiet Sunday with their grandparents. (Rev: BCCB 10/96; BL 11/15/96; SLJ 1/97)

3872 Sandburg, Carl. *The Huckabuck Family and How They Raised Popcorn in Nebraska and Quit and Came Back* (K–3). Illus. by David Small. 1999, Farrar $16.00 (0-374-33511-7). 40pp. This story, part of the author's *Rootabaga Stories,* tells of the Huckabuck family, their trials and tribulations, travels, and eventual return to their farm. (Rev: BCCB 9/99; BL 9/15/99; HB 9–10/99; HBG 3/00; SLJ 8/99)

3873 Sasso, Sandy Eisenberg. *For Heaven's Sake* (K–3). Illus. by Kathryn Kunz Finney. 1999, Jewish Lights $16.95 (1-58023-054-7). 32pp. Young Isaiah wonders where heaven is and discovers, through his wise grandmother, that it is all around you. (Rev: BL 10/1/99; SLJ 1/00)

3874 Say, Allen. *Grandfather's Journey* (PS–3). Illus. by author. 1993, Houghton $16.95 (0-395-57035-2). 32pp. An autobiographical story that chronicles the passages of generations of the author's family as they moved between Japan and the United States. Winner of the 1994 Caldecott Medal. (Rev: BL 7/93*; SLJ 9/98)

3875 Say, Allen. *The Lost Lake* (2–4). Illus. 1989, Houghton $16.00 (0-395-50933-5). 32pp. Realizing that he is not paying sufficient attention to his son, Dad takes him on a camping trip. (Rev: BCCB 1/90; BL 10/1/89; HB 1–2/90; SLJ 12/89*)

3876 Schaefer, Carole L. *The Copper Tin Cup* (PS–3). Illus. by Stan Fellows. 2000, Candlewick $15.99 (0-7636-0471-2). 32pp. Sammy Carl realizes that his favorite cup, made of copper and tin, is actually a family heirloom that has been used by different generations since his grandfather's older sister brought it from the old country. (Rev: BL 5/15/00; HBG 10/00; SLJ 5/00)

3877 Schaefer, Carole L. *Sometimes Moon* (PS–2). Illus. by Pierre Morgan. 1999, Crown LB $18.99 (0-517-70981-3). 32pp. A little girl named Selene, her family, and their activities are reminiscent of the Moon and its phases. (Rev: BL 8/99; HBG 3/00; SLJ 9/99)

3878 Schertle, Alice. *Down the Road* (PS–3). Illus. by E. B. Lewis. 1995, Harcourt $16.00 (0-15-276622-7). 40pp. Hetty accidentally breaks the eggs that she has been carefully carrying from the store for her family's breakfast. (Rev: BCCB 12/95; BL 9/15/95*; SLJ 4/96)

3879 Schindel, John. *Dear Daddy* (K–3). Illus. by Dorothy Donohue. 1995, Albert Whitman LB $13.95 (0-8075-1531-0). 32pp. Jesse longs to see his dad, who lives miles away. Finally, in a telephone conversation, they plan for a summer visit. (Rev: BL 5/1/95; SLJ 5/95)

3880 Schindel, John. *Frog Face: My Little Sister and Me* (PS–1). Illus. by Janet Delaney. 1998, Holt $14.95 (0-8050-5546-0). Photos show the conflicting emotions that a preschooler feels about her new baby sister: delighted one minute and jealous the next. (Rev: BL 11/1/98; HB 9–10/98; HBG 3/99; SLJ 11/98)

3881 Schlessinger, Laura C., and Martha L. Lambert. *Why Do You Love Me?* (PS–1). Illus. by Paul Meisel. 1999, HarperCollins $15.95 (0-06-027866-8). 40pp. A reassuring story in which a mother tells her young son that in spite of his mischievous behavior she still loves him. (Rev: HBG 10/99; SLJ 4/99)

3882 Schwartz, Amy. *A Teeny Tiny Baby* (PS–1). Illus. 1994, Orchard LB $17.99 (0-531-08668-2). 32pp. A teeny tiny baby tells about all the things he likes and dislikes about his status. (Rev: BCCB 9/94; BL 7/94*; SLJ 9/94*)

3883 Segal, Lore. *Tell Me a Mitzi* (K–2). Illus. by Harriet Pincus. 1982, Farrar paper $5.95 (0-374-47502-4). 40pp. Three hilarious stories about the antics of a city family: a mad trip to Grandma's house, coming down with a cold, and a meeting with the president.

3884 Selway, Martina. *Don't Forget to Write* (PS–2). Illus. 1992, Ideals $12.95 (0-8249-8543-5). 28pp. On a visit to Grandad's farm, Rosie writes letters daily to her mother. (Rev: BL 6/1/92; SLJ 8/92)

3885 Senisi, Ellen B. *For My Family, Love, Allie* (PS–2). Illus. 1998, Albert Whitman $14.95 (0-8075-2539-1). 30pp. In this photo-essay, young

Allie helps prepare a barbecue with her large, biracial, loving family. (Rev: BL 9/1/98; HBG 3/99; SLJ 12/98)

3886 Shannon, David. *No, David!* (PS–K). Illus. 1998, Scholastic $14.95 (0-590-93002-8). 32pp. It seems that everything young David does is met with a "No!" from his mother, but in spite of her criticism, he knows she loves him. (Rev: BCCB 9/98; BL 9/1/98; HBG 3/99; SLJ 8/98)

3887 Shannon, George. *This Is the Bird* (K–3). Illus. by David Soman. 1997, Houghton $15.95 (0-395-72037-0). 32pp. Eight generations of the women in a family are connected to each other by a family heirloom: a wooden carving of a bird. (Rev: BL 2/15/97; SLJ 4/97)

3888 Sharratt, Nick. *Snazzy Aunties* (PS). Illus. 1994, Candlewick $8.95 (1-56402-214-5). 24pp. A boy is visited by his seven eccentric aunts. (Rev: BL 6/1–15/94; SLJ 9/94)

3889 Sherkin-Langer, Ferne. *When Mommy Is Sick* (PS–2). Illus. by Kay Life. 1995, Albert Whitman $12.95 (1-8075-8894-6). 32pp. A first-person narrative about the emptiness a young girl feels when her mother is hospitalized. (Rev: BL 3/15/95; SLJ 5/95)

3890 Shields, Carol D. *Lucky Pennies and Hot Chocolate* (PS–2). Illus. by Hiroe Nakata. 2000, Dutton $13.99 (0-525-46450-6). 32pp. A little boy is looking forward to a visit from his favorite person who turns out to be his grandfather. (Rev: BCCB 9/00; BL 8/00; HBG 3/01; SLJ 9/00)

3891 Shough, Carol Gandee. *All the Mamas: A True Love Story for Mothers and Daughters of All Ages* (K–2). Illus. 1998, Summerhouse $16.95 (1-887714-29-4). 32pp. The never-ending cycle of mother love is traced in one family as a contemporary mother holds and kisses her baby, just as her mother did to her and just as preceding generations of mothers held and kissed their babies. (Rev: BL 8/98; SLJ 9/98)

3892 Shough, Carol Gandee. *All the Papas: A True Love Story for Fathers and Their Children* (K–4). Illus. by author. 1999, Summerhouse $16.95 (1-887714-36-7). 32pp. Based on the author's family history, this book pictures eight generations of fathers and their loving relationships with their families. (Rev: SLJ 7/99)

3893 Showers, Paul. *The Listening Walk* (K–2). Illus. by Aliki. 1991, HarperCollins LB $15.89 (0-06-021638-7). A boy and his father listen to the sounds around them as they walk. (Rev: SLJ 7/91)

3894 Shulevitz, Uri. *The Treasure* (K–2). Illus. by author. 1979, Farrar $16.00 (0-374-37740-5); paper $5.95 (0-374-47955-0). 32pp. A man discovers that the most valuable things in life are usually found at home.

3895 Shute, Linda. *How I Named the Baby* (K–3). Illus. 1993, Whitman LB $14.95 (0-8075-3417-X). 32pp. During the nine-month wait for the baby to be born, all the members of the family suggest various names depending on the season. (Rev: BL 6/1–15/93; SLJ 7/93)

3896 Singer, Marilyn. *The One and Only Me* (PS–K). Illus. by Nicole Rubel. 2000, HarperFestival $9.95

(0-694-01279-3). A little girl explains how she is like various members of her extended family in this charming family story illustrated with brightly colored cartoons. (Rev: HBG 10/00; SLJ 7/00)

3897 Slier, Deborah. *Hello Baby* (PS). Illus. 1988, Checkerboard $2.95 (1-56288-087-X). 12pp. A board book that shows basic actions, such as sitting and crying, for the toddler. Also use: *Baby's Words; Busy Baby* (both 1988). (Rev: BCCB 7–8/88; BL 7/88)

3898 Smalls, Irene. *Dawn and the Round To-It* (PS–1). Illus. by Tyrone Geter. 1994, Simon & Schuster paper $15.00 (0-671-87166-8). 28pp. When Dawn is promised by family members that they will play with her when they get around to it, she misunderstands and draws her own "round to-it." (Rev: BL 7/94; SLJ 9/94)

3899 Smalls, Irene. *Kevin and His Dad* (PS–1). Illus. by Michael Hays. 1999, Little, Brown $15.95 (0-316-79899-1). 32pp. An African American boy and his dad spend a day together — first helping around the house, then playing baseball, and going to a movie. (Rev: BCCB 5/99; BL 2/15/99; HBG 10/99; SLJ 5/99)

3900 Smythe, Anne. *Islands* (K–2). Illus. by Laszlo Gal. 1996, Douglas & McIntyre $14.95 (0-88899-238-6). 32pp. A mother and a daughter skate across a frozen lake to three small islands and examine wildlife in this quiet picture book. (Rev: BL 12/1/96)

3901 Snyder, Carol. *One Up, One Down* (PS–K). Illus. by Maxie Chambliss. 1995, Simon & Schuster $15.00 (0-689-31828-6). 32pp. A little girl helps her parents take care of twin baby brothers until they are able to walk. (Rev: BL 6/1–15/95; SLJ 5/95)

3902 Soto, Gary. *Big Bushy Mustache* (PS–1). Illus. by Joe Cepeda. 1998, Random LB $17.99 (0-679-98030-X). 32pp. In the Cinco de Mayo play, Ricky gets to wear a fake mustache, just like his father's, but he loses it on the way home to show him. (Rev: BL 6/1–15/98; HBG 10/98; SLJ 9/98)

3903 Spinelli, Eileen. *When Mama Comes Home Tonight* (PS–1). Illus. by Jane Dyer. 1998, Simon & Schuster $14.00 (0-689-81065-2). 32pp. A touching picture book that describes the activities that a mother and child engage in when the two are reunited after Mother gets home from work. (Rev: BL 7/98*; HBG 3/99; SLJ 11/98)

3904 Steptoe, John. *Baby Says* (PS). Illus. by author. 1988, Lothrop LB $15.89 (0-688-07424-3). 32pp. An almost wordless picture book catching the exchange between a baby and a big brother. (Rev: BL 4/1/88; HB 7–8/88; SLJ 3/88)

3905 Steptoe, John. *Stevie* (PS–2). Illus. by author. 1969, HarperCollins paper $6.95 (0-06-443122-3). 32pp. A small African American boy eloquently expresses his resentment at having to share his possessions and mother with a temporary younger boarder who becomes "kinda like a little brother"; illustrated in bold line and color.

3906 Stevenson, Harvey. *Grandpa's House* (PS–1). Illus. by author. 1994, Hyperion LB $15.49 (1-56282-589-5). A simple text is used with effective

pictures to convey the fine time young Woody has during a visit with his grandfather. (Rev: SLJ 6/94)

3907 Stiles, Martha Bennett. *Island Magic* (K–2). Illus. by Daniel San Souci. 1999, Simon & Schuster $16.00 (0-689-80588-8). 32pp. A quiet story about a young boy named David who helps his grandfather adjust to the move from his farm to live with David's family. (Rev: BL 2/1/00; HBG 3/00; SLJ 1/00)

3908 Stilz, Carol C. *Grandma Buffalo, May and Me* (K–3). Illus. by Constance R. Bergum. 1995, Sasquatch $14.95 (1-57061-015-0). 32pp. Poppy visits parts of Montana where her great-grandmother once lived and does the same things her ancestor did, like plant an apple tree and feed the buffalo. (Rev: BL 10/1/95; SLJ 12/95)

3909 Suen, Anastasia. *Window Music* (PS). Illus. by Wade Zahares. 1998, Viking $15.99 (0-670-87287-3). A beautifully illustrated story of a girl and her mother and the rail journey they take from her grandmother's house to their big city home, where her father awaits them. (Rev: HB 11–12/98; HBG 3/99; SLJ 12/98)

3910 Sweeney, Joan. *Me and My Family Tree* (PS–2). Illus. by Annette Cable. 1999, Crown $13.00 (0-517-70966-X). 28pp. Using her family tree as an example, a little girl diagrams her family and finds her place within it. (Rev: BL 8/99; HBG 10/99; SLJ 6/99) [929]

3911 Taulbert, Clifton L. *Little Cliff and the Porch People* (PS–3). Illus. by E. B. Lewis. 1999, Dial LB $15.89 (0-8037-2175-7). 32pp. Little Cliff, living with his grandparents in the Mississippi Delta during the 1950s, goes from house to house, gathering the ingredients for his grandmother's famous candied potatoes. (Rev: BCCB 3/99; BL 2/15/99; HBG 10/99; SLJ 3/99)

3912 Taylor, Ann. *Baby Dance* (PS). Illus. by Marjorie van Heerden. Series: Harper Growing Tree. 1999, HarperFestival $5.95 (0-694-01206-8). In this board book, an African American dad and his baby daughter play to a series of catchy rhymes. (Rev: BCCB 5/99; SLJ 3/99)

3913 Thiesing, Lisa. *Me and You: A Mother-Daughter Album* (PS–K). Illus. 1998, Hyperion LB $15.49 (0-7868-2338-0). 24pp. A mother places her black-and-white childhood photos opposite her daughter's color snapshots, providing an interesting contrast that reveals similarities and differences in this photo-album picture book. (Rev: BL 7/98; HBG 10/98; SLJ 7/98)

3914 Thomas, Elizabeth. *Green Beans* (PS–2). Illus. by Vicki Jo Redenbaugh. 1992, Carolrhoda LB $15.95 (0-87614-708-2). 32pp. Gramma, who is trying too hard to make her green beans grow, lets granddaughter Dorothea take over. (Rev: BCCB 2/93; BL 9/15/92; SLJ 1/93)

3915 Thomas, Jane Resh. *Saying Good-bye to Grandma* (2–4). Illus. by Marcia Sewall. 1988, Houghton paper $7.95 (0-395-54779-2). 40pp. Seven-year-old Suzie attends Grandma's funeral. (Rev: BL 10/15/88; HB 9–10/88; SLJ 2/89)

3916 Thomas, Naturi. *Uh-oh! It's Mama's Birthday!* (PS–3). Illus. by Keinyo White. 1997, Albert Whitman LB $13.95 (0-8075-8268-9). 24pp. An African American boy gives his mother what she really wants on her birthday: a big hug. (Rev: BL 2/15/97; HB 3–4/97; SLJ 5/97)

3917 Thompson, Mary. *Gran's Bees* (PS–2). Illus. by Donna Peterson. 1996, Millbrook LB $21.90 (1-56294-652-8). 32pp. Jessie, her dad, and her grandmother harvest the summer's last honey on Gran's farm. (Rev: BL 2/15/96; SLJ 4/96)

3918 Thompson, Mary. *My Brother Matthew* (K–4). Illus. 1992, Woodbine $14.95 (0-933149-47-6). 28pp. The family member who adjusts best to the baby who is born with physical problems is young David. (Rev: BL 2/15/93; SLJ 6/92)

3919 Tiffault, Benette W. *A Quilt for Elizabeth* (1–4). Illus. by Mary McConnell. 1992, Centering paper $8.95 (1-56123-034-0). After Elizabeth accepts her father's death, she and her grandmother begin a quilt using patches of his clothing. (Rev: SLJ 8/92)

3920 Tompert, Ann. *Will You Come Back for Me?* (PS). Illus. by Robin Kramer. 1988, Whitman LB $14.95 (0-8075-9112-2); paper $5.95 (0-8075-9113-0). 32pp. Her mother must go to work and the little girl must go to day care, but she worries that her mother won't come back for her. (Rev: BCCB 12/88; BL 11/1/88; SLJ 1/89)

3921 Torres, Leyla. *Liliana's Grandmothers* (PS–2). Illus. 1998, Farrar $16.00 (0-374-35105-8). 32pp. Liliana compares the lives of her two grandmothers — one lives nearby in America and the other lives in another country and speaks only Spanish. (Rev: BL 7/98; HBG 3/99; SLJ 3/99)

3922 Tunnell, Michael O. *Mailing May* (K–3). Illus. by Ted Rand. 1997, Morrow LB $15.89 (0-688-12879-3). 32pp. Unable to afford a rail ticket, May's father sends her parcel post to visit her grandmother. (Rev: BL 8/97; HB 9–10/97; HBG 3/98; SLJ 9/97)

3923 Turner, Ann. *Through Moon and Stars and Night Skies* (PS–2). Illus. by James G. Hale. 1990, HarperCollins LB $15.89 (0-06-026190-0). 32pp. An Asian boy recalls all of the steps in being adopted into his happy American home. (Rev: BL 5/15/90; HB 5–6/90; SLJ 5/90)

3924 Turner, Barbara J. *A Little Bit of Rob* (1–3). Illus. by Marni Backer. 1996, Albert Whitman LB $14.95 (0-8075-4577-5). 32pp. A family tries unsuccessfully to forget the death of a son by going on a crabbing expedition. (Rev: BL 10/15/96; SLJ 12/96)

3925 Uff, Caroline. *Hello, Lulu* (PS–1). Illus. 1999, Walker $14.95 (0-8027-8712-6). 24pp. A multiracial family and their activities are introduced in this story about little Lulu and her day. (Rev: BL 9/1/99; HBG 3/00; SLJ 9/99)

3926 Van Leeuwen, Jean. *The Tickle Stories* (PS–2). Illus. by Mary Whyte. 1998, Dial $15.99 (0-8037-2048-3). 32pp. At bedtime, a grandfather tells his grandchildren three tall tales about life on the family farm when he was growing up. (Rev: BL 5/1/98; HBG 10/98; SLJ 7/98)

3927 Viorst, Judith. *Alexander and the Terrible, Horrible, No Good, Very Bad Day* (K–3). Illus. by Ray Cruz. 1972, Macmillan LB $14.00 (0-689-30072-7); paper $4.99 (0-689-71173-5). Alexander wakes up to a bad day and things get progressively worse as the hours wear on, until he thinks he may escape it all and go to Australia.

3928 Viorst, Judith. *Alexander, Who's Not (Do You Hear Me? I Mean It!) Going to Move* (PS–3). Illus. by Robin P. Glasser. 1995, Simon & Schuster LB $15.00 (0-689-31958-4). 42pp. Alexander of bad-day fame, faces another crisis when he adamantly refuses to move to the family's new home. (Rev: BCCB 11/95; BL 8/95*; SLJ 10/95*)

3929 Viorst, Judith. *I'll Fix Anthony* (PS–3). Illus. by Arnold Lobel. 1969, Macmillan paper $4.99 (0-689-71202-2). 32pp. A young boy has a field day planning revenge on an older brother.

3930 Waboose, Jan B. *Firedancers* (1–4). Illus. by C. J. Taylor. 2000, Stoddart $14.95 (0-7737-3138-5). 32pp. A young Ojibwa girl visits Smooth Rock Island at night and joins her grandmother as a Firedancer. (Rev: BL 7/00)

3931 Waddell, Martin. *Rosie's Babies* (PS). Illus. by Penny Dale. 1999, Candlewick $15.99 (0-7636-0718-5). While her mother takes care of her new baby, Rosie, age four, also takes care of her family, a stuffed toy rabbit and a bear. (Rev: HBG 10/99; SLJ 3/99)

3932 Waddell, Martin. *When the Teddy Bears Came* (PS–K). Illus. by Penny Dale. 1995, Candlewick $15.99 (1-56402-529-2). 32pp. When baby comes, all the friends and family bring teddy bears as gifts. (Rev: BL 8/95; SLJ 6/95*)

3933 Wahl, Jan. *Mabel Ran Away with the Toys* (PS–2). Illus. by Liza Woodruff. 2000, Charlesbridge $16.95 (1-58089-059-8); paper $6.95 (1-58089-067-9). Little Mabel has problems adjusting when a new baby disrupts her schedule. (Rev: HBG 3/01; SLJ 9/00)

3934 Wallace, Ian. *Duncan's Way* (2–4). Illus. 2000, DK $15.95 (0-7894-2679-X). 32pp. When Duncan's father, a Newfoundland fisherman, becomes unemployed, the boy persuades him to convert their boat into a floating bakery that makes regular deliveries. (Rev: BL 2/15/00; HBG 3/01; SLJ 3/00)

3935 Wardlaw, Lee. *Saturday Night Jamboree* (PS–3). Illus. by Barry Root. 2000, Dial $15.99 (0-8037-2189-7). 32pp. A little girl enjoys the babysitters she has when her parents go out dancing, but the best times are when Mama and Daddy do their dancing at home. (Rev: BCCB 11/00; BL 12/15/00; HBG 3/01; SLJ 9/00)

3936 Wellington, Monica, and Andrew Kupfer. *Night City* (PS–3). Illus. by Monica Wellington. 1998, Dutton $14.99 (0-525-45948-0). 32pp. An imaginatively illustrated picture book that describes the activities in a city, such as baking and fire fighting, that occur after children go to bed. (Rev: BL 7/98*; HBG 10/98; SLJ 7/98)

3937 Weninger, Brigitte. *Special Delivery* (PS–). Trans. from German by J. Alison James. Illus. by Alexander Reichstein. 2000, North-South $15.95 (0-7358-1318-3). In this flap book, Mother receives a surprise gift in the mail and it turns out to be a baby. (Rev: HBG 3/01; SLJ 12/00)

3938 Weston, Martha. *Apple Juice Tea* (PS–K). Illus. 1994, Clarion $14.95 (0-395-65480-7). 32pp. Polly scarcely remembers her grandmother; but when they are reunited, they have a great time together. (Rev: BL 11/1/94; SLJ 9/94)

3939 Weston, Martha. *Bad Baby Brother* (K–2). Illus. 1997, Clarion $14.95 (0-395-72103-2). 32pp. In spite of all her overtures of friendship, Tessa finds that her new baby brother doesn't respond to her. (Rev: BL 4/15/97; SLJ 6/97)

3940 Whitman, Candace. *Now It Is Morning* (PS–K). Illus. 1999, Farrar $15.00 (0-374-35527-4). 32pp. An attractive picture book that traces the morning activities of three families in different settings — one on a farm, one in a town, and another in a big city. (Rev: BL 2/15/99; HBG 10/99; SLJ 3/99)

3941 Whybrow, Ian. *A Baby for Grace* (PS–1). Illus. by Christian Birmingham. 1998, Kingfisher $14.95 (0-7534-5142-5). 32pp. Everything that a young girl tries to do to be helpful around the house, including holding the new baby, is greeted with the same response, "No, Grace." (Rev: BL 10/1/98; HBG 3/99; SLJ 1/99)

3942 Wild, Margaret. *All the Better to See You With!* (K–3). Illus. by Pat Reynolds. 1993, Whitman LB $14.95 (0-8075-0284-7). 32pp. A girl who is always outshone by her four brothers and sisters gains attention when she needs glasses. (Rev: BL 7/93; SLJ 8/93)

3943 Wild, Margaret. *Big Cat Dreaming* (K–3). Illus. by Anne Spudvilas. 1997, Annick $16.95 (1-55037-493-1). 32pp. Two grandchildren enjoy visiting their grandmother, partly because of her wonderful pets. (Rev: BL 2/1/98; SLJ 2/98)

3944 Wild, Margaret. *Our Granny* (PS–1). Illus. by Julie Vivas. 1994, Ticknor $14.95 (0-395-67023-3). 32pp. All kinds of grandmothers from the glamorous and kinky to cuddly and plain are celebrated in this lively picture book. (Rev: BCCB 5/94; BL 1/15/94*; HB 5–6/94; SLJ 4/94*)

3945 Wild, Margaret. *Remember Me* (PS–2). Illus. by Dee Huxley. 1995, Albert Whitman LB $14.95 (0-8075-6934-8). 32pp. In spite of her increasing forgetfulness, Grandma remembers the good times she spent with Ellie, her granddaughter. (Rev: BL 2/1/96; SLJ 1/96)

3946 Willhoite, Michael. *Daddy's Roommate* (PS–2). Illus. 1990, Alyson paper $10.95 (1-55583-118-4). 32pp. After his parents' divorce, a young boy finds that his father has a male partner and on weekends the boy enjoys visiting the two of them. (Rev: BCCB 2/91; BL 3/1/91; SLJ 4/91)

3947 Willhoite, Michael. *Daddy's Wedding* (PS–3). Illus. 1996, Alyson $15.95 (1-55583-350-0). 32pp. Nick is best man when his father marries his male roommate. A sequel to *Daddy's Roommate* (1991). (Rev: BCCB 6/96; BL 7/96)

3948 Williams, Vera B. *A Chair for My Mother* (PS–2). Illus. by author. 1982, Greenwillow $15.93 (0-688-00915-8). 32pp. After fire destroys their home, Rose and her mother and grandmother save to buy a nice new chair. Two sequels are: *Something Special for Me* (1983); *Music, Music for Everyone* (1984).

3949 Williams, Vera B. *Lucky Song* (PS–K). Illus. 1997, Greenwillow $14.93 (0-688-14460-8). 24pp. Evie is a lucky girl because all of her wants and needs are satisfied by her loving family. (Rev: BL 10/1/97*; HB 9–10/97; HBG 3/98; SLJ 8/97*)

3950 Williams-Garcia, Rita. *Catching the Wild Waiyuuzee* (PS–1). Illus. by Mike Reed. 2000, Simon & Schuster $16.00 (0-689-82601-X). 32pp. The elusive creature called the Wild Waiyuuzee who runs away easily, is actually an African American child who is avoiding having her mother comb and braid her hair. (Rev: BCCB 12/00; BL 11/15/00; HBG 3/01; SLJ 11/00)

3951 Winch, John. *Keeping Up with Grandma* (PS–3). Illus. 2000, Holiday $16.95 (0-8234-1563-5). 32pp. Grandma wants to start mountain climbing, whitewater canoeing, and hot-air ballooning but she and Grandpa later decide that their usual quiet life is better. (Rev: BL 11/15/00; HBG 3/01; SLJ 11/00)

3952 Wing, Natasha L. *Jalapeno Bagels* (PS–2). Illus. by Robert Casilla. 1996, Simon & Schuster $15.00 (0-689-80530-6). 32pp. Pablo, who comes from a racially mixed family, finds his life is enriched by both cultures. (Rev: BL 6/1–15/96; SLJ 7/96)

3953 Winter, Susan. *I Can* (PS–K). Illus. by author. 1993, DK $9.95 (1-56458-197-7). An older brother tells of his accomplishments and compares them to those of his younger sister. The sister's side of the story is told in a companion volume, *Me, Too* (1993). (Rev: SLJ 2/94)

3954 Winthrop, Elizabeth. *I'm the Boss!* (PS–1). Illus. by Mary Morgan. 1994, Holiday LB $15.95 (0-8234-1113-3). 32pp. Julia is tired of being bossed around and wants her chance to be a dictator. (Rev: BL 5/1/94; SLJ 7/94)

3955 Winthrop, Elizabeth. *Promises* (1–3). Illus. by Betsy Lewin. 2000, Clarion $16.00 (0-395-82272-6). 32pp. Sarah's mother is very ill with cancer and the young girl misses the good times they had before she became sick. (Rev: BL 6/1–15/00; HBG 10/00; SLJ 6/00)

3956 Wittmann, Patricia. *Scrabble Creek* (1–3). Illus. by Nancy Poydar. 1993, Macmillan LB $14.95 (0-02-793225-7). 32pp. Too old to sleep with her parents, a young girl must move to the bunkhouse at her family's summer camp. (Rev: BCCB 3/93; BL 3/15/93; SLJ 5/93)

3957 Wood, Douglas. *Grandad's Prayers of the Earth* (K–3). Illus. by P. J. Lynch. 1999, Candlewick $16.99 (0-7636-0660-X). 32pp. A boy and his grandfather talk about prayer, and after the old man's death, the boy remembers his gentle ways and his loving faith. (Rev: BL 12/1/99; HBG 3/00; SLJ 1/00)

3958 Woodson, Jacqueline. *We Had a Picnic This Sunday Past* (PS–3). Illus. by Diane Greenseid. 1998, Hyperion LB $15.49 (0-7868-2192-2). 32pp. Young Teeka describes her African American family's Sunday picnic. (Rev: BCCB 9/98; BL 8/98; HBG 10/98; SLJ 5/98)

3959 Woodtor, Dee Parmer. *Big Meeting* (K–3). Illus. by Dolores Johnson. 1996, Simon & Schuster $16.00 (0-689-31993-9). 32pp. A celebration of a down-home family reunion is chronicled in this joyous book. (Rev: BL 9/1/96; SLJ 9/96)

3960 Wyse, Lois, and Molly Rose Goldman. *How to Take Your Grandmother to the Museum* (1–3). Illus. by Marie-Louise Gay. 1998, Workman $12.95 (0-7611-0990-0). 48pp. When a young boy discovers that his grandmother has never been to New York City's American Museum of Natural History, he takes her on his own special guided tour. (Rev: BL 1/1–15/99; HBG 3/99; SLJ 12/98)

3961 Yektai, Niki. *Triplets* (PS–2). Illus. 1998, Millbrook LB $21.40 (0-7613-0351-0). 32pp. This lively picture book explores the rivalry among three siblings and its humorous consequences. (Rev: BL 5/15/98; HBG 10/98; SLJ 8/98)

3962 Zagwyn, Deborah Turney. *Apple Batter* (K–3). Illus. 1999, Tricycle Pr. $14.95 (1-883672-92-9). 32pp. Loretta plants and cares for three apple trees while her young son develops an interest in baseball in this picture book that ends with both interests converging. (Rev: BL 1/1–15/00; HBG 3/00; SLJ 12/99)

3963 Zalben, Jane Breskin. *Beni's First Wedding* (K–3). Illus. by author. 1998, Holt $14.95 (0-8050-4846-4). In this story about a Jewish wedding in which Beni is the page boy and Sara the flower girl, many Jewish wedding customs are explained, and a recipe is given for a wedding cake. (Rev: HBG 10/98; SLJ 5/98)

3964 Zalben, Jane Breskin. *Pearl's Marigolds for Grandpa* (PS–2). Illus. 1997, Simon & Schuster paper $15.00 (0-689-80448-2). 32pp. When her grandfather dies, Pearl decides that one way to remember him is to plant some marigold seeds as the two always did in the past. (Rev: BL 11/1/97; HBG 3/98; SLJ 9/97)

3965 Zamorano, Ana. *Let's Eat!* (PS–2). Illus. by Julie Vivas. 1997, Scholastic $15.95 (0-590-13444-2). 32pp. A loving Spanish family enjoys Mama's food even more when she returns home from the hospital with baby Rosa. (Rev: BCCB 4/97; BL 5/15/97; SLJ 4/97*)

3966 Zapater, Beatriz M. *Fiesta!* (K–3). Illus. by Jose Ortega. 1993, Simon & Schuster paper $4.95 (0-671-79842-1). 26pp. Chucho and his family, from Colombia, plan a fiesta in their new home in America. (Rev: BL 3/15/93)

3967 Zemach, Harve. *Mommy, Buy Me a China Doll* (K–3). Illus. by Margot Zemach. 1989, Farrar paper $4.95 (0-374-45286-5). 32pp. This adaptation of the Ozark song tells how Eliza Lou and her mother make plans to buy a doll. A reissue.

3968 Ziefert, Harriet. *Clara Ann Cookie* (PS–1). Illus. by Emily Bolam. 1999, Houghton $15.00 (0-395-92324-7). 32pp. After waking, Clara Ann is in a terrible mood until Mom makes a game of getting dressed and preparing to face the world. (Rev: BL 3/1/99; HBG 10/99; SLJ 4/99)

3969 Ziefert, Harriet. *A New Coat for Anna* (K–3). Illus. by Anita Lobel. 1986, Knopf paper $6.99 (0-394-89861-3). 40pp. It's been a long time since Anna has had a new coat, and her mother vows to get one for her in this story of post-World War II Europe. (Rev: BCCB 3/87; BL 12/15/86; SLJ 12/86)

3970 Ziefert, Harriet. *Talk, Baby!* (PS). Illus. by Emily Bolam. 1999, Holt $13.95 (0-8050-6144-4). A flap book that tells of a young boy who is trying to get his little baby sister to start talking. (Rev: HBG 3/00; SLJ 10/99)

3971 Ziefert, Harriet. *Waiting for Baby* (PS–K). Illus. by Emily Bolam. 1998, Holt $13.95 (0-8050-5929-6). After weeks of suspense, Max gets so tired of waiting for his brother to be born that he goes out to play and then, of course, the blessed event occurs. (Rev: BL 12/15/98; HBG 3/99; SLJ 5/99)

3972 Zolotow, Charlotte. *Do You Know What I'll Do?* (PS–2). Illus. by Javaka Steptoe. 2000, HarperCollins LB $15.89 (0-06-027880-3). 32pp. An African American girl cherishes, bosses, dazzles, and comforts her baby brother in this portrait of loving siblings. (Rev: BCCB 1/01; BL 9/15/00*; HBG 3/01; SLJ 9/00)

3973 Zolotow, Charlotte. *The Quarreling Book* (K–2). Illus. by Arnold Lobel. 1963, HarperCollins paper $5.95 (0-06-443034-0). 32pp. Father's failure to kiss mother one morning triggers a series of quarrels, but the pet dog sets things right. Also use: *The Hating Book* (1969).

3974 Zolotow, Charlotte. *Some Things Go Together* (PS–1). Illus. by Ashley Wolff. Series: Harper Growing Tree. 1999, HarperFestival $9.95 (0-694-01197-5). Family love is pictured in this tender story about belonging that is also suitable as a bedtime book. (Rev: HBG 10/99; SLJ 3/99)

3975 Zolotow, Charlotte. *This Quiet Lady* (PS–2). Illus. by Anita Lobel. 1992, Greenwillow LB $13.93 (0-688-09306-X). 24pp. In this celebration of life, a little girl looks at photos of her mother from babyhood to motherhood. (Rev: BCCB 6/92; BL 5/1/92*; SLJ 6/92)

3976 Zolotow, Charlotte. *William's Doll* (PS–3). Illus. by William Pene du Bois. 1972, HarperCollins LB $15.89 (0-06-027048-9); paper $5.95 (0-06-443067-7). 32pp. William wanted a doll, much to his father's dismay; but when Grandma comes to visit she presents William with a doll, saying that now he will have an opportunity to practice being a good father.

FRIENDSHIP STORIES

3977 Aliki. *Best Friends Together Again* (PS–3). Illus. 1995, Greenwillow $14.89 (0-688-13754-7). 32pp. Peter and Robert, two dear friends, are reunited after Peter comes for a visit after he had to move. (Rev: BL 8/95; HB 9–10/95; SLJ 9/95)

3978 Aliki. *We Are Best Friends* (K–3). Illus. by author. 1982, Morrow paper $5.95 (0-688-07037-X). 32pp. Robert is at a loss when his best friend moves away.

3979 Belton, Sandra. *May'naise Sandwiches and Sunshine Tea* (K–3). Illus. by Gail G. Carter. 1994, Four Winds paper $14.95 (0-02-709035-3). Big Mama recalls growing up in a poor but loving household and visiting friend Bettie Jean, who belonged to a middle-class African American family and lived in a much nicer neighborhood. (Rev: SLJ 12/94)

3980 Blegvad, Lenore. *Anna Banana and Me* (K–3). Illus. by Erik Blegvad. 1985, Macmillan LB $13.95 (0-689-50274-5); paper $5.99 (0-689-71114-X). 32pp. A young boy who is afraid of everything takes brave Anna Banana's advice when he is stranded alone. (Rev: BCCB 3/85; BL 7/85; HB 5–6/85)

3981 Bluthenthal, Diana Cain. *Matilda the Moocher* (PS–2). Illus. 1997, Orchard LB $16.99 (0-531-33003-6). 32pp. Libby gets tired of her friend Matilda's constant borrowing of her possessions and money. (Rev: BL 3/15/97; SLJ 5/97)

3982 Boelts, Maribeth. *Grace and Joe* (K–3). Illus. by Martine Gourbault. 1994, Albert Whitman LB $14.95 (0-8075-3019-0). Grace, a lonely preschooler, forms a friendship with Joe, a mail carrier, and follows him around on his route. (Rev: SLJ 12/94)

3983 Brown, Laurie Krasny. *How to Be a Friend: A Guide to Making Friends and Keeping Them* (K–3). Illus. by Marc Brown. 1998, Little, Brown $14.95 (0-316-10913-4). 32pp. Using humanlike dinosaurs as subjects, this practical guide shows how to make friends and keep their friendship. (Rev: BL 10/15/98; HB 11–12/98; HBG 3/99; SLJ 9/98)

3984 Brown, Marc. *The True Francine* (1–3). Illus. by author. 1981, Little, Brown $15.95 (0-316-11212-7). Francine discovers the meaning of friendship when she is accused of cheating.

3985 Buchholz, Quint. *The Collector of Moments* (1–4). Trans. by Peter F. Neumeyer. Illus. 1999, Farrar $18.00 (0-374-31520-5). 48pp. A young boy growing up in a big city forms a friendship with Max, an artist, who lives in an apartment in the same building. (Rev: BCCB 2/00; BL 11/15/99*; HBG 3/00; SLJ 10/99)

3986 Carlstrom, Nancy White. *Blow Me a Kiss, Miss Lilly* (K–2). Illus. by Amy Schwartz. 1990, HarperCollins LB $15.89 (0-06-021013-3). 32pp. The story of a special friendship between an elderly lady and little Sara. (Rev: BCCB 5/90; BL 4/15/90; HB 5–6/90; SLJ 7/90)

3987 Carr, Jan. *Frozen Noses* (PS–K). Illus. by Dorothy Donohue. 1999, Holiday $15.95 (0-8234-1462-0). 32pp. Collage illustrations and an interesting text are used to describe three friends having fun outdoors on a cold winter's day. (Rev: BL 9/15/99; HBG 3/00; SLJ 9/99)

3988 Champion, Joyce. *Emily and Alice Again* (PS–2). Illus. by Sucie Stevenson. 1995, Harcourt $14.00 (0-15-200439-4). 32pp. Three episodes that

tell of the everyday activities of two friends, Emily and Alice. (Rev: BL 3/15/95; HB 5–6/95; SLJ 5/95)

3989 Christiansen, C. B. *Sycamore Street* (1–3). Illus. by Melissa Sweet. 1993, Macmillan $13.95 (0-689-31784-0). 48pp. When best friend Angel goes on vacation, Chloe is forced to play with a newcomer. (Rev: BL 8/93)

3990 Cole, Joanna. *Don't Tell the Whole World!* (K–3). Illus. by Kate Duke. 1992, HarperCollins paper $4.95 (0-064-43292-0). 32pp. A husband tricks his wife into keeping secret the fact that they have found a buried treasure. (Rev: BL 11/1/90; HB 11–12/90; SLJ 12/90)

3991 Cote, Nancy. *Palm Trees* (PS–2). Illus. 1993, Macmillan LB $14.95 (0-02-724760-0). 32pp. Renne makes fun of Millie's hairstyle, but in time tries it herself. (Rev: BL 2/15/93; SLJ 7/93)

3992 Davies, Sally J. K. *When William Went Away* (K–3). Illus. 1999, Carolrhoda $15.95 (1-57505-303-9). 32pp. When Matthew's best friend William moves away, the boy is lost until Mary moves in next door, and William finds out that girls can also be friends. (Rev: BL 8/99; HBG 3/00; SLJ 7/99)

3993 Denslow, Sharon P. *Bus Riders* (PS–2). Illus. by Nancy Carpenter. 1993, Macmillan $14.95 (0-02-728682-7). 32pp. When their regular school bus driver becomes ill, the children cannot adjust to the substitute. (Rev: BL 3/15/93; HB 5–6/93; SLJ 7/93)

3994 English, Karen. *Neeny Coming, Neeny Going* (PS–3). Illus. by Synthia Saint James. 1996, Troll $14.95 (0-8167-3796-7). 32pp. Two friends are reunited on an island off the coast of South Carolina but can't resume their relationship. (Rev: BL 5/15/96; HB 7–8/96; SLJ 7/96)

3995 Fox, Mem. *Wilfrid Gordon McDonald Partridge* (K–2). Illus. by Julie Vivas. 1989, Kane/Miller $13.95 (0-916291-04-9); paper $7.95 (0-916291-26-X). 32pp. The heartwarming story of the boy with four names who collects memorabilia in a box to take to his friend with four names who is losing her memory. (Rev: BL 2/15/86; HB 1–2/86; SLJ 2/86)

3996 Gauch, Patricia L. *Christina Katerina and Fats and the Great Neighborhood War* (PS–2). Illus. by Stacey Schuett. 1997, Putnam $15.95 (0-399-22651-6). 32pp. When friend Fats doesn't support Christina when she needs it, she begins a feud with him. (Rev: BCCB 6/97; BL 3/1/97; SLJ 3/97)

3997 Gauch, Patricia L. *Tanya and Emily in a Dance for Two* (PS–3). Illus. by Satomi Ichikawa. 1994, Putnam $16.99 (0-399-22688-5). 32pp. Though they have different approaches to ballet, two young girls become friendly at dance class. (Rev: BCCB 1/95; BL 10/15/94*; HB 11–12/94; SLJ 9/94*)

3998 Gray, Libba M. *Miss Tizzy* (K–4). Illus. by Jada Rowland. 1993, Simon & Schuster $15.00 (0-671-77590-1). 31pp. Miss Tizzy is the one person the neighborhood people can count on for kind acts and expressions of concern and love. (Rev: BL 6/1–15/93)

3999 Greenfield, Eloise. *Honey, I Love* (PS–K). Illus. by Jan S. Gilchrist. 1995, HarperFestival

$7.95 (0-694-00579-7). 20pp. With illustrations of African American children, this simple picture book describes various forms of love. Also use *On My Horse* (1995). (Rev: BL 2/1/95; HB 3–4/95; SLJ 2/95)

4000 Haseley, Dennis. *Crosby* (K–3). Illus. by Jonathan Green. 1996, Harcourt $15.00 (0-15-200829-2). While fixing a kite and flying it, a young African American boy finds a new friend. (Rev: SLJ 9/96)

4001 Havill, Juanita. *Jamaica and Brianna* (PS–1). Illus. by Anne S. O'Brien. 1993, Houghton $16.00 (0-395-64489-5). 32pp. Jamaica is upset when her friend, Brianna, makes fun of her hand-me-down boots. (Rev: BCCB 11/93; BL 10/15/93; HB 11–12/93; SLJ 10/93)

4002 Havill, Juanita. *Jamaica's Blue Marker* (PS–1). Illus. by Anne S. O'Brien. 1995, Houghton $16.00 (0-395-72036-2). 32pp. Jamaica feels annoyance toward a classmate until she finds out he is moving. (Rev: BCCB 10/95; BL 7/95; SLJ 1/96)

4003 Hazen, Barbara S. *That Toad Is Mine!* (PS–1). Illus. by Jane Manning. Series: Growing Tree. 1998, HarperFestival $9.95 (0-694-01035-9). 24pp. Two young friends argue over custody of a toad they find. After the toad escapes, they realize that their friendship is more important than who keeps the toad. (Rev: BL 11/15/98; HBG 3/99; SLJ 1/99)

4004 Henkes, Kevin. *Chester's Way* (PS–2). Illus. by author. 1988, Greenwillow $15.89 (0-688-07608-4). 32pp. Chester and Wilson are best friends and will have nothing to do with new girl Lilly, until she bails them out of trouble. (Rev: BL 9/1/88; HB 9–10/88; SLJ 9/88)

4005 Hess, Debra. *Wilson Sat Alone* (K–3). Illus. by Diane Greenseid. 1994, Simon & Schuster $14.00 (0-671-87046-7). A boy with a reputation for being a loner responds to offers of friendship from a new girl in his class. (Rev: SLJ 11/94)

4006 Hilton, Nette. *Andrew Jessup* (K–3). Illus. by Cathy Wilcox. 1993, Ticknor $13.95 (0-395-66900-6). 32pp. Andrew was a wonderful, considerate friend; and when he moves away, his buddy is convinced that no one can take his place. (Rev: BL 12/15/93; SLJ 10/93)

4007 Himmelman, John. *Honest Tulio* (PS–2). Illus. 1997, Troll $14.95 (0-8167-3812-2). 32pp. People are so impressed with Tulio's honesty that they shower him with presents as a reward. (Rev: BL 6/1–15/97; SLJ 7/97)

4008 Howard, Arthur. *When I Was Five* (PS–1). Illus. 1996, Harcourt $15.00 (0-15-200261-8). 40pp. A 6-year-old boy finds that he has changed a lot in a year, except that he still has the same best friend. (Rev: BL 5/1/96*; HB 9–10/96; SLJ 5/96*)

4009 Jahn-Clough, Lisa. *Missing Molly* (PS). Illus. 2000, Houghton $15.00 (0-618-00980-9). 32pp. In a hide-and-seek game with Simon, Molly pretends to be missing while making an appearance in a disguise to fool her friend. (Rev: BL 2/1/00; HBG 10/00; SLJ 4/00)

4010 Jahn-Clough, Lisa. *My Friend and I* (PS). Illus. 1999, Houghton $15.00 (0-395-93545-8).

32pp. A little girl and her friend quarrel after one of their toys breaks, but soon they make up. (Rev: BL 4/15/99; HBG 10/99; SLJ 5/99)

4011 Jam, Teddy. *The Stoneboat* (1–3). Illus. by Ange Zhang. 1999, Douglas & McIntyre $15.95 (0-88899-368-4). 32pp. In this Canadian story, a boy and his older brother save the life of their cranky neighbor and gradually break down the barriers of race and prejudice that separate them. (Rev: BCCB 12/99; BL 1/1–15/00; HBG 10/00; SLJ 1/00)

4012 James, Simon. *Leon and Bob* (PS–1). Illus. 1997, Candlewick $15.99 (1-56402-991-3). 32pp. Leon loses his imaginary playmate when he forms a new, real friendship. (Rev: BCCB 3/97; BL 2/1/97; SLJ 4/97)

4013 Jones, Rebecca C. *Matthew and Tilly* (PS–2). Illus. by Beth Peck. 1995, Puffin paper $5.99 (0-14-055640-0). 32pp. Matthew, a white boy, and Tilly, a black girl, resume their close friendship after an argument. (Rev: BL 1/15/91; SLJ 3/91)

4014 Keats, Ezra Jack. *Apt. 3* (PS–3). Illus. by author. 1986, Macmillan paper $5.99 (0-689-71059-3). 32pp. Two brothers, investigating the various sounds of an apartment building, find a friend in Mr. Muntz, the blind man behind the door of Apt. 3.

4015 Keats, Ezra Jack. *Goggles!* (K–3). Illus. by author. 1987, Macmillan paper $4.95 (0-689-71157-3). 40pp. Dachshund Willie outmaneuvers some neighborhood bullies trying to confiscate the motorcycle goggles found by Peter. Bold collage paintings perfectly capture inner-city neighborhood scenes.

4016 Keats, Ezra Jack. *Whistle for Willie* (PS–1). Illus. by author. 1964, Puffin paper $5.99 (0-14-050202-5). After many false starts, Peter at last learns to whistle.

4017 King, Stephen M. *Henry and Amy (right-way-round and upside down)* (PS–1). Illus. 1999, Walker LB $16.85 (0-8027-8687-1). 32pp. Henry, who can't get anything right, meets Amy, who never makes mistakes, and they become friends. (Rev: BL 6/1–15/99; HBG 10/99; SLJ 6/99)

4018 Kline, Suzy. *Horrible Harry and the Ant Invasion* (2–4). Illus. by Frank Remkiewicz. 1989, Viking $13.99 (0-670-82469-0). 64pp. Horrible Harry becomes class monitor for the ant farm. (Rev: BL 12/1/89; SLJ 3/90)

4019 Kolar, Bob. *Do You Want to Play? A Book About Being Friends* (K–3). Illus. 1999, Dutton $16.99 (0-525-45938-3). 32pp. Two young boys enjoy each other's company when they visit Friendship Park. (Rev: BCCB 6/99; BL 7/99; HBG 10/99; SLJ 7/99)

4020 Komaiko, Leah. *Earl's Too Cool for Me* (K–2). Illus. by Laura Cornell. 1988, HarperCollins $14.00 (0-06-023281-1); paper $5.95 (0-06-443245-9). 40pp. A rhyming, outlandish story about Earl, the coolest kid around. (Rev: BL 12/1/88; HB 9–10/88; SLJ 11/88)

4021 Kroll, Virginia. *Pink Paper Swans* (K–4). Illus. by Nancy L. Clouse. 1994, Eerdmans $15.00 (0-8028-5081-2). 32pp. In this account of how Janetta Jackson began helping Mrs. Tsujimoto, an origami expert, there are instructions for making a pink swan. (Rev: BCCB 10/94; BL 7/94; SLJ 8/94)

4022 Lester, Alison. *Tessa Snaps Snakes* (K–2). Illus. by author. 1991, Houghton paper $13.95 (0-685-52551-1). In double-page spreads, seven little children reveal their secrets and pet dislikes. (Rev: HB 11–12/91; SLJ 12/91)

4023 Lewis, Kim. *Friends* (PS–1). Illus. 1998, Candlewick $15.99 (0-7636-0346-5). 32pp. When Alice visits Sam on his parents' farm, the two youngsters quarrel over a hen's egg but later make up. (Rev: BL 4/15/98; HBG 10/98; SLJ 7/98)

4024 Lonborg, Rosemary. *Helpin' Bugs* (PS–2). Illus. by Diane R. Houghton. 1995, Little Friend $14.95 (0-9641285-2-7). 32pp. Lonely Hanna finds happiness helping her neighbor Douglas create a bug village. (Rev: BL 1/1–15/96; SLJ 2/96)

4025 Lyon, George E. *Together* (PS–2). Illus. by Vera Rosenberry. 1989, Orchard $15.95 (0-531-05831-X); paper $5.95 (0-531-07047-6). 32pp. Short poems explore the meaning of togetherness and friendship. (Rev: BL 9/15/89; HB 11–12/89; SLJ 9/89) [811]

4026 McBratney, Sam. *I'm Sorry* (PS–2). Illus. by Jennifer Eachus. 2000, HarperCollins $15.95 (0-06-028686-5). 40pp. Two best friends part after having a violent quarrel but the boy feels very sad at losing his friend and wonders if she feels sad too. (Rev: BL 8/00; HBG 10/00; SLJ 6/00)

4027 McKay, Hilary. *Pirates Ahoy!* (PS–2). Illus. by Alex Ayliffe. 2000, Simon & Schuster $16.00 (0-689-83114-5). 32pp. Age differences disappear when two cousins — Peter, 6, and Simon, 3 — imagine embarking on a series of adventures together. (Rev: BCCB 6/00; BL 5/15/00; HBG 10/00; SLJ 6/00)

4028 Miller, Margaret. *Big and Little* (PS). Illus. 1998, Greenwillow LB $14.93 (0-688-14749-6). 24pp. The concept of relative size is shown using double-page spreads and clear color photos. (Rev: BL 6/1–15/98; HBG 10/98; SLJ 7/98) [153.7]

4029 Mills, Claudia. *A Visit to Amy-Claire* (PS–K). Illus. by Sheila Hamanaka. 1992, Macmillan $14.95 (0-02-766991-2). 32pp. Rachel becomes jealous when her younger sister becomes cousin Amy-Claire's favorite. (Rev: BCCB 2/92; BL 2/1/92; SLJ 6/92*)

4030 Munson, Derek. *Enemy Pie* (K–3). Illus. by Tara Calahan King. 2000, Chronicle $14.95 (0-8118-2778-X). A young boy is nice to a boy he doesn't like and ends up having a good time. (Rev: BCCB 1/01; HBG 3/01; SLJ 12/00)

4031 Narahashi, Keiko. *Two Girls Can!* (PS–K). Illus. 2000, Simon & Schuster $16.00 (0-689-82618-4). 32pp. This book explores what two girls can do together including climb a tree, share a joke, get mad at each other, and make up. (Rev: BCCB 6/00; BL 3/15/00; HBG 10/00; SLJ 6/00)

4032 Pinkwater, Daniel. *Doodle Flute* (1–4). Illus. 1991, Macmillan LB $13.95 (0-02-774635-6). 32pp. Spoiled Kevin Spoon wants Mason Mintz's doodle flute in this story about sharing and friendship. (Rev: BL 2/1/91; HB 5–6/91; SLJ 6/91)

4033 Polacco, Patricia. *The Bee Tree* (K–3). Illus. 1993, Putnam $16.99 (0-399-21965-X). 32pp. After gathering honey from the bee tree with his granddaughter, Grampa explains that sweet things also can be found in books. (Rev: BL 3/1/93; HB 5–6/93; SLJ 6/93*)

4034 Polacco, Patricia. *Mrs. Katz and Tush* (K–4). Illus. 1992, Bantam $15.00 (0-553-08122-5). 32pp. A lonely Jewish widow is befriended by an African American boy who brings her a kitten to love. (Rev: BCCB 7–8/92; BL 4/15/92; HB 11–12/92; SLJ 7/92)

4035 Pomerantz, Charlotte. *You're Not My Best Friend Anymore* (PS–4). Illus. by David Soman. 1998, Dial LB $15.89 (0-8037-1560-9). 32pp. Grade-schoolers Molly and Ben, one white and one black, are good friends, but on occasion they quarrel and make up. (Rev: BCCB 6/98; BL 4/15/98; HBG 3/99; SLJ 7/98)

4036 Raschka, Chris. *Yo! Yes?* (K–4). Illus. 1993, Orchard LB $16.99 (0-531-08619-4). 32pp. This picture book consists of a conversation between two boys, one white, one African American. (Rev: BCCB 4/93; BL 3/15/93; HB 5–6/93; SLJ 5/93*)

4037 Recknagel, Friedrich. *Meg's Wish* (PS–2). Trans. by Sibylle Kazeroid. Illus. by Ilse van Garderen. 1999, North-South LB $15.88 (0-7358-1117-2). Meg wishes on a shooting star that she will make friends at her new school, and her wish comes true. (Rev: HBG 3/00; SLJ 12/99)

4038 Schaefer, Carole L. *Snow Pumpkin* (PS–1). Illus. by Pierre Morgan. 2000, Crown $14.95 (0-517-80015-2). 32pp. Lily, a young Asian narrator, uses all the available snow when she and friend Jesse begin to build a snowman so they must use an old pumpkin for the head. (Rev: BCCB 10/00; BL 9/15/00; HBG 3/01; SLJ 9/00)

4039 Schick, Eleanor. *My Navajo Sister* (K–3). Illus. 1996, Simon & Schuster $16.00 (0-689-80529-2). 30pp. The author, as a child, and her friend Genni share some wonderful experiences on their Navajo land. (Rev: BL 12/1/96; SLJ 12/96)

4040 Schotter, Roni. *Captain Snap and the Children of Vinegar Lane* (K–3). Illus. by Marcia Sewall. 1989, Orchard paper $5.95 (0-531-07038-7). 32pp. A bitter old man frightens the children away with his snapping fingers, until one day they discover he is ill. (Rev: BL 5/1/89; SLJ 5/89)

4041 Schubert, Ingrid, and Dieter Schubert. *Wild Will* (K–2). Illus. 1994, Carolrhoda LB $19.95 (0-87614-816-X). 32pp. Gradually, young Frank breaks down the hostility that a retired pirate feels toward people. (Rev: BL 9/15/94; SLJ 8/94)

4042 Schwartz, Ellen. *Mr. Belinsky's Bagels* (PS–2). Illus. by Stefan Czernecki. 1998, Charlesbridge LB $15.95 (0-88106-256-1). 32pp. Mr. Belinsky, the neighborhood bagel maker, loses some of his friends when he decides to branch out into cakes and cookies to compete with the new bakery across the street. (Rev: BL 7/98; HBG 3/99)

4043 Shannon, George. *Seeds* (PS–2). Illus. by Steve Bjorkman. 1994, Houghton $13.95 (0-395-66990-1). 32pp. Little Warren enjoys being with his older buddy Bill and is crushed when Bill and his family move away. (Rev: BL 6/1–15/94; SLJ 4/94)

4044 Slaughter, Hope. *A Cozy Place* (PS–K). Illus. by Susan Torrence. 1991, Red Hen LB $15.95 (0-931093-13-9). 32pp. Two girls discover that it is each other's presence that makes a place cozy. (Rev: BL 6/1/91)

4045 Snihura, Ulana. *I Miss Franklin P. Shuckles* (K–3). Illus. by Leanne Franson. 1998, Annick LB $15.95 (1-55037-517-2); paper $5.95 (1-55037-516-4). When school starts, Molly decides to drop Franklin as a friend, but when she does she realizes how much she misses him. (Rev: SLJ 6/98)

4046 Starkman, Neal. *The Riddle* (K–2). Illus. by Ellen Sasaki. 1990, Comprehensive Health paper $10.00 (0-935529-13-6). 50pp. When a class assignment matches them together, Maria and a shy boy named Pete become friends. (Rev: BL 9/1/90)

4047 Steptoe, John. *Creativity* (PS–3). Illus. by E. B. Lewis. 1997, Clarion $15.95 (0-395-68706-3). 32pp. An African American boy wonders why a new class member who is as dark-skinned as himself can only speak Spanish. (Rev: BL 2/15/97; SLJ 4/97)

4048 Stone, Phoebe. *Go Away, Shelley Boo!* (1–3). Illus. by author. 1999, Little, Brown $15.95 (0-316-81677-9). A young girl imagines that her new neighbor next door is a real hellion, but she turns out to be a great friend. (Rev: HBG 3/00; SLJ 11/99)

4049 Stroud, Bettye. *Down Home at Miss Dessa's* (PS–3). Illus. by Felicia Marshall. 1996, Lee & Low $14.95 (1-880000-39-3). 32pp. When Miss Dessa is injured, neighborhood children help her in this story of African Americans in the South. (Rev: BCCB 12/96; BL 12/15/96; SLJ 1/97)

4050 Tusa, Tricia. *Stay Away from the Junkyard* (PS–1). Illus. by author. 1988, Macmillan LB $14.95 (0-02-789541-6); paper $5.99 (0-689-71626-5). 32pp. Theodora is told to stay away from the junkyard because Old Man Crampton is "mad," but Theo discovers he isn't mad at all. (Rev: BL 5/1/88; SLJ 8/88)

4051 Udry, Janice May. *Let's Be Enemies* (PS–2). Illus. by Maurice Sendak. 1961, HarperCollins LB $14.89 (0-06-026131-5). 32pp. John is tired of James and his bossiness and decides to tell him so, but things are patched up and they remain friends.

4052 Viorst, Judith. *Rosie and Michael* (1–3). Illus. by Lorna Tomei. 1974, Macmillan $15.00 (0-689-30439-0); paper $4.99 (0-689-71272-3). 40pp. In spite of the many tricks they play on one another, Rosie and Michael are still friends.

4053 Vizurraga, Susan. *Miss Opal's Auction* (1–3). Illus. by Mark Graham. 2000, Holt $16.00 (0-8050-5891-5). As an auctioneer sells Miss Opal's possessions before she enters a retirement apartment, a young white girl remembers all the great times she and her elderly African American friend shared. (Rev: HBG 3/01; SLJ 11/00)

4054 Von Konigslow, Andrea Wayne. *Bing and Chutney* (PS–K). Illus. by author. 1999, Annick LB $16.95 (1-55037-609-6); paper $5.95 (1-55037-608-

X). Two female friends separate to seek their own fortunes and, after each is successful, they are reunited. (Rev: SLJ 1/00)

4055 Vulliamy, Clara. *Ellen and Penguin* (PS–K). Illus. by author. 1993, Candlewick $13.95 (1-56402-193-9). Ellen and her plush penguin conquer their fears and begin to play with a young girl who is accompanied by her toy monkey. (Rev: SLJ 12/93)

4056 Waber, Bernard. *Gina* (PS–3). Illus. 1995, Houghton $14.95 (0-395-74279-X). 32pp. Gina's skill at baseball helps her make friends when she moves to a new neighborhood in Queens where there are just boys. (Rev: BL 9/15/95; SLJ 10/95)

4057 Wallace, Nancy E. *Paperwhite* (PS–1). Illus. 2000, Houghton $14.00 (0-618-04283-0). 32pp. In spite of their age differences, Lucy and neighbor Miss Mamie enjoy each other's company and engage in such activities as planting narcissus bulbs for the spring. (Rev: BCCB 11/00; BL 11/15/00; HBG 3/01; SLJ 10/00)

4058 Wells, Rosemary. *Yoko* (PS–2). Illus. 1998, Hyperion LB $15.49 (0-7868-2345-3). 32pp. Only Timothy is brave enough to try Yoko's sushi during their class's International Day feast. As a result, they become close friends. (Rev: BL 11/15/98*; HBG 3/99; SLJ 10/98)

4059 Whitcomb, Mary E. *Odd Velvet* (K–3). Illus. by Tara Calahan King. 1998, Chronicle $13.95 (0-8118-2004-1). 32pp. Because she dresses and behaves differently than other children in her school, Velvet is ignored by them, but gradually they change their ways. (Rev: BCCB 1/99; BL 11/1/98; HBG 3/99; SLJ 1/99)

4060 Wild, Margaret. *Mr. Nick's Knitting* (K–2). Illus. by Dee Huxley. 1989, Harcourt $12.95 (0-15-200518-8). 32pp. Mr. Nick and Mrs. Jolley always knit together on the morning train, but one day Mrs. Jolley doesn't appear. (Rev: BL 10/1/89; HB 11–12/89; SLJ 10/89)

4061 Wiles, Deborah. *Freedom Summer* (K–3). Illus. by Jerome Lagarrigue. 2001, Simon & Schuster $16.00 (0-689-83016-5). 32pp. Set in the South during desegregation, this is the story of the friendship between John Henry Waddell, an African American boy, and the narrator, who is white. (Rev: BCCB 2/01; BL 2/15/01; SLJ 2/01)

4062 Williams, Suzanne. *Secret Pal Surprises* (1–3). Illus. by Jackie Snider. Series: Hyperion Chapters. 1999, Hyperion paper $3.99 (0-7868-1219-2). 54pp. In this beginning chapter book, Tommy Chen has two problems. The first involves the accidental damage of his friend's property and the second, his suspicions that Jake, a new kid, is stealing. (Rev: SLJ 9/99)

4063 Woodson, Jacqueline. *The Other Side* (K–3). Illus. by E. B. Lewis. 2001, Putnam $16.99 (0-399-23116-1). 32pp. The story of a white girl and a black girl who form a friendship despite the barrier between their houses. (Rev: BCCB 2/01; BL 2/15/01*; SLJ 1/01)

4064 Yee, Brenda Shannon. *Sand Castle* (PS–2). Illus. by Thea Kliros. 1999, Greenwillow $15.00 (0-

688-16194-4). As Jen builds a sandcastle, other children come to help and add distinctive parts in this story about cooperation and friendship. (Rev: HB 7–8/99; HBG 10/99; SLJ 6/99)

4065 Yezerski, Thomas F. *Together in Pinecone Patch* (K–4). Illus. 1998, Farrar $16.00 (0-374-37647-6). 32pp. Two poor immigrant children, one from Poland and the other from Ireland, meet and fall in love and marry. (Rev: BL 2/1/98; HBG 10/98; SLJ 3/98)

4066 Yolen, Jane. *Miz Berlin Walks* (K–4). Illus. by Floyd Cooper. 1997, Putnam $15.95 (0-399-22938-8). 32pp. During her nightly walk, an older white woman tells stories to an African American girl who follows her. (Rev: BL 9/15/97; HBG 3/98; SLJ 10/97)

4067 Zarin, Cynthia. *Rose and Sebastian* (PS–K). Illus. by Sarah Durham. 1997, Houghton $16.00 (0-395-75920-X). Rose meets her upstairs neighbor, a noisy, ill-mannered boy named Sebastian. (Rev: HB 9–10/97; HBG 3/98; SLJ 9/97)

4068 Ziegler, Jack. *Mr. Knocky* (1–3). Illus. by author. 1993, Macmillan LB $14.95 (0-02-793725-9). All the kids think that Mr. Knocky is only a big bore until they begin to see him in a new light. (Rev: SLJ 12/93)

4069 Zolotow, Charlotte. *I Know a Lady* (PS–2). Illus. by James Stevenson. 1984, Morrow paper $4.95 (0-688-11519-5). 24pp. Sally loves a kind old lady who lives in the neighborhood.

4070 Zolotow, Charlotte. *My Friend John* (PS–2). Illus. by Amanda Harvey. 2000, Doubleday $14.95 (0-385-32651-3). 32pp. This picture book tells the story of the friendship between two boys and how they share one another's feelings and fears. (Rev: BL 7/00; HBG 3/01; SLJ 7/00)

HUMOROUS STORIES

4071 Adinolfi, JoAnn. *Tina's Diner* (PS–1). Illus. by author. 1997, Simon & Schuster paper $16.00 (0-689-80634-5). When the sink in Tina's diner gets clogged, an enterprising boy sets out to find the plumber. (Rev: SLJ 6/97)

4072 Agee, Jon. *The Return of Freddy Legrand* (PS–1). Illus. 1992, Farrar $15.00 (0-374-36249-1). 32pp. The famous aviator Freddy Legrand is helped by Sophie and Albert when his plane crashes on their farm. (Rev: BL 11/1/92; HB 1–2/93; SLJ 11/92*)

4073 Ahrens, Robin Isabel. *Dee and Bee* (PS–1). Illus. by Amanda Haley. 2000, Winslow $14.95 (1-890817-26-0). 32pp. Identical twin sisters often switch identities to fool their friends and family and, sometimes, even the reader. (Rev: BL 4/15/00)

4074 Alarcon, Karen Beaumont. *Louella Mae, She's Run Away!* (PS–2). Illus. by Rosanne Litzinger. 1997, Holt $15.95 (0-8050-3532-X). 32pp. In this merry barnyard romp a farm family turns out in full force to have a search when the mysterious Louella Mae is missing. (Rev: BL 6/1–15/97; HB 5–6/97; SLJ 5/97)

4075 Alda, Arlene. *Hurry Granny Annie* (K–3). Illus. by Eve Aldridge. 1999, Tricycle Pr. $14.95 (1-883672-72-4). 32pp. A long entourage, including granddaughter Ruthie, other children, and some animals, follows Granny, who is in a hurry to catch the sunset. (Rev: BL 8/99; HBG 3/00; SLJ 1/00)

4076 Allan, Nicholas. *The Bird* (K–3). Illus. by author. 1998, Doubleday $7.95 (0-385-32573-8). After a hermit living on a desert island drives off an annoying bird, the results are unexpected. (Rev: SLJ 7/98)

4077 Allard, Harry. *The Stupids Have a Ball* (K–3). Illus. by James Marshall. 1984, Houghton $18.00 (0-395-26497-9); paper $5.95 (0-395-36169-9). The whole Stupid family decides to celebrate when the children bring home terrible report cards from school. Two others in the series: *The Stupids Step Out* (1974); *The Stupids Die* (1981).

4078 Allard, Harry. *The Stupids Take Off* (K–3). Illus. by James Marshall. 1989, Houghton $16.00 (0-395-50068-0). 32pp. The irresistible noodleheads set off on a fourth adventure, this time to avoid a visit from Uncle Carbuncle. (Rev: BCCB 10/89; BL 10/1/89; SLJ 10/89)

4079 Armstrong, Jennifer. *Pierre's Dream* (PS–3). Illus. by Susan Gaber. 1999, Dial $15.99 (0-8037-1700-8). 32pp. While Pierre is sleeping, a circus pitches its tent around him. On awakening, he thinks he is still dreaming and becomes a star performer. (Rev: BCCB 7–8/99; BL 8/99; HBG 10/99; SLJ 6/99)

4080 Baehr, Patricia. *Mouse in the House* (PS–1). Illus. by Laura Lydecker. 1994, Holiday LB $15.95 (0-8234-1102-8). When a mouse moves into Mrs. Teapot's house, she tries a number of unsuccessful ploys to get rid of it. (Rev: SLJ 9/94)

4081 Baker, Keith. *Hide and Snake* (PS–K). Illus. 1991, Harcourt $15.00 (0-15-233986-8). 32pp. A snake hides in each of the double-page spreads depicting everyday life. (Rev: BL 11/15/91; SLJ 12/91*)

4082 Barrett, Judith. *Animals Should Definitely Not Wear Clothing* (PS–1). Illus. by Ron Barrett. 1970, Macmillan $13.95 (0-689-20592-9); paper $5.99 (0-689-70807-6). 32pp. Humorous idea expressed in brief text and comic drawings. A sequel is: *Animals Should Definitely Not Act Like People* (Simon & Schuster 1988).

4083 Barton, Byron. *Wee Little Woman* (PS–K). Illus. 1995, HarperCollins LB $14.89 (0-06-023388-5). 32pp. The milk that a wee woman gets from her wee cow is stolen by a cat. (Rev: BCCB 6/95; BL 7/95; SLJ 8/95*)

4084 Bauer, Steven. *The Strange and Wonderful Tale of Robert McDoodle* (K–3). Illus. by Brad Sneed. 1999, Simon & Schuster $16.00 (0-689-80619-1). 32pp. An appealing farce in which a little boy decides he would rather be a dog than a human. (Rev: BL 9/1/99; HBG 3/00; SLJ 10/99)

4085 Birdseye, Tom, and Debbie H. Birdseye. *She'll Be Comin' Round the Mountain* (K–3). Illus. by Andrew Glass. 1994, Holiday LB $15.95 (0-8234-1032-3). 32pp. A variation on the old song that tells about a group of mountain folk who are awaiting

ʼmin' round the mountain for a visit. ⌐4; SLJ 9/94)

⌐irney, Betty G. *Pie's in the Oven* (PS–1). Illus. by Holly Meade. 1996, Houghton $15.95 (0-395-76501-3). 32pp. A boy's family, friends, and neighbors line up to get a piece of his grandmother's famous pie. (Rev: BL 7/96; SLJ 9/96)

4087 Bishop, Claire Huchet. *Five Chinese Brothers* (1–3). Illus. by Kurt Wiese. 1988, Putnam paper $5.99 (0-698-11357-8). 64pp. Physically identical in every way, each of the five Chinese brothers has one distinguishing trait that saves the lives of all of them.

4088 Blake, Quentin. *Mrs. Armitage and the Big Wave* (PS–2). Illus. 1998, Harcourt $15.00 (0-15-201642-2). 32pp. While patiently waiting in the surf for the Big Wave, Mrs. Armitage and her dog make sure they are fully prepared by taking several trips back to the shore for such provisions as a hat, an umbrella, a wind sock, and a megaphone. (Rev: BCCB 5/98; BL 4/1/98; HBG 10/98; SLJ 5/98)

4089 Bloom, Suzanne. *The Bus for Us* (PS–K). Illus. 2001, Boyds Mills $10.95 (1-56397-932-2). 32pp. A humorous story that describes children waiting to be picked up on the first day of school. (Rev: BL 3/15/01*)

4090 Borton, Lady. *Junk Pile!* (PS–3). Illus. by Kimberly B. Root. 1997, Putnam $15.95 (0-399-22728-8). 32pp. Jamie, who collects parts from her father's automobile junkyard, is able to repair the school bus when it gets stuck. (Rev: BCCB 5/97; BL 4/15/97; SLJ 4/97)

4091 Bourgeois, Paulette. *Too Many Chickens!* (PS–3). Illus. by Bill Slavin. 1990, General Dist. Services paper $4.95 (1-550-74067-9). 32pp. A gift of chicken eggs to a class of elementary school children brings unexpected results. (Rev: BL 8/91; SLJ 6/91)

4092 Bowie, C. W. *Busy Toes* (PS). Illus. by Fred Willingham. 1998, Whispering Coyote $15.95 (1-879085-72-0). 32pp. This energetic picture book shows a group of children performing all sorts of activities with their feet and toes, including digging, playing, and writing. (Rev: BL 1/1–15/99; HBG 3/99; SLJ 12/98)

4093 Bradman, Tony. *Michael* (PS–3). Illus. by Tony Ross. 1998, Trafalgar paper $9.95 (0-86264-759-2). 32pp. Brainy Michael won't pay attention in class; he just wants to learn about spacecraft. (Rev: BL 1/15/91; SLJ 3/91)

4094 Braybrooks, Ann. *Plenty of Pockets* (PS–2). Illus. by Scott Menchin. 2000, Harcourt $17.00 (0-15-202173-6). 32pp. A family can't find anything because of the clutter in the house, so father decides to sew pockets on all their clothes to store important things. (Rev: BCCB 6/00; BL 7/00; HBG 10/00; SLJ 5/00)

4095 Brown, Marc. *Arthur and the Crunch Cereal Contest* (2–4). Illus. 1998, Little, Brown $12.95 (0-316-11552-5); paper $3.95 (0-316-11553-3). 64pp. Arthur tries to compose a winning entry for the Crunch Cereal Jingle Contest, but it is his young sis-

ter, D. W., who supplies the inspiration. (Rev: BL 11/1/98; HBG 10/98; SLJ 10/98)

4096 Brown, Ruth. *The Big Sneeze* (PS–K). Illus. by author. 1997, Morrow paper $4.95 (0-688-15282-1). 32pp. A fly lands on a farmer's nose; he sneezes, and havoc breaks out in the barnyard. (Rev: BCCB 2/86; BL 9/15/85; SLJ 10/85)

4097 Buckley, Helen E. *Where Did Josie Go?* (PS–K). Illus. by Jan Ormerod. 1999, Lothrop LB $15.93 (0-688-16508-7). 24pp. A family searches for its youngest member, Josie, and the only clues are the petals that drop from her bouquet of flowers. (Rev: BL 5/15/99; HB 7–8/99; HBG 10/99; SLJ 5/99)

4098 Bunting, Eve. *My Backpack* (PS–K). Illus. 1997, Boyds Mills $14.95 (1-56397-433-9). 32pp. A young boy thinks he is doing everyone a favor when he gathers a lot of objects around the house and stores them in his backpack for safekeeping. (Rev: BL 5/1/97; SLJ 4/98)

4099 Busser, Marianne, and Ron Schroder. *King Bobble* (K–3). Illus. by Hans de Beer. Series: Easy-to-Read. 1996, North-South LB $13.88 (1-55858-592-3). 62pp. Ten delightfully zany stories about the daffy King and Queen Bobble. (Rev: BL 5/15/96; SLJ 7/96)

4100 Butler, Dorothy. *Another Happy Tale* (PS–2). Illus. by John Hurford. 1992, Crocodile $12.95 (0-940793-88-1). Mabel and Ned are so ill prepared to bring up their baby girl that they accidentally sell her as part of a litter of pigs. (Rev: SLJ 4/92)

4101 Byars, Betsy. *The Golly Sisters Go West* (1–3). Illus. by Sue Truesdell. 1986, HarperCollins LB $15.89 (0-06-020884-8); paper $3.95 (0-06-444132-6). 64pp. In six stories, two adventurous women take on frontier life and the Wild West. (Rev: BCCB 11/86)

4102 Cabrera, Jane. *Rory and the Lion* (PS). Illus. by author. Series: DK Toddler Storybook. 1999, DK $9.95 (0-7894-4843-2). Rory, who loves to dress up and roar in his lion costume, thinks he hears a real lion roaring outside his house. (Rev: HBG 3/00; SLJ 12/99)

4103 Cannon, Ann Edwards. *I Know What You Do When I Go to School* (K–3). Illus. by Jennifer Mazzucco. 1996, Gibbs Smith $14.95 (0-87905-743-2). Howie thinks he is missing good times at home when he goes to school, but his mother convinces him otherwise. (Rev: SLJ 12/96)

4104 Carrick, Carol. *Big Old Bones: A Dinosaur Tale* (PS–3). Illus. by Donald Carrick. 1992, Houghton paper $6.95 (0-395-61582-8). 32pp. Professor Potts finds a bunch of old bones to take back East to assemble. (Rev: BL 3/1/89; HB 5–6/89; SLJ 5/89)

4105 Cecil, Ivon. *Kirby Kelvin and the Not-Laughing Lessons* (1–3). Illus. by Judy Love. 1998, Whispering Coyote $14.95 (1-879085-95-X); paper $5.95 (1-879085-39-9). 32pp. When Kirby Kelvin gets a fit of the giggles during a spelling test, he is taken to Mr. Gloomsmith's office to get not-laughing lessons from a man who hasn't laughed in 29 years. (Rev: BL 5/15/98; HBG 10/98; SLJ 7/98)

4106 Charlip, Remy. *Why I Will Never Ever Ever Have Enough Time to Read This Book* (K–3). Illus. by Jon J. Muth. 2000, Tricycle Pr. $14.95 (1-58246-018-3). 40pp. A humorous book about a little girl who has so many things to do, like homework and calling friends, that she will never to able to finish the big book that is always at her side. (Rev: BL 1/1–15/01; HBG 3/01; SLJ 9/00)

4107 Child, Lauren. *Clarice Bean, Guess Who's Babysitting?* (1–4). Illus. by author. 2001, Candlewick $16.99 (0-7636-1373-8). While her firefighter Uncle Ted is looking after Clarice and her siblings, their pet guinea pig escapes in this uproarious picture book. (Rev: SLJ 3/01*)

4108 Child, Lauren. *I Want a Pet* (PS–1). Illus. 1999, Tricycle Pr. $13.95 (1-883672-82-1). 24pp. A hilarious story about a family that cannot agree on the perfect pet. (Rev: BL 4/15/99; HB 5–6/99; HBG 10/99; SLJ 5/99)

4109 Child, Lauren. *I Will Never Not Ever Eat a Tomato* (PS–2). Illus. by author. 2000, Candlewick $15.99 (0-7636-1188-3). Charlie gets his fussy little sister to eat by calling the food by exotic names. (Rev: HBG 3/01; SLJ 11/00)

4110 Choldenko, Gennifer. *Moonstruck: The True Story of the Cow Who Jumped over the Moon* (K–2). Illus. by Paul Yalowitz. 1997, Hyperion LB $15.49 (0-7868-2130-2). 32pp. A horse supplies details about the amazing feat accomplished by a cow that jumped over the moon. (Rev: BL 3/1/97; SLJ 4/97)

4111 Christelow, Eileen. *The Five-Dog Night* (PS–3). Illus. 1993, Clarion $14.95 (0-395-62399-5). 36pp. On cold nights, cranky old Ezra finds an unusual use for his five pet dogs. (Rev: BL 9/15/93; SLJ 10/93)

4112 Cibula, Matt. *The Contrary Kid* (2–4). Illus. by Brian Strassburg. 1995, Zino $16.95 (1-55933-177-1). 32pp. Cartoons and rhymes are used to tell about the antics of a kooky kid who revels in being different. (Rev: BL 1/1–15/96; SLJ 7/96)

4113 Clark, Emma C. *Across the Blue Mountains* (K–3). Illus. 1993, Harcourt $14.95 (0-15-201220-6). 32pp. Miss Bilberry sets out to find a new home but mistakenly moves back into her old house, which she finds is "perfection." (Rev: BL 10/15/93; SLJ 1/94)

4114 Clarke, Gus. *Nothing But Trouble* (PS–2). Illus. by author. 1998, Andersen paper $9.95 (0-86264-841-6). Maisie's day begins with her baby brother rudely wakening her, and her mother spilling cereal on her head — then things go from bad to worse. (Rev: SLJ 3/99)

4115 Clement, Rod. *Frank's Great Museum Adventure* (K–3). Illus. 1999, HarperCollins LB $14.89 (0-06-027674-6). 32pp. A little boy and his dog walk through a historical museum's exhibits and draw amusing and telling parallels between ancient times and today. (Rev: BL 7/99; HBG 10/99; SLJ 12/99)

4116 Clement, Rod. *Grandpa's Teeth* (PS–3). Illus. 1998, HarperCollins $15.95 (0-06-027671-1). 32pp. When Grandpa's false teeth are stolen, a nationwide search is begun. (Rev: BL 2/15/98; HBG 10/98; SLJ 3/98*)

4117 Clements, Andrew. *Double Trouble in Walla Walla* (1–3). Illus. by Sal Murdocca. 1997, Millbrook LB $21.90 (0-7613-0306-5). A girl is sent to the principal's office when she can't stop speaking in hyphenated words, like mish-mash. (Rev: HBG 3/98; SLJ 1/98)

4118 Cocca-Leffler, Maryann. *Clams All Year* (PS–3). Illus. 1996, Boyds Mills $14.95 (1-56397-469-X). 32pp. A family goes clamming and is so successful that soon their swimming pool is filled with clams. (Rev: BL 6/1–15/96; SLJ 7/96)

4119 Cole, Babette. *Bad Habits! (or The Taming of Lucretzia Crum)* (K–3). Illus. 1999, Dial $14.99 (0-8037-2432-2). 32pp. It takes a perfectly horrible solution devised by her parents to change Lucretzia Crum's terrible behavior. (Rev: BL 7/99; HBG 10/99; SLJ 8/99)

4120 Cole, Brock. *Buttons* (K–3). Illus. 2000, Farrar $16.00 (0-374-31001-7). 32pp. When their father bursts his buttons, three daughters set out separately to bring him new ones, in this charming, humorous tale. (Rev: BCCB 3/00; BL 2/15/00*; HB 3–4/00; HBG 10/00; SLJ 4/00)

4121 Cummings, Pat. *Clean Your Room, Harvey Moon!* (PS–3). Illus. 1991, Macmillan LB $16.95 (0-02-725511-5). 32pp. Harvey's mother orders him to clean up his room in this humorous tale. (Rev: BL 2/15/91; SLJ 4/91)

4122 Cuyler, Margery. *That's Good! That's Bad!* (PS–K). Illus. by David Catrow. 1993, Holt paper $6.95 (0-8050-2954-0). 32pp. A boy's red balloon whisks him aloft for a series of adventures. (Rev: BCCB 12/91; BL 12/1/91; SLJ 11/91)

4123 Cyrus, Kurt. *Tangle Town* (PS–2). Illus. 1997, Farrar $16.00 (0-374-37384-1). 32pp. A fast-moving, humorous book about a series of misunderstandings that gradually involve an entire town. (Rev: BCCB 3/97; BL 5/1/97; SLJ 3/97)

4124 Dale, Penny. *All About Alice* (PS–K). Illus. 1993, Candlewick $13.95 (1-56402-171-8). 32pp. In this book about a preschooler, the reader is able to participate by identifying familiar objects in the pictures. (Rev: BL 6/1–15/93; SLJ 7/93)

4125 DeFelice, Cynthia. *Willy's Silly Grandma* (K–3). Illus. by Shelley Jackson. 1997, Orchard LB $16.99 (0-531-33012-5). Willy's Grandma spouts a lot of silly superstitions, but she is right in telling Willy not to go by the Old Swamp at night. (Rev: BCCB 6/97; HB 5–6/97; SLJ 4/97*)

4126 Delton, Judy. *Blue Skies, French Fries* (2–3). Illus. by Alan Tiegreen. 1988, Dell paper $3.99 (0-440-40064-3). 80pp. The Pee Wee scouts earn badges. Also use: *Lucky Dog Days; Peanut Butter Pilgrims; Camp Ghost-Away* (all 1988). (Rev: BL 2/15/89)

4127 dePaola, Tomie. *Helga's Dowry: A Troll Love Story* (K–2). Illus. by author. 1977, Harcourt paper $6.00 (0-15-640010-3). 32pp. Helga cannot marry Lars because she has no dowry, but this humorous account tells how she acquires one.

4128 dePaola, Tomie. *Pancakes for Breakfast* (PS–2). Illus. by author. 1978, Harcourt $14.95 (0-15-259455-8); paper $5.00 (0-15-670768-3). 32pp. The trials and travails of a country woman who decides to make some pancakes.

4129 Derby, Sally. *King Kenrick's Splinter* (K–3). Illus. by Leonid Gore. 1994, Walker LB $15.85 (0-8027-8323-6). 32pp. King Kenrick is afraid to have a splinter removed from his big toe. (Rev: BL 11/1/94; SLJ 1/95)

4130 De Regniers, Beatrice S. *May I Bring a Friend?* (PS–2). Illus. by Beni Montresor. 1971, Macmillan LB $16.95 (0-689-20615-1); paper $5.99 (0-689-71353-3). 48pp. The king and queen invite a small boy to tea, and each time he goes, he takes a friend — a seal, a hippopotamus, and several lions. Caldecott Medal winner, 1965.

4131 Dodds, Dayle Ann. *Sing, Sophie!* (PS–1). Illus. by Rosanne Litzinger. 1997, Candlewick $15.99 (0-7836-0131-4). 32pp. Everyone ignores Sophie's singing talent except her baby brother, who prefers it to the sound of thunder. (Rev: BL 5/15/97; SLJ 6/97)

4132 Dorrie, Doris. *Lottie's Princess Dress* (PS–K). Illus. by Julia Kaergel. 1999, Dial $15.99 (0-8037-2388-1). A good-humored book about a little girl who wants to go to kindergarten dressed as a princess. (Rev: BCCB 11/99; HB 7–8/99; HBG 3/00; SLJ 9/99)

4133 Downey, Lynn. *Sing, Henrietta! Sing!* (PS–3). Illus. by Tony Sansevero. 1997, Ideals $14.95 (1-57102-103-5). George loves his dear friend Henrietta, but he finds her singing earsplitting. (Rev: SLJ 7/97)

4134 Dragonwagon, Crescent. *The Bat in the Dining Room* (1–4). Illus. by S. D. Schindler. 1997, Marshall Cavendish $15.95 (0-7614-5007-6). 32pp. When a bat causes havoc after flying into the crowded dining room, Melissa gently coaxes the creature out. (Rev: BL 10/1/97; HBG 3/98; SLJ 9/97)

4135 Drescher, Henrik. *Klutz* (PS–3). Illus. by author. 1996, Hyperion LB $16.49 (0-7868-2182-5). The accident-prone Klutz family finds its calling in a traveling circus. (Rev: SLJ 12/96)

4136 Duncan, Alice Faye. *Miss Viola and Uncle Ed Lee* (PS–3). Illus. by Catherine Stock. 1999, Simon & Schuster $16.00 (0-689-80476-8). 40pp. Bradley recalls the role he played in the courtship of his two neighbors, neat Miss Viola and messy Uncle Ed Lee. (Rev: BL 2/15/99; HBG 10/99; SLJ 2/99)

4137 Dunrea, Olivier. *Eppie M. Says . . .* (K–2). Illus. 1990, Macmillan LB $14.95 (0-02-733205-5). Little brother Ben believes everything his older sister tells him, even the preposterous parts. (Rev: BL 2/1/90*; HB 1–2/91; SLJ 10/90)

4138 Dunrea, Olivier. *The Painter Who Loved Chickens* (PS–3). Illus. 1995, Farrar $15.00 (0-374-35729-3). 32pp. An artist who wants only to paint chickens moves to a farm where he can raise them. (Rev: BCCB 4/95; BL 3/1/95; HB 7–8/95; SLJ 6/95)

4139 Egan, Tim. *Chestnut Cove* (PS–3). Illus. 1995, Houghton $16.00 (0-395-69823-5). 32pp. A once-happy community becomes divided when people compete to grow the biggest watermelon. (Rev: BL 3/15/95; HB 11–12/95; SLJ 3/95*)

4140 English, Karen. *Just Right Stew* (PS–1). Illus. by Anna Rich. 1998, Boyds Mills $15.95 (1-56397-487-8). Friends and relatives offer advice concerning ingredients as Victoria's mother and aunt try to prepare oxtail soup. (Rev: BL 2/15/98; HBG 10/98; SLJ 3/98)

4141 Ernst, Lisa Campbell. *The Luckiest Kid on the Planet* (K–2). Illus. 1994, Bradbury paper $14.95 (0-02-733566-6). 40pp. When Lucky finds out that this is not his real first name, he believes that his luck will change. (Rev: BL 9/1/94; HB 11–12/94; SLJ 11/94)

4142 Ernst, Lisa Campbell. *Miss Penny and Mr. Grubbs* (PS–3). Illus. 1995, Simon & Schuster paper $4.95 (0-689-80035-5). 40pp. Mr. Grubbs decides to sabotage Miss Penny's garden by putting some rabbits in it. (Rev: BCCB 4/91; BL 3/15/91*; SLJ 6/91)

4143 Ernst, Lisa Campbell. *Stella Louella's Runaway Book* (PS–2). Illus. 1998, Simon & Schuster $16.00 (0-689-81883-1). 40pp. Stella Louella traces the whereabouts of her lost library book by questioning various townspeople who have read it and passed it along. (Rev: BCCB 12/98; BL 8/98; HBG 3/99; SLJ 9/98)

4144 Evans, Nate. *The Mixed-Up Zoo of Professor Yahoo* (K–3). Illus. 1993, Junior League of Kansas City $14.95 (0-9607076-3-8). 32pp. In nonsense verse, this book describes a bumbling professor's attempts to create the best zoo in the land. (Rev: BL 7/93) [811]

4145 Everett, Percival. *The One That Got Away* (1–3). Illus. by Dirk Zimmer. 1992, Houghton $14.95 (0-395-56437-9). 32pp. The number one figures prominently in this spoof of westerns. (Rev: BL 4/15/92; SLJ 4/92)

4146 Everitt, Betsy. *Mean Soup* (PS–1). Illus. 1992, Harcourt $16.00 (0-15-253146-7). 32pp. Horace gets rid of his nasty thoughts and feelings by throwing them into a pot and making mean soup. (Rev: BL 3/15/92*; SLJ 7/92)

4147 Fleming, Candace. *Westward Ho, Carlotta!* (PS–3). Illus. by David Catrow. 1998, Simon & Schuster $16.00 (0-689-81063-6). 32pp. Carlotta Carusa, famous opera singer, takes a trip into the Wild West and has a series of amazing adventures. (Rev: BCCB 9/98; BL 5/1/98; HBG 10/98; SLJ 7/98)

4148 Fox, Mem. *Guess What?* (PS–2). Illus. by Vivienne Goodman. 1990, Harcourt $15.00 (0-15-200452-1). 32pp. Through a series of questions, a strange lady, who is a witch, is introduced. (Rev: BL 9/1/90; HB 11–12/91; SLJ 11/90)

4149 Fox, Mem. *Shoes from Grandpa* (PS–K). Illus. by Patricia Mullins. 1992, Orchard paper $6.95 (0-531-07031-X). 32pp. A cumulative story about buying clothes for a growing Jessie. (Rev: BL 2/15/90; HB 3–4/90; SLJ 4/90*)

4150 Freeman, Don. *Mop Top* (K–2). Illus. by author. 1978, Puffin paper $5.99 (0-14-050326-9). 48pp. Moppy changes his mind about a haircut after being mistaken for a floor mop by a nearsighted shopper.

4151 French, Vivian. *Oliver's Vegetables* (PS–2). Illus. by Alison Bartlett. 1995, Orchard $14.95 (0-531-09462-6). 32pp. Longing for some French fries, Oliver promises to eat anything he finds in his Grandpa's vegetable garden, hoping to find potatoes. (Rev: BL 9/15/95; SLJ 10/95)

4152 French, Vivian, and Alex Ayliffe. *Let's Go, Anna!* (PS). 2000, David & Charles $14.95 (1-86233-074-3). 32pp. A flap book that relates Anna's hilarious misadventures during a shopping trip and at the same time gives youngsters a chance to count to five and learn the concept of size. (Rev: BL 1/1–15/01; SLJ 3/01)

4153 Frienz, D. J. *Where Will Nana Go Next? An Illustrated Tour of 19 Places to Go and Things to Do Across America and the World* (PS–1). Illus. by Sean Garber. 1999, Howling at the Moon $15.95 (0-9654333-0-7). Feisty Nana and her dog Spike visit some of America's tourist sights, in this book illustrated with bright, humorous cartoons. (Rev: SLJ 8/99)

4154 Gage, Wilson. *My Stars, It's Mrs. Gaddy: The Three Mrs. Gaddy Stories* (1–4). Illus. by Marylin Hafner. 1991, Greenwillow $15.95 (0-688-10514-9). 96pp. Mrs. Gaddy has a number of humorous adventures on her farm. (Rev: BL 10/15/91)

4155 Garrison, Susan. *How Emily Blair Got Her Fabulous Hair* (K–3). Illus. by Marjorie Priceman. 1995, Troll $14.95 (0-8167-3496-8). 32pp. Emily longs to have curly hair but settles for arranging her straight locks into braids. (Rev: BL 1/1–15/96; SLJ 1/96)

4156 Gay, Marie-Louise. *Fat Charlie's Circus* (PS–2). Illus. by author. Series: Cranky Nell Books. 1997, Kane/Miller $12.95 (0-916291-73-1). A circus-crazy youngster decides to dive into a cup of water from the top of a tall tree. (Rev: SLJ 6/97)

4157 Geoghegan, Adrienne. *Dogs Don't Wear Glasses* (PS–1). Illus. 1996, Crocodile $14.95 (1-56656-208-2). 32pp. Nanny Needle discovers it is her poor eyesight and not that of her dog's that is causing a series of mishaps. (Rev: BL 4/1/96; SLJ 5/96)

4158 Geringer, Laura. *A Three Hat Day* (PS–1). Illus. by Arnold Lobel. 1985, HarperCollins LB $15.89 (0-06-021989-0); paper $5.95 (0-06-443157-6). 32pp. R. R. Pottle the Third is a gentleman who loves hats in this tale of loneliness and finding someone who cares. (Rev: BCCB 1/86; BL 9/15/85; HB 11–12/85)

4159 Gibala-Broxholm, Janice. *Let Me Do It!* (PS). Illus. by Diane Paterson. 1994, Bradbury $14.95 (0-02-735827-5). 32pp. A youngster's desire to do things on her own creates chaos. (Rev: BL 1/15/94; SLJ 5/94)

4160 Gibbons, Faye. *Mama and Me and the Model T* (PS–3). Illus. by Ted Rand. 1999, Morrow LB $15.93 (0-688-15299-6). 40pp. In this delightful sequel to *Mountain Wedding,* Mama shows that it's not just the menfolk who can drive the new Model T around the farm. (Rev: BL 11/15/99; HBG 3/00; SLJ 11/99)

4161 Gibbons, Faye. *Mountain Wedding* (K–4). Illus. by Ted Rand. 1996, Morrow $16.89 (0-688-11349-4). 40pp. A series of humorous mishaps delay the wedding of widow Searcy and widower Long. (Rev: BCCB 9/96; BL 4/1/96; HB 5–6/96; SLJ 4/96)

4162 Gillmor, Don. *The Fabulous Song* (PS–2). Illus. by Marie-Louise Gay. 1998, Kane/Miller $12.95 (0-916291-80-4). A musical spoof in which a young boy who has no talent for playing an instrument finds he is a born orchestra conductor. (Rev: HBG 10/98; SLJ 7/98)

4163 Golembe, Carla. *Dog Magic* (PS–2). Illus. 1997, Houghton $15.00 (0-395-81662-9). 32pp. Molly Gail thinks that the new slippers she received for her birthday have magically cured her fear of dogs. (Rev: BL 11/1/97; HBG 3/98; SLJ 9/97)

4164 Gosney, Joy. *Naughty Parents* (PS). Illus. by author. 2000, Millbrook LB $21.90 (0-7613-1823-2). In this humorous tale of role reversal, a little girl must take care of her parents when they spend an afternoon in the park, including finding them at the "Missing Parents Booth." (Rev: HBG 10/00; SLJ 5/00)

4165 Gottlieb, Dale. *Where Jamaica Go?* (PS–1). Illus. 1996, Orchard LB $15.99 (0-531-08875-8). 32pp. In Afro-Caribbean jargon, Jamaica travels downtown, to the beach, and on a trip in her father's van. (Rev: BL 10/1/96; SLJ 11/96)

4166 Grambling, Lois G. *Can I Have a Stegosaurus, Mom? Can I? Please!?* (PS–1). Illus. by H. Lewis. 1995, Troll $15.95 (0-8167-3386-4). 32pp. A boy points out all the advantages of having a dinosaur for a pet, including eating all his distasteful vegetables. (Rev: BCCB 12/94; BL 1/15/95; SLJ 6/95)

4167 Gray, Kes. *Eat Your Peas* (PS–3). Illus. by Nick Sharratt. 2000, DK $14.95 (0-7894-2667-6). 32pp. A lively farce, in which a mother increases to ridiculous lengths the inducements to get her daughter Daisy to eat her peas. (Rev: BL 9/1/00; HBG 3/01; SLJ 9/00)

4168 Greene, Carol. *The Golden Locket* (K–3). Illus. by Marcia Sewall. 1992, Harcourt $13.95 (0-15-231220-X); paper $5.00 (0-15-201008-4). 32pp. Miss Teaberry's generosity leads to amusing complications in this picture book. (Rev: BCCB 7–8/92; BL 4/1/92; HB 5–6/92; SLJ 5/92)

4169 Grossman, Bill. *Donna O'Neeshuck Was Chased by Some Cows* (K–3). Illus. by Sue Truesdell. 1988, HarperCollins paper $5.95 (0-06-443255-6). 40pp. A farcical rhyming story of a red-haired girl. (Rev: BL 11/15/88; HB 9–10/88; SLJ 2/89)

4170 Grossman, Bill. *Timothy Tunny Swallowed a Bunny* (PS–2). Illus. by Kevin Hawkes. 2001, HarperCollins $14.95 (0-06-028010-7). 32pp. Eighteen nonsense poems explore comic situations, such as the boy who grew a new nose every year. (Rev: BCCB 2/01; BL 2/15/01; SLJ 3/01)

4171 Gukova, Julia. *All Mixed-Up! A Mixed-Up Matching Book* (PS–3). Illus. by author. 2000, North-South $9.95 (0-7358-1300-0). In this interactive book, readers are invited to assemble 13 characters — such as a cat and a wart hog — whose bodies have been divided into three parts: heads, bodies, and legs. (Rev: SLJ 6/00)

4172 Hafner, Marylin. *Mommies Don't Get Sick* (PS–1). Illus. 1995, Candlewick $14.95 (1-56402-287-0). 32pp. Everything goes wrong when young Abby is left alone for a few minutes to take care of her baby brother. (Rev: BCCB 11/95; BL 9/1/95; SLJ 10/95)

4173 Hafner, Marylin. *A Year with Molly and Emmett* (PS–1). Illus. 1997, Candlewick $15.99 (1-56402-966-2). 32pp. Through the seasons with Molly and her cat Emmett in this humorous picture book filled with delightful adventures. (Rev: BL 7/97; SLJ 6/97)

4174 Halperin, Wendy A. *When Chickens Grow Teeth* (K–3). Illus. 1996, Orchard LB $16.99 (0-531-08876-6). 32pp. Confined to bed because of an accident, Toine makes himself useful by hatching some chicken eggs. (Rev: BL 10/15/96; SLJ 9/96)

4175 Harper, Jessica. *I Forgot My Shoes* (PS–1). Illus. by Kathy Osborn. 1999, Putnam $15.99 (0-399-23149-8). 32pp. A whimsical picture book about a very forgetful family and town. (Rev: BL 11/1/99; HBG 3/00; SLJ 10/99)

4176 Harper, Jo. *Outrageous, Bodacious Boliver Boggs!* (2–3). Illus. by JoAnn Adinolfi. 1996, Simon & Schuster paper $16.00 (0-689-80504-7). Boliver Boggs invents a number of outrageous stories to explain why he is late for school. (Rev: SLJ 4/96)

4177 Hartmann, Wendy, and Niki Daly. *The Dinosaurs Are Back and It's All Your Fault Edward!* (PS–2). Illus. by Niki Daly. 1997, Simon & Schuster $16.00 (0-689-81152-7). 32pp. An older brother persuades Edward that the rock under his bed is really a dinosaur egg about to hatch. (Rev: BL 6/1–15/97; SLJ 6/97)

4178 Hartry, Nancy. *Jocelyn and the Ballerina* (PS–3). Illus. by Linda Hendry. 2000, Fitzhenry & Whiteside $14.95 (1-55041-649-9). 32pp. Jocelyn is so attached to her tutu that she puts it on under the beautiful pink dress she has to wear to a wedding. (Rev: BL 12/15/00; SLJ 1/01)

4179 Hassett, John, and Ann Hassett. *Cat Up a Tree* (PS–2). Illus. 1998, Houghton $15.00 (0-395-88415-2). 32pp. As the number of cats increases in a tree outside her house, Nana Quimby tries several sources for help, starting with the firehouse and the police station and ending with the post office and the library, but finally she has do something about it herself. (Rev: BCCB 11/98; BL 10/15/98*; HBG 3/99; SLJ 10/98)

4180 Himmelman, John. *J.J. Versus the Baby-sitter* (K–2). Illus. by author. 1996, BridgeWater $13.95 (0-8167-3800-9). An entertaining read about a baby-sitter who doesn't realize that her charge has an identical twin. (Rev: SLJ 5/96)

4181 Himmelman, John. *Lights Out!* (K–2). Illus. 1995, Troll $13.95 (0-8167-3450-X). 32pp. A humorous story about the terrible creatures the six Badger Scouts believe await them at summer camp. (Rev: BL 4/1/95; SLJ 8/95)

4182 Hoberman, Mary Ann. *The Seven Silly Eaters* (PS–3). Illus. by Marla Frazee. 1997, Harcourt $16.00 (0-15-200096-8). 40pp. A humorous picture book about Mrs. Peters and her brood of picky eaters. (Rev: BCCB 5/97; BL 3/1/97; HB 5–6/97; SLJ 3/97)

4183 Hoff, Syd. *Arturo's Baton* (PS–3). Illus. 1995, Clarion $13.95 (0-395-71020-0). 32pp. When a famous conductor loses his favorite baton, he no longer can perform. (Rev: BL 9/1/95; SLJ 9/95)

4184 Hubbell, Patricia. *Pots and Pans* (PS). Illus. by Diane De Groat. 1998, HarperFestival $9.95 (0-694-01072-3). Baby clears out the kitchen cupboards, producing chaos and a mad clattering as the child bangs away at the pots and pans. (Rev: BCCB 9/98; BL 8/98; HBG 10/98; SLJ 6/98)

4185 Huliska-Beith, Laura. *The Book of Bad Ideas* (K–3). Illus. by author. 2000, Little, Brown $14.95 (0-316-08748-3). A humorous book of bad ideas — like jumping off the high dive to show off your new bathing suit. (Rev: BCCB 11/00; HBG 3/01; SLJ 9/00)

4186 Hutchins, Pat. *Don't Forget the Bacon!* (K–3). Illus. by author. 1976, Morrow paper $4.95 (0-688-08743-4). 32pp. A young boy mixes up the shopping list on a trip to the grocery store.

4187 Inkpen, Mick. *Billy's Beetle* (PS–2). Illus. 1992, Harcourt $13.95 (0-15-200427-0). 32pp. Even with the help of a trained dog, Billy is not able to find his lost beetle. (Rev: BL 4/15/92; SLJ 8/92)

4188 Isaacs, Anne. *Swamp Angel* (K–4). Illus. by Paul O. Zelinsky. 1994, Dutton $15.99 (0-525-45271-0). 40pp. Angelica Longrider is a true tall-tale heroine because, among her many accomplishments, she is able to lasso a tornado. (Rev: BCCB 11/94; BL 10/15/94*; SLJ 12/94*)

4189 Isadora, Rachael. *Max* (K–2). Illus. by Rachel Isadora. 1976, Macmillan LB $13.95 (0-02-747450-X); paper $4.99 (0-02-043800-1). 32pp. Max, an avid baseball player, finds that joining his sister's dancing class makes an excellent warm-up for the game.

4190 Jam, Teddy. *The Charlotte Stories* (1–3). Illus. by Harvey Chan. 1996, Groundwood $14.95 (0-88899-210-6). 48pp. Charlotte is a candid 7-year-old who can't avoid trouble because of her open, honest nature. (Rev: SLJ 12/96)

4191 Jay, Betsy. *Jane vs. the Tooth Fairy* (K–3). Illus. by Lori Osiecki. 2000, Rising Moon $15.95 (0-87358-769-3). 32pp. A young girl doesn't want to lose her loose tooth and takes such measures as closing her bedroom window so the Tooth Fairy can't get in. (Rev: BL 11/15/00; SLJ 11/00)

4192 Johnson, Arden. *The Lost Tooth Club* (K–2). Illus. by author. 1998, Tricycle Pr. $13.95 (1-883672-55-4). Olivia tries various methods to lose her loose front tooth, so she can join the exclusive Lost Tooth Club. (Rev: HBG 10/98; SLJ 6/98)

4193 Johnson, Doug. *Never Ride Your Elephant to School* (PS–3). Illus. by Abby Carter. 1995, Holt $16.95 (0-8050-2880-3). 32pp. This cautionary tale describes all the catastrophes that can occur when you take an elephant to school. (Rev: BL 9/15/95; SLJ 12/95)

4194 Johnson, Paul B. *Mr. Persnickety and Cat Lady* (K–2). Illus. by Paul Johnson. 2000, Orchard LB $16.99 (0-531-33283-7). A humorous story about Mr. Persnickety who tries to get rid of his neighbor's 37 cats until his house is infested with mice. (Rev: BCCB 7–8/00; HBG 3/01; SLJ 11/00)

4195 Jonas, Ann. *Round Trip* (PS–4). Illus. by author. 1983, Morrow paper $4.95 (0-688-09986-6). 32pp. A book to read forward, backward, and then upside down.

4196 Jonas, Ann. *Watch William Walk* (PS–K). Illus. 1997, Greenwillow $14.89 (0-688-14175-7). 24pp. An alphabet adventure in which the entire story is told with words that begin with *w*. (Rev: BL 4/1/97; HB 7–8/97; SLJ 4/97)

4197 Jonell, Lynne. *I Need a Snake* (PS–K). Illus. by Petra Mathers. 1998, Putnam $12.99 (0-399-23176-5). 32pp. Robbie is frustrated when his mother refuses to get him a snake for a pet, so he imagines snakes in common household items like his mother's shoelaces and his dad's belt. (Rev: BL 5/15/98; HBG 10/98; SLJ 6/98)

4198 Karas, G. Brian. *Bebe's Bad Dream* (PS–2). Illus. 2000, Greenwillow $15.95 (0-688-16182-0). 32pp. Bebe is convinced that aliens visit her every night but afterward realizes it is just a dream. (Rev: BCCB 6/00; BL 6/1–15/00; HB 7–8/00; HBG 10/00; SLJ 6/00)

4199 Kastner, Jill. *Barnyard Big Top* (PS–1). Illus. 1997, Simon & Schuster paper $16.00 (0-689-80484-9). 32pp. When Uncle Julius and his Two Ring Extravaganza suddenly arrive, young Ben's farm becomes a bustling circus. (Rev: BL 11/1/97; HBG 3/98; SLJ 11/97)

4200 Keats, Ezra Jack. *Jennie's Hat* (K–2). Illus. by author. 1966, HarperCollins paper $6.95 (0-06-443072-3). 32pp. Jennie's drab new hat is decorated by her bird friends, who become its trimming.

4201 Kelley, Marty. *The Rules* (K–3). Illus. by author. 2000, Zino $12.95 (1-55933-284-0). Though the text offers many important dos and don'ts, the pictures show children humorously breaking each of the rules. (Rev: SLJ 12/00)

4202 Ketteman, Helen. *Shoeshine Whittaker* (1–3). Illus. by Scott Goto. 1999, Walker LB $16.85 (0-8027-8715-0). 32pp. In Mudville, Shoeshine guarantees how long his shine will last — and lives to regret it. (Rev: BL 10/15/99; HBG 3/00; SLJ 10/99)

4203 Kimmel, Eric A. *I Took My Frog to the Library* (PS–K). Illus. by Blanche Sims. 1992, Puffin paper $5.99 (0-14-050916-X). 32pp. A number of different animals create havoc when they visit the library. (Rev: BL 2/15/90; SLJ 3/90)

4204 Kiser, Kevin. *Buzzy Widget* (1–4). Illus. by John O'Brien. 1999, Marshall Cavendish $15.95 (0-7614-5057-2). Buzzy, a compulsive inventor, creates mechanical helpmates including CHEF, MAID, and WIFE. (Rev: HBG 3/00; SLJ 10/99)

4205 Kulman, Andrew. *Red Light Stop, Green Light Go* (PS–1). Illus. 1993, Simon & Schuster paper $15.00 (0-671-79493-0). A nonsense book about cars, people, and animals — all waiting for the green light. (Rev: SLJ 7/93)

4206 Laden, Nina. *Peek-a-Who?* (PS). Illus. by author. 2000, Chronicle $6.95 (0-8118-2602-3). A board book that uses die-cut windows so the reader can play a game of peek-a-boo. (Rev: SLJ 7/00)

4207 Landstrom, Olof, and Lena Landstrom. *Will Gets a Haircut* (K–2). Trans. from Swedish by Elisabeth Dyssegaard. Illus. by authors. 1993, R&S $13.00 (91-29-62075-9). Will's new hairdo, in the shape of a corkscrew, creates a sensation at school. (Rev: SLJ 2/94)

4208 La Prise, Larry, et al. *The Hokey Pokey* (PS–3). Illus. by Sheila Hamanaka. 1997, Simon & Schuster $16.00 (0-689-80519-5). 32pp. A lively picture book about a variety of people caught in action dancing the hokey pokey. (Rev: BL 2/1/97*; SLJ 3/97)

4209 Lattimore, Deborah N. *The Lady with the Ship on Her Head* (PS–2). Illus. 1990, Harcourt $14.95 (0-15-243525-5). 32pp. In 18th-century France, Madame Pompenstance is unaware that a ship has landed on her hair. (Rev: BL 3/15/90; SLJ 6/90)

4210 Lawston, Lisa. *A Pair of Red Sneakers* (PS–2). Illus. by B. B. Sams. 1998, Orchard LB $16.99 (0-531-33104-0). 32pp. Miles imagines all the wonderful things he could do with a new pair of red sneakers, only to discover the store is out of them. (Rev: BL 10/1/98; HBG 3/99; SLJ 9/98)

4211 Lester, Helen. *It Wasn't My Fault* (PS–1). Illus. by Lynn Munsinger. 1985, Houghton $16.00 (0-395-35629-6). 32pp. Nerdy Murdley Gurdson tries to discover why an ostrich laid an egg on his head. (Rev: BCCB 6/85; BL 3/1/85; SLJ 5/85)

4212 Levitin, Sonia. *A Single Speckled Egg* (K–3). Illus. by John Larrecq. 1976, Houghton $6.95 (0-87466-074-2). 40pp. Three foolish farmers are outwitted by their wives in this ridiculous tale told in the folk tradition.

4213 Lewis, J. Patrick. *The Boat of Many Rooms: The Story of Noah in Verse* (K–3). Illus. by Reg Cartwright. 1997, Simon & Schuster $16.00 (0-689-80118-1). 28pp. A whimsical look at the overcrowding that existed on Noah's Ark. (Rev: BCCB 2/97; BL 2/1/97; SLJ 3/97)

4214 Lithgow, John. *The Remarkable Farkle McBride* (K–2). Illus. by C. F. Payne. 2000, Simon & Schuster $16.00 (0-689-83340-7). Farkle McBride tires of each musical instrument he tries until he realizes he was born to become a conductor. (Rev: BCCB 6/00; HBG 3/01; SLJ 9/00)

4215 Lobel, Arnold. *Ming Lo Moves the Mountain* (PS–3). Illus. by author. 1982, Morrow paper $5.95 (0-688-10995-0). 32pp. A humorous tale about a man's attempt to move a mountain away from his house.

4216 London, Sara. *Firehorse Max* (PS–1). Illus. 1997, HarperCollins LB $14.00 (0-06-205095-8).

32pp. Grandpa Lev's new horse, a former horse at the firehouse, has a behavioral problem when fire bells ring. (Rev: BL 10/1/97; SLJ 10/97)

4217 Long, Melinda. *Hiccup Snickup* (PS–3). Illus. by Thor Wickstrom. 2001, Simon & Schuster $16.00 (0-689-82245-6). 32pp. Everyone in the family tries to help Hattie get rid of her hiccups by suggesting sure cures that don't seem to work. (Rev: BCCB 3/01; BL 3/1/01)

4218 Lord, John Vernon. *The Giant Jam Sandwich* (PS–2). Illus. by author. 1987, Houghton $17.00 (0-395-16033-2); paper $5.95 (0-395-44237-0). A rhymed verse about the citizens of Itching Down who make a giant jam sandwich to attract wasps.

4219 Lowell, Susan. *Little Red Cowboy Hat* (K–3). Illus. by Randy Cecil. 1997, Holt $16.95 (0-8050-3508-7). 32pp. A humorous retelling of *Little Red Riding Hood* using the Wild West as the setting. (Rev: BCCB 6/97; BL 4/15/97; SLJ 5/97*)

4220 Lyon, George E. *A Regular Rolling Noah* (PS–1). Illus. by Stephen Gammell. 1986, Macmillan paper $4.95 (0-689-71449-1). 32pp. A farmhand tells how he once helped a family move its entire farm to Canada. (Rev: BL 9/1/86; HB 11–12/86; SLJ 11/86)

4221 McCloskey, Robert. *Burt Dow, Deep-Water Man* (K–3). Illus. by author. 1963, Puffin paper $5.99 (0-14-050978-X). 64pp. The humorous tale of an old Maine fisherman who caught a whale by the tail and then used a multicolored Band-Aid to cover the hole.

4222 McCloskey, Robert. *Lentil* (K–3). Illus. by author. 1940, Puffin paper $5.99 (0-14-050287-4). 64pp. Tale of a boy who can't carry a tune, yet learns to play the harmonica.

4223 McCully, Emily Arnold. *Popcorn at the Palace* (K–3). Illus. 1997, Harcourt $16.00 (0-15-277699-0). 40pp. The Ferris family is considered odd by Illinois neighbors in the mid-1800s because they go to England to demonstrate corn popping for the queen. (Rev: BL 9/15/97; HBG 3/98; SLJ 10/97)

4224 MacDonald, Amy. *Cousin Ruth's Tooth* (PS–1). Illus. by Marjorie Priceman. 1996, Houghton $16.00 (0-395-71253-X). 32pp. When Ruth loses a tooth, the whole family mounts a search to find it. (Rev: BCCB 6/96; BL 4/1/96; SLJ 5/96)

4225 MacDonald, Amy. *Rachel Fister's Blister* (PS–2). Illus. by Marjorie Priceman. 1990, Houghton $15.00 (0-395-52152-1); paper $5.95 (0-395-65744-X). 32pp. A doctor, pastor, rabbi, postman, and others have different suggestions to treat Rachel's blister. (Rev: BL 10/1/90; HB 11–12/90; SLJ 11/90)

4226 McElligott, Matthew. *Uncle Frank's Pit* (K–3). Illus. 1998, Viking $15.99 (0-670-87737-9). 32pp. Zany Uncle Frank gradually moves all his furniture into the huge hole he is digging, where he hopes one day to find dinosaur bones. (Rev: BL 11/1/98; HBG 3/99; SLJ 10/98)

4227 McEvoy, Greg. *The Ice Cream King* (K–3). Illus. by author. 1998, Stoddart $13.95 (0-7737-3069-9). After graduating from King School, Lionel finds there are few openings, so he compromises

and becomes an ice-cream seller known as "The Ice Cream King." (Rev: SLJ 12/98)

4228 Mangas, Brian. *Follow That Puppy!* (PS–2). Illus. by R. W. Alley. 1991, Simon & Schuster paper $12.95 (0-671-70780-9). When Puppy escapes his elderly owner while out for a walk, an exciting chase occurs. (Rev: SLJ 11/91)

4229 Marshak, Samuel. *The Absentminded Fellow* (PS–3). Trans. by Richard Pevear. Illus. by Marc Rosenthal. 1999, Farrar $16.00 (0-374-30013-5). 32pp. A nonsense story about an absentminded fellow who puts on his landlady's cat, instead of a hat, and uses his trouser legs as sleeves. (Rev: BL 7/99; HB 3–4/99; HBG 10/99; SLJ 3/99)

4230 Martin, Bill, Jr. *The Maestro Plays* (PS–K). Illus. by Vladimir Radunsky. 1994, Holt $15.95 (0-8050-1746-1). 38pp. A circus setting is used to show all the different instruments the maestro plays. (Rev: BCCB 12/94; BL 11/1/94; SLJ 11/94*)

4231 Marx, Patricia. *Meet My Staff* (K–2). Illus. by Roz Chast. 1998, HarperCollins $14.95 (0-06-027484-0). 40pp. Young Walter has his staff do all the things he hates, such as eating revolting vegetables, but what happens when the staff takes a day off? (Rev: BCCB 12/98; BL 8/98; HBG 3/99; SLJ 12/98)

4232 Marzollo, Jean. *I Spy Funhouse: A Book of Picture Riddles* (PS–3). Photos by Walter Wick. 1993, Scholastic $12.95 (0-590-46293-8). 40pp. This entertaining book consists of a series of picture puzzles involving an amusement park fun house and of a series of rhyming word clues. (Rev: BL 5/15/93; SLJ 4/93) [793]

4233 Mazer, Anne. *The Fixits* (PS–3). Illus. by Paul Meisel. 1999, Hyperion LB $13.49 (0-7868-2202-3). 24pp. When the Fixits arrive to help Augusta and her brother mend a cracked plate, they create havoc by breaking everything in sight. (Rev: BL 4/1/99; HBG 10/99; SLJ 6/99)

4234 Mazer, Anne. *The No-Nothings and Their Baby* (PS–3). Illus. by Ross Collins. 2000, Scholastic $15.95 (0-590-68049-8). 40pp. Three goofy stories about Mr. and Mrs. No-Nothing and their misguided efforts to bring up a baby. (Rev: BL 1/1–15/01; HBG 3/01; SLJ 11/00)

4235 Meister, Cari. *Busy, Busy City Street* (PS–2). Illus. by Steven Guarnaccia. 2000, Viking $15.99 (0-670-88944-X). A wacky tale about all the different reasons for noise in a big city — fire trucks rushing to burning buildings, dumpsters losing their loads, and cars with square wheels. (Rev: BCCB 2/01; SLJ 2/01)

4236 Miller, Margaret. *Guess Who?* (PS–K). Illus. 1994, Greenwillow LB $14.93 (0-688-12784-3). 40pp. A series of simple questions get ridiculous answers, but finally the correct one is given. (Rev: BCCB 9/94; BL 8/94*; SLJ 10/94)

4237 Minters, Frances. *Sleepless Beauty* (K–4). Illus. by G. Brian Karas. 1996, Viking $14.99 (0-670-87033-1). 32pp. *Sleeping Beauty* is retold to a hip-hop beat. (Rev: BCCB 11/96; BL 11/1/96; HB 11–12/96; SLJ 9/96)

4238 Most, Bernard. *Whatever Happened to the Dinosaurs?* (1–3). Illus. by author. 1984, Harcourt $16.00 (0-15-295295-0); paper $4.95 (0-15-295296-9). 32pp. Fantastic explanations to the title question.

4239 Munsch, Robert. *Alligator Baby* (PS–2). Illus. by Michael Martchenko. 1997, Scholastic $10.95 (0-590-21101-3). 29pp. An amusing story about overwrought parents who bring different baby animals home from the zoo, thinking each is their child. (Rev: HBG 3/98; SLJ 11/97)

4240 Munsch, Robert. *Andrew's Loose Tooth* (1–2). Illus. by Michael Martchenko. 1998, Scholastic $10.95 (0-590-21102-1). 32pp. Even the Tooth Fairy who arrives on her motorcycle can't dislodge Andrew's stubborn loose tooth. (Rev: BCCB 7–8/98; BL 3/15/98; HBG 10/98; SLJ 5/98)

4241 Munsch, Robert. *Get Out of Bed!* (PS–2). Illus. by Alan Daniel and Lea Daniel. 1998, Scholastic $10.95 (0-590-76977-4). 32pp. Because she has watched television all night, Amy can't get out of bed in the morning, so her family takes her to school in her bed, with humorous results. (Rev: BL 9/15/98; HBG 3/99; SLJ 9/98)

4242 Munsch, Robert. *Munschworks: The First Munsch Collection* (PS–3). Illus. by Michael Martchenko. 1998, Annick $19.95 (1-55037-523-7). 128pp. This omnibus volume includes five of Robert Munsch's popular picture books, including *The Paper Bag Princess, David's Father,* and *Thomas' Snowsuit.* (Rev: BL 1/1–15/99)

4243 Munsch, Robert. *Munschworks 2: The Second Munsch Treasury* (PS–2). Illus. by Michael Martchenko and Helene Desputeaux. 1999, Annick $19.95 (1-55037-553-9). 136pp. This anthology contains five of Robert Munsch's picture books including *Purple, Green and Yellow*, *Pigs*, and *Something Good.* (Rev: BL 1/1–15/00; HBG 3/00)

4244 Munsch, Robert. *Stephanie's Ponytail* (1–3). Illus. by Michael Martchenko. 1996, Firefly $16.95 (1-55037-485-0); paper $5.95 (1-55037-484-2). Stephanie is annoyed when every one of her style changes is copied by class members and her teacher. (Rev: SLJ 11/96)

4245 Munsch, Robert, and Michael Kusugak. *Munschworks 3: The Third Munsch Treasury* (PS–2). Illus. by Vladyana Krykorka and Michael Martchenko. 2000, Annick $19.95 (1-55037-633-0). 144pp. A large book that is a compilation of five of Munsch's previously published picture books including *Stephanie's Ponytail* (1986), *Angela's Airplane* (1988), and *A Promise Is a Promise* (1988). (Rev: BL 2/1/01) [813]

4246 Murphy, Jill. *The Last Noo-Noo* (PS–1). Illus. 1995, Candlewick $14.95 (1-56402-581-0). 32pp. Members of his family finally convince Marlon that it is time to give up using his pacifier. (Rev: BL 11/1/95; SLJ 1/96)

4247 Myers, Lynne B., and Christopher Myers. *Turnip Soup* (PS–2). Illus. by Katie Keller. 1994, Hyperion LB $14.49 (1-56282-446-5). 32pp. George is afraid that there is a Komodo dragon in his basement, and he is right. (Rev: BL 11/15/94; SLJ 2/95)

4248 Naylor, Phyllis Reynolds. *"I Can't Take You Anywhere!"* (PS–2). Illus. by Jef Kaminsky. 1997, Simon & Schuster $15.00 (0-689-31966-5). 32pp. On every outing, Amy Audrey gets into so much trouble that everyone agrees they can't take her anywhere. (Rev: BL 10/1/97; HBG 3/98; SLJ 10/97)

4249 Nielsen, Laura F. *Jeremy's Muffler* (PS–3). Illus. by Christine M. Schneider. 1995, Simon & Schuster $15.00 (0-689-80319-2). 32pp. Jeremy's aunt knits him a muffler that is so long people make fun of it. (Rev: BL 12/15/95; SLJ 12/95)

4250 Nikola-Lisa, W. *Can You Top That?* (K–3). Illus. by Hector Viveros Lee. 2000, Lee & Low $15.95 (1-880000-99-7). 32pp. A group of children try to outdo each other by naming the strange animals they have at home, but a young African American tops them all by claiming he can produce an elephant — and he can, a little stuffed one. (Rev: BL 9/15/00; SLJ 12/00)

4251 Noble, Trinka Hakes. *Meanwhile, Back at the Ranch* (PS–1). Illus. by Tony Ross. 1987, Puffin paper $5.99 (0-14-054564-6). 32pp. A humorous Western adventure concerning Rancher Hicks and his drive into Sleepy Gulch for some excitement. (Rev: BL 4/1/87; SLJ 5/87)

4252 Nolan, Lucy. *The Lizard Man of Crabtree County* (K–3). Illus. by Jill Kastner. 1999, Marshall Cavendish $15.95 (0-7614-5049-1). 32pp. A young boy, who dresses up as a bush, causes a commotion when he is mistaken for the Lizard Man. (Rev: BCCB 10/99; BL 11/15/99; HBG 3/00; SLJ 10/99)

4253 Novak, Matt. *The Pillow War* (PS–2). Illus. 1998, Orchard LB $16.99 (0-531-33048-6). 32pp. Millie and Fred have a pillow fight over who will sleep with Sam the dog, but Sam has other plans. (Rev: BL 2/15/98; HBG 10/98; SLJ 3/98)

4254 Numeroff, Laura. *Why a Disguise?* (PS–3). Illus. by David McPhail. 1996, Simon & Schuster $14.00 (0-689-80513-6). 32pp. A little boy dons a series of disguises to fool his parents. (Rev: BL 4/15/96*; SLJ 7/96)

4255 Numeroff, Laura, and Barney Saltzberg. *Two for Stew* (1–3). Illus. by Sal Murdocca. 1996, Simon & Schuster $15.00 (0-689-80571-3). 32pp. A young woman and her poodle are disappointed at a restaurant when told there is no more stew. (Rev: BL 9/15/96; SLJ 12/96)

4256 O'Neill, Alexis. *Loud Emily* (PS–3). Illus. by Nancy Carpenter. 1998, Simon & Schuster $16.00 (0-689-81078-4). 40pp. Although her family abhors their daughter's booming voice, Emily finds many uses for it, such as serenading whales and saving endangered ships at sea. (Rev: BCCB 10/98; BL 10/15/98; HBG 3/99; SLJ 10/98)

4257 Oppenheim, Shulamith Levey. *What Is the Full Moon Full Of?* (PS–2). Illus. by Cyd Moore. 1997, Boyds Mills $14.95 (1-56397-479-7). 32pp. Every one of the animals has a different answer when Jonas asks what the moon is full of. (Rev: BL 12/1/97; HBG 3/98; SLJ 12/97)

4258 Palatini, Margie. *Bedhead* (K–3). Illus. by Jack E. Davis. 2000, Simon & Schuster $16.00 (0-689-82397-5). No one can tame Oliver's wild hair and so he must wear his trusty blue baseball hat to school. (Rev: BCCB 10/00; HBG 3/01; SLJ 7/00)

4259 Palatini, Margie. *Good as Goldie* (PS–2). Illus. by author. 2000, Hyperion LB $15.49 (0-7868-2435-2). In this amusing picture book, Goldie delights in reporting on all the shortcomings of her baby brother, little realizing that she shares many of the same traits and behavior patterns. (Rev: BCCB 3/00; HBG 10/00; SLJ 5/00)

4260 Parr, Todd. *The Feelings Book* (PS–2). Illus. by author. 2000, Little, Brown $5.95 (0-316-69131-3). A humorous, simple book about how feelings change quickly. Also use *Underwear Do's and Don'ts* (2000). (Rev: HBG 3/01; SLJ 12/00)

4261 Patschke, Steve. *The Spooky Book* (K–3). Illus. by Matt McElligott. 1999, Walker LB $16.85 (0-8027-8693-6). 32pp. Two children, in separate houses, don't realize that they are reading scary books about each other and their spooky homes. (Rev: BCCB 9/99; BL 10/15/99; HBG 3/00; SLJ 11/99)

4262 Pearson, Tracey Campbell. *The Purple Hat* (PS–2). Illus. 1997, Farrar $16.00 (0-374-36153-3). 32pp. When Annie loses her new purple hat, the whole town turns out to help find it. (Rev: BCCB 3/97; BL 2/1/97; SLJ 4/97)

4263 Peters, Lisa Westberg. *Purple Delicious Blackberry Jam* (PS–3). Illus. by Barbara McGregor. 1992, Arcade $14.95 (1-55970-167-6). 32pp. Two children persuade their grandmother to make blackberry jam, but the results are not as expected. (Rev: BL 12/1/92; SLJ 3/93)

4264 Pinkwater, Daniel. *Author's Day* (1–4). Illus. 1993, Macmillan $14.00 (0-02-774642-9). 32pp. An author visits a school where a series of hilarious misadventures occurs. (Rev: BCCB 4/93; BL 3/15/93; SLJ 7/93)

4265 Pinkwater, Daniel. *The Big Orange Splot* (K–2). Illus. by author. 1992, Scholastic paper $4.99 (0-590-44510-3). 32pp. A cumulative story about the effects of dropping a can of orange paint on the roof of Mr. Plumbean's house.

4266 Pinkwater, Daniel. *Rainy Morning* (PS–2). Illus. by Jill Pinkwater. 1999, Simon & Schuster $16.00 (0-689-81143-8). 32pp. During a rainstorm, Mr. and Mrs. Submarine open their kitchen to all sorts of creatures, and soon it is filled with everything from a wildebeest to Ludwig van Beethoven and the U.S. Marine Band. (Rev: BCCB 3/99; BL 3/1/99; HBG 10/99; SLJ 3/99)

4267 Plourde, Lynn. *Pigs in the Mud in the Middle of the Rud* (PS–2). Illus. by John Schoenherr. 1997, Scholastic $15.95 (0-590-56863-9). A farm family in their Model T Ford can't budge because of the animals in their way, including some pigs wallowing in the mud. (Rev: BCCB 2/97; SLJ 3/97*)

4268 Polacco, Patricia. *In Enzo's Splendid Gardens* (1–4). Illus. 1997, Putnam $16.99 (0-399-23107-2). 32pp. A cumulative tale of chaos in an outdoor Italian restaurant begun by an innocent bee. (Rev: BL 8/97; SLJ 5/97)

4269 Polisar, Barry L. *Don't Do That! A Child's Guide to Bad Manners, Ridiculous Rules, and Inad-*

equate Etiquette. Rev. ed. (K–4). Illus. by David Clark. 1995, Rainbow Morning Music $14.95 (0-938663-20-8). An irreverent book of manners that, for example, tells how to pick one's nose properly in public. (Rev: SLJ 8/95)

4270 Pomerantz, Charlotte. *Serena Katz* (K–2). Illus. by R. W. Alley. 1992, Macmillan LB $13.95 (0-02-774901-0). 32pp. The Duncan family visits the amazing, multitalented Serena Katz of New York City. (Rev: BCCB 6/92; BL 4/15/92; SLJ 6/92)

4271 Porte, Barbara Ann. *Chickens! Chickens!* (PS–2). Illus. by Greg Henry. 1995, Orchard LB $15.99 (0-531-08727-1). 32pp. A humorous tale of a man who achieves fame through his many paintings of chickens. (Rev: BCCB 4/95; BL 2/1/95; HB 3–4/95; SLJ 4/95)

4272 Powell, Polly. *Just Dessert* (PS–1). Illus. 1996, Harcourt $15.00 (0-15-200383-5). 32pp. Patsy Apple creeps downstairs to eat the last piece of delicious yellow cake that is in the fridge. (Rev: BL 5/1/96; SLJ 8/96)

4273 Poydar, Nancy. *Busy Bea* (PS–3). Illus. 1994, Macmillan paper $14.95 (0-689-50592-2). 32pp. Bea is always losing things, but she retrieves everything at the school's lost and found. (Rev: BL 11/1/94; SLJ 12/94)

4274 Poydar, Nancy. *Mailbox Magic* (PS–2). Illus. 2000, Holiday $15.95 (0-8234-1525-2). 32pp. Will, who longs to get mail, collects box tops to send away for a cereal bowl. (Rev: BL 6/1–15/00; SLJ 9/00)

4275 Priest, Robert. *The Old Pirate of Central Park* (PS–2). Illus. 1999, Houghton $15.00 (0-395-90505-2). 32pp. Old Pirate launches a replica of his ship, the *Laughing Dog,* in Central Park's sailboat pond, only to find that a retired queen wants to do the same with her ocean liner, the S.S. *Uppity Princess.* (Rev: BCCB 9/99; BL 4/1/99; HBG 10/99; SLJ 6/99)

4276 Proimos, James. *The Loudness of Sam* (K–3). Illus. 1999, Harcourt $13.00 (0-15-202087-X). 32pp. Sam likes to do everything in a big way, and soon his aunt, whom he is visiting, is behaving the same way. (Rev: BCCB 4/99; BL 7/99; HBG 10/99; SLJ 5/99)

4277 Pulver, Robin. *Axle Annie* (PS–3). Illus. by Tedd Arnold. 1999, Dial $15.99 (0-8037-2096-3). 32pp. Shifty Rhodes and friends conspire to get extra ice and snow on a steep hill so that the school bus, driven by Axle Annie, will not be able to make it and there will be, at long last, a snow day in Burskyville. (Rev: BL 2/15/00; HBG 3/00; SLJ 10/99)

4278 Pulver, Robin. *Mrs. Toggle's Beautiful Blue Shoe* (PS–2). Illus. by R. W. Alley. 1994, Four Winds paper $13.95 (0-02-775456-1). 32pp. Members of Mrs. Toggle's class help her retrieve her shoe when she accidentally sends it flying into a tree. (Rev: BL 3/1/94; SLJ 5/94)

4279 Pulver, Robin. *Mrs. Toggle's Zipper* (K–2). Illus. by R. W. Alley. 1990, Macmillan LB $13.95 (0-02-775451-0). 32pp. When Mrs. Toggle's zipper gets stuck, everyone at her school tries to help her out of her coat. (Rev: BCCB 3/90; BL 3/1/90; SLJ 5/90)

4280 Radunsky, Vladimir, and Eugenia Radunsky. *Yucka Drucka Droni* (1–3). Illus. 1998, Scholastic $15.95 (0-590-09837-3). 40pp. A European tale that is a tongue twister about three brothers who marry three sisters and have children with strange names. (Rev: BCCB 7–8/98; BL 2/1/98; HBG 10/98; SLJ 3/98*)

4281 Rattigan, Jama Kim. *Truman's Aunt Farm* (PS–3). Illus. by G. Brian Karas. 1994, Houghton $14.95 (0-395-65661-3). 32pp. In a mix-up, Truman gets a colony of 50 aunts, not ants, from his mail order firm. (Rev: BCCB 3/94; BL 2/15/94; SLJ 6/94*)

4282 Robart, Rose. *The Cake That Mack Ate* (PS–K). Illus. by Maryann Kovalski. 1991, Little, Brown paper $5.95 (0-316-74891-9). A cumulative tale featuring a festive party table. (Rev: BL 3/1/87; SLJ 6–7/87)

4283 Rodda, Emily. *Power and Glory* (PS–2). Illus. by Geoff Kelly. 1996, Greenwillow $15.00 (0-688-14214-1). 32pp. After a series of unwanted interruptions, a young boy, now accompanied by his whole family, plays his video game, "Power and Glory." (Rev: BL 4/15/96*; SLJ 5/96)

4284 Rodda, Emily. *Yay!* (PS–2). Illus. by Craig Smith. 1997, Greenwillow $15.00 (0-688-15255-4). 40pp. A young boy manages to survive all the rides at an amusement park while members of his family drop out, one by one. (Rev: BL 9/1/97; HBG 3/98; SLJ 8/97)

4285 Root, Phyllis. *Aunt Nancy and Cousin Lazybones* (1–4). Illus. by David Parkins. 1998, Candlewick $16.99 (1-56402-425-3). 32pp. Silver-haired Nancy gets rid of a shiftless cousin, Lazybones, by reeling off a list of chores that must be done. (Rev: BCCB 12/98; BL 11/15/98; HB 1–2/99; HBG 3/99; SLJ 11/98)

4286 Root, Phyllis. *Turnover Tuesday* (PS). Illus. by Helen Craig. 1998, Candlewick $10.99 (0-7636-0447-X); paper $3.29 (0-7636-0455-0). 32pp. After Bonnie Bumble eats five turnovers, everything in her life turns around — she wears gloves on her feet and shoes on her hands — but luckily the sixth turnover sets things to rights. (Rev: BL 10/15/98; HBG 3/99; SLJ 11/98)

4287 Rosen, Michael. *Rover* (K–3). Illus. by Neal Layton. 1999, Doubleday $14.95 (0-385-32677-7). 28pp. The dog narrator in this humorous picture book notes the absurdities of human behavior. (Rev: BCCB 6/99; BL 7/99; HBG 10/99; SLJ 6/99)

4288 Ross, Tony. *I Want My Dinner* (PS). Illus. by author. 1996, Harcourt $12.00 (0-15-200972-8). A humorous look at an ill-mannered girl who throws temper tantrums when she doesn't get her way. (Rev: SLJ 5/96)

4289 Ross, Tony. *I Want to Be* (PS–1). Illus. by author. 1993, Kane/Miller $11.95 (0-916291-46-4). A little princess seeks advice from others so that she will grow up to be a perfect adult. (Rev: SLJ 3/94)

4290 Roth, Roger. *Fishing for Methuselah* (PS–3). Illus. 1998, HarperCollins $14.95 (0-06-027592-8). 32pp. Each of two great rivals in the North Country vows that he will catch the biggest fish in the lake, Methuselah, during the annual Winter Carnival. (Rev: BCCB 11/98; BL 11/15/98; HBG 3/99; SLJ 12/98)

4291 Rubel, Nicole. *A Cowboy Named Ernestine* (PS–3). Illus. by author. 2001, Dial $15.99 (0-8037-2152-8). To avoid marriage to a man she can't bear, Ernestine O'Reilly disguises herself and becomes Ernest T. O'Reilly, a cowboy. (Rev: SLJ 3/01)

4292 Ryan-Lush, Geraldine. *Hairs on Bears* (K–3). Illus. by Normand Cousineau. 1994, Annick LB $14.95 (1-55037-351-X); paper $4.95 (1-55037-352-8). A humorous picture book about the problems caused when the family pooch begins to shed his hair. (Rev: SLJ 12/94)

4293 Sadler, Marilyn. *Alistair's Time Machine* (K–2). Illus. by Roger Bollen. 1986, Simon & Schuster paper $5.95 (0-671-68493-0). 40pp. Alistair invents a time machine and has wondrous travels, but when he returns home and enters it in a science contest, he loses. (Rev: BL 7/86; SLJ 9/86)

4294 Sadu, Itah. *Christopher Changes His Name* (1–3). Illus. by Roy Condy. 1998, Firefly $15.95 (1-55209-216-X); paper $5.95 (1-55209-214-3). 29pp. An African American boy is unhappy with his name and decides to change it to something more distinctive and impressive. (Rev: SLJ 6/98)

4295 Saenz, Benjamin Alire. *Grandma Fina and Her Wonderful Umbrellas/La Abuelita Fina y Sus Sombrillas Maravillosas* (K–2). Trans. by Pilar Herrera. Illus. by Geronimo Garcia. 1999, Cinco Puntos $15.95 (0-938317-46-6). 31pp. In this bilingual book, Grandma Fina is given a total on nine new umbrellas on her birthday, but she knows exactly what to do with each of them. (Rev: HBG 3/00; SLJ 10/99)

4296 Sage, James. *Sassy Gracie* (PS–1). Illus. by Pierre Pratt. 1998, Dutton $15.99 (0-525-45885-9). 32pp. Gracie, the cook's helper, works up such an appetite dancing in her big red shoes that she eats the two plump chickens intended for her master and his guest. However, ingenious Gracie thinks up a solution. (Rev: BCCB 7–8/98; BL 6/1–15/98; HBG 10/98; SLJ 8/98)

4297 Saltzberg, Barney. *The Flying Garbanzos* (PS–1). Illus. 1998, Crown LB $17.99 (0-517-70979-1). 40pp. A wacky glimpse at the daily life of a family of acrobats, known as the Flying Garbanzos, and their home filled with trapezes, high wires, and trampolines. (Rev: BL 9/15/98; SLJ 9/98)

4298 Saltzberg, Barney. *The Soccer Mom from Outer Space* (K–2). Illus. by author. 2000, Crown LB $17.99 (0-517-80064-0). A humorous story about parents who let their enthusiasm carry them away when their daughter plays in her first soccer game. (Rev: BCCB 6/00; HBG 3/01; SLJ 8/00)

4299 Saltzberg, Barney. *Where, Oh, Where Is My Underwear? A Pop-Up Book* (PS–K). Illus. 1994, Hyperion $9.95 (1-56282-694-8). 12pp. A search for underwear leads to great fun pulling tabs and lifting flaps in this interactive book. (Rev: BL 11/15/94)

4300 Samuels, Barbara. *Aloha, Dolores* (PS–2). Illus. 2000, DK $15.95 (0-7894-2508-4). 32pp. A humorous story in which a young girl goes to great lengths to make sure her cat wins a trip to Hawaii. (Rev: BL 3/1/00; HBG 10/00; SLJ 4/00)

4301 Sanfield, Steve. *Bit by Bit* (PS–1). Illus. by Susan Gaber. 1995, Putnam $16.99 (0-399-22736-9). 32pp. Zundel the tailor continually recycles his beloved coat until it becomes only a button. (Rev: BCCB 5/95; BL 3/15/95; SLJ 8/95*)

4302 Scheer, Julian. *Rain Makes Applesauce* (K–2). Illus. by Marvin Bileck. 1964, Holiday $16.95 (0-8234-0091-3). 36pp. A series of silly statements nonsensically presented and accompanied by humorous detailed pictures.

4303 Schneider, Christine M. *Picky Mrs. Pickle* (K–2). Illus. by author. 1999, Walker LB $16.85 (0-8027-8703-7). Mrs. Pickle has a pickle fetish and her stubborn niece tries to introduce her to other tastes. (Rev: HBG 3/00; SLJ 9/99)

4304 Schwartz, Amy. *How to Catch an Elephant* (PS–2). Illus. 1999, DK $15.95 (0-7894-2579-3). A silly, offbeat story about how to catch an elephant, using three cakes, two raisins, one telescope, and tweezers. (Rev: BL 11/15/99; HBG 3/00; SLJ 2/00)

4305 Scieszka, Jon. *The Stinky Cheese Man: And Other Fairly Stupid Tales* (2–6). Illus. by Lane Smith. 1992, Viking $16.99 (0-670-84487-X). 56pp. Lots of fun with fractured fairy tales. (Rev: BCCB 10/92*; BL 9/1/92; HB 11–12/92*; SLJ 9/92*)

4306 Segal, Lore. *All the Way Home* (K–3). Illus. by James Marshall. 1988, Farrar paper $3.95 (0-374-40355-4). 32pp. Juliet's wailing attracts the attention of some animal friends in this amusing story of a day in the park.

4307 Selgin, Peter. *S.S. Gigantic Across the Atlantic: The Story of the World's Biggest Ocean Liner Ever! And Its Disastrous Maiden Voyage* (1–5). Illus. 1999, Simon & Schuster $16.00 (0-689-82467-X). 40pp. A hilarious tale about the SS *Gigantic* — so big it sinks an iceberg but, nevertheless, meets its end on its maiden voyage. (Rev: BCCB 9/99; BL 6/1–15/99; HBG 10/99; SLJ 6/99)

4308 Sendak, Maurice. *Chicken Soup with Rice: A Book of Months* (K–3). Illus. by author. 1962, HarperCollins LB $15.89 (0-06-025535-8). 48pp. A rhyming story that takes one through each of the months with the always suitable chicken soup with rice.

4309 Seuss, Dr., and Jack Prelutsky. *Hooray for Diffendoofer Day!* (K–4). Illus. by Lane Smith. 1998, Knopf LB $18.99 (0-679-99008-9). 56pp. With this story about an unusual teacher named Miss Bonkers, Prelutsky and Smith complete the sketches Dr. Seuss left when he died in 1991. (Rev: BCCB 6/98; BL 5/1/98; HBG 10/98; SLJ 6/98)

4310 Seymour, Tres. *I Love My Buzzard* (K–3). Illus. by S. D. Schindler. 1994, Orchard LB $16.99 (0-531-08669-0). 32pp. Mom gives up and decides to leave when her young son's menagerie grows and grows. (Rev: BL 1/15/94; SLJ 4/94)

4311 Seymour, Tres. *Jake Johnson: The Story of a Mule* (PS–3). Illus. by Marsha Gray Carrington. 1999, DK $15.95 (0-7894-2563-7). 32pp. When Farmer Puckett's stubborn mule won't budge to deliver the Fourth of July fireworks, he and his wife must think of a plan to make him move. (Rev: BCCB 4/99; BL 7/99; HBG 10/99; SLJ 4/99)

4312 Seymour, Tres. *Too Quiet for These Old Bones* (PS–1). Illus. by Paul Johnson. 1997, Orchard LB $16.99 (0-531-33052-4). 32pp. To their surprise, four children discover that Granny doesn't really want the quiet they expect and instead would like to make a racket. (Rev: BL 11/15/97; HBG 3/98; SLJ 10/97)

4313 Shannon, David. *The Rain Came Down* (PS–2). Illus. 2000, Scholastic $15.95 (0-439-05021-9). 32pp. Rain creates chaos in a big city as every living thing reacts in surprise. (Rev: BCCB 12/00; BL 10/15/00; HB 9–10/00; HBG 3/01; SLJ 10/00)

4314 Sharmat, Marjorie W. *Gila Monsters Meet You at the Airport* (PS–2). Illus. by Byron Barton. 1980, Macmillan $16.00 (0-02-782450-0); paper $4.95 (0-689-71383-5). 32pp. A young boy imagines all sorts of horrible things about his move from New York City.

4315 Sharratt, Nick. *Mrs. Pirate* (PS–1). Illus. by author. 1994, Candlewick $8.95 (1-56402-249-8). In this small book, Mrs. Pirate goes off on a shopping spree to prepare for her sea journey. (Rev: SLJ 9/94)

4316 Silverman, Erica. *Mrs. Peachtree's Bicycle* (K–3). Illus. by Ellen Beier. 1996, Simon & Schuster $15.00 (0-689-80477-6). In turn-of-the-century New York, old Mrs. Peachtree masters the art of bicycle riding so well that she gets a speeding ticket. (Rev: SLJ 7/96)

4317 Simms, Laura. *Rotten Teeth* (K–3). Illus. by David Catrow. 1998, Houghton $15.00 (0-395-82850-3). 32pp. Melissa has many things she could bring to school for show-and-tell, such as the alligator that lives in her family's doghouse. But her final choice is so disgusting that she will be remembered forever in the school's history. (Rev: BCCB 12/98; BL 9/1/98; HBG 3/99; SLJ 9/98)

4318 Sloat, Teri. *The Thing That Bothered Farmer Brown* (PS–1). Illus. by Nadine Bernard Westcott. 1995, Orchard LB $16.99 (0-531-08733-6). 32pp. A pesky mosquito keeps Farmer Brown and all the farm animals awake. (Rev: BL 2/1/95; SLJ 3/95)

4319 Slobodkina, Esphyr. *Caps for Sale* (K–3). Illus. by author. 1947, HarperCollins LB $15.89 (0-06-025778-4); paper $5.95 (0-06-443143-6). 48pp. When some monkeys engage in a bit of monkey business, the cap peddler must use his imagination to retrieve his wares.

4320 Spence, Rob, and Amy Spence. *Clickety Clack* (PS–1). Illus. by Margaret Spengler. 1999, Viking $15.99 (0-670-87946-0). 32pp. Each of the passengers picked up by a little black train makes so much noise that Driver Zack must take stern measures. (Rev: BL 7/99; HBG 10/99; SLJ 8/99)

4321 Spurr, Elizabeth. *The Long, Long Letter* (K–3). Illus. by David Catrow. 1996, Hyperion LB $15.49

(0-7868-2100-0). 32pp. Aunt Hetta longs to receive a letter, so her sister obliges with the longest one ever. (Rev: BL 4/15/96; SLJ 8/96)

4322 Stadler, John. *The Cats of Mrs. Calamari* (PS–2). Illus. 1997, Orchard $15.95 (0-531-30020-X). 32pp. When Mrs. Calamari discovers that her new landlord hates cats, she must think of unusual ways to save her large brood. (Rev: BL 3/1/97*; SLJ 5/97)

4323 Stanley, Diane. *Raising Sweetness* (PS–3). Illus. by G. Brian Karas. 1999, Putnam $15.99 (0-399-23225-7). 32pp. The kindly sheriff of Possum Trot adopts Sweetness and seven other orphans, and to show her appreciation, Sweetness arranges a reunion between the sheriff and his girlfriend. (Rev: BCCB 2/99; BL 2/15/99; HB 3–4/99; HBG 10/99; SLJ 1/99*)

4324 Stanley, Diane. *Saving Sweetness* (PS–3). Illus. by G. Brian Karas. 1996, Putnam $16.99 (0-399-22645-1). 32pp. After she runs away from an orphanage, Sweetness must save the sheriff who has been trying to catch her. (Rev: BCCB 11/96; BL 1/1–15/97*; HB 9–10/96; SLJ 11/96*)

4325 Steig, William. *The Amazing Bone* (K–2). Illus. by author. 1983, Farrar $17.00 (0-374-30248-0). 32pp. A bone that talks saves a piglet from being eaten by a fox in this nonsensical and witty story.

4326 Steig, William. *CDB!* Rev. ed. (PS–4). Illus. 2000, Simon & Schuster $16.00 (0-689-83160-9). 48pp. The great word-game book of 30 years ago is now reissued with color drawings. (Rev: BL 4/1/00; HBG 10/00) [793.734]

4327 Steig, William. *Pete's a Pizza* (PS–K). Illus. 1998, HarperCollins $13.95 (0-06-205157-1). 32pp. Pete is in a terrible mood until his parents pretend he is a pizza and begin kneading him, tossing him in the air, and sprinkling him with flour. (Rev: BL 10/1/98*; HB 9–10/98; HBG 3/99; SLJ 11/98)

4328 Stevens, Jan R. *Carlos and the Skunk: Carlos y el Zorrillo* (1–4). Illus. by Jeanne Arnold. 1997, Northland LB $15.95 (0-87358-591-7). 32pp. A bilingual book in which Carlos tangles with a skunk. (Rev: BL 5/15/97; HBG 3/98)

4329 Stevens, Kathleen. *Aunt Skilly and the Stranger* (PS–3). Illus. by Robert Andrew Parker. 1994, Ticknor $14.95 (0-395-68712-8). 32pp. A stranger, whom Aunt Skilly helps, comes back at night to steal her valuable quilts in this story of Appalachian Mountain life. (Rev: BL 10/1/94; HB 11–12/94; SLJ 10/94)

4330 Stevenson, James. *Don't Make Me Laugh* (PS–1). Illus. 1999, Farrar $16.00 (0-374-31827-1). 32pp. A cartoon-illustrated, interactive book full of animal characters who get into trouble — thanks to the activities of the reader. (Rev: BL 6/1–15/99; HBG 3/00; SLJ 9/99)

4331 Stevenson, James. *Worse Than the Worst* (K–3). Illus. 1994, Greenwillow LB $13.93 (0-688-12250-7). 32pp. Worst, the most cranky person ever, meets his match when his disagreeable grand-nephew Warren comes to stay. (Rev: BCCB 7–8/94; BL 3/1/94; HB 5–6/94; SLJ 7/94)

4332 Stevenson, James. *Yard Sale* (2–4). Illus. 1996, Greenwillow $14.89 (0-688-14127-7). 32pp. All of the creatures of Mud Flat participate in an unusual yard sale. (Rev: BL 3/15/96; HB 7–8/96; SLJ 7/96*)

4333 Stewart, Dianne. *Gift of the Sun* (PS–3). Illus. by Jude Daly. 1996, Farrar $15.00 (0-374-32425-5). 30pp. Thulani loves his wife but is too lazy to do the chores around their farm. (Rev: BCCB 12/96; BL 9/1/96; HB 11–12/96; SLJ 9/96*)

4334 Stuart, Chad. *The Ballymara Flood* (PS–3). Illus. by George Booth. 1996, Harcourt $15.00 (0-15-205698-X). 40pp. A boy's innocent bath time ritual ends in a flood. (Rev: BL 4/1/96; SLJ 6/96)

4335 Tafuri, Nancy. *This Is the Farmer* (PS). Illus. 1994, Morrow $16.95 (0-688-09468-6). 24pp. A series of amusing cause-and-effect situations begin when a farmer gives a good-morning kiss to his wife. (Rev: BL 5/15/94; HB 9–10/94; SLJ 5/94)

4336 Teague, Mark. *Baby Tamer* (PS–3). Illus. 1997, Scholastic $15.95 (0-590-67712-8). 32pp. Amanda, the new baby-sitter, proves unflappable when tested by the Eggmont children. (Rev: BL 8/97; HBG 3/98; SLJ 10/97)

4337 Thomas, Valerie. *Winnie Flies Again* (PS–3). Illus. by Korky Paul. 2000, Kane/Miller $7.95 (0-916291-95-2). Winnie the Witch has accidents no matter what form of transportation she uses and finally discovers she needs glasses. (Rev: SLJ 7/00)

4338 Tucker, Kathy. *Do Cowboys Ride Bikes?* (PS–2). Illus. by Nadine Bernard Westcott. 1997, Albert Whitman LB $15.95 (0-8075-1693-7). 32pp. A humorous picture book that explores cowboy behavior in a delightful series of questions and answers with droll illustrations. (Rev: BCCB 6/97; BL 4/1/97; HBG 3/98; SLJ 6/97)

4339 Van Laan, Nancy. *Round and Round Again* (PS–1). Illus. by Nadine Bernard Westcott. 1994, Hyperion LB $14.49 (0-7868-2005-5). 32pp. Mama is a collector of discarded objects that she plans to reuse in ingenious ways. (Rev: BL 10/1/94; SLJ 12/94)

4340 Viorst, Judith. *Earrings!* (K–3). Illus. by Nola L. Malone. 1990, Macmillan $16.95 (0-689-31615-1). 32pp. A young heroine wants pierced ears so she can wear a wide variety of earrings. (Rev: BCCB 1/91; BL 10/1/90; HB 11–12/90; SLJ 11/90)

4341 Viorst, Judith. *My Mama Says There Aren't Any Zombies, Ghosts, Vampires, Creatures, Demons, Monsters, Fiends, Goblins, or Things* (PS–1). Illus. by Kay Chorao. 1973, Macmillan $16.00 (0-689-30102-2); paper $5.99 (0-689-71204-9). 48pp. A humorous story concerned with a child's vivid description of imaginary monsters and his mother's reassurance that they don't exist.

4342 Viorst, Judith. *Super-Completely and Totally the Messiest* (K–4). Illus. by Robin P. Glasser. 2001, Simon & Schuster $16.00 (0-689-82941-8). 32pp. Olivia describes the antics of her baby sister, who deserves the title "The Messiest." (Rev: BL 2/1/01; SLJ 3/01)

4343 Waber, Bernard. *Do You See a Mouse?* (PS–1). Illus. 1995, Houghton $14.95 (0-395-72292-6). 32pp. Every one of the characters in this humorous picture book fails to see the mouse that is apparent to the reader. (Rev: BL 4/1/95; HB 7–8/95; SLJ 9/95)

4344 Walsh, Melanie. *Do Pigs Have Stripes?* (PS–1). Illus. 1996, Houghton $12.95 (0-395-73976-4). 40pp. Nonsensical questions about animals (like the title) produce equally entertaining answers. (Rev: BL 3/1/96; HB 5–6/96; SLJ 4/96)

4345 Walter, Virginia. *"Hi, Pizza Man!"* (PS–2). Illus. by Ponder Goembel. 1995, Orchard LB $16.99 (0-531-08735-2). 32pp. Vivian wonders what sort of messenger will deliver the pizza that she and her mother have ordered. (Rev: BL 1/15/95; HB 3–4/95; SLJ 3/95)

4346 Walton, Rick. *Little Dogs Say "Rough!"* (PS–K). Illus. by Henry Cole. 2000, Putnam $12.99 (0-399-23228-1). Animal sounds are the subject of this humorous picture book that features wacky word plays for the actual sounds (for example, a horse's "neigh" becomes "nay"). (Rev: HBG 10/00; SLJ 8/00)

4347 Walton, Rick. *Why the Banana Split* (1–4). Illus. by Jimmy Holder. 1998, Gibbs Smith $15.95 (0-87905-853-6). A book of verbal puns that tells how everyone and everything leave town when dinosaur Rex visits; for example, even the frogs hop a train. (Rev: SLJ 1/99)

4348 Weeks, Sarah. *Mrs. McNosh Hangs Up Her Wash* (PS–K). Illus. by Nadine Bernard Westcott. 1998, HarperCollins $9.95 (0-694-01076-6). 24pp. On wash day, Mrs. McNosh gets carried away and begins hanging out such items as the newspaper, the dog, and the phone to dry. (Rev: BCCB 5/98; BL 4/15/98; HBG 10/98; SLJ 7/98)

4349 Westcott, Nadine Bernard. *Peanut Butter and Jelly: A Play Rhyme* (PS–K). Illus. by author. 1987, Puffin paper $5.99 (0-14-054852-1). 32pp. A play rhyme describes the making of this food that is a children's favorite. (Rev: BL 10/1/87; SLJ 9/87)

4350 Whatley, Bruce, and Rosie Smith. *Captain Pajamas* (PS–2). Illus. by Bruce Whatley. 2000, HarperCollins LB $15.89 (0-06-026614-7). 32pp. Late one night Brian believes that aliens have landed, but the sounds he hears are only his dog trying to get into the fridge. (Rev: BCCB 9/00; BL 5/15/00; HBG 10/00; SLJ 6/00)

4351 White, Linda. *Too Many Pumpkins* (PS–2). Illus. by Megan Lloyd. 1996, Holiday LB $16.95 (0-8234-1245-8). 28pp. Rebecca Estelle, who hates pumpkins, finds she has a bumper crop in her garden. (Rev: BCCB 12/96; BL 9/15/96; SLJ 11/96)

4352 White, Linda Arms. *Comes a Wind* (PS–3). Illus. by Tom Curry. 2000, DK $15.95 (0-7894-2601-3). 32pp. In this tall tale, two fiercely competitive brothers learn to cooperate when their mother gets blown away by a mighty Texas wind. (Rev: BCCB 3/00; BL 3/15/00; HBG 10/00; SLJ 5/00)

4353 Williams, Jay. *Everyone Knows What a Dragon Looks Like* (K–3). Illus. by Mercer Mayer. 1984, Macmillan paper $6.95 (0-02-045600-X). 32pp. In this humorous tale told in the folk tradition, the leaders argue about what a dragon looks like, but the people know — "a small, fat, bald old man."

4354 Williams, Vera B. *"More More More," Said the Baby: 3 Love Stories* (PS). Illus. 1990, Greenwillow $15.89 (0-688-09174-1). 32pp. All the ways that parents and grandparents play with youngsters are portrayed in this humorous picture book. (Rev: BCCB 10/90; BL 10/1/90; HB 11–12/90; SLJ 10/90*)

4355 Wishinsky, Frieda. *Oonga Boonga* (PS–K). Illus. by Carol Thompson. 1999, Dutton $15.99 (0-525-46095-0). 32pp. No one can quiet howling Baby Louise until big brother comes home from school and says "oonga boonga" to her. (Rev: BL 5/1/99; HBG 10/99; SLJ 6/99)

4356 Wood, Audrey. *King Bidgood's in the Bathtub* (PS–2). Illus. by Don Wood. 1985, Harcourt $16.00 (0-15-242730-9). 32pp. No one can get the king out of his bathtub, until the young page thinks of pulling the plug. (Rev: BCCB 1/86; BL 10/1/85; SLJ 11/85)

4357 Wood, Audrey. *The Napping House* (PS–2). Illus. by Don Wood. 1984, Harcourt $16.00 (0-15-256708-9). 32pp. A cumulative story about all the members of a household taking a nap except for a flea.

4358 Wood, Audrey. *Red Racer* (PS–2). Illus. 1996, Simon & Schuster $16.00 (0-689-80553-5). 30pp. Nona tries unsuccessfully to get rid of her old bicycle so she can get a new red racer. (Rev: BCCB 7–8/96; BL 9/1/96; SLJ 9/96*)

4359 Wood, Jakki. *Across the Big Blue Sea: An Ocean Wildlife Book* (PS–2). Illus. 1998, National Geographic $14.95 (0-7922-7308-7). 32pp. The story of a tiny toy boat's adventures on a long journey from a California beach to the coast of Great Britain. (Rev: BL 5/1/98; HBG 10/98; SLJ 4/98)

4360 Yaccarino, Dan. *An Octopus Followed Me Home* (PS–2). Illus. 1997, Viking $15.99 (0-670-87401-9). 32pp. After allowing his daughter to keep a menagerie of pets, a father draws the line at an octopus. (Rev: BL 8/97; HBG 3/98; SLJ 1/98)

4361 Yee, Wong H. *Eek! There's a Mouse in the House* (PS–K). Illus. by author. 1992, Houghton $16.00 (0-395-62303-0). A young girl sends for larger and larger animals to rid her house of a mouse. (Rev: SLJ 10/92)

4362 Yorinks, Arthur. *Oh, Brother* (K–3). Illus. by Richard Egielski. 1989, Farrar $15.95 (0-374-35599-1). 40pp. In this humorous tale, two orphan boys continue to quarrel regardless of what situation they are in. (Rev: BCCB 11/89; BL 10/15/89*; SLJ 12/89*)

4363 Yorinks, Arthur. *Whitefish Will Rides Again!* (K–4). Illus. by Mort Drucker. 1994, HarperCollins LB $14.89 (0-06-205038-9). 32pp. Whitefish Will, a retired sheriff, is brought back to town to take care of evil Bart, who is terrorizing the citizenry. (Rev: BCCB 1/95; BL 11/15/94; SLJ 10/94)

4364 Zemach, Harve. *A Penny a Look: An Old Story Retold* (K–3). Illus. by Margot Zemach. 1971, Farrar $16.00 (0-374-35793-5); paper $4.95 (0-374-45758-1). 48pp. A rascal tries to exploit his brother in a wild money-making scheme.

4365 Ziefert, Harriet. *I Swapped My Dog* (PS–1). Illus. by Emily Bolam. 1998, Houghton $15.00 (0-

395-89159-0). 32pp. A cumulative story about a man who swaps each animal he receives for what he thinks is a better one, but ends up with his original faithful dog. (Rev: BL 3/1/98; HB 7–8/98; HBG 10/98; SLJ 5/98)

4366 Ziefert, Harriet. *Someday We'll Have Very Good Manners* (PS–3). Illus. by Chris L. Demarest. 2001, Putnam $15.99 (0-399-23558-2). 32pp. A merry book juxtaposing future proper behavior with current boorishness. (Rev: BL 2/15/01; SLJ 2/01)

4367 Ziefert, Harriet. *When I First Came to This Land* (K–2). Illus. by Simms Taback. 1998, Putnam $15.99 (0-399-23044-0). 32pp. A bouncy, rhyming saga about the misadventures of an early Pennsylvania farmer and his problems with such animals as the cow named No-milk-now. (Rev: BCCB 9/98; BL 6/1–15/98; HBG 10/98; SLJ 6/98)

4368 Zimelman, Nathan. *How the Second Grade Got $8,205.50 to Visit the Statue of Liberty* (K–3). Illus. by Bill Slavin. 1992, Whitman LB $14.95 (0-8075-3431-5). 32pp. Second-graders try to raise money for a field trip, with humorous results. (Rev: BL 9/15/92)

NATURE AND SCIENCE

4369 Albert, Burton. *Windsongs and Rainbows* (PS–2). Illus. by Susan Stillman. 1993, Simon & Schuster paper $14.00 (0-671-76004-1). Changes in the weather, including a rainstorm, are depicted. (Rev: SLJ 8/93)

4370 Aldridge, Josephine Haskell. *A Possible Tree* (K–3). Illus. by Daniel San Souci. 1993, Macmillan LB $16.00 (0-02-700407-4). 32pp. All the pests around Joe Bracken's farm — like a blue jay, raccoon, and squirrel — take refuge in a small fir tree so that at Christmas it looks like a living Christmas wreath. (Rev: BL 10/1/93)

4371 Allen, Marjorie. *Changes* (PS–K). Illus. by Shelley Rotner. 1991, Macmillan paper $14.00 (0-02-700252-7). This photo-essay shows the changes that occur in nature, such as the opening of a flower. (Rev: BCCB 3/91; BL 6/15/91; SLJ 7/91)

4372 Anderson, David A. *The Rebellion of Humans: An African Spiritual Journey* (K–4). Illus. by Claude Joachim. 1994, Sights $18.95 (0-9629978-6-2). 32pp. This ecological tale tells about an African tribe that forgets the lessons of the past and creates a wasteland by destroying the forests. A sequel to *The Origin of Life on Earth* (1992). (Rev: BL 10/1/94)

4373 Arnosky, Jim. *Beaver Pond, Moose Pond* (PS–K). Illus. 2000, National Geographic $15.95 (0-7922-7692-2). 32pp. A brief text showing how a beaver works on his pond at night, and while he is sleeping during the day the visitors include a heron, a moose, and ducks. (Rev: BL 1/1–15/01; HBG 3/01; SLJ 11/00)

4374 Arnosky, Jim. *Crinkleroot's Guide to Knowing the Birds* (K–4). Illus. 1992, Macmillan $15.00 (0-02-705857-3). 32pp. The lovable woodsman offers tips on all sorts of nature know-how. (Rev: BL 10/15/92; SLJ 11/92) [598]

4375 Arnosky, Jim. *Crinkleroot's Guide to Walking in Wild Places* (1–3). Illus. 1990, Macmillan $15.00

(0-02-705842-5). 32pp. How-to for a leisurely walk through the woods. (Rev: BL 8/90; HB 11–12/90; SLJ 11/90) [796.5]

4376 Arnosky, Jim. *Crinkleroot's Visit to Crinkle Cove* (K–2). Illus. 1998, Simon & Schuster $14.00 (0-689-81602-2). 32pp. Crinkleroot, the nature guide and woodsman, introduces various plants and animals while he wanders through the woods searching for his beloved snake, Sassafras. (Rev: BL 8/98; HBG 3/99; SLJ 8/98)

4377 Asch, Frank. *The Earth and I* (PS–2). Illus. 1994, Harcourt $15.00 (0-15-200443-2). 32pp. A young boy shares many thoughts and activities with his friend the earth. (Rev: BL 1/15/95; SLJ 10/94)

4378 Asch, Frank. *The Sun Is My Favorite Star* (PS–1). Illus. 2000, Harcourt $15.00 (0-15-202127-2). 32pp. A little girl sings the praises of the sun and the light that it gives her. (Rev: BL 11/1/00; HBG 3/01; SLJ 10/00)

4379 Aschenbrenner, Gerald. *Jack, the Seal and the Sea* (1–4). Illus. by author. 1988, Silver Burdett LB $12.95 (0-382-09985-0); paper $4.95 (0-382-09986-9). 30pp. Jack rescues a seal who leads him to bountiful fishing grounds. (Rev: BL 1/15/89; SLJ 3/89)

4380 Atwell, Debby. *River* (K–3). Illus. 1999, Houghton $15.00 (0-395-93546-6). 32pp. This book describes the changes that occur to an American river over time, and the reader gets an antipollution lesson along the way. (Rev: BL 11/1/99; HBG 3/00; SLJ 11/99)

4381 Aylesworth, Jim. *Wake Up, Little Children: A Rise-and-Shine Rhyme* (PS–2). Illus. by Walter L. Krudop. 1996, Simon & Schuster $16.00 (0-689-31857-X). The flora and fauna of the countryside are pictured, with an invitation for children to come out and enjoy nature. (Rev: SLJ 4/96)

4382 Baker, Sanna Anderson. *Mississippi Going North* (K–3). Illus. by Bill Farnsworth. 1996, Albert Whitman LB $15.95 (0-8075-5164-3). A picture book about a family that explores the northern part of the Mississippi River by canoe and sees many animals and birds. (Rev: SLJ 10/96)

4383 Bang, Molly. *Common Ground: The Water, Earth, and Air We Share* (PS–3). Illus. 1997, Scholastic $12.95 (0-590-10056-4). 32pp. A parable in which villagers misuse their grazing areas points out the modern environmental problem of wasting the earth's resources. (Rev: BL 10/1/97*; HB 11–12/97; HBG 3/98; SLJ 10/97)

4384 Baskwill, Jane. *Somewhere* (PS–1). Illus. by Trish Hill. 1996, Mondo $13.95 (1-57255-131-3). A simple rhyme and drawings of simple outdoor scenes are used to introduce the beauty and variety of nature. (Rev: SLJ 5/96)

4385 Bauer, Marion Dane. *When I Go Camping with Grandma* (PS–2). Illus. by Allen Garns. 1995, Troll $15.95 (0-8167-3448-8). 32pp. A mood piece that lovingly describes a camping trip with a child and grandmother. (Rev: BL 1/1/95; SLJ 4/95)

4386 Baylor, Byrd. *If You Are a Hunter of Fossils* (PS–1). Illus. by Peter Parnall. 1984, Simon & Schuster paper $5.99 (0-689-70773-8). 32pp. A story that introduces a sense of long ago.

4387 Below, Halina. *Chestnut Dreams* (PS–1). Illus. by author. 2000, Fitzhenry & Whiteside $14.95 (1-55041-545-X). 40pp. The life cycle of a horse chestnut tree is explored in this picture book that shows a girl and her grandmother enjoying and observing the tree through several seasons. (Rev: SLJ 1/01)

4388 Bess, Clayton. *The Truth About the Moon* (K–3). Illus. by Rosekrans Hoffman. 1983, Houghton paper $6.95 (0-395-64371-6). 48pp. A young African boy hears both realistic and fanciful explanations for the moon.

4389 Bogacki, Tomek. *My First Garden* (K–3). Illus. 2000, Farrar $16.00 (0-374-32518-9). 40pp. In this book about the power of nature, a young boy turns a courtyard into a beautiful garden that all the neighbors enjoy. (Rev: BCCB 2/00; BL 2/15/00; HBG 10/00; SLJ 4/00)

4390 Borden, Louise. *Caps, Hats, Socks, and Mittens: A Book About the Four Seasons* (PS–K). Illus. by Lillian Hoban. 1989, Scholastic paper $4.99 (0-590-44872-2). Children are introduced to the uniqueness of each season. (Rev: BL 2/15/89; SLJ 4/89)

4391 Brady, Kimberley Smith. *Keeper for the Sea* (PS–1). Illus. by Peter M. Fiore. 1996, Simon & Schuster $16.00 (0-689-80472-5). 30pp. A boy and his grandfather creep out at night to catch bluefish on the seashore. (Rev: BL 10/15/96; SLJ 12/96)

4392 Brandt, Keith. *Wonders of the Seasons* (1–3). Illus. by James Watling. 1982, Troll LB $17.25 (0-89375-580-X); paper $3.50 (0-89375-581-8). 32pp. A simple introduction to the four seasons and the characteristics of each.

4393 Brinckloe, Julie. *Fireflies!* (PS–1). Illus. by author. 1986, Simon & Schuster paper $4.99 (0-689-71055-0). 32pp. A boy catches fireflies one evening, but when their light grows dim, he releases them. (Rev: BL 5/1/85; HB 9–10/85; SLJ 4/85)

4394 Brown, Margaret Wise. *Wait Till the Moon Is Full* (PS–1). Illus. by Garth Williams. 1948, HarperCollins paper $5.95 (0-06-443222-X). 32pp. The fears of night are dispelled in this tender story about raccoons.

4395 Buchanan, Ken. *This House Is Made of Mud* (PS–1). Illus. by Libba Tracy. 1994, Northland LB $14.95 (0-87358-593-3); paper $6.95 (0-87358-580-1). 32pp. A child describes his adobe house in the Sonoran Desert and the plants and animal life around it. (Rev: BL 9/15/91)

4396 Bunting, Eve. *Butterfly House* (K–2). Illus. by Greg Shed. 1999, Scholastic $15.95 (0-590-84884-4). 32pp. A young girl and her grandfather rescue a caterpillar and observe it change into a butterfly. (Rev: BL 6/1–15/99; HBG 10/99; SLJ 4/99)

4397 Bunting, Eve. *Secret Place* (K–3). Illus. by Ted Rand. 1996, Clarion $15.00 (0-395-64367-8). 32pp. A young boy finds a place in the city where wildlife still exists. (Rev: BL 9/1/96; SLJ 9/96)

4398 Bunting, Eve. *Someday a Tree* (PS–3). Illus. by Ronald Himler. 1993, Houghton $15.00 (0-395-61309-4). 32pp. In spite of attention from friends, a sick tree continues to die. (Rev: BL 3/1/93; SLJ 5/93)

4399 Bunting, Eve. *Sunflower House* (PS–2). Illus. by Kathryn Hewitt. 1996, Harcourt $15.00 (0-15-200483-1). 32pp. A boy plants some sunflower seeds and witnesses the dramatic miracle of plant growth. (Rev: BL 4/1/96; SLJ 5/96)

4400 Burns, Kate. *Hide and Seek: In the Snow* (PS–K). Illus. by Dawn Apperley. 1996, Little, Brown $9.95 (0-316-11820-6). Pulling tabs in this book reveals various residents of Northern habitats. (Rev: BL 12/15/96; SLJ 1/97)

4401 Cannon, Annie. *The Bat in the Boot* (PS–2). Illus. 1996, Orchard LB $16.99 (0-531-08795-6). 32pp. Two children nurture a baby bat until its mother comes to rescue it. (Rev: BL 4/1/96; SLJ 6/96)

4402 Carle, Eric. *The Tiny Seed* (K–2). Illus. by author. 1991, Picture Book $16.00 (0-88708-015-4). 32pp. A tiny seed travels by the wind, survives all sorts of perils, and grows into a flower. A reissue.

4403 Carlstrom, Nancy White. *Wild Wild Sunflower Child Anna* (PS–1). Illus. by Jerry Pinkney. 1987, Macmillan LB $14.95 (0-02-717360-7). 32pp. Watercolor illustrations highlight Little Anna's romp through a summer day. (Rev: BL 10/1/87; HB 11–12/87)

4404 Cherry, Lynne. *The Great Kapok Tree: A Tale of the Amazon Rain Forest* (K–3). Illus. 1990, Harcourt $16.00 (0-15-200520-X). 32pp. A carefully researched picture book of the Amazon rain forest. (Rev: BL 3/15/90; HB 5–6/90; SLJ 5/90)

4405 Christian, Peggy. *If You Find a Rock* (1–3). Illus. by Barbara Hirsch Lember. 2000, Harcourt $16.00 (0-15-239339-0). 32pp. This book illustrated with photographs tells of the varieties and purposes of rocks, such as rocks for skipping across ponds or for hiding little creatures. (Rev: BCCB 7–8/00; BL 4/1/00; HBG 10/00; SLJ 4/00)

4406 Cole, Henry. *I Took a Walk* (PS–K). Illus. 1998, Greenwillow $15.00 (0-688-15115-9). 28pp. A boy narrates his walk through woods and a meadow, by a stream and a pond, as he observes an assortment of animals, plants, and insects. (Rev: BCCB 3/98; BL 5/1/98; HB 5–6/98; HBG 10/98; SLJ 5/98)

4407 Condra, Estelle. *See the Ocean* (K–2). Illus. by Linda Crockett-Blassingame. 1994, Ideals $14.95 (1-57102-005-5). 32pp. A blind girl, using her inner feelings, is the first to detect the ocean. (Rev: BL 10/15/94; SLJ 10/94)

4408 Cordova, Amy. *Abuelita's Heart* (K–3). Illus. 1997, Simon & Schuster $16.00 (0-689-80181-5). 32pp. A grandmother takes her granddaughter on a tour around their home in the Southwest to point out nature's beauty. (Rev: BL 8/97; HBG 3/98; SLJ 9/97)

4409 Coucher, Helen. *Rain Forest* (K–2). Illus. by author. 1988, Farrar $15.00 (0-374-36167-3). 32pp. A machine cuts down the trees in the rain forest, and when the rains come, with no trees to hold the soil in place, the river bursts its banks. (Rev: BL 1/15/89; SLJ 2/89)

4410 Davol, Marguerite W. *The Heart of the Wood* (PS–1). Illus. by Sheila Hamanaka. 1992, Simon &

Schuster paper $15.00 (0-671-74778-9). 32pp. A tree that is chopped down continues to give pleasure when it becomes a violin. (Rev: BCCB 2/93; BL 12/1/92; SLJ 10/92)

4411 Demas, Corinne. *The Disappearing Island* (1–3). Illus. by Ted Lewin. 2000, Simon & Schuster $16.00 (0-689-80539-X). 32pp. Carrie and her grandmother visit Billingsgate, an island off Cape Cod that appears only during a low tide. (Rev: BCCB 5/00; BL 6/1–15/00; HBG 10/00; SLJ 7/00)

4412 Demunn, Michael. *The Earth Is Good: A Chant in Praise of Nature* (PS–1). Illus. by Jim McMullan. 1999, Scholastic $15.95 (0-590-35010-2). Accompanied by her puppy, a little girl explores the earth, including mountains, fields, an ocean, and forests. (Rev: HBG 10/99; SLJ 8/99)

4413 Denslow, Sharon P. *On the Trail with Miss Pace* (K–2). Illus. by G. Brian Karas. 1995, Simon & Schuster paper $15.00 (0-02-728688-6). 32pp. Two of her pupils join school teacher Miss Pace during her summer vacation out West. (Rev: BL 6/1–15/95; SLJ 6/95)

4414 dePaola, Tomie. *Charlie Needs a Cloak* (PS–1). Illus. by author. 1982, Simon & Schuster paper $5.95 (0-671-66467-0). The facts about cloth making are humorously presented in this story of Charlie, a shepherd.

4415 dePaola, Tomie. *The Cloud Book* (K–3). Illus. by author. 1975, Holiday LB $15.95 (0-8234-0259-2); paper $6.95 (0-8234-0531-1). 32pp. The ten most common clouds, along with related myths and sayings.

4416 dePaola, Tomie. *The Quicksand Book* (1–3). Illus. by author. 1977, Holiday LB $15.95 (0-8234-0291-6); paper $6.95 (0-8234-0532-X). 32pp. Science is both informative and entertaining in this story of Jungle Girl, who falls into a patch of quicksand.

4417 Desimini, Lisa, et al. *All Year Round* (PS–1). Illus. 1997, Scholastic $15.95 (0-590-36097-3). 32pp. Four artists have contributed their illustrations and short poems to this book about the seasons. (Rev: BL 12/15/97; HBG 3/98)

4418 Dorros, Arthur. *Feel the Wind* (PS–2). Illus. by author. 1989, HarperCollins LB $15.89 (0-690-04741-X); paper $4.95 (0-06-445095-3). 32pp. Defining what causes the wind to blow. (Rev: BL 4/1/89; SLJ 6/89)

4419 Downing, Julie. *White Snow, Blue Feather* (PS–1). Illus. by author. 1989, Macmillan $14.95 (0-02-732530-X). A little boy explores the countryside in the dead of winter. (Rev: SLJ 11/89)

4420 Doyle, Malachy. *Jody's Beans* (PS–1). Illus. by Judith Allibone. 1999, Candlewick $15.95 (0-7636-0687-1). 32pp. This simple family story is also a gardening book in which Jody's Granda plants runner beans and shows her how to care for them until the plants mature and produce food. (Rev: BL 7/99; HB 3–4/99; HBG 10/99; SLJ 6/99)

4421 Dunn, Judy. *The Little Rabbit* (K–2). Illus. by Phoebe Dunn. 1980, Random paper $3.25 (0-394-84377-0). 32pp. A real rabbit family is introduced in photographs.

4422 Dunn, Phoebe. *Farm Animals* (PS). Illus. by author. 1984, Random $3.99 (0-394-86254-6). 28pp. An introduction to more than 15 farm animals.

4423 Easwaran, Eknath. *The Monkey and the Mango: Stories of My Granny* (K–2). Illus. by Ilka Jerabek. 1996, Nilgiri Pr. $14.95 (0-915132-82-6). 29pp. In the southern Indian state of Kerala, a grandmother tells her grandson a number of stories that tell about the wonders of nature, creation, and humankind's relation to all creatures. (Rev: SLJ 8/96)

4424 Ehlert, Lois. *Feathers for Lunch* (PS–2). Illus. 1990, Harcourt $16.00 (0-15-230550-5). 32pp. A wide variety of American birds are introduced by way of a cat's stalking activities. (Rev: BCCB 1/91; BL 9/1/90; HB 11–12/90*; SLJ 12/90)

4425 Ehlert, Lois. *Red Leaf, Yellow Leaf* (PS–2). Illus. 1991, Harcourt $16.00 (0-15-266197-2). 32pp. A child tells of buying, planting, and caring for a sugar maple tree. (Rev: BCCB 10/91; BL 10/1/91*; HB 11–12/91*; SLJ 11/91)

4426 Evans, Lezlie. *Rain Song* (PS–1). Illus. by Cynthia Jabar. 1995, Houghton $14.95 (0-395-69865-0). 32pp. Two girls enjoy the sounds and the excitement of a rainstorm. (Rev: BCCB 3/95; BL 3/15/95; SLJ 7/95)

4427 Fife, Dale H. *Empty Lot* (K–3). Illus. by Jim Arnosky. 1996, Sierra Club paper $6.95 (0-871-56859-4). Harry realizes that his empty country lot is actually alive with all kinds of wildlife. (Rev: SLJ 8/91)

4428 Fisher, Leonard Everett. *Sky, Sea, the Jetty, and Me* (1–3). Illus. 2001, Marshall Cavendish $15.95 (0-7614-5082-3). 32pp. A young narrator at the seashore experiences the excitement and violence of a sudden storm. (Rev: BL 3/15/01)

4429 Fleming, Denise. *In the Small, Small Pond* (PS–K). Illus. 1993, Holt $16.95 (0-8050-2264-3); paper $6.95 (0-8050-5983-0). 30pp. In a series of collages, a frog views a year of changing seasons in a small pond. (Rev: BL 9/1/93; HB 9–10/93; SLJ 9/93*)

4430 Fletcher, Ralph. *Twilight Comes Twice* (K–2). Illus. by Kate Kiesler. 1997, Clarion $15.00 (0-395-84826-1). 32pp. In radiant illustrations, the author describes two times of day: the evening at twilight and dawn, when twilight colors are again present. (Rev: BL 10/15/97; HBG 3/98; SLJ 10/97)

4431 Florian, Douglas. *A Summer Day* (PS–K). Illus. by author. 1988, Greenwillow LB $12.88 (0-688-07565-7). 24pp. A city family is on the way to the country for some fun. Also use: *A Winter Day* (1987). (Rev: BL 3/1/88; SLJ 5/88)

4432 Ford, Miela. *Sunflower* (PS). Illus. by Sally Noll. 1995, Greenwillow $15.93 (0-688-13302-9). 24pp. A young girl plants and cares for a single seed that grows into a massive sunflower. (Rev: BL 2/15/95; HB 5–6/95; SLJ 5/95)

4433 Franklin, Kristine L. *The Gift* (PS–2). Illus. by Barbara Lavallee. 1999, Chronicle $14.95 (0-8118-0447-X). In this sea story set in the Pacific Northwest, a young fisherman throws the Chinook salmon he has just caught back into the ocean to be food for a passing pod of killer whales. (Rev: HBG 3/00; SLJ 1/00)

4434 Franklin, Kristine L. *When the Monkeys Came Back* (K–3). Illus. by Robert Roth. 1994, Atheneum $14.95 (0-689-31807-3). 32pp. When the Costa Rican forest in which Marta lives is destroyed by developers, she misses the monkeys who used to live there. (Rev: BL 1/1/95; SLJ 12/94)

4435 Frasier, Debra. *On the Day You Were Born* (K–2). Illus. 1991, Harcourt $16.00 (0-15-257995-8). 32pp. The wonders of nature and the interdependence of all living things are celebrated in this book that introduces science in a personalized way. (Rev: BL 6/15/91; SLJ 6/91*)

4436 Frasier, Debra. *Out of the Ocean* (PS–3). Illus. 1998, Harcourt $16.00 (0-15-258849-3). 40pp. A mother and her child explore the many gifts that the ocean can give, such as a seashell or pelican feathers. (Rev: BL 4/15/98; HBG 10/98; SLJ 8/98)

4437 Gackenbach, Dick. *Mighty Tree* (PS). Illus. 1992, Harcourt $13.95 (0-15-200519-6). 32pp. This large picture book presents the uses and wonder of trees. (Rev: BL 4/1/92; SLJ 6/92) [582.16]

4438 George, Jean Craighead. *Dear Katie, the Volcano Is a Girl* (1–3). Illus. by Daniel Powers. 1998, Hyperion $14.95 (0-7868-0314-2). 32pp. On the slopes of Hawaii's Kilauea volcano crater, Katie's grandmother gives her the scientific explanation for volcanic action, but Katie maintains that it is really the work of Pele, the goddess of fire, quarreling with her sister. (Rev: BL 11/1/98; HBG 3/99; SLJ 12/98)

4439 George, Lindsay Barrett. *Around the Pond: Who's Been Here?* (PS–2). Illus. 1996, Greenwillow $15.93 (0-688-14377-6). 40pp. Creatures and objects around a pond are revealed through clues. (Rev: BL 9/15/96; SLJ 9/96)

4440 George, Lindsay Barrett. *In the Snow: Who's Been Here?* (PS–1). Illus. 1995, Greenwillow $16.89 (0-688-12321-X). 40pp. On their way to go sledding, two children discover clues showing that various animals are present in this nature book that supplies interesting explanations. (Rev: BL 12/1/95; SLJ 12/95)

4441 George, William T. *Box Turtle at Long Pond* (2–3). Illus. by Lindsay B. George. 1989, Greenwillow LB $15.89 (0-688-08185-1). 24pp. Box Turtle ambles out from a rotting log on Long Pond at the beginning of the day. (Rev: BL 9/1/89; SLJ 10/89*)

4442 Gibbons, Gail. *The Reasons for Seasons* (K–3). Illus. 1995, Holiday LB $16.95 (0-8234-1174-5). 32pp. The seasons, their causes, and the changes they produce are introduced. (Rev: BL 4/1/95; SLJ 5/95) [525]

4443 Gibbons, Gail. *The Seasons of Arnold's Apple Tree* (PS–1). Illus. by author. 1984, Harcourt $15.00 (0-15-271246-1); paper $6.00 (0-15-271245-3). 32pp. Arnold's apple tree is useful in all seasons.

4444 Glaser, Omri. *Round the Garden* (K–3). Illus. by Byron Glaser and Sandra Higashi. 2000, Abrams $15.95 (0-8109-4137-6). 34pp. This easily read text explains the water cycle through the journey of a tear that eventually becomes a drop of rain that

helps an onion grow. (Rev: BCCB 11/00; BL 6/1–15/00; HBG 10/00; SLJ 5/00)

4445 Goble, Paul. *I Sing for the Animals* (PS–2). Illus. by author. 1991, Macmillan LB $9.95 (0-02-737725-3). 32pp. The relationship of humankind to the natural world and the creator. (Rev: BL 11/1/91; SLJ 10/91) [242.62]

4446 Goldsen, Louise. *Weather* (K–2). Illus. by Sophie Kniffke. 1991, Scholastic $12.95 (0-590-45234-7). Various changes in the weather are illustrated through the use of overlays. (Rev: SLJ 5/92) [551.6]

4447 Gomi, Taro. *Spring Is Here* (2–4). Illus. 1995, Chronicle paper $4.95 (0-811-81022-4). 32pp. For the very young, this is a delightful introduction to the spring season. (Rev: BL 8/89; HB 11–12/89; SLJ 10/89)

4448 Griese, Arnold. *Anna's Athabaskan Summer* (K–3). Illus. by Charles Ragins. 1995, Boyds Mills $14.95 (1-56397-232-8). 32pp. A young Athapaskan Indian girl enjoys all the activities of being part of a summer fishing camp. (Rev: BL 6/1–15/95; SLJ 5/95)

4449 Guiberson, Brenda Z. *Cactus Hotel* (PS–3). Illus. by Megan Lloyd. 1991, Holt $16.95 (0-8050-1333-4). 32pp. The life cycle of the giant saguaro cactus. (Rev: BL 6/15/91; SLJ 7/91) [574.5]

4450 Haas, Jessie. *Sugaring* (PS–2). Illus. by Joseph A. Smith. 1996, Greenwillow $15.00 (0-688-14200-1). 24pp. The stages of making maple sugar and syrup are examined when Nora decides to help her grandfather in this late winter ritual. A sequel to *Mowing* (1994) and *No Foal Yet* (1995). (Rev: BL 11/15/96; SLJ 10/96)

4451 Hader, Berta, and Elmer Hader. *The Big Snow* (PS–3). Illus. by authors. 1972, Macmillan LB $17.00 (0-02-737910-8); paper $6.95 (0-689-71757-1). 48pp. How all the little animals of a country hillside survive a heavy winter storm. Caldecott Medal winner, 1949.

4452 Hague, Kathleen. *Calendarbears: A Book of Months* (PS–1). Illus. by Michael Hague. 1997, Holt $14.95 (0-8050-3818-3). 32pp. Twelve engaging bears highlight activities associated with each of the months. (Rev: BL 3/15/97; SLJ 7/97)

4453 Hall, Zoe. *The Apple Pie Tree* (PS–2). Illus. by Shari Halpern. 1996, Scholastic $15.95 (0-590-62382-6). 32pp. The changes that occur to an apple tree during one year are described by two sisters. (Rev: BCCB 12/96; BL 10/1/96; SLJ 12/96)

4454 Hall, Zoe. *Fall Leaves Fall!* (PS). Illus. by Shari Halpern. 2000, Scholastic $15.95 (0-590-10079-X). 40pp. In autumn, two children play with leaves and engage in activities like kicking them, comparing their shapes, and raking them into piles. (Rev: BL 12/15/00; HBG 3/01; SLJ 9/00)

4455 Hall, Zoe. *The Surprise Garden* (PS–1). Illus. by Shari Halpern. 1998, Scholastic $15.95 (0-590-10075-0). 32pp. A charming book in which children plant seeds and tend their gardens until the plants grow into marvelous vegetables. (Rev: BCCB 3/98; BL 1/1–15/98; HBG 10/98; SLJ 3/98)

4456 Heller, Ruth. *Chickens Aren't the Only Ones* (K–2). Illus. by author. 1981, Putnam $16.99 (0-448-01872-1). 48pp. All kinds of animals that lay eggs are introduced.

4457 Henderson, Kathy. *The Storm* (PS–1). Illus. by author. 1999, Candlewick $15.99 (0-7636-0904-8). When a fierce storm hits the seashore, young Jim realizes the power and strength of nature. (Rev: HB 11–12/99; HBG 3/00; SLJ 12/99)

4458 Henderson, Kathy. *A Year in the City* (PS–2). Illus. by Paul Howard. 1996, Candlewick $15.99 (1-56402-872-0). 32pp. A celebration of the seasons as experienced by a city child. (Rev: BL 1/1–15/97; HB 11–12/96; SLJ 1/97)

4459 Hirschi, Ron. *Spring* (PS–K). Illus. by Thomas D. Mangelsen. 1990, Dutton $15.99 (0-525-65037-7). 32pp. Photos focus on spring as a time of renewal. (Rev: BL 10/15/90; HB 1–2/91; SLJ 11/90) [508]

4460 Hiscock, Bruce. *When Will It Snow?* (PS–K). Illus. 1995, Simon & Schuster $15.00 (0-689-31937-1). 32pp. As a young boy awaits the year's first snowfall, animals and humans are making necessary preparations. (Rev: BL 12/1/95; SLJ 12/95)

4461 Hooper, Meredith. *River Story* (K–3). Illus. by Bee Willey. 2000, Candlewick $15.99 (0-7636-0792-4). 32pp. This picture book traces the course of a river from its beginning as a mountain stream to its emptying into the ocean. (Rev: BL 7/00; HBG 10/00; SLJ 8/00)

4462 *How Big Is the Ocean? First Questions and Answers About the Beach* (PS–3). Illus. Series: First Questions and Answers. 1994, Time Life $14.95 (0-7835-0897-2). 48pp. Basic questions about the ocean — such as "Why is it blue?" — are answered in this picture book. (Rev: BL 3/1/95) [508]

4463 Howell, Will C. *I Call It Sky* (K–3). Illus. by John Ward. 1999, Walker LB $16.85 (0-8027-8678-2). Concepts of weather are explored as children play through snow, rain, fog, and other weather phenomena. (Rev: BL 5/1/99; HBG 10/99; SLJ 6/99)

4464 Hughes, Shirley. *Out and About* (PS–1). Illus. 1988, Lothrop $16.00 (0-688-07690-4). 48pp. A colorful journey through the seasons in a picture book of poems. (Rev: BCCB 6/88; BL 3/15/88; SLJ 5/88)

4465 Jackson, Ellen. *Brown Cow, Green Grass, Yellow Mellow Sun* (K–2). Illus. by Victoria Raymond. 1995, Hyperion LB $14.89 (0-7867-2006-3). 32pp. The process of getting milk from a cow and turning it into butter is the subject of this picture book illustrated with photos of objects made from modeling clay. (Rev: BL 6/1–15/95; SLJ 5/95)

4466 Jessup, Harley. *Grandma Summer* (PS–1). Illus. 1999, Viking $15.99 (0-670-88260-7). 32pp. In this happy picture book, a boy stays with his upbeat grandmother at her beach cottage and discovers the wonders of the seashore. (Rev: BL 8/99; HBG 10/99; SLJ 7/99)

4467 Johnston, Tony. *Desert Song* (K–3). Illus. by Ed Young. 2000, Sierra Club $15.95 (0-87156-491-2). 32pp. A lyrical volume that describes the sights and sounds of the desert in a book-length poem

filled with glowing illustrations. (Rev: BL 10/1/00*; SLJ 12/00)

4468 Jones, Betty, comp. *A Child's Seasonal Treasury* (PS–2). Illus. by Betty Jones. 1997, Tricycle Pr. $22.95 (1-883672-30-9). 136pp. For each of the seasons, a collection of poems, songs, fingerplays, and activities. (Rev: SLJ 10/97)

4469 Joosse, Barbara M. *Snow Day!* (K–2). Illus. by Jennifer Plecas. 1995, Clarion $14.95 (0-395-66588-4). 31pp. Activities to engage in on a snow day are pictured, including a family snow fight. (Rev: SLJ 9/95*)

4470 Kalan, Robert. *Rain* (PS–1). Illus. by Donald Crews. 1978, Greenwillow $16.89 (0-688-84139-2); Morrow paper $5.95 (0-688-10479-7). 24pp. A rainstorm described in pictures and brief text.

4471 Keats, Ezra Jack. *The Snowy Day* (PS–1). Illus. by author. 1962, Puffin paper $5.99 (0-14-050182-7). 40pp. A young African American boy's delight during his first snowfall. Caldecott Medal winner, 1963.

4472 Kerins, Tony. *Little Clancy's New Drum* (PS–K). Illus. by author. 1996, Candlewick $9.99 (0-7636-0061-X). Even when his new drum is taken away from him by people who want to sleep, Little Clancy goes around thumping and pounding on any object he can find. (Rev: SLJ 1/97)

4473 Killion, Bette. *The Same Wind* (2–5). Illus. by Barbara B. Falk. 1992, HarperCollins LB $14.89 (0-06-021051-6). 32pp. The many kinds of winds and their uses are explored in this picture book. (Rev: BL 1/1/93)

4474 Kinsey-Warnock, Natalie. *When Spring Comes* (K–2). Illus. by Stacey Schuett. 1993, Dutton $16.99 (0-525-45008-4). 32pp. Looking out on a winter landscape, a young girl remembers all the activities connected with spring. (Rev: BL 3/1/93; SLJ 4/93)

4475 Koch, Michelle. *World Water Watch* (K–2). Illus. 1993, Greenwillow $15.93 (0-688-11465-2). 32pp. Simple prose and beautiful watercolors introduce six endangered aquatic animals, such as the Chilean fur seal and the Alaskan sea otter. (Rev: BL 6/1–15/93; SLJ 4/93*) [639.9]

4476 Krauss, Ruth. *The Growing Story* (PS–2). Illus. by Phyllis Rowand. 1947, HarperCollins $8.95 (0-06-023380-X). 32pp. A little boy watches things grow but doesn't realize until fall that he, too, has grown.

4477 Kroll, Virginia. *The Seasons and Someone* (K–3). Illus. by Tatsuro Kiuchi. 1994, Harcourt $15.00 (0-15-271233-X). 32pp. In this exquisite picture book, a little Eskimo girl watches the changes of seasons from her Northern home. (Rev: BL 12/1/94; SLJ 1/95*)

4478 Lakin, Patricia. *Hurricane!* (1–3). Illus. by Vanessa Lubach. 2000, Millbrook LB $21.90 (0-7613-1616-7). 32pp. A girl and her father make preparations to withstand Hurricane Bob and after the storm has passed survey the damage. (Rev: BL 10/15/00; HBG 3/01; SLJ 1/01)

4479 LaMarche, Jim. *The Raft* (2–4). Illus. 2000, HarperCollins LB $15.89 (0-688-13978-7). 40pp.

Nicky is unhappy spending the summer with his grandmother in the country until he learns the joy of camping outdoors and the wonders of the animal life around him. (Rev: BCCB 7–8/00; BL 5/1/00; HBG 10/00; SLJ 5/00)

4480 Laser, Michael. *The Rain* (K–3). Illus. by Jeffrey Greene. 1997, Simon & Schuster paper $16.00 (0-689-80506-3). 32pp. Three adults and two children react in various ways to being out in the rain. (Rev: BCCB 6/97; BL 4/1/97; SLJ 5/97)

4481 Lasky, Kathryn. *Pond Year* (K–3). Illus. by Mike Bostock. 1995, Candlewick $14.99 (1-56402-187-4). 32pp. Two girls share fascinating experiences as they explore the life in a local pond. (Rev: BL 5/15/95; SLJ 9/95)

4482 Lawson, Julie. *Midnight in the Mountains* (K–3). Illus. by Sheena Lott. 1998, Orca $14.95 (1-55143-113-0). After spending her first day in the mountains during winter, a young girl who is too excited to sleep thinks about all the fun she had that day, like making snow angels. (Rev: HBG 3/99; SLJ 1/99)

4483 Leedy, Loreen. *Blast Off to Earth! A Look at Geography* (PS–3). Illus. 1992, Holiday LB $16.95 (0-8234-0973-2). 32pp. An alien teacher and his students take a class trip to Earth. (Rev: BL 11/1/92; SLJ 1/93) [910]

4484 Levine, Evan. *Not the Piano, Mrs. Medley!* (PS–2). Illus. by S. D. Schindler. 1991, Watts LB $16.99 (0-531-08556-2). 32pp. Mrs. Medley, Max, and Word the dog pack just about everything — except bathing suits — to go to the beach. (Rev: BL 7/91*; HB 9–10/91; SLJ 11/91*)

4485 Lindbergh, Reeve. *North Country Spring* (K–2). Illus. by Liz Sivertson. 1997, Houghton $15.95 (0-395-82819-8). 32pp. Vivid rhyming couplets and expressive paintings evoke the changes that spring brings to the northern United States. (Rev: BL 5/15/97; SLJ 4/97)

4486 Lobb, Janice. *Splish! Splosh! Why Do We Wash?* (K–2). Illus. by Peter Utton. 2000, Kingfisher $10.95 (0-7534-5244-8). 32pp. Using bathroom furnishings, this activity book answers such questions as "Why does soap float?' and "What happens when one flushes a toilet?" (Rev: BL 7/00; HBG 3/01; SLJ 8/00) [500]

4487 London, Jonathan. *Dream Weaver* (PS–2). Illus. by Rocco Baviera. 1998, Harcourt $16.00 (0-15-200944-2). 32pp. A boy watches a spider on its web and later dreams of weaving his own web to catch falling stars. (Rev: BL 4/1/98; HBG 10/98; SLJ 7/98)

4488 Luenn, Nancy. *Mother Earth* (PS–3). Illus. by Neil Waldman. 1992, Macmillan $15.00 (0-689-31668-2). 32pp. The cycle of the seasons and their variety of life are celebrated in this tribute to Mother Earth. (Rev: BL 2/1/92; SLJ 3/92)

4489 Maass, Robert. *When Autumn Comes* (PS–2). Illus. 1990, Holt paper $6.95 (0-8050-2349-6). 32pp. What people do as autumn progresses, with large, handsome photos. (Rev: BL 10/1/90; SLJ 9/90) [508]

4490 Maass, Robert. *When Summer Comes* (K–2). Illus. 1993, Holt paper $5.95 (0-8050-4706-9). 30pp. In this tribute to the joys of summer, many of the activities associated with this season are pictured in photographs. (Rev: BL 6/1–15/93; SLJ 6/93) [508]

4491 McCloskey, Robert. *Time of Wonder* (1–4). Illus. by author. 1957, Puffin paper $5.99 (0-14-050201-7). 64pp. Full-color watercolors illustrate this poetic text describing a summer on the Maine coast and the hurricane that hits it. Caldecott Medal winner, 1958.

4492 McCurdy, Michael. *Hannah's Farm: The Seasons on an Early American Homestead* (1–3). Illus. by author. 1988, Holiday LB $12.95 (0-8234-0700-4). 32pp. The seasons are presented on this 19th-century farm in Massachusetts. (Rev: BL 11/15/88; SLJ 2/89)

4493 McNulty, Faith. *Orphan: The Story of a Baby Woodchuck* (K–3). Illus. by Darby Morrell. 1992, Scholastic $11.95 (0-590-43838-7). 48pp. The author befriends a baby woodchuck on her Rhode Island farm and then realizes she must teach it to return to the wild. (Rev: BL 4/15/92; SLJ 9/92) [599.32]

4494 Maestro, Betsy. *Snow Day* (PS–2). Illus. by Giulio Maestro. 1992, Scholastic paper $4.95 (0-590-46083-8). 32pp. While families stay home because of the heavy snow, snow removal crews are doing their job. (Rev: BCCB 10/89; BL 11/1/89; SLJ 1/90) [628]

4495 Magdanz, James. *Go Home, River* (K–2). Illus. by Dianne Widom. 1996, Alaska Northwest $15.95 (0-88240-476-8). 32pp. The place of a river in the life of a group of Inupiat people in Alaska is portrayed in this picture book set in 1875. (Rev: BL 11/1/96; SLJ 1/97)

4496 Major, Beverly. *Over Back* (1–3). Illus. by Thomas B. Allen. 1993, HarperCollins LB $14.89 (0-06-020287-4). A young African American girl takes the reader on a nature tour behind her house. (Rev: BL 2/1/93; SLJ 3/93)

4497 Malone, Peter. *Star Shapes* (PS–3). Illus. 1997, Chronicle $15.95 (0-8118-0726-6). 26pp. In this enchanting picture book, the shapes of many constellations are pictured with their earthly counterparts looking on. (Rev: BL 10/1/97; HBG 3/98; SLJ 11/97)

4498 Manuel, Lynn. *The Night the Moon Blew Kisses* (PS–2). Illus. by Robin Spowart. 1996, Houghton $14.95 (0-395-73979-9). An atmospheric tale of a walk through a nocturnal winter landscape by a girl and her grandmother. (Rev: SLJ 11/96)

4499 Marshall, Janet. *A Honey of a Day* (PS–1). Illus. 2000, Greenwillow $23.95 (0-688-16917-1). 24pp. A pleasant story about an outdoor wedding is used to introduce and picture 28 lovely flowers including sweet william and black-eyed susan. (Rev: BL 7/00; HBG 10/00; SLJ 5/00)

4500 Michels, Tilde. *What a Beautiful Day!* (PS–2). Illus. by Thomas Muller. 1992, Carolrhoda LB $18.95 (0-87614-739-2). 32pp. On a beautiful summer morning, young Peter enjoys nature as he walks in the woods. (Rev: BL 1/15/93; SLJ 4/93)

4501 Mockford, Caroline. *What's This?* (PS–1). Illus. 2000, Barefoot $15.95 (1-84148-018-5). 32pp. This simple picture book describes the cultivation and growth of a sunflower seed and plant by a little girl and brown bird. (Rev: BL 5/1/00; SLJ 8/00) [631.5]

4502 Mora, Pat. *Listen to the Desert/Oye al Desierto* (PS–2). Illus. by Francisco Mora. 1994, Clarion $16.00 (0-395-67292-9). Using double-page spreads, this book in English and Spanish introduces the animals and sounds found in a Southwestern desert. (Rev: SLJ 10/94) [574.5]

4503 Otten, Charlotte F. *January Rides the Wind: A Book of Months* (PS–2). Illus. by Todd L. W. Doney. 1997, Lothrop LB $15.93 (0-688-12557-3). 32pp. Short poems and evocative paintings capture the essence of the outdoor world during each month of the year. (Rev: BL 10/15/97*; HBG 3/98; SLJ 10/97)

4504 Pallotta, Jerry. *Dory Story* (PS–4). Illus. by David Biedrzycki. 2000, Charlesbridge $15.95 (0-88106-075-5). 32pp. An ocean food chain from krill-eating plankton to huge orcas eating tuna is explored in this story of a boy's imaginary dory trip into the depths. (Rev: BL 2/1/00*; HBG 10/00; SLJ 3/00)

4505 Pearson, Susan. *Silver Morning* (PS–2). Illus. by David Christiana. 1998, Harcourt $16.00 (0-15-274786-9). 32pp. An atmospheric account of a boy and his mother taking a walk in the woods on a very foggy morning. (Rev: BL 3/15/98; HBG 10/98; SLJ 4/98)

4506 Peet, Bill. *The Wump World* (1–3). Illus. by author. 1981, Houghton $16.00 (0-395-19841-0); paper $6.95 (0-395-31129-2). An animal parable in which pollution and the waste of natural resources are the main themes.

4507 Perkins, Lynne Rae. *Home Lovely* (1–4). Illus. 1995, Greenwillow $14.93 (0-688-13688-5). 32pp. Tiffany, who is left alone while her mother works, learns a great deal about gardening, particularly from the friendly mail carrier. (Rev: BCCB 9/95; BL 1/1–15/96*; HB 11–12/95)

4508 Peters, Lisa Westberg. *October Smiled Back* (PS–2). Illus. by Ed Young. 1996, Holt $14.95 (0-8050-1776-3). 28pp. Each month is personified in this poem, accompanied by bold color illustrations. (Rev: BL 11/1/96; SLJ 10/96*)

4509 Peters, Lisa Westberg. *The Sun, the Wind, and the Rain* (K–3). Illus. by Ted Rand. 1988, Holt paper $6.95 (0-8050-1481-0). 48pp. The creation and evolution of mountains using the analogy of a little girl at the beach. (Rev: BL 10/15/88; HB 11–12/88; SLJ 10/88)

4510 Petit, Genevieve. *The Seventh Walnut* (K–3). Illus. by Joelle Boucher. 1992, Wellington $13.95 (0-922984-10-7). 32pp. The story of how a walnut, dropped on the ground, grows into a tree; translated from the French. (Rev: BCCB 10/92; BL 12/1/92) [574]

4511 Prelutsky, Jack. *It's Snowing! It's Snowing!* (1–4). Illus. by Jeanne Titherington. 1984, Greenwillow $17.93 (0-688-01513-1). 48pp. A few story poems on the experiences and joys of winter.

4512 Priddy, Roger. *My Big Book of Everything* (PS–1). Illus. 1996, DK $14.95 (0-7894-0998-4). 61pp. A variety of subjects — like toys, concepts, and the body — are covered in more than 800 color photographs. (Rev: BL 12/15/96; SLJ 1/97) [413.1]

4513 Rand, Gloria. *Fighting for the Forest* (K–3). Illus. by Ted Rand. 1999, Holt $15.95 (0-8050-5466-9). 32pp. A boy and his father fail to save a forest they love from a logging company. But they raise public awareness and find another woods to love and guard. (Rev: HBG 10/99; SLJ 4/99)

4514 Ray, Mary L. *Mud* (PS–2). Illus. by Lauren Stringer. 1996, Harcourt $16.00 (0-15-256263-X). In the period between winter and spring, it is the season of mud, and this book joyfully explores it. (Rev: SLJ 6/96*)

4515 Riha, Susanne. *Animals and the Seasons: The Cycle of Nature* (1–3). Trans. from German by Annette Betz. Illus. by author. 2000, Blackbirch $17.95 (1-56711-429-6). 30pp. This book of stunning illustrations and text takes the reader through the four seasons and depicts the flora and fauna of each. (Rev: HBG 10/00; SLJ 9/00)

4516 Ripley, Catherine. *Why Do Stars Twinkle? and Other Nighttime Questions* (PS–3). Illus. by Scot Ritchie. Series: Question and Answer Storybook. 1996, Owl $17.95 (1-895688-41-8); paper $6.95 (1-895688-42-6). 32pp. In a question-and-answer format, facts about night, bedtime, and sleep are covered. (Rev: BL 12/1/96) [500]

4517 Rockwell, Anne. *Bumblebee, Bumblebee, Do You Know Me? A Garden Guessing Game* (PS–1). Illus. 1999, HarperCollins $14.95 (0-06-027330-5). 24pp. Each double-page spread introduces a different plant with a riddle-and-response discussion. (Rev: BL 3/15/99; HBG 10/99; SLJ 2/99)

4518 Rockwell, Anne. *Ducklings and Pollywogs* (1–3). Illus. by Lizzy Rockwell. 1994, Macmillan paper $14.95 (0-02-777452-X). 32pp. A girl and her father visit a pond and watch all the changes that the four seasons bring. (Rev: BL 12/15/94; SLJ 1/95)

4519 Rockwell, Anne. *The Storm* (K–3). Illus. by Robert Sauber. 1994, Hyperion LB $16.49 (0-7868-2013-6). The morning after a violent storm hits their coastal home, a young girl and her mother walk the beach and view all the accumulated debris. (Rev: SLJ 11/94)

4520 Rockwell, Anne, and Harlow Rockwell. *The First Snowfall* (PS–1). Illus. by authors. 1987, Macmillan LB $13.95 (0-02-777770-7); paper $5.99 (0-689-71614-1). 24pp. The fun and beauty of the first snow as seen by a young girl. (Rev: BL 11/1/87; HB 11–12/87)

4521 Rosenberry, Vera. *Who Is in the Garden?* (PS–2). Illus. 2001, Holiday $16.95 (0-8234-1529-5). 32pp. A little boy tours a garden and finds such wonders as wrens in a birch tree, a snake in a grape vine, and a turtle under the rhubarb. (Rev: BL 3/1/01) [577.5]

4522 Rotner, Shelley, and Steve Calcagnino. *The Body Book* (PS–K). Illus. 2000, Orchard LB $16.99 (0-531-33256-X). 32pp. As well as pointing out the different parts of the body, this picture book shows that people are basically the same even though they come in different sizes, shapes, and colors. (Rev: BL 3/1/00; HBG 10/00; SLJ 5/00) [611]

4523 Rotner, Shelley, and Ken Kreisler. *Nature Spy* (2–6). Illus. by Shelley Rotner. 1992, Macmillan LB $14.95 (0-02-777885-1). 32pp. Vivid fall photos invite young readers to look closely at nature. (Rev: BL 9/15/92; SLJ 10/92) [508]

4524 Rotner, Shelley, and Ken Kreisler. *Ocean Day* (PS–K). Illus. by Shelley Rotner. 1993, Macmillan $14.95 (0-02-777886-X). 32pp. In this photo-essay, a young girl finds all sorts of sea life swelling in a tidal pool. (Rev: BL 4/1/93; SLJ 6/93)

4525 Rucki, Ani. *When the Earth Wakes* (PS–1). Illus. 1998, Scholastic $15.95 (0-590-05951-3). 32pp. The text describes the changes that occur in the spring, and the pictures show a bear cub and its mother waking up and entering the world again. (Rev: BL 3/1/98; HBG 10/98; SLJ 3/98)

4526 Ryan, Pam M. *Hello Ocean* (PS–2). Illus. by Mark Astrella. 2001, Charlesbridge $16.95 (0-88106-987-6); paper $6.95 (0-88106-988-4). 32pp. A young girl who is visiting an ocean beach describes how this experience affects her senses. (Rev: BL 3/1/01*)

4527 Ryder, Joanne. *Each Living Thing* (PS–3). Illus. by Ashley Wolff. 2000, Harcourt $16.00 (0-15-201898-0). 32pp. In a gentle, rhyming text, the author cautions readers to respect and protect all living things. (Rev: BL 4/15/00; HBG 10/00; SLJ 4/00)

4528 Ryder, Joanne. *Earthdance* (K–4). Illus. by Norman Gorbaty. 1996, Holt $16.95 (0-8050-2678-9). 32pp. The earth and its wonders are celebrated in this brief poem with accompanying drawings. (Rev: BCCB 7–8/96; BL 4/1/96; SLJ 5/96*) [811]

4529 Ryder, Joanne. *A Fawn in the Grass* (PS–K). Illus. by Keiko Narahashi. 2001, Holt $16.95 (0-8050-6236-X). 32pp. A child's sense of wonder is conveyed in this quiet picture book about a pre-schooler's walk in a meadow, where he sees such sights as a fawn, insects, squirrels, worms, a hawk, and a mole. (Rev: BL 3/1/01)

4530 Rylant, Cynthia. *In November* (PS–2). Illus. by Jill Kastner. 2000, Harcourt $16.00 (0-15-201076-9). 32pp. Lovely oil paintings and poetic language are used to evoke November atmosphere and activities, including a Thanksgiving feast and the coming of winter. (Rev: BL 9/1/00*; HBG 3/01; SLJ 9/00)

4531 Rylant, Cynthia. *This Year's Garden* (PS–K). Illus. by Mary Szilagyi. 1984, Macmillan paper $4.95 (0-689-71122-0). 32pp. A year in the garden in drawings and gentle text.

4532 Rylant, Cynthia. *The Whales* (PS–3). Illus. 1996, Scholastic $15.95 (0-590-58285-2). 40pp. The behavior and thoughts of whales are depicted in words and illustrations. (Rev: BL 4/1/96; SLJ 3/96)

4533 Sanders, Scott R. *Crawdad Creek* (PS–1). Illus. by Robert Hynes. 1999, National Geographic $15.95 (0-7922-7097-5). 32pp. A girl and her brother find fossils, birds, fish, and animal tracks during a visit to a creek. (Rev: BL 12/1/99; HBG 3/00; SLJ 10/99)

4534 Sanders, Scott R. *Meeting Trees* (PS–2). Illus. by Robert Hynes. 1997, National Geographic $16.00 (0-7922-4140-1). During a walk in the woods with his father, a boy learns to identify a number of trees by their shapes, bark, and leaves. (Rev: SLJ 7/97)

4535 Schaefer, Lola M. *This Is the Sunflower* (PS–3). Illus. by Donald Crews. 2000, Greenwillow LB $15.89 (0-688-16414-5). 24pp. A cumulative rhyme that describes the life of a sunflower plant from seed to flower. (Rev: BCCB 5/00; BL 7/00; HB 7–8/00; HBG 10/00; SLJ 5/00)

4536 Schnur, Steven. *Spring Thaw* (K–3). Illus. by Stacey Schuett. 2000, Viking $15.99 (0-670-87961-4). 32pp. A poetic picture book that depicts signs of spring in a rural setting. (Rev: BL 3/1/00; HBG 10/00; SLJ 2/00)

4537 Schoen, Mark. *Bellybuttons Are Navels* (PS–2). Illus. by M. J. Quay. 1990, Prometheus $17.95 (0-87975-585-7). 40pp. While bathing naked, two preschoolers recite all the visible parts of their bodies. (Rev: BL 6/1/90; SLJ 11/90) [612]

4538 Serfozo, Mary. *Rain Talk* (PS–K). Illus. by Keiko Narahashi. 1990, Macmillan LB $15.00 (0-689-50496-9). 32pp. An African American girl and her dog enjoy listening to the various sounds that rain makes. (Rev: BL 10/1/90; SLJ 12/90*)

4539 Seuss, Dr. *The Lorax* (K–3). Illus. by author. 1971, Random LB $16.99 (0-394-92337-5). 64pp. The Lorax, a little brown creature, has tried in vain to ward off pollution and ecological blight, but Onceler, who wanted the trees for his business, would not heed the warning.

4540 Shea, Pegi Deitz. *New Moon* (PS–1). Illus. by Cathryn Falwell. 1996, Boyds Mills $14.95 (1-56397-410-X). 24pp. Vinnie and her big brother explore the various phases of the moon. (Rev: BL 1/1–15/97; SLJ 10/96)

4541 Shetterly, Susan Hand. *Shelterwood* (K–3). Illus. by Rebecca Haley McCall. 1999, Tilbury $16.95 (0-88448-210-3). 40pp. Set in Maine, this picture book shows the lessons a girl learned from her grandfather about nature and how to preserve the earth's riches. (Rev: BL 3/1/00; SLJ 3/00)

4542 Shulevitz, Uri. *Dawn* (PS–2). Illus. by author. 1974, Farrar $16.00 (0-374-31707-0); paper $5.95 (0-374-41689-3). 32pp. A rare, beautiful book describing in simple poetic terms the coming of dawn.

4543 Shulevitz, Uri. *Rain Rain Rivers* (PS–2). Illus. by author. 1969, Farrar $16.00 (0-374-36171-1); paper $3.95 (0-374-46195-3). 32pp. A little girl sits in her attic bedroom while the rain falls, and her imagination takes her to the places touched by the rain — the city, streams, and the sea.

4544 Siddals, Mary M. *Tell Me a Season* (PS–K). Illus. by Petra Mathers. 1997, Clarion $12.95 (0-395-71021-9). 26pp. A cheerful picture book that explores the seasons and describes each in terms of colors. (Rev: BCCB 7–8/97; BL 4/1/97; SLJ 5/97)

4545 Silsbe, Brenda. *Just One More Color* (PS–1). Illus. by Shawn Steffler. 1992, Firefly LB $14.95 (1-55037-133-9); paper $4.95 (1-55037-136-3). Mr. Hall tries to change the exterior of his house to suit each season. (Rev: SLJ 4/92)

4546 Sommerdorf, Norma. *An Elm Tree and Three Sisters* (K–3). Illus. by Erika Weihs. 2001, Viking $15.99 (0-670-89308-0). 32pp. A gentle picture book about an elm tree that is raised by three sisters who love it and care for it through the years. (Rev: BCCB 2/01; BL 2/1/01; SLJ 2/01)

4547 Stynes, Barbara W. *Walking with Mama* (PS–K). Illus. 1997, Dawn $14.95 (1-883220-56-4); paper $6.95 (1-883220-57-2). 24pp. A nature walk through the forest with his mother is described by a toddler. (Rev: BL 9/15/97)

4548 Sweetland, Nancy. *God's Quiet Things* (PS–K). Illus. by Rick Stevens. 1994, Eerdmans $15.00 (0-8028-5082-0). 32pp. Quiet things in nature, like butterflies flying, are celebrated in this thoughtful picture book. (Rev: BL 1/1/95; SLJ 1/95)

4549 Swope, Sam. *Gotta Go! Gotta Go!* (PS–2). Illus. by Sue Riddle. 2000, Farrar $12.00 (0-374-32757-2). 32pp. The story of the caterpillar who turns into a monarch butterfly and travels three thousand miles from the U.S. to Mexico because he's "gotta go." (Rev: BCCB 5/00; BL 3/1/00*; HB 5–6/00; HBG 10/00; SLJ 5/00)

4550 Tafuri, Nancy. *Snowy Flowy Blowy: A Twelve Months Rhyme* (PS–2). Illus. by author. 1999, Scholastic $15.95 (0-590-18973-5). The months of the year are presented in double-page spreads with illustrations that picture the seasons. (Rev: HBG 3/00; SLJ 10/99)

4551 Tamar, Erika. *The Garden of Happiness* (PS–3). Illus. by Barbara Lambase. 1996, Harcourt $16.00 (0-15-230582-3). 40pp. Marisol's seed, planted in a New York City cracked sidewalk, grows into a huge sunflower. (Rev: BL 7/96*; SLJ 5/96)

4552 Titherington, Jeanne. *Pumpkin Pumpkin* (PS–1). Illus. by author. 1986, Greenwillow $16.89 (0-688-05696-2); Morrow paper $4.95 (0-688-09930-0). 24pp. A simple, rhythmic picture book about the facts of plant life. (Rev: BCCB 3/86; BL 3/15/86; SLJ 4/86)

4553 Tresselt, Alvin. *Hide and Seek Fog* (K–2). Illus. by Roger Duvoisin. 1965, Lothrop LB $15.93 (0-688-51169-4); Morrow paper $5.95 (0-688-07813-3). 32pp. Pastel watercolors quietly reflect obscure seashore scenes as the mysterious, deepening fog rolls in from the sea.

4554 Tresselt, Alvin. *Rain Drop Splash* (K–3). Illus. by Leonard Weisgard. 1946, Morrow paper $4.95 (0-688-09352-3). 28pp. How the raindrops form a puddle that grows from pond to river and finally joins the sea.

4555 Turner, Ann. *Apple Valley Year* (K–3). Illus. by Sandi W. Resnick. 1993, Macmillan $14.95 (0-02-789281-6). 32pp. A year on an apple farm as spent some time ago by the hardworking Clark fam-

ily and an equally diligent family of foxes. (Rev: BL 9/1/93)

4556 Udry, Janice May. *A Tree Is Nice* (PS). Illus. by Marc Simont. 1957, HarperCollins LB $15.89 (0-06-026156-0); paper $5.95 (0-06-443147-9). 32pp. The many delights to be had in, with, or under a tree: picking apples, raking leaves, swinging, or just sitting in the shade. Caldecott Medal winner, 1957.

4557 verDorn, Bethea. *Day Breaks* (PS–3). Illus. by Thomas Graham. 1992, Arcade $14.95 (1-55970-187-0). A gentle picture book that presents various scenes of morning as it is experienced across the United States. (Rev: SLJ 9/92)

4558 Waboose, Jan B. *Morning on the Lake* (K–3). Illus. by Karen Reczuch. 1998, Kids Can $15.95 (1-55074-373-2). 32pp. Three stories about an Ojibwa grandfather and his young grandson, their walks in a forest, and the mystical bond they feel with nature. (Rev: BL 3/15/98; HBG 10/98; SLJ 5/98)

4559 Waddell, Martin. *The Big Big Sea* (PS–3). Illus. by Jennifer Eachus. 1994, Candlewick $15.95 (1-56402-066-5). 32pp. Under a full moon, a little girl and her mother take a walk by the sea. (Rev: BL 9/15/94; SLJ 9/94)

4560 Widman, Christine. *The Willow Umbrella* (K–3). Illus. by Catherine Stock. 1993, Macmillan LB $14.95 (0-02-792760-1). 32pp. Two friends share a walk through a rainy countryside. (Rev: BL 3/15/93; SLJ 6/93)

4561 Wildsmith, Brian. *Seasons* (PS–3). Illus. by author. 1980, Oxford paper $9.95 (0-19-272175-5). 32pp. A sense of the marvels of the seasons is conveyed in this picture book.

4562 Wilson-Max, Ken. *Max Loves Sunflowers* (PS). Illus. by author. 1999, Hyperion $12.95 (0-7868-0413-0). Using tabs, this book covers the life cycle of a sunflower, beginning with preschooler Max planting a seed. (Rev: SLJ 12/99)

4563 Wood, Audrey. *Birdsong* (PS–2). Illus. by Robert Florczak. 1997, Harcourt $16.00 (0-15-200014-3). 32pp. An impressive picture book that identifies a state bird and a flower through the experiences of children in different parts of the United States. (Rev: BL 10/1/97; HBG 3/98; SLJ 10/97)

4564 Yerxa, Leo. *Last Leaf First Snowflake to Fall* (K–3). Illus. 1994, Orchard LB $14.99 (0-531-08674-7). 32pp. Two Indians explore the countryside and canoe across a pond in this picture book that explores the coming of winter. (Rev: BL 10/1/94; SLJ 12/94)

4565 Yolen, Jane. *Nocturne* (PS–2). Illus. by Anne Hunter. 1997, Harcourt $15.00 (0-15-201458-6). 32pp. Accompanied by his mother and his dog, a young boy explores the night sky and the world of nocturnal creatures. (Rev: BL 10/1/97; HBG 3/98; SLJ 11/97)

4566 Yolen, Jane. *Welcome to the Green House* (PS–3). Illus. by Laura Regan. 1993, Putnam LB $16.99 (0-399-22335-5). 32pp. Through a simple text and double-page paintings, a rain forest is introduced with a plea to save this kind of habitat. (Rev: BL 4/1/93; SLJ 4/93) [574]

OTHER TIMES, OTHER PLACES

4567 Ackerman, Karen. *Araminta's Paint Box* (K–3). Illus. by Betsy Lewin. 1998, Aladdin paper $5.99 (0-689-82091-7). 32pp. The Darling family is heading west to California by wagon. (Rev: BCCB 3/90; BL 2/1/90; SLJ 3/90)

4568 Ackerman, Karen. *The Tin Heart* (1–3). Illus. by Michael Hays. 1990, Macmillan $13.95 (0-689-31461-2). 32pp. Even the Civil War cannot split the friendship of two girls from families of different sides. (Rev: BCCB 11/90; BL 12/15/90; SLJ 9/90)

4569 Adams, Jeanie. *Going for Oysters* (K–3). Illus. by author. 1993, Albert Whitman LB $15.95 (0-8075-2978-8). A picture book that uses a simple story to introduce Australian aboriginal life by depicting life in a native outback community. (Rev: SLJ 1/94)

4570 Addy, Sharon Hart. *Right Here on This Spot* (PS–3). Illus. 1999, Houghton $15.00 (0-395-73091-0). 32pp. This book focuses on a single piece of land and what happened on that spot from prehistoric times to the present. (Rev: BL 10/15/99; HBG 3/00; SLJ 11/99)

4571 Adler, David A. *The Babe and I* (PS–2). Illus. by Terry Widener. 1999, Harcourt $16.00 (0-15-201378-4). 32pp. During the Great Depression, the young narrator sells newspapers on the street, and one day Babe Ruth buys a paper from him. (Rev: BCCB 6/99; BL 3/15/99*; HB 3–4/99; HBG 10/99; SLJ 5/99)

4572 Alexander, Sue. *Behold the Trees* (K–3). Illus. by Leonid Gore. 2001, Scholastic $16.95 (0-590-76211-7). 48pp. This picture book is about the trees of Israel, how the forests were cut down years ago, and how people began planting trees after World War I. (Rev: BCCB 3/01; BL 3/1/01*; SLJ 3/01)

4573 Aliki. *Marianthe's Story: Painted Words / Spoken Memories* (K–3). Illus. by author. 1998, Greenwillow LB $15.93 (0-688-15662-2). In this book combining two stories, the first tells how Mari, a young immigrant girl, expresses herself in her paintings; in the second, Mari relates life in her native land. (Rev: BCCB 1/99; HB 9–10/98; HBG 3/99; SLJ 10/98)

4574 Alrawi, Karim. *The Girl Who Lost Her Smile* (1–4). Illus. by Stefan Czernecki. 2000, Winslow $16.95 (1-890817-17-1). 40pp. A Middle Eastern tale about a young girl who has lost her smile and is told she will only get it back when a great artist paints a picture she likes. (Rev: BL 11/1/00; HBG 3/01; SLJ 12/00)

4575 Ancona, George. *Fiesta Fireworks* (1–3). Photos by author. 1998, Lothrop LB $15.93 (0-688-14818-2). A photo-essay describing a feast day in the city of Tultepec, Mexico, where some of the world's greatest fireworks are made. (Rev: BL 4/1/98; HB 5–6/98; HBG 10/98; SLJ 3/98)

4576 Andrews, Jan. *Very Last First Time* (PS–1). Illus. by Ian Wallace. 1986, Macmillan $17.00 (0-689-50388-1). 32pp. Eva's first time alone under the ice searching for the shellfish that her Inuit people of northern Canada eat nearly turns into disaster

when she dallies too long. (Rev: BCCB 9/86; BL 6/15/86; SLJ 5/86)

4577 Anholt, Laurence. *Camille and the Sunflowers: A Story About Vincent van Gogh* (PS–3). Illus. 1994, Barron's $14.95 (0-8120-6409-7). 32pp. Young Camille befriends the artist van Gogh when he comes to paint in his village in the Netherlands. (Rev: BL 12/1/94; SLJ 2/95)

4578 Arcellana, Francisco. *The Mats* (K–4). Illus. by Hermes Alegre. 1999, Kane/Miller $13.95 (0-916291-86-3). 24pp. A tender story about a Philippine family whose father returns home and brings a gift for each member of the group, including those children who have died. (Rev: BL 5/1/99; HBG 10/99; SLJ 9/99)

4579 Arnold, Marsha Diane. *The Pumpkin Runner* (K–3). Illus. by Brad Sneed. 1998, Dial $15.99 (0-8037-2124-2). 32pp. Based on a true story, this picture book tells of a 61-year-old Australian farmer who eats pumpkins for energy and wins a footrace against younger, better-trained opponents. (Rev: BCCB 11/98; BL 11/1/98; HBG 3/99; SLJ 12/98)

4580 Atwell, Debby. *Barn* (PS–3). Illus. 1996, Houghton $15.95 (0-395-78568-5). 32pp. Events in the life of a barn, from its erection in the late 1700s to the present day. (Rev: BL 10/1/96; SLJ 8/96*)

4581 Avi. *Finding Providence: The Story of Roger Williams* (2–3). Illus. by James Watling. 1997, HarperCollins LB $15.89 (0-06-025294-4). 48pp. An easy-to-read book that tells, through the eyes of Roger Williams's daughter, the story of Williams's Boston trial and escape to the wilderness. (Rev: BCCB 3/97; BL 2/1/97; HB 5–6/97; SLJ 3/97)

4582 Babbitt, Natalie. *Phoebe's Revolt* (K–3). Illus. by author. 1988, Farrar paper $3.95 (0-374-45792-1). 40pp. The story of a stubborn little girl set in the gaslight era.

4583 Baker, Jeannie. *The Story of Rosy Dock* (K–3). Illus. 1995, Greenwillow $14.89 (0-688-11493-8). 32pp. In the outback of Australia, the plant ecology is disturbed when settlers introduce rosy dock, a plant with distinctive red seedpods. (Rev: BCCB 3/95; BL 4/1/95*; SLJ 5/95) [508.94]

4584 Baker, Leslie. *Paris Cat* (PS–1). Illus. 1999, Little, Brown $15.95 (0-316-07309-1). 32pp. While on a visit to Paris with her young owner, Alice the cat chases a mouse and finds she is visiting the famous sights of the City of Lights. (Rev: BL 5/1/99; HBG 10/99; SLJ 6/99)

4585 Banim, Lisa. *American Dreams* (2–3). Illus. Series: Stories of the States. 1993, Silver Moon LB $14.95 (1-881889-34-3). 80pp. In this story set in California, the friendship between Jeannie and Amy, a Japanese American girl, is shattered when World War II breaks out. (Rev: SLJ 12/93)

4586 Banks, Sara H. *A Net to Catch Time* (K–3). Illus. by Scott Cook. 1996, Knopf LB $17.99 (0-679-96673-0). 28pp. A typical day in the life of a boy living on the Sea Islands off Georgia. (Rev: BL 12/1/96; SLJ 1/97)

4587 Bartone, Elisa. *Peppe the Lamplighter* (2–4). Illus. by Ted Lewin. 1993, Lothrop LB $15.89 (0-688-10269-7); Morrow paper $4.95 (0-688-15469-

7). 32pp. The story of an immigrant Italian boy who is a lamplighter in turn-of-the-century New York City. (Rev: BCCB 5/93; BL 4/15/93; SLJ 7/93)

4588 Baylor, Byrd. *One Small Blue Bead* (1–4). Illus. by Ronald Himler. 1992, Macmillan $16.00 (0-684-19334-5). 32pp. A story of an early tribe of cave dwellers in the American Southwest. First published in 1965. (Rev: BL 3/1/92; SLJ 4/92)

4589 Bell, Lili. *The Sea Maidens of Japan* (K–4). Illus. by Erin M. Brammer. 1997, Ideals $14.95 (1-57102-095-0). 32pp. A Japanese girl who is afraid of diving is expected to become an ama — a woman who dives to the ocean floor to harvest seafood. (Rev: BCCB 5/97; BL 6/1–15/97; SLJ 6/97)

4590 Bemelmans, Ludwig. *Madeline* (PS–3). Illus. by author. 1987, Viking $16.99 (0-670-81667-1). 32pp. The unforgettable Madeline in a pop-up-book format. (Rev: BL 11/15/87)

4591 Bemelmans, Ludwig, and John Bemelmans Marciano. *Madeline in America and Other Holiday Tales* (PS–3). Illus. 1999, Scholastic $19.95 (0-590-03910-5). This Madeline tale was completed by the author's grandson. The book also contains a few other short stories, including one about Christmas. (Rev: BL 11/15/99; HBG 10/00; SLJ 2/00)

4592 Benchley, Nathaniel. *George the Drummer Boy* (1–2). Illus. by Don Bolognese. 1977, HarperCollins LB $15.89 (0-06-020501-6). 64pp. The beginning of the American Revolution from the viewpoint of a young British soldier, told simply and dramatically.

4593 Benchley, Nathaniel. *Sam the Minuteman* (2–4). Illus. by Arnold Lobel. 1969, HarperCollins LB $15.89 (0-06-020480-X); paper $3.95 (0-06-444107-5). 64pp. An easy-to-read book that gives information on the way of life at the beginning of the Revolution.

4594 Beskow, Elsa. *Pelle's New Suit* (PS–3). Illus. by author. 1989, Gryphon $15.95 (0-86315-092-6). 16pp. A Swedish story of the steps in getting a new suit for a small boy, from shearing the lamb to tailoring.

4595 Blos, Joan W. *The Heroine of the Titanic: A Tale Both True and Otherwise of the Life of Molly Brown* (1–4). Illus. by Tennessee Dixon. 1991, Morrow $16.00 (0-688-07546-0). 40pp. A picture-book biography of the boisterous survivor of the Titanic who later became a Colorado legend. (Rev: BCCB 9/91; BL 8/91; SLJ 9/91)

4596 Blumberg, Rhoda. *Bloomers!* (K–4). Illus. by Mary Morgan. 1993, Macmillan LB $14.95 (0-02-711684-0). 32pp. A story that is based on fact of women who tried to become liberated by wearing balloon trousers, later called "bloomers." (Rev: BL 8/93) [305.42]

4597 Booth, David. *The Dust Bowl* (K–4). Illus. by Karen Reczuch. 1997, Kids Can $16.95 (1-55074-295-7). 32pp. A story about a poor Canadian farm family living in a Western dust bowl during the 1930s. (Rev: BL 9/1/97; SLJ 12/97)

4598 Borden, Louise. *A. Lincoln and Me* (1–4). Illus. by Ted Lewin. 1999, Scholastic $15.95 (0-590-45714-4). 32pp. A young boy named Abe, who

shares a birthday with Abraham Lincoln, thinks about himself and his famous namesake. (Rev: BL 11/15/99*; HBG 3/00; SLJ 10/99)

4599 Borden, Louise. *Good-bye, Charles Lindbergh* (K–4). Illus. by Thomas B. Allen. 1998, Simon & Schuster paper $16.00 (0-689-81536-0). 40pp. Based on a true incident, this picture book tells of a young boy from Canton, Mississippi, and his encounter with the legendary Charles Lindbergh. (Rev: BCCB 5/98; BL 3/1/98*; HBG 10/98; SLJ 3/98)

4600 Boulton, Jane. *Only Opal: The Diary of a Young Girl* (1–4). Illus. by Barbara Cooney. 1994, Putnam $15.95 (0-399-21990-0). 32pp. This book is based on a real journal kept by a very young girl growing up in rural Oregon with a foster family at the turn of the century. (Rev: BCCB 6/94; BL 3/15/94*; HB 5–6/94; SLJ 5/94) [973]

4601 Brace, Steve. *From Beans to Batteries* (PS–2). Illus. by Annie Kubler. Series: One World. 1999, Child's Play paper $6.99 (0-85953-799-4). Village life in Peru is depicted in this tale about a boy who walks to a market to trade beans for batteries to use in his radio. (Rev: SLJ 6/99)

4602 Bradby, Marie. *Momma, Where Are You From?* (PS–3). Illus. by Chris K. Soentpiet. 2000, Orchard LB $17.99 (0-531-33105-9). 32pp. At her daughter's request, an African American woman describes her life in the rural South during segregation. (Rev: BCCB 3/00; BL 2/15/00; HBG 10/00; SLJ 4/00)

4603 Bradby, Marie. *More Than Anything Else* (K–3). Illus. by Chris K. Soentpiet. 1996, Orchard LB $16.99 (0-531-08764-6). 32pp. A fictionalized account of the childhood of Booker T. Washington, told in a picture book format. (Rev: BL 7/95; SLJ 11/95*)

4604 Bresnick-Perry, Roslyn. *Leaving for America* (K–3). Illus. by Mira Reisberg. 1992, Children's Book Pr. $14.95 (0-89239-105-7). 32pp. Remembrances by the author, who left Russia in 1929 as a young child. (Rev: BCCB 2/93; BL 1/15/93; SLJ 2/93) [947]

4605 Brooks, Nigel, and Abigail Horner. *Town Mouse House: How We Lived One Hundred Years Ago* (PS–2). Illus. 2000, Walker $15.95 (0-8027-8732-0). 32pp. Using mice as the central characters, this book shows how the gentry lived in England a century ago. (Rev: BL 5/1/00; HBG 10/00; SLJ 5/00)

4606 Brownlow, Mike. *Way Out West with a Baby* (K–3). Illus. by author. 2000, Ragged Bears $13.95 (1-929927-04-5). Three cowpokes discover a baby and risk their lives to return it to its mother who is on a wagon train. (Rev: HBG 3/01; SLJ 12/00)

4607 Bunting, Eve. *Dreaming of America* (K–4). Illus. by Ben F. Stahl. 2000, Troll $15.95 (0-8167-6520-0). 32pp. Based on a true story, this picture book tells of Annie Moore, her trip from Ireland to America in 1892, and the distinction of being the first Irish immigrant processed on Ellis Island. (Rev: BL 4/1/00; SLJ 5/00)

4608 Bunting, Eve. *Going Home* (K–3). Illus. by David Diaz. 1996, HarperCollins LB $15.89 (0-06-026297-4). 32pp. Carlos and his family leave their adopted home in California to visit their original home in Mexico. (Rev: BCCB 12/96; BL 10/1/96; SLJ 9/96)

4609 Bunting, Eve. *I Have an Olive Tree* (PS–3). Illus. by Karen Barbour. 1999, HarperCollins LB $16.98 (0-06-027574-X). Sophia, a Greek American girl, and her mother go to Greece to revisit their family home and the olive tree that Sophia's grandfather planted before he died. (Rev: BCCB 5/99; BL 5/15/99; HB 7–8/99; HBG 10/99; SLJ 5/99)

4610 Bunting, Eve. *Market Day* (PS–2). Illus. by Holly Berry. 1996, HarperCollins LB $15.89 (0-06-025368-1). 32pp. Market day in a small Irish town is an exciting event, particularly when the young narrator is given a penny by her father to spend. (Rev: BL 2/15/96*; SLJ 4/96)

4611 Bunting, Eve. *So Far from the Sea* (K–4). Illus. by Chris K. Soentpiet. 1998, Clarion $15.00 (0-395-72095-8). 32pp. A young Japanese-American girl and her family visit the former internment camp of Manzanar and recall the family's hardships and experiences during their imprisonment from 1942 to the end of World War II. (Rev: BCCB 7–8/98; BL 5/1/98; HB 5–6/98; HBG 10/98; SLJ 6/98)

4612 Burke, Timothy R. *Tugboats in Action* (PS–2). Illus. 1993, Albert Whitman LB $15.95 (0-8075-8112-7). 32pp. Life aboard a tugboat on its journey on the Buffalo River to Lake Erie. (Rev: BCCB 12/93; BL 10/15/93; SLJ 1/94)

4613 Burleigh, Robert. *Lookin' for Bird in the Big City* (2–4). Illus. by Marek Los. 2001, Harcourt $16.00 (0-15-202031-4). 32pp. In this fictionalized story, teenage Miles Davis journeys to New York City to meet his idol, Charlie the "Bird" Parker, with whom he would later play jazz. (Rev: BL 2/15/01)

4614 Butler, Philippa. *Pawprints in Time* (K–3). Illus. by George Smith. 1998, Viking $14.99 (0-670-87177-X). 32pp. An ancient cat tells of her past lives and transports the reader to ancient Egypt, China, Rome, and Tibet. (Rev: BL 6/1–15/98; HBG 10/98; SLJ 9/98)

4615 Carling, Amelia Lau. *Mama and Papa Have a Store* (PS–2). Illus. 1998, Dial LB $15.89 (0-8037-2045-9). 32pp. A young Chinese girl describes a typical day at her parents' general store in Guatemala City. (Rev: BL 7/98; HBG 10/98; SLJ 8/98)

4616 Castaneda, Omar S. *Abuela's Weave* (K–3). Illus. by Enrique O. Sanchez. 1993, Lee & Low $15.95 (1-880000-00-8). 32pp. In Guatemala, a young girl and her grandmother take their handicrafts to sell at a fiesta. (Rev: BL 8/93; SLJ 7/93)

4617 Cech, John. *My Grandmother's Journey* (K–3). Illus. by Sharon McGinley-Nally. 1991, Macmillan LB $16.00 (0-02-718135-9). 40pp. A grandmother recalls the terrible life she had in Russia during the Revolution and World War II and how she came to freedom in the West. (Rev: BCCB 11/91; BL 8/91; SLJ 5/92)

4618 Chanin, Michael. *The Chief's Blanket* (PS–4). Illus. by Kim Howard. 1998, H.J. Kramer $14.95 (0-915811-78-2). 32pp. Using Navajo life during the 1800s as a background, this picture book tells how a young Indian girl weaves a blanket to buy horses so her grandmother will be able to travel in comfort. (Rev: BL 4/15/98; SLJ 7/98)

4619 Cherry, Lynne, and Mark J. Plotkin. *The Shaman's Apprentice* (K–4). Illus. 1998, Harcourt $16.00 (0-15-201281-8). 40pp. In the Amazon rain forest, young Kamanya hopes to become his tribe's new shaman, but new diseases brought in by foreigners challenge the powers of his traditional medicines. (Rev: BL 4/1/98; HBG 10/98; SLJ 5/98)

4620 Choi, Sook N. *Yunmi and Halmoni's Trip* (K–3). Illus. by Karen M. Dugan. 1997, Houghton $15.00 (0-395-81180-5). 32pp. Yunmi, a Korean American girl, goes to Korea for a visit with her grandmother. (Rev: BL 9/15/97; HBG 3/98; SLJ 10/97)

4621 Claverie, Jean. *Little Lou* (2–3). Illus. 1990, Creative Ed. $22.60 (0-88682-329-3). 48pp. Little Lou describes how he was introduced to blues music when he was a child in the thirties. (Rev: BL 4/15/91)

4622 Clements, Andrew. *Temple Cat* (K–3). Illus. by Kate Kiesler. 1996, Clarion $14.95 (0-395-69842-1). 32pp. A pampered temple cat in ancient Egypt finds happiness with a fisherman's family. (Rev: BCCB 2/96; BL 2/1/96; SLJ 3/96)

4623 Cohen, Miriam. *Mimmy and Sophie* (PS–3). Illus. by Thomas F. Yezerski. 1999, Farrar $16.00 (0-374-34988-6). 40pp. Four sweet, sentimental vignettes about the activities of two young sisters in Depression-era Brooklyn. (Rev: BL 8/99; HBG 10/99; SLJ 3/99)

4624 Coleman, Evelyn. *White Socks Only* (K–3). Illus. by Tyrone Geter. 1996, Albert Whitman LB $15.95 (0-8075-8955-1). 30pp. An elderly African American tells her granddaughter about her childhood in the segregated South. (Rev: BCCB 4/96; BL 2/15/96; SLJ 6/96)

4625 Collier, Mary Jo, and Peter Collier. *The King's Giraffe* (1–3). Illus. by Stephane Poulin. 1996, Simon & Schuster $16.00 (0-689-80679-5). 40pp. In 1826, the pasha of Egypt sent the King of France an unusual gift: a giraffe. (Rev: BCCB 3/96; BL 6/1–15/96; SLJ 3/96)

4626 Cooney, Barbara. *Hattie and the Wild Waves: A Story from Brooklyn* (1–5). Illus. 1990, Viking $15.99 (0-670-83056-9). 40pp. A re-creation of a young girl's life growing up in turn-of-the-century Brooklyn and Manhattan. (Rev: BCCB 12/90*; BL 11/1/90*; HB 1–2/91*; SLJ 12/90)

4627 Corey, Shana. *You Forgot Your Skirt, Amelia Bloomer!* (1–3). Illus. by Chesley McLaren. 2000, Scholastic $16.95 (0-439-07819-9). The story of Amelia Bloomer, how she founded a newspaper, worked for women's rights, and started a dress craze. (Rev: BCCB 2/00; BL 2/1/00*; HBG 10/00; SLJ 3/00)

4628 Corpi, Lucha. *Where Fireflies Dance* (K–4). Illus. by Mira Reisberg. 1997, Children's Book Pr.

$15.95 (0-89239-145-6). 32pp. The author remembers everyday incidents in her life growing up in a Mexican town. (Rev: BL 1/1–15/98; HBG 3/98; SLJ 12/97)

4629 Cowcher, Helen. *Whistling Thorn* (PS–3). Illus. 1993, Scholastic $14.95 (0-590-47299-2). 40pp. A nonfiction account of why the thorn trees of Africa's grasslands whistle when the wind blows through them. (Rev: BL 10/15/93; SLJ 10/93) [583]

4630 Cowen-Fletcher, Jane. *It Takes a Village* (PS–1). Illus. 1994, Scholastic $15.95 (0-590-46573-2). 32pp. Yemi realizes that all the townspeople are concerned when her young brother wanders off at market time in this book that explores life in a West African village. (Rev: BL 1/1/94; SLJ 3/94)

4631 Cutler, Jane. *The Cello of Mr. O* (1–4). Illus. by Greg Couch. 1999, Dutton $15.99 (0-525-46119-1). 32pp. In a war-torn city where food is scarce and all the men are at the front, there is a tiny ray of hope from the music that Mr. O plays in the town square every day. (Rev: BCCB 12/99; BL 12/15/99*; HBG 3/00; SLJ 11/99)

4632 Daly, Niki. *Bravo, Zan Angelo!* (K–3). Illus. 1998, Farrar $16.00 (0-374-30953-1). 36pp. In 18th-century Venice, Angelo wants to be a famous commedia dell'arte clown like his famous grandfather and, through determination and the help of strangers, he proves that he can do it. (Rev: BL 8/98; HBG 3/99; SLJ 9/98)

4633 Daly, Niki. *Jamela's Dress* (PS–2). Illus. 1999, Farrar $16.00 (0-374-33667-9). 32pp. In this picture book set in a South African township, a young girl gets into trouble when she soils some cloth that her mother bought for a new dress. (Rev: BCCB 6/99; BL 3/15/99; HB 7–8/99; HBG 10/99; SLJ 8/99)

4634 Daly, Niki. *Not So Fast, Songololo* (PS–K). Illus. by author. 1986, Simon & Schuster $16.00 (0-689-50367-9); Puffin paper $4.95 (0-689-80154-8). 32pp. A South African boy who does everything slowly puts on a pair of red-striped sneakers and walks fast and proud. (Rev: BCCB 4/86; BL 4/1/86; SLJ 5/86)

4635 Day, Marie. *Quennu and the Cave Bear* (K–3). Illus. by author. 1999, Owl $17.95 (1-895688-86-8); paper $6.95 (1-895688-87-6). 32pp. A young girl conquers her fear of cave bears and paints one on the wall during a prehistoric ceremony; includes accurate information about cave art. (Rev: HBG 10/99; SLJ 5/99)

4636 Deetlefs, Rene. *The Song of Six Birds* (PS–K). Illus. by Lyn Gilbert. 1999, Dutton $15.99 (0-525-46314-3). 32pp. Lindewe finds that local birdsong provides perfect musical material for her new flute. (Rev: BL 12/15/99; HBG 10/00; SLJ 2/00)

4637 Delgado, María Isabel. *Chave's Memories/Los Recuerdos de Chave* (PS–3). Illus. by Yvonne Symank. 1996, Piñata $14.95 (1-55885-084-8). A bilingual picture book in which a woman recalls her trips as a child from Brownsville, Texas, to her grandparents' ranch in northern Mexico. (Rev: SLJ 12/96)

4638 Drummond, Allan. *Casey Jones* (K–3). Illus. 2001, Farrar $16.00 (0-374-31175-7). 32pp. Inspired by railroading in the 1800s, this is the story of Casey, his fateful trip, and the fiery wreck that was his train. (Rev: BL 2/15/01)

4639 Edwards, Pamela Duncan. *Barefoot: Escape on the Underground Railroad* (K–4). Illus. by Henry Cole. 1997, HarperCollins LB $15.89 (0-06-027138-8). 32pp. The birds and other animals in a forest seem to work together to help an escaped slave. (Rev: BL 2/15/97; SLJ 2/97*)

4640 Emberley, Rebecca. *Taking a Walk/Caminando: A Book in Two Languages/Una Libra en Dos Lenguas* (1–3). Illus. 1994, Little, Brown paper $6.95 (0-316-23471-0). 32pp. Bright artwork and simple phrases introduce Spanish to English readers, and vice versa. Also use the bilingual *My House/Mi Casa* (1990). (Rev: BL 6/15/90; HB 9–10/90; SLJ 8/90)

4641 Ernst, Lisa Campbell. *Sam Johnson and the Blue Ribbon Quilt* (K–3). Illus. by author. 1983, Lothrop LB $15.89 (0-688-01517-4); Morrow paper $4.95 (0-688-11505-5). 32pp. The men and the women vie for honors in the quilting contest.

4642 Eversole, Robyn. *The Gift Stone* (K–3). Illus. by Allen Garns. 1998, Knopf LB $17.99 (0-679-98684-7). 32pp. Jean is unhappy when she must leave her grandparents to live with her father in a South Australia opal-mining town, but her discovery of a large opal changes her future prospects. (Rev: BL 8/98; HBG 3/99; SLJ 10/98)

4643 Fagan, Cary. *Gogol's Coat* (1–3). Illus. by Regolo Ricci. 1998, Tundra $14.95 (0-88776-429-0). 62pp. When a coat, which Gogol spent years saving for, is stolen, the thief is shamed into returning it. (Rev: BL 2/1/99; HBG 3/99; SLJ 4/99)

4644 Feder, Paula K. *The Feather-Bed Journey* (K–3). Illus. by Stacey Schuett. 1995, Albert Whitman LB $15.95 (0-8075-2330-5). 32pp. Grandma tells her grandchildren how her favorite feather pillow was once part of a large feather bed that kept her warm in a Jewish ghetto during World War II. (Rev: BCCB 12/95; BL 10/15/95; SLJ 11/95)

4645 Feeney, Stephanie. *A Is for Aloha* (PS–K). Photos by Jeff Reese. 1985, Univ. of Hawaii Pr. $11.95 (0-8248-0722-7). A simple introduction to Hawaii and its many cultures.

4646 Fleming, Candace. *A Big Cheese for the White House: The True Tale of a Tremendous Cheddar* (PS–3). Illus. by S. D. Schindler. 1999, DK $16.95 (0-7894-2573-4). In this fact-based story, residents of Cheshire, Massachusetts, produce a 1,235-pound cheese and present it to President Jefferson. (Rev: BCCB 9/99; BL 11/1/99; HB 9–10/99; HBG 3/00; SLJ 8/99)

4647 Fleming, Candace. *Gabriella's Song* (PS–3). Illus. by Giselle Potter. 1997, Simon & Schuster $16.00 (0-689-80973-5). 40pp. The song that Gabriella hums on the streets of Venice, Italy, is so infectious that soon everyone is singing it. (Rev: BL 12/1/97; HBG 3/98; SLJ 11/97*)

4648 Flora, James. *The Fabulous Firework Family* (K–2). Illus. 1994, Macmillan paper $14.95 (0-689-

50596-5). 32pp. The Fabulous Firework Family makes fireworks for a village's saint's day in this happy picture book set in Mexico. (Rev: BL 5/1/94; SLJ 4/94)

4649 Freschet, Gina. *Naty's Parade* (K–2). Illus. 2000, Farrar $16.00 (0-374-35500-2). 32pp. Naty, dressed in a big mouse costume, gets lost during the Mexican Guelaguetza parade but the sounds and smells lead her back to it. (Rev: BL 5/15/00; HBG 10/00; SLJ 3/00)

4650 Friedrich, Elizabeth. *Leah's Pony* (K–3). Illus. by Michael Garland. 1996, Boyds Mills $14.95 (1-56397-189-5). 32pp. Conditions in the Dust Bowl are so bad for Leah's family that they must sell their stock and equipment to survive. (Rev: BL 3/1/96; SLJ 3/96*)

4651 Garaway, Margaret K. *Ashkii and His Grandfather* (K–3). Illus. by Harry Warren. 1995, Old Hogan $14.95 (0-963-88517-0); paper $8.95 (0-963-88516-2). 33pp. A young Navajo boy helps his grandfather at summer sheep camp. (Rev: BL 3/1/90)

4652 Garay, Luis. *The Long Road* (PS–4). Illus. 1997, Tundra $15.95 (0-88776-408-8). 32pp. The experiences of a Latin American boy and his mother, who are forced to flee their village and seek asylum in another country. (Rev: BL 11/1/97; HBG 3/98; SLJ 1/98)

4653 Garay, Luis. *Pedrito's Day* (K–3). Illus. 1997, Orchard $14.95 (0-531-09522-3). 32pp. Pedrito, a Mexican boy, is heartbroken when he loses the money he had saved to buy a bicycle. (Rev: BL 3/1/97; SLJ 4/97)

4654 Garne, S. T. *By a Blazing Blue Sea* (PS–2). Illus. by Lori Lohstoeter. 1999, Harcourt $16.00 (0-15-201780-1). 32pp. A friendly parrot takes the reader on a tour of a tropical island and provides a glimpse of a beachcomber's life. (Rev: BL 7/99; HBG 10/99; SLJ 7/99)

4655 George, Jean Craighead. *Arctic Son* (K–2). Illus. by Wendell Minor. 1997, Hyperion LB $15.49 (0-7868-2255-4). 32pp. Luke, whose Eskimo name is Kupaaq, participates in many of his people's activities during the period of the Arctic sun. (Rev: BL 9/1/97; HBG 3/98; SLJ 11/97)

4656 George, Jean Craighead. *Nutik, the Wolf Pup* (PS–3). Illus. by Ted Rand. 2001, HarperCollins LB $15.89 (0-06-028165-0). 40pp. Amaroq nurses a wolf pup back to health and then must give him up and return him to the pack. (Rev: BL 2/1/01; SLJ 3/01)

4657 Germein, Katrina. *Big Rain Coming* (PS–2). Illus. by Bronwyn Bancroft. 2000, Clarion $15.00 (0-618-08344-8). 32pp. In the Australian Outback where it gets very hot, every living creature is waiting for the rain that Old Joseph claims is on its way. (Rev: BL 8/00; HBG 3/01; SLJ 9/00)

4658 Gerrard, Roy. *Croco'Nile* (K–3). Illus. 1994, Farrar $15.00 (0-374-31659-7). 32pp. A picture book about two talented youngsters growing up in ancient Egypt. (Rev: BCCB 1/95; BL 10/15/94; SLJ 11/94)

4659 Gerrard, Roy. *The Roman Twins* (K–3). Illus. 1998, Farrar $16.00 (0-374-36339-0). 32pp. In ancient Rome, two slave children named Maximus and Vanilla save the city from the Ostrogoths with the help of a horse named Polydox. (Rev: BCCB 10/98; BL 10/15/98; HB 11–12/98; HBG 3/99; SLJ 9/98)

4660 Gerrard, Roy. *Sir Cedric* (1–4). Illus. by author. 1984, Farrar paper $4.95 (0-374-46659-9). 32pp. A spoof on knights and the age of chivalry.

4661 Gershator, Phillis, and David Gershator. *Greetings, Sun* (PS–2). Illus. by Synthia Saint James. 1998, DK $15.95 (0-7894-2482-7). In this book set on a Caribbean island, two black children greet all of the things in life that they love. (Rev: BCCB 4/98; BL 3/15/98; HBG 10/98; SLJ 5/98)

4662 Gerstein, Mordicai. *The Mountains of Tibet* (K–3). Illus. by author. 1989, HarperCollins paper $6.95 (0-06-443211-4). 32pp. A woodcutter spends his life in a Tibetan valley in this story of reincarnation. (Rev: BL 11/15/87; HB 11–12/87; SLJ 11/87)

4663 Gerstein, Mordicai. *The Wild Boy* (1–3). Illus. 1998, Farrar $16.00 (0-374-38431-2). 40pp. Based on fact, this is the story of Victor, the wild child captured in 1800 near the village of Saint-Semin in France, and of the efforts to tame and civilize him while he yearns for his old life in the wilderness. (Rev: BCCB 12/98; BL 10/1/98*; HB 11–12/98; HBG 3/99; SLJ 10/98) [155.45]

4664 Glass, Andrew. *Bewildered for Three Days: As to Why Daniel Boone Never Wore His Coonskin Cap* (2–3). Illus. 2000, Holiday $16.95 (0-8234-1446-9). 32pp. After several hair-raising adventures including spending a night in a hollow log with a mother raccoon, Daniel Boone swears off wearing his coonskin cap forever. (Rev: BCCB 11/00; BL 9/1/00; SLJ 10/00)

4665 Goble, Paul. *Death of the Iron Horse* (K–2). Illus. by author. 1993, Simon & Schuster paper $5.99 (0-689-71686-9). 32pp. Rail sabotage from the Indian point of view, set in 1867. (Rev: BCCB 4/87; BL 4/1/87; HB 5–6/87)

4666 Godard, Alex. *Idora* (2–3). Trans. by Laura McKenna. Illus. 1999, Kane/Miller $14.95 (0-916291-89-8). 30pp. Idora is a lonely girl growing up in Paris, but finally she manages to leave her troubles behind for a stay on France's beautiful southern coast. (Rev: BL 12/1/99; HBG 3/00; SLJ 12/99)

4667 Goodall, John S. *The Story of a Farm* (2–5). Illus. by author. 1989, Macmillan $14.95 (0-689-50479-9). Detailing the changing centuries on an English farm. (Rev: BL 5/15/89; HB 5–6/89; SLJ 5/89)

4668 Graham, Christine. *When Pioneer Wagons Rumbled West* (PS–2). Illus. by Sherry Meidell. 1998, Deseret $14.95 (1-57345-272-6). 26pp. This picture book illustrates the hardships faced by Mormon families and the importance of prayer in their lives as they journeyed to settle land for their new home in Utah. (Rev: BL 9/15/98; SLJ 12/98)

4669 Graham, Steve. *Dear Old Donegal* (PS–2). Illus. by John O'Brien. 1996, Clarion $15.95 (0-

395-68187-1). 32pp. A colorful picture book version of the song about the Irishman who succeeded in the New World and later was welcomed back to his former home in Donegal. (Rev: BL 2/1/96; SLJ 4/96)

4670 Green, Norma B. *The Hole in the Dike* (K–2). Illus. by Eric Carle. 1975, Scholastic paper $4.95 (0-590-46146-X). 32pp. Brilliant illustrations accompany this simple retelling of the Mary Mapes Dodge story of the boy who put his finger in the dike and saved his Dutch town.

4671 Greenfield, Eloise. *Africa Dream* (K–3). Illus. by Carole Byard. 1989, HarperCollins LB $15.89 (0-690-04776-2); paper $5.95 (0-06-443277-7). 32pp. In this reissued picture book, a young black girl dreams about visiting her granddaddy's African village.

4672 Guarnieri, Paolo. *A Boy Named Giotto* (K–3). Trans. by Jonathan Galassi. Illus. by Bimba Landmann. 1999, Farrar $17.00 (0-374-30931-0). 32pp. A fictional story about how the painter Giotto found his profession through the teachings of the master artist Cimabue. (Rev: BCCB 1/00*; BL 12/15/99; HBG 3/00; SLJ 10/99)

4673 Haddon, Mark. *The Sea of Tranquillity* (1–3). Illus. by Christian Birmingham. 1996, Harcourt $16.00 (0-15-201285-0). 32pp. A man looks back at his childhood, when one night he stayed up late to watch the moon landing on TV. (Rev: SLJ 9/96)

4674 Hall, Donald. *Ox-Cart Man* (K–3). Illus. by Barbara Cooney. 1979, Puffin paper $6.99 (0-14-050441-9). 40pp. The cycle of production and sale of goods in 19th-century New England is pictured in human terms. Caldecott Medal winner, 1980.

4675 Hanson, Regina. *The Face at the Window* (1–3). Illus. by Linda Saport. 1997, Clarion $14.95 (0-395-78625-8). 32pp. A little girl in Jamaica is afraid of the old neighbor lady until her parents take the youngster to meet her. (Rev: BCCB 5/97; BL 6/1–15/97; SLJ 6/97)

4676 Harper, Jo, and Josephine Harper. *Prairie Dog Pioneers* (PS–3). Illus. by Craig Spearing. 1998, Turtle $16.95 (1-890515-10-8). 48pp. This historical adventure story tells of the experiences of Mae Dean and her family as they travel by covered wagon to their new home in the Texas panhandle. (Rev: BL 9/15/98; HBG 3/99; SLJ 10/98)

4677 Hathorn, Libby. *Sky Sash So Blue* (K–3). Illus. by Benny Andrews. 1998, Simon & Schuster $16.00 (0-689-81090-3). 32pp. A slave secretly sews for her daughter a wedding dress made out of scraps. (Rev: BCCB 5/98; BL 2/15/98; HB 7–8/98; HBG 10/98; SLJ 6/98)

4678 Heide, Florence Parry, and Judith Heide Gilliland. *The Day of Ahmed's Secret* (PS–3). Illus. by Ted Lewin. 1990, Lothrop LB $15.93 (0-688-08895-3). 32pp. Ahmed, a young boy in present-day Cairo, has a job delivering bottled gas. (Rev: BCCB 10/90; BL 9/1/90*; HB 11–12/90; SLJ 8/90*)

4679 Heide, Florence Parry, and Judith Heide Gilliland. *Sami and the Time of the Troubles* (1–4). Illus. by Ted Lewin. 1992, Houghton $15.95 (0-395-55964-2). 40pp. This compelling picture book shows a modern Beirut family caught up in the horrors of war. (Rev: BL 4/1/92*; HB 7–8/92; SLJ 5/92*)

4680 Hidaka, Masako. *Girl from the Snow Country* (K–2). Trans. by Amanda Mayer Stinchecum. Illus. 1986, Kane/Miller $13.95 (0-916291-06-5). 32pp. Her wish comes true when Mi-chan makes snow bunnies and needs something to make red eyes. (Rev: BL 2/1/87; SLJ 1/87)

4681 Hippely, Hilary H. *A Song for Lena* (PS–2). Illus. by Leslie Baker. 1996, Simon & Schuster paper $16.00 (0-689-80763-5). 32pp. In old Hungary, a mother gives a beggar a sample of her delicious strudel, with unforeseen consequences. (Rev: BL 11/1/96; SLJ 10/96)

4682 Hodges, Margaret. *Brother Francis and the Friendly Beasts* (K–3). Illus. by Ted Lewin. 1991, Macmillan $13.95 (0-684-19173-3). 32pp. The story of the son of a merchant who rejected riches for prayer. (Rev: BCCB 11/91; BL 8/91; HB 9–10/91; SLJ 12/91) [271]

4683 Hoffman, Mary. *Boundless Grace* (PS–3). Illus. by Caroline Binch. 1995, Dial $16.99 (0-8037-1715-6). 32pp. Grace's father sends airplane tickets for her to visit him in Gambia and meet his new family. (Rev: BCCB 6/95; BL 4/15/95; HB 7–8/95; SLJ 5/95*)

4684 Hong, Lily T. *The Empress and the Silkworm* (PS–3). Illus. 1995, Albert Whitman LB $16.95 (0-8075-2009-8). 32pp. A Chinese empress uses the silk threads she finds when she discovers the cocoons of silkworms to make a robe for the emperor. (Rev: BCCB 12/95; BL 9/15/95; SLJ 11/95)

4685 Hopkinson, Deborah. *Maria's Comet* (1–3). Illus. by Deborah Lanino. 1999, Simon & Schuster $16.00 (0-689-81501-8). 32pp. A fictionalized story of astronomer Maria Mitchell's childhood in the early 1800s. (Rev: BCCB 1/00; BL 9/15/99; HBG 3/00; SLJ 10/99)

4686 Howard, Elizabeth F. *Papa Tells Chita a Story* (PS–1). Illus. by Floyd Cooper. 1995, Simon & Schuster paper $15.00 (0-02-744623-9). 28pp. Papa tells Chita of his experiences during the Spanish-American War. A sequel to *Chita's Christmas Tree* (1989). (Rev: BL 4/1/95; HB 9–10/95; SLJ 6/95)

4687 Howard, Ellen. *The Log Cabin Quilt* (K–3). Illus. by Ronald Himler. 1996, Holiday LB $16.95 (0-8234-1247-4). 28pp. Quilting scraps help chink the holes in a log cabin in this story of Western pioneers. (Rev: BCCB 10/96; BL 12/15/96; SLJ 10/96)

4688 Hubbard, Louise Garff. *Grandfather's Gold Watch* (K–4). Illus. 1998, Shadow Mountain $11.95 (1-57345-242-4). 32pp. When Peter and his family leave Denmark for America in 1850, his grandfather gives him his gold watch and asks the boy to question himself each year on how he has spent his time. (Rev: BL 11/15/98; SLJ 2/99)

4689 Hughes, Monica. *A Handful of Seeds* (K–3). Illus. by Luis Garay. 1996, Orchard $14.95 (0-531-09498-7). 32pp. When Concepcion moves from the country to the city, she brings some seeds with her to start a garden in the barrio. (Rev: BCCB 6/96; BL 4/1/96; SLJ 3/96)

4690 Isadora, Rachael. *Caribbean Dream* (PS–1). Illus. 1998, Putnam $15.99 (0-399-23230-3). 32pp. Lively pictures and spare, poetic text are used to illustrate the actions of four island children and evoke the mood of the Caribbean. (Rev: BL 11/1/98; HBG 3/99; SLJ 4/99)

4691 Isom, Joan Shaddox. *The First Starry Night* (K–3). Illus. 1998, Whispering Coyote $15.95 (1-879085-96-8). 32pp. Jacques becomes a friend of Vincent van Gogh when the artist boards in the young boy's house in Arles. (Rev: BL 4/15/98; HBG 10/98; SLJ 6/98)

4692 James, J. Alison. *The Drums of Noto Hanto* (K–3). Illus. by Tsukushi. 1999, DK $16.95 (0-7894-2574-2). Based on an incident that occurred in Japan 400 years ago, this book tells how a group of villagers frighten off a fleet of invading samurai with loud noises and scary masks. (Rev: BL 9/1/99; HBG 3/00; SLJ 8/99)

4693 Johnson, Angela. *The Rolling Store* (K–3). Illus. by Peter Catalanotto. 1997, Orchard LB $16.99 (0-531-33015-X). 32pp. A young African American girl tells her friend about the traveling store in a truck that used to visit their community during her grandfather's childhood. (Rev: BCCB 5/97; BL 2/15/97; SLJ 4/97)

4694 Johnson, Dinah. *All Around Town: The Photographs of Richard Samuel Roberts* (K–4). Photos by Richard S. Roberts. 1998, Holt $15.95 (0-8050-5456-1). 32pp. This album of photos depicts the daily lives of African Americans living in Columbia, South Carolina, during the 1920s and 1930s. (Rev: BCCB 4/98; BL 2/15/98; HB 3–4/98; HBG 10/98; SLJ 3/98) [779]

4695 Johnson, Dinah. *Quinnie Blue* (PS–2). Illus. by James E. Ransome. 2000, Holt $16.95 (0-8050-4378-0). 32pp. An African American girl imagines what life was like when her grandmother was growing up. (Rev: BL 4/15/00; HBG 10/00; SLJ 6/00)

4696 Johnson, Dolores. *Now Let Me Fly: The Story of a Slave Family* (K–4). Illus. 1993, Macmillan LB $15.00 (0-02-747699-5). 32pp. The inhuman story of an African girl who is sold into slavery in the United States, where she raises a family. (Rev: BCCB 11/93; BL 10/15/93; SLJ 3/94)

4697 Johnson, Dolores. *Seminole Diary: Remembrances of a Slave* (1–3). Illus. 1994, Macmillan paper $16.00 (0-02-747848-3). 32pp. Excerpts from a diary kept by a slave girl who escaped to southern Florida, where she lived with the Seminole Indians. (Rev: BCCB 10/94; BL 12/1/94; SLJ 11/94) [975.9]

4698 Johnston, Tony. *How Many Miles to Jacksonville?* (PS–3). Illus. by Bart Forbes. 1996, Putnam $15.95 (0-399-22615-X). 32pp. Simple pleasures from bygone times are featured in this story set in the East Texas town of Jacksonville. (Rev: BL 10/15/96; SLJ 12/96)

4699 Johnston, Tony. *The Magic Maguey* (PS–3). Illus. by Elisa Kleven. 1996, Harcourt $16.00 (0-15-250988-7). 32pp. Miguel tries to save from destruction the wonderful maguey tree, which supplies so many comforts for his family. (Rev: BL 10/15/96)

4700 Johnston, Tony. *The Wagon* (2–3). Illus. by James E. Ransome. 1996, Morrow LB $15.93 (0-688-13537-4). 40pp. A boy born into slavery celebrates his freedom at the time of Lincoln's tragic death. (Rev: BCCB 9/96; BL 1/1–15/97; SLJ 3/97)

4701 Joosse, Barbara M. *Lewis and Papa: Adventure on the Santa Fe Trail* (2–4). Illus. by Jon Van Zyle. 1998, Chronicle $14.95 (0-8118-1959-0). 40pp. During an adventurous wagon-train journey across the Great Plains with his father, young Lewis learns that sometimes being afraid and crying are natural parts of life. (Rev: BL 6/1–15/98; HBG 10/98; SLJ 10/98)

4702 Joseph, Lynn. *Jump Up Time: A Trinidad Carnival Story* (K–3). Illus. by Lynn Saport. 1998, Clarion $16.00 (0-395-65012-7). 32pp. Lily helps her big sister overcome stage fight when it's time to perform in her lovely hummingbird costume during carnival. (Rev: BCCB 1/99; BL 10/15/98; HBG 3/99; SLJ 11/98)

4703 Kalman, Maira. *Sayonara, Mrs. Kackleman* (K–3). Illus. 1989, Viking $16.99 (0-670-82945-5). 40pp. Japan is introduced through the wild and woolly adventures of an American tourist. (Rev: BCCB 11/89; BL 11/15/89; SLJ 1/90)

4704 Karim, Roberta. *Kindle Me a Riddle* (K–2). Illus. by Bethanne Andersen. 1999, Greenwillow LB $15.93 (0-688-16204-5). 40pp. In frontier America, a family traces the origins of their simple pioneer home and its contents, such as the candles that were once beeswax. (Rev: BL 9/1/99; HBG 3/00; SLJ 1/00)

4705 Kay, Verla. *Covered Wagons, Bumpy Trails* (PS–3). Illus. by S. D. Schindler. 2000, Putnam $15.99 (0-399-22928-0). A rhyming tale with excellent paintings that depicts the hardships and triumphs of a pioneer family and their journey to California. (Rev: HB 1–2/01; HBG 3/01; SLJ 11/00)

4706 Kay, Verla. *Gold Fever* (K–3). Illus. by S. D. Schindler. 1999, Putnam $15.99 (0-399-23027-0). 32pp. A young man encounters many obstacles while traveling to the California Gold Rush but, when he doesn't find gold, must go home disappointed. (Rev: BL 1/1–15/99; HB 3–4/99; HBG 10/99; SLJ 3/99)

4707 Keefer, Janice Kulyk. *Anna's Goat* (2–4). Illus. by Janet Wilson. 2001, Orca $15.95 (1-55143-153-X). 32pp. Based on a true story, a nanny goat helps ease the pain and loneliness of two refugee children. (Rev: BL 3/15/01)

4708 Kellerhals-Stewart, Heather. *Brave Highland Heart* (PS–1). Illus. by Werner Zimmerman. 1999, Stoddart $15.95 (0-7737-3099-0). 32pp. A little Scottish girl fears she will be denied permission to go the ceilidh, a traditional Scottish party that will be held in the family barn, but her father allows her to stay up and enjoy the fun and dancing. (Rev: BL 8/99; SLJ 6/99)

4709 Kerley, Barbara. *Songs of Papa's Island* (K–3). Illus. by Katherine Tillotson. 1995, Houghton $14.95 (0-395-71548-2). 59pp. A mother tells her child about the wildlife on the island in the

Pacific where she lived while she was pregnant. (Rev: SLJ 10/95)

4710 Kessler, Cristina. *My Great-Grandmother's Gourd* (K–3). Illus. by Walter L. Krudop. 2000, Orchard $16.95 (0-531-30284-9). 32pp. A lyrically told story set in a Sudanese village about an elderly grandmother who wisely continues to store water in the old-fashioned way even though a new water pump has been installed. (Rev: BCCB 12/00; BL 1/1–15/01; HBG 3/01; SLJ 12/00)

4711 Ketcham, Sallie. *Bach's Big Adventure* (PS–3). Illus. by Timothy Bush. 1999, Orchard LB $17.99 (0-531-33140-7). 32pp. Ten-year-old Bach journeys to Hamburg to hear the man who is supposedly the greatest organist in the world. (Rev: BCCB 5/99; BL 4/1/99; HBG 10/99; SLJ 6/99)

4712 Khan, Rukhsana. *The Roses in My Carpets* (1–4). Illus. by Ronald Himler. 1998, Holiday $15.95 (0-8234-1399-3). 32pp. A young Afghan boy who lives in a refugee camp dreams of freedom and a place without bombs or warfare as he learns to weave carpets. (Rev: BL 11/15/98; HBG 3/99; SLJ 11/98)

4713 Kidd, Richard. *Almost Famous Daisy!* (PS–3). Illus. 1996, Simon & Schuster paper $16.00 (0-689-80390-7). 32pp. Daisy visits the sites where painters like van Gogh and Monet found their inspiration so that she can begin work on her own masterpiece. (Rev: BL 4/15/96; SLJ 9/96)

4714 Kirk, Daniel. *Breakfast at the Liberty Diner* (K–3). Illus. 1997, Hyperion LB $15.49 (0-7868-2243-0). 32pp. Bobby and his mother and baby brother have a meal at a busy diner during the 1940s and are surprised by a visit from President Roosevelt. (Rev: BL 11/1/97; HBG 3/98; SLJ 11/97)

4715 Koscielniak, Bruce. *Hear, Hear, Mr. Shakespeare: Story, Illustrations, and Selections from Shakespeare's Plays* (1–4). Illus. by author. 1998, Houghton $15.00 (0-395-87495-5). In Stratford-on-Avon, Shakespeare must suddenly write a play for a troupe of visiting players, and Queen Elizabeth is very impressed. (Rev: HBG 10/98; SLJ 5/98)

4716 Kroeger, Mary Kay, and Louise Borden. *Paperboy* (K–4). Illus. by Ted Lewin. 1996, Clarion $16.95 (0-395-64482-8). 32pp. In 1927 Cincinnati, a young paperboy has trouble selling his newspapers when boxing champ Jack Dempsey loses the prizefight. (Rev: BCCB 3/96; BL 3/15/96; HB 9–10/96; SLJ 8/96*)

4717 Kroll, Virginia. *Africa Brothers and Sisters* (PS–2). Illus. by Vanessa French. 1992, Macmillan $15.00 (0-02-751166-9). 32pp. Father and son engage in a conservation/fact-finding game regarding contemporary Africa. (Rev: BL 2/15/93)

4718 Kroll, Virginia. *Sweet Magnolia* (1–3). Illus. by Laura Jacques. 1995, Charlesbridge paper $6.95 (0-88106-414-9). When Denise visits her grandmother, a naturalist, in Louisiana, she learns about the flora and fauna of the swamps and tastes Cajun food. (Rev: SLJ 2/96)

4719 Krull, Kathleen, and Enrique O. Sanchez. *Maria Molina and the Days of the Dead* (PS–2). Illus. 1994, Macmillan paper $15.95 (0-02-750999-

0). 32pp. A Mexican family prepares for the celebration of the Day of the Dead and then participates in the festivities. (Rev: BL 10/15/94; SLJ 12/94)

4720 Krupinski, Loretta. *Best Friends* (K–3). Illus. 1998, Hyperion LB $15.49 (0-7868-2356-9). 32pp. Charlotte gives up her prized possession, her doll, in order to send a message to her friend, a young Nez Perce girl, that soldiers plan to forcibly relocate her tribe. (Rev: BL 6/1–15/98; HBG 10/98; SLJ 7/98)

4721 Kurtz, Jane, and Christopher Kurtz. *Only a Pigeon* (PS–4). Illus. by E. B. Lewis. 1997, Simon & Schuster paper $16.00 (0-689-80077-0). 40pp. A little boy growing up in Addis Ababa, Ethiopia, takes pride in caring for some homing pigeons. (Rev: BCCB 7–8/97; BL 6/1–15/97; SLJ 6/97)

4722 Kusugak, Michael A. *Arctic Stories* (2–4). Illus. by Vladyana Krykorka. 1998, Annick $18.95 (1-55037-452-4); paper $6.95 (1-55037-453-2). 40pp. Three stories about an Inuit girl growing up in a village around northern Hudson Bay are simply told with full-page watercolors. (Rev: BL 11/1/98; SLJ 3/99)

4723 Lamorisse, Albert. *The Red Balloon* (1–3). Illus. by author. 1967, Doubleday $16.95 (0-385-00343-9); paper $10.95 (0-385-14297-8). 45pp. Pascal possesses a magic balloon that leads him on a tour of Paris, and he must defend the balloon from a gang of boys bent on bursting it.

4724 Lanteigne, Helen. *The Seven Chairs* (K–3). Illus. by Maryann Kovalski. 1998, Orchard $14.95 (0-531-30110-9). 32pp. A picture book that traces the history of seven chairs that were carved by a woodworker in England several centuries ago. (Rev: BL 9/1/98; HBG 3/99; SLJ 11/98)

4725 Lattimore, Eleanor F. *Little Pear* (K–3). Illus. by author. 1992, Buccaneer LB $14.95 (0-89966-917-4); Harcourt paper $3.95 (0-15-652799-5). 106pp. A young boy growing up in China during the 1920s.

4726 Lawson, Julie. *Emma and the Silk Train* (1–5). Illus. by Paul Mombourquette. 1998, Kids Can $15.95 (1-55074-388-0). 32pp. When a train carrying bales of silk is derailed, Emma joins the search for the lost silk, finds a bale, and gets stuck on a small island. Based on the true story of a "silker" derailment in 1927. (Rev: BL 11/1/98; HBG 3/99; SLJ 10/98)

4727 Lester, Alison. *My Farm* (K–4). Illus. 1994, Houghton $14.95 (0-395-68193-6). 32pp. The author recalls her childhood on an Australian farm — the chores, the cattle, and the joy of receiving a palomino pony at Christmas. (Rev: BCCB 7–8/94; BL 7/94; SLJ 9/94*) [630]

4728 Lester, Julius. *Black Cowboy, Wild Horses: A True Story* (K–4). Illus. by Jerry Pinkney. 1998, Dial LB $16.89 (0-8037-1788-1). 40pp. Based on true incidents, this is the story of cowboy Bob Lemmons, a former slave who helped tame the Wild West and had a series of exciting adventures. (Rev: BCCB 5/98; BL 5/1/98; HB 7–8/98; HBG 10/98; SLJ 6/98)

4729 Le Tord, Bijou. *A Bird or Two: A Story About Henri Matisse* (K–3). Illus. 1999, Eerdmans $17.00

(0-8028-5184-3). 32pp. Using Matisse-like paintings, this picture book tells about the artist and the south of France that he loved. (Rev: BL 11/15/99; HBG 3/00; SLJ 2/00)

4730 Levine, Ellen. *The Tree That Would Not Die* (1–4). Illus. by Ted Rand. 1995, Scholastic $14.95 (0-590-43724-0). 32pp. The story of the 400-year-old Treaty Oak in Texas and the important historical events that it witnessed. (Rev: BCCB 10/95; BL 11/1/95*; SLJ 12/95) [813]

4731 Levitin, Sonia. *Boom Town* (PS–3). Illus. by Cat B. Smith. 1998, Orchard LB $17.99 (0-531-33043-5). 40pp. In Gold Rush California, Amanda gets rich making wonderful gooseberry pies. A companion to *Nine for California* (1996). (Rev: BCCB 5/98; BL 2/15/98; HB 3–4/98; HBG 10/98; SLJ 3/98)

4732 Levitin, Sonia. *Taking Charge* (K–3). Illus. by Cat B. Smith. 1999, Orchard LB $17.99 (0-531-33149-0). 32pp. In this story about a California pioneer family, young Amanda must take over caring for baby Nathan after their mother is called away on an emergency. (Rev: BL 4/15/99; HB 3–4/99; HBG 10/99; SLJ 4/99)

4733 Lewin, Hugh. *Jafta* (K–3). Illus. by Lisa Kopper. 1983, Lerner paper $4.95 (0-87614-494-6). 24pp. There are six volumes in this set that are about a black South African child and his father. Others are: *Jafta's Father* (1983); *Jafta's Mother* (1983); *Jafta: The Journey* (1984); *Jafta: The Town* (1984); *Jafta and the Wedding* (1988).

4734 Lewin, Ted. *The Storytellers* (K–3). Illus. 1998, Lothrop $16.00 (0-688-15178-7). 40pp. In the ancient Moroccan city of Fez, Abdul and his grandfather wander through the colorful streets until they find a suitable spot to entertain people with their intriguing stories. (Rev: BL 4/1/98; HBG 10/98; SLJ 4/98)

4735 Lewis, Rose. *I Love You Like Crazy Cakes* (PS–3). Illus. by Jane Dyer. 2000, Little, Brown $14.95 (0-316-52538-3). 32pp. The author, an American, presents a fictional account of her trip to China to adopt a baby girl. (Rev: BL 9/1/00; SLJ 10/00)

4736 Lieberman, Syd. *The Wise Shoemaker of Studena* (K–3). Illus. by Martin Lemelman. 1994, Jewish Publication Soc. $15.95 (0-8276-0509-9). 32pp. Samuel learns not to judge people by their appearances when he offends the disreputable-looking wise man Yossi. (Rev: BL 10/15/94)

4737 Lied, Kate. *Potato: A Tale from the Great Depression* (K–3). Illus. by Lisa Campbell Ernst. 1997, National Geographic $16.00 (0-7922-3521-5). 32pp. A story about the Great Depression in which a family is forced to leave its home to pick potatoes in Idaho. (Rev: BL 4/1/97; HB 5–6, 9–10/97; SLJ 7/97)

4738 Lindgren, Astrid. *The Tomten* (PS–2). Illus. by Harald Wiberg. 1997, Putnam paper $5.99 (0-698-11591-0). 32pp. The friendly troll speaks in Tomten language only animals and children understand. By the same author, illustrator, and publisher: *The Tomten and the Fox* (1989).

4739 Little, Mimi O. *Yoshiko and the Foreigner* (K–4). Illus. 1996, Farrar $16.00 (0-374-32448-4). 32pp. A love story about an African American soldier and the Japanese girl he meets in Tokyo. (Rev: BL 11/15/96; HB 11–12/96; SLJ 1/97)

4740 Littlesugar, Amy. *Freedom School, Yes!* (PS–3). Illus. by Floyd Cooper. 2001, Putnam $16.99 (0-399-23006-8). 40pp. Based on fact, this is the story of volunteers who came South during the civil rights struggle in 1964 and set up "freedom schools." (Rev: BCCB 2/01; BL 2/15/01; SLJ 1/01)

4741 Littlesugar, Amy. *Jonkonnu* (2–4). Illus. by Ian Schoenherr. 1997, Putnam $15.95 (0-399-22831-4). 32pp. A story, based on fact, about a trip the artist Winslow Homer took to Virginia to make studies of African Americans for a painting he was planning. (Rev: BL 1/1–15/98; HBG 10/98; SLJ 2/98)

4742 Littlesugar, Amy. *Tree of Hope* (PS–3). Illus. by Floyd Cooper. 1999, Putnam $16.99 (0-399-23300-8). 40pp. During the Depression, Florrie's dad, who has a job frying doughnuts, gets a part in Orson Welles's all-black production of *Macbeth*. (Rev: BL 12/15/99; HBG 3/00; SLJ 11/99)

4743 London, Jonathan. *Ali, Child of the Desert* (K–4). Illus. by Ted Lewin. 1997, Lothrop LB $15.93 (0-688-12561-1). 32pp. Ali and his camel, Jabad, survive in the desert after a terrible dust storm separates them from the rest of their party. (Rev: BCCB 6/97; BL 3/1/97; SLJ 5/97)

4744 London, Jonathan. *Hurricane!* (K–3). Illus. by Henri Sorensen. 1998, Lothrop $16.00 (0-688-12977-3). 32pp. Two boys experience the fierceness of a hurricane when it strikes their Puerto Rico home. (Rev: BL 8/98; HBG 3/99; SLJ 1/99)

4745 London, Jonathan. *Moshi Moshi* (K–5). Illus. by Yoshi Miyake. 1998, Millbrook LB $21.40 (0-7613-0110-0). 32pp. Japan and its customs are seen through the eyes of a young American boy who is visiting his Japanese pen pal, Kenji, for the summer. (Rev: BL 11/1/98; HBG 3/99; SLJ 1/99)

4746 Luenn, Nancy. *A Gift for Abuelita: Celebrating the Day of the Dead: Un regalo para Abuelita: En celebración del Día de los Muertos* (K–3). Illus. by Robert Chapman. 1998, Rising Moon $15.95 (0-87358-688-3). 32pp. Told in English and Spanish, this picture book relates Rosita's tribute to her grandmother on the Day of the Dead. (Rev: BCCB 1/99; BL 3/15/99; HBG 3/99; SLJ 3/99)

4747 Luenn, Nancy. *Nessa's Fish* (PS–3). Illus. by Neil Waldman. 1990, Macmillan $15.00 (0-689-31477-9). 32pp. When her grandmother becomes ill during an ice-fishing expedition, an Inuit girl must fight off the attacks of several animals. (Rev: BL 3/1/90*; SLJ 3/90)

4748 Luenn, Nancy. *Nessa's Story* (K–3). Illus. by Neil Waldman. 1994, Atheneum $14.95 (0-689-31782-4). While walking in the tundra, an Inuit girl uses her imagination and makes up a story similar to the ones that her grandmother frequently tells. (Rev: SLJ 4/94)

4749 Lyon, George E. *Dreamplace* (K–4). Illus. by Peter Catalanotto. 1993, Orchard $15.95 (0-531-05466-7); paper $6.95 (0-531-07101-4). 32pp. A poetic text about a girl who sees the 800-year-old site of the Anasazi and dreams of when the tribe lived there long ago. (Rev: BCCB 3/93; BL 3/15/93*; HB 3–4/93; SLJ 3/93*)

4750 McBrier, Page. *Beatrice's Goat* (K–3). Illus. by Lori Lohstoeter. 2001, Simon & Schuster $16.00 (0-689-82460-2). 40pp. Beatrice longs to attend school in her Ugandan village, and when her family gets a goat from an aid organization, it provides enough income to send her there. (Rev: BCCB 2/01; BL 2/15/01; SLJ 2/01)

4751 McClintock, Barbara. *The Fantastic Drawings of Danielle* (PS–2). Illus. 1996, Houghton $17.00 (0-395-73980-2). 32pp. In 19th-century Paris, Danielle astounds everyone with her imaginative drawings. (Rev: BCCB 2/97; BL 10/15/96; SLJ 9/96)

4752 McCully, Emily Arnold. *Beautiful Warrior: The Legend of the Nun's Kung Fu* (K–4). Illus. 1998, Scholastic $16.95 (0-590-37487-7). 40pp. In this beautiful picture book, two women learn kung fu and use it in different ways in 17th-century China. (Rev: BCCB 3/98; BL 2/1/98; SLJ 2/98*)

4753 McCully, Emily Arnold. *Mirette and Bellini Cross Niagara Falls* (PS–3). Illus. 2000, Putnam $15.99 (0-399-23348-2). 32pp. A thrilling adventure story in which young Mirette and her guardian, the high-wire-artist, Bellini, come to the States for the ultimate stunt, crossing Niagara Falls on a wire. (Rev: BCCB 1/01; BL 11/15/00; SLJ 11/00)

4754 McCully, Emily Arnold. *Mirette on the High Wire* (PS–2). Illus. 1992, Putnam $16.99 (0-399-22130-1). 32pp. Set in Paris 100 years ago, this is the story of how a young girl helps a high-wire performer regain his courage. Caldecott Medal winner, 1993. (Rev: BCCB 10/92*; BL 11/15/92; SLJ 10/92)

4755 MacDonald, Suse. *Nanta's Lion: A Search and Find Adventure* (PS–1). Illus. 1995, Morrow $15.00 (0-688-13125-5). 24pp. An interactive book about an African girl who sets out to find the lion that has been stealing cattle from her village. (Rev: BL 4/15/95; SLJ 5/95)

4756 McKay, Lawrence, Jr. *Caravan* (1–4). Illus. by Darryl Ligasan. 1995, Lee & Low $14.95 (1-880000-23-7). A boy tells about going on his first caravan through the mountains in Afghanistan to trade his family's furs for grain. (Rev: SLJ 12/95)

4757 McKissack, Patricia. *Ma Dear's Aprons* (PS–3). Illus. by Floyd Cooper. 1997, Simon & Schuster $16.00 (0-689-81051-2). 32pp. During the early 1900s in Alabama, Ma Dear must support her family by doing domestic work. (Rev: BCCB 6/97; BL 2/15/97; HB 5–6/97; SLJ 6/97)

4758 MacLachlan, Patricia. *Three Names* (K–3). Illus. by Alexander Pertzoff. 1991, HarperCollins LB $16.89 (0-06-024036-9). 32pp. A boy repeats the stories that his great-grandfather told him of growing up in pioneer days. (Rev: BCCB 1/92; BL 8/91; HB 9–10/91; SLJ 7/91)

4759 Madrigal, Antonio H. *Erandi's Braids* (PS–3). Illus. by Tomie dePaola. 1999, Putnam $15.99 (0-399-23212-5). 32pp. Erandi, a young member of a

poor 1950s Mexican family, reluctantly decides to sell her beautiful hair to help her family. (Rev: BL 1/1–15/99*; HBG 10/99; SLJ 2/99)

4760 Manson, Ainslie. *A Dog Came, Too: A True Story* (1–3). Illus. by Ann Blades. 1993, Macmillan $13.95 (0-689-50567-1). 32pp. In a fictionalized format, this is the story of the dog that accompanied explorer Alexander Mackenzie across Canada to the Pacific Ocean. (Rev: BCCB 3/93; BL 5/1/93) [917.1]

4761 Manson, Ainslie. *Just Like New* (1–4). Illus. by Karen Reczuch. 1996, Douglas & McIntyre $14.95 (0-88899-228-9). 32pp. During World War II, a Canadian girl sends her favorite doll to a deprived English youngster at Christmas. (Rev: BCCB 1/97; BL 11/15/96; SLJ 12/96)

4762 Markun, Patricia M. *The Little Painter of Sabana Granda* (K–2). Illus. by Robert Casilla. 1993, Macmillan $14.95 (0-02-762205-3). 32pp. A young Panamanian boy paints pictures on the walls of his family's home. (Rev: BL 3/1/93; SLJ 7/93)

4763 Martin, C. L. G. *The Blueberry Train* (PS–2). Illus. by Angela T. Thomas. 1995, Atheneum $15.00 (0-689-80304-4). This story set in Minnesota at the turn of the century tells about a boy who longs to make money so that he can buy his first long pants. (Rev: HB 11–12/95; SLJ 12/95)

4764 Martin, Nora. *The Stone Dancers* (K–3). Illus. by Jill Kastner. 1995, Simon & Schuster $15.00 (0-689-80312-5). 32pp. A French grandfather tells his granddaughter how, many years ago, a king created a community for unwanted people. (Rev: BL 1/1–15/96; SLJ 12/95)

4765 Marton, Jirina. *You Can Go Home Again* (K–3). Illus. by author. 1994, Annick LB $15.95 (1-55037-991-7); paper $5.95 (1-55037-990-9). Annie and her mother visit Prague, the city that had been the home of their family before World War II. (Rev: SLJ 11/94)

4766 Medearis, Angela Shelf. *Rum-a-Tum-Tum* (PS–3). Illus. by James E. Ransome. 1997, Holiday LB $16.95 (0-8234-1143-5). 32pp. All the color, excitement, and sound of a market in the French Quarter of New Orleans at the turn of the century are captured in this picture book. (Rev: BCCB 7–8/97; BL 5/1/97; SLJ 7/97)

4767 Melmed, Laura K. *Little Oh* (K–4). Illus. by Jim LaMarche. 1997, Lothrop LB $15.93 (0-688-14209-5). 32pp. In this story set in Japan, a potter makes an origami girl come to life. (Rev: BL 9/1/97; HB 9–10/97; HBG 3/98; SLJ 11/97*)

4768 Millen, C. M. *A Symphony for the Sheep* (K–3). Illus. by Mary Azarian. 1996, Houghton $14.95 (0-395-76503-X). 32pp. The old-fashioned way of making woolen clothes is shown in this rhyme set in the Irish countryside. (Rev: BCCB 12/96; BL 8/96; SLJ 1/97)

4769 Miller, William. *The Bus Ride* (PS–1). Illus. by John Ward. 1998, Lee & Low $15.95 (1-880000-60-1). 32pp. Set in the segregated South during the 1950s, this picture book tells of the consequences faced by a young girl when she dares to sit in the front of a bus. (Rev: BL 8/98; HBG 3/99; SLJ 10/98)

4770 Miller, William. *The Piano* (K–3). Illus. by Susan Keeter. 2000, Lee & Low $15.95 (1-880000-98-9). 32pp. In the segregated South in the early 1900s, music-loving Tia is taught to play the piano by the elderly woman for whom she cleans house. (Rev: BCCB 10/00; BL 7/00; HBG 10/00; SLJ 7/00)

4771 Miller, William. *Richard Wright and the Library Card* (K–4). Illus. by Gregory Christie. 1997, Lee & Low $15.95 (1-880000-57-1). 32pp. In this story based on fact, African American Richard Wright, growing up in the segregated South, borrows books from the all-white library by pretending he is taking them to his white boss. (Rev: BCCB 3/98; BL 12/1/97; HBG 3/98; SLJ 2/98)

4772 Mollel, Tololwa M. *Big Boy* (PS–3). Illus. by E. B. Lewis. 1995, Clarion $14.95 (0-395-67403-4). 28pp. In Tanzania, a boy named Oli dreams of what it would be like to be a giant. (Rev: BCCB 3/95; BL 3/1/95; HB 7–8/95; SLJ 6/95)

4773 Mollel, Tololwa M. *My Rows and Piles of Coins* (PS–3). Illus. by E. B. Lewis. 1999, Clarion $15.00 (0-395-75186-1). 32pp. Saruni, a Tanzanian boy, scrimps and saves to buy a bicycle, so he can help his mother with her chores. (Rev: BCCB 10/99; BL 8/99; HBG 3/00; SLJ 8/99)

4774 Montes, Marisa. *Juan Bobo Goes to Work* (PS–3). Illus. by Joe Cepeda. 2000, HarperCollins LB $15.89 (0-688-16234-7). 32pp. A charming story — set in Puerto Rico and using many Spanish words and phrases — about Juan Bobo who makes a rich girl laugh and is rewarded with a ham every Sunday. (Rev: BL 2/1/01; HBG 3/01; SLJ 10/00)

4775 Myers, Tim. *Basho and the Fox* (K–3). Illus. by Oki S. Han. 2000, Marshall Cavendish $15.95 (0-7614-5068-8). 32pp. Basho, Japan's famous haiku poet, meets a fox who promises not to eat the poet's cherries if he can produce a poem that the fox thinks is worthy. (Rev: BL 9/15/00; HB 9–10/00; HBG 3/01; SLJ 10/00)

4776 Namioka, Lensey. *The Laziest Boy in the World* (K–3). Illus. by Yongsheng Xuan. 1998, Holiday $16.95 (0-8234-1330-6). 32pp. A humorous story about a Chinese boy who is so lazy he washes alternate sides of his face each day, and the thief who makes him change his ways. (Rev: BL 11/1/98; HBG 3/99; SLJ 10/98)

4777 Namioka, Lensey. *The Loyal Cat* (K–3). Illus. by Aki Sogabe. 1995, Harcourt $15.00 (0-15-200092-5). 40pp. A wise cat tries to publicize the worth of her pious master, a Japanese priest. (Rev: BCCB 11/95; BL 9/15/95; SLJ 10/95)

4778 Nerlove, Miriam. *Flowers on the Wall* (1–4). Illus. 1996, Simon & Schuster paper $16.00 (0-689-50614-7). 32pp. A Polish Jewish girl suffers persecution during World War II and ends up being deported to the Treblinka concentration camp. (Rev: BCCB 3/96; BL 4/15/96; HB 5–6/96; SLJ 4/96)

4779 Nivola, Claire A. *Elisabeth* (K–4). Illus. 1997, Farrar $16.00 (0-374-32085-3). 32pp. Ruth's Jewish family flees pre-war Germany, leaving everything, including her doll, Elisabeth, behind. (Rev: BCCB 3/97; BL 2/1/97; HB 5–6/97; SLJ 4/97)

4780 Nomura, Takaaki. *Grandpa's Town* (PS–3). Trans. by Amanda Mayer Stinchecum. Illus. 1991, Kane/Miller $13.95 (0-916291-36-7). 32pp. A story of rural Japan in which a family is afraid that their grandfather is very lonely after his wife's death. (Rev: BCCB 12/91*; HB 1–2/92; SLJ 1/92)

4781 Nye, Naomi S. *Sitti's Secrets* (PS–3). Illus. by Nancy Carpenter. 1994, Four Winds paper $16.00 (0-02-768460-1). 32pp. A small American girl misses her sitti — Arabic for *grandmother* — who lives at home in her Palestinian village. (Rev: BCCB 3/94; BL 3/15/94; HB 5–6/94; SLJ 6/94*)

4782 Oberman, Sheldon. *The Always Prayer Shawl* (1–4). Illus. by Ted Lewin. 1994, Boyds Mills $15.95 (1-878093-22-3). 32pp. Adam takes his grandfather's prayer shawl when he emigrates from Russia to the United States, where he wears it into manhood. (Rev: BL 12/15/93*; SLJ 3/94)

4783 Olaleye, Isaac. *Bitter Bananas* (PS–3). Illus. by Ed Young. 1994, Boyds Mills $14.95 (1-56397-039-2). 32pp. Yusuf thinks of an ingenious scheme to deter the baboons from eating his palm sap in this story set in Nigeria. (Rev: BCCB 10/94; BL 9/15/94; SLJ 8/94*)

4784 Olaleye, Isaac. *Lake of the Big Snake: An African Rain Forest Adventure* (K–3). Illus. by Claudia Shepard. 1998, Boyds Mills $15.95 (1-56397-096-1). In this story set in an African rain forest, two boys disobey their mothers, wander away from home, and encounter a giant snake. (Rev: BL 10/15/98; HBG 3/99; SLJ 11/98)

4785 Onyefulu, Ifeoma. *Chidi Only Likes Blue: An African Book of Colors* (PS–3). Illus. 1997, Dutton $14.99 (0-525-65243-4). 30pp. The significance of various colors in the everyday life of a Nigerian village is shown in text and photos. (Rev: BL 9/15/97; HB 7–8/97; HBG 3/98; SLJ 8/97)

4786 Onyefulu, Ifeoma. *Grandfather's Work: A Traditional Healer in Nigeria* (K–2). Illus. 1998, Millbrook LB $19.90 (0-7613-0412-6). 32pp. The reader meets each member of a young Nigerian boy's family and learns of the work they do, with particular emphasis on his grandfather who is a medicine man. (Rev: BL 1/1–15/99; HB 1–2/99; HBG 3/99; SLJ 1/99)

4787 Oppenheim, Shulamith Levey. *Yanni Rubbish* (K–3). Illus. by Doug Chayka. 1999, Boyds Mills $15.95 (1-56397-668-4). 28pp. Yanni, a young Greek trash collector, is embarrassed when his friends make fun of him and his dusty wagon, until he and his mother paint and decorate his cart so it becomes the pride of the town. (Rev: BL 3/1/99; HBG 10/99; SLJ 8/99)

4788 Orr, Katherine. *My Grandpa and the Sea* (K–3). Illus. 1990, Carolrhoda LB $19.95 (0-87614-409-1). 32pp. When Grandpa loses his fishing business to modern-day fishermen, he finds a new way of earning a living. (Rev: BCCB 11/90; BL 10/1/90)

4789 Otto, Carolyn. *Pioneer Church* (1–3). Illus. 1999, Holt $16.95 (0-8050-2554-5). 32pp. Based on fact, this is a history of the Old Zion Church in central Pennsylvania, from colonial days to the present. (Rev: BCCB 12/99; BL 10/1/99; HBG 3/00; SLJ 12/99)

4790 Pace, Lorenzo. *Jalani and the Lock* (PS–K). Illus. 2001, Rosen $15.95 (0-8239-9700-6). 32pp. A young African boy named Jalani, who spends years as a slave, passes the lock from his chains on to his grandchildren. (Rev: BL 2/15/01)

4791 Pacilio, V. J. *Ling Cho and His Three Friends* (1–3). Illus. by Scott Cook. 2000, Farrar $16.00 (0-374-34545-7). 32pp. A clever picture book about a prosperous Chinese farmer who wants to share his wealth with his neighbors without injuring their pride. (Rev: BL 3/1/00; HBG 10/00; SLJ 5/00)

4792 Parillo, Tony. *Michelangelo's Surprise* (K–3). Illus. 1998, Farrar $16.00 (0-374-34961-4). 32pp. After a rare snowstorm in Florence, Piero de' Medici sends for Michelangelo to make a snow sculpture, and the reader is taken on a wonderful tour of Renaissance Florence. (Rev: BL 9/15/98; HBG 3/99; SLJ 3/99)

4793 Park, Frances, and Ginger Park. *The Royal Bee* (K–3). Illus. by Christopher Zhong-Yuan Zhang. 2000, Boyds Mills $15.95 (1-56397-614-5). A simple tale about a poor Korean boy growing up in the the late 19th century and his efforts to get an education so he can lift himself and his mother out of poverty. (Rev: HBG 10/00; SLJ 4/00)

4794 Partridge, Elizabeth. *Oranges on Golden Mountain* (K–3). Illus. by Aki Sogabe. 2001, Dutton $16.99 (0-525-46453-0). 40pp. Jo Lee is sent to live with an uncle who is a fisherman on the California coast and there the little boy often dreams of China and his mother. (Rev: BCCB 2/01; BL 1/1–15/01; SLJ 3/01)

4795 Pilegard, Virginia Walton. *The Warlord's Puzzle* (K–3). Illus. by Nicolas Debon. 2000, Pelican $14.95 (1-56554-495-1). 32pp. A handsome tile given to a Chinese warlord is broken into various geometric shapes and only a simple peasant can solve the puzzle and put it together again. (Rev: BL 4/1/00; HBG 10/00; SLJ 6/00)

4796 Polacco, Patricia. *Babushka Baba Yaga* (PS–3). Illus. 1993, Putnam $15.95 (0-399-22531-5). 32pp. In this reversal of the traditional Russian folklore, the witch Baba Yaga is really a kindly grandmother named Babushka. (Rev: BL 8/93)

4797 Polacco, Patricia. *The Butterfly* (K–4). Illus. 2000, Putnam $16.99 (0-399-23170-6). 32pp. Based on a true story, this picture book tells of a little girl growing up in France during World War II who becomes aware that her family is hiding a Jewish family in the cellar. (Rev: BCCB 6/00; BL 4/1/00; HBG 10/00; SLJ 5/00)

4798 Pomeranc, Marion Hess. *The Hand-Me-Down Horse* (1–3). Illus. by Joanna Yardley. 1996, Albert Whitman LB $15.95 (0-8075-3141-3). Before a Jewish refugee boy can go to the United States after World War II, he makes the trip many times in his imagination on a rocking horse. (Rev: SLJ 1/97)

4799 Porte, Barbara Ann. *Ma Jiang and the Orange Ants* (K–3). Illus. by Annie Cannon. 2000, Orchard LB $17.99 (0-531-33241-1). 32pp. Ma Jiang devis-

es an unusual way to catch carnivorous "orange" ants to sell to fruit growers for pest control. (Rev: BL 10/15/00; HBG 3/01; SLJ 12/00)

4800 Pryor, Bonnie. *The House on Maple Street* (PS–1). Illus. by Beth Peck. 1987, Morrow paper $5.95 (0-688-12031-8). 32pp. Chris and Jenny find a small china cup and begin a kind of history exploration from the house on Maple Street. (Rev: BL 4/1/87; SLJ 5/87)

4801 Rabin, Staton. *Casey Over There* (K–3). Illus. by Greg Shed. 1994, Harcourt $14.95 (0-15-253186-6). 32pp. In this picture book, Aubrey's brother is fighting in the trenches, while he is growing up in Brooklyn during World War I. (Rev: BL 3/15/94; SLJ 5/94)

4802 Rael, Elsa O. *What Zeesie Saw on Delancey Street* (K–3). Illus. by Marjorie Priceman. 1996, Simon & Schuster $16.00 (0-689-80549-7). 28pp. Young Zeesie realizes the meaning of community while growing up in a Jewish American family on the Lower East Side of Manhattan in the early 1900s. (Rev: BCCB 12/96; BL 9/1/96; HB 11–12/96)

4803 Rand, Gloria. *Baby in a Basket* (PS–3). Illus. by Ted Rand. 1997, Dutton $15.99 (0-525-65233-7). 32pp. Based on an event that occurred in Alaska in 1917, this picture book tells of the amazing rescue of a baby believed to be lost. (Rev: BL 11/15/97; HBG 3/98; SLJ 11/97)

4804 Ransom, Candice. *The Promise Quilt* (K–3). Illus. by Ellen Beier. 1999, Walker LB $16.85 (0-8027-8695-2). 32pp. In this picture book set in the South during the Civil War, Addie loses her father when he joins General Lee and his fight for "the cause." (Rev: BL 11/1/99; HBG 3/00; SLJ 11/99)

4805 Rappaport, Doreen, and Lyndall Callan. *Dirt on Their Skirts: The Story of the Young Women Who Won the World Championship* (PS–3). Illus. by E. B. Lewis. 2000, Dial $16.99 (0-8037-2042-4). 40pp. A fictionalized account of the 1946 championship game of the All-American Girls Professional Baseball League. (Rev: BCCB 2/00; BL 1/1–15/00; HBG 10/00; SLJ 3/00)

4806 Ray, Mary L. *Basket Moon* (K–3). Illus. by Barbara Cooney. 1999, Little, Brown $15.95 (0-316-73521-3). 32pp. A 19th-century boy is embarrassed when townspeople call him and his father, a basket weaver, "hillbillies," but gradually he is able to reaffirm the love he feels for his dad. (Rev: BCCB 9/99; BL 6/1–15/99; HB 11–12/99; HBG 3/00; SLJ 9/99)

4807 Ray, Mary L. *Shaker Boy* (K–3). Illus. by Jeanette Winter. 1994, Harcourt $15.95 (0-15-276921-8). 48pp. The life story of a man who spent his life with the Shakers after being brought to them as a child after the Civil War. (Rev: BCCB 11/94; BL 11/15/94; SLJ 11/94)

4808 Reddix, Valerie. *Dragon Kite of the Autumn Moon* (K–3). Illus. by Jean Tseng. 1992, Lothrop LB $13.93 (0-688-11031-2). 32pp. When Grandfather becomes sick, Tad-Tin must fly his kite alone in this tale set in Formosa. (Rev: BL 5/15/92; SLJ 8/92)

4809 Reiser, Lynn. *Tortillas and Lullabies: Tortillas y cancioncitas* (PS–3). Illus. by Corazones Valientes. 1998, Greenwillow $16.00 (0-688-14628-7). 40pp. Three generations of Latin American women are depicted in this bilingual story of how love and gifts have been exchanged in a family through the years. (Rev: BL 4/1/98; HB 5–6/98; SLJ 4/98)

4810 Reynolds, Marilyn. *The Prairie Fire* (1–3). Illus. by Don Kilby. 1999, Orca $14.95 (1-55143-137-8). 32pp. While his parents are out tending to a fire break, young Percy douses sparks from a brush fire and saves his home from destruction in this story set in pioneer America. (Rev: BCCB 11/99; BL 1/1–15/00; HBG 3/00; SLJ 1/00)

4811 Richardson, Jean. *The Courage Seed* (2–3). Illus. by Pat Finney. 1993, Eakin $14.95 (0-89015-902-5). 71pp. When her parents are killed, a young Navajo girl is fearful that she will lose her tribal ways when she goes to live with an aunt in Houston. (Rev: SLJ 2/94)

4812 Roop, Peter, and Connie Roop. *Buttons for General Washington* (2–3). Illus. by Peter E. Hanson. 1986, Carolrhoda LB $21.27 (0-87614-294-3); paper $5.95 (0-87614-476-8). 48pp. Based on incidents from the life of John Darragh, this is the story of a 14-year-old boy who carries secret messages to George Washington hidden in his coat buttons during the Revolution. (Rev: BCCB 12/86; BL 12/1/86)

4813 Rosenblum, Richard. *Brooklyn Dodger Days* (1–4). Illus. 1991, Macmillan $13.95 (0-689-31512-0). 32pp. Re-creating a 1946 game between the Brooklyn Dodgers and the New York Giants. (Rev: BCCB 2/91; BL 1/1/91; SLJ 7/91) [796.357]

4814 Rumford, James. *The Cloudmakers* (1–4). Illus. 1996, Houghton $15.95 (0-395-76505-6). 32pp. A Chinese grandfather and his grandson are commanded by a sultan to produce rain clouds. (Rev: BL 9/15/96; SLJ 9/96)

4815 Rush, Ken. *The Seltzer Man* (PS–3). Illus. 1993, Macmillan LB $14.95 (0-02-777917-3). 32pp. Before he retires from his route in New York City, Eli, the friendly seltzer man, is accompanied on his route by two young girls. (Rev: BL 6/1–15/93; SLJ 7/93)

4816 Ryan, Pam M. *Amelia and Eleanor Go for a Ride: Based on a True Story* (2–4). Illus. by Brian Selznick. 1999, Scholastic $16.95 (0-590-96075-X). 40pp. An interesting, if exaggerated, variation on the story of Amelia Earhart and Eleanor Roosevelt's shared plane ride. (Rev: BL 10/15/99; HBG 3/00; SLJ 9/99)

4817 Ryder, Joanne. *Where Butterflies Grow* (PS–3). Illus. by Lynne Cherry. 1989, Dutton $15.99 (0-525-67284-2). 32pp. Detailed illustrations and poetic text explain the life cycle of a black swallowtail butterfly. (Rev: BL 11/1/89*; SLJ 9/89*) [595]

4818 Saltzman, David. *The Jester Has Lost His Jingle* (1–3). Illus. 1995, Jester $20.00 (0-9644563-0-3). 64pp. A jester who is out of work because he isn't funny sets out to discover laughter in the world. (Rev: BL 10/15/95; SLJ 10/95)

4819 Sanders, Scott R. *Aurora Means Dawn* (K–3). Illus. by Jill Kastner. 1989, Macmillan $16.00 (0-

02-778270-0). 32pp. A pioneer family's journey westward is temporarily halted when a fallen tree blocks their path. (Rev: BCCB 12/89; BL 9/15/89*; HB 9–10/89; SLJ 11/89)

4820 Sanders, Scott R. *The Floating House* (K–3). Illus. by Helen Cogancherry. 1995, Simon & Schuster paper $17.00 (0-02-778137-2). 32pp. The story of the McClure family, their trip by flatboat on the Ohio River in 1815, and their relocation to a farm in Indiana. (Rev: BL 6/1–15/95; SLJ 6/95)

4821 Sanders, Scott R. *Here Comes the Mystery Man* (K–3). Illus. by Helen Cogancherry. 1993, Bradbury $15.95 (0-02-778145-3). 32pp. A pioneer family is delighted when a traveling peddler visits their log cabin. (Rev: BL 11/15/93; SLJ 10/93)

4822 Sanders, Scott R. *A Place Called Freedom* (K–3). Illus. by Thomas B. Allen. 1997, Simon & Schuster $16.00 (0-689-80470-9). 32pp. Beginning with a single family of freed slaves who travel from the South to Indiana, others arrive and found a town called Freedom. (Rev: BCCB 7–8/97; BL 6/1–15/97; SLJ 8/97)

4823 Sandin, Joan. *The Long Way to a New Land* (1–3). Illus. by author. 1981, HarperCollins paper $3.95 (0-06-444100-8). 64pp. An easy-to-read account of a Swedish family's journey to New York in the late 1860s.

4824 Sandoval, Dolores. *Be Patient, Abdul* (1–4). Illus. 1996, Simon & Schuster paper $15.00 (0-689-50607-4). 30pp. In Sierra Leone, 7-year-old Abdul saves his money so that he can go to school. (Rev: BL 9/15/96; SLJ 8/96)

4825 Say, Allen. *The Bicycle Man* (K–3). Illus. by author. 1982, Houghton $11.95 (0-685-05704-6); paper $5.95 (0-395-50652-2). 48pp. Two American soldiers in Japan put on a show for a school.

4826 Schick, Eleanor. *Navajo Wedding Day: A Dine Marriage Ceremony* (1–3). Illus. 1999, Marshall Cavendish $15.95 (0-7614-5031-9). 40pp. A realistic picture book that describes a marriage ceremony in Navajo country. (Rev: BL 4/15/99; HBG 10/99; SLJ 4/99)

4827 Schrier, Jeffrey. *On the Wings of Eagles: An Ethiopian Boy's Story* (1–4). Illus. 1998, Millbrook LB $20.90 (0-7613-0004-X). 32pp. Using photographs and collages, this book introduces Isaiah, a young Ethiopian Jew, who uses his flute to tell the story of his people — from Solomon and Sheba to the hardships of modern times. (Rev: BCCB 5/98; BL 6/1–15/98; HBG 10/98; SLJ 12/98)

4828 Scott, Ann H. *On Mother's Lap* (PS–K). Illus. by Glo Coalson. 1992, Houghton $15.00 (0-395-58920-7); paper $6.95 (0-395-62976-4). 32pp. A warm, tender story of an Eskimo family and of a young boy's realization that there is enough room on mother's lap for both him and his sister.

4829 Seabrooke, Brenda. *The Boy Who Saved the Town* (2–4). Illus. by Howard M. Burns. 1990, Tidewater $7.95 (0-87033-405-0). 28pp. This legend tells how the town of St. Michaels escaped bombardment by the British in the War of 1812. (Rev: BL 9/1/90)

4830 Shank, Ned. *The Sanyasin's First Day* (K–3). Illus. by Catherine Stock. 1999, Marshall Cavendish $15.95 (0-7614-5055-6). 32pp. The lives of several people intersect in this story set in modern India about a holy man who begs on the streets and is given alms by a child. (Rev: BL 10/1/99; HBG 3/00; SLJ 11/99)

4831 Simon, Norma. *All Kinds of Children* (PS–K). Illus. by Diane Paterson. 1999, Albert Whitman $15.95 (0-8075-0281-2). 32pp. This book emphasizes how children around the world have different lifestyles and homes but similar needs. (Rev: BL 3/15/99; HBG 10/99; SLJ 6/99) [305.23]

4832 Sisulu, Elinor B. *The Day Gogo Went to Vote* (PS–4). Illus. by Sharon Wilson. 1996, Little, Brown $15.95 (0-316-70267-6). 32pp. Thembi tells how her great-grandmother voted for the first time in Soweto, South Africa, in 1994. (Rev: BCCB 3/96; BL 2/15/96; SLJ 5/96*)

4833 Smalls, Irene. *Irene Jennie and the Christmas Masquerade: The Johnkankus* (K–4). Illus. by Melodye Rosales. 1996, Little, Brown $15.95 (0-316-79878-9). 32pp. In the times of slavery, young Irene Jennie hopes her parents, on loan to another plantation, will return for Christmas. (Rev: BCCB 11/96; BL 9/15/96)

4834 Smalls, Irene. *A Strawbeater's Thanksgiving* (2–5). Illus. by Melodye Rosales. 1998, Little, Brown $15.95 (0-316-79866-5). 32pp. This picture book, based on slave narratives, depicts a corn-husking party celebrating the harvest and the efforts of 7-year-old Jess to become the straw beater and play with the band. (Rev: BL 9/1/98; HBG 3/99; SLJ 10/98)

4835 Sorel, Edward, and Cheryl Carlesimo. *The Saturday Kid* (K–3). Illus. 2000, Simon & Schuster $18.00 (0-689-82399-1). 32pp. Set in New York City in a different era, this picture book tells how Leo gets the best of the bully Morty when he plays the violin and meets the mayor, two events that Morty and his parents are surprised to see in a newsreel at the local movie theater. (Rev: BL 12/15/00; HBG 3/01; SLJ 9/00)

4836 Soto, Gary. *The Old Man and His Door* (PS–2). Illus. by Joe Cepeda. 1996, Putnam $15.99 (0-399-22700-8). 32pp. In a Mexican setting, this fable tells of an old fool's adventures on the way to a barbeque. (Rev: BCCB 9/96; BL 4/1/96; HB 7–8/96; SLJ 6/96)

4837 Stanley, Sanna. *Monkey Sunday: A Story from a Congolese Village* (1–3). Illus. by author. 1998, Farrar $16.00 (0-374-35018-3). In this picture book set in the Congo, a little girl finds it difficult to sit still during her father's preaching at a Thanksgiving service; then a playful monkey threatens to disrupt everything. (Rev: BCCB 4/98; HBG 10/98; SLJ 4/98)

4838 Steiner, Barbara. *Whale Brother* (K–3). Illus. by Gretchen Will Mayo. 1988, Walker LB $13.85 (0-8027-6805-9). The touching story of an Inuit boy who wants to be an artist and his protective love for animals. (Rev: BCCB 1/89)

4839 Stevens, Jan R. *Carlos and the Cornfield/Carlos y la Milpa de Maiz* (K–3). Illus. by Jeanne Arnold. 1995, Northland LB $14.95 (0-87358-596-8). 32pp. Carlos learns some truths about gardening when he plants corn to earn enough money to buy a pocketknife. (Rev: BL 9/1/95; SLJ 9/95)

4840 Stevenson, James. *Don't You Know There's a War On?* (K–3). Illus. 1992, Greenwillow $15.93 (0-688-11384-2). 32pp. Remembrances of what it was like to be an American child growing up in a small town during World War II. (Rev: BCCB 11/92*; BL 11/1/92*; HB 1–2/93*; SLJ 10/92) [940.53]

4841 Stewart, Sarah. *The Gardener* (K–3). Illus. by David Small. 1997, Farrar $16.00 (0-374-32517-0). 40pp. During the Depression, a little girl is sent off to live with a cold, somber uncle, but gradually she wins him over. (Rev: BL 6/1–15/97; HB 11–12/97; HBG 3/98; SLJ 8/97*)

4842 Stock, Catherine. *Gugu's House* (1–3). Illus. 2001, Clarion $14.00 (0-618-00389-4). 32pp. Set in Zimbabwe, this is the story of a loving grandmother whose talents include creating paintings and sculptures, as well as telling stories to granddaughter Kukamba. (Rev: BL 2/15/01*)

4843 Stroud, Bettye. *The Leaving* (K–3). Illus. by Cedric Lucas. 2001, Marshall Cavendish $15.95 (0-7614-5067-X). 32pp. Five years after emancipation, a young girl helps her parents escape from bondage. (Rev: BL 2/15/01)

4844 Stuve-Bodeen, Stephanie. *Elizabeti's Doll* (PS–1). Illus. by Christy Hale. 1998, Lee & Low $15.95 (1-880000-70-9). 32pp. In Tanzania, Elizabeti lacks a doll to copy her mother's activities with her new baby, so the little girl uses a rock instead. (Rev: BL 10/1/98; HB 11–12/98; HBG 3/99; SLJ 9/98)

4845 Stuve-Bodeen, Stephanie. *Mama Elizabeti* (1–3). Illus. by Christy Hale. 2000, Lee & Low $15.95 (1-58430-002-7). 32pp. Set in contemporary Tanzania, this story involves Elizabeti and her problems caring for her toddler brother. (Rev: BCCB 9/00; BL 8/00; HB 7–8/00; HBG 10/00; SLJ 7/00)

4846 Sweeney, Joan. *Bijou, Bonbon and Beau: The Kittens Who Danced for Degas* (K–3). Illus. by Leslie Wu. 1998, Chronicle $12.95 (0-8118-1975-2). Three kittens are saved by artist Edgar Degas when the stage manager threatens to throw them out of the theater that they have called home. (Rev: BCCB 7–8/98; BL 7/98; HBG 10/98; SLJ 6/98)

4847 Sweeney, Joan. *Suzette and the Puppy: A Story About Mary Cassatt* (PS–3). Illus. by Jennifer Heyd Wharton. 2000, Barron's $12.95 (0-7641-5294-7). A fictionalized story of a little French girl and how Mary Cassatt came to paint her as the "Little Girl in a Blue Armchair." (Rev: SLJ 1/01)

4848 Tarbescu, Edith. *Annushka's Voyage* (PS–3). Illus. by Lydia Dabcovich. 1998, Clarion $15.00 (0-395-64366-X). 32pp. A picture book that depicts the experiences of two young Jewish girls, Anya and her young sister, Tanya, when they leave their village in Russia to join their father in America. (Rev: BL 9/1/98; HBG 3/99; SLJ 12/98)

4849 Tchana, Katrin, and Louise T. Pami. *Oh, No, Toto!* (K–3). Illus. by Colin Bootman. 1997, Scholastic $15.95 (0-590-46585-6). 32pp. Toto, a young African boy, tastes exotic Cameroon food when his mother takes him to the market. (Rev: BCCB 3/97; BL 3/1/97; SLJ 3/97)

4850 Thaxter, Celia. *Celia's Island Journal* (PS–3). Illus. by Loretta Krupinski. 1992, Little, Brown $15.95 (0-316-83921-3). 32pp. The author's life on White Island off the New England coast. (Rev: BL 12/1/92; HB 11–12/92; SLJ 10/92) [974.1]

4851 Thomassie, Tynia. *Cajun: Through and Through* (2–4). Illus. by Andrew Glass. 2000, Little, Brown $14.95 (0-316-84189-7). 32pp. TiBoy and Baptiste are Cajun brothers who resent the visit of Cousin Remington from the big city, until they discover that he has a little Cajun in him and can share their proud heritage. (Rev: BL 3/15/00; HBG 10/00; SLJ 5/00)

4852 Torres, Leyla. *Saturday Sancocho* (K–3). Illus. 1995, Farrar $16.00 (0-374-36418-4). 32pp. A South American girl and her grandmother visit a market with their eggs to barter for the ingredients of a chicken stew. (Rev: BL 4/15/95; SLJ 5/95)

4853 Trottier, Maxine. *Flags* (1–4). Illus. by Paul Morin. 1999, Stoddart $16.95 (0-7737-3136-9). When their Japanese American neighbor, Mr. Hiroshi, is sent to an internment camp after Pearl Harbor, Mary saves some stones and some bulbs from his garden to start one of her own. (Rev: SLJ 3/00)

4854 Trottier, Maxine. *Little Dog Moon* (K–5). Illus. by Laura Fernandez and Rick Jacobson. 2000, Stoddart $14.95 (0-7737-3220-9). Moon, a young Tibetan terrier, helps guide two Tibetan children across the border to freedom in Nepal. (Rev: SLJ 3/01)

4855 Trottier, Maxine. *Prairie Willow* (K–3). Illus. by Laura Fernandez and Rick Jacobson. 1998, Stoddart $15.95 (0-7737-3067-2). 24pp. After the harvest, Emily, who lives with her family in a sod house on the Canadian prairie, is allowed to choose a gift for herself. She buys a weeping willow tree, which she and her family nurture for many years. (Rev: BL 9/15/98; SLJ 2/99)

4856 Trottier, Maxine. *The Walking Stick* (K–3). Illus. by Annouchka Gravel Galouchko. 1999, Stoddart $15.95 (0-7737-3101-6). A story about a walking stick fashioned by a Buddhist monk in Vietnam for a young boy who carries it throughout his life, even when he must leave his native land and come to America. (Rev: SLJ 9/99)

4857 Turner, Ann. *Dakota Dugout* (PS–1). Illus. by Ronald Himler. 1985, Macmillan $15.00 (0-02-789700-1); paper $4.99 (0-689-71296-0). 32pp. Rich images prevail as a lady tells of life on the prairie long ago. (Rev: BCCB 10/85; BL 12/1/85; HB 1–2/86)

4858 Turner, Ann. *Katie's Trunk* (1–5). Illus. by Ronald Himler. 1992, Macmillan LB $15.00 (0-02-789512-2). When raiders attack Katie's house during the American Revolution, she tries to save her family's possessions. (Rev: BCCB 11–12/92; SLJ 11/92)

4859 Turner, Ann. *Red Flower Goes West* (K–4). Illus. by Dennis Nolan. 1999, Hyperion LB $15.49 (0-7868-2253-8). 32pp. A red geranium becomes a symbol of hope in this story of the hardships faced by a family making a covered-wagon trek to the California gold fields. (Rev: BCCB 7–8/99; BL 5/1/99; HB 9–10/99; HBG 10/99; SLJ 6/99)

4860 Van Leeuwen, Jean. *Nothing Here But Trees* (PS–3). Illus. by Phil Boatwright. 1998, Dial LB $15.89 (0-8037-2180-3). 32pp. This story, set in the Ohio forests of the 19th century and told from the perspective of a young boy, depicts pioneer family life, as two brothers help Pa clear the woods to make way for a house, a farm, and a fence. The arrival of another family helps lessen their loneliness and isolation. (Rev: BL 9/1/98; HBG 3/99; SLJ 11/98)

4861 Van Nutt, Julia. *Pumpkins from the Sky? A Cobtown Story: From the Diaries of Lucky Hart* (K–3). Illus. by Robert Van Nutt. 1999, Doubleday $15.95 (0-385-32568-1). When a fallen tree makes her pumpkin patch inaccessible, Aunt Heddy wonders how she will bake pies for the annual pie-eating contest at the 1845 Cobtown Harvest Festival. (Rev: HBG 3/00; SLJ 10/99)

4862 Van West, Patricia E. *The Crab Man* (1–3). Illus. by Cedric Lucas. 1998, Turtle $15.95 (1-890515-08-6). 40pp. A young Jamaican boy must decide whether or not he should continue to sell hermit crabs after he discovers that they are being cruelly treated. (Rev: BL 10/1/98; HBG 3/99; SLJ 11/98)

4863 Von Ahnen, Katherine. *Charlie Young Bear* (2–3). Illus. by Paulette L. Lambert. Series: Council for Indian Education. 1994, Roberts Rinehart paper $4.95 (1-57098-001-2). 42pp. After the U.S. government agrees on a cash settlement with the Mesquakie Indians in 1955, Charlie Young Bear hopes his share will be a bike. (Rev: SLJ 4/95)

4864 Wallace, Ian. *Boy of the Deeps* (K–4). Illus. 1999, DK $16.95 (0-7894-2569-6). 32pp. At the dawn of the 20th century, young James joins his father and other miners for his first day of work in a coal mine on Nova Scotia's Cape Breton Island. (Rev: BCCB 4/99; BL 3/15/99; HBG 10/99; SLJ 7/99)

4865 Wallner, Alexandra. *Sergio and the Hurricane* (K–3). Illus. 2000, Holt $16.00 (0-8050-6203-3). 32pp. Sergio learns about the destructive power of a hurricane when it hits the Puerto Rican town in which he lives. (Rev: BCCB 10/00; BL 9/15/00; HBG 3/01; SLJ 11/00)

4866 Walton, Rick. *Dance, Pioneer, Dance!* (K–3). Illus. by Brad Teare. 1998, Deseret $14.95 (1-57345-243-2). 28pp. Brigham Young calls a square dance in which humans and animals take part. His whimsical verses recall the journey of the first Mormons to Utah in 1847. (Rev: BL 9/15/98; SLJ 8/98)

4867 Ward, Leila. *I Am Eyes Ni Macho* (PS–1). Illus. by Nonny Hogrogian. 1987, Scholastic paper $3.95 (0-590-40990-5). 32pp. A new day and all of nature's wonders are greeted by a Kenyan child. A reissue of the 1978 edition.

4868 Warner, Sunny. *The Magic Sewing Machine* (PS–3). Illus. 1997, Houghton $16.00 (0-395-82747-7). 32pp. Two orphaned children take their sewing machine to the orphanage in this story set in Dickensian London. (Rev: BL 9/15/97; HBG 3/98; SLJ 9/97)

4869 Waterton, Betty. *Pettranella* (K–3). Illus. by Ann Blades. 1991, Firefly paper $4.95 (0-88899-108-8). 32pp. An immigrant girl grows flowers from seeds she brought from Europe.

4870 Watkins, Sherrin. *Green Snake Ceremony* (PS–2). Illus. by Kim Doner. Series: The Greyfeather. 1996, Council Oak $17.95 (0-933031-89-0). Neither a Shawnee girl nor the green snake that lives under the porch want to participate in the traditional snake ceremony that involves the young girl putting the snake in her mouth. (Rev: SLJ 12/96)

4871 Watson, Mary. *The Butterfly Seeds* (K–4). Illus. 1995, Morrow LB $15.93 (0-688-14133-1). 32pp. Jake, a new immigrant to the US, plants the seeds his grandfather back home gave him in a windowbox in his tenement building. (Rev: BL 9/1/95; SLJ 11/95)

4872 Watson, Pete. *The Market Lady and the Mango Tree* (K–3). Illus. by Mary Watson. 1994, Morrow $14.00 (0-688-12970-6). 32pp. When Market Lady places nets around the mango tree so that children will have to buy the fruit rather than pick it from the ground, she realizes that this is an act of selfishness. (Rev: BL 2/15/94; SLJ 6/94)

4873 Webb, Denise. *The Same Sun Was in the Sky* (1–4). Illus. by Walter Porter. 1995, Northland LB $14.95 (0-87358-602-6). 32pp. A boy and his grandfather think about the prehistoric Indians of the Southwest and the amazing rock paintings that they produced. (Rev: BL 8/95)

4874 Weeks, Sarah. *Piece of Jungle* (PS–1). Illus. by Suzanne Duranceau. 1999, HarperCollins $15.95 (0-06-028409-9). 32pp. Through song lyrics (found on the accompanying cassette), young children are introduced to a rain forest and the plants and animals found there. (Rev: BL 8/99)

4875 Weitzman, Jacqueline Preiss. *You Can't Take a Balloon into the National Gallery* (PS–3). Illus. by Robin P. Glasser. 2000, Dial $16.99 (0-8037-2303-2). 40pp. A balloon gets loose in Washington, D.C., and takes the reader on a tour of the capital's sights. (Rev: BL 4/15/00; HB 5–6/00; HBG 10/00; SLJ 6/00)

4876 Wells, Rosemary. *The Language of Doves* (K–2). Illus. by Greg Shed. 1996, Dial $14.89 (0-8037-1472-6). 48pp. Grandfather tells of an incident during World War II in which a pigeon saved the lives of eight men. (Rev: BCCB 9/96; BL 8/96; SLJ 9/96*)

4877 Wilder, Laura Ingalls. *Going to Town* (PS–1). Illus. by Renee Graef. Series: My First Little House Books. 1995, HarperCollins LB $11.89 (0-06-023013-4). A picture book abridgment of a chapter from *Little House in the Big Woods* in which the

Wilders prepare for a trip into town. (Rev: SLJ 12/95)

4878 Williams, Karen L. *Painted Dreams* (PS–1). Illus. by Catherine Stock. 1998, Lothrop LB $15.93 (0-688-13902-7). 40pp. Set in the slums of Haiti, this picture book tells of little Ti Marie, who finds some discarded paints in an artist's trash and, with his help, cultivates her artistic talent. (Rev: BL 9/15/98; HBG 3/99; SLJ 10/98)

4879 Williams, Karen L. *Tap-Tap* (PS–1). Illus. by Catherine Stock. 1994, Clarion $14.95 (0-395-65617-6). 34pp. After a day selling flowers in a Haitian market, young Sasifi treats herself to a ride home in a jitney. (Rev: BCCB 3/94; BL 4/15/94; HB 7–8/94; SLJ 6/94)

4880 Williams, Karen L. *When Africa Was Home* (PS–2). Illus. by Floyd Cooper. 1991, Orchard LB $16.99 (0-531-08525-2). 32pp. A white boy is so at home in Africa with his black friends that he feels lost when he has to go to America. (Rev: BCCB 2/92; BL 1/15/91*; SLJ 4/91)

4881 Williams, Laura E. *Torch Fishing with the Sun* (K–3). Illus. by Fabricio Vandenbroeck. 1999, Boyds Mills $15.95 (1-56397-685-4). 32pp. Young Makoa's grandfather tells him that he uses the sun as a torch while he fishes, but the boy has doubts when others claim that the old man actually buys his catch from another fisherman. (Rev: BL 3/15/99; HBG 10/99; SLJ 6/99)

4882 Willow, Diane. *At Home in the Rain Forest* (PS–3). Illus. by Laura Jacques. 1991, Charlesbridge $15.95 (0-88106-485-8). 32pp. The flora and fauna of the Amazon rain forest are explored in text and color paintings. (Rev: BL 6/1/91) [574]

4883 Winnick, Karen B. *Mr. Lincoln's Whiskers* (1–3). Illus. 1996, Boyds Mills $15.95 (1-56397-485-1). 32pp. A young girl writes to Lincoln to suggest that he would gain votes if he grew whiskers. (Rev: BL 12/15/96; SLJ 1/97)

4884 Winnick, Karen B. *Sybil's Night Ride* (K–3). Illus. 2000, Boyds Mills $15.95 (1-56397-697-8). 32pp. This picture book re-creates the historic ride of 16-year-old Sybil Ludington who, during the American Revolution, raced on her horse to warn her father's troops that the British were burning Danbury, New York. (Rev: BL 3/1/00; HBG 10/00)

4885 Winslow, Barbara. *Dance on a Sealskin* (1–3). Illus. by Teri Sloat. 1995, Alaska Northwest $15.95 (0-88240-443-1). 32pp. Annie is thrilled at being able to dance as a coming-of-age ritual at the Inuit potlatch. (Rev: BL 8/95; SLJ 12/95)

4886 Winter, Jeanette. *Follow the Drinking Gourd* (K–3). Illus. by author. 1988, Knopf paper $5.99 (0-679-81997-5). 48pp. The story of Peg Leg Pete who helps slaves escape to the North. (Rev: BCCB 1/89; BL 12/15/88; SLJ 5/89)

4887 Winter, Jeanette. *My Baby* (K–2). Illus. 2001, Farrar $16.00 (0-374-35103-1). 32pp. Set in Mali, this is the story of a woman who makes a special mud-dyed cloth for the baby she is expecting. (Rev: BL 2/15/01)

4888 Wisniewski, David. *Rain Player* (K–3). Illus. 1991, Houghton $17.00 (0-395-55112-9). 32pp.

Young Pik challenges the rain god in this story based on Mayan folklore. (Rev: BCCB 11/91; BL 10/15/91*; HB 1–2/92; SLJ 10/91)

4889 Wittmann, Patricia. *Buffalo Thunder* (K–4). Illus. by Bert Dodson. 1997, Marshall Cavendish $15.95 (0-7614-5001-7). 32pp. A young boy and his family share many adventures when they travel west in their prairie schooner. (Rev: BL 9/15/97; HBG 3/98; SLJ 9/97)

4890 Wong, Janet S. *The Trip Back Home* (PS–2). Illus. by Bo Jia. 2000, Harcourt $16.00 (0-15-200784-9). 32pp. The food and fun involved when the author visited her grandparents in rural Korea when she was a child are recalled in this tender story of family love. (Rev: BL 11/15/00; HBG 3/01; SLJ 12/00)

4891 Woodruff, Elvira. *The Memory Coat* (K–4). Illus. by Michael Dooling. 1999, Scholastic $15.95 (0-590-67717-9). 32pp. This story of a Jewish family's migration from Russia to America focuses on Rachel and her orphaned cousin, Grisha. (Rev: BL 1/1–15/99; HBG 10/99; SLJ 3/99)

4892 Wright, Courtni C. *Jumping the Broom* (K–3). Illus. by Gershom Griffith. 1994, Holiday LB $15.95 (0-8234-1042-0). A picture book set in the days of slavery about the marriage celebration known as "jumping the broom." (Rev: BCCB 7–8/94; SLJ 4/94)

4893 Yacowitz, Caryn. *Pumpkin Fiesta* (PS–1). Illus. by Joe Cepeda. 1998, HarperCollins $14.95 (0-06-027658-4). 32pp. Foolish Fernando tries by fair and foul means to rob Old Juana of the glory of winning the fiesta's special prize for her extraordinary pumpkins, but justice triumphs. (Rev: BL 9/1/98; HB 11–12/98; HBG 3/99; SLJ 9/98)

4894 Yaroshevskaya, Kim. *Little Kim's Doll* (K–3). Illus. by Luc Melanson. 1999, Groundwood $14.95 (0-88899-353-6). Growing up in Communist Russia during the 1930s, young Kim longs for a doll but her parents want to give her a more practical gift like a toy rifle. (Rev: SLJ 8/99)

4895 Yin. *Coolies* (K–4). Illus. by Chris K. Soentpiet. 2001, Putnam $16.99 (0-399-23227-3). 40pp. The experiences of two Chinese brothers who migrate to America to work on the Transcontinental Railroad reveal the courage and integrity of these Chinese Americans and the racism they endured. (Rev: BCCB 2/01; BL 2/1/01; SLJ 3/01)

PERSONAL PROBLEMS

4896 Ada, Alma F. *The Gold Coin* (K–3). Trans. by Bernice Randall. Illus. by Neil Waldman. 1991, Macmillan LB $16.00 (0-689-31633-X). Juan, who has been a thief all his life, redeems himself in this gentle story translated from the Spanish. (Rev: BL 3/1/92; SLJ 4/91)

4897 Adams, Eric J., and Kathleen Adams. *On the Day His Daddy Left* (1–3). Illus. by Layne Johnson. 2000, Albert Whitman $14.95 (0-8075-6072-3). 32pp. When his father moves out in preparation for a divorce, a small boy wonders if it is his fault. (Rev: BL 11/15/00; HBG 3/01; SLJ 12/00)

4898 Allen, Debbie. *Dancing in the Wings* (K–3). Illus. by Kadir Nelson. 2000, Dial $16.99 (0-8037-2501-9). 32pp. Sassy is afraid that she is too tall and lanky to become a ballerina, but a Russian ballet master chooses her to dance in a festival. (Rev: BCCB 11/00; BL 11/15/00; HBG 3/01; SLJ 9/00)

4899 Altman, Linda Jacobs. *Amelia's Road* (PS–3). Illus. by Enrique O. Sanchez. 1993, Lee & Low $15.95 (1-880000-04-0). 32pp. Amelia, the daughter of migrant workers, cries every time her father takes out a map because it means her family will move again. (Rev: BL 9/15/93; SLJ 12/93)

4900 Atkins, Jeannine. *A Name on the Quilt: A Story of Remembrance* (1–4). Illus. by Tad Hills. 1999, Simon & Schuster $16.00 (0-689-81592-1). 32pp. Family and friends gather at Lauren's home to make a memorial quilt in honor of her beloved Uncle Ron who has died of AIDS. (Rev: BL 1/1–15/99; HBG 10/99; SLJ 3/99)

4901 Bahr, Mary. *If Nathan Were Here* (K–2). Illus. by Karen A. Jerome. 2000, Eerdmans $16.00 (0-8028-5187-8). 32pp. A boy imagines all the things he could do if Nathan were there but, as the reader learns, Nathan is dead and his friend misses him. (Rev: BL 4/15/00; HBG 10/00; SLJ 8/00)

4902 Bang, Molly. *When Sophie Gets Angry — Really, Really Angry* (PS–3). Illus. 1999, Scholastic $15.95 (0-590-18979-4). 40pp. This book describes in drawings and text what happens to Sophie when she becomes angry. (Rev: BCCB 4/99; BL 2/1/99; HBG 10/99; SLJ 1/99*)

4903 Barron, T. A. *Where Is Grandpa?* (PS–3). Illus. by Chris K. Soentpiet. 2000, Putnam $15.99 (0-399-23037-8). 32pp. A young boy believes his dead grandfather is enjoying all the beauties of nature that he loved. (Rev: BL 5/1/00; HBG 10/00; SLJ 2/00)

4904 Bat-Ami, Miriam. *Sea, Salt, and Air* (2–5). Illus. by Mary O. Young. 1993, Smithmark $4.98 (0-765-10095-9). 32pp. During a summer visit to her grandparents at the beach, a young girl ponders how she will develop in the future. (Rev: BL 5/15/93; SLJ 6/93)

4905 Battle-Lavert, Gwendolyn. *Off to School* (K–3). Illus. by Gershom Griffith. 1995, Holiday LB $15.95 (0-8234-1185-0). 32pp. A migrant worker's child, Wezielee, longs to go to school but must stay at the camp and cook for the laborers. (Rev: BL 10/15/95; SLJ 1/96)

4906 Baumgart, Klaus. *Don't Be Afraid, Tommy* (PS–1). Illus. by author. 1998, Little Tiger $14.95 (1-888444-32-0). Tommy learns to conquer his own fears when he is given a toy dog and told to teach him not to be afraid. (Rev: HBG 10/98; SLJ 7/98)

4907 Bernstein, Sharon C. *A Family That Fights* (PS–3). Illus. by Karen Ritz. 1991, Whitman LB $13.95 (0-8075-2248-1). 32pp. A quiet story that deals with three children who live in a family where the father hits their mother and threatens them when he is angry. (Rev: BL 11/15/91; SLJ 2/92)

4908 Best, Cari. *Getting Used to Harry* (PS–3). Illus. by Diane Palmisciano. 1996, Orchard LB $16.99 (0-531-08794-8). 32pp. Cynthia gradually adjusts to her mother's new husband, Harry the shoe man. (Rev: BCCB 10/96; BL 11/1/96; SLJ 10/96)

4909 Blegvad, Lenore. *A Sound of Leaves* (2–4). Illus. 1996, Simon & Schuster paper $15.00 (0-689-80038-X). 58pp. A 9-year-old is fearful of going to the beach for the first time but discovers that it is fun. (Rev: BCCB 5/96; BL 5/1/96; HB 9–10/96; SLJ 5/96)

4910 Blumenthal, Deborah. *The Chocolate-Covered-Cookie Tantrum* (PS–K). Illus. by Harvey Stevenson. 1996, Clarion $15.00 (0-395-68699-7). 32pp. When she can't get the cookie she wants, a little girl stages a temper tantrum. (Rev: SLJ 9/96)

4911 Bottner, Barbara. *Bootsie Barker Bites* (PS–3). Illus. by Peggy Rathmann. 1992, Putnam $15.95 (0-399-22125-5). 32pp. The young narrator stands just so much from bully Bootsie Barker and finally stands up for herself. (Rev: BCCB 9/92; BL 10/1/92*; HB 3–4/93; SLJ 2/93*)

4912 Brandt, Amy. *Benjamin Comes Back/Benjamin regresa* (PS–K). 2000, Child Care Books for Kids paper $11.95 (1-884834-79-5). 32pp. A bilingual book about day care in which Benjamin misses his mother so much that he needs to be reassured that she will be coming for him after school. (Rev: SLJ 10/00)

4913 Brown, Tricia. *Someone Special, Just Like You* (PS–2). Photos by Fran Ortiz. 1984, Holt $16.95 (0-8050-0481-5). 64pp. A book that shows that children are children even if they are handicapped.

4914 Bulla, Clyde Robert. *The Chalk Box Kid* (2–3). Illus. by Thomas B. Allen. 1987, Random LB $11.99 (0-394-99102-8); paper $3.99 (0-394-89102-3). 64pp. Miffed because Uncle Max is sharing his room, Gregory sets out to explore his new neighborhood. (Rev: BCCB 9/87; BL 12/1/87; SLJ 12/87)

4915 Bunnett, Rochelle. *Friends in the Park* (PS–K). Illus. by Carl Sahlhoff. 1993, Checkerboard $7.95 (1-56288-347-X). 32pp. In this book of photographs and text, disabled kids are shown enjoying all the activities that youngsters like. (Rev: BL 4/15/93) [305.9]

4916 Bunting, Eve. *Fly Away Home* (K–3). Illus. by Ronald Himler. 1991, Houghton $16.00 (0-395-55962-6). 32pp. The airport serves as a home for two homeless people — a boy and his father. (Rev: BCCB 5/92; BL 4/1/91*; HB 7–8/91; SLJ 6/91*)

4917 Bunting, Eve. *Ghost's Hour, Spook's Hour* (PS–2). Illus. by Donald Carrick. 1987, Houghton $16.00 (0-89919-484-2); paper $6.95 (0-395-51583-1). 32pp. A boy and his dog, Biff, search the house for Mom and Dad when they hear noises that frighten them. (Rev: BCCB 10/87; BL 8/87; SLJ 9/87)

4918 Bunting, Eve. *On Call Back Mountain* (1–3). Illus. by Barry Moser. 1997, Scholastic $15.95 (0-590-25929-6). Two young brothers adjust to the death of an elderly man who has worked as a fire spotter in a tower close to their home. (Rev: SLJ 3/97)

4919 Bunting, Eve. *Twinnies* (PS–1). Illus. by Nancy Carpenter. 1997, Harcourt $15.00 (0-15-291592-3). 32pp. A girl feels jealous when her twin sisters get all the attention. (Rev: BL 9/15/97; HBG 3/98; SLJ 10/97)

4920 Burnett, Frances Hodgson. *A Little Princess* (K–2). Illus. by Barbara McClintock. 2000, Harper-Collins LB $16.89 (0-06-029010-2). 32pp. A retelling in a shortened form of Burnett's beloved classic story of a privileged child who turned pauper and back again. (Rev: BL 1/1–15/01; HBG 3/01)

4921 Canfield, Jack, and Mark V. Hansen. *Chicken Soup for Little Souls: The Best Night Out with Dad* (K–4). Illus. by Bert Dodson. Series: Chicken Soup for Little Souls. 1997, Health Communications $14.95 (1-55874-508-4). 32pp. This slight story teaches the value of being unselfish and giving to others. Also use *Chicken Soup for Little Souls: The Goodness Gorilla* and *Chicken Soup for Little Souls: The Never-Forgotten Doll* (1997). (Rev: BL 11/15/97; HBG 3/98; SLJ 1/98)

4922 Carlson, Nancy. *Arnie and the New Kid* (PS–2). Illus. 1992, Puffin paper $5.99 (0-14-050945-3). 32pp. When Arnie has an accident, he realizes what life is like for newcomer Philip, who is confined to a wheelchair. (Rev: BCCB 5/90; BL 5/15/90)

4923 Carr, Jan. *Dark Day, Light Night* (PS–2). Illus. by James E. Ransome. 1996, Hyperion LB $15.49 (0-7868-2014-4). 32pp. When 'Manda claims there is nothing in the world she really likes, Aunt Ruby compiles a list of her own favorite things. (Rev: BL 2/15/96; HB 5–6/96; SLJ 6/96)

4924 Carrick, Carol. *The Accident* (K–3). Illus. by Donald Carrick. 1981, Houghton paper $6.95 (0-89919-041-3). 32pp. A story that deals sympathetically and realistically with a child's reaction to the death of his pet dog.

4925 Carrick, Carol. *Patrick's Dinosaurs* (PS–3). Illus. by Donald Carrick. 1983, Houghton $15.00 (0-89919-189-4); paper $5.95 (0-89919-402-8). 32pp. Patrick is frightened when his brother tells him about dinosaurs.

4926 Carrier, Roch. *The Boxing Champion* (1–2). Trans. by Sheila Fischman. Illus. by Sheldon Cohen. 1991, Tundra $15.95 (0-88776-249-2). Young Rock wants to go into training so he can become a powerful boxer. (Rev: SLJ 7/91)

4927 Carter, Alden R. *Seeing Things My Way* (1–3). Illus. 1998, Albert Whitman $14.95 (0-8075-7296-9). 32pp. The story of a 7-year-old girl who is visually impaired, how she copes with her problem, and the aids that help her live a more normal life. (Rev: BL 11/15/98; HBG 3/99; SLJ 11/98) [362.4]

4928 Carter, Dorothy. *Bye, Mis' Lela* (K–3). Illus. by Harvey Stevenson. 1998, Farrar $16.00 (0-374-31013-0). 32pp. An African American girl must cope with the death of her beloved baby sitter, Mis' Lela. (Rev: BL 2/15/98; HBG 10/98; SLJ 3/98)

4929 Caseley, Judith. *Priscilla Twice* (K–2). Illus. 1995, Greenwillow LB $14.93 (0-688-13306-1). 32pp. After her parents divorce, Priscilla finds that she now has two of everything, including two sets of clothes. (Rev: BL 8/95; SLJ 9/95)

4930 Child, Lauren. *Clarice Bean, That's Me* (PS–2). Illus. by author. 1999, Candlewick $16.99 (0-7636-0961-7). Clarice Bean's house is so crowded that she hopes she will be sent to her room as a punishment so she can be alone for a while. (Rev: HBG 3/00; SLJ 12/99)

4931 Cocca-Leffler, Maryann. *Missing: One Stuffed Rabbit* (K–3). Illus. 1998, Albert Whitman LB $14.95 (0-8075-5161-9). 32pp. Janine is frantic when she loses the class mascot, a stuffed rabbit named Coco, at a shopping mall. (Rev: BL 3/15/98; HBG 10/98; SLJ 5/98)

4932 Cohn, Janice. *Molly's Rosebush* (PS–2). Illus. by Gail Owens. 1994, Albert Whitman LB $14.95 (0-8075-5213-5). 32pp. Grandma helps Molly get over her grief at the loss of her mother's baby by miscarriage. (Rev: BL 1/15/95; SLJ 3/95)

4933 Cole, Babette. *The Un-Wedding* (PS–2). Illus. 1998, Knopf $17.00 (0-679-88898-5). 32pp. A lighthearted look at marital discord in which two children encourage their quarreling parents to live in adjoining houses so they can visit each of them easily. (Rev: BCCB 5/98; BL 6/1–15/98; HBG 10/98; SLJ 5/98)

4934 Cosby, Bill. *The Day I Was Rich* (1–3). Illus. by Varnette P. Honeywood. Series: Little Bill. 1999, Scholastic $15.95 (0-590-52172-1); paper $3.99 (0-590-52173-X). In this beginning chapter book, Little Bill discovers that the object he found is not a diamond but only a glass paperweight. Also use *The Worst Day of My Life* (1999). (Rev: HBG 3/00; SLJ 2/00)

4935 Coville, Bruce. *My Grandfather's House* (K–3). Illus. by Henri Sorensen. 1996, Troll $14.95 (0-8167-3804-1). 32pp. A young boy painfully adjusts to his grandfather's death. (Rev: BL 6/1–15/96; SLJ 8/96)

4936 Cowley, Joy. *Big Moon Tortilla* (PS–3). Illus. by Dyanne Strongbow. 1998, Boyds Mills $14.95 (1-56397-601-3). When Marta Enos has a bad day at home on the Papago reservation in southern Arizona, her grandmother tells her a traditional tale to help her cope with problems. (Rev: BL 10/15/98; HBG 10/99; SLJ 11/98)

4937 Crary, Elizabeth. *I'm Frustrated* (PS–1). Illus. by Jean Whitney. 1992, Parenting Pr. LB $16.95 (0-943990-65-3). 30pp. In this slim book, a child is faced with a difficult situation and must work through his feelings. Others in this series are: *I'm Mad; I'm Proud* (both 1992). (Rev: SLJ 6/92)

4938 Crew, Gary. *Bright Star* (1–3). Illus. by Anne Spudvilas. 1997, Kane/Miller $13.95 (0-916291-15-8). 32pp. In this Australian picture book, a young girl finds the freedom she wants when she develops an interest in astronomy. (Rev: BL 10/15/97; HBG 3/98; SLJ 2/98)

4939 Cristaldi, Kathryn. *Samantha the Snob* (1–3). Illus. by Denise Brunkus. Series: Step into Reading. 1994, Random LB $11.99 (0-679-94640-3); paper $3.99 (0-679-84640-9). 48pp. Everyone thinks that the new girl in their class is a snob and showoff, but her birthday party shows that they are wrong. (Rev: SLJ 11/94)

4940 Curtis, Jamie Lee. *Today I Feel Silly: And Other Moods That Make My Day* (PS–2). Illus. by Laura Cornell. 1998, HarperCollins $14.95 (0-06-024560-3). 32pp. In this lighthearted picture book, the young narrator describes how she feels on different days and the ways she copes with emotional ups and downs. (Rev: BL 10/15/98; HBG 3/99; SLJ 12/98)

4941 Czech, Jan M. *An American Face* (PS–2). Illus. by Frances Clancy. 2000, Child & Family paper $8.95 (0-87868-718-1). 32pp. Korean-born Jessie believes that when he becomes an American citizen he will get a new face like his adoptive American parents. (Rev: BL 5/15/00; SLJ 8/00)

4942 Daly, Niki. *My Dad* (1–4). Illus. 1995, Simon & Schuster paper $16.00 (0-689-50620-1). 32pp. Two siblings react with embarrassment and fear when their father abuses alcohol. (Rev: BCCB 6/95; BL 5/1/95; SLJ 6/95)

4943 Davies, Sally J. K. *Why Did We Have to Move Here?* (K–3). Illus. 1997, Carolrhoda $15.95 (1-57505-046-3). 32pp. After William and his family move to a new home, he has difficulty making friends. (Rev: BL 12/15/97; HBG 3/98)

4944 Dengler, Marianna. *Fiddlin' Sam* (K–3). Illus. by Sibyl G. Gerig. 1999, Northland $15.95 (0-87358-742-1). 32pp. Sam, who wants to pass his gift of music on to someone else, finally finds a successor. (Rev: BL 11/15/99; HBG 3/00; SLJ 12/99)

4945 dePaola, Tomie. *Now One Foot, Now the Other* (K–3). Illus. by author. 1981, Putnam $13.95 (0-399-20774-0). 48pp. Bobby helps his grandfather recover from a stroke.

4946 dePaola, Tomie. *Oliver Button Is a Sissy* (K–3). Illus. by author. 1979, Harcourt $14.00 (0-15-257852-8); paper $6.00 (0-15-668140-4). 48pp. People think Oliver is a sissy until he shines in a talent show as a fine tap dancer.

4947 Dunrea, Olivier. *Appearing Tonight! Mary Heather Elizabeth Livingstone* (PS–4). Illus. 2000, Farrar $15.00 (0-374-30455-6). 32pp. The story of a famous stage star and beauty who becomes plump from eating chocolates, loses her grand position, and must adjust to a new lifestyle. (Rev: BL 8/00; HBG 10/00; SLJ 5/00)

4948 Edwards, Becky. *My Brother Sammy* (PS–2). Illus. by David Armitage. 1999, Millbrook LB $21.90 (0-7613-1417-2). An older boy has troubles adjusting to the erratic behavior of his autistic younger brother, Sammy. (Rev: HBG 10/99; SLJ 7/99)

4949 Edwards, Michelle. *A Baker's Portrait* (PS–3). Illus. 1991, Smithmark paper $3.95 (0-831-73218-0). 32pp. Michelin has problems when she is commissioned to paint portraits of her aunt and uncle. (Rev: BCCB 2/92; BL 10/15/91; SLJ 10/91)

4950 Ehrlich, Amy. *Lucy's Winter Tale* (K–4). Illus. by Troy Howell. 1999, NAL paper $4.99 (0-140-55581-1). 32pp. A young girl runs away with a circus juggler who is looking for his lost love. (Rev: BCCB 1/93; BL 7/92; SLJ 9/92)

4951 Ehrlich, H. M. *Louie's Goose* (PS–3). Illus. by Emily Bolam. 2000, Houghton $15.00 (0-618-03023-9). 32pp. Louie is so attached to his stuffed goose, Rosie, that, although it is falling apart and needs constant repair, he can't part with it. (Rev: BL 3/1/00; HBG 10/00; SLJ 3/00)

4952 England, Linda. *The Old Cotton Blues* (PS–2). Illus. by Teresa Flavin. 1998, Simon & Schuster $16.00 (0-689-81074-1). 32pp. Dexter loves the sound of the clarinet, but his mother tells him that the little money they have must go for rent instead of musical instruments. (Rev: BCCB 7–8/98; BL 2/15/98; HBG 10/98; SLJ 7/98)

4953 Falwell, Cathryn. *Dragon Tooth* (K–2). Illus. 1996, Clarion $14.95 (0-395-56916-8). 32pp. Sara gradually convinces herself that it is all right to have her father pull her loose tooth. (Rev: BL 4/15/96; SLJ 4/96)

4954 Fernandes, Eugenie. *A Difficult Day* (K–2). Illus. 1999, Kids Can $14.95 (0-921103-17-4). 32pp. Poor Melinda has a bad day and a temper tantrum, but it ends with cookies and hugs from an understanding mom. (Rev: BL 5/15/99; HBG 10/99)

4955 Figueredo, D. H. *When This World Was New* (PS–3). Illus. by Enrique O. Sanchez. 1999, Lee & Low $15.95 (1-880000-86-5). 32pp. Danilito leaves his warm Caribbean island to migrate with his parents to the U.S., and there he has many unsettling experiences but one outstanding joy — seeing the city transformed by snow. (Rev: BL 6/1–15/99; HBG 10/99; SLJ 7/99)

4956 Fine, Edith Hope. *Under the Lemon Moon* (K–3). Illus. by René King Moreno. 1999, Lee & Low $15.95 (1-880000-69-5). 32pp. Young Rosalinda learns to cope with loss when a thief steals all the lemons from her pet tree and damages it as well. (Rev: BL 5/15/99; HBG 10/99; SLJ 4/99)

4957 Fleming, Virginia. *Be Good to Eddie Lee* (K–3). Illus. by Floyd Cooper. 1993, Putnam $16.99 (0-399-21993-5). 30pp. Eddie Lee, a boy with Down's syndrome, teaches his neighbor, Christy, to look at the world differently. (Rev: BL 1/15/94; SLJ 2/94)

4958 Foreman, Michael. *Seal Surfer* (K–4). Illus. 1997, Harcourt $16.00 (0-15-201399-7). 36pp. A disabled boy and his grandfather form an unusual bond between themselves and a seal pup. (Rev: BCCB 5/97; BL 5/1/97; SLJ 3/97*)

4959 Fox, Mem. *Harriet, You'll Drive Me Wild!* (PS). Illus. by Marla Frazee. 2000, Harcourt $16.00 (0-15-201977-4). 32pp. Harriet is such a pest that her usually patient mother begins to shout at her but then they kiss and make up. (Rev: BCCB 6/00; BL 3/1/00; HB 3–4/00; HBG 10/00; SLJ 4/00)

4960 Fraustino, Lisa Rowe. *The Hickory Chair* (PS–3). Illus. by Benny Andrews. 2001, Scholastic $15.95 (0-590-52248-5). 32pp. Although Louis was born blind, he seems to have a sixth sense. For example, after his beloved grandmother dies, it is Louis who finds her notes about the disposal of her property. (Rev: BCCB 3/01*; BL 3/1/01; SLJ 2/01)

4961 Freymann, Saxton, and Joost Elffers. *How Are You Peeling? Foods with Moods* (PS–1). Illus. 1999, Scholastic $15.95 (0-439-10431-9). 48pp. Collages of fruits and vegetables are used to portray human emotions. (Rev: BL 2/1/00; HBG 3/00; SLJ 1/00) [152.4]

4962 Gauch, Patricia L. *Bravo, Tanya* (PS–2). Illus. by Satomi Ichikawa. 1992, Putnam $15.99 (0-399-22145-X). 32pp. Young Tanya encounters difficulties when she begins taking ballet lessons. (Rev: BL 5/1/92; SLJ 3/92*)

4963 Gauch, Patricia L. *Presenting Tanya, the Ugly Duckling* (PS–3). Illus. by Satomi Ichikawa. 1999, Putnam $16.99 (0-399-23200-1). 32pp. Dancing the lead in *The Ugly Duckling* gives Tanya the confidence she needs to turn from an awkward dancer into a graceful swan. (Rev: BL 7/99*; HBG 10/99; SLJ 6/99)

4964 Gehret, Jeanne. *The Don't-Give-Up-Kid and Learning Differences* (K–3). Illus. by Sandra A. DePauw. 1992, Verbal Images paper $9.95 (0-884-28110-9). 32pp. A first-grader receives special attention to help his dyslexia. (Rev: BL 6/1/90)

4965 Gifaldi, David. *Ben, King of the River* (K–3). Illus. by Layne Johnson. 2001, Albert Whitman $14.95 (0-8075-0635-4). 32pp. An older boy is afraid his disabled brother will spoil the family's first camping trip. (Rev: BL 3/1/01)

4966 Giff, Patricia Reilly. *Ronald Morgan Goes to Bat* (PS–3). Illus. by Susanna Natti. 1988, Puffin paper $5.99 (0-14-050669-1). 32pp. Ronald is so bad a batter that he closes his eyes when the ball comes, but his spirit is unbeatable. Also use: *Watch Out, Ronald Morgan!* (1985). (Rev: BL 6/1/88; HB 9–10/88; SLJ 9/88)

4967 Gomi, Taro. *I Lost My Dad* (PS–2). Illus. 2001, Kane/Miller $12.95 (0-916291-04-2). 32pp. This book explores a young boy's panic and fear when he is separated from his dad in a large department store. (Rev: BL 3/1/01)

4968 Grifalconi, Ann. *Tiny's Hat* (K–3). Illus. by author. 1999, HarperCollins LB $14.89 (0-06-027655-X). When Tiny's father, a blues player, goes away, the little girl dons her daddy's big black hat and begins to sing the blues. (Rev: HBG 10/99; SLJ 1/99)

4969 Grimm, Edward. *The Doorman* (K–3). Illus. by Ted Lewin. 2000, Orchard LB $17.99 (0-531-33280-2). 32pp. Residents in a New York City apartment building mourn the death of the doorman who meant so much to them. (Rev: BCCB 7–8/00; BL 7/00; HBG 3/01; SLJ 10/00)

4970 Grindley, Sally. *A New Room for William* (K–3). Illus. by Carol Thompson. 2000, Candlewick $15.99 (0-7636-1196-4). 32pp. William, a child of divorce, gradually gets used to his new home alone with his mother, particularly after she lets him pick wallpaper for his new room. (Rev: BCCB 12/00; BL 1/1–15/01; HBG 3/01; SLJ 11/00)

4971 Hamilton, DeWitt. *Sad Days, Glad Days: A Story About Depression* (K–3). Illus. by Gail Owens. 1995, Albert Whitman LB $14.95 (0-8075-7200-4). 32pp. An honest account of a girl facing the problems caused by her mother's fits of depression. (Rev: BL 4/15/95; SLJ 5/95)

4972 Hanson, Regina. *The Tangerine Tree* (PS–3). Illus. by Harvey Stevenson. 1995, Clarion $14.95 (0-395-68963-5). 32pp. Ida's Jamaican family is torn apart when her father must become a migrant worker in New York City. (Rev: BL 7/95; SLJ 9/95)

4973 Harrison, Troon. *Aaron's Awful Allergies* (PS–1). Illus. by Eugenie Fernandes. 1998, Kids Can $12.95 (1-55074-299-X). Aaron is unhappy when he has to get rid of his pets because of his allergies. (Rev: HBG 10/98; SLJ 3/98)

4974 Harshman, Marc. *The Storm* (K–3). Illus. by Mark Mohr. 1995, Dutton $15.99 (0-525-65150-0). 32pp. Wheelchair-bound Jonathan finds himself in the path of a deadly tornado. (Rev: BL 5/1/95; SLJ 7/95)

4975 Hasler, Eveline. *The Giantess* (K–3). Trans. by Laura McKenna. Illus. by Renate Seelig. 1997, Kane/Miller $12.95 (0-916291-76-6). 24pp. A giantess named Emmeline finds happiness when she joins a traveling carnival. (Rev: BL 12/1/97; HBG 3/98; SLJ 12/97)

4976 Heide, Florence Parry, and Roxanne H. Pierce. *Oh, Grow Up!* (K–4). Illus. by Nadine Bernard Westcott. 1996, Orchard LB $16.99 (0-531-08771-9). 32pp. Humorous verses and imaginative drawings illustrate everyday problems in growing up, such as dealing with brothers and sisters. (Rev: BCCB 3/96; BL 3/1/96; SLJ 4/96)

4977 Heitler, Susan M. *David Decides About Thumbsucking: A Motivating Story for Children and an Informative Guide for Parents* (PS–3). Illus. by Paula Singer. 1996, Reading Matters paper $13.95 (0-9614780-2-0). 52pp. This photo-essay concentrates on David and his decision to give up his thumb sucking. (Rev: BL 11/1/85; SLJ 2/86)

4978 Hickman, Martha W. *When Andy's Father Went to Prison* (K–5). Illus. by Larry Raymond. 1990, Whitman LB $13.95 (0-8075-8874-1). Andy faces a personal crisis when he learns that his father has been sent to jail. (Rev: BCCB 1/91; SLJ 2/91)

4979 Holcomb, Nan. *Andy Finds a Turtle* (K–3). Illus. by Dot Yoder. Series: Turtle Books. 1992, Jason LB $14.95 (0-944727-13-1); paper $8.95 (0-944727-02-6). 32pp. The story of Andy, a young boy with cerebral palsy. Two other books about children with physical problems are: *Danny and the Merry-Go-Round* and *How about a Hug* (both 1992). All three are reissues.

4980 Hopkins, Beverly H. *Changes: My Family and Me* (PS–2). Illus. by Sarah K. Hoctor. 1999, Child & Family $8.95 (0-87868-723-8). As seen through the eyes of the oldest child in a family, this account tells of the changes that a family experiences when parents divorce, remarry, and have both stepchildren and children of their own. (Rev: SLJ 6/99)

4981 Howard, Elizabeth F. *Virgie Goes to School with Us Boys* (K–2). Illus. by E. B. Lewis. 2000, Simon & Schuster $16.00 (0-689-80076-2). 32pp. Virgie, youngest in a family of boys, vows that she will accompany her brothers when they walk the seven miles to school every Monday morning. (Rev: BCCB 2/00; BL 11/1/99*; HBG 10/00; SLJ 3/00)

4982 Hru, Dakari. *Joshua's Masai Mask* (K–3). Illus. by Anna Rich. 1993, Lee & Low $14.95 (1-880000-02-4). 32pp. By playing the kalimba, an African musical instrument, in his school's talent show, Joshua gains self-esteem. (Rev: BL 4/1/93)

4983 Hughes, Shirley. *Alfie and the Birthday Surprise* (PS–K). Illus. 1998, Lothrop $16.00 (0-688-15187-6). 32pp. Alfie, an English toddler, helps his neighbors adjust to the death of their pet cat, Smoky. (Rev: BCCB 3/98; BL 3/1/98; HB 5–6/98; HBG 10/98; SLJ 3/98)

4984 Hughes, Shirley. *Dogger* (PS–K). Illus. by author. 1988, Lothrop LB $15.93 (0-688-07981-4); Morrow paper $6.95 (0-688-11704-X). 32pp. Dave's lost stuffed dog turns up at a fair booth, but Dave doesn't have the money to buy it back — until sister comes to the rescue. (Rev: BL 9/1/88)

4985 Hutchins, Hazel. *Believing Sophie* (K–3). Illus. by Dorothy Donohue. 1995, Albert Whitman LB $14.95 (0-8075-0625-7). 32pp. Sophie is falsely accused of stealing cough drops from her local store. (Rev: BL 9/1/95; SLJ 1/96)

4986 Isadora, Rachael. *Ben's Trumpet* (K–3). Illus. by Rachel Isadora. 1979, Greenwillow $16.95 (0-688-80194-3); Morrow paper $6.95 (0-688-10988-8). 32pp. A young African American boy dreams of becoming a trumpet player and eventually is taken to a jazz club by a musician.

4987 Isherwood, Shirley. *Flora the Frog* (K–3). Illus. by Anna C. Leplar. 2000, Peachtree $16.95 (1-56145-223-8). 32pp. Flora is so upset at playing a frog in the class play, that she throws away the frog costume that her mother and aunt have made. (Rev: BCCB 11/00; BL 9/15/00; HBG 3/01; SLJ 10/00)

4988 Jay, Betsy. *Swimming Lessons* (PS–2). Illus. by Lori Osiecki. 1998, Northland $15.95 (0-87358-685-9). 32pp. When her neighbor Jimmy taunts her because she won't go swimming, Jane seeks revenge. She not only becomes a fine swimmer but also manages to separate Jimmy from his swim trunks! (Rev: BCCB 9/98; BL 6/1–15/98; HBG 10/98; SLJ 9/98)

4989 Jimenez, Francisco. *La Mariposa* (K–3). Illus. by Simon Silva. 1998, Houghton $16.00 (0-395-81663-7). 40pp. Francisco becomes adept at drawing butterflies and, as a gesture of reconciliation, offers one of his drawings to the boy who beat him up on the playground. (Rev: BL 3/1/99; HBG 3/99; SLJ 11/98)

4990 Jordan, Deloris, and Roslyn M. Jordan. *Salt in His Shoes: Michael Jordan in Pursuit of a Dream* (K–4). Illus. by Kadir Nelson. 2000, Simon & Schuster $16.95 (0-689-83371-7). 32pp. A fictionalized tale about a youthful Michael Jordan whose mother (the author) encourages him to pursue his basketball dreams even though he's the shortest boy on the team. (Rev: BL 2/1/01; HBG 3/01)

4991 Joslin, Sesyle. *What Do You Say, Dear?* (1–3). Illus. by Maurice Sendak. 1958, HarperCollins LB $15.89 (0-06-023074-6); paper $5.95 (0-06-443112-6). 48pp. Humorous handbook on manners for young ladies and gentlemen of 6 to 8. Also use: *What Do You Do, Dear?* (1958).

4992 Karas, G. Brian. *Home on the Bayou: A Cowboy's Story* (K–3). Illus. 1996, Simon & Schuster paper $15.00 (0-689-80156-4). 32pp. Ned has to contend with a new home on the bayou and Big Head Ed, the school bully. (Rev: BCCB 1/97; BL 9/15/96; SLJ 10/96*)

4993 Karkowsku, Nancy. *Grandma's Soup* (PS–3). Illus. by Shelly O. Haas. 1989, Kar-Ben paper $5.95 (0-930494-99-7). Several grandchildren gradually adjust to the fact that their grandmother has Alzheimer's disease. (Rev: SLJ 12/89)

4994 Karlins, Mark. *Music over Manhattan* (K–3). Illus. by Jack E. Davis. 1998, Doubleday $15.95 (0-385-32225-9). 32pp. Bernie is discouraged because he is constantly compared to his perfect cousin Herbert. Then he becomes a star trumpeter and changes everything. (Rev: BL 8/98; HBG 3/99; SLJ 8/98)

4995 Keats, Ezra Jack. *Louie* (PS–K). Illus. by author. 1983, Greenwillow $14.89 (0-688-02383-5). 32pp. Louie, a silent child, makes his first friend, a puppet, and is allowed to keep it for his very own.

4996 Keller, Holly. *Jacob's Tree* (PS–1). Illus. 1999, Greenwillow LB $14.93 (0-688-15996-6). 24pp. Jacob tried everything including vegetables, vitamins, and exercise to speed up his growth. (Rev: BL 7/99; HB 3–4/99; HBG 10/99; SLJ 5/99)

4997 Kibbey, Marsha. *My Grammy: A Book About Alzheimer's Disease* (1–3). Illus. by Karen Ritz. 1988, Carolrhoda paper $4.95 (0-87614-544-6). 32pp. Eight-year-old Amy and her family must cope with Grammy's worsening Alzheimer's disease. (Rev: BL 7/88; SLJ 10/88)

4998 Klassen, Heather. *I Don't Want to Go to Justin's House Anymore* (PS–2). Illus. by Beth Jepson. 1999, Child & Family paper $6.95 (0-87868-724-6). Collin witnesses child abuse at friend Justin's house, and gets his mother to promise to get help. (Rev: SLJ 3/00)

4999 Kolbisen, Irene M. *Wiggle-Butts and Up-Faces* (PS–K). Illus. by Sandy D. Zmolek. 1989, I Think I Can LB $14.95 (1-877863-00-9). 32pp. Ingrid's young brother is afraid of taking beginner swimming lessons. (Rev: BL 12/1/89)

5000 Koski, Mary. *Impatient Pamela Asks: Why Are My Feet So Huge?* (K–2). Illus. by Dan Brown. 1999, Trellis LB $15.95 (0-9663281-2-4). Pamela is self-conscious about her big feet until she realizes they can be an asset. (Rev: SLJ 10/99)

5001 Krauss, Ruth. *A Very Special House* (PS–K). Illus. by Maurice Sendak. 1953, HarperCollins LB $17.89 (0-06-023456-3). 32pp. A little boy tells what it would be like in his very special house — no one would ever say "Stop, Stop."

5002 Krisher, Trudy. *Kathy's Hats: A Story of Hope* (PS–3). Illus. by Nadine Bernard Westcott. 1992, Whitman LB $14.95 (0-8075-4116-8). 32pp. When Kathy undergoes chemotherapy for cancer, she finds a new reason to wear her hats. (Rev: BCCB 10/92; BL 10/1/92; SLJ 6/91)

5003 Kroll, Virginia. *Can You Dance, Dalila?* (PS–3). Illus. by Nancy Carpenter. 1996, Simon & Schuster paper $15.00 (0-689-80551-9). 32pp. An African American child who can't master social dancing shines during a folk dance performance. (Rev: BL 11/15/96; SLJ 2/97)

5004 Kroll, Virginia. *Fireflies, Peach Pies and Lullabies* (PS–3). Illus. by Nancy Cote. 1995, Simon & Schuster $15.00 (0-689-80291-9). 32pp. At Great-Granny Annabel's wake, Francie asks each family member to relate a remembrance of her. The list is read at the funeral service and becomes a celebration of Great-Granny's life. (Rev: BL 12/15/95; SLJ 4/96)

5005 Lachner, Dorothea. *Danny, the Angry Lion* (PS–K). Trans. by J. Alison James. Illus. by Gusti. 2000, North-South $15.95 (0-7358-1386-8). 32pp. A charming story about a boy who storms out of the house in a fit of anger and how he gradually calms down. (Rev: BL 12/15/00; HBG 3/01; SLJ 11/00)

5006 Lagercrantz, Rose, and Samuel Lagercrantz. *Is It Magic?* (K–3). Trans. by Paul Norlen. Illus. by Eva Eriksson. 1991, R&S $13.95 (91-29-59182-1). Young Pete and Cilla are in love until the class bully steps in. (Rev: SLJ 3/91)

5007 Lampert, Emily. *A Little Touch of Monster* (PS–1). Illus. by Melanie Kroupa. 1986, Little, Brown LB $12.95 (0-316-51287-7). 32pp. No one listens to Parker, so he turns into a bit of a monster; then they listen to him too much, granting almost his every wish. (Rev: BCCB 5/86; BL 3/15/86; HB 5–6/86)

5008 Lasker, Joe. *Nick Joins In* (K–3). Illus. by author. 1980, Whitman LB $14.95 (0-8075-5612-2). 32pp. Wheelchair-bound Nicky wonders what will happen to him when he goes to a regular school.

5009 Lasky, Kathryn. *The Tantrum* (PS–1). Illus. by Bobette McCarthy. 1993, Macmillan LB $13.95 (0-02-751661-X). 32pp. Gracie tells about her terrible temper tantrum and how everyone responded to it. (Rev: BL 4/1/93)

5010 Leach, Norman. *My Wicked Stepmother* (PS–3). Illus. by Jane Browne. 1993, Macmillan LB $13.95 (0-02-754700-0). 32pp. At first, Tom hates his stepmother, but when he deliberately hurts her and she cries, his hate turns to love. (Rev: BCCB 7–8/93; BL 2/15/93; SLJ 3/93)

5011 Lears, Laurie. *Ian's Walk: A Story About Autism* (2–3). Illus. by Karen Ritz. 1998, Whitman $14.95 (0-8075-3480-3). 32pp. Narrator Julie and her sister Tara take their autistic younger brother, Ian, for a walk. Although they are disturbed by his unusual reactions to events and have ambivalent feelings toward him, they show their love by rescuing him when he wanders away. (Rev: BL 4/1/98; HB 5–6/98; HBG 10/98; SLJ 9/98)

5012 Lears, Laurie. *Waiting for Mr. Goose* (K–3). Illus. by Karen Ritz. 1999, Albert Whitman $14.95 (0-8075-8628-5). Stephen, a young boy who can't keep still or pay attention in school, finds a mission in life when he rescues a goose caught in a trap. (Rev: BL 12/1/99; HBG 3/00; SLJ 1/00)

5013 Levy, Janice. *Totally Uncool* (K–3). Illus. by Chris Monroe. 1998, Carolrhoda $15.95 (1-57505-306-3). 32pp. Alex is not impressed with Elizabeth, Dad's new girlfriend, until Elizabeth helps cure her headaches and designs a prize-winning costume for her. (Rev: BCCB 2/99; BL 2/15/99; HBG 10/99; SLJ 3/99)

5014 Lindgren, Barbro. *Sam's Ball* (PS). Illus. by Eva Eriksson. 1983, Morrow paper $6.95 (0-688-02359-2). 32pp. A book in which a toddler shares his toy with a kitty. Four others in this series are: *Sam's Car; Sam's Cookie; Sam's Teddy Bear* (all 1982); *Sam's Bath* (1983).

5015 Litchfield, Ada B. *Words in Our Hands* (2–4). Illus. by Helen Cogancherry. 1980, Whitman LB $14.95 (0-8075-9212-9). Michael describes his life with his deaf parents.

5016 Littlesugar, Amy. *Shake Rag: From the Life of Elvis Presley* (1–4). Illus. by Floyd Cooper. 1998, Philomel LB $16.99 (0-399-23005-X). A story about Elvis Presley's poor childhood and how he came to realize the power of music. (Rev: HBG 3/99; SLJ 10/98)

5017 Lobby, Ted. *Jessica and the Wolf: A Story for Children Who Have Bad Dreams* (PS–1). Illus. by Tennessee Dixon. 1990, Brunner $11.95 (0-945354-22-3); paper $8.95 (0-945354-21-5). 32pp. Parents help their daughter when she has a recurring nightmare about a wolf. (Rev: BL 9/1/90)

5018 London, Jonathan. *The Lion Who Has Asthma* (PS–2). Illus. by Nadine Bernard Westcott. 1992, Whitman LB $14.95 (0-8075-4559-7). In his imagination, asthmatic Sean becomes a variety of animals to suit different situations. (Rev: SLJ 6/92)

5019 Lottridge, Celia B. *Something Might Be Hiding* (PS–K). Illus. by Paul Zwolak. 1996, Douglas & McIntyre $14.95 (0-88899-176-2). 24pp. A child feels the stress of moving to a new house. (Rev: BL 8/96; SLJ 6/96)

5020 Luthardt, Kevin. *Mine!* (PS–1). Illus. 2001, Simon & Schuster $14.00 (0-689-83237-0). 32pp. A nearly wordless picture book in which each of two brothers claims sole possession of a toy dinosaur received as a joint present. (Rev: BCCB 1/01; BL 2/1/01; SLJ 2/01)

5021 McCourt, Lisa. *Chicken Soup for Little Souls: The New Kid and the Cookie Thief* (K–2). Illus. by Mary O. Young. Series: Chicken Soup for Little Souls. 1998, Health Communications $14.95 (1-55874-588-2). 32pp. Julie mistakenly thinks that the boy next to her on the school bus has eaten her cookies and forces herself to apologize. (Rev: BL 2/1/99; HBG 3/99; SLJ 12/98)

5022 McCully, Emily Arnold. *Mouse Practice* (PS–3). Illus. 1999, Scholastic $15.95 (0-590-68220-2). 32pp. Monk lacks the necessary skills to play baseball with the big kids until he figures out a way to improve his skills. (Rev: BCCB 2/99; BL 4/15/99; HB 3–4/99; HBG 10/99; SLJ 3/99)

5023 McKissack, Patricia. *The Honest-to-Goodness Truth* (PS–3). Illus. by Giselle Potter. 2000, Simon & Schuster $16.00 (0-689-82668-0). 32pp. When Libby tells the honest truth to her friends and classmates, she finds that she can hurt their feelings. (Rev: BCCB 2/00; BL 12/15/99; HBG 10/00; SLJ 1/00)

5024 McMahon, Patricia. *Listen for the Bus: David's Story* (K–4). Photos by John Godt. 1995, Boyds Mills $15.95 (1-56397-368-5). 48pp. In this photoessay, a blind boy who also has hearing problems

nevertheless takes great joy in the simple things in life. (Rev: BL 11/1/95; SLJ 10/95) [362.41]

5025 Magorian, Michelle. *Who's Going to Take Care of Me?* (PS–K). Illus. by James G. Hale. 1990, HarperCollins $13.95 (0-06-024105-5). 32pp. When Eric's older sister starts school, he wonders who will take care of him. (Rev: BL 11/15/90; HB 1–2/91; SLJ 12/90)

5026 Martin, C. L. G. *Down Dairy Farm Road* (K–3). Illus. by Diane D. Hearn. 1994, Macmillan paper $14.95 (0-02-762450-1). 32pp. Junie Mae can't afford the beauty parlor curls her rich friend Lucinda has, so she settles for attractive braids instead. (Rev: BL 6/1–15/94; SLJ 5/94)

5027 Mauser, Pat Rhoads. *Patti's Pet Gorilla* (2–4). Illus. by Diane Palmisciano. 1991, Avon paper $2.95 (0-380-71039-0). 64pp. Patti wants to impress her classmates at show-and-tell, so she tells them she has a pet gorilla. (Rev: BCCB 9/87; BL 3/15/87; SLJ 8/87)

5028 Mayer, Mercer. *You're the Scaredy-Cat* (K–2). Illus. by author. 1991, Rain Bird paper $5.95 (1-879920-01-8). 40pp. Two young boys decide to spend the night camping out in the backyard.

5029 Maynard, Bill. *Quiet, Wyatt!* (PS–1). Illus. by Frank Remkiewicz. 1999, Putnam $15.99 (0-399-23217-6). 32pp. Wyatt conquers rejection when he saves a puppy and gains the respect of others who now invite him to join in their activities. (Rev: BCCB 10/99; BL 6/1–15/99; HBG 10/99; SLJ 7/99)

5030 Medearis, Angela Shelf. *Annie's Gifts* (K–3). Illus. by Anna Rich. 1995, Just Us $14.95 (0-940975-30-0); paper $6.95 (0-940975-31-9). Annie is upset because everyone in her family except her is musically talented. (Rev: BCCB 4/95; SLJ 9/95)

5031 Merriam, Eve, and Pam Pollack. *Where's That Cat?* (PS–2). Illus. by Joanna Harrison. 2000, Simon & Schuster $16.00 (0-689-82904-3). 32pp. The engaging story of a little girl who sets out to find her lost cat, Jitterbugs. (Rev: BL 12/15/00; HBG 3/01; SLJ 11/00)

5032 Miller, Elizabeth I. *Just Like Home: Como en Mi Tierra* (PS–3). Illus. by Mira Reisberg. 1999, Albert Whitman $14.95 (0-8075-4068-4). 32pp. A Hispanic girl gradually fits into American life in this bilingual picture book. (Rev: BL 12/1/99; HBG 3/00; SLJ 12/99)

5033 Miller, Kathryn Ann. *Did My First Mother Love Me? A Story for an Adopted Child* (K–3). Illus. by Jami Moffett. 1994, Morning Glory $12.95 (0-930934-85-7); paper $5.95 (0-930934-84-9). 47pp. A girl learns the reasons why her real mother put her up for adoption and is comforted by this knowledge. (Rev: SLJ 7/94)

5034 Miller, William. *Night Golf* (1–3). Illus. by Cedric Lucas. 1999, Lee & Low $15.95 (1-880000-79-2). This is the story of an African American boy in the late 1950s, the prejudice he encounters when he wants to play golf on an all-white course, and how he perseveres and overcomes this problem. (Rev: HBG 10/99; SLJ 6/99)

5035 Millman, Isaac. *Moses Goes to a Concert* (K–4). Illus. 1998, Farrar $16.00 (0-374-35067-1).

40pp. This picture book, written in both English and American Sign Language, portrays the everyday experiences of a deaf child, Moses, and of a special occasion when he and his classmates go to a concert. (Rev: BL 4/15/98*; HBG 10/98; SLJ 4/98)

5036 Millman, Isaac. *Moses Goes to School* (PS–3). Illus. 2000, Farrar $16.00 (0-374-35069-8). 32pp. This story, written in both English and sign language, tells how Moses and his friends learn at their special school for the deaf. (Rev: BL 8/00; HBG 3/01; SLJ 8/00)

5037 Mochizuki, Ken. *Baseball Saved Us* (2–4). Illus. by Dom Lee. 1993, Lee & Low $15.95 (1-880000-01-6). 32pp. A Japanese American boy gains acceptance playing an excellent game of baseball learned while an internee during World War II. (Rev: BCCB 5/93; BL 4/15/93; HB 7–8/93; SLJ 6/93)

5038 Mora, Pat. *The Rainbow Tulip* (PS–4). Illus. by Elizabeth Sayles. 1999, Viking $15.99 (0-670-87291-1). 32pp. A Mexican American child feels torn between her family traditions and the alien Anglo world, but she learns through experience that it is all right to be different. (Rev: BCCB 12/99; BL 11/1/99; HBG 3/00; SLJ 11/99)

5039 Moss, Deborah M. *Lee, the Rabbit with Epilepsy* (PS–1). Illus. by Carol Schwartz. 1989, Woodbine LB $12.95 (0-933149-32-8). 24pp. While fishing with her grandfather, Lee, a young rabbit, has her first epileptic seizure. A companion book is: *Shelley, the Hyperactive Turtle* (1989). (Rev: BL 12/1/89)

5040 Munsch, Robert, and Saoussan Askar. *From Far Away* (K–3). Illus. by Michael Martchenko. 1995, Firefly LB $16.95 (1-55037-397-8); paper $5.95 (1-55037-396-X). 24pp. Saoussan, a war refugee, has problems adjusting to her new home in Canada. (Rev: BL 1/1–15/96; SLJ 3/96)

5041 Naylor, Phyllis Reynolds. *King of the Playground* (K–3). Illus. by Nola L. Malone. 1991, Macmillan $16.00 (0-689-31558-9). 32pp. After some advice from his dad, Kevin is able to stand up to the playground bully. (Rev: BL 9/1/91; HB 9–10/91; SLJ 1/92)

5042 Ness, Evaline. *Sam, Bangs and Moonshine* (K–2). Illus. by author. 1966, Holt $15.95 (0-8050-0314-2); paper $6.95 (0-8050-0315-0). 48pp. A little girl learns to distinguish truth from "moonshine" only after her cat and playmate nearly meet tragedy. Caldecott Medal winner, 1967.

5043 Newman, Leslea. *Saturday Is Pattyday* (PS–3). Illus. by Annette Hegel. 1993, New Victoria LB $14.95 (0-934678-52-9); paper $6.95 (0-934678-51-0). 24pp. Frankie is unhappy when his two moms break up and one moves to her own apartment. (Rev: BCCB 11/93; BL 11/1/93)

5044 Newman, Leslea. *Too Far Away to Touch* (K–4). Illus. by Catherine Stock. 1995, Clarion $14.95 (0-395-68968-6). 32pp. Uncle Leonard, who has AIDS, tries to prepare his young niece Zoe for his imminent death. (Rev: BCCB 5/95; BL 3/15/95; HB 5–6/95; SLJ 9/95)

5045 Old, Wendie C. *Stacy Had a Little Sister* (PS–2). Illus. by Judith Friedman. 1995, Albert Whitman LB $14.95 (0-8075-7598-4). 32pp. When Stacy's baby sister dies of SIDS, she feels confused and guilty. (Rev: BCCB 5/95; BL 1/1/95; SLJ 2/95)

5046 Paterson, Katherine. *The Smallest Cow in the World* (PS–2). Illus. by Jane Brown. 1991, HarperCollins LB $14.89 (0-06-024691-X); paper $3.95 (0-06-444164-4). 64pp. When he and his family move to another farm, Marvin misses Rosie, the cow he left behind. (Rev: BCCB 1/92*; BL 9/15/91; HB 9–10/91; SLJ 1/92*)

5047 Peacock, Carol Antoinette. *Mommy Far, Mommy Near: An Adoption Story* (K–2). Illus. by Shawn Costello Brownell. 2000, Albert Whitman $14.95 (0-8075-5234-8). 32pp. In spite of her loving Caucasian American family, Elizabeth, an adopted Chinese girl, sometimes wonders why her real mother gave her up and why there wasn't enough room for her in China. (Rev: BL 3/15/00; HBG 10/00; SLJ 5/00)

5048 Peterson, Jeanne Whitehouse. *I Have a Sister, My Sister Is Deaf* (1–3). Illus. by Deborah Kogan Ray. 1977, HarperCollins LB $15.89 (0-06-024702-9); paper $5.95 (0-06-443059-6). 32pp. About a young girl's adjustment to deafness.

5049 Pinkney, Brian. *Jojo's Flying Side Kick* (K–4). Illus. 1995, Simon & Schuster $15.00 (0-689-80283-8). 32pp. Everyone offers advice to Jojo to help her win her yellow belt, which involves breaking a board with a flying side kick. (Rev: BCCB 12/95; BL 10/15/95; HB 9–10/95; SLJ 9/95)

5050 Polacco, Patricia. *Thank You, Mr. Falker* (K–4). Illus. 1998, Putnam $15.99 (0-399-23166-8). 40pp. Based on the author's personal experiences, this is the story of Trisha, who was able to draw beautifully but hid the fact that she couldn't read until she got special help in the fifth grade. (Rev: BCCB 6/98; BL 5/1/98; HBG 10/98; SLJ 6/98)

5051 Pollack, Eileen. *Whisper Whisper Jesse, Whisper Whisper Josh: A Story About AIDS* (K–4). Illus. by Bruce Gilfoy. 1992, Advantage LB $16.95 (0-9624828-4-6); paper $5.95 (0-9624828-3-8). 32pp. Jesse's uncle, Josh, who is dying of AIDS, comes to stay with Jesse's family. (Rev: BL 3/15/93)

5052 Pulver, Robin. *Way to Go, Alex!* (PS–3). Illus. by Elizabeth Wolf. 1999, Albert Whitman $14.95 (0-8075-1583-3). 32pp. Carly is unhappy with her older brother who is mentally handicapped but helps him train after her parents enroll him in the Special Olympics. (Rev: BL 1/1–15/00; HBG 3/00; SLJ 11/99)

5053 Ransom, Jeanie Franz. *I Don't Want to Talk About It* (K–3). Illus. by Kathryn Kunz Finney. 2000, Magination $14.95 (1-55798-664-9); paper $8.95 (1-55798-703-3). 28pp. A young girl whose parents are divorcing talks about her feelings and means of coping. (Rev: SLJ 2/01)

5054 Rathmann, Peggy. *Ruby the Copycat* (K–3). Illus. 1991, Scholastic $14.95 (0-590-43747-X). 32pp. At first, Angela is flattered when a new girl, Ruby, copies everything she does; then it becomes annoying. (Rev: BL 11/15/91; SLJ 1/92*)

5055 Reynolds, Marilyn. *The Magnificent Piano Recital* (K–3). Illus. by Laura Fernandez and Rick Jacobson. 2001, Orca $15.95 (1-55143-180-7). 32pp. When Arabella moves to a new town, she feels lonely and unwanted until she triumphs at a piano recital. (Rev: BL 3/1/01)

5056 Rheingrover, Jean S. *Veronica's First Year* (K–3). Illus. by Kay Life. 1996, Albert Whitman LB $13.95 (0-8075-8474-6). When Nathan's long-awaited sister arrives and is diagnosed as having Down's syndrome, his parents explain the situation to him and make plans for this special child. (Rev: BCCB 12/96; SLJ 10/96)

5057 Riecken, Nancy. *Today Is the Day* (PS–3). Illus. by Catherine Stock. 1996, Houghton $14.95 (0-395-73917-9). 32pp. Yese awaits her father's return from the big city, where he has been working for six months, to their rural Mexican home. (Rev: BCCB 9/96; BL 9/15/96; SLJ 8/96)

5058 Rockwell, Anne. *No! No! No!* (PS–K). Illus. 1995, Simon & Schuster paper $14.00 (0-02-777782-0). 32pp. Everything seems to go wrong for a young boy whose bad mood continues throughout a whole day. (Rev: BL 5/1/95; SLJ 7/95)

5059 Rodell, Susanna. *Dear Fred* (PS–2). Illus. by Kim Gamble. 1995, Ticknor $14.95 (0-395-71544-X). 32pp. Grace writes to her half-brother, who has been separated from her because of divorce and relocation. (Rev: BL 8/95; SLJ 4/95)

5060 Rodgers, Frank. *Who's Afraid of the Ghost Train?* (PS–K). Illus. by author. 1989, Harcourt $12.95 (0-15-200642-7). Robert uses his imagination to conquer his fears, including riding the carnival Ghost Train. (Rev: SLJ 10/89)

5061 Rodriguez, Bobbie. *Sarah's Sleepover* (1–3). Illus. by Mark Graham. 2000, Viking $15.99 (0-670-87750-6). 32pp. Sarah, who is blind, helps her visiting cousins by leading them to safety when the lights go out. (Rev: BL 4/1/00; HBG 10/00; SLJ 5/00)

5062 Rodriguez, Luis J. *America Is Her Name* (2–4). Illus. by Carlos Vazquez. 1998, Curbstone $15.95 (1-880684-40-3). Lonely in her barrio home in Chicago, America Soliz learns to express herself in poetry. (Rev: HBG 10/98; SLJ 9/98)

5063 Rosen, Michael. *This Is Our House* (PS–2). Illus. by Bob Graham. 1996, Candlewick $15.99 (1-56402-870-4). 32pp. George learns to share when his friends exclude him because of his selfish ways. (Rev: BL 11/1/96; HB 7–8/96; SLJ 7/96)

5064 Rosenberry, Vera. *Vera Runs Away* (PS–3). Illus. 2000, Holt $16.00 (0-8050-6267-X). 32pp. Vera feels so underappreciated at home when she receives a straight-A report card that she decides to run away. (Rev: BL 10/15/00; HBG 3/01; SLJ 11/00)

5065 Ross, Kent, and Alice Ross. *Cemetery Quilt* (K–3). Illus. by Rosanne Kaloustian. 1995, Houghton $14.95 (0-395-70948-2). 32pp. A young girl tries to avoid going to the funeral of the grandmother she loved dearly. (Rev: BL 9/15/95; SLJ 9/95)

5066 Sakai, Kimiko. *Sachiko Means Happiness* (K–3). Illus. by Tomie Arai. 1990, Children's Book

Pr. $14.95 (0-89239-065-4). 32pp. A young Japanese American girl has difficulty adjusting to the changes in her grandmother, who has Alzheimer's disease. (Rev: BCCB 1/91; BL 12/1/90; HB 1–2/91; SLJ 3/91)

5067 Saltzberg, Barney. *Mrs. Morgan's Lawn* (K–3). Illus. 1993, Hyperion LB $14.49 (1-56282-424-4). 32pp. With an act of kindness, a boy melts the heart of mean old Mrs. Morgan. (Rev: BL 12/1/93)

5068 Say, Allen. *Allison* (PS–3). Illus. 1997, Houghton $17.00 (0-395-85895-X). 32pp. Little Allison, an Asian girl, is upset when she learns that she has been adopted by her Caucasian parents. (Rev: BL 12/15/97*; HBG 3/98; SLJ 10/97)

5069 Say, Allen. *Emma's Rug* (PS–3). Illus. 1996, Houghton $16.95 (0-395-74294-3). 32pp. Emma is inconsolable when she loses the rug that has been the inspiration for her art. (Rev: BCCB 11/96; BL 10/1/96; HB 9–10/96; SLJ 9/96)

5070 Schick, Eleanor. *Mama* (K–3). Illus. 2000, Marshall Cavendish $15.95 (0-7614-5060-2). 32pp. A mother's death and the ensuing sorrow, acceptance, and cherishing of memories are the subjects of this picture book, seen through a young daughter's eyes. (Rev: BL 2/15/00; HBG 10/00; SLJ 5/00)

5071 Schneider, Antonie. *Good-Bye, Vivi!* (PS–2). Trans. by J. Alison James. Illus. by Maja Dusikova. 1998, North-South $15.95 (1-55858-985-6). 28pp. Two young children become acquainted with death when Granny's pet canary dies and later so does their beloved grandmother. (Rev: BL 1/1–15/99; HBG 3/99; SLJ 1/99)

5072 Sendak, Maurice. *Pierre: A Cautionary Tale in Five Chapters and a Prologue* (K–3). Illus. by author. 1962, HarperCollins LB $15.89 (0-06-025965-5). 48pp. The story about a young boy whose motto is "I don't care."

5073 Sgouros, Charissa. *A Pillow for My Mom* (K–2). Illus. by Christine Ross. 1998, Houghton $15.00 (0-395-82280-7). A little girl's mother is seriously ill in hospital, and to comfort her, the girl sews a colorful pillow for her hospital bed. (Rev: HBG 10/98; SLJ 5/98)

5074 Shange, Ntozake. *White Wash* (PS–2). Illus. by Michael Sporn. 1997, Walker $15.95 (0-8027-8490-9). Helene-Angel and her brother are attacked by a group of white thugs who cover her face with white paint and traumatize her so much that she doesn't want to return to school. (Rev: HBG 3/98; SLJ 5/98)

5075 Shannon, David. *A Bad Case of Stripes* (1–3). Illus. 1998, Scholastic $15.95 (0-590-92997-6). 32pp. Camilla's desire to please and be popular causes her some problems. (Rev: BCCB 3/98; BL 1/1–15/98; HBG 10/98; SLJ 3/98)

5076 Shavick, Andrea. *You'll Grow Soon, Alex* (PS–1). Illus. by Russell Ayto. 2000, Walker $15.95 (0-8027-8736-3). 32pp. Alex tries everything including diet and exercise to hasten his growth but later decides that being tall has its disadvantages. (Rev: BL 10/15/00; SLJ 10/00)

5077 Simon, Norma. *I Am Not a Crybaby* (K–3). Illus. by Helen Cogancherry. 1989, Whitman LB

$14.95 (0-8075-3447-1). 40pp. A comforting book on emotions for primary grades. (Rev: BCCB 4/89; BL 4/15/89)

5078 Simon, Norma. *I Was So Mad!* (K–3). Illus. by Dora Leder. 1974, Whitman LB $13.95 (0-8075-3520-6); paper $5.95 (0-8075-3519-2). 40pp. Children catalog the things that make them mad and learn that adults get angry too.

5079 Simon, Norma. *I Wish I Had My Father* (2–4). Illus. by Arieh Zeldich. 1983, Whitman LB $13.95 (0-8075-3522-2). 32pp. A young boy wishes his divorced father was back with him.

5080 Slepian, Jan. *Emily Just in Time* (PS–1). Illus. by Glo Coalson. 1998, Putnam $15.99 (0-399-23043-2). 32pp. This picture book shows how little Emily masters new skills and abilities through maturation and conquering her fears. (Rev: BCCB 5/98; BL 4/15/98; HBG 10/98; SLJ 5/98)

5081 Smalls, Irene. *Because You're Lucky* (PS–3). Illus. by Michael Hays. 1997, Little, Brown $15.95 (0-316-79867-3). 32pp. A young boy goes to live with his aunt's family and arouses the hostility of his cousin. (Rev: BL 9/1/97; HBG 3/98; SLJ 10/97)

5082 Spalding, Andrea, and Janet Wilson. *Me and Mr. Mah* (K–3). Illus. 2000, Orca $14.95 (1-55143-168-8). 32pp. Young Ian misses his divorced father and the farm where he lived. When he shares these feelings with Mr. Mah, a Chinese neighbor, and shows him some treasures he has kept from the farm, the old man in turn shows Ian a box of small mementos from China. (Rev: BL 3/15/00; HBG 10/00; SLJ 3/00)

5083 Spelman, Cornelia Maude. *After Charlotte's Mom Died* (K–2). Illus. by Judith Friedman. 1996, Albert Whitman LB $13.95 (0-8075-0196-4). 32pp. Charlotte feels conflicting emotions, such as anger and fear, as she adjusts to her mother's death. (Rev: BL 4/15/96; SLJ 8/96)

5084 Spelman, Cornelia Maude. *Mama and Daddy Bear's Divorce* (PS–1). Illus. by Kathy Parkinson. 1998, Albert Whitman $13.95 (0-8075-5221-6). 32pp. Though animals are used as characters, this is a realistic story about the effects of divorce. It offers the comforting message that love continues even through separation. (Rev: BL 12/1/98; HBG 3/99; SLJ 9/98)

5085 Spinelli, Eileen. *Somebody Loves You, Mr. Hatch* (K–3). Illus. by Paul Yalowitz. 1991, Macmillan LB $16.00 (0-02-786015-9). 32pp. An antisocial man receives a huge box of chocolates from an unknown admirer. (Rev: BL 11/15/91; HB 11–12/91; SLJ 2/92)

5086 Stanek, Muriel. *All Alone After School* (2–3). Illus. by Gay Owens. 1985, Whitman $13.95 (0-8075-0278-2). 32pp. At first, Josh needs a lucky stone to help him cope with being alone after school while his mother works. (Rev: BCCB 4/85; BL 3/15/85; SLJ 9/85)

5087 Stanek, Muriel. *Don't Hurt Me, Mama* (1–3). Illus. by Helen Cogancherry. 1983, Whitman LB $13.95 (0-8075-1689-9). 32pp. A simple story of child abuse as seen through the eyes of a child.

5088 Steig, William. *Spinky Sulks* (K–3). Illus. 1988, Farrar paper $4.95 (0-374-46990-3). 32pp. Spinky is a first-class sulker but is forced to reconsider his position. (Rev: BCCB 12/88; BL 1/15/89; HB 3–4/89)

5089 Stein, Sara Bonnett. *About Dying* (1–3). Illus. by author. 1974, Walker $10.95 (0-8027-6172-0); paper $8.95 (0-8027-7223-4). 48pp. Sensitive portrayal of the death of a bird and of a grandfather. Also use: *About Handicaps* (1974); *Making Babies* (1974); *About Phobias; The Adopted One; On Divorce* (all 1979).

5090 Stolz, Mary. *Storm in the Night* (K–3). Illus. by Pat Cummings. 1988, HarperCollins LB $15.89 (0-06-025913-2); paper $5.95 (0-06-443256-4). 32pp. Grandfather tells Thomas, a young African American boy, of a time when he was afraid, in order to calm the child's fears about a dark, stormy night. (Rev: BL 2/1/88; HB 7–8/88; SLJ 3/88)

5091 Thompson, Mary. *Andy and His Yellow Frisbee* (1–3). Illus. by author. 1996, Woodbine $14.95 (0-933149-83-2). The story of an autistic child as seen through the eyes of a young classmate. (Rev: SLJ 1/97)

5092 Trottier, Maxine. *A Safe Place* (K–3). Illus. by Judith Friedman. 1997, Albert Whitman LB $13.95 (0-8075-7212-8). 24pp. At night, a little girl and her mother seek safety from an abusive daddy by going to a safe place, the white house on the hill. (Rev: BL 6/1–15/97; SLJ 5/97)

5093 Trottier, Maxine. *The Tiny Kite of Eddie Wing* (PS–2). Illus. by Al Van Mil. 1996, Kane/Miller $13.95 (0-916291-66-9). 28pp. Eddie Wing's family is so poor that they can't afford to buy him a kite. (Rev: BL 11/15/96; SLJ 12/96)

5094 Verniero, Joan C. *You Can Call Me Willy: A Story for Children About AIDS* (K–3). Illus. by Verdon Flory. Series: Books to Help Parents Help Their Children. 1995, Magination paper $8.95 (0-945354-60-6). A touching story of a third-grader who has AIDS and the intolerance and misunderstandings she faces at school. (Rev: SLJ 9/95)

5095 Vigna, Judith. *I Wish Daddy Didn't Drink So Much* (PS). Illus. by author. 1988, Whitman paper $5.95 (0-8075-3526-5). 32pp. A Christmas story told by a little girl whose father is an alcoholic. (Rev: BL 10/1/88; SLJ 1/89)

5096 Vigna, Judith. *My Two Uncles* (2–4). Illus. 1995, Albert Whitman LB $14.95 (0-8075-5507-X). 32pp. A little girl has difficulty understanding the hostility her grandfather feels toward her gay Uncle Ned and his partner, Phil. (Rev: BCCB 5/95; BL 4/15/95; SLJ 6/95)

5097 Vigna, Judith. *Saying Goodbye to Daddy* (K–2). Illus. 1991, Whitman LB $14.95 (0-8075-7253-5). 32pp. When her father is killed in a car accident, Clare goes through the phases of grieving. (Rev: BL 2/1/91; SLJ 3/91)

5098 Vigna, Judith. *When Eric's Mom Fought Cancer* (PS–3). Illus. 1993, Albert Whitman LB $14.95 (0-8075-8883-0). 32pp. Eric is frightened, confused, and, at times, angry when his mother undergoes various cancer treatments. (Rev: BL 10/1/93; SLJ 10/93)

5099 Viorst, Judith. *The Good-bye Book* (PS–K). Illus. by Kay Chorao. 1988, Macmillan $16.00 (0-689-31308-X). A young boy is absolutely dead set against his parents going out — until they leave and the baby-sitter reads aloud. (Rev: BL 2/15/88; SLJ 8/88)

5100 Viorst, Judith. *The Tenth Good Thing About Barney* (K–2). Illus. by Erik Blegvad. 1971, Macmillan $14.00 (0-689-20688-7); paper $4.99 (0-689-71203-0). 32pp. At a backyard funeral, a little boy tries to think of ten good things to say about his cat, Barney — but can come up with only nine.

5101 Waber, Bernard. *Ira Sleeps Over* (PS–2). Illus. by author. 1973, Houghton $15.00 (0-395-13893-0); paper $5.95 (0-395-20503-4). 48pp. When Ira is invited to sleep overnight at Reggie's house, he wants to go, but should he or shouldn't he take along his teddy bear?

5102 Watts, Jeri Hanel. *Keepers* (K–3). Illus. by Felicia Marshall. 1997, Lee & Low $15.95 (1-880000-58-X). 32pp. Kenyon feels guilty because he has bought a baseball glove with the money intended for Grandmother's 90th birthday present. (Rev: BL 1/1–15/98; HBG 3/98; SLJ 1/98)

5103 Williams, Sherley A. *Girls Together* (PS–3). Illus. by Synthia Saint James. 1999, Harcourt $16.00 (0-15-230982-9). 32pp. Set in a California housing project, this moving picture book describes the harsh living conditions that a migrant child faces every day. (Rev: BCCB 5/99; BL 2/15/99; HB 3–4/99; HBG 10/99; SLJ 6/99)

5104 Willis, Jeanne. *Susan Laughs* (PS–K). Illus. 2000, Holt $15.00 (0-8050-6501-6). 32pp. Susan is presented in a series of activities — laughing, singing, and swimming, for example — and on the last page is shown in her wheelchair. (Rev: BCCB 10/00; BL 8/00; HBG 3/01; SLJ 11/00)

5105 Winthrop, Elizabeth. *As the Crow Flies* (PS–3). Illus. by Joan Sandin. 1998, Clarion $15.00 (0-395-77612-0). 32pp. Michael spends an ideal week with his divorced father when Dad comes to visit him at his new home in Arizona. (Rev: BL 4/1/98; HBG 10/98; SLJ 6/98)

5106 Winton, Tim. *The Deep* (PS–2). Illus. by Karen Louise. 2000, Tricycle Pr. $14.95 (1-58246-024-8). 32pp. Alice is afraid to swim in the deep water near her home until some playful dolphins help her to overcome her fears. (Rev: BL 5/15/00; HBG 10/00; SLJ 7/00)

5107 Wishinsky, Frieda. *Each One Special* (PS–2). Illus. by H. Werner Zimmermann. 1999, Orca $14.95 (1-55143-122-X). 32pp. When a creative cake decorator is fired from his job, he takes up a related field — sculpting. (Rev: BL 1/1–15/99; HBG 10/99; SLJ 7/99)

5108 Woodson, Jacqueline. *Sweet, Sweet Memory* (K–3). Illus. by Floyd Cooper. 2001, Hyperion $14.99 (0-7868-0241-3). 32pp. Even though Grandpa is dead and she grieves for him, a young African American girl follows his advice that life must go on. (Rev: BL 2/15/01)

5109 Yolen, Jane. *Grandad Bill's Song* (K–2). Illus. by Melissa Mathis. 1994, Putnam $16.99 (0-399-21802-5). 32pp. After his grandfather's death, a young boy asks different members of his family what they remember most about him. (Rev: BL 7/94; SLJ 7/94)

5110 Zolotow, Charlotte. *The Old Dog* (PS–2). Illus. by James E. Ransome. 1995, HarperCollins LB $15.89 (0-06-024412-7). 32pp. Ben has problems coping with the death of his beloved dog. (Rev: BL 9/1/95; HB 11–12/95; SLJ 12/95)

REAL AND ALMOST REAL ANIMALS

5111 Abercrombie, Barbara. *Charlie Anderson* (PS–3). Illus. by Mark Graham. 1990, Macmillan LB $16.00 (0-689-50486-1). 32pp. Sarah and Elizabeth discover that the cat that spends only the night with them is leading a double life. (Rev: BCCB 11/90; BL 10/15/90; SLJ 12/90)

5112 Abercrombie, Barbara. *Michael and the Cats* (PS–2). Illus. by Mark Graham. 1993, Macmillan LB $13.95 (0-689-50543-4). 32pp. Michael has to use psychology to gain the friendship of his aunt's two cats. (Rev: BL 12/15/93; SLJ 10/93)

5113 Adlerman, Daniel. *Africa Calling: Nighttime Falling* (PS–1). Illus. by Kimberly Adlerman. 1996, Whispering Coyote $15.95 (1-879085-98-4). 32pp. A young girl tries to imagine her stuffed animals in their native African habitats. (Rev: BL 10/1/96; SLJ 9/96)

5114 Aliki. *At Mary Bloom's* (K–2). Illus. by author. 1983, Greenwillow LB $15.93 (0-688-02481-5). 32pp. When her pet mouse has babies, a little girl shares the excitement with a neighbor's household.

5115 Allen, Judy. *Seal* (K–3). Illus. by Tudor Humphries. 1994, Candlewick $14.95 (1-56402-145-9). 32pp. While vacationing on the coast of Greece, Jenny discovers a cave containing a colony of endangered Mediterranean monk seals. (Rev: BL 5/1/94; SLJ 4/94)

5116 Ancona, George, and Mary Beth Ancona. *Handtalk Zoo* (1–4). Illus. 1989, Macmillan $14.95 (0-02-700801-0). 32pp. Children with hearing problems sign the names of various animals during a fun day at the zoo. (Rev: BCCB 1/90; BL 10/1/89*; HB 11–12/89; SLJ 10/89)

5117 *Animal Homes* (PS–2). Illus. Series: What's Inside? 1993, DK $8.95 (1-56458-218-3). 17pp. After seeing a picture of the exterior of an animal habitation, readers get an inside view by peeling back the diagram. (Rev: BL 8/93) [591]

5118 Aragon, Jane C. *Salt Hands* (K–2). Illus. by Ted Rand. 1994, Puffin paper $5.99 (0-140-50321-8). 24pp. When a little girl sprinkles salt on her palm, a deer comes to her. (Rev: BL 9/15/89; SLJ 11/89)

5119 Archambault, John. *The Birth of a Whale* (K–2). Illus. by Janet Skiles. 1996, Silver Burdett LB $18.95 (0-382-39566-2). 48pp. In rhythmic verse and watercolor illustrations, the birth of a humpback whale is chronicled. (Rev: BL 3/15/96; SLJ 3/96) [599.5]

5120 Arno, Iris Hiskey. *I Like a Snack on an Iceberg* (PS). Illus. by John Sandford. 1999, Harper-Festival $9.95 (0-694-01176-2). 24pp. This picture book for preschoolers introduces a number of animals and their favorite foods. (Rev: BL 11/1/99; HBG 3/00; SLJ 11/99)

5121 Arnosky, Jim. *Big Jim and the White-Legged Moose* (PS–3). Illus. 1999, Lothrop LB $15.93 (0-688-10865-2). 32pp. An artist, Big Jim, is treed by a moose in this fact-based story. (Rev: BL 8/99; HBG 10/99; SLJ 6/99)

5122 Arnosky, Jim. *Little Lions* (PS). Illus. 1998, Putnam $15.99 (0-399-22944-2). 32pp. A simple picture book that reports on the playful activities of two mountain lion cubs and their ever-watchful mother. (Rev: BL 3/1/98; HBG 10/98; SLJ 3/98)

5123 Arnosky, Jim. *A Manatee Morning* (PS–1). Illus. 2000, Simon & Schuster $16.00 (0-689-81604-9). 32pp. A manatee mother and her baby enjoy playing in the waters of Florida's Crystal River. (Rev: BL 10/15/00; HBG 3/01; SLJ 9/00)

5124 Arnosky, Jim. *Otters Under Water* (PS–1). Illus. 1992, Putnam $14.95 (0-399-22339-8). 32pp. Minimal text and full-color artwork tell of two young otters swimming in the pond with mother watching. (Rev: BL 9/1/92; SLJ 8/92) [599.74]

5125 Arrigoni, Patricia. *Harpo: The Baby Harp Seal* (2–3). Illus. 1995, Travel Publishers $16.95 (0-9625468-8-7). 32pp. Harpo, a baby harp seal, is rescued by a little girl when he is separated from his mother. (Rev: BL 2/1/96)

5126 Asch, Frank. *The Last Puppy* (PS–2). Illus. by author. 1989, Simon & Schuster paper $4.95 (0-671-66687-8). 32pp. An enchanting story of the puppy born last in a large litter.

5127 Asher, Sandy. *Stella's Dancing Days* (PS–1). Illus. by Kathryn Brown. 2001, Harcourt $16.00 (0-15-201613-9). 32pp. A cat's view of a family, from her arrival as a kitten until she has a litter of her own. (Rev: BL 3/15/01)

5128 Ashman, Linda. *Castles, Caves, and Honeycombs* (PS–K). Illus. by Lauren Stringer. 2001, Harcourt $16.00 (0-15-202211-2). 32pp. Animal homes — nests, shells, dens, or hollow logs — are pictured in drawings and rhyming verse. (Rev: BL 3/15/01*)

5129 Baker, Karen Lee. *Seneca* (PS–3). Illus. 1997l, Greenwillow $15.00 (0-688-14030-0). 32pp. In this picture book, a young girl tells how she has chosen her horse and how she rides him and takes care of him. (Rev: BCCB 3/97; BL 4/1/97; SLJ 4/97)

5130 Balian, Lorna. *Amelia's Nine Lives* (PS–K). Illus. by author. 1986, Humbug LB $13.95 (0-687-01250-3). 32pp. Nora's black cat, Amelia, is missing, but when friends keep bringing black cats to replace it, Nora knows the difference. (Rev: BL 12/1/86; SLJ 2/87)

5131 Banks, Kate. *Baboon* (PS–K). Illus. by Georg Hallensleben. 1997, Farrar $14.00 (0-374-30474-2). 32pp. A mother introduces her baby baboon to the intricacies of the great world. (Rev: BCCB 4/97; BL 3/1/97*; HB 5–6/97; SLJ 3/97)

5132 Banks, Merry. *Animals of the Night* (PS–2). Illus. by Ronald Himler. 1990, Macmillan $13.95 (0-684-19093-1). 32pp. A parade of nocturnal animals is pictured in soft, dusky colors. (Rev: BCCB 6/90; BL 3/1/90; HB 3–4/90; SLJ 5/90) [599]

5133 Barner, Bob. *Fish Wish* (PS–K). Illus. 2000, Holiday $16.95 (0-8234-1482-5). 32pp. Collages are used to illustrate this fanciful picture book about a boy who dreams of being a fish and encountering all the creatures in a coral reef. (Rev: BL 2/1/00; HBG 10/00; SLJ 5/00)

5134 Barton, Byron. *Bones, Bones, Dinosaur Bones* (PS–K). Illus. 1990, HarperCollins LB $15.89 (0-690-04827-0). 32pp. Paleontologists collect a number of bones and reconstruct a dinosaur. (Rev: BL 10/15/90; HB 11–12/90*; SLJ 9/90)

5135 Bernard, Robin. *Juma and the Honey Guide* (PS–3). Illus. by Nneka Bennett. 1996, Dillon LB $18.95 (0-382-39162-4); paper $5.95 (0-382-39164-0). 32pp. A young African boy and his father share a honeycomb with a small bird that has led them to the beehive. (Rev: BL 8/96; SLJ 8/96)

5136 Blake, Robert J. *Akiak: A Tale from the Iditarod* (PS–3). Illus. 1997, Putnam $16.99 (0-399-22798-9). 32pp. An aging sled dog named Akiak participates in the Iditarod sled race for the last time. (Rev: BL 9/1/97; HBG 3/98; SLJ 9/97*)

5137 Blake, Robert J. *Dog* (K–3). Illus. 1994, Putnam $14.95 (0-399-22019-4). 32pp. Gradually, a stray dog insinuates itself into the life of a grumpy old man in this story set in Ireland. (Rev: BL 3/15/94; SLJ 5/94)

5138 Blake, Robert J. *Fledgling* (PS–3). Illus. 2000, Putnam $15.99 (0-399-23321-0). 32pp. A fledgling kestrel spends an exciting day in New York City when he takes his first flight. (Rev: BL 12/15/00; HB 1–2/01; HBG 3/01; SLJ 10/00)

5139 Blanc, Esther S. *Berchick* (1–3). Illus. by Tennessee Dixon. 1989, Volcano $14.95 (0-912078-81-2). Mama takes care of a colt found beside its dead mother. (Rev: SLJ 11/89)

5140 Braun, Trudi. *My Goose Betsy* (PS–1). Illus. by John Bendall-Brunello. 1999, Candlewick $16.99 (0-7636-0449-6). 32pp. A young narrator introduces readers to his pet goose and her behavioral habits, such as settling on her nest to hatch her eggs. (Rev: BCCB 6/99; BL 4/1/99*; HB 5–6/99; HBG 10/99; SLJ 4/99)

5141 Brenner, Barbara, and Julia Takaya. *Chibi: A True Story from Japan* (K–3). Illus. by June Otani. 1996, Clarion $14.95 (0-395-69623-2). 63pp. In this photographic essay, an actual wild duck family upsets daily life when it decides to change homes in downtown Tokyo. (Rev: BL 2/15/96; HB 7–8/96; SLJ 3/96*) [598.4]

5142 Breslow, Susan, and Sally Blakemore. *I Really Want a Dog* (PS–3). Illus. by True Kelley. 1993, Puffin paper $4.99 (0-140-54941-2). 40pp. A youth confronts an enormous doglike cloud in the sky. (Rev: BL 6/1/90; HB 7–8/90; SLJ 7/90)

5143 Brown, Alan. *The Windhover* (K–3). Illus. by Christian Birmingham. 1997, Harcourt $17.00 (0-15-201187-0). 32pp. Told from the falcon's, or windhover's, point of view, this story tells how the young bird is captured by a boy who wants to make him his pet. (Rev: BL 11/1/97; HBG 3/98; SLJ 1/98)

5144 Brown, Margaret Wise. *Big Red Barn* (PS–1). Illus. by Felicia Bond. 1989, HarperCollins LB $15.95 (0-06-020749-3). 32pp. The big red barn contains lots and lots of animals and their offspring. (Rev: BL 3/1/89; SLJ 6/89)

5145 Brown, Margaret Wise. *Bumble Bee* (PS). Illus. by Victoria Raymond. Series: Harper Growing Tree. 1999, HarperFestival $5.95 (0-694-01749-3). This 1959 poem about an active bumblebee is now in a board book format with bright illustrations. (Rev: SLJ 7/99)

5146 Brown, Margaret Wise. *Wheel on the Chimney* (PS–3). Illus. by Tibor Gergely. 1954, Harper-Collins LB $13.00 (0-397-30296-7). 32pp. Hungarian storks return each spring from Africa to nest on farmers' chimneys. A 1955 Caldecott Honor Book.

5147 Browne, Philippa-Alys. *Kangaroos Have Joeys* (PS–1). Illus. 1996, Simon & Schuster $15.00 (0-689-81040-7). 26pp. The offspring of animals — e.g., "moose have calves," "rabbits have kits" — are described and pictured. (Rev: BL 11/1/96; SLJ 11/96) [591.3]

5148 Buck, Nola. *Oh, Cats!* (PS–1). Illus. by Nadine Bernard Westcott. 1997, HarperCollins LB $12.89 (0-06-025374-6). 32pp. A little girl tries to befriend three very independent cats. (Rev: BL 11/15/96; SLJ 2/97)

5149 Bunting, Eve. *Red Fox Running* (PS–3). Illus. by Wendell Minor. 1993, Houghton $15.95 (0-395-58919-3). 30pp. A story about a hungry fox that hunts until it kills a bobcat to bring home to his family. (Rev: BL 11/15/93; SLJ 12/93)

5150 Burningham, John. *Hey! Get Off Our Train* (K–3). Illus. 1990, Crown paper $7.99 (0-517-88204-3). 48pp. A boy's dream takes him on a train trip around the world where he sees environmental dangers. (Rev: BCCB 4/90; BL 5/15/90; HB 5–6/90; SLJ 5/90)

5151 Bushey, Jeanne. *A Sled Dog for Moshi* (K–3). Illus. by Germaine Arnaktauyok. 1994, Hyperion LB $15.49 (1-56282-632-8). 40pp. A sled dog saves two Inuit children during a storm. (Rev: BL 1/15/95; SLJ 1/95)

5152 Bushnell, Jack. *Circus of the Wolves* (1–3). Illus. by Robert Andrew Parker. 1994, Lothrop $15.00 (0-688-12554-9). 32pp. The story of Kael, a timber wolf, and his life after being captured to become part of a traveling circus. (Rev: BL 4/1/94; SLJ 4/94)

5153 Bushnell, Jack. *Sky Dancer* (K–3). Illus. by Jan Ormerod. 1996, Lothrop LB $15.93 (0-688-05289-4). 32pp. Jenny tries to save a red-tailed hawk from being shot by local farmers. (Rev: BL 9/15/96; SLJ 9/96)

5154 Butler, John. *Pi-Shu, the Little Panda* (K–2). Illus. 2001, Peachtree $15.95 (1-56145-242-4). 32pp. The daily activities of a baby panda named Pi-shu are recounted in this picture book that also gives information on why this is an endangered species. (Rev: BL 3/15/01)

5155 Cameron, Alice. *The Cat Sat on the Mat* (PS–K). Illus. by Carol Jones. 1994, Houghton $13.95 (0-395-68392-0). 32pp. In this interactive book, a restless cat has difficulty settling down. (Rev: BL 12/15/94; SLJ 10/94)

5156 Campbell, Rod. *Dear Zoo* (PS). Illus. by author. 1983, Puffin paper $4.95 (0-317-62180-7). 22pp. A youngster keeps sending back the pets requested from a zoo until a puppy arrives.

5157 Capucilli, Alyssa Satin. *Inside a Barn in the Country: A Rebus Read-Along Story* (PS–K). Illus. by Tedd Arnold. 1995, Scholastic $10.95 (0-590-46999-1). 32pp. Using simple verses, this game book also teaches the sounds that animals make. (Rev: BL 1/15/95; SLJ 4/95)

5158 Carle, Eric. *Does a Kangaroo Have a Mother, Too?* (PS–1). Illus. 2000, HarperCollins LB $16.89 (0-06-028767-5). 32pp. In this simple book about wildlife, 12 young animals are presented along with their mothers. (Rev: BCCB 4/00; BL 1/1–15/00; HBG 10/00; SLJ 4/00) [591.3]

5159 Carle, Eric. *Have You Seen My Cat?* (PS–2). Illus. by author. 1991, Picture Book $16.00 (0-88708-054-5). A small boy loses his cat, sees many other felines, and returns home to find that his cat has had kittens. A reissue of a 1973 title.

5160 Carle, Eric. *The Very Hungry Caterpillar* (PS–2). Illus. by author. 1981, Putnam $19.99 (0-399-20853-4). 32pp. A caterpillar eats a great deal and then spins its cocoon.

5161 Carrick, Carol. *Lost in the Storm* (K–3). Illus. by Donald Carrick. 1987, Houghton paper $6.95 (0-89919-493-1). 32pp. The story of a dog, lost overnight in a storm, who is found in the morning by his owner and safely sheltered under a flight of stairs.

5162 Carrick, Carol. *Mothers Are Like That* (PS–1). Illus. by Paul Carrick. 2000, Clarion $15.00 (0-395-88351-2). 32pp. This tender picture book shows how various animals keep their offspring clean including a human mother and child. (Rev: BL 3/15/00; HB 3–4/00; HBG 10/00; SLJ 5/00)

5163 Caseley, Judith. *Mr. Green Peas* (PS–K). Illus. 1995, Greenwillow $14.93 (0-688-12860-2). 32pp. Norman's classmates won't believe him when he tells them he has a pet iguana at home. (Rev: BL 2/15/95; SLJ 4/95)

5164 Chekhov, Anton. *Kashtanka* (K–3). Illus. by Gennady Spirin. 1995, Gulliver $16.00 (0-15-200539-0). In this story set in 19th-century Russia, a lost dog is found by a circus performer. (Rev: SLJ 12/95)

5165 Christian, Peggy. *Chocolate, a Glacier Grizzly* (K–3). Illus. by Carol Cottone-Kolthoff. 1997, Benefactory $12.95 (1-882728-63-7). 32pp. The story of a female grizzly bear in Glacier National Park from her birth to the birth of her own cubs years later. (Rev: SLJ 11/97)

5166 Cimarusti, Marie Torres. *Peek-a-Moo!* (PS). Illus. by Stephanie Peterson. 1998, Dutton $9.99 (0-525-46083-7). A flap book that introduces seven familiar farm animals and the sounds they make. (Rev: SLJ 11/98)

5167 Climo, Lindee. *Chester's Barn* (2–4). Illus. by author. 1995, Tundra paper $6.95 (0-88776-351-0). The story in words and pictures of life in a Prince Edward Island barn on a winter afternoon.

5168 Coffelt, Nancy. *Good Night, Sigmund* (PS–1). Illus. 1992, Harcourt $13.95 (0-15-200464-5). 40pp. The artwork is a show stealer in this story of a young boy and his pet cat. (Rev: BL 2/15/92; SLJ 5/92)

5169 Cole, Joanna. *My New Kitten* (PS–1). Illus. by Margaret Miller. 1995, Morrow $14.93 (0-688-12902-1). 40pp. A photo-essay about a young girl getting to know and love her new kitten. (Rev: BCCB 6/95; BL 3/1/95; HB 5–6/95; SLJ 4/95) [636.8]

5170 Cole, William. *Have I Got Dogs!* (PS–1). Illus. by Margot Apple. 1996, Puffin paper $4.99 (0-140-54195-0). 32pp. Different dogs are introduced in rhyming couplets and engaging cartoonlike drawings. (Rev: BL 8/93)

5171 Cowcher, Helen. *Jaguar* (K–2). Illus. 1997, Scholastic $15.95 (0-590-29937-9). 32pp. When an armed hunter finally corners the jaguar that has been killing his cattle, he is so enthralled by its beauty that he cannot shoot it. (Rev: BL 10/15/97; HBG 3/98; SLJ 8/97)

5172 Cowcher, Helen. *Tigress* (PS–1). Illus. 1991, Farrar $14.95 (0-374-37567-4). 40pp. A park ranger must do his best to save the life of a marauding tigress. (Rev: BCCB 11/91; BL 12/1/91; HB 1–2/92; SLJ 12/91*)

5173 Cummings, Pat. *Purrrrr* (PS). Illus. by author. Series: Harper Growing Tree. 1999, HarperFestival $5.95 (0-694-01056-1). In this board book, an African American boy tries to get his lazy cat to join him in his various activities. (Rev: SLJ 8/99)

5174 Cutler, Jane. *Mr. Carey's Garden* (K–3). Illus. by G. Brian Karas. 1996, Houghton $14.95 (0-395-68191-X). 32pp. Eveyone offers free advice on how Mr. Carey can rid his garden of snails. (Rev: BL 3/15/96; HB 5–6/96; SLJ 5/96)

5175 Dalgliesh, Alice. *The Bears on Hemlock Mountain* (1–4). Illus. by Helen Sewell. 1990, Macmillan paper $4.99 (0-689-71604-4). 64pp. Jonathan ventured over the mountain by himself after dark and discovered the reality of bear existence!

5176 Davenport, Zoe. *Animals* (PS). Illus. 1995, Ticknor $5.95 (0-395-71537-7). 16pp. A simple concept book that introduces vocabulary related to various animals. (Rev: BL 2/1/95; SLJ 8/95) [599]

5177 Davis, Katie. *Who Hoots?* (PS–K). Illus. 2000, Harcourt $14.00 (0-15-202312-7). 36pp. This fun book delightfully presents animals that hoot, buzz, squeak, roar, and quack, and those that don't. (Rev: BL 10/1/00; HBG 3/01; SLJ 12/00)

5178 Davis, Patricia A. *Brian's Bird* (K–3). Illus. by Layne Johnson. 2000, Albert Whitman $14.95 (0-8075-0881-0). 32pp. Brian, a visually impaired youngster, is devastated when his pet bird, Scratchy, flies away, but with the help of his older brother he is able to recapture him. (Rev: BL 2/15/00; HBG 10/00; SLJ 5/00)

5179 Day, Nancy Raines. *A Kitten's Year* (PS–1). Illus. by Anne Mortimer. 2000, HarperCollins LB $14.89 (0-06-027231-7). 32pp. Using realistic paintings and a simple text, this lovely picture book traces the development of a kitten over a 12-month period. (Rev: BL 12/15/99*; HBG 10/00; SLJ 4/00)

5180 DeFelice, Cynthia. *Clever Crow* (PS–1). Illus. by S. D. Schindler. 1998, Simon & Schuster $16.00 (0-689-80671-X). 32pp. A young girl outsmarts a crow into dropping a set of car keys it has stolen, but the clever bird has other tricks to play. (Rev: BL 5/1/98; HBG 10/98; SLJ 6/98)

5181 Denslow, Sharon P. *Hazel's Circle* (PS–2). Illus. by Sharon McGinley-Nally. 1992, Macmillan $14.95 (0-02-728683-5). 32pp. A young girl named Hazel takes her pet rooster, Ike, for a walk to visit her neighbors. (Rev: BL 5/1/92; SLJ 1/93)

5182 De Zutter, Hank. *Who Says a Dog Goes Bow-Wow?* (PS–K). Illus. by Suse MacDonald. 1997, Dell paper $5.99 (0-440-41338-9). 32pp. Various animal sounds as they are interpreted in various languages are presented. (Rev: BL 5/15/93; SLJ 8/93) [418]

5183 DiSalvo-Ryan, DyAnne. *A Dog Like Jack* (PS–2). Illus. 1999, Holiday $15.95 (0-8234-1369-1). 32pp. Mike and his dog Jack share many years together, and when the dog dies, Mike grieves but learns to celebrate his friend's life. (Rev: BL 3/1/99; HBG 10/99; SLJ 4/99)

5184 Disher, Garry. *Switch Cat* (PS–2). Illus. by Andrew McLean. 1995, Ticknor $14.95 (0-395-71643-8). 32pp. Two very different girls have equally mismatched cats as pets. (Rev: BL 3/15/95; SLJ 3/95*)

5185 Dixon, Ann. *Blueberry Shoe* (PS–3). Illus. by Evon Zerbetz. 1999, Alaska Northwest $15.95 (0-88240-518-7); paper $8.95 (0-88240-519-5). 32pp. Several Alaskan animals are introduced in this story of a lost red sneaker and how each of the animals that finds it changes it. (Rev: BL 10/15/99; HBG 3/00; SLJ 12/99)

5186 Doherty, Berlie. *Paddiwak and Cozy* (PS–1). Illus. by Alison Bartlett. 1999, Orchard $14.95 (0-531-30180-X). 32pp. Instant dislike develops when new cat Cozy is introduced into Sally's house and meets Paddiwak, the cat-in-residence. (Rev: BL 8/99; HBG 3/00; SLJ 10/99)

5187 Doner, Kim. *Buffalo Dreams* (K–4). 1999, Graphic Arts $16.95 (1-55868-475-1); paper $9.95 (1-55868-476-X). 40pp. When her little brother angers the mother of a rare white buffalo, Sarah must summon up the courage to rescue him. (Rev: BL 1/1–15/00; HBG 3/00; SLJ 2/00)

5188 Donohue, Dorothy. *Big and Little on the Farm* (PS). Illus. 1999, Golden Bks. $9.95 (0-307-10225-4). 24pp. Each pair of pages shows a different adult farm animal followed by a picture of its baby. (Rev: BL 4/1/99; HBG 10/99; SLJ 4/99)

5189 Doyle, Malachy. *Well, a Crocodile Can! Flip-up Flaps and Pop-up Tricks* (PS–K). Illus. by Britta Teckentrup. 1999, Millbrook $12.95 (0-7613-1032-0). Pop-ups and flaps are used to show a variety of different animals performing amazing tricks that are true to their nature — like an elephant wiggling its ears. (Rev: SLJ 3/00)

5190 Duffey, Betsy. *A Boy in the Doghouse* (2–4). Illus. by Leslie Morrill. 1993, Simon & Schuster paper $3.95 (0-671-86698-2). 56pp. George must train his dog, Lucky, or face having him be returned to the pound. (Rev: BL 12/1/91; SLJ 9/91)

5191 Duffey, Betsy. *The Wild Things* (1–3). Illus. by Susanna Natti. Series: Duffey's Pet Patrol. 1995, Puffin paper $3.99 (0-140-34998-7). 80pp. Megan and Evie get involved in solving who or what is getting into the trash cans. (Rev: BL 3/1/93; SLJ 4/93)

5192 Dunbar, Joyce. *Four Fierce Kittens* (PS–K). Illus. by Jakki Wood. 1992, Scholastic $13.95 (0-590-45535-4). 32pp. Four kittens think they are fierce but cannot frighten the other farm animals. (Rev: BL 6/1/92; SLJ 4/92)

5193 Dunn, Judy. *The Little Puppy* (PS–K). Illus. by Phoebe Dunn. 1984, Random paper $3.25 (0-394-86595-2). 32pp. The story of a little boy who must care for his first puppy.

5194 Ericsson, Jennifer A. *No Milk!* (PS–2). Illus. by Ora Eitan. 1993, Morrow $15.93 (0-688-11307-9). A dairy cow refuses to be persuaded by a city boy to give milk. (Rev: SLJ 6/93*)

5195 Erlbruch, Wolf. *Mrs. Meyer the Bird* (PS–2). Illus. 1997, Orchard LB $15.99 (0-531-33017-6). 32pp. Mrs. Meyer is a born worrier until she finds an injured bird to take care of and take her mind off her problems. (Rev: BCCB 5/97; BL 4/1/97; SLJ 4/97)

5196 Ernst, Lisa Campbell. *Cat's Play* (PS). Illus. 2000, Viking $5.99 (0-670-89116-9). 14pp. A young toddler enjoys playful activities with a cat in this board book. (Rev: BCCB 4/00; BL 10/1/00; SLJ 7/00)

5197 Ets, Marie Hall. *Just Me* (PS–K). Illus. by author. 1965, Puffin paper $5.99 (0-14-050325-0). 32pp. A little boy imagines he can match the antics of his animal friends as he spends an afternoon at solitary play.

5198 Ets, Marie Hall. *Play with Me* (PS–K). Illus. by author. 1955, Puffin paper $5.99 (0-14-050178-9). 32pp. A little girl finds a playmate among the meadow creatures when she finally learns to sit quietly and not frighten them.

5199 Evans, Katie. *Hunky Dory Ate It* (PS). Illus. by Janet M. Stoeke. 1996, Puffin paper $4.99 (0-140-55856-X). 32pp. A pup named Hunky Dory gets into trouble because of his uncontrollable appetite. (Rev: BL 2/1/92; SLJ 3/92)

5200 *Farm Animals* (PS). Illus. Series: Eye Openers. 1991, Macmillan $8.99 (0-689-71403-3). 24pp. In eight double-page spreads, eight farm animals are introduced with many smaller drawings and accompanying text. Also use in this series: *Zoo Animals* (1991). (Rev: BL 6/15/91) [636]

5201 Faulkner, Keith. *The Big Yawn* (PS–1). Illus. by Jonathan Lambert. 1999, Millbrook $9.95 (0-7613-1029-0). Using tabs and cutaways, this interactive book pictures the creatures of a rain forest and how they settle in for the night. (Rev: BCCB 12/99; SLJ 11/99)

5202 Faulkner, Keith. *David Dreaming of Dinosaurs* (K–2). Illus. by Jonathan Lambert. 1992, Fantasy $13.00 (1-56021-182-2). 12pp. David dreams of dinosaurs and they appear in foldout illustrations. (Rev: BL 11/15/92)

5203 Flack, Marjorie. *Angus and the Ducks* (K–2). Illus. by author. 1997, Farrar paper $5.95 (0-374-40385-6). 40pp. Angus, the Scottish terrier, and his amusing adventures. Other titles in this series are: *Angus and the Cat* and *Angus Lost* (both 1989).

5204 Fleming, Denise. *Barnyard Banter* (PS–1). Illus. 1994, Holt $16.95 (0-8050-1957-X). 32pp. All the farm animals greet Goose with their appropriate sounds as she tours the farmyard. (Rev: BCCB 5/94; BL 5/1/94; HB 5–6/94; SLJ 5/94*)

5205 Fleming, Denise. *In the Tall, Tall Grass* (PS–1). Illus. 1991, Holt $16.95 (0-8050-1635-X). 32pp. An excellent story-hour book in which a caterpillar munches through the tall, tall grass, watching nature along the way. (Rev: BL 10/1/91*; HB 1–2/92*; SLJ 9/91*)

5206 Florian, Douglas. *Turtle Day* (PS–2). Illus. 1989, HarperCollins LB $15.89 (0-690-04745-2). 32pp. A day in the life of a turtle. (Rev: BL 10/15/89; HB 11–12/89; SLJ 11/89)

5207 Ford, Miela. *Bear Play* (PS–1). Illus. 1995, Greenwillow $14.89 (0-688-13833-0). 24pp. The antics of two playful polar bear cubs are captured in a simple text and large color photographs. (Rev: BL 1/1–15/96; SLJ 11/95)

5208 Ford, Miela. *Little Elephant* (PS–K). Illus. by Tana Hoban. 1994, Greenwillow LB $14.93 (0-688-13141-7). 24pp. A baby zoo elephant decides to go into the pool in his cage by himself in this book illustrated with amazing color photos. (Rev: BL 6/1–15/94; HB 5–6/94; SLJ 7/94*)

5209 Ford, Miela. *Mom and Me* (PS–3). Illus. 1998, Greenwillow $15.00 (0-688-15889-7). 24pp. Using amazing photographs, this simple picture book depicts the playful antics of a mother polar bear and her cub. (Rev: BL 8/98; HBG 3/99; SLJ 9/98)

5210 Fox, Mem. *Zoo-Looking* (PS–1). Illus. by Candace Whitman. 1996, Mondo $14.95 (1-57255-010-4). 28pp. Flora is happy when the animals at the zoo seem to look back at her. (Rev: BCCB 7–8/96; BL 6/1–15/96; SLJ 7/96)

5211 Fox-Davies, Sarah. *Little Caribou* (PS–2). Illus. 1996, Candlewick $14.99 (1-56402-923-9). 32pp. The first year in the life of a caribou is traced, with details on the behavior of the herd. (Rev: BL 12/1/96; SLJ 12/96)

5212 French, Vivian. *Growing Frogs* (K–3). Illus. by Alison Bartlett. 2000, Candlewick $15.99 (0-7636-0317-1). 29pp. A nicely illustrated story about a mother and daughter who gather frog spawn and cultivate it until there are adult frogs to return to their pond. (Rev: HB 5–6/00; HBG 10/00; SLJ 5/00)

5213 French, Vivian. *Whale Journey* (K–3). Illus. by Lisa Flather. 1998, Zero to Ten $14.95 (1-84089-022-3). 32pp. Beginning with his birth, this book traces the journey north to Alaskan waters of gray whale Little Grey and his mother and a friend. (Rev: BL 1/1–15/99; HBG 3/99)

5214 Frost, Jonathan. *Gowanus Dogs* (K–4). Illus. 1999, Farrar $16.00 (0-374-31058-0). 48pp. Wild, hungry dogs and a homeless man help one another in this tale set under an expressway in Brooklyn, New York. (Rev: BL 4/15/99; HBG 10/99; SLJ 6/99)

5215 Gackenbach, Dick. *A Bag Full of Pups* (PS–1). Illus. by author. 1983, Houghton paper $5.95 (0-89919-179-7). 32pp. A little boy would like one of the pups Mr. Mullen is giving away.

5216 Gag, Wanda. *Millions of Cats* (PS–1). Illus. by author. 1996, Putnam paper $5.99 (0-698-11363-2). 112pp. A wonderful picture book about an old man looking for a cat who suddenly finds himself with millions.

5217 Galvin, Laura Gates. *Bumblebee at Apple Tree Lane* (1–3). Illus. by Kristin Kest. 2000, Soundprints $15.95 (1-56899-820-1). 31pp. This fictional account of the queen bumblebee follows her life from waking from hibernation in the spring to crawling underground when winter approaches. (Rev: HBG 3/01; SLJ 3/01)

5218 Gammell, Stephen. *Once Upon MacDonald's Farm . . .* (K–3). Illus. by author. 1990, Simon & Schuster paper $4.95 (0-689-71379-7). 32pp. MacDonald tries to populate his farm with circus animals. Originally published in 1981.

5219 Garrett, Ann, and Gene-Michael Higney. *What's for Lunch?* (PS–K). Illus. 1999, Dutton $9.99 (0-525-46251-1). Each spread contains a picture of an animal and clues about its food; then a flap can be pulled to get the answer. (Rev: BL 12/15/99; HBG 3/00; SLJ 12/99)

5220 Geeslin, Campbell. *On Ramon's Farm: Five Tales of Mexico* (PS–2). Illus. by Petra Mathers. 1998, Simon & Schuster $16.00 (0-689-81134-9). 48pp. A bilingual book of short stories involving Ramon, his farm animals, and his daily chores. (Rev: BL 12/15/98; SLJ 3/99)

5221 George, Jean Craighead. *Elephant Walk* (PS–2). Illus. by Anna Vojtech. Series: Animal Kingdom. 1998, Disney $13.95 (0-7868-3163-4). 32pp. As a baby elephant, his mother, and other elephants walk through the savanna, the reader learns about elephant behavior and an important habitat. (Rev: BL 12/1/98; HBG 3/99)

5222 George, Jean Craighead. *Giraffe Trouble* (K–2). Illus. by Anna Vojtech. Series: Animal Kingdom. 1998, Disney $12.95 (0-7868-3167-7). 32pp. Cam, a young giraffe, strays too far from home and is almost eaten by a lion. (Rev: BL 8/98; HBG 10/98; SLJ 3/99)

5223 George, Jean Craighead. *Look to the North: A Wolf Pup Diary* (K–4). Illus. by Lucia Washburn. 1997, HarperCollins LB $15.89 (0-06-023640-X). 32pp. A description of a year in the lives of three wolf cubs and how they adjust to each of the seasons. (Rev: BL 4/15/97; SLJ 4/97)

5224 George, Jean Craighead. *Rhino Romp* (K–2). Illus. by Stacey Schuett. 1998, Disney $12.95 (0-7868-3164-2). 32pp. This is the story of little Simu,

a young rhino who gets lost while playfully chasing other animals. (Rev: BL 8/98; HBG 10/98; SLJ 3/99)

5225 George, Jean Craighead. *Snow Bear* (K–3). Illus. by Wendell Minor. 1999, Hyperion $15.99 (0-7868-0456-4). 32pp. Bessie, an Inuit child, and a polar bear cub play together under the watchful eyes of the bear's mother and the child's older brother. (Rev: BL 8/99; HBG 3/00; SLJ 9/99)

5226 George, Lindsay Barrett. *Around the World: Who's Been Here?* (K–3). Illus. 1999, Greenwillow LB $15.93 (0-688-15269-4). 40pp. Different animals are introduced in this question-and-answer game involving a trip around the world and a series of different locales. (Rev: BL 8/99; HB 3–4/99; HBG 10/99; SLJ 4/99)

5227 Gill, Shelly. *Alaska's Three Bears* (PS–2). Illus. by Shannon Cartwright. 1990, Paws Four $15.95 (0-934007-10-1); paper $8.95 (0-934007-11-X). 32pp. In a folklike tale, three types of Alaskan bears — polar bears, black bears, and grizzlies — are introduced. (Rev: BL 3/1/91)

5228 Gliori, Debi. *The Snow Lambs* (PS–3). Illus. 1996, Scholastic $15.95 (0-590-20304-5). 40pp. Young Sam worries about the safety of the family's sheepdog during severe winter weather. (Rev: BCCB 2/97; BL 11/15/96*; SLJ 10/96)

5229 Goble, Paul. *The Girl Who Loved Wild Horses* (K–2). Illus. by author. 1982, Macmillan LB $17.00 (0-02-736570-0); paper $5.99 (0-689-71696-6). 32pp. A mystical story of a girl and her love for a black stallion. Caldecott Medal winner, 1979.

5230 Golembe, Carla. *Annabelle's Big Move* (PS–1). Illus. 1999, Houghton $12.00 (0-395-91543-0). 32pp. When the family she lives with moves, Annabelle the dog is confused and a little frightened by all the activity, including being put in a crate that goes on an airplane. (Rev: BL 4/15/99; HBG 10/99; SLJ 5/99)

5231 Gove, Doris. *One Rainy Night* (K–4). Illus. by Walter L. Krudop. 1994, Atheneum $14.95 (0-689-31800-6). 32pp. During a nocturnal walk in the Blue Ridge Mountains, a boy and his mother gather small animals, like a baby box turtle and salamanders, for her nature center. (Rev: BL 3/15/94; SLJ 6/94)

5232 Graham, Bob. *Queenie, One of the Family* (PS–1). Illus. 1997, Candlewick $15.99 (0-7636-0359-7). 32pp. When Caitlin's dad rescues a hen from the lake, the family doesn't realize that they have acquired a faithful pet. (Rev: BL 1/1–15/98*; HBG 3/98; SLJ 11/97*)

5233 Graham, John. *I Love You, Mouse* (K–2). Illus. by Tomie dePaola. 1990, Harcourt paper $3.95 (0-15-644106-3). 32pp. A tender book about how a young boy would feel if he were several different animals.

5234 Greene, Carol. *Where Is That Cat?* (PS–K). Illus. by Loretta Krupinski. 1999, Hyperion $14.99 (0-7868-0457-2). 32pp. Miss Perkins brings home a stray cat she names Fitz, and when various people come to see if it is their cat, Fitz hides, although an observant reader can spot him. (Rev: BL 9/1/99; HBG 3/00; SLJ 8/99)

5235 Griffith, Helen V. *"Mine Will," Said John* (PS–3). Illus. by Joseph A. Smith. 1992, Greenwillow LB $13.93 (0-688-10958-6). 32pp. John's parents try different pets until they hit on the perfect one, a puppy. (Rev: BL 10/1/92; SLJ 10/92)

5236 Grindley, Sally. *Little Elephant Thunderfoot* (K–2). Illus. by John Butler. 1999, Peachtree $15.95 (1-56145-180-0). After his grandmother is killed by poachers in an African savanna, Little Elephant must find a new home and adjust to a new herd. (Rev: HBG 3/00; SLJ 2/00)

5237 Grindley, Sally. *Little Sibu: An Orangutan Tale* (PS–2). Illus. by John Butler. 1999, Peachtree $15.95 (1-56145-196-7). Little Sibu is now 7 and his mother must force him to leave her and live on his own as other male orangutans do. (Rev: HBG 10/99; SLJ 5/99)

5238 Grindley, Sally. *Polar Star* (K–3). Illus. by John Butler. 1998, Peachtree $15.95 (1-56145-181-9). A beautifully illustrated story about Polar Star, her cubs, and their activities in the cold land they call home. (Rev: HBG 3/99; SLJ 12/98)

5239 Grooms, Molly. *We Are Bears* (PS–1). Illus. by Lucia Guarnotta. 2000, NorthWord $12.95 (1-55971-747-5). 32pp. A mother bear takes her two cubs out on a nature walk. (Rev: BL 12/15/00)

5240 Guthrie, Arlo. *Mooses Come Walking* (PS–K). Illus. by Alice M. Brock. 1995, Chronicle $11.95 (0-8118-1051-8). 32pp. A picture book that gives advice to youngsters when moose come visiting at night. (Rev: BL 12/15/95)

5241 Haas, Jessie. *Chipmunk!* (PS–2). Illus. by Joseph A. Smith. 1993, Greenwillow $13.93 (0-688-11875-5). 24pp. When a chipmunk enters a household and wants to escape, mayhem results. (Rev: BL 10/15/93; SLJ 2/94)

5242 Haas, Jessie. *Mowing* (PS–1). Illus. by Joseph A. Smith. 1994, Greenwillow $14.00 (0-688-11680-9). 32pp. While Gramp and Nora mow a field with a horse-drawn mower, they leave spaces uncut to protect a fawn and a killdeer nest. (Rev: BL 6/1–15/94; HB 5–6/94; SLJ 7/94)

5243 Haas, Jessie. *No Foal Yet* (1–3). Illus. by Joseph A. Smith. 1995, Greenwillow LB $15.93 (0-688-12956-9). 24pp. Nora becomes impatient waiting for her horse Bonnie to give birth; but when it finally happens, no one is around. (Rev: BL 5/15/95; HB 5–6/95; SLJ 6/95)

5244 Hale, Irina. *The Naughty Crow* (K–3). Illus. 1992, Macmillan LB $14.95 (0-689-50546-9). 32pp. In a story set in czarist Russia, a naughty crow is banished from the household that has adopted him. (Rev: BL 11/5/92; SLJ 10/92)

5245 Hall, Derek. *Baby Animals: Five Stories of Endangered Species* (PS–1). Illus. by John Butler. 1992, Candlewick $14.95 (1-56402-004-5). 64pp. Each of the five stories in this volume features a young animal from a different habitat and tells how each is separated from and then reunited with its parents. (Rev: BL 3/15/92)

5246 Hall, Jacque. *What Does the Rabbit Say?* (PS–K). Illus. by Reg Cartwright. 2000, Doubleday $15.95 (0-385-32552-5). A merry picture book that

introduces all the different sounds that animals make. (Rev: HBG 10/00; SLJ 4/00)

5247 Hardy, Tad. *Lost Cat* (PS–2). Illus. by David Goldin. 1996, Houghton $14.95 (0-395-73574-2). A lost cat produces different reactions in the distraught master who has lost her and in the man who finds her. (Rev: HB 7–8/96; SLJ 6/96)

5248 Harjo, Joy. *The Good Luck Cat* (PS–3). Illus. by Paul Lee. 2000, Harcourt $16.00 (0-15-232197-7). Having used up eight of her nine lives, Woogie, a cat, disappears and everyone fears the worse. (Rev: BCCB 4/00; HBG 10/00; SLJ 4/00)

5249 Harper, Isabelle. *My Cats Nick and Nora* (PS–1). Illus. by Barry Moser. 1995, Scholastic $14.95 (0-590-47620-3). 32pp. Isabelle and cousin Emmie spend every Sunday taking care of the family pets, Nick and Nora. A sequel to *My Dog Rosie* (1994). (Rev: BL 10/1/95; SLJ 10/95)

5250 Harper, Isabelle. *Our New Puppy* (PS–1). Illus. by Barry Moser. 1996, Scholastic $14.95 (0-590-56926-0). 32pp. Rosie gradually grows to love the family's new puppy. (Rev: BL 9/1/96; SLJ 10/96)

5251 Hazen, Barbara S. *Stay, Fang* (K–3). Illus. by Leslie Morrill. 1990, Macmillan LB $13.95 (0-689-31599-6). 32pp. Large, furry Fang can't bear to be parted from his young master. (Rev: BL 2/15/90; SLJ 6/90)

5252 Hazen, Barbara S. *Tight Times* (2–3). Illus. by Trina S. Hyman. 1979, Puffin paper $5.99 (0-14-050442-7). 32pp. A child is allowed to keep a stray kitten even though there are hard times in the household.

5253 Heinz, Brian J. *Nanuk: Lord of the Ice* (1–3). Illus. by Gregory Manchess. 1998, Dial $15.99 (0-8037-2194-3). 27pp. Nanuk, a polar bear, feels he is lord of the ice until a boy, his dogs, and hunting sled pursue him. Luckily he escapes to become, once again, lord of the ice. (Rev: BCCB 12/98; BL 1/1–15/99; HBG 3/99; SLJ 11/98)

5254 Helmer, Marilyn. *Fog Cat* (PS–2). Illus. by Paul Mombourquette. 1999, Kids Can $14.95 (1-55074-460-7). 32pp. Hannah manages, in foggy weather, to get a wild cat to come indoors — but only long enough to have her litter and leave again. (Rev: BL 3/15/99; HBG 10/99; SLJ 5/99)

5255 Helmer, Marilyn. *Mr. McGratt and the Ornery Cat* (PS–3). Illus. by Martine Gourbault. 1999, Kids Can $14.95 (1-55074-564-6). At first Mr. McGratt wants to get rid of the cat that has moved in but, in time, he realizes he has found the perfect pet. (Rev: HBG 3/00; SLJ 12/99)

5256 Hendry, Diana. *Dog Donovan* (PS–2). Illus. by Margaret Chamberlain. 1995, Candlewick $13.95 (1-56402-537-3). 32pp. Members of the Donovan family conquer their fears when they find a dog they must protect. (Rev: BL 3/1/95; SLJ 4/95)

5257 Herriot, James. *Blossom Comes Home* (1–3). Illus. by Ruth Brown. 1988, St. Martin's paper $6.95 (0-312-09131-1). 32pp. Farmer Dakin is sad to sell Blossom the cow, but happy when she escapes and returns home. (Rev: BL 12/1/88; HB 1–2/89)

5258 Herriot, James. *Moses the Kitten* (PS–3). Illus. by Peter Barrett. 1984, St. Martin's paper $6.95 (0-312-06419-5). 32pp. The story of a stray black kitten and how it was saved.

5259 Herriot, James. *Smudge, the Little Lost Lamb* (1–3). Illus. by Ruth Brown. 1991, St. Martin's $12.95 (0-312-06404-7). 32pp. Smudge, a new twin lamb, gets into trouble when he pushes under the fence and goes free. (Rev: BL 1/15/92)

5260 Herzig, Alison C. *Bronco Busters* (PS–3). Illus. by Kimberly B. Root. 1998, Putnam $15.99 (0-399-22917-5). 32pp. When three tough bronco-busters are unable to tame a black pony, a small cowboy succeeds simply by using kindness. (Rev: BCCB 10/98; BL 9/15/98; HBG 3/99; SLJ 1/99)

5261 Hindley, Judy. *The Best Thing About a Puppy* (PS–1). Illus. by Patricia Casey. 1998, Candlewick $10.99 (0-7636-0596-4); paper $3.29 (0-7636-0597-2). 24pp. Detailed artwork helps emphasize all the fun in this picture book in which a little boy describes what he likes most — and least — about his puppy. (Rev: BL 11/1/98; HBG 3/99; SLJ 10/98)

5262 Hines-Stephens, Sarah. *Bean's Games* (PS). Illus. by Anna Grossnickle Hines. 1998, Harcourt $4.95 (0-15-201606-6). A board book showing Bean, a small black cat, in various activities. (Rev: SLJ 7/98)

5263 Hirschi, Ron. *What Is a Cat?* (PS–K). Illus. by Linda Q. Younker. 1991, Walker LB $14.85 (0-8027-8123-3). 32pp. An attractive book for young browsers to enjoy. (Rev: BL 1/15/92; SLJ 11/91) [599.7]

5264 Hirschi, Ron. *What Is a Horse?* (PS–2). Illus. by Linda Q. Younker and Ron Hirschi. 1989, Walker LB $12.85 (0-8027-6877-6). 32pp. This introduction includes material on structure, habits, and uses of the horse. Also use: *Where Do Horses Live?* (1989). (Rev: BL 8/89; SLJ 1/90) [636.1]

5265 Hirschi, Ron. *Where Do Cats Live?* (PS–K). Illus. by Linda Q. Younker. 1991, Walker LB $14.85 (0-8027-8110-1). 32pp. A visually appealing book that shows cats living alone, together, indoors, outdoors, everywhere. (Rev: BL 1/15/92; SLJ 11/91) [636.8]

5266 Holsonback, Anita. *Monkey See, Monkey Do: An Animal Exercise Book for You!* (PS–K). Illus. by Leo Timmers. 1997, Millbrook LB $20.90 (0-7613-0260-3). Each page features an animal in its natural habitat along with a drawing of a boy and girl who mimic the way the creature moves and a verse. (Rev: HBG 3/98; SLJ 1/98)

5267 Hooper, Meredith. *Tom's Rabbit: A Surprise on the Way to Antarctica* (K–3). Illus. by Bert Kitchen. 1998, National Geographic $15.95 (0-7922-7070-3). 32pp. Based on fact, this is the story of a pet rabbit that was on Robert Scott's expedition to Antarctica in December 1910 and how she gave birth to 17 babies on Christmas Day. (Rev: BL 11/1/98; HBG 3/99; SLJ 10/98)

5268 Horowitz, Ruth. *Crab Moon* (K–4). Illus. by Kate Kiesler. 2000, Candlewick $15.99 (0-7636-0709-6). 32pp. During the first full moon in June, Daniel and his mother go down to the beach to watch the horseshoe crabs fertilize and bury their eggs. (Rev: BL 8/00; HBG 10/00; SLJ 5/00)

5269 Houk, Randy. *Chessie, the Travelin' Man* (K–3). Illus. by Paula Bartlett. 1997, Benefactory $12.95 (1-882728-56-4). 32pp. The story of a Florida manatee and his trips from the South to Port Judith, Rhode Island, in 1994 and 1995. (Rev: SLJ 11/97)

5270 Hubbell, Patricia. *Bouncing Time* (PS). Illus. by Melissa Sweet. 2000, HarperCollins LB $15.89 (0-688-17377-2). 32pp. A delightful rhyming poem about a mother with a child in a backpack who visit a zoo and watch the animals at play. (Rev: BCCB 5/00; BL 4/1/00; HBG 10/00; SLJ 7/00)

5271 Huneck, Stephen. *Sally Goes to the Beach* (K–3). Illus. 2000, Abrams $17.95 (0-8109-4186-4). 38pp. Simple color woodcuts are used to illustrate this dog's-eye view of a day at the beach. (Rev: BCCB 11/00; BL 5/15/00; HBG 10/00; SLJ 6/00)

5272 Hutchins, Hazel. *One Duck* (K–2). Illus. by Ruth Ohi. 1999, Annick LB $18.95 (1-55037-561-X); paper $6.95 (1-55037-560-1). A duck whose nest is in the way of an oncoming tractor is helped by a considerate farmer. (Rev: HBG 3/00; SLJ 10/99)

5273 Ingman, Bruce. *Lost Property* (PS–3). Illus. 1998, Houghton $15.00 (0-395-88900-6). 32pp. When things get lost in Maurice's house, everyone wants to blame Mac, the dog, but is he the culprit? (Rev: BL 4/15/98; HBG 10/98; SLJ 4/98)

5274 Isadora, Rachael. *A South African Night* (PS–K). Illus. 1998, Greenwillow $14.89 (0-688-11390-7). 24pp. As the people of Johannesburg go home after a day's work and prepare for bed, many of the animals in the Kruger National Park begin their nocturnal activities. (Rev: BCCB 4/98; BL 2/15/98; HBG 10/98; SLJ 8/98)

5275 James, Ellen Foley. *Little Bull: Growing Up in Africa's Elephant Kingdom* (K–3). Illus. 1998, Sterling $12.95 (0-8069-2098-X). 48pp. This picture book uses color photographs to chronicle the first experiences of a young elephant — standing up, playing with his family, and observing other animals on the plains. (Rev: BL 9/15/98; HBG 10/99; SLJ 11/98)

5276 James, Shirley K. *Going to a Horse Farm* (1–3). Illus. by Laura Jacques. 1992, Charlesbridge $15.95 (0-88106-477-7). 32pp. Two children visit a horse farm to see a new foal. (Rev: BL 6/1/92) [636.1]

5277 James, Simon. *The Wild Woods* (PS–1). Illus. 1993, Candlewick $13.95 (1-56402-219-6). 32pp. Jess realizes that the squirrel she would like to keep as a pet should remain free in the woods. (Rev: BL 10/15/93; SLJ 10/93)

5278 Johnson, Herschel. *A Visit to the Country* (1–3). Illus. by Romare Bearden. 1989, HarperCollins $13.95 (0-06-022849-0). 32pp. Mike nurses an injured cardinal back to health but knows he must return it to the wild. (Rev: BL 9/15/89; SLJ 12/89)

5279 Johnson, Paul B., and Celeste Lewis. *Lost* (PS–2). Illus. by Paul Johnson. 1996, Orchard LB $16.99 (0-531-08851-0). 32pp. While camping out in Arizona's Tonto National Forest, a young girl's dog wanders off and gets lost. (Rev: BCCB 3/96; BL 4/1/96; SLJ 4/96*)

5280 Johnston, Tony. *The Barn Owls* (PS–3). Illus. by Deborah Kogan Ray. 2000, Charlesbridge $15.95 (0-88106-981-7). 32pp. Eloquent pictures and text describe the activities of a family of barn owls. (Rev: BL 2/15/00; HBG 10/00; SLJ 3/00)

5281 Jonas, Ann. *Bird Talk* (K–2). Illus. 1999, Greenwillow LB $14.93 (0-688-14173-0). 32pp. About 65 different species of birds comment on a garden being seeded, with each bird identified by name at the back of this imaginative nature book. (Rev: BCCB 5/99; BL 6/1–15/99; HBG 10/99; SLJ 4/99)

5282 Jonas, Ann. *Two Bear Cubs* (1–3). Illus. by author. 1982, Greenwillow $15.93 (0-688-01408-9). 24pp. A mother bear shepherds her two cubs through some everyday adventures.

5283 Joosse, Barbara M. *Nugget and Darling* (K–3). Illus. by Sue Truesdell. 1997, Clarion $14.95 (0-395-64571-9). 32pp. The dog Nugget becomes jealous when his young mistress pays attention to a stray kitten. (Rev: BL 3/1/97; SLJ 4/97)

5284 Kasperson, James. *Little Brother Moose* (PS–3). Illus. by Karlyn Holman. 1995, Dawn paper $7.95 (1-883220-33-5). 32pp. A young moose who wanders into town finds his way home by following migrating geese. (Rev: BL 7/95; SLJ 10/95)

5285 Kasza, Keiko. *When the Elephant Walks* (PS–K). Illus. 1997, Putnam paper $5.95 (0-698-11430-2). 32pp. In this cumulative tale, each animal has another bigger than himself to be frightened of. (Rev: BCCB 5/90; BL 3/1/90; HB 5–6/91; SLJ 6/90)

5286 Kerr, Janet. *The Quiet Little Farm* (PS–1). Illus. 2000, Holt $15.95 (0-8050-5869-9). 32pp. Tinted photographs show how a quiet farm is transformed in the spring when new animals are born. (Rev: BL 4/1/00; HBG 10/00; SLJ 8/00)

5287 Kessler, Cristina. *Jubela* (PS–3). Illus. by JoEllen M. Stammen. 2001, Simon & Schuster $16.00 (0-689-81895-5). 32pp. Based on a true story, this handsome picture book tells how an orphaned baby rhino is cared for by a surrogate mother who teaches him survival skills. (Rev: BL 2/1/01; SLJ 3/01)

5288 Ketteman, Helen. *Grandma's Cat* (PS–K). Illus. by Marsha Winborn. 1996, Houghton $16.00 (0-395-73094-5). 32pp. A little girl has trouble befriending her grandmother's independent cat. (Rev: BL 4/1/96; SLJ 5/96)

5289 Killilea, Maria. *Newf* (PS–3). Illus. by Ian Schoenherr. 1992, Putnam $14.95 (0-399-21875-0). 32pp. This picture book tells about a loving relationship between a kitten and a large Newfoundland dog. (Rev: BCCB 10/92; BL 12/1/92; SLJ 10/92)

5290 King, Deborah. *The Flight of the Snow Geese* (K–2). Illus. 1998, Orchard $15.95 (0-531-30088-9). 32pp. In verses accompanied by watercolor paintings, the author tells of the annual journey of snow geese from their tundra home to warmer climates. (Rev: BL 9/15/98; HBG 3/99; SLJ 11/98)

5291 King-Smith, Dick. *All Pigs Are Beautiful* (PS–3). Illus. by Anita Jeram. 1993, Candlewick $14.95 (1-56402-148-3). 32pp. In simple prose and watercolors, the habits and behavior of pigs are introduced. (Rev: BCCB 5/93; BL 5/1/93; HB 7–8/93*) [636.4]

5292 Koralek, Jenny. *Cat and Kit* (PS–2). Illus. by Patricia MacCarthy. 1995, Hyperion LB $14.49 (0-7868-2030-6). 32pp. Cat rescues Kit, but in time the young kitten returns to the wild where he belongs. (Rev: BL 7/95; SLJ 9/95)

5293 Kroll, Steven. *Andrew Wants a Dog* (2–4). Illus. by Molly Delaney. 1992, Little, Brown LB $12.49 (1-56282-119-9). 54pp. Seven-year-old Andrew wants a dog so much that he dresses up like one to get his parents to agree. (Rev: BL 5/15/92; SLJ 7/92)

5294 Kroll, Steven. *Oh, Tucker!* (PS–K). Illus. by Scott Nash. 1998, Candlewick $15.99 (0-7636-0429-1). 32pp. A loving, very large pup bounds through the house leaving destruction and mayhem behind in his quest for his human family. (Rev: BL 5/1/98; HBG 10/98; SLJ 7/98)

5295 Kroll, Steven. *Patches Lost and Found* (K–3). Illus. by Barry Gott. 2001, Winslow $16.95 (1-890817-53-8). 32pp. Jenny loves to draw pictures but can't write stories, so she draws pictures of her pet hamster and fills in the words of a story afterward. (Rev: BL 3/1/01*)

5296 Kroll, Virginia. *Motherlove* (PS–2). Illus. by Lucia Washburn. 1998, Dawn $16.95 (1-883220-81-5); paper $7.95 (1-883220-80-7). In rhyming text, the role of mothers in the animal kingdom is explored with paintings of various animal mothers and their offspring. (Rev: HBG 3/99; SLJ 3/99) [591.56]

5297 Kvasnosky, Laura McGee. *Mr. Chips!* (PS–2). Illus. 1996, Farrar $15.00 (0-374-35092-2). 32pp. Ellie is distraught when her dog, Mr. Chips, gets lost and the family must move without him. (Rev: BCCB 11/96; BL 7/96; SLJ 8/96)

5298 Lawson, Julie. *Bear on the Train* (PS–2). Illus. by Brian Deines. 1999, Kids Can $14.95 (1-55074-560-3). 32pp. Bear enters the hopper of a train to eat some grain and becomes so comfortable that he hibernates there all winter. (Rev: BL 10/15/99; HBG 3/00; SLJ 11/99)

5299 Leedy, Loreen. *Mapping Penny's World* (PS–2). Illus. 2000, Holt $17.00 (0-8050-6178-9). 32pp. Using her newly learned map skills, Penny draws maps of the territory covered by her pet boxer, Lisa. (Rev: BCCB 9/00; BL 7/00; HBG 3/01; SLJ 9/00)

5300 Lesser, Carolyn. *Dig Hole, Soft Mole* (K–3). Illus. by Laura Regan. 1996, Harcourt $15.00 (0-15-223491-8). 32pp. A marsh mole has many underground and underwater adventures and meets a number of other marshland creatures. (Rev: BL 10/1/96; SLJ 12/96)

5301 Lesser, Carolyn. *Great Crystal Bear* (K–3). Illus. by William Noonan. 1996, Harcourt $15.00 (0-15-200667-2). 32pp. The author pictures how polar bears survive their hostile environment. (Rev: BL 5/1/96; SLJ 6/96)

5302 Lewin, Betsy. *Booby Hatch* (PS–2). Illus. 1995, Clarion $14.95 (0-395-68703-9). 32pp. The life of the Galapagos Islands' booby is told in charming double-page spreads. (Rev: BL 3/1/95; SLJ 5/95*)

5303 Lewin, Ted. *Nilo and the Tortoise* (K–3). Illus. by author. 1999, Scholastic $16.95 (0-590-69004-0). Young Nilo is stranded overnight on one of the Galapagos Islands and shares sleeping quarters with a giant tortoise. (Rev: BL 8/99; SLJ 4/99)

5304 Lewis, Kim. *Emma's Lamb* (PS–K). Illus. 1998, Candlewick $15.99 (0-7636-0424-0). 32pp. Even though Emma showers her pet lamb with affection, she realizes he needs his mother. (Rev: BL 3/15/91; HBG 10/98; SLJ 7/91)

5305 Lewis, Kim. *Floss* (PS–3). 1992, Candlewick $14.95 (1-56402-010-X). 32pp. A young Border collie has some trouble learning to be a sheep herder. (Rev: BL 2/15/92; SLJ 4/92)

5306 Lewis, Kim. *Just Like Floss* (PS–1). Illus. 1998, Candlewick $15.99 (0-7636-0684-7). 32pp. When father says that the family can keep only one of Floss's pups, they choose Sam because he behaves just like his mother. (Rev: BCCB 11/98; BL 1/1–15/99; HB 11–12/98; HBG 3/99; SLJ 1/99)

5307 Lewis, Kim. *Little Calf* (PS). Illus. 2000, Candlewick $9.99 (0-7636-0899-8). 24pp. A little girl plays with a newborn calf, strokes its face, touches its nose, and sees it take its first steps. Also use *Little Lamb* and *Little Puppy*. (Rev: BL 3/15/00; HBG 10/00; SLJ 6/00)

5308 Lindenbaum, Pija. *Boodil, My Dog* (K–3). 1992, Holt $14.95 (0-8050-1444-1); paper $5.95 (0-8050-3940-6). 48pp. Bull terrier Boodil is spoiled rotten, but to the young narrator, she can do no wrong. (Rev: BCCB 12/92*; BL 12/1/92; SLJ 2/93)

5309 Lindgren, Barbro. *Rosa: Perpetual Motion Machine* (PS–2). Illus. by Eva Eriksson. 1996, Douglas & McIntyre $14.95 (1-55054-241-9). 32pp. A mischievous pup breaks her lease, runs away, and gets lost. (Rev: BL 6/1–15/96; SLJ 7/96)

5310 Lipkind, William, and Nicolas Mordvinoff. *Finders Keepers* (K–3). Illus. by Nicolas Mordvinoff. 1951, Harcourt $14.95 (0-15-227529-0); paper $7.00 (0-15-630950-5). 32pp. Two dogs have a dispute over one bone but unite against a common enemy. Caldecott Medal winner, 1952.

5311 Lobel, Arnold. *The Rose in My Garden* (PS–3). Illus. by Anita Lobel. 1984, Morrow paper $6.95 (0-688-12265-5). 40pp. A cumulative tale that starts with a bee sleeping on a rose.

5312 London, Jonathan. *At the Edge of the Forest* (PS–K). Illus. by Barbara Firth. 1998, Candlewick $15.99 (0-7636-0014-8). 32pp. A young boy tells how his father gets a shepherd dog instead of killing the coyote that is destroying their sheep. (Rev: BL 12/1/98; HBG 3/99; SLJ 11/98)

5313 London, Jonathan. *Baby Whale's Journey* (1–3). Illus. by Jon Van Zyle. 1999, Chronicle $14.95 (0-8118-2496-9). 35pp. A poetic introduction to the life of a sperm whale from its birth through weaning to final acceptance by the pod as they feed on a giant squid. (Rev: BL 11/1/99; HBG 3/00; SLJ 1/00)

5314 London, Jonathan. *Ice Bear and Little Fox* (K–3). Illus. by Daniel San Souci. 1998, Dutton $15.99 (0-525-45907-3). 40pp. A realistic story of a polar bear's first year without its mother and the symbiotic relationship it develops with an arctic fox. (Rev: BL 1/1–15/99; HBG 3/99; SLJ 1/99)

5315 London, Jonathan. *Phantom of the Prairie: Year of the Black-footed Ferret* (PS–2). Illus. by Barbara Bash. 1998, Sierra Club $16.95 (0-87156-387-8). 32pp. Though the animals are anthropomorphized, this story of Phantom, a black-footed ferret, gives authentic details of the animal's life cycle. (Rev: BL 7/98; HBG 10/98; SLJ 8/98)

5316 London, Jonathan. *Red Wolf Country* (PS–2). Illus. by Daniel San Souci. 1996, Dutton $15.99 (0-525-45191-9). 32pp. She-Wolf and her mate search for a place to make a den so that she may safely have her litter. (Rev: BCCB 6/96; BL 1/1–15/96; SLJ 3/96*)

5317 London, Jonathan. *Wiggle Waggle* (PS). Illus. by Michael Rex. 1999, Harcourt $13.00 (0-15-201940-5). 32pp. Using double-page spreads, this book amusingly explains how various animals walk. (Rev: BL 5/15/99; HBG 10/99; SLJ 6/99)

5318 Longfellow, Layne. *Imaginary Menagerie* (PS–1). Illus. by Woodleigh Hubbard. 1997, Chronicle $10.95 (0-8118-0797-5). A puzzle book in which readers look through a cut-out square and guess what the animal is on the following page. (Rev: BL 1/1–15/98; HBG 3/98; SLJ 2/98)

5319 Losordo, Stephen. *Cow Moo Me* (PS). Illus. by Jane Conteh-Morgan. Series: Harper Growing Tree. 1998, HarperFestival $5.95 (0-694-01108-8). In a series of two-page spreads, common animals engage in humorous activities with accompanying rhyming text. (Rev: BL 12/15/98; SLJ 2/99)

5320 Luenn, Nancy. *Otter Play* (PS–2). Illus. by Anna Vojtech. 1998, Simon & Schuster $16.00 (0-689-81126-8). 32pp. A family of otters and a human family seem to echo each other's actions in this gentle picture book. (Rev: BL 3/15/98; HBG 10/98; SLJ 7/98)

5321 Lyon, George E. *Ada's Pal* (PS–1). Illus. by Marguerite Casparian. 1996, Orchard LB $16.99 (0-531-08878-2). 32pp. Ada pines away when her companion, the other dog in the family, dies. (Rev: BL 9/15/96; SLJ 9/96)

5322 Lyon, George E. *A Traveling Cat* (PS–1). Illus. by Paul Johnson. 1998, Orchard $15.95 (0-531-30102-8). 32pp. A little girl cares for a stray cat and tends to her litter. When the cat later disappears, the girl realizes that she is a born traveler. (Rev: BL 11/15/98; HB 11–12/98; HBG 3/99; SLJ 9/98)

5323 McDonald, Megan. *Insects Are My Life* (PS–2). Illus. by Paul Johnson. 1995, Orchard LB $16.99 (0-531-08724-7). 32pp. No one seems to understand

Amanda's fascination with insects. (Rev: BCCB 4/95; BL 3/1/95; HB 3–4/95; SLJ 3/95*)

5324 McDonald, Megan. *Whoo-oo Is It?* (PS–1). Illus. by S. D. Schindler. 1992, Orchard LB $16.99 (0-531-08574-0). 32pp. A mother owl oversees the hatching of her egg in this book that explores the sounds of the night. (Rev: BL 2/1/92; HB 5–6/92; SLJ 4/92)

5325 McGeorge, Constance W. *Boomer Goes to School* (PS–K). Illus. by Mary Whyte. 1996, Chronicle $14.95 (0-8118-1117-4). 32pp. Boomer, a golden retriever, becomes a hero during show-and-tell when he visits his young master's school. (Rev: BL 4/15/96; SLJ 7/96)

5326 McGeorge, Constance W. *Boomer's Big Day* (PS–2). Illus. by Mary Whyte. 1994, Chronicle $14.95 (0-8118-0526-3). 32pp. Boomer, a dog, is a bystander as the family prepares to move, but eventually he is transported to his new home. (Rev: BL 7/94)

5327 McGraw, Sheila. *Pussycats Everywhere!* (PS–2). Illus. by author. 2000, Firefly LB $19.95 (1-55209-346-8); paper $6.95 (1-55209-348-4). When Karen's cat wanders away and she places lost-cat posters everywhere, 37 cats are brought to her house. (Rev: HBG 3/01; SLJ 12/00)

5328 McGuirk, Leslie. *Tucker Flips!* (PS–K). Illus. 1999, Dutton $9.99 (0-525-46259-7). 32pp. Tucker is the most adventurous of the three new puppies, particularly when he hops on a sled and does a flip after the sled hits a bump. (Rev: BL 1/1–15/00; HBG 3/00; SLJ 12/99)

5329 McKenna, Virginia. *Back to the Blue* (K–3). Illus. by Ian Andrew. Series: Born Free Wildlife Book/Templar Book. 1998, Millbrook LB $21.40 (0-7613-0409-6). Based on fact, these are accounts of real animal rescue and relocation projects run by the conservation charity Born Free Foundation. (Rev: BL 8/98; HBG 10/98; SLJ 3/98)

5330 MacLeod, Elizabeth. *I Heard a Little Baa* (PS). Illus. by Louise Phillips. 1998, Kids Can $7.95 (1-55074-496-8). 24pp. An animal guessing game in which different animal riddles-in-rhyme are solved by unfolding pages. (Rev: HBG 3/99; SLJ 12/98)

5331 McMillan, Bruce. *Gletta the Foal* (PS–2). Illus. 1998, Marshall Cavendish $14.95 (0-7614-5039-4). 32pp. An Icelandic foal tells her own story as she plays with other horses, adjusts to her family, and experiences new emotions. Captivating photos accompany the imaginative text. (Rev: BL 9/15/98; HBG 3/99; SLJ 12/98)

5332 McNeal, Tom, and Laura McNeal. *The Dog Who Lost His Bob* (K–2). Illus. by John Sandford. 1996, Albert Whitman LB $15.95 (0-8075-1662-7). 32pp. Phil, a dog that hates baths, escapes this ordeal but becomes lost as a result. (Rev: BCCB 10/96; BL 9/1/96; SLJ 11/96)

5333 McNulty, Faith. *The Lady and the Spider* (K–3). Illus. by Bob Marstall. 1986, HarperCollins $15.00 (0-06-024191-8); paper $5.95 (0-06-443152-5). 48pp. The reader enters the small world of the

spider, who lives on a head of lettuce in a garden and feels part of it. (Rev: BL 3/15/86; SLJ 9/86)

5334 McNulty, Faith. *A Snake in the House* (K–4). Illus. by Ted Rand. 1994, Scholastic $14.95 (0-590-44758-0). 32pp. A captured garter snake escapes in a boy's house and eventually is successful in getting back to his pond. (Rev: BCCB 2/94; BL 5/1/94; SLJ 3/94)

5335 Madrigal, Antonio H. *Blanca's Feather* (1–4). Illus. by Gerardo Suzan. 2000, Rising Moon $15.95 (0-87358-743-X). 32pp. On Saint Francis of Assisi's Day, Rosalia can't find her hen to take to church to be blessed and brings one of her feathers instead. (Rev: BL 4/15/00; HBG 10/00; SLJ 7/00)

5336 Mahy, Margaret. *Making Friends* (K–4). Illus. by Wendy Smith. 1990, Macmillan $13.95 (0-689-50498-5). Two dogs bring their lonely owners together. (Rev: HB 5–6/90; SLJ 8/90)

5337 Mantegazza, Giovanna. *The Hippopotamus* (PS–1). Illus. by Paola Marchi. 1992, Boyds Mills $6.95 (1-56397-033-3). 12pp. Absorbing facts about hippos for young readers in this Italian board book. (Rev: BL 6/15/92; SLJ 8/92) [599.734]

5338 Marsh, T. J., and Jennifer Ward. *Way Out in the Desert* (PS–2). Illus. by Kenneth J. Spengler. 1998, Rising Moon $15.95 (0-87358-687-5). 32pp. Using double-page spreads, familiar animals of the desert are presented in a delightful takeoff on "Over in the Meadow." (Rev: BCCB 5/98; HBG 10/98; SLJ 6/98)

5339 Martin, Ann M. *Leo the Magnificat* (K–3). Illus. by Emily Arnold McCully. 1996, Scholastic $15.95 (0-590-48498-2). 32pp. A nomadic cat finds a home in a community church. (Rev: BCCB 12/96; BL 9/1/96; SLJ 11/96)

5340 Martin, Bill, Jr. *Polar Bear, Polar Bear, What Do You Hear?* (PS–K). Illus. by Eric Carle. 1991, Holt $15.95 (0-8050-1759-3). 32pp. Animal sounds from ten different animals are featured in this picture book. (Rev: BCCB 12/91; BL 11/15/91; HB 1–2/92; SLJ 11/91*)

5341 Martin, Jacqueline B. *Washing the Willow Tree Loon* (2–4). Illus. by Nancy Carpenter. 1995, Simon & Schuster $16.00 (0-689-80415-6). 40pp. A fictionalized account of how an oil-slicked loon is saved by a woman who, with others, tries to save animals after an oil barge hits a bridge. (Rev: BL 12/15/95; HB 9–10/95; SLJ 10/95)

5342 Marzollo, Jean. *Mama Mama* (PS). Illus. by Laura Regan. Series: Harper Growing Tree. 1999, HarperFestival $5.95 (0-694-01245-9). This board book celebrates the tender mother-child relations that exist with such animals as a lioness, leopard, chimpanzee, panda, elephant, and sea otter. (Rev: SLJ 11/99)

5343 Masurel, Claire. *No, No, Titus!* (PS–K). Illus. by Shari Halpern. 1997, North-South LB $15.88 (1-55858-726-8). 28pp. When the dog Titus wonders what his role will be on the farm his owners have moved to, he finds it is to frighten off the fox. (Rev: BL 6/1–15/97)

5344 Mazer, Anne. *The Salamander Room* (PS–1). Illus. by Steve Johnson. 1991, Knopf LB $17.99 (0-

394-92945-4). 32pp. A young boy tries to get permission from his mother to keep a salamander. (Rev: BL 2/15/91; SLJ 4/91)

5345 Meeker, Clare Hodgson. *Who Wakes Rooster?* (PS). Illus. by Megan Halsey. 1996, Simon & Schuster $13.00 (0-689-80541-1). 32pp. Only when the rooster finally crows does the day officially begin and all the farm animals waken. (Rev: BL 11/1/96; SLJ 9/96)

5346 Meggs, Libby Phillips. *Go Home! The True Story of James the Cat* (K–3). Illus. 2000, Albert Whitman $15.95 (0-8075-2975-3). 32pp. This picture book, based on a true story, chronicles the plight of a lost cat that survives in a hostile environment through a winter and into late summer. (Rev: BL 3/1/00; HBG 10/00; SLJ 8/00)

5347 Miller, Edna. *Patches Finds a New Home* (K–2). Illus. by author. 1989, Simon & Schuster paper $12.95 (0-671-66266-X). 40pp. A mother cat searches for a new home for herself and her kittens. (Rev: BL 6/15/89; SLJ 6/89)

5348 Miller, Ruth. *I Went to the Bay* (PS–1). Illus. by Martine Gourbault. 1999, Kids Can $12.95 (1-55074-498-4). 24pp. A young boy searches above and below water for frogs but finds only a variety of other marine animals. (Rev: BL 3/15/99; HBG 10/99; SLJ 6/99) [629]

5349 Mitchell, Adrian, and Daniel Pudles. *Twice My Size* (PS–1). Illus. 1999, Millbrook LB $21.40 (0-7613-1423-7). 32pp. A series of animals each introduces another animal friend that is bigger than it is. (Rev: BL 4/15/99; HBG 10/99; SLJ 6/99)

5350 Mockford, Caroline. *Cleo the Cat* (PS). Illus. by author. 2000, Barefoot $14.99 (1-84148-259-5). A charming story about a cat named Cleo who finds a home and a friend. (Rev: HBG 3/01; SLJ 12/00)

5351 Morpurgo, Michael. *The Silver Swan* (K–3). Illus. by Christian Birmingham. 2000, Penguin $16.99 (0-8037-2543-4). 32pp. A young boy tames a female swan and after she is killed by a fox, he watches over the cygnets and their pining father. (Rev: BL 11/15/00; HBG 3/01; SLJ 12/00)

5352 Most, Bernard. *A Dinosaur Named After Me* (PS–2). Illus. 1991, Harcourt $12.95 (0-15-223494-2). 32pp. On each page is a dinosaur and a child who adds information about the beast. (Rev: BL 4/1/91; SLJ 5/91) [597.9]

5353 Murphy, Mary. *Here Comes Spring: and Summer and Fall and Winter* (PS). Illus. 1999, DK $9.95 (0-7894-3484-9). 32pp. A young dog and its mother display their favorite activities in each of the seasons. (Rev: BL 6/1–15/99; HBG 10/99; SLJ 6/99)

5354 Nethery, Mary. *Hannah and Jack* (PS–1). Illus. by Mary Morgan. 1996, Simon & Schuster $15.00 (0-689-80533-0). 32pp. Hannah misses her pet cat, Jack, so much when she visits Grandma that she sends him postcards. (Rev: BL 5/1/96; HB 7–8/96; SLJ 3/96)

5355 Nethery, Mary. *Mary Veronica's Egg* (PS–2). Illus. by Paul Yalowitz. 1999, Orchard LB $16.99 (0-531-33134-2). 32pp. Mary Veronica finds a large

egg that, to her delight, later hatches into a duckling. (Rev: BCCB 2/99; BL 7/99; HBG 10/99; SLJ 3/99)

5356 Newsome, Jill. *Shadow* (PS–2). Illus. by Claudio Munoz. 1999, DK $15.95 (0-7894-2631-5). 32pp. Unhappy because of a family move, a young girl discovers an interest in sheltering an injured rabbit she finds in the woods. (Rev: BL 10/15/99; HBG 3/00; SLJ 9/99)

5357 Okimoto, Jean D. *Blumpoe the Grumpoe Meets Arnold the Cat* (PS–3). Illus. by Howie Schneider. 1990, Little, Brown $13.95 (0-316-63811-0). 32pp. In an accommodating hotel, a grumpy old man is offered a cat to keep him company. (Rev: BL 5/15/90; HB 7–8/90; SLJ 7/90)

5358 Orr, Katherine. *Story of a Dolphin* (K–4). Illus. 1993, Carolrhoda LB $15.95 (0-87614-777-5). 32pp. Tourists on a Caribbean island mistreat the dolphin that Laura and her father have grown to love and understand. (Rev: BL 9/15/93; SLJ 10/93)

5359 Patent, Dorothy Hinshaw. *Baby Horses* (PS–1). Illus. by William Munoz. 1991, Carolrhoda LB $22.60 (0-87614-690-6). 56pp. A new edition presenting the first months of a foal's life in simple text and color photos. (Rev: BL 1/1/92) [636.1]

5360 Paulsen, Gary. *Canoe Days* (PS–3). Illus. by Ruth W. Paulsen. 1999, Doubleday $16.95 (0-385-32524-X). 32pp. From a canoe in the middle of a lake, the boater can see fish, ducks, deer, foxes, raccoons, and other marvels of nature. (Rev: BL 2/1/99; HBG 10/99; SLJ 3/99)

5361 Penner, Lucille R. *Dinosaur Babies* (PS–1). Illus. by Peter Barrett. Series: Step into Reading. 1991, Random paper $3.99 (0-679-81207-5). 32pp. An easily read introduction to dinosaurs and their babies in large type with many illustrations. (Rev: BL 2/1/92; SLJ 1/92) [567.9]

5362 Perrow, Angeli. *Lighthouse Dog to the Rescue* (K–3). Illus. by Emily Harris. 2000, Down East $15.95 (0-89272-487-0). 32pp. Based on a real incident in Maine during the 1930s, a dog that lives in a lighthouse brings a mail boat's captain safely home during a terrible blizzard. (Rev: BL 3/1/01)

5363 Phillips, Mildred. *And the Cow Said Moo!* (PS). Illus. by Sonja Lamut. 2000, Greenwillow LB $15.89 (0-688-16803-5). A charming rhyming guide to a few farm animals and the sounds they make. (Rev: HBG 10/00; SLJ 7/00)

5364 Pilkey, Dav. *Dogzilla* (K–3). Illus. 1993, Harcourt $13.00 (0-15-223944-8); paper $7.00 (0-15-223945-6). 32pp. Using retouched photos of the author's pets as illustrations, this zany story tells of Dreadful Dogzilla, whose breath could send everyone running. Also use *Kat Kong* (1993). (Rev: BL 9/1/93; SLJ 12/93)

5365 Pirotta, Saviour. *Turtle Bay* (PS–3). Illus. by Nilesh Mistry. 1997, Farrar $15.00 (0-374-37888-6). In this picture book set on a Japanese beach, two children witness the laying of eggs by sea turtles. Eight weeks later, they see the baby turtles hatch. (Rev: HBG 3/98; SLJ 11/97)

5366 Pitcher, Caroline. *The Time of the Lion* (PS–3). Illus. by Jackie Morris. 1998, Beyond Words $15.95 (1-885223-83-8). 32pp. In an African savanna,

Joseph becomes friendly with a lion whose cubs are later saved by Joseph's father. (Rev: BL 1/1–15/99; HBG 3/99; SLJ 12/98)

5367 Polacco, Patricia. *Mrs. Mack* (K–4). Illus. 1998, Putnam $16.99 (0-399-23167-6). 40pp. Drawing on incidents in the author's childhood, this is the story of Mrs. Mack, who allowed the author to work around horses and gain self-confidence. (Rev: BL 11/15/98; HBG 3/99; SLJ 12/98)

5368 Politi, Leo. *Song of the Swallows* (K–3). Illus. by author. 1987, Macmillan LB $15.00 (0-684-18831-7); paper $5.99 (0-689-71140-9). 32pp. Juan rings the mission's bells to welcome the swallows back to San Juan Capistrano. Caldecott Medal winner, 1950.

5369 Pomerantz, Charlotte. *Where's the Bear?* (PS). Illus. by Byron Barton. 1984, Greenwillow $15.93 (0-688-01753-3); Morrow paper $3.95 (0-688-10999-3). 32pp. A picture book involving the search for a bear; the text uses only seven words.

5370 Porte, Barbara Ann. *Tale of a Tadpole* (PS–3). Illus. by Annie Cannon. 1997, Orchard LB $16.99 (0-531-33049-4). 32pp. Francine watches the changes that occur to a tadpole until it becomes a toad. (Rev: BL 8/97; HBG 3/98; SLJ 9/97)

5371 Posey, Lee. *Night Rabbits* (PS–3). Illus. by Michael G. Montgomery. 1999, Peachtree $15.95 (1-56145-164-9). 32pp. A little girl who can't get to sleep watches the rabbits on the lawn, but in the morning she's always ready for her father's arms. (Rev: BL 5/1/99; HBG 10/99; SLJ 5/99)

5372 Preller, James. *Cardinal and Sunflower* (PS–2). Illus. by Huy Voun Lee. 1998, HarperCollins $14.95 (0-06-026222-2). 32pp. Sunflower seeds scattered during the winter by a mother and daughter feed a pair of cardinals. They raise a family the following spring and feed on a sunflower that has grown from one of the overlooked seeds. (Rev: BL 6/1–15/98; HBG 10/98; SLJ 6/98)

5373 Pringle, Laurence. *Naming the Cat* (K–3). Illus. by Katherine Potter. 1997, Walker LB $16.85 (0-8027-8622-7). 32pp. A family ponders what the best name would be for their new cat. After watching its escapades, they decide to call him Lucky. (Rev: BL 10/1/97; HBG 3/98; SLJ 11/97)

5374 Radcliffe, Theresa. *Bashi, Elephant Baby* (PS–3). Illus. by John Butler. 1998, Viking $15.99 (0-670-87054-4). 32pp. When her baby gets stuck in a watering hole, a mother elephant must think fast to foil an attack by some hungry lionesses. (Rev: BCCB 3/98; BL 2/1/98; HBG 10/98; SLJ 2/98)

5375 Radcliffe, Theresa. *Maya, Tiger Cub* (PS–2). Illus. by John Butler. 1999, Viking $14.99 (0-670-87894-4). Double-page paintings re-create a day in the life of a tiger cub in an Indian forest. (Rev: HBG 10/00; SLJ 3/00)

5376 Rand, Gloria. *A Home for Spooky* (K–4). Illus. by Ted Rand. 1998, Holt $15.95 (0-8050-4611-9). 32pp. Annie shares her school lunch with a stray dog she names Spooky and eventually gets permission to bring the dog home. Based on a true story. (Rev: BL 4/1/98; HBG 10/98; SLJ 6/98)

5377 Ranville, Myrelene. *Tex* (PS–2). Illus. by Clive Dobson. 1999, Firefly $16.95 (1-55209-294-1); paper $6.95 (1-55209-291-7). 31pp. Tex, the runt of a litter of English foxhounds, is sent to the pound but eventually finds a happy home. (Rev: HBG 10/99; SLJ 11/99)

5378 Rathmann, Peggy. *Officer Buckle and Gloria* (PS–2). Illus. 1995, Putnam $16.99 (0-399-22616-8). 32pp. A police dog named Gloria steals the show when Officer Buckle gives a presentation on safety to local school children. Caldecott Medal winner, 1996. (Rev: BCCB 10/95; BL 11/1/95*; HB 11–12/95; SLJ 9/95*)

5379 Reeves, Mona R. *The Spooky Eerie Night Noise* (K–2). Illus. by Paul Yalowitz. 1989, Macmillan LB $13.95 (0-02-775732-3). 32pp. At night a little girl hears a strange noise from outside and finds it is caused by skunks. (Rev: BL 8/89; SLJ 9/89)

5380 Reiser, Lynn. *My Cat Tuna: A Book About the Five Senses* (PS). Illus. by author. 2001, Greenwillow $9.95 (0-688-16874-4). This flap book explores what a cat sees, hears, smells, tastes, and feels in the house and in the garden. The same from a dog's point of view is found in *My Dog Truffle: A Book About the Five Senses*. (Rev: SLJ 3/01)

5381 Reiser, Lynn. *The Surprise Family* (PS–2). Illus. 1994, Greenwillow $16.00 (0-688-11671-X). 32pp. Despite obvious differences, a chicken loves the little ducks she has hatched. (Rev: BL 6/1–15/94; SLJ 7/94*)

5382 Rice, Eve. *Sam Who Never Forgets* (PS–1). Illus. by author. 1977, Morrow paper $5.95 (0-688-07335-2). 32pp. Sam, the zookeeper, feeds all the animals each day, but one day there appears to be nothing for the elephant.

5383 Robertus, Polly M. *The Dog Who Had Kittens* (PS–2). Illus. by Janet Stevens. 1991, Holiday LB $16.95 (0-8234-0860-4). 32pp. Baxter, a basset hound, decides that he can help raise the new family of Eloise the cat. (Rev: BL 3/15/91; SLJ 5/91)

5384 Rockwell, Anne. *Our Yard Is Full of Birds* (PS–1). Illus. by Lizzy Rockwell. 1992, Macmillan LB $14.00 (0-02-777273-X). 32pp. A little boy observes and describes the birds that come into the yard. (Rev: BCCB 3/92; BL 1/15/92; SLJ 4/92) [598]

5385 Rosen, Michael J. *Bonesy and Isabel* (PS–4). Illus. by James E. Ransome. 1995, Harcourt $15.00 (0-15-209813-5). 32pp. A newly adopted girl from El Salvador feels a terrible loss when the farm dog she has grown to love dies. (Rev: BL 4/15/95; SLJ 6/95)

5386 Rossiter, Nan P. *The Way Home* (K–3). Illus. 1999, Dutton $15.99 (0-525-45767-4). 32pp. Samuel cares for an injured Canada goose, whom he names Chicory, and eventually sees his pet fly away with his mate as winter approaches. (Rev: BL 9/15/99; HBG 3/00; SLJ 11/99)

5387 Rotner, Shelley, and Cheo Garcia. *Pick a Pet* (PS–1). Illus. 1999, Orchard LB $16.99 (0-531-33147-4). 32pp. Using alliteration, this story involves Patty's search for a pet, such as a freckled frog, or a plump pig, or even one of the fanciful creatures Patty imagines. (Rev: BL 7/99; HBG 10/99; SLJ 4/99)

5388 Rounds, Glen. *Once We Had a Horse* (K–2). Illus. 1996, Holiday $15.95 (0-8234-1241-5). 32pp. One summer, a boy and his sister learn to ride a gentle farm horse. (Rev: BL 6/1–15/96; SLJ 7/96*)

5389 Rounds, Glen. *Wild Horses* (1–4). Illus. 1993, Holiday LB $14.95 (0-8234-1019-6). 32pp. The lives of wild horses in the West are explored in text and beautiful drawings. (Rev: BL 4/1/93) [599.72]

5390 Rowe, Jeannette. *Whose Feet?* (PS–K). Illus. by author. 1999, Little, Brown $7.95 (0-316-75934-1). In this flap book, readers must match animal bodies with the correct feet. Also use *Whose Nose?* (1999). (Rev: HBG 3/00; SLJ 1/00)

5391 Roy, Ron. *Three Ducks Went Wandering* (PS–1). Illus. by Paul Galdone. 1987, Ticknor paper $5.96 (0-89919-494-X). Three ducks are oblivious to the dangers all around them when they take a walk.

5392 Royston, Angela. *Baby Animals* (PS). Illus. by Andrew Aloof. Series: Eye Openers. 1992, Macmillan paper $8.99 (0-689-71563-3). 24pp. Numerous photographs in color help introduce a variety of baby animals to preschoolers. (Rev: BL 8/92; SLJ 10/92) [599]

5393 Royston, Angela. *Jungle Animals* (PS–2). Illus. by Martine Blaney and Dave Hopkins. Series: Eye Openers. 1991, Macmillan $8.99 (0-689-71519-6). 21pp. A number of jungle animals are introduced. (Rev: BL 9/15/91; SLJ 1/92) [581]

5394 Royston, Angela. *Sea Animals* (PS). Illus. by Stephen Shott. Series: Eye Openers. 1992, Macmillan paper $8.99 (0-689-71565-X). 32pp. In full-color photographs, a number of marine animals are identified for the very young. (Rev: BL 8/92; SLJ 10/92) [591]

5395 Rush, Ken. *What About Emma?* (PS–3). Illus. 1996, Orchard LB $16.99 (0-531-08884-7). 32pp. Even though her farm family must sell their stock to survive, Sue is allowed to keep her favorite cow, Emma. (Rev: BL 9/1/96; SLJ 9/96)

5396 Ryder, Joanne. *Jaguar in the Rain Forest* (K–4). Illus. by Michael Rothman. 1996, Morrow $15.89 (0-688-12991-9). 32pp. The home and habits of the graceful jaguar are explored in this sumptuous picture book. (Rev: BL 3/15/96; SLJ 3/96)

5397 Rylant, Cynthia. *The Bookshop Dog* (PS–K). Illus. 1996, Scholastic $15.95 (0-590-54331-8). 40pp. A dog named Martha Jane becomes the mascot at her owner's bookshop. (Rev: BL 9/1/96; SLJ 9/96)

5398 Rylant, Cynthia. *Dog Heaven* (PS–1). Illus. 1995, Scholastic $15.95 (0-590-41701-0). 32pp. In dog heaven, dogs run and play and wait for their absent friends. (Rev: BCCB 10/95; BL 8/95; SLJ 10/95)

5399 Rylant, Cynthia. *The Old Woman Who Named Things* (PS–3). Illus. by Kathryn Brown. 1996, Harcourt $16.00 (0-15-257809-9). 32pp. An old lady who only names things that will outlive her doesn't

name the pup she adopts. (Rev: BL 5/1/96*; HB 5–6/98; SLJ 10/96*)

5400 Samuels, Barbara. *Duncan and Dolores* (K–2). Illus. by author. 1986, Macmillan paper $4.99 (0-689-71294-4). 32pp. Dolores learns a lesson when she smothers Duncan the cat with too much love and attention and he runs away from her. (Rev: BCCB 3/87; BL 10/15/86; HB 1–2/87)

5401 Schindel, John. *Busy Penguins* (PS). Illus. by Jonathan Chester. 2000, Tricycle Pr. $6.95 (1-58246-016-7). 20pp. A board book that shows penguins in various activities — jumping, sliding, diving, bumping, and even pooping. (Rev: BL 3/15/00; SLJ 8/00)

5402 Schneider, Antonie. *Luke the Lionhearted* (PS–2). Trans. from German by J. Alison James. Illus. by Cristina Kadmon. 1998, North-South LB $15.88 (1-55858-977-5). In this picture book story about overcoming fears, Luke helps the local zoo director recapture an escaped lion. (Rev: HBG 3/99; SLJ 1/99)

5403 Schoenherr, John. *Rebel* (K–2). Illus. 1995, Putnam $15.95 (0-399-22727-X). 32pp. A pair of wild geese raise a family, including a rebel gosling that tends to wander away from its family. (Rev: BCCB 12/95; BL 12/15/95*; SLJ 10/95*)

5404 Schubert, Leda. *Winnie All Day Long* (PS–1). Illus. by William Benedict. 2000, Candlewick $10.99 (0-7636-1041-0). 40pp. Four brief, humorous stories about Annie, a toddler, and her huge dog, Winnie, are contained in this book for beginning readers. Also use *Winnie Plays Ball* (2000). (Rev: HBG 10/00; SLJ 7/00)

5405 Schuch, Steve. *A Symphony of Whales* (1–4). Illus. by Peter Sylvada. 1999, Harcourt $16.00 (0-15-201670-8). 32pp. Based on fact, this is the story of a Siberian girl whose ability to reproduce the song of the whales helps save a group of Beluga whales trapped in a bay. (Rev: BCCB 11/99; BL 1/1–15/00; HBG 3/00; SLJ 11/99)

5406 Scuderi, Lucia. *To Fly* (PS–1). Trans. by Phillis Gershator and Robin Blum. Illus. by author. Series: Cranky Nell Books. 1998, Kane/Miller $12.95 (0-916291-79-0). Three young crows learn the lesson that you can't fly unless you try. (Rev: HBG 10/98; SLJ 6/98)

5407 Seeber, Dorothea P. *A Pup Just for Me/A Boy Just for Me* (PS–2). Illus. by Ed Young. 2000, Putnam $16.99 (0-399-23403-9). 40pp. Two parallel stories about a boy who longs for a dog and a dog who longs for an owner are printed front to back and back to front so that they meet in the middle. (Rev: BL 4/15/00; HBG 10/00; SLJ 5/00)

5408 Sewell, Anna. *Black Beauty* (1–3). Adapted by Robin McKinley. Illus. by Susan Jeffers. 1986, Random LB $20.99 (0-394-96575-2). 72pp. A smooth adaptation of the classic horse tale. (Rev: BCCB 1/87; BL 12/1/86; SLJ 12/86)

5409 Seymour, Tres. *Hunting the White Cow* (PS–3). Illus. by Wendy A. Halperin. 1993, Orchard LB $17.99 (0-531-08646-1). 32pp. After a white cow has escaped from the farm, several people try unsuccessfully to catch her. (Rev: BCCB 10/93; BL 9/1/93; HB 11–12/93; SLJ 12/93*)

5410 Shapiro, Arnold L. *Mice Squeak, We Speak* (PS–K). Illus. by Tomie dePaola. 1997, Putnam $13.99 (0-399-23202-8). 32pp. Three friends introduce the different sounds made by a variety of animals. (Rev: BL 9/15/97*; HBG 3/98; SLJ 10/97)

5411 Sheehan, Patty. *Shadow and the Ready Time* (K–3). Illus. by Itoko Maeno. 1994, Advocacy $14.95 (0-911655-13-1). 38pp. A wolf cub is raised by an older, lame wolf when he is separated from his pack. (Rev: SLJ 12/94)

5412 Sheppard, Jeff. *Splash, Splash* (PS–1). Illus. by Dennis Panek. 1994, Macmillan paper $15.00 (0-02-782455-1). 40pp. Different animals fall in the pond, make different sounds, and have different reactions. (Rev: BL 6/1–15/94; HB 5–6/94; SLJ 5/94)

5413 Simmons, Jane. *Ebb and Flo and the Greedy Gulls* (PS–2). Illus. Series: Ebb and Flo. 2000, Simon & Schuster $14.95 (0-689-82484-X). 32pp. When Flo and her mother go to the seashore for a picnic, Ebb, her dog, is wrongfully accused of eating the sandwiches and pastries. (Rev: BL 4/15/00; HBG 10/00; SLJ 5/00)

5414 Simon, Norma. *Fire Fighters* (PS–K). Illus. by Pamela Paparone. 1995, Simon & Schuster paper $14.00 (0-689-80280-3). 32pp. A day in the life of firefighters who are actually dalmatians. (Rev: BL 9/15/95; SLJ 12/95)

5415 Simon, Norma. *Oh, That Cat!* (K–3). Illus. by Dora Leder. 1986, Whitman LB $13.95 (0-8075-5919-9). 32pp. Max may be obnoxious in some ways, but he's special too. (Rev: BL 4/15/86; SLJ 8/86)

5416 Simont, Marc. *The Stray Dog* (PS–3). Illus. 2001, HarperCollins LB $15.89 (0-06-028934-1). 32pp. A family goes back to a picnic ground to bring home the stray dog they saw the week before in this tender animal story. (Rev: BCCB 3/01; BL 1/1–15/01; SLJ 2/01)

5417 Singer, Marilyn. *Good Day, Good Night* (PS–2). Illus. by Ponder Goembel. 1998, Marshall Cavendish $15.95 (0-7614-5018-1). An interesting book that describes, in rhyme, how various animals spend their days and nights. (Rev: BCCB 7–8/98; HBG 10/98; SLJ 6/98)

5418 Sis, Peter. *Komodo!* (PS–2). Illus. 1993, Greenwillow $15.89 (0-688-11584-5). 32pp. On a trip to Indonesia, a young boy encounters the animal he has been fascinated with, the Komodo dragon. (Rev: BCCB 6/93; BL 4/15/93*; HB 5–6/93*; SLJ 7/93*)

5419 Slepian, Jan. *Lost Moose* (PS–2). Illus. by Ted Lewin. 1995, Putnam $15.95 (0-399-22749-0). 32pp. A small boy tracks a lost baby moose, and eventually both find their mothers. (Rev: BL 3/1/95; SLJ 8/95)

5420 Slier, Deborah. *Farm Animals* (PS). Illus. 1988, Checkerboard $2.95 (1-56288-084-5). 12pp. Farm creatures for the toddler to admire. (Rev: BCCB 7–8/88; BL 7/88)

5421 Smith, Maggie. *Desser the Best Ever Cat* (PS–1). Illus. 2001, Knopf $14.95 (0-375-81056-0). 32pp. An engaging picture book arranged like a scrapbook of memories that tells the life story of a family's beloved cat from the day he was adopted as a stray. (Rev: BL 2/15/01)

5422 Stern, Maggie. *Acorn Magic* (K–2). Illus. by Donna Ruff. 1998, Greenwillow $15.00 (0-688-15699-1). 32pp. Simon is so busy picking up acorns in the woods that he misses seeing a fine array of animals and birds, but when he throws away the acorns in anger, the animals come back to partake of the feast. (Rev: BL 11/15/98; HBG 3/99; SLJ 10/98)

5423 Stern, Maggie. *The Missing Sunflowers* (PS–2). Illus. by Donna Ruff. 1997, Greenwillow $15.00 (0-688-14873-5). 32pp. Simon wonders who has stolen the heads from his sunflower plants and finds that a hungry squirrel is the culprit. (Rev: BCCB 4/97; BL 5/15/97; SLJ 4/97)

5424 Stockdale, Susan. *Some Sleep Standing Up* (PS–K). Illus. 1996, Simon & Schuster paper $13.00 (0-689-80509-8). 32pp. Two-page spreads illustrate the ways in which various animals sleep. (Rev: BL 9/1/96; SLJ 4/96) [591.52]

5425 Strete, Craig Kee. *They Thought They Saw Him* (PS–1). Illus. by Jose Aruego and Ariane Dewey. 1996, Greenwillow $14.93 (0-688-14195-1). 32pp. A chameleon escapes many dangers by changing color in this clever picture book. (Rev: BL 4/15/96; HB 7–8/96; SLJ 5/96*)

5426 Swinburne, Stephen R. *Swallows in the Birdhouse* (K–3). Illus. by Robin Brickman. 1996, Millbrook LB $21.90 (1-56294-182-8). 32pp. Two tree swallows create a nest and raise a family after moving into a small birdhouse. (Rev: BL 6/1–15/96; SLJ 6/96) [598.2]

5427 Tafuri, Nancy. *The Barn Party* (PS–1). Illus. 1995, Greenwillow $15.00 (0-688-04616-9). 32pp. At a memorable barn party, children enjoy petting the animals until the creatures are frightened away by a balloon popping. (Rev: BL 9/1/95; SLJ 10/95)

5428 Tan, Amy. *The Chinese Siamese Cat* (1–4). Illus. by Gretchen Schields. 1994, Macmillan paper $16.95 (0-02-788835-5). 32pp. A Chinese tale that explains how cats got their markings. (Rev: BL 10/1/94; SLJ 11/94)

5429 Taylor, Livingston. *Can I Be Good?* (PS–3). Illus. by Ted Rand. 1993, Harcourt $15.00 (0-15-200436-X). 32pp. Though he claims he is trying to be good, a golden retriever seems to be always causing confusion and disorder. (Rev: BL 9/15/93; SLJ 10/93)

5430 Thomas, Jane Resh. *Scaredy Dog* (1–3). Illus. by Marilyn Mets. 1996, Hyperion $13.95 (0-7868-0278-2); paper $3.95 (0-7868-1148-X). 43pp. In the pet shelter, Erin picks a fearful pup that has been mistreated and wins him over through love and attention. (Rev: SLJ 11/96)

5431 Thompson, Colin. *Unknown* (2–3). Illus. by Anna Pignataro. 2000, Walker LB $16.85 (0-8027-8731-2). 32pp. A small stray dog labeled "Unknown" in the animal shelter is able to warn the keeper about a dangerous fire. (Rev: BCCB 5/00; BL 5/1/00; HBG 10/00; SLJ 7/00)

5432 Tildes, Phyllis L. *Animals: Black and White* (PS–2). Illus. by author. 1996, Charlesbridge paper $6.95 (0-88106-959-0). This picture puzzle book consists of guessing games in which several black-and-white animals describe themselves and show parts of their bodies before their identities are revealed. (Rev: SLJ 1/97)

5433 Timmel, Carol Ann. *Tabitha: The Fabulous Flying Feline* (PS–1). Illus. by Laura Kelly. 1996, Walker paper $16.85 (0-8027-8449-6). 32pp. Tabitha the cat remains undiscovered for 13 days in the cargo hold of a large airplane. (Rev: BL 10/15/96; SLJ 11/96)

5434 Toriseva, JoNelle. *Rodeo Day* (1–3). Illus. by Robert Casilla. 1994, Bradbury paper $14.95 (0-02-789405-3). 32pp. Lacey is filled with fear and apprehension as she prepares herself and her horse for her first rodeo. (Rev: BL 11/1/94; SLJ 11/94)

5435 Trapani, Iza. *What Am I? An Animal Guessing Game* (PS–1). Illus. 1992, Whispering Coyote $14.95 (1-879085-76-3). 30pp. An animal is described, and young readers must guess the identity. (Rev: BL 12/15/92; SLJ 1/93) [591.2]

5436 Travers, Will. *The Elephant Truck* (K–3). Illus. by Lawrie Taylor. Series: Born Free Wildlife Book/Templar Book. 1998, Millbrook LB $21.40 (0-7613-0408-8). This picture book presents a fictionalized account of the first relocation of elephants in Kenya's translocation project. (Rev: BL 8/98; HBG 10/98; SLJ 3/98)

5437 Tregebov, Rhea. *The Big Storm* (PS–2). Illus. by Maryann Kovalski. 1993, Hyperion LB $14.49 (1-56282-462-7). 32pp. The promise of tasty latkes from a neighbor makes Jeanette forget about caring for her cat, Kitty Doyle. (Rev: BL 12/15/93; SLJ 1/94)

5438 Tsubakiyama, Margaret. *Mei-Mei Loves the Morning* (PS–3). Illus. by Cornelius Van Wright and Ying-Hwa Hu. 1999, Albert Whitman $15.95 (0-8075-5039-6). In modern, urban China, Mei-Mei and her grandfather participate in the family's daily routines, such as feeding the bird, eating breakfast, going to the park, and shopping at the market. (Rev: BCCB 5/99; BL 3/15/99; HBG 10/99; SLJ 5/99)

5439 Turner, Ann. *Let's Be Animals* (PS). Illus. by Rick Brown. 1998, HarperFestival $9.95 (0-694-01154-1). 24pp. A rhyming picture book in which a group of children visit a farm, meet many different animals, and pretend to be each of them. (Rev: BL 12/15/98; HBG 3/99; SLJ 1/99)

5440 Van Camp, Richard. *What's the Most Beautiful Thing You Know About Horses?* (K–3). Illus. by George Littlechild. 1998, Children's Book Pr. $15.95 (0-89239-154-5). A little child living in Canada's Northwest Territories asks about the beauty of horses. (Rev: HBG 3/99; SLJ 10/98)

5441 Van Laan, Nancy. *When Winter Comes* (PS–2). Illus. by Susan Gaber. 2000, Simon & Schuster $16.00 (0-689-81778-9). As a family walks through the woods during an early snowfall, they wonder about the animals cope during the winter; the illus-

trations reveal the answers. (Rev: HBG 3/01; SLJ 11/00)

5442 Vargo, Vanessa. *Zebra Talk* (PS–1). Illus. 1991, Child's Play paper $5.99 (0-85953-395-6). 20pp. A mother zebra explains how life was years ago when thousands of zebras roamed the plains of Africa. (Rev: BL 3/1/91)

5443 Voake, Charlotte. *Ginger* (PS–3). Illus. 1997, Candlewick $16.99 (0-7636-0108-X). 40pp. Ginger the cat is upset when a new kitten is introduced into the household. (Rev: BCCB 4/97; BL 2/1/97; SLJ 4/97)

5444 Waite, Judy. *The Storm Seal* (K–3). Illus. by Neil Reed. 1998, Crocodile $14.95 (1-56656-292-9). Peter, a retired sailor, saves a seal pup and after nursing it back to health returns it to its natural habitat. (Rev: HBG 3/99; SLJ 12/98)

5445 Wallace, Karen. *Imagine You Are a Crocodile* (PS–1). Illus. by Mike Bostock. 1997, Holt $14.95 (0-8050-4637-2). A picture book that gives the reader a crocodile's views of the world and its swampy habitat. (Rev: BL 5/1/97*; SLJ 7/97)

5446 Walsh, Melanie. *Do Donkeys Dance?* (PS). Illus. 2000, Houghton $15.00 (0-618-00330-4). 40pp. Using questions and answers, this simple picture book reveals the distinctive qualities of various animals. (Rev: BCCB 4/00; BL 4/15/00; HB 7–8/00; HBG 10/00; SLJ 4/00)

5447 Walsh, Melanie. *Do Monkeys Tweet?* (PS). Illus. 1997, Houghton $15.00 (0-395-85081-9). 40pp. A funny picture book that answers such questions as "Do horses bark?" (Rev: BL 9/1/97; HB 11–12/97; HBG 3/98; SLJ 10/97) [591.59]

5448 Weller, Frances W. *Riptide* (PS–3). Illus. by Robert J. Blake. 1990, Putnam $15.95 (0-399-21675-8). 32pp. A dog named Riptide acts as a lifeguard on Cape Cod. (Rev: BL 3/15/90*; HB 7–8/90; SLJ 4/90*)

5449 Wells, Rosemary. *McDuff and the Baby* (PS–1). Illus. by Susan Jeffers. 1997, Hyperion LB $12.89 (0-7868-2258-9). 24pp. McDuff, a terrier, loses status when a new baby arrives in his home. (Rev: BL 9/15/97; HBG 3/98; SLJ 10/97)

5450 Wells, Rosemary. *McDuff Comes Home* (PS–K). Illus. by Susan Jeffers. 1997, Hyperion LB $13.49 (0-7868-2259-7). 32pp. McDuff the white terrier gets lost when he chases a rabbit but, through the help of matronly Mrs. Higgins, finds his way home again. (Rev: BL 6/1–15/97; HB 7–8/97; SLJ 7/97)

5451 Wells, Rosemary. *McDuff Moves In* (PS–2). Illus. by Susan Jeffers. 1997, Hyperion LB $13.49 (0-7868-2257-0); paper $4.99 (0-7868-1190-0). 32pp. A little dog jumps out of a dog catcher's truck and finds himself a new home with a sympathetic couple. (Rev: BCCB 4/97; BL 4/1/97*; HB 7–8/97; SLJ 5/97*)

5452 Wheeler, Cindy. *Bookstore Cat* (1–2). Illus. by author. Series: Step into Reading. 1994, Random paper $3.99 (0-394-84109-3). 32pp. Mulligan, a cat that lives in a bookstore, is kept busy when a pigeon gets into the store. (Rev: SLJ 4/95)

5453 Wieler, Diana. *To the Mountains by Morning* (K–3). Illus. by Ange Zhang. 1996, Douglas &

McIntyre $14.95 (0-88899-227-0). 32pp. Knowing she is going to be disposed of because of her age, Old Bailey the mare runs away. (Rev: BL 7/96; SLJ 6/96)

5454 Wildsmith, Brian, and Rebecca Wildsmith. *Wake Up, Wake Up!* (PS–1). Illus. 1993, Harcourt $6.95 (0-15-200685-0). 16pp. One by one, the animals wake up until, finally, the farmer also wakes up to feed them. (Rev: BL 3/15/93)

5455 Wilhelm, Hans. *I'll Always Love You* (PS–2). Illus. by author. 1988, Crown $17.00 (0-517-55648-0); paper $6.99 (0-517-57265-6). 32pp. The affection between boy and dog and the sadness when a beloved pet grows old and dies. (Rev: BCCB 1/86; BL 11/1/85)

5456 Winters, Kay. *Tiger Trail* (PS–3). Illus. by Laura Regan. 2000, Simon & Schuster $16.95 (0-689-82323-1). 32pp. This dramatic picture book describes how a mother tiger cares for her kits and gives them milk, after which she must hunt for herself. (Rev: BL 10/15/00; HBG 3/01; SLJ 1/01)

5457 Winters, Kay. *Wolf Watch* (K–3). Illus. by Laura Regan. 1997, Simon & Schuster paper $16.00 (0-689-80218-8). 32pp. Lyrical verses and striking paintings depict wolves and their pups engaging in many activities, including playing and searching for food. (Rev: BL 11/1/97; HBG 3/98; SLJ 11/97)

5458 Wood, A. J. *Amazing Animals* (PS–K). Illus. 1991, Boyds Mills $8.95 (1-878093-46-0). With spare prose and double-page spreads, ten different animals are introduced. (Rev: SLJ 11/91) [591]

5459 Wood, A. J. *Beautiful Birds* (PS–K). Illus. 1991, Boyds Mills $8.95 (1-878093-47-9). In attactive pictures and short statements, ten different birds are introduced. (Rev: SLJ 11/91) [591]

5460 Wood, Ellen. *Hundreds of Fish* (1–4). Illus. by Monique Felix. 2000, Creative Co. $17.95 (1-56846-162-3). 40pp. The food chain is explored in this picture book set in Alaska about a young girl who, while ice fishing, catches a pike that she saw eating three ducklings months before. (Rev: HBG 10/00; SLJ 9/00)

5461 Wundrow, Deanna. *Jungle Drum* (PS–1). Illus. by Susan Swan. 1999, Millbrook LB $19.90 (0-7613-1270-6). 24pp. When a group of jungle animals hear the distant beating of drums, each joins in with its own distinctive sound. (Rev: BL 3/15/99; HBG 10/99; SLJ 10/99)

5462 Yaccarino, Dan. *So Big!* (PS). Illus. 2001, HarperFestival $7.95 (0-694-01509-1). 12pp. This book explores the sizes of various baby animals through a series of fold-up flaps. (Rev: BL 1/1–15/01)

5463 Yolen, Jane. *Owl Moon* (PS–2). Illus. by John Schoenherr. 1987, Putnam $16.99 (0-399-21457-7). 32pp. Winner of the 1988 Caldecott Medal, this is the poetic story of a little girl and her father on an owl adventure in winter. (Rev: BL 12/15/87; SLJ 12/87)

5464 Zagwyn, Deborah Turney. *Turtle Spring* (PS–1). Illus. 1998, Tricycle Pr. $15.95 (1-883672-53-8). 32pp. Clee is happy to have a pet turtle to play with instead of her baby brother. Over the winter, though, she thinks the turtle has died, and she

comes to love her brother. In spring, Clee's turtle wakes from its hibernation and she has both brother and turtle to love. (Rev: BL 7/98*; HBG 10/98; SLJ 8/98)

5465 Zimmerman, Andrea, and David Clemesha. *My Dog Toby* (PS–2). Illus. by True Kelley. 2000, Harcourt $15.00 (0-15-202014-4). 32pp. The little girl who owns Toby is convinced that he is a bright dog and Toby proves she is right. (Rev: BCCB 6/00; BL 5/1/00*; HBG 10/00; SLJ 5/00)

SCHOOL STORIES

5466 Allard, Harry. *Miss Nelson Has a Field Day* (1–3). Illus. by James Marshall. 1985, Houghton $15.00 (0-395-36690-9); paper $5.95 (0-395-48654-8). 32pp. The plucky Miss Nelson gets a losing football team into shape. (Rev: BCCB 7/85; BL 5/15/85; HB 5–6/85)

5467 Allard, Harry. *Miss Nelson Is Missing!* (K–2). Illus. by James Marshall. 1985, Houghton $16.00 (0-395-25296-2); paper $5.95 (0-395-40146-1). When Miss Nelson's students in Room 207 misbehave, she disappears and is replaced by a martinet. A sequel is: *Miss Nelson Is Back* (1985).

5468 Anholt, Laurence. *Billy and the Big New School* (PS–2). Illus. by Catherine Anholt. 1999, Albert Whitman $14.95 (0-8075-0743-1). 32pp. Billy is afraid to start school, but like a sparrow he helps fly away, he realizes he must learn to be independent. (Rev: BCCB 5/99; BL 3/1/99; HBG 10/99; SLJ 3/99)

5469 Aseltine, Lorraine. *First Grade Can Wait* (K–2). Illus. by Virginia Wright-Frierson. 1988, Whitman LB $13.95 (0-8075-2451-4). 32pp. At 6, Luke isn't mature enough to start school, so his parents decide to hold him out for a year. (Rev: BL 3/15/88; SLJ 7/88)

5470 Ashley, Bernard. *Cleversticks* (PS–1). Illus. by Derek Brazell. 1995, Crown paper $6.99 (0-517-88332-5). 32pp. Ling Sung is a nobody at school until he reveals he can use chopsticks. (Rev: BCCB 7–8/92; BL 11/15/92; SLJ 3/93)

5471 Baehr, Patricia. *School Isn't Fair* (PS). Illus. by R. W. Alley. 1989, Macmillan LB $13.95 (0-02-708130-3). Edward gets into trouble in his nursery school, mainly because of a bully. (Rev: SLJ 8/89)

5472 Baker, Barbara. *Third Grade Is Terrible* (2–4). Illus. by Roni Shepherd. 1991, Pocket paper $3.99 (0-671-70379-X). 80pp. Lisa looked forward to third grade until she realized her teacher is mean Mrs. Rumford. (Rev: BCCB 5/89; BL 2/1/89)

5473 Bercaw, Edna Coe. *Halmoni's Day* (K–3). Illus. by Robert Hunt. 2000, Dial $15.99 (0-8037-2444-6). 32pp. Jennifer is afraid her Korean grandmother, who wears her native clothes and speaks no English, will embarrass her when they go to her school's Grandparents' Day. (Rev: BL 11/1/00; HBG 3/01; SLJ 8/00)

5474 Bianchi, John. *Welcome Back to Pokeweed Public School* (PS–1). Illus. 1996, Firefly $15.95 (0-921285-45-0); paper $4.95 (0-921285-44-2). 24pp. The new computers at Pokeweed Public contain a few unexplained glitches. (Rev: BL 2/1/97)

5475 Boelts, Maribeth. *Little Bunny's Preschool Countdown* (PS). Illus. by Kathy Parkinson. 1996, Albert Whitman LB $14.95 (0-8075-4582-1). 32pp. LB, a rabbit, begins to dread his first day at preschool. (Rev: BL 9/15/96; SLJ 11/96)

5476 Boelts, Maribeth. *Summer's End* (K–3). Illus. by Ellen Kandoian. 1995, Houghton $14.95 (0-395-70559-2). 32pp. As summer draws to a close, a young girl becomes apprehensive about entering the second grade. (Rev: BCCB 3/95; BL 4/1/95; SLJ 4/95)

5477 Borden, Louise. *Good Luck, Mrs. K.!* (1–3). Illus. by Adam Gustavson. 1999, Simon & Schuster $15.00 (0-689-82147-6). 32pp. The remarkable influence Mrs. Kempczinski has over her class continues, even after she is forced to leave them because of cancer. (Rev: BCCB 6/99; BL 7/99*; HBG 10/99; SLJ 5/99)

5478 Brandt, Amy. *When Katie Was Our Teacher/ Cuando Katie era nuestra maestra* (PS–K). 2000, Child Care Books for Kids $11.95 (1-884834-78-7). 32pp. In this bilingual book about day care, Katie and her friends miss their teacher when she leaves. (Rev: SLJ 10/00)

5479 Bunting, Eve. *Our Teacher's Having a Baby* (K–2). Illus. by Diane De Groat. 1992, Houghton $15.00 (0-395-60470-2). 32pp. Mrs. Neal explains to her class that she is going to have a baby, and together they prepare for the event. (Rev: BL 9/15/92; SLJ 3/93)

5480 Carlson, Nancy. *Hooray for Grandparents' Day!* (PS–2). Illus. 2000, Viking $15.99 (0-670-88876-1). 32pp. Arnie has no grandparents to bring to school on Grandparents' Day and he feels left out. (Rev: BL 6/1–15/00; HBG 3/01; SLJ 8/00)

5481 Carlson, Nancy. *Look Out Kindergarten, Here I Come!* (PS–K). Illus. 1999, Viking $15.99 (0-670-88378-6). 32pp. Henry is excited about his first day in kindergarten, particularly after he makes a new friend. (Rev: BL 6/1–15/99; HBG 10/99; SLJ 7/99)

5482 Carter, Alden R. *Dustin's Big School Day* (K–2). Illus. by Dan Young and Carol S. Carter. 1999, Albert Whitman $14.95 (0-8075-1741-0). 32pp. Photographs are used to document Dustin's day in school, when a ventriloquist visits as a special treat. (Rev: BCCB 3/99; BL 4/15/99; HBG 10/99; SLJ 6/99)

5483 Caseley, Judith. *Field Day Friday* (PS–2). Illus. 2000, Greenwillow LB $15.89 (0-688-16762-4). 32pp. At his school's field day, Mickey's sneaker comes off during the 50-yard dash and the wretched youngster comes in last. (Rev: BL 5/1/00; HBG 10/00; SLJ 5/00)

5484 Caseley, Judith. *Mickey's Class Play* (PS–2). Illus. 1998, Greenwillow LB $14.93 (0-688-15406-9). 32pp. Mickey is very excited to be cast as a duck in the class play — so excited that he forgets his costume in the yard and it is ruined. (Rev: BL 8/98; HBG 3/99; SLJ 9/98)

5485 Caudill, Rebecca. *A Pocketful of Cricket* (1–3). Illus. by Evaline Ness. 1989, Holt paper $5.95 (0-8050-1275-3). 48pp. A small boy delights in the countryside around his home, and one day his pet cricket goes to school in his pocket.

5486 Chardiet, Bernice, and Grace Maccarone. *The Best Teacher in the World* (PS–2). Illus. by G. Brian Karas. 1991, Scholastic paper $2.50 (0-590-43307-5). 32pp. Bunny is selected by her favorite teacher to run an errand. (Rev: BL 1/1/90; SLJ 10/90)

5487 Cocca-Leffler, Maryann. *Mr. Tanen's Ties* (PS–2). Illus. 1999, Albert Whitman LB $14.95 (0-8075-5301-8). 32pp. Mr. Tanen wears different ties to school each day to mark various occasions, but Mr. Apple, the superintendent of schools, doesn't like it. (Rev: BL 5/15/99; HBG 10/99; SLJ 3/99)

5488 Cohen, Miriam. *Best Friends* (PS–K). Illus. by Lillian Hoban. 1971, Macmillan LB $15.00 (0-02-722800-2); paper $5.99 (0-689-71334-7). 32pp. Kindergarten is the setting for this story of the friendship and disagreements between two boys. By the same author: *First Grade Takes a Test* (1983, Dell); *See You Tomorrow, Charles* (1989, Dell).

5489 Cohen, Miriam. *Will I Have a Friend?* (PS–2). Illus. by Lillian Hoban. 1967, Macmillan paper $4.99 (0-689-71333-9). 32pp. Jim, a kindergartner, lives out the actual concern that small children have about finding a friend on the first day of school. By the same author and publisher: *No Good in Art* (1980); *So What?* (1982); *Jim's Dog Muffins* (1986); *Jim Meets the Thing* (1989).

5490 Conlin, Susan, and Susan L. Friedman. *All My Feelings at Preschool: Nathan's Day* (PS–K). Illus. by Kathryn M. Smith. 1991, Parenting Pr. LB $16.95 (0-943990-61-0); paper $6.95 (0-943990-60-2). 32pp. This picture book describes a day in the life of Nathan at his nursery school. (Rev: BL 6/1/91)

5491 Couric, Katie. *The Brand New Kid* (K–2). Illus. by Marjorie Priceman. 2000, Doubleday $15.95 (0-385-50030-0). Lazlo S. Gasky is unhappy and friendless at his new school, until a classmate decides to help him. (Rev: SLJ 2/01)

5492 Crebbin, June. *Danny's Duck* (PS–K). Illus. by Clara Vulliamy. 1995, Candlewick $13.95 (1-56402-536-5). 32pp. Danny secretly visits a duck's nest at the edge of the schoolyard and each time draws a picture of what he has seen. (Rev: BL 6/1–15/95; SLJ 5/95)

5493 Daniels, Teri. *The Feet in the Gym* (K–3). Illus. by Travis Foster. 1999, Winslow $15.95 (1-890817-12-4). 32pp. The humorous story of how a poor school custodian tries to keep the school clean, in spite of different groups of children, each producing its own terrible mess. (Rev: BL 7/99; SLJ 6/99)

5494 Davis, Gibbs. *The Other Emily* (K–2). Illus. by Linda Shute. 1990, Harcourt paper $4.95 (0-395-54947-7). 32pp. Emily loves her name until she encounters another Emily in her class.

5495 dePaola, Tomie. *The Art Lesson* (K–3). Illus. by author. 1989, Putnam $16.99 (0-399-21688-X). 32pp. Tommy just keeps on drawing and drawing and drawing. (Rev: BCCB 3/89; BL 3/1/89; SLJ 4/89)

5496 Fain, Moira. *Snow Day* (K–3). Illus. 1996, Walker LB $16.85 (0-8027-8410-0). 32pp. Maggie

Murphy escapes a school punishment when a snow day is declared the following day. (Rev: BCCB 10/96; BL 10/15/96; SLJ 10/96*)

5497 Finchler, Judy. *Miss Malarkey Doesn't Live in Room 10* (K–3). Illus. by Kevin O'Malley. 1995, Walker LB $15.85 (0-8027-8387-2). 32pp. A young boy is convinced that his teacher lives at school until she moves into his apartment building. (Rev: BL 11/15/95; SLJ 12/95)

5498 Finchler, Judy. *Miss Malarkey Won't Be In Today* (1–3). Illus. by Kevin O'Malley. 1998, Walker LB $16.85 (0-8027-8653-7). 32pp. Miss Malarkey is too sick to go to school, but she worries about the reception different substitute teachers will get. When she returns, she is surprised to find out who took her place. (Rev: BL 9/1/98; HBG 3/99; SLJ 10/98)

5499 Finchler, Judy. *Testing Miss Malarkey* (1–4). Illus. by Kevin O'Malley. 2000, Walker LB $16.85 (0-8027-8737-8). 32pp. A humorous story in which kids are being prepared for standardized tests that they eventually pass with flying colors. (Rev: BL 10/1/00)

5500 Flood, Nancy Bo. *I'll Go to School If . . .* (PS–K). Illus. by Ronnie W. Shipman. 1997, Fairview $14.95 (1-57749-024-X). 32pp. A fearful little boy panics at the thought of his first day of school and thinks of ways he can impress his school chums. (Rev: BL 6/1–15/97; HBG 3/98)

5501 Giff, Patricia Reilly. *Pet Parade* (1–3). Illus. 1996, Dell paper $3.99 (0-440-41232-3). 100pp. Ms. Rooney's class prepares for the day each child can bring a pet to school. (Rev: BL 9/15/96; SLJ 8/96)

5502 Giff, Patricia Reilly. *Today Was a Terrible Day* (2–3). Illus. by Susanna Natti. 1980, Puffin paper $5.99 (0-14-050453-2). 32pp. Ronald is having a terrible day until his teacher writes him an understanding note.

5503 Hathorn, Libby. *Freya's Fantastic Surprise* (1–3). Illus. by Sharon Thompson. 1989, Scholastic $12.95 (0-590-42442-4). 32pp. Freya makes up so many surprises at News Time in school that her classmates become hostile. (Rev: HB 3–4/89)

5504 Havill, Juanita. *Jamaica and the Substitute Teacher* (PS–3). Illus. by Anne S. O'Brien. 1999, Houghton $15.00 (0-395-90503-6). 32pp. Jamaica is so ashamed of cheating on a spelling test that she can't cope with the guilt and decides to confess. (Rev: BL 2/15/99; HB 5–6/99; HBG 10/99; SLJ 5/99)

5505 Henkes, Kevin. *Lilly's Purple Plastic Purse* (PS–K). Illus. 1996, Greenwillow $14.89 (0-688-12898-X). 32pp. Lilly runs afoul of her teacher, Mr. Slinger, whom she adores. A sequel to *Julius, the Baby of the World* (1990). (Rev: BCCB 10/96; BL 8/96*; HB 9–10/96; SLJ 8/96*)

5506 Howe, James. *When You Go to Kindergarten* (PS–1). Photos by Betsy Imershein. 1994, Morrow LB $15.93 (0-688-12913-7). 48pp. With color photos and a simple text, this book tells what a child can expect when he or she goes to kindergarten. (Rev: BL 9/1/94; SLJ 9/94) [372.21]

5507 Howlett, Bud. *I'm New Here* (K–4). Illus. 1993, Houghton $16.00 (0-395-64049-0). 32pp. A photo-essay about a fifth-grader from El Salvador and her first experiences in an American school. (Rev: BL 10/1/93; SLJ 9/93)

5508 Jocelyn, Marthe. *Hannah's Collections* (PS–K). Illus. 2000, Dutton $14.99 (0-525-46442-5). 24pp. Hannah is facing a dilemma choosing which of her collections — buttons, feathers, or rings — she should share with her class. (Rev: BL 9/15/00*; HBG 3/01; SLJ 10/00)

5509 Johnson, Dolores. *My Mom Is My Show-and-Tell* (K–3). Illus. 1999, Marshall Cavendish $15.95 (0-7614-5041-6). 32pp. Brian, an African American boy who is the class clown, is anxious about his mother's visit on Parents' Day. (Rev: BL 4/15/99; HBG 10/99; SLJ 5/99)

5510 Kline, Suzy. *Horrible Harry Goes to the Moon* (2–3). Illus. by Frank Remkiewicz. 2000, Viking $13.99 (0-670-88764-1). 64pp. In this story about Horrible Harry, Miss Mackle's third-grade class decides to hold a bake sale to buy a used telescope. (Rev: HBG 10/00; SLJ 2/00)

5511 Kline, Suzy. *Song Lee in Room 2B* (1–3). Illus. 1993, Viking $13.99 (0-670-84772-0). 64pp. This episodic story about the kids in Miss Mackle's Room 2B features a Korean-born girl, Song Lee. (Rev: BL 4/15/93)

5512 Krensky, Stephen. *My Teacher's Secret Life* (PS–3). Illus. by JoAnn Adinolfi. 1996, Simon & Schuster paper $15.00 (0-689-80271-4). 28pp. A young school child discovers that his teacher really has a life outside of school. (Rev: BCCB 12/96; BL 11/15/96; SLJ 10/96)

5513 Lasky, Kathryn. *Show and Tell Bunnies* (PS–2). Illus. by Marylin Hafner. 1998, Candlewick $15.99 (0-7636-0396-1). 32pp. Clyde's mysterious contribution to show-and-tell turns out to be a cocoon filled with baby spiders that hatch, spin their silk, and sail out the classroom window. (Rev: BL 12/1/98; HBG 3/99; SLJ 2/99)

5514 Lawlor, Laurie. *How to Survive Third Grade* (2–4). Illus. by Joyce A. Zarins. 1988, Whitman LB $9.95 (0-8075-3433-1); Pocket paper $3.99 (0-671-67713-6). 72pp. Ernest isn't sure about third grade until he makes friends with Jomo from Kenya. (Rev: BCCB 11/88; BL 6/15/88; SLJ 9/88)

5515 Lehn, Barbara. *What Is a Teacher?* (K–2). Photos by Carol Krauss. 2000, Millbrook LB $19.90 (0-7613-1713-9). The characteristics of a good teacher are acted out in a series of captioned photos showing children in the teacher's role. (Rev: HBG 3/01; SLJ 1/01)

5516 Lindgren, Astrid. *I Want to Go to School, Too!* (PS–1). Trans. by Barbara Lucas. Illus. by Ilon Wikland. 1987, Farrar $10.95 (91-29-58328-4). 32pp. Lena, 5, visits school for a day with 7-year-old Peter and learns what it's all about. (Rev: BL 12/1/87)

5517 Lorbiecki, Marybeth. *Sister Anne's Hands* (K–3). Illus. by K. Wendy Popp. 1998, Dial LB $15.89 (0-8037-2039-4). 40pp. In a small-town parochial school during the 1960s, an African American nun, Sister Anne, comes to teach second grade and finds that her students need to know the lessons of segregation and persecution. (Rev: BCCB 11/98; BL 10/1/98; HBG 3/99; SLJ 1/99)

5518 McCourt, Lisa. *It's Time for School, Stinky Face* (PS–1). Illus. by Cyd Moore. 2000, Troll $15.95 (0-8167-6961-3). 32pp. A little boy who is wildly imagining the worst things that could happen to him on his first day at school is reassured by his mother. (Rev: BL 10/15/00; HBG 3/01; SLJ 10/00)

5519 Moon, Nicola. *Something Special* (K–2). Illus. by Alex Ayliffe. 1997, Peachtree $14.95 (1-56145-137-1). 32pp. Charlie decides to bring his new baby sister to school for a special show-and-tell. (Rev: BL 6/1–15/97; SLJ 6/97)

5520 Moss, Marissa. *Regina's Big Mistake* (PS–2). Illus. 1990, Houghton $16.00 (0-395-55330-X). 32pp. At first, Regina is unable to get an inspiration for an art assignment, but gradually the drawing takes shape. (Rev: BCCB 10/90; BL 11/1/90; SLJ 1/91)

5521 Munsch, Robert. *We Share Everything!* (PS–1). Illus. by Michael Martchenko. 1999, Scholastic $11.95 (0-590-89600-8). 32pp. In kindergarten, the high jinks of Amanda and Jeremiah prove to be too much for their long-suffering teacher. (Rev: BCCB 11/99; BL 9/1/99; HBG 3/00; SLJ 9/99)

5522 Musgrave, Susan, and Marie-Louise Gay. *Dreams Are More Real than Bathtubs* (K–3). Illus. 1999, Orca $14.95 (1-55143-107-6). 32pp. A little girl shares her thoughts about her family, her pet stuffed lion, fears, and starting first grade. (Rev: BL 7/99; HBG 10/99; SLJ 8/99)

5523 Ormerod, Jan. *Ms. MacDonald Has a Class* (PS–2). Illus. 1996, Clarion $15.95 (0-395-77611-2). 32pp. After a visit to a farm, Ms. MacDonald's class prepares a pageant. (Rev: BCCB 10/96; BL 9/15/96; SLJ 8/96)

5524 Poydar, Nancy. *First Day, Hooray!* (PS–1). Illus. 1999, Holiday $15.95 (0-8234-1437-X). 32pp. Young Ivy Green is worried about her first day at school, but so are others involved in the school's opening, including the bus driver and the principal. (Rev: BL 10/15/99; HBG 3/00; SLJ 8/99)

5525 Poydar, Nancy. *Snip, Snip . . . Snow!* (PS–1). Illus. 1997, Holiday LB $15.95 (0-8234-1328-4). 32pp. Sophie is so disappointed at the lack of snow that she persuades her teacher to let the class make paper snowflakes. (Rev: BL 11/1/97; HBG 3/98; SLJ 10/97)

5526 Reiser, Lynn. *Earthdance* (PS–3). Illus. 1999, Greenwillow LB $15.93 (0-688-16327-0). 32pp. While Terra is at school preparing for a show, her astronaut mother is traveling to the end of the universe. (Rev: BL 12/1/99; HBG 3/00; SLJ 10/99)

5527 Rockwell, Anne. *Career Day* (PS–K). Illus. by Lizzy Rockwell. 2000, HarperCollins $14.95 (0-06-027565-0). 32pp. During Mrs. Madoff's classroom Career Day presentations, ten children introduce a parent or grandparent who talks about his or her occupation. (Rev: BL 5/1/00; HBG 10/00; SLJ 7/00)

5528 Rockwell, Anne. *Show and Tell Day* (PS–K). Illus. by Lizzy Rockwell. 1997, HarperCollins LB $14.89 (0-06-027301-1). 32pp. In this show-and-tell story, ten young boys and girls show their treasures to each other and a sympathetic teacher. (Rev: BL 4/1/97; SLJ 5/97)

5529 Rogers, Jacqueline. *Tiptoe into Kindergarten* (PS–1). Illus. 1999, Scholastic $10.95 (0-590-46653-4). 32pp. A preschooler steals into her brother's kindergarten class and soon becomes part of the activities. (Rev: BL 8/99; HBG 3/00; SLJ 9/99)

5530 Rosenberry, Vera. *Vera's First Day of School* (PS–1). Illus. 1999, Holt $15.95 (0-8050-5936-9). 32pp. On her first day of school, Vera gets confused, and when she finds the school doors closed, she runs home where her mother comforts her. (Rev: BL 9/15/99; HB 9–10/99; HBG 3/00; SLJ 9/99)

5531 Russo, Marisabina. *I Don't Want to Go Back to School* (PS–2). Illus. 1994, Greenwillow $15.89 (0-688-04602-9). 32pp. A little boy worries about his reception when he returns to school after summer vacation. (Rev: BL 9/1/94; SLJ 7/94*)

5532 Saltzberg, Barney. *Phoebe and the Spelling Bee* (PS–2). Illus. 1997, Hyperion LB $15.49 (0-7868-2114-0). 32pp. Phoebe is an uninterested student who hates spelling bees, but in time she learns a new way to achieve success in the classroom. (Rev: BL 10/1/97; HBG 3/98)

5533 Saltzberg, Barney. *Show-and-Tell* (K–3). Illus. 1994, Hyperion LB $15.49 (0-7868-2016-0). 32pp. Young Phoebe's parents always interfere with her school plans and create something grand out of a simple assignment. (Rev: BL 10/15/94; SLJ 10/94)

5534 Schwartz, Amy. *Annabelle Swift, Kindergartner* (PS–K). Illus. by author. 1988, Orchard paper $6.95 (0-531-07027-1). 32pp. A good match of art and text tells the story of Annabelle, who finds that school isn't as much fun as she had thought — until it's time to count the milk money. (Rev: BCCB 5/88; BL 2/1/88; HB 3–4/88)

5535 Scieszka, Jon. *Math Curse* (1–4). Illus. by Lane Smith. 1995, Viking $16.99 (0-670-86194-4). 32pp. All sorts of math problems and riddles, from the practical to the absurd are presented in this school story. (Rev: BCCB 10/95; BL 11/1/95*; HB 11–12/95; SLJ 9/95*)

5536 Senisi, Ellen B. *Hurray for Pre-K!* (PS–K). Illus. 2000, HarperCollins LB $13.99 (0-06-028897-3). 32pp. Using double-page spreads and photographs of a pre-kindergarten classroom in New York State, this charming picture book highlights the activities that take place during a typical day. (Rev: BL 9/15/00; HBG 3/01; SLJ 9/00)

5537 Senisi, Ellen B. *Kindergarten Kids* (PS–K). Illus. 1994, Scholastic paper $2.50 (0-590-47614-9). 32pp. A photo-essay that describes a typical day in a kindergarten class in Schenectady, New York. (Rev: BL 11/1/94) [372.21]

5538 Serfozo, Mary. *Benjamin Bigfoot* (PS–2). Illus. by Joseph A. Smith. 1993, Macmillan $14.95 (0-689-50570-1). 32pp. Benjamin enjoys wearing his father's shoes so much that he wants to wear them when he starts kindergarten. (Rev: BL 4/15/93; SLJ 8/93)

5539 Shannon, David. *David Goes to School* (PS–K). Illus. 1999, Scholastic $14.95 (0-590-48087-1). 32pp. David, an imaginative nonconformist, has difficulty doing the right thing when he begins school. (Rev: BCCB 1/00; BL 8/99*; HBG 3/00; SLJ 9/99)

5540 Simon, Norma. *I'm Busy, Too* (PS–1). Illus. by Dora Leder. 1980, Whitman LB $13.95 (0-8075-3464-1). A day-care-center child realizes that every member of the family has an important role to play.

5541 Slate, Joseph. *Miss Bindergarten Stays Home from Kindergarten* (PS–2). Illus. by Ashley Wolff. 2000, Dutton $16.99 (0-525-46396-8). Miss Bindergarten catches the flu and has to stay home; progressively the students and even the substitute, Mr. Tusky, are also infected. (Rev: HBG 3/01; SLJ 11/00)

5542 Tester, Sylvia Root. *We Laughed a Lot, My First Day of School* (PS–1). Illus. by Frances Hook. 1979, Child's World LB $14.95 (0-685-55556-9). A Mexican American boy has an unexpectedly pleasant first day at school.

5543 Tolstoy, Leo. *Philipok* (PS–3). Illus. by Gennady Spirin. 2000, Putnam $16.99 (0-399-23482-9). 32pp. Philipok is too young to attend school but he decides to go anyway in this story adapted from Tolstoy by Ann Beneduce. (Rev: BL 12/1/00; HBG 3/01; SLJ 1/01)

5544 Vazquez, Sarah. *The School Mural* (2–4). Illus. by Melinda Levine. 1998, Raintree Steck-Vaughn LB $19.97 (0-8172-5160-X). 24pp. Mrs. Sanchez's students get community support for their plan to create a mural celebrating their school's 50th anniversary. (Rev: HBG 3/98; SLJ 7/98)

5545 Yashima, Taro. *Crow Boy* (K–3). Illus. by author. 1955, Puffin paper $5.99 (0-14-050172-X). 40pp. Distinguished picture book about a shy little Japanese boy who feels like an outsider at school.

TRANSPORTATION AND MACHINES

5546 Baer, Edith. *This Is the Way We Go to School* (PS–2). Illus. by Steve Bjorkman. 1994, Scholastic paper $5.99 (0-590-49443-0). 40pp. How children around the world go to school is told in rhyming couplets. (Rev: BCCB 10/90; BL 10/1/90; SLJ 7/90*) [629]

5547 Barton, Byron. *Airport* (PS–1). Illus. by author. 1982, HarperCollins LB $14.89 (0-690-04169-1); paper $5.95 (0-06-443145-2). 32pp. Common sights at an airport, reproduced in drawings and text.

5548 *Bikes, Cars, Trucks and Trains* (PS–1). Illus. 1997, Scholastic $19.95 (0-590-47653-X). Overlays are used to explore the interiors of cars and other vehicles. Also use *Boats and Ships* (1997). (Rev: BL 12/15/97) [388.09]

5549 Borden, Louise. *The Neighborhood Trucker* (PS–2). Illus. by Sandra Speidel. 1997, Scholastic paper $3.95 (0-590-46037-4). 32pp. A boy is entranced with trucks, particularly a cement truck driven by Slim. (Rev: BCCB 12/90; BL 9/1/90; SLJ 10/90)

5550 Brown, Margaret Wise. *The Diggers* (PS–K). Illus. by Daniel Kirk. 1995, Hyperion LB $15.49 (0-

7868-2001-2). 32pp. A newly illustrated edition of the book that deals with steam shovels and other earth movers in a set of poems. (Rev: BL 5/1/95; SLJ 7/95) [811]

5551 Burton, Virginia Lee. *Mike Mulligan and His Steam Shovel* (1–3). Illus. by author. 1939, Houghton LB $11.95 (0-395-06681-6); paper $5.95 (0-395-25939-8). Thrilling race against time as Mike Mulligan and his steam shovel dig a cellar in one day. Also use: *Katy and the Big Snow* (1973).

5552 Coulter, Hope N. *Uncle Chuck's Truck* (PS). Illus. by Rick Brown. 1993, Macmillan LB $13.95 (0-02-724825-9). 32pp. A youngster rides in a farm truck to feed the cows. (Rev: BL 1/15/93; SLJ 3/93)

5553 Cowley, Joy. *The Rusty, Trusty Tractor* (K–2). Illus. by Olivier Dunrea. 1999, Boyds Mills $14.95 (1-56397-565-3). 40pp. In spite of a tractor salesman's dire predictions, Micah's grandfather's 50-year-old tractor takes the old man through another season on the farm. (Rev: BCCB 3/99; BL 3/15/99; HBG 10/99; SLJ 5/99)

5554 Crews, Donald. *Bicycle Race* (PS–K). Illus. by author. 1985, Greenwillow $15.89 (0-688-05172-3). 24pp. A counting book that features 12 bicyclists in yellow numbered helmets, with a flat tire added for drama. (Rev: BL 9/15/85; SLJ 11/85)

5555 Crews, Donald. *Flying* (PS). Illus. by author. 1986, Greenwillow $15.93 (0-688-04319-4); Morrow paper $5.95 (0-688-09235-7). 32pp. Brief text and full-color art highlight this study in movement as a plane takes off, flies over different landscapes, and lands. (Rev: BL 9/1/86; SLJ 10/86)

5556 Crews, Donald. *Harbor* (K–2). Illus. by author. 1982, Greenwillow $15.93 (0-688-00862-3); Morrow paper $4.95 (0-688-07332-8). 32pp. The activities and objects associated with harbors and harbor activities are illustrated.

5557 Crews, Donald. *Inside Freight Train* (PS). Illus. 2001, HarperCollins $9.95 (0-688-17087-0). 12pp. A well-designed board book that makes Crews's famous 1978 book interactive by using split pages that slip sideways to reveal smaller pages. (Rev: BL 12/15/00*)

5558 Crews, Donald. *School Bus* (PS–1). Illus. by author. 1984, Greenwillow $15.89 (0-688-02808-X); Morrow paper $5.95 (0-688-12267-1). 32pp. Many kinds of school buses pick up children for school.

5559 Crowther, Robert. *Dump Trucks and Diggers* (PS–K). Illus. 1996, Candlewick $7.99 (0-7636-0008-3). 12pp. Dump trucks and other heavy machinery move in this book when tabs are pulled. (Rev: BL 12/15/96)

5560 Cuetara, Mittie. *The Crazy Crawler Crane and Other Very Short Truck Stories* (K–2). Illus. 1998, Dutton $14.99 (0-525-45951-0). 32pp. Fourteen breezy short stories introduce a variety of trucks, including a tow truck, a school bus, and a cement mixer. (Rev: BCCB 10/98; BL 10/1/98; HBG 3/99; SLJ 9/98)

5561 Delafosse, Claude. *Tools* (PS–1). Trans. from French by Wendy Barish. Illus. by Daniel Moignot. Series: First Discovery. 1999, Scholastic $12.95 (0-

439-04404-9). This book covers such common tools as pliers, wall anchors, saws, and hammers. (Rev: HBG 3/00; SLJ 1/00)

5562 Demarest, Chris L. *Train* (PS). Illus. 1996, Harcourt paper $4.95 (0-15-200809-8). 16pp. Trains and what they do are introduced in this attractive board book. (Rev: BL 4/1/96; SLJ 8/96)

5563 Eick, Jean. *Bulldozers* (PS). Series: Big Machines at Work. 1999, Child's World LB $13.95 (1-56766-525-X). 32pp. This book for the very young introduces (in text and photos) bulldozers, their functions, and their parts. (Rev: BL 4/15/98; HBG 10/99; SLJ 6/99) [629]

5564 Eick, Jean. *Concrete Mixers* (PS). Series: Big Machines at Work. 1999, Child's World LB $13.95 (1-56766-527-6). 32pp. The basics of concrete mixers, how they work, and their fundamental parts are described in simple text and photographs. (Rev: BL 4/15/98; HBG 10/99; SLJ 6/99) [629]

5565 Floca, Brian. *Five Trucks* (PS). Illus. 1999, DK $15.95 (0-7894-2561-0). 32pp. Illustrated, double-page spreads show five different kinds of trucks and explain the function of each. (Rev: BL 6/1–15/99; HB 3–4/99; HBG 10/99; SLJ 5/99)

5566 Gibbons, Gail. *Boat Book* (PS–1). Illus. by author. 1983, Holiday LB $16.95 (0-8234-0478-1); paper $5.95 (0-8234-0709-8). 32pp. An illustration of all sorts of boats in simple drawings.

5567 Gibbons, Gail. *Emergency!* (PS–1). Illus. 1994, Holiday LB $16.95 (0-8234-1128-1). 32pp. This picture book shows how a number of people are saved through the use of such vehicles as fire engines, Coast Guard boats, and police cars. (Rev: BCCB 11/94; BL 10/15/94; SLJ 11/94) [363.3]

5568 Gibbons, Gail. *New Road!* (K–2). Illus. by author. 1983, HarperCollins LB $15.89 (0-690-04343-0). 32pp. The process of road construction from start to finish.

5569 Gramatky, Hardie. *Little Toot* (K–3). Illus. by author. 1939, Putnam $16.99 (0-399-22419-X); paper $6.99 (0-698-11576-7). 96pp. Little Toot, son of the mightiest tug in the harbor, had no ambition until he became a hero during a raging storm.

5570 Gray, Libba M. *The Little Black Truck* (K–2). Illus. by Elizabeth Sayles. 1994, Simon & Schuster $15.00 (0-671-78105-7). 32pp. Left to rust after years of service, a little black truck named Mary Ann gets a new lease on life when a young man decides to restore her. (Rev: BL 6/1–15/94; SLJ 8/94)

5571 Hennessy, B. G. *Road Builders* (PS–1). Illus. by Simms Taback. 1994, Viking $14.99 (0-670-83390-8). 32pp. A picture book that shows how different kinds of machines and vehicles are used in building a road. (Rev: BL 5/1/94; SLJ 9/94) [625.7]

5572 Hill, Lee S. *Get Around in the City* (1–3). Series: Get Around Book. 1999, Carolrhoda LB $15.95 (1-57505-307-1). 32pp. An attractive, practical book that depicts in photos and text different kinds of urban transportation including cars, buses, gondolas, and elephants. A companion volume is *Get Around in the Country* (1999). (Rev: HBG 10/99; SLJ 7/99) [629.04]

5573 Hindley, Judy. *The Big Red Bus* (PS). Illus. by William Benedict. 1995, Candlewick $15.99 (1-56402-639-6). 32pp. A simple picture book about a road jam caused by a big red bus that has a wheel caught in a large pothole. (Rev: BL 10/15/95; SLJ 1/96)

5574 Hoban, Tana. *Construction Zone* (PS–1). Illus. 1997, Greenwillow $15.89 (0-688-12285-X). 32pp. Thirteen construction machines like the bulldozer, backhoe, and forklift are introduced in pictures and a simple text. (Rev: BCCB 4/97; BL 4/1/97; SLJ 3/97) [624]

5575 Imershein, Betsy. *Trucks* (PS). Illus. 2000, Simon & Schuster $4.99 (0-689-82887-X). 14pp. This board book gives information about eight different trucks. (Rev: BCCB 9/00; BL 6/1–15/00; HBG 10/00)

5576 Jennings, Dana A. *Me, Dad, and Number 6* (K–2). Illus. by Goro Sasaki. 1997, Harcourt $15.00 (0-15-200085-2). A reminiscence about a boy and his father who restore an old 1937 Pontiac coupe, which Dad later races at the stock car track. (Rev: BCCB 5/97; SLJ 4/97)

5577 Johnson, Angela. *Those Building Men* (1–4). Illus. by Barry Moser. 2001, Scholastic $16.95 (0-590-66521-9). 32pp. This poem pays tribute to builders and construction workers who move earth for canals, lay steel for railroads, and cut down trees for building. (Rev: BCCB 2/01; BL 2/1/01; SLJ 3/01)

5578 Katz, Bobbi. *Truck Talk: Rhymes on Wheels* (PS–1). Illus. 1997, Scholastic $10.95 (0-590-69328-X). 32pp. Each of the trucks pictured — e.g., tow trucks, ambulances, and garbage trucks — describes its function in its own words. (Rev: BL 4/1/97; SLJ 3/97) [811]

5579 Kuklin, Susan. *Fighting Fires* (K–2). Illus. 1993, Macmillan LB $15.00 (0-02-751238-X). 32pp. In clear color photos, the daily life and equipment of fire fighters are described. (Rev: BL 7/93) [628.9]

5580 Lewis, Kevin. *Chugga-Chugga Choo Choo* (PS–K). Illus. by Daniel Kirk. 1999, Hyperion LB $15.49 (0-7868-2379-8). 32pp. A day in the life of a busy freight train as it travels through different locales from morning until night. (Rev: BL 10/15/99; SLJ 9/99)

5581 Lewis, Kevin. *The Lot at the End of My Block* (PS–2). Illus. by Reg Cartwright. 2001, Hyperion LB $16.49 (0-7868-2512-X). Using a rhyme similar to "The House That Jack Built" a young boy tells how an empty lot is transformed into an apartment building. (Rev: SLJ 3/01)

5582 Litowinsky, Olga. *Boats for Bedtime* (PS). Illus. by Melanie Hope Greenberg. 1999, Clarion $12.00 (0-395-89128-0). 32pp. An appealing mouse introduces a series of different boats, including tugboats, tankers, kayaks, sailboats, and freighters. (Rev: HBG 3/00; SLJ 8/99)

5583 Lyon, David. *The Biggest Truck* (PS–1). Illus. by author. 1988, Lothrop LB $13.88 (0-688-05514-1). 32pp. Jim the truck driver goes to work when everyone else is going to bed. (Rev: BL 11/1/88; SLJ 1/89)

5584 Maccarone, Grace. *Cars! Cars! Cars!* (PS). Illus. by David A. Carter. 1995, Scholastic $6.95 (0-590-47572-X). 24pp. The concept of different styles, colors, and models of cars is introduced in this very simple picture book. (Rev: BL 1/15/95; SLJ 12/95)

5585 McDonnell, Flora. *I Love Boats* (PS–1). Illus. 1995, Candlewick $15.95 (1-56402-539-X). 32pp. A picture book that introduces all kinds of boats, from a rowboat to a big ship. (Rev: BL 8/95; HB 7–8/95; SLJ 8/95)

5586 McGough, Roger. *Until I Met Dudley: How Everyday Things Really Work* (K–4). Illus. by Chris Riddell. 1997, Walker $15.95 (0-8027-8623-5). An amusing story that explains how five common appliances, like a toaster, work. (Rev: HBG 3/98; SLJ 11/97)

5587 Maestro, Betsy, and Ellen DelVecchio. *Big City Port* (PS–2). Illus. by Giulio Maestro. 1984, Macmillan LB $14.95 (0-02-762110-3); Scholastic paper $4.95 (0-590-41577-8). 32pp. A picture book that shows activities in a big-city port.

5588 Miranda, Anne. *Beep! Beep!* (PS). Illus. by David Murphy. 1999, Turtle $15.95 (1-890515-14-0). All kinds of vehicles are shown in this picture book about a boy who imagines that he is riding in each of them. (Rev: HBG 3/00; SLJ 6/99)

5589 Moignot, Daniel. *Fire Fighting* (PS–1). Trans. from French by Wendy Barish. Illus. by author. Series: First Discovery. 1999, Scholastic $12.95 (0-439-04403-0). Using one sentence per page, this simple account introduces fire fighting equipment such as trucks, ladders, and protective clothing. (Rev: HBG 3/00; SLJ 1/00)

5590 Mott, Evelyn Clarke. *Steam Train Ride* (PS–K). Illus. 1991, Walker LB $14.85 (0-8027-6996-9). A delightful ride for train lovers on Engine 89. (Rev: BL 5/15/91; SLJ 8/91) [625.2]

5591 Neitzel, Shirley. *I'm Taking a Trip on My Train* (PS–1). Illus. by Nancy Winslow Parker. 1999, Greenwillow LB $14.93 (0-688-15834-X). 32pp. A boy pretends he is an engineer on his toy train in this picture book, which uses rebus drawings to introduce parts of a train and a freight yard. (Rev: BL 4/15/99; HBG 10/99; SLJ 3/99)

5592 Piper, Watty. *The Little Engine That Could* (K–2). Illus. by George Hauman and Doris Hauman. 1930, Putnam $7.99 (0-448-40520-2). 48pp. Little Engine saves the day.

5593 Relf, Patricia. *Tonka Big Book of Trucks* (PS–3). Illus. by Thomas La Padula. 1996, Scholastic $12.95 (0-590-84572-1). 48pp. Double-page spreads are used to describe a variety of trucks and their drivers. (Rev: BL 10/1/96; SLJ 9/96) [629.2]

5594 Rex, Michael. *My Race Car* (PS–2). Illus. 2000, Holt $15.95 (0-8050-6101-0). 32pp. In this fantasy, a young boy imagines being on a racetrack in his car and, after checking the car, participating in an exciting race at top speed. (Rev: BCCB 9/00; BL 5/1/00; HBG 10/00; SLJ 7/00) [629.228]

5595 Rex, Michael. *Who Builds?* (PS). Illus. 1999, HarperFestival $6.95 (0-694-01249-1). 16pp. A lift-the-flap book that explores the world of construction, using both human and animal builders. (Rev: BL 5/1/99; SLJ 7/99)

5596 Rex, Michael. *Who Digs?* (PS). Illus. 1999, HarperFestival $6.95 (0-694-01254-8). 16pp. Animals and humans are used in this flap book, which describes different kinds of digging projects. (Rev: BL 5/1/99; SLJ 7/99)

5597 Rotner, Shelley. *Wheels Around* (PS–1). Illus. 1995, Houghton $13.95 (0-395-71815-5). 32pp. All kinds of wheeled vehicles from fire and mail trucks to small trailers and wheelchairs are featured. (Rev: BL 11/1/95; SLJ 10/95) [621.8]

5598 Royston, Angela. *Cars* (PS–2). Illus. by Jane Cradock-Watson and Dave Hopkins. Series: Eye Openers. 1991, Macmillan paper $8.99 (0-689-71517-X). 21pp. Double-page spreads introduce a variety of cars. Also use: *Diggers and Dump Trucks* (1991). (Rev: BL 9/15/91; SLJ 1/92) [629]

5599 Siebert, Diane. *Train Song* (PS–2). Illus. by Mike Wimmer. 1990, HarperCollins LB $16.89 (0-690-04728-2). 32pp. This poem portrays trains as they travel across America. (Rev: BCCB 12/90; BL 10/1/90; SLJ 9/90*)

5600 Siebert, Diane. *Truck Song* (PS–1). Illus. by Byron Barton. 1984, HarperCollins LB $15.89 (0-690-04411-9); paper $6.95 (0-06-443134-7). 32pp. Simple rhymes tell of trucks traveling cross-country.

5601 Sis, Peter. *Trucks Trucks Trucks* (PS). Illus. 1999, Greenwillow $14.95 (0-688-16276-2). 24pp. Matt enters an imaginary world where he operates a number of massive trucks and oversees their many operations. (Rev: BCCB 5/99; BL 6/1–15/99; HB 5–6/99; HBG 10/99; SLJ 5/99)

5602 Stickland, Paul. *Truck Jam* (PS–K). Illus. 2000, Ragged Bears $16.95 (1-929927-03-7). A pop-up book whose pages are filled with dump trucks, tow trucks, and pickups. (Rev: BL 12/1/00)

5603 Swift, Hildegarde, and Lynd Ward. *Little Red Lighthouse and the Great Gray Bridge* (1–3). Illus. by Lynd Ward. 1942, Harcourt $17.00 (0-15-247040-9); paper $8.00 (0-15-652840-1). 52pp. The beacon of the little red lighthouse at the base of the George Washington Bridge in New York City is still needed even after the bridge is built.

5604 *Trucks* (PS). Illus. Series: Eye Openers. 1991, Macmillan $7.95 (0-689-71405-X). 24pp. Double-page spreads feature clear photos of a single object. (Rev: BL 6/15/91) [629.2]

5605 Wilson-Max, Ken. *Little Green Tow Truck* (PS–2). Illus. 1997, Scholastic paper $14.95 (0-590-89802-7). 14pp. Tabs and flaps are featured in this book about the parts and uses of tow trucks. Also use *Big Red Fire Truck* (1997). (Rev: BL 12/15/97) [629]

5606 Wilson-Max, Ken. *Little Red Plane* (PS–1). Illus. 1995, Scholastic $14.95 (0-590-43008-4). 14pp. By pulling tabs, the reader can make this airplane perform all sorts of stunts. (Rev: BL 2/1/96)

5607 Wolf, Sallie. *Peter's Trucks* (PS–K). Illus. by Cat B. Smith. 1992, Whitman LB $14.95 (0-8075-6519-9). 24pp. A variety of trucks are introduced as Peter inquires about the contents of each. (Rev: BCCB 3/92; BL 3/1/92; SLJ 6/92)

5608 Ziefert, Harriet. *Train Song* (PS). Illus. by Donald Saaf. 2000, Orchard $14.95 (0-531-30204-0). 32pp. A little boy watches a freight train go by and sees the contents of all the cars: logs, pigs, ducks, cows, and so on. (Rev: BL 4/1/00; HBG 10/00; SLJ 4/00)

Stories About Holidays and Holy Days

GENERAL AND MISCELLANEOUS

5609 Anderson, Laurie Halse. *No Time for Mother's Day* (K–3). Illus. by Dorothy Donohue. 1999, Albert Whitman $14.95 (0-8075-4955-X). As a special treat for her mother on Mother's Day, Charity turns off all the phones, faxes, and so on, so her mother can have a day of rest. (Rev: BCCB 4/99; BL 2/15/99; HBG 10/99; SLJ 4/99)

5610 Barker, Margot. *What Is Martin Luther King, Jr. Day?* (K–2). Illus. by Matthew Bates. Series: Understanding Holidays. 1990, Children's paper $4.95 (0-516-43784-4). 48pp. Two white classmates learn from their African American friends who Martin Luther King, Jr., was and why we celebrate his birthday. (Rev: SLJ 2/91) [921]

5611 Bouchard, David. *The Dragon New Year: A Chinese Legend* (PS–3). Illus. by Zhong-Yang Huang. 1999, Peachtree $16.95 (1-56145-210-6). 32pp. A Chinese grandmother explains to her frightened grandchild the origin of the noisy Dragon Dance at New Year's and how it was intended to frighten a real dragon who lived at the bottom of the sea. (Rev: BL 9/1/99; HBG 3/00; SLJ 11/99)

5612 Brown, Marc. *Arthur's April Fool* (PS–2). Illus. by author. 1985, Little, Brown $15.95 (0-316-11196-1); paper $5.95 (0-316-11234-8). 32pp. Arthur is afraid he will forget his magic tricks prepared for the April Fools' Day show.

5613 Bunting, Eve. *The Mother's Day Mice* (PS–1). Illus. by Jan Brett. 1986, Houghton $15.00 (0-89919-387-0); paper $5.95 (0-89919-702-7). Three little mice go out to seek presents for Mother's Day; the smallest one brings home a song he heard a human sing. (Rev: BCCB 4/86; BL 4/1/86; SLJ 3/86)

5614 Bunting, Eve. *A Perfect Father's Day* (PS–1). Illus. by Susan Meddaugh. 1993, Houghton paper $5.95 (0-395-66416-0). 32pp. Susie plans a perfect time for her father on Father's Day. (Rev: BL 4/15/91; SLJ 5/91)

5615 Bunting, Eve. *St. Patrick's Day in the Morning* (PS–2). Illus. by Jan Brett. 1983, Houghton $15.00 (0-395-29098-8); paper $5.95 (0-89919-162-2). 32pp. Jamie is too small to parade to the top of the hill with the rest of his family, so he rises early and has a St. Patrick's Day adventure of his own.

5616 Carrier, Roch. *A Happy New Year's Day* (2–4). Illus. by Gilles Pelletier. 1991, Tundra $14.95 (0-88776-267-0). This is a happy recollection of a New Year's Day spent in a French Canadian town during World War II. (Rev: SLJ 2/92)

5617 Chall, Marsha Wilson. *Happy Birthday, America!* (K–2). Illus. by Guy Porfirio. 2000, Harper-Collins LB $15.89 (0-688-13052-6). 32pp. Seen through the eyes of an 8-year-old narrator, a family celebrates the traditions and customs associated with the Fourth of July. (Rev: BL 5/1/00; HBG 10/00; SLJ 6/00)

5618 Chin, Steven A. *Dragon Parade: A Chinese New Year Story* (PS–3). Illus. by Mou-Sien Tseng. 1993, Raintree Steck-Vaughn LB $22.83 (0-8114-7215-9). 32pp. This is a fictionalized account of the Chinese immigrant Noram Ah Sing, who started the first big New Year's Parade in San Francisco. (Rev: BL 5/1/93; SLJ 7/93) [394.2]

5619 Chocolate, Deborah M. *My First Kwanzaa Book* (PS–2). Illus. by Cal Massey. 1992, Scholastic $10.95 (0-590-45762-4). 32pp. A celebration of African American cultural heritage for the very young. (Rev: BCCB 2/93; BL 9/1/92) [394.2]

5620 Compestine, Ying Chang. *The Runaway Rice Cake* (PS–3). Illus. by Tungwai Chau. 2001, Simon & Schuster $16.95 (0-689-82972-8). 40pp. As part of the Chinese New Year's Eve celebration, Mooma Chang cooks a rice cake that comes to life and runs away. (Rev: BL 2/1/01; SLJ 2/01)

5621 Demi. *Happy New Year! Kung-Hsi Fa-Ts' Ai!* (PS–3). Illus. 1997, Crown $16.00 (0-517-70957-0). 36pp. This joyous picture book shows all the preparations and celebrations that accompany the Chinese New Year festival. (Rev: BL 2/15/98; HBG 10/98; SLJ 3/98)

5622 dePaola, Tomie. *The Lady of Guadalupe* (K–3). Illus. by author. 1980, Holiday LB $16.95 (0-8234-0373-4); paper $8.95 (0-8234-0403-X). 48pp. The legend of the patron saint of Mexico is retold in this excellent picture book.

5623 Dillon, Jana. *Lucky O'Leprechaun* (K–2). Illus. by author. 1998, Pelican $14.95 (1-56554-333-5). On St. Patrick's Day weekend, Meg and Sean are determined to catch the leprechaun that lives under a thorn bush in the garden. (Rev: HBG 3/99; SLJ 1/99)

5624 *The 11th Commandment: Wisdom from Our Children* (PS–3). Illus. 1996, Jewish Lights $16.95 (1-879045-46-X). 48pp. The results of a survey of a group of children from different faiths who were asked to suggest an 11th commandment. (Rev: BL 10/1/96) [170]

5625 English, Karen. *Nadia's Hands* (K–4). Illus. by Jonathan Weiner. 1999, Boyds Mills $15.95 (1-56397-667-6). 32pp. A Pakistani American girl learns to appreciate the rich traditions of marriage in her faith when she is asked to be a flower girl at her aunt's wedding. (Rev: BCCB 4/99; BL 3/1/99; HBG 10/99; SLJ 4/99)

5626 Ford, Juwanda G. *K Is for Kwanzaa: A Kwanzaa Alphabet Book* (K–3). Illus. by Ken Wilson-Max. 1997, Scholastic $10.95 (0-590-92200-9). 32pp. Arranged alphabetically various objects, customs, and rituals connected with Kwanzaa are introduced. (Rev: BL 9/1/97; HBG 3/98; SLJ 10/97) [394.261]

5627 Ghazi, Suhaib Hamid. *Ramadan* (K–4). Illus. by Omar Rayyan. 1996, Holiday $16.95 (0-8234-1254-7). 32pp. The Islamic month of Ramadan, with its fasting and prayers, as seen through the eyes of a young boy. (Rev: BCCB 12/96; BL 10/1/96; SLJ 10/96) [297]

5628 Johnston, Tony. *Day of the Dead* (K–4). Illus. by Jeanette Winter. 1997, Harcourt $14.00 (0-15-222863-2). 56pp. A Mexican family makes preparations for the holiday Day of the Dead and celebrates it festively. (Rev: BL 9/15/97; HBG 3/98; SLJ 9/97)

5629 Koller, Jackie F. *Mole and Shrew: All Year Through* (2–3). 1997, Random paper $3.99 (0-679-88666-4). 80pp. Best friends Mole and Shrew have great times celebrating such holidays as Christmas, Thanksgiving, New Years Eve and Easter. (Rev: BL 2/1/98; HBG 3/98)

5630 Kroll, Steven. *Happy Father's Day* (K–2). Illus. by Marylin Hafner. 1996, Silhouette paper $3.99 (0-373-24033-3). 32pp. A healthy breakfast is the first of several special treats for Dad. (Rev: BCCB 6/88; BL 4/1/88; SLJ 5/88)

5631 Kroll, Steven. *It's Groundhog Day!* (PS–2). Illus. by Jeni Bassett. 1987, Scholastic paper $3.25 (0-590-44669-X). 32pp. Godfrey Groundhog will not see his shadow come February 2, and this very much upsets Roland Raccoon, who owns a ski lodge. (Rev: BL 10/15/87; SLJ 11/87)

5632 Kroll, Steven. *Mary McLean and the St. Patrick's Day Parade* (1–3). Illus. by Michael Dooling. 1991, Scholastic $15.95 (0-590-43701-1). 32pp. A young Irish girl newly arrived in the United States is visited by a leprechaun on St. Patrick's Day. (Rev: BCCB 2/91; BL 1/1/91; SLJ 6/91)

5633 Levine, Abby. *Gretchen Groundhog, It's Your Day!* (PS–K). Illus. by Nancy Cote. 1998, Albert Whitman $15.95 (0-8075-3058-1). This book about Groundhog Day tells of Gretchen Groundhog, who is too shy to appear in front of people to look at her shadow. (Rev: BL 12/1/98; HBG 3/99; SLJ 1/99)

5634 Levy, Janice. *The Spirit of Tio Fernando: A Day of the Dead Story/El Espiritu de Tio Fernando: Una Historia del Dia de los Muertos* (1–3). Trans. by Teresa Mlawer. Illus. by Morella Fuenmayor. 1995, Albert Whitman $14.95 (0-8075-7585-2); paper $6.95 (0-8075-7586-0). 32pp. On the Day of the Dead, Nando remembers his Uncle Fernando, who died six months before. (Rev: BL 11/15/95; SLJ 11/95)

5635 Low, William. *Chinatown* (K–1). Illus. 1997, Holt paper $15.95 (0-8050-4214-8). 32pp. At Chinese New Year's, a boy and his grandmother take a tour through their Chinatown. (Rev: BL 9/15/97; HBG 3/98; SLJ 9/97)

5636 Lowery, Linda. *Earth Day* (2–3). Illus. by Mary Bergherr. 1991, Carolrhoda LB $21.27 (0-87614-662-0). 48pp. The significance of the 1990 Earth Day celebration is explained in simple terms. (Rev: BL 6/15/91; SLJ 8/91) [333.7]

5637 Medearis, Angela Shelf. *Seven Spools of Thread: A Kwanzaa Story* (K–3). Illus. by Daniel

Minter. 2000, Albert Whitman $15.95 (0-8075-7315-9). 40pp. An original folktale that takes place in a Ghanaian village and effectively introduces the seven principles of Kwanzaa. (Rev: BL 9/15/00; HBG 3/01)

5638 Mills, Claudia. *Phoebe's Parade* (PS–1). Illus. by Carolyn Ewing. 1994, Macmillan paper $14.95 (0-02-767012-0). 32pp. Phoebe's plan to shine on the Fourth of July backfires. (Rev: BL 3/1/94; SLJ 6/94)

5639 Moore, Elizabeth, and Alice Couvillon. *Mimi and Jean-Paul's Cajun Mardi Gras* (1–3). Illus. by Marilyn C. Rougelot. 1996, Pelican $14.95 (1-56554-069-7). The unique Courir (Run) de Mardi Gras celebrated in Cajun country is experienced by a young girl. (Rev: SLJ 3/96)

5640 Moorman, Margaret. *Light the Lights! A Story About Celebrating Hanukkah and Christmas* (K–3). Illus. 1994, Scholastic $12.95 (0-590-47003-5). 32pp. This book celebrates the spirit of both Christmas and Hanukkah and shows similarities in these holidays and their traditions. (Rev: BL 8/94) [394.26]

5641 Morris, Ann. *Weddings* (PS–2). Illus. 1995, Lothrop LB $14.93 (0-688-13273-1). 32pp. Different wedding customs and clothing from around the world are pictured and discussed. (Rev: BCCB 10/95; BL 10/1/95; SLJ 1/96) [391.5]

5642 O'Donnell, Elizabeth Lee. *Patrick's Day* (K–2). Illus. by Jacqueline Rogers. 1994, Morrow $15.00 (0-688-07853-2). 32pp. When Patrick, who is growing up in an Irish village, realizes that St. Patrick's Day is not in his honor, he becomes very grumpy. (Rev: BL 4/1/94; SLJ 5/94)

5643 Paraskevas, Betty. *On the Day the Tall Ships Sailed* (PS–3). Illus. by Michael Paraskevas. 2000, Simon & Schuster $16.00 (0-689-82864-0). 32pp. This enchanting picture book depicts a single eagle soaring over the tall ships that are sailing up the Hudson River on the Fourth of July. (Rev: BL 10/15/00; HBG 10/00; SLJ 10/00)

5644 Patrick, Diane. *Family Celebrations* (2–5). Illus. by Michael Bryant. 1993, Silver Moon LB $14.95 (1-881889-04-1). 62pp. Portrays a variety of family gatherings that are associated with such occasions as birth, marriage, and death as they are observed in many cultures. (Rev: BL 6/1–15/93) [392]

5645 Rattigan, Jama Kim. *Dumpling Soup* (PS–3). Illus. by Lillian Hsu-Flanders. 1993, Little, Brown $16.95 (0-316-73445-4). 32pp. Marisa attempts to make dumplings when her extended, multiracial family celebrates New Year's Eve in this story set in Hawaii. (Rev: BCCB 10/93; BL 9/15/93; HB 11–12/93; SLJ 12/93)

5646 Rosen, Michael J. *Elijah's Angel: A Story for Chanukah and Christmas* (K–3). Illus. by Aminah Robinson. 1992, Harcourt $16.00 (0-15-225394-7). 32pp. The story of an unusual friendship between an elderly African American man and a 9-year-old Jewish boy. (Rev: BCCB 11/92; BL 8/92*; HB 11–12/92*)

5647 Ross, Kathy. *Crafts for Kwanzaa* (1–3). Illus. by Sharon L. Holm. 1994, Millbrook LB $21.90 (1-56294-412-6). 48pp. A history of Kwanzaa is given, plus instructions for a number of projects using simple materials. (Rev: BL 10/15/94) [745]

5648 Saint James, Synthia. *The Gifts of Kwanzaa* (PS–2). Illus. 1994, Albert Whitman LB $14.95 (0-8075-2907-9). 32pp. Explains the origins of Kwanzaa and identifies the Seven Principles as well as giving information about rituals. (Rev: BL 11/15/94) [394.2]

5649 Sasso, Sandy Eisenberg. *A Prayer for the Earth: The Story of Naamah, Noah's Wife* (PS–2). Illus. by Bethanne Andersen. 1997, Jewish Lights $16.95 (1-879045-60-5). 32pp. Noah's wife, Naamah, is given the job of bringing samples of each of the earth's plants into Noah's Ark. (Rev: BCCB 7–8/97; BL 2/15/97; SLJ 6/97)

5650 Shaik, Fatima. *On Mardi Gras Day* (K–3). Illus. by Floyd Cooper. 1999, Dial $16.99 (0-8037-1442-4). 32pp. An African American girl explains how she celebrates Mardi Gras in the South — by dressing up, watching parades, and sharing a feast with the family. (Rev: BL 3/1/99; HBG 10/99; SLJ 4/99)

5651 Swartz, Nancy Sohn. *In Our Image: God's First Creatures* (PS–2). Illus. by Melanie Hall. 1998, Jewish Lights $16.95 (1-879045-99-0). 32pp. Several animals reveal characteristics that God would want humans to possess, such as the bravery of the tiger and the gentleness of the lamb. (Rev: BL 10/1/98; HBG 3/99; SLJ 3/99) [296.3]

5652 Thomas, Jane Resh. *Celebration!* (K–3). Illus. by Raul Colon. 1997, Hyperion LB $15.49 (0-7868-2160-4). 32pp. Everyone is celebrating the Fourth of July at Maggie's house, including a chagrined Maurice, who has been caught stealing candy from a drugstore. (Rev: BL 5/15/97; SLJ 7/97)

5653 Tucker, Kathy. *The Leprechaun in the Basement* (PS–2). Illus. by John Sandford. 1999, Albert Whitman $18.95 (0-8075-4450-7). 32pp. On St. Patrick's Day, Michael meets a leprechaun and the two learn a lesson from each other about relationships. (Rev: BL 1/1–15/99; HBG 10/99; SLJ 12/98)

5654 Vaughan, Marcia. *The Dancing Dragon* (K–2). Illus. by Stanley Wong Hoo Foon. 1996, Mondo paper $5.95 (1-57255-134-8). In rhyming couplets, a Chinese American child describes preparations for Chinese New Year celebrations, including the dragon parade. (Rev: SLJ 12/96)

5655 Walter, Mildred P. *Kwanzaa: A Family Affair* (PS–2). Illus. by Cheryl Carrington. 1995, Lothrop $15.00 (0-688-11553-5). 80pp. Background material, ways of celebrating the holiday, and crafts and gifts are all covered in this introduction to Kwanzaa. (Rev: BL 9/15/95) [394.2]

5656 Waters, Kate, and Madeline Slovenz-Low. *Lion Dancer: Ernie Wan's Chinese New Year* (PS–3). 1990, Scholastic paper $4.99 (0-590-43047-5). 32pp. This account describes how a Chinese-American family celebrates the lunar New Year. (Rev: HB 7–8/90; SLJ 2/90) [391.2]

5657 Watson, Wendy. *Hurray for the Fourth of July* (PS–2). Illus. 1992, Houghton $16.00 (0-395-53627-8). 32pp. This picture book shows and tells how a New England family celebrates the Fourth of July in their village. (Rev: BL 4/1/92; SLJ 6/92)

5658 Wong, Janet S. *This Next New Year* (PS–3). Illus. by Yangsook Choi. 2000, Farrar $16.00 (0-374-35503-7). 32pp. A little boy who is half Korean prepares to celebrate Chinese New Year and describes the traditional and modern customs involved. (Rev: BCCB 9/00; BL 9/15/00; HB 11–12/00; HBG 3/01; SLJ 10/00)

5659 Yolen, Jane. *The Three Bears Holiday Rhyme Book* (PS–2). Illus. by Jane Dyer. 1995, Harcourt $15.00 (0-15-200932-9). 32pp. Fifteen poems featuring Goldilocks and the Three Bears are used to introduce such holidays as Valentine's Day, Arbor Day, and Groundhog Day. (Rev: BL 3/15/95; SLJ 6/95) [811.54]

5660 Ziefert, Harriet. *Hats Off for the Fourth of July!* (PS–2). Illus. by Gus Miller. 2000, Viking $15.99 (0-670-89118-5). 32pp. A description in words and illustrations of a New England Fourth of July parade complete with cowboys, floats, and patriots with muskets. (Rev: BCCB 6/00; BL 4/15/00; HBG 10/00; SLJ 6/00)

BIRTHDAYS

5661 Bailey, Debbie. *Happy Birthday* (PS). Photos by Susan Huszar. Series: Talk-About-Books. 1999, Annick $5.95 (1-55037-559-8). In this board book, full-color illustrations are used to show different ways of celebrating children's birthdays. (Rev: SLJ 9/99)

5662 Barker, Marjorie. *Magical Hands* (2–4). Illus. by Yoshi. 1989, Picture Book $16.00 (0-88708-103-7). 28pp. William does his friends' work, hoping they will think it is magic, and then finds that his work is done too! (Rev: BL 2/1/90)

5663 Barrett, Judith. *Benjamin's 365 Birthdays* (K–2). Illus. by Ron Barrett. 1992, Simon & Schuster paper $4.95 (0-689-71635-4). 40pp. Benjamin the bear is so delighted with his birthday presents that he decides to rewrap them so that he can enjoy one each day throughout the ensuing months.

5664 Beck, Andrea. *Elliot Bakes a Cake* (PS–1). Illus. 1999, Kids Can $12.95 (1-55074-443-7). 32pp. Elliot Moose and his stuffed toy friends converge on the kitchen to bake a birthday cake for their pal Lionel Lion. (Rev: BL 10/1/99; HBG 3/00; SLJ 12/99)

5665 Best, Cari. *Three Cheers for Catherine the Great!* (PS–3). Illus. by Giselle Potter. 1999, DK $16.95 (0-7894-2622-6). Sarah decides that the perfect birthday present for her Russian grandmother would be to help her learn to read and write English. (Rev: BCCB 1/00; BL 9/15/99*; HB 11–12/99; HBG 3/00; SLJ 8/99)

5666 Brown, Marc. *Arthur's Birthday* (K–2). Illus. 1989, Little, Brown $15.95 (0-316-11073-6); paper $5.95 (0-316-11074-4). Muffy is upset to learn that Arthur's birthday is the same day as hers. (Rev: BL 4/15/89; HB 5–6/89)

5667 Brown, Tricia. *Hello, Amigos!* (K–2). Illus. by Fran Ortiz. 1992, Holt paper $7.95 (0-8050-1891-3). 48pp. The anticipation and excitement of Frankie Valdez's birthday. (Rev: BCCB 1/87; BL 12/15/86; SLJ 4/87)

5668 Butler, Dorothy. *My Brown Bear Barney at the Party* (PS–2). Illus. by Elizabeth Fuller. 2001, Greenwillow LB $15.89 (0-688-17549-X). 24pp. At Barney Hinkel's birthday party his little sister claims that Barney Bear is hers, much to the consternation of the toy's real owner. (Rev: BL 2/1/01; SLJ 2/01)

5669 Cameron, Ann. *Julian, Dream Doctor* (2–4). Illus. by Ann Strugnell. Series: Stepping Stone. 1990, Random LB $11.99 (0-679-90524-3); paper $3.99 (0-679-80524-9). 40pp. In this warm story of an African American family, Julian wants to discover Dad's idea of a dream birthday present. (Rev: BCCB 3/90; BL 5/15/90; HB 9–10/90; SLJ 7/90)

5670 Capucilli, Alyssa Satin. *Happy Birthday, Biscuit!* (PS). Illus. by Pat Schories. Series: I Can Read. 1999, HarperCollins LB $12.89 (0-06-028361-0). 24pp. A frisky puppy named Biscuit enjoys a birthday romp with his friends in this book for beginning readers. (Rev: BL 6/1–15/99; HBG 10/99; SLJ 6/99)

5671 Carle, Eric. *The Secret Birthday Message* (PS–1). Illus. by author. 1972, HarperCollins LB $15.89 (0-690-72348-2); paper $6.95 (0-06-443099-5). 26pp. In a brightly illustrated picture book with intriguing cutouts, a little boy has to decipher the coded message to find his birthday present.

5672 Carlstrom, Nancy White. *Happy Birthday, Jesse Bear!* (PS–K). Illus. by Bruce Degen. 1994, Macmillan $15.00 (0-02-717277-5). 32pp. Jesse Bear arranges for his birthday party, which turns out to be a big success. (Rev: BL 11/1/94; SLJ 12/94)

5673 Charlip, Remy, et al. *Handtalk Birthday: A Number and Story Book in Sign Language* (1–4). Illus. by George Ancona. 1987, Simon & Schuster $15.95 (0-02-718080-8). 48pp. A happy birthday book in sign language that tells about a surprise party for Mary Beth. (Rev: BL 3/15/87; HB 9–10/87; SLJ 5/87)

5674 Chavarria-Chairez, Becky. *Magda's Tortillas/ Las tortillas de Magda* (K–2). Trans. by Julia Mercedes Castilla. Illus. by Anne Vega. 2000, Piñata $14.95 (1-55885-286-7). On her birthday, Magda produces tortillas in different shapes in this bilingual book. (Rev: SLJ 10/00)

5675 Cooke, Trish. *So Much* (PS–K). Illus. by Helen Oxenbury. 1994, Candlewick $16.99 (1-56402-344-3). 32pp. Relatives arrive for Daddy's surprise birthday party, but it is the baby who is the center of attention. (Rev: BCCB 1/95; BL 3/1/95*; HB 11–12/94; SLJ 1/95)

5676 Corey, Dorothy. *Will It Ever Be My Birthday?* (PS–K). Illus. by Eileen Christelow. 1986, Whitman LB $14.95 (0-8075-9106-8). 32pp. Rabbit gets an invitation to Bear's birthday party and wonders if his will ever come. (Rev: BL 10/1/86; SLJ 3/86)

5677 Cousins, Lucy. *Happy Birthday, Maisy* (PS–1). Illus. by author. 1998, Candlewick $12.99 (0-7636-0577-8). In this interactive book with flaps and tabs,

little mouse Maisy enjoys her birthday. (Rev: SLJ 10/98)

5678 Day, Alexandra. *Carl's Birthday* (PS–2). Illus. 1995, Farrar $12.95 (0-374-31144-7). 32pp. In this almost wordless picture book, Madeline and her beloved Rottweiler, Carl, secretly help prepare a surprise birthday party for the dog. (Rev: BL 1/1–15/96; SLJ 12/95)

5679 De Groat, Diane. *Happy Birthday to You, You Belong in a Zoo* (PS–1). Illus. 1999, Morrow $15.00 (0-688-16544-3). 32pp. Gilbert wants to get even with bully Lewis by giving him a dumb gift at his birthday party, but Mom saves the day. (Rev: BL 8/99; HBG 3/00; SLJ 10/99)

5680 Dickinson, Rebecca. *Monster Cake* (PS–3). Illus. by author. 2000, Scholastic paper $5.99 (0-439-06752-9). Monster children make a delicious birthday cake for their mother that consists of worms, slugs, and bugs. (Rev: SLJ 3/01)

5681 Dorflinger, Carolyn. *Tomorrow Is Mom's Birthday* (PS–1). Illus. by Iza Trapani. 1994, Whispering Coyote $14.95 (1-879085-84-4). 32pp. Tyler thinks of all sorts of things to give to his mother on her birthday, but he decides to paint a family portrait. (Rev: BCCB 4/94; BL 5/1/94)

5682 Edmiston, Jim. *The Emperor Who Forgot His Birthday* (PS–1). Illus. by author. Series: A Barefoot Beginner Book. 1999, Barefoot $14.95 (1-84148-015-0). An emperor wakes up and finds that his cat, family, and servants are all missing, little knowing that they are preparing a surprise birthday party for him. (Rev: SLJ 12/99)

5683 Ellwand, David. *Alfred's Party: A Collection of Picture Puzzles* (1–3). Illus. 2000, Dutton $15.99 (0-525-46385-2). 32pp. On his birthday, Alfred, a dog, realizes that he has forgotten to organize a party and gets a group of children to help with the last-minute preparations. (Rev: BL 5/15/00; HBG 10/00; SLJ 12/00)

5684 Estes, Kristyn Rehling. *Manuela's Gift* (K–2). Illus. by Claire B. Cotts. 1999, Chronicle $15.95 (0-8118-2085-8). Manuela dreams of having a beautiful yellow dress but, when she doesn't receive it because her family is poor, she gradually accepts the situation. (Rev: BL 6/1–15/99; HBG 10/99; SLJ 10/99)

5685 Fox, Mem. *Night Noises* (PS–2). Illus. by Terry Denton. 1989, Harcourt $16.00 (0-15-200543-9); paper $4.95 (0-15-257421-2). 32pp. An old lady's dog becomes agitated at the commotion he hears outside while the woman sleeps, which turns out to be relatives arriving for a surprise ninetieth birthday party. (Rev: BL 11/15/89; HB 11–12/89*; SLJ 9/89*)

5686 Gantos, Jack. *Happy Birthday, Rotten Ralph* (PS–3). Illus. by Nicole Rubel. 1990, Houghton $13.95 (0-395-53766-5). 32pp. Rotten Ralph, a cat, is so rotten that even sweet Sarah decides he doesn't deserve a birthday party. (Rev: BL 10/1/90; HB 1–2/90; SLJ 10/90)

5687 Giff, Patricia Reilly. *Happy Birthday, Ronald Morgan!* (2–3). Illus. by Susanna Natti. 1988, Puffin paper $5.99 (0-14-050668-3). 32pp. The day goes from bad to worse for Ronald, but ends up delightfully with a surprise birthday party. (Rev: BL 10/15/86; SLJ 4/87)

5688 Goldstein, Bobbye S., sel. *Birthday Rhymes, Special Times* (PS–3). Illus. by Jose Aruego and Ariane Dewey. 1995, Dell paper $5.99 (0-440-41018-5). 48pp. Poems that are amusingly illustrated deal with some aspect of birthdays. (Rev: SLJ 6/93) [811]

5689 Griffith, Helen V. *How Many Candles?* (K–3). Illus. by Sonja Lamut. 1999, Greenwillow $16.00 (0-688-16258-4). 24pp. Different animals help celebrate Robbie's tenth birthday, although each realizes that its life cycle span differs from that of humans. (Rev: BL 10/15/99; HBG 3/00; SLJ 9/99)

5690 Hershenhorn, Esther. *There Goes Lowell's Party!* (K–3). Illus. by Jacqueline Rogers. 1998, Holiday LB $15.95 (0-8234-1313-6). In this tale set in the Ozarks, Lowell is afraid that rain will spoil his birthday party. (Rev: BCCB 4/98; HBG 10/98; SLJ 3/98)

5691 Hest, Amy. *Gabby Growing Up* (K–3). Illus. by Amy Schwartz. 1998, Simon & Schuster $16.00 (0-689-80573-X). 32pp. Gabby and her mother go to Manhattan, where they celebrate Grandpa's birthday with him at a skating rink. (Rev: BL 1/1–15/98; HBG 10/98; SLJ 3/98)

5692 Hest, Amy. *Nana's Birthday Party* (K–4). Illus. by Amy Schwartz. 1993, Morrow $15.95 (0-688-07497-9). 32pp. Maggie wants to write a story for her grandmother for her birthday, but she lacks the inspiration. (Rev: BL 8/93*)

5693 Hobbie, Holly. *Toot and Puddle: A Present for Toot* (PS–1). Illus. 1998, Little, Brown $12.95 (0-316-36556-4). 32pp. Puddle, a pig, is in a quandary about buying a birthday present for friend Toot, another pig. (Rev: BL 11/1/98; HBG 3/99; SLJ 10/98)

5694 Hopkins, Lee Bennett, ed. *Happy Birthday* (K–4). Illus. by Hilary Knight. 1991, Simon & Schuster paper $11.95 (0-671-70973-9). This collection of poems about birthdays also contains a list of birthdays of famous people. (Rev: SLJ 10/91) [811]

5695 Howard, Elizabeth F. *Lulu's Birthday* (PS–1). Illus. by Pat Cummings. 2001, Greenwillow LB $15.89 (0-688-15945-1). 24pp. A delightful picture book in which two children are part of the plan to surprise Aunt Lulu with a birthday party. (Rev: BL 1/1–15/01; SLJ 2/01)

5696 Howe, James. *Creepy-Crawly Birthday* (PS–3). Illus. by Leslie Morrill. 1991, Morrow LB $13.88 (0-688-09688-3). 48pp. Toby's pet dog and cat have an unexpected surprise for him at his birthday party. (Rev: BL 11/15/91; SLJ 11/91)

5697 Hutchins, Pat. *Happy Birthday, Sam* (1–3). Illus. by author. 1978, Morrow paper $5.95 (0-688-10482-7). 32pp. Sam is disappointed on his birthday morning to discover that he hasn't grown at all.

5698 Hutchins, Pat. *It's My Birthday* (PS–2). 1999, Greenwillow LB $14.93 (0-688-09664-6). 32pp. Monster Billy acts so selfishly about his birthday presents that he finds it difficult to get anyone to

play with him. (Rev: BL 6/1–15/99; HBG 10/99; SLJ 3/99)

5699 Jeram, Anita. *Birthday Happy, Contrary Mary* (PS–K). Illus. 1998, Candlewick $9.99 (0-7636-0448-8); paper $3.29 (0-7636-0456-9). 24pp. Contrary Mary, a little mouse who does things her own way, engages in some strange birthday behavior. (Rev: BCCB 5/98; BL 5/15/98; HBG 10/98; SLJ 5/98)

5700 Jocelyn, Marthe. *Hannah and the Seven Dresses* (PS–K). Illus. 1999, Dutton $14.99 (0-525-46113-2). 32pp. Hannah has a special dress for each day of the week, but when her birthday comes, she must think of something even more special. (Rev: BL 7/99; HBG 10/99; SLJ 7/99)

5701 Jonell, Lynne. *It's My Birthday, Too!* (PS–3). Illus. by Petra Mathers. 1999, Putnam $12.99 (0-399-23323-7). 32pp. Christopher doesn't want his younger brother at his birthday party, but he lives to regret it. (Rev: BCCB 4/99; BL 3/1/99*; HB 5–6/99; HBG 10/99; SLJ 5/99)

5702 Keselman, Gabriela. *The Gift* (PS–2). Illus. by Pep Montserrat. Series: Cranky Nell Books. 1999, Kane/Miller $15.95 (0-916291-91-X). Mikie's response to what he wants for his birthday is cryptic, but eventually his parents examine each clue and correctly decide it is a hug. (Rev: BCCB 1/00; HBG 3/00; SLJ 12/99)

5703 Kleven, Elisa. *Hooray, A Piñata!* (PS–2). Illus. 1996, Dutton $16.99 (0-525-45605-8). 32pp. Clara doesn't want her piñata, the image of a small dog, to be destroyed. (Rev: BL 9/15/96*; SLJ 11/96)

5704 Klinting, Lars. *Bruno the Baker* (PS–2). Illus. 1997, Holt $15.95 (0-8050-5506-1). In this step-by-step picture book, Bruno the beaver bakes his own birthday cake with the help of his friend Felix. (Rev: BL 1/1–15/98; HBG 3/98; SLJ 10/97)

5705 Kulling, Monica. *Edgar Badger's Balloon Day* (K–3). Illus. by Carol O'Malia. 1997, Mondo paper $4.50 (1-57255-220-4). 46pp. Edgar Badger is afraid that his friends have forgotten that his birthday is approaching. (Rev: SLJ 1/98)

5706 Lascaro, Rita. *Down on the Farm* (1–2). Illus. Series: Easy Reader. 1999, Harcourt paper $3.95 (0-15-202000-4). 20pp. Shawn and his dog, Keeper, prepare for the birthday they share in this book for beginning readers. (Rev: BL 10/1/99; SLJ 4/99)

5707 Lobe, Mira. *Christoph Wants a Party* (1–3). Retold by Marcia Lane. Illus. by Winfried Opgenoorth. 1995, Kane/Miller $15.95 (0-916291-59-6). In a six-page foldout section, Christoph imagines an extravagant fifth birthday party. (Rev: SLJ 2/96)

5708 Lodge, Bernard. *Mouldylocks* (K–3). Illus. 1998, Houghton $15.00 (0-395-90945-7). 32pp. Mouldylocks, a witch, attends her surprise birthday party, where she plays such games as Snakes and Ladders with real snakes and ladders. When things get out of hand, she has to use her new book of spells to turn her guests back into themselves. (Rev: BL 9/1/98; HBG 3/99; SLJ 10/98)

5709 Lopez, Loretta. *The Birthday Swap* (PS–3). Illus. 1997, Lee & Low $15.95 (1-880000-47-4). 32pp. A young Mexican American girl enjoys the annual reunion of family from both sides of the border, when everyone comes to celebrate her older sister's birthday. (Rev: BCCB 6/97; BL 5/1/97; SLJ 6/97)

5710 McCourt, Lisa, adapt. *Della Splatnuk, Birthday Girl* (K–3). Illus. by Pat G. Porter. Series: Chicken Soup for Little Souls. 1999, Health Communications $14.95 (1-55874-600-5). Carrie realizes how cruel her classmates are when she is the only one to attend Della's birthday party because the others think she is weird. (Rev: BL 5/1/99; HBG 10/99; SLJ 9/99)

5711 McLarey, Kristina Thermaenius, and Myra McLarey. *When You Take a Pig to a Party* (PS–3). Illus. by Marjory Wunsch. 2000, Orchard LB $16.99 (0-531-33257-8). 32pp. When Adelaide is invited to Ethan's birthday party she makes the mistake of bringing her pet pig, Sherman, along. (Rev: BL 4/15/00; HBG 10/00; SLJ 4/00)

5712 Moon, Nicola. *Happy Birthday, Amelia* (K–2). Illus. by Jenny Jones. 2000, Pavilion $17.95 (1-86205-208-5). 32pp. On her birthday, Amelia follows clues that take her around her farmyard home and eventually to the orchard where everyone is waiting for her party to begin. (Rev: BL 7/00)

5713 Mora, Pat. *A Birthday Basket for Tia* (PS–1). Illus. by Cecily Lang. 1992, Macmillan LB $16.00 (0-02-767400-2). 32pp. Cecila decides on what is the perfect present for her great-aunt's ninetieth birthday. (Rev: BL 9/15/92; HB 1–2/93; SLJ 1/93)

5714 Mueller, Virginia. *Monster's Birthday Hiccups* (PS–K). Illus. by Lynn Munsinger. 1992, Whitman LB $13.95 (0-8075-5267-4). 24pp. Monster cures his hiccups at his birthday party by blowing out the candles on his cake and granting his own wish. (Rev: BL 1/15/92)

5715 Oram, Hiawyn. *Badger's Bring Something Party* (PS–2). Illus. by Susan Varley. 1995, Lothrop $15.00 (0-688-14082-3). 32pp. Mole feels out of place at Badger's birthday party because he didn't have a gift to bring. A prequel to *Badger's Parting Gifts* (1984). (Rev: BL 4/15/95; HB 5–6/95; SLJ 7/95)

5716 Oxenbury, Helen. *It's My Birthday* (PS). Illus. 1994, Candlewick $9.99 (1-56402-412-1). 24pp. A group of animal friends help a boy make a cake for his birthday by contributing ingredients. (Rev: BL 7/94; SLJ 11/94)

5717 Pfister, Marcus. *Make a Wish, Honey Bear!* (PS–K). Illus. 1999, North-South LB $15.88 (0-7358-1244-6). 32pp. When it's time to blow out the candles on his birthday cake, Honey Bear doesn't know what to wish for, so everyone in the family offers a suggestion. (Rev: BL 11/1/99; HBG 3/00; SLJ 11/99)

5718 Polacco, Patricia. *Some Birthday!* (K–3). Illus. 1991, Simon & Schuster paper $16.00 (0-671-72750-8). Patricia thinks everyone has forgotten about her sixth birthday, until the surprise comes in the evening. (Rev: BL 1/1/92*; SLJ 10/91)

5719 Pomerantz, Charlotte. *The Birthday Letters* (K–3). Illus. by JoAnn Adinolfi. 2000, Greenwillow LB $15.89 (0-688-16336-X). Tom decides to disin-

vite Emilia from his dog's birthday party when he learns she is going to bring her pet gerbils. (Rev: HBG 10/00; SLJ 6/00)

5720 Quattlebaum, Mary. *Aunt CeeCee, Aunt Belle, and Mama's Surprise* (K–4). Illus. by Michael Chesworth. 1999, Doubleday $15.95 (0-385-32275-5). A young girl narrates this simple story about her problems in arranging a surprise birthday party for her mother. (Rev: BCCB 6/99; HBG 10/99; SLJ 7/99)

5721 Roth, Susan L. *Happy Birthday Mr. Kang* (2–4). Illus. 2001, National Geographic $16.95 (0-7922-7723-6). 32pp. When Mr. Kang's grandson Sam asks if the old man's hua mei bird wants its freedom, Mr. Kang releases it with surprising results in this birthday story. (Rev: BL 1/1–15/01; SLJ 2/01)

5722 Scamell, Ragnhild. *Toby's Doll's House* (PS–3). Illus. by Adrian Reynolds. 1999, Levinson $14.95 (1-86233-026-3). Toby takes all the boxes in which his birthday gifts were packed and turns them into the doll's house that he really wanted. (Rev: SLJ 9/99)

5723 Shaw, Nancy. *Sheep in a Shop* (PS–1). Illus. by Margot Apple. 1991, Houghton $14.00 (0-395-53681-2). 32pp. Five sheep are a little short of cash when they shop for a present for a friend. (Rev: HB 5–6/91*; SLJ 2/91)

5724 Soto, Gary. *Chato and the Party Animals* (PS–3). Illus. by Susan Guevara. 2000, Putnam $15.99 (0-399-23159-5). 32pp. Because he is from a pound, Novio Boy doesn't know his birthday, so Chato the Cat organizes a special surprise birthday party for him. (Rev: BL 8/00; HBG 3/01; SLJ 7/00)

5725 Spirn, Michele. *A Know-Nothing Birthday* (K–2). Illus. by R. W. Alley. Series: An I Can Read Book. 1997, HarperCollins LB $14.89 (0-06-027274-0). 48pp. An easy-to-read book about the Know-Nothings — Boris, Norris, Doris, and Morris — and the birthday party Boris gives himself. (Rev: SLJ 6/97)

5726 Stevens, Jan R. *Carlos and the Carnival: Carlos y la Feria* (K–3). Illus. by Jeanne Arnold. 1999, Northland $15.95 (0-87358-733-2). 32pp. In this bilingual book, Carlos receives some money for his birthday but does not need his father's advice about spending it wisely. (Rev: BL 8/99; HBG 3/00; SLJ 7/99)

5727 Stewart, Paul. *The Birthday Presents* (PS–2). Illus. by Chris Riddell. 2000, HarperCollins $12.95 (0-06-028279-7). Rabbit and Hedgehog don't know their birthdays so they decide to have a joint birthday party the next day so they can exchange presents. (Rev: HBG 10/00; SLJ 2/00)

5728 Stock, Catherine. *Birthday Present* (PS–1). Illus. Series: Festive Year. 1991, Macmillan paper $11.95 (0-02-788401-5). 32pp. A boy takes special care in selecting a present for his friend Maria. (Rev: BCCB 3/91; BL 2/1/91; SLJ 9/91)

5729 Theroux, Phyllis. *Serefina under the Circumstances* (K–3). Illus. by Marjorie Priceman. 1999, Greenwillow $16.00 (0-688-15942-7). 32pp. Serefina imagines that the everyday metaphors that people use are really true (e.g., someone is beside himself), and this literal-minded girl tries to keep her young brother's surprise birthday party a secret. (Rev: BCCB 10/99; BL 9/1/99; HBG 3/00; SLJ 9/99)

5730 Tryon, Leslie. *Albert's Birthday* (K–3). 1999, Simon & Schuster $16.00 (0-689-82296-0). 48pp. Patsy Pig plans a lavish birthday party for her friend Albert Duck but, unfortunately, forgets to invite the guest of honor. (Rev: BL 10/1/99; HBG 3/00; SLJ 1/00)

5731 Uff, Caroline. *Happy Birthday, Lulu!* (PS). Illus. 2000, Walker $14.95 (0-8027-8751-7). 24pp. Lulu celebrates her birthday in many ways, receiving cards, opening presents, getting a special phone call from Grandpa, and having a big party. (Rev: BL 12/1/00)

5732 Wadsworth, Ginger. *Tomorrow Is Daddy's Birthday* (PS–1). Illus. by Maxie Chambliss. 1994, Boyds Mills $14.95 (1-56397-042-2). Rachel wants to surprise her father with a gift on his birthday, so she tells every living thing that she encounters not to give away her secret. (Rev: SLJ 11/94)

5733 Wallace, John. *Tiny Rabbit Goes to a Birthday Party* (PS–K). Illus. 2000, Holiday $16.95 (0-8234-1489-2). 32pp. Tiny Rabbit is worried about going to his first birthday party but, when he has a good time, he starts to make plans for his own party. (Rev: BL 2/1/00; HBG 10/00; SLJ 4/00)

5734 Wallace, Nancy E. *Tell-A-Bunny* (PS–1). Illus. 2000, Winslow $15.95 (1-890817-29-5). 32pp. When bunnies phone each other about a surprise birthday party, the message gets garbled as it is passed from one bunny to another. (Rev: BL 5/15/00; HBG 10/00; SLJ 5/00)

5735 Wardlaw, Lee. *Bow-Wow Birthday* (PS–3). Illus. by Arden Johnson-Petrov. 1998, Boyds Mills $15.95 (1-56397-489-4). A humorous story about a group of children who hold a birthday party for an ancient dog who only wants to sleep in his favorite closet. (Rev: BCCB 4/98; BL 3/1/98; HBG 10/98; SLJ 5/98)

5736 Weninger, Brigitte. *Happy Birthday, Davy!* (PS–2). Trans. by Rosemary Lanning. Illus. by Eve Tharlet. 2000, North-South LB $15.88 (0-7358-1346-9). 32pp. Bunny Davy gets his birthday wish — having people pay attention to him — when his grandparents come to visit. (Rev: BL 12/15/00; HBG 3/01; SLJ 12/00)

5737 Whittington, Mary K. *The Patchwork Lady* (K–2). Illus. by Jane Dyer. 1991, Harcourt $13.95 (0-15-259580-5). A woman whose house and dress look like a patchwork quilt decides to hold a birthday party for herself. (Rev: SLJ 6/91)

5738 Willis, Jeanne. *Sloth's Shoes* (PS–3). Illus. by Tony Ross. 1998, Kane/Miller $13.95 (0-916291-78-2). 28pp. All the jungle animals prepare for Sloth's birthday party, but Sloth is so slow he misses it by a year. (Rev: BL 6/1–15/98; HBG 10/98; SLJ 8/98)

5739 Wormell, Mary. *Hilda Hen's Happy Birthday* (PS–K). Illus. 1995, Harcourt $14.00 (0-15-200299-5). 32pp. A hen finds presents in the most unusual places in this humorous picture book. (Rev: BL 4/1/95; HB 5–6/95; SLJ 4/95)

5740 Yezerski, Thomas F. *Queen of the World* (PS–3). Illus. 2000, Farrar $16.00 (0-374-36165-7). 32pp. Constant quarreling by the narrator and her sisters ruin their mother's birthday party, but they try to make amends the next day. (Rev: BCCB 11/00; BL 9/1/00; HB 9–10/00; HBG 3/01; SLJ 10/00)

CHRISTMAS

5741 Ada, Alma F. *The Christmas Tree/El Arbol de Navidad* (1–3). Illus. by Terry Ybanez. 1997, Hyperion LB $15.49 (0-7868-2123-X). A bilingual book about the joy a Christmas tree brings to those who decorate it. (Rev: SLJ 10/97)

5742 Adams, Adrienne. *The Christmas Party* (1–3). Illus. by author. 1978, Macmillan paper $3.95 (0-689-71630-3). 32pp. An Easter bunny helps prepare for a Christmas party.

5743 Aliki. *Christmas Tree Memories* (PS–2). Illus. 1991, HarperCollins LB $14.89 (0-06-020008-1). 32pp. This is a remembrance of Christmases past and the activities associated with celebrations years ago. (Rev: BL 7/91; HB 11–12/91)

5744 Ammon, Richard. *An Amish Christmas* (K–3). Illus. by Pamela Patrick. 1996, Simon & Schuster $17.00 (0-689-80377-X). 32pp. Many of the celebrations and holiday customs associated with an Amish Christmas are described. (Rev: BL 9/1/96)

5745 Anaya, Rudolfo A. *Farolitos for Abuelo* (1–4). Illus. by Edward Gonzales. 1999, Hyperion LB $16.49 (0-7868-2186-8). A touching story about Liz and how she remembers her beloved Grandfather Abuelo after his death by placing farolitos around his grave at Christmastime. (Rev: HBG 3/00; SLJ 10/99)

5746 Anaya, Rudolfo A. *The Farolitos of Christmas* (K–3). Illus. by Edward Gonzales. 1995, Hyperion LB $16.49 (0-7868-2047-0). 32pp. In a New Mexico setting, a Chicano family makes do in spite of the absence of their father, who has not yet returned from World War II. (Rev: BL 9/15/95; HB 11–12/95)

5747 Antle, Nancy. *Sam's Wild West Christmas* (1–2). Illus. 2000, Dial $13.99 (0-8037-2199-4). 40pp. In this easy reader, Sam and Rosie, two cowpokes, try to catch train robbers who have stolen the passengers' Christmas presents. (Rev: BCCB 10/00; BL 9/1/00; HBG 3/01)

5748 Arnold, Katya. *The Adventures of Snowwoman* (PS–3). Illus. 1998, Holiday $15.95 (0-8234-1390-X). 32pp. Children build Snowwoman to take a message to Santa to bring them a tree. (Rev: BL 12/1/98; HBG 3/99; SLJ 3/99)

5749 Auch, Mary Jane. *The Nutquacker* (K–3). Illus. 1999, Holiday $16.95 (0-8234-1524-4). 32pp. Clara the duck wanders off to find something called "Christmas," which she hears is on its way, only to find that Christmas is a time for being with people who love you. (Rev: BL 11/1/99; HBG 3/00; SLJ 10/99)

5750 Barrett, Mary Brigid. *The Man of the House at Huffington Row: A Christmas Story* (K–3). Illus.

1998, Harcourt $16.00 (0-15-201580-9). 32pp. In this sentimental Christmas story set during the Depression, Katherine Mary and her brother Francis are mourning the loss of their father. Francis cheers Katherine Mary up with the help of the other residents of Huffington Row. (Rev: BL 9/1/98; HBG 3/99; SLJ 10/98)

5751 Barry, Robert. *Mr. Willowby's Christmas Tree* (PS–2). Illus. 2000, Doubleday $15.95 (0-385-32721-8). 32pp. A Christmas tree makes the rounds of seven different homes. In each case it is chopped down a little to fit the house, until the last part is so small that three little mice find it just right. (Rev: BL 9/1/00)

5752 Bauer, Marion Dane. *Christmas in the Forest* (2–3). Illus. 1998, Holiday $15.95 (0-8234-1371-3). 48pp. The spirit of Christmas pervades the animal kingdom and makes friends out of traditional enemies in this beginning reader. (Rev: BL 12/1/98; HBG 3/99; SLJ 10/98)

5753 Baumgart, Klaus. *Laura's Christmas Star* (1–3). Trans. from German by Judy Waite. Illus. by author. 1999, Little Tiger $16.95 (1-888444-59-2). Facing a treeless Christmas, young Laura finds a small, raggedy tree in the street and brings it home. (Rev: HBG 3/00; SLJ 10/99)

5754 Becker, Bonny. *The Christmas Crocodile* (PS–1). Illus. by David Small. 1998, Simon & Schuster $16.00 (0-689-81503-4). 40pp. Alice Jayne finds a crocodile under the Christmas tree. He destroys the family's Christmas by eating all the presents and ruining the living room, but order is restored when they take him to a petting zoo. (Rev: BL 9/1/98; HBG 3/99; SLJ 10/98)

5755 Berger, Barbara Helen. *The Donkey's Dream* (K–3). Illus. by author. 1985, Putnam $16.95 (0-399-21233-7). 32pp. The story of a donkey who at Christmas time carried "a lady full of heaven" to a stable. (Rev: HB 11–12/85; SLJ 10/85)

5756 Bond, Michael. *Paddington Bear and the Christmas Surprise* (K–2). Illus. by R. W. Alley. 1997, HarperCollins $11.95 (0-694-00897-4). Paddington's visit with his family to a department store at Christmas is not the joyful occasion he had hoped for. (Rev: BL 9/15/97; SLJ 10/97)

5757 Borden, Louise. *Just in Time for Christmas* (1–4). Illus. by Ted Lewin. 1994, Scholastic $14.95 (0-590-45355-6). 32pp. Christmas time for Will in Kentucky is a happy time except that he is fearful that Great Gram is becoming too forgetful. (Rev: BL 8/94)

5758 Boynton, Sandra. *Bob: And 6 More Christmas Stories* (PS–K). Illus. by author. 1999, Simon & Schuster $7.99 (0-689-82568-4). A humorous book that consists of seven double-page stories about animals celebrating Christmas. (Rev: SLJ 10/99)

5759 Brett, Jan. *Christmas Trolls* (K–3). Illus. 1993, Putnam LB $16.99 (0-399-22507-2). 32pp. Treva discovers that the mysterious disappearance of objects from her house is the work of trolls. (Rev: BL 7/93)

5760 Brett, Jan. *The Wild Christmas Reindeer* (K–2). Illus. 1990, Putnam $16.99 (0-399-22192-1).

32pp. Santa has a whole new crew of wild reindeer that might not want to work on Christmas Eve. (Rev: BL 9/15/90*)

5761 Briggs, Raymond. *Father Christmas* (K–3). Illus. by author. 1997, Random $18.99 (0-679-88776-8). 32pp. Christmas Eve, as Santa sees it, is pictured by the author-artist (winner of the Kate Greenaway Medal) in full-color, comic-strip style.

5762 Brimner, Larry. *Merry Christmas, Old Armadillo* (PS–2). Illus. by Dominic Catalano. 1995, Boyds Mills $15.95 (1-56397-354-5). 32pp. When Armadillo returns home, his friends plan a Christmas surprise to welcome him. (Rev: BL 9/15/95; SLJ 10/95*)

5763 Brown, Ken. *Mucky Pup's Christmas* (PS–1). Illus. 1999, Dutton $16.99 (0-525-46141-8). 32pp. Mucky, a puppy, messes up the family Christmas with such activities as knocking over the tree, but he receives a present anyway. (Rev: BL 9/15/99; HBG 3/00; SLJ 10/99)

5764 Brown, Marc. *Arthur's Christmas* (K–2). Illus. by author. 1984, Little, Brown $15.95 (0-316-11180-5). Arthur, an anteater, has a series of Christmas adventures.

5765 Brown, Ruth. *Holly: The True Story of a Cat* (PS–K). Illus. 2000, Holt $14.95 (0-8050-6500-8). 32pp. At Christmas a stray cat, whom the family names Holly, is taken in and soon becomes a necessary part of the household. (Rev: BCCB 12/00; BL 9/1/00; HBG 3/01)

5766 Buck, Nola. *Santa's Short Suit Shrunk: and Other Christmas Tongue Twisters* (1–3). Illus. by Sue Truesdell. Series: I Can Read. 1997, HarperCollins LB $14.89 (0-06-026663-5). 32pp. A grab bag of tongue twisters about Christmas topics like shopping, feasting, and opening presents. (Rev: BL 9/15/97; HB 11–12/97; HBG 3/98; SLJ 10/97)

5767 Bunting, Eve. *The Day Before Christmas* (1–3). Illus. by Beth Peck. 1992, Houghton $16.00 (0-89919-866-X). 32pp. Allie's grandfather takes her to see The Nutcracker, just as he had taken her deceased mother. (Rev: BL 11/1/92; HB 11–12/92)

5768 Bunting, Eve. *December* (K–3). Illus. by David Diaz. 1997, Harcourt $16.00 (0-15-201434-9). 40pp. A miracle occurs when a homeless mother and her son allow an old lady to sleep in their cardboard home at Christmas time. (Rev: BL 9/1/97*; HBG 3/98; SLJ 10/97*)

5769 Bunting, Eve. *Night Tree* (PS–3). Illus. by Ted Rand. 1991, Harcourt $13.95 (0-15-257425-5). 32pp. On the night before Christmas, a family drives into the woods and decorates a tree. (Rev: BCCB 10/91; BL 9/15/91; HB 11–12/91)

5770 Bunting, Eve. *Who Was Born This Special Day?* (PS–1). Illus. by Leonid Gore. 2000, Simon & Schuster $16.00 (0-689-82302-9). 32pp. The narrator asks each animal if it is his birthday but the answer is always "no" because it is the birthday of the child in the manger. (Rev: BCCB 10/00; BL 9/1/00; HBG 3/01)

5771 Butterworth, Nick. *Jingle Bells* (PS–2). Illus. 1998, Orchard $15.95 (0-531-30124-9). 32pp. At Christmastime two little mice, Lottie and Jack, give their tormentor, a house cat named Angus, a bell. Angus's owner likes it so much he insists the cat wear it. (Rev: BL 12/1/98; HBG 3/99; SLJ 10/98)

5772 Byrd, Robert. *Saint Francis and the Christmas Donkey* (K–4). Illus. 2000, Dutton $15.99 (0-525-46480-8). 40pp. Saint Francis tells a donkey two stories to make him feel better about his lot in life; one about the donkey that carried Mary to Bethlehem. (Rev: BCCB 11/00; BL 9/1/00*; HB 11–12/00; HBG 3/01)

5773 Carle, Eric. *Dream Snow* (PS–1). Illus. 2000, Philomel $21.99 (0-399-23579-5). 32pp. In this counting book set at Christmastime, a farmer dreams that a gentle snow covers all his animals. (Rev: BCCB 10/00; BL 9/1/00; HBG 3/01)

5774 Carlson, Lori M. *Hurray for Three Kings' Day!* (PS–3). Illus. by Ed Martinez. 1999, Morrow LB $15.93 (0-688-16240-1). 32pp. The traditional Latin American holiday is the setting for this story about Anita and her older brothers, who dress as the Christmas kings and carry make-believe gifts around the town. (Rev: BL 9/1/99; HBG 3/00; SLJ 10/99)

5775 Carlstrom, Nancy White. *Where Is Christmas, Jesse Bear?* (PS–K). Illus. by Bruce Degen. 2000, Simon & Schuster $15.00 (0-689-81962-5). 32pp. Jesse Bear won't hibernate because he wants to experience all the joys of Christmas. (Rev: BL 11/15/00; HBG 3/01)

5776 Carrier, Lark. *A Christmas Promise* (PS–2). Illus. by author. 1991, Simon & Schuster $15.95 (0-88708-032-4). 36pp. Amy nurtures her small tree, planning to bring it inside for Christmas, and then can't bear to cut it down. (Rev: BL 11/1/86)

5777 Catalano, Dominic. *Santa and the Three Bears* (PS–K). Illus. 2000, Boyds Mills $15.95 (1-56397-864-4). 32pp. Mama, Papa, and Baby Bear seek shelter in Santa's house while he is out delivering gifts and the three intruders wreak mayhem before falling asleep. (Rev: BL 9/1/00; HBG 3/01)

5778 Cecil, Mirabel. *Ruby the Christmas Donkey* (K–3). Illus. by Christina Gascoigne. 1999, Candlewick paper $3.99 (0-7636-0716-9). For beginning readers, this is a Christmas story about Ruby, a donkey, and the part she plays in a Nativity play. (Rev: SLJ 10/99)

5779 Chmielarz, Sharon. *Down at Angel's* (PS–3). Illus. by Jill Kastner. 1994, Ticknor $14.95 (0-395-65993-0). 32pp. At Christmas time, two children and their mother deliver a box of goodies to their friend, a woodcarver named Angel. (Rev: BCCB 12/94; BL 8/94; HB 11–12/94)

5780 Chorao, Kay. *The Christmas Story* (PS–3). Illus. 1996, Holiday LB $16.95 (0-8234-1251-2). 28pp. The biblical account of Christmas from the King James version is illustrated in Renaissance-like paintings. (Rev: BL 9/1/96)

5781 Christelow, Eileen. *Not Until Christmas, Walter!* (PS–2). Illus. 1997, Clarion $15.00 (0-395-82273-4). 40pp. Walter, a dog who has ruined a family's Christmas presents, redeems himself by tracking a lost person. (Rev: BL 9/1/97; HBG 3/98; SLJ 10/97)

5782 *Christmas Stories for the Very Young* (PS–2). Ed. by Sally Grindley. Illus. by Helen Cooper. 1998, Kingfisher paper $6.95 (0-7534-5168-9). 40pp. This oversized illustrated paperback contains six engaging Christmas stories by English writers. (Rev: BL 9/1/98)

5783 Ciavonne, Jean. *Carlos, Light the Farolito* (PS–3). Illus. by Donna Clair. 1995, Clarion $14.95 (0-395-66759-3). 32pp. Carlos is a small boy who enjoys the tradition of lighting the farolito, a lantern that guides pilgrims at Christmas. (Rev: BL 9/15/95)

5784 Clements, Andrew. *Bright Christmas: An Angel Remembers* (PS–3). Illus. by Kate Kiesler. 1996, Clarion $16.00 (0-395-72096-6). 30pp. The Christmas story as seen through the eyes of an angel. (Rev: BCCB 11/96; BL 9/1/96)

5785 Clifton, Lucille. *Everett Anderson's Christmas Coming* (PS–2). Illus. by Jan S. Gilchrist. 1991, HarperCollins $14.95 (0-8050-1549-3). 32pp. This book describes how Christmas comes for a young African American boy, Everett Anderson. (Rev: BCCB 9/91; BL 10/1/91)

5786 Climo, Shirley. *The Cobweb Christmas* (K–3). Illus. by Joe Lasker. 1982, HarperCollins LB $15.89 (0-690-04216-7); paper $5.95 (0-06-443110-X). 32pp. Spiders turn Tante's Christmas tree into a glistening thing of beauty.

5787 Colle, Gisela. *The Star Tree* (K–2). Illus. 1997, North-South LB $15.88 (1-55858-742-X). 24pp. An old man produces an old-fashioned Christmas tree for his neighbors. (Rev: BL 9/1/97; HBG 3/98; SLJ 10/97)

5788 Conrad, Pam. *The Tub People's Christmas* (PS–K). Illus. by Richard Egielski. 1999, Harper-Collins LB $15.89 (0-06-026029-7). 32pp. Small wooden toys named the Tub People are confused when they become ornaments on a Christmas tree. (Rev: BL 9/1/99; HBG 3/00; SLJ 10/99)

5789 Cooper, Susan. *Danny and the Kings* (PS–1). Illus. by Joseph A. Smith. 1993, Macmillan $14.95 (0-689-50577-9). 32pp. Steve's tree, a gift to a poor friend at Christmas time, is ruined when a truck runs over it. (Rev: BCCB 2/94; BL 10/15/93; HB 11–12/93)

5790 Corrin, Sara, and Stephen Corrin, eds. *Round the Christmas Tree* (K–4). Illus. by Jill Bennett. 1983, Puffin paper $3.95 (0-317-62263-3). Sixteen stories, many of them fairy tales, about Christmas.

5791 Currey, Anna. *Truffle's Christmas* (PS–1). Illus. 2000, Orchard $15.95 (0-531-30266-0). 32pp. Truffle, a mouse, is sorry he asked Santa for a hula hoop for Christmas because he knows the family needs a new blanket more. (Rev: BL 9/15/00; HBG 3/01)

5792 Cuyler, Margery. *Fat Santa* (PS–1). Illus. by Marsha Winborn. 1989, Holt paper $4.95 (0-8050-1167-6). 32pp. Santa gets stuck in the chimney and resourceful Molly rescues him. (Rev: BCCB 11/87; BL 11/1/87)

5793 Czernecki, Stefan, and Timothy Rhodes. *Pancho's Pinata* (PS–2). Illus. by Stefan Czernecki. 1992, Hyperion $14.95 (1-562-82277-2); paper $4.95 (0-786-81007-6). 40pp. The fanciful story of how the first pinata was invented, in the village of San Miguel. (Rev: BL 11/1/92) [398.2]

5794 D'Allance, Mireille. *Bear's Christmas Star* (PS–1). Illus. 2000, Simon & Schuster $12.95 (0-684-83826-3). 28pp. Bear wants to help trim the Christmas tree but Papa says he is just too small; however, at the end, it takes both of them to put the star on the top of the tree. (Rev: BL 11/1/00)

5795 Day, Alexandra, and Cooper Edens. *The Christmas We Moved to the Barn* (PS–3). Illus. by Alexandra Day. 1997, HarperCollins $14.95 (0-06-205149-0). 32pp. A woman and her family get help from different animals when they are forced to move to a barn at Christmas. (Rev: BL 9/1/97; HBG 3/98; SLJ 10/97)

5796 De Groat, Diane. *Jingle Bells, Homework Smells* (K–2). Illus. 2000, HarperCollins LB $15.99 (0-688-17544-9). 32pp. Around the Christmas holiday season, Gilbert the possum puts off doing his school assignment until it is too late. (Rev: BL 9/1/00; HBG 3/01)

5797 Delton, Judy. *The Perfect Christmas Gift* (PS–2). Illus. by Lisa McCue. 1992, Macmillan LB $13.95 (0-02-728471-9). 32pp. Bear has a difficult time finding a suitable Christmas present for her friend Duck. (Rev: BL 10/1/92)

5798 dePaola, Tomie, ed. *The Clown of God* (K–3). Illus. by Tomie dePaola. 1978, Harcourt $16.00 (0-15-219175-5); paper $7.00 (0-15-618192-4). 45pp. On Christmas Eve, a juggler gives to a statue of Christ his only possession, the gift of his art.

5799 dePaola, Tomie. *Country Angel Christmas* (PS–1). Illus. 1995, Putnam $16.95 (0-399-22817-9). 32pp. Three little angels think they have been forgotten in the preparations for Christmas, but St. Nicholas comes to the rescue. (Rev: BCCB 11/95; BL 9/15/95)

5800 dePaola, Tomie. *An Early American Christmas* (K–2). Illus. by author. 1987, Holiday $16.95 (0-8234-0617-2); paper $6.95 (0-8234-0979-1). 32pp. What it might have been like for a German family of long ago to move to a New England village where most of the people did not celebrate Christmas. (Rev: BCCB 11/87; BL 9/1/87)

5801 dePaola, Tomie, reteller. *The Legend of Old Befana* (PS–3). Illus. by Tomie dePaola. 1980, Harcourt $16.00 (0-15-243816-5); paper $6.00 (0-15-243817-3). 32pp. The legend of the old lady who is still searching for the Christ child.

5802 dePaola, Tomie. *Merry Christmas, Strega Nona* (PS–3). Illus. by author. 1986, Harcourt $16.00 (0-15-253183-1); paper $7.00 (0-15-253184-X). 32pp. Strega Nona is worried because her helper Big Anthony doesn't seem to be helping her to prepare for Christmas at all. (Rev: BL 11/1/86; HB 11–12/86)

5803 dePaola, Tomie. *The Night of Las Posadas* (K–4). Illus. 1999, Putnam $15.99 (0-399-23400-4). 32pp. During the festival of Las Posadas, a Spanish custom that celebrates the search for shelter by Joseph and Mary, a miracle occurs in this fantasy set in Santa Fe, New Mexico. (Rev: BL 9/1/99; HBG 3/00; SLJ 10/99)

5804 Donnelly, Liza. *Dinosaurs' Christmas* (PS–2). Illus. 1994, Scholastic paper $2.99 (0-590-44798-X). 32pp. Rex and his dog Bones travel by dinosaur to the North Pole just before Christmas. (Rev: BL 7/91)

5805 Dooley, Norah. *Everybody Serves Soup* (2–4). Illus. by Peter J. Thornton. 2000, Carolrhoda $15.95 (1-57505-422-1). 40pp. When Carrie tastes her neighbors' soups, she gets an idea for a unique Christmas present for her mother. (Rev: BL 1/1–15/01; HBG 3/01)

5806 Dunbar, Joyce. *This Is the Star* (K–3). Illus. by Gary Blythe. 1996, Harcourt $16.00 (0-15-200851-9). 36pp. A cumulative tale using the story of the Nativity as a framework. (Rev: BL 9/1/96)

5807 Dunrea, Olivier. *Bear Noel* (PS–2). Illus. 2000, Farrar $16.00 (0-374-39990-5). 32pp. On Christmas Eve, Hare, Fox, Wolf, and other animals await the arrival of Bear Noel and the wonderful things he will bring. (Rev: BCCB 11/00; BL 9/1/00; HBG 3/01)

5808 Edens, Cooper. *Nicholi* (PS–2). Illus. by A. Scott Banfill. 1997, Simon & Schuster paper $16.00 (0-689-80495-4). 40pp. A mysterious stranger brings to life all the snow sculptures in a village in this Christmas story. (Rev: BL 9/1/97; HBG 3/98; SLJ 10/97)

5809 Edens, Cooper. *Santa Cows* (1–4). Illus. by Daniel Lane. 1991, Simon & Schuster $14.00 (0-671-74863-7). 32pp. In this spoof, it is cows that come down the chimney at Christmas. (Rev: BL 1/1/91)

5810 Ets, Marie Hall, and Aurora Labastida. *Nine Days to Christmas* (K–2). Illus. by Marie Hall Ets. 1959, Puffin paper $4.99 (0-14-054442-9). 48pp. Kindergartner Ceci is old enough to have her first posada — one of the nine special parties held in Mexico, one a day preceding the day of Christmas. Caldecott Medal winner, 1960.

5811 Facklam, Margery. *Only a Star* (K–3). Illus. by Nancy Carpenter. 1996, Eerdmans $15.00 (0-8028-5122-3). 32pp. The Christmas star magically transforms all creatures and objects that it illuminates. (Rev: BL 10/15/96; SLJ 10/96*)

5812 Falwell, Cathryn. *Christmas for 10* (PS–K). Illus. 1998, Clarion $15.00 (0-395-85581-0). 32pp. A Christmas counting book that shows an African American family engaged in a number of holiday activities. (Rev: BL 9/1/98; HBG 3/99; SLJ 10/98)

5813 Fearnley, Jan. *Little Robin's Christmas* (K–2). Illus. 1998, Little Tiger $14.95 (1-888444-40-1). 32pp. When Little Robin gives away all of his vests to shivering animals, Santa Claus gives him a new red one for Christmas and also gives him a new name, Little Robin Redbreast. (Rev: BL 9/15/98; HBG 3/99; SLJ 10/98)

5814 Fearrington, Ann. *Christmas Lights* (PS–2). Illus. 1996, Houghton $15.95 (0-395-71036-7). 32pp. On Christmas night, a family drives around the city to see all the Christmas lights. (Rev: BL 9/1/96)

5815 Foreman, Michael. *The Little Reindeer* (PS–2). Illus. 1997, Dial $15.99 (0-8037-2184-6). 32pp.

One of Santa's tiny reindeer is accidentally wrapped as a Christmas present and delivered to a boy. (Rev: BL 9/1/97; HBG 3/98; SLJ 10/97)

5816 Forward, Toby. *Ben's Christmas Carol* (K–4). Illus. by Ruth Brown. 1996, Dutton $15.99 (0-525-45593-0). 48pp. A reworking of Dickens's famous tale using a miserly mouse that lives in Scrooge's house as the central character. (Rev: BL 9/1/96; HB 11–12/96; SLJ 10/96*)

5817 Fox, Mem. *Wombat Divine* (PS–3). Illus. by Kerry Argent. 1996, Harcourt $15.00 (0-15-201416-0). 32pp. A sleepy wombat gets to play baby Jesus in the Christmas Nativity play. (Rev: BL 10/15/96; SLJ 10/96*)

5818 French, Vivian. *A Christmas Star Called Hannah* (PS–3). Illus. by Anne Y. Gilbert. 1997, Candlewick $9.99 (0-7636-0397-X). 32pp. Hannah saves the day when she offers her brother as the Baby Jesus in the Christmas pageant. (Rev: BL 11/1/97; HBG 3/98; SLJ 10/97)

5819 Gackenbach, Dick. *Claude the Dog: A Christmas Story* (K–3). Illus. by author. 1984, Houghton paper $5.95 (0-89919-124-X). 32pp. Claude gives away all his presents but gets an even better one from his master. A related title is: *What's Claude Doing?* (1984).

5820 Gammell, Stephen. *Wake Up, Bear . . . It's Christmas!* (PS–1). Illus. by author. 1981, Morrow paper $4.95 (0-688-09934-3). 32pp. A bear is afraid he will sleep through Christmas.

5821 Gantos, Jack. *Rotten Ralph's Rotten Christmas* (K–2). Illus. by Nicole Rubel. 1984, Houghton $15.00 (0-395-35380-7); paper $4.95 (0-395-45685-1). 32pp. This miserable cat is determined that Sarah's Christmas will also be miserable.

5822 Garland, Michael. *An Elf for Christmas* (PS–1). Illus. 1999, Dutton $15.99 (0-525-46212-0). 32pp. When one of Santa's elves is accidentally delivered as part of a Christmas gift, he must find his way back to the North Pole. (Rev: BL 11/1/99; HBG 3/00; SLJ 10/99)

5823 Gibbons, Gail. *Santa Who?* (K–4). Illus. 1999, Morrow LB $15.93 (0-688-15529-4). 32pp. This book traces the legend of Santa Claus — from Saint Nicholas in Europe, the bringing of Sinter Cleas to America by the Dutch, and its evolution in modern times. (Rev: BCCB 10/99; BL 9/1/99; HBG 3/00; SLJ 10/99)

5824 Gillmor, Don. *The Christmas Orange* (K–2). Illus. by Marie-Louise Gay. 1999, Stoddart $15.95 (0-7737-3100-8). 32pp. When Anton receives only an orange for Christmas, he sues Santa for breach of promise. (Rev: BL 1/1–15/00)

5825 Gleeson, Brian. *The Savior Is Born* (K–3). Illus. by Robert Van Nutt. 1996, Simon & Schuster paper $19.95 (0-689-81098-9). 40pp. The Christmas story is retold using illustrations that resemble stained-glass windows. (Rev: BL 11/15/96) [232.92]

5826 Gliori, Debi. *What Can I Give Him?* (PS–3). Illus. 1998, Holiday $15.95 (0-8234-1392-6). 32pp. Using double-page spreads — one depicting a contemporary girl with her loving family at Christmastime and the other a poor servant girl in the stable where Jesus was born — this book explores the question of what one should give as a loving present. (Rev: BL 9/1/98; HBG 3/99; SLJ 10/98)

5827 Greene, Rhonda Gowler. *The Stable Where Jesus Was Born* (PS–1). Illus. by Susan Gaber. 1999, Simon & Schuster $16.00 (0-689-81258-2). 40pp. A cumulative rhyme that describes the stable where Jesus was born, the animals, visitors, and his parents. (Rev: BL 9/1/99; HBG 3/00; SLJ 10/99) [232.92]

5828 Greenfield, Monica. *Waiting for Christmas* (PS–1). Illus. by Jan S. Gilchrist. 1996, Scholastic $15.95 (0-590-52700-2). 32pp. An African American brother and sister look forward to the excitement of Christmas. (Rev: BL 9/1/96)

5829 Grosz, Peter. *The Special Gifts* (PS–2). Illus. by Giuliano Lunelli. 1998, North-South LB $15.88 (1-55858-962-7). 32pp. This vividly illustrated picture book tells how three elderly friends, a poet, a carpenter, and a stonemason, create toys for poor children who live nearby. (Rev: BL 9/1/98; HBG 3/99; SLJ 10/98)

5830 Hague, Michael. *The Perfect Present* (PS–1). Illus. 1996, Morrow $16.00 (0-688-10880-6). 48pp. Jack, a rabbit, goes to Big Bear's Toy Shoppe to find a Christmas present for his girlfriend. (Rev: BL 9/1/96)

5831 Hall, Donald. *Lucy's Christmas* (K–3). Illus. by Michael McCurdy. 1994, Harcourt $14.95 (0-15-276870-X). 40pp. Everyday life of a New England family in 1909 from late fall through the celebration of Christmas. (Rev: BCCB 10/94; BL 8/94; HB 11–12/94)

5832 Harvey, Brett. *My Prairie Christmas* (1–3). Illus. by Deborah Kogan Ray. 1990, Holiday LB $16.95 (0-8234-0827-2). 32pp. Young Eleanor wonders what sort of Christmas her pioneering family can have in their new Dakota home. (Rev: BCCB 11/90; BL 10/1/90)

5833 Hayes, Sarah. *Happy Christmas, Gemma* (PS–1). Illus. by Jan Ormerod. 1986, Lothrop $15.00 (0-688-06508-2). 32pp. Christmas is warmly celebrated by this Jamaican immigrant family. (Rev: BCCB 11/86; BL 11/15/86; HB 11–12/86)

5834 Heath, Amy. *Sofie's Role* (PS–2). Illus. 1992, Macmillan LB $14.95 (0-02-743505-9). 36pp. On the day before Christmas, a young girl helps her parents in their bakery. (Rev: BCCB 12/92; BL 7/92)

5835 Helldorfer, M. C. *Daniel's Gift* (K–3). Illus. by Julie Downing. 1987, Macmillan paper $4.95 (0-689-71440-8). 32pp. The shepherd boy Daniel is the focus of this Nativity story set in the Middle Ages. (Rev: BL 11/1/87; SLJ 12/87)

5836 High, Linda O. *A Christmas Star* (K–3). Illus. by Ronald Himler. 1997, Holiday LB $15.95 (0-8234-1301-2). 32pp. Stolen gifts are miraculously returned to a church in this Christmas tale set during the Depression. (Rev: BL 9/1/97; HBG 3/98; SLJ 10/97)

5837 Hill, Susan. *King of Kings* (1–4). Illus. by John Lawrence. 1993, Candlewick $14.95 (1-56402-210-

2). 32pp. On Christmas Eve, Mr. Hegarty, a recluse, discovers a baby on his doorstep. (Rev: BL 10/1/93)

5838 Hines, Gary. *A Christmas Tree in the White House* (K–2). Illus. by Alexandra Wallner. 1998, Holt $15.95 (0-8050-5076-0). 32pp. Based on a true story, the sons of President Theodore Roosevelt sneak a small Christmas tree into their room in spite of their conservationist father's refusal to have a Christmas tree in the White House. (Rev: BL 10/1/98; HBG 3/99; SLJ 10/98)

5839 Hoban, Lillian. *Arthur's Christmas Cookies* (1–2). Illus. by author. 1972, HarperCollins LB $15.89 (0-06-022368-5); paper $3.95 (0-06-444055-9). 64pp. What can Arthur give his parents for Christmas? Christmas cookies such as he learned to bake in Cub Scouts are the answer, but a hilarious mix-up occurs when salt is used instead of sugar.

5840 Hodges, Margaret. *Silent Night: The Song and Its Story* (PS–3). Illus. by Tim Ladwig. 1997, Eerdmans $17.00 (0-8028-5138-X). 32pp. A dramatic retelling of the 1818 creation of this much-loved Christmas carol. (Rev: BL 9/1/97; HBG 3/98; SLJ 10/97)

5841 Hoff, Syd. *Where's Prancer?* (PS–1). Illus. 1997, HarperCollins LB $13.00 (0-06-027601-0). 32pp. After making his rounds, Santa discovers that Prancer is missing. (Rev: BL 9/1/97; HBG 3/98)

5842 Hoffman, Mary. *An Angel Just Like Me* (PS–2). Illus. by Cornelius Van Wright and Ying-Hwa Hu. 1997, Dial $14.99 (0-8037-2265-6). 32pp. When the Christmas tree angel breaks, a young African American boy named Tyler wants a replacement that looks like himself. (Rev: BCCB 3/98; BL 11/1/97; HBG 3/98; SLJ 12/97)

5843 Hoffman, Mary. *Three Wise Women* (1–4). Illus. by Lynne Russell. 1999, Penguin $16.99 (0-8037-2466-7). In this variation on the Magi story, three women from different parts of the world come to visit the baby Jesus. (Rev: HBG 3/00; SLJ 10/99)

5844 Hooks, William H. *The Legend of the Christmas Rose* (K–4). Illus. by Richard A. Williams. 1999, HarperCollins LB $14.89 (0-06-027103-5). 32pp. Dorothy has no presents to offer the infant Jesus, but an angel provides her with the flower now known as the Christmas Rose. (Rev: BL 9/1/99; HBG 3/00)

5845 Hooper, Maureen B. *The Christmas Drum* (PS–1). Illus. by Diane Paterson. 1994, Boyds Mills $14.95 (1-56397-105-4). 28pp. Set in Romania, this Christmas story tells of a boy who wishes for his father's return so that he will not have to take his place as drum beater in the village rituals. (Rev: BL 10/1/94)

5846 Howard, Elizabeth F. *Chita's Christmas Tree* (K–3). Illus. by Floyd Cooper. 1989, Macmillan LB $14.95 (0-02-744621-2). 32pp. Set in turn-of-the-century Baltimore, this book celebrates the holiday season and family life. (Rev: BCCB 9/89; BL 9/1/89*)

5847 Howard, Ellen. *The Log Cabin Christmas* (K–3). Illus. by Ronald Himler. 2000, Holiday $16.95 (0-8234-1381-0). 32pp. Set in Michigan during pioneer times, Elvirey and her family are afraid

there will be no Christmas now that Mam's dead, but the young girl decides she can save the day. (Rev: BCCB 11/00; BL 11/15/00; HBG 3/01)

5848 Hudson, Cheryl W. *Hold Christmas in Your Heart: African-American Songs, Poems, and Stories for the Holidays* (K–2). Illus. 1995, Scholastic $10.95 (0-590-48024-3). 32pp. Poems, stories, and songs from African American authors are found in this fine anthology. (Rev: BL 9/15/95)

5849 Hughes, Langston. *Carol of the Brown King* (PS–3). Illus. by Ashley Bryan. 1998, Simon & Schuster $16.00 (0-689-81877-7). 32pp. A colorful picture book that presents six short poems about Christmas — five by Langston Hughes plus one poem he translated from a Puerto Rican Christmas card. (Rev: BL 9/1/98; HB 9–10/98; HBG 3/99; SLJ 10/98) [811]

5850 Hurd, Thacher. *Santa Mouse and the Ratdeer* (PS–1). Illus. 1998, HarperCollins $14.95 (0-06-027694-0). 40pp. Santa Mouse has a bad day when he can't find his clothes and his sleigh crashes, but little Rosie Mouse comes to the rescue. (Rev: BL 11/1/98; HBG 10/99; SLJ 10/98)

5851 Inkpen, Mick. *Kipper's Christmas Eve* (PS–2). Illus. 2000, Harcourt $13.95 (0-15-202660-6). 32pp. Kipper the puppy engages in all sorts of activities to find out which is better — Christmas Day or Christmas Eve — in this charming book with an electric device that flashes. (Rev: BL 9/15/00; HBG 3/01)

5852 Janovitz, Marilyn. *What Could Be Keeping Santa?* (PS–1). Illus. 1997, North-South LB $15.88 (1-55858-820-5). 32pp. The sleigh is packed and the stockings are hung, but where's Santa? (Rev: BL 10/1/97; HBG 3/98; SLJ 10/97)

5853 Jimenez, Francisco. *The Christmas Gift: El regalo de Navidad* (K–4). Illus. by Claire B. Cotts. 2000, Houghton $15.00 (0-395-92869-9). 32pp. In this bilingual book, Panchito is disappointed because there is no money to buy him the red ball he wants for Christmas. (Rev: BCCB 12/00; BL 9/1/00; HBG 3/01)

5854 Johnston, Tony. *Pages of Music* (K–3). Illus. by Tomie dePaola. 1988, Putnam LB $13.95 (0-399-21436-4). 32pp. In Sardinia a shepherd fills Paolo with the joy of his music. (Rev: BL 10/15/88; SLJ 2/89)

5855 Joyce, William. *Snowie Rolie* (PS–2). Illus. 2000, HarperCollins $15.95 (0-06-029285-7). 40pp. When the snowman Rolie the robot builds begins to melt, he whisks it off to leave it in safety with Santa Claus. (Rev: BL 9/1/00)

5856 Keller, Holly. *Merry Christmas, Geraldine* (PS–1). Illus. 1997, Greenwillow $14.89 (0-688-14501-9). 32pp. Two young pigs go out to choose the family Christmas tree. (Rev: BL 9/1/97; HBG 3/98; SLJ 10/97)

5857 Kennedy, Pamela. *A Christmas Carol* (K–3). Illus. by Carol Heyer. 1995, Ideals $14.95 (1-57102-047-0). 32pp. With vibrant paintings and a simple text, the classic story is retold for a young audience. (Rev: BL 11/15/95)

5858 Kline, Suzy. *Horrible Harry and the Christmas Surprise* (K–2). Illus. by Frank Remkiewicz.

1991, Viking $13.99 (0-670-83357-6). 64pp. While reading a story to the class, Miss Mackle, the teacher in 2B, falls and is sent to the hospital. (Rev: BL 7/91)

5859 Knowlton, Laurie L. *The Nativity: Mary Remembers* (K–3). Illus. by Kasi Kubiak. 1998, Boyds Mills $14.95 (1-56397-714-1). 32pp. The story of the Nativity is retold through the eyes of Mary, who wonders how she could have been chosen to bear the child who will be the Messiah. (Rev: BCCB 11/98; BL 9/15/98; HBG 10/99; SLJ 10/98)

5860 Kroeber, Theodora. *A Green Christmas* (K–3). Illus. by John Larrecq. 1967, Houghton $6.95 (0-87466-047-5). Children new to California discover that Santa Claus will visit places without snow.

5861 Kvasnosky, Laura McGee. *Zelda and Ivy One Christmas* (K–3). Illus. 2000, Candlewick $15.99 (0-7636-1000-3). 48pp. The fox sisters and their recently widowed neighbor prepare for Christmas by baking gingerbread cookies and looking through catalogs for presents. (Rev: BCCB 12/00; BL 11/15/00; HB 11–12/00; HBG 3/01)

5862 Landa, Norbert. *Little Bear's Christmas* (PS–K). Illus. by Marlis Scharff-Kniemeyer. 1999, Little Tiger $14.95 (1-888444-60-6). 32pp. Little Bear sets the alarm clock so he will not hibernate through Christmas and miss seeing Santa Claus. (Rev: BL 10/1/99; HBG 3/00; SLJ 10/99)

5863 Lindgren, Astrid. *Christmas in the Stable* (PS–2). Illus. by Harald Wiberg. 1998, Putnam paper $5.99 (0-698-11664-X). 32pp. A mother tells her child the story of the birth of Jesus, and the child projects the tale into her own present-day farm-life setting.

5864 Lindgren, Astrid. *Lotta's Christmas Surprise* (PS–2). Illus. by Ilon Wikland. 1990, R&S $13.95 (91-29-59782-X). 32pp. In this Christmas story, Lotta overcomes many trials and tribulations. (Rev: BL 12/1/90)

5865 Lindgren, Astrid. *Pippi Longstocking's After-Christmas Party* (K–2). Illus. by Michael Chesworth. 1996, Viking $13.99 (0-670-86790-X). 32pp. An episodic story about Pippi's party in an igloo after Christmas. (Rev: BL 9/1/96)

5866 Low, Alice, ed. *The Family Read-Aloud Christmas Treasury* (K–5). Illus. by Marc Brown. 1995, Little, Brown paper $12.95 (0-316-53284-3). 137pp. A rich compilation of Christmas read-aloud material. (Rev: BL 11/1/89*) [394.268]

5867 McCaughrean, Geraldine. *How the Reindeer Got Their Antlers* (1–3). Illus. by Heather Holland. 2000, Holiday $16.95 (0-8234-1562-7). 32pp. The reindeer is ashamed of its twisted antlers, until Santa uses them to save the day when his sleigh slips on ice. (Rev: BL 9/1/00; HBG 3/01)

5868 McCutcheon, Marc. *Grandfather's Christmas Camp* (K–3). Illus. by Kate Kiesler. 1995, Clarion $15.95 (0-395-69626-7). 32pp. In her search for an old, lost mongrel dog, Lizzie spends a Christmas sleeping in an igloo with her grandfather. (Rev: BCCB 11/95; BL 9/15/95; SLJ 10/95*)

5869 McDonald, Megan. *Tundra Mouse: A Story-knife Tale* (PS–2). Illus. by S. D. Schindler. 1997, Orchard LB $16.99 (0-531-33047-8). 32pp. Tundra Mouse and House Mouse think they are doing people a favor when they tidy up by stripping a Christmas tree of its ornaments, little knowing it's the night before Christmas. (Rev: BL 1/1–15/98; HBG 3/98; SLJ 10/97)

5870 McGovern, Ann. *The Lady in the Box* (K–3). Illus. by Marni Backer. 1997, Turtle $14.95 (1-890515-01-9). 32pp. At Christmas time, two youngsters help a homeless woman who is living over a hot-air vent. (Rev: BL 9/1/97; SLJ 10/97)

5871 McPhail, David. *Santa's Book of Names* (K–3). Illus. 1993, Little, Brown $14.95 (0-316-56335-8). 27pp. Edward learns to read names while helping Santa deliver presents to other children. (Rev: BL 8/93)

5872 McQuade, Jacqueline. *Christmas with Teddy Bear* (PS–K). Illus. 1996, Dial $13.99 (0-8037-2075-0). 32pp. Christmas traditions like carol singing are introduced through the activities of a teddy bear. (Rev: BL 9/1/96)

5873 Mahy, Margaret. *The Christmas Tree Tangle* (PS–2). Illus. by Tony Kerins. 1994, Macmillan paper $16.00 (0-689-50616-3). 32pp. One animal after another gets stuck on the Christmas tree trying to rescue a kitten that has climbed to the top. (Rev: BL 8/94)

5874 Maloney, Peter, and Felicia Zekauskas. *Redbird at Rockefeller Center* (1–4). Illus. 1997, Dial $14.89 (0-8037-2257-5). 32pp. Hundreds of toy birds that decorate the Christmas tree at Rockefeller Center come to life and fly the tree back to its original home. (Rev: BL 11/1/97; HBG 3/98; SLJ 12/97)

5875 Manushkin, Fran. *The Perfect Christmas Picture* (PS–3). Illus. by Karen Ann Weinhaus. 1980, HarperCollins $11.95 (0-06-024068-7). 64pp. An easily read story of Mr. Green, who wants to photograph his family for a Christmas picture.

5876 Marzollo, Jean. *I Spy Christmas: A Book of Picture Riddles* (PS–3). Illus. by Walter Wick. 1992, Scholastic $12.95 (0-590-45846-9). 40pp. Full-color photos illustrate 13 scenes of Christmas. (Rev: BCCB 11/92; BL 11/1/92) [793.73]

5877 Masurel, Claire. *Christmas Is Coming!* (PS–2). Illus. by Marie H. Henry. 1998, Chronicle $14.95 (0-8118-2106-4). 40pp. Juliette experiences Christmas Eve activities like making cookies and, the next morning, the joy of opening presents. (Rev: BCCB 11/98; BL 9/1/98; HBG 3/99; SLJ 10/98)

5878 Mattingley, Christobel. *The Magic Saddle* (PS–3). Illus. by Patricia Mullins. 1996, Simon & Schuster $16.00 (0-689-80959-X). 32pp. An Australian Christmas story about a boy who receives a magical gingerbread horse that transports him to faraway places. (Rev: BL 9/1/96)

5879 Mayper, Monica. *Come and See: A Christmas Story* (PS–1). Illus. by Stacey Schuett. 1999, HarperCollins LB $14.89 (0-06-023527-6). 32pp. Shepherds waken the townsfolk in the middle of the night to accompany them to the stable where the joyful Christmas celebration takes place. (Rev: BL 9/1/99; HBG 3/00; SLJ 10/99)

5880 Medearis, Angela Shelf. *Poppa's Itchy Christmas* (PS–1). Illus. by John Ward. 1998, Holiday $15.95 (0-8234-1298-9). 32pp. George, an African American youngster, is not happy with the scarf and red long underwear he receives for Christmas, but when he falls through the ice while trying out his new skates, they are the two items that help save his life. (Rev: BL 9/1/98; HBG 10/99; SLJ 10/98)

5881 Mendez, Phil. *The Black Snowman* (K–4). Illus. by Carole Byard. 1989, Scholastic $15.95 (0-590-40552-7). 48pp. An African American learns a little about his heritage from a snowman that comes to life. (Rev: BCCB 11/89; BL 10/1/89; SLJ 9/89)

5882 Menotti, Gian Carlo. *Amahl and the Night Visitors* (K–3). Illus. by Michele Lemieux. 1986, Morrow LB $19.88 (0-688-05427-7). 64pp. A lavish edition of the story of this touching opera. (Rev: BCCB 10/86; HB 11–12/86)

5883 Mills, Claudia. *One Small Lost Sheep* (PS–3). Illus. by Walter L. Krudop. 1997, Farrar $16.00 (0-374-35649-1). 32pp. A lost sheep leads a young shepherd to the manger at the first Christmas. (Rev: BL 9/1/97; HBG 3/98; SLJ 10/97)

5884 Moeri, Louise. *Star Mother's Youngest Child* (PS–2). Illus. by Trina S. Hyman. 1975, Houghton $14.95 (0-395-21406-8); paper $5.95 (0-395-29929-2). 48pp. An old woman and a star child celebrate Christmas.

5885 Moore, Clement Clarke. *A Visit from Saint Nicholas and Santa Mouse, Too!* (PS–K). Illus. by Loretta Krupinski. 1998, Hyperion LB $13.49 (0-7868-2252-X). 32pp. Making slight changes in the text of the classic poem, this story becomes the night before Christmas as experienced by a tiny mouse. (Rev: BL 9/1/98; HBG 3/99; SLJ 10/98)

5886 Morrissey, Dean. *The Christmas Ship* (K–4). Illus. 2000, HarperCollins LB $16.89 (0-06-028576-1). 40pp. On Christmas Eve, toy maker Sam Thatcher helps Santa by delivering toys from his boat, which soars through the night sky. (Rev: BL 10/1/00; HBG 3/01)

5887 Moses, Will. *Silent Night* (1–4). Illus. 1997, Putnam $16.99 (0-399-23100-5). 40pp. Using the words of the carol as chapter headings, this is the story of a family's exciting Christmas in rural Vermont. (Rev: BL 9/1/97; HBG 3/98; SLJ 10/97)

5888 *My First Christmas Board Book* (PS). Series: DK My First Book. 1999, DK $6.95 (0-7894-4735-5). A simple board book that introduces the symbols and meaning of Christmas with material on a manger, animals of the stable, and so on. (Rev: SLJ 10/99)

5889 Naylor, Phyllis Reynolds. *Keeping a Christmas Secret* (PS–K). Illus. by Lena Shiffman. 1989, Macmillan $15.00 (0-689-31447-7). 32pp. Michael inadvertently tells Dad what the family has given him for Christmas. (Rev: BCCB 10/89; BL 9/1/89; HB 11–12/89)

5890 Naylor, Phyllis Reynolds. *Old Sadie and the Christmas Bear* (K–3). Illus. by Patricia Montgomery Newton. 1984, Macmillan $15.00 (0-689-31052-8). 32pp. Amos, a hibernating bear, wakens to share a Christmas with Old Sadie.

5891 Neugebauer, Charise. *Santa's Gift* (PS–2). Illus. by Barbara Nascimbeni. 1999, North-South LB $15.88 (0-7358-1146-6). 32pp. With the help of his only friend, Humphrey the hippo, selfish kitten Timmy learns at Christmastime that it is as much fun to give as to receive. (Rev: BL 9/1/99; HBG 3/00; SLJ 10/99)

5892 Nikola-Lisa, W. *Hallelujah! A Christmas Celebration* (PS–1). Illus. by Synthia Saint James. 2000, Atheneum $16.00 (0-689-81673-1). 32pp. A joyous Nativity picture book in which all of the characters including the Holy Family and the shepherds are black. (Rev: BL 9/1/00*; HBG 3/01)

5893 O'Brien, John. *Mother Hubbard's Christmas* (K–2). Illus. 1996, Boyds Mills $14.95 (1-56397-139-9). 28pp. This hilarious variation on the standard nursery rhyme tells how Mother Hubbard prepares for Christmas. (Rev: BL 10/15/96)

5894 Palatini, Margie. *Moosletoe* (PS–1). Illus. by Henry Cole. 2000, Hyperion $15.99 (0-7868-0567-6). 32pp. The moose with the remarkable mustache allows it to be decked with ornaments to preserve the spirit of the Christmas season. (Rev: BL 9/1/00; HBG 3/01)

5895 Parish, Peggy. *Merry Christmas, Amelia Bedelia* (1–2). Illus. by Lynn Sweat. 1986, Greenwillow $15.89 (0-688-06102-8); Avon paper $3.99 (0-380-70325-4). 64pp. Christmas fun with silly Amelia Bedelia, the maid with nonsensical assumptions. (Rev: BCCB 10/86; BL 10/1/86)

5896 Paterson, Katherine. *Marvin's Best Christmas Present Ever* (1–2). Illus. by Jane Brown. 1997, HarperCollins LB $14.89 (0-06-027160-4). 48pp. Marvin is so happy with the Christmas wreath he has made for the family's trailer door that he doesn't want to take it down. (Rev: BL 9/1/97; HB 11–12/97; HBG 3/98; SLJ 10/97*)

5897 Pearson, Tracey Campbell. *Where Does Joe Go?* (PS–1). Illus. 1999, Farrar $16.00 (0-374-38319-7). 32pp. Everyone in town has a different theory concerning where fat Joe with his snow white beard spends his winters, but no one guesses that he is really Santa Claus and his winter home is the North Pole. (Rev: BL 11/1/99*; HBG 3/00; SLJ 10/99)

5898 Pilkey, Dav. *Dragon's Merry Christmas* (1–2). Illus. 1991, Orchard LB $16.99 (0-531-08557-0). 48pp. The Christmas tree that Dragon finds in the forest is too perfect to cut down. (Rev: BL 7/91)

5899 Pinkwater, Daniel. *Wolf Christmas* (PS–3). Illus. by Jill Pinkwater. 1998, Marshall Cavendish $15.95 (0-7614-5030-0). 32pp. On the longest night of the year, three wolf pups are taken by their Uncle Louis to see a human village and witness how this other animal species acts during their winter holidays. (Rev: BL 9/1/98; HBG 3/99; SLJ 10/98)

5900 Pittman, Helena Clare. *The Angel Tree* (PS–3). Illus. by JoEllen M. Stammen. 1998, Dial $15.99 (0-8037-1939-6). 32pp. Kindly Mr. McCafferty usually buys the biggest spruce from the Christmas tree lot and invites all the neighborhood children to decorate it at his house, but since he has moved away,

Jake and his father buy the tree, and angels decorate it. (Rev: BL 10/15/98; HBG 3/99; SLJ 10/98)

5901 Polacco, Patricia. *The Trees of the Dancing Goats* (PS–3). Illus. 1996, Simon & Schuster $16.00 (0-689-80862-3). 32pp. A Jewish family delivers Christmas trees to needy Christian families. (Rev: BL 11/1/96; SLJ 2/97)

5902 Polacco, Patricia. *Uncle Vova's Tree* (K–2). Illus. 1989, Putnam $15.95 (0-399-21617-0). 32pp. Old Christmas customs are described when a young girl spends Christmas with elderly Russian relatives. (Rev: BL 9/15/89; HB 11–12/89)

5903 Polacco, Patricia. *Welcome Comfort* (K–3). Illus. by author. 1999, Philomel LB $16.99 (0-399-23169-2). Welcome Comfort, an overweight foster child, gets a special surprise at Christmas. (Rev: BCCB 11/99; HBG 3/00; SLJ 10/99)

5904 Powell, Consie. *Old Dog Cora and the Christmas Tree* (PS–1). Illus. 1999, Albert Whitman $15.95 (0-8075-5968-7). 32pp. Written from the standpoint of Cora, the family's oldest dog, this is the story of a faithful pet who, in spite of her age, wants to help drag the Christmas tree home. (Rev: BL 9/1/99; HBG 3/00; SLJ 10/99)

5905 Price, Moe. *The Reindeer Christmas* (K–3). Illus. by Atsuko Morozumi. 1993, Harcourt $15.95 (0-15-266199-9). 32pp. A delightful Christmas story that tells why Santa decided that reindeer should be the animals to pull his sleigh. (Rev: BL 9/15/93)

5906 Primavera, Elise. *Auntie Claus* (PS–2). Illus. 1999, Harcourt $16.00 (0-15-201909-X). 40pp. Sophie Crinkle follows her Aunt Claus to a snowy land and there discovers that her relative is the real force behind Christmas. (Rev: BCCB 12/99; BL 9/1/99; HBG 3/00; SLJ 10/99)

5907 Rahaman, Vashanti. *O Christmas Tree* (K–3). Illus. by Frane Lessac. 1996, Boyds Mills $14.95 (1-56397-237-9). 26pp. Anslem has problems believing in a traditional Christmas with snow and Christmas trees in his Caribbean home. (Rev: BCCB 11/96; BL 9/1/96*)

5908 Ransom, Candice. *The Christmas Dolls* (K–3). Illus. by Moira Fain. 1998, Walker LB $16.85 (0-8027-8661-8). 32pp. Claire is sad because her father will be absent for Christmas. She is comforted by helping her mother repair dolls to give to poor children and by making a rag doll that she will give her mother on Christmas morning. (Rev: BL 9/1/98; HBG 3/99; SLJ 10/98)

5909 Ransom, Candice. *One Christmas Dawn* (K–3). Illus. by Peter M. Fiore. 1996, Troll $15.95 (0-8167-3384-8). 32pp. In 1917 Appalachia, a young girl awaits the promised arrival of her father for Christmas. (Rev: BL 10/15/96)

5910 Repchuk, Caroline. *The Snow Tree* (PS–1). Illus. by Josephine Martin. 1997, Dutton $15.99 (0-525-45903-0). 32pp. Animals offer to a little bear many colorful objects to decorate his Christmas tree. (Rev: BL 9/1/97; HBG 3/98)

5911 Riggio, Anita. *A Moon in My Teacup* (PS–2). Illus. 1993, Boyds Mills LB $14.95 (1-56397-008-2). 32pp. On a visit to her Italian American grand-

parents, a young girl sings "Silent Night" to the baby figure she finds in the stable of a miniature village that belongs to her grandfather. (Rev: BL 10/15/93)

5912 Root, Phyllis. *All for the Newborn Baby* (PS–K). Illus. by Nicola Bayley. 2000, Candlewick $12.99 (0-7636-0093-8). 40pp. A lovely picture book that imagines the lullaby that Mary sang to Jesus. (Rev: BL 9/1/00; HBG 3/01)

5913 Rylant, Cynthia. *Mr. Putter and Tabby Bake the Cake* (1–3). Illus. by Arthur Howard. 1994, Harcourt $13.00 (0-15-200205-7); paper $6.00 (0-15-200214-6). 44pp. Mr. Putter bakes a Christmas cake for his neighbor, Mrs. Teaberry, in this easily read book. (Rev: BL 10/15/94; HB 9–10/94; SLJ 12/94)

5914 Rylant, Cynthia. *Silver Packages: An Appalachian Christmas Story* (K–3). Illus. by Chris K. Soentpiet. 1997, Orchard LB $16.99 (0-531-33051-6). 32pp. At Christmas time, a young doctor tries to repay an Appalachian community for the gifts that were given to him in the past. (Rev: BL 9/1/97; HBG 3/98; SLJ 10/97)

5915 Say, Allen. *Tree of Cranes* (PS–3). Illus. 1991, Houghton $17.95 (0-395-52024-X). 32pp. A Japanese woman brings a tree indoors because it reminds her of the Christmas she spent years ago in California. (Rev: BCCB 9/91*; BL 9/15/91; HB 11–12/91*)

5916 Schachner, Judith Byron. *Willy and May* (PS–3). Illus. 1995, Dutton $14.99 (0-525-45347-4). 32pp. May thinks of an unusual solution when a snowstorm prevents her great niece from visiting her at Christmas. (Rev: BL 11/1/95*; SLJ 10/95*)

5917 Seuss, Dr. *How the Grinch Stole Christmas* (K–3). Illus. by author. 1957, Random $15.99 (0-394-90079-0). A rhyming book about a queer creature, the Grinch, who plans to do away with Christmas.

5918 Shannon, David. *The Amazing Christmas Extravaganza* (K–3). Illus. 1995, Scholastic $15.95 (0-590-48090-1). 32pp. A parable about Mr. Merriweather and how he alienates his neighbors at Christmas time. (Rev: BL 9/15/95)

5919 Shepard, Aaron. *The Baker's Dozen: A Saint Nicholas Tale* (PS–2). Illus. by Wendy Edelson. 1995, Simon & Schuster $15.00 (0-689-80298-6). 32pp. A baker learns the meaning of being generous at the same time he finds out what is meant by a baker's dozen in this story about a visit from Saint Nicholas. (Rev: BL 9/15/95) [398.2]

5920 Slate, Joseph. *The Secret Stars* (PS–2). Illus. by Felipe Davalos. 1998, Marshall Cavendish $15.95 (0-7614-5027-0). 32pp. On the Night of the Three Kings holiday, the weather in New Mexico is so bad that Pepe and Sila worry that the kings will not be able to deliver their presents. (Rev: BL 9/15/98; HBG 3/99; SLJ 10/98)

5921 Soto, Gary. *Too Many Tamales* (PS–1). Illus. by Ed Martinez. 1993, Putnam $15.95 (0-399-22146-8). 32pp. A Hispanic child enthusiastically enters into the cooking and other rituals that surround her family's celebration of Christmas. (Rev: BCCB 10/93; BL 9/15/93; HB 11–12/93)

5922 Spinelli, Eileen. *Coming Through the Blizzard* (PS–2). Illus. by Jenny Tylden-Wright. 1999, Simon & Schuster $16.00 (0-689-81490-9). 32pp. On a very snowy Christmas Eve, a minister wonders if anyone will come out to church, but has a most pleasant surprise. (Rev: BL 9/1/99; HBG 3/00; SLJ 10/99)

5923 Spirin, Gennady. *The Christmas Story: According to the Gospels of Matthew and Luke from the King James Bible* (1–6). Illus. 1998, Holt $19.95 (0-8050-5292-5). 32pp. A beautifully illustrated version of the Nativity that incorporates verses from the Gospels of Matthew and Luke from the King James version of the Bible. (Rev: BL 11/15/98; HBG 3/99; SLJ 10/98) [232.9]

5924 Spowart, Robin. *Inside, Outside Christmas* (PS). Illus. 1998, Holiday $15.95 (0-8234-1370-5). 32pp. Using double-page spreads and short rhyming phrases, this picture book depicts inside and outside activities of a loving mouse family at Christmas. (Rev: BL 9/1/98; HBG 3/99; SLJ 10/98)

5925 Steven, Kenneth. *The Bearer of Gifts* (PS–2). Illus. by Lily Moon. 1998, Dial $12.99 (0-8037-2374-1). 26pp. This book tells how Santa Claus, a simple woodcarver, dedicates his life to giving gifts to children after he visits the stable where the infant Jesus lies in a manger. (Rev: BCCB 12/98; BL 10/15/98; HBG 3/99; SLJ 10/98)

5926 Stevenson, James. *Christmas at Mud Flat* (1–3). Illus. 2000, HarperCollins LB $15.89 (0-688-17302-0). 48pp. It's a week before Christmas and everyone in Mud Flat is making hasty preparations for the big event. (Rev: BCCB 11/00; BL 9/1/00; HBG 3/01)

5927 Stickland, Henrietta. *The Christmas Bear* (PS–2). Illus. by Paul Stickland. 1993, Dutton $15.99 (0-525-45062-9). 32pp. When a bear cub accidentally falls into Santa's home, he is taken on a tour of the premises. (Rev: BL 10/1/93)

5928 Stone, Phoebe. *What Night Do the Angels Wander?* (PS–2). Illus. 1998, Little, Brown $15.95 (0-316-81439-3). 32pp. This magical picture book depicts Christmas night, when angels spread good works and good cheer around the world. (Rev: BL 9/1/98; HBG 3/99; SLJ 10/98)

5929 Strand, Keith. *Grandfather's Christmas Tree* (PS–3). Illus. by Thomas Locker. 1999, Harcourt $16.00 (0-15-201821-2). 32pp. A lovely Christmas story about a pioneer family who are saved from having to chop down their last spruce tree for firewood and, thus, are able to save a pair of geese that have taken shelter in it. (Rev: BL 9/1/99; HBG 3/00; SLJ 10/99)

5930 Summers, Susan. *The Fourth Wise Man: Based on the Story of Henry Van Dyke* (K–4). Illus. by Jackie Morris. 1998, Dial $16.99 (0-8037-2312-1). 34pp. Because he stops along the way to Bethlehem to help people in need, Artaban, the fourth wise man, misses seeing the Christ child, but he is rewarded at the end of his life for his good deeds. (Rev: BCCB 12/98; BL 10/1/98; HBG 3/99; SLJ 10/98)

5931 Sundvall, Viveca L. *Santa's Winter Vacation* (K–3). Trans. by Kjersti Board. Illus. by Olof Landstrom. 1995, Farrar $13.00 (91-29-62953-5). 32pp. At Christmas, Reuben Stormfoot becomes Santa Stormfoot and teaches a lesson to the loud, rude Sandworm children, whom he has encountered on his vacation. (Rev: BL 9/15/95)

5932 Sykes, Julie. *Hurry, Santa!* (PS–K). Illus. by Tim Warnes. 1998, Little Tiger $14.95 (1-888444-37-1). 32pp. Santa oversleeps and Christmas Eve becomes a big rush, rush, rush to get everything done in time. (Rev: BL 9/1/98; HBG 3/99; SLJ 10/98)

5933 Tafuri, Nancy. *Counting to Christmas* (PS–K). Illus. 1998, Scholastic $15.95 (0-590-27143-1). 40pp. In the weeks leading up to Christmas, a little girl engages in various crafts, such as making ornaments. Directions for her projects appear at the end of the book. (Rev: BCCB 11/98; BL 9/15/98; HBG 3/99; SLJ 10/98)

5934 Tews, Susan. *The Gingerbread Doll* (K–3). Illus. by Megan Lloyd. 1993, Clarion $16.00 (0-395-56438-7). 32pp. Starting as a poor youngster during the Great Depression when she gets a gingerbread doll, Rebecca finds that her Christmas presents change as her family gets more prosperous. (Rev: BL 9/1/93)

5935 Thayer, Jane. *The Puppy Who Wanted a Boy* (1–3). Illus. by Lisa McCue. 1986, Morrow paper $5.95 (0-688-08293-9). 48pp. Petey the puppy doesn't get a boy for Christmas as he wished, but he does find 50 boys in a Home for Boys to whom he can give his love. (Rev: BL 4/1/86; SLJ 5/86)

5936 Thompson, Kay. *Eloise at Christmastime* (PS–3). Illus. by Hilary Knight. 199, Simon $17.50 (0-689-83039-4). A reissue of the book about the little girl who lives in the Plaza Hotel in New York City and her adventures at Christmas. (Rev: BL 11/15/99; HBG 3/00)

5937 Thompson, Lauren. *Mouse's First Christmas* (PS). Illus. by Buket Erdogan. 1999, Simon & Schuster $12.00 (0-689-82325-8). 32pp. A little mouse explores the house on Christmas Eve and finds all sorts of treats, including a meeting with Santa Claus. (Rev: BCCB 11/99; BL 9/1/99; HBG 3/00; SLJ 10/99)

5938 Thomson, Pat. *Beware of the Aunts!* (PS–2). Illus. by Emma C. Clark. 1992, Macmillan $14.95 (0-689-50538-8). Nine unusual aunts and Christmas gift giving are the subjects of this humorous book. (Rev: SLJ 7/92)

5939 Tompert, Ann. *A Carol for Christmas* (K–3). Illus. by Laura Kelly. 1994, Macmillan paper $16.00 (0-02-789402-9). 32pp. A mouse witnesses the composition of the carol "Silent Night" from the comfort of a pastor's coat pocket. (Rev: BL 10/15/94)

5940 Trivas, Irene. *Emma's Christmas* (PS–4). Illus. 1988, Orchard paper $6.95 (0-531-07022-0). 32pp. When Emma, the farmer's daughter, declines the prince's offer of marriage, he begins to send her gifts. (Rev: BCCB 10/88; BL 9/15/88; HB 11–12/88)

5941 Tryon, Leslie. *Albert's Christmas* (K–2). Illus. by author. 1997, Simon & Schuster $16.00 (0-689-

81034-2). In this Christmas story, the animals of Pleasant Valley, led by Albert the duck, work hard to feed the reindeer, etc., when Santa makes a pit stop in their town. (Rev: HBG 3/98; SLJ 10/97)

5942 Vainio, Pirkko. *The Christmas Angel* (K–2). Trans. by Anthea Bell. Illus. 1995, North-South LB $15.88 (1-55858-500-1); paper $6.95 (1-55858-774-8). 32pp. Through good works at Christmas time, a young girl helps a music box angel get her wings. (Rev: BL 12/15/95)

5943 Van Allsburg, Chris. *The Polar Express* (K–2). Illus. by author. 1985, Houghton $18.95 (0-395-38949-6). 32pp. Whisked aboard the Polar Express to the North Pole on Christmas Eve, a young boy gets to receive the first gift of Christmas. Caldecott Medal winner, 1986. (Rev: BCCB 10/85; BL 10/1/85; SLJ 10/85)

5944 Waber, Bernard. *Lyle at Christmas* (K–3). Illus. 1998, Houghton $16.00 (0-395-91304-7). 48pp. At Christmastime, Lyle, the lovable crocodile, tries to cheer up Mr. Grumps, who is in the dumps, by finding his beloved cat, Loretta. (Rev: BL 9/1/98; HB 11–12/98; HBG 3/99; SLJ 10/98)

5945 Waldron, Jan L. *Angel Pig and the Hidden Christmas* (PS–2). Illus. by David McPhail. 1997, Dutton $14.99 (0-525-45744-5). 32pp. Six little pigs are getting excited about Christmas, but they have no money for presents. (Rev: BL 9/1/97*; HBG 3/98; SLJ 10/97)

5946 Wallner, Alexandra. *An Alcott Family Christmas* (K–2). Illus. 1996, Holiday LB $15.95 (0-8234-1265-2). 30pp. A fictionalized account of how Louisa May Alcott's family might have observed Christmas as the March family did in *Little Women*. (Rev: BL 9/1/96)

5947 Walsh, Vivian, and J. Otto Seibold. *Olive, the Other Reindeer* (1–3). Illus. 1997, Chronicle $13.95 (0-8118-1807-1). 32pp. A little dog believes that she is really a reindeer and heads to the North Pole to give Santa a hand. (Rev: BL 10/15/97; HBG 3/98)

5948 Watts, Bernadette. *Harvey Hare's Christmas* (PS–K). Illus. 1999, North-South LB $15.88 (0-7358-1059-1). 32pp. The animals think of all sorts of ways to help Harvey Hare, the postman, at Christmastime, but none of them work. (Rev: BL 9/1/99; HBG 3/00; SLJ 10/99)

5949 Weller, Frances W. *The Angel of Mill Street* (K–3). Illus. by Robert J. Blake. 1998, Putnam $15.99 (0-399-23133-1). 32pp. On his way to visit his niece on a snowy Christmas Eve, disabled Uncle Ambrose falls into a snowbank and is rescued by a mysterious black dog in this tale set 100 years ago. (Rev: BCCB 12/98; BL 9/1/98; HBG 3/99; SLJ 2/99)

5950 Wells, Rosemary. *McDuff's New Friend* (PS–K). Illus. by Susan Jeffers. 1998, Hyperion $12.95 (0-7868-0386-X). In this sweet tale, McDuff, a terrier, and his owner dig a tunnel after a severe snowstorm and find Santa stuck in a snowdrift. (Rev: BL 12/1/98; HBG 3/99; SLJ 10/98)

5951 Wells, Rosemary. *Morris's Disappearing Bag* (PS–1). Illus. 1999, Viking $15.99 (0-670-88721-8).

40pp. A young rabbit is disappointed with the stuffed bear he gets for Christmas but is delighted with another present that contains a Disappearing Bag. (Rev: BL 1/1–15/00; HBG 3/00)

5952 Weninger, Brigitte. *A Letter to Santa Claus* (K–3). Trans. by Sibylle Kazeroid. Illus. by Anne Moller. 2000, North-South LB $15.88 (0-7358-1360-4). 32pp. A sweet tale about a poor boy whose letter to Santa is answered in an amazing way. (Rev: BL 9/1/00; HBG 3/01)

5953 Weninger, Brigitte. *Merry Christmas, Davy!* (PS–3). Trans. by Rosemary Lanning. Illus. by Eve Tharlet. 1998, North-South LB $15.88 (1-55858-981-3). 32pp. Davy, a little rabbit, believes in the spirit of sharing at Christmas and, to his family's dismay, gives away all the food that they have stored for the winter. (Rev: BL 9/1/98; HBG 3/99; SLJ 10/98)

5954 Wild, Margaret. *Thank You, Santa* (PS–3). Illus. by Kerry Argent. 1992, Scholastic $12.95 (0-590-45805-1). 32pp. After Christmas, a young girl in Australia begins a correspondence with Santa Claus. (Rev: BCCB 11/92; BL 11/1/92)

5955 Williams, Sam. *Teddy Bears Trim the Tree* (PS–K). Illus. by Jacqueline McQuade. 2000, Scholastic $14.95 (0-439-19285-4). An interactive book about a group of teddy bears who find a Christmas tree, bring it in, and decorate it in time for Santa's arrival. (Rev: BL 12/1/00)

5956 Winthrop, Elizabeth. *Bear's Christmas Surprise* (PS–2). Illus. by Patience Brewster. 1991, Holiday LB $14.95 (0-8234-0888-4). 32pp. While playing hide-and-seek, Bear accidentally discovers some Christmas presents hidden in a closet and opens them. (Rev: BL 9/15/91)

5957 Wojciechowski, Susan. *The Christmas Miracle of Jonathan Toomey* (PS–4). Illus. by P. J. Lynch. 1995, Candlewick $18.99 (1-56402-320-6). 40pp. Mean old Jonathan Toomey is transformed at Christmas time when a widowed mother and her son ask him to build a Christmas creche for them. (Rev: BL 9/15/95; SLJ 10/95*)

5958 Wood, Audrey. *The Christmas Adventure of Space Elf Sam* (PS–3). Illus. by Bruce Robert Wood. 1998, Scholastic $15.95 (0-590-03143-0). 40pp. When families from Earth colonize outer space, Santa Claus needs help to perform his Christmas Eve duties. (Rev: BL 9/1/98; HBG 3/99; SLJ 10/98)

5959 Wright, Cliff. *Santa's Ark* (K–3). Illus. 1997, Millbrook LB $22.40 (0-7613-0314-6). 36pp. Different animals from around the world stow away in Santa's sleigh when he makes his stops. (Rev: BL 12/15/97; HBG 3/98; SLJ 10/97)

5960 Zagwyn, Deborah Turney. *The Winter Gift* (K–3). Illus. 2000, Tricycle Pr. $15.95 (1-883672-93-7). 32pp. Grandma is selling all her furniture before moving into an apartment, but she gives her piano to her grandchildren to continue the tradition of playing it at Christmas. (Rev: BL 9/1/00*; HBG 3/01)

5961 Ziefert, Harriet. *Presents for Santa* (K–1). Illus. by Laura Rader. 2000, Viking $13.89 (0-670-

88390-5); paper $3.99 (0-14-038186-4). 32pp. In this easy-to-read book, nine mousekins suggest gifts for Santa — such as a bike and a pony — and the next morning find that those are the gifts they have received. (Rev: BL 12/1/00; HBG 3/01)

EASTER

5962 Adams, Adrienne. *The Easter Egg Artists* (PS–2). 1991, Simon & Schuster paper $5.99 (0-689-71481-5). 32pp. A rabbit family paints 100 dozen eggs for Easter, helped greatly by the son's flair for comic design.

5963 Bishop, Adela. *The Easter Wolf* (PS–2). Illus. by Carole Dzapla. 1991, Dot $12.95 (0-9625620-1-7). 28pp. When he is saved from drowning by the Easter Rabbit, a hungry wolf reforms. (Rev: BL 3/15/91)

5964 Denim, Sue. *The Dumb Bunnies' Easter* (K–2). Illus. by Dav Pilkey. 1995, Scholastic $12.95 (0-590-20241-3). 32pp. The Dumb Bunnies have a very distorted view of what to expect from the Easter Bunny. (Rev: BL 2/1/95; SLJ 2/95)

5965 Devlin, Wende, and Harry Devlin. *Cranberry Easter* (PS–3). Illus. by Harry Devlin. 1990, Macmillan LB $15.00 (0-02-729935-X). In the town of Cranberryport, friends help each other and the result is a happy Easter. (Rev: SLJ 3/90)

5966 Friedrich, Priscilla, and Otto Friedrich. *The Easter Bunny That Overslept* (PS–1). Illus. by Adrienne Adams. 1983, Morrow paper $4.95 (0-688-07038-8). 40pp. Santa Claus helps a tardy Easter Bunny who has trouble getting up on time.

5967 Gibbons, Gail. *Easter* (PS–2). Illus. by author. 1989, Holiday LB $16.95 (0-8234-0737-3); paper $6.95 (0-8234-0866-3). 32pp. Biblical, pagan, and modern aspects of the holiday are described. (Rev: BL 4/1/89; SLJ 3/89)

5968 Heyward, DuBose. *The Country Bunny and the Little Gold Shoes* (K–3). Illus. by Marjorie Flack. 1939, Houghton $15.00 (0-395-15990-3); paper $5.95 (0-395-18557-2). 48pp. Cottontail, the mother of 21 bunnies, finally realizes her great ambition to be an Easter Bunny.

5969 Houselander, Caryll. *Petook: An Easter Story* (K–3). Illus. by Tomie dePaola. 1988, Holiday LB $16.95 (0-8234-0681-4). 32pp. The rooster, Petook, and a simple story of Easter. (Rev: BL 4/15/88; SLJ 5/88)

5970 Lindgren, Astrid. *Lotta's Easter Surprise* (K–2). Trans. by Barbara Lucas. Illus. by Ilon Wikland. 1991, R&S $13.95 (91-29-59862-1). 32pp. When her local candy store goes out of business, Lotta must settle for Christmas candies at Easter. (Rev: BCCB 4/91; BL 3/15/91)

5971 Modesitt, Jeanne. *Little Bunny's Easter Surprise* (PS–K). Illus. by Robin Spowart. 1999, Simon & Schuster $12.95 (0-689-82491-2). 32pp. To the family's surprise, on Easter morning Little Bunny says she has hidden Easter baskets for them and her baby brother. (Rev: BL 2/1/99; HBG 10/99; SLJ 2/99)

5972 Nerlove, Miriam. *Easter* (PS–1). Illus. 1989, Whitman paper $4.95 (0-8075-1872-7). 24pp. This major religious holiday is described in rhyming text. (Rev: BL 1/15/90; SLJ 4/90)

5973 Paraskevas, Betty. *Nibbles O'Hare* (PS–2). Illus. by Michael Paraskevas. 2001, Simon & Schuster $16.00 (0-689-82865-9). 32pp. A cunning rabbit named Nibbles O'Hare flees to the country after his thieving ways have been exposed, and there he cons the locals into thinking he is the Easter Bunny. (Rev: BL 12/15/00)

5974 Polacco, Patricia. *Chicken Sunday* (PS–3). Illus. 1992, Putnam $15.95 (0-399-22133-6). 32pp. Three youngsters of different races and religions unite to help Miss Eula have a good Easter. (Rev: BCCB 7–8/92; BL 3/15/92*; SLJ 5/92*)

5975 Stock, Catherine. *Easter Surprise* (PS–1). Illus. Series: Festive Year. 1991, Macmillan LB $13.00 (0-02-788371-X). 32pp. A girl and her older brother engage in such Easter activities as hunting for eggs. (Rev: BCCB 3/91; BL 2/1/91; SLJ 9/91)

5976 Watson, Wendy. *Happy Easter Day!* (PS–2). Illus. 1993, Houghton $14.95 (0-395-53629-4). A family prepares for Easter by participating in such activities as baking hot-cross buns. (Rev: SLJ 4/93) [263]

5977 Wiencirz, Gerlinde. *Teddy's Easter Secret* (PS–2). Trans. by J. Alison James. Illus. by Giuliano Lunelli. 2001, North-South LB $15.88 (0-7358-1358-2). 32pp. During an excursion in the woods, Teddy, a stuffed toy, meets the Easter Bunny and brings home some colored eggs for his young owner. (Rev: BL 3/15/01)

5978 Winters, Kay. *How Will the Easter Bunny Know?* (1–2). Illus. by Martha Weston. 1999, Delacorte $13.95 (0-385-32596-7); paper $4.50 (0-440-41499-7). 48pp. When Mike goes to Grandma's for Easter, he leaves a map so the Easter Bunny will be able to find him, in this book for beginning readers. (Rev: BL 3/15/99; HBG 10/99; SLJ 4/99)

5979 Zolotow, Charlotte. *The Bunny Who Found Easter* (PS–2). Illus. by Helen Craig. 1998, Houghton $15.00 (0-395-86265-5). 32pp. A new edition of the story about a bunny who wanders through a year searching for Easter so he can enjoy the company of other bunnies. The 1959 edition is illustrated by Betty Peterson. (Rev: BL 3/1/98; HBG 3/99; SLJ 9/98)

HALLOWEEN

5980 Adams, Adrienne. *A Woggle of Witches* (PS–3). Illus. by author. 1971, Macmillan paper $5.99 (0-689-71050-X). 32pp. The activities of a group of witches on Halloween night as they go about their business of dining on bat stew and riding on a broom.

5981 Beard, Darleen Bailey. *The Pumpkin Man from Piney Creek* (PS–3). Illus. by Laura Kelly. 1995, Simon & Schuster $15.00 (0-689-80315-X). 32pp. Hattie is sad because all of her father's pumpkins have been promised to the Pumpkin Man and she will not have one from which to carve a jack-o'-lantern. (Rev: BL 9/15/95; SLJ 10/95)

5982 Bridwell, Norman. *Clifford's Halloween* (PS–1). Illus. by author. 1970, Scholastic paper

$2.99 (0-590-44287-2). 32pp. Halloween adventures of a big red dog.

5983 Brown, Marc. *Arthur's Halloween* (PS–2). Illus. by author. 1983, Little, Brown $15.95 (0-316-11116-3); paper $5.95 (0-316-11059-0). 32pp. Arthur must find courage to help his sister on Halloween.

5984 Broyles, Anne. *Shy Mama's Halloween* (2–4). Illus. by Leane Morin. 2000, Tilbury $16.95 (0-88448-218-9). 40pp. Recently arrived from Russia, Anya and her siblings are taken out on Halloween by their mother and suddenly feel more at home in their new country. (Rev: BL 11/15/00; HBG 3/01; SLJ 1/01)

5985 Bunting, Eve. *Scary, Scary Halloween* (PS–1). Illus. by Jan Brett. 1986, Houghton $15.00 (0-89919-414-1); paper $5.95 (0-89919-799-X). 32pp. A scary poem tells of a parade of creatures on Halloween night. (Rev: BCCB 9/86; BL 9/1/86; HB 11–12/86)

5986 Capucilli, Alyssa Satin. *Inside a House That Is Haunted: A Rebus Read-Along Story* (PS–3). Illus. by Tedd Arnold. 1998, Scholastic $11.95 (0-590-99716-5). On Halloween night the ghostly inhabitants of a haunted house are terrified when they hear a knock on the door. (Rev: HBG 3/99; SLJ 9/98)

5987 Carlson, Nancy. *Harriet's Halloween Candy* (PS–K). Illus. by author. 1982, Carolrhoda LB $15.95 (0-87614-182-3); Lerner paper $4.95 (0-87614-850-X). 32pp. A childlike dog overeats on Halloween candy.

5988 Carlstrom, Nancy White. *What a Scare, Jesse Bear* (PS–K). Illus. by Bruce Degen. 1999, Simon & Schuster $15.00 (0-689-81961-7). 32pp. Jesse Bear has fun and a few scares when he ventures out alone on Halloween. (Rev: BL 9/1/99; HBG 3/00; SLJ 10/99)

5989 Caseley, Judith. *Witch Mama* (PS–2). Illus. 1996, Greenwillow LB $14.93 (0-688-14458-6). 32pp. On Halloween, Mama becomes Witch Mama, but she still cares for her two children. (Rev: BL 9/1/96; SLJ 8/96)

5990 Cazet, Denys. *Never Poke a Squid* (PS–2). Illus. 2000, Orchard LB $17.99 (0-531-33279-9). 32pp. When the school principal pins an award on the Halloween squid costume that Arnie and friend Raymond are wearing, ink pours out — to the delight of all the first-grade kids. (Rev: BCCB 9/00; BL 9/1/00; HBG 3/01; SLJ 9/00)

5991 Cocca-Leffler, Maryann. *Jungle Halloween* (PS). Illus. 2000, Albert Whitman $14.95 (0-8075-4056-0). 32pp. A group of jungle animals dress up as monsters and participate in a big, boisterous Halloween party. (Rev: BL 9/1/00; HBG 3/01; SLJ 9/00)

5992 Cushman, Doug. *Aunt Eater's Mystery Halloween* (1–2). Illus. Series: I Can Read. 1998, HarperCollins LB $14.89 (0-06-027804-8). 64pp. Four short mysteries about Halloween are solved by Aunt Eater, the anteater who dresses like Sherlock Holmes. (Rev: BL 9/1/98; HBG 3/99; SLJ 10/98)

5993 De Groat, Diane. *Trick or Treat, Smell My Feet* (PS–3). Illus. 1998, Morrow LB $14.93 (0-

688-15767-X). 32pp. Gilbert takes his sister's Halloween costume to the school parade instead of his own by mistake and finds that he has to dress as a ballerina instead of a Martian space pilot. (Rev: BL 9/1/98; HBG 3/99; SLJ 10/98)

5994 Diviny, Sean. *Halloween Motel* (K–3). Illus. by Joe Rocco. 2000, HarperCollins LB $15.89 (0-06-028816-7). 32pp. In this humorous Halloween story, a boy and his family check into a hotel where the bellhop is Frankie Stein and the guests are monsters. (Rev: BL 9/1/00; HBG 3/01; SLJ 9/00)

5995 Dodds, Dayle Ann. *Ghost and Pete* (K–3). Illus. by Matt Novak. Series: Step into Reading. 1995, Random LB $11.99 (0-679-96199-2); paper $3.99 (0-679-86199-8). 48pp. When Pete moves into his new house, he becomes friendly with Ghost, who lives in the attic, in this Halloween story. (Rev: SLJ 3/96)

5996 Enderle, Judith R., and Stephanie G. Tessler. *Six Creepy Sheep* (PS–1). Illus. by John O'Brien. 1992, Boyds Mills LB $12.95 (1-56397-092-9). 24pp. Six sheep go out on Halloween dressed as ghosts. (Rev: BL 9/1/92; HB 3–4/93; SLJ 10/92)

5997 *Five Little Pumpkins* (PS). Illus. by Dan Yaccarino. 1998, HarperFestival $5.95 (0-694-01177-0). 16pp. A board book that illustrates the old rhyme about five little pumpkins sitting on a gate. (Rev: BL 12/15/98; HBG 3/99; SLJ 2/99)

5998 Gantos, Jack. *Rotten Ralph's Trick or Treat* (K–3). Illus. by Nicole Rubel. 1986, Houghton $15.00 (0-395-38943-7); paper $6.95 (0-395-48655-6). 32pp. Ralph the cat and waitress Sarah exchange identities at a Halloween party. (Rev: HB 9–10/86; SLJ 10/86)

5999 Gordon, Lynn. *The Witch's Revenge* (K–4). Illus. by Val Martino. Series: Lights Out. 1997, Simon & Schuster $9.99 (0-689-81679-0). In this interactive book — which contains images that can be projected on walls using a flashlight — a witch plans to get even for a trick played on her at Halloween. (Rev: SLJ 1/98)

6000 Gralley, Jean. *Hogula: Dread Pig of Night* (PS–1). Illus. 1999, Holt $15.95 (0-8050-5700-5). 32pp. A Halloween story about Hogula, a vampire pig, who lives on Grimey Pork Chop Hill and likes to snort on human necks. (Rev: BCCB 10/99; BL 11/15/99; HBG 3/00; SLJ 11/99)

6001 Grambling, Louis. *Miss Hildy's Missing Cape Caper* (1–3). Illus. by Bridget S. Taylor. Series: Step into Reading. 2000, Random $3.99 (0-375-80196-0). 48pp. In this beginning reader, detective Hildy sets out to discover who stole her witch's cape and hat on Halloween. (Rev: BL 10/1/00)

6002 Greene, Carol. *The 13 Days of Halloween* (PS–3). Illus. by Tim Raglin. 2000, Troll $15.95 (0-8167-6965-6). 32pp. A dapper ghoul tries to woo his friend with such gifts as a vulture in a dead tree in this take-off on the Christmas carol. (Rev: BL 9/1/00; SLJ 9/00)

6003 Hall, Zoe. *It's Pumpkin Time!* (K–3). Illus. by Shari Halpern. 1994, Scholastic $14.95 (0-590-47833-8). This picture book describes how two children plant a pumpkin seed and care for it so that it will be useful at Halloween. (Rev: SLJ 11/94)

6004 Hautzig, Deborah. *Little Witch's Big Night* (1–2). Illus. by Marc Brown. 1984, Random paper $3.99 (0-394-86587-1). 48pp. Little Witch has a better Halloween than she expected.

6005 Heinz, Brian J. *The Monsters' Test* (K–2). Illus. by Sal Murdocca. 1996, Millbrook LB $23.90 (0-7613-0050-3). A group of scary monsters are frightened by some trick-or-treaters. (Rev: SLJ 10/96)

6006 Hennessy, B. G. *Corduroy's Halloween: A Lift-the-Flap Book* (PS–K). Illus. by Lisa McCue. 1995, Viking $11.99 (0-670-86193-6). Flaps that lift add surprise to this story of how a little bear spends his Halloween. (Rev: SLJ 10/95)

6007 Hines, Anna Grossnickle. *When the Goblins Came Knocking* (PS–K). Illus. 1995, Greenwillow LB $15.93 (0-688-13736-9). 24pp. A young boy decides that, unlike other Halloweens, this time he will be the one to frighten others. (Rev: BL 9/15/95; SLJ 9/95)

6008 Hoban, Lillian. *Arthur's Halloween Costume* (1–3). Illus. by author. 1984, HarperCollins LB $15.89 (0-06-022391-X); paper $3.95 (0-06-444101-6). 64pp. Arthur is annoyed because no one understands his Halloween costume.

6009 Holub, Joan. *Boo Who? A Spooky Lift-the-Flap Book* (PS–1). Illus. by author. Series: Spooky Lift-the-Flap Book. 1997, Scholastic $6.95 (0-590-05905-X). Rhymes and flaps are used to introduce the objects and creatures associated with Halloween. (Rev: SLJ 10/97)

6010 Howe, James. *Scared Silly: A Halloween Treat* (K–2). Illus. by Leslie Morrill. 1989, Morrow $16.00 (0-688-07666-1); paper $4.95 (0-688-16322-X). A really scary story featuring Chester and the crew from the Bunnicula series. (Rev: BL 8/89; SLJ 8/89*)

6011 Hubbard, Patricia. *Trick or Treat Countdown* (PS). Illus. by Michael Letzig. 1999, Holiday $15.95 (0-8234-1367-5). A simple counting rhyme goes from one to 12 and back again, using Halloween symbols and general spookiness. (Rev: BCCB 10/99; BL 9/1/99; HBG 3/00; SLJ 9/99)

6012 Hubbell, Patricia. *Boo! Halloween Poems and Limericks* (K–4). Illus. by Jeff Spackman. 1998, Marshall Cavendish $15.95 (0-7614-5023-8). 32pp. Witty original poems and limericks about Halloween are presented with suitably lurid illustrations. (Rev: BL 9/1/98; HBG 3/99; SLJ 9/98) [811]

6013 Hubbell, Will. *Pumpkin Jack* (PS–2). Illus. 2000, Albert Whitman $15.95 (0-8075-6665-9). 32pp. After Halloween, Tim reluctantly throws away the jack-o'-lantern he has craved only to find, in the spring, that a sprout has appeared to bear more pumpkins for next Halloween. (Rev: BL 9/1/00; HBG 3/01; SLJ 9/00)

6014 Hulme, Joy N. *Eerie Feary Feeling: A Hairy Scary Pop-Up Book* (K–2). Illus. by Paul Ely. 1998, Orchard $13.95 (0-531-30086-2). Cats, bats, witches, ghosts, and ghouls are all featured in this interactive pop-up book. (Rev: SLJ 12/98)

6015 Hutchins, Pat. *Which Witch Is Which?* (PS–K). Illus. 1989, Greenwillow $15.89 (0-688-06358-6). 24pp. Identical twins dress as witches on Halloween. (Rev: BL 9/1/89; SLJ 8/89*)

6016 Jane, Pamela. *Halloween Hide-and-Seek* (1–3). Illus. by Julie Durrell. Series: A Yearling First Choice Chapter Book. 1997, Delacorte paper $3.99 (0-440-41219-6). 48pp. Jonathan is unhappy because he has to wear last year's pirate costume to Leo's Halloween party. (Rev: HBG 3/98; SLJ 12/97)

6017 Johnston, Tony. *The Soup Bone* (PS–3). Illus. by Margot Tomes. 1990, Harcourt $12.95 (0-15-277255-3). 32pp. A witch looking for a soup bone uncovers a whole skeleton. (Rev: BL 10/15/90; HB 11–12/90; SLJ 1/91)

6018 Johnston, Tony. *The Vanishing Pumpkin* (PS–2). Illus. by Tomie dePaola. 1996, Putnam paper $5.99 (0-698-11414-0). 32pp. An old man and an old woman set out on Halloween to find their pumpkin.

6019 Johnston, Tony. *Very Scary* (PS–K). Illus. by Douglas Florian. 1995, Harcourt $14.00 (0-15-293625-4). 32pp. When a girl carves a pumpkin into a jack-o'-lantern, it shouts "Boo" and frightens everyone. (Rev: BL 9/15/95; SLJ 11/95)

6020 Keats, Ezra Jack. *The Trip* (1–3). Illus. by author. 1978, Greenwillow $15.93 (0-688-84123-6); Morrow paper $5.95 (0-688-07328-X). 32pp. Halloween proves to be a time when Louis isn't lonely anymore.

6021 Kraus, Robert. *How Spider Saved Halloween* (K–3). Illus. by author. 1988, Scholastic paper $2.99 (0-590-42117-4). 32pp. Spider saves the fun of Halloween by creating an ingenious disguise.

6022 Kroll, Steven. *The Biggest Pumpkin Ever* (PS–2). Illus. by Jeni Bassett. 1984, Holiday LB $16.95 (0-8234-0505-2); Scholastic paper $2.50 (0-590-41113-6). 32pp. Two mice hope to grow the largest pumpkin ever for Halloween.

6023 Kutner, Merrily. *Z Is for Zombie* (PS–2). Illus. by John Manders. 1999, Albert Whitman $15.95 (0-8075-9490-3). 32pp. This rhyming alphabet book uses scary Halloween illustrations and spooky creatures. (Rev: BL 9/1/99; HBG 3/00; SLJ 10/99)

6024 Lattimore, Deborah N. *Cinderhazel: The Cinderella of Halloween* (PS–2). Illus. 1997, Scholastic $15.95 (0-590-20232-4). 32pp. A parody on the famous fairy tale, with a feminist twist and a Halloween setting. (Rev: BL 9/1/97; HBG 3/98; SLJ 10/97)

6025 Leedy, Loreen. *The Dragon Halloween Party* (PS–2). Illus. by author. 1986, Holiday paper $5.95 (0-8234-0765-9). 32pp. Ten children and their mother Ma Dragon get ready for their Halloween party, in short rhyming verse. (Rev: BL 9/15/86; SLJ 12/86)

6026 Leedy, Loreen. *2 x 2=Boo! A Set of Spooky Multiplication Stories* (1–4). Illus. 1995, Holiday LB $16.95 (0-8234-1190-7). 32pp. Halloween creatures and objects are used in a series of scary stories to demonstrate the principles of multiplication. (Rev: BL 9/15/95; SLJ 11/95)

6027 Levine, Abby. *This Is the Pumpkin* (PS–K). Illus. by Paige Billin-Frye. 1997, Albert Whitman LB $13.95 (0-8075-7886-X). 24pp. All of the fun and excitement of Halloween, first at school then trick-or-treating, is captured in a catchy cumulative verse. (Rev: BL 9/1/97; HBG 3/98; SLJ 9/97)

6028 Lewis, J. Patrick. *The House of Boo* (K–3). Illus. by Katya Krenina. 1998, Simon & Schuster $16.00 (0-689-80356-7). 32pp. An unusual Halloween poem about three children who explore Boo Scoggins's scary house and, after they are frightened away, discover a fresh grave with his name on it. (Rev: BL 9/1/98; HBG 3/99; SLJ 9/98)

6029 London, Jonathan. *Froggy's Halloween* (PS–1). Illus. by Frank Remkiewicz. 1999, Viking $15.99 (0-670-88449-9). 32pp. Froggy decides to dress as the Frog Prince on Halloween and looks so handsome that, to his dismay, Frogilina wants to kiss him. (Rev: BL 9/1/99; HBG 3/00; SLJ 9/99)

6030 Mangas, Brian. *You Don't Get a Carrot Unless You're a Bunny* (PS–2). Illus. by Sidney Levitt. 1989, Simon & Schuster paper $5.95 (0-671-67201-0). Two rabbits dressed as a duck and a bear go out trick-or-treating. (Rev: SLJ 2/90)

6031 Martin, Bill, Jr. *Old Devil Wind* (K–3). Illus. by Barry Root. 1993, Harcourt $13.95 (0-15-257768-8). 32pp. A cumulative Halloween story about events in a haunted house. (Rev: BL 10/1/93)

6032 Martin, Bill, Jr., and John Archambault. *The Magic Pumpkin* (PS–2). Illus. by Robert J. Lee. 1989, Holt $15.95 (0-8050-1134-X). 32pp. A carved pumpkin proves to be a menace to the young narrator in this scary story. (Rev: BL 9/1/89; SLJ 12/89)

6033 Meddaugh, Susan. *The Witches' Supermarket* (PS–3). Illus. 1991, Houghton $13.95 (0-395-57034-4). 32pp. On Halloween, Helen finds herself in a strange supermarket offering such goodies as scum milk and bug bars. (Rev: BCCB 9/91; BL 8/91; SLJ 11/91)

6034 Minor, Wendell. *Pumpkin Heads!* (PS–1). Illus. 2000, Scholastic $15.95 (0-590-52105-5). 32pp. Jack-o'-lanterns appear everywhere, including unexpected places, in this delightful picture book that captures Halloween's excitement. (Rev: BCCB 9/00; BL 9/1/00; HBG 3/01; SLJ 9/00)

6035 Nerlove, Miriam. *Halloween* (PS–1). Illus. 1989, Whitman paper $4.95 (0-8075-3130-8). 24pp. A family gets ready for Halloween through such activities as carving a pumpkin. (Rev: BL 7/89; SLJ 9/89)

6036 Nikola-Lisa, W. *Shake Dem Halloween Bones* (PS–2). Illus. by Mike Reed. 1997, Houghton $16.00 (0-395-73095-3). 32pp. Fairy tale characters shake, rattle, and roll at a super Halloween party. (Rev: BL 10/1/97; HBG 3/98)

6037 O'Malley, Kevin. *Velcome* (2–4). Illus. 1997, Walker LB $16.95 (0-8027-8629-4). 32pp. A picture book of jokes and scary stories for Halloween that are narrated by a host who "velcomes" you into his house. (Rev: BL 9/1/97; HBG 3/98; SLJ 9/97)

6038 Passen, Lisa. *Attack of the 50-Foot Teacher* (K–3). Illus. 2000, Holt $16.00 (0-8050-6100-2). 32pp. Miss Birmbaum assigns homework on Hal-loween but, after an encounter with space aliens and a visit with her principal, she realizes that nobody gives homework on a holiday like this. (Rev: BL 11/15/00; HBG 3/01; SLJ 12/00)

6039 Pilkey, Dav. *The Hallo-Wiener* (PS–2). Illus. 1995, Scholastic $14.95 (0-590-41703-7). 32pp. At Halloween, Oscar the dachshund earns a change in his nickname from Wiener Dog to Hero Sandwich. (Rev: BCCB 10/95; BL 9/15/95; SLJ 10/95*)

6040 Polacco, Patricia. *Picnic at Mudsock Meadow* (K–3). Illus. 1992, Putnam $15.95 (0-399-21811-4). 32pp. During the Halloween festivities, William is a failure until he has courage enough to investigate a scary swamp. (Rev: BL 11/15/92; HB 11–12/92; SLJ 10/92)

6041 Poploff, Michelle. *Bat Bones and Spider Stew* (K–2). Illus. by Bill Basso. Series: A Yearling First Choice Chapter Book. 1998, Bantam $13.95 (0-385-32557-6); paper $4.50 (0-440-41440-7). 48pp. Henry is a little frightened when he receives an invitation to spend Halloween with his friend Artie Doomsday, whose house is rumored to be haunted. (Rev: HBG 3/99; SLJ 12/98)

6042 Reeves, Howard W. *There Was an Old Witch* (PS–4). Illus. by David Catrow. 1998, Hyperion $9.95 (0-7868-0438-6). 24pp. This variation on "I know an old lady who swallowed a fly" uses a Halloween motif and characters including a witch, a cat, a bat, and an owl. (Rev: BL 12/15/98; HBG 3/99; SLJ 3/99)

6043 Rex, Michael. *Brooms Are for Flying!* (PS). Illus. by author. 2000, Holt $16.00 (0-8050-6410-9). A pretty little witch leads a group of kids in Halloween costumes in simple appropriate exercises like showing the skeleton how to shake one's bones. (Rev: HB 9–10/00; HBG 3/01; SLJ 9/00)

6044 Roberts, Bethany. *Halloween Mice!* (PS–1). Illus. by Doug Cushman. 1995, Clarion $13.00 (0-395-67064-0). 32pp. At Halloween, a group of mice turn the tables and frighten a cat. (Rev: BL 9/15/95; SLJ 9/95)

6045 Rockwell, Anne. *Halloween Day* (PS–K). Illus. by Lizzy Rockwell. 1997, HarperCollins LB $14.89 (0-06-027568-5). 40pp. Nineteen children create Halloween costumes at home and come to school in their creations. (Rev: BL 9/1/97; SLJ 9/97)

6046 Ross, Eileen. *The Halloween Showdown* (K–2). Illus. by Lynn Rowe Reed. 1999, Holiday $15.95 (0-8234-1395-0). At Halloween, Grandmother Katt enlists the help of her animal friends to save a kitty that has been stolen by a witch named Grizzorka. (Rev: BCCB 10/99; HBG 3/00; SLJ 9/99)

6047 Roy, Ron. *The Bald Bandit* (2–4). Illus. by John S. Gurney. Series: A to Z Mysteries. 1997, Random LB $11.99 (0-679-98449-6); paper $3.99 (0-679-88449-1). 70pp. A short Halloween story about three youngsters who are trying to find a videotape of a bank robbery. (Rev: HBG 3/98; SLJ 1/98)

6048 Shaw, Nancy. *Sheep Trick or Treat* (PS–1). Illus. by Margot Apple. 1997, Houghton $14.00 (0-

395-84168-2). 32pp. Sheep in costumes go trick-or-treating at Halloween and have unexpected adventures. (Rev: BL 9/1/97; HB 9–10/97; HBG 3/98; SLJ 9/97)

6049 Sierra, Judy. *The House That Drac Built* (K–2). Illus. by Will Hillenbrand. 1995, Harcourt $14.00 (0-15-200015-1). 40pp. Halloween misadventures occur to a number of animals in the house that Drac built. (Rev: BCCB 10/95; BL 9/15/95; SLJ 9/95)

6050 Silverman, Erica. *The Halloween House* (PS–3). Illus. by Jon Agee. 1997, Farrar $16.00 (0-374-33270-3). 32pp. A counting book that uses monsters, vampires, bats, and other Halloween trappings as subjects. (Rev: BL 9/1/97; HB 9–10/97; HBG 3/98; SLJ 11/97)

6051 Smalls, Irene. *Jenny Reen and the Jack Muh Lantern* (PS–3). Illus. by Keinyo White. 1996, Simon & Schuster $16.00 (0-689-31875-8). 32pp. Jenny Reen, a slave child, is frightened by a wild creature she sees in the woods in this Halloween tale. (Rev: BCCB 12/96; BL 9/1/96; SLJ 12/96)

6052 Spirn, Michele. *A Know-Nothing Halloween* (1–2). Illus. Series: I Can Read. 2000, HarperCollins LB $15.99 (0-06-028186-6). 48pp. Four friends and a dog named Floris learn some Halloween tricks and scare themselves in this book for beginning readers. (Rev: BL 9/1/00)

6053 Stock, Catherine. *Halloween Monster* (PS–K). Illus. 1990, Macmillan paper $13.00 (0-02-788404-X). 32pp. A young African American boy is apprehensive about monsters he will meet on Halloween. (Rev: BCCB 11/90; BL 10/1/90; SLJ 10/90)

6054 Teague, Mark. *One Halloween Night* (PS–3). Illus. 1999, Scholastic $14.95 (0-590-84625-6). 32pp. When a black cat crosses their path on Halloween night, a trio of tricksters fear that they are in for a bad night and, for a while, they are absolutely correct. (Rev: BCCB 9/99; BL 9/1/99; HBG 3/00; SLJ 9/99)

6055 Thompson, Lauren. *Mouse's First Halloween* (PS–K). Illus. by Buket Erdogan. 2000, Simon & Schuster $12.95 (0-689-83176-5). 32pp. On his first Halloween, Mouse has a few scary adventures. (Rev: BL 9/1/00; HBG 3/01; SLJ 8/00)

6056 Tunnell, Michael O. *Halloween Pie* (PS–2). Illus. by Kevin O'Malley. 1999, Lothrop LB $14.93 (0-688-16805-1). 24pp. A scary story about Halloween creatures who eat a witch's pumpkin pie while she is away and magically become the ingredients for another pie. (Rev: BCCB 9/99; BL 9/15/99; HBG 3/00; SLJ 9/99)

6057 Updike, David. *An Autumn Tale* (2–4). Illus. by Robert Andrew Parker. 1988, Pippin $15.95 (0-945912-02-1). 40pp. A magical Halloween tale of young Homer and his dog Sophocles. (Rev: BCCB 5/89; BL 10/15/88; SLJ 11/88)

6058 Van Rynbach, Iris. *Five Little Pumpkins* (PS–K). Illus. 1995, Boyds Mills $7.95 (1-56397-452-5). 24pp. At Halloween, five little jack-o'-lanterns come alive and join in the holiday celebrations. (Rev: BL 9/15/95; SLJ 10/95)

6059 Waldron, Jan L. *John Pig's Halloween* (PS–1). Illus. by David McPhail. 1998, Dutton $15.99 (0-525-45941-3). 32pp. Afraid to go out on Halloween, John Pig stays home, where he enjoys himself helping a witch prepare a feast for her monster friends. (Rev: BCCB 10/98; BL 9/1/98; HBG 3/99; SLJ 1/99)

6060 Watson, Wendy. *Boo! It's Halloween* (PS–3). Illus. 1992, Houghton $14.95 (0-395-53628-6). 32pp. A family prepares for Halloween, and after the school party it's at last time for trick or treating. (Rev: BL 9/1/92)

6061 West, Kipling. *A Rattle of Bones: A Halloween Book of Collective Nouns* (K–2). Illus. 1999, Orchard $15.95 (0-531-30196-6). 32pp. In a series of rhyming couplets, collective nouns are effectively introduced to describe groups of creatures associated with Halloween, such as a cloud of bats, a venom of spiders, and a wake of vultures. (Rev: BL 9/1/99; HBG 3/00; SLJ 9/99)

6062 Winters, Kay. *The Teeny Tiny Ghost* (PS–1). Illus. by Lynn Munsinger. 1997, HarperCollins LB $14.89 (0-06-025684-2). 32pp. A tiny ghost passes the test of not being frightened on Halloween. (Rev: BL 9/1/97; HBG 3/98; SLJ 11/97)

6063 Winters, Kay. *Whooo's Haunting the Teeny Tiny Ghost?* (PS–1). Illus. by Lynn Munsinger. 1999, HarperCollins $14.95 (0-06-027358-5). 32pp. The teeny tiny ghost finds that someone is haunting his house and later discovers that it is his cousin practicing his haunting techniques. (Rev: BL 9/1/99; HBG 3/00; SLJ 9/99)

6064 Wojciechowski, Susan. *The Best Halloween of All* (PS–2). Illus. by Susan Meddaugh. 1998, Candlewick $9.99 (0-7636-0458-5). 28pp. At Halloween, the 7-year-old narrator decides he needs a new costume and fashions one to his own tastes. (Rev: BL 10/1/98; HBG 3/99; SLJ 9/98)

6065 Yolen, Jane. *Child of Faerie, Child of Earth* (K–3). Illus. by Jane Dyer. 1997, Little, Brown $15.95 (0-316-96897-8). 32pp. On Halloween, a little girl is transported to a magical fairy land but, in time, realizes that she must go home. (Rev: BL 1/1–15/98; HBG 3/98; SLJ 1/98)

6066 Ziefert, Harriet. *Two Little Witches: A Halloween Counting Story* (PS–K). Illus. by Simms Taback. 1996, Candlewick $9.99 (1-56402-621-3). 32pp. A counting book that uses Halloween symbols like pumpkins and witches. (Rev: BL 9/1/96; SLJ 12/96)

JEWISH HOLY DAYS

6067 Adler, David A. *Chanukah in Chelm* (K–3). Illus. by Kevin O'Malley. 1997, Lothrop LB $15.89 (0-688-09953-X). 32pp. A bumbling synagogue keeper is the central character in this story set at Hanukkah. (Rev: BL 9/1/97; HB 9–10/97; HBG 3/98; SLJ 10/97*)

6068 Brodmann, Aliana. *The Gift* (K–3). Illus. by Anthony Carnabuci. 1993, Simon & Schuster paper $15.00 (0-671-75110-7). 32pp. At Hanukkah, a young girl discovers that giving can be better than receiving. (Rev: BL 7/93)

6069 Cohen, Barbara. *Here Come the Purim Players!* (K–3). Illus. by Shoshana Mekibel. 1998, UAHC $12.95 (0-8074-0645-7). In medieval Prague, the Jews in the ghetto celebrate Purim at the rabbi's house with a performance of the story of Esther. (Rev: SLJ 6/98)

6070 Fishman, Cathy G. *On Passover* (PS–2). Illus. by Melanie Hall. 1997, Simon & Schuster $16.00 (0-689-80528-4). 40pp. Through the eyes of a young Jewish girl, the reader experiences the wonder and rituals of a traditional Passover. (Rev: BL 3/1/97; SLJ 4/97) [296.4]

6071 Gelman, Rita G. *Queen Esther Saves Her People* (K–3). Illus. by Frane Lessac. 1998, Scholastic $15.95 (0-590-47025-6). 40pp. A personalized account of the Jewish girl Esther and how she saved her people at the court of the Persian king. (Rev: BCCB 3/98; BL 3/1/98; HBG 10/98; SLJ 2/98) [222]

6072 Glaser, Linda. *The Borrowed Hanukkah Latkes* (K–3). Illus. by Nancy Cote. 1997, Albert Whitman LB $15.95 (0-8075-0841-1). 32pp. Gradually, Rachel persuades the family's neighbor Mrs. Greenberg to join them for Hanukkah. (Rev: BL 9/1/97; HBG 3/98; SLJ 10/97)

6073 Gold-Vukson, Marji. *The Colors of My Jewish Year* (PS). Illus. by Madeline Wikler. 1998, Kar-Ben $4.95 (1-58013-011-9). This concept book introduces the colors of the rainbow (plus a few others) while describing the Jewish holidays associated with each. (Rev: SLJ 11/98)

6074 Goldin, Barbara D. *A Mountain of Blintzes* (K–3). Illus. by Anik McGrory. 2001, Harcourt $16.00 (0-15-201902-2). 32pp. In the Catskills in the 1920s, two Jewish children secretly earn money so the family can have a specially enjoyable Shavuot. (Rev: BL 3/1/01)

6075 Goldin, Barbara D. *The World's Birthday: A Rosh Hashanah Story* (PS–3). Illus. by Jeanette Winter. 1990, Harcourt $13.95 (0-15-299648-6). 32pp. On Rosh Hashanah, the celebration of the birth of the world, Daniel wants to invite the world over to its birthday party. (Rev: BL 9/1/90; HB 11–12/90; SLJ 2/91)

6076 Greenberg, Melanie H. *Blessings: Our Jewish Ceremonies* (PS–3). Illus. 1995, Jewish Publication Soc. $16.95 (0-8276-0540-4). 32pp. Various ceremonies and rituals connected with the Jewish faith are explained. (Rev: BL 2/1/96) [296.4]

6077 Groner, Judye, and Madeline Wikler. *All About Hanukkah: In Story and Song.* Rev. ed. (K–3). Illus. by Kinny Kreiswirth. 1999, Kar-Ben paper $12.95 (1-58013-057-7). 32pp. This story on the origins of Hanukkah tells of struggles of the Jewish people of 2000 years ago to regain their religious freedom by opposing the power of a Syrian king. (Rev: SLJ 10/99) [286]

6078 Herman, Charlotte. *How Yussel Caught the Gefilte Fish: A Shabbos Story* (K–3). Illus. by Katya Krenina. 1999, Dutton $16.99 (0-525-45449-7). 32pp. Young Yussel wants to catch a gefilte fish until his mother tells him the truth and allows him to help change an ordinary fish into his favorite tasty treat. (Rev: BL 2/1/99; HBG 10/99; SLJ 7/99)

6079 Hirsh, Marilyn. *Potato Pancakes All Around: A Hanukkah Tale* (1–3). Illus. 1982, Jewish Publication Soc. paper $4.95 (0-8276-0217-0). 34pp. A humorous story about making potato pancakes for Hanukkah.

6080 Howland, Naomi. *Latkes, Latkes, Good to Eat: A Chanukah Story* (PS–1). Illus. 1999, Clarion $15.99 (0-395-89903-6). 32pp. As a reward for helping an old lady, Sadie is given a magic frying pan, which will produce as many latkes at Hanukkah as she wants. (Rev: BL 9/1/99; HBG 3/00; SLJ 10/99)

6081 Jaffe, Nina. *In the Month of Kislev: A Story for Hanukkah* (PS–3). Illus. by Louise August. 1992, Viking $15.00 (0-670-82863-7). 32pp. Unable to afford the potatoes for Hanukkah latkes, three poor sisters must content themselves with the delicious smell of a neighbor's cooking. (Rev: BCCB 11/92; BL 8/92; HB 11–12/92)

6082 Kimmel, Eric A. *Asher and the Capmakers: A Hanukkah Story* (K–3). Illus. by Will Hillenbrand. 1993, Holiday LB $15.95 (0-8234-1031-5). 32pp. Asher has many adventures when he sets out to borrow an egg for the family's latkes. (Rev: BL 7/93)

6083 Kimmel, Eric A. *The Chanukkah Guest* (PS–2). Illus. by Giora Carmi. 1990, Holiday LB $16.95 (0-8234-0788-8); paper $6.95 (0-8234-0978-3). 32pp. Bubba Brayna is making potato latkes for the rabbi. (Rev: BCCB 12/90; BL 9/15/90*)

6084 Kimmel, Eric A. *Hershel and the Hanukkah Goblins* (K–3). Illus. by Trina S. Hyman. 1989, Holiday LB $16.95 (0-8234-0769-1). 32pp. In this tale set in Eastern Europe, Hershel is looking forward to Hanukkah until he finds that the synagogue is haunted by goblins. (Rev: BCCB 10/89; BL 9/1/89; HB 1–2/90)

6085 Kimmel, Eric A. *The Magic Dreidels: A Hanukkah Story* (PS–3). Illus. by Katya Krenina. 1996, Holiday LB $16.95 (0-8234-1256-3). 28pp. In this Hanukkah story, Jacob receives a magic dreidel from a goblin. (Rev: BCCB 11/96; BL 9/1/96)

6086 Kimmel, Eric A. *When Mindy Saved Hanukkah* (PS–2). Illus. by Barbara McClintock. 1998, Scholastic $15.95 (0-590-37136-3). 32pp. Mindy and Zayde, members of the miniature Klein family who live in the historic Eldridge Street Synagogue in New York, evade the huge synagogue cat and bring home a Hanukkah candle, showing that they are as brave as the heroes of old, the Maccabees. (Rev: BCCB 1/99; BL 9/1/98; HBG 3/99; SLJ 10/98)

6087 Kimmelman, Leslie. *The Runaway Latkes* (PS). Illus. by Paul Yalowitz. 2000, Albert Whitman $15.95 (0-8075-7176-8). 32pp. In this humorous Hanukkah version of "The Gingerbread Man," three latkes jump out of the pan and roll off to see the town. (Rev: BL 9/1/00; HBG 3/01)

6088 Kimmelman, Leslie. *Sound the Shofar! A Story for Rosh Hashanah and Yom Kippur* (PS–1). Illus. by John Himmelman. 1998, HarperCollins $12.95 (0-06-027501-4). 32pp. A young girl describes the family's activities during Rosh Hashanah and Yom Kippur while her uncle blows the ram's horn, known as the shofar. (Rev: BL 10/1/98; HBG 3/99; SLJ 1/99)

6089 Kobre, Faige. *A Sense of Shabbat* (PS–K). Illus. 1990, Torah $14.95 (0-933873-44-1). 32pp. This Jewish holiday is shown from a preschooler's sensory perspective. (Rev: BCCB 3/91; BL 1/1/91) [296.4]

6090 Kress, Camille. *Purim!* (PS). Illus. by author. 1999, UAHC $5.95 (0-8074-0654-6). A brief text and quiet illustrations depict a group of children acting out the story of Purim. (Rev: SLJ 8/99)

6091 Kress, Camille. *Tot Shabbat* (PS). Illus. 1996, UAHC $5.95 (0-8074-0607-4). 7pp. In this simple board book, the Jewish Sabbath is introduced. (Rev: BL 2/1/97; SLJ 9/97)

6092 Krulik, Nancy. *Is It Hanukkah Yet?* (K–1). Illus. by DyAnne DiSalvo-Ryan. Series: Step into Reading. 2000, Random $3.99 (0-375-80286-X). 48pp. This easy-to-read book follows the last-minute preparations for Hanukkah and the first night's activities as seen through the eyes of a little girl. (Rev: BL 9/1/00)

6093 Lamstein, Sarah M. *Annie's Shabbat* (PS–3). Illus. by Cecily Lang. 1997, Albert Whitman LB $15.95 (0-8075-0376-2). 40pp. This first-person account describes the wonder and fun involved in the celebration of the Jewish Sabbath. (Rev: BL 10/1/97*; HBG 3/98; SLJ 12/97) [296.4]

6094 Manushkin, Fran. *The Matzah That Papa Brought Home* (PS–1). Illus. by Ned Bittinger. 1995, Scholastic $14.95 (0-590-47146-5). 32pp. A cumulative tale that introduces symbols associated with Passover. (Rev: BL 1/15/95; SLJ 2/95)

6095 Manushkin, Fran. *Starlight and Candles: The Joys of the Sabbath* (K–3). Illus. by Jacqueline Chwast. 1995, Simon & Schuster paper $15.00 (0-689-80274-9). 32pp. Using one family's activities as examples, the traditions of the Jewish Sabbath are introduced. (Rev: BL 9/1/95; SLJ 12/95)

6096 Melmed, Laura K. *Moishe's Miracle: A Hanukkah Story* (K–3). Illus. by David Slonim. 2000, HarperCollins LB $15.98 (0-688-14683-X). 32pp. Moishe's generosity at Hanukkah results in a gift of a magical pan that makes pancakes for all. (Rev: BL 9/1/00; HB 9–10/00; HBG 3/01)

6097 Michelson, Richard. *Grandpa's Gamble* (PS–4). Illus. by Barry Moser. 1999, Marshall Cavendish $15.95 (0-7614-5034-3). 32pp. At Passover, Grandpa, a Jewish immigrant of many years ago, regrets that he lied and cheated to get ahead and tells how he changed his wicked ways. (Rev: BCCB 4/99; BL 3/15/99; HBG 10/99; SLJ 6/99)

6098 Modesitt, Jeanne. *It's Hanukkah!* (PS–1). Illus. by Robin Spowart. 1999, Holiday $15.95 (0-8234-1451-5). A family of mice enjoy all the activities associated with Hanukkah, including lighting the Menorah and eating latkes. (Rev: HBG 3/00; SLJ 10/99)

6099 Nerlove, Miriam. *Hanukkah* (PS–1). Illus. 1989, Whitman paper $5.95 (0-8075-3142-1). 24pp. A brief history and explanation of the customs and activities of Hanukkah in verse. (Rev: BL 7/89; SLJ 9/89)

6100 Nerlove, Miriam. *Passover* (PS–1). Illus. 1989, Whitman LB $13.95 (0-8075-6360-9). 24pp. A description of this Jewish holy day in rhyming text. (Rev: BL 1/15/90; SLJ 4/90)

6101 Nerlove, Miriam. *Purim* (PS–1). Illus. 1992, Whitman LB $13.95 (0-8075-6682-9). 24pp. Watercolors and simple text explain the joyful observance of Purim. (Rev: BL 1/1/92; SLJ 9/92)

6102 Nerlove, Miriam. *Shabbat* (PS–1). Illus. 1998, Whitman $13.95 (0-8075-7324-8). 24pp. Using a simple rhyming text and gentle watercolors, this book shows how a happy, traditional family observes Shabbat, the Jewish Sabbath, both at home and at the synagogue. (Rev: BL 10/1/98; HBG 3/99; SLJ 10/98) [296.4]

6103 Newman, Leslea. *Matzo Ball Moon* (PS–3). Illus. by Elaine Greenstein. 1998, Clarion $15.00 (0-395-71530-X). 32pp. At Passover, all of Eleanor's family enjoy the matzo balls of her grandmother, Bubbe, and when Eleanor opens the door to welcome the prophet Elijah, she sees a full moon and imagines it to be another of Bubbe's yummy creations. (Rev: BL 4/1/98; HBG 10/98; SLJ 6/98)

6104 Oberman, Sheldon. *By the Hanukkah Light* (1–4). Illus. by Neil Waldman. 1997, Boyds Mills $15.95 (1-56397-658-7). 32pp. As Rachel and her grandfather polish the menorah at Hanukkah, he tells her about the Holocaust and its meaning for the Jewish people. (Rev: BL 9/1/97*; HBG 3/98; SLJ 10/97)

6105 Portnoy, Mindy A. *Matzah Ball: A Passover Story* (PS–3). Illus. by Katherine J. Kahn. 1994, Kar-Ben paper $6.95 (0-929371-69-0). While attending a baseball game during Passover, Aaron meets an elderly man (Elijah perhaps?) who tells him about Jewish fans going to games at Ebbets Field. (Rev: SLJ 8/94)

6106 Rael, Elsa O. *When Zaydeh Danced on Eldridge Street* (PS–3). Illus. by Marjorie Priceman. 1997, Simon & Schuster $16.00 (0-689-80451-2). 40pp. Zeesie is taken to the synagogue by her grandfather in this explanation of the religious holiday of Simchas Torah. (Rev: BL 10/1/97; HB 11–12/97; HBG 3/98; SLJ 10/97)

6107 Rosen, Michael J. *Our Eight Nights of Hanukkah* (K–3). Illus. by DyAnne DiSalvo-Ryan. 2000, Holiday $16.95 (0-8234-1476-0). 32pp. The activities of a Jewish family are chronicled as they celebrate the eight nights of Hanukkah. (Rev: BL 9/1/00; HBG 3/01)

6108 Ross, Kathy. *The Jewish Holiday Craft Book* (PS–1). Illus. 1997, Millbrook LB $25.90 (0-7613-0055-4); paper $12.95 (0-7613-0175-5). 96pp. Using simple materials, craft projects, such as making a Yom Kippur doll, celebrate and explain Jewish traditions and holidays. (Rev: BL 3/1/97; SLJ 4/97) [296.4]

6109 Rothenberg, Joan. *Inside-Out Grandma* (K–3). Illus. 1995, Hyperion LB $15.49 (0-7868-2092-6). 32pp. A circuitous story about the relationship between a grandmother wearing her clothes inside out and making potato pancakes at Hanukkah. (Rev: BCCB 11/95; BL 9/15/95)

6110 Rothenberg, Joan. *Matzah Ball Soup* (PS–2). Illus. 1999, Hyperion LB $15.49 (0-7868-2170-1). 32pp. Explaining to Rosie why they have four matzah balls in their soup, Grandma tells the story of how she and her three sisters from Hungary used different recipes for their matzah balls. (Rev: BL 10/1/99; HBG 3/00; SLJ 9/99)

6111 Rouss, Sylvia A. *Sammy Spider's First Passover* (PS–K). Illus. by Katherine J. Kahn. 1995, Kar-Ben paper $6.95 (0-929371-82-8). A pleasant story about a little spider that watches the Shapiro family make preparations for Passover. (Rev: SLJ 7/95)

6112 Rouss, Sylvia A. *Sammy Spider's First Rosh Hashanah* (PS–1). Illus. by Katherine J. Kahn. 1996, Kar-Ben paper $6.95 (0-929371-99-2). Mother Spider explains to her son Sammy the holiday customs and symbols associated with the Jewish New Year. (Rev: SLJ 5/97)

6113 Rouss, Sylvia A. *Sammy Spider's First Shabbat* (K–2). Illus. by Katherine J. Kahn. 1998, Kar-Ben $14.95 (1-58013-007-0); paper $5.95 (1-58013-006-2). Sammy Spider observes the Shapiro family's preparations for the Shabbat, including braiding the challah. (Rev: SLJ 6/98)

6114 Schotter, Roni. *Purim Play* (PS–3). Illus. by Marylin Hafner. 1998, Little, Brown $15.95 (0-316-77518-5). 32pp. In spite of illness, Fannie and her cousins put on the Purim play in which Queen Esther saves the Jewish people from wicked Haman. (Rev: BL 2/1/98; HBG 10/98; SLJ 4/98)

6115 Schur, Maxine R. *The Peddler's Gift* (K–4). Illus. by Kimberly B. Root. 1999, Dial $15.99 (0-8037-1978-7). 32pp. A boy, Leibush, discovers that the much-derided peddler Shimon is actually a wise, kind man who understands the mysteries of the Jewish faith. (Rev: BL 10/1/99; HBG 3/00; SLJ 10/99)

6116 Schweiger-Dmi'el, Itzhak. *Hanna's Sabbath Dress* (PS–2). Trans. by Razi Dmi'el, et al. Illus. by Ora Eitan. 1996, Simon & Schuster $15.00 (0-689-80517-9). 30pp. In an act of unselfishness, Hanna helps an old man but ruins her special Sabbath dress. (Rev: BL 10/1/96; SLJ 11/96)

6117 Simon, Norma. *The Story of Hanukkah* (K–3). Illus. by Leonid Gore. 1997, HarperCollins LB $14.00 (0-06-027420-4). 32pp. Legend and history are delineated in this book on the origins of Hanukkah. (Rev: BL 9/1/97; HBG 3/98; SLJ 10/97) [296.4]

6118 Snyder, Carol. *God Must Like Cookies, Too* (PS–1). Illus. by Beth Glick. 1993, Jewish Publication Soc. $16.95 (0-8276-0423-8). 32pp. A young girl attends a Shabbat service at temple and looks forward to the three cookies she has been promised after the service. (Rev: BL 1/15/94; SLJ 10/93)

6119 Stillerman, Marci. *Nine Spoons: A Chanukah Story* (K–2). Illus. by Pesach Gerber. 1998, Hachai $11.95 (0-922613-84-2). In a Nazi concentration camp, Raizel shows her ingenuity by fashioning a menorah out of nine spoons so that Hanukkah can

be celebrated. (Rev: HB 1–2/99; HBG 3/99; SLJ 10/98)

6120 Topek, Susan Remick. *A Costume for Noah: A Purim Story* (PS–K). Illus. by Sally Springer. 1996, Kar-Ben $13.95 (0-929371-91-7); paper $5.95 (0-929371-90-9). Traditional terms and customs are introduced in this simple story of a boy preparing with his friends to celebrate Purim. (Rev: SLJ 5/96)

6121 Topek, Susan Remick. *Shalom Shabbat: A Book for Havdalah* (PS). Illus. by Shelly Schonebaum Ephraim. 1998, Kar-Ben $4.95 (1-58013-010-0). This simple board book celebrates the ceremony of Havdalah that takes place at the end of the Jewish Sabbath. (Rev: SLJ 2/99)

6122 Weilerstein, Sadie R. *K'tonton's Yom Kippur Kitten* (K–2). Illus. by Joe Boddy. 1995, Jewish Publication Soc. $12.95 (0-8276-0541-2). 36pp. K'tonton learns the true meaning of Yom Kippur when he tries to blame a kitten for the problems he has created. (Rev: BL 11/15/95; SLJ 3/96)

6123 Wilkowski, Susan. *Baby's Bris* (PS–1). Illus. by Judith Friedman. 1999, Karben $16.95 (1-58013-052-6); paper $6.95 (1-58013-053-4). 32pp. A young girl grows to love her baby brother particularly through an understanding of the bris ceremony when the boy is circumcised. (Rev: BL 1/1–15/00; HBG 3/00; SLJ 1/00)

6124 Yorinks, Arthur. *The Flying Latke* (1–3). Photos by Paul Colin and Arthur Yorinks. Illus. by William Steig. 1999, Simon & Schuster $16.95 (0-689-82597-8). A humorous Hanukkah story about a quarrel that results in a latke flying over New Jersey and a family being trapped for eight days and nights. (Rev: BCCB 11/99; HBG 3/00; SLJ 10/99)

6125 Zalben, Jane Breskin. *Beni's First Chanukah* (PS–K). Illus. by author. 1988, Holt $12.95 (0-8050-0479-3). 32pp. Beni Bear's first Hanukkah is filled with happy moments. (Rev: BL 12/15/88)

6126 Zalben, Jane Breskin. *Happy New Year, Beni* (PS–3). Illus. 1993, Holt $13.95 (0-8050-1961-8). 28pp. A tender picture book showing an extended Jewish family celebrating the New Year. (Rev: BL 7/93)

6127 Zalben, Jane Breskin. *Leo and Blossom's Sukkah* (PS–1). Illus. 1990, Holt $13.95 (0-8050-1226-5). 32pp. In spite of many problems, all ends well for two bears who decide to build their own sukkah. (Rev: BL 9/15/90; SLJ 2/92)

6128 Zalben, Jane Breskin. *Papa's Latkes* (PS–1). Illus. 1996, Holt $13.95 (0-8050-4634-8). 32pp. When Beni the Bear's mother decides not to make latkes at Hanukkah, the rest of the family tries to prepare them instead. (Rev: BL 9/1/96)

6129 Zalben, Jane Breskin. *Pearl's Eight Days of Chanukah* (PS–3). Illus. 1998, Simon & Schuster $16.00 (0-689-81488-7). 48pp. Pearl's family of rams are visited by cousins Harry and Sophie, and together they engage in Hanukkah activities and crafts, with accompanying directions and recipes. (Rev: BL 9/1/98; HBG 3/99; SLJ 10/98) [296.4]

6130 Ziefert, Harriet. *Eight Days of Hanukkah* (PS–K). Illus. by Melinda Levine. 1997, Viking paper $10.99 (0-670-87326-8). 24pp. The traditions and significance of Hanukkah are explored in this picture book. (Rev: BL 9/15/97; HBG 3/98; SLJ 10/97)

6131 Zolkower, Edie Stoltz. *Too Many Cooks: A Passover Parable* (PS–2). Illus. by Shauna Mooney Kawasaki. 2000, Kar-Ben paper $5.95 (1-58013-063-1). At Passover, everyone in the family decides to add a special ingredient to Bubbie's charoses for the seder. (Rev: SLJ 12/00)

THANKSGIVING

6132 Anderson, Laurie Halse. *Turkey Pox* (PS–2). Illus. by Dorothy Donohue. 1996, Albert Whitman LB $14.95 (0-8075-8127-5). 30pp. Charity's Thanksgiving is almost spoiled when it is discovered that she has chicken pox. (Rev: BCCB 11/96; BL 9/1/96; SLJ 10/96)

6133 Borden, Louise. *Thanksgiving Is . . .* (1–2). Illus. by Steve Bjorkman. 1997, Scholastic $3.99 (0-590-33128-0). 32pp. In this easy reader, the story of the *Mayflower*, its passengers, and the first Thanksgiving are told in an interesting, fact-filled narrative. (Rev: BL 2/1/98; SLJ 3/98)

6134 Brown, Marc. *Arthur's Thanksgiving* (K–3). Illus. by author. 1983, Little, Brown paper $5.95 (0-316-11232-1). 32pp. Arthur is made director of his class Thanksgiving play.

6135 Bunting, Eve. *How Many Days to America? A Thanksgiving Story* (2–4). Illus. by Beth Peck. 1988, Houghton $16.00 (0-89919-521-0); paper $5.95 (0-395-54777-6). 32pp. A family flees oppression on a Caribbean island and heads for the United States. (Rev: BL 11/1/88; SLJ 10/88)

6136 Bunting, Eve. *A Turkey for Thanksgiving* (PS–1). Illus. by Diane De Groat. 1991, Houghton $15.00 (0-89919-793-0). 32pp. After bringing a live turkey home at Thanksgiving, Mr. and Mrs. Moose decide to have a vegetarian meal. (Rev: BCCB 9/91; BL 10/1/91; SLJ 9/91)

6137 Capucilli, Alyssa Satin. *Happy Thanksgiving, Biscuit!* (PS). Illus. by Pat Schories. 1999, Harper-Festival paper $6.95 (0-694-01221-1). In this flap book, Biscuit, an endearing puppy, enjoys the fuss surrounding Thanksgiving. (Rev: SLJ 12/99)

6138 Carlstrom, Nancy White. *Thanksgiving Day at Our House* (PS–3). Illus. by R. W. Alley. 1999, Simon & Schuster $15.00 (0-689-80360-5). 32pp. A family's Thanksgiving, their activities, and their prayers are explored in these original poems. (Rev: BL 9/1/99; HBG 3/00; SLJ 10/99) [811]

6139 Cazet, Denys. *Minnie and Moo and the Thanksgiving Tree* (1–2). Illus. 2000, DK $12.95 (0-7894-2654-4); paper $3.95 (0-7894-2655-2). 418pp. At Thanksgiving, Minnie and Moo help the animals (starting with the turkeys) escape by hiding them in a tree only to discover that the farmer and his family are vegetarians. (Rev: BL 9/1/00; HB 9–10/00; HBG 3/01; SLJ 9/00)

6140 Child, Lydia M. *Over the River and Through the Wood* (PS–2). Illus. by David Catrow. 1996, Holt $16.95 (0-8050-3825-6). 32pp. At Thanksgiving, a New York City family faces traffic jams on

the way to Grandma's house. (Rev: BCCB 11/96; BL 9/1/96; SLJ 10/96)

6141 Cowley, Joy. *Gracias, the Thanksgiving Turkey* (PS–2). Illus. by Joe Cepeda. 1996, Scholastic $15.95 (0-590-46976-2). 32pp. A New York City boy dreads Thanksgiving, when his pet turkey, Gracias, will be killed. (Rev: BCCB 11/96; BL 9/1/96; SLJ 12/96)

6142 Dalgliesh, Alice. *The Thanksgiving Story* (K–3). Illus. by Helen Sewell. 1988, Macmillan $16.00 (0-684-18999-2); paper $5.99 (0-689-71053-4). 32pp. This reissued 1954 Caldecott Honor Book tells of the Hopkins family's experiences from the Mayflower voyage to the first Thanksgiving.

6143 Hennessy, B. G. *One Little, Two Little, Three Little Pilgrims* (PS–1). Illus. by Lynne W. Cravath. 1999, Viking $15.99 (0-670-87779-4). 32pp. The traditional rhyme is used to show how ten Pilgrim children and ten Wampanoag Indian children celebrate the Thanksgiving feast in the Plimoth colony. (Rev: BL 9/1/99; HBG 3/00; SLJ 9/99)

6144 Hoban, Lillian. *Silly Tilly's Thanksgiving Dinner* (K–3). Illus. 1990, HarperCollins LB $15.89 (0-06-022423-1). 64pp. Forgetful Silly Tilly sends out recipe cards instead of invitations for Thanksgiving dinner. (Rev: BL 10/15/90; SLJ 9/90)

6145 Jackson, Alison. *I Know an Old Lady Who Swallowed a Pie* (PS–2). Illus. by Judith Byron Schachner. 1997, Dutton $15.99 (0-525-45645-7). 32pp. This favorite folk song is given a new twist by using foods associated with Thanksgiving. (Rev: BL 9/1/97; HBG 3/98; SLJ 11/97)

6146 Koller, Jackie F. *Nickommoh! A Thanksgiving Celebration* (K–3). Illus. by Marcia Sewall. 1999, Simon & Schuster $16.00 (0-689-81094-6). 32pp. Long before the Puritans arrived, the Narragansett tribe of Native Americans celebrated their own harvest festival during the Moon of the Falling Leaves. (Rev: BL 11/15/99; HBG 3/00; SLJ 10/99) [394.26]

6147 Kroll, Steven. *Oh, What a Thanksgiving!* (K–2). Illus. by S. D. Schindler. 1988, Scholastic paper $3.95 (0-590-40616-7). 32pp. David imagines himself at Plymouth in 1620. (Rev: BL 9/15/88; SLJ 9/88)

6148 Levine, Abby. *This Is the Turkey* (PS–K). Illus. by Paige Billin-Frye. 2000, Albert Whitman $14.95 (0-8075-7888-6). 32pp. A humorous Thanksgiving story that tells how the roast turkey fell into the goldfish tank at Max's house. (Rev: BL 9/1/00; HBG 3/01; SLJ 9/00)

6149 Nerlove, Miriam. *Thanksgiving* (PS–1). Illus. 1990, Whitman LB $13.95 (0-8075-7818-5). 24pp. Discusses origins and customs of Thanksgiving in verse. (Rev: BL 7/90; SLJ 10/90)

6150 Pomeranc, Marion Hess. *The Can-Do Thanksgiving* (K–2). Illus. by Nancy Cote. 1998, Albert Whitman $14.95 (0-8075-1054-8). 32pp. Through a school food drive and a contribution of a can of peas, Dee is chosen to help serve a Thanksgiving meal and, there, meets a new friend. (Rev: BL 11/1/98; HBG 3/99; SLJ 9/98)

6151 Rockwell, Anne. *Thanksgiving Day* (PS–K). Illus. by Lizzy Rockwell. 1999, HarperCollins LB

$14.89 (0-06-028388-2). 40pp. In a series of double-page spreads, a preschooler and his classmates perform a short play that tells what they have learned about the first Thanksgiving and the Pilgrims. (Rev: BL 9/1/99; HBG 3/00; SLJ 10/99)

6152 Roop, Peter, and Connie Roop. *Let's Celebrate Thanksgiving* (1–4). Illus. by Gwen Connelly. 1999, Millbrook LB $19.90 (0-7613-0973-X); paper $5.95 (0-7613-0429-0). 32pp. An easy-to-read explanation of Thanksgiving's origination and how it is celebrated, along with some related jokes and projects. (Rev: BL 9/15/99; HBG 3/00; SLJ 11/99) [394.2649]

6153 Rosen, Michael J. *A Thanksgiving Wish* (1–4). Illus. by John Thompson. 1999, Scholastic $16.95 (0-590-25563-0). 32pp. A poignant story of the first Thanksgiving celebrated by an extended family since the death of their beloved grandmother, Bubbe. (Rev: BCCB 10/99; BL 9/1/99; HBG 3/00; SLJ 10/99)

6154 Ruelle, Karen G. *The Thanksgiving Beast Feast* (1–2). Illus. 1999, Holiday $14.95 (0-8234-1511-2). 32pp. At Thanksgiving, Harry Cat and his sister, Emily, decide to show their thanks by preparing food for the birds, squirrels, and chipmunks in their neighborhood. (Rev: BL 9/1/99; HB 9–10/99; HBG 3/00; SLJ 9/99)

6155 Spinelli, Eileen. *Thanksgiving at the Tappletons'* (K–2). Illus. by Maryann Cocca-Leffler. 1992, HarperCollins LB $16.89 (0-06-020872-4). 32pp. Through a series of accidents, the Tappletons ruin their Thanksgiving dinner. (Rev: BL 10/1/92)

6156 Spirn, Michele. *The Know-Nothings Talk Turkey* (1–2). Illus. Series: I Can Read. 2000, HarperCollins $14.95 (0-06-028183-9). 48pp. In his easy-to-read book, four friends and their dog Floris decide to serve a turkey at Thanksgiving so they invite one to their dinner. (Rev: BL 9/1/00; HBG 3/01; SLJ 10/00)

6157 Stock, Catherine. *Thanksgiving Treat* (PS–K). Illus. 1990, Macmillan LB $13.00 (0-02-788402-3). 32pp. When a young boy tries to help out at Thanksgiving, he finds he is only in the way. (Rev: BCCB 11/90; BL 10/1/90; SLJ 10/90)

6158 Tryon, Leslie. *Albert's Thanksgiving* (K–2). Illus. 1994, Atheneum $16.00 (0-689-31865-0). 32pp. Poor Albert the duck seems to be the only one who is working hard to prepare for the PTA Thanksgiving feast. (Rev: BL 8/94; SLJ 10/94)

6159 Willey, Margaret. *Thanksgiving with Me* (PS–2). Illus. by Lloyd Bloom. 1998, HarperCollins $14.95 (0-06-027113-2). 32pp. While her mother describes each of her six brothers, a little girl waits with great anticipation for the arrival of her uncles at Thanksgiving time. (Rev: BCCB 11/98; BL 9/1/98; HBG 3/99; SLJ 9/98)

VALENTINE'S DAY

6160 Adams, Adrienne. *The Great Valentine's Day Balloon Race* (K–3). Illus. by author. 1980, Macmillan $14.95 (0-684-16640-2); paper $4.00 (0-689-71847-0). 32pp. Two rabbits plus the Abbot family construct a balloon for a Valentine's Day race.

6161 Balian, Lorna. *A Sweetheart for Valentine* (K–3). Illus. by author. 1988, Humbug $12.95 (0-687-37109-0). 32pp. An original, highly imaginative explanation of the origins of Valentine's Day.

6162 Brown, Marc. *Arthur's Valentine* (K–3). Illus. by author. 1980, Little, Brown $15.95 (0-316-11062-0); Avon paper $5.95 (0-316-11187-2). 32pp. Who is sending Arthur valentines?

6163 Bunting, Eve. *The Valentine Bears* (K–3). Illus. by Jan Brett. 1983, Houghton $15.00 (0-89919-138-X); paper $5.95 (0-89919-313-7). 32pp. Mr. and Mrs. Bear decide not to sleep through Valentine's Day this year.

6164 Capucilli, Alyssa Satin. *Biscuit's Valentine's Day* (PS). Illus. by Pat Schories. 2000, HarperFestival $6.95 (0-694-01222-X). 20pp. While his young owner is preparing for Valentine's Day, Biscuit the dog is engaged in all sorts of activities that are revealed when the reader lifts the flaps in this interactive book. (Rev: BL 2/15/01)

6165 De Groat, Diane. *Roses Are Pink, Your Feet Really Stink* (PS–3). Illus. 1996, Morrow LB $14.93 (0-688-13605-2). 32pp. A chipmunklike youngster writes mean valentines to the people he dislikes; but in the end, all is forgiven. (Rev: BCCB 2/96; BL 3/1/96; SLJ 4/96)

6166 Devlin, Wende, and Harry Devlin. *Cranberry Valentine* (PS–1). Illus. 1992, Simon & Schuster paper $5.99 (0-689-71509-9). 40pp. Mr. Whiskers, the town's bearded old salt, is surprised and at first dismayed to discover he's received so many valentines. (Rev: BL 10/15/86; SLJ 1/87)

6167 Gantos, Jack. *Rotten Ralph's Rotten Romance* (PS–1). Illus. by Nicole Rubel. 1997, Houghton $14.95 (0-395-73978-0). 32pp. Rotten Ralph decides to be completely unlovable on Valentine's Day. (Rev: BL 11/15/96; SLJ 2/97)

6168 Grambling, Lois G. *Happy Valentine's Day, Miss Hildy!* (2–3). Illus. by Bridget S. Taylor. 1997, Random LB $11.99 (0-679-98870-X); paper $3.99 (0-679-88870-5). 48pp. In this easily read story, Miss Hildy tries to determine who has sent her a gift of 12 pink flamingos for Valentine's Day. (Rev: BL 2/1/98; HBG 10/98)

6169 Gregory, Valiska. *A Valentine for Norman Noggs* (PS–2). Illus. by Marsha Winborn. 1999, HarperCollins LB $14.89 (0-06-027657-6). 32pp. Hamster Norman faces possible trouble when he ignores the threats of bullies Richard and Arthur and delivers a valentine to Wilhemina. (Rev: BCCB 2/99; BL 4/1/99; HBG 10/99; SLJ 1/99)

6170 Hoban, Lillian. *Arthur's Great Big Valentine* (1–2). Illus. by author. 1989, HarperCollins LB $15.89 (0-06-022407-X); paper $3.95 (0-06-444149-0). 64pp. Arthur wants to celebrate Valentine's Day, but he's mad at his best friend. (Rev: BL 3/1/89; HB 3–4/89)

6171 Hoban, Lillian. *Silly Tilly's Valentine* (K–2). Illus. by author. Series: I Can Read. 1998, HarperCollins LB $14.89 (0-06-027401-8). 47pp. Tilly the mole is so excited about a snowfall that she forgets it is Valentine's Day. (Rev: HBG 10/98; SLJ 2/98)

6172 Hurd, Thacher. *Little Mouse's Big Valentine* (PS–1). Illus. 1990, HarperCollins $13.95 (0-06-026192-7); paper $5.95 (0-06-443281-5). 32pp. Little Mouse makes a valentine so big that nobody wants it. (Rev: BL 1/1/90)

6173 Lexau, Joan M. *Don't Be My Valentine: A Classroom Mystery* (1–2). Illus. by Syd Hoff. 1999, HarperCollins $14.95 (0-06-028239-8). 64pp. In this easy-to-read book, Amy Lou keeps butting into Sam's affairs, so he sends her a not-so-nice valentine that, unfortunately, is received by his teacher. (Rev: BL 3/15/99; HBG 10/99)

6174 Modell, Frank. *One Zillion Valentines* (PS–2). Illus. by author. 1987, Morrow paper $4.95 (0-688-07329-8). 32pp. Milton and Marvin distribute their homemade hearts to the neighborhood.

6175 Roberts, Bethany. *Valentine Mice!* (PS–K). Illus. by Doug Cushman. 1998, Clarion $13.00 (0-395-77518-3). 32pp. A group of mice are so busy delivering valentines in a snowy forest that they don't realize the smallest one of them is missing. (Rev: BL 12/15/97; HBG 10/98; SLJ 1/98)

6176 Rockwell, Anne. *Valentine's Day* (K–2). Illus. by Lizzy Rockwell. 2000, HarperCollins LB $14.89 (0-06-028515-X). 40pp. Mrs. Madoff's class make and send valentines to their friend, Michido, who is back in Japan and, on Valentine's Day, a package arrives from her filled with origami valentines. (Rev: BL 1/1–15/01)

6177 Roop, Peter, and Connie Roop. *Let's Celebrate Valentine's Day* (2–4). Illus. by Katy K. Arnsteen. Series: Let's Celebrate. 1999, Millbrook LB $19.90 (0-7613-0972-1); paper $5.95 (0-7913-0428-2). 32pp. Discusses the origins of Valentine's Day, describes how it is celebrated, and includes many related jokes and riddles. (Rev: BL 2/15/99; HBG 10/99; SLJ 4/99) [394.2618]

6178 Ruelle, Karen G. *Snow Valentines* (1–2). Illus. Series: Holiday House Readers. 2000, Holiday $14.95 (0-8234-1533-3). 32pp. A book for beginning readers that describes how two little cats solve the problem of what to get their parents for Valentine's Day. (Rev: BL 7/00; SLJ 9/00)

Books for Beginning Readers

6179 Adler, David A. *Young Cam Jansen and the Baseball Mystery* (1–2). Illus. by Susanna Natti. Series: A Viking Easy-to-Read Book. 1999, Viking $13.99 (0-670-88481-2). 32pp. Cam Jansen, the girl with the amazing memory, tackles the problem of a missing baseball. (Rev: BL 10/1/99; HBG 10/99; SLJ 6/99)

6180 Adler, David A. *Young Cam Jansen and the Dinosaur Game* (1–2). Illus. 1996, Viking $13.99 (0-670-86399-8). 32pp. Cam discovers that a boy has cheated in order to win a prize. (Rev: BCCB 5/96; BL 8/96; SLJ 7/96)

6181 Adler, David A. *Young Cam Jansen and the Ice Skate Mystery* (1–2). Illus. by Susanna Natti. Series: Easy-to-Read. 1998, Viking $13.99 (0-670-87791-3). 32pp. In this mystery story, young Cam Jansen helps her friend Eric find the lost key to his locker in the ice rink. (Rev: BL 5/1/98; SLJ 8/98)

6182 Adler, David A. *Young Cam Jansen and the Missing Cookie* (1–2). Illus. 1996, Viking $13.99 (0-670-86772-1). 32pp. Jason, Cam's friend, has a cookie stolen from his school lunchbox. (Rev: BL 8/96; SLJ 7/96)

6183 Adler, David A. *Young Cam Jansen and the Pizza Shop Mystery* (1–2). Illus. by Susanna Natti. Series: Easy-to-Read. 2000, Viking $13.99 (0-670-88861-3). 32pp. Cam Jansen uses her photographic memory to determine who stole her jacket and why in this book for beginning readers. (Rev: BL 4/15/00; HBG 10/00; SLJ 5/00)

6184 Ahlberg, Allan. *The Ghost Train* (1–2). Illus. by Andre Amstutz. Series: Funnybones. 1992, Morrow paper $3.95 (0-688-11659-0). 32pp. Three skeletons known as the Funnybones take a train ride to a ghost town. (Rev: BL 10/1/92)

6185 Albee, Sarah. *The Dragon's Scales* (1–2). Illus. by John Manders. Series: Step into Reading + Math. 1998, Random LB $11.99 (0-679-98381-3); paper $3.99 (0-679-88381-9). 48pp. While telling an exciting story about a clever girl who outwits a dragon, this book also explains the concept of weights and measures. (Rev: BL 7/98)

6186 Albee, Sarah. *I Can Do It!* (PS–K). Illus. by Larry DiFiori. Series: Step into Reading. 1997, Random LB $11.99 (0-679-98687-1); paper $3.99 (0-679-88687-7). 30pp. A beginning reader featuring the Muppets, with the purpose of building self-confidence in children. (Rev: SLJ 2/98)

6187 Albert, Shirley. *Doll Party* (1–2). Illus. by Amy Flynn. 1994, Putnam paper $3.99 (0-448-40182-7). 32pp. An easy-to-read book about Becky and her new doll. (Rev: BL 1/1/95)

6188 Alexander, Sue. *World Famous Muriel and the Magic Mystery* (2–3). Illus. by Marla Frazee. 1990, HarperCollins LB $12.89 (0-690-04789-4). 32pp. Muriel, known for her tightrope walking and incredible smarts, is after a missing magician. (Rev: BL 3/15/90; SLJ 7/90)

6189 Allen, Laura J. *Rollo and Tweedy and the Ghost at Dougal Castle* (1–2). Illus. Series: I Can Read. 1992, HarperCollins LB $15.89 (0-06-020107-X). 64pp. A mouse detective and his assistant catch the ghost that is haunting a Scottish castle. (Rev: BCCB 9/92*; BL 6/15/92; HB 9–10/92; SLJ 10/92)

6190 Anderson, Peggy Perry. *To the Tub* (PS–1). Illus. by author. 1996, Houghton $13.95 (0-395-77614-7). 32pp. In this easily read book, a young frog and his father enjoy a mud bath together. (Rev: SLJ 10/96)

6191 Armstrong, Jennifer. *Sunshine, Moonshine* (1–2). Illus. by Lucia Washburn. 1997, Random paper $3.99 (0-679-86442-3). 32pp. A busy day in the life of a young boy is chronicled in this easy-to-read book. (Rev: BL 5/1/97; SLJ 8/97)

6192 Backstein, Karen. *The Blind Men and the Elephant* (1–2). Illus. by Annie Mitra. 1992, Scholastic paper $3.50 (0-590-45813-2). 48pp. The Indian folktale about the blind men who each see the nature of the elephant in a different way. (Rev: BL 3/1/93) [398.2]

6193 Baker, Alan. *Little Rabbits' First Word Book* (PS). Illus. 1996, Kingfisher $10.95 (0-7534-5020-8). 40pp. For beginning readers, basic words are given for everyday objects. (Rev: BL 11/1/96) [428.1]

6194 Baker, Barbara. *Digby and Kate and the Beautiful Day* (1–2). Illus. by Marsha Winborn. Series: Dutton Easy Reader. 1998, Dutton $13.99 (0-525-45855-7). 48pp. In this easy reader, dog Digby and cat Kate find that, like all true friends, they sometimes have their differences. (Rev: BL 2/1/98; HBG 10/98; SLJ 3/98*)

6195 Baker, Barbara. *N-O Spells No!* (1–3). Illus. by Nola L. Malone. 1993, Scholastic paper $3.99 (0-590-44186-8). 64pp. In this book illustrated with cartoons, there are five short stories about Annie and her big brother. (Rev: BL 6/1/91; SLJ 8/91)

6196 Baker, Barbara. *One Saturday Afternoon* (2–3). Illus. by Kate Duke. 1999, Dutton $13.99 (0-525-45882-4). 48pp. Six short stories about a bear family and their Saturday afternoon activities. (Rev: BL 5/15/99; HBG 10/99; SLJ 8/99)

6197 Baker, Keith. *Sometimes* (1–2). Illus. 1999, Harcourt paper $3.95 (0-15-202002-0). 20pp. The moods and personality of a cartoon alligator are revealed in this easy reader that uses just 70 different words in repeated patterns. (Rev: BL 10/1/99; SLJ 5/99)

6198 Bauer, Marion Dane. *Bear's Hiccups* (1–2). Illus. by Diane D. Hearn. Series: Holiday House Readers. 1998, Holiday $14.95 (0-8234-1339-X). 48pp. A group of animals demands to know if Bear, a grouch who wants to dominate the forest pond, is responsible for the disappearance of Frog. (Rev: BCCB 6/98; BL 5/1/98; HBG 10/98; SLJ 6/98)

6199 Bauer, Marion Dane. *Turtle Dreams* (1–2). Illus. by Diane D. Hearn. Series: Holiday House Readers. 1997, Holiday LB $14.95 (0-8234-1322-5). 48pp. In this easy reader, Turtle goes to sleep for the winter and finds that he has wonderful dreams. (Rev: BL 2/1/98; HBG 3/98; SLJ 1/98)

6200 Bechtold, Lisze. *Buster, the Very Shy Dog* (2). Illus. 1999, Houghton $16.00 (0-395-85008-8). 48pp. An easy reader about how shy puppy Buster adjusts to his new home and to Phoebe, an older dog. (Rev: BCCB 3/99; BL 5/15/99; HB 7–8/99; HBG 10/99; SLJ 5/99)

6201 Benchley, Nathaniel. *A Ghost Named Fred* (1–3). Illus. by Ben Shecter. 1968, HarperCollins LB $15.89 (0-06-020474-5). 64pp. To get out of the rain, George enters an empty house and meets Fred, an absentminded ghost.

6202 Benchley, Nathaniel. *Oscar Otter* (K–2). Illus. by Arnold Lobel. 1966, HarperCollins LB $15.89 (0-06-020472-9); paper $3.95 (0-06-444025-7). 64pp. Hilarious words and pictures describe Oscar's fun on the long and perilous slide he builds to get to his pool.

6203 Benchley, Nathaniel. *Red Fox and His Canoe* (1–2). Illus. by Arnold Lobel. 1964, HarperCollins LB $15.89 (0-06-020476-1); paper $3.95 (0-06-444075-3). 64pp. Red Fox gets himself a large canoe and picks up so many unusual passengers that it capsizes. Also from the same author and publisher: *The Strange Disappearance of Arthur Cluck* (1967).

6204 Berenstain, Stan, and Jan Berenstain. *Bears in the Night* (1–2). Illus. by authors. 1971, Random LB $11.99 (0-394-92286-7). Bear cubs go on a rampage after being put to bed. The lively cartoon style and simple phrases make this a good book for beginning readers. Also from the same authors and publisher: *Bears on Wheels* (1969).

6205 Bernstein, Margery. *My Brother, the Pest* (1–2). Illus. by Dorothy Handelman. Series: Real Kids Readers. 1999, Millbrook LB $16.90 (0-7613-2055-5); paper $3.99 (0-7613-2080-6). 32pp. A rhyming story of sibling rivalry involving two sisters who quarrel and make up. (Rev: BL 5/15/99; SLJ 8/99)

6206 Black, Sonia. *Hanging Out with Mom* (1–2). Illus. by George Ford. 2000, Scholastic paper $3.99 (0-590-86636-2). 32pp. A beginning reader about a day that an African American boy and his mother spend in the park. (Rev: BL 10/1/00)

6207 Blackstone, Stella. *Bear on a Bike* (PS–1). Illus. by Debbie Harter. Series: A Barefoot Beginner Book. 1999, Barefoot $13.95 (1-901223-49-3). A bear, accompanied by a young African American boy, takes off in a variety of vehicles to see the world and its wonders. (Rev: SLJ 3/99)

6208 Blegvad, Lenore. *First Friends* (PS). Illus. by Erik Blegvad. Series: Growing Tree. 2000, HarperFestival $9.95 (0-694-01273-4). 24pp. In this beginning reader, children at preschool play alone and then gradually come together as friends. (Rev: BL 4/15/00; HBG 10/00; SLJ 7/00)

6209 Bliss, Corinne D. *Snow Day* (1–3). Illus. by Nancy Poydar. Series: Step into Reading. 1998, Random LB $11.99 (0-679-98222-1). 48pp. Snow closes her school, giving Emily some unexpected outdoor activities and a topic for her school paper. (Rev: BL 3/15/99; SLJ 3/99)

6210 Blocksma, Mary. *Yoo Hoo, Moon!* (1–3). Illus. by Patience Brewster. Series: Bank Street Ready-to-Read. 1992, Bantam paper $4.50 (0-553-35212-1). 32pp. Bear can't sleep because there is no moon visible. (Rev: BL 4/1/92; SLJ 3/92)

6211 Bonsall, Crosby. *The Case of the Scaredy Cats* (1–2). Illus. by author. 1971, HarperCollins LB $15.89 (0-06-020566-0); paper $3.95 (0-06-444047-8). 64pp. What do you do when you find a bevy of girls in your secret clubhouse? Four other mysteries by the same author and publisher are: *The Case of the Hungry Stranger* (1963); *The Case of the Cat's Meow* (1965); *The Case of the Dumb Bells* (1966); *The Case of the Double Cross* (1980).

6212 Bonsall, Crosby. *Mine's the Best* (1–2). Illus. by author. 1997, HarperCollins paper $3.75 (0-064-44213-6). 32pp. Two small boys discover they have identical balloons, and then begins the argument — whose is the best?

6213 Bonsall, Crosby. *Piggle* (1–2). Illus. by author. 1973, HarperCollins LB $15.89 (0-06-020580-6).

64pp. Homer goes in search of someone to play games with and finds Bear, who enjoys "Piggle" with him. This rhyming spree of nonsense words will please beginning readers.

6214 Bonsall, Crosby. *Tell Me Some More* (1–3). Illus. by Fritz Siebel. 1961, HarperCollins LB $15.89 (0-06-020601-2). 64pp. Andrew introduces his friend to the magic of the library.

6215 Bonsall, Crosby. *Who's a Pest?* (1–3). Illus. by author. 1962, HarperCollins LB $15.89 (0-06-020621-7); paper $3.95 (0-06-444099-0). 64pp. Even though his four sisters, a lizard, a rabbit, and a chipmunk insist that he's a pest, Homer refuses to believe it.

6216 Bonsall, Crosby. *Who's Afraid of the Dark?* (1–3). Illus. by author. 1980, HarperCollins LB $15.89 (0-06-020599-7); paper $3.95 (0-06-444071-0). 32pp. A little boy talks about how Stella, his dog, is afraid of the dark.

6217 Bottner, Barbara. *Bootsie Barker Ballerina* (1–2). Illus. by G. Brian Karas. 1997, HarperCollins LB $14.89 (0-06-027101-9). 40pp. Bootsie Barker gets her comeuppance when she tries to bully everyone in her ballet class, including the teacher. (Rev: BL 5/1/97; SLJ 6/97)

6218 Bottner, Barbara. *Marsha Is Only a Flower* (1–3). Illus. by Denise Brunkus. Series: Road to Reading. 2000, Golden Bks. paper $3.99 (0-307-26330-4). 48pp. In this beginning reader, Lulu's moment of glory at a dance recital is threatened when her younger sister gets some unwanted attention. (Rev: SLJ 3/01)

6219 Bottner, Barbara. *Two Messy Friends* (K–2). Illus. by author. Series: Hello Reader! 1999, Scholastic paper $3.50 (0-590-63285-X). In this beginning reader, two very different friends accommodate their differences because they value their friendship. (Rev: SLJ 8/99)

6220 Brenner, Barbara. *Beavers Beware!* (1–3). Illus. by Emily Arnold McCully. Series: Bank Street Ready-to-Read. 1992, Gareth Stevens LB $19.93 (0-8368-1769-9); Bantam paper $4.50 (0-553-35386-1). 32pp. A family who lives by a river discovers that beavers are constructing a lodge using their dock as a platform. (Rev: BL 4/1/92; HBG 10/99; SLJ 3/92)

6221 Brenner, Barbara. *The Color Wizard* (1–3). Illus. by Leo Dillon and Diane Dillon. 1989, Bantam paper $4.50 (0-553-34690-3). 32pp. Wizard Gray forms a number of new colors from red, blue, and yellow. Also use: *Annie's Pet* (1989). (Rev: BL 9/15/89; SLJ 11/89)

6222 Brenner, Barbara. *Wagon Wheels* (1–3). Illus. by Don Bolognese. 1993, HarperCollins LB $15.89 (0-06-020669-1); paper $3.95 (0-06-444052-4). 64pp. The adventures of an African American family in Kansas in the 1870s.

6223 Bridwell, Norman. *Clifford Makes a Friend* (1). Illus. Series: Hello Reader! 1998, Scholastic paper $3.50 (0-590-37930-5). 32pp. Clifford, the beloved shaggy dog, meets a boy and, after copying his actions, becomes his friend. (Rev: BL 3/15/99)

6224 Brill, Marlene T. *Allen Jay and the Underground Railroad* (1–2). Illus. by Janice L. Porter. Series: On My Own. 1993, Carolrhoda LB $21.27 (0-87614-776-7); paper $5.95 (0-87614-605-1). 48pp. This story, which is based on fact, tells how a young Quaker child helped a slave to freedom. (Rev: BL 7/93; SLJ 8/93)

6225 Brimner, Larry. *Cats!* (1). Illus. by Tom Payne. 2000, Children's $15.00 (0-516-22010-1); paper $4.95 (0-516-27075-3). 24pp. After a little girl lets nine cats into her room, they oblige by playing with her in this book for beginning readers. (Rev: BL 2/15/01)

6226 Brimner, Larry. *Cowboy Up!* (PS–2). Illus. by Susan Miller. Series: Rookie Readers. 1999, Children's LB $17.00 (0-516-21199-4). 31pp. A beginning reader that tells, in simple text and pictures, of a cowboy's day at the rodeo. (Rev: HBG 10/99; SLJ 8/99)

6227 Brimner, Larry. *Dinosaurs Dance* (PS–K). Series: Rookie Readers. 1998, Children's LB $17.00 (0-516-20752-0). 32pp. Gaily colored cartoons show dinosaurs performing a series of dances in this beginning reader. (Rev: HBG 10/98; SLJ 7/98)

6228 Brisson, Pat. *Hot Fudge Hero* (1–3). Illus. by Diana C. Bluthenthal. 1997, Holt $15.95 (0-8050-4551-1). 73pp. A simple chapter book about the adventures of Bertie, a likable second-grade kid, who always gets a hot fudge sundae when he succeeds in his endeavors. (Rev: BCCB 6/97; BL 4/1/97; HB 7–8/97; SLJ 7/97)

6229 Brisson, Pat. *Little Sister, Big Sister* (2–3). Illus. 1999, Holt $15.95 (0-8050-5887-7). 56pp. Two sisters, Zelda and Ivy, are sometimes friends and sometimes enemies in these four stories for beginning readers. (Rev: BCCB 3/99; BL 4/15/99; HBG 10/99; SLJ 7/99)

6230 Brown, Laurie Krasny. *Rex and Lilly Family Time* (1). Illus. by Marc Brown. Series: Dino Easy Reader. 1995, Little, Brown $12.95 (0-316-11385-9). 32pp. Dinosaur Lilly and brother Rex make a mess of their mother's birthday in this easy-to-read book. Also use *Rex and Lilly Playtime* (1995). (Rev: BL 4/15/95; SLJ 8/95)

6231 Brown, Laurie Krasny. *Rex and Lilly Schooltime* (1–2). Illus. by Marc Brown. 1997, Little, Brown $13.95 (0-316-10920-7). 32pp. In this easy reader, dino Rex goes to school and participates in a show-and-tell exercise. (Rev: BL 5/1/97)

6232 Brown, Marc. *Arthur Accused* (2–4). Illus. 1998, Little, Brown $12.95 (0-316-11554-1); paper $3.95 (0-316-11556-8). 64pp. In this Arthur chapter book, the beloved aardvark is wrongfully accused of stealing quarters from a fund drive and is helped by brand-new private eye Buster Baxter who solves the crime. (Rev: BL 7/98; HBG 10/98; SLJ 12/98)

6233 Brown, Marc. *Arthur and the Scare-Your-Pants-Off Club* (2–4). Illus. 1998, Little, Brown $12.00 (0-316-11548-7); paper $3.95 (0-316-11549-5). 64pp. In this simple chapter book, beloved Arthur encounters censorship when a group of parents take a popular scary book series off the library shelves. (Rev: BL 8/98; HBG 10/98; SLJ 6/98)

6234 Brown, Marc. *Arthur Makes the Team* (2–4). Illus. 1998, Little, Brown $12.95 (0-316-11550-9); paper $3.95 (0-316-11551-7). 64pp. Everyone learns the value of teamwork after Arthur joins the baseball team. (Rev: BL 8/98; HBG 10/98; SLJ 10/98)

6235 Brown, Marc. *There's No Place Like Home* (1–3). Illus. Series: Step into Reading. 1991, Parents $5.00 (0-8193-1125-1). 40pp. In this easy reader, various kinds of homes are introduced in verse. (Rev: BL 12/1/91)

6236 Brown, Margaret Wise. *I Like Stars* (1). Illus. by Joan Paley. Series: Road to Reading. 1998, Golden Bks. paper $3.99 (0-307-26105-0). 32pp. A little rabbit leaves his bed and joins in play with a frog, a bird, and a mouse in this easy-to-read book. (Rev: BL 3/15/99)

6237 Buck, Nola. *Sid and Sam* (PS–K). Illus. Series: My First I Can Read Book. 1996, HarperCollins LB $14.89 (0-06-025372-X). 32pp. Sid's song is so long that his friend Sam says, "So long." (Rev: BCCB 7–8/96; BL 8/96; SLJ 6/96)

6238 Bulla, Clyde Robert. *Daniel's Duck* (1–3). Illus. by Joan Sandin. 1979, HarperCollins LB $15.89 (0-06-020909-7); paper $3.95 (0-06-444031-1). 64pp. In this story for beginning readers, a young boy is hurt when people make fun of his wood carving of a duck.

6239 Bulla, Clyde Robert. *Singing Sam* (2–3). Illus. by Susan Magurn. 1989, Random LB $11.99 (0-394-91977-7); paper $3.99 (0-394-81977-2). 48pp. Amy takes in Sam, a dog, when his owner, spoiled Rob, decides he wants a pony instead. (Rev: BL 6/1/89)

6240 Buller, Jon, and Susan Schade. *Captain Zap and the Evil Baron von Fishhead* (2–3). Illus. Series: Step-into-Reading. 2000, Random LB $11.99 (0-679-99461-0); paper $3.99 (0-679-89461-6). 48pp. In this easy reader, everything that Perry and Cosmo draw with their magic pencils comes to life. (Rev: BL 2/15/01)

6241 Buller, Jon, and Susan Schade. *Felix and the 400 Frogs* (2–3). Illus. 1996, Random LB $12.00 (0-679-96745-1); paper $3.99 (0-679-86745-7). 48pp. Felix helps a frog recapture a magic stone from a neighbor's yard. (Rev: BCCB 4/96; BL 9/15/96)

6242 Burke, Jennifer S. *Cloudy Days* (PS–1). Series: Weather Report. 2000, Children's LB $13.50 (0-516-23117-0); paper $4.95 (0-516-23042-5). 24pp. In this beginning reader, a young girl decides what she will do and wear on a cloudy day. Also use *Sunny Days* (2000). (Rev: SLJ 3/01)

6243 Butler, Kristi T. *Rip's Secret Spot* (K–1). Illus. by Joe Cepeda. Series: Green Light. 2000, Harcourt $10.95 (0-15-202640-1); paper $3.95 (0-15-202646-0). 20pp. Family members, each of whom has lost something, find them when they uncover their dog's "secret spot" in the garden in this beginning reader. (Rev: HBG 3/01; SLJ 10/00)

6244 Byars, Betsy. *Ant Plays Bear* (1–3). Illus. by Marc Simont. 1997, Viking $13.99 (0-670-86776-4). 32pp. An easy-to-read book that explores in four stories the relationship between a boy and his younger brother, Ant. (Rev: BL 9/1/97*; HB 7–8/97; HBG 3/98; SLJ 6/97)

6245 Byars, Betsy. *The Golly Sisters Ride Again* (1–3). Illus. by Sue Truesdell. 1994, HarperCollins LB $15.89 (0-06-021564-X). 64pp. Easily read stories about the Golly sisters, who run a traveling show in the old West. (Rev: BCCB 6/94; BL 4/1/94; HB 7–8/94; SLJ 6/94*)

6246 Byars, Betsy. *Hooray for the Golly Sisters!* (1–3). Illus. by Sue Truesdell. 1990, HarperCollins LB $15.89 (0-06-020899-6). 64pp. Five funny stories about the two fearless pioneer sisters and their adventures. (Rev: BCCB 10/90; BL 9/15/90; HB 1–2/91; SLJ 9/90*)

6247 Byars, Betsy. *My Brother, Ant* (1–3). Illus. by Marc Simont. 1996, Viking $13.99 (0-670-86664-4). 32pp. A charming, amusing, easy chapter book in which a boy details some of the antics of his younger brother, Anthony — Ant, for short. (Rev: BL 1/1–15/96*; HB 7–8/96; SLJ 4/96)

6248 Calmenson, Stephanie. *Marigold and Grandma on the Town* (1–2). Illus. by Mary Chalmers. Series: I Can Read. 1994, HarperCollins LB $15.89 (0-06-020813-9). 64pp. Marigold, a bunny, learns to make the wind her friend in this gentle, easy-to-read book. (Rev: BCCB 3/94; BL 2/1/94; HB 3–4/94; SLJ 4/94)

6249 Calmenson, Stephanie. *My Dog's the Best!* (1–2). Illus. by Marcy Ramsey. 1997, Scholastic $3.99 (0-590-33072-1). 32pp. An easy-to-read book in which a number of children tell why they think their dog is best. (Rev: BL 2/1/98)

6250 Calmenson, Stephanie. *Roller Skates!* (1–2). Illus. by True Kelley. 1992, Scholastic paper $3.99 (0-590-45716-0). 32pp. A young boy accidentally receives a shipment of 52 pairs of roller skates, so he decides to have a sale. (Rev: BL 3/1/93)

6251 Cameron, Ann. *Julian's Glorious Summer* (2–3). Illus. by Dora Leder. 1987, Random paper $3.99 (0-394-89117-1). 64pp. Troubles begin for Julian when he lies because he is afraid to ride a bike. Also use two other stories about the ups and downs of this warm African American family: *More Stories Julian Tells* (Knopf 1986); *Julian, Secret Agent* (Random 1988). (Rev: BCCB 12/87; BL 12/15/87; SLJ 12/87)

6252 Caple, Kathy. *The Friendship Tree* (1–2). Illus. Series: Holiday House Readers. 2000, Holiday $14.95 (0-8234-1376-4). 32pp. Blanche and Otis are sheep in this easy reader that consists of four stories about trees and forests. (Rev: BL 2/15/00; HB 7–8/00; HBG 10/00; SLJ 4/00)

6253 Caple, Kathy. *Well Done, Worm!* (K–1). Illus. Series: Brand New Reader. 2000, Candlewick $10.99 (0-7636-1146-8). 32pp. Four very short stories featuring a lovable worm are contained in this beginning reader. (Rev: BL 10/1/00; HBG 3/01; SLJ 3/01)

6254 Cappetta, Cynthia. *Chairs, Chairs, Chairs!* (PS–2). Illus. by Rick Stromoski. Series: Rookie Readers. 1999, Children's LB $17.00 (0-516-21542-6). 31pp. A beginning reader that introduces different kinds of chairs, their sizes and shapes, and tells where they can be found. (Rev: HBG 10/99; SLJ 8/99)

6255 Capucilli, Alyssa Satin. *Bathtime for Biscuit* (1). Illus. by Pat Schories. 1998, HarperCollins LB $12.89 (0-06-027938-9). 32pp. A simple story about the problems a little boy has getting his little dog, Biscuit, into the bath. (Rev: BL 11/1/98; HBG 3/99; SLJ 10/98)

6256 Capucilli, Alyssa Satin. *Biscuit* (K–1). Illus. 1996, HarperCollins LB $14.89 (0-06-026198-6). 32pp. A dog named Biscuit tries to make his wants known. (Rev: BL 8/96; SLJ 7/96)

6257 Capucilli, Alyssa Satin. *Biscuit Finds a Friend* (1–2). Illus. by Pat Schories. 1997, HarperCollins LB $14.89 (0-06-027413-1). 24pp. In this easy reader, a puppy named Biscuit finds a lost baby duckling. (Rev: BL 5/1/97; SLJ 6/97)

6258 Capucilli, Alyssa Satin. *Biscuit's New Trick* (K–1). Illus. by Pat Schories. Series: I Can Read. 2000, HarperCollins $12.95 (0-06-028067-0). 32pp. A little girl thinks she is a failure at trying to get Biscuit, a puppy, to fetch a ball in this simple beginner's story. (Rev: BL 4/15/00; HBG 10/00; SLJ 6/00)

6259 Capucilli, Alyssa Satin. *Inside a Zoo in the City: A Rebus Read-Along Story* (PS–K). Illus. by Tedd Arnold. 2000, Scholastic $11.95 (0-590-99715-7). 32pp. Told with pictures that substitute for the names of various animals, this simple rebus book tells how the animals in a zoo actually live in apartments and have to get up in the morning and go to work like other people. (Rev: BL 12/15/00; SLJ 3/01)

6260 Carle, Eric. *My Very First Book of Words* (PS–1). Illus. by author. 1985, HarperCollins $2.95 (0-690-57368-5). 10pp. A nicely illustrated beginning word book, printed on heavy stock cards.

6261 Cazet, Denys. *Minnie and Moo and the Musk of Zorro* (1–2). Illus. 2000, DK $12.95 (0-7894-2652-8); paper $3.95 (0-7894-2653-6). 48pp. Minnie and Moo, cows who are best friends, masquerade as Zorro to save the farm from a fox in this book for beginning readers. (Rev: BL 12/1/00; HB 9–10/00; HBG 3/01; SLJ 11/00)

6262 Cazet, Denys. *Minnie and Moo Go Dancing* (1–2). Illus. 1998, DK $12.95 (0-7894-2515-7); paper $3.95 (0-7894-2536-X). 48pp. In this easy reader, unexpected things happen when cows Minnie and Moo dress up to go dancing. (Rev: BCCB 9/98; BL 7/98; HBG 3/99; SLJ 11/98)

6263 Cazet, Denys. *Minnie and Moo Go to Paris* (1–2). Illus. 1999, DK $12.95 (0-7894-2595-5). 48pp. Two fun-loving cows commandeer a tour bus that takes them to China, Paris, and a safari park. Also use *Minnie and Moo Save the Earth* (1999). (Rev: BCCB 10/99; BL 12/1/99; HBG 3/00)

6264 Cazet, Denys. *Minnie and Moo Go to the Moon* (1–2). Illus. 1998, DK $12.95 (0-7894-2516-

5); paper $3.95 (0-7894-2537-8). 48pp. Two cows, Minnie and Moo, have an exciting adventure after Moo decides she would like to drive a tractor. (Rev: BCCB 9/98; BL 7/98; HB 9–10/98; HBG 3/99; SLJ 11/98)

6265 Chorao, Kay. *Here Comes Kate* (1–2). Illus. by author. 2000, Dutton $13.99 (0-525-46443-3). 48pp. This book for beginning readers tells of the daily problems facing Kate, a young elephant, such as getting annoyed with her brother and losing a toy. (Rev: HBG 3/01; SLJ 2/01)

6266 Christian, Mary Blount. *The Toady and Dr. Miracle* (1–4). Illus. by Christine Jenny. Series: Ready-to-Read. 1997, Simon & Schuster $15.00 (0-689-80890-9); paper $3.99 (0-689-80891-7). 40pp. A beginning reader in which Luther is able to trick Dr. Miracle, a phony medicine man. (Rev: SLJ 9/97)

6267 Cleary, Beverly. *Muggie Maggie* (2–3). Illus. by Kay Life. 1990, Avon paper $4.95 (0-380-71087-0). 80pp. Third-grader Maggie decides that learning to write is not necessary for a girl who can use a computer. (Rev: BCCB 6/90; BL 3/15/90; HB 11–12/90; SLJ 6/90)

6268 Clifford, Eth. *Flatfoot Fox and the Case of the Missing Schoolhouse* (2–3). Illus. by Brian Lies. 1997, Houghton $15.00 (0-395-81446-4). 48pp. An easy read in which Flatfoot Fox and sidekick Secretary Bird foil the schemes of Wacky Weasel. (Rev: BL 3/15/97; SLJ 4/97)

6269 Clifford, Eth. *Flatfoot Fox and the Case of the Nosy Otter* (2–4). Illus. by Brian Lies. 1992, Houghton $15.00 (0-395-60289-0). 32pp. Flatfoot Fox is hot on the trail of Nosy, Mrs. Chatterbox Otter's missing son. Also use: *Flatfoot Fox and the Case of the Missing Eye* (1991). (Rev: BCCB 11/92; BL 9/1/92; SLJ 9/92)

6270 Cobb, Annie. *Wheels!* (PS–K). Illus. Series: Early Step into Reading. 1996, Random LB $11.99 (0-679-96445-2); paper $3.99 (0-679-86445-8). 32pp. All sorts of wheels are shown in this beginning reader. (Rev: BL 8/96; SLJ 7/96)

6271 Cocca-Leffler, Maryann. *Ice-Cold Birthday* (K–1). Illus. Series: All Aboard Reading. 1992, Putnam paper $3.95 (0-448-40380-3). 32pp. A young girl has a delightful birthday in spite of a power blackout. (Rev: BL 10/1/92; SLJ 9/92)

6272 Coerr, Eleanor. *The Big Balloon Race* (1–3). Illus. by Carolyn Croll. 1992, HarperCollins LB $15.89 (0-06-021353-1); paper $3.95 (0-06-444053-2). 64pp. Arill and her mother fly their balloon in a suspenseful race.

6273 Coerr, Eleanor. *Buffalo Bill and the Pony Express* (2–4). Illus. by Don Bolognese. 1995, HarperCollins LB $15.89 (0-06-023373-7). 64pp. Billy outsmarts some Indians and scares off a pack of wolves in this easily read adventure. (Rev: BCCB 4/95; BL 4/15/95; HB 7–8/95; SLJ 5/95)

6274 Coerr, Eleanor. *Chang's Paper Pony* (1–3). Illus. by author. 1988, HarperCollins LB $15.89 (0-06-021329-9); paper $3.95 (0-06-444163-6). 64pp. A young Chinese boy longs for a pony in the California Gold Rush days. (Rev: BL 7/88; SLJ 12/88)

6275 Coerr, Eleanor. *The Josefina Story Quilt* (1–3). Illus. by Bruce Degen. 1986, HarperCollins LB $15.89 (0-06-021349-3); paper $3.95 (0-06-444129-6). 64pp. Faith's sorrow at the death of her pet hen during their trip west to California is softened by the quilt she sews in remembrance. (Rev: BCCB 5/86; BL 3/15/86; SLJ 5/86)

6276 Cohen, Caron L. *How Many Fish?* (1–2). Illus. by S. D. Schindler. Series: My First I Can Read Book. 1998, HarperCollins paper $12.95 (0-06-027713-0). 32pp. A fish is trapped under a child's upside-down pail, but later it is freed in this easy-to-read adventure. (Rev: BL 2/1/98; HBG 10/98; SLJ 2/98)

6277 Cole, Joanna. *Bully Trouble* (1–3). Illus. by Marylin Hafner. 1989, Random paper $3.99 (0-394-84949-3). 48pp. Two friends concoct a plan to get even with a bully. (Rev: BL 2/1/90; SLJ 2/90)

6278 Cole, Joanna. *The Missing Tooth* (1–3). Illus. by Marylin Hafner. 1989, Random paper $3.99 (0-394-89279-8). 48pp. Arlo is upset when best friend Robby loses a second tooth and he doesn't. (Rev: BL 3/1/89; SLJ 5/89)

6279 Cole, Joanna. *Norma Jean, Jumping Bean* (1–3). Illus. 1987, Random paper $3.99 (0-394-88668-2). 48pp. Norma Jean, a kangaroo child, stops jumping when her feelings are ruffled, until field day at school. (Rev: BCCB 6/87; BL 6/1/87; SLJ 6–7/87)

6280 Cole, Joanna, and Stephanie Calmenson, eds. *Ready . . . Set . . . Read! The Beginning Reader's Treasury* (K–2). Illus. 1990, Doubleday $17.95 (0-385-41416-1). 144pp. This is an easily read collection of stories by such writers as Dr. Seuss and Maurice Sendak. (Rev: BL 12/1/90; SLJ 9/90*)

6281 Cosby, Bill. *One Dark and Scary Night* (K–2). Illus. by Varnette P. Honeywood. Series: Little Bill. 1999, Scholastic $15.95 (0-590-51475-X); paper $3.99 (0-590-51476-8). In this beginning reader, Little Bill learns to conquer his fears concerning noises he hears in the night. (Rev: HBG 10/99; SLJ 7/99)

6282 Cosby, Bill. *Shipwreck Saturday* (2–4). Illus. Series: Little Bill. 1998, Scholastic $13.95 (0-590-16400-7); paper $3.99 (0-590-95620-5). 40pp. Although Little Bill's boat is destroyed on its first voyage, a friend uses its parts for a kite. (Rev: BL 5/15/98; SLJ 6/98)

6283 Cosby, Bill. *Super-Fine Valentine* (2–4). Illus. Series: Little Bill. 1998, Scholastic $13.95 (0-590-16401-5); paper $3.99 (0-590-95622-1). 40pp. Using eye-catching artwork, this is the simple story of Little Bill who is reluctant to give his friend Mia a Valentine until some of his other friends give her one first. (Rev: BL 5/15/98; SLJ 6/98)

6284 Cottle, Joan. *Emily's Shoes* (1). Illus. 1999, Children's LB $17.50 (0-516-21585-X). 32pp. In this simple reader, Emily imagines all sorts of activities that she can engage in, along with the shoes that each would require. (Rev: BL 10/1/99)

6285 Cottringer, Anne. *Movie Magic: A Star Is Born* (2–4). Illus. by Roger Stewart. Series: Eyewitness Reader. 1999, DK $12.95 (0-7894-4009-1); paper $3.95 (0-7894-4008-3). 48pp. In this easy reader, which uses color photos to show the movie-making process, a young African American girl gets a part in a science fiction movie. (Rev: SLJ 8/99)

6286 Cousins, Lucy. *Maisy's Pool* (PS–1). Illus. by author. 1999, Candlewick $9.99 (0-7636-0886-6); paper $3.29 (0-7636-0907-2). Maisy, a mouse, repairs a wading pool with her friend Tallulah and, together with Eddie the elephant, they enjoy a dip. Also use *Maisy's Bedtime* (1999). (Rev: HBG 3/00; SLJ 9/99)

6287 Cowley, Joy. *Agapanthus Hum and Major Bark* (K–2). Illus. by Jennifer Plecas. 2001, Putnam $13.99 (0-399-23322-9). 48pp. In this easy-to-read chapter book, Agapanthus Hum enters her dog, Major Bark, in a dog show where he wins as the dog with the smallest eyes. (Rev: BCCB 3/01; BL 2/15/01; SLJ 2/01)

6288 Cox, Phil Roxbee. *Ted in a Red Bed* (K–1). Illus. by Stephen Cartwright. Series: Easy Words to Read. 1999, EDC paper $7.95 (0-7460-3023-1). 16pp. A beginning reader with flaps about a bear who buys a bed and falls asleep on it in the store. (Rev: SLJ 12/99)

6289 Coxe, Molly. *Big Egg* (1–2). Illus. 1997, Random LB $11.99 (0-679-98126-8); paper $3.99 (0-679-88126-3). 32pp. For the beginning reader, this story tells what happens after Hen finds a huge egg among her little ones. (Rev: BL 5/1/97)

6290 Coxe, Molly. *Hot Dog* (1). Illus. Series: Road to Reading. 1998, Golden Bks. paper $3.99 (0-307-26101-8). 32pp. A dog who is trying to fight the heat, irritates a cat, skunk, pig, and others in this beginning reader. (Rev: BCCB 2/99; BL 3/15/99)

6291 Coxe, Molly. *R Is for Radish!* (1–2). Illus. 1997, Random LB $11.99 (0-679-98574-3); paper $3.99 (0-679-88574-9). 48pp. Three easily read stories about Radish Rabbit, who finds it is easy to remember spelling words if you invent a rap routine about them while you study. (Rev: BL 2/1/98)

6292 Crews, Donald. *Cloudy Day Sunny Day* (1). Illus. Series: Green Light. 1999, Harcourt paper $3.95 (0-15-201997-9). 20pp. In this easy reader, two African American children find plenty to do regardless of the weather. (Rev: BL 5/15/99)

6293 Cristaldi, Kathryn. *Baseball Ballerina* (1–3). Illus. by Abby Carter. Series: Step into Reading. 1992, Random paper $3.99 (0-679-81734-4). 48pp. A young girl who loves baseball is afraid that her friends will find out she is taking ballet lessons. (Rev: BCCB 6/92; BL 6/1/92; SLJ 9/92)

6294 Cristaldi, Kathryn. *Baseball Ballerina Strikes Out!* (1–2). Illus. by Abby Carter. Series: Step into Reading. 2000, Random $11.99 (0-679-99132-8); paper $3.99 (0-679-89132-3). 48pp. The baseball-playing, ballet-student narrator must cope with two bullies who are teasing her in this book for beginning readers. (Rev: HBG 10/00; SLJ 9/00)

6295 Cristaldi, Kathryn. *Princess Lulu Goes to Camp* (1–2). Illus. by Heather H. Maione. 1997, Putnam paper $3.99 (0-448-41125-3). 48pp. An easy reader about the obnoxious Princess Lulu at a summer camp. (Rev: BL 8/97; SLJ 12/97)

6296 Croll, Carolyn. *Too Many Babas* (PS–3). Illus. Series: I Can Read. 1994, HarperCollins LB $15.89 (0-06-021384-1). 64pp. Too many cooks spoil the broth in this easy-to-read book with a Russian setting. (Rev: BL 2/1/94)

6297 Crummel, Susan Stevens. *Tumbleweed Stew* (1–2). Illus. by Janet Stevens. Series: Green Light. 2000, Harcourt $10.95 (0-15-202673-8); paper $3.95 (0-15-202628-2). 20pp. Rabbit tricks all the animals into bringing the ingredients for tumbleweed stew in this humorous easy reader. (Rev: BL 10/1/00; HBG 3/01; SLJ 1/01)

6298 Cushman, Doug. *Aunt Eater Loves a Mystery* (1–2). Illus. by author. 1987, HarperCollins LB $15.89 (0-06-021327-2); paper $3.95 (0-06-444126-1). 64pp. Grandmotherly Aunt Eater, an anteater, loves to solve mysteries. (Rev: BL 10/1/87; SLJ 12/87)

6299 Cushman, Doug. *Aunt Eater's Mystery Vacation* (1–2). Illus. 1992, HarperCollins LB $15.89 (0-06-020514-8). 64pp. Amateur detective Aunt Eater finds mystery and adventure on what was promised to be a relaxing cruise. (Rev: BL 4/1/92; SLJ 6/92)

6300 Cushman, Doug. *Inspector Hopper* (1–3). Illus. Series: I Can Read. 2000, HarperCollins LB $14.89 (0-06-028383-1). 64pp. Inspector Grasshopper and sidekick McBugg solve two mysteries in this easy-to-read book. (Rev: BL 4/15/00; HB 7–8/00; HBG 10/00; SLJ 10/00)

6301 Daniel, Claire. *The Chick That Wouldn't Hatch* (1–2). Illus. by Lisa Campbell Ernst. Series: Green Light. 1999, Harcourt $10.95 (0-15-202337-2); paper $3.95 (0-15-202269-4). 20pp. In this easy reader, Mother Hen's one egg that won't hatch rolls down the hill, chased by all the barnyard animals. (Rev: BL 12/1/99; HBG 3/00; SLJ 11/99)

6302 Danziger, Paula. *It's Justin Time, Amber Brown* (1–3). Illus. by Tony Ross. 2001, Putnam $12.99 (0-399-23470-5). 48pp. In this beginning reader, Amber Brown, age 7, gets her wish of a watch for her birthday now that she has learned to tell the time. (Rev: SLJ 3/01)

6303 Davis, Tim. *Mice of the Westing Wind: Book One* (2–3). Illus. by author. 1998, Journey Bks. paper $6.49 (1-57924-065-8). 114pp. Two mouse spies, Charles and Oliver, join a group out to capture a crew of pirate sea dogs who have escaped from prison. Also use *The Mouse of the Westing Wind: Book Two* (1998). (Rev: SLJ 5/99)

6304 Delton, Judy. *Cookies and Crutches* (1–2). Illus. by Alan Tiegreen. 1988, Dell paper $3.99 (0-440-40010-4). 80pp. Molly and her friends find out that baking at home isn't quite as easy as it looks. (Rev: BL 6/1/88)

6305 dePaola, Tomie. *Kit and Kat* (1–2). Illus. 1994, Putnam paper $3.99 (0-448-40748-5). 32pp. Three easily read stories about the everyday adventures of Kit and Kat, the Kitten Kids. (Rev: BL 1/1/95)

6306 deRubertis, Barbara. *Deena's Lucky Penny* (1–2). Illus. by Joan Holub and Cynthia Fisher. Series: Math Matters. 1999, Kane paper $4.95 (1-57565-091-6). 32pp. This easy reader introduces the simple arithmetic of counting money, through the story of a young girl who saves to buy her mother a birthday present. (Rev: BL 12/1/99)

6307 Dobkin, Bonnie. *Everybody Says* (1–2). Illus. by Keith Neely. 1993, Children's $18.00 (0-516-02019-6). 32pp. In this easy-to-read book, a young boy's opinions differ from those of everyone else. (Rev: BL 12/1/93)

6308 Dodd, Lynley. *Hairy Maclary and Zachary Quack* (PS–2). Illus. by author. Series: Gold Star First Reader. 2000, Gareth Stevens LB $15.95 (0-8368-2676-0). 31pp. Harry the dog has a joyful day playing with Zachary Quack in this delightful first reader. Also use, in the same series, *Sniff-Snuff-Snap!* (2000), the story of a bossy wart hog. (Rev: SLJ 2/01)

6309 Dodds, Siobhan. *Words and Pictures* (PS–1). Illus. 1992, Candlewick $14.95 (1-56402-042-8). 32pp. This "first picture book dictionary" offers 12 well-known childhood experiences, explained in simple sentences. (Rev: BL 7/92; SLJ 8/92)

6310 Donnelly, Judy. *The Titanic: Lost . . . and Found* (2–4). Illus. by Keith Kohler. 1987, Random paper $3.99 (0-394-88669-0). 48pp. In a simple account the author describes the sinking of the Titanic and its rediscovery. (Rev: BCCB 6/87; BL 6/1/87; SLJ 6–7/87)

6311 Donnelly, Judy. *Tut's Mummy: Lost . . . and Found* (2–3). Illus. by James Watling. 1988, Random paper $3.99 (0-394-89189-9). 48pp. The story of the 20th-century discovery of King Tut's tomb. (Rev: BL 10/1/88; SLJ 10/88)

6312 Dotlich, Rebecca. *Away We Go!* (PS). Illus. by Dan Yaccarino. Series: Growing Tree. 2000, HarperFestival $9.95 (0-694-01393-5). 24pp. All kinds of vehicles — from a school bus and jumbo jet to a wheelchair and sled — are pictured along with people in motion in this easy-to-read book. (Rev: BL 9/1/00; HBG 3/01; SLJ 11/00)

6313 Douglas, Eric. *Get That Pest!* (1–2). Illus. by Wong H. Yee. Series: Green Light. 2000, Harcourt $10.95 (0-15-202548-0); paper $3.95 (0-15-202554-5). 20pp. Mom and Pop discover that the wolf who has been stealing their eggs is secretly painting them rather than eating them. (Rev: BL 2/15/00; HBG 10/00; SLJ 7/00)

6314 Dragonwagon, Crescent. *Annie Flies the Birthday Bike* (K–3). Illus. by Emily Arnold McCully. 1993, Macmillan LB $14.95 (0-02-733155-5). 32pp. Annie finally learns to ride her birthday present, a two-wheel bike. (Rev: BL 3/1/93; SLJ 7/93)

6315 Driscoll, Laura. *The Bravest Cat! The True Story of Scarlett* (K–2). Illus. by DyAnne DiSalvo-Ryan. Series: All Aboard Reading. 1997, Grosset LB $13.99 (0-448-41720-0); paper $3.95 (0-448-41703-0). 32pp. Based on a true story, this easy reader tells how a mother cat saved her kittens from a fire in an old garage in 1996. (Rev: HBG 3/98; SLJ 2/98)

6316 Dubowski, Cathy E. *Pirate School* (1–3). Illus. by Mark Dubowski. Series: All Aboard Reading. 1996, Grosset paper $3.95 (0-448-41132-6). 48pp. An easy-to-read adventure about a boy who attends pirate school. (Rev: SLJ 4/97)

6317 Dubowski, Cathy E., and Mark Dubowski. *Snug Bug* (PS–1). Illus. 1995, Putnam paper $3.99 (0-448-40849-X). 32pp. An easily read book about a little bug that prepares for bed. (Rev: BL 7/95)

6318 Duffey, Betsy. *How to Be Cool in the Third Grade* (1–3). Illus. by Janet Wilson. 1993, Viking $13.99 (0-670-84798-4). 80pp. Robbie wants to be a "cool dude" at school, but circumstances — including a run-in with the class bully — thwart his plans. (Rev: BCCB 10/93; BL 9/1/93; SLJ 9/93)

6319 Eastman, P. D. *Are You My Mother?* (1–3). Illus. by author. 1960, Random LB $13.99 (0-394-90018-9). 64pp. A bird falls from the nest and looks for its mother.

6320 Eastman, Patricia. *Sometimes Things Change* (K–1). Illus. by Seymour Fleishman. 1983, Children's LB $18.00 (0-516-02044-7); paper $4.95 (0-516-42044-5). 32pp. A story of how things in nature change.

6321 Eaton, Deborah. *The Rainy Day Grump* (K–2). Illus. by Dorothy Handelman. Series: Real Kids Readers. 1998, Millbrook LB $16.90 (0-7613-2018-0); paper $3.99 (0-7613-2043-1). 32pp. In this easy reader illustrated by color photographs, Rosie tries to amuse her brother Clay who is grumpy because it's raining and he can't go out to play. (Rev: BL 11/1/98)

6322 Edwards, Frank B. *Is the Spaghetti Ready?* (K–1). Illus. by John Bianchi. Series: Bungalo Books New Reader. 1998, Firefly LB $16.95 (0-921285-67-1); paper $5.95 (0-921285-66-3). A zoo full of animal friends are ready for feeding time in this clever beginning reader. (Rev: SLJ 9/98)

6323 Edwards, Frank B. *New at the Zoo* (K–1). Illus. by John Bianchi. Series: Bungalo Books New Reader. 1998, Firefly LB $16.95 (0-921285-70-1); paper $5.95 (0-921285-69-8). This brightly colored book uses several zoo animals to introduce its friendship theme. (Rev: SLJ 9/98)

6324 Edwards, Frank B. *Troubles with Bubbles* (K–1). Illus. by John Bianchi. Series: Bungalo Books New Reader. 1998, Firefly LB $16.95 (0-921285-63-9); paper $5.95 (0-921285-64-7). A brightly illustrated, easy-to-read book in which a group of animal friends get rid of the day's dirt and grime. (Rev: SLJ 9/98)

6325 Edwards, Roberta. *Five Silly Fishermen* (K–2). Illus. by Sylvie Wickstrom. 1989, Random LB $11.99 (0-679-90092-6); paper $3.99 (0-679-80092-1). 48pp. A simple version of the folktale about five fishermen who mistakenly believe one of them is missing. (Rev: BL 2/1/90; SLJ 4/90)

6326 Ehrlich, Amy. *Leo, Zack, and Emmie* (1–3). Illus. by Steven Kellogg. 1997, Puffin paper $3.99 (0-140-36199-5). 64pp. An easily read story of the friendship shared by three people.

6327 Ehrlich, Fred. *A Class Play with Ms. Vanilla* (1–2). Illus. by Martha Gradisher. 1992, Puffin paper $3.50 (0-140-54580-8). 32pp. Primary graders put on their version of Red Riding Hood. (Rev: BL 12/1/92)

6328 Elste, Joan. *True Blue* (2–3). Illus. by DyAnne DiSalvo-Ryan. 1996, Putnam paper $3.99 (0-448-41264-0). 48pp. J.D. worries when his faithful dog Blue disappears. (Rev: BL 11/15/96)

6329 Erickson, John R. *Hank the Cowdog: The Case of the Haystack Kitties* (2–3). Illus. by Gerald L. Holmes. Series: Hank the Cowdog. 1998, Gulf $14.95 (0-87719-338-X). 113pp. Hank's many adventures on the ranch include being threatened by a bull and saving a family of kittens. (Rev: SLJ 11/98)

6330 Etra, Jonathan, and Stephanie Spinner. *Aliens for Lunch* (2–4). Illus. by Steve Bjorkman. 1991, Random $11.99 (0-679-91056-5); paper $3.99 (0-679-81056-0). 39pp. Richard and Henry are called upon to help stop an evil planet's scheme to steal the dessert resources of the earth. (Rev: BL 6/1/91)

6331 Farber, Erica, and J. R. Sansevere. *Ooey Gooey* (PS–2). Illus. by Mercer Mayer. Series: Mercer Mayer's Critters of the Night/Step into Reading. 1998, Random LB $11.99 (0-679-98991-9); paper $3.99 (0-679-88991-4). 32pp. In search of his gold tooth, Captain Short Bob, a pirate, takes a trip underwater in this beginning reader. (Rev: SLJ 7/98)

6332 Feder, Paula K. *Where Does the Teacher Live?* (1–2). Illus. by Lillian Hoban. 1996, Viking paper $3.99 (0-14-038119-8). 48pp. Three young people try to find out where their teacher lives.

6333 Finch, Margo. *The Lunch Bunch* (K–2). Photos by Dorothy Handelman. Series: Real Kids Readers. 1998, Millbrook LB $16.90 (0-7613-2005-9); paper $3.99 (0-7613-2030-X). 32pp. A new girl at school searches for friends in this enjoyable beginning reader. (Rev: SLJ 7/98)

6334 Floyd, Lucy. *Rabbit and Turtle Go to School* (K–1). Illus. by Christopher Denise. Series: Green Light. 2000, Harcourt $10.95 (0-15-202679-7); paper $3.95 (0-15-202685-1). 20pp. A delightful book for beginning readers about still another race between the rabbit and the turtle. (Rev: BL 10/1/00; SLJ 10/00)

6335 Ford, Miela. *Watch Us Play* (PS–1). Photos by author. 1998, Greenwillow LB $14.93 (0-688-15607-X). Full-color photographs show the playful antics of two lion cubs who finally tire and take a nap. (Rev: SLJ 5/98)

6336 Franco, Betsy. *Why the Frog Has Big Eyes* (1–2). Illus. by Joung Un Kim. 2000, Harcourt $10.95 (0-15-202536-7). 20pp. This easy-to-read pourquoi story tells how Frog's eyes grew to be so big. (Rev: BL 10/1/00; HBG 3/01; SLJ 1/01)

6337 Friend, Catherine. *Silly Ruby* (PS–1). Illus. by Rachel Merriman. Series: Brand New Reader. 2000, Candlewick $10.99 (0-7636-1072-0). 40pp. Silly Ruby, a sheep, has all sorts of misfortunes in this easy reader including getting buried in a mound of apples. (Rev: HBG 3/01; SLJ 3/01)

6338 Galbraith, Kathryn O. *Roommates* (2–3). Illus. by Mark Graham. 1990, Macmillan LB $18.00 (0-689-50487-X). 48pp. Mimi and Beth must share a room because the new baby is coming, and they're not happy. A sequel is: *Roommates and Rachel* (1991). (Rev: BL 3/1/90; SLJ 3/90)

6339 Garcia, Carolyn. *Moonboy* (PS–2). Illus. by author. 1999, Beyond Words $15.95 (1-885223-81-

1). Because of his unusual appearance, Moonboy is shunned by all except a boy named Ed, who wants him as a friend. (Rev: HBG 3/00; SLJ 8/99)

6340 Gelman, Rita G. *Pizza Pat* (PS–1). Illus. by Will Terry. Series: Step into Reading. 1999, Random LB $11.99 (0-679-99134-4); paper $3.99 (0-679-89134-X). 25pp. An easy reader that consists of a joyful cumulative rhyme about the ingredients in a pizza. (Rev: HBG 10/99; SLJ 9/99)

6341 Ghigna, Charles. *Mice Are Nice* (1). Illus. by Jon Goodell. Series: Step into Reading. 1999, Random LB $11.99 (0-679-98929-3); paper $3.99 (0-679-88929-9). 32pp. In a pet store, a small mouse tells a little girl why mice make the best pets compared with other animals. (Rev: BL 10/1/99; HBG 3/00)

6342 Giff, Patricia Reilly. *The Beast in Ms. Rooney's Room* (2–4). Illus. by Blanche Sims. 1984, Dell paper $4.50 (0-440-40485-1). 80pp. A volume in the Kids of the Polk Street School series. Another title is: *Fish Face* (1984).

6343 Giff, Patricia Reilly. *Garbage Juice for Breakfast* (2–3). Illus. by Blanche Sims. 1989, Bantam paper $3.99 (0-440-40207-7). 156pp. Dawn hopes to beat her rival at finding the hidden treasure at summer camp. (Rev: BL 12/15/89)

6344 Giff, Patricia Reilly. *Good Luck, Ronald Morgan!* (K–2). Illus. by Susanna Natti. 1996, Viking $14.99 (0-670-86303-3). 26pp. Ronald, who has just gotten a new dog, wonders if he can get along with his neighbor, who has a cat. (Rev: BCCB 10/96; SLJ 9/96)

6345 Giff, Patricia Reilly. *In the Dinosaur's Paw* (2–4). Illus. by Blanche Sims. 1985, Dell paper $3.99 (0-440-44150-1). 80pp. The Polk Street School kids in the month of February. Also use: *The Candy Corn Contest* (1984); *December Secrets* (1984); *The Valentine Star* (1985); *All about Stacy* (1988). (Rev: BL 4/15/85)

6346 Giff, Patricia Reilly. *Next Stop, New York City! The Polk Street Kids on Tour* (2–4). Illus. by Blanche Sims. Series: Polk Street Special. 1997, Dell paper $3.99 (0-440-41362-1). 119pp. When Ms. Rooney and the Polk Street crowd visit New York City, Emily Arrow is upset because she has been dubbed an expert on the Big Apple, but she really knows nothing about it. (Rev: SLJ 10/97)

6347 Giff, Patricia Reilly. *The Powder Puff Puzzle* (1–2). Illus. by Blanche Sims. 1987, Dell paper $3.50 (0-440-47180-X). The class detective follows clues to find her missing cat. Also use: *The Riddle of the Red Purse; The Secret at the Polk Street School* (both 1987). (Rev: BL 4/1/88)

6348 Giff, Patricia Reilly. *Purple Climbing Days* (1–3). Illus. by Blanche Sims. 1985, Bantam paper $3.99 (0-440-47309-8). 80pp. Richard "Beast" Best of the Polk Street School is afraid to climb the floor-to-ceiling rope in gym. Two others in this series are: *Lazy Lions, Lucky Lambs; Snaggle Doodles* (both 1985). (Rev: BL 8/85; SLJ 11/85)

6349 Giff, Patricia Reilly. *Sunny-Side Up* (1–3). Illus. by Blanche Sims. 1986, Dell paper $3.99 (0-440-48406-5). 74pp. The Polk Street School kids

are in summer school and have to deal with Matthew's announcement that he is moving away. Another in this series is: *Spectacular Stone Soup* (1989). (Rev: BL 10/1/86; SLJ 3/87)

6350 Godwin, Laura. *Forest* (1–2). Illus. by Stacey Schuett. Series: I Can Read. 1998, HarperCollins $14.95 (0-06-026664-3). 48pp. A young girl and her mother find a lost fawn in the forest and bring it home before turning it over to an agency that cares for wild animals. (Rev: BL 5/1/98; HB 5–6/98; HBG 10/98; SLJ 6/98)

6351 Godwin, Laura. *Happy and Honey* (1–2). Illus. by Jane Chapman. 2000, Simon & Schuster $12.95 (0-689-83406-3). 32pp. Honey, a cat that likes to play, tries to get a sleeping dog named Happy to join her in this easy reader. (Rev: BL 12/1/00; HBG 3/01; SLJ 12/00)

6352 Godwin, Laura. *Honey Helps* (PS–1). Illus. by Jane Chapman. Series: Happy Honey. 2000, Simon & Schuster $12.95 (0-689-83407-1). A beginning reader about an energetic cat named Honey who wants to help her doggy friend Happy chew his bone. (Rev: HBG 3/01; SLJ 12/00)

6353 Goode, Molly. *Mama Loves* (PS–1). Illus. by Lisa McCue. Series: Bright and Early Books for Beginning Beginners. 1999, Random LB $11.99 (0-679-99462-9). An easy-to-read bedtime story that shows how animal mothers take care of their young. (Rev: SLJ 8/99)

6354 Graves, Bonnie. *No Copycats Allowed!* (1–3). Illus. by Abby Carter. Series: Hyperion Chapters. 1998, Hyperion LB $14.49 (0-7868-2235-X); paper $3.95 (0-7868-1166-8). 51pp. A young girl, new to her class, decides to fit in by copying the interests, dress, and manners of others. (Rev: HBG 10/98; SLJ 6/98)

6355 Greene, Carol. *Hi, Clouds* (K–2). Illus. by Gene Sharp. 1983, Children's LB $18.00 (0-516-02036-6); paper $4.95 (0-516-42036-4). 32pp. Two children see many objects in clouds in this easy-to-read book. Two others in this series are: *Ice Is . . . Whee!; Shine, Sun!* (both 1983).

6356 Greer, Gery, and Bob Ruddick. *Billy the Ghost and Me* (2–4). Illus. by Roger Roth. Series: I Can Read. 1997, HarperCollins LB $15.89 (0-06-026783-6). 48pp. Sarah and friend Billy the Ghost capture a gang of bank robbers. (Rev: BL 11/15/96; SLJ 3/97)

6357 Griffith, Helen V. *Alex and the Cat* (2–3). Illus. 1997, Greenwillow $15.00 (0-688-15241-4). 56pp. Contains seven charming short stories about the adventures of Alex the dog and his cat friend. (Rev: BL 10/15/97; HBG 3/98; SLJ 10/97)

6358 Grimes, Nikki. *Wild, Wild Hair* (1–2). Illus. by George Ford. Series: Hello Reader! 1997, Scholastic $3.99 (0-590-26590-3). A young African American girl dreads Monday, when her hair is braided, in this easy-to-read book. (Rev: BL 5/1/97; SLJ 4/97)

6359 Grindley, Sally. *The Giant Postman* (K–3). Illus. by Wendy Smith. Series: I Am Reading. 2000, Kingfisher paper $3.95 (0-7534-5319-3). 44pp. An oversize postman causes damage in the neighborhood until a brave young boy solves the problem. (Rev: SLJ 2/01)

6360 Gruber, Wilhelm. *The Upside-Down Reader* (2–3). Trans. from German by J. Alison James. Illus. by Marlies Rieper-Bastian. 1998, North-South LB $13.88 (1-55858-975-9). 60pp. A beginning chapter book in which Tim's older sister is learning to read, and he decides to try as well. (Rev: HBG 3/99; SLJ 12/98)

6361 Guilfoile, Elizabeth. *Nobody Listens to Andrew* (1–3). Illus. by Mary Stevens. 1957, Modern Curriculum paper $5.10 (0-8136-5959-0). The reaction of Andrew's elders when he tells them there is a bear in his bed.

6362 Gutelle, Andrew. *Baseball's Best: Five True Stories* (2–4). Illus. by Cliff Spohn. 1990, Random paper $3.99 (0-394-80983-1). 48pp. Special moments in the careers of five famous players. (Rev: BCCB 6/90; BL 6/1/90) [796.357]

6363 Hall, Kirsten. *At the Carnival* (K–1). Illus. by Laura Rader. 1996, Scholastic $3.99 (0-590-68994-0). 32pp. An easy reader that uses detachable pages and a trip to the carnival to introduce language. (Rev: BL 2/1/97)

6364 Hall, Lynn. *Barry: The Bravest Saint Bernard* (2–4). Illus. by Antonio Castro. Series: Step into Reading. 1992, Random paper $3.99 (0-679-83054-5). 48pp. The true story of a Saint Bernard dog that saved 40 lives in Switzerland. (Rev: BL 3/1/93) [636.7]

6365 Hanel, Wolfram. *Mia the Beach Cat* (1–3). Trans. from German by J. Alison James. Illus. by Kirsten Hocker. Series: Michael Neugebauer Books. 1994, North-South LB $12.88 (1-55858-315-7). 45pp. In this easy-to-read story, a little girl gradually persuades her parents to let her keep a kitten she has found on the beach. (Rev: BCCB 1/95; SLJ 12/94)

6366 Hanel, Wolfram. *Old Mahony and the Bear Family* (1–3). Trans. by Rosemary Lanning. Illus. 1997, North-South LB $13.88 (1-55858-714-4). 46pp. Old Mahony enjoys salmon fishing with Big Bill the bear; but when Bill's family appears, he wonders about their future together. (Rev: BL 9/15/97; SLJ 7/97)

6367 Harshman, Terry Webb. *Porcupine's Pajama Party* (1–3). Illus. by Doug Cushman. 1988, Harper-Collins $9.00 (0-06-022248-4); paper $3.95 (0-06-444140-7). 64pp. Porcupine, Otter, and Owl can't sleep after watching a scary movie. (Rev: BL 7/88; SLJ 10/88)

6368 Haskins, Lori. *Ducks in Muck* (K–1). Illus. by Valeria Petrone. Series: Step into Reading. 2000, Random paper $3.99 (0-679-89166-8). 32pp. A simple humorous tale about ducks that escape from trucks stuck in muck. (Rev: BL 4/15/00; HBG 10/00; SLJ 2/01)

6369 Hathorn, Elizabeth. *The Tram to Bondi Beach* (1–3). Illus. by Julie Vivas. 1989, Kane/Miller $12.95 (0-916291-20-0). 32pp. Paperboy Keiran decides that one day he will be the driver of the tram. (Rev: BL 6/1/89; HB 7–8/89)

6370 Hautzig, Deborah. *Little Witch Goes to School* (K–3). Illus. by Sylvie Wickstrom. Series: Step into Reading. 1998, Random paper $3.99 (0-679-88738-5). 47pp. When she promises to be bad, Little Witch is allowed to go to school, where she breaks her promise by being a good and cooperative student. (Rev: SLJ 1/99)

6371 Hautzig, Deborah. *The Nutcracker Ballet* (1–3). Illus. by Carolyn Ewing. 1992, Random paper $3.99 (0-679-82385-9). 48pp. In a simple narrative, this is the story of the Nutcracker. (Rev: BL 12/1/92)

6372 Hayes, Geoffrey. *The Secret of Foghorn Island* (2–3). Illus. by author. 1988, Random paper $3.99 (0-394-89614-9). 48pp. Otto and Uncle Tooth investigate four shipwrecks on the island. (Rev: BL 10/1/88; SLJ 12/88)

6373 Hayes, Geoffrey. *Treasure of the Lost Lagoon* (2–3). Illus. Series: Step into Reading. 1992, Random paper $3.99 (0-679-81484-1). 48pp. Otto tries to befriend sad Ducky Doodle by taking him on a picnic. (Rev: SLJ 4/92)

6374 Hayward, Linda. *Baker, Baker, Cookie Maker* (PS–K). Illus. by Tom Brannon. Series: Step into Reading. 1998, CTW paper $3.99 (0-679-88379-7). 23pp. In this easy-reader, Sesame Street's Cookie Monster bakes tray after tray of cookies, but there are never any cookies left for him. (Rev: SLJ 2/99)

6375 Hazen, Barbara S. *Digby* (1). Illus. by Barbara J. Phillips-Duke. Series: I Can Read. 1997, Harper-Collins LB $15.89 (0-06-026254-0). 32pp. A boy finds that the family dog is getting too old to play with him. (Rev: BL 11/15/96; SLJ 2/97)

6376 Heilbroner, Joan. *Tom the TV Cat* (1–2). Illus. by Sal Murdocca. 1984, Random paper $3.59 (0-394-86708-4). 48pp. Tom wants to do all the things he sees on TV.

6377 Hennessy, B. G. *Busy Dinah Dinosaur* (K–1). Illus. by Ana Martín Larrañaga. Series: Brand New Reader. 2000, Candlewick $10.99 (0-7636-1140-9). 40pp. There are four simple stories in this beginning reader about Dinah Dinosaur and her daily activities, like playing in the mud. (Rev: BL 12/1/00; HBG 3/01; SLJ 3/01)

6378 Hennessy, B. G. *Meet Dinah Dinosaur* (K–1). Illus. by Ana Martín Larrañaga. Series: Brand New Reader. 2000, Candlewick $10.99 (0-7636-1133-6). 32pp. This small easy-to-read book contains four very short stories about Dinah Dinosaur and her friend Doug. (Rev: BL 10/1/00; HBG 3/01; SLJ 2/01)

6379 Herman, Gail. *Double-Header* (1–2). Illus. by Jerry Smath. 1993, Putnam paper $3.95 (0-448-40157-6). 32pp. Monsters Bob and Rob, who share the same body, but with two heads, discuss their dilemma. (Rev: BL 12/1/93; SLJ 2/94)

6380 Herman, Gail. *Flower Girl* (PS–2). Illus. by Paige Billin-Frye. Series: All Aboard Reading. 1996, Putnam LB $13.99 (0-448-41107-5); paper $3.99 (0-448-41108-3). 48pp. A beginning reader about an unsentimental girl who finds that her lucky ring saves her wedding day from being a disaster. (Rev: BCCB 9/96; SLJ 8/96)

6381 Herman, Gail. *My Dog Talks* (PS–2). Illus. by Ron Fritz. Series: Hello Reader! 1995, Scholastic paper $3.99 (0-590-22196-5). A beginning reader that describes the bond between a boy and his dog as so close that they seem to talk to each other. (Rev: SLJ 9/95)

6382 Herman, R. A. *Pal the Pony* (1–2). Illus. 1996, Putnam paper $3.99 (0-448-41257-8). 32pp. A pony named Pal shows his true talents at a rodeo. (Rev: BL 8/96; SLJ 7/96)

6383 Hill, Eric. *Spot Goes to School* (PS). Illus. by author. 1984, Putnam paper $12.99 (0-399-21073-3). 22pp. A book that tells the story of a young dog. Two others in this series are: *Spot's First Walk* (1981); *Spot's Birthday Party* (1982).

6384 Hill, Eric. *Spot Goes to the Circus* (PS). Illus. by author. 1986, Putnam $12.99 (0-399-21317-1). 22pp. Spot loses his ball at the circus, and readers help him peer into the lion's jaws or the tiger's cage to find it. Also use: *Spot Goes to the Beach* (1985). (Rev: BL 8/86; HB 11–12/86; SLJ 12/86)

6385 Himmelman, John. *The Animal Rescue Club* (1–3). Illus. by author. Series: An I Can Read Book. 1998, HarperCollins LB $14.89 (0-06-027409-3). 46pp. In this easy reader, members of the Animal Rescue Club take a number of creatures in distress to a hospital and later return them to their natural habitats. (Rev: HBG 10/98; SLJ 6/98)

6386 Himmelman, John. *The Clover County Carrot Contest* (1–2). Illus. 1991, Silver Burdett paper $3.50 (0-671-69641-6). 48pp. Each member of a family of inventive bears tries to grow the best carrot. Also use: *The Super Camper Caper* (1991). (Rev: BL 6/1/91; SLJ 10/91)

6387 Himmelman, John. *The Ups and Downs of Simpson Snail* (1–3). Illus. 1997, Puffin paper $3.99 (0-14-038726-9). 48pp. In four easily read chapters, the innocent Simpson Snail has many adventures. (Rev: BL 12/1/89; SLJ 12/89)

6388 Hoban, Julia. *Quick Chick* (2–3). Illus. by Lillian Hoban. 1995, Puffin paper $3.99 (0-14-036664-4). 32pp. Quick Chick earns his name when the cat arrives. (Rev: BL 6/1/89)

6389 Hoban, Lillian. *Arthur's Back to School Day* (1–2). Illus. Series: I Can Read. 1996, Harper-Collins LB $15.89 (0-06-024956-0). 48pp. Arthur and friends are confused by a lunch box mix-up on the first day at school. (Rev: BL 9/15/96; SLJ 9/96)

6390 Hoban, Lillian. *Arthur's Birthday Party* (1–2). Illus. 1999, HarperCollins $14.95 (0-06-027798-X). 64pp. As expected at Arthur's birthday party, all his friends perform amazing gymnastic tricks, but Arthur wins the best all-round gymnast award. (Rev: BL 3/15/99; HB 1–2/99; HBG 10/99; SLJ 2/99)

6391 Hoban, Lillian. *Arthur's Camp-Out* (1–2). Illus. 1993, HarperCollins LB $15.89 (0-06-020526-1). 64pp. Arthur the chimp camps out by himself with unfortunate results. (Rev: BL 3/1/93; SLJ 4/93)

6392 Hoban, Lillian. *Arthur's Honey Bear* (1–3). Illus. by author. 1974, HarperCollins LB $15.89 (0-06-022370-7); paper $3.95 (0-06-444033-8). 64pp. Arthur, a chimp, decides to sell all his old toys except his bear, but his sisters bribe him into parting with Honey Bear. Three others in the series are: *Arthur's Pen Pal* (1976); *Arthur's Prize Reader* (1978); *Arthur's Funny Money* (1981).

6393 Hoban, Lillian. *Arthur's Loose Tooth* (1–3). Illus. by author. 1985, HarperCollins LB $15.89 (0-06-022354-5); paper $3.95 (0-06-444093-1). 64pp. Brave Arthur the chimp is afraid of blood, so how does he get rid of his loose tooth in order to eat taffy apples? (Rev: BL 10/15/85; HB 11–12/85; SLJ 12/85)

6394 Hoban, Lillian, and Phoebe Hoban. *Ready . . . Set . . . Robot!* (2–3). Illus. by Lillian Hoban. 1982, HarperCollins $11.95 (0-06-022345-6). 64pp. A robot, Sol-1, competes in a space race.

6395 Hoban, Russell. *Bedtime for Frances* (1–2). Illus. by Garth Williams. 1960, HarperCollins LB $13.89 (0-06-022351-0); paper $5.95 (0-06-443451-6). 32pp. Frances, a badger, tries every familiar trick to tease her way past bedtime. Others in the series: *Bread and Jam for Frances* (1965); *A Bargain for Frances* (1970).

6396 Hoban, Russell. *Best Friends for Frances* (1–2). Illus. by Lillian Hoban. 1969, HarperCollins LB $15.89 (0-06-022328-6); paper $5.95 (0-06-443008-1). 32pp. When friend Albert decides that he must exclude girls from his "wondering day" and baseball game, Frances chooses younger sister Gloria as a companion. Also use: *A Baby Sister for Frances* (1964).

6397 Hoff, Syd. *Albert the Albatross* (1–2). Illus. by author. 1961, HarperCollins LB $15.89 (0-06-022446-0). 32pp. A seabird's unsuccessful search for the ocean is rewarded by accompanying a lady who is going on an ocean trip.

6398 Hoff, Syd. *Barkley* (1–3). Illus. by author. 1975, HarperCollins LB $15.89 (0-06-022448-7). 32pp. An easily read story about a forcibly retired, aging circus dog.

6399 Hoff, Syd. *Barney's Horse* (1–3). Illus. by author. 1987, HarperCollins LB $15.89 (0-06-022450-9); paper $3.95 (0-06-444142-3). 32pp. Barney the peddler and his horse delight children, but elevated trains soon begin to rumble overhead. (Rev: BCCB 11/87; BL 10/1/87)

6400 Hoff, Syd. *Danny and the Dinosaur* (K–2). Illus. by author. 1958, HarperCollins LB $15.89 (0-06-022466-5); paper $3.95 (0-06-444002-8). 64pp. Danny wanted to play and so did the dinosaur. What could have been more natural than for them to leave the museum together? Also from the same author and publisher: *Sammy the Seal* (1959).

6401 Hoff, Syd. *Danny and the Dinosaur Go to Camp* (1–3). Illus. 1996, HarperCollins LB $15.89 (0-06-026440-3). 32pp. At summer camp, a dinosaur provides transportation for tired boys and girls. (Rev: BL 8/96; SLJ 6/96)

6402 Hoff, Syd. *Grizzwold* (1–2). Illus. by author. 1963, HarperCollins LB $15.89 (0-06-022481-9); paper $3.95 (0-06-444057-5). 64pp. After foresters have destroyed his home, a bear sets out to find a new one.

6403 Hoff, Syd. *Happy Birthday, Danny and the Dinosaur!* (1–3). Illus. 1995, HarperCollins LB $15.89 (0-06-026438-1). 32pp. Danny invites his friend the dinosaur to his birthday party in this easy-to-read book. (Rev: BCCB 10/95; BL 10/1/95; SLJ 9/95)

6404 Hoff, Syd. *The Lighthouse Children* (1–2). Illus. Series: I Can Read. 1994, HarperCollins LB $15.89 (0-06-022959-4). 32pp. After a storm destroys their lighthouse, two children must leave the seagulls they feed in this easy-to-read book. (Rev: BL 2/1/94; SLJ 4/94)

6405 Hoff, Syd. *Mrs. Brice's Mice* (PS–2). Illus. by author. 1988, HarperCollins LB $15.89 (0-06-022452-5); paper $3.95 (0-06-444145-8). 32pp. Mrs. Brice has 25 mice — one is an individualist. (Rev: BCCB 12/88; BL 12/1/88; SLJ 4/89)

6406 Hoff, Syd. *Sammy the Seal* (K–1). Illus. Series: I Can Read. 2000, HarperCollins LB $14.89 (0-06-028546-X). 64pp. After wandering from the zoo, a small seal discovers there is no place like home. (Rev: BL 12/1/99; HBG 10/00)

6407 Hoff, Syd. *Stanley* (1–3). Illus. by author. 1992, HarperCollins LB $15.89 (0-06-022536-X); paper $3.95 (0-06-444010-9). 64pp. A caveman finds a new home in this inventive tale.

6408 Hood, Susan. *I Am Mad!* (PS–1). Photos by Dorothy Handelman. Series: Real Kids Readers. 1999, Millbrook LB $16.90 (0-7613-2061-X); paper $3.99 (0-7613-2086-5). 28pp. For very beginning readers, this is a simple story of a bullying older sister. (Rev: SLJ 1/00)

6409 Hood, Susan. *Look! I Can Read!* (1). Illus. by Amy Wummer. Series: All Aboard Reading. 2000, Putnam $13.89 (0-448-42282-4); paper $3.99 (0-448-41967-X). 32pp. A little girl is thrilled as she passes from one stage to another in her mastery of reading. (Rev: BL 12/1/00; HBG 3/01)

6410 Hood, Susan. *The New Kid* (K–1). Illus. by Dorothy Handelman. Series: Real Kids Readers. 1998, Millbrook LB $16.90 (0-7613-2014-8); paper $3.99 (0-7613-2039-3). 32pp. Sid, a newcomer at school, acts strangely because he is uncomfortable, but one boy, who understands the situation, makes the effort to become his friend. (Rev: BL 11/1/98; SLJ 1/99)

6411 Hooks, William H. *Mr. Baseball* (2–3). Illus. by Paul Meisel. 1998, Gareth Stevens LB $18.60 (0-8368-1765-6); Bantam paper $4.50 (0-553-35303-9). 48pp. Five-year-old Eddie wants to get involved in baseball, but can't find his niche. (Rev: BCCB 11/91; BL 12/1/91; HBG 10/98)

6412 Hooks, William H. *Mr. Big Brother* (1–2). Illus. by Kate Duke. Series: Bank Street Ready-to-Read. 1999, Gareth Stevens $14.95 (0-8368-2417-2). 32pp. Eli is looking forward to having a new baby brother; when the baby arrives and it is a girl, Eli needs some time to adjust. (Rev: BL 2/15/00; HBG 10/00; SLJ 9/99)

6413 Howe, James. *Pinky and Rex and the Mean Old Witch* (2–3). Illus. by Melissa Sweet. 1991, Macmillan $15.00 (0-689-31617-8). 40pp. Rex wants to get even with mean Mrs. Morgan, but

Pinky thinks the old lady needs kindness. Also use: *Pinky and Rex and the Spelling Bee* (1991). (Rev: BL 4/15/91; SLJ 7/91)

6414 Howe, James. *Pinky and Rex and the New Baby* (K–3). Illus. by Melissa Sweet. 1994, Avon paper $3.99 (0-380-12083-3). 48pp. Rex and her best friend are nervous about the new baby Rex's parents are planning to adopt. (Rev: BL 3/1/93; SLJ 6/93)

6415 Howe, James. *Pinky and Rex and the New Neighbors* (1–3). Illus. by Melissa Sweet. 1997, Simon & Schuster $15.00 (0-689-80022-3); paper $3.99 (0-689-81296-5). 48pp. For beginning readers, this story tells how Rex worries about who will move next door when his beloved neighbor leaves. (Rev: BL 5/1/97; SLJ 6/97)

6416 Howe, James. *Pinky and Rex and the School Play* (2–3). Illus. by Melissa Sweet. 1998, Simon & Schuster $15.00 (0-689-31872-3); paper $3.99 (0-689-81704-5). 48pp. Pinky, who would like to be an actor, is angry when his best friend Rex, who has never shown an interest in acting, gets the star part in the school play. (Rev: BL 5/1/98; HBG 10/98; SLJ 5/98)

6417 Howe, James. *Pinky and Rex Get Married* (K–3). Illus. by Melissa Sweet. 1990, Simon & Schuster LB $11.95 (0-685-58512-3). 48pp. Two young friends, a 7-year-old girl and a boy named Pinky, are so close that they decide to get married. Also use: *Pinky and Rex* (1990). (Rev: BCCB 4/90; BL 4/15/90*; HB 3–4/90; SLJ 5/90)

6418 Howe, James. *Pinky and Rex Go to Camp* (2–3). Illus. by Melissa Sweet. 1992, Macmillan $12.95 (0-689-31718-2). 40pp. Pinky and Rex tackle the ups and downs of friendship when they get ready for sleep-away camp. (Rev: BL 4/1/92; SLJ 4/92)

6419 Hudson, Wade. *Jamal's Busy Day* (PS–1). Illus. by George Ford. 1991, Just Us LB $12.95 (0-940975-21-1); paper $6.95 (0-940975-24-6). Jamal, an African American boy, prepares with his parents for a busy day — he will spend his at school and they at work. (Rev: SLJ 2/92)

6420 Hurwitz, Johanna. *The Adventures of Ali Baba Bernstein* (2–4). Illus. 1985, Morrow $16.95 (0-688-04161-2); Avon paper $4.95 (0-380-72349-2). 96pp. Episodes in the life of David Bernstein, an 8-year-old who changes what he thinks is his boring name. Also use: *Hurray for Ali Baba Bernstein* (1989). (Rev: BCCB 6/85; BL 5/15/85; HB 5–6/85)

6421 Jewell, Nancy. *Two Silly Trolls* (1–2). Illus. by Lisa Thiesing. Series: I Can Read. 1994, HarperCollins paper $3.95 (0-06-444173-3). 64pp. Four simple stories about the trolls Nip and Tuck. (Rev: BL 6/15/92; SLJ 2/93)

6422 Johansen, K. V. *Pippin and the Bones* (PS–2). Illus. by Bernice Lum. 2000, Kids Can $12.95 (1-55074-629-4). 32pp. For beginning readers, this is the story of a dog named Pippin who digs up some huge bones that his master gives to the museum. (Rev: BL 8/00; HBG 10/00; SLJ 8/00)

6423 Johnson, Crockett. *Harold and the Purple Crayon* (K–2). Illus. by author. 1958, HarperCollins paper $5.95 (0-06-443022-7). 64pp. A little boy draws all of the things necessary for him to go for a walk. Three sequels are: *Harold's Trip to the Sky* (1957); *Harold's Circus* (1959); *A Picture for Harold's Room* (1960).

6424 Johnston, Tony. *The Bull and the Fire Truck* (1–2). Illus. by R. W. Alley. 1996, Scholastic $3.99 (0-590-47597-5). 32pp. An easily read book about how a community accommodates a bull that hates the color red. (Rev: BL 2/1/97)

6425 Johnston, Tony. *Sparky and Eddie: The First Day of School* (1–2). Illus. by Susannah Ryan. Series: Hello Reader! 1997, Scholastic $13.95 (0-590-47978-4); paper $3.99 (0-590-47979-2). 32pp. In this easy reader, friends Sparky and Eddie decide that they won't start school if they can't be in the same rooms. (Rev: BL 8/97; HBG 3/98; SLJ 9/97)

6426 Johnston, Tony. *Sparky and Eddie: Wild, Wild Rodeo* (1–2). Illus. by Susannah Ryan. Series: Hello Reader! 1998, Scholastic $13.95 (0-590-47984-9). 40pp. Two friends, Sparky and Eddie, are crushed when their class doesn't win the school rodeo contests, such as roping teddy bears. (Rev: BL 5/1/98; HBG 10/98; SLJ 5/98)

6427 Jordan, Taylor. *Hiccup* (1). Illus. by Frank Remkiewicz. 1998, Golden Bks. paper $3.99 (0-307-26103-4). 32pp. Hippo tries everything to rid himself of the hiccups and finally finds the solution — wearing a chicken costume. (Rev: BL 3/15/99)

6428 Karlin, Nurit. *The Fat Cat Sat on the Mat* (1–2). Illus. 1996, HarperCollins LB $14.89 (0-06-026674-0). 32pp. A witch's rat can't budge a cat from a favorite resting place, the mat. (Rev: BCCB 10/96; BL 9/15/96; SLJ 12/96)

6429 Keenan, Sheila. *More or Less a Mess* (1–2). Illus. by Patrick Girouard. Series: Hello Math Reader. 1997, Scholastic $3.99 (0-590-60248-9). When a girl is told by her mother to tidy up her room, she doesn't know where to begin, so she puts everything under the covers of her bed. (Rev: BL 5/1/97)

6430 Keller, Holly. *A Bed Full of Cats* (1–2). Illus. Series: Green Light. 1999, Harcourt $10.95 (0-15-202331-3); paper $3.95 (0-15-202262-7). 20pp. Lee's cat, Flora, likes to sleep on his bed, but one night she disappears, and later Lee discovers it is to have her kittens. (Rev: BL 10/1/99; HBG 3/00; SLJ 11/99)

6431 Keller, Holly. *What I See* (1). Illus. Series: Green Light. 1999, Harcourt paper $3.95 (0-15-201996-0). 20pp. A young boy sees all sorts of things during his walk, including his reflection in a pond. (Rev: BL 5/15/99)

6432 Kessler, Ethel, and Leonard Kessler. *Stan the Hot Dog Man* (1–3). Illus. 1990, HarperCollins LB $15.89 (0-06-023280-3). 64pp. In all kinds of weather, Stan sells his hot dogs to satisfied customers. (Rev: BCCB 3/90; BL 4/1/90; SLJ 7/90)

6433 Kessler, Leonard. *Here Comes the Strikeout* (1–2). Illus. by author. 1992, HarperCollins LB $15.89 (0-06-023156-4); paper $3.95 (0-06-444011-7). 64pp. Bobby always strikes out at bat until his friend Willie helps him to improve his game. Two other sports stories by the same author and publisher

are: *Kick, Pass and Run* (1966); *Last One in Is a Rotten Egg* (1969). (Rev: BL 12/1/92)

6434 Kessler, Leonard. *Last One In Is a Rotten Egg* (1–2). Illus. Series: I Can Read. 1999, HarperCollins LB $14.89 (0-06-028485-4). 64pp. After Freddy takes swimming lessons, he can go into the deep end of the pool without fear. (Rev: BL 10/1/99; HBG 3/00)

6435 Krensky, Stephen. *Buster's Dino Dilemma* (1–3). Illus. by Marc Brown. Series: A Marc Brown Arthur Chapter Book. 1998, Little, Brown paper $3.95 (0-316-11560-6). 58pp. Based on scripts used in the PBS series, this easy chapter book involves Arthur and a fossil he has found during a school field trip. Also use *Locked in the Library!* (1998). (Rev: HBG 10/98; SLJ 11/98)

6436 Krensky, Stephen. *Lionel at School* (K–2). Illus. by Susanna Natti. Series: Easy-to-Read. 2000, Dial $13.99 (0-8037-2457-8). 48pp. The four easy-to-read stories in this book about Lionel focus on his experiences at school. (Rev: BL 10/1/00; HBG 3/01; SLJ 9/00)

6437 Krensky, Stephen. *Lionel in the Spring* (1–3). Illus. by Susanna Natti. Series: Easy-to-Read. 1997, Viking paper $3.99 (0-14-038463-4). In the spring of the year, Lionel engages in all sorts of activities. (Rev: BL 4/1/90; HB 7–8/90; SLJ 3/90)

6438 Krensky, Stephen. *Lionel in the Summer* (1–2). Illus. by Susanna Natti. Series: Dial Easy-to-Read. 1998, Dial LB $13.89 (0-8037-2244-3). 48pp. This book features four short stories about Lionel and his everyday adventures — some with his sister Louise. (Rev: BL 7/98; HBG 10/98; SLJ 9/98)

6439 Krensky, Stephen. *My Loose Tooth* (1). Illus. by Hideko Takahashi. Series: Step into Reading. 1999, Random LB $11.99 (0-679-98847-5). 32pp. In this easily read story, a young boy discovers, while brushing his teeth, that he has a loose tooth, and soon he can't forget it. (Rev: BL 3/15/99; HBG 10/99; SLJ 8/99)

6440 Krensky, Stephen. *We Just Moved!* (1–2). Illus. by Larry DiFiori. Series: Hello Reader! 1998, Scholastic paper $3.50 (0-590-33127-2). 32pp. Set during the Middle Ages, this humorous story tells of a young boy's move to a new castle and how this compares with a change of homes in modern times. (Rev: BL 7/98)

6441 Kueffner, Sue. *Our New Baby* (PS–1). Illus. by Dorothy Stott. Series: All-Star Readers. 1999, Reader's Digest paper $3.99 (1-57584-292-0). 31pp. A beginning reader about the upheaval caused by the arrival of a new baby as seen by her older sister. (Rev: SLJ 7/99)

6442 Kuskin, Karla. *Soap Soup and Other Verses* (1–3). Illus. 1994, HarperCollins paper $3.50 (0-06-444174-1). 64pp. This easily read book contains simple poems about a variety of everyday objects and experiences. (Rev: BCCB 6/92; BL 4/1/92; SLJ 4/92) [811]

6443 Kwitz, Mary D. *Gumshoe Goose, Private Eye* (2–3). Illus. by Lisa Campbell Ernst. 1996, Puffin paper $3.99 (0-14-036194-4). 48pp. Gumshoe

Goose to the rescue of the kidnapped Baby Chick-Chick. (Rev: BL 12/1/88; SLJ 12/88)

6444 Larson, Kirby. *Cody and Quinn, Sitting in a Tree* (2–3). Illus. 1996, Holiday $14.95 (0-8234-1227-X). 64pp. Cody is teased by a bully because of his friendship with a girl, Quinn. (Rev: BCCB 9/96; BL 4/1/96; SLJ 4/96)

6445 Lavis, Steve. *Little Mouse Has a Busy Day* (PS–K). Illus. by author. 2000, Ragged Bears $6.95 (1-929766-10-X). This book for beginning readers traces the hour-by-hour activities of Little Mouse from getting up at 8 A.M. to bedtime at 6. Also use *Little Mouse Has an Adventure.* (Rev: SLJ 1/01)

6446 Lawlor, Laurie. *The Worst Kid Who Ever Lived on Eighth Avenue* (1–2). Illus. by Cynthia Fisher. 1998, Holiday $14.95 (0-8234-1350-0). 48pp. Mary Lou and her friends are convinced that big bad Leroy is up to no good when he buries a large bag in his backyard. (Rev: BL 5/1/98; HBG 10/98; SLJ 4/98)

6447 Leonard, Marcia. *Best Friends* (PS–1). Photos by Dorothy Handelman. Series: Real Kids Readers. 1999, Millbrook LB $16.90 (0-7613-2064-4); paper $3.99 (0-7613-2089-X). 30pp. In this simple story for very beginning readers that is illustrated with photographs, two girls describe their similarities and differences. (Rev: SLJ 1/00)

6448 Leonard, Marcia. *Dan and Dan* (PS–1). Photos by Dorothy Handelman. Series: Real Kids Readers. 1998, Millbrook LB $16.90 (0-7613-2003-2); paper $3.99 (0-7613-2028-8). 31pp. A beginning reader that tells of the loving relationship between a young boy and his namesake and grandfather. (Rev: SLJ 6/98)

6449 Leonard, Marcia. *Get the Ball, Slim* (1). Illus. by Dorothy Handelman. Series: Real Kids Readers. 1998, Millbrook LB $16.90 (0-7613-2000-8); paper $3.99 (0-7613-2025-3). 32pp. Using photographs for illustrations, this simple reader tells about African American twins Tim and Jim and their dog Slim. (Rev: BL 5/1/98; HBG 10/98; SLJ 6/98)

6450 Leonard, Marcia. *I Like Mess* (1). Illus. by Dorothy Handelman. Series: Real Kids Readers. 1998, Millbrook LB $16.90 (0-7613-2002-4); paper $3.99 (0-7613-2027-X). 32pp. In this simple reader illustrated with photographs, a young girl tries to please her mother by cleaning up the mess she has created. (Rev: BL 5/1/98; SLJ 6/98)

6451 Leonard, Marcia. *My Pal Al* (PS–1). Photos by Dorothy Handelman. Series: Real Kids Readers. 1998, Millbrook LB $16.90 (0-7613-2001-6); paper $3.99 (0-7613-2026-1). 31pp. A beginning reader that describes how a little African American girl loves her favorite toy. (Rev: SLJ 6/98)

6452 Leonard, Marcia. *No New Pants!* (1). Illus. by Dorothy Handelman. Series: Real Kids Readers. 1999, Millbrook LB $16.90 (0-7613-2063-6); paper $3.99 (0-7613-2088-1). 32pp. A young African American child doesn't want to go shopping for pants with his mother, but he enjoys getting a pair of hand-me-downs from his brother. (Rev: BL 12/1/99; HBG 3/00)

6453 Le Sieg, Theo. *Ten Apples Up on Top* (K–2). Illus. 1961, Random LB $11.99 (0-394-90019-7). 72pp. Three bears try to pile apples on their heads in this nonsense story. Also from the same author and publisher: *I Wish That I Had Duck Feet* (1965); *Eye Book* (1968).

6454 Levinson, Nancy S. *Clara and the Bookwagon* (1–2). Illus. by Carolyn Croll. 1988, HarperCollins LB $15.89 (0-06-023838-0); paper $3.95 (0-06-444134-2). 64pp. A real-life story about a young girl who wants to read despite her father's objections. (Rev: BL 4/1/88; SLJ 7/88)

6455 Levy, Elizabeth. *The Creepy Computer Mystery* (2–3). Illus. by Denise Brunkus. 1996, Scholastic paper $3.99 (0-590-60322-1). 48pp. The trio Invisible Ink solves the mystery of the online intruder. (Rev: BL 9/15/96)

6456 Levy, Elizabeth. *The Karate Class Mystery* (2–4). Illus. by Denise Brunkus. 1996, Scholastic $3.99 (0-590-60323-X). 48pp. A mystery in which Justin's karate belt disappears and the culprit must be caught. (Rev: BL 2/1/97)

6457 Levy, Elizabeth. *The Mystery of the Missing Dog* (2–3). Illus. 1995, Scholastic paper $3.99 (0-590-47484-7). 44pp. Invisible Chip loses his invisible dog, Max, but solves a mystery with the help of friends Justin and Charlene. (Rev: BL 1/1–15/96)

6458 Levy, Elizabeth. *Parents' Night Fright* (2–4). Illus. by Denise Brunkus. 1998, Scholastic paper $3.99 (0-590-60324-8). 48pp. When Charlene's prize-winning story disappears, she and buddies Justin, who is deaf, and the invisible Chip set out to solve the mystery. (Rev: BL 7/98; SLJ 9/98)

6459 Lewin, Betsy. *Wiley Learns to Spell* (PS–1). Illus. by author. Series: Hello Reader! 1998, Scholastic paper $3.50 (0-590-10835-2). In this easy reader, Wiley, a mischievous monster, makes words out of an armload of colorful block letters. (Rev: SLJ 2/99)

6460 Lewis, Rob. *Grandpa at the Beach* (2–3). Illus. 1998, Mondo paper $4.50 (1-57255-552-1). 47pp. A grandfather bear and his grandson, Finley, investigate the reports that a beach house contains a monster and discover it is only Dad. (Rev: BL 7/98)

6461 Lewis, Rob. *Too Much Trouble for Grandpa* (2–3). Illus. 1998, Mondo paper $4.50 (1-57255-551-3). 47pp. Grandpa Bear brings home things he believes will not cause problems, such as a cat and a girlfriend, but in each case he is wrong. (Rev: BL 7/98)

6462 Little, Jean. *Emma's Magic Winter* (1–2). Illus. by Jennifer Plecas. 1998, HarperCollins $14.95 (0-06-025389-4). 64pp. Though Emma is basically very shy, she is brave enough to make a good friend of Sally, the new girl next door. (Rev: BCCB 10/98; BL 11/1/98; HB 9–10/98*; HBG 3/99; SLJ 10/98)

6463 Little, Jean. *Emma's Yucky Brother* (1–2). Illus. by Jennifer Plecas. Series: I Can Read. 2001, HarperCollins LB $14.89 (0-06-028349-1). 64pp. In this book for beginning readers, Emma has mixed feelings when her family adopts a 4-year-old boy. (Rev: BL 12/1/00; SLJ 1/01)

6464 Lobel, Arnold. *Frog and Toad Are Friends* (K–2). Illus. by author. 1970, HarperCollins LB $15.89 (0-06-023958-1); paper $3.90 (0-06-444020-6). 64pp. Two new friends for the independent reader. Three sequels are: *Frog and Toad Together* (1972); *Frog and Toad All Year* (1976); *Days with Frog and Toad* (1979).

6465 Lobel, Arnold. *Grasshopper on the Road* (1–2). Illus. by author. 1978, HarperCollins LB $15.89 (0-06-023962-X); paper $3.95 (0-06-444094-X). 64pp. A series of short stories, each with a vital message.

6466 Lobel, Arnold. *Mouse Soup* (1–2). Illus. by author. 1977, HarperCollins LB $15.89 (0-06-023968-9); paper $3.95 (0-06-444041-9). 64pp. When Mouse is caught by Weasel, who plans to use him for soup, he convinces his captor that "mouse soup must be mixed with stones to make it taste really good."

6467 Lobel, Arnold. *Mouse Tales* (1–2). Illus. by author. 1972, HarperCollins LB $15.89 (0-06-023942-5); paper $3.95 (0-06-444013-3). 64pp. Seven bedtime stories told by Papa Mouse to his seven sons. Lively little drawings add to the humor.

6468 Lobel, Arnold. *Owl at Home* (1–2). Illus. by author. 1975, HarperCollins LB $15.89 (0-06-023949-2); paper $3.95 (0-06-444034-6). 64pp. Five stories dealing with the humorous and bungling attempts of Owl to be helpful.

6469 Lobel, Arnold. *Small Pig* (K–2). Illus. by author. 1969, HarperCollins LB $15.89 (0-06-023932-8); paper $3.95 (0-06-444120-2). 64pp. A dirty little pig in a search for mud ends up in cement.

6470 Lobel, Arnold. *Uncle Elephant* (K–3). Illus. by author. 1981, HarperCollins LB $15.89 (0-06-023980-8); paper $3.95 (0-06-444104-0). 64pp. A nephew and uncle elephant form a friendship.

6471 Loehr, Mallory, adapt. *Babe: A Little Pig Goes a Long Way* (1–2). Illus. by Christopher Moroney. Series: Beginner Books. 1999, Random $7.99 (0-375-80110-3). This *Babe* movie tie-in is a version of the pig's life written for beginning readers. (Rev: HBG 10/99; SLJ 9/99)

6472 London, Jonathan. *Shawn and Keeper and the Birthday Party* (1). Illus. by Renee Williams-Andriani. Series: Green Light. 1999, Dutton $13.99 (0-525-46115-9). 32pp. An easy reader in which a little girl imitates the actions of a number of farm animals. (Rev: BL 10/1/99; HBG 3/00; SLJ 11/99)

6473 London, Jonathan. *Shawn and Keeper Show-and-Tell* (1–2). Illus. by Renee Williams-Andriani. 2000, Dutton $13.99 (0-525-46114-0). 32pp. In this easy reader, Shawn makes a bad mistake when he decides to take his dog to school to show off the tricks he has taught him. (Rev: BL 4/15/00; SLJ 9/00)

6474 Lopshire, Robert. *Put Me in the Zoo* (1–3). Illus. by author. 1960, Beginner Books $7.99 (0-394-80017-6). 72pp. An unusual dog thinks he should be in the zoo, but his talents really mean he should be in a circus.

6475 Lunn, Carolyn. *A Whisper Is Quiet* (1–2). Illus. by Clovis Martin. 1989, Children's LB $18.00 (0-516-02087-0); paper $4.95 (0-516-42087-9). 32pp. A concept book introduces opposites. (Rev: BL 3/1/89)

6476 Maccarone, Grace. *The Gym Day Winner* (PS–1). Illus. 1996, Scholastic paper $3.99 (0-590-26263-7). 32pp. A youngster finds a sport at which he excels. (Rev: BL 8/96; SLJ 1/97)

6477 Maccarone, Grace. *I Shop with My Daddy* (1). Illus. by Denise Brunkus. Series: Hello Reader! 1998, Scholastic paper $3.50 (0-590-50196-8). 32pp. A little girl and her father go shopping, and as a last item, he allows her something sweet — a frozen yogurt. (Rev: BL 7/98)

6478 Maccarone, Grace. *The Lunch Box Surprise* (1). Illus. by Betsy Lewin. 1995, Scholastic paper $3.99 (0-590-26267-X). 32pp. First-grader Sam is surprised at school when he finds that his mother hasn't packed his lunch. (Rev: BL 1/1–15/96)

6479 Maccarone, Grace. *My Tooth Is About to Fall Out* (1–2). Illus. by Betsy Lewin. 1995, Scholastic $3.99 (0-590-48376-5). 32pp. An easy-to-read book about the problems of having a loose tooth. (Rev: BL 7/95)

6480 Maccarone, Grace. *Recess Mess* (1–2). Illus. by Betsy Lewin. Series: Hello Reader! 1996, Scholastic paper $3.99 (0-590-73878-X). 32pp. Sam has trouble determining which bathroom is for boys in this easily read school story. (Rev: BL 2/1/97)

6481 Maccarone, Grace. *Sharing Time Troubles* (PS–1). Illus. by Betsy Lewin. Series: Hello Reader! 1997, Scholastic paper $3.50 (0-590-73879-8). For a school show-and-tell session, Sam gets a brilliant idea and brings his pesky younger brother. (Rev: BL 5/1/97; SLJ 7/97)

6482 McClintock, Mike. *Stop That Ball!* (1–3). Illus. by Fritz Siebel. 1959, Beginner Books $7.99 (0-394-80010-9). Chasing a bouncing ball becomes a big adventure in this reissued picture book.

6483 McCully, Emily Arnold. *The Grandma Mix-Up* (1–3). Illus. by author. 1988, HarperCollins LB $15.89 (0-06-024202-7); paper $3.95 (0-06-444150-4). 64pp. Two grandmothers with very different ways arrive to baby-sit. (Rev: BL 12/1/89; SLJ 3/89)

6484 McCully, Emily Arnold. *Grandmas at Bat* (1–2). Illus. 1993, HarperCollins paper $3.95 (0-06-444193-8). 64pp. Pip's two grandmothers, last-minute replacements, coach his baseball team. (Rev: BL 3/1/93; HB 7–8/93; SLJ 6/93)

6485 McCully, Emily Arnold. *Grandma's at the Lake* (1–3). Illus. 1990, HarperCollins $10.95 (0-06-024126-8); paper $3.95 (0-06-444177-6). 64pp. While sharing a lakeside cabin, Nan and Sal find it hard to accept their grandma's advice. (Rev: BCCB 5/90; BL 4/1/90; SLJ 6/90)

6486 MacDonald, Maryann. *Hedgehog Bakes a Cake* (K–2). Illus. by Lynn Munsinger. Series: Bank Street Ready-to-Read. 1990, Bantam paper $4.50 (0-553-34890-6). There is mayhem when Hedgehog's friends help him bake a cake. (Rev: SLJ 5/91)

6487 McDonald, Megan. *Beezy and Funnybone* (1–2). Illus. by Nancy Poydar. Series: Beezy. 2000, Orchard LB $15.99 (0-531-33211-X); paper $4.95 (0-531-07161-8). 48pp. A book for beginning readers that contains three simple stories about a little girl and her dog Funnybone. (Rev: BL 7/00; HBG 10/00; SLJ 9/00)

6488 McDonald, Megan. *Beezy at Bat* (1–2). Illus. by Nancy Poydar. 1998, Orchard LB $14.99 (0-531-33085-0). 48pp. In this, the third book about Beezy, she plays baseball, exchanges riddles with Gran, and scares a friend with a snake. (Rev: BL 11/1/98; HBG 3/99; SLJ 9/98)

6489 McDonald, Megan. *Beezy Magic* (2–4). Illus. by Nancy Poydar. 1997, Orchard LB $14.99 (0-531-33064-8). 48pp. Three easily read short stories involving carrot-haired Beezy, her family, and her dog. (Rev: BL 7/98; HBG 10/98; SLJ 4/98)

6490 McDonald, Megan. *Lucky Star* (1–3). Illus. by Andrea Wallace. Series: Road to Reading. 2000, Golden Bks. paper $3.99 (0-307-26329-0). 48pp. When Star accidentally damages her library book, she decides to earn money to replace it. (Rev: SLJ 3/01)

6491 McKay, Sindy. *Ben and Becky in the Haunted House* (1–3). Illus. by Meredith Johnson. Series: We Both Read. 1999, Treasure Bay $7.99 (1-891327-14-3); paper $3.99 (1-891327-18-6). The story of two children who are forced to spend a night in a haunted house is told with two texts, one for adults and the other for beginning readers. (Rev: SLJ 11/99)

6492 McKissack, Patricia. *Monkey-Monkey's Trick: Based on an African Folk Tale* (1–3). Illus. by Paul Meisel. 1988, Random paper $3.99 (0-394-89173-2). 48pp. Monkey-Monkey needs help building his new house in this amusing fable. (Rev: BL 3/1/89)

6493 McKissack, Patricia, and Fredrick McKissack. *Messy Bessey's Family Reunion* (K–1). Illus. by Dana Regan. Series: Rookie Readers. 2000, Children's LB $18.00 (0-516-20830-6); paper $4.95 (0-516-26552-0). 32pp. In this easy reader, Messy Bessey is so upset at the mess she and her relatives have made at an outdoor picnic that she organizes them into a clean-up squad. (Rev: BL 12/1/00)

6494 McKissack, Patricia, and Fredrick McKissack. *Messy Bessey's Holidays* (PS–2). Illus. by Dana Regan. Series: Rookie Readers. 1999, Children's LB $17.00 (0-516-20829-2). 30pp. In this beginning reader, a child bakes cookies for her friends for Hanukkah, Christmas, and Kwanzaa. (Rev: HBG 10/99; SLJ 8/99)

6495 McPhail, David. *Big Brown Bear* (1–2). Illus. Series: Green Light. 1999, Harcourt paper $3.95 (0-15-201999-5). 20pp. Big Bear has bad luck every time he tries to paint his tree house in this easy-to-read, humorous story. (Rev: BL 5/15/99; SLJ 4/99)

6496 McPhail, David. *A Bug, a Bear, and a Boy* (1–2). Illus. 1998, Scholastic paper $3.50 (0-590-14904-0). 32pp. A young boy spends an enjoyable day with his two companions, a bear and a bug. (Rev: BL 11/1/98)

6497 McPhail, David. *The Day the Sheep Showed Up* (1–2). Illus. Series: Hello Reader! 1998, Scholastic paper $3.50 (0-590-84910-7). 32pp. An uproarious farce in which the other animals try to find out what sort of being is a sheep after it unexpectedly joins the farm community. (Rev: BL 5/1/98)

6498 McPhail, David. *A Girl, a Goat, and a Goose* (1). Illus. 2000, Scholastic paper $3.99 (0-439-09978-1). 32pp. Three good friends — a girl, a goose, and a goat — share four amiable adventures in this book for beginning readers. (Rev: BL 12/1/00)

6499 McPhail, David. *The Great Race* (1–2). Illus. Series: Hello Reader! 1998, Scholastic paper $3.50 (0-590-84909-3). 32pp. In this humorous easy reader, the animals have a race and, in spite of many mistakes, end together — each one a winner! (Rev: BL 5/1/98)

6500 McPhail, David. *Snow Lion* (PS–2). Illus. by author. 1983, Parents LB $5.00 (0-8193-1098-0). 48pp. A lion finds it's too hot for him to stay in the jungle.

6501 Mahr, Juli. *The Mailbox Mice Mystery* (K–2). Illus. by Graham Percy. 1999, Random $12.99 (0-679-88603-6). A humorous tale for beginning readers about Watson Mouse and his efforts to solve the mystery of the missing cheese. (Rev: SLJ 4/00)

6502 Maitland, Barbara. *The Bookstore Ghost* (1–2). Illus. by Nadine Bernard Westcott. 1998, Dutton $13.89 (0-525-46049-7). 32pp. A mouse-loving cat thinks up a scheme to save her master's bookshop when it becomes infested with mice. (Rev: BL 11/1/98; HBG 3/99; SLJ 11/98)

6503 Marshall, Edward. *Three by the Sea* (1–3). Illus. by James Marshall. 1981, Puffin paper $3.99 (0-14-037004-8). 48pp. Three friends, Lolly, Spider, and Sam, tell stories by the seashore.

6504 Marshall, James. *Fox Outfoxed* (2–3). Illus. 1992, Viking paper $3.99 (0-14-038113-9). 48pp. Three easily read stories about Fox and how his careful plans misfire. (Rev: BCCB 4/92; BL 4/1/92; HB 7–8/92; SLJ 5/92*)

6505 Martin, David. *Monkey Business* (K–1). Series: Brand New Reader. 2000, Candlewick $10.99 (0-7636-1178-6). A little monkey has a series of adventures including losing a tooth. Also use *Monkey Trouble* (2000). (Rev: HBG 10/00; SLJ 8/00)

6506 Marzollo, Jean. *I Am an Apple* (PS–1). Illus. by Judith Moffatt. Series: Hello Reader! 1997, Scholastic $3.99 (0-590-37223-8). A beginning reader that details the life of an apple from flower to fruit to market to table. (Rev: SLJ 1/98)

6507 Marzollo, Jean. *I'm a Caterpillar* (K–2). Illus. by Judith Moffatt. Series: Hello Reader! 1997, Scholastic $3.50 (0-590-84779-1). A beginning reader that presents, in story form, the life cycle of a caterpillar. (Rev: SLJ 11/97)

6508 Marzollo, Jean. *Once upon a Springtime* (1–2). Illus. by Jacqueline Rogers. Series: Hello Reader! 1998, Scholastic paper $3.50 (0-590-46017-X). 30pp. A fawn and its mother stay together during the first year of its life and observe humans and their comparable annual activities. (Rev: BL 5/1/98)

6509 Marzollo, Jean. *Soccer Cousins* (2–4). Illus. by Irene Trivas. Series: Hello Reader! 1997, Scholastic $3.99 (0-590-74254-X). 32pp. In this easy-to-read book David is afraid that he is not a good soccer player, but he is thrilled with the invitation to go to Mexico to see his cousin play. (Rev: BL 2/1/98; SLJ 6/98)

6510 Marzollo, Jean. *Soccer Sam* (1–2). Illus. by Blanche Sims. 1987, Random paper $3.99 (0-394-88406-X). 48pp. Marco from Mexico spends a year with his friend Sam in the United States, and the boys organize a soccer team. (Rev: BL 8/87; SLJ 9/87)

6511 Marzollo, Jean, et al. *Football Friends* (1–2). Illus. by True Kelley. Series: Hello Reader! 1997, Scholastic $3.99 (0-590-38395-7). 32pp. Freddy becomes so angry with his friend Mark when they choose teams for playing football that he begins using his fists and feet in this easy-to-read sports book. (Rev: BL 2/1/98; SLJ 3/98)

6512 Marzollo, Jean, and Dan Marzollo. *Basketball Buddies* (1–2). Illus. by True Kelley. 1998, Scholastic paper $3.99 (0-590-38401-5). 32pp. Although Paul is tall he is not a good basketball player, but with his teammate's help, he improves. (Rev: BL 3/15/99; SLJ 4/99)

6513 Mason, Jane B. *Hellow, Two-Wheeler!* (1–2). Illus. by David Monteith. 1995, Putnam paper $3.95 (0-448-40853-8). 48pp. A boy accidentally learns to ride his bike without its training wheels. (Rev: BL 7/95)

6514 Matthias, Catherine. *I Love Cats* (K–1). Illus. by Tom Dunnington. 1983, Children's LB $18.00 (0-516-02041-2); paper $4.95 (0-516-42041-0). 32pp. The narrator likes many things, but cats are best.

6515 May, Kara. *Joe Lion's Big Boots* (K–3). Illus. by Jonathan Allen. Series: I Am Reading. 2000, Kingfisher paper $3.95 (0-7534-5318-5). 42pp. Little Joe Lion buys a pair of oversize boots so he can appear to be as tall as his friends. (Rev: SLJ 2/01)

6516 Medearis, Angela Shelf. *Here Comes the Snow* (1). Illus. 1996, Scholastic paper $3.99 (0-590-26266-1). 32pp. Kids enjoy all of the fun of a first snowfall. (Rev: BL 8/96; SLJ 9/96)

6517 Meister, Cari. *Tiny Goes to the Library* (1). Illus. by Rich Davis. 2000, Viking $13.89 (0-670-88556-8). 32pp. Tiny, an enormous dog, helps his young master by pulling home the wagon that the boy has overfilled with library books. (Rev: BCCB 7–8/00; BL 4/15/00; HBG 10/00; SLJ 7/00)

6518 Meister, Cari. *Tiny's Bath* (K–1). Illus. by Rich Davis. 1999, Viking $13.89 (0-670-87962-2). 32pp. A boy tries to give his huge dog a bath but finds he has to use the backyard pool. (Rev: BCCB 4/99; BL 3/15/99; HB 5–6/99; HBG 10/99; SLJ 5/99)

6519 Meister, Cari. *When Tiny Was Tiny* (1). Illus. by Rich Davis. Series: Easy-to-Read. 1999, Viking LB $13.89 (0-670-88058-2). 32pp. A simple story

about a boy and his dog, Tiny, who is no longer so. (Rev: BL 10/1/99; HBG 3/00; SLJ 12/99)

6520 Merriam, Eve. *On My Street* (PS). Illus. by Melanie Hope Greenberg. Series: Growing Tree. 2000, HarperFestival $9.95 (0-694-01258-0). 24pp. Using simple rhymes, this easy-reader introduces various people in the neighborhood as seen through a preschooler's eyes. (Rev: BL 4/15/00; HBG 10/00; SLJ 7/00)

6521 Miles, Betty. *The Sky Is Falling!* (PS–1). Illus. by Cynthia Fisher. Series: Ready-to-Read. 1998, Simon & Schuster $15.00 (0-689-81790-8). 31pp. For beginning readers, a version of the classic tale in which Chicken Licken and several of her friends are certain that the sky is falling. (Rev: HBG 10/98; SLJ 7/98)

6522 Milgrim, David. *Why Benny Barks* (1–2). Illus. Series: Step into Reading. 1994, Random LB $11.99 (0-679-96157-7); paper $3.99 (0-679-86157-2). 32pp. In this easily read book, a child tries to figure out why his dog barks. (Rev: BL 1/1/95)

6523 Miller, Sara S. *Three More Stories You Can Read to Your Dog* (2–3). Illus. 2000, Houghton $15.00 (0-395-92293-3). 48pp. Three amusing easy-to-read stories that will amuse children, even if they don't have a dog. (Rev: BL 3/15/00; HBG 10/00; SLJ 4/00)

6524 Miller, Sara S. *Three Stories You Can Read to Your Cat* (1–3). Illus. by True Kelley. 1997, Houghton $13.95 (0-395-78831-5). 48pp. An easy-to-read book about Kelley's playful, adventurous cat. (Rev: BL 3/1/97; SLJ 5/97)

6525 Miller, Sara S. *Three Stories You Can Read to Your Dog* (2–4). Illus. by True Kelley. 1995, Houghton $15.00 (0-395-69938-X). 42pp. Three easy-to-read stories that feature a muddle-headed dog that doesn't know how to behave. (Rev: BCCB 3/95; BL 4/15/95; SLJ 4/95)

6526 Mills, Claudia. *Gus and Grandpa* (1). Illus. by Catherine Stock. 1997, Farrar $13.00 (0-374-32824-2). 48pp. Three easily read stories about Gus, who is 6, and the fun he has with his grandfather. (Rev: BL 2/1/97; SLJ 4/97)

6527 Mills, Claudia. *Gus and Grandpa and Show-and-Tell* (1–2). Illus. by Catherine Stock. Series: Gus and Grandpa. 2000, Farrar $13.00 (0-374-32819-6). 48pp. Gus doesn't shine at show-and-tell until he brings his grandfather to school to talk about history in this delightful easy-to-read story. (Rev: BL 10/1/00; HBG 3/01; SLJ 8/00)

6528 Mills, Claudia. *Gus and Grandpa and the Christmas Cookies* (1–2). Illus. by Catherine Stock. 1997, Farrar $13.00 (0-374-32823-4). 48pp. At Christmas time, Gus and his grandfather receive so many cookies that they decide to give some away. (Rev: BL 9/15/97; HBG 3/98; SLJ 10/97)

6529 Mills, Claudia. *Gus and Grandpa at the Hospital* (1–3). Illus. by Catherine Stock. 1998, Farrar $13.00 (0-374-32827-7). 48pp. Gus, who regards his Grandpa as a pal, is upset when he learns that Grandpa is in the hospital after a heart attack. (Rev: BL 11/1/98; HBG 3/99; SLJ 9/98)

6530 Mills, Claudia. *Gus and Grandpa Ride the Train* (1–2). Illus. by Catherine Stock. 1998, Farrar $13.00 (0-374-32826-9). 46pp. In the three short stories in this beginning reader, Gus and his Grandpa share their love of trains and train travel. (Rev: BL 5/1/98; HBG 10/98; SLJ 5/98)

6531 Milton, Joyce. *Whales: The Gentle Giants* (2–3). Illus. by Alton Langford. 1989, Random paper $3.99 (0-394-89809-5). 48pp. A sailor named Brendan steps on the back of a whale. (Rev: BL 6/1/89)

6532 Milton, Joyce. *Wild, Wild Wolves* (2–3). Illus. by Larry Schwinger. 1992, Random LB $11.99 (0-679-91052-2); paper $3.99 (0-679-81052-8). 48pp. This easy-to-read science book contains a wealth of information about wolves and how they live. (Rev: BCCB 5/92; BL 4/1/92; SLJ 8/92) [599.74]

6533 Minarik, Else Holmelund. *Little Bear* (K–2). Illus. by Maurice Sendak. 1957, HarperCollins LB $15.89 (0-06-024241-8); paper $3.95 (0-06-444004-4). 64pp. Humorous adventure stories of Mother Bear and Little Bear. Others in the series: *Little Bear's Friend* (1960); *Little Bear's Visit* (1961); *A Kiss for Little Bear* (1968).

6534 Minarik, Else Holmelund. *No Fighting, No Biting!* (PS–3). Illus. by Maurice Sendak. 1958, HarperCollins LB $15.89 (0-06-024291-4); paper $3.95 (0-06-444015-X). 64pp. Light-foot and Quick-foot, two little alligators, teach Rosa and Willy a lesson.

6535 Minters, Frances. *Chicken for a Day* (1–2). Illus. by Diane Greenseid. 2000, Random LB $11.99 (0-679-99133-6); paper $3.95 (0-679-89133-1). 48pp. In this beginning reader, Daisy wakes up to find she has been turned into a chicken who shortly thereafter has to contend with a fox. (Rev: BL 12/1/00)

6536 Moffatt, Judith. *Who Stole the Cookies?* (1–2). Illus. 1996, Putnam paper $3.99 (0-448-41127-X). 32pp. A cast of animal characters ask who stole the cookies in this rhyming first reader. (Rev: BL 8/96; SLJ 9/96)

6537 Moran, Alex. *Popcorn* (1). Illus. by Betsy Everitt. Series: Green Light. 1999, Harcourt paper $3.95 (0-15-201998-7). 20pp. A lighthearted, simple reader about a little girl who makes popcorn with her friends, including a large pink rabbit. (Rev: BL 5/15/99; SLJ 4/99)

6538 Morris, Kim. *Molly in the Middle* (2–3). Illus. by Dorothy Handelman. Series: Real Kids Readers. 1999, Millbrook LB $17.90 (0-7613-2059-8); paper $3.99 (0-7613-2084-9). 48pp. Molly, a middle child, decides that if she can't be the youngest or oldest, she will be the "est" in some other way, such as being the loudest or funniest. (Rev: BL 5/15/99; SLJ 8/99)

6539 Most, Bernard. *Catch Me If You Can!* (1). Illus. Series: Green Light. 1999, Harcourt paper $3.95 (0-15-202001-2). 20pp. A little dinosaur is the only one not afraid of the great big dinosaur because he is her Grandpa. (Rev: BL 5/15/99; SLJ 5/99)

6540 Most, Bernard. *The Very Boastful Kangaroo* (1–2). Illus. Series: Green Light. 1999, Harcourt $10.95 (0-15-202349-6); paper $3.95 (0-15-202266-X). 20pp. Pride goes before a downfall when a boastful kangaroo is cut down to size by a tiny member of its species. (Rev: BL 10/1/99; HBG 3/00; SLJ 11/99)

6541 Neasi, Barbara J. *Just Like Me* (K–1). Illus. by Lois Axeman. 1984, Children's LB $18.00 (0-516-02047-1); paper $4.95 (0-516-42047-X). 32pp. Twins explore their similarities and differences.

6542 Neitzel, Shirley. *The Dress I'll Wear to the Party* (PS–K). Illus. by Nancy Winslow Parker. 1992, Greenwillow $13.89 (0-688-09960-2). 32pp. A girl dresses up in her mother's clothes for a party, but later her mother has different ideas on what is suitable attire. (Rev: BL 10/15/92; SLJ 10/92)

6543 Nodset, Joan L. *Come Here, Cat* (K–3). Illus. by Steven Kellogg. 1973, HarperCollins $10.00 (0-06-024557-3). 32pp. A young girl chases a cat around her house and onto the roof in this simple but enjoyable story.

6544 Nodset, Joan L. *Go Away, Dog* (1–2). Illus. by Paul Meisel. 1997, HarperCollins LB $12.89 (0-06-027503-0). 32pp. A boy finds that he can't get rid of the dog that is following him in this easy-to-read book. (Rev: BL 8/97; HBG 3/98; SLJ 10/97)

6545 Nodset, Joan L. *Who Took the Farmer's Hat?* (1–2). Illus. by Fritz Siebel. 1963, HarperCollins LB $15.89 (0-06-024566-2); paper $6.95 (0-06-443174-6). 32pp. When the wind blows away the farmer's hat, all of the animals think they saw it.

6546 Noonan, Julia. *Hare and Rabbit: Friends Forever* (1–2). Illus. by author. 2000, Scholastic paper $3.99 (0-439-08753-8). Hare and Rabbit share a house and enjoy three simple adventures together. (Rev: SLJ 11/00)

6547 O'Connor, Jane. *Kate Skates* (PS–1). Illus. by DyAnne DiSalvo-Ryan. 1995, Putnam paper $3.99 (0-448-40935-6). 48pp. Tiny Jen easily learns to skate on her double blades, but older sister Kate has problems with her grownup single blades. (Rev: BL 1/1–15/96; SLJ 5/96)

6548 O'Connor, Jane. *Molly the Brave and Me* (1–3). Illus. by Sheila Hamanaka. 1990, Random paper $3.99 (0-394-84175-1). 48pp. Molly seems fearless, but in time of trouble Beth leads the way. (Rev: BCCB 6/90; BL 6/1/90; SLJ 8/90)

6549 O'Connor, Jane. *Nina, Nina Ballerina* (PS–1). Illus. by DyAnne DiSalvo-Ryan. 1993, Putnam paper $3.99 (0-448-40511-3). 32pp. When Nina breaks her arm, she worries that she will not be able to perform in her ballet class show. (Rev: BL 7/93; SLJ 8/93)

6550 O'Connor, Jane. *Nina, Nina, Star Ballerina* (1–2). Illus. by DyAnne DiSalvo-Ryan. 1997, Putnam LB $13.99 (0-448-41611-5). 32pp. A young girl is playing a star but not *the* star in the ballet *Night Sky*. (Rev: BL 8/97)

6551 O'Connor, Jane. *The Teeny Tiny Woman* (K–2). Illus. by R. W. Alley. 1986, Random $11.99 (0-394-98320-3); paper $3.99 (0-394-88320-9). 32pp. The familiar folktale retold. By the same author, another easy reader, *Sir Small and the Dragonfly* (1988). (Rev: BL 12/1/86)

6552 Oechsli, Kelly. *Mice at Bat* (1–2). Illus. by author. 1986, HarperCollins $11.95 (0-06-024623-5); paper $3.95 (0-06-444139-3). 64pp. Two baseball teams (of mice) who are traditional rivals prepare for the big game. (Rev: BCCB 10/86; SLJ 5/86)

6553 Oppenheim, Joanne. *The Show-and-Tell Frog* (1–2). Illus. by Kate Duke. Series: Ready-to-Read. 1998, Gareth Stevens LB $18.60 (0-8368-1762-1); Bantam paper $4.50 (0-553-35147-8). 32pp. A little green frog has some amazing adventures in this easily read book. (Rev: BL 6/1/92; HBG 10/98)

6554 Osborne, Mary Pope. *Dinosaurs Before Dark* (1–2). Illus. by Sal Murdocca. 1992, Random LB $11.99 (0-679-92411-6). 68pp. Jack and his sister time-travel to the days of the dinosaurs. (Rev: BL 10/1/92; SLJ 9/92)

6555 Packard, Mary. *When I Am Big* (PS–1). Illus. by Laura Rader. Series: All-Star Readers. 1999, Reader's Digest paper $3.99 (1-57584-294-7). 31pp. A beginning reader about a young boy's dreams of the future and achieving athletic glory. (Rev: SLJ 7/99)

6556 Papademetriou, Lisa. *My Pen Pal, Pat* (1–3). Photos by Dorothy Handelman. Series: Real Kids Readers. 1998, Millbrook LB $17.90 (0-7613-2023-7); paper $3.99 (0-7613-2048-2). 45pp. Two pen pals named Pat finally meet and discover that one is a boy and the other a girl. (Rev: HBG 3/99; SLJ 12/98)

6557 Papademetriou, Lisa. *You're in Big Trouble, Brad!* (1–3). Photos by Dorothy Handelman. Series: Real Kids Readers. 1998, Millbrook LB $17.90 (0-7613-2022-9); paper $3.99 (0-7613-2047-4). 44pp. When Brad is called to the principal's office, he thinks that he is facing big trouble, but actually he just forgot his lunch. (Rev: SLJ 12/98)

6558 Parish, Herman. *Amelia Bedelia 4 Mayor* (2–3). Illus. 1999, Greenwillow $15.00 (0-688-16721-7). 48pp. The literal-minded housekeeper decides to throw her hat in the ring (and does just that!) when she plans to run for mayor. (Rev: BL 8/99; HBG 3/00; SLJ 9/99)

6559 Parish, Herman. *Bravo, Amelia Bedelia!* (1–3). Illus. by Lynn Sweat. 1997, Greenwillow $11.95 (0-688-15155-8). 40pp. Literal-minded Amelia Bedelia creates havoc at a school concert in this beginning reader. (Rev: BL 5/1/97; SLJ 4/97)

6560 Parish, Herman. *Good Driving, Amelia Bedelia* (1–2). Illus. by Lynn Sweat. 1995, Greenwillow $15.89 (0-688-13359-2). 40pp. The literal-minded Amelia Bedelia practices her driving with hilarious results. (Rev: BCCB 3/95; BL 4/15/95; SLJ 4/95)

6561 Parish, Peggy. *Amelia Bedelia* (1–3). Illus. by Fritz Siebel. 1992, HarperCollins LB $15.89 (0-06-020187-8); paper $3.95 (0-06-444155-5). 64pp. The adventures of a literal-minded housekeeper, in a newly illustrated edition. Other series titles are: *Amelia Bedelia and the Surprise Shower* (1966); *Thank You, Amelia Bedelia* (1993).

6562 Parish, Peggy. *Amelia Bedelia Goes Camping* (2–4). Illus. by Lynn Sweat. 1985, Greenwillow $16.00 (0-688-04057-8); Avon paper $3.99 (0-380-

70067-0). 56pp. Amelia's camping trip is the occasion for all kinds of mistakes. Also use: *Amelia Bedelia's Family Album* (1988). (Rev: BCCB 7/85; BL 3/15/85; SLJ 5/85)

6563 Parish, Peggy. *The Cats' Burglar* (1–2). Illus. by Lynn Sweat. 1983, Greenwillow LB $15.93 (0-688-01826-2); Avon paper $3.99 (0-380-72973-3). 64pp. Aunt Emma's nine cats foil a burglary attempt.

6564 Parish, Peggy. *Good Hunting, Blue Sky* (1–3). Illus. by James Watts. 1988, HarperCollins LB $15.89 (0-06-024662-6); paper $3.95 (0-06-444148-2). 64pp. Blue Sky intends to bring home some meat with his new bow and arrow. (Rev: BL 12/1/88)

6565 Parish, Peggy. *No More Monsters for Me!* (K–3). Illus. by Marc Simont. 1981, HarperCollins LB $15.89 (0-06-024658-8); paper $3.95 (0-06-444109-1). 64pp. A young girl wants to keep a monster for a pet.

6566 Parish, Peggy. *Play Ball, Amelia Bedelia* (1–3). Illus. by Wallace Tripp. 1972, HarperCollins LB $14.89 (0-06-024656-1); paper $3.95 (0-06-444205-5). 64pp. Amelia Bedelia has trouble with baseball lingo. Other series titles are: *Come Back, Amelia Bedelia* (1971); *Teach Us, Amelia Bedelia* (1977, Greenwillow); *Amelia Bedelia Helps Out* (1979, Greenwillow); *Amelia Bedelia and the Baby* (1981, Greenwillow).

6567 Parish, Peggy. *Scruffy* (1–2). Illus. by Kelly Oechsli. 1988, HarperCollins LB $15.89 (0-06-024660-X); paper $3.95 (0-06-444137-7). 64pp. A small boy learns how to choose and care for his first pet — a kitten. (Rev: BL 2/1/88; SLJ 7/88)

6568 Park, Barbara. *Junie B. Jones Has a Monster Under Her Bed* (2–3). Illus. by Denise Brunkus. Series: Stepping Stone. 1997, Random $11.99 (0-679-96697-8). 80pp. An easy reader in which little Junie is convinced that an invisible monster lives under her bed. Also use *Junie B. Jones Is Not a Crook* (1997). (Rev: HB 7–8/97; SLJ 11/97)

6569 Park, Barbara. *Junie B. Jones Loves Handsome Warren* (1–2). Illus. by Denise Brunkus. 1996, Random LB $11.99 (0-679-96696-X); paper $3.99 (0-679-86696-5). 71pp. Junie falls in love with a new boy in her kindergarten class in this easy-to-read book. (Rev: BL 2/1/97)

6570 Paul, Ann W. *Silly Sadie, Silly Samuel* (K–1). Illus. by Sylvie Wickstrom. Series: Ready-to-Read. 2000, Simon & Schuster $15.00 (0-689-81689-8). 40pp. Slapstick nonsense is featured in this easy reader about Sadie and Samuel, an old-fashioned farm couple. (Rev: BL 12/1/99; HBG 10/00; SLJ 3/00)

6571 Pearson, Susan. *Eagle-Eye Ernie Comes to Town* (2–3). Illus. by Gioia Fiammenghi. 1990, Simon & Schuster paper $11.95 (0-671-70564-4). 70pp. Ernestine earns the admiration of her classmates when she solves the mystery of items missing from lunch bags. (Rev: BCCB 12/92; BL 10/1/90; SLJ 4/91)

6572 Pearson, Susan. *The Green Magician Puzzle* (1–3). Illus. by Gioia Fiammenghi. 1991, Simon &

Schuster paper $11.95 (0-671-74054-7). 88pp. Ernie and her classmates must solve a series of riddles to become the Green Magicians of the Earth Day parade. (Rev: SLJ 12/91)

6573 *Pet Stories: You Don't Have to Walk* (1–2). Illus. 2000, North-South LB $14.88 (1-58717-032-9); paper $3.99 (1-58717-031-0). 64pp. A book for beginning readers that features stories and excerpts from well-known easy-to-read books like Cynthia Rylant's Henry and Mudge stories. A companion book is *School Stories: Your Dog Didn't Eat* (2000). (Rev: BL 7/00; HBG 3/01)

6574 Petrie, Catherine. *Joshua James Likes Trucks* (PS–1). Illus. by Jerry Warshaw. 1982, Children's paper $4.95 (0-516-43525-6). 32pp. A description of all the trucks that Joshua likes.

6575 Phillips, Joan. *My New Boy* (K–2). Illus. by Lynn Munsinger. 1986, Random paper $3.99 (0-394-88277-6). 32pp. A pet store puppy searches for just the right owner. Also use: *Lucky Bear* (1986). (Rev: BCCB 1/87; BL 12/1/86)

6576 Pilkey, Dav. *Big Dog and Little Dog Making a Mistake* (PS–K). Illus. by author. Series: A Big Dog and Little Dog Book. 1999, Harcourt $5.95 (0-15-200354-1). This board book for beginning readers tells what happens when two doggy friends mistake a skunk for a kitten. (Rev: SLJ 6/99)

6577 Pinkney, Andrea D. *Solo Girl* (2–3). Illus. by Nneka Bennett. Series: Hyperion Chapters. 1997, Hyperion LB $14.49 (0-7868-2265-1); paper $3.95 (0-7868-1216-8). 56pp. A third-grader realizes that her superior math abilities can help her make friends when she moves to a new neighborhood. (Rev: SLJ 10/97)

6578 Pinkwater, Daniel. *Second-Grade Ape* (2–3). Illus. by Jill Pinkwater. Series: Hello Reader! 1998, Scholastic paper $3.99 (0-590-37261-0). 48pp. Young Flash Fleetwood mistakes a gorilla hiding in the bushes for a cat and takes him home as a pet. (Rev: BL 5/1/98; SLJ 9/98)

6579 Platt, Kin. *Big Max* (1–2). Illus. by Robert Lopshire. Series: I Can Read. 1992, HarperCollins LB $15.89 (0-06-024751-7); paper $3.95 (0-06-444006-0). 64pp. A modest detective unravels the case of the king's missing elephant in this newly illustrated I Can Read Book.

6580 Pomerantz, Charlotte. *The Outside Dog* (1–3). Illus. by Jennifer Plecas. 1993, HarperCollins LB $15.89 (0-06-024783-5). 64pp. An easy-reader that tells how Marisol gradually breaks down her grandfather's opposition to having a dog as a pet. (Rev: BCCB 10/93; BL 9/15/93*; SLJ 11/93*)

6581 Poploff, Michelle. *Tea Party for Two* (2–3). Illus. by Maryann Cocca-Leffler. Series: Yearling First Choice Chapter Book. 1997, Delacorte paper $3.99 (0-440-41334-6). 41pp. Two girls plan a party and find that a boy and his dog have eaten all their food. (Rev: HBG 3/98; SLJ 2/98)

6582 Porte, Barbara Ann. *Harry in Trouble* (1–3). Illus. by Yossi Abolafia. 1989, Dell paper $4.99 (0-440-80210-5). 48pp. Harry's third library card has disappeared! (Rev: BCCB 2/89; BL 3/1/89; SLJ 3/89)

6583 Porte, Barbara Ann. *Harry's Pony* (1–2). Illus. by Yossi Abolafia. 1997, Greenwillow $14.93 (0-688-14826-3). 56pp. Harry wins a pony in a contest, but his father won't let him keep it in this easily read book. (Rev: BL 8/97; HB 9–10/97; HBG 3/98; SLJ 8/97)

6584 Prager, Annabelle. *The Baseball Birthday Party* (1–2). Illus. by Marilyn Mets. 1995, Random paper $3.99 (0-679-84171-7). 48pp. A boy throws a baseball party, but none of his friends show up in this easily read story. (Rev: BL 7/95)

6585 Prager, Annabelle. *The Surprise Party* (1–3). Illus. by Tomie dePaola. 1988, Random paper $3.99 (0-394-89596-7). 48pp. Nicky plans his own surprise party but receives a real surprise in this easily read picture book.

6586 Pragoff, Fiona. *Where Is Alice's Bear?* (PS–1). Photos by author. 1999, Doubleday $12.95 (0-385-32625-4). A pop-up book for beginning readers that tells of a little girl's search for her teddy bear. (Rev: SLJ 10/99)

6587 *The Random House Book of Easy-to-Read Stories* (K–2). Illus. 1993, Random $19.95 (0-679-83438-9). 252pp. Easy-to-read stories from 16 authors, including Dr. Seuss, the Berenstains, and P. D. Eastman. (Rev: BCCB 1/94; BL 2/1/94; SLJ 3/94)

6588 Ransom, Candice. *Danger at Sand Cave* (1–3). Illus. by Den Schofield. Series: On My Own History. 2000, Carolrhoda LB $21.27 (1-57505-379-9); paper $5.95 (1-57505-454-X). 46pp. A fictitious 10-year-old boy helps in the unsuccessful efforts to rescue Floyd Collins from a cave in 1925. (Rev: HB 7–8/00; HBG 10/00; SLJ 8/00)

6589 Rau, Dana Meachen. *A Box Can Be Many Things* (1–2). Illus. by Paige Billin-Frye. Series: Rookie Readers. 1997, Children's $18.00 (0-516-20317-7). 32pp. Two children rescue a big box from the garbage and use it in many imaginative ways in this beginning reader. (Rev: BL 5/1/97)

6590 Rau, Dana Meachen. *Purple Is Best* (1). Illus. by Mik Cressy. Series: Rookie Readers. 1999, Children's LB $17.50 (0-516-21638-4). 32pp. Sue who loves blue and Fred who paints in red get together and produce purple in this easy reader. (Rev: BL 12/1/99)

6591 Robins, Joan. *Addie Meets Max* (1–3). Illus. by Sue Truesdell. 1985, HarperCollins $9.95 (0-06-025063-1). 32pp. Addie is sure she won't like her new neighbor until mother invites him in for pizza. Also use: *Addie Runs Away* (1989). (Rev: BCCB 5/85; BL 4/15/85; SLJ 5/85)

6592 Rocklin, Joanne. *The Case of the Backyard Treasure* (1–2). Illus. by John Speirs. 1998, Scholastic paper $3.99 (0-590-30872-6). Liz the Whiz, her brother Henry, and their dog follow a series of clues that lead them to a treasure — a stack of cookies. (Rev: BL 7/98)

6593 Rocklin, Joanne. *Jake and the Copycats* (K–2). Illus. by Janet Pedersen. Series: A Yearling First Choice Chapter Book. 1998, Bantam $13.95 (0-385-32530-4); paper $4.50 (0-440-41408-3). 48pp. Pete devises a brilliant plan to save Jake's cat, which is stranded in a tree, thus redeeming himself in his older brother's eyes. (Rev: BCCB 12/98; HBG 3/99; SLJ 12/98)

6594 Rockwell, Anne. *The Story Snail* (2–3). Illus. by Theresa Smith. 1997, Simon & Schuster $15.00 (0-689-81221-3); paper $3.99 (0-689-81220-5). 48pp. Unpopular John finds a magic snail that gives him interesting stories to tell in this easy reader. (Rev: BL 5/1/97; SLJ 9/97)

6595 Rockwell, Anne. *Sweet Potato Pie* (PS–K). Illus. Series: Early Step into Reading. 1996, Random LB $11.99 (0-679-96440-1); paper $3.99 (0-679-86440-7). 32pp. Every member of a family stops what each is doing when Grandma bakes a sweet potato pie. (Rev: BL 8/96)

6596 Roland, Timothy. *Come Down Now, Flying Cow!* (K–2). Illus. by author. Series: Beginner Books. 1997, Random LB $11.99 (0-679-98110-1). In this book for beginning readers, Beth the Cow and her bird companion share adventures during a trip in a hot-air balloon. (Rev: HBG 3/98; SLJ 10/97)

6597 Roop, Peter, and Connie Roop. *Keep the Lights Burning, Abbie* (1–3). Illus. by Peter E. Hanson. 1985, Carolrhoda LB $21.27 (0-87614-275-7); paper $5.95 (0-87614-454-7). 40pp. The true story of Abbie Burgess, who keeps the lighthouse lights ablaze for four storm-filled weeks while her father is on the mainland. (Rev: BCCB 1/86; BL 1/15/86) [387.1]

6598 Root, Phyllis. *Here Comes Tabby Cat* (K–1). Illus. by Katharine McEwen. Series: Brand New Reader. 2000, Candlewick $10.99 (0-7636-1038-0). 40pp. Four simple stories that involve an orange-striped cat and everyday adventures like searching for a mouse and playing with yarn. Also use *Hey, Tabby Cat!* (2000). (Rev: HBG 10/00; SLJ 8/00)

6599 Ross, Alice, and Kent Ross. *The Copper Lady* (1–3). Illus. by Leslie Bowman. 1997, Carolrhoda LB $21.27 (0-87614-934-4). 48pp. An easy-to-read book about a young Parisian who watches the construction of the Statue of Liberty and stows away on the ship that is taking it to the United States. (Rev: BCCB 7–8/97; BL 8/97; SLJ 9/97)

6600 Rylant, Cynthia. *The Case of the Climbing Cat* (1–2). Illus. by G. Brian Karas. Series: High Rise Private Eyes. 2000, Greenwillow LB $14.89 (0-688-16309-2). 48pp. An easy-to-read mystery in which Bunny, a rabbit, and Jack, a raccoon, help a neighbor find her stolen binoculars. Also use *The Case of the Missing Monkey* (2000). (Rev: BCCB 11/00; BL 10/1/00; HBG 3/01; SLJ 8/00)

6601 Rylant, Cynthia. *Henry and Mudge and Annie's Good Move* (2–3). Illus. by Sucie Stevenson. 1998, Simon & Schuster $14.00 (0-689-81174-8). 40pp. Henry and his dog Mudge are both excited to hear that Henry's cousin, Annie, is going to move next door. (Rev: BL 7/98; HBG 3/99; SLJ 10/98)

6602 Rylant, Cynthia. *Henry and Mudge and Annie's Perfect Pet* (2–3). Illus. by Sucie Stevenson. Series: Ready-to-Read. 2000, Simon & Schuster $15.00 (0-689-81177-2). 48pp. Henry's cousin Annie wants a pet so much that he takes her to a pet store where

they buy a rabbit. (Rev: BL 12/1/99; HBG 10/00; SLJ 4/00)

6603 Rylant, Cynthia. *Henry and Mudge and the Careful Cousin* (1–3). Illus. by Sucie Stevenson. 1994, Bradbury $14.00 (0-02-778021-X). 48pp. At first, Annie finds lots to dislike about her cousin Henry and his dog Mudge, but gradually she comes around. (Rev: BL 2/1/94; HB 3–4/94; SLJ 4/94*)

6604 Rylant, Cynthia. *Henry and Mudge and the Sneaky Crackers* (1–2). Illus. by Sucie Stevenson. 1998, Simon & Schuster paper $14.00 (0-689-81176-4). 40pp. Henry and his dog Mudge have fun with a new spy kit in this easily read book. (Rev: BCCB 3/98; BL 2/1/98; HBG 10/98; SLJ 8/98)

6605 Rylant, Cynthia. *Henry and Mudge and the Starry Night* (1). Illus. by Sucie Stevenson. Series: Ready-to-Read. 1998, Simon & Schuster $14.00 (0-689-81175-6). 48pp. Henry, his dog Mudge, and Henry's parents go camping where they witness such wonders as a deer, a waterfall, a rainbow, and a starry night. (Rev: BL 5/1/98; HBG 10/98; SLJ 4/98)

6606 Rylant, Cynthia. *Henry and Mudge and the Wild Wind: The Twelfth Book of Their Adventures* (1–2). Illus. by Sucie Stevenson. 1993, Macmillan paper $13.00 (0-02-778014-7). 40pp. Henry and his dog don't like thunderstorms. (Rev: BL 7/93; HB 7–8/93; SLJ 6/93)

6607 Rylant, Cynthia. *Henry and Mudge and Their Snowman Plan: The Nineteenth Book of Their Adventures* (1–2). Illus. by Sucie Stevenson. Series: Ready-to-Read. 1999, Simon & Schuster $14.00 (0-689-81169-1). 40pp. After a snowstorm, Henry and his dog Mudge entry a snowman-building competition and win third prize. (Rev: BL 10/1/99; HBG 3/00; SLJ 3/00)

6608 Rylant, Cynthia. *Henry and Mudge in the Family Trees* (1–2). Illus. by Sucie Stevenson. 1997, Simon & Schuster $14.00 (0-689-81179-9). 48pp. In this easy reader, Henry is afraid that his new relatives won't like his dog, Mudge. (Rev: BL 8/97; HBG 3/98; SLJ 9/97)

6609 Rylant, Cynthia. *Mr. Putter and Tabby Fly the Plane* (1–2). Illus. by Arthur Howard. 1997, Harcourt $11.00 (0-15-256253-2); paper $5.95 (0-15-201060-2). 44pp. For beginning readers, this humorous story tells about Mr. Putter's purchase of a radio-controlled biplane. Also use *Mr. Putter and Tabby Row the Boat* (1997). (Rev: BL 4/1/97; SLJ 4/97)

6610 Rylant, Cynthia. *Mr. Putter and Tabby Pick the Pears* (1–3). Illus. by Arthur Howard. 1995, Harcourt $13.00 (0-15-200245-6); paper $6.00 (0-15-200246-4). 44pp. Mr. Putter experiments with an alternative method to harvest pears from his tree. (Rev: BL 1/1–15/96; SLJ 10/95)

6611 Rylant, Cynthia. *Mr. Putter and Tabby Pour the Tea* (1–2). Illus. by Arthur Howard. 1994, Harcourt $13.00 (0-15-256255-9); paper $5.95 (0-15-200901-9). 44pp. Lonely Mr. Putter finds a friend when he adopts a cat from the local pound. Also use *Mr. Putter and Tabby Walk the Dog* (1994). (Rev: BL 2/1/94; HB 5–6/94; SLJ 4/94)

6612 Rylant, Cynthia. *Mr. Putter and Tabby Take the Train* (1–2). Illus. by Arthur Howard. 1998, Harcourt $13.00 (0-15-201786-0). 44pp. Mr. Putter and Mrs. Teaberry decide to take a train ride with their pets, but they learn that animals are not allowed on the train. (Rev: BL 11/1/98; HBG 3/99; SLJ 9/98)

6613 Rylant, Cynthia. *Mr. Putter and Tabby Toot the Horn* (1–3). Illus. by Arthur Howard. 1998, Harcourt $13.00 (0-15-200244-8). 44pp. Elderly Mr. Putter heeds the advice of his neighbor, Mrs. Teaberry, and joins a band with amusing results. (Rev: BL 5/1/98; HBG 10/98; SLJ 4/98)

6614 Rylant, Cynthia. *Poppleton* (1–2). Illus. by Mark Teague. 1997, Scholastic $15.95 (0-590-84782-1). 48pp. Poppleton the pig has three adventures, including one in which he helps a friend take his medicine. (Rev: BL 2/1/97; SLJ 3/97)

6615 Rylant, Cynthia. *Poppleton and Friends* (1–3). Illus. by Mark Teague. 1997, Scholastic $15.95 (0-590-84786-4). 48pp. Three stories about the friendship of Poppleton pig with his buddies Hudson and Cherry Sue. (Rev: BL 8/97; HBG 3/98; SLJ 9/97)

6616 Rylant, Cynthia. *Poppleton Everyday* (PS–2). Illus. by Mark Teague. 1998, Scholastic $14.95 (0-590-84845-3). 48pp. A beginning reader that presents Poppleton the pig in three humorous stories about his misadventures. (Rev: BCCB 4/98; HBG 10/98; SLJ 5/98)

6617 Rylant, Cynthia. *Poppleton Forever* (1–2). Illus. by Mark Teague. 1998, Scholastic $14.95 (0-590-84843-7). 56pp. In this easy reader, Poppleton the pig and friend Cherry Pie, a llama, share three adventures — one involving getting Poppleton's newly planted tree to grow. (Rev: BL 7/98; HBG 3/99; SLJ 9/98)

6618 Rylant, Cynthia. *Poppleton in Fall* (1–2). Illus. by Mark Teague. 1999, Scholastic $14.95 (0-590-84789-9); paper $3.99 (0-590-84794-5). 56pp. In these three episodes, Poppleton Pig is always helped out of troubling situations by his dear friend Cherry Sue, the llama. (Rev: BL 10/15/99; HBG 3/00; SLJ 9/99)

6619 Rylant, Cynthia. *Poppleton in Spring* (K–2). Illus. by Mark Teague. Series: Poppleton. 1999, Scholastic paper $3.99 (0-590-84822-4). 48pp. Three adventures involving the popular pig, Poppleton, and his springtime activities. (Rev: HBG 10/99; SLJ 3/99)

6620 Sachar, Louis. *Marvin Redpost: Kidnapped at Birth?* (1–3). Illus. by Neal Hughes. Series: Stepping Stone. 1992, Random LB $11.99 (0-679-91946-5); paper $3.99 (0-679-81946-0). 68pp. Marvin Redpost secretly believes that he is the kidnapped son of the king. (Rev: BCCB 10/92; BL 12/1/92; SLJ 3/93)

6621 Sadler, Marilyn. *The Parakeet Girl* (1–3). Illus. by Roger Bollen. Series: Step into Reading. 1997, Random paper $3.99 (0-679-87289-2). 48pp. Emma is happy with her parakeet until her brother also gets one in this easy reader. (Rev: BCCB 7–8/97; BL 5/1/97; SLJ 9/97)

6622 Sandin, Joan. *Pioneer Bear* (2–3). Illus. Series: Step into Reading. 1995, Random LB $11.99 (0-679-96050-3); paper $3.99 (0-679-86050-9). 43pp. Using a pioneer setting, this is the story of a photographer who hopes to take pictures of a pet bear. (Rev: BCCB 7–8/95; BL 7/95; SLJ 10/95)

6623 Sathre, Vivian. *Leroy Potts Meets the McCrooks* (2–3). Illus. Series: Yearling First Choice Chapter Book. 1997, Bantam paper $3.99 (0-440-41137-8). 48pp. When Leroy gets struck by lightning, he loses his memory in this humorous beginning reader. (Rev: BL 5/1/97; SLJ 9/97)

6624 Sathre, Vivian. *Slender Ella and Her Fairy Hogfather* (2–3). Illus. by Sally Anne Lambert. Series: First Choice Chapter Book. 1999, Delacorte $13.95 (0-385-32516-9); paper $4.50 (0-440-41397-4). 48pp. This easily read chapter book is a variation on the Cinderella story, using a contemporary setting with pigs as characters. (Rev: BCCB 4/99; BL 3/15/99; HBG 10/99; SLJ 6/99)

6625 Scarry, Richard. *Lowly Worm Joins the Circus* (1–2). Illus. 1998, Simon & Schuster paper $3.99 (0-689-81625-1). 32pp. In spite of an unexpected success in the circus, Lowly Worm decides to stay behind when the circus moves on. (Rev: BL 5/1/98)

6626 Scarry, Richard. *Mr. Fixit's Magnet Machine* (1–2). Illus. Series: Ready-to-Read. 1998, Simon & Schuster paper $3.99 (0-671-81624-3). 32pp. When Huckle, Lowly, and Mr. Frumble notice metal objects flying into the air, they trace this phenomenon to Mr. Fixit's new magnet machine. (Rev: BL 7/98)

6627 *Scary Stories to Read When It's Dark* (1–3). Illus. Series: Reading Rainbow Reader. 2000, North-South LB $14.88 (1-58717-036-1); paper $3.99 (1-58717-035-3). 64pp. Seven easy-to-read scary stories by such writers as Arnold Lobel, Betsy Byars, and Alvin Schwartz. (Rev: BL 10/1/00; HBG 3/01)

6628 Schade, Susan. *Space Rock* (2–3). Illus. 1989, Random paper $3.99 (0-394-89384-0). 48pp. Bob finds a purple rock that talks. (Rev: BL 3/1/89)

6629 Schade, Susan, and Jon Buller. *Toad on the Road* (1). Illus. 1992, Random paper $3.99 (0-679-82689-0). 32pp. Toad and his friends go out in his car for a series of pleasant experiences. (Rev: BL 6/15/92)

6630 Schade, Susan, and Jon Buller. *Toad Takes Off* (1–2). Illus. 1997, Random paper $3.99 (0-679-86935-2). 32pp. Toad takes his friends Pig and Cow on an airplane ride in this charming easy reader. (Rev: BL 5/1/97; SLJ 8/97)

6631 Schecter, Ellen. *I Love to Sneeze* (K–1). Illus. by Gioia Fiammenghi. 1992, Bantam paper $4.50 (0-553-35159-1). 32pp. The effects of a little girl's giant sneeze include blowing the fleas off a dog. (Rev: BL 10/1/92)

6632 Scheffler, Ursel. *Be Brave, Little Lion!* (1–3). Illus. 2000, North-South LB $13.88 (0-7358-1265-9). 48pp. In this beginning reader, lion cub Lea learns that being afraid is often beneficial when she wanders away to explore on her own. (Rev: BL 6/1–15/00; HBG 10/00)

6633 Scherer, Jeffrey. *One Snowy Day* (1–2). Illus. 1997, Scholastic $3.50 (0-590-74240-X). 32pp. When snow arrives, a bear, kitten, and deer come together to build a snowman. (Rev: BL 2/1/98)

6634 Schneider, Antonie. *The Birthday Bear* (PS–3). Trans. from German by J. Alison James. Illus. by Uli Waas. 1996, North-South LB $13.88 (1-55858-656-3). An easy-to-read book about a family camping trip that is interrupted by the arrival of a bear. (Rev: SLJ 12/96)

6635 Schubert, Ulli. *Harry's Got a Girlfriend!* (1–3). Trans. from German by J. Alison James. Illus. by Wolfgang Slawski. 1999, North-South LB $13.88 (0-7358-1106-7). 61pp. In this beginning reader, Harry is embarrassed that friends think Michelle is his girlfriend, but finds that, nevertheless, he enjoys himself at her birthday party. (Rev: HBG 10/99; SLJ 5/99)

6636 Schwartz, Alvin. *Busy Buzzing Bumblebees and Other Tongue Twisters* (1–3). Illus. by Paul Meisel. 1992, HarperCollins LB $15.89 (0-06-025269-3). 64pp. A collection of nonsensical tongue twisters, illustrated with watercolors, for beginning readers. (Rev: BL 4/1/92; SLJ 6/92) [818]

6637 Schwartz, Alvin. *Ghosts! Ghostly Tales from Folklore* (K–2). Illus. by Victoria Chess. 1991, HarperCollins LB $15.89 (0-06-021797-9); paper $3.95 (0-06-444170-9). 64pp. Contains a number of suspenseful ghost stories written for the beginning reader. (Rev: BCCB 9/91; BL 9/15/91; HB 9–10/91; SLJ 9/91)

6638 Schwartz, Alvin. *I Saw You in the Bathtub and Other Folk Rhymes* (1–3). Illus. by Syd Hoff. 1989, HarperCollins paper $3.95 (0-06-444151-2). 64pp. An amusing assortment of folk rhymes. Also use: *All of Our Noses Are Here and Other Noodle Tales* (1985). (Rev: BCCB 4/89; BL 3/1/89; SLJ 5/89)

6639 Serfozo, Mary. *A Head Is For Hats* (1–2). Illus. by Katy Bratun. 2000, Scholastic paper $3.99 (0-439-09909-9). 32pp. Using simple, easy-to-read verses, this book explains what ears, eyes, noses, mouths, hands, and feet are for. (Rev: BL 10/1/00)

6640 Seuss, Dr. *The Cat in the Hat* (1–3). Illus. by author. 1957, Random LB $11.99 (0-394-90001-4). 72pp. The story of the fabulous cat that came to visit one rainy day when Mother was away. Also from the same author and publisher: *The Cat in the Hat Comes Back!* (1958); *Foot Book* (1968).

6641 Seuss, Dr. *Green Eggs and Ham* (K–3). Illus. by author. 1960, Random $11.99 (0-394-90016-2). 72pp. A charming nonsense book.

6642 Seuss, Dr. *Hop on Pop* (1–2). Illus. by author. 1963, Random LB $11.99 (0-394-90029-4). 72pp. One of the many entertaining, controlled vocabulary stories of Dr. Seuss. Also use: *One Fish, Two Fish, Red Fish, Blue Fish* (1960); *Fox in Socks* (1965).

6643 Seuss, Dr. *I Am Not Going to Get Up Today!* (1–2). Illus. by James Stevenson. 1987, Random LB $11.99 (0-394-99217-2). 48pp. A rhyming story about a little boy who refuses to get up in the morning. (Rev: BL 12/1/87)

6644 Seuss, Dr. *I Can Lick Thirty Tigers Today and Other Stories* (K–3). Illus. by author. 1969, Random $14.95 (0-394-80094-X). The Cat in the Hat tells three zany stories.

6645 Seuss, Dr. *I Can Read with My Eyes Shut!* (1–2). Illus. by author. 1978, Random LB $11.99 (0-394-93912-3). The Cat in the Hat tells us of all the joys of reading.

6646 Seuss, Dr. *Oh Say Can You Say?* (1–3). Illus. by author. 1979, Random LB $11.99 (0-394-94255-8). Tongue-twisting verses presented by a variety of imaginative creatures.

6647 Sharmat, Marjorie W. *Nate the Great* (1–3). Illus. by Marc Simont. 1986, Dell paper $4.50 (0-440-46126-X). 48pp. Nate, a boy detective, puts on his Sherlock Holmes outfit and sets out confidently to solve the mystery of the missing painting. Other titles in the series: *Nate the Great Goes Undercover* (1977); *Nate the Great and the Lost List* (1976); *Nate the Great and the Phony Clue* (1981); *Nate the Great and the Sticky Case* (1981); *Nate the Great and the Missing Key* (1981); *Nate the Great and the Snowy Trail* (1982).

6648 Sharmat, Marjorie W. *Nate the Great and Me* (1–2). Illus. by Marc Simont. 1998, Delacorte $9.95 (0-385-32601-7). 64pp. In this installment of the popular series, the reader gets to solve some of the puzzles, but Nate gets to unravel the mystery of the missing dog, Fang. (Rev: BL 7/98; HBG 3/99; SLJ 12/98)

6649 Sharmat, Marjorie W. *Nate the Great and the Fishy Prize* (1–3). Illus. by Marc Simont. 1988, Dell paper $4.50 (0-440-40039-2). Nate the Great and his dog Sludge solve the mystery of the stolen prize. Also use: *Nate the Great Stalks Stupidweed* (1986); *Nate the Great Goes Down in the Dumps* (1989). (Rev: BL 8/85; SLJ 9/85)

6650 Sharmat, Marjorie W. *Nate the Great and the Monster Mess* (1–3). Illus. by Martha Weston. 1999, Delacorte $14.95 (0-385-32114-7). 45pp. In this beginning reader mystery, Nate and his dog, Sludge, set out to find his mother's missing recipe for monster cookies. (Rev: HBG 3/00; SLJ 12/99)

6651 Sharmat, Marjorie W. *Nate the Great Saves the King of Sweden* (1–3). Illus. by Marc Simont. 1997, Delacorte $14.95 (0-385-32120-1). 42pp. Although he doesn't leave home, Nate solves a crime in Sweden in this easy-to-read mystery story. (Rev: BL 2/1/98; HBG 3/98; SLJ 10/97)

6652 Sharmat, Marjorie W., and Craig Sharmat. *Nate the Great and the Tardy Tortoise* (1–3). Illus. by Marc Simont. 1995, Delacorte $13.95 (0-385-32111-2). 48pp. Using a trail of half-eaten plants as a guide, Nate the Great is able to return a lost turtle to its owner. (Rev: BL 10/1/95; SLJ 10/95)

6653 Sharmat, Marjorie W., and Mitchell Sharmat. *Nate the Great: San Francisco Detective* (1–3). Illus. by Martha Weston. 2000, Delacorte LB $15.99 (0-385-90000-7). 48pp. Nate the Great and his dog Sludge solve the mystery of a lost joke book in this easy-reader. (Rev: BL 7/00)

6654 Shaw, Nancy. *Sheep in a Jeep* (K–2). Illus. by Margot Apple. 1986, Houghton $14.00 (0-395-41105-X); paper $4.95 (0-395-47030-7). 32pp. Silly sheep in a silly tale; they fall down, Jeep and all, and land in a muddy pool. Also use: *Sheep on a Ship* (1989). (Rev: BL 9/15/86; HB 11–12/86)

6655 Shaw, Nancy. *Sheep Out to Eat* (PS–1). Illus. by Margot Apple. 1992, Houghton $14.00 (0-395-61128-8). 32pp. Several sheep are asked to leave a tea shop after they misbehave in this amusing story in rhyme. (Rev: BL 9/15/92; SLJ 9/92)

6656 Shea, George. *Amazing Rescues* (2–3). Illus. by Marshall H. Peck. 1992, Random paper $3.99 (0-679-81107-9). 48pp. There are three thrilling true-life rescue stories in this easily read book. (Rev: BCCB 11/92; BL 3/1/93; SLJ 4/93) [628.9]

6657 Shea, George. *First Flight: The Story of Tom Tate and the Wright Brothers* (2–3). Illus. by Don Bolognese. Series: I Can Read. 1997, HarperCollins LB $15.89 (0-06-024504-2). 48pp. A fictional account of a boy who is a friend of Orville and Wilbur Wright and participates in their flights. (Rev: BL 11/15/96; HB 3–4/97; SLJ 1/97)

6658 *Silly Stories to Tickle Your Funny Bone* (1–2). Illus. Series: Reading Rainbow Reader. 2000, North-South LB $14.88 (1-58717-034-5); paper $3.99 (1-58717-033-7). 64pp. This is an excellent collection of previously published simple, humorous stories for beginning readers by such writers as James Marshall, Cynthia Rylant, and Arnold Lobel. (Rev: BL 12/1/00)

6659 Simon, Charnan. *Come! Sit! Speak!* (PS–2). Illus. by Bari Weissman. Series: Rookie Readers. 1997, Children's LB $18.00 (0-516-20397-5). 32pp. A humorous beginning reader about a girl who wanted a puppy but got a baby sister instead. (Rev: HBG 3/98; SLJ 2/98)

6660 Simon, Charnan. *I Like to Win!* (PS–1). Photos by Dorothy Handelman. Series: Real Kids Readers. 1999, Millbrook LB $16.90 (0-7613-2062-8); paper $3.99 (0-7613-2087-3). 31pp. An African American girl and boy resolve their differences about winning at board games in this book for the very beginning reader. (Rev: SLJ 1/00)

6661 Simon, Charnan. *Mud!* (1). Illus. by Dorothy Handelman. Series: Real Kids Readers. 1999, Millbrook LB $16.90 (0-7613-2051-2); paper $3.99 (0-7613-2076-8). 32pp. Color photographs are used to illustrate this easy-to-read story about three boys playing in the mud. (Rev: BL 5/15/99)

6662 Singer, Bill. *The Fox with Cold Feet* (K–2). Illus. by Dennis Kendrick. 1980, Parents LB $5.95 (0-8193-1022-0). 48pp. A fox sets out to get a pair of boots to help cure his cold feet.

6663 Singer, Marilyn. *Solomon Sneezes* (PS–1). Illus. by Brian Floca. Series: Harper Growing Tree. 1999, HarperFestival $9.95 (0-694-01748-5). In this beginning reader, Solomon Snorkel's sneezes are so powerful they can knock down skiers and topple a giant. (Rev: HBG 3/00; SLJ 9/99)

6664 Siracusa, Catherine. *No Mail for Mitchell* (K–1). Illus. 1990, Random LB $11.99 (0-679-90476-X); paper $3.99 (0-679-80476-5). 32pp. The postman, a dog named Mitchell, never gets any letters for himself. (Rev: BL 12/1/90)

6665 Skofield, James. *Detective Dinosaur* (1–3). Illus. 1996, HarperCollins LB $14.89 (0-06-024908-

0). 48pp. Three uncomplicated mysteries are included in this easily read book. (Rev: BL 8/96; SLJ 8/96)

6666 Skofield, James. *Detective Dinosaur Lost and Found* (1–2). Illus. by R. W. Alley. Series: I Can Read. 1998, HarperCollins $14.95 (0-06-026784-4). 48pp. There are three humorous cases involving Detective Dinosaur in this easy-to-read book. (Rev: BL 2/1/98; HBG 10/98; SLJ 3/98)

6667 Slaughter, Hope. *Buckley and Wilberta* (2–3). Illus. Series: I'm Reading Now. 1996, Red Hen LB $14.95 (0-931093-15-5). 64pp. Two friends, Buckley the Hedgehog and Wilberta Rabbit, are featured in four stories. (Rev: BL 4/1/96)

6668 Smath, Jerry. *Pretzel and Pop's Closetful of Stories* (2–3). Illus. 1991, Silver Burdett LB $7.95 (0-671-72231-X). 64pp. Pop rabbit tells his daughter Pretzel stories about her relatives. (Rev: BL 12/1/91)

6669 Smith, Janice Lee. *Wizard and Wart at Sea* (1–2). Illus. 1995, HarperCollins LB $15.89 (0-06-024755-X). 48pp. Though on a holiday, Wizard insists on casting spells on various animals in this easy-to-read story. (Rev: BCCB 9/95; BL 7/95; SLJ 12/95)

6670 Smith, Janice Lee. *Wizard and Wart in Trouble* (1–2). Illus. by Paul Meisel. Series: I Can Read. 1998, HarperCollins LB $14.89 (0-06-027762-9). 48pp. Wizard and his dog Wart straighten out problems with the use of magic spells. (Rev: BL 5/1/98; HBG 10/98; SLJ 6/98)

6671 Spohn, Kate. *Dog and Cat Shake a Leg* (K–1). Illus. 1996, Viking $13.99 (0-670-86758-6). 32pp. Dog and Cat share many everyday activities and have good times in this easily read book. (Rev: BL 1/1–15/96; SLJ 4/96)

6672 Spohn, Kate. *Turtle and Snake at Work* (1). Illus. 1999, Viking $13.89 (0-670-88258-5); paper $3.99 (0-14-130270-4). 32pp. This brief story tells how Turtle, a crossing guard, and Snake, a chef, spend their days. (Rev: BL 3/15/99; HBG 3/00; SLJ 5/99)

6673 Spohn, Kate. *Turtle and Snake Go Camping* (K–2). Illus. Series: Easy-to-Read. 2000, Viking $13.89. (0-670-88866-4). When Turtle and Snake go camping, they are frightened by an owl's call and head for home. (Rev: BL 4/15/00; HBG 10/00; SLJ 7/00)

6674 Stadler, John. *The Adventures of Snail at School* (1–2). Illus. 1993, HarperCollins LB $15.89 (0-06-021042-7). 64pp. Snail has an unexpected adventure when he volunteers to pick up books at the school library. (Rev: BL 9/15/93)

6675 Stadler, John. *Ready, Set, Go!* (1–2). Illus. Series: I Can Read. 1996, HarperCollins LB $15.89 (0-06-024947-1). 32pp. Little Sasha, a dog, must contend with the scorn of her big cousin Oliver. (Rev: BL 9/15/96; SLJ 12/96)

6676 Stamper, Judith B. *Five Creepy Creatures* (2–3). Illus. by Tim Raglin. Series: Hello Reader! 1998, Scholastic paper $3.99 (0-590-92154-1). 48pp. Five scary short stories are contained in this amusing book for beginning readers. (Rev: BL 3/15/99)

6677 Stamper, Judith B. *Five Goofy Ghosts* (2–3). Illus. by Tim Raglin. Series: Hello Reader! 1997, Scholastic $3.99 (0-590-92152-5). 32pp. Five horror stories that are also humorous are contained in this simple beginning reader. (Rev: BL 2/1/98)

6678 Stamper, Judith B. *Space Race* (K–1). Illus. by Jerry Zimmerman. Series: Hello Reader! 1999, Scholastic paper $3.50 (0-590-76267-2). An easy reader that introduces imaginative space vehicles and alien-type characters. (Rev: SLJ 9/99)

6679 Stamper, Judith B. *Tic-Tac-Toe: Three in a Row* (K–1). Illus. by Ken Wilson-Max. Series: Hello Math Reader. 1998, Scholastic paper $3.50 (0-590-39963-2). This book explains, in a beginning-reader format with a simple story, how one can always win at tic-tac-toe. (Rev: BL 11/1/98; SLJ 7/98)

6680 Standiford, Natalie. *The Bravest Dog Ever: The True Story of Balto* (1–3). Illus. by Donald Cook. 1989, Random paper $3.99 (0-394-89695-5). 48pp. In easy-to-read format, this is the true story of an amazing dog who guided a sled team carrying medicine to Nome, Alaska. (Rev: BCCB 1/90; BL 2/1/90; SLJ 2/90) [636.7]

6681 Stanley, George E. *Ghost Horse* (1–3). Illus. by Ann Barrow. Series: Road to Reading. 2000, Golden Bks. paper $3.99 (0-307-26500-5). 69pp. With the help of a new friend, Emily solves the mystery of a ghost horse she spies from her bedroom window. (Rev: SLJ 3/01)

6682 Stanley, George E. *Snake Camp* (1–2). Illus. by Jared Lee. Series: Road to Reading. 2000, Golden Bks. $10.99 (0-307-46406-7); paper $3.99 (0-307-26406-8). 32pp. In this easy-reader, Stevie mistakenly is sent to a snake camp instead of a computer camp and, unfortunately, Stevie is terrified of snakes. (Rev: BL 12/1/00; HBG 3/01)

6683 Stern, Maggie. *George and Diggety* (2–3). Illus. 2000, Orchard LB $15.99 (0-531-33295-0). 48pp. A humorous, easy-to-read book about a good-hearted kid named George and his dog Diggety. (Rev: BL 9/1/00; HB 9–10/00; HBG 3/01)

6684 Stevens, Janet, and Susan Stevens Crummel. *Shoe Town* (1). Illus. Series: Green Light. 1999, Harcourt paper $3.95 (0-15-201994-4). 24pp. Mama Mouse wants to relax in her empty nest, but several fairy-tale friends come to share her space. (Rev: BL 5/15/99; SLJ 5/99)

6685 Stevenson, James. *Mud Flat April Fool* (1–3). Illus. 1998, Greenwillow $15.89 (0-688-15164-7). 48pp. A humorous book for beginning readers in which the animal residents of Mud Flat have fun playing jokes on April Fools' Day. (Rev: BL 2/15/98; HB 5–6/98; HBG 10/98; SLJ 3/98)

6686 Stolz, Mary. *Emmett's Pig* (1–3). Illus. by Garth Williams. 1959, HarperCollins LB $15.89 (0-06-025856-X). 64pp. Although he lives in a city apartment, Emmett's greatest wish is to own his own pig.

6687 Suen, Anastasia. *Willie's Birthday* (K–2). Illus. by Allan Eitzen. 2001, Viking $13.99 (0-670-

88943-1). 32pp. A beginning reader in which mayhem results when Peter invites his friends and their pets to help celebrate the birthday of his dachshund, Willie. (Rev: SLJ 3/01)

6688 Swanson, June. *I Pledge Allegiance* (1–3). Illus. by Rick Hanson. 1990, Carolrhoda LB $21.27 (0-87614-393-1). 40pp. The difficult words in the Pledge of Allegiance are explained and its history is traced. (Rev: BCCB 6/90; BL 6/1/90; SLJ 7/90) [323.6]

6689 Sweeney, Jacqueline. *Critter Day* (K–2). Series: We Can Read! 2000, Marshall Cavendish $21.36 (0-7614-1119-4). After a day of games, each animal has won one of the events. Also use *Molly's Store*, *Homesick*, and *What About Bettie*, all in the same series for beginning readers (all 2000). (Rev: HBG 3/01; SLJ 11/00)

6690 Tafuri, Nancy. *Spots, Feathers, and Curly Tails* (PS). Illus. by author. 1988, Greenwillow $15.93 (0-688-07537-1). 32pp. A concept book that makes a mystery of identifying familiar animals from the barnyard. (Rev: BL 8/88; HB 11–12/88; SLJ 12/88)

6691 Tafuri, Nancy. *Will You Be My Friend?* (PS–K). Illus. 2000, Scholastic $15.95 (0-590-63782-7). 32pp. In this easy reader, a young bunny and his friends help Bird rebuild his home when his nest is ruined in a rainstorm. (Rev: BL 1/1–15/00; HBG 10/00; SLJ 3/00)

6692 Thomas, Shelley M. *Good Night, Good Knight* (1–3). Illus. by Jennifer Plecas. Series: Dutton Easy Reader. 2000, Dutton $13.99 (0-525-46326-7). 48pp. A gentle knight discovers three young dragons who want to be tucked in for the night in this charming bedtime book for beginning readers. (Rev: BCCB 2/00; BL 2/15/00; HBG 10/00; SLJ 3/00)

6693 Thompson, Carol. *Piggy Goes to Bed* (PS–1). Illus. by author. 1998, Candlewick paper $3.99 (0-7636-0428-3). Piggy takes us on a tour of his room, introducing us to such furniture as a chair, a bookcase, a toy box, and a bed. (Rev: SLJ 12/98)

6694 Tidd, Louise Vitellaro. *The Best Pet Yet* (K–2). Photos by Dorothy Handelman. Series: Real Kids Readers. 1998, Millbrook LB $16.90 (0-7613-2006-7); paper $3.99 (0-7613-2031-8). 32pp. A boy selects his first pet in this beginning reader with photographs. (Rev: HBG 10/98; SLJ 7/98)

6695 Tidd, Louise Vitellaro. *I'll Do It Later* (1–2). Illus. by Dorothy Handelman. Series: Real Kids Readers. 1999, Millbrook LB $16.90 (0-7613-2066-0); paper $3.99 (0-7613-2091-1). 32pp. In this easy reader, a snow day provides a lazy boy with a reprieve from submitting a school assignment. (Rev: BL 12/1/99; SLJ 11/99)

6696 Tidd, Louise Vitellaro. *Let Me Help!* (1–2). Illus. by Dorothy Handelman. Series: Real Kids Readers. 1999, Millbrook LB $16.90 (0-7613-2067-9); paper $3.99 (0-7613-2092-X). 32pp. In spite of Tara's good intentions, her efforts to help her father always end disastrously. (Rev: BL 10/1/99; HBG 3/00)

6697 Tidd, Louise Vitellaro. *Lost and Found* (PS–2). Photos by Dorothy Handelman. Series: Real Kids

Readers. 1998, Millbrook LB $16.90 (0-7613-2020-2); paper $3.99 (0-7613-2045-8). 31pp. Using engaging photos and double-page spreads, this easy-reader tells about the search for a lost sneaker. (Rev: SLJ 1/99)

6698 Trimble, Patti. *Lost!* (K–1). Illus. by Daniel Moreton. Series: Green Light. 2000, Harcourt $10.95 (0-15-202667-3); paper $3.95 (0-15-202634-7). 20pp. A lost ant wanders around the house until he finally finds his home in this beginning reader. (Rev: HBG 3/01; SLJ 10/00)

6699 Trimble, Patti. *What Day Is It?* (1). Illus. by Daniel Moreton. 2000, Harcourt $10.95 (0-15-202500-6); paper $3.95 (0-15-202506-5). 20pp. Gil thinks everyone has forgotten his birthday but he is mistaken in this beginning reader. (Rev: BL 4/15/00; HBG 10/00; SLJ 8/00)

6700 Turner, Ann. *Dust for Dinner* (1–2). Illus. by Robert Barrett. 1995, HarperCollins LB $15.89 (0-06-023377-X). 64pp. An easy-to-read book about an Oklahoma family ruined by drought and the Depression. (Rev: BCCB 9/95; BL 7/95; SLJ 10/95)

6701 Udry, Janice May. *Thump and Plunk* (K–1). Illus. by Geoffrey Hayes. Series: My First I Can Read Book. 2000, HarperCollins LB $12.89 (0-06-028529-X). 23pp. A tongue-twisting book in which two duckling siblings play with their frog dolls Thumpit and Plunkit. (Rev: HBG 3/01; SLJ 1/00)

6702 Van Laan, Nancy. *Moose Tales* (1–2). Illus. by Amy Rusch. 1999, Houghton $15.00 (0-395-90863-9). 48pp. An easy chapter book that involves Moose and his adventures with friend Beaver. (Rev: BL 10/15/99; HBG 3/00; SLJ 12/99)

6703 Van Leeuwen, Jean. *Amanda Pig and Her Best Friend Lollipop* (1–2). Illus. by Ann Schweninger. 1998, Dial LB $13.89 (0-8037-1983-3). 48pp. Four short stories in which Lollipop comes to play at Amanda Pig's house, and Amanda visits Lollipop's home. (Rev: BL 7/98; HBG 10/98; SLJ 7/98)

6704 Van Leeuwen, Jean. *Oliver and Albert, Friends Forever* (1–2). Illus. by Ann Schweninger. Series: Easy-to-Read. 2000, Penguin $13.99 (0-8037-2517-5). 48pp. Albert is teased because he can't play ball, so Oliver helps him with his game while Albert shares with Oliver his skill in reading. (Rev: BL 12/1/00; HB 9–10/00; HBG 3/01; SLJ 11/00)

6705 Vaughan, Marcia. *Lemonade Stand* (1–2). Illus. by Tom Payne. Series: All Aboard Reading. 1999, Putnam paper $3.99 (0-448-41977-7). 32pp. With hopes of buying boats and sports cars, Boomer the bear and his mouse friend set up a lemonade stand in this humorous easy reader. (Rev: BL 10/1/99)

6706 Viorst, Judith. *Alexander, Who Used to Be Rich Last Sunday* (K–2). Illus. by Ray Cruz. 1978, Macmillan LB $16.00 (0-689-30602-4); paper $4.99 (0-689-71199-9). 32pp. Alexander spends his dollar gift foolishly penny by penny.

6707 Wallace, Karen. *A Bed for the Winter* (PS–3). Series: DK Reader. 2000, DK $12.95 (0-7894-5706-7); paper $3.95 (0-7894-5707-5). 32pp. In this beginning reader, a dormouse searches for a winter home and sees other animals doing the same thing. (Rev: HBG 3/01; SLJ 1/01)

6708 Wardlaw, Lee. *Hector's Hiccups* (1–2). Illus. by Joan Holub. Series: Step into Reading. 1999, Random LB $11.99 (0-679-99200-6); paper $3.99 (0-679-89200-1). 48pp. Two Hispanic children try to rid their younger brother of the hiccups, using all the usual methods, in this easy reader. (Rev: HBG 3/00; SLJ 12/99)

6709 Weeks, Sarah. *Drip, Drop* (K–2). Illus. by Jane Manning. Series: I Can Read. 2000, HarperCollins LB $14.89 (0-06-028524-9). 32pp. The noise of water dripping from a leaky roof causes Pip Squeak. a little mouse, to lose sleep in this easy-to-read book. (Rev: BL 7/00; HBG 3/01; SLJ 9/00)

6710 Weeks, Sarah. *Splish, Splash!* (1). Illus. by Ashley Wolff. 1999, HarperCollins $12.95 (0-06-027892-7). 32pp. In his bathtub, Chub the fish is joined by many friends who want to frolic with him. (Rev: BL 3/15/99; HBG 10/99; SLJ 2/99)

6711 Weiss, Ellen. *My First Day at Camp* (1). Illus. by Rebecca M. Thornburgh. Series: Bank Street Easy-to-Read. 1999, Bantam paper $4.50 (0-553-37587-3). 32pp. Anna is frightened on her first day of camp but soon joins in the activities and enjoys herself. (Rev: BL 5/15/99; SLJ 9/99)

6712 Welch, Catherine A. *Danger at the Breaker* (1–4). Illus. by Andrea Shine. 1992, Carolrhoda LB $17.50 (0-87614-693-0); paper $5.95 (0-87614-564-0). 48pp. In the 1880s, 8-year-old Andrew must leave school to work in the coal mines. (Rev: BL 3/1/93; SLJ 9/92)

6713 Weston, Martha. *Cats Are Like That* (1–2). Illus. 1999, Holiday LB $14.95 (0-8234-1419-1). 32pp. Fuzzy the cat is jealous when Dot begins showering her attentions on her new pet fish. (Rev: BL 3/15/99; HBG 10/99; SLJ 6/99)

6714 Weston, Martha. *Space Guys* (K–1). Illus. Series: Holiday House Readers. 2000, Holiday $14.95 (0-8234-1487-6). 32pp. A group of space travelers spend a riotous night in an average American home in this science fiction easy-reader. (Rev: BL 4/15/00; HBG 10/00; SLJ 5/00)

6715 Wetterer, Margaret K. *Kate Shelley and the Midnight Express* (2–3). Illus. by Karen Ritz. 1990, Carolrhoda LB $21.27 (0-87614-425-3). 48pp. Based on a true story, the tale of a young girl who saved a train from disaster. (Rev: BCCB 11/90; BL 9/15/90; SLJ 1/91)

6716 Wheeler, Cindy. *The Emperor's Birthday Suit* (1–3). Illus. by R. W. Alley. 1996, Random paper $3.99 (0-679-87424-0). 48pp. A hilarious variation on the familiar Hans Christian Andersen tale. (Rev: BL 9/15/96)

6717 Wilhelm, Hans. *I Lost My Tooth!* (PS–1). Illus. by author. Series: Hello Reader! 1999, Scholastic paper $3.50 (0-590-64230-8). A little puppy plans to leave his loose tooth for the Tooth Fairy when it falls out, but he accidentally swallows it. (Rev: SLJ 9/99)

6718 Wilhelm, Hans. *It's Too Windy!* (1). 2000, Scholastic paper $3.99 (0-439-10849-7). 32pp. An easy-to-read book about a shaggy white dog who saves a baby when its stroller rolls away. (Rev: BL 7/00)

6719 Willis, Jeanne. *Be Quiet, Parrot!* (1–2). Illus. by Mark Birchall. 2000, Carolrhoda $7.95 (1-57505-492-2). 32pp. In this beginning reader, a noisy parrot interrupts everyone and everything with his constant talking. Also use *Take Turns, Penguin!* (2000), an additional story about sharing and self-ishness. (Rev: BL 12/1/00; HBG 3/01; SLJ 1/01)

6720 Wiseman, Bernard. *Barber Bear* (2–3). Illus. by author. 1987, Little, Brown paper $11.95 (0-316-94859-4). 48pp. Puns aplenty in this story of Barber Bear. (Rev: BL 8/87; SLJ 8/87)

6721 Wiseman, Bernard. *Morris and Boris at the Circus* (1–2). Illus. by author. 1988, HarperCollins LB $15.89 (0-06-026478-0); paper $3.95 (0-06-444143-1). 64pp. Two friends, a moose and a bear, attend the circus. Also use: *Morris Goes to School* (1983). (Rev: BL 12/1/88; SLJ 2/89)

6722 Wolff, Ferida. *Watch Out for Bears! The Adventures of Henry and Bruno* (1–2). Illus. by Brad Sneed. Series: Step into Reading. 1999, Random LB $11.99 (0-679-98761-4); paper $3.99 (0-679-88761-X). 48pp. Three stories for beginning readers about Henry, a loner, and his friend, a polite bear named Bruno. (Rev: HBG 3/00; SLJ 12/99)

6723 Wyeth, Sharon D. *Ginger Brown: The Nobody Boy* (2–3). Illus. by Cornelius Van Wright. 1997, Random paper $3.99 (0-679-85645-5). 71pp. Ginger Brown becomes friends with a boy who is sad because of his parents' separation in this easy-to-read book. (Rev: BL 5/1/97)

6724 Wyeth, Sharon D. *Tomboy Trouble* (2–3). Illus. by Lynne W. Cravath. Series: Step into Reading. 1998, Random LB $11.99 (0-679-98127-6); paper $3.99 (0-679-88127-1). 48pp. Because she has short hair, Georgia is teased by some children at her new school, but new-made friends and a sympathetic teacher help her confront the bullies. (Rev: SLJ 3/99)

6725 Ziefert, Harriet. *April Fool!* (1–2). Illus. by Chris L. Demarest. Series: Viking Easy-to-Read. 2000, Viking $13.89 (0-670-88762-5). 32pp. On April Fool's Day, Will tells a tall tale to his friends about an acrobatic elephant he claims to have seen. (Rev: BL 2/15/00; HBG 10/00; SLJ 3/00)

6726 Ziefert, Harriet. *The Snow Child* (1–2). Illus. by Julia Zanes. Series: Easy-to-Read. 2000, Penguin $13.89 (0-670-88748-X); paper $3.99 (0-14-130577-0). 32pp. A childless couple makes a child out of snow that returns to them every winter, in this easy-to-read fantasy. (Rev: BL 12/1/00; HBG 3/01; SLJ 3/01)

Fiction for Older Readers

Adventure and Mystery

6727 Abbott, Kate. *Mystery at Echo Cliffs* (4–6). Illus. by Faith DeLong. 1994, Red Crane Bks. paper $11.95 (1-878610-37-6). 183pp. After the death of their parents, two Navajo youngsters move back to the reservation, where they help track down a gang of pottery thieves. (Rev: SLJ 12/94)

6728 Abbott, Tony. *Danger Guys* (2–4). Illus. 1994, HarperCollins paper $4.25 (0-06-440519-2). 80pp. Zeek and Noodle have some wild adventures before they outwit thieves at a temple site. Also use *Danger Guys Blast Off!* (1994). (Rev: BL 8/94)

6729 Adler, David A. *Cam Jansen and the Barking Treasure Mystery* (2–4). Illus. 1999, Viking $13.99 (0-670-88516-9). 64pp. Cam and her best friend solve the mystery of a missing dog. (Rev: BL 10/15/99; HBG 3/00; SLJ 12/99)

6730 Adler, David A. *Cam Jansen and the Birthday Mystery* (2–4). Illus. 2000, Viking $13.99 (0-670-88877-X). 64pp. In this beginning chapter book, Cam, with her photographic memory, solves the mystery of who stole her grandparents' luggage at the airport. (Rev: BL 11/1/00; HBG 3/01; SLJ 1/01)

6731 Adler, David A. *Cam Jansen and the Catnapping Mystery* (2–3). Illus. 1998, Viking $13.99 (0-670-88044-2). 47pp. Cam Jansen, super girl detective, helps police track down the thief who posed as a bellhop and stole an elderly woman's luggage and pet cat from the Royal Hotel. (Rev: BL 11/15/98; HBG 3/99; SLJ 1/99)

6732 Adler, David A. *Cam Jansen and the Ghostly Mystery* (2–4). Illus. 1996, Viking $12.99 (0-670-86872-8). 64pp. Cam Jansen and her friend Eric are involved in the robbery of a ticket booth at a rock concert. (Rev: BL 1/1–15/97; SLJ 12/96)

6733 Adler, David A. *Cam Jansen and the Mystery at the Haunted House* (2–4). Illus. by Susanna Natti. 1992, Viking $13.99 (0-670-83419-X). 58pp. Cam uses her photographic memory to uncover the thief who stole her aunt's wallet at an amusement park. (Rev: BL 4/1/92; SLJ 4/92)

6734 Adler, David A. *Cam Jansen and the Mystery of Flight 54* (3–4). Illus. by Susanna Natti. 1989, Viking $13.99 (0-670-81841-0). 64pp. Cam uses her photographic memory to find a missing French girl. (Rev: BL 11/15/89; SLJ 11/89)

6735 Adler, David A. *Cam Jansen and the Mystery of the Chocolate Fudge Sale* (2–4). Illus. by Susanna Natti. 1993, Viking $11.99 (0-670-84968-5). 64pp. Cam springs into action when she spots a suspicious woman around a vacant house. (Rev: BL 10/15/93; SLJ 9/93)

6736 Adler, David A. *Cam Jansen and the Scary Snake Mystery* (2–4). Illus. 1997, Viking $13.99 (0-670-87517-1). 64pp. Cam solves a mystery in which her mother's video camera is stolen after it had been used to photograph someone's pet snake. (Rev: BL 11/15/97; SLJ 12/97)

6737 Adler, David A. *Cam Jansen and the Triceratops Pops Mystery* (2–4). Illus. 1995, Viking $13.99 (0-670-86027-1). 64pp. Cam and her friend Eric solve the mystery of the missing CDs. (Rev: BL 11/1/95; SLJ 12/95)

6738 Adler, David A. *Parachuting Hamsters and Andy Russell* (2–4). Illus. 2000, Harcourt $14.00 (0-15-202185-X). 144pp. A beginning chapter book in which Andy Russell solves the mystery of the parachuting hamsters when he visits his friend Tamika's aunt and uncle in a big city apartment building. (Rev: BL 11/1/00; SLJ 10/00)

6739 Aiken, Joan. *Dangerous Games* (4–7). 1999, Delacorte $15.95 (0-385-32661-0). 251pp. Dido Twite sets out on an adventurous quest to find Lord Herodsfoot, whose knowledge of clever games could be used to help cheer the ailing King James. (Rev: BL 3/1/99; HB 1–2/99; HBG 10/99; SLJ 1/99)

6740 Aiken, Joan. *The Wolves of Willoughby Chase* (4–6). Illus. by Pat Marriott. 1987, Dell paper $4.99 (0-440-49603-9). 168pp. A Victorian melodrama about two little girls who outwit their wicked governess-guardian. A reissue of the 1963 edition. Two sequels are: *Black Hearts in Battersea* (1981) and *Nightbirds on Nantucket* (1969).

6741 Alcock, Vivien. *Stranger at the Window* (4–6). 1998, Houghton $16.00 (0-395-81661-0). 208pp. Eleven-year-old Lesley discovers that the three youngsters living next door to her London home are hiding a young illegal immigrant in the attic of their house. (Rev: BCCB 5/98; BL 5/15/98; HB 5–6/98; HBG 10/98; SLJ 6/98)

6742 Alcock, Vivien. *The Trial of Anna Cotman* (5–8). 1990, Houghton paper $6.95 (0-395-81649-1). 160pp. Anna finds that the secret society to which she belongs is gradually becoming an instrument of terror. (Rev: SLJ 2/90)

6743 Alexander, Lloyd. *The Drackenberg Adventure* (5–8). 1988, Dell paper $3.99 (0-440-40296-4). 160pp. This atypical heroine deals with villains and gypsies and attends the diamond jubilee of Maria-Sophia of Drackenberg. Part of series that includes: *The Illyrian Adventure* (Bantam 1995); *The El Dorado Adventure* (Bantam 1990). (Rev: BCCB 6/88)

6744 Alexander, Lloyd. *Gypsy Rizka* (4–7). 1999, Dutton $16.99 (0-525-46121-3). 176pp. Rizka, who is an outcast living on the edge of town, draws the good elements in the area together to fight the stupid authorities. (Rev: BL 3/15/99*; HB 3–4/99; HBG 10/99; SLJ 3/99)

6745 Alexander, Lloyd. *The Jedera Adventure* (5–8). 1989, Dell paper $4.50 (0-440-40295-6). 208pp. Vesper decides to return a valuable library book borrowed by her late father, but the library is in the mythical kingdom of Jedera. (Rev: BL 6/1/89)

6746 Alexander, Nina. *Alison Rides the Rapids* (3–5). Illus. by Gabriel Picart and Rich Grot. Series: Magic Attic Club. 1998, Magic Attic LB $16.40 (1-57513-141-2); paper $5.95 (1-57513-121-8). 75pp. When she dons a life jacket she finds in an old trunk, Alison, who is dyslexic, is transported magically to a whitewater adventure. (Rev: SLJ 4/99)

6747 Anastasio, Dina. *The Case of the Glacier Park Swallow* (4–7). Illus. 1994, Roberts Rinehart $6.95 (1-879373-85-8). 80pp. Juliet, who wants to be a veterinarian, stumbles upon a drug-smuggling ring in this tightly knit mystery. (Rev: BL 12/1/94; SLJ 10/94)

6748 Anastasio, Dina. *The Case of the Grand Canyon Eagle* (5–8). Series: Juliet Stone Environmental Mystery. 1994, Roberts Rinehart paper $6.95 (1-879373-84-X). 73pp. In this ecological mystery, 17-year-old Juliet Stone investigates the disappearance of eagle eggs. Also use *The Case of the Glacier Park Swallow* (1994). (Rev: SLJ 10/94)

6749 Anderson, Mary. *Suzy's Secret Snoop Society* (4–6). 1990, Avon paper $2.95 (0-380-75917-9). 112pp. Two new friends accidentally uncover a criminal plot. (Rev: BL 12/15/90)

6750 Andrews, Jean F. *The Secret in the Dorm Attic* (3–5). 1990, Gallaudet Univ. paper $4.95 (0-930323-66-1). 100pp. At a school for the deaf, some boys uncover stolen jewels and become the victims of a kidnapping. (Rev: BL 10/1/90)

6751 *Ask the Bones: Scary Stories from Around the World* (5–9). Ed. by Arielle North Olson and Howard Schwartz. Illus. 1999, Viking $15.99 (0-670-87581-3). 160pp. A collection of 22 scary stories about subjects ranging from ghosts to witches and voodoo spells, accompanied by spooky illustrations. (Rev: BCCB 4/99; BL 5/1/99; HB 5–6/99; HBG 10/99; SLJ 4/99)

6752 Avi. *Captain Grey* (5–8). 1993, Morrow paper $4.95 (0-688-12234-5). 160pp. In 1783, young Kevin is captured by pirates. A reissue.

6753 Avi. *The Christmas Rat* (4–7). 2000, Simon & Schuster $16.00 (0-689-83842-5). 144pp. Eric finds that he is on the side of the rat that is hiding in a basement storage area and is being hunted by a mysterious exterminator. (Rev: BCCB 10/00; BL 9/1/00; HB 11–12/00; HBG 3/01)

6754 Avi. *Man from the Sky* (4–6). Illus. by David Wiesner. 1992, Morrow paper $4.95 (0-688-11897-6). 96pp. Eleven-year-old Jamie spots a thief parachuting from an airplane.

6755 Avi. *Something Upstairs: A Tale of Ghosts* (5–7). 1988, Orchard LB $16.99 (0-531-08382-9); Avon paper $4.99 (0-380-70853-1). 128pp. Kenny moves into a house in Rhode Island that is haunted by the ghost of a slave who was murdered in 1800. (Rev: BCCB 9/88; BL 11/1/88; SLJ 10/88)

6756 Avi. *Who Stole the Wizard of Oz?* (4–6). Illus. by Derek James. 1990, McKay paper $4.99 (0-394-84992-2). 128pp. Several books disappear from the Chickertown Library book sale.

6757 Avi. *Windcatcher* (4–7). 1991, Macmillan $16.00 (0-02-707761-6); Avon paper $4.99 (0-380-71805-7). 128pp. Eleven-year-old Tony dreads a summer by the sea, but ends up finding a sailing adventure. (Rev: BCCB 5/91; BL 3/1/91; HB 5–6/91; SLJ 4/91)

6758 Babbitt, Natalie. *Goody Hall* (4–6). Illus. by author. 1986, Farrar paper $4.95 (0-374-42767-4). 176pp. Gothic mystery told with suspense and humor, centering around the magnificent home of the Goody family.

6759 Babbitt, Natalie. *Kneeknock Rise* (4–7). Illus. by author. 1970, Farrar paper $4.95 (0-374-44260-6). 96pp. Young Egan sets out to see the people-eating Megrimum.

6760 Bacon, Katharine Jay. *Finn* (5–9). 1998, Simon & Schuster $16.00 (0-689-82216-2). 176pp. After a traumatizing plane crash that killed his family, 15-year-old Finn refuses to talk until encounters with drug dealers force him to choose between remaining silent or saving his few remaining loved ones. (Rev: BCCB 11/98; BL 12/1/98; HBG 3/99; SLJ 11/98)

6761 Bailey, Linda. *How Can I Be a Detective If I Have to Baby-Sit?* (4–6). 1996, Albert Whitman LB $13.95 (0-8075-3404-8); paper $4.50 (0-8075-3405-6). 157pp. Stevie and Jessie find that their baby-sitting charge is involved in a mystery. (Rev: BL 3/15/96; SLJ 7/96)

6762 Bailey, Linda. *How Come the Best Clues Are Always in the Garbage?* (4–6). Series: Stevie Diamond Mystery. 1996, Albert Whitman LB $13.95 (0-8075-3409-9); paper $4.50 (0-8075-3410-2). 175pp. When Stevie's mother leads a crusade against a fast-food restaurant, their apartment is burglarized in this fast-moving mystery. (Rev: SLJ 5/96)

6763 Bailey, Linda. *What's a Daring Detective Like Me Doing in the Doghouse?* (4–5). Series: Stevie Diamond Mystery. 1997, Albert Whitman LB $13.95 (0-8075-8834-2); paper $4.50 (0-8075-8835-0). 185pp. Stevie and her friend Jesse set out to find the culprit who has stolen the president's dog. (Rev: HBG 3/98; SLJ 1/98)

6764 Banks, Kate. *Howie Bowles, Secret Agent* (2–3). Illus. 1999, Farrar $15.00 (0-374-33500-1). 96pp. In this easy chapter book, Howie Banks decides to become a secret agent to solve the mystery of who is putting gum in the school's water fountains. (Rev: BCCB 12/99; BL 12/15/99; HB 11–12/99; HBG 3/00; SLJ 10/99)

6765 Bartholomew, Lois Thompson. *The White Dove* (5–8). 2000, Houghton $15.00 (0-618-00464-5). 208pp. In this adventure story set in a mythical kingdom, Princess Tasha escapes from the evil Com and must undertake a dangerous mission to help overthrow the tyrant. (Rev: BL 3/1/00; HBG 10/00)

6766 Barton, Byron. *I Want to Be an Astronaut* (2–4). Illus. by author. 1988, HarperCollins LB $15.89 (0-690-04744-4); paper $6.95 (0-06-443280-7). 32pp. Simple text explains a child's desire to go into outer space. (Rev: BCCB 10/88; BL 5/15/88; SLJ 5/88)

6767 Base, Graeme. *The Eleventh Hour: A Curious Mystery* (4–6). Illus. 1989, Abrams $18.95 (0-8109-0851-4). 32pp. An elaborate picture-book mystery written in verse. (Rev: BL 11/1/89; SLJ 2/90)

6768 Bauer, Marion Dane. *On My Honor* (5–7). 1986, Houghton $15.00 (0-89919-439-7); Dell paper $4.99 (0-440-46633-4). 96pp. The powerful story of 12-year-old Joel who goes along with one of his friend Tony's schemes, which causes Tony's death, and how Joel realizes that he is responsible for his own choices. (Rev: BCCB 10/86; BL 9/1/86; SLJ 11/86)

6769 Blades, Ann. *A Boy of Tache* (3–5). Illus. 1995, Tundra paper $5.95 (0-88776-350-2). A novel of life in Tache, an Indian reservation in northwest Canada, which focuses on a young boy and a trapping expedition.

6770 Blatchford, Claire H. *Nick's Mission* (4–6). 1995, Lerner LB $19.95 (0-8225-0740-4). 144pp. A hearing-impaired boy happens on a gang of smugglers who are illegally bringing macaws into the United States from Mexico. (Rev: BL 11/15/95; SLJ 10/96)

6771 Blatchford, Claire H. *Nick's Secret* (5–7). 2000, Lerner $14.95 (0-8225-0743-9). 168pp. When 13-year-old Nick, who is deaf, is summoned to a motel by Darryl Smythe and his gang of vandals, the boy knows he is in for trouble. (Rev: BL 9/15/00; HBG 3/01; SLJ 12/00)

6772 Bledsoe, Lucy Jane. *Tracks in the Snow* (3–6). 1997, Holiday paper $15.95 (0-8234-1309-8). 96pp. A survival story about two girls caught in the woods during a violent snowstorm. (Rev: BL 8/97; HBG 3/98; SLJ 7/97)

6773 Bodett, Tom. *Williwaw* (5–8). 1999, Knopf LB $17.99 (0-679-99030-5). 192pp. The story of two youngsters — 13-year-old September Crane and her 12-year-old brother Ivan — and their life in the wilds of Alaska, where they are often left alone by their fisherman father. (Rev: BCCB 6/99; BL 4/1/99; HBG 10/99; SLJ 5/99)

6774 Booth, Martin. *Panther* (4–7). 2001, Simon & Schuster $15.00 (0-689-82976-0). 96pp. In this fast-moving plot set in England's West Country, Simon and Pati are convinced that there's a panther around and set out to track it. (Rev: BCCB 3/01; BL 2/1/01)

6775 Brittain, Bill. *Dr. Dredd's Wagon of Wonders* (4–6). Illus. by Andrew Glass. 1987, HarperCollins LB $15.89 (0-06-020714-0). 160pp. Set in a remote New England town. Dr. Dredd comes to Coven Tree to cure the drought and causes havoc in this spooky tale. (Rev: SLJ 8/87)

6776 Brittain, Bill. *Who Knew There'd Be Ghosts?* (4–6). Illus. by Michele Chessare. 1985, Harper-Collins paper $4.95 (0-06-440224-X). 128pp. Tommy, the narrator, relates how he discovers ghosts Essie and Horace and how they help him solve a mystery. (Rev: BL 6/1/85; HB 7–8/85; SLJ 5/85)

6777 Brontë, Charlotte. *Jane Eyre* (6–8). Illus. by Kathy Mitchell. 1983, Putnam $16.99 (0-448-06031-0); Bantam paper $4.95 (0-553-21140-4). 576pp. The immortal love story of Jane and Mr. Rochester.

6778 Bunting, Eve. *Coffin on a Case* (4–6). 1992, HarperCollins $14.95 (0-06-020273-4). 108pp. The daughter of a woman who has disappeared enlists the aid of a private detective's son to find her. (Rev: BCCB 11/92; BL 10/1/92; SLJ 10/92)

6779 Bunting, Eve. *The Hideout* (5–7). 1991, Harcourt $14.95 (0-15-233990-6). 144pp. Andy decides to stage his own kidnapping so he can join his father in England. (Rev: BCCB 4/91; BL 4/1/91; SLJ 5/91)

6780 Bunting, Eve. *Someone Is Hiding on Alcatraz Island* (5–8). 1986, Berkley paper $4.99 (0-425-10294-7). 144pp. A boy and a young woman ranger are trapped by a gang of thugs on Alcatraz.

6781 Byars, Betsy. *The Dark Stairs: A Herculeah Jones Mystery* (4–6). 1994, Viking $13.99 (0-670-85487-5). 128pp. Pesky but brave Herculeah Jones and her sidekick, Meat, solve the mystery surrounding a creepy old house. (Rev: BCCB 11/94; BL 8/94; HB 11–12/94; SLJ 9/94)

6782 Byars, Betsy. *Dead Letter* (4–6). 1996, Viking $14.99 (0-670-86860-4). 128pp. Herculeah Jones finds a mysterious message in a coat she has bought in a used-clothing shop. (Rev: BCCB 7–8/96; BL 6/1–15/96; SLJ 7/96)

6783 Byars, Betsy. *Death's Door* (4–6). 1997, Viking $14.99 (0-670-87423-X). 128pp. Herculeah Jones and her partner, Meat, try to find out who is trying to kill Meat's uncle Neiman. (Rev: BCCB 6/97; BL 3/1/97; SLJ 6/97)

6784 Byars, Betsy. *Tarot Says Beware* (4–6). Illus. 1995, Viking $14.99 (0-670-85575-8). 128pp. Herculeah and sidekick Meat discover a palmist's body with a knife in her chest and try to solve the mystery themselves. (Rev: BL 7/95; HB 11–12/95; SLJ 8/95)

6785 Cadwallader, Sharon. *Cookie McCorkle and the Case of the Emerald Earrings* (3–5). Illus. by Patrick Chapin. 1991, Avon paper $2.95 (0-380-76098-3). 128pp. Ten-year-old Cookie and her dog Moriarity solve a mystery in the Holmesian manner. Followed by: *Cookie McCorkle and the Case of the Polka-Dot Safecracker* (1991). (Rev: BL 9/15/91)

6786 Carey, Peter. *The Big Bazoohley* (4–6). Illus. 1995, Holt $14.95 (0-8050-3855-8). 115pp. Sam is kidnapped by two crooks who disguise him to look like their son in this adventure set in Toronto. (Rev: BCCB 12/95; BL 11/1/95; SLJ 10/95)

6787 Carlyle, Carolyn. *Mercy Hospital: Crisis!* (5–8). 1993, Avon paper $3.50 (0-380-76846-1). 128pp. Three friends volunteer at a local hospital. (Rev: SLJ 7/93)

6788 Casanova, Mary. *Moose Tracks* (4–6). 1995, Hyperion LB $15.49 (0-7868-2035-7). 128pp. During a moose hunt, Seth and friend Matt stumble onto a pair of dangerous poachers. (Rev: BCCB 7–8/95; BL 7/95; SLJ 6/95)

6789 Casanova, Mary. *Wolf Shadows* (5–7). 1997, Hyperion LB $15.49 (0-7868-2269-4). 192pp. In this outdoor story, a sequel to *Moose Tracks*, Seth and his friend Matt quarrel over wolf-protection programs but are brought together when a severe blizzard occurs on the first day of hunting season. (Rev: BL 10/1/97; HBG 3/98; SLJ 10/97)

6790 Cavanagh, Helen. *The Last Piper* (4–7). 1996, Simon & Schuster paper $16.00 (0-689-80481-4). 123pp. While on a trip to Scotland, Christine comes to believe that her brother is the reincarnation of an innocent man executed years before. (Rev: BCCB 5/96; BL 7/96; SLJ 5/96)

6791 Chocolate, Deborah M. *NEATE to the Rescue!* (4–7). 1992, Just Us paper $3.95 (0-940975-42-4). 98pp. A 13-year-old African American girl and her friends help out when her mother's seat on the local council is put in doubt by a racist. (Rev: BCCB 3/93; BL 3/15/93)

6792 Christian, Mary Blount. *Sebastian (Super Sleuth) and the Bone to Pick Mystery* (3–5). Illus. by Lisa McCue. 1983, Simon & Schuster LB $12.00 (0-02-718440-4). 64pp. Sebastian, an English sheepdog, and master John Jones at a fossil dig. Also use: *Sebastian (Super Sleuth) and the Crummy Yummies Caper* (1983).

6793 Christian, Mary Blount. *Sebastian (Super Sleuth) and the Copycat Crime* (3–5). 1993, Macmillan LB $13.00 (0-02-718211-8). 64pp. Sebastian the dog detective once again comes to the rescue and this time solves the mystery of the stolen manuscript. (Rev: BL 1/1/94; SLJ 3/94)

6794 Clark, Clara Gillow. *Willie and the Rattlesnake King* (5–7). 1997, Boyds Mills $14.95 (1-56397-

654-4). 167pp. When 13-year-old Willie joins a traveling medicine show he finds that life on the road isn't as glamorous as expected. (Rev: BL 12/1/97; HBG 3/98; SLJ 11/97)

6795 Clifford, Eth. *Harvey's Mystifying Raccoon Mix-Up* (3–5). 1994, Houghton $14.95 (0-395-68714-4). 112pp. Nora and Harvey solve the mystery of the prowler who is terrorizing a neighborhood. (Rev: BL 9/15/94; SLJ 10/94)

6796 Clifford, Eth. *Help! I'm a Prisoner in the Library* (3–5). Illus. by George Hughes. 1979, Houghton $16.00 (0-395-28478-3); Scholastic paper $4.50 (0-590-44351-8). 112pp. Two youngsters are locked in a library after it closes. Two sequels are: *The Dastardly Murder of Dirty Pete* (1981); *Just Tell Me When We're Dead!* (1983).

6797 Clifford, Eth. *Scared Silly* (3–5). Illus. by George Hughes. 1989, Scholastic paper $2.75 (0-590-42382-7). 128pp. Mary Rose and Jo-Beth encounter a mysterious Walk-Your-Way-Around-the-World Museum. (Rev: BCCB 4/88; BL 4/1/88; SLJ 6–7/88)

6798 Cohen, Daniel. *Great Ghosts* (3–6). Illus. by David Linn. 1990, Dutton $14.99 (0-525-65039-3). 48pp. Nine ghost stories, all concerning British-type haunted houses. (Rev: BL 10/1/90; SLJ 11/90)

6799 Coleman, Michael. *Escape Key* (4–6). Illus. 1997, Bantam paper $3.99 (0-553-48621-7). 128pp. The Internet Detectives, two boys and a girl, solve the mystery of the criminal who is selling via the computer a chess game that doesn't exist. Also use *Net Bandits* (1997). (Rev: BL 3/1/98)

6800 Coleman, Michael. *Weirdo's War* (5–8). 1998, Orchard LB $17.99 (0-531-33103-2). 192pp. Noted for being the class misfit, Daniel is paired with Tozer, his nemesis, on a class excursion in this life-or-death survival story. (Rev: BCCB 11/98; BL 8/98; HB 9–10/98*; HBG 3/99)

6801 Conford, Ellen. *A Case for Jenny Archer* (2–4). Illus. by Diane Palmisciano. 1990, Little, Brown paper $4.50 (0-316-15352-4). Jenny, who longs to become a detective, inadvertently foils a burglary. (Rev: BL 1/15/89; SLJ 3/89)

6802 Cooper, Ilene. *Lucy on the Loose* (2–4). Illus. Series: Road to Reading. 2000, Golden Bks. $10.99 (0-307-46508-X); paper $3.99 (0-307-26508-0). 80pp. Bobby must overcome shyness to retrieve his beagle, which has taken off after a cat in this easy chapter book. (Rev: BL 10/1/00)

6803 Coville, Bruce. *The Ghost Wore Grey* (4–6). 1988, Bantam paper $4.50 (0-553-15610-1). 128pp. Sixth-graders unravel a 100-year-old mystery at a country inn. Also use: *The Ghost in the Third Row* (1987); *How I Survived My Summer Vacation* (1988, Pocket). (Rev: SLJ 9/88)

6804 Cray, Jordan. *Dead Man's Hand* (5–9). Series: danger.com. 1998, Simon & Schuster paper $3.99 (0-689-82383-5). 210pp. With the help of cyberspace and modern technology, Nick and his stepsister Annie solve a murder. (Rev: SLJ 2/99)

6805 Cray, Jordan. *Shiver* (5–8). Series: danger.com. 1998, Simon & Schuster paper $3.99 (0-689-82384-3). 203pp. Six drama students are spending a weekend in the Green Mountains of Vermont, when one of the group is murdered. (Rev: SLJ 2/99)

6806 Creech, Sharon. *The Wanderer* (5–9). Illus. by David Diaz. 2000, HarperCollins LB $15.89 (0-06-027731-9). 288pp. In this Newbery honor book, 13-year-old Sophie, her two cousins, and three uncles sail across the Atlantic Ocean to England in a 45-foot sailboat. (Rev: BCCB 4/00*; HB 5–6/00; HBG 10/00; SLJ 4/00*)

6807 Crossman, David A. *The Secret of the Missing Grave* (5–8). Series: A Bean and Ab Mystery. 1999, Down East $16.95 (0-89272-456-0). 184pp. Two girls investigate a haunted house and get involved in a mystery concerning a missing treasure and some stolen paintings in this fast-paced novel set in Maine. (Rev: HBG 3/00; SLJ 1/00)

6808 Curry, Jane L. *The Big Smith Snatch* (5–7). 1989, Macmillan LB $16.00 (0-689-50478-0). 192pp. The Smith children discover that they have been kidnapped. (Rev: BL 9/1/89; SLJ 10/89)

6809 Curry, Jane L. *The Great Smith House Hustle* (4–7). 1993, Macmillan $14.95 (0-689-50580-9). 192pp. The Smith children uncover a real estate scam and help save their grandmother's house from being sold. (Rev: BL 5/1/93; SLJ 8/93)

6810 Cushman, Doug. *The Mystery of King Karfu* (2–4). Illus. 1996, HarperCollins $14.95 (0-06-024796-7). 32pp. Wombat detective Seymour Sleuth and sidekick Abbott Muggs, a mouse, solve the mystery of a stolen stone chicken. (Rev: BL 1/1–15/97; SLJ 2/97*)

6811 Cushman, Doug. *The Mystery of the Monkey's Maze* (1–4). Illus. 1999, HarperCollins LB $14.89 (0-06-027720-3). 32pp. After receiving threatening notes, Dr. Irene A. Tann, who is in Borneo on the trail of a flower that will cure hiccups, asks Seymour Sleuth and his sidekick Abbott Moggs to crack the case. (Rev: BL 6/1–15/99; HBG 10/99; SLJ 5/99)

6812 Dahl, Michael. *The Horizontal Man: A Finnegan Zwake Mystery* (5–9). 1999, Pocket paper $3.99 (0-671-03269-0). 183pp. When a rodent-eaten body is discovered in the basement, 12-year-old Finnegan and his mystery-writer uncle set out to solve the crime. (Rev: BL 3/15/00; SLJ 12/99)

6813 DeClements, Barthe. *Wake Me at Midnight* (4–6). 1993, Puffin paper $3.99 (0-140-36486-2). 154pp. Caitlin's problems include the responsibility for her baby brother, nasty neighbors, and the fact that the boy next door is acting strangely. (Rev: BCCB 9/91; BL 8/91; SLJ 11/91)

6814 Deedy, Carmen A. *The Secret of Old Zeb* (2–3). Illus. by Michael P. White. 1997, Peachtree $16.95 (1-56145-115-0). An adventure novel in which Uncle Walter tells his niece about a summer when he found that his next-door neighbor was building a ship in his basement. (Rev: HBG 3/98; SLJ 3/98)

6815 DeFelice, Cynthia. *Death at Devil's Bridge* (5–8). 2000, Farrar $16.00 (0-374-31723-2). 181pp. This mystery, set on Martha's Vineyard, tells of 13-year-old Ben Daggett and his investigation of the

death of a teenager suspected of dealing in drugs. (Rev: BCCB 9/00; HBG 3/01; SLJ 9/00)

6816 DeFelice, Cynthia. *Devil's Bridge* (4–6). 1992, Macmillan paper $14.00 (0-02-726465-3). 96pp. Ben and his mother's new boyfriend become involved in a plot to rig the Martha's Vineyard Striped Bass Derby. (Rev: BCCB 11/92; BL 12/1/92; SLJ 11/92)

6817 DeFelice, Cynthia. *Lostman's River* (5–7). 1994, Macmillan LB $15.00 (0-02-726466-1). 160pp. Tyler's trust is betrayed when he takes an eccentric scientist to a secret rookery in the Everglades and the man reveals himself to be an unscrupulous plume hunter. (Rev: BCCB 6/94; BL 5/15/94; HB 9–10/94; SLJ 7/94)

6818 Delaney, Mark. *The Vanishing Chip* (5–8). Series: Misfits, Inc. 1998, Peachtree paper $5.95 (1-56145-176-2). 188pp. Four teens who don't fit in at school investigate the disappearance of the world's most powerful computer chip. (Rev: SLJ 2/99)

6819 Delaney, Michael. *Deep Doo-Doo and the Mysterious E-mail* (4–6). 2001, Dutton $15.99 (0-525-46530-8). 128pp. When a pumpkin suddenly appears on top of the town hall flagpole, third-graders Bennett and Pete, with the help of Elizabeth and e-mail from the Mad Poet, solve the mystery. (Rev: BL 3/1/01; SLJ 3/01)

6820 Demers, Barbara. *Willa's New World* (5–8). 2000, Coteau paper $6.95 (1-55050-150-X). 192pp. An adventure story set in Canada around 1800 in which 15-year-old Willa is sent to a trading post on Hudson's Bay. (Rev: BL 9/15/00)

6821 Dexter, Catherine. *I Dream of Murder* (5–8). 1997, Morrow $15.00 (0-688-13182-4). 153pp. A strange-looking man who works at the zoo appears in a boy's recurring nightmare in this gripping mystery. (Rev: BCCB 3/97; SLJ 5/97)

6822 Doyle, Brian. *Spud Sweetgrass* (5–8). 1996, Douglas & McIntyre $14.95 (0-88899-164-9). 128pp. Spud and two friends solve the mystery of who is dumping grease in the Ottawa River. A sequel to *Spud in Winter* (1996). (Rev: BCCB 7–8/96; BL 6/1–15/96; SLJ 9/96)

6823 Draper, Sharon M. *Lost in the Tunnel of Time* (3–6). Illus. by Michael Bryant. Series: Ziggy and the Black Dinosaurs. 1996, Just Us paper $6.00 (0-940975-63-7). 96pp. While exploring tunnels used by the Underground Railroad, boys are trapped underground when one of the tunnels collapses. (Rev: SLJ 8/96)

6824 Draper, Sharon M. *Shadows of Caesar's Creek* (3–5). Series: Ziggy and the Black Dinosaurs. 1997, Just Us paper $6.00 (0-940975-76-9). 91pp. A group of African American kids get lost in a state park and are rescued by a Shawnee chief. (Rev: SLJ 6/98)

6825 Duey, Kathleen, and Karen A. Bale. *Flood: Mississippi, 1927* (4–6). Series: Survival! 1998, Simon & Schuster paper $3.99 (0-689-82116-6). 169pp. Two children living on the banks of the Mississippi set out to rescue their hard-earned, hidden money before it is swept away in a flood. (Rev: SLJ 12/98)

6826 Duey, Kathleen, and Karen A. Bale. *Train Wreck: Kansas, 1892* (4–7). Series: Survival! 1999, Simon & Schuster paper $3.99 (0-689-82543-9). 172pp. An adventure story about two youngsters who are apprentices in a circus that seems prone to misfortunes. (Rev: SLJ 6/99)

6827 Dygard, Thomas J. *River Danger* (5–9). 1998, Morrow $15.00 (0-688-14852-2). 151pp. An adventure story in which two brothers happen on a car-theft ring while they're on a canoe trip in Arkansas. (Rev: HBG 10/98; SLJ 5/98)

6828 Easley, Maryann. *I Am the Ice Worm* (4–6). 1996, Boyds Mills $15.95 (1-56397-412-6). 127pp. A California girl is rescued by Inupiats when she is stranded in Alaska after a plane crash. (Rev: BL 10/15/96; SLJ 11/96)

6829 Easton, Patricia H. *A Week at the Fair: A Country Celebration* (2–5). Photos by Herb Ferguso. 1995, Millbrook LB $20.90 (1-56294-527-0). A week's activities at a county fair in western Pennsylvania are seen through the eyes of a 12-year-old girl. (Rev: SLJ 2/96)

6830 Elmer, Robert. *Far from the Storm* (4–7). Series: Young Underground. 1995, Bethany paper $5.99 (0-55661-377-6). 174pp. At the end of World War II, Danish twins Peter and Elise set out to find the culprit who set their uncle's boat on fire. (Rev: BL 2/15/96)

6831 Elmer, Robert. *Follow the Star* (5–8). Series: Young Underground. 1997, Bethany paper $5.99 (1-55661-660-0). 178pp. In post–World War II Denmark, Henrik believes that his mother is being held captive by the Russians, who believe she is a spy. (Rev: SLJ 2/98)

6832 Emerson, Kathy L. *The Mystery of the Missing Bagpipes* (5–7). 1991, Avon paper $2.95 (0-380-76138-6). 128pp. Kim tries to find out who is the real culprit when a young boy is wrongfully accused of stealing a set of ancient bagpipes and some precious daggers. (Rev: BL 9/15/91)

6833 Engh, M. J. *The House in the Snow* (4–6). Illus. 1990, Scholastic paper $2.75 (0-590-42658-3). 144pp. Orphan Benjamin lands in a house of robbers who have cloaks that make them invisible. With the help of the other boys, he plans to take over the house. (Rev: BL 11/1/87; SLJ 9/87)

6834 Enright, Elizabeth. *Gone-Away Lake* (4–6). Illus. by Beth Krush and Joe Krush. 1990, Harcourt paper $6.00 (0-15-231649-3). 256pp. An abandoned summer colony bordering a swamp leads to a vacation of glorious exploration for Julian and Portia.

6835 Farley, Carol. *The Case of the Haunted Health Club* (4–6). 1991, Avon paper $2.95 (0-380-75918-7). 112pp. Two sisters solve a mystery involving a health club. (Rev: BL 3/15/91)

6836 Farley, Carol. *The Case of the Vanishing Villain* (5–6). Illus. 1986, Avon paper $2.95 (0-380-89959-0). 80pp. A 10-year-old solves the mystery of the escaped convict's disappearance. Also use: *Mystery of the Melted Diamonds* (1986); *The Case of the Lost Lookalike* (1988). (Rev: BL 9/15/86; SLJ 11/86)

6837 Fazzi, Maura, and Peter Kuhner. *The Circus of Mystery* (3–6). Trans. by Rosemary Lanning. 1999, North-South $15.95 (0-7358-1168-7). 30pp. A beautifully illustrated picture book for older readers about the organization of a circus by a young clown. (Rev: BL 12/1/99; HBG 3/00; SLJ 3/00)

6838 Ferguson, Dwayne. *Kid Caramel, Private Investigator: The Werewolf of PS 40* (3–5). Series: Kid Caramel. 1998, Just Us paper $4.50 (0-940975-82-3). 68pp. When animals begin to disappear from his town, Kid Caramel and his sidekick, Earnie, set out to find the culprit. (Rev: SLJ 3/99)

6839 Ferguson, Dwayne J. *Case of the Missing Ankh* (2–4). Series: Kid Caramel. 1997, Just Us paper $4.50 (0-940975-71-8). 59pp. Two junior detectives solve the mystery of the stolen museum treasure. (Rev: SLJ 9/97)

6840 Fields, T. S. *Danger in the Desert* (5–7). 1997, Rising Moon $12.95 (0-87358-666-2); paper $6.95 (0-87358-664-6). 126pp. A survival story about two boys who endure great hardships when they are left without food or supplies in the desert. (Rev: HBG 3/98; SLJ 11/97)

6841 Fields, T. S. *Missing in the Mountains* (4–6). 1999, Rising Moon paper $6.95 (0-87358-741-3). 108pp. While trying to escape a bully on a ski slope, two children are buried in snow by an avalanche and must find their way to safety. (Rev: SLJ 12/99)

6842 Fleck, Earl. *Chasing Bears: A Canoe-Country Adventure* (5–8). Illus. by author. 1999, Holy Cow paper $12.95 (0-930100-90-5). 135pp. An adventure story set near the Minnesota-Canada border that involves Danny, a 12-year-old who is on a canoe trip with his father and older brother. (Rev: SLJ 12/99)

6843 Fleischman, Paul. *The Half-a-Moon Inn* (5–7). Illus. by Kathryn Jacobi. 1991, HarperCollins paper $4.95 (0-06-440364-5). 96pp. A young mute boy sets out to find his mother lost in a violent snowstorm.

6844 Fleischman, Sid. *The Whipping Boy* (5–7). Illus. 1986, Greenwillow $16.00 (0-688-06216-4); Troll paper $4.95 (0-8167-1038-4). 96pp. Prince Brat and his whipping boy, Jemmy, who takes the blame for all the bad things the prince does, find their roles reversed when they meet up with CutWater and Hold-Your-Nose Billy. Newbery Medal winner, 1987. (Rev: BCCB 3/86; BL 3/1/86; SLJ 5/86)

6845 Flora, James. *Grandpa's Ghost Stories* (2–4). Illus. by author. 1980, Macmillan $13.95 (0-689-50112-9). 32pp. Three grisly short stories told by an old man to his grandson.

6846 Fox, Paula. *How Many Miles to Babylon?* (4–6). Illus. by Paul Giovanopoulos. 1982, Macmillan $13.95 (0-02-735590-X). 128pp. Tension and suspense when 10-year-old James Douglas is kidnapped by teenage dog thieves and held captive in an abandoned Coney Island fun house.

6847 Galbraith, Kathryn O. *Something Suspicious* (4–6). 1987, Avon paper $2.50 (0-380-70253-3). 128pp. Lizzie and her friend Ivy are on the trail of the bank robber known as the Green Pillowcase Bandit. (Rev: BCCB 1/86; BL 10/1/85)

6848 Gantos, Jack. *Heads or Tails: Stories from the Sixth Grade* (5–8). 1994, Farrar $16.00 (0-374-32909-5). 176pp. A collection of eight unusual short stories about a born survivor, a sixth-grader named Jack, who overcomes amazing obstacles in this book set in Fort Lauderdale. (Rev: BCCB 7–8/94; HB 7–8/94; SLJ 6/94*)

6849 Gantos, Jack. *Jack on the Tracks: Four Seasons of Fifth Grade* (5–7). 1999, Farrar $16.00 (0-374-33665-2). 192pp. An episodic novel (the fourth about Jack Henry) in which Jack, a preadolescent, has several innocent adventures while growing up. (Rev: BCCB 9/99; BL 9/1/99; HB 11–12/99; HBG 3/00; SLJ 10/99)

6850 Gardiner, John Reynolds. *General Butterfingers* (4–6). Illus. by Cat B. Smith. 1993, Puffin paper $4.99 (0-14-036355-6). 96pp. Walter, at 11, outwits the nasty nephew who wants to evict the trio of elderly veterans of World War II. (Rev: BCCB 2/89; BL 1/15/87)

6851 Garland, Sherry. *The Silent Storm* (4–7). 1993, Harcourt $14.95 (0-15-274170-4). 240pp. Alyssa, who has lost both of her parents in a violent storm and has become mute because of the trauma, hears that another hurricane is approaching. (Rev: BCCB 4/93; BL 6/1–15/93)

6852 George, Jean Craighead. *Julie* (4–6). Illus. 1994, HarperCollins LB $15.89 (0-06-023529-2). 240pp. Julie must choose between her Inuit ways and those of the white men in this sequel to *Julie of the Wolves* (1972). (Rev: BCCB 6/94; BL 10/15/94*; HB 3–4/94, 11–12/94; SLJ 10/94)

6853 George, Jean Craighead. *Julie of the Wolves* (5–8). Illus. by John Schoenherr. 1974, HarperCollins LB $15.89 (0-06-021944-0); paper $5.95 (0-06-440058-1). 180pp. Julie (Inuit name, Miyax) begins a trek across frozen Alaska and is saved only by the friendship of a pack of wolves. Newbery Award winner, 1973.

6854 George, Jean Craighead. *Julie's Wolf Pack* (5–7). Illus. Series: Julie of the Wolves. 1997, HarperCollins LB $15.89 (0-06-027407-7). 208pp. The life of Julie's wolf pack in the wild and how their lives become entwined with Julie's when Kapu, the leader, is captured by researchers. (Rev: BL 9/1/97; HBG 3/98; SLJ 9/97)

6855 George, Jean Craighead. *The Talking Earth* (6–8). 1983, HarperCollins LB $15.89 (0-06-021976-9); paper $4.95 (0-06-440212-6). 160pp. A young Seminole girl spends three months in the Everglades alone.

6856 George, Twig C. *Swimming with Sharks* (4–6). Illus. 1999, HarperCollins LB $13.89 (0-06-027758-0). 96pp. Sarah and her grandfather, a shark expert, are on the trail of a "finner" — someone who cuts off sharks' fins and leaves them to die. (Rev: BL 7/99; HBG 10/99; SLJ 7/99)

6857 Gerson, Corinne. *My Grandfather the Spy* (5–7). 1990, Walker $14.95 (0-8027-6955-1). 120pp. When a man arrives on the family farm in Vermont with a briefcase full of money, Danny suspects his grandfather is a spy. (Rev: BL 6/15/90; SLJ 8/90)

6858 Giff, Patricia Reilly. *Have You Seen Hyacinth Macaw?* (4–6). Illus. 1982, Bantam paper $4.50 (0-440-43450-5). 128pp. Abby Jones, a would-be detective, misunderstands clues and thinks her brother is a thief. A sequel is: *Loretta P. Sweeney, Where Are You?* (1983).

6859 Giff, Patricia Reilly. *Kidnap at the Catfish Cafe* (2–4). Illus. 1998, Viking $13.99 (0-670-88180-5). 63pp. When Minnie finds both a cat named Max and an amber ring, she finds she has two cases to solve in this witty mystery. (Rev: BL 11/1/98; HBG 3/99; SLJ 1/99)

6860 Giff, Patricia Reilly. *Mary Moon Is Missing* (3–5). Illus. 1998, Viking $13.99 (0-670-88182-1). 80pp. When Mary Moon, a prize racing pigeon, disappears, Minnie, with friend Cash and cat Max, begins an investigation. (Rev: BL 10/15/98; HBG 3/99; SLJ 1/99)

6861 Gilson, Jamie. *Soccer Circus: Featuring Hobie Hanson* (4–6). Illus. by Dee deRosa. 1993, Lothrop $15.00 (0-688-12021-0). 148pp. On a harmless overnight soccer trip, Hobie manages to get into a great deal of trouble. (Rev: BL 4/1/93; SLJ 6/93)

6862 Godden, Rumer. *The Rocking Horse Secret* (4–6). Illus. by Juliet Stanwell Smith. 1988, Puffin paper $3.95 (0-317-69650-5). 64pp. Tibby solves many problems when she finds a will hidden in a rocking horse.

6863 Gorman, Carol. *Jennifer-the-Jerk Is Missing* (4–6). 1994, Simon & Schuster $15.00 (0-671-86578-1). 135pp. Amy wonders whether Malcolm, her baby-sitting charge, is telling the truth about seeing a kidnapping. (Rev: BCCB 5/94; BL 6/1–15/94; SLJ 6/94)

6864 Greenberg, Martin H., and Charles G. Waugh, eds. *A Newbery Halloween: A Dozen Scary Stories by Newbery Award-Winning Authors* (3–6). 1993, Delacorte $16.95 (0-385-31028-5). 208pp. Twelve spooky short stories or excerpts from longer works by such Newbery winners as Naylor, Cleary, and Konigsburg. (Rev: BL 9/1/93; SLJ 10/93)

6865 Greene, Stephanie. *Owen Foote, Frontiersman* (2–4). Illus. 1999, Clarion $14.00 (0-395-61578-X). 96pp. In this beginning chapter book, Owen and his pal Joseph must rescue their tree fort from two older boys who threaten to destroy it. (Rev: BL 10/15/99; HB 9–10/99; HBG 3/00; SLJ 10/99)

6866 Griffin, Peni R. *The Brick House Burglars* (4–6). 1994, Macmillan $14.95 (0-689-50579-5). 144pp. Four sixth-grade girls discover that someone is trying to burn down the abandoned building they are using as a club house. (Rev: BL 3/1/94; SLJ 6/94)

6867 Griffin, Peni R. *The Treasure Bird* (4–6). 1992, Macmillan paper $14.00 (0-689-50554-X). 144pp. In this story set in Texas, 10-year-old Jessy thinks Goldie the parrot might have the clue to a jar of gold coins. (Rev: BCCB 2/93; BL 9/1/92; SLJ 11/92)

6868 Grover, Wayne. *Dolphin Freedom* (3–5). Illus. 1999, Greenwillow $15.00 (0-688-16010-7). 112pp.

Diver Wayne Grover tries to save dolphins that are the target of a poaching ring working off the coast of Florida. (Rev: BL 5/15/99; HBG 10/99; SLJ 6/99)

6869 Grover, Wayne. *Dolphin Treasure* (3–5). Illus. 1996, Greenwillow $14.00 (0-688-14343-1). 48pp. Three veteran divers ignore warning signs in their exploration of a sunken Spanish galleon. (Rev: BL 8/96; SLJ 7/96)

6870 Hahn, Mary D. *Following the Mystery Man* (5–7). 1988, Avon paper $4.99 (0-380-70677-6). 192pp. Madigan is certain that her grandmother's new boarder is none other than her missing father. (Rev: BL 3/15/88; HB 7–8/88; SLJ 4/88)

6871 Hahn, Mary D. *The Spanish Kidnapping Disaster* (5–7). 1991, Houghton $15.00 (0-395-55696-1); Avon paper $4.50 (0-380-71712-3). 132pp. Felix is tagging along on her mother's honeymoon in Spain and isn't having a good time. (Rev: BCCB 5/91; BL 3/15/91; SLJ 5/91)

6872 Hamilton, Virginia. *The House of Dies Drear* (5–8). Illus. by Eros Keith. 1984, Macmillan $17.00 (0-02-742500-2); paper $4.99 (0-02-043520-7). 256pp. First-rate suspense as history professor Small and his young son Thomas investigate their rented house, formerly a station on the Underground Railroad, unlocking the secrets and dangers from attitudes dating back to the Civil War.

6873 Hamilton, Virginia. *The Mystery of Drear House* (5–7). 1987, Greenwillow $15.95 (0-688-04026-8); Scholastic paper $4.99 (0-590-95627-2). 224pp. The story of Thomas Small and the threat to the treasure of Drear House. The conclusion of the Dies Drear Chronicle. (Rev: BCCB 5/87; BL 6/15/87; SLJ 6–7/87)

6874 Hanel, Wolfram. *Rescue at Sea!* (2–3). Trans. by Rosemary Lanning. Illus. 1999, North-South LB $15.88 (0-7358-1046-X). 62pp. Paul's acts of heroism during a storm convince his father that he can keep the dog he has saved. (Rev: BCCB 7–8/99; BL 6/1–15/99; HBG 10/99; SLJ 7/99)

6875 Harding, Donal. *The Leaving Summer* (4–6). 1996, Morrow $15.00 (0-688-13893-4). 177pp. An 11-year-old boy and his aunt hide an injured escaped convict in their basement and nurse him back to health in this coming-of-age story. (Rev: BCCB 9/96; SLJ 4/96)

6876 Harlow, Joan Hiat. *Star in the Storm* (4–7). Illus. 2000, Simon & Schuster $16.00 (0-689-82905-1). 160pp. This novel, set in Newfoundland in 1912, tells how a girl and her dog save a ship full of stranded passengers. (Rev: BCCB 3/00; BL 1/1–15/00; HB 3–4/00; HBG 10/00; SLJ 4/00)

6877 Harrison, Ted. *Children of the Yukon* (2–4). Illus. by author. 1977, Tundra paper $6.95 (0-88776-163-1). Life in present-day Yukon with a little historical material.

6878 Hart, Alison. *Hostage* (3–5). Illus. 2000, Random LB $12.99 (0-679-99366-5); paper $5.99 (0-679-89366-0). 96pp. The inner workings of a police squad are shown through a fictional story about a botched bank robbery in which hostages are taken. (Rev: BL 4/15/00; HBG 10/00; SLJ 10/00)

6879 Hartas, Leo. *Haunted Castle: An Interactive Adventure Book* (4–7). Illus. by author. 1997, DK $14.95 (0-7894-2464-9). A choose-your-own-adventure tale in which the reader accompanies two boys as they explore tumbledown Grizzlemyst Castle. (Rev: SLJ 1/98)

6880 Haugaard, Erik C. *Under the Black Flag* (5–7). 1994, Roberts Rinehart paper $8.95 (1-879373-63-7). 170pp. Fourteen-year-old William is captured by the pirate Blackbeard and held for ransom in this 18th-century yarn. (Rev: BL 4/1/94; HB 9–10/94; SLJ 5/94)

6881 Hawks, Robert. *The Richest Kid in the World* (4–8). 1992, Avon paper $2.99 (0-380-76241-2). 136pp. Josh is kidnapped and taken to the estate of billionaire Grizzle Welch. (Rev: SLJ 5/92)

6882 Hearne, Betsy. *Eli's Ghost* (5–7). Illus. by Ronald Himler. 1987, Macmillan $13.95 (0-689-50420-9). 112pp. Eli learns that his mother is not dead but has fled into the swamp, and he goes in search of her. (Rev: BCCB 3/87; BL 4/1/87; SLJ 4/87)

6883 Hearne, Betsy. *Who's in the Hall? A Mystery in Four Chapters* (2–4). Illus. 2000, Greenwillow LB $15.89 (0-688-16262-2). 32pp. Three different sets of kids in the same apartment building are troubled by a stranger who knocks at their doors asking to be let in. (Rev: BCCB 1/01; BL 9/15/00; HBG 3/01; SLJ 8/00)

6884 Heisel, Sharon E. *Wrapped in a Riddle* (4–6). 1993, Houghton $14.95 (0-395-65026-7). 140pp. When a series of unexplained events occur at her grandmother's bed-and-breakfast, Miranda becomes a sleuth intent on solving the mysteries. (Rev: BCCB 11/93; BL 10/1/93; SLJ 2/94)

6885 Helldorfer, M. C. *Spook House* (5–7). 1989, Pocket paper $2.99 (0-671-72326-X). 160pp. Will and friends decide to give guided tours of an old abandoned house in their eastern shore Maryland town. (Rev: BL 10/1/89; HB 11–12/92; SLJ 10/89)

6886 Henderson, Aileen K. *The Monkey Thief* (5–7). 1997, Milkweed $14.95 (1-57131-612-4). 144pp. While working with his uncle in the Costa Rican rain forest, Ron uncovers a plot to plunder ancient burial sites. (Rev: BL 11/1/97; HBG 3/98; SLJ 12/97)

6887 Henderson, Aileen K. *The Summer of the Bonepile Monster* (3–5). Illus. 1995, Milkweed $15.95 (1-57131-603-5); paper $6.95 (1-57131-602-7). 140pp. Hollis changes into a self-reliant young man during a summer spent in the country during which he solves a community mystery. (Rev: BCCB 7–8/95; BL 5/1/95; SLJ 7/95)

6888 Herndon, Ernest. *The Secret of Lizard Island* (3–5). 1994, HarperCollins paper $5.99 (0-310-38251-3). 128pp. Through a misunderstanding, Eric, a typical 12-year-old, is sent to a South Pacific island where scientists are growing huge lizards. (Rev: BL 9/1/94)

6889 Herzig, Alison C., and Jane L. Mali. *Mystery on October Road* (3–5). 1993, Puffin paper $4.99 (0-14-034614-7). 96pp. Casey wonders why his neighbor wears a bandanna over his face until he discovers that Mr. Smith has been disfigured in a fire. (Rev: BL 7/91; SLJ 9/91)

6890 Hildick, E. W. *The Case of the Absent Author* (4–6). 1995, Macmillan paper $14.00 (0-02-743821-X). 144pp. McGurk and Co., young detectives, realize that the disappearance of the famous author William Le Grand has been staged. (Rev: BL 8/95; SLJ 7/95)

6891 Hildick, E. W. *The Case of the Wiggling Wig* (4–6). 1996, Simon & Schuster paper $15.00 (0-689-80082-7). 154pp. A broken leg doesn't stop McGurk from his detective work. (Rev: BL 5/15/96; SLJ 5/96)

6892 Hildick, E. W. *The Purloined Corn Popper* (4–6). 1997, Marshall Cavendish $14.95 (0-7614-5010-6). 160pp. In this new mystery series, Tim Kowalski and his friend investigate the disappearance of a corn popper that contained Mrs. Kowalski's money. Also use *Sneak Thief* (1997). (Rev: BL 1/1–15/98; HBG 10/98; SLJ 2/98)

6893 Hilgartner, Beth. *A Murder for Her Majesty* (5–8). 1986, Houghton paper $5.95 (0-395-61619-0). 256pp. Alice disguises herself as a boy to escape her father's murderers. (Rev: BCCB 9/86; SLJ 10/86)

6894 Hill, Kirkpatrick. *Toughboy and Sister* (4–6). 1990, Macmillan paper $15.00 (0-689-50506-X). 128pp. A survival story set in an Alaskan native village. (Rev: BCCB 11/90*; BL 9/15/90; HB 3–4/91*; SLJ 10/90)

6895 Hill, Kirkpatrick. *Winter Camp* (4–6). 1993, Macmillan paper $15.00 (0-689-50588-4). 192pp. To teach them the ways of the wild, Natasha, an Athapascan Indian, and her two stepchildren spend a winter in an Alaskan bush camp. (Rev: BCCB 11/93; BL 10/1/93; SLJ 10/93)

6896 Hobbs, Will. *Jason's Gold* (5–9). 1999, Morrow $16.00 (0-688-15093-4). 192pp. In this sharply realistic novel, 15-year-old Jason leaves Seattle in 1897 and, with a dog he has saved, heads for the Klondike and gold. (Rev: BL 8/99; HB 9–10/99; HBG 3/00; SLJ 11/99)

6897 Holcomb, Jerry Kimble. *The Chinquapin Tree* (5–8). 1998, Marshall Cavendish $14.95 (0-7614-5028-9). 189pp. Faced with being sent back to their abusive mother, three youngsters head for the wilderness in this survival story set in Oregon. (Rev: HBG 10/98; SLJ 5/98)

6898 Holman, Felice. *Slake's Limbo* (5–7). 1974, Macmillan $16.00 (0-684-13926-X); paper $4.99 (0-689-71066-6). 126pp. Thirteen-year-old Artemis Slake finds an ideal hideaway for four months in the labyrinth of the New York City subway.

6899 Hopper, Nancy J. *Ape Ears and Beaky* (4–7). 1987, Avon paper $2.50 (0-380-70270-3). 112pp. Scott and Beaky solve the mystery of the robberies in a condominium.

6900 Houston, James. *Frozen Fire* (6–8). Illus. by author. 1977, Macmillan $16.99 (0-689-50083-1); paper $4.95 (0-689-71612-5). 160pp. Two boys — one white and one Inuit — set out on a rescue mission in the Far North.

6901 Howard, Milly. *The Case of the Dognapped Cat* (2–4). Illus. 1997, Bob Jones Univ. paper $6.49 (0-89084-936-6). 144pp. Three Florida youngsters call themselves Crimebusters and, in this adventure, solve the mystery of a cat that has been kidnapped. (Rev: BL 1/1–15/98)

6902 Howe, James. *Bunnicula Escapes! A Pop-Up Adventure* (2–3). Illus. by Alan Daniel and Lea Daniel. 1994, Morrow paper $14.95 (0-688-13212-X). 12pp. In this Bunnicula adventure at a county fair, most of the fun comes from the amazing pop-ups. (Rev: BL 11/15/94)

6903 Howe, James. *Dew Drop Dead: A Sebastian Barth Mystery* (4–7). 1990, Macmillan $16.00 (0-689-31425-6). 160pp. Sebastian Barth finds a body in the abandoned Dew Drop Inn, but before he can investigate, it disappears. (Rev: SLJ 4/90)

6904 Hughes, Dean. *Nutty and the Case of the Ski-Slope Spy* (4–6). 1985, Macmillan $15.00 (0-689-31126-5). 144pp. Student council president Nutty Nutsell takes his show on the road this time as he organizes a student ski trip and runs into a case of stolen computer documents. (Rev: BL 11/1/85; SLJ 1/86)

6905 Hyde, Dayton O. *Mr. Beans* (5–7). 2000, Boyds Mills $14.95 (1-56397-866-0). 160pp. In a small town in Oregon in the early 1940s, bully Mugsy wrongfully accuses a tame bear of attacking him, and timid Chirp frees the bear and takes off with him on a wilderness journey. (Rev: BL 11/15/00)

6906 Hyland, Hilary. *The Wreck of the Ethie* (4–7). Illus. by Paul Bachem. 1999, Peachtree paper $7.95 (1-56145-198-3). 115pp. Told through the eyes of two youngsters, this is a novelization of a true incident in which a dog was responsible for saving passengers stranded after their ship sank off the coast of Newfoundland during a violent storm in 1919. (Rev: SLJ 4/00)

6907 Irwin, Hadley. *The Original Freddie Ackerman* (5–7). Illus. by James Hosten. 1992, Macmillan $15.00 (0-689-50562-0). 184pp. Twelve-year-old Trevor is dismayed to find himself on a Maine isle with two unknown great-aunts, no television, no theaters, and no malls. (Rev: BCCB 9/92; BL 1/1/92; SLJ 8/92*)

6908 Jam, Teddy. *ttuM* (2–4). Illus. by Harvey Chan. Series: A Charlotte Novel Series. 1999, Groundwood $14.95 (0-88899-373-0); paper $5.95 (0-88899-374-9). 109pp. In this beginning chapter book, a little girl who speaks to her dog, ttuM, in reverse, solves a mystery about a strange person in black seen canoeing on the village lake. (Rev: SLJ 3/00)

6909 Johnson, Annabel, and Edgar Johnson. *The Grizzly* (5–7). Illus. by Gilbert Riswold. 1964, HarperCollins paper $4.95 (0-06-440036-0). 194pp. A perceptive story of a father-son relationship in which David, on a camping trip, saves his father's life when a grizzly bear attacks.

6910 Joosse, Barbara M. *Alien Brain Fryout* (2–5). Illus. Series: Wild Willy Mystery. 2000, Clarion $15.00 (0-395-68964-3). 96pp. When the behavior of the neighborhood bully changes radically for the better, Willie and his friends think he might be under the control of extraterrestrials. (Rev: BL 9/15/00; HBG 3/01; SLJ 9/00)

6911 Joosse, Barbara M. *Ghost Trap: A Wild Willie Mystery* (3–5). Illus. 1998, Clarion $15.00 (0-395-66587-6). 69pp. An easily read mystery about three friends, Willie, Kyle, and Lucy, and mysterious happenings that occur in a house formerly owned by an amateur detective and now the home of Kyle and his family. (Rev: BCCB 7–8/98; BL 6/1–15/98; HB 7–8/98; HBG 10/98; SLJ 6/98)

6912 Karas, Phyllis. *For Lucky's Sake* (5–8). 1997, Avon paper $3.99 (0-380-78647-8). 153pp. In this mystery with an animal rights theme, Benjy investigates a mysterious fire in which two greyhounds, which have been rescued from a research lab, are killed. (Rev: BL 10/1/97)

6913 Keep, Linda Lowery. *Hannah and the Angels: Mission Down Under* (4–6). Illus. 1998, Random paper $3.99 (0-679-89081-5). 127pp. Sixth-grader Hannah is whisked off by her angels to Australia where she is to help a boy named Ian to track down poachers. (Rev: BL 7/98; SLJ 11/98)

6914 Kehret, Peg. *Danger at the Fair* (5–8). 1995, Pocket paper $3.99 (0-671-52939-0). 136pp. Ellen's brother Corey gets into trouble after he spots a pickpocket at a county fair. (Rev: BCCB 2/95; BL 12/1/94; SLJ 2/95)

6915 Kehret, Peg. *Don't Tell Anyone* (4–7). 2000, Dutton $15.99 (0-525-46388-7). 144pp. After Megan sees a hit-and-run accident, she receives a threatening message in this adventure that also contains forgery, arson, and a kidnapping. (Rev: BCCB 5/00; BL 8/00; HBG 10/00; SLJ 4/00)

6916 Kehret, Peg. *Earthquake Terror* (4–7). 1996, Dutton $14.99 (0-525-65226-4). 144pp. A violent earthquake strikes the small island on which 12-year-old Jonathan is alone with his younger sister, Abby. (Rev: BCCB 3/96; BL 1/1–15/96; SLJ 2/96)

6917 Kehret, Peg. *Frightmares: Don't Go Near Mrs. Tallie* (3–6). 1995, Pocket paper $3.99 (0-671-89191-X). 131pp. Rosie and Kayo suspect that their elderly neighbor, Mrs. Tallie, is slowly being poisoned. (Rev: BL 10/1/95; SLJ 12/95)

6918 Kehret, Peg. *Searching for Candlestick Park* (5–8). 1997, Dutton $14.99 (0-525-65256-6). 160pp. An adventure story about a boy who sets out from Seattle to find his father in San Francisco. (Rev: BL 8/97; HBG 3/98; SLJ 9/97)

6919 Kelleher, D. V. *Defenders of the Universe* (3–6). Illus. by Jane Brown. 1993, Houghton $16.00 (0-395-60515-6). 128pp. Rachel is asked to join a crime-fighting club at her new school. (Rev: BL 3/15/93; SLJ 4/93)

6920 Keller, Holly. *Angela's Top-Secret Computer Club* (2–4). Illus. 1998, Greenwillow $15.00 (0-688-15571-5). 64pp. In this sequel to *I Am Angela,* some unknown student hackers have ruined the school computer program and Angela and friends must solve the mystery. (Rev: BCCB 3/98; BL 8/98; HBG 10/98; SLJ 6/98)

6921 King-Smith, Dick. *Harry's Mad* (4–6). Illus. 1990, Macmillan $15.95 (0-7451-1101-7); Knopf paper $4.99 (0-679-88688-5). Mad the talking parrot is stolen, but the sharp-witted bird finally makes it back home. (Rev: BCCB 5/87; BL 7/87; SLJ 5/87)

6922 Kingman, Lee. *The Luck of the Miss L* (5–7). 1986, Houghton $12.95 (0-685-11813-4). 160pp. Alec faces obstacles at every turn as he practices rowing for the Junior Rowers Race. (Rev: BCCB 9/86; BL 8/86; HB 5–6/86)

6923 Kline, Suzy. *Orp and the FBI* (3–6). 1995, Putnam $14.95 (0-399-22664-8). 112pp. The rival detective agencies formed by Orp and his sister Chloe compete to solve the mystery of strange sounds that come from a neighbor's house. (Rev: BL 4/15/95; SLJ 5/95)

6924 Konigsburg, E. L. *Father's Arcane Daughter* (5–8). 1976, Macmillan LB $15.00 (0-689-30524-9). 128pp. When Caroline reappears after an absence of 17 years, everyone wonders if she is really an imposter in this complex suspense tale.

6925 Konigsburg, E. L. *From the Mixed-Up Files of Mrs. Basil E. Frankweiler* (5–7). Illus. by author. 1967, Macmillan $16.00 (0-689-20586-4); Dell paper $5.50 (0-440-43180-8). 168pp. Adventure, suspense, detection, and humor are involved when 12-year-old Claudia and her younger brother elude the security guards and live for a week in New York's Metropolitan Museum of Art. Newbery Award winner, 1968.

6926 Konigsburg, E. L. *Silent to the Bone* (5–9). 2000, Simon & Schuster $16.00 (0-689-83601-5). 272pp. A mystery story filled with suspense about a baby who's been dropped and a 13-year-old suspect who has lost his ability to speak. (Rev: BL 8/00*; HB 11–12/00; HBG 3/01)

6927 Kotzwinkle, William. *Trouble in Bugland: A Collection of Inspector Mantis Mysteries* (6–8). Illus. by Joe Servello. 1996, Godine paper $14.95 (1-56792-070-5). 160pp. An all-insect cast in a takeoff on Sherlock Holmes mysteries. A reissue.

6928 Krupinski, Loretta. *Lost in the Fog* (3–4). Illus. 1990, Little, Brown $14.95 (0-316-07462-4). 32pp. When their boat loaded with geese overturns, Mother Tipton thinks of a novel plan to save herself and Willie. (Rev: BL 5/1/90)

6929 Labatt, Mary. *The Ghost of Captain Briggs* (3–5). Illus. by Troy Hill-Jackson. Series: Sam, Dog Detective. 1999, Kids Can $12.95 (1-55074-638-3); paper $4.95 (1-55074-636-7). 116pp. Jenny learns to read the thoughts of sheepdog Samantha, and together they investigate a haunted house. Also use *Spying on Dracula* (1999). (Rev: HBG 3/00; SLJ 2/00)

6930 Lachtman, Ofelia Dumas. *Call Me Consuelo* (4–6). 1997, Arte Publico paper $9.95 (1-55885-187-9). 147pp. Consuelo, a recent arrival in Los Angeles, becomes involved in finding the criminals who are committing mysterious local robberies. (Rev: SLJ 7/97)

6931 Landon, Lucinda. *Meg Mackintosh and the Mystery at the Medieval Castle: A Solve-It-Yourself Mystery* (3–6). Illus. by author. 1989, Little, Brown paper $4.95 (0-316-51376-8). 64pp. While Meg and her class visit a castle, a jewel-encrusted chalice is stolen. Also use: *Meg Mackintosh and the Case of the Curious Whale Watch* (1987). (Rev: BL 6/15/89)

6932 Landon, Lucinda. *Meg Mackintosh and the Mystery at the Soccer Match* (3–6). Illus. by author. Series: Solve-It-Yourself Mystery. 1997, Secret Passage paper $4.95 (1-888695-05-6). 48pp. Detective Meg and her soccer team are competing for a gold medal that suddenly disappears from the awards table. (Rev: SLJ 3/98)

6933 Landon, Lucinda. *Meg Mackintosh and the Mystery in the Locked Library: A Solve-It-Yourself Mystery* (3–6). Illus. 1996, Secret Passage paper $4.95 (1-888695-04-8). 48pp. Along with Meg Mackintosh, readers are asked to solve the mystery of the stolen rare book. (Rev: BL 2/1/93; SLJ 3/93)

6934 Lawson, Julie. *Goldstone* (5–7). 1998, Stoddart paper $6.95 (0-7737-5891-7). 176pp. A suspenseful adventure set in British Columbia at the turn of the century in which 12-year-old Karen, who is coping with her mother's death in a landslide, dreams that there soon will be another, more deadly one. (Rev: BL 7/98; SLJ 5/98)

6935 Lee, Marie G. *Night of the Chupacabras* (3–6). 1998, Avon $14.00 (0-380-97706-0). 128pp. Korean Americans Mi-Sun and her brother Ju-Won go with their friend Lupe to a ranch in Mexico where they uncover a mystery involving strange puncture wounds found on vegetables and animals. (Rev: BL 11/15/98; HBG 3/99; SLJ 12/98)

6936 Lehr, Norma. *The Secret of the Floating Phantom* (3–6). 1994, Lerner LB $19.93 (0-8225-0736-6). 192pp. Kathy's special psychic powers help her locate a buried treasure. (Rev: BL 12/1/94; SLJ 12/94)

6937 Lehr, Norma. *The Shimmering Ghost of Riversend* (5–7). 1991, Lerner LB $19.95 (0-8225-0732-3). 168pp. An engaging mystery concerning an old family mansion in gold-rush country where Kathy has gone to spend the summer with her aunt. (Rev: BL 10/1/91)

6938 Leroe, Ellen. *Racetrack Robbery* (2–4). Illus. 1996, Hyperion $13.95 (0-7868-0093-3); paper $3.95 (0-7868-1092-0). 64pp. With their invisible Ghost Dog, Artie and little sister Sarah solve the mystery of a missing coin. (Rev: BL 4/1/96; SLJ 5/96)

6939 Leroux, Gaston. *The Phantom of the Opera* (3–6). Illus. by Paul Jennis. 1989, Random paper $3.99 (0-394-83847-5). 48pp. An abridgment of this horror story about a defaced man who lives in the depths of an opera house. (Rev: SLJ 1/90)

6940 Lester, Alison. *The Quicksand Pony* (4–6). 1998, Houghton $15.00 (0-395-93749-3). 160pp. When Biddy joins her parents on a cattle roundup in the Australian wilderness, she encounters a young orphan boy who has been surviving alone in the wilds. (Rev: BCCB 10/98; BL 12/15/98; HB 1–2/99; HBG 3/99; SLJ 10/98)

6941 Levin, Betty. *Fire in the Wind* (4–8). 1995, Greenwillow $15.00 (0-688-14299-0). 137pp. Meg, a self-sufficient girl who cares for her younger brother and backward cousin, faces a crisis when a raging fire threatens her home. (Rev: BCCB 1/96; SLJ 10/95)

6942 Levin, Betty. *Island Bound* (5–7). Illus. 1997, Greenwillow $15.00 (0-688-15217-1). 224pp. Two teenagers uncover the truth behind a 150-year-old tragedy while they spend time on a tiny Maine island. (Rev: BL 7/97; HBG 3/98; SLJ 10/97)

6943 Levin, Betty. *Shadow-Catcher* (4–7). 2000, Greenwillow $15.95 (0-688-17862-6). 160pp. In Maine during the 1890s young Jonathan Capewell has the opportunity to act the detective in a local mystery and behave like the heroes in the dime novels he reads. (Rev: BL 5/15/00*; HB 7–8/00; HBG 10/00; SLJ 6/00)

6944 Levy, Elizabeth. *Frankenstein Moved In on the Fourth Floor* (2–4). Illus. by Mordicai Gerstein. 1979, HarperCollins paper $4.95 (0-06-440122-7). 64pp. Is the strange Mr. Frank really Frankenstein? A sequel is: *Dracula Is a Pain in the Neck* (1983).

6945 Levy, Elizabeth. *A Mammoth Mix-Up* (2–5). Illus. 1995, HarperCollins LB $12.89 (0-06-024815-7). 96pp. Brian and his sister Penny solve the mystery of the mammoth tusk they have found in their garden. (Rev: BL 9/15/95; SLJ 12/95)

6946 Levy, Elizabeth. *Something Queer at the Library: A Mystery* (2–4). Illus. by Mordicai Gerstein. 1989, Dell paper $3.50 (0-440-48120-1). 48pp. Jill and Gwen try to track down the person who is mutilating books in the library. Sequels are: *Something Queer on Vacation* (1980, Delacorte); *Something Queer at the Haunted School* (1982, Delacorte); *Something Queer Is Going On* (1982); *Something Queer at the Ball Park* (1984).

6947 Levy, Elizabeth. *Something Queer in the Wild West* (2–5). Illus. by Mordicai Gerstein. 1997, Hyperion $14.95 (0-7868-0258-8); paper $4.95 (0-7868-1117-X). 48pp. A lighthearted mystery in which friends Gwen and Jill visit a ranch in New Mexico and discover a haunted barn. (Rev: BL 4/15/97; SLJ 5/97)

6948 Lindbergh, Anne. *The Worry Week* (5–7). Illus. by Kathryn Hewitt. 1985, Harcourt $12.95 (0-15-299675-3); Avon paper $2.95 (0-380-70394-7). 144pp. Left alone with her sisters for a week in Maine, 11-year-old "Legs" spends most of her time tending to and worrying about her siblings. (Rev: BL 6/1/85; HB 9–10/85; SLJ 8/85)

6949 Lindgren, Astrid. *Pippi to the Rescue* (K–2). Illus. by Michael Chesworth. Series: Pippi Longstocking Storybooks. 2000, Viking $13.99 (0-670-88074-4). 32pp. This heavily illustrated episode from the original Pippi Longstocking tells about the rescue of two children from a burning building. (Rev: BL 10/1/00; HBG 10/00)

6950 Lisle, Janet T. *A Message from the Match Girl* (4–6). Series: Investigators of the Unknown. 1995, Orchard LB $16.99 (0-531-08787-5). 128pp. Georgina and Poco wonder if the messages and mementos that Walter is receiving from the past are genuine. (Rev: BCCB 11/95; BL 10/1/95; SLJ 10/95*)

6951 Little, Kimberly Griffiths. *Enchanted Runner* (5–7). 1999, Avon $15.00 (0-380-97623-4). 160pp.

Twelve-year-old Kendall, who is half Native American, hopes to excel in running as his ancestors did, and is given an unusual opportunity to test himself. (Rev: BCCB 9/99; BL 9/1/99; HBG 3/00; SLJ 12/99)

6952 Lloyd, Emily. *Catch of the Day: The Case of the Helpless Humpbacks* (4–6). Series: Kinetic City Super Crew. 1997, McGraw-Hill paper $4.25 (0-07-006390-7). 166pp. The Kinetic City Super Crew faces opposition from some fishermen when its members try various methods to discourage whales from swimming into fishing nets off the coast of Nova Scotia. (Rev: SLJ 7/98)

6953 Lloyd, Emily. *Forest Slump: The Case of the Pilfered Pine Needles* (3–5). 1997, McGraw-Hill paper $4.25 (0-07-006388-5). 150pp. Using a message from science as a basis, this novel tells how four youngsters solve the mystery of who has stolen the pine needles from the forest floor. (Rev: BL 2/15/98; SLJ 4/98)

6954 Lourie, Peter. *The Lost Treasure of Captain Kidd* (5–8). Illus. 1996, Shawangunk Pr. paper $10.95 (1-885482-03-5). 136pp. Friends Killian and Alex set out to discover Captain Kidd's treasure buried on the banks of the Hudson River centuries ago. (Rev: BL 2/15/96; SLJ 6/96)

6955 McClain, Margaret S. *Bellboy: A Mule Train Journey* (4–6). Illus. by Sara Brown Stuart. 1989, New Mexico Publg. $17.95 (0-9622468-1-6). 192pp. A young boy takes a job leading a mule train into isolated towns in northern California in the 1870s. (Rev: BL 3/1/90)

6956 McGraw, Eloise. *Tangled Webb* (5–7). 1993, Macmillan $13.95 (0-689-50573-6). 154pp. Twelve-year-old Juniper has the feeling that her new stepmother is hiding something from her past, and she sets out to find out what it is. (Rev: BCCB 6/93; BL 6/1–15/93)

6957 Macken, Walter. *Island of the Great Yellow Ox* (4–7). 1991, Simon & Schuster paper $14.00 (0-671-73800-3). 192pp. Four boys are marooned on an Irish island where the golden ox of the Druids is hidden. (Rev: SLJ 10/91)

6958 Mahy, Margaret. *Clancy's Cabin* (3–5). Illus. by Barbara Steadman. 1995, Overlook $14.95 (0-87951-592-9). 95pp. Two brothers and a sister spend a summer in a cabin in New Zealand and have great adventures, one of which involves finding a treasure. (Rev: SLJ 1/96)

6959 Mahy, Margaret. *The Pirate Uncle* (3–6). Illus. 1995, Overlook $14.95 (0-87951-555-4). 128pp. Nick and sister Caroline vacation with Uncle Ludovic, a pirate who is trying to reform. (Rev: BCCB 5/95; BL 4/15/95; SLJ 5/95)

6960 Mahy, Margaret. *Tangled Fortunes* (4–6). Illus. 1994, Delacorte $14.95 (0-385-32066-3). 105pp. The friendship between a brother and sister is explored in this mystery set in New Zealand. (Rev: BL 10/1/94; SLJ 11/94*)

6961 Maifair, Linda Lee. *The Case of the Bashed-Up Bicycle* (2–4). 1996, Zondervan paper $3.99 (0-310-20736-3). 64pp. Tomboy Darcy solves the mystery of who stripped down her brother's new bicycle. Also use *The Case of the Nearsighted Neighbor* (1996). (Rev: BL 11/15/96)

6962 Markham, Marion M. *The April Fool's Day Mystery* (2–4). Illus. by Pau Estrada. 1991, Avon paper $3.50 (0-380-71716-6). 42pp. The detective twins Kate and Micky Dixon try to clear the name of Billy Wade, wrongfully accused of putting a snake in the school cafeteria's flour bin. (Rev: BL 7/91; SLJ 9/91)

6963 Markham, Marion M. *The Halloween Candy Mystery* (2–4). Illus. by Emily Arnold McCully. 1982, Avon paper $2.95 (0-380-70965-1). 48pp. The Dixon twins and their brother solve the mystery of a Halloween thief. Another mystery is: *The Christmas Present Mystery* (1984).

6964 Markham, Marion M. *The St. Patrick's Day Shamrock Mystery* (2–4). Illus. 1995, Houghton $15.00 (0-395-72137-7). 48pp. Someone has painted a large shamrock on their neighbor's front door, and the Dixon twins set out to find the culprit. (Rev: BL 9/15/95; SLJ 12/95)

6965 Markham, Marion M. *The Thanksgiving Day Parade Mystery* (3–4). Illus. 1986, Avon paper $2.95 (0-380-70967-8). 48pp. Twins Kate and Mickey track down the disappearance of the school band on the way to the Macy's Thanksgiving Day Parade. Also use: *The Birthday Party Mystery* (1989). (Rev: BCCB 11/86; BL 9/15/86; SLJ 11/86)

6966 Martin, Les. *Humbug* (5–8). Series: The X-Files. 1996, HarperTrophy paper $3.95 (0-06-440627-X). 103pp. Even for veteran FBI agents Fox Mulder and Dana Scully, the murder of "The Alligator Man" is bizarre. (Rev: SLJ 6/96)

6967 Martin, Terri. *A Family Trait* (5–7). 1999, Holiday $15.95 (0-8234-1467-1). 156pp. In this fast-paced story, 11-year-old Iris has a number of mysteries to solve while trying to finish a book report. (Rev: BL 10/1/99; HBG 3/00; SLJ 10/99)

6968 Maynard, Bill. *Pondfire* (4–6). 2000, Putnam $15.99 (0-399-23439-X). 96pp. Jeb Webster is falsely accused of a series of arsons in his small town and sets out to find the real culprit. (Rev: BCCB 3/00; BL 2/15/00; HBG 10/00; SLJ 5/00)

6969 Maynard, Bill. *Rock River* (4–6). 1998, Putnam $15.99 (0-399-23224-9). 112pp. Eleven-year-old Luke, still grieving over the death of his older brother, shares outdoor adventures with pal Milo and learns the meaning of courage when he saves Milo's life. (Rev: BCCB 10/98; HBG 3/99; SLJ 10/98)

6970 Mazer, Harry. *Snow Bound* (5–7). 1987, Dell $18.50 (0-8446-6240-2); paper $4.99 (0-440-96134-3). In this survival story, Tony and Cindy spend 11 days together snowbound.

6971 Mazer, Harry. *The Wild Kid* (4–6). 1998, Simon & Schuster $15.00 (0-689-80751-1). 112pp. While lost in a forest preserve, Sammy, a 12-year-old with Down syndrome, stumbles on the hideout of Kevin, a reform-school escapee. (Rev: BCCB 11/98; BL 8/98; HB 9–10/98*; HBG 3/99; SLJ 10/98)

6972 Meacham, Margaret. *Oyster Moon* (3–6). Illus. by Marcy Ramsey. 1996, Cornell Maritime paper

$9.95 (0-87033-459-X). 112pp. Anna, who is able to communicate through telepathy with her twin brother, Toby, receives messages indicating that he is in danger. (Rev: SLJ 11/96)

6973 Medearis, Angela Shelf. *The Spray-Paint Mystery* (3–5). 1996, Scholastic paper $3.99 (0-590-48474-5). 102pp. A young African American third-grader sets out to find the culprit who is spray-painting a wall in his school. (Rev: BL 2/15/97; SLJ 4/97)

6974 Miller, Dorothy R. *The Clearing: A Mystery* (4–6). 1996, Simon & Schuster $15.00 (0-689-80997-2). 119pp. An 11-year-old girl becomes involved in an unsolved mystery in rural Pennsylvania. (Rev: BCCB 11/96; BL 11/1/96; SLJ 10/96)

6975 Mitchell, Nancy. *Global Warning: Attack on the Pacific Rim!* (5–8). Illus. by Darren Wiebe and Ryan T. Fong. Series: The Changing Earth Trilogy. 1999, Lightstream paper $5.95 (1-892713-02-0). 191pp. A thrilling adventure story about Jenny Powers, a wheelchair-bound youngster, who must warn the authorities of an impending biological disaster at her school. (Rev: SLJ 10/99)

6976 Monsell, Mary Elise. *The Mysterious Cases of Mr. Pin* (2–4). Illus. by Eileen Christelow. 1992, Pocket paper $3.50 (0-671-74084-9). 64pp. Mr. Pin is a penguin and he has come to Chicago from the South Pole to be a detective. (Rev: BL 5/15/89; SLJ 6/89)

6977 Murphy, Elspeth C. *The Mystery of the Dancing Angels* (2–5). Illus. 1995, Bethany paper $3.99 (1-55661-408-X). 64pp. The Three Cousins Detective Club sets out to solve the mystery involving a 4-year-old distant cousin and a family riddle. (Rev: BL 10/1/95; SLJ 9/95)

6978 Murphy, Elspeth C. *The Mystery of the Eagle Feather* (2–4). Illus. by Joe Nordstrom. Series: Three Cousins Detective Club. 1995, Bethany paper $3.99 (1-55661-413-6). 64pp. Timothy, Titus, and Sarah-Jane attend a powwow and solve the mystery of some missing feathers. (Rev: BL 2/15/96)

6979 Murphy, Elspeth C. *The Mystery of the Haunted Lighthouse* (2–4). Illus. by Joe Nordstrom. Series: Three Cousins Detective Club. 1995, Bethany paper $3.99 (1-55661-411-X). 64pp. The Three Cousins Detective Club visits an abandoned lighthouse and decides it is haunted. (Rev: BL 12/15/95)

6980 Murphy, Elspeth C. *The Mystery of the Hobo's Message* (2–4). Illus. 1995, Bethany paper $3.99 (1-55661-409-8). 64pp. Five youngsters use coded messages to foil a plot by developers to take over property dishonestly. (Rev: BL 10/15/95; SLJ 11/95)

6981 Murrow, Liza Ketchum. *The Ghost of Lost Island* (4–6). 1991, Holiday $15.95 (0-8234-0874-4). 176pp. Gabe and his sister try to solve the mystery of a drowned dairymaid on Lost Island. (Rev: BCCB 5/91; BL 4/15/91; SLJ 5/91)

6982 Myers, Edward. *Hostage* (5–7). 1996, Hyperion $15.95 (0-7868-0115-8). 192pp. During a hiking trip in Dinosaur National Monument, two youngsters are held hostage by a man who has stolen a dinosaur egg. (Rev: BCCB 2/96; BL 4/15/96; SLJ 4/96)

6983 Naylor, Phyllis Reynolds. *The Bodies in the Bessledorf Hotel* (4–6). 1986, Macmillan LB $15.00 (0-689-31304-7); Avon paper $2.99 (0-380-70485-4). 144pp. Bodies keep appearing in the hotel rooms, and Bernie is afraid his father will lose his manager's job. (Rev: BCCB 1/87; BL 10/1/86; SLJ 12/86)

6984 Naylor, Phyllis Reynolds. *The Bomb in the Bessledorf Bus Depot* (4–6). 1996, Simon & Schuster $15.00 (0-689-80461-X). 136pp. Bernie and friends try to clear his sister from charges that she was involved in some local bombings. (Rev: BL 4/1/96; SLJ 5/96)

6985 Naylor, Phyllis Reynolds. *Carlotta's Kittens and the Club of Mysteries* (3–6). Illus. Series: Club of Mysteries. 2000, Simon & Schuster $16.00 (0-689-83269-9). 144pp. The male members of the Club of Mysteries share many adventures when they take care of five kittens until the young ones can be delivered to their new home. (Rev: BL 11/15/00; HBG 3/01; SLJ 1/01)

6986 Naylor, Phyllis Reynolds. *The Face in the Bessledorf Funeral Parlor* (4–6). 1993, Atheneum $14.00 (0-689-31802-2). 144pp. A zany mystery that involves a new, improved funeral parlor, missing retirement funds, and a chuck roast. (Rev: BL 10/15/93; SLJ 10/93)

6987 Naylor, Phyllis Reynolds. *The Fear Place* (5–7). 1994, Atheneum $16.95 (0-689-31866-9). 128pp. When two brothers are left alone in a remote mountain camp for a few days, their mounting dislike of each other explodes in this gripping survival story. (Rev: BCCB 1/95; BL 12/15/94; SLJ 12/94)

6988 Naylor, Phyllis Reynolds. *One of the Third-Grade Thonkers* (4–6). Illus. 1988, Macmillan $16.95 (0-689-31424-8); Dell paper $4.50 (0-440-40407-X). 144pp. Jimmy and his third-grade pals form an elite macho club, but it takes a wreck on the Mississippi for them to learn what bravery is really about. (Rev: BL 10/1/88; SLJ 12/88)

6989 Naylor, Phyllis Reynolds. *Peril in the Bessledorf Parachute Factory* (4–6). 2000, Simon & Schuster $16.00 (0-689-82539-0). 148pp. In this Bessledorf Hotel adventure, Bernie Magruder tries to marry off his sister so he can have her room. (Rev: BL 1/1–15/00; HBG 3/01; SLJ 2/00)

6990 Naylor, Phyllis Reynolds. *The Treasure of Bessledorf Hill* (3–5). 1998, Simon & Schuster $15.00 (0-689-81337-6). 136pp. In this Bessledorf mystery, Bernie decides to follow clues he hopes will lead to buried treasure. (Rev: BL 1/1–15/98; HBG 10/98; SLJ 3/98)

6991 Newman, Robert. *The Case of the Baker Street Irregular: A Sherlock Holmes Story* (4–6). 1984, Macmillan paper $4.95 (0-689-70766-5). Young Andrew unexpectedly finds himself teamed up with Sherlock Holmes.

6992 Nixon, Joan Lowery. *Ghost Town* (4–7). 2000, Delacorte $14.95 (0-385-32681-5). 149pp. This collection of stories combines the author's flair for writing mysteries with an interest in the Wild West. (Rev: BL 9/1/00; HBG 3/01; SLJ 10/00)

6993 Nixon, Joan Lowery. *Search for the Shadow-man* (4–6). 1996, Delacorte $15.95 (0-385-32203-8). 149pp. Using computer research, Andy tries to clear the name of a long-dead relative accused of treachery. (Rev: BCCB 1/97; BL 10/1/96; SLJ 11/96)

6994 Nixon, Joan Lowery. *Who Are You?* (5–9). 1999, Delacorte $15.95 (0-385-32566-5). 184pp. Kristi gets involved in a frightening adventure when she discovers that a mysterious man who has been keeping a file on her is a target for murder. (Rev: HBG 10/99; SLJ 6/99)

6995 Nolan, Peggy. *The Spy Who Came in from the Sea* (4–8). 1999, Pineapple $14.95 (1-56164-186-3). 129pp. In this adventure story set in World War II Florida, 14-year-old Frank, who has a reputation for lying, is not believed when he claims to have seen a German sub off the coast. (Rev: HBG 3/00; SLJ 1/00)

6996 O'Dell, Scott. *Black Star, Bright Dawn* (5–8). 1988, Houghton $16.00 (0-395-47778-6); Fawcett paper $4.50 (0-449-70340-1). 144pp. An Inuit girl decides to run the 1,197-mile sled dog race called the Iditarod. (Rev: BCCB 6/88; BL 4/1/88; SLJ 5/88)

6997 O'Dell, Scott. *Island of the Blue Dolphins* (5–8). 1960, Houghton $16.00 (0-395-06962-9); Dell paper $5.99 (0-440-43988-4). 192pp. An Indian girl spends 18 years alone on an island off the coast of California in the 1800s. Newbery Award winner, 1961. A sequel is: *Zia* (1976).

6998 O'Malley, Kevin. *Who Killed Cock Robin?* (2–4). Illus. 1993, Lothrop LB $14.93 (0-688-12431-3). 32pp. In this complex mystery, Cock Robin fakes his own death to steal some precious jewels. (Rev: BL 11/15/93)

6999 Orr, Wendy. *Nim's Island* (2–5). Illus. by Kerry Millard. 2001, Knopf LB $16.99 (0-375-91123-5). 144pp. When her father leaves their isolated island to study plankton, Nim is left alone with a marine iguana, a sea lion, and her trusty computer to keep her company. (Rev: SLJ 2/01)

7000 Osborne, Mary Pope. *Spider Kane and the Mystery Under the May-Apple* (3–5). Illus. by Victoria Chess. 1992, Knopf LB $11.99 (0-679-90855-2). 128pp. Nature details embellish the story of butterflies who seek the advice of sleuth Spider Kane. (Rev: BCCB 5/92; BL 5/1/92; HBG 3/00; SLJ 4/92)

7001 Otis, James. *Toby Tyler: Or Ten Weeks with a Circus* (4–6). 1981, Buccaneer LB $25.95 (0-89966-363-X); Dover paper $2.00 (0-486-29349-1). 152pp. A perennial favorite about a subject popular with most children.

7002 Page, Katherine H. *Christie and Company in the Year of the Dragon* (5–8). 1997, Avon $14.00 (0-380-97397-9). 144pp. When their Chinese American schoolmate is threatened with deportation, three teenage amateur sleuths come to her aid. (Rev: HBG 10/98; SLJ 5/98)

7003 Patneaude, David. *Someone Was Watching* (5–8). Illus. by Paul Micich. 1993, Whitman LB $14.95 (0-8075-7531-3). 221pp. Chris and his friend disobey parental orders and fly to Florida to rescue Chris's younger sister from kidnappers. (Rev: SLJ 7/93)

7004 Paulsen, Gary. *Escape from Fire Mountain* (4–6). Series: Culpepper Adventure. 1995, Dell paper $3.99 (0-440-41025-8). 67pp. An adventure story in which a young girl faces incredible challenges to rescue two lost children. (Rev: SLJ 7/95)

7005 Paulsen, Gary. *The Legend of Red Horse Cavern* (4–6). Series: World of Adventure. 1994, Dell paper $3.99 (0-440-41023-1). 55pp. After two youngsters find a treasure chest, they become the targets of a gang of villains in this Western story. (Rev: SLJ 12/94)

7006 Paulsen, Gary. *The Rock Jockeys* (4–6). Series: World of Adventure. 1995, Dell paper $3.99 (0-440-41026-6). 66pp. An adventure story in which three boys, the Rock Jockeys, set out to climb Devil's Wall to find the remains of a World War II bomber. (Rev: SLJ 10/95)

7007 Pearce, Philippa. *Who's Afraid? And Other Strange Stories* (5–7). 1987, Greenwillow $11.95 (0-688-06895-2). 160pp. Eleven ghost stories, mostly in the supernatural category. (Rev: BCCB 4/87; BL 4/1/87; HB 5–6/87)

7008 Peck, Robert Newton. *The Cowboy Ghost* (5–9). 1999, HarperCollins LB $15.89 (0-06-028211-8). 240pp. In order to prove his maturity to his overly critical father, 16-year-old Titus decides to help his brother in a grueling cattle drive across Florida. (Rev: BL 6/1–15/99; HBG 10/99)

7009 Peck, Robert Newton. *Nine Man Tree* (5–8). 1998, Random $17.00 (0-679-89257-5). 176pp. Two children of a kind mother and an abusive father become involved in a hunt for a wild 500-pound boarhog in this novel set in the Florida wetlands. (Rev: BCCB 12/98; BL 8/98; HBG 3/99; SLJ 11/98)

7010 Petersen, P. J. *Liars* (5–8). 1992, Simon & Schuster $15.00 (0-671-75035-6). 146pp. Sam learns that he has the unusual ability to detect when people are not telling the truth. (Rev: SLJ 4/92*)

7011 Petersen, P. J. *White Water* (4–6). 1997, Simon & Schuster paper $15.00 (0-689-80664-7). 112pp. When his father is bitten by a rattlesnake, timid Greg finds he is in charge in this white-water rafting adventure. (Rev: BCCB 6/97; BL 6/1–15/97; SLJ 5/97)

7012 Peterson, Melissa. *Hasta La Vista, Blarney!* (3–6). Illus. 1997, HarperCollins paper $4.50 (0-06-440665-2). 144pp. Young detectives Ben and Maya globetrot while trying to follow clues left by Carmen Sandiego. (Rev: BL 2/1/97; SLJ 2/97)

7013 Pilling, Ann. *The Year of the Worm* (5–7). 2000, Lion paper $7.50 (0-7459-4294-6). 172pp. Lonely Peter Wrigley, who is mourning his father's death, gets his chance to become a hero when he uncovers a group of birds'-nest poachers in this English novel set in the Lake District. (Rev: SLJ 3/01)

7014 Pryor, Bonnie. *Marvelous Marvin and the Wolfman Mystery* (3–5). Illus. by Melissa Sweet. 1994, Morrow $15.00 (0-688-12866-1). 128pp. Marvin stumbles on some real crooks when he investigates the rumor that his new neighbor is a werewolf. (Rev: BL 3/15/94; SLJ 5/94)

7015 Ransome, Arthur. *Swallows and Amazons* (4–7). Illus. by author. 1985, Godine paper $14.95 (0-87923-573-X). 352pp. These adventures of the four Walker children have been read for many years. A reissue. Others in the series: *Swallowdale* (1985); *Peter Duck* (1987).

7016 Ransome, Arthur. *Winter Holiday* (4–7). Illus. by author. 1989, Godine paper $14.95 (0-87923-661-2). Further adventures of the Swallows and Amazons. A reissue. A sequel is: *Coot Club* (1989).

7017 Rau, Dana Meachen. *One Giant Leap* (3–5). Illus. by Thomas Buchs. Series: Odyssey. 1996, Smithsonian Institution $14.95 (1-56899-343-9); paper $5.95 (1-58899-344-7). 32pp. The first moon landing is described in a fictional account in which a young boy believes he is Neil Armstrong. (Rev: BL 10/15/96)

7018 *Read for Your Life: Tales of Survival from the Editors of Read Magazine* (5–8). Series: Best of Read. 1998, Millbrook LB $22.40 (0-7613-0362-6); paper $5.95 (0-7613-0344-8). 160pp. This a collection of thrilling adventure and survival stories culled from 50 years of publication. (Rev: BL 8/98)

7019 Rees, Celia. *The Truth Out There* (5–7). 2000, DK $16.95 (0-7894-2668-4). 217pp. Josh, who loves computer games, uncovers one that could only have been created by his long-dead uncle. (Rev: BCCB 11/00; BL 11/1/00; HBG 3/01)

7020 Repp, Gloria. *Mik-Shrok* (4–8). Illus. by Jim Brooks. 1998, Bob Jones Univ. paper $6.49 (1-57924-069-0). 133pp. A married missionary couple journey to a remote Alaska village in 1950, where they begin their work and, in time, acquire a dog team led by Mik-Shrok. (Rev: BL 3/1/99)

7021 Riehecky, Janet. *The Mystery of the Missing Money* (4–6). Illus. 1996, Forest House LB $12.95 (1-56674-087-8); paper $5.95 (1-56674-701-2). 120pp. Twins Karen and Kyle investigate strange lights and noises in an empty old house. (Rev: BL 7/96; SLJ 7/96)

7022 Riehecky, Janet. *The Mystery of the UFO* (4–6). Illus. 1996, Forest House LB $12.95 (1-56674-088-6); paper $6.95 (1-56674-702-3). 128pp. Rumors of UFO sightings bring twins Karen and Kyle to a campground to investigate. (Rev: BL 7/96; SLJ 7/96)

7023 Roach, Marilynne K. *Encounters with the Invisible World* (5–7). Illus. by author. 1977, Amereon $18.95 (0-89190-874-9). For this reworking of traditional stories, there are ten stories of ghosts, witches, and the devil.

7024 Roberts, Willo Davis. *The Absolutely True Story: My Trip to Yellowstone Park with the Terrible Rupes (No Names Have Been Changed to Protect the Guilty) by Lewis Q. Dodge* (4–7). 1994, Atheneum $15.00 (0-689-31939-8). 160pp. A humorous mystery about a trip to Yellowstone Park by Lewis and sister Alison with the strange Rupes family. (Rev: BCCB 2/95; BL 1/15/95; SLJ 3/95)

7025 Roberts, Willo. *Baby-Sitting Is a Dangerous Job* (5–7). 1987, Fawcett paper $4.50 (0-449-70177-8). 192pp. Darcy tries to cope with three bratty children, but a kidnapping puts her and her charges in the hands of three dangerous men. (Rev: BCCB 3/85; BL 5/1/85; SLJ 5/85)

7026 Roberts, Willo Davis. *Caught!* (4–7). 1994, Atheneum $16.00 (0-689-31903-7). 160pp. Vickie and her younger sister run away to join heir father in California, where they confront an intriguing mystery. (Rev: BL 4/1/94; SLJ 5/94)

7027 Roberts, Willo Davis. *Hostage* (4–7). Illus. 2000, Simon & Schuster $16.00 (0-689-81669-3). 144pp. When she returns home unexpectedly from school, Kaci is taken hostage, along with a snoopy neighbor, by a gang of thieves. (Rev: BCCB 2/00; BL 2/1/00; HBG 3/01; SLJ 2/00)

7028 Roberts, Willo Davis. *The Kidnappers* (4–7). 1998, Simon & Schuster $15.00 (0-689-81394-5). 144pp. Joel Bishop, a private-school student, can't get anyone to believe him when he witnesses a kidnapping. (Rev: BCCB 3/98; BL 2/1/98; HBG 10/98; SLJ 3/98)

7029 Roberts, Willo Davis. *Megan's Island* (5–7). 1988, Macmillan LB $14.95 (0-689-31397-7). 192pp. Eleven-year-old Megan and her brother are alarmed to discover that someone is following their family. (Rev: BCCB 4/88; BL 5/1/88; SLJ 4/88)

7030 Roberts, Willo Davis. *The Pet-Sitting Peril* (4–6). 1990, Simon & Schuster paper $4.99 (0-689-71427-0). 176pp. Nick and friend Stan happen upon a gang of arsonists.

7031 Roberts, Willo Davis. *Scared Stiff* (4–7). 1991, Macmillan $16.00 (0-689-31692-5). 160pp. Stories for middle readers set in an amusement park. (Rev: BCCB 2/91; BL 2/15/91)

7032 Roberts, Willo Davis. *What Could Go Wrong?* (4–6). 1989, Macmillan $15.00 (0-689-31438-8); paper $4.99 (0-689-71690-7). 176pp. Three cousins find mystery and adventure on a plane trip to San Francisco. (Rev: HB 5–6/89)

7033 Robinson, Mary. *The Amazing Valvano and the Mystery of the Hooded Rat* (4–6). 1990, Avon paper $2.75 (0-380-70713-6). 168pp. Maria's plans for her great magic act go astray when Lester the rat is stolen. (Rev: BL 6/15/88; SLJ 4/88)

7034 Rocklin, Joanne. *Sonia Begonia* (4–6). Illus. by Julie Downing. 1986, Avon paper $2.50 (0-380-70307-6). 96pp. Sonia Begley wants to follow in her family's footsteps and open her own business, which she does with some amusing results. (Rev: BCCB 3/86; BL 3/15/86; SLJ 5/86)

7035 Rogo, Thomas Paul. *A Surfrider's Odyssey* (5–8). Illus. by author. 1999, Bess Pr. $19.95 (1-57306-082-8). 64pp. Set in the 1940s, this old-fashioned novel tells how a boy teaches himself to surf and later becomes a hero when he rescues a woman whose sailboat has capsized. (Rev: HBG 10/99; SLJ 8/99)

7036 Roos, Stephen. *My Favorite Ghost* (5–7). Illus. by Dee deRosa. 1988, Macmillan LB $13.95 (0-

689-31301-2). 128pp. Thirteen-year-old Derek's money-making scheme involves the legend of a local ghost. A Plymouth Island story. (Rev: BL 4/15/88; HB 5–6/88; SLJ 4/88)

7037 Roy, Ron. *The Deadly Dungeon* (2–4). Illus. by John S. Gurney. Series: A to Z Mysteries. 1998, Random LB $11.99 (0-679-98755-X); paper $3.99 (0-679-88755-5). 86pp. Dink, Josh, and Ruth Rose uncover a mystery when they travel to Maine to visit a castle. (Rev: SLJ 10/98)

7038 Roy, Ron. *The Goose's Gold* (2–4). Illus. by John S. Gurney. Series: Stepping Stone. 1999, Random paper $3.99 (0-679-89078-5). 86pp. An easy chapter book mystery in which three young sleuths overhear a man planning a robbery and set out to foil his plot. (Rev: BL 10/15/99; HBG 10/99; SLJ 7/99)

7039 Ruckman, Ivy. *Night of the Twisters* (4–6). 1984, HarperCollins LB $15.89 (0-690-04409-7); paper $4.95 (0-06-440176-6). 160pp. An 11-year-old boy witnesses a series of tornadoes that destroy his Nebraska town.

7040 Ruckman, Ivy. *Spell It M-U-R-D-E-R* (4–6). 1994, Bantam paper $3.50 (0-553-48175-4). 160pp. Two girls stumble upon a murderer when they try to escape from a summer camp they detest. (Rev: BL 7/94; SLJ 8/94)

7041 Sachar, Louis. *Holes* (5–8). 1998, Farrar $16.00 (0-374-33265-7). 240pp. This Newbery Award-winning novel describes unfortunate Stanley Yelnats's stay at a juvenile detention home after he has been wrongfully found guilty of stealing a pair of sneakers. (Rev: HB 9–10/98*; HBG 3/99; SLJ 9/98*)

7042 Saunders, Susan. *The Curse of the Cat Mummy* (2–4). Series: The Black Cat Club. 1997, Harper-Trophy paper $3.95 (0-06-442037-X). 73pp. When the children of the Black Cat Club visit an exhibit of artifacts from ancient Egypt, the cat Mittens falls under a mysterious spell. (Rev: SLJ 3/97)

7043 Saunders, Susan. *The Ghost Who Ate Chocolate* (2–4). Illus. 1996, HarperCollins paper $3.95 (0-06-442035-3). 80pp. The four members of the Black Cat Club befriend the library ghost, Alice. A sequel is *The Haunted Skateboard* (1996). (Rev: BL 12/15/96; SLJ 11/96)

7044 Scheffler, Ursel. *The Man with the Black Glove* (2–5). Illus. 1999, North-South LB $13.88 (0-7358-1179-2). 62pp. After Martin and Pauline find a glove that a mysterious stranger has dropped, they suddenly are involved in a series of robberies. (Rev: BL 11/15/99; HBG 3/00; SLJ 12/99)

7045 Scheffler, Ursel. *The Spy in the Attic* (2–4). Trans. by Marianne Martens. Illus. 1997, North-South $13.95 (1-55858-727-6). 62pp. In this mystery adventure, Martin and his friends think that their new neighbor is a spy. (Rev: BL 6/1–15/97; SLJ 4/97)

7046 Schwartz, Alvin. *Scary Stories 3: More Tales to Chill Your Bones* (4–7). Illus. by Stephen Gammell. 1991, HarperCollins LB $15.89 (0-06-021795-2); paper $4.95 (0-06-440418-8). 128pp. A modern-

ized version of spooky tales handed down through the years. (Rev: BL 8/91; HB 11–12/91; SLJ 11/91)

7047 Scieszka, Jon. *Knights of the Kitchen Table* (3–5). Illus. by Lane Smith. 1991, Viking $14.99 (0-670-83622-2). 64pp. The Time Warp Trio hangs out with Lancelot and his pals. Also use: *The Not-So-Jolly Roger* (1991). (Rev: BCCB 7–8/91; BL 5/1/91; SLJ 8/91*)

7048 Seabrooke, Brenda. *The Haunting at Stratton Falls* (5–8). 2000, Dutton $15.99 (0-525-46389-5). 150pp. Eleven-year-old Abby, who has recently moved to Stratton Falls, New York, while her father is fighting in Germany during World War II, sees wet footprints in the hall and wonders if the stories about the house being haunted are true. (Rev: BCCB 9/00; BL 7/00; HBG 3/01; SLJ 8/00)

7049 Selznick, Brian. *The Boy of a Thousand Faces* (4–7). Illus. 2000, HarperCollins $14.95 (0-06-026265-6). 48pp. Ten-year-old Alonzo King has a fixation on horror movies and makeup disguises, both of which help him when the The Beast comes to town. (Rev: BL 9/15/00; HBG 3/01; SLJ 9/00)

7050 Service, Pamela F. *Phantom Victory* (4–6). 1994, Scribners paper $16.00 (0-684-19441-4). 128pp. Two friends on South Bass Island in Ohio try to find a fabulous necklace that was hidden years ago. (Rev: BL 5/15/94; SLJ 7/94)

7051 Shahan, Sherry. *Frozen Stiff* (4–7). 1998, Delacorte $14.95 (0-385-32303-4). 151pp. This is an exciting survival story set in Alaska that involves two cousins, Cody and Derek, and their ill-fated kayak trip into the wilderness. (Rev: BCCB 5/98; BL 7/98; HBG 3/99; SLJ 8/98)

7052 Sharpe, Susan. *Spirit Quest* (4–6). Illus. 1991, Macmillan LB $13.95 (0-02-782355-5). 128pp. As part of their spirit quests, two young Indian boys go on a two-night camping trip. (Rev: BCCB 9/91; BL 9/1/91; SLJ 10/91)

7053 Sharpe, Susan. *Waterman's Boy* (3–6). 1990, Macmillan paper $16.00 (0-02-782351-2). 96pp. Ten-year-old Ben helps an environmentalist track down the culprits who are polluting Chesapeake Bay. (Rev: BCCB 7–8/90; BL 5/1/90; SLJ 4/90)

7054 Sherlock, Patti. *Four of a Kind* (4–6). 1991, Holiday $13.95 (0-8234-0913-9). 160pp. Eleven-year-old Andy has only one dream: to drive a draft horse team in a pulling contest. (Rev: SLJ 10/91)

7055 Shura, Mary Francis. *Don't Call Me Toad!* (4–6). Illus. by Jacqueline Rogers. 1987, Avon paper $2.95 (0-380-70496-X). Jane and Dinah have a rocky relationship at first and become involved in a mystery about robberies that sweep a town. (Rev: BCCB 7–8/87; BL 5/15/87; SLJ 4/87)

7056 Simon, Seymour. *The On-Line Spaceman and Other Cases* (3–6). Illus. 1997, Morrow $15.00 (0-688-14433-0). 96pp. Using deduction and an advanced knowledge of science, 12-year-old Einstein Anderson solves ten short mysteries. (Rev: BL 5/1/97; SLJ 4/97)

7057 Skurzynski, Gloria. *Lost in the Devil's Desert* (4–6). Illus. by Joseph M. Scrofani. 1993, Morrow paper $3.95 (0-688-04593-6). 96pp. In this adventure story, Kevin is trapped in an ex-con's getaway car. A reissue.

7058 Skurzynski, Gloria, and Alane Ferguson. *Cliff-Hanger* (4–7). 1999, National Geographic $15.95 (0-7922-7036-3). 152pp. In Mesa Verde National Park, the Landon family encounters two problems — a foster care girl named Lucky, who is deceitful, and a rampaging cougar. (Rev: BL 4/15/99; HBG 10/99)

7059 Skurzynski, Gloria, and Alane Ferguson. *Deadly Waters* (4–7). Illus. Series: National Parks Mystery. 1999, National Geographic $15.95 (0-7922-7037-1). 160pp. The Landon kids — Jack, Ashley, and foster brother, Bridger — travel to the Florida Everglades where their parents are investigating the mysterious deaths of some manatees. (Rev: BL 10/15/99; HBG 3/00; SLJ 10/99)

7060 Skurzynski, Gloria, and Alane Ferguson. *Ghost Horses* (4–6). Illus. Series: National Parks Mystery. 2000, National Geographic $15.95 (0-7922-7055-X). 152pp. Horses that are behaving strangely, a flash flood, and interpersonal conflicts are three of the elements in this mystery story set in Utah's Zion National Park. (Rev: BL 12/15/00; HBG 3/01; SLJ 11/00)

7061 Skurzynski, Gloria, and Alane Ferguson. *The Hunted* (5–8). Illus. Series: National Parks Mystery. 2000, National Geographic $15.95 (0-7922-7053-3). 160pp. The Landon family sets out to discover why young grizzly bears are disappearing from Glacier National Park. (Rev: BL 6/1–15/00; HBG 10/00; SLJ 8/00)

7062 Skurzynski, Gloria, and Alane Ferguson. *Rage of Fire* (4–6). Illus. Series: National Parks Mystery. 1998, National Geographic $15.95 (0-7922-7035-5). 160pp. While visiting Devastation Trail in Hawaii Volcanoes National Park, Jack Landon, his sister, and their friend, a Vietnamese youngster, realize they are being stalked by a mysterious woman in red. (Rev: BL 6/1–15/98; HBG 10/98; SLJ 7/98)

7063 Skurzynski, Gloria, and Alane Ferguson. *Wolf Stalker* (4–6). Illus. 1997, National Geographic $15.00 (0-7922-7034-7). 154pp. Three youngsters solve the mystery of who is killing the wolves in Yellowstone Park. (Rev: BL 12/15/97; HBG 3/98; SLJ 1/98)

7064 Smith, Roland. *Jaguar* (5–8). 1997, Hyperion LB $16.49 (0-7868-2226-0). 192pp. When Jake visits his zoologist father at a jaguar preserve in Brazil, he gets involved in a mystery and, at one point, must survive alone in the Amazon jungle. (Rev: BL 5/15/97; SLJ 6/97)

7065 Smith, Roland. *The Last Lobo* (5–9). 1999, Hyperion LB $16.50 (0-7868-2378-X). 178pp. When Jake returns to his Hopi reservation in northern Arizona, he discovers that the tribe thinks that a Mexican wolf-lobo is killing their livestock. (Rev: HBG 3/00; SLJ 11/99)

7066 Smith, Roland. *Sasquatch* (4–7). 1998, Hyperion $15.95 (0-7868-0368-1). 176pp. In this thrilling adventure story set on Mount St, Helens on the eve of its eruption, Dylan and a retired biologist set out to find Sasquatch, who has been sighted in the area. (Rev: BL 4/15/98; HBG 10/98; SLJ 6/98)

7067 Snicket, Lemony. *The Bad Beginning* (4–7). Illus. 1999, HarperCollins paper $8.95 (0-06-440766-7). 192pp. A humorous story about the ill-fated Beaudelaire orphans and the creepy, wicked villains they never seem to avoid. (Rev: BL 12/1/99; HBG 3/00; SLJ 11/99)

7068 Snicket, Lemony. *The Miserable Mill* (4–6). Series: A Series of Unfortunate Events. 2000, HarperCollins LB $14.89 (0-06-028315-7). 128pp. The unfortunate Baudelaire orphans are forced to work in a lumber mill in this entertaining segment of the ongoing melodrama set in mock-Victorian times. (Rev: BL 5/1/00; HBG 10/00; SLJ 7/00)

7069 Snicket, Lemony. *The Wide Window* (4–7). Illus. 2000, HarperCollins LB $14.89 (0-06-028314-9); paper $8.95 (0-06-440768-3). 128pp. The three Baudelaire children have a new guardian, timid cousin Josephine, but they are pursued by former keeper Count Olaf. (Rev: BL 2/1/00; HBG 10/00; SLJ 1/00)

7070 Snyder, Zilpha Keatley. *The Headless Cupid* (4–7). 1971, Macmillan $17.00 (0-689-20687-9); Dell paper $4.99 (0-440-43507-2). 208pp. Amanda, a student of the occult, upsets her new family. A sequel is: *The Famous Stanley Kidnapping Case* (1985).

7071 Sobol, Donald J. *Encyclopedia Brown and the Case of the Disgusting Sneakers* (3–5). Illus. by Gail Owens. 1990, Morrow $15.95 (0-688-09012-5). 68pp. Ten new cases just as hard to solve and as much fun as previous brainteasers. (Rev: BCCB 12/90; BL 9/15/90; SLJ 1/91)

7072 Sobol, Donald J. *Encyclopedia Brown and the Case of the Mysterious Handprints* (3–5). Illus. 1985, Morrow $16.00 (0-688-04626-6). 96pp. Matching wits with the 10-year-old sleuth in ten more crime cases. Also use: *Encyclopedia Brown and the Case of the Secret Pitch* (1978, Bantam); *Encyclopedia Brown Lends a Hand* (1979, Dutton); *Encyclopedia Brown and the Case of the Treasure Hunt* (1988). (Rev: BL 11/15/85; SLJ 2/86)

7073 Sobol, Donald J. *Encyclopedia Brown and the Case of the Sleeping Dog* (3–5). Illus. by Warren Chang. 1998, Delacorte $14.95 (0-385-32576-2). 70pp. The fifth-grade crime buster reappears in a series of mysteries involving himself and junior partner, Sally Kimball. (Rev: HBG 3/99; SLJ 11/98)

7074 Sobol, Donald J. *Encyclopedia Brown and the Case of the Slippery Salamander* (3–5). Illus. 1999, Delacorte $14.95 (0-385-32579-7). 76pp. Ten mysteries are presented in this new book of Leroy Brown's adventures. (Rev: BL 9/1/99; HBG 3/00; SLJ 11/99)

7075 Sobol, Donald J. *Encyclopedia Brown, Boy Detective* (3–5). Illus. by Leonard Shortall and Lillian Brandi. 1979, Bantam paper $4.50 (0-553-15724-8). 96pp. Ten-year-old Leroy Brown opens his own detective agency and solves ten crimes. Some sequels are: *Encyclopedia Brown and the Case of the Dead Eagles* (1977); *Encyclopedia Brown Finds the Clues; Encyclopedia Brown Gets*

His Man; Encyclopedia Brown Keeps the Peace (all 1979); *Encyclopedia Brown Sets the Pace* (1984).

7076 Soto, Gary. *Crazy Weekend* (4–7). 1994, Scholastic $13.95 (0-590-47814-1). 143pp. Two boys are being pursued by some crooks in this fast-moving adventure story. (Rev: BCCB 7–8/94; SLJ 3/94)

7077 Sperry, Armstrong. *Call It Courage* (5–8). Illus. by author. 1968, Macmillan $16.00 (0-02-786030-2); paper $4.99 (0-689-71391-6). 96pp. The "Crusoe" theme is interwoven with this story of a Polynesian boy's courage in facing the sea he feared. Newbery Award winner, 1941.

7078 Spinelli, Jerry. *Blue Ribbon Blues* (3–4). Illus. by Donna Nelson. Series: Stepping Stone. 1998, Random LB $11.99 (0-679-98753-3); paper $3.99 (0-679-88753-9). 69pp. Because of her brother's tricks, Tooter loses her chance to show her pet goat at the county fair, but in a reversal of fortune she becomes a popular heroine through an act of courage. (Rev: SLJ 5/98)

7079 Spirn, Michele. *The Bridges in London: Going to London* (5–7). Series: Going To. 2000, Four Corners paper $7.95 (1-893577-00-7). 96pp. When two sisters fly to London with their parents, they become involved in a mystery when they find a suitcase full of knives. (Rev: SLJ 3/00)

7080 Stanley, George E. *The Clue of the Left-Handed Envelope* (2–3). Illus. by Sal Murdocca. Series: Third-Grade Detectives. 2000, Simon & Schuster paper $3.99 (0-689-82194-8). 80pp. Noelle and Todd together with the other third graders and their teacher, Mr. Merlin, unmask the identity of the person who has sent Amber Lee a secret-admirer letter. (Rev: BCCB 12/00; SLJ 2/01)

7081 Steiner, Barbara. *Foghorn Flattery and the Dancing Horses* (4–6). 1991, Avon paper $2.95 (0-380-76147-5). 108pp. Carly and brother Foghorn travel to Vienna and encounter a mystery. (Rev: BL 6/15/91)

7082 Stem, Jacqueline. *The Cellar in the Woods* (4–6). 1997, Eakin $14.95 (1-57168-115-9). 145pp. In East Texas, three cousins explore a deserted house and encounter danger. (Rev: SLJ 1/98)

7083 Stevenson, James. *The Bones in the Cliff* (4–7). 1995, Greenwillow $16.00 (0-688-13745-8). 128pp. Pete is sure that a hit man is stalking his father at their home on Cutlass Island. (Rev: BCCB 6/95; BL 5/1/95*; HB 7–8/95; SLJ 4/95)

7084 Stevenson, James. *The Unprotected Witness* (4–7). 1997, Greenwillow $15.00 (0-688-15133-7). 176pp. In this sequel to *The Bones in the Cliff*, Pete and his friend Rootie try to unravel the mystery of where a treasure is buried by seeking cludes in a letter from Pete's dead father. (Rev: BL 10/1/97*; HB 11–12/97; HBG 3/98; SLJ 9/97)

7085 Stolz, Mary. *Casebook of a Private (Cat's) Eye* (3–5). Illus. 1999, Front Street $14.95 (0-8126-2650-8). 128pp. Eileen O'Kelly, a cat detective from Boston, solves a number of short mysteries in this novel set in 1912. (Rev: BCCB 6/99; BL 4/15/99; HBG 10/99; SLJ 6/99)

7086 Strasser, Todd. *Gator Prey* (4–6). Series: Against the Odds. 1999, Pocket paper $3.99 (0-671-02312-8). 160pp. An exciting adventure story about Justin, his mother, her boyfriend Bill, and Bill's daughter Rachel, and their dangerous journey to safety after their small plane crashes in the Everglades. (Rev: BL 3/1/99; SLJ 5/99)

7087 Strasser, Todd. *Shark Bite* (5–8). 1998, Pocket paper $3.99 (0-671-02309-8). 147pp. An action-packed sea adventure in which 12-year-old Ian must take command of a sailboat during a freak storm that critically injures his leader. (Rev: BL 2/15/99; SLJ 12/98)

7088 Stray, P. J. *Secrets of the Mayan Ruins* (4–6). Series: Passport to Mystery. 1995, Silver Burdett LB $13.95 (0-382-24704-3); paper $4.95 (0-382-24705-1). 139pp. Three teenagers join forces to solve the mystery of the stolen Mayan artifacts in this mystery set in Mexico. (Rev: SLJ 9/95)

7089 Strickland, Brad. *The Beast Under the Wizard's Bridge* (3–6). 2000, Dial $16.99 (0-8037-2220-6). 160pp. A fast-paced mystery involving Lewis, Rosa, Rita, Mrs. Zimmerman, and Uncle Jonathan, who seems strangely upset at the news that an old iron bridge is to be torn down. (Rev: BL 11/1/00; SLJ 12/00)

7090 Strickland, Brad. *The Specter from the Magician's Museum* (4–6). 1998, Dial $15.99 (0-8037-2202-8). 160pp. When Rose Rita is imprisoned in a tomb by a believer in an ancient Egyptian cult, Jonathan and Florence come to her rescue. (Rev: BL 10/1/98; HBG 3/99; SLJ 11/98)

7091 Sukach, Jim. *Clever Quicksolve Whodunit Puzzles* (4–7). Illus. by Lucy Corvino. Series: Mini-Mysteries for You to Solve. 1999, Sterling $14.95 (0-8069-6569-X). 96pp. Thirty-five mini-mysteries are presented with answers appended. (Rev: SLJ 1/00)

7092 Talbert, Marc. *Small Change* (5–9). 2000, DK $16.95 (0-7894-2531-9). 170pp. A suspenseful novel set in Mexico and involving two kidnapped boys, one Mexican and the other American. (Rev: BCCB 6/00; HBG 10/00; SLJ 6/00)

7093 Talbott, Hudson, and Mark Greenberg. *Amazon Diary: The Jungle Adventures of Alex Winters* (4–6). Photos by Mark Greenberg. Illus. by Hudson Talbott. 1996, Putnam $15.95 (0-399-22916-7). While traveling in the Amazon rain forest, a young boy gets to know the Yanomami people and how they live. (Rev: BCCB 1/97; SLJ 9/96)

7094 Tanaka, Shelley. *On Board the Titanic* (5–7). Illus. by Ken Marschall. 1996, Hyperion $16.95 (0-7868-0283-9). 48pp. Real-life characters are re-created in this story of 17-year-old Jack Thayer and his voyage on the *Titanic* with his parents. (Rev: BCCB 9/96; BL 9/1/96; SLJ 10/96)

7095 Taylor, Cora. *Vanishing Act* (4–6). Series: Northern Lights Young Novels. 1998, Orca paper $7.95 (0-88995-165-9). 199pp. A suspenseful adventure story in which Jennifer, who can make herself invisible, gets the help of her twin sister Maggie and her best friend, Samuel, to solve the mystery of her father's disappearance. (Rev: SLJ 7/98)

7096 Taylor, Theodore. *The Odyssey of Ben O'Neal* (6–8). Illus. by Richard Cuffari. 1991, Avon paper $3.99 (0-380-71026-9). 224pp. Action and humor are skillfully combined in this story of a trip by Ben and his friend Tee to England at the turn of the century. Two others in the series: *Teetoncey; Teetoncey and Ben O'Neal* (both 1981).

7097 Taylor, Theodore. *Timothy of the Cay: A Prequel-Sequel* (5–7). 1993, Harcourt $13.95 (0-15-288358-4). 160pp. This tells what happened to the two main characters from the author's *The Cay* before their shipwreck on the Caribbean island and what happened after they were saved. (Rev: BCCB 11/93; BL 9/15/93; SLJ 10/93)

7098 Taylor, William. *Numbskulls* (4–6). 1995, Scholastic $14.95 (0-590-22629-0). 144pp. To help his younger sister, Chas submits to the ordeal of being placed in evil Alice's learning machine. A sequel to *Knitwits* (1992). (Rev: BL 10/15/95; SLJ 10/95)

7099 Thomas, Jane Resh. *Courage at Indian Deep* (5–7). 1984, Houghton paper $6.95 (0-395-55699-6). 128pp. A young boy must help save a ship caught in a sudden storm.

7100 Thomas, Jane Resh. *Fox in a Trap* (3–5). Illus. by Troy Howell. 1987, Houghton paper $5.95 (0-395-54426-2). 96pp. Daniel changes his mind about trapping once he accompanies his Uncle Pete. (Rev: BCCB 4/87; BL 4/1/87; SLJ 6–7/87)

7101 *A Treasury of Pirate Stories* (3–5). Ed. by Tony Bradman. Illus. 1999, Kingfisher paper $6.95 (0-7534-5190-5). 160pp. A collection of witty and varied pirate stories from such writers as Ransome, Mahy, Stevenson, Barrie, and Joan Aiken. (Rev: BL 7/99)

7102 Tuitel, Johnnie, and Sharon Lamson. *The Barn at Gun Lake* (4–6). Series: The Gun Lake Adventure. 1999, Cedar Tree paper $5.99 (0-9658075-0-9). 103pp. Wheelchair-bound Johnnie, who has cerebral palsy, stumbles onto a CD-pirating ring and tries to find its leader. Also use *Mystery Explosion!* (1999). (Rev: SLJ 8/99)

7103 Twain, Mark. *The Stolen White Elephant* (4–8). Illus. 1882, Ayer $19.95 (0-8369-3486-5). A tale of the elephant's guardian, who naively is impressed by a corrupt police detective. (Rev: BL 5/1/88; SLJ 2/88)

7104 Updike, David. *A Spring Story* (3–5). Illus. by Robert Andrew Parker. 1989, Pippin LB $15.95 (0-945912-06-4). 40pp. When spring comes, the ice breaks up and two adventurous boys are stranded on an ice floe. (Rev: BCCB 3/90; BL 1/15/90; SLJ 1/90)

7105 Valgardson, W. D. *Winter Rescue* (4–6). Illus. by Ange Zhang. 1995, Simon & Schuster paper $15.00 (0-689-80094-0). An adventure story that involves a young boy and the Icelandic-Canadian fishermen around Lake Winnipeg. (Rev: BCCB 12/95; SLJ 11/95)

7106 Vanasse, Deb. *Out of the Wilderness* (5–8). 1999, Clarion $15.00 (0-395-91421-3). 176pp. Fif-teen-year-old Josh, his father, and his older half brother move to Willow Creek, Alaska, where they build a cabin and try to live off the land. (Rev: BL 3/15/99; HBG 10/99)

7107 Van Draanen, Wendelin. *Sammy Keyes and the Hollywood Mummy* (5–8). Illus. by Dan Yaccarino. 2001, Knopf LB $16.99 (0-375-90266-X). 272pp. Sammy is visiting her mother in Hollywood when one of her mother's house mates is murdered. (Rev: SLJ 2/01)

7108 Van Draanen, Wendelin. *Sammy Keyes and the Hotel Thief* (4–6). 1998, Knopf LB $16.99 (0-679-98839-4). 163pp. Samantha Keyes witnesses a robbery, but the police won't believe her so she must catch the criminal herself. (Rev: BCCB 7–8/98; HBG 10/98; SLJ 7/98)

7109 Van Draanen, Wendelin. *Sammy Keyes and the Sisters of Mercy* (4–6). 1999, Knopf LB $16.99 (0-679-98852-1). 224pp. While doing detention time at St. Mary's Church, junior-high sleuth Sammy discovers that a valuable ivory cross has been stolen. (Rev: BL 4/1/99; HBG 10/99; SLJ 7/99)

7110 Van Draanen, Wendelin. *Sammy Keyes and the Skeleton Man* (4–7). 1998, Knopf LB $16.99 (0-679-98850-5). 180pp. On Halloween, Sammy and his friends witness a mugging and burglary and set out to find the culprit. (Rev: BL 9/1/98; HBG 3/99; SLJ 9/98)

7111 Verne, Jules. *Around the World in Eighty Days* (5–8). Trans. by George Makepeace Towle. Illus. by Barry Moser. 1988, Morrow $22.00 (0-688-07508-8). 256pp. An 1829 world map as endpapers highlights this handsome edition of the classic. (Rev: BL 2/15/89)

7112 Verne, Jules. *Twenty Thousand Leagues Under the Sea* (3–6). Illus. by Wayne Geehan. 1990, Troll LB $19.95 (0-8167-1879-2); paper $5.95 (0-8167-1880-6). 48pp. The fantastic adventures of Captain Nemo with a submarine in the 1860s.

7113 Vigor, John. *Danger, Dolphins, and Ginger Beer* (5–7). 1993, Macmillan $16.00 (0-689-31817-0). 192pp. In the British Virgin Islands, Sally joins some island children to capture a gang of drug smugglers. (Rev: BL 8/93; SLJ 7/93)

7114 Voigt, Cynthia. *The Callender Papers* (5–8). 1983, Fawcett paper $4.50 (0-449-70184-0). 224pp. Jean takes a summer job in the Berkshire hills of Massachusetts and finds adventure and mystery.

7115 Wallace, Barbara Brooks. *Cousins in the Castle* (4–6). 1996, Simon & Schuster $15.00 (0-689-80637-X). 152pp. A thrilling mystery set in Victorian times about Amelia and her life in the United States and the danger she faces. (Rev: BCCB 4/96; BL 4/1/96*; SLJ 5/96)

7116 Wallace, Barbara Brooks. *Ghosts in the Gallery* (5–7). 2000, Simon & Schuster $16.00 (0-689-83175-7). 144pp. Orphaned 11-year-old Jenny is sent to live with her wealthy grandfather in England and must work like a servant in a mansion where she is sure someone wants to kill her. (Rev: BCCB 7–8/00; BL 4/1/00; HB 7–8/00; HBG 10/00; SLJ 7/00)

7117 Wallace, Barbara Brooks. *Peppermints in the Parlor* (4–6). 1993, Macmillan paper $4.99 (0-689-71680-X). 208pp. Emily encounters mystery and terror when she goes to her aunt's home in San Francisco.

7118 Wallace, Barbara Brooks. *The Twin in the Tavern* (4–6). 1993, Atheneum $15.00 (0-689-31846-4). 192pp. In this mystery story, orphaned Taddy sets out to find his twin in Dickensian London. (Rev: BL 11/1/93; SLJ 10/93*)

7119 Wallace, Bill. *Blackwater Swamp* (4–6). Illus. 1994, Holiday $15.95 (0-8234-1120-6). 185pp. A woman, known by all to be a witch, helps Ted catch a group of crooks responsible for some local robberies. (Rev: BCCB 5/94; BL 6/1–15/94; SLJ 4/94)

7120 Wallace, Bill. *Danger in Quicksand Swamp* (4–7). 1989, Holiday $15.95 (0-8234-0786-1). 181pp. While searching for buried treasure, Ben and Jake become stranded on an island near Quicksand Swamp. (Rev: BL 1/1/90; SLJ 10/89)

7121 Wallace, Bill. *Eye of the Great Bear* (4–6). 1999, Pocket $14.00 (0-671-02504-X). 162pp. A fearful 12-year-old boy who is growing up in pioneer Texas gains courage when he encounters a big grizzly. (Rev: BL 2/1/99; HBG 10/99; SLJ 5/99)

7122 Wallace, Bill. *Trapped in Death Cave* (5–8). 1984, Holiday $15.95 (0-8234-0516-8). 176pp. Gary is convinced his grandpa was murdered to secure a map indicating where some gold is buried.

7123 Warner, Gertrude C. *The Mystery of the Hidden Painting* (3–5). Illus. by Charles Tang. Series: Boxcar Children Mystery. 1992, Whitman LB $13.95 (0-8075-5383-2). 117pp. Four children are determined to find the missing necklace once owned by their grandmother. (Rev: SLJ 9/92)

7124 Waysman, Dvora. *Back of Beyond: A Bar Mitzvah Journey* (5–7). Illus. 1996, Pitspopany paper $4.95 (0-943706-54-8). 140pp. On his trip to Australia, a 12-year-old Jewish boy becomes involved in the Aborigine culture and witnesses a ritual of manhood similar to a bar mitzvah. (Rev: SLJ 5/96)

7125 Weiss, Ellen, and Mel Friedman. *Color Me Criminal* (3–6). Illus. 1997, HarperCollins paper $4.50 (0-06-440663-6). 144pp. Based on the television show, two young detectives travel around the United States in search of Carmen Sandiego. (Rev: BL 2/1/97; SLJ 2/97)

7126 Whatley, Bruce, and Rosie Smith. *Whatley's Quest* (5–8). Illus. 1995, HarperCollins LB $14.89 (0-06-026292-3). 48pp. An oversize picture book that creates questing stories, each involving a letter of the alphabet and objects that begin with that letter. (Rev: BL 9/15/95; SLJ 1/96) [421]

7127 Wilson, Eric. *Murder on the Canadian: A Tom Austen Mystery* (4–8). Illus. by Richard Row. 2000, Orca paper $4.99 (1-55143-151-3). 95pp. A fast-moving mystery starring an intrepid hero who is also featured in *Vancouver Nightmare: A Tom Austen Mystery* (2000). (Rev: SLJ 1/01)

7128 Woodman, Nancy. *Sea-Fari Deep* (3–5). Illus. 1999, National Geographic $17.95 (0-7922-7340-0). 48pp. Using a fictionalized format, a participant in

the JASON Project describes how a young girl named Dusty was part of the expedition that explored the Sea of Cortez. (Rev: BL 4/1/99; HBG 10/99; SLJ 3/99)

7129 Woodruff, Elvira. *Ghosts Don't Get Goose Bumps* (4–6). Illus. by Joel Iskowitz. 1993, Holiday $15.95 (0-8234-1035-8). 96pp. On her visit to West Virginia, Jenna befriends an impish girl and is soon involved in a haunted marble factory and a mysterious disappearance. (Rev: BL 11/15/93; SLJ 10/93)

7130 Wright, Betty R. *The Dollhouse Murders* (4–7). 1983, Holiday $15.95 (0-8234-0497-8). 160pp. Dolls in a dollhouse come to life in this mystery about long-ago murders.

7131 Wright, Betty R. *A Ghost in the Family* (4–6). 1998, Scholastic $15.95 (0-590-02955-X). 176pp. Friends Chad and Jeannie are spending two weeks visiting Jeannie's aunt at her boardinghouse in Milwaukee where a psychic warns Chad that he is in danger. (Rev: BL 6/1–15/98; HBG 10/98; SLJ 9/98)

7132 Wright, Betty R. *Too Many Secrets* (3–5). 1997, Scholastic $14.95 (0-590-25235-6). 128pp. Chad and his friend Jeannie decide to investigate without telling others when they hear a prowler in a neighbor's house. (Rev: BL 10/1/97; HB 7–8/97; HBG 3/98; SLJ 8/97)

7133 Wright, Susan K. *Dead Letters* (4–6). Series: Dead-End Road Mysteries. 1996, Herald Pr. paper $6.99 (0-8361-9036-X). 176pp. Nellie and her friends set out to catch the culprit who is stealing mail from the boxes outside the Lucky Clover trailer park. (Rev: SLJ 9/96)

7134 Wright, Susan K. *The Secret of the Old Graveyard* (5–7). 1993, Herald Pr. paper $6.99 (0-8361-3627-6). 183pp. Nellie forgets the trouble she has accepting her hippielike parents when mysterious events occur in an old graveyard. (Rev: SLJ 11/93)

7135 Wyeth, Sharon D. *The Dinosaur Tooth* (3–4). Illus. 1990, Bantam paper $2.75 (0-553-15815-5). 96pp. The loss of Gregory's tooth causes problems when 9-year-old Annie is rehearsing neighborhood kids in her play. (Rev: BL 10/1/90)

7136 Wyss, Johann D. *Swiss Family Robinson* (5–8). Illus. by Lynd Ward. 1949, Putnam $16.99 (0-448-06022-1). 400pp. A family is shipwrecked in this classic story.

7137 Yep, Laurence. *The Case of the Firecrackers* (4–7). 1999, HarperCollins LB $14.89 (0-06-024452-6). 144pp. In this Chinatown mystery, Tiger Lil and her great-niece, Lily, investigate an attempt on a movie star's life and confront the accusation that Lily's brother did it. (Rev: BL 9/15/99; HBG 3/00; SLJ 9/99)

7138 Yep, Laurence. *The Case of the Goblin Pearls* (5–7). 1997, HarperCollins LB $15.89 (0-06-024446-1). 192pp. Lily and her Auntie Tiger Lil, a former actress, solve the mystery of the stolen pearls. (Rev: BCCB 5/97; BL 1/1–15/97; SLJ 3/97)

7139 Yep, Laurence. *The Case of the Lion Dance* (4–6). Series: Chinatown Mystery. 1998, HarperCollins LB $14.89 (0-06-024448-8). 224pp. Lily and her great aunt Tiger Lil, a public relations expert, try to find out who is responsible for ruining the opening of a new restaurant and stealing money meant for a charity. (Rev: BL 10/15/98; HBG 3/99; SLJ 11/98)

7140 Yep, Laurence. *Cockroach Cooties* (3–5). 2000, Hyperion LB $16.49 (0-7868-2419-0). 144pp. Brothers Teddy and Bobby join forces to fight the school bully, Arnie. (Rev: BCCB 6/00; BL 5/1/00; HBG 10/00; SLJ 5/00)

7141 Yolen, Jane, and Heidi E. Y. Stemple. *An Unsolved Mystery from History: The Mary Celeste* (3–5). Illus. 1999, Simon & Schuster $16.00 (0-689-81079-2). 32pp. The young narrator of this novel tackles the baffling true mystery of the *Mary Celeste,* a ship that was found floating in 1872 without its captain, his family, or crew members. (Rev: BCCB 11/99; BL 10/15/99; HBG 3/00; SLJ 11/99)

7142 *The Young Oxford Book of Nasty Endings* (5–10). Ed. by Dennis Pepper. Illus. 1998, Oxford $22.99 (0-19-278151-0). 224pp. A quality collection of horror stories beginning with a retelling of a Chaucer tale and progressing to contemporaries like Ray Bradbury and Evan Hunter. (Rev: BL 10/15/98)

7143 Zambreno, Mary F. *Journeyman Wizard* (4–7). 1994, Harcourt $16.95 (0-15-200022-4); Hyperion paper $5.95 (0-7868-1127-7). 240pp. Student wizard Jeremy is studying the casting of spells with Lady Allons when an unfortunate death occurs and he is accused of murder. (Rev: BL 5/1/94; SLJ 6/94)

7144 Zindel, Paul. *Raptor* (5–9). 1998, Hyperion LB $15.49 (0-7868-2374-7). 176pp. While on a paleontology dig, two friends discover a mysterious egg that hatches into a raptor. Mayhem follows when its mother attempts to save her baby — and herself — from the mercenary director of the dig. (Rev: BL 9/1/98; HBG 3/99)

7145 Zoehfeld, Kathleen W. *Fossil Fever* (2–4). Illus. 2000, Golden Bks. $10.99 (0-307-46400-8); paper $3.99 (0-307-26400-9). 48pp. A fictionalized version of a fossil-hunting expedition and a young boy who finds an important dinosaur bone. (Rev: BL 5/15/00; SLJ 11/00)

Animal Stories

7146 Adler, C. S. *More Than a Horse* (5–7). 1997, Clarion $14.95 (0-395-79769-1). 192pp. Leeann and her mother move to a dude ranch in Arizona, where the young girl develops a love of horses. (Rev: BCCB 3/97; BL 3/15/97; SLJ 4/97)

7147 Adler, C. S. *One Unhappy Horse* (5–7). 2001, Clarion $15.00 (0-618-04912-6). 155pp. Set on a small ranch near Tucson, this novel features 12-year-old Jan, her horse, Dove, an old lady in a retirement home, and Jan's new friend, Lisa. (Rev: BL 3/1/01)

7148 Adoff, Arnold. *The Return of Rex and Ethel* (2–4). Illus. by Catherine Deeter. 2000, Harcourt $16.00 (0-15-266367-3). When their dogs die, Pepper and Belle decide to undertake a memorial project, a shelter for wild animals. (Rev: HBG 10/00; SLJ 6/00)

7149 Alter, Judith. *Maggie and a Horse Named Devildust* (5–7). 1989, Ellen C. Temple paper $5.95 (0-936650-08-7). 160pp. Maggie is determined to ride her spirited horse in the Wild West show in this historical horse story. (Rev: BL 4/15/89)

7150 Alter, Judith. *Maggie and the Search for Devildust* (5–7). 1989, Ellen C. Temple paper $5.95 (0-936650-09-5). 159pp. Maggie, a gorgeous girl of the Old West, sets out to find her horse, which has been stolen. (Rev: BL 10/1/89)

7151 Anderson, Laurie Halse. *Fight for Life* (4–6). Series: Wild at Heart. 2000, Pleasant paper $4.95 (1-58485-043-4). 123pp. When ten sick puppies arrive at the animal clinic run by her grandmother, 11-year-old Maggie believes that a puppy mill is responsible and sets out to find who's behind it. (Rev: BL 5/1/00; SLJ 7/00)

7152 Arnosky, Jim. *Long Spikes* (4–7). Illus. 1992, Houghton $13.00 (0-395-58830-8). 90pp. As spring turns to summer, a yearling buck and his twin sister travel together after the death of their mother. (Rev: BCCB 4/92; BL 5/1/92; SLJ 5/92)

7153 Bagnold, Enid. *National Velvet* (5–8). Illus. by Ted Lewin. 1985, Avon paper $4.99 (0-380-71235-0). 272pp. A reissue of one of the most famous horse stories ever written, to celebrate its 50th anniversary. (Rev: BL 12/15/85)

7154 Barber, Phyllis. *Legs: The Story of a Giraffe* (4–6). 1991, Macmillan $13.95 (0-689-50526-4). 80pp. The story of a giraffe born in Kenya that reveals much about the lives of these fascinating animals. (Rev: BL 12/15/91; SLJ 1/92)

7155 Bauer, Marion Dane. *Alison's Puppy* (2–4). Illus. 1997, Hyperion LB $14.49 (0-7868-2237-6); paper $3.95 (0-7868-1140-4). 48pp. When a hoped-for puppy does not appear on her birthday, Alison settles for a kitten. (Rev: BL 5/1/97; SLJ 8/97)

7156 Baylor, Byrd. *Hawk, I'm Your Brother* (3–5). Illus. by Peter Parnall. 1976, Macmillan $16.00 (0-684-14571-5); paper $5.99 (0-689-71102-6). 48pp. A desert boy captures a young hawk, hoping it will teach him how to fly.

7157 Beales, Valerie. *Emma and Freckles* (3–6). Illus. by Jacqueline Rogers. 1992, Simon & Schuster paper $13.00 (0-671-74686-3). 176pp. Emma gets her wish with Freckles the pony, who turns out to be a little too much for an 11-year-old. (Rev: BCCB 5/92; BL 7/92; SLJ 6/92)

7158 Berends, Polly. *The Case of the Elevator Duck* (3–5). Illus. by Diane Allison. 1989, Random paper $3.99 (0-394-82646-9). 64pp. In spite of the rule that no pets are allowed in his housing development, little Gilbert decides to keep a duck in an elevator.

7159 Bograd, Larry, and Coleen Hubbard. *Colorado Summer* (3–6). Illus. by Sandy Rabinowitz. Series: Treasured Horses Collection. 1999, Gareth Stevens LB $14.95 (0-8368-2277-3). 128pp. Eleven-year-old Carrie is spending a summer on her aunt's ranch in Colorado when she becomes interested in competing in a rodeo because of her joy in riding Georgia, a fabulous horse. (Rev: SLJ 8/99)

7160 Brandenburg, Jim. *Scruffy: A Wolf Finds His Place in the Pack* (2–4). Illus. 1996, Walker LB

$16.85 (0-8027-8446-1). 32pp. A photo-essay about an outcast wolf that gradually finds status in the pack. (Rev: BCCB 10/96; BL 9/1/96; SLJ 12/96)

7161 Branford, Henrietta. *White Wolf* (4–6). Illus. 1999, Candlewick $16.99 (0-7636-0748-7). 96pp. Told by a white wolf, this wilderness story relates how he was raised by white settlers, escaped into the wild, and regained his lost wolf heritage. (Rev: BL 8/99; HBG 10/99; SLJ 6/99)

7162 Briggs-Bunting, Jane. *Laddie of the Light* (4–6). Illus. 1997, Black River Trading $17.00 (0-9649083-1-X). 43pp. Jessie adjusts to her parents' approaching divorce with the help of two dogs, one real and the other a fictitious one that her grandfather tells her about. (Rev: BL 7/97)

7163 Brooke, Lauren. *Heartland: Coming Home* (4–7). 2000, Scholastic paper $4.50 (0-439-13020-4). 144pp. When her mother dies, Amy works through her grief by helping horses with behavioral problems in this novel set on a Virginia horse farm. (Rev: BL 9/15/00)

7164 Brown, F. K. *Last Hurdle* (4–6). Illus. by Peter Spier. 1988, Shoe String LB $18.50 (0-208-02212-0). 202pp. Kathy spends her savings on a broken-down horse, but manages to restore him in this book originally published in 1953.

7165 Bryant, Bonnie. *Horse Crazy* (4–6). 1996, Bantam paper $4.50 (0-553-48402-8). 144pp. Three girls become friends at a riding stable. Also use: *Horse Shy* (1996). (Rev: BL 2/15/89)

7166 Bunting, Eve. *Some Frog!* (2–4). Illus. 1998, Harcourt $15.00 (0-15-277082-8). 48pp. An easily read book about a boy who, together with his mom, captures a large frog to enter in the frog-jumping contest at school. (Rev: BL 9/15/98; HBG 3/99; SLJ 10/98)

7167 Burgess, Melvin. *The Cry of the Wolf* (5–8). 1994, Morrow $16.95 (0-397-30693-8). 128pp. Young Ben Tilley insists that wolves run past his farm in rural Surrey, even though they have supposedly been gone from England for 500 years. (Rev: BL 10/15/92; SLJ 9/92)

7168 Burgess, Melvin. *Kite* (5–8). 2000, Farrar $16.00 (0-374-34228-8). 181pp. In this novel set in rural England in 1964, Taylor's father, a games keeper on a large estate, must stand up to his employer who is cruel to animals and wants to eliminate some rare birds. (Rev: BCCB 6/00; HBG 10/00; SLJ 4/00)

7169 Byars, Betsy. *The Midnight Fox* (4–6). Illus. by Ann Grifalconi. 1968, Puffin paper $4.99 (0-14-031450-4). 160pp. When Tom spends two months on a farm with his aunt and uncle, he never expects that a black fox will become the focus of his life.

7170 Byars, Betsy. *Tornado* (3–5). Illus. 1996, HarperCollins LB $14.89 (0-06-026452-7). 64pp. To pass the time during a tornado watch, Pete, a farmhand, tells about another Tornado, an unusual dog. (Rev: BCCB 11/96; BL 9/15/96; HB 11–12/96; SLJ 11/96)

7171 Byars, Betsy, et al. *My Dog, My Hero* (3–6). Illus. 2000, Holt $16.00 (0-8050-6327-7). 48pp. Author Byars and her two daughters collaborated on this collection of eight stories about heroic dogs. (Rev: BL 1/1–15/01; HBG 3/01; SLJ 1/01)

7172 Carlson, Nolan. *Summer and Shiner* (5–8). 1992, Hearth paper $6.95 (0-9627947-4-0). 160pp. In a small Kansas town in the 1940s, 12-year-old Carley adopts a raccoon called Shiner. (Rev: BL 9/15/92)

7173 Carnell, Suzanne, ed. *A Treasury of Pet Stories* (3–5). Illus. 1997, Kingfisher $6.95 (0-7534-5074-7). 160pp. Some of the authors represented in this fine collection are Beverly Cleary, Joan Aiken, Betsy Byars, and Judy Blume. (Rev: BL 8/97; SLJ 12/97)

7174 Carris, Joan. *Just a Little Ham* (4–6). Illus. by Dora Leder. 1993, Pocket paper $3.99 (0-671-74783-5). 144pp. The entire family soon becomes enamored of pet piglet Pandora. (Rev: BCCB 11/89; BL 1/15/90; SLJ 2/90)

7175 Casanova, Mary. *Stealing Thunder* (4–7). 1999, Hyperion LB $15.49 (0-7868-2268-6). 136pp. A fast-paced adventure in which Libby plans to kidnap Thunder, a horse that is being abused by his owner. (Rev: HBG 10/99; SLJ 10/99)

7176 Cole, Joanna, and Stephanie Calmenson, eds. *Give a Dog a Bone: Stories, Poems, Jokes, and Riddles About Dogs* (2–3). Illus. 1996, Scholastic $16.95 (0-590-46374-8). 96pp. An anthology of writings, anecdotes, and jokes about dogs. (Rev: BL 2/1/96; SLJ 3/96)

7177 Cone, Molly. *Mishmash* (3–5). Illus. by Leonard Shortall. 1962, Houghton $16.00 (0-395-06711-1). 128pp. A dog, Mishmash, moves in, takes over, and then helps his owner to adjust to a new home. Other series titles are: *Mishmash and the Sauerkraut Mystery* (1974); *Mishmash and the Robot* (1991).

7178 Conrad, Pam. *Don't Go Near That Rabbit, Frank!* (3–5). Illus. 1998, HarperCollins $14.95 (0-06-021514-3). 48pp. Philip and his sister are horrified when their pet dog, Frank, kills neighbor Oscar Hoover's pet rabbit and are mystified at a seeming resurrection. (Rev: BL 6/1–15/98; HBG 10/98; SLJ 10/98)

7179 Crisp, Marty. *My Dog, Cat* (3–6). Illus. 2000, Holiday $15.95 (0-8234-1537-6). 64pp. Even though he always wanted a big dog, Abbie finds that size doesn't matter when he takes care of a little Yorkie while its owner is away. (Rev: BCCB 12/00; BL 1/1–15/01; SLJ 1/01)

7180 Crisp, Marty. *Ratzo* (4–7). 1998, Northland $12.95 (0-87358-722-7); paper $6.95 (0-87358-723-5). 160pp. When a boy finds some racing greyhounds that have been abandoned, he is determined to bring the culprits to justice. (Rev: BL 2/15/99; HBG 3/99; SLJ 4/99)

7181 Dana, Barbara. *Zucchini Out West* (3–5). Illus. 1997, HarperCollins LB $14.89 (0-06-024898-X). 192pp. Ten-year-old Bill and his sister and pet ferret, Zucchini, travel west to spend time visiting ferret experts in Wyoming. (Rev: BL 7/97; SLJ 7/97)

7182 Dann, Colin. *Nobody's Dog* (5–7). 2000, Hutchinson $22.95 (0-09-176900-0). 136pp. After a series of adventures, an abandoned Border collie finds a permanent home with a loving master. (Rev: SLJ 1/01)

7183 DeJong, Meindert. *Along Came a Dog* (4–7). Illus. by Maurice Sendak. 1958, HarperCollins paper $4.95 (0-06-440114-6). 192pp. The friendship of a timid, lonely dog and a toeless little red hen is the basis for a very moving story, full of suspense.

7184 DeJong, Meindert. *Hurry Home, Candy* (4–6). Illus. by Maurice Sendak. 1953, HarperCollins LB $15.89 (0-06-021486-4); paper $6.95 (0-06-440025-5). 244pp. Candy is a little dog who, after many adventures, finds a home.

7185 Duffey, Betsy. *Puppy Love* (2–4). Illus. by Susanna Natti. Series: Pet Patrol. 1994, Puffin paper $3.99 (0-140-34997-9). 64pp. Evie and Megan have trouble placing Flea, the runt of the litter, in a good home. (Rev: BL 10/1/92; SLJ 9/92)

7186 Eckert, Allan W. *Incident at Hawk's Hill* (6–8). Illus. by John Schoenherr. 1995, Bantam paper $5.95 (0-316-20948-1). 173pp. A 6-year-old boy wanders away from home and is nurtured and protected by a badger.

7187 Edwards, Julie Andrews. *Little Bo* (3–5). Illus. 1999, Hyperion LB $20.49 (0-7868-2449-2). 90pp. Bo, a little kitten, is taken aboard a fishing trawler by a young sailor who is unaware that his skipper is allergic to cats. (Rev: BL 2/15/00; HBG 3/00; SLJ 12/99)

7188 Erickson, John R. *The Case of the Vanishing Fishhook* (3–6). Illus. by Gerald L. Holmes. Series: Hank the Cowdog. 1999, Viking $14.99 (0-670-88438-3); paper $4.99 (0-14-130356-5). 144pp. When Hank, a lovable dog, eats the liver that his young owner is using for fish bait, he realizes that he has also eaten a fish hook. (Rev: HBG 10/99; SLJ 4/99)

7189 Farley, Steven. *The Black Stallion's Shadow* (5–7). 1996, Random $16.00 (0-679-85004-X). 182pp. The Black Stallion develops a fear of shadows and trainer Alec Ramsay hopes for a cure. (Rev: BCCB 9/96; BL 9/15/96)

7190 Farley, Walter. *Black Stallion* (5–8). Illus. by Keith Ward. 1944, Random $11.99 (0-394-90601-2). A wild Arabian stallion and the boy who trained him. Other series titles: *The Black Stallion Returns; Son of the Black Stallion* (both 1977).

7191 Feldman, Eve B. *That Cat!* (2–4). Illus. 1994, Morrow $14.00 (0-688-13310-X). 112pp. Molly is devastated when her cat disappears, and she tries many tactics to get him home. (Rev: BL 10/1/94; SLJ 9/94)

7192 Gasque, Dale Blackwell. *Pony Trouble* (2–4). Illus. 1998, Hyperion paper $3.95 (0-7868-1218-4). 64pp. Amy is constantly in the shadow of her talented cousin Rebecca, but Amy knows she has one special skill, her horsemanship. (Rev: BL 7/98; SLJ 9/98)

7193 George, Jean Craighead. *The Cry of the Crow* (5–7). 1980, HarperCollins paper $4.95 (0-06-440131-6). 160pp. Mandy finds a helpless baby crow in the woods and tames it.

7194 George, Jean Craighead. *Frightful's Mountain* (5–8). 1999, Dutton $15.99 (0-525-46166-3).

176pp. Frightful, the falcon that appears in stories about Sam Gribley, such as *My Side of the Mountain,* is the central character in this novel in which she is torn between life in the wild and life with her master. (Rev: BL 9/1/99; HBG 3/00; SLJ 9/99)

7195 George, Jean Craighead. *There's an Owl in the Shower* (3–5). Illus. 1995, HarperCollins $14.95 (0-06-024891-2). 144pp. Borden hates the spotted owl because his father lost his logging job through conservation efforts to save it, but later he finds himself caring for a young owl he has rescued. (Rev: BL 9/1/95; SLJ 11/95)

7196 George, Twig C. *A Dolphin Named Bob* (2–5). Illus. 1996, HarperCollins LB $13.89 (0-06-025363-0). 64pp. Presents, in a fictional format, the life cycle of a dolphin at the Maryland State Aquarium. (Rev: BL 2/1/96; SLJ 5/96)

7197 Ghent, Natale. *Piper* (5–7). 2001, Orca paper $6.95 (1-55143-167-X). 176pp. The love and attention young Wesley showers on a tiny Australian shepherd puppy helps her recover from the death of her father. (Rev: BL 3/1/01)

7198 Gilbert, Suzie. *Hawk Hill* (3–5). Illus. by Sylvia Long. 1996, Chronicle $14.95 (0-8118-0839-4). 40pp. In this picture book, a young boy finds a new interest in caring for injured birds of prey. (Rev: BCCB 12/96; BL 11/1/96; SLJ 11/96)

7199 Gipson, Fred. *Old Yeller* (6–8). Illus. by Carl Burger. 1956, HarperCollins $23.00 (0-06-011545-9); paper $4.95 (0-06-440382-3). 176pp. A powerful story set in the Texas hill country about a 14-year-old boy and the ugly stray dog he comes to love. Also use: *Savage Sam* (1976).

7200 Graeber, Charlotte. *Fudge* (3–5). Illus. by Cheryl Harness. 1989, Pocket paper $3.99 (0-671-70288-2). 128pp. Chad Garcia's parents say he can have a puppy, but no one has time to train it, so Chad must prove himself responsible. (Rev: BCCB 7–8/87; BL 8/87)

7201 Graeber, Charlotte. *Nobody's Dog* (2–4). Illus. 1998, Hyperion LB $13.49 (0-7868-2093-4). 32pp. An abandoned pup outwits Miss Pepper and finds a home with her in spite of her initial dislike of the engaging canine. (Rev: BCCB 9/98; BL 8/98; HBG 10/98; SLJ 6/98)

7202 Greenberg, Martin H., and Charles G. Waugh, eds. *A Newbery Zoo: A Dozen Animal Stories by Newbery Award-Winning Authors* (4–7). 1995, Delacorte $16.95 (0-385-32263-1). 143pp. Twelve animal stories by such Newbery winners as Beverly Cleary, Betsy Byars, and Jean Craighead George. (Rev: BL 1/15/95; SLJ 4/95)

7203 Griffith, Helen V. *Foxy* (4–6). 1984, Greenwillow $15.00 (0-688-02567-6). 144pp. Jeff believes his dog Foxy is dead, but his neighbor, Amber, knows this isn't true.

7204 Haas, Jessie. *Be Well, Beware* (2–5). Illus. by Joseph A. Smith. 1996, Greenwillow $15.00 (0-688-14545-0). 72pp. Lily nurses her beloved horse, Beware, through a deadly attack of colic. (Rev: BCCB 3/96; BL 5/1/96; SLJ 4/96)

7205 Haas, Jessie. *Beware and Stogie* (2–5). Illus. 1998, Greenwillow $15.00 (0-688-15605-3). 80pp.

Lilly and her mare, Beware, face a great challenge in attempting to round up missing livestock during a violent storm. (Rev: BCCB 10/98; BL 8/98; HB 9–10/98; HBG 3/99; SLJ 11/98)

7206 Haas, Jessie. *A Blue for Beware* (2–4). Illus. 1995, Greenwillow $14.00 (0-688-13678-8). 64pp. Lily and her horse Beware compete in their first horse show. A sequel to *Beware the Mare* (1993). (Rev: BCCB 3/95; BL 5/15/95; HB 5–6/95; SLJ 5/95)

7207 Haas, Jessie. *A Horse Like Barney* (4–6). 1993, Greenwillow $13.00 (0-688-12415-1). 176pp. When Sarah narrows her choice of a horse to two, she must make some painful decisions. (Rev: BL 9/15/93; HB 11–12/93; SLJ 10/93)

7208 Hall, Elizabeth. *Child of the Wolves* (4–7). 1996, Houghton $16.00 (0-395-76502-1). 176pp. Granite, a Siberian husky pup, must survive in the wilderness when he is separated from his family. (Rev: BCCB 3/96; BL 4/1/96)

7209 Hall, Lynn. *Windsong* (4–6). 1992, Macmillan paper $12.95 (0-684-19439-2). 80pp. Looks like the only way Marty might be able to have a dog at home is if her parents divorce. (Rev: BCCB 2/93; BL 11/1/92)

7210 Hanel, Wolfram. *Abby* (2–4). Illus. by Alan Marks. 1996, North-South LB $13.88 (1-55858-649-0). 60pp. Moira's beloved pet dog, Abby, becomes ill after eating poisoned meat in this story set on an island near Ireland. (Rev: BL 12/1/96*; SLJ 1/97)

7211 Hanel, Wolfram. *Mary and the Mystery Dog* (2–4). Trans. by J. Alison James. Illus. by Kirsten Hocker. 1999, North-South LB $13.88 (0-7358-1044-3). 48pp. Mary finds a dog on the beach, and though he belongs to a local fisherman, he becomes her close companion. (Rev: BL 4/15/99; HBG 10/99; SLJ 5/99)

7212 Hart, Alison. *Shadow Horse* (4–8). 1999, Random $15.00 (0-679-88642-7). 230pp. When Jan begins caring for Shadow, a neglected horse, she uncovers suspicious facts about her old horse, which died a mysterious death. (Rev: BL 7/99; HBG 10/99; SLJ 10/99)

7213 Hearne, Betsy. *Eliza's Dog* (3–5). 1996, Simon & Schuster paper $16.00 (0-689-80704-X). 151pp. Eliza shares many adventures with her sheepdog pup, Panda. (Rev: BCCB 3/96; BL 4/1/96; HB 9–10/96; SLJ 5/96)

7214 Henkes, Kevin. *Protecting Marie* (5–7). 1995, Greenwillow $15.95 (0-688-13958-2). 208pp. Fanny is afraid that she will lose her pet dog if her temperamental father decides the dog must go. (Rev: BCCB 3/95; BL 3/15/95; HB 7–8/95; SLJ 5/95*)

7215 Henry, Marguerite. *Brown Sunshine* (4–6). Illus. 1996, Simon & Schuster paper $16.00 (0-689-80364-8). 93pp. At first, Molly is unhappy with the old mare she has bought, but gradually she grows to love Lady Sue. (Rev: BCCB 10/96; BL 10/1/96; SLJ 9/96)

7216 Henry, Marguerite. *King of the Wind* (5–8). Illus. by Wesley Dennis. 1990, Macmillan LB $16.95 (0-02-743629-2); Aladdin paper $4.99 (0-689-71486-6). 176pp. The horse Godolphin Arabian, ancestor of Man O'War and founder of the thoroughbred strain. Newbery Award winner, 1949. Also use: *Black Gold; Born to Trot* (both 1987).

7217 Henry, Marguerite. *Misty of Chincoteague* (4–7). Illus. by Wesley Dennis. 1990, Simon & Schuster LB $16.95 (0-02-743622-5); paper $2.65 (0-689-82170-0). 176pp. A horse story. Two sequels are: *Sea Star; Stormy, Misty's Foal* (both 1991).

7218 Henry, Marguerite. *Mustang, Wild Spirit of the West* (6–8). Illus. by Robert Lougheed. 1992, Macmillan paper $4.99 (0-689-71601-X). 224pp. An excellent horse story written by a master.

7219 Henry, Marguerite. *San Domingo: The Medicine Hat Stallion* (4–6). Illus. by Robert Lougheed. 1992, Macmillan paper $4.99 (0-689-71631-1). 240pp. Set in the West during the mid-19th century, this is the story of a young man who rights a wrong inflicted on his father. Also from the same author and publisher: *Brighty of the Grand Canyon; Justin Morgan Had a Horse* (both 1991).

7220 Herriot, James. *Only One Woof* (2–4). Illus. by Peter Barrett. 1985, St. Martin's $13.00 (0-312-58583-7); paper $6.95 (0-312-09129-X). 32pp. The sentimental story of two sheepdogs and the one and only time one of them barks. (Rev: BL 1/1/86; HB 3–4/86; SLJ 1/86)

7221 Hesse, Karen. *Sable* (2–4). Illus. by Marcia Sewall. 1994, Holt $15.95 (0-8050-2416-6). 60pp. Tate is sure that her dog, Sable, who has been given away for misbehaving, will return. (Rev: BCCB 5/94; BL 6/1–15/94; HB 7–8/94; SLJ 5/94*)

7222 High, Linda O. *Hound Heaven* (5–7). 1995, Holiday $15.95 (0-8234-1195-8). 194pp. More than anything in the world, Silver Iris wants a dog, but her grandfather, with whom she lives, won't allow it. (Rev: BCCB 12/95; SLJ 11/95)

7223 Howard, Ellen. *Murphy and Kate* (2–4). Illus. by Mark Graham. 1995, Simon & Schuster paper $15.00 (0-671-79775-1). 32pp. Kate and her dog, Murphy, grow up together; but when they were both age 14, death separates them and the young girl grieves the loss of her beloved friend. (Rev: BL 5/1/95; SLJ 6/95)

7224 Howe, James. *Pinky and Rex and the Just-Right Pet* (2–3). Illus. 2001, Simon & Schuster $15.00 (0-689-82861-6). 48pp. Pinky gives the new family kitten to his little sister Amanda, but when he becomes attached to the cat he regrets his generosity in this beginning chapter book. (Rev: BL 3/1/01)

7225 Hurwitz, Johanna. *A Llama in the Family* (2–4). Illus. 1994, Morrow $16.00 (0-688-13388-6). 96pp. Instead of the bike he has been hoping for as a surprise from his parents, Adam receives a llama. (Rev: BCCB 9/94; BL 9/1/94; SLJ 9/94)

7226 Hurwitz, Johanna. *Llama in the Library* (3–6). Illus. 1999, Morrow $15.00 (0-688-16138-3). 144pp. Ten-year-old Adam continues to care for his pet llama while adjusting to first love and to a new baby in the family. (Rev: BCCB 3/99; BL 5/1/99; HBG 10/99; SLJ 6/99)

7227 Hurwitz, Johanna. *One Small Dog* (3–5). 2000, HarperCollins LB $15.89 (0-06-029220-2). 128pp. Curtis has always wanted a dog and finally gets one, but the small cocker spaniel causes enormous problems. (Rev: BCCB 9/00; BL 10/15/00; HB 9–10/00; HBG 3/01; SLJ 11/00)

7228 Intrater, Roberta G. *The Christmas Puppy* (3–6). Illus. 1999, Scholastic $10.95 (0-439-08285-4). 64pp. Zach's beloved dog Tina runs away, and when she is finally located weeks later, she has become the pet of a homeless man. (Rev: BL 12/1/99; HBG 3/00; SLJ 10/99)

7229 Jimenez, Juan Ramon. *Platero y Yo/Platero and I* (5–7). Trans. by Myra Cohn Livingston and Joseph F. Dominguez. Illus. by Antonio Frasconi. 1994, Clarion $14.95 (0-395-62365-0). 47pp. Using both Spanish and English texts, this book contains excerpts from the prose poem about a writer and his donkey. (Rev: BL 6/1–15/94) [863]

7230 Joyce, William. *Buddy* (4–6). Illus. 1997, HarperCollins LB $15.00 (0-06-027661-4). 96pp. Gertrude Lintz buys a gorilla and treats it like a human. (Rev: BL 8/97; SLJ 8/97)

7231 Karwoski, Gail L. *Seaman: The Dog Who Explored the West with Lewis and Clark* (4–8). Illus. 1999, Peachtree paper $8.95 (1-56145-190-8). 192pp. The story of Seaman, the Newfoundland dog on the Lewis and Clark expedition, and how he proved to be a valuable member of the group. (Rev: BL 8/99; SLJ 10/99)

7232 Keehn, Sally M. *The First Horse I See* (5–8). 1999, Putnam $16.99 (0-399-23351-2). 224pp. In this story filled with personal and family problems, the central issue involves Willo and the horse she has purchased in spite of its wild nature. (Rev: BCCB 9/99; BL 9/1/99; HBG 10/99; SLJ 7/99)

7233 Kehret, Peg. *Frightmares: Bone Breath and the Vandals* (4–6). 1995, Pocket paper $3.50 (0-671-89189-8). 113pp. Rosie's dog, Bone Breath, is instrumental in capturing a gang of vandals who have been destroying school property. (Rev: BL 5/1/95; SLJ 5/95)

7234 Keith, Harold. *Chico and Dan* (4–6). Illus. by Scott Arbuckle. 1998, Eakin $15.95 (1-57168-216-3). In 1915, eleven-year-old Dan gets a job working on his great-uncle's cattle ranch in Nevada, where he tames a wild colt and teaches him to be a cow horse. (Rev: HBG 3/99; SLJ 10/98)

7235 Kendall, Sarita. *Ransom for a River Dolphin* (5–8). 1993, Lerner LB $19.95 (0-8225-0735-8). 128pp. Carmenza nurses back to health a river dolphin wounded by her stepfather in this novel set on the banks of the Amazon River. (Rev: BL 2/1/94; SLJ 3/94)

7236 King-Smith, Dick. *The Cuckoo Child* (3–6). Illus. by Leslie Bowman. 1995, Hyperion paper $3.95 (0-7868-1001-7). 128pp. Jack oversees the hatching of an ostrich egg and tends the offspring, Oliver, for two years in this humorous story. (Rev: BL 4/15/93; SLJ 4/93*)

7237 King-Smith, Dick. *The Invisible Dog* (2–4). Illus. by Roger Roth. 1995, Random paper $4.99 (0-679-87041-5). Janie can't have a pet dog so she

invents one. (Rev: BCCB 4/93; BL 3/1/93; HB 5–6/93; SLJ 5/93)

7238 King-Smith, Dick. *Jenius: The Amazing Guinea Pig* (2–3). Illus. 1996, Hyperion $13.95 (0-7868-0243-X); paper $3.95 (0-7868-1135-8). 64pp. Judy is convinced that her pet guinea pig is a "Jenius." (Rev: BL 10/1/96; SLJ 11/96)

7239 King-Smith, Dick. *Smasher* (2–4). Illus. 1997, Random LB $11.99 (0-679-98330-9); paper $3.99 (0-679-88330-4). 72pp. Smasher is a pup that causes so much trouble that Farmer Buzzard and his wife don't know how to control him. (Rev: BL 1/1–15/98)

7240 King-Smith, Dick. *Sophie Hits Six* (2–4). Illus. by David Parkins. 1993, Candlewick $15.95 (1-56402-216-1). 128pp. Sophie hopes to become a farmer when she grows up and prepares for it by taking good care of her pets. (Rev: BL 11/1/93; SLJ 12/93)

7241 King-Smith, Dick. *Sophie's Lucky* (3–4). Illus. 1996, Candlewick $14.99 (1-56402-869-0). 112pp. Sophie's dream of becoming a farmer comes closer to reality in this, Sophie's last book. (Rev: BCCB 2/96; BL 5/1/96; SLJ 4/96)

7242 Kipling, Rudyard. *The Beginning of the Armadilloes* (1–5). Illus. by Lorinda Bryan Cauley. 1985, Harcourt $14.95 (0-15-206380-3); paper $6.00 (0-15-206381-1). 48pp. One of the lesser-known Just So Stories.

7243 Kipling, Rudyard. *The Jungle Book* (5–8). Illus. by Christian Broutin. Series: The Whole Story. 1996, Viking $22.99 (0-670-86919-8). 210pp. The original text is reprinted in this handsome edition, with period illustrations and newly commissioned paintings. (Rev: HB 1–2/96; SLJ 7/96)

7244 Kipling, Rudyard. *The Jungle Book: The Mowgli Stories* (4–7). Illus. by Jerry Pinkney. 1995, Morrow $20.00 (0-688-09979-3). 272pp. Eight stories about Mowgli are reprinted with 18 handsome watercolors. (Rev: BCCB 6/96; BL 10/15/95; SLJ 11/95)

7245 Kipling, Rudyard. *Just So Stories* (3–5). Illus. by David Frampton. 1991, HarperCollins $19.95 (0-06-023294-3). 128pp. Woodcuts enhance the retelling of these old favorites. (Rev: BL 11/15/91; HB 1–2/92; SLJ 11/91)

7246 Kipling, Rudyard. *Just So Stories* (4–6). Illus. by Barry Moser. 1996, Morrow $21.95 (0-688-13957-4). 160pp. Twelve classic stories are featured in this well-illustrated edition of Kipling favorites. (Rev: BL 11/1/96)

7247 Kjelgaard, James A. *Big Red* (6–8). Illus. by Bob Kuhn. 1945, Holiday $19.95 (0-8234-0007-7); Bantam paper $5.50 (0-553-15434-6). 254pp. Adventures of a champion Irish setter and a trapper's son. Also use: *Irish Red: Son of Big Red* (1951); *Outlaw Red* (1953).

7248 Knight, Dawn. *Mischief, Mad Mary, and Me* (2–4). Illus. 1997, Greenwillow $15.00 (0-688-14865-4). 112pp. Brit, who lives with her poor family in an underground house in Minnesota, befriends a dog that she hopes one day to own. (Rev: BL 5/15/97; SLJ 5/97)

7249 Lantz, Francess. *Mom, There's a Pig in My Bed!* (4–6). 1992, Avon paper $3.50 (0-380-76112-2). 144pp. Mr. Ewing, fired from his job, moves to rural Kansas to raise seeing-eye pigs for blind people who are allergic to dogs, not realizing that pigs have poor eyesight too. (Rev: BL 4/15/92; SLJ 1/93)

7250 Lattimore, Deborah N. *Frida María: A Story of the Old Southwest* (2–4). Illus. by author. 1994, Harcourt $14.95 (0-15-276636-7). In this horse story set in Old California, Frida tries to be a conventional girl to please her mother, but her adventurous spirit prevails. (Rev: SLJ 5/94)

7251 Lawson, Julie. *Cougar Cove* (4–6). Illus. by David Powell. 1996, Orca paper $6.95 (1-55143-072-X). 138pp. An animal adventure involving a girl who is visiting relatives on Vancouver Island, Canada. (Rev: SLJ 9/96)

7252 Levin, Betty. *Away to Me, Moss* (5–7). 1994, Greenwillow $15.00 (0-688-13439-4). 192pp. When his master has a stroke, Moss, a border collie, runs out of control. (Rev: BCCB 12/94; BL 10/1/94; SLJ 10/94)

7253 Levin, Betty. *Creature Crossing* (3–5). 1999, Greenwillow $15.00 (0-688-16220-7). 96pp. Ben finds a strange animal he thinks is a dinosaur. When he discovers it is a salamander — an endangered species — Ben and his friends try to make their community more aware of their environment. (Rev: BL 3/1/99; HB 5–6/99; HBG 10/99; SLJ 6/99)

7254 Levin, Betty. *Gift Horse* (4–6). Illus. 1996, Greenwillow $15.00 (0-688-14698-8). 176pp. Uncle Oliver fulfills his promise and gives Matt a horse. (Rev: BCCB 11/96; BL 10/1/96; SLJ 11/96)

7255 Levin, Betty. *Look Back, Moss* (5–8). 1998, Greenwillow $15.00 (0-688-15696-7). 160pp. Young Moss, disturbed by his mother's lack of attention and his own weight problems, welcomes an injured sheepdog into the family. (Rev: BCCB 10/98; BL 8/98; HB 1–2/99; HBG 3/99; SLJ 11/98)

7256 Lewis, J. Patrick. *One Dog Day* (3–6). Illus. by Marcy Ramsey. 1993, Macmillan $12.95 (0-689-31808-1). 64pp. In spite of the derision of others, Jilly enters her pet collie in the county's annual coon dog contest. (Rev: BL 4/15/93; SLJ 6/93)

7257 Lindquist, Susan H. *Wander* (3–6). 1998, Delacorte $14.95 (0-385-32563-0). 133pp. Still grieving for their dead mother, James and his sister Sary find solace in a stray dog they befriend and hope will be allowed to be a family pet. (Rev: BCCB 11/98; BL 9/15/98; HBG 3/99; SLJ 9/98)

7258 Little, Jean. *Different Dragons* (4–6). Illus. 1987, Puffin paper $4.99 (0-14-031998-0). 144pp. Ben, who fears everything, especially his aunt's dog, learns that everyone sometimes has something to fear. (Rev: BCCB 7–8/87; BL 6/1/87; SLJ 6–7/87)

7259 Loggia, Wendy. *A Puppy of My Own* (3–5). Series: Woof! 2001, Bantam paper $4.50 (0-553-48733-7). 106pp. In this beginning chapter book, three friends hope to get dogs and, by the book's end, two have been granted their wishes. (Rev: BL 1/1–15/01)

7260 London, Jack. *White Fang* (5–8). 1964, Airmont paper $4.10 (0-8049-0036-1). The classic dog story in one of many editions available. A reissue of the 1935 edition.

7261 London, Jonathan. *The Eyes of Gray Wolf* (K–5). Illus. by Jon Van Zyle. 1993, Chronicle $14.95 (0-8118-0285-X). 32pp. After losing his mate to hunters, Grey Wolf is consoled when he encounters a wolf pack with a white wolf that will be his future mate. (Rev: BL 11/1/93*; SLJ 1/94)

7262 McKay, Hilary. *Dog Friday* (4–6). 1995, Simon & Schuster paper $15.00 (0-689-80383-4). 134pp. In spite of his fear of dogs, Robin plans to nurse back to health a dog he has found on a beach. Also use by the same author: *The Exiles* (1993) and *The Exiles at Home* (1994). (Rev: BCCB 10/95; BL 11/15/95; SLJ 10/95*)

7263 Malterre, Elona. *The Last Wolf of Ireland* (5–7). 1990, Houghton $15.00 (0-395-54381-9). 124pp. Devin and his friend Katey hide wolf pups when the pups are threatened. (Rev: BCCB 10/90; BL 9/15/90*; SLJ 10/90)

7264 Maynard, Meredy. *Dreamcatcher* (5–7). 1995, Polestar paper $7.50 (1-896095-01-1). 137pp. With the help of an American Indian girl, a 13-year-old boy secretly raises a baby raccoon that was abandoned in the woods. (Rev: SLJ 5/96)

7265 Moeyaert, Bart. *Bare Hands* (3–7). Trans. by David Colmer. 1999, Front Street $14.95 (1-886910-32-4). 112pp. In this translation of a powerful novel from the Netherlands, Young Ward seeks revenge when the village loner, who is also his mother's suitor, kills his dog. (Rev: BL 12/15/98*; HBG 10/99; SLJ 2/99)

7266 Morehead, Debby. *A Special Place for Charlee: A Child's Companion Through Pet Loss* (3–6). Illus. by Karen Cannon. 1996, Partners in Publishing paper $6.95 (0-9654049-0-0). 36pp. Mark gets help and counseling when the dog he has grown up with dies. (Rev: BL 11/15/96)

7267 Morey, Walt. *Gentle Ben* (5–7). Illus. by John Schoenherr. 1965, Puffin paper $4.99 (0-14-036035-2). 192pp. A warm story of the deep trust and friendship between a boy and an Alaskan bear.

7268 Morey, Walt. *Scrub Dog of Alaska* (4–8). 1989, Blue Heron paper $7.95 (0-936085-13-4). 160pp. A pup, abandoned because of his small size, turns out to be a winner. Also use: *Kavik the Wolf Dog* (1977, Dutton).

7269 Morey, Walt. *Year of the Black Pony* (5–7). Illus. by Fredrika Spillman. 1989, Blue Heron paper $6.95 (0-936085-14-2). 160pp. A family story about a boy's love for his pony in rural Oregon at the turn of the century.

7270 Morpurgo, Michael. *The Butterfly Lion* (4–6). 1997, Viking $14.99 (0-670-87461-2). 96pp. In this novel set in South Africa, a young boy is determined to find his pet white lion, which has been sold by his father. (Rev: BL 6/1–15/97; SLJ 8/97)

7271 Morris, Judy K. *Nightwalkers* (4–6). Illus. 1996, HarperCollins $14.95 (0-06-027200-7).

144pp. James is doing a school report on elephants when Daisy, a pachyderm that has escaped from a zoo, adopts him. (Rev: BCCB 12/96; BL 12/1/96; SLJ 12/96)

7272 Mowat, Farley. *The Dog Who Wouldn't Be* (4–7). Illus. by Paul Galdone. 1957, Bantam paper $4.99 (0-553-27928-9). 208pp. The humorous story of Mutt, a dog of character and personality, and his boy.

7273 Mukerji, Dhan Gopal. *Gay-Neck: The Story of a Pigeon* (4–8). Illus. by Boris Artzybasheff. 1968, Dutton $15.99 (0-525-30400-2). 192pp. This Newbery Award winner, 1928, is the story of a boy from India and his brave carrier pigeon during World War I.

7274 Myers, Anna. *Red-Dirt Jessie* (4–7). 1992, Walker $13.95 (0-8027-8172-1). 120pp. In this tale of the Depression era in Oklahoma, 12-year-old Jessie helps keep her family together. (Rev: BCCB 10/92; BL 1/15/93; HB 1–2/93; SLJ 11/92*)

7275 Myers, Anna. *Spotting the Leopard* (4–6). 1996, Walker $15.95 (0-8027-8459-3). 160pp. In this sequel to *Red-Dirt Jessie* (1992), a young boy tries to save an escaped zoo leopard from recapture and possible death. (Rev: BCCB 2/97; BL 10/15/96; SLJ 11/96)

7276 Myers, Christopher. *Black Cat* (3–8). Illus. 1999, Scholastic $15.95 (0-590-03375-1). 40pp. An intriguing picture book with rap rhythm that tells of a black cat's progress walking through a city's streets. (Rev: BCCB 2/99; BL 4/15/99; HB 3–4/99; HBG 10/99; SLJ 3/99)

7277 Naylor, Phyllis Reynolds. *Saving Shiloh* (4–7). 1997, Simon & Schuster $15.00 (0-689-81460-7). 144pp. In this sequel to the Newbery Award–winning *Shiloh* and *Shiloh Season*, Marty again encounters the evil Judd Travers, who has been accused of murder. (Rev: BL 9/1/97*; HB 9–10/97; HBG 3/98; SLJ 9/97)

7278 Naylor, Phyllis Reynolds. *Shiloh* (4–8). 1991, Macmillan $15.00 (0-689-31614-3); Dell paper $5.50 (0-440-40752-4). 144pp. When a beagle follows him home, Marty, from a West Virginia family with a strict code of honor, learns a painful lesson about right and wrong. Newbery Award winner, 1992. (Rev: BCCB 10/91; BL 12/1/91*; HB 1–2/92; SLJ 9/91)

7279 Naylor, Phyllis Reynolds. *Shiloh Season* (4–8). 1996, Simon & Schuster $15.00 (0-689-80647-7). 120pp. The evil Judd Travers wants his dog back from the Prestons in this sequel to *Shiloh* (1991). (Rev: BCCB 12/96; BL 11/15/96*; HB 11–12/96; SLJ 11/96)

7280 *The Necessary Cat: A Celebration of Cats in Picture and Word* (3–7). Ed. by Nicola Bayley. Illus. 1998, Candlewick $17.99 (0-7636-0571-9). 80pp. This book collects all sorts of cat pictures and lore in the form of poems, stories, nonfiction material, and a cat alphabet. (Rev: BL 10/15/98; HBG 10/99; SLJ 10/98)

7281 Nielsen, Virginia. *Batty Hattie* (4–6). 1999, Marshall Cavendish $14.95 (0-7614-5047-5). 142pp. When her mother goes on tour with a jazz band, Harriet is left alone with her uncle and feels extreme loneliness until she rescues a helpless baby bat she finds on the ground. (Rev: BCCB 4/99; BL 3/1/99; HBG 10/99; SLJ 4/99)

7282 North, Sterling. *Rascal: A Memoir of a Better Era* (6–8). Illus. by John Schoenherr. 1984, Puffin paper $4.99 (0-14-034445-4). 192pp. Autobiographical memoir of the beauties of nature as experienced by an 11-year-old and his pet raccoon.

7283 Orr, Wendy. *Ark in the Park* (2–3). Illus. 2000, Holt $15.95 (0-8050-6221-1). 78pp. Seven-year-old Sophie desperately wants a pet and is delighted when she gets a chance to help Mr. and Mrs. Noah in their pet shop. (Rev: BCCB 9/00; BL 9/15/00; HBG 10/00; SLJ 6/00)

7284 Parker, Cam. *A Horse in New York* (4–8). 1989, Avon paper $2.75 (0-380-75704-4). 135pp. To save Blue, the horse she rode at summer camp, from destruction, Tiffin has to convince her parents to board him for the winter. (Rev: BL 12/15/89)

7285 Patent, Dorothy Hinshaw. *Return of the Wolf* (4–6). Illus. by Jared T. Williams. 1995, Clarion $15.95 (0-395-72100-8). 67pp. A female wolf banished from her pack finds a new mate and a territory where she can begin a new pack. (Rev: BCCB 7–8/95; SLJ 7/95)

7286 Platt, Chris. *Race the Wind!* (5–7). 2000, Random $15.00 (0-679-88657-5). 221pp. Kate wants to ride her horse, Willow King, in the Kentucky Derby but she is afraid that she will not get her license in time and rival Mark, a jockey, will ride instead. (Rev: HBG 3/01; SLJ 9/00)

7287 Platt, Chris. *Willow King* (4–6). 1998, Random $15.00 (0-679-88655-9). 208pp. Katie saves a colt that, like her, had been born with a bad leg and eventually turns it into a champion racehorse. (Rev: BL 4/15/98; HBG 10/98; SLJ 7/98)

7288 Pullein-Thompson, Diana, ed. *Classic Horse and Pony Stories: The World's Best Horse and Pony Stories in Their Real-life Settings* (4–6). Illus. by Neal Puddephatt. 1999, DK $16.95 (0-7894-4896-3). 96pp. Drawing on the work of such writers as Marguerite Henry, Anna Sewell, Lewis Carroll, and Walter Farley, this is an outstanding collection of 11 classic horse stories. (Rev: HBG 3/00; SLJ 2/00)

7289 Rawlings, Marjorie Kinnan. *The Yearling* (6–8). Illus. by N. C. Wyeth. 1985, Macmillan $28.00 (0-684-18461-3). 416pp. The contemporary classic of a boy and a fawn growing up together in the backwoods of Florida. A reissue of the 1938 edition.

7290 Rawls, Wilson. *Summer of the Monkeys* (4–6). 1989, Doubleday $15.95 (0-385-11450-8); Bantam paper $5.99 (0-553-29818-6). 358pp. Jay and his dog spend a summer chasing 29 escaped monkeys.

7291 Reeve, Kirk. *Lolo and Red-Legs* (4–6). 1998, Northland $12.95 (0-87358-683-2); paper $6.95 (0-87358-684-0). 122pp. Mexican American Lolo Garcia is excited about showing his giant tarantula at the Los Angeles County Fair, but he discovers that local teenagers have stolen his pet. (Rev: BL 4/15/98; HBG 10/98; SLJ 7/98)

7292 Rodowsky, Colby. *Not My Dog* (2–4). Illus. 1999, Farrar $15.00 (0-374-35531-2). 80pp. In this beginning chapter book, Ellie, who has been promised a puppy, has to settle for Preston, an older dog that her grandmother has to give up. (Rev: BCCB 3/99; BL 2/1/99; HB 3–4/99; SLJ 4/99)

7293 Rounds, Glen. *The Blind Colt* (3–6). Illus. by author. 1989, Holiday $16.95 (0-8234-0010-7); paper $5.95 (0-8234-0758-6). 84pp. The story of the colt that overcame his blindness and the boy who saved him. A reissue.

7294 Ruepp, Krista. *Horses in the Fog* (2–4). Trans. by Alison James. 1997, North-South $13.88 (1-55858-805-1). 58pp. A young girl living on an island gets to ride a neighbor's Arabian stallion and finds a new riding companion in Mona. A sequel to *Midnight Rider* (1995). (Rev: BL 2/1/98; HBG 3/98)

7295 Ruepp, Krista. *Midnight Rider* (2–5). Trans. by J. Alison James. Illus. 1995, North-South LB $13.88 (1-55858-495-1). 62pp. Charlie has an accident while secretly riding her sullen neighbor's horse, Starbright. (Rev: BCCB 10/95; BL 12/1/95; SLJ 12/95)

7296 Rylant, Cynthia. *Every Living Thing* (5–7). Illus. by S. D. Schindler. 1985, Macmillan LB $14.00 (0-02-777200-4); paper $4.99 (0-689-71263-4). 96pp. Twelve short stories that describe the effects that a bird or an animal has on disinterested humans. (Rev: HB 3–4/86)

7297 Sachar, Louis. *Marvin Redpost: Alone in His Teacher's House* (2–4). 1994, Random LB $11.99 (0-679-91949-X); paper $3.99 (0-679-81949-5). 83pp. Marvin is upset and confused when the dog he is taking care of dies. (Rev: BL 6/1–15/94)

7298 Sachs, Betsy. *The Boy Who Ate Dog Biscuits* (2–4). Illus. by Margot Apple. 1989, Random paper $3.99 (0-394-84778-4). 64pp. Billy, who helps out at the vet's office and likes dog biscuits, prefers dogs to his baby sister. (Rev: BL 1/15/90)

7299 Salten, Felix. *Bambi* (2–4). Adapted by Janet Schulman. Illus. by Steve Johnson and Lou Fancher. 1999, Simon & Schuster $18.00 (0-689-81954-4). 47pp. A shortened version of this classic tale now made accessible to younger readers. (Rev: HBG 3/00; SLJ 10/99)

7300 Salten, Felix. *Bambi: A Life in the Woods* (5–8). 1926, Pocket paper $4.99 (0-671-66607-X). The growing to maturity of an Austrian deer.

7301 Saunders, Susan. *Lucky Lady* (3–7). 2000, HarperCollins $14.95 (0-380-97784-2). 144pp. The lives of 12-year-old Jennie and her dispirited grandfather change for the better when the girl buys a wild buckskin filly named Lucky Lady. (Rev: BCCB 5/00; BL 8/00; HBG 10/00; SLJ 7/00)

7302 Schecter, Ellen. *The Pet-Sitters* (2–4). Illus. by Bob Dorsey. Series: West Side Kids. 1996, Hyperion paper $3.95 (0-7868-1046-7). 74pp. When the West Side Kids want more pets than their apartments can hold, they decide on the next best thing: a pet-sitting service. (Rev: SLJ 3/97)

7303 Schlein, Miriam. *The Year of the Panda* (3–5). Illus. by Kam Mak. 1990, HarperCollins LB $15.89 (0-690-04866-1). 96pp. A Chinese farm boy cares for an orphaned baby panda. (Rev: BCCB 11/90; BL 9/15/90; HB 11–12/90; SLJ 10/90)

7304 Scott, Ann H. *A Brand Is Forever* (3–5). Illus. by Ronald Himler. 1993, Houghton $12.95 (0-395-60118-5). 48pp. Annie hates the idea of branding her pet calf named Doodle. (Rev: BCCB 4/93; BL 4/1/93; HB 5–6/93; SLJ 5/93)

7305 Seidler, Tor. *The Silent Spillbills* (5–8). 1998, HarperCollins LB $14.89 (0-06-205181-4). 224pp. Katrina faces problems trying to overcome her stuttering but stands up to her tyrannical grandfather to help save from extinction a rare bird known as the silent spillbill. (Rev: BCCB 1/99; BL 12/15/98; HBG 3/99; SLJ 4/99)

7306 Silverstein, Shel. *Lafcadio, the Lion Who Shot Back* (3–6). Illus. by author. 1963, HarperCollins LB $15.89 (0-06-025676-1). 112pp. His marksmanship makes him a success, but Lafcadio discovers it's not to his liking.

7307 Smith, Susan M. *The Booford Summer* (3–6). Illus. 1994, Clarion $13.95 (0-395-66590-6). 144pp. A girl takes pity on Booford, a neighbor's dog, and begins taking him for walks. (Rev: BL 9/15/94; SLJ 11/94)

7308 Stewart, Elisabeth J. *Bimmi Finds a Cat* (3–4). Illus. by James E. Ransome. 1996, Clarion $14.95 (0-395-64652-9). 32pp. A Creole boy tries to find the owner of the cat that he has befriended. (Rev: BL 10/15/96; SLJ 8/97)

7309 Stowe, Cynthia. *Not-So-Normal Norman* (3–5). 1995, Albert Whitman LB $13.95 (0-8075-5767-6). 127pp. Anthony's first client in the pet-sitting service he has started is a tarantula named Norman. (Rev: BL 1/15/95; SLJ 3/95)

7310 Strickland, Brad. *When Mack Came Back* (3–6). 2000, Dial $15.99 (0-8037-2498-5). 112pp. Set in World War II Georgia, this is the story of 10-year-old Maury and the injured black dog he finds in the woods. (Rev: BCCB 5/00; BL 10/15/00; HBG 10/00; SLJ 6/00)

7311 Talbert, Marc. *The Trap* (4–6). 1999, DK $15.95 (0-7894-2599-8). 144pp. When Ellie sets a metal trap to catch coyotes and kills a stray dog instead, she begins lying to cover up her guilt. (Rev: BCCB 10/99; BL 11/15/99; HBG 3/00; SLJ 10/99)

7312 Taylor, Theodore. *The Hostage* (5–8). 1988, Dell paper $3.99 (0-440-20923-4). 176pp. Fourteen-year-old Jamie in Canada is stunned when his efforts to capture a trapped whale are misinterpreted. (Rev: BL 2/15/88; SLJ 3/88)

7313 Taylor, Theodore. *The Trouble with Tuck* (5–8). 1989, Doubleday $15.95 (0-385-17774-7). 96pp. The story of a golden Labrador retriever who becomes blind.

7314 Taylor, Theodore. *Tuck Triumphant* (4–7). 1991, Avon paper $4.99 (0-380-71323-3). 150pp. A 1950s novel about a blind dog in a loving family and the deaf Korean boy they adopt. (Rev: BL 2/1/91)

7315 Taylor, William. *Agnes the Sheep* (5–7). 1991, Scholastic $13.95 (0-590-43365-2). 132pp. A wild and woolly story about an ornery and ill-kempt sheep and the two middle-graders who must care for her. (Rev: BCCB 3/91*; BL 5/15/91*)

7316 Updike, David. *The Sounds of Summer* (3–5). Illus. by Robert Andrew Parker. 1993, Pippin $15.95 (0-945912-20-X). 40pp. After Homer's dog, Sophocles, dies, the boy remembers the good times they had together. (Rev: BCCB 10/93; BL 9/1/93; SLJ 10/93)

7317 Ure, Jean. *Muddy Four Paws* (4–6). Series: We Love Animals. 1999, Barron's paper $3.95 (0-7641-0968-5). 128pp. In this English story, 11-year-old Clara is upset when her mother will not let her adopt a puppy she has found in a ditch. (Rev: SLJ 6/99)

7318 Vincent, Gabrielle. *A Day, a Dog* (PS–4). Illus. 2000, Front Street $16.95 (1-886910-51-0). 72pp. A wordless book that tells the story of a dog that is dumped by its owners and how it learns to survive. (Rev: BCCB 4/00; BL 7/00; HB 5–6/00; HBG 10/00; SLJ 6/00)

7319 Wallace, Bill. *Coyote Autumn* (4–6). 2000, Holiday $16.95 (0-8234-1628-3). 201pp. During his first autumn in rural Oklahoma, Brad finds an orphan coyote pup that he raises. (Rev: BCCB 11/00; BL 12/15/00; SLJ 10/00)

7320 Wallace, Bill. *A Dog Called Kitty* (4–7). 1980, Holiday $15.95 (0-8234-0376-9); Pocket paper $3.99 (0-671-77081-0). 160pp. A boy tries to overcome his fear of dogs so he can help a stray.

7321 Wells, Rosemary. *Lassie Come-Home: Eric Knight's Original 1938 Classic* (3–5). Illus. by Susan Jeffers. 1995, Holt $16.95 (0-8050-3794-2). 48pp. A simplified picture-book version of Eric Knight's classic dog story set in the Scottish countryside. (Rev: BCCB 2/96; BL 12/1/95; SLJ 11/95*)

7322 Whelan, Gloria. *Silver* (2–4). Illus. by Stephen Marchesi. 1988, Random paper $3.99 (0-394-89611-4). 64pp. Rachel wants to compete in the Alaska Iditarod sled race, and she thinks she can win with her lead dog, Silver. (Rev: BCCB 7–8/88; BL 7/88; SLJ 10/88)

7323 Wiebe, Trina. *Hamsters Don't Glow in the Dark* (2–4). Illus. by Marisol Sarrazin. 2000, Lobster paper $5.95 (1-894222-15-6). 32pp. Abby brings the class hamster home for spring break and discovers that Mr. Nibbles was misnamed because she has given birth to eight babies. (Rev: SLJ 2/01)

7324 Wilbur, Frances. *The Dog with Golden Eyes* (4–7). Illus. 1998, Milkweed $14.95 (1-57131-614-0); paper $6.95 (1-57131-615-9). 160pp. Cassie befriends a white dog that turns out to be an arctic wolf, and she must find his owners before he becomes a target for the police or hunters. (Rev: BCCB 9/98; BL 9/1/98; HBG 3/99; SLJ 7/98)

7325 Williams, Laura E. *The Ghost Stallion* (5–7). 1999, Holt $15.95 (0-8050-6193-2). 104pp. On a horse ranch in rural Oregon in 1959, Mary Elizabeth participates in a hunt to capture a renegade stallion while still trying to adjust to the absence of her mother. (Rev: BCCB 1/00; BL 11/1/99; HBG 3/00; SLJ 11/99)

7326 Wittbold, Maureen. *Mending Peter's Heart* (K–6). Illus. by Larry Salk. 1995, Portunus paper $8.95 (0-9641330-2-4). 32pp. Peter needs consolation when his pet husky, Mishka, dies. (Rev: SLJ 11/95)

7327 Woods, Shirley. *Black Nell: The Adventures of a Coyote* (3–5). Illus. 1998, Douglas & McIntyre $14.95 (0-88899-318-8). 96pp. Nell the coyote survives such disasters as a forest fire, being hit by a car, caught in a trap, and wounded by a hunter, in this novel that explores in detail the life cycle and habits of coyotes. (Rev: BL 11/1/98)

7328 Woods, Shirley. *Kit: The Adventures of a Raccoon* (2–5). Illus. by Celia Godkin. 2000, Groundwood $14.95 (0-88899-375-7). 92pp. This story follows a young raccoon from his birth to maturity during which time he learns to survive and live in the wild. (Rev: HBG 10/00; SLJ 7/00)

7329 Wright, Lynn F. *Flick* (3–5). Illus. by Tony Waters. 1995, Worry Wart $13.95 (1-881519-02-3); paper $7.95 (1-881519-03-1). 68pp. Jack nurses back to health a badly injured puppy he has found on the railroad tracks. (Rev: SLJ 2/96)

7330 Yep, Laurence. *Later, Gator* (4–6). 1995, Hyperion LB $14.49 (0-7868-2083-7). 128pp. Teddy is surprised when his young brother is delighted at his birthday gift, a baby alligator. (Rev: BCCB 7–8/95; BL 5/1/95; HB 7–8/95; SLJ 7/95*)

Ethnic Groups

7331 Ada, Alma F. *My Name Is Maria Isabel* (3–5). Trans. by Ana M. Cerro. Illus. by K. Dyble Thompson. 1993, Macmillan $13.00 (0-689-31517-1). 64pp. A Puerto Rican girl in the United States resents the fact that her teacher calls her Mary instead of Maria. (Rev: BCCB 6/93; BL 6/1–15/93; SLJ 4/93)

7332 Asher, Sandy, ed. *With All My Heart, With All My Mind: Thirteen Stories About Growing Up Jewish* (5–9). 1999, Simon & Schuster $18.00 (0-689-82012-7). 176pp. Thirteen contemporary young adult writers have contributed stories on the meaning of being Jewish in both the past and present. (Rev: BL 10/1/99; HBG 3/00)

7333 Balgassi, Haemi. *Tae's Sonata* (5–8). 1997, Clarion $14.00 (0-395-84314-6). 122pp. When Tae, a Korean American, is given a school assignment on Korea she must come to terms with her native culture and the memories she has of her homeland. (Rev: BL 10/15/97; HBG 3/98; SLJ 9/97)

7334 Bernier-Grand, Carmen T. *In the Shade of the Nispero Tree* (4–7). 1999, Orchard LB $16.99 (0-531-33154-7). 192pp. Prejudice and racism separate two friends in this story set in Ponce, Puerto Rico, during 1961. (Rev: BCCB 3/99; BL 4/1/99; HBG 10/99; SLJ 3/99)

7335 Blume, Judy. *Iggie's House* (4–7). 1970, Macmillan LB $16.00 (0-02-711040-0); Dell paper $4.50 (0-440-44062-9). 128pp. An African American family moves into Iggie's old house.

7336 Buss, Fran L. *Journey of the Sparrows* (5–8). 1993, Dell paper $4.50 (0-440-40785-0). 160pp. The plight of illegal aliens in the United States is the focus of this novel about three Salvadoran children. (Rev: BCCB 1/92; HB 11–12/91; SLJ 10/91)

7337 Curtis, Christopher Paul. *The Watsons Go to Birmingham — 1963* (4–8). 1995, Delacorte $15.95 (0-385-32175-9); Dell paper $5.99 (0-440-41412-1). 210pp. An African American family returns to Alabama from Michigan to place their troubled son with his grandmother. (Rev: BL 8/95; SLJ 10/95*)

7338 English, Karen. *Francie* (5–8). 1999, Farrar $16.00 (0-374-32456-5). 208pp. Growing up in the segregated South, 12-year-old Francie, who lives a life of poverty with her mother, helps a friend on the run from a racist employer and places her own family in danger. (Rev: BCCB 10/99; HB 9–10/99; HBG 3/00; SLJ 9/99)

7339 Fleischman, Paul. *Seedfolks* (4–8). Illus. by Judy Pedersen. 1997, HarperCollins LB $14.89 (0-06-027472-7). 69pp. Thirteen people from many cultures explain why they have planted their gardens in a vacant lot in Cleveland, Ohio. (Rev: BCCB 7–8/97; HB 5–6/97; SLJ 5/97*)

7340 Gardiner, John Reynolds. *Stone Fox* (3–6). Illus. by Marcia Sewall. 1980, HarperCollins LB $15.89 (0-690-03984-0); paper $4.95 (0-06-440132-4). 96pp. Ten-year-old Willy competes against the Indian mountain man, Stone Fox, in the national dogsled races.

7341 Garland, Sherry. *The Lotus Seed* (K–5). Illus. by Tatsuro Kluchi. 1993, Harcourt $16.00 (0-15-249465-0). 32pp. A young narrator tells of fleeing her Vietnamese homeland to settle with her family in America. (Rev: BL 3/15/93*; HB 5–6/93; SLJ 7/93)

7342 Greenfield, Eloise. *Easter Parade* (2–4). Illus. by Jan S. Gilchrist. 1998, Hyperion LB $14.49 (0-7868-2271-6). 64pp. Two African American cousins — one in Washington and the other in Chicago — anticipate their Easter parades in this simple chapter book set in 1943. (Rev: BCCB 6/98; BL 4/1/98; HB 9–10/98; HBG 10/98; SLJ 8/98)

7343 Greenfield, Eloise. *Koya DeLaney and the Good Girl Blues* (4–6). 1995, Scholastic paper $4.50 (0-590-43299-0). 176pp. Sixth-grader Koya DeLaney, whose talent is a gift of laughter, has some growing up to do when family conflicts arise. (Rev: BCCB 3/92; BL 2/15/92; SLJ 3/92)

7344 Haugaard, Kay. *No Place* (4–6). 1998, Milkweed $15.95 (1-57131-616-7); paper $6.95 (1-57131-617-5). 175pp. Based on fact, this is the story of a yearlong project in which Arturo and his friends turn a junk-filled barrio lot in Los Angeles into a park. (Rev: BL 11/15/98; HBG 3/99)

7345 Hooks, William H. *Circle of Fire* (5–8). 1982, Macmillan LB $15.00 (0-689-50241-9). 144pp. Three boys — one white and two African American — try to thwart an attack on some Irish gypsies by the Ku Klux Klan.

7346 Hopkinson, Deborah. *A Band of Angels: A Story Inspired by the Jubilee Singers* (2–4). Illus. by Raul Colon. 1999, Simon & Schuster $16.00 (0-689-81062-8). 40pp. A fictionalized account of the Fisk University Jubilee Singers and how they sang their people's spirituals to raise money for their col-

lege. (Rev: BCCB 2/99; BL 4/15/99*; HB 3–4/99; HBG 10/99; SLJ 2/99)

7347 Hoyt-Goldsmith, Diane. *Day of the Dead: A Mexican-American Celebration* (4–6). Illus. 1994, Holiday LB $16.95 (0-8234-1094-3). 32pp. The Hispanic Day of the Dead celebration as seen through the experiences of an American family living in a Mexican American community. (Rev: BL 7/94; SLJ 9/94)

7348 Kidd, Diana. *Onion Tears* (3–5). Illus. by Lucy Montgomery. 1991, Orchard LB $16.99 (0-531-08470-1); Morrow paper $3.95 (0-688-11862-3). 72pp. A Vietnamese girl tries to adjust to her new life with a foster mother. (Rev: BL 3/15/91; HB 5–6/91; SLJ 6/91)

7349 Lee, Lauren. *Stella: On the Edge of Popularity* (5–7). 1994, Polychrome $10.95 (1-879965-08-9). 178pp. A Korean American girl has to choose between being popular and being loyal to her Korean culture. (Rev: BCCB 7–8/94; SLJ 9/94)

7350 Lester, Julius. *Long Journey Home* (6–8). 1998, Viking paper $4.99 (0-14-038981-4). 160pp. Six based-on-fact stories concerning slaves, ex-slaves, and their lives in a hostile America.

7351 Littlesugar, Amy. *A Portrait of Spotted Deer's Grandfather* (2–4). Illus. 1997, Albert Whitman LB $15.95 (0-8075-6622-5). 32pp. Spotted Deer's grandfather, Moose Horn, is afraid that if he has his portrait painted he will lose his spirit. (Rev: BL 1/1–15/98; HBG 3/98; SLJ 9/97)

7352 Lord, Bette Bao. *In the Year of the Boar and Jackie Robinson* (4–6). Illus. by Marc Simont. 1984, HarperCollins paper $4.95 (0-06-440175-8). 176pp. The story of a Chinese girl who leaves China to join her father in New York in 1947.

7353 Martin, Bill, Jr., and John Archambault. *Knots on a Counting Rope* (PS–5). Illus. by Ted Rand. 1987, Holt $16.95 (0-8050-0571-4). 32pp. Each time his grandson asks him to repeat the story of Boy-Strength of Blue-Horses, Grandfather adds another knot in the counting rope, a metaphor for the passage of time. (Rev: BCCB 11/87; BL 11/15/87; SLJ 12/87)

7354 Matthews, Mary. *Magid Fasts for Ramadan* (3–6). Illus. 1996, Clarion $15.95 (0-395-66589-2). 48pp. Eight-year-old Magid wants to fast as his family does during the holy month for Moslems, Ramadan. (Rev: BCCB 2/96; BL 3/1/96; HB 7–8/96; SLJ 7/96)

7355 Mazer, Anne, ed. *America Street: A Multicultural Anthology of Stories* (5–8). 1993, Persea paper $7.95 (0-89255-191-7). 160pp. A collection of 14 stories, each one dealing with a different American ethnic group. (Rev: BCCB 11/93; BL 9/1/93; SLJ 11/93)

7356 Medearis, Michael, and Angela Shelf Medearis. *Daisy and the Doll* (2–4). Illus. 2000, Vermont Folklife Center $14.95 (0-916718-15-8). 32pp. Daisy, an African American girl, is embarrassed when her classroom teacher gives her a black doll to hold during a program on different countries and nationalities. (Rev: BL 9/15/00; SLJ 9/00)

7357 Meyer, Carolyn. *Rio Grande Stories* (4–6). 1994, Harcourt $12.00 (0-15-200548-X); paper $6.00 (0-15-200066-6). 224pp. Twelve children in a middle school in Albuquerque, New Mexico, investigate their origins through oral histories and documents. (Rev: BCCB 9/94; BL 10/1/94; SLJ 6/94)

7358 Mochizuki, Ken. *Heroes* (2–4). Illus. by Dom Lee. 1995, Lee & Low $15.95 (1-880000-16-4). 32pp. During the Vietnam War, a Japanese American child becomes the butt of other children's bullying. (Rev: BL 3/15/95; HB 5–6/95; SLJ 7/95)

7359 Murphy, Rita. *Black Angels* (5–7). 2001, Delacorte $14.95 (0-385-32776-5). 152pp. In this exciting novel set in Mystic, Georgia, in 1961, an 11-year-old girl is caught up in the struggle that pits the freedom riders and black leaders against racists including the Klan. (Rev: BCCB 3/01; BL 2/15/01)

7360 Myers, Walter Dean. *145th Street: Stories* (5–9). 2000, Delacorte $15.95 (0-385-32137-6). 150pp. A Harlem neighborhood is the setting for this collection of short stories dealing with a wide range of human emotions. (Rev: BL 12/15/99; HB 3–4/00; HBG 10/00)

7361 Naidoo, Beverley. *Journey to Jo'burg: A South African Story* (4–6). Illus. by Eric Velasquez. 1986, HarperCollins LB $15.89 (0-397-32169-4); paper $4.95 (0-06-440237-1). 96pp. The story of Naledi, from a South African village, who travels to the city with her brother to seek their mother, who works in the home of whites, because their baby sister is dying. (Rev: BCCB 5/86; BL 3/25/86; SLJ 8/86)

7362 Nelson, Vaunda M. *Beyond Mayfield* (3–5). 1999, Putnam $15.99 (0-399-23355-5). 144pp. In this sequel to *Mayfield Crossing*, also set in a small Pennsylvania town in the 1960s, the children are still encountering problems being bused to school where African Americans are not accepted and their older friend Sam Wood is trying to register black voters. (Rev: BCCB 11/99; HBG 3/00; SLJ 8/99)

7363 Nelson, Vaunda M. *Mayfield Crossing* (4–6). Illus. by Leonard Jenkins. 1993, Putnam $14.95 (0-399-22331-2). 82pp. A group of children from Mayfield Crossing encounter racial prejudice when they enter a newer, bigger school at Parview. (Rev: BCCB 3/93; BL 4/1/93*)

7364 Pinkney, Andrea D. *Hold Fast to Dreams* (5–8). 1995, Morrow $16.00 (0-688-12832-7). 112pp. A bright, resourceful African American girl faces problems when she finds she is the only black student in her new middle school. (Rev: BCCB 5/95; BL 2/15/95; HB 9–10/95; SLJ 4/95)

7365 Pitts, Paul. *Racing the Sun* (5–7). 1988, Avon paper $4.95 (0-380-75496-7). 160pp. Brandon begins to understand his Navajo heritage after his grandfather comes to live with him. (Rev: BL 9/15/88; SLJ 2/89)

7366 Robinet, Harriette G. *Walking to the Bus-Rider Blues* (3–6). 2000, Simon & Schuster $16.00 (0-689-83191-9). 147pp. In 1956 at the time of the bus boycotts, African American Alfa Merryfield is involved both in the civil rights movement and a mystery involving a thief who has been stealing the family's meager savings. (Rev: BL 5/1/00; HBG 10/00; SLJ 5/00)

7367 Rodriguez, Luis J. *It Doesn't Have to Be This Way: A Barrio Story/No tiene que ser asi: una historia del barrio* (3–7). Illus. by Daniel Galvez. 1999, Children's Book Pr. $15.95 (0-89239-161-8). 32pp. In this bilingual book, Monchi, a young resident of the barrio, gradually sinks into the violence and crime of gang life, until a sudden death brings him to his senses. (Rev: BL 8/99; HBG 3/00; SLJ 10/99)

7368 Roseman, Kenneth. *The Other Side of the Hudson: A Jewish Immigrant Adventure* (5–8). Illus. Series: Do-It-Yourself Adventure. 1993, UAHC paper $8.95 (0-8074-0506-X). 140pp. Using an interactive format, readers can choose various destinations for a young male Jewish immigrant after he arrives in New York City from Germany in 1851. (Rev: SLJ 6/94)

7369 Rosen, Sybil. *Speed of Light* (5–9). 1999, Simon & Schuster $16.00 (0-689-82437-8). 176pp. When Audrey's father, a Jewish worker in a small Virginia town in 1956, supports the appointment of the first black police officer in town, it unleashes a flood of anti-Semitism. (Rev: BL 8/99; HBG 3/00; SLJ 8/99)

7370 Schecter, Ellen. *The Big Idea* (2–5). Illus. 1996, Hyperion LB $14.49 (0-7868-2085-3); paper $3.95 (0-7868-1043-2). 80pp. Young Luzita wants to transform a vacant lot into a neighborhood garden. (Rev: BCCB 4/96; BL 1/1–15/97; SLJ 4/96)

7371 Sing, Rachel. *Chinese New Year's Dragon* (3–5). Illus. by Shao Wei Liu. 1994, Simon & Schuster paper $5.99 (0-671-88602-9). 23pp. A young girl works with her family to prepare for the Chinese New Year and then enjoys participating in the joyous festival. (Rev: BL 4/15/94)

7372 Smothers, Ethel Footman. *Moriah's Pond* (4–7). 1995, Knopf $16.00 (0-679-84504-6). 112pp. In this sequel to *In the Piney Woods* (1992), racial tensions surround African American youngsters growing up in rural Georgia in the 1950s. (Rev: BCCB 4/95; BL 1/15/95; SLJ 2/95)

7373 Soto, Gary. *Local News* (4–7). 1993, Harcourt $14.00 (0-15-248117-6). 144pp. This collection of 13 short stories deals with a number of Mexican American youngsters at home, school, and play. (Rev: BL 4/15/93; HB 7–8/93*)

7374 Soto, Gary. *Petty Crimes* (5–8). 1998, Harcourt $16.00 (0-15-201658-9). 176pp. Ten short stories about young Mexican American kids in California's Central Valley that deal with some humorous situations but more often, gangs, violence, and poverty. (Rev: BL 3/15/98; HBG 10/98; SLJ 5/98)

7375 Soto, Gary. *Taking Sides* (5–7). 1991, Harcourt $17.00 (0-15-284076-1). 160pp. An unhappy Hispanic American youngster, whose family has recently moved to a new neighborhood, meets problems on the basketball team. (Rev: SLJ 11/91)

7376 Stanek, Muriel. *I Speak English for My Mom* (3–5). Illus. by Judith Friedman. 1989, Whitman LB $13.95 (0-8075-3659-8). 32pp. A young Mexican

American translates for her mother, who can't read English. (Rev: BCCB 2/89; BL 3/1/89; SLJ 5/89)

7377 Tolliver, Ruby C. *Sarita, Be Brave* (3–6). 1999, Eakin $14.95 (1-57168-184-1). 144pp. After the deaths of her grandmother and mother, 12-year-old Sara leaves Honduras for an eventful truck trip to Texas where she encounters problems and hardships before making a good adjustment. (Rev: HBG 3/00; SLJ 8/99)

7378 Uchida, Yoshiko. *Journey Home* (4–6). Illus. by Charles Robinson. 1978, Macmillan $16.00 (0-689-50126-9); paper $4.99 (0-689-71641-9). 144pp. Life of a Japanese American family after its release from a World War II internment camp.

7379 Uchida, Yoshiko. *Journey to Topaz: A Story of the Japanese-American Evacuation* (4–7). Illus. by Donald Carrick. 1985, Creative Arts paper $9.95 (0-916870-85-5). 160pp. In this reissue of a 1971 title, 11-year-old Yuki and her family endure shameful treatment after Pearl Harbor.

7380 Yep, Laurence. *Thief of Hearts* (5–8). 1995, HarperCollins LB $15.89 (0-06-025342-8). 197pp. Stacy, who is half Chinese, goes back to San Francisco's Chinatown to trace her family roots. (Rev: BCCB 9/95; BL 7/95; SLJ 8/95)

Family Stories

7381 Adler, C. S. *Her Blue Straw Hat* (4–7). 1997, Harcourt $16.00 (0-15-201466-7). 112pp. Rachel has an opportunity to meet her stepfather's daughter during a summer vacation. (Rev: BL 9/1/97; HBG 3/98; SLJ 9/97)

7382 Adler, C. S. *One Sister Too Many* (5–7). 1989, Macmillan paper $3.95 (0-689-71521-8). 176pp. Casey and her reunited family are being driven crazy by the newest addition — a colicky baby. (Rev: BCCB 3/89; BL 3/15/89; SLJ 4/89)

7383 Adler, David A. *Andy and Tamika* (2–4). Illus. 1999, Harcourt $14.00 (0-15-201735-6). 144pp. While befriending a stray kitten and preparing for the fourth-grade carnival, young Andy Russell, along with his sister, tries to trick his parents into revealing the gender of the baby that is soon to arrive. (Rev: BL 3/1/99; HBG 10/99; SLJ 5/99)

7384 Alcott, Louisa May. *Little Women* (4–7). Illus. by Louis Jambor. 1947, Putnam $18.99 (0-448-06019-1). 656pp. One of the many fine editions of this enduring story. Two sequels are: *Little Men* (Knopf 1995); *Jo's Boys* (Viking 1996).

7385 Aliki. *The Two of Them* (K–4). Illus. by author. 1987, Morrow paper $4.95 (0-688-07337-9). 32pp. A moving story of a tender relationship between a child and her grandfather and of the death of the old man.

7386 Alvarez, Julia. *How Tia Lola Came to ~~Visit~~ Stay* (4–7). 2001, Knopf $15.95 (0-375-80215-0). 160pp. Aunt Lola from the Dominican Republic comes to visit 10-year-old Miguel and his family in Vermont and everywhere she goes she spreads friendliness, enthusiasm, stories, and surprise parties. (Rev: BL 2/15/01; SLJ 3/01)

7387 Armstrong, William H. *Sounder* (6–8). Illus. by James Barkley. 1969, HarperCollins LB $15.89 (0-06-020144-4); paper $5.95 (0-06-440020-4). 128pp. Harsh customs and hard circumstances cripple the bodies of both the dog Sounder and his master. Newbery Award winner, 1970. A sequel is: *Sour Land* (1971).

7388 Babbitt, Natalie. *The Eyes of the Amaryllis* (4–6). 1977, Farrar $15.00 (0-374-32241-4); paper $4.95 (0-374-42238-9). 160pp. In this story set in an Atlantic coastal village during the late 19th century, an 11-year-old girl is drawn into her grandmother's obsession.

7389 Baker, Barbara. *Oh, Emma* (3–5). Illus. by Catherine Stock. 1993, Puffin paper $3.99 (0-140-36357-2). 96pp. When Emma learns that a fourth child is expected in their already cramped, low-income apartment, she becomes very upset. (Rev: BCCB 1/92; BL 11/15/91; SLJ 2/92)

7390 Bawden, Nina. *Granny the Pag* (5–7). 1996, Clarion $14.95 (0-935-77604-X). 192pp. Catriona is embarrassed by her grandmother's eccentric ways, such as riding motorbikes and wearing leather jackets. (Rev: BCCB 3/96; BL 4/1/96; HB 9–10/96; SLJ 4/96*)

7391 Bawden, Nina. *Humbug* (4–6). 1992, Houghton $13.95 (0-395-62149-6). 136pp. First there was her parents' trip to Japan, then her grandmother's trip to the hospital; it's all humbug, which Cora likes to think of as a magic word. (Rev: BCCB 11/92*; BL 10/1/92*; HB 3–4/93; SLJ 10/92*)

7392 Bechard, Margaret. *My Mom Married the Principal* (5–8). 1998, Viking $14.99 (0-670-87394-2). 144pp. For Jonah the eighth grade is the pits and having his stepfather as principal doesn't help. (Rev: BCCB 4/98; BL 3/1/98; HBG 10/98; SLJ 3/98)

7393 Bertrand, Diane Gonzales. *Alicia's Treasure* (4–6). 1996, Arte Publico paper $7.95 (1-55885-086-4). 125pp. Ten-year-old Alicia spends her first weekend at the beach, thanks to her brother's girlfriend. (Rev: BL 5/1/96; SLJ 7/96)

7394 Borders, Christine. *Gram Makes a House Call* (2–4). Illus. by author. 1999, Greenhills paper $5.95 (0-9671160-0-7). 77pp. A simple chapter book about the good times a boy has with his unconventional grandmother. (Rev: SLJ 1/00)

7395 Burch, Robert. *Ida Early Comes over the Mountain* (4–7). 1990, Puffin paper $4.99 (0-14-034534-5). 144pp. Ida Early becomes the housekeeper for four motherless children.

7396 Burnett, Frances Hodgson. *A Little Princess* (4–6). Illus. by Tasha Tudor. 1987, HarperCollins paper $3.95 (0-064-40187-1). 240pp. Sad story of a penniless orphan whose fortune is finally restored.

7397 Byars, Betsy. *Beans on the Roof* (3–5). Illus. 1990, Dell paper $3.99 (0-440-40314-6). 80pp. George's sister and the whole family are writing roof poems and George feels awful until he can write one too. (Rev: BCCB 11/88; BL 11/1/88; SLJ 11/88)

7398 Byars, Betsy. *The Blossoms and the Green Phantom* (5–7). Illus. 1987, Dell paper $3.99 (0-

440-40069-4). 160pp. Junior is about to launch his greatest invention — a hot-air balloon that he hopes will be mistaken for a flying saucer. The three other books about the Blossoms are: *The Blossoms Meet the Vulture Lady; The Not-Just-Anybody Family* (both Bantam 1987); *A Blossom Promise* (Delacorte 1987). (Rev: BCCB 4/87; BL 3/15/87; HB 3–4/87)

7399 Byars, Betsy. *The Glory Girl* (6–8). 1985, Puffin paper $4.99 (0-14-031785-6). 144pp. Anna is the nonsinging member of a family of gospel singers.

7400 Cameron, Ann. *The Stories Julian Tells* (3–5). Illus. by Ann Strugnell. 1981, Pantheon $15.99 (0-394-94301-5); Knopf paper $4.99 (0-394-82892-5). 96pp. Six short stories chiefly about the home life of Julian and his family.

7401 Canfield, Dorothy. *Understood Betsy* (4–6). Illus. by Martha Alexander. 1981, Buccaneer LB $25.95 (0-89966-342-7). 219pp. A new edition of the old favorite about Elizabeth Ann and the fearful new way of life that awaits her when she goes to live in the wilds of Vermont.

7402 Carlson, Margaret. *The Canning Season* (4–6). Illus. 1999, Carolrhoda paper $7.95 (1-57505-283-0). Peggie's family's prejudice threatens her friendship with an African American girl in 1950s Minnesota. (Rev: BL 2/15; HBG 3/00; SLJ 3/99)

7403 Caseley, Judith. *Harry and Arney* (2–4). 1994, Greenwillow $14.00 (0-688-12140-3). 144pp. An episodic story about Harry Kane growing up in a loving Jewish family that is adjusting to a new baby. (Rev: BL 9/1/94; SLJ 9/94)

7404 Caseley, Judith. *Starring Dorothy Kane* (3–5). 1992, Greenwillow $13.00 (0-688-10182-8). 160pp. Dorothy does not want to move, does not want to go to a new school, and does not like being the middle child. (Rev: BCCB 5/92; BL 3/15/92; SLJ 5/92)

7405 Christiansen, C. B. *I See the Moon* (5–7). 1994, Atheneum $14.95 (0-689-31928-2). 128pp. Grown-up Bitte looks back at being 12, the year her unmarried older sister became pregnant. (Rev: BCCB 1/95; BL 2/1/95; SLJ 1/95)

7406 Cleary, Beverly. *Ramona the Pest* (3–5). Illus. by Louis Darling. 1968, Morrow $15.89 (0-688-31721-9). 192pp. The fine addition to this popular series follows spirited Ramona Quimby, sister to Beezus and neighbor to Henry, through her kindergarten escapades. Also use: *Beezus and Ramona* (1955); *Ribsy* (1964).

7407 Cleary, Beverly. *Ramona's World* (3–6). Illus. 1999, Morrow LB $14.93 (0-688-16818-3). 192pp. Ramona, now in fourth grade, has a new baby sister, enjoys having a best friend, and feels twinges of love for her old buddy, Yard Ape. (Rev: BCCB 9/99; BL 6/1–15/99*; HB 9–10/99; HBG 3/00; SLJ 8/99)

7408 Cleary, Beverly. *Sister of the Bride* (6–8). Illus. by Beth Krush and Joe Krush. 1963, Morrow $16.89 (0-688-31742-1); Avon paper $4.95 (0-380-72807-9). 256pp. All the excitement and confusion an approaching wedding brings to a household.

7409 Cleary, Beverly. *Socks* (4–6). Illus. by Beatrice Darwin. 1973, Morrow $15.93 (0-688-30067-7); Avon paper $4.99 (0-380-70926-0). 160pp. What

happens when the family cat Socks realizes that his position of importance is threatened by the arrival of a baby.

7410 Clifton, Lucille. *The Lucky Stone* (3–5). Illus. by Dale Payson. 1986, Dell paper $3.99 (0-440-45110-8). 64pp. Several stories in the life of a girl's great-grandmother linked by the power of a stone.

7411 Clough, B. W. *An Impossumble Summer* (4–6). 1992, Walker $14.95 (0-8027-8150-0). 146pp. Rianne and her siblings discover their grumpy opossum can speak and grant wishes. (Rev: BL 3/1/92; SLJ 4/92)

7412 Clymer, Eleanor. *My Mother Is the Smartest Woman in the World* (4–6). Illus. by Nancy Kincade. 1982, Macmillan $13.95 (0-689-30916-3). 96pp. Kathleen's mom runs for mayor.

7413 Cohen, Barbara. *The Carp in the Bathtub* (3–4). Illus. by Joan Halpern. 1972, Kar-Ben paper $5.95 (0-930494-67-9). 48pp. Two Jewish children decide that the carp in the bathtub should be rescued before it becomes Passover gefilte fish.

7414 Conford, Ellen. *And This Is Laura* (4–6). 1992, Little, Brown paper $4.95 (0-316-15354-0). 192pp. A very ordinary girl discovers that she possesses psychic powers.

7415 Conrad, Pam. *Our House: The Stories of Levittown* (4–7). Illus. by Brian Selznick. 1995, Scholastic $14.95 (0-590-46523-6). 96pp. The history of the middle-class community Levittown, New York, is traced through a series of fictional vignettes. (Rev: BCCB 12/95; BL 1/1–15/96; HB 11–12/95; SLJ 11/95)

7416 Corcoran, Barbara. *Family Secrets* (5–8). 1992, Macmillan LB $13.95 (0-689-31744-1). 136pp. After a move to New England with her family, 13-year-old Tracy discovers she is adopted. (Rev: BL 3/1/92; SLJ 2/92)

7417 de Anda, Diane. *The Ice Dove and Other Stories* (3–5). 1997, Arte Publico paper $7.95 (1-55885-189-5). 72pp. In these four stories, two involving Christmas and two the classroom, Hispanic American youngsters gain the strength to face problems through help from their loving extended families. (Rev: BL 10/1/97)

7418 DeGross, Monalisa. *Donavan's Word Jar* (2–3). Illus. 1994, HarperCollins LB $14.89 (0-06-020191-6). 80pp. Whereas his friends collect coins or comics, Donavan collects interesting words and puts them in a jar. (Rev: BL 6/1–15/94; SLJ 8/94)

7419 Delacre, Lulu. *Salsa Stories* (4–7). Illus. 2000, Scholastic $15.95 (0-590-63118-7). 112pp. After each of her relatives tells a childhood story about a favorite food, Carmen Teresa records them and supplies appropriate recipes. (Rev: BCCB 5/00; BL 5/1/00; HBG 10/00; SLJ 3/00)

7420 Delton, Judy. *Angel Bites the Bullet* (3–5). Illus. 2000, Houghton $15.00 (0-618-04085-4). 144pp. Angel and her best friend try everything to get rid of the unwanted guest who's sharing Angel's room. (Rev: BL 11/1/00; HBG 3/01; SLJ 10/00)

7421 Delton, Judy. *Angel's Mother's Baby* (4–6). Illus. by Margot Apple. 1989, Houghton $16.00 (0-395-50926-2). 112pp. Angel is content with her new stepfather in the family, but she had not counted on a new baby. (Rev: BL 9/15/89; HB 11–12/89; SLJ 10/89)

7422 Delton, Judy. *Angel's Mother's Boyfriend* (3–5). Illus. by Margot Apple. 1986, Houghton $16.00 (0-395-39968-8). 176pp. Angel and brother Rags are dismayed to discover that their mother has a boyfriend, and doubly dismayed to discover that he is a clown — a real one! Also use: *Angel in Charge* (1985); *Angel's Mother's Wedding* (1987). (Rev: BL 4/1/86; HB 7–8/86; SLJ 8/86)

7423 Delton, Judy. *Back Yard Angel* (3–5). Illus. by Leslie Morrill. 1983, Houghton $16.00 (0-395-33883-2). 112pp. Ten-year-old Angel O'Leary is saddled with taking care of her little brother.

7424 Dowell, Frances O'Roark. *Dovey Coe* (4–7). 2000, Simon & Schuster $16.00 (0-689-83174-9). 192pp. The mountain country of North Carolina in 1928 is the setting of this story of a plucky girl who cares for her siblings and who gets involved in a murder trial. (Rev: HBG 10/00; SLJ 5/00)

7425 Duncan, Jane. *Brave Janet Reachfar* (4–6). Illus. by Mairi Hedderwick. 1975, Houghton $7.95 (0-8164-3130-2). 32pp. Scottish farm life is depicted through the adventures of young Janet and her relationship with her tyrannical grandmother.

7426 Dunlop, Eileen. *Finn's Island* (4–6). 1992, Holiday $13.95 (0-8234-0910-4). 128pp. Bored and grieving, Finn takes a trip from Scotland to the Hebrides island of his grandfather's birth, where he learns to see the man more realistically. (Rev: BL 2/1/92; SLJ 6/92)

7427 Engel, Diana. *Holding On* (4–6). 1997, Marshall Cavendish $14.95 (0-7614-5016-5). 96pp. Tommy is fearful about spending two weeks with his erratic great-uncle, but slowly they become friends. (Rev: BL 9/15/97; HBG 3/98; SLJ 11/97)

7428 Enright, Elizabeth. *Thimble Summer* (4–6). Illus. by author. 1938, Holt $17.95 (0-8050-0306-1); Dell paper $4.99 (0-440-48681-5). 124pp. A small girl on a Wisconsin farm finds a magic thimble. Newbery Award winner, 1939.

7429 Fakih, Kimberly O. *High on the Hog* (4–7). 1994, Farrar $16.00 (0-374-33209-6). 166pp. A 12-year-old girl stays with her great-grandparents on a farm in Iowa and discovers a family secret. (Rev: BCCB 7–8/94; BL 6/1–15/94; SLJ 5/94*)

7430 Fenner, Carol. *Yolonda's Genius* (4–6). 1995, Simon & Schuster paper $17.00 (0-689-80001-0). 153pp. African American Yolonda tries to prove that her young brother, who does poorly at school, is really a musical genius. (Rev: BL 6/1–15/95; SLJ 7/95)

7431 Fine, Anne. *Step by Wicked Step* (4–6). 1996, Little, Brown $15.95 (0-316-28345-2). 138pp. Five children share stories about their stepfamilies. (Rev: BCCB 5/96; BL 5/15/96; HB 7–8/96; SLJ 6/96*)

7432 Fitzhugh, Louise. *Nobody's Family Is Going to Change* (5–8). Illus. by author. 1986, Farrar paper $5.95 (0-374-45523-6). 221pp. There is considerable misunderstanding within a middle-class African American family but also much humor and warmth.

7433 Fletcher, Ralph. *Fig Pudding* (5–7). 1995, Clarion $15.00 (0-395-71125-8). 160pp. A year that brings both tragedy and hilarity in the life of a family of six children. (Rev: BCCB 5/95; BL 5/15/95; SLJ 7/95)

7434 Fox, Paula. *Maurice's Room* (3–5). Illus. by Ingrid Fetz. 1985, Macmillan LB $13.95 (0-02-735490-3); paper $4.50 (0-689-71216-2). 64pp. An 8-year-old campaigns to protect his bedroom full of junk. A reissue.

7435 Galbraith, Kathryn O. *Holding onto Sunday* (2–3). Illus. 1995, Simon & Schuster paper $14.00 (0-689-50623-6). 48pp. A child looks forward to Sundays, when she spends the whole day with her single-parent father. (Rev: BL 5/15/95; SLJ 9/95)

7436 Gates, Doris. *Blue Willow* (4–6). Illus. by Paul Lantz. 1940, Puffin paper $5.99 (0-14-030924-1). 176pp. Janey, a child of migrant workers in the San Joaquin Valley of California, longs for a lasting home to "stay" in.

7437 Giff, Patricia Reilly. *A Glass Slipper for Rosie* (3–4). Illus. Series: Ballet Slippers. 1997, Viking $13.99 (0-670-87469-8). 80pp. Rosie plans a special surprise for her Grandfather on his birthday involving a ballet in which she will be performing, but she discovers, to her disappointment, that he will be away on a trip. (Rev: BL 10/1/97; HBG 3/98; SLJ 12/97)

7438 Greenfield, Eloise. *Sister* (5–7). Illus. by Moneta Barnett. 1974, HarperCollins $15.95 (0-690-00497-4); paper $4.95 (0-06-440199-5). 96pp. Four years in an African American girl's life, as revealed through scattered diary entries, during which she shows maturation, particularly in her attitude toward her sister.

7439 Griffith, Helen V. *Grandaddy and Janetta Together: The Three Stories in One Book* (2–5). Illus. 2001, Greenwillow LB $15.89 (0-06-029238-5). 80pp. Three great picture books — *Grandaddy's Place* (1987), *Grandaddy and Janetta* (1993), and *Grandaddy's Stars* (1995) — are reprinted in one volume that tells the continuing story of the bond between a city girl and her country grandfather. (Rev: BL 12/15/00)

7440 Hall, Donald. *Old Home Day* (3–6). Illus. by Emily Arnold McCully. 1996, Harcourt $16.00 (0-15-276896-3). 48pp. The changes in Blackwater Pond in New Hampshire from the Ice Age to the present, with emphasis on the time after the first settlers arrived in 1799. (Rev: BCCB 10/96; BL 9/1/96*; HB 11–12/96; SLJ 10/96)

7441 Hamilton, Morse. *The Garden of Eden Motel* (4–6). 1999, Greenwillow $16.00 (0-688-16814-0). 160pp. Dal, an 11-year-old, spends the summer of 1952 with his new stepfather in the Garden of Eden Motel in Eden, Idaho. (Rev: BCCB 11/99; BL 12/1/99; HBG 3/00; SLJ 10/99)

7442 Hamilton, Virginia. *Bluish* (4–6). 1999, Scholastic $15.95 (0-590-28879-2). 128pp. Dreenie tries to become friends with a girl nicknamed Bluish, wheelchair-ridden and suffering from cancer, who is in Dreenie's fifth-grade class. (Rev: BCCB 10/99; BL 9/15/99; HBG 3/00; SLJ 11/99)

7443 Hamilton, Virginia. *Justice and Her Brothers* (6–8). 1992, Harcourt paper $3.95 (0-15-241640-4). A slow-moving but compelling study of a young girl's relationship with her older twin brothers. Two sequels: *Dustland* (1980, Greenwillow); *The Gathering* (1989).

7444 Hamilton, Virginia. *M. C. Higgins, the Great* (6–8). 1974, Macmillan LB $17.00 (0-02-742480-4); paper $4.99 (0-02-043490-1). 288pp. The Newbery Award winner (1975) about a 13-year-old African American boy growing up in Appalachia as part of a loving family whose future is threatened by a possible mountain slide.

7445 Harrison, Maggie. *Angels on Roller Skates* (2–4). Illus. 1992, Candlewick $14.95 (1-56402-003-7). 112pp. Bigun, Middlun, and Littun are the stars in six tales about family life in England. (Rev: BCCB 6/92; BL 5/1/92)

7446 Harrison, Maggie. *Lizzie's List* (3–6). Illus. by Bethan Matthews. 1993, Candlewick $14.95 (1-56402-197-1). 112pp. Lizzie lacks the large family that her friends have, and so she sets out to create her own grandparents. (Rev: BL 10/1/93; SLJ 11/93)

7447 Hehrlich, Gretel. *A Blizzard Year: Timmy's Almanac of the Seasons* (4–7). Illus. by Kate Kiesler. 1999, Hyperion LB $15.49 (0-7868-2309-7). 122pp. Using a diary format, this novel covers a year in the life of 13-year-old Timmy, who is growing up with her family on a ranch in Wyoming. (Rev: HBG 3/00; SLJ 2/00)

7448 Henkes, Kevin. *The Zebra Wall* (4–6). 1988, Greenwillow $15.95 (0-688-07568-1); Puffin paper $4.99 (0-14-032969-2). 160pp. Adine and her sisters await the sixth child in the family. (Rev: BCCB 4/88; BL 4/15/88; SLJ 4/88)

7449 Hickcox, Ruth. *Great-grandmother's Treasure* (2–6). Illus. by David Soman. 1998, Dial $15.99 (0-8037-1513-7). 32pp. The life story, from birth to death, of a caring, giving woman who enjoyed making her friends and family happy. (Rev: BL 11/1/98; HBG 3/99; SLJ 1/99)

7450 Hickman, Janet. *Jericho* (5–8). 1994, Greenwillow $15.00 (0-688-13398-3). 144pp. When Angela takes care of her grandmother during her last illness, she learns about the many disappointments the old lady faced during her life. (Rev: BCCB 11/94; BL 9/1/94; HB 11–12/94; SLJ 9/94)

7451 Holl, Kristi D. *Just Like a Real Family* (4–6). 1997, Royal Fireworks paper $6.99 (0-88092-430-6). 132pp. June Finch, a 12-year-old, gets involved in a class project to adopt grandparents from a retirement home.

7452 Holl, Kristi D. *No Strings Attached* (5–7). 1998, Royal Fireworks paper $6.99 (0-88092-434-9). 128pp. June finds some difficulties in adjustment when she and her mother move in with crabby old Franklin Cooper. (Rev: BCCB 5/88; BL 6/15/88; SLJ 4/88)

7453 Holm, Jenni. *Our Only May Amelia* (4–6). 1999, HarperCollins LB $15.89 (0-06-028354-8). 160pp. Told in diary form, this is the story of 12-year-old May Amelia, who lives with her large family in Washington State in the late 1800s, and of her troubles when her grandmother comes to stay. (Rev: BCCB 9/99; BL 9/1/99; HBG 10/99; SLJ 9/99)

7454 Holt, Kimberly Willis. *Dancing in Cadillac Light* (5–7). 2001, Putnam $15.99 (0-399-23402-0). 176pp. A strong, tender story about 11-year-old Jaynell, a tomboy who is growing up in Moon, Texas, in 1968. (Rev: BCCB 3/01; BL 2/1/01; SLJ 3/01)

7455 Horvath, Betty. *Sir Galahad, Mr. Longfellow, and Me* (3–6). 1998, Simon & Schuster $15.00 (0-689-81470-4). 144pp. A quiet family story set in Missouri in 1938 that tells of a sixth-grade girl and how her writing abilities are fostered by her new schoolteacher. (Rev: BCCB 5/98; BL 6/1–15/98; HBG 10/98; SLJ 6/98)

7456 Howe, James. *Pinky and Rex and the Double-Dad Weekend* (2–4). Illus. by Melissa Sweet. 1995, Atheneum $14.00 (0-689-31871-5). 42pp. Pinky and Rex won't let a little rain spoil the camping trip they have planned with their dads. (Rev: BL 4/15/95; SLJ 8/95)

7457 Hurwitz, Johanna. *The Down and Up Fall* (4–6). Illus. 1996, Morrow $15.00 (0-688-14568-X). 128pp. An 11-year-old girl adjusts to living with her great-aunt and -uncle while her parents are away. (Rev: BCCB 9/96; BL 10/15/96; SLJ 9/96)

7458 Hurwitz, Johanna. *"E" Is for Elisa* (2–4). Illus. by Lillian Hoban. 1991, Morrow $12.88 (0-688-10440-1). 80pp. Episodes of everyday life with 8-year-old Russell who loves to tease his 4-year-old sister. (Rev: BCCB 9/91; BL 9/1/91*; HB 9–10/91; SLJ 8/91)

7459 Hurwitz, Johanna. *School's Out* (2–4). Illus. by Sheila Hamanaka. 1991, Morrow $15.00 (0-688-09938-6). 128pp. Lucas looks forward to the arrival of the French girl who has been hired to take care of his younger twin brothers. (Rev: BCCB 4/91; BL 1/15/91; HB 7–8/91; SLJ 5/91)

7460 Jarrow, Gail. *If Phyllis Were Here* (5–7). 1989, Avon paper $2.75 (0-380-70634-2). 144pp. Libby, age 11, has to learn to adjust to living without her best friend — her grandmother who moves to Florida. (Rev: BL 10/15/87; SLJ 9/87)

7461 Kehret, Peg. *Sisters Long Ago* (5–8). 1992, Pocket paper $3.99 (0-671-78433-4). 149pp. While surviving a near drowning, Willow has a glimpse of herself living another life in ancient Egypt. (Rev: SLJ 3/90)

7462 Kennedy, Trish. *Baseball Card Crazy* (3–5). Illus. by Timothy Schodorf. 1993, Macmillan $11.95 (0-684-19536-4). 80pp. Oliver is obsessed with the idea of finding his dad's old baseball cards. (Rev: BL 3/15/93; SLJ 5/93)

7463 King-Smith, Dick. *The Stray* (3–6). Illus. 1996, Crown LB $17.99 (0-517-70935-X). 128pp. At age 75, Henny leaves her old-folks home to find independence and freedom. (Rev: BL 9/15/96; SLJ 11/96)

7464 Klein, Norma. *Mom, the Wolfman and Me* (5–8). 1972, Avon paper $3.50 (0-380-00791-6). 160pp. Brett has a most unusual mother and, therefore, doesn't mind the state of being fatherless, but the Wolfman changes things.

7465 Klein, Robin. *The Sky in Silver Lace* (6–8). 1996, Viking $13.00 (0-670-86266-5). 184pp. The four Melling sisters and their mother move to a large city in Australia to find better times in this sequel to *All in the Blue Unclouded Weather* (1992). (Rev: BCCB 2/96; BL 2/15/96; HB 5–6/96; SLJ 2/96)

7466 L'Engle, Madeleine. *Meet the Austins* (5–7). 1997, Farrar $16.00 (0-374-34929-0); Dell paper $4.99 (0-440-95777-X). The story of a country doctor's family, told by the 12-year-old daughter, and their reaction to having Maggie, a spoiled orphan, come to live with them.

7467 Levitin, Sonia. *Annie's Promise* (5–8). 1993, Macmillan $15.00 (0-689-31752-2). 192pp. In this third book about the Platt family that escaped from Nazi Germany to America, Annie, now 13, goes to a Quaker-run summer camp. (Rev: BCCB 3/93; SLJ 4/93*)

7468 Levoy, Myron. *The Witch of Fourth Street and Other Stories* (4–7). Illus. 1991, Peter Smith $15.25 (0-8446-6450-2); HarperCollins paper $4.95 (0-06-440059-X). 128pp. Eight stories about growing up poor on the Lower East Side of New York City.

7469 Levy, Elizabeth. *Wolfman Sam* (3–5). Illus. 1996, HarperCollins paper $3.95 (0-06-442048-5). 128pp. Young Robert resents his older brother's entry into puberty. (Rev: BL 11/15/96; SLJ 4/97)

7470 Lewis, Beverly. *The Chicken Pox Panic* (2–4). Illus. Series: Cul-de-Sac Kids. 1995, Bethany paper $3.99 (1-55661-626-0). 80pp. While recovering from chicken pox, Abby plans a birthday party for her Korean brother; but when he arrives, everyone has chicken pox. Also in the series: *The Double Dabble Surprise* (1995). (Rev: BL 9/1/95)

7471 Lexau, Joan M. *Striped Ice Cream* (2–5). Illus. by John Wilson. 1968, HarperCollins LB $14.89 (0-397-31047-1). 96pp. The conquest of poverty is realistically portrayed in this warmly told story about a fatherless African American family as they work together.

7472 Lindquist, Jennie D. *The Little Silver House* (3–5). Illus. by Garth Williams. 1986, Peter Smith $16.00 (0-8446-6190-2). A 9-year-old girl is intrigued by a mysterious boarded-up house. A reissue of a 1959 title.

7473 Loredo, Betsy. *Faraway Families* (2–4). Illus. by Monisha Raja. Series: Family Ties. 1995, Silver Moon LB $14.95 (1-881889-61-0). 56pp. Five short stories, each dealing with a different racial minority, explore the emotional problems that result after families are separated. (Rev: SLJ 8/95)

7474 Lowry, Lois. *Us and Uncle Fraud* (4–6). 1984, Houghton $16.00 (0-395-36633-X). 192pp. Two children become disillusioned with their Uncle Claude.

7475 McKay, Hilary. *Dolphin Luck* (4–6). 1999, Simon & Schuster $16.00 (0-689-82376-2). 160pp. When the Robinson parents are away, Beany and Sun Dance stay with neighbors and have several adventures, including searching for a magical sword

that will grant wishes. (Rev: BCCB 6/99; BL 7/99*; HB 7–8/99; HBG 10/99; SLJ 7/99)

7476 McKay, Hilary. *The Exiles* (4–7). 1992, Macmillan $17.99 (0-689-50555-8). 208pp. The four Conroe sisters are shipped off to Big Grandma's for the summer. She thinks they "read too much, answer back, and never do anything to help." (Rev: BCCB 11/92*; BL 1/1/93; HB 1–2/93*; SLJ 10/92)

7477 McKay, Hilary. *The Exiles at Home* (4–7). 1994, Macmillan paper $15.95 (0-689-50610-4). 208pp. In this sequel to *The Exiles*, the four Conway sisters sponsor the schooling of a young African boy and must find the money to pay for their generosity. (Rev: BCCB 1/95; BL 1/15/95*; SLJ 2/95)

7478 McKay, Hilary. *The Exiles in Love* (4–7). 1998, Simon & Schuster $16.00 (0-689-81752-5). 176pp. Because of their grandmother's scheming, the four Conway sisters are able to spent their spring break on a farm in Brittany. (Rev: BCCB 4/98; BL 5/1/98*; HB 5–6/98*; HBG 10/98; SLJ 5/98)

7479 MacLachlan, Patricia. *All the Places to Love* (5–8). Illus. by Mike Wimmer. 1994, HarperCollins LB $16.89 (0-06-021099-0). 32pp. This picture book celebrates the love found in an extended rural family and the joy that a new arrival brings. (Rev: BCCB 7–8/94; BL 6/1–15/94*; SLJ 6/94)

7480 MacLachlan, Patricia. *Cassie Binegar* (4–7). 1982, HarperCollins LB $14.89 (0-06-024034-2); paper $4.95 (0-06-440195-2). 128pp. Cassie is not happy with the disorder in her family situation.

7481 MacLachlan, Patricia. *Seven Kisses in a Row* (2–4). Illus. by Maria Pia Marrella. 1983, HarperCollins LB $14.89 (0-06-024084-9); paper $4.95 (0-06-440231-2). 64pp. Seven stories about two youngsters who are cared for by an aunt and uncle.

7482 Martin, Ann M. *Ten Kids, No Pets* (4–7). 1988, Scholastic paper $3.50 (0-590-43620-1). 184pp. The Rosso family — 12 strong — moves to New Jersey and a 100-year-old farmhouse. (Rev: BL 6/15/88; SLJ 5/88)

7483 Mathis, Sharon Bell. *The Hundred Penny Box* (3–5). Illus. by Leo Dillon and Diane Dillon. 1975, Puffin paper $5.99 (0-14-032169-1). 48pp. Old and frail Aunt Dew tells Michael about her experiences through a box that contains a penny for each year of her life.

7484 Meyer, Carolyn. *Jubilee Journey* (5–7). 1997, Harcourt $13.00 (0-15-201377-6). 256pp. A biracial girl finds her spiritual identity when she visits her African American relatives in Texas. (Rev: BL 9/1/97; HBG 3/98; SLJ 1/98)

7485 Miles, Betty. *Just the Beginning* (4–7). 1978, Avon paper $2.50 (0-380-01913-2). 148pp. Being relatively poor in an upper-class neighborhood causes problems for 13-year-old Catherine Myers.

7486 Morpurgo, Michael. *Escape from Shangri-La* (5–7). 1998, Putnam $16.99 (0-399-23311-3). 240pp. In this English novel, Cessie gradually forms a close relationship with an old boatman in a nursing home whom she believes to be her grandfather. (Rev: BCCB 12/98; BL 9/15/98; HBG 3/99; SLJ 11/98)

7487 Mulford, Philippa Greene. *The Holly Sisters on Their Own* (4–6). 1998, Marshall Cavendish $14.95 (0-7614-5022-X). 158pp. Charmaine, age 11, is not happy at the prospect of her older half sister's arrival to spend the summer in New York City, but time produces a friendship. (Rev: BCCB 7–8/98; BL 5/1/98; HBG 10/98; SLJ 4/98)

7488 Namioka, Lensey. *Yang the Eldest and His Odd Jobs* (3–7). Illus. 2000, Little, Brown $15.95 (0-316-59011-8). 128pp. In this story about the Yangs, a family of new Chinese Americans, First Brother, who wants to buy a violin, takes odd jobs — babysitting, waiting tables, and so forth — to make money. (Rev: BL 2/15/00; HBG 10/00; SLJ 4/00)

7489 Naylor, Phyllis Reynolds, and Lura Schield Reynolds. *Maudie in the Middle* (3–5). Illus. by Judith G. Brown. 1988, Macmillan LB $16.00 (0-689-31395-0). 176pp. Eight-year-old Maudie, the middle of seven children in the 1900s, longs to be "first" with someone. (Rev: BCCB 5/88; BL 4/1/88; SLJ 5/88)

7490 Paterson, Katherine. *Come Sing, Jimmy Jo* (5–7). 1985, Avon paper $3.99 (0-380-70052-2). 208pp. The family decides it's time to include James in their singing group. (Rev: BL 9/1/87)

7491 Paterson, Katherine. *Jacob Have I Loved* (6–8). 1980, HarperCollins LB $15.89 (0-690-04079-2); paper $5.95 (0-06-440368-8). 228pp. A story set in the Chesapeake Bay region about the rivalry between two sisters. Newbery Award winner, 1981.

7492 Peck, Richard. *A Year Down Yonder* (5–8). 2000, Dial $16.99 (0-8037-2518-3). 130pp. In this Newbery medal winner, 15-year-old Mary Alice visits her feisty, independent, but lovable Grandma Dowdel in rural Illinois during the Great Depression. A sequel to the honor book *A Long Way from Chicago* (1998). (Rev: BCCB 1/01; HB 11–12/00; HBG 3/01; SLJ 9/00)

7493 Pfeffer, Susan Beth. *Kid Power* (4–6). Illus. by Leigh Grant. 1991, Scholastic paper $3.99 (0-590-42607-9). 121pp. A spunky young girl organizes an employment agency for herself and friends when her mother loses her job.

7494 Porte, Barbara A. *If You Ever Get Lost* (3–4). Illus. 2000, Greenwillow $15.95 (0-688-16947-3). 80pp. A simple chapter book about the daily activities of Julia and her little brother, Evan. (Rev: BCCB 5/00; BL 6/1–15/00; HBG 10/00; SLJ 7/00)

7495 Porte, Barbara Ann. *Fat Fanny, Beanpole Bertha and the Boys* (4–6). Illus. by Maxie Chambliss. 1991, Orchard LB $16.99 (0-531-08528-7). 112pp. Fanny and Bertha are best friends despite their differences. (Rev: BCCB 4/91*; BL 3/1/91; HB 7–8/91; SLJ 2/91*)

7496 Pryor, Bonnie. *Toenails, Tonsils, and Tornadoes* (3–5). Illus. 1997, Morrow $15.00 (0-688-14885-9). 160pp. Fourth-grader Martin is not too happy when his Aunt Henrietta visits, principally because he has to give up his room. (Rev: BCCB 6/97; BL 5/15/97; SLJ 5/97)

7497 Regan, Dian C. *The Friendship of Milly and Tug* (2–3). Illus. by Jennifer Danza. Series: A Redfeather Chapter Book. 1999, Holt $15.95 (0-8050-5935-0). 61pp. A beginning chapter book about two sisters and how the older one is put in her place after she starts to get bossy. (Rev: HBG 10/99; SLJ 7/99)

7498 Robinson, Nancy K. *Angela and the Broken Heart* (3–5). 1991, Scholastic $12.95 (0-590-43212-5). 144pp. A warm story of family problems with Angela, who, in the second grade, wonders whether she is engaged or not, and her suddenly stuck-up brother. (Rev: BL 4/1/91; SLJ 4/91)

7499 Rocklin, Joanne. *Strudel Stories* (4–6). 1999, Delacorte $14.95 (0-385-32602-5). 131pp. A series of vignettes reveals a Jewish family baking strudel over a period of 100 years — with episodes in Odessa in 1894 and involving migration to America and Holocaust survival. (Rev: BCCB 5/99; BL 1/1–15/99; HBG 10/99; SLJ 1/99*)

7500 Ross, Lillian H. *Sarah, Also Known as Hannah* (4–6). Illus. by Helen Cogancherry. 1994, Albert Whitman LB $13.95 (0-8075-7237-3). 64pp. At age 12, Hannah is sent by her Jewish mother in the Ukraine to live in safety with her uncle in the United States. (Rev: BCCB 3/94; BL 4/1/94; SLJ 5/94)

7501 Rylant, Cynthia. *The Blue Hill Meadows* (2–5). Illus. 1997, Harcourt $16.00 (0-15-201404-7). 48pp. Four gentle stories about everyday life with Willie and his family. (Rev: BL 9/1/97; HBG 3/98; SLJ 10/97)

7502 Rylant, Cynthia. *In Aunt Lucy's Kitchen* (2–4). Illus. Series: Cobble Street Cousins. 1998, Simon & Schuster $15.00 (0-689-81711-8). 54pp. Three cousins start their own cookie company and find a boyfriend for their wonderful Aunt Lucy. (Rev: BCCB 1/99; BL 1/1–15/99; HBG 3/99; SLJ 2/99)

7503 Rylant, Cynthia. *A Little Shopping* (2–4). Illus. Series: Cobble Street Cousins. 1998, Simon & Schuster $14.00 (0-689-81710-X). 64pp. Charming cousins Rosie, Lily, and Tess surprise their lovable Aunt Lucy with a model of her shop — complete with miniature furniture. (Rev: BCCB 1/99; BL 1/1–15/99; HBG 3/99; SLJ 2/99)

7504 Rylant, Cynthia. *Some Good News* (3–5). Illus. Series: Cobble Street Cousins. 1999, Simon & Schuster $14.00 (0-689-81713-4). 55pp. Three cousins, who are living with their Aunt Lucy, start a Cobble Street newspaper in this low-key story. (Rev: BL 6/1–15/99; HBG 10/99; SLJ 6/99)

7505 Rylant, Cynthia. *Special Gifts* (3–5). Illus. Series: Cobble Street Cousins. 1999, Simon & Schuster $14.00 (0-689-81714-2). 55pp. Three cousins, who are staying with their aunt, are out of school for the summer and take up sewing as a hobby. (Rev: BL 6/1–15/99; HBG 10/99; SLJ 6/99)

7506 Sachs, Marilyn. *JoJo and Winnie: Sister Stories* (2–4). Illus. 1999, Dutton $14.99 (0-525-46005-5). 80pp. Self-contained chapters describe a sibling relationship between two sisters, from the birth of the younger child until she begins school. (Rev: BL 9/15/99; HBG 10/99; SLJ 7/99)

7507 Sachs, Marilyn. *JoJo and Winnie Again: More Sister Stories* (2–4). Illus. 2000, Dutton $15.99 (0-525-46393-3). 80pp. In this easy chapter book, sibling rivalry is rampant between JoJo and Winnie but there is also mutual support and friendship. (Rev: BL 8/00; HBG 3/01; SLJ 9/00)

7508 Sachs, Marilyn. *Surprise Party* (5–7). 1998, Dutton $15.99 (0-525-45962-6). 192pp. Sixth-grader Gen, who resents the fuss made over her attention-seeking younger brother, nevertheless works with him to plan a surprise anniversary party for their parents. (Rev: BL 6/1–15/98; HBG 10/98; SLJ 5/98)

7509 Scheffler, Ursel. *Grandpa's Amazing Computer* (2–4). Illus. by Ruth Scholte van Mast. 1997, North-South LB $13.88 (1-55858-796-9). 46pp. Ollie's grandfather tells the young boy why a sunflower seed can perform more amazing feats than a computer. (Rev: BL 2/15/98)

7510 Sendak, Philip. *In Grandpa's House* (4–6). Trans. by Seymour Barofsky. Illus. by Maurice Sendak. 1985, HarperCollins LB $9.89 (0-06-025463-7). 48pp. Translated from Yiddish, these are stories of an Eastern European Jewish immigrant and the family he created in America. (Rev: HB 1–2/86; SLJ 10/85)

7511 Sheldon, Dyan. *My Brother Is a Superhero* (4–6). Illus. 1996, Candlewick $15.99 (1-56402-624-8). 128pp. Adam is reluctant to call on his overbearing older brother for help in fighting three teenage bullies. (Rev: BCCB 2/96; BL 5/1/96; SLJ 4/96)

7512 Shreve, Susan. *Goodbye, Amanda the Good* (4–7). 2000, Knopf LB $18.99 (0-679-99241-3). 144pp. Between the sixth and seventh grades, Amanda, who has always been angelic, rebels, changes her ways, and becomes a hellion. (Rev: BCCB 2/00; BL 2/1/00; HBG 10/00)

7513 Sidney, Margaret. *The Five Little Peppers and How They Grew* (4–6). 1981, Buccaneer LB $27.95 (0-89966-340-0). 302pp. The classic of five children growing up many decades ago.

7514 Simon, Norma. *How Do I Feel?* (4–6). Illus. by Joe Lasker. 1970, Whitman LB $14.95 (0-8075-3414-5). A small boy has tangled, emotional problems with his twin and his older brother.

7515 Slepian, Jan. *The Broccoli Tapes* (5–7). 1989, Putnam $14.95 (0-399-21712-6); Scholastic paper $3.50 (0-590-43473-X). Sara uses tapes during her stay in Hawaii to keep up with her class oral history project. (Rev: BCCB 4/89; SLJ 4/89)

7516 Smith, Janice Lee. *The Monster in the Third Dresser Drawer and Other Stories About Adam Joshua* (3–5). Illus. by Dick Gackenbach. 1981, HarperCollins LB $15.89 (0-06-025739-3); paper $4.25 (0-06-440223-1). 96pp. Adam Joshua faces many everyday problems, including a new baby sister, in these six stories. A sequel is: *The Kid Next Door and Other Headaches: Stories about Adam Joshua* (1984).

7517 Smith, Robert K. *The War with Grandpa* (4–6). Illus. by Richard Lauter. 1984, Dell paper $4.99 (0-440-49276-9). 128pp. Peter resents giving up his bedroom to his grandfather.

7518 Sorensen, Virginia. *Miracles on Maple Hill* (4–6). 1990, Harcourt paper $4.95 (0-15-254561-1). 232pp. The story of a troubled family drawn together by the experience of a year of country living. Newbery Award winner, 1957.

7519 Spinelli, Jerry. *Crash* (5–7). 1996, Knopf $16.00 (0-679-87957-9). 162pp. Athlete Crash Coogan changes his bullying ways after his grandfather suffers a stroke. (Rev: BCCB 5/96; BL 6/1–15/96; HB 9–10/96; SLJ 6/96*)

7520 Spurr, Elizabeth. *Mama's Birthday Surprise* (3–4). Illus. 1996, Hyperion paper $3.95 (0-7868-1124-2). 64pp. Three children discover that many of the stories about their mother's Mexican childhood are false. (Rev: BCCB 12/96; BL 11/1/96; HB 11–12/96; SLJ 11/96)

7521 Stewart, Sarah. *The Journey* (2–4). Illus. by David Small. 2001, Farrar $16.00 (0-374-33905-8). 40pp. A young Amish girl from the country keeps a diary about her exciting visit to Chicago with her mother. (Rev: BL 3/15/01; SLJ 3/01)

7522 Stolz, Mary. *Go Fish* (3–5). Illus. by Pat Cummings. 1991, HarperCollins LB $14.89 (0-06-025822-5). 80pp. Thomas and his grandfather spend warm times together. (Rev: BCCB 5/91; BL 5/15/91; HB 7–8/91; SLJ 5/91*)

7523 Stone, B. J. *Ola's Wake* (3–6). 2000, Holt $15.95 (0-8050-6157-6). 100pp. When 10-year-old Josie attends the funeral of a great-grandmother she never met, she learns that she and the old woman had many things in common. (Rev: BCCB 6/00; HB 7–8/00; HBG 10/00; SLJ 7/00)

7524 Talbert, Marc. *A Sunburned Prayer* (4–6). 1995, Simon & Schuster paper $14.00 (0-689-80125-4). 112pp. Eloy knows that if he can make a pilgrimage to a local shrine he can save his grandmother from dying. (Rev: BCCB 7–8/95; BL 8/95; SLJ 7/95*)

7525 Tashjian, Janet. *Tru Confessions* (5–7). 1997, Holt $15.95 (0-8050-5254-2). 160pp. Tru hatches a plan to get her own TV show and also help her mentally disabled twin brother. (Rev: BL 1/1–15/98; HBG 3/98; SLJ 12/97)

7526 Taylor, Mildred D. *Roll of Thunder, Hear My Cry* (6–8). Illus. by Jerry Pinkney. 1976, Bantam paper $3.50 (0-553-25450-2). Set in rural Mississippi during the Depression, this Newbery Award winner (1977) continues the story about African American Cassie Logan and her family. Begun in: *Song of the Trees* (1975); continued in: *Let the Circle Be Unbroken* (1981).

7527 Taylor, Sydney. *All-of-a-Kind Family* (3–6). Illus. by Helen John. 1980, Peter Smith $19.50 (0-8446-6253-4); Dell paper $4.99 (0-440-40059-7). 192pp. Warm and moving stories of Jewish family life in New York City. Also use: *Ella of All-of-a-Kind Family* (1980, Dell paper).

7528 Tomey, Ingrid. *Grandfather's Day* (3–5). Illus. by Robert A. McKay. 1992, Boyds Mills LB $12.95 (1-56397-022-8). 62pp. Nine-year-old Raydeen tries to mend grandfather's broken heart when he comes to live with them after the death of his wife. (Rev: BL 9/15/92; SLJ 10/92)

7529 Uchida, Yoshiko. *The Happiest Ending* (4–6). 1985, Macmillan $15.00 (0-689-50326-1). 120pp. Twelve-year-old Rinko tries to stop an arranged marriage in this story of a Japanese American family during the Great Depression. (Rev: SLJ 11/85)

7530 Uchida, Yoshiko. *A Jar of Dreams* (4–7). 1981, Macmillan $16.00 (0-689-50210-9); paper $4.99 (0-689-71672-9). 144pp. A Japanese American family is disillusioned until Aunt Waka arrives. A sequel is: *The Best Bad Thing* (1983).

7531 Van Steenwyk, Elizabeth. *Three Dog Winter* (5–8). 1987, Walker $13.95 (0-8027-6718-4). A story of dog racing, this family tale tells of 12-year-old Scott and his Malamute, Kaylah. (Rev: BL 2/1/88; SLJ 12/87)

7532 Voigt, Cynthia. *Dicey's Song* (5–8). 1982, Macmillan $17.00 (0-689-30944-9); Fawcett paper $5.99 (0-449-70276-6). 204pp. This story of Dicey's life with her "Gram" in Maryland won a Newbery Award (1983). Preceding it was: *Homecoming* (1981); a sequel is: *A Solitary Blue* (1983).

7533 Wallace, Bill. *Beauty* (5–7). 1988, Holiday $16.95 (0-8234-0715-2). 192pp. Luke finds the adjustment difficult when he and his mother go to live on his grandfather's Oklahoma farm. (Rev: BCCB 11/88; BL 2/1/89; SLJ 10/88)

7534 Welch, Sheila K. *The Shadowed Unicorn* (4–6). 2000, Front Street $15.95 (0-8126-2895-0). 192pp. Identical twins Brendan and Nick join their older, bossy sister Arni on a hunt for a black unicorn in this family story that borders on fantasy. (Rev: BCCB 10/00; BL 4/15/00; HBG 10/00; SLJ 7/00)

7535 Wesley, Valerie W. *Freedom's Gifts: A Juneteenth Story* (3–6). Illus. by Sharon Wilson. 1997, Simon & Schuster paper $16.00 (0-689-80269-2). 32pp. Set in 1943, this novel about African Americans celebrating a holiday commemorating the end of slavery points out that the battle for civil rights isn't over. (Rev: BCCB 6/97; BL 5/1/97; SLJ 6/97)

7536 Wiggin, Kate Douglas. *Rebecca of Sunnybrook Farm* (4–7). Illus. by Lawrence Beall Smith. 1986, Dell paper $3.99 (0-440-47533-3). Rebecca is a spunky, curious girl living in a quiet Maine community of the 19th century. One of many editions.

7537 Wilder, Laura Ingalls. *Little House in the Big Woods* (4–7). Illus. by Garth Williams. 1953, HarperCollins LB $16.89 (0-06-026431-4); paper $5.95 (0-06-440001-8). 238pp. Outstanding story of a log-cabin family in Wisconsin in the late 1800s. Also use: *By the Shores of Silver Lake; Farmer Boy; Little House on the Prairie; Long Winter; On the Banks of Plum Creek; These Happy Golden Years* (all 1953); *Little Town on the Prairie* (1961); *The First Four Years* (1971).

7538 Wilder, Laura Ingalls. *West from Home: Letters of Laura Ingalls Wilder, San Francisco, 1915* (6–8). 1974, HarperCollins paper $4.95 (0-06-440081-6). 176pp. Laura visited her daughter Rose in San Francisco in the year that the city was preparing a world's fair, and she wrote about her experiences to her husband.

7539 Willis, Patricia. *The Barn Burner* (5–8). 2000, Clarion $15.00 (0-395-98409-2). 208pp. In 1933, 14-year-old Ross, a runaway, becomes involved with the Warfield family whose father is away looking for work. (Rev: BCCB 5/00; BL 4/15/00; HBG 10/00; SLJ 7/00)

7540 Wilson, Jacqueline. *Double Act* (3–6). Illus. 1998, Delacorte $14.95 (0-385-32312-3). 185pp. In this English story, Ruby and Garnet are identical twins on the outside but very different inside, as their father's new girlfriend finds out. (Rev: BL 1/1–15/98*; HBG 10/98; SLJ 3/98)

7541 Woodruff, Elvira. *"Dear Napoleon, I Know You're Dead, But . . ."* (3–5). Illus. 1992, Holiday $15.95 (0-8234-0962-7). 220pp. Marty is astounded when he receives a reply to his letter to Napoleon, after Gramps tells him about a courier at his nursing home who can deliver messages to the dead. (Rev: BCCB 12/92; BL 12/15/92; SLJ 10/92)

7542 Young, Ronder T. *Learning by Heart* (5–7). 1993, Houghton $14.95 (0-395-65369-X). 172pp. Race relations and friendship become important to 10-year-old Rachel, who is growing up in a small Southern town in the 1960s with the family's African American maid, whom she adores. (Rev: BCCB 12/93; BL 12/15/93; SLJ 10/93*)

7543 Zucker, David. *Uncle Carmello* (3–6). Illus. by Lyle Miller. 1993, Macmillan LB $14.95 (0-02-793760-7). 32pp. On one special day, David gets to know forbidding Uncle Carmello, who speaks with a thick Italian accent. (Rev: BL 3/15/93; SLJ 7/93)

Fantasy and the Supernatural

7544 Adams, Richard. *Watership Down* (6–8). Illus. 1974, Macmillan $40.00 (0-02-700030-3); Avon paper $12.00 (0-380-00428-3). 444pp. Rabbits, frightened by the coming destruction of their warren, journey across the English downs in search of a new home.

7545 Adler, C. S. *Ghost Brother* (5–7). 1990, Houghton $15.00 (0-395-52592-6). 150pp. After his older brother dies in an accident, 11-year-old Wally finds comfort in his ghost. (Rev: BCCB 5/90; BL 5/15/90; SLJ 5/90)

7546 Adler, C. S. *Good-bye Pink Pig* (5–7). 1986, Avon paper $2.75 (0-380-70175-8). 176pp. Shy Amanda takes comfort in the make-believe world of her miniature pink pig — away from the elegant world of her mother and easygoing life of her brother — until trouble enters her real and imaginary worlds and she learns to assert herself. (Rev: BCCB 2/86; BL 12/15/85)

7547 Adler, C. S. *Help, Pink Pig!* (5–7). 1991, Avon paper $2.95 (0-380-71156-7). 176pp. Unsure of herself with her mother, Amanda retreats into the world of her miniature pink pig. (Rev: BL 5/1/90; SLJ 5/90)

7548 Alcock, Vivien. *The Haunting of Cassie Palmer* (5–8). 1997, Houghton paper $6.95 (0-395-

81653-X). 160pp. Cassie finds she is blessed with second sight.

7549 Alcock, Vivien. *The Red-Eared Ghosts* (5–7). 1997, Houghton $15.95 (0-395-81660-2). 272pp. Mary Frewin travels through time to solve a mystery concerning her great-great-grandmother. (Rev: BL 3/1/97; SLJ 4/97)

7550 Alcock, Vivien. *The Stonewalkers* (5–8). 1998, Houghton paper $4.95 (0-395-81652-1). 192pp. Statues come to life and begin stalking two girls.

7551 Alexander, Lloyd. *The Book of Three* (5–8). 1964, Dell paper $5.99 (0-440-40702-8). 224pp. Welsh legend and universal mythology are blended in the tale of an assistant pig keeper who becomes a hero. Newbery Award winner, 1969. Others in the Prydain cycle: *The Black Cauldron; The Castle of Llyr; Taran Wanderer; The High King* (all Holt 1995).

7552 Alexander, Lloyd. *The Cat Who Wished to Be a Man* (5–6). 1973, Dell paper $3.99 (0-440-40580-7). A cat named Lionel, turned into a man by a magician, begins combating the corrupt mayor of the town.

7553 Alexander, Lloyd. *The First Two Lives of Lukas-Kasha* (5–7). 1998, Puffin paper $4.99 (0-141-30057-4). 224pp. Lukas awakens to find himself in a strange land.

7554 Alexander, Lloyd. *Time Cat: The Remarkable Journeys of Jason and Gareth* (4–6). Illus. by Bill Sokol. 1996, Puffin paper $3.99 (0-140-37827-8). Jason's cat takes him to various times and places.

7555 Alexander, Lloyd. *The Wizard in the Tree* (4–6). Illus. by Laszlo Kubinyi. 1998, Viking paper $4.50 (0-140-38801-X). 144pp. A delightful fantasy of a good-versus-evil struggle involving an orphan, Mallory, his wizard, and their battle against Mrs. Parsel and Squire Scrupnor.

7556 Almond, David. *Heaven Eyes* (5–8). 2001, Delacorte $15.95 (0-385-32770-6). 240pp. A very ambitious novel about three young escapees from a detention center in England and the life they live in a forgotten warehouse where the watchman is a deranged man known as Heaven Eyes. (Rev: BL 1/1–15/01*)

7557 Almond, David. *Skellig* (5–8). 1998, Delacorte $15.95 (0-385-32653-X). 182pp. In this Printz honor book, which becomes part fantasy, part mystery, and part family story, Michael discovers a ragged man in his garage existing on dead flies. (Rev: BL 2/1/99*; HB 5–6/99; HBG 10/99; SLJ 2/99)

7558 Alphin, Elaine M. *Tournament of Time* (4–6). 1994, Bluegrass paper $3.95 (0-9643683-0-7). 125pp. A young American girl in York, England, solves a historic murder mystery with the help of ghosts. (Rev: BL 3/15/95)

7559 Amato, Mary. *The Word Eater* (4–6). Illus. 2000, Holiday $15.95 (0-8234-1468-X). 146pp. Lerner's pet worm Fip likes eating paper, but when he eats paper with an object's name on it, the object itself disappears in this comic fantasy. (Rev: BCCB 9/00; BL 10/15/00; HBG 3/01; SLJ 10/00)

7560 Amoss, Berthe. *Lost Magic* (5–7). 1993, Hyperion $14.95 (1-56282-573-9). 192pp. Fantasy and history mingle in this story set in the Middle Ages about a young girl who knows how to use both healing herbs and magic. (Rev: BL 11/1/93)

7561 Angeletti, Roberta. *The Minotaur of Knossos* (2–4). Illus. Series: A Journey Through Time. 1999, Oxford $16.95 (0-19-521557-5). 32pp. In this fantasy, a young boy visits the Palace at Knossos and has a close encounter with the Minotaur. (Rev: BL 1/1–15/00; HBG 3/00; SLJ 2/00)

7562 Anzaldua, Gloria. *Prietita and the Ghost Woman* (3–6). Illus. by Christina Gonzalez. 1996, Children's Book Pr. $15.95 (0-89239-136-7). While looking for an herb to cure her mother, Prietita gets lost in the woods in this English-Spanish fantasy. (Rev: BCCB 4/96; SLJ 7/96)

7563 Arkin, Alan. *Cassie Loves Beethoven* (4–7). 2000, Hyperion LB $17.49 (0-7868-2489-1). 175pp. A delightful story about the Kennedy family and an adopted cow that learns to play Beethoven on the piano. (Rev: BCCB 2/01; BL 12/15/00; SLJ 2/01)

7564 Arkin, Alan. *The Lemming Condition* (4–7). Illus. by Joan Sandin. 1989, HarperCollins paper $9.00 (0-062-50048-1). 64pp. Bubber opposes the mass suicide of his companions in this interesting fable.

7565 Atwood, Margaret. *Princess Prunella and the Purple Peanut* (3–5). Illus. by Maryann Kovalski. 1995, Workman $13.95 (0-7611-0166-7). 32pp. Words beginning with the letter P are used to tell this story of pampered Prunella and the purple peanut that grows on her nose. (Rev: BL 12/15/95)

7566 Avi. *Ereth's Birthday: A Tale from Dimwood Forest* (3–5). 2000, HarperCollins $15.95 (0-380-97734-6). 192pp. Ereth, a cranky porcupine, gets more than he bargained for when he looks after three little foxes after their mother dies. (Rev: BCCB 7–8/00; BL 4/1/00; HB 5–6/00; HBG 10/00; SLJ 5/00)

7567 Avi. *Perloo the Bold* (4–7). 1998, Scholastic $16.95 (0-590-11002-0). 240pp. Perloo, a member of the jackrabbitlike Montmer tribe, is the unlikely hero of this fantasy about the rivalry between the Montmers and the Felbarts, a coyotelike tribe. (Rev: BCCB 11/98; BL 12/15/98; HB 1–2/99; HBG 3/99; SLJ 11/98)

7568 Avi. *Poppy* (4–6). Illus. 1995, Orchard LB $16.99 (0-531-08783-2). 160pp. Tragedy occurs when a young deer mouse named Poppy disobeys her father and ventures out into the night with her boyfriend. (Rev: BCCB 1/96; BL 10/15/95*; SLJ 12/95*)

7569 Avi. *Poppy and Rye* (4–6). Illus. 1998, Avon $14.00 (0-380-97638-2). 160pp. Fearless deer mouse Poppy travels to visit another mouse family, where she foils the plans of some beavers to build a dam and also falls in love with another mouse named Rye. (Rev: BL 5/15/98; HB 7–8/98; HBG 10/98; SLJ 6/98)

7570 Avi. *Ragweed* (4–6). Illus. 1999, Avon $15.00 (0-380-97690-0). 192pp. Ragweed, a brave young mouse, becomes friends with members of a hip band and leads the opposition against Silversides, an angry white cat. (Rev: BCCB 10/99; BL 5/15/99; HBG 10/99; SLJ 7/99)

7571 Avi. *Tom, Babette, and Simon: Three Tales of Transformation* (4–6). Illus. 1995, Simon & Schuster paper $15.00 (0-02-707765-9). 43pp. Three stories about the unusual consequences that occur when three youngsters are transformed into different beings. (Rev: BCCB 7–8/95; BL 5/15/95; SLJ 6/95)

7572 Babbitt, Natalie. *The Devil's Other Storybook* (4–6). Illus. by author. 1987, Farrar paper $4.95 (0-374-41704-0). 112pp. The devil generally fouls up things in these humorous tales, but sometimes does an unintentional good deed. (Rev: BCCB 7–8/87; BL 8/87; SLJ 8/87)

7573 Babbitt, Natalie. *The Devil's Storybook* (4–6). Illus. by author. 1974, Farrar $13.00 (0-374-31770-4); paper $4.95 (0-374-41708-3). 102pp. Ten stories about outwitting the devil, in this case personified as a middle-aged, vain, but crafty adversary.

7574 Babbitt, Natalie. *The Search for Delicious* (4–7). Illus. by author. 1969, Farrar $16.00 (0-374-36534-2). 176pp. The innocent task of polling the kingdom's subjects for personal food preferences provokes civil war in a zestful spoof of taste and society.

7575 Babbitt, Natalie. *Tuck Everlasting* (4–6). 1975, Farrar $16.00 (0-374-37848-7); paper $4.95 (0-374-48009-5). 160pp. Violence erupts when the Tuck family members discover that their secret about a spring that brings immortality has been discovered.

7576 Bailey, Carolyn Sherwin. *Miss Hickory* (4–6). Illus. by Ruth Gannett. 1946, Puffin paper $4.99 (0-14-030956-X). 128pp. The adventures of a doll made from an apple branch with a hickory nut head. Newbery Award winner, 1947.

7577 Bailey, Linda. *Adventures in the Middle Ages* (3–6). Illus. by Bill Slavin. 2000, Kids Can $14.95 (1-55074-538-7); paper $7.95 (1-55074-540-9). 48pp. A slapstick story about twins Josh and Emma and their trip to the Middle Ages via a yellowing guidebook that gives basic information about the period. (Rev: HBG 3/01; SLJ 12/00)

7578 Baker, Jeannie. *The Hidden Forest* (2–4). Illus. 2000, Greenwillow LB $16.89 (0-688-15761-0). 32pp. In this fantasy, Ben is led by his friend Sophie into the underwater world of a kelp forest where they encounter a whale. (Rev: BL 9/1/00; HB 7–8/00; HBG 10/00; SLJ 5/00)

7579 Baker, Jeannie. *Where the Forest Meets the Sea* (K–4). Illus. by author. 1988, Greenwillow $15.93 (0-688-06364-0). 32pp. A young boy travels through a reef and arrives in the rain forest in Australia and pretends he has gone back in time. (Rev: BCCB 5/88; BL 6/15/88; SLJ 7/88)

7580 Balan, Bruce. *Buoy: Home at Sea* (3–4). Illus. by Raul Colon. 1998, Delacorte $14.95 (0-385-32539-8). 70pp. In this novel, Buoy, who is anchored to the ocean floor, enjoys life on the sea, especially when he can guide big ships with the help of his friends Gull and Seal. (Rev: BCCB 7–8/98; BL 6/1–15/98; HBG 10/98; SLJ 6/98)

7581 Banks, Lynne Reid. *Angela and Diabola* (5–8). 1997, Avon $14.00 (0-380-97562-9). 164pp. A wicked romp that chronicles the lives of twin sisters, the angelic Angela and the truly horrible and destructive Diabola. (Rev: SLJ 7/97)

7582 Banks, Lynne Reid. *Harry the Poisonous Centipede: A Story to Make You Squirm* (3–5). Illus. 1997, Morrow $15.00 (0-688-14711-9). 160pp. A fantasy about the many dangers facing Harry, a young centipede. (Rev: BL 9/15/97; HBG 3/98; SLJ 9/97)

7583 Banks, Lynne Reid. *The Indian in the Cupboard* (3–5). Illus. by Brock Cole. 1985, Doubleday $16.95 (0-385-17051-3); Avon paper $4.99 (0-380-60012-9). 192pp. A magical cupboard turns toys into living things.

7584 Banks, Lynne Reid. *The Key to the Indian* (4–8). Illus. 1998, Avon $16.00 (0-380-97717-6). 240pp. In the fifth book of the Indian in the Cupboard series, Omri and Dad return to the time of Little Bear to help the Iroquois deal with European meddlers. (Rev: BL 11/15/98; HBG 3/99; SLJ 12/98)

7585 Banks, Lynne Reid. *The Mystery of the Cupboard* (5–8). Illus. by Tom Newsom. 1993, Morrow $15.93 (0-688-12635-9). 256pp. In this, the fourth of the Cupboard series, the young hero Omri uncovers a diary that reveals secrets about his magical cupboard. (Rev: BCCB 6/93; BL 4/1/93; HB 7–8/93; SLJ 6/93)

7586 Banks, Lynne Reid. *The Return of the Indian* (5–7). Illus. by William Celdart. 1986, Doubleday $15.95 (0-385-23497-X); Avon paper $4.99 (0-380-70284-3). 192pp. Omri brings his plastic Indian figures to life and discovers that his friend Little Bear has been wounded and needs his help. (Rev: BL 9/15/86; HB 11–12/86; SLJ 11/86)

7587 Banks, Lynne Reid. *The Secret of the Indian* (4–6). Illus. by Ted Lewin. 1989, Doubleday $15.95 (0-385-26292-2). 160pp. Once again, Omri's magic cupboard brings toy figures to life, and in this novel, friend Patrick travels back in time to the Old West. (Rev: BCCB 1/90; BL 9/15/89; HB 3–4/90; SLJ 10/89)

7588 Barber, Antonia. *The Ghosts* (4–6). 1989, Pocket paper $3.50 (0-671-70714-0). Two youngsters meet ghosts from another country in their garden.

7589 Barrie, J. M. *Peter Pan* (4–6). Illus. by Michael Hague. 1987, Holt $19.95 (0-8050-0276-6). Color illustrations give the flavor of the Victorian era in this classic tale. (Rev: BL 12/15/87)

7590 Barrie, J. M. *Peter Pan* (5–7). Illus. 2000, Chronicle $19.95 (0-8118-2297-4). 173pp. Using illustrations from 15 different artists, this is an unusual, unabridged edition of Barrie's classic fantasy. (Rev: BL 11/1/00; HBG 3/01; SLJ 12/00)

7591 Bauer, Marion Dane. *Ghost Eye* (3–6). Illus. by Trina S. Hyman. 1992, Scholastic $13.95 (0-590-45298-3). 64pp. Popcorn, a Cornish rex show cat who sees ghosts, leads a tantalizing cast of characters. (Rev: BL 9/15/92; SLJ 10/92)

7592 Bauer, Marion Dane. *A Taste of Smoke* (5–7). 1993, Clarion $14.95 (0-395-64341-4). 106pp. On a camping trip with her sister, Caitlin encounters the ghost of a boy killed a century before. (Rev: BCCB 1/94; BL 10/15/93; SLJ 12/93)

7593 Bauer, Marion Dane. *Touch the Moon* (5–7). Illus. by Alix Berenzy. 1987, Houghton $15.00 (0-89919-526-1). 96pp. Angry over not getting a real horse, Jennifer throws away her toy horse gift and learns a lesson in responsibility. (Rev: BCCB 9/87; BL 9/15/87; HB 9–10/87)

7594 Bauer, Steven. *A Cat of a Different Color* (3–6). Illus. 2000, Delacorte $15.95 (0-385-32710-2). 197pp. An inspiring fantasy about Ulwazzer the cat who organizes the people and animals of a village to fight the greedy new mayor. (Rev: BCCB 7–8/00; BL 6/1–15/00; HB 7–8/00; HBG 10/00; SLJ 8/00)

7595 Baum, L. Frank. *The Marvelous Land of Oz* (4–6). Illus. by John R. Neill. 1985, Morrow $22.95 (0-688-05439-0). 288pp. This is a facsimile of the original 1904 edition with the illustrations in both color and black and white. Other titles in this series are published by Peter Smith and Amereon in hard cover and Dover and Puffin in paperback.

7596 Baum, L. Frank. *The Wizard of Oz* (3–5). Illus. by Michael Hague. 1982, Holt $29.95 (0-8050-0221-9). 232pp. One of many editions.

7597 Baum, L. Frank. *The Wizard of Oz* (PS–4). Illus. by Charles Santore. 1986, Ballantine paper $5.99 (0-345-33590-2). 96pp. For a younger audience than the original, this is an abridged, heavily illustrated version of the Baum classic. (Rev: SLJ 12/91)

7598 Baum, L. Frank. *The Wizard of Oz* (4–8). Illus. by Michael Hague. 2000, Holt $29.95 (0-8050-6430-3). 220pp. A gorgeous edition of the classic fantasy that is a reissue of the 1982 version with a few new illustrations. (Rev: BL 12/1/00; HBG 10/00)

7599 Baum, L. Frank. *The Wonderful Wizard of Oz* (4–8). Illus. by W. W. Denslow. 1987, Morrow $21.95 (0-688-06944-4). 316pp. A reissue of the 1900 classic with original colorplates. (Rev: BL 11/1/87)

7600 Baum, L. Frank. *The Wonderful Wizard of Oz* (4–8). Illus. by W. W. Denslow. 2000, HarperCollins $24.95 (0-06-029323-3). 267pp. A handsome facsimile of the 1900 publication on high-quality paper and featuring 24 original color plates and 130 two-color drawings. (Rev: BL 12/1/00)

7601 Baum, L. Frank. *The Wonderful Wizard of Oz: A Commemorative Pop-Up* (4–8). Illus. by Robert Sabuda. 2001, Simon & Schuster $24.95 (0-689-81751-7). An extraordinary pop-up version of the classic fantasy told in a condensed text. (Rev: BL 12/1/00; HB 9–10/00; HBG 3/01; SLJ 11/00)

7602 Baum, Roger S. *Dorothy of Oz* (4–6). Illus. by Elizabeth Miles. 1989, Morrow $17.00 (0-688-07848-6). 176pp. A story true to the original in which Dorothy is called back to Oz because the Tin Woodman, the Scarecrow, and the Cowardly Lion need help. (Rev: BL 1/1/90; SLJ 10/89)

7603 Bellairs, John. *The Curse of the Blue Figurine* (5–8). 1984, Bantam paper $3.50 (0-553-15540-7). 208pp. A boy steals an ancient book from a church and evil spells begin working. Two sequels are: *The Mummy, the Will, and the Crypt* (1985); *The Spell of the Sorcerer's Skull* (Puffin 1997).

7604 Bellairs, John. *The Ghost in the Mirror* (5–8). 1994, Puffin paper $4.50 (0-140-34934-0). 176pp. Fourteen-year-old Rose and white witch Mrs. Zimmerman are transported in time to 1828 on a secret mission. (Rev: SLJ 3/93)

7605 Bellairs, John. *The Mansion in the Mist* (5–7). 1992, Puffin paper $3.99 (0-140-34933-2). 176pp. Anthony Monday finds mystery and adventure on a remote island in northern Canada. (Rev: BL 8/92; SLJ 6/92)

7606 Bender, Robert, comp. *Lima Beans Would Be Illegal: Children's Ideas of a Perfect World* (2–5). Illus. by Robert Bender. 2000, Dial $12.00 (0-8037-2532-9). An appealing fantasy in which children describe what a perfect world would be like. (Rev: HBG 10/00; SLJ 7/00)

7607 Bennett, David, ed. *A Treasury of Witches and Wizards* (4–6). Illus. 1996, Kingfisher paper $5.95 (1-85697-678-5). 160pp. A collection of supernatural tales by such writers as Diana Wynne Jones, Alan Garner, and Helen Cresswell. (Rev: BL 6/1–15/96)

7608 Berger, Barbara Helen. *Gwinna* (4–8). Illus. 1990, Putnam $22.95 (0-399-21738-X). 126pp. A mystic coming-of-age fable when a couple's wish for a child is granted in the form of a daughter who grows wings. (Rev: BL 10/15/90; SLJ 12/90)

7609 Bial, Raymond. *The Fresh Grave: And Other Ghostly Stories* (5–7). 1997, Midwest Traditions $18.95 (1-883953-23-5); paper $13.95 (1-883953-22-7). 162pp. A series of ten adventure stories featuring two teenage heroes and their escapades in a small midwestern town. (Rev: SLJ 12/97)

7610 Bial, Raymond. *The Ghost of Honeymoon Creek* (5–8). Illus. 2000, Midwest Traditions $18.95 (1-883953-28-6). 176pp. While investigating a strange light in a neighboring farm, 15-year-old Hank encounters a ghost. (Rev: BL 9/1/00; HBG 3/01; SLJ 1/01)

7611 Billingsley, Franny. *The Folk Keeper* (5–8). 1999, Simon & Schuster $16.00 (0-689-82876-4). 162pp. Orphaned Corinna disguises herself as a boy to become a Folk Keeper, one who tends the fierce Folk who live underground, so they will not cause trouble. (Rev: BCCB 10/99; BL 9/1/99; HB 11–12/99; HBG 3/00; SLJ 10/99)

7612 Billingsley, Franny. *Well Wished* (5–8). 1997, Simon & Schuster $16.00 (0-689-81210-8). 176pp. An intriguing fantasy that involves a lonely girl and a wishing well that grants each person a single wish. (Rev: BCCB 4/97; BL 6/1–15/97; HB 5–6/97; SLJ 5/97*)

7613 Birdseye, Tom. *The Eye of the Stone* (4–6). 2000, Holiday $15.95 (0-8234-1564-3). 165pp. Jackson, a fearful 13-year-old boy, is transported to a primitive society where he must find the courage to fight a monster and bring peace to his people. (Rev: BL 2/15/01; SLJ 12/00)

7614 Blair, Margaret Whitman. *Brothers at War* (4–7). 1997, White Mane paper $7.95 (1-57249-049-7). 145pp. Two brothers and their friend Sarah find themselves transported back in time to the Battle of Antietam in 1862. (Rev: BL 8/97)

7615 Bliss, Corinne D. *Matthew's Meadow* (3–6). Illus. by Ted Lewin. 1997, Harcourt paper $7.00 (0-152-01500-0). 40pp. Nine-year-old Matthew returns each year to a meadow where he learns to communicate with a red-tailed hawk. (Rev: BL 3/15/92; SLJ 8/92)

7616 Bodkin, Odds. *Ghost of the Southern Belle: A Sea Tale* (3–6). Illus. 1999, Little, Brown $15.95 (0-316-02608-5). 32pp. After the *Southern Belle* sinks on the rocks on All Hallow's Eve, it becomes a ghost ship under Captain LeNoir and lures other ships to their doom. (Rev: BCCB 10/99; BL 9/15/99; HBG 3/00; SLJ 9/99)

7617 Bomans, Godfried. *Eric in the Land of the Insects* (4–6). Illus. by Mark Richardson. 1994, Houghton $14.95 (0-395-65231-6). 197pp. Eric learns a great deal about the secret lives of insects when he enters their world in this fantasy. (Rev: BCCB 6/94; BL 3/15/94; SLJ 3/94)

7618 Bond, Adrienne. *Sugarcane House and Other Stories About Mr. Fat* (4–6). Illus. 1997, Harcourt $16.00 (0-15-201446-2). 80pp. Ma Minnie loves telling stories about Mr. Fat, a.k.a. John Fortune, a Georgia trickster, and his strong-minded talking mule, Brownie. (Rev: BL 12/1/97; HB 11–12/97; HBG 3/98; SLJ 1/98)

7619 *The Book of Fairies* (3–6). Ed. by Michael Hague. Illus. 2000, HarperCollins $19.95 (0-688-10881-4). 128pp. Eight stories, songs, and poems celebrate this unworldly creature in a beautiful book illustrated by Michael Hague. (Rev: BL 12/15/00; HBG 3/01) [808.8]

7620 Bos, Burny. *Fun with the Molesons* (2–4). Illus. 2000, North-South $13.95 (0-7358-1353-1). 48pp. A beginning chapter book that contains six stories about a family of moles. (Rev: BL 1/1–15/01; SLJ 1/01)

7621 Bradshaw, Gillian. *The Land of Gold* (5–8). Illus. 1992, Greenwillow $14.00 (0-688-10576-9). 160pp. Prahotep, sidekick Baki, and Hathor the dragon save a Nubian princess in ancient Egypt. A sequel to *Dragon and the Thief* (1991). (Rev: BCCB 10/92; BL 9/15/92; HB 3–4/93; SLJ 10/92)

7622 Breathed, Berkeley. *The Last Basselope: One Ferocious Story* (4–7). Illus. 1992, Little, Brown $14.95 (0-316-10761-1). 32pp. In this imaginative picture book for older readers, Opus and his reluctant adventurers are after the nearly extinct basselope. (Rev: BCCB 1/93; BL 12/15/92; SLJ 1/93)

7623 Brittain, Bill. *All the Money in the World* (4–6). Illus. by Charles Robinson. 1992, HarperCollins paper $4.95 (0-06-440128-6). 160pp. A leprechaun grants Quentin Stowe his wish for all the money in the world.

7624 Brittain, Bill. *Devil's Donkey* (3–6). Illus. by Andrew Glass. 1981, HarperCollins LB $14.89 (0-06-020683-7). 128pp. Dan'l defies the witches and is turned into a donkey. A sequel is: *The Wish Giver: Three Tales of Coven Tree* (1983).

7625 Brittain, Bill. *The Ghost from Beneath the Sea* (4–6). Illus. by Michele Chessare. 1994, HarperCollins paper $4.50 (0-064-40526-5). 128pp. Tommy, Books, and Harry must prove a poker game on the Titanic was rigged in order to save their ghost friends. (Rev: BL 12/1/92; HB 1–2/93; SLJ 1/93)

7626 Brittain, Bill. *The Mystery of the Several Sevens* (3–6). Illus. by James Warhola. 1994, HarperCollins LB $12.89 (0-06-024462-3). 96pp. Mr. Merlin, a substitute teacher, takes two of his pupils to a land where they must solve mysteries. (Rev: BL 11/15/94; SLJ 12/94)

7627 Brittain, Bill. *Wings* (5–7). 1995, HarperCollins paper $4.50 (0-064-40612-1). 144pp. Troubles really begin for 12-year-old Ian when he sprouts wings. (Rev: BCCB 11/91; BL 1/1/91; SLJ 10/91)

7628 Brooks, Bruce. *Throwing Smoke* (4–7). 2000, HarperCollins LB $15.89 (0-06-028320-3). 144pp. Whiz discovers that winning isn't everything when his dream team comes to life in this baseball fantasy. (Rev: BCCB 5/00; BL 5/15/00; HB 5–6/00; HBG 10/00; SLJ 6/00)

7629 Brown, Calef. *Polkabats and Octopus Slacks: 14 Stories* (3–5). Illus. 1998, Houghton $15.00 (0-395-85403-2). 32pp. Nonsense verses introduce some wacky characters, including Kansas City Octopus, who goes out on the town in four-legged bell bottoms. (Rev: BL 3/15/98; HBG 10/98; SLJ 5/98)

7630 Brown, Marc. *Scared Silly! A Book for the Brave* (3–6). Illus. 1994, Little, Brown $18.95 (0-316-11360-3). 64pp. As well as containing a fine collection of spooky, but humorous, stories, this book provides suggestions for activities to frighten friends. (Rev: BL 10/1/94; HB 11–12/94; SLJ 9/94*)

7631 Buchwald, Emilie. *Gildaen: The Heroic Adventures of a Most Unusual Rabbit* (4–6). Illus. by Barbara Flynn. 1993, Milkweed paper $6.95 (0-915-94375-1). 184pp. This fantasy set in medieval times deals with the meek triumphing over might. A reissue.

7632 Buffie, Margaret. *The Watcher* (5–8). 2000, Kids Can $16.95 (1-55074-829-7). 264pp. Sixteen-year-old Emma discovers that she is really a changeling, a Watcher, whose mission is to protect her younger sister from warring factions. (Rev: BL 11/1/00; HBG 3/01)

7633 Burgess, Melvin. *The Earth Giant* (3–6). 1997, Putnam $15.95 (0-399-23187-0). 160pp. After a terrible storm, an extraterrestrial giant is unearthed by Amy, who must protect it from being discovered by others. (Rev: BL 10/1/97; HBG 3/98)

7634 Burnard, Damon. *The Amazing Adventures of Soupy Boy!* (2–4). Illus. 1998, Houghton paper $4.50 (0-395-91225-3). 96pp. After he falls into a vat of radioactive tomato juice, Ashley Fugg develops "Soupy Powers," which enable him to become a master crime fighter in this cartoon adventure. (Rev: BL 1/1–15/99; SLJ 1/99)

7635 Burnard, Damon. *Burger!* (2–5). Illus. by author. 1998, Houghton paper $4.50 (0-395-91315-2). 118pp. Clementine helps a space alien, Jeff, devise a new kind of burger, so the boy will be freed by his master Gluttor. (Rev: SLJ 12/98)

7636 Burnard, Damon. *Pork and Beef's Great Adventure* (2–4). Illus. 1998, Houghton $15.00 (0-395-86765-7). 48pp. Pork the pig and Beef the cow attach feathers to themselves and fly to the moon. (Rev: BL 3/1/98; HBG 10/98; SLJ 4/98)

7637 Bush, Lawrence. *Emma Ansky-Levine and Her Mitzvah Machine* (4–6). Illus. by Joel Iskowitz. 1991, UAHC paper $7.95 (0-8074-0458-6). 115pp. Emma receives a machine from her uncle in Jerusalem that gives her personal guidance. (Rev: SLJ 7/91)

7638 Byars, Betsy. *McMummy* (4–6). 1993, Viking $14.99 (0-670-84995-2). 176pp. A boy named Mozie believes he is being threatened by a giant, humming pea pod in this exciting fantasy. (Rev: BL 11/1/93; SLJ 9/93)

7639 Byars, Betsy. *The Winged Colt of Casa Mia* (4–6). Illus. by Richard Cuffari. 1981, Avon paper $2.95 (0-380-00201-9). 132pp. In this fantasy, a young boy visits the Texas ranch of his uncle, an ex-stuntman, and encounters a colt with supernatural powers.

7640 Cameron, Eleanor. *The Court of the Stone Children* (5–7). 1990, Puffin paper $4.99 (0-14-034289-3). 192pp. Nina's move with her family to San Francisco is a disaster until she encounters a young ghost in a small museum.

7641 Cardo, Horacio. *The Story of Chess* (3–5). Illus. 1998, Abbeville $16.95 (0-7892-0250-6). 45pp. After their countries destroyed each other in a war, two kings listen to a war historian who uses the first chess set to explain every participant and every move. (Rev: BL 11/15/98; HBG 3/99; SLJ 4/99)

7642 Carroll, Lewis. *Alice in Wonderland* (3–6). Illus. by Lisbeth Zwerger. 1999, North-South $19.95 (0-7358-1166-0). 103pp. A newly illustrated edition of this beloved fantasy. (Rev: BL 11/1/99; SLJ 10/99)

7643 Carroll, Lewis. *Alice's Adventures in Wonderland* (4–6). Illus. by Abelardo Morell. 1998, Dutton $19.99 (0-525-46094-2). 115pp. This is a superior edition with a good format, clear typeface, and the traditional Tenniel illustrations. (Rev: BL 4/1/99; HBG 10/99)

7644 Carroll, Lewis. *Alice's Adventures in Wonderland* (3–6). Illus. by Helen Oxenbury. 1999, Candlewick $24.99 (0-7636-0804-1). 208pp. A fine edition of the Carroll classic illustrated by well-known British artist Helen Oxenbury. (Rev: BL 1/1–15/00; HBG 3/00; SLJ 1/00)

7645 Carroll, Lewis. *Alice's Adventures in Wonderland* (5–7). Illus. 2000, Chronicle $19.95 (0-8118-2274-5). 140pp. This oversize edition of the complete text of Carroll's classic contains examples of illustrations from 29 artists. (Rev: BL 11/1/00; HBG 3/01; SLJ 11/00)

7646 Carroll, Lewis. *Alice's Adventures in Wonderland and Through the Looking Glass* (4–7). Illus. by John Tenniel. 1963, Putnam $16.99 (0-448-06004-3). One of many recommended editions of these enduring fantasies.

7647 Carroll, Lewis. *Through the Looking Glass, and What Alice Found There* (4–7). Illus. by John Tenniel. 1977, St. Martin's $14.95 (0-312-80374-5). 224pp. Sequel to *Alice's Adventures in Wonderland*. One of many editions.

7648 Carroll, Thomas. *The Colony* (4–7). 2000, Sunstone $18.95 (0-86534-295-4). 152pp. Tony, a fifth-grader, and his arch-enemy, the bully Lawrence, are shrunk to the size of ants by a Navajo charm and in their new environment join opposing forces. (Rev: HBG 3/01; SLJ 7/00)

7649 Carus, Marianne, ed. *That's Ghosts for You: 13 Scary Stories* (4–7). Illus. by Yongsheng Xuan. 2000, Front Street $15.95 (0-8126-2675-3). 131pp. A fine collection of 13 chilling stories each with a supernatural twist. (Rev: BL 12/1/00; HBG 3/01; SLJ 12/00)

7650 Carusone, Al. *Don't Open the Door After the Sun Goes Down* (3–6). Illus. 1994, Clarion $13.95 (0-395-65225-1); Hyperion paper $3.95 (0-7868-1086-6). 83pp. A collection of nine scary stories, many of which deal with the supernatural. (Rev: BL 9/1/94; SLJ 9/94)

7651 Carusone, Albert R. *The Boy with Dinosaur Hands* (4–7). Illus. 1998, Clarion $14.00 (0-395-77515-9). 96pp. An eerie collection of nine original horror stories — most with surprise endings. (Rev: BL 8/98; HBG 10/98; SLJ 7/98)

7652 Cassedy, Sylvia. *Behind the Attic Wall* (6–8). 1983, HarperCollins LB $15.89 (0-690-04337-6). 320pp. Maggie Turner, a difficult girl, is contacted by ghosts in the large house where two great-aunts live.

7653 Christian, Peggy. *The Bookstore Mouse* (4–6). Illus. by Gary Lippincott. 1995, Harcourt $16.00 (0-15-200203-0). 126pp. Cervantes, a bookstore mouse, is transported by a book to a medieval English monastery, where he meets Sigfried, a young scribe. (Rev: SLJ 11/95)

7654 Clark, Margaret, comp. *A Treasury of Dragon Stories* (2–5). Illus. by Mark Robertson. Series: Treasury. 1997, Kingfisher paper $6.95 (0-7534-5114-X). 156pp. A collection of 15 previously published stories or excerpts from books that deal with dragons. (Rev: SLJ 1/98)

7655 Clifford, Eth. *Flatfoot Fox and the Case of the Bashful Beaver* (2–4). Illus. by Brian Lies. 1995, Houghton $16.00 (0-395-70560-6). 47pp. Flatfoot Fox and Secretary Bird solve the mystery of strange thefts involving forest animals. (Rev: BL 3/1/95; SLJ 4/95)

7656 Cohen, Daniel. *Dangerous Ghosts* (5–7). 1996, Putnam $14.99 (0-399-22913-2). 96pp. Seventeen ghost stories, many with historical backgrounds. (Rev: BL 11/15/96; SLJ 4/97)

7657 Cohen, Daniel. *Ghostly Tales of Love and Revenge* (5–8). 1995, Pocket paper $3.50 (0-671-79523-6). 95pp. An international collection of ghost

LITERATURE

stories that deal with vengeance and unhappy loves. (Rev: SLJ 7/92)

7658 Cole, Joanna. *Doctor Change* (2–4). Illus. by Donald Carrick. 1986, Morrow LB $12.88 (0-688-06136-2). 32pp. Young Tom discovers that Doctor Change can turn himself into a variety of objects; he learns the man's secrets and confronts the evil magic. (Rev: BCCB 10/86; BL 9/15/86; SLJ 10/86)

7659 Coleman, Janet W. *Fast Eddie* (3–4). Illus. by Alec Gillman. 1993, Macmillan LB $13.95 (0-02-722815-0). 144pp. Eddie the raccoon faces danger when he plays tricks on humans. (Rev: SLJ 6/93)

7660 Collodi, Carlo. *The Adventures of Pinocchio* (3–6). Illus. by Fritz Kredel. 1996, Putnam $15.95 (0-448-41479-1). 272pp. One of many recommended editions.

7661 Collodi, Carlo. *Pinocchio* (4–7). Retold by James Riordan. Illus. by Victor G. Ambrus. 1996, Oxford paper $11.95 (0-192-72287-5). 96pp. A lighthearted rendition of the classic tale. (Rev: BL 11/15/88)

7662 Collodi, Carlo. *Pinocchio* (3–5). Illus. by Ed Young. 1996, Putnam $18.95 (0-399-22941-8). 48pp. An abridged version of this classic that nevertheless captures its flavor and excitement. (Rev: BL 11/15/96; SLJ 10/96)

7663 Conly, Jane L. *R-T, Margaret, and the Rats of NIMH* (4–6). Illus. by Leonard Lubin. 1990, HarperCollins LB $14.89 (0-06-021364-7); paper $4.95 (0-06-440387-4). 288pp. The third installment of the brilliant rodents, in which two human children star. (Rev: BCCB 6/90; BL 5/15/90; SLJ 6/90)

7664 Conly, Jane L. *Racso and the Rats of NIMH* (5–7). Illus. by Leonard Lubin. 1986, HarperCollins LB $16.89 (0-06-021362-0). 288pp. This sequel to the Newbery Medal winner involves once again the smart rodents who wish to live in peace in Thorn Valley. (Rev: BCCB 6/86; BL 6/1/86; SLJ 4/86)

7665 Conrad, Pam. *Stonewords: A Ghost Story* (5–8). 1990, HarperCollins LB $15.89 (0-06-021316-7); paper $4.95 (0-06-440354-8). 144pp. Zoe moves to her grandparents' home and finds a playmate, from another century, already living there. (Rev: BCCB 5/90; BL 3/1/90; HB 7–8/90; SLJ 5/90*)

7666 Conrad, Pam. *Zoe Rising* (4–7). 1996, HarperCollins LB $14.89 (0-06-027218-X). 128pp. In a sequel to *Stonewords* (1990), Zoe's time traveling brings her an experience that almost causes her death. (Rev: BCCB 10/96; BL 8/96; HB 11–12/96; SLJ 11/96)

7667 Cooper, Susan. *The Boggart* (4–6). 1993, Macmillan $15.00 (0-689-50576-0). 200pp. An old desk unleashes the Boggart, a mischievous spirit who has lived in a Scottish castle for centuries. (Rev: BCCB 3/93; BL 1/15/93; HB 5–6/93*; SLJ 1/93)

7668 Cooper, Susan. *The Boggart and the Monster* (4–6). 1997, Simon & Schuster paper $16.00 (0-689-81330-9). 192pp. The Boggart, a Scottish spirit-creature, wants to accompany young Jessup and Emily when they go to Loch Ness to find the mon-

ster. (Rev: BCCB 5/97; BL 3/1/97; HB 5–6/97; SLJ 5/97)

7669 Cooper, Susan. *King of Shadows* (5–8). Illus. by John Clapp. 1999, Simon & Schuster $16.00 (0-689-82817-9). 192pp. Nat Field time-travels to 1599 London and assumes the child-actor role of Puck in *A Midsummer Night's Dream*. (Rev: BL 10/15/99*; HB 11–12/99; HBG 3/00; SLJ 11/99)

7670 Cooper, Susan. *Seaward* (5–8). 1983, Macmillan LB $16.00 (0-689-50275-3); paper $4.99 (0-02-042190-7). 180pp. West follows his mother's dying words and heads seaward to his father.

7671 Cooper, Susan. *Silver on the Tree* (5–7). 1980, Macmillan $17.00 (0-689-50088-2); paper $4.99 (0-689-71152-2). 256pp. The fifth and last volume of the series that tells of the final struggle waged by Will Stanton and his friends against the Dark, the powers of evil. The first four volumes are: *Over Sea, Under Stone* (1966); *The Dark Is Rising* (1973); *The Grey King* (1975); *Greenwitch* (1985). The Grey King was the winner of the 1976 Newbery Medal.

7672 Coville, Bruce. *The Dragonslayers* (4–6). Illus. 1994, Pocket $14.00 (0-671-89036-0); paper $3.99 (0-671-79832-4). 70pp. When a king promises the hand of his daughter to the person who kills a pesky dragon, his daughter disguises herself and joins the hunt. (Rev: BL 12/1/94; SLJ 2/95)

7673 Coville, Bruce. *The Ghost in the Big Brass Bed* (4–6). 1991, Bantam paper $4.50 (0-553-15827-9). 184pp. Two ghosts appeal for help to Chris and Nina, who try to solve the mystery surrounding them. (Rev: SLJ 1/92)

7674 Coville, Bruce. *Goblins in the Castle* (5–7). Illus. 1992, Pocket paper $4.99 (0-671-72711-7). 166pp. William, now 11, has grown up in Toad-in-a-Cage Castle and knows many of its secret passages. (Rev: BL 2/1/93)

7675 Coville, Bruce. *Into the Land of the Unicorns* (4–6). 1994, Scholastic $12.95 (0-590-45955-4); paper $4.50 (0-590-45956-2). 176pp. A fantasy in which a girl, trying to escape pursuers, is helped by a unicorn. (Rev: BL 10/1/94; SLJ 10/94)

7676 Coville, Bruce. *Jennifer Murdley's Toad* (3–5). Illus. by Gary Lippincott. 1992, Harcourt $16.95 (0-15-200745-8); Pocket paper $3.99 (0-671-79401-9). 160pp. Jennifer's magical adventures begin when she buys Bufo, a discounted toad, at a mysterious store. (Rev: BL 3/15/92; SLJ 9/92)

7677 Coville, Bruce. *Jeremy Thatcher, Dragon Hatcher* (4–6). Illus. by Gary Lippincott. 1991, Harcourt $16.95 (0-15-200748-2); Pocket paper $4.99 (0-671-74782-7). 160pp. Jeremy buys a small ball that turns out to be a dragon egg. (Rev: BL 5/15/91; SLJ 5/91)

7678 Coville, Bruce. *The Monster's Ring* (4–6). Illus. by Katherine Coville. 1989, Pocket paper $3.99 (0-671-69389-1). 96pp. A boy finds a ring that turns him into a monster.

7679 Coville, Bruce. *Odder Than Ever* (5–9). 1999, Harcourt $16.00 (0-15-201747-X). 146pp. A satisfying anthology of nine stories from this master of science fiction and fantasy. (Rev: HBG 10/99; SLJ 6/99)

7680 Coville, Bruce. *The Skull of Truth* (5–7). Illus. Series: Magic Shop Books. 1997, Harcourt $17.00 (0-15-275457-1). 176pp. A fantasy in which compulsive liar Charlie learns to tell the truth through the efforts of a wisecracking skull. (Rev: BL 10/1/97; HBG 3/98; SLJ 10/97*)

7681 Coville, Bruce. *Song of the Wanderer* (5–8). Series: Unicorn Chronicles. 1999, Scholastic $16.95 (0-590-45953-8). 336pp. Cara and her friends undertake a dangerous mission — returning to Earth to bring her grandmother, the Wanderer, back to Luster. This is a sequel to *Into the Land of the Unicorn.* (Rev: BL 3/1/00; HBG 3/00; SLJ 12/99)

7682 Coville, Bruce. *The World's Worst Fairy Godmother* (3–5). Illus. 1996, Pocket $14.00 (0-671-00229-5); paper $3.99 (0-671-00228-7). 112pp. A klutz of a fairy godmother gets an unusual assignment to make a dislikable girl popular. (Rev: BL 1/1–15/97)

7683 Craddock, Sonia. *Sleeping Boy* (5–8). 1999, Simon & Schuster $16.95 (0-689-81763-0). 40pp. This version of the Sleeping Beauty is set in Berlin around World War II. A wicked general curses a baby boy who is later saved from going to war by an aunt who puts him to sleep. (Rev: BL 2/1/00; HBG 3/00; SLJ 9/99)

7684 Creech, Sharon. *Pleasing the Ghost* (3–6). 1996, HarperCollins LB $14.89 (0-06-026986-3). 128pp. Dennis, who is visited by ghosts, has difficulty understanding the garbled language of the newest visitor, Uncle Arvie. (Rev: BCCB 10/96; BL 9/1/96; SLJ 11/96)

7685 Cresswell, Helen. *The Secret World of Polly Flint* (5–7). Illus. by Shirley Felts. 1994, Peter Smith $18.00 (0-844-66760-9). 176pp. In this English fantasy, a young girl meets some inhabitants of a village that disappeared centuries ago.

7686 Cresswell, Helen. *Time Out* (3–6). Illus. by Peter Elwell. 1997, Parkwest $12.95 (0-718-82658-2). 80pp. In 1887, a family is transported to 1987 for an unnerving vacation. (Rev: BL 2/1/90; SLJ 6/90)

7687 Cresswell, Helen. *The Watchers* (4–6). 1994, Macmillan paper $15.95 (0-02-725371-6). 160pp. Katy and Josh run away from a children's home and hide out in an amusement park. (Rev: BCCB 2/95; BL 12/15/94; SLJ 2/95)

7688 Cross, Gillian. *Pictures in the Dark* (5–8). 1996, Holiday $16.95 (0-8234-1267-9). 224pp. A boy whose life is miserable uses supernatural means to escape the pressures. (Rev: BCCB 1/97; BL 1/1–15/97)

7689 Crosse, Joanna. *A Child's Book of Angels* (3–5). Illus. by Olwyn Whelan. 2000, Barefoot LB $19.99 (1-84148-082-7). 64pp. A young boy's guardian angel takes him on a tour of heaven where he meets different kinds of angels and learns about their responsibilities — looking after the seasons, for example, or healing. (Rev: SLJ 2/01)

7690 Curry, Jane L. *Moon Window* (5–8). 1996, Simon & Schuster $16.00 (0-689-80945-X). 170pp.

Joellen travels back in time and meets several of her ancestors. (Rev: BCCB 11/96; BL 10/15/96; SLJ 12/96)

7691 Cuyler, Margery. *The Battlefield Ghost* (2–4). Illus. 1999, Scholastic $15.95 (0-590-10848-4). 112pp. In this easy chapter book, a family moves to a Princeton house that is haunted by the ghost of a Revolutionary War soldier. (Rev: BL 11/15/99; HBG 3/00; SLJ 12/99)

7692 Cuyler, Margery. *Weird Wolf* (3–6). Illus. by Dirk Zimmer. 1991, Holt paper $6.95 (0-8050-1643-0). 72pp. Nine-year-old Harry Walpole has to find out how to rid himself of being a werewolf, just like his grandfather. (Rev: BCCB 1/90; BL 12/1/89; SLJ 4/90)

7693 Dadey, Debbie, and Marcia T. Jones. *Leprechauns Don't Play Basketball* (5–8). Illus. by John S. Gurney. 1992, Scholastic paper $3.99 (0-590-44822-6). 70pp. The Bailey Elementary third grade thinks the gym teacher is a leprechaun. (Rev: BL 9/15/92)

7694 Dahl, Roald. *Charlie and the Chocolate Factory* (4–6). Illus. by Joseph Schindelman. 1964, Knopf LB $18.99 (0-394-91011-7); Puffin paper $4.99 (0-140-32869-6). A rather morbid tale of Charlie and four of his nasty friends who tour Willy Wonka's extraordinary chocolate factory. They all meet disaster except for Charlie, for he has obeyed orders. A sequel is: *Charlie and the Great Glass Elevator* (1984, Bantam).

7695 Dahl, Roald. *George's Marvelous Medicine* (4–6). Illus. by Quentin Blake. 1998, Puffin paper $4.99 (0-14-130111-2). 96pp. George concocts medicine that shrinks his mean grandmother.

7696 Dahl, Roald. *James and the Giant Peach* (3–5). Illus. by Lane Smith. 1996, Knopf LB $17.99 (0-679-98090-3). 144pp. James is unhappy living with his mean aunts until a magic potion produces an enormous peach, which becomes a home for him. (Rev: BL 5/1/96)

7697 Dahl, Roald. *Magic Finger* (3–5). Illus. by William Pene du Bois. 1966, HarperCollins $15.00 (0-060-21381-7). 48pp. An 8-year-old girl mysteriously has the power to punish people for wrongdoing by pointing her finger at them.

7698 Dahl, Roald. *The Witches* (3–6). Illus. by Quentin Blake. 1983, Farrar $16.00 (0-374-38457-6); Puffin paper $3.95 (0-14-031730-9). 208pp. A boy and his grandmamma save English children from being turned into mice by witches.

7699 Dahl, Roald. *The Wonderful Story of Henry Sugar and Six More* (4–6). 1977, Puffin paper $4.99 (0-14-032874-2). 224pp. Seven tales of fantasy and fun.

7700 Deem, James M. *The Very Real Ghost Book of Christina Rose* (4–6). Illus. 1996, Houghton $15.00 (0-395-76128-X). 176pp. Twins Christina and Danny feel they are being visited by their mother's ghost when they move to a new house in California. (Rev: BL 5/1/96; SLJ 5/96)

7701 DeFelice, Cynthia. *Cold Feet* (2–4). Illus. by Robert Andrew Parker. 2000, DK $15.95 (0-7894-2636-6). 32pp. A poor Scottish bagpiper with great holes in his shoes stumbles on a dead body with a nice pair of boots in this ghost story told in a picture book for older readers. (Rev: BCCB 11/00; BL 9/1/00; HB 9–10/00; HBG 3/01; SLJ 9/00)

7702 DeFelice, Cynthia. *The Ghost of Fossil Glen* (4–6). 1998, Farrar $16.00 (0-374-31787-9). 176pp. Allie has been chosen by the ghost of a young girl to avenge her death in this tense thriller. (Rev: BCCB 3/98; BL 3/15/98; HB 9–10/98; HBG 10/98; SLJ 7/98)

7703 Del Negro, Janice. *Lucy Dove* (3–6). Illus. by Leonid Gore. 1998, DK $16.95 (0-7894-2514-9). 32pp. In this adventure set in Scotland and based loosely on several folktales, seamstress Lucy Dove is determined to win a sackful of gold by sewing a pair of trousers in a graveyard occupied by a scary monster. (Rev: BCCB 9/98; BL 9/1/98; HB 9–10/98; HBG 3/99; SLJ 11/98)

7704 Derby, Sally. *Jacob and the Stranger* (3–5). Illus. 1994, Ticknor $11.95 (0-395-66897-2). 32pp. Jacob takes care of a plant that sprouts miniature animals that become his companions. (Rev: BL 9/1/94; HB 9–10/94; SLJ 9/94)

7705 Dexter, Catherine. *A Is for Apple, W Is for Witch* (3–5). Illus. by Capucine Mazille. 1996, Candlewick $14.99 (1-56402-541-1). 160pp. Apple learns a spell from her witch-mother and turns classmate Barnaby into a frog. (Rev: BCCB 2/96; BL 9/15/96; SLJ 7/96)

7706 Dickens, Charles. *The Magic Fish-bone* (3–5). Illus. by Robert Florczak. 2000, Harcourt $17.00 (0-15-201080-7). 40pp. Although she possesses a magic fishbone, Princess Alicia declines to use it unless it is absolutely necessary. (Rev: BL 1/1–15/01; HBG 3/01; SLJ 11/00)

7707 Dickinson, Peter. *Chuck and Danielle* (4–6). Illus. by Kees de Kiefte. 1996, Delacorte paper $3.99 (0-440-41087-8). A fantasy about an independent-minded whippet, Church, and his owner, Danielle, who wants to train him for an agility competition. (Rev: SLJ 2/00)

7708 Doyle, Debra, and James D. MacDonald. *Knight's Wyrd* (5–8). 1992, Harcourt $16.95 (0-15-200764-4). 176pp. Young Will learns from a wizard that he will soon meet his death. (Rev: SLJ 11/92)

7709 Doyle, Roddy. *The Giggler Treatment* (2–5). Illus. by Brian Ajhar. 2000, Scholastic $14.95 (0-439-16299-8). 112pp. A nonsense story about several well-wishers who rush to warn Mister Mack that there is "dog poo" in the path where he is walking that has been placed there by furry little creatures named Gigglers. (Rev: HBG 3/01; SLJ 11/00)

7710 Drexler, Sam, and Fay Shelby. *Lost in Spillville* (5–9). Series: Erika and Oz Adventures in American History. 2000, Aunt Strawberry paper $6.99 (0-9669988-1-2). 150pp. Two teenagers accidentally are transported to the 1930s and must locate an important clock maker to be returned to the 1990s. (Rev: SLJ 11/00)

7711 Duane, Diane. *Deep Wizardry* (5–8). 1996, Harcourt paper $6.00 (0-152-01240-0). 288pp. Nita and Kit, the two young wizards of *So You Want to*

Be a Wizard, again use their powers to prevent a great catastrophe. (Rev: HB 5–6/85)

7712 Duane, Diane. *So You Want to Be a Wizard* (5–8). 1996, Harcourt paper $6.00 (0-152-01239-7). 288pp. Nita and friends embark on a journey to retrieve the Book of Night with Moon.

7713 Dunlop, Eileen. *The Ghost by the Sea* (4–6). 1996, Holiday $15.95 (0-8234-1264-4). 192pp. Robin uncovers details of a death that occurred 80 years ago and is haunted by a restless ghost. (Rev: BCCB 3/97; BL 1/1–15/97; SLJ 3/97)

7714 Dunlop, Eileen. *Websters' Leap* (4–7). 1995, Holiday $15.95 (0-8234-1193-1). 160pp. In this time-slip fantasy, Jill gets involved with people who owned a Scottish castle 400 years before. (Rev: BL 10/1/95; SLJ 10/95)

7715 Duquennoy, Jacques. *Operation Ghost* (2–4). Illus. by author. 1999, Harcourt $13.00 (0-15-202182-5); paper $6.00 (0-15-202203-1). Henry, a ghost who has health problems, goes to a doctor who adjusts his inner clock. (Rev: HB 11–12/99; HBG 3/00; SLJ 10/99)

7716 Einhorn, Edward. *Paradox in Oz* (4–6). Illus. 2000, Hungry Tiger $24.95 (1-929527-01-2). 240pp. This new Oz adventure is true to the famous series and contains familiar characters including Ozma and Glinda, the Good Witch of the South. (Rev: BL 4/15/00; SLJ 8/00)

7717 Ephron, Delia. *The Girl Who Changed the World* (3–6). 1993, Ticknor $13.95 (0-395-66139-0). 160pp. Tired of being bullied by her older brother, Violet rebels and organizes other sibling victims to do the same. (Rev: BCCB 10/93; BL 11/15/93; SLJ 11/93)

7718 Erickson, John R. *Moonlight Madness* (3–7). Series: Hank the Cowdog. 1994, Gulf $11.95 (0-87719-252-9); paper $6.95 (0-87719-251-0). Hank the Cowdog has his hands full with a pet raccoon that tells tall tales. (Rev: SLJ 2/00)

7719 Etchemendy, Nancy. *The Power of Un* (4–7). 2000, Front Street $14.95 (0-8126-2850-0). 160pp. Gib, a young boy, meets a strange old man who gives him an "unner," which can send him back in time in this thought-provoking fantasy. (Rev: BCCB 7–8/00; BL 5/1/00; HBG 10/00; SLJ 6/00)

7720 Faulkner, Matt. *Black Belt* (2–4). Illus. 2000, Knopf $15.95 (0-375-80157-X). 40pp. In this time travel story a Japanese boy goes back in time to learn karate so he can deal with the schoolyard bullies. (Rev: BL 5/1/00; HBG 3/01; SLJ 6/00)

7721 Favole, Robert J. *Through the Wormhole* (5–8). 2001, Flywheel $17.95 (1-930826-00-1). 192pp. Michael and Kate time-travel to Colonial America to aid Lafayette's attack on the British and to save one of Michael's ancestors. (Rev: BL 3/1/01)

7722 Fawcett, Melissa Jayne, and Joseph Bruchac. *Makiawisug: The Gift of the Little People* (3–5). Illus. by David Wagner. 1997, Little People $19.95 (0-9656933-2-5). 28pp. The story of the antics of the American Indian "little people," the Makiawisug. (Rev: BL 9/15/97)

7723 Field, Rachel. *Hitty: Her First Hundred Years* (4–6). Illus. by Dorothy P. Lathrop. 1969, Macmillan $17.00 (0-02-734840-7); Dell paper $4.99 (0-440-40337-5). 220pp. America 100 years ago seen through the adventures of a wooden doll. A reissue of the 1930 Newbery Award winner.

7724 Findon, Joanne. *When Night Eats the Moon* (4–7). 2000, Red Deer paper $7.95 (0-88995-212-4). 176pp. Her flute music and some magic take Holly, a Canadian girl visiting England, back to prehistoric times at Stonehenge when the locals are being threatened with a Celtic invasion. (Rev: BL 8/00)

7725 Fine, Anne. *Bad Dreams* (4–6). 2000, Delacorte $15.95 (0-385-32757-9). 134pp. Mel discovers that her new friend Imogene can absorb the contents of a book by placing her hand on it. (Rev: BCCB 6/00; BL 5/1/00; HBG 10/00; SLJ 6/00)

7726 Fleischman, Sid. *The Midnight Horse* (3–6). Illus. by Peter Sis. 1990, Greenwillow $16.00 (0-688-09441-4). 84pp. An orphan boy named Touch, accompanied by a friendly ghost, is the center of this 19th-century tale. (Rev: BCCB 12/90; BL 8/90; HB 11–12/90; SLJ 9/90)

7727 Fleischman, Sid. *The 13th Floor: A Ghost Story* (4–6). Illus. 1995, Greenwillow $15.00 (0-688-14216-8). 144pp. When a ghost who lived in the 17th century asks for his help, Bud obligingly travels back in time. (Rev: BL 10/1/95; HB 11–12/95; SLJ 10/95)

7728 Fleming, Ian. *Chitty Chitty Bang Bang* (4–6). Illus. by John Burningham. 1964, Amereon LB $22.72 (0-88411-983-1). 159pp. Chitty Chitty Bang Bang, a magical racing car, flies, floats, and has a real talent for getting the Pott family in and out of trouble.

7729 Fletcher, Susan. *Flight of the Dragon Kyn* (5–7). 1993, Atheneum $17.00 (0-689-31880-4). 224pp. A girl with a special talent to call down birds uses it to attract dragons for the king and his hunters. (Rev: BL 1/15/94; SLJ 11/93)

7730 Fletcher, Susan. *Sign of the Dove* (5–7). 1996, Simon & Schuster $17.00 (0-689-80460-1). 214pp. Lyf tries to save some dragons from the evil queen, who wants to cut out their hearts. A sequel to *Dragon's Milk* (1989). (Rev: BL 5/1/96; HB 9–10/96; SLJ 5/96)

7731 Foster, Elizabeth. *Gigi: The Story of a Merry-Go-Round Horse* (3–6). Illus. by Ilse Bischoff. 1983, North Atlantic paper $9.95 (0-913028-55-X). 124pp. The beloved fantasy now reissued after many years. A sequel is: *Gigi in America: The Further Adventures of a Merry-Go-Round Horse* (1983).

7732 Foster, Evelyn, and Olwyn Whelan. *The Mermaid of Cafur* (1–5). 1999, Barefoot LB $15.95 (1-902283-40-6). Through the courage of Meaghan, the evil power of the mermaid queen of Cafur is broken and her captive children are set free. (Rev: SLJ 3/99)

7733 French, Vivian. *Under the Moon* (3–5). Illus. by Chris Fisher. 1994, Candlewick $14.95 (1-56402-330-3). 96pp. Three stories (one based on a folktale) that tell about fantastic beings and present timeless themes. (Rev: BL 3/15/94; SLJ 6/94)

7734 Fromental, Jean-Luc. *Broadway Chicken* (5–8). Trans. by Suzi Baker. Illus. by Miles Hyman. 1995, Hyperion LB $15.49 (0-7868-2048-9). 40pp. After a leg operation, Charlie, the famous dancing chicken, finds that he will never dance again. (Rev: BL 12/15/95; SLJ 2/96)

7735 Froud, Wendy, and Terri Windling. *A Midsummer Night's Faery Tale* (4–6). Illus. 1999, Simon & Schuster $18.00 (0-684-85559-3). 52pp. A young fairy named Sneezle sets out on a dangerous quest to save the life of his queen, Titania. (Rev: BL 2/1/00)

7736 Gaarder, Jostein. *Hello? Is Anybody There?* (3–5). Trans. by James Anderson. Illus. 1998, Farrar $15.00 (0-374-32948-6). 144pp. When a shooting star turns into a boy named Mika, young Joe introduces him to our world and its wonders. (Rev: BL 12/15/98; HBG 3/99; SLJ 12/98)

7737 Garland, Sherry. *Cabin 102* (5–8). 1995, Harcourt $11.00 (0-15-200663-X); paper $6.00 (0-15-200662-1). 224pp. On a cruise ship with his family, Dusty encounters a mysterious girl from the extinct Taino tribe. (Rev: BL 11/15/95; SLJ 12/95)

7738 Garner, Alan. *The Well of the Wind* (4–7). Illus. by Herve Blondon. 1998, DK $14.95 (0-7894-2519-X). 45pp. In this fantasy, a young girl sets out to find her brother who has fallen under the spell of an evil witch. (Rev: BCCB 11/98; BL 8/98; HBG 10/99; SLJ 11/98)

7739 Geras, Adele. *The Fabulous Fantoras, Book Two: Family Photographs* (4–6). 1999, Avon $15.00 (0-380-97546-7). 160pp. The family cat narrates this story of the Fantoras as they prepare for Auntie Varvara's upcoming marriage to an Italian werewolf. (Rev: BL 6/1–15/99; HBG 10/99)

7740 Gerstein, Mordicai. *The Giant* (3–5). Illus. 1995, Hyperion LB $14.49 (0-7868-2104-3). 40pp. When three children rebuff a giant's attempts to become friends with them, later that night they hear him sobbing. (Rev: BL 10/15/95; SLJ 11/95)

7741 Gibbons, Faye. *Hook Moon Night: Spooky Stories from the Georgia Mountains* (3–6). Illus. 1997, Morrow $15.00 (0-688-14504-3). 128pp. In his Georgia home, Grandpa tells ghost stories, including one in which a sick woman is buried alive by her son-in-law. (Rev: BL 11/1/97; HBG 3/98; SLJ 10/97)

7742 *A Glory of Unicorns* (5–8). Ed. by Bruce Coville. Illus. 1998, Scholastic $16.95 (0-590-95943-3). 208pp. This is a collection of stories set in the past and present about unicorns and their magical powers. (Rev: BL 6/1–15/98; HBG 10/98; SLJ 5/98)

7743 Gogol, Nikolai. *The Nose* (3–8). Illus. by Gennady Spirin. 1993, Godine $17.95 (0-87923-963-8). In this novel of the absurd set in St. Petersburg, Kovaliov finds that his nose has disappeared. (Rev: SLJ 8/93)

7744 Goldsmith, Howard. *The Twiddle Twins' Haunted House* (2–3). Illus. 1997, Mondo paper $4.50 (1-57255-222-0). 40pp. Hippo twins suspect a ghost when they are awakened one night by a tapping sound. Also use *Twiddle Twins' Music Box Mystery* (1997). (Rev: BL 2/1/98)

7745 Gollub, Matthew. *The Twenty-Five Mixtec Cats* (4–6). Illus. by Leovigildo Martinez. 1993, Morrow LB $15.93 (0-688-11640-X). 32pp. Roughly based on a Mexican folktale, this is the amusing story of a healer in an Oaxacan village who returns from market with 25 cats. (Rev: BL 4/1/93; SLJ 6/93)

7746 Gormley, Beatrice. *Best Friend Insurance* (5–7). Illus. by Emily Arnold McCully. 1988, Avon paper $2.50 (0-380-69854-4). 160pp. Maureen finds that her mother has been transformed into a new friend named Kitty.

7747 Gormley, Beatrice. *Fifth Grade Magic* (4–6). Illus. by Emily Arnold McCully. 1982, Avon paper $3.50 (0-380-67439-4). 128pp. Gretchen uses the help of an inept fairy godmother to get the lead in the school play.

7748 Gormley, Beatrice. *Mail-Order Wings* (3–5). Illus. by Emily Arnold McCully. 1984, Avon paper $2.95 (0-380-67421-1). 164pp. Andrea finds her Wonda-Wings are gradually transforming her into a bird.

7749 Gormley, Beatrice. *More Fifth Grade Magic* (3–5). Illus. by Emily Arnold McCully. 1990, Avon paper $3.50 (0-380-70883-3). 128pp. Amy uses the magical powers she finds in a calendar to grant her wishes. (Rev: BL 8/89)

7750 Gorog, Judith. *In a Messy, Messy Room* (4–6). Illus. by Kimberly B. Root. 1990, Putnam $14.95 (0-399-22218-9). 48pp. Eerie tales for the younger set. (Rev: BCCB 6/90; BL 6/90; SLJ 7/90)

7751 Grahame, Kenneth. *The Adventures of Mr. Toad: From The Wind in the Willows* (3–5). Illus. 1998, Candlewick $21.99 (0-7636-0581-6). 86pp. This is an abridgement of the parts of *The Wind in the Willows* that feature Mr. Toad. (Rev: BL 3/15/99; HBG 3/99; SLJ 3/99)

7752 Grahame, Kenneth. *The River Bank: And Other Stories from The Wind in the Willows* (2–4). Illus. by Inga Moore. 1996, Candlewick $21.99 (0-7636-0059-8). 93pp. A charming retelling of five stories from *The Wind in the Willows*, with rich-toned illustrations. (Rev: SLJ 1/97)

7753 Grahame, Kenneth. *The Wind in the Willows* (4–7). Illus. by E. H. Shepard. 1983, Macmillan $19.95 (0-684-17957-1). 256pp. The classic that introduced Mole, Ratty, and Mr. Toad. Two of many other editions are: illus. by Michael Hague (1980, Henry Holt); illus. by John Burningham (1983, Viking).

7754 Grahame, Kenneth. *The Wind in the Willows* (4–6). Illus. by Patrick Benson. 1995, St. Martin's $19.95 (0-312-13624-2). 272pp. A brilliantly illustrated edition of this classic, with pictures that rival the work of Ernest H. Shepard. (Rev: BL 2/1/96)

7755 Grahame, Kenneth. *The Wind in the Willows: The Gates of Dawn. Vol. 3* (2–5). Trans. from French by Joe Johnson. Adapted by Michel Plessix. Illus. by author. 2000, NBM $15.95 (1-56163-245-7). 31pp. A graphic novel that retells key episodes from Chapters 7, 8, and 9 of *The Wind in the Willows*. (Rev: HBG 3/01; SLJ 7/00)

7756 Gray, Luli. *Falcon's Egg* (3–5). 1995, Houghton $13.95 (0-395-71128-2). 144pp. A young girl hatches an egg she finds in Central Park and, as a result, is transported to a world of magical creatures. (Rev: BCCB 10/95; BL 9/15/95; SLJ 9/95*)

7757 Greenburg, Dan. *Dr. Jekyll, Orthodontist* (3–4). Illus. by Jack E. Davis. Series: The Zack Files. 1997, Grosset LB $11.99 (0-448-41584-4); paper $3.95 (0-448-41338-8). 57pp. Zack drinks some mouthwash at his dentist's office, and his teeth begin to grow. Also use *I'm Out of My Body . . . Please Leave a Message* (1996). (Rev: SLJ 3/97)

7758 Greenburg, Dan. *A Ghost Named Wanda* (3–5). Illus. by Jack E. Davis. Series: Zack Files. 1996, Grosset paper $3.99 (0-448-41261-6). 59pp. The story of Zack, a 10-year-old with the knack of getting into unusual situations. Also use *Zap! I'm a Mind Reader* (1996). (Rev: SLJ 2/97)

7759 Greenburg, Dan. *Great-Grandpa's in the Litter Box* (3–5). Illus. 1996, Putnam paper $3.95 (0-448-41260-8). 61pp. Zack adopts a cat that not only talks but also claims to be a relative. Zack has further adventures in *Through the Medicine Cabinet* (1996). (Rev: BL 1/1–15/97; SLJ 2/97)

7760 Greer, Gery, and Bob Ruddick. *Max and Me and the Time Machine* (5–8). 1983, HarperCollins paper $4.95 (0-06-440222-3). 140pp. Steve and Max travel back in time to England during the Middle Ages.

7761 Gregory, Valiska. *When Stories Fell Like Shooting Stars* (3–6). Illus. by Stefano Vitale. 1996, Simon & Schuster paper $16.00 (0-689-80012-6). 32pp. Two allegorical tales involving animals with supernatural powers. (Rev: BCCB 2/97; BL 1/1–15/97; SLJ 10/96)

7762 Griffin, Peni R. *A Dig in Time* (4–7). 1991, Macmillan $14.95 (0-689-50525-6). 192pp. Twelve-year-old Nan and her brother spend the summer in San Antonio with their grandmother and find they can travel back in time to witness events in their family's history. (Rev: BCCB 10/91; BL 6/15/91; SLJ 6/91)

7763 Griffin, Peni R. *Margo's House* (3–6). 1996, Simon & Schuster $16.00 (0-689-80944-1). 122pp. A girl and her father project themselves into the bodies of two dolls. (Rev: BCCB 11/96; BL 9/1/96; SLJ 10/96)

7764 Griffith, Helen V. *Cougar* (4–6). 1999, Greenwillow $15.00 (0-688-16337-8). 112pp. In this engaging fantasy, Nickel, a neglected youngster, gets help from a ghost horse to cope with bully Robbo. (Rev: BCCB 3/99; BL 4/1/99; HB 5–6/99; HBG 10/99; SLJ 5/99)

7765 Griffith, Helen V. *Dinosaur Habitat* (4–6). Illus. 1998, Greenwillow $15.00 (0-688-15324-0). 112pp. Through a freak accident, Nathan and his young brother land in a dinosaur terrarium where all the beasts suddenly come to life. (Rev: BL 3/15/98; HBG 10/98; SLJ 6/98)

7766 Grindley, Sally. *Breaking the Spell: Tales of Enchantment* (3–5). Illus. 1997, Kingfisher $17.95 (0-7534-5002-X). 80pp. Seven original folk and fairy tales set in exotic locales and written by both established and new writers. (Rev: BL 1/1–15/98; HBG 3/98; SLJ 12/97)

7767 Guiberson, Brenda Z. *Tales of the Haunted Deep* (3–6). Illus. 2000, Holt $15.95 (0-8050-6057-X). 70pp. This collection of ghost stories of the sea contains tales of monsters, pirates, lighthouses, and ships, many of them from folklore. (Rev: BCCB 9/00; BL 6/1–15/00; HBG 10/00; SLJ 11/00)

7768 Gutman, Dan. *Babe and Me* (4–7). Illus. 2000, Avon $15.00 (0-380-97739-7). 160pp. Joe and his dad time-travel to the 1932 World Series to witness a historic moment with hitter Babe Ruth. (Rev: BL 2/1/00; HBG 10/00; SLJ 2/00)

7769 Gutman, Dan. *Honus and Me: A Baseball Card Adventure* (4–7). 1997, Avon paper $4.95 (0-380-78878-0). 160pp. Young Joe Stoshack finds a magical baseball card that allows him to travel through time and participate in the 1909 World Series. (Rev: BL 4/15/97; SLJ 6/97)

7770 Gutman, Dan. *Jackie and Me: A Baseball Card Adventure* (4–7). Illus. 1999, Avon $15.00 (0-380-97685-4). 144pp. While time-traveling to research a paper on Jackie Robinson, Joe Stoshack becomes an African American and experiences prejudice first hand. (Rev: BL 2/1/99; HBG 10/99; SLJ 3/99)

7771 Haddix, Margaret P. *Running Out of Time* (4–7). 1995, Simon & Schuster paper $16.00 (0-689-80084-3). 185pp. Living in a historical site where the time is the 1840s, Jessie escapes into the present in this fantasy. (Rev: BCCB 11/95; BL 10/1/95; SLJ 10/95*)

7772 Hague, Michael, ed. *The Book of Dragons* (4–7). Illus. by Michael Hague. 1995, Morrow $21.95 (0-688-10879-2). 160pp. Seventeen classic tales about dragons by such authors as Tolkien and Kenneth Grahame are included in this interesting anthology. (Rev: BL 10/1/95; SLJ 10/95)

7773 Hague, Michael. *Michael Hague's Magical World of Unicorns* (3–5). Illus. by author. 1999, Simon & Schuster $16.00 (0-689-82849-7). This collection of medieval legends, poetry, and prose about unicorns is exquisitely illustrated. (Rev: HBG 3/00; SLJ 12/99)

7774 Hahn, Mary D. *The Doll in the Garden: A Ghost Story* (4–6). Illus. 1989, Houghton $15.00 (0-89919-848-1). 160pp. Ten-year-old Ashley and her mother try to start a new life in a house owned by a grouchy octogenarian. (Rev: BCCB 3/89; BL 3/15/89; SLJ 5/89)

7775 Hahn, Mary D. *Time for Andrew: A Ghost Story* (4–6). 1994, Clarion $14.95 (0-395-66556-6). 167pp. Drew changes places with his look-alike distant relative and travels back to 1910. (Rev: BCCB 4/94; BL 4/1/94; SLJ 5/94)

7776 Hahn, Mary D. *Wait Till Helen Comes: A Ghost Story* (5–7). 1986, Houghton $15.00 (0-89919-453-2); Avon paper $4.99 (0-380-70442-0). 192pp. Things go from bad to worse for Molly and

Michael and their stepsister Heather when Heather becomes involved in a frightening relationship with the ghost of a dead child. (Rev: BCCB 10/86; BL 9/1/86; SLJ 10/86)

7777 Hale, Bruce. *The Chameleon Wore Chartreuse* (3–6). Illus. 2000, Harcourt $14.00 (0-15-202281-3). 112pp. Using a private-eye style of writing, this humorous mystery involves Chet Gecko, a fourth-grade lizard/investigator, who uncovers a plot to steal the team mascot. (Rev: BCCB 6/00; BL 5/15/00; HBG 3/01; SLJ 8/00)

7778 Hale, Bruce. *Farewell, My Lunchbag* (2–5). Illus. 2001, Harcourt $14.00 (0-15-202275-9). 128pp. Detective Chet Gecko investigates the problem of the mystery food snatcher who is operating in his elementary school. (Rev: BL 3/15/01)

7779 Hale, Bruce. *The Mystery of Mr. Nice* (4–6). 2000, Harcourt $14.00 (0-15-202271-6). 112pp. Chet Gecko, the lizard detective, sets out to discover why his school principal is suddenly acting very nicely toward everyone. (Rev: BL 11/1/00; HBG 3/01; SLJ 12/00)

7780 Hall, Elizabeth, and Scott O'Dell. *Venus Among the Fishes* (4–6). 1995, Houghton $15.95 (0-395-70561-4). 143pp. A dolphin who is trained to rescue divers in trouble falls in love with a human. (Rev: BCCB 4/95; BL 4/15/95; SLJ 6/95)

7781 Hamilton, Virginia. *The All Jahdu Storybook* (3–5). Illus. by Barry Moser. 1991, Harcourt $19.95 (0-15-239498-2). 108pp. A retelling of Jahdu stories about a shape-changing trickster. (Rev: BCCB 1/92; BL 12/1/91; SLJ 1/92)

7782 Hamilton, Virginia. *Jaguarundi* (2–5). Illus. by Floyd Cooper. 1994, Scholastic $14.95 (0-590-47366-2). 40pp. A wildcat (jaguarundi) persuades a coati to flee across the river to find a new home. (Rev: BCCB 2/95; BL 12/15/94; SLJ 12/94)

7783 Hansen, Brooks. *Caesar's Antlers* (5–7). Illus. 1997, Farrar $16.00 (0-374-31024-6). 224pp. In this animal fantasy, Caesar the reindeer and his friend Bette the sparrow and her two offspring set out to contact some human friends to get help for the winter. (Rev: BL 10/1/97; HBG 3/98; SLJ 11/97)

7784 Hansen, Ron. *The Shadowmaker* (4–6). Illus. by Margot Tomes. 1987, HarperCollins paper $4.95 (0-06-440287-8). 80pp. Drizzle and her brother Soot save the day when they outwit Shadowmaker, who is selling the wrong shadows to everyone. (Rev: BL 5/15/87; HB 9–10/87; SLJ 8/87)

7785 Haseley, Dennis. *Ghost Catcher* (3–5). Illus. by Lloyd Bloom. 1991, HarperCollins $15.95 (0-06-022244-1). 40pp. A man who can get close to ghosts without turning into one needs the help of his friends when he visits the shadow village. (Rev: BL 10/1/91; SLJ 11/91)

7786 Hatrick, Gloria. *Masks* (4–6). 1996, Orchard LB $16.99 (0-531-08864-2). 128pp. In this fantasy, Pete uses animal masks to communicate with his paralyzed older brother. (Rev: BCCB 3/96; BL 4/15/96; SLJ 5/96)

7787 Hayes, Sarah. *Crumbling Castle* (3–6). Illus. by Helen Craig. 1992, Candlewick $13.95 (1-56402-108-4). 80pp. A wizard moves into a castle that's been empty for 100 years, but it's his talkative crow who solves the mystery of why it's crumbling. (Rev: BL 12/15/92; SLJ 10/92)

7788 Hearne, Betsy. *Wishes, Kisses, and Pigs* (4–6). 2001, Simon & Schuster $16.00 (0-689-84122-1). 133pp. In this fantasy, Louise's pesky older brother disappears and suddenly there is a new white pig on the farm. (Rev: BL 3/1/01)

7789 Hench, Larry L. *Boing-Boing the Bionic Cat* (2–4). Illus. by Ruth Denise Lear. 2000, American Ceramic Society $17.00 (1-57498-109-9). 48pp. A chapter book in picture-book format about a man with allergies who accepts a bionic cat because he can't live with a real one. (Rev: HBG 10/00; SLJ 8/00)

7790 Herman, Gail. *Tooth Fairy Travels* (2–4). Illus. by Fran Gianfriddo. Series: Fairy School. 1999, Bantam paper $3.99 (0-553-48679-9). 90pp. An easy chapter book about Belinda Dentalette, who is going to school to become a tooth fairy. (Rev: SLJ 8/99)

7791 Hill, Margaret Bateson. *Masha and the Fire-bird* (PS–3). Illus. by Anne Wilson. 2000, Zero to Ten $17.95 (1-84089-134-3). 32pp. In this original folk tale set in Russia, a brave girl confronts witch Baba Yaga to save the stolen egg of the Firebird. (Rev: BL 1/1–15/01)

7792 Hiser, Constance. *Night of the Werepoodle* (2–4). Illus. 1994, Holiday $14.95 (0-8234-1116-8). 122pp. After being bitten by a poodle, Jonathan turns into a "werepoodle" and must find some wolf-bane to become a boy again. (Rev: BL 6/1–15/94; SLJ 6/94)

7793 Hoban, Russell. *Trouble on Thunder Mountain* (2–4). Illus. 2000, Orchard $14.95 (0-531-30206-7). 40pp. When a family of dinosaurs are evicted from Thunder Mountain to make room for an amusement park, they vow to fight back. (Rev: BCCB 9/00; BL 6/1–15/00; HBG 10/00; SLJ 7/00)

7794 Hodges, Margaret, ed. *Comus* (4–6). Illus. by Trina S. Hyman. 1996, Holiday $16.95 (0-8234-1146-X). 32pp. In this retelling of a work by John Milton, Alice resists the enchantment of the evil magician Comus. (Rev: BCCB 10/94; BL 3/1/96; SLJ 3/96)

7795 Hodges, Margaret. *Gulliver in Lilliput: From Gulliver's Travels by Jonathan Swift* (4–7). Illus. by Kimberly B. Root. 1995, Holiday LB $16.95 (0-8234-1147-8). 32pp. The story of Gulliver in the land of the little people is retold with bright, detailed illustrations. (Rev: BCCB 6/95; BL 4/15/95; HB 7–8/95; SLJ 6/95*)

7796 Hoffman, Alice. *Aquamarine* (4–7). 2001, Scholastic $16.95 (0-439-09863-7). 112pp. Twelve-year-old friends Hailey and Claire find a lonely mermaid named Aquamarine, and they try to give her love and adventure. (Rev: BCCB 2/01; BL 3/1/01; SLJ 3/01)

7797 Holch, Gregory. *The Things with Wings* (4–6). Illus. 1998, Scholastic $15.95 (0-590-93501-1). 160pp. Newton is astonished when his friend Vanessa, who shares his interest in the emerald rainbow butterfly, samples the fruit from a strange tree

and becomes one. (Rev: BL 8/98; HB 7–8/98; HBG 10/98; SLJ 5/98)

7798 Howe, James. *Morgan's Zoo* (4–6). Illus. by Leslie Morrill. 1984, Macmillan $16.00 (0-689-31046-3); Avon paper $3.99 (0-380-69994-X). 192pp. Morgan, a set of twins, and a number of animals band together to save a zoo.

7799 Hughes, Carol. *Jack Black and the Ship of Thieves* (4–6). 2000, Random LB $17.99 (0-375-90472-7). 240pp. In this old-fashioned adventure fantasy, young Jack becomes involved in a series of escapades involving airships, pirates, volcanoes, and a sea monster. (Rev: BCCB 9/00; BL 10/15/00; HB 9–10/00; HBG 3/01)

7800 Hughes, Carol. *Toots and the Upside-Down House* (4–6). Illus. 1997, Random LB $18.99 (0-679-98653-7). 141pp. In this fantasy, Toots is captured by fairies and reduced to their size. (Rev: BL 9/1/97; SLJ 10/97)

7801 Hughes, Dean. *Nutty's Ghost* (5–7). 1993, Macmillan $13.95 (0-689-31743-3). 136pp. Nutty finds a ghost is sabotaging the completion of the movie in which he is appearing. (Rev: SLJ 5/93)

7802 Hughes, Monica, sel. *What If? Amazing Stories* (5–10). 1998, Tundra paper $6.95 (0-88776-458-4). 199pp. Fourteen fantasy and science fiction short stories by noted Canadian writers are included in this anthology, plus a few related poems. (Rev: SLJ 6/99)

7803 Hughes, Shirley. *Enchantment in the Garden* (3–5). Illus. 1997, Lothrop $18.00 (0-688-14597-3). 64pp. In this fantasy, a rich little girl in Italy during the 1920s brings to life the statue of a sea god's son. (Rev: BCCB 7–8/97; BL 5/15/97; HB 3–4/97; SLJ 5/97)

7804 Hunter, Mollie. *The Mermaid Summer* (5–8). 1988, HarperCollins LB $15.89 (0-06-022628-5); paper $4.95 (0-06-440344-0). 160pp. Eric Anderson leaves his Scottish fishing village after his boat is dashed to pieces on the rocks, but he sends wonderful gifts back to his grandchildren. (Rev: BCCB 5/88; BL 6/1/88; SLJ 6–7/88)

7805 Hurmence, Belinda. *A Girl Called Boy* (5–8). 1982, Houghton paper $5.95 (0-395-55698-8). 180pp. A contemporary African American girl travels back to the time of slavery.

7806 Hurwitz, Johanna. *PeeWee's Tale* (2–5). Illus. 2000, North-South $13.95 (1-58717-027-2). 96pp. PeeWee is a little guinea pig whose intelligence and ability to read help him escape danger when he is left in a park. (Rev: BL 10/1/00; HBG 3/01; SLJ 10/00)

7807 Hutchins, Hazel. *The Prince of Tarn* (3–5). Illus. 1997, Annick $14.95 (1-55037-439-7). 143pp. The spoiled prince created by his author mother in one of her fantasies comes to life and takes Fred to his kingdom. (Rev: BL 2/15/98; SLJ 2/98)

7808 Ibbotson, Eva. *Island of the Aunts* (5–8). 2000, Dutton $15.99 (0-525-46484-0). 276pp. Three elderly sisters kidnap three children to help them take care of their collection of exotic creatures, including mermaids. (Rev: BCCB 2/01; BL 12/1/00; HBG 3/01; SLJ 11/00)

7809 Ibbotson, Eva. *The Secret of Platform 13* (4–7). Illus. 1998, Dutton $15.99 (0-525-45929-4). 224pp. In this fantasy, three unusual creatures — a wizard, an ogre, and a hag — set out to rescue from their enchanted kingdom a prince who has been kidnapped. (Rev: BL 2/15/98; HBG 10/98; SLJ 3/98*)

7810 Ibbotson, Eva. *Which Witch?* (5–8). 1999, Dutton $15.99 (0-525-46164-7). 224pp. This British fantasy involves a wizard who holds a competition to find a wife, a sweet witch who wants to win the wizard's heart, and orphan Terence who is looking for a home. (Rev: BCCB 9/99; BL 8/99; HBG 3/00; SLJ 8/99)

7811 Icanberry, Mark. *Picnic on a Cloud* (3–5). Illus. by Mark Icanberry and Arthur Mount. Series: Look, Learn and Do. 2000, Tricycle Pr. $14.95 (1-893327-00-0); paper $7.95 (1-893327-02-7). 47pp. David, his dog Newton, and friend Jessica construct a blimp using 289 balloons and take a ride during which they picnic on a cloud. The trio build a greenhouse in *Super Salads* (2000). (Rev: SLJ 1/01)

7812 Irving, Washington. *The Legend of Sleepy Hollow* (3–5). Retold by Robert D. San Souci. Illus. by Daniel San Souci. 1995, Bantam paper $6.99 (0-440-41074-6). 32pp. A retelling that retains the atmosphere and sense of character. (Rev: BL 1/15/87; SLJ 12/86)

7813 Irving, Washington. *The Legend of Sleepy Hollow: Found Among the Papers of the Late Diedrich Knickerbocker* (4–6). Illus. 1999, Ideals $16.95 (0-8249-4160-8). 64pp. A well-illustrated edition of this perennial favorite about Ichabod Crane, the Headless Horseman, and the heiress Katrina Van Tassel. (Rev: BL 10/1/99)

7814 Irving, Washington. *Rip Van Winkle* (5–7). Illus. by N. C. Wyeth. 1987, Morrow $21.95 (0-688-07459-6). 110pp. Distinguished illustrations highlight this 1921 edition. (Rev: BL 9/1/87)

7815 Irving, Washington. *Rip Van Winkle* (3–5). Adapted and illus. by Rick Meyerowitz. 1995, Rabbit Ears $19.95 (0-689-80193-9). A delightful retelling of this classic tale, with illustrations of many historical occurrences of the era. (Rev: SLJ 12/95)

7816 Irving, Washington. *Rip Van Winkle and the Legend of Sleepy Hollow* (5–7). Illus. by Felix O. Darley. 1980, Sleepy Hollow $19.95 (0-912882-42-5). 152pp. A handsome edition of these two classics.

7817 Jacques, Brian. *The Bellmaker* (5–7). Illus. 1995, Putnam $22.99 (0-399-22805-5). 352pp. This seventh tale in the Redwall series of animal fantasies features Mariel, a courageous, outspoken mouse. (Rev: BCCB 4/95; BL 4/1/95; HB 5–6/95; SLJ 8/95)

7818 Jacques, Brian. *Castaways of the Flying Dutchman* (5–9). 2001, Putnam $22.95 (0-399-23601-5). 318pp. A mute boy stows away on the *Flying Dutchman*, a ship that is condemned to sail the seas forever, and there he meets the ghostly crew and the crazed captain in this story in which the boy has many adventures and eventually gains

the power of speech and the gift of staying young forever. (Rev: BCCB 3/01; BL 3/1/01; SLJ 3/01)

7819 Jacques, Brian. *The Great Redwall Feast* (4–6). Illus. by Christopher Denise. 1996, Putnam $18.99 (0-399-22707-5). 64pp. In this illustrated storybook, the creatures of Redwall prepare a magnificent feast. (Rev: BL 10/15/96; SLJ 12/96)

7820 Jacques, Brian. *The Legend of Luke: A Tale from Redwall* (5–8). Illus. 2000, Putnam $22.95 (0-399-23490-X). 384pp. This Redwall book focuses on the building of the abbey, Martin's search for his father Luke, and Luke's heroic career. (Rev: BL 12/15/99; HBG 10/00; SLJ 2/00)

7821 Jacques, Brian. *The Long Patrol* (5–8). Illus. 1998, Putnam $22.99 (0-399-23165-X). 368pp. In this tenth Redwall adventure, the villainous Rapscallions decide to attack the peaceful Abbey of Redwall. (Rev: BCCB 4/98; BL 12/15/97; HB 3–4/98; HBG 10/98; SLJ 1/98)

7822 Jacques, Brian. *Lord Brocktree* (5–8). 2000, Putnam $22.95 (0-399-23590-6). 320pp. In this installment of the Redwall saga, the villainous Ungatt Trunn and his Blue Hordes invade and capture the mountain fortress Salamandastron. (Rev: BCCB 9/00; BL 9/1/00; HB 9–10/00; HBG 3/01; SLJ 9/00)

7823 Jacques, Brian. *Mariel of Redwall* (5–7). Illus. by Gary Chalk. 1992, Putnam $22.99 (0-399-22144-1). 400pp. Fourth in the saga of the animals of Redwall Abbey, this story tells how the great Joseph Bell is brought to the abbey. (Rev: BCCB 3/92; BL 1/15/92*; HB 9–10/92; SLJ 3/92)

7824 Jacques, Brian. *Marlfox* (5–8). Illus. 1999, Putnam $22.99 (0-399-23307-5). 400pp. The famous tapestry depicting Martin and Warrior has been stolen from Redwall Abbey, and four young would-be heroes set out to recover it. (Rev: BL 12/15/98; HB 1–2/99; HBG 10/99; SLJ 4/99)

7825 Jacques, Brian. *Martin the Warrior* (5–7). Illus. by Gary Chalk. Series: Redwall. 1994, Putnam $22.99 (0-399-22670-2). 375pp. This Redwall book tells how the mouse Martin the Warrior became the bold, courageous fighter that he is. (Rev: BCCB 1/94; BL 3/1/94; HB 9–10/94; SLJ 1/94)

7826 Jacques, Brian. *Mattimeo* (4–6). 1990, Putnam $22.99 (0-399-21741-X). 448pp. The son of Matthias, the hero of Redwall, overcomes the treachery of Slager, a sly fox. (Rev: BCCB 4/90; BL 4/15/90; SLJ 9/90)

7827 Jacques, Brian. *Mossflower* (5–7). Illus. by Gary Chalk. 1988, Putnam $22.99 (0-399-21549-2); Avon paper $5.99 (0-380-70828-0). 432pp. How a brave and resourceful mouse took power from the evil wildcat. (Rev: BCCB 12/88; BL 11/1/88; SLJ 11/88)

7828 Jacques, Brian. *Outcast of Redwall* (5–7). Illus. by Allan Curless. 1996, Putnam $22.99 (0-399-22914-0). 360pp. This episode in the Redwall saga involves the badger Sunflash the Mace and his enemy, the ferret Swartt Sixclaw. (Rev: BCCB 3/96; BL 3/1/96; SLJ 5/96)

7829 Jacques, Brian. *The Pearls of Lutra* (5–8). 1997, Putnam $22.99 (0-399-22946-9). 408pp. The evil marten Mad Eyes threatens the peaceful Red-wall Abbey in this book, the ninth in the series. (Rev: BCCB 4/97; BL 2/15/97; SLJ 3/97*)

7830 Jacques, Brian. *Salamandastron* (5–7). Illus. by Gary Chalk. 1993, Putnam $22.99 (0-399-21992-7). 400pp. Tales centered on the badgers and hares of the castle of Salamandastron near the sea. (Rev: BCCB 7–8/93; BL 3/15/93; HB 5–6/93; SLJ 3/93)

7831 Jacques, Brian. *Seven Strange and Ghostly Tales* (4–7). 1991, Putnam $15.99 (0-399-22103-4); Avon paper $3.99 (0-380-71906-1). 137pp. Seven genuinely scary stories with touches of humor. (Rev: BCCB 12/91; BL 1/1/91*; HB 5–6/92; SLJ 12/91)

7832 James, Mary. *Shoebag* (3–7). 1990, Scholastic $13.95 (0-590-43029-7); paper $3.99 (0-590-43030-0). 144pp. Shoebag, a cockroach named after his place of birth, turns into a boy. (Rev: BCCB 3/90; BL 4/15/90; SLJ 6/90*)

7833 James, Mary. *The Shuteyes* (4–7). 1994, Scholastic paper $3.25 (0-590-45070-0). 176pp. Chester has some unusual experiences when he journeys to Alert, a land where no one sleeps. (Rev: SLJ 4/93)

7834 Jane, Pamela. *Noelle of the Nutcracker* (3–5). Illus. by Jan Brett. 1997, Houghton $17.00 (0-395-39969-6); Bantam paper $3.99 (0-440-41418-0). 64pp. Ilyana wants Noelle the ballerina doll, but her rich arch rival Mary Jane is bound to get her. (Rev: BCCB 10/86; BL 9/15/86)

7835 Jarrell, Randall. *The Bat-Poet* (3–6). Illus. by Maurice Sendak. 1997, HarperCollins $13.95 (0-06-205084-2); paper $6.95 (0-06-205905-X). 44pp. A little-known bat makes up poems during the day to recite to his fellows.

7836 Jarvis, Robin. *The Dark Portal: Book One of The Deptford Mice* (5–8). 2000, North-South $17.95 (1-58717-021-3). 240pp. In this tale of horror, valor, and adventure, Albert, one of the mice living in an old, empty house in Deptford, London, must leave his household and enter the slimy sewers inhabited by deadly rats. (Rev: BL 10/15/00; HBG 3/01; SLJ 12/00)

7837 Jennings, Patrick. *Faith and the Electric Dogs* (3–6). Illus. 1996, Scholastic $15.95 (0-590-69768-4). 128pp. Unhappy in Mexico and longing for the United States, Faith gets some comfort from a very unusual dog. (Rev: BCCB 1/97; BL 12/1/96*; SLJ 12/96)

7838 Jennings, Patrick. *Faith and the Rocket Cat* (4–6). 1998, Scholastic $15.95 (0-590-11004-7). 232pp. Faith and her dog Eddie, who can read and write in several languages, move from Mexico to San Francisco where they take an exciting rocket trip. (Rev: BL 9/15/98; HBG 3/99; SLJ 9/98)

7839 Jennings, Richard W. *Orwell's Luck* (4–7). 2000, Houghton $15.00 (0-618-03628-8). 146pp. After a 12-year-old girl saves a rabbit's life she begins receiving coded messages from him that change her life. (Rev: BCCB 11/00; BL 10/15/00*; HB 9–10/00; HBG 3/01; SLJ 10/00)

7840 Jensen, Dorothea. *The Riddle of Penncroft Farm* (5–7). 1989, Harcourt $21.00 (0-15-200574-

9). 192pp. Lars finds a ghost from the American Revolution when his family moves to rural Pennsylvania near Valley Forge. (Rev: BCCB 11/89; BL 10/1/89; SLJ 10/89)

7841 Jeppson, Ann-Sofie. *Here Comes Pontus!* (2–4). Trans. from Swedish by Frances Corry. Illus. by Catarina Kruusval. 2000, R&S $14.00 (91-29-64561-1). 29pp. A 3-year-old pony adjusts to its new home and has experiences like escaping from its stall, being in a barn fire, making friends with a cat, and meeting his brother. (Rev: BCCB 7–8/00; HBG 10/00; SLJ 7/00)

7842 Jocelyn, Marthe. *Invisible Day* (3–5). Illus. 1997, Dutton $14.99 (0-525-45908-1). 128pp. In Manhattan, a young girl uses a magic makeup kit that makes her invisible to get the privacy she longs for. (Rev: BL 1/1–15/98; HBG 10/98; SLJ 3/98)

7843 Jocelyn, Marthe. *The Invisible Harry* (3–5). Illus. 1998, Dutton $14.99 (0-525-46078-0). 144pp. Jodie, who can make things disappear, helps fifth-grader Billie who wants to adopt a puppy, by making the dog temporarily vanish. (Rev: BL 11/15/98; HBG 3/99; SLJ 12/98)

7844 Johansen, Hanna. *Dinosaur with an Attitude* (4–6). Trans. by Elisabetta Maccari. Illus. 1994, RDR Bks. $12.95 (1-57143-018-0). 144pp. In this fantasy, a boy faces problems caused by a dinosaur that hatched from one of his Easter eggs. (Rev: BL 8/94; SLJ 8/94)

7845 Johnson, Annabel. *I Am Leaper* (3–5). Illus. by Stella Ormai. 1992, Scholastic paper $2.99 (0-590-43399-7). 128pp. A talking kangaroo mouse leaves her burrow to warn humans that a monster is destroying the desert. (Rev: BL 11/15/90; SLJ 1/91)

7846 Johnson, Charles. *Pieces of Eight* (5–7). Illus. by Jennie Anne Nelson. 1989, Discovery $9.95 (0-944770-00-2). 110pp. David and Mitchell rouse a sea captain's ghost and get to meet Blackbeard the pirate. (Rev: BL 3/15/89)

7847 Jones, Diana Wynne. *Charmed Life* (4–6). 1998, Morrow paper $5.95 (0-688-15546-4). 224pp. Gwendole tries to obtain supernatural powers from her mysterious guardian. A sequel is: *Witch Week* (1988).

7848 Joyce, William. *George Shrinks* (4–6). Illus. by author. 1985, HarperCollins LB $14.89 (0-06-023071-1); paper $5.95 (0-06-443129-0). 32pp. George wakes up to find he is small and must learn to cope with some strange situations. (Rev: BCCB 12/85; BL 1/15/86; SLJ 10/85)

7849 Juster, Norton. *The Phantom Tollbooth* (4–6). Illus. by Jules Feiffer. 1972, Knopf $19.95 (0-394-81500-9); paper $5.50 (0-394-82037-1). 256pp. When Milo receives a tollbooth as a gift, he finds that it admits him to a land where many adventures take place. A favorite fantasy.

7850 Kalman, Maira. *Swami on Rye: Max in India* (4–8). Illus. 1995, Viking $14.99 (0-670-84646-0). 40pp. A sophisticated comic novel about a dog who goes to India to find the meaning of life. (Rev: BL 10/15/95; SLJ 11/95)

7851 Karon, Jan. *Jeremy: The Tale of an Honest Bunny* (3–5). Illus. 2000, Viking $15.99 (0-670-

88104-X). 82pp. A sweet tale about a toy bunny and his adventures traveling from a small English cottage to his new home in North Carolina. (Rev: BL 4/15/00; HBG 10/00; SLJ 9/00)

7852 Kassem, Lou. *A Summer for Secrets* (5–7). 1989, Avon paper $2.95 (0-380-75759-1). 105pp. Laura's ability to communicate with animals causes complications. (Rev: BL 10/1/89)

7853 Keefauver, John. *The Three-Day Traffic Jam* (3–6). 1992, Simon & Schuster paper $13.00 (0-671-75599-4). 89pp. In the near future, when traffic jams around Los Angeles can last for months, Henry gets caught in one with his father's new car. (Rev: SLJ 6/92)

7854 Kehret, Peg. *The Blizzard Disaster* (4–6). 1998, Pocket $14.00 (0-671-00963-X). 138pp. Sixth-graders Warren and Betsy time-travel to 1940 Minnesota to research a terrible blizzard in which they encounter 12-year-old Janis and her beloved horse Pansy. (Rev: BL 7/98; SLJ 8/98)

7855 Kehret, Peg. *The Volcano Disaster* (4–6). Series: Frightmares. 1998, Pocket $14.00 (0-671-00969-9). 136pp. While working on a school assignment on volcanoes, Warren is transported to the 1980 eruption of Mount St. Helens and must rely on his friend Betsy to bring him back alive. (Rev: BL 8/98; SLJ 7/98)

7856 Kelley, Ellen A. *The Lucky Lizard* (3–5). Illus. 2000, Dutton $14.99 (0-525-46142-6). 96pp. Bima, the narrator of this story, is a lizard who gets into lots of trouble but helps third-grader Todd get over his fear of riding a two-wheeler as well as helping him to form a new friendship. (Rev: BL 10/1/00; HBG 3/01; SLJ 10/00)

7857 Kempton, Kate. *The World Beyond the Waves: An Environmental Adventure* (5–7). Illus. 1995, Portunus $14.95 (0-9641330-6-7); paper $8.95 (0-9641330-1-6). 88pp. After being washed overboard during a violent storm, Sam visits a land where she meets ocean animals that have been misused by humans. (Rev: BL 4/15/95; SLJ 3/95)

7858 Kendall, Carol. *The Gammage Cup* (4–7). Illus. by Erik Blegvad. 1990, Harcourt paper $6.00 (0-15-230575-0). 283pp. Fantasy of the Minnipins, a small people of the "land between the mountains."

7859 Kennedy, Richard. *Amy's Eyes* (5–6). Illus. by Richard Egielski. 1985, HarperCollins $15.00 (0-06-023219-6). 448pp. Amy's doll, Captain, comes alive and runs away to sea. Before he returns, Amy herself changes into a doll, and the Captain takes her with him for a journey of high adventure. (Rev: BCCB 4/85; BL 5/1/85; SLJ 5/85)

7860 Kennedy, X. J. *The Eagle as Wide as the World* (3–6). 1997, Simon & Schuster $16.00 (0-689-81157-8). 173pp. A young boy is kidnapped by giant honeybees and taken to April Fool Isle, home of Meadea, queen of the bees. (Rev: SLJ 12/97)

7861 Kimmel, Elizabeth C. *In the Stone Circle* (4–8). 1998, Scholastic $15.95 (0-590-21308-3). 160pp. When 14-year-old Cris leaves Ohio to spend a summer in Wales with her historian father, she becomes involved with a number of hauntings, including encounters with a ghostly girl related to a 13th-century Welsh ruler. (Rev: BCCB 3/98; BL 4/15/98; HBG 10/98; SLJ 4/98)

7862 Kimmel, Eric A. *Website of the Warped Wizard* (4–6). Illus. by Jeff Shelly. 2001, Dutton $14.99 (0-525-46656-8). 128pp. Through their new computer game, Jessica and friend Matt enter a different world where they meet Sir Lancelot, Merlin, and King Arthur, and confront an unknown dictator. (Rev: BCCB 3/01; SLJ 3/01)

7863 King-Smith, Dick. *Animal Stories* (3–5). Illus. 1998, Orchard $18.95 (0-531-30099-4). 128pp. A collection of animal stories, including an excerpt from *Babe: the Gallant Pig* and a story involving Max, the heroic hedgehog. (Rev: BL 9/1/98; HBG 3/99; SLJ 11/98)

7864 King-Smith, Dick. *Charlie Muffin's Miracle Mouse* (3–5). Illus. 1999, Crown LB $17.99 (0-517-80034-9). 112pp. Because his girlfriend says she will marry him if he creates a green mouse, Charlie Muffin, a mouse breeder, does the impossible in the name of love. (Rev: BL 4/15/99; HBG 10/99; SLJ 6/99)

7865 King-Smith, Dick. *Hogsel and Gruntel and Other Animal Stories* (3–4). Illus. 1999, Orchard $18.95 (0-531-30208-3). 128pp. A collection of 15 amusing and exciting imaginary animal tales. (Rev: BL 11/1/99; HBG 3/00; SLJ 10/99)

7866 King-Smith, Dick. *A Mouse Called Wolf* (2–4). Illus. 1997, Crown $16.00 (0-517-70973-2). 98pp. Mary Mouse is convinced that her son, whom she has named Wolfgang Amadeus, is a musical genius. (Rev: BL 10/1/97; HBG 3/98; SLJ 12/97)

7867 King-Smith, Dick. *Pigs Might Fly* (3–5). Illus. by Mary Rayner. 1990, Puffin paper $4.99 (0-14-034537-X). 168pp. A pig named Daggie Dogfoot saves the day because he can swim.

7868 King-Smith, Dick. *The Roundhill* (5–7). Illus. 2000, Crown LB $17.99 (0-517-80048-9). 96pp. In the English countryside in 1936, 14-year-old Evan meets a mysterious girl who seems to be the Alice of *Alice in Wonderland*. (Rev: BL 1/1–15/01; HBG 3/01; SLJ 12/00)

7869 King-Smith, Dick. *The School Mouse* (3–5). Illus. 1995, Hyperion LB $14.49 (0-7868-2029-2). 124pp. Flora's ability to read saves her illiterate mouse parents from eating poison that has been placed around the school where they live. (Rev: BCCB 1/96; BL 10/15/95; SLJ 12/95*)

7870 King-Smith, Dick. *The Water Horse* (3–5). Illus. 1998, Crown LB $17.99 (0-517-80027-6). 108pp. When the egg that Kirstie finds on the beach hatches into a water horse of Scottish legend, the family decides that a good home for the creature would be Loch Ness. (Rev: BL 9/15/98; HB 11–12/98; HBG 3/99; SLJ 10/98)

7871 Kinsey-Warnock, Natalie. *As Long As There Are Mountains* (5–8). 1997, Dutton $14.99 (0-525-65236-1). 144pp. When her father is injured, Iris, age 13, wants to retain the family farm, but her older brother wants to sell it. (Rev: BL 8/97; HBG 3/98; SLJ 8/97*)

7872 Kipling, Rudyard. *Rikki-Tikki-Tavi* (3–5). Illus. by Jerry Pinkney. 1997, Morrow $15.93 (0-688-

14321-0). 40pp. In this classic tale, a mongoose repays a debt of kindness after he has been saved from drowning. (Rev: BL 9/1/97*; HBG 3/98; SLJ 8/97*)

7873 Kline, Suzy. *Horrible Harry and the Purple People* (2–4). Illus. by Frank Remkiewicz. 1997, Viking $13.99 (0-670-87035-8). 64pp. Harry maintains that there are invisible purple people in the classroom and plans to invite one to a class tea party to prove it. (Rev: HBG 3/98; SLJ 9/97)

7874 Koller, Jackie F. *Dragon Quest* (3–5). Illus. 1997, Pocket paper $3.50 (0-671-00193-0). 87pp. Darek's jealousy leads to a dragon hunt in this sequel to *The Dragonling* (1991) and *A Dragon in the Family* (1993). (Rev: BL 3/1/97)

7875 Koller, Jackie F. *The Dragonling* (2–4). Illus. by Judith Mitchell. 1995, Pocket paper $3.99 (0-671-86790-3). 64pp. Darek befriends a young dragon that has been orphaned. (Rev: BL 1/1/91; SLJ 2/91)

7876 Koller, Jackie F. *If I Had One Wish . . .* (5–8). 1991, Little, Brown $14.95 (0-316-50150-6). 161pp. Alex wishes that his pesky young brother had never been born; to his amazement, his wish is granted. (Rev: BCCB 12/91; SLJ 11/91)

7877 Kortum, Jeanie. *Ghost Vision* (5–8). Illus. by Dugald Stermer. n.d., Scholastic paper $3.50 (0-614-19197-1). 160pp. A Greenland Inuit realizes that his son has special mystical powers.

7878 Kraan, Hanna. *Flowers for the Wicked Witch* (3–5). Trans. by Wanda Boeke. Illus. Series: Wicked Witch. 1998, Front Street $15.95 (1-886910-35-9). 128pp. A collection of charming stories about the relationship between a wicked witch and different forest animals, including a hare, a hedgehog, and an owl. (Rev: BL 11/15/98; HBG 10/99; SLJ 2/99)

7879 Kraan, Hanna. *Tales of the Wicked Witch* (3–5). Illus. by Annemarie van Haeringen. 1995, Front Street $14.95 (1-886910-04-9). 128pp. Fourteen short stories about several forest creatures who have problems with the resident witch. (Rev: BL 1/1–15/96; SLJ 1/96)

7880 Kraan, Hanna. *The Wicked Witch Is at It Again* (3–5). Trans. by Wanda Boeke. Illus. 1997, Front Street $14.95 (1-886910-18-9). 128pp. Fourteen brief stories about the relationship between a wicked witch and the forest animals that live nearby. (Rev: BL 9/15/97; SLJ 7/97*)

7881 Krensky, Stephen. *Arthur and the Big Blow-Up* (2–4). Illus. 2000, Little, Brown $12.95 (0-316-12129-0); paper $3.95 (0-316-12203-3). 64pp. A quarrel between Francine and the Brain threatens the future of their soccer team, so Arthur intervenes to reconcile the two. (Rev: BL 6/1–15/00; HBG 10/00)

7882 Kretzer-Malvehy, Terry. *Passage to Little Bighorn* (5–8). 1999, Rising Moon paper $6.95 (0-87358-713-8). 217pp. A biracial boy with Caucasian and Native American parents is visiting the site of the Battle of Little Bighorn when he is suddenly transported back in time to the 1870s and the events that surround the battle. (Rev: HBG 10/99; SLJ 6/99)

7883 Labatt, Mary. *Aliens in Woodford* (2–4). Illus. by Troy Hill-Jackson. 2000, Kids Can $12.95 (1-55074-611-1); paper $4.95 (1-55074-607-3). 110pp. Sam, a sheepdog, and her master, Jennie, who can understand the dog's thoughts, solve the mystery of strange nighttime activities at an abandoned airfield. (Rev: HBG 3/01; SLJ 12/00)

7884 Labatt, Mary. *Strange Neighbors* (2–4). 2000, Kids Can $12.95 (1-55074-605-7); paper $4.95 (1-55074-603-0). 116pp. Sam, the talking sheepdog who can only be understood by Jennie, is convinced that the three old ladies who have moved to their neighborhood are witches. (Rev: BL 5/1/00; HBG 10/00; SLJ 9/00)

7885 Lally, Soinbhe. *A Hive for the Honeybee* (5–8). Illus. by Patience Brewster. 1999, Scholastic $16.95 (0-590-51038-X). 224pp. This clever, thought-provoking fantasy is set in a beehive and explores the life and roles of several workers and drones. (Rev: HB 3–4/99; HBG 10/99; SLJ 5/99*)

7886 Langton, Jane. *The Fledgling* (5–7). 1980, HarperCollins LB $15.89 (0-06-023679-5); paper $5.95 (0-06-440121-9). 192pp. A young girl learns to fly with her Goose Prince. A sequel is: *The Fragile Flag* (1984). Also use: *The Diamond in the Window* (1962).

7887 Langton, Jane. *The Time Bike* (4–6). 2000, HarperCollins LB $15.89 (0-06-028438-2). 176pp. Eddy Hall and his older sister Eleanor time-travel and experience great adventure on their magic bicycle. (Rev: BCCB 7–8/00; HBG 10/00; SLJ 6/00)

7888 Lansky, Bruce, ed. *Newfangled Fairy Tales, Book 1* (3–5). 1998, Meadowbrook Pr. LB $3.95 (0-671-57704-2). 110pp. These fractured fairy tales involve such characters as a backpacking Sleeping Beauty and King Midas as a workaholic banker. (Rev: BL 3/1/98)

7889 Lasky, Kathryn. *Double Trouble Squared* (5–7). 1991, Harcourt paper $8.00 (0-15-224127-2). 232pp. The first in a series concerning the lively Starbuck family, with youngsters who can read one another's minds. (Rev: BCCB 2/92; BL 1/15/92; SLJ 2/92)

7890 Lasky, Kathryn. *Shadows in the Water: A Starbuck Family Adventure* (4–6). 1992, Harcourt paper $8.00 (0-15-273534-8). 192pp. The Starbucks in a new adventure, this time investigating toxic waste dumping in the Florida Keys. (Rev: BL 1/15/93; SLJ 1/93)

7891 Lassig, Jurgen. *Spiny* (2–4). Trans. by J. Alison James. Illus. 1995, North-South LB $13.88 (1-55858-402-1). 58pp. A young dinosaur's baby-sitter saves him from being eaten by the dreaded tyrannosaurus. (Rev: BL 5/1/95; SLJ 6/95)

7892 Lauber, Patricia. *Purrfectly Purrfect: Life at the Acatemy* (3–6). Illus. by Betsy Lewin. 2000, HarperCollins LB $15.89 (0-06-029209-1). 78pp. A witty, well-illustrated story about cats who attend a school, the Acatemy, where they learn to be "purrfect" by studying the "purriculum." (Rev: BCCB 12/00; HBG 3/01; SLJ 12/00)

7893 Lawrence, Michael. *The Poppykettle Papers* (5–9). Illus. by Robert Ingpen. 2000, Pavilion $22.95 (1-86205-282-4). 120pp. Two boys discover an ancient manuscript that tells of an adventure-filled voyage taken by five tiny people in a poppykettle, a vessel used to make tea for the gods. (Rev: SLJ 3/00)

7894 Lawson, Robert. *The Fabulous Flight* (4–6). Illus. by author. 1984, Little, Brown paper $5.95 (0-316-51731-3). 152pp. Peter becomes so small he can take a trip via a pet seagull.

7895 Lawson, Robert. *Rabbit Hill* (4–7). Illus. by author. 1944, Puffin paper $4.99 (0-14-031010-X). 128pp. The small creatures of a Connecticut countryside — each with a distinct personality — create a warm and humorous story. Newbery Award winner, 1945.

7896 Layefsky, Virginia. *Impossible Things* (5–8). 1998, Marshall Cavendish $14.95 (0-7614-5038-6). 207pp. Twelve-year-old Brady has several personal and family problems to solve along with taking care of the dragonlike creature that he is hiding. (Rev: HBG 3/99; SLJ 11/98)

7897 Lee, Tanith. *Islands in the Sky* (4–7). Series: Voyage of the Basset. 1999, Random paper $3.99 (0-679-89127-7). 249pp. In this fantasy a boy and a girl are transported from Victorian England to a land where mythological beasts, gods, and people come to life. (Rev: SLJ 1/00)

7898 Lee, Tanith. *Wolf Tower* (5–8). 2000, Dutton $15.99 (0-525-46394-1). 240pp. In this adventure-filled fantasy, a 16-year-old slave girl is chosen to rescue a young man captured when his hot-air balloon is shot down. (Rev: BL 4/15/00; HBG 10/00)

7899 Le Guin, Ursula K. *Catwings* (2–4). Illus. by S. D. Schindler. 1998, Orchard $14.95 (0-531-05759-3); Scholastic paper $2.95 (0-590-46072-2). 48pp. Four kittens are born with wings into a city neighborhood, but their mother urges them to strike out on their own for safety. Also use *Catwings Return* (1989). (Rev: BCCB 9/88; BL 8/88; HB 11–12/88)

7900 Le Guin, Ursula K. *Jane on Her Own* (2–4). Illus. Series: Catwings. 1999, Orchard LB $15.99 (0-531-33133-4). 48pp. This fourth installment of the Catwings series features Jane, one of the winged cats, and her experiences when she leaves home to find adventure and friends. (Rev: BCCB 7–8/99; BL 2/1/99; HBG 10/99; SLJ 4/99)

7901 Le Guin, Ursula K. *Wonderful Alexander and the Catwings* (2–4). Illus. Series: Catwings. 1994, Orchard LB $15.99 (0-531-08701-8). 48pp. Alexander the kitten helps Jane — one of the flying cats called Catwings — regain her power of speech. (Rev: BL 9/15/94; SLJ 9/94)

7902 Lehr, Norma. *Dance of the Crystal Skull* (4–6). 1999, Northland paper $6.95 (0-87358-725-1). 160pp. When 11-year-old Cathy is sent to spend a summer with family friend Concha, she meets some interesting Western characters, including several contemporary Native Americans, and encounters mysterious sightings of a crystal skull relic. (Rev: BL 6/1–15/99; HBG 10/99; SLJ 8/99)

7903 Lehr, Norma. *Haunting at Black Water Cove* (4–6). 2000, Rising Moon paper $6.95 (0-87358-750-2). 119pp. Through the help of a ghost, Kathy Wicklow solves a mystery concerning a local girl who was thought to have drowned in 1906. (Rev: BCCB 6/00; SLJ 7/00)

7904 Lennon, Joan. *There's a Kangaroo in My Soup!* (2–3). Illus. by Wendy Rasmussen. 2000, Front Street $15.95 (0-8126-2898-5). 128pp. Gloria, a runaway circus kangaroo, brings young Kevin out of his shell in this beginning chapter book fantasy. (Rev: SLJ 12/00)

7905 Leroe, E. W. *Monster Vision* (4–7). Series: Friendly Corners. 1996, Hyperion paper $3.95 (0-7868-1095-5). 125pp. Ghosts of people killed when a meteorite struck at Friendly Corners return to haunt the residents. Others in this series are *Nasty the Snowman*, *Pizza Zombies*, and *Hairy Horror* (all 1966). (Rev: SLJ 5/97)

7906 Leroe, Ellen. *Ghost Dog* (3–5). Illus. by Bill Basso. 1993, Hyperion $12.95 (1-56282-268-3). 64pp. On a visit to his grandfather's, Artie encounters a ghost dog, and together they foil a thief intent on stealing a valuable baseball card. (Rev: BL 4/1/93; SLJ 6/93)

7907 Leroe, Ellen. *H.O.W.L. High* (4–7). 1991, Pocket paper $2.95 (0-671-68568-6). 132pp. His classmates at H.O.W.L. Junior High do not realize that Drac is really a warlock. (Rev: SLJ 1/92)

7908 Levin, Betty. *The Banished* (5–8). 1999, Greenwillow $16.00 (0-688-16602-4). 160pp. In this engaging prequel to *The Ice Bear,* Siri must make a dangerous sea journey to deliver an ice bear to her people's king. (Rev: BL 8/99; HB 11–12/99; HBG 3/00; SLJ 10/99)

7909 Levine, Gail C. *The Wish* (4–7). 2000, HarperCollins LB $15.89 (0-06-027901-X). 208pp. When a kindly old lady grants Wilma's wish to become popular at school, the girl forgets that she is graduating in only three weeks. (Rev: BCCB 5/00; BL 4/1/00; HBG 10/00; SLJ 5/00)

7910 Lewis, C. S. *The Lion, the Witch and the Wardrobe* (3–5). Illus. by Robin Lawrie. 1995, HarperCollins paper $11.95 (0-06-443399-4). 64pp. Using an elegant comic book format, the first of the Narnia books is abridged for young readers. (Rev: BCCB 6/95; SLJ 8/95)

7911 Lewis, C. S. *The Lion, the Witch and the Wardrobe: A Story for Children* (4–7). Illus. by Pauline Baynes. 1988, Macmillan paper $7.95 (0-02-044490-7). 160pp. A beautifully written modern tale of the adventures of four children who go into the magical land of Narnia. A special edition with illustrations by Michael Hague was published in 1983. Some sequels are: *The Silver Chair; The Last Battle; Prince Caspian; The Voyage of the "Dawn Treader"; The Magician's Nephew* (all 1969); *The Horse and His Boy* (1986).

7912 Lindbergh, Anne. *Bailey's Window* (3–6). Illus. by Kinuko Craft. 1984, Harcourt $14.95 (0-15-205642-4); Avon paper $3.50 (0-380-70767-5). 115pp. A young boy paints a scene into which he enters.

7913 Lindbergh, Anne. *The Hunky-Dory Dairy* (5–7). Illus. by Julie Brinckloe. 1986, Harcourt $14.95 (0-15-237449-3); Dell paper $2.75 (0-380-70320-3). 147pp. Zannah visits a community magically removed from the 20th century and enjoys introducing the people to bubble gum, tacos, and other "modern" things. (Rev: BCCB 9/86; BL 4/1/86; SLJ 8/86)

7914 Lindbergh, Anne. *The People in Pineapple Place* (4–6). 1982, Harcourt $14.95 (0-15-260517-7); Avon paper $2.95 (0-380-70766-7). 153pp. August Brown is still adjusting to his parents' divorce when he meets some people only he can see.

7915 Lindbergh, Anne. *The Prisoner of Pineapple Place* (5–7). 1988, Harcourt $13.95 (0-15-263559-9); Avon paper $2.95 (0-380-70765-9). 173pp. Pineapple Place is invisible to everyone except the inhabitants, and somehow finds itself landing in Connecticut. (Rev: BL 7/88; SLJ 8/88)

7916 Lindbergh, Anne. *Three Lives to Live* (5–8). 1995, Pocket paper $3.50 (0-671-86732-6). 183pp. Garet is visited by Daisy, who is really her grandmother of 50 years before. (Rev: SLJ 6/92)

7917 Lindgren, Astrid. *Ronia, the Robber's Daughter* (4–7). 1985, Puffin paper $4.99 (0-14-031720-1). 176pp. Ronia becomes friendly with the son of her father's rival in this fantasy.

7918 Lindsay, Janice. *The Milly Stories: Corpses, Carnations, the Weirdness Index, and, of Course, Aunt Gloria* (4–6). 1998, DK $15.95 (0-7894-2491-6). 131pp. Milly, an orphan who lives with her undertaker uncle, helps a ghost find peace and forms a close friendship with a girl in her writing class, both with the help of advice from her dead aunt. (Rev: BCCB 5/98; BL 4/1/98; HBG 10/98; SLJ 4/98)

7919 Lisle, Janet T. *Afternoon of the Elves* (4–6). 1989, Orchard LB $16.99 (0-531-08437-X). 128pp. Hilary discovers that the strange girl named Sara-Kate has a garden inhabited by elves. (Rev: BCCB 10/89; BL 8/89*; HB 9–10/89; SLJ 9/89*)

7920 Lisle, Janet T. *The Gold Dust Letters* (4–6). 1994, Orchard LB $16.99 (0-531-08680-1). 128pp. Angela's father fools her into believing that she is receiving messages from a fairy in an effort to effect a reconciliation. (Rev: BCCB 7–8/94; BL 2/1/94; SLJ 4/94)

7921 Lisle, Janet T. *The Lampfish of Twill* (4–8). Illus. by Wendy A. Halperin. 1991, Orchard $16.95 (0-531-05963-4). 176pp. Orphaned Eric faces forces of danger as he lives in the mysterious country of Twill. (Rev: BCCB 10/91; HB 1–2/92; SLJ 9/91*)

7922 Lisle, Janet T. *Looking for Juliette* (4–6). 1994, Orchard LB $16.99 (0-531-08720-4). 128pp. Georgina and her friend Poco believe that the strange Miss Bone is responsible for running down their cat Juliette. (Rev: BCCB 12/94; BL 9/15/94; SLJ 8/94*)

7923 Lisle, Janet T. *The Lost Flower Children* (4–6). Illus. 1999, Putnam $16.99 (0-399-23393-8). 112pp. Youngsters Olivia and Nellie discover a storybook in which children are turned into flowers

and must find a way to break the spell. (Rev: BCCB 7–8/99; BL 5/15/99; HB 5–6/99; HBG 10/99; SLJ 6/99)

7924 Loehr, Mallory. *Water Wishes* (2–5). 1999, Random LB $11.99 (0-679-99216-2); paper $3.99 (0-679-89216-8). 128pp. Sam and his sister,10-year-old Polly, quarrel with their older brother over the possession of a green bottle that can grant wishes. (Rev: BL 6/1–15/99; HBG 10/99; SLJ 7/99)

7925 Lofting, Hugh. *The Story of Doctor Dolittle* (3–6). Illus. by author. 1996, Dover paper $1.00 (0-486-29350-5). 144pp. Reissue of the 1970 edition, reedited to remove racially offensive passages. Also use the similarly edited 1923 Newbery Medal winner *The Voyages of Doctor Dolittle* (1988, Dell). (Rev: BL 7/88)

7926 Lowry, Lois. *Gathering Blue* (5–9). 2000, Houghton $15.00 (0-618-05581-9). 224pp. In an inhospitable future world, young Kira must use her courage and her artistic talents. (Rev: BL 6/1–15/00*; HB 9–10/00; HBG 3/01; SLJ 8/00*)

7927 Lowry, Lois. *Stay! Keeper's Story* (5–8). Illus. 1997, Houghton $15.00 (0-395-87048-8). 128pp. A dog named Keeper narrates this story about his puppyhood and the three different masters he has had. (Rev: BL 11/1/97; HBG 3/98; SLJ 10/97)

7928 Lubar, David. *Hidden Talents* (5–8). 1999, Tor $26.95 (0-312-86646-1). 224pp. Five misfits, who are attending the last-resort Edgeview Alternative School, become friends and discover extrasensory talents they can use against the school bully. (Rev: BL 9/15/99; HBG 10/99)

7929 Lytle, Robert A. *Three Rivers Crossing* (5–8). 2000, River Road $15.95 (0-938682-55-5). 208pp. After he suffers an accident while fishing, seventh-grader Walker wakes to find he is in the 1820s village of his ancestors. (Rev: BL 5/15/00)

7930 Macaulay, David. *BAAA* (5–7). Illus. by author. 1985, Houghton $13.95 (0-395-38948-8); paper $5.95 (0-395-39588-7). 64pp. A sophisticated fantasy about a world inhabited by humanlike sheep. (Rev: SLJ 10/85)

7931 McCaughrean, Geraldine. *A Pack of Lies* (5–7). 1990, Macmillan $16.95 (0-7451-1154-8). 168pp. Stories told by mysterious M.C.C. Berkshire, who wanders into an antique store run by adolescent Ailsa and her mother. (Rev: BCCB 5/89)

7932 McCaughrean, Geraldine. *The Stones Are Hatching* (5–8). 2000, HarperCollins LB $15.89 (0-06-028766-7). 230pp. Eleven-year-old Phelim Green begins a quest with strange friends to kill the Stoor Worm and thus save the world. (Rev: HB 7–8/00; HBG 10/00; SLJ 6/00)

7933 McCusker, Paul. *Arin's Judgment* (5–8). 1999, Tommy Nelson paper $6.99 (1-56179-774-X). 180pp. In 1945, while awaiting word about his father who is missing in action, Wade is transported to another world where his knowledge of World War II places him at risk. (Rev: SLJ 4/00)

7934 MacDonald, Betty. *Hello, Mrs. Piggle-Wiggle* (3–5). Illus. by Hilary Knight. 1957, HarperCollins $15.95 (0-397-31715-8); paper $4.95 (0-06-440149-9). 132pp. Introducing the lady who loves all children, good or bad. Further adventures are: *Mrs. Piggle-Wiggle's Farm* (1954); *Mrs. Piggle-Wiggle* (1957); *Mrs. Piggle-Wiggle's Magic* (1957).

7935 MacDonald, George. *At the Back of the North Wind* (4–7). Illus. by Jessie Willcox Smith. 1989, Morrow $22.00 (0-688-07808-7). 352pp. A facsimile edition of the 1919 printing of this classic fantasy.

7936 McDonald, Megan. *The Bone Keeper* (3–5). Illus. by G. Brian Karas. 1999, DK $16.95 (0-7894-2559-9). 32pp. A fantasy in which a woman collects bones and, in her cave, assembles them into a wolf's skeleton that comes to life. (Rev: BCCB 3/99; BL 4/15/99; HBG 10/99; SLJ 5/99)

7937 McFarland, Lyn Rossiter. *The Pirate's Parrot* (2–4). Illus. 2000, Tricycle Pr. $14.95 (1-58246-014-0). 40pp. Near-blind pirate Captain Cur mistakes a bear for his new parrot in this farcical sea story. (Rev: BL 5/15/00; HBG 10/00; SLJ 5/00)

7938 McGraw, Eloise. *The Moorchild* (4–6). 1996, Simon & Schuster LB $17.00 (0-689-80654-X). 242pp. Set in the Middle Ages, this fantasy tells of Moql, who is born half human and half fairy, and her difficulties fitting into either world. (Rev: BCCB 6/96; BL 3/1/96*; HB 9–10/96; SLJ 4/96*)

7939 McKay, Hilary. *The Amber Cat* (4–6). 1997, Simon & Schuster $15.00 (0-689-81360-0). 114pp. The supernatural is evoked in this story in which a mother tells about her childhood experiences and the mysterious girl named Harriet who would join her and her brothers from time to time. (Rev: BL 11/15/97*; HB 11–12/97; SLJ 11/97*)

7940 McKean, Thomas. *The Secret of the Seven Willows* (4–6). 1991, Simon & Schuster paper $12.95 (0-671-72997-7). 160pp. Tad uses a magic ring to travel back in time to find out his family's past. (Rev: SLJ 10/91)

7941 McKelvey, Douglas Kaine. *The Angel Knew Papa and the Dog* (3–5). 1996, Putnam $14.95 (0-399-23042-4). 96pp. An angel helps rescue Evangeline when she is threatened by rising flood waters. (Rev: BCCB 9/96; BL 9/15/96)

7942 MacLachlan, Patricia. *Tomorrow's Wizard* (3–5). Illus. by Kathryn Jacobi. 1982, HarperCollins LB $13.89 (0-06-024074-1). 96pp. Six short stories about a wizard, an apprentice, and their horse.

7943 McMullan, Kate. *The New Kid at School* (3–6). Illus. 1997, Putnam LB $13.89 (0-448-41727-8); paper $3.99 (0-448-41592-5). 32pp. A clever fantasy about a boy who hates violence and his mission to kill the hated dragon Gorzil. (Rev: BL 12/1/97; HBG 3/98)

7944 Maguire, Gregory. *Four Stupid Cupids* (4–6). Series: Hamlet Chronicles. 2000, Clarion $15.00 (0-395-83895-9). 184pp. A far-fetched comedy about four cupids who are freed when the magical vase that Fawn Petros brings to her Vermont school breaks. (Rev: BL 12/1/00; HBG 3/01; SLJ 10/00)

7945 Maguire, Gregory. *Seven Spiders Spinning* (4–6). Illus. by Dirk Zimmer. 1994, Clarion $15.00 (0-395-68965-1). 144pp. In this farce, seven tarantulas invade a classroom and go on their separate quests. (Rev: BCCB 10/94; BL 9/15/94; SLJ 10/94)

7946 Mahy, Margaret. *The Blood-and-Thunder Adventure on Hurricane Peak* (4–6). Illus. by Wendy Smith. 1989, Macmillan $13.95 (0-689-50488-8). 132pp. Huxley and Zaza find fantastic adventures at Unexpected School on Hurricane Peak. (Rev: BCCB 10/89; BL 10/15/89; HB 11–12/89*; SLJ 10/89)

7947 Mahy, Margaret. *The Five Sisters* (3–5). Illus. 1997, Viking $14.99 (0-670-87042-0). 80pp. Five paper dolls have a series of adventures that reveal their different personalities. (Rev: BCCB 5/97; BL 2/1/97; HB 3–4/97; SLJ 3/97*)

7948 Mahy, Margaret. *The Horribly Haunted School* (3–6). Illus. by Robert Staermose. 1998, Viking $14.99 (0-670-87490-6). 119pp. The ghost of a former principal of Monty's school enlists the boy's help in tracking down some former pupils. (Rev: SLJ 7/98)

7949 Mahy, Margaret. *A Tall Story and Other Tales* (3–5). Illus. by Jan Nesbitt. 1992, Macmillan $15.95 (0-689-50547-7). 96pp. Eleven stories combine witches and monsters and such with everyday life. (Rev: BL 2/1/92; SLJ 3/92)

7950 Marston, Elsa. *The Fox Maiden* (1–5). Illus. by Tatsuro Kiuchi. 1996, Simon & Schuster paper $16.00 (0-689-80107-6). An original fantasy set in ancient Japan about a fox who changes her shape to that of a human. (Rev: SLJ 12/96)

7951 Martin, Ann M., and Laura Godwin. *The Doll People* (3–6). Illus. 2000, Hyperion $15.99 (0-7868-0361-4). 272pp. In this fantasy about dolls that are alive, Annabelle Doll tries to solve the mystery of the disappearance of Aunt Sarah Doll in 1955. (Rev: BCCB 1/01; BL 8/00; HBG 3/01; SLJ 11/00)

7952 Masson, Sophie. *Serafin* (5–8). 2000, Saint Mary's paper $5.50 (0-88489-567-X). 140pp. After he saves Calou from being lynched as a witch, Frederick is forced to flee his 17th-century French village with Calou and soon afterward realizes that the girl is a matagot, a half-angel half-human creature. (Rev: SLJ 8/00)

7953 Matas, Carol, and Perry Nodelman. *Of Two Minds* (5–8). 1995, Simon & Schuster paper $16.00 (0-689-80138-6). 202pp. The adventure of Lenora, a princess with supernatural powers, and Coren, the shy prince who has been chosen to be her husband. (Rev: SLJ 10/95*)

7954 Matas, Carol, and Perry Nodelman. *Out of Their Minds* (5–8). 1998, Simon & Schuster $16.00 (0-689-81946-3). 184pp. In this sequel to *Of Two Minds* and *More Minds* (1996), Princess Lenora and Prince Coren journey to Coren's kingdom where they hope to be married. (Rev: HBG 3/99; SLJ 9/98)

7955 Mather, Karen Trella. *Silas: The Bookstore Cat* (2–4). Illus. by Chris Van Dusen. 1994, Down East $14.95 (0-89272-352-2). 32pp. Silas, the bookstore cat, helps his master find books about his favorite subject, soccer. (Rev: BL 2/1/95; SLJ 3/95)

7956 Mayne, William. *The Book of Hob Stories* (3–5). Illus. by Patrick Benson. 1997, Candlewick $17.99 (0-7636-0390-2). 93pp. This book includes all 20 of the previously published stories about Hob, the helpful household spirit. (Rev: BL 11/1/97; HBG 3/98; SLJ 11/97)

7957 Mayne, William. *Hob and the Goblins* (3–5). Illus. by Norman Messenger. 1994, DK $12.95 (1-56458-713-4). 140pp. Hob, a spirit, must save the family he protects when they move into a house containing an evil force at work. (Rev: BCCB 12/94; BL 11/1/94; SLJ 11/94*)

7958 Mayne, William. *Hob and the Peddler* (3–6). 1997, DK $15.95 (0-7894-2462-2). 128pp. Hob the helpful sprite finds something strange lurking in the pond behind the house where he lives. (Rev: BL 1/1–15/98; HBG 3/98; SLJ 12/97)

7959 Mazer, Anne. *A Sliver of Glass and Other Uncommon Tales* (3–5). 1996, Hyperion LB $14.49 (0-7868-2165-5). 80pp. Eleven intriguing stories of horror and mystery. (Rev: BCCB 11/96; BL 9/15/96; SLJ 2/97)

7960 Medearis, Angela Shelf. *Haunts: Five Hair-Raising Tales* (4–7). Illus. by Trina S. Hyman. 1996, Holiday LB $15.95 (0-8234-1280-6). 37pp. Five stories that contain elements of horror and the supernatural. (Rev: BL 2/1/97; SLJ 4/97)

7961 Meeks, Arone R. *Enora and the Black Crane* (4–6). 1993, Scholastic $14.95 (0-590-46375-6). 32pp. Enora, growing up in a rain forest, spoils the mystical experiences he has had in the wilds by killing a crane. (Rev: BL 10/1/93)

7962 Milne, A. A. *Pooh's Bedtime Book* (PS–3). Illus. by E. H. Shepard. 1980, Dutton $13.99 (0-525-44895-0). 48pp. Excerpts from *When We Were Very Young* and others.

7963 Milne, A. A. *The World of Pooh: The Complete Winnie-the-Pooh; and the House at Pooh Corner* (1–4). Illus. by E. H. Shepard. 1988, Dutton $21.99 (0-525-44447-5). 320pp. A pleasing combination volume.

7964 Monsell, Mary Elise. *Toohy and Wood* (3–5). Illus. 1992, Macmillan $12.95 (0-689-31721-2). 80pp. Toohy the lizard is devastated by the death of Pearl, a musical dove, in this story of a world inhabited by affectionate animals. (Rev: BCCB 12/92; BL 10/1/92; SLJ 10/92)

7965 Montes, Marisa. *Something Wicked's in Those Woods* (4–7). 2000, Harcourt $17.00 (0-15-202391-7). 224pp. Javier is lonely after leaving Puerto Rico and relocating in northern California until he meets the ghost of a boy killed decades ago in an unsolved crime. (Rev: BCCB 10/00; BL 10/15/00)

7966 Moore, Lillian. *Don't Be Afraid, Amanda* (2–5). Illus. by Kathleen G. McCord. 1992, Macmillan $12.95 (0-689-31725-5). 80pp. Amanda Mouse is off to the country to see her pen pal, Adam Mouse. (Rev: BL 6/1/92; HB 7–8/92; SLJ 9/92)

7967 Morgan, Jill. *Blood Brothers* (4–6). 1996, HarperCollins paper $4.50 (0-06-440562-1). 144pp. A fast-paced adventure in which identical twins are turned into vampires. (Rev: BL 12/1/96; SLJ 1/97)

7968 Moroney, Lynn. *Moontellers: Myths of the Moon from Around the World* (3–5). Illus. by Greg Shed. 1995, Northland LB $14.95 (0-87358-601-8). A collection of stories that reflect the attitudes of various cultures — such as the Aztecs and the Chi-

nese — toward the moon, with a final section on modern astronomers. (Rev: SLJ 9/95)

7969 Morris, Gerald. *The Savage Damsel and the Dwarf* (5–8). 2000, Houghton $15.00 (0-395-97126-8). 224pp. Sixteen-year-old Lady Lynet travels to Camelot, in the company of a dwarf, to ask King Arthur's aid in defeating her sister's suitor. (Rev: BL 3/1/00; HB 5–6/00; HBG 10/00)

7970 Morris, Gilbert. *Journey to Freedom* (4–8). 2000, Crossway $14.99 (1-58134-191-1). 256pp. Chip, an ordinary white-foot mouse, is chosen to lead his people against the invasions of warlike brown rats. (Rev: BL 12/15/00)

7971 Morris, Gilbert. *Vanishing Clues* (4–6). Series: Time Navigators. 1996, Bethany paper $5.99 (1-55661-396-2). 138pp. Danny and Dixie Fortune travel back to the time of the French and Indian Wars in this story that emphasizes religious principles. (Rev: BL 10/1/96)

7972 Morrison, Toni, and Slade Morrison. *The Big Box* (2–4). Illus. by Giselle Potter. 1999, Hyperion $19.99 (0-7868-0416-5). 48pp. In this fantasy, three youngsters are imprisoned because their nonconformist thoughts threaten the adult world. (Rev: BCCB 2/00; BL 8/99; HB 9–10/99; HBG 3/00; SLJ 9/99)

7973 Moses, Will. *The Legend of Sleepy Hollow* (3–5). Illus. 1995, Putnam $18.99 (0-399-22687-7). 48pp. A simple retelling of this classic tale, with paintings of various sizes and shapes. (Rev: BL 10/1/95; SLJ 10/95)

7974 Moses, Will. *Rip Van Winkle* (3–5). Illus. 1999, Putnam $16.99 (0-399-23152-8). 48pp. This large-format book is a handsome, somewhat simplified version of the classic fantasy by Washington Irving. (Rev: BCCB 12/99; BL 11/1/99; HBG 3/00; SLJ 10/99)

7975 Mullarkey, Lisa Geurdes. *The Witch's Portraits* (4–7). 1998, Dial $15.99 (0-8037-2337-7). 192pp. Twelve-year-old Laura's best friend is Cara, who believes that the strange artist Mrs. Blackert is holding people prisoner in her portraits. (Rev: BL 9/15/98; HBG 3/99; SLJ 10/98)

7976 Mullin, Caryl Cude. *A Riddle of Roses* (4–7). 2000, Second Story Pr. paper $6.95 (1-896764-28-2). 180pp. Meryl, who has been expelled from school for a year, goes on a quest to Avalon to find her own wisdom. (Rev: BL 2/15/01)

7977 Murphy, Jill. *The Worst Witch* (4–6). 1982, Avon paper $2.50 (0-380-60665-8). 72pp. Mildred's first year at Miss Cackle's Academy for Witches is a disaster. A sequel is: *The Worst Witch Strikes Again* (1987).

7978 Murphy, Rita. *Night Flying* (5–9). 2000, Delacorte $14.95 (0-385-32748-X). 130pp. Like all the females in the Hansen family, 16-year-old Georgia has the ability to fly and with it comes some unusual responsibilities. (Rev: HB 9–10/00; HBG 3/01; SLJ 11/00)

7979 Napoli, Donna Jo. *Jimmy, the Pickpocket of the Palace* (4–6). Illus. 1995, Dutton $14.99 (0-525-45357-1). 176pp. Jimmy the frog has trouble adjusting when he becomes a boy. (Rev: BCCB 6/95; BL 3/15/95; SLJ 6/95*)

7980 Napoli, Donna Jo. *The Prince of the Pond: Otherwise Known as De Fawg Pin* (3–6). Illus. by Judith Byron Schachner. 1992, Dutton $15.99 (0-525-44976-0). 112pp. In this "different" telling of the frog prince tale, Jade, a female frog, meets the prince under his enchantment and never quite catches on that he really isn't a frog. (Rev: BCCB 1/93; BL 1/15/93; SLJ 10/92)

7981 Naylor, Phyllis Reynolds. *Bernie and the Bessledorf Ghost* (4–6). 1990, Macmillan $15.00 (0-689-31499-X). 128pp. Bernie and his family discover that the hotel they operate has a ghost. (Rev: BL 4/15/90; SLJ 7/90)

7982 Naylor, Phyllis Reynolds. *The Grand Escape* (5–7). Illus. 1993, Macmillan $16.00 (0-689-31722-0). 144pp. Two adventurous cats must solve three mysteries before they can join the Cats' Club of Mysteries. (Rev: BL 7/93; SLJ 8/93)

7983 Naylor, Phyllis Reynolds. *The Healing of Texas Jake* (3–6). Illus. 1997, Simon & Schuster $15.00 (0-689-81124-1). 128pp. Each of the cats who are members of the Club of Mystery rally around their leader, Texas Jake, when he is injured in a brawl. (Rev: BL 5/1/97; SLJ 4/97)

7984 Naylor, Phyllis Reynolds. *Jade Green: A Ghost Story* (5–8). 2000, Simon & Schuster $16.00 (0-689-82005-4). 176pp. Set in South Carolina about 100 years ago, this ghost story involves Judith Sparrow, age 15, and the mystery surrounding the gruesome death of a girl named Jade Green. (Rev: HBG 10/00; SLJ 2/00)

7985 Nesbit, Edith. *The Deliverers of Their Country* (3–5). Illus. by Lisbeth Zwerger. 1985, Picture Book paper $15.95 (0-88708-005-7). 32pp. Two children seek the advice of St. George, England's great dragon slayer, to rid the land of a plague of dragons. (Rev: BCCB 1/86; BL 1/15/86; HB 3–4/86)

7986 Nesbit, Edith. *The Enchanted Castle* (4–6). Illus. by Paul O. Zelinsky. 1992, Morrow $22.95 (0-688-05435-8). 304pp. A handsome volume that showcases Nesbit's fantasy about four English children and their adventures with a magic ring, first published in 1907. (Rev: BL 12/15/92)

7987 Nesbit, Edith. *Five Children and It* (4–6). Illus. by H. R. Miller. 1981, Buccaneer LB $25.95 (0-89966-362-1). 188pp. An enchanting story about a group of children who discover a Psammead, a sand fairy, who both enlivens and confuses their lives. Two more stories about the children: *The Phoenix and the Carpet* (1985); *The Story of the Amulet* (1986).

7988 Newman, Robert. *Merlin's Mistake* (4–6). Illus. by Richard Lebenson. 1986, Peter Smith $16.25 (0-8446-6187-2). Sixteen-year-old Brian and his friend Tertius set out to find Merlin in this fantasy originally published in 1970. Followed by: *The Testing of Tertius* (1986).

7989 Nichol, Barbara. *Dippers* (3–5). Illus. by Barry Moser. 1997, Tundra $15.95 (0-88776-396-0). A fantasy about a sick child in Toronto in 1912 and

about her sister, who sees dippers, creatures that look like prairie dogs with wings. (Rev: SLJ 9/97)

7990 Nicholson, William. *The Wind Singer* (5–7). Illus. 2000, Hyperion $17.99 (0-7868-0569-2). 384pp. In the structured community of Amaranth, ruled by a caste system, twin brother and sister Kestrel and Bowman rebel and try to get help from the Wind Singer. (Rev: BL 10/15/00; SLJ 12/00)

7991 Nimmo, Jenny. *Orchard of the Crescent Moon* (5–7). 1990, Troll paper $2.95 (0-8167-2265-X). 170pp. Nia has begun to believe it when her family says "Nia-can't-do-nothing." (Rev: BL 8/89)

7992 Nixon, Joan Lowery. *Gus and Gertie and the Missing Pearl* (2–4). Illus. 2000, North-South LB $15.88 (1-58717-023-X). 48pp. When penguins Gertie and Gus enter a seedy hotel on a tropical island, Gertie's necklace is stolen and they must solve the mystery and catch the thief. (Rev: BL 11/1/00; HBG 3/01; SLJ 10/00)

7993 Nodelman, Perry. *A Completely Different Place* (5–8). 1997, Simon & Schuster paper $16.00 (0-689-80836-4). 192pp. Johnny awakes from a nightmare and finds that he has shrunk in size and is in the land of the green-skinned Strangers. (Rev: BL 7/97; SLJ 6/97)

7994 Noonan, R. A. *Enter at Your Own Risk* (4–5). Series: Monsterville. 1995, Simon & Schuster paper $3.95 (0-689-71863-2). 155pp. In this horror tale, Darcy and her two cousins discover Monsterville, a refuge for supernatural creatures. Also use *Don't Go into the Graveyard!* (1995). (Rev: SLJ 3/96)

7995 Norton, Andre, and Phyllis Miller. *House of Shadows* (5–7). 1985, Tor paper $2.95 (0-8125-4743-8). 256pp. While staying with a great-aunt, three children learn about the family curse.

7996 Norton, Mary. *Are All the Giants Dead?* (4–6). Illus. by Brian Froud. 1978, Harcourt paper $9.95 (0-15-607888-0). James journeys to the fairy-tale world of princes, giants, and witches.

7997 Norton, Mary. *The Borrowers* (4–6). Illus. by Beth Krush and Joe Krush. 1953, Harcourt $17.00 (0-15-209987-5); paper $6.00 (0-15-209990-5). 180pp. Little people, no taller than a pencil, live in old houses and borrow what they need from humans. Some sequels are: *The Borrowers Afield* (1955); *The Borrowers Afloat* (1959); *The Borrowers Aloft* (1961); *The Borrowers Avenged* (1982).

7998 Norton, Mary. *Poor Stainless: A New Story About the Borrowers* (2–4). Illus. by Beth Krush and Joe Krush. 1985, Harcourt $7.95 (0-15-263221-2). 32pp. The tiny people called The Borrowers are back in print.

7999 O'Brien, Robert C. *Mrs. Frisby and the Rats of NIMH* (5–7). Illus. by Zena Bernstein. 1971, Macmillan $17.00 (0-689-20651-8); paper $5.50 (0-689-71068-2). 240pp. Saga of a group of rats made literate and given human intelligence by a series of experiments, who escape from their laboratory to found their own community. Newbery Award winner, 1972.

8000 Oppel, Kenneth. *Peg and the Whale* (K–3). Illus. by Terry Widener. 2000, Simon & Schuster $16.95 (0-689-82423-8). 40pp. Seven-year-old Peg sets out to catch a whale and is swallowed by one instead in this humorous tall tale. (Rev: BCCB 7–8/00; BL 11/15/00*; HB 7–8/00; HBG 3/01; SLJ 11/00)

8001 Oppel, Kenneth. *Silverwing* (4–6). 1997, Simon & Schuster paper $16.00 (0-689-81529-8). 217pp. The young hero Slade, who is an undersized bat, must save his colony from invaders. (Rev: HB 11–12/97; HBG 3/98; SLJ 10/97)

8002 Oppel, Kenneth. *Sunwing* (5–8). 2000, Simon & Schuster $17.00 (0-689-82674-5). 272pp. In this sequel to *Silverwing*, Shade, the Silverwing bat, sets out to find his father and has a series of adventures including confronting the forces of evil. (Rev: BCCB 5/00; BL 1/1–15/00; HB 3–4/00; HBG 10/00; SLJ 2/00)

8003 O'Rourke, Frank. *Burton and Stanley* (4–6). Illus. by Jonathan Allen. 1993, Godine $15.95 (0-87923-824-0). 56pp. Two talking birds from Africa are transported by a tornado to a small town in the Midwest. (Rev: BL 5/15/93; SLJ 5/93)

8004 O'Shea, Pat. *The Hounds of the Morrigan* (5–8). 1986, Holiday $16.95 (0-8234-0595-8). 469pp. A fantasy about 10-year-old Pidge and his little sister, both of whom are drawn into a battle between Irish spirits. (Rev: BCCB 7–8/86; HB 7–8/86; SLJ 3/86)

8005 Parish, Peggy. *Haunted House* (4–6). 1991, Peter Smith $18.50 (0-8446-6391-3); Dell paper $3.99 (0-440-43459-9). The Roberts family believes a ghost is loose and nearby.

8006 Paterson, Katherine. *The Field of the Dogs* (3–5). Illus. by Emily Arnold McCully. 2001, HarperCollins LB $14.89 (0-06-029475-2). 96pp. Josh, beset by bullies in the Vermont town where he has moved with his mother, discovers that he can understand the language of dogs. (Rev: BCCB 2/01; SLJ 2/01)

8007 Patneaude, David. *Dark Starry Morning: Stories of This World and Beyond* (5–8). 1995, Albert Whitman LB $13.95 (0-8075-1474-8). 128pp. Six eerie tales about encounters with the unknown and the supernatural. (Rev: BL 9/1/95; SLJ 9/95)

8008 Pattison, Darcy. *The Wayfinder* (4–6). 2000, Greenwillow LB $15.89 (0-06-029157-5). 208pp. An adventure-fantasy in which a young boy is sent on a quest to find the Well of Life, whose waters can help stop a deadly plague. (Rev: BCCB 1/01; BL 12/15/00; HBG 3/01; SLJ 1/01)

8009 Pearce, Philippa. *Tom's Midnight Garden* (4–7). Illus. by Susan Einzig. 1959, HarperCollins LB $15.89 (0-397-30477-3); Dell paper $5.95 (0-06-440445-5). 240pp. When the clock strikes 13, Tom visits his garden and meets Hatty, a strange mid-Victorian girl.

8010 Peck, Richard. *The Ghost Belonged to Me* (5–8). 1997, Viking paper $4.99 (0-14-038671-8). 184pp. Richard unwillingly receives the aid of his nemesis, Blossom Culp, in trying to solve the mystery behind the ghost of a young girl. Two sequels are: *Ghosts I Have Been* (1977); *The Dreadful Future of Blossom Culp* (1983).

8011 Perez, L. King. *Ghoststalking* (3–6). Illus. 1995, Carolrhoda LB $19.95 (0-87614-821-6). 56pp. Chuy and Emilio camp outdoors to find the ghost of La Llorona, a woman who has drowned her children in this Latino tale of the supernatural. (Rev: BL 9/15/95; SLJ 12/95)

8012 Perrin, Randy, et al. *Time Like a River* (5–7). 1997, RDR Bks. $14.95 (1-57143-061-X). 139pp. Margie travels back in time to find a cure for her mother's mysterious illness. (Rev: HBG 3/98; SLJ 3/98)

8013 Peterson, Beth. *No Turning Back* (4–6). 1996, Simon & Schuster $14.00 (0-689-31914-2). 103pp. In an attempt to help his injured friend, Dillon travels through an enchanted forest filled with talking animals. (Rev: BL 5/1/96; SLJ 5/96)

8014 Pierce, Tamora. *Briar's Book* (5–8). Series: Circle of Magic. 1999, Scholastic $15.95 (0-590-55359-3). 272pp. Briar, one of the four mages-in-training in this series, seeks the help of her friends when a mysterious plague threatens to destroy their city. (Rev: HBG 10/99; SLJ 3/99)

8015 Pierce, Tamora. *The Circle Opens: Magic Steps* (5–9). Series: Circle Opens. 2000, Scholastic $16.95 (0-590-39588-2). 272pp. Fourteen-year-old Sandry and her friend Pasco use their magic to stop the murders of local merchants. (Rev: BCCB 3/00; BL 3/1/00; HB 5–6/00; HBG 10/00; SLJ 4/00)

8016 Pierce, Tamora. *Daja's Book* (5–9). Series: Circle of Magic. 1998, Scholastic $15.95 (0-590-55358-5). 234pp. Daja, a mage-in-training, uses her magical powers to create a living vine out of metal, and soon members of the Nomadic Traders want to possess it. (Rev: BCCB 12/98; HBG 3/99; SLJ 12/98)

8017 Pierce, Tamora. *First Test* (4–7). 1999, Random LB $17.99 (0-679-98914-5). 224pp. Keladry uses her wits and intelligence to conquer the many obstacles she encounters during her first year in knight training. (Rev: BL 6/1–15/99; HBG 10/99; SLJ 7/99)

8018 Pierce, Tamora. *Tris's Book* (5–9). Series: Circle of Magic. 1998, Scholastic $15.95 (0-590-55357-7). 251pp. Tris and her three fellow mages combine forces to fight the pirates who are threatening to destroy their home. (Rev: BCCB 4/98; HBG 10/98; SLJ 4/98)

8019 Pinkwater, Daniel. *The Magic Pretzel* (3–5). Illus. Series: Werewolf Club. 2000, Simon & Schuster $15.00 (0-689-83800-X). 64pp. Members of the Werewolf Club, including newcomer Norman Gnormal, search for a magic pretzel to lift a curse that has been placed on mysterious Mr. Talbot. (Rev: BCCB 9/00; BL 7/00; HBG 3/01; SLJ 11/00)

8020 Pipe, Jim. *The Werewolf* (4–7). Illus. Series: In the Footsteps Of. 1996, Millbrook LB $23.90 (0-7613-0450-9). 40pp. A horror story in which Bernard, a werewolf, commits terrible acts under the influence of a full moon. (Rev: SLJ 7/96)

8021 Place, François. *The Last Giants* (4–6). Trans. from French by William Rodarmor. Illus. by author. 1993, Godine $15.95 (0-87923-990-5). 74pp. This novel tells of the fearless explorer Archibald Ruth-more and his journey into the Land of the Giants. It is part fable, part fantasy, and part exciting adventure story. (Rev: HB 11–12/93; SLJ 12/93)

8022 Polacco, Patricia. *I Can Hear the Sun* (2–4). Illus. by author. 1996, Putnam $16.99 (0-399-22520-X). A fantasy in which a misunderstood, troubled boy accepts an invitation from the geese and flies away with them. (Rev: BL 11/1/96; SLJ 11/96)

8023 Preussler, Otfried. *The Satanic Mill* (5–8). 1987, Peter Smith $19.50 (0-8446-6196-1). 256pp. A young apprentice outwits a strange magician in this fantasy first published in 1972. (Rev: BL 6/1–15/98)

8024 Price, Reynolds. *A Perfect Friend* (5–8). 2000, Simon & Schuster $16.00 (0-689-83029-7). 128pp. Set in the early part of the 20th century, this story tells how Ben, whose mother has died, communes with a young circus elephant who has also just lost a loved one. (Rev: BCCB 10/00; BL 11/15/00; HB 9–10/00; HBG 3/01; SLJ 2/01)

8025 Priceman, Marjorie. *My Nine Lives: by Clio* (3–6). Illus. 1998, Simon & Schuster $16.00 (0-689-81135-7). 48pp. Clio the cat shares information about her nine lives, beginning with being an astronomer in Mesopotamia and working through other incarnations where, for example, she made the Mona Lisa smile. (Rev: BL 11/15/98; HBG 3/99; SLJ 10/98)

8026 Priest, Robert. *The Town That Got Out of Town* (2–5). Illus. 1989, Godine $14.95 (0-87923-786-4). 48pp. One Labor Day, the city of Boston decides to pay a visit to Portland, Maine. (Rev: BL 1/1/90; SLJ 5/90)

8027 Proysen, Alf. *Little Old Mrs. Pepperpot and Other Stories* (3–5). 1960, Astor-Honor $14.95 (0-8392-3021-4). The story of a woman who can shrink to the size of a pepper pot.

8028 Pryor, Bonnie. *Marvelous Marvin and the Pioneer Ghost* (3–6). Illus. 1995, Morrow $15.00 (0-688-13886-1). 144pp. With the help of a ghost, Marvin and his friends find out who is polluting Liberty Creek. (Rev: BL 5/1/95; SLJ 7/95)

8029 Pullman, Philip. *Clockwork* (4–7). Illus. by Leonid Gore. 1998, Scholastic $16.95 (0-590-12999-6). 128pp. Reality and fantasy interact when characters in a storyteller's tale come to life in this story set in a bygone German inn. (Rev: BCCB 12/98; BL 9/15/98*; HB 11–12/98; HBG 3/99; SLJ 10/98)

8030 Pullman, Philip. *Count Karlstein* (5–8). 1998, Knopf LB $18.99 (0-679-99255-3). 243pp. A Gothic thriller about a teenage maidservant in a castle where the owner, Count Karlstein, is preparing to offer his two nieces to the Demon Huntsman as part of an old bargain. (Rev: BCCB 10/98; HB 9–10/98; HBG 3/99; SLJ 9/98)

8031 Pullman, Philip. *The Firework-Maker's Daughter* (3–6). Illus. 1999, Scholastic $15.95 (0-590-18719-8). 112pp. In a fanciful historical land, Lila sets out on a dangerous quest to find royal sulfur, a substance that will enable her to become a true fire-

works maker. (Rev: BCCB 1/00; BL 9/15/99*; HBG 3/00; SLJ 11/99)

8032 Pullman, Philip. *I Was a Rat!* (4–6). 2000, Knopf LB $17.99 (0-375-90176-0). 192pp. A humorous spinoff on the Cinderella story in which a young foundling finds a home with an elderly couple, in spite of the fact that he keeps insisting he is a rat. (Rev: BCCB 2/00; BL 2/1/00; HBG 10/00; SLJ 3/00)

8033 Pyle, Howard. *The Garden Behind the Moon: A Real Story of the Moon Angel* (4–6). Illus. by author. 1988, Parabola paper $10.95 (0-930407-22-9). 180pp. A boy follows the path of the moonlight and visits the Moon-Angel and the Man-in-the-Moon in this fantasy. A reissue of the 1895 edition.

8034 Quindlen, Anna. *Happily Ever After* (2–4). Illus. by James Stevenson. 1997, Viking $13.99 (0-670-86961-9). 64pp. Spunky fourth-grader Kate reverses stereotypes when she magically becomes a fairytale princess. (Rev: BL 2/1/97; SLJ 3/97)

8035 Raschka, Chris. *Elizabeth Imagined an Iceberg* (K–6). Illus. by author. Series: Richard Jackson Books. 1994, Orchard LB $15.99 (0-531-08667-4). Elizabeth meets an unusual, frightening woman and is able to repulse her advances in this unsettling picture book. (Rev: BCCB 5/94; SLJ 4/94)

8036 Raskin, Ellen. *Figgs and Phantoms* (4–6). Illus. by author. 1989, Puffin paper $5.99 (0-14-032944-7). 160pp. The family of Figg-Newton has always dreamed of going to Capri, and in this fantasy, heroine Mona Lisa fulfills the wish.

8037 Ratnett, Michael. *Dracula Steps Out* (3–5). Illus. by June Goulding. 1998, Orchard $19.95 (0-531-30100-1). Dracula riddles and jokes are included in this interactive book where Dracula pops up in different places. (Rev: BL 1/1–15/99)

8038 Redmond, Shirley-Raye. *Grampa and the Ghost* (3–5). 1994, Avon paper $3.50 (0-380-77382-1). 82pp. When Mark and Sibyl advertise for a ghost writer, they get an assistant from beyond the grave named Tallulah. (Rev: SLJ 7/94)

8039 Regan, Dian C. *Monsters and My One True Love* (4–6). Illus. 1998, Holt $15.95 (0-8050-4676-3). 198pp. In this Monster-of-the-Month story, 13-year-old Rilla is about to meet her long-lost father at Christmastime, when she receives the December monster that comes to life at unpredictable times. (Rev: BL 4/15/98; HBG 10/98; SLJ 6/98)

8040 Regan, Dian C. *Monsters in the Attic* (4–6). Illus. 1995, Holt $14.95 (0-8050-3709-8). 186pp. Life becomes complicated for Rilla when she joins the Monster of the Month Club. (Rev: BL 10/15/95; SLJ 11/95)

8041 *Ribbiting Tales* (5–7). Ed. by Nancy Springer. Illus. 2000, Putnam $16.99 (0-399-23312-1). 128pp. This is an anthology of eight stories about frogs by such authors as Janet Taylor Lisle, Robert J. Harris, and Bruce Coville. (Rev: BL 11/1/00; SLJ 1/01)

8042 Richardson, Bill. *After Hamelin* (4–8). 2000, Annick $19.95 (1-55037-629-2). 144pp. In this entertaining fantasy that is a follow-up to the Pied Piper of Hamelin story, Penelope gets the gift of Deep Dreaming and is able to enter the Piper's secret world in the hope of rescuing the children. (Rev: BL 2/15/01)

8043 Richemont, Enid. *The Glass Bird* (3–5). Illus. by Caroline Anstey. 1993, Candlewick $14.95 (1-56402-195-5). 112pp. Adam and Gary form a lasting friendship as a result of a magical glass bird that appears to Adam after he wishes on a chestnut. (Rev: BL 10/15/93; SLJ 10/93)

8044 Richemont, Enid. *The Time Tree* (4–6). 1990, Little, Brown $12.95 (0-316-74452-2). 96pp. A girl from the 16th century visits the 20th and takes back the skills she has learned. (Rev: BCCB 5/90; BL 8/90; SLJ 6/90)

8045 Rodda, Emily. *The Pigs Are Flying* (4–6). Illus. by Noela Young. 1988, Greenwillow paper $2.95 (0-380-70555-9). 160pp. Rachel's friend Burt, who has come to cheer her when she has a cold, makes her believe in the impossible. (Rev: BL 10/1/88; HB 11–12/88)

8046 Roden, Katie. *The Mummy* (3–6). Illus. Series: In the Footsteps Of. 1996, Millbrook LB $21.90 (0-7613-0451-7). 40pp. Fiction and fact mix in this account of mummification and a horror story about King Tut's tomb. (Rev: SLJ 5/96)

8047 Ross, Gaby. *Damien the Dragon* (3–5). Illus. by Carla Daly. 1990, Poolbeg paper $6.95 (1-85371-078-4). 92pp. Alan and the residents of Gravellonia construct a companion for Lady Silk Dragon. (Rev: BL 12/15/90)

8048 Rowling, J. K. *Harry Potter and the Chamber of Secrets* (4–8). 1999, Scholastic $17.95 (0-439-06486-4). 352pp. During his second year at Hogwarts School of Witchcraft and Wizardry, Harry is baffled when he hears noises no one else can. (Rev: BCCB 9/99; BL 5/15/99*; HB 7–8/99; HBG 10/99; SLJ 7/99)

8049 Rowling, J. K. *Harry Potter and the Goblet of Fire* (4–9). 2000, Scholastic $25.95 (0-439-13959-7). 734pp. This, the fourth installment of Harry Potter's adventures, begins when Voldemort tries to regain the power he lost in his failed attempt to kill Harry. (Rev: BL 8/00*; HB 11–12/00; HBG 3/01; SLJ 8/00)

8050 Rowling, J. K. *Harry Potter and the Prisoner of Azkaban* (4–8). Illus. by Mary GrandPré. 1999, Scholastic $19.95 (0-439-13635-0). 448pp. The third thrilling installment of Harry Potter's adventures at Hogwarts School of Witchcraft and Wizardry. (Rev: BCCB 10/99; BL 9/1/99*; HB 11–12/99; HBG 3/00; SLJ 10/99)

8051 Rowling, J. K. *Harry Potter and the Sorcerer's Stone* (4–8). Illus. 1998, Scholastic $16.95 (0-590-35340-3). 320pp. This is the first volume of the hugely successful fantasy series. In this volume Harry completes an eventful first year at Hogwarts School of Witchcraft and Wizardry. (Rev: BCCB 11/98; BL 9/15/98*; HB 1–2/99; HBG 3/99; SLJ 10/98)

8052 Ruiz, Joseph J. *The Little Ghost Who Wouldn't Go Away/El pequeño fantasma que no quería irse* (2–4). Trans. by Juan S. Lucero. Illus. by Kris Hotvedt. 2000, Sunstone paper $10.95 (0-86534-303-9). 95pp. The ghost of a young boy gets the

help of Rebecca Garcia to locate his missing tombstone so he can rest in peace in this story in both Spanish and English. (Rev: SLJ 1/01)

8053 Rupp, Rebecca. *The Dragon of Lonely Island* (4–6). 1998, Candlewick $16.99 (0-7636-0408-9). 160pp. Three children, ages 12, 10, and 8, are new arrivals on Lonely Island where they befriend a three-headed dragon who tells them a story from each of its heads. (Rev: BCCB 12/98; BL 2/1/99; HBG 3/99; SLJ 11/98)

8054 Ruskin, John. *King of the Golden River or the Black Brother* (5–8). Illus. by Richard Doyle. 1974, Dover paper $3.50 (0-486-20066-3). 56pp. Two mean brothers incur the wrath of the South-West Wind, Esquire.

8055 Russell, Barbara T. *Blue Lightning* (5–7). 1997, Viking $14.99 (0-670-87023-4). 128pp. When Rory dies, he comes back to haunt Cal Doogan, whom he met in a hospital emergency room. (Rev: BCCB 2/97; BL 2/15/97; HB 5–6/97; SLJ 2/97)

8056 Rylant, Cynthia. *The Bird House* (2–4). Illus. by Barry Moser. 1998, Scholastic $15.95 (0-590-47345-X). 32pp. In this charming fantasy, a young girl gradually forms a friendship with an old lady because of birds' intervention. (Rev: BL 10/15/98; HBG 3/99; SLJ 9/98)

8057 Rylant, Cynthia. *Gooseberry Park* (4–6). Illus. 1995, Harcourt $15.00 (0-15-232242-6). 144pp. A group of animals bands together to feed the squirrel Stumpy's babies after she disappears. (Rev: BCCB 2/96; BL 10/1/95; SLJ 12/95)

8058 Rylant, Cynthia. *The Heavenly Village* (4–7). 1999, Scholastic $15.95 (0-439-04096-5). 96pp. A special book about the Heavenly Village — a place where some people stay who are not sure about going to heaven — and about some of the people who live in this in-between world. (Rev: BL 12/1/99*; HBG 3/00)

8059 Rylant, Cynthia. *The High-Rise Private Eyes: The Case of the Puzzling Possum* (2–4). Illus. by G. Brian Karas. 2001, Greenwillow $14.95 (0-688-16308-4). 48pp. In this beginning chapter book, the mystery of why a trombone is continually stolen and returned is solved by detective Bunny Brown and her bumbling sidekick, the raccoon named Jack. (Rev: BL 12/1/00)

8060 Rylant, Cynthia. *The Islander* (5–8). 1998, DK $14.95 (0-7894-2490-8). 97pp. Growing up on a lonely island off the coast of British Columbia with his grandfather, Daniel encounters a mermaid and, through her, learns about his family. (Rev: BCCB 5/98; BL 2/1/98*; HB 5–6/98; HBG 10/98; SLJ 3/98)

8061 Rylant, Cynthia. *The Van Gogh Cafe* (4–6). 1995, Harcourt $14.00 (0-15-200843-8). 64pp. Seven vignettes about the people who frequent the Van Gogh Cafe situated off Highway 70 in Flowers, Kansas. (Rev: BCCB 9/95; BL 6/1–15/95; SLJ 7/95)

8062 Salsitz, Rhoni V. *The Twilight Gate* (5–8). Illus. by Alan M. Clark. 1993, Walker $16.95 (0-8027-8213-2). 192pp. Siblings are being pursued by man-beasts called weevils in this unusual and complex fantasy. (Rev: SLJ 5/93)

8063 San Souci, Robert D., reteller. *A Terrifying Taste of Short and Shivery: Thirty Creepy Tales* (5–9). Illus. by Lenny Wooden. Series: Short and shivery. 1998, Delacorte $14.95 (0-385-32635-1). 159pp. A scary collection of 30 tales from around the world that deal with ghosts and the supernatural. (Rev: HBG 3/99; SLJ 11/98)

8064 Sanvoisin, Eric. *The Ink Drinker* (2–3). Trans. by Georges Moroz. Illus. 1998, Delacorte $9.95 (0-385-32591-6). 35pp. A young boy trapped in his father's bookshop is turned into a Draculink by a vampire who, allergic to blood, feeds on ink sucked from the pages of books. (Rev: BL 12/15/98; HBG 3/99; SLJ 1/99)

8065 Sanvoisin, Eric. *A Straw for Two* (2–4). Illus. 1999, Delacorte $9.95 (0-385-32702-1). 48pp. Odilon, a vampire who drinks ink, meets Carmilla, who is a fellow follower of Draculink. (Rev: BL 12/1/99; HBG 3/00)

8066 Sargent, Sarah. *Weird Henry Berg* (4–6). 1993, Knopf paper $3.50 (0-679-80703-9). 120pp. Henry, his pet lizard Vincent, friend Millie, and a dragon named Aelf are the main characters in this fantasy.

8067 Say, Allen. *Stranger in the Mirror* (3–6). Illus. 1995, Houghton $16.95 (0-395-61590-9). 32pp. In this fantasy, Sam one morning discovers that he has the face of an old, wrinkled man. (Rev: BCCB 11/95; BL 10/1/95; SLJ 10/95*)

8068 Schaeffer, Susan F. *The Dragons of North Chittendon* (5–7). Illus. by Darcy May. 1986, Simon & Schuster paper $2.95 (0-685-14462-3). The story of Arthur, an unruly dragon, and his ESP relationship with the boy Patrick in a story of humans and dragons in and above North Chittendon, Vermont. (Rev: BL 8/86; SLJ 9/86)

8069 Schmidt, Annie M. G. *Minnie* (3–6). Trans. by Lance Salway. Illus. 1994, Milkweed $14.95 (1-57131-601-9); paper $6.95 (1-57131-600-0). 164pp. Mr. Tibbs, a reporter, and Miss Minnie, formerly a cat, try to get a villain to confess to his crime. (Rev: BL 9/1/94; SLJ 9/94)

8070 Schmidt, Gary D. *Pilgrim's Progress* (4–7). Illus. by Barry Moser. 1994, Eerdmans $20.00 (0-8028-5080-4). 88pp. A simple retelling of the classic in which Christian leaves his home to find the Celestial City. (Rev: BL 11/1/94; SLJ 12/94)

8071 Schnur, Steven. *The Shadow Children* (4–7). Illus. by Herbert Tauss. 1994, Morrow $15.93 (0-688-13831-4). 86pp. The experiences of the Holocaust are relived by a boy when he visits an area in France where Jewish refugees lived before being sent to the death camps. (Rev: BCCB 12/94; BL 11/15/94; SLJ 10/94)

8072 Scieszka, Jon. *It's All Greek to Me* (4–6). 1999, Viking $13.99 (0-670-88596-7). 80pp. The Time Warp Trio discover they are in ancient Greece where they must contend with the three-headed dog, Cerberus, and meet the gods of Mount Olympus. (Rev: BL 11/15/99; HBG 3/00; SLJ 10/99)

8073 Scieszka, Jon. *Summer Reading Is Killing Me* (3–6). Illus. by Lane Smith. 1998, Viking $13.99 (0-670-88041-8). 80pp. In this hilarious adventure, the Time Warp Trio get mixed up with characters from books on a summer reading list, such as Dracula, Winnie the Pooh, Long John Silver, and Frankenstein. (Rev: BL 6/1–15/98; HBG 3/99; SLJ 8/98)

8074 Scieszka, Jon. *Tut, Tut* (4–6). Illus. by Lane Smith. 1996, Viking $13.99 (0-670-84832-8). 80pp. The Time Warp Trio find themselves in ancient Egypt in the clutches of the pharaoh's evil priest. (Rev: BL 10/1/96)

8075 Scott, Deborah. *The Kid Who Got Zapped Through Time* (4–7). 1997, Avon $14.00 (0-380-97356-1). 160pp. In this humorous time-travel fantasy, Flattop Kincaid is transported to England during the Middle Ages, where he becomes a serf. (Rev: BL 11/1/97; SLJ 9/97)

8076 Seabrooke, Brenda. *The Care and Feeding of Dragons* (3–5). 1998, Dutton $15.99 (0-525-65252-3). 128pp. A humorous story about a young boy who has a pet dragon that he claims is really a rare dog. A sequel to *Seabrooke's Dragon That Ate Summer* (1992). (Rev: BL 2/1/98; HBG 10/98; SLJ 2/98)

8077 Seabrooke, Brenda. *The Vampire in My Bathtub* (4–7). 1999, Holiday $15.95 (0-8234-1505-8). 150pp. After 13-year-old Jeff moves to a new home with his mother, he finds a friendly vampire hidden inside an old trunk. (Rev: BL 1/1–15/00; HBG 3/00; SLJ 12/99)

8078 Sedgwick, Marcus. *Floodland* (5–8). Illus. by author. 2001, Delacorte $15.95 (0-385-32801-X). 148pp. In this fantasy set in an England undergoing terrible floods, young Zoe is swept away to an island where she is held prisoner by people who have reverted to primitive ways. (Rev: BCCB 3/01; SLJ 3/01)

8079 Seidler, Tor. *Mean Margaret* (4–6). Illus. by Jon Agee. 1997, HarperCollins LB $14.00 (0-06-205091-5). 176pp. Two newly married woodchucks decide to adopt a human child who has made her parents' life miserable. (Rev: BL 12/1/97; SLJ 11/97*)

8080 Seidler, Tor. *The Wainscott Weasel* (4–6). Illus. by Fred Marcellino. 1993, HarperCollins LB $19.89 (0-06-205033-8). 200pp. Although his girl friend, a fish, spurns him, a weasel named Bagley Brown, Jr. is determined to help when her pond is threatened. (Rev: BCCB 11/93; BL 11/1/93*; HB 11–12/93; SLJ 12/93)

8081 Selden, George. *The Cricket in Times Square* (3–6). Illus. by Garth Williams. 1960, Farrar $16.00 (0-374-31650-3); Dell paper $5.50 (0-440-41563-2). 160pp. A Connecticut cricket is transported in a picnic basket to New York's Times Square. Two sequels are: *Tucker's Countryside* (1969); *Harry Cat's Pet Puppy* (1974).

8082 Selden, George. *The Genie of Sutton Place* (5–6). 1985, Farrar paper $4.95 (0-374-42530-2). The summer Tim lives with his Aunt Lucy on Sutton Place in New York City, he evokes his own magical genie who works not only miracles but mishaps.

8083 Selden, George. *Harry Kitten and Tucker Mouse* (3–5). Illus. by Garth Williams. 1986, Farrar $16.00 (0-374-32860-9); Dell paper $3.99 (0-440-40124-0). 64pp. Harry and Tucker meet and set up housekeeping in the Times Square subway station in New York City. (Rev: BL 2/15/87; SLJ 2/87)

8084 Sendak, Maurice. *Higglety Pigglety Pop! or There Must Be More to Life* (K–4). Illus. by author. 1967, HarperCollins $15.00 (0-06-025487-4); paper $7.95 (0-06-443021-9). 80pp. Jennie, a Sealyham terrier who has everything but wants more, leaves home in search of experience.

8085 Service, Pamela F. *Storm at the Edge of Time* (4–6). 1994, Walker $16.95 (0-8027-8306-6). 192pp. Three children from different time periods are summoned to help Urkar, a Neolithic wise man. (Rev: BL 10/15/94; SLJ 12/94)

8086 Service, Pamela F. *Vision Quest* (5–7). 1989, Fawcett paper $3.99 (0-449-70372-X). 160pp. Mourning the death of her father, Kate is changed by an ancient Indian charm-stone. (Rev: BCCB 5/89; BL 4/15/89; SLJ 3/89)

8087 Shakespeare, William. *The Tempest* (3–6). Retold by Ann Keay Beneduce. Illus. by Gennady Spirin. 1996, Philomel $16.99 (0-399-22764-4). 32pp. A well-executed retelling of Shakespeare's play using paintings that suggest the Italian Renaissance. (Rev: BCCB 7–8/96; HB 5–6/96; SLJ 5/96)

8088 Shalant, Phyllis. *Bartleby of the Mighty Mississippi* (4–6). 2000, Dutton $15.99 (0-525-46033-0). 160pp. The story of a brave, loyal, small turtle named Bartleby who begins an adventure-filled journey down the Mississippi. (Rev: BL 5/15/00; HBG 10/00; SLJ 8/00)

8089 Shearer, Alex. *Professor Sniff and the Lost Spring Breezes* (4–6). Illus. 1998, Orchard $14.95 (0-531-30079-X). 112pp. Sam and Lorna discover that the wind cannot blow and seek the help of Professor Sniff who owns a hurricane he brought back from Florida. (Rev: BL 4/1/98; HBG 10/98; SLJ 4/98)

8090 Shearer, Alex. *The Summer Sisters and the Dance Disaster* (3–5). Illus. 1998, Orchard LB $15.99 (0-531-33080-X). 112pp. The three summer sisters decide to use magic to create different kinds of weather but unfortunately get their spells mixed up. (Rev: BL 4/15/98; HBG 10/98; SLJ 5/98)

8091 Shipton, Paul. *The Mighty Skink* (4–6). 2000, HarperCollins $15.95 (0-688-17420-5). 192pp. Kaz, a fearful rhesus monkey, joins up with fast-talking newcomer Skink and together they escape from their zoo to explore the outside world. (Rev: BCCB 5/00; BL 8/00; HBG 10/00; SLJ 6/00)

8092 Shreve, Susan. *Ghost Cats* (4–7). 1999, Scholastic $14.95 (0-590-37131-2). 128pp. A boy, who is trying to adjust to a new family home and the loss of his five cats, is helped when the cats return as ghosts. (Rev: BCCB 12/99; BL 9/1/99; HBG 3/00; SLJ 11/99)

8093 Shulevitz, Uri. *The Strange and Exciting Adventures of Jeremiah Hash* (4–6). Illus. by author. 1986, Farrar $14.00 (0-374-33656-3). 96pp. Jeremiah the lonely monkey spends a disappointing evening in a singles' club. (Rev: BCCB 3/87; BL 2/1/87; SLJ 2/87)

8094 Sims, J. Michael. *Young Claus: Legend of the Boy Who Became Santa* (2–4). 1995, Cygnet Trumpeter $12.95 (0-9645976-6-7). 112pp. A fantasy about a young orphan who encounters many adventures in his mission to be Santa. (Rev: BL 11/15/95)

8095 Sincic, Alan. *Edward Is Only a Fish* (3–5). Illus. 1996, Holt paper $4.95 (0-8050-4906-1). 56pp. When the Billingsly home is flooded because of running bathwater, Edward the goldfish has a field day and a free tour of the house. (Rev: BL 1/15/95; SLJ 2/95)

8096 Singer, Marilyn. *The Circus Lunicus* (3–6). 2000, Holt $17.00 (0-8050-6268-8). 168pp. When Solly disobeys his mean stepmother and sneaks off to the circus, he encounters a mystery involving a sinister ringmaster, a weeping girl, and some singing alligators. (Rev: BL 12/1/00; SLJ 12/00)

8097 Sinykin, Sheri C. *A Matter of Time* (4–6). 1998, Marshall Cavendish $14.95 (0-7614-5019-X). 207pp. Jody, wanting to spend more time with his dad to understand him better, gets his wish when he time-travels back to 1958 and meets his father as a youngster. (Rev: BL 5/15/98; HBG 10/98; SLJ 5/98)

8098 Slade, Arthur G. *The Haunting of Drang Island* (5–7). 1999, Orca paper $6.95 (1-55143-111-4). 160pp. In this sequel to *Draugr* (1998), 14-year-old Michael and his writer father are on Drang Island, off the coast of British Columbia, when they become involved with an undead sorcerer and creatures from Icelandic mythology. (Rev: BL 4/1/99; SLJ 8/99)

8099 Sleator, William. *The Beasties* (5–7). 1997, Dutton $15.99 (0-525-45598-1). 192pp. In this modern horror tale, Doug and his younger sister discover a hidden tunnel where a race of weird underground people live. (Rev: BL 10/1/97; HB 9–10/97; HBG 3/98; SLJ 12/97)

8100 Sleator, William. *The Boxes* (5–7). 1998, Dutton $15.99 (0-525-46012-8). 189pp. In spite of warnings from her Uncle Marco, Annie opens two mysterious boxes he has left her and, as a result, finds herself swept into a different set of relationships that will change her life. (Rev: BCCB 7–8/98; BL 6/1–15/98; HB 5–6/98; HBG 10/98; SLJ 6/98)

8101 Sleator, William. *Rewind* (4–6). 1999, Dutton $14.99 (0-525-46130-2). 128pp. Peter travels back in time to try and change the events that led to his death after being hit by a neighbor's car. (Rev: BL 10/15/99; HB 7–8/99; HBG 3/00; SLJ 8/99)

8102 Slepian, Jan. *Back to Before* (5–7). 1994, Scholastic paper $3.25 (0-590-48459-1). 144pp. Cousins Linny and Hilary travel back to a time before Linny's mother's death and Hilary's parents' separation. (Rev: BCCB 9/93; BL 9/1/93*; SLJ 10/93)

8103 Small, David. *Fenwick's Suit* (4–8). Illus. 1996, Farrar $16.00 (0-374-32298-8). 30pp. Fenwick discovers that the new suit he has purchased has a life of its own. (Rev: BCCB 10/96; BL 9/15/96; SLJ 9/96)

8104 Small, David. *George Washington's Cows* (3–4). Illus. 1994, Farrar $15.00 (0-374-32535-9). 32pp. Humorous rhymes that depict daily life of the animals at George Washington's Mount Vernon. (Rev: BL 11/1/94; SLJ 1/95*)

8105 Smith, Dodie. *The Hundred and One Dalmatians* (3–5). 1981, Avon paper $2.95 (0-380-00895-5). 208pp. Pongo and Missis must save the Dalmatian puppies captured by Cruella de Vil.

8106 Smith, L. J. *Heart of Valor* (5–7). 1990, Macmillan $14.95 (0-02-785861-8). 224pp. Claudia, in her third-grade classroom, realizes an earthquake is imminent. (Rev: BL 2/15/90; SLJ 12/90)

8107 Smith, Sherwood. *Court Duel* (5–8). 1998, Harcourt $18.00 (0-15-201609-0). 256pp. In this fantasy, Meliara has problems at court when she can't distinguish friends from enemies. (Rev: BL 3/1/98; HBG 10/98; SLJ 4/98)

8108 Smith, Sherwood. *Crown Duel* (5–8). 1997, Harcourt $17.00 (0-15-201608-2). 272 pp. Young Meliara and her brother Bran lead a small band of friends against the wicked King Galdran to protect their land. (Rev: BCCB 7–8/97; BL 4/15/97; SLJ 8/97)

8109 Smith, Sherwood. *Wren's War* (5–8). 1995, Harcourt $17.00 (0-15-200977-9). 208pp. Princess Teresa uses the help of Wren to prevent her kingdom from being taken over by evil forces. (Rev: BL 3/1/95*; SLJ 5/95)

8110 Sneve, Virginia Driving Hawk. *The Trickster and the Troll* (3–6). 1997, Univ. of Nebraska Pr. $25.00 (0-8032-4261-1). 110pp. An American Indian trickster meets a Norwegian troll in this fantasy. (Rev: BL 9/15/97; HBG 3/98; SLJ 12/97)

8111 Snyder, Zilpha Keatley. *The Trespassers* (5–7). 1995, Delacorte $15.95 (0-385-31055-2). 200pp. Grub, a 7-year-old, forms a friendship with a ghost after he and his older sister, Neely, explore a deserted mansion. (Rev: BCCB 10/95; BL 6/1–15/95; SLJ 8/95)

8112 Somary, Wolfgang. *Night and the Candlemaker* (4–8). Illus. 2000, Barefoot $15.99 (1-84148-137-8). 32pp. In this allegory, a candle maker continues with his trade in spite of threats he receives from Night. (Rev: BL 9/15/00; SLJ 1/01)

8113 Sonenklar, Carol. *Bug Boy* (3–6). Illus. 1997, Holt $15.95 (0-8050-4794-8). 100pp. Charlie, who is nuts about bugs, gets a gift of a device that turns him into a number of different insects. (Rev: BCCB 5/97; BL 4/1/97; SLJ 7/97)

8114 Sonenklar, Carol. *Bug Girl* (3–6). Illus. 1998, Holt $15.95 (0-8050-5821-4). 103pp. When Charlie looks through his Bug-a-View, he becomes a beetle and is caught by his nemesis Raymond. (Rev: BL 11/1/98; HBG 3/99; SLJ 10/98)

8115 Soto, Gary. *The Cat's Meow* (2–5). Illus. 1995, Scholastic $13.95 (0-590-47001-9). 80pp. Graciela's cat, Pip, astounds everyone by suddenly speaking in Spanish. (Rev: BL 12/1/95; SLJ 10/95)

8116 Spalding, Andrea. *The Keeper and the Crows* (3–6). Illus. 2000, Orca paper $4.50 (1-55143-141-6). 119pp. Misha sets out to retrieve a key to a magic box that contains Hope, in this fantasy that is a spinoff on the Greek myth about Pandora's Box. (Rev: BL 11/15/00)

8117 Spinner, Stephanie, and Ellen Weiss. *Born to Be Wild* (2–4). Series: Weebie Zone No. 3. 1997, HarperTrophy LB $13.89 (0-06-027338-0). 60pp. Garth and the gerbil with whom he communicates plan to help rescue a runaway bunny. (Rev: SLJ 2/97)

8118 Spires, Elizabeth. *The Mouse of Amherst* (2–5). Illus. 1999, Farrar $15.00 (0-374-35083-3). 64pp. A tiny mouse, Emmaline, who lives in Emily Dickinson's house, is so impressed with the poetry she reads that she begins writing her own. (Rev: BL 3/15/99; HBG 10/99; SLJ 5/99)

8119 Springer, Nancy. *I Am Mordred: A Tale from Camelot* (5–8). 1998, Philomel $16.99 (0-399-23143-9). 184pp. The story of King Arthur's son, Mordred, who fights the prophecy that he will kill his father. (Rev: HB 3–4/98; HBG 10/98; SLJ 5/98)

8120 Springer, Nancy. *Red Wizard* (4–7). 1990, Macmillan $13.95 (0-689-31485-X). 138pp. In this fantasy, Ryan is summoned to an alternative world by a bumbling wizard. (Rev: SLJ 7/90)

8121 Springer, Nancy. *Sky Rider* (5–8). 1999, Avon $15.00 (0-380-97604-8). 128pp. Beset with personal problems involving her family and a sick horse, Dusty Grove encounters the ghost of a teenage boy recently killed on her father's property. (Rev: BCCB 10/99; HBG 3/00; SLJ 8/99)

8122 Stamaty, Mark Alan. *Too Many Time Machines: Or, the Incredible Story of How I Went Back in Time, Met Babe Ruth, and Discovered the Secret of Homerun Hitting* (3–6). Illus. by author. 1999, Viking $13.99 (0-670-88477-4); paper $6.99 (0-670-88635-1). A time-travel novel that involves Roger getting some much-needed baseball tips from the Babe himself. (Rev: HBG 10/99; SLJ 7/99)

8123 Stanley, Diane. *Roughing It on the Oregon Trail* (2–4). Illus. by Holly Berry. 2000, Harper-Collins $15.95 (0-06-027065-9). 48pp. Lenny and Liz, with their grandmother and her magic hat, travel back in time to 1843 to join a relative on the Oregon Trail. (Rev: BCCB 6/00; BL 4/1/00; HBG 10/00; SLJ 6/00)

8124 Stanley, George E. *The Day the Ants Got Really Mad* (2–4). Illus. 1996, Simon & Schuster paper $3.99 (0-689-80858-5). 74pp. A colony of ants seeks revenge when Michael's family builds a house over their anthill. (Rev: BL 4/1/96; SLJ 8/96)

8125 Steele, Mary Q. *Journey Outside* (5–8). Illus. by Rocco Negri. 1984, Peter Smith $18.25 (0-8446-6169-4); Puffin paper $4.99 (0-14-030588-2). 144pp. Young Dilar, believing that his Raft People in seeking a "Better Place" have been circling endlessly, sets out to discover the origin and fate of his kind.

8126 Steig, William. *Abel's Island* (4–6). Illus. by author. 1976, Farrar $15.00 (0-374-30010-0); paper $4.95 (0-374-40016-4). 128pp. A tale of a pampered mouse who must fend for himself after being marooned on an isolated island.

8127 Steig, William. *Dominic* (4–6). Illus. by author. 1984, Farrar paper $4.95 (0-374-41826-8).

160pp. A resourceful and engaging hound dog helps a group of animals overcome the wicked Doomsday Gang.

8128 Steig, William. *The Real Thief* (4–5). Illus. by author. 1976, Farrar paper $3.95 (0-374-46208-9). 64pp. Gawain, a goose, is disgraced when gold and jewels begin disappearing from the Royal Treasury where he is the guard.

8129 Stevenson, James. *The Mud Flat Mystery* (2–4). Illus. 1997, Greenwillow $14.93 (0-688-14966-9). 56pp. All the animals of Mud Flat are curious to know about the contents of a large box delivered to Duncan. (Rev: BL 9/15/97; HB 9–10/97; HBG 3/98; SLJ 8/97)

8130 Stevenson, Robert Louis. *The Bottle Imp* (4–7). Illus. by Jacqueline Mair. 1996, Clarion $16.95 (0-395-72101-6). 60pp. The classic story of the mixed blessings of owning a magic bottle that will grant wishes. (Rev: BCCB 2/96; BL 2/15/96; SLJ 5/96)

8131 Stewart, Jennifer J. *If That Breathes Fire, We're Toast!* (4–6). 1999, Holiday $15.95 (0-8234-1430-2). 117pp. Mrs. Yang, a dragon, takes Rick and friend Natalie on several trips through time and imagination. (Rev: BCCB 9/99; BL 8/99; HBG 10/99; SLJ 12/99)

8132 Stine, R. L. *Nightmare Hour* (4–7). Illus. 1999, HarperCollins $9.95 (0-06-028688-1). 148pp. Ten scary stories by a master of mystery, with characters that include aliens, sorcerers, werewolves, witches, and ghosts. (Rev: BL 10/15/99; HBG 3/00; SLJ 12/99)

8133 Strasser, Todd. *Help! I'm Trapped in Obedience School* (5–8). 1995, Scholastic paper $4.50 (0-590-54209-5). 126pp. Andy, trapped in a dog's body, must adjust to eating dog food and engaging in other typical canine activities. (Rev: BL 2/1/96; SLJ 2/96)

8134 Strasser, Todd. *Hey Dad, Get a Life!* (5–8). 1996, Holiday $15.95 (0-8234-1278-4). 160pp. Kelly and Sasha train the ghost of their father to be helpful around the house. (Rev: BCCB 3/97; BL 2/15/97; SLJ 3/97)

8135 Strasser, Todd. *Pastabilities* (5–8). 2000, Pocket paper $4.99 (0-671-03628-9). 165pp. Heavenly Litebody, a modern-day nanny with mysterious powers, travels with her five charges to Italy for a vacation. (Rev: SLJ 8/00)

8136 Strauss, Linda Leopold. *A Fairy Called Hilary* (2–4). Illus. 1999, Holiday $15.95 (0-8234-1418-3). 113pp. Nine related stories about Caroline, her family, and their adopted fairy, Hilary. (Rev: BL 3/1/99; HBG 10/99; SLJ 3/99)

8137 Strickland, Brad. *The Wrath of the Grinning Ghost* (5–8). 1999, Dial $15.99 (0-8037-2222-2). 176pp. Johnny Dixon discovers that an evil spirit is trying to overpower his dad in order to destroy the world. (Rev: BL 9/15/99; HBG 3/00; SLJ 10/99)

8138 Templeton, Ty. *Batman Gotham Adventures* (5–10). 2000, DC Comics paper $15.95 (1-56389-616-8). 144pp. This graphic novel offers six short stories about Batman, Catwoman, Robin, and the usual villains, drawn by Rick Burkett and others. (Rev: BL 12/1/00)

8139 Thomas, Jane Resh. *The Princess in the Pigpen* (4–6). 1989, Houghton $15.00 (0-395-51587-4). 124pp. In a reverse time travel story, a girl is transported from 17th-century England to present-day America. (Rev: BL 9/15/89; SLJ 11/89)

8140 Thomas, Joyce C. *The Bowlegged Rooster and Other Tales That Signify* (2–5). Illus. 2000, HarperCollins LB $15.89 (0-06-025378-9). 112pp. Five original folktales in which animals mirror the human condition but solve their problems in a whimsical fashion. (Rev: BCCB 12/00; BL 10/1/00; HBG 3/01; SLJ 11/00)

8141 Thompson, Colin. *The Last Alchemist* (3–5). Illus. 1999, Knopf $17.00 (0-375-80156-1). 32pp. A fantasy about an alchemist who finds the ultimate gold in a wondrous glow of sunshine. (Rev: BL 7/99; HBG 10/00; SLJ 9/99)

8142 Thompson, Colin. *Looking for Atlantis* (4–6). Illus. 1994, Knopf paper $6.99 (0-679-88547-1). 32pp. A 10-year-old boy's grandfather returns to the sea on his final voyage, but not before telling the boy that he must learn to look for Atlantis. (Rev: BL 4/1/94; SLJ 5/94)

8143 Thompson, Kate. *Switchers* (5–7). 1998, Hyperion LB $15.49 (0-7868-2328-3). 224pp. A young shape-changing girl and her friend save the world from a new ice age in this fast-moving fantasy. (Rev: BCCB 9/98; BL 3/15/98; HBG 10/98; SLJ 5/98)

8144 Thompson, Kate. *Wild Blood* (5–8). 2000, Hyperion LB $16.49 (0-7868-2497-2). 272pp. On her 15th birthday, Tess must choose the form she will retain for the rest of her life because, on that day, she will lose the power to "switch" and become other creatures. (Rev: HBG 10/00; SLJ 7/00)

8145 Thornton, Duncan. *Kalifax* (5–9). Illus. by Yves Noblet. 2000, Coteau paper $8.95 (1-55050-152-6). 168pp. In this fantasy novel, young Tom, with the help of Grandfather Frost, saves the crew of his ship after it becomes trapped in ice. (Rev: SLJ 1/01)

8146 Thurber, James. *The Great Quillow* (3–5). Illus. by Steven Kellogg. 1994, Harcourt $17.95 (0-15-232544-1). 56pp. A little toy maker becomes a hero when he outwits a giant. (Rev: BL 12/1/94*; HB 11–12/94; SLJ 11/94)

8147 Tibo, Gilles. *The Cowboy Kid* (2–5). Illus. 2000, Tundra $16.95 (0-88776-511-4). 24pp. In this fantasy, a youngster named the Cowboy Kid finds a horse and together they ride through the sky rescuing other horses from statues and paintings. (Rev: BL 6/1–15/00)

8148 Titus, Eve. *Basil of Baker Street* (4–6). Illus. by Paul Galdone. 1958, Pocket paper $2.50 (0-318-37408-0). A clever mystery about a mouse who moves to 221 Baker Street out of admiration for Mr. Holmes. Another in the series: *Basil in the Wild West* (1990).

8149 Tolan, Stephanie S. *The Face in the Mirror* (5–8). 1998, Morrow $15.00 (0-688-15394-1). 208pp. When Jared goes to live with his actor father, he becomes interested in acting and in making friends with a ghost who haunts the theater. (Rev: BCCB 9/98; HBG 3/99; SLJ 11/98)

8150 Tolan, Stephanie S. *Who's There?* (5–8). 1994, Morrow $15.00 (0-688-04611-8); paper $4.95 (0-688-15289-9). 240pp. Fourteen-year-old Drew is convinced that there is a ghost in her crusty grandfather's house, where she and her brother Evan, who has been mute since their parents' deaths, are currently living. (Rev: BCCB 12/94; BL 9/1/94; SLJ 10/94)

8151 Tolkien, J. R. R. *The Hobbit* (5–7). Illus. by author. 1938, Houghton $14.95 (0-395-07122-4); Ballantine paper $6.99 (0-345-33968-1). 320pp. A saga of dwarfs and elves, goblins and trolls in a far-off, long ago land. There is a special edition illustrated by Michael Hague (1984).

8152 Tolkien, J. R. R. *Roverandom* (4–9). Illus. 1998, Houghton $17.00 (0-395-89871-4). 128pp. This fantasy deals with a dog named Roverandom who has the misfortune of insulting a wizard and having to pay the consequences. (Rev: BL 7/98; SLJ 6/98)

8153 Townsend, Tom. *The Trouble with an Elf* (5–8). Series: Fairie Ring. 1999, Royal Fireworks paper $7.99 (0-88092-525-6). 158pp. The adopted daughter of the king of the elves, Elazandra, journeys through a ring of mushrooms to the world of humans to stop the evil that will destroy both worlds. (Rev: SLJ 4/00)

8154 Tudor, Tasha. *The Great Corgiville Kidnapping* (4–6). Illus. 1997, Little, Brown $15.95 (0-316-85583-9). 48pp. Caleb Corgi, a dog detective, must save Babe the rooster when he is kidnapped by some no-good raccoons. (Rev: BL 10/15/97; HBG 3/98; SLJ 12/97)

8155 Tunnell, Michael O. *School Spirits* (4–6). 1997, Holiday LB $15.95 (0-8234-1310-1). 201pp. Patrick and his new friend Nairen encounter a ghost that they believe wants to harm them. (Rev: BCCB 3/98; BL 2/15/98; HBG 3/98; SLJ 3/98)

8156 Turner, Ann. *Elfsong* (3–7). 1995, Harcourt $16.00 (0-15-200826-8). 208pp. Maddy and Grandpa discover a forest where elves live and they can hear birds and other animals speak. (Rev: BCCB 12/95; BL 10/1/95; SLJ 10/95)

8157 Turner, Ann. *Finding Walter* (3–6). 1997, Harcourt $16.00 (0-15-200212-X). 176pp. While visiting their grandmother's house, two sisters investigate an old dollhouse in which the dolls are able to transmit thoughts. (Rev: BL 10/15/97; HBG 3/98; SLJ 10/97)

8158 Turner, Megan W. *Instead of Three Wishes* (4–6). 1995, Greenwillow $15.00 (0-688-13922-1); Viking paper $4.99 (0-14-038672-6). 144pp. Everyday lives of ordinary people and fairy tale situations intermingle in these seven stories involving magic. (Rev: BCCB 10/95; BL 10/1/95*; SLJ 9/95)

8159 Turner, Megan W. *The Queen of Attolia* (5–8). 2000, Greenwillow $15.95 (0-688-17423-X). 288pp. In this sequel to *The Thief*, Gen, a slippery rogue, once more gets involved in the rivalry

between two city states. (Rev: BL 4/15/00; HB 7–8/00; HBG 10/00)

8160 Turner, Megan W. *The Thief* (5–8). 1996, Greenwillow $15.95 (0-688-14627-9). 224pp. To escape life imprisonment, Gen must steal a legendary stone in this historical novel. (Rev: BCCB 11/96; BL 1/1–15/97; HB 11–12/96; SLJ 10/96)

8161 Twain, Mark. *A Connecticut Yankee in King Arthur's Court* (5–8). Illus. by Trina S. Hyman. 1988, Morrow $23.00 (0-688-06346-2). 384pp. A smooth talker finds himself time traveling to Arthurian England. A reissued edition.

8162 Uhlberg, Myron. *Flying over Brooklyn* (3–6). Illus. 1999, Peachtree $16.95 (1-56145-194-0). 32pp. Set in Brooklyn in 1947, this dreamlike fantasy tells of a boy who dons a new coat that gives him the power to fly over the city's buildings. (Rev: BL 12/1/99; HBG 3/00; SLJ 12/99)

8163 Ure, Jean. *The Children Next Door* (4–6). 1996, Scholastic $14.95 (0-590-22293-7). 144pp. In this time-travel fantasy, Laura discovers the truth about two mysterious children who play in the garden next door. (Rev: BCCB 5/96; BL 1/1–15/96; SLJ 3/96)

8164 Ure, Jean. *The Wizard in the Woods* (3–5). Illus. by David Amstey. 1992, Candlewick $14.95 (1-56402-110-6). 176pp. After a botched-up spell, Ben-Muzzy is transported to Three Penny Wood, near the home of twins Joel and Gemma. (Rev: BL 12/1/92; SLJ 10/92)

8165 Ure, Jean. *Wizard in Wonderland* (3–5). Illus. by David Anstey. 1993, Candlewick $14.95 (1-56402-138-6). 176pp. Twins Joel and Gemma take a tour of Wonderland. (Rev: SLJ 7/93)

8166 *Vampire and Werewolf Stories* (5–10). Ed. by Alan Durant. Illus. Series: Kingfisher Story Library. 1998, Kingfisher paper $6.95 (0-7534-5152-2). 224pp. Eighteen stories, many written originally for an adult audience, make up this classic Gothic horror anthology about vampires and werewolves. (Rev: BL 1/1–15/99)

8167 Van Allsburg, Chris. *The Sweetest Fig* (3–6). Illus. 1993, Houghton $17.95 (0-395-67346-1). 32pp. All of his wildest dreams come true when a cruel dentist eats the figs given him in payment by a poor woman. (Rev: BCCB 11/93; BL 10/1/93*; SLJ 11/93*)

8168 Van Allsburg, Chris. *The Wreck of the Zephyr* (2–5). Illus. by author. 1983, Houghton $17.95 (0-395-33075-0). 32pp. The story behind the wreck of a sailboat.

8169 Vande Velde, Vivian. *A Coming Evil* (5–9). 1998, Houghton $16.00 (0-395-90012-3). Through encounters with the ghost of a 14th-century knight at her aunt's home in Nazi-occupied France, Lizette gains the courage to help her aunt hide several Jewish and Gypsy children. (Rev: BCCB 9/98; BL 10/1/98; HBG 3/99; SLJ 11/98)

8170 Vande Velde, Vivian. *Ghost of a Hanged Man* (3–6). 1998, Marshall Cavendish $14.95 (0-7614-5015-7). 96pp. A town falls under the deathly curse placed on it by murderous Jake Barnett before he was hanged, and now 11-year-old Ben and his sister

Annabelle believe they are next to be murdered by Jake's ghost. (Rev: BCCB 10/98; BL 11/15/98; HB 11–12/98; HBG 3/99; SLJ 10/98)

8171 Vande Velde, Vivian. *Smart Dog* (4–6). 1998, Harcourt $16.00 (0-15-201847-6). 144pp. When Amy tries to help a talking dog who is fleeing from lab experiments, her life becomes a confused muddle in this humorous fantasy. (Rev: BCCB 11/98; BL 9/1/98; HB 11–12/98; HBG 3/99; SLJ 11/98)

8172 Vande Velde, Vivian. *There's a Dead Person Following My Sister Around* (4–7). 1999, Harcourt $16.00 (0-15-202100-0). 160pp. In this historical ghost story, 11-year-old Ted discovers that his house in Rochester, New York, is haunted by the ghosts of two runaway slaves who drowned in the Erie Canal. (Rev: BCCB 10/99; HBG 3/00; SLJ 9/99)

8173 Van Leeuwen, Jean. *The Great Rescue Operation* (3–5). Illus. by Margot Apple. 1982, Dial LB $10.89 (0-685-01456-8). 144pp. Two mice try to locate their friend who has disappeared in Macy's department store.

8174 Van Leeuwen, Jean. *The Great Summer Camp Catastrophe* (4–6). Illus. by Diane De Groat. 1992, Dial $12.89 (0-8037-1107-7). 192pp. Marvin the mouse and rodent buddies Raymond and Fats end up at summer camp after hiding in a box that is shipped to Vermont. (Rev: BL 5/1/92; SLJ 4/92)

8175 Vansickle, Lisa. *The Secret Little City* (5–8). 2000, Palmae $15.95 (1-930167-11-3). 230pp. When 11-year-old Mackenzie moves with her family to a small town in Oregon, she discovers a whole civilization of inch-high people living beneath the floorboards of her new room. (Rev: SLJ 8/00)

8176 Vaugelade, Anais. *The War* (3–5). Trans. by Marie-Christine Rouffiac and Tom Streissguth. Illus. 2001, Carolrhoda $15.95 (1-57505-562-7). 32pp. In this picture-book allegory about the futility of war, a young idealist tricks the kings of the two warring sides into believing they have a common enemy and, therefore, must declare peace. (Rev: BL 3/15/01)

8177 Venokur, Ross. *The Amazing Frecktacle* (4–7). 1998, Delacorte $14.95 (0-385-32621-1). 136pp. Nicholas Bells, tired of being teased because of his abundant freckles, strikes a bargain with the villainous Mr. Piddlesticks to remove them, little knowing that his freckles are magical. (Rev: BCCB 9/98; BL 8/98; HBG 10/99; SLJ 9/98)

8178 Venokur, Ross. *The Cookie Company* (4–7). 2000, Delacorte $14.95 (0-385-32680-7). 181pp. After eating a strange fortune cookie, Alex is transported to another world where he meets some odd characters. (Rev: BCCB 2/00; BL 1/1–15/00; HBG 10/00; SLJ 2/00)

8179 Vivelo, Jackie. *Chills in the Night: Tales That Will Haunt You* (5–8). 1997, DK $14.95 (0-7894-2463-0). 123pp. Everyday experiences become strange and fearsome in this collection of bizarre, sometimes scary, stories. (Rev: BL 1/1–15/98; HBG 3/98; SLJ 1/98)

8180 Wagener, Gerda. *The Ghost in the Classroom* (2–4). Trans. by J. Alison James. Illus. 1997, North-

South LB $13.88 (1-55858-800-0). 46pp. A mischievous ghost named Otto helps Tina get the cat that she wants. (Rev: BL 1/1–15/98; HBG 10/98)

8181 Wallace, Bill. *Snot Stew* (4–6). Illus. by Lisa McCue. 1989, Holiday $15.95 (0-8234-0745-4); Pocket paper $3.99 (0-671-69335-2). 96pp. The amusing tale of how Mama Cat moves her kittens out into the world. (Rev: BL 5/15/89; SLJ 4/89)

8182 Wallace, Bill. *Totally Disgusting* (4–6). Illus. by Leslie Morrill. 1991, Holiday $15.95 (0-8234-0873-6); Pocket paper $3.99 (0-671-75416-5). 120pp. Feline Mewkiss wants to be brave and strong but isn't at all sure that he'll make it. (Rev: BCCB 6/91; BL 4/1/91; SLJ 6/91)

8183 Wallace, Bill. *Upchuck and the Rotten Willy: Running Wild* (3–6). Illus. by John S. Gurney. 2000, Pocket $17.00 (0-7434-0026-7); paper $3.99 (0-7434-0027-5). 99pp. Chuck, a cat, must choose between staying friends with Willy, a rottweiler, or making new friends with the two new cats in town who hate dogs. (Rev: SLJ 1/01)

8184 Wallace, Bill. *Watchdog and the Coyotes* (3–5). Illus. 1995, Pocket $14.00 (0-671-53620-6); paper $3.99 (0-671-89075-1). 105pp. A Great Dane learns to be more assertive when he becomes friends with an Irish setter and a beagle. (Rev: BL 12/15/95; SLJ 11/95)

8185 Wallace, Carol, and Bill Wallace. *The Flying Flea, Callie, and Me* (2–5). Illus. by David Slonim. 1999, Pocket $15.00 (0-671-02505-8). 86pp. A beginning chapter book about a kitten who takes care of an abandoned baby mockingbird that has a fear of flying. (Rev: HBG 10/99; SLJ 8/99)

8186 Wallace, Carol, and Bill Wallace. *That Furball Puppy and Me* (2–5). Illus. by Jason Wolff. 1999, Pocket $16.00 (0-671-02506-6). 83pp. An easy chapter book that tells the story of a kitten who is so jealous of a new puppy that he maneuvers to have him banished to the barn. (Rev: SLJ 4/00)

8187 Walsh, Jill Paton. *Pepi and the Secret Names* (3–5). Illus. by Fiona French. 1995, Lothrop $15.00 (0-688-13428-9). 32pp. In this fantasy set in ancient Egypt, Pepi gets animals to pose for her artist father by guessing their secret names. (Rev: BL 4/15/95; SLJ 4/95)

8188 Watson, Patrick. *Ahmek* (5–6). Illus. by Tracy Thomson. 1999, Stoddart $14.95 (0-7737-3145-8). 167pp. Ahmek, a beaver, is forced to leave his beloved pond and travel north to find a new home and a mate for life. (Rev: SLJ 4/00)

8189 Waugh, Sylvia. *The Mennyms* (4–8). 1994, Greenwillow $16.00 (0-688-13070-4). 212pp. When their owner dies, a family of rag dolls comes to life and takes over her house in this beginning volume of an extensive series. (Rev: BCCB 5/94; HB 7–8/94; SLJ 4/94)

8190 Waugh, Sylvia. *Mennyms Alive* (4–6). 1997, Greenwillow $16.00 (0-688-15201-5). 224pp. The last book about the Mennyms, rag dolls who have problems finding a permanent home. (Rev: BL 9/15/97; HB 11–12/97; HBG 3/98; SLJ 9/97)

8191 Waugh, Sylvia. *Mennyms Alone* (4–6). 1996, Greenwillow $16.00 (0-688-14702-X). 208pp. The rag doll creatures known as the Mennyms prepare for the end of their existence. (Rev: BCCB 11/96; BL 9/15/96; SLJ 9/96)

8192 Waugh, Sylvia. *Mennyms in the Wilderness* (4–6). 1995, Greenwillow $15.00 (0-688-13820-9). 256pp. The Mennyms, a family of lively rag dolls, fight the highway construction that threatens to destroy their home. A sequel to *The Mennyms*. (Rev: BCCB 3/95; BL 5/1/95; HB 7–8/95; SLJ 5/95)

8193 Waxman, Sydell, reteller. *The Rooster Prince* (2–5). Illus. by Giora Carmi. 2000, Pitspopany $16.95 (0-943706-45-9); paper $9.95 (0-943706-49-1). 40pp. In 18th-century Russia, a village boy is given the task of curing a prince who is behaving like rooster. (Rev: SLJ 1/01)

8194 Weinberg, Karen. *Window of Time* (5–7). Illus. by Annelle W. Ratcliffe. 1991, White Mane paper $9.95 (0-942597-18-4). 166pp. Ben climbs through a window and finds himself 125 years back in time. (Rev: SLJ 7/91)

8195 Welch, R. C. *Scary Stories for Stormy Nights* (5–7). Illus. 1995, Lowell House paper $5.95 (1-56565-262-2). 128pp. Ten contemporary horror stories that involve such characters as a werewolf and some pirates. (Rev: BL 5/1/95)

8196 Wells, Rosemary. *Rachel Field's Hitty: Her First Hundred Years* (4–6). Illus. by Susan Jeffers. 1999, Simon $21.95 (0-689-81716-9). Part abridgement, part extension of specific incidents with new material, this is an interesting and original look at Field's classic, now issued with bright illustrations. (Rev: BL 11/15/99; HBG 3/00; SLJ 1/00)

8197 Wesley, Mary. *Haphazard House* (5–7). 1993, Overlook $14.95 (0-87951-470-1). 150pp. An artist's magic hat enables him to make money betting on the Derby race during a visit to England. (Rev: BCCB 10/93; BL 1/1/94)

8198 West, Tracey. *Voyage of the Half Moon* (3–5). Illus. Series: Stories of the States. 1993, Silver Moon LB $14.95 (1-881889-18-1). 55pp. When Gwen is sent to live with a new foster family, she is haunted by a ghost that no one else can see. (Rev: SLJ 9/93)

8199 Westall, Robert. *Ghost Abbey* (5–7). 1989, Scholastic paper $3.25 (0-590-41693-6). Twelve-year-old Maggi is in charge of her small English household since her mother died. (Rev: BCCB 2/89; BL 2/1/89; SLJ 3/89)

8200 White, E. B. *Charlotte's Web* (3–5). Illus. by Garth Williams. 1952, HarperCollins LB $16.89 (0-06-026386-5); paper $5.95 (0-06-440055-7). 184pp. Classic, whimsical barnyard fable about a spider who saves the life of Wilbur the pig. Read about the ever-engaging mouse in: *Stuart Little* (1945).

8201 White, E. B. *The Trumpet of the Swan* (3–6). Illus. by Edward Frascino. 1970, HarperCollins LB $16.89 (0-06-026398-9); paper $5.95 (0-06-440048-4). 222pp. Louis, a voiceless trumpeter swan, is befriended by Sam, learns to play a trumpet, and finds fame, fortune, and fatherhood.

8202 Whitmore, Arvella. *Trapped between the Lash and the Gun: A Boy's Journey* (5–8). 1999, Dial

$15.99 (0-8037-2384-9). 192pp. Jordan, an African American boy of 12, changes after he travels back in time and experiences the horror and terror of slavery and a trip to freedom on the Underground Railroad. (Rev: BCCB 2/99; BL 11/15/98; HBG 10/99; SLJ 1/99)

8203 Whybrow, Ian. *Little Wolf's Diary of Daring Deeds* (2–4). Illus. by Tony Ross. 2000, Carolrhoda LB $12.95 (1-57505-411-6). 127pp. A beginning chapter book told in hilarious letters by Little Wolf, who is trying to found a school called Adventure Academy with his cousin Yeller. (Rev: HBG 10/00; SLJ 6/00)

8204 Whybrow, Ian. *Little Wolf's Haunted Hall for Small Horrors* (2–4). Illus. by Tony Ross. 2000, Carolrhoda $12.95 (1-57505-412-4). 128pp. Little Wolf, his friend Yeller, and younger brother Smellybreff encounter the ghost of Little Wolf's uncle Bigbad Wolf in this amusing animal fantasy told through letters. (Rev: HBG 3/01; SLJ 9/00)

8205 Willard, Nancy. *The High Rise Glorious Skittle Skat Roarious Sky Pie Angel Food Cake* (3–5). Illus. by Richard J. Watson. 1990, Harcourt $15.95 (0-15-234332-6). 64pp. Grandma's cake has mysterious ingredients — an odd spell and the special help of angels. (Rev: BCCB 12/90; BL 9/1/90; SLJ 11/90*)

8206 Willard, Nancy. *The Marzipan Moon* (4–5). Illus. by Marcia Sewall. 1981, Harcourt paper $3.95 (0-15-252963-2). 46pp. A cracked pot given to a parish priest has miraculous powers.

8207 Willard, Nancy. *The Tortilla Cat* (3–5). Illus. by Jeanette Winter. 1998, Harcourt $16.00 (0-15-289587-6). 48pp. Dr. Romero is convinced that the little cat that helps his children get better when they are ill is only a dream. (Rev: BCCB 5/98; BL 3/1/98; HBG 10/98; SLJ 3/98)

8208 Willard, Nancy. *Uncle Terrible: More Adventures of Anatole* (4–6). Illus. by David McPhail. 1985, Harcourt paper $5.95 (0-15-292794-8). 120pp. A boy's visit to Uncle Terrible, so named because he is so terribly nice.

8209 Williams, Margery. *The Velveteen Rabbit: Or, How Toys Become Real* (2–4). Illus. by Michael Hague. 1983, Holt $16.95 (0-8050-0209-X). 48pp. Love brings a toy rabbit to life. One of many fine editions.

8210 Winter, Laurel. *Growing Wings* (4–6). 2000, Houghton $15.00 (0-618-07405-8). 224pp. When 11-year-old Linnet begins to grow wings, her mother abandons her and she is taken in by a colony of winged people. (Rev: BL 10/15/00; HBG 3/01; SLJ 10/00)

8211 Winthrop, Elizabeth. *The Battle for the Castle* (4–7). 1993, Holiday $15.95 (0-8234-1010-2). 216pp. William and friend Jason time-travel to the Middle Ages, where they become involved in a struggle to prevent the return of evil as a ruling power. A sequel to *The Castle in the Attic* (1985). (Rev: BL 9/1/93; HB 7–8/93; SLJ 5/93)

8212 Winthrop, Elizabeth. *The Castle in the Attic* (5–7). 1985, Holiday $15.95 (0-8234-0579-6). 192pp. In an effort to keep his sitter from returning to England, William miniaturizes her and then must find a way to undo the deed. (Rev: BCCB 10/85; BL 1/15/86; SLJ 2/86)

8213 Wiseman, David. *Jeremy Visick* (5–8). 1981, Houghton paper $7.95 (0-395-56153-1). Matthew helps the ghost of young Jeremy find rest.

8214 Wojciechowski, Susan. *Beany (Not Beanhead) and the Magic Crystal* (2–4). Illus. 1997, Candlewick $15.99 (0-7636-0052-0). 96pp. In this light-hearted story, Beany thinks that a crystal from a chandelier might be magical and wonders what would be the perfect wish. (Rev: BL 7/97; HBG 3/98; SLJ 7/97)

8215 Wood, Beverley, and Chris Wood. *Dogstar* (5–7). 1998, Orca paper $6.95 (1-896095-37-2). 256pp. On a trip to Juneau, Alaska, young Jeff follows a stray dog who takes him back in time to the 1930s and an adventure involving sunken ships and lost treasure. (Rev: BL 4/1/98; SLJ 8/98)

8216 Woodruff, Elvira. *Awfully Short for the Fourth Grade* (3–6). Illus. by Will Hillenbrand. 1989, Holiday $15.95 (0-8234-0785-3). 112pp. Noah's toy soldiers and superheroes come to life and he becomes their size when he uses a special dust from his magic kit. (Rev: BL 1/1/90; SLJ 11/89)

8217 Woodruff, Elvira. *The Ghost of Lizard Light* (4–6). Illus. by Elaine Clayton. 1999, Knopf LB $16.99 (0-679-99281-2). 176pp. Set in Maine, this novel tells 10-year-old Jack Carlton's troubles with his strict father and what happens when Jack is contacted by the ghost of a boy who died 150 years ago. (Rev: HBG 3/00; SLJ 1/00)

8218 Woodruff, Elvira. *Orphan of Ellis Island* (4–7). 1997, Scholastic $15.95 (0-590-48245-9). 192pp. Left alone on Ellis Island, Dominic finds himself transported in time to the village in Italy his family came from. (Rev: BCCB 3/97; BL 6/1–15/97; SLJ 5/97)

8219 Woodruff, Elvira. *The Summer I Shrank My Grandmother* (4–6). Illus. by Katherine Coville. 1992, Bantam paper $3.99 (0-440-40640-4). 160pp. Nelly finds an ancient chemistry set and changes her grandmother into a gorgeous 30-year-old who keeps getting younger. (Rev: BL 1/1/91; SLJ 12/90)

8220 Wrede, Patricia C. *Book of Enchantments* (5–8). 1996, Harcourt $17.00 (0-15-201255-9). 240pp. A collection of stories with various settings, each dealing with an enchantment. (Rev: BCCB 5/96; BL 5/15/96; SLJ 6/96)

8221 Wright, Betty R. *Christina's Ghost* (4–6). 1985, Holiday $15.95 (0-8234-0581-8). 128pp. Dismayed at having to spend the summer with grumpy Uncle Ralph in his Victorian mansion, Christina is even more dismayed to discover a ghost in the house. (Rev: BCCB 2/86; BL 2/1/86)

8222 Wright, Betty R. *The Ghost Comes Calling* (3–6). 1994, Scholastic $14.95 (0-590-47353-0). 128pp. When Chad encounters the ghost that built the shabby log cabin his father has just bought, he sets out to right a wrong and let the ghost rest. (Rev: BCCB 3/94; BL 2/15/94; HB 9–10/94; SLJ 4/94)

8223 Wright, Betty R. *The Ghost in Room 11* (2–4). 1997, Holiday $15.95 (0-8234-1318-7). 112pp. Matt can't convince his classmates that he is being visited

by the ghost of an old school teacher. (Rev: BCCB 4/98; BL 3/1/98; HBG 10/98; SLJ 3/98)

8224 Wright, Betty R. *A Ghost in the House* (5–7). 1991, Scholastic $13.95 (0-590-43606-6). 160pp. Bizarre happenings take place when Sarah's elderly aunt moves in. (Rev: BCCB 11/91; BL 1/1/91; SLJ 11/91)

8225 Wright, Betty R. *The Ghost of Popcorn Hill* (2–4). Illus. by Karen Ritz. 1993, Holiday $15.95 (0-8234-1009-9). 96pp. Martin and Peter are frightened by the ghost who visits their bedroom each night in their rustic home on Popcorn Hill. (Rev: BCCB 6/93; BL 2/15/93; HB 7–8/93; SLJ 5/93)

8226 Wright, Betty R. *Haunted Summer* (4–6). 1996, Scholastic $14.95 (0-590-47355-7). 128pp. Abby discovers that a wicked witch wants possession of a music box that Abby's aunt has sent as a gift. (Rev: BCCB 4/96; BL 4/1/96; HB 7–8/96; SLJ 5/96)

8227 Wright, Betty R. *The Moonlight Man* (4–6). 2000, Scholastic $15.95 (0-590-25237-2). 176pp. Jenny Joslin, 15, has moved to a new house with her father and younger sister, which they discover is haunted by a vindictive ghost. (Rev: HBG 10/00; SLJ 2/00)

8228 Wright, Betty R. *Out of the Dark* (4–6). 1995, Scholastic $14.95 (0-590-43598-1). 128pp. Jessica's stay in her grandmother's home in the country becomes unexpectedly horrifying when she encounters a ghost. (Rev: BCCB 2/95; BL 12/1/94; SLJ 1/95)

8229 Wynne Jones, Diana. *Fantasy Stories* (4–8). Illus. 1994, Kingfisher paper $7.95 (1-85697-982-2). 256pp. A selection of fantasies from such authors as Kipling, C. S. Lewis, and Jane Yolen. (Rev: BL 3/1/95; SLJ 11/94)

8230 Wynne-Jones, Tim. *Some of the Kinder Planets* (5–8). 1995, Orchard LB $16.99 (0-531-08751-4). 144pp. Nine imaginative stories about young people in unusual situations. (Rev: BCCB 5/95; BL 3/1/95*; HB 5–6/95, 9–10/95, 1-2/95; SLJ 4/95*)

8231 Yee, Paul. *Ghost Train* (3–5). Illus. by Harvey Chan. 1996, Douglas & McIntyre $15.95 (0-88899-257-2). 32pp. In this historical fantasy, a Chinese girl comes to the United States and discovers that her father has been killed while working as a railroad construction laborer. (Rev: BCCB 2/97; BL 11/1/96)

8232 Yep, Laurence. *Dragon of the Lost Sea* (5–8). 1982, HarperCollins paper $5.95 (0-06-440227-4). 224pp. Shimmer, a dragon, in the company of a boy, Thorn, sets out to destroy the villain Civet.

8233 Yep, Laurence. *The Imp That Ate My Homework* (3–7). Illus. 1998, HarperCollins LB $14.89 (0-06-027689-4). 96pp. A six-foot-tall, four-armed ancient creature enters Jim's life and creates havoc in this novel set in San Francisco's Chinatown. (Rev: BCCB 4/98; BL 12/15/97; HB 5–6/98; HBG 10/98; SLJ 3/98)

8234 Yep, Laurence. *The Magic Paintbrush* (3–5). Illus. 2000, HarperCollins LB $13.89 (0-06-028200-2). 96pp. A young Chinese American boy discovers a new life when everything he paints with his new paintbrush becomes real. (Rev: BCCB 4/00; BL 2/1/00; SLJ 3/00)

8235 Yolen, Jane. *Boots and the Seven Leaguers: A Rock-and-Troll Novel* (5–8). 2000, Harcourt $17.00 (0-15-202557-X). 192pp. In this fantasy with a contemporary twist, Gog and best friend Pook set out on a quest in the New Forest to rescue Gog's kidnapped little brother, Magog. (Rev: HBG 3/01; SLJ 10/00)

8236 Yolen, Jane. *Here There Be Dragons* (3–8). Illus. by David Wilgus. Series: Jane Yolen Books. 1993, Harcourt $16.95 (0-15-209888-7); paper $10.00 (0-15-201705-4). 160pp. This original collection of pieces about dragons contains eight stories and five poems. (Rev: SLJ 12/93)

8237 Yolen, Jane. *Here There Be Ghosts* (5–9). Illus. by David Wilgus. Series: Here There Be. 1998, Harcourt $19.00 (0-15-201566-3). 122pp. A collection of short stories and a few poems about ghosts and lost souls. (Rev: HBG 3/99; SLJ 11/98)

8238 Yolen, Jane. *Merlin* (5–8). 1997, Harcourt $15.00 (0-15-200814-4). 112pp. In this concluding volume of the Young Merlin trilogy, Hawk-Hobby, alias Merlin, escapes from his enemies with a young friend who will later become King Arthur. (Rev: BL 4/15/97; SLJ 5/97)

8239 Yolen, Jane. *Passager: The Young Merlin Trilogy, Book One* (4–7). 1996, Harcourt $15.00 (0-15-200391-6). 96pp. In medieval England, an abandoned 8-year-old boy named Merlin is taken in by a friendly man who becomes his master. Book two of the trilogy is *Hobby* (1996). (Rev: BL 5/1/96; HB 7–8/96; SLJ 5/96*)

8240 Yolen, Jane. *The Pictish Child* (3–6). Series: Tartan Magic. 1999, Harcourt $15.00 (0-15-202261-9). 144pp. Molly receives a talisman that begins a series of events involving Jennifer, a young Pict girl, who has time-traveled to modern times from ninth-century Britain. (Rev: BL 11/15/99; HBG 3/00; SLJ 12/99)

8241 Yolen, Jane. *The Sea Man* (3–5). Illus. 1998, Putnam $14.99 (0-399-22939-6). 48pp. After a 1663 sailing ship catches a merman in its nets and the lieutenant in charge rescues him, the young sailor is rewarded in an unusual way. (Rev: BL 11/1/98; HBG 10/98; SLJ 10/98)

8242 Yolen, Jane. *Wizard's Hall* (4–6). 1991, Harcourt $13.95 (0-15-298132-2). 144pp. Henry, an 11-year-old novice wizard, can't seem to get anything right. (Rev: BCCB 7–8/91; BL 3/15/91; SLJ 7/91)

8243 Yolen, Jane. *The Wizard's Map* (3–6). Series: Tartan Magic. 1999, Harcourt $15.00 (0-15-202067-5). 144pp. Thirteen-year-old twins, Jennifer and Peter, and younger sister Molly are in Scotland visiting relatives when they encounter an evil sorcerer. (Rev: BL 5/15/99; HBG 10/99; SLJ 5/99)

8244 Yoshi. *The Butterfly Hunt* (5–8). Illus. 1991, Picture Book paper $14.95 (0-88708-137-1). In this fantasy, a young boy releases a butterfly and forevermore it becomes his own. (Rev: SLJ 6/91)

8245 Zadrzynska, Ewa. *The Peaceable Kingdom* (4–6). Illus. by Tomek Olbinski. 1994, M.M. Art Bks. $14.95 (0-9638904-0-9). 32pp. In this fantasy, visitors to Brooklyn find that the three animals pictured in Hicks's painting "The Peaceable Kingdom," hanging in the Brooklyn Museum, are sitting in the park. (Rev: BL 7/94; SLJ 9/94)

Friendship Stories

8246 Adler, C. S. *Always and Forever Friends* (5–7). 1990, Avon paper $3.99 (0-380-70687-3). 176pp. Wendy, at 11, is having a painful struggle making new friends after Meg moves away until she meets Honor, who is African American and very hesitant about accepting Wendy. (Rev: BCCB 4/88; BL 4/1/88; SLJ 4/88)

8247 Adler, C. S. *The Magic of the Glits* (5–7). Illus. by Ati Forberg. 1987, Avon paper $2.50 (0-380-70403-X). 96pp. Jeremy, age 12, takes care of 7-year-old Lynette for the summer. A reissue of the 1979 edition. Also use: *Some Other Summer* (1988).

8248 Adler, C. S. *Not Just a Summer Crush* (5–7). 1998, Clarion $15.00 (0-395-88532-9). 128pp. Lonely and misunderstood, 12-year-old Hana forms a friendship with a former teacher but Hana's mother discovers this relationship and moves to end it. (Rev: BCCB 10/98; BL 11/15/98; HB 11–12/98; HBG 3/99; SLJ 11/98)

8249 Angell, Judie. *The Buffalo Nickel Blues Band* (5–8). 1991, Macmillan paper $3.95 (0-689-71448-3). 192pp. Five youngsters join together to form a band.

8250 Appelbaum, Diana. *Cocoa Ice* (2–5). Illus. by Holly Meade. 1997, Orchard LB $17.99 (0-531-33040-0). 56pp. Two girls, one in Santo Domingo and the other in Maine, are linked by world trade, which brings chocolate to one and ice to the other. (Rev: BCCB 3/98; BL 11/1/97*; HBG 3/98; SLJ 1/98*)

8251 Armistead, John. *The $66 Summer* (5–9). 2000, Milkweed $15.95 (1-57131-626-4); paper $6.95 (1-57131-625-6). 234pp. In 1955, 12-year-old George is spending a summer with his grandmother in Alabama where he makes friends with two African American boys and joins them in solving a mystery involving racism and tragedy. (Rev: BL 5/1/00; HBG 10/00; SLJ 5/00)

8252 Bauer, Marion Dane. *A Dream of Queens and Castles* (4–6). 1990, Houghton $13.95 (0-395-51330-8). 103pp. Except for the fact that she can meet the Princess of Wales, Diana is not happy to be going to England for a year. (Rev: BCCB 6/90; BL 2/15/90; HB 7–8/90; SLJ 5/90)

8253 Bedard, Michael. *Emily* (3–5). Illus. by Barbara Cooney. 1992, Doubleday $16.95 (0-385-30697-0). A young girl visits her neighbor, the reclusive Emily Dickinson. (Rev: BCCB 1/93; BL 2/1/93; HB 1–2/93; SLJ 11/92)

8254 Bellingham, Brenda. *Lilly's Good Deed* (3–4). Illus. by Kathy Kaulbach. Series: First Novels. 1999, Formac paper $3.99 (0-88780-460-8). 64pp. A beginning chapter book from Canada in which Lilly discovers that first impressions can be wrong when she realizes the value of the friendship of a clumsy classmate. (Rev: SLJ 8/99)

8255 Belton, Sandra. *Ernestine and Amanda* (4–6). 1996, Simon & Schuster $16.00 (0-689-80848-8). 150pp. Two young African American girls tell of their misunderstandings in alternating chapters. (Rev: BL 1/1–15/97; SLJ 11/96)

8256 Belton, Sandra. *Ernestine and Amanda: Summer Camp, Ready or Not!* (4–6). 1997, Simon & Schuster $16.00 (0-689-80846-1). 176pp. Two African American girls, who are friends, are sent to different summer camps and report on their experiences. (Rev: BCCB 1/97; BL 8/97; SLJ 8/97)

8257 Belton, Sandra. *Members of the C.L.U.B* (4–7). 1997, Simon & Schuster paper $16.00 (0-689-81611-1). 176pp. The friendship of Ernestine and Amanda, two African American girls from different backgrounds, seems to have ended permanently when one forms a club and excludes the other. (Rev: BL 11/15/97; HBG 3/98; SLJ 11/97)

8258 Belton, Sandra. *Mysteries on Monroe Street* (4–7). Illus. by Nancy Carpenter. 1998, Simon & Schuster $16.00 (0-689-81612-X). 160pp. In this, the fourth book in the Ernestine and Amanda series set in the late 1950s (told in alternating chapters by each of these African American friends), the focus is on adolescent problems, family tensions, and racial integration. (Rev: BL 7/98; HBG 10/98; SLJ 6/98)

8259 Bonners, Susan. *The Silver Balloon* (3–5). Illus. 1997, Farrar $14.00 (0-374-36913-5). 80pp. Two pen pals reveal facts about each other through a series of mystery gifts they exchange. (Rev: BL 9/15/97; SLJ 10/97)

8260 Brockmann, Carolee. *Going for Great* (4–6). Series: AG Fiction. 1999, Pleasant $9.95 (1-56247-847-8); paper $5.95 (1-56247-752-8). 119pp. Two sixth-grade girls, who have been friends all their lives, find they are drifting apart because of different interests. (Rev: HBG 3/00; SLJ 2/00)

8261 Brooks, Bruce. *Everywhere* (5–8). 1990, HarperCollins LB $15.89 (0-06-020729-9). 80pp. Eleven-year-old Dooley, who is African American, helps a 10-year-old white boy live through the emotional trauma of waiting to see if his beloved grandfather will recover from a heart attack. (Rev: BCCB 10/90; BL 10/15/90*; SLJ 9/90*)

8262 Bunting, Eve. *Summer Wheels* (3–5). Illus. by Thomas B. Allen. 1992, Harcourt $14.95 (0-15-207000-1). 48pp. Lawrence and Brady are annoyed by the new kid, who signs out a bike from the Bicycle Man with the clear intention of not returning it. (Rev: BCCB 3/92; BL 4/15/92; HB 7–8/92; SLJ 8/92)

8263 Burnett, Frances Hodgson. *The Secret Garden* (4–6). Illus. by Tasha Tudor. 1987, HarperCollins paper $4.95 (0-06-440188-X). 256pp. Three children find a secret garden and make it bloom again; the garden, in turn, changes the children. One of many fine editions.

8264 Buscaglia, Leo. *A Memory for Tino* (4–6). Illus. by Carol Newsom. 1988, Slack $12.95 (1-556-42020-X). 50pp. Tino becomes friends with elderly

Mrs. Sunday, and gives her his family's TV set. (Rev: BL 4/1/88; SLJ 5/88)

8265 Byars, Betsy. *The Animal, the Vegetable and John D. Jones* (5–8). Illus. by Ruth Sanderson. 1983, Dell paper $3.99 (0-440-40356-1). 160pp. Clara and Deanie must share their vacation with the brainy John D.

8266 Byars, Betsy. *The Pinballs* (5–7). 1977, HarperCollins LB $15.89 (0-06-020918-6). 144pp. Three misfits in a foster home band together to help lessen their problems.

8267 Carlson, Natalie Savage. *The Family Under the Bridge* (3–5). Illus. by Garth Williams. 1958, HarperCollins LB $15.89 (0-06-020991-7); paper $5.95 (0-06-440250-9). 112pp. Old Armand, a Paris hobo, finds three children huddled in his hideaway under the bridge and befriends them.

8268 Choyce, Lesley. *Carrie's Crowd* (3–4). Illus. by Mark Thurman. Series: First Novels. 1999, Formac paper $3.99 (0-88780-464-0). 64pp. A beginning chapter book in which Carrie realizes that making a friend of Giselle, a member of the "in" crowd, was a mistake because Giselle is rude and lacks respect for others. (Rev: SLJ 8/99)

8269 Christiansen, C. B. *A Snowman on Sycamore Street* (2–4). Illus. 1996, Simon & Schuster $15.00 (0-689-31927-4). 30pp. In this sequel to *Sycamore Street* (1993), the three friends — Angel, Chloe, and Rupert — continue to have good times together. (Rev: BL 10/1/96; SLJ 11/96)

8270 Cooper, Ilene. *Queen of the Sixth Grade* (4–6). 1990, Puffin paper $3.95 (0-140-34028-9). 128pp. Robin and Veronica, acknowledged leader of the sixth grade, fight, and Robin learns about being an outsider. (Rev: BCCB 11/88; BL 9/1/88; SLJ 11/88)

8271 Cooper, Susan. *Dawn of Fear* (5–6). Illus. by Margery Gill. 1989, Simon & Schuster paper $4.99 (0-689-71327-4). 157pp. Reality must be faced by a group of English boys when one of their friends is killed in an air raid during World War II.

8272 Cosby, Bill. *The Best Way to Play* (2–4). Illus. 1997, Scholastic $13.95 (0-590-13756-5); paper $3.99 (0-590-95617-5). 40pp. Little Bill wants a $50 video game but finds that he can have more fun making up a game with his friends. Also use *The Meanest Thing To Say* and *The Treasure Hunt* (both 1997). (Rev: BL 2/15/98; HBG 3/98; SLJ 12/97)

8273 Cruise, Robin. *Fiona's Private Pages* (5–7). 2000, Harcourt $15.00 (0-15-202210-4). 160pp. In her journal Fiona explores the meaning of friendship, what makes a good friend, and how friends can help each other. (Rev: BL 5/15/00; HBG 10/00; SLJ 6/00)

8274 Danziger, Paula, and Ann M. Martin. *P.S. Longer Letter Later* (5–7). 1998, Scholastic $15.95 (0-590-21310-5). 240pp. This epistolary novel consists of letters between two recently separated girlfriends — one who is adjusting well and the other who is facing family problems after her father loses his job and the family must change their lifestyle. (Rev: BL 6/1–15/98; HBG 10/98; SLJ 5/98)

8275 Danziger, Paula, and Ann M. Martin. *Snail Mail No More* (5–7). 2000, Scholastic $16.95 (0-

439-06335-3). 336pp. Two 13-year-old friends correspond by e-mail and reveal funny, thought-provoking experiences that involve family and social problems. (Rev: BCCB 4/00; BL 3/15/00; HBG 10/00)

8276 DeFelice, Cynthia. *The Light on Hogback Hill* (4–8). 1993, Macmillan paper $15.00 (0-02-726453-X). 144pp. Two friends explore the haunted Hogback Hill and make a friend of the recluse they find living there. (Rev: BCCB 12/93; BL 11/1/93; SLJ 11/93)

8277 Duffy, James. *Uncle Shamus* (4–6). 1992, Macmillan LB $13.95 (0-684-19434-1). 144pp. Two children form an unusual friendship with an elderly African American man, returned after 30 years in prison. (Rev: BCCB 5/92; BL 3/1/92; SLJ 7/92)

8278 Dunlop, Eileen. *Finn's Search* (4–7). 1994, Holiday $14.95 (0-8234-1099-4). 128pp. Two Scottish boys try to save a gravel pit from local developers. (Rev: BCCB 12/94; BL 10/1/94; SLJ 10/94)

8279 Elliott, David. *The Cool Crazy Crickets* (2–3). 2000, Candlewick $15.99 (0-7636-0601-4). 48pp. In this easy chapter book, four interracial girls decide to form a club that they call the Cool Crazy Crickets. (Rev: BL 9/15/00; HBG 10/00; SLJ 8/00)

8280 England, Linda. *3 Kids Dreamin'* (2–5). Illus. by Dena Schutzer. 1997, Simon & Schuster paper $16.00 (0-689-80866-6). Three youngsters form a rap group and become a big success. (Rev: SLJ 6/97)

8281 Farrell, Mame. *Marrying Malcolm Murgatroyd* (5–7). 1995, Farrar $14.00 (0-374-34838-3). 122pp. Hannah defends the class nerd because he has been kind to her handicapped younger brother. (Rev: BCCB 12/95; BL 11/1/95; SLJ 11/95)

8282 Feuer, Elizabeth. *Lost Summer* (5–8). 1995, Farrar $16.00 (0-374-31020-3). 185pp. Lydia has difficulties adjusting to her cabinmates at summer camp. (Rev: BCCB 4/95; BL 5/15/95; SLJ 5/95)

8283 Fields, Julia. *The Green Lion of Zion Street* (4–6). Illus. by Jerry Pinkney. 1988, Simon & Schuster $14.95 (0-689-50414-4). 32pp. A group of African American children cautiously approach a stone lion in a fog-shrouded park. (Rev: BCCB 6/88; BL 4/15/88; SLJ 5/88)

8284 Fogelin, Adrian. *Crossing Jordan* (5–8). Illus. by Suzy Schultz. 2000, Peachtree $14.95 (1-56145-215-7). 140pp. Set in contemporary Florida, this novel tells how 12-year-old Cass must keep her friendship with African American Jemmie a secret from her racist father. (Rev: BCCB 4/00; HBG 10/00; SLJ 6/00)

8285 Fowler, Susi G. *Albertina the Practically Perfect* (2–4). Illus. 1998, Greenwillow $15.00 (0-688-15829-3). 80pp. When Molly moves across town, she is desperate to make new friends and, as a result, makes some mistakes in evaluating people. (Rev: BCCB 10/98; BL 10/15/98; HB 9–10/98; HBG 3/99; SLJ 10/98)

8286 Gabhart, Ann. *Two of a Kind* (3–6). 1992, Avon paper $3.50 (0-380-76153-X). 170pp. Birdie decides it's better to be aloof, even with her likable aunt and uncle, so she won't feel so bad when she's sent to another foster home. (Rev: BL 8/92)

8287 Galbraith, Kathryn O. *Roommates Again* (2–4). Illus. 1994, Macmillan paper $13.00 (0-689-50597-3). 48pp. Two sisters go to summer camp together and find they each must conquer private fears involving new situations. (Rev: BL 8/94; SLJ 8/94)

8288 Giff, Patricia Reilly. *Love, from the Fifth-Grade Celebrity* (4–6). Illus. by Leslie Morrill. 1998, Bantam paper $3.99 (0-440-44948-0). 144pp. Casey and Tracy get involved in tattling on each other and realize the error of their ways. (Rev: BL 9/1/86)

8289 Gilson, Jamie. *Hello, My Name Is Scrambled Eggs* (5–7). Illus. by John Wallner. 1985, Lothrop $16.00 (0-688-04095-0). 160pp. Harvey looks forward to the arrival of a Vietnam refugee family and their son, but runs into trouble with the prejudice of his American friend Quint. (Rev: BCCB 7/85; BL 4/14/85; SLJ 8/85)

8290 Greene, Bette. *Philip Hall Likes Me, I Reckon Maybe* (4–6). Illus. by Charles Lilly. 1975, Dell paper $4.99 (0-440-45755-6). 144pp. Beth finds that letting Philip Hall get first place in their class turns out not to be the best way to gain his affection.

8291 Greene, Carol. *The Jenny Summer* (2–4). Illus. by Ellen Eagle. 1988, HarperCollins $11.95 (0-06-022208-5). 80pp. Robin learns a lot about friendship during one summer. (Rev: BL 6/15/88; SLJ 8/88)

8292 Greene, Constance C. *A Girl Called Al* (5–7). Illus. by Byron Barton. 1991, Puffin paper $5.99 (0-14-034786-0). 128pp. The friendship between two seventh graders and their apartment building superintendent is humorously and deftly recounted.

8293 Gregory, Deborah. *Wishing on a Star* (5–8). Series: The Cheetah Girls. 1999, Hyperion paper $3.99 (0-7868-1384-9). 120pp. A light novel about five girls in New York City who form a singing group, the Cheetah Girls, and are soon signed up for an important gig. (Rev: SLJ 1/00)

8294 Grove, Vicki. *The Crystal Garden* (5–8). 1995, Putnam $16.99 (0-399-21813-0). 217pp. When she moves to a small town in Missouri, Eliza is determined to become part of the rich girls' clique. (Rev: BCCB 6/95; BL 9/1/95; SLJ 5/95*)

8295 Grove, Vicki. *Reaching Dustin* (4–6). 1998, Putnam $15.99 (0-399-23008-4). 208pp. Carly, a sixth-grader growing up in a quiet Missouri farming community, is given the tough assignment of interviewing the class bully, Dustin Groat, whose gun-carrying family is rumored to be manufacturing illegal drugs. (Rev: BCCB 3/98; BL 5/1/98; HB 3–4/98; HBG 10/98; SLJ 5/98)

8296 Hahn, Mary D. *Daphne's Book* (6–8). 1983, Houghton $15.00 (0-89919-183-5); Avon paper $4.50 (0-380-72355-7). 192pp. The story of a friendship between two very different girls.

8297 Hansen, Joyce. *The Gift-Giver* (4–7). 1980, Houghton paper $6.95 (0-89919-852-X). 128pp. Doris forms a friendship with a quiet boy, Amir.

8298 Hansen, Joyce. *Yellow Bird and Me* (4–6). 1986, Houghton paper $6.95 (0-395-55388-1).

128pp. The continuing story of the growing up of Doris, an African American girl in the Bronx, New York, and her friendship with Yellow Bird, who suffers from dyslexia. (Rev: BCCB 4/86; BL 4/1/86; SLJ 5/86)

8299 Herman, Charlotte. *Max Malone Makes a Million* (3–5). Illus. 1991, Holt paper $6.95 (0-8050-2328-3). 77pp. Max wants to make a fortune, but learns a lesson in generosity instead. Also use: *Max Malone and the Great Cereal Rip-Off* (1990). (Rev: BCCB 6/91; BL 3/1/91; SLJ 6/91)

8300 Hermes, Patricia. *I Hate Being Gifted* (5–8). 1992, Pocket paper $3.50 (0-671-74786-X). 144pp. Everybody says it's an honor to be in the Learning Enrichment Activity Program, but KT thinks it can ruin her entire sixth-grade year. (Rev: BL 12/1/90)

8301 Hirsch, Karen. *Ellen Anders on Her Own* (4–6). 1994, Macmillan paper $15.00 (0-02-743975-5). 96pp. Ellen learns about friendship through reading a journal kept by her mother years before she died. (Rev: BL 5/1/94; SLJ 6/94)

8302 Hoffman, Mary. *Starring Grace* (2–4). Illus. by Caroline Binch. 2000, Penguin $13.99 (0-8037-2559-0). 96pp. A lively chapter book about young Grace and her many summer adventures with friends, culminating in walk-on roles in a theatrical production. (Rev: BCCB 9/00; BL 2/15/00; HB 3–4/00; HBG 10/00; SLJ 7/00)

8303 Holt, Kimberly Willis. *When Zachary Beaver Came to Town* (5–8). 1999, Holt $16.95 (0-8050-6116-9). 227pp. Thirteen-year-old Toby Wilson learns the value of love and friendship when he gets to know Zachary Beaver, a 643-pound teen who has been abandoned by his guardian. (Rev: BCCB 12/99; HB 11–12/99; HBG 3/00; SLJ 11/99*)

8304 Honeycutt, Natalie. *Josie's Beau* (5–7). 1988, Avon paper $2.95 (0-380-70524-9). 128pp. Beau's mother doesn't want him fighting, so Josie offers to say she's the one who fights — but the lie backfires. (Rev: BCCB 12/87; BL 12/1/87; SLJ 12/87)

8305 Hossack, Sylvie. *Green Mango Magic* (4–7). 1999, Avon $14.00 (0-380-97613-7). 128pp. Maile, who lives alone with her grandmother in Hawaii since her father abandoned her, finds a friend in Brooke, from Seattle, who is a recovering cancer patient. (Rev: BCCB 12/98; BL 5/1/99; HBG 10/99; SLJ 2/99)

8306 Hossack, Sylvie A. *The Flying Chickens of Paradise Lane* (3–6). 1994, Avon paper $3.50 (0-380-72201-1). 144pp. Ten-year-old Brenda, who desperately wants to learn to fly, forms a secret club with friends and practices jumping from ever-increasing heights. (Rev: BL 3/1/93; SLJ 3/93)

8307 Hurwitz, Johanna. *The Cold and Hot Winter* (4–6). Illus. by Carolyn Ewing. 1988, Morrow $14.95 (0-688-07839-7). 144pp. The relationship of three children is strained because one may be a thief. (Rev: BCCB 11/88; BL 10/15/88; SLJ 9/88)

8308 Hurwitz, Johanna. *The Hot and Cold Summer* (4–6). Illus. by Gail Owens. 1984, Morrow $16.00 (0-688-02746-6); Scholastic paper $4.50 (0-590-42858-6). 176pp. Roddy and Derek wonder about

their neighbor's niece, who is spending the summer with her aunt.

8309 Hurwitz, Johanna. *The Just Desserts Club* (3–5). 1999, Morrow $16.00 (0-688-16266-5). 144pp. In four short stories, Cricket and her friends engage in cooking activities and provide tasty recipes for this book. (Rev: BL 8/99; HBG 3/00; SLJ 10/99)

8310 Hurwitz, Johanna. *Ozzie on His Own* (2–4). Illus. by Eileen McKeating. 1995, Morrow $15.00 (0-688-13742-3). 128pp. When Ozzie finds an abandoned chicken coop, he soon forms a club and makes new friends. (Rev: BCCB 3/95; BL 3/1/95; SLJ 6/95)

8311 Hurwitz, Johanna. *Spring Break* (3–5). Illus. 1997, Morrow $15.00 (0-688-14937-5). 144pp. An appealing novel about Cricket and her adventures when she is unable to go with her class to Washington, D.C., during spring break because of a broken ankle. (Rev: BCCB 4/97; BL 4/15/97; SLJ 5/97)

8312 Hurwitz, Johanna. *The Up and Down Spring* (3–6). Illus. by Gail Owens. 1993, Morrow $14.00 (0-688-11922-0). 112pp. On a trip to Ithaca, New York, Roddy has trouble keeping his fear of flying a secret in this sequel to *The Hot and Cold Summer* (1984). (Rev: BCCB 4/93; BL 2/15/93; SLJ 7/93)

8313 Johnson, Angela. *Maniac Monkeys on Magnolia Street* (3–5). 1998, Knopf $16.00 (0-679-89053-X). 112pp. Charlie enjoys living on her new street, meeting her neighbors, and sharing some innocent adventures with her new friend Billy. (Rev: BL 1/1–15/99; HBG 3/99; SLJ 2/99)

8314 Johnson, Angela. *When Mules Flew on Magnolia Street* (2–4). 2000, Knopf LB $16.99 (0-679-99077-1). 112pp. Everyday events that happen to Charlie and her friends on Magnolia Street are reported in this episodic beginning chapter book. (Rev: BL 1/1–15/01; HBG 3/01; SLJ 1/01)

8315 Jukes, Mavis. *Getting Even* (5–7). 1988, Knopf paper $3.99 (0-679-86570-5). 160pp. Maggie seems unable to stop the nasty pranks of classmate Corky, and receives differing advice from her divorced parents. (Rev: BCCB 5/88; BL 4/1/88; SLJ 5/88)

8316 Kaye, Marilyn. *Cabin Six Plays Cupid* (4–6). 1989, Avon paper $2.95 (0-380-75701-X). 116pp. Five friends in Cabin 6 at Camp Sunnyside try to help their counselor's love life. Also use: *No Boys Allowed* (1989). (Rev: BL 7/89; SLJ 9/89)

8317 Kaye, Marilyn. *A Friend Like Phoebe* (4–6). 1989, Harcourt $13.95 (0-15-200450-5). 144pp. Phoebe's best friend is chosen for an honor that Phoebe wanted, which causes a crisis in their friendship. A sequel to *Phoebe* (1987). (Rev: BL 8/89; SLJ 11/89)

8318 Keillor, Garrison, and Jenny L. Nilsson. *The Sandy Bottom Orchestra* (5–8). 1996, Hyperion LB $15.49 (0-7868-2145-0). 263pp. Rachel, age 14, faces some problems in growing up, including the ending of a treasured friendship. (Rev: BCCB 2/97; BL 1/1–15/97; SLJ 1/97)

8319 King-Smith, Dick. *Mysterious Miss Slade* (3–5). Illus. 2000, Crown LB $17.99 (0-517-80046-2). 128pp. Smelly, lonely Miss Slade, a reclusive eccentric, tries to change her life after she becomes friendly with two children who live nearby. (Rev: BL 8/00; HB 7–8/00; HBG 10/00; SLJ 7/00)

8320 Kline, Suzy. *Herbie Jones and the Dark Attic* (3–5). Illus. by Richard Williams. 1992, Putnam $13.95 (0-399-21838-6). 112pp. Herbie is not sure he can go through with it when he volunteers to sleep in the attic when Grandpa comes. (Rev: BL 11/15/92; SLJ 12/92)

8321 Koertge, Ron. *The Heart of the City* (5–7). 1998, Orchard LB $16.99 (0-531-33078-8). 144pp. Apprehensive about moving to the big city of Los Angeles, 10-year-old Joy soon finds a friend in a young African American girl and together they fight the takeover of an abandoned house by hoods. (Rev: BCCB 4/98; BL 4/1/98; HBG 10/98)

8322 Koller, Jackie F. *Impy for Always* (2–4). Illus. by Carol Newsom. 1989, Little, Brown $9.95 (0-316-50147-6); paper $3.95 (0-316-50149-2). 64pp. Eight-year-old Imogene's thoughts of another fun summer are dashed when 12-year-old cousin Christina arrives all grown up. (Rev: BL 6/15/59)

8323 Konigsburg, E. L. *Jennifer, Hecate, Macbeth, William McKinley, and Me, Elizabeth* (4–6). Illus. by author. 1971, Macmillan $15.00 (0-689-30007-7); Dell paper $5.50 (0-440-44162-5). 128pp. African American Jennifer hazes white newcomer Elizabeth, her apprentice witch, and their amusing amateur sorcery leads to the magic of a firm friendship for two loners.

8324 Konigsburg, E. L. *The View from Saturday* (5–7). 1996, Simon & Schuster $16.00 (0-689-80993-X). 163pp. A complicated tale about four sixth-graders who are contestants in an Academic Bowl competition. Newbery Medal winner, 1997. (Rev: BCCB 11/96; BL 10/15/96; SLJ 9/96*)

8325 Kornblatt, Marc. *Understanding Buddy* (3–5). 2001, Simon & Schuster $16.00 (0-689-83215-X). 115pp. A novel about friendship that involves two fifth-grade boys: Sam, a sensitive Jewish boy, and Buddy who, except for playing soccer, has retreated into isolation after his mother's death. (Rev: BCCB 3/01; BL 2/1/01)

8326 Koss, Amy Goldman. *The Trouble with Zinny Weston* (3–5). 1998, Dial $15.99 (0-8037-2287-7). 112pp. Ava, the fifth-grade daughter of veterinarians, and her best friend, Zinny, quarrel about a case of animal cruelty, but their friendship survives. (Rev: BL 5/15/98; HBG 10/98; SLJ 7/98)

8327 Kroll, Steven. *Patrick's Tree House* (3–4). Illus. by Roberta Wilson. 1994, Macmillan paper $13.95 (0-02-751005-0). 64pp. Patrick and Sarah don't know what to do when two older children take over their treehouse. (Rev: BL 5/1/94; SLJ 8/94)

8328 Kuhn, Betsy. *Not Exactly Nashville* (3–6). 1998, Delacorte $14.95 (0-385-32589-4). 136pp. Two 11-year-old friends, Ellen and Valery, decide to enter a star-search contest sponsored by their favorite country and western singer. (Rev: BCCB 9/98; BL 4/15/98; HBG 10/98; SLJ 6/98)

8329 Lafaye, A. *Strawberry Hill* (5–8). 1999, Simon & Schuster $16.95 (0-689-82441-6). 272pp. Raleia, a 12-year-old girl who is old-fashioned in her atti-

tudes and interests, spends a summer in a Maine coastal town and finds a friend in an old man who is also old-fashioned. (Rev: BCCB 5/99; BL 8/99; HBG 10/99; SLJ 8/99)

8330 Lamb, Nancy. *The Great Mosquito, Bull, and Coffin Caper* (3–5). Illus. by Frank Remkiewicz. 1994, Morrow paper $4.95 (0-688-12944-7). 120pp. To make sure they will not forget each other when one moves away, two friends face three dares, each tougher than the last. (Rev: BL 10/15/92; SLJ 11/92)

8331 Lantz, Francess. *A Royal Kiss* (5–8). 2000, Simon & Schuster paper $3.99 (0-689-83422-5). 121pp. In this light romance 14-year-old Samantha Simms meets and falls in love with a real Prince who sweeps her off her feet. (Rev: SLJ 8/00)

8332 Leverich, Kathleen. *Best Enemies Forever* (2–4). Illus. 1995, Greenwillow $14.00 (0-688-13963-9). 100pp. Rivals Priscilla and Felicity clash over a do-gooders club that Priscilla has founded. (Rev: BL 8/95; SLJ 10/95)

8333 Levin, Betty. *Starshine and Sunglow* (3–5). Illus. by Joseph A. Smith. 1994, Greenwillow $14.00 (0-688-12806-8). 96pp. In this picture book, neighbors "adopt" two scarecrows and help three children in their battle to save corn plants from raiders like birds and raccoons. (Rev: BL 5/1/94*; HB 9–10/94; SLJ 6/94)

8334 Levy, Elizabeth. *Third Grade Bullies* (2–3). 1998, Hyperion LB $14.49 (0-7868-2264-3); paper $3.95 (0-7868-1214-1). 64pp. An easy chapter book that tells how the rivalry between two third-graders, Jane Powell and Sally Shapiro, is resolved after a bullying fourth-grader starts pushing Sally around. (Rev: BL 4/15/98; HBG 10/98; SLJ 7/98)

8335 Lewis, Beverly. *Holly's First Love* (4–6). Series: Holly's Heart. 1993, Zondervan paper $6.99 (0-310-38051-0). 160pp. Holly and Andie's friendship is strained when they both find they are attracted to the new boy in town. Also use *Secret Summer Dreams* (1993). (Rev: SLJ 12/93)

8336 Lindberg, Becky T. *Chelsea Martin Turns Green* (3–4). Illus. by Nancy Poydar. 1993, Whitman LB $13.95 (0-8075-1134-X). 123pp. Chelsea is afraid that Abigail is trying to steal her best friend. (Rev: SLJ 7/93)

8337 McGuigan, Mary Ann. *Where You Belong* (5–8). 1997, Simon & Schuster $16.00 (0-689-81250-7). 176pp. In 1963 in the Bronx, a lonely white girl growing up in poverty forms a friendship with an African American girl. (Rev: BCCB 5/97; BL 6/1–15/97; SLJ 7/97)

8338 McKenna, Colleen O'Shaughnessy. *Camp Murphy* (5–7). 1993, Scholastic $13.95 (0-590-45807-8). 160pp. It's harder than it looks when Collette and friends decide to run a week-long day camp for the neighborhood kids. (Rev: BCCB 3/93; BL 3/15/93; SLJ 4/93)

8339 Maguire, Gregory. *Six Haunted Hairdos* (4–6). Illus. 1997, Clarion $15.00 (0-395-78626-6). 148pp. A funny story about two rival school groups, the boys' Copycats and the girls' Tattletales, and how they amuse themselves by telling ghost stories. The sequel to *Seven Spiders Spinning* (1994). (Rev: BL 11/1/97; HBG 3/98; SLJ 9/97)

8340 Makris, Kathryn. *The Five Cat Club* (4–6). Series: Eco-Kids. 1994, Avon paper $3.50 (0-380-77049-0). 156pp. Three junior high girls find homes for five abandoned kittens and become interested in animal rights and environmental issues. Also use *The Green Team* and *The Clean-up Crew* (both 1994). (Rev: SLJ 9/94)

8341 Mazer, Norma Fox. *Mrs. Fish, Ape and Me, the Dump Queen* (5–7). 1981, Avon paper $3.50 (0-380-69153-1). 144pp. Three misfits band together in friendship.

8342 Medearis, Angela Shelf. *The Adventures of Sugar and Junior* (2–3). Illus. by Nancy Poydar. 1995, Holiday LB $15.95 (0-8234-1182-6). 32pp. A simple story of a friendship between a Hispanic American and an African American youngster and their happy times together. (Rev: BL 10/15/95; SLJ 12/95)

8343 Miller, Judi. *My Crazy Cousin Courtney* (5–7). 1993, Pocket paper $2.99 (0-671-73821-6). Cathy is shocked to discover how much she and her California cousin are alike. (Rev: BL 3/1/93)

8344 Moore, Martha. *Under the Mermaid Angel* (5–8). 1995, Delacorte $14.95 (0-385-32160-0). 168pp. Thirteen-year-old Jesse is fascinated by her new neighbor, fast-talking, brash Roxanne. (Rev: BCCB 12/95; BL 8/95; SLJ 10/95)

8345 Mosher, Richard. *The Taxi Navigator* (5–7). 1996, Putnam $15.95 (0-399-23104-8). 144pp. Nine-year-old Kyle shares many adventures with his taxi-driving Uncle Hank. (Rev: BL 9/15/96; SLJ 1/97)

8346 Moss, Marissa. *The All-New Amelia* (3–5). Illus. 1999, Pleasant $12.95 (1-56247-784-0); paper $5.95 (1-56247-822-2). 32pp. Using diary entries and letters to tell the story, this novel's central character, Amelia, falls under the spell of a new girl in class and tries for a time to copy her in every way. (Rev: BL 11/1/99; HBG 3/00; SLJ 10/99)

8347 Moss, Marissa. *Luv, Amelia Luv, Nadia* (3–5). Illus. Series: Amelia. 1999, Pleasant $14.95 (1-56247-839-7); paper $7.95 (1-56247-823-0). 32pp. Two girls exchange letters about their families and mutual problems. Some of the letters are pull-outs inside envelopes. (Rev: BL 11/1/99; HBG 3/00; SLJ 10/99)

8348 Myers, Laurie. *Surviving Brick Johnson* (3–5). Illus. 2000, Clarion $15.00 (0-395-98031-3). 80pp. Fifth-grader Alex believes that newcomer Brick is a big bully, but when they both sign up for karate classes, he finds that he is wrong. (Rev: BCCB 11/00; BL 9/15/00; HBG 3/01; SLJ 10/00)

8349 Nagda, Ann Whitehead. *Dear Whiskers* (2–4). Illus. 2000, Holiday $15.95 (0-8234-1495-7). 64pp. For a school assignment, Jenny writes to a younger Saudi Arabian girl in her school and gradually forms a friendship with this reclusive girl who knows little English. (Rev: BCCB 2/01; BL 11/15/00; SLJ 1/01)

8350 Naylor, Phyllis Reynolds. *Josie's Troubles* (3–5). 1992, Macmillan $13.95 (0-689-31659-3).

112pp. Josephine discovers that if your relationship is strong enough, there's room for other friends in it. (Rev: BL 9/1/92; SLJ 11/92)

8351 Nelson, Theresa. *The Empress of Elsewhere* (4–6). 1998, DK $17.95 (0-7894-2498-3). 288pp. In this novel set in east Texas, three youngsters — 11-year-old Jim, his little sister Mary Al, and feisty J. D. — try to save a capuchin monkey that J. D.'s father had acquired before his death in an automobile accident. (Rev: BCCB 12/98; BL 9/1/98; HB 1–2/99; HBG 3/99; SLJ 11/98)

8352 Nicholson, Peggy, and John F. Warner. *The Case of the Furtive Firebug* (3–5). 1994, Lerner LB $14.95 (0-8225-0709-9). 120pp. Halley and her little brother Jason try to help a Vietnamese American girl who is falsely accused of arson. (Rev: BL 3/1/95)

8353 O'Connor, Barbara. *Me and Rupert Goody* (5–7). 1999, Farrar $15.00 (0-374-34904-5). 112pp. Set in Appalachia, this novel deals with the problems of young Jennalee, how she becomes friendly with the local store owner, and how this friendship is endangered when the owner's son moves into town. (Rev: BCCB 10/99; BL 11/1/99; HB 9–10/99; HBG 3/00; SLJ 10/99)

8354 Park, Barbara. *Buddies* (5–8). 1986, Avon paper $2.95 (0-380-69992-3). 144pp. Dinah's two weeks in camp are the subject of this first-person narrative. (Rev: BCCB 5/85; SLJ 5/85)

8355 Paterson, Katherine. *Bridge to Terabithia* (6–8). Illus. by Donna Diamond. 1977, HarperCollins LB $15.89 (0-690-04635-9); paper $5.95 (0-06-440184-7). 144pp. Jess becomes a close friend of Leslie, a new girl in his school, and suffers agony after her accidental death. Newbery Award winner, 1978. (Rev: SLJ 1/00)

8356 Patneaude, David. *The Last Man's Reward* (5–8). 1996, Albert Whitman LB $14.95 (0-8075-4370-5). 185pp. In this adventure, a group of boys agree to a pact rewarding the last to leave the neighborhood. (Rev: BL 6/1–15/96; SLJ 7/96)

8357 Paulsen, Gary. *The Schernoff Discoveries* (5–7). 1997, Delacorte $15.95 (0-385-32194-5). 103pp. A humorous novel about the misadventures of two friends, both self-confessed geeks. (Rev: BCCB 7–8/97; BL 6/1–15/97; SLJ 7/97)

8358 Peck, Robert Newton. *Soup* (5–7). Illus. by Charles C. Gehm. 1974, Knopf LB $15.99 (0-394-92700-1); Dell paper $4.50 (0-440-48186-4). 104pp. Rural Vermont in the 1920s is re-created in these reminiscences of the author of the times he spent with his friend Soup. Also use: *Soup for President* (1978); *Soup in the Saddle* (1983).

8359 Perkins, Lynne Rae. *All Alone in the Universe* (5–8). 1999, Greenwillow $16.00 (0-688-16881-7). 160pp. Debbie is crushed when her friend of many years drops her for another, but she has the courage to adjust and reach out to others. (Rev: BCCB 10/99; BL 9/1/99*; HB 9–10/99; HBG 3/00; SLJ 10/99)

8360 Peters, Julie A. *How Do You Spell G-E-E-K?* (4–7). 1996, Little, Brown $12.95 (0-316-70266-8). 112pp. Kim feels left out when her best friend, Ann, befriends Lurlene, a new student. (Rev: BCCB 10/96; BL 9/15/96; SLJ 10/96)

8361 Petersen, P. J. *My Worst Friend* (2–4). Illus. 1998, Dutton $14.99 (0-525-46028-4). 80pp. The friendship of Jenny and Sara is based on rivalry and playing tricks on each other — until Sara becomes seriously ill with a brain tumor. (Rev: BCCB 10/98; BL 10/15/98; HBG 3/99; SLJ 10/98)

8362 Pryor, Bonnie. *The Plum Tree War* (2–5). Illus. by Dora Leder. 1989, Morrow $14.00 (0-688-08142-8). 128pp. Nine-year-old Robert isn't happy when a cousin comes to stay for a year. (Rev: BL 6/15/89; SLJ 4/89)

8363 Radin, Ruth Yaffe. *Tac's Island* (3–6). Illus. by Gail Owens. 1989, Troll paper $2.95 (0-8167-1320-0). 80pp. The growing friendship between Tac, a year-round island boy, and Steve, vacationing on the coastal Virginia island. (Rev: BL 5/1/86; SLJ 8/86)

8364 Radley, Gail. *Odd Man Out* (4–6). 1995, Simon & Schuster paper $14.00 (0-02-775792-7). 144pp. The deep friendship of sixth-grader twins is tested when they differ about the friends each has made. (Rev: BCCB 9/95; BL 8/95; SLJ 6/95)

8365 Rosner, Ruth. *I Hate My Best Friend* (2–4). Illus. 1997, Hyperion LB $14.49 (0-7868-2079-9); paper $3.95 (0-7868-1169-2). 64pp. When Nina begins to act cruelly toward Annie, the two best friends become enemies. (Rev: BL 4/15/97; SLJ 8/97)

8366 Sachar, Louis. *Sixth Grade Secrets* (4–6). 1987, Scholastic paper $4.50 (0-590-46075-7). 208pp. Laura starts a club called Pig City, which eventually ends up by telling everyone's secrets. (Rev: BL 11/1/87; SLJ 9/87)

8367 Scott, C. Anne. *Lizard Meets Ivana the Terrible* (3–5). Illus. 1999, Holt $15.95 (0-8050-6093-6). 115pp. A newcomer to the school, third-grader Lizzie is anxious to make a friend but doesn't count on its being the strange girl nicknamed "Ivana the Terrible." (Rev: BCCB 1/00; BL 11/1/99; HBG 3/00; SLJ 11/99)

8368 Shura, Mary Francis. *The Josie Gambit* (5–7). 1986, Avon paper $2.50 (0-380-70497-8). 160pp. Josie's friend Tory behaves in an inexplicable way to his new friend Greg. (Rev: BCCB 5/86; SLJ 9/86)

8369 Skurzynski, Gloria. *Good-bye, Billy Radish* (5–7). Illus. 1992, Macmillan LB $15.00 (0-02-782921-9). 176pp. Vignettes set against the backdrop of World War I Pennsylvania describe the friendship between two boys of different backgrounds. (Rev: BL 10/15/92; HB 11–12/92; SLJ 12/92*)

8370 Smith, Jane D. *Charlie Is a Chicken* (3–5). 1998, HarperCollins $14.95 (0-06-027594-4). 176pp. In order to gain the friendship of popular Jessica, Maddie secretly joins a conspiracy against her best friend Charlie and, later, he finds out about Maddie's treachery. (Rev: BCCB 11/98; BL 11/1/98; HBG 10/99; SLJ 11/98)

8371 Snyder, Zilpha Keatley. *The Egypt Game* (5–7). Illus. by Alton Raible. 1967, Macmillan

$17.00 (0-689-30006-9); Dell paper $5.99 (0-440-42225-6). 224pp. Humor and suspense mark an outstanding story of city children whose safety, while playing at an unsupervised re-creation of an Egyptian ritual, is threatened by a violent lunatic.

8372 Snyder, Zilpha Keatley. *The Gypsy Game* (4–6). 1997, Delacorte $15.95 (0-385-32266-6). 217pp. In this sequel to *The Egypt Game* (1967), five friends decide to become gypsies, but their plans change when one of them disappears. (Rev: BCCB 2/97; BL 2/1/97; HB 3–4/97; SLJ 2/97)

8373 Staunton, Ted. *Two False Moves* (3–5). 2000, Red Deer paper $4.95 (0-88995-205-1). 64pp. Relations between classmates Nick and Lindsey deteriorate when Lindsey's parents become prospective buyers of the rented home where Nick and his family live. (Rev: BL 2/15/01)

8374 Steele, Mary. *Featherbys* (4–6). 1996, Peachtree paper $6.95 (1-56145-135-5). 180pp. Sixth-graders Jess and Vicky befriend two elderly sisters and help them fight a menacing relative. (Rev: BL 12/15/96)

8375 Stolz, Mary. *The Bully of Barkham Street* (4–8). Illus. by Leonard Shortall. 1963, HarperCollins paper $4.95 (0-06-440159-6). 224pp. Eleven-year-old Martin goes through a typical phase of growing up — feeling misunderstood. Also use: *A Dog on Barkham Street* (1960).

8376 Stolz, Mary. *The Noonday Friends* (4–6). Illus. by Louis Glanzman. 1965, HarperCollins LB $15.89 (0-06-025946-9); paper $4.95 (0-06-440009-3). 192pp. Eleven-year-old Franny's unskilled father is out of work, and the demanded family teamwork leaves her free from chores only during lunch periods.

8377 Taylor, Theodore. *The Cay* (5–8). 1987, Doubleday $16.95 (0-385-07906-0); Avon paper $4.99 (0-380-00142-X). 160pp. Themes of growing up and survival — black versus white, innocence and distrust versus wisdom and respect — are deftly woven into the saga of a young blind American boy and an old West Indian native, both stranded on a Caribbean cay.

8378 Vail, Rachel. *If You Only Knew* (4–7). Series: Friendship Ring. 1998, Scholastic $14.95 (0-590-03370-0). 240pp. In this book shaped like a CD, Zoe Grandon, a seventh-grader, gives up a boy she likes to pursue a friendship. (Rev: BCCB 10/98; BL 10/15/98; HBG 3/99; SLJ 10/98)

8379 Vail, Rachel. *Please, Please, Please* (4–7). Series: Friendship Ring. 1998, Scholastic $14.95 (0-590-00327-5). 288pp. CJ Hurley has to overcome a controlling mother in order to hang out with her friends in this book shaped like a CD. (Rev: BCCB 10/98; BL 10/15/98; HBG 3/99; SLJ 12/98)

8380 Waggoner, Karen. *Partners* (3–5). Illus. 1995, Simon & Schuster $13.00 (0-671-86466-1). 95pp. Jamie balks at being partners with his brother in a scheme to raise mice for snake food. (Rev: BCCB 9/95; BL 5/15/95; HB 11–12/95; SLJ 6/95)

8381 Walsh, Jill Paton. *Gaffer Samson's Luck* (4–6). Illus. by Brock Cole. 1984, Farrar paper $4.95 (0-374-42513-2). 112pp. Out to retrieve a good luck stone for his elderly friend Gaffer, James runs into the school bully and learns about different kinds of friendship.

8382 Warner, Sally. *Leftover Lily* (2–4). Illus. 1999, Knopf LB $16.99 (0-679-99139-5). 160pp. First-grader Lily quarrels with friends LaVon and Daisy and is afraid that she will get only a few valentines on Valentine's Day. (Rev: BL 7/99; HBG 3/00; SLJ 7/99)

8383 Warner, Sally. *Sort of Forever* (5–8). 1998, Knopf $16.00 (0-679-88648-6). 144pp. Twelve-year-old Cady discovers that her friend-for-life Nana has leukemia and that she has only a short time to live. (Rev: BL 6/1–15/98; HBG 10/98; SLJ 7/98)

8384 Williams, Carol L. *My Angelica* (5–9). 1999, Delacorte $15.95 (0-385-32622-X). 148pp. Sage is disappointed when her writing efforts are criticized but finds solace in her growing romantic feelings for her best friend, George. (Rev: BL 12/15/98; HB 1–2/99; HBG 10/99)

8385 Williams, Vera B. *Scooter* (4–6). Illus. 1993, Greenwillow $14.89 (0-688-09377-9). 160pp. Elana Rose explores her new urban neighborhood and finds that it is filled with new friends and new experiences. (Rev: BCCB 10/93; BL 11/15/93; SLJ 10/93)

8386 Willner-Pardo, Gina. *Figuring Out Frances* (4–6). 1999, Clarion $14.00 (0-395-91510-4). 144pp. In middle school, Abigail, who is coping with personal problems such as her grandmother's Alzheimer's disease, is dismayed when her long-time friend Travis drifts away and prefers the company of boys. (Rev: BCCB 10/99; BL 9/15/99; HBG 3/00; SLJ 9/99)

8387 Willner-Pardo, Gina. *When Jane-Marie Told My Secret* (3–4). Illus. 1995, Clarion $14.95 (0-395-66382-2). 40pp. Carolyn can't forgive her dear friend Jane-Marie after she has given away one of their secrets. (Rev: BL 8/95; SLJ 9/95)

8388 Wilson, Nancy H. *Old People, Frogs, and Albert* (3–4). Illus. 1997, Farrar $14.00 (0-374-35625-4). 64pp. Albert loses his fear of a nursing home when he has to visit a friend there who has had a stroke. (Rev: BL 9/15/97; SLJ 11/97)

8389 Winkler, David. *Scotty and the Gypsy Bandit* (5–8). 2000, Farrar $16.00 (0-374-36420-6). 208pp. After his father's death, Scotty forms a tentative friendship with an eccentric boy and together they complete a tree house. (Rev: BCCB 5/00; HB 3–4/00; HBG 10/00; SLJ 4/00)

8390 Withrow, Sarah. *Bat Summer* (4–7). 1999, Douglas & McIntyre $15.95 (0-88899-351-X). 160pp. Out of loneliness, Terrence mingles with Lucy, the strange neighbor who wears a cape and pretends she is a bat. (Rev: BCCB 5/99; BL 7/99)

8391 Wittlinger, Ellen. *Gracie's Girl* (4–7). 2000, Simon & Schuster $16.00 (0-689-82249-9). 192pp. Bess and her best friend Ethan, both middle schoolers, get involved with a homeless old lady. (Rev: BCCB 2/01; BL 9/15/00; HBG 3/01; SLJ 11/00)

8392 Wood, June R. *About Face* (4–6). 1999, Putnam $19.99 (0-399-23419-5). 272pp. Shy Glory

Bea Goode gains self-confidence after her brief friendship with brassy Marvalene Zulig, who is part of a carnival that has come to town for three days. (Rev: BCCB 11/99; BL 10/15/99; HBG 3/00)

8393 Wright, Betty R. *The Summer of Mrs. Mac-Gregor* (5–8). 1986, Holiday $15.95 (0-8234-0628-8). 160pp. Caroline becomes disillusioned with her new friend, "Mrs. MacGregor," a 17-year-old sophisticate from New York. (Rev: BCCB 12/86; SLJ 11/86)

8394 York, Carol B. *The Key to the Playhouse* (2–4). Illus. by John Speirs. 1994, Scholastic $13.95 (0-590-46258-X). 69pp. Cousins Alice Ann and Megan behave cruelly toward their neighbor Cissie and later regret their actions. (Rev: BCCB 4/94; HB 9–10/94; SLJ 6/94)

Growing into Maturity

Family Problems

8395 Ackerman, Karen. *The Leaves in October* (4–6). 1991, Macmillan $13.95 (0-689-31583-X). 128pp. A docunovel about 9-year-old Livvy, her little brother, and unemployed father. (Rev: BL 2/1/91)

8396 Adler, C. S. *The Silver Coach* (4–6). 1988, Avon paper $2.50 (0-380-75498-3). 112pp. Chris and her sister adjust to their parents' imminent divorce during a summer with their grandmother. A reissue.

8397 Banks, Lynne Reid. *Alice-by-Accident* (4–8). 2000, HarperCollins $14.95 (0-380-97865-2). 144pp. Through school compositions and diaries, 9-year-old Alice describes her life, her mother — a lawyer and single parent, and her paternal grandmother. (Rev: BCCB 9/00; BL 6/1–15/00; HB 5–6/00; HBG 10/00; SLJ 6/00)

8398 Bawden, Nina. *The Real Plato Jones* (5–8). 1993, Clarion $13.95 (0-395-66972-3). 166pp. Plato Jones discovers that his Greek grandfather might have been a coward during World War II. (Rev: BCCB 11/93; BL 10/15/93; SLJ 11/93*)

8399 Betancourt, Jeanne. *Puppy Love* (5–6). Illus. 1986, Avon paper $2.50 (0-380-89958-2). Aviva is having trouble dealing with her divorced parents' new lives and her own crush on Bob Hanley. (Rev: BL 8/86; SLJ 12/86)

8400 Birdseye, Tom. *Just Call Me Stupid* (4–6). 1993, Holiday $15.95 (0-8234-1045-5). 128pp. Patrick's reading problems are complicated by an unfortunate home situation and his feelings of unworthiness. (Rev: BL 1/15/94; SLJ 10/93)

8401 Birdseye, Tom. *Tucker* (4–6). 1990, Holiday $15.95 (0-8234-0813-2). 112pp. Tucker's 9-year-old sister comes to live with him and his father after an absence of seven years. (Rev: BL 7/90; SLJ 6/90)

8402 Blume, Judy. *It's Not the End of the World* (4–7). 1982, Macmillan LB $17.00 (0-02-711050-8); Dell paper $5.50 (0-440-44158-7). 176pp. Twelve-year-old Karen's world seems to end when her parents are divorced and her older brother runs away.

8403 Bohlmeijer, Arno. *Something Very Sorry* (4–6). 1996, Houghton $15.00 (0-395-74679-5). 176pp. A terrible automobile accident in which Rose and her family are involved changes the young girl's life forever. (Rev: BCCB 3/96; BL 4/1/96; SLJ 7/96*)

8404 Bowdish, Lynea. *Living with My Stepfather Is like Living with a Moose* (3–5). Illus. 1997, Farrar $14.00 (0-374-34630-5). 64pp. Matt finds that he and his new stepfather have little in common. (Rev: BL 3/1/97; SLJ 4/97)

8405 Boyd, Candy Dawson. *Charlie Pippin* (5–7). 1988, Puffin paper $4.99 (0-14-032587-5). 192pp. A daughter tries to find out why her father is so embittered about his war experiences in Vietnam. (Rev: BCCB 5/87; BL 4/15/87; SLJ 4/87)

8406 Brown, Susan M. *You're Dead, David Borelli* (5–7). 1995, Simon & Schuster $15.00 (0-689-31959-2). 155pp. From a sheltered rich-kid life, David is suddenly thrown into a foster home in a rough neighborhood when his mother dies and his father disappears. (Rev: BL 6/1–15/95; SLJ 7/95)

8407 Bunting, Eve. *Is Anybody There?* (4–7). 1990, HarperCollins paper $4.95 (0-06-440347-5). 176pp. His latchkey disappears and things are stolen, and Marcus is both scared and angry. (Rev: BCCB 10/88; BL 12/15/88; SLJ 12/88)

8408 Bunting, Eve. *Sharing Susan* (5–7). 1994, HarperCollins paper $3.95 (0-064-40430-7). 128pp. The nightmarish story of two families whose daughters were switched in the hospital at birth. (Rev: BL 9/15/91; HB 1–2/92; SLJ 10/91)

8409 Byars, Betsy. *Cracker Jackson* (5–6). 1986, Puffin paper $4.99 (0-14-031881-X). 168pp. Eleven-year-old Cracker proves a caring friend to his ex-baby-sitter when he suspects she is a victim of wife beating. (Rev: BL 4/1/85; HB 5–6/85; SLJ 5/85)

8410 Byars, Betsy. *The Two-Thousand-Pound Goldfish* (4–6). 1982, HarperCollins LB $14.89 (0-06-020890-2). 160pp. Warren can't accept the fact that his mother has rejected him.

8411 Calhoun, Mary. *Katie John* (4–6). Illus. by Paul Frame. 1960, HarperCollins LB $14.89 (0-06-020951-8). 128pp. In spite of her worst fears, Katie John has a pleasant time and makes new friends during a summer in a small Southern town. Two sequels are: *Depend on Katie John; Katie John and Heathcliff* (both 1981).

8412 Calvert, Patricia. *Glennis, Before and After* (5–8). 1996, Simon & Schuster $16.00 (0-689-80641-8). 150pp. Glennis must face many harsh realities when her father is sent to prison for white-collar crime and her mother has a nervous breakdown. (Rev: BCCB 10/96; SLJ 9/96)

8413 Chambers, Veronica. *Marisol and Magdalena: The Sound of Our Sisterhood* (5–8). 1998, Hyperion LB $15.49 (0-7868-2385-8). 141pp. Hispanic American Marisol is sent to live with her grandmother in Panama for a year, and hopes to track down her absent father. (Rev: SLJ 12/98)

8414 Clifford, Eth. *Family for Sale* (3–5). 1996, Houghton $15.00 (0-395-73571-8). 112pp. Four

young siblings, left in the charge of a 17-year-old sister, quarrel over who should make decisions. (Rev: BCCB 3/96; BL 2/1/96; SLJ 4/96)

8415 Clifford, Eth. *The Remembering Box* (4–6). Illus. 1985, Houghton $16.00 (0-395-38476-1); Morrow paper $4.95 (0-688-11777-5). 64pp. Joshua enjoys a special relationship with his grandmother, who shortly before her death gives him a "remembering box" in which she places a girlhood picture of herself. (Rev: BCCB 12/85; BL 12/1/85; HB 3–4/86)

8416 Coman, Carolyn. *What Jamie Saw* (5–8). 1995, Front Street $13.95 (1-886910-02-2). 128pp. In this novel seen through the eyes of a young boy, a mother and her family flee her physically abusive husband. (Rev: BCCB 12/95; BL 12/15/95*; SLJ 12/95*)

8417 Couloumbis, Audrey. *Getting Near to Baby* (5–9). 1999, Putnam $17.99 (0-399-23389-X). 224pp. When their baby sister dies and their mother sinks into a depression, 12-year-old Willa Jo and Little Sister go to live with a bossy aunt in this story set in North Carolina. (Rev: BCCB 11/99; BL 11/1/99; HB 11–12/99; HBG 3/00)

8418 Cullen, Lynn. *The Three Lives of Harris Harper* (5–7). 1996, Clarion $14.95 (0-395-73680-3). 160pp. Harris Harper's family is an embarrassment to him, unlike the seemingly perfect Benya family for whom he works. (Rev: BCCB 4/96; BL 4/1/96; SLJ 3/96)

8419 Danziger, Paula. *Amber Brown Wants Extra Credit* (3–5). Illus. 1996, Putnam $14.99 (0-399-22900-0). 112pp. Troubled by her parents' divorce, Amber begins having problems with her schoolwork. (Rev: BCCB 10/96; BL 6/1–15/96; SLJ 8/96)

8420 Danziger, Paula. *Forever Amber Brown* (2–4). Illus. 1996, Putnam $14.99 (0-399-22932-9). 101pp. Amber's divorced mother is being courted by Max, and the young girl is concerned. (Rev: BL 11/15/96; SLJ 2/97)

8421 Dewey, Jennifer O. *Navajo Summer* (5–8). Illus. 1998, Boyds Mills $14.95 (1-56397-248-4). 143pp. When family life becomes intolerable for 12-year-old Janie, she runs away to spend time with the Wilsons, a close-knit Navajo family she met when horse-trading with her father. (Rev: BCCB 11/98; BL 10/1/98; HBG 3/99; SLJ 11/98)

8422 Doren, Marion. *Nell of Blue Harbor* (4–6). 1990, Harcourt $15.95 (0-15-256889-1). 160pp. From a commune in Vermont, 11-year-old Nell finds it difficult to adjust to life in Maine. (Rev: BCCB 1/91; BL 9/1/90; SLJ 11/90)

8423 Doucet, Sharon Arms. *Fiddle Fever* (4–7). 2000, Clarion $15.00 (0-618-04324-1). 176pp. Felix disobeys his mother, who hates fiddle playing, and builds one out of a cigar box and practices in secret. (Rev: BL 9/1/00; HB 9–10/00; HBG 3/01; SLJ 10/00)

8424 Duffey, Betsy. *Coaster* (4–8). 1994, Viking $13.99 (0-670-85480-8). 128pp. Hart is not too happy about his parents' divorce and that his father doesn't come around much anymore. (Rev: BCCB 10/94; BL 8/94; SLJ 9/94)

8425 Duncan, Lois. *A Gift of Magic* (5–8). Illus. by Arvis Stewart. 1990, Pocket paper $3.99 (0-671-72649-8). A young girl, gifted with extrasensory perception, adjusts to her parents' divorce.

8426 Ellis, Sarah. *Out of the Blue* (5–7). Illus. 1995, Simon & Schuster paper $15.00 (0-689-80025-8). 120pp. Twelve-year-old Megan discovers that she has a 24-year-old half-sister whom her mother gave up for adoption years ago. (Rev: BCCB 4/95; BL 5/1/95; HB 7–8/95; SLJ 5/95)

8427 Fletcher, Susan. *The Stuttgart Nanny Mafia* (4–6). 1991, Macmillan LB $14.95 (0-689-31709-3). 160pp. When her mother marries a dentist, Aurora realizes that her life is about to be "taken over." (Rev: BCCB 9/91; BL 12/15/91; SLJ 10/91)

8428 Foggo, Cheryl. *One Thing That's True* (5–8). 1998, Kids Can $14.95 (1-55074-411-9). 128pp. Roxanne is heartbroken when her older brother runs away after learning that he is adopted. (Rev: BCCB 5/98; BL 2/15/98; HBG 10/98; SLJ 4/98)

8429 Fox, Paula. *One-Eyed Cat* (6–8). Illus. by Irene Trivas. 1984, Macmillan $14.95 (0-02-735540-3); Dell paper $5.50 (0-440-46641-5). 192pp. A story about a boy growing up in upstate New York and a gift of an air rifle.

8430 Franklin, Kristine L. *Dove Song* (5–8). 1999, Candlewick $16.99 (0-7636-0409-7). 190pp. After young Bobbie Lynn's father is declared missing in Vietnam, the girl's already-depressed mother retreats into a world where she sleeps all day. (Rev: BCCB 11/99; HBG 3/00; SLJ 9/99)

8431 Franklin, Kristine L. *Lone Wolf* (4–7). 1997, Candlewick $16.99 (1-56402-935-2). 224pp. Perry has problems with his father when the two move to the north woods of Minnesota and Perry faces a life of isolation. (Rev: BCCB 5/97; BL 7/97; SLJ 6/97*)

8432 French, Simon. *Change the Locks* (5–7). 1993, Scholastic $13.95 (0-590-45593-1). 112pp. Steven wants to know about his past, but his single-parent mother remains silent on the topic. (Rev: BCCB 5–6/93; BL 5/1/93)

8433 Giff, Patricia Reilly. *Rat Teeth* (4–6). Illus. by Leslie Morrill. 1989, Bantam paper $3.99 (0-440-47457-4). 144pp. Radcliffe can't adjust to both his parents' divorce and a new school.

8434 Gilliland, Hap, and William Walters. *Flint's Rock* (5–7). 1996, Roberts Rinehart paper $8.95 (1-879373-82-3). 144pp. Flint, a young Cheyenne, faces problems when he moves with his parents from the reservation to Butte, Montana. (Rev: BCCB 5/96; BL 5/1/96)

8435 Gilmore, Rachna. *Mina's Spring of Colors* (4–7). 2000, Fitzhenry & Whiteside $15.95 (1-55041-549-2); paper $7.95 (1-55041-534-4). 150pp. Mina is happy when her grandfather comes from India, but with his arrival comes a culture clash that troubles the girl. (Rev: BL 6/1–15/00; SLJ 9/00)

8436 Gleitzman, Morris. *Puppy Fat* (5–7). 1996, Harcourt $11.00 (0-15-200047-X); paper $5.00 (0-15-200052-6). 144pp. Beset by quarreling parents, Keith discovers that his father is attracted to his friend's mother. A sequel to *Misery Guts* and *Worry*

Worts (both 1993). (Rev: BCCB 7–8/96; BL 6/1–15/96; SLJ 5/96)

8437 Gold, Carolyn J. *Dragonfly Secret* (3–6). 1997, Simon & Schuster $15.00 (0-689-31938-X). 144pp. Even though Gramps has his faults, the family rallies around to prevent Aunt Louise from sending him to a retirement home. (Rev: BL 7/97; SLJ 7/97)

8438 Goodman, Joan E. *Songs from Home* (5–7). Illus. 1994, Harcourt paper $4.95 (0-15-203591-5). 224pp. Anna discovers the truth about her father, who has become a drifter in Italy singing for tips in restaurants. (Rev: BCCB 12/94; BL 9/1/94; SLJ 10/94)

8439 Green, Connie J. *Emmy* (5–8). 1992, Macmillan $13.95 (0-689-50556-6). 160pp. This is the story of 11-year-old Emmy and her family after her father is injured in a Kentucky mine cave-in in 1924. (Rev: BCCB 2/92; BL 12/1/92; HB 1–2/93; SLJ 12/92)

8440 Griffin, Adele. *Dive* (5–8). 1999, Hyperion LB $15.49 (0-7868-2389-5). 160pp. A tangled family story in which 11-year-old Ben tries to become friends with his stepbrother, Dustin. (Rev: BL 9/15/99; HB 11–12/99; HBG 3/00)

8441 Griffin, Adele. *The Other Shepards* (5–8). 1998, Hyperion LB $15.49 (0-7868-2370-4). 240pp. The two Shepard children live under the specter of the death of their three older siblings before they were born, but then Annie arrives in the household and gives them a new lease on life. (Rev: BL 8/98; HBG 3/99)

8442 Griffin, Adele. *Sons of Liberty* (4–6). 1997, Hyperion LB $15.49 (0-7868-2292-9). 176pp. Two brothers differ on how they should cope with an abusive, domineering father. (Rev: BL 9/15/97; HBG 3/98; SLJ 11/97)

8443 Griffin, Adele. *Split Just Right* (5–8). 1997, Hyperion LB $15.49 (0-7868-2288-0). 160pp. Even though Danny's father has been gone as long as she can remember, she still wonders about him. (Rev: BL 6/1–15/97; HB 7–8/97; SLJ 6/97)

8444 Hahn, Mary D. *Following My Own Footsteps* (5–8). 1996, Clarion $15.00 (0-395-76477-7). 192pp. Living with a grandmother to escape a drunken father, William has problems adjusting. (Rev: BCCB 10/96; BL 9/15/96; HB 9–10/96; SLJ 11/96)

8445 Hahn, Mary D. *The Jellyfish Season* (5–7). 1992, Avon paper $4.99 (0-380-71635-6). 176pp. Kathleen must learn to cope with change: a move to Chesapeake Bay, a hostile cousin, her father's drinking, and her mother's pregnancy. (Rev: BCCB 2/86; BL 10/1/85; SLJ 10/85)

8446 Hahn, Mary D. *Tallahassee Higgins* (5–7). 1987, Avon paper $4.99 (0-380-70500-1). 192pp. With her mother gone to Hollywood with a boyfriend, 12-year-old Tallahassee is stuck in her mother's hometown, where she finds out a lot about her mother's childhood. (Rev: BCCB 4/87; BL 3/1/87; HB 5–6/87)

8447 Hamilton, Virginia. *Plain City* (5–7). 1993, Scholastic $13.95 (0-590-47364-6). 194pp. Buhlaire's life changes dramatically when the father she believed to be dead unexpectedly arrives in town. (Rev: BCCB 11/93; BL 9/15/93*; SLJ 11/93*)

8448 Henkes, Kevin. *The Birthday Room* (5–7). 1999, Greenwillow $16.00 (0-688-16733-0). 176pp. Ben travels to Oregon with his mother to visit Uncle Ian who was responsible for Ben's losing his little finger in an accident. (Rev: BCCB 9/99; BL 7/99; HB 9–10/99; HBG 3/00; SLJ 10/99)

8449 Henkes, Kevin. *Two Under Par* (4–6). Illus. by author. 1987, Greenwillow $15.95 (0-688-06708-5). 128pp. Wedge doesn't like his new stepfather — the miniature golf king! — and he's doubly unhappy with the prospect of a new baby. (Rev: BL 6/1/87; HB 7–8/87; SLJ 6–7/87)

8450 Hermes, Patricia. *Cheat the Moon* (5–8). 1998, Little, Brown $15.95 (0-316-35929-7). 176pp. After her mother's death, 12-year-old Gabby takes care of herself and her younger brother, with occasional help from her alcoholic father. (Rev: BL 6/1–15/98; HB 9–10/98; HBG 10/98; SLJ 6/98)

8451 Hermes, Patricia. *Heads, I Win* (4–7). Illus. 1988, Pocket paper $2.99 (0-671-67408-0). 132pp. Bailey is foster-home smart; she always leaves before someone can dump her. (Rev: BL 6/15/88; SLJ 8/88)

8452 Hermes, Patricia. *You Shouldn't Have to Say Good-bye* (5–8). 1982, Harcourt $11.95 (0-15-299944-2); Scholastic paper $3.25 (0-590-43174-9). 117pp. Sarah's mother is dying of cancer.

8453 Herschler, Mildred Barger. *The Darkest Corner* (5–9). 2000, Front Street $16.95 (1-886910-54-5). 240pp. In this novel set in the Deep South of the 1960s, 10-year-old Teddy is shocked to discover that her beloved dad participated in the lynching of her best friend's father. (Rev: BL 1/1–15/01; HBG 3/01)

8454 High, Linda O. *Maizie* (4–8). 1995, Holiday $14.95 (0-8234-1161-3). 177pp. Maizie, a survivor, succeeds in spite of being abandoned by her mother and left with an alcoholic father. (Rev: BCCB 4/95; BL 4/15/95; HB 5–6/95; SLJ 4/95)

8455 High, Linda O. *A Stone's Throw from Paradise* (4–6). 1997, Eerdmans $15.00 (0-8028-5147-9); paper $5.00 (0-8028-5142-8). 128pp. Lizzie, whose parents were excommunicated from an Amish community, is spending a summer with her Amish Granny Zook. (Rev: BL 6/1–15/97; SLJ 12/97)

8456 Hobbs, Valerie. *Charlie's Run* (4–7). 2000, Farrar $16.00 (0-374-34994-0). 176pp. To escape his parents' impending separation, 11-year-old Joey hits the road and finds there are worse things in life than divorce. (Rev: BCCB 3/00; HB 3–4/00; HBG 10/00; SLJ 3/00)

8457 Holl, Kristi D. *Hidden in the Fog* (5–7). 1997, Royal Fireworks paper $6.99 (0-88092-436-5). 144pp. Set on a Mississippi steamboat, this story tells how Nikki worries that a fading tourist season will bring back her father's depression. (Rev: BCCB 3/89)

8458 Holt, Kimberly Willis. *Mister and Me* (3–6). Illus. 1998, Putnam $13.99 (0-399-23215-X). 80pp. Jolene resents the fact that her widowed mother

plans to remarry, but as she gets to know her mother's boyfriend, she gradually changes her attitude. (Rev: BL 11/15/98; HB 11–12/98; HBG 3/99; SLJ 11/98)

8459 Honeycutt, Natalie. *Twilight in Grace Falls* (5–8). 1997, Orchard LB $17.99 (0-531-33007-9). 192pp. A moving novel about the closing of a lumber mill that brings unemployment to the father of 11-year-old Dasie Jenson. (Rev: BCCB 6/97; BL 3/15/97*; HB 7–8/97; SLJ 5/97)

8460 Hunter, Evan. *Me and Mr. Stenner* (5–8). 1976, HarperCollins $11.95 (0-397-31689-5). 128pp. Abby's attitudes toward her new stepfather gradually change from resentment to love.

8461 Hurwitz, Johanna. *DeDe Takes Charge!* (5–7). Illus. by Diane De Groat. 1984, Morrow $16.00 (0-688-03853-0). 128pp. DeDe's life is not the same A.D. (after divorce).

8462 Hutchins, Hazel. *Tess* (3–5). Illus. by Ruth Ohi. 1995, Annick LB $16.95 (1-55037-395-1); paper $5.95 (1-55037-394-3). 32pp. Set during the Great Depression in western Canada, this story tells how Tess and her family cope with extreme poverty. (Rev: BL 12/15/95)

8463 James, Mary. *Frankenlouse* (5–8). 1994, Scholastic $13.95 (0-590-46528-7). 176pp. Nick and his father clash at the military academy where Nick is a student and his father a teacher. (Rev: BCCB 11/94; BL 10/15/94; SLJ 11/94)

8464 Jennings, Patrick. *Putnam and Pennyroyal* (4–7). 1999, Scholastic $15.95 (0-439-07965-9). 176pp. Family tensions cause Cora to doubt that she will continue to spend Christmas with her Uncle Frank, but a parable about two grebes that Frank tells helps ease the situation. (Rev: BCCB 12/99; BL 11/15/99; HBG 3/00; SLJ 3/00)

8465 Johnson, Angela. *Songs of Faith* (5–8). 1998, Orchard LB $16.99 (0-531-33023-0). 112pp. Doreen is a child of divorce who is particularly upset at seeing her younger brother's problems in adjusting after their father moves away. (Rev: BCCB 6/98; BL 2/15/98; HBG 10/98; SLJ 3/98)

8466 Jordan, Mary K. *Losing Uncle Tim* (2–4). Illus. by Judith Friedman. 1989, Whitman LB $14.95 (0-8075-4756-5). 32pp. A little boy remembers the fine times he had with Uncle Tim, who died of AIDS. (Rev: BCCB 11/89; BL 12/1/89; HB 1–2/90; SLJ 1/90)

8467 Katz, Susan. *Snowdrops for Cousin Ruth* (4–7). 1998, Simon & Schuster $16.00 (0-689-81391-0). 192pp. The arrival of an elderly relative helps fill the void left after the death of 9-year-old Johanna's brother and eases the sorrow that her family feels. (Rev: BCCB 5/98; BL 7/98*; HB 5–6/98; HBG 10/98; SLJ 6/98)

8468 Kaye, Marilyn. *Happily Ever After* (4–6). 1992, Avon paper $3.50 (0-380-76555-1). 116pp. When two friends become stepsisters, adjustment problems begin. (Rev: SLJ 4/92)

8469 Koss, Amy Goldman. *The Ashwater Experiment* (5–8). 1999, Dial $15.99 (0-8037-2391-1). 160pp. After Hillary spends nine months in Ashwater, California, she doesn't want to leave when her

nomadic, hippie parents decide to move on. (Rev:
BCCB 6/99; BL 6/1–15/99; HB 7–8/99; HBG
10/99; SLJ 8/99)

8470 Koss, Amy Goldman. *Stranger in Dadland*
(4–6). 2001, Dial $16.99 (0-8037-2563-9). 128pp.
Twelve-year-old John is not optimistic when he
goes to L.A. for his annual visit to his dad but a crisis brings the two closer. (Rev: BCCB 2/01; BL
3/1/01; SLJ 3/01)

8471 Lafaye, A. *The Year of the Sawdust Man*
(4–6). 1998, Simon & Schuster $16.00 (0-689-
81513-1). 224pp. In a small Louisiana town in
1934, Nissa's mama — an outspoken, unconven-
tional woman — runs away from home leaving a
bewildered and resentful Nissa behind. (Rev: BCCB
7–8/98; BL 6/1–15/98; HBG 10/98)

8472 Lantz, Francess. *Stepsister from the Planet
Weird* (5–8). 1997, Random LB $11.99 (0-679-
97330-3); paper $3.99 (0-679-87330-9). 170pp.
Megan and her almost-stepsister Ariel conspire to
prevent their parents from marrying. (Rev: SLJ
2/98)

8473 Lawson, Julie. *Turns on a Dime* (5–8). Series:
Goldstone Trilogy. 1999, Stoddart paper $6.95 (0-
7737-5942-5). 173pp. In frustration after discovering that she is adopted, Jo retreats to her grandparents house to sort things out. (Rev: SLJ 6/99)

8474 Levinson, Marilyn. *No Boys Allowed* (5–8).
1993, Troll paper $13.95 (0-8167-3135-7). 128pp.
Cassie, her father's pet, is crushed when he divorces
her mother and moves to Kentucky. (Rev: BL
10/1/93; SLJ 11/93)

8475 Lewis, Beverly. *Whispers down the Lane*
(5–8). Series: Summerhill Secrets. 1995, Bethany
paper $5.99 (1-55661-476-4). 144pp. An Amish girl
agrees to hide Lissa, who has run away from her
father's abusive treatment. (Rev: BL 9/1/95; SLJ
2/96)

8476 Lindbergh, Anne. *Nobody's Orphan* (4–6).
1983, Avon paper $2.95 (0-380-70395-5). Martha
believes that she is adopted, though she has no
proof.

8477 Loftis, Chris. *The Boy Who Sat by the Window*
(3–6). Illus. by Catharine Gallagher. 1997, New
Horizon Pr. paper $12.95 (0-88282-147-4). 52pp.
Using free verse, the author tells the story of a boy
who has been randomly shot while riding his bike to
school. (Rev: BL 6/1–15/97; SLJ 8/97)

8478 Lowery, Linda. *Laurie Tells* (4–6). 1994, Carolrhoda LB $19.93 (0-87614-790-2). 40pp. Eleven-
year-old Laurie is ignored by her mother when she
tells her of being sexually abused by her father.
(Rev: BL 6/1–15/94; SLJ 7/94)

8479 Luger, Harriett. *Bye, Bye, Bali Kai* (5–7).
1996, Harcourt $11.00 (0-15-200862-4); paper
$5.00 (0-15-200863-2). 192pp. Suzie's family hits
rock bottom when they are evicted and forced to
live in an abandoned building. (Rev: BCCB 3/96;
BL 6/1–15/96; SLJ 6/96)

8480 Mack, Tracy. *Drawing Lessons* (5–8). 2000,
Scholastic $15.95 (0-439-11202-8). 176pp. Aurora,
who adores her artist father, must adjust her expectations when she catches him in a compromising

position with one of his models. (Rev: BCCB 3/00;
BL 3/15/00; HBG 10/00)

8481 MacLachlan, Patricia. *Journey* (5–7). Illus. by
Barry Moser. 1991, Delacorte $14.95 (0-385-30427-
7). 83pp. A boy named Journey and his sister Cat
must make a new life for themselves on their grandparents' farm. (Rev: BCCB 10/91; BL 9/15/91; HB
11–12/91*; SLJ 9/91)

8482 Marino, Jan. *For the Love of Pete* (5–8). 1994,
Avon paper $3.50 (0-380-72281-X). 197pp. Three
devoted servants take Olivia on a journey to find the
father she has never met. (Rev: BCCB 7–8/93; SLJ
5/93*)

8483 Martin, Patricia A. *Memory Jug* (5–7). 1998,
Hyperion LB $16.49 (0-7868-2368-2). 276pp.
Mack, who still misses her dead father, feels she is
losing contact with the rest of her family when her
mother finds a new boyfriend, her younger sister
makes a new friend, and bossy Aunt Sydney moves
in. (Rev: BCCB 11/98; BL 11/1/98; SLJ 11/98)

8484 Martin, Patricia A. *Travels with Rainie Marie*
(5–7). 1997, Hyperion LB $16.49 (0-7868-2212-0).
192pp. When there is no one to care for her and her
five brothers and sisters, Rainie Marie is afraid that
her bossy aunt will try to split up the family among
various relatives. (Rev: BL 5/15/97; SLJ 7/97)

8485 Mead, Alice. *Junebug* (4–7). 1995, Farrar
$15.00 (0-374-33964-3). 112pp. Junebug, a young
boy, realizes that the only hope for his family is to
move from the city project where they live. (Rev:
BCCB 12/95; BL 9/15/95; SLJ 11/95)

8486 Mead, Alice. *Junebug and the Reverend* (4–6).
1998, Farrar $16.00 (0-374-33965-1). 192pp. Juneb-
ug, now out of the projects with his family, faces
new problems like coping with his mother's new
boyfriend and bullies at school, while accepting the
responsibility of walking an old emphysema patient,
nicknamed the Reverend. (Rev: BL 9/1/98; HB
9–10/98; HBG 3/99; SLJ 9/98)

8487 Mead, Alice. *Soldier Mom* (5–7). 1999, Farrar
$16.00 (0-374-37124-5). 160pp. Jasmyn's life —
including her basketball game — suffers when her
mother, an army reservist, is called up during the
Persian Gulf War and Jake, her mother's fiance,
takes over managing the house. (Rev: BCCB 12/99;
BL 9/1/99*; HB 9–10/99; HBG 3/00; SLJ 9/99)

8488 Mead, Alice. *Walking the Edge* (5–8). 1995,
Albert Whitman LB $14.95 (0-8075-8649-8).
190pp. Scott escapes the abuse of his drunken father
by throwing himself into his 4-H science project.
(Rev: SLJ 12/95)

8489 Metzger, Lois. *Barry's Sister* (4–7). 1992,
Macmillan $15.95 (0-689-31521-X). 227pp. When
Ellen's new brother develops cerebral palsy, she
blames herself because she didn't want a baby
brother. (Rev: SLJ 6/92)

8490 Metzger, Lois. *Missing Girls* (5–8). 1999,
Viking $15.99 (0-670-87777-8). 208pp. Carrie
Schmidt, age 13, is unhappy at home and still miss-
es her dead mother, but she finds a new life when
she idealizes her friend's family. (Rev: BCCB 2/99;
BL 2/1/99; HB 5–6/99; HBG 10/99)

8491 Meyer, Carolyn. *Gideon's People* (5–7). 1996, Harcourt $12.00 (0-15-200303-7); paper $6.00 (0-15-200304-5). 320pp. Similarities and differences in religious practices become apparent when an Orthodox Jewish boy spends time on an Amish farm in 1911. (Rev: BCCB 5/96; BL 5/1/96; SLJ 4/96)

8492 Miller, Dorothy R. *Home Wars* (5–8). 1997, Simon & Schuster $16.00 (0-689-81411-9). 176pp. Halley has misgivings when her father brings home three rifles, one for himself and the others for her two brothers. (Rev: BL 9/1/97; HBG 3/98; SLJ 10/97)

8493 Miller, Judi. *Purple Is My Game, Morgan Is My Name* (4–7). 1998, Pocket paper $3.99 (0-671-00280-5). 119pp. In this humorous novel, young Morgan has two goals — to find a suitable career goal and to reunite her separated parents. (Rev: SLJ 11/98)

8494 Moss, Marissa. *Amelia's Family Ties* (3–5). Illus. Series: Amelia's Notebook. 2000, Pleasant $12.95 (1-58485-079-5); paper $5.95 (1-58485-078-7). 40pp. After years of silence, Amelia receives a letter from her divorced father and goes to visit him and her stepmother in Chicago. (Rev: BL 2/15/00; HBG 10/00; SLJ 6/00)

8495 Myers, Anna. *Rosie's Tiger* (4–8). 1994, Walker $14.95 (0-8027-8305-8). 128pp. Rosie is filled with jealousy when her beloved brother returns home from the Korean War with a wife and child. (Rev: BL 9/15/94; SLJ 11/94)

8496 Namioka, Lensey. *Yang the Second and Her Secret Admirers* (4–6). Illus. 1998, Little, Brown $15.95 (0-316-59731-7). 144pp. The oldest girl in a Chinese American family living in Seattle has trouble fitting in and clings desperately to her Chinese heritage. (Rev: BL 9/15/98; HBG 10/98; SLJ 8/98)

8497 Namioka, Lensey. *Yang the Third and Her Impossible Family* (4–7). Illus. by Kees de Kiefte. 1996, Bantam paper $4.50 (0-440-41231-5). 144pp. Mary, part of a Chinese family newly arrived in Seattle, is embarrassed by her parents' old-country ways in this humorous story. (Rev: BCCB 5/95; BL 4/15/95; SLJ 8/95)

8498 Napoli, Donna Jo. *Changing Tunes* (4–6). 1998, Dutton $15.99 (0-525-45861-1). 160pp. After her father leaves with the family piano, Eileen gets help from her friend Stephanie as she begins adjusting to her parents' divorce and to the fact that she has to practice on an old school piano. (Rev: BCCB 9/98; BL 5/15/98; HBG 10/98; SLJ 8/98)

8499 Naylor, Phyllis Reynolds. *Being Danny's Dog* (4–7). 1995, Simon & Schuster $15.00 (0-689-31756-5). 150pp. T.R.'s strong bond with his older brother, Danny, is tested when he discovers that Danny is involved in an unsavory plot. (Rev: BCCB 1/96; BL 10/1/95; SLJ 10/95)

8500 Naylor, Phyllis Reynolds. *Reluctantly Alice* (5–8). 1991, Macmillan $15.00 (0-689-31681-X). 192pp. Alice's life in the seventh grade seems full of embarrassment. (Rev: BCCB 4/91*; BL 2/1/91; HB 7–8/91)

8501 Nixon, Joan Lowery. *Maggie Forevermore* (5–7). 1987, Harcourt $13.95 (0-15-250345-5).

112pp. Maggie spends Christmas with her father and his new bride at their beach house in Malibu. Two other Maggie stories are: *Maggie, Too* (1985); *And Maggie Makes Three* (1986). (Rev: BCCB 4/87; BL 3/1/87; SLJ 3/87)

8502 O'Connor, Barbara. *Beethoven in Paradise* (5–8). 1997, Farrar $16.00 (0-374-30666-4). 176pp. Martin, who wants to be a musician, clashes with his father, who prefers to see him play baseball. (Rev: BCCB 5/97; BL 4/15/97; SLJ 4/97)

8503 Park, Barbara. *Don't Make Me Smile* (4–6). 1981, Avon paper $2.95 (0-380-61994-6). Charles refuses to face the fact of his parents' divorce.

8504 Park, Barbara. *The Graduation of Jake Moon* (5–8). 2000, Simon & Schuster $15.00 (0-689-83912-X). 115pp. Jake Moon finds it impossible to cope with his grandfather's gradual disintegration from Alzheimer's disease. (Rev: BCCB 12/00; BL 6/1–15/00; HB 9–10/00; HBG 3/01; SLJ 9/00)

8505 Paterson, Katherine. *Park's Quest* (4–7). 1989, Puffin paper $4.99 (0-14-034262-1). 160pp. A boy searches for the cause of his father's death in Vietnam. (Rev: BCCB 4/88; HB 7–8/88; SLJ 5/88)

8506 Pearson, Kit. *A Handful of Time* (4–7). 1988, Puffin paper $6.99 (0-14-032268-X). 192pp. Patricia is ill at ease staying with her aunt and cousins while her parents work out a divorce. (Rev: HB 7–8/88)

8507 Peck, Richard. *Strays Like Us* (5–8). 1998, Dial $15.99 (0-8037-2291-5). 160pp. Two unwanted youngsters, each living with relatives in a small Missouri town, together face family problems and the trauma of junior high school. (Rev: BCCB 4/98; BL 4/1/98*; HB 5–6/98; HBG 10/98)

8508 Petersen, P. J. *I Want Answers and a Parachute* (4–6). Illus. by Anna DiVito. 1993, Simon & Schuster paper $13.00 (0-671-86577-3). 112pp. Jason and older brother Matt are apprehensive about meeting their father's new wife and her young daughter. (Rev: BCCB 9/93; BL 10/1/93; SLJ 12/93)

8509 Pevsner, Stella. *Would My Fortune Cookie Lie?* (5–8). 1996, Clarion $14.95 (0-395-73082-1). 192pp. Alexis, already upset by her parents' separation, learns a shattering secret from a mysterious stranger. (Rev: BCCB 3/96; BL 2/15/96; SLJ 4/96)

8510 Pfeffer, Susan Beth. *Devil's Den* (4–7). 1998, Walker $15.95 (0-8027-8650-2). 128pp. Joey faces the pain of rejection when he seeks out his real father, discovers he is not wanted by him, and must accept living permanently with his mom and loving stepfather. (Rev: BCCB 5/98; BL 5/15/98; HBG 10/98; SLJ 6/98)

8511 Philbrick, Rodman. *The Fire Pony* (5–8). 1996, Scholastic $14.95 (0-590-55251-1). 175pp. Rescued from a foster home by his half-brother Joe, Roy hopes that life will be better on the ranch where Joe finds work. (Rev: BCCB 7–8/96; BL 5/1/96; HB 7–8/96; SLJ 9/96)

8512 Polikoff, Barbara G. *Life's a Funny Proposition, Horatio* (4–7). 1992, Holt $14.95 (0-8050-1972-3). 103pp. When his father dies, Horatio and his mother move to Wisconsin. (Rev: SLJ 8/92*)

8513 Rinn, Miriam. *The Saturday Secret* (4–7). Illus. 1998, Alef Design Group paper $7.95 (1-881283-26-7). 144pp. Jason's resentment and anger at having to obey the strict rules imposed by his devout Orthodox Jewish stepfather are made more intense because of his grief at the death of his beloved father. (Rev: BL 10/1/98; SLJ 2/99)

8514 Roberts, Willo Davis. *Pawns* (5–8). 1998, Simon & Schuster $16.00 (0-689-81668-5). 160pp. Pregnant Dori claims to be the wife of Mamie's dead son, but Teddi, whom Mamie has raised, thinks that Dori is lying and sets out to prove that she is right. (Rev: BL 11/15/98; HBG 3/99)

8515 Roberts, Willo Davis. *What Are We Going to Do About David?* (5–8). 1993, Macmillan $16.00 (0-689-31793-X). 176pp. A realistic story about 11-year-old David and what happens when his parents prepare to separate. (Rev: BL 3/15/93; SLJ 4/93)

8516 Rodowsky, Colby. *Hannah in Between* (5–8). 1994, Farrar $15.00 (0-374-32837-4). 158pp. Hannah slowly realizes that her mother is sinking into alcoholism and wonders what to do about it. (Rev: BL 4/1/94; HB 9–10/94; SLJ 5/94)

8517 Rodowsky, Colby. *Spindrift* (5–8). 2000, Farrar $15.00 (0-374-37155-5). 112pp. A realistic family story about 13-year-old Cassie who lives at Spindrift, a seaside bed-and-breakfast run by her grandmother, and who tries to reunite her sister and estranged husband. (Rev: BCCB 3/00; BL 2/15/00; HBG 10/00; SLJ 3/00)

8518 Ross, Adrienne. *In the Quiet* (3–6). 2000, Delacorte $14.95 (0-385-32678-5). 150pp. Neither 11-year-old Samantha nor her father have openly grieved over the death of her recently deceased mother, but when Aunt Constance becomes part of the household, all three must come to terms with the situation. (Rev: BCCB 4/00*; BL 3/1/00; HB 3–4/00; HBG 10/00)

8519 Ross, Ramon R. *The Dancing Tree* (5–7). 1995, Simon & Schuster $14.00 (0-689-80072-X). 59pp. Zeenie's grandmother helps her cope with the sudden disappearance of her mother, who hopes to sort out her life. (Rev: BL 9/1/95; SLJ 2/96)

8520 Sachs, Marilyn. *Fran Ellen's House* (4–6). 1989, Avon paper $2.75 (0-380-70583-4). Although her family is back together, Fran Ellen's baby sister won't talk to her and their house is in a shambles. A sequel to: *The Bears' House* (1987). (Rev: BCCB 11/87; BL 11/1/87; SLJ 10/87)

8521 Shawver, Margaret. *What's Wrong with Grandma? A Family's Experience with Alzheimer's* (3–6). Illus. 1996, Prometheus $14.95 (1-57392-107-6). 63pp. Ellen is confused and sometimes terrified when her grandmother begins to exhibit the erratic behavior associated with Alzheimer's disease. (Rev: BL 4/15/97)

8522 Shreve, Susan. *The Formerly Great Alexander Family* (3–5). Illus. by Chris Cart. 1995, Tambourine $13.00 (0-688-13551-X). 91pp. The security and happiness of 10-year-old Liam Alexander come to an end when his parents announce they're divorcing. (Rev: HB 1–12/95; SLJ 9/95)

8523 Siebold, Jan. *Rope Burn* (4–6). Illus. 1998, Albert Whitman $12.95 (0-8075-7109-1). 82pp. To fulfill a school writing assignment, 11-year-old Richard writes about the terrible effects his parents' divorce has had on him, his difficulties making new friends, and his problems communicating with his mother. (Rev: BCCB 6/98; BL 6/1–15/98; SLJ 6/98)

8524 Slate, Joseph. *Crossing the Trestle* (5–8). 1999, Marshall Cavendish $14.95 (0-7614-5053-X). 144pp. Set in West Virginia in 1944, this novel centers on 11-year-old Petey and the problems he and his family face after their father is killed in an accident. (Rev: BCCB 12/99; BL 1/1–15/00; HBG 3/00; SLJ 10/99)

8525 Snyder, Zilpha Keatley. *Cat Running* (4–6). 1994, Delacorte $15.95 (0-385-31056-0). 168pp. To spite her father, Cat Kinsey, a fast runner, refuses to participate in the annual school sports fair. (Rev: BCCB 1/95; BL 9/1/94; SLJ 11/94*)

8526 Stevenson, Laura C. *Happily After All* (4–7). 1990, Houghton $15.95 (0-395-50216-0). 256pp. Becca goes to live with her mother, who she believes abandoned her when she was young. (Rev: BCCB 5/90; BL 4/15/90; HB 5–6/90; SLJ 6/90)

8527 Stone, Phoebe. *All the Blue Moons at the Wallace Hotel* (5–7). 2000, Little, Brown $15.95 (0-316-81645-0). 208pp. This story about family love and problems centers around 11-year-old Fiona, her lively younger sister, their withdrawn mother, and the memories of the wealth the family once had. (Rev: BCCB 12/00; BL 12/1/00; HBG 3/01; SLJ 12/00)

8528 Strete, Craig Kee. *The World in Grandfather's Hands* (5–7). 1995, Clarion $13.95 (0-395-72102-4). 135pp. An 11-year-old American Indian boy faces problems when he and his mother leave their pueblo and move to the city. (Rev: BCCB 10/95; SLJ 9/95*)

8529 Thesman, Jean. *When the Road Ends* (5–8). 1992, Houghton $16.00 (0-395-59507-X). 184pp. Mary tells how she and other foster children spend a summer in a remote cabin with a sick adult. (Rev: BCCB 4/92; HB 5–6/92; SLJ 4/92)

8530 Tolan, Stephanie S. *Save Halloween!* (4–7). 1993, Morrow $16.00 (0-688-12168-3). 176pp. Johnna, the daughter of a preacher, is forbidden to take part in any of the rituals and parties connected with Halloween. (Rev: BCCB 10/93; BL 9/1/93*; SLJ 10/93)

8531 Traylor, Betty. *Buckaroo* (4–6). 1999, Delacorte $14.95 (0-385-32637-8). 196pp. This story set in 1958 involves Preston Davis, nicknamed Buckaroo, who is sent to live with his aunt in a small Arkansas town where he makes friends with an African American boy. (Rev: BCCB 9/99; BL 9/15/99; HBG 3/00; SLJ 8/99)

8532 Van Leeuwen, Jean. *Dear Mom, You're Ruining My Life* (4–6). Illus. 1989, Puffin paper $4.99 (0-14-034386-5). 160pp. Samantha's sixth-grade year is filled with ups and downs. (Rev: BCCB 5/89; BL 5/1/89; HB 6/89)

8533 Viglucci, Patricia C. *Sun Dance at Turtle Rock* (5–7). 1996, Patri paper $10.75 (0-9645914-9-9).

128pp. The child of a racially mixed marriage feels uncomfortable when he visits his white grandfather. (Rev: BL 4/15/96)

8534 Wallace, Bill. *True Friends* (4–7). 1994, Holiday $15.95 (0-8234-1141-9). 160pp. Everything in Courtney's life becomes a shambles and she must rely on her new friend Judy to help her. (Rev: BCCB 11/94; BL 10/15/94; SLJ 10/94)

8535 Walter, Mildred P. *Mariah Keeps Cool* (3–6). 1990, Macmillan LB $15.00 (0-02-792295-2). 140pp. Mariah, who is preoccupied with an upcoming swimming meet, finds she has new problems when her half-sister moves in. (Rev: BCCB 4/90; BL 4/15/90; SLJ 6/90)

8536 Walton, Darwin McBeth. *Dance, Kayla!* (4–6). 1998, Albert Whitman $14.95 (0-8075-1453-5). 155pp. When her beloved Gran dies and her father is still absent, Kayla is sent from her grandparents' farm to Chicago to live with an aunt and uncle. (Rev: BL 9/1/98; HBG 10/98; SLJ 8/98)

8537 Ware, Cheryl. *Catty-Cornered* (4–6). Illus. by Paul Yalowitz. 1998, Orchard LB $16.99 (0-531-33067-2). 106pp. A smart, curious, and funny girl keeps a journal of the two months she had to spend with her grandmother in a trailer park. (Rev: BL 4/1/98; HBG 10/98; SLJ 3/98)

8538 Warner, Sally. *How to Be a Real Person (in Just One Day)* (5–8). 2001, Knopf $15.95 (0-375-80434-X). 128pp. Kara puts up a brave front when she is with her classmates but she is facing huge problems because her father has left and her mother has sunk into a depression. (Rev: BCCB 3/01; BL 2/15/01; SLJ 2/01)

8539 Williams, Laura E. *Up a Creek* (5–8). 2001, Holt $17.00 (0-8050-6453-2). 135pp. Thirteen-year-old Starshine Bott, daughter of a young, single-mother activist, wonders if her mother cares more for her social causes than she does for her. (Rev: BCCB 2/01; SLJ 1/01)

8540 Willner-Pardo, Gina. *Spider Storch's Carpool Catastrophe* (2–4). Illus. by Nick Sharratt. 1997, Albert Whitman LB $11.95 (0-8075-7575-5); paper $3.95 (0-8075-7576-3). 60pp. Joey, nicknamed Spider, is afraid that his mother's friendship with Mrs. Brennerman will mean that he will have to get involved with her unpopular daughter. (Rev: HBG 3/98; SLJ 11/97)

8541 Wilson, Jacqueline. *Elsa, Star of the Shelter* (4–6). Illus. 1996, Albert Whitman LB $14.95 (0-8075-1981-2). 208pp. The grim life of a homeless English family as seen through the eyes of courageous 10-year-old Elsa. (Rev: BCCB 2/96; BL 1/1–15/96; SLJ 2/96)

8542 Wilson, Nancy H. *Becoming Felix* (4–6). 1996, Farrar $16.00 (0-374-30664-8). 184pp. Twelve-year-old JJ makes sacrifices to help save the family farm. (Rev: BCCB 1/97; BL 10/15/96; SLJ 10/96)

8543 Wilson, Nancy H. *The Reason for Janey* (5–7). Illus. 1994, Macmillan paper $15.00 (0-02-793127-7). 176pp. A mentally disabled woman helps Janie adjust to her parents' divorce and her father's departure. (Rev: BCCB 6/94; BL 4/15/94; HB 7–8/94; SLJ 5/94*)

8544 Wolitzer, Hilma. *Wish You Were Here* (5–8). 1984, Farrar paper $3.45 (0-374-48412-0). Bernie does not want to live with his stepfather and decides to move to Florida with his grandfather.

8545 Woodbury, Mary. *Brad's Universe* (5–8). 1998, Orca paper $7.95 (1-55143-120-3). 191pp. Fourteen-year-old Brad is happy in the small Canadian town to which he and his mother have moved, but when his father joins them, Brad discovers that his dad is a child molester. (Rev: SLJ 2/99)

8546 Yep, Laurence. *The Amah* (4–6). 1999, Putnam $16.99 (0-399-23040-8). 192pp. Amy Chin begins to act like the wicked stepsister (a role she plays in her ballet school's Cinderella) when she has to take on more responsibility caring for her four younger siblings. (Rev: BL 5/15/99; HBG 10/99; SLJ 7/99)

8547 Yep, Laurence. *Dream Soul* (5–8). 2000, HarperCollins LB $14.89 (0-06-028309-4). 256pp. In this sequel to *Star Fisher* (1991), the Lees, a family of Chinese immigrants who live in Clarksburg, West Virginia, in 1927, face conflicts when the children want to celebrate Christmas. (Rev: BL 12/1/00)

8548 Yep, Laurence. *Ribbons* (5–7). 1996, Putnam $15.95 (0-399-22906-X). 192pp. Robin begins to understand and sympathize with her Chinese grandmother after she learns the woman's secret. (Rev: BCCB 2/96; BL 1/1–15/96; SLJ 2/96)

8549 Young, Ronder T. *Moving Mama to Town* (5–8). 1997, Orchard LB $18.99 (0-531-33025-7). 224pp. Although his father is a gambler and a failure, Fred never loses faith in him in this story of a boy who must help support his family though he's only 13. (Rev: BL 6/1–15/97; HB 7–8/97; SLJ 6/97)

Personal Problems

8550 Adler, C. S. *Daddy's Climbing Tree* (5–7). 1993, Houghton $15.00 (0-395-63032-0). 134pp. Jessica cannot adjust to the death of her father in a hit-and-run accident. (Rev: BCCB 7–8/93; BL 6/1–15/93; HB 7–8/93; SLJ 5/93)

8551 Adler, C. S. *The Lump in the Middle* (5–7). 1991, Avon paper $3.50 (0-380-71176-1). 160pp. Kelsey, the middle child, struggles for her identity after dad loses his job. (Rev: BL 10/1/89; SLJ 10/89)

8552 Adler, C. S. *What's to Be Scared Of, Suki?* (4–7). 1996, Clarion $13.95 (0-395-77600-7). 176pp. A neighbor's handsome 13-year-old son helps Suki overcome her fears. (Rev: BL 11/1/96; SLJ 10/96)

8553 Adler, C. S. *Willie, the Frog Prince* (4–7). 1994, Clarion $15.00 (0-395-65615-X). 163pp. Willie's inability to accept responsibility almost causes the loss of his dog, Booboo. (Rev: BL 4/15/94; SLJ 6/94)

8554 Adler, David A. *The Many Troubles of Andy Russell* (2–5). Illus. 1998, Harcourt $14.00 (0-15-201295-8). 144pp. The story, in a simple chapter book format, of fourth-grader Andy Russell who faces many problems including a pregnant mother, a pet gerbil that escapes, and a friend who needs a new foster family. (Rev: BL 8/98; HBG 3/99; SLJ 12/98)

8555 Appelt, Kathi. *Kissing Tennessee: And Other Stories from the Stardust Dance* (5–9). 2000, Harcourt $15.00 (0-15-202249-X). 144pp. Eight short stories follow several graduating eighth-graders on the night of their last junior high dance and explore the many adolescent problems they face. (Rev: BL 6/1–15/00; HBG 10/00)

8556 Armstrong, Robb. *Drew and the Bub Daddy Showdown* (3–5). 1996, HarperCollins paper $4.25 (0-06-442030-2). 96pp. Drew Taylor finds he has artistic ability and soon creates his own comic book hero. (Rev: BL 9/15/96; SLJ 8/96)

8557 Auch, Mary Jane. *Seven Long Years Until College* (4–7). 1991, Holiday $13.95 (0-8234-0901-5). 160pp. Unhappy at home, Natalie runs away to join her older sister at college. (Rev: BCCB 1/92; SLJ 10/91)

8558 Avi. *What Do Fish Have to Do with Anything?* (5–8). Illus. 1997, Candlewick $16.99 (0-7636-0329-5); paper $5.99 (0-7636-0412-7). 208pp. Seven excellent stories about youngsters facing the first pangs of adolescence. (Rev: BL 11/15/97; HB 11–12/97; HBG 3/98; SLJ 12/97*)

8559 Barnes, Joyce Annette. *Promise Me the Moon* (5–8). 1997, Dial $14.99 (0-8037-1798-9). 176pp. Annie faces many problems in eighth grade, including being labeled an egghead, in this sequel to *The Baby Grand, the Moon in July, and Me* (1994). (Rev: BCCB 2/97; BL 11/15/96; SLJ 2/97)

8560 Belton, Sandra. *McKendree* (5–8). 2000, Greenwillow $15.95 (0-688-15950-8). 256pp. Tilara, the 14-year-old child of a mixed marriage, spends a summer in a West Virginia town where she does volunteer work in a home for the elderly and falls in love with a quiet, soft-spoken boy who is also a volunteer. (Rev: BL 8/00; HBG 10/00; SLJ 6/00)

8561 Benjamin, Carol Lea. *The Wicked Stepdog* (4–7). Illus. by author. 1982, Avon paper $2.50 (0-380-70089-1). Louise is in the midst of puberty problems and her father's remarriage.

8562 Birdseye, Tom. *Tarantula Shoes* (3–6). 1995, Holiday $15.95 (0-8234-1179-6); Puffin paper $4.99 (0-14-037955-X). 96pp. With the help of a new friend and his pet tarantula, Ryan is able to buy the basketball shoes of his dreams. (Rev: BL 4/15/95; SLJ 5/95)

8563 Blades, Ann. *Mary of Mile 18* (2–4). Illus. by author. 1971, Tundra paper $8.99 (0-88776-059-7). Mile 18 is in reality a Mennonite community in Canada, and Mary was a student in the school where the author taught.

8564 Blume, Judy. *Are You There God? It's Me, Margaret* (4–6). 1990, Macmillan LB $16.00 (0-02-710991-7); Dell paper $5.50 (0-440-40419-3). 156pp. Eleven-year-old Margaret is the daughter of a Jewish father and a Catholic mother.

8565 Blume, Judy. *Blubber* (4–6). 1982, Macmillan LB $16.99 (0-02-711010-9); Dell paper $4.99 (0-440-40707-9). 160pp. Jill finds out what it's like to

be an outsider when she defends Linda, a classmate who is teased because of her obesity.

8566 Blume, Judy. *Otherwise Known as Sheila the Great* (4–6). 1972, Dell paper $4.99 (0-440-46701-2). 128pp. During a summer in New York, Sheila learns a great deal about herself and how to overcome her feelings of inferiority.

8567 Blume, Judy. *Then Again, Maybe I Won't* (5–7). 1971, Dell paper $4.99 (0-440-48659-9). 176pp. Thirteen-year-old Tony adjusts with difficulty to his family's move to a home in the affluent suburbs of Long Island, New York.

8568 Blume, Judy. *Tiger Eyes: A Novel* (6–8). 1981, Dell paper $4.99 (0-440-98469-6). 256pp. Davey must deal with reactions to her father's murder.

8569 Bonners, Susan. *Edwina Victorious* (3–5). Illus. by author. 2000, Farrar $16.00 (0-374-31968-5). 131pp. A charming story about a girl who forges her great-grandaunt's signature on letters to the mayor to try to win much-needed reforms. (Rev: BCCB 10/00; HBG 3/01; SLJ 10/00)

8570 Bowdish, Lynea. *Brooklyn, Bugsy, and Me* (3–5). Illus. 2000, Farrar $15.00 (0-374-30993-0). 96pp. In 1953, 9-year-old Sam has problems adjusting to the move from his beloved West Virginia to Brooklyn. (Rev: BCCB 4/00; BL 2/15/00; HB 5–6/00; HBG 10/00; SLJ 6/00)

8571 Brisson, Pat. *Sky Memories* (4–7). Illus. 1999, Delacorte $14.95 (0-385-32606-8). 71pp. Ten-year-old Emily and her mother share a special bond that cannot be broken, even when her mother has terminal cancer. (Rev: BCCB 7–8/99; BL 5/15/99; HBG 10/99; SLJ 8/99)

8572 Brokaw, Nancy Steele. *Leaving Emma* (4–7). 1999, Clarion $15.00 (0-395-90699-7). 144pp. When Emma's best friend moves away and her father is sent to work overseas, the young girl is left with a mother who suffers from bouts of depression. (Rev: BCCB 3/99; BL 3/1/99; HBG 10/99; SLJ 5/99)

8573 Buck, Pearl. *The Big Wave* (4–6). 1973, HarperCollins LB $16.89 (0-381-99923-8); paper $4.95 (0-06-440171-5). 88pp. The loss of family and home in a tidal wave reveals the courage of a little Japanese boy.

8574 Bulla, Clyde Robert. *The Paint Brush Kid* (2–4). Illus. by Ellen Beier. 1999, Random LB $11.99 (0-679-99282-0); paper $3.99 (0-679-89282-6). 64pp. In this beginning chapter book, the pictures Gregory has painted on a house depicting his uncle's life in Mexico are going to be destroyed because the house is slated for demolition. (Rev: HBG 10/99; SLJ 8/99)

8575 Bulla, Clyde Robert. *Shoeshine Girl* (3–5). Illus. by Leigh Grant. 1975, HarperCollins LB $15.89 (0-690-04830-0); paper $4.50 (0-06-440228-2). 80pp. A somewhat indolent 10-year-old girl matures during a summer working for Al at his shoeshine stand.

8576 Bunting, Eve. *Blackwater* (5–8). 1999, HarperCollins LB $15.89 (0-06-027843-9). 160pp. Brodie feels responsible for the drowning deaths of two young teenagers, but is unable to tell the truth and admit his guilt. (Rev: HBG 3/00; SLJ 8/99)

8577 Bunting, Eve. *Doll Baby* (5–10). Illus. by Catherine Stock. 2000, Clarion $15.00 (0-395-93094-4). 48pp. A simple, direct narrative in which 15-year-old Ellie explains how being pregnant and having a baby radically changed her life. (Rev: BL 11/1/00; HB 9–10/00; HBG 3/01; SLJ 10/00)

8578 Bunting, Eve. *Your Move* (2–5). Illus. by James E. Ransome. 1998, Harcourt $16.00 (0-15-200181-6). 32pp. A 10-year-old boy and his young brother are caught up in the violence that accompanies the rivalry between street gangs. (Rev: BCCB 6/98; BL 2/15/98; HBG 10/98; SLJ 5/98)

8579 Burch, Robert. *Queenie Peavy* (4–7). Illus. by Jerry Lazare. 1987, Puffin paper $4.99 (0-14-032305-8). 160pp. A defiant 13-year-old rescues her future from reform school in a Georgia town of the 1930s.

8580 Busby, Cylin. *The Chicken-Fried Rat: Tales Too Gross to Be True* (4–6). Illus. by Phoebe Gloeckner. 1998, HarperTrophy paper $4.95 (0-06-440701-2). 112pp. Told in short vignettes, this novel traces the problems Eric faces on his first day of summer vacation. (Rev: BCCB 11/98; SLJ 2/99)

8581 Butcher, Kristin. *The Runaways* (4–7). 1998, Kids Can $14.95 (1-55074-413-5). 168pp. Two youngsters with problems — 12-year-old Nick who is coping with his mother's remarriage and street urchin Luther — form an unusual friendship. (Rev: BL 4/15/98; HBG 10/98; SLJ 4/98)

8582 Byars, Betsy. *The Cartoonist* (4–6). Illus. by Richard Cuffari. 1978, Puffin paper $3.99 (0-14-032309-0). 128pp. Alfie's refuge in his attic room with his cartoons is disrupted by his brother's return.

8583 Byars, Betsy. *The House of Wings* (4–6). Illus. by Daniel Schwartz. 1972, Puffin paper $4.99 (0-14-031523-3). 148pp. Sammy is distraught when he is left alone with his grandfather, but things get better when a wounded crane is found and must be taken care of.

8584 Byars, Betsy. *The Night Swimmers* (5–6). Illus. by Troy Howell. 1983, Bantam paper $4.50 (0-440-45857-9). 160pp. An enterprising girl tries to be a housekeeper and to take care of her two brothers.

8585 Caldwell, V. M. *The Ocean Within* (5–7). 1999, Milkweed $15.95 (1-57131-623-X); paper $6.95 (1-57131-624-8). 273pp. Elizabeth, who is on her third set of foster parents since she was orphaned five years before, has built walls of silence around herself that are impossible to penetrate. (Rev: BCCB 1/00; BL 9/1/99; HBG 3/00)

8586 Calhoun, Mary. *Flood* (PS–3). Illus. by Erick Ingraham. 1997, Morrow $15.89 (0-688-13920-5). 40pp. A story set during the Mississippi River flood of 1993 that tells how a family lost its home. (Rev: BCCB 4/97; BL 3/15/97*; SLJ 5/97)

8587 Calvert, Patricia. *Michael, Wait for Me* (4–6). 2000, Simon & Schuster $16.00 (0-689-82102-6). 160pp. A tragic story of the futile efforts of sixth-grader Sarah to help a guilt-ridden young man who has accidentally killed his brother. An additional

theme involves Sarah's involvement with the dogs her father prepares for showing. (Rev: BCCB 4/00; BL 2/1/00; HBG 10/00; SLJ 4/00)

8588 Calvert, Patricia. *Writing to Richie* (4–6). Illus. 1994, Scribners $13.95 (0-684-19764-2). 128pp. With the help of an ill-tempered young girl who has come to his foster home, David learns to grieve for his dead younger brother. (Rev: BL 12/15/94; SLJ 1/95)

8589 Cameron, Ann. *Gloria's Way* (2–4). 2000, Farrar $15.00 (0-374-32670-3). 112pp. In this easy chapter book, readers meet African American Gloria and, in six short episodes, learn about her problems with friendships and family. (Rev: BCCB 2/00; BL 2/15/00; HB 3–4/00; HBG 10/00; SLJ 3/00)

8590 Cameron, Ann. *The Secret Life of Amanda K. Woods* (4–6). 1998, Farrar $16.00 (0-374-36702-7). 208pp. A perceptive, realistic novel about a fifth-grade girl's efforts to ease her loneliness while growing up outside a small Wisconsin town with only her pony for company. (Rev: BCCB 5/98; BL 4/15/98; HBG 10/98; SLJ 5/98)

8591 *Camy Baker's How to be Popular in the Sixth Grade: 30 Cool Rules to Rule the School* (4–6). 1998, Bantam paper $3.99 (0-553-48655-1). 135pp. Sixth-grader Camy Baker dispenses sound advice about behavior and illustrates each with incidents from her life in Beverly Hills. (Rev: SLJ 12/98)

8592 Capote, Truman. *The Thanksgiving Visitor* (5–7). Illus. by Beth Peck. 1996, Knopf $19.00 (0-679-83898-8). 32pp. Buddy conquers his loneliness and fear of a bully, Odd Henderson, through his friendship with Miss Sook. (Rev: BL 10/15/96; SLJ 12/96)

8593 Carrick, Carol. *The Upside-Down Cake* (2–5). Illus. 1999, Clarion $14.00 (0-395-84151-8). 62pp. A young boy gradually adjusts to the death of the father he loved. (Rev: BL 11/1/99; HBG 3/00; SLJ 10/99)

8594 Casanova, Mary. *Riot* (5–8). 1996, Hyperion LB $14.49 (0-7868-2204-X). 128pp. Young Bryan is caught up in his father's conflict concerning the hiring of nonunion workers at his workplace. (Rev: BCCB 1/97; BL 11/1/96; SLJ 10/96)

8595 Caseley, Judith. *Chloe in the Know* (3–5). 1993, Greenwillow $14.00 (0-688-11055-X). 144pp. In this sequel to *Hurricane Harry* (1991) and *Starring Dorothy Kane* (1992), Chloe, big sister to Harry and Dorothy, is upset when she finds out that her mother is pregnant again. (Rev: BCCB 4/93; BL 4/15/93; SLJ 4/93)

8596 Caseley, Judith. *Dorothy's Darkest Days* (2–4). Illus. 1997, Greenwillow $15.00 (0-688-13422-X). 144pp. Dorothy is filled with guilt when her disliked classmate is killed in a car accident. (Rev: BL 8/97; HBG 3/98; SLJ 8/97)

8597 Caseley, Judith. *Jorah's Journal* (2–4). Illus. 1997, Greenwillow $15.00 (0-688-14879-4). 64pp. Jorah has problems adjusting to her family's move to a different city and becoming the new girl in her class. (Rev: BL 5/1/97; SLJ 6/97)

8598 Caseley, Judith. *Praying to A. L* (5–8). 2000, Greenwillow $15.95 (0-688-15934-6). 192pp. After her father dies, 12-year-old Sierra transfers all her love to a portrait of Abraham Lincoln given to her by her father. (Rev: BL 5/15/00; HBG 10/00; SLJ 6/00)

8599 Cavanagh, Helen. *Panther Glade* (4–6). 1993, Simon & Schuster paper $16.00 (0-671-75617-6). 147pp. Bill gains a little self-confidence during a summer with an aunt who is an archaeologist. (Rev: SLJ 6/93)

8600 Cleary, Beverly. *Dear Mr. Henshaw* (4–7). Illus. by Paul O. Zelinsky. 1983, Morrow $15.89 (0-688-02406-8); Dell paper $3.99 (0-440-41794-5). 144pp. A Newbery Award winner (1984) about a boy who pours out his problems in letters to a writer he greatly admires.

8601 Cleary, Beverly. *Strider* (4–8). Illus. by Paul O. Zelinsky. 1991, Morrow $15.89 (0-688-09901-7). 192pp. In this sequel to the 1984 Newbery winner *Dear Mr. Henshaw,* Leigh Botts is beginning high school and finding himself, aided by his beloved dog Strider. (Rev: BCCB 10/91; BL 7/91*; HB 9–10/91; SLJ 9/91)

8602 Cleaver, Vera, and Bill Cleaver. *Grover* (4–7). Illus. by Fred Marvin. 1970, HarperCollins $13.95 (0-397-31118-4). 128pp. After his mother's suicide and his father's resultant breakdown, 10-year-old Grover must face the hard reality of death and trouble.

8603 Colman, Hila. *Diary of a Frantic Kid Sister* (4–6). 1973, Archway paper $2.95 (0-671-61926-8). Sarah has trouble communicating with her family, so she pours out her soul to her diary.

8604 Conford, Ellen. *Hail, Hail Camp Timberwood* (5–7). Illus. by Gail Owens. 1978, Little, Brown $14.95 (0-316-15291-9). Thirteen-year-old Melanie's first summer at camp.

8605 Conly, Jane L. *Crazy Lady!* (5–8). 1993, HarperCollins LB $15.89 (0-06-021360-4). 196pp. In a city slum Vernon forms a friendship with an eccentric lady who cares for her disabled teenage son. (Rev: BCCB 7–8/93; BL 5/15/93*; SLJ 4/93*)

8606 Conly, Jane L. *What Happened on Planet Kid* (4–8). 2000, Holt $16.95 (0-8050-6065-0). 216pp. Twelve-year-old Dawn learns a lot about life, herself, and her dreams of becoming a major league pitcher during the summer she spends on a farm with her aunt and uncle. (Rev: BCCB 4/00; BL 5/15/00; HB 5–6/00; HBG 10/00; SLJ 5/00)

8607 Conly, Jane L. *While No One Was Watching* (5–7). 1998, Holt $16.95 (0-8050-3934-1). 233pp. Three siblings face personal problems when they are forced to spend a summer with their Aunt Lulu in a squalid city row house. (Rev: BCCB 9/98; BL 5/15/98; HB 7–8/98*; HBG 10/98; SLJ 7/98)

8608 Conrad, Pam. *Prairie Songs* (5–8). Illus. by Darryl S. Zudeck. 1985, HarperCollins $17.02 (0-060-21336-1); paper $4.95 (0-06-440206-1). 176pp. Louise's family thrives despite the harshness of the prairie land, but the life there is unendurable for others. (Rev: SLJ 10/85)

8609 Conrad, Pam. *Staying Nine* (4–6). Illus. by Mike Wimmer. 1988, HarperCollins paper $4.25 (0-06-440377-7). 80pp. A private few days in the life of a young girl who doesn't want to be ten. (Rev: BCCB 10/88; BL 11/15/88; SLJ 12/88)

8610 Coolidge, Susan. *What Katy Did* (4–6). 1988, Buccaneer LB $19.95 (0-899-66585-3). Tomboy Katy Carr overcomes a tragic accident in this classic story.

8611 Cooper, Ilene. *Absolutely Lucy* (2–4). Illus. Series: Read to Reading. 2000, Golden Bks. LB $10.99 (0-307-48502-0); paper $3.99 (0-307-26502-1). 76pp. An easy chapter book about a boy whose beagle puppy helps him conquer his shyness. (Rev: BCCB 5/00; BL 3/15/00; SLJ 3/01)

8612 Corbin, William. *Me and the End of the World* (5–7). 1991, Simon & Schuster paper $15.00 (0-671-74223-X). 256pp. Fearful that the world is soon ending, 13-year-old-Tom decides to do things he has always wanted to do. (Rev: SLJ 9/91)

8613 Corcoran, Barbara. *The Potato Kid* (5–8). 1993, Avon paper $3.50 (0-380-71213-X). 192pp. In spite of her protests, Ellis is chosen to take care of an underprivileged girl her mother takes in for the summer. (Rev: BCCB 11/89; HB 1–2/90; SLJ 10/89)

8614 Cosby, Bill. *My Big Lie* (2–4). Illus. 1999, Scholastic $15.95 (0-590-52160-8); paper $3.99 (0-590-52161-6). 40pp. Late for dinner because of a baseball game, Little Bill tells a lie to protect himself and only gets into worse trouble. (Rev: BL 10/15/99; HBG 10/99; SLJ 8/99)

8615 Cottonwood, Joe. *Danny Ain't* (5–8). 1992, Scholastic $13.95 (0-590-45067-0). 240pp. When Danny's father, a Vietnam War vet, is taken to a VA hospital, the boy tries to survive on his own. (Rev: SLJ 10/92)

8616 Cox, Judy. *Mean, Mean Maureen Green* (2–5). Illus. 1999, Holiday $15.95 (0-8234-1502-3). 88pp. Lilley is a fearful person who dreads going to school because of a mean neighborhood dog, a school bully, and her new bike without training wheels. (Rev: BCCB 2/00; BL 12/1/99; HBG 10/00; SLJ 3/00)

8617 Creech, Sharon. *Absolutely Normal Chaos* (5–8). 1995, HarperCollins LB $15.89 (0-06-026992-8). 208pp. Mary Lou keeps a journal during her 13th absolutely normal summer and chronicles such events as her first kiss and her summer reading assignments. (Rev: BCCB 11/95; BL 10/1/95; SLJ 11/95)

8618 Creech, Sharon. *Chasing Redbird* (5–8). 1997, HarperCollins $15.89 (0-06-026988-X). 261pp. Thirteen-year-old Zinny, who lives in Appalachia, is trying to understand herself while adjusting to the death of her beloved Aunt Jessie. (Rev: HB 5–6/97; SLJ 4/97*)

8619 Creel, Ann Howard. *Nowhere, Now Here* (5–7). 2000, Pleasant $12.95 (1-58485-200-3). 149pp. Twelve-year-old Laney is unhappy when she and her parents move from Florida to Colorado, where they plan to raise alpacas. (Rev: BL 9/15/00; SLJ 1/01)

8620 Cruise, Robin. *The Top-Secret Journal of Fiona Claire Jardin* (4–7). 1998, Harcourt $13.00 (0-15-201383-0). 160pp. At the advice of her therapist, Fiona, age 11, keeps a journal about her problems, chiefly coping with her parents' divorce and living under a joint-custody agreement. (Rev: BL 4/15/98; HBG 10/98; SLJ 4/98)

8621 Cummings, Priscilla. *A Face First* (5–8). 2001, Dutton $15.99 (0-525-46522-7). 224pp. After being severely burned in a car accident, Kelly sinks into a terrible depression particularly after she is told that she will have to wear a plastic face mask for two years. (Rev: BCCB 2/01; BL 2/1/01)

8622 Curtis, Christopher Paul. *Bud, Not Buddy* (4–6). 1999, Delacorte $15.95 (0-385-32306-9). 272pp. In this Newbery Medal winner set in Michigan during the Great Depression, 10-year-old Bud, on the run from his orphanage and his latest foster parents, is determined to find his father. (Rev: BCCB 11/99; BL 9/1/99; HB 11–12/99; HBG 3/00; SLJ 9/99)

8623 Curtis, Sandra R. *Gabriel's Ark* (2–5). Illus. 1998, Alef Design Group paper $7.95 (1-881283-22-4). 64pp. Gabe, who was born disabled, celebrates his bar mitzvah in his own way, thanks to a supportive family and an understanding rabbi. (Rev: BL 10/1/98; SLJ 1/99)

8624 DiCamillo, Kate. *Because of Winn-Dixie* (4–6). 2000, Candlewick $15.99 (0-7636-0776-2). 184pp. In this Newbery Honor book, lonely 10-year-old India Opal Buloni adopts a stray dog, named Winn-Dixie, who changes her life. (Rev: BCCB 6/00; BL 5/1/00; HB 7–8/00; HBG 10/00; SLJ 6/00)

8625 DiCamillo, Kate. *The Tiger Rising* (4–6). 2001, Candlewick $12.99 (0-7636-0911-0). 128pp. This novel of grieving, friendship, and animal love involves Rob whose mother has just died, an outsider named Sistine with whom he becomes friends, and a caged tiger. (Rev: SLJ 3/01)

8626 Dorman, N. B. *Petey and Miss Magic* (3–5). 1993, Shoe String LB $16.00 (0-208-02345-3). 99pp. A lonely boy who longs for a pet finds a worm that he begins to care for. (Rev: SLJ 3/93)

8627 Dragonwagon, Crescent. *Winter Holding Spring* (3–6). Illus. by Ronald Himler. 1990, Macmillan paper $15.00 (0-02-733122-9). 32pp. Father and daughter talk about their feelings over the death of their wife and mother. (Rev: BL 4/1/90)

8628 Dreyer, Ellen. *Speechless in New York: Going to New York* (5–8). Series: Going To. 2000, Four Corners paper $7.95 (1-893577-01-5). 96pp. Jessie is beset with personal problems when she flies to New York from Minnesota with the Prairie Youth Chorale. (Rev: SLJ 3/00)

8629 Duffey, Betsy. *Spotlight on Cody* (2–4). Illus. 1998, Viking $14.99 (0-670-88077-9). 96pp. A beginning chapter book in which Cody Michaels, who has to perform in his third-grade talent show, is convinced he has nothing to offer. (Rev: BL 10/1/98; HB 11–12/98; HBG 3/99; SLJ 11/98)

8630 Duffey, Betsy. *Utterly Yours, Booker Jones* (5–7). Illus. 1995, Viking $14.99 (0-670-86007-7).

128pp. Twelve-year-old Booker faces many problems: finishing his science fiction novel, having to sleep under the dining room table, and coping with an impossible older sister. (Rev: BCCB 10/95; BL 9/15/95; HB 11–12/95; SLJ 9/95)

8631 Dunmore, Helen. *Brother Brother, Sister Sister* (5–8). 2000, Scholastic paper $4.50 (0-439-11322-9). 116pp. Written in diary format, this is the story of Tanya, once an only child and now surrounded by babies after her mother has quadruplets. (Rev: SLJ 8/00)

8632 Durant, Penny R. *When Heroes Die* (5–8). 1992, Macmillan $15.00 (0-689-31764-6). 144pp. Gary learns that the uncle he loves has AIDS. (Rev: SLJ 11/92)

8633 Eige, Lillian. *Dangling* (4–6). 2001, Simon & Schuster $16.00 (0-689-83581-7). 176pp. Eleven-year-old Ben describes how he learns that his best friend, Ring, was in foster care and wonders whether his supposed drowning was real or staged. (Rev: BCCB 3/01; BL 2/1/01)

8634 Enderle, Judith R., and Stephanie G. Tessler. *What's the Matter, Kelly Beans?* (2–4). 1996, Candlewick $14.99 (1-56402-534-9). 112pp. Eight-year-old Kelly is unhappy after the family moves and she has to share her room with her kid sister, Erin. (Rev: BL 10/1/96; SLJ 10/96)

8635 Evans, Douglas. *So What Do You Do?* (4–6). 1997, Front Street $14.95 (1-886910-20-0). 124pp. Two middle-schoolers try to help their beloved former teacher, who has become a hopeless drunk. (Rev: BCCB 3/98; BL 11/1/97; HBG 3/98; SLJ 1/98)

8636 Evans, Mari. *Dear Corinne, Tell Somebody! A Book About Secrets* (3–7). 1999, Just Us $12.95 (0-940975-81-5). 48pp. A book of letters in which Corinne's friends try to get her to seek help for her problem, which is later revealed as child abuse. (Rev: HBG 3/00; SLJ 12/99)

8637 Fagan, Cary. *The Market Wedding* (2–5). Illus. by Regolo Ricci. 2000, Tundra $16.95 (0-88776-492-4). The guests that Minnie and Morris invite to their wedding are so in awe of the luxurious trappings that they are afraid to attend. (Rev: BCCB 10/00; BL 12/1/00; HBG 3/01; SLJ 3/01)

8638 Fenner, Carol. *The King of Dragons* (4–6). 1998, Simon & Schuster $17.00 (0-689-82217-0). 224pp. A group of people arrive to convert an empty courthouse into a gallery to house a kite exhibition, threatening homeless Ian, who thinks he is about 11, with the loss of his shelter. (Rev: BCCB 1/99; BL 11/15/98*; HB 1–2/99; HBG 3/99; SLJ 12/98)

8639 Fenner, Carol. *Randall's Wall* (3–6). 1991, Macmillan $15.00 (0-689-50518-3). 96pp. Fifth-grader Randall Lord is so dirty that no one wants to sit near him, so he imagines himself behind an invisible wall that keeps others out. (Rev: BCCB 7–8/91; BL 4/1/91; HB 7–8/91; SLJ 4/91)

8640 Ferguson, Alane. *Stardust* (4–6). 1993, Macmillan LB $14.00 (0-02-734527-0). 160pp. A former television child star returns to a normal life in her small hometown. (Rev: BCCB 4/93; BL 5/15/93; SLJ 6/93)

8641 Fletcher, Ralph. *Spider Boy* (5–8). 1997, Clarion $15.00 (0-395-77606-6). 192pp. Bobby — whose nickname is Spider Boy because he knows so much about spiders — has problems adjusting to his new life in New Paltz, New York. (Rev: BCCB 4/97; BL 6/1–15/97; HB 7–8/97; SLJ 7/97)

8642 Fletcher, Ralph. *Tommy Trouble and the Magic Marble* (3–4). Illus. 2000, Holt $16.00 (0-8050-6387-0). 47pp. A beginning chapter book about a boy who tries to collect ten dollars to buy a ring that is supposed to protect him from nightmares. (Rev: BL 8/00; SLJ 9/00)

8643 Fox, Paula. *Monkey Island* (5–8). 1991, Watts LB $16.99 (0-531-08562-7). 160pp. At age 11, Clay finds himself homeless in New York City and struggles for the basics of life. (Rev: BCCB 10/91*; BL 9/1/91; HB 9–10/91*; SLJ 8/91)

8644 Fox, Paula. *Radiance Descending* (4–7). 1997, DK $14.95 (0-7894-2467-3). 101pp. Paul learns the true meaning of love when he gradually accepts his younger brother, who has Down's syndrome. (Rev: BL 9/1/97; HB 9–10/97; HBG 3/98; SLJ 9/97)

8645 Fox, Paula. *The Stone-Faced Boy* (4–7). Illus. by Donald MacKay. 1982, Simon & Schuster LB $13.95 (0-02-735570-5). 112pp. Gus, a sensitive and timid middle child in a family of five, learns to mask his feelings and present a "stone face" to the world.

8646 Fox, Paula. *The Village by the Sea* (5–8). 1988, Orchard $16.95 (0-531-05788-7); Dell paper $4.50 (0-440-40299-9). Emma is staying with an aunt and uncle while her father has heart surgery, and the three interact in complex ways. Also use the reissued *A Likely Place* (Simon & Schuster 1997). (Rev: BCCB 7–8/88; HB 9–10/88; SLJ 8/88)

8647 Fox, Paula. *Western Wind* (5–8). 1993, Orchard LB $17.99 (0-531-08652-6). 201pp. At first resentful of being sent to spend a summer with her grandmother on a Maine island, Elizabeth gradually adjusts and learns a great deal about herself. (Rev: BCCB 9/93; SLJ 12/93*)

8648 Frasier, Debra. *Miss Alaineus: A Vocabulary Disaster* (3–5). Illus. 2000, Harcourt $16.00 (0-15-202163-9). 32pp. Fifth-grader Sage mistakes the word *miscellaneous* for *Miss Alaineus* but turns this embarrassment into a triumph. (Rev: BL 9/15/00; HBG 3/01; SLJ 9/00)

8649 Freeman, Martha. *The Trouble with Cats* (2–4). 2000, Holiday $15.95 (0-8234-1479-5). 76pp. A beginning chapter book about Holly, who is adjusting to a new life in San Francisco with a new stepfather and a new school situation. (Rev: BCCB 4/00; BL 3/15/00; HBG 10/00; SLJ 7/00)

8650 Freeman, Suzanne. *The Cuckoo's Child* (5–8). 1996, Greenwillow $15.00 (0-688-14290-7). 256pp. Because her parents are missing, Mia leaves Lebanon to live with her aunt in Tennessee. (Rev: BCCB 3/96; BL 3/15/96*; HB 7–8/96; SLJ 4/96*)

8651 Friedman, Aileen. *A Cloak for the Dreamer* (3–5). Illus. by Kim Howard. 1995, Scholastic $15.95 (0-590-48987-9). 15pp. Misha sets out to

find his fortune in an amazing cloak designed by his father and brothers. (Rev: BL 2/1/95; SLJ 4/95)

8652 Friesen, Gayle. *Men of Stone* (5–8). 2000, Kids Can $16.95 (1-55074-781-9). 216pp. While Ben Conrad traces his own family roots, he confronts a local bully in this story of a boy's journey to maturity. (Rev: HBG 3/01; SLJ 10/00)

8653 Fromm, Pete. *Monkey Tag* (4–7). 1994, Scholastic $14.95 (0-590-46525-2). 352pp. When his twin is paralyzed from an accident, Eli feels partly responsible. (Rev: BCCB 12/94; BL 10/15/94; SLJ 10/94)

8654 Gantos, Jack. *Joey Pigza Loses Control* (4–7). 2000, Farrar $16.00 (0-374-39989-1). 208pp. Joey, a hyperactive kid, tries to please his father but goes haywire when his father destroys his medication in this Newbery Award honor book. (Rev: BCCB 9/00*; BL 9/1/00*; HB 9–10/00; HBG 3/01; SLJ 9/00)

8655 Garden, Nancy. *Holly's Secret* (5–8). 2000, Farrar $16.00 (0-374-33273-8). 144pp. When Holly and her family move to western Massachusetts, she decides to hide from her new classmates the fact that her parents are lesbians. (Rev: BCCB 9/00; BL 10/15/00; HB 9–10/00; HBG 3/01; SLJ 9/00)

8656 George, Jean Craighead. *The Summer of the Falcon* (5–8). 1992, Peter Smith $18.00 (0-8446-6503-7); HarperCollins paper $4.95 (0-06-440095-6). 153pp. June learns to take responsibility and discipline when she trains her own falcons.

8657 Gifaldi, David. *Toby Scudder, Ultimate Warrior* (4–6). 1993, Clarion $15.00 (0-395-66400-4). 201pp. A new teacher helps overweight Toby find the self-esteem he lacks. (Rev: BCCB 11/93; BL 10/15/93; SLJ 10/93*)

8658 Giff, Patricia Reilly. *The Gift of the Pirate Queen* (4–6). Illus. by Jenny Rutherford. 1983, Dell paper $4.50 (0-440-43046-1). 160pp. Grace is looking forward to the arrival of Fiona from Ireland to take care of her family.

8659 Giff, Patricia Reilly. *Poopsie Pomerantz, Pick Up Your Feet* (3–5). Illus. by Leslie Morrill. 1998, Bantam paper $3.99 (0-440-40287-5). 147pp. Poopsie's self-confidence really fades when she's chosen to play the pig in a performance of The Ugly Duckling. (Rev: BL 3/1/89; HB 5–6/89)

8660 Giff, Patricia Reilly. *Starring Rosie* (2–4). Illus. by Julie Durrell. 1997, Viking $13.99 (0-670-86967-8). 96pp. Rosie is crushed when she is cast as the wicked fairy in the class production of *Sleeping Beauty*. (Rev: BL 12/15/96; SLJ 3/97)

8661 Girard, Linda Walvoord. *Alex, the Kid with AIDS* (3–5). 1991, Whitman LB $14.95 (0-8075-0245-6). 32pp. Alex, who has AIDS, gets special treatment in class and uses the sympathy of adults to manipulate them. (Rev: BL 4/1/91; SLJ 6/91)

8662 Girard, Linda Walvoord. *At Daddy's on Saturdays* (1–4). Illus. by Judith Friedman. 1987, Whitman LB $14.95 (0-8075-0475-0); paper $6.95 (0-8075-0473-4). 32pp. The emotions and concerns of young Katie as her father moves out one Saturday after the divorce and returns for their outing the next. (Rev: BL 11/15/87; SLJ 12/87)

8663 Glaser, Linda. *Tanya's Big Green Dream* (3–5). Illus. 1994, Macmillan paper $13.95 (0-02-735994-8). 48pp. Tanya overcomes many obstacles to have a tree planted in a public park on Earth Day. (Rev: BL 5/15/94; SLJ 8/94)

8664 Glassman, Miriam. *Box Top Dreams* (4–7). 1998, Delacorte $14.95 (0-385-32532-0). 184pp. Ari is devastated when her best friend moves away; but through this experience she learns independence. (Rev: BCCB 3/98; BL 2/1/98; HB 5–6/98; HBG 10/98; SLJ 3/98)

8665 Godden, Rumer. *Listen to the Nightingale* (4–6). Illus. 1994, Puffin paper $3.99 (0-140-36091-3). 192pp. Finding a puppy alters the plans of 10-year-old Lottie to become a ballerina. (Rev: BCCB 11/92; BL 12/15/92*; HB 11–12/92; SLJ 12/92)

8666 Golding, Theresa Martin. *Kat's Surrender* (5–8). 1999, Boyds Mills $14.95 (1-56397-755-9). 179pp. Thirteen-year-old Kat misses her deceased mother terribly, but she tries to hide it in her friendships for an old man and a wacky girl. (Rev: BL 10/15/99; HBG 3/00; SLJ 11/99)

8667 Gordon, Amy. *When JFK Was My Father* (5–8). 1999, Houghton $15.00 (0-395-91364-0). 208pp. Georgia, who often imagines that President Kennedy is her caring father, has several problems including divorcing parents and adjustment to a Connecticut boarding school. (Rev: HB 7–8/99; HBG 10/99; SLJ 4/99)

8668 Gosselin, Kim. *Smoking Stinks!!* (2–4). Illus. by Thom Buttner. 1997, JayJo $16.95 (0-9639449-5-9). When Maddie's grandfather comes to school to tell her class why he smokes, he agrees that smoking stinks. (Rev: BL 4/1/98; SLJ 1/98)

8669 Gray, Dianne E. *Holding Up the Earth* (5–8). 2000, Houghton $15.00 (0-618-00703-2). 224pp. Sarah, a foster child now living on a Nebraska farm, does some research and uncovers stories of the many generations of women who preceded her on the farm and their struggles and problems. (Rev: BL 1/1–15/01; HB 9–10/00; HBG 3/01; SLJ 10/00)

8670 Greene, Constance C. *Beat the Turtle Drum* (4–6). Illus. by Donna Diamond. 1994, Puffin paper $4.99 (0-14-036850-7). 128pp. A young girl must adjust to the accidental death of her beloved younger sister.

8671 Greenwald, Sheila. *My Fabulous New Life* (4–6). 1993, Harcourt $10.95 (0-15-277693-1); paper $3.95 (0-15-276716-9). 160pp. Shocked by all the poor people she sees around her new home in Manhattan, Alison tries to find a way to help them. (Rev: BL 10/1/93; SLJ 10/93)

8672 Groth, B. L., and Thomas Wray, eds. *Home Is Where We Live* (3–5). Illus. 1995, Cornerstone paper $7.95 (0-940895-34-X). 32pp. A simple story told in photos and narrative of a homeless child in a Chicago shelter. (Rev: BL 10/15/95; SLJ 12/95)

8673 Grove, Vicki. *Destiny* (5–9). 2000, Putnam $16.99 (0-399-23449-7). 176pp. Destiny Louise, age 12, who is growing up in poverty with a mother who only watches TV, finds an outlet in her interest in art and two teachers who befriend her. (Rev: BCCB 9/00; BL 5/1/00; HBG 3/01; SLJ 4/00)

8674 Guest, Elissa Haden. *Iris and Walter* (1–3). Illus. 2000, Harcourt $14.00 (0-15-202122-1). 44pp. It takes time, but gradually Iris comes to enjoy living in the country far from the city activities she loved, in this beginning chapter book. (Rev: BCCB 12/00*; BL 10/15/00; HBG 3/01; SLJ 11/00)

8675 Haas, Jessie. *Unbroken: A Novel* (5–8). 1999, HarperCollins $14.95 (0-688-16260-6). 192pp. A powerful story of a 13-year-old girl's adjustment to her mother's death and her efforts to train a stubborn colt so that she can ride him to school. (Rev: HB 7–8/99; HBG 10/99; SLJ 4/99*)

8676 Haas, Jessie. *Will You, Won't You?* (5–8). 2000, Greenwillow LB $15.89 (0-06-029197-4). 192pp. Mad (short for Madison) is a shy middleschooler who comes out of her shell during a summer she spends with her wise grandmother in the country. (Rev: BCCB 10/00; BL 2/1/01; HBG 3/01)

8677 Hahn, Mary D. *Anna on the Farm* (3–5). Illus. 2001, Clarion $15.00 (0-618-03605-9). 152pp. When 9-year-old Anna arrives at her aunt and uncle's farm for a week, she finds they have taken in an orphan named Theodore, and a hearty rivalry begins. (Rev: BL 2/15/01; SLJ 3/01)

8678 Hahn, Mary D. *As Ever, Gordy* (5–8). 1998, Clarion $15.00 (0-395-83627-1). 192pp. After his grandmother's death, 13-year-old Gordy must move back to his hometown to live with his older brother, and there he finds himself in a downward spiral with friends who betray him. (Rev: BCCB 6/98; BL 5/1/98; HBG 10/98; SLJ 7/98)

8679 Hamilton, Virginia. *Cousins* (5–8). 1990, Putnam $16.99 (0-399-22164-6). 125pp. Cammy faces both guilt and grief when her cousin Patty Ann drowns. (Rev: BCCB 11/90*; HB 3–4/91; SLJ 12/90)

8680 Hamilton, Virginia. *Drylongso* (3–5). Illus. by Jerry Pinkney. 1992, Harcourt $18.95 (0-15-224241-4). 64pp. During a great duststorm on the prairie in 1975, a tall boy appears who helps Lindy and her family find water. (Rev: BCCB 10/92*; BL 7/92*; HB 9–10/92; SLJ 1/93)

8681 Hamilton, Virginia. *Second Cousins* (5–8). 1998, Scholastic $14.95 (0-590-47368-9). 176pp. In this sequel to *Cousins*, 12-year-old Cammy learns a family secret during a family reunion in her small Ohio town. (Rev: BCCB 11/98; BL 8/98; HB 1–2/99; HBG 3/99; SLJ 11/98)

8682 Hamilton, Virginia. *Zeely* (4–6). Illus. by Symeon Shimin. 1967, Macmillan $17.00 (0-02-742470-7); paper $4.99 (0-689-71695-8). 128pp. An 11-year-old African American city girl is lightly guided from her daydreams to reality by Zeely, who is as kind as she is tall and beautiful.

8683 Harrah, Madge. *The Nobody Club* (4–6). 1989, Avon paper $2.50 (0-380-75631-5). 166pp. Three misunderstood girls form a club to help solve one another's problems. (Rev: SLJ 8/89)

8684 Hartling, Peter. *Ben Loves Anna* (4–6). Trans. by J. H. Auerbach. Illus. by Ellen Weinstein. 1990, Overlook $12.95 (0-87951-401-9). 96pp. The feelings of a lovestruck 10-year-old boy are captured by one of Germany's most distinguished children's writers. (Rev: BCCB 4/91; BL 6/15/91; SLJ 5/91)

8685 Hearne, Betsy. *Listening for Leroy* (4–7). 1998, Simon & Schuster $16.00 (0-689-82218-9). 224pp. When her family, dominated by her strict doctor father, moves from Alabama to Tennessee in the 1950s, Alice finds she doesn't fit in at school either physically (she is too tall and doesn't dress conventionally) or emotionally. (Rev: BL 11/15/98*; HBG 3/99; SLJ 11/98)

8686 Henderson, Aileen K. *Treasure of Panther Peak* (4–7). Illus. 1998, Milkweed $15.95 (1-57131-618-3); paper $6.95 (1-57131-619-1). 184pp. Twelve-year-old Ellie Williams gradually adjusts to her new home when her mother, fleeing an abusive husband, moves to Big Bend National Park to teach in a one-room school. (Rev: BL 12/1/98; HBG 3/99)

8687 Henkes, Kevin. *Sun and Spoon* (3–5). 1997, Greenwillow $15.00 (0-688-15232-5). 144pp. Spoon takes his dead grandmother's solitaire cards as a memento, but later he regrets his action. (Rev: BL 8/97; HB 9–10/97; HBG 3/98; SLJ 7/97*)

8688 Herman, Gail. *Just Like Mike* (3–5). 2000, Delacorte $13.95 (0-385-32542-8). 59pp. When his mother remarries, Michael Brown becomes Michael Jordan but unfortunately he is completely unlike his namesake and this causes him some problems. (Rev: BCCB 3/00; BL 2/15/00; HBG 10/00; SLJ 3/00)

8689 Hermes, Patricia. *The Cousins Club: Everything Stinks* (4–6). 1995, Pocket paper $3.50 (0-671-87967-7). 147pp. Jennifer and twin Amy are in the fifth grade and facing the problems of becoming adolescents. (Rev: BL 1/15/95; SLJ 3/95)

8690 Hesse, Karen. *Just Juice* (3–5). Illus. 1998, Scholastic $14.95 (0-590-03382-4). 144pp. Nine-year-old Juice, the middle child of five sisters growing up in a poor rural family, would rather stay home and help Pa in his machine shop and her diabetic mother instead of attending school where she has problems learning to read. (Rev: BCCB 12/98; BL 11/1/98; HB 11–12/98; HBG 3/99; SLJ 10/98)

8691 Hest, Amy. *The Great Green Notebook of Katie Roberts: Who Just Turned 12 on Monday* (3–5). Illus. 1998, Candlewick $14.99 (0-7636-0464-X). 112pp. Katie, now 12 and entering seventh grade, confides in her journal that she is suffering many of the problems of early adolescence. (Rev: BL 11/15/98; HB 1–2/99; HBG 3/99; SLJ 9/98)

8692 Hest, Amy. *The Private Notebook of Katie Roberts, Age 11* (4–6). Illus. 1995, Candlewick $14.99 (1-56402-474-1). 80pp. Katie confides in her diary about problems adjusting to her new Texas home and about her many questions concerning the difficulties of growing up. (Rev: BL 7/95*; HB 9–10/95; SLJ 9/95)

8693 High, Linda O. *The Summer of the Great Divide* (5–8). 1996, Holiday $15.95 (0-8234-1228-8). 176pp. During the summer of 1969, 13-year-old Wheezie sorts herself out at her relative's farm. (Rev: BCCB 7–8/96; BL 6/1–15/96; SLJ 4/96)

8694 Hobbs, Valerie. *Carolina Crow Girl* (4–6). 1999, Farrar $16.00 (0-374-31153-6). 144pp. Carolina, who lives with her mother in an old school bus, finds a way out of her problems through saving a young crow and forming a friendship with a wheelchair-bound man. (Rev: BCCB 6/99; BL 2/15/99; HBG 10/99; SLJ 4/99)

8695 Holden, Dwight. *Grand-Gran's Best Trick* (3–5). Illus. by Michael Chesworth. 1989, Brunner paper $8.95 (0-945354-16-9). 48pp. A young girl faces the sad experience of her beloved grandfather's death. (Rev: BL 12/1/89)

8696 Holl, Kristi D. *First Things First* (5–7). 1997, Royal Fireworks paper $6.99 (0-88092-432-2). Informed that the family can't afford to send her to camp this year, Shelley decides to earn her own money. (Rev: BL 5/1/86; SLJ 5/86)

8697 Horvath, Penny. *Everything on a Waffle* (5–7). 2001, Farrar $16.00 (0-374-32236-8). 160pp. Eleven-year-old Primrose Squarp does not believe her parents drowned during a storm. In the meantime she is moved from pillar to post, ending up as a foster child to an elderly couple. (Rev: BCCB 3/01*; BL 2/15/01)

8698 Howe, James. *A Night Without Stars* (5–7). 1983, Macmillan $13.95 (0-689-30957-0); Avon paper $2.95 (0-380-69877-3). 192pp. A novel about a young girl's hospitalization and serious operation.

8699 Howe, James. *Pinky and Rex and the Bully* (2–4). Illus. 1996, Simon & Schuster $15.00 (0-689-80021-5); paper $3.99 (0-689-80834-8). 40pp. When the local bully calls him a sissy, Pinky wonders if he should change his ways. (Rev: BL 4/1/96; SLJ 4/96)

8700 Howe, James. *Pinky and Rex and the Perfect Pumpkin* (2–4). Illus. 1998, Simon & Schuster $15.00 (0-689-81782-7); paper $3.99 (0-689-81777-0). 48pp. Rex feels left out of the fun on the annual search for the perfect pumpkin when Abby makes sure that Rex knows she is not part of the family. (Rev: BL 9/1/98; HBG 3/99; SLJ 10/98)

8701 Hughes, Dean. *Family Pose* (5–8). 1989, Macmillan LB $14.95 (0-689-31396-9). 192pp. A novel of an 11-year-old runaway and his growing attachment to a "new family." (Rev: BL 4/1/89; SLJ 4/89)

8702 Hunt, Irene. *No Promises in the Wind* (5–8). 1987, Berkley paper $4.99 (0-425-09969-5). 100pp. During the Great Depression, Josh Grondowski is forced to make his own way in life.

8703 Hurwitz, Johanna. *Once I Was a Plum Tree* (4–5). Illus. by Ingrid Fetz. 1992, Morrow paper $3.95 (0-688-11848-8). 160pp. In spite of her parents' indifference, Geraldine becomes aware of her Jewish inheritance.

8704 Hurwitz, Johanna. *Summer with Elisa* (2–4). Illus. 2000, HarperCollins $15.95 (0-688-17095-1). 96pp. Using a separate chapter for each incident, this book tells about a series of crises that a young girl faces during her summer vacation. (Rev: BL 9/15/00; HBG 3/01; SLJ 9/00)

8705 Hurwitz, Johanna. *Yellow Blue Jay* (3–5). Illus. by Donald Carrick. 1986, Morrow paper $4.95 (0-688-12278-7). 128pp. Shy city-boy Jay finds that two weeks at a Vermont cabin is not as bad as he feared. (Rev: BCCB 6/86; BL 6/15/86; SLJ 8/86)

8706 Huser, Glen. *Touch of the Clown* (5–9). 1999, Groundwood $15.95 (0-88899-343-9). 223pp. Since her mother's death, Barbara and her younger sister have been living with her abusive father and grandmother, both alcoholics, but her life seems to turn around when she secretly attends a clown workshop for teens and becomes friendly with the teacher. (Rev: SLJ 11/99)

8707 Hyppolite, Joanne. *Ola Shakes It Up* (4–8). Illus. 1998, Delacorte $14.95 (0-385-32235-6). 166pp. A spunky girl tries to prevent her parents from moving to a neighborhood where she will be the only African American in school. (Rev: BL 2/15/98; HB 3–4/98; HBG 10/98; SLJ 2/98)

8708 Irwin, Hadley. *The Lilith Summer* (6–8). 1979, Feminist Pr. $8.95 (0-912670-52-5). 126pp. Twelve-year-old Ellen learns about old age when she "lady sits" with 77-year-old Lilith Adams.

8709 Janover, Caroline. *How Many Days Until Tomorrow?* (4–6). 2000, Woodbine paper $11.95 (1-890-62722-4). 122pp. At first 12-year-old Josh, who is dyslexic, wants to run away from the Maine island where he is spending a month with his grandparents, but gradually he learns to adjust. (Rev: BL 1/1–15/01)

8710 Jarrow, Gail. *Beyond the Magic Sphere* (4–6). 1994, Harcourt $15.95 (0-15-200193-X). 192pp. S. B.'s only ray of hope during the summer she is spending with her unsympathetic cousin is meeting Cally, who plays a strange fantasy game. (Rev: BL 10/15/94; SLJ 11/94)

8711 Jarzyna, Dave. *Slump* (5–8). 1999, Delacorte $14.95 (0-385-32618-1). 137pp. When Mitchie's life seems in a tailspin, including his quitting the soccer team, he vows to turn things around. (Rev: BCCB 9/99; HBG 3/00; SLJ 8/99)

8712 Johnson, Emily Rhoads. *Write Me If You Dare!* (4–6). 2000, Front Street $15.95 (0-8126-2944-2). 208pp. While coping with her mother's death and her father's new girlfriend, 11-year-old Maddie decides that her pen pal is really a ghost. (Rev: BCCB 12/00; BL 11/1/00; HB 1–2/01; HBG 3/01; SLJ 11/00)

8713 Joosse, Barbara M. *Anna and the Cat Lady* (3–6). Illus. by Gretchen Will Mayo. 1992, HarperCollins LB $13.89 (0-06-020243-2). 176pp. Two third-graders rescue a kitten and meet an elderly eccentric woman who they later realize needs their help to survive. (Rev: BCCB 2/92; BL 1/1/92; SLJ 3/92)

8714 Joosse, Barbara M. *Pieces of the Picture* (5–8). 1989, HarperCollins LB $12.89 (0-397-32343-3); paper $3.50 (0-06-440310-6). 144pp. Emily finds life unhappy when she and her mother move to Wisconsin from Chicago after her father's death. (Rev: BL 6/1/89; SLJ 4/89)

8715 Joseph, Lynn. *The Color of My Words* (4–6). 2000, HarperCollins LB $14.89 (0-06-028233-9). 144pp. Growing up in the Dominican Republic, Ana Rosa has an eventful 12th year, including the discovery that the man she thought was her father is not. (Rev: BCCB 10/00; BL 10/15/00*; HB 9–10/00; HBG 3/01; SLJ 9/00)

8716 Katz, Welwyn W. *Out of the Dark* (5–8). 1996, Simon & Schuster $16.00 (0-689-80947-6). 176pp. A young boy escapes the painful present by imagining himself as a Viking shipbuilder. (Rev: BL 10/15/96; HB 11–12/96; SLJ 9/96)

8717 Kaye, Marilyn. *Real Heroes* (5–7). 1993, Avon paper $3.50 (0-380-72283-6). 144pp. Kevin finds he is in the middle of a situation involving quarrels between parents and between best friends, and a controversy about a teacher who is HIV positive. (Rev: BCCB 5/93; BL 4/1/93)

8718 Keene, Carolyn. *Love Times Three* (5–8). Series: River Heights. 1991, Pocket paper $3.50 (0-671-96703-7). 156pp. Nikki has a crush on Tim, but Brittany wants him too. (Rev: BL 12/15/89)

8719 Kehret, Peg. *I'm Not Who You Think I Am* (5–8). 1999, Penguin $15.99 (0-525-46153-1). 144pp. Thirteen-year-old Ginger has two problems, one concerning a deranged woman who thinks she is her daughter and the other involving her favorite teacher who is being harassed by a parent. (Rev: BCCB 3/99; HBG 10/99; SLJ 4/99)

8720 Kehret, Peg. *My Brother Made Me Do It* (4–6). 2000, Pocket $16.00 (0-671-03418-9). 132pp. Written as a series of letters from 11-year-old Julie to a nursing home resident, this novel tells of Julie's problems with rheumatoid arthritis. (Rev: BL 6/1–15/00; HBG 10/00; SLJ 9/00)

8721 Killien, Christi. *Artie's Brief: The Whole Truth, and Nothing But* (5–7). 1989, Avon paper $2.95 (0-380-71108-7). 112pp. Sixth-grader Artie deals with the suicide of his older brother. (Rev: BL 5/15/89)

8722 King-Smith, Dick. *Sophie Is Seven* (2–4). Illus. 1995, Candlewick $14.95 (1-56402-542-X). 123pp. A classroom unit on life helps promote Sophie's determination to own a farm one day. (Rev: BCCB 5/95; BL 7/95; SLJ 7/95)

8723 Kinsey-Warnock, Natalie. *The Canada Geese Quilt* (4–6). Illus. by Leslie Bowman. 1989, Dutton $14.99 (0-525-65004-0). 64pp. Ariel and her grandmother adjust to the elderly woman's stroke and to a new baby in the family. (Rev: BCCB 1/90; BL 10/1/89*; SLJ 11/89*)

8724 Kinsey-Warnock, Natalie. *In the Language of Loons* (4–7). 1998, Cobblehill $15.99 (0-525-65237-X). 105pp. During a summer on his grandfather's farm, Arlis gains self-confidence and learns how to tap his potential. (Rev: BCCB 4/98; HBG 10/98; SLJ 3/98)

8725 Klass, Sheila S. *Kool Ada* (5–7). 1991, Scholastic $13.95 (0-590-43902-2). 176pp. Ada reacts only with her fists when she is sent to live in inner-city Chicago. (Rev: BL 10/15/91; SLJ 8/91*)

8726 Klass, Sheila S. *Little Women Next Door* (3–6). 2000, Holiday $15.95 (0-8234-1472-8). 144pp. Lonely 11-year-old Susan Wilson's life changes when a group experimenting with communal life moves into the neighborhood. (Rev: HBG 3/01; SLJ 11/00)

8727 Klass, Sheila S. *The Uncivil War* (4–6). 1998, Holiday $15.95 (0-8234-1329-2). 162pp. After she is taunted by the class bully, middle schooler Asa decides to mend her ways and, among other things, lose weight. (Rev: HBG 10/98; SLJ 4/98)

8728 Kline, Suzy. *Marvin and the Mean Words* (2–4). Illus. 1997, Putnam $14.99 (0-399-23009-2). 80pp. Marvin, the second-grade class bully, gets a taste of his own medicine. (Rev: BL 4/1/97; SLJ 5/97)

8729 Kline, Suzy. *Mary Marony and the Chocolate Surprise* (2–4). Illus. 1995, Putnam $14.99 (0-399-22829-2). 86pp. Mary Marony cheats to become a contest winner and later wonders if it was worth it. (Rev: BL 12/1/95; SLJ 12/95)

8730 Konigsburg, E. L. *Altogether, One at a Time* (4–6). Illus. by Gail E. Haley. 1971, Macmillan paper $4.99 (0-689-71290-1). 88pp. Four short stories by the Newbery Medal-winning writer, each of which explores the theme that compromise is often necessary to appreciate life fully.

8731 Konigsburg, E. L. *T-Backs, T-Shirts, Coat, and Suit* (5–8). Series: Jean Karl Books. 1993, Atheneum $14.00 (0-689-31855-3). 160pp. When Chloé goes to visit her former flower-child sister, she becomes part of a struggle for individual rights in the workplace. (Rev: BCCB 11/93; SLJ 10/93*)

8732 Korman, Gordon. *Liar, Liar, Pants on Fire* (2–4). Illus. by JoAnn Adinolfi. 1997, Scholastic $14.95 (0-590-27142-3). 84pp. Third-grader Zoe lies so much that no one believes her when she tells the truth. (Rev: HBG 3/98; SLJ 9/97)

8733 Koss, Amy Goldman. *The Girls* (5–9). 2000, Dial $16.99 (0-8037-2494-2). 128pp. In chapters narrated by different protagonists, this book tells of Maya who has been dropped for no apparent reason from a clique of five popular girls in the middle school she attends. (Rev: BCCB 6/00; BL 8/00; HB 7–8/00; HBG 10/00; SLJ 6/00)

8734 Koss, Amy Goldman. *Smoke Screen* (5–8). 2000, Pleasant $12.95 (1-58485-202-X). 139pp. A harmless fib gets out of control when Mitzi lies in order to impress a boy. (Rev: BL 9/15/00; SLJ 11/00)

8735 Krumgold, Joseph. *Onion John* (5–8). Illus. by Symeon Shimin. 1959, HarperCollins LB $15.89 (0-690-04698-7); paper $5.95 (0-06-440144-8). 248pp. A Newbery Medal winner (1960) about a boy's friendship with an old man. Also use the Newbery Award winner . . . *And Now Miguel* (1954).

8736 Lafaye, A. *Nissa's Place* (5–7). 1999, Simon & Schuster $16.00 (0-689-82610-9). 245pp. In the 1930s, young Nissa visits her divorced mother in Chicago and sorts out her feelings about her mother, father, and pregnant stepmother, and her attitudes about life. (Rev: BCCB 10/99; BL 10/15/99; HBG 3/00)

8737 Laser, Michael. *6–321* (4–7). 2001, Simon & Schuster $15.00 (0-689-83372-5). 115pp. In this autobiographical novel set in 1963, sixth-grader Marc Chaikin falls in love, experiences his parents' divorce, and reacts to the assassination of John F. Kennedy. (Rev: BCCB 2/01; BL 1/1–15/01)

8738 Layton, George. *The Swap* (5–8). 1997, Putnam $16.95 (0-399-23148-X). 192pp. A series of stories narrated by an 11-year-old working-class boy in the north of England, who is troubled by bullying and growing up without a father. (Rev: BL 10/1/97; HBG 3/98; SLJ 9/97)

8739 Lears, Laurie. *Ben Has Something to Say: A Story About Stuttering* (K–5). Illus. by Karen Ritz. 2000, Albert Whitman LB $14.95 (0-8075-0633-8). Ben, who has a stutter, gains some self-confidence when he summons up the courage to ask a junk dealer if he can adopt the dog that the man is planning to get rid of. (Rev: HBG 3/01; SLJ 11/00)

8740 Lemieux, Michele. *Stormy Night* (4–8). Illus. by author. 1999, Kids Can $15.95 (1-55074-692-8). 240pp. A long picture book in which a young girl who can't sleep ponders questions that are common to preteen girls. (Rev: HBG 3/00; SLJ 12/99)

8741 Leverich, Kathleen. *Daisy* (2–4). Illus. 1997, HarperCollins paper $4.25 (0-06-442019-1). 96pp. Daisy is unhappy when she discovers she will be only one of several flower girls at an upcoming wedding. Other stories about flower girls are *Violet, Rose,* and *Heather* (all 1997). (Rev: BL 7/97; HB 5–6/97; SLJ 4/97)

8742 Leverich, Kathleen. *The New You* (5–7). 1998, Greenwillow $15.00 (0-688-16076-X). 128pp. Abby, who recently moved to New York City and entered a new school, is unhappy and friendless until she begins to share her experiences with others. (Rev: BL 11/1/98; HBG 3/99)

8743 Levy, Elizabeth. *My Life as a Fifth-Grade Comedian* (4–6). Illus. 1997, HarperCollins $15.95 (0-06-026602-3). 128pp. Jimmy, a born joker, has problems at home and finds that his grades are slipping at school. (Rev: BL 8/97; HBG 3/98; SLJ 9/97)

8744 Lewis, Beverly. *Catch a Falling Star* (5–8). 1995, Bethany paper $5.99 (1-55661-478-0). 144pp. An Amish boy faces excommunication when he begins paying too much attention to a non-Amish girl. (Rev: BL 3/15/96)

8745 Lewis, Beverly. *Night of the Fireflies* (5–8). 1995, Bethany paper $5.99 (1-55661-479-9). 144pp. In this sequel to *Catch a Falling Star* (1995), Levi, an Amish boy, tries to save his young sister, who has been struck by a car. (Rev: BL 3/15/96)

8746 Lewis, Maggie. *Morgy Makes His Move* (3–5). Illus. 1999, Houghton $15.00 (0-395-92284-4). 80pp. A pleasant novel that tells of third-grader Morgan and his adjustment to his new home in Massachusetts, which involves coping with a bully named Ferguson. (Rev: BCCB 10/99; BL 12/15/99; HBG 3/00; SLJ 11/99)

8747 Little, Jean. *The Belonging Place* (4–6). 1997, Viking $13.99 (0-670-87593-7). 144pp. Already uprooted once because of the death of her parents, Elspet Mary is upset when her aunt and uncle with whom she has been living decide to move up to the Canadian wilderness. (Rev: BL 11/15/97; HBG 3/98; SLJ 11/97)

8748 Love, D. Anne. *My Lone Star Summer* (4–6). 1996, Holiday $15.95 (0-8234-1235-0). 192pp. Jill experiences the first problems of adolescence when she spends her 12th summer visiting her grandmother's ranch. (Rev: BCCB 7–8/96; BL 5/1/96; SLJ 3/96)

8749 Lowery, Linda. *Somebody Somewhere Knows My Name* (3–5). Illus. by John E. Karpinski. 1995, Carolrhoda LB $19.93 (0-87614-946-8). 40pp. Grace and her 8-year-old brother are abandoned by their mother and taken to a shelter for the homeless. (Rev: BL 12/1/95; SLJ 11/95)

8750 McDonnell, Christine. *It's a Deal, Dogboy* (2–4). Illus. 1998, Viking $14.99 (0-670-83264-2). 80pp. Leo, alias Dogboy, feels his summer is ruined when his mother wants him to do some housework, his baseball team goes coed, and he finds his pesky sister and cousin are going to be around. (Rev: BL 11/1/98; HB 11–12/98; HBG 3/99; SLJ 11/98)

8751 McElfresh, Lynn E. *Can You Feel the Thunder?* (4–8). 1999, Simon & Schuster $16.00 (0-689-82324-X). 138pp. Mic, a seventh grader, has trouble adjusting to his blind and deaf older sister and also finds that if he doesn't master mathematical fractions, he won't be allowed to play baseball at school. (Rev: BCCB 9/99; BL 6/1–15/99; HBG 10/99)

8752 McKenna, Colleen O'Shaughnessy. *Fifth Grade: Here Comes Trouble* (4–6). 1991, Scholastic paper $3.25 (0-590-41734-7). 128pp. Collette feels insecure when her rich friend invites her to her first boy-girl party. (Rev: BCCB 10/89; SLJ 9/89)

8753 MacLachlan, Patricia. *The Facts and Fictions of Minna Pratt* (5–7). 1988, HarperCollins LB $14.89 (0-06-024117-9); paper $4.95 (0-06-440265-7). 144pp. A budding young cellist on the verge of adolescence experiences her first boyfriend. (Rev: BCCB 4/88; BL 6/15/88; SLJ 6–7/88)

8754 MacLachlan, Patricia. *Unclaimed Treasures* (5–8). 1984, HarperCollins paper $4.95 (0-06-440189-8). 128pp. A romantic story of a young girl finding herself.

8755 McNamee, Graham. *Nothing Wrong with a Three-Legged Dog* (4–6). 2000, Delacorte $14.95 (0-385-32755-2). 134pp. Keath, the worst student and only white boy in his class, has problems with a bully and with helping a three-legged dog he cares for. (Rev: BCCB 9/00; BL 8/00; HBG 3/01; SLJ 9/00)

8756 Masterman-Smith, Virginia. *First Mate Tate* (5–9). 2000, Marshall Cavendish $14.95 (0-7614-5075-0). 204pp. The story of a young girl in Atlantic City and her parents who are addicted to gambling. (Rev: HBG 3/01; SLJ 9/00)

8757 Miles, Miska. *Annie and the Old One* (2–5). Illus. by Peter Parnall. 1972, Little, Brown $16.95 (0-316-57117-2); paper $7.95 (0-316-57120-2). Annie, a young Navajo girl, realizes her wonderful grandmother is dying and tries to put off the inevitable.

8758 Miles, Miska. *Gertrude's Pocket* (3–5). Illus. by Emily Arnold McCully. 1984, Peter Smith $15.75 (0-8446-6164-3). A reissue of a 1970 title in which Gertrude's tormentor gets his comeuppance in a story about poor folk in Appalachia.

8759 Mills, Claudia. *Cally's Enterprise* (4–6). 1989, Avon paper $2.75 (0-380-70693-8). 128pp. Cally, the daughter of overachievers, breaks her foot and can't go to ballet and gym, and to her surprise learns that she likes being a businesswoman when her friend Chuck gets her to sell magazines. (Rev: BCCB 4/88; BL 6/1/88; SLJ 5/88)

8760 Mills, Claudia. *Dinah Forever* (5–7). 1995, Farrar $14.00 (0-374-31788-7). 144pp. Dinah, who is a competitive achiever, questions her values when an elderly friend dies. (Rev: BCCB 11/95; BL 10/1/95; SLJ 11/95*)

8761 Mills, Claudia. *Gus and Grandpa and the Two-Wheeled Bike* (1–3). Illus. 1999, Farrar $13.00 (0-374-32821-8). 48pp. An easy chapter book about Gus who doesn't feel confident in trying to ride his new bike without, at least, training wheels. (Rev: BL 2/1/99; HB 3–4/99; HBG 10/99; SLJ 4/99)

8762 Mills, Lauren. *The Rag Coat* (3–5). Illus. 1991, Little, Brown $16.95 (0-316-57407-4). 32pp. A picture book that celebrates Appalachia. (Rev: BCCB 1/92; BL 10/15/91; HB 11–12/91; SLJ 11/91*)

8763 Mohr, Nicholasa. *The Magic Shell* (2–4). Illus. 1995, Scholastic $13.95 (0-590-47110-4). 112pp. A young boy is not happy in his new home in New York City and misses his native land, the Dominican Republic. (Rev: BCCB 12/95; BL 8/95; SLJ 10/95)

8764 Montgomery, L. M. *Anne of Green Gables* (5–8). Illus. by Jody Lee. 1983, Putnam $15.99 (0-448-06030-2). 384pp. The old-fashioned story of an orphan girl and her adventures. Others in this series are available in paperback from Bantam.

8765 Moon, Pat. *The Spying Game* (5–8). 1999, Putnam $16.99 (0-399-23354-7). 208pp. After Joe's father is killed in an automobile accident, the 12-year-old boy begins to stalk the man he thinks is responsible. (Rev: BCCB 10/99; HBG 3/00; SLJ 8/99)

8766 Moore, Emily. *Whose Side Are You On?* (5–7). 1988, Farrar paper $4.95 (0-374-48373-6). 128pp. Barbra is dismayed to find out that her math tutor is none other than T.J., the class pest. (Rev: BCCB 10/88; BL 1/15/89; SLJ 10/88)

8767 Moss, Marissa. *Amelia Takes Command* (3–5). Illus. 1998, Tricycle Pr. $14.95 (1-883672-70-8). 40pp. In this installment of Amelia's continuing journal, she faces two problems beginning the fifth grade — an inconsistent friend and a problem bully — but gains confidence through experiences at Space Camp during winter break. (Rev: BL 9/1/98; HBG 3/99; SLJ 10/98)

8768 Moss, Marissa. *Amelia Works It Out* (3–5). Illus. Series: Amelia's Notebook. 2000, Pleasant $12.95 (1-58485-081-7). 44pp. In this novel in journal form, Amelia tries different jobs in an effort to make enough money to buy an expensive pair of shoes that her mother refuses to get for her. (Rev: BL 9/1/00; HBG 3/01; SLJ 9/00)

8769 Myers, Anna. *When the Bough Breaks* (5–8). 2000, Walker $16.95 (0-8027-8725-8). 170pp. The story of a foster child, her elderly neighbor, and the terrible secrets that each is hiding. (Rev: HB 1–2/01; HBG 3/01; SLJ 12/00)

8770 Naylor, Phyllis Reynolds. *The Agony of Alice* (5–7). 1985, Macmillan $16.00 (0-689-31143-5); Dell paper $4.99 (0-689-81672-3). 144pp. Sixth-grader Alice is motherless and longing for a female model, which she finally finds in her teacher, Mrs. Plotkin, whom she hates. (Rev: BL 10/1/85; SLJ 1/86)

8771 Naylor, Phyllis Reynolds. *Alice in April* (5–8). 1993, Macmillan $16.00 (0-689-31805-7). Al faces problems at school and at home, all related to her growing up. (Rev: SLJ 6/93)

8772 Naylor, Phyllis Reynolds. *Alice the Brave* (5–7). 1995, Simon & Schuster $15.00 (0-689-80095-9); paper $4.50 (0-689-80598-5). 131pp. Alice conquers her fear of deep water and also feels the pangs of growing up in this amusing continuation of a popular series. (Rev: BCCB 4/95; BL 5/1/95; HB 7–8/95; SLJ 5/95)

8773 Naylor, Phyllis Reynolds. *All But Alice* (5–8). 1992, Macmillan $15.00 (0-689-31773-5). 128pp. Alice, now a seventh-grader and still motherless, looks for guidance by joining in the activities of her peer group. (Rev: BCCB 5/92; HB 7–8/92; SLJ 5/92)

8774 Naylor, Phyllis Reynolds. *Eddie, Incorporated* (4–6). Illus. by Blanche Sims. 1980, Macmillan $15.00 (0-689-30754-3). After many tries, a sixth-grader finally finds a way to make money.

8775 Naylor, Phyllis Reynolds. *Night Cry* (5–8). 1984, Macmillan $17.00 (0-689-31017-X); Dell paper $3.99 (0-440-40017-1). 168pp. A 13-year-old Mississippi girl lives alone in the backwoods.

8776 Nilsson, Ulf. *If You Didn't Have Me* (3–5). Trans. by George Blecher. Illus. by Eva Eriksson. 1987, Macmillan $16.00 (0-689-50406-3). While his parents are building a house in town, a Swedish boy spends a lonely summer on his grandparents' farm. (Rev: BCCB 4/87; BL 4/15/87; HB 5–6/87)

8777 Orgel, Doris. *Don't Call Me Slob-o* (2–5). Illus. 1996, Hyperion LB $14.49 (0-7868-2086-1); paper $3.95 (0-7868-1044-0). 80pp. Shrimp, once the target of the neighborhood kids' jokes, loses that status when a new kid, Slob-o, comes to town. (Rev: BL 1/1–15/97; SLJ 7/96)

8778 Palatini, Margie. *The Wonder Worm Wars* (4–6). 1997, Hyperion LB $15.49 (0-7868-2295-3). 144pp. Elliot faces a dismal summer after he breaks his arm and discovers that his next-door neighbor, a girl, is a better athlete than he is. (Rev: BL 10/1/97; HBG 3/98; SLJ 12/97)

8779 Paterson, Katherine. *The Great Gilly Hopkins* (4–6). 1978, HarperCollins LB $15.89 (0-690-03838-0); paper $5.95 (0-06-440201-0). 192pp. Precocious Gilly bounces from one foster home to another.

8780 Paterson, Katherine. *Preacher's Boy* (5–7). 1999, Clarion $15.00 (0-395-83897-5). 176pp. At the turn of the 20th century, Robbie, the son of a minister, becomes tired of trying to please God and decides to make his own moral choices in this disturbing but entertaining novel. (Rev: BCCB 10/99; BL 8/99*; HB 9–10/99; HBG 3/00; SLJ 8/99)

8781 Paulsen, Gary. *Alida's Song* (5–8). 1999, Delacorte $15.95 (0-385-32586-X). 88pp. In this story about reaching maturity, a 14-year-old boy gets a summer job working on a farm run by two Norwe-

gian brothers. A sequel to *The Cookcamp*. (Rev: HBG 10/99; SLJ 7/99)

8782 Paulsen, Gary. *Brian's Return* (5–8). 1999, Delacorte $15.95 (0-385-32500-2). 117pp. Brian, the hero of *Brian's Winter*, becomes so disheartened with life at school away from the wilderness that he decides to leave society behind forever. (Rev: BL 2/1/99; HB 1–2/99; HBG 10/99)

8783 Paulsen, Gary. *The Cookcamp* (5–7). 1991, Orchard $15.95 (0-531-05927-8). 128pp. After a 5-year-old boy discovers his mother is having an affair, he is sent off to northern Minnesota in this World War II story. (Rev: BCCB 3/91; BL 3/1/91; HB 3–4/91; SLJ 2/91*)

8784 Pearson, Gayle. *The Secret Box* (5–8). 1997, Simon & Schuster $15.00 (0-689-81379-1). 128pp. Five short stories about the pangs of growing up, set in Oakland, California. (Rev: BCCB 7–8/97; BL 8/97; HBG 3/98; SLJ 6/97)

8785 Peters, Julie A. *Revenge of the Snob Squad* (4–6). 1998, Little, Brown $13.95 (0-316-70603-5). 144pp. A moving story about four girls who are social outcasts at school because of weight and other problems and how they form the Snob Squad to combat the school bullies who exclude and make fun of them. (Rev: BCCB 9/98; BL 9/15/98; HBG 10/98; SLJ 7/98)

8786 Peterseil, Tehila. *The Safe Place* (5–8). 1996, Pitspopany $16.95 (0-943706-71-8); paper $12.95 (0-943706-72-6). 136pp. A moving story of an Israeli girl and the problems she faces at school because of a learning disability. (Rev: SLJ 12/96)

8787 Pevsner, Stella. *Is Everyone Moonburned But Me?* (4–7). 2000, Clarion $15.00 (0-395-95770-2). 208pp. In this lighthearted look at adolescent problems, 13-year-old Hannah shoulders many household responsibilities when her parents divorce. (Rev: BCCB 6/00; BL 5/1/00; HBG 10/00; SLJ 7/00)

8788 Pinkney, Andrea D. *Raven in a Dove House* (5–8). 1998, Harcourt $16.00 (0-15-201461-6). 208pp. Twelve-year-old Nell, who is spending the summer with an aunt in upstate New York, is terrified when her male cousin, Foley, takes up with a smooth-talking boy who hides a gun in her dollhouse. (Rev: BCCB 5/98; HBG 10/98; SLJ 5/98)

8789 Porter, Tracey. *Treasures in the Dust* (5–7). 1997, HarperCollins LB $14.89 (0-06-027564-2). 160pp. With alternating points of view, two girls from poor families in Oklahoma's Dust Bowl tell their stories. (Rev: BL 8/97; HB 9–10/97; HBG 3/98; SLJ 12/97*)

8790 Radin, Ruth Yaffe. *All Joseph Wanted* (3–7). Illus. by Deborah Kogan Ray. 1991, Macmillan $14.00 (0-02-775641-6). 80pp. When 11-year-old Joseph persuades his mother to learn to read at a literacy program at the public library, he is freed from adult responsibilities and reclaims time for friends and school work. (Rev: BCCB 11/91; BL 1/1/91; SLJ 1/92)

8791 Ray, Karen. *The T.F. Letters* (2–4). 1998, DK $15.95 (0-7894-2530-0). 160pp. After Alex loses her first tooth, she writes to the tooth fairy and thus begins an interesting correspondence in which the young girl talks honestly about her concerns. (Rev: BCCB 9/98; BL 11/1/98; HBG 3/99; SLJ 8/98)

8792 Reiss, Kathryn. *Paperquake* (3–6). 1998, Harcourt $17.00 (0-15-201183-8). 288pp. Eighth-grader Violet, the least popular of triplets, is fearful of another earthquake hitting her California home and begins collecting documents about three young people who lived through the earthquake of 1906. (Rev: BCCB 6/98; BL 5/15/98; HBG 10/98; SLJ 6/98)

8793 Richardson, Judith B. *David's Landing* (4–6). Illus. by Molly Bang. 1984, Woods Hole $10.95 (0-9611374-1-X). 150pp. A boy troubled by his parents' divorce is healed in this old-fashioned story of life in a small town. (Rev: BL 8/85; HB 9–10/85)

8794 Richardson, Sandy. *The Girl Who Ate Chicken Feet* (4–6). 1998, Dial $15.99 (0-8037-2254-0). 144pp. The story of Sissy and her problems being an adolescent in a Southern town during the 1960s. (Rev: BL 3/1/98; HBG 10/98; SLJ 3/98)

8795 Roberts, Willo Davis. *Don't Hurt Laurie!* (4–6). Illus. by Ruth Sanderson. 1977, Macmillan $16.00 (0-689-30571-0); paper $4.99 (0-689-71206-5). 176pp. Seen from the viewpoint of 11-year-old Laurie, this is a harrowing story of child abuse.

8796 Roberts, Willo Davis. *Secrets at Hidden Valley* (5–7). 1997, Simon & Schuster $16.00 (0-689-81166-7). 160pp. Gradually, 11-year-old Steffi learns to fit in when she is sent to northern Michigan to live with a grandfather she has never met. (Rev: BL 3/15/97; SLJ 6/97)

8797 Robinson, Nancy K. *Countess Veronica* (4–6). 1994, Scholastic $13.95 (0-590-44485-9). 176pp. Pesky Veronica Schmidt tries to marry off her father to the local librarian. (Rev: BL 2/1/94; SLJ 4/94)

8798 Rodowsky, Colby. *The Turnabout Shop* (4–6). 1998, Farrar $16.00 (0-374-37889-4). 135pp. Livvy has a difficult time fitting in when, after her mother's death, she is sent to live with her mother's old college friend, whom the girl has never met. (Rev: BL 6/1–15/98; HBG 10/98; SLJ 3/98*)

8799 Rosen, Michael J. *The Blessing of the Animals* (3–6). 2000, Farrar $15.00 (0-374-30838-1). 96pp. A Jewish boy wants to take his dog to be blessed at the St. Francis Festival and consults a number of people about whether this is a proper thing for him to do. (Rev: BL 11/1/00; HBG 3/01; SLJ 11/00)

8800 Rottman, S. L. *Hero* (5–7). 1997, Peachtree $14.95 (1-56145-159-2). 144pp. When his home life becomes unbearable, Sean is sent to Carbondale Ranch, where his sense of self-worth gradually grows. (Rev: BL 12/1/97; HBG 3/98; SLJ 12/97)

8801 Russell, Barbara T. *Last Left Standing* (5–7). 1996, Houghton $14.95 (0-395-71037-5). 144pp. Gradually, Josh is able to accept the reality of his brother's death. (Rev: BL 11/15/96; SLJ 10/96)

8802 Ryan, Mary C. *The Voice from the Mendelsohns' Maple* (5–7). Illus. by Irena Roman. 1990, Little, Brown $13.95 (0-316-76360-8). 132pp. Penny tries to cope with many problems, including finding out who the woman is who is hiding in the neighbor's maple tree. (Rev: SLJ 12/89)

8803 Ryan, Mary E. *Me, My Sister, and I* (4–7). 1992, Simon & Schuster paper $15.00 (0-671-73851-8). 160pp. Mattie is in a dilemma about whom to ask to the Sadie Hawkins dance in this story of the ups and downs of being twins. (Rev: BL 12/15/92)

8804 Ryden, Hope. *Wild Horse Summer* (5–8). Illus. 1997, Clarion $15.00 (0-395-77519-1). 155pp. During a summer on her relatives' Wyoming ranch, Alison overcomes her anxieties and fears. (Rev: BL 8/97; HBG 3/98; SLJ 9/97)

8805 Rylant, Cynthia. *A Blue-Eyed Daisy* (5–7). 1985, Macmillan LB $15.00 (0-02-777960-2); Dell paper $3.25 (0-440-40927-6). 112pp. One year in the rather sad and troubled world of 11-year-old Ellie. (Rev: BCCB 9/85; HB 7–8/85; SLJ 4/85)

8806 Rylant, Cynthia. *Missing May* (5–8). 1992, Orchard LB $15.99 (0-531-08596-1); Dell paper $5.50 (0-440-40865-2). 96pp. Caring about each other is the tender message in this story of 12-year-old Summer, who, along with her uncle, must cope with the death of her beloved aunt. Newbery Award winner, 1993. (Rev: BCCB 3/92*; BL 2/15/92*; HB 3–4/92; SLJ 3/92*)

8807 Sachar, Louis. *Marvin Redpost: Why Pick on Me?* (2–4). Illus. by Barbara Sullivan. 1993, Random LB $11.99 (0-679-91947-3); paper $3.99 (0-679-81947-9). 40pp. Marvin becomes a social outcast after he is wrongfully accused of picking his nose. (Rev: BCCB 2/93; BL 5/1/93)

8808 Salisbury, Graham. *Jungle Dogs* (5–9). 1998, Delacorte $15.95 (0-385-32187-2). 183pp. Set in a poor Hawaiian village, this is the story of Boy, his school experiences, and his confrontations with the "jungle" dogs, a gang of bullies who torment him when he tries to deliver the morning papers. (Rev: BL 9/1/98; HB 9–10/98; HBG 3/99)

8809 Say, Allen. *The Sign Painter* (5–9). Illus. 2000, Houghton $17.00 (0-395-97974-9). 32pp. An Asian American youth who wants to be a serious artist gets a job painting signboards scattered through the desert. (Rev: BL 10/1/00; HB 9–10/00; HBG 3/01; SLJ 9/00)

8810 Shreve, Susan. *Jonah, the Whale* (4–6). 1998, Scholastic $14.95 (0-590-37133-9). 128pp. After his family moves to New Haven, Connecticut, overweight 11-year-old Jonah finds friendship with another outsider, the sassy Blister, and achieves fulfillment by fantasizing that he is a famous TV personality. (Rev: BCCB 4/98; BL 5/1/98; HBG 10/98; SLJ 4/98)

8811 Shura, Mary Francis. *The Search for Grissi* (4–6). Illus. by Ted Lewin. 1987, Avon paper $3.50 (0-380-70305-X). Eleven-year-old Peter has difficulty adjusting to life in Peoria until his little sister involves him in a search for her lost cat. (Rev: BCCB 7/85; BL 3/15/85; SLJ 5/85)

8812 Shura, Mary Francis. *The Sunday Doll* (5–7). 1988, Avon paper $2.95 (0-380-70618-0). 112pp. Thirteen-year-old Emmy is miffed when the family won't tell her what has happened to upset her older sister Jayne, until she learns that Jayne's boyfriend has committed suicide. (Rev: BCCB 7–8/88; BL 7/88; SLJ 8/88)

8813 Slepian, Jan. *The Mind Reader* (5–7). 1997, Putnam $15.95 (0-399-23150-1). 208pp. A 12-year-old clairvoyant runs away from vaudeville and a drunken father to live with a cousin he has never met. (Rev: BL 9/15/97; HB 9–10/97; HBG 3/98; SLJ 9/97)

8814 Smith, Doris Buchanan. *A Taste of Blackberries* (4–6). Illus. by Charles Robinson. 1973, HarperCollins LB $14.89 (0-690-80512-8); paper $4.95 (0-06-440238-X). 64pp. Young Jamie dies unexpectedly of a bee sting, and his friends adjust to this loss.

8815 Smith, Robert K. *Jelly Belly* (4–6). Illus. by Bob Jones. 1982, Dell paper $4.50 (0-440-44207-9). 160pp. A boy is sent to a weight-loss camp by his parents.

8816 Snyder, Zilpha Keatley. *The Diamond War* (4–6). Series: Castle Court. 1995, Dell paper $3.50 (0-440-40985-3). 119pp. It's the boys versus the girls in this story about whether the trees in the only vacant lot in the area should be chopped down to make a baseball diamond. (Rev: BL 9/1/95; SLJ 8/95)

8817 Snyder, Zilpha Keatley. *The Runaways* (4–8). 1999, Delacorte $15.95 (0-385-32599-1). 264pp. Twelve-year-old Dani O'Donnell, angry at her mother for moving them to a desert town where she feels lost, makes plans to run away. (Rev: BL 1/1–15/99; HBG 10/99; SLJ 3/99)

8818 Sonenklar, Carol. *Mighty Boy* (3–6). 1999, Orchard LB $16.99 (0-531-33203-9). 128pp. Transplanted to New York City, lonely 9-year-old Howard Weinstein retreats into a fantasy world when the class bully harasses him. (Rev: BCCB 1/00; BL 10/15/99; HBG 3/00; SLJ 10/99)

8819 Sonenklar, Carol. *My Own Worst Enemy* (5–8). 1999, Holiday $15.95 (0-8234-1456-6). 149pp. In this first-person narrative, Eve Belkin finds there is a price to pay when she outdoes herself to be popular in her new school. (Rev: BL 5/15/99; HBG 10/99; SLJ 8/99)

8820 Sorensen, Virginia. *Plain Girl* (4–6). Illus. by Charles Geer. 1988, Harcourt paper $7.00 (0-15-262437-6). An Amish girl finds it difficult to accept both her cultural heritage and the world around her.

8821 Soto, Gary. *The Pool Party* (4–7). Illus. by Robert Casilla. 1992, Delacorte $13.95 (0-385-30890-6). 112pp. Rudy, part of a Mexican-American family, has growing-up problems. (Rev: SLJ 6/93)

8822 Speregen, Devra. *Phone Call from a Flamingo* (5–7). Series: Full House. 1993, Pocket paper $3.99 (0-671-88004-7). 134pp. Stephanie decides that the price of being popular with the in crowd is too high when it involves hurting others. Based on the TV series *Full House*. (Rev: SLJ 11/93)

8823 Spinelli, Jerry. *Maniac Magee* (5–7). 1990, Little, Brown $15.95 (0-316-80722-2). 192pp. This Newbery Medal winner (1991) tells of an amazing boy who can help others but needs help himself. (Rev: BL 6/1/90*)

8824 Spinelli, Jerry. *Wringer* (4–7). 1997, HarperCollins LB $15.89 (0-06-024914-5). 192pp. A sensitive boy must participate in the massacre of thousands of pigeons released at an annual fair. (Rev: BL 9/1/97*; HB 9–10/97; HBG 3/98; SLJ 9/97*)

8825 Spurr, Elizabeth. *Lupe and Me* (3–4). Illus. by Enrique O. Sanchez. 1995, Harcourt $13.00 (0-15-200522-6). 40pp. Susan is upset when her mother's housekeeper, 16-year-old Lupe, has to return to Mexico because she is an illegal alien. (Rev: BL 6/1–15/95; SLJ 6/95)

8826 Stiles, Martha Bennett. *Sarah the Dragon Lady* (4–6). 1986, Avon paper $2.75 (0-380-70471-4). 96pp. Sarah tries to adjust to life in a small Kentucky town and face the fact of trouble in her parents' marriage. (Rev: BCCB 2/87; BL 1/1/87; SLJ 12/86)

8827 Tabor, Nancy María Grande. *Bottles Break* (1–4). Illus. by author. 1999, Charlesbridge LB $15.95 (0-88106-317-7); paper $6.95 (0-88106-318-5). A young narrator, the child of an alcoholic mother, tells about his fears, confusion, and low self-esteem and about the help he receives from an understanding teacher. (Rev: HBG 10/99; SLJ 5/99)

8828 Talbert, Marc. *Star of Luis* (5–9). 1999, Clarion $16.00 (0-395-91423-X). 192pp. Racial prejudice is the theme of this story, set in New Mexico during World War II, about a Hispanic American boy who discovers he is Jewish. (Rev: BCCB 5/99; BL 3/1/99; HBG 10/99)

8829 Tashjian, Janet. *Multiple Choice* (5–9). 1999, Holt $16.95 (0-8050-6086-3). 186pp. Fourteen-year-old Monica realizes she needs outside help when her attempts to cope with her obsessive drive for perfection spin out of control with almost tragic consequences. (Rev: BL 6/1–15/99; HB 7–8/99; HBG 10/99)

8830 Testa, Maria. *Nine Candles* (3–5). Illus. 1996, Carolrhoda LB $19.93 (0-87614-940-9). 32pp. Raymond is looking forward to visiting his mother, who is in prison. (Rev: BCCB 9/96; BL 7/96; SLJ 9/96)

8831 Testa, Maria. *Someplace to Go* (3–5). Illus. 1996, Albert Whitman LB $14.95 (0-8075-7524-0). 32pp. Unlike his classmates, Davey has no home to return to after school. (Rev: BCCB 3/96; BL 4/15/96; SLJ 5/96)

8832 Thesman, Jean. *Calling the Swan* (5–8). 2000, Viking $15.99 (0-670-88874-5). 176pp. A troubled girl gets help when she forms a tentative friendship with kids in her summer school English class. (Rev: BL 6/1–15/00; HB 7–8/00; HBG 10/00)

8833 Tolan, Stephanie S. *Ordinary Miracles* (5–9). 1999, Morrow $16.00 (0-688-16269-X). 221pp. Mark, the twin son of a preacher, suffers a crisis of faith and wonders if his future plans to enter the ministry are wise. (Rev: BCCB 10/99; HBG 3/00; SLJ 10/99)

8834 Tolliver, Ruby C. *I Love You, Daisy Phew* (4–6). 1994, Hendrick-Long LB $14.95 (0-937460-86-9). 168pp. Blake finds an unusual pet in a goat named Daisy Phew when the troubled boy goes to live with his grandfather in Texas. (Rev: BL 1/15/95)

8835 Towne, Mary. *Steve the Sure* (4–6). 1990, Macmillan LB $13.95 (0-689-31646-1). 144pp. During his stay in Vermont one summer, know-it-all Steve arranges a talent show. (Rev: SLJ 12/90)

8836 Trueman, Terry. *Stuck in Neutral* (5–9). 2000, HarperCollins LB $14.89 (0-06-028518-4). 114pp. Shawn McDaniel, a 14-year-old who appears to be retarded because of cerebral palsy, narrates this novel in a way that shows the reader he is really a near-genius. (Rev: HB 5–6/00; HBG 10/00; SLJ 7/00)

8837 Ure, Jean. *Skinny Melon and Me* (5–7). Illus. 2001, Holt $16.00 (0-8050-6359-5). 202pp. An interesting British novel about a young Cherry Waterton, who keeps a diary; her mother's boyfriend who sends Cherry rebus letters to win her over; and Cherry's teacher, who writes to a friend about the girl's problem behavior. (Rev: BCCB 3/01; BL 1/1–15/01; SLJ 1/01)

8838 Vail, Rachel. *Daring to Be Abigail* (4–6). 1996, Orchard LB $16.99 (0-531-08867-7). 144pp. At summer camp, Abigail deliberately misbehaves so she won't be considered an outsider by the in-crowd. (Rev: BCCB 2/96; BL 3/1/96; HB 5–6/96; SLJ 3/96*)

8839 Vail, Rachel. *Ever After* (5–8). 1994, Orchard LB $16.99 (0-531-08688-7). 176pp. Fourteen-year-old Molly is trying to act maturely but always seems to mess things up. (Rev: BCCB 4/94; BL 3/1/94; HB 5–6/94, 7–8/94; SLJ 5/94*)

8840 Van Oosting, James. *The Last Payback* (5–8). 1997, HarperCollins $14.95 (0-06-027491-3). 144pp. The story of how Dimple gradually accepts the death of her twin brother, who has died of a gunshot wound. (Rev: BCCB 6/97; BL 6/1–15/97; HB 7–8/97; SLJ 7/97)

8841 Wagner, Jane. *J.T.* (4–6). Photos by Gordon Parks. 1972, Dell paper $4.99 (0-440-44275-3). 128pp. J. T. Gamble lives in Harlem, and his most prized possessions are a tiny portable radio and a stray cat, for whom he has made a home.

8842 Wainwright, Richard M. *Mountains to Climb* (3–5). Illus. by Jack Crompton. 1991, Family Life $18.00 (0-9619566-3-1). 56pp. During his two-year stay in the United States, a young Ecuadoran boy gradually wins his classmates' acceptance. (Rev: BL 12/15/91; SLJ 1/92)

8843 Walker, Alice. *To Hell with Dying* (4–7). Illus. 1988, Harcourt paper $8.00 (0-15-289074-2). The Walker family won't let old Mr. Sweet die. (Rev: BCCB 4/88; BL 4/15/88; HB 7–8/88)

8844 Walker, Pamela. *Pray Hard* (5–8). 2001, Scholastic $15.99 (0-439-21586-2). 177pp. After Amelia Forest's father dies in an airplane accident for which she feels responsible, her life and that of her family fall apart. (Rev: BL 3/1/01)

8845 Walpole, Peter. *The Healer of Harrow Point* (4–7). 2000, Hampton Roads paper $11.95 (1-57174-167-4). 131pp. A novel of love and compassion about a boy who is promised a hunting trip for his twelfth birthday but wonders if he can kill a

deer, particularly after seeing one killed by poachers and after meeting Emma, who can heal animals with her touch. (Rev: SLJ 10/00)

8846 Walter, Mildred P. *Justin and the Best Biscuits in the World* (3–5). Illus. by Catherine Stock. 1986, Lothrop $16.00 (0-688-06645-3); Knopf paper $3.25 (0-679-80346-7). 128pp. Justin thinks some things are "women's work" until his grandfather shows him differently. (Rev: BCCB 12/86; BL 10/15/86; SLJ 11/86)

8847 Walter, Virginia. *Making Up Megaboy* (5–8). Illus. by Katrina Roeckelein. 1998, DK $16.95 (0-7894-2488-6). 62pp. Using multiple points of view, this is the gritty story of a 13-year-old boy who is accused of shooting an elderly Korean liquor store owner. (Rev: BCCB 5/98; HBG 10/98; SLJ 4/98)

8848 Warner, Sally. *Accidental Lily* (2–3). Illus. 1999, Knopf $15.00 (0-679-89138-2). 96pp. Lily, who is 6, still wets the bed and is embarrassed about it. (Rev: BL 3/15/99; HBG 10/99; SLJ 7/99)

8849 Warner, Sally. *Totally Confidential* (4–7). 2000, HarperCollins LB $14.89 (0-06-028262-2). 160pp. Twelve-year-old Quinney has a talent for giving good advice to others but this gift brings unforeseen responsibilities and problems. (Rev: BCCB 5/00; BL 6/1–15/00; HBG 10/00; SLJ 6/00)

8850 White Deer of Autumn. *The Great Change* (3–5). Illus. by Carol Grigg. 1992, Beyond Words $14.95 (0-941831-79-5). After Grandfather's death, a Native American woman explains the circle of life to her granddaughter. (Rev: SLJ 12/92)

8851 Williams, Carol L. *Carolina Autumn* (5–8). 2000, Delacorte $14.95 (0-385-32716-1). 146pp. A finely crafted novel in which 14-year-old Carolina copes with the death of her father and sister, sorts out her feelings for a neighborhood boy, and tries to fathom the resentment she feels toward her mother. (Rev: SLJ 9/00)

8852 Williams, Carol L. *Christmas in Heaven* (5–8). 2000, Putnam $16.99 (0-399-23436-5). 160pp. Honey DeLoach, a resident of Heaven, Florida, finds that her life does not necessarily improve when movie star Miriam Season moves into town with her daughters, Easter and Christmas. (Rev: BCCB 5/00; BL 6/1–15/00; HBG 10/00; SLJ 6/00)

8853 Williams, Carol L. *If I Forget, You Remember* (5–8). 1998, Delacorte $15.95 (0-385-32534-7). 200pp. A first-person narrative about a self-centered seventh-grade girl who gains maturity after her grandmother, who is suffering from Alzheimer's disease, moves in. (Rev: BL 4/15/98; HBG 10/98)

8854 Williams, Karen L. *One Thing I'm Good At* (3–5). 1999, Lothrop $15.00 (0-688-16846-9). 144pp. Julie is developing an inferiority complex, but her ability to shoot marbles helps her gain a feeling of self-worth. (Rev: BCCB 12/99; BL 10/15/99; HBG 3/00; SLJ 12/99)

8855 Willis, Patricia. *Out of the Storm* (4–7). 1995, Clarion $15.00 (0-395-68708-X). 160pp. In 1946, Mandy's family moves in with her difficult Aunt Bess, who makes her tend a flock of sheep. (Rev: BCCB 5/95; BL 4/15/95; SLJ 4/95)

8856 Willner-Pardo, Gina. *Daphne Eloise Slater, Who's Tall for Her Age* (3–5). Illus. 1997, Clarion $15.00 (0-395-73080-5). 40pp. After a cruel classmate calls her a giraffe, Daphne becomes painfully aware of her height. (Rev: BL 8/97; HB 9–10/97; HBG 3/98; SLJ 10/97)

8857 Willner-Pardo, Gina. *Jumping into Nothing* (3–5). Illus. 1999, Clarion $14.00 (0-395-84130-5). 64pp. Sophie is afraid to jump off the high board at the local pool, but gradually she overcomes her fear. (Rev: BCCB 4/99; BL 3/15/99; HB 5–6/99; HBG 10/99; SLJ 5/99)

8858 Wilson, Jacqueline. *Bad Girls* (3–6). Illus. 2001, Delacorte $15.95 (0-385-72916-2). 176pp. Ten-year-old Mandy is a slightly immature, pampered little girl who is constantly being teased by two older, more sophisticated classmates. (Rev: BCCB 3/01; BL 1/1–15/01; SLJ 3/01)

8859 Wilson, Jacqueline. *The Lottie Project* (4–6). Illus. 1999, Delacorte $15.95 (0-385-32718-8). 214pp. In this astute English novel, Charlotte, nicknamed Charlie, is growing up with a single mother and must contend with numerous problems, such as her mother's new boyfriend. (Rev: BCCB 12/99; BL 10/1/99; HB 11–12/99; HBG 3/00; SLJ 11/99)

8860 Wilson, Johnniece M. *Poor Girl* (5–7). 1992, Scholastic $13.95 (0-590-44732-7). 176pp. A first-person story about Miranda, who spends the summer trying to earn money for contact lenses before the fall. (Rev: BCCB 4/92; BL 8/92; SLJ 4/92)

8861 Wilson, Johnniece M. *Robin on His Own* (4–6). 1992, Scholastic paper $2.95 (0-590-41809-2). 144pp. Watusi the cat comforts a young black boy when his mother dies. (Rev: BL 10/15/90; SLJ 1/91)

8862 Wilson, Nancy H. *Flapjack Waltzes* (4–6). 1998, Farrar $16.00 (0-374-32345-3). 144pp. Two years after her brother was killed in an automobile accident, 12-year-old Natalie still feels its effects — in the lost friendship of a girl whose brother survived the accident and in the emotional upheaval within her family. (Rev: BCCB 9/98; BL 8/98; HBG 3/99; SLJ 8/98)

8863 Wohl, Lauren L. *Christopher Davis's Best Year Yet* (2–4). Illus. 1995, Hyperion paper $3.95 (0-7868-1083-1). 64pp. Second-grader Christopher solves a series of minor personal problems in the course of a year. (Rev: BL 4/1/96; SLJ 4/96)

8864 Wojciechowska, Maia. *Shadow of a Bull* (5–7). Illus. by Alvin Smith. 1964, Macmillan $16.00 (0-689-30042-5); paper $4.99 (0-689-71567-6). 160pp. Manolo, surviving son of a great bullfighter, has his own "moment of truth" when he faces his first bull. Newbery Award winner, 1965.

8865 Wojciechowski, Susan. *Beany and the Dreaded Wedding* (3–5). Illus. 2000, Candlewick $15.99 (0-7636-0924-2). 128pp. Beany is worried about everything involving her role as flower girl at her cousin's wedding. (Rev: BCCB 12/00; BL 11/15/00; HBG 3/01; SLJ 10/00)

8866 Wood, June R. *The Man Who Loved Clowns* (5–8). 1992, Putnam $16.99 (0-399-21888-2). 192pp. When Delrita's parents are killed in an auto

accident, she grows close to her uncle, an adult with Down's syndrome. (Rev: BL 11/15/92; SLJ 9/92)

8867 Wood, June R. *Turtle on a Fence Post* (5–8). 1997, Putnam $16.99 (0-399-23184-6). 260pp. After the deaths of her parents and an uncle, Delrita, now living with an aunt and her husband, is so emotionally upset that it seems she will never love anyone again. A sequel to *The Man Who Loved Clowns* (1992). (Rev: BL 11/15/97; HBG 3/98; SLJ 9/97)

8868 Wood, June R. *When Pigs Fly* (5–8). 1995, Putnam $16.95 (0-399-22911-6). 240pp. In a family-living project, Buddy and her classmates are assigned hard-boiled eggs to take care of as though they were their parents. (Rev: BCCB 11/95; BL 12/1/95; SLJ 10/95)

8869 Woodruff, Elvira. *The Secret Funeral of Slim Jim the Snake* (4–5). 1993, Holiday $15.95 (0-8234-1014-5). 144pp. Nick lives over a funeral home and faces some problems with humorous solutions. (Rev: SLJ 3/93)

8870 Wright, Betty R. *The Wish Master* (3–6). 2000, Holiday $15.95 (0-8234-1611-9). 112pp. Transported to his grandparents' home in Wisconsin for the summer, unhappy Corby wishes on a pile of rocks known as the Wish Master for a way to go home. (Rev: BCCB 1/01; BL 11/1/00; SLJ 12/00)

8871 Wyeth, Sharon D. *A Piece of Heaven* (4–7). 2001, Knopf LB $16.99 (0-679-98535-2). 160pp. Mahalia Moon, a 13-year-old New Yorker whose mother is having a nervous breakdown, finds friendship and a job when she begins to clean up the swept-dirt backyard of a neighbor. (Rev: BCCB 3/01; SLJ 2/01)

8872 Wynne-Jones, Tim. *Lord of the Fries: And Other Stories* (4–8). 1999, DK $17.95 (0-7894-2623-4). 224pp. Seven stories about young people and the decisions they make that change their lives. (Rev: BCCB 3/99; HB 7–8/99; HBG 10/99; SLJ 4/99)

8873 Yang, Dori Jones. *The Secret Voice of Gina Zhang* (4–6). 2000, Pleasant $12.95 (1-58485-204-6); paper $5.95 (1-58485-203-8). 220pp. A Chinese immigrant girl loses her voice and retreats into a fantasy world where she is finally reached by a friendless outsider named Priscilla. (Rev: BL 10/1/00; HBG 3/01; SLJ 10/00)

Physical and Emotional Problems

8874 Abbott, Deborah, and Henry Kisor. *One TV Blasting and a Pig Outdoors* (3–5). Illus. 1994, Albert Whitman LB $14.95 (0-8075-6075-8). 40pp. A book that describes what it's like to live in a household where the father is deaf. (Rev: BL 9/15/94; SLJ 12/94)

8875 Banks, Jacqueline T. *Egg-Drop Blues* (4–6). 1995, Houghton $15.00 (0-395-70931-8). 128pp. Judge Jenkins, a dyslexic, faces problems when his mother threatens to send him to a different school if he doesn't do better where he is. A sequel to Banks' *Project Wheels* (1993) and *The New One* (1994). (Rev: BCCB 5/95; BL 4/15/95; HB 7–8/95; SLJ 8/95)

8876 Bauer, Marion Dane. *An Early Winter* (4–7). 1999, Clarion $15.00 (0-395-90372-6). 128pp. When he convinces him to go on a camping trip, Tim doesn't realize that his Grandad is suffering from Alzheimer's disease. (Rev: BCCB 10/99; BL 12/1/99; HBG 3/00; SLJ 10/99)

8877 Bennett, Cherie. *Zink* (5–7). Illus. 1999, Delacorte $15.95 (0-385-32669-6). 222pp. The moving story of 10-year-old Becky, her struggle with a fatal case of leukemia, and her dreams of a herd of zebra and their heroic leader named Zink. (Rev: BL 8/99; HBG 3/00; SLJ 2/00)

8878 Betancourt, Jeanne. *My Name Is Brain/Brian* (4–6). 1993, Scholastic $14.95 (0-590-44921-4). 176pp. Brian, a sixth-grader who is dyslexic, matures and changes his attitudes toward his friends and teachers. (Rev: BCCB 4/93; BL 4/1/93; SLJ 4/93)

8879 Blatchford, Claire H. *Going with the Flow* (2–4). Illus. 1998, Carolrhoda LB $14.95 (1-57505-069-2). 40pp. When he has difficulty adjusting to his new school, where he is the only deaf child, fifth-grader Mark is helped by a friend and by becoming part of the basketball team. (Rev: BL 6/1–15/98; HBG 10/98; SLJ 6/98)

8880 Blue, Rose. *Me and Einstein: Breaking Through the Reading Barrier* (4–6). Illus. by Peggy Luks. 1984, Human Sciences $16.95 (0-87705-388-X); paper $10.95 (0-89885-185-8). Bobby, a dyslexic youngster, tries to hide the fact that he can't read.

8881 Blume, Judy. *Deenie* (5–7). 1982, Macmillan LB $17.00 (0-02-711020-6); Dell paper $4.99 (0-440-93259-9). 192pp. Instead of becoming a model, as her mother wishes, Deenie must cope with scoliosis and wearing a spinal brace.

8882 Brooks, Bruce. *Vanishing* (5–8). 1999, HarperCollins LB $14.89 (0-06-028237-1). 160pp. A challenging novel about a hospitalized girl, who gives up eating so she can't be sent home to her dysfunctional family, and the boy she meets who is in remission from a fatal disease. (Rev: BL 5/15/99*; HB 5–6/99; HBG 10/99)

8883 Butts, Nancy. *Cheshire Moon* (5–7). 1996, Front Street $14.95 (1-886910-08-1). 105pp. A friendless deaf girl grieves for a cousin who has drowned at sea in this novel in an island setting. (Rev: BL 10/15/96; SLJ 11/96)

8884 Byars, Betsy. *The Summer of the Swans* (5–7). Illus. by Ted Coconis. 1970, Puffin paper $4.99 (0-14-031420-2). 144pp. The story of a 14-year-old named Sara — moody, unpredictable, and on the brink of womanhood — and how her life changes when her younger, mentally retarded brother disappears. Newbery Award winner, 1971.

8885 Cunningham, Julia. *Burnish Me Bright* (4–6). 1980, Peter Smith $18.75 (0-8446-6252-6). An imaginative mute boy named Auguste is scorned by the inhabitants of the French village where he lives.

8886 Cutler, Jane. *Spaceman* (4–6). 1997, Dutton $14.99 (0-525-45636-8). 144pp. Gary, who has a learning disability, is about to give up when he is sent to a special school. (Rev: BCCB 5/97; BL 3/15/97; SLJ 5/97)

8887 Farnes, Catherine. *Snow* (5–9). 1999, Bob Jones Univ. paper $6.49 (1-57924-199-9). 158pp. A thoughtful novel about an albino girl's problems being accepted, even among students who profess to have Christian charity. (Rev: BL 7/99)

8888 Fassler, Joan. *Howie Helps Himself* (2–4). Illus. by Joe Lasker. 1975, Whitman LB $14.95 (0-8075-3422-6). 32pp. Howie adjusts to cerebral palsy and the use of his wheelchair.

8889 Fine, Anne. *The Tulip Touch* (4–8). 1997, Little, Brown $15.95 (0-316-28325-8). 160pp. Natalie forms a dangerous friendship with Tulip, a girl going completely out of control. (Rev: BL 9/15/97*; HB 9–10, 11–12/97; HBG 3/98; SLJ 9/97*)

8890 Gantos, Jack. *Joey Pigza Swallowed the Key* (4–7). 1998, Farrar $16.00 (0-374-33664-4). 192pp. Joey, who lives with his eccentric grandmother, is mystified by his uncontrollable manic behavior until it is found he has attention deficit hyperactivity disorder (ADHD). (Rev: BCCB 11/98; BL 12/15/98; HB 11–12/98; HBG 3/99; SLJ 12/98)

8891 Garfield, James B. *Follow My Leader* (4–6). Illus. 1994, Puffin paper $4.99 (0-140-36485-4). 192pp. With the aid of friends and a guide dog, an 11-year-old boy resumes his life.

8892 Gleitzman, Morris. *Sticky Beak* (4–6). 1995, Harcourt $11.00 (0-15-200366-5); paper $5.00 (0-15-200367-3). 160pp. Rowena, a mute from birth, faces having a new sibling and caring for a foul-mouthed cockatoo in this humorous novel from Australia. (Rev: BCCB 4/95; BL 6/1–15/95; SLJ 6/95)

8893 Gould, Marilyn. *Golden Daffodils* (5–7). 1991, Allied Crafts paper $10.95 (0-9632305-1-4). 17pp. Janis adjusts to her handicap resulting from cerebral palsy.

8894 Howard, Ellen. *Edith, Herself* (5–7). 1987, Macmillan $15.00 (0-689-31314-4). 144pp. In the 1890s, young Edith is sent to live with her married sister when their mother dies; there her life is complicated by epileptic seizures. (Rev: BCCB 5/87; BL 4/1/87; SLJ 4/87)

8895 Janover, Caroline. *Zipper: The Kid with ADHD* (4–7). Illus. 1997, Woodbine paper $11.95 (0-933149-95-6). 164pp. Zipper Wilson suffers from attention deficit hyperactivity disorder and gradually learns to cope with it. (Rev: BL 2/1/98; SLJ 3/98)

8896 Kachur, Wanda G. *The Nautilus* (5–7). 1997, Peytral paper $7.95 (0-9644271-5-X). 171pp. A compassionate novel about a girl's rehabilitation after receiving spinal cord injuries in an automobile accident. (Rev: SLJ 9/97)

8897 King-Smith, Dick. *Spider Sparrow* (3–5). Illus. 2000, Crown LB $18.99 (0-517-80044-6). 176pp. A moving story of a foundling nicknamed Spider, who is both physically and mentally impaired, and his short life on the farm of the kindly Sparrow family in England. (Rev: BL 1/1–15/00; HBG 10/00; SLJ 3/00)

8898 Laird, Elizabeth. *Secret Friends* (5–8). 1999, Putnam $14.99 (0-399-23334-2). 80pp. Lucy tells the story of her ill-fated friendship with the class outsider who has been nicknamed Earwig because of protruding ears. (Rev: BCCB 2/99; BL 1/1–15/99; HBG 10/99)

8899 Lasker, Joe. *He's My Brother* (2–4). Illus. by author. 1974, Whitman LB $14.95 (0-8075-3218-5). 40pp. A family's attitudes and their wonderful treatment of their retarded family member, Jamie, are told by his older brother.

8900 Levine, Edna S. *Lisa and Her Soundless World* (3–5). Illus. by Gloria Kamen. 1984, Human Sciences $14.95 (0-87705-104-6); paper $10.95 (0-89885-204-8). The plight of a deaf girl is explored in this gripping, realistic story of Lisa and her problems.

8901 Litchfield, Ada B. *A Cane in Her Hand* (2–4). Ed. by Caroline Rubin. Illus. by Eleanor Mill. 1977, Whitman LB $14.95 (0-8075-1056-4). A partially sighted girl must adjust to using a cane.

8902 Little, Jean. *From Anna* (4–6). Illus. by Joan Sandin. 1972, HarperCollins paper $4.95 (0-06-440044-1). 208pp. Anna's family emigrates to Canada to escape Nazi persecution, and this opens up a new world and a wonderful change for the partially sighted girl.

8903 McDaniel, Lurlene. *To Live Again* (5–9). 2001, Bantam paper $4.99 (0-553-57151-6). 152pp. After three years of remission from leukemia, 16-year-old Dawn suffers a stroke that produces a terrible bout of depression. (Rev: BL 3/1/01)

8904 McLaren, Clemence. *Dance for the Land* (5–6). 1999, Simon & Schuster $16.00 (0-689-82393-2). 160pp. A child of mixed parentage, moving back to Hawaii with her father, faces prejudice from relatives because of her light skin. (Rev: BL 2/15/99; HBG 10/99; SLJ 6/99)

8905 McMahon, Patricia. *Summer Tunes: A Martha's Vineyard Vacation* (3–6). Photos by Peter Simon. 1996, Boyds Mills $16.95 (1-56397-572-6). 47pp. A photo-essay about Conor, a 10-year-old physically handicapped boy, and his family, who go to Martha's Vineyard for a vacation. (Rev: SLJ 10/96)

8906 Marino, Jan. *Eighty-Eight Steps to September* (5–7). 1989, Avon paper $2.95 (0-380-71001-3). 162pp. Amy and Robbie have the usual sibling rivalry, until Robbie develops leukemia. (Rev: BCCB 5/89; BL 8/89)

8907 Morpurgo, Michael. *The Ghost of Grania O'Malley* (4–6). 1996, Viking $15.99 (0-670-86861-2). 144pp. On an island close to Ireland, Jessie, who has cerebral palsy, witnesses two factions quarrel over custody of a beautiful hill. (Rev: BL 6/1–15/96; SLJ 7/96)

8908 Osofsky, Audrey. *My Buddy* (3–6). Illus. by Ted Rand. 1992, Holt $15.95 (0-8050-1747-X). 32pp. A boy with muscular dystrophy talks of his best friend, Buddy, a golden retriever service dog. (Rev: BCCB 10/92; BL 2/1/93)

8909 Riskind, Mary. *Apple Is My Sign* (5–6). 1995, Houghton paper $5.95 (0-395-65747-4). 160pp. A deaf and mute boy is sent to a special school in the early 1900s.

8910 Roberts, Willo Davis. *Sugar Isn't Everything* (4–6). 1987, Macmillan $16.00 (0-689-31316-0);

paper $4.95 (0-689-71225-1). 192pp. A story that presents the facts of diabetes for young readers. (Rev: BCCB 4/87; BL 3/1/87; SLJ 5/87)

8911 Roos, Stephen. *The Gypsies Never Came* (4–7). 2001, Simon & Schuster $15.00 (0-689-83147-1). 128pp. Augie Knapp, who was born without a left hand, slowly develops confidence with the help of Lydie Rose, an eccentric outsider. (Rev: BL 3/1/01; SLJ 2/01)

8912 Senisi, Ellen B. *Just Kids: Visiting a Class for Children with Special Needs* (3–5). Illus. 1998, Dutton $16.99 (0-525-45646-5). 40pp. In this book illustrated with color photographs, young Cindy spends time in her school's special-needs classroom and learns about autism, Down syndrome, ADHD, epilepsy, and more. (Rev: BCCB 7–8/98; BL 5/1/98*; HBG 10/98; SLJ 4/98)

8913 Shyer, Marlene Fanta. *Welcome Home, Jellybean* (5–7). 1978, Macmillan paper $4.99 (0-689-71213-8). 160pp. Twelve-year-old Neil encounters a near-tragic situation when his older retarded sister comes home to stay.

8914 Slote, Alfred. *Hang Tough, Paul Mather* (4–7). 1973, HarperCollins paper $4.95 (0-06-440153-7). 160pp. Paul recollects from his hospital bed the details of his struggle with leukemia. Told candidly and without sentimentality.

8915 Smith, Mark. *Pay Attention, Slosh!* (3–4). Illus. 1997, Albert Whitman LB $11.95 (0-8075-6378-1). 54pp. Using a fictional format, this is the story of a boy who is suffering from attention deficit disorder and how his condition is treated. (Rev: BL 12/1/97; HBG 3/98; SLJ 10/97)

8916 Snyder, Zilpha Keatley. *The Witches of Worm* (5–8). Illus. by Alton Raible. 1972, Macmillan $17.00 (0-689-30066-2); Dell paper $5.50 (0-440-49727-2). 192pp. A deeply disturbed girl believes that her selfish and destructive acts are caused by bewitchment.

8917 Strachan, Ian. *The Flawed Glass* (5–8). 1990, Little, Brown $14.95 (0-316-81813-5). 208pp. Physically disabled Shona makes friends with an American boy on an island off the Scottish coast. (Rev: BCCB 11/90; BL 12/1/90; SLJ 1/91)

8918 Testa, Maria. *Thumbs Up, Rico!* (3–4). Illus. 1994, Albert Whitman LB $14.95 (0-8075-7906-8). 40pp. Rico, a boy with Down's syndrome, tells about his trials and triumphs in this simple chapter book. (Rev: BL 4/15/94; SLJ 7/94)

8919 Wanous, Suzanne. *Sara's Secret* (2–4). Illus. by Shelly O. Haas. 1995, Carolrhoda LB $19.93 (0-87614-856-9). 40pp. Sara's secret is that she has a brother who is a victim of cerebral palsy and is mentally retarded. (Rev: BL 7/95; SLJ 8/95)

8920 Welch, Sheila K. *Don't Call Me Marda* (4–6). Illus. 1991, Our Child Pr. $16.95 (0-9611872-3-9); paper $12.95 (0-9611872-4-7). 138pp. Marsha is disappointed when the girl her parents adopt is mentally handicapped. (Rev: SLJ 3/91)

8921 Werlin, Nancy. *Are You Alone on Purpose?* (5–8). 1994, Houghton $16.00 (0-395-67350-X). 176pp. When Harry Roth, a rabbi's son, is confined to a wheelchair after an accident, Alison becomes interested in being a friend of this overbearing boy. (Rev: BCCB 12/94; BL 8/94; SLJ 9/94)

8922 Whelan, Gloria. *Hannah* (3–5). Illus. by Leslie Bowman. 1991, Knopf LB $11.99 (0-679-91397-1). 42pp. In northern Michigan in 1887, 9-year-old Hannah is encouraged by the new teacher to attend school despite her blindness. (Rev: BCCB 6/91; BL 3/1/91; HB 5–6/91; SLJ 6/91)

8923 Wilson, Nancy H. *Bringing Nettie Back* (5–7). 1992, Macmillan $15.00 (0-02-793075-0). 160pp. The story of a friendship between two "opposites" and of Nettie's illness. (Rev: BL 1/1/93; SLJ 10/92)

8924 Wright, Betty R. *Rosie and the Dance of the Dinosaurs* (4–6). 1989, Holiday $15.95 (0-8234-0782-9). 112pp. Rosie, who has only nine fingers, is worried about the piano recital in which she must perform. (Rev: BCCB 2/90; BL 11/15/89; HB 3–4/90)

Historical Fiction and Foreign Lands

General and Miscellaneous

8925 Bernard, Virginia. *Eliza Down Under: Going to Sydney* (5–8). Series: Going To. 2000, Four Corners paper $7.95 (1-893577-02-3). 96pp. This novel deals with Eliza's adventures in Australia when she accompanies her mother to the 2000 Olympic Games in Sydney. (Rev: SLJ 3/00)

8926 Carmi, Daniella. *Samir and Yonatan* (4–8). Trans. from Hebrew by Yael Lotan. 2000, Scholastic $15.95 (0-439-13504-4). 192pp. Samir, a young Palestinian, is sent to a Jewish hospital for surgery and there he meets some Jewish contemporaries. (Rev: BCCB 4/00; HBG 10/00; SLJ 3/00)

8927 Conrad, Pam. *Pedro's Journal: A Voyage with Christopher Columbus* (3–5). Illus. by Peter Koeppen. 1991, Boyds Mills $17.95 (1-878093-17-7). 81pp. The journal of a "ship boy" aboard the Santa Maria, dated August 3, 1492, to February 14, 1493. (Rev: BCCB 2/92; BL 10/15/92; SLJ 2/92)

8928 Durbin, William. *The Broken Blade* (5–8). 1997, Delacorte $14.95 (0-385-32224-0). 163pp. To help his family, 13-year-old Pierre becomes a *voyageur*, a fur trader in old Quebec. (Rev: BCCB 2/97; BL 3/1/97; SLJ 2/97)

8929 Curtis, Chara M. *No One Walks on My Father's Moon* (4–8). Illus. by Rebecca Hyland. 1996, Voyage LB $16.95 (0-9649454-1-X). 26pp. A Turkish boy is accused of blasphemy when he states that a man has walked on the moon. (Rev: BL 11/15/96)

8930 Disher, Garry. *The Bamboo Flute* (3–6). 1993, Ticknor $10.95 (0-395-66595-7). 96pp. Growing up in terrible poverty in rural Australia during 1932, young Paul forms a friendship with a drifter named Eric the Red. (Rev: BL 9/1/93; SLJ 9/93*)

8931 Durbin, William. *Wintering* (5–8). 1999, Delacorte $14.95 (0-385-32598-3). 191pp. In this companion to *The Broken Blade,* young Pierre LaPage again lives the exciting life of a *voyageur* and spends a winter in the Great Lakes area transporting furs. (Rev: BL 2/15/99*; HBG 10/99; SLJ 2/99)

8932 Hammer, Loretta J., and Gail L. Karwoski. *The Tree That Owns Itself: And Other Adventure Tales from Out of the Past* (3–6). Illus. by James Watling. 1996, Peachtree paper $8.95 (1-56145-120-7). 149pp. In these 12 stories, famous characters associated with the history of Georgia come to life and interact with fictitious young heroes and heroines. (Rev: SLJ 7/96)

8933 Hesse, Karen. *Stowaway* (5–8). Illus. 2000, Simon & Schuster $17.00 (0-689-83987-1). 319pp. Told by an 11-year-old stowaway, this adventurous sea story tells of Captain Cook's two-and-a-half-year voyage around the world beginning in 1768. (Rev: BL 12/15/00; HB 1–2/01; HBG 3/01; SLJ 11/00)

8934 Hill, Anthony. *The Burnt Stick* (4–7). Illus. 1995, Houghton $12.95 (0-395-73974-8). 64pp. The moving story of a boy who, at age 5, is taken from his Aborigine mother in Australia and raised in a white missionary community. (Rev: BCCB 9/95; BL 7/95; HB 11–12/95; SLJ 10/95)

8935 Holeman, Linda. *Promise Song* (5–8). 1997, Tundra paper $6.95 (0-88776-387-1). 264pp. In 1900, Rosetta, an English orphan who has been sent to Canada, becomes an indentured servant. (Rev: BL 6/1–15/97; SLJ 10/97)

8936 Levine, Anna. *Running on Eggs* (5–9). 1999, Front Street $15.95 (0-8126-2875-6). 136pp. The story of two girls — one Jewish and the other Palestinian — and a friendship that withstands cultural and political differences. (Rev: BCCB 11/99; BL 1/1–15/00; HBG 3/00; SLJ 12/99)

8937 Lottridge, Celia B. *Ticket to Canada* (4–6). Illus. 1995, Silver Burdett LB $17.95 (0-382-39145-4). 144pp. In 1915, Sam and his family relocate from Iowa to rural Alberta and must build their own house. (Rev: BL 2/1/96; SLJ 2/96)

8938 Miklowitz, Gloria D. *Masada: The Last Fortress* (5–8). 1998, Eerdmans $16.00 (0-8028-5165-7). 188pp. The siege of Masada comes alive as seen through the eyes of 19-year-old Simon. (Rev: HBG 3/99; SLJ 12/98)

8939 Napoli, Donna Jo. *Trouble on the Tracks* (5–7). 1997, Scholastic $14.95 (0-590-13447-7). 190pp. Zach and his younger sister are embroiled in an Australian adventure involving smugglers and survival in a desert. (Rev: BCCB 3/97; BL 2/1/97; SLJ 3/97)

8940 Nunes, Susan. *To Find the Way* (4–6). Illus. by Cissy Gray. 1992, Univ. of Hawaii Pr. $12.95 (0-8248-1376-6). 48pp. A picture story of the amazing voyage by the ancient Polynesians from Tahiti to Hawaii, seen through a child's eyes. (Rev: BL 1/15/93)

8941 Rubalcaba, Jill. *The Wadjet Eye* (5–8). 2000, Clarion $15.00 (0-395-68942-2). 128pp. After mummifying his dead mother, Damon sets off to find his father and is later hired by Cleopatra as a spy in this action-filled novel set in the Roman Empire of 45 B.C. (Rev: BL 5/15/00; HBG 10/00; SLJ 6/00)

8942 Schneider, Mical. *Between the Dragon and the Eagle* (5–8). 1997, Carolrhoda LB $21.27 (0-87614-

649-3). 151pp. A historical novel that follows a piece of silk from China to Rome. (Rev: BCCB 3/97; BL 2/1/97; SLJ 4/97)

8943 Southern, Randy. *Ruled Out* (3–5). 2000, Bethany paper $5.99 (1-56179-884-3). 112pp. In this story with a biblical basis, Ethan and his family remain faithful to the god of Moses when others have begun to worship the golden calf. (Rev: SLJ 2/01)

8944 Speare, Elizabeth G. *The Bronze Bow* (6–8). 1961, Houghton paper $6.95 (0-395-13719-5). 256pp. A Jewish boy seeks revenge against the Romans who killed his parents, but he finally loses his hatred after he hears the messages and teachings of Jesus. Newbery Medal winner, 1962.

8945 Trottier, Maxine. *A Circle of Silver* (5–8). 2000, Stoddart paper $7.95 (0-7737-6055-5). 216pp. Set in the 1760s, this is the story of 13-year-old John MacNeil who is sent to Canada by his father to toughen him up. (Rev: SLJ 9/00)

8946 Valgardson, W. D. *Sarah and the People of Sand River* (3–5). Illus. by Ian Wallace. 1996, Douglas & McIntyre $16.95 (0-88899-255-6). 56pp. An Icelandic family, now relocated in Manitoba, Canada, is helped by Cree Indians. (Rev: BCCB 12/96; BL 11/1/96*; SLJ 12/96) [398.2]

8947 Walters, Eric. *War of the Eagles* (5–7). 1998, Orca $14.00 (1-55143-118-1); paper $8.95 (1-55143-099-1). 224pp. During the opening months of the war against Japan, a West Coast Canadian boy witnesses the growing prejudice against Japanese Canadians and also becomes aware of his own Indian heritage. (Rev: BL 12/15/98; HBG 3/99)

8948 Ware, Jim. *Crazy Jacob* (3–5). Series: KidWitness Tales. 2000, Bethany paper $5.99 (1-56179-885-1). 115pp. Based on a Bible story, this novel features Crazy Jacob whose demons are cast out by Jesus and turned into swine. (Rev: SLJ 2/01)

8949 Weir, Joan. *The Witcher* (5–7). 1998, Polestar paper $6.95 (1-896095-44-5). 157pp. In Canada's Gold Rush country, 12-year-old Lion and his older sister help their father solve the custody issues surrounding a young girl who possesses divining powers. (Rev: SLJ 3/99)

Prehistory

8950 Caselli, Giovanni. *An Ice Age Hunter* (3–5). 1992, Bedrick LB $12.95 (0-87226-103-4). 30pp. The story of a year in the life of an ice-age family as experienced by a young girl. (Rev: SLJ 7/92)

8951 Cowley, Marjorie. *Anooka's Answer* (5–8). Illus. 1998, Clarion $16.00 (0-395-88530-2). 160pp. Set in prehistoric times, this sequel to *Dar and the Spear Thrower* introduces 13-year-old Anooka and her quest to find her missing mother. (Rev: BL 11/15/98; HBG 3/99; SLJ 12/98)

8952 Cowley, Marjorie. *Dar and the Spear-Thrower* (5–7). 1994, Clarion $13.95 (0-395-68132-4). 118pp. This is the story of Dar, a boy growing up in the Cro-Magnon period, and the problems he faces when beginning to accept adult responsibilities. (Rev: BL 8/94; SLJ 9/94)

8953 Craig, Ruth. *Malu's Wolf* (4–6). 1995, Orchard LB $16.99 (0-531-08784-0). 192pp. Set in Stone Age Europe, this novel tells how Malu domesticated a wolf cub named Kono. (Rev: BL 12/15/95; SLJ 10/95)

8954 Denzel, Justin. *Boy of the Painted Cave* (5–7). 1988, Putnam $14.95 (0-399-21559-X). 160pp. The story of a boy who longs to be a cave artist, set in Cro Magnon times. (Rev: BL 11/1/88; SLJ 11/88)

8955 Dickinson, Peter. *Noli's Story* (4–7). Series: The Kin. 1998, Putnam paper $3.99 (0-448-41710-3). 216pp. Noli, his friend Suth, and three other orphaned children of a prehistoric clan experience many adventures before they are eventually reunited with the adults of their society. (Rev: BL 8/98; HBG 3/99; SLJ 1/99)

8956 Dickinson, Peter. *Suth's Story* (4–7). Series: The Kin. 1998, Grosset $14.99 (0-399-23327-X); paper $3.99 (0-448-41709-X). 211pp. In this opening volume of The Kin series, two orphans, Suth and Noli, along with some other children, find a lush new home in the crater of a volcano. (Rev: BL 8/98; HBG 3/99; SLJ 1/99)

8957 Heide, Florence Parry, and Judith Heide Gilliland. *House of Wisdom* (3–5). Illus. 1999, DK $16.95 (0-7894-2562-9). 40pp. An exotic tale, set in Baghdad in the ninth century, about a young man who travels far and wide to buy rare books for the Caliph and his House of Wisdom. (Rev: BCCB 9/99; BL 9/15/99; HBG 3/00; SLJ 1/00)

8958 Nolan, Dennis. *Wolf Child* (3–5). Illus. 1989, Macmillan paper $16.00 (0-02-768141-6). 40pp. A young boy's affection for an orphaned wolf cub is the focus of this prehistoric tale. (Rev: BL 12/15/89; SLJ 12/89)

8959 Turnbull, Ann. *Maroo of the Winter Caves* (4–7). 1984, Houghton paper $6.95 (0-395-54795-4). 144pp. A story centered on seminomadic people who lived in southern Europe during the last Ice Age.

Africa

8960 Bunting, Eve. *I Am the Mummy Heb-Nefert* (3–6). Illus. by David Christiana. 1997, Harcourt $15.00 (0-15-200479-3). 32pp. A touching picture book in which a female mummy tells of her life as the wife of the pharaoh's brother and of her death and how her body was preserved. (Rev: BCCB 5/97; BL 5/15/97; SLJ 8/97)

8961 Ellis, Veronica F. *Afro-Bets First Book About Africa* (2–5). Illus. by George Ford. 1990, Just Us LB $13.95 (0-940975-12-2); paper $6.95 (0-940975-03-3). 32pp. A classroom of African Americans learns about the history and culture of Africa. (Rev: BL 3/1/90*; SLJ 5/90)

8962 Farmer, Nancy. *Do You Know Me?* (4–6). Illus. by Shelley Jackson. 1993, Orchard LB $16.99 (0-531-08624-0). 112pp. There are culture clashes (many amusing) when 9-year-old Tapiwa's uncle comes from rural Mozambique to live with her family in the city. (Rev: BL 4/1/93; SLJ 4/93)

8963 Gormley, Beatrice. *Miriam* (4–6). 1999, Eerdmans paper $6.00 (0-8028-5156-8). 192pp. The story of 11-year-old Miriam, Moses' elder sister, who manages to get her baby brother into an Egyptian princess's house and her mother hired to care for him. (Rev: SLJ 5/99)

8964 Gregory, Kristiana. *Cleopatra VII: Daughter of the Nile* (5–8). Series: Royal Diaries. 1999, Scholastic $10.95 (0-590-81975-5). 224pp. This mock-diary recounts various events in the life of 12-year-old Cleopatra who, even at that age, was involved in palace intrigue. (Rev: BL 1/1–15/00; HBG 3/00; SLJ 10/99)

8965 Havill, Juanita. *Sato and the Elephants* (2–4). Illus. by Jean Tseng and Mou-Sien Tseng. 1993, Lothrop LB $14.93 (0-688-11156-4). 32pp. A young ivory carver realizes that animals must be killed to supply him with material and therefore decides to try working in stone the next time. (Rev: BL 10/15/93; SLJ 4/94)

8966 Kehret, Peg. *The Secret Journey* (4–7). 1999, Pocket $16.00 (0-671-03416-2). 138pp. In 1834, 12-year-old stowaway Emma is washed ashore on the coast of Liberia and must survive by learning from the chimps she observes. (Rev: BL 1/1–15/00; HBG 10/00; SLJ 3/00)

8967 Kroll, Virginia. *Masai and I* (2–4). Illus. by Nancy Carpenter. 1992, Macmillan LB $16.00 (0-02-751165-0). A young African American girl contrasts her life with the life of the Masai in Africa. (Rev: SLJ 10/92)

8968 Kurtz, Jane. *The Storyteller's Beads* (5–7). 1998, Harcourt $15.00 (0-15-201074-2). 128pp. Two young girls, both Ethiopian refugees, gradually become friends despite cultural differences during a grueling journey to hoped-for freedom and safety. (Rev: BCCB 9/98; BL 5/1/98; HBG 10/98; SLJ 7/98)

8969 Lattimore, Deborah N. *The Winged Cat: A Tale of Ancient Egypt* (3–6). Illus. 1992, HarperCollins $15.00 (0-06-023635-3). 32pp. A serving girl witnesses the killing of the sacred cat Bast in this handsomely illustrated tale of ancient Egypt. (Rev: BL 9/1/92; SLJ 4/92)

8970 Levitin, Sonia. *Dream Freedom* (5–9). 2000, Harcourt $17.00 (0-15-202404-2). 288pp. A novel that graphically portrays the plight of Sudanese slaves, juxtaposed with the story of an American fifth-grade class that joins the fight to free them. (Rev: BL 11/1/00; HBG 3/01; SLJ 10/00)

8971 McKissack, Patricia. *Nzingha: Warrior Queen of Matamba* (5–8). Illus. Series: Royal Diaries. 2000, Scholastic $10.95 (0-439-11210-9). 144pp. Based on fact, this is the story of 17th-century African queen Nzingha who, in present-day Angola, resisted the Portuguese colonizers and slave traders. (Rev: BL 11/1/00; HBG 3/01; SLJ 12/00)

8972 Marie, D. *Tears for Ashan* (3–6). Illus. by Norman Childers. 1989, Creative $12.95 (0-9621681-0-6). 32pp. Set in Africa years ago, Kumasi sees his best friend taken captive by slave traders. (Rev: BL 12/1/89)

8973 Mollel, Tololwa M. *Shadow Dance* (PS–3). Illus. by Donna Perrone. 1998, Clarion $15.00 (0-395-82909-7). 32pp. In this African folktale, Salome must outwit an ungrateful crocodile who threatens to eat her after she has saved him from a deep gully. (Rev: BCCB 1/99; BL 11/15/98; HBG 3/99; SLJ 12/98) [398.2]

8974 Moore, Miriam, and Penny Taylor. *Koi's Python* (2–4). Illus. Series: Hyperion Chapters. 1998, Hyperion LB $14.49 (0-7868-2285-6); paper $3.95 (0-7868-1227-3). 64pp. A beginning chapter book about a young boy of the Batetela tribe in Central Africa who stands up to the local bully and learns from an old hunter how to kill a python. (Rev: BL 1/1–15/99; SLJ 2/99)

8975 Naidoo, Beverley. *No Turning Back* (5–8). 1997, HarperCollins LB $15.89 (0-06-027506-5). 160pp. Jaabu, a homeless African boy, looks for shelter in contemporary Johannesburg. (Rev: BCCB 2/97; BL 12/15/96*; HB 3–4/97; SLJ 2/97)

8976 Posner, Mitch. *Kai, a Big Decision: Africa, 1440* (4–6). Illus. 1997, Simon & Schuster paper $5.99 (0-689-80990-5). 72pp. Kai must decide if she can face leaving her Nigerian village to become an honored member of a craft guild. (Rev: BL 5/1/97)

8977 Rubalcaba, Jill. *A Place in the Sun* (3–6). 1997, Clarion $13.95 (0-395-82645-4). 96pp. Set in 13th-century-B.C. Egypt, this fast-moving novel describes the fate of a boy who is exiled to the gold mines of Nubia. (Rev: BL 4/1/97; SLJ 4/97)

8978 Rupert, Rona. *Straw Sense* (K–3). Illus. by Michael Dooling. 1993, Simon & Schuster paper $14.00 (0-671-77047-0). 32pp. In this story set in South Africa, young Goolam-Habib finds the courage to speak through the friendship he develops with an old man. (Rev: BCCB 1/94; BL 11/15/93; SLJ 2/94)

8979 Thomas, Dawn C. *Kai: A Mission for Her Village* (3–6). Illus. by Vanessa Holley. Series: Girlhood Journeys. 1996, Simon & Schuster paper $13.00 (0-689-81140-3). 71pp. This novel, set in 15th-century Africa, features a young girl who longs to become an artisan, even though women were banned from this work. (Rev: SLJ 3/97)

8980 Welch, Leona N. *Kai: The Lost Statue* (3–6). Illus. Series: Girlhood Journeys. 1997, Simon & Schuster paper $5.99 (0-689-81571-9). 72pp. In this historical novel set in southwestern Nigeria, Kai encounters problems when she becomes an apprentice to a sculptor. (Rev: BL 4/1/98; SLJ 4/98)

8981 Zemser, Amy Bronwen. *Beyond the Mango Tree* (4–8). 1998, Greenwillow $15.00 (0-688-16005-0). 176pp. Sarina, a white American living with her mother in Liberia, feels trapped between her erratic mother's behavior and an alien outside world. (Rev: HB 11–12/98; HBG 3/99; SLJ 10/98)

Asia

8982 Atkins, Jeannine. *Aani and the Tree Huggers* (2–5). Illus. by Venantius J. Pinto. 1995, Lee & Low $14.95 (1-880000-24-5). In this tale set in

India, a village woman tries to save a tree from big-city developers by throwing her arms around it. (Rev: SLJ 12/95)

8983 Axworthy, Anni. *Anni's India Diary* (3–5). Illus. 1992, Whispering Coyote $16.95 (1-879085-59-3). 32pp. In diary form, an account of a girl's three-month trip through India. (Rev: BL 11/1/92; SLJ 12/92)

8984 Balgassi, Haemi. *Peacebound Trains* (3–5). Illus. by Chris K. Soentpiet. 1996, Clarion $14.95 (0-395-72093-1). 47pp. Sumi's grandmother tells about the perilous journey she took to escape the Communists during the Korean War. (Rev: BCCB 10/96; BL 9/15/96; SLJ 1/97)

8985 Bond, Ruskin. *Binya's Blue Umbrella* (2–5). Illus. by Vera Rosenberry. 1995, Boyds Mills $12.95 (1-56397-135-6). 68pp. In this novel set in India, Binya acquires a wonderful umbrella that everyone envies. (Rev: BL 3/15/95; SLJ 3/95)

8986 Breckler, Rosemary K. *Sweet Dried Apples: A Vietnamese Wartime Childhood* (3–5). Illus. by Deborah Kogan Ray. 1996, Houghton $15.95 (0-395-73570-X). 32pp. Using a picture-book format, a childhood in war-torn Vietnam is examined. (Rev: BL 9/1/96; SLJ 3/97)

8987 Choi, Sook N. *Echoes of the White Giraffe* (5–8). 1993, Houghton $14.95 (0-395-64721-5). 144pp. In this sequel to *Year of Impossible Goodbyes* (1991), Sookan and her family once again are separated, this time by the Korean War. (Rev: SLJ 5/93)

8988 Chrisman, Arthur B. *Shen of the Sea* (4–6). Illus. by Else Hasselriis. 1968, Dutton $16.99 (0-525-39244-0). 224pp. These engaging short stories of Chinese life received the Newbery Award, 1926.

8989 Coerr, Eleanor. *Mieko and the Fifth Treasure* (4–7). 1993, Putnam $14.99 (0-399-22434-3). 78pp. A Japanese girl believes that she will never draw again after she is injured during the atomic bomb attack on Nagasaki. (Rev: BCCB 4/93; BL 4/1/93*; SLJ 7/93)

8990 Conrad, Pam. *Blue Willow* (4–6). Illus. by S. Saelig Gallagher. 1999, Putnam $16.99 (0-399-22904-3). 32pp. Using a Chinese setting, this folktale-like story tells of When Kung Shi Fair and her tragic love for a local fisherman. (Rev: BCCB 12/99; BL 10/15/99; HBG 3/00; SLJ 8/99)

8991 Crofford, Emily. *Born in the Year of Courage* (5–8). 1992, Carolrhoda LB $21.27 (0-87614-679-5). 160pp. Based on fact, this story tells of a Japanese fisherman, educated in America, who participated in the California Gold Rush. (Rev: SLJ 12/92)

8992 Ellis, Deborah. *The Breadwinner* (5–7). 2001, Groundwood $15.95 (0-88899-419-2). 170pp. In Kabul under the strict rule of the Taliban, Parvana dresses as a boy so she can work to feed the remaining women in her family. (Rev: BL 3/1/01)

8993 Fletcher, Susan. *Shadow Spinner* (5–9). 1998, Simon & Schuster $17.00 (0-689-81852-1). 221pp. Marjan leaves the harem in search of someone who can tell her the ending of a story that Shahrazad is telling the Sultan as part of her 1,001-night cycle.

(Rev: BCCB 7–8/98; HB 7–8/98; HBG 10/98; SLJ 6/98)

8994 Giles, Gail. *Breath of the Dragon* (4–7). Illus. 1997, Clarion $14.95 (0-395-76476-9). 112pp. In this story set in Thailand, Malila faces rejection and loneliness because her father was a thief. (Rev: BCCB 4/97; BL 4/1/97; SLJ 6/97)

8995 Glass, Tom. *Even a Little Is Something: Stories of Nong* (4–6). Illus. by Elena Gerard. 1997, Linnet LB $16.95 (0-208-02457-3). 119pp. Accurately depicts the daily struggle of peasants living hand-to-mouth in northeastern Thailand. (Rev: HBG 3/98; SLJ 2/98)

8996 Godden, Rumer. *Premlata and the Festival of Lights* (4–6). Illus. by Ian Andrew. 1997, Greenwillow $15.00 (0-688-15136-1). 58pp. The story of a poor family in the Bengal region of India and how they plan to celebrate the festival of light, Diwali, to honor the goddess Kali. (Rev: HB 5–6/97; SLJ 5/97)

8997 Hill, Elizabeth S. *Bird Boy* (2–4). Illus. 1999, Farrar $15.00 (0-374-30723-7). 64pp. Chang, a mute Chinese boy, learns a bitter lesson about friendship and trust when he raises a cormorant chick and involves others in his project. (Rev: BCCB 7–8/99; BL 4/15/99; HBG 10/99; SLJ 6/99)

8998 Huynh, Quang Nhuong. *The Land I Lost: Adventures of a Boy in Vietnam* (5–8). Illus. by Mai Vo-Dinh. 1990, HarperCollins LB $15.89 (0-397-32448-0); paper $4.95 (0-06-440183-9). 128pp. The story of a boy's growing up in rural Vietnam before the war.

8999 Kamal, Aleph. *The Bird Who Was an Elephant* (3–5). Illus. by Frane Lessac. 1990, HarperCollins LB $14.89 (0-397-32446-4). 32pp. The story of what a bird sees as it flies over an Indian village. (Rev: BCCB 7–8/90; BL 4/15/90; SLJ 8/90)

9000 Lattimore, Deborah N. *Fool and the Phoenix: A Tale of Ancient Japan* (3–6). Illus. 1997, HarperCollins LB $14.89 (0-06-026211-7). 40pp. Hideo, a mute, falls in love with the phoenix bird of Japan and catches her in a net. (Rev: BL 8/97; HBG 3/98; SLJ 9/97)

9001 Lewis, Elizabeth Foreman. *Young Fu of the Upper Yangtze* (5–8). Illus. by Ed Young. 1973, Dell paper $5.50 (0-440-49043-X). 268pp. Young Fu must pay back a debt of $5 or face public shame. Newbery Medal winner, 1933.

9002 McKibbon, Hugh William. *The Token Gift* (3–5). Illus. by Scott Cameron. 1996, Annick $16.95 (1-55037-499-0); paper $6.95 (1-55037-498-2). 32pp. Set in ancient India, this is the story of Mohan, the boy who invented chess. (Rev: BL 2/1/97; SLJ 1/97)

9003 Neuberger, Anne E. *The Girl-Son* (3–6). Illus. 1994, Carolrhoda LB $21.27 (0-87614-846-1). 132pp. Based on fact, this is the story of a Korean girl born in 1896 and her fight for women's rights. (Rev: BCCB 2/95; BL 1/1/95; SLJ 2/95)

9004 Park, Linda Sue. *The Kite Fighters* (4–6). 2000, Clarion $15.00 (0-395-94041-9). 144pp. Contests involving kite flying are the subject of this exciting novel set in 15th-century Korea. (Rev:

BCCB 6/00; BL 4/1/00; HB 5–6/00; HBG 10/00; SLJ 6/00)

9005 Park, Linda Sue. *Seesaw Girl* (4–7). Illus. 1999, Clarion $14.00 (0-395-91514-7). 90pp. In 17th-century Korea, 12-year-old Jade Blossom wanders away from her aristocratic palace and discovers the reality and poverty of the world outside. (Rev: BCCB 12/99; BL 9/1/99; HBG 3/00; SLJ 9/99)

9006 Paterson, Katherine. *The Master Puppeteer* (4–7). Illus. by Haru Wells. 1989, HarperCollins paper $4.95 (0-06-440281-9). 192pp. Feudal Japan is the setting for this story about a young apprentice puppeteer and his search for a mysterious bandit.

9007 Paterson, Katherine. *Of Nightingales That Weep* (4–7). Illus. by Haru Wells. 1974, Harper-Collins $14.00 (0-690-00485-0); paper $4.95 (0-06-440282-7). 192pp. A story set in feudal Japan tells of Takiko, a samurai's daughter, who is sent to the royal court when her mother remarries.

9008 Paterson, Katherine. *The Sign of the Chrysanthemum* (5–7). Illus. by Peter Landa. 1973, HarperCollins LB $14.89 (0-690-04913-7); paper $4.95 (0-06-440232-0). 128pp. At the death of his mother, a young boy sets out to find his samurai father in 12th-century Japan.

9009 Pevsner, Stella, and Fay Tang. *Sing for Your Father, Su Phan* (4–6). 1997, Clarion $14.00 (0-395-82267-X). 112pp. A fictional memoir of a North Vietnamese girl's experience and hardships during the Vietnam War. (Rev: BL 1/1–15/98; HBG 3/98; SLJ 12/97)

9010 Russell, Ching Yeung. *Child Bride* (4–7). Illus. 1999, Boyds Mills $15.95 (1-56397-748-6). 133pp. Set in China in the early 1940s, this is the story of 11-year-old Ying, her arranged marriage, and an understanding bridegroom who allows her to go home to her ailing grandmother. (Rev: BL 3/1/99; HBG 10/99; SLJ 4/99)

9011 Russell, Ching Yeung. *First Apple* (3–5). Illus. 1994, Boyds Mills $15.95 (1-56397-206-9). 127pp. In this tale set in China, Ying is determined to buy her grandmother a birthday gift that she has never had before, an apple. (Rev: BCCB 1/95; BL 11/1/94; SLJ 9/94)

9012 Russell, Ching Yeung. *Lichee Tree* (4–7). 1997, Boyds Mills $14.95 (1-56397-629-3). 182pp. Growing up in China during the 1940s, Ying dreams of selling lichee nuts and visiting Canton. (Rev: BCCB 4/97; BL 3/15/97; SLJ 6/97)

9013 Russell, Ching Yeung. *Water Ghost* (3–5). Illus. 1995, Boyds Mills $14.95 (1-56397-413-4). 192pp. Ying, age 10 and growing up in China, faces the scorn of her family when she helps an aged grandmother. (Rev: BL 10/15/95; SLJ 12/95)

9014 Schaeffer, Edith. *Mei Fuh: Memories from China* (3–6). Illus. 1998, Houghton $16.00 (0-395-72290-X). 96pp. A fictionalized memoir of a young American girl growing up in China in the 1910s and of her eventual trip to America with her parents. (Rev: BCCB 9/98; BL 7/98; HBG 10/98; SLJ 7/98)

9015 Spivak, Dawnine. *Grass Sandals: The Travels of Basho* (3–5). Illus. by Demi. 1997, Simon & Schuster $16.00 (0-689-80776-7). 40pp. An outstanding picture book about the 17th-century poet and his travels around Japan. (Rev: BCCB 7–8/97; BL 5/1/97*; HBG 3/98; SLJ 4/97) [895.6]

9016 Sreenivasan, Jyotsna. *Aruna's Journeys* (4–7). Illus. 1997, Smooth Stone paper $6.95 (0-9619401-7-4). 136pp. Aruna denies her Indian heritage until she spends a summer in Bangalore, India. (Rev: BL 7/97)

9017 Tan, Amy. *The Moon Lady* (4–6). Illus. by Gretchen Schields. 1992, Macmillan LB $16.95 (0-02-788830-4). 32pp. A grandmother in the United States remembers her childhood in China in this story adapted from the adult best-seller *The Joy Luck Club*. (Rev: BCCB 11/92; BL 9/1/92; SLJ 9/92)

9018 Wartski, Maureen C. *A Boat to Nowhere* (4–5). 1981, NAL paper $4.99 (0-451-16285-4). 160pp. An adventure story about the Vietnamese "boat people."

9019 Whelan, Gloria. *Homeless Bird* (5–8). 2000, HarperCollins LB $14.89 (0-06-028452-8). 192pp. A novel set in contemporary India about a young girl and her arranged marriage to a young man who is dying of tuberculosis. (Rev: HBG 10/00; SLJ 2/00)

9020 Whitesel, Cheryl Aylward. *Rebel: A Tibetan Odyssey* (5–8). 2000, HarperCollins $15.95 (0-688-16735-7). 190pp. In Tibet about one hundred years ago, Thunder, a young boy, is sent to live with his uncle, an important lama in a Buddhist monastery. (Rev: BCCB 5/00; HBG 3/01; SLJ 7/00)

9021 Wu, Priscilla. *The Abacus Contest: Stories from Taiwan and China* (5–8). Illus. 1996, Fulcrum $15.95 (1-55591-243-5). 55pp. Six simple short stories explore life in a city on Taiwan. (Rev: BL 7/96; SLJ 6/96)

9022 Yumoto, Kazumi. *The Friends* (5–7). Trans. by Cathy Hirano. 1996, Farrar $15.00 (0-374-32460-3). 176pp. Three young friends witness the gradual death of their dear friend, an old man, in this novel set in Japan. (Rev: BCCB 2/97; BL 10/15/96; HB 11–12/96; SLJ 12/96)

Europe

9023 Alcock, Vivien. *Singer to the Sea God* (5–8). 1995, Dell paper $3.99 (0-440-41003-7). 208pp. This historical tale, which is set in Greece during mythological times, tells of the adventurous escape from King Polydectes' court. (Rev: BCCB 2/93; HB 7–8/93; SLJ 3/93)

9024 Anderson, Margaret J. *Children of Summer: Henri Fabre's Insects* (4–7). Illus. 1997, Farrar $15.00 (0-374-31243-5). 112pp. A fictionalized biography of the French naturalist Jean Henri Fabre and his work with insects. (Rev: BCCB 6/97; BL 3/1/97; HB 7–8/97; SLJ 9/97)

9025 Anholt, Laurence. *Leonardo and the Flying Boy* (2–4). Illus. 2000, Barron's $13.95 (0-7641-5225-4). 32pp. A fictionalized account of da Vinci's life and accomplishments as reflected in anecdotes about his young apprentices. (Rev: BL 1/1–15/01; SLJ 2/01)

9026 Avi. *Midnight Magic* (5–8). 1999, Scholastic $15.95 (0-590-36035-3). 256pp. During the Middle Ages, a magician and his young servant boy become involved in castle intrigue when they investigate the sighting of a ghost by 10-year-old Princess Teresina. (Rev: BCCB 12/99; BL 9/15/99; HB 11–12/99; HBG 3/00; SLJ 10/99)

9027 Barrett, Tracy. *Anna of Byzantium* (5–7). 1999, Delacorte $14.95 (0-385-32626-2). 210pp. Based on fact, this is the story of Anna Commena who, in ninth-century Constantinople, was being groomed to become the sovereign of the Byzantine empire when a baby brother was born. (Rev: BL 4/1/99; HB 7–8/99; HBG 10/99)

9028 Björk, Christina. *Vendela in Venice* (4–7). Illus. 1999, R&S $18.00 (91-29-64559-X). 93pp. A book about the wonders and excitement of Venice as experienced by Vendela, who travels there with her father during Easter break. (Rev: BL 11/15/99; HB 11–12/99; HBG 3/00; SLJ 1/00)

9029 Blacklock, Dyan. *Pankration: The Ultimate Game* (5–8). 1999, Albert Whitman LB $15.95 (0-8075-6323-4). 192pp. An exciting, far-fetched story set in ancient Greece about two friends, separated by a shipwreck, who are reunited at the Olympic Games at the time of the Pankration, a combination wrestling and boxing sport. (Rev: BCCB 6/99; HBG 10/99; SLJ 4/99)

9030 Casanova, Mary. *Curse of a Winter Moon* (5–8). 2000, Hyperion $15.99 (0-7868-0547-1). 144pp. Set in 16th-century France, this novel tells of the conflict between the Huguenots and the Roman Catholics as seen from the point of view of young Marius. (Rev: BL 10/15/00; HBG 3/01; SLJ 10/00)

9031 Celenza, Anna Harwell. *The Farewell Symphony* (2–4). Illus. by JoAnn E. Kitchel. 2000, Charlesbridge LB $19.95 (1-57091-406-0). A fictional version of the story behind Haydn's "Farewell Symphony" and the effect it had on Prince Nicholas, the composer's sponsor. (Rev: HBG 3/01; SLJ 7/00)

9032 DeJong, Meindert. *Wheel on the School* (4–7). Illus. by Maurice Sendak. 1954, HarperCollins LB $15.89 (0-06-021586-0); paper $5.95 (0-06-440021-2). 256pp. The storks are brought back to their island by the schoolchildren in a Dutch village. Newbery Medal winner, 1955.

9033 Delton, Judy. *Angel Spreads Her Wings* (3–5). Illus. 1999, Houghton $15.00 (0-395-91006-4). 160pp. Angel flourishes when her stepdad takes the family to visit his hometown in Greece and live in a house without electricity. (Rev: BL 5/1/99; HB 7–8/99; HBG 10/99; SLJ 4/99)

9034 de Trevino, Elizabeth. *I, Juan de Pareja* (5–8). 1965, Farrar $13.95 (0-374-33531-1); paper $4.95 (0-374-43525-1). 192pp. Through the eyes of his devoted black slave, Juan de Pareja, the character of the artist Velasquez is revealed. Newbery Medal winner, 1966.

9035 Deverell, Catherine. *Stradivari's Singing Violin* (3–5). Illus. by Andrea Shine. 1992, Carolrhoda LB $21.27 (0-87614-732-5). 48pp. A fictional account of the historical figure behind what is per-

haps the world's best-known musical instrument. (Rev: BL 2/15/93)

9036 Dexter, Catherine. *Safe Return* (5–7). 1996, Candlewick $15.99 (0-7636-0005-9). 96pp. On her island home in the Baltic Sea in 1824, an orphan anxiously awaits the return of her aunt, who has sailed to Stockholm, Sweden. (Rev: BCCB 11/96; BL 10/15/96; HB 11–12/96; SLJ 12/96)

9037 Early, Margaret. *Romeo and Juliet* (4–6). Illus. 1998, Abrams $18.95 (0-8109-3799-9). 32pp. This retelling of the Shakespeare classic often uses lines from the play and is illustrated with dazzling Renaissance-type paintings. (Rev: BL 5/1/98; HBG 10/98; SLJ 6/98)

9038 Eisner, Will. *The Last Knight: An Introduction to Don Quixote by Miguel de Cervantes* (4–8). Illus. 2000, NBM $15.95 (1-56163-251-1). 32pp. Using an engaging text and a comic-book format, this is a fine retelling of Cervantes' classic. (Rev: BL 6/1–15/00; HBG 10/00; SLJ 7/00)

9039 Elmer, Robert. *Chasing the Wind* (4–7). Series: Young Underground. 1996, Bethany paper $5.99 (1-55661-658-9). 187pp. Three Danish children discover that after the Germans surrender some Nazis are still in their town diving for sunken treasure. (Rev: BL 5/1/96)

9040 Gray, Elizabeth Janet. *Adam of the Road* (5–8). Illus. by Robert Lawson. 1942, Puffin paper $5.99 (0-14-032464-X). 320pp. Adventures of a 13th-century minstrel boy. Newbery Medal winner, 1943.

9041 Greene, Jacqueline D. *Marie: Summer in the Country* (3–6). Illus. Series: Girlhood Journeys. 1997, Simon & Schuster paper $5.99 (0-689-81562-X). 72pp. In this historical novel set in France, Marie plots to save her country cousin from being sent away to work as a servant. (Rev: BL 4/1/98; SLJ 4/98)

9042 Greene, Jacqueline D. *One Foot Ashore* (4–6). 1994, Walker $16.95 (0-8027-8281-7). 208pp. To escape servitude in Brazil, Maria stows away on a boat bound for Amsterdam, where she finds work in the home of Rembrandt. (Rev: BCCB 6/94; BL 4/1/94; HB 7–8/94; SLJ 6/94)

9043 Hest, Amy. *When Jessie Came Across the Sea* (2–4). Illus. by P. J. Lynch. 1997, Candlewick $16.99 (0-7636-0094-6). 40pp. A Jewish girl living in an Eastern European shtetl gets an opportunity to come to the United States, but she will have to leave her wonderful grandmother behind. (Rev: BCCB 3/98; BL 2/1/98; HBG 3/98; SLJ 11/97)

9044 Hodges, Margaret, ed. *Don Quixote and Sancho Panza* (4–6). Illus. by Stephen Marchesi. 1992, Macmillan $16.95 (0-684-19235-7). 80pp. Abridged episodes from the Cervantes novel suitable for young readers. (Rev: BCCB 2/93; BL 12/1/92; HB 3–4/93; SLJ 11/92)

9045 Hugo, Victor. *The Hunchback of Notre Dame* (4–6). Retold by Tim Wynne-Jones. Illus. by Bill Slavin. 1997, Orchard $15.95 (0-531-30055-2). This abridgement of the Hugo classic captures the spirit of Paris in the Middle Ages and Quasimodo's love for Esmeralda. (Rev: HBG 3/98; SLJ 4/98)

9046 Hunt, Jonathan. *Leif's Saga: A Viking Tale* (3–5). Illus. by author. 1996, Simon & Schuster paper $16.00 (0-689-80492-X). In this novel set in Viking times, Sigrid hears her father tell of Leif Eriksson's famed voyage to North America. (Rev: BCCB 3/96; SLJ 5/96)

9047 Jackson, Dave, and Neta Jackson. *The Betrayer's Fortune* (3–6). Illus. 1994, Bethany paper $5.99 (1-55661-467-5). 144pp. During the persecution of the Anabaptists in the 16th century, a young boy discovers he possesses great reserves of courage. (Rev: BL 4/1/95)

9048 Jones, Terry. *The Lady and the Squire* (5–7). Illus. 2001, Pavilion $22.95 (1-86205-417-7). 304pp. A beautiful aristocrat joins Tom and Ann as they make their way through a war torn countryside to the papal court at Avignon. (Rev: BL 2/15/01; SLJ 3/01)

9049 Juster, Norton. *Alberic the Wise* (4–8). Illus. by Leonard Baskin. 1992, Picture Book $16.95 (0-88708-243-2). 32pp. In this picture book set in the Renaissance, Alberic becomes an apprentice to a stained-glass maker. (Rev: BCCB 2/93; BL 1/15/93; SLJ 3/93)

9050 Kanefield, Teri. *Rivka's Way* (4–8). 2001, Front Street $15.95 (0-8126-2870-5). 144pp. Daily life inside and outside the Prague ghetto in 1778 is explored in this novel about an unconventional Jewish girl, 15-year-old Rivka Liebermann. (Rev: SLJ 3/01)

9051 Kelly, Eric P. *The Trumpeter of Krakow* (5–8). Illus. by Janina Domanska. 1966, Macmillan LB $17.00 (0-02-750140-X); paper $4.99 (0-689-71571-4). 224pp. Mystery surrounds a precious jewel and the youthful patriot who stands watch over it in a church tower in this novel of 15th-century Poland. Newbery Medal winner, 1929.

9052 Kimmel, Eric A. *Count Silvernose: A Story from Italy* (3–6). Illus. by Omar Rayyan. 1996, Holiday $15.95 (0-8234-1216-4). 30pp. Set in the late Renaissance, this adventure story tells how Assunta sets out to find her sisters, who have been abducted by Count Silvernose. (Rev: BCCB 7–8/96; BL 3/15/96*; HB 7–8/96; SLJ 3/96)

9053 Knight, Joan MacPhail. *Charlotte in Giverny* (4–6). Illus. 2000, Chronicle $15.95 (0-8118-2383-0). 64pp. In this novel set in France in the 1890s a young American girl gets to know many of the American artists who are studying with Monet at Giverny and even meets the reclusive painter himself. (Rev: BL 7/00; HBG 10/00; SLJ 6/00)

9054 Korman, Susan. *Megan in Ancient Greece* (3–5). Illus. by Bill Dodge and Catherine Huert. Series: Magic Attic Club. 1998, Magic Attic LB $17.40 (1-57513-143-9); paper $5.95 (1-57513-127-7). 71pp. Using a toga she finds in a magic trunk, Megan is transported to ancient Greece where she helps solve a mystery and also learns about living conditions in ancient times. (Rev: SLJ 4/99)

9055 Kramer, Stephen. *Theodoric's Rainbow* (4–6). Illus. by Daniel Duffy. 1995, Scientific American paper $17.95 (0-7167-6603-5). 32pp. A picture book for middle-graders that tells the story of Theodoric, a 13th-century monk who experiments with the wonders of rainbows. (Rev: BCCB 2/96; BL 1/1–15/96)

9056 Lasky, Kathryn. *Marie Antoinette: Princess of Versailles* (5–8). Series: Royal Diaries. 2000, Scholastic $10.95 (0-439-07666-8). 240pp. This fictional diary covers two years in the life of Marie Antoinette, beginning in 1769 when the 13-year-old was preparing for her fateful marriage. (Rev: BL 4/15/00; HBG 10/00; SLJ 5/00)

9057 Lasky, Kathryn. *The Night Journey* (4–7). Illus. by Trina S. Hyman. 1986, Puffin paper $4.99 (0-14-032048-2). 152pp. Nana tells her great-granddaughter about her escape from Czarist Russia.

9058 Littlesugar, Amy. *Marie in Fourth Position: The Story of Degas' "The Little Dancer"* (1–3). Illus. by Ian Schoenherr. 1996, Philomel $16.99 (0-399-22794-6). The story of a young ballet student who modeled for Degas to get money for her poor parents. (Rev: SLJ 10/96*)

9059 Macaulay, David. *Rome Antics* (4–8). Illus. 1997, Houghton $17.00 (0-395-82289-3). 80pp. The reader gets a pigeon-eye view of vistas and building as the bird flies over Rome. (Rev: BL 9/15/97; SLJ 11/97*)

9060 McKay, Sharon E. *Charlie Wilcox* (5–8). 2000, Stoddart paper $7.95 (0-7737-6093-8). 221pp. This is the story of a 14-year-old Canadian boy who becomes involved in the trench warfare in France during World War I. (Rev: SLJ 11/00)

9061 Mead, Alice. *Girl of Kosovo* (5–10). 2001, Farrar $16.00 (0-374-32620-7). 128pp. A moving novel about the ethnic wars in Kosovo as seen through the eyes of an 11-year-old Albanian girl who has witnessed the death of her father and two brothers and whose foot is smashed during the fighting. (Rev: BL 3/15/01*; SLJ 3/01)

9062 Menick, Stephen. *The Muffin Child* (5–7). 1998, Putnam $17.99 (0-399-23303-2). 208pp. In a Balkan village, Tanya, an outcast at age 11, is wrongfully accused of kidnapping a child, but when she places blame on a band of Gypsies, she inadvertently causes a massacre in this tale of cruelty and kindness. (Rev: BCCB 10/98; BL 9/15/98; HB 1–2/99; HBG 3/99; SLJ 9/98)

9063 Meyer, Carolyn. *Anastasia: The Last Grand Duchess, Russia, 1914* (4–8). Series: Royal Diaries. 2000, Scholastic $10.95 (0-439-12908-7). 224pp. Anastasia's fictional diary that begins when she is 12 in 1914 and ends with her captivity in 1918. (Rev: SLJ 10/00)

9064 Morrison, Taylor. *The Neptune Fountain: The Apprenticeship of a Renaissance Sculptor* (3–6). Illus. 1997, Holiday LB $15.95 (0-8234-1293-8). 32pp. The creation of a marble sculpture is described in this novel about an apprentice to a famous sculptor in 17th-century Rome. (Rev: BL 6/1–15/97; SLJ 6/97)

9065 Nichol, Barbara. *Beethoven Lives Upstairs* (3–6). Illus. by Scott Cameron. 1994, Orchard $15.95 (0-531-06828-5). 48pp. When Beethoven moves into his house, young Christoph gradually learns to sympathize with the agonies suffered by

Beethoven because of his deafness. (Rev: BCCB 2/94; BL 1/1/94*; HB 7–8/94; SLJ 4/94)

9066 Pernoud, Regine. *A Day with a Miller* (4–7). Trans. by Dominique Clift. Illus. by Giorgio Bacchin. 1997, Runestone LB $22.60 (0-8225-1914-3). 48pp. A description of the life of a miller and his family in the 12th century and how hydraulic energy was being introduced at that time. (Rev: HBG 3/98; SLJ 3/98)

9067 Pyle, Howard. *Otto of the Silver Hand* (6–8). Illus. by author. 1967, Dover paper $8.95 (0-486-21784-1). 173pp. Life in feudal Germany, the turbulence and cruelty of robber barons, and the peaceful, scholarly pursuits of the monks are presented in the story of the kidnapped son of a robber baron.

9068 Robertson, Bruce. *Marguerite Makes a Book* (3–6). 1999, Getty Museum $18.95 (0-89236-372-X). 48pp. A stunning picture book for older readers, set in 15th-century Paris, in which young Marguerite takes over her father's book-painting craft when the old man become too infirm to work. (Rev: BL 11/15/99; HBG 3/00; SLJ 1/00)

9069 Schwartz, Ellen. *Jesse's Star* (2–5). Illus. 2000, Orca paper $4.50 (1-55143-143-2). 108pp. Jesse travels back in time and becomes his great-great-grandfather, a Jewish boy growing up in Russia, reliving his part in helping villagers and himself escape the pogroms and make their way to Canada. (Rev: BL 7/00; SLJ 11/00)

9070 Seredy, Kate. *The Good Master* (4–6). Illus. by author. 1986, Puffin paper $4.99 (0-14-030133-X). 196pp. Warm and humorous story of a city girl on her uncle's farm in prewar Hungary.

9071 Skurzynski, Gloria. *The Minstrel in the Tower* (3–4). Illus. by Julek Heller. 1988, Random paper $3.99 (0-394-89598-3). 64pp. Alice and Roger search for their uncle after their father has been killed in the Crusades, in this story of life in the Middle Ages. (Rev: BCCB 7–8/88; BL 7/88)

9072 Visconti, Guido. *The Genius of Leonardo* (3–6). Trans. by Mark Roberts. Illus. 2000, Barefoot $16.99 (1-84148-301-X). 40pp. Using many quotes from the writings of Leonardo da Vinci, this novel tries to re-create this great man's in the eyes of his servant, Giacomo. (Rev: BCCB 10/00; BL 9/15/00; SLJ 9/00)

9073 Vos, Ida. *Dancing on the Bridge at Avignon* (5–8). Trans. by Terese Edlstein and Inez Smidt. 1995, Houghton $14.95 (0-395-72039-7). 144pp. Rosa, a Jewish girl in the Netherlands during World War II, lives in constant fear that the Nazis will deport her and her family. (Rev: BCCB 2/96; BL 10/15/95; SLJ 10/95)

9074 Watts, Irene N. *Good-Bye Marianne* (5–8). 1998, Tundra paper $7.95 (0-88776-445-2). 112pp. In this autobiographical novel, 11-year-old Marianne Kohn is Jewish and experiencing Nazi persecution in 1938 Berlin when her parents decide to sent her to Britain as part of the Kindertransport rescue operation. (Rev: BCCB 7–8/98; BL 8/98; SLJ 8/98)

9075 Weston, Carol. *The Diary of Melanie Martin; or, How I Survived Matt the Brat, Michelangelo,*

and the Leaning Tower of Pizza (4–6). 2000, Knopf LB $17.99 (0-375-90509-X). 144pp. Ten-year-old Melanie tells her diary about an eventful trip to Italy with her parents and kid brother. (Rev: BCCB 6/00; BL 5/1/00; HBG 10/00; SLJ 6/00)

9076 Wild, Margaret. *Let the Celebrations Begin!* (3–6). Illus. by Julie Vivas. 1991, Watts LB $14.99 (0-531-08537-6). 32pp. A picture book for older children about a group of Polish women in the Belsen death camp who organized a party for the surviving children after liberation. (Rev: BCCB 9/91; BL 8/91; SLJ 7/91)

9077 Williams, Laura E. *Behind the Bedroom Wall* (5–8). Illus. 1996, Milkweed $15.95 (1-57131-607-8); paper $6.95 (1-57131-606-X). 176pp. Korinna, a young Nazi, discovers that her parents are hiding a Jewish couple. (Rev: BL 8/96; SLJ 9/96)

9078 Williams, Laura E. *The Spider's Web* (5–7). Illus. 1999, Milkweed $15.95 (1-57131-621-3); paper $6.95 (1-57131-622-1). 134pp. Lexi, a modern German girl, joins a racist skinhead organization and discovers the consequences of irrational hatred — from her own actions and from speaking with an older woman who was once a member of Hitler's Youth. (Rev: BL 6/1–15/99; HBG 10/99)

Great Britain and Ireland

9079 Blackwood, Gary L. *The Shakespeare Stealer* (5–8). 1998, Dutton $15.99 (0-525-45863-8). 208pp. A 14-year-old apprentice at the Globe theater is sent by a rival company to steal Shakespeare's plays. (Rev: BL 6/1–15/98; HB 7–8/98; HBG 10/98; SLJ 6/98)

9080 Blackwood, Gary L. *Shakespeare's Scribe* (5–8). 2000, Dutton $15.99 (0-525-46444-1). 224pp. Set in Elizabethan England, this is the story of how young Widge discovers his true identity while traveling outside London with a theatrical troupe. (Rev: BL 9/1/00; HB 11–12/00; HBG 3/01; SLJ 9/00)

9081 Borden, Louise. *The Little Ships: The Heroic Rescue at Dunkirk in World War II* (3–5). Illus. by Michael Foreman. 1997, Simon & Schuster $15.00 (0-689-80827-5). 32pp. A young English girl and her father help during the evacuation of Dunkirk (Dunkerque), France during World War II. (Rev: BCCB 4/97; BL 3/1/97; HB 5–6/97; SLJ 4/97*)

9082 Branford, Henrietta. *Fire, Bed, and Bone* (5–8). 1998, Candlewick $16.99 (0-7636-0338-4). 128pp. This unusual novel, narrated from a dog's point of view, tells about the oppression of the peasants in late 14th-century England and of the revolt led by Wat Tyler and the preacher John Ball. (Rev: BCCB 5/98; BL 3/15/98; HBG 10/98)

9083 Bulla, Clyde Robert. *The Sword in the Tree* (2–5). Illus. by Paul Galdone. 1962, HarperCollins LB $15.89 (0-690-79909-8). 128pp. A simply written account of knighthood at the time of King Arthur.

9084 Burgess, Melvin. *The Copper Treasure* (3–6). Illus. 2000, Holt $15.95 (0-8050-6381-1). 104pp. Set in 19th-century London, this is an adventure story involving 11-year-old Jeremy and two friends who try to salvage a roll of copper that has sunk to the bottom of the Thames. (Rev: BCCB 7–8/00; BL 6/1–15/00; HB 7–8/00; HBG 10/00; SLJ 7/00)

9085 Chaucer, Geoffrey. *Canterbury Tales* (4–8). Adapted by Barbara Cohen. Illus. by Trina S. Hyman. 1988, Lothrop $21.95 (0-688-06201-6). 96pp. Beautiful edition of selected stories including: The Pardoner's Tale and The Wife of Bath's Tale. (Rev: BL 9/1/88; SLJ 8/88)

9086 Cheaney, J. B. *The Playmaker* (5–8). 2000, Knopf LB $17.99 (0-375-90577-4). 256pp. A well-written historical adventure story set in Elizabethan England and featuring a teenage boy caught up in dangerous political plots. (Rev: HBG 3/01; SLJ 12/00)

9087 Clayton, Elaine. *The Yeoman's Daring Daughter and the Princes in the Tower* (K–4). Illus. 1999, Crown LB $18.99 (0-517-70985-6). 40pp. A reworking of history in which the princes in the Tower of London are not murdered by an order from Richard III, but saved through the efforts of the daughter of a yeoman. (Rev: BL 4/1/99; HBG 10/99; SLJ 6/99)

9088 Conlon-McKenna, Marita. *Fields of Home* (5–7). Illus. by Donald Teskey. 1997, Holiday paper $15.95 (0-8234-1295-4). 189pp. The story of the effects of the 19th-century potato famine in Ireland and the grinding poverty it produced on the young daughter of one of the survivers. (Rev: BCCB 7–8/97; SLJ 6/97)

9089 Conlon-McKenna, Marita. *Under the Hawthorn Tree* (4–6). 1990, Holiday $13.95 (0-8234-0838-8). 153pp. This story is set during the Great Famine in Ireland in the late 1840s. A sequel is: *Wildflower Girl* (1992). (Rev: BCCB 12/90; BL 11/15/90; SLJ 12/90)

9090 Cushman, Karen. *Matilda Bone* (4–8). 2000, Clarion $15.00 (0-395-88156-0). 176pp. Set in the 14th century, this novel describes the development of Matilda, 13, who serves as an assistant to the local bone setter in exchange for food and shelter. (Rev: BCCB 12/00; HB 11–12/00; HBG 3/01; SLJ 9/00*)

9091 De Angeli, Marguerite. *The Door in the Wall* (5–7). Illus. by author. 1990, Dell paper $4.99 (0-440-40283-2). Crippled Robin proves his courage in plague-ridden 19th-century London. Newbery Medal winner, 1950.

9092 Doherty, Berlie. *Street Child* (5–7). 1994, Orchard LB $16.99 (0-531-08714-X). 160pp. The story of a street urchin in Victorian London who is forced to work on a river barge until he escapes. (Rev: BCCB 11/94; BL 9/1/94; SLJ 10/94)

9093 Flegg, Aubrey. *Katie's War* (5–8). 2000, O'Brien paper $7.95 (0-86278-525-1). 192pp. Set during Ireland's fight for independence from England, this story shows a girl torn between two sides when her father wants peace and her brother is preparing to use force. (Rev: BL 12/1/00)

9094 Giff, Patricia Reilly. *Nory Ryan's Song* (4–7). 2000, Delacorte $15.95 (0-385-32141-4). 176pp. Set in Ireland at the time of the great famine, 12-year-old Nory must fight starvation as well as care for her younger brother. (Rev: BL 9/15/00*; HB 1–2/01; HBG 3/01; SLJ 8/00)

9095 Goodman, Joan E. *The Winter Hare* (4–8). Illus. 1996, Houghton $15.95 (0-395-78569-3). 240pp. In 12th-century England, Will becomes a page to the wicked Earl Aubrey. (Rev: BCCB 2/97; BL 11/15/96; SLJ 11/96)

9096 Graham, Harriet. *A Boy and His Bear* (4–6). 1996, Simon & Schuster $16.00 (0-689-80943-3). 196pp. In Elizabethan England, Dickon is determined to save his pet bear from being killed in a bear-baiting competition. (Rev: BCCB 2/97; BL 10/15/96; SLJ 11/96*)

9097 Graves, Robert. *An Ancient Castle* (4–6). Illus. by Elizabeth Graves. 1991, Michael Kesend paper $8.95 (0-935576-33-9). 72pp. A novel of heroes, villains, and buried treasures set in pre-World War I Britain.

9098 Harrison, Cora. *The Famine Secret* (5–7). Illus. by Orla Roche. Series: Drumshee Timeline. 1998, Irish American paper $6.95 (0-86327-649-0). 128pp. In 1847 the four McMahon children are orphaned and sent to an Irish workhouse, but their determination prevails and they are soon plotting to regain their home. (Rev: SLJ 12/98)

9099 Harrison, Cora. *The Secret of Drumshee Castle* (5–7). Illus. by Orla Roche. Series: Drumshee Timeline. 1998, Irish American paper $6.95 (0-86327-632-6). 128pp. Grace Barry, the orphaned heiress to a castle in Ireland during Elizabethan times, flees to England to escape threats by her acquisitive guardians. (Rev: SLJ 12/98)

9100 Harrison, Cora. *The Secret of the Seven Crosses* (4–7). Illus. 1998, Wolfhound paper $6.95 (0-86327-616-4). 128pp. In medieval Ireland, three youngsters hope to find hidden treasure by examining sources in their monastery library. Preceded by *Nuala and Her Secret Wolf* and followed by *The Secret of Drumshee Castle*. (Rev: BL 12/15/98)

9101 Haugaard, Erik C. *A Boy's Will* (4–6). Illus. by Troy Howell. 1983, Houghton paper $6.95 (0-395-54962-0). A novel set on a coastal Irish island during the American Revolution.

9102 Horowitz, Anthony. *The Devil and His Boy* (5–8). 2000, Putnam $15.99 (0-399-23432-2). 128pp. In Elizabethan England, young Tom Falconer, a boy of the streets, ends up saving his queen. (Rev: BCCB 3/00; BL 1/1–15/00; HBG 10/00; SLJ 4/00)

9103 Howard, Ellen. *The Gate in the Wall* (5–7). 1999, Simon & Schuster $16.00 (0-689-82295-2). 160pp. In Victorian England, 10-year-old orphan Emma escapes the drudgery of factory work and gets a job on a canal boat where she helps load the cargo. (Rev: BCCB 5/99; BL 2/15/99; HB 3–4/99; HBG 10/99; SLJ 3/99)

9104 Kirwan, Anna. *Juliet: A Dream Takes Flight* (3–6). Illus. by Lynne Marshall. Series: Girlhood Journeys. 1996, Simon & Schuster $13.00 (0-689-81137-3); paper $5.99 (0-689-80983-2). 71pp. Set in England in 1339, this story tells of the place of women and their difficulties as seen through the experiences of young Juliet. (Rev: BCCB 11/96; SLJ 9/96)

9105 Lasky, Kathryn. *Elizabeth I: Red Rose of the House of Tudor* (4–7). Series: Royal Diaries. 1999, Scholastic $10.95 (0-590-68484-1). 192pp. Told in diary form, this is a fictionalized account of Elizabeth I's childhood after her mother was killed and she lived with her father, Henry VIII, and Catherine Parr. (Rev: BCCB 12/99; BL 9/15/99; HBG 3/00; SLJ 10/99)

9106 Lawrence, Iain. *The Smugglers* (5–8). 1999, Delacorte $15.95 (0-385-32663-7). 178pp. In this continuation of *The Wreckers,* 16-year-old John Spencer faces more adventures aboard the *Dragon,* where he faces powerful enemies and must bring the ship safely to port. (Rev: BCCB 7–8/99; BL 4/1/99*; HB 5–6/99; HBG 10/99; SLJ 6/99)

9107 Lawrence, Iain. *The Wreckers* (5–8). 1998, Delacorte $15.95 (0-385-32535-5). 191pp. In this historical novel, young John Spencer narrowly escapes with his life after the ship on which he is traveling is wrecked off the Cornish coast, lured to its destruction by a gang seeking to plunder its cargo. (Rev: BCCB 6/98; BL 6/1–15/98*; HB 7–8/98*; HBG 10/98)

9108 McAllister, Margaret. *Hold My Hand and Run* (4–6). 2000, Dutton $15.99 (0-525-46391-7). 160pp. In 17th-century England, a 13-year-old girl runs away from the impossible conditions in the home of her harsh aunt only to find more hardship on the road. (Rev: BCCB 9/00; BL 4/1/00; HBG 10/00; SLJ 7/00)

9109 MacDonald, George. *Sir Gibbie* (4–6). 1987, Sunrise $27.50 (0-940652-55-2). The story of a Scottish waif and the triumph of love over hardship.

9110 Mayer, Marianna. *The Prince and the Pauper* (3–5). Illus. 1999, Dial $17.99 (0-8037-2099-8). 48pp. In picture-book format, this is a retelling of the Mark Twain story of two look-alike boys, one a prince and the other a pauper, who switch places in 16th-century England. (Rev: BL 11/1/99; HBG 10/00; SLJ 11/99)

9111 Merrill, Linda, and Sarah Ridley. *The Princess and the Peacocks: Or, The Story of the Room* (4–6). Illus. by Tennessee Dixon. 1993, Hyperion LB $15.49 (1-56282-328-0). 32pp. For older readers, this fictionalized account tells how the painter Whistler decorated his famous Peacock Room. (Rev: BL 6/1–15/93; SLJ 8/93)

9112 Meyer, Carolyn. *Beware, Princess Elizabeth* (5–8). Series: Young Royals. 2001, Harcourt $17.00 (0-15-202659-2). 224pp. A first-person account of the youth of Elizabeth I, whose mother was murdered by her father, Henry VIII, and whose life is surrounded with intrigue after Henry's death. (Rev: BL 3/1/01)

9113 Morris, Gerald. *The Squire, His Knight, and His Lady* (5–9). 1999, Houghton $15.00 (0-395-91211-3). 240pp. This is a retelling, from the perspective of a knight's squire, of the classic story of Sir Gawain and the Green Knight. (Rev: BL 5/1/99; HBG 10/99; SLJ 5/99)

9114 Morris, Gerald. *The Squire's Tale* (5–9). 1998, Houghton $15.00 (0-395-86959-5). 212pp. Terence, a 14-year-old boy, becomes Gawain's squire and helps him earn his knighthood and a place at the Round Table. (Rev: HB 7–8/98; SLJ 7/98)

9115 O'Brien, Patrick. *The Making of a Knight: How Sir James Earned His Armor* (3–6). Illus. 1998, Charlesbridge $15.95 (0-88106-354-1); paper $6.95 (0-88106-355-X). 32pp. This novel traces the studies, training, and experiences of young James and his journey from page to squire and finally to knight in medieval England. (Rev: BL 8/98; HBG 3/99; SLJ 9/98)

9116 Osborne, Mary Pope. *Kate and the Beanstalk* (PS–3). Illus. by Giselle Potter. 2000, Atheneum $16.00 (0-689-82550-1). 40pp. Kate, the daughter of a knight killed by the giant, is the heroine of this delightful version of Jack and the Beanstalk. (Rev: BCCB 1/01; BL 11/15/00*; HBG 3/01; SLJ 10/00) [398.2]

9117 Pierce, Tamora. *Page: Protector of the Small* (5–8). 2000, Random $16.00 (0-679-88915-9). 240pp. After successfully passing her first year of knight's training, Keladry moves on to the next three years as a page. (Rev: BCCB 9/00; BL 8/00; HBG 10/00; SLJ 8/00)

9118 Platt, Richard. *Castle Diary: The Journal of Tobias Burgess, Page* (3–5). Illus. 1999, Candlewick $21.99 (0-7636-0489-5). 64pp. In 1285 Tobias, an 11-year-old who is spending a year as a page at his uncle's castle, keeps a diary of the events he witnesses and his general impressions. (Rev: BCCB 12/99; BL 11/15/99; HBG 3/00; SLJ 12/99*)

9119 Pyle, Howard. *Men of Iron* (5–8). Adapted by Earle Hitchner. Illus. 1930, Troll paper $5.95 (0-8167-1872-5). 48pp. Brave deeds and knightly adventure in England — an old favorite.

9120 Robins, Deri, and Jim Robins. *The Stone in the Sword: The Quest for a Stolen Emerald* (2–4). Illus. 1998, Candlewick $12.99 (0-7636-0313-9). 32pp. This oversize volume with illustrations, which contain hidden visual clues, is set in the Middle Ages and tells of a valuable emerald that is missing from a knight's sword. (Rev: BL 4/1/98; HBG 10/98; SLJ 7/98)

9121 Rosen, Sidney, and Dorothy S. Rosen. *The Magician's Apprentice* (5–8). 1994, Carolrhoda LB $21.27 (0-87614-809-7). 155pp. An orphaned 15-year-old boy is sent by the Inquisition to spy on the English scientist Roger Bacon to see if he is performing black magic. (Rev: BL 5/1/94; SLJ 6/94)

9122 Schmidt, Gary D. *Anson's Way* (5–9). 1999, Clarion $16.00 (0-395-91529-5). 224pp. When young Anson Granville is sent from England to Ireland as a drummer boy in the Staffordshire Fencibles, he realizes the injustices that the British are perpetrating in Ireland. (Rev: BL 4/1/99*; HBG 10/99; SLJ 4/99)

9123 Snicket, Lemony. *The Austere Academy* (4–6). Illus. Series: Unfortunate Events. 2000, HarperTrophy LB $14.89 (0-06-028884-0). 240pp. The Baudelaire orphans endure horrible hardships when they enroll as students at Prufrock Academy, where their only friends — the Quagmire orphans — are kidnapped by wicked Count Olaf. (Rev: BL 10/15/00)

9124 Sturtevant, Katherine. *At the Sign of the Star* (4–8). 2000, Farrar $16.00 (0-374-30449-1). 144pp. Growing up with her bookseller father in London during 1677, high-spirited Meg finds it difficult to adjust when her father remarries. (Rev: BCCB 1/01; BL 10/15/00*; HB 9–10/00; HBG 3/01; SLJ 9/00)

9125 Tomlinson, Theresa. *Child of the May* (5–9). 1998, Orchard LB $16.99 (0-531-33118-0). 120pp. A historical novel, set in the Middle Ages, about forest people and their struggle against FitzRanulf, an evil mercenary. (Rev: HB 11–12/98; HBG 3/99; SLJ 11/98)

9126 Wallace, Barbara Brooks. *Sparrows in the Scullery* (5–7). 1997, Simon & Schuster $15.00 (0-689-81585-9). 160pp. Without explanation, Colley finds himself in an orphan home in this novel set in the London of Dickens. (Rev: BL 9/15/97; HBG 3/98; SLJ 11/97)

9127 Williams, Laura. *The Executioner's Daughter* (5–8). 2000, Holt $15.95 (0-8050-6234-3). 136pp. Set in England during the Middle Ages, this is the story of poor Lily who, after her mother dies, must assume the position of helping her father, an official executioner. (Rev: BCCB 5/00; BL 4/1/00; HBG 10/00)

9128 Wise, William. *Nell of Branford Hall* (4–6). 1999, Dial $16.99 (0-8037-2393-8). 144pp. Set in rural 17th-century England at the time of the bubonic plague, this novel tells of 13-year-old Nell and her adventures. (Rev: BL 11/1/99; HBG 3/00; SLJ 10/99)

9129 Yolen, Jane, ed. *Sherwood: Original Stories from the World of Robin Hood* (4–9). Illus. by Dennis Nolan. 2000, Philomel $19.99 (0-399-23182-X). 134pp. Nine short stories using Robin Hood and his men as the central characters. (Rev: BCCB 9/00; HBG 10/00; SLJ 8/00)

Latin America

9130 Belpré, Pura. *Firefly Summer* (5–7). 1996, Piñata paper $7.95 (1-55885-180-1). 205pp. In this novel set in turn-of-the-century Puerto Rico, two girls uncover the identity of an orphaned boy who has grown up on their finca (estate). (Rev: SLJ 2/97)

9131 Eboch, Chris. *The Well of Sacrifice* (5–8). Illus. 1999, Clarion $16.00 (0-395-90374-2). 240pp. Details of Mayan life come alive in this novel about Eveningstar Macaw and her mission to avenge the death of her brother, Smoke Shell. (Rev: BL 4/1/99; HBG 10/99; SLJ 5/99)

9132 Gantos, Jack. *Jack's New Power: Stories from a Caribbean Year* (5–8). 1995, Farrar $16.00 (0-374-33657-1); paper $4.95 (0-374-43715-7). 214pp. Eight stories about the interesting people Jack meets when his family moves to the Caribbean. A sequel to *Heads or Tales* (1994). (Rev: BCCB 12/95; BL 12/1/95; SLJ 11/95*)

9133 Head, Judith. *Culebra Cut* (4–6). 1995, Carolrhoda LB $21.27 (0-87614-878-X). 153pp. William witnesses the building of the Panama Canal when his doctor father is transferred to the area in 1911. (Rev: BCCB 12/95; BL 11/1/95; SLJ 1/96)

9134 Lattimore, Deborah N. *The Flame of Peace: A Tale of the Aztecs* (4–6). Illus. 1987, HarperCollins paper $7.95 (0-06-443272-6). 48pp. Details about Aztec life are compiled in this folklorelike story. (Rev: BL 11/15/87; SLJ 11/87)

9135 Newman, Shirlee P. *Isabella: A Wish for Miguel* (3–6). Illus. Series: Girlhood Journeys. 1997, Simon & Schuster paper $5.99 (0-689-81572-7). 72pp. In this historical novel set in Peru during Spanish colonial times, Isabella tries to save a young male servant from being sent to work in the mines. (Rev: BL 4/1/98; SLJ 4/98)

9136 O'Dell, Scott. *My Name Is Not Angelica* (5–7). 1989, Houghton $18.00 (0-395-51061-9). 144pp. A fictionalized account of the slave revolt in the Virgin Islands in 1733–34. (Rev: BL 11/15/89*)

9137 Robinet, Harriette G. *If You Please, President Lincoln* (4–6). 1995, Simon & Schuster $16.00 (0-689-31969-X). 147pp. In 1863, Moses, an escaped slave, is shanghaied to Haiti by a madman who plans to form his own colony there. (Rev: BCCB 9/95; BL 8/95; SLJ 6/95)

9138 Rohmer, Harriet. *Uncle Nacho's Hat* (3–6). Illus. by Mira Reisberg. 1993, Children's Book Pr. $15.95 (0-89239-043-3); paper $7.95 (0-89239-112-X). 32pp. This bilingual book tells a Nicaraguan tale about how hard it is to break habits. A reissue.

9139 Skarmeta, Antonio. *The Composition* (3–5). Trans. by Elisa Amado. Illus. 2000, Douglas & McIntyre $14.95 (0-88899-390-0). 32pp. Set in a police state in Latin America, this picture book tells of a young boy who is under pressure from the police to betray his parents. (Rev: BL 5/1/00; HB 9–10/00; HBG 10/00; SLJ 8/00)

9140 Stanley, Diane. *Elena* (3–5). Illus. 1996, Hyperion LB $14.49 (0-7868-2211-2). 56pp. A daughter recalls the life of her Mexican mother, who defied authority and took her family on a dangerous journey to the United States. (Rev: BCCB 3/96; BL 4/1/96; SLJ 6/96)

9141 Vande Griek, Susan. *A Gift for Ampato* (5–8). Illus. by Mary Jane Gerber. 1999, Groundwood $14.95 (0-88899-358-7). 109pp. Set in the days of the ancient Incas, this story tells about a young girl, Tinta, who has been chosen to be a human sacrifice to the gods. (Rev: BCCB 1/00; SLJ 12/99)

9142 Yolen, Jane. *Encounter* (2–5). Illus. by David Shannon. 1992, Harcourt $16.00 (0-15-225962-7). 32pp. From the viewpoint of a Taino Indian boy, this picture book tells of the first meeting between Native Americans and Columbus. (Rev: BCCB 5/92; BL 3/1/92; SLJ 5/92)

United States

NATIVE AMERICANS

9143 Ackerman, Ned. *Spirit Horse* (4–6). 1998, Scholastic $15.95 (0-590-39650-1). 176pp. Set in the northern Great Plains 200 years old, this is the story of a young Native American, Running Crane, his search for the legendary "spirit horse," and his passage into manhood. (Rev: BCCB 3/98; BL 6/1–15/98; HBG 10/98; SLJ 4/98)

9144 Armstrong, Nancy M. *Navajo Long Walk* (4–7). Illus. 1994, Roberts Rinehart paper $8.95 (1-879373-56-4). 120pp. The story of the Long Walk of the Navajo in 1864 and their confinement in an internment camp are vividly told. (Rev: BL 10/1/94; SLJ 1/95)

9145 Bird, E. J. *The Rainmakers* (4–6). Illus. 1993, Carolrhoda LB $21.27 (0-87614-748-1). 120pp. This novel about a young Indian boy and his pet bear is centered around the life of the Anasazi Indians, who disappeared from the Southwest around A.D. 1300. (Rev: BL 6/1–15/93)

9146 Bruchac, Joseph. *A Boy Called Slow: The True Story of Sitting Bull* (5–8). Illus. by Rocco Baviera. 1995, Putnam $15.95 (0-399-22692-3). 32pp. The story of the boyhood of Sitting Bull, who, because of his sluggishness, had been called Slow. (Rev: BCCB 4/95; BL 3/15/95; HB 9–10/95; SLJ 10/95)

9147 Bruchac, Joseph. *Crazy Horse's Vision* (2–4). Illus. by S. D. Nelson. 2000, Lee & Low $16.95 (1-880000-94-6). 40pp. This is the story of how a young Native American boy, nicknamed Curly, gained the name Crazy Horse and became a leader of the Lakota. (Rev: BCCB 9/00; BL 5/15/00; HB 7–8/00; HBG 10/00; SLJ 7/00)

9148 Bruchac, Joseph. *The Heart of a Chief* (5–8). 1998, Dial $15.99 (0-8037-2276-1). 160pp. Chris, an 11-year-old Penacook Indian, fights against three evils that beset his people: racial slurs, alcoholism, and gambling, in this novel about a boy trying to prove his identity. (Rev: BL 10/15/98; HBG 3/99; SLJ 12/98)

9149 Bunting, Eve. *Cheyenne Again* (3–5). Illus. by Irving Toddy. 1995, Clarion $14.95 (0-395-70364-6). 32pp. In the 1880s, a young Cheyenne boy is taken from the reservation and sent to a white boarding school. (Rev: BCCB 9/95; BL 8/95; SLJ 12/95)

9150 Chanin, Michael. *Grandfather Four Winds and Rising Moon* (3–5). Illus. by Sally J. Smith. 1994, H.J. Kramer $14.95 (0-915811-47-2). Grandfather Four Winds introduces young Rising Moon to the sacred "Tree of Our People" to help him stop worrying about the future. (Rev: SLJ 12/94)

9151 Cooper, James Fenimore. *Last of the Mohicans* (3–5). Adapted by Les Martin. Illus. by Shannon Stirnweis. Series: Step-Up Classics. 1993, Random paper $3.99 (0-679-84706-5). 96pp. A simplified version of the Cooper classic that illuminates details and abridges the plot for young readers. (Rev: SLJ 10/93)

9152 Cornelissen, Cornelia. *Soft Rain: A Story of the Cherokee Trail of Tears* (4–7). 1998, Delacorte $14.95 (0-385-32253-4). 115pp. Told from a Cherokee child's point of view, this novel tells how Soft Rain's family was separated, of the brutal roundups by white soldiers, and of the long, forced march west from North Carolina in 1838. (Rev: BL 8/98; HBG 10/99; SLJ 10/98)

9153 Curry, Jane L. *Back in the Beforetime: Tales of the California Indians* (4–6). Illus. by James Watts. 1987, Macmillan $16.00 (0-689-50410-1). 144pp. A loose narrative containing traditional tales from many native tribes of California. (Rev: BCCB 5/87; BL 6/15/87; SLJ 4/87)

9154 Dadey, Debbie. *Cherokee Sister* (4–7). 2000, Delacorte $14.95 (0-385-32703-X). 120pp. In 1838, Cherokees are forced on a terrible march and, by mistake, include a 12-year-old white girl named Allie. (Rev: BL 4/1/00; HBG 3/01; SLJ 4/00)

9155 Dorris, Michael. *Sees Behind Trees* (3–6). 1996, Hyperion LB $15.49 (0-7868-2215-5). 128pp. Set in 16th-century America, this story tells about a young Indian boy who earned the name Sees Behind Trees. (Rev: BCCB 1/97; BL 9/15/96*; HB 9–10/96; SLJ 10/96*)

9156 Duey, Kathleen. *Celou Sudden Shout, Idaho, 1826* (4–8). Series: American Diaries. 1998, Simon & Schuster paper $3.99 (0-689-81622-7). 150pp. Crow Indians kidnap Celou's mother, who is a Shoshone, and Celou follows the raiding party, hoping to effect a rescue. (Rev: SLJ 6/98)

9157 Durrant, Lynda. *The Beaded Moccasins: The Story of Mary Campbell* (5–8). 1998, Clarion $15.00 (0-395-85398-2). 185pp. Based on fact, this is the story of Mary Campbell's first year of captivity with the Delaware Indians in 1759. (Rev: BCCB 5/98; HBG 10/98; SLJ 6/98)

9158 Eckert, Allan W. *Return to Hawk's Hill* (5–7). 1998, Little, Brown $15.95 (0-316-21593-7). 192pp. In this sequel to *Incident at Hawk's Hill*, 7-year-old Ben is cast adrift on a river, is rescued by a Metis youth, and has many adventures before being reunited with his family. (Rev: BCCB 7–8/98; HBG 3/99; SLJ 6/98)

9159 Erdrich, Louise. *The Birchbark House* (4–8). Illus. 1999, Hyperion LB $15.49 (0-7868-2241-4). 235pp. An Ojibwa Indian child living on an island in Lake Superior in 1847 describes the problems that began when white people arrived to take over their land. (Rev: BL 4/1/99; HB 5–6/99; HBG 10/99)

9160 Grutman, Jewel H., and Gay Matthaei. *The Ledgerbook of Thomas Blue Eagle* (4–8). Illus. by Adam Cvijanovic. 1994, Thomasson-Grant $18.95 (1-56566-063-3). 72pp. A young Native American boy attends a white man's school but tries to retain his own identity and culture in this story that takes place in the West 100 years ago. (Rev: SLJ 12/94)

9161 Hamm, Diane J. *Daughter of Suqua* (3–6). 1997, Albert Whitman LB $14.95 (0-8075-1477-2). 153pp. In 1905, Ida's life in the Puget Sound area is changed when the government forces her Indian family to relocate. (Rev: BL 9/1/97; SLJ 10/97)

9162 Harrell, Beatrice O. *Longwalker's Journey: A Novel of the Choctaw Trail of Tears* (3–6). Illus. 1999, Dial $15.99 (0-8037-2380-6). 144pp. Ten-year old Minko Ushi, a Choctaw, takes comfort in the fact that his faithful pony is following him and his people while they are enduring the hardships of the forced march from their Mississippi homes to Oklahoma in 1831. (Rev: BL 3/1/99; HBG 10/99; SLJ 4/99)

9163 Hirschfelder, Arlene, and Beverly R. Singer, eds. *Rising Voices: Writings of Young Native Americans* (5–8). 1992, Macmillan $14.00 (0-684-19207-

1). 115pp. This anthology of poems, stories, songs, and essays presents the writings of modern young Native Americans. (Rev: BCCB 9/92; SLJ 12/92*)

9164 Hudson, Jan. *Sweetgrass* (5–8). 1989, Scholastic paper $3.99 (0-590-43486-1). 160pp. A description of the culture of the Dakota Indians in the 1830s. (Rev: BCCB 4/89; BL 4/1/89; SLJ 4/89)

9165 Hunter, Sara H. *The Unbreakable Code* (2–4). Illus. by Julia Miner. 1996, Northland LB $15.95 (0-87358-638-7). A Navajo man reassures his grandson that he will adjust successfully to a move off the reservation with his mother and new stepfather. (Rev: SLJ 8/96)

9166 Keehn, Sally M. *I Am Regina* (5–8). 1991, Putnam $16.99 (0-399-21797-5). 219pp. Set in the mid-18th century, this is the story of a young girl's years of captivity by Indians. (Rev: SLJ 6/91)

9167 Lunge-Larsen, Lise, and Margi Preus. *The Legend of the Lady Slipper: An Ojibwe Tale* (PS–3). Illus. by Andrea Arroyo. 1999, Houghton $15.00 (0-395-90512-5). 32pp. An Ojibwa tale about how a young girl's moccasins are turned into the plant known as lady slippers, as a reward for her saving her village from a plague. (Rev: BCCB 7–8/99; BL 4/15/99; HBG 10/99; SLJ 5/99) [398.2]

9168 McLain, Gary. *The Indian Way: Learning to Communicate with Mother Earth* (3–6). Illus. by Michael Taylor. 1990, John Muir paper $9.95 (0-945465-73-4). 114pp. Stories told by an Indian grandfather, all with ecological themes. (Rev: BCCB 3/91; BL 12/1/90)

9169 Marchand, Peter. *What Good Is a Cactus?* (3–5). Illus. by Craig Brown. 1994, Roberts Rinehart paper $7.95 (1-879373-83-1). Through talking to a wise Native American and observing nature, a scientist realizes the importance of all living things and the role each plays. (Rev: SLJ 11/94)

9170 Mead, Alice. *Crossing the Starlight Bridge* (3–5). 1994, Bradbury LB $15.00 (0-02-765950-X). 128pp. Rayanne, a young Penobscot girl, gets inspiration from her Gram when the youngster leaves the reservation on a Maine Island and goes to live on the mainland. (Rev: BCCB 6/94; BL 6/1–15/94*; HB 9–10/94; SLJ 6/94)

9171 Nikcolai, Margaret. *Kitaq Goes Ice Fishing* (2–4). Illus. by David Rubin. 1998, Alaska Northwest $15.95 (0-88240-504-7). 32pp. An advanced picture book, set in Alaska, about the first ice-fishing experience of young Kitaq and how he catches enough fish to feed his family. (Rev: BCCB 1/99; BL 11/15/98; HBG 3/99; SLJ 1/99)

9172 Osborne, Mary Pope. *Standing in the Light: The Captive Diary of Catharine Carey Logan* (3–6). Illus. Series: Dear America. 1998, Scholastic $9.95 (0-590-13462-0). 192pp. After 13-year-old Caty and her younger brother are captured by Lenape Indians in rural Pennsylvania in 1763, they gradually learn to appreciate the values in this foreign culture. (Rev: BL 10/15/98; HBG 3/99; SLJ 1/99)

9173 Raczek, Linda Theresa. *Rainy's Powwow* (3–5). Illus. by Gary Bennett. 1999, Northland $15.95 (0-87358-686-7). 32pp. Lorraine is seeking to develop her own special dance at the powwow,

when an eagle feather changes her hopes. (Rev: BL 4/1/99; HBG 10/99; SLJ 6/99)

9174 Richter, Conrad. *Light in the Forest* (6–8). Illus. by Warren Chappell. 1966, Fawcett paper $5.99 (0-449-70437-8). A young white boy is captured by Indians and, after becoming a true tribe member, is suddenly returned to his parents.

9175 Rinaldi, Ann. *My Heart Is on the Ground: The Diary of Nannie Little Rose, a Sioux Girl* (4–6). Illus. 1999, Scholastic $10.95 (0-590-14922-9). 208pp. Told in diary entries, this is the story of 12-year-old Nannie Little Rose, a Sioux girl, and her life in a Pennsylvania boarding school for Indian children in 1897–98. (Rev: BL 4/1/99; SLJ 4/99)

9176 Rodolph, Stormy. *Quest for Courage* (4–7). Illus. by Paulette L. Lambert. 1993, Roberts Rinehart paper $8.95 (1-879373-57-2). 104pp. A boy nicknamed Lame Bear because of the injury that made him a cripple is not able to join hunting parties with his friends. (Rev: BL 3/15/94)

9177 Roop, Peter. *The Buffalo Jump* (2–4). Illus. by Bill Farnsworth. 1996, Northland LB $14.95 (0-87358-616-6). Little Blaze, a Native American boy, saves his older brother's life during a buffalo hunt. (Rev: SLJ 2/97)

9178 Santiago, Chiori. *Home to Medicine Mountain* (3–6). Illus. by Judith Lowry. 1998, Children's Book Pr. $15.95 (0-89239-155-3). 32pp. In the 1930s, two Native American children are separated from their families and forced to attend a government-run boarding house far from their home. (Rev: BL 8/98; HBG 3/99; SLJ 11/98)

9179 Stewart, Elisabeth J. *On the Long Trail Home* (5–7). 1994, Clarion $15.00 (0-395-68361-0). 106pp. A Cherokee girl escapes from the Trail of Tears and makes her way back to the Appalachian Mountains during the 1830s. (Rev: BCCB 12/94; BL 10/15/94; SLJ 12/94)

9180 Strasser, Todd. *The Diving Bell* (4–7). Illus. 1992, Scholastic $13.95 (0-590-44620-7). 192pp. When Spanish ships ladened with gold sink close to their island, some natives try to salvage them in this story set in the New World during the Spanish conquest. (Rev: SLJ 6/92)

9181 Tapahonso, Luci. *Songs of Shiprock Fair* (2–4). Illus. by Anthony Chee Emerson. 1999, Kiva $15.95 (1-885772-11-4). This is the story of the oldest fair in the Navajo Nation at Shiprock, New Mexico, as seen through the eyes of a little girl who experiences it from the early preparations to the ceremonial dances on the last night. (Rev: HBG 3/00; SLJ 4/00)

9182 Turner, Ann. *The Girl Who Chased Away Sorrow: The Diary of Sarah Nita, a Navajo Girl* (5–8). Illus. 1999, Scholastic $10.95 (0-590-97216-2). 208pp. In diary form, this novel tells of a young Navajo girl, the Long Walk in 1864, and the settlement her people eventually reached with the white man. (Rev: BL 11/15/99; HBG 3/00; SLJ 2/00)

9183 Vick, Helen H. *Shadow* (5–7). Series: Courage of the Stone. 1998, Roberts Rinehart $15.95 (1-57098-218-X); paper $9.95 (1-57098-195-7). 122pp. Shadow, an independent Pueblo Indian girl in pre-Columbian Arizona, leaves her home to rescue her father. (Rev: SLJ 10/98)

9184 Von Ahnen, Katherine. *Heart of Naosaqua* (4–6). Illus. 1996, Roberts Rinehart paper $9.95 (1-57098-010-1). 160pp. In 1823, Naosaqua and her people, the Mesquakie Indians, must find a new home. (Rev: BL 7/96)

COLONIAL PERIOD

9185 Borden, Louise. *Sleds on Boston Common: A Story of the American Revolution* (3–5). Illus. 2000, Simon & Schuster $17.00 (0-689-82812-8). 40pp. Just before the Revolution, 9-year-old Henry Price and his brothers confront British soldiers on Boston Common and ask them to move so they can use the sled runs. (Rev: BCCB 7–8/00; BL 7/00; HB 11–12/00; HBG 3/01; SLJ 12/00)

9186 Bulla, Clyde Robert. *A Lion to Guard Us* (3–6). Illus. by Michele Chessare. 1981, Harper-Collins LB $14.89 (0-690-04097-0); paper $4.95 (0-06-440333-5). 128pp. Three motherless children sail for America to be united with their father in the Jamestown, Virginia, colony.

9187 Collier, James Lincoln. *The Corn Raid: A Story of the Jamestown Settlement* (5–9). 2000, Jamestown paper $5.95 (0-8092-0619-6). 142pp. History and fiction mix in this adventure tale set in the Jamestown settlement and featuring a 12-year-old indentured servant and his cruel master. (Rev: SLJ 4/00)

9188 Curry, Jane L. *A Stolen Life* (5–8). 1999, Simon & Schuster $16.00 (0-689-82932-9). 208pp. A young Scottish teenager is kidnapped in 1758 and sent to America where she has a number of adventures before returning home. (Rev: BCCB 11/99; BL 11/1/99; HBG 3/00; SLJ 11/99)

9189 Dalgliesh, Alice. *Courage of Sarah Noble* (3–5). Illus. by Leonard Weisgard. 1954, Macmillan $15.99 (0-684-18830-9); paper $4.99 (0-689-71540-4). 64pp. The true story of a brave little girl who in 1707 went with her father into the wilds of Connecticut.

9190 Duey, Kathleen. *Sarah Anne Hartford* (4–7). Series: American Diaries. 1996, Simon & Schuster paper $4.50 (0-689-80384-2). 137pp. A story set in Puritan New England about two girls who are placed in a pillory for playing on the Sabbath. (Rev: BCCB 5/96; BL 5/15/96; HB 9–10/96; SLJ 6/96)

9191 Durrant, Lynda. *Echohawk* (5–9). 1996, Clarion $14.95 (0-395-74430-X). Raised by Mohican Indians after the death of his family in 1738, Jonathan Starr, renamed Echohawk, is eventually sent to a white teacher to learn English and become reacquainted with his true heritage. (Rev: BL 9/1/99)

9192 Durrant, Lynda. *Turtle Clan Journey* (5–9). 1999, Clarion $15.00 (0-395-90369-6). 192pp. In this sequel to *Echohawk,* Jonathan is forced to leave the Indians who raised him and is sent to live in Albany with an aunt he doesn't know. (Rev: BL 5/1/99; HBG 10/99; SLJ 6/99)

9193 Edmonds, Walter. *The Matchlock Gun* (5–7). Illus. by Paul Lantz. 1941, Putnam $16.99 (0-399-

21911-0). 64pp. Exciting, true story of a courageous boy who protected his mother and sister from the Indians of the Hudson Valley. Newbery Medal winner, 1942.

9194 Field, Rachel. *Calico Bush* (5–7). Illus. by Allen Louis. 1987, Macmillan $16.00 (0-02-734610-2); Bantam paper $4.99 (0-440-40368-5). 224pp. This 1932 Newbery Honor Book is an adventure story of a French girl "loaned" to a family of American pioneers in Maine in the 1740s.

9195 Forrester, Sandra. *Wheel of the Moon* (5–8). 2000, HarperCollins LB $15.89 (0-06-029203-2). 176pp. The story of Pen, a 14-year-old orphan, who is kidnapped from the streets of London and shipped to Virginia where she is sold at auction as an indentured servant. (Rev: BL 11/15/00; HBG 3/01)

9196 Harness, Cheryl. *Three Young Pilgrims* (3–5). Illus. by author. 1992, Macmillan paper $16.00 (0-02-742643-2). 40pp. This is a fictionalized account of the voyage of the Pilgrims as experienced by three children. (Rev: SLJ 9/92)

9197 Hermes, Patricia. *Our Strange New Land: Elizabeth's Diary, Jamestown, Virginia, 1609* (3–5). Series: My America. 2000, Scholastic $8.95 (0-439-11208-7). Told in a diary format, this book describes how 9-year-old Elizabeth and other colonists adjust to the weather and other trying conditions in the Jamestown Colony. (Rev: HBG 10/00; SLJ 8/00)

9198 Hildick, E. W. *Hester Bidgood: Investigatrix of Evill Deedes* (4–6). 1994, Macmillan paper $14.95 (0-02-743966-6). 160pp. Two young residents in a 17th-century New England village set out to find who branded a cat with the sign of the cross. (Rev: BCCB 12/94; BL 11/15/94; SLJ 12/94)

9199 Hoobler, Dorothy, and Thomas Hoobler. *Priscilla Foster: The Story of a Salem Girl* (3–6). Illus. 1997, Silver Burdett LB $17.95 (0-382-39640-5); paper $4.95 (0-382-39641-3). 128pp. A grandmother takes her granddaughter to Salem, Massachusetts, and tells her about the witch trials of 1692. (Rev: BL 8/97; SLJ 8/97)

9200 Howard, Ginger. *William's House* (K–3). Illus. by Larry Day. 2001, Millbrook LB $22.90 (0-7613-1674-4). 32pp. An informative story that describes how a colonist built a house like the one he left behind in England and gradually had to change and modify it to adjust to a new climate and environment. (Rev: BL 3/15/01*; SLJ 3/01)

9201 Kirkpatrick, Katherine. *Trouble's Daughter: The Story of Susanna Hutchinson, Indian Captive* (5–8). 1998, Delacorte $14.95 (0-385-32600-9). 247pp. Based on fact, this outstanding historical novel recounts Susanna Hutchinson's life after she is kidnapped by Lenape Indians who massacre her family on Long Island in 1663. (Rev: BL 8/98*; HBG 3/99)

9202 Lasky, Kathryn. *A Journey to the New World: The Diary of Remember Patience Whipple* (4–7). Series: Dear America. 1996, Scholastic $10.95 (0-590-50214-X). 144pp. Using diary entries as a format, this is the story of 12-year-old Mem Whipple, her journey on the *Mayflower,* and her first year in the New World. (Rev: BCCB 10/96; HB 9–10/96; SLJ 8/96)

9203 Littlesugar, Amy. *The Spinner's Daughter* (3–5). Illus. 1994, Pippin LB $14.95 (0-945912-22-6). 32pp. In her strict Puritan community in Connecticut, Elspeth is considered sinful because she has a cornhusk doll. (Rev: BL 9/1/94; SLJ 9/94)

9204 Martin, Jacqueline B. *Grandmother Bryant's Pocket* (2–4). Illus. by Petra Mathers. 1996, Houghton $14.95 (0-395-68984-8). 48pp. Set in Maine during 1787, this is the story of how a young girl's grandmother helps her adjust to the death of her dog. (Rev: BCCB 7–8/96; BL 5/15/96; HB 7–8/96; SLJ 6/96*)

9205 Nixon, Joan Lowery. *Ann's Story: 1747* (4–6). Series: Young Americans: Colonial Williamsburg. 2000, Delacorte $9.95 (0-385-32673-4). 151pp. Nine-year-old Ann McKenzie, who longs to be a doctor like her father, is caught in troubling events in colonial Williamsburg that result in the burning of the city and a smallpox epidemic. (Rev: HBG 10/00; SLJ 4/00)

9206 Nixon, Joan Lowery. *Caesar's Story: 1759* (4–6). Illus. Series: Young Americans: Colonial Williamsburg. 2000, Random $9.95 (0-385-32676-9). 144pp. Nine-year-old Caesar realizes the meaning of slavery when he becomes personal servant to Nat, once a playmate, in this novel set in Colonial Williamsburg. (Rev: BL 6/1–15/00; HBG 10/00; SLJ 8/00)

9207 Nixon, Joan Lowery. *Nancy's Story: 1765* (4–6). Series: Young Americans: Colonial Williamsburg. 2000, Delacorte $9.95 (0-385-32679-3). 160pp. Based on fact, this is the story of young Nancy Geddy, daughter of a silversmith in the days immediately preceding the Revolution. (Rev: BL 12/15/00)

9208 Ovecka, Janice. *Cave of Falling Water* (4–8). Illus. by David K. Fadden. 1992, New England Pr. paper $10.95 (0-933050-98-4). 116pp. A cave in the hills of Vermont plays a part in the lives of three girls, one an Indian and one white, both from colonial times, and the last, a contemporary adolescent. (Rev: BL 5/1/93)

9209 Petry, Ann. *Tituba of Salem Village* (6–8). 1988, HarperCollins paper $5.95 (0-06-440403-X). 254pp. The story of the slave Tituba and her husband, John Indian, from the day they were sold in the Barbados until the tragic Salem witchcraft trials.

9210 Pryor, Bonnie. *Thomas in Danger* (4–6). 1999, Morrow $15.00 (0-688-16518-4). 160pp. After discovering a Tory plot, Thomas is kidnapped and left, desperately ill, with Iroquois who nurse him back to health. (Rev: BL 10/1/99; HBG 3/00; SLJ 12/99)

9211 Rinaldi, Ann. *The Journal of Jasper Jonathan Pierce: A Pilgrim Boy, Plymouth, 1620* (4–8). 2000, Scholastic $10.95 (0-590-51078-9). 155pp. This fictionalized account of the Pilgrims in journal format follows the adventures of a 14-year-old indentured servant aboard the *Mayflower* and during his first year in the New World. (Rev: BL 2/15/00; HBG 10/00; SLJ 7/00)

9212 Speare, Elizabeth G. *The Sign of the Beaver* (6–8). 1983, Houghton $16.00 (0-395-33890-5); Dell paper $5.50 (0-440-47900-2). 144pp. In Maine in 1768, Matt, though only 12, must protect his family.

9213 Speare, Elizabeth G. *The Witch of Blackbird Pond* (6–8). 1958, Houghton $16.00 (0-395-07114-3); Dell paper $5.99 (0-440-99577-9). 256pp. Historical romance set in Puritan Connecticut with the theme of witchcraft. Newbery Medal winner, 1959. Also use: *Calico Captive* (1957).

9214 Tripp, Valerie. *Changes for Felicity: A Winter Story* (2–5). Illus. by Dan Andreasen. Series: American Girl. 1992, Pleasant $12.95 (1-56247-038-8); paper $5.95 (1-56247-037-X). 34pp. In this story of a girl who lives in colonial Williamsburg, the father of her best friend is jailed as a Loyalist. Also use: *Felicity Saves the Day: A Summer Story;* and *Happy Birthday, Felicity* (both 1992). (Rev: BL 5/1/92)

9215 Tripp, Valerie. *Felicity Learns a Lesson: A School Story* (3–5). Illus. by Dan Andreasen. Series: American Girl. 1991, Pleasant paper $5.95 (1-56247-007-8). 69pp. Felicity learns to control her temper in this story set in colonial Williamsburg. (Rev: BL 1/1/91; SLJ 1/92)

9216 Tripp, Valerie. *Felicity's Surprise: A Christmas Story* (3–5). Illus. by Dan Andreasen. Series: American Girl. 1991, Pleasant paper $5.95 (1-56247-010-8). 69pp. The family must depend more on Felicity when her mother is ill, in this story of colonial Williamsburg. (Rev: BL 1/1/91; SLJ 1/92)

9217 Waters, Kate. *Mary Geddy's Day: A Colonial Girl in Williamsburg* (3–5). Illus. 1999, Scholastic $16.95 (0-590-92925-9). 40pp. Set in Williamsburg on May 15, 1776, young Mary Geddy is the central character in this description of a day in colonial America. (Rev: BL 10/15/99; HBG 3/00; SLJ 9/99)

9218 Wisler, G. Clifton. *This New Land* (5–8). 1987, Walker LB $14.85 (0-8027-6727-3). Twelve-year-old Richard and his family begin a new life in Plymouth, Massachusetts, in 1620. (Rev: BL 3/15/88)

9219 Wyeth, Sharon D. *Once on This River* (5–8). 1998, Knopf LB $17.99 (0-679-98350-3). 150pp. In this historical novel set in 1760, 11-year-old Monday de Groot accompanies her mother from Madagascar to colonial New York to save her brother who has been wrongfully sold into slavery. (Rev: BCCB 4/98; HBG 10/98; SLJ 4/98)

THE REVOLUTION

9220 Avi. *The Fighting Ground* (5–7). Illus. by Ellen Thompson. 1984, HarperCollins $15.89 (0-397-32074-4); paper $4.95 (0-06-440185-5). 160pp. Thirteen-year-old Jonathan marches off to fight the British.

9221 Banim, Lisa. *Drums at Saratoga* (3–5). Series: Stories of the States. 1993, Silver Moon LB $14.95 (1-881889-20-3). 58pp. Young Nathaniel Phillips and a black servant are captured by the American forces during the Revolutionary War. (Rev: SLJ 10/93)

9222 Banim, Lisa. *The Hessian's Secret Diary* (3–5). Illus. 1997, Silver Moon LB $14.95 (1-881889-86-6). 80pp. In 1776, a young Brooklyn resident helps a wounded Hessian soldier, even though this endangers her family's safety. (Rev: BL 5/1/97; SLJ 4/97)

9223 Banim, Lisa. *A Spy in the King's Colony* (3–5). Illus. by Tatyana Yuditskaya. Series: Mysteries in Time. 1994, Silver Moon $14.95 (1-881889-54-8). 76pp. In 1775, 11-year-old Emily Parker is living in British-occupied Boston, where spies for both sides abound. (Rev: SLJ 7/94)

9224 Berleth, Richard. *Samuel's Choice* (4–6). Illus. by James Watling. 1990, Whitman LB $14.95 (0-8075-7218-7). 40pp. Samuel, 14, is a young black slave in Brooklyn who plays a heroic role in the Battle of Long Island during the American Revolution. (Rev: BCCB 1/91; BL 1/1/91; SLJ 4/91)

9225 Bruchac, Joseph. *The Arrow over the Door* (4–7). Illus. 1998, Dial $15.99 (0-8037-2078-5). 96pp. Two boys, one a Quaker and the other a Native American, share the narration of this story that takes place immediately before the Battle of Saratoga in 1777. (Rev: BCCB 4/98; BL 2/15/98; HBG 10/98; SLJ 4/98)

9226 Collier, James Lincoln, and Christopher Collier. *My Brother Sam Is Dead* (6–8). 1984, Simon & Schuster LB $17.00 (0-02-722980-7); Scholastic paper $4.50 (0-590-42792-X). 224pp. The story, based partially on fact, of a Connecticut family divided in loyalties during the Revolutionary War.

9227 Denenberg, Barry. *The Journal of William Thomas Emerson: A Revolutionary War Patriot* (4–7). Illus. 1998, Scholastic $9.95 (0-590-31350-9). 160pp. This historical novel consists of journal entries kept in 1774 by 12-year-old Will, who has become involved with people in the revolutionary movement. (Rev: BCCB 11/98; BL 11/1/98; HBG 3/99; SLJ 5/99)

9228 Durrant, Lynda. *Betsy Zane, the Rose of Fort Henry* (5–8). 2000, Clarion $15.00 (0-395-97899-8). 176pp. Toward the end of the Revolutionary War, Betsy sets out alone from Philadelphia to rejoin her five brothers in western Virginia. (Rev: BCCB 10/00; BL 9/15/00; HBG 3/01)

9229 Fleming, Candace. *The Hatmaker's Sign: A Story by Benjamin Franklin* (3–5). Illus. by Robert Andrew Parker. 1998, Orchard $16.95 (0-531-30075-7). 40pp. When Jefferson complains to Dr. Franklin about the mutilation of his Declaration of Independence by Congress, the good doctor tells him a comforting parable. (Rev: BL 2/15/98; HB 3–4/98; HBG 10/98; SLJ 4/98)

9230 Forbes, Esther. *Johnny Tremain: A Novel for Old and Young* (6–8). Illus. by Lynd Ward. 1943, Houghton $15.00 (0-395-06766-9); Dell paper $6.50 (0-440-94250-0). 272pp. Story of a young silversmith's apprentice, who plays an important part in the American Revolution. Newbery Medal winner, 1944.

9231 Fritz, Jean. *The Cabin Faced West* (3–6). Illus. by Feodor Rojankovsky. 1958, Putnam $15.99 (0-399-23223-0); Puffin paper $5.99 (0-14-032256-6).

128pp. The western Pennsylvania territory of 1784 is a very lonely place for Ann until General Washington comes to visit.

9232 Fritz, Jean. *George Washington's Breakfast* (3–5). Illus. by Paul Galdone. 1998, Putnam paper $5.99 (0-698-11611-9). 43pp. George W. Allen knows all there is to know about our first president — except what he had for breakfast.

9233 Gauch, Patricia L. *This Time, Tempe Wick?* (2–5). 1992, Putnam $13.95 (0-399-21880-7). 48pp. Tempe (Temperance) Wick helped the Revolutionary soldiers who camped on her farm in New Jersey in 1780, until they tried to steal her horse, and then she got mad.

9234 Goodman, Joan E. *Hope's Crossing* (5–8). 1998, Houghton $15.00 (0-395-86195-0). 160pp. Kidnapped by British loyalists during the Revolution, Hope must try to escape and find her way home. (Rev: BCCB 7–8/98; BL 6/1–15/98; HBG 10/98; SLJ 5/98)

9235 Gregory, Kristiana. *Five Smooth Stones: Hope's Diary* (3–5). Series: My America. 2001, Scholastic $8.95 (0-439-14827-8). 112pp. Set in 1776 Philadelphia and told in diary format, this novel tells of a 9-year-old girl and her family's problems at the beginning of the Revolutionary War. (Rev: BL 1/1–15/01)

9236 Gregory, Kristiana. *The Winter of Red Snow: The Revolutionary War Diary of Abigail Jane Stewart* (5–8). Series: Dear America. 1996, Scholastic $10.95 (0-590-22653-3). 176pp. The hardships faced by the Revolutionary Army at Valley Forge in 1777–1778 are seen through the eyes of young girl who lives close to the encampment. (Rev: BCCB 10/96; HB 9–10/96; SLJ 9/96)

9237 Harrah, Madge. *My Brother, My Enemy* (4–7). 1997, Simon & Schuster paper $16.00 (0-689-80968-9). 144pp. Using Bacon's Rebellion in 1676 as a background, this novel involves a 14-year-old whose family is killed during an Indian raid on their cabin. (Rev: BCCB 7–8/97; BL 5/1/97; SLJ 7/97)

9238 Jacobs, Paul S. *James Printer: A Novel of Rebellion* (5–8). 1997, Scholastic $15.95 (0-590-16381-7). 224pp. During colonial times, an Indian boy who was raised in Cambridge, Massachusetts, agonizes over his divided loyalties when the English and the Indians go to war. (Rev: BCCB 3/97; BL 4/15/97; SLJ 6/97)

9239 Kirkpatrick, Katherine. *Redcoats and Petticoats* (3–5). Illus. by Ronald Himler. 1999, Holiday $15.95 (0-8234-1416-7). 32pp. When 13-year-old Thomas Strong is sent on some unusual errands, he is unaware at first that he is part of a spy network conveying messages to the forces of George Washington during the Revolutionary War. (Rev: BL 3/1/99; HBG 10/99; SLJ 4/99)

9240 Lunn, Janet. *The Hollow Tree* (5–9). 2000, Viking $15.99 (0-670-88949-0). 208pp. Torn between feelings for both the rebels and the Tories, Phoebe finally decides to join the refugees heading to Canada and safety. (Rev: BCCB 6/00; HBG 10/00; SLJ 6/00)

9241 Massie, Elizabeth. *Patsy's Discovery* (3–5). 1997, Pocket paper $3.99 (0-671-00132-9). 135pp. Thirteen-year-old Patsy Black is growing up in Philadelphia during the Continental Congress meetings of 1776. (Rev: BL 12/1/97; SLJ 8/97)

9242 Moore, Ruth Nulton. *Distant Thunder* (5–8). Illus. by Allan Eitzen. 1991, Herald Pr. paper $6.99 (0-8361-3557-1). 160pp. During the Revolution, when wounded Americans are sent to Pennsylvania to recover, young Kate experiences the horrors of war. (Rev: BCCB 1/92; SLJ 1/92)

9243 Moss, Marissa. *Emma's Journal* (3–5). Illus. Series: Young America Voices. 1999, Harcourt $15.00 (0-15-202025-X). 56pp. Set in journal format, this novel tells the story of 10-year-old Emma who helps the patriots in revolutionary Boston. (Rev: BL 9/15/99; HBG 3/00; SLJ 12/99)

9244 Myers, Anna. *The Keeping Room* (4–7). 1997, Walker $15.95 (0-8027-8641-3). 144pp. In this tale set during the Revolutionary War, Joseph's home is taken over by the Redcoats after his father goes off to war. (Rev: BL 11/1/97; HBG 3/98; SLJ 12/97)

9245 O'Dell, Scott. *Sarah Bishop* (5–8). 1980, Houghton $16.00 (0-395-29185-2); Scholastic paper $4.99 (0-590-44651-7). 240pp. A first-person narrative of a girl who lived through the American Revolution and its toll of suffering and misery. (Rev: BL 2/15/98; HBG 10/98; SLJ 3/98)

9246 Pryor, Bonnie. *Thomas* (4–6). Illus. by Bert Dodson. Series: American Adventures. 1998, Morrow $15.00 (0-688-15669-X). 144pp. Set in Pennsylvania during the Revolutionary War, this is the story of 10-year-old Thomas Bowden and the spying mission in which he becomes involved. (Rev: HBG 3/99; SLJ 10/98)

9247 Rinaldi, Ann. *Cast Two Shadows* (5–9). Series: Great Episodes. 1998, Harcourt $16.00 (0-15-200881-0). 288pp. When the Revolutionary War reaches her home in Camden, South Carolina, life changes for 14-year-old Caroline Whitaker, whose family is divided in its allegiances. (Rev: BCCB 9/98; HBG 10/99; SLJ 9/98)

9248 Roop, Peter, and Connie Roop. *An Eye for an Eye: A Story of the Revolutionary War* (5–9). 2000, Jamestown paper $5.95 (0-8092-0628-5). 168pp. During the Revolutionary War, Samantha, disguised as boy, sets out to save her brother who is being held prisoner on a British ship. (Rev: BCCB 7–8/00; SLJ 4/00)

9249 Schurfranz, Vivian. *A Message for General Washington* (3–4). Illus. by John F. Martin. Series: Stories of the States. 1998, Silver Moon LB $13.95 (1-881889-89-0). 92pp. Hannah, age 12, undertakes a perilous journey from Yorktown to Williamsburg, where she delivers a message to General Washington. (Rev: HBG 10/98; SLJ 11/98)

9250 Sweetzer, Anna Leah. *Treason Stops at Oyster Bay* (4–6). Illus. 1999, Silver Moon LB $13.95 (1-893110-03-6). 96pp. Sally is attracted to Colonel Simcoe, a British officer billeted in her family's house on Long Island, and must decide if she should pass on vital information she has overheard to her brother who is a Patriot spy. (Rev: BL 8/99; HBG 3/00)

9251 Van Leeuwen, Jean. *Hannah of Fairfield* (3–5). Illus. 1999, Dial LB $14.89 (0-8037-2336-9). 96pp. Set in Fairfield, Connecticut, in the early days of the Revolutionary War, this story involves 9-year-old Hannah, her family, and her older brother who leaves to join George Washington's army. (Rev: BL 3/1/99; SLJ 5/99)

9252 Van Leeuwen, Jean. *Hannah's Helping Hands* (2–5). Illus. 1999, Penguin $13.99 (0-8037-2447-0). 96pp. Hannah Perley and her family live in Fairfield, Connecticut, in 1779 when the British attack. (Rev: BL 9/15/99; HBG 3/00; SLJ 11/99)

9253 Van Leeuwen, Jean. *Hannah's Winter of Hope* (4–8). Illus. Series: Pioneer Daughters. 2000, Penguin $13.99 (0-8037-2492-6). 96pp. After the British burn down their home, the Perley family suffers even more privations in this story told from the viewpoint of 11-year-old Hannah Perley. (Rev: BL 8/00; HBG 10/00; SLJ 7/00)

9254 Walker, Sally M. *The 18 Penny Goose* (2–4). Illus. by Ellen Beier. Series: I Can Read. 1998, HarperCollins LB $14.89 (0-06-027557-X). 64pp. In this easy reader based on fact, a little girl is afraid that the British army raiders will eat her pet goose during the Revolutionary War. (Rev: BL 2/1/98; HB 5–6/98; HBG 10/98; SLJ 3/98)

9255 Waters, John F. *Night Raiders Along the Cape* (3–5). Illus. 1998, Silver Moon LB $14.95 (1-881889-85-8). 96pp. Asa rows from his island home to warn the mainlanders of a British plot in this novel set in Massachusetts during the American Revolution. (Rev: BL 2/15/98; HBG 10/98; SLJ 7/98)

THE YOUNG NATION, 1789–1861

9256 Arbuckle, Scott. *Zeb, the Cow's on the Roof Again! And Other Tales of Early Texas Dwellings* (3–7). Illus. by author. 1996, Eakin $17.75 (1-57168-102-7). 128pp. Four youngsters tell about their dwellings in stories that take place at various times in Texas history. (Rev: SLJ 4/97)

9257 Armstrong, Jennifer. *Steal Away* (5–8). 1992, Scholastic paper $3.99 (0-590-46921-5). 224pp. Susannah, who hates slavery, is given a slave when she moves to Virginia to live with her uncle and his family. (Rev: SLJ 2/92)

9258 Auch, Mary Jane. *Frozen Summer* (4–7). 1998, Holt $16.95 (0-8050-4923-1). 202pp. The summer of 1816 for Mem and her family, introduced in *Journey to Nowhere,* is full of problems complicated by several early frosts and Mama's slow descent into madness. (Rev: BCCB 1/99; BL 1/1–15/99; HB 1–2/99; HBG 3/99; SLJ 12/98)

9259 Auch, Mary Jane. *Journey to Nowhere* (4–7). 1997, Holt $16.95 (0-8050-4922-3). 202pp. In 1815, 11-year-old Mem and her family relocate from Connecticut to Genesee County in western New York. (Rev: BCCB 6/97; BL 4/15/97; HB 7–8/97; SLJ 5/97)

9260 Auch, Mary Jane. *The Road to Home* (5–8). 2000, Holt $16.95 (0-8050-4921-5). 216pp. In this sequel to *Journey to Nowhere* and *Frozen Summer,* Mem, now 13, and two siblings live in a boarding house in Rome, New York, while their father goes to work on the building of the Erie Canal. (Rev: BCCB 6/00; BL 4/1/00; HB 7–8/00; HBG 3/01; SLJ 7/00)

9261 Berleth, Richard. *Mary Patten's Voyage* (4–6). Illus. by Ben Otero. 1994, Albert Whitman LB $14.95 (0-8075-4987-8). 40pp. Based on facts involving an 1856 clipper ship race, this is the story of Mary Patten, who took command when her captain husband became ill. (Rev: BCCB 12/94; BL 1/1/95; SLJ 12/94)

9262 Blos, Joan W. *A Gathering of Days: A New England Girl's Journal, 1830–32* (6–8). 1979, Macmillan $15.00 (0-684-16340-3); paper $4.99 (0-689-71419-X). 144pp. A fictional diary kept by 13-year-old Catherine Cabot, who is growing up in the town of Meredith, New Hampshire. Newbery Medal winner, 1980.

9263 Bradley, Kimberly Brubaker. *Weaver's Daughter* (5–7). 2000, Delacorte $14.95 (0-385-32769-2). 166pp. Set in the South in the 1790s, this is the story of 10-year-old Lizzy Baker who suffers from asthma that is so severe that she is sent to live with a family in Charleston, to be near the sea air. (Rev: BCCB 11/00; BL 8/00; HBG 3/01; SLJ 10/00)

9264 Bryant, Louella. *The Black Bonnet* (5–7). 1996, New England Pr. paper $12.95 (1-881535-22-3). 160pp. Two sisters are smuggled out of the South via the Underground Railroad to Burlington, Vermont. (Rev: BL 2/1/97; SLJ 2/97)

9265 Carrick, Carol. *Stay Away from Simon!* (4–6). Illus. by Donald Carrick. 1985, Houghton paper $5.95 (0-89919-849-X). 64pp. Mentally handicapped Simon has a reputation of being dangerous, but Lucy discovers he also has a generous heart in this story set in Martha's Vineyard in the 1830s. (Rev: BCCB 11/85; BL 8/85; SLJ 4/85)

9266 Coleman, Evelyn. *The Foot Warmer and the Crow* (2–5). Illus. by Daniel Minter. 1994, Macmillan paper $14.95 (0-02-722816-9). With the help of a crow, the slave Nezekiah outwits his cruel master and gains his freedom. (Rev: BCCB 12/94; SLJ 11/94)

9267 Collier, James Lincoln, and Christopher Collier. *The Clock* (5–7). Illus. by Maddox Kelly. 1995, Dell paper $4.99 (0-440-40999-3). 176pp. Fifteen-year-old Annie Steele contends with the harsh life of mill work in Connecticut in 1810. (Rev: BCCB 4/92; BL 2/1/92; HB 3–4/92)

9268 Connelly, Bernardine. *Follow the Drinking Gourd: A Story of the Underground Railroad. with CD* (3–7). Illus. by Yvonne Buchanan. 1997, Simon & Schuster paper $22.00 (0-689-80242-0). The infamous days of slavery and the heroism and courage involved in the operation of the Underground Railroad are combined in this story about Mary Prentice and her escape to freedom with her family. (Rev: SLJ 3/98)

9269 Curry, Jane L. *What the Dickens!* (4–6). 1991, Macmillan LB $13.95 (0-689-50524-8). 160pp. It is Pennsylvania in 1842 and 11-year-old Cherry and her twin brother are chasing Charles Dickens to

recover a stolen manuscript. (Rev: BL 10/1/91; SLJ 9/91)

9270 DeFelice, Cynthia. *The Apprenticeship of Lucas Whitaker* (5–8). 1996, Farrar $15.00 (0-374-34669-0). 152pp. In the mid-1800s, orphan Lucas becomes an apprentice to the local dentist/barber/undertaker, Dr. Uriah M. Beecher. (Rev: BCCB 10/96; BL 10/1/96; SLJ 8/96*)

9271 Demas, Corinne. *If Ever I Return Again* (5–8). 2000, HarperCollins LB $15.89 (0-06-028718-7). 224pp. Twelve-year-old Celia describes life aboard a whaling ship in letters home to her cousin. (Rev: BCCB 6/00; BL 4/1/00; HBG 10/00; SLJ 8/00)

9272 Duey, Kathleen. *Evie Peach: St. Louis, 1857* (3–6). Series: American Diaries. 1997, Simon & Schuster paper $4.50 (0-689-81621-9). 144pp. In pre–Civil War St. Louis, freed slaves Evie Peach and her father are saving money to buy the freedom of Evie's mother. (Rev: BL 2/15/98; SLJ 3/98)

9273 Duey, Kathleen, and Karen A. Bale. *Cave-In: St. Claire, Pennsylvania, 1859* (4–6). Series: Survival! 1998, Simon & Schuster paper $3.99 (0-689-82350-9). 158pp. In this survival story set in the coal mines of Pennsylvania during 1859, two boys and their landlady's daughter are trapped underground in a mine after a cave-in. (Rev: SLJ 2/99)

9274 Duey, Kathleen, and Karen A. Bale. *Hurricane: Open Seas, 1844* (5–7). Series: Survival! 1999, Simon & Schuster paper $3.99 (0-689-82544-7). 169pp. This exciting sea story, set in 1844, tells of two youngsters who are on a whaler when a killer hurricane strikes. (Rev: SLJ 8/99)

9275 Forrester, Sandra. *Dust from Old Bones* (5–7). 1999, Morrow $16.00 (0-688-16202-9). 144pp. In this novel set in New Orleans before the Civil War, young Simone resents her mother's strict discipline and instead likes to hang out with an aunt from Paris who persuades her to help two slaves escape. (Rev: BCCB 10/99; BL 8/99; HBG 3/00)

9276 Fox, Paula. *The Slave Dancer* (6–8). Illus. by Eros Keith. 1982, Macmillan $16.95 (0-02-735560-8); Dell paper $5.50 (0-440-96132-7). 192pp. Fourteen-year-old Jessie is kidnapped and press-ganged aboard an American slave ship bound for Africa. Newbery Medal winner, 1974.

9277 Fritz, Jean. *Brady* (4–7). Illus. by Lynd Ward. 1960, Puffin paper $4.99 (0-14-032258-2). 224pp. When Brady discovers his father is an Underground Railroad agent, he learns to control his tongue and form his own opinion about slavery.

9278 Gaeddert, Louann. *Breaking Free* (5–8). 1994, Atheneum paper $16.00 (0-689-31883-9). 144pp. In upstate New York in 1800, orphaned Richard is upset that there are slaves on his uncle's farm and is determined to help one escape. (Rev: BL 4/1/94; HB 9–10/94; SLJ 5/94)

9279 Garland, Sherry. *A Line in the Sand: The Alamo Diary of Lucinda Lawrence* (4–7). Illus. Series: Dear America. 1998, Scholastic $9.95 (0-590-39466-5). 208pp. Lucinda relates events in Gonzales, Texas, in 1835, which led to the Texas War of Independence and to the massacre at the Alamo. (Rev: BL 3/1/99; HBG 3/99; SLJ 1/99)

9280 Givens, Steven J. *Levi Dust: A Tale from the Kerry Patch* (2–4). 1997, New Canaan paper $4.95 (1-889658-07-3). 56pp. Ten-year-old twins get lost on the streets of St. Louis in the 1850s and are brought home by a kindly bell ringer. (Rev: BL 2/1/98)

9281 Greenwood, Barbara. *The Last Safe House: A Story of the Underground Railroad* (3–6). Illus. by Heather Collins. 1998, Kids Can $16.95 (1-55074-507-7); paper $9.95 (1-55074-509-3). 119pp. Using a Canadian family's participation in the Underground Railroad in 1856 as a framework, this book supplies good background on the railroad's organization, accomplishments, and the fight against slavery. (Rev: HBG 3/99; SLJ 1/99)

9282 Gregory, Kristiana. *The Stowaway: A Tale of California Pirates* (4–6). 1995, Scholastic $3.99 (0-590-48822-8). 144pp. Carlito must endure the squalid life of being a pirate's captive in this tale set on the California coast during the early 1800s. (Rev: BCCB 10/95; BL 9/15/95; SLJ 9/95)

9283 Hansen, Joyce. *The Captive* (5–8). 1994, Scholastic $13.95 (0-590-41625-1). 195pp. The exciting story based on fact of a young African boy sold into slavery in Massachusetts and how he eventually escaped. (Rev: BCCB 3/94; HB 1–2/94; 5–6/94; SLJ 1/94)

9284 Hausman, Gerald. *Tom Cringle: Battle on the High Seas* (4–8). Illus. by Tad Hills. 2000, Simon & Schuster $16.95 (0-689-82810-1). 185pp. Set during the War of 1812, this novel tells of a young midshipman who is rescued by a pirate ship when his vessel sinks. (Rev: BCCB 7–8/00; HBG 3/01; SLJ 11/00)

9285 Hermann, Spring. *Seeing Lessons* (4–6). 1998, Holt $15.95 (0-8050-5706-4). 164pp. In this first-person narrative, 10-year-old Abigail Carter leaves her farm near Boston in 1832 to attend Perkins School, the first school for the blind in America. (Rev: BL 12/1/98; HBG 3/99; SLJ 11/99)

9286 Hill, Donna. *Shipwreck Season* (5–8). 1998, Clarion $15.00 (0-395-86614-6). 215pp. In the 1800s, 16-year-old Daniel joins a crew of seamen who patrol America's eastern coastline, rescuing people and cargo from shipwrecks. (Rev: BCCB 7–8/98; HBG 3/99; SLJ 6/98)

9287 Hilts, Len. *Timmy O'Dowd and the Big Ditch: A Story of the Glory Days on the Old Erie Canal* (5–7). 1988, Harcourt $13.95 (0-15-200606-0). 91pp. Timmy and his cousin Dennis don't get along, but when the canals threaten to flood, they realize each other's strengths and stamina. (Rev: BCCB 12/88; BL 10/1/88; SLJ 12/88)

9288 Holland, Isabelle. *The Promised Land* (4–6). 1996, Scholastic $15.95 (0-590-47176-7). 156pp. Orphaned Maggie and Annie, who have been happily living with the Russell family on the Kansas frontier, are visited by an uncle who wants them to come home with him. A sequel to *The Journey Home* (1990). (Rev: BCCB 4/96; BL 4/15/96; SLJ 8/96)

9289 Hooks, William H. *Freedom's Fruit* (2–4). Illus. by James E. Ransome. 1995, Knopf LB $17.99 (0-679-92438-8). 42pp. Using her sorcery and spells, Mama Marina plots to free several slaves, including her daughter, Sheba. (Rev: BL 2/15/96; SLJ 2/96)

9290 Hopkinson, Deborah. *Sweet Clara and the Freedom Quilt* (3–5). Illus. by James E. Ransome. 1993, Knopf LB $16.99 (0-679-92311-X). 36pp. In this picture book for older readers, a slave girl maps out her escape to Canada on a brightly colored quilt. (Rev: BCCB 7–8/93; BL 4/15/93; HB 5–6/93*; SLJ 6/93)

9291 Houston, Gloria. *Bright Freedom's Song: A Story of the Underground Railroad* (4–7). 1998, Harcourt $16.00 (0-15-201812-3). 145pp. A tense, dramatic story about a girl who helps her parents operate a North Carolina station on the Underground Railroad and discovers that her father, a Scottish immigrant, is also a fugitive. (Rev: BCCB 1/99; BL 11/1/98; HBG 3/99; SLJ 12/98)

9292 Jackson, Dave, and Neta Jackson. *The Runaway's Revenge* (4–6). Series: Trailblazer. 1995, Bethany paper $5.99 (1-55661-471-3). 144pp. A novel about the life of John Newton, a slave trader who later became a minister and wrote such hymns as "Amazing Grace." (Rev: BL 1/1–15/96)

9293 Jackson, Dave, and Neta Jackson. *The Thieves of Tyburn Square* (3–6). Series: Trailblazer. 1995, Bethany paper $5.99 (1-55661-470-5). 144pp. In this fictionalized account set in the early 1800s, the Quaker Elizabeth Fry helps two youngsters caught picking pockets. (Rev: BL 3/15/96)

9294 Jakes, John. *Susanna of the Alamo: A True Story* (3–5). Illus. by Paul Bacon. 1986, Harcourt $13.95 (0-15-200592-7); paper $7.00 (0-15-200595-1). 32pp. Only women, children, and slaves were spared by the Mexicans at the battle of the Alamo in 1836, and one, Susanna Dickinson, was spared to inform Sam Houston of the outcome. (Rev: BCCB 6/86; BL 6/15/86; SLJ 8/86)

9295 Johnson, Lois W. *Escape into the Night* (4–6). Illus. 1995, Bethany paper $5.99 (1-55661-351-2). 160pp. On a Mississippi River steamboat, young Libby must rethink her attitudes toward slavery when she encounters a conductor on the Underground Railroad. (Rev: BL 11/15/95; SLJ 10/95)

9296 Johnson, Lois W. *Midnight Rescue* (4–6). 1996, Bethany paper $5.99 (1-55661-353-9). 160pp. Twelve-year-old Libby, a riverboat captain's daughter, becomes involved with the Underground Railroad and an escaped slave. (Rev: BL 1/1–15/97)

9297 Johnston, Norma. *Over Jordan* (5–9). 1999, Avon $15.00 (0-380-97635-8). 192pp. Fourteen-year-old Roxana takes her attendant, Joss, and Joss's beau, escaped slave Gideon, upriver to Cincinnati in the hope of finding refuge for them through the Underground Railroad. (Rev: BL 12/15/99; HBG 3/00; SLJ 12/99)

9298 Karr, Kathleen. *The Great Turkey Walk* (4–8). 1998, Farrar $16.00 (0-374-32773-4). 199pp. A good-humored tale about a pioneer entrepreneur who decides to buy turkeys in the Midwest to sell in Denver, where the price is sky-high. (Rev: BCCB 5/98; HBG 10/98; SLJ 3/98*)

9299 Karr, Kathleen. *Skullduggery* (5–7). 2000, Hyperion LB $16.49 (0-7868-2439-5). 160pp. Set in New York in the 19th century, this is the story of a young orphan boy whose job with a phrenologist involves digging up skulls for the doctor's research. (Rev: BCCB 4/00; BL 4/1/00; HB 5–6/00; HBG 10/00; SLJ 3/00)

9300 Ketchum, Liza. *Orphan Journey Home* (5–7). Illus. 2000, Avon $15.00 (0-380-97811-3). 162pp. When their parents die in southern Illinois in 1828, Jesse and her three siblings must find their way to their grandmother in eastern Kentucky. (Rev: BCCB 6/00; BL 6/1–15/00; HBG 10/00; SLJ 8/00)

9301 Killcoyne, Hope Lourie. *The Lost Village of Central Park* (3–5). Illus. by Mary Lee Majno. Series: Mysteries in Time. 1999, Silver Moon LB $13.95 (1-893110-02-8). 89pp. An exciting story about life in Seneca Village, an African American settlement in 19th-century New York City, and the slave catchers that terrorized its people. (Rev: HBG 10/00; SLJ 2/00)

9302 Kohl, Susan. *The Ghost of Gracie Mansion* (3–5). Illus. by Ned Butterfield. Series: Mysteries in Time. 1999, Silver Moon LB $13.95 (1-893110-04-4). 96pp. When the Gracie family move to their new mansion in northern Manhattan in 1803, they encounter a mystery concerning disappearing objects. (Rev: SLJ 2/00)

9303 Lottridge, Celia B. *The Wind Wagon* (2–4). Illus. by Daniel Clifford. 1995, Silver Burdett LB $12.95 (0-382-24927-5); paper $4.95 (0-382-24929-1). 56pp. A fictionalized account of Sam Peppard and his invention of a wagon powered by the wind in Kansas in 1860. (Rev: SLJ 8/95)

9304 McCaughrean, Geraldine, adapt. *Moby Dick* (5–8). Illus. by Victor G. Ambrus. 1997, Oxford $25.00 (0-19-274156-X). 100pp. A shortened version of this classic that does not sacrifice the quality of the original. (Rev: SLJ 5/97*)

9305 McKissack, Patricia. *A Picture of Freedom: The Diary of Clotee, a Slave Girl* (4–6). 1997, Scholastic $9.95 (0-614-25386-1). 208pp. Using a diary format, this novel describes the life of slaves on a Southern plantation as seen through the eyes of a young slave girl. (Rev: BL 4/15/97; SLJ 9/97)

9306 McKissack, Patricia, and Fredrick McKissack. *Let My People Go* (5–8). Illus. by James E. Ransome. 1998, Simon & Schuster $20.00 (0-689-80856-9). 144pp. This novel set in the early 19th century combines Bible stories and the hardships endured by slaves as told by Price Jefferson, a former slave who is now an abolitionist living in South Carolina. (Rev: BCCB 12/98; BL 10/1/98*; HBG 3/99; SLJ 11/98)

9307 Minahan, John A. *Abigail's Drum* (2–5). Illus. 1995, Pippin $15.95 (0-945912-25-0). 64pp. During the War of 1812, Rebecca and Abigail try to save their father, who has been captured by the British. (Rev: BCCB 2/96; BL 2/15/96; SLJ 2/96)

9308 Monjo, F. N. *The Drinking Gourd* (2–4). Illus. by Fred Brenner. 1970, HarperCollins LB $15.89 (0-06-024330-9); paper $3.95 (0-06-444042-7).

64pp. A New England white boy helps a black family escape on the Underground Railroad.

9309 Paterson, Katherine. *Jip, His Story* (5–8). 1996, Dutton $15.99 (0-525-67543-4). 208pp. An orphan boy who works on a poor farm in Vermont in the 1850s finds a stranger is stalking him. (Rev: BCCB 12/96; BL 9/1/96*; HB 11–12/96; SLJ 10/96*)

9310 Patrick, Denise Lewis. *The Adventures of Midnight Son* (5–8). 1997, Holt $16.00 (0-8050-4714-X). 152pp. Fleeing slavery on a horse given to him by his parents, Midnight rides to Mexico and freedom. (Rev: BL 12/15/97; HBG 3/98; SLJ 12/97)

9311 Pryor, Bonnie. *Luke on the High Seas: The American Adventure Series* (4–6). Illus. 2000, HarperCollins $14.95 (0-688-17134-6). 192pp. When Luke and his friend Toby leave Boston on a clipper ship bound for California, they don't realize that soon they will be encountering storms, sharks, and pirates. (Rev: BL 7/00; HBG 10/00; SLJ 8/00)

9312 Rappaport, Doreen. *Freedom River* (3–5). Illus. 2000, Hyperion $14.99 (0-7868-0350-9). 32pp. Based on fact, this is a picture book for older readers that tells how John Parker, an ex-slave, helped a family to escape from Kentucky via the Underground Railroad. (Rev: BL 10/1/00; HBG 3/01; SLJ 10/00)

9313 Rinaldi, Ann. *The Blue Door* (5–8). 1996, Scholastic $15.95 (0-590-46051-X). 272pp. In this, the third volume of the Quilt trilogy — following *A Stitch in Time* (1994) and *Broken Days* (1995) — Amanda is forced to take a mill job in Lowell, Massachusetts, because of an identity misunderstanding. (Rev: BL 11/1/96)

9314 Robinet, Harriette G. *The Twins, the Pirates, and the Battle of New Orleans* (4–6). 1997, Simon & Schuster $15.00 (0-689-81208-6). 144pp. Twins Andrew and Pierre, who have been rescued from slavery, are left alone in a Louisiana swamp, where they battle alligators, pirates, and bounty hunters. (Rev: BL 11/15/97; HBG 3/98; SLJ 12/97)

9315 Robinet, Harriette G. *Washington City Is Burning* (5–7). 1996, Simon & Schuster $16.00 (0-689-80773-2). 149pp. In this historical novel set in the Washington, D.C., of James and Dolley Madison, young Virginia helps slaves escape. (Rev: BCCB 12/96; BL 11/1/96; SLJ 11/96)

9316 Roop, Peter, and Connie Roop. *Good-Bye for Today: The Diary of a Young Girl at Sea* (2–5). Illus. 2000, Simon & Schuster $16.00 (0-689-82222-7). 48pp. In diary format, this story of a young girl's adventures on her father's 19th-century whaling ship gives a realistic picture of life at sea. (Rev: BCCB 4/00; BL 6/1–15/00; HBG 10/00; SLJ 12/00)

9317 Rosen, Michael J. *A School for Pompey Walker* (4–6). Illus. 1995, Harcourt $16.00 (0-15-200114-X). 48pp. This story, based on fact, tells about a slave who sold himself several times into slavery to get the money to open a school for black children. (Rev: BCCB 1/96; BL 10/15/95; SLJ 11/95)

9318 Rosenburg, John. *William Parker: Rebel Without Rights* (5–7). 1996, Millbrook LB $21.90 (1-56294-139-9). 144pp. A fictionalized account of William Parker, an escaped slave, who led the Christiana Riot in Pennsylvania in 1851 to prevent the return of slaves to the South. (Rev: BL 2/15/96; SLJ 5/96)

9319 Schwartz, Virginia Frances. *Send One Angel Down* (5–8). 2000, Holiday $15.95 (0-8234-1484-1). 163pp. This is the story of a young slave girl, Eliza, the skills she learns on the plantation, and how this knowledge helps her when she gains freedom. (Rev: BL 6/1–15/00; HB 7–8/00; HBG 10/00; SLJ 8/00)

9320 Siegelson, Kim L. *Escape South* (2–4). Illus. by Shelley Jackson. Series: Road to Reading. 2000, Golden Bks. $10.99 (0-307-46504-7). This easy chapter book tells, in fictionalized form, how some runaway slaves were given shelter and land by the Seminole Indians in Florida and later left for land out west. (Rev: BL 2/15/01; HBG 3/01)

9321 Siegelson, Kim L. *In the Time of the Drums* (2–5). Illus. by Brian Pinkney. 1999, Hyperion LB $16.49 (0-7686-2386-0). 32pp. Told from the standpoint of a young African American, this is the legend of the slave rebellion at Ibo's Landing in South Carolina's Sea Islands. (Rev: BL 4/1/99)

9322 Smucker, Barbara. *Runaway to Freedom* (3–5). Illus. by Charles Lilly. 1978, HarperCollins paper $4.95 (0-06-440106-5). 160pp. Two slave girls try to reach Canada and freedom.

9323 Sterman, Betsy. *Saratoga Secret* (5–8). 1998, Dial $15.99 (0-8037-2332-6). 256pp. In the Upper Hudson River Valley in 1777, young Amity must warn the Continentals of an impending attack by General Burgoyne. (Rev: BL 11/1/98; HBG 3/99; SLJ 11/98)

9324 Stowe, Cynthia M. *The Second Escape of Arthur Cooper* (5–7). 2000, Marshall Cavendish $14.95 (0-7614-5069-6). 112pp. Based on a true story, this novel tells of Arthur Cooper, an escaped slave, and the Quakers on Nantucket Island who saved him from slave catchers in 1822. (Rev: BL 8/00; HBG 3/01; SLJ 10/00)

9325 Thomas, Velma M. *Lest We Forget: The Passage from Africa to Slavery and Emancipation* (5–8). Illus. 1997, Crown $29.95 (0-609-60030-3). An interactive book about slavery based on material from the Black Holocaust Museum. (Rev: BL 12/15/97) [973.6]

9326 Turner, Glennette Tilley. *Running for Our Lives* (5–7). Illus. 1994, Holiday $16.95 (0-8234-1121-4). 198pp. A thoroughly researched novel about a boy and his family who escape slavery in the 1850s and traveled on the Underground Railroad to Canada. (Rev: BCCB 6/94; BL 6/1–15/94; SLJ 4/94)

9327 Van Nutt, Julia. *A Cobtown Christmas: From the Diaries of Lucky Hart* (3–4). Illus. by Robert Van Nutt. 1998, Doubleday $15.95 (0-385-32556-8). 34pp. Written in diary format, this is the story of Lucky Hart who, in 1845, is a resident of the village of Cobtown where preparations for Christmas are being made, and Lucky is trying to reunite a blind man with his dog. (Rev: BCCB 12/98; BL 10/1/98; HBG 3/99; SLJ 10/98)

9328 Van Nutt, Julia. *The Mystery of Mineral Gorge* (2–4). Illus. 1999, Doubleday $15.95 (0-385-32562-2). 48pp. Set in a small town in the 1840s, this novel tells how Lucky joins her friends and other townspeople who are investigating horrible screams that are heard at night. (Rev: BL 8/99; HBG 10/99; SLJ 7/99)

9329 Vaughan, Marcia K. *Abbie Against the Storm: The True Story of a Young Heroine and a Lighthouse* (2–4). Illus. 1999, Beyond Words $15.95 (1-58270-007-9). 32pp. Based on fact, this elegant picture book tells how 17-year-old Abigail Burgess cared for her family's Maine lighthouse during a terrible storm in 1856. (Rev: BL 4/1/00; HBG 3/00; SLJ 7/00)

9330 Wall, Bill. *The Cove of Cork* (5–9). 1999, Irish American paper $7.95 (0-85635-225-0). 144pp. In this novel about the War of 1812, an Irish lad, the first mate on an American schooner, sees action in a battle against a British vessel and wins the hand of the one he loves. (Rev: SLJ 7/99)

9331 Weitzman, David. *Old Ironsides* (3–6). Illus. 1997, Houghton $15.95 (0-395-74678-7). 32pp. A fictionalized account of the building of the ship in President Washington's time that would protect merchant ships from pirates. (Rev: BCCB 6/97; BL 5/1/97; HB 5–6/97; SLJ 4/97*)

9332 West, Tracey. *Mr. Peale's Bones* (4–6). Series: Stories of the States. 1994, Silver Moon LB $14.95 (1-881889-50-5). 63pp. In this novel, set in upstate New York in 1801, Will and his estranged father find a new bond when they help Charles Willson Peale and his excavation of mammoth bones. (Rev: SLJ 7/94)

9333 Whelan, Gloria. *Farewell to the Island* (5–8). 1998, HarperCollins $14.95 (0-06-027751-3). 192pp. In this sequel to *Once on This Island,* Mary leaves her Michigan home after the War of 1812 and travels to England where she falls in love with Lord Lindsay. (Rev: BL 12/1/98; HBG 3/99; SLJ 1/99)

9334 Whelan, Gloria. *Once on This Island* (4–7). 1995, HarperCollins LB $14.89 (0-06-026249-4). 224pp. In 1812, Mary and her older brother and sister must tend the family farm on Mackinac Island when their father goes off to war. (Rev: BCCB 11/95; BL 10/1/95; SLJ 11/95)

9335 Wiley, Melissa. *On Tide Mill Lane* (4–8). Illus. 2001, HarperCollins $15.95 (0-06-027013-6). 208pp. Charlotte experiences a number of household crises in Roxbury, Massachusetts, where she lives with her blacksmith father at the time of the War of 1812. (Rev: BL 2/15/01)

9336 Wisler, G. Clifton. *Caleb's Choice* (5–8). 1996, Dutton $14.99 (0-525-67526-4). 160pp. During 1858 in northern Texas, 13-year-old Caleb helps two escaped slaves. (Rev: BCCB 9/96; BL 8/96; SLJ 8/96)

9337 Woodruff, Elvira. *Dear Austin: Letters from the Underground Railroad* (4–6). Illus. 1998, Knopf

LB $17.99 (0-679-98594-8). 128pp. In 1853 when young Darcy is captured by slave catchers, her brother Jupiter and white friend Levi set out to save her in an adventure that involves the Underground Railroad. (Rev: BL 11/15/98; HBG 3/99; SLJ 10/98)

9338 Wright, Courtni C. *Journey to Freedom: A Story of the Underground Railroad* (3–5). Illus. by Griffith Gershom. 1994, Holiday LB $16.95 (0-8234-1096-X). 28pp. A picture book that tells of 8-year-old Joshua and his flight to freedom on the Underground Railroad. (Rev: BL 11/15/94; SLJ 1/95)

PIONEERS AND WESTWARD EXPANSION

9339 Altman, Linda Jacobs. *The Legend of Freedom Hill* (2–4). Illus. by Cornelius Van Wright and Ying-Hwa Hu. 2000, Lee & Low $15.95 (1-58430-003-5). 32pp. Set in Gold Rush California, this novel tells how Rosabel, the daughter of a runaway slave, and her Jewish friend Sophia pan enough gold to buy the freedom of Rosabel's mother. (Rev: BL 11/1/00; HBG 3/01; SLJ 8/00)

9340 Anderson, Joan. *Pioneer Children of Appalachia* (4–6). Illus. 1986, Houghton paper $7.95 (0-395-54792-X). The Davis family is shown in everyday life in Appalachia of the early 1800s. (Rev: BCCB 12/86; BL 11/1/86; SLJ 10/86)

9341 Applegate, Stan. *The Devil's Highway* (5–8). Illus. by James Watling. 1998, Peachtree paper $8.95 (1-56145-184-3). 148pp. In this adventure novel set in the early 1800s, 14-year-old Zeb and his horse, Christmas, set out on the bandit-infested Natchez Trail to search for his grandfather. (Rev: SLJ 2/99)

9342 Arrington, Frances. *Bluestem* (4–6). 2000, Putnam $16.99 (0-399-23564-7). 140pp. Eleven-year-old Polly and her younger sister must fend for themselves on the American frontier after their mother wanders away. (Rev: BCCB 9/00; BL 4/1/00; HB 5–6/00; HBG 10/00; SLJ 6/00)

9343 Avi. *The Barn* (3–6). Series: Richard Jackson Books. 1994, Orchard LB $15.99 (0-531-08711-5). 106pp. In this novel set in 1855 Oregon, three motherless children try to run the family farm after their father becomes sick. (Rev: SLJ 10/94)

9344 Ayres, Katherine. *Silver Dollar Girl* (4–8). 2000, Delacorte $14.95 (0-385-32763-3). 195pp. Set in the silver rush days of the 1880s, this story tells how Valentine Harper disguises herself as a boy and sets out from Pittsburgh to find her father in Colorado. (Rev: BL 11/15/00; SLJ 11/00)

9345 Bailer, Darice. *The Last Rail* (3–5). Illus. by Bill Farnsworth. Series: Odyssey. 1996, Smithsonian Institution $14.95 (1-56899-362-5); paper $5.95 (1-56899-363-3). 32pp. Using a fictional format, this book tells about a young girl who witnesses the building of the first transcontinental railroad. (Rev: BL 10/15/96)

9346 Blakeslee, Ann R. *A Different Kind of Hero* (5–7). 1997, Marshall Cavendish LB $14.95 (0-7614-5000-9). 144pp. In 1881 Colorado, Renny is criticized for befriending and helping a Chinese boy

new to town. (Rev: BL 9/1/97; HBG 3/98; SLJ 1/98)

9347 Buchanan, Jane. *Gratefully Yours* (3–6). 1997, Farrar $15.00 (0-374-32775-0). 128pp. After her parents die in a fire, Hattie rides the Orphan Train west to find a new family. (Rev: BL 10/15/97; HBG 3/98; SLJ 12/97)

9348 Bunting, Eve. *Train to Somewhere* (2–5). Illus. by Ronald Himler. 1996, Clarion $16.00 (0-395-71325-0). 32pp. The story of the Orphan Train as seen from the point of view of Marianne, a homeless girl who travels west in 1878 to find an adoptive family. (Rev: BCCB 3/96; BL 2/1/96*; SLJ 3/96*)

9349 Burks, Brian. *Wrango* (5–8). 1999, Harcourt $16.00 (0-15-201815-8). 128pp. In this historical novel, George, an African American boy, is forced out of town by the Klan and turns to the adventurous life of a cowboy. (Rev: BL 9/1/99; HBG 3/00; SLJ 12/99)

9350 Byars, Betsy. *Trouble River* (3–6). Illus. by Rocco Negri. 1989, Puffin paper $4.99 (0-14-034243-5). 160pp. Dewey uses his canoe to escape Indians.

9351 Calvert, Patricia. *Bigger* (5–8). 1994, Scribners paper $16.00 (0-684-19685-9). 144pp. After the Civil War, 12-year-old Tyler travels from Missouri to the Rio Grande in search of his soldier-father. (Rev: BCCB 3/94; BL 4/1/94; HB 7–8/94; SLJ 4/94)

9352 Calvert, Patricia. *Sooner* (5–9). 1998, Simon & Schuster $16.00 (0-689-81114-4). 176pp. After the Civil War, Tyler's father leaves the family to seek his fortune in Mexico and 13-year-old Tyler must assume adult responsibilities in this prequel to *Bigger*. (Rev: BCCB 6/98; BL 6/1–15/98; HBG 10/98; SLJ 6/98)

9353 Coville, Bruce. *Fortune's Journey* (5–8). 1995, Troll $13.95 (0-8167-3650-2). 256pp. A historical novel about a troupe of actors heading west in pioneer days, led by feisty Fortune Plunkett, age 16. (Rev: BL 10/15/95; SLJ 11/95)

9354 Creel, Ann Howard. *Water at the Blue Earth* (4–6). 1998, Roberts Rinehart $14.95 (1-57098-209-0); paper $8.95 (1-57098-224-4). 141pp. In 1854, 12-year-old Wren Taylor, a recent arrival at Fort Massachusetts in New Mexico territory, befriends a blind Ute boy and finds that her loyalties are soon divided. (Rev: HBG 3/99; SLJ 2/99)

9355 Cushman, Karen. *The Ballad of Lucy Whipple* (5–8). 1996, Clarion $15.00 (0-395-72806-1). 208pp. Lucy hates being stuck in the California wilderness with an overbearing mother who runs a boarding house. (Rev: BCCB 9/96; BL 8/96; HB 9–10/96; SLJ 8/96*)

9356 DeFelice, Cynthia. *Weasel* (4–6). 1990, Macmillan paper $15.00 (0-02-726457-2). 112pp. A stranger appears at the cabin door of Nathan and his sister Molly with a locket that could have come only from their missing father. (Rev: BCCB 5/90; BL 5/15/90; SLJ 5/90*)

9357 Duey, Kathleen. *Anisett Lundberg: California, 1851* (4–7). Series: American Diaries. 1996, Simon

& Schuster paper $4.50 (0-689-80386-9). 139pp. An adventure story featuring Anisett and her family, who live in the fold-mining region of California in 1851. (Rev: HB 9–10/96; SLJ 12/96)

9358 Duey, Kathleen. *Willow Chase: Kansas Territory, 1847* (4–6). 1997, Simon & Schuster paper $4.50 (0-689-81355-4). 144pp. When accidently swept down the Platte River, Willow Chase must find her way back to the family's wagon train. (Rev: BL 3/1/97; SLJ 4/97)

9359 Duey, Kathleen, and Karen A. Bale. *Death Valley: California, 1849* (4–6). Series: Survival! 1998, Simon & Schuster paper $3.99 (0-689-82117-4). 168pp. This survival story tells how the family of Jess and Will encounter a number of obstacles while crossing the American West in a wagon train bound for California and the promise of gold. (Rev: SLJ 1/99)

9360 Durbin, William. *The Journal of Sean Sullivan: A Transcontinental Railroad Worker, Nebraska and Points West, 1867* (5–8). Series: My Name Is America. 1999, Scholastic $10.95 (0-439-04994-6). 188pp. This novel describes the early days of railroad construction in America as seen through the eyes of young Sean, who works his way up from a "water carrier" to "spiker." (Rev: HBG 3/00; SLJ 11/99)

9361 Ernst, Kathleen. *Trouble at Fort La Pointe* (4–8). 2000, Pleasant $9.95 (1-58485-087-6). 165pp. In a fur trading post near Lake Superior in the early 18th century, 12-year-old Suzette sets out to investigate who is plotting against her father. (Rev: BL 10/1/00; SLJ 12/00)

9362 Finley, Mary Peace. *White Grizzly* (5–9). 2000, Filter $15.95 (0-86541-053-4); paper $6.95 (0-86541-058-5). 215pp. Fifteen-year-old Julio sets out on an arduous journey along the Santa Fe Trail to discover his true identity. (Rev: SLJ 1/01)

9363 Fleischman, Paul. *The Borning Room* (5–8). 1991, HarperCollins paper $4.95 (0-06-447099-7). 80pp. In Georgina's family house in Ohio, there is a room for birthing and a room for dying as the images of life unfold. (Rev: BCCB 9/91; BL 10/1/91*; HB 11–12/91*)

9364 Fleischman, Sid. *Bandit's Moon* (3–6). Illus. 1998, Greenwillow $15.00 (0-688-15830-7). 144pp. Based partly on fact, this is a humorous adventure story about Annyrose, a young girl who, disguised as a boy, joins a band of Mexican bandits led by Wakeen, the notorious robber. (Rev: BCCB 11/98; BL 10/1/98*; HB 11–12/98; HBG 3/99; SLJ 9/98)

9365 Fleischman, Sid. *Jim Ugly* (4–6). Illus. by Joseph A. Smith. 1992, Greenwillow $16.00 (0-688-10886-5). 144pp. In the time of the Old West, Jake — accompanied by his dad's mongrel dog — sets off in search of his missing father. (Rev: BCCB 3/92*; BL 5/15/92; SLJ 4/92)

9366 Gaeddert, Louann. *Hope* (5–7). 1995, Simon & Schuster $14.00 (0-689-80128-9). 165pp. While their father is panning for gold in California, Hope and brother John move to a Shaker community. (Rev: BL 12/15/95; SLJ 11/95)

9367 Glass, Andrew. *A Right Fine Life: Kit Carson on the Santa Fe Trail* (3–5). Illus. 1997, Holiday LB $16.95 (0-8234-1326-8). 48pp. This tall tale tells about 16-year-old Kit Carson's first journey west and his many adventures along the way. (Rev: BL 2/1/98; HBG 3/98; SLJ 2/98)

9368 Glaze, Lynn. *Seasons of the Trail* (4–6). Illus. by Matthew Archambault. 2000, Silver Moon LB $14.95 (1-893110-20-6). 92pp. To avoid the oncoming Civil War, 14-year-old Lucy Scott and her family leave their home in Missouri and journey to California by covered wagon. (Rev: HBG 3/01; SLJ 1/01)

9369 Gregory, Kristiana. *Across the Wide and Lonesome Prairie: The Oregon Trail Diary of Hattie Campbell* (4–7). Illus. Series: Dear America. 1997, Scholastic $10.95 (0-590-22651-7). 149pp. In a diary format, this novel chronicles the hardships that pioneers endured during a trip west on the Oregon Trail. (Rev: SLJ 3/97)

9370 Gregory, Kristiana. *The Great Railroad Race: The Diary of Libby West* (4–8). Illus. 1999, Scholastic $10.95 (0-590-10991-X). 208pp. The story of the building of the transcontinental railroad as seen through the eyes of a 14-year-old girl whose father is a reporter following this massive undertaking. (Rev: BL 4/1/99; HBG 10/99; SLJ 8/99)

9371 Hahn, Mary D. *The Gentleman Outlaw and Me-Eli: A Story of the Old West* (5–8). 1996, Clarion $15.00 (0-395-73083-X). 224pp. In frontier days, Eliza, masquerading as a boy, travels west in search of her father. (Rev: BCCB 4/96; BL 4/1/96; HB 9–10/96; SLJ 5/96)

9372 Heisel, Sharon E. *Precious Gold, Precious Jade* (5–8). 2000, Holiday $16.95 (0-8234-1432-9). 185pp. At the end of the Gold Rush in southern Oregon, two sisters create hostilities when they befriend a Chinese family that has moved to town. (Rev: BCCB 4/00; HBG 10/00; SLJ 4/00)

9373 Helldorfer, M. C. *Hog Music* (K–4). Illus. by S. D. Schindler. 2000, Viking $15.99 (0-670-87182-6). Set in the first half of the 19th century, this book chronicles the routes and vehicles involved in transporting a hat from the east to Illinois. (Rev: BCCB 9/00; HBG 10/00; SLJ 5/00)

9374 Henry, Joanne L. *A Clearing in the Forest: A Story About a Real Settler Boy* (3–5). Illus. by Charles Robinson. 1992, Macmillan $14.95 (0-02-743671-3). 44pp. Action highlights this historical novel about growing up in Indianapolis in the 1830s. (Rev: BCCB 6/92; BL 3/1/92; SLJ 3/92)

9375 Hermes, Patricia. *Calling Me Home* (4–7). 1998, Avon $15.00 (0-380-97451-7). 144pp. In the late 1850s, Abbie and her family are living in their sod house in Missouri when a cholera epidemic strikes and her brother dies. (Rev: BL 1/1–15/99; HBG 3/99; SLJ 12/98)

9376 Hermes, Patricia. *Westward to Home: Joshua's Diary* (3–5). 2001, Scholastic $8.95 (0-439-11209-5). 112pp. The hardships of pioneers are revealed in this novel in journal form about a 9-year-old boy on a wagon train from Missouri to the Oregon Territory. (Rev: BL 2/1/01)

9377 Hickman, Janet. *Susannah* (4–6). 1998, Greenwillow $15.00 (0-688-14854-9). 144pp. In the early 1800s, 14-year-old Susannah and her father join an Ohio Shaker community where the young girl faces problems of adjustment and the Shakers encounter opposition from other settlers. (Rev: BCCB 11/98; BL 10/15/98; HB 1–2/99; HBG 3/99; SLJ 10/98)

9378 Hite, Sid. *Stick and Whittle* (5–8). 2000, Scholastic $16.95 (0-439-09828-9). 208pp. At the end of the Civil War, two young men, who adopt the nicknames Stick and Whittle, travel together in Comanche Territory and encounter kidnapping, romance, Indians, and a tornado. (Rev: BCCB 10/00; BL 11/1/00; HB 1–2/01; HBG 3/01; SLJ 9/00)

9379 Hoff, Carol. *Johnny Texas* (4–6). Illus. by Bob Meyers. 1992, Hendrick-Long paper $13.95 (0-937460-81-8). 160pp. Texas history is interwoven into this story of a pioneer German family. A reissue.

9380 Holland, Isabelle. *The Journey Home* (4–6). 1990, Scholastic $13.95 (0-590-43110-2). 192pp. Two orphaned girls start life anew in the second half of the 19th century when they are adopted by a couple in Kansas. (Rev: BCCB 12/90; SLJ 12/90)

9381 Holling, Holling C. *Tree in the Trail* (4–7). Illus. by author. 1942, Houghton $20.00 (0-395-18228-X); paper $9.95 (0-395-54534-X). 64pp. The history of the Santa Fe Trail, described through the life of a cottonwood tree, a 200-year-old landmark to travelers and a symbol of peace to the Indians.

9382 Hooks, William H. *Pioneer Cat* (2–4). Illus. by Charles Robinson. 1988, Random paper $3.99 (0-394-82038-X). 64pp. Kate smuggles a cat aboard the prairie schooner as the family heads west on the Oregon Trail. (Rev: BCCB 12/88; BL 1/15/89; SLJ 3/89)

9383 Howard, Ellen. *The Chickenhouse House* (3–5). Illus. by Nancy Oleksa. 1991, Macmillan LB $13.00 (0-689-31695-X). 64pp. A pioneer family builds a home on the prairie. (Rev: BCCB 5/91; BL 5/15/91; HB 7–8/91; SLJ 7/91)

9384 Irwin, Hadley. *Jim-Dandy* (5–7). 1994, Macmillan LB $15.00 (0-689-50594-9). 144pp. When his father sells his horse to the army, Caleb joins Custer's Cavalry to be near his pet in this story set in the Kansas frontier. (Rev: BCCB 4/94; BL 4/15/94; HB 7–8/94; SLJ 5/94)

9385 Jackson, Dave, and Neta Jackson. *Abandoned on the Wild Frontier* (4–6). 1995, Bethany paper $5.99 (1-55661-468-3). 144pp. Based on fact, this is the story of a young boy's search for his mother, who has been carried off by Indians after the War of 1812. (Rev: BL 9/1/95)

9386 Karr, Kathleen. *Gold-Rush Phoebe* (5–8). Series: The Petticoat Party. 1998, HarperTrophy paper $4.95 (0-06-440498-6). 208pp. An adventure-filled historical novel in which Phoebe, disguised as a boy, leaves Oregon with her friend Robbie to find wealth in Gold-Rush California. (Rev: SLJ 1/99)

9387 Karr, Kathleen. *Oregon, Sweet Oregon* (4–6). Series: Petticoat Party. 1998, HarperCollins paper $4.95 (0-06-440497-8). 208pp. Phoebe Brown and

her family arrive in Oregon City after a series of wagon-train adventures in this light historical novel. (Rev: BL 7/98; SLJ 7/98)

9388 Kent, Peter. *Quest for the West: In Search of Gold* (3–6). Illus. 1997, Millbrook LB $21.40 (0-7613-0302-2). 32pp. The Hornik family leave their Czech homeland in 1849 to find a new life in the United States in this novel with excellent pen-and-ink and watercolor illustrations. (Rev: BL 12/1/97; SLJ 6/98)

9389 Kerr, Rita. *Texas Footprints* (4–7). Illus. 1988, Eakin $13.95 (0-89015-676-X). 80pp. A tale of the author's great-great-grandparents who went to Texas in 1823. (Rev: BL 3/1/89)

9390 Kramer, Sydelle. *Wagon Train* (2–4). Illus. by Deborah Kogan Ray. Series: All Aboard Reading. 1997, Putnam paper $3.99 (0-448-41334-5). 48pp. This easy-to-read book follows a family as it crosses the United States wagon in 1848. (Rev: BL 2/1/98)

9391 Kurtz, Jane. *I'm Sorry, Almira Ann* (3–5). Illus. 1999, Holt $15.95 (0-8050-6094-4). 119pp. Eight-year-old Sarah and her friend Almira Ann find adventure when their families go west on the Oregon Trail. (Rev: BCCB 12/99; BL 11/15/99; HB 3–4/00; HBG 3/00; SLJ 11/99)

9392 Lasky, Kathryn. *Alice Rose and Sam* (4–7). 1998, Hyperion LB $15.49 (0-7868-2277-5). 208pp. While growing up in Virginia City, Nevada, in 1863, 12-year-old Alice Rose Tucker witnesses a murder and seeks help from young Samuel Clemens, who works on her father's newspaper. (Rev: BCCB 5/98; BL 4/15/98; HBG 10/98)

9393 Laurgaard, Rachel K. *Patty Reed's Doll: The Story of the Donner Party* (3–6). Illus. by Elizabeth Michaels. 1989, Tomato Enterprises paper $7.95 (0-9617357-2-4). 144pp. A fantasy seen through the eyes of a doll about a survivor of the Donner Party. A reissue. (Rev: SLJ 11/89)

9394 Lawlor, Laurie. *Addie Across the Prairie* (3–5). Illus. 1986, Whitman LB $13.95 (0-8075-0165-4); Pocket paper $3.99 (0-671-70147-9). 128pp. Nine-year-old Addie learns about sod houses and curious Indians as her family travels cross-country to the Dakota Territory. (Rev: BL 8/86; SLJ 10/86)

9395 Lawlor, Laurie. *Addie's Dakota Winter* (3–5). Illus. by Toby Gowing. 1989, Whitman LB $13.95 (0-8075-0171-9). 160pp. Addie is disappointed when her only possibility for a friend turns out to be a boastful immigrant child. (Rev: BCCB 12/89; BL 11/15/89; SLJ 1/90)

9396 Lawlor, Laurie. *Addie's Long Summer* (5–7). Illus. by Toby Gowing. 1992, Whitman $13.95 (0-8075-0167-0). 174pp. Addie is disappointed to find that her cousins do not fit into pioneer farm life. (Rev: BCCB 11/92; BL 8/92; SLJ 11/92)

9397 Lawlor, Laurie. *Adventure on the Wilderness Road* (4–6). Series: American Sisters. 1999, Pocket $9.00 (0-671-01553-2). 186pp. Told from the standpoint of an 11-year-old girl, this is the story of the Poage family and their harrowing journey through the wilderness in 1775 to join Daniel Boone's settlement in Kentucky. (Rev: BL 4/1/99; HBG 3/00; SLJ 11/99)

9398 Lawlor, Laurie. *Gold in the Hills* (4–6). 1995, Walker $15.95 (0-8027-8371-6). 152pp. When their father sets out to find gold, Hattie and her brother must stay with bitter, tyrannical cousin Tirzah in this novel set in Colorado during frontier days. (Rev: BCCB 7–8/95; BL 6/1–15/95; SLJ 8/95)

9399 Lawlor, Laurie. *West Along the Wagon Road, 1852* (4–6). Series: American Sisters. 1998, Pocket $9.00 (0-671-01551-6). 183pp. Eleven-year-old Harriet Scott, along with her parents and her eight siblings, endures hardships, hunger, and threats of attack in this story about a family on the Oregon Trail. (Rev: BL 12/1/98; HBG 10/99; SLJ 12/98)

9400 Leland, Dorothy K. *Sallie Fox: The Story of a Pioneer Girl* (4–6). 1995, Tomato Enterprises paper $8.95 (0-9617357-6-7). 115pp. A fictionalized account of the trek of 12-year-old Sallie Fox by wagon train with her family from Iowa to California in the mid 1800s. (Rev: SLJ 2/96)

9401 Love, D. Anne. *Bess's Log Cabin Quilt* (2–5). Illus. by Ronald Himler. 1995, Holiday $15.95 (0-8234-1178-8). 72pp. In frontier Oregon, Bess hopes that by winning a quilt contest she can help ease her family's financial problems. (Rev: BCCB 6/95; BL 2/15/95; SLJ 6/95)

9402 Loveday, John. *Goodbye, Buffalo Sky* (5–8). 1997, Simon & Schuster $16.00 (0-689-81370-8). 176pp. Two girls are kidnapped by a vengeful Sioux warrior in this exciting adventure set in the Great Plains during the 1870s. (Rev: BL 1/1–15/98; HBG 3/98; SLJ 11/97)

9403 MacBride, Roger L. *In the Land of the Big Red Apple* (3–7). Illus. by David Gilleece. 1995, Harper-Collins LB $15.89 (0-06-024964-1). 352pp. In the mid-1890s, the farm at Rocky Ridge, where Rose Wilder Lane is growing up, gradually prospers. (Rev: BL 5/15/95; SLJ 9/95)

9404 MacBride, Roger L. *Little Farm in the Ozarks* (3–6). Illus. 1994, HarperCollins paper $5.95 (0-06-440510-9). 304pp. Based on the journals of Rose Wilder Lane, this novel tells about the Wilder family's first spring and summer in Mansfield, Missouri. (Rev: BL 5/1/94)

9405 MacBride, Roger L. *Little House on Rocky Edge* (3–7). Illus. by David Gilleece. 1993, Harper-Collins paper $4.95 (0-06-440478-1). 304pp. This reworking of Laura Ingalls Wilder's material tells the story from Rose's perspective of the Wilder family's move from South Dakota to Missouri. This is the first part of a projected five-part series. (Rev: BL 6/1–15/93)

9406 MacBride, Roger L. *New Dawn on Rocky Ridge* (4–7). Illus. Series: Rocky Ridge. 1997, HarperCollins $15.95 (0-06-024971-4); paper $4.95 (0-06-440581-8). 320pp. This part of the Wilder family story covers 1900–1903 and focuses on Rose's difficult early teen years. (Rev: BL 11/1/97; HBG 3/98; SLJ 2/98)

9407 McCully, Emily Arnold. *An Outlaw Thanksgiving* (2–5). Illus. 1998, Dial LB $15.89 (0-8037-2198-6). 37pp. Told from the standpoint of young

Clara, whose family is en route to California in the 1890s, this is the story of the lavish Thanksgiving banquet given by Butch Cassidy and his outlaws. (Rev: BCCB 10/98; BL 9/1/98; HBG 3/99; SLJ 11/98)

9408 McDonald, Brix. *Riding on the Wind* (5–10). 1998, Avenue paper $5.95 (0-9661306-0-X). 243pp. In frontier Wyoming during the early 1860s, 15-year-old Carrie Sutton is determined to become a rider in the Pony Express after her family's ranch has been chosen as a relay station. (Rev: SLJ 1/99)

9409 McKissack, Patricia. *Run Away Home* (4–7). 1997, Scholastic $14.95 (0-590-46751-4). 176pp. In 1888 rural Alabama, a young African American girl helps shelter a fugitive Apache boy. (Rev: BL 10/1/97; HB 11–12/97; HBG 3/98; SLJ 11/97)

9410 MacLachlan, Patricia. *Sarah, Plain and Tall* (3–5). Illus. by Marcia Sewall. 1985, HarperCollins LB $14.89 (0-06-024102-0); paper $4.95 (0-06-440205-3). 64pp. Two children wait on the prairie for the arrival of their new stepmother, who has answered their father's ad for a wife. Newbery Medal winner, 1986. (Rev: BCCB 5/85; BL 5/1/89; SLJ 5/85)

9411 MacLachlan, Patricia. *Skylark* (4–6). 1994, HarperCollins LB $12.89 (0-06-023333-8). 64pp. In this sequel to *Sarah, Plain and Tall* (1985), Sarah goes back east with her children, leaving Jacob, her husband, to take care of the farm. (Rev: BCCB 2/94; BL 1/1/94; HB 7–8/94; SLJ 3/94)

9412 Mercati, Cynthia. *Wagons Ho! A Diary of the Oregon Trail* (3–5). Illus. 2000, Perfection Learning $13.95 (0-7807-9011-1). 56pp. A simple read in diary form about young Lisa and her adventures in a Conestoga wagon heading west with her family in 1849. (Rev: BL 10/15/00)

9413 Miller, Robert H. *A Pony for Jeremiah* (3–6). Illus. by Nneka Bennett. 1996, Silver Burdett LB $22.00 (0-382-39459-3); paper $4.95 (0-382-39460-7). 64pp. A historial novel about a runaway slave and his family who settle in Nebraska. (Rev: BL 2/15/97; SLJ 3/97)

9414 Milligan, Bryce. *With the Wind, Kevin Dolan: A Novel of Ireland and Texas* (5–7). Illus. 1987, Corona paper $7.95 (0-931722-45-4). 194pp. The story of Kevin and Tom, brothers who leave the famine in Ireland in the 1830s and head for America. (Rev: BL 8/87; SLJ 9/87)

9415 Moeri, Louise. *Save Queen of Sheba* (5–7). 1990, Avon paper $3.50 (0-380-71154-0). 112pp. Young David survives a wagon train massacre and must take care of his young sister.

9416 Moss, Marissa. *Rachel's Journal* (3–6). Illus. 1998, Harcourt $15.00 (0-15-201806-9). 48pp. In journal format, this is the record of Rachel's travels west to California in 1850, with descriptions of crossing the Missouri River, tramping through deserts, and the birth of a sister en route. (Rev: BL 10/1/98; HBG 3/99; SLJ 9/98)

9417 Moss, Marissa. *True Heart* (2–4). Illus. 1999, Harcourt $16.00 (0-15-201344-X). 32pp. When the train's engineer is wounded by bandits, Bee gets her chance to take over in this tale set in the Wild West during the 1890s. (Rev: BCCB 4/99; BL 4/1/99; HBG 10/99; SLJ 4/99)

9418 Murphy, Jim. *West to a Land of Plenty: The Diary of Teresa Angelino Viscardi* (4–6). Illus. Series: Dear America. 1998, Scholastic $9.95 (0-590-73888-7). 208pp. In this diary account, an Italian American family from New Jersey treks across country by train and covered wagon. (Rev: BCCB 3/98; BL 4/1/98; HBG 10/98; SLJ 4/98)

9419 Myers, Walter Dean. *The Journal of Joshua Loper: A Black Cowboy* (4–6). Illus. Series: My Name Is America. 1999, Scholastic paper $10.95 (0-590-02691-1). 160pp. Joshua, a young African American cowboy, earns his spurs when he joins a cattle drive on the Chisholm Trail in 1871. (Rev: BL 2/15/99; HBG 10/99; SLJ 4/99)

9420 Nixon, Joan Lowery. *Aggie's Home* (3–6). Illus. Series: Orphan Train Children. 1998, Delacorte $9.95 (0-385-32295-X). 116pp. Orphan Aggie is sent west when she is 12 to be adopted by the eccentric Bradon family. (Rev: BL 1/1–15/99; HBG 3/99; SLJ 12/98)

9421 Nixon, Joan Lowery. *Circle of Love* (4–6). 1997, Delacorte $15.95 (0-385-32280-1). 176pp. While waiting for her boyfriend to marry her, Frances agrees to chaperone 30 children to the West, where they hope to find families. (Rev: BL 4/1/97; SLJ 5/97)

9422 Nixon, Joan Lowery. *David's Search* (3–6). Series: Orphan Train Children. 1998, Delacorte $9.95 (0-385-32296-8). 127pp. David, an adoptee from the Orphan Train, fits in well with the Bauers of Missouri on their farm, and becomes friendly with an African American hired hand. (Rev: HBG 3/99; SLJ 2/99)

9423 Nixon, Joan Lowery. *Will's Choice* (4–6). Series: Orphan Train Children. 1998, Delacorte $9.95 (0-385-32294-1). 119pp. Twelve-year-old Will who was sent West by his father and adopted by a loving family, now must choose between staying with his stepfamily or returning to the East. (Rev: HBG 10/98; SLJ 6/98)

9424 O'Dell, Scott. *Streams to the River, River to the Sea: A Novel of Sacagawea* (5–8). 1986, Houghton $16.00 (0-395-40430-4); Fawcett paper $5.99 (0-449-70244-8). 191pp. A fictionalized portrait of the real-life Indian woman who traveled west with Lewis and Clark on their famous journey. (Rev: BL 3/15/86; HB 9–10/86)

9425 Osborne, Mary Pope. *Adaline Falling Star* (4–6). 2000, Scholastic $16.95 (0-439-05947-X). 176pp. Adaline Falling Star, the daughter of Kit Carson and an Arapaho Indian woman, sets out to find her father who is on an expedition through the Rockies. (Rev: BCCB 3/00; BL 2/15/00; HB 5–6/00; HBG 10/00; SLJ 3/00)

9426 Paulsen, Gary. *Call Me Francis Tucket* (5–8). 1995, Delacorte $15.95 (0-385-32116-3). 97pp. Fifteen-year-old Francis becomes separated from the wagon train to Oregon that he has joined and later becomes hopelessly lost in the wilderness. (Rev: BL 7/95; SLJ 6/95)

9427 Paulsen, Gary. *Tucket's Gold* (4–6). Series: Tucket Adventures. 1999, Delacorte $15.95 (0-385-32501-0). 100pp. The fourth installment in the saga of Tucket and his adopted family making their way back to the Oregon Trail. (Rev: BL 12/1/99; HBG 3/00; SLJ 10/99)

9428 Paulsen, Gary. *Tucket's Home* (4–8). 2000, Delacorte $15.95 (0-385-32648-3). 90pp. In this, the fifth and last installment of the Tucket Adventures, Francis, Lottie, and Billy continue their journey on the Oregon Trail where they meet an English adventurer and his servants. (Rev: BL 9/1/00; HBG 3/01; SLJ 9/00)

9429 Paulsen, Gary. *Tucket's Ride* (4–7). 1997, Delacorte $15.95 (0-385-32199-6). 86pp. Fifteen-year-old Francis Tucket faces hair-raising dangers while traveling into the Old West with orphans Lottie and Billy. (Rev: BL 12/15/96; SLJ 3/97)

9430 Pryor, Bonnie. *Luke: 1849 — On the Golden Trail* (3–6). Illus. 1999, Morrow $15.00 (0-688-15670-3). 160pp. Luke's pioneer family has such misfortune farming that the boy decides to leave and accompany his wealthy uncle to Boston. (Rev: BL 8/99; HBG 10/99; SLJ 8/99)

9431 Rinaldi, Ann. *The Second Bend in the River* (5–8). 1997, Scholastic $15.95 (0-590-74258-2). 288pp. A novel set in colonial Ohio in which the Indian chief Tecumseh falls in love with a white settler, Rebecca Galloway. (Rev: BCCB 3/97; BL 2/15/97; HBG 3/98; SLJ 6/97)

9432 Rinaldi, Ann. *The Staircase* (5–7). 2000, Harcourt $16.00 (0-15-202430-1). 256pp. The exciting story of a 19-century teenager named Lizzy who is attending a Catholic girls' school where she rooms with conniving Elinora. (Rev: BL 11/1/00; HBG 3/01)

9433 Roberts, Willo Davis. *Jo and the Bandit* (4–6). 1992, Macmillan $16.00 (0-689-31745-X). 192pp. Jo's life is in danger when the bandits who robbed the stagecoach in which she was a passenger find out she can draw accurate likenesses of them. (Rev: BL 6/1/92; SLJ 7/92)

9434 Roop, Peter, and Connie Roop. *Girl of the Shining Mountains: Sacagawea's Story* (5–8). 1999, Hyperion LB $15.49 (0-7868-2422-0). 178pp. In this fictionalized account, Sacagawea tells her son about her life and the remarkable expedition of Lewis and Clark. (Rev: HBG 3/00; SLJ 3/00)

9435 Rounds, Glen. *Sod Houses on the Great Plains* (K–3). Illus. 1995, Holiday LB $16.95 (0-8234-1162-1). 32pp. An illustrated account of the construction and utilization of a sod house, home of many prairie pioneers. (Rev: BCCB 3/95; BL 3/1/95*; HB 5–6/95; SLJ 3/95*) [693]

9436 Ryan, Pam M. *Riding Freedom* (3–6). Illus. 1998, Scholastic $15.95 (0-590-95766-X). 144pp. Based on fact, this is the story of a girl who lived her life as a man in mid-19th-century America. (Rev: BCCB 5/98; BL 1/1–15/98; HBG 10/98; SLJ 3/98)

9437 Shaw, Janet. *Happy Birthday Kirsten!* (3–5). Illus. 1987, Pleasant $12.95 (0-937295-88-4); paper $5.95 (0-937295-33-7). 72pp. It is 1854 in Minnesota and Kirsten looks forward to the gift of a day off from household chores. Also use: *Changes for Kirsten; Kirsten Saves the Day* (both 1988). (Rev: BL 4/1/88)

9438 Shaw, Janet. *Kirsten Learns a Lesson: A School Story* (3–5). Illus. 1986, Pleasant LB $12.95 (0-937295-82-5); paper $5.95 (0-937295-10-8). 72pp. Kirsten, a young immigrant girl, lives with her Swedish family in 1854 Minnesota. Others in this series are: *Kirsten's Surprise: A Christmas Story; Meet Kirsten: An American Girl* (both 1986). (Rev: BL 12/1/86)

9439 Shefelman, Janice. *Comanche Song* (5–8). Illus. by Tom Shefelman. 2000, Eakin $17.95 (1-57168-397-6). 255pp. The story of 16-year-old Tsena, son of a Comanche peace chief, and events that lead to the Battle of Plum Creek during the 1840s in Texas. (Rev: SLJ 10/00)

9440 Smith, Roland. *The Captain's Dog: My Journey with the Lewis and Clark Tribe* (5–8). 1999, Harcourt $17.00 (0-15-201989-8). 208pp. This is the story of the Lewis and Clark expedition as experienced by the Newfoundland dog that accompanied the two explorers. (Rev: HBG 3/00; SLJ 11/99)

9441 Stevens, Carla. *Trouble for Lucy* (4–6). Illus. by Ronald Himler. 1979, Houghton paper $5.95 (0-89919-523-7). 80pp. Lucy's pup Finn causes trouble during a wagon trip to the Oregon Territory.

9442 Tamar, Erika. *The Midnight Train Home* (5–7). 2000, Knopf LB $18.99 (0-375-90159-0). 208pp. Diedre O'Roarke, age 11, is adopted from the Orphan Train but her new home situation with a minister and his wife is far from happy. (Rev: BCCB 5/00; BL 4/1/00; HB 7–8/00; HBG 10/00; SLJ 7/00)

9443 Thomas, Joyce C. *I Have Heard of a Land* (3–6). Illus. by Floyd Cooper. 1998, HarperCollins LB $14.89 (0-06-023478-4). 32pp. This tribute to the pioneer spirit tells, through the eyes of a black woman, what it was like to come to the untamed frontier, build a home, and put down roots. (Rev: BCCB 6/98; BL 2/15/98*; HBG 10/98; SLJ 7/98)

9444 Travis, Lucille. *Redheaded Orphan* (4–7). 1995, Baker Book House paper $5.99 (0-8010-4023-X). 152pp. In 1864, Ben Abee and his family move from New York City to Minnesota, where Ben befriends orphaned Jamie. (Rev: BL 2/15/96)

9445 Tripp, Valerie. *Happy Birthday, Josefina! A Springtime Story* (3–5). Series: American Girls. 1998, Pleasant $12.99 (1-56247-588-6); paper $5.95 (1-56247-587-8). 68pp. In the New Mexico of 1824, Josefina discovers she can become a healer after she cures a friend bitten by a rattlesnake. (Rev: BL 8/98; HBG 3/99)

9446 Tripp, Valerie. *Josefina Saves the Day: A Summer Story* (3–5). Illus. Series: American Girls. 1998, Pleasant $12.95 (1-56247-590-8); paper $5.95 (1-56247-589-4). 68pp. A heavily illustrated novel, set in the New Mexico of 1824, in which young Josefina's father must decide whether or not to trust an American trader. (Rev: BL 8/98; HBG 3/99)

9447 Tripp, Valerie. *Meet Josefina: An American Girl* (3–5). Illus. Series: American Girls. 1997,

Pleasant paper $5.95 (1-56247-515-0). 85pp. In this story set in 1824 on a Mexican ranch in what is now New Mexico, the young heroine helps manage the ranch after her mother's death. Also use *Josefina Learns a Lesson: A School Story* (1997). (Rev: BL 10/1/97; HBG 3/98; SLJ 12/97)

9448 Turner, Ann. *Grasshopper Summer* (4–6). 1989, Troll paper $3.95 (0-8167-2262-5). 144pp. Sam's father moves his family from Kentucky to the Dakota Territory. (Rev: BCCB 4/89; BL 6/15/89)

9449 Waddell, Martin. *Little Obie and the Flood* (3–6). Illus. 1992, Candlewick $13.95 (1-56402-106-8). 80pp. The story of Obie and his grandparents, who have little worldly goods but always room for one more. (Rev: BL 9/1/92; SLJ 11/92)

9450 Waddell, Martin. *Little Obie and the Kidnap* (3–5). Illus. by Elsie Lennox. 1994, Candlewick $14.95 (1-56402-352-4). 79pp. A pioneer story in which a community unites to care for two orphan boys who are found with their dead mother in a stranded wagon. (Rev: SLJ 10/94)

9451 Wallace, Bill. *Red Dog* (4–6). 1987, Holiday $16.95 (0-8234-0650-4); Pocket paper $4.50 (0-671-70141-X). 192pp. Adam and his dog Ruff defy gold speculators in this story of the Wyoming Territory in the 1860s. (Rev: BL 6/1/87; SLJ 6–7/87)

9452 Welch, Catherine A. *Clouds of Terror* (2–4). Illus. by Laurie K. Johnson. 1994, Carolrhoda LB $21.27 (0-87614-771-6). 48pp. The harm caused by hordes of grasshoppers is depicted in this story set on a Minnesota farm during the 1870s. (Rev: BL 9/15/94; SLJ 8/94)

9453 Whalen, Sharla S. *Friends on Ice* (3–5). Illus. 1997, ABDO paper $5.95 (1-56239-901-2). 64pp. This is a story about four friends growing up on the Illinois prairie in the 1890s and of their preparations for the Winter Entertainment festivities. (Rev: BL 2/1/98)

9454 Whelan, Gloria. *Miranda's Last Stand* (4–7). 1999, HarperCollins LB $14.89 (0-06-028252-5). 128pp. After her husband was killed at Little Big Horn, Miranda's mother can't bear to be around Indians, including Sitting Bull who works with her at Buffalo Bill's Wild West Show. (Rev: BL 11/1/99; HBG 3/00; SLJ 11/99)

9455 Whelan, Gloria. *Next Spring an Oriole* (2–4). Illus. 1987, Random LB $6.99 (0-394-99125-7); paper $3.99 (0-394-89125-2). 64pp. The story of 10-year-old Libby who journeys to Michigan from Virginia in a covered wagon with her family in 1837. (Rev: BCCB 10/87; BL 10/1/87)

9456 Whelan, Gloria. *Return to the Island* (4–7). 2000, HarperCollins LB $14.89 (0-06-028254-1). 192pp. In the early 19th century on Mackinac Island, Mary must decide between two men who love her: White Hawk, an orphan raised by a white family, and James, an English painter. (Rev: BL 1/1–15/01; HBG 3/01; SLJ 12/00)

9457 Wilkes, Maria D. *Little Clearing in the Woods* (3–6). Illus. by Dan Andreasen. Series: The Caroline Years. 1998, HarperCollins LB $15.89 (0-06-026998-7). 315pp. Caroline Quiner (the mother of Laura Ingalls Wilder) and her family move to a small cabin in the woods, where her widowed mother takes a job cooking for neighborhood laborers. (Rev: HBG 10/98; SLJ 10/98)

9458 Wilkes, Maria D. *Little House in Brookfield* (3–6). Illus. by Dan Andreasen. Series: The Brookfield Years. 1996, HarperCollins paper $4.95 (0-06-440610-5). 298pp. This spinoff from the *Little House* books tells of the childhood in Brookfield, Wisconsin, of Caroline Quiner, who much later would become the mother of Laura Ingalls Wilder. (Rev: SLJ 8/96)

9459 Wilkes, Maria D. *Little Town at the Crossroads* (3–6). Illus. 1997, HarperCollins LB $15.89 (0-06-026996-0). 368pp. The fictionalized story of Laura Ingalls Wilder's mother and her growing up in Brookfield, Wisconsin, in 1846–1847. (Rev: BL 4/15/97; SLJ 7/97)

9460 Wills, Patricia. *Danger Along the Ohio* (4–7). 1997, Clarion $15.00 (0-395-77044-0). 192pp. This action-packed historical novel set in Ohio in 1795 tells how Amos and his younger brother and sister are captured by Indians. (Rev: BCCB 5/97; BL 5/1/97; SLJ 5/97)

9461 Wilson, Laura. *How I Survived the Oregon Trail: The Journal of Jesse Adams* (3–6). Series: Time Travelers. 1999, Morrow paper $9.95 (0-688-17276-8). 38pp. Beginning on April 29, 1852, this fictionalized diary account of a 10-year-old's journey with his family from Iowa to Oregon contains excellent illustrations and a fold-out map. (Rev: SLJ 2/00)

9462 Wisler, G. Clifton. *All for Texas: A Story of Texas Liberation* (4–8). 2000, Jamestown paper $5.95 (0-8092-0629-3). 140pp. A thirteen-year-old boy tells about moving west with his family in 1838 to Texas, where his father has been promised land if he will fight against Mexico. (Rev: BCCB 7–8/00; SLJ 8/00)

THE CIVIL WAR

9463 Banks, Sara H. *Abraham's Battle: A Novel of Gettysburg* (4–7). 1999, Simon & Schuster $15.00 (0-689-81779-7). 96pp. After the Battle of Gettysburg, Abraham Small, a former slave and ambulance driver, helps a wounded Confederate soldier whom he met prior to the battle. (Rev: BCCB 4/99; BL 3/1/99; HBG 10/99; SLJ 7/99)

9464 Bartoletti, Susan Campbell. *No Man's Land: A Young Soldier's Story* (5–9). 1999, Scholastic $15.95 (0-590-38371-X). 176pp. The story of a young boy's life as a Confederate soldier after he lies about his age and joins the Okefenokee Rifles in 1861. (Rev: BCCB 6/99; BL 4/1/99; HBG 10/99; SLJ 6/99)

9465 Beatty, Patricia. *Who Comes with Cannons?* (5–7). 1992, Morrow $15.95 (0-688-11028-2). 192pp. The Civil War brings danger to Truth Hopkins and her Quaker family because they are pacifists. (Rev: BCCB 10/92; BL 1/1/93; HB 1–2/93; SLJ 10/92)

9466 Berry, Carrie. *A Confederate Girl: The Diary of Carrie Berry, 1864* (4–6). Ed. by Christy Steel and Anne Todd. Series: Diaries, Letters, and Memoirs. 2000, Capstone LB $22.60 (0-7368-0343-2). 32pp. These excerpts from the diary of a 10-year-old Confederate girl describe everyday life and problems behind the front lines and are supplemented by informative sidebars that give good background information. (Rev: BL 10/15/00; HBG 10/00; SLJ 9/00) [973.7]

9467 Bircher, William. *A Civil War Drummer Boy: The Diary of William Bircher, 1861–1865* (4–6). Ed. by Shelley Swanson Sateren. Illus. Series: Diaries, Letters, and Memoirs. 2000, Capstone $22.60 (0-7368-0348-3). Excerpts from a 15-year-old's diary tell what it was like for a young man to face death in the Civil War; this account also contains period photographs, a timeline, maps, and sidebars. (Rev: BL 10/15/00; HBG 10/00; SLJ 9/00) [973.7]

9468 Brill, Marlene T. *Diary of a Drummer Boy* (4–7). 1998, Millbrook LB $21.90 (0-7613-0118-6). 48pp. Using a diary format, this novel tells of a 12-year-old's experiences as a drummer in the Union Army during the Civil War. (Rev: BL 3/1/98; HBG 10/98; SLJ 5/98)

9469 Bunting, Eve. *The Blue and the Gray* (3–5). Illus. by Ned Bittinger. 1996, Scholastic $14.95 (0-590-60197-0). 32pp. Using free verse, the author recreates a Civil War battle and points out what we have learned from this terrible conflict. (Rev: BCCB 2/97; BL 11/15/96; SLJ 12/96)

9470 Crist-Evans, Craig. *Moon over Tennessee: A Boy's Civil War Journal* (4–7). 1999, Houghton $15.00 (0-395-91208-3). 64pp. In free-verse diary entries, 13-year-old Crist-Evans reports on the Civil War from his vantage point in a camp behind the front lines. (Rev: BCCB 6/99; BL 5/15/99; HBG 10/99)

9471 Donahue, John. *An Island Far from Home* (4–7). 1994, Carolrhoda LB $21.27 (0-87614-859-3). 180pp. Joshua, a Union supporter, forms an unusual friendship through corresponding with a young Southern soldier who is a prisoner of war. (Rev: BCCB 2/95; BL 2/15/95; SLJ 2/95)

9472 Duey, Kathleen. *Amelina Carrett: Bayou Grand Coeur, Louisiana, 1863* (5–8). Series: American Diaries. 1999, Simon & Schuster paper $3.99 (0-689-82402-5). 137pp. Growing up in Cajun country during the Civil War, Amelina has to make a difficult decision when she finds a wounded Yankee soldier hiding in the bayou. (Rev: SLJ 9/99)

9473 Ellison, Suzanne Pierson. *Best of Enemies* (5–7). 1998, Rising Moon $12.95 (0-87358-714-6); paper $6.95 (0-87358-717-0). 200pp. During the Civil War, three young people, a wealthy New Mexican boy, a young Confederate soldier, and a Navajo slave girl, are thrown together in a quest for survival. (Rev: HBG 3/99; SLJ 5/99)

9474 Ernst, Kathleen. *Retreat from Gettysburg* (5–8). Illus. 2000, White Mane $17.95 (1-57249-187-6). 142pp. When a doctor orders 14-year-old Chig and his mother to care for a wounded Confederate soldier, the boy finds it hard to be kind to a man who belongs to the side that killed his father and brothers. (Rev: BL 9/15/00)

9475 Forman, James D. *Becca's Story* (5–8). 1992, Macmillan LB $15.00 (0-684-19332-9). 192pp. The story of the courtship between Becca, in Michigan, and Alex, in the Union Army, during the Civil War. (Rev: BL 12/1/92)

9476 Freedman, Florence B. *Two Tickets to Freedom: The True Story of Ellen and William Craft, Fugitive Slaves* (4–8). Illus. by Ezra Jack Keats. 1971, Bedrick $12.95 (0-87226-330-4); paper $5.95 (0-87226-221-9). 96pp. An exciting story of slavery, escape, and pursuit that is based on fact. A reissue.

9477 Garrity, Jennifer Johnson. *The Bushwhacker: A Civil War Adventure* (5–8). Illus. by Paul Bachem. 1999, Peachtree paper $8.95 (1-56145-201-7). 196pp. The clash of divided loyalties is the main conflict in this story of a boy torn between his Unionist feelings and the friendship he feels towards his protector, a Confederate sympathizer. (Rev: SLJ 4/00)

9478 Hahn, Mary D. *Promises to the Dead* (4–6). 2000, Clarion $15.00 (0-395-96394-X). 202pp. When 12-year-old Jesse sets out to travel north to Baltimore to take the son of a dead slave to relatives, he doesn't anticipate the outbreak of the Civil War. (Rev: BCCB 5/00; HBG 10/00; SLJ 6/00)

9479 Hesse, Karen. *A Light in the Storm: The Civil War Diary of Amelia Martin* (4–7). Series: Dear America. 1999, Scholastic $10.95 (0-590-56733-0). 176pp. The story of Amelia Martin, the 15-year-old daughter of a lighthouse keeper in Delaware, and how her family became involved in the oncoming Civil War. (Rev: BL 10/15/99; HBG 3/00; SLJ 11/99)

9480 Hoobler, Thomas, and Dorothy Hoobler. *Sally Bradford: The Story of a Rebel Girl* (4–7). Illus. 1997, Silver Burdett LB $17.95 (0-382-39258-2); paper $4.95 (0-382-39259-0). 128pp. The Civil War changes the lives of Sally Bradford and her family, who operate a farm without slaves in Norfolk, Virginia. (Rev: BL 6/1–15/97; SLJ 8/97)

9481 Houston, Gloria. *Mountain Valor* (4–7). Illus. by Thomas B. Allen. 1994, Putnam $15.95 (0-399-22519-6). 224pp. In this Civil War novel, Valor lives up to her name by recovering the family's supplies after they have been stolen by Yankee soldiers. (Rev: BCCB 6/94; BL 4/1/94; SLJ 6/94)

9482 Hunt, Irene. *Across Five Aprils* (6–8). 1993, Silver Burdett paper $5.00 (0-8136-7202-3). 100pp. A young boy's experiences during the Civil War in the backwoods of southern Illinois. One brother joins the Union forces, the other the Confederacy, and the family is divided.

9483 Jones, Elizabeth McDavid. *Watcher in the Piney Woods* (5–7). Illus. by Jean-Paul Tibbles and Greg Dearth. Series: History Mysteries. 2000, Pleasant $9.95 (1-58485-091-4); paper $5.95 (1-58485-090-6). 144pp. In southern Virginia during the last year of the Civil War, 12-year-old Cassie sets out to solve the mystery of objects disappearing from her home and farm. (Rev: SLJ 1/01)

9484 Karr, Kathleen. *Spy in the Sky* (2–4). Illus. by Thomas F. Yezerski. Series: Hyperion Chapters.

1997, Hyperion LB $14.49 (0-7868-2239-2); paper $3.95 (0-7868-1165-X). 60pp. An exciting, simple novel that uses as background the exploits of Thaddeus Lowe and his Balloon Corps on the Union side of the Civil War. (Rev: SLJ 8/97)

9485 Keith, Harold. *Rifles for Watie* (6–8). 1991, HarperCollins LB $15.89 (0-690-04907-2); paper $5.95 (0-06-447030-X). 332pp. Life of a Union soldier and spy fighting the Civil War in the West. Newbery Medal winner, 1958.

9486 Love, D. Anne. *Three Against the Tide* (5–8). 1998, Holiday $15.95 (0-8234-1400-0). 162pp. In this Civil War novel, 12-year-old Confederate Susanna Simons must care for her two younger brothers when Yankee troops invade South Carolina. (Rev: BL 12/1/98; HBG 10/99; SLJ 1/99)

9487 Lyons, Mary E., and Muriel M. Branch. *Dear Ellen Bee: A Civil War Scrapbook of Two Union Spies* (5–8). Illus. 2000, Atheneum $17.00 (0-689-82379-7). 161pp. Set in Richmond, Virginia, before and during the Civil War, this novel, based on fact, tells how a strong-willed lady and her emancipated slave get involved in a spying adventure. (Rev: BCCB 10/00; BL 11/1/00; HBG 3/01; SLJ 10/00)

9488 Murphy, Jim. *The Journal of James Edmond Pease: A Civil War Union Soldier, Virginia, 1863* (5–8). Series: My Name Is America. 1998, Scholastic $9.95 (0-590-43814-X). 173pp. This novel takes the form of a journal kept by a 16-year-old private in the New York Volunteers during the Civil War and tells of his experiences, including the time he was lost behind enemy lines. (Rev: BCCB 11/98; HBG 3/99; SLJ 7/99)

9489 O'Dell, Scott. *Sing Down the Moon* (5–8). 1970, Houghton $17.00 (0-395-10919-1); Dell paper $5.50 (0-440-97975-7). 138pp. The tragic forced march of the Indians to Fort Sumter in 1864, told by a young Navajo girl.

9490 Osborne, Mary Pope. *My Brother's Keeper: Virginia's Diary* (2–5). Illus. Series: My America. 2000, Scholastic $8.95 (0-439-15307-7). 112pp. Told in journal format, this presents a young girl's reactions to the bloody battle at Gettysburg and Lincoln's famous address. (Rev: BL 10/1/00; HBG 10/00; SLJ 8/00)

9491 Owens, L. L. *The Code of the Drum* (3–6). Illus. by Margaret Sanfilippo. Series: Cover-to-Cover Books. 2000, Perfection Learning $13.95 (0-7807-9654-3); paper $8.95 (0-7891-5310-6). 54pp. When his father is killed in the Civil War, 12-year-old Jacob McCoy joins his dad's Union regiment as a drummer boy. (Rev: SLJ 12/00)

9492 Patrick, Denise Lewis. *The Longest Ride* (5–7). 1999, Holt $15.95 (0-8050-4715-8). 164pp. This sequel to *The Adventures of Midnight Son* explores slavery and Indian-black relations when a teenaged runaway slave is helped by a band of Arapaho Indians at the time of the Civil War. (Rev: HBG 3/00; SLJ 12/99)

9493 Paulsen, Gary. *Soldier's Heart* (5–8). 1998, Delacorte $15.95 (0-385-32498-7). 144pp. A powerful novel about the agony of the Civil War, based on the real-life experiences of a Union soldier who was only 15 when he went to war. (Rev: BCCB 9/98; BL 6/1–15/98*; HB 11–12/98; HBG 3/99)

9494 Pinkney, Andrea D. *Silent Thunder: A Civil War Story* (5–8). 1999, Hyperion LB $15.49 (0-7868-2388-7). 208pp. The brutal oppression of slavery is revealed in this story told by two black children living on a Virginia plantation during the Civil War. (Rev: BL 9/1/99; HBG 3/00; SLJ 12/99)

9495 Polacco, Patricia. *Pink and Say* (K–5). Illus. 1994, Putnam $16.99 (0-399-22671-0). 32pp. Based on a true incident during the Civil War, this book tells of the friendship of two Union soldiers: Say, a white man who is rescued by a black man, Pinkus, known as Pink. (Rev: BCCB 9/94; BL 9/1/94; HB 11–12/94; SLJ 10/94*)

9496 Porter, Connie. *Addy Learns a Lesson* (3–6). Illus. by Melodye Rosales. Series: American Girls Collection. 1993, Pleasant $12.95 (1-56247-078-7); paper $5.95 (1-56247-077-9). 70pp. In the year 1864, young Addy and her mother try to escape slavery by fleeing to the North after her father is sold again and they are separated. (Rev: BL 8/93; SLJ 1/94)

9497 Pryor, Bonnie. *Joseph: 1861 — A Rumble of War* (3–7). Illus. 1999, Morrow $15.00 (0-688-15671-1). 160pp. Growing up in Kentucky in 1861, Joseph decides to join the abolitionist cause when he sees how inhumanely slaves are treated. (Rev: BL 7/99; HBG 10/99; SLJ 8/99)

9498 Pryor, Bonnie. *Joseph's Choice — 1861* (3–5). Illus. Series: American Adventures. 2000, HarperCollins LB $14.89 (0-06-029226-1). 176pp. At the beginning of the Civil War in a small Kentucky town, young Joseph realizes that he must take sides. (Rev: BL 12/15/00; SLJ 10/00)

9499 Reeder, Carolyn. *Across the Lines* (4–7). 1997, Simon & Schuster $17.00 (0-689-81133-0). 224pp. Edward and his slave friend, Simon, are separated when Yankees capture their Virginia plantation in this Civil War novel. (Rev: BCCB 6/97; BL 4/1/97*; SLJ 6/97)

9500 Reeder, Carolyn. *Captain Kate* (4–7). 1999, Avon $15.00 (0-380-97628-5). 192pp. Set during the Civil War, this novel tells how 12-year-old Kate and her stepbrother navigate the 184 miles of the Cumberland and Ohio Canal on the family's canal boat. (Rev: HBG 10/99; SLJ 1/99)

9501 Reeder, Carolyn. *Shades of Gray* (4–7). 1989, Macmillan LB $16.00 (0-02-775810-9). 152pp. The story of 12-year-old Will, the last surviving member of his family from the South during the Civil War. (Rev: BCCB 1/90; BL 1/15/90; HB 3–4/90; SLJ 1/90)

9502 Rinaldi, Ann. *Amelia's War* (5–8). 1999, Scholastic $15.95 (0-590-11744-0). 272pp. During the Civil War, young Amelia Grafton secretly finds a way to prevent the Confederate forces from destroying her town in Maryland. (Rev: BL 11/15/99; HBG 3/00)

9503 Roop, Peter, and Connie Roop. *Grace's Letter to Lincoln* (2–4). Illus. by Stacey Schuett. Series: Hyperion Chapters. 1998, Hyperion LB $14.49 (0-7868-2375-5); paper $3.95 (0-7868-1296-6). 68pp.

In this easy chapter book based on fact, a little girl writes to Lincoln suggesting that he would get more votes in the upcoming election if he grew a beard. (Rev: SLJ 1/99)

9504 Stolz, Mary. *A Ballad of the Civil War* (4–6). Illus. 1997, HarperCollins LB $13.89 (0-06-027363-1). 64pp. Based on a Civil War ballad, this is the story of two Southern brothers who enlist on opposite sides. (Rev: BL 10/1/97; SLJ 2/98)

9505 Turner, Ann. *Drummer Boy: Marching to the Civil War* (3–5). Illus. by Mark Hess. 1998, HarperCollins LB $14.89 (0-06-027697-5). 32pp. In this first-person account, a 13-year-old runs away from home to become a drummer boy during the Civil War and later encounters the reality of war and death. (Rev: BCCB 11/98; BL 9/15/98; HBG 3/99; SLJ 11/98)

9506 Wisler, G. Clifton. *The Drummer Boy of Vicksburg* (4–6). 1997, Dutton $15.99 (0-525-67537-X). 144pp. The story of a drummer boy who is in the Union Army during the Civil War. (Rev: BL 12/1/96; SLJ 3/97)

9507 Wisler, G. Clifton. *Mr. Lincoln's Drummer* (5–7). 1994, Dutton $15.99 (0-525-67463-2). 144pp. Eleven-year-old Willie, a Vermonter, joins the Union Army as a drummer boy when his father enlists. (Rev: BCCB 1/95; BL 1/15/95)

9508 . Wisler, G. Clifton. *Mustang Flats* (5–8). 1997, Dutton $14.99 (0-525-67544-2). 128pp. Abby wants to help his family when his father returns from the Civil War a broken, bitter man. (Rev: BL 8/97; HBG 3/98; SLJ 7/97)

9509 Wisler, G. Clifton. *Run the Blockade* (5–8). 2000, HarperCollins LB $15.89 (0-06-029208-3). 128pp. An Irish lad signs aboard the steamship *Banshee*, whose mission is to try to break the Union shipping blockade during the Civil War. (Rev: BCCB 10/00; BL 9/15/00; HBG 3/01)

9510 Zeinert, Karen. *Those Courageous Women of the Civil War* (5–8). Illus. 1998, Millbrook LB $27.40 (0-7613-0212-3). 96pp. This account relates the contributions of women during the Civil War, with details on how they served as nurses, spies, writers, and workers on the home front. (Rev: BL 6/1–15/98; HBG 3/99) [973.7]

RECONSTRUCTION TO WORLD WAR II, 1865–1941

9511 Adler, Susan S. *Meet Samantha: An American Girl* (3–5). Illus. 1986, Pleasant LB $12.95 (0-937295-80-9); paper $5.95 (0-937295-04-3). 72pp. Samantha is an orphan living with her wealthy grandmother in the America of 1904. Two others in the series are: *Samantha Learns a Lesson; Samantha's Surprise* (both 1986). (Rev: BL 12/1/86)

9512 Alter, Judith. *Luke and the Van Zandt County War* (5–8). Illus. 1984, Christian Univ. $14.95 (0-912646-88-8). 132pp. Life in Reconstruction Texas as seen through the eyes of two 14-year-olds. (Rev: SLJ 3/85)

9513 Armstrong, Jennifer. *Theodore Roosevelt: Letters from a Young Coal Miner* (3–6). Illus. Series: Dear Mr. President. 2000, Winslow $8.95 (1-

890817-27-9). 128pp. Using fictional letters between a 13-year-old Pennsylvania coal miner and Teddy Roosevelt, this book introduces the hardships of a miner's life as well as the character and administration of President Roosevelt. (Rev: BL 3/1/01)

9514 Avi. *Abigail Takes the Wheel* (2–4). Illus. by Don Bolognese. Series: I Can Read. 1999, Harper-Collins LB $14.89 (0-06-027663-0). 64pp. In this easily read story set in the 1880s, young Abigail steers a freight boat up the Hudson after the mate gets sick. (Rev: BCCB 6/99; BL 4/1/99; HB 3–4/99; HBG 10/99; SLJ 5/99)

9515 Ayres, Katherine. *Under Copp's Hill* (4–6). Illus. by Troy Howell and Laszlo Kubinyi. Series: History Mysteries. 2000, Pleasant $9.95 (1-58485-089-2); paper $5.95 (1-58485-088-4). 163pp. In 1908 Boston, Innie and her cousin Teresa are alarmed when books begin disappearing from their settlement house library. (Rev: SLJ 3/01)

9516 Bader, Bonnie. *East Side Story* (3–5). Series: Stories of the States. 1993, Silver Moon LB $14.95 (1-881889-22-X). 72pp. The story of an 11-year-old Jewish immigrant girl and her sister, both of whom work in the Triangle Shirtwaist Factory in New York City during the early 1900s. (Rev: SLJ 2/94)

9517 Baier, Joan Foley. *Luvella's Promise* (3–5). 1999, Writers Club paper $9.95 (1-893652-04-1). 83pp. Luvella is growing up with her family in a logging town in Pennsylvania in 1905 when typhoid fever strikes. (Rev: SLJ 11/99)

9518 Barasch, Lynne. *Radio Rescue* (2–5). Illus. 2000, Farrar $16.00 (0-374-36166-5). 40pp. Based on fact, this novel set in New York in 1923 tells how a young amateur radio operator saved Florida hurricane victims by picking up their distress signals. (Rev: BCCB 7–8/00; BL 9/15/00; HB 9–10/00; HBG 3/01; SLJ 10/00)

9519 Bartoletti, Susan Campbell. *A Coal Miner's Bride: The Diary of Anetka Kaminska* (5–9). Illus. 2000, Scholastic paper $10.95 (0-439-05386-2). 224pp. Based on a series of true events, this gripping historical novel tells of a young Polish immigrant girl and her struggle to survive in a coal mining town in Pennsylvania in the late 1890s. (Rev: BL 4/1/00; HBG 10/00; SLJ 8/00)

9520 Bartoletti, Susan Campbell. *Dancing with Dziadziu* (3–6). Illus. by Annika Nelson. 1997, Harcourt $15.00 (0-15-200675-3). 40pp. Gabriella's grandmother, now in failing health, remembers her experiences as an immigrant in this country and the joys of dancing with her husband. (Rev: BCCB 5/97; BL 3/15/97*; SLJ 5/97)

9521 Blackwood, Gary L. *Moonshine* (5–8). 1999, Marshall Cavendish $14.95 (0-7614-5056-4). 158pp. Thirteen-year-old Thad, growing up with his mother in rural Mississippi during the Depression, makes a little extra money by running an illegal still that produces moonshine for the locals. (Rev: BCCB 11/99; BL 9/1/99; HBG 3/00)

9522 Blakeslee, Ann R. *Summer Battles* (5–8). 2000, Marshall Cavendish $14.95 (0-7614-5064-5). 127pp. The story of Kath, age 11, growing up in a small town in Indiana in 1926 and of her father, a preacher, who is attacked for opposing the Ku Klux Klan. (Rev: BCCB 3/00; BL 4/1/00; HBG 10/00; SLJ 4/00)

9523 Blos, Joan W. *Brooklyn Doesn't Rhyme* (5–7). Illus. 1994, Scribners paper $16.00 (0-684-19694-8). 96pp. A young girl narrates this episodic story about a Polish-Jewish family new to New York City in the early 1900s. (Rev: BCCB 11/94; BL 9/15/94; HB 9–10/94; SLJ 9/94)

9524 Bradley, Kimberly Brubaker. *One-of-a-Kind Mallie* (3–5). 1999, Delacorte $15.95 (0-385-32694-7). 149pp. During World War I in a small Midwestern town, Mallie resents being a twin and always paired with her sister. (Rev: BCCB 9/99; BL 8/99; HBG 3/00; SLJ 9/99)

9525 Bradley, Kimberly Brubaker. *Ruthie's Gift* (3–5). Illus. 1998, Delacorte $14.95 (0-385-32525-8). 143pp. This honest, moving novel describes a girl's feelings and actions as she grows up on a farm in Indiana around 1915. (Rev: BCCB 5/98; BL 1/1–15/98; HBG 10/98; SLJ 2/98*)

9526 Bunting, Eve. *Dandelions* (2–4). Illus. by Greg Shed. 1995, Harcourt $16.00 (0-15-200050-X). 48pp. Zoe compares the dandelions she sees growing wild in a meadow to her family, which has just traveled west to the Nebraska Territory by covered wagon. (Rev: BCCB 9/95; BL 9/15/95; SLJ 11/95*)

9527 Burandt, Harriet, and Shelley Dale. *Tales from the Homeplace: Adventures of a Texas Farm Girl* (4–8). 1997, Holt $15.95 (0-8050-5075-2). 158pp. A family story that takes place on a Texas cotton farm during the Depression and features a spunky heroine, 12-year-old Irene, and her six brothers and sisters. (Rev: BCCB 7–8/97; HB 5–6/97; SLJ 4/97*)

9528 Carbone, Elisa. *Storm Warriors* (4–8). 2001, Knopf LB $18.99 (0-375-90664-9). 176pp. An exciting adventure story set on the Outer Banks of North Carolina in 1895, about a boy who wants to become part of the nearby rescue station that is manned by an African American crew. (Rev: BL 1/1–15/01; SLJ 2/01)

9529 Carter, Alden R. *Crescent Moon* (5–8). 1999, Holiday $16.95 (0-8234-1521-X). 153pp. In early part of the 20th century, Jeremy joins Great-Uncle Mac on a log drive where they become friends with a Native American and his daughter and, through them, experience the shame of racial prejudice. (Rev: BCCB 1/00; BL 2/15/00; HB 3–4/00; HBG 10/00; SLJ 3/00)

9530 Clifton, Lucille. *The Times They Used to Be* (4–9). Illus. 2000, Delacorte $12.95 (0-385-32126-0). 39pp. In this narrative poem, Mama tells her African American children about the days when she was growing up in the segregated South through a series of stories that deal with happiness, sorrow, yearning, and humor. (Rev: BL 1/1–15/01)

9531 Crofford, Emily. *A Place to Belong* (5–7). Illus. 1994, Carolrhoda LB $21.27 (0-87614-808-9). 160pp. During the Depression, clubfooted Talmadge and his family lose their home and must become cotton pickers in Arkansas. (Rev: BCCB 7–8/94; BL 5/15/94; SLJ 6/94)

9532 Cross, Gillian. *The Great American Elephant Chase* (5–8). 1993, Holiday $16.95 (0-8234-1016-1). 194pp. A heartwarming story of a lonely orphan and his journey with an elephant in 1881 America. (Rev: BCCB 6/93; BL 3/15/93*; SLJ 5/93*)

9533 Cutler, Jane. *The Song of the Molimo* (5–7). 1998, Farrar $16.00 (0-374-37141-5). 192pp. During the St. Louis World's Fair of 1904, 12-year-old Harry gets to know a group of pygmies who are on exhibit and encounters questions of race, intelligence, and fair play. (Rev: BCCB 10/98; BL 10/15/98; HBG 3/99; SLJ 11/98)

9534 De Angeli, Marguerite. *Copper-Toed Boots* (3–6). Illus. by author. 1996, Wayne State Univ. Pr. paper $15.95 (0-814-32654-4). 96pp. American family life in the early 20th century.

9535 DeClements, Barthe. *The Bite of the Gold Bug: A Story of the Alaskan Gold Rush* (3–6). Illus. by Dan Andreasen. Series: Once upon America. 1994, Puffin paper $4.99 (0-140-36081-6). 64pp. The story of 12-year-old Bucky who spends six months in the gold fields with his father and uncle. (Rev: BCCB 5/92; BL 5/15/92; SLJ 8/92)

9536 DeFelice, Cynthia. *Nowhere to Call Home* (5–8). 1999, Farrar $16.00 (0-374-35552-5). 208pp. During the Great Depression, and after her father has committed suicide, 12-year-old Frances decides to dress as a boy and ride the rails like the hobos she has heard about. (Rev: BL 4/1/99; HB 3–4/99; HBG 10/99; SLJ 4/99)

9537 Denenberg, Barry. *So Far from Home: The Diary of Mary Driscoll, an Irish Mill Girl* (4–8). 1997, Scholastic $10.95 (0-590-92667-5). 176pp. Using a diary format, this novel tells the story of Mary Driscoll's journey to the United States from Ireland and her ordeals as a worker in a Massachusetts textile mill in the 1800s. (Rev: BL 12/15/97; HBG 3/98; SLJ 10/97)

9538 De Young, C. Coco. *A Letter to Mrs. Roosevelt* (3–5). 1999, Delacorte $14.95 (0-385-32633-5). 105pp. By writing a letter to Mrs. Roosevelt during the Great Depression, 11-year-old Margo Bandini is able to help prevent the foreclosure on the family home. (Rev: BCCB 3/99; BL 2/1/99; HBG 10/99; SLJ 3/99)

9539 Duey, Kathleen. *Agnes May Gleason: Walsenburg, Colorado, 1933* (4–7). Series: American Diaries. 1998, Simon & Schuster paper $3.99 (0-689-82329-0). 137pp. Set during the Great Depression, this novel tells how 12-year-old Agnes and her family strive to keep their dairy farm operating. (Rev: SLJ 1/99)

9540 Duey, Kathleen. *Ellen Elizabeth Hawkins: Mobeetie, Texas, 1886* (4–7). Series: American Diaries. 1997, Simon & Schuster paper $4.50 (0-689-81409-7). 141pp. In this novel set on a Texas cattle ranch in 1886, young Ellen wants to be a rancher in spite of her father's objections. (Rev: SLJ 8/97)

9541 Duey, Kathleen. *Nell Dunne: Ellis Island, 1904* (4–8). 2000, Simon & Schuster paper $4.50 (0-689-83555-8). 138pp. This tells the story of an Irish immigrant family's trip across the Atlantic and their reception at Ellis Island. (Rev: SLJ 10/00)

9542 Duey, Kathleen. *Rosa Moreno: Hollywood, California, 1928* (4–6). 1999, Simon & Schuster paper $4.50 (0-689-83126-9). 140pp. A novel, set in Hollywood from 1928 to 1934, about young Rosa Moreno and her efforts to become a motion picture star like Shirley Temple. (Rev: SLJ 6/00)

9543 Duey, Kathleen, and Karen A. Bale. *Fire: Chicago, 1871* (4–7). Series: Survival! 1998, Simon & Schuster paper $3.99 (0-689-81310-4). 172pp. The tragic fire of 1871 that swept through Chicago is experienced by Nate Cooper, an orphan, and Julie Flynn, daughter of an important merchant. (Rev: SLJ 9/98)

9544 Duey, Kathleen, and Karen A. Bale. *Shipwreck: The Titanic, 1912* (4–7). Series: Survival! 1998, Simon & Schuster paper $3.99 (0-689-81311-2). 175pp. The voyage of the *Titanic*, as experienced by Gavin Reilly, who is working his way to America, and by Karolina Green, who is returning to the United States after the death of her parents in England. (Rev: SLJ 9/98)

9545 Duffy, James. *Radical Red* (5–8). 1993, Scribners $16.95 (0-684-19533-X). 160pp. Connor O'Shea joins a demonstration for women's rights when Susan B. Anthony comes to Albany in 1894. (Rev: BCCB 1/94; BL 12/1/93; SLJ 1/94)

9546 Gregory, Kristiana. *Orphan Runaways* (5–7). 1998, Scholastic $15.95 (0-590-60366-3). 160pp. Two brothers run away from a San Francisco orphanage in 1879 to look for an uncle in the gold fields. (Rev: BCCB 3/98; BL 2/15/98; HBG 10/98; SLJ 3/98)

9547 Hahn, Mary D. *Anna All Year Round* (3–5). Illus. 1999, Clarion $15.00 (0-395-86975-7). 144pp. Using an early 1900s urban setting, this warm family story tells about German immigrants and their children adjusting to America. (Rev: BCCB 6/99; BL 3/15/99; HB 7–8/99; HBG 10/99; SLJ 5/99)

9548 Hall, Donald. *The Milkman's Boy* (3–5). Illus. 1997, Walker LB $16.85 (0-8027-8465-8). 32pp. Around the time of World War I, Paul's father, a milkman, does not believe in the necessity of pasteurization. (Rev: BL 9/1/97; HBG 3/98; SLJ 9/97)

9549 Hansen, Joyce. *I Thought My Soul Would Rise and Fly: The Diary of Patsy, a Freed Girl* (4–8). 1997, Scholastic $10.95 (0-590-84913-1). 208pp. In this novel in the form of a diary, a freed slave girl wonders what to do with her life after leaving the plantation. (Rev: BL 12/15/97; HBG 3/98; SLJ 11/97)

9550 Hesse, Karen. *Letters from Rifka* (4–8). 1992, Holt $16.95 (0-8050-1964-2). 148pp. The harrowing story of a young Russian Jew's journey to America in 1919. (Rev: BCCB 10/92; HB 9–10/92*; SLJ 8/92*)

9551 Hesse, Karen. *A Time of Angels* (5–8). 1995, Hyperion LB $16.49 (0-7868-2072-1). 224pp. Through the experience of Hannah and her sisters in New England, the terrible effects of the flu epidemic of 1918 are re-created. (Rev: BCCB 1/96; BL 12/1/95; SLJ 12/95)

9552 Holland, Isabelle. *Paperboy* (4–6). 1999, Holiday $15.95 (0-8234-1422-1). 137pp. Growing up in a New York City slum in 1881, 12-year-old Kevin O'Donnell helps out his family by getting a job as a messenger for the owner of the *New York Chronicle*. (Rev: BCCB 10/99; HBG 3/00; SLJ 9/99)

9553 Hoobler, Dorothy, and Thomas Hoobler. *The First Decade: Curtain Going Up* (4–6). Illus. Series: Century Kids. 2000, Millbrook LB $21.90 (0-7613-1600-0). 160pp. Presents the first decade of the 20th century in the life of the Aldriches, a theatrical family living in Maine. (Rev: BCCB 7–8/00; BL 5/1/00; HBG 10/00; SLJ 7/00)

9554 Hoobler, Dorothy, and Thomas Hoobler. *Florence Robinson: The Story of a Jazz Age Girl* (3–6). Illus. by Robert Sauber. Series: Her Story. 1997, Silver Burdett LB $17.95 (0-382-39644-8); paper $4.95 (0-382-39645-6). 123pp. In the 1920s, an African American family moves north to Chicago in pursuit of freedom and a better life. (Rev: SLJ 8/97)

9555 Hoobler, Dorothy, and Tom Hoobler. *The Second Decade: Voyages* (4–6). Illus. Series: Century Kids. 2000, Millbrook LB $21.90 (0-7613-1601-9). 160pp. In the second decade of the 20th century, Peggy Aldrich and her sister photograph the factory workers in Lowell, Massachusetts, explore issues involving child labor and women's suffrage, and feel the effects of the sinking of the *Titanic*. (Rev: BCCB 7–8/00; BL 5/1/00; HBG 10/00; SLJ 7/00)

9556 Houston, Gloria. *Littlejim* (4–6). Illus. by Thomas B. Allen. 1990, Putnam $14.95 (0-399-22220-0). 176pp. In this story of Appalachia, sensitive Littlejim tries to gain attention from his macho father. (Rev: BL 11/1/90; SLJ 2/91)

9557 Houston, Gloria. *Littlejim's Dreams* (5–8). Illus. by Thomas B. Allen. 1997, Harcourt $16.00 (0-15-201509-4). 231pp. Littlejim wants to become a writer, but his father thinks he should be a farmer and logger like himself, in this novel set in Appalachia in 1920. A sequel to *Littlejim* (1990). (Rev: SLJ 7/97)

9558 Hulme, Joy N. *Through the Open Door* (4–6). 2000, HarperCollins $14.95 (0-380-97870-9). 162pp. Told by 9-year-old Dora Cookson, this is an appealing story of a Mormon family and their move from Utah to homestead in New Mexico in 1910. (Rev: BCCB 6/00; HBG 3/01; SLJ 8/00)

9559 Hurst, Carol Otis. *Through the Lock* (5–8). 2001, Houghton $15.00 (0-618-03036-0). 172pp. In this novel set in Connecticut in the first half of the 19th century, a young orphan named Etta shares many adventures with a boy who lives in an abandoned cabin by a canal. (Rev: BCCB 3/01; SLJ 3/01)

9560 Hurwitz, Johanna. *Faraway Summer* (5–7). Illus. by Mary Azarian. 1998, Morrow $14.95 (0-688-15334-8). 112pp. In 1910, a Jewish orphan who lives in a tenement in New York City is thrilled at the thought of spending two weeks on a farm in Vermont, thanks to the Fresh Air Fund. (Rev: BL 3/1/98; HB 7–8/98; HBG 10/98; SLJ 5/98)

9561 Hyatt, Patricia Rusch. *Coast to Coast with Alice* (3–6). Illus. 1995, Carolrhoda LB $21.27 (0-87614-789-9). 72pp. A fictionalized account of the first automobile cross-country trip by a woman in 1909. (Rev: BCCB 9/95; BL 7/95; HB 11–12/95; SLJ 8/95)

9562 Isaacs, Anne. *Treehouse Tales* (3–5). Illus. 1997, Dutton $14.99 (0-525-45611-2). 96pp. This book, set in Pennsylvania in the 1880s, contains three stories, one for each of the Barrett children. (Rev: BL 9/15/97; HB 9–10/97; HBG 3/98; SLJ 7/97)

9563 Jaspersohn, William. *The Two Brothers* (2–4). Illus. Series: Family Heritage. 2000, Vermont Folklife Center $14.95 (0-916718-16-6). 32pp. Based on a true story, this novel tells of two German brothers who immigrated separately to the United States in the 1880s and were miraculously reunited. (Rev: BL 11/1/00; SLJ 9/00)

9564 Jocelyn, Marthe. *Earthly Astonishments* (4–8). 2000, Dutton $15.99 (0-525-46263-5). 179pp. The setting is New York City in the 1880s and the novel involves a girl who is only 22 inches tall and her career in a glorified freak show. (Rev: BCCB 2/00; HBG 10/00; SLJ 4/00)

9565 Jones, Elizabeth McDavid. *Secrets on 26th Street* (3–6). Illus. by Greg Dearth. 1999, Pleasant $9.95 (1-56247-816-8); paper $5.95 (1-56247-760-9). 144pp. This novel affords an interesting behind-the-scenes look at the suffragette movement in New York during 1914 when the heroine's mother is arrested during a demonstration. (Rev: HBG 3/00; SLJ 4/00)

9566 Kalman, Esther. *Tchaikovsky Discovers America* (3–5). Illus. by Laura Fernandez and Rick Jacobson. 1995, Orchard $16.95 (0-531-06894-3). 32pp. Through a diary kept by 11-year-old Eugenia, the reader learns about Tchaikovsky's trip to the United States in 1891. (Rev: BL 3/15/95; HB 1–2/95, 5–6/95; SLJ 4/95)

9567 Karr, Kathleen. *The Lighthouse Mermaid* (2–4). Illus. 1998, Hyperion LB $14.49 (0-7868-2297-X); paper $3.95 (0-7868-1232-X). 64pp. This novel set during the 19th century tells of spunky Kate, the daughter of a lighthouse keeper, and of her responsibility to keep the beacon shining when her father is away. (Rev: BCCB 6/98; BL 6/1–15/98; HBG 10/98; SLJ 8/98)

9568 Karr, Kathleen. *Man of the Family* (4–6). 1999, Farrar $16.00 (0-374-34764-6). 192pp. Told by a 10-year-old boy, this is the story of an immigrant Hungarian family trying to make a home on a chicken farm in southern New Jersey in the 1920s. (Rev: BCCB 11/99; BL 9/15/99; HB 11–12/99; HBG 3/00; SLJ 11/99)

9569 Kendall, Jane. *Miranda Goes to Hollywood: Adventures in the Land of Palm Trees, Cowboys, and Moving Pictures* (5–7). 1999, Harcourt $16.00 (0-15-202059-4). 256pp. In 1915, young Miranda goes to Hollywood, hoping to become a star, and there she gets involved with personalities such as D.W. Griffith and Fatty Arbuckle. (Rev: BL 4/1/99; HBG 10/99; SLJ 6/99)

9570 Kinsey-Warnock, Natalie. *If Wishes Were Horses* (3–6). 2000, Dutton $15.99 (0-525-46448-

4). 112pp. In 1932, during the Great Depression, the money that Lily hopes her family will spend on a horse for her is diverted when her sister contracts polio. (Rev: BL 11/15/00; HBG 3/01; SLJ 12/00)

9571 Klass, Sheila S. *A Shooting Star: A Novel About Annie Oakley* (5–7). 1996, Holiday $15.95 (0-8234-1279-2). 192pp. A fictionalized biography of the woman who rose from poverty to become a famous show business sharpshooter. (Rev: BL 12/15/96; SLJ 5/97)

9572 Koller, Jackie F. *Nothing to Fear* (5–7). 1991, Harcourt $14.95 (0-15-200544-7); paper $8.00 (0-15-257582-0). 288pp. The focus is on Danny Garvey, first-generation Catholic Irish American, growing up in New York City in the 1930s. (Rev: BCCB 3/91; BL 3/1/91; SLJ 5/91)

9573 Kroll, Steven. *When I Dream of Heaven: Angelina's Story* (5–8). Series: Jamestown's American Portraits. 2000, Jamestown paper $5.95 (0-8092-0623-4). 155pp. Set at the beginning of the 20th century in New York City, this novel tells of a young Italian American girl who works in a sweatshop but longs for an education. (Rev: SLJ 9/00)

9574 Kudlinski, Kathleen V. *Shannon: A Chinatown Adventure* (3–6). Illus. by Bill Farnsworth. Series: Girlhood Journeys. 1996, Simon & Schuster $13.00 (0-689-81138-1); paper $5.99 (0-689-80984-0). 71pp. Set in San Francisco in 1880, this novel tells about a lonely Irish American girl and her efforts to help another girl she has seen in Chinatown. (Rev: BCCB 11/96; SLJ 9/96)

9575 Kudlinski, Kathleen V. *Shannon: The Schoolmarm Mysteries, San Francisco, 1880* (3–5). Illus. by Bill Farnsworth. Series: Girlhood Journeys. 1997, Simon & Schuster paper $5.99 (0-689-81561-1). 71pp. This mystery features Shannon O'Brien, a recent Irish immigrant living in San Francisco in 1880. (Rev: SLJ 4/98)

9576 Kudlinski, Kathleen V. *Shannon, Lost and Found: San Francisco, 1880* (4–6). Illus. 1997, Simon & Schuster paper $5.99 (0-689-80988-3). 72pp. In 1880, Shannon and her friend Mi Ling become involved in collecting books for the new San Francisco Public Library. (Rev: BCCB 11/96; BL 5/1/97)

9577 Lasky, Kathryn. *Dreams in the Golden Country: The Diary of Zipporah Feldman, a Jewish Immigrant Girl* (4–6). Illus. Series: Dear America. 1998, Scholastic $9.95 (0-590-02973-8). 192pp. In diary format, this novel traces the problems and joys of a Russian Jewish immigrant family in New York City in 1903, as reflected in a young girl's impressions. (Rev: BL 4/1/98; HBG 10/98; SLJ 5/98)

9578 Lawlor, Laurie. *Addie's Forever Friend* (2–4). Illus. Series: Addie. 1997, Albert Whitman LB $13.95 (0-8075-0164-6). 126pp. While Addie's father is out west looking for a homestead, she lives with an aunt and forms a friendship that changes her life. (Rev: BL 11/15/97; HBG 3/98; SLJ 2/98)

9579 Lawlor, Laurie. *Come Away with Me: Book 1* (3–6). Series: Heartland. 1996, Pocket paper $3.99 (0-671-53716-4). 184pp. In the early 1900s in a small Wisconsin town, Moe has trouble growing up

in a household with a controlling mother and older sister. Also use *Take to the Sky: Book 2* (1996). (Rev: SLJ 11/96)

9580 Lehrman, Robert. *The Store That Mama Built* (4–7). 1992, Macmillan LB $13.95 (0-02-754632-2). 128pp. The story of a Russian immigrant family in Pennsylvania in 1917. (Rev: BCCB 5/92; BL 4/15/92; SLJ 7/92)

9581 Lenski, Lois. *Strawberry Girl* (4–6). Illus. by author. 1945, HarperCollins LB $17.89 (0-397-30110-3); paper $5.95 (0-06-440585-0). 192pp. Lively adventures of a little girl, full of the flavor of the Florida lake country. Newbery Medal winner, 1946.

9582 Levine, Gail C. *Dave at Night* (5–7). 1999, HarperCollins LB $15.89 (0-06-028154-5). 272pp. In 1926, Dave, an orphan and resident of the Hebrew Home for Boys (also known as Hell Hole for Brats) sneaks out and meets Solly, a free spirit, who introduces the boy to the jazz world of the Harlem Renaissance. (Rev: BCCB 9/99; BL 6/1–15/99; HBG 3/00; SLJ 9/99)

9583 Lewis, Zoe. *Keisha Discovers Harlem* (3–5). Illus. by Dan Burr and Rich Grot. Series: Magic Attic Club. 1999, Magic Attic LB $17.40 (1-57513-144-7). 74pp. Keisha puts on a flapper costume and finds herself transported to New York City during the Harlem Renaissance. (Rev: SLJ 4/99)

9584 Lindquist, Susan H. *Summer Soldiers* (4–6). 1999, Delacorte $14.95 (0-385-32641-6). 177pp. When his father goes to fight in 1918, 11-year-old Joe Farrington is left to become the man of the family in this novel that deals with friendship, bravery, and bullies in World War I California. (Rev: BCCB 7–8/99; BL 5/15/99; HBG 10/99; SLJ 6/99)

9585 Litchman, Kristin Embry. *All Is Well* (3–5). 1998, Delacorte $14.95 (0-385-32592-4). 107pp. In Salt Lake City during the late 1800s, Miranda becomes friends with her 10-year-old neighbor, Emmy, whose Mormon father has two wives. (Rev: BCCB 9/98; BL 5/15/98; HBG 3/99; SLJ 6/98)

9586 Littlefield, Holly. *Fire at the Triangle Factory* (4–6). Illus. 1996, Carolrhoda LB $21.27 (0-87614-868-2); paper $5.95 (0-87614-970-0). 48pp. Two young workers — Jewish Minnie and Catholic Tessa — work at the Triangle Shirtwaist Company at the time of the fire of 1911. (Rev: BL 8/96; SLJ 10/96)

9587 Love, D. Anne. *I Remember the Alamo* (4–6). 2000, Holiday $15.95 (0-8234-1426-4). 156pp. The McCann family moves to San Antonio and becomes embroiled in the battle of the Alamo and its aftermath in this historical novel. (Rev: BL 1/1–15/00; HB 3–4/00; HBG 3/00; SLJ 1/00)

9588 Love, D. Anne. *A Year Without Rain* (4–6). 2000, Holiday $15.95 (0-8234-1488-4). 118pp. Set in the late 19th century, this novel tells how Rachel, who lives on the Dakota prairie, tries to thwart her father's plans to remarry. (Rev: BCCB 7–8/00; BL 4/1/00; HB 7–8/00; HBG 10/00; SLJ 9/00)

9589 Lowell, Susan. *I Am Lavina Cumming* (5–7). Illus. by Paul Mirocha. 1993, Milkweed $14.95 (0-915943-39-5); paper $6.95 (0-915943-77-8). 198pp.

Ten-year-old Lavina encounters a number of challenging adjustments when she is sent to live with an aunt in San Francisco at the time of the earthquake. (Rev: BCCB 2/94; SLJ 1/94)

9590 McDonough, Yona Z. *The Dollhouse Magic* (3–5). Illus. 2000, Holt $15.00 (0-8050-6464-8). 86pp. Set in the 1930s during the Great Depression, this beginning chapter book, tells how two sisters, Lila and Jane, inherit a dollhouse when their elderly friend dies. (Rev: BCCB 12/00; BL 11/15/00; HBG 3/01; SLJ 2/01)

9591 Machlin, Mikki. *My Name Is Not Gussie* (3–5). Illus. 1999, Houghton $15.00 (0-395-95646-3). 32pp. A series of vignettes about a young girl who immigrated to the United States early in the 20th century. (Rev: BL 11/1/99; HBG 3/00; SLJ 10/99)

9592 McKissack, Patricia. *Color Me Dark: The Diary of Nellie Lee Love, the Great Migration North* (4–6). Series: Dear America. 2000, Scholastic $10.95 (0-590-51159-9). 224pp. Told in diary form, this is the fictional story of African American Nellie Lee Love, whose family moves from Tennessee to Chicago in 1919 and encounters prejudice, corruption, and race riots. (Rev: BL 2/15/00; HBG 10/00; SLJ 7/00)

9593 Marvin, Isabel R. *A Bride for Anna's Papa* (5–7). 1994, Milkweed paper $6.95 (0-915943-93-X). 136pp. In this novel set in Minnesota in 1907, 13-year-old Anna takes over managing the household after her mother's death and tries to find a new bride for her father. (Rev: SLJ 7/94)

9594 Mattern, Joanne. *Coming to America: The Story of Immigration* (4–8). Illus. by Margaret Sanfilippo. 2000, Perfection Learning $14.95 (0-7807-9715-9); paper $8.95 (0-7891-2851-9). 64pp. A fictional presentation centering on the Martini family and their journey from Italy at the turn of the 20th century to experience Ellis Island before finding a new home in America. (Rev: HBG 3/01; SLJ 2/01)

9595 Mayerson, Evelyn Wilde. *The Cat Who Escaped from Steerage* (4–6). 1990, Macmillan $15.00 (0-684-19209-8). 64pp. The story of a two-week steerage voyage to the United States by Polish immigrants. (Rev: BL 10/1/90; HB 1–2/91; SLJ 2/91)

9596 Medearis, Angela Shelf, reteller. *Treemonisha* (2–6). Illus. by Michael Bryant. 1995, Holt $15.95 (0-8050-1748-8). 37pp. Set in Arkansas in 1884, this book, based on Scott Joplin's opera, tells about the lives and hopes of former slaves. (Rev: BCCB 2/96; SLJ 1/96)

9597 Mills, Judith C. *The Stonehook Schooner* (2–4). Illus. by author. 1997, Firefly $14.95 (1-55013-653-4); paper $4.95 (1-55013-719-0). In this story, set on a ship in Lake Ontario in the early 1900s, young Matthew ties himself to the mast to help sight land during a violent storm. (Rev: SLJ 8/97)

9598 Mitchell, Margaree King. *Uncle Jed's Barber Shop* (2–5). Illus. by James E. Ransome. 1993, Simon & Schuster $16.00 (0-671-76969-3); paper $6.99 (0-689-81913-7). 40pp. Uncle Jed, an African American barber in the 1920s, hopes to open his

own shop, but his generosity always prevents him from saving enough money. (Rev: BCCB 9/93; BL 9/1/93; HB 11–12/93; SLJ 10/93)

9599 Moeri, Louise. *The Devil in Ol' Rosie* (4–6). 2001, Atheneum $16.00 (0-689-82614-1). 208pp. Wart, a 12-year-old boy, has to get back the horses that a mean old mare has led from the family ranch in Oregon in this novel set in 1909. (Rev: BCCB 3/01; BL 2/15/01; HB 1–2/01; SLJ 3/01)

9600 Moss, Marissa. *Hannah's Journal: The Story of an Immigrant Girl* (3–5). Illus. 2000, Harcourt $15.00 (0-15-202155-8). 56pp. This novel in diary form tells about a 10-year-old Jewish girl who leaves her home in Lithuania in 1901, voyages to New York, is processed at Ellis Island, and begins work in the big city. (Rev: BL 10/1/00; HBG 3/01; SLJ 11/00)

9601 Myers, Anna. *Graveyard Girl* (5–8). 1995, Walker $14.95 (0-8027-8260-4). 125pp. During the yellow-fever epidemic in Memphis in 1878, young Eli, whose family has been decimated, forms a friendship with Grace, who rings the bell for the dead at the graveyard. (Rev: SLJ 10/95)

9602 Oneal, Zibby. *A Long Way to Go* (3–5). Illus. by Michael Dooling. 1992, Puffin paper $4.99 (0-14-032950-1). 64pp. Lila's life changes when her grandmother is jailed for fighting for women's rights in 1917 America. (Rev: BCCB 9/90; BL 3/1/90; HB 7–8/90; SLJ 9/90)

9603 Pastore, Clare. *Fiona McGilray's Story: A Voyage from Ireland in 1849* (5–8). Series: Journey to America. 2001, Berkley $9.95 (0-425-17783-1). 184pp. To escape the Irish potato famine, Fiona McGilray and her brother emigrate to America where Fiona is befriended by a wealthy woman. (Rev: BL 3/15/01)

9604 Peck, Richard. *A Long Way from Chicago: A Novel in Stories* (4–8). 1998, Dial $15.99 (0-8037-2290-7). 148pp. In the 1930s Joe and Mary Alice Dowdel spend part of their summers with an eccentric, high-spirited grandmother in this fast-paced, humorous novel set in rural Illinois. (Rev: BCCB 10/98; HB 11–12/98; HBG 3/99; SLJ 10/98*)

9605 Peck, Robert Newton. *A Day No Pigs Would Die* (6–8). 1972, Knopf $24.00 (0-394-48235-2). 144pp. A gentle story about a 12-year-old Vermont farm boy.

9606 Perez, N. A. *Breaker* (4–6). 1988, Houghton $16.00 (0-395-45537-5). 216pp. The story of a 14-year-old slate picker in a Pennsylvania coal-mining town. (Rev: BCCB 7–8/88; SLJ 8/88)

9607 Pfitsch, Patricia C. *Keeper of the Light* (4–6). 1997, Simon & Schuster $16.00 (0-689-81492-5). 137pp. Set in the 1870s, this is the exciting story of Faith, a lighthouse keeper's daughter who, in a race against time, saves the lives of two people. (Rev: HBG 3/98; SLJ 5/98)

9608 Porter, Connie. *Addy Saves the Day: A Summer Story* (2–4). Illus. by Bradford Brown. 1994, Pleasant paper $5.95 (1-56247-083-3). 59pp. In this novel set in Philadelphia in 1864, Addy, a former slave, and her family try to make money to search for relatives lost in the Civil War. Also use *Happy*

Birthday, Addy! (1994). (Rev: BL 11/1/94; SLJ 11/94)

9609 Rabe, Berniece. *Hiding Mr. McMulty* (5–8). 1997, Harcourt $18.00 (0-15-201330-X). 256pp. This novel, set in southeast Missouri in 1937, tells of both race and class conflicts as experienced by 11-year-old Rass. (Rev: BL 10/15/97; HBG 3/98; SLJ 12/97)

9610 Ransom, Candice. *Fire in the Sky* (3–5). Illus. 1997, Carolrhoda LB $19.93 (0-87614-867-4). 72pp. In the late 1930s in New Jersey, Stenny becomes involved in the flight of the dirigible *Hindenburg* and the rescue operation after it burns. (Rev: BL 5/1/97; SLJ 8/97)

9611 Ransom, Candice. *Jimmy Crack Corn* (3–5). Illus. 1994, Carolrhoda LB $19.93 (0-87614-786-4). 56pp. The beginning of the Great Depression as seen through the experiences of a farm family sinking into poverty with no hope for the future. (Rev: BCCB 6/94; BL 7/94; SLJ 6/94)

9612 Raven, Margot T. *Angels in the Dust* (3–6). Illus. by Roger Essley. 1997, Troll $15.95 (0-8167-3806-8). 32pp. Based on a true story, this picture book describes the hardships of an Oklahoma family living in the 1930s Dust Bowl. (Rev: BL 4/15/97; SLJ 6/97)

9613 Recorvits, Helen. *Goodbye, Walter Malinski* (5–7). Illus. 1999, Farrar $15.00 (0-374-32747-5). 96pp. This family story, told from the viewpoint of fifth-grader Wanda Malinski, tells of the devastating effects of the Great Depression on her family and of a terrible accident that almost tears them apart. (Rev: BL 5/1/99; HB 5–6/99; HBG 10/99; SLJ 6/99)

9614 Robinet, Harriette G. *Children of the Fire* (4–7). 1991, Macmillan $16.00 (0-689-31655-0). 144pp. Hallelujah, born into slavery, escapes to Chicago, where she spends one night following the path of the Great Fire. (Rev: BCCB 9/91; BL 10/15/91; SLJ 10/91)

9615 Robinet, Harriette G. *Forty Acres and Maybe a Mule* (4–7). 1998, Simon & Schuster $16.00 (0-689-82078-X). 144pp. After the Civil War, Gideon and other freed slaves begin working the 40 acres of land each has been promised in spite of the opposition of white settlers. (Rev: BL 1/1–15/99; HBG 3/99; SLJ 11/98)

9616 Rose, Deborah L. *The Rose Horse* (3–4). Illus. 1995, Harcourt $16.00 (0-15-200068-2). 80pp. The story of the Jewish immigrant community in Coney Island, Brooklyn, at the turn of the century. (Rev: BCCB 11/95; BL 9/1/95; SLJ 1/96)

9617 Ross, Pat. *Hannah's Fancy Notions* (3–6). Illus. by Bert Dodson. 1992, Puffin paper $4.99 (0-14-032389-9). 64pp. The story of Hannah and the folk art of making band boxes. (Rev: BL 10/1/88; SLJ 1/89)

9618 Rossiter, Phyllis. *Moxie* (4–7). 1990, Macmillan $14.95 (0-02-777831-2). 185pp. The story of a gallant family's fight against drought and foreclosure in the Dust Bowl of the 1930s. (Rev: SLJ 12/90)

9619 Ruckman, Ivy. *In Care of Cassie Tucker* (4–6). 1998, Delacorte $14.95 (0-385-32514-2). 165pp. Orphan Evan, a fiercely independent young boy, comes to live with the family of 11-year-old Cassie Tucker in the town of Blue Hills, Nebraska, in 1899, and clashes with the strict puritanism of Cassie's preacher father. (Rev: BCCB 10/98; BL 8/98; HBG 3/99; SLJ 10/98)

9620 Ryan, Pam M. *Esperanza Rising* (5–8). 2000, Scholastic $15.95 (0-439-12041-1). 272pp. During the Great Depression, Esperanza and her mother are forced by poverty to leave Mexico to work in a agricultural labor camp in California. (Rev: BCCB 12/00; BL 12/1/00; HB 1–2/01; HBG 3/01)

9621 Sandin, Joan. *The Long Way Westward* (2–4). Illus. 1989, HarperCollins paper $3.95 (0-06-444198-9). 64pp. In this continuation of *A Long Way to a New Land* (1981), the immigrant Swedish family continues its journey to Minnesota. (Rev: BCCB 11/89; BL 9/15/89; HB 9–10/89; SLJ 9/89)

9622 Sawyer, Ruth. *Roller Skates* (4–6). Illus. by Valenti Angelo. 1988, Peter Smith $18.75 (0-8446-6343-3). 192pp. A little girl explores New York City on roller skates in the 1890s. Newbery Honor book, 1937.

9623 Schachner, Judith Byron. *Mr. Emerson's Cook* (2–4). Illus. 1998, Dutton $15.99 (0-525-45884-0). 32pp. When young Annie, fresh from Ireland, goes to work as a cook for Ralph Waldo Emerson, both discover they can profit from this arrangement. (Rev: BL 11/1/98; HBG 3/99; SLJ 1/99)

9624 Sebestyen, Ouida. *Words by Heart* (5–7). 1979, Little, Brown $15.95 (0-316-77931-8). 144pp. Race relations are explored when an African American family moves to an all-white community during the Reconstruction Era.

9625 Sherman, Eileen B. *Independence Avenue* (5–8). 1990, Jewish Publication Soc. $13.95 (0-8276-0367-3). 145pp. A 14-year-old Jewish boy from Russia is all alone in the United States of 1907. (Rev: SLJ 1/91)

9626 Skolsky, Mindy W. *Love from Your Friend, Hannah* (4–6). Illus. 1998, DK $17.95 (0-7894-2492-4). 246pp. In this epistolary novel set in the the mid-1930s — a continuation of earlier Hannah books — the sensitive heroine carries on a correspondence with different friends, including President Roosevelt. (Rev: BCCB 4/98; BL 4/1/98; HBG 10/98; SLJ 4/98)

9627 Snyder, Zilpha Keatley. *Gib and the Gray Ghost* (4–7). 2000, Delacorte $15.95 (0-385-32609-2). 230pp. In this companion volume to *Gib Rides Home* 11-year-old Gib returns to the Thornton ranch where he attends school, encounters bullies, and trains a horse that turns up at the ranch during a snowstorm. (Rev: BCCB 2/00; BL 1/1–15/00*; HB 5–6/00; HBG 10/00; SLJ 3/00)

9628 Snyder, Zilpha Keatley. *Gib Rides Home* (5–8). 1998, Delacorte $15.95 (0-385-32267-4). 246pp. Set in post–World War I America, this is the story of an orphan boy and how he conquered hardships and deprivations. (Rev: BL 1/1–15/98; HB 3–4/98; HBG 10/98; SLJ 1/98*)

9629 Tolliver, Ruby C. *Boomer's Kids* (4–6). Illus. by Lyle Miller. 1992, Hendrick-Long paper $10.95 (0-885777-22-1). 128pp. Teenagers Andy and Ellie are tired of moving, as the family follows their father, a "boomer" in the oil fields in 1901. (Rev: BL 8/92)

9630 Tripp, Valerie. *Changes for Samantha: A Winter Story* (3–5). Illus. by Robert Grace and Nancy Niles. 1988, Pleasant LB $12.95 (0-937295-95-7); paper $5.95 (0-937295-47-7). 72pp. Wealthy New Yorker Samantha now lives with her aunt and uncle in a series that takes place in 1904 and includes: *Happy Birthday Samantha* (1987); *Samantha Saves the Day* (1988). (Rev: BL 1/1/89; SLJ 2/89)

9631 Tripp, Valerie. *Kit Learns a Lesson: A School Story* (3–5). Illus. 2000, Pleasant $12.99 (1-58485-121-X). 67pp. As the Great Depression grows more serious, it affects all facets of Kit Kittredge's life including her family and school. (Rev: BL 9/1/00; HBG 3/01; SLJ 12/00)

9632 Tripp, Valerie. *Meet Kit: An American Girl* (3–5). Illus. by Walter Rane. Series: American Girls. 2000, Pleasant $12.99 (1-58485-017-5). 70pp. In 1934, Kit Kittredge and her family feel the effects of the Great Depression when her father loses his job and her mother takes in boarders. (Rev: BL 9/1/00; HBG 3/01; SLJ 12/00)

9633 Tucker, Terry Ward. *Moonlight and Mill Whistles* (5–7). 1998, Summerhouse $15.00 (1-887714-32-4). 120pp. Thirteen-year-old Tommy is unaware how his life will change after he meets a gypsy girl named Rhona in this novel set in an early 1900s South Carolina cotton mill town. (Rev: BL 3/1/99)

9634 Uchida, Yoshiko. *Samurai of Gold Hill* (5–8). Illus. by Ati Forberg. 1984, Creative Arts paper $8.95 (0-916870-86-3). 128pp. In this reissue of a 1972 title, a group of Japanese colonists try to farm an arid stretch of California in 1869.

9635 Wax, Wendy. *Empire Dreams* (3–6). Illus. by Todd Doney. Series: Adventures in America. 2000, Silver Moon LB $14.95 (1-893110-19-2). 91pp. Eleven-year-old Julie, growing up in New York during the construction of the Empire State Building, secretly takes a job to help out her family after her father becomes unemployed. (Rev: HBG 3/01; SLJ 3/01)

9636 West, Tracey. *Fire in the Valley* (3–5). Illus. Series: Stories of the States. 1993, Silver Moon LB $14.95 (1-881889-32-7). 80pp. Eleven-year-old Sarah becomes involved in mob violence concerning water rights in this novel set in 1905 California. (Rev: SLJ 12/93)

9637 Whalen, Sharla S. *Meet the Friends* (3–5). Illus. 1997, ABDO paper $5.95 (1-56239-900-4). 64pp. Set in 1896, this is the story of four very different girlfriends. (Rev: BL 5/15/97)

9638 White, Ellen E. *Voyage on the Great Titanic: The Diary of Margaret Ann Brady* (3–6). Illus. Series: Dear America. 1998, Scholastic $9.95 (0-590-96273-6). 197pp. Orphaned Margaret Brady accepts an opportunity to act as a companion to a wealthy American on the maiden voyage of the *Titanic*. (Rev: BL 10/15/98; HBG 3/99; SLJ 12/98)

9639 Whitmore, Arvella. *The Bread Winner* (4–6). 1990, Houghton $16.00 (0-395-53705-3). 144pp. In this Depression-era story, the Pucketts are forced to sell their farm. (Rev: BCCB 1/91; BL 11/1/90; SLJ 10/90)

9640 Wolfert, Adrienne. *Making Tracks* (5–7). Illus. Series: Adventures in America. 2000, Silver Moon LB $14.95 (1-893110-16-8). 96pp. In this novel set in the Depression, young Henry leaves his foster home to ride the rails to Chicago to find his father. (Rev: BL 7/00; HBG 3/01; SLJ 11/00)

9641 Yep, Laurence. *The Journal of Wong Ming-Chung* (4–7). Illus. 2000, Scholastic paper $10.95 (0-590-38607-7). 224pp. Told in diary format beginning in October 1851, this is the story of a Chinese boy nicknamed Runt who travels from his native country to join an uncle in the gold mining fields of America. (Rev: BL 4/1/00; HBG 10/00; SLJ 4/00)

9642 Yolen, Jane. *Tea with an Old Dragon: A Story of Sophia Smith, Founder of Smith College* (2–4). Illus. by Monica Vachula. 1998, Boyds Mills $15.95 (1-56397-657-9). In this historical story set in a 19th-century New England town, a little girl becomes friends with Miss Sophy Smith, the founder of Smith College. (Rev: HBG 3/99; SLJ 10/98)

World War II and After

9643 Avi. *Who Was That Masked Man, Anyway?* (5–7). 1992, Orchard LB $16.99 (0-531-08607-0). 176pp. In a story told through dialogue, sixth-grader Frankie lives through World War II by immersing himself in his beloved radio serials. (Rev: BCCB 10/92*; BL 8/92*; HB 3–4/93; SLJ 10/92*)

9644 Ayres, Katherine. *Voices at Whisper Bend* (3–6). Illus. by Greg Dearth and Dahl Taylor. Series: History Mysteries. 1999, Pleasant $9.95 (1-56247-817-6); paper $5.95 (1-56247-761-7). 162pp. During World War II in Pennsylvania, young Charlotte leads a drive to collect scrap metal and, later, must solve a mystery when it is stolen. (Rev: HBG 3/00; SLJ 2/00)

9645 Banks, Sara H. *Under the Shadow of Wings* (4–8). 1997, Simon & Schuster $15.00 (0-689-81207-8). 147pp. In this novel set in rural Alabama near the end of World War II, 11-year-old Tattnall is filled with grief and guilt when his 15-year-old brain-damaged cousin dies. (Rev: SLJ 6/97)

9646 Bishop, Claire Huchet. *Twenty and Ten* (4–6). Illus. by William Pene du Bois. 1984, Peter Smith $17.75 (0-8446-6168-6); Puffin paper $4.99 (0-14-031076-2). A nun and 20 French children hide ten young refugees from the Nazis.

9647 Buckvar, Felice. *Dangerous Dream* (4–6). Ed. by Myrna Kemnitz. 1998, Royal Fireworks paper $6.99 (0-88092-277-X). 123pp. A 13-year-old Holocaust survivor is suspicious of the man who claims to be her father. (Rev: SLJ 4/99)

9648 Carey, Janet. *Molly's Fire* (4–7). 2000, Simon & Schuster $16.00 (0-689-82612-5). 208pp. During World War II, Molly learns that her father's plane has been shot down but she refuses to believe he is dead. (Rev: BCCB 4/00; BL 4/15/00; HBG 10/00; SLJ 5/00)

9649 Chang, Margaret, and Raymond Chang. *In the Eye of War* (5–7). 1990, Macmillan $13.95 (0-689-50503-5). 224pp. A novel based on true experiences of growing up in Shanghai during World War II. (Rev: BCCB 4/90; BL 3/15/90; SLJ 8/90)

9650 Cutler, Jane. *My Wartime Summers* (5–7). 1994, Farrar $15.00 (0-374-35111-2). 158pp. This novel contrasts home front life during World War II with the story of a girl's older brother, who is a soldier. (Rev: BCCB 11/94; BL 10/1/94*; SLJ 11/94)

9651 Dahlberg, Maurine F. *Play to the Angel* (5–9). 2000, Farrar $16.00 (0-374-35994-6). 192pp. When Hitler invades Austria in 1938, Greta must help her Jewish music teacher escape. (Rev: BL 7/00; HBG 3/01; SLJ 9/00)

9652 Deedy, Carmen A. *The Yellow Star: The Legend of King Christian X of Denmark* (3–5). 2000, Peachtree $16.95 (1-56145-208-4). Although in real life it did not happen, this picture book tells how the King of Denmark wore a Jewish star in World War II to show Hitler that in his country there are only Danes. (Rev: BCCB 11/00; BL 7/00; HBG 3/01; SLJ 9/00)

9653 DeJong, Meindert. *The House of Sixty Fathers* (6–8). Illus. by Maurice Sendak. 1956, HarperCollins LB $15.89 (0-06-021481-3); paper $5.95 (0-06-440200-2). 192pp. Tien Pao and his pig, Glory-of-the-Republic, journey to find his parents in Japanese-occupied China.

9654 Denenberg, Barry. *The Journal of Ben Uchida: Citizen 13559 Mirror Lake Internment Camp* (5–8). Illus. Series: Dear America. 1999, Scholastic $10.95 (0-590-48531-8). 160pp. In his fictional diary, Ben Uchida and his Japanese American family are shipped off to an internment camp after Pearl Harbor. (Rev: BL 12/15/99; HBG 3/00)

9655 Denenberg, Barry. *One Eye Laughing, The Other Weeping* (5–7). Series: Dear America. 2000, Scholastic $12.95 (0-439-09518-2). 256pp. Thirteen-year-old Julie Weiss is able to flee Austria when the Nazis invade and travel to America to stay with her aunt, a famous stage star. (Rev: BL 7/00; HBG 3/01; SLJ 12/00)

9656 Douglas, Kirk. *The Broken Mirror* (5–8). 1997, Simon & Schuster paper $13.00 (0-689-81493-3). 96pp. This short novel by the famous actor depicts the despair and loss of faith that occurs to a Jewish child who has lost all his loved ones in the Holocaust. (Rev: BL 10/1/97; HBG 3/98; SLJ 9/97)

9657 Duey, Kathleen. *Josie Poe: Palouse, Washington, 1943* (4–7). Series: American Diaries. 1999, Simon & Schuster paper $4.50 (0-689-82930-2). 139pp. Josie's diary entries during World War II depict life on the home front and also include a mystery concerning her older brother's strange behavior. (Rev: SLJ 1/00)

9658 Elmer, Robert. *Into the Flames* (5–7). Series: Young Underground. 1995, Bethany paper $5.99 (1-55661-376-8). 144pp. Danish twins are captured by the Gestapo while trying to rescue their uncle during World War II. (Rev: BL 5/15/95; SLJ 8/95)

9659 Garrigue, Sheila. *The Eternal Spring of Mr. Ito* (4–6). 1994, Simon & Schuster paper $4.99 (0-689-71809-8). 176pp. This sequel to *All the Children Were Sent Away* (o.p.) continues the story of a young girl evacuated from London to Vancouver, British Columbia, during World War II. (Rev: BCCB 12/85; HB 1–2/86; SLJ 11/85)

9660 Giff, Patricia Reilly. *Lily's Crossing* (5–8). 1997, Delacorte $15.95 (0-385-32142-2). 180pp. During World War II, motherless Lily must say good-bye to her father when he is sent to fight in France. (Rev: BCCB 4/97; BL 2/1/97; HB 3–4/97; SLJ 2/97)

9661 Hahn, Mary D. *Stepping on the Cracks* (5–8). 1991, Houghton $16.00 (0-395-58507-4); Avon paper $4.99 (0-380-71900-2). 218pp. The compelling story of a sixth-grade girl during World War II and her painful decision to help a pacifist deserter. (Rev: BCCB 12/91*; BL 10/15/91*; HB 11–12/91; SLJ 12/91*)

9662 Harrison, Barbara. *Theo* (5–9). 1999, Clarion $15.00 (0-395-19959-3). 176pp. A realistic war novel that tells of an orphan boy wandering alone in Greece during World War II, after his older brother has been executed. (Rev: SLJ 9/99)

9663 Heneghan, James. *Wish Me Luck* (5–8). 1997, Farrar $16.00 (0-374-38453-3). 208pp. When Jamie is evacuated to Canada from England during World War II, the ship he is on is sunk by a German U-boat. (Rev: BCCB 4/97; BL 6/1–15/97; HB 9–10/97; SLJ 6/97)

9664 Hoestlandt, Jo. *Star of Fear, Star of Hope* (2–4). Trans. by Mark Polizzotti. Illus. by Johanna Kang. 1995, Walker LB $16.85 (0-8027-8374-0). 32pp. In World War II–occupied France, Helen witnesses the growing persecution of her Jewish friend Lydia. (Rev: BCCB 6/95; BL 5/1/95; HB 9–10/95; SLJ 8/95)

9665 Holm, Anne. *North to Freedom* (6–8). 1984, Harcourt paper $6.00 (0-15-257553-7). 239pp. A boy who has never known anything except life in a concentration camp makes his way across Europe alone and escapes to freedom.

9666 Hopper, Nancy J. *Cassandra — Live at Carnegie Hall!* (5–7). Illus. 1998, Dial $15.99 (0-8037-2329-6). 160pp. Set in New York City during World War II, this novel tells about 13-year-old Cassandra and her sisters, who must move from Connecticut to Carnegie Hall to live with their bandleader father and pretend to be his cousins to protect his dashing image. (Rev: BL 6/1–15/98; HBG 10/98; SLJ 8/98)

9667 Hughes, Shirley. *The Lion and the Unicorn* (4–6). Illus. 1999, DK $17.95 (0-7894-2555-6). During the London Blitz of World War II, a young Jewish boy is sent with other children to live in a great country house where he is extremely unhappy until he meets a wounded war vet. (Rev: BL 4/1/99; HBG 10/99; SLJ 4/99)

9668 Kudlinski, Kathleen V. *Pearl Harbor Is Burning! The Story of World War II* (4–6). Illus. by Ronald Himler. 1993, Puffin paper $4.99 (0-14-

034509-4). 64pp. Historical events are brought into perspective in a fictional framework as Frank, a newcomer to Hawaii, must learn to adjust to island living. (Rev: BCCB 10/91; BL 11/15/91; SLJ 2/92)

9669 Lee, Milly. *Nim and the War Effort* (2–5). Illus. by Yangsook Choi. 1997, Farrar $16.00 (0-374-35523-1). 32pp. Nim, who is growing up in San Francisco's Chinatown during World War II, wants to help in the war effort. (Rev: BCCB 3/97; BL 2/1/97; HB 3–4/97; SLJ 3/97)

9670 Levitin, Sonia. *Journey to America* (5–8). Illus. by Charles Robinson. 1970, Macmillan $16.00 (0-689-31829-4); paper $4.99 (0-689-71130-1). 160pp. A Jewish mother and her three daughters flee Nazi Germany in 1938 for a long and difficult journey to join their father in America. (Rev: BL 9/1/93)

9671 Lisle, Janet T. *The Art of Keeping Cool* (5–8). 2000, Simon & Schuster $17.00 (0-689-83787-9). 216pp. Robert is staying with his grandparents in New England during World War II and forms a friendship with his cousin, Eliot, who is helping an outcast German painter whom Robert thinks might be a spy. (Rev: BL 9/15/00*; HB 11–12/00; HBG 3/01; SLJ 10/00)

9672 Lowry, Lois. *Number the Stars* (5–7). 1989, Houghton $16.00 (0-395-51060-0); Dell paper $5.99 (0-440-40327-8). 160pp. The story of war-torn Denmark and best friends Annemarie Johansen and Ellen Rosen. Newbery Medal winner, 1990. (Rev: BCCB 3/89; BL 3/1/89; SLJ 3/89)

9673 McSwigan, Marie. *Snow Treasure* (4–7). Illus. by Andre Le Blanc. 1986, Scholastic paper $4.50 (0-590-42537-4). 156pp. Children smuggle gold out of occupied Norway on their sleds.

9674 Maguire, Gregory. *The Good Liar* (4–6). 1999, Clarion $15.00 (0-395-90697-0). 129pp. A first-person novel about a boy growing up in occupied France during World War II and the deception involved when his parents hide a Jewish woman and her daughter. (Rev: BCCB 3/99; BL 4/15/99*; HB 7–8/99; HBG 10/99; SLJ 5/99)

9675 Mazer, Norma Fox. *Good Night, Maman* (5–9). 1999, Harcourt $16.00 (0-15-201468-3). 176pp. The fictionalized account of two young Jewish refugees who travel to the U.S. in 1944 and are placed in a camp in Oswego where they become Americanized. (Rev: BCCB 12/99; BL 8/99*; HB 11–12/99; HBG 3/00; SLJ 12/99)

9676 Michener, James A. *South Pacific* (5–8). Illus. by Michael Hague. 1992, Harcourt $16.95 (0-15-200618-4). 40pp. The famous author retells the story of his Tales from the South Pacific, on which the musical and movie South Pacific were based. (Rev: BCCB 11/92; BL 9/1/92; SLJ 11/92)

9677 Mori, Hana. *Jirohattan* (3–6). Trans. from Japanese by Tamiko Kurosaki and Elizabeth Crowe. Illus. by Elizabeth Crowe. 1993, Bess Pr. paper $6.95 (1-880188-69-4). 76pp. In this tale set in World War II Japan, a slow-witted boy named Jiro-hattan helps others but is unable to comprehend death. (Rev: BCCB 2/94; SLJ 5/94)

9678 Myers, Anna. *Captain's Command* (4–8). Illus. 1999, Walker $15.95 (0-8027-8706-1). 144pp. In Oklahoma during 1943, 12-year-old Gail and her family cope with problems caused by World War II, including the news that their father has been declared missing in action in France. (Rev: BL 12/15/99; HBG 3/00; SLJ 10/99)

9679 Myers, Walter Dean. *The Journal of Scott Pendleton Collins: A World War II Soldier* (5–8). Illus. Series: My Name Is America. 1999, Scholastic $10.95 (0-439-05013-8). 144pp. Through a series of letters, readers get to know 17-year-old Collins, an American soldier, who participated in the D-Day invasion of Europe. (Rev: BL 6/1–15/99; HBG 10/99)

9680 Napoli, Donna Jo. *Stones in Water* (5–8). 1997, Dutton $15.99 (0-525-45842-5). 154pp. The exciting story of two Italian boys, one of whom is Jewish, who have been transported to work camps by the Nazis during World War II. (Rev: BL 10/1/97; HBG 3/98; SLJ 11/97*)

9681 Orlev, Uri. *The Island on Bird Street* (5–7). 1984, Houghton $16.00 (0-395-33887-5); paper $5.95 (0-395-61623-9). 176pp. A young Jewish boy inside the Warsaw ghetto during World War II.

9682 Osborne, Mary Pope. *My Secret War: The World War II Diary of Madeline Beck* (5–9). Illus. Series: Dear America. 2000, Scholastic $10.95 (0-590-68715-8). 192pp. Using a diary format, this novel set on Long Island during World War II tells of an eighth-grade girl who forms a club to help in the war effort. (Rev: BL 10/1/00; HBG 3/01; SLJ 10/00)

9683 Propp, Vera W. *When the Soldiers Were Gone* (4–9). 1999, Putnam $15.99 (0-399-23325-3). 101pp. The heartrending story of a young Jewish boy who, after World War II, must return to his own people and leave behind the loving farm family in Holland who had protected him and saved his life. (Rev: BCCB 2/99; BL 1/1–15/99; HB 7–8/99; HBG 10/99; SLJ 2/99)

9684 Radin, Ruth Yaffe. *Escape to the Forest: Based on a True Story of the Holocaust* (4–6). Illus. by Janet Hamlin. 2000, HarperCollins LB $13.89 (0-06-028521-4). 80pp. A realistic story of a Jewish girl named Sarah and her part in resistance against the Nazis during World War II. (Rev: BCCB 3/00; HBG 10/00; SLJ 3/00)

9685 Reiss, Johanna. *The Upstairs Room* (5–8). 1972, HarperCollins $15.95 (0-690-85127-8); paper $5.95 (0-06-440370-X). 196pp. Two young Jewish girls are hidden for over two years in the home of a simple Dutch peasant during the German occupation. A sequel is: The Journey Back (1976).

9686 Rinaldi, Ann. *Keep Smiling Through* (4–6). 1996, Harcourt $12.00 (0-15-200768-7); paper $6.00 (0-15-201072-6). 208pp. Life on the home front during World War II as seen through the eyes of Kay, a lonely 10-year-old. (Rev: BCCB 4/96; BL 7/96*; SLJ 6/96)

9687 Serraillier, Ian. *The Silver Sword* (6–8). Illus. by C. Walter Hodges. 1959, Phillips $18.00 (0-87599-104-1). A World War II story of Polish children who are separated from their parents and finally reunited.

9688 Shemin, Margaretha. *The Little Riders* (4–6). Illus. by Peter Spier. 1988, Morrow paper $4.95 (0-688-12499-2). 80pp. An 11-year-old girl is trapped in German-occupied Netherlands during World War II. A reissue.

9689 Sim, Dorrith M. *In My Pocket* (3–6). Illus. by Gerald Fitzgerald. 1997, Harcourt $16.00 (0-15-201357-1). 32pp. A picture book about a small girl who was one of the 10,000 Jewish children taken from Nazi Europe to Great Britain. (Rev: BCCB 6/97; BL 4/15/97; SLJ 5/97)

9690 Taylor, Marilyn. *Faraway Home* (5–8). 2000, O'Brien paper $7.95 (0-86278-643-6). 221pp. Taken from his Austrian homeland by the "kindertransport," 13-year-old Karl is sent to County Down in Ireland where he endures the hardship of country life and the hostility of the locals. (Rev: BL 3/1/01)

9691 Tripp, Valerie. *Meet Molly: An American Girl* (3–5). Illus. by C. F. Payne. 1986, Pleasant LB $12.95 (0-937295-81-7); paper $5.95 (0-937295-07-8). 72pp. Molly is growing up without a father during World War II in America. Others in the series are: *Molly Learns a Lesson* (1986); *Molly's Surprise* (1986); *Molly Saves the Day* (1988); *Happy Birthday, Molly!* (1987); *Changes for Molly* (1988). (Rev: BL 12/1/86)

9692 Uchida, Yoshiko. *The Bracelet* (1–5). Illus. by Joanna Yardley. 1993, Putnam $16.99 (0-399-22503-X). 32pp. Emi, a Japanese American girl, is confused and frightened when she is interned in a prison camp during World War II. (Rev: BCCB 9/93; BL 9/15/93; HB 11–12/93; SLJ 12/93)

9693 Vander Els, Betty. *The Bombers' Moon* (5–7). 1992, Farrar paper $4.50 (0-374-30877-7). 168pp. Missionary children Ruth and Simeon are evacuated to escape the Japanese invasion of China; they will not see their parents for four years. A sequel is: *Leaving Point* (1987). (Rev: BCCB 9/85; BL 11/1/85; HB 9–10/85)

9694 Vos, Ida. *Anna Is Still Here* (5–7). Trans. by Terese Edelstein and Inez Smidt. 1993, Houghton $13.95 (0-395-65368-1). 144pp. The story of a survivor of the Holocaust and her adjustment to freedom after years of solitude and terror. (Rev: BL 4/15/93*; HB 7–8/93; SLJ 5/93)

9695 Vos, Ida. *Hide and Seek* (4–8). Trans. by Terese Edelstein and Inez Smidt. 1991, Houghton $13.95 (0-395-56470-0). 144pp. A first-person narrative of a Jewish girl in Holland during the Nazi occupation. (Rev: BCCB 3/91; BL 3/15/91*; HB 5–6/91; SLJ 5/91)

9696 Vos, Ida. *The Key Is Lost* (5–9). Trans. by Terese Eddelstein. 2000, HarperCollins $15.95 (0-688-16283-5). 192pp. Based on the author's experiences as a child, this novel tells the story of a young Jewish girl and her sister who survive World War II in hiding in Holland. (Rev: BCCB 9/00; BL 4/1/00; HBG 10/00; SLJ 6/00)

9697 Walsh, Jill Paton. *Fireweed* (5–8). 1970, Farrar paper $4.95 (0-374-42316-4). 144pp. Teenagers Bill and Julie meet during a London blitz.

9698 Watts, Irene N. *Remember Me: A Search for Refuge in Wartime Britain* (5–8). 2000, Tundra paper $6.95 (0-88776-519-X). 176pp. A heart-tugging story of an 11-year-old Jewish girl who, at the beginning of World War II, is transported from her home in Berlin to live in a Welsh mining town where she knows no one and speaks no English. (Rev: BL 12/1/00; SLJ 1/01)

9699 Winkler, Allan M. *Cassie's War* (4–6). 1994, Royal Fireworks paper $9.99 (0-88092-106-4). 94pp. Cassie is growing up in California during World War II, which brings internment to her Japanese American friend and death to her soldier father. (Rev: BL 2/1/95)

9700 Yep, Laurence. *Hiroshima* (4–7). 1995, Scholastic $9.95 (0-590-20832-2). 64pp. A powerful fiction work that explores the bombing of Hiroshima in 1945 and its aftermath. (Rev: BCCB 6/95; BL 3/15/95*; HB 9–10/95; SLJ 5/95)

9701 Yolen, Jane. *The Devil's Arithmetic* (4–8). 1988, Puffin paper $4.99 (0-14-034535-3). 160pp. This time-warp story transports a young Jewish girl back to Poland in the 1940s, conveying the horrors of the Holocaust. (Rev: SLJ 8/88)

9702 Zeinert, Karen. *To Touch the Stars: A Story of World War II* (5–8). Series: Jamestown's American Portraits. 2000, Jamestown paper $5.95 (0-8092-0630-7). 126pp. Eighteen-year-old Liz Erickson, who loves to fly airplanes, longs for independence while she investigates possible sabotage in the Women's Airforce Service pilots program in 1942 during World War II. (Rev: SLJ 9/00)

Holidays and Holy Days

9703 Alcott, Louisa May. *An Old Fashioned Thanksgiving* (4–5). Illus. by Jody Wheeler. 1990, Applewood paper $5.95 (1-55709-135-8). 40pp. The happenings in a New Hampshire farm family in the 1820s, first published in 1881. (Rev: BL 10/1/89; SLJ 10/89)

9704 Alcott, Louisa May. *The Quiet Little Woman: A Christmas Story* (4–7). Illus. by C. Michael Dudash. 1999, Honor Bks. $14.99 (1-56292-616-0). 128pp. Three Christmas stories from old children's magazines that recapture the atmosphere of Louisa May Alcott's work. (Rev: SLJ 10/99)

9705 Allan, Nicholas. *Jesus' Christmas Party* (3–6). Illus. 1997, Bantam $8.95 (0-385-32521-5). 32pp. The nativity story, as told from the point of view of the innkeeper. (Rev: BL 7/92; HBG 3/98)

9706 Ames, Mildred. *Grandpa Jake and the Grand Christmas* (3–5). 1990, Macmillan $15.00 (0-684-19241-1). 96pp. Long-lost Grandpa Jake turns up for a Christmas visit. (Rev: BCCB 11/90; BL 11/15/90; SLJ 3/91*)

9707 Axelrod, Amy. *Pigs Go to Market: Halloween Fun with Math and Shopping* (2–4). Illus. by Sharon McGinley-Nally. 1997, Simon & Schuster paper $14.00 (0-689-81069-5). At Halloween, the Pig family eats all the candy before the guests arrive. (Rev: HBG 3/98; SLJ 9/97)

9708 Bauer, Caroline Feller, ed. *Halloween: Stories and Poems* (3–6). Illus. by Peter Sis. 1989, Harper-Collins LB $14.89 (0-397-32301-8). 96pp. An anthology with spooky happenings for reading on Halloween, although not directly related to the holiday. (Rev: BL 9/1/89; SLJ 10/89)

9709 Burch, Robert. *Christmas with Ida Early* (5–7). 1985, Puffin paper $4.99 (0-14-031971-9). 144pp. A preacher involves Ida in a Christmas pageant in this amusing story.

9710 Burden-Patmon, Denise. *Imani's Gift at Kwanzaa* (3–5). Illus. by Floyd Cooper. 1993, Simon & Schuster paper $4.95 (0-671-79841-3). 26pp. Imani isn't sure she wants a new girl to join her family's Kwanzaa celebration. (Rev: BL 1/15/93)

9711 Burton, Tim. *The Nightmare Before Christmas* (3–5). Illus. 1993, Hyperion $15.95 (1-56282-411-2). 40pp. Based on the movie of the same name, this book tells of Jack Skellington's diabolical decision to trade places with Santa. (Rev: BL 10/1/93)

9712 Capote, Truman. *A Christmas Memory* (3–6). Illus. by Beth Peck. 1989, Knopf $19.00 (0-679-80040-9). A tender story about Christmas preparations in a parentless, poor household. (Rev: HB 3–4/90; SLJ 12/89)

9713 Caudill, Rebecca. *A Certain Small Shepherd* (3–6). Illus. by William Pene du Bois. 1997, Holt paper $6.95 (0-805-05392-1). A mute boy gets an opportunity to play one of the shepherds in a Christmas pageant.

9714 Collington, Peter. *A Small Miracle* (2–5). Illus. 1997, Knopf $18.00 (0-679-88725-3). 32pp. An old woman who has rescued Nativity scene figures from the hands of a thief is in turn helped by them when she collapses in the snow. (Rev: BL 10/15/97*; HB 11–12/97; HBG 3/98; SLJ 10/97)

9715 Davies, Valentine. *Miracle on 34th Street* (3–6). Illus. by Tomie dePaola. 1987, Harcourt paper $13.00 (0-15-254528-X). 120pp. An old man named Kris Kringle is hired as the Macy's Santa Claus.

9716 Delton, Judy. *Halloween Helpers* (2–4). Illus. by Alan Tiegreen. Series: Pee Wee Scouts /Yearling Book. 1997, Bantam paper $3.99 (0-440-41330-3). 115pp. When their leader leaves temporarily, the Pee Wee Scouts are afraid that they won't have their usual Halloween party. (Rev: SLJ 1/98)

9717 Delton, Judy. *Tricks and Treats* (2–3). Illus. 1994, Dell paper $3.99 (0-440-40976-4). 87pp. In this story set at Halloween, young Molly worries about what will happen to her family because her father has unexpectedly lost his job. (Rev: BL 9/15/94)

9718 Dickens, Charles. *A Christmas Carol* (6–8). Illus. by Trina S. Hyman. 1983, Holiday $18.95 (0-8234-0486-2). 128pp. A handsome edition of this classic.

9719 Dickens, Charles. *A Christmas Carol* (3–6). Illus. by Lisbeth Zwerger. 1991, Picture Book $19.95 (0-88708-069-3). 60pp. The classic tale with distinctive illustrations. (Rev: HB 11–12/88)

9720 Dickens, Charles. *A Christmas Carol* (4–8). Illus. by Quentin Blake. 1995, Simon & Schuster

paper $19.95 (0-689-80213-7). 144pp. The classic Christmas story illustrated by a master. (Rev: BL 10/15/95)

9721 Dickens, Charles. *A Christmas Carol* (5–8). Illus. by Carter Goodrich. 1996, Morrow $18.00 (0-688-13606-0). 64pp. An abridged version of Dickens's performance text, with excellent illustrations. (Rev: BL 9/1/96; HB 1–2/96)

9722 Gietzen, Jean. *If You're Missing Baby Jesus: A True Story That Embraces the Spirit of Christmas* (2–4). Illus. by Vicki Shuck. 1999, Multnomah paper $9.99 (1-57673-498-6). 48pp. The story of how a good deed helped a poor family in North Dakota during the bitterly cold winter of 1943. (Rev: SLJ 10/99)

9723 Giff, Patricia Reilly. *Turkey Trouble* (2–4). Illus. 1994, Dell paper $3.99 (0-440-40955-1). 31pp. Emily is preparing for a school Thanksgiving party and also preparing her younger sister for the arrival of a new baby in their household. (Rev: BL 12/1/94)

9724 Goldin, Barbara D. *While the Candles Burn: Eight Stories for Hanukkah* (3–6). Illus. 1996, Viking $16.99 (0-670-85875-7). 64pp. Eight short stories highlight the various traditions of Hanukkah. (Rev: BCCB 11/96; BL 9/15/96)

9725 Grahame, Kenneth. *A Wind in the Willows Christmas* (3–5). Illus. 2000, North-South LB $15.88 (1-58717-007-8). 48pp. This is the Christmas chapter from *A Wind in the Willows*, abridged and turned into a charming Christmas book illustrated by Michael Hague. (Rev: BL 9/15/00; HBG 3/01)

9726 Greenberg, Martin H., and Charles G. Waugh, eds. *A Newbery Christmas: Fourteen Stories of Christmas* (4–6). 1991, Delacorte $19.95 (0-385-30485-4). 194pp. Newbery Award winners offer stories about the holiday. (Rev: BCCB 12/91; BL 11/15/91)

9727 Hague, Michael. *Michael Hague's Family Christmas Treasury* (4–6). Illus. 1995, Holt $19.95 (0-8050-1011-4). 32pp. A selection of the author's favorite stories, poems, and carols about Christmas. (Rev: BL 11/1/95) [394]

9728 Hall, Lynn. *Here Comes Zelda Claus and Other Holiday Disasters* (4–6). 1989, Harcourt $16.00 (0-15-233790-3). 144pp. Each of the five stories about Zelda Claus in this collection deals with a different holiday. (Rev: BL 10/1/89; HB 3–4/90; SLJ 10/89)

9729 Hamilton, Virginia. *The Bells of Christmas* (3–5). Illus. by Lambert Davis. 1989, Harcourt $19.00 (0-15-206450-8). 60pp. A century ago a young boy celebrates the holiday with his family in Ohio. (Rev: BCCB 11/89; BL 10/1/89*; HB 11–12/89)

9730 Hardy, Sian. *A Treasury of Christmas Stories* (3–5). Illus. 1994, Kingfisher paper $7.95 (1-85697-985-7). 160pp. A fine collection of stories by such writers as Cleary, Andersen, and Aiken. (Rev: BL 10/1/94)

9731 Henry, O. *The Gift of the Magi* (5–8). Illus. by Carol Heyer. 1994, Ideals $14.95 (1-57102-003-9). 32pp. The classic story of unselfish love at Christmas gets some handsome illustrations. Another fine edition is illus. by Kevin King (1988, Simon & Schuster). (Rev: BL 8/94)

9732 Hill, Susan. *The Christmas Collection* (4–7). Illus. by John Lawrence. 1994, Candlewick $19.95 (1-56402-341-9). 96pp. Four moving Christmas stories and a poem compose this holiday anthology. (Rev: BL 10/15/94)

9733 Hill, Susan. *The Glass Angels* (3–6). Illus. by Valerie Littlewood. 1992, Candlewick $17.95 (1-56402-111-4). 96pp. A sentimental story of post-World War II England and the life of Tilly and her widowed mother. (Rev: BCCB 11/92; BL 9/15/92*)

9734 Houston, Gloria. *Littlejim's Gift: An Appalachian Christmas Story* (2–4). Illus. by Thomas B. Allen. 1994, Putnam $16.99 (0-399-22696-6). 32pp. Set in Appalachia in 1917, this novel explores father-son relationships and tells how Littlejim uses his hard-earned money to buy a doll for his sister at Christmas. A sequel to *Littlejim* (1990). (Rev: BL 8/94; HB 11–12/94)

9735 Joseph, Lynn. *An Island Christmas* (2–6). Illus. by Catherine Stock. 1992, Houghton $14.95 (0-395-58761-1). 32pp. Memories of island life in the Caribbean are enhanced by muted watercolors. (Rev: BCCB 11/92; BL 9/15/92)

9736 *Joy to the World: A Family Christmas Treasury* (4–6). Ed. by Ann Keay Beneduce. Illus. by Gennady Spirin. 2000, Simon & Schuster $25.00 (0-689-82113-1). 192pp. A handsome volume that contains a fine selection of Christmas stories including an adaptation of O. Henry's "The Gift of the Magi." (Rev: BL 9/1/00; HBG 3/01)

9737 Kertes, Joseph. *The Gift* (3–5). Illus. 1996, Douglas & McIntyre $12.95 (0-88899-235-1). 48pp. An immigrant Jewish boy gives an inappropriate Christmas gift to a friend. (Rev: BL 11/1/96)

9738 Kimmel, Eric A. *The Spotted Pony: A Collection of Hanukkah Stories* (3–6). Illus. by Leonard Everett Fisher. 1992, Holiday $15.95 (0-8234-0936-8). 70pp. A collection of wonderfully earthy and joyous Jewish folktales. (Rev: BL 11/15/92)

9739 Kingman, Lee. *The Best Christmas* (3–5). Illus. by Barbara Cooney. 1984, Peter Smith $17.00 (0-8446-6160-0). 96pp. First published in 1949, this reissue is about a Finnish family and their concerns over an absent son at Christmas time.

9740 Koller, Jackie F. *The Promise* (3–6). Illus. 1999, Knopf LB $17.99 (0-679-98484-X). 80pp. When Matt goes out with his dog one Christmas to feed suet to the birds, they are chased by a bear. (Rev: BL 9/1/99)

9741 Koss, Amy Goldman. *How I Saved Hanukkah* (3–6). Illus. 1998, Dial $15.99 (0-8037-2241-9). 96pp. When Marla Feinstein, the only Jewish kid in her fourth-grade class, decides to research the meaning of Hanukkah, she, her family, and her friends catch the Hanukkah spirit. (Rev: BL 10/1/98; HB 11–12/98; SLJ 10/98)

9742 Krensky, Stephen. *How Santa Got His Job* (2–4). Illus. by S. D. Schindler. 1998, Simon & Schuster $15.00 (0-689-80697-3). 32pp. A humorous picture book that traces Santa's career from chimney sweep to becoming a fixture at Christmas. (Rev: BL 9/1/98*; HBG 3/99; SLJ 10/98)

9743 L'Engle, Madeleine. *The Twenty-Four Days Before Christmas: An Austin Family Story* (3–5). Illus. by Joe DeVelasco. 1984, Harold Shaw $11.99 (0-87788-843-4); Dell paper $3.99 (0-440-40105-4). 48pp. Things work out for 7-year-old Vicky, who worries that she will be an awkward angel in the play and that her mother will be in the hospital having a baby on Christmas Day.

9744 Lewis, Beverly. *The Crazy Christmas Angel Mystery* (2–4). Series: Cul-de-Sac Kids. 1995, Bethany paper $3.99 (1-55661-627-9). 62pp. Eric is convinced that his strange new neighbor is dancing with angels in this holiday mystery story. (Rev: BL 9/15/95)

9745 Lovelace, Maud H. *The Trees Kneel at Christmas* (4–6). Illus. by Marie-Claude Monchaux. 1994, ABDO LB $16.98 (1-56239-999-3). 110pp. Afify and her young brother go to a Brooklyn park to see if trees really bow down on Christmas Eve, as the legend says. (Rev: BL 8/94)

9746 Low, Alice. *The Witch Who Was Afraid of Witches* (2–4). Illus. Series: I Can Read. 1999, HarperCollins LB $14.89 (0-06-028306-8). 48pp. In this easy chapter book, Wendy, a witch who doubts her own powers, gains confidence one Halloween night. (Rev: BL 9/1/99; HBG 3/00; SLJ 12/99)

9747 Maguire, Gregory. *Five Alien Elves* (3–5). Illus. by Elaine Clayton. 1998, Clarion $15.00 (0-395-83894-0). 176pp. On Christmas Eve, five space aliens kidnap the town mayor, and two rival clubs — the Copycats and the Tattletales — join forces to rescue him. (Rev: HBG 3/99; SLJ 10/98)

9748 Matthews, Caitlin. *While the Bear Sleeps: Winter Tales and Traditions* (4–6). Illus. 1999, Barefoot $19.95 (1-902283-81-3). 80pp. A satisfying anthology of tales about winter holidays and customs, including Hanukkah, Kwanzaa, Christmas, and Twelfth Night, tied together by a story involving a little girl and her guide, a bear. (Rev: BL 11/15/99; SLJ 10/99)

9749 Montgomery, L. M. *Christmas with Anne and Other Holiday Stories* (4–7). 1996, Delacorte paper $16.95 (0-385-32288-7). 214pp. A collection of 16 short pieces and stories (two from the Anne books) that deal with Christmas. (Rev: BL 9/1/96)

9750 Moore, Miriam, and Penny Taylor. *The Kwanzaa Contest* (2–4). Illus. by Laurie Spencer. 1996, Hyperion $13.95 (0-7868-0261-8); paper $3.95 (0-7868-1122-6). 64pp. Ronald, a third-grader, is determined to win a Kwanzaa contest. (Rev: BL 9/15/96)

9751 Moser, Barry. *Good and Perfect Gifts: An Illustrated Retelling of O. Henry's The Gift of the Magi* (3–6). Illus. 1997, Little, Brown $14.95 (0-316-58543-2). 32pp. Set in a modern Appalachian community, this is a retelling of O. Henry's story, with a number of fresh twists. (Rev: BL 9/1/97; HBG 3/98; SLJ 10/97)

9752 Norris, Leslie. *Albert and the Angels* (4–6). Illus. by Mordicai Gerstein. 2000, Farrar $16.00 (0-374-30192-1). 48pp. When Albert loses the medallion he has bought for his mother at Christmas, he is magically transported to a warehouse where a Santa-like proprietor returns it to him. (Rev: BCCB 12/00; BL 9/15/00; HB 11–12/00; HBG 3/01)

9753 Paterson, Katherine. *Angels and Other Strangers: Family Christmas Stories* (5–8). 1991, HarperCollins LB $13.89 (0-690-04911-0); paper $4.95 (0-06-440283-5). 128pp. Nine stories that explore various meanings of Christmas and what it should represent to people.

9754 Pearl, Sydelle. *Elijah's Tears: Stories for the Jewish Holidays* (3–5). Illus. 1996, Holt $14.95 (0-8050-4627-5). 62pp. These stories feature four Jewish holidays in which the prophet Elijah appears. (Rev: BCCB 11/96; BL 9/15/96; SLJ 1/97)

9755 Penn, Malka. *The Hanukkah Ghosts* (3–5). 1995, Holiday $14.95 (0-8234-1145-1). 88pp. Susan — who is living with an elderly aunt on an English moor during Hanukkah — is visited by children who lived there during World War II. (Rev: BL 9/15/95)

9756 Pirotta, Saviour, reteller. *Joy to the World: Christmas Stories from Around the World* (3–4). Illus. by Sheila Moxley. 1998, HarperCollins $15.95 (0-06-027902-8). 44pp. This book retells five Christmas stories, one each from Syria, Malta, Mexico, Ghana, and Russia. (Rev: HBG 10/99; SLJ 10/98) [398.2]

9757 Robinson, Barbara. *The Best Christmas Pageant Ever* (4–6). Illus. by Judith G. Brown. 1972, HarperCollins LB $15.89 (0-06-025044-5); paper $4.95 (0-06-440275-4). 96pp. When a family of unrestrained children takes over the church Christmas pageant, the results are hilarious.

9758 Rocklin, Joanne. *The Very Best Hanukkah Gift* (2–4). Illus. 1999, Delacorte $14.95 (0-385-32656-4). 112pp. At Hanukkah, Daniel is able to conquer his fears of the new dog next door. (Rev: BL 9/1/99; HBG 3/00; SLJ 10/99)

9759 Russell, Ching Yeung. *Moon Festival* (3–5). Illus. by Christopher Zhong-Yuan. 1997, Boyds Mills $15.95 (1-56397-596-3). 32pp. Ying and her friends celebrate the summer Moon Festival in many ways, including making paper lanterns. (Rev: BL 9/15/97; HBG 3/98)

9760 Rylant, Cynthia. *Children of Christmas: Stories for the Season* (4–6). Illus. by S. D. Schindler. 1987, Orchard paper $6.95 (0-531-07042-5). 48pp. Six quiet stories about the emotions of Christmas. (Rev: BCCB 10/87; BL 9/1/87)

9761 Singer, Isaac Bashevis. *The Power of Light* (4–7). Illus. by Irene Lieblich. 1980, Avon paper $2.50 (0-380-60103-6). 80pp. A collection of eight charming, original stories celebrating Hanukkah, the Festival of Lights.

9762 Sussman, Susan. *There's No Such Thing as a Chanukah Bush, Sandy Goldstein* (3–5). Illus. by Charles Robinson. 1983, Whitman LB $8.95 (0-8075-7862-2). 48pp. The difference between believing in a holiday and helping others celebrate is brought out in this story.

9763 Thury, Fredrick H. *The Last Straw* (2–3). Illus. 1999, Charlesbridge $15.95 (0-88106-152-2). 32pp.

An ailing, aged camel is too proud to refuse to carry any of the gifts, regardless of their weight, to the child in Bethlehem. (Rev: BL 9/1/99; HBG 3/00; SLJ 10/99)

9764 Van Draanen, Wendelin. *Sammy Keyes and the Runaway Elf* (4–7). Illus. 1999, Knopf LB $16.99 (0-679-98854-8). 208pp. At Christmastime, 13-year-old Samantha Keyes unravels the strands of a complicated mystery. (Rev: BL 9/1/99; HBG 3/00; SLJ 9/99)

9765 Van Leeuwen, Jean. *The Great Christmas Kidnapping Caper* (3–5). Illus. by Steven Kellogg. 1975, Dial $12.95 (0-685-01454-1). 144pp. A group of mice who live in a dollhouse at Macy's solve the mystery of the disappearance of Santa Claus.

9766 Walter, Mildred P. *Have a Happy . . .* (3–5). Illus. by Carole Byard. 1989, Avon paper $3.99 (0-380-71314-4). 144pp. In this story set during Kwanzaa, a week after Christmas, the fortunes of a struggling African American family are told. (Rev: BCCB 12/89; BL 9/1/89; HB 11–12/89)

9767 Weatherford, Carole Boston. *Juneteenth Jamboree* (2–4). Illus. by Yvonne Buchanan. 1995, Lee & Low $15.95 (1-880000-18-0). Two youngsters, new to Texas, celebrate Juneteenth, which commemorates the day Texas slaves learned that the Emancipation Proclamation freed them. (Rev: SLJ 1/96)

9768 Wiggin, Kate Douglas. *The Birds' Christmas Carol* (3–5). Illus. by Jessie Gillespie. 1941, Houghton $9.95 (0-395-07205-0). A beautiful edition of a story first published in 1888.

9769 Williams, Karen L. *A Real Christmas This Year* (5–8). 1995, Clarion $13.95 (0-395-70115-5). 164pp. Megan hopes for a "real" Christmas in spite of the many problems she faces both at home and at school. (Rev: BCCB 11/95; BL 9/15/95; HB 11–12/95)

Humorous Stories

9770 Alford, Jan. *I Can't Believe I Have to Do This* (4–7). 1997, Putnam $16.95 (0-399-23130-7). 192pp. When Dean turns 12, his mother gives him a diary, and the entries he makes are funny, terse, and authentic. (Rev: BL 10/15/97; HBG 3/98; SLJ 9/97)

9771 Allan, Jonathan. *Don't Wake the Baby! An Interactive Book with Sounds* (2–4). Illus. 2000, Candlewick $19.99 (0-7636-0891-2). In this interactive book with sound effects, Dad has a hard time keeping quiet as he trips on a rug, steps on the cat's tail, etc. (Rev: BL 12/1/00; SLJ 12/00)

9772 Atwater, Richard, and Florence Atwater. *Mr. Popper's Penguins* (4–6). Illus. by Robert Lawson. 1938, Little, Brown $16.95 (0-316-05842-4). 144pp. Mr. Popper has to get a penguin from the zoo to keep his homesick penguin company; soon there are 12.

9773 Auch, Mary Jane. *I Was a Third Grade Science Project* (2–4). Illus. by Herm Auch. 1998, Holiday $15.95 (0-8234-1357-8). 94pp. Brian tries to hypnotize his dog into believing he's a cat, but the spell works on one of Brian's classmates instead. (Rev: BL 3/15/98; HBG 10/98; SLJ 5/98)

9774 Banks, Kate. *Howie Bowles and Uncle Sam* (2–4). Illus. 2000, Farrar $15.00 (0-374-35116-3). 96pp. A delightful story in which third-grader Howie believes that he owes the IRS more than a hundred dollars and will soon be sent to jail because he can't produce the cash. (Rev: BCCB 1/01; BL 10/15/00; HBG 3/01; SLJ 12/00)

9775 Base, Graeme. *The Discovery of Dragons* (5–8). Illus. 1996, Abrams $17.95 (0-8109-3237-7). 32pp. A humorous account of the three pioneers in dragon research. (Rev: BL 11/15/96; SLJ 11/96)

9776 Bateman, Teresa. *The Ring of Truth* (3–6). Illus. by Omar Rayyan. 1997, Holiday $16.95 (0-8234-1255-5). 32pp. In this picture book with an Irish flavor, a famous fibber, who is also a car salesman, is denied the right to lie. (Rev: BCCB 5/97; BL 7/97; SLJ 5/97)

9777 Beard, Darleen Bailey. *The Flimflam Man* (2–4). Illus. 1998, Farrar $15.00 (0-374-32346-1). 96pp. On a hot day in 1950, an advance man for a circus begins selling tickets for future performances, but some townspeople think that he is a fraud. (Rev: BCCB 5/98; BL 2/15/98; HB 3–4/98; HBG 10/98; SLJ 3/98)

9778 Belloc, Hilaire. *Jim, Who Ran Away from His Nurse, and Was Eaten by a Lion* (3–5). Illus. by Victoria Chess. 1987, Little, Brown paper $4.95 (0-316-13816-9). Spoiled young Jim runs away from nanny at the zoo — with dire consequences. (Rev: BL 5/1/87; HB 5–6/87; SLJ 6–7/87)

9779 Birdseye, Tom. *I'm Going to Be Famous* (4–6). 1986, Holiday $15.95 (0-8234-0630-X). 144pp. Fifth-grader Arlo Moore is going to break the Guinness Book of World Records' time for eating bananas. (Rev: BCCB 1/87; BL 12/1/86)

9780 Bliss, Corinne D. *Electra and the Charlotte Russe* (2–4). Illus. by Michael Garland. 1997, Boyds Mills $14.95 (1-56397-436-3). When she trips and upsets the cream on the pastries she is taking home, Electra tries to reshape them with her tongue. (Rev: HBG 3/98; SLJ 10/97)

9781 Blume, Judy. *Freckle Juice* (2–5). Illus. by Sonia O. Lisker. 1971, Macmillan $15.00 (0-02-711690-5); Dell paper $4.50 (0-440-42813-0). 40pp. A gullible second-grader pays 50c/ for a recipe to grow freckles.

9782 Blume, Judy. *Fudge-a-Mania* (4–6). 1990, Dutton $14.99 (0-525-44672-9). 128pp. Brother Peter and Fudge must spend the summer with the dreaded Sheila the Great. (Rev: BCCB 11/90; BL 10/15/90; HB 1–2/91; SLJ 12/90)

9783 Blume, Judy. *Starring Sally J. Freedman as Herself* (4–7). 1977, Macmillan LB $17.00 (0-02-711070-2); Dell paper $5.50 (0-440-48253-4). 296pp. A story of a fifth-grader's adventures in New Jersey and Florida in the late 1940s.

9784 Blume, Judy. *Tales of a Fourth Grade Nothing* (3–4). Illus. by Roy Doty. 1972, Dell paper $4.99 (0-440-48474-X). 128pp. Peter Hatcher's trials and tribulations, most of which are caused by his two-

year-old pesky brother, Fudge. A sequel is: *Superfudge* (Bantam 1994).

9785 Bond, Michael. *A Bear Called Paddington* (3–6). Illus. by Peggy Fortnum. 1960, Dell paper $4.99 (0-440-40483-5). 128pp. An endearing bear with a talent for getting into trouble. Some sequels (published by Houghton and Dell) are: *More about Paddington* (1979); *Paddington at Work* (1967); *Paddington Goes to Town* (1977); *Paddington Abroad* (1973); *Paddington Helps Out* (1973).

9786 Bond, Michael. *Paddington at Large*. Rev. ed. (3–7). Illus. 1998, Houghton $15.00 (0-395-91294-6). 144pp. This reissue of the 1962 classic features beloved Paddington in some of his most famous adventures. (Rev: BL 8/98; HBG 10/98)

9787 Bond, Michael. *Paddington's Storybook* (3–5). Illus. by Peggy Fortnum. 1984, Houghton $23.00 (0-395-36667-4). 160pp. A selection of some of the very best stories published over the past 25 years.

9788 Brisson, Pat. *Bertie's Picture Day* (2–3). Illus. 2000, Holt $16.00 (0-8050-6281-5). 70pp. In this easy chapter book, Bertie looks awful in his school picture after he loses a front tooth, gets a black eye, and is given a terrible haircut by his young sister. (Rev: BCCB 2/01; BL 12/1/00; SLJ 9/00)

9789 Brooke, William J. *A Is for AARRGH!* (5–8). 1999, HarperCollins LB $14.89 (0-06-023394-X). 160pp. A humorous story about a prehistoric boy, Mog, and his amazing discoveries about language and communication. (Rev: BCCB 11/99; BL 10/15/99; HB 9–10/99; HBG 3/00; SLJ 9/99)

9790 Browne, Anthony. *Willy's Pictures* (5–8). Illus. 2000, Candlewick LB $16.99 (0-7636-1323-1). 32pp. In this imaginative picture book for older children, the author/artist changes famous paintings to tell new and wild stories. (Rev: BL 12/15/00; SLJ 12/00)

9791 Bunting, Eve. *Nasty, Stinky Sneakers* (4–6). Illus. 1994, HarperCollins LB $14.89 (0-06-024237-X). 128pp. Colin thinks his sneakers are so smelly that they will win a prize, and then they suddenly disappear. (Rev: BL 5/1/94; SLJ 6/94)

9792 Butterworth, Oliver. *The Enormous Egg* (3–6). Illus. by Louis Darling. 1995, Houghton $9.00 (0-395-73249-2). The story of a boy whose hen lays a large egg, which hatches a triceratops!

9793 Byars, Betsy. *The Cybil War* (4–6). Illus. by Gail Owens. 1981, Puffin paper $4.99 (0-14-034356-3). 144pp. A humorous story about the relationship between two boys and a girl, Cybil.

9794 Byars, Betsy. *Me Tarzan* (3–5). 2000, HarperCollins LB $14.89 (0-06-028707-1). 96pp. Dorothy's Tarzan yell is so effective that she wins the part of Tarzan in the school play, and also finds that animals respond to her call. (Rev: BCCB 6/00; BL 3/15/00; HB 5–6/00; HBG 10/00; SLJ 7/00)

9795 Byars, Betsy. *The Seven Treasure Hunts* (3–5). Illus. by Jennifer Barrett. 1992, HarperCollins paper $4.25 (0-06-440435-8). 80pp. Readers giggle and guess their way through the story of Jackson and friend Goat who are into treasure hunts. (Rev: BCCB 4/91; BL 3/15/91; HB 7–8/91; SLJ 6/91)

9796 Callen, Larry. *Who Kidnapped the Sheriff? Tales from Tickfaw* (4–6). Illus. by Stephen Gammell. 1985, Little, Brown $14.95 (0-316-12499-0). 176pp. The small town of Tickfaw has lots of characters, who are introduced in these related short stories. (Rev: BL 6/1/85; HB 5–6/85; SLJ 8/85)

9797 Calmenson, Stephanie, and Joanna Cole. *Gator Halloween* (2–4). Illus. 1999, Morrow LB $14.93 (0-688-14785-2). 64pp. Amy and Allie's plan to win the best Halloween costume prize gets sidetracked when they try to find a lost pet. (Rev: BL 9/1/99; HBG 3/00; SLJ 9/99)

9798 Calmenson, Stephanie, and Joanna Cole. *Get Well, Gators!* (2–4). Illus. Series: Gator Girls. 1998, Morrow LB $15.93 (0-688-14787-9). 64pp. When Allie, who was to sing a duet with Amy at the Swamp Town fair, comes down with swamp flu, Amy is afraid to sing solo in this simple, humorous story. (Rev: BL 11/15/98; HBG 3/99; SLJ 10/98)

9799 Cameron, Ann. *More Stories Huey Tells* (2–4). Illus. 1997, Farrar $13.00 (0-374-35065-5). 128pp. Some humorous everyday adventures experienced by a bright, eager 7-year-old named Huey. (Rev: BCCB 7–8/97; BL 4/15/97; HB 7–8/97; SLJ 6/97)

9800 Cleary, Beverly. *Ellen Tebbits* (3–5). Illus. by Louis Darling. 1951, Morrow $15.89 (0-688-31264-0); Avon paper $4.99 (0-380-70913-9). 160pp. Eight-year-old Ellen has braces on her teeth, takes ballet lessons, and, worst of all, wears long woolen underwear.

9801 Cleary, Beverly. *Emily's Runaway Imagination* (3–6). Illus. by Beth Krush and Joe Krush. 1961, Morrow $15.89 (0-688-31267-5); Avon paper $4.95 (0-380-70923-6). 224pp. Emily's imagination helps get a library for Pitchfork, Oregon, in the 1920s.

9802 Cleary, Beverly. *Henry Huggins* (3–5). Illus. by Louis Darling. 1950, Morrow $14.89 (0-688-31385-X); Avon paper $4.99 (0-380-70912-0). 160pp. Henry is a small boy with a knack for creating hilarious situations. Others in the series: *Henry and Beezus* (1952); *Henry and Ribsy* (1954); *Henry and the Paper Route* (1957); *Henry and the Clubhouse* (1962).

9803 Cleary, Beverly. *Otis Spofford* (3–6). Illus. by Louis Darling. 1953, Avon paper $4.99 (0-380-70919-8). 192pp. This story of Otis stirring up a little excitement at school is full of humor.

9804 Cleary, Beverly. *Runaway Ralph* (3–5). Illus. by Louis Darling. 1970, Morrow $15.93 (0-688-31701-4). 176pp. A motorcyclist mouse finds family life too stifling so he takes to his wheels, only to find that freedom is an evasive thing. Two others in the series: *The Mouse and the Motorcycle* (1965); *Ralph S. Mouse* (1982).

9805 Clifford, Eth. *Harvey's Horrible Snake Disaster* (3–5). 1984, Houghton $15.00 (0-395-35378-5). 128pp. Harvey tries to disguise the fact that he is petrified of snakes.

9806 Conford, Ellen. *Annabel the Actress Starring in Gorilla My Dreams* (2–4). Illus. by Renee W. Andriani. 1999, Simon & Schuster $14.00 (0-689-81404-6). 64pp. A humorous beginning chapter book that introduces clever young Annabel, who aspires to be a fine actress and who advertises that no part is too big or too small. (Rev: BCCB 7–8/99; BL 7/99; HBG 10/99; SLJ 7/99)

9807 Conford, Ellen. *Annabel the Actress Starring in Just a Little Extra* (2–4). Illus. 2000, Simon & Schuster $15.00 (0-689-81405-4). 64pp. A humorous story about Annabel, a would-be actress, who gets a job as a screaming extra in a crowd scene. (Rev: BL 9/15/00; HBG 3/01; SLJ 12/00)

9808 Conford, Ellen. *The Frog Princess of Pelham* (5–7). 1997, Little, Brown $15.95 (0-316-15246-3). 112pp. When Chandler is turned into a frog after kissing the local heartthrob, she tries all sorts of ways to solve this problem. (Rev: BCCB 7–8/97; BL 3/15/97; SLJ 6/97)

9809 Conford, Ellen. *Jenny Archer to the Rescue* (3–5). Illus. by Diane Palmisciano. 1992, Little, Brown paper $4.95 (0-316-15369-9). 64pp. Jenny wants to be a hero, so she hunts for someone to save. Also use: *Can Do, Jenny Archer* (1991). (Rev: BL 11/1/90; SLJ 12/90)

9810 Conford, Ellen. *A Job for Jenny Archer* (2–4). Illus. by Diane Palmisciano. 1990, Little, Brown paper $4.50 (0-316-15349-4). Jenny's plans for an expensive present for her mother's birthday backfire, but she learns that small gifts can be precious, too. (Rev: BL 4/1/88; HB 7–8/88; SLJ 4/88)

9811 Conford, Ellen. *My Sister the Witch* (3–5). Illus. by Tim Jacobus. Series: Norman Newman. 1996, Troll LB $15.35 (0-8167-3815-7). 92pp. Norman mistakes his sister's readings from *Macbeth* as proof that she is practicing witchcraft. (Rev: SLJ 6/96)

9812 Conford, Ellen. *Nibble, Nibble, Jenny Archer* (2–4). Illus. by Diane Palmisciano. 1993, Little, Brown $14.95 (0-316-15371-0). 62pp. Jenny's enthusiasm and pride in being part of a TV commercial fades when she sees the final ad. (Rev: BCCB 7–8/93; BL 9/15/93; SLJ 7/93)

9813 Conford, Ellen. *What's Cooking, Jenny Archer?* (2–4). Illus. by Diane Palmisciano. 1991, Little, Brown paper $4.95 (0-316-15357-5). 80pp. Jenny is inspired to make her own lunches after watching a cooking show. (Rev: BL 1/15/90; SLJ 1/90)

9814 Corbett, Scott. *The Lemonade Trick* (3–5). Illus. by Paul Galdone. 1988, Scholastic paper $4.50 (0-590-32197-8). 96pp. Kirby and his wonderful chemistry change good boys into bad boys and vice versa.

9815 Cowley, Joy. *Agapanthus Hum and the Eyeglasses* (K–3). Illus. by Jennifer Plecas. 1999, Putnam $13.99 (0-399-23211-7). 48pp. The young heroine of this easy chapter book is always rushing around and dropping her glasses. (Rev: BCCB 4/99; HBG 10/99; SLJ 4/99)

9816 Cox, Judy. *Third Grade Pet* (2–3). Illus. 1998, Holiday $15.95 (0-8234-1379-9). 93pp. In this easy chapter book, Rosemary takes her class's pet rat home to save him from the class bully and has problems keeping him hidden and safe. (Rev: BCCB 2/99; BL 12/15/98; HBG 3/99; SLJ 2/99)

9817 Cox, Judy. *Weird Stories from the Lonesome Cafe* (2–5). Illus. 2000, Harcourt $15.00 (0-15-202134-5). 80pp. An easy chapter book in which Sam and his uncle open a roadside cafe to which celebrities come incognito. (Rev: BCCB 4/00; BL 4/15/00; HBG 10/00; SLJ 6/00)

9818 Crebbin, June. *Cows in the Kitchen* (PS). Illus. by Katharine McEwen. 1998, Candlewick $15.99 (0-7636-0645-6). 32pp. While a farmer sleeps in the haystack, his farm animals invade his house causing chaos and great fun. (Rev: BCCB 10/98; BL 9/1/98; HBG 3/99; SLJ 9/98)

9819 Cresswell, Helen. *Posy Bates, Again!* (3–5). 1994, Macmillan paper $13.95 (0-02-725372-4). 112pp. Posy is determined to keep the stray dog left behind after her pet show. (Rev: BL 5/15/94; HB 7–8/94; SLJ 6/94)

9820 Cutler, Jane. *'Gator Aid* (3–5). Illus. 1999, Farrar $16.00 (0-374-32502-2). 144pp. Second-grader Edward, who has a vivid imagination, claims he has seen a baby alligator in a local lake, and soon the rumor gets out of hand. (Rev: BCCB 9/99; BL 8/99; HB 9–10/99; HBG 3/00; SLJ 9/99)

9821 Cutler, Jane. *No Dogs Allowed* (3–5). Illus. by Tracey Campbell Pearson. 1992, Farrar $14.00 (0-374-35526-6). 112pp. Edward and his older brother cannot have a dog because they are allergic, so Edward decides that he is a dog. (Rev: BL 10/15/92*; HB 1–2/93*; SLJ 12/92)

9822 Cutler, Jane. *Rats!* (3–5). Illus. 1996, Farrar $14.00 (0-374-36181-9). 114pp. Two brothers, one in the fourth grade and the other in the first grade, face everyday crises with amusing results in this sequel to *No Dogs Allowed* (1992). (Rev: BL 2/1/96; HB 5–6/96; SLJ 4/96*)

9823 Danziger, Paula. *Amber Brown Goes Fourth* (2–4). Illus. 1995, Putnam $14.99 (0-399-22849-7). 112pp. Amber Brown, a fourth-grader unsure of herself, doesn't know how to react to her divorced mother's new boyfriend. (Rev: BCCB 11/95; BL 10/15/95; HB 11–12/95; SLJ 10/95*)

9824 Danziger, Paula. *Amber Brown Is Feeling Blue* (3–5). Illus. 1998, Putnam $14.99 (0-399-23179-X). 32pp. Amber's humorous adventures continue when her divorced mother takes a new boyfriend, her father returns from Paris, and a new girl in her class also has a color-name, Kelly Green. (Rev: BL 12/1/98; SLJ 11/98)

9825 Danziger, Paula. *Amber Brown Is Not a Crayon* (2–4). Illus. by Tony Ross. 1994, Putnam $13.99 (0-399-22509-9). 80pp. Amber Brown's close friendship with Justin Daniels will end soon because Justin's family is moving. (Rev: BCCB 6/94; BL 4/15/94; HB 7–8/94; SLJ 5/94*)

9826 Danziger, Paula. *Amber Brown Sees Red* (2–4). Illus. 1997, Putnam $14.99 (0-399-22901-9). 120pp. Amber Brown is now in the fourth grade and is increasingly upset with her parents' custody battles involving her. (Rev: BL 5/15/97; SLJ 7/97)

9827 Danziger, Paula. *I, Amber Brown* (3–6). Illus. by Tony Ross. 1999, Putnam $14.99 (0-399-23180-3). 140pp. Amber Brown, daughter of divorced parents, gets her ears pierced when she is with her father, in spite of her mother's objections. (Rev: BL 10/15/99; HBG 3/00; SLJ 11/99)

9828 Danziger, Paula. *You Can't Eat Your Chicken Pox, Amber Brown* (2–4). Illus. by Tony Ross. 1995, Putnam $14.99 (0-399-22702-4). 112pp. Amber visits London with her aunt while her parents are getting a divorce. A sequel to *Amber Brown Is Not a Crayon* (1994). (Rev: BCCB 4/95; BL 3/15/95; SLJ 6/95*)

9829 Davol, Marguerite W. *Papa Alonzo Leatherby: A Collection of Tall Tales from the Best Storyteller in Carroll County* (3–6). 1995, Simon & Schuster paper $14.00 (0-689-80278-1). 70pp. Tall tales from New England that involve the Alonzo family, Papa, his wife Lulie, and nine children. (Rev: SLJ 10/95)

9830 De Groat, Diane. *Annie Pitts, Burger Kid* (2–5). Illus. 2000, North-South $14.95 (1-58717-015-9). 80pp. Annie is certain that she will be the new poster kid for her favorite restaurant, Burger Barn, in this funny novel about the everyday life of an energetic kid. (Rev: BCCB 1/01; BL 10/1/00; HBG 3/01; SLJ 10/00)

9831 du Bois, William Pene. *Twenty-One Balloons* (4–6). Illus. by author. 1947, Puffin paper $5.99 (0-14-032097-0). 184pp. Truth and fiction are combined in the adventures of a professor who sails around the world in a balloon. Newbery Medal winner, 1948.

9832 Duffey, Betsy. *Alien for Rent* (3–5). 1999, Delacorte $14.95 (0-385-32572-X). 66pp. When Lexie and her buddy J.P. rent a tiny green and furry alien, Bork, to tame the class bully, they find he has already done the job. (Rev: BCCB 2/99; BL 1/1–15/99; HB 1–2/99; HBG 10/99; SLJ 3/99)

9833 Duffey, Betsy. *Cody Unplugged* (2–6). Illus. 1999, Viking $14.99 (0-670-88592-4). 96pp. Cody, who is addicted to television and computers, doesn't think he will survive a summer at Camp Bear where there is no electricity. (Rev: BL 6/1–15/99; HB 5–6/99; HBG 10/99; SLJ 7/99)

9834 Duffey, Betsy. *Cody's Secret Admirer* (2–3). Illus. 1998, Viking $13.99 (0-670-87400-0). 80pp. A humorous story about 9-year-old Cody, who regards getting a valentine from a secret admirer as "gross." (Rev: BCCB 5/98; BL 2/1/98; HBG 10/98; SLJ 10/98)

9835 Duffey, Betsy. *The Gadget War* (2–4). Illus. by Janet Wilson. 1991, Viking $13.99 (0-670-84152-8). 64pp. When Albert Einstein Jones comes to third grade, it is hate at first sight for Kelly, undisputed gadget champ. (Rev: BCCB 9/91; BL 10/1/91*; SLJ 11/91)

9836 Duffey, Betsy. *Hey, New Kid!* (2–4). Illus. 1996, Viking $13.99 (0-670-86760-8). 80pp. When third-grader Cody and his family move, the boy decides that it is a perfect time to create a new image. (Rev: BL 4/1/96; HB 7–8/96; SLJ 4/96)

9837 Duffey, Betsy. *Virtual Cody* (2–4). Illus. 1997, Viking $13.99 (0-670-87470-1). 80pp. When Cody learns he was named after a dog, he is fearful that people, particularly P.J. and her friends, will make fun of him. (Rev: BCCB 6/97; BL 6/1–15/97; HB 7–8/97; SLJ 7/97)

9838 Evans, Douglas. *Apple Island; or, the Truth About Teachers* (4–6). Illus. 1998, Front Street $14.95 (1-886910-25-1). 144pp. Young Bradley finds a teacher-training camp on Apple Island where all the mean teachers are plotting to take over the schools. (Rev: BL 1/1–15/99; HBG 10/99; SLJ 1/99)

9839 Evans, Douglas. *The Elevator Family* (2–4). 2000, Delacorte $14.95 (0-385-32723-4). 87pp. A lighthearted story about a family who is forced to live in a hotel elevator when they discover there are no vacant rooms. (Rev: BCCB 7–8/00; BL 5/1/00; HBG 10/00)

9840 Evans, Douglas. *Math Rashes and Other Classroom Tales* (2–4). Illus. 2000, Front Street $15.95 (1-886910-66-9). 112pp. Wacky third-grade experiences are the subject of this collection of original short stories. (Rev: BL 12/15/00; HBG 3/01; SLJ 11/00)

9841 Feiffer, Jules. *The Man in the Ceiling* (5–7). Illus. 1993, HarperCollins $15.95 (0-06-205035-4); paper $6.95 (0-06-205907-6). 192pp. Jimmy turns to cartooning in an effort to gain some recognition in a family that is intent on ignoring him. (Rev: BCCB 12/93; BL 11/15/93; SLJ 2/94*)

9842 Ferguson, Alane. *The Practical Joke War* (3–6). 1993, Avon paper $3.50 (0-380-71721-2). 160pp. All-out war is declared when the Dillon children — lovers of practical jokes — are left to themselves one summer. (Rev: BCCB 7–8/91; BL 4/1/91; SLJ 6/91)

9843 Fitzgerald, John D. *The Great Brain* (4–7). Illus. by Mercer Mayer. 1985, Dial LB $11.89 (0-803-73076-4); Dell paper $4.99 (0-440-43071-2). 192pp. A witty and tender novel in which narrator John recalls the escapades of older brother Tom whose perceptive and crafty schemes set him apart. Some sequels are: *More Adventures of the Great Brain* (1969); *Me and My Little Brain* (1971); *The Great Brain at the Academy* (1972); *The Great Brain Reforms* (1973); *The Return of the Great Brain* (1974); *The Great Brain Does It Again* (1975).

9844 Fleischman, Sid. *By the Great Horn Spoon* (4–6). Illus. by Eric Von Schmidt. 1988, Little, Brown $16.95 (0-316-28577-3); paper $5.95 (0-316-28612-5). Accompanied by Praiseworthy, the butler, an orphan boy named Jack Fogg runs away and becomes involved in the California gold rush of 1849 in this hilarious adventure story.

9845 Fleischman, Sid. *A Carnival of Animals* (3–6). Illus. 2000, Greenwillow $15.95 (0-688-16948-1). 48pp. A tall tale about a tornado that causes weird changes in the farm animals. (Rev: BCCB 1/01; BL 9/1/00; HBG 3/01; SLJ 10/00)

9846 Fleischman, Sid. *Chancy and the Grand Rascal* (5–7). Illus. by Eric Von Schmidt. 1966, Little, Brown $14.95 (0-316-28575-7); paper $4.95 (0-316-26012-6). 190pp. The boy and his uncle, the grand rascal, combine hard work and quick wits to outsmart a scoundrel, hoodwink a miser, and capture a band of outlaws.

9847 Fleischman, Sid. *The Ghost in the Noonday Sun* (5–7). Illus. by Warren Chappell. 1989, Greenwillow $16.00 (0-688-08410-9); Scholastic paper $3.50 (0-590-43662-7). 144pp. Pirate story with all the standard ingredients of shanghaied boy, villainous captain, and buried treasure.

9848 Fleischman, Sid. *The Ghost on Saturday Night* (3–5). Illus. by Eric Von Schmidt. 1974, Little, Brown $14.95 (0-316-28583-8). 64pp. Ten-year-old Opie's efforts to raise money for a saddle involve him in a ghost-raising session and the recovery of money stolen from a bank.

9849 Fleischman, Sid. *Humbug Mountain* (4–6). Illus. by Eric Von Schmidt. 1998, Bantam paper $4.50 (0-440-41403-2). A madcap tall tale adventure in the wild West.

9850 Fleischman, Sid. *McBroom Tells the Truth* (3–5). Illus. by Walter Lorraine. 1981, Little, Brown $12.45 (0-316-28550-1). 48pp. A tall tale about a New England farmer named McBroom. Also use: *McBroom and the Great Race* (1980).

9851 Fleischman, Sid. *Mr. Mysterious and Company* (3–5). Illus. by Eric Von Schmidt. 1997, Greenwillow $15.00 (0-688-14921-9); paper $4.95 (0-688-14922-7). A traveling magic show during the 1880s makes for an entertaining family story that is also an excellent historical novel.

9852 Foley, June. *Susanna Siegelbaum Gives Up Guys* (5–8). 1992, Scholastic paper $3.25 (0-590-43700-3). 160pp. Susanna, a flirt, makes a bet that she can give up guys for three months. (Rev: SLJ 8/91)

9853 Fowler, Susi G. *Albertina, the Animals, and Me* (3–5). Illus. 2000, Greenwillow LB $14.89 (0-06-029160-5). 96pp. A humorous story of two friends, Molly and Albertina, who try various schemes to get their parents to allow them to have pets. (Rev: BL 12/15/00; HBG 3/01; SLJ 12/00)

9854 Franklin, Kristine L. *Nerd No More* (4–6). 1996, Candlewick $15.99 (1-56402-674-4). 144pp. Wiggie sets out to correct his nerdish image by changing his personality. (Rev: BCCB 10/96; BL 10/15/96; HB 11–12/96; SLJ 10/96)

9855 Freeman, Martha. *The Polyester Grandpa* (4–5). 1998, Holiday $15.95 (0-8234-1398-5). 145pp. Grandma turns up with a new husband — brash, uncouth Jimmy Barkenfalt — and 10-year-old Morgan Knight's family has a fit. (Rev: BCCB 1/99; BL 12/1/98; HBG 3/99; SLJ 12/98)

9856 Friedman, Robin. *How I Survived My Summer Vacation: And Lived to Write the Story* (5–9). 2000, Front Street $15.95 (0-8126-2738-5). 160pp. A humorous story about 13-year-old Jackie Monterey, his friends, family, and the vow he has made to write the great American novel. (Rev: HBG 10/00; SLJ 6/00)

9857 Gannett, Ruth. *My Father's Dragon* (4–6). Illus. by author. 1986, Knopf paper $4.99 (0-394-89048-5). 88pp. Hilarious adventures of Elmer Elevator. Also use: *The Dragons of Blueland* (1963); *Elmer and the Dragon* (1987).

9858 Gardiner, John Reynolds. *Top Secret* (4–6). Illus. by Marc Simont. 1995, Little, Brown paper

$4.95 (0-316-30363-1). 129pp. Allen is convinced he can solve the world's hunger problem, and when no one believes him he goes to the president of the United States. (Rev: BCCB 11/85; BL 1/15/86; SLJ 11/85)

9859 Geras, Adele. *The Fabulous Fantoras: Book One: Family Files* (4–6). 1998, Avon $14.00 (0-380-97547-5). 144pp. The antics of an eccentric English family, in which each member has a special zany talent, are recorded by the family cat, Ozymandias, or Ozzy for short. (Rev: BL 11/1/98; HBG 3/99; SLJ 1/99)

9860 Getz, David. *Almost Famous* (3–5). Illus. 1994, Holt paper $5.95 (0-805-03464-1). 182pp. Overbearing Maxine knows she's destined to be an inventor, but for now, she has to team up with Toni the troublemaker for an invention contest partner. (Rev: BL 12/15/92*; SLJ 2/93)

9861 Giff, Patricia Reilly. *Not-So-Perfect Rosie* (2–4). Illus. 1997, Viking $13.99 (0-670-86968-6). 80pp. Rosie's summer is a busy one, with her planned ballet performance and a visit with a cousin from Ireland. (Rev: BL 5/1/97; SLJ 10/97)

9862 Gondosch, Linda. *The Monsters of Marble Avenue* (2–4). Illus. by Cat B. Smith. 1988, Little, Brown $10.95 (0-316-31991-0). 64pp. Luke learns the meaning of "the show must go on" when the puppets for his upcoming show are given away by mistake. (Rev: BL 4/1/87; SLJ 8/88)

9863 Gorman, Carol. *Dork in Disguise* (3–7). 1999, HarperCollins LB $15.89 (0-06-024867-X). 160pp. A hilarious novel about a boy who decides to sacrifice anything to be part of the "in" crowd. (Rev: BCCB 9/99; BL 9/1/99; HBG 3/00; SLJ 9/99)

9864 Gorman, Carol. *Lizard Flanagan, Supermodel??* (4–7). 1998, HarperCollins $14.95 (0-06-024868-8). 160pp. Sixth-grader Lizard Flanagan will do anything to make enough money to go by bus from her home in Iowa to a game in Wrigley Field, but is entering a local fashion show for teens going too far? (Rev: BL 11/15/98; HBG 3/99; SLJ 10/98)

9865 Gormley, Beatrice. *The Magic Mean Machine* (4–6). Illus. by Emily Arnold McCully. 1989, Avon paper $2.95 (0-380-75519-X). 128pp. Marvin invents a special machine to ensure that friend Alison will beat bully Spencer at chess. (Rev: BL 7/89)

9866 Greene, Stephanie. *Owen Foote, Money Man* (2–4). Illus. by Martha Weston. 2000, Clarion $14.00 (0-618-02369-0). 96pp. In this beginning chapter book, young Owen helps his neighbor, Mr. White, build a backyard goldfish pond so he can earn enough money to buy a whoopee cushion and some plastic vomit. (Rev: BCCB 10/00; BL 9/1/00; HB 9–10/00; HBG 3/01; SLJ 9/00)

9867 Greenwald, Sheila. *Mariah Delany's Author-of-the-Month Club* (4–6). 1990, Troll paper $2.95 (0-8167-3000-8). 124pp. Mariah is back in business with an author-of-the-month club. (Rev: BL 12/1/90; SLJ 12/91)

9868 Greer, Gery, and Bob Ruddick. *This Island Isn't Big Enough for the Four of Us!* (4–6). 1987, HarperCollins paper $4.95 (0-06-440203-7). 160pp.

It's boys against girls in this tale of too many camping out on Turtle Island. (Rev: BCCB 9/87; BL 7/87; SLJ 8/87)

9869 Gutman, Dan. *The Kid Who Ran for President* (4–6). 1996, Scholastic $15.95 (0-590-93987-4). 144pp. A 12-year-old boy runs an outrageous campaign when he decides to run for U.S. president. (Rev: BCCB 11/96; BL 11/1/96; SLJ 11/96)

9870 Haas, Dorothy. *Burton and the Giggle Machine* (3–6). Illus. by Cathy Bobak. 1996, Pocket paper $3.50 (0-671-79897-9). 160pp. Can the scion of the famous family of inventors produce a giggle machine that will make his friends happy enough to forget their problems? (Rev: BCCB 4/92; BL 2/15/92; SLJ 4/92)

9871 Haas, Jessie. *Clean House* (2–4). 1996, Greenwillow $15.00 (0-688-14079-3). 56pp. When relatives visit Tess's newly cleaned house, she makes them feel at home by returning it to its usual state. (Rev: BCCB 3/96; BL 4/15/96; HB 5–6/96; SLJ 5/96)

9872 Hall, Lynn. *The Secret Life of Dagmar Schultz* (4–6). 1988, Macmillan LB $13.95 (0-684-18915-1). 96pp. Dagmar, oldest of six, longs for something of her own, so when best friend Shelly gets a boyfriend, Dagmar makes up one for herself. (Rev: BL 6/1/88; HB 7–8/88; SLJ 4/88)

9873 Hayes, Daniel. *Eye of the Beholder* (5–8). 1998, Fawcett paper $5.99 (0-449-00235-7). 192pp. Two eighth-graders, looking for the lost work of a famous sculptor, try their hand at the art. (Rev: BL 2/1/93; SLJ 12/92)

9874 Heide, Florence Parry. *The Shrinking of Treehorn* (2–5). Illus. by Edward Gorey. 1971, Holiday LB $16.95 (0-8234-0189-8); paper $6.95 (0-8234-0975-9). 64pp. Treehorn has a special talent — he can become smaller by the moment — but nobody notices. A sequel is: *The Adventures of Treehorn* (1983).

9875 Hermes, Patricia. *Kevin Corbett Eats Flies* (4–6). Illus. 1986, Harcourt $13.95 (0-15-242290-0); Pocket paper $3.99 (0-671-69183-X). 160pp. Kevin and his father move around whenever the mood strikes; now Kevin doesn't want to move anymore and thinks that if his father fell in love, he wouldn't want to either. (Rev: BCCB 9/86; BL 8/86; SLJ 5/86)

9876 Hermes, Patricia. *Nothing but Trouble* (4–6). 1994, Scholastic $13.95 (0-590-43499-3). 160pp. A humorous story about a fifth-grader who wants to prove herself as a baby-sitter. (Rev: BL 3/15/94; SLJ 4/94)

9877 Hodgman, Ann. *My Babysitter Is a Vampire* (3–6). Illus. by John Pierard. 1991, Pocket paper $3.50 (0-671-64751-2). 121pp. Meg and Trevor do research on how to get rid of Vincent Graver, their baby-sitter, who they believe is a vampire. (Rev: SLJ 12/91)

9878 Honey, Elizabeth. *Don't Pat the Wombat* (4–7). Illus. 2000, Knopf LB $16.99 (0-375-90578-2). 144pp. This Aussie import tells the breezy story of a group of kids at school and at summer camp.

(Rev: BCCB 9/00; BL 5/15/00; HB 5–6/00; HBG 10/00; SLJ 7/00)

9879 Honey, Elizabeth. *Stella Street, and Everything That Happened* (4–6). Illus. 1998, Annick $12.95 (1-55037-515-6); paper $5.95 (1-55037-514-8). 184pp. A very funny tale told by a 12-year-old girl about her neighbors on Stella Street in an Australian community. When an obnoxious new family moves in, it isn't long before they become known as the Phonies. (Rev: BL 6/1–15/98; SLJ 9/98)

9880 Honeycutt, Natalie. *Granville Jones: Commando* (2–5). 1998, Farrar $15.00 (0-374-32764-5). 112pp. Young Granville, a friend of Jonas Twist (hero of several preceding volumes), encounters many problems, including having his room painted a sissy blue, his combat boots giving him blisters, and his attempt to gain fame backfiring. (Rev: BCCB 6/98; BL 4/1/98; HBG 10/98; SLJ 5/98)

9881 Horvath, Polly. *The Happy Yellow Car* (5–7). 1994, Farrar $15.00 (0-374-32845-5). 150pp. In a small Missouri town, where this humorous story takes place, 12-year-old Betty Grunt must find a dollar if she wants to be elected Pork-Fry Queen. (Rev: BCCB 11/94; BL 8/94; SLJ 9/94)

9882 Horvath, Polly. *An Occasional Cow* (4–6). Illus. by Gioia Fiammenghi. 1989, Farrar paper $4.95 (0-374-45573-2). 112pp. Imogene's camp burns down, so she is shipped off to Iowa to stay with relatives. (Rev: BCCB 5/89; BL 5/15/89; HB 6/89)

9883 Horvath, Polly. *The Trolls* (3–6). Illus. by Wendy A. Halperin. 1999, Farrar $16.00 (0-364-37787-1). 144pp. Aunt Sally spins some fanciful tales when she entertains two nieces and a nephew left in her care. (Rev: BL 3/1/99*; SLJ 4/99)

9884 Horvath, Polly. *When the Circus Came to Town* (5–8). 1996, Farrar $15.00 (0-374-38308-1). 144pp. Ivy witnesses her town develop divided loyalties when a circus troupe decides to relocate there. (Rev: BCCB 12/96; BL 11/15/96; SLJ 12/96*)

9885 Howe, Deborah, and James Howe. *Bunnicula: A Rabbit Tale of Mystery* (4–6). Illus. by Alan Daniel. 1979, Macmillan LB $16.00 (0-689-30700-4); Avon paper $3.99 (0-380-51094-4). 112pp. A dog named Harold tells the story of a rabbit many believe to be a vampire. Two sequels by James Howe are: *Howliday Inn* (1982); *The Celery Stalks at Midnight* (1983).

9886 Howe, James. *Bunnicula Strikes Again!* (3–6). 1999, Simon & Schuster $15.00 (0-689-81463-1). 128pp. In this sequel to *Bunnicula*, the fanged rabbit, who needs a diet of carrot juice, is again pursued by Chester, who is afraid other vegetables might be endangered. (Rev: BL 10/1/99; HBG 3/00; SLJ 12/99)

9887 Howe, James. *The New Nick Kramer; or, My Life as a Baby-sitter* (5–8). 1995, Hyperion LB $14.49 (0-7868-2053-5). 120pp. Nick and rival Mitch make an unusual bet on who will win the affections of newcomer Jennifer. (Rev: BL 12/15/95; SLJ 1/96)

9888 Howe, James. *Nighty-Nightmare* (3–6). Illus. by Leslie Morrill. 1987, Macmillan $15.00 (0-689-

31207-5); Avon paper $3.99 (0-380-70490-0). 128pp. Harold the canine and friends set out on a camping trip. (Rev: BCCB 4/87; BL 3/1/87; SLJ 4/87)

9889 Howe, James. *Return to Howliday Inn* (3–6). Illus. by Alan Daniel. 1992, Macmillan $15.00 (0-689-31661-5). 174pp. With the vampire bunny off with friends, the focus is on the Chateau Bow-Wow where the family boards their cat and dogs. (Rev: BL 5/1/92; HB 7–8/92; SLJ 5/92)

9890 Hughes, Dean. *Nutty, the Movie Star* (4–6). 1989, Macmillan $12.95 (0-689-31509-0); paper $3.95 (0-689-71524-2). 144pp. Friend William gets Nutty a job in Hollywood. (Rev: BL 10/15/89; SLJ 10/89)

9891 Hurwitz, Johanna. *Aldo Applesauce* (3–5). Illus. by John Wallner. 1979, Morrow $15.89 (0-688-32199-2); Puffin paper $4.99 (0-14-034083-1). 128pp. Aldo moves to New York City and acquires a new nickname and a strange friend. Two others in the series are: *Much Ado About Aldo* (1978); *Aldo Ice Cream* (1981).

9892 Hurwitz, Johanna. *Elisa in the Middle* (2–4). Illus. by Lillian Hoban. Series: Russell and Elisa. 1995, Morrow $15.00 (0-688-14050-5). 64pp. In her efforts to help members of her family, Elisa often causes mayhem and catastrophe in this humorous beginning chapter book. (Rev: BCCB 10/95; BL 9/1/95; HB 11–12/95; SLJ 10/95)

9893 Jones, Jennifer B. *Dear Mrs. Ryan, You're Ruining My Life* (4–6). 2000, Walker $15.95 (0-8027-8728-2). 132pp. Harry's mother, a writer of children's books, embarrasses the boy when she becomes interested in his widowed school principal. (Rev: BCCB 4/00; BL 4/1/00; HBG 10/00; SLJ 5/00)

9894 Keller, Beverly. *Desdemona: Twelve Going on Desperate* (5–7). 1986, HarperCollins paper $4.95 (0-06-440226-6). 160pp. Mishap after mishap befalls Desdemona, including running into the handsomest boy in school. A sequel is: *Fowl Play, Desdemona* (1989). (Rev: BCCB 12/86; BL 10/1/86; SLJ 11/86)

9895 Kerr, M. E. *Dinky Hocker Shoots Smack!* (6–8). 1972, HarperCollins paper $4.95 (0-06-447006-7). 204pp. Dinky, a compulsive eater, tries many ways to gain her parents' attention.

9896 Kharms, Daniil. *It Happened Like This* (4–6). Trans. by Ian Frazier. Illus. by Katya Arnold. 1998, Farrar $17.00 (0-374-33635-0). 48pp. A collection of ten humorous pieces by the Russian absurdist who was imprisoned by the Communists. (Rev: BL 12/1/98; HBG 3/99; SLJ 2/99)

9897 Kidd, Ronald. *Sammy Carducci's Guide to Women* (5–7). 1995, Dramatic Publg. $3.50 (0-87129-522-9). 112pp. A somewhat sexist sixth-grader discovers that, where women are concerned, perhaps he is not as irresistible as he thinks he is. (Rev: BCCB 1/92; BL 1/1/92; SLJ 1/92)

9898 Kinerk, Robert. *Slim and Miss Prim* (3–5). Illus. by Jim Harris. 1998, Northland $15.95 (0-87358-689-1). 32pp. When Miss Marigold Prim, along with cowboy Slim and her cattle, is captured by rustlers, her boring, never-ending diatribes on lawlessness and sin cause the fatigued outlaws to set them all free. (Rev: BL 11/1/98; HBG 10/99; SLJ 12/98)

9899 King-Smith, Dick. *Mr. Ape* (3–5). Illus. 1998, Crown LB $17.99 (0-517-70987-2). 128pp. Mr. Ape, alone and in his 70s, turns his home into a menagerie with hens, rabbits, guinea pigs, and canaries. (Rev: BCCB 7–8/98; BL 5/1/98; SLJ 9/98)

9900 Kline, Suzy. *Molly's in a Mess* (2–3). Illus. 1999, Putnam $13.99 (0-399-23131-5). 80pp. Molly is out to get the girl who tattles on her about accidentally knocking off the principal's hairpiece. (Rev: BL 8/99; HBG 3/00; SLJ 8/99)

9901 Kline, Suzy. *Orp* (4–6). 1989, Putnam $13.95 (0-399-21639-1); Avon paper $3.50 (0-380-71038-2). 94pp. Orville is so discontented with his name that he forms the I Hate My Name Club. (Rev: BL 7/89)

9902 Kline, Suzy. *Orp and the Chop Suey Burgers* (4–6). 1990, Putnam $14.95 (0-399-22185-9); Avon paper $3.50 (0-380-71359-4). 94pp. Orville Rudemeyer Pyugenski, Jr., enters a cooking contest for a trip to Disney World. (Rev: BL 6/1/90; SLJ 9/90)

9903 Kline, Suzy. *Orp Goes to the Hoop* (5–7). 1993, Avon paper $3.50 (0-380-71829-4). 109pp. Seventh-grader Orp gets a chance to play a big part in the basketball team's big game. (Rev: BCCB 7–8/91; BL 7/91; SLJ 7/91)

9904 Kline, Suzy. *Who's Orp's Girlfriend?* (5–7). 1993, Putnam $13.95 (0-399-22431-9). 94pp. Orp, who is attracted to two girls, makes a date with both of them for the same night. (Rev: BL 8/93; SLJ 7/93)

9905 Klise, Kate. *Letters from Camp* (5–8). Illus. 1999, Avon $15.00 (0-380-97539-4). 178pp. A humorous mystery about three sets of quarreling siblings who are sent to Camp Happy Harmony to learn to get along. The story is told entirely through letters, memos, journal entries, telegrams, receipts, lists, and drawings. (Rev: BL 7/99; HBG 10/99; SLJ 6/99)

9906 Klise, Kate. *Regarding the Fountain: A Tale, in Letters, of Liars and Leaks* (4–6). Illus. 1998, Avon $14.00 (0-380-97538-6). 144pp. Dry Creek's school needs a new water fountain, causing a flurry of letters, memos, and other communications involving the school and fountain designer, Florence Waters. (Rev: BL 8/98; HB 5–6/98; HBG 10/98; SLJ 6/98)

9907 Komaiko, Leah. *Annie Bananie and the Pain Sisters* (2–4). Illus. 1998, Delacorte $14.95 (0-385-32118-X). 96pp. In order to impress her friends, Libby "borrows" her dead grandfather's gallbladder stones, claiming they are her own. However, when Libby loses the stones, she doesn't know how to break the news to her grandmother. (Rev: BL 11/1/98; HBG 10/99; SLJ 1/99)

9908 Konigsburg, E. L. *About the B'nai Bagels* (3–6). Illus. by author. 1971, Dell paper $4.50 (0-440-40034-1). 176pp. Poor Mark — his mother is the manager of the Little League baseball team on which he plays, and his older brother is the coach.

9909 Konigsburg, E. L. *Samuel Todd's Book of Great Inventions* (3–6). Illus. 1991, Macmillan $13.95 (0-689-31680-1). 32pp. Samuel Todd explains why certain inventions are his favorites, such as training wheels, step stools, and backpacks. (Rev: BL 8/91; HB 1–2/92; SLJ 10/91) [608]

9910 Korman, Gordon. *The Chicken Doesn't Skate* (4–6). 1996, Scholastic $14.95 (0-590-85300-7). 192pp. As part of his science fair project on food chains, Milo plans to eat Henrietta, a chicken who has become the school mascot. (Rev: BL 11/15/96; SLJ 11/96)

9911 Krensky, Stephen. *Louise Goes Wild* (2–4). Illus. 1999, Dial $13.99 (0-8037-2307-5). 80pp. Louise thinks that she is too predictable and therefore decides to change her behavior, but it doesn't work because she hasn't changed inwardly. (Rev: BL 7/99; HBG 10/99; SLJ 7/99)

9912 Lawson, Robert. *Ben and Me* (5–8). Illus. by author. 1939, Little, Brown $16.95 (0-316-51732-1); paper $5.95 (0-316-51730-5). The events of Benjamin Franklin's life, as told by his good mouse Amos, who lived in his old fur cap.

9913 Lawson, Robert. *Captain Kidd's Cat* (3–5). Illus. by author. 1984, Little, Brown paper $7.95 (0-316-51735-6). A narrative recount by McDermot, faithful cat of Captain William Kidd.

9914 Lawson, Robert. *Mr. Revere and I* (5–8). Illus. by author. 1953, Little, Brown paper $5.95 (0-316-51729-1). 152pp. A delightful account of certain episodes in Revere's life, as revealed by his horse Scheherazade.

9915 Levoy, Myron. *The Magic Hat of Mortimer Wintergreen* (4–6). 1988, HarperCollins $11.95 (0-06-023841-0). 224pp. Joshua and Amy escape from creepy Aunt Vootch with a magician and search for their grandparents. (Rev: BL 2/15/88; SLJ 3/88)

9916 Lewis, Cynthia C. *Dilly's Summer Camp Diary* (3–5). Illus. by Cynthia Copeland Lewis. 1999, Millbrook LB $19.90 (0-7613-1416-4). Told in diary form, this is the humorous story of Dilly's three weeks at summer camp with all its delights and trials. (Rev: HBG 10/99; SLJ 6/99)

9917 Lindgren, Astrid. *Pippi Longstocking* (4–6). Trans. by Florence Lamborn. Illus. by Louis Glanzman. 1950, Puffin paper $4.99 (0-14-030957-8). 158pp. A little Swedish tomboy who has a monkey and a horse for companions. Also use: *Pippi Goes on Board* (1957); *Pippi in the South Seas* (1959).

9918 Lindgren, Astrid. *Pippi's Extraordinary Ordinary Day* (2–3). Illus. by Michael Chesworth. Series: Pippi Longstocking Storybooks. 1999, Viking $13.99 (0-670-88073-6). 32pp. Chapters from the original *Pippi Longstocking* are included in this newly illustrated edition for younger readers. (Rev: BL 10/15/99; HBG 3/00)

9919 Lowry, Lois. *Anastasia, Absolutely* (4–6). Series: Anastasia Krupnik. 1995, Houghton $16.00 (0-395-74521-7); Bantam paper $3.99 (0-440-41222-6). 176pp. Anastasia absentmindedly throws a bag filled with her dog's poop into a mailbox and incurs an investigation by the police. (Rev: BCCB 9/95; BL 10/1/95; HB 11–12/95; SLJ 10/95)

9920 Lowry, Lois. *Anastasia at This Address* (5–8). 1991, Houghton $16.00 (0-395-56263-5). 112pp. Seventh-grader Anastasia Krupnik answers a personal ad, using her mother's picture instead of her own. (Rev: BCCB 3/91; BL 4/1/91; SLJ 8/91)

9921 Lowry, Lois. *Anastasia on Her Own* (5–7). Illus. 1985, Houghton $16.00 (0-395-38133-9); Dell paper $4.50 (0-440-40291-3). 131pp. Seventh-grader Anastasia Krupnik must face both domestic crisis and romance. Another chapter in Anastasia's busy life is recounted in *Anastasia Has the Answers* (1986). (Rev: BL 5/15/85; HB 9–10/85; SLJ 8/85)

9922 Lowry, Lois. *Anastasia's Chosen Career* (5–7). 1987, Houghton $16.00 (0-395-42506-9); Bantam paper $4.50 (0-440-40100-3). Thirteen-year-old Anastasia gets some surprises when she begs to go to charm school to change her freaky looks. Anastasia's baby brother is featured in *All About Sam* (1988). (Rev: BCCB 9/87; BL 9/1/87; SLJ 9/87)

9923 Lowry, Lois. *Attaboy, Sam!* (2–5). Illus. by Diane De Groat. 1992, Houghton $16.00 (0-395-61588-7). 116pp. Anastasia Krupnik's little brother, Sam, decides to make perfume for his mother's birthday. (Rev: BCCB 4/92; BL 2/15/92*; HB 7–8/92*; SLJ 5/92*)

9924 Lowry, Lois. *The One Hundredth Thing About Caroline* (5–7). 1983, Houghton $16.00 (0-395-34829-3); Dell paper $4.50 (0-440-46625-3). 160pp. Caroline tries everything and anything to break up her mother's new romance.

9925 Lowry, Lois. *See You Around, Sam!* (3–6). Illus. by Diane De Groat. 1996, Houghton $15.00 (0-395-81664-5). 144pp. Sam decides to run away to Alaska because his mother won't let him wear his plastic fangs. (Rev: BCCB 11/96; BL 10/1/96*; HB 9–10/96; SLJ 10/96*)

9926 Lowry, Lois. *Switcharound* (5–7). 1985, Houghton $16.00 (0-395-39536-4); Dell paper $4.50 (0-440-48415-4). Caroline and her nemesis brother J.P. must spend the summer with their divorced father's new family in Des Moines. A sequel to: *The One Hundredth Thing About Caroline* (1983). (Rev: BCCB 1/86; BL 10/1/85; HB 1–2/86)

9927 Lowry, Lois. *Zooman Sam* (3–5). Illus. 1999, Houghton $15.00 (0-395-97393-7). 160pp. Sam Krupnick is in seventh heaven when he learns to read in his nursery school. (Rev: BCCB 9/99; BL 7/99; HB 9–10/99; HBG 3/00; SLJ 9/99)

9928 Lynch, Chris. *The Wolf Gang* (3–7). 1998, HarperCollins LB $14.89 (0-06-027418-2); paper $4.50 (0-06-440659-8). 112pp. Wolf, former leader of the He-Man Women Haters Club, forms a new club for girls only that has its headquarters in, of all places, a beauty parlor. (Rev: BL 8/98; HBG 10/98; SLJ 6/98)

9929 McCloskey, Robert. *Homer Price* (3–6). Illus. by author. 1943, Puffin paper $4.99 (0-14-030927-6). 160pp. Popular and preposterous adventures of a Midwestern boy. Continued in: *Centerburg Tales* (1951).

9930 MacDonald, Amy. *No More Nice* (4–7). Illus. 1996, Orchard LB $15.99 (0-531-08892-8). 128pp.

A humorous story about a spring vacation spent by a boy with his eccentric great-aunt and -uncle. (Rev: BCCB 10/96; BL 9/1/96; SLJ 9/96)

9931 Mackay, Claire, sel. *Laughs* (5–8). 1997, Tundra paper $6.95 (0-88776-393-6). 199pp. An anthology of humorous stories from well-known Canadian writers. (Rev: SLJ 9/97)

9932 McKenna, Colleen O'Shaughnessy. *Mother Murphy* (5–7). 1993, Scholastic paper $2.95 (0-590-44856-0). 160pp. With her mother confined to bed, 12-year-old Collette volunteers as mother-for-a-day with disasterous and funny results. (Rev: BCCB 2/92; BL 2/1/92; SLJ 2/92)

9933 MacLachlan, Patricia. *Arthur, for the Very First Time* (4–6). Illus. by Lloyd Bloom. 1980, HarperCollins LB $15.89 (0-06-024047-4); paper $4.95 (0-06-440288-6). 128pp. Arthur spends a summer on the farm of his aunt and uncle.

9934 Manes, Stephen. *Chocolate-Covered Ants* (4–6). 1993, Scholastic paper $2.95 (0-590-40961-1). 128pp. Max bets his brother that people do eat chocolate-covered ants. (Rev: BCCB 12/92; BL 9/1/90; SLJ 12/90)

9935 Manes, Stephen. *Make Four Million Dollars by Next Thursday!* (3–6). Illus. by George Ulrich. 1996, Bantam paper $4.50 (0-440-41370-2). 112pp. Would-be millionaire Jazon Nozzle finds a book that tells him how to do it. (Rev: BCCB 2/91; BL 2/15/91; SLJ 6/91)

9936 Merrill, Jean. *The Pushcart War* (5–7). Illus. by Ronni Solbert. 1987, Dell paper $4.99 (0-440-47147-8). 224pp. Mack, driving a Mighty Mammoth, runs down a pushcart belonging to Morris the Florist, and a most unusual war is on!

9937 Merrill, Jean. *The Toothpaste Millionaire* (4–6). Illus. by Jan Palmer. 1974, Houghton $16.00 (0-395-18511-4). 96pp. Kate tells the delightful story of an African American boy, Rufus, who challenges the entire business community by marketing a product called simply "toothpaste."

9938 Mills, Claudia. *Dinah in Love* (4–7). 1993, Macmillan LB $14.00 (0-02-766998-X). 148pp. Dinah can't believe that boorish Nick, who continually insults her, really likes her. (Rev: BL 11/15/93; SLJ 12/93)

9939 Mills, Claudia. *You're a Brave Man, Julius Zimmerman* (5–7). 1999, Farrar $16.00 (0-374-38708-7). 160pp. Julius Zimmerman, of *Losers, Inc.* fame, has a busy summer ahead of him, taking French classes and babysitting Edison who isn't toilet-trained. (Rev: BCCB 9/99; BL 10/15/99; HB 9–10/99; HBG 3/00; SLJ 9/99)

9940 Morgenstern, Susie. *Secret Letters from 0 to 10* (4–7). Trans. by Gill Rosner. Illus. 1998, Viking $15.99 (0-670-88007-8). 208pp. Ten-year-old Ernest Morlaisse, whose mother is dead and father gone, is living a bleak existence with a grim grandfather, until he meets Victoria and her 13 outgoing brothers. (Rev: BCCB 10/98; BL 10/1/98*; HB 11–12/98; HBG 3/99; SLJ 10/98)

9941 Murphy, Jill. *Jeffrey Strangeways* (3–5). Illus. 1992, Candlewick $14.95 (1-56402-018-5). 140pp. Eleven-year-old Jeffrey, who unfortunately is very clumsy, wants nothing more than to become a knight. (Rev: BCCB 9/92; BL 6/15/92; SLJ 5/92)

9942 Naylor, Phyllis Reynolds. *Alice In-Between* (5–7). 1994, Atheneum $16.00 (0-689-31890-1). 160pp. Alice, now 13, along with her friends, is becoming very aware of her changing body and of boys in this humorous look at early adolescence. (Rev: BCCB 5/94; BL 5/1/94; HB 7–8/94; SLJ 6/94)

9943 Naylor, Phyllis Reynolds. *Alice in Rapture, Sort Of* (4–7). 1989, Macmillan LB $16.00 (0-689-31466-3); Dell paper $3.99 (0-440-40462-2). 176pp. Alice and her friends vow to find boyfriends before summer's end. (Rev: HB 5–6/89; SLJ 4/89)

9944 Naylor, Phyllis Reynolds. *Beetles, Lightly Toasted* (4–6). 1987, Macmillan $16.00 (0-689-31355-1). 144pp. Andy must test his essay premise that beetles are good eating. (Rev: BCCB 11/87; BL 9/1/87; SLJ 10/87)

9945 Naylor, Phyllis Reynolds. *Boys Against Girls* (4–6). 1994, Delacorte $14.95 (0-385-32081-7). 147pp. Boys and girls try to trick each other into believing that a strange monster exists, and maybe they are right. (Rev: BCCB 11/94; BL 9/1/94; SLJ 11/94)

9946 Naylor, Phyllis Reynolds. *Danny's Desert Rats* (4–6). 1998, Simon & Schuster $16.00 (0-689-81776-2). 144pp. Ten-year-old T. R. and his brother Danny help their friend Paul hide his cat Bonkers in their condo complex, where pets are forbidden. A sequel to *Being Danny's Dog*. (Rev: BL 6/1–15/98; HBG 10/98; SLJ 7/98)

9947 Naylor, Phyllis Reynolds. *The Girls' Revenge* (3–5). 1998, Delacorte $15.95 (0-385-32334-4). 150pp. The Hatford boys and the Malloy girls continue their feud, but when 8-year-old Caroline chooses Wally to be her partner in a school project, there seems to be a tentative truce. (Rev: BL 9/1/98; HBG 3/99; SLJ 9/98)

9948 Naylor, Phyllis Reynolds. *Outrageously Alice* (5–8). 1997, Simon & Schuster $15.00 (0-689-80354-0). 133pp. Thirteen-year-old Alice, now in the eighth grade, decides that she is too ordinary and wants to do something about it. (Rev: BCCB 7–8/97; HB 7–8/98; SLJ 6/97)

9949 Naylor, Phyllis Reynolds. *A Spy Among the Girls* (4–6). 2000, Delacorte $15.95 (0-385-32336-0). 135pp. Beth Malloy and Josh Haltford are involved in puppy love and a mysterious animal is stalking the town in this humorous installment of the Malloy/Hatford series. (Rev: BL 9/1/00; HBG 3/01; SLJ 9/00)

9950 Naylor, Phyllis Reynolds. *A Traitor Among the Boys* (4–6). 1999, Delacorte $15.95 (0-385-32335-2). 118pp. The feud between the Hatford boys and the Malloy girls gets hot once more when Peter innocently tells the boys' secret plans to the girls. (Rev: BL 9/1/99; HBG 3/00; SLJ 9/99)

9951 Park, Barbara. *Junie B. Jones and a Little Monkey Business* (2–3). Illus. by Denise Brunkus. 1993, Random paper $3.99 (0-679-83886-4). 46pp. Junie is amazed to learn that her new brother is a monkey after grandmother declares, "He's the cutest monkey I've ever seen!" (Rev: BL 3/1/93)

9952 Park, Barbara. *Junie B. Jones and Some Sneaky Peeky Spying* (2–4). Illus. 1994, Random $11.99 (0-679-95101-6); paper $3.99 (0-679-85101-1). 66pp. Junie's flair for sleuthing and misinterpreting ordinary occurrences gets her into trouble. (Rev: BL 11/15/94; SLJ 10/94)

9953 Park, Barbara. *Junie B. Jones and the Stupid Smelly Bus* (2–3). Illus. by Denise Brunkus. 1992, Random $11.99 (0-679-92642-9); paper $3.99 (0-679-82642-4). 70pp. Junie B. is a cross between Lily Tomlin's Edith Ann and Eloise in this funny story of a youngster on her way to kindergarten. (Rev: BL 12/1/92; SLJ 11/92)

9954 Park, Barbara. *Junie B. Jones Is a Beauty Shop Guy* (2–3). 1998, Random LB $11.99 (0-679-98939-5); paper $3.99 (0-679-88931-0). 67pp. Junie B. Jones believes she has a calling to become a barber and, after practicing on various stuffed animals, decides to move on to a human subject — herself. (Rev: BL 11/15/98; SLJ 12/98)

9955 Park, Barbara. *Junie B. Jones Smells Something Fishy* (2–4). Illus. 1998, Random paper $3.99 (0-679-89130-7). 67pp. When all her plans to take a pet to school fail, a disappointed Junie brings a fish stick instead and wins a prize for the most well-behaved pet. (Rev: BL 3/15/99)

9956 Park, Barbara. *The Kid in the Red Jacket* (4–6). 1988, Knopf paper $3.99 (0-394-80571-2). 128pp. Ten-year-old Howard is having some trouble adjusting to life in Massachusetts when his family moves from Arizona. (Rev: BCCB 3/87; BL 2/15/87; SLJ 3/87)

9957 Park, Barbara. *Operation: Dump the Chump* (3–6). Illus. by Robert Sauber. 1989, Knopf paper $4.99 (0-394-82592-6). 128pp. Oscar Winkle devises a plan to get rid of his young brother.

9958 Paulsen, Gary. *Harris and Me: A Summer Remembered* (5–8). 1993, Harcourt $13.95 (0-15-292877-4); paper $4.99 (0-440-40994-2). A humorous story in which the narrator often gets the blame for mischief caused by troublemaker Harris. (Rev: SLJ 2/00)

9959 Peck, Robert Newton. *Higbee's Halloween* (5–7). 1990, Walker LB $14.85 (0-8027-6969-1). 101pp. Higbee decides something must be done about the unruly Striker children. (Rev: SLJ 10/90)

9960 Peters, Julie A. *Romance of the Snob Squad* (4–6). 1999, Little, Brown $13.95 (0-316-70627-2). 144pp. The continuing saga of four sixth-grade misfit girls, two of whom have crushes on classmates. Also use *Revenge of the Snob Squad* (1998). (Rev: BL 4/1/99; HBG 3/00; SLJ 6/99)

9961 Petersen, P. J. *I Hate Weddings* (2–5). Illus. 2000, Dutton $15.99 (0-525-46327-5). 96pp. A humorous story about Dan who must not only participate in his divorced father's wedding but also move into his stepmother's home after the marriage. (Rev: BCCB 3/00; BL 3/1/00; HBG 10/00; SLJ 6/00)

9962 Pilkey, Dav. *The Adventures of Captain Underpants* (2–4). Illus. 1997, Scholastic $16.95 (0-

590-84627-2). 128pp. A superhero spoof in which two boys capture their principal and turn him into Captain Underpants. (Rev: BL 7/97; HBG 3/98; SLJ 12/97)

9963 Pilkey, Dav. *Captain Underpants and the Attack of the Talking Toilets* (3–5). Illus. 1999, Scholastic $16.95 (0-590-63136-5). 144pp. George, Harold, and their school principal, who is also Captain Underpants, get involved in an army of teacher-eating toilets led by supercommode Turbo Toilet 2000. (Rev: BCCB 5/99; BL 5/1/99; HBG 10/99; SLJ 6/99)

9964 Pilkey, Dav. *Captain Underpants and the Invasion of the Incredibly Naughty Cafeteria Ladies from Outer Space (and the Subsequent Assault of the Equally Evil Lunchroom Zombie Nerds)* (4–6). Illus. 1999, Scholastic $16.95 (0-439-04995-4). 144pp. Another wacky adventure featuring fourth-graders George and Harold, their principal who becomes Captain Underpants, and a threat from outer space. (Rev: BL 9/15/99; HBG 3/00; SLJ 11/99)

9965 Pilkey, Dav. *Captain Underpants and the Perilous Plot of Professor Poopypants* (3–5). Illus. 2000, Scholastic $16.95 (0-439-04997-0). 160pp. Captain Underpants, aka Mr. Krupp, an elementary school principal, and students George and Harold combat a mad scientific genius, Pippy Pee-pee Poopypants. (Rev: BL 2/15/00; HBG 10/00; SLJ 5/00)

9966 Pinkwater, Daniel. *Fat Men from Space* (3–6). Illus. by author. 1977, Dell paper $3.99 (0-440-44542-6). 64pp. Among other adventures, William encounters raiders of junk food from outer space in this nutrition-conscious farce.

9967 Pinkwater, Daniel. *The Hoboken Chicken Emergency* (3–7). 1977, Simon & Schuster LB $4.95 (0-671-66447-6). 94pp. A young boy buys a 6-foot, 260-pound chicken in this humorous story.

9968 Pinkwater, Daniel. *The Werewolf Club: The Lunchroom of Doom* (3–4). Illus. 2000, Atheneum $15.00 (0-689-83846-8). 64pp. In this easy chapter book, the members of the Watson Elementary School's Werewolf Club have trouble convincing people that they really are werewolves. (Rev: BL 1/1–15/01; HBG 3/01)

9969 Poploff, Michelle. *Busy O'Brien and the Great Bubble Gum Blowout* (3–5). Illus. by Abby Carter. 1990, Walker LB $13.85 (0-8027-6984-5). 80pp. Ten-year-old Busy O'Brien wishes she had more time to spend with her mom so she devises a plan. (Rev: BL 12/15/90; SLJ 10/90)

9970 Pryor, Bonnie. *Vinegar Pancakes and Vanishing Cream* (2–4). Illus. by Gail Owens. 1987, Morrow $16.00 (0-688-06728-X). 128pp. The ups and downs of life for Martin Elwood Snodgrass, who has too-successful older siblings and a too-cute baby brother. (Rev: BL 6/15/87; SLJ 6–7/87)

9971 Raskin, Ellen. *The Mysterious Disappearance of Leon (I Mean Noel)* (4–6). Illus. by author. 1989, Puffin paper $5.99 (0-14-032945-5). 160pp. Humorous saga of Mrs. Carillon's search for her husband

Leon (or Noel), who is the joint heir to a soup fortune.

9972 Richler, Mordecai. *Jacob Two-Two's First Spy Case* (4–5). Illus. 1997, Farrar $16.00 (0-374-33659-8). 152pp. Jacob Two-Two and a friend discover that the new headmaster at their school has his hands in the till in this humorous adventure. (Rev: BL 8/97; HB 7–8/97; SLJ 8/97)

9973 Robertson, Keith. *Henry Reed, Inc.* (5–7). Illus. by Robert McCloskey. 1989, Puffin paper $4.99 (0-14-034144-7). 240pp. Told deadpan in diary form, this story of Henry's enterprising summer in New Jersey presents one of the most amusing boys since Tom and Huck. Others in the series: *Henry Reed's Journey* (1963); *Henry Reed's Baby-Sitting Service* (1966); *Henry Reed's Big Show* (1970).

9974 Robinson, Barbara. *The Best School Year Ever* (3–5). 1994, HarperCollins LB $14.89 (0-06-023043-6). 128pp. Beth has to write a complimentary composition about a classmate who appears to have no redeeming qualities. (Rev: BL 10/15/94; HB 11–12/94; SLJ 10/94)

9975 Robinson, Barbara. *My Brother Louis Measures Worms and Other Louis Stories* (3–6). 1988, HarperCollins LB $15.89 (0-06-025083-6); paper $4.95 (0-06-440362-9). 160pp. Events in ten stories of the wild Lawson family. (Rev: BCCB 12/88; BL 11/1/88; SLJ 12/88)

9976 Rockwell, Thomas. *How to Eat Fried Worms* (4–6). Illus. by Emily Arnold McCully. 1973, Watts LB $25.00 (0-531-02631-0); Dell paper $4.99 (0-440-44545-0). 128pp. In this very humorous story, Billy takes on a bet — he will eat 15 worms in 15 days. His family and friends help devise ways to cook them.

9977 Rodgers, Mary. *Freaky Friday* (4–7). 1972, HarperCollins LB $15.89 (0-06-025049-6); paper $4.95 (0-06-440046-8). 156pp. Thirteen-year-old Annabel learns some valuable lessons during the day she becomes her mother. Two sequels are: *A Billion for Boris* (1974); *Summer Switch* (1982).

9978 Roos, Stephen. *Twelve-Year-Old Vows Revenge After Being Dumped by Extraterrestrial on First Date* (5–6). Illus. 1991, Dell paper $3.25 (0-440-40465-7). 119pp. The rivalry between two girls reaches such a point that they take the matter to court. (Rev: BL 5/15/90; SLJ 7/90)

9979 Rosenthal, Paul. *Yo, Aesop! Get a Load of These Fables* (2–5). Illus. by Marc Rosenthal. 1998, Simon & Schuster $16.00 (0-689-80100-9). 64pp. An updated collection of variations on traditional Aesop's fables — each more zany than the next. (Rev: BCCB 6/98; BL 4/1/98; HBG 10/98)

9980 Ryan, Mary C. *My Friend, O'Connell* (3–5). Illus. by Patrick Chapin. 1991, Avon paper $2.95 (0-380-76145-9). 104pp. In this humorous story, Bradley and friend O'Connell get involved in such situations as running a golf tournament and organizing a school cafeteria boycott. (Rev: BL 6/15/91)

9981 Rylant, Cynthia. *Mr. Putter and Tabby Paint the Porch* (2–3). Illus. by Arthur Howard. 2000, Harcourt $13.00 (0-15-201787-9). 44pp. An easy chapter book in which Mr. Putter's project to paint the porch is almost ruined when different animals walk across the wet paint. (Rev: BL 4/15/00; HBG 10/00; SLJ 7/00)

9982 Sachar, Louis. *Marvin Redpost: Is He a Girl?* (2–4). Illus. by Barbara Sullivan. 1993, Random LB $11.99 (0-679-91948-1); paper $3.99 (0-679-81948-7). 74pp. Marvin wonders if he is turning into a girl because he seems to be developing feminine interests. (Rev: BCCB 6/94; BL 11/15/93)

9983 Sachar, Louis. *Sideways Arithmetic from Wayside School* (4–8). Series: Wayside School. 1992, Scholastic paper $4.50 (0-590-45726-8). 89pp. Sue learns a new kind of math and encounters some humorous brainteasers when she transfers to Wayside School. (Rev: BL 12/15/89)

9984 Sandburg, Carl. *Rootabaga Stories* (4–6). Illus. by Michael Hague. 1988, Harcourt paper $7.00 (0-15-269065-4). 192pp. A reissued collection of modern tales from Rootabaga country.

9985 Sandburg, Carl. *Rootabaga Stories: Part Two* (3–6). Illus. by Michael Hague. 1989, Harcourt $19.95 (0-15-269062-X); paper $7.00 (0-15-269063-8). 179pp. Twenty-four nonsense stories first published in 1923. A companion volume to Part One (1988). (Rev: BL 8/89; SLJ 6/89)

9986 Scieszka, Jon. *Squids Will Be Squids: Fresh Morals, Beastly Fables* (2–6). Illus. by Lane Smith. 1998, Viking $17.99 (0-670-88135-X). 48pp. This book by the author of the *Stinky Cheese Man* presents 18 contemporary, goofy fables, each with a silly moral attached. (Rev: BCCB 11/98; BL 9/15/98; HB 11–12/98; HBG 3/99; SLJ 10/98)

9987 Scrimger, Richard. *The Nose from Jupiter* (5–8). 1998, Tundra paper $7.95 (0-88776-428-2). 160pp. Norbert, a tiny alien from Jupiter, takes up residency in Alan Dingwall's nose, where he often speaks his mind and causes trouble for poor Alan. (Rev: BL 7/98)

9988 Scrimger, Richard. *The Way to Schenectady* (4–6). Illus. 1999, Tundra paper $5.95 (0-88776-427-4). 168pp. A girl who is traveling from Ontario to Massachusetts with her family takes pity on a homeless man and hides him in the back of the van. (Rev: BL 5/1/99; SLJ 6/99)

9989 Seuling, Barbara. *Oh No, It's Robert* (2–4). Illus. 1999, Front Street $14.95 (0-8126-2934-5). 128pp. Robert is anxious to excel at something, but things always go wrong, especially when he lets the class hamster loose in his living room. (Rev: BL 7/99; HBG 10/99; SLJ 7/99)

9990 Siegel, Bruce H. *Coming of Age* (5–7). Illus. 1998, Alef Design Group paper $7.95 (1-881283-29-1). 96pp. In amusing diary entries, Faith Blackman chronicles her opposition to a bat mitzvah and her dislike of the stand-in student rabbi Michael Baskin. (Rev: BL 10/1/98)

9991 Singer, Marilyn. *Josie to the Rescue* (3–4). Illus. 1999, Scholastic $14.95 (0-590-76339-3). 96pp. Second-grader Josie tries several schemes to help supplement the family income, but they all fail in a comical fashion. (Rev: BL 5/1/99; HBG 10/99; SLJ 6/99)

9992 Smith, Lane. *Glasses: Who Needs 'Em?* (3–4). Illus. 1991, Viking $15.99 (0-670-84160-9). 32pp. A nutty optometrist uses extreme measures to get a young boy to wear his glasses. (Rev: BL 9/1/91; HB 11–12/91; SLJ 10/91)

9993 Smith, Robert K. *Chocolate Fever* (4–6). Illus. by Gioia Fiammenghi. 1989, Putnam $11.99 (0-399-61224-6); Dell paper $4.50 (0-440-41369-9). 96pp. Henry Green develops the first recorded case of chocolate fever in this reissued story.

9994 Soto, Gary. *Summer on Wheels* (5–8). 1995, Scholastic $13.95 (0-590-48365-X). 144pp. In this sequel to *Crazy Weekend* (1994), Hector and Mando take a bike ride from their barrio home in Los Angeles to Santa Monica. (Rev: BL 1/15/95; SLJ 4/95)

9995 Spinelli, Eileen. *Lizzie Logan Gets Married* (2–4). 1997, Simon & Schuster paper $15.00 (0-689-81066-0). 96pp. A humorous novel about Lizzie Logan, her friends, and her mother's upcoming wedding. (Rev: BL 8/97; HBG 3/98; SLJ 6/97)

9996 Spinelli, Eileen. *Lizzie Logan, Second Banana* (2–5). 1998, Simon & Schuster $15.00 (0-689-81510-7). 96pp. In order to ensure that her pregnant mother will continue to love her after the new baby arrives, Lizzie decides she must win the Miss Seafood Pageant. (Rev: BL 7/98; HBG 10/98; SLJ 8/98)

9997 Spinelli, Eileen. *Lizzie Logan Wears Purple Sunglasses* (2–4). Illus. 1995, Simon & Schuster $14.00 (0-671-74685-5). 122pp. The rocky friendship between 8-year-old Heather and Lizzie, a bossy 10-year-old, is re-created in this humorous novel. (Rev: BL 5/15/95; HB 9–10/95; SLJ 6/95)

9998 Spinelli, Jerry. *The Bathwater Gang* (2–4). Illus. by Meredith Johnson. 1990, Little, Brown $10.95 (0-316-80720-6). 59pp. Bertie is bored, so she forms a Girls Only gang, and the boys retaliate. (Rev: BCCB 9/90; BL 6/15/90; SLJ 5/90)

9999 Spinelli, Jerry. *The Library Card* (5–7). 1997, Scholastic $15.95 (0-590-46731-X). 160pp. Four humorous, poignant stories about how books changed the lives of several youngsters. (Rev: BCCB 3/97; BL 2/1/97; HB 3–4/97; SLJ 3/97)

10000 Spinelli, Jerry. *Tooter Pepperday* (3–5). Illus. 1995, Random LB $11.99 (0-679-94702-7); paper $3.99 (0-679-84702-2). 85pp. Tooter has some hilarious adventures while adjusting to life on a farm far from her beloved city. (Rev: BCCB 6/95; BL 5/1/95; HB 9–10/95; SLJ 7/95)

10001 Stanley, George E. *Hershell Cobwell and the Miraculous Tattoo* (4–8). 1991, Avon paper $2.95 (0-380-75897-0). 128pp. A junior high boy decides to gain popularity by getting a tattoo. (Rev: BL 3/15/91)

10002 Steiner, Barbara. *Oliver Dibbs to the Rescue!* (4–6). Illus. 1985, Avon paper $2.50 (0-380-70465-X). 96pp. To save threatened wildlife, Oliver paints his dog Dolby as a tiger and exhibits him in a shopping mall. When Dolby "escapes," Oliver lands in the police station. Also use: *Oliver Dibbs and the Dinosaur Cause* (1986). (Rev: BL 12/1/85; SLJ 3/86)

10003 Strasser, Todd. *Here Comes Heavenly* (5–8). Series: Here Comes Heavenly. 1999, Pocket paper $4.99 (0-671-03626-2). 177pp. A slight story about a bizarre-looking nanny named Heavenly Litebody and how she manages to tame a family of five unruly children while their parents are away. (Rev: SLJ 12/99)

10004 Strasser, Todd. *Kidnap Kids* (5–7). 1998, Putnam $15.99 (0-399-23111-0). 208pp. Because two brothers rarely see their busy parents, they hatch a plan to kidnap them. (Rev: BCCB 3/98; BL 1/1–15/98; HBG 10/98; SLJ 3/98)

10005 Todd, Pamela. *Pig and the Shrink* (5–7). 1999, Delacorte $14.95 (0-385-32657-2). 185pp. A humorous story in which Tucker, a seventh-grader, uses his fat friend, Angelo Pighetti, as a subject for his science project on nutrition. (Rev: BCCB 11/99; BL 10/1/99; HBG 3/00; SLJ 9/99)

10006 Trahey, Jane. *The Clovis Caper* (5–8). 1990, Avon paper $2.95 (0-380-75914-4). 138pp. Martin is so upset at leaving his dog, Clovis, when going to England that Aunt Hortense plots to smuggle the dog out of the country. (Rev: BL 7/90)

10007 Twain, Mark. *Adventures of Huckleberry Finn* (6–8). 1993, Random $16.50 (0-679-42470-9). One of many editions.

10008 Van Nutt, Julia. *The Monster in the Shadows* (3–4). Illus. 2000, Doubleday $23.95 (0-385-32565-7). 32pp. This picture book for older children spins a story, set in rural America more than 100 years ago, about a stranger who comes into town and tricks the locals into believing that he has captured a giant. (Rev: BL 11/15/00; SLJ 12/00)

10009 Van Nutt, Julia. *Pignapped!* (3–4). 2000, Doubleday $15.95 (0-385-32559-2). 32pp. In this picture book in the Cobtown series, three foolish scientists seeking a specimen for their museum mistakenly capture Aunt Heddy's beloved wild pig. (Rev: BL 4/15/00; HBG 10/00; SLJ 8/00)

10010 Voigt, Cynthia. *Bad, Badder, Baddest* (5–8). 1997, Scholastic $16.95 (0-590-60136-9). 272pp. A hilarious mix of funny situations and outrageous dialogue is featured in this novel about two sixth-grade outsiders who deserve their reputation for being bad. A sequel to *Bad Girls*. (Rev: BL 11/1/97; HBG 3/98; SLJ 11/97)

10011 Voigt, Cynthia. *Bad Girls* (4–6). 1996, Scholastic $16.95 (0-590-60134-2). 256pp. Mikey and Margalo, two fifth-graders with reputations for causing trouble, test their limits. (Rev: BCCB 4/96; BL 4/1/96; HB 7–8/96; SLJ 5/96)

10012 Wallace, Bill. *Ferret in the Bedroom, Lizards in the Fridge* (4–6). 1986, Holiday $15.95 (0-8234-0600-8). 144pp. Liz would certainly win the sixth-grade presidency if it weren't that her zoology teacher-father keeps so many unusual animals around the house and scares away her friends. (Rev: BCCB 7–8/86; BL 6/15/86)

10013 Wardlaw, Lee. *101 Ways to Bug Your Parents* (3–6). 1996, Dial $15.99 (0-8037-1901-9). 208pp. Sneeze Wyatt uses a summer session at school to compile a book on how to annoy parents. (Rev: BCCB 11/96; BL 10/1/96; SLJ 10/96)

10014 Ware, Cheryl. *Venola in Love* (4–7). Illus. by Kristin Sorra. 2000, Orchard LB $16.99 (0-531-33306-X). 160pp. Told through diary entries, e-mail messages, and class notes, this humorous novel tells how seventh-grader Venola discovers the problems of falling in love. (Rev: BCCB 10/00; SLJ 10/00)

10015 Warner, Sally. *Private Lily* (2–4). Illus. 1998, Knopf LB $16.99 (0-679-99137-9). 96pp. Lily, who lives in a tiny apartment with her mother and 12-year-old brother, tries different ways to secure privacy with humorous results. (Rev: BCCB 9/98; BL 9/15/98; HBG 3/99; SLJ 10/98)

10016 Weeks, Sarah. *Guy Time* (5–7). 2000, HarperCollins LB $14.89 (0-06-028366-1). 176pp. A humorous story about 13-year-old Guy, his separated parents, his mother who is constantly dating, and the girl who has a crush on him. (Rev: BCCB 5/00; BL 8/00; HB 5–6/00; HBG 10/00; SLJ 6/00)

10017 Weeks, Sarah. *Regular Guy* (4–6). 1999, HarperCollins LB $14.89 (0-06-028368-8). 128pp. In this humorous book, Guy is so unhappy with the wild behavior of his hippy parents that he tries to switch them for another pair. (Rev: BCCB 7–8/99; BL 9/1/99; HB 5–6/99; HBG 10/99; SLJ 6/99)

10018 Willner-Pardo, Gina. *Spider Storch's Desperate Deal* (2–4). Illus. 1999, Albert Whitman $11.95 (0-8075-7588-7); paper $3.95 (0-8075-7589-5). 69pp. Joey, also known as Spider, is afraid of the teasing he will get when his friends find out he will be an attendant at a wedding, so he tries to get his fellow attendant, Mary Grace, not to tell. (Rev: BCCB 12/99; BL 1/1–15/00; HBG 3/00; SLJ 1/00)

10019 Willner-Pardo, Gina. *Spider Storch's Fumbled Field Trip* (2–3). Illus. by Nick Sharratt. 1998, Albert Whitman LB $11.95 (0-8075-7581-X); paper $3.95 (0-8075-7582-8). 68pp. Joey "Spider" Storch falls into a tidal pool on a field trip to an aquarium and is sent back to the bus in this easy chapter book. (Rev: HBG 3/99; SLJ 3/99)

10020 Winton, Tim. *Lockie Leonard, Scumbuster* (5–9). 1999, Simon & Schuster $16.00 (0-689-82247-2). 144pp. A humorous story about a likable young Australian surfer, Lockie, who, with his friend Egg, engages in a crusade against local polluters who are destroying the quality of the water in his harbor. (Rev: BCCB 6/99; HB 11–12/99; HBG 10/99; SLJ 6/99)

10021 Wisniewski, David. *The Secret Knowledge of Grown-ups* (3–5). Illus. 1998, Lothrop LB $16.89 (0-688-15340-2). 48pp. A zany book that explores the truth behind such parental directives as "Drink your milk" and "Don't bite your fingernails." (Rev: BCCB 7–8/98; BL 3/1/98; HBG 10/98; SLJ 3/98)

10022 Wojciechowski, Susan. *Don't Call Me Beanhead!* (3–5). Illus. 1994, Candlewick $15.99 (1-56402-319-2). 80pp. Five humorous stories about a little worrywart named Beany. (Rev: BL 10/15/94; SLJ 10/94)

10023 Yep, Laurence. *The Cook's Family* (4–6). 1998, Putnam $15.99 (0-399-22907-8). 192pp. In order to get a Chinese cook to do his work, Robin and her grandmother must pretend to be the man's relatives. (Rev: BCCB 5/98; BL 1/1–15/98; HBG 10/98; SLJ 4/98)

School Stories

10024 Adler, David A. *School Trouble for Andy Russell* (2–4). Illus. 1999, Harcourt $14.00 (0-15-202190-6). 144pp. In this third installment of the Andy Russell series, Andy has problems at school, first with his math teacher, Ms. Roman, and then with her replacement, Ms. Salmon, who seems to be out to get him. (Rev: BL 1/1–15/00; HBG 3/00; SLJ 11/99)

10025 Asch, Frank. *Hands Around Lincoln School* (4–6). 1994, Scholastic $13.95 (0-590-44149-3). 217pp. Amy, a sixth-grader, decides to start a Save the Earth Club in her school to fight pollution and help save the environment. (Rev: BL 1/15/94; SLJ 3/94)

10026 Bartlett, Susan. *Seal Island School* (2–4). Illus. 1999, Viking $13.99 (0-670-88349-2). 80pp. A beginning chapter book about a little girl attending school on Maine's Seal Island, where the school population is six. (Rev: BCCB 3/99; BL 3/15/99; HBG 10/99; SLJ 5/99)

10027 Bechard, Margaret. *My Sister, My Science Report* (5–7). 1990, Puffin paper $4.99 (0-14-034408-X). 96pp. In this humorous novel, Tess's sister becomes the object of a scientific study for a school project. (Rev: BL 5/15/90; HB 5/90 & 9–10/90; SLJ 5/90)

10028 Benjamin, Saragail Katzman. *My Dog Ate It* (4–6). 1994, Holiday $14.95 (0-8234-1047-1). 166pp. Danny dislikes homework so much that he decides to go on strike, but his teacher comes up with a novel solution. (Rev: SLJ 5/94)

10029 Borden, Louise. *The Day Eddie Met the Author* (2–4). Illus. 2001, Simon & Schuster $15.00 (0-689-83405-5). 40pp. Third-grader Eddie gets his wish to ask a question of his favorite author when she visits his school. (Rev: BL 3/1/01)

10030 Byars, Betsy. *The Burning Questions of Bingo Brown* (6–8). 1990, Puffin paper $4.99 (0-14-032479-8). 160pp. During Bingo's sixth-grade year, he falls in love three times for starters. (Rev: BCCB 4/88; BL 4/15/88; SLJ 5/88)

10031 Byars, Betsy. *The 18th Emergency* (4–6). Illus. by Robert Grossman. 1981, Puffin paper $4.99 (0-14-031451-2). 128pp. A young boy, nicknamed Mousi, incurs the wrath of the school bully and awaits his inevitable punishment with fear.

10032 Carbone, Elisa. *Sarah and the Naked Truth* (3–5). 2000, Knopf LB $17.99 (0-375-90264-3). 144pp. Friends Sarah and Christina welcome Olivia, a new classmate from Trinidad who has a physical disability. (Rev: BCCB 2/00; BL 3/15/00; HBG 10/00; SLJ 4/00)

10033 Carbone, Elisa. *Starting School with an Enemy* (3–5). 1998, Knopf LB $17.99 (0-679-98639-1). 112pp. Sarah, a newcomer in the fifth grade, becomes so obsessed with getting even with the class bully, Eric, that it almost costs her the loss

of her friend Christina. (Rev: BCCB 4/98; BL 9/15/98; HBG 10/98; SLJ 7/98)

10034 Caudill, Rebecca. *Did You Carry the Flag Today, Charley?* (2–5). Illus. by Nancy Grossman. 1966, Holt $16.95 (0-8050-1201-X); Dell paper $4.50 (0-440-40092-9). 96pp. Contemporary Appalachia is the setting for the activities of Charley, an irrepressibly curious kindergartner, who finally achieves the honor of carrying the school flag for his class.

10035 Cleary, Beverly. *Mitch and Amy* (3–5). Illus. by Bob Marstall. 1991, Morrow $15.00 (0-688-10806-7); Avon paper $4.99 (0-380-70925-2). 224pp. Twins Mitch and Amy squabble their way through fourth grade.

10036 Clements, Andrew. *Frindle* (3–6). Illus. 1996, Simon & Schuster $15.00 (0-689-80669-8). 105pp. Nick's desire to get even with a teacher gets out of hand. (Rev: BL 9/1/96; HB 11–12/96; SLJ 9/96)

10037 Clements, Andrew. *The Janitor's Boy* (3–7). 2000, Simon & Schuster $15.00 (0-689-81818-1). 144pp. Jack Rankin is ashamed that his father is the janitor in the middle school that he is attending. Once his classmates find out about his father, the teasing begins. (Rev: BCCB 9/00; BL 3/1/00; HB 7–8/00; HBG 10/00; SLJ 5/00)

10038 Clements, Andrew. *The Landry News* (3–7). Illus. 1999, Simon & Schuster $15.00 (0-689-81817-3). 128pp. When Cara's editorial about a lazy teacher causes him to lose his job, issues of responsibility and freedom of the press emerge. (Rev: BCCB 6/99; BL 6/1–15/99; HB 7–8/99; HBG 10/99; SLJ 7/99)

10039 Cohen, Barbara. *Two Hundred Thirteen Valentines* (3–5). Illus. by Wil Clay. 1993, Holt paper $4.95 (0-805-02627-4). 55pp. Two African American children who transfer to a school for the gifted must rethink their attitudes. (Rev: BCCB 1/92; BL 9/1/91; HB 3–4/92; SLJ 11/91)

10040 Conford, Ellen. *Dear Lovey Hart, I Am Desperate* (6–7). 1975, Little, Brown $14.95 (0-316-15306-0). 224pp. Freshman reporter Carrie Wasserman gets into trouble with her advice column in the school newspaper.

10041 Coville, Bruce. *Aliens Ate My Homework* (4–6). Illus. by Katherine Coville. 1993, Pocket $14.00 (0-671-87249-4). 180pp. No one believes Ron when he maintains that an alien ate his homework, even though it is the truth. (Rev: BL 1/15/94)

10042 Creech, Sharon. *Bloomability* (5–7). 1998, HarperCollins LB $14.89 (0-06-026994-4). 288pp. Although she has lived in 13 states in 12 years, Dinnie is not prepared to spend a year at the American School in Lugano, Switzerland, where her uncle is the headmaster. (Rev: BCCB 10/98; BL 9/15/98; HB 9–10/98; HBG 3/99; SLJ 10/98)

10043 Cullen, Lynn. *Stink Bomb* (4–6). 1998, Avon $14.00 (0-380-97647-1). 120pp. When Kenny breaks wind during gym class, he blames it on the class nerd, Alice Glowers, who becomes known as "Stink Bomb." (Rev: HBG 10/98; SLJ 3/98)

10044 Dadey, Debbie. *King of the Kooties* (3–4). Illus. 1999, Walker $15.95 (0-8027-8709-6). 112pp. Nate and his friend Donald clash with the class bully, Louisa, who finally gets her comeuppance. (Rev: BCCB 11/99; BL 9/15/99; HBG 3/00; SLJ 11/99)

10045 Dahl, Roald. *Matilda* (4–8). Illus. by Quentin Blake. 1988, Puffin paper $4.99 (0-14-034294-X). 224pp. Superbright first-grader Matilda deals with the evil school principal Miss Trunchbutt. (Rev: BCCB 10/88; HB 1–2/89; SLJ 10/88)

10046 DeClements, Barthe. *Liar, Liar* (4–6). 1998, Marshall Cavendish $14.95 (0-7614-5021-1). 144pp. Sixth-grader Gretchen finds her secure and happy social and school life ends when newcomer Marybelle begins her scheming ways. (Rev: BCCB 7–8/98; BL 8/98; HB 7–8/98; HBG 10/98)

10047 DeClements, Barthe. *Nothing's Fair in Fifth Grade* (4–6). 1981, Puffin paper $4.99 (0-14-034443-8). 144pp. Overweight Elsie steals lunch money to feed her habits. A sequel is: *Seventeen and In-Between* (1984).

10048 DeClements, Barthe. *Sixth Grade Can Really Kill You* (4–6). 1995, Puffin paper $3.99 (0-140-37130-3). 146pp. "Bad Helen" acts up to cover her embarrassment about her reading problem in this portrayal of life for a learning-disabled child. (Rev: BCCB 12/85; BL 11/1/85; SLJ 11/85)

10049 Delton, Judy. *Kitty from the Start* (4–6). 1987, Houghton $16.00 (0-395-42847-5). 141pp. The story of Kitty, a Catholic girl growing up in the 1940s, and her life in third grade. (Rev: BL 4/1/87; HB 5–6/87; SLJ 5/87)

10050 Dugan, Barbara. *Good-bye, Hello* (4–6). 1994, Greenwillow $13.00 (0-688-12447-X). 160pp. Bobbie thinks she has more than her share of problems at school until she discovers that her grandmother is dying. (Rev: BL 4/1/94; HB 7–8/94; SLJ 5/94)

10051 Duncan, Lois. *Wonder Kid Meets the Evil Lunch Snatcher* (2–4). Illus. 1990, Little, Brown paper $4.95 (0-316-19561-8). 76pp. Brian and his friend Robbie devise Wonder Kid, who can take care of any bully at school. (Rev: BL 6/1/88; SLJ 5/88)

10052 Edwards, Michelle. *Pa Lia's First Day* (2–4). Illus. 1999, Harcourt $14.00 (0-15-201974-X). 56pp. A beginning chapter book that tells about the problems and joys of a second-grader's first day in a new school. (Rev: BL 11/15/99; HBG 3/00; SLJ 11/99)

10053 Ellerbee, Linda. *Girl Reporter Blows Lid Off Town!* (4–7). Series: Get Real. 2000, HarperCollins LB $14.89 (0-06-028245-2); paper $3.99 (0-06-440755-1). 224pp. Casey Smith, a sixth-grade reporter, discovers the thrill of tracking down stories and getting at the truth in this lighthearted story set in a small town in the Berkshires. Also use: *Girl Reporter Sinks School!* (Rev: BL 3/1/00; HBG 10/00; SLJ 6/00)

10054 Estes, Eleanor. *The Hundred Dresses* (3–5). Illus. by Louis Slobodkin. 1944, Harcourt $16.00 (0-15-237374-8); paper $6.00 (0-15-642350-2).

32pp. A little Polish girl in an American school finally wins acceptance by her classmates.

10055 Fitzhugh, Louise. *Harriet the Spy* (4–6). Illus. by author. 1964, HarperCollins paper $4.50 (0-064-40660-1). 224pp. Precocious, overprivileged Harriet darts around her Manhattan neighborhood ferreting out and writing down the worst and best on her scene, sparing no one. A provocative sequel, primarily about Harriet's friend Beth, is: *The Long Secret* (1965).

10056 Flake, Sharon. *The Skin I'm In* (5–9). 1998, Hyperion LB $15.49 (0-7868-2392-5). 192pp. Maleeka Madison feels like an outsider in her new inner-city middle school, and she is led into delinquent behavior by bully Charlese. (Rev: BL 9/1/98; HBG 3/99)

10057 Fletcher, Ralph. *Flying Solo* (5–8). 1998, Clarion $15.00 (0-395-87323-1). 144pp. This novel answers the question "What will a sixth-grade class do if their substitute teacher fails to appear, and they are left alone for a whole day?" (Rev: BCCB 9/98; BL 8/98*; HB 11–12/98; HBG 3/99; SLJ 10/98)

10058 Floca, Brian. *The Frightful Story of Harry Walfish* (2–4). Illus. 1997, Orchard LB $16.99 (0-531-33008-7). 32pp. When Ms. Leonard-Brakhurst's class misbehaves at the natural-history museum, she tells them a cautionary tale that quiets them down. (Rev: BL 4/1/97; SLJ 3/97)

10059 Freeman, Martha. *Fourth Grade Weirdo* (3–5). 1999, Holiday $16.95 (0-8234-1460-4). 147pp. Even though Dexter thinks he is the weirdest kid in Mr. Dizwinkle's fourth-grade class, he is able to catch the thief whose robberies have cast suspicions on his teacher. (Rev: HBG 3/00; SLJ 1/00)

10060 Gauthier, Gail. *The Hero of Ticonderoga* (4–6). 2001, Putnam $16.99 (0-399-23559-0). 240pp. Therese, an outcast in the sixth grade, delivers a stunning oral report on Ethan Allen, part of which is spoken during a class trip to Fort Ticonderoga. (Rev: BCCB 3/01; SLJ 2/01)

10061 Gauthier, Gail. *A Year with Butch and Spike* (4–6). 1998, Putnam $15.99 (0-399-23216-8). 208pp. Jasper Gordon, pet of all his teachers, plans on staying that way; however, when he enters the sixth grade, he finds he is seated between the Couture cousins, whose favorite activity is bugging their teachers. (Rev: BCCB 6/98; BL 6/1–15/98; HB 5–6/98*; HBG 10/98; SLJ 6/98)

10062 Giff, Patricia Reilly. *Fourth Grade Celebrity* (3–5). Illus. by Leslie Morrill. 1989, Bantam paper $4.50 (0-440-42676-6). 128pp. Casey decides that she wants to become famous, and she does, in a most surprising way. Two sequels are: *The Girl Who Knew It All* (1979); *The Winter Worm Business* (1981).

10063 Giff, Patricia Reilly. *Look Out, Washington, D.C.!* (2–4). Illus. 1995, Dell paper $3.99 (0-440-40934-9). 118pp. A series of setbacks dull Emily's enthusiasm for the field trip the Polk Street School class is taking to Washington, D.C. (Rev: BCCB 7–8/95; BL 6/1–15/95; SLJ 10/95)

10064 Gilson, Jamie. *Bug in a Rug* (2–4). Illus. 1998, Clarion $15.00 (0-395-86616-2). 69pp. In this easily read chapter book, the reader follows Richard through a day in the second grade, including the embarrassment of having to wear purple pants — a gift from his visiting Aunt Nannie. (Rev: BL 4/15/98; HBG 10/98; SLJ 6/98)

10065 Gilson, Jamie. *It Goes Eeeeeeeeeeee!* (2–4). Illus. by Diane De Groat. 1994, Clarion $15.00 (0-395-67063-2). 68pp. Patrick, a conceited new boy in school, is put in his place when he spreads misinformation about bats in class and is corrected by Dawn Marie. (Rev: BCCB 5/94; BL 4/1/94; SLJ 6/94)

10066 Gilson, Jamie. *Thirteen Ways to Sink a Sub* (4–7). Illus. by Linda Strauss Edwards. 1982, Lothrop $16.00 (0-688-01304-X). 144pp. The girls in Room 4A challenge the boys to see who can first make their substitute teacher cry. A sequel is: *4B Goes Wild* (1983).

10067 Graves, Bonnie. *The Best Worst Day* (2–3). Illus. by Nelle Davis. 1996, Hyperion $13.95 (0-7868-0167-0); paper $3.95 (0-7868-1090-4). 64pp. During a typical school day, Lucy tries to make friends with the new girl in her class. (Rev: SLJ 7/96)

10068 Greene, Stephanie. *Owen Foote, Second Grade Strongman* (2–3). Illus. 1996, Clarion $15.00 (0-395-72098-2). 96pp. When Owen openly criticizes the school nurse, Mrs. Jackson, he gets into trouble with the principal and his parents. (Rev: BCCB 3/96; BL 4/15/96; HB 5–6/96; SLJ 4/96)

10069 Greene, Stephanie. *Show and Tell* (2–3). Illus. 1998, Clarion $15.00 (0-395-88898-0). 96pp. Substitute teacher Miss Plunkett is not amused when Woody brings a dead fish to a show-and-tell session in his second-grade classroom. (Rev: BL 11/1/98; HBG 3/99; SLJ 10/98)

10070 Greenwald, Sheila. *Stucksville* (3–5). 2000, DK $16.95 (0-7894-2675-7). 152pp. A likable story about a girl whose school assignment gives her a new interest in her surroundings — and a new comfort. (Rev: BCCB 1/01; BL 11/1/00; HBG 3/01; SLJ 10/00)

10071 Guthrie, Donna. *Frankie Murphy's Kiss List* (5–7). 1993, Simon & Schuster paper $15.00 (0-671-75624-9). 144pp. Frankie Murphy accepts a bet that he can kiss all six girls in his sixth-grade class. (Rev: SLJ 9/93)

10072 Hall, Katy, and Lisa Eisenberg. *The Paxton Cheerleaders: Go for It, Patti!* (4–7). 1994, Simon & Schuster paper $3.50 (0-671-89490-X). 137pp. Four seventh-grade girls from different backgrounds make the cheerleading team in their junior high school. (Rev: BL 2/1/95)

10073 Haywood, Carolyn. *"B" Is for Betsy* (3–4). Illus. by author. 1939, Harcourt $15.00 (0-15-204975-4); paper $6.00 (0-15-204977-0). 159pp. Betsy's adventures in the first grade. Others in the series: *Betsy and Billy* (1941); *Back to School with Betsy* (1943); *Betsy and the Boys* (1945).

10074 Herrera, Juan Felipe. *The Upside Down Boy/El niño de cabeza* (2–5). Illus. by Elizabeth Gomez. 2000, Children's Book Pr. $15.95 (0-89239-162-6). 31pp. Juanito, a young Hispanic American, is afraid that he won't fit into his new

Anglo school, but he is pleasantly surprised. (Rev: BCCB 4/00; HB 9–10/00; HBG 10/00; SLJ 3/00)

10075 Hill, Kirkpatrick. *The Year of Miss Agnes* (4–6). 2000, Simon & Schuster $16.00 (0-689-82933-7). 128pp. Set in northern Canada, this is a gentle story about a schoolteacher named Miss Agnes and the changes she makes in her pupils during the year she teaches in a one-room schoolhouse. (Rev: BCCB 11/00; BL 10/15/00; HB 11–12/00; HBG 3/01; SLJ 9/00)

10076 Holmes, Barbara W. *Charlotte Shakespeare and Annie the Great* (4–6). Illus. by John Himmelman. 1989, HarperCollins $12.95 (0-06-022614-5); paper $3.95 (0-06-440385-8). 126pp. Charlotte writes a Halloween school play and gets jealous because of all the attention the leading lady receives. (Rev: BCCB 11/89; BL 11/15/89; SLJ 11/89)

10077 Honeycutt, Natalie. *The All New Jonah Twist* (4–6). Illus. 1987, Avon paper $3.50 (0-380-70317-3). 128pp. Jonah is determined to change his image at the start of third grade — he'll no longer be inattentive in class, and he'll prove himself responsible enough for a pet. A sequel is: *The Best-Laid Plans of Jonah Twist* (1988). (Rev: BL 5/15/86; SLJ 8/86)

10078 Honeycutt, Natalie. *Invisible Lissa* (4–6). Illus. 1986, Avon paper $2.75 (0-380-70120-0). 192pp. Lissa challenges the student power structure in her fifth-grade class. (Rev: BCCB 7/85; BL 4/1/85; SLJ 8/85)

10079 Hudson, Wade. *Anthony's Big Surprise* (5–7). Series: NEATE. 1998, Just Us paper $3.95 (0-940975-42-6). 89pp. Interracial tensions erupt in junior high school when some African American students are suspended and Anthony, who is also trying to cope with a family crisis, must deal with both problems. (Rev: SLJ 6/99)

10080 Hughes, Dean. *Re-Elect Nutty!* (4–6). 1995, Simon & Schuster $14.00 (0-671-31862-6). 122pp. In this humorous novel, Nutty decides to run for reelection even though he was considered the worst student council president his school has ever had. (Rev: BL 5/1/95; SLJ 6/95)

10081 Hurwitz, Johanna. *Class Clown* (3–5). Illus. by Sheila Hamanaka. 1987, Morrow $15.95 (0-688-06723-9); Scholastic paper $3.99 (0-590-41821-1). 112pp. Lucas the class clown learns that there is a right and wrong way to use his humor. A sequel is: *Teacher's Pet* (1988). (Rev: BCCB 4/87; BL 5/15/87; HB 5–6/87)

10082 Hurwitz, Johanna. *Class President* (3–5). Illus. by Sheila Hamanaka. 1990, Morrow $15.95 (0-688-09114-8); Scholastic paper $4.50 (0-590-44064-0). 160pp. Julio works to get his friend elected class president, but discovers that he's the one with leadership qualities. (Rev: BCCB 5/90; BL 4/1/90; HB 7–8/90; SLJ 5/90)

10083 Hurwitz, Johanna. *Ever-Clever Elisa* (2–4). Illus. by Lillian Hoban. 1997, Morrow $15.00 (0-688-15189-2). 64pp. Six short episodes about Elisa in first grade, including one in which she gives her mother's engagement ring to her teacher as a sign of love. (Rev: BL 7/97; HB 9–10/97; HBG 3/98; SLJ 11/97)

10084 Hurwitz, Johanna. *School Spirit* (3–5). Illus. by Karen M. Dugan. 1994, Morrow $14.00 (0-688-12825-4). 144pp. Julio is annoyed when another boy hogs the spotlight as leader of a protest to save their school from being closed. (Rev: BL 5/1/94; HB 7–8/94; SLJ 5/94)

10085 Hurwitz, Johanna. *Starting School* (2–4). Illus. 1998, Morrow $15.00 (0-688-15685-1). 144pp. Twins Marcus and Marius decide to switch kindergarten classes to test the quality of each other's teacher, little knowing their teachers have also decided to do the same thing. (Rev: BL 8/98; HB 9–10/98; HBG 3/99; SLJ 9/98)

10086 Hurwitz, Johanna. *Tough-Luck Karen* (4–6). Illus. by Diane De Groat. 1982, Morrow $15.95 (0-688-01485-2). 160pp. Karen prefers housework to homework.

10087 Kline, Suzy. *Herbie Jones* (3–5). Illus. 1985, Putnam $13.95 (0-399-21183-7); Puffin paper $3.99 (0-14-032071-7). 96pp. Herbie and Raymond are determined to get out of the lowest reading group in the third grade. Other books about Herbie are: *What's the Matter with Herbie Jones?* (1986); *Herbie Jones and the Class Gift* (1987); *Herbie Jones and the Monster Ball* (1988). (Rev: BCCB 9/85; BL 8/85; SLJ 10/85)

10088 Kline, Suzy. *Horrible Harry at Halloween* (2–3). Illus. 2000, Viking $13.99 (0-670-88864-8). 38pp. At Halloween, Harry must solve the mystery of a stolen party costume in this story about Class 3B. (Rev: BL 9/15/00; HBG 3/01; SLJ 9/00)

10089 Kline, Suzy. *Horrible Harry Moves Up to Third Grade* (2–3). Illus. 1998, Viking $13.99 (0-670-87873-1). 128pp. During a third-grade field trip to an underground mine, Harry has to conquer his fears and also find his nemesis, Sidney, who suddenly disappears. (Rev: BL 10/15/98; HBG 3/99; SLJ 9/98)

10090 Kline, Suzy. *Marvin and the Meanest Girl* (2–4). Illus. 2000, Putnam $14.99 (0-399-23409-8). 70pp. An easy chapter book about a boy who discovers that the classmate he has been bugging is really grieving for her dead grandfather. (Rev: BL 11/1/00; HBG 3/01; SLJ 12/00)

10091 Kline, Suzy. *Song Lee and the "I Hate You" Notes* (2–4). Illus. 1999, Viking $13.99 (0-670-87887-1). 64pp. Song Lee, the nicest girl in Doug's third-grade class, is hurt when she receives hate notes, but she learns how to strike back. (Rev: BL 5/1/99; HBG 10/99; SLJ 6/99)

10092 Koehler-Pentacoff, Elizabeth. *Louise the One and Only* (3–5). Illus. 1996, Troll paper $2.95 (0-8167-3757-6). 64pp. In kindergarten, Louise longs to be the best at something. (Rev: BL 7/96; SLJ 8/96)

10093 Korman, Gordon. *The 6th Grade Nickname Game* (4–6). 1998, Hyperion LB $15.49 (0-7868-2382-7). 160pp. Typical problems encountered in the sixth grade are faced by Wiley and Jeff along with the anxiety of mounting a campaign to save the substitute teacher, Mr. Hughes. (Rev: BL 10/15/98)

10094 Korman, Gordon. *Something Fishy at Macdonald Hall* (4–6). 1995, Scholastic $14.95 (0-590-

25521-5). 198pp. At Macdonald Hall School, Boots and Bruno are accused of pranks they didn't commit and so they set out to find the real culprit. (Rev: BL 8/95; SLJ 9/95)

10095 Korman, Gordon. *The Twinkle Squad* (5–7). 1992, Scholastic $13.95 (0-590-45249-5). 160pp. A bossy, insecure sixth-grader and a defender of weaker kids are sentenced to the school's Special Discussion Group. (Rev: BCCB 11/92; BL 9/15/92; SLJ 9/92)

10096 Korman, Gordon. *The Zucchini Warriors* (4–6). 1991, Scholastic paper $4.50 (0-590-44174-4). 208pp. The boys at a Canadian boarding school have a wild and woolly adventure. (Rev: BL 1/1/89; SLJ 9/88)

10097 Krensky, Stephen. *Louise Takes Charge* (2–4). Illus. 1998, Dial $13.99 (0-8037-2305-9). 80pp. When Jasper returns to school in the fall, he has turned into a bully, so Louise and her classmates devise a scheme to make him change his ways. (Rev: BL 10/1/98; HBG 3/99; SLJ 10/98)

10098 Lauture, Denizé. *Running the Road to ABC* (1–5). Illus. by Reynold Ruffins. 1996, Simon & Schuster paper $16.00 (0-689-80507-1). A joyous picture book about a group of Haitian children happily going to school, where they hope to learn to read. (Rev: BCCB 3/96; HB 5–6/96; SLJ 6/96)

10099 Levy, Elizabeth. *Keep Ms. Sugarman in the Fourth Grade* (3–5). 1991, HarperCollins LB $14.89 (0-06-020427-3). 96pp. Smart-alecky and disruptive Jackie meets her match in Ms. Sugarman, a gifted teacher. (Rev: BL 12/1/91; SLJ 1/92)

10100 Levy, Elizabeth. *Seventh Grade Tango* (5–7). 2000, Hyperion LB $16.49 (0-7868-2427-1). 144pp. Seventh-grader Rebecca gets into a ballroom dancing program with her friend Scott, who is being chased by Samantha, much to Rebecca's annoyance. (Rev: BCCB 3/00; BL 3/1/00; HBG 10/00; SLJ 4/00)

10101 Lewis, Beverly. *Frog Power* (2–5). Illus. 1995, Bethany paper $3.99 (1-55661-645-7). 80pp. Stacy, who is afraid of frogs, is dismayed when she learns that Jason has brought his pet frog to school. (Rev: BL 10/1/95)

10102 Lindberg, Becky T. *Thomas Tuttle, Just in Time* (2–4). Illus. 1994, Albert Whitman LB $13.95 (0-8075-7898-3). 112pp. Thomas, a third-grader, might do a little better if he would only get organized. (Rev: BL 11/15/94; SLJ 10/94)

10103 Lovelace, Maud H. *Betsy-Tacy* (3–4). Illus. by Lois Lenski. 1940, HarperCollins paper $5.95 (0-06-440096-4). 113pp. Two 5-year-olds are inseparable at school and at play. One of a popular series. Five sequels are: *Betsy-Tacy and Tib* (1941); *Betsy and Tacy Go over the Big Hill* (1942); *Betsy and Tacy Go Downtown* (1943); *Heaven to Betsy* (1945); *Betsy in Spite of Herself* (1946).

10104 Low, Alice, ed. *Stories to Tell a Six-Year-Old* (K–3). Illus. 1997, Little, Brown paper $8.95 (0-316-53418-8). 192pp. A delightful anthology of 20 folktales, short stories, picture book texts, and chapters from books like *Mary Poppins*. (Rev: BL 3/1/98; SLJ 10/97)

10105 Lurie, Jon. *Allison's Story: A Book About Homeschooling* (2–4). Illus. by Rebecca Dallinger. 1996, Lerner $21.27 (0-8225-2579-8). 40pp. A photo-essay about an 8-year-old's experiences with home schooling. (Rev: BL 11/1/96; SLJ 12/96) [649]

10106 MacDonald, Maryann. *Secondhand Star* (2–5). Illus. by Eileen Christelow. 1994, Hyperion $11.95 (1-56282-616-6). 64pp. Francie, who is cast as Toto in the school production of "The Wizard of Oz," becomes a last-minute replacement for an ill Dorothy. (Rev: BL 7/94; SLJ 7/94)

10107 McDonald, Megan. *Judy Moody* (2–4). Illus. 2000, Candlewick $15.99 (0-7636-0685-5). 196pp. A beginning chapter book about Judy Moody, a third-grader, and her everyday trials and tribulations. (Rev: BCCB 5/00; BL 7/00; HBG 10/00; SLJ 7/00)

10108 McKenna, Colleen O'Shaughnessy. *Live from the Fifth Grade* (4–6). Illus. 1994, Scholastic $13.95 (0-590-46684-4). 145pp. Practical joker Roger Friday becomes serious when a friendly custodian at his school is accused of theft. (Rev: BL 11/15/94; SLJ 10/94)

10109 Matson, Nancy. *The Boy Trap* (4–6). Illus. 1999, Front Street $14.95 (0-8126-2663-X). 112pp. Emma decides that by entering the best project in her fifth-grade class's science fair, she will be able to prove that girls are better than boys. (Rev: BL 1/1–15/00; HBG 10/00; SLJ 11/99)

10110 Mills, Claudia. *Dinah for President* (3–6). 1992, Macmillan LB $14.00 (0-02-766999-8). 128pp. Conflicting emotions in a middle schooler form the basis of this believable story. (Rev: BCCB 4/92; BL 7/92; HB 7–8/92; SLJ 5/92*)

10111 Mills, Claudia. *Lizzie at Last* (4–6). 2000, Farrar $16.00 (0-374-34659-3). 160pp. Lizzie compromises her individuality to become popular with her classmates, but she comes to regret it. (Rev: BCCB 10/00; BL 11/1/00; HB 11–12/00; HBG 3/01; SLJ 11/00)

10112 Mills, Claudia. *Losers, Inc* (5–7). 1997, Farrar $16.00 (0-374-34661-5). 160pp. Ethan develops a crush on his new student teacher and tries every way possible to impress her. (Rev: BCCB 4/97; BL 3/1/97; SLJ 4/97)

10113 Mills, Claudia. *Standing Up to Mr. O* (4–7). 1998, Farrar $16.00 (0-374-34721-2). 176pp. In spite of opposition from friends and teachers, Maggie McIntosh refuses to dissect specimens in biology class, even though she risks getting an F. (Rev: BCCB 10/98; BL 10/15/98; HB 9–10/98; HBG 3/99; SLJ 12/98)

10114 Morris, Judy K. *The Kid Who Ran for Principal* (4–6). 1989, HarperCollins $12.00 (0-397-32360-3). 212pp. Sixth-grader Gail persuades Bonnie to be a candidate for interim principal in their school. (Rev: BCCB 1/90; BL 11/15/89; SLJ 10/89)

10115 Myers, Laurie. *Earthquake in the Third Grade* (2–4). Illus. by Karen Ritz. 1993, Clarion $15.00 (0-395-65360-6). 63pp. John and his friends try to reverse their teacher's decision to move away. (Rev: BL 12/1/93)

10116 Myers, Laurie. *Guinea Pigs Don't Talk* (2–4). Illus. 1994, Clarion $13.95 (0-395-68967-8). 68pp. Two students play pranks on Lisa, the new student in class, but she retaliates. (Rev: BL 10/15/94; SLJ 10/94)

10117 Napoli, Donna Jo. *Shelley Shock* (3–6). 2000, Dutton $15.99 (0-525-46452-2). 160pp. Sixth-grade life as experienced by Adam, whose chief competition for a spot on the soccer team is a girl, is the main subject of this novel. (Rev: BCCB 11/00; BL 9/15/00; SLJ 11/00)

10118 Park, Barbara. *Junie B. Jones and her Big Fat Mouth* (2–4). Illus. by Denise Brunkus. 1993, Random $11.99 (0-679-94407-9); paper $3.99 (0-679-84407-4). 72pp. In this hilarious story of kindergartner Junie B. Jones, the little girl has trouble with the Pledge of Allegiance, keeping quiet in class, and deciding what to be on Job Day. (Rev: BL 11/15/93)

10119 Park, Barbara. *Junie B. Jones and the Yucky Blucky Fruitcake* (2–4). Illus. by Denise Brunkus. Series: Junie B. Jones. 1995, Random paper $3.99 (0-679-86694-9). 71pp. A young kindergartner tells about her many troubles at school, where she is always a loser. (Rev: BL 12/15/95)

10120 Peck, Robert Newton. *Arly* (5–8). 1989, Walker $16.95 (0-8027-6856-3). 151pp. In this story set in 1927 in Florida, Arly has few hopes of learning to read until a teacher named Miss Binie appears. (Rev: BL 7/89)

10121 Petersen, P. J. *Can You Keep a Secret?* (3–5). Illus. 1997, Dutton $15.99 (0-525-45840-9). 80pp. Mike, who has a reputation for not being able to keep a secret, finds he is being made a confidant by his friend Amy and wonders if he can keep her trust. (Rev: BL 10/1/97; HBG 3/98; SLJ 1/98)

10122 Pryor, Bonnie. *Poison Ivy and Eyebrow Wigs* (3–5). Illus. by Gail Owens. 1993, Morrow $15.00 (0-688-11200-5). 156pp. Martin's problems in the fourth grade include wanting to be popular and having a crush on his teacher. (Rev: BL 4/15/93; SLJ 6/93)

10123 Ragz, M. M. *French Fries up Your Nose* (5–8). 1994, Pocket paper $2.99 (0-671-88410-7). 74pp. Though most people think it is a joke, Iggy Sands really wants to win the election and become student council president. (Rev: BL 3/15/94)

10124 Rocklin, Joanne. *For Your Eyes Only* (4–6). 1997, Scholastic $14.95 (0-590-67447-1). 144pp. Sixth-grader Lucy blossoms under the attention of Mr. Moffat, a substitute teacher. (Rev: BCCB 4/97; BL 3/1/97; HBG 3/98; SLJ 3/97*)

10125 Sachar, Louis. *Marvin Redpost: Class President* (2–4). Illus. 1999, Random LB $11.99 (0-679-98999-4); paper $3.99 (0-679-88999-X). 80pp. In this beginning chapter book, Marvin's third-grade class has a surprise visit from the president of the United States. (Rev: BCCB 4/99; BL 4/15/99; HBG 10/99; SLJ 6/99)

10126 Sachar, Louis. *Wayside School Is Falling Down* (3–6). Illus. by Joel Schick. 1989, Lothrop $15.95 (0-688-07868-0); Avon paper $4.99 (0-380-

75484-3). 192pp. Episodes with the children who inhabit the world's wackiest elementary school. (Rev: BL 5/1/89; SLJ 5/89)

10127 Sachs, Marilyn. *The Bears' House* (4–7). Illus. by Louis Glanzman. 1987, Avon paper $2.99 (0-380-70582-6). 80pp. A poor girl escapes from reality by living in a fantasy in her classroom. A reissue of the 1971 edition.

10128 Sathre, Vivian. *J. B. Wigglebottom and the Parade of Pets* (3–5). Illus. by Catharine O'Neill. 1993, Macmillan $12.95 (0-689-31811-1). 96pp. J. B. gets back at Buddy the bully. (Rev: BL 3/1/93; SLJ 7/93)

10129 Schenker, Dona. *The Secret Circle* (5–8). 1998, Knopf $16.00 (0-679-88989-2). 176pp. When Jamie wants to join the exclusive Secret Circle at her new private school, she finds the tests she must pass are against her principles. (Rev: BCCB 10/98; BL 11/1/98; HBG 3/99; SLJ 10/98)

10130 Schlieper, Anne. *The Best Fight* (3–5). Illus. 1995, Albert Whitman LB $10.95 (0-8075-0662-1). 63pp. Jamie, who has a reading disability and often gets into fights at school, gets good advice from his principal. (Rev: BL 3/15/95; SLJ 7/95)

10131 Sharmat, Marjorie W. *Getting Something on Maggie Marmelstein* (3–5). Illus. by Ben Shecter. 1971, HarperCollins LB $14.89 (0-06-025552-8). 110pp. When Thad's mortal enemy, Maggie, sees him cooking and begins teasing him, Thad must find some way of blackmailing her into silence. Two sequels are: *Maggie Marmelstein for President* (1975); *Mysteriously Yours, Maggie Marmelstein* (1982).

10132 Shreve, Susan. *Joshua T. Bates in Trouble Again* (3–5). Illus. 1997, Knopf $17.00 (0-679-88520-X). 90pp. At school, Joshua has trouble with bullies, but he decides that standing up to them is the only solution. A sequel to *The Flunking of Joshua T. Bates* (1984) and *Joshua T. Bates Takes Charge* (1993). (Rev: BL 2/1/98; HBG 3/98; SLJ 1/98)

10133 Vail, Rachel. *Not That I Care* (4–7). Series: Friendship Ring. 1998, Scholastic $14.95 (0-590-03476-6). 240pp. For a classroom presentation on ten items that reveal who you are, Morgan Miller remembers crucial incidents in her life but, in her final report, glosses over the truth. (Rev: BCCB 12/98; BL 11/15/98; HBG 3/99; SLJ 12/98)

10134 Vogiel, Eva. *Invisible Chains* (5–8). 2000, Judaica Pr. $19.95 (1-880582-57-0). 280pp. In 1948, 14-year-old Frumie is sent with her crippled younger sister, Judy, to a boarding school for religiously observant Jewish girls. (Rev: BL 7/00; HBG 10/00)

10135 Voigt, Cynthia. *It's Not Easy Being Bad* (5–7). 2000, Simon & Schuster $16.00 (0-689-82473-4). 256pp. Seventh-graders Mikey and Margalo, who have reputations for being bad, come up with several plans for getting in with the popular set at school. (Rev: BCCB 12/00*; BL 11/15/00; HB 1–2/01; HBG 3/01; SLJ 11/00)

10136 Warner, Sally. *Finding Hattie* (5–8). 2001, HarperCollins $14.95 (0-06-028464-1). 234pp. Hat-

tie Knowlton's 1882 journal describes Miss Bulkey's school in Tarrytown, New York, and the people she meets there, including her sophisticated, shallow but popular cousin Sophie. (Rev: BL 2/1/01; SLJ 2/01)

10137 Warner, Sally. *Sweet and Sour Lily* (2–3). Illus. 1998, Knopf $15.00 (0-679-89136-6). 96pp. Lily Hill, whose brother is Case of *Dog Years*, tries to impress two girls in her first-grade class by breaking the rules and bringing her favorite doll to school. (Rev: BL 8/98; HBG 3/99; SLJ 10/98)

10138 Whelan, Gloria. *Welcome to Starvation Lake* (3–4). Illus. 2000, Golden Bks. $10.99 (0-307-46506-3); paper $3.99 (0-307-26506-4). 71pp. An easy chapter book in which a rock band, the Putrid Armpits, volunteer to give a benefit concert to help the school library in tiny Starvation Lake. (Rev: BL 12/1/00; HBG 3/01)

10139 Willner-Pardo, Gina. *Spider Storch's Music Mess* (2–3). Illus. by Nick Sharratt. 1998, Albert Whitman LB $11.95 (0-8075-7583-6); paper $3.95 (0-8075-7584-4). 76pp. In this easy chapter book, Spider tries to get out of music class, but when he succeeds in getting bounced, he finds he misses it. (Rev: HBG 3/99; SLJ 3/99)

10140 Willner-Pardo, Gina. *Spider Storch's Teacher Torture* (2–4). Illus. 1997, Albert Whitman LB $11.95 (0-8075-7577-1); paper $3.95 (0-8075-7578-X). 60pp. Spider Storch thinks up some wild schemes to prevent his beloved teacher from retiring. (Rev: BL 1/1–15/98; HBG 3/98; SLJ 11/97)

Science Fiction

10141 Anderson, Kevin J., and Ralph McQuarrie. *Stars Wars: Jabba's Palace Pop-Up Book* (2–4). Illus. 1996, Little, Brown $19.45 (0-316-53513-3). 14pp. A pop-up book using sound and pictures to illustrate parts of the *Star Wars* films. (Rev: BL 12/15/96)

10142 Archer, Chris. *Alien Blood* (4–6). 1997, Pocket paper $3.99 (0-671-01483-8). 118pp. A chilling story narrated by a 13-year-old who is experiencing strange and frightening events. Also use *Alien Terror* (1997). (Rev: BL 12/15/97; SLJ 3/98)

10143 Asimov, Janet. *Norby and the Terrified Taxi* (3–5). Illus. 1997, Walker $15.95 (0-8027-8642-1). 144pp. Using time travel and brains, Norby the Robot and Jeff are able to foil the nasty Garc the Great. (Rev: BL 1/1–15/98; SLJ 12/97)

10144 Asimov, Janet. *The Package in Hyperspace* (5–7). Illus. 1988, Walker LB $14.85 (0-8027-6823-7). 84pp. Two space-wrecked children must fend for themselves as they try to reach Merkina. (Rev: BL 1/1/89; SLJ 11/88)

10145 Asimov, Janet, and Isaac Asimov. *Norby and the Court Jester* (4–6). 1991, Walker LB $15.85 (0-8027-8132-2); Ace paper $5.50 (0-441-00341-9). 118pp. Jeff, his robot Norby, and the head of a space academy travel to the planet Izz. (Rev: SLJ 2/92)

10146 Asimov, Janet, and Isaac Asimov. *Norby and the Invaders* (5–8). 1985, Walker LB $10.85 (0-

8027-6607-2). 138pp. In a fast-paced adventure, Jeff and his robot, Norby, are off to the planet Jamya to the rescue of Norby's ancestor. (Rev: BL 3/1/86; SLJ 2/86)

10147 Asimov, Janet, and Isaac Asimov. *Norby and the Oldest Dragon* (3–5). 1990, Walker LB $15.85 (0-8027-6910-1). 110pp. When Jeff visits the planet Jamyn, he finds that a mysterious vapor surrounds him and other residents. (Rev: SLJ 7/90)

10148 Asimov, Janet, and Isaac Asimov. *Norby Finds a Villain* (4–8). 1987, Walker LB $13.85 (0-8027-6711-7). 102pp. Norby the robot and his human friends set out to free Pera, who has been robot-napped by the traitor Ing, in this sixth book of the Norby series. Also use: *Norby and the Queen's Necklace* (1986). (Rev: BL 1/1/88; SLJ 11/87)

10149 Asimov, Janet, and Isaac Asimov. *Norby, the Mixed-up Robot* (4–6). 1984, Walker LB $10.85 (0-8027-6496-7). 96pp. Jeff, his brother Fargo, and a robot named Norby combat Ing the Ingrate. A sequel is: *Norby's Other Secret* (1984).

10150 Base, Graeme. *The Worst Band in the Universe: A Totally Cosmic Musical Adventure* (4–7). Illus. 1999, Abrams $19.95 (0-8109-3998-3). 48pp. A resourceful 13-year-old musician uses music to power his spaceship back to his home planet and a confrontation with the evil Musical Inquisitor. (Rev: BL 9/15/99; HBG 3/00; SLJ 12/99)

10151 Bawden, Nina. *Off the Road* (5–9). 1998, Clarion $16.00 (0-395-91321-7). 192pp. In this science fiction novel set in a time when the elderly are exterminated, 11-year-old Tom follows his grandfather into the "savage jungle" Outside the Wall where the old man hopes to escape his fate and, instead, discovers a much different kind of society. (Rev: BCCB 10/98; BL 9/15/98; HBG 10/99; SLJ 11/98)

10152 Bell, Hilari. *Songs of Power* (5–8). 2000, Hyperion LB $16.49 (0-7868-2487-5). 224pp. In this science fiction novel, young Annis, who is living with her parents in an undersea station, is convinced that a series of accidents are caused by spells not saboteurs. (Rev: HBG 10/00; SLJ 5/00)

10153 Brennan, Herbie. *The Mystery Machine* (3–5). 1995, Simon & Schuster paper $14.00 (0-689-50615-5). 52pp. Herbie discovers that his neighbor is actually an alien preparing to take over the world. (Rev: BL 5/1/95; HB 9–10/95; SLJ 7/95)

10154 Butler, Susan. *The Hermit Thrush Sings* (5–8). 1999, DK $17.95 (0-7894-2489-4). 282pp. Leora, who is living in a future civilization in North America, must leave the safety of her walled village, controlled by the Rulers, and find rebels who are working to overthrow the government. (Rev: BCCB 4/99; BL 2/15/99*; HBG 10/99; SLJ 4/99)

10155 Butts, Nancy. *The Door in the Lake* (5–8). 1998, Front Street $15.95 (1-886910-27-8). 160pp. Twenty-seven months after being abducted by aliens, Joey, now age 14, returns home to find that everything has changed while he has remained the same. (Rev: BCCB 7–8/98; BL 5/15/98; HBG 10/98; SLJ 6/98)

10156 Byars, Betsy. *The Computer Nut* (4–6). 1984, Puffin paper $4.99 (0-14-032086-5). 144pp. Through her computer, Kate encounters an extraterrestrial being.

10157 Cameron, Eleanor. *Mr. Bass's Planetoid* (4–6). Illus. by Louis Darling. 1958, Little, Brown $14.95 (0-316-12525-3). A further story about the Mushroom Planet, Mr. Bass, and two young heroes. Also use: *Stowaway to the Mushroom Planet* (1956).

10158 Cameron, Eleanor. *The Wonderful Flight to the Mushroom Planet* (4–6). Illus. by Robert Henneberger. 1988, Little, Brown paper $7.95 (0-316-12540-7). Science fiction combined with magic in the story of two boys who take off on a spaceship with a magical man named Tyco Bass.

10159 Christopher, John. *When the Tripods Came* (5–8). 1990, Macmillan paper $4.99 (0-02-042575-9). 160pp. How the Tripods came to Earth and imposed a new order. (Rev: BCCB 7–8/88; BL 7/88; HB 9–10/88)

10160 Christopher, John. *The White Mountains* (6–8). 1967, Simon & Schuster LB $17.00 (0-02-718360-2); Macmillan paper $4.99 (0-02-042711-5). 192pp. The first volume of a trilogy in which a young boy escapes from a futuristically mechanized tyranny. The other volumes are: *City of Gold and Lead* (1967); *Pool of Fire* (1968). (Rev: BL 9/15/98)

10161 Ciencin, Scott. *Dinoverse* (5–8). Illus. 1999, Random $18.00 (0-679-88842-X). 304pp. Bertram's science project really works and he and his three schoolmates are caught in a time warp in which they become dinosaurs. (Rev: BL 4/1/99; HBG 10/99; SLJ 4/99)

10162 Conford, Ellen. *Diary of a Monster's Son* (2–4). Illus. 1999, Little, Brown $14.95 (0-316-15245-5). 76pp. A humorous story, told in diary form, about a boy whose father is a monster. (Rev: BCCB 6/99; BL 7/99; HBG 10/99; SLJ 7/99)

10163 Cousins, Steven. *Frankenbug* (4–6). 2000, Holiday $15.95 (0-8234-1496-5). 151pp. Adam gets revenge on the bully, Jeb, by creating a super bug by sewing together parts of insects he has bought through a mail-order catalog and, then, frightening his tormentor. (Rev: SLJ 3/01)

10164 Coville, Bruce. *Aliens Stole My Body* (4–7). Illus. Series: Alien Adventure. 1998, Pocket $14.00 (0-671-02414-0). 220pp. A science fiction thriller in which Rod's body is held by the evil BKR while his brain is in Seymour, an alien with six legs, one eye, and no mouth. (Rev: BL 11/1/98; SLJ 2/99)

10165 Coville, Bruce. *The Attack of the Two-Inch Teacher* (3–6). Illus. by Tony Sansevero. Series: I Was a Sixth Grade Alien. 1999, Pocket paper $3.99 (0-671-02651-8). 165pp. Pleskit, a visiting alien, accidentally shrinks his sixth-grade teacher and best friend to matchbox size. (Rev: SLJ 2/00)

10166 Coville, Bruce, ed. *Bruce Coville's Alien Visitors* (4–7). 1999, Avon paper $4.99 (0-380-80254-6). 209pp. A collection of 14 short stories about aliens and alien encounters by such writers as Ray Bradbury. (Rev: BL 11/15/99)

10167 Coville, Bruce, comp. and ed. *Bruce Coville's UFOs* (4–8). Illus. by Ernie Colon and John Nyberg. 2000, HarperCollins paper $4.99 (0-380-80257-0). 212pp. A collection of 13 new and previously published science fiction short stories by well-known authors. (Rev: SLJ 11/00)

10168 Coville, Bruce. *I Left My Sneakers in Dimension X* (4–6). Illus. by Katherine Coville. 1994, Pocket $14.00 (0-671-89072-7); paper $3.99 (0-671-79833-2). 180pp. Rod is kidnapped by an alien monster and must save the universe from destruction. This is a sequel to *Aliens Ate My Homework* (1993). (Rev: BL 1/15/95; SLJ 3/95)

10169 Coville, Bruce. *I Was a Sixth Grade Alien* (3–6). Illus. 1999, Pocket $16.00 (0-671-03651-3); paper $3.99 (0-671-02650-X). 180pp. Tim Tompkins's attempts to befriend an alien in his sixth-grade class get him involved in a science fiction mystery. (Rev: BL 10/15/99; SLJ 10/99)

10170 Coville, Bruce. *My Teacher Fried My Brains* (3–6). Illus. by John Pierard. 1991, Pocket paper $4.50 (0-671-72710-9). 136pp. Duncan is convinced his teacher is an alien when he finds a fake hand in a dumpster. (Rev: BL 9/15/91)

10171 Coville, Bruce. *Space Brat 4: Planet of the Dips* (3–5). Illus. Series: Space Brat. 1995, Pocket $14.00 (0-671-50090-2); paper $3.99 (0-671-50092-9). 72pp. Lunk's spaceship goes off course, and he finds himself on the loony planet of the Dips. (Rev: BL 11/1/95; SLJ 12/95)

10172 Cowley, Joy. *Starbright and the Dream Eater* (5–8). 2000, HarperCollins LB $14.89 (0-06-028420-X). 144pp. A child born to a mentally disabled teenage mother and named Starbright is destined to save the earth from the Dream Eater. (Rev: BCCB 7–8/00; BL 4/15/00; HBG 10/00; SLJ 6/00)

10173 Crilley, Mark. *Akiko in the Sprubly Islands* (3–5). 2000, Delacorte $9.95 (0-385-32726-9). 176pp. A fourth-grader leads her crew across the Moonguzzit Sea to rescue Prince Froptoppit in this far-fetched science fiction fantasy. (Rev: BL 1/1–15/01; HBG 3/01; SLJ 11/00)

10174 Crilley, Mark. *Akiko on the Planet Smoo* (4–7). Illus. 2000, Delacorte $12.95 (0-385-32724-2). 176pp. A fast-paced science fiction novel about Akiko, a fourth-grader, and her flight into space to find the kidnapped son of King Froptoppit. (Rev: BL 3/1/00; HBG 10/00; SLJ 2/00)

10175 DeFelice, Cynthia. *The Strange Night Writing of Jessamine Colter* (4–6). Illus. 1988, Macmillan paper $13.95 (0-02-726451-3). 56pp. Jessie feels compelled to write things she knows nothing about, and realizes that her strange writing predicts the future. (Rev: BCCB 9/88; BL 10/1/88; SLJ 11/88)

10176 Dexter, Catherine. *Alien Game* (5–8). 1995, Morrow $15.00 (0-688-11332-X). 208pp. Zoe is convinced that the new girl in the eighth grade is really an alien. (Rev: BCCB 3/95; BL 5/1/95; HB 9–10/95; SLJ 4/95)

10177 Doyle, Debra, and James D. MacDonald. *Groogleman* (5–8). 1996, Harcourt $15.00 (0-15-200235-9). 112pp. A science fiction novel about a boy who is pitted against the groogleman, the person who collects the heads of plague victims. (Rev: BCCB 12/96; SLJ 12/96)

10178 Etra, Jonathan, and Stephanie Spinner. *Aliens for Breakfast* (3–5). Illus. 1988, Random $11.99 (0-394-92093-7); paper $3.99 (0-394-82093-2). 64pp. Richard meets an alien who needs help to find a secret weapon. (Rev: BCCB 12/88; BL 1/15/89; SLJ 3/89)

10179 Evans, Douglas. *The Classroom at the End of the Hall* (2–4). Illus. 1996, Front Street $14.95 (1-886910-07-3). 128pp. Typical third-graders have some atypical adventures in these 11 stories. (Rev: BCCB 9/96; BL 8/96; SLJ 10/96)

10180 Finch, Sheila. *Tiger in the Sky* (4–8). Series: Out of Time. 1999, Avon paper $4.99 (0-380-79971-5). 256pp. In the mid-2300s, three youngsters are sent to the edge of the solar system to deal with a plague of furry animals that are endangering a scientific station. (Rev: BL 9/1/99)

10181 Follett, Ken. *The Power Twins* (4–8). 1991, Scholastic paper $2.75 (0-590-42507-2). 90pp. Three youngsters travel to a planet where large, gentle worms live. (Rev: SLJ 1/91)

10182 Foster, Alan Dean. *The Hand of Dinotopia* (5–8). Illus. by James Gurne. Series: Dinotopia. 1999, HarperCollins $22.95 (0-06-028005-0). 416pp. A lengthy sequel to *Dinotopia Lost* (1998) that deals with Will and Sylvia and their trip through a harsh desert to a steamy rain forest where intelligent dinosaurs dwell. (Rev: HBG 10/99; SLJ 4/99)

10183 Gauthier, Gail. *Club Earth* (4–7). 1999, Putnam LB $15.99 (0-399-23373-3). 160pp. When the Denis home is chosen to be an interstellar resort, the family finds that each alien visitor has an unusual talent in this humorous science fiction novel. (Rev: HB 5–6/99; HBG 10/99; SLJ 8/99)

10184 Gauthier, Gail. *My Life Among the Aliens* (3–6). 1996, Putnam $14.95 (0-399-22945-0). 104pp. In this episodic book, Will and his friends encounter aliens in a variety of situations. (Rev: BCCB 6/96; SLJ 6/96)

10185 Gilden, Mel. *Outer Space and All That Junk* (5–7). Illus. 1989, HarperCollins LB $12.00 (0-397-32307-7). 176pp. Myron's uncle is collecting junk, which he believes will help aliens return to their home in outer space. (Rev: BL 12/1/89; SLJ 12/89)

10186 Gilden, Mel. *The Pumpkins of Time* (4–7). 1994, Harcourt $10.95 (0-15-276603-0); paper $4.95 (0-15-200889-6). 192pp. Myron, his friend Princess, and their cat do some stylish time-traveling. (Rev: BL 10/15/94; SLJ 10/94)

10187 Gormley, Beatrice. *Paul's Volcano* (4–6). Illus. 1988, Avon paper $2.50 (0-380-70562-1). 143pp. Adam and new kid Paul tangle over a science-fair volcano model that seems to have a mind of its own. (Rev: BL 5/15/87; SLJ 3/87)

10188 Gormley, Beatrice. *Wanted: UFO* (3–6). Illus. by Emily Arnold McCully. 1992, Avon paper $2.99 (0-380-71313-6). 128pp. Elise and Nick discover two aliens in the backyard. (Rev: BCCB 6/90; BL 7/90; SLJ 7/90)

10189 Greenburg, Dan. *My Son, the Time Traveler* (2–4). Illus. by Jack E. Davis. Series: Zack Files. 1997, Grosset LB $12.99 (0-448-41587-9); paper $3.95 (0-448-41341-8). 57pp. In this time-travel story, Zack, a fifth-grader, meets his future son. (Rev: SLJ 10/97)

10190 Greer, Gery, and Bob Ruddick. *Max and Me and the Wild West* (4–6). 1988, Harcourt $12.95 (0-15-253136-X). 138pp. Professor Flybender's time machine once more lands Steve and Max in the middle of an adventure — this time in 1882 Arizona Territory. (Rev: BL 2/15/88)

10191 Griffin, Peni R. *Switching Well* (5–8). 1993, Macmillan $17.00 (0-689-50581-7). 224pp. Two girls from different centuries trade places. (Rev: BCCB 7–8/93; SLJ 6/93*)

10192 Gutman, Dan. *Virtually Perfect* (4–6). 1998, Hyperion $13.95 (0-7868-0394-0). 128pp. Seventh-grader Yip Turner uses his father's software to create a virtual teen who starts out as a friend and later wants to assassinate the president. (Rev: BL 6/1–15/98; HBG 10/98; SLJ 8/98)

10193 Haddix, Margaret P. *Among the Hidden* (5–8). 1998, Simon & Schuster $16.00 (0-689-81700-2). 154pp. In a society where only two children are allowed per family, Luke, the third, endures a secret life hidden from authorities. (Rev: HBG 3/99; SLJ 9/98)

10194 Harwood, Chuck. *Hot-Tempered Farmers: The Case of the Barbecued Barns* (4–6). Series: Kinetic City Super Crew. 1997, McGraw-Hill paper $4.25 (0-07-006389-3). 164pp. Set in the near future, Super Crew members use their sophisticated technology to solve the mystery of two barn burnings. (Rev: SLJ 5/98)

10195 Heintze, Ty. *Valley of the Eels* (5–8). Illus. 1993, Eakin $15.95 (0-89015-904-1). 156pp. In the Gulf of Mexico, Billy and Shawn discover an underwater station where aliens live in this novel about pollution and scuba diving. (Rev: BL 3/1/94)

10196 Hill, William. *The Magic Bicycle* (5–8). 1998, Otter Creek paper $13.95 (1-890611-00-X). 326pp. For helping an alien escape, Danny receives a magical bicycle that is capable of transporting him through time and space. (Rev: BL 1/1–15/98; SLJ 3/98)

10197 Hooks, William H. *The Girl Who Could Fly* (3–4). Illus. by Kees de Kiefte. 1995, Macmillan paper $14.00 (0-02-744433-3). 53pp. Tom, a girl, is actually an alien from outer space who can perform amazing feats like stopping a ball in midair. (Rev: BCCB 7–8/95; BL 8/95; SLJ 7/95)

10198 Hughes, Monica. *The Golden Aquarians* (4–6). 1995, Simon & Schuster paper $15.00 (0-671-50543-2). 186pp. Walt is sent by his father to the planet Aqua with the hope of making a man of him. (Rev: BCCB 10/95; BL 5/1/95; HB 9–10/95; SLJ 8/95)

10199 Kahn, Sharon. *Kacy and the Space Shuttle Secret: A Space Adventure for Young Readers* (4–6). Illus. by Mark Mitchell. 1996, Eakin $17.75

(1-57168-025-X). 128pp. An exciting science fiction adventure in which a young would-be scientist helps launch a space shuttle. (Rev: SLJ 4/96)

10200 Katz, Welwyn W. *Time Ghost* (4–6). 1995, Simon & Schuster paper $16.00 (0-689-80027-4). 171pp. In a heavily polluted 21st-century environment, Sara time-travels to the 1990s, when the world was still green. (Rev: BCCB 5/95; BL 5/1/95; SLJ 5/95)

10201 Kaye, Marilyn. *Amy, Number Seven* (4–7). Series: Replica. 1998, Bantam paper $0.99 (0-553-49238-1). 197pp. Amy Candler discovers that she has unusual abilities because she is the product of a government-sponsored lab experiment. (Rev: SLJ 10/98)

10202 Key, Alexander. *The Forgotten Door* (5–7). 1986, Scholastic paper $2.95 (0-590-43130-7). 144pp. When little Jon falls to earth from another planet, he encounters suspicion and hostility as well as sympathy.

10203 King-Smith, Dick. *Harriet's Hare* (2–4). Illus. 1995, Crown LB $16.99 (0-517-59831-0). 128pp. Harriet shares an adventurous summer with a hare who is actually a space alien. (Rev: BCCB 6/95; BL 4/15/95*; SLJ 6/95)

10204 Korman, Gordon. *Nose Pickers from Outer Space!* (2–5). Illus. 1999, Hyperion LB $13.49 (0-7868-2431-X). 128pp. Ten-year-old Devin discovers that his nose-picking exchange student, Stan, is actually operating a nose computer to try and save the planet Earth. (Rev: BL 8/99; HBG 3/00; SLJ 1/00)

10205 Kress, Nancy. *Yanked!* (4–8). Series: Out of Time. 1999, Avon paper $4.99 (0-380-79968-5). 246pp. Teenagers Jason and Sharon are "yanked" from the 1990s to the 2300s to help save some youngsters lost on an alien planet. (Rev: BL 9/1/99)

10206 Kurts, Charles. *These Are the Voyages: A Three-Dimensional Star Trek Album* (4–7). Illus. 1996, Simon & Schuster $35.00 (0-671-55139-6). Pop-ups are used to re-create the Starfleet ships, including the U.S.S. *Enterprise*. (Rev: BL 12/15/97)

10207 L'Engle, Madeleine. *A Wrinkle in Time* (6–8). 1962, Farrar $17.00 (0-374-38613-7); Dell paper $6.50 (0-440-49805-8). 224pp. A provocative fantasy-science fiction tale of a brother and sister in search of their father, who is lost in the fifth dimension. Newbery Medal winner, 1963. Also use: *Wind in the Door* (1973); *A Swiftly Tilting Planet* (1978); *A Ring of Endless Light* (1981).

10208 Levy, Robert. *Escape from Exile* (4–8). 1993, Houghton $16.00 (0-395-64379-1). 176pp. After being knocked unconscious by a strange bolt of lightning, Daniel wakes up in a strange land. (Rev: SLJ 5/93)

10209 Lisle, Janet T. *Angela's Aliens* (4–6). Series: Unknown. 1996, Orchard LB $15.99 (0-531-08891-X). 128pp. Angela is abducted by mysterious aliens in the fourth and final volume of the Unknown series. (Rev: BL 11/1/96; SLJ 11/96)

10210 Lowenstein, Sallie. *Evan's Voice* (5–8). Illus. 1998, Lion Stone paper $15.00 (0-9658486-1-2). 187pp. Teenager Jake cares for his catatonic younger brother while seeking civilization's last chance for survival in an area known as the Dead Zone. (Rev: BL 3/1/99)

10211 MacGrory, Yvonne. *The Secret of the Ruby Ring* (4–6). Illus. by Terry Myler. 1994, Milkweed paper $6.95 (0-915943-92-1). 192pp. A fantasy about a young Irish girl who time-travels to live in a nearby castle over a century ago. (Rev: BCCB 5/94; BL 3/1/94; SLJ 3/94)

10212 Mackel, Kathy. *Can of Worms* (4–7). 1999, Avon $14.00 (0-380-97681-1). 144pp. Mike Pillsbury, an alien, can't seem to solve his many problems on earth so he sends out an intergalactic cry for help in this entertaining science fiction adventure. (Rev: HB 5–6/99; HBG 10/99; SLJ 6/99)

10213 Mackel, Kathy. *Eggs in One Basket* (5–7). 2000, HarperCollins LB $14.89 (0-06-029213-X). 144pp. Scott Schreiber has hallucinations that lead him to a birdlike alien who is being watched by a dangerous race of conquerors. (Rev: BL 9/15/00; HB 9–10/00; HBG 3/01; SLJ 11/00)

10214 Mahy, Margaret. *Raging Robots and Unruly Uncles* (4–6). Illus. by Peter Stevenson. 1993, Overlook $13.95 (0-87951-469-8). 94pp. Twin uncles — one bad, one good — are saddled with children they regard as unsatisfactory. (Rev: BL 3/1/93; SLJ 3/93)

10215 Matas, Carol, and Perry Nodelman. *A Meeting of the Minds* (5–9). 1999, Simon & Schuster $17.00 (0-689-81947-1). 208pp. Princess Lenora and fiance Prince Coren, strangers from a different universe, find themselves trapped in a shopping mall. (Rev: BL 12/1/99; HBG 3/00; SLJ 11/99)

10216 Morris, Gilbert. *The Dangerous Voyage* (4–6). Series: Time Navigators. 1995, Bethany paper $5.99 (1-55661-395-4). 160pp. In order to help their ailing young brother, twins Danny and Dixie volunteer to travel through time in this book, the first of the series. (Rev: BL 1/1–15/96; SLJ 1/96)

10217 Mould, Chris. *Frankenstein* (4–7). Illus. 1998, Oxford $16.95 (0-19-279020-X). 32pp. Using a cartoon style, this is a retelling of Mary Shelley's thriller about the creation of a lonely, misunderstood monster. (Rev: BL 9/1/98; HBG 10/98)

10218 Orr, Wendy. *A Light in Space* (5–6). Series: Young Novels. 1994, Annick paper $5.95 (1-55037-975-5). 188pp. Andrew makes contact with a space alien who plans to use Earth as a colony for her people. (Rev: SLJ 2/95)

10219 Paulsen, Gary. *The Transall Saga* (5–7). 1998, Delacorte $15.95 (0-385-32196-1). 248pp. Mark is involved in a series of time-warp adventures before he decides to stay in the 1990s. (Rev: BCCB 7–8/98; HBG 10/98; SLJ 5/98)

10220 Peck, Richard. *The Great Interactive Dream Machine* (4–6). 1996, Dial $14.99 (0-8037-1989-2). 160pp. In this sequel to *Lost in Cyberspace* (1995), Josh and his friend Aaron travel again through time and space. (Rev: BCCB 9/96; BL 9/1/96; SLJ 9/96)

10221 Philbrick, Rodman. *REM World* (4–6). 2000, Scholastic $16.95 (0-439-08362-1). 192pp. Ten-year-old Arthur gets stuck in the REM world when he tries to use a REM sleep machine to lose weight.

(Rev: BCCB 6/00; BL 5/1/00; HBG 10/00; SLJ 5/00)

10222 Pinkwater, Daniel. *Borgel* (5–7). 1990, Macmillan LB $15.00 (0-02-774671-2). 160pp. An unusual visitor takes young Melvin on a trip to the stars. (Rev: BCCB 7–8/90; BL 5/1/90; SLJ 3/90)

10223 Pinkwater, Daniel. *Mush, a Dog from Space* (2–5). Illus. 1995, Simon & Schuster $15.00 (0-689-80317-6). 40pp. In spite of her parents, Kelly is determined to keep the dog from outer space that she has found. (Rev: BL 10/1/95; HB 11–12/95; SLJ 11/95)

10224 Pinkwater, Daniel. *Ned Feldman, Space Pirate* (3–5). Illus. 1994, Macmillan paper $14.95 (0-02-774633-X). 48pp. Captain Bugbeard takes Ned on a galactic trip to a planet where giant chickens live. (Rev: BCCB 10/94; BL 11/1/94; SLJ 12/94)

10225 Pinkwater, Daniel. *Wallpaper from Space* (2–4). Illus. by Jill Pinkwater. 1996, Simon & Schuster $15.00 (0-689-80764-3). 32pp. A spaceship on Steven's new wallpaper takes him on a zany space trip. (Rev: BCCB 10/96; BL 9/1/96; SLJ 10/96)

10226 Regan, Dian C. *Monsters in Cyberspace* (4–6). Illus. 1997, Holt $14.95 (0-8050-4677-1). 178pp. A 13-year-old girl and her Monster of the Month enjoy running up bills surfing the Net. (Rev: BCCB 7–8/97; BL 6/1–15/97; SLJ 9/97)

10227 Regan, Dian C. *Princess Nevermore* (5–7). 1995, Scholastic $14.95 (0-590-47582-6). 232pp. A princess from another world gets her wish to visit Earth, where she is befriended by two teenagers, Sarah and Adam. (Rev: BCCB 11/95; SLJ 9/95)

10228 Rodda, Emily. *Finders Keepers* (4–7). Illus. by Noela Young. 1991, Greenwillow $12.95 (0-688-10516-5). 192pp. Patrick is transported onto the set of a quiz show in a parallel world beyond the "great barrier." (Rev: BCCB 12/91; BL 11/15/91; SLJ 8/91)

10229 Rubinstein, Gillian. *Under the Cat's Eye* (5–7). 1998, Simon & Schuster $16.00 (0-689-81800-9). 208pp. Jai is sent by his parents to a boarding school where the fiendish headmaster uses technology to steal the future of his pupils and deprive them of hope and a sense of purpose. (Rev: BL 8/98; HB 11–12/98; HBG 3/99; SLJ 10/98)

10230 Sadler, Marilyn. *Bobo Crazy* (2–4). Illus. by Roger Bollen. 2001, Random LB $11.99 (0-679-99249-9); paper $3.99 (0-679-89249-4). 93pp. This beginning chapter book set on a space station in 2049 tells of a girl who wants a robot dog for a pet like her friends have. (Rev: SLJ 2/01)

10231 Scieszka, Jon. *See You Later, Gladiator* (4–6). Illus. 2000, Viking $13.99 (0-670-89340-4). 80pp. The three members of the Time Warp Trio travel back to ancient Rome, where they attend gladiator school and fight in the Colosseum in this hilarious spoof. (Rev: BL 1/1–15/01; HBG 3/01; SLJ 11/00)

10232 Scrimger, Richard. *A Nose for Adventure* (3–6). 2001, Tundra paper $6.95 (0-88776-499-1). 184pp. After meeting on a plane to New York City,

13-year-old Alan and sassy, wheelchair-bound Frieda get involved in a smuggling plot at the airport and encounter Norbert, a small alien from Jupiter. (Rev: BL 2/15/01)

10233 Service, Pamela F. *Stinker from Space* (3–6). 1988, Macmillan $12.95 (0-684-18910-1); Fawcett paper $5.50 (0-449-70330-4). 96pp. When his spaceship crashes to earth, Tsyng Tyr from the Sylon Confederacy takes over the body of a skunk. (Rev: BL 3/1/88; HB 9–10/88)

10234 Service, Pamela F. *Stinker's Return* (4–6). 1993, Macmillan $12.95 (0-684-19542-9). 96pp. In this sequel to *Stinker from Space* (1990), alien Tsyng Yr again returns to earth as a skunk, and with Jonathan and Karen has many adventures in Washington, D.C. (Rev: BCCB 6/93; BL 4/1/93; SLJ 5/93)

10235 Sheldon, Dyan. *Harry the Explorer* (4–6). Illus. by Sue Heap. 1992, Candlewick $13.95 (1-56402-109-2). 80pp. Adventures of the girl Chicken and Harry, her cat, who is really a visitor from another planet. (Rev: BL 10/15/92; SLJ 9/92)

10236 Simons, Jamie, and E. W. Scollon. *Goners: RU1:2* (4–7). Illus. 1998, Avon paper $3.99 (0-380-79729-1). 149pp. In this science fiction comedy, four teenage aliens from the planet Roma time-travel to a modern-day high school. (Rev: BL 5/15/98)

10237 Simons, Jamie, and E. W. Scollon. *Goners: The Hunt Is On* (4–7). Illus. 1998, Avon paper $3.99 (0-380-79730-5). 150pp. Four alien teens from the planet Roma time-travel to Monticello to fetch Thomas Jefferson. (Rev: BL 5/15/98)

10238 Sleator, William. *Boltzmon!* (5–8). 1999, Dutton $15.99 (0-525-46131-0). 150pp. A subatomic particle transports Chris to an alternate universe where he must complete dangerous quests to prevent his own death on earth. (Rev: HBG 3/00; SLJ 11/99)

10239 Slote, Alfred. *My Robot Buddy* (4–6). Illus. by Joel Schick. 1975, HarperCollins paper $4.95 (0-06-440165-0). 80pp. For his tenth birthday, Jack's parents get him his very own Robot Buddy. Sequels are: *My Trip to Alpha I* (1978); *Omega Station* (1983).

10240 Sobol, Donald J. *My Name Is Amelia* (4–8). 1994, Atheneum $14.00 (0-689-31970-3). 128pp. Lisa is cast ashore on a strange island governed by a mad scientist with plans to inhabit a distant galaxy. (Rev: BCCB 2/95; BL 1/1/95; SLJ 1/95)

10241 Spinner, Stephanie, and Terry Bisson. *Be First in the Universe* (4–6). 2000, Delacorte $14.95 (0-385-32687-4). 135pp. While staying with their hippie grandparents, twins Tod and Tessa explore a mall and encounter two young aliens who are trying to save their planet. (Rev: BCCB 2/00; BL 1/1–15/00; HBG 10/00; SLJ 2/00)

10242 Standiford, Natalie. *Space Dog and the Pet Show* (3–4). Illus. by Kelly Oechsli. 1990, Avon paper $2.95 (0-380-75954-3). 76pp. A literate dog from outer space is entered into a competition by his new owner. Further adventures of Space Dog are found in *Space Dog in Trouble* (1991). (Rev: BL 12/15/90)

10243 Stevenson, Robert Louis. *The Strange Case of Dr. Jekyll and Mr. Hyde* (5–8). Illus. Series: Whole Story. 2000, Viking $25.99 (0-670-88865-6). 112pp. Using lively ink-and-watercolor illustrations, this book offers the complete text of the classic in an attractive format. (Rev: BL 5/1/00; HBG 10/00)

10244 Walsh, Jill Paton. *The Green Book* (4–7). Illus. by Lloyd Bloom. 1982, Farrar paper $3.95 (0-374-42802-6). 80pp. The exodus of a group of Britons from dying earth to another planet.

10245 Waugh, Sylvia. *Space Race* (4–6). 2000, Delacorte $15.95 (0-385-32766-8). 242pp. Thomas, a young alien, does not want to leave Earth to return to his native planet. (Rev: BCCB 7–8/00; BL 7/00; HB 7–8/00; HBG 3/01; SLJ 8/00)

10246 Wells, H. G. *The Time Machine* (3–5). Adapted by Les Martin. Illus. by John Edens. 1990, Random paper $3.99 (0-679-80371-8). 93pp. A clever adaptation of a classic science fiction story about a time traveler and his friends. (Rev: SLJ 4/91)

10247 Whitman, John. *Star Wars: The Death Star* (2–5). Illus. by Barbara Gibson. 1997, Little, Brown $15.95 (0-316-93592-1). 12pp. Action-packed science fiction is featured in this pop-up book. Also use *Millennium Falcon* (1997). (Rev: BL 12/15/97)

10248 Wismer, Donald. *Starluck* (6–8). 1982, Ultramarine $20.00 (0-89366-255-0). 186pp. Paul becomes a threat to the Emperor of the Three Hundred Suns.

10249 Yolen, Jane. *Commander Toad and the Voyage Home* (2–4). Illus. 1998, Putnam $15.99 (0-399-23122-6). 64pp. Anxious to get home, Commander Toad, aboard the *Star Warts*, unfortunately steers the spacecraft toward an unknown planet. (Rev: BL 11/1/98; HBG 3/99)

10250 *The Young Oxford Book of Aliens* (5–10). Ed. by Dennis Pepper. Illus. 1999, Oxford $22.95 (0-19-278155-3). 215pp. A collection of well-crafted stories by notable authors about a variety of aliens from the wicked to the kind. (Rev: BL 4/1/99)

Short Stories and Anthologies

10251 Baylor, Byrd. *I'm in Charge of Celebrations* (4–6). Illus. 1986, Macmillan $17.00 (0-684-18579-2). 32pp. Poetic prose about rainbows, cactus greens, and desert browns. (Rev: BL 11/1/86; HB 1–2/87)

10252 Bennett, William J., ed. *The Book of Virtues for Young People: A Treasury of Great Moral Stories* (4–6). 1995, Silver Burdett LB $16.95 (0-382-24923-2). 384pp. A book of readings organized under such themes as friendship, self-discipline, work, and honesty. (Rev: BL 8/95; SLJ 8/95) [808.8]

10253 Castor, Harriet, ed. *Ballet Stories* (4–6). Illus. 1997, Kingfisher $7.95 (0-7534-5073-9). 224pp. Fifteen stories (two from autobiographies) tell about the joys, sorrows, and conflicts that young people face when they study ballet seriously. (Rev: BL 7/97; SLJ 1/98)

10254 *Chicken Soup for the Kid's Soul: 101 Stories of Courage, Hope and Laughter* (4–7). Ed. by Jack Canfield and others. 1998, Health Communications paper $12.95 (1-55874-609-9). 396pp. A collection of inspiring true stories, some by well-known people, but mostly by children who sent them to the editors. (Rev: BL 9/1/98; HBG 3/99) [158.1]

10255 Clay, Julie. *The Stars That Shine* (4–7). Illus. 2000, Simon & Schuster $24.95 (0-689-82202-2). 112pp. This is an attractive collection of 12 inspirational short stories suggested by celebrities including Dolly Parton, LeAnn Rimes, and Willy Nelson. (Rev: BL 1/1–15/01; HBG 3/01; SLJ 12/00)

10256 Dahl, Roald. *The Roald Dahl Treasury* (4–6). Illus. 1997, Viking $35.00 (0-670-87769-7). 448pp. An omnibus volume that features a generous selection of excerpts from Dahl's novels, autobiographies, and poetry, all handsomely illustrated by well-known artists. (Rev: BL 12/1/97; HBG 3/98) [820]

10257 *Great Girl Stories: A Treasury of Classics from Children's Literature* (4–6). Ed. by Rosemary Sandberg. Illus. 1999, Kingfisher $18.95 (0-7534-5207-3). 160pp. A lavish gift book containing excerpts from 16 stories with central girl characters, including *Heidi, Anne of Green Gables,* and *The Great Gilly Hopkins.* (Rev: BL 10/15/99; HBG 3/00; SLJ 12/99)

10258 Highlights for Children, eds. *Ashanti Festival* (3–5). 1996, Boyds Mills paper $3.95 (1-56397-608-0). 96pp. Sixteen excellent short stories taken from the pages of *Highlights for Children.* (Rev: SLJ 1/97)

10259 Hurwitz, Johanna, ed. *Birthday Surprises: Ten Great Stories to Unwrap* (4–6). 1995, Morrow $16.00 (0-688-13194-8). 128pp. Ten short stories by such writers as Richard Peck and Ellen Conford deal with presents in containers that are empty. (Rev: BCCB 5/95; BL 4/15/95; SLJ 4/95*)

10260 Jennings, Paul. *Unreal! Eight Surprising Stories* (4–8). 1995, Puffin paper $3.99 (0-14-037577-5). 112pp. A good assortment of short stories from an Australian writer. (Rev: BCCB 9/91; BL 8/91; SLJ 12/91*)

10261 Kantor, Susan, ed. *One-Hundred-and-One African-American Read-Aloud Stories* (3–8). 1998, Black Dog & Leventhal $12.98 (1-57912-039-3). 416pp. This book includes folktales, excerpts from novels, biographies, and history books, plus a sampling of songs, poetry, and chants all about African Americans and their heritage. (Rev: SLJ 6/99)

10262 Macaulay, David. *Black and White* (2–6). Illus. 1990, Houghton $17.00 (0-395-52151-3). 32pp. With thought-provoking illustrations, four short stories are presented. Caldecott Medal winner, 1991. (Rev: BCCB 5/90; BL 4/1/90*; HB 9–10/90)

10263 *My Wish for Tomorrow: Words and Pictures from Children Around the World* (K–5). Illus. 1995, Morrow LB $15.93 (0-688-14456-X). 48pp. To celebrate the 50th birthday of the United Nations, this is a collection of writing and art by children ages 4 to 14 from around the world. (Rev: BL 10/15/95; SLJ 10/95)

10264 *Newbery Girls: Selections from Fifteen Newbery Award–Winning Books Chosen Especially for Girls* (4–8). Ed. by Heather Dietz. 2000, Simon & Schuster $18.00 (0-689-83931-6). 208pp. Fifteen chapters from Newbery winners and honor books that stand almost as short stories are reprinted in this interesting anthology for girls. (Rev: BL 11/1/00; HBG 3/01; SLJ 10/00)

10265 Speed, Toby. *Water Voices* (2–4). Illus. by Julie Downing. 1998, Putnam $12.99 (0-399-22631-1). 32pp. A group of verses that are riddles describing the nature of water in various places and situations. (Rev: BL 2/1/98; HBG 10/98; SLJ 4/98)

10266 Valgardson, W. D. *Garbage Creek and Other Stories* (4–6). Illus. 1997, Douglas & McIntyre $15.95 (0-88899-297-1). 132pp. These eight short stories deal with such themes as moving, poverty, absent fathers, and protecting nature. (Rev: BL 1/1–15/98)

Sports Stories

10267 Adler, C. S. *Winning* (5–8). 1999, Clarion $14.00 (0-395-65017-8). 160pp. Eighth-grader Vicky, who lacks self-esteem, doesn't challenge her tennis doubles partner, who she knows is cheating. (Rev: BCCB 10/99; HBG 3/00; SLJ 9/99)

10268 Alter, Judith. *Callie Shaw, Stable Boy* (4–6). 1996, Eakin $19.00 (1-57168-092-6). 188pp. During the Great Depression, Callie, disguised as a boy, works in a stable and uncovers a race-fixing racket. (Rev: BL 2/1/97; SLJ 8/97)

10269 Alvord, Douglas. *Sarah's Boat: A Young Girl Learns the Art of Sailing* (3–6). Illus. 1994, Tilbury $16.95 (0-88448-117-4). 44pp. Sarah learns how to sail from her grandfather and enters her *Bluejay* sloop in the Labor Day race. (Rev: BL 7/94)

10270 Armstrong, Jennifer. *Patrick Doyle Is Full of Blarney* (2–4). Illus. 1996, Random LB $17.99 (0-679-97285-4). 80pp. In the Hell's Kitchen section of New York City in 1915, Patrick Doyle secures access to a baseball diamond through his skill and the help of the Giants hitter Larry Doyle. (Rev: BCCB 4/96; BL 5/1/96; SLJ 8/96)

10271 Armstrong, Robb. *Runnin' with the Big Dawgs* (3–5). Illus. 1998, HarperCollins paper $3.99 (0-06-107067-X). 64pp. Twelve-year-old Patrick faces some ethical problems when he tries to join the coolest basketball team in town, the great Sky Walkers, led by their star, Dwayne "Dawg" Brewerton. (Rev: BL 9/1/98)

10272 Auch, Mary Jane. *Angel and Me and the Bayside Bombers* (2–4). Illus. by Cat B. Smith. 1989, Little, Brown $9.95 (0-316-05914-5); paper $2.95 (0-316-05915-3). 60pp. A poor soccer player, Brian bribes his way onto the team. (Rev: BL 1/15/90; HB 3–4/90; SLJ 3/90)

10273 Avi. *S.O.R. Losers* (5–7). 1984, Macmillan $15.00 (0-02-793410-1). 112pp. The most inept soccer team in the history of the South Orange River Middle School is formed.

10274 Barwin, Steven, and Gabriel David Tick. *Slam Dunk* (5–7). Series: Sports Stories. 1999, Orca paper $5.50 (1-55028-598-X). 88pp. An easy read about a junior high basketball team in Canada that goes coed and the problems that result. (Rev: SLJ 1/00)

10275 Bledsoe, Lucy Jane. *The Big Bike Race* (2–4). 1995, Holiday $15.95 (0-8234-1206-7). 80pp. Though disappointed that he did not receive the bike of his dreams for his birthday, Ernie trains for the Citywide Cup race. (Rev: BCCB 12/95; BL 10/1/95; SLJ 11/95)

10276 *The Blue Darter and Other Sports Stories* (4–6). 1995, Boyds Mills paper $3.95 (1-56397-446-0). 96pp. A collection of 11 sports stories from *Highlights for Children* that deals with various sports. (Rev: BL 10/1/95)

10277 Bo, Ben. *The Edge* (5–8). 1999, Lerner LB $14.95 (0-8225-3307-3). 139pp. Conflicted Declan is sent to a rehabilitation program in Canada's Glacier National Park, where he learns to snowboard and is drawn into a duel with the local champion. (Rev: BCCB 1/00; HBG 3/00; SLJ 1/00)

10278 Bowen, Fred. *The Final Cut* (4–7). Illus. by Ann Barrow. Series: AllStar Sport Story. 1999, Peachtree paper $4.95 (1-56145-192-4). 102pp. A fast-paced novel about four friends and their efforts to make the junior high school basketball team. (Rev: SLJ 7/99)

10279 Bowen, Fred. *Full Court Fever* (3–6). Illus. by Ann Barrow. Series: AllStar Sport Story. 1998, Peachtree paper $4.95 (1-56145-160-6). 103pp. Michael and the rest of the seventh-grade basketball team are fearful about the coming match against the eighth graders. (Rev: SLJ 12/98)

10280 Bowen, Fred. *On the Line* (4–7). Illus. by Ann Barrow. 1999, Peachtree paper $4.95 (1-56145-199-1). 103pp. A young boy learns about self-image and open-mindedness while trying to improve his foul shots in this novel about an eighth-grader and his basketball skills. (Rev: SLJ 4/00)

10281 Bowen, Fred. *Playoff Dreams* (3–5). Illus. 1997, Peachtree paper $4.95 (1-56145-155-X). 112pp. When Brendan begins to feel that he is the only salvation open to his baseball team, Uncle Jack steps in with some good advice. (Rev: BL 11/1/97; SLJ 3/98)

10282 Bowen, Fred. *T.J.'s Secret Pitch* (3–5). Illus. by Jim Thorpe. Series: AllStar Sport Story. 1996, Peachtree paper $4.95 (1-56145-119-3). 104pp. A young Little Leaguer copies the famous pitch of the legendary Truett "Rip" Sewell and achieves fame. (Rev: SLJ 7/96)

10283 Bowman, Crystal. *Ivan and the Dynamos* (4–6). 1997, Eerdmans $15.00 (0-8028-5087-1); paper $5.00 (0-8028-5090-1). 140pp. An 11-year-old boy is unhappy about being traded to a new hockey team, particularly when he learns that the coach is eccentric. (Rev: SLJ 9/97)

10284 Brooks, Bruce. *Billy* (4–8). Series: The Wolfbay Wings. 1998, HarperCollins LB $14.89 (0-06-027899-4); paper $4.50 (0-06-440707-1). 93pp. Billy, part of the Wolfbay Wings hockey team, wor-

ries that his overbearing father will refuse him permission to join the gang at the beach during summer vacation. (Rev: HBG 3/99; SLJ 7/98)

10285 Brooks, Bruce. *Boot* (4–7). Series: The Wolfbay Wings. 1998, HarperCollins LB $14.89 (0-06-027569-3); paper $4.50 (0-06-440680-6). 122pp. In this hockey story, a foster child named The Boot is reluctant to "hit" his opponents. (Rev: HBG 10/98; SLJ 3/98)

10286 Brooks, Bruce. *Cody* (4–6). Series: The Wolfbay Wings. 1997, HarperCollins LB $14.89 (0-06-027541-3); paper $4.50 (0-06-440599-0). 101pp. In this hockey story, Cody must defy his father, the coach, for the good of the team. (Rev: HBG 3/98; SLJ 12/97)

10287 Brooks, Bruce. *Dooby* (5–8). Series: The Wolfbay Wings. 1998, HarperCollins LB $14.89 (0-06-027898-6); paper $4.50 (0-06-440708-X). 120pp. Dooby, a member of a Peewee hockey team, the Wolfbay Wings, is upset when a girl is elected as captain of the team, a position he was hoping to get. (Rev: HBG 3/99; SLJ 2/99)

10288 Brooks, Bruce. *Prince* (5–8). Series: The Wolfbay Wings. 1998, HarperCollins LB $14.89 (0-06-027542-1); paper $4.50 (0-06-440600-8). 122pp. Prince, the only African American boy on the Wolfbay Wings hockey team, is pressured by his middle-school coach to give up hockey and take up basketball. (Rev: HBG 10/98; SLJ 6/98)

10289 Brooks, Bruce. *Reed* (5–8). Series: The Wolfbay Wings. 1998, HarperCollins LB $14.89 (0-06-028055-7); paper $4.50 (0-06-440726-8). 128pp. Reed, a member of the Wolfbay Wings hockey team, is considered a "puck-hog" and must learn to be more of a team player. (Rev: HBG 3/99; SLJ 2/99)

10290 Brooks, Bruce. *Shark* (5–8). Series: The Wolfbay Wings. 1998, HarperCollins LB $14.89 (0-06-027570-7); paper $4.50 (0-06-440681-4). 118pp. Shark is happy being the fattest, slowest member of the Wolfbay Wings hockey team until the hockey bug takes over. (Rev: HBG 10/98; SLJ 6/98)

10291 Brooks, Bruce. *Woodsie* (4–6). 1997, HarperCollins paper $4.50 (0-06-440597-4). 144pp. In this sports novel about the Wolfbay Wings Squirt A hockey team, Woodsie finds he is in a no-win situation. Also use *Zip* (1997). (Rev: BL 1/1–15/98; HBG 3/98; SLJ 12/97)

10292 Cadnum, Michael. *Heat* (5–8). 1998, Viking $15.99 (0-670-87886-3). 195pp. While Bonnie is recovering from a diving accident, she learns that her father has been arrested for defrauding his clients. (Rev: HBG 3/99; SLJ 9/98)

10293 Charbonnet, Gabrielle. *Competition Fever* (5–7). 1996, Bantam paper $3.50 (0-553-48295-5). 138pp. In this novel, rivalry between two girls endangers a team's chances of victory in gymnastics competitions. (Rev: BL 9/1/96; SLJ 6/96)

10294 Christopher, Matt. *Baseball Turnaround* (4–6). 1977, Little, Brown paper $4.50 (0-316-14264-6). 160pp. After Sandy has had a brush with the law, he tries to keep this part of his past a secret from his teammates. (Rev: BL 6/1–15/97; SLJ 8/97)

10295 Christopher, Matt. *The Captain Contest* (2–3). Illus. 1999, Little, Brown $13.95 (0-316-14169-0). 64pp. A soccer story in which 10-year-old Danny faces an unusual problem because he doesn't want to become the team captain. (Rev: BL 6/1–15/99; HBG 10/99; SLJ 8/99)

10296 Christopher, Matt. *The Catcher's Mask* (2–4). Illus. Series: Peach Street Mudders. 1998, Little, Brown $13.95 (0-316-14186-0). 64pp. Young Rudy Calhoun's catching skills seem to improve when he buys a used catcher's mask that he thinks might have belonged to Yogi Berra. (Rev: BL 10/1/98; HBG 10/98; SLJ 5/98)

10297 Christopher, Matt. *Center Court Sting* (3–5). 1998, Little, Brown $15.95 (0-316-14278-6). 160pp. Daren McCall, the star forward of his basketball team, alienates his teammates with his sharp tongue and hot temper. (Rev: BL 1/1–15/99; HBG 3/99; SLJ 1/99)

10298 Christopher, Matt. *The Comeback Challenge* (4–6). Illus. 1996, Little, Brown $15.95 (0-316-14090-2); paper $4.50 (0-316-14152-6). 160pp. Twelve-year-old Mark has problems with Vince, the captain of his soccer team. (Rev: BL 1/1–15/96; SLJ 1/96)

10299 Christopher, Matt. *Dirt Bike Racer* (3–5). Illus. by Barry Bomzer. 1986, Little, Brown paper $4.50 (0-316-14053-8). Ron finds a bike at the bottom of a lake and begins dirt bike racing. Another sports story from the same author is: *Dirt Bike Runaway* (1989).

10300 Christopher, Matt. *The Dog That Called the Pitch* (1–3). Illus. 1998, Little, Brown $14.95 (0-316-14207-7). 48pp. An easily read story about baseball, young Mike, his telepathic dog Harry, and the discovery that an umpire can also read minds. (Rev: BL 5/15/98; HBG 10/98; SLJ 9/98)

10301 Christopher, Matt. *The Dog That Pitched a No-Hitter* (2–4). Illus. by Daniel Vasconcellos. 1993, Little, Brown paper $3.95 (0-316-14103-8). 42pp. Mike's dog Harry has powers of ESP and helps Mike with his pitching game. (Rev: BL 5/15/88; SLJ 8/88)

10302 Christopher, Matt. *Hat Trick* (2–4). Illus. by Daniel Vasconcellos. Series: Soccer Cats. 2000, Little, Brown $13.95 (0-316-10669-0). 64pp. Stookie is determined to score three goals per soccer game regardless of the methods used. Also use *Secret Weapon* (2000), another soccer story by this author. (Rev: HBG 10/00; SLJ 4/00)

10303 Christopher, Matt. *The Hit-Away Kid* (2–5). Illus. 1988, Little, Brown paper $4.50 (0-316-14007-4). 55pp. Barry McGee, left fielder for the Peach Street Mudders, learns a lesson in sportsmanship and telling the truth. Two other baseball stories are: *Supercharged Infield* (1985); *The Spy on Third Base* (1988). (Rev: BCCB 5/88; BL 4/1/88; SLJ 5/88)

10304 Christopher, Matt. *The Hockey Machine* (3–5). Illus. 1986, Little, Brown $15.95 (0-316-14055-4); paper $4.50 (0-316-14087-2). 137pp. Thirteen-year-old Steve Crandall finds himself kidnapped and spirited away to a secluded camp

because of his hockey skills. (Rev: BCCB 12/86; BL 1/1/87)

10305 Christopher, Matt. *Mountain Bike Mania* (5–7). 1998, Little, Brown paper $3.95 (0-316-14292-1). 160pp. Will is at loose ends with no after-school activities until he becomes involved in a mountain bike club. (Rev: BL 2/1/99; HBG 10/99; SLJ 3/99)

10306 Christopher, Matt. *Operation Baby-Sitter* (1–4). Illus. by Daniel Vasconcellos. Series: Soccer Cats. 1999, Little, Brown $13.95 (0-316-13723-5). 56pp. A soccer story that is also a beginning chapter book in which 10-year-old Buddy discovers that his baby-sitter is a soccer fan. (Rev: HBG 10/99; SLJ 7/99)

10307 Christopher, Matt. *Penalty Shot* (3–5). Illus. 1997, Little, Brown $15.95 (0-316-13787-1); paper $3.95 (0-316-14190-9). 134pp. Kevin is thrown off the hockey team for bad grades but is determined to get back on. (Rev: BL 1/1–15/97; SLJ 2/97)

10308 Christopher, Matt. *Prime-Time Pitcher* (4–7). 1998, Little, Brown $15.95 (0-316-14215-8); paper $3.95 (0-316-14213-1). 138pp. Koby Caplin becomes arrogant about his winning streak on the baseball team and soon loses games because of his lack of teamwork. (Rev: HBG 3/99; SLJ 12/98)

10309 Christopher, Matt. *Red-Hot Hightops* (4–6). Illus. 1992, Little, Brown paper $4.50 (0-316-14089-9). 128pp. Shyness prevents Kelly from showing off her basketball skills or speaking to a boy she likes until she finds a pair of red sneakers in her locker. (Rev: BL 1/15/88)

10310 Christopher, Matt. *Return of the Home Run Kid* (4–7). Illus. by Paul Casale. 1994, Little, Brown paper $4.50 (0-316-14273-5). 176pp. In this sequel to *The Kid Who Only Hit Homers* (1972), Sylvester learns to be more aggressive on the field but gets criticism from his friends. (Rev: BL 4/15/92; SLJ 5/92)

10311 Christopher, Matt. *Roller Hockey Radicals* (3–7). 1998, Little, Brown $15.95 (0-316-13739-1); paper $3.95 (0-316-13675-1). 153pp. Kirby wants to play roller hockey with a gang of street kids but his parents object. (Rev: HBG 10/98; SLJ 10/98)

10312 Christopher, Matt. *Shortstop from Tokyo* (3–5). Illus. by Harvey Kidder. 1988, Little, Brown paper $3.95 (0-316-13992-0). Stogie feels resentment when a Japanese boy takes his place on the baseball team. Also from the same author and publisher: *The Kid Who Only Hit Homers* (1972); *The Fox Steals Home* (1985); *The Year Mom Won the Pennant* (1986); *No Arm in Left Field* (1987).

10313 Christopher, Matt. *Snowboard Maverick* (4–7). 1997, Little, Brown $15.95 (0-316-14261-1); paper $3.95 (0-316-14203-4). 152pp. Dennis overcomes his fears and begins snowboarding. (Rev: BL 4/1/98; HBG 3/98; SLJ 3/98)

10314 Christopher, Matt. *Soccer Halfback* (4–6). Illus. by Larry Johnson. 1985, Little, Brown paper $4.50 (0-316-13981-5). Everyone wants Jabber to play football, but his favorite sport is soccer.

10315 Christopher, Matt. *Soccer Scoop* (3–6). 1998, Little, Brown $15.95 (0-316-14206-9). 160pp. A soccer story in which the team's star goalie becomes the target of a series of unflattering cartoons. (Rev: BL 2/15/98; HBG 10/98; SLJ 5/98)

10316 Christopher, Matt. *Spike It!* (5–8). 1999, Little, Brown $15.95 (0-316-13451-1); paper $3.95 (0-316-13401-5). 147pp. Eighth-grader Jamie must adjust to her new stepsister, Michaela, and to the fact that she is planning on joining Jamie's volleyball team. (Rev: HBG 10/99; SLJ 6/99)

10317 Christopher, Matt. *Stranger in Right Field* (2–4). Illus. 1997, Little, Brown $13.95 (0-316-14111-9). 61pp. Alfie is afraid that a new player on his baseball team is being groomed to take his place. (Rev: BL 9/1/97; SLJ 10/97)

10318 Christopher, Matt. *Tennis Ace* (3–6). 2000, Little, Brown $15.95 (0-316-13519-4); paper $3.95 (0-316-13491-0). 116pp. Steve, 12, and his sister Ginny, 14, both play tennis, but Ginny is serious about her game and Steve is not. (Rev: HBG 10/00; SLJ 8/00)

10319 Cohen, Barbara. *Thank You, Jackie Robinson* (4–6). Illus. by Richard Cuffari. 1989, Scholastic paper $3.50 (0-590-42378-9). A memoir written by Sam about his friendship with an old man and his devotion as a boy to the Brooklyn Dodgers and Ebbets Field.

10320 Cooper, Ilene. *Choosing Sides* (4–6). 1990, Morrow $15.00 (0-688-07934-2). 224pp. Jonathan wants to quit the basketball team but does not want to disappoint his dad. (Rev: BCCB 9/90; BL 2/15/90; SLJ 5/90)

10321 Coy, John. *Strong to the Hoop* (2–5). Illus. 1999, Lee & Low $16.95 (1-880000-80-6). 32pp. In this basketball story, 10-year-old James is drafted to play with the older kids when one of their teammates hurts his ankle. (Rev: BL 12/15/99; HBG 10/00; SLJ 10/99)

10322 Curtis, Gavin. *The Bat Boy and His Violin* (3–5). Illus. by E. B. Lewis. 1998, Simon & Schuster $16.00 (0-689-80099-1). 32pp. In 1948 young Reginald heeds his father's orders and becomes batboy for the Dukes, a team in the Negro League, where he beguiles the players with his violin playing. (Rev: BL 6/1–15/98; HBG 10/98; SLJ 7/98)

10323 Drumtra, Stacy. *Face-Off* (4–8). 1992, Avon paper $3.50 (0-380-76863-1). 118pp. T.J. and his twin Brad become rivals both for friends and for status on the hockey team. (Rev: BL 4/1/93)

10324 Durant, Alan, sel. *Sports Stories* (5–9). Illus. by David Kearney. Series: Story Library. 2000, Kingfisher $14.95 (0-7534-5322-3). 221pp. A collection of 21 previously published short stories by well-known authors dealing with a variety of sports. (Rev: SLJ 11/00)

10325 Dygard, Thomas J. *Second Stringer* (5–8). 1998, Morrow $15.00 (0-688-15981-8). 174pp. Kevin, a second stringer, must learn confidence and earn the respect of his teammates when he takes over the school's football team after the star quarterback is injured. (Rev: HBG 3/99; SLJ 12/98)

10326 Farrell, Mame. *Bradley and the Billboard* (5–8). 1998, Farrar $16.00 (0-374-30949-3). 224pp. Brad Wilson, a precocious kid who plays amazing

baseball, finds a new life when he enters the modeling world. (Rev: BCCB 4/98; BL 7/98*; HB 7–8/98; HBG 10/98)

10327 Giff, Patricia Reilly. *Left-Handed Shortstop* (4–6). Illus. by Leslie Morrill. 1997, Bantam paper $3.99 (0-440-44672-4). 128pp. Walter tries everything possible not to play baseball.

10328 Greene, Stephanie. *Owen Foote, Soccer Star* (2–4). Illus. 1998, Clarion $14.00 (0-395-86143-8). 88pp. When Owen joins a local soccer team, he is not prepared for the powerhouse players he meets. A sequel to *Owen Foote, Second Grade Strongman* (1996). (Rev: BL 3/15/98; HB 5–6/98; HBG 10/98; SLJ 7/98)

10329 Hall, Donald. *When Willard Met Babe Ruth* (4–6). Illus. by Barry Moser. 1996, Harcourt $16.00 (0-15-200273-1). 48pp. A young New Hampshire farm boy and his father have a chance meeting with Babe Ruth. (Rev: BCCB 6/96; BL 3/15/96*; HB 9–10/96; SLJ 5/96)

10330 Heymsfeld, Carla. *Coaching Ms. Parker* (3–5). Illus. by Jane O'Connor. 1992, Macmillan LB $13.00 (0-02-743715-9). 96pp. Fourth-graders face the challenge of teaching Ms. Parker baseball in time for the faculty versus sixth-grade game. (Rev: BCCB 6/92; BL 6/15/92; SLJ 7/92)

10331 Holohan, Maureen. *Catch Shorty by Rosie* (4–8). Series: The Broadway Ballplayers. 1999, Broadway Ballplayers paper $6.95 (0-9659091-6-6). 160pp. Sixth-grader Rosie Jones devotes her time to organizing an all-girls football league while coping with a series of minor personal problems at home and school. (Rev: SLJ 3/00)

10332 Holohan, Maureen. *Everybody's Favorite* (4–6). Series: The Broadway Ballplayers. 1998, Broadway Ballplayers paper $6.95 (0-9659091-2-3). 107pp. Capable young Penny finds she is thrust into a position of responsibility when she and the Broadway Ballplayers (sports-loving neighborhood girls) try to earn money for a soccer camp. (Rev: BL 4/15/98)

10333 Holohan, Maureen. *Left Out* (4–6). Series: The Broadway Ballplayers. 1998, Broadway Ballplayers paper $6.95 (0-9659091-1-5). 160pp. The narrator, shy and nonacademic Rosie, tells about the summer she joined the All Star baseball team and encountered a coach who didn't want to give her a chance. (Rev: BL 4/15/98)

10334 Hughes, Dean. *Brad and Butter Play Ball* (2–4). Illus. by Layne Johnson. Series: Stepping Stone. 1998, Random LB $11.99 (0-679-98355-4); paper $3.99 (0-679-88355-X). 78pp. Brad's baseball game is dominated by his perfectionist dad, but it improves when he adopts the more casual approach of his friend Butter. (Rev: HBG 10/98; SLJ 6/98)

10335 Hughes, Dean. *End of the Race* (5–7). 1993, Atheneum $13.95 (0-689-31779-4). 160pp. Both Jared and his African American track team competitor, Davin, are pressured by their parents to win. (Rev: BL 11/1/93; SLJ 12/93)

10336 Hughes, Dean. *Home Run Hero* (3–6). Series: Scrappers. 1999, Simon & Schuster $14.00 (0-689-81925-0); paper $3.99 (0-689-81964-X). 119pp.

Conflicts within the Scrappers baseball team thrust Wilson, the team's catcher, into the center of the problem. (Rev: BL 6/1–15/99; HBG 10/99; SLJ 6/99)

10337 Hughes, Dean. *Now We're Talking* (3–6). Series: Scrappers. 1999, Simon & Schuster $14.00 (0-689-81927-7); paper $3.99 (0-689-81937-4). 117pp. Ollie, the pitcher for the Scrappers, announces his pitches before throwing them, which causes Gloria, a shortstop, to make fun of him. (Rev: HBG 10/99; SLJ 8/99)

10338 Hughes, Dean. *Play Ball* (3–6). Series: Scrappers. 1999, Simon & Schuster $14.00 (0-689-81924-2); paper $3.99 (0-689-81933-1). 123pp. Robbie and Trent must find seven more players, a coach, and a sponsor to enter their team in a summer baseball league. (Rev: BL 6/1–15/99; HBG 10/99; SLJ 4/99)

10339 Hurwitz, Johanna. *Baseball Fever* (3–6). Illus. by Ray Cruz. 1981, Morrow paper $3.95 (0-688-10495-9). 128pp. Mr. Feldman loathes baseball, but his son Ezra loves it.

10340 Johnson, Scott. *Safe at Second* (5–8). 1999, Putnam $16.99 (0-399-23365-2). 224pp. The story of the friendship between Paulie and Todd, their love of baseball, and what happens after Todd is hit during a game and loses an eye. (Rev: BL 6/1–15/99; HBG 10/99)

10341 Joosse, Barbara M. *The Losers Fight Back* (3–6). Illus. 1994, Clarion $15.00 (0-395-62335-9). 128pp. When the Bruisers, a losing soccer team, bribe Chuckie to join them, they find that he takes over their games. (Rev: BL 9/15/94; SLJ 11/94)

10342 Knudson, R. R. *Rinehart Lifts* (4–6). 1982, Avon paper $1.95 (0-380-57059-9). 88pp. A failure at all sports, Rinehart finds he can excel in weight lifting.

10343 Krensky, Stephen. *Louise, Soccer Star?* (2–4). Illus. 2000, Dial $13.99 (0-8037-2495-0). 80pp. Louise is sure she will be the star of this year's soccer team until she is upstaged by a newcomer who also happens to be sweet and likable. (Rev: BL 3/1/01; HBG 3/01; SLJ 1/01)

10344 Kroll, Steven. *New Kid in Town* (2–4). Illus. 1992, Avon paper $3.50 (0-380-76407-5). 80pp. Phil finally makes the Raymondtown Rockets baseball team, only to find his happiness threatened because his father may be transferred. (Rev: BL 3/15/92)

10345 Lynch, Chris. *Gold Dust* (5–8). 2000, HarperCollins LB $15.89 (0-06-028175-8). 208pp. Richard comes from a Boston working-class family and Napoleon is the son of a visiting professor from the Dominican Republic in this novel about friendship, baseball, and racial tensions. (Rev: BCCB 11/00; BL 9/1/00; HBG 3/01; SLJ 10/00)

10346 Mackel, Kathy. *A Season of Comebacks* (4–7). 1997, Putnam $15.99 (0-399-23026-2). 112pp. Molly is jealous of her sister Allie, who plays a better game of baseball than she does. (Rev: BCCB 4/97; BL 8/97; SLJ 7/97)

10347 Maifair, Linda Lee. *Batter Up, Bailey Benson!* (3–5). 1997, Zondervan paper $3.99 (0-310-20705-3). 64pp. Bailey faces jealousy problems when she finds that she is on a different baseball team than her friend Nicole. (Rev: BL 3/15/97)

10348 Maifair, Linda Lee. *Go Figure, Gabriella Grant!* (3–5). 1997, Zondervan paper $3.99 (0-310-20702-9). 64pp. Gabriella has problems budgeting her time when she takes up figure skating. (Rev: BL 3/15/97)

10349 Manes, Stephen. *An Almost Perfect Game* (4–7). 1995, Scholastic $14.95 (0-590-44432-8). 163pp. Jake and Randy enjoy visiting their grandparents each summer because all of them are avid baseball fans. (Rev: BL 6/1–15/95; SLJ 6/95)

10350 Marzollo, Jean. *Slam Dunk Saturday* (2–4). Illus. 1994, Random LB $11.99 (0-679-92366-7); paper $3.99 (0-679-82366-2). 79pp. Billy is nervous about the outcome of a basketball-shooting contest he has entered. (Rev: BL 1/1/95)

10351 Mathis, Sharon Bell. *Running Girl: The Diary of Ebonee Rose* (3–5). Illus. 1997, Harcourt $17.00 (0-15-200674-5). 64pp. Ebonee Rose, a star runner, looks forward to the All-City Track Meet. (Rev: BL 9/1/97; HBG 3/98; SLJ 10/97)

10352 Mazer, Abby. *The Amazing Days of Abby Hayes* (3–6). 2000, Scholastic paper $4.95 (0-439-14977-0). 144pp. Told in prose, journal entries, and drawings, this is the story of Abby Hayes, who tries without much success to shine at soccer. (Rev: BL 8/00)

10353 Myers, Walter Dean. *The Journal of Biddy Owens* (5–7). Series: My Name Is America. 2001, Scholastic $10.95 (0-439-09503-4). 142pp. A fictional journal that tells of the last year of the Negro Leagues, and of 17-year-old Biddy Owens and his involvement with the Birmingham Black Barons. (Rev: BL 2/15/01)

10354 Myers, Walter Dean. *Me, Mop, and the Moondance Kid* (5–7). Illus. 1988, Dell paper $4.99 (0-440-40396-0). 128pp. The efforts of T.J. and Moondance to get their friend Mop adopted. (Rev: BCCB 12/88; BL 2/1/89; SLJ 1/88)

10355 Patneaude, David. *Haunting at Home Plate* (4–7). 2000, Albert Whitman $14.95 (0-8075-3181-2). Twelve-year-old Nelson is amazed when mysterious instructions are left on the playing field in this baseball novel about a losing team that suddenly seems to be getting help from a ghost. (Rev: BCCB 11/00; BL 9/1/00; HBG 3/01; SLJ 9/00)

10356 Peers, Judi. *Shark Attack* (5–7). Series: Sports Stories. 1999, Orca paper $5.50 (1-55028-620-X). 74pp. An easily read story set in Canada, in which a young baseball player wants to impress his father but doesn't think he can ever reach his older brother's record. (Rev: SLJ 1/00)

10357 Ritter, John H. *Choosing Up Sides* (5–9). 1998, Putnam $15.99 (0-399-23185-4). 176pp. Jake is a great southpaw in baseball. But his father, a preacher, forbids him to use his left hand for pitching because he believes it is the instrument of Satan. (Rev: BCCB 6/98; BL 5/1/98; HBG 10/98; SLJ 6/98)

10358 Rivers, Karen. *Waiting to Dive* (4–6). 2001, Orca paper $6.95 (1-55143-159-9). 106pp. When her best friend breaks her back in a diving accident, Carly, 10, loses her desire to become a diving champion and sinks into grief and depression. (Rev: BL 3/1/01)

10359 Schnur, Steven. *The Koufax Dilemma* (4–6). Illus. 1997, Morrow $15.00 (0-688-14221-4). 192pp. Danny faces problems because of his parents' divorce and the fact that his mother won't let him play baseball in the big game on Passover. (Rev: BCCB 5/97; BL 3/15/97; SLJ 5/97)

10360 Scholz, Jackson. *The Football Rebels* (5–7). 1993, Morrow paper $4.95 (0-688-12643-X). 256pp. Clint does his best on the intramural football team when he doesn't make the varsity. Also use: *Rookie Quarterback* (1993). Both are reissues.

10361 Shannon, David. *How Georgie Radbourn Saved Baseball* (1–5). Illus. 1994, Scholastic $14.95 (0-590-47410-3). 32pp. A rich and powerful wheeler-dealer decides to ban baseball, and it's up to young Georgie Radbourn to save it. (Rev: BL 1/15/94; SLJ 4/94*)

10362 Slote, Alfred. *Finding Buck McHenry* (4–6). 1991, HarperCollins LB $15.89 (0-06-021653-0). 256pp. Is Jason's baseball coach really the former great player he sees on a baseball card? (Rev: BCCB 5/91; BL 3/15/91; SLJ 5/91)

10363 Smith, Charles R. *Tall Tales: Six Amazing Basketball Dreams* (5–8). Illus. 2000, Dutton $15.99 (0-525-46172-8). 40pp. This book consists of six fantasy short stories about basketball. In one, for example, people find out that the best player in the neighborhood is blind. (Rev: BCCB 5/00; BL 3/1/00; HBG 10/00; SLJ 9/00)

10364 Spinelli, Jerry. *There's a Girl in My Hammerlock* (5–8). 1991, Simon & Schuster paper $14.00 (0-671-74684-7). 200pp. At 105 pounds, Maisie Potter is going out for junior high wrestling. (Rev: BCCB 9/91; BL 10/15/91; HB 9–10/91; SLJ 9/91*)

10365 Sullivan, Ann. *Molly Maguire: Wide Receiver* (4–6). 1992, Avon paper $2.99 (0-380-76114-9). 104pp. Molly wants to show a certain bully that she can play football, with the help of her next-door neighbor, who played for Notre Dame. (Rev: BL 10/1/92)

10366 Tamar, Erika. *Soccer Mania!* (2–4). Illus. by Dee deRosa. 1993, Random paper $3.99 (0-679-83396-X). 63pp. Pete and his friends are happy that parents are going to sponsor their soccer team, but they are dismayed at the rules they impose. (Rev: BL 9/15/93)

10367 Trembath, Don. *Frog Face and the Three Boys* (4–7). Series: Black Belt. 2001, Orca paper $6.95 (1-55143-165-3). 157pp. Three very different seventh-graders are enrolled in a karate class to teach them discipline. (Rev: BL 3/1/01)

10368 Tunis, John R. *The Kid from Tomkinsville* (5–8). 1990, Harcourt $14.95 (0-15-242568-3); paper $6.00 (0-15-242567-5). "Kid" Tucker's rookie year with the 1940 Brooklyn Dodgers. Other Tunis classics are: *Rookie of the Year; Keystone Kids* (both 1990). (Rev: BL 8/87)

10369 Wallace, Bill. *Never Say Quit* (5–7). 1993, Holiday $15.95 (0-8234-1013-7). 212pp. A group of misfits who don't make the soccer team decide to form one of their own. (Rev: BL 4/15/93)

10370 Walter, Mildren P. *Suitcase* (3–6). 1999, Lothrop $15.00 (0-688-16547-8). 112pp. Xander, a tall African American boy with great artistic talent, disappoints his father when he proves to be inept at basketball, but regains his affection as a star pitcher on the baseball team. (Rev: BCCB 10/99; BL 9/15/99; HB 11–12/99; HBG 3/00; SLJ 9/99)

10371 Walters, Eric. *Three on Three* (3–5). Illus. 2000, Orca paper $4.50 (1-55143-170-X). 122pp. Third-graders Nick and Kia, excellent basketball players, get the best player in school to join them for a 3-on-3 tournament, but unforeseen problems arise. (Rev: BCCB 6/00; BL 6/1–15/00)

10372 Webster-Doyle, Terrence. *Breaking the Chains of the Ancient Warrior: Tests of Wisdom for Young Martial Artists* (5–8). Illus. by Rod Cameron. 1995, Martial Arts for Peace paper $14.95 (0-942941-32-2). 176pp. A collection of karate parables and tests that promote ethical behavior, with accompanying follow-up questions for the reader and a message for adults. (Rev: SLJ 1/96)

10373 Wolff, Virginia E. *Bat 6* (5–9). 1998, Scholastic $16.95 (0-590-89799-3). 240pp. In this novel narrated by the members of the opposing teams, a Japanese American girl, who has just spent six years in an internment camp, meets a bitter girl whose father was killed at Pearl Harbor, and the two become rivals in baseball. (Rev: BCCB 6/98; BL 5/1/98*; HBG 10/98; SLJ 5/98)

10374 Zirpoli, Jane. *Roots in the Outfield* (5–7). 1988, Houghton $16.00 (0-395-45184-1). 133pp. Josh spends a summer with his newly married father in Wisconsin and discovers some baseball memorabilia that help him overcome his own fears and ineptness in right field. (Rev: BL 4/1/88; SLJ 5/88)

Fairy Tales

10375 Ada, Alma F. *The Malachite Palace* (PS–3). Trans. by Rosa Zubizarreta. Illus. by Leonid Gore. 1998, Simon & Schuster $16.00 (0-689-31972-X). 32pp. In this original Spanish fairy tale, an overly protected princess learns about freedom from a bird who flies into her room, and manages to set herself free. (Rev: BCCB 3/98; BL 5/15/98; HBG 10/98; SLJ 5/98)

10376 Allen, Debbie. *Brothers of the Knight* (K–3). Illus. by Kadir Nelson. 1999, Dial $15.99 (0-8037-2488-8). 40pp. Set in Harlem, this variation on *The Twelve Dancing Princesses* involves a clergyman's 12 sons who sneak out every night to dance. (Rev: BL 11/15/99; HBG 3/00; SLJ 10/99) [398.2]

10377 Andersen, Hans Christian. *The Emperor and the Nightingale* (K–6). Illus. by Meilo So. 1995, Simon & Schuster paper $10.95 (0-689-80363-X). This is a streamlined but very effective retelling of the Andersen tale. (Rev: SLJ 10/92)

10378 Andersen, Hans Christian. *The Emperor's New Clothes* (K–3). Retold by Anthea Bell. Illus. by Dorothee Duntze. 1986, North-South $16.95 (1-55858-036-0). 32pp. A formal, slightly oversize rendition of the famous tale. (Rev: BL 10/15/86; SLJ 1/87)

10379 Andersen, Hans Christian. *The Emperor's New Clothes* (1–3). Trans. by Naomi Lewis. Illus. by Angela Barrett. 1997, Candlewick $15.99 (0-7636-0119-5). 32pp. In this version of the Andersen tale, two con men persuade the emperor to order a magical suit that will expose the incompetence of those who can't see it. (Rev: BL 12/15/97; HB 11–12/97; SLJ 11/97*)

10380 Andersen, Hans Christian. *The Emperor's New Clothes* (1–2). Adapted by Sindy McKay. Illus. by Toni Goffe. Series: We Both Read. 1998, Treasure Bay $7.99 (1-891327-03-8). This adaption of the famous fairy tale contains a simple text for children to read on one page and, opposite it, the full text for parents. (Rev: SLJ 3/99)

10381 Andersen, Hans Christian. *The Emperor's New Clothes* (PS–3). Trans. by Rosemary Lanning.

Illus. by Eve Tharlet. 2000, North-South LB $15.88 (0-7358-1341-8). 32pp. Detailed, high-spirited illustrations are the highlight of this playful retelling of the Andersen tale. (Rev: BL 5/15/00; HBG 3/01; SLJ 10/00)

10382 Andersen, Hans Christian. *The Fir Tree* (2–4). Illus. by Bernadette Watts. 1990, North-South $14.95 (1-55858-093-X). 32pp. A large-format edition of the classic tale. (Rev: BL 1/1/91)

10383 Andersen, Hans Christian. *Hans Christian Andersen Fairy Tales* (1–5). Trans. by Anthea Bell. Illus. by Lisbeth Zwerger. 1992, Picture Book $19.95 (0-88708-182-7). 70pp. This is a collection of eight of Andersen's tales, some familiar, others not. (Rev: BL 11/15/92)

10384 Andersen, Hans Christian. *The Little Match Girl* (4–6). Illus. by Blair Lent. 1975, Houghton paper $1.95 (0-685-02294-3). The touching story of the lonely, shivering little match girl who sees visions in the flames of the matches she cannot sell.

10385 Andersen, Hans Christian. *The Little Mermaid* (K–3). Illus. by Rachel Isadora. 1998, Putnam $15.99 (0-399-22813-6). 32pp. A shortened version of the Andersen tale illustrated with dazzling Impressionistic paintings. (Rev: BCCB 7–8/98; BL 6/1–15/98; HBG 10/98; SLJ 8/98)

10386 Andersen, Hans Christian. *The Little Mermaid and Other Fairy Tales* (4–6). Ed. by Neil Philip. Illus. 1998, Viking $21.99 (0-670-87840-5). 144pp. An authentic retelling of some of Andersen's classic tales including "The Emperor's New Clothes" and the original "Little Match Girl." (Rev: BL 12/1/98; HBG 3/99; SLJ 4/99)

10387 Andersen, Hans Christian. *The Snow Queen* (K–3). Trans. and retold by Anthea Bell. Illus. by Bernadette Watts. 1987, North-South $14.95 (1-55858-053-0). 32pp. A large-format edition of this beloved fairy tale. (Rev: BL 11/1/87; SLJ 10/87)

10388 Andersen, Hans Christian. *The Steadfast Tin Soldier* (K–4). Retold by Tor Seidler. Illus. by Fred Marcellino. 1997, HarperCollins paper $5.95 (0-062-05900-9). 32pp. This version of the popular tale sticks to the traditional story and acknowledges the author. (Rev: BL 12/1/92*; HB 3–4/93; SLJ 2/93)

10389 Andersen, Hans Christian. *Stories from Hans Christian Andersen* (2–4). Retold by Andrew Matthews. Illus. by Alan Snow. 1993, Orchard $18.95 (0-531-05463-2). 96pp. Eleven popular Andersen fairy tales, like *The Steadfast Tin Soldier* and *The Little Mermaid*, are retold in a simplified, conversational manner. (Rev: SLJ 12/93) [398.2]

10390 Andersen, Hans Christian. *The Swan's Stories* (3–5). Trans. by Brian Alderson. Illus. by Chris Riddell. 1997, Candlewick $22.99 (1-56402-894-1). 144pp. A handsome, large-format book in which there are graceful retellings of 13 of Andersen's tales, some of which are widely known. (Rev: BL 12/15/97; HB 11–12/97; HBG 3/98; SLJ 9/97)

10391 Andersen, Hans Christian. *Thumbelina* (1–3). Trans. by Erik Haugaard. Illus. by Arlene Graston. Series: Children's Classics. 1997, Delacorte $16.95 (0-385-32251-8). 32pp. With captivating illustrations, this book includes the complete text of the engaging fairy tale. (Rev: BL 11/15/97; HBG 3/98; SLJ 9/97*)

10392 Andersen, Hans Christian. *Thumbeline* (PS–2). Illus. by Lisbeth Zwerger. 1986, Simon & Schuster $16.00 (0-88708-006-5). 28pp. Adventures of a girl no bigger than a thumb and her animal friends. (Rev: BL 1/1/86; SLJ 2/86)

10393 Andersen, Hans Christian. *The Tinderbox* (1–4). Illus. by Warwick Hutton. 1988, Macmillan paper $14.95 (0-689-50458-6). 32pp. The tale of a soldier and how power and prosperity come to him through a witch's tinderbox. (Rev: BL 10/1/88; HB 11–12/88; SLJ 12/88)

10394 Andersen, Hans Christian. *The Tinderbox* (PS–3). Retold by Peggy Tomson. Illus. by James Warhola. 1991, Simon & Schuster paper $14.95 (0-671-70546-6). A retelling that omits some of the violence but keeps the flavor of the tale. (Rev: BL 9/1/91; SLJ 11/91)

10395 Andersen, Hans Christian. *The Top and the Ball* (K–2). Illus. by Elisabeth Nyman. 1992, Ideals LB $15.00 (0-8249-8583-4). 32pp. In the 19th century, a wooden top loves a ball in a boy's toy box. (Rev: BL 10/15/92)

10396 Andersen, Hans Christian. *The Ugly Duckling* (PS–3). Illus. by Bernadette Watts. 2000, North-South LB $15.88 (0-7358-1389-2). The double-page illustrations are outstanding in this retelling of the Andersen classic. (Rev: BL 5/15/00)

10397 Balcells, Jacqueline. *The Enchanted Raisin* (3–6). Trans. by Elizabeth G. Miller. Illus. 1989, Latin American Literary Review Pr. paper $11.00 (0-935480-38-2). 103pp. Ten contemporary fairy stories by a noted Chilean writer for children. (Rev: BL 12/1/89)

10398 Banks, Lynne Reid. *The Fairy Rebel* (4–6). Illus. by William Geldart. 1989, Avon paper $4.50 (0-380-70650-4). 128pp. A modern-day fairy tale of a woman who wants to have a child and a fairy who grants her wish and offends the all-powerful fairy queen. (Rev: BL 12/1/88; SLJ 10/88)

10399 Barber, Antonia. *Catkin* (K–3). Illus. by P. J. Lynch. 1994, Candlewick $17.99 (1-56402-485-7). 48pp. When Carrie is kidnapped by the Little People, her faithful cat sets out to find her in this modern fairy tale. (Rev: BL 1/1/95; SLJ 1/95) [398.2]

10400 Bazilian, Barbara. *The Red Shoes* (K–2). Illus. 1997, Whispering Coyote $15.95 (1-879085-56-9). 40pp. This attractive retelling of Andersen's story has been changed to make it less preachy and gory. (Rev: BL 11/1/97; HBG 3/98; SLJ 10/97)

10401 Berenzy, Alix. *A Frog Prince* (K–3). Illus. 1989, Holt $16.95 (0-8050-0426-2). 32pp. This classic tale is told from the frog's point of view. (Rev: BCCB 10/89; BL 12/1/89; SLJ 10/89*)

10402 Branford, Henrietta. *Prosper's Mountain* (PS–2). Illus. by Chris Baker. 2000, Trafalgar $19.95 (0-09-176636-2). 32pp. In this fairy tale, young Prosper is persecuted because he has grown wings and the villagers hate anyone who is different. (Rev: BL 8/00)

10403 Brown, Marc. *Arthur's Really Helpful Bedtime Book* (PS–2). Adapted by Stephen Krensky. Illus. by author. 1998, Random LB $15.99 (0-679-88468-2). 44pp. The characters from the Arthur books are featured in these retellings of ten classic stories including "The Princess and the Pea," "The Three Little Pigs," and "The Frog Prince." (Rev: SLJ 3/99)

10404 Campbell, Ann. *Once upon a Princess and a Pea* (PS–3). Illus. by Kathy O. Young. 1993, Stewart, Tabori & Chang $14.95 (1-55670-289-2). 32pp. In a modern version of this fairy tale, a runaway princess must prove her sensitivity. (Rev: BL 8/93)

10405 Cash, Rosanne. *Penelope Jane: A Fairy's Tale* (PS–3). Illus. by G. Brian Karas. 2000, HarperCollins $15.95 (0-06-027543-X). 32pp. Penelope Jane, a little fairy, causes trouble when she visits the school that her friend Carrie attends. (Rev: BL 6/1–15/00; HBG 10/00; SLJ 6/00)

10406 Charles, Veronika M. *The Crane Girl* (K–2). Illus. 1995, Orchard paper $6.95 (0-773-75718-X). 32pp. After she feels rejected by her parents, Yoshiko begs the cranes to transform her into one of them so she can fly away. (Rev: BL 5/1/93; SLJ 7/93)

10407 Climo, Shirley. *The Persian Cinderella* (PS–4). Illus. by Robert Florczak. 1999, HarperCollins LB $15.89 (0-06-026765-8). 32pp. In this Persian variation on the Cinderella story, the heroine, Settareh, has a pari — a kind of fairy — who lives in a blue jar and turns Settareh into a turtledove. (Rev: BL 7/99; HBG 10/99; SLJ 6/99) [398.2]

10408 Climo, Shirley, comp. and reteller. *A Pride of Princesses: Princess Tales from Around the World* (3–5). Illus. by Angelo Tillery. 1999, HarperTrophy paper $4.25 (0-06-442102-3). 96pp. Issued first as a picture book, these seven stories involving characters such as Psyche and a frog princess are now in a chapter-book format. Also use *A Serenade of Mermaids* (1999), which contains seven more stories from around the world. (Rev: SLJ 6/99)

10409 Coatsworth, Elizabeth. *The Cat Who Went to Heaven* (4–6). Illus. by Lynd Ward. 1990, Simon &

Schuster LB $17.00 (0-02-719710-7); Macmillan paper $4.99 (0-689-71433-5). 72pp. A charming legend of a Japanese artist, his cat, and a Buddhist miracle. Newbery Medal winner, 1931.

10410 Cole, Brock. *The Giant's Toe* (K–2). Illus. by author. 1986, Farrar paper $5.95 (0-374-42557-4). 32pp. A "revisionist" version of Jack and the Beanstalk, with a grandfatherly giant and a teeny boy. (Rev: BCCB 7–8/86; BL 8/86; SLJ 10/86)

10411 Craft, K. Y. *Cinderella* (2–4). Illus. 2000, North-South LB $15.88 (1-58717-005-1). 32pp. An exquisite version of Cinderella based on the Lang and Rackham text and accompanied by wonderful oil-over-watercolor paintings. (Rev: BCCB 11/00; BL 11/1/00*; HBG 3/01; SLJ 11/00)

10412 Curry, Jane L. *Little Little Sister* (K–3). Illus. by Erik Blegvad. 1989, Macmillan $12.95 (0-689-50459-4). A Thumbelina-size girl saves the day when she brings her brother back home. (Rev: BCCB 11/89; BL 12/1/89; HB 11–12/89; SLJ 11/89)

10413 Daly, Jude. *Fair, Brown and Trembling: An Irish Cinderella Story* (PS–2). Illus. 2000, Farrar $16.00 (0-374-32247-3). 32pp. This is the traditional Cinderella story but set in Ireland. The ugly stepsisters are called Fair and Brown and the heroine's name is not Cinderella but Trembling. (Rev: BCCB 7–8/00; BL 9/1/00; HBG 3/01; SLJ 9/00)

10414 Datlow, Ellen, and Terri Windling, eds. *A Wolf at the Door: And Other Retold Fairy Tales* (5–8). 2000, Simon & Schuster $16.00 (0-689-82138-7). 166pp. These are interesting variations on standard fairy tales that have been written in imaginative ways by well-known authors. (Rev: HBG 3/01; SLJ 8/00)

10415 Demi. *The Emperor's New Clothes* (PS–3). Illus. 2000, Simon & Schuster $19.95 (0-689-83068-8). 42pp. Employing a Chinese motif in the illustrations, this is a new, interesting, multicultural retelling of the Andersen tale. (Rev: BL 6/1–15/00; HB 5–6/00; HBG 10/00; SLJ 6/00)

10416 Doherty, Berlie. *Fairy Tales* (3–6). Illus. 2000, Candlewick $19.99 (0-7636-0997-8). 224pp. This retelling of 12 favorite tales, like those about Sleeping Beauty and Aladdin, is modern in language but true to the original stories. (Rev: BL 11/15/00; HBG 3/01; SLJ 10/00)

10417 Eisner, Will. *The Princess and the Frog: By the Grimm Brothers* (4–7). Illus. 1999, NBM $15.95 (1-56163-244-9). 32pp. A retelling of the familiar fairy tale in graphic-novel style. (Rev: BL 12/15/99; HBG 3/00) [398.2]

10418 Ernst, Lisa Campbell. *Goldilocks Returns* (K–2). Illus. 2000, Simon & Schuster $16.00 (0-689-82537-4). 40pp. Middle-aged Goldilocks tries to make up for the harm she did to the bears 50 years before, giving them a new lock for the door and some healthy food and redecorating for them. (Rev: BCCB 5/00; BL 4/1/00; HBG 10/00; SLJ 5/00)

10419 *Fairy Tales of Oscar Wilde* (5–8). Illus. by P. Craig Russell. 1992, Nantier $15.95 (1-56163-056-

X). 46pp. Cartoon art enlivens the retelling of two of Wilde's short stories. (Rev: BL 1/15/93)

10420 French, Vivian. *The Kingfisher Book of Fairy Tales* (4–6). Illus. 2000, Kingfisher $19.95 (0-7534-5223-5). 96pp. Seven standard fairy tales like "Jack and the Beanstalk," "Cinderella," and "Beauty and the Beast" are retold and accompanied by elegant illustrations. (Rev: BL 11/15/00; SLJ 1/01)

10421 French, Vivian. *The Thistle Princess* (K–3). Illus. by Elizabeth Harbour. 1998, Candlewick $16.99 (0-7636-0307-4). A king and queen open up their home to the children of their kingdom after the fairy child they have cared for dies. (Rev: HBG 3/99; SLJ 11/98)

10422 Goode, Diane. *Cinderella: The Dog and Her Little Glass Slipper* (K–3). Illus. 2000, Scholastic $15.95 (0-439-07166-6). 40pp. A tongue-in-cheek version of Cinderella in which all the characters are dogs. (Rev: BL 11/1/00; HBG 3/01; SLJ 9/00)

10423 Goode, Diane. *The Dinosaur's New Clothes* (PS–1). Illus. 1999, Scholastic $15.95 (0-590-38360-4). 40pp. This variation on the Andersen tale is set in the Palace of Versailles and features dinosaurs as characters. (Rev: BCCB 12/99; BL 11/15/99; HBG 3/00; SLJ 9/99)

10424 Grahame, Kenneth. *The Reluctant Dragon* (2–4). Illus. by E. H. Shepard. 1938, Holiday $14.95 (0-8234-0093-X); paper $6.95 (0-8234-0755-1). 58pp. Tongue-in-cheek story of a boy who makes friends with a peace-loving dragon. Another fine edition is: Illus. by Michael Hague (1983, Holt).

10425 Greaves, Margaret. *Sarah's Lion* (PS–3). 1995, Barron's paper $5.95 (0-812-09272-4). 32pp. A spirited princess rebels at always being staid and proper. (Rev: BL 12/1/92; SLJ 5/93)

10426 Gregory, Philippa. *Florizella and the Wolves* (4–6). Illus. by Patrice Aggs. 1993, Candlewick $14.95 (1-56402-126-2). 80pp. A princess adopts four orphaned wolf cubs, and eventually one of them saves her life. (Rev: BL 5/1/93; SLJ 5/93)

10427 Grimm Brothers. *The Frog Prince* (1–2). Adapted by Sindy McKay. Illus. by George Ulrich. Series: We Both Read. 1998, Treasure Bay $7.99 (1-891327-02-X). This fairy tale is retold twice — with an adult's and a child's vocabulary. (Rev: SLJ 12/98)

10428 Hautzig, Deborah. *Beauty and the Beast* (2–3). Illus. by Kathy Mitchell. 1995, Random LB $11.99 (0-679-95296-9); paper $3.99 (0-679-85296-4). 48pp. A simple version of this familiar fairy tale prepared for beginning readers. (Rev: BL 7/95) [398.2]

10429 Hayes, Sarah. *The Candlewick Book of Fairy Tales* (K–4). Illus. by P. J. Lynch. 1993, Candlewick $16.95 (1-56402-260-9). 92pp. Ten famous fairy tales from Perrault and the Grimm Brothers, like *Cinderella* and *Rapunzel,* are retold in an abridged format with attractive illustrations. (Rev: SLJ 12/93) [398.2]

10430 Helldorfer, M. C. *Cabbage Rose* (K–3). Illus. by Julie Downing. 1993, Macmillan $14.95 (0-02-743513-X). 32pp. Cabbage, a serving girl, is given a magic paintbrush that can bring to life everything it paints. (Rev: BL 2/1/93)

10431 Helldorfer, M. C. *Night of the White Stag* (K–4). Illus. by Yvonne Gilbert. 1999, Random $16.95 (0-385-32261-5). 32pp. In this fairy tale set in medieval times, young Finder helps an old, blind man in his quest for the mythical white stag. (Rev: BL 12/1/99; HBG 3/00; SLJ 11/99)

10432 Helldorfer, M. C. *Phoebe and the River Flute* (K–3). Illus. by Paul Hess. 2000, Doubleday $15.95 (0-385-32338-7). 32pp. In this fairy tale, Phoebe works in the king's aviary and sets a rare bird free, incurring the anger of the keeper but earning the love of a prince. (Rev: BL 3/1/00; HBG 10/00; SLJ 3/00)

10433 Hoffman, Mary. *The Barefoot Book of Brother and Sister Tales* (2–5). Illus. 2000, Barefoot $19.99 (1-84148-029-0). 63pp. An anthology of uplifting original stories about children who suffer hardships resulting from such problems as cruel queens, witches, and stepmothers. (Rev: BL 11/15/00; HBG 3/01; SLJ 1/01)

10434 Hopkins, Jackie Mims. *The Horned Toad Prince* (PS–2). Illus. by Michael Austin. 2000, Peachtree $15.95 (1-56145-195-9). 32pp. This breezy update of the fairy tale is set in the Southwest and features a frog who demands that the heroine feed him chili. (Rev: BCCB 7–8/00; BL 5/15/00; HBG 10/00; SLJ 4/00)

10435 Impey, Rose. *Read Me a Fairy Tale: A Child's Book of Classic Fairy Tales* (3–6). Illus. by Ian Beck. 1993, Scholastic $16.95 (0-590-49431-7). 128pp. A collection of 14 favorite fairy tales told in an informal style. (Rev: BL 1/15/94; SLJ 2/94)

10436 Isadora, Rachael, reteller. *The Steadfast Tin Soldier* (PS–2). Illus. by Rachel Isadora. 1996, Putnam $15.95 (0-399-22676-1). 32pp. After a series of adventures, a one-legged tin soldier returns home to his beloved ballerina in this story based on the Hans Christian Andersen's original. (Rev: BCCB 1/97; BL 4/15/96*; SLJ 4/96) [398.2]

10437 Jackson, Ellen. *Cinder Edna* (PS–3). Illus. by Kevin O'Malley. 1994, Lothrop $16.00 (0-688-12322-8). 32pp. Whereas Cinderella is a passive wimp, Cinder Edna is a spirited girl who mows lawns to make money so she can attend the ball. In this book, the two stories are told side by side. (Rev: BL 3/15/94; SLJ 4/94)

10438 Johnston, Tony. *Bigfoot Cinderrrrella* (K–4). Illus. by James Warhola. 1998, Putnam $15.99 (0-399-23021-1). 32pp. In this humorous backwoods version of Cinderella, Bigfoot Rrrrrella gets help from her beary godfather to roll Prince Bigfoot off his log and, thus, win his heart. (Rev: BL 12/1/98; HBG 3/99; SLJ 11/98) [398.2]

10439 Johnston, Tony. *The Cowboy and the Black-Eyed Pea* (PS–3). Illus. by Warren Ludwig. 1992, Putnam $15.99 (0-399-22330-4). 32pp. Farethee Well decides to try a reversal of the "princess and the pea" story to find a suitably sensitive husband. (Rev: BL 11/15/92; SLJ 12/92)

10440 Kroll, Steven. *Queen of the May* (PS–3). Illus. by Patience Brewster. 1993, Holiday LB $15.95 (0-8234-1004-8). 32pp. Sylvie becomes Queen of the May in spite of her meddling stepmother and stepsister. (Rev: BL 4/1/93; SLJ 7/93)

10441 Lamm, C. Drew. *The Prog Frince: A Mixed-Up Tale* (2–4). Illus. 1999, Orchard LB $17.99 (0-531-33135-0). 32pp. This is a humorous version of the fairy tale in which a prince is turned into a frog for loving a stable girl. (Rev: BCCB 2/99; BL 2/1/99; HB 3–4/99; HBG 10/99; SLJ 3/99)

10442 Lang, Andrew, ed. *Blue Fairy Book* (4–6). 1965, Dover paper $8.95 (0-486-21437-0). 390pp. A fine edition of this classic collection. There are 11 other "color" Fairy Books. Some are: *Green Fairy Book* (1965); *Yellow Fairy Book* (1966); *Grey Fairy Book; Orange Fairy Book; Red Fairy Book* (all 1968).

10443 Langton, Jane. *The Queen's Necklace: A Swedish Folktale* (3–5). Illus. by Ilse Plume. 1994, Hyperion LB $16.49 (0-7868-2007-1). 40pp. When a queen gives away pearls to help the poor, her cruel king demands her life. (Rev: BL 10/1/94; SLJ 10/94)

10444 Lattimore, Deborah N. *The Dragon's Robe* (K–3). Illus. 1990, HarperCollins $15.00 (0-06-023719-8). 32pp. A story about an orphan and a poor weaver set in 13th-century China. (Rev: BCCB 6/90; BL 4/1/90; SLJ 5/90)

10445 Levine, Gail C. *Cinderellis and the Glass Hill* (4–6). Illus. 2000, HarperCollins LB $8.89 (0-06-028337-8). 96pp. This humorous variation on the Cinderella story has as its central character a boy named Ellis who is ignored by his older brothers but eventually wins the princess Marigold. (Rev: BL 1/1–15/00; HBG 10/00)

10446 Levine, Gail C. *Ella Enchanted* (5–8). 1997, HarperCollins LB $15.89 (0-06-027511-1). 240pp. A spirited retelling of the Cinderella story in which Ella is finally paired with the Prince Charmant. (Rev: BCCB 5/97; BL 4/15/97*; HB 5/6/97; SLJ 4/97*)

10447 Levine, Gail C. *The Fairy's Mistake* (3–6). Illus. 1999, HarperCollins LB $8.89 (0-06-028061-1). 80pp. This is a reworking of a traditional fairy tale from France in which a fairy is disappointed in her evaluation of two sisters. (Rev: BCCB 5/99; BL 4/15/99; HB 5–6/99; HBG 10/99; SLJ 5/99)

10448 Levine, Gail C. *Princess Sonora and the Long Sleep* (4–6). Illus. Series: Princess Tales. 1999, HarperCollins LB $8.89 (0-06-028065-4). 96pp. This retelling of the *Sleeping Beauty* story involves Princess Sonora, who is so brilliant she reads books while having her diaper changed. (Rev: BCCB 10/99; BL 11/15/99; HBG 3/00; SLJ 10/99)

10449 Levine, Gail C. *The Princess Test* (3–6). Illus. 1999, HarperCollins LB $8.89 (0-06-028063-0). 80pp. In this variation on *The Princess and the Pea*, a blacksmith's daughter turns out to be more sensitive than a princess. (Rev: BL 4/15/99)

10450 Lewis, Naomi, reteller. *Elf Hill: Tales from Hans Christian Andersen* (K–3). Illus. by Emma C. Clark. 1999, Star Bright $17.95 (1-887734-70-8). 68pp. A straightforward retelling of nine tales from the familiar "The Princess and the Pea" to the unfamiliar "The Money-Box Pig." (Rev: SLJ 1/00)

10451 Lobel, Anita. *The Dwarf Giant* (1–3). Illus. 1996, Greenwillow $16.00 (0-688-14407-1); Morrow paper $4.95 (0-688-14408-X). 32pp. The life of a bored prince becomes more interesting when a dwarf arrives. (Rev: BCCB 4/91; BL 4/1/91)

10452 Lowell, Susan. *Cindy Ellen: A Wild Western Cinderella* (K–3). Illus. by Jane Manning. 2000, HarperCollins LB $16.99 (0-06-027447-6). 40pp. This version of the Cinderella story features a mean stepmother, a godmother with a six-gun, and a cowboy hero named Joe Prince. (Rev: BCCB 9/00; BL 5/15/00; HBG 10/00)

10453 McCaughrean, Geraldine. *My First Oxford Book of Stories* (2–4). Illus. by Ruby Green. 2000, Oxford $19.95 (0-19-278115-4). 96pp. A dozen of the most famous fairy tales, like "Little Red Riding Hood," are retold and illustrated with charming pictures. (Rev: BL 7/00; HBG 3/01; SLJ 9/00)

10454 MacDonald, George. *The Golden Key* (2–6). Illus. by Maurice Sendak. 1993, Farrar paper $6.95 (0-374-42590-6). 96pp. In this classic fairy tale, two young people search for a keyhole where their golden key will fit.

10455 MacDonald, George. *The Light Princess* (3–6). Illus. by Maurice Sendak. 1984, Farrar paper $5.95 (0-374-44458-7). 120pp. The story of the princess without gravity and the prince who saves her.

10456 MacDonald, George. *The Light Princess* (1–6). Adapted by Robin McKinley. Illus. by Katie T. Treherne. 1988, Harcourt $13.95 (0-15-245300-8). 44pp. A prince breaks the spell of a princess who has been deprived of gravity. (Rev: BL 7/88)

10457 MacDonald, George. *The Princess and the Goblin* (4–7). Illus. by Jessie Willcox Smith. 1986, Morrow $22.95 (0-688-06604-6). 208pp. Full-color edition of the 1920 classic about the princess who is protected by the goblins beneath the castle. (Rev: BL 10/15/86)

10458 MacDonald, Margaret Read. *The Old Woman Who Lived in a Vinegar Bottle: A British Fairy Tale* (PS–2). Illus. by Nancy D. Fowlkes. 1995, August House $15.95 (0-87483-415-5). 32pp. In this English folktale, a fairy discovers that there is no pleasing some people when she supplies better housing for an old woman who had been living in a vinegar bottle. (Rev: BL 10/1/95; SLJ 1/96) [398.2]

10459 McKinley, Robin. *The Door in the Hedge* (6–8). 1981, Greenwillow $15.00 (0-688-00312-5). 224pp. A sensitive retelling of four fairy tales.

10460 Mahy, Margaret. *The Chewing-Gum Rescue* (3–4). Illus. by Jan Ormerod. 1992, Overlook $19.95 (0-87951-424-8). 141pp. A collection of 11 short stories, most of which are fairy tales or contain elements of fantasy. (Rev: SLJ 2/92)

10461 Matthews, Caitlin. *The Barefoot Book of Princesses* (4–6). Illus. 1998, Barefoot $17.95 (1-901223-74-4). 64pp. In a collection of fairy tales from around the world, the reader meets a number of princesses (some familiar, such as Sleeping Beauty, others not) and their challenging situations. (Rev: BL 11/15/98; SLJ 11/98) [398.2]

10462 Maugham, W. Somerset. *Princess September and the Nightingale* (K–3). Illus. by Richard C. Jones. 1998, Oxford $16.95 (0-19-512480-4). 40pp. A fairy tale about a Siamese princess who grants freedom to a nightingale that is so unhappy in captivity that it is near death. (Rev: BL 11/15/98; HBG 3/99; SLJ 2/99)

10463 Melmed, Laura K. *The Rainbabies* (PS–2). Illus. by Jim LaMarche. 1992, Lothrop LB $15.93 (0-688-10756-7). 32pp. An elderly couple care for 12 teeny babies they find in the grass. (Rev: BL 11/1/92; HB 3–4/93; SLJ 12/92)

10464 Milne, A. A. *The Magic Hill* (PS–2). Illus. by Isabel Bodor Brown. 2000, Dutton $14.99 (0-525-46147-7). 32pp. Originally written in 1925, this is the charming tale of a princess named Daffodil who causes flowers to grow wherever she walks. (Rev: BL 4/1/00; HBG 10/00; SLJ 4/00)

10465 Minters, Frances. *Cinder-Elly* (K–3). Illus. by G. Brian Karas. 1994, Viking $15.99 (0-670-84417-9). 32pp. A present-day version of Cinderella, with the heroine living in New York City and her godmother changing a garbage can into a bicycle so that Elly can go to an important basketball game. (Rev: BCCB 4/94; BL 1/15/94; SLJ 6/94) [398.2]

10466 Mitchell, Adrian. *The Ugly Duckling: Hans Christian Andersen* (1–3). Retold by Adrian Mitchell. Illus. by Jonathan Heale. 1994, DK $14.95 (1-56458-557-3). 32pp. A retelling of the Andersen fairy tale that retains the quality of the original. (Rev: BL 7/94; SLJ 7/94)

10467 Murphy, Shirley Rousseau. *Wind Child* (K–4). Illus. by The Dillons. 1999, HarperCollins LB $15.89 (0-06-024904-8). 40pp. A romantic fairy tale about a lonely girl whose extraordinary weaving skills attract a prince who falls in love with her. (Rev: BL 6/1–15/99; HBG 10/99; SLJ 4/99)

10468 Nesbit, Edith. *Melisande* (K–3). Illus. by P. J. Lynch. 1989, Harcourt $13.95 (0-15-253164-5). 48pp. The fairies take their revenge when a royal family excludes them from the daughter's christening party. (Rev: BL 10/1/89*; HB 11–12/89; SLJ 1/90)

10469 Nikly, Michelle. *The Perfume of Memory* (3–7). Illus. by Jean Claverie. 1999, Scholastic $16.95 (0-439-08206-4). In this fairy tale, a young child uses various perfumes to restore the memory of the queen. (Rev: HBG 3/00; SLJ 11/99)

10470 Nones, Eric Jon. *The Canary Prince* (1–3). Illus. 1991, Farrar $16.00 (0-374-31029-7). 32pp. A princess is locked in a tower by her wicked stepmother in this little-known tale from Italy. (Rev: BL 8/91)

10471 Ogburn, Jacqueline K. *The Magic Nesting Doll* (PS–3). Illus. by Laurel Long. 2000, Dial $16.99 (0-8037-2414-4). 32pp. An original fairy tale set in Russia about a girl who inherits a set of nesting dolls with magical powers. (Rev: BL 9/15/00; HBG 3/01; SLJ 12/00)

10472 O'Neal, Shaquille. *Shaq and the Beanstalk: And Other Very Tall Tales* (K–4). Illus. by Shane

W. Evans. 1999, Scholastic $15.95 (0-590-91823-0). 80pp. A collection of fractured fairy tales that feature Shaq O'Neal and such characters as the Big Bad Wolf, the three bears, and a hen that lays golden basketballs. (Rev: HBG 10/00; SLJ 2/00)

10473 Opie, Iona, and Peter Opie, eds. *The Classic Fairy Tales* (4–8). Illus. 1992, Oxford paper $15.95 (0-19-520219-8). 256pp. Contains the earliest published text of these tales.

10474 Paterson, Katherine. *The Wide-Awake Princess* (2–5). Illus. 2000, Clarion $15.00 (0-395-53777-0). 48pp. The story of a princess who leaves her castle to find out about the common people in her kingdom and how they live. (Rev: BL 3/15/00; HBG 10/00; SLJ 7/00)

10475 Perrault, Charles. *Cinderella* (PS–3). Trans. by Anthea Bell. Illus. by Loek Koopmans. 1999, North-South LB $15.88 (0-7358-1052-4). 24pp. Delicate watercolors illustrate this charming retelling of the Cinderella story in which the protagonists are children. (Rev: BL 8/99; HBG 10/99)

10476 Perrault, Charles, reteller. *Cinderella, Puss in Boots, and Other Favorite Tales* (K–4). Trans. from French by A. E. Johnson. 2000, Abrams $24.95 (0-8109-4014-0). 163pp. A colorful, new translation of such Perrault favorites as "Little Red Riding Hood," "Puss in Boots," "Cinderella," and "Blue Beard." (Rev: HBG 10/00; SLJ 8/00)

10477 Philip, Neil, ed. *Christmas Fairy Tales* (4–6). 1996, Viking $19.99 (0-670-86805-1). 144pp. Twelve stories about Christmas and the spirit that it represents. (Rev: BL 9/1/96; SLJ 10/96*)

10478 Philip, Neil, ed. *The Fairy Tales of Oscar Wilde* (4–6). Illus. by Isabelle Brent. 1994, Viking $19.99 (0-670-85585-5). 144pp. A splendid edition of these fairy tales with two or three illustrations per story. (Rev: BL 12/1/94; SLJ 3/95)

10479 Pinkney, Jerry. *The Little Match Girl* (3–5). Illus. 1999, Penguin $16.99 (0-8037-2314-8). 32pp. A beautifully illustrated version of the tragic tale by Han Christian Andersen about the little girl who is sent out to sell artificial flowers and matches on New Year's Eve. (Rev: BL 10/15/99*; HBG 3/00; SLJ 10/99)

10480 Pinkney, Jerry. *The Ugly Duckling* (PS–3). 1999, Morrow LB $15.93 (0-688-15933-8). 40pp. Gorgeous double-page spreads are used in this handsome retelling of Hans Christian Andersen's classic story. (Rev: BCCB 3/99; BL 3/1/99*; HB 5–6/99; HBG 10/99; SLJ 5/99)

10481 Prokofiev, Sergei. *Peter and the Wolf* (1–4). Illus. by Barbara Cooney. 1986, Viking $19.99 (0-670-80849-0). 10pp. A three-dimensional celebration of the famous tale. (Rev: BL 6/1/86; SLJ 5/86)

10482 Pyle, Howard. *The Swan Maiden* (K–3). Illus. by Robert Sauber. 1994, Holiday LB $15.95 (0-8234-1088-9). 28pp. In this fairy tale, one of the king's sons discovers that a swan maiden is stealing pears from his father's pear tree. (Rev: BL 10/15/94; SLJ 1/95)

10483 Pyle, Howard. *The Wonder Clock: Or Four and Twenty Marvelous Tales* (4–6). Illus. by author. 1915, Dover paper $8.95 (0-486-21446-X). 319pp.

Tales for each hour in the day, told by figures on a clock.

10484 Rae, Jennifer. *Dog Tales* (1–3). Illus. by Rose Cowles. 1999, Tricycle Pr. $14.95 (1-58246-011-6). 28pp. Six fractured fairy tales are told using dogs as characters. One example is "The Doberman's New Clothes." (Rev: HBG 10/00; SLJ 12/99)

10485 Riggio, Anita. *Beware the Brindlebeast* (K–2). Illus. 1994, Boyds Mills $16.95 (1-56397-133-X). 32pp. A courageous old lady finds a cast-iron kettle that changes into the fierce Brindlebeast in this English fairy tale. (Rev: BL 9/15/94; SLJ 10/94) [398.2]

10486 Ringgold, Faith. *The Invisible Princess* (K–3). Illus. 1998, Crown LB $19.99 (0-517-80025-X). When slaves Mama and Papa Love give their daughter, the Invisible Princess, to the Great Lady of Peace for protection, they do not anticipate the wrath of their wicked plantation owner. (Rev: BCCB 3/99; BL 12/1/98; HBG 3/99; SLJ 12/98)

10487 Russell, P. Craig. *The Fairy Tales of Oscar Wilde, v. 3: The Birthday of the Infanta* (5–8). Illus. 1998, NBM $15.95 (1-56163-213-9). 32pp. A retelling of Wilde's fairy tale about the misshapen dwarf who dies of a broken heart over his love of a princess. (Rev: BL 4/1/99) [741.5]

10488 Sand, George. *The Castle of Pictures and Other Stories: A Grandmother's Tale*, Vol. 1 (4–6). Trans. by Holly Erskine Hirko. Illus. 1995, Feminist Pr. $22.25 (1-55861-091-X); paper $9.95 (1-55861-092-8). 176pp. Four fairy tales written in the 19th century by this distinguished French novelist for her grandchildren. (Rev: BL 5/15/95; SLJ 5/95)

10489 Sanderson, Ruth. *Papa Gatto: An Italian Fairy Tale* (4–6). Illus. 1995, Little, Brown $15.95 (0-316-77073-6). 32pp. A male cat advertises for a nanny to take care of his brood with mixed results. (Rev: BCCB 12/95; BL 12/1/95*; SLJ 10/95) [398.2]

10490 Sanderson, Ruth. *Rose Red and Snow White: A Grimms Fairy Tale* (1–3). Illus. 1997, Little, Brown $15.95 (0-316-77094-9). 32pp. A handsome edition of the Grimm Brothers' tale about two loving sisters, their enchanted forest, and the dwarf that brings evil into their lives. (Rev: BL 4/15/97; SLJ 5/97)

10491 San Jose, Christine, reteller. *Cinderella* (3–4). Illus. by Debrah Santini. 1994, Boyds Mills $15.95 (1-56397-152-6). This well-written, imaginative version of Cinderella is set in Manhattan during the Gay Nineties. (Rev: SLJ 9/94)

10492 San Jose, Christine, reteller. *The Emperor's New Clothes* (PS–3). Illus. by Anastassija Archipowa. 1998, Boyds Mills $15.95 (1-56397-699-4). 32pp. A new version of Andersen's familiar story in a large-format picture book with graceful watercolor pictures. (Rev: BL 4/1/98; HBG 10/98; SLJ 4/98)

10493 San Jose, Christine. *The Little Match Girl* (K–3). Illus. by Anastassija Archipowa. 1995, Boyds Mills $14.95 (1-56397-470-3). 32pp. A retelling of Andersen's fairy tale about the poor match girl who sees visions in the flames of her matches but dies alone in the snow. (Rev: BL 9/15/95; SLJ 11/95) [398.2]

10494 San Jose, Christine. *Sleeping Beauty* (K–3). Illus. by Dominic Catalano. 1997, Boyds Mills $14.95 (1-56397-636-6). 32pp. Dormouse characters are used in this successful retelling of the traditional fairy tale. (Rev: BL 10/15/97; HBG 3/98; SLJ 9/97) [398]

10495 San Souci, Robert D. *Cendrillon: A Caribbean Cinderella* (PS–3). Illus. by Brian Pinkney. 1998, Simon & Schuster $16.00 (0-689-80668-X). 40pp. An enchanting new version of the Cinderella story that is based on a French Creole tale and uses Martinique as its setting. (Rev: BCCB 1/99; BL 10/15/98; HB 11–12/98; HBG 3/99; SLJ 9/98) [398.2]

10496 San Souci, Robert D. *Cinderella Skeleton* (3–5). Illus. by David Catrow. 2000, Harcourt $16.00 (0-15-202003-9). 32pp. A macabre variation on the Cinderella story in which the heroine is a stick-figure skeleton who lives in Boneyard Acres and falls in love with Prince Charnel. (Rev: BCCB 10/00; BL 9/1/00; HB 9–10/00; HBG 3/01; SLJ 9/00)

10497 San Souci, Robert D. *Little Gold Star: A Spanish American Cinderella Tale. by* (2–4). Illus. 2000, HarperCollins LB $15.89 (0-688-14781-X). 32pp. Using a Southwestern setting, this Cinderella retelling involves Teresa, who tends the Holy Infant for Mary and is rewarded with the help she needs to marry her Prince Charming, Don Miguel. (Rev: BCCB 12/00; BL 10/1/00; HBG 3/01; SLJ 10/00)

10498 San Souci, Robert D., reteller. *The White Cat: An Old French Fairy Tale* (3–4). Illus. by Gennady Spirin. 1990, Orchard LB $17.99 (0-531-08409-4). 32pp. The retelling of the story of three princes who vie for their father's kingdom. (Rev: BCCB 11/90; BL 9/1/90; HB 11–12/90; SLJ 10/90)

10499 Scieszka, Jon. *The Frog Prince Continued* (1–4). Illus. by Steve Johnson. 1991, Viking $14.95 (0-670-83421-1). 32pp. After the princess and the former frog are married, he still keeps hopping about and wonders if he should change back into a frog. (Rev: BCCB 5/91; BL 6/1/91; HB 7–8/91; SLJ 5/91)

10500 Scott-Mitchell, Clare. *Cinderella* (PS–2). Illus. by Gordon Fitchett. 2001, Penguin $16.99 (0-8037-2577-8). 32pp. In this fresh version of Cinderella all the characters are animals, including the heroine, who is a black-and white cat. (Rev: BL 1/1–15/01; SLJ 2/01)

10501 Setterington, Ken. *Hans Christian Andersen's The Snow Queen* (3–5). Illus. by Nelly Hofer and Ernst Hofer. 2000, Tundra $16.95 (0-88776-497-5). 48pp. A secular retelling of the Andersen story illustrated with old-fashioned black-and-white silhouettes. (Rev: BL 12/15/00; SLJ 3/01)

10502 Sierra, Judy. *The Gift of the Crocodile* (PS–3). Illus. by Reynold Ruffins. 2000, Simon & Schuster $17.00 (0-689-82188-3). 40pp. This is an exotic version of Cinderella, set in the Spice Islands, with a river crocodile serving as Grandmother Croc-

odile, the fairy godmother. (Rev: BCCB 12/00; BL 1/1–15/01; HB 1–2/01; HBG 3/01; SLJ 11/00)

10503 Singer, Marilyn. *In the Palace of the Ocean King* (K–3). Illus. by Ted Rand. 1995, Simon & Schuster $15.00 (0-689-31755-7). 32pp. Roles are reviewed in this modern fairy tale about a gallant girl who dives to the Ocean King's realm to rescue her true love, a prince. (Rev: BL 7/95; SLJ 8/95)

10504 Spiegelman, Art. *Little Lit: Folklore and Fairy Tale Funnies* (4–9). Illus. 2000, HarperCollins $19.95 (0-06-028624-5). 64pp. In this presentation in graphic format, 15 different artists create brilliant variations on standard fairy and folk tales. (Rev: BL 1/1–15/01*; HB 9–10/00; HBG 3/01; SLJ 12/00)

10505 Stanley, Diane. *Rumpelstiltskin's Daughter* (K–4). Illus. 1997, Morrow $15.89 (0-688-14328-8). 32pp. Like her mother, Rumpelstiltskin's daughter must spin straw into gold, but her solutions to this problem are unique. (Rev: BCCB 7–8/97; BL 3/1/97I; SLJ 3/97*)

10506 *The Starlight Princess and Other Princess Stories* (4–8). Ed. by Annie Dalton. Illus. 1999, DK $19.95 (0-7894-2632-3). 110pp. Eight tales about princesses are featured, including old favorites like "Sleeping Beauty" and "The Princess and the Pea." (Rev: BL 2/1/00*; HBG 3/00; SLJ 1/00) [398.2]

10507 Steer, Dugald. *Just One More Story* (PS–2). Illus. by Elisabeth Moseng. 1999, Dutton $14.99 (0-525-46215-5). Several variations on standard fairy tales are included in this collection of stories that feature pigs as central characters (e.g., "The Ugly Piglet"), with each story appearing as a little booklet glued onto a double-page spread. (Rev: HBG 3/00; SLJ 11/99)

10508 Steig, Jeanne. *A Handful of Beans* (PS–3). Illus. by William Steig. 1998, HarperCollins $17.95 (0-06-205162-8). 144pp. Six favorite fairy tales, including *Rumpelstiltskin, Hansel and Gretel,* and *Jack and the Beanstalk,* are informally retold with cartoon-style drawings. (Rev: BL 11/15/98*; HB 1–2/99; HBG 3/99; SLJ 12/98)

10509 *Tales of Wonder and Magic* (5–8). Ed. by Berlie Doherty. Illus. 1998, Candlewick $21.99 (1-56402-891-7). 108pp. An elegantly illustrated anthology of ten fairy tales: nine traditional ones from many world cultures and one by the editor. (Rev: BCCB 6/98; BL 5/15/98; HBG 10/98; SLJ 7/98) [398.2]

10510 Thompson, Lauren. *One Riddle, One Answer* (K–3). Illus. by Linda S. Wingerter. 2001, Scholastic $15.95 (0-590-31333-5). 32pp. In this original fairy tale, a sultan's daughter gets permission from her father to a pose a riddle to each of her prospective husbands. (Rev: BL 2/1/01)

10511 Thurber, James. *Many Moons* (2–4). Illus. by Marc Simont. 1990, Harcourt $14.95 (0-15-251872-X). 48pp. A sick princess asks her father for the moon to help her get better. The original edition, illustrated by Louis Slobodkin, was the 1944 Caldecott Medal winner. (Rev: BL 9/15/90; HB 1–2/90*; SLJ 1/91)

10512 Thurber, James. *The White Deer* (6–7). Illus. by author. 1968, Harcourt paper $9.00 (0-15-696264-0). 115pp. Three princes, a princess, and magic occurrences in this modern fairy tale.

10513 Townley, Roderick. *The Great Good Thing* (4–6). 2001, Simon & Schuster $17.00 (0-689-84324-0). 216pp. In this fairy tale, all the characters, including heroine Princess Sophie, live in a book and only come to life when a Reader opens it. (Rev: BL 3/15/01)

10514 Treherne, Katie T., reteller. *The Little Mermaid* (1–5). Illus. by Katie T. Treherne. 1989, Harcourt $15.95 (0-15-246320-8). 48pp. A retelling of Andersen's familiar story of the mermaid who falls in love with a prince. (Rev: BL 1/1/90; SLJ 11/89)

10515 Vande Velde, Vivian. *The Rumpelstiltskin Problem* (4–6). 2000, Houghton $15.00 (0-618-05523-1). 116pp. After a criticism of the logic behind this famous fairy tale, the author presents six new versions of the tale that, supposedly, make more sense. (Rev: BCCB 2/01; HBG 3/01; SLJ 11/00)

10516 Wallis, Diz, reteller. *Something Nasty in the Cabbages* (2–6). Illus. by Diz Wallis. 1991, Boyds Mills $15.95 (1-878093-10-X). 32pp. This adaptation of the Chanticleer and the Fox story contains many new variations and stunning illustrations. (Rev: BCCB 2/92; SLJ 12/91)

10517 Waters, Fiona. *The Emperor and the Nightingale* (PS–3). Illus. by Paul Birkbeck. 2000, Bloomsbury $19.95 (0-7475-3559-0). 32pp. A fine retelling of this classic fairy tale with lavish illustrations and sensitive language. (Rev: BL 11/15/00; SLJ 1/01)

10518 Waters, Fiona. *Oscar Wilde's The Selfish Giant* (K–4). Illus. by Fabian Negrin. 2000, Knopf LB $17.99 (0-375-90319-4). 32pp. A simplified retelling of Oscar Wilde's tale of the giant who banishes children from his beautiful garden. (Rev: BL 12/15/99; HBG 10/00; SLJ 2/00)

10519 Wegman, William. *Cinderella* (PS–2). Illus. 1993, Hyperion $16.95 (1-56282-348-5). 38pp. The characters in this reworking of the Cinderella story are all dogs, but the story remains the same. (Rev: BCCB 7–8/93; BL 5/15/93; SLJ 4/93)

10520 Wells, Rosemary. *The Fisherman and His Wife* (K–3). Illus. by Eleanor Hubbard. 1998, Dial LB $15.89 (0-8037-1851-9). 32pp. The Grimm tale of the fisherman who regrets catching a wish-granting fish is transplanted to the fjords of Norway in this fine retelling. (Rev: BL 7/98; HBG 3/99; SLJ 8/98) [398.2]

10521 Wenzel, David, and Doug Wheeler. *Fairy Tales of the Brothers Grimm* (4–6). Illus. 1995, NBM $15.95 (1-56163-130-2). 48pp. Using a comic book format, some of the best-known tales of the Grimm Brothers are retold, with an emphasis on story-telling pictures. (Rev: BL 4/15/96) [398.2]

10522 Wilde, Oscar. *Happy Prince* (3–5). Illus. by Ed Young. 1992, Simon & Schuster paper $5.95 (0-671-77819-6). 32pp. The lovely story of the prince-statue and the swallow who gives his life for the Happy Prince. (Rev: BL 6/15/89)

10523 Wisniewski, David. *The Warrior and the Wise Man* (3–5). Illus. by author. 1989, Lothrop LB $15.93 (0-688-07890-7). 32pp. Twin sons of the emperor of Japan search for five magical elements of the world. (Rev: BL 5/1/89; HB 7–8/89; SLJ 4/89)

10524 Wood, Audrey. *Heckedy Peg* (PS–2). Illus. by Don Wood. 1987, Harcourt $16.00 (0-15-233678-8); paper $7.00 (0-15-233679-6). 32pp. Mother promises gifts to her seven children, all named for days of the week, taken from a 16th-century game still played in England. (Rev: BCCB 12/87; BL 9/15/87; SLJ 11/87)

10525 Yep, Laurence. *The Ghost Fox* (3–5). Illus. by Jean Tseng and Mou-Sien Tseng. 1994, Scholastic $13.95 (0-590-47204-6). 70pp. In this Chinese fairy tale, Little Lee must save his mother from a dangerous ghost fox that is stealing her soul. (Rev: BCCB 3/94; BL 11/15/93; SLJ 5/94)

10526 Yolen, Jane. *King Long Shanks* (PS–4). Illus. by Victoria Chess. 1998, Houghton $15.00 (0-15-200013-5). 32pp. A charming retelling of Andersen's *The Emperor's New Clothes* in which all of the characters are frogs. (Rev: BL 4/1/98; HBG 10/98; SLJ 6/98)

10527 Ziefert, Harriet, reteller. *The Princess and the Pea* (K–1). Illus. by Emily Bolam. Series: Easy-to-Read. 1996, Viking $13.99 (0-670-86054-9). An easy-to-read version of the classic fairy tale by Andersen about a supersensitive princess. (Rev: SLJ 8/96)

Folklore

General

10528 Adler, Naomi. *Play Me a Story: Nine Tales About Musical Instruments* (3–6). Illus. 1998, Millbrook LB $23.40 (0-7613-0401-0). 80pp. Beginning with the tale of the Pied Piper of Hamelin, this book contains nine stories about musical instruments from different countries, including a Native American story and a myth from ancient Greece. (Rev: BL 7/98; HBG 10/98; SLJ 4/98) [398]

10529 Batt, Tanya. *The Fabrics of Fairytale: Stories Spun from Far and Wide* (4–6). Illus. 2000, Barefoot $19.99 (1-84148-061-4). 80pp. This book contains seven retold folktales, each related to a different kind of fabric or an article of clothing, like silk brocade, a patchwork coat, or a feather cloak. Patchwork illustrations are reminiscent of a story quilt. (Rev: BL 11/15/00; SLJ 11/00) [398.23]

10530 *Bear Tales: Three Treasured Stories* (PS–1). Ed. by Vlasta van Kampen. Illus. 2000, Annick LB $18.95 (1-55037-619-5); paper $6.95 (1-55037-618-7). 40pp. Three bear stories are retold here, one from Czech sources, one from Russian, and one from Native American folklore. (Rev: BL 6/1–15/00; HBG 10/00; SLJ 10/00) [398.2]

10531 Beeler, Selby B. *Throw Your Tooth on the Roof: Tooth Traditions from Around the World* (PS–3). Illus. by G. Brian Karas. 1998, Houghton $16.00 (0-395-89108-6). 32pp. As well as some basic facts about teeth, this book outlines lost-tooth traditions from around the world, each of which makes placing the tooth under a pillow to get money from the tooth fairy seem very tame. (Rev: BCCB 11/98; BL 7/98; HBG 3/99; SLJ 9/98) [398]

10532 Bevan, Finn. *Beneath the Earth: The Facts and the Fables* (3–5). Illus. Series: Landscapes and Legends. 1998, Children's LB $20.00 (0-516-20954-X). 32pp. This work compares folktales about natural phenomena, such as volcanoes and underwater springs, with the scientific facts we

know today. (Rev: BL 1/1–15/99; HBG 3/99) [398.2]

10533 Bevan, Finn. *Cities of Splendor: The Facts and the Fables* (3–5). Illus. 1998, Children's LB $20.00 (0-516-20955-8). 32pp. Folktales associated with such fabled cities as Jerusalem and Mecca are retold and then compared with known facts about the cities. (Rev: BL 1/1–15/99; HBG 3/99) [291.3]

10534 Bini, Renata, reteller. *A World Treasury of Myths, Legends, and Folktales: Stories from Six Continents* (3–6). Trans. from Italian by Alexandra Bonfante-Warren. Illus. by Mikhail Fiodorov. 2000, Abrams $24.95 (0-8109-4554-1). 126pp. These brief retellings of tales from around the world cover many cultures and times; about one-quarter are from Native American sources. (Rev: HBG 3/01; SLJ 12/00) [398.2]

10535 Borlenghi, Patricia. *Chaucer the Cat and the Animal Pilgrims* (3–6). Illus. by Giles Greenfield. 2000, Bloomsbury $22.95 (0-7475-4491-3). 77pp. A group of animal pilgrims from around the world led by Chaucer the Cat from London tell folk tales on their way to honor Saint Francis at Assisi. (Rev: SLJ 1/01) [398.2]

10536 Brill, Marlene T. *Tooth Tales from Around the World* (K–2). Illus. by Katya Krenina. 1998, Charlesbridge LB $15.95 (0-88106-398-3); paper $6.95 (0-88106-399-1). 32pp. An outline of the many traditions and beliefs from around the world concerning lost teeth. For example, ancient Egyptians threw their teeth to the sun in the belief that the sun made teeth strong. (Rev: BL 7/98; HBG 10/98) [398]

10537 Caduto, Michael J. *Earth Tales from Around the World* (5–8). Illus. 1997, Fulcrum paper $17.95 (1-55591-968-5). 192pp. This collection of 48 folktales from around the world emphasizes respect for the natural world and explores humankind's relationship to the earth. (Rev: BL 4/1/98) [398.27]

10538 Carle, Eric. *Eric Carle's Treasury of Classic Stories for Children by Aesop, Hans Christian Andersen, and the Brothers Grimm* (2–4). Illus. by author. 1988, Orchard $24.95 (0-531-05742-9). 160pp. Familiar stories with Carle's distinctive mark. (Rev: BCCB 6/88; BL 3/1/88; SLJ 4/88) [398.2]

10539 Climo, Shirley. *King of the Birds* (PS–3). Illus. by Ruth Heller. 1991, HarperCollins paper $5.95 (0-06-443273-4). 32pp. The long-ago legend of how the birds chose a king. (Rev: BL 2/15/88; SLJ 8/88) [398.2]

10540 Climo, Shirley. *A Treasury of Mermaids: Mermaid Tales from Around the World* (4–8). Illus. by Jean Tseng and Mou-Sien Tseng. 1997, Harper-Collins $16.95 (0-06-023876-3). 80pp. A fine retelling of eight folktales from around the world about mermaids and other enchanted sea creatures. (Rev: BL 11/15/97; HBG 3/98; SLJ 10/97) [398.2]

10541 Cook, Joel. *The Rats' Daughter* (K–3). Illus. 1992, Boyds Mills $14.95 (1-56397-140-2). 32pp. The lovely daughter of a prominent rat family is torn between her parents' wishes and her love for a handsome rat boy. (Rev: BL 1/15/93; SLJ 5/93) [398.2]

10542 Cooling, Wendy. *Farmyard Tales from Far and Wide* (PS–2). Illus. by Rosslyn Moran. 1998, Barefoot $15.95 (1-901223-38-8). 48pp. Each of these seven folktales deals with common farmyard animals and comes from the folklore of a different country. (Rev: BL 11/1/98; SLJ 11/98) [398.2]

10543 Craig, Helen. *The Random House Book of Nursery Stories* (PS–2). Illus. 2000, Random $19.95 (0-375-80586-9). 96pp. Ten favorite folktales, among them "Little Red Riding Hood," "The Three Little Pigs," and "The Gingerbread Man," are retold with bright line drawings. (Rev: BL 12/1/00; HBG 3/01; SLJ 12/00) [398.2]

10544 Czarnota, Lorna MacDonald. *Medieval Tales That Kids Can Read and Tell* (3–6). Series: World Folktale Collections. 2000, August House $21.95 (0-87483-589-5); paper $12.95 (0-87483-588-7). 96pp. This collection of folk tales suitable for children to tell features such characters as Robin Hood, William Tell, Robert Bruce, Joan of Arc, and Beowulf. (Rev: HBG 10/00; SLJ 2/01) [398.2]

10545 dePaola, Tomie, ed. *Tomie dePaola's Favorite Nursery Tales* (PS–3). Illus. by Tomie dePaola. 1986, Putnam $24.95 (0-399-21319-8). 128pp. The artist's favorite childhood remembrances in an attractive package. (Rev: BCCB 2/87; BL 11/1/86; SLJ 1/87) [398.2]

10546 DeSpain, Pleasant, reteller. *Thirty-Three Multicultural Tales to Tell* (3–7). Illus. by Joe Shlichta. Series: American Folklore and Storytelling. 1993, August House paper $15.00 (0-87483-266-7). 126pp. An interesting international collection of folktales that span a number of subjects and moods. (Rev: SLJ 6/94) [398.2]

10547 Evetts-Secker, Josephine. *The Barefoot Book of Father and Son Tales* (3–6). Illus. 1999, Barefoot $19.95 (1-902283-32-5). 80pp. Father-son relationships are explored in this collection of folktales that includes the Daedalus-Icarus myth. (Rev: BL 4/1/99; SLJ 6/99) [398.27]

10548 Evetts-Secker, Josephine. *The Barefoot Book of Mother and Son Tales* (3–6). 1999, Barefoot $19.95 (1-902283-05-8). 80pp. Using colorful illustrations and a choice of tales from the world's folklore, this collection explores mother-son relationships. (Rev: BL 4/1/99; SLJ 6/99) [398.27]

10549 Forest, Heather. *Wisdom Tales from Around the World* (4–7). 1996, August House $27.95 (0-87483-478-3); paper $17.95 (0-87483-479-1). 160pp. Fifty fables, folktales, and myths from around the world. (Rev: BCCB 2/97; BL 3/1/97) [398.2]

10550 Forest, Heather. *Wonder Tales from Around the World* (4–6). Illus. 1995, August House paper $16.95 (0-87483-422-8). 160pp. A collection of 27 traditional stories, some familiar and others never anthologized before. (Rev: BL 11/15/95; SLJ 4/96) [398.2]

10551 Garner, Alan. *Once upon a Time: Though It Wasn't in Your Time, and It Wasn't in My Time, and It Wasn't in Anybody Else's Time . . .* (K–3). Illus. by Norman Messenger. 1993, DK $12.95 (1-56458-381-3). 32pp. Three traditional tales told with simplicity, with evocative watercolors. (Rev: BCCB 1/94; BL 12/1/93; SLJ 3/94) [398.21]

10552 Gibbons, Gail. *Behold . . . the Dragons!* (K–3). Illus. 1999, Morrow LB $15.93 (0-688-15527-8). 32pp. Drawing on the world's folklore, this book follows dragons through different cultures and times. (Rev: BL 5/1/99; HBG 10/99; SLJ 4/99) [398]

10553 Gilchrist, Cherry. *A Calendar of Festivals* (3–7). Illus. 1998, Barefoot $18.95 (1-901223-68-X). 80pp. This anthology includes folktales and stories for many of the major holidays celebrated annually around the world. (Rev: BL 9/15/98; SLJ 12/98) [394.2]

10554 Gilchrist, Cherry. *Stories from the Silk Road* (3–7). Illus. 1999, Barefoot $19.95 (1-902283-25-2). 80pp. Seven exotic folktales represent the culture and history of the countries along the fabled Silk Road that stretched from China to Persia. (Rev: BL 9/15/99; SLJ 11/99) [398.27]

10555 Gilchrist, Cherry. *Sun-Day, Moon-Day: How the Week Was Made* (3–5). Illus. by Amanda Hall. 1998, Barefoot $18.95 (1-901223-63-9). 80pp. Each day of the week is highlighted, with background information and a tale from Greek, Norse, Roman, Babylonian, and other folklore traditions. (Rev: SLJ 9/98) [398.2]

10556 Hamilton, Martha, and Mitch Weiss. *How and Why Stories: World Tales Kids Can Read and Tell* (5–10). Illus. 1999, August House $21.95 (0-87483-562-3); paper $12.95 (0-87483-561-5). 96pp. This excellent collection of 25 pourquoi (how and why) stories from around the world also contains a useful introduction on folklore plus tips on delivering each of the tales. (Rev: BL 5/15/00; HBG 3/00; SLJ 1/00) [398.2]

10557 Hamilton, Martha, and Mitch Weiss. *Noodlehead Stories: World Tales Kids Can Read and Tell* (3–5). Illus. 2000, August House $21.95 (0-87483-584-4); paper $12.95 (0-87483-585-2). 96pp.

Includes 23 humorous stories from around the world, with tips on effective delivery and general storytelling advice. (Rev: BL 2/15/01; SLJ 1/01) [389.2]

10558 Hamilton, Virginia. *A Ring of Tricksters: Animal Tales from North America, the West Indies, and Africa* (3–6). Illus. by Barry Moser. 1997, Scholastic $19.95 (0-590-47374-3). 112pp. This is a stunning collection of trickster tales, many from Africa and others that were adapted by slaves to reflect conditions in the West Indies and the United States. (Rev: BL 1/1–15/98; HBG 3/98; SLJ 11/97) [398.2]

10559 Hausman, Gerald, and Loretta Hausman. *Cats of Myth* (3–6). Illus. 2000, Simon & Schuster $19.95 (0-689-82320-7). 96pp. This is a fine collection of nine folktales about cats from many cultures and historical periods. (Rev: BL 12/15/00; SLJ 12/00) [398.24]

10560 Hausman, Gerald, and Loretta Hausman. *Dogs of Myth* (3–5). Illus. 1999, Simon & Schuster $19.95 (0-689-80696-5). 96pp. A picture book for older readers that contains 13 folktales about dogs, culled from world mythology and legend. (Rev: BL 11/1/99; HBG 3/00; SLJ 3/00) [398.24]

10561 Hodges, Margaret, ed. *Hauntings: Ghosts and Ghouls from Around the World* (5–8). Illus. by David Wenzel. 1991, Little, Brown $16.95 (0-316-36796-6). 144pp. Sixteen meaty retellings of stories of the supernatural. (Rev: BL 11/15/91; HB 11–12/91; SLJ 11/91) [398.2]

10562 Hoffman, Mary, reteller. *A First Book of Myths: Myths and Legends for the Very Young from Around the World* (K–2). Illus. by Roger Langton and Kevin Kimber. 1999, DK $9.95 (0-7894-3973-5). 48pp. This collection of folktales consists of retellings from different geographical areas including ancient Greece and Rome, America, Aztec Mexico, Australia, Egypt, and Japan. (Rev: HBG 10/99; SLJ 9/99) [398.2]

10563 Hoffman, Mary. *Sun, Moon, and Stars* (3–6). Illus. by Jane Ray. 1998, Dutton $22.50 (0-525-46004-7). 96pp. Facts and ancient lore about the sun, moon, and stars are combined in a gloriously illustrated book that retells folktales from around the world. (Rev: BL 11/1/98; HBG 3/99; SLJ 10/98) [398.26]

10564 Hoffman, Mary. *A Twist in the Tail: Animal Stories from Around the World* (K–3). Illus. by Jan Ormerod. 1998, Holt $18.95 (0-8050-5945-6). 68pp. Ten lively folktales about animals from such places as India, China, Malaysia, and Nigeria are included in this anthology. (Rev: BL 11/15/98; SLJ 11/98) [398.245]

10565 Holt, David, and Bill Mooney, eds. *More Ready-to-Tell Tales from Around the World* (4–10). 2000, August House $24.95 (0-87483-592-5); paper $14.95 (0-87483-583-6). 256pp. Well-known storytellers have chosen a total of 45 pieces that are certain crowd-pleasers. (Rev: SLJ 11/00) [398.2]

10566 Hutchinson, Duane. *The Gunny Wolf and Other Fairy Tales* (4–6). Illus. 1993, Foundation paper $6.95 (0-934988-29-3). 88pp. A total of seven folktales, including Tom Thumb and The Six Swans, are included in this collection. (Rev: BL 5/15/93) [398.2]

10567 Jaffe, Nina, and Steve Zeitlin. *The Cow of No Color: Riddle Stories and Justice Tales from Around the World* (5–8). Illus. 1998, Holt $16.95 (0-8050-3736-5). 160pp. A collection of folktales from around the world that deal with the theme of justice. (Rev: BCCB 12/98; BL 11/1/98; HBG 3/99; SLJ 12/98) [398.2]

10568 Kneen, Maggie. *"Too Many Cooks . . ." and Other Proverbs* (PS–3). Illus. by author. 1992, Simon & Schuster $13.00 (0-671-78120-0). 32pp. Twenty-five proverbs, most of them familiar to older readers, are attractively presented. (Rev: BL 9/15/92; SLJ 10/92) [398.2]

10569 Krishnaswami, Uma. *Stories of the Flood* (4–6). Illus. 1994, Roberts Rinehart $15.95 (1-57098-007-1). 41pp. In a picture-book format, nine flood myths from such places as ancient Sumeria and Hawaii are retold. (Rev: BL 2/1/95; SLJ 2/95) [291.13]

10570 Lansky, Bruce, sel. *Girls to the Rescue: Tales of Clever, Courageous Girls from Around the World* (3–6). 1995, Meadowbrook Pr. paper $3.95 (0-88166-215-1). 100pp. A collection of stories about resourceful young women, many of which originated in the world's folklore. (Rev: SLJ 12/95) [398.2]

10571 Lansky, Bruce, ed. *Girls to the Rescue Book 2: Tales of Clever, Courageous Girls from Around the World* (3–6). 1996, Meadowbrook Pr. LB $3.95 (0-671-57375-6). 103pp. In each of the folktales gathered from around the world, young women must rely on their ingenuity to overcome obstacles. (Rev: SLJ 2/97) [398.2]

10572 Lottridge, Celia B. *Ten Small Tales* (PS–K). Illus. by Joanne Fitzgerald. 1994, Macmillan paper $15.95 (0-689-50568-X). 64pp. These simple folktales move quickly, have simple dialogue, and use rhyme and repetition effectively. (Rev: BCCB 5/94; BL 3/15/94; HB 1–2/94; SLJ 6/94) [398.2]

10573 Lupton, Hugh, reteller. *Tales of Wisdom and Wonder* (2–6). Illus. by Niamh Sharkey. 1998, Barefoot $18.95 (1-901223-09-4). 64pp. Seven traditional stories from different cultures, such as Haitian, Cree, West African, Russian, and Irish, are retold in this anthology. (Rev: SLJ 10/98) [398.2]

10574 McCaughrean, Geraldine. *The Bronze Cauldron* (5–6). Illus. 1998, Simon & Schuster $19.95 (0-689-81758-4). 144pp. Twenty-six myths and legends, such as the rise and fall of Faust, a Viking legend about the founding of London, and the story of Cupid and Psyche, are retold in this delightful collection. (Rev: BCCB 7–8/98; BL 5/15/98; HBG 10/98; SLJ 7/98) [398.2]

10575 McCaughrean, Geraldine. *The Crystal Pool* (4–5). Illus. 1999, Simon & Schuster $20.00 (0-689-82266-9). 144pp. A superior collection of folktales from around the world that includes creation myths, flood stories, and trickster tales. (Rev: BCCB 9/99; BL 5/15/99; HBG 3/00; SLJ 8/99) [398.2]

10576 McCaughrean, Geraldine. *The Silver Treasure: Myths and Legends of the World* (5–8). Illus.

by Bee Willey. 1997, Simon & Schuster paper $19.95 (0-689-81322-8). 144pp. A collection of 23 myths and legends, some well known, like *Rip Van Winkle*, and others unfamiliar, like a Bolivian legend on how the natives outsmarted their Spanish conquerors. (Rev: BCCB 6/97; BL 4/15/97; HBG 3/98; SLJ 4/97*) [398.2]

10577 McCaughrean, Geraldine. *Starry Tales* (3–6). Illus. 2001, Simon & Schuster $21.00 (0-689-83015-7). 112pp. From different cultures and countries, this is a collection of 15 stories that explain the existence of the sun, moon, and stars. (Rev: BL 2/15/01) [398.2]

10578 MacDonald, Margaret Read, comp. *Earth Care: World Folktales to Talk About* (3–7). 1999, Linnet LB $26.50 (0-208-02416-6); paper $17.50 (0-208-02426-3). 161pp. These 41 folk stories from 30 countries deal with humans and their relationship to nature. (Rev: HBG 3/00; SLJ 4/00) [398.2]

10579 MacDonald, Margaret Read. *Peace Tales: World Folktales to Talk About* (5–7). Illus. 1992, Shoe String LB $25.00 (0-208-02328-3); paper $17.50 (0-208-02329-1). 114pp. Stories and proverbs directed toward achieving world peace. (Rev: BL 6/15/92; SLJ 10/92) [398.2]

10580 Mama, Raouf. *The Barefoot Book of Tropical Tales* (3–5). Illus. 2000, Barefoot $19.95 (1-902283-21-X). 64pp. Backed up by extensive source notes, this book contains eight folktales that come from either African or Afro-Caribbean traditions. (Rev: BL 4/1/00; SLJ 9/00) [398.2]

10581 Martin, Rafe. *Mysterious Tales of Japan* (4–7). Illus. by Tatsuro Kiuchi. 1996, Putnam $19.99 (0-399-22677-X). 80pp. Ten haunting folktales about the spiritual powers in nature, such as the story of a priest who lived three days as a carp. (Rev: BL 3/15/96; HB 9–10/96; SLJ 4/96*) [398.2]

10582 Matthews, Andrew. *Marduk the Mighty and Other Stories of Creation* (4–6). Illus. by Sheila Moxley. 1997, Millbrook LB $22.40 (0-7613-0204-2). 96pp. A collection of 24 creation stories, beginning with Genesis and ending with a Norse myth about the fall of the gods. (Rev: BCCB 6/97; BL 6/1–15/97; SLJ 7/97) [291.1]

10583 Matthews, John. *Giants, Ghosts and Goblins* (4–6). Illus. 1999, Barefoot $19.95 (1-902283-27-9). 80pp. Nine stories of ghosts, some of them friendly, from such faraway places as Australia. (Rev: BL 10/15/99; SLJ 10/99) [398.2]

10584 Matthews, John, and Caitlin Matthews. *The Wizard King and Other Spellbinding Tales* (3–6). Illus. 1998, Barefoot $18.95 (1-901223-84-1). 80pp. An interesting collection of nine folk and fairy stories from around the world that feature dragons, monsters, spells, and wizards. (Rev: BL 10/15/98; SLJ 12/98) [398.2]

10585 Mayer, Marianna. *Iron John* (K–3). Illus. by Winslow Pels. 1999, Morrow LB $14.93 (0-688-11555-1). 40pp. Elements from traditional folk and fairy tales are used in this story of a young boy, Hans, who frees a wild man named Iron John and follows him like a son into an enchanted forest. (Rev: BL 9/1/99; HBG 3/00; SLJ 9/99) [398.2]

10586 Mayer, Marianna. *Women Warriors: Myths and Legends of Heroic Women* (4–7). Illus. 1999, Morrow $18.00 (0-688-15522-7). 80pp. Using stories from folklore as well as history, this book profiles 12 female warriors from around the world. (Rev: BCCB 10/99; BL 9/15/99; HBG 3/00; SLJ 9/99) [398]

10587 Mayo, Margaret, reteller. *Magical Tales from Many Lands* (3–6). Illus. by Jane Ray. 1993, Dutton $22.99 (0-525-45017-3). 128pp. A collection of 14 traditional tales, each from a different culture. (Rev: BL 11/1/93; SLJ 9/93) [398.2]

10588 Mayo, Margaret. *When the World Was Young: Creation and Pourquoi Tales* (4–7). Illus. by Louise Brierley. 1996, Simon & Schuster $19.95 (0-689-80867-4). 75pp. Age-old questions are answered in this collection of folktales that give explanations for natural phenomena. (Rev: BCCB 2/97; BL 9/1/96; SLJ 12/96) [398.2]

10589 Milord, Susan. *Bird Tales from Near and Far* (1–5). Illus. 1999, Williamson $14.95 (1-885593-18-X). 96pp. From many cultures, this collection of folktales about a variety of birds also contains factual information, projects, and crafts. (Rev: BL 2/15/99; SLJ 11/98) [398.2]

10590 Milord, Susan. *Tales Alive! Ten Multicultural Folktales with Activities* (4–6). Illus. 1995, Williamson paper $15.95 (0-913589-79-9). 128pp. This book contains 19 folktales plus such related material as riddles, puzzles, and craft projects. (Rev: BL 4/15/95; SLJ 3/95) [398.2]

10591 Milord, Susan, reteller. *Tales of the Shimmering Sky: Ten Global Folktales with Activities* (3–6). Illus. by JoAnn E. Kitchel. Series: A Williamson Tales Alive! Book. 1996, Williamson paper $15.95 (1-885593-01-5). 128pp. Ten folktales from different cultures explore such topics as the sky, wind, seasons, colors, and the weather, with additional background material and many suggested projects. (Rev: SLJ 2/97) [398.2]

10592 Minard, Rosemary, ed. *Womenfolk and Fairy Tales* (4–6). Illus. by Suzanna Klein. 1975, Houghton $18.00 (0-395-20276-0). 176pp. In each of these 18 stories, the female characters triumph because of wit, spunk, and courage. [398.2]

10593 Muten, Burleigh. *Grandmothers' Stories: Wise Woman Tales from Many Cultures* (3–5). Illus. 1999, Barefoot $19.95 (1-902283-24-4). 80pp. An anthology of folktales from around the world that portray older women in a favorable light. (Rev: BL 11/15/99; SLJ 3/00) [398.27]

10594 *Not One Damsel in Distress: World Folktales for Strong Girls* (3–6). Ed. by Jane Yolen. Illus. 2000, Harcourt $17.00 (0-15-202047-0). 112pp. A collection of folktales from such different locales as Argentina, Romania, and Germany in which girls face obstacles difficult to surmount. (Rev: BCCB 4/00; BL 3/1/00; HBG 10/00; SLJ 7/00) [398.22]

10595 Oram, Hiawyn. *Not-So-Grizzly Bear Stories* (3–4). 1998, Little Tiger $16.95 (1-888444-41-X). 96pp. An exciting retelling of ten folktales about bears from around the world. (Rev: BL 3/1/99; HBG 3/99; SLJ 4/99) [398.24]

10596 Osborne, Mary Pope. *Favorite Medieval Tales* (4–6). Illus. 1998, Scholastic $17.95 (0-590-60042-7). 96pp. A retelling of nine European folktales (e.g., a Robin Hood story, part of the French Roland saga, and tales from Ireland and Germany) from the Middle Ages in a handsome large-size edition with full-page paintings. (Rev: BL 5/1/98; HBG 10/98; SLJ 8/98) [398.2]

10597 Osborne, Mary Pope, ed. *Mermaid Tales from Around the World* (3–6). Illus. by Troy Howell. 1993, Scholastic $16.95 (0-590-44377-1). 96pp. Twelve stories about mermaids collected from the world's folklore. (Rev: BCCB 2/94; BL 10/15/93; SLJ 11/93) [398.21]

10598 *The Oxford Treasury of World Stories* (3–6). Ed. by Michael Harrison and Christopher Stuart-Clark. Illus. 1999, Oxford $25.00 (0-19-278144-8). 144pp. A collection of 23 traditional tales from around the world are included in this attractive volume. (Rev: BL 6/1–15/99; HBG 3/00; SLJ 5/99) [398.2]

10599 Pearson, Maggie. *The Fox and the Rooster and Other Tales* (K–3). Illus. by Joanne Moss. 1997, Little Tiger $14.95 (1-888444-17-7). 77pp. Fourteen countries — e.g., Norway, Japan, and Ireland — are represented in this collection of folktales. (Rev: BCCB 3/98; BL 2/15/98; HBG 10/98) [398.2]

10600 Pearson, Maggie. *The Headless Horseman and Other Ghoulish Tales* (4–7). Illus. 2001, Interlink $18.95 (1-56656-377-1). 96pp. From Bluebeard to Baba Yaga and Ichabod Crane, this is a collection of 14 tales about eerie beings. (Rev: BL 3/1/01; SLJ 1/01) [398.2]

10601 Peters, Andrew F. *Strange and Spooky Stories* (3–6). Illus. 1997, Millbrook LB $23.90 (0-7613-0321-9). 80pp. Nine unusual but appealing tales from North America, the British Isles, Central Europe, and the Czech Republic. (Rev: BL 2/1/98; HBG 3/98) [398.2]

10602 Phelps, Ethel Johnston. *The Maid of the North: Feminist Folk Tales from Around the World* (2–6). 1981, Holt paper $9.95 (0-8050-0679-6). 196pp. A collection of folktales from around the world. [398.2]

10603 Phelps, Ethel Johnston. *Tatterhood and Other Tales* (3–6). Illus. by Pamela Baldwin-Ford. 1978, Feminist Pr. paper $9.95 (0-912670-50-9). 192pp. Tales in which women play a vital and decisive role. [398.2]

10604 Pilling, Ann. *Creation: Read-Aloud Stories from Many Lands* (3–5). Illus. 1997, Candlewick $19.99 (1-56402-888-7). 96pp. A retelling of 16 creation stories that come from such sources as the Bible, Greek mythology, and Chinese and Norse folklore. (Rev: BL 9/1/97; HBG 3/98; SLJ 10/97) [291.2]

10605 Polacco, Patricia. *Babushka's Mother Goose* (PS–1). Illus. 1995, Putnam $18.99 (0-399-22747-4). 64pp. A retelling of the stories and legends told by a babushka (grandmother) to her granddaughter. (Rev: BL 10/15/95; SLJ 10/95) [398.8]

10606 Reneaux, J. J. *How Animals Saved the People* (4–8). Illus. 2001, HarperCollins LB $17.89 (0-688-16254-1). 64pp. Eighty lively, evocative folk tales are included in this anthology about a variety of animals and and their ingenious schemes. (Rev: BCCB 3/01; BL 2/15/01; SLJ 1/01) [398.2]

10607 Riordan, James. *The Storytelling Star: Tales of the Sun, Moon and Stars* (K–6). Illus. by Amanda Hall. 2000, Pavilion $19.95 (1-86205-202-6). 60pp. A collection of nine folktales each from a different culture including Norse, Inca, Greek, Chinese, Chippewa, Aztec, and Seneca. (Rev: SLJ 11/00) [398.2]

10608 Rosen, Michael J. *How the Animals Got Their Colors* (5–8). Illus. by John Clemenston. 1992, Harcourt $14.95 (0-15-236783-7). 48pp. Tales from around the world that explain such things as a leopard's spots and the green on a frog's back. (Rev: BCCB 7–8/92; BL 6/15/92; SLJ 9/91) [398.2]

10609 Rosen, Michael J., ed. *South and North, East and West: The Oxfam Book of Children's Stories* (K–8). Illus. 1992, Candlewick $19.95 (1-56402-117-3). 96pp. Around the world in 25 stories showing the lore and wisdom of the native peoples. (Rev: BCCB 12/92; BL 9/15/92; SLJ 12/92) [398.2]

10610 Sanderson, Ruth. *The Crystal Mountain* (2–4). Illus. 1999, Little, Brown $15.95 (0-316-77092-2). 32pp. Combining stories from both Chinese and Norwegian folklore, this tells of a beautiful woven tapestry and three men's quest to retrieve it after it is stolen. (Rev: BL 9/1/99; HBG 3/00; SLJ 10/99) [398.2]

10611 San Souci, Robert D. *Even More Short and Shivery: Thirty Spine-Tingling Stories* (5–8). Illus. by Jacqueline Rogers. 1997, Delacorte $14.95 (0-385-32252-6). 140pp. A collection of 30 scary stories, mostly folktales from around the world, that are great for reading or giving presentations before a group. (Rev: BL 7/97; HBG 3/98; SLJ 10/97) [398.2]

10612 Shannon, George. *Still More Stories to Solve: Fourteen Folktales from Around the World* (4–6). Illus. 1994, Greenwillow $15.00 (0-688-04619-3). 64pp. Each of these folktales from around the world also contains the answer to a riddle. (Rev: BL 10/1/94; HB 11–12/94; SLJ 9/94) [398.2]

10613 Shannon, George. *Stories to Solve: Folktales from Around the World* (4–6). Illus. by Peter Sis. 1985, Morrow paper $4.95 (0-688-10496-7). 56pp. Fourteen stories combine puzzles and folklore asking readers how the problem was figured out or the mystery solved. (Rev: BL 12/1/85; HB 9–10/85; SLJ 9/85) [398.2]

10614 Shannon, George. *True Lies: 18 Tales for You to Judge* (4–6). Illus. 1997, Greenwillow $15.00 (0-688-14483-7). 48pp. Short folktales are used to explore the various meanings of truth. (Rev: BL 5/15/97; HB 7–8/97; SLJ 6/97) [398.2]

10615 Sherman, Josepha. *Merlin's Kin: World Tales of the Heroic Magician* (5–8). 1998, August House $21.95 (0-87483-523-2); paper $11.95 (0-87483-519-4). 192pp. An international collection of folktales featuring heroic magicians. (Rev: BL 4/15/99; SLJ 3/99) [398.21]

10616 Sherman, Josepha. *Told Tales: Nine Folktales from Around the World* (4–6). Illus. 1995, Silver Moon LB $14.95 (1-881889-64-5). 80pp. A general introduction for beginning storytellers that uses a question-and-answer technique and supplies nine folktales from around the world. (Rev: BL 2/1/96; SLJ 1/96) [398.2]

10617 Shulevitz, Uri. *The Secret Room* (PS–2). Illus. 1993, Farrar $15.00 (0-374-34169-9). 32pp. A jealous chief counselor to the king tries to get rid of a wise old man who seems to be taking his place. (Rev: BCCB 2/94; BL 11/15/93; HB 1–2/93; SLJ 1/94) [398.2]

10618 Sierra, Judy, ed. *Nursery Tales Around the World* (4–6). Illus. by Stefano Vitale. 1996, Clarion $20.00 (0-395-67894-3). 114pp. This fascinating work retells folktales with similar themes as they exist in different cultures. (Rev: BCCB 2/96; BL 3/1/96; HB 5–6/96; SLJ 4/96) [398.2]

10619 Singh, Rina, and Debbie Lush. *Moon Tales: Myths of the Moon from Around the World* (3–6). 2000, Bloomsbury $22.95 (0-7475-4112-4). 77pp. A stylish retelling of folk tales from around the world dealing with the moon and its powers. (Rev: SLJ 3/01) [398.2]

10620 *The Songs of Birds: Stories and Poems from Many Cultures* (4–7). Ed. by Hugh Lupton. Illus. 2000, Barefoot $19.95 (1-84148-045-2). 80pp. A beautifully illustrated collection of stories (mostly creation myths) and poems about birds culled from a wide range of cultures. (Rev: BL 3/15/00; SLJ 9/00) [808.819]

10621 Thompson, Stith, ed. *One Hundred Favorite Folktales* (5–8). Illus. by Franz Altschuler. 1968, Indiana Univ. Pr. $39.95 (0-253-15940-7); paper $18.95 (0-253-20172-1). 456pp. A selection from an international store of folktales. [398.2]

10622 Vogel, Carole G. *Legends of Landforms: Native American Lore and the Geology of the Land* (4–6). Illus. 1999, Millbrook LB $27.90 (0-7613-0272-7). 96pp. This book contains 14 legends about such geological formations as the Grand Canyon and Martha's Vineyard, with scientific background material on each. (Rev: BL 11/15/99; HBG 10/00; SLJ 1/00) [398.2]

10623 Walker, Paul R. *Giants! Stories from Around the World* (3–6). Illus. 1995, Harcourt $17.00 (0-15-200883-7). 80pp. A collection of seven stories about giants, some obscure and others as familiar as "Jack and the Beanstalk." (Rev: BL 11/1/95; SLJ 2/96) [398.2]

10624 Walker, Paul R. *Little Folk: Stories from Around the World* (K–4). Illus. by James Bernardin. 1997, Harcourt $17.00 (0-15-200327-4). 80pp. The retelling of eight tales about pixies, including *Rumpelstiltskin* and a story about a leprechaun. (Rev: BCCB 7–8/97; BL 3/15/97; HBG 3/98; SLJ 4/97) [398.2]

10625 Walker, Richard. *The Barefoot Book of Pirates* (4–6). Illus. 1998, Barefoot $17.95 (1-901223-79-5). 64pp. Pirates and robbers from folklore, including Robin Hood and Pirate Grace, are included in this entertaining collection of folktales from around the world. (Rev: BL 11/15/98; SLJ 9/98) [398.2]

10626 Walker, Richard. *The Barefoot Book of Trickster Tales* (3–6). Illus. 1998, Barefoot $18.95 (1-902283-08-2). 80pp. A collection of trickster tales from around the world, including an Anansi story, a Jack tale, a Brer Rabbit adventure, and a Red Riding Hood story from Bengal. (Rev: BL 1/1–15/99; SLJ 11/98) [398]

10627 Ward, Helen. *The King of the Birds* (PS–3). Illus. 1997, Millbrook LB $24.90 (0-7613-0313-8). 40pp. In this folktale about determining who is the king of the birds, it is the humble wren and not the eagle who wins. (Rev: BL 10/15/97; HBG 3/98; SLJ 1/98) [398.2]

10628 Williams, Rose. *The Book of Fairies: Nature Spirits from Around the World* (5–7). Illus. 1997, Beyond Words $18.95 (1-885223-56-0). 80pp. Fairies play a major role in these eight stories from such countries as France, Ireland, and India. (Rev: BL 1/1–15/98; HBG 3/98; SLJ 1/98) [398.2]

10629 Yep, Laurence. *Tree of Dreams: Ten Tales from the Garden of Night* (3–6). Illus. by Isadore Seltzer. 1995, Troll $13.95 (0-8167-3498-4). 96pp. Folktales from China, Greece, Brazil, and other countries explore the world of sleep. (Rev: BCCB 4/95; BL 1/15/95; HB 11–12/95; SLJ 3/95) [398.2]

10630 Yolen, Jane. *Fairies' Ring: A Book of Fairy Stories and Poems* (3–5). Illus. 1999, Dutton $21.99 (0-525-46045-4). 96pp. An international collection of stories and poems about fairies from such diverse sources as the folklore of Persia and New Zealand. (Rev: BCCB 1/00; BL 11/1/99; HBG 3/00) [808.8]

10631 Yolen, Jane. *Once upon a Bedtime Story* (K–3). Illus. by Ruth T. Councell. 1997, Boyds Mills $17.95 (1-57397-484-3). 96pp. This is a charming collection of 16 folktales, fairy tales, and fables, chiefly from Europe. (Rev: BL 11/15/97; SLJ 9/97) [398.2]

10632 Young, Ed. *Donkey Trouble* (PS–3). Illus. 1995, Simon & Schuster $16.00 (0-689-31854-5). 32pp. A man and his grandson eventually find that the advice offered by people to them on their journey to market with their donkey is not helpful. (Rev: BL 11/15/95*; SLJ 12/95) [392.2]

10633 Young, Richard, and Judy D. Young, eds. *Stories from the Days of Christopher Columbus* (5–8). 1992, August House paper $8.95 (0-87483-198-9). 160pp. This collection of folktales comes from a variety of sources, including Italian, Spanish, Portuguese, and North and South American Indians. (Rev: SLJ 7/92)

10634 *The Young Oxford Book of Folk Tales* (5–8). Ed. by Kevin Crossley-Holland. Illus. 1999, Oxford $22.95 (0-19-278141-3). 213pp. A delightful collection of folktales from around the world, with accompanying notes on their origins. (Rev: BL 5/15/99; HBG 3/00; SLJ 10/99) [398.2]

10635 Zeitlin, Steve. *The Four Corners of the Sky: Creation Stories and Cosmologies from Around the World* (5–10). Illus. by Chris Raschka. 2000, Holt

$17.00 (0-8050-4816-2). 135pp. Theories and beliefs about the creation of the world from 16 ancient cultures, with a folktale illustrating each one. (Rev: HB 1–2/01; HBG 3/01; SLJ 12/00) [398.2]

10636 Zerner, Amy, and Jessie S. Zerner, retellers. *Scheherazade's Cat: And Other Fables from Around the World* (3–6). Illus. by Amy Zerner and Jessie S. Zerner. 1994, Tuttle $16.95 (0-8048-1807-X). 115pp. A collection of nine folktales, including one originally in the *1001 Nights* anthology about a wise cat. (Rev: SLJ 4/94) [398.2]

Africa

10637 Aardema, Verna. *Anansi Does the Impossible!* (K–4). Illus. by Lisa Desimini. 1997, Simon & Schuster $16.00 (0-689-81092-X). 32pp. In this Ashanti tale, Anansi the spider performs three difficult tasks to get stories from the Sky God. (Rev: BL 12/1/97; HBG 3/98; SLJ 9/97*) [398.2]

10638 Aardema, Verna. *Bimwili and the Zimwi: A Tale from Zanzibar* (K–3). Illus. by Susan Meddaugh. 1985, Puffin paper $5.99 (0-14-054608-1). 32pp. The story of little Bimwili, who finds a shell, loses it, is captured by the ogrelike Zimwi, and then outwits him to escape. (Rev: BL 12/1/85; SLJ 11/85) [398.2]

10639 Aardema, Verna, reteller. *Bringing the Rain to Kapiti Plain: A Nandi Tale* (PS–2). Illus. by Beatriz Vidal. 1981, Puffin paper $5.99 (0-14-054616-2). 32pp. A rhyming book on how the rain was brought to an African plain. [398.2]

10640 Aardema, Verna. *Koi and the Kola Nuts: A Tale from Liberia* (PS–3). Illus. by Joe Cepeda. 1999, Simon & Schuster $16.95 (0-689-81760-6). 32pp. When Koi, a chieftain's son, sets out on a quest for a bride, the animals he has helped return his kindness. (Rev: BCCB 1/00; BL 10/15/99; HBG 3/00; SLJ 11/99) [398.2]

10641 Aardema, Verna. *The Lonely Lioness and the Ostrich Chicks* (PS–2). Illus. by Yumi Heo. 1996, Knopf LB $18.99 (0-679-96934-0). 32pp. In this Masai story, a lonely lioness is determined to raise an ostrich's four chicks. (Rev: BCCB 2/97; BL 11/15/96; SLJ 12/96*) [398.2]

10642 Aardema, Verna. *Rabbit Makes a Monkey of Lion* (K–1). Illus. by Jerry Pinkney. 1989, Puffin paper $5.99 (0-14-054593-X). 32pp. A Swahili tale of a wily little rabbit outwitting the big brawny lion. (Rev: BL 3/1/89; HB 5–6/89; SLJ 6/89) [398.2]

10643 Aardema, Verna. *Sebgugugu the Glutton: A Bantu Tale from Rwanda, Africa* (4–6). Illus. by Nancy L. Clouse. 1993, Africa World $14.95 (0-86543-377-1). 32pp. In this Rwandian folktale, a foolish man loses everything because of his greed. (Rev: BL 4/1/93; SLJ 6/93) [398.2]

10644 Aardema, Verna, ed. *Why Mosquitoes Buzz in People's Ears: A West African Tale* (K–3). Illus. by Leo Dillon and Diane Dillon. 1992, Puffin paper $6.99 (0-14-054905-6). 32pp. Bold, stylized paintings illustrate this tale of a mosquito who tells a whopping lie, thus setting off a chain of events. Caldecott Medal winner, 1976. [398.2]

10645 Anderson, David A. *The Origin of Life on Earth: An African Creation Myth* (2–6). Illus. by Kathleen A. Wilson. 1991, Sights LB $18.95 (0-9629978-5-4). This African myth tells how earthly creatures were formed and how the world began spinning. (Rev: SLJ 7/92) [398.2]

10646 Appiah, Peggy. *Tales of an Ashanti Father* (2–7). Illus. by Mora Dickson. 1989, Beacon paper $7.95 (0-8070-8313-5). 160pp. Twenty-two stories about trickster Ananse. [398.2]

10647 Araujo, Frank P. *The Perfect Orange: A Tale from Ethiopia* (K–3). Illus. by Xiao Jun Li. Series: Toucan Tales. 1994, Rayve $16.95 (1-877810-94-0). In this Ethiopian folktale, a simple girl impresses a king with her generosity, and he rewards her with gold and jewels. (Rev: SLJ 3/95) [398.2]

10648 Arkhurst, Joyce Cooper. *The Adventures of Spider: West African Folktales* (4–7). Illus. by Jerry Pinkney. 1992, Little, Brown paper $8.95 (0-316-05107-1). Six humorous stories featuring the crafty spider. [398.2]

10649 Ashabranner, Brent, and Russell Davis. *The Lion's Whiskers and Other Ethiopian Tales* (4–7). Illus. 1997, Linnet LB $19.95 (0-208-02429-8). 96pp. A classic collection of 16 Ethiopian folktales originally published in 1995. (Rev: BL 10/1/97; SLJ 5/97*) [398.2]

10650 Barbosa, Rogerio Andrade. *African Animal Tales* (4–6). Trans. by Feliz Guthrie. Illus. by Cica Fittipaldi. 1993, Volcano $17.95 (0-912078-96-0). 63pp. Weak, small animals outwit stronger animals in this collection of ten African folktales. (Rev: BL 2/15/94) [398.2]

10651 Berry, James. *Don't Leave an Elephant to Go and Chase a Bird* (PS–1). Illus. by Ann Grifalconi. 1996, Simon & Schuster $16.00 (0-689-80464-4). 32pp. A group of elephants conspire to out-trick the cunning Anancy Spiderman in this folktale from Ghana. (Rev: BCCB 1/96; BL 2/15/96; SLJ 3/96) [398.2]

10652 Berry, James. *First Palm Trees* (PS–4). Illus. by Greg Couch. 1997, Simon & Schuster $17.00 (0-689-81060-1). 40pp. In this West African tale, Anansi the spider seeks help to make palm trees so that he can collect a reward from the king. (Rev: BL 12/15/97; HBG 3/98; SLJ 12/97) [398.2]

10653 Bryan, Ashley. *Beat the Story-Drum, Pum-Pum* (K–4). Illus. by author. 1987, Macmillan paper $8.95 (0-689-71107-7). 80pp. A retelling of five Nigerian folktales. [398.2]

10654 Bryan, Ashley. *Lion and the Ostrich Chicks and Other African Folk Tales* (3–5). Illus. 1996, Simon & Schuster paper $6.95 (0-689-80713-9). 96pp. Spirited retelling of African folktales involving the triumph of the underdog. (Rev: BCCB 2/87; BL 2/1/87; SLJ 1/87) [398.2]

10655 Bryan, Ashley. *The Night Has Ears: African Proverbs* (K–3). Illus. 1999, Simon & Schuster $16.00 (0-689-82427-0). 32pp. Presenting one proverb per page, this is a collection of 26 aphorisms from various African tribes. (Rev: BL 9/15/99; HBG 3/00; SLJ 1/00) [398.9]

10656 Bryan, Ashley. *The Story of Lightning and Thunder* (3–6). Illus. 1993, Atheneum $16.00 (0-689-31836-7). 32pp. In this African folktale, Thunder, a sheep, and her son Lightning are banished to the sky when Lightning becomes too destructive. (Rev: BCCB 10/93; BL 9/15/93; SLJ 9/93*) [398.2]

10657 Chocolate, Deborah M. *Imani in the Belly* (PS–3). Illus. by Alex Boies. 1994, Troll $14.95 (0-8167-3466-6). 32pp. Imani sets out to catch Simba the lion, who has taken her children. (Rev: BL 10/15/94; SLJ 12/94) [398.2]

10658 Climo, Shirley. *The Egyptian Cinderella* (1–4). Illus. by Ruth Heller. 1989, HarperCollins LB $15.89 (0-690-04824-6). 32pp. A tale based on fact about a Greek girl who was kidnapped and brought to Egypt is one of the world's first Cinderella stories. (Rev: BCCB 10/89; BL 9/1/89; SLJ 10/89*) [398.2]

10659 Courlander, Harold, and George Herzog. *The Cow-Tail Switch: And Other West African Stories* (4–6). Illus. by Madye Lee Chastain. 1988, Holt paper $9.95 (0-8050-0298-7). 160pp. Originally published in 1947, this is a fine collection of folktales about foolish and wise men and animals. [398.2]

10660 Day, Nancy Raines. *The Lion's Whiskers: An Ethiopian Folktale* (PS–2). Illus. by Ann Grifalconi. 1995, Scholastic $14.95 (0-590-45803-5). 32pp. A stepmother seeks the aid of a medicine man in her efforts to win the affection of the stepson who rejects her. (Rev: BCCB 3/95; BL 2/15/95; SLJ 4/95*) [398.2]

10661 Dee, Ruby. *Two Ways to Count to Ten: A Liberian Folktale* (PS–1). Illus. by Susan Meddaugh. 1990, Holt paper $6.95 (0-8050-1314-8). 32pp. The antelope outsmarts them all when the king advertises for a successor. (Rev: BL 7/88; SLJ 6–7/88) [398.2]

10662 Diakite, Baba Wague, reteller. *The Hatseller and the Monkeys* (K–3). Illus. by Baba Wague Diakite. 1999, Scholastic $15.95 (0-590-96069-5). This is an interesting West African version of the traditional tale about a peddler whose hats are stolen by a group of monkeys. (Rev: BCCB 2/99; HB 5–6/99; HBG 10/99; SLJ 2/99) [398.2]

10663 Diakite, Baba Wague. *The Hunterman and the Crocodile: A West African Folktale* (K–3). Illus. 1997, Scholastic $15.95 (0-590-89828-0). 32pp. A West African folktale about the Hunterman who runs afoul of Bamba the Crocodile and is helped by Rabbit. (Rev: BCCB 2/97; BL 3/15/97; SLJ 3/97) [398.2]

10664 Echewa, T. Obinkaram. *The Magic Tree: A Folktale from Nigeria* (PS–3). Illus. by E. B. Lewis. 1999, Morrow LB $15.93 (0-688-16232-0). 32pp. In this Nigerian folktale, a young outsider gains power and prestige when a magic udara tree gives him fruit and obeys his commands. (Rev: BCCB 4/99; BL 6/1–15/99*; HBG 10/99; SLJ 8/99) [398.2]

10665 Farris, Pamela J. *Young Mouse and Elephant: An East African Folktale* (PS–2). Illus. by Valeri Gorbachev. 1996, Houghton $14.95 (0-395-73977-2). 32pp. Young Mouse believes he is the strongest animal alive and sets off across the African plains to prove to Elephant that he is right. (Rev: BL 5/1/96; SLJ 4/96) [398.2]

10666 Gershator, Phillis. *Only One Cowry* (K–3). Illus. by David Soman. 2000, Orchard LB $17.99 (0-531-33288-8). 32pp. This African folktale in picture-book format tells about tricksters, weddings, and dowries and employs collages made of cut and torn paper to illustrate its events. (Rev: BCCB 1/01; BL 10/15/00; HBG 3/01; SLJ 9/00) [398.2]

10667 Gershator, Phillis. *Zzzng! Zzzng! Zzzng! A Yoruba Tale* (PS–1). Illus. by Theresa Smith. 1998, Orchard LB $16.99 (0-531-08873-1). 32pp. In this Yoruba folktale from Nigeria, Mosquito faces rejection when he tries to marry above his station and takes out his anger by buzzing and biting. (Rev: BCCB 10/98; BL 8/98; HBG 3/99; SLJ 10/98) [398.2]

10668 Greaves, Nick. *When Hippo Was Hairy: And Other Tales from Africa* (4–8). Illus. 1988, Barron's paper $11.95 (0-8120-4548-3). 144pp. Thirty-one traditional African tales, a combination of folklore and fact. (Rev: BL 2/15/89; SLJ 2/89) [398.2]

10669 Greger, C. Shana. *Cry of the Benu Bird: An Egyptian Creation Story* (4–6). Illus. 1996, Houghton $14.95 (0-395-73573-4). 32pp. In this book based on an Egyptian creation myth, an enchanted bird fights the darkness of Chaos to help the beginnings of human life. (Rev: BL 3/15/96; SLJ 4/96) [398.2]

10670 Gregorowski, Christopher. *Fly, Eagle, Fly!* (K–4). Illus. by Niki Daly. 2000, Simon & Schuster $16.00 (0-689-82398-3). 32pp. This Ghanaian folktale tells how an eagle is raised as a chicken but eventually finds its native environment and freedom. (Rev: BL 1/1–15/00; HBG 10/00; SLJ 3/00) [398.2]

10671 Grifalconi, Ann. *The Village of Round and Square Houses* (PS–2). Illus. by author. 1986, Little, Brown $16.95 (0-316-32862-6). 32pp. This blend of fiction, anthropology, and folklore centers around the central African remote village of Tos. (Rev: BCCB 6/86; BL 6/15/86; SLJ 8/86) [398.2]

10672 Haley, Gail E. *A Story, a Story* (1–4). Illus. by author. 1970, Macmillan LB $17.00 (0-689-20511-2); paper $5.99 (0-689-71201-4). 36pp. How African "spider stories" began is traced back to the time when Ananse, the Spider Man, made a bargain with the Sky God. Caldecott Medal winner, 1971. [398.2]

10673 *The Honey Hunters* (PS–3). Illus. by Francesca Martin. 1992, Candlewick $14.95 (1-56402-086-X). 32pp. The tale of a time long ago when all earth animals were friends and they all liked honey. (Rev: BL 11/15/92) [398.2]

10674 Hull, Robert, reteller. *Egyptian Stories* (4–6). Illus. by Noel Bateman and Barbara Loftus. Series: Tales from Around the World. 1994, Thomson Learning LB $24.26 (1-56847-155-6). 48pp. Introduces seven traditional tales, including a creation story, as well as life in ancient Egypt. (Rev: SLJ 8/94) [398.2]

10675 Kimmel, Eric A. *Anansi and the Moss-Covered Rock* (PS–3). Illus. by Janet Stevens. 1988, Holiday LB $16.95 (0-8234-0689-X); paper $6.95 (0-8234-0798-5). 32pp. Anansi the trickster discovers a magic rock that knocks animals out, and then he steals their food. (Rev: BCCB 10/88; BL 10/1/88; SLJ 11/88) [398.2]

10676 Kimmel, Eric A. *Anansi and the Talking Melon* (PS–3). Illus. by Janet Stevens. 1994, Holiday LB $16.95 (0-8234-1104-4). 32pp. Hiding inside a melon, Anansi the Spider tricks all the animals into believing that the melon can speak in this African folktale. (Rev: BCCB 6/94; BL 2/15/94; SLJ 3/94*) [398.2]

10677 Kimmel, Eric A. *Anansi Goes Fishing* (K–3). Illus. by Janet Stevens. 1992, Holiday LB $16.95 (0-8234-0918-X). 32pp. Lazy but lovable trickster Anansi is outwitted by the clever turtle in this contemporary rendition of an old tale. (Rev: BL 3/15/92; SLJ 5/92) [398.2]

10678 Kimmel, Eric A. *Rimonah of the Flashing Sword: A North African Tale* (K–3). Illus. by Omar Rayyan. 1995, Holiday LB $15.95 (0-8234-1093-5). 32pp. An Egyptian folktale that is a variation on the Snow White story about a princess fleeing the wrath of a wicked stepmother. (Rev: BL 3/1/95; SLJ 3/95) [398.2]

10679 Knutson, Barbara. *How the Guinea Fowl Got Her Spots: A Swahili Tale of Friendship* (PS–2). Illus. 1990, Carolrhoda LB $19.95 (0-87614-416-4). 24pp. Cow returns a favor given by Nganga the Guinea Fowl by giving her spots that can help her hide from enemies. (Rev: BCCB 7–8/90*; BL 6/15/90; HB 9–10/90; SLJ 9/90) [398.2]

10680 Kurtz, Jane. *Fire on the Mountain* (1–4). Illus. by E. B. Lewis. 1994, Simon & Schuster paper $16.00 (0-671-88268-6). 32pp. A young boy and his sister trick a wealthy man into paying his debts in this Ethiopian folktale. (Rev: BCCB 10/94; BL 10/15/94; HB 11–12/94; SLJ 12/94*) [398.2]

10681 Kurtz, Jane. *Pulling the Lion's Tail* (PS–3). Illus. by Floyd Cooper. 1995, Simon & Schuster paper $15.00 (0-689-80324-9). 32pp. A child's grandfather gives an unusual prescription for gaining her stepmother's love in this Ethiopian folktale. (Rev: BL 9/1/95; SLJ 12/95) [398.2]

10682 Kurtz, Jane. *Trouble* (4–7). Illus. by Durga Bernhard. 1997, Harcourt $15.00 (0-15-200219-7). 40pp. An Eritrean story about a young goatherd who has a knack for getting into trouble. (Rev: BL 3/15/97; SLJ 4/97) [398.2]

10683 Laird, Elizabeth. *When the World Began: Stories Collected in Ethiopia* (3–6). Illus. 2000, Oxford $25.00 (0-19-274535-2). 96pp. This book contains retellings of 20 Ethiopian folktales that introduce a variety of villains, heroes, animals, and monsters. (Rev: BL 2/15/01; SLJ 11/00) [398.2]

10684 Lake, Mary D., reteller. *The Royal Drum: An Ashanti Tale* (K–2). Illus. by Carol O'Malia. 1996, Mondo $14.95 (1-57255-140-2). Using a rebus approach, this tale from Ghana tells how Anansi the

spider gets all of the animals to participate in making a drum for Lion the king. (Rev: SLJ 11/96) [398.2]

10685 Lester, Julius. *How Many Spots Does a Leopard Have?* (K–5). Illus. by David Shannon. 1994, Scholastic paper $5.95 (0-590-41972-2). 72pp. This is a splendid retelling of 12 folktales, ten of which are African and the other two Jewish. (Rev: BCCB 9/89; BL 11/15/89; HB 1–2/90; SLJ 11/89) [398.2]

10686 Lester, Julius. *What a Truly Cool World* (PS–3). Illus. by Joe Cepeda. 1999, Scholastic $15.95 (0-590-86468-8). 40pp. In this African creation myth, God, with the help of the angel Shaniqua, adds the finishing touches to the world he has made. (Rev: BCCB 2/99; BL 2/15/99; HBG 10/99; SLJ 4/99) [398.2]

10687 Lilly, Melinda. *Kwian and the Lazy Sun: African Tales and Myths* (K–3). Series: African Tales and Myths. 1998, Rourke LB $19.95 (1-57103-243-6). In this South African tale, a young girl figures out how to get the sun and the moon into the sky. Also use from the same series and author *Tamba and the Chief: A Tenne Tale* and *Warrior Son of a Warrior Son: A Masai Tale* (both 1998). (Rev: SLJ 4/99) [398.2]

10688 Lilly, Melinda, reteller. *Spider and His Son Find Wisdom: An Akan Tale* (2–4). Illus. by Charles Reasoner. Series: African Tales and Myths. 1998, Rourke LB $16.95 (1-57103-244-4). 31pp. The spider, Anansi, tries to retrieve all the good advice he has given to unappreciative villagers in this Akan tale told in a picture-book format. (Rev: SLJ 3/99) [398.2]

10689 Lilly, Melinda, reteller. *Wanyana and Matchmaker Frog: A Bagandan Tale* (2–4). Illus. by Charles Reasoner. Series: African Tales and Myths. 1998, Rourke LB $16.95 (1-57103-247-9). 31pp. To repay a kindness he received when in distress, a frog gives a young girl good advice in choosing a husband in this African folk tale. (Rev: SLJ 3/99) [398.2]

10690 Lilly, Melinda, reteller. *Zimani's Drum: A Malawian Tale* (2–4). Illus. by Charles Reasoner. Series: African Tales and Myths. 1998, Rourke LB $16.95 (1-57103-248-7). 31pp. Blind Zimani rescues his brother and two sisters from the clutches of Mkango the Lion. (Rev: SLJ 3/99) [398.2]

10691 Lottridge, Celia B., reteller. *The Name of the Tree* (K–5). Illus. by Ian Wallace. 1990, Macmillan $16.00 (0-689-50490-X). This Bantu tale begins with hungry animals finding a tree laden with every fruit imaginable. (Rev: BCCB 4/90; SLJ 3/90) [398.2]

10692 McDermott, Gerald. *Anansi, the Spider: A Tale from the Ashanti* (K–3). Illus. by author. 1972, Holt LB $16.95 (0-8050-0310-X); paper $6.95 (0-8050-0311-8). 48pp. Because Anansi and his sons quarrel, the moon remains in the sky. [398.2]

10693 McDermott, Gerald. *Zomo the Rabbit: A Trickster Tale from West Africa* (PS–3). Illus. 1992, Harcourt $14.95 (0-15-299967-1). 32pp. An enduring Nigerian tale of a trickster who is cunning but not always wise. (Rev: BCCB 9/92*; BL 9/15/92*; SLJ 11/92*) [398.2]

10694 Mama, Raouf. *Why Goats Smell Bad and Other Stories from Benin* (4–6). Illus. 1998, Linnet LB $21.50 (0-208-02469-7). 138pp. This interesting collection of African folktales from Benin contains stories about children, spirits, animals, and tricksters. (Rev: BCCB 5/98; BL 2/15/98; HBG 10/98; SLJ 4/98) [398.2]

10695 Martin, Francesca. *Clever Tortoise* (2–3). Illus. 2000, Candlewick $14.99 (0-7636-0506-9). 32pp. In this East African folktale, Tortoise outsmarts the bullies Hippopotamus and Elephant. (Rev: BL 5/15/00; SLJ 9/00) [398.2]

10696 Medearis, Angela Shelf. *The Singing Man* (PS–3). Illus. by Terea D. Shaffer. 1994, Holiday LB $16.95 (0-8234-1103-6). 36pp. Banzar is scorned in his Nigerian village because he wants to become a musician, but eventually he returns to his home in triumph. (Rev: BL 7/94; SLJ 9/94) [398.2]

10697 Medearis, Angela Shelf. *Too Much Talk* (PS–2). Illus. by Stefano Vitale. 1995, Candlewick $15.95 (1-56402-323-0). 32pp. A cumulative West African folktale about a group of people who discover that inanimate objects and animals can speak their language. (Rev: BCCB 12/95; BL 1/1–15/96; HB 11–12/95; SLJ 12/95) [398.2]

10698 Medlicott, Mary, ed. and sel. *The River That Went to the Sky: Twelve Tales by African Storytellers* (4–7). Illus. by Ademola Akintola. 1995, Kingfisher $16.95 (1-85697-608-4). 90pp. Twelve excellent folktales represent 11 geographical areas of Africa. (Rev: SLJ 4/96) [398.2]

10699 Mollel, Tololwa M. *Ananse's Feast: An Ashanti Tale* (K–3). Illus. by Andrew Glass. 1997, Clarion $14.95 (0-395-67402-6). 32pp. Akye the turtle gets revenge on Ananse the spider in this gentle Ashanti tale. (Rev: BL 4/15/97; SLJ 5/97) [398.2]

10700 Mollel, Tololwa M. *The Flying Tortoise* (3–5). Illus. by Barbara Spurll. 1994, Clarion $14.95 (0-395-68845-0). 32pp. A Nigerian folktale about how a crafty tortoise gets his cracked shell. (Rev: BCCB 10/94; BL 11/15/94; SLJ 9/94) [398.2]

10701 Mollel, Tololwa M. *The King and the Tortoise* (K–3). Illus. by Kathy Blankley. 1993, Houghton $14.95 (0-395-64480-1). 32pp. In this folktale from Cameroon, a clever tortoise is able to make a robe of smoke for a proud king. (Rev: BL 4/1/93) [398.2]

10702 Mollel, Tololwa M. *Kitoto the Mighty* (K–3). Illus. by Kristi Frost. 1998, Stoddart $14.95 (0-7737-3019-2). An African folktale about Kitoto, a mouse who sets out to find a force strong enough to protect him from a hawk. (Rev: BCCB 11/98; SLJ 2/99) [398.2]

10703 Mollel, Tololwa M. *The Orphan Boy* (K–3). Illus. by Paul Morin. 1991, Houghton $16.00 (0-89919-985-2). 32pp. In this Masai folktale, an old man takes in an orphan boy who is actually the planet Venus. (Rev: BCCB 4/91*; BL 5/1/91; SLJ 7/91*) [398.2]

10704 Mollel, Tololwa M. *Song Bird* (K–4). Illus. by Rosanne Litzinger. 1999, Clarion $15.00 (0-395-82908-9). 32pp. Adapted from African folktales, this story involves Mariamu and her family, who are trying to live off the land, and a magical bird that serenades them. (Rev: BCCB 2/99; BL 2/15/99; HBG 10/99; SLJ 4/99) [398.2]

10705 Mollel, Tololwa M. *Subira Subira* (PS–2). Illus. by Linda Saport. 2000, Clarion $15.00 (0-395-91809-X). 32pp. A Tanzanian folktale in which a brave young girl named Tatu is given advice by a spirit woman on how to control her difficult younger brother. (Rev: BCCB 5/00; BL 2/15/00; HBG 10/00; SLJ 4/00) [398.22]

10706 Mollel, Tololwa M. *To Dinner, for Dinner* (PS–3). Illus. by Synthia Saint James. 2000, Holiday $16.95 (0-8234-1527-9). 32pp. Based on a Tanzanian story, this tale tells of a rabbit, Juhudi, and his tricks to keep from becoming Leopard's dinner. (Rev: BL 9/1/00; SLJ 8/00) [398.2]

10707 Musgrove, Margaret. *The Spider Weaver: A Legend of Kente Cloth* (PS–3). Illus. by Julia Cairns. 2001, Scholastic $16.95 (0-590-98787-9). 40pp. In this Ghanaian folk tale, two weavers learn from a spider complicated patterns that they use in their kente cloth. (Rev: BCCB 3/01; BL 2/15/01; SLJ 2/01) [398.2]

10708 Olaleye, Isaac. *In the Rainfield: Who Is the Greatest?* (K–3). Illus. by Ann Grifalconi. 2000, Scholastic $16.95 (0-590-48363-3). 32pp. In this folktale from Nigeria, three elements — Wind, Fire, and Rain — compete to see which is greatest. (Rev: BCCB 2/00; BL 2/15/00; HBG 10/00; SLJ 4/00) [398.2]

10709 Oram, Hiawyn, reteller. *Counting Leopard's Spots: Animal Stories from Africa* (K–4). Illus. by Tim Warnes. 1998, Little Tiger $16.95 (1-888444-31-2). 96pp. A handsome book that contains a variety of tales from Africa, including cautionary, pourquoi, and trickster stories. (Rev: BL 8/98; HBG 10/98; SLJ 12/98) [398.2]

10710 Paye, Won-Ldy, and Margaret H. Lippert. *Why Leopard Has Spots: Dan Stories from Liberia* (3–6). Illus. by Ashley Bryan. 1998, Fulcrum $15.95 (1-55591-344-X). 50pp. A collection of inviting African folktales, including several about a lazy spider that are reminiscent of the Anansi stories. (Rev: BCCB 11/98; BL 9/1/98; HBG 10/99; SLJ 12/98) [398.2]

10711 Riordan, James. *The Coming of Night: A Yoruba Tale from West Africa* (K–3). Illus. by Jenny Stow. 1999, Millbrook LB $21.40 (0-7613-1358-3). 32pp. This folktale from Africa tells how night and its creatures came into being. (Rev: BL 2/15/99; HBG 10/99; SLJ 5/99) [398.2]

10712 Savory, Phyllis. *Zulu Fireside Tales* (4–6). Illus. by Sylvia Baxter. 1993, Carol Publg. paper $9.95 (0-8065-1380-2). 240pp. This is an authentic collection of ten Zulu tales that originated in the area now known as Kwazulu. (Rev: BL 5/1/93) [398.2]

10713 Seeger, Pete, adapt. *Abiyoyo: Based on a South African Lullaby and Folk Story* (PS–1). Illus.

by Michael Hays. 1986, Macmillan LB $16.00 (0-02-781490-4). 48pp. An ostracized father and little boy who plays the ukelele find a way to best the giant Abiyoyo. (Rev: BCCB 6/86; BL 5/1/86; SLJ 8/86) [398.2]

10714 Shepard, Aaron. *Master Man: A Tall Tale of Nigeria* (PS–3). Illus. by David Wisniewski. 2001, HarperCollins LB $15.89 (0-688-13784-9). 32pp. The origins of thunder are explained in this Nigerian folk tale about a man who claims to be the strongest on earth. (Rev: BCCB 2/01; BL 1/1–15/01; SLJ 2/01) [398.2]

10715 Steptoe, John. *Mufaro's Beautiful Daughters: An African Tale* (PS–2). Illus. by author. 1987, Lothrop LB $15.89 (0-688-04046-2). 32pp. Two sisters of opposite natures vie for the hand of the king. (Rev: BCCB 4/87; BL 4/15/87; SLJ 6–7/87) [398.2]

10716 *Tales from Africa* (2–5). Ed. by Mary Medlicott. Illus. 2000, Kingfisher paper $11.95 (0-7534-5290-1). 96pp. Writers from 12 different African nations contributed a variety of folktales to this volume, including trickster stories and animal fables. (Rev: BL 5/15/00) [398.2]

10717 Tchana, Katrin. *The Serpent Slayer and Other Stories of Strong Women* (4–7). Illus. 2000, Little, Brown $21.95 (0-316-38701-0). 128pp. A collection of 18 folktales from around the world featuring brave, creative, and strong women and girls. (Rev: BCCB 11/00*; BL 12/15/00; HB 11–12/00; HBG 3/01; SLJ 11/00) [398.2]

10718 Wisniewski, David. *Sundiata: Lion King of Mali* (K–5). Illus. 1992, Houghton $17.00 (0-395-61302-7). 32pp. The dying king gives his kingdom to a sickly prince who cannot walk or speak, but in time, he becomes a great and brave leader. (Rev: BL 12/1/92*; HB 3–4/93; SLJ 10/92*) [398.2]

Asia

General and Miscellaneous

10719 Asian Cultural Center for Unesco, ed. *Folk Tales from Asia for Children Everywhere: Book Three* (2–5). Illus. 1976, Weatherhill $6.50 (0-8348-1034-4). 60pp. Nine tales with a wide range of folk themes. [398.2]

10720 Chodzin, Sherab, and Alexandra Kohn. *The Wisdom of the Crows and Other Buddhist Tales* (3–5). Illus. 1998, Tricycle Pr. $16.95 (1-883672-68-6). 80pp. This collection of Asian folktales illustrated with clear watercolors represents various facets of Buddhist thought and beliefs. (Rev: BL 6/1–15/98) [294]

10721 Climo, Shirley. *The Korean Cinderella* (K–3). Illus. by Ruth Heller. 1993, HarperCollins $15.95 (0-06-020432-X). 48pp. After Pear Blossom's mother dies and her father remarries, she is mistreated by her stepmother and stepsister. (Rev: BCCB 6/93; BL 5/1/93; SLJ 8/93) [398.2]

10722 Davison, Katherine. *Moon Magic: Stories from Asia* (3–5). Illus. 1994, Carolrhoda LB $19.95 (0-87614-751-1). 56pp. A retelling of four Asian myths that deal with the moon and its phases. (Rev: BL 5/15/94; SLJ 6/94) [398.2]

10723 Demi. *The Donkey and the Rock* (PS–3). Illus. 1999, Holt $16.95 (0-8050-5959-8). 32pp. An Asian folktale — probably Buddhist in origin — of the consequences that result when one man's donkey accidentally shatters another man's jar of oil. (Rev: BL 6/1–15/99; HBG 10/99; SLJ 3/99) [398.2]

10724 Farley, Carol. *Mr. Pak Buys a Story* (K–3). Illus. by Benrei Huang. 1997, Albert Whitman LB $15.95 (0-8075-5178-3). 32pp. A Korean folktale about a servant who is sent by a wealthy couple to buy a story in the big city. (Rev: BCCB 5/97; BL 4/15/97; HB 7–8/97; SLJ 4/97) [398.2]

10725 Froese, Deborah. *The Wise Washerman: A Folktale from Burma* (K–3). Illus. by Wang Kui. 1996, Hyperion LB $15.49 (0-7868-2232-5). A jealous neighbor tries to get an industrious washerwoman into trouble in this Burmese folktale. (Rev: BCCB 12/96; SLJ 1/97) [398.2]

10726 Ginsburg, Mirra. *The Chinese Mirror* (1–3). Illus. by Margot Zemach. 1991, Harcourt paper $6.00 (0-15-217508-3). 26pp. An old folktale from Korea tells of a man who brings home a mirror — unknown to his fellow villagers — from a trip to China. (Rev: BCCB 5/88; BL 4/15/88; SLJ 4/88) [398.2]

10727 Han, Suzanne C. *The Rabbit's Tail: A Story from Korea* (K–3). Illus. by Richard Wehrman. 1999, Holt $15.95 (0-8050-4580-5). 32pp. A charming folktale in which Tiger, through a series of misunderstandings, becomes involved with a rabbit that loses its tail. (Rev: BCCB 6/99; BL 2/15/99; HBG 10/99; SLJ 3/99) [398.2]

10728 Heo, Yumi. *The Green Frogs* (K–3). Illus. 1996, Houghton $14.95 (0-395-68378-5). 32pp. Two disobedient frogs decide to honor their mother's last wish in this Korean folktale. (Rev: BCCB 10/96; BL 7/96; HB 11–12/96) [398.2]

10729 Holt, Daniel D., sel. *Tigers, Frogs, and Rice Cakes: A Book of Korean Proverbs* (2–4). Illus. by Soma Han Stickler. 1999, Shen's $15.95 (1-885008-10-4). Each of the 20 Korean proverbs included are given in both English and Korean, with explanations. (Rev: BCCB 5/99; HBG 10/99; SLJ 6/99) [398.2]

10730 *Kindness: A Treasury of Buddhist Wisdom for Children and Parents* (4–7). Ed. by Sarah Conover. Illus. 2001, Eastern Washington Univ. paper $19.95 (0-910055-67-X). 164pp. Thirty-one stories related to Buddhism, including Jataka tales about the Buddha's incarnations, have been effectively translated and adapted for this anthology. (Rev: BL 2/15/01) [294.3]

10731 Mi-ae, Lee. *The Two Love Stars: The Story of Kyonu and Chingyo* (K–3). Trans. by Lee Chunoc and John Harvey. Illus. by Yoo Ae-ro. 1998, Borim $14.95 (89-433-0332-7). 32pp. In this Korean folktale, two stars who are lovers are separated by an angry king but reunited by birds who build a bridge to bring them together. (Rev: BL 7/98) [398.26]

10732 O'Brien, Anne S. *The Princess and the Beggar: A Korean Folktale* (K–3). Illus. 1993, Scholastic $14.95 (0-590-46092-7). 32pp. In this Korean folktale, a princess is banished from her father's castle because she refuses to marry a man she doesn't love. (Rev: BCCB 6/93; BL 4/15/93; SLJ 5/93) [398.2]

10733 Rhee, Nami. *Magic Spring: A Korean Folktale* (K–3). Illus. 1993, Putnam LB $15.95 (0-399-22420-3). 32pp. A Korean folktale about an elderly couple who find a magical spring that returns their youth. (Rev: BCCB 6/93; BL 4/1/93; SLJ 7/93*) [398.2]

10734 Riordan, James, reteller. *Korean Folk-Tales* (4–8). Series: Oxford Myths and Legends. 1995, Oxford paper $12.95 (0-19-274160-8). 133pp. A clear and interesting retelling of 20 well-known Korean folktales. (Rev: SLJ 3/95) [398.2]

10735 San Souci, Daniel. *In the Moonlight Mist: A Korean Tale* (PS–3). Illus. by Eujin Kim Neilan. 1999, Boyds Mills $15.95 (1-56397-754-0). 32pp. In this Korean tale, a poor woodcutter saves a deer and, as a reward, is granted his wish to have a wife who loves him. (Rev: BCCB 4/99; BL 3/1/99; HBG 10/99; SLJ 4/99) [398.2]

10736 Seros, Kathleen, adapt. *Sun and Moon: Fairy Tales from Korea* (2–5). Illus. by Norman Sibley and Robert Krause. 1983, Hollym $18.50 (0-930878-25-6). 61pp. A collection of seven stories from Korea. [398.2]

10737 Yep, Laurence. *The Khan's Daughter* (K–3). Illus. by Jean Tseng and Mou-Sien Tseng. 1997, Scholastic $16.95 (0-590-48389-7). 32pp. A Mongolian folktale in which the hero's most formidable opponent is the khan's daughter. (Rev: BCCB 3/97; BL 2/1/97*; HB 3–4/97; SLJ 2/97*) [398.2]

China

10738 Bouchard, David. *The Great Race* (3–6). Illus. by Zhong-Yang Huang. 1997, Millbrook LB $21.40 (0-7613-0305-7). 32pp. This folktale tells that the order of the animals in the Chinese zodiac was determined by a great race. (Rev: BL 2/1/98; HBG 3/98; SLJ 1/98) [398.2]

10739 Carpenter, F. R. *Tales of a Chinese Grandmother* (5–7). Illus. by Malthe Hasselriis. 1973, Amereon LB $24.95 (0-89190-481-6); Tuttle paper $8.95 (0-8048-1042-7). 293pp. A boy and a girl listen to 30 classic Chinese tales. [398.2]

10740 Casanova, Mary. *The Hunter* (PS–3). Illus. by Ed Young. 2000, Simon & Schuster $16.95 (0-689-82906-X). 32pp. This is a Chinese tale of a simple hunter who is granted the ability to understand the language of animals. He bravely tells his people that a great flood is coming and that he has learned of it from the animals, but he is turned to stone for divulging his secret ability. (Rev: BCCB 11/00*; BL 5/15/00; SLJ 8/00) [398.2]

10741 Chang, Margaret, and Raymond Chang. *The Beggar's Magic* (1–3). Illus. by David Johnson. 1997, Simon & Schuster paper $16.00 (0-689-81340-6). 32pp. In this Chinese folktale, when a wise man is denied a pear by a stingy farmer, he plants a tree that will bear enough fruit to feed a vil-

lage. (Rev: BL 10/15/97; HB 11–12/97; HBG 3/98; SLJ 12/97*) [398.2]

10742 Chang, Margaret, and Raymond Chang. *The Cricket Warrior: A Chinese Tale* (K–4). Illus. by Warwick Hutton. 1994, Macmillan paper $14.95 (0-689-50605-8). 32pp. A boy is transformed into a cricket and saves his family in this Chinese folktale. (Rev: BCCB 10/94; BL 11/1/94; SLJ 1/95) [398.2]

10743 Chang, Margaret, and Raymond Chang. *Da Wei's Treasure: A Chinese Tale* (K–4). Illus. by Lori McElrath-Eslick. 1999, Simon & Schuster $16.00 (0-689-81835-1). 32pp. Da Wei follows a magic cart to a grand house where he dines with an orange kitten that turns into an enchanted lady and becomes his wife. (Rev: BL 5/15/99; HBG 10/99; SLJ 6/99) [398.2]

10744 Chen, Kerstin. *Lord of the Cranes: A Chinese Tale* (PS–3). Illus. by Jian Jiang Chen. 2000, North-South LB $15.88 (0-7358-1193-8). 36pp. In this Chinese folktale, a poor man is rewarded for his kindness toward a magician disguised as a beggar. (Rev: BL 4/15/00; HBG 3/01; SLJ 7/00) [398.2]

10745 Chin, Charlie. *China's Bravest Girl: The Legend of Hua Mu Lan* (1–3). Illus. by Tomie Arai. 1993, Children's Book Pr. $14.95 (0-89239-120-0). 31pp. A Chinese girl disguised as a man becomes a distinguished warrior in this folktale told in both English and Mandarin Chinese. (Rev: BL 3/1/94; SLJ 3/94) [398.21]

10746 Chin, Yin-lien C., ed. *Traditional Chinese Folktales* (5–8). Illus. by Lu Wang. 1989, East Gate $41.95 (0-87332-507-9). 180pp. This is a collection of 12 Chinese folktales that express a variety of themes and genres from faithful lovers to trickster tales. (Rev: SLJ 8/89) [398.2]

10747 Czernecki, Stefan. *The Cricket's Cage: A Chinese Folktale* (1–4). Illus. 1997, Hyperion LB $15.49 (0-7868-2234-1). 32pp. In this Chinese folktale, a cricket helps a kindly carpenter design the watchtowers in the Forbidden City. (Rev: BCCB 6/97; BL 4/15/97; SLJ 6/97) [398.2]

10748 Demi. *The Dragon's Tale and Other Animal Fables of the Chinese Zodiac* (3–6). Illus. 1996, Holt $18.95 (0-8050-3446-3). 26pp. A collection of 12 fables that involve the animals in the Chinese zodiac. (Rev: BCCB 1/97; BL 9/15/96; SLJ 10/96) [398.2]

10749 Demi. *The Empty Pot* (K–2). Illus. by author. 1990, Holt $16.95 (0-8050-1217-6). 32pp. Young Ping finds out that honesty pays when the emperor gives seeds to each child in the kingdom to produce the best flower. (Rev: BL 4/1/90; HB 5–6/90 & 1-2/91; SLJ 7/90) [398.2]

10750 Demi. *The Greatest Treasure* (PS–3). Illus. 1998, Scholastic $16.95 (0-590-31339-8). 32pp. In this retelling of a traditional Chinese folktale, poor peasant Li receives a gift of money from his rich neighbor and his lifestyle changes as he begins to worry about how to care for his newfound wealth. (Rev: BL 8/98*; HBG 3/99; SLJ 9/98) [398.2]

10751 Fang, Linda. *The Ch'i-lin Purse: A Collection of Ancient Chinese Stories* (3–5). Illus. by Jeanne M. Lee. 1995, Farrar $16.00 (0-374-31241-

9). 127pp. Nine folktales from ancient China are dramatically retold, each with an accompanying illustration. (Rev: BCCB 4/95; BL 1/15/95*; HB 5–6/95; SLJ 3/95) [398.2]

10752 Gao, R. L. *Adventures of Monkey King* (PS–2). Illus. by Marylys Barton. 1997, Victory paper $6.95 (0-9620765-1-1). 132pp. An action-packed story of Monkey King's journey from China to India, translated from a Chinese folktale that is over 400 years old. (Rev: BL 3/1/90) [398.2]

10753 Granfield, Linda. *The Legend of the Panda* (1–3). Illus. by Song Nan Zhang. 1998, Tundra $15.95 (0-88776-421-5). 24pp. This Chinese tale of how the panda got its black markings tells of a beautiful young shepherdess and how she allowed a white bear to join her flock. (Rev: BL 12/15/98; HBG 3/99; SLJ 11/98) [398.2]

10754 Han, Carolyn. *Why Snails Have Shells: Minority and Han Folktales from China* (4–6). Trans. by Jay Han. Illus. 1994, Univ. of Hawaii Pr. $14.95 (0-8248-1505-X). 73pp. Attractive paintings accompany this splendid collection of 20 folktales from China. (Rev: BL 8/94) [398.2]

10755 Heyer, Marilee. *The Weaving of a Dream: A Chinese Folktale* (3–5). Illus. by author. 1989, Puffin paper $5.99 (0-14-050528-8). 32pp. The third of an old widow's sons retrieves her precious brocade, from whence steps the Red Fairy, and all three live happily ever after. (Rev: BL 4/15/86; SLJ 4/86) [398.2]

10756 Hong, Lily T. *How the Ox Star Fell from Heaven* (PS–3). Illus. 1995, Whitman paper $6.95 (0-8075-3429-3). 32pp. A retelling of the Chinese folktale of how oxen first lolled about the celestial home of the emperor of All the Heavens. (Rev: BL 4/1/91; SLJ 7/91*) [398.2]

10757 Hong, Lily T. *Two of Everything: A Chinese Folktale* (K–3). Illus. 1993, Whitman LB $15.95 (0-8075-8157-7). 32pp. Elderly Mr. Haktak finds a magical brass pot in his garden. (Rev: BL 3/15/93*; HB 7–8/93*; SLJ 6/93*) [398.2]

10758 Hume, Lotta Carswell. *Favorite Children's Stories from China and Tibet* (3–6). Illus. by Lo Koon-Chiu. 1962, Tuttle paper $16.95 (0-8048-1605-0). 120pp. An enjoyable retelling of 19 tales from the East, many with an uncanny resemblance to Western counterparts. [398.2]

10759 Kendall, Carol, and Li Yao-wen. *Sweet and Sour: Tales from China* (5–7). Illus. 1990, Houghton paper $7.95 (0-395-54798-9). 112pp. A choice collection of some enchanting Chinese folktales. [398.2]

10760 Kimmel, Eric A. *The Rooster's Antlers: A Story of the Chinese Zodiac* (PS–3). Illus. by Yongsheng Xuan. 1999, Holiday $16.95 (0-8234-1385-3). This Chinese folktale tells how Rooster gets his revenge when he isn't chosen by the emperor to be part of the Chinese calendar. (Rev: BCCB 10/99; BL 12/15/99; HBG 3/00; SLJ 10/99) [398.2]

10761 Kimmel, Eric A. *Ten Suns: A Chinese Legend* (K–3). Illus. by Yongsheng Xuan. 1998, Holiday $15.95 (0-8234-1317-9). 32pp. When the ten sons (suns) of Di Jun decide that they will no longer

make their solitary journeys across the sky each day but instead walk together, their father is afraid the combined heat will destroy the earth. (Rev: BCCB 6/98; BL 5/1/98; HBG 10/98; SLJ 5/98) [398.2]

10762 Lawson, Julie. *The Dragon's Pearl* (PS–3). Illus. by Paul Morin. 1993, Houghton $15.95 (0-395-63623-X). 36pp. Fearful that robbers will steal his magic pearl, a young boy swallows it and turns into a dragon. (Rev: BCCB 5/93; BL 4/15/93; SLJ 7/93) [398.2]

10763 Lee, Jeanne M. *The Song of Mu Lan* (5–8). Illus. 1995, Front Street $15.95 (1-886910-00-6). 32pp. Mu Lan disguises herself as a boy and joins the emperor's army in this traditional Chinese tale. (Rev: BL 11/15/95; SLJ 12/95) [398.2]

10764 Louie, Ai-Ling, reteller. *Yeh-Shen: A Cinderella Story from China* (2–6). Illus. by Ed Young. 1982, Putnam $16.99 (0-399-20900-X). 32pp. A Chinese story about a poor girl living with her cruel stepmother and stepsisters. [398.2]

10765 Mahy, Margaret. *The Seven Chinese Brothers* (K–3). Illus. by Jean Tseng. 1992, Scholastic paper $5.99 (0-590-42057-7). 40pp. Each of seven Chinese brothers has an amazing gift, used to help one another. (Rev: BCCB 7–8/90; BL 4/1/90; HB 7–8/90; SLJ 3/90*) [398.2]

10766 Mosel, Arlene. *Tikki Tikki Tembo* (K–2). Illus. by Blair Lent. 1968, Holt $16.95 (0-8050-0662-1); paper $6.95 (0-8050-1166-8). 32pp. Explains why the Chinese no longer honor their firstborn with an unusually long name. [398.2]

10767 Poole, Amy Lowry. *How the Rooster Got His Crown* (K–3). Illus. 1999, Holiday $15.95 (0-8234-1389-6). 32pp. A little rooster persuades a sun to leave its cave and is rewarded with a crown in this Chinese pourquoi tale. (Rev: BL 4/15/99; HB 5–6/99; HBG 10/99; SLJ 5/99) [398.2]

10768 Porte, Barbara Ann. *Hearsay: Strange Tales from the Middle Kingdom* (5–9). Illus. by Rosemary Feit Covey. 1998, Greenwillow $15.00 (0-688-15381-X). 136pp. Using themes and elements found in Chinese folklore, the author has written 15 short, original fantasies involving subjects such as dragons, crickets, magicians, and ghosts. (Rev: BCCB 5/98; HBG 10/98; SLJ 6/98)

10769 Sanfield, Steve. *Just Rewards, or Who Is That Man in the Moon and What's He Doing Up There Anyway?* (PS–3). Illus. by Emily Lisker. 1996, Orchard LB $15.99 (0-531-08885-5). 32pp. The origin of the belief that there is a man in the moon is retold in this Chinese folktale. (Rev: BL 10/1/96; HB 11–12/96; SLJ 9/96*) [398.2]

10770 Tseng, Grace. *White Tiger, Blue Serpent* (K–3). Illus. by Jean Tseng and Mou-Sien Tseng. 1999, Lothrop $16.00 (0-688-12515-8). 32pp. A Chinese folktale in which a young peasant, Kai, faces many dangers while journeying to the palace of the goddess Qin to retrieve a silk brocade. (Rev: BL 8/99; HBG 10/99; SLJ 7/99) [398.2]

10771 Wang, Rosalind C. *The Magical Starfruit Tree: A Chinese Folktale* (K–2). Illus. by Shao Wei Liu. 1994, Beyond Words $14.95 (0-941831-89-2). 30pp. In this Chinese tale, a stranger rewards a young acrobat for his kindness and punishes a miser for his nastiness. (Rev: BL 7/94) [398.2]

10772 Wang, Rosalind C. *The Treasure Chest: A Chinese Tale* (PS–3). Illus. by Will Hillenbrand. 1995, Holiday LB $15.95 (0-8234-1114-1). 32pp. In this Chinese tale, a humble peasant gets help from the Ocean King to fight an evil despot. (Rev: BL 6/1–15/95; SLJ 6/95) [398.2]

10773 Wilson, Barbara K., reteller. *Wishbones* (K–6). Illus. by Meilo So. 1993, Bradbury paper $14.95 (0-02-793125-0). In this Chinese folktale, a wicked stepmother kills and eats a young girl's magical fish, but its bones continue to help her. (Rev: SLJ 3/94) [398.2]

10774 Xuan, Yong-Sheng. *The Dragon Lover and Other Chinese Proverbs* (K–3). 1999, Shen's $16.95 (1-885008-11-2). 32pp. Illustrated with Chinese paper cuts, this lovely book contains the stories behind five well-known Chinese proverbs. (Rev: BCCB 7–8/99; BL 5/15/99; HBG 10/99; SLJ 8/99) [398.2]

10775 Ye, Ting-xing. *Three Monks, No Water* (K–3). Illus. by Harvey Chan. 1997, Annick LB $16.95 (1-55037-443-5); paper $6.95 (1-55037-442-7). 32pp. This story supposedly explains the origin of the Chinese expression "Three monks, no water," which is used when children try to avoid chores. (Rev: BL 2/1/98; SLJ 12/97) [398.2]

10776 Yep, Laurence. *The Dragon Prince: A Chinese Beauty and the Beast Tale* (4–6). Illus. by Kam Mak. 1997, HarperCollins LB $14.89 (0-06-024393-7). 32pp. A Chinese fairy tale in which a farmer's life can be saved only if one of his daughters marries a dragon. (Rev: BL 7/97; SLJ 10/97) [398.2]

10777 Yep, Laurence. *The Junior Thunder Lord* (K–3). Illus. by Robert Van Nutt. 1994, Troll $15.95 (0-8167-3454-2). 32pp. Yue's chance kindness toward a stranger helps saves his village from drought in this Chinese folktale. (Rev: BCCB 12/94; BL 11/1/94; SLJ 10/94) [398.2]

10778 Yep, Laurence. *The Man Who Tricked a Ghost* (K–3). Illus. by Isadore Seltzer. 1993, Troll $15.95 (0-8167-3030-X). 32pp. In ancient China, a fearless boy encounters a ghost. (Rev: BL 6/1–15/93*) [398.2]

10779 Yep, Laurence. *Tiger Woman* (PS–4). Illus. by Robert Roth. 1995, BridgeWater $15.95 (0-8167-3464-X). In this version of a Shantung folk song, a selfish old woman won't share her food with a beggar. (Rev: SLJ 2/96) [398.2]

10780 Yolen, Jane. *The Emperor and the Kite* (K–3). Illus. by Ed Young. 1988, Putnam $16.99 (0-399-21499-2). 32pp. Oriental-like paper cuts illustrate this Chinese legend about the unshakable loyalty of the emperor's smallest daughter. First published in 1967. [398.2]

10781 Young, Ed. *Lon Po Po: A Red-Riding-Hood Story from China* (2–4). Illus. 1989, Putnam $16.99 (0-399-21619-7). 32pp. In this variation of the Red Riding Hood story, Mother visits Grandmother, leaving her three children in danger from a marauding wolf. Caldecott Medal winner, 1990. (Rev: BCCB 11/89*; BL 11/15/89; HB 1–2/90*; SLJ 12/89*) [398.2]

10782 Young, Ed. *The Lost Horse: A Chinese Folktale* (K–3). Illus. 1998, Harcourt $18.00 (0-15-201016-5). 32pp. Every sad or happy event in a Chinese peasant's life brings the same response in this Chinese folktale about a man who accepts his fate stoically. (Rev: BL 3/15/98; SLJ 4/98) [398.2]

10783 Young, Ed. *Mouse Match: A Chinese Folktale* (PS–2). Illus. 1997, Harcourt $20.00 (0-15-201453-5). 26pp. In this Chinese folktale, a young mouse waits for her doting parents to decide who is the best choice in a husband for her. (Rev: BL 10/15/97*; HB 11–12/97; HBG 3/98; SLJ 10/97*) [398.2]

10784 Young, Ed. *Night Visitors* (PS–3). Illus. 1995, Putnam $15.95 (0-399-22731-8). 32pp. Ho Kuan dreams that he has become part of an ant colony in this Chinese folktale. (Rev: BCCB 1/96; BL 9/15/95; SLJ 10/95*) [398.2]

10785 Zhang, Song Nan. *A Time of Golden Dragons* (3–6). Illus. 2000, Tundra LB $16.95 (0-88776-506-8). 24pp. This is a collection of dragon lore from China that includes material and stories about the dragon's origin, dragon homes, dragon boat races, and other bits of dragon information. (Rev: BL 11/1/00; SLJ 10/00) [398.2]

India

10786 Arenson, Roberta. *Manu and the Talking Fish* (PS–3). Illus. 2000, Barefoot $15.95 (1-84148-032-0). 32pp. This Indian variation on the Noah story tells of Manu, a prince, who rescues a fish. When the fish grows up, he warns Manu of an impending flood that will destroy the world. (Rev: BL 4/1/00; SLJ 6/00) [398.2]

10787 Beach, Milo Cleveland. *The Adventures of Rama* (4–6). Illus. 1983, Smithsonian Institution $15.00 (0-934686-51-3). 64pp. Tales from the Hindu epic Ramayana. [398.2]

10788 Birch, David. *The King's Chessboard* (3–5). Illus. by Devis Grebu. 1988, Puffin paper $6.99 (0-14-054880-7). 32pp. A wise man outsmarts a vain king when he is offered a reward. (Rev: BL 5/15/88; SLJ 4/88) [398.2]

10789 Demi. *One Grain of Rice* (3–6). Illus. 1997, Scholastic $19.95 (0-590-93998-X). 40pp. Rani outwits the rajah to gain food for her people in this Indian folktale. (Rev: BCCB 2/97; BL 3/1/97*; SLJ 3/97*) [398.2]

10790 Ernst, Judith, reteller. *The Golden Goose King: A Tale Told by the Buddha* (3–6). Illus. by Judith Ernst. 1995, Parvardigar $19.95 (0-9644362-0-5). A Jataka tale about a queen who captures the Golden Goose King, who is actually Buddha. (Rev: BL 9/1/95; SLJ 9/95) [398.2]

10791 French, Fiona, reteller. *Jamil's Clever Cat: A Folk Tale from Bengal* (PS–2). Illus. by Fiona French and Dick Newby. 1999, Star Bright $13.95 (1-887734-72-4). In this tale from Bengal, a cat helps his master gain riches and a bride. (Rev: SLJ 3/00) [398.2]

10792 Galdone, Paul. *The Monkey and the Crocodile: A Jataka Tale from India* (K–3). Illus. by author. 1969, Houghton paper $6.95 (0-89919-524-5). 32pp. A crocodile decides he will catch a monkey. [398.2]

10793 *Heart of Gold* (2–4). Illus. by Rosalyn White. 1989, Dharma paper $7.95 (0-89800-193-5). In this retelling of a Jataka story, a wealthy man gives away all his possessions. Another Jataka story is: *The Rabbit in the Moon* (1989). (Rev: BL 8/89) [294.3]

10794 Jacobs, Joseph. *Indian Fairy Tales* (3–6). Illus. by John D. Batten. 1969, Dover paper $9.95 (0-486-21828-7). 255pp. A standard collection by the well-known authority. [398.2]

10795 Jaffrey, Madhur. *Seasons of Splendor: Tales, Myths, and Legends from India* (5–8). Illus. by Michael Foreman. 1985, Puffin paper $7.95 (0-317-62172-6). 128pp. Folktales and family stories as well as accounts of Rama and Krishna. (Rev: BCCB 1/86; BL 1/15/86) [398.2]

10796 Jendresen, Erik, and Joshua M. Greene, re-tellers. *Hanuman: Based on Valmiki's Ramayana* (3–6). Illus. by Li Ming. 1998, Tricycle Pr. $15.95 (1-883672-78-3). A retelling of the section of the Ramayana in which the monkey clan under Hanuman helps Rama rescue his wife Sita. (Rev: BCCB 3/99; HBG 10/99; SLJ 11/98) [398.2]

10797 Kajpust, Melissa. *The Peacock's Pride* (PS–2). Illus. by Jo'Anne Kelly. 1997, Hyperion LB $15.49 (0-7868-2233-3). 32pp. In this Indian folktale, a proud, strutting peacock is put in his place by a little bird. (Rev: BL 1/1–15/98) [398.2]

10798 Krishnaswami, Uma, reteller. *Shower of Gold: Girls and Women in the Stories of India* (5–9). Illus. by Maniam Selven. 1999, Linnet LB $19.95 (0-208-02484-0). 125pp. All of the enchanting tales in this fine collection of Indian folklore feature wise and powerful women. (Rev: BCCB 5/99; HBG 3/00; SLJ 8/99) [398.2]

10799 Lee, Jeanne M. *I Once Was a Monkey: Stories Buddha Told* (2–4). Illus. 1999, Farrar $16.00 (0-374-33548-6). 40pp. This handsome volume contains six *Jatakas* or birth stories from the Buddhist faith. (Rev: BCCB 4/99; BL 3/15/99; HBG 10/99; SLJ 3/99) [294.3]

10800 Martin, Rafe. *The Brave Little Parrot* (K–3). Illus. by Susan Gaber. 1998, Putnam $15.99 (0-399-22825-X). 32pp. As a reward for trying to put out a forest fire, a little parrot is given colored plumage in this Indian jataka tale. (Rev: BCCB 3/98; BL 2/15/98; SLJ 5/98) [298.2]

10801 Martin, Rafe. *Foolish Rabbit's Big Mistake* (PS–2). Illus. by Ed Young. 1985, Putnam $16.99 (0-399-21178-0). 32pp. A tale from India reminiscent of Chicken Little, about a little rabbit who fears the end of the world and tells everyone that the earth is breaking up. A Jataka tale. (Rev: BCCB 12/85; BL 12/15/85; HB 3–4/86) [398.2]

10802 Martin, Rafe. *The Monkey Bridge* (1–4). Illus. by Fahimeh Amiri. 1997, Knopf $17.00 (0-679-88106-9). 32pp. A Buddhist tale from India that tells how the monkey king gave his life to protect his tribe from human invaders. (Rev: BL 5/15/97; SLJ 7/97) [398.2]

10803 Ness, Caroline. *The Ocean of Story: Fairy Tales from India* (4–6). Illus. 1996, Lothrop $17.00 (0-688-13584-6). 128pp. Eighteen fairy tales from India that have been collected from unusual and often obscure source materials. (Rev: BCCB 5/96; BL 4/15/96; SLJ 4/96) [398.2]

10804 Rao, Sandhya, reteller. *And Land Was Born* (1–4). Illus. by Uma Krishnaswamy. Series: Visual Expressions. 1999, Banyan Tree $19.99 (81-86895-13-2). A delightful creation story from central India that tells how a tortoise helps produce land in a world where only water existed. (Rev: SLJ 7/99) [398.2]

10805 Shepard, Aaron. *The Gifts of Wali Dad* (1–3). Illus. by Daniel San Souci. 1995, Atheneum paper $16.00 (0-684-19445-7). 32pp. Although Wali Dad gains great wealth, he only wants to remain a simple grass cutter in this folktale from India. (Rev: BL 5/1/95; SLJ 8/95) [398.2]

10806 Shepard, Aaron, reteller. *Savitri: A Tale of Ancient India* (3–6). Illus. by Vera Rosenberry. 1992, Whitman LB $16.95 (0-8075-7251-9). 40pp. In picture-book format, the retelling of India's epic poem, the Mahabharata. (Rev: BCCB 3/92; BL 3/15/92; SLJ 5/92) [398.2]

10807 Singh, Rina. *The Foolish Men of Agra: And Other Tales of Mogul India* (2–5). Illus. 1998, Key Porter $14.95 (1-55013-771-9). 48pp. These ten tales from Mogul India focus on the trusted adviser of emperor Akbar and how he is able to outsmart his enemies. (Rev: BL 6/1–15/98; SLJ 6/98) [398.2]

10808 Souhami, Jessica, reteller. *Rama and the Demon King: An Ancient Tale from India* (K–3). Illus. by Jessica Souhami. 1997, DK $14.95 (0-7894-2450-9). A retelling of the important incidents in this Hindu epic about the journeys of the exiled Prince Rama, who was accompanied by his wife, Sita, and brother, Lakshman. (Rev: HBG 3/98; SLJ 9/97) [398.2]

10809 Wolf, Gita. *The Very Hungry Lion: A Folktale* (PS–1). Illus. by Indrapramit Roy. 1996, Annick $24.95 (1-55037-461-3). 32pp. In this folktale from western India, a lion is too lazy to go out to hunt. (Rev: BL 11/1/96; SLJ 1/97) [398.24]

10810 Young, Ed. *Seven Blind Mice* (PS–3). Illus. 1992, Putnam $17.99 (0-399-22261-8). 44pp. A stunning picture book illustrating a version of the old Indian folktale about seven blind men and one elephant. (Rev: BCCB 3/92*; BL 4/1/92*; HB 3–4/92; SLJ 4/92) [398.2]

Japan

10811 Bodkin, Odds. *The Crane Wife* (K–4). Illus. by Gennady Spirin. 1998, Harcourt $16.00 (0-15-201407-1). 32pp. This well-known Japanese folktale tells how a poor sail maker saves a crane who returns as a beautiful maiden whom he marries but later loses when she sacrifices herself to save him. (Rev: BCCB 10/98; BL 11/15/98*; HB 11–12/98; HBG 3/99; SLJ 10/98) [398.2]

10812 Edmonds, I. G. *Ooka the Wise: Tales of Old Japan* (3–6). Illus. by Sanae Yamazaki. 1994, Linnet LB $16.00 (0-208-02379-8). 96pp. A collection of 17 Japanese folktales featuring the legendary judge Ooka Tadasuke, who is devoted to the cause of justice. (Rev: BL 5/15/94) [398.2]

10813 Garrison, Christian. *The Dream Eater* (K–2). Illus. by Diane Goode. 1978, Macmillan paper $4.95 (0-689-71058-5). 32pp. Yukio meets a creature who eats bad dreams in this Japanese folktale. [398.2]

10814 Hamilton, Morse. *Belching Hill* (1–3). Illus. by Forest Rogers. 1997, Greenwillow $15.00 (0-688-14561-2). 32pp. A variation on the Japanese folktale about a little old woman who outsmarts some disgusting monsters. (Rev: BL 4/15/97; SLJ 4/97) [398.2]

10815 Hedlund, Irene. *Mighty Mountain and the Three Strong Women* (PS–3). Trans. by Judith Elkin. Illus. 1990, Volcano $14.95 (0-912078-86-3). 32pp. A sumo wrestler meets three women who surpass him in strength. (Rev: BL 6/1/90; SLJ 10/90) [398.2]

10816 Johnston, Tony. *The Badger and the Magic Fan: A Japanese Folktale* (PS–3). Illus. by Tomie dePaola. 1990, Putnam $13.95 (0-399-21945-5). 32pp. A greedy badger steals the Japanese goblin's magic fan. (Rev: BCCB 4/90; BL 5/1/90*; HB 9–10/90; SLJ 6/90) [398.2]

10817 Kajikawa, Kimiko. *Yoshi's Feast* (PS–3). Illus. by Yumi Heo. 2000, DK $15.95 (0-7894-2607-2). 32pp. In this Japanese folktale, Sabu, a cook, wants to charge his neighbor, Yoshi, for inhaling the wonderful odors from his fragrant eels as they are broiling. (Rev: BL 3/1/00*; HB 5–6/00; HBG 10/00; SLJ 5/00) [398.2]

10818 Kimmel, Eric A. *The Greatest of All: A Japanese Folktale* (PS–3). Illus. by Giora Carmi. 1991, Holiday LB $16.95 (0-8234-0885-X). 32pp. The father of Chuko Mouse is not happy when she tells him she wants to marry a humble, but handsome, field mouse. (Rev: BL 10/15/91; SLJ 10/91) [398.2]

10819 Kimmel, Eric A. *Sword of the Samurai: Adventure Stories from Japan* (4–6). Illus. 1999, Harcourt $15.00 (0-15-201985-5). 80pp. Eleven stories, some of them fantasies, that deal with the samurai warriors of Japan and their adventures. (Rev: BCCB 4/99; BL 3/15/99; HBG 10/99; SLJ 6/99) [398.2]

10820 Kudler, David. *The Seven Gods of Luck* (PS–3). Illus. by Linda Finch. 1997, Houghton $15.00 (0-395-78830-7). 32pp. In this traditional Japanese tale, as a reward for cleaning the snow off the statues of the Seven Gods of Luck, two girls are rewarded with a feast. (Rev: BL 12/15/97; HBG 3/98; SLJ 10/97) [398.2]

10821 *Lady Kaguya's Secret: A Japanese Folktale* (3–7). Illus. by Jirina Marton. 1997, Annick $19.95 (1-55037-441-9). 48pp. A foundling grows into a beautiful, bright young woman, but she wonders about her origins in this Japanese folktale. (Rev: BL 1/1–15/98; SLJ 2/98) [398.2]

10822 McCarthy, Ralph F. *The Inch-High Samurai* (K–3). Illus. by Shiro Kasamatsu. 1993, Kodansha $19.95 (4-7700-1758-8). 48pp. Pint-sized Inchy Bo performs some mighty deeds, including fighting an ogre, in this Japanese folktale. (Rev: BL 12/15/93; SLJ 2/94) [398.2]

10823 McCarthy, Ralph F. *The Moon Princess* (3–6). Illus. by Kancho Oda. Series: Children's Classics. 1993, Kodansha $19.95 (4-7700-1756-1). 48pp. Retellings in verse of three Japanese folktales, one about a virtuous old man and his dog, another a Tom Thumb–like character, and another, the title story, about a couple who find a tiny girl inside a bamboo. (Rev: SLJ 2/94) [398.2]

10824 McDermott, Gerald. *The Stonecutter: A Japanese Folk Tale* (K–3). Illus. by author. 1975, Puffin paper $5.99 (0-14-050289-0). 32pp. The familiar tale of the stonecutter who kept demanding greater power is brilliantly illustrated with colorful, stylized collage paintings. [398.2]

10825 Merrill, Jean. *The Girl Who Loved Caterpillars: A Twelfth-Century Tale from Japan* (5–8). Illus. by Floyd Cooper. 1992, Putnam $16.99 (0-399-21871-8). 32pp. The story of a young Izumi who has no interest in lute playing or writing poetry but is fascinated with "creepy crawlies" instead. (Rev: BCCB 11/92; BL 9/1/92*; SLJ 9/92) [398.2]

10826 Paterson, Katherine. *The Tale of the Mandarin Ducks* (K–4). Illus. by Leo Dillon and Diane Dillon. 1990, Dutton $16.99 (0-525-67283-4). 36pp. Because they have helped free a caged duck, a Japanese girl and her beloved are rewarded with freedom from a sentence of death. (Rev: BCCB 9/90*; BL 9/1/90*; HB 11–12/90*; SLJ 10/90*) [398.2]

10827 Sakade, Florence, ed. *Japanese Children's Favorite Stories* (2–4). Illus. by Yoshio Kurosaki. 1958, Tuttle $16.95 (0-8048-0284-X). 120pp. Twenty folktales traditionally told to Japanese children. [398.2]

10828 Schroeder, Alan. *The Tale of Willie Monroe* (1–3). Illus. by Andrew Glass. 1999, Clarion $15.00 (0-395-69852-9). 32pp. An adaptation of the Japanese folktale that uses a hillbilly hero instead of a Japanese wrestler. (Rev: BCCB 6/99; BL 4/15/99; HB 3–4/99; HBG 10/99; SLJ 6/99) [398.2]

10829 Sierra, Judy. *Tasty Baby Belly Buttons* (K–2). Illus. by Meilo So. 1999, Knopf LB $18.99 (0-679-99369-X). 40pp. A childless Japanese couple find a baby in a melon and later have to rescue it when it is kidnapped by an evil spirit. (Rev: BCCB 6/99; BL 5/1/99; SLJ 5/99) [398.2]

10830 Snyder, Dianne. *The Boy of the Three-Year Nap* (K–3). Illus. by Allen Say. 1988, Houghton $16.95 (0-395-44090-4). 32pp. In this Japanese folktale adaptation, Taro, who does nothing but eat and sleep, schemes to marry his rich neighbor's daughter. (Rev: BCCB 4/88; BL 4/1/88; HB 5–6/88) [398.2]

10831 Takamado, Princess. *Katie and the Dream-Eater* (PS–2). Illus. by Brian Wildsmith. 1997, Oxford $18.95 (0-19-279005-6). 32pp. This variation on a Japanese folktale tells the story of Baby

Baku, one of the dream eaters, the shy creatures who eat bad dreams. (Rev: BL 6/1–15/98; HBG 3/98) [398.2]

10832 Uchida, Yoshiko. *Magic Listening Cap* (4–6). Illus. by author. 1987, Creative Arts paper $8.95 (0-88739-016-1). 160pp. Japanese folktales retold with charm and simplicity. [398.2]

10833 Uchida, Yoshiko. *The Magic Purse* (K–3). Illus. by Keiko Narahashi. 1993, Macmillan $15.95 (0-689-50559-0). 32pp. A poor Japanese farmer is rewarded when he carries a message to the parents of a girl who is held captive by the lord of the Black Swamp. (Rev: BL 10/1/93) [398.2]

10834 Uchida, Yoshiko. *The Wise Old Woman* (K–3). Illus. by Martin Springett. 1994, Macmillan paper $14.95 (0-689-50582-5). 32pp. The wisdom of an old lady, who has been condemned to die because of her age, saves the people of her village in this Japanese folktale. (Rev: BL 11/15/94; SLJ 7/95*) [398.2]

10835 Wells, Ruth. *The Farmer and the Poor God: A Folktale from Japan* (PS–2). Illus. by Yoshi. 1996, Simon & Schuster $16.00 (0-689-80214-5). 32pp. A Japanese folktale in which a family blames the Poor God, who lives with them, for their plight. (Rev: BL 4/1/96; SLJ 5/96*) [398.2]

10836 Williams, Carol Ann. *Tsubu the Little Snail* (K–3). Illus. by Tatsuro Kiuchi. 1995, Simon & Schuster $15.00 (0-671-87167-6). 24pp. Love transforms a snail into a handsome young man in this Japanese folktale. (Rev: BL 6/1–15/95) [398.2]

Southeast Asia

10837 Coburn, Jewell Reinhart, and Tzexa Cherta Lee, adapt. *Jouanah: A Hmong Cinderella* (K–3). Illus. by Anne S. O'Brien. 1996, Shen's $15.95 (1-885008-01-5). This version of the Cinderella story from the Hmong of Southeast Asia takes place in a peasant village. (Rev: BCCB 12/96; SLJ 3/97) [398.2]

10838 Day, Noreha Yussof. *Kancil and the Crocodiles: A Tale from Malaysia* (K–3). Illus. by Britta Teckentrup. 1996, Simon & Schuster paper $16.00 (0-689-80954-9). 32pp. Kancil, a trickster mouse, fools the crocodiles so that he can have a delicious meal. (Rev: BCCB 1/97; BL 12/15/96; SLJ 12/96) [398.2]

10839 Lee, Jeanne M., reteller. *Toad Is the Uncle of Heaven: A Vietnamese Folk Tale* (4–7). Illus. by Jeanne M. Lee. 1985, Holt paper $5.95 (0-8050-1147-1). 32pp. This book tells the story of Toad who collects companions on his way to see the King of Heaven, who makes rain. (Rev: BL 11/1/85; HB 3–4/86) [398.2]

10840 MacDonald, Margaret Read, reteller. *The Girl Who Wore Too Much: A Folktale from Thailand* (PS–3). Illus. by Yvonne Davis. 1998, August House $15.95 (0-87483-503-8). In this updated folktale from Thailand, a young girl learns the value of simplicity when she wears all her beautiful dresses to a dance and is so weighted down she can't

keep up with her friends. (Rev: HBG 10/98; SLJ 6/98) [398.2]

10841 Meeker, Clare Hodgson. *A Tale of Two Rice Birds: A Folktale from Thailand* (4–8). Illus. by Christine Lamb. 1994, Sasquatch $14.95 (1-57061-008-8). 32pp. Two rice birds are reincarnated as a princess and a farmer's son in this Thai folktale. (Rev: BL 1/15/95; SLJ 11/94) [398.2]

10842 Shepard, Aaron. *The Crystal Heart: A Vietnamese Legend* (K–3). Illus. by Joseph Daniel Fiedler. 1998, Simon & Schuster $16.00 (0-689-81551-4). 32pp. In this Vietnamese folktale, Mi Nuong's rejection of a suitor causes his death; however, her tears set his spirit free. (Rev: BCCB 7–8/98; BL 10/1/98; HBG 3/99; SLJ 11/98) [398.2]

10843 Souhami, Jessica. *No Dinner! The Story of the Old Woman and the Pumpkin* (PS–1). Illus. 2000, Marshall Cavendish $15.95 (0-7614-5059-9). 32pp. In this South Asian folktale, Grandma outwits a wolf, a tiger, and a bear on her way to and from visiting her granddaughter in the forest. (Rev: BCCB 3/00; BL 3/1/00; HBG 10/00; SLJ 4/00) [823.914]

10844 Spagnoli, Cathy. *Judge Rabbit and the Tree Spirit: A Folktale from Cambodia* (PS–2). Illus. by Nancy Hom. 1991, Children's Book Pr. $14.95 (0-89239-071-9). 32pp. A tree spirit takes the shape of an absent husband. (Rev: BL 9/15/91; SLJ 8/91) [398.2]

10845 Vuong, Lynette Dyer. *The Brocaded Slipper and Other Vietnamese Tales* (5–7). Illus. by Vo-Dinh Mai. 1982, HarperCollins paper $4.50 (0-06-440440-4). 96pp. Five Vietnamese fairytales, some of which are similar to our own. [398.2]

10846 Xiong, Blia. *Nine-in-One, Grr! Grr!* (3–6). Adapted by Cathy Spagnoli. Illus. by Nancy Hom. 1993, Children's Book Pr. $14.95 (0-89239-048-4); paper $7.95 (0-89239-110-3). 32pp. In this folktale from Laos, Bird comes up with a trick to prevent the earth from being overpopulated with tigers. A reissue. [398.2]

Australia and the Pacific Islands

10847 Galdone, Paul. *The Turtle and the Monkey: A Philippine Tale* (K–2). Illus. by author. 1990, Houghton paper $6.95 (0-395-54425-4). 32pp. Turtle asks monkey to help him save a banana tree. [398.2]

10848 Gittins, Anne. *Tales from the South Pacific Islands* (4–6). Illus. by Frank Rocca. 1977, Stemmer $12.95 (0-916144-02-X). 96pp. Twenty-two folktales from such places as Fiji and Samoa in which the sea and its creatures play prominent roles. [398.3]

10849 Morin, Paul. *Animal Dreaming: An Aboriginal Dreamtime Story* (3–6). Illus. by author. 1998, Harcourt $16.00 (0-15-200054-2). A folktale from Australia that tells how three animals — a kangaroo, a turtle, and an emu — try to bring peace to a warring world. (Rev: HBG 10/98; SLJ 3/98) [398.2]

10850 Roth, Susan L. *The Biggest Frog in Australia* (K–2). Illus. 1996, Simon & Schuster paper $15.00 (0-689-80490-3). 30pp. A parched frog swallows all the water on the continent and in the rain clouds to slake his great thirst. (Rev: BL 6/1–15/96; SLJ 6/96*) [398.2]

10851 Sierra, Judy. *The Dancing Pig* (PS–3). Illus. by Jesse Sweetwater. 1999, Harcourt $16.00 (0-15-201594-9). 32pp. In this Balinesian tale, to save her children a mother must use a dancing pig to outwit an ogress named Rangsasa. (Rev: BCCB 11/99; BL 9/15/99; HBG 3/00; SLJ 10/99) [398.2]

10852 Wolfson, Margaret O. *Turtle Songs: A Tale for Mothers and Daughters* (K–3). Illus. by Karla Sachi. 1999, Beyond Words $15.95 (1-885223-95-1). 32pp. Set on a Fijian island, this folktale tells how an island princess and her daughter were turned into sea turtles. (Rev: BL 8/99; HBG 3/00; SLJ 7/99) [398.2]

Europe

General and Miscellaneous

10853 Bodnar, Judit Z. *A Wagonload of Fish* (PS–2). Illus. by Alexi Natchev. 1996, Lothrop LB $14.93 (0-688-12173-X). 32pp. In this Hungarian folktale, a nagging wife demands that her husband bring her some fish to eat. (Rev: BL 4/1/96; SLJ 5/96) [398.21]

10854 Brett, Jan. *The Mitten* (PS–2). Illus. 1990, Putnam $16.99 (0-399-21920-X). In this Ukrainian folktale, Nicki loses in the snow one of the mittens that his grandmother knit him. (Rev: BCCB 12/89; BL 9/15/89*; HB 11–12/89; SLJ 11/89) [398.2]

10855 Early, Margaret. *William Tell* (K–4). Illus. 1991, Abrams $17.95 (0-8109-3854-5). 32pp. An enchanting, full-color retelling of the story of this famous and good man who triumphed over evil. (Rev: BCCB 2/92; BL 11/15/91*; HB 1–2/92; SLJ 1/91*) [398.2]

10856 Fisher, Leonard Everett. *Kinderdike* (K–3). Illus. 1994, Macmillan paper $15.95 (0-02-735365-6). 32pp. A Dutch folktale about how villagers found the strength to rebuild after a flood destroyed their homes. (Rev: BL 1/1/94; SLJ 4/94) [398.2]

10857 Fisher, Leonard Everett. *William Tell* (1–3). Illus. 1996, Farrar $16.00 (0-374-38436-3). 32pp. The legend of William Tell and his struggle against tyranny are well retold in this attractive picture book. (Rev: BL 2/15/96; SLJ 3/96*) [398]

10858 Gorbachev, Valeri. *Fool of the World and the Flying Ship* (1–3). Illus. by author. 1998, Star Bright $15.95 (1-887734-19-8). 40pp. A new adaptation of the Ukrainian tale about a tsar who promises his daughter in marriage to the man who brings him a flying ship. (Rev: SLJ 4/99) [398.2]

10859 Hogrogian, Nonny. *One Fine Day* (K–3). Illus. by author. 1971, Macmillan $16.00 (0-02-744000-1); paper $5.99 (0-02-043620-3). 32pp. Based on an Armenian folktale, this cumulative story is ideal for reading aloud. Caldecott Medal winner, 1972. [398.2]

10860 Kimmel, Eric A. *Sirko and the Wolf* (K–3). Illus. by Robert Sauber. 1997, Holiday LB $15.95 (0-8234-1257-1). 32pp. When a dog grows too old to be useful, he strikes a bargain with a wolf in this Ukrainian folktale. (Rev: BL 9/15/97; HBG 3/98; SLJ 11/97) [398.2]

10861 Larson, Jean Russell. *The Fish Bride and Other Gypsy Tales* (4–6). Illus. 2000, Linnet $22.50 (0-208-02474-3). 90pp. Sixteen tales of romance, adventure, and humor from the rich traditions of Rom or Gypsies are attractively retold in this entertaining collection. (Rev: BL 11/1/00; HB 11–12/00; HBG 3/01; SLJ 9/00) [398.2]

10862 Peters, Andrew. *Salt Is Sweeter Than Gold* (1–3). Illus. by Zdenka Kabatova-Taborska. 1994, Shambhala $16.00 (1-56957-933-4). 32pp. A Czech folktale in which a king asks his three daughters how much they love him. (Rev: BL 1/1/95) [398.2]

10863 San Souci, Robert D., reteller. *A Weave of Words* (2–5). Illus. by Raul Colon. 1998, Orchard LB $17.99 (0-531-33053-2). In this Armenian tale, an imprisoned king uses his weaving skills to communicate with his wife. (Rev: BCCB 4/98; HBG 10/98; SLJ 3/98) [398.2]

10864 Tresselt, Alvin, ed. *The Mitten* (K–2). Illus. by Yaroslava Mills. 1964, Lothrop LB $14.93 (0-688-51053-1); paper $5.95 (0-688-09238-1). 30pp. An old Ukrainian folktale about a little boy and his lost mitten. [398.2]

10865 Walker, Barbara K., ed. *A Treasury of Turkish Folktales for Children* (4–7). 1988, Shoe String LB $25.00 (0-208-02206-6). 155pp. A witty collection interspersed with riddles. (Rev: BL 10/15/88; SLJ 10/88) [398.2]

France

10866 Brett, Jan, reteller. *Beauty and the Beast* (PS–3). Illus. 1989, Houghton $16.00 (0-89919-497-4). 32pp. A smooth, brief retelling of the old classic. (Rev: BCCB 12/89; BL 10/1/89; SLJ 11/89) [398.2]

10867 Brown, Marcia. *Stone Soup* (1–4). Illus. by author. 1979, Macmillan $16.00 (0-684-92296-7); paper $5.99 (0-689-71103-4). 48pp. An old French tale about three soldiers who make soup from stones. [398.2]

10868 DeFelice, Cynthia, and Mary DeMarsh. *Three Perfect Peaches* (K–2). Illus. by Irene Trivas. 1995, Orchard LB $16.99 (0-531-08722-0). 32pp. In this French folktale, a young farmboy claims the hand of a princess he helped save from death. (Rev: BCCB 4/95; BL 1/15/95; SLJ 4/95) [398.2]

10869 Early, Margaret. *Sleeping Beauty* (1–4). Illus. 1993, Abrams $17.95 (0-8109-3835-9). 32pp. A retelling of the Perrault classic, with dramatic illustrations. (Rev: BL 12/1/93; SLJ 1/94) [398]

10870 Forest, Heather. *Stone Soup* (PS–3). Illus. by Susan Gaber. 1998, August House $15.95 (0-87483-498-8). 32pp. Using a contemporary village as its setting, this is a handsome retelling of the ancient tale that originated in France and, in a different version, Sweden. (Rev: BL 9/1/98; HBG 10/98; SLJ 5/98) [398.2]

10871 Huck, Charlotte. *Toads and Diamonds* (K–3). Illus. by Anita Lobel. 1996, Greenwillow $15.89 (0-688-13681-8). 32pp. A downtrodden girl is rewarded for her kindness in this retelling of a folktale. (Rev: BCCB 1/97; BL 11/1/96*; HB 11–12/96; SLJ 9/96) [398.2]

10872 Kimmel, Eric A. *Three Sacks of Truth: A Story from France* (PS–3). Illus. by Robert Rayevsky. 1993, Holiday LB $15.95 (0-8234-0921-X). 32pp. In this French folktale, a king promises his daughter to the man who can bring him the perfect peach. (Rev: BCCB 7–8/93; BL 4/15/93; SLJ 7/93) [398.2]

10873 Kirsten, Lincoln, adapt. *Puss in Boots* (K–3). Illus. by Alain Vaes. 1994, Little, Brown paper $7.95 (0-316-89501-6). 32pp. Full-color paintings highlight this retelling of Perrault's classic tale. (Rev: BCCB 4/92*; BL 5/15/92; SLJ 4/92*) [398.2]

10874 McGovern, Ann, adapt. *Stone Soup* (PS–1). Illus. by Winslow Pels. 1986, Scholastic paper $3.25 (0-590-41602-2). 32pp. The old story of the young man who asks for food and is refused by the old woman, then he asks her for a stone. (Rev: BCCB 2/87; BL 10/15/86; SLJ 11/86) [398.2]

10875 Mayer, Marianna. *Beauty and the Beast* (3–5). Illus. by author. 1987, Simon & Schuster paper $6.95 (0-689-71151-4). 48pp. A fine retelling made memorable by dazzling pictures. Another version is: *Beauty and the Beast* by Deborah Apy, illus. by Michael Hague (1995, Henry Holt). [398.2]

10876 Perrault, Charles. *The Complete Fairy Tales of Charles Perrault* (4–6). Trans. by Neil Philip and Nicoletta Simborowski. Illus. by Sally Holmes. 1993, Clarion $24.00 (0-395-57002-6). 156pp. Eleven tales by Perrault, newly translated and illustrated with watercolors and printed with fine historical notes. (Rev: BL 11/1/93; SLJ 9/93) [398]

10877 Perrault, Charles. *Perrault's Fairy Tales* (4–6). Illus. by Gustave Dore. 1969, Dover paper $7.95 (0-486-22311-6). 117pp. A classic edition with illustrations by the French master. [398.2]

10878 Perrault, Charles. *Puss in Boots* (K–3). Illus. by Paul Galdone. 1983, Houghton paper $6.95 (0-89919-192-4). 32pp. A favorite French folktale. [398.2]

10879 Perrault, Charles. *Puss in Boots* (K–4). Illus. by Fred Marcellino. 1990, Farrar $16.00 (0-374-36160-6). 32pp. A handsomely illustrated version of this classic tale. (Rev: BCCB 12/90; BL 12/1/90*; HB 3–4/91*; SLJ 1/91) [398.2]

10880 Perrault, Charles. *Puss in Boots* (K–2). Trans. by Anthea Bell. Illus. by Giuliano Lunelli. 1999, North-South LB $15.88 (0-7358-1159-8). 25pp. A lively retelling of Perrault's tale of a son who inherits a mere cat, not realizing how resourceful that feline will be. (Rev: BL 11/1/99; HBG 3/00; SLJ 12/99) [398.2]

10881 Shannon, Mark. *The Acrobat and the Angel* (K–3). Illus. by David Shannon. 1999, Putnam $15.99 (0-399-22918-3). 32pp. In this French folktale, a young boy in medieval France brings a statue

of an angel to life with his skill as an acrobat. (Rev: BL 10/1/99*; HBG 3/00; SLJ 12/99) [398.2]

Germany

10882 Andreasen, Dan. *Rose Red and the Bear Prince* (PS–1). Illus. 2000, HarperCollins LB $16.89 (0-06-027967-2). 40pp. In this version of the Brothers Grimm tale, Rose Red helps a wandering bear to break the enchantment that has turned him from a prince to this animal. (Rev: BL 1/1–15/00; HBG 10/00; SLJ 2/00) [398.2]

10883 Babbitt, Natalie. *Ouch!* (2–4). Illus. by Fred Marcellino. 1998, HarperCollins $14.95 (0-06-205066-4). 32pp. In this retelling of a Grimm Brothers story, a king sets a baby boy afloat in a river after he hears a prediction that the baby will eventually marry his daughter. (Rev: BL 11/15/98; HB 1–2/99; HBG 3/99; SLJ 12/98) [398.2]

10884 Bell, Anthea. *Jack in Luck* (PS–2). Illus. by Eve Tharlet. 1992, Picture Book paper $14.95 (0-88708-249-1). 32pp. Winsome watercolors highlight this retelling of the classic tale about a simple lad who starts with a fortune and goes downhill from there. (Rev: BL 1/15/93; SLJ 4/93) [398]

10885 Carter, David, and Noelle Carter. *The Nutcracker* (4–6). Illus. 2000, Simon & Schuster $19.95 (0-689-83285-0). A pop-up version of the E. T. A. Hoffman classic story. (Rev: BL 12/1/00) [398.2]

10886 de la Mare, Walter. *The Turnip* (1–4). Illus. by Kevin Hawkes. 1992, Godine $18.95 (0-87923-934-4). 32pp. Based on a Grimm brothers tale, the story of a good but poor man with an enormous turnip and his greedy, rich half-brother. (Rev: BL 11/15/92; HB 1–2/93; SLJ 12/92) [398.2]

10887 Dugina, Olga, and Andrej Dugin. *The Brave Little Tailor* (PS–3). Illus. 2000, Abrams $15.95 (0-8109-4113-9). 32pp. The classic tale from the Brothers Grimm about the little tailor that kills seven flies with one blow and, as a result, becomes king, is handsomely retold. (Rev: BL 12/1/00; HBG 3/01; SLJ 11/00) [398.2]

10888 Fitchett, Gordon. *The Twelve Princesses* (PS–3). Illus. 2000, Penguin $15.99 (0-8037-2474-8). 32pp. Using ducks as the main characters, this is a faithful retelling of the Brothers Grimm tale about the beauties who dance all night. (Rev: BL 2/1/00; HBG 10/00; SLJ 7/00) [398.2]

10889 Foreman, Michael. *Rock-A-Doodle-Do!* (K–2). Illus. 2000, Andersen $16.95 (0-86264-951-X). 32pp. This entertaining version of *The Bremen Town Musicians* takes place in the American Southwest in the 1950s. (Rev: BL 3/1/01)

10890 Gay, Marie-Louise, adapt. *Rumpelstiltskin* (PS–2). Illus. by Marie-Louise Gay. 1997, Groundwood $15.95 (0-88899-279-3). This childlike version of the tale will appeal to youngsters. (Rev: SLJ 11/97) [389.2]

10891 Grimm Brothers. *The Brave Little Tailor* (K–4). Retold by Anthea Bell. Illus. by Eve Tharlet. 1989, Picture Book paper $14.95 (0-88708-091-X). A charming retelling of the folktale about a fearless tailor and his encounter with a giant. (Rev: SLJ 9/89) [398.2]

10892 Grimm Brothers. *The Bremem Town Musicians* (PS–2). Illus. by Hans Fischer. 1998, North-South $15.95 (1-55858-893-0). 32pp. This new translation of the classic folktale has illustrations by the famous Swiss artist Hans Fischer. (Rev: BL 4/15/98; HBG 10/98) [398.2]

10893 Grimm Brothers. *The Complete Grimm's Fairy Tales* (4–6). Illus. by Josef Scharl. 1974, Pantheon paper $18.00 (0-394-70930-6). Based on Margaret Hunt's translation, this has become the standard edition of these perennial favorites. [398.2]

10894 Grimm Brothers. *Dear Mili* (1–3). Illus. by Maurice Sendak. 1988, Farrar $16.95 (0-374-31762-3). 40pp. A mother sends her only child into the forest to escape the war that is raging. (Rev: BCCB 11/88; BL 11/1/88; SLJ 11/88) [398.2]

10895 Grimm Brothers. *The Elves and the Shoemaker* (PS–K). Retold and illus. by Paul Galdone. 1984, Houghton paper $6.95 (0-89919-422-2). 32pp. A poor shoemaker is visited by elves at night. [398.2]

10896 Grimm Brothers. *The Elves and the Shoemaker* (PS–2). Illus. by Margaret Walty. 1998, Barefoot $15.95 (1-901223-69-8). A fine retelling of the familiar tale of a poor craftsman and his wife who are aided by two selfless elves. (Rev: SLJ 3/99) [398.2]

10897 Grimm Brothers. *The Fisherman and His Wife* (2–4). Adapted by Eric Metaxas. Illus. by Diana Bryan. 1991, Rabbit Ears $19.95 (0-88708-123-1). Unusual illustrations with cutout silhouettes adorn this age-old story. (Rev: SLJ 9/91) [398.2]

10898 Grimm Brothers. *The Frog Prince: Or, Iron Henry* (2–3). Trans. by Naomi Lewis. Illus. by Binette Schroeder. 1989, North-South $15.95 (1-55858-015-8). 32pp. Fancy special effects highlight this retelling of the classic tale. (Rev: BL 1/15/90; HB 1–2/90; SLJ 12/89) [398.2]

10899 Grimm Brothers. *Household Stories of the Brothers Grimm* (4–7). Illus. by Walter Crane. n.d., Dover paper $7.95 (0-486-21080-4). 269pp. First published in the United States in 1883. [398.2]

10900 Grimm Brothers. *Little Red Riding Hood/ Caperucita roja: A Bilingual Book* (K–2). Trans. by James Surges. Illus. by Pau Estrada. 1999, Chronicle $12.95 (0-8118-2561-2); paper $6.95 (0-8118-2562-0). A bilingual version of the favorite folktale with charming yet scary illustrations. (Rev: SLJ 2/00) [398.2]

10901 Grimm Brothers. *Nibble Nibble Mousekin* (K–3). Illus. by Joan Walsh Anglund. 1962, Harcourt $10.95 (0-15-257400-X); paper $4.95 (0-15-665588-8). 32pp. A version of the Hansel and Gretel story. [398.2]

10902 Grimm Brothers. *Rapunzel* (1–4). Illus. by Trina S. Hyman. 1982, Holiday paper $5.95 (0-8234-0652-0). 32pp. The famous tale of the captive princess and her fabulous hair. Another version is: Illus. by Michael Hague (1984, Creative Ed.). [398.2]

10903 Grimm Brothers. *Rapunzel* (K–3). Trans. by Anthea Bell. Illus. by Maja Dusikova. 1997, North-

South LB $15.88 (1-55858-685-7). 25pp. A fine retelling of the classic fairy tale, with exquisite artwork. (Rev: BL 8/97) [398.2]

10904 Grimm Brothers. *Rumpelstiltskin* (PS–1). Illus. by Paul Galdone. 1985, Houghton $16.00 (0-89919-266-1); paper $6.95 (0-395-52599-3). 32pp. Bold drawings highlight this straightfoward version of the little man who spins straw into gold. Another fine edition is: Illus. by John Wallner (1984, Prentice). (Rev: BL 6/1/ 5; SLJ 8/85) [398.2]

10905 Grimm Brothers. *Rumpelstiltskin* (PS–2). Retold and illus. by Paul O. Zelinsky. 1986, Dutton $16.99 (0-525-44265-0). 40pp. Closeups and much detail in the illustrations highlight the retelling of this old favorite. (Rev: BCCB 10/86; BL 9/1/86; SLJ 10/86) [398.2]

10906 Grimm Brothers. *The Shoemaker and the Elves* (K–2). Illus. by Adrienne Adams. 1982, Evanescent $60.00 (0-945303-04-1). 16pp. A favorite German tale illustrated with soft watercolors. [398.2]

10907 Grimm Brothers. *The Shoemaker and the Elves* (K–2). Retold and illus. by Ilse Plume. 1991, Harcourt $14.95 (0-15-274050-3). This folktale is relocated to Renaissance Italy, but the plot is the same except that the elves now number four. (Rev: SLJ 1/92) [398.2]

10908 Grimm Brothers. *The Six Swans* (3–6). Trans. from German by Anthea Bell. Illus. by Dorothee Duntze. 1998, North-South LB $16.88 (1-55858-983-X). In this traditional version of the Grimm brothers' tale, a sister rescues her six brothers, who have been turned into swans by a cruel stepmother. (Rev: HBG 3/99; SLJ 12/98) [398.2]

10909 Grimm Brothers. *Snow White and the Seven Dwarves* (1–4). Trans. and adapted by Anthea Bell. Illus. by Chihiro Iwasaki. 1991, Picture Book $15.95 (0-88708-012-X). 40pp. A good translation and light-hearted artwork highlight this interpretation of the classic tale. (Rev: BL 1/1/86; SLJ 3/86) [398.2]

10910 Grimm Brothers. *The Three Feathers* (5–8). Illus. by Eleonore Schmid. 1984, Creative Ed. LB $13.95 (0-87191-941-9). 32pp. A version for older readers that is faithful to the original. [398.2]

10911 Grimm Brothers. *The Three Languages* (3–5). Illus. by Ivan Chermayeff. 1984, Creative Ed. LB $13.95 (0-87191-940-0). 32pp. The tale of the seemingly foolish son who ends up as Pope of Rome. [398.2]

10912 Grimm Brothers. *The Water of Life: A Tale from the Brothers Grimm* (PS–3). Retold by Barbara Rogasky. Illus. by Trina S. Hyman. 1986, Holiday LB $15.95 (0-8234-0552-4). 40pp. Three brothers journey to find the water of life for their ailing father. (Rev: BCCB 11/86; BL 9/15/86; HB 3–4/87) [398.2]

10913 Grimm Brothers. *The Wolf and the Seven Little Kids* (PS–3). Illus. by Bernadette Watts. 1995, North-South LB $15.88 (1-55858-446-3). 28pp. Even though her kids have been eaten by the wicked wolf, ingenious Mother Goat is able to save them. (Rev: BL 1/1–15/96; SLJ 1/96) [398.2]

10914 Hamilton, Virginia. *The Girl Who Spun Gold* (PS–3). Illus. by Leo Dillon and Diane Dillon. 2000, Scholastic $16.95 (0-590-47378-6). 40pp. Stunning illustrations and stirring prose mark this outstanding retelling of the Rumpelstiltskin folktale using a West Indian setting. (Rev: BCCB 12/00; BL 8/00*; HB 9–10/00; HBG 3/01; SLJ 9/00) [398.2]

10915 Hodges, Margaret. *The Hero of Bremen* (3–6). Illus. by Charles Mikolaycak. 1993, Holiday LB $16.95 (0-8234-0934-1). 32pp. In this German folktale, a disabled cobbler is helped by the ghost of Roland, the legendary knight who saved the city of Bremen centuries before. (Rev: BCCB 10/93; BL 10/15/93; HB 11–12/93; SLJ 10/93) [398.2]

10916 Hoffman, E. T. A. *The Nutcracker* (4–6). Trans. by Ralph Manheim. Illus. by Maurice Sendak. 1984, Crown paper $20.00 (0-517-58659-2). 120pp. A brilliant, new rendition of this favorite story. [398.2]

10917 Hoffman, E. T. A. *The Strange Child* (3–5). Adapted by Anthea Bell. Illus. by Lisbeth Zwerger. 1984, Picture Book paper $16.95 (0-907234-60-7). 28pp. A reworking of the Hoffman story of two children who fall under magic spells. [398.2]

10918 Holden, Robert. *The Pied Piper of Hamelin* (PS–4). Illus. by Drahos Zak. 1998, Houghton $15.00 (0-395-89918-4). 32pp. A brilliant version of this folktale in which both the rats and the residents of Hamelin, Germany are equally ugly. (Rev: BCCB 5/98; BL 3/1/98*; HBG 10/98; SLJ 5/98) [398.2]

10919 Jackson, Bobby L., reteller. *Little Red Ronnika* (1–4). Illus. by Rhonda Mitchell. 1998, Multicultural Publns. LB $16.95 (1-884242-80-4). 32pp. In this version of Little Red Riding Hood, the characters are all African Americans. Granny is a hip senior and the wolf is a rapper. (Rev: SLJ 1/99) [398.2]

10920 Kajpust, Melissa. *A Dozen Silk Diapers: A Christmas Story* (PS–2). Illus. by Veselina Tomova. 1993, Hyperion LB $14.49 (1-56282-457-0). 32pp. In this German folktale, a young spider who has come to visit the child Jesus falls into the manger. (Rev: BL 9/1/93) [598.2]

10921 Kimmel, Eric A. *The Four Gallant Sisters* (PS–3). Illus. by Tatyana Yuditskaya. 1992, Holt $16.95 (0-8050-1901-4). 32pp. Adapted from the Grimm brothers stories, this is a feminist fairy tale about sisters who disguise themselves as men to find work and independence. (Rev: BL 5/1/92; SLJ 5/92) [398.2]

10922 Kimmel, Eric A. *The Goose Girl: A Story from the Brothers Grimm* (4–6). Illus. by Robert Sauber. 1995, Holiday LB $15.95 (0-8234-1074-9). 32pp. A retelling of the Brothers Grimm tale of the young princess who is cheated out of her birthright by a greedy serving girl. (Rev: BL 10/15/95; SLJ 10/95) [398.2]

10923 Kimmel, Eric A. *Iron John* (K–4). Illus. by Trina S. Hyman. 1994, Holiday LB $16.95 (0-8234-1073-0). 32pp. An adaptation of a Grimm tale about Prince Walter, who meets Iron John in the forest and breaks a spell that has been cast over him. (Rev: BCCB 12/94; BL 11/1/94; SLJ 12/94) [398.2]

10924 Kimmel, Eric A. *Seven at One Blow: A Tale from the Brothers Grimm* (PS–1). Illus. by Megan Lloyd. 1998, Holiday $16.95 (0-8234-1383-7). 32pp. After amazing himself by killing seven flies on his jelly sandwich with one blow, a little tailor sets out to seek his fortune in this tale from the Brothers Grimm. (Rev: BL 11/15/98; HB 1–2/99; HBG 3/99; SLJ 12/98) [398.2]

10925 Kinter, Judith. *King of Magic, Man of Glass: A German Folk Tale* (PS–3). Illus. by Dirk Zimmer. 1998, Clarion $16.00 (0-395-79730-6). 42pp. In this German folktale, Rudolf finds that after receiving unlimited riches he becomes so jaded that he would like to go back to his simple life in the Black Forest. (Rev: BL 11/15/98; HB 1–2/99; HBG 3/99; SLJ 12/98) [398.2]

10926 Latimer, Jim. *The Irish Piper* (3–5). Illus. by John O'Brien. 1991, Macmillan $13.95 (0-684-19130-X). 32pp. A retelling of this legend combines fantasy and contemporary nonsense in a medieval setting. (Rev: BCCB 1/92; BL 1/1/91*; SLJ 12/91) [398.2]

10927 McDermott, Dennis. *The Golden Goose* (PS–2). Illus. 2000, HarperCollins LB $15.89 (0-688-11403-2). 32pp. In this version of the Grimm Brothers tale, young Hans is rewarded for helping a troll by the gift of a talking golden goose. (Rev: BL 5/15/00; HBG 10/00; SLJ 7/00) [398.2]

10928 Marshall, James, reteller. *Hansel and Gretel* (K–3). Illus. 1990, Puffin paper $5.99 (0-14-050836-8). A retelling of the famous story with innovative, often humorous, illustrations. (Rev: SLJ 12/90*) [398.2]

10929 Ray, Jane, reteller. *Hansel and Gretel* (K–3). Illus. by Jane Ray. 1997, Candlewick $15.99 (0-7636-0358-9). A graceful retelling of this familiar German folktale. (Rev: BL 12/1/97; HBG 3/98; SLJ 11/97) [398.2]

10930 Ross, Tony, reteller. *Hansel and Gretel* (K–3). Illus. 1990, Trafalgar $15.95 (0-86264-210-8). Humorous, imaginative details are added to the famous tale. (Rev: SLJ 8/90) [398.2]

10931 Shulevitz, Uri. *The Golden Goose* (PS–3). Illus. 1995, Farrar $16.00 (0-374-32695-9). 32pp. When he aids an old man that his brothers have shunned, a simpleton is rewarded with the gift of a gold-feathered goose in this tale from the Grimm Brothers. (Rev: BCCB 1/96; BL 11/15/95; SLJ 12/95) [398.2]

10932 Shulman, Janet. *The Nutcracker* (K–5). Illus. by Renee Graef. 1999, HarperCollins $19.95 (0-06-027814-5). 48pp. An adaptation of Hoffman's story *The Nutcracker and the Mouse King*, with a CD consisting of the narration and some excerpts from the Tchaikovsky ballet. (Rev: BL 9/1/99; HBG 3/00; SLJ 10/99)

10933 Vande Velde, Vivian. *Tales from the Brothers Grimm and the Sisters Weird* (4–8). Illus. by Brad Weinman. Series: Jane Yolen Books. 1995, Harcourt $17.00 (0-15-200220-0). 128pp. Using a role-reversal technique, the author examines the nature of good and evil in some of the standard tales from the Brothers Grimm. (Rev: BCCB 10/95; SLJ 1/96) [398.2]

10934 Wallace, Ian. *Hansel and Gretel* (2–4). Illus. 1996, Douglas & McIntyre $14.95 (0-88899-212-2). 32pp. A scary retelling in a contemporary setting of the famous Grimm folktale. (Rev: BL 6/1–15/96; SLJ 5/96) [398.2]

10935 Wallis, Diz. *Battle of the Beasts* (2–5). Illus. 2000, Ragged Bears $16.95 (1-929927-15-0). 32pp. An oversize, elegant book that retells the folk tale from the Brothers Grimm about the problems in the animals kingdom when a bear insults the King of Birds, the wren. (Rev: BL 12/1/00; SLJ 1/01) [398.2]

10936 Wegman, William, et al. *Little Red Riding Hood* (2–4). Illus. 1993, Hyperion LB $17.49 (1-56282-417-1). 40pp. The famous fairy tale is retold with some new plot twists and using the author's weimaraners dressed in clothes as models. (Rev: BL 12/1/93; SLJ 3/94) [398.21]

10937 Wildsmith, Brian. *The Bremen Town Band* (PS–1). Illus. 2000, Oxford $16.95 (0-19-279034-X). 32pp. This is a charming retelling of the Grimms' tale about four farm animals who route some thieves from a house as they travel to Bremen. (Rev: BL 6/1–15/00; HBG 10/00; SLJ 8/00) [398.2]

10938 Wolkstein, Diane, reteller. *The Glass Mountain* (K–4). Illus. by Louisa Bauer. 1999, Morrow LB $15.93 (0-688-14848-4). A lesser-known Grimm Brothers tale in which a young girl is held prisoner in an underground cave by an unpleasant old man named Old Rinkrank. (Rev: BCCB 3/99; HBG 10/99; SLJ 7/99) [398.2]

10939 Yolen, Jane. *The Musicians of Bremen: A Tale from Germany* (PS–2). Illus. by John Segal. 1996, Simon & Schuster paper $14.00 (0-689-80501-2). 32pp. The popular German folktale is retold with some humorous twists. (Rev: BL 7/96; HB 5–6/96; SLJ 7/96) [398.2]

10940 Zelinsky, Paul O. *Rapunzel* (3–5). Illus. 1997, Dutton $16.99 (0-525-45607-4). 48pp. Rich oil paintings illustrate this tale of the enduring power of love. Caldecott Medal winner, 1998. (Rev: BL 11/15/97*; HBG 3/98; SLJ 11/97*) [398.2]

10941 Zemach, Margot. *The Three Wishes: An Old Story* (PS–2). Illus. by author. 1986, Farrar $16.00 (0-374-37529-1). 32pp. The story of a poor wood-cutter and his wife who are granted three wishes — and squander them. (Rev: BCCB 3/87; BL 1/1/87; SLJ 12/86) [398.2]

10942 Ziefert, Harriet. *Little Red Riding Hood* (1–2). Illus. by Emily Bolam. Series: Viking Easy-to-Read. 2000, Viking $13.89 (0-670-88389-1). 32pp. A retelling of the Little Red Riding Hood story for beginning readers that warns children not to talk to strangers. (Rev: BL 2/15/00; HBG 10/00; SLJ 4/00) [398.2]

Great Britain and Ireland

10943 Alderson, Brian, reteller. *The Tale of the Turnip* (K–2). Illus. by Fritz Wegner. 1999, Candlewick $12.99 (0-7636-0494-1). In this folktale a

king rewards a poor farmer for his gift of a large turnip. (Rev: BCCB 11/99; HB 11–12/99; HBG 3/00; SLJ 10/99) [398.2]

10944 Asch, Frank. *Ziggy Piggy and the Three Little Pigs* (PS–1). Illus. 1998, Kids Can $14.95 (1-55074-515-8). 32pp. A variation on the story of the three little pigs in which a fourth little pig, Ziggy, rescues his brothers from the wolf and takes them to a raft he made from driftwood. (Rev: BL 11/15/98; HB 11–12/98; HBG 3/99) [398.2]

10945 Aylesworth, Jim. *The Gingerbread Man* (PS–2). Illus. by Barbara McClintock. 1998, Scholastic $15.95 (0-590-97219-7). 32pp. A traditional retelling of the old folktale about the cheerful elderly couple who created a gingerbread man who comes to life and leads them a merry chase. (Rev: BL 4/1/98; HBG 10/98; SLJ 4/98) [398.21]

10946 Barton, Byron. *The Little Red Hen* (PS–2). Illus. 1993, HarperCollins LB $15.89 (0-06-021676-X). 32pp. A new interpretation of this favorite story of the industrious hen, with appealing illustrations. (Rev: BL 5/1/93; SLJ 7/93) [398.2]

10947 Barton, Byron. *The Three Bears* (PS). Illus. 1991, HarperCollins LB $15.89 (0-06-020424-9). 32pp. For the very young, this is a retelling of the story of Goldilocks and the Three Bears. (Rev: BL 1/1/91; SLJ 11/91) [398.2]

10948 Behan, Brendan. *The King of Ireland's Son* (3–5). Illus. by P. J. Lynch. 1997, Orchard $16.95 (0-531-09549-5). 32pp. A rich retelling of the Irish folktale about three princes who set out to find the origin of the heavenly music that is heard in their land. (Rev: BCCB 4/97; BL 4/15/97; SLJ 6/97) [398.2]

10949 Beneduce, Ann Keay. *Jack and the Beanstalk* (1–3). Illus. by Gennady Spirin. 1999, Putnam $15.99 (0-399-23118-8). 32pp. An expanded version of the classic tale, based on a Victorian retelling, in which a fairy figures prominently as Jack's helper. (Rev: BCCB 12/99; BL 11/1/99; HBG 3/00; SLJ 11/99) [398.2]

10950 Bofill, Francesc. *Jack and the Beanstalk/Juan y los frijoles magicos* (2–4). 1998, Chronicle $13.95 (0-8118-2062-9). 32pp. Using an easy English/ Spanish text, this is an attractive retelling of the classic folktale. (Rev: BL 11/15/98; SLJ 8/98) [398.2]

10951 Brett, Jan. *Gingerbread Baby* (PS–3). Illus. 1999, Putnam $16.99 (0-399-23444-6). 32pp. In this updated version of the old tale, Gingerbread Baby escapes and wreaks havoc in the Swiss village where he had been baked. (Rev: BL 11/15/99; HBG 3/00; SLJ 11/99)

10952 Brown, Marcia. *Dick Whittington and His Cat* (K–3). Illus. by author. 1988, Macmillan $16.00 (0-684-18998-4). 32pp. A reissue of a Caldecott Honor Book published in 1950 about the boy who went to London to seek his fortune. [398.2]

10953 Byrd, Robert. *Finn MacCoul and His Fearless Wife: A Giant of a Tale from Ireland* (K–3). Illus. 1999, Dutton $16.99 (0-525-45971-5). 40pp. A traditional tale from Ireland about the giant Finn MacCoul, his wife Oonagh, and the bully and outsider, Cucullin. (Rev: BL 1/1–15/99; HBG 10/99; SLJ 2/99) [398.2]

10954 Calmenson, Stephanie. *The Teeny Tiny Teacher* (PS–K). Illus. by Denis Roche. 1998, Scholastic $15.95 (0-590-37123-1). 32pp. In this English folktale, a teeny tiny teacher takes her teeny tiny class for a walk in a teeny tiny park and finds a teeny tiny bone that belongs to a ghost that is not teeny tiny. (Rev: BCCB 10/98; BL 8/98; HB 9–10/98; HBG 3/99; SLJ 11/98) [398.2]

10955 Carpenter, Stephen. *The Three Billy Goats Gruff* (PS). Illus. Series: Harper Growing Tree. 1998, HarperFestival $9.95 (0-694-01033-2). 24pp. For the very young, this is a simple but accurate retelling of the old English folktale using double-page pictures. (Rev: BL 5/15/98; HBG 10/98; SLJ 7/98) [398.2]

10956 Climo, Shirley. *Magic and Mischief: Tales from Cornwall* (3–7). Illus. 1999, Clarion $17.00 (0-395-86968-4). 127pp. A brilliant retelling of ten Cornish folktales about enchantment, the sea, and supernatural beings. (Rev: BCCB 10/99; BL 8/99; HBG 3/00; SLJ 8/99) [398.2]

10957 *The Cock, the Mouse, and the Little Red Hen* (PS–2). Illus. by Graham Percy. 1992, Candlewick $14.95 (1-56402-008-8). 32pp. The little red hen story retold with the added ingredient of five foxes. (Rev: BL 2/1/92) [398.2]

10958 Cohen, Carol Lee. *Digger Pig and the Turnip* (1–2). Illus. by Christopher Denise. Series: Green Light. 2000, Harcourt $10.95 (0-15-202524-3); paper $3.95 (0-15-202530-8). 20pp. This easy-reader is a simple variation on "The Little Red Hen" using Digger Pig who gets no help from her animals friends in making a large turnip pie. (Rev: BL 2/15/00; HBG 10/00; SLJ 7/00) [398.24]

10959 Collins, Sheila Hebert. *Jolie Blonde and the Three Heberts: A Cajun Twist to an Old Tale* (K–4). Illus. by Patrick Soper. 1999, Pelican $14.95 (1-56554-324-6). In this Cajun version of Goldilocks, the heroine is Jolie Blonde and the bears are three humans named Hebert whose gumbo is eaten while they are away. (Rev: HBG 10/99; SLJ 6/99) [398.2]

10960 Collins, Sheila Hebert, reteller. *Les Trois Cochons* (2–5). Illus. by Patrick Soper. 1999, Pelican $14.95 (1-56554-325-4). A Cajun rendering of the "Three Little Pigs" that contains a number of Cajun phases that are fun but can be confusing. (Rev: SLJ 4/00) [398.2]

10961 Cooper, Susan, reteller. *The Selkie Girl* (3–5). Illus. by Warwick Hutton. 1986, Macmillan paper $4.95 (0-689-71467-X). 32pp. A Scottish tale about a seal who sheds its skin and takes human form on land. (Rev: BL 9/15/86; HB 11–12/86; SLJ 11/86) [398.2]

10962 Cooper, Susan, reteller. *The Silver Cow: A Welsh Tale* (K–4). Illus. by Warwick Hutton. 1991, Simon & Schuster paper $5.99 (0-689-71512-9). 32pp. A greedy farmer inherits a silver cow from his son, who received it for his harp playing. [398.2]

10963 Cooper, Susan. *Tam Lin* (3–6). Illus. by Warwick Hutton. 1991, Macmillan $13.95 (0-689-50505-1). 32pp. A retelling of the old Scottish

ballad with ethereal illustrations. (Rev: BL 2/15/91; HB 5–6/91; SLJ 5/91) [398.2]

10964 Creswick, Paul. *Robin Hood* (6–8). Illus. by N. C. Wyeth. 1984, Macmillan $28.00 (0-684-18162-2). 362pp. A classic edition now reissued. [398.2]

10965 Crossley-Holland, Kevin. *The World of King Arthur and His Court: People, Places, Legend, and Lore* (5–7). Illus. 1999, Dutton $25.00 (0-525-46167-1). 128pp. A beautifully illustrated book that presents material about King Arthur, his loves, his knights, and his feats of chivalry. (Rev: BL 11/15/99; HBG 10/00; SLJ 1/00) [942.01]

10966 Cullen, Lynn. *The Mightiest Heart* (3–5). Illus. by Laurel Long. 1998, Dial $16.99 (0-8037-2292-3). 31pp. A retelling of the Welsh legend about young Prince Llywelyn who, mistakenly believing that his hound, Gelert, has attacked his baby son, banishes the faithful dog. (Rev: BCCB 11/98; BL 12/15/98*; HBG 3/99; SLJ 11/98) [398.2]

10967 Curry, Jane L. *The Christmas Knight* (K–4). Illus. by DyAnne DiSalvo-Ryan. 1993, Macmillan $14.95 (0-689-50572-8). 32pp. Sir Cleges so pleases King Uther that he is given a castle in Wales where he can distribute food to the poor each Christmas. (Rev: BL 9/15/93) [398.2]

10968 Curry, Jane L. *Robin Hood and His Merry Men* (3–5). Illus. by John Lytle. 1994, Macmillan paper $13.95 (0-689-50609-0). 48pp. The traditional tales of Robin Hood, Little John, the Sheriff of Nottingham, et al., told in a modern version. (Rev: BL 1/15/95; SLJ 4/95) [398.2]

10969 Curry, Jane L. *Robin Hood in the Greenwood* (3–5). Illus. 1995, Simon & Schuster paper $15.00 (0-689-80147-5). 50pp. Seven traditional stories about Robin Hood that end with him going to London to live at the court of his king. (Rev: BL 11/15/95; SLJ 1/96) [398.2]

10970 dePaola, Tomie, reteller. *Fin M'Coul: The Giant of Knockmany Hill* (PS–3). Illus. by Tomie dePaola. 1981, Holiday LB $16.95 (0-8234-0384-X); paper $6.95 (0-8234-0385-8). 32pp. Fin's wife saves him from the most feared giant in Ireland. [398.2]

10971 dePaola, Tomie. *Jamie O'Rourke and the Big Potato: An Irish Folktale* (PS–3). Illus. 1992, Putnam $16.99 (0-399-22257-X). 32pp. Lazy Jamie gets a seed from a leprechaun and produces an enormous potato. (Rev: BL 2/15/92; SLJ 4/92) [398.2]

10972 Doyle, Malachy. *Tales from Old Ireland* (3–6). Illus. 2000, Barefoot $19.99 (1-902283-97-X). 96pp. A heady collection of traditional Irish tales that includes the familiar "Children of Lir" and "The Soul Cages." (Rev: BL 11/15/00; SLJ 11/00) [398.2]

10973 Early, Margaret. *Robin Hood* (3–5). Illus. 1996, Abrams $17.95 (0-8109-4428-6). 32pp. A lavishly illustrated edition of 14 of the most popular stories about Robin Hood and his Merry Men. (Rev: BL 6/1–15/96; SLJ 8/96) [398.22]

10974 Egielski, Richard. *The Gingerbread Boy* (PS–4). Illus. 1997, HarperCollins LB $14.89 (0-06-

026031-9). 32pp. This traditional folktale is transported to the streets of New York City, and the chase now involves the subway, among other landmarks. (Rev: BL 10/15/97; HB 9–10/97; HBG 3/98; SLJ 9/97*) [398.2]

10975 Finch, Mary. *The Little Red Hen and the Ear of Wheat* (PS–K). Illus. by Elisabeth Bell. Series: A Barefoot Beginner Book. 1999, Barefoot $15.95 (1-902283-47-3). A retelling of the famous folktale about the little red hen who can't find helpers to prepare a loaf of bread. (Rev: SLJ 5/99) [398.2]

10976 Forest, Heather. *The Woman Who Flummoxed the Fairies: An Old Tale from Scotland* (K–3). Illus. by Susan Gaber. 1990, Harcourt $14.95 (0-15-299150-6). In this retelling of a tale from Scotland, the fairies kidnap a baker so she will make cakes only for them. (Rev: BL 4/1/90; SLJ 6/90) [398.2]

10977 Foster, Joanna. *The Magpies' Nest* (K–3). Illus. by Julie Downing. 1995, Clarion $15.95 (0-395-62155-0). 32pp. An English folktale that compares how various birds build their nests. (Rev: BL 2/1/96; SLJ 3/96) [398.2]

10978 Galdone, Paul. *The Gingerbread Boy* (PS–1). Illus. by author. 1983, Houghton $16.00 (0-395-28799-5); paper $6.95 (0-89919-163-0). 40pp. Humorous and vigorous illustrations enhance this favorite folktale of the adventures of a runaway gingerbread boy. [398.2]

10979 Galdone, Paul. *Henny Penny* (K–2). Illus. by author. 1979, Houghton $16.00 (0-395-28800-2); paper $6.95 (0-89919-225-4). 32pp. A retelling of the favorite cumulative folktale of the hen who thought the sky was falling. [398.2]

10980 Galdone, Paul. *The Little Red Hen* (K–2). Illus. by author. 1979, Houghton $15.00 (0-395-28803-7); paper $5.95 (0-89919-349-8). A little hen works for her lazy housemates in this reworking of the old tale. Another fine edition is: *The Little Red Hen: An Old Story,* illus. by Margot Zemach (1983, Farrar). [398.2]

10981 Galdone, Paul. *The Three Bears* (K–2). Illus. by author. 1979, Houghton $15.00 (0-395-28811-8); paper $6.95 (0-89919-401-X). 32pp. The illustrations for this familiar story are large, colorful, and humorous; excellent to use with a group. [398.2]

10982 Galdone, Paul. *The Three Little Pigs* (PS–1). Illus. by author. 1979, Houghton $15.00 (0-395-28813-4). The old folktale told in verse. Another recommended edition is: Illus. by Erik Blegvad (1980, Macmillan). [398.2]

10983 Garner, Alan, reteller. *The Little Red Hen* (PS–2). Illus. by Norman Messenger. 1997, DK $8.95 (0-7894-1171-7). 32pp. A retelling of this folktale by one of England's great writers for children. (Rev: BL 11/1/97; HBG 3/98; SLJ 12/97) [398.2]

10984 *The Gingerbread Boy* (PS). Illus. by Kathy Wilburn. 1984, Putnam $3.99 (0-448-10217-X). 18pp. A favorite folktale with color illustrations in sturdy books for thumbing by toddlers. [398.2]

10985 Gleeson, Brian. *Finn McCoul: The Legendary Irish Folk Hero* (1–4). Illus. by Peter de Seve. 1995, Simon & Schuster $19.95 (0-689-80201-3). The exploits of the legendary Irish giant as told by his wife, Oonagh, who appears to be his match in every way. (Rev: SLJ 3/96) [398.2]

10986 *Goldilocks and the Three Bears* (PS–K). Illus. by Mireille Levert. 2000, Golden Bks. $9.95 (0-307-10235-1). 24pp. A straight-forward retelling of the traditional tale that makes Goldilocks a modern-day girl who rides a bike. (Rev: BL 6/1–15/00) [398.2]

10987 *Goldilocks and the Three Bears: A Tale Moderne* (PS–3). Illus. by Steven Guarnaccia. 2000, Abrams $15.95 (0-8109-4139-2). 32pp. Goldilocks is a con artist in this hip version of an old favorite. (Rev: BL 5/15/00; HBG 10/00; SLJ 4/00) [398.2]

10988 Green, Roger L. *Adventures of Robin Hood* (4–6). 1995, Puffin paper $3.99 (0-140-36700-4). 256pp. A classic retelling of stories involving Robin and his merry men. [398.2]

10989 Greene, Ellin. *Billy Beg and His Bull* (K–3). Illus. by Kimberly B. Root. 1994, Holiday LB $15.95 (0-8234-1100-1). 32pp. Using gifts he has received from a magic bull, Billy Beg defeats giants and wins a princess in this Irish folktale. (Rev: BCCB 4/94; BL 3/1/94; SLJ 7/94) [398.21]

10990 Greene, Ellin. *The Little Golden Lamb* (PS–2). Illus. by Rosanne Litzinger. 2000, Clarion $15.00 (0-395-71526-1). 32pp. Anyone who touches the lamb with a golden fleece becomes stuck to it in this amusing folktale. (Rev: BCCB 5/00; BL 3/15/00; HB 5–6/00; HBG 10/00; SLJ 6/00) [398.22]

10991 Gross, Gwen, ed. *Knights of the Round Table* (2–5). Illus. by Norman Green. 1992, Random paper $3.99 (0-394-87579-6). 112pp. A retelling of many of the most popular Arthurian legends. (Rev: BCCB 9/85; SLJ 2/86) [398.2]

10992 Harris, Jim, reteller. *The Three Little Dinosaurs* (K–3). Illus. by Jim Harris. 1999, Pelican $14.95 (1-56554-371-8). In this version the three little pigs folktale, three young brachiosaurs build different homes to withstand the big bad Tyrannosaurus rex. (Rev: HBG 3/00; SLJ 2/00) [398.2]

10993 Hastings, Selina, reteller. *Sir Gawain and the Loathly Lady* (5–8). Illus. by Juan Wijngaard. 1987, Lothrop paper $4.95 (0-688-07046-9). 32pp. Noble Sir Gawain agrees to honor a pledge for a husband to a deformed old hag and discovers that he has broken an old spell and released a beautiful woman. (Rev: BCCB 11/85; BL 11/15/85) [398.2]

10994 Heaney, Marie, reteller. *The Names Upon the Harp: Irish Myth and Legend* (4–9). Illus. by P. J. Lynch. 2000, Scholastic $19.95 (0-590-68052-8). 95pp. Using a sampling of stories from various periods of Irish folklore, this is a solid collection of representative myths and legends. (Rev: BCCB 3/01; HBG 3/01; SLJ 1/01) [398.2]

10995 Hewitt, Kathryn, adapt. *The Three Sillies* (K–3). Illus. by Kathryn Hewitt. 1989, Harcourt paper $3.95 (0-15-286856-9). A suitor sets out to find three sillier people than his betrothed's family. (Rev: BCCB 5/86; BL 4/1/86; SLJ 5/86) [398.2]

10996 Heyer, Carol, reteller. *Robin Hood* (2–4). Illus. by Carol Heyer. 1993, Ideals LB $15.00 (0-

8249-8648-2). This handsome book retells the most famous of Robin Hood's exploits, culminating in the King's pardon. (Rev: SLJ 11/93) [398.2]

10997 Hodges, Margaret, reteller. *The Kitchen Knight: A Tale of King Arthur* (3–6). Illus. by Trina S. Hyman. 1990, Holiday LB $15.95 (0-8234-0787-X). A lavishly illustrated version of the story of the king who hides his identity to work in the kitchen at King Arthur's court. (Rev: BCCB 11/90*; HB 3–4/91; SLJ 1/91) [398.2]

10998 Hodges, Margaret. *St. George and the Dragon: A Golden Legend* (2–5). Illus. by Trina S. Hyman. 1984, Little, Brown $16.95 (0-316-36789-3). A reworking of the English tale as it appeared in Edmund Spenser's Fairie Queen. Caldecott Medal winner, 1985. [398.2]

10999 Hodges, Margaret. *Up the Chimney* (K–2). Illus. by Amanda Harvey. 1998, Holiday $15.95 (0-8234-1354-3). 32pp. When a girl goes out to seek her fortune, she is helped by all the objects and animals she has helped in the past, but when her uncharitable, cruel sister goes out, her fate is different. (Rev: BCCB 12/98; BL 11/15/98; HBG 3/99; SLJ 1/99) [398.2]

11000 Hodges, Margaret, and Margery Evernden, retellers. *Of Swords and Sorcerers: The Adventures of King Arthur and His Knights* (4–8). Illus. by David Frampton. 1993, Macmillan $15.00 (0-684-19437-6). 96pp. From Merlin as a young boy to the last battle, this is the story of King Arthur and the knights and ladies connected with his court. (Rev: SLJ 8/93) [398.2]

11001 Howe, John. *Jack and the Beanstalk* (K–2). Illus. 1998, Little, Brown paper $5.95 (0-316-37562-4). 32pp. This fine retelling includes realistic paintings. (Rev: BCCB 11/89; BL 10/15/89; HB 11–12/89; SLJ 2/90) [398.2]

11002 Hunter, Mollie. *Gilly Martin the Fox* (PS–1). Illus. by Dennis McDermott. 1994, Hyperion $15.95 (1-56282-517-8). 40pp. A Scottish folktale about a fox that helps a young prince win the hand of a beautiful princess. (Rev: BL 4/1/94; SLJ 6/94) [398.2]

11003 Jacobs, Joseph. *Celtic Fairy Tales* (3–6). Illus. by John D. Batten. 1968, Peter Smith $22.25 (0-8446-2302-4); Dover paper $6.95 (0-486-21826-0). 267pp. A classic collection. Followed by: *More Celtic Fairy Tales* (1969, Dover paper). [398.2]

11004 Jacobs, Joseph. *English Fairy Tales* (3–6). Illus. by John D. Batten. 1969, Peter Smith $21.75 (0-8446-2303-2); Dover paper $7.95 (0-486-21818-X). A standard collection by a master storyteller. [398.2]

11005 Kellogg, Steven. *Jack and the Beanstalk* (PS–2). Illus. 1991, Morrow $16.89 (0-688-10251-4). 40pp. A well-known artist's version of the classic folktale. (Rev: BL 10/15/91; HB 1–2/92; SLJ 12/91*) [398.2]

11006 Kellogg, Steven. *The Three Little Pigs* (K–3). Illus. 1997, Morrow $15.93 (0-688-08732-9). 32pp. A humorous retelling of the old story, with inventive new details sure to please. (Rev: BL 8/97*; HBG 3/98; SLJ 9/97) [398.2]

11007 Kellogg, Steven. *The Three Sillies* (PS–3). Illus. 1999, Candlewick $16.99 (0-7636-0811-4). 40pp. In this classic English folktale, a man decides that he can't marry a farmer's daughter until he finds three people who are sillier than the girl and her parents. (Rev: BL 11/1/99; HBG 3/00; SLJ 11/99) [398.2]

11008 Kimmel, Eric A. *The Gingerbread Man* (PS–K). Illus. by Megan Lloyd. 1993, Holiday LB $16.95 (0-8234-0824-8). 32pp. This is a modern version of a classic tale about the cookie that says he can't be caught. (Rev: BL 3/15/93; SLJ 6/93*) [398.2]

11009 Kimmel, Eric A. *The Old Woman and Her Pig* (PS–3). Illus. by Giora Carmi. 1992, Holiday LB $16.95 (0-8234-0970-8). 32pp. An excellent retelling of the classic British folktale. (Rev: BL 1/1/93; SLJ 10/92) [398.2]

11010 Leavy, Una. *Irish Fairy Tales and Legends* (4–8). Illus. 1997, Roberts Rinehart $18.95 (1-57098-177-9). 96pp. An attractive book that contains ten Irish legends, some going back 2,000 years. (Rev: BL 2/1/98; HBG 10/98; SLJ 2/98) [398.2]

11011 McBratney, Sam, reteller. *Celtic Myths* (3–5). Illus. by Stephen Playe. Series: Myths of the World. 1998, NTC $22.50 (0-87226-561-7). 96pp. Using haunting watercolors, this book contains 15 magical, entertaining stories from Ireland and Britain that date back to the early history of these lands. (Rev: HBG 10/98; SLJ 4/99) [398.2]

11012 McClure, Gillian. *Selkie* (K–3). Illus. 1999, Farrar $16.00 (0-374-36709-4). 32pp. In this version of the Selkie legend, young Peter helps a Selkie — a seal that can transform itself into a girl — escape after she has been captured by an oysterman. (Rev: BL 12/15/99; HBG 3/00; SLJ 11/99) [398.2]

11013 MacDonald, Margaret Read. *Slop! A Welsh Folktale* (K–2). Illus. by Yvonne Davis. 1997, Fulcrum $15.95 (1-55591-352-0). 24pp. In this Welsh folktale, fairies become annoyed when their neighbor continually empties his slop bucket on top of their cottage. (Rev: BL 11/1/97; HBG 3/98; SLJ 11/97) [398.2]

11014 McGovern, Ann. *Too Much Noise* (K–3). Illus. by Simms Taback. 1967, Houghton $16.00 (0-395-18110-0); paper $6.95 (0-395-62985-3). 48pp. An old man follows the advice of the village wise man when he complains that his house is too noisy. [398.2]

11015 McKay, Sindy, adapt. *Jack and the Beanstalk* (1–2). Illus. by Lydia Halverson. Series: We Both Read. 1998, Treasure Bay $7.99 (1-891327-00-3). This traditional English folktale is told twice — with an adult's and a child's vocabulary. (Rev: SLJ 12/98) [398.2]

11016 Mata, Marta. *Goldilocks and the Three Bears/ Ricitos de Oro y los tres osos* (2–4). Trans. by Alis Alejandro. 1988, Chronicle $12.95 (0-8118-2075-0). 32pp. Using a bilingual format in English and Spanish, and bold, contemporary illustrations, this is an easy retelling of the English folktale. (Rev: BL 11/15/98; SLJ 8/98) [398.2]

11017 Miles, Betty. *Goldilocks and the Three Bears* (1). Illus. by Bari Weissman. 1998, Simon & Schuster $15.00 (0-689-81787-8). 32pp. For beginning readers, this is a charming, very simple retelling of the traditional English folktale. (Rev: BL 11/1/98; HBG 3/99; SLJ 1/99) [398.2]

11018 Miles, Betty. *The Three Little Pigs* (1). Illus. by Paul Meisel. 1998, Simon & Schuster $15.00 (0-689-81788-6). 32pp. In this version of the English folktale for beginning readers, the wolf makes an escape from the wily little pigs at the end. (Rev: BL 11/1/98; HBG 3/99; SLJ 1/99) [398.2]

11019 Morpurgo, Michael. *Arthur: High King of Britain* (4–7). Illus. by Michael Foreman. 1995, Harcourt $22.00 (0-15-200080-1). 144pp. King Arthur tells nine stories of his exploits to a 12-year-old boy. (Rev: BCCB 5/95; BL 8/95; SLJ 7/95)

11020 Murphy, Church. *Jack and the Beanstalk: A Classic Collectible Pop-Up* (PS–K). Illus. 1998, Simon $19.95 (0-689-82207-3). Pop-up giants, trees, and castles are a few of the surprises in this interactive version of the classic folktale. (Rev: BL 1/1–15/99) [398.2]

11021 Paterson, Katherine. *Parzival: The Quest of the Grail Knight* (5–8). Illus. 1998, Dutton $15.99 (0-525-67579-5). 128pp. A retelling of the epic poem about the quest for the Holy Grail and the sin that caused the knight Parzival to wander the world looking for peace. (Rev: BL 3/1/98; HBG 10/98; SLJ 2/98*) [398.2]

11022 Philip, Neil. *Celtic Fairy Tales* (4–8). Illus. 1999, Viking $21.99 (0-670-88387-5). 144pp. The 20 stories in this fine anthology originated in Ireland, Scotland, Brittany, Wales, Cornwall, and the Isle of Man. (Rev: BL 11/15/99; HBG 10/00) [398.2]

11023 Pyle, Howard. *The Merry Adventures of Robin Hood* (5–8). Illus. by author. 1968, Dover paper $9.95 (0-486-22043-5). 296pp. Stories about Robin Hood and the inhabitants of Sherwood Forest. [398.2]

11024 Pyle, Howard. *The Story of King Arthur and His Knights* (6–8). Illus. by author. 1966, Dover paper $8.95 (0-486-21445-1). One of the most famous editions of these classic stories. A sequel is: *The Story of the Champions of the Round Table* (1968). [398.2]

11025 Pyle, Howard. *The Story of the Grail and the Passing of Arthur* (5–8). Illus. by author. 1985, Macmillan paper $8.95 (0-486-27361-X). 340pp. The last title of a four-volume King Arthur series, first published in 1910. (Rev: BL 12/15/85) [398.2]

11026 Riordan, James. *King Arthur* (5–7). Illus. 1998, Oxford $19.95 (0-19-274176-4). 96pp. A large-format book that retells the Arthurian legends with emphasis on his beginnings and his death. (Rev: BL 10/1/98; SLJ 4/99) [398.2]

11027 Robins, Arthur. *The Teeny Tiny Woman* (PS–2). Illus. 1998, Candlewick $10.99 (0-7636-0444-5); paper $3.29 (0-7936-0452-6). 32pp. A humorous, suspenseful retelling of the famous English folktale, illustrated with cartoon-like drawings.

(Rev: BCCB 10/98; BL 12/15/98; HBG 3/99; SLJ 9/98) [398.2]

11028 Rosales, Melodye Benson. *Leola and the Honeybears: An African-American Retelling of Goldilocks and the Three Bears* (PS–1). Illus. 1999, Scholastic $15.95 (0-590-38358-2). 38pp. The changes in the text of this classic tale are minor, but the paintings are outstanding in this version of Goldilocks in which the heroine is an African American. (Rev: BCCB 10/99; BL 11/1/99; HBG 3/00; SLJ 11/99) [398.22]

11029 Ross, Tony, reteller. *Goldilocks and the Three Bears* (K–3). Illus. 1992, Viking $13.95 (0-87951-453-1). 28pp. An enjoyable retelling of the old classic with modern updating. (Rev: BL 2/15/93) [398.2]

11030 Sabuda, Robert. *Arthur and the Sword* (2–5). Illus. 1995, Simon & Schuster $16.00 (0-689-31987-8). 32pp. The story of young King Arthur and how he pulled the sword Excalibur from the anvil. (Rev: BL 11/1/95; SLJ 11/95)

11031 San Souci, Robert D. *Brave Margaret: An Irish Adventure* (1–4). Illus. by Sally Wern Comport. 1999, Simon & Schuster $17.00 (0-689-81072-5). 40pp. An intrepid girl survives a shipwreck, challenges a giant, and saves her boyfriend in this adaptation of an Irish folktale. (Rev: BCCB 5/99; BL 3/1/99; HBG 10/99; SLJ 9/99) [398.2]

11032 San Souci, Robert D. *Young Arthur* (1–3). Illus. by Jamichael Henterly. 1997, Doubleday $16.95 (0-385-32268-2). 32pp. This account of the youth of King Arthur ends after he has received the sword Excalibur and has won his first battle. (Rev: BL 11/1/97; HBG 3/98; SLJ 10/97) [398.2]

11033 Scieszka, Jon. *The True Story of the Three Little Pigs: By A. Wolf* (PS–2). Illus. 1989, Viking $16.99 (0-670-82759-2). 32pp. A hip and funny version, from the wolf's point of view. (Rev: BCCB 9/89*; BL 9/1/89; HB 1–2/90; SLJ 10/89) [398.2]

11034 Sewall, Marcia. *The Green Mist* (K–4). Illus. 1999, Houghton $15.00 (0-395-90013-1). 32pp. A retelling of the Lincolnshire folktale in which people await the coming of the Green Mist, which signals the arrival of spring. (Rev: BCCB 6/99; BL 4/1/99; HB 3–4/99; HBG 10/99; SLJ 4/99) [398.2]

11035 Singer, Marilyn. *The Maiden on the Moor* (1–3). Illus. by Troy Howell. 1995, Morrow LB $14.93 (0-688-08765-6). 40pp. In this English ballad, two shepherd brothers discover a young woman lying unconscious and must decide if they should care for her. (Rev: BL 4/15/95; SLJ 4/95) [398.2]

11036 Sturges, Philemon. *The Little Red Hen (Makes a Pizza)* (PS–2). Illus. by Amy Ward. 1999, Dutton $15.99 (0-525-45953-7). 32pp. In this variation on the classic folktale, the industrious Little Red Hen makes pizza instead of bread. (Rev: BCCB 2/00; BL 11/15/99; HBG 3/00; SLJ 12/99*) [398.2]

11037 Sutcliff, Rosemary, reteller. *Beowulf* (5–8). Illus. by Charles Keeping. 1984, Smith $22.50 (0-8446-6165-1). This is a reissue of the Anglo-Saxon tale published originally in 1962. Also use the King Arthur story, *The Sword and the Circle* (1981, Dutton). [398.2]

11038 Talbott, Hudson, reteller. *King Arthur and the Round Table* (2–4). Illus. by Hudson Talbott. Series: Tales of King Arthur. 1995, Morrow $15.89 (0-688-11341-9). Three stories about King Arthur in which he forms the Round Table and marries Guinevere. (Rev: SLJ 12/95) [398.2]

11039 Talbott, Hudson. *Lancelot* (5–7). Illus. 1999, Morrow LB $15.93 (0-688-14833-6). 40pp. A retelling of the life of Lancelot, from his rescue as a child by the Lady of the Lake to his love for Guinevere, marriage to Elaine, and fathering of Galahad. (Rev: BL 9/1/99; HBG 3/00; SLJ 10/99) [398.2]

11040 Thomas, Gwyn, and Kevin Crossley-Holland. *Tales from the Mabinogion* (5–8). Illus. by Margaret Jones. 1985, Overlook $19.95 (0-87951-987-8). 88pp. A translation of Welsh hero tales. (Rev: BCCB 6/85; BL 4/1/85) [398.2]

11041 Wahl, Jan. *Little Johnny Buttermilk* (PS–1). Illus. by Jennifer Mazzucco. 1999, August House $15.95 (0-87483-559-3). 32pp. An English tale about Little Johnny and how he escapes from a witch after being captured on his way to market. (Rev: BL 12/15/99; HBG 3/00; SLJ 2/00) [398.2]

11042 Wattenberg, Jane. *Henny-Penny* (PS–3). Illus. 2000, Scholastic $15.95 (0-439-07817-2). 40pp. An updated, hilarious version of the story of the hen and her friends who decide to warn the king that the sky is falling. (Rev: BCCB 5/00; BL 4/15/00; HBG 10/00; SLJ 4/00) [398.24]

11043 Wells, Rosemary, reteller. *Jack and the Beanstalk* (PS–2). Illus. by Norman Messenger. 1997, DK $8.95 (0-7894-1170-9). 32pp. In this version of the folktale, Jack not only confronts the giant but also frees his father from his captors. (Rev: BL 11/1/97; HBG 3/98; SLJ 12/97) [398.2]

11044 White, Carolyn. *Whuppity Stoorie: A Scottish Folktale* (PS–2). Illus. by S. D. Schindler. 1997, Putnam $15.95 (0-399-22903-5). 32pp. In this Scottish folktale, a mysterious woman asks a high price for nursing a pig back to health. (Rev: BCCB 7–8/97; BL 9/1/97; SLJ 7/97) [398.2]

11045 Williams, Marcia. *The Adventures of Robin Hood* (3–5). Illus. 1995, Candlewick $17.95 (1-56402-535-7); paper $7.99 (0-7636-0275-2). 32pp. Eleven of the most famous exploits of Robin Hood are retold using a bold comic strip style. (Rev: BL 3/15/95; SLJ 4/95) [398.22]

11046 Yolen, Jane, ed. *Camelot* (4–7). Illus. 1995, Putnam $19.99 (0-399-22540-4). 198pp. Ten stories and one song explore various facets of the life of King Arthur and the circle of friends and enemies that surrounded him. (Rev: BL 2/1/96; SLJ 1/96) [398.2]

11047 Zemach, Harve. *Duffy and the Devil: A Cornish Tale Retold* (1–3). Illus. by Margot Zemach. 1973, Farrar $17.00 (0-374-31887-5); paper $6.95 (0-374-41897-7). 40pp. A variant of "Rumpelstiltskin," this folktale is told with humor and verve and boldly illustrated. Caldecott Medal winner, 1974. [398.2]

Greece and Italy

11048 Aesop. *The Aesop for Children* (3–5). Illus. by Milo Winter. 1984, Checkerboard $12.95 (1-56288-039-X); paper $5.99 (0-590-47977-6). This edition, reissued with the original artwork, includes 126 tales. [398.2]

11049 Aesop. *Aesop's Fables* (3–5). Illus. by Fulvio Testa. 1989, Barron's $14.95 (0-8120-5958-1). 48pp. Twenty familiar tales illustrated with paintings that use a Middle East oasis as a setting. (Rev: BCCB 5/89; HB 7–8/89) [398.2]

11050 Aesop. *Aesop's Fables* (1–3). Illus. by Lisbeth Zwerger. 1989, Picture Book $16.00 (0-88708-108-8). 28pp. Twelve familiar tales are interpreted with watercolor paintings. (Rev: BCCB 2/90; BL 11/15/89; SLJ 12/89) [398.2]

11051 Aesop. *Fables of Aesop* (4–6). Illus. by David Levine. 1984, Harvard Common $13.95 (0-87645-074-5); paper $8.95 (0-87645-116-4). 108pp. One of many recommended editions of this classic. [398.2]

11052 Aesop. *The Tortoise and the Hare: An Aesop Fable* (PS–K). Illus. by Janet Stevens. 1984, Holiday LB $15.95 (0-8234-0510-9); paper $6.95 (0-8234-0564-8). 32pp. An updated, charming retelling of the classic fable. [398.2]

11053 Aesop. *The Town Mouse and the Country Mouse* (PS–1). Illus. by T. R. Garcia. 1979, Troll LB $15.95 (0-89375-131-6); paper $3.95 (0-89375-109-X). 32pp. The classic story faithfully and entertainingly retold. [398.2]

11054 Ash, Russell, and Bernard A. Higton, eds. *Aesop's Fables* (3–6). Illus. 1991, Chronicle $17.95 (0-87701-780-8). 95pp. More than 50 fables reprinted and illustrated with artists from the past. (Rev: SLJ 3/91) [398.2]

11055 Barnes-Murphy, Frances. *The Fables of Aesop* (3–5). Illus. 1994, Lothrop $19.95 (0-688-07051-5). 96pp. An extensive collection of more than 100 fables with lively illustrations. (Rev: BL 12/1/94; SLJ 10/94) [398.2]

11056 Craig, Helen. *The Town Mouse and the Country Mouse* (K–3). Illus. 1992, Candlewick $13.95 (1-56402-102-5). 32pp. A refreshing variation on the Aesop fable with embellishments that add a new flavor. (Rev: BCCB 1/93; BL 11/15/92; HB 1–2/93; SLJ 3/93) [398.2]

11057 dePaola, Tomie. *Days of the Blackbird: A Tale of Northern Italy* (K–3). Illus. 1997, Putnam $15.99 (0-399-22929-9). 32pp. An Italian tale about a faithful bird that stays through the winter to sing for an ailing duke. (Rev: BL 3/15/97; HB 3–4/97; SLJ 3/97*)

11058 dePaola, Tomie. *The Mysterious Giant of Barletta: An Italian Folktale* (K–3). Illus. by author. 1988, Harcourt paper $6.00 (0-15-256349-0). 32pp. A statue of an old lady saves the town from marauders. [398.2]

11059 dePaola, Tomie. *Strega Nona* (PS–2). Illus. by author. 1979, Simon & Schuster paper $6.95 (0-671-66606-1). 32pp. The old Italian folktale retold.

Also use: *Big Anthony and the Magic Ring* (1979) and *Strega Nona's Magic Lessons* (1982). [398.2]

11060 dePaola, Tomie. *Strega Nona: Her Story* (PS–3). Illus. 1996, Putnam $16.99 (0-399-22818-7). 32pp. This book supplies background information on the birth and youth of Nona and how she became the village strega. (Rev: BL 9/15/96; HB 11–12/96; SLJ 10/96) [398.2]

11061 dePaola, Tomie. *Tony's Bread: An Italian Folktale* (K–3). Illus. 1989, Putnam $15.95 (0-399-21693-6). 32pp. A Milano nobleman hopes to win Serafina by setting her father up in business in the city. (Rev: BL 10/1/89; HB 1–2/90; SLJ 11/89) [398.2]

11062 Fox, Paula. *Amzat and His Brothers: Three Italian Tales* (3–5). Illus. by Emily Arnold McCully. 1993, Orchard $16.95 (0-531-05462-4). 80pp. Tales retold from a grandfather who lived in a small Italian village. (Rev: BCCB 3/93*; BL 3/15/93; HB 7–8/93; SLJ 7/93) [398.2]

11063 Gal, Laszlo, and Raffaella Gal. *The Parrot* (K–3). Illus. 1997, Douglas & McIntyre $16.95 (0-88899-287-4). 32pp. In this Italian folktale, a prince assumes the identity of a parrot to help a princess. (Rev: BL 9/15/97; SLJ 10/97) [398.2]

11064 Herman, Gail, reteller. *The Lion and the Mouse* (1). Illus. by Lisa McCue. Series: Early Step into Reading. 1998, Random paper $3.99 (0-679-88674-5). 32pp. The classic Aesop fable is retold dramatically in a simple text suitable for beginning readers. (Rev: BL 11/1/98; SLJ 2/99) [398.2]

11065 Jones, Carol. *The Hare and the Tortoise* (K–3). Illus. 1996, Houghton $13.95 (0-395-81368-9). 32pp. Peepholes and detailed illustrations are used in this retelling of the famous Aesop fable. (Rev: BL 9/1/96; SLJ 9/96) [398.24]

11066 Lowell, Susan. *The Tortoise and the Jackrabbit* (PS–2). Illus. by Jim Harris. 1994, Northland LB $15.95 (0-87358-586-0). 32pp. This favorite Aesop fable is retold with the tortoise an aged grandmother and the hare a conceited egocentric. (Rev: BL 1/15/95; SLJ 2/95)

11067 Lynch, Tom, adapt. *Fables from Aesop* (3–5). Illus. by Tom Lynch. 2000, Viking $15.99 (0-670-88948-2). A striking presentation of 13 of the most famous fables from Aesop. (Rev: SLJ 10/00) [398.2]

11068 McClintock, Barbara. *Animal Fables from Aesop* (4–6). Illus. 1991, Godine $18.95 (0-87923-913-1). 48pp. The text is an expansion of nine fables complete with dialogue and dramatic situations. (Rev: BCCB 1/92; BL 1/1/92; HB 1–2/92; SLJ 1/92) [398.2]

11069 McDermott, Gerald. *The Fox and the Stork* (1–2). Illus. Series: Green Light. 1999, Harcourt $10.95 (0-15-202343-7); paper $3.95 (0-15-202267-8). 20pp. This is a simple retelling in an easy-reader format of the fable about the stork and the fox who learn that being kind to each other is proper behavior. (Rev: BL 10/1/99; HBG 3/00) [398.2]

11070 Manna, Anthony L., and Christodoula Mitakidou. *Mr. Semolina-Semolinus: A Greek Folktale* (1–4). Illus. by Giselle Potter. 1997, Simon &

Schuster $16.00 (0-689-81093-8). 40pp. Areti creates the perfect man for herself, but he is stolen by an evil queen. (Rev: BCCB 7–8/97; BL 4/15/97; HB 5–6/97; SLJ 4/97) [398.2]

11071 Miles, Betty. *The Tortoise and the Hare* (1). Illus. by Paul Meisel. Series: Starting to Read. 1998, Simon & Schuster $15.00 (0-689-81792-4). 32pp. A sprightly retelling of the Aesop fable in an easy-to-read format with pen and watercolor illustrations. (Rev: BL 5/1/98; HBG 10/98; SLJ 5/98) [398.2]

11072 Orgel, Doris. *The Lion and the Mouse and Other Aesop's Fables* (K–3). Illus. by Bert Kitchen. 2000, DK $16.95 (0-7894-2665-X). 32pp. An oversize picture book that retells Aesop's most famous fables, including "The Boy Who Cried Wolf" and "The Hare and the Tortoise." (Rev: BL 10/1/00; SLJ 10/00) [398.2]

11073 Pinkney, Jerry. *Aesop's Fables* (2–4). Illus. 2000, North-South $19.95 (1-58717-000-0). 96pp. A first-rate collection of 60 of Aesop's tales retold and illustrated by this acclaimed artist. (Rev: BCCB 12/00; BL 12/15/00*; HB 1–2/01; HBG 3/01; SLJ 10/00) [398.24]

11074 Poole, Amy Lowry. *The Ant and the Grasshopper* (PS–1). Illus. 2000, Holiday $16.95 (0-8234-1477-9). 32pp. This version of Aesop's fable is transported to China, and the ink and gouache illustrations on rice paper impart a quaint Oriental look. (Rev: BCCB 12/00; BL 8/00; HBG 3/01; SLJ 9/00) [398.24]

11075 Santangelo, Colony Elliot. *Brother Wolf of Gubbio: A Legend of Saint Francis* (K–3). Illus. 2000, Handprint $15.95 (1-929766-07-6). 32pp. In this old Italian tale, Saint Francis tames a wolf that has been terrorizing a village. (Rev: BCCB 1/01; BL 1/1–15/01; HBG 3/01; SLJ 2/01) [398.2]

11076 Sogabe, Aki, reteller. *Aesop's Fox* (K–3). Illus. by Aki Sogabe. 1999, Harcourt $16.00 (0-15-201671-6). Several of Aesop's fables involving the fox are interwoven into a single narrative with striking pictures. (Rev: BCCB 11/99; HBG 3/00; SLJ 12/99) [398.2]

11077 Ward, Helen. *The Hare and the Tortoise* (PS–3). Illus. 1999, Millbrook LB $23.90 (0-7613-1318-4). 40pp. A witty, straightforward retelling of the fable, illustrated with outstanding watercolor paintings. (Rev: BCCB 6/99; BL 5/15/99*; HBG 10/99; SLJ 7/99) [398.24]

11078 Watts, Bernadette, reteller. *The Lion and the Mouse: An Aesop Fable* (PS–2). Illus. by Bernadette Watts. 2000, North-South LB $15.88 (0-7358-1221-7). An expansion of the traditional Aesop fable that is illustrated with paintings of jungle scenes. (Rev: HBG 10/00; SLJ 8/00) [398.2]

11079 Watts, Bernadette. *The Town Mouse and the Country Mouse: An Aesop Fable* (PS–2). Illus. 1998, North-South LB $15.88 (1-55858-988-0). 28pp. A delightful version of the old Aesop fable about two mice that visit each other and discover that home is best. (Rev: BL 11/15/98; HBG 3/99; SLJ 3/99) [398.2]

Russia

11080 Afanasyev, Alexander, ed. *Russian Fairy Tales* (4–7). Illus. by Alexander Alexeieff. 1976, Pantheon paper $18.00 (0-394-73090-9). The definitive collection of folktales reissued in the 1945 edition. [398.2]

11081 Arnold, Katya, reteller. *That Apple Is Mine!* (PS–1). Illus. by Katya Arnold. 2000, Holiday $15.95 (0-8234-1629-1). In this Russian folktale, Bear teaches the animals to share when they all want the same apple. (Rev: HB 1–2/01; HBG 3/01; SLJ 12/00) [398.2]

11082 Cech, John. *First Snow, Magic Snow* (K–3). Illus. by Sharon McGinley-Nally. 1992, Macmillan LB $14.95 (0-02-717971-0). In this Russian folktale, a childless woodsman makes a baby from snow. (Rev: BCCB 11/92; HB 11–12/92; SLJ 12/92) [398.2]

11083 Cecil, Laura. *The Frog Princess* (PS–3). Illus. by Emma C. Clark. 1995, Greenwillow $16.00 (0-688-13506-4). 32pp. In this variation on a Russian folktale, a young prince falls in love with a little green frog. (Rev: BCCB 4/95; BL 2/1/95; SLJ 4/95*) [398.2]

11084 Cole, Joanna. *Bony-Legs* (1–4). Illus. by Dirk Zimmer. 1983, Macmillan $16.00 (0-02-722970-X); Scholastic paper $3.99 (0-590-40516-0). 48pp. A simply read story based on the Russian Baba Yaga. [398.2]

11085 Crouch, Marcus. *Ivan: Stories of Old Russia* (3–5). Illus. by Bob Dewar. 1989, Oxford $20.00 (0-19-274135-7). 80pp. Simple Ivan wins in the end in these Russian tales. (Rev: BCCB 5/89; BL 7/89; SLJ 9/89) [398.2]

11086 Davis, Aubrey. *The Enormous Potato* (PS–1). Illus. by Dusan Petricic. 1998, Kids Can $14.95 (1-55074-386-4). 32pp. This variation on the Russian tale about a turnip uses a gigantic potato that again requires the help of everyone, including a tiny mouse, to get it out of the ground. (Rev: BCCB 10/98; BL 11/1/98; HBG 3/99; SLJ 11/98) [398.2]

11087 De Regniers, Beatrice S. *Little Sister and the Month Brothers* (K–3). Illus. by Margot Tomes. 1976, Houghton $8.95 (0-8164-3147-7). 48pp. A delightful retelling of an old Slavic tale reminiscent of the Cinderella theme. [398.2]

11088 Ginsburg, Mirra. *Clay Boy* (PS–3). Illus. by Joseph A. Smith. 1997, Greenwillow $15.89 (0-688-14410-1). 32pp. In this Russian folktale, a grandpa makes a clay boy who comes to life and has a voracious appetite. (Rev: BL 4/15/97*; HB 3–4/97; SLJ 5/97) [398.2]

11089 Ginsburg, Mirra. *Good Morning, Chick* (PS–K). Illus. by Byron Barton. 1980, Greenwillow $15.89 (0-688-84284-4); Morrow paper $5.95 (0-688-08741-8). 32pp. A Russian folktale about a chick who must learn his identity. [398.2]

11090 Hoffman, Mary. *Clever Katya: A Fairy Tale from Old Russia* (K–3). Illus. by Marie Cameron. 1998, Barefoot $15.95 (1-901223-64-7). 32pp. In this Russian folktale, 7-year-old Katya so impresses the czar with her intelligence that he asks her to visit him in his palace. (Rev: BL 10/1/98; SLJ 10/98) [398.2]

11091 Hogrogian, Nonny. *The Contest* (3–5). Illus. by author. 1976, Greenwillow $15.89 (0-688-84042-6). 32pp. Adaptation of the folktale about two robbers who discover that they are engaged to the same girl. [398.2]

11092 Jackson, Ellen. *The Impossible Riddle* (K–3). Illus. by Alison Winfield. 1995, Whispering Coyote $14.95 (1-879085-93-3). 32pp. In this Russian folktale, a czar hopes to prevent his daughter's marriage by demanding that prospective suitors answer an impossible riddle. (Rev: BL 1/1–15/96) [398.2]

11093 Kimmel, Eric A. *Baba Yaga: A Russian Folktale* (K–3). Illus. by Megan Lloyd. 1991, Holiday LB $16.95 (0-8234-0854-X). 32pp. A traditional Russian folktale about Marina, whose wicked stepmother sends her to the forest witch. (Rev: BL 5/1/91; SLJ 6/91) [398.2]

11094 Kimmel, Eric A. *Bearhead: A Russian Folktale* (K–3). Illus. by Charles Mikolaycak. 1991, Holiday LB $16.95 (0-8234-0902-3). 32pp. A peasant woman finds an odd-looking foundling with the body of a human and the head of a bear. (Rev: BCCB 12/91; BL 9/1/91; SLJ 10/91) [398.2]

11095 Kimmel, Eric A. *The Birds' Gift: A Ukrainian Easter Story* (PS–3). Illus. by Katya Krenina. 1999, Holiday $16.95 (0-8234-1384-5). 34pp. After saving a group of birds, on Easter morning townspeople find beautifully decorated eggs left behind as gifts. (Rev: BL 4/15/99; HBG 10/99; SLJ 6/99) [398.2]

11096 Kimmel, Eric A. *I Know Not What, I Know Not Where: A Russian Tale* (4–6). Illus. by Robert Sauber. 1994, Holiday LB $16.95 (0-8234-1020-X). 64pp. In this Russian fairy tale, a hunter is rewarded for saving an enchanted dove's life by getting help to perform tasks demanded by the czar. (Rev: BCCB 7–8/94; BL 3/1/94; SLJ 6/94) [398.2]

11097 Kimmel, Eric A. *One Eye, Two Eyes, Three Eyes: A Hutzul Tale* (PS–3). Illus. by Dirk Zimmer. 1996, Holiday LB $15.95 (0-8234-1183-4). 32pp. A traveler unwittingly bargains away his daughter in this Ukrainian tale. (Rev: BL 11/1/96; SLJ 1/97) [398.2]

11098 Langton, Jane. *Salt: From a Russian Folktale* (K–3). Trans. by Alice Plume. Illus. by Ilse Plume. 1992, Hyperion $14.95 (1-56282-178-4). 48pp. A Russian folktale about three brothers who go to sea to seek their fortunes. (Rev: BCCB 1/93; BL 10/15/92; SLJ 12/92) [398.2]

11099 Lewis, J. Patrick. *At the Wish of the Fish: A Russian Folktale* (1–4). Illus. by Katya Krenina. 1999, Simon & Schuster $16.00 (0-689-81336-8). 32pp. The life of Emelya, a lazy simpleton, changes when he catches a magic fish that will grant his wishes. (Rev: BL 6/1–15/99; HBG 10/99; SLJ 5/99) [398.2]

11100 Lottridge, Celia B. *Music for the Tsar of the Sea* (K–3). Illus. by Harvey Chan. 1998, Douglas & McIntyre $16.95 (0-88899-328-5). 32pp. A lengthy retelling of the Russian folktale about musician Sadko and the Tsar of the Sea, who takes an unwilling Sadko to his underwater kingdom to play for him forever. (Rev: BL 1/1–15/99; SLJ 1/99) [398.2]

11101 Lurie, Alison. *The Black Geese: A Baba Yaga Story from Russia* (PS–3). Illus. by Jessica Souhami. 1999, DK $14.95 (0-7894-2558-0). 32pp. While rushing to save her baby brother from the clutches of fearful Baba Yaga, Elena stops to help different animals in need and they, in turn, help her in her quest. (Rev: BCCB 5/99; BL 6/1–15/99; HB 5–6/99; HBG 10/99; SLJ 6/99) [398.2]

11102 McCaughrean, Geraldine. *Grandma Chickenlegs* (K–3). Illus. by Moira Kemp. 1999, Carolrhoda $15.95 (1-57505-415-9). 32pp. In this classic Russian folktale, young Tatia is sent to the witch's house to borrow a needle and is soon a prisoner of the horrible Baba Yaga. (Rev: BL 10/15/99; HBG 3/00; SLJ 1/00) [398.2]

11103 Marshak, Samuel, reteller. *The Month-Brothers: A Slavic Tale* (K–4). Illus. by Diane Stanley. 1983, Morrow $15.93 (0-688-01510-7). 32pp. A folktale involving such familiar elements as a girl and a mean stepmother. [398.2]

11104 Martin, Rafe. *The Language of Birds* (1–4). Illus. by Susan Gaber. 2000, Putnam $15.99 (0-399-22925-6). 32pp. In this Russian folktale, young Vasilii saves his brothers at sea when he learns the language of the birds. (Rev: BCCB 10/00; BL 5/15/00; HB 7–8/00; HBG 3/01; SLJ 7/00) [398.2]

11105 Mayer, Marianna. *Baba Yaga and Vasilisa the Brave* (PS–3). Illus. by Kinuko Craft. 1994, Morrow $16.95 (0-688-08500-8). 40pp. Vasilisa survives both the schemes of her wicked stepmother and a visit to the witch Baba Yaga and finally marries the czar. (Rev: BL 6/1–15/94; SLJ 7/94*) [398.2]

11106 Polacco, Patricia. *Luba and the Wren* (1–3). Illus. 1999, Putnam $16.99 (0-399-23168-4). 32pp. In this Russian folktale, Luba wants none of the wishes given her after saving an enchanted wren, but her parents want wealth and power. (Rev: BL 5/15/99; HBG 10/99; SLJ 6/99) [398.2]

11107 Prokofiev, Sergei. *Peter and the Wolf* (4–8). Adapted by Miguelanxo Prado. Illus. by author. 1998, NBM $15.95 (1-56163-200-7). 22pp. A somber version of the Russian folktale filled with menacing situations and scary settings. (Rev: HBG 10/98; SLJ 6/98) [398.2]

11108 Ransome, Arthur. *The Fool of the World and the Flying Ship* (1–4). Illus. by Uri Shulevitz. 1968, Farrar $16.00 (0-374-32442-5); paper $6.95 (0-374-42438-1). 48pp. Colorful, panoramic scenes extend this retelling of a popular Russian folktale about a simple peasant boy who acquires a flying ship. Caldecott Medal winner, 1969. [398.2]

11109 Reyher, Becky. *My Mother Is the Most Beautiful Woman in the World* (2–5). Illus. by Ruth Gannett. 1945, Lothrop LB $16.93 (0-688-51251-8). 40pp. A girl tries to find her mother in this Russian setting. [398.2]

11110 Robbins, Ruth. *Baboushka and the Three Kings* (2–4). Illus. by Nicholas Sidjakov. 1960, Houghton $16.00 (0-395-27673-X); paper $6.95 (0-395-42647-2). 32pp. The Russian legend of the old woman who refused to follow the three kings in search of the Holy Child. Caldecott Medal winner, 1961. [398.2]

11111 San Souci, Robert D. *Peter and the Blue Witch Baby* (K–3). Illus. by Alexi Natchev. 2000, Doubleday $15.95 (0-385-32269-0). 32pp. In this Russian folktale, Tsar Peter must get the help of three giants to rid his palace of a powerful witch. (Rev: BCCB 11/00; BL 11/1/00; HBG 3/01; SLJ 11/00) [398.2]

11112 Shepard, Aaron. *The Sea King's Daughter: A Russian Legend* (4–6). Illus. by Gennady Spirin. 1997, Simon & Schuster $17.00 (0-689-80759-7). 40pp. In this Russian folktale Sadko, a talented musician, must decide whether he loves the daughter of the King of the Sea enough to remain in the underwater kingdom for the rest of his life. (Rev: BL 11/15/97; HBG 3/98; SLJ 12/97) [398.2]

11113 Sherman, Josepha. *Vassilisa the Wise: A Tale of Medieval Russia* (K–3). Illus. by Daniel San Souci. 1988, Harcourt $16.00 (0-15-293240-2). 26pp. Staver, a merchant, brags that his wife, Vassilisa, is more clever than any woman at the royal court, which makes the prince angry. (Rev: BL 4/15/88; HB 7–8/88; SLJ 9/88) [398.2]

11114 Tolstoy, Aleksei. *The Gigantic Turnip* (PS–2). Illus. by Niamh Sharkey. Series: Barefoot Beginner. 2000, Barefoot $15.95 (1-902283-12-0). 40pp. A rather complicated retelling of the popular Russian folktale about a husband and wife who need help to uproot a huge turnip. (Rev: BCCB 7–8/99; SLJ 4/99) [398.2]

11115 Vagin, Vladimir. *Peter and the Wolf* (PS–3). Illus. 2000, Scholastic $15.95 (0-590-38608-5). 32pp. This retelling of the musical fairy tale makes a few changes, for example, the duck is saved and the wolf ends up in a zoo. (Rev: BL 11/15/00; SLJ 11/00) [398.2]

11116 Winthrop, Elizabeth. *The Little Humpbacked Horse: A Russian Tale* (4–6). Illus. by Alexander Koshkin. 1997, Clarion $14.95 (0-395-65361-4). 24pp. A retelling of the Russian tale about a boy whose mentor is a humpbacked colt. (Rev: BCCB 5/97; BL 3/1/97; SLJ 4/97*) [398.2]

Scandinavia

11117 Arnold, Tim. *The Three Billy Goats Gruff* (PS–1). Illus. 1993, Macmillan LB $14.95 (0-689-50575-2). 32pp. This Norwegian folktale is retold with a Rocky Mountain setting and a few modern touches. (Rev: BL 12/1/93; HB 7–8/93; SLJ 10/93) [398.2]

11118 Asbjornsen, Peter C. *The Three Billy Goats Gruff* (PS–2). Retold by Glen Rounds. Illus. 1993, Holiday LB $16.95 (0-8234-1015-3). 32pp. This veteran illustrator noted for animal drawings illustrates and retells this famous Norwegian folktale. (Rev: BL 4/15/93; HB 7–8/93; SLJ 6/93*) [398.2]

11119 Asbjornsen, Peter C., and Jorgen Moe. *The Man Who Kept House* (PS–3). Illus. by Svend Otto S. 1992, Macmillan $13.95 (0-689-50560-4). 32pp. A farmer and his wife swap jobs for the day; he never again complains about his wife's housekeeping. (Rev: BL 2/1/93; HB 1–2/93; SLJ 1/93) [398.2]

11120 Asbjornsen, Peter C., and Jorgen Moe. *Norwegian Folk Tales* (3–6). Illus. by Erik Werenskiold and Theodor Kittelsen. 1978, Pantheon paper $14.00 (0-394-71054-1). This edition retains the original illustrations from the 1845 edition. [398.2]

11121 *East o' the Sun and West o' the Moon* (3–6). Trans. by George Webbe. Illus. by P. J. Lynch. 1992, Candlewick $15.95 (1-56402-049-5). 48pp. A striking picture-book version of a beloved Norwegian folktale. (Rev: BL 9/15/92*; SLJ 9/92) [398.2]

11122 Emberley, Rebecca. *Three Cool Kids* (K–3). Illus. 1995, Little, Brown $15.95 (0-316-23666-7). 32pp. A variation on "The Three Billy Goats Gruff" featuring three sibling goats who live in an inner-city area. (Rev: BCCB 4/95; BL 3/1/95; SLJ 3/95*) [398.2]

11123 French, Vivian. *Why the Sea Is Salty* (K–3). Illus. by Patrice Aggs. 1993, Candlewick $14.95 (1-56402-183-1). 32pp. In this Norwegian folktale, the misuse of wishes by a miser produces enough salt to make the oceans salty. (Rev: BL 6/1–15/93; SLJ 8/93) [398.2]

11124 Galdone, Paul. *The Three Billy Goats Gruff* (PS–3). Illus. by author. 1973, Houghton $16.00 (0-395-28812-6). 32pp. A troll meets his match. [398.2]

11125 Huth, Holly Young. *The Son of the Sun and the Daughter of the Moon* (3–5). Illus. by Anna Vojtech. 2000, Simon & Schuster $17.00 (0-689-82482-3). 32pp. This poignant folktale from the Saami people of northern Scandinavia tells of the conflict between the sun and the moon about the marriage of their children. (Rev: BL 5/15/00; HBG 10/00; SLJ 7/00) [398.2]

11126 Katz, Welwyn W. *Beowulf* (4–6). Illus. 1999, Douglas & McIntyre $19.95 (0-88899-365-X). 64pp. A retelling of the Beowulf legend, including his defeat of Grendel and the monster's mother. (Rev: BL 12/1/99) [813.54]

11127 Kimmel, Eric A. *Boots and His Brothers: A Norwegian Tale* (PS–3). Illus. by Kimberly B. Root. 1992, Holiday LB $14.95 (0-8234-0886-8). 32pp. In this Norwegian folktale, three brothers set out to seek their fortunes, but only the youngest, Boots, succeeds. (Rev: BCCB 3/92; BL 3/1/92) [398.2]

11128 Kimmel, Eric A. *Easy Work! An Old Tale* (PS–3). Illus. by Andrew Glass. 1998, Holiday $15.95 (0-8234-1349-7). 32pp. In this variation on the classic Norwegian folktale, farmer McTeague and his wife decide to exchange roles for a day, with disastrous results. (Rev: BL 4/15/98; HBG 10/98; SLJ 6/98) [398.2]

11129 Lunge-Larsen, Lise. *The Troll with No Heart in His Body* (2–4). Illus. 1999, Houghton $18.00 (0-395-91371-3). 96pp. A collection of nine Norwegian folktales, including "Three Billy Goats Gruff." (Rev: BCCB 1/00; BL 9/1/99; HB 11–12/99; HBG 3/00; SLJ 11/99) [398.2]

11130 Mayer, Mercer. *East of the Sun and West of the Moon* (3–5). Illus. by author. 1980, Macmillan paper $6.99 (0-689-71113-1). 48pp. A poor farmer gives his daughter to a strange white bear in this Norwegian folktale. [398.2]

11131 Shepard, Aaron. *The Maiden of Northland: A Hero Tale of Finland* (3–7). Illus. by Carol Schwartz. 1996, Simon & Schuster $16.00 (0-689-80485-7). In this tale from the Finnish epic the Kalevala, Aila, the maiden of Northland, is courted by two suitors. (Rev: SLJ 4/96) [398.2]

11132 Wisniewski, David. *Elfwyn's Saga* (4–5). Illus. 1990, Viking LB $13.89 (0-688-09590-9). 32pp. Boldly colored dramatic artwork provides the scene for these Icelandic sagas. (Rev: BL 11/1/90; HB 11–12/90; SLJ 10/90*) [398.2]

Spain and Portugal

11133 Ada, Alma F. *The Three Golden Oranges* (K–3). Illus. by Reg Cartwright. 1999, Simon & Schuster $16.00 (0-689-80775-9). 32pp. A retelling of the Spanish folktale about the three princes who want wives, and to get them must bring three oranges to a wise old woman. (Rev: BCCB 7–8/99; BL 5/15/99; HBG 10/99; SLJ 7/99) [398.2]

11134 Araujo, Frank P. *Nekane, the Lamina and the Bear: A Tale of the Basque Pyrenees* (K–2). Illus. by Xiao Jun Li. 1993, Rayve $20.25 (1-877810-01-0). 32pp. In this Basque version of the standard fairy tale, Red Riding Hood becomes Nekane, who is stopped by a forest spirit on her way to her uncle's home. (Rev: BCCB 3/94; BL 2/1/94; SLJ 5/94) [398.2]

11135 Cruz Martinez, Alejandro. *The Woman Who Outshone the Sun: The Legend of Lucia Zenteno* (K–3). Trans. by Rosalma Zubizarreta. Illus. by Fernando Olivera. 1991, Children's Book Pr. $14.95 (0-89239-101-4). 30pp. This Hispanic folktale in English and Spanish tells about a woman who is misunderstood because of her great bond with nature. (Rev: BCCB 2/92; SLJ 3/92) [398.2]

11136 Kimmel, Eric A. *Bernal and Florinda: A Spanish Tale* (K–3). Illus. by Robert Rayevsky. 1994, Holiday LB $15.95 (0-8234-1089-7). 32pp. A comic fairy tale about two Spanish lovers who are united in marriage despite the objections of the bride's father. (Rev: BCCB 9/94; BL 9/15/94; SLJ 11/94) [398.2]

11137 Kimmel, Eric A. *Squash It! A True and Ridiculous Tale* (3–5). Illus. by Robert Rayevsky. 1997, Holiday LB $15.95 (0-8234-1299-7). 32pp. The Spanish tale of the king who adopted a louse as his favorite pet. (Rev: BL 6/1–15/97; HB 7–8/97; SLJ 7/97) [398.2]

11138 Robbins, Sandra. *The Firefly Star: A Hispanic Folk Tale* (PS–3). Illus. by Iku Oseki. 1995, See-More's Workshop paper $6.95 (1-882601-23-8). 32pp. In this Spanish folktale, the important holiday Three Kings' Day almost doesn't take place until a mouse and a ladybug intervene. (Rev: BL 12/1/95; SLJ 2/96) [398.2]

11139 Sierra, Judy. *The Beautiful Butterfly: A Folktale from Spain* (K–3). Illus. by Victoria Chess. 2000, Clarion $15.00 (0-395-90015-8). 32pp. This popular Spanish folktale ends happily when the fish that had swallowed Butterfly's new husband — a mouse — spits him out, thus reuniting the happy pair. (Rev: BCCB 5/00; BL 3/15/00; HBG 10/00; SLJ 8/00) [398.2]

Jewish Folklore

11140 Aroner, Miriam. *The Kingdom of Singing Birds* (K–5). Illus. by Shelly O. Haas. 1993, Kar-Ben $13.95 (0-929371-43-7); paper $5.95 (0-929371-44-5). In this Jewish folktale, a rabbi tells a king that the only way to get his birds to sing is to set them free. (Rev: SLJ 9/93) [398.2]

11141 Blades, Ann. *Too Small* (K–2). Illus. by author. 2000, Groundwood $15.95 (0-88899-400-1). A variation on the traditional Yiddish tale about a house that becomes crowded when a lot of friends and animals are invited in. (Rev: HBG 3/01; SLJ 10/00) [398.2]

11142 Brodmann, Aliana, reteller. *Such a Noise! A Jewish Folktale* (K–3). Trans. by Aliana Brodmann and David Filingham. Illus. by Hans Poppel. 1989, Kane/Miller $11.95 (0-916291-25-1). A man tries to drown out the noise in his household by bringing farm animals inside. (Rev: SLJ 12/89) [398.2]

11143 Clement, Gary. *Just Stay Put: A Chelm Story* (K–4). Illus. 1996, Douglas & McIntyre $14.95 (0-88899-239-4). 32pp. A resident of Chelm, Poland, mistakes his hometown for Warsaw. (Rev: BL 9/15/96; SLJ 6/96) [398.2]

11144 Davis, Aubrey. *Bone Button Borscht* (K–3). Illus. by Dusan Petricic. 1997, Kids Can $15.95 (1-55074-224-8). 32pp. An Eastern European version of *Stone Soup*, in which a beggar persuades the synagogue caretaker to let him make borscht from his coat buttons. (Rev: BL 11/1/97; SLJ 11/97) [398.2]

11145 Freedman, Florence B. *It Happened in Chelm: A Story of the Legendary Town of Fools* (K–4). Illus. by Nik Krevitsky. 1990, Shapolsky paper $9.95 (0-933503-22-9). A retelling of one of the Jewish folktales about the fools who live in Chelm. (Rev: SLJ 3/91) [398.2]

11146 Gerstein, Mordicai. *The Shadow of a Flying Bird: A Legend from the Kurdistani Jews* (1–5). Illus. 1994, Hyperion LB $16.49 (0-7868-2012-8). 32pp. God comes to earth to claim the life of his faithful servant Moses in this Jewish folktale. (Rev: BL 10/1/94; SLJ 9/94) [398.2]

11147 Gilman, Phoebe. *Something from Nothing* (PS–3). Illus. 1993, Scholastic $15.95 (0-590-47280-1). 32pp. This folktale tells how a frugal grandfather recycles the material from a jacket to ever smaller objects, ending with the covering for a button. (Rev: BCCB 2/94; BL 9/1/93; HB 11–12/93; SLJ 1/94) [398.2]

11148 Gordon, Ruth. *Feathers* (K–4). Illus. by Lydia Dabcovich. 1993, Macmillan LB $14.95 (0-02-736511-5). 32pp. The foolish men of Chelm botch the plan to collect money for a new bathhouse in this Jewish folktale. (Rev: BCCB 12/93; BL 10/15/93) [398.21]

11149 Harber, Frances. *The Brothers' Promise* (4–6). Illus. by Thor Wickstrom. 1998, Albert Whitman LB $15.95 (0-8075-0900-0). 32pp. In this traditional Jewish tale, two brothers secretly sacrifice to help each other and fulfill their father's wishes. (Rev: BCCB 4/98; BL 3/15/98; HBG 10/98; SLJ 5/98) [398.2]

11150 Jaffe, Nina. *Tales for the Seventh Day: A Collection of Sabbath Stories* (3–7). Illus. by Kelly Stribling Sutherland. 2000, Scholastic $15.95 (0-590-12054-9). 73pp. A collection of Jewish tales that honor the traditions and the celebration of the Sabbath. (Rev: BL 12/15/00; HBG 3/01; SLJ 11/00) [398.2]

11151 Jaffe, Nina. *The Way Meat Loves Salt: A Cinderella Tale from the Jewish Tradition* (PS–2). Illus. by Louise August. 1998, Holt $15.95 (0-8050-4384-5). A Yiddish folktale that combines King Lear with Cinderella and casts Elijah the Prophet in the role of fairy godmother. (Rev: BCCB 11/98; BL 10/1/98; HB 9–10/98; HBG 3/99; SLJ 9/98) [398.2]

11152 *A Journey to Paradise: And Other Jewish Tales* (1–4). Ed. by Howard Schwartz. Illus. by Giora Carmi. 2000, Pitspopany $16.95 (0-943706-21-1); paper $9.95 (0-943706-16-5). 48pp. A collection of eight Jewish folktales that revolve around mystery, magic, and life after death. (Rev: BL 4/15/00; HBG 10/00; SLJ 6/00) [296.1]

11153 Kimmel, Eric A. *The Adventures of Hershel of Ostropol* (K–4). Illus. by Trina S. Hyman. 1995, Holiday $15.95 (0-8234-1210-5). 64pp. Ten Jewish folktales that use as a locale a village community in the Ukraine during the 19th century. (Rev: BL 10/15/95; SLJ 11/95) [398.2]

11154 Kimmel, Eric A. *Gershon's Monster* (2–4). Illus. by Jon J. Muth. 2000, Scholastic $16.95 (0-439-10839-X). 32pp. Based on an early Hasidic legend, this is the story of Gershon and how his sins catch up with him. (Rev: BCCB 10/00; BL 10/1/00; HB 9–10/00; HBG 3/01; SLJ 9/00) [398.2]

11155 Kimmel, Eric A. *The Jar of Fools: Eight Hanukkah Stories from Chelm* (PS–3). Illus. by Mordicai Gerstein. 2000, Holiday $18.95 (0-8234-1463-9). 56pp. This collection of eight stories — some original plus some traditional Fools of Chelm tales — is filled with silliness and slapstick. (Rev: BL 9/1/00; HB 9–10/00; HBG 3/01)

11156 Kimmel, Eric A. *Onions and Garlic* (PS–3). Illus. by Katya Arnold. 1996, Holiday $15.95 (0-8234-1222-9). 32pp. In this Hebrew folktale, young Getzel is able to use a sackful of onions to obtain a fortune in diamonds. (Rev: BCCB 6/96; BL 4/1/96; SLJ 7/96) [398.2]

11157 Patterson, Jose. *Angels, Prophets, Rabbis and Kings: From the Stories of the Jewish People* (3–6). Illus. by Claire Bushe. 1991, Bedrick LB $24.95 (0-87226-912-4). 144pp. A treasure chest of stories and parables. (Rev: BL 9/15/91; SLJ 8/91) [398.2]

11158 Podwal, Mark. *Golem: A Giant Made of Mud* (K–4). Illus. 1995, Greenwillow LB $14.93 (0-688-13812-X). 32pp. A collection of stories about the mysterious shape-changing creature that is associated with Prague. (Rev: BL 10/1/95; SLJ 11/95) [398.2]

11159 Prose, Francine. *The Angel's Mistake: Stories of Chelm* (PS–4). Illus. by Mark Podwal. 1997, Greenwillow $14.89 (0-688-14906-5). 24pp. A series of anecdotes about the city of Chelm — where fools reside — its creation and eventual destruction. (Rev: BCCB 7–8/97; BL 3/1/97; HB 7–8/97; SLJ 4/97) [398.2]

11160 Prose, Francine. *The Demons' Mistake: A Story from Chelm* (PS–3). Illus. by Mark Podwal. 2000, Greenwillow LB $15.89 (0-688-17566-X). 32pp. This retelling of the traditional Yiddish tale is set in modern New York City, where the demons of Chelm have come because they believe the streets are paved with gold. (Rev: BCCB 11/00; BL 8/00; HBG 3/01; SLJ 10/00) [398.2]

11161 Prose, Francine. *You Never Know: A Legend of the Lamed-vavniks* (K–4). Illus. by Mark Podwal. 1998, Greenwillow LB $14.93 (0-688-15807-2). 24pp. Gradually the town of Plotchnik realizes that poor Schmuel the Shoemaker is one of God's holy Lamed-vavniks — 36 righteous people living in secret throughout the world. (Rev: BCCB 7–8/98; BL 6/1–15/98; HBG 10/98; SLJ 8/98) [398.2]

11162 Rogasky, Barbara. *The Golem* (4–6). Illus. by Trina S. Hyman. 1996, Holiday $18.95 (0-8234-0964-3). 96pp. The story of the giant monster of the 16th century and its use to help protect the Jewish people in Prague from persecution. (Rev: BCCB 9/96; BL 10/1/96*; HB 1–2/96; SLJ 10/96) [398.2]

11163 Rossel, Seymour. *Sefer Ha-Aggadah: The Book of Legends for Young Readers* (4–7). Illus. by Judy Dick. 1996, UAHC paper $14.00 (0-8074-0603-1). 67pp. A collection of legends based on stories about the Jewish people from the Old Testament. (Rev: SLJ 3/97) [398.2]

11164 Rothenberg, Joan. *Yettele's Feathers* (PS–3). Illus. 1995, Hyperion LB $15.49 (0-7868-2081-0). 40pp. A rabbi makes Yettele realize how harmful her gossiping can be. (Rev: BL 5/1/95; SLJ 4/95) [398.2]

11165 Schram, Peninnah. *Ten Classic Jewish Children's Stories* (3–6). Illus. 1998, Pitspopany $16.95 (0-943706-96-3). 48pp. A volume that contains the retelling of ten traditional Jewish tales — many that illustrate situations in the Torah — with questions to reflect on the lessons taught. (Rev: BL 11/15/98; SLJ 3/99) [296.1]

11166 Schwartz, Howard. *The Day the Rabbi Disappeared: Jewish Holiday Tales of Magic* (4–7). Illus. by Monique Passicot. 2000, Viking $15.99 (0-670-88733-1). 80pp. A collection of short folktales that explore Jewish heritage and the role of mysticism in the religion. (Rev: BL 10/1/00*; HB 7–8/00; HBG 3/01) [398.2]

11167 Schwartz, Howard, and Barbara Rush, sels. and retellers. *A Coat for the Moon and Other Jewish Tales* (2–5). Illus. by Michael Iofin. 1999, Jewish Publication Soc. $14.95 (0-8276-0596-X). 81pp. An engaging collection of 15 folktales from Europe and the Middle East, many from the Israel Folktale

Archive. (Rev: HB 11–12/99; HBG 3/00; SLJ 10/99) [398.2]

11168 Sherman, Josepha. *Rachel the Clever and Other Jewish Folktales* (4–6). Illus. 1993, August House paper $10.95 (0-87483-307-8). 176pp. Jewish tales gathered from many lands. (Rev: BL 3/15/93) [398.2]

11169 Shollar, Leah. *A Thread of Kindness: A Tzedaka Story* (2–4). Illus. by Shoshana Mekibel. 2000, Hachai $9.95 (1-929628-01-3). 32pp. This traditional tale tells of a poor but virtuous farmer who gains wealth through his kindness to others. (Rev: BL 10/1/00; SLJ 1/01) [398.2]

11170 Silverman, Erica. *Raisel's Riddle* (K–4). Illus. by Susan Gaber. 1999, Farrar $16.00 (0-374-36168-1). 40pp. This variation on the Cinderella story tells of a poor Jewish girl in Poland who helps an old woman and, as a reward, is granted three wishes. (Rev: BCCB 2/99; BL 5/1/99*; HB 3–4/99; HBG 10/99; SLJ 3/99) [398.2]

11171 Singer, Isaac Bashevis. *Elijah the Slave* (PS–3). Illus. by Antonio Frasconi. 1970, Farrar $16.00 (0-374-32084-5); paper $4.95 (0-374-42047-5). 32pp. Retelling of a Hebrew legend. [398.2]

11172 Singer, Isaac Bashevis. *The Fools of Chelm and Their History* (5–6). Illus. by Uri Shulevitz. 1973, Farrar $14.00 (0-374-32444-1). 64pp. Nonsense stories about the village that is the setting of other Singer tales. [398.2]

11173 Singer, Isaac Bashevis. *Stories for Children* (4–7). 1984, Farrar paper $14.00 (0-374-46489-8). 338pp. A collection of stories that draw on Yiddish folklore. [398.2]

11174 Singer, Isaac Bashevis. *When Shlemiel Went to Warsaw and Other Stories* (4–7). Illus. by Margot Zemach. 1986, Farrar paper $4.95 (0-374-48365-5). 161pp. Illustrations and the eight stories retold here delightfully reveal the distinctive people of Chelm and their extraordinary, universally exportable wisdom. (Rev: BL 6/1–15/98) [398.2]

11175 Singer, Isaac Bashevis. *Zlateh the Goat and Other Stories* (4–6). Illus. by Maurice Sendak. 1966, HarperCollins $16.00 (0-06-025698-2); paper $6.95 (0-06-440147-2). 96pp. Warm, humorous, and ironical stories based on middle European Jewish folklore and on the author's childhood memories. [398.2]

11176 Taback, Simms. *Joseph Had a Little Overcoat* (PS–2). Illus. 1999, Viking $15.99 (0-670-87855-3). 40pp. The many uses of a piece of cloth — from an overcoat to only enough material to cover a button — is the subject of this picture book based on an old Yiddish song. The mixed-media and collage illustrations are warm and lively. (Rev: BCCB 3/00; BL 1/1–15/00; HBG 3/00; SLJ 1/00) [398.2]

11177 Tarbescu, Edith. *The Boy Who Stuck Out His Tongue: A Yiddish Folktale* (PS–1). Illus. by Judith C. Mills. 2000, Barefoot $16.99 (1-84148-067-3). 32pp. A disobedient son sticks out his tongue and it freezes to a cold iron fence. All the villagers try to free him in this Jewish folktale. (Rev: BCCB 11/00; BL 5/15/00; HBG 3/01; SLJ 9/00) [398.2]

11178 Wisniewski, David. *Golem* (3–6). Illus. 1996, Clarion $15.95 (0-395-72618-2). 30pp. The terrifying story of the golem, who was created by Rabbi Loew in the 16th century to help protect his people in the Prague ghetto. Caldecott Medal winner, 1997. (Rev: BCCB 9/96; BL 10/1/96*; SLJ 10/96) [398.2]

11179 Zemach, Margot. *It Could Always Be Worse: A Yiddish Folktale* (K–3). Illus. by author. 1976, Scholastic paper $4.95 (0-374-43636-3). 32pp. A Yiddish version of an old tale with colorful, humorous illustrations. [398.2]

Middle East

11180 Alderson, Brian. *The Arabian Nights; or, Tales Told by Sheherezade During a Thousand Nights and One Night* (4–8). Illus. by Michael Foreman. 1995, Morrow $20.00 (0-688-14219-2). 192pp. A fine collection of more than 30 tales that includes parts from the stories of Sinbad, Ali Baba, and Aladdin. (Rev: BL 10/15/95; SLJ 9/95) [398.22]

11181 Balouch, Kristen. *The King and the Three Thieves: A Persian Tale* (PS–3). Illus. 2000, Viking $15.99 (0-670-88059-0). 32pp. A Persian king who leaves his palace to find some poor people to feed instead finds three thieves who are plotting to steal from the royal treasury. (Rev: BCCB 1/01; BL 12/1/00; HBG 3/01; SLJ 1/01) [398.2]

11182 Ben-Ezer, Ehud. *Hosni the Dreamer: An Arabian Tale* (K–3). Illus. by Uri Shulevitz. 1997, Farrar $16.00 (0-374-33340-8). 32pp. This old Arabian folktale about a young shepherd who buys a life-changing verse from a wise man. (Rev: BL 11/1/97; HB 9–10/97; HBG 3/98; SLJ 12/97*) [398.2]

11183 Bower, Tamara. *The Shipwrecked Sailor: An Egyptian Tale with Hieroglyphs* (3–5). Illus. 2000, Simon & Schuster $17.00 (0-689-83046-7). 32pp. Based on a story found on a 4,000-year-old papyrus scroll, this is a folktale about a shipwrecked sailor who is helped by a huge serpent. (Rev: BL 11/1/00; HBG 3/01; SLJ 10/00) [398.2]

11184 dePaola, Tomie. *The Legend of the Persian Carpet* (K–3). Illus. by Claire Ewart. 1993, Putnam $15.99 (0-399-22415-7). 32pp. When his prize diamond is stolen and shattered, a Persian king finds solace in a beautiful new carpet woven for him. (Rev: BL 10/1/93; SLJ 1/94) [398.2]

11185 Hickox, Rebecca. *The Golden Sandal: A Middle Eastern Cinderella Story* (K–3). Illus. by Will Hillenbrand. 1998, Holiday $15.95 (0-8234-1331-4). 32pp. A vivid retelling with atmospheric illustrations of an Iraqi folktale that is a variation of the Cinderella story. (Rev: BCCB 6/98; BL 4/1/98; HB 3–4/98; HBG 10/98; SLJ 4/98) [398.2]

11186 Hofmeyr, Dianne. *The Star-Bearer: A Creation Myth from Ancient Egypt* (3–5). Illus. by Judy Daly. 2001, Farrar $16.00 (0-374-37481-4). 32pp. In this picture book for older readers, a creation myth from Egypt is retold in which the god of rain and dew and the god of air emerge from a lotus bud. (Rev: BCCB 3/01; BL 2/15/01) [299]

11187 Hofmeyr, Dianne. *The Stone: A Persian Legend of the Magi* (K–3). Illus. by Jude Daly. 1998, Farrar $16.00 (0-374-37198-9). 32pp. Based on a 13th-century Persian legend retold by Marco Polo, this is the story of the three magi who visit a holy child with gifts. (Rev: BL 10/1/98; HBG 3/99; SLJ 10/98) [398.2]

11188 Kherdian, David. *The Golden Bracelet* (K–4). Illus. by Nonny Hogrogian. 1998, Holiday $16.95 (0-8234-1362-4). 32pp. An Armenian story about a prince who uses his skill as a weaver to send a message to his wife when he is held prisoner by an evil sorcerer. (Rev: BL 6/1–15/98; HBG 10/98; SLJ 8/98) [398.2]

11189 Kimmel, Eric A. *The Tale of Aladdin and the Wonderful Lamp: A Story from the Arabian Nights* (PS–3). Illus. by Ju-Hong Chen. 1992, Holiday LB $14.95 (0-8234-0938-4). 32pp. A humorous retelling of the famous story. (Rev: BL 11/1/92; SLJ 12/92) [398.2]

11190 Kimmel, Eric A. *The Three Princes* (K–3). Illus. by Leonard Everett Fisher. 1994, Holiday LB $16.95 (0-8234-1115-X). 30pp. A beautiful princess shows great wisdom in choosing her husband from the three noble cousins who are her suitors in this Middle Eastern folktale. (Rev: BCCB 4/94; BL 3/1/94*; SLJ 3/94) [398.2]

11191 Lang, Andrew, ed. *The Arabian Nights Entertainments* (5–8). Illus. 1969, Dover paper $8.95 (0-486-22289-6). 424pp. Fairy tales, folktales, and legends of Arabia and the East. [398.2]

11192 Lattimore, Deborah N. *Arabian Nights: Three Tales* (1–5). Illus. 1995, HarperCollins LB $16.89 (0-06-024734-7). 64pp. The three stories masterfully retold are "Aladdin," "The Queen of the Serpents," and "Ubar, the Lost City of Brass." (Rev: BL 10/15/95; SLJ 9/95) [398.2]

11193 McVilly, Walter, reteller. *Ali Baba and the Forty Thieves* (K–4). Illus. by Margaret Early. 1989, Abrams $17.95 (0-8109-1888-9). 32pp. Vivid re-creation of the most famous story of the Thousand and One Nights. (Rev: BL 5/15/89; HB 7–8/89) [398.2]

11194 Oppenheim, Shulamith Levey. *Iblis* (1–4). Illus. by Ed Young. 1994, Harcourt $15.95 (0-15-238016-7). 32pp. In this Islamic version of Adam and Eve's expulsion from Eden, the devil is called Iblis. (Rev: BCCB 4/94; BL 3/15/94; SLJ 4/94) [297]

11195 Philip, Neil. *The Arabian Nights* (4–6). Illus. by Sheila Moxley. 1994, Orchard $19.95 (0-531-06868-4). 160pp. With lovely paintings and colorful prose, this is an excellent retelling of 16 of the Arabian Nights stories, including Ali Baba, Scheherazade, and Aladdin. (Rev: BL 12/15/94; HB 5–6/94; SLJ 12/94*) [398.2]

11196 Shah, Idries. *The Boy Without a Name* (PS–2). Illus. by Mona Caron. 2000, Hoopoe $17.00 (1-883536-20-0). 32pp. Based on an Islamic story, this folktale tells of a boy who visits a wise man to get a name. (Rev: BL 12/1/00; SLJ 2/01) [398.22]

11197 Shah, Idries. *The Clever Boy and the Terrible, Dangerous Animal* (1–4). Illus. by Rose Mary

Santiago. 2000, Hoopoe $17.00 (1-883536-18-9). In this Middle Eastern folktale, a young boy quiets some villagers by explaining that the animal they fear is really just a melon. (Rev: SLJ 12/00) [398.2]

11198 Shah, Idries. *The Lion Who Saw Himself in the Water* (PS–2). Illus. by Ingrid Rodriguez. 1998, Hoopoe $17.00 (1-883536-12-X). 32pp. In this Sufi tale from Islam, a lion is so frightened by his reflection in the water that he can't drink from the pool until a friendly butterfly helps him conquer his fear. (Rev: BL 10/1/98; SLJ 12/98) [398.24]

11199 Shah, Idries. *The Magic Horse* (3–5). Illus. by Julie Freeman. 1998, Hoopoe $17.00 (1-883536-11-1). 34pp. This picture-book version of a Muslim Sufi tale involves two brothers and their separate quests. (Rev: SLJ 2/99) [398.2]

11200 Shah, Idries. *Neem the Half-Boy* (PS–2). Illus. by Midori Mori and Robert Revels. 1998, Hoopoe $17.00 (1-883536-10-3). 32pp. In this story based on an ancient Sufi tale from Islam, Neem remains a half-boy until he successfully confronts a dragon in his lair. (Rev: BL 10/1/98; SLJ 1/99) [398.22]

11201 Shepard, Aaron. *Forty Fortunes: A Tale of Iran* (2–4). Illus. by Alisher Dianov. 1999, Clarion $15.00 (0-395-81133-3). 32pp. Ahmed turns to fortune telling to make extra money in this Iranian folktale, but the plan backfires. (Rev: HBG 3/00; SLJ 8/99) [398.2]

11202 Yeoman, John. *The Seven Voyages of Sinbad the Sailor* (4–7). Illus. by Quentin Blake. 1997, Simon & Schuster $19.95 (0-689-81368-6). 128pp. In these adaptations of stories from *Arabian Nights*, Sinbad tells about the seven amazing voyages that brought him horror, disaster, adventure, and eventually wealth. (Rev: BL 1/1–15/98; HB 3–4/98; HBG 3/98; SLJ 12/97) [398.2]

11203 Zeman, Ludmila. *Sindbad: From the Tales of the Thousand and One Nights* (3–5). Illus. 1999, Tundra $17.95 (0-88776-460-6). 32pp. Using extraordinary illustrations, the author-artist tells the stories of two of the famous voyages of Sinbad, one involving a giant whale and the other featuring a huge bird. (Rev: BL 1/1–15/00*; SLJ 1/00) [813.54]

North America

Inuit

11204 Bierhorst, John, ed. *The Dancing Fox: Arctic Folktales* (4–6). Illus. 1997, Morrow $15.00 (0-688-14406-3). 192pp. After an introduction to the land and people of the American Arctic, the author presents 18 Inuit folktales. (Rev: BCCB 7–8/97; BL 4/15/97; HB 5–6/97; SLJ 6/97) [398.2]

11205 Dabcovich, Lydia, reteller. *The Polar Bear Son: An Inuit Tale* (K–2). Illus. by Lydia Dabcovich. 1997, Clarion $16.00 (0-395-72766-9). 37pp. In this Inuit tale, the men of a village want to kill the polar bear that one of their women had adopted when it was an orphaned cub. (Rev: SLJ 6/97) [398.2]

11206 Houston, James. *Tikta'liktak: An Eskimo Legend* (4–6). Illus. by author. 1990, Harcourt paper $10.00 (0-15-287748-7). 63pp. Legend of a young Inuit hunter who is carried out to sea on a drifting ice floe with only his bow and arrows and a harpoon. Also use: *The White Archer: An Eskimo Legend* (1990). [398.2]

11207 Martin, Rafe. *The Eagle's Gift* (K–4). Illus. by Tatsuro Kiuchi. 1997, Putnam $15.95 (0-399-22923-X). 32pp. An eagle transformed into a man helps Marten learn the gift of joy in this Inuit folktale. (Rev: BL 9/15/97; HBG 3/98; SLJ 2/98) [398.2]

11208 Murphy, Claire R. *Caribou Girl* (K–3). Illus. by Linda Russell. 1998, Roberts Rinehart $16.95 (1-57098-145-0). A young Inuit changes into a caribou to bring the herd to her starving people. (Rev: HBG 10/98; SLJ 7/98) [398.2]

11209 Norman, Howard. *The Girl Who Dreamed Only Geese and Other Stories of the Far North* (4–8). Illus. by Leo Dillon and Diane Dillon. 1997, Harcourt $22.00 (0-15-230979-9). 164pp. A fine collection of Inuit tales, enhanced by illustrations resembling stone carvings. (Rev: BL 9/15/97*; SLJ 11/97*) [398.2]

Native Americans

11210 Ata, Te. *Baby Rattlesnake* (PS–K). Adapted by Lynn Moroney. Illus. by Veg Reisberg. 1990, Children's Book Pr. $14.95 (0-89239-049-2); paper $7.95 (0-89239-111-1). 32pp. A baby rattlesnake doesn't know how to behave when he is given a rattle before reaching maturity. (Rev: BL 3/1/90; SLJ 4/90) [398.2]

11211 Baylor, Byrd. *Moon Song* (1–3). Illus. by Ronald Himler. 1982, Macmillan LB $13.95 (0-684-17463-4). 24pp. Why the coyote and descendants gather in the night and sing to the moon. [398.2]

11212 Bierhorst, John, ed. *The Deetkatoo: Native American Stories About Little People* (3–7). Illus. by Ron Hilbert Coy. 1998, Morrow $16.00 (0-688-14837-9). 153pp. Twenty-two Native American folktales that deal with little people and their interactions with normal-sized humans. (Rev: BCCB 7–8/98; HBG 10/98; SLJ 9/98) [398.2]

11213 Bierhorst, John, sel. *On the Road of Stars: Native American Night Poems and Sleep Charms* (2–6). Illus. by Judy Pedersen. 1994, Macmillan paper $15.95 (0-02-709735-8). An unusual, charming collection of more than 50 night songs and lullabies from different Native American cultures. (Rev: BCCB 3/94; HB 7–8/94; SLJ 5/94) [398.2]

11214 Bierhorst, John. *The Woman Who Fell from the Sky: The Iroquois Story of Creation* (K–4). Illus. by Robert Andrew Parker. 1993, Morrow LB $14.93 (0-688-10681-1). 32pp. Sky Woman, with the help of her two sons, creates the earth. (Rev: BCCB 5/93; BL 3/15/93; HB 5–6/93; SLJ 4/93) [398.2]

11215 Bruchac, Joseph. *Between Earth and Sky: Legends of Native American Sacred Places* (2–5).

Illus. by Thomas Locker. 1996, Harcourt $16.00 (0-15-200042-9). 32pp. A retelling of ten legends dealing with sacred places from various Native American tribes. (Rev: BL 4/1/96; HB 5–6/96; SLJ 7/96) [398.2]

11216 Bruchac, Joseph. *Dog People: Native Dog Stories* (3–6). Illus. by Murv Jacob. 1995, Fulcrum $14.95 (1-55591-228-1). 63pp. This book contains five very readable stories about the Abenaki Indian children and their dogs. (Rev: SLJ 1/96) [398.2]

11217 Bruchac, Joseph. *Flying with the Eagle, Racing the Great Bear: Stories from Native North America* (5–8). Illus. 1993, Troll $13.95 (0-8167-3026-1). 144pp. Sixteen stories, arranged geographically, introduce coming-of-age rites for males in Native American cultures. (Rev: BL 12/15/93; SLJ 9/93) [398.2]

11218 Bruchac, Joseph. *Gluskabe and the Four Wishes* (PS–3). Illus. by Christine N. Shrader. 1995, Dutton $15.99 (0-525-65164-0). 32pp. A legend that explains why Gluskabe is considered a hero by the Abnaki Indians of New England. (Rev: BCCB 2/95; BL 12/15/94; HB 3–4/95; SLJ 2/95) [398.2]

11219 Bruchac, Joseph. *Native American Animal Stories* (1–5). Illus. by John K. Fadden and David K. Fadden. 1992, Fulcrum paper $12.95 (1-55591-127-7). 160pp. Includes 24 engrossing animal tales from tribes across North America. (Rev: SLJ 11/92) [398.2]

11220 Bruchac, Joseph. *Native Plant Stories* (4–8). Illus. 1995, Fulcrum paper $12.95 (1-55591-212-5). 128pp. A collection of stories about plants that come from various Native American cultures in North and Central America. (Rev: BL 9/1/95) [398.24]

11221 Bruchac, Joseph, and James Bruchac. *How Chipmunk Got His Stripes: A Tale of Bragging and Teasing* (1–3). Illus. by Ariane Dewey and Jose Aruego. 2001, Dial $15.99 (0-8037-2404-7). 32pp. In this Native American story, squirrel is punished for teasing Big Bear by having the now-familiar chipmunk stripe placed on his back. (Rev: BCCB 3/01; BL 2/1/01; SLJ 2/01) [398.24]

11222 Bruchac, Joseph, and James Bruchac. *When the Chenoo Howls* (3–6). Illus. 1998, Walker $15.95 (0-8027-8638-3). 128pp. This anthology consists of 12 scary stories from the Northeast woodland Native Americans — most of them traditional folktales together with a few original stories that incorporate legendary characters. (Rev: BCCB 9/98; BL 8/98; HBG 3/99; SLJ 12/98) [398.2]

11223 Cohen, Caron L. *The Mud Pony: A Traditional Skidi Pawnee Tale* (K–3). Illus. by Shonto Begay. 1988, Scholastic $15.95 (0-590-41525-5). 32pp. The moving story of a boy too poor to have a pony of his own who grows up to become chief of his people. (Rev: BCCB 12/88; BL 12/1/88; SLJ 1/89) [398.2]

11224 Connolly, James E. *Why the Possum's Tail Is Bare: And Other North American Indian Nature Tales* (4–7). Illus. 1992, Stemmer $15.95 (0-88045-069-X); paper $7.95 (0-88045-107-6). 64pp. Nature

and folklore are combined in 13 Native American animal tales. (Rev: BL 9/1/85; SLJ 10/85) [398.2]

11225 Crook, Connie Brummel. *Maple Moon* (K–4). Illus. by Scott Cameron. 1998, Stoddart $15.95 (0-7737-3017-6). 32pp. A crippled young Mississauga boy accidentally discovers tree sap as a source of food for his people in this adaptation of two Native American folktales. (Rev: BL 4/15/98; SLJ 4/98)

11226 Curry, Jane L. *Turtle Island* (3–7). Illus. 1999, Simon & Schuster $17.00 (0-689-82233-2). 160pp. A collection of 27 tales from the culture of the Algonquin nations, including creation stories, pourquoi tales, and legends of heroes and tricksters. (Rev: BL 6/1–15/99; HBG 3/00; SLJ 7/99) [398.2]

11227 De Montano, Marty Kreipe. *Coyote in Love with a Star* (PS–3). Illus. by Tom Coffin. 1998, Abbeville $14.95 (0-7892-0162-3). 31pp. In this updated pourquoi tale that explains why coyotes howl at the moon, Coyote travels to New York City and there falls in love with a star. (Rev: BL 12/1/98; HB 3–4/99; HBG 3/99; SLJ 2/99) [398.2]

11228 Dengler, Marianna. *The Worry Stone* (3–5). Illus. by Sibyl G. Gerig. 1996, Northland LB $15.95 (0-87358-642-5). 34pp. When her grandfather dies, Amanda finds that she gets comfort from rubbing a stone that the old man had given to her. (Rev: BL 12/15/96; SLJ 1/97) [398.2]

11229 dePaola, Tomie, reteller. *The Legend of the Bluebonnet: An Old Tale of Texas* (K–3). Illus. by Tomie dePaola. 1983, Putnam $16.99 (0-399-20937-9). 32pp. This book retells the Comanche Indian story of the origin of the Texas bluebonnet flower. [398.2]

11230 Dominic, Gloria, adapt. *Brave Bear and the Ghosts: A Sioux Legend* (2–4). Illus. by Charles Reasoner. Series: Native American Lore and Legends. 1996, Rourke LB $16.95 (0-86593-429-0). 47pp. A charming trickster tale with a surprise ending from the Sioux. Also use *Coyote and the Grasshoppers: A Pomo Legend* and *Song of the Hermit Thrush: An Iroquois Legend* (both 1996). (Rev: SLJ 3/97) [398.2]

11231 Drucker, Malka. *The Sea Monster's Secret* (PS–3). Illus. by Christopher Aja. 1999, Harcourt $16.00 (0-15-200619-2). 32pp. A folktale from Alaska that tells how an unassuming hero secretly supplies his village with food. (Rev: BL 10/15/99; HBG 10/99; SLJ 6/99) [398.24]

11232 Dwyer, Mindy, reteller. *Coyote in Love* (PS–3). Illus. by Mindy Dwyer. 1997, Alaska Northwest $15.95 (0-88240-485-7). This Native American tale of how Crater Lake was formed tells of Coyote's unrequited love for a star. (Rev: SLJ 7/97) [398.2]

11233 Eagle Walking Turtle. *Full Moon Stories: Thirteen Native American Legends* (3–6). Illus. 1997, Hyperion LB $16.49 (0-7868-2175-2). 48pp. A wonderful collection of legends that were told to the author by his grandfather years ago. (Rev: BL 6/1–15/97; HBG 3/98; SLJ 7/97) [398.2]

11234 Esbensen, Barbara J. *Ladder to the Sky: How the Gift of Healing Came to the Ojibway Nation* (K–3). Illus. by Helen K. Davie. 1989, Little, Brown

$15.95 (0-316-24952-1). 32pp. Although the Ojibwa (Chippewa) lost their direct connection to the Great Spirit, they were granted healing powers. (Rev: BCCB 2/90; BL 11/1/89; SLJ 10/89) [398.2]

11235 Esbensen, Barbara J. *The Star Maiden: An Ojibway Tale* (3–5). Illus. by Helen K. Davie. 1991, Little, Brown paper $5.95 (0-316-24955-6). 32pp. A star appears in a dream to a young brave, falls to earth, and becomes a water lily. (Rev: BCCB 4/88; BL 4/1/88; SLJ 6–7/88) [398.2]

11236 French, Fiona. *Lord of the Animals: A Miwok Indian Creation Myth* (PS–3). Illus. 1997, Millbrook $15.95 (0-7613-0112-7). 32pp. In this Native American myth, Coyote creates man to be Lord of the Animals. (Rev: BCCB 6/97; BL 6/1–15/97; SLJ 9/97) [398.2]

11237 Goble, Paul. *Adopted by the Eagles* (3–5). Illus. 1994, Bradbury paper $15.95 (0-02-736575-1). 40pp. One friend betrays another when they both fall in love with the same maiden in this Dakota Indian folktale. (Rev: BL 11/1/94; SLJ 1/95) [398.2]

11238 Goble, Paul. *Buffalo Woman* (4–6). Illus. by author. 1984, Macmillan $16.00 (0-02-737720-2); paper $5.99 (0-689-71109-3). 32pp. A legend from the Plains Indians about a buffalo that turns into a beautiful girl. [398.2]

11239 Goble, Paul. *Crow Chief: A Plains Indian Story* (K–3). Illus. by author. 1992, Orchard LB $17.99 (0-531-08547-3). 32pp. This Plains Indian legend explains why crows have black feathers. (Rev: BCCB 4/92; BL 2/15/92; HB 3–4/92; SLJ 3/92) [398.2]

11240 Goble, Paul. *The Gift of the Sacred Dog* (2–4). Illus. by author. 1982, Macmillan LB $15.00 (0-02-736560-3). 32pp. A boy brings to his starving people the gift of horses. [398.2]

11241 Goble, Paul. *The Great Race: Of the Birds and Animals* (K–3). Illus. by author. 1991, Simon & Schuster paper $5.99 (0-689-71452-1). 32pp. The story of the great race between the animals and humans in which the people won and now have responsibility to care for animals. (Rev: BCCB 9/85; BL 9/15/85; SLJ 9/85) [398.2]

11242 Goble, Paul. *Her Seven Brothers* (K–3). Illus. by author. 1988, Macmillan $14.95 (0-02-737960-4); paper $5.99 (0-689-71730-X). 32pp. The Cheyenne legend that tells of the origin of the Big Dipper. (Rev: BCCB 4/88; BL 4/15/88; SLJ 6–7/88) [398.2]

11243 Goble, Paul. *Iktomi and the Berries: A Plains Indian Story* (K–2). Illus. by author. 1992, Orchard paper $6.95 (0-531-07029-8). 32pp. A witty folktale about a disreputable hero. (Rev: BCCB 12/89*; BL 9/15/89; HB 11–12/89; SLJ 9/89*) [398.2]

11244 Goble, Paul. *Iktomi and the Boulder: A Plains Indian Story* (3–5). Illus. by author. 1988, Orchard $16.95 (0-531-05760-7); paper $6.95 (0-531-07023-9). 32pp. Iktomi, a trickster, is the hero of many humorous adventures in these Sioux tales. (Rev: BCCB 7–8/88; BL 8/88; HB 9–10/88) [398.2]

11245 Goble, Paul. *Iktomi and the Buffalo Skull: A Plains Indian Story* (K–3). Illus. by author. 1996, Orchard paper $5.95 (0-531-07077-8). 32pp. Iktomi

the trickster tries to impress girls but ends up with his head stuck in a buffalo skull. (Rev: BL 2/1/91; HB 5–6/91; SLJ 3/91) [398.2]

11246 Goble, Paul. *Iktomi and the Coyote: A Plains Indian Story* (3–5). Illus. by author. 1998, Orchard LB $17.99 (0-531-33108-3). Iktomi, a trickster, thinks he has found himself a meal of prairie dog, but he is outwitted by a clever coyote. (Rev: BCCB 1/99; HBG 3/99; SLJ 11/98) [398.2]

11247 Goble, Paul. *Iktomi Loses His Eyes: A Plains Indian Story* (K–4). Illus. 1999, Orchard LB $17.99 (0-531-33200-4). 32pp. In this trickster tale, Bad Guy fools Iktomi into giving up his land for the ability to throw his eyes out of his head. (Rev: BL 8/99; HBG 3/00; SLJ 9/99) [398.2]

11248 Goble, Paul. *The Legend of the White Buffalo Woman* (4–8). Illus. 1998, National Geographic $16.95 (0-7922-7074-6). 32pp. After a great flood, an earth woman and an eagle mate to produce a new people in this Lakota tale. (Rev: BL 3/15/98; HBG 10/98) [398.2]

11249 Goble, Paul. *The Lost Children* (3–5). Illus. 1993, Macmillan $14.95 (0-02-736555-7). An Indian legend about six orphaned boys who journey to the sky and become the Pleiades. (Rev: BCCB 6/93; SLJ 5/93) [398.2]

11250 Goble, Paul. *Love Flute* (3–8). Illus. by author. 1992, Macmillan $16.00 (0-02-736261-2). 32pp. From the legends of the Plains Indians, this is a love story about a young man too shy to woo the woman he loves. (Rev: BCCB 12/92; BL 8/92*; HB 3–4/93; SLJ 10/92) [398.2]

11251 Goble, Paul. *Remaking the Earth: A Creation Story from the Great Plains of North America* (3–6). Illus. 1996, Orchard LB $16.99 (0-531-08874-X). 32pp. In this creation myth, Earth Maker re-creates the land after a destructive flood. (Rev: BL 9/15/96; SLJ 10/96) [398.2]

11252 Goble, Paul. *The Return of the Buffaloes: A Plains Indian Story About Famine and Renewal of the Earth* (K–3). Illus. 1996, National Geographic $15.95 (0-7922-2714-X). 32pp. A Lakota myth about a woman with magical powers who saves her people. (Rev: BL 6/1–15/96; HB 7–8/96; SLJ 7/96) [398.2]

11253 Goble, Paul, reteller. *Star Boy* (2–4). 1991, Simon & Schuster paper $5.99 (0-689-71499-8). 32pp. The legend of how Star Boy was able to rid himself of a disfiguring scar. [398.2]

11254 Goldin, Barbara D. *Coyote and the Fire Stick: A Pacific Northwest Indian Tale* (3–5). Illus. by Will Hillenbrand. 1996, Harcourt $16.00 (0-15-200438-6). 40pp. In this Pacific Northwest tale, a coyote sets out to steal fire from three ugly evil spirits. (Rev: BL 10/1/96; HB 11–12/96; SLJ 10/96) [398.2]

11255 Goldin, Barbara D. *The Girl Who Lived with the Bears* (4–6). Illus. by Andrew Plewes. 1997, Harcourt $15.00 (0-15-200684-2). 40pp. A folktale from the Pacific Northwest Indians about a chief's daughter who insulted the bear people and was later forced to live with them as their slave. (Rev: BL 4/15/97; SLJ 4/97) [398.2]

11256 Hausman, Gerald. *The Story of Blue Elk* (K–4). Illus. by Kristina Rodanas. 1998, Clarion $15.00 (0-395-84512-2). 32pp. In this Pueblo Indian legend, a voiceless boy is able to communicate by using a flute fashioned from a cedar tree that grew from the antlers of Blue Elk. (Rev: BL 5/15/98; HBG 10/98; SLJ 8/98) [398.2]

11257 Highwater, Jamake. *Anpao: An American Indian Odyssey* (5–8). Illus. by Fritz Scholder. 1993, HarperCollins paper $7.95 (0-06-440437-4). 256pp. A young hero encounters great danger on his way to meet his father, the Sun, in this dramatic Native American folktale. [398.2]

11258 Hillerman, Tony, ed. *The Boy Who Made Dragonfly: A Zuni Myth* (5–7). Illus. by Laszlo Kubinyi. 1986, Univ. of New Mexico Pr. paper $8.95 (0-8263-0910-0). 85pp. A Zuni boy and his little sister are left behind by their tribe and survive hunger and deprivation through the intervention of the Cornstalk Being. [398.2]

11259 Jackson, Ellen. *The Precious Gift: A Navaho Creation Myth* (1–3). Illus. by Woodleigh Hubbard. 1996, Simon & Schuster paper $16.00 (0-689-80480-6). In this part of the creation myth of the Navajo, water is brought to the arid earth. (Rev: BCCB 6/96; SLJ 5/96) [398.2]

11260 Jones, Jennifer B. *Heetunka's Harvest: A Tale of the Plains Indians* (K–3). Illus. by Shannon Keegan. 1995, Roberts Rinehart $15.95 (1-879373-17-3). 32pp. Nature takes revenge on a thieving Dakota Indian woman who steals from Heetunka the bean mouse. (Rev: BL 1/1/95; SLJ 4/95) [398.2]

11261 Larrabee, Lisa. *Grandmother Five Baskets* (2–4). Illus. by Lori Sawyer. 1993, Harbinger paper $9.95 (0-943173-90-6). 60pp. Using five baskets that have been made by a Poarch Creek Indian woman as a metaphor, different stages of life are explained. (Rev: SLJ 3/94)

11262 Lasky, Kathryn. *Cloud Eyes* (K–4). Illus. by Barry Moser. 1994, Harcourt $14.95 (0-15-219168-2). In this folklike story, a young Native American is able to subdue both a hiveful of bees and some greedy bears to provide honey for his people. (Rev: SLJ 10/94) [398.2]

11263 Lavitt, Edward, and Robert E. McDowell. *Nihancan's Feast of Beaver: Animal Tales of the North American Indians* (2–6). Illus. by Bunny P. Huffman. 1990, Museum of New Mexico paper $12.95 (0-89013-211-9). 120pp. This handsome book contains 36 tales from nine different cultural areas in North America. (Rev: BL 3/1/91) [398.2]

11264 Lelooska, Chief. *Echoes of the Elders: The Stories and Paintings of Chief Lelooska* (1–4). Illus. by author. 1997, DK $24.95 (0-7894-2455-X). 38pp. Five Native American tales that reveal a profound respect for nature and the role of the supernatural in everyday life. (Rev: HB 11–12/97; HBG 3/98; SLJ 11/97*) [398.2]

11265 Luenn, Nancy. *The Miser on the Mountain: A Nisqually Legend of Mount Rainier* (3–6). Illus. by Pierre Morgan. 1997, Sasquatch $15.95 (1-57061-082-7). 32pp. A legend set on Ta-co-bet, or Mount Rainier, in which greed leads to a man's downfall. (Rev: BL 9/15/97; HBG 3/98; SLJ 1/98) [398.2]

11266 McDermott, Gerald. *Coyote: A Trickster Tale from the American Southwest* (PS–K). Illus. 1994, Harcourt $15.00 (0-15-220724-4). 32pp. Obnoxious Coyote has a comedown when he tries to fly with the crows. (Rev: BCCB 11/94; BL 8/94*; SLJ 11/94) [398.2]

11267 McDermott, Gerald. *Raven: A Trickster Tale from the Pacific Northwest* (K–4). Illus. by author. 1993, Harcourt $16.00 (0-15-265661-8). 32pp. A traditional tale told by the tribes of the area and illustrated by a Caldecott Medal winner. (Rev: BCCB 6/93*; BL 3/1/93*; HB 7–8/93*; SLJ 5/93*) [398]

11268 Malotki, Ekkehart, comp. *The Magic Hummingbird: A Hopi Folktale* (2–4). Illus. by Michael Lacapa. 1996, Kiva $15.95 (1-885772-04-1). In this Hopi tale, a boy makes a toy hummingbird that comes to life and helps end a drought by taking the boy and his sister to the fertility god. (Rev: SLJ 11/96) [398.2]

11269 Manitonquat. *The Children of the Morning Light: Wampanoag Tales* (3–5). Illus. 1994, Macmillan paper $16.95 (0-02-765905-4). 80pp. Several creation stories and four other legends from the Wampanoag Indians of Massachusetts are retold. (Rev: BCCB 6/94; BL 4/15/94; HB 7–8/94; SLJ 4/94) [398.2]

11270 Martin, Rafe. *The Boy Who Lived with the Seals* (4–6). Illus. by David Shannon. 1993, Putnam LB $16.99 (0-399-22413-0). 32pp. A boy vanishes and goes to live with the seals, becoming one of them. (Rev: BCCB 6/93; BL 3/15/93*; HB 7–8/93; SLJ 4/93) [398.2]

11271 Martin, Rafe. *The Rough-Face Girl* (1–4). Illus. by David Shannon. 1992, Putnam LB $16.99 (0-399-21859-9). 32pp. This variation on the Cinderella tale takes place in an Algonquin village on the shores of Lake Ontario. (Rev: BL 4/15/92; HB 7–8/92; SLJ 5/92) [398.2]

11272 Max, Jill, ed. *Spider Spins a Story: Fourteen Legends from Native America* (3–6). Illus. 1997, Northland $16.95 (0-87358-611-5). 72pp. Spider plays a prominent role in these folktales, illustrated by six Native American artists. (Rev: BL 12/15/97; HBG 10/98; SLJ 1/98) [398.2]

11273 Mayo, Gretchen Will, reteller. *Big Trouble for Tricky Rabbit!* (2–4). Illus. by Gretchen Will Mayo. Series: Native American Trickster Tales. 1994, Walker LB $13.85 (0-8027-8276-0). 38pp. Using simple vocabulary and short sentences, the author retells five trickster tales from Native American folklore, all involving Rabbit. (Rev: BCCB 6/94; SLJ 7/94) [398.2]

11274 Mayo, Gretchen Will. *Earthmaker's Tales: North American Indian Stories About Earth Happenings* (4–6). Illus. 1989, Walker LB $13.85 (0-8027-6840-7). 96pp. Legends that center on the earth itself. (Rev: BL 3/1/89) [398.2]

11275 Mayo, Gretchen Will. *Here Comes Tricky Rabbit!* (2–4). Illus. Series: Native American Trickster Tales. 1994, Walker LB $13.85 (0-8027-8274-

4). 48pp. These five folktales reveal Rabbit to be a wily trickster. (Rev: BCCB 6/94; BL 8/94; SLJ 7/94) [398.2]

11276 Mayo, Gretchen Will, reteller. *Meet Tricky Coyote!* (2–5). Illus. by Gretchen Will Mayo. Series: Native American Trickster Tales. 1993, Walker LB $13.85 (0-8027-8199-3). 36pp. A retelling of some short, humorous stories about the clever trickster coyote. Companion volumes are *That Tricky Coyote!* and *Magical Tales from Many Lands* (both 1993). (Rev: SLJ 9/93) [398.2]

11277 Mayo, Gretchen Will. *Star Tales: North American Indian Stories About the Stars* (4–7). Illus. by author. 1987, Walker LB $13.85 (0-8027-6673-0). 96pp. Fourteen tales, each introduced by a one-page commentary on a constellation. (Rev: BL 6/15/87; SLJ 5/87) [398.2]

11278 Mayo, Gretchen Will. *That Tricky Coyote!* (PS–3). Illus. 1993, Walker LB $13.85 (0-8027-8201-9). 32pp. Five short stories from different tribes that deal with the escapades of the trickster Coyote. (Rev: BL 9/1/93; SLJ 9/93) [398.2]

11279 Medicine Crow, Joe. *Brave Wolf and the Thunderbird* (PS–3). Illus. by Linda R. Martin. 1998, Abbeville $14.95 (0-7892-0160-7). 31pp. Written and illustrated by Native Americans, this is the traditional tale of the kidnapping of Brave Wolf by Thunderbird to assist in the rescue of Thunderbird's chicks from a sea monster. (Rev: BL 12/1/98; HBG 3/99; SLJ 4/99) [398.2]

11280 Monroe, Jean Guard, and Ray A. Williamson. *They Dance in the Sky: Native American Star Myths* (4–8). Illus. 1987, Houghton $16.00 (0-395-39970-X). 130pp. Numerous Native American legends about stars. (Rev: BL 9/1/87; SLJ 9/87) [398.2]

11281 Nelson, S. D. *Gift Horse: A Lakota Story* (PS–3). Illus. 1999, Abrams $14.95 (0-8109-4127-9). 40pp. Flying Cloud earns his status as a Lakota warrior when he joins a raiding party to return horses stolen by Crow enemies. (Rev: BL 12/1/99; HBG 3/00; SLJ 11/99) [978]

11282 Norman, Howard. *Trickster and the Fainting Birds* (4–7). Illus. by Tom Pohrt. 1999, Harcourt $20.00 (0-15-200888-8). 82pp. In these seven Algonquian tales from Manitoba, the trickster often takes the form of a man but it can also change its shape into various animal forms. (Rev: BCCB 1/00; BL 1/1–15/00; HB 11–12/99; HBG 3/00; SLJ 12/99) [398.2]

11283 Normandin, Christine, ed. *Spirit of the Cedar People: More Stories and Paintings of Chief Lelooska* (2–6). 1998, DK $24.95 (0-7894-2571-8). 38pp. A collection of effectively illustrated, authentic tales from the Pacific Northwest that also contains a CD read by the editor. (Rev: BCCB 12/98; HB 1–2/99; HBG 3/99; SLJ 12/98) [398.2]

11284 Oliviero, Jamie. *The Day Sun Was Stolen* (K–3). Illus. by Sharon Hitchcock. 1995, Hyperion LB $15.49 (0-7868-2026-8). 32pp. In this Haida Indian story, Bear, who is hot in his heavy coat, hides the sun in his cave to keep cool. (Rev: BL 11/1/95; SLJ 12/95) [398.2]

11285 Oughton, Jerrie. *How the Stars Fell into the Sky: A Navajo Legend* (PS–3). Illus. by Lisa Desimini. 1992, Houghton $16.00 (0-395-58798-0). 32pp. In this Navajo legend, the trickster coyote brings chaos to the night sky. (Rev: BCCB 6/92; BL 3/15/92*; SLJ 5/92) [398.2]

11286 Oughton, Jerrie. *The Magic Weaver of Rugs: A Tale of the Navajo* (2–5). Illus. by Lisa Desimini. 1994, Houghton $16.00 (0-395-66140-4). 32pp. This Navajo folktale explains how the gift of weaving came to the tribe through the help of the Spider Woman. (Rev: BL 3/1/94; SLJ 8/94) [398.2]

11287 *The People with Five Fingers: A Native Californian Creation Tale* (K–3). Ed. by John Bierhorst. Illus. by Robert Andrew Parker. 2000, Marshall Cavendish $15.95 (0-7614-5058-0). 32pp. A Native American creation tale about how Coyote put the animals to work to prepare for the arrival of humans in the world. (Rev: BCCB 3/00; BL 4/1/00; HBG 10/00; SLJ 6/00) [398.2]

11288 *Pia Toya: A Goshute Indian Legend* (PS–2). Retold by the children and teachers of Ibapah Elementary School. Illus. 2000, Univ. of Utah $11.95 (0-87480-661-5). In this Native American legend, Coyote is responsible for the creation of the mountain Pia Toya because he tricked Hawk out of her breakfast. (Rev: SLJ 2/01) [398.2]

11289 Pohrt, Tom. *Coyote Goes Walking* (PS–3). Illus. 1995, Farrar $16.00 (0-374-31628-7). 32pp. Different aspects of Coyote's personality are explored in these four tales from the Plains Indians. (Rev: BCCB 12/95; BL 12/15/95; SLJ 12/95) [398.2]

11290 Pollock, Penny. *The Turkey Girl: A Zuni Cinderella Story* (4–6). Illus. by Ed Young. 1996, Little, Brown $16.95 (0-316-71314-7). 32pp. In this Zuni folktale, Turkey Girl's magical transformation ends in disaster when she forgets her promise to return to her flock of birds. (Rev: BCCB 4/96; BL 4/15/96; HB 5–6/96; SLJ 5/96) [398.2]

11291 Raczek, Linda. *Stories from Native North America* (2–4). Illus. by Richard Hook. Series: Multicultural Stories. 2000, Raintree Steck-Vaughn LB $27.12 (0-7398-1336-6). 48pp. A fine collection of Native American folktales that represents many geographical locations. (Rev: HBG 10/00; SLJ 11/00) [398.2]

11292 Renner, Michelle. *The Girl Who Swam with the Fish* (K–3). Illus. by Christine Cox. 1995, Alaska Northwest $15.95 (0-88240-442-3). 32pp. In this fantasy, a curious girl gets to run with the salmon. (Rev: BL 10/15/95; SLJ 10/95) [398.2]

11293 Riordan, James. *The Songs My Paddle Sings* (2–5). Illus. 1998, Pavilion paper $16.95 (1-86205-076-7). 128pp. An anthology of 20 legends from various Native American peoples, including creation stories, hero legends, and cautionary tales. (Rev: BL 3/15/98; SLJ 5/98) [398.2]

11294 Rodanas, Kristina, adapt. *The Dragonfly's Tale* (PS–3). Illus. 1992, Houghton $14.95 (0-395-57003-4). 28pp. The Ashiwi's waste of food causes the Corn Maiden to bring famine to the village, but a boy and his sister find a way to harvest a successful crop. (Rev: BCCB 6/92; BL 4/1/92; SLJ 7/92) [398.2]

11295 Rosen, Michael J. *The Dog Who Walked with God* (K–4). Illus. by Stan Fellows. 1998, Candlewick $16.99 (0-7636-0470-4). 40pp. A Native American creation story that tells how the Great Traveler, accompanied by his dog, reshapes the world after a devastating flood. (Rev: BCCB 4/98; BL 3/15/98; HBG 10/98; SLJ 6/98) [398.2]

11296 Runningwolf, Michael, and Patrick Clark Smith. *On the Trail of Elder Brother* (3–6). Illus. 2000, Persea $16.95 (0-89255-248-4). 128pp. Sixteen tales including creation myths and pourquoi stories are included in this collection of Micmac folktales about Glous'gap, called Elder Brother, the embodiment of the Great Spirit. (Rev: BCCB 6/00; BL 7/00; HBG 10/00) [398.2]

11297 Sage, James. *Coyote Makes Man* (PS–3). Illus. by Britta Teckentrup. 1995, Simon & Schuster $15.00 (0-689-80011-8). 32pp. In this Crow Indian tale, Coyote sets out to create the first human. (Rev: BCCB 7–8/95; BL 5/15/95; SLJ 6/95) [398.2]

11298 San Souci, Robert D. *Two Bear Cubs* (K–4). Illus. by Daniel San Souci. 1997, Yosemite $14.95 (0-939666-87-1). Two bear cubs fall asleep on a rock that grows into a mountain in this Native American folktale that explains the rock formation known as El Capitan in Yosemite National Park. (Rev: BCCB 3/98; BL 1/1–15/98; SLJ 4/98) [398.2]

11299 Shenandoah-Tekalihwa: Khwa, Joanne, and Douglas M. George-Kanentiio. *Skywoman: Legends of the Iroquois* (4–8). Illus. by John Kahionhes Fadden and David K. Fadden. 1998, Clear Light $14.95 (0-940666-99-5). 108pp. Several of these nine traditional Iroquois tales deal with creation myths, while others deal with the origins of constellations and trees. (Rev: HBG 10/99; SLJ 2/99) [398.2]

11300 Simms, Laura. *The Bone Man* (2–4). Illus. by Michael McCurdy. 1997, Hyperion LB $15.49 (0-7868-2074-8). 32pp. This is the story of a young Native American who must fulfill his grandmother's prediction and confront a horrible monster, the Bone Man. (Rev: BL 11/1/97; HBG 3/98; SLJ 11/97) [398.2]

11301 Steptoe, John, reteller. *The Story of Jumping Mouse: A Native American Legend* (1–4). 1984, Morrow paper $5.95 (0-688-08740-X). 40pp. The legend of the mouse who, because of good acts, is transformed into an eagle. [398.2]

11302 Stevens, Janet. *Coyote Steals the Blanket: A Ute Tale* (4–6). Illus. 1993, Holiday LB $16.95 (0-8234-0996-1). 32pp. In this amusing legend, a rock chases a coyote after the animal steals a blanket that had covered it. (Rev: BCCB 5/93*; BL 4/1/93; SLJ 6/93) [398.2]

11303 Stevens, Janet. *Old Bag of Bones: A Coyote Tale* (K–4). Illus. 1996, Holiday LB $16.95 (0-8234-1215-6). 32pp. Coyote, who resents growing old, persuades Young Buffalo to share his youth with him in this Shoshone tale. (Rev: BCCB 5/96; BL 5/1/96; HB 7–8/96; SLJ 5/96*) [398.24]

11304 Strauss, Susan. *Coyote Stories for Children* (2–7). Illus. by Gary Lund. 1992, Beyond Words paper $7.95 (0-941831-62-0). A collection of four stories from Native American cultures that tell about the trickster coyote. (Rev: SLJ 4/92) [398.2]

11305 Swamp, Chief Jake. *Giving Thanks: A Native American Good Morning Message* (PS–1). Illus. by Erwin Printup. 1995, Lee & Low $15.95 (1-880000-15-6). 24pp. A Mohawk chieftain gives thanks for Mother Earth and the universe that surrounds her. (Rev: BL 10/15/95; SLJ 11/95) [299]

11306 Taylor, C. J. *The Ghost and Lone Warrior: An Arapaho Legend* (2–5). Illus. by author. 1991, Tundra $13.95 (0-88776-263-8). When he is injured, Lone Warrior is left behind by his hunting party and must survive in the wilderness alone. (Rev: BCCB 2/92; SLJ 2/92) [398.2]

11307 Taylor, C. J. *How We Saw the World: Nine Native Stories of the Way Things Began* (4–6). Illus. 1993, Tundra $17.99 (0-88776-302-2). 32pp. These nine stories from various tribes explain the origin of several animals, like horses, and geographical landmarks, like Niagara Falls. (Rev: BL 11/1/93; SLJ 2/94) [398.3]

11308 Taylor, C. J. *The Secret of the White Buffalo* (K–3). Illus. 1993, Tundra paper $13.95 (0-88776-321-9). 24pp. Two Native American scouts encounter a beautiful woman when they set out to track buffalo in this Oglala folktale. (Rev: BL 1/1/94) [398.2]

11309 Taylor, Harriet P. *Brother Wolf: A Seneca Tale* (PS–3). Illus. 1996, Farrar $15.00 (0-374-30997-3). 32pp. A Seneca folktale concerning the consequences of a rivalry between Wolf and Raccoon. (Rev: BL 11/1/96; SLJ 10/96) [398.24]

11310 Taylor, Harriet P. *Coyote and the Laughing Butterflies* (1–3). Illus. 1995, Simon & Schuster paper $15.00 (0-02-788846-0). 32pp. Butterflies always carry Coyote home before he can gather the bag of salt he sets out to get. (Rev: BL 7/95; SLJ 8/95) [398.2]

11311 Taylor, Harriet P. *Coyote Places the Stars* (K–2). Illus. 1993, Bradbury LB $16.00 (0-02-788845-2). 32pp. A clever coyote rearranges the stars in the sky so they resemble the shapes of his animal friends in this Wasco Indian folktale. (Rev: BL 11/15/93; SLJ 12/93) [398.2]

11312 Taylor, Harriet P. *When Bear Stole the Chinook* (K–3). Illus. 1997, Farrar $16.00 (0-374-30589-7). 32pp. In this Blackfoot Indian folktale, an orphan boy and his animal friends investigate why the spring warm winds don't come. (Rev: BL 1/1–15/98; SLJ 10/97) [398.2]

11313 Toye, William. *The Loon's Necklace* (K–3). Illus. by Elizabeth Cleaver. 1990, Oxford paper $7.95 (0-19-540675-3). 24pp. In this reissue of a 1977 picture book of a Native American legend, an old man rewards a loon with a necklace for helping him regain his sight. [398.2]

11314 Van Laan, Nancy. *In a Circle Long Ago: A Treasury of Native Lore from North America* (3–5). Illus. 1995, Knopf LB $21.99 (0-679-95807-5). 128pp. Nature is explored in 25 geographically arranged tales, with an introduction to their cultural origins. (Rev: BL 11/15/95; SLJ 11/95) [392.2]

11315 Van Laan, Nancy. *Shingebiss: An Ojibwe Legend* (3–4). Illus. by Betsy Bowen. 1997, Houghton $16.00 (0-395-82745-0). 32pp. In this Ojibwa (Chippewa) legend, it appears that Shingebiss, a duck, will freeze during the winter because he has only four logs to heat his lodge. (Rev: BL 7/97; HB 11–12/97; SLJ 10/97) [398.2]

11316 Waboose, Jan B. *SkySisters* (PS–2). Illus. by Brian Deines. 2000, Kids Can $15.95 (1-55074-697-9). 32pp. Two Ojibwa sisters encounter three guardian spirits — a rabbit, a deer, and a coyote — as they venture out one night to see the Northern Lights. (Rev: BL 11/15/00; HBG 3/01; SLJ 1/01) [398.2]

11317 Wisniewski, David. *The Wave of the Sea-Wolf* (3–6). Illus. by author. 1994, Clarion $17.00 (0-395-66478-0). This Tlingit Indian legend tells how Princess Kchokeen saves her people by luring destructive white traders to their death. (Rev: BCCB 11/94; SLJ 10/94) [398.2]

11318 Wood, Audrey. *The Rainbow Bridge: Inspired by a Chumash Tale* (1–4). Illus. by Robert Florczak. 1995, Harcourt $16.00 (0-15-265475-5). 32pp. In this Chumash tale, earth goddess Hutash turns some of her people into dolphins to save them from drowning. (Rev: BCCB 12/95; BL 12/1/95; SLJ 10/95) [398.24]

11319 Wood, Douglas. *Rabbit and the Moon* (PS–3). Illus. by Leslie Baker. 1998, Simon & Schuster $15.00 (0-689-80769-4). 40pp. In this Cree Indian tale, Rabbit persuades Crane to take him on a flight so that he can get a moon's eye view of the world. (Rev: BL 2/15/98; HBG 10/98; SLJ 7/98) [398.2]

11320 Wood, Douglas. *The Windigo's Return: A North Woods Story* (3–6). Illus. by Greg Couch. 1996, Simon & Schuster paper $16.00 (0-689-80065-7). 32pp. An exciting, imaginative version of the Indian legend of how the first mosquitoes came to be. (Rev: BCCB 11/96; BL 9/15/96; SLJ 11/96) [398.2]

11321 Wood, Nancy. *The Girl Who Loved Coyotes: Stories of the Southwest* (K–4). Illus. by Diana Bryer. 1995, Morrow $16.00 (0-688-13981-7). 48pp. Twelve stories about the coyote who manages to survive in its native habitat in spite of the invasions of strangers of many cultures. (Rev: BL 9/15/95; SLJ 12/95) [398.2]

11322 Young, Richard, and Judy D. Young, eds. *Race with Buffalo: And Other Native American Stories for Young Readers* (3–7). Illus. by Wendell E. Hall. 1994, August House $19.95 (0-87483-343-4); paper $9.95 (0-87483-342-6). 175pp. This collection of 32 American Indian folktales includes such genres as creation and trickster stories. (Rev: SLJ 8/94) [398.2]

United States

11323 Anaya, Rudolfo A. *My Land Sings: Stories from the Rio Grande* (5–9). Illus. 1999, Morrow $17.00 (0-688-15078-0). 144pp. A magical collection of ten stories — some original and some from Mexican and Native American folklore — set mostly in New Mexico. (Rev: BL 8/99; HBG 10/00; SLJ 9/99) [398.2]

11324 Bang, Molly. *Wiley and the Hairy Man* (2–4). Illus. by author. 1996, Simon & Schuster $14.00 (0-689-81141-1); paper $3.99 (0-689-81142-X). 64pp. In this story from Alabama, Wiley's mother helps him outwit the Hairy Man, a terrible swamp creature. Adapted from an American folktale. [398.2]

11325 Birdseye, Tom. *Soap! Soap! Don't Forget the Soap! An Appalachian Folktale* (3–6). Illus. by Andrew Glass. 1993, Holiday LB $16.95 (0-8234-1005-6). 32pp. An adaptation of a familiar story about a forgetful hero sent to the store by his mother. (Rev: BCCB 6/93; BL 3/15/93; HB 5–6/93) [398.2]

11326 Brown, Marcia. *Backbone of the King: The Story of Paka'a and His Son Ku* (5–7). Illus. by author. 1984, Univ. of Hawaii Pr. $12.95 (0-8248-0963-7). 180pp. A reissue of the book based on a Hawaiian legend of a boy who wants to help his exiled father. [398.2]

11327 Cech, John. *Django* (K–3). Illus. by Sharon McGinley-Nally. 1994, Four Winds paper $15.95 (0-02-765705-1). 40pp. A fiddler named Django saves the animals of a Florida swamp when he warns them by playing his instrument during a hurricane. (Rev: BL 12/1/94; SLJ 12/94) [398.21]

11328 Chase, Richard. *Grandfather Tales* (4–6). Illus. by Berkeley Williams. 1948, Houghton $18.00 (0-395-06692-1); paper $7.95 (0-395-56150-7). 240pp. Folktales gathered from the South. Also use: *The Jack Tales* (1943). [398.2]

11329 Cohen, Daniel. *Railway Ghosts and Highway Horrors* (3–5). Illus. by Stephen Marchesi. 1993, Scholastic paper $2.95 (0-590-45423-4). 112pp. Phantom hitchhikers and accident victims fill this anthology of American and British travelers' lore. (Rev: BL 11/15/91) [133.1]

11330 Cohen, Daniel. *Southern Fried Rat and Other Gruesome Tales* (6–8). Illus. by Peggy Brier. 1989, Avon paper $3.50 (0-380-70655-5). 128pp. Grisly folktales — some funny, some gruesome. [398.2]

11331 Davis, Aubrey. *Sody Salleratus* (PS–2). Illus. by Alan Daniel and Lea Daniel. 1998, Kids Can $14.95 (1-55074-281-7). 32pp. In this American folktale, a wise squirrel solves the problem of having a bear in town that delights in eating everyone. (Rev: BL 3/15/98; HBG 10/98; SLJ 4/98) [398.2]

11332 Davis, Donald. *Jack and the Animals* (PS–2). Illus. by Kitty Harvill. 1995, August House $15.95 (0-87483-413-9). 32pp. Jack and a group of unhappy animals outwit a gang of robbers in this Appalachian tale. (Rev: BL 10/1/95; SLJ 1/96)

11333 DeFelice, Cynthia. *The Dancing Skeleton* (1–3). Illus. by Robert Andrew Parker. 1996, Simon & Schuster paper $5.99 (0-689-80453-9). 32pp. Old Aaron refuses to stay in his coffin until he "feels dead." (Rev: BCCB 10/89; BL 9/1/89; HB 1–2/90; SLJ 9/89*) [398.2]

11334 DeSpain, Pleasant. *Sweet Land of Story: Thirty-Six American Tales to Tell* (4–6). Illus. 2000, August House $19.95 (0-87483-569-0). 176pp. This anthology of 36 American folktales ranges from tall tales and Native American stories to Jack tales and traditional ghost stories. (Rev: BL 12/15/00; SLJ 12/00) [398.2]

11335 Doucet, Sharon Arms. *Why Lapin's Ears Are Long and Other Tales from the Louisiana Bayou* (4–6). Illus. by David Catrow. 1997, Orchard LB $19.99 (0-531-33041-9). 64pp. Three entertaining folktales from Cajun country that feature the trickster rabbit. (Rev: BL 8/97; HB 9–10/97; HBG 3/98; SLJ 9/97) [398.2]

11336 Farmer, Nancy. *Casey Jones's Fireman: The Story of Sim Webb* (PS–3). Illus. by James Bernardin. 1999, Penguin $15.99 (0-8037-1929-9). 40pp. A retelling of the story of the legendary train wreck as experienced by Sim Webb, the black fireman on Casey Jones's Cannonball Express. (Rev: BCCB 1/00; BL 9/15/99*; HBG 3/00; SLJ 10/99) [398.2]

11337 Forest, Heather. *The Baker's Dozen: A Colonial American Tale* (PS–2). Illus. by Susan Gaber. 1993, Harcourt paper $5.00 (0-152-05687-4). 28pp. A baker in colonial New York State cuts back on his cookie recipe, and when a woman demands 13 cookies for the dozen and he refuses, his baking is cursed. (Rev: BCCB 10/88; BL 9/15/88; SLJ 4/89) [398.2]

11338 Galdone, Joanna. *The Tailypo: A Ghost Story* (1–3). Illus. by Paul Galdone. 1984, Houghton paper $6.95 (0-395-30084-3). In this ghostly story, a mysterious creature returns to retrieve his tail, cut off by an old man. [398.2]

11339 Goodall, Jane. *The Eagle and the Wren* (K–3). Illus. by Alexander Reichstein. 2000, North-South LB $15.88 (0-7358-1381-7). 40pp. An appealing tale about several different birds who hold a contest to see which of them can fly the highest. (Rev: BL 12/1/00; SLJ 11/00) [398.2]

11340 Hamilton, Virginia. *Her Stories: African American Folktales, Fairy Tales, and True Tales* (5–8). Illus. by Leo Dillon and Diane Dillon. 1995, Scholastic $19.95 (0-590-47370-0). 144pp. A collection of 19 folktales about African American women. (Rev: BL 11/1/95*; SLJ 11/95*) [398.2]

11341 Hamilton, Virginia. *The People Could Fly: American Black Folk Tales* (4–8). Illus. by Leo Dillon and Diane Dillon. 1985, Knopf LB $18.99 (0-394-96925-1); paper $13.00 (0-679-84336-1). 192pp. These 24 folktales include such familiar titles as Tar Baby and lesser-known stories from Africa. (Rev: BCCB 7/85; BL 7/85; SLJ 11/85) [398.2]

11342 Hamilton, Virginia. *When Birds Could Talk and Bats Could Sing: The Adventures of Bruh Sparrow, Sis Wren, and Their Friends* (4–6). Illus. by Barry Moser. 1996, Scholastic $17.95 (0-590-47372-7). 72pp. Each of these eight tales from the American South deals with unpleasant, often foolish birds, and each ends with an important moral. (Rev: BCCB 6/96; BL 4/15/96*; HB 9–10/96; SLJ 5/96*) [398.2]

11343 Harris, Jim. *Jack and the Giant: A Story Full of Beans* (K–4). Illus. 1997, Northland LB $15.95 (0-87358-680-8). 32pp. This version of "Jack and the Beanstalk" had Jack living on a ranch in Arizona with his mother, Annie Okey-Dokey. (Rev: BL 2/1/98; HBG 3/98; SLJ 2/98) [398.2]

11344 Harris, Joel Chandler. *Brer Rabbit and Boss Lion* (PS–4). Retold by Brad Kessler. Illus. by Bill Mayer. 1996, Simon & Schuster paper $10.95 (0-689-80606-X). When a lion begins to eat the inhabitants of Brer Village, Brer Rabbit decides to take on the beast. (Rev: SLJ 1/97) [398.2]

11345 Harris, Joel Chandler. *Jump! The Adventures of Brer Rabbit* (3–5). Adapted by Van Dyke Parks and Malcolm Jones. Illus. by Barry Moser. 1986, Harcourt $15.95 (0-15-241350-2); paper $7.00 (0-15-201493-4). 40pp. An edition with tracings of the stories' roots in oral tradition. (Rev: BCCB 11/86; BL 1/1/87; SLJ 11/86) [398.2]

11346 Hayes, Joe. *Little Gold Star/Estrellita de oro: A Cinderella Cuento* (PS–3). Illus. by Gloria Osuna Perez and Lucia Angela Perez. 2000, Cinco Puntos $15.95 (0-938317-49-0). 32pp. Told in English and Spanish, this is an interesting version of the Cinderella story that is popular in the mountain communities of New Mexico. (Rev: BCCB 7–8/00; BL 5/15/00; HBG 10/00; SLJ 6/00) [398.2]

11347 Hayward, Linda. *All Stuck Up* (1–3). Illus. by Normand Chartier. 1990, Random paper $3.99 (0-679-80216-9). 32pp. The tar baby story featuring Brer Rabbit is retold. (Rev: BCCB 7–8/92; BL 6/1/90; SLJ 8/90) [398.2]

11348 Hayward, Linda. *Hello, House!* (1–2). Illus. by Lynn Munsinger. 1988, Random paper $3.99 (0-394-88864-2). 32pp. The Uncle Remus tale in which Brer Rabbit outsmarts sly Brer Wolf. (Rev: BL 10/1/88) [398.2]

11349 Hicks, Ray, and Lynn Salsi. *The Jack Tales* (3–5). Illus. 2000, Callaway $24.95 (0-935112-58-8). 40pp. Two different versions of each of three plucky Jack tales are effectively presented in print and on a CD. (Rev: BL 11/15/00*; HBG 3/01; SLJ 11/00) [398.2]

11350 Hoberman, Mary Ann. *Miss Mary Mack: A Hand-Clapping Rhyme* (K–3). Illus. by Nadine Bernard Westcott. 1998, Little, Brown $14.95 (0-316-93118-7). 32pp. A catchy hand-clapping rhyme that uses appropriate cartoon illustrations. (Rev: BCCB 5/98; BL 3/15/98; HBG 10/98; SLJ 5/98) [398.2]

11351 Hooks, William H. *Snowbear Whittington: An Appalachian Beauty and the Beast* (1–4). Illus. by Victoria Lisi. 1994, Macmillan paper $15.95 (0-02-744355-8). 56pp. To save her father, a young girl agrees to accompany a large white bear to his castle in this American folktale. (Rev: BL 10/15/94; SLJ 11/94) [398.2]

11352 Hooks, William H. *The Three Little Pigs and the Fox* (PS–2). Illus. by S. D. Schindler. 1997, Simon & Schuster paper $5.99 (0-689-80962-X). 32pp. A refreshing version drawn from Appalachian sources. (Rev: BCCB 1/90*; BL 9/1/89; HB 3–4/90; SLJ 10/89) [398.2]

11353 Hunt, Angela E. *The Tale of Three Trees: A Traditional Folktale* (K–2). Illus. by Tim Jonke. 1989, Lion $14.99 (0-7459-1743-7). 32pp. A folktale about three trees — a manger for the Christ child, a fishing boat that carries Jesus, and timbers that become the cross. (Rev: BL 11/1/89) [398.2]

11354 Jacobs, Jimmy. *Moonlight Through the Pines: Tales from Georgia Evenings* (5–7). Illus. 2000, Franklin-Sarrett paper $11.95 (0-9637477-3-8). 115pp. A collection of humorous reminiscences, family stories, tall tales, and other examples of folklore, all from the South. (Rev: BL 8/00) [398.2]

11355 Johnson, Paul B. *Old Dry Frye: A Deliciously Funny Tall Tale* (K–3). Illus. 1999, Scholastic $15.95 (0-590-37658-6). 40pp. An Appalachian tale about the body of Old Dry Frye and how the townspeople try to hide it in case they will be accused of his death. (Rev: BL 12/1/99; HBG 3/00; SLJ 9/99) [398.2]

11356 Keats, Ezra Jack. *John Henry: An American Legend* (1–3). Illus. by author. 1965, Knopf paper $5.99 (0-394-89052-3). 32pp. Large, bold figures capture the spirit of the hero who died with a hammer in his hand. [398.2]

11357 Kellogg, Steven. *Paul Bunyan* (K–4). Illus. by author. 1984, Morrow $16.89 (0-688-03850-6); paper $5.95 (0-688-05800-0). 40pp. Several stories about Paul and the blue ox Babe, all wittily illustrated. [398.2]

11358 Kellogg, Steven, reteller. *Pecos Bill* (K–3). Illus. by Steven Kellogg. 1986, Scholastic paper $5.95 (0-688-09924-6). 32pp. Humor permeates these tall tales of the American folk hero. (Rev: BCCB 11/86; BL 9/1/86; SLJ 9/86) [398.2]

11359 Kellogg, Steven. *Sally Ann Thunder Ann Whirlwind Crockett* (PS–3). Illus. 1995, Morrow $16.89 (0-688-14043-2). 48pp. A humorous look at the life of Davy Crockett's wife and her equally amazing exploits. (Rev: BCCB 9/95; BL 8/95; SLJ 10/95) [398.2]

11360 Kidd, Ronald, ed. *On Top of Old Smoky: A Collection of Songs and Stories from Appalachia* (4–6). Illus. by Linda Anderson. 1992, Ideals $13.95 (0-8249-8569-9). 38pp. A handsome collection of songs and stories from Appalachia with distinctive illustrations. (Rev: BL 12/1/92) [782]

11361 Kimmel, Eric A. *Billy Lazroe and the King of the Sea: A Tale of the Northwest* (2–4). Illus. by Michael Steirnagle. 1996, Harcourt $16.00 (0-15-200108-5). 40pp. A Russian folktale reset in Oregon, about Billy's love of the sea and its consequences. (Rev: BCCB 12/96; BL 12/15/96; SLJ 12/96) [398.2]

11362 Kimmel, Eric A. *The Runaway Tortilla* (K–2). Illus. by Randy Cecil. 2000, Winslow $16.95 (1-890817-18-X). A silly tortilla runs away but is finally caught and eaten by Señor Coyote. (Rev: BCCB 12/00; SLJ 10/00) [398.2]

11363 Liddell, Janice. *Imani and the Flying Africans* (2–5). Illus. by Linda Nickens. 1994, Africa World $14.95 (0-86543-365-8); paper $6.95 (0-86543-366-6). After hearing about the Flying Africans, who could rise into the air and escape slavery, young Imani dreams that he is captured by kidnappers and uses the same method to achieve freedom. (Rev: SLJ 11/94) [398.2]

11364 Lyons, Mary E., ed. *Raw Head, Bloody Bones: African-American Tales of the Supernatural* (5–7). 1991, Macmillan $15.00 (0-684-19333-7). 112pp. A bone-chiller full of ghosts, devils, and ogres as well as less familiar demons such as Plat-Eye and the monstrous night doctor. (Rev: BCCB 2/92; BL 1/1/92; HB 1–2/92; SLJ 12/91*) [398.2]

11365 McCormick, Dell J. *Paul Bunyan Swings His Axe* (4–6). Illus. by author. 1936, Caxton $15.95 (0-87004-093-6). The stories of the giant woodsman and his great blue ox named Babe are favorites among American folktales. [398.2]

11366 McKissack, Patricia. *The Dark-Thirty: Southern Tales of the Supernatural* (4–8). Illus. by Brian Pinkney. 1992, Knopf LB $17.99 (0-679-91863-9). 124pp. Ten tales "rooted in African-American history and the oral storytelling tradition." (Rev: BCCB 12/92; BL 12/15/92; HB 3–4/93; SLJ 12/92) [398.2]

11367 Mathews, Judith, and Fay Robinson. *Nathaniel Willy, Scared Silly* (PS–2). Illus. by Alexi Natchev. 1994, Bradbury paper $15.00 (0-02-765285-8). 32pp. Gramma brings in a variety of animals to comfort young Nathaniel who can't get to sleep because of a squeaky door. (Rev: BCCB 2/94; BL 5/15/94; SLJ 5/94) [398.2]

11368 Medearis, Angela Shelf. *Tailypo: A Newfangled Tall Tale* (K–3). Illus. by Sterling Brown. 1996, Holiday LB $15.95 (0-8234-1249-0). 32pp. A variation on the folktale about a monster that leaves its tail behind in the cabin of an African American boy. (Rev: BL 11/1/96; SLJ 1/97) [398.2]

11369 Metaxas, Eric. *Stormalong: The Legendary Sea Captain* (1–4). Illus. by Don Vanderbeek. 1995, Rabbit Ears paper $19.95 (0-689-80194-7). An amusing retelling of the tall tale about the legendary New England sea captain. (Rev: SLJ 12/95) [398.2]

11370 Osborne, Mary Pope. *American Tall Tales* (4–7). Illus. by Michael McCurdy. 1991, Knopf LB $23.99 (0-679-90089-6). 115pp. Nine tall tales perfect for telling to all ages. (Rev: BCCB 1/92; BL 3/15/92; SLJ 12/91*) [398.2]

11371 Reneaux, J. J. *Haunted Bayou: And Other Cajun Ghost Stories* (4–8). 1994, August House paper $9.95 (0-87483-385-X). 158pp. Thirteen scary, entertaining folktales from Cajun country are retold effectively. (Rev: SLJ 12/94) [398.2]

11372 Reneaux, J. J. *Why Alligator Hates Dog* (1–3). Illus. by Donnie Lee Green. 1995, August House $15.95 (0-87483-412-0). 32pp. Dog loves to torment Alligator, but the wily reptile plots his revenge. (Rev: BL 10/15/95; SLJ 1/96) [398.3]

11373 Rounds, Glen. *Ol' Paul, the Mighty Logger* (3–6). Illus. by author. 1976, Holiday paper $5.95 (0-8234-0713-6). 96pp. An account of the incredible exploits of one of our national folk heroes. [398.2]

11374 Rumford, James. *The Island-Below-the-Star* (1–3). Illus. 1998, Houghton $15.00 (0-395-85159-9). 32pp. A folk-like story about five adventurous brothers who set out to find a new island home. (Rev: BCCB 7–8/98; BL 3/15/98; HBG 10/98; SLJ 6/98) [398.2]

11375 San Souci, Robert D. *Callie Ann and Mistah Bear* (K–3). Illus. by Don Daily. 2000, Dial $15.99

(0-8037-1766-0). 32pp. In this folktale from the American South, a young girl discovers that the attractive stranger who is courting her mother is really a bear. (Rev: BL 12/1/00; HBG 3/01; SLJ 10/00) [398.2]

11376 San Souci, Robert D. *Cut from the Same Cloth: American Women of Myth, Legend and Tall Tale* (4–6). Illus. by Brian Pinkney. 1993, Putnam $19.99 (0-399-21987-0). 142pp. This is a lively collection of folktales retold by the author, each of which features a female central character. (Rev: BCCB 6/93*; BL 4/15/93; SLJ 6/93) [398.2]

11377 San Souci, Robert D. *The Secret of the Stones* (2–4). Illus. by James E. Ransome. 1999, Penguin $16.99 (0-8037-1640-0). 40pp. In this folktale with roots in both Arkansas and Zaire, a childless couple tries to rescue two orphans who have been turned into pebbles. (Rev: BCCB 1/00; BL 1/1–15/00; HBG 3/00; SLJ 2/00) [398.2]

11378 San Souci, Robert D. *Six Foolish Fishermen* (PS–3). Illus. by Doug Kennedy. 2000, Hyperion LB $15.49 (0-7868-2335-6). 32pp. The author has combined and expanded several "noodle" stories from around the world and presented them in a goofy tale set in Cajun country. (Rev: BL 5/15/00; HBG 10/00; SLJ 7/00) [398.2]

11379 San Souci, Robert D., reteller. *Sukey and the Mermaid* (K–3). Illus. by Brian Pinkney. 1992, Macmillan LB $16.00 (0-02-778141-0). 32pp. Drawing from African tradition, this is the story of a rare black mermaid and how she saves a poor unhappy girl. (Rev: BCCB 3/92*; BL 2/1/92; SLJ 5/92*) [398.2]

11380 Schwartz, Alvin. *More Scary Stories to Tell in the Dark* (4–7). Illus. by Stephen Gammell. 1984, HarperCollins LB $14.89 (0-397-32082-5); paper $4.95 (0-06-440177-4). 128pp. Brief tales from folk stories and hearsay with a scary bent. [398.2]

11381 Schwartz, Alvin, ed. *Scary Stories to Tell in the Dark* (3–8). Illus. by Stephen Gammell. 1981, HarperCollins LB $15.89 (0-397-31927-4); paper $4.95 (0-06-440170-7). 128pp. Ghost stories collected from American folklore. [398.2]

11382 Schwartz, Alvin, ed. *Whoppers: Tall Tales and Other Lies* (3–5). Illus. 1975, HarperCollins paper $7.95 (0-06-446091-6). 128pp. A collection of long and short humorous tales from a number of sources. [398.2]

11383 Shapiro, Irwin. *Joe Magarac and His U.S.A. Citizen Papers* (5–7). Illus. by James Daugherty. 1979, Univ. of Pittsburgh Pr. paper $7.95 (0-8229-5305-6). 58pp. Tall tale of the Hungarian-born hero to the steel mills of Pennsylvania. [398.2]

11384 Shepard, Aaron. *The Legend of Slappy Hooper: An American Tall Tale* (K–3). Illus. by Toni Goffe. 1993, Scribners $14.95 (0-684-19535-6). 32pp. Slappy Hooper's paintings of animals and plants are so realistic that they come to life. (Rev: BL 11/1/93) [398.21]

11385 Stevens, Janet. *Tops and Bottoms* (PS–2). Illus. 1995, Harcourt $16.00 (0-15-292851-0). 32pp. An African American folktale about how Hare takes unfair advantage of Bear in a garden project. (Rev: BCCB 4/95; BL 3/15/95*; HB 5–6/95; SLJ 5/95) [398.2]

11386 *Stockings of Buttermilk: American Folktales* (4–5). Ed. by Neil Philip. Illus. 1999, Clarion $20.00 (0-395-84980-2). 124pp. A collection of 18 folktales that had their roots in Europe (e.g., "Jack and the Beanstalk") but were changed when imported into America — often by African American storytellers. (Rev: BL 9/1/99; HB 11–12/99; HBG 3/00; SLJ 10/99) [398.2]

11387 Vagin, Vladimir. *The Enormous Carrot* (K–2). Illus. 1998, Scholastic $15.95 (0-590-45491-9). 32pp. A reworking of the old folktale "The Enormous Turnip," with an engaging cast of animal characters. (Rev: BCCB 6/98; BL 3/1/98; HBG 10/98; SLJ 3/98) [398.2]

11388 Van Laan, Nancy. *With a Whoop and a Holler: A Bushel of Lore from Way Down South* (3–6). Illus. 1998, Simon & Schuster $19.95 (0-689-81061-X). 112pp. A priceless collection of rhymes, folktales, superstitions, and riddles from the South. (Rev: BCCB 9/98; BL 3/1/98*; HBG 10/98; SLJ 4/98) [398]

11389 Walker, Paul R. *Big Men, Big Country: A Collection of American Tall Tales* (4–6). Illus. by James Bernardin. 1993, Harcourt $16.95 (0-15-207136-9). 80pp. After an introduction on the origins of American tales, there is a rollicking, retelling of the exploits of such characters as Davy Crockett, Paul Bunyan, and lesser-known figures like Gib Morgan and Big Mose. (Rev: BCCB 6/93; BL 4/1/93; SLJ 5/93) [398.2]

11390 Washington, Donna. *A Big, Spooky House* (1–5). Illus. by Jacqueline Rogers. 2000, Hyperion $15.99 (0-7868-0349-5). A traditional African American folktale in which a strong man who has taken refuge in a spooky house is warned by cats of the arrival of big bad John. (Rev: BCCB 1/01; BL 9/15/00; HBG 3/01; SLJ 9/00) [398.2]

11391 Wooldridge, Connie N. *Wicked Jack* (K–3). Illus. by Will Hillenbrand. 1995, Holiday LB $16.95 (0-8234-1101-X). 32pp. A retelling of the Southern tale about a mean blacksmith who outwits the Devil and his young sons. (Rev: BCCB 12/95; BL 11/1/95; SLJ 12/95*) [398.2]

South and Central America

Mexico and Other Central American Lands

11392 Ada, Alma F. *The Lizard and the Sun* (K–3). Illus. by Felipe Davalos. 1997, Doubleday $16.95 (0-385-32121-X). 40pp. In this Mexican tale told in both English and Spanish, a lizard, with the help of an emperor and a woodpecker, frees the sun that is trapped inside a rock. (Rev: BL 12/15/97; HBG 3/98; SLJ 8/97) [398.2]

11393 Anaya, Rudolfo A. *Maya's Children: The Story of La Llorona* (1–4). Illus. by Maria Baca. 1997, Hyperion LB $15.49 (0-7868-2124-8). 32pp. A retelling of the Latin American tale of Maya, the daughter of the sun god, who has been given the gift of immortality. (Rev: BCCB 7–8/97; BL 5/1/97; SLJ 6/97) [398.2]

11394 Bierhorst, John. *Doctor Coyote: A Native American Aesop's Fables* (3–5). Illus. by Wendy Watson. 1987, Macmillan LB $15.95 (0-02-709780-3). 48pp. Aesop's fables as they were translated into Spanish in the New World. (Rev: BCCB 3/87; BL 3/15/87; SLJ 5/87) [398.2]

11395 Bierhorst, John, ed. *The Monkey's Haircut: And Other Stories Told by the Maya* (4–6). Illus. by Robert Andrew Parker. 1986, Morrow $16.00 (0-688-04269-4). 160pp. Forms of folklore in a collection of Maya legends, most from the early 1900s. (Rev: BCCB 5/86; BL 7/86; SLJ 8/86) [398.2]

11396 Climo, Shirley, reteller. *The Little Red Ant and the Great Big Crumb* (PS–2). Illus. by Francisco Mora. 1995, Clarion $16.00 (0-395-70732-3). 39pp. A tiny ant seeks help in vain from other animals to move a heavy crumb in this Mexican tale. (Rev: SLJ 11/95) [398.2]

11397 Coburn, Jewell Reinhart. *Domitila: A Cinderella Tale from the Mexican Tradition* (3–5). Illus. 2000, Shen's $16.95 (1-885008-13-9). 32pp. This variation on the story of Cinderella comes from the folklore of Hidalgo, Mexico. (Rev: BL 5/15/00; HBG 10/00; SLJ 7/00) [398.2]

11398 Czernecki, Stefan, and Timothy Rhodes. *The Sleeping Bread* (1–3). Illus. by Stefan Czernecki. 1992, Hyperion $14.95 (1-562-82183-0). 40pp. In this Central American folktale, the tears of a beggar who is driven out of town change the village's bread when they are added to the dough. (Rev: BCCB 9/92; BL 4/15/92; SLJ 8/92) [398.2]

11399 dePaola, Tomie. *The Legend of the Poinsettia* (K–4). Illus. 1994, Putnam LB $16.99 (0-399-21692-8). 32pp. Lucinda is unhappy because she has ruined the blanket that was intended for use in a Christmas procession. (Rev: BL 8/94; HB 11–12/94) [398.2]

11400 de Sauza, James. *Brother Anansi and the Cattle Ranch/El Hermano Anansi y el Rancho de Ganada* (3–6). Adapted by Harriet Rohmer. Illus. by Stephen Von Mason. 1989, Children's Book Pr. $14.95 (0-89239-044-1). 32pp. A bilingual retelling of the ancient folktale about the trickster spider, now transplanted to Nicaragua. Two others in this dual-language series are: *Mr. Sugar Came to Town/La Visita del Señor Azucar* (1989); *Uncle Nacho's Hat/El Sombrero de Tio Nacho* (1989). (Rev: BL 11/15/89) [398.2]

11401 Ehlert, Lois. *Cuckoo/Cucu* (PS–2). Trans. by Gloria de Aragon Andujar. Illus. 1997, Harcourt $16.00 (0-15-200274-X). 40pp. In this Mayan tale, Cuckoo saves the annual harvest of seeds on which the other birds live during the winter. (Rev: BCCB 6/97; BL 4/1/97*; HBG 3/98; SLJ 3/97) [398.2]

11402 Harper, Jo. *The Legend of Mexicatl* (K–3). Illus. by Robert Casilla. 1998, Turtle $15.95 (1-890515-05-1). 32pp. A handsome retelling of the Mexican legend about the teenage boy who is destined to lead his people out of the desert. (Rev: BL 4/15/98) [398.2]

11403 Johnston, Tony. *The Tale of Rabbit and Coyote* (PS–3). Illus. by Tomie dePaola. 1994, Putnam $15.99 (0-399-22258-8). 32pp. Trickster Rabbit always is able to get the best of foolish Coyote in this tale from Mexico. (Rev: BCCB 7–8/94; BL 5/15/94*; HB 5–6/94; SLJ 6/94) [398.2]

11404 Kimmel, Eric A. *Montezuma and the Fall of the Aztecs* (2–5). Illus. by Daniel San Souci. 2000, Holiday $16.95 (0-8234-1452-3). 32pp. After introducing the history and culture of the Aztecs, this picture book covers the reign of Montezuma, the coming of Cortes, and the Aztec leader's defeat. (Rev: BL 1/1–15/00; HBG 10/00; SLJ 3/00) [972]

11405 Kimmel, Eric A. *The Two Mountains: An Aztec Legend* (3–5). Illus. 2000, Holiday $16.95 (0-8234-1504-X). 32pp. This Aztec legend tells how two young lovers are transformed into the two mountains that overlook the Valley of Mexico. (Rev: BL 5/15/00; HBG 10/00; SLJ 4/00) [398.2]

11406 Lewis, Richard. *All of You Was Singing* (PS–3). Illus. by Ed Young. 1991, Macmillan $13.95 (0-689-31596-1). 32pp. This creation myth from the Aztecs is retold in simple text and mystical illustrations. (Rev: BCCB 7–8/91; BL 1/15/91) [398.2]

11407 Love, Hallie N., and Bonni Larson, retellers. *Watakame's Journey: The Story of the Great Flood and the New World: A Huichol Indian Tale* (2–6). Illus. 1999, Clear Light $14.95 (1-56416-029-X). 84pp. This is a Mexican version of the Noah story featuring a young boy who is selected by the goddess of all growing things to build a boat to withstand the coming flood. (Rev: SLJ 12/99) [398.2]

11408 McDermott, Gerald. *Musicians of the Sun* (PS–3). Illus. 1997, Simon & Schuster paper $17.00 (0-689-80706-6). 40pp. In this Aztec creation story, Wind is sent to free the colors Red, Yellow, Blue, and Green, who are being held prisoner by the Sun. (Rev: BL 11/1/97*; HBG 3/98; SLJ 12/97*) [389.2]

11409 Madrigal, Antonio H. *The Eagle and the Rainbow: Timeless Tales from México* (4–7). Illus. by Tomie dePaola. 1997, Fulcrum $15.95 (1-55591-317-2). 56pp. A collection of wise, wonderful, but little-known folktales from Mexico. (Rev: BL 7/97) [398.2]

11410 Marcos, Subcomandante. *The Story of Colors/La Historia de los Colores: A Folktale from the Jungles of Chiapas* (K–4). Trans. by Anne Bar Din. Illus. by Domitila Domínguez. 1999, Cinco Puntos $15.95 (0-938317-45-8). This folktale told in both Spanish and English explains the origins of the colors in the world and how the macaw got its bright plumage. (Rev: HBG 10/99; SLJ 5/99) [398.2]

11411 Montejo, Victor, reteller. *Popol Vuh: A Sacred Book of the Maya* (5–8). Trans. by David Under. Illus. by Luis Garay. 1999, Groundwood $19.95 (0-88899-334-X). 85pp. A creation story from the Mayans in a beautifully designed book that features gods, giants, mortals, and animals. (Rev: HBG 3/00; SLJ 12/99) [398.2]

11412 Mora, Pat. *The Night the Moon Fell* (PS–K). Illus. by Domi. 2000, Douglas & McIntyre $16.95 (0-88899-398-6). 32pp. A Mayan myth about how Luna, the moon, is shattered when she falls from the sky and how she gathers strength to repair herself and return to her home. (Rev: BL 9/1/00; HBG 3/01; SLJ 11/00) [398.2]

11413 Ober, Hal. *How Music Came to the World: An Ancient Mexican Myth* (1–4). Illus. by Carol Ober. 1994, Houghton $17.00 (0-395-67523-5). 32pp. How music came to the world is the subject of this folktale dating to pre-Columbian times. (Rev: BL 3/15/94; SLJ 10/94) [398.2]

11414 Rockwell, Anne. *The Boy Who Wouldn't Obey* (2–4). Illus. 2000, Greenwillow $15.95 (0-688-14881-6). 24pp. In this Mayan legend a young boy steals the tools of Chac, the god of the sky, but doesn't know how to control them. (Rev: BCCB 7–8/00; BL 5/15/00; HBG 10/00; SLJ 6/00) [398.2]

11415 Shetterly, Susan Hand. *The Dwarf-Wizard of Uxmal* (4–6). Illus. by Robert Shetterly. 1990, Macmillan LB $13.95 (0-689-31455-8). 32pp. This Mayan legend tells how the great temple at Uxmal originated as a large tortilla pyramid. (Rev: BL 3/15/90; SLJ 4/90) [398.2]

11416 Strauss, Susan. *When Woman Became the Sea: A Costa Rican Creation Myth* (K–3). Illus. by Cristina Acosta. 1998, Beyond Words $14.95 (1-885223-85-4). 32pp. A retelling of the Costa Rican folktale that tells how Thunder's pregnant wife, Sea, is killed by a snake and how her body splits and produces all the waters of the world. (Rev: BL 10/15/98; HBG 3/99; SLJ 11/98) [398.2]

Puerto Rico and Other Caribbean Islands

11417 Alvarez, Julia. *The Secret Footprints* (1–4). Illus. by Fabian Negrin. 2000, Knopf $16.95 (0-679-89309-1). 32pp. A folktale from the Taino Indians of the Dominican Republic about the ciguapas, beautiful humanlike creatures whose feet are on backwards and who have a great fear of humans. (Rev: BCCB 10/00; BL 8/00; HBG 3/01; SLJ 9/00) [398.2]

11418 Breinburg, Petronella. *Stories from the Caribbean* (2–4). Illus. by Syrah Arnold and Tina Barber. Series: Multicultural Stories. 2000, Raintree Steck-Vaughn LB $27.12 (0-7398-1334-X). 48pp. Ghost stories, creation fables, and animal stories are included in this interesting anthology. (Rev: HBG 10/00; SLJ 11/00) [398.2]

11419 Bryan, Ashley. *Turtle Knows Your Name* (K–3). Illus. 1989, Macmillan $12.95 (0-689-31578-3). 32pp. A fine retelling of a West Indies folktale that points out the importance of names in this culture. (Rev: BCCB 2/90; BL 10/1/89; HB 1–2/90; SLJ 10/89) [398.2]

11420 Comissiong, Lynette. *Mind Me Good Now!* (PS–3). Illus. by Marie Lafrance. 1997, Annick $16.95 (1-55037-483-4); paper $6.95 (1-55037-482-6). 32pp. A Hansel and Gretel–like Caribbean folktale about Tina, her brother Dalby, and a wicked witch, Cocoya, who loves eating boys. (Rev: BL 1/1–15/98; SLJ 7/98) [398.2]

11421 Gershator, Phillis. *Tukama Tootles the Flute* (PS–3). Illus. by Synthia Saint James. 1994, Orchard LB $16.99 (0-531-08661-5). 32pp. A flute-playing youngster uses his music to escape the clutches of a giant in this folktale from the Virgin Islands. (Rev: BCCB 4/94; BL 5/1/94; HB 5–6/94; SLJ 4/94) [398.2]

11422 Gonzalez, Lucia M. *The Bossy Gallito* (K–3). Illus. by Lulu Delacre. 1994, Scholastic $15.95 (0-590-46843-X). 32pp. In this cumulative tale from Cuba, a rooster must involve a great number of animals in order to get his beak cleaned. (Rev: BCCB 7–8/94; BL 5/15/94; HB 9–10/94; SLJ 4/94) [398.2]

11423 Hausman, Gerald. *Doctor Bird: Three Lookin' Up Tales from Jamaica* (3–5). Illus. by Ashley Wolff. 1998, Putnam $15.99 (0-399-22744-X). 40pp. These three animal stories from the north coast of Jamaica feature a hummingbird, a dim-witted owl, a houseless mouse, and a mongoose. (Rev: BL 6/1–15/98; HBG 10/98; SLJ 9/98) [398.2]

11424 Izcoa, Carmen Rivera, adapt. *Mediopollito/ Half-a-Chick* (K–3). Illus. by Nívea O. Montáñez. 1996, Ediciones Huracan $10.50 (0-929157-43-5). A Puerto Rican folktale about a bird that punishes the king for being mean and selfish. (Rev: SLJ 11/97) [398.2]

11425 Jaffe, Nina. *The Golden Flower: A Taino Myth from Puerto Rico* (K–3). Illus. by Enrique O. Sanchez. 1996, Simon & Schuster $16.95 (0-689-80469-5). 32pp. The creation of the island of Puerto Rico is told in this Taino myth about a magical pumpkin. (Rev: BCCB 6/96; BL 6/1–15/96; SLJ 7/96) [398.2]

11426 Joseph, Lynn. *The Mermaid's Twin Sister: More Stories from Trinidad* (3–7). Illus. 1994, Clarion $13.95 (0-395-64365-1). 65pp. A retelling in the native patois of some folktales from Trinidad, many of them scary. (Rev: BCCB 6/94; BL 4/15/94; HB 7–8/94; SLJ 6/94) [398.2]

11427 Joseph, Lynn. *A Wave in Her Pocket: Stories from Trinidad* (3–5). Illus. by Brian Pinkney. 1991, Houghton $15.00 (0-395-54432-7). 50pp. Traditional folklore is combined with a child's view of island life in these six stories. (Rev: BCCB 7–8/91; BL 5/15/91*; SLJ 7/91*) [398.2]

11428 Keens-Douglas, Richard. *Mama God, Papa God: A Caribbean Tale* (K–2). Illus. by Stefan Czernecki. 1999, Crocodile LB $15.95 (1-56656-307-0). A Caribbean Island folktale attractively illustrated that tells a creation story centering around Mama God and Papa God and how they created diversity in the people that they made. (Rev: HBG 10/99; SLJ 7/99) [398.2]

11429 Linzer, Lila. *Once Upon an Island* (2–5). 1999, Front Street $15.95 (1-886910-10-3). 76pp. Four tales about animals (including bees, goats, and doves) from the island of St. Croix are retold in a dialect that captures the lilting rhythms of West Indian English. (Rev: HBG 10/99; SLJ 4/99) [398.2]

11430 Moreton, Daniel. *La Cucaracha Martina: A Caribbean Folktale* (PS–2). Illus. 1997, Turtle $14.95 (1-890515-03-5). 32pp. A refined cockroach finally finds her mate, a handsome cricket, in this Caribbean folktale. (Rev: BL 1/1–15/98; SLJ 11/97) [398.2]

11431 San Souci, Robert D. *The Faithful Friend* (K–4). Illus. by Brian Pinkney. 1995, Simon &

Schuster paper $16.00 (0-02-786131-7). 40pp. On the island of Martinique, Hippolyte tries to save his friend's wedding from destruction by the bride's evil uncle. (Rev: BCCB 9/95; BL 4/15/95*; HB 9–10/95; SLJ 6/95) [398.2]

11432 Sherlock, Philip M., ed. *West Indian Folk Tales* (3–6). Illus. by Joan Kiddell-Monroe. 1978, Oxford paper $12.95 (0-19-274127-6). 151pp. Tales from the Caribbean including those about the spider, Anansi. [398.2]

11433 Wolkstein, Diane. *Bouki Dances the Kokioko: A Comical Tale from Haiti* (K–3). Illus. by Jesse Sweetwater. 1997, Harcourt $15.00 (0-15-200034-8). 32pp. In this Haitian trickster tale, a king invents a dance and offers a large reward for anyone who can master it. (Rev: BL 9/15/97; HBG 3/98; SLJ 11/97) [398.2]

South America

11434 Aldana, Patricia, ed. *Jade and Iron: Latin American Tales from Two Cultures* (5–8). Trans. by Hugh Hazelton. Illus. 1996, Douglas & McIntyre $18.95 (0-88899-256-4). 64pp. Fourteen folktales on a variety of subjects and from many regions in Latin America are retold in this large-format picture book. (Rev: BCCB 1/97; BL 12/1/96) [398.2]

11435 Delacre, Lulu. *Golden Tales: Myths, Legends and Folktales from Latin America* (4–6). Illus. 1996, Scholastic $18.95 (0-590-48186-X). 80pp. Twelve important Latin American folktales from before and after the time of Columbus are clearly presented. (Rev: BCCB 1/97; BL 12/15/96; SLJ 9/96) [398.2]

11436 DeSpain, Pleasant. *The Dancing Turtle: A Folktale from Brazil* (K–3). Illus. by David Boston. 1998, August House $15.95 (0-87483-502-X). 32pp. Through trickery, wily Turtle escapes from her human captors in this Brazilian folktale set in a tropical rain forest. (Rev: BL 5/1/98; HBG 10/98; SLJ 5/98) [398.2]

11437 Dorson, Mercedes, and Jeanne Wilmot. *Tales from the Rain Forest: Myths and Legends from the Amazonian Indians of Brazil* (5–8). Illus. 1997, Ecco $18.00 (0-88001-567-5). 133pp. Ten entertaining folktales from the Amazonian Indians of Brazil. (Rev: BL 2/15/98; HB 3–4/98; HBG 10/98) [398.2]

11438 Ehlert, Lois. *Moon Rope: A Peruvian Folktale* (4–8). Illus. 1992, Harcourt $17.00 (0-15-255343-6). 40pp. In both English and Spanish, this is the story of Fox, who wants to go to the moon and persuades his friend Mole to go along. (Rev:

BCCB 12/92; BL 10/15/92*; HB 11–12/92; SLJ 10/92*) [398.2]

11439 Gonzalez, Lucia M. *Señor Cat's Romance and Other Favorite Stories from Latin America* (1–3). Illus. by Lulu Delacre. 1997, Scholastic $17.95 (0-590-48537-7). 48pp. Six enchanting folktales popular in Latin America. (Rev: BCCB 4/97; BL 2/1/97; HB 3–4/97; SLJ 2/97) [398.2]

11440 Jendresen, Erik, and Alberto Villoldo. *The First Story Ever Told* (1–3). Illus. by Yoshi. 1996, Simon & Schuster $16.00 (0-689-80515-2). 32pp. An explorer dreams about the creation of the earth and life in this tale from the Incas. (Rev: BL 12/15/96; SLJ 12/96) [398.2]

11441 Munduruku, Daniel. *Tales of the Amazon: How the Munduruku Indians Live* (5–8). Trans. by Jane Springer. Illus. by Laurabeatriz. 2000, Groundwood $18.95 (0-88899-392-7). 56pp. This is an interesting view of the life of the human inhabitants of the Amazon rain forest with material on lifestyles, houses, languages, myths, and marriage. (Rev: HBG 3/01; SLJ 9/00) [981]

11442 Pitcher, Caroline. *Mariana and the Merchild: A Folk Tale from Chile* (PS–3). Illus. by Jackie Morris. 2000, Eerdmans $17.00 (0-8028-5204-1). 32pp. In this Chilean folktale, Mariana, who lives alone on the beach, raises an infant mermaid until she is old enough to survive in the sea. (Rev: BL 3/1/00; HBG 10/00; SLJ 5/00) [398.2]

11443 Van Laan, Nancy. *The Magic Bean Tree: A Legend from Argentina* (PS–3). Illus. by Beatriz Vidal. 1998, Houghton $15.00 (0-395-82746-9). 32pp. In this Argentinian folktale, young Topec must frighten away the evil Bird of the Underworld so that rain will return to the pampas and save his beloved carob tree. (Rev: BCCB 7–8/98; BL 4/1/98; HBG 10/98; SLJ 6/98) [398.2]

11444 Van Laan, Nancy. *So Say the Little Monkeys* (PS–2). Illus. by Yumi Heo. 1998, Simon & Schuster $16.00 (0-689-81038-5). 40pp. The small "blackmouth" monkeys of Brazil have so much fun playing that they neglect to build a shelter for themselves against the rain in this Brazilian folktale. (Rev: BCCB 9/98; BL 9/1/98; HBG 3/99; SLJ 9/98) [398.2]

11445 Weiss, Jacqueline Shachter. *Young Brer Rabbit: And Other Trickster Tales from the Americas* (4–6). Illus. 1985, Stemmer $14.95 (0-88045-037-1); paper $9.95 (0-88045-138-6). 80pp. Fifteen stories translated from Spanish, French, and Portuguese. (Rev: BCCB 1/86; BL 3/1/86; SLJ 1/86) [398.2]

Mythology

General and Miscellaneous

11446 Fisher, Leonard Everett. *Gods and Goddesses of the Ancient Maya* (4–7). Illus. 1999, Holiday $16.95 (0-8234-1427-2). 36pp. This book provides a fascinating introduction to Mayan mythology by describing ten gods and two goddesses. (Rev: BL 2/1/00; HBG 3/00; SLJ 12/99) [299]

11447 Harris, Geraldine. *Gods and Pharaohs from Egyptian Mythology* (5–8). Illus. by David O'Connor and John Sibbick. 1992, Bedrick LB $24.95 (0-87226-907-8). 132pp. A collection of myths and legends from ancient Egypt. [398.2]

11448 January, Brendan. *The New York Public Library Amazing Mythology: A Book of Answers for Kids* (5–8). Illus. 2000, Wiley paper $12.95 (0-471-33205-4). 169pp. This compendium of information covers Middle Eastern, African, Mediterranean, Asian, Pacific, Northern European, and North and Central American mythology. (Rev: BL 11/1/00) [291.1]

11449 Koenig, Viviane. *A Family Treasury of Myths from Around the World* (PS–3). Trans. by Anthony Zielonka. Illus. 1998, Abrams $29.95 (0-8109-4380-8). 160pp. This attractive retelling of ten myths from around the world includes stories from ancient Egypt, the legend of Romulus and Remus, Ulysses's adventure with the Sirens, and the epic of Moses in Egypt. (Rev: BL 1/1–15/99; HBG 3/99) [398.2]

11450 Leeming, David A., ed. *The Children's Dictionary of Mythology* (4–7). 1999, Watts LB $32.00 (0-531-11708-1). 128pp. A basic introduction to world mythology through alphabetically arranged characters, stories, and motifs from a wide variety of cultures. (Rev: SLJ 11/99) [291.1]

11451 McCaughrean, Geraldine. *The Golden Hoard: Myths and Legends of the World* (4–6). Illus. by Bee Willey. 1996, Simon & Schuster $19.95 (0-689-80741-4). 130pp. Twenty-two myths from around the world are retold in imaginative, often colloquial

prose. (Rev: BCCB 7–8/96; BL 5/1/96; HB 5–6/96; SLJ 3/96*) [883]

11452 Martell, Hazel M. *Myths and Civilization of the Celts* (3–6). Illus. 2000, Bedrick $16.95 (0-87226-591-9). 48pp. Using double-page spreads, Celtic myths are retold and followed by historical and cultural background material. (Rev: BL 3/1/00) [299]

11453 Morley, Jacqueline. *Egyptian Myths* (4–6). 2000, Bedrick $22.50 (0-87226-589-7). 64pp. With illustrations that take their cues from ancient Egyptian art, this handsome volume contains several Egyptian myths involving such characters as Osiris and Isis. (Rev: BL 4/1/00; HBG 10/00; SLJ 3/00) [299]

11454 O'Neill, Cynthia, ed. *Goddesses, Heroes and Shamans: The Young People's Guide to World Mythology* (5–8). Illus. 1997, Kingfisher paper $17.95 (0-7534-5058-5). 160pp. Using a geographical arrangement, this book introduces world mythology, with coverage on characters, purpose, and significance. (Rev: BL 10/1/97) [291.1]

11455 Philip, Neil. *The Illustrated Book of Myths: Tales and Legends of the World* (5–8). Illus. by Nilesh Mistry. 1995, DK $19.95 (0-7894-0202-5). 192pp. Ancient myths from both the Old World and the New World have been collected under such headings as creation, destruction, and fertility. (Rev: BL 12/1/95; SLJ 12/95) [291.1]

11456 Philip, Neil. *Mythology* (4–9). Series: Eyewitness Books. 1999, Knopf $19.00 (0-375-80135-9). 59pp. Using lavish photographs and a concise text, this is an introduction to topics in world mythology such as creation, fertility, birth, ancestor worship, tricksters, idols, mythical beasts, death, and the end of the world. (Rev: HBG 3/00; SLJ 9/99) [291.1]

11457 Waldherr, Kris. *The Book of Goddesses* (4–7). Illus. 1996, Beyond Words $17.95 (1-885223-30-7). 64pp. In an oversize volume, 26 goddesses from mythology are profiled. (Rev: BL 4/1/96; SLJ 5/96) [291.2]

11458 Williams, Marcia. *Fabulous Monsters* (3–5). Illus. 1999, Candlewick $15.99 (0-7636-0791-6). 32pp. This book tells the stories of some of the famous monsters from mythology, like Grendel and his mother, the Chimera, and the Australian Bunyip. (Rev: BL 1/1–15/00; HBG 3/00; SLJ 11/99) [398.21]

Classical

11459 Balit, Christina. *Atlantis* (3–5). Illus. 2000, Holt $16.95 (0-8050-6334-X). 32pp. Adapted from ancient sources, this is the story of how Poseidon built the city of Atlantis and later destroyed it by sinking it to the ocean floor. (Rev: BCCB 9/00; BL 5/15/00*; HBG 10/00; SLJ 5/00) [398.23]

11460 Barber, Antonia, reteller. *Apollo and Daphne: Masterpieces of Greek Mythology* (5–9). 1998, Getty Museum $16.95 (0-89236-504-8). 45pp. A stunning book that retells famous Greek myths, including stories of the Trojan War and the return of Odysseus, with full-page reproductions of 19 splendid paintings inspired by these myths. (Rev: HBG 3/99; SLJ 9/98) [398.2]

11461 Burleigh, Robert. *Hercules* (3–6). Illus. by Raul Colon. 1999, Harcourt $16.00 (0-15-201667-8). 32pp. After an introduction to Hercules and his 12 labors, this superbly illustrated book describes in detail his last labor — the journey to Hades. (Rev: BCCB 11/99; BL 8/99; HBG 3/00; SLJ 10/99) [398.2]

11462 Claybourne, Anna, and Kamini Khanduri, retellers. *Greek Myths: Ulysses and the Trojan War* (5–10). Illus. by Jeff Anderson. 1999, EDC $24.95 (0-7460-3361-3). 160pp. The events surrounding the Trojan War are retold, plus an account of Ulysses' adventures and voyage home. (Rev: HBG 3/00; SLJ 6/99) [398.2]

11463 Clement-Davies, David. *Trojan Horse: The World's Greatest Adventure* (2–5). Series: Eyewitness Reader. 1999, DK $12.95 (0-7894-4474-7); paper $3.95 (0-7894-4475-5). 48pp. This account uses sidebars and dramatic drawings to present the story of the *Iliad* from the quarrel over the golden apple to the fall of Troy. (Rev: SLJ 8/99) [398.2]

11464 Climo, Shirley. *Atalanta's Race: A Greek Myth* (3–5). Illus. by Alexander Koshkin. 1995, Clarion $16.00 (0-395-67322-4). 32pp. A retelling of the Greek myth about Atalanta, who, abandoned at birth, becomes the world's fastest runner. (Rev: BCCB 6/95; BL 4/15/95; SLJ 4/95*) [398.21]

11465 Colum, Padraic. *The Children's Homer: The Adventures of Odysseus and the Tale of Troy* (4–6). Illus. by Willy Pogany. 1982, Macmillan paper $9.95 (0-02-042520-1). 256pp. First published in 1918, the engrossing tales of Homer. [398.2]

11466 Colum, Padraic. *The Golden Fleece and the Heroes Who Lived Before Achilles* (5–7). Illus. by Willy Pogany. 1983, Macmillan LB $18.00 (0-02-723620-X); paper $9.95 (0-02-042260-1). 320pp. Jason's search for the Golden Fleece incorporates some of the best-known myths and legends of ancient Greece. [398.2]

11467 Coolidge, Olivia. *Greek Myths* (4–7). Illus. by Eduard Sandoz. 1949, Houghton $16.00 (0-395-06721-9). 256pp. Twenty-seven well-known myths dramatically retold with accompanying illustrations. [398.2]

11468 Craft, Charlotte. *King Midas and the Golden Touch* (1–3). Illus. by Kinuko Craft. 1999, Morrow LB $15.93 (0-688-13166-2). 32pp. A traditional retelling of the story of King Midas, using the Middle Ages as a setting. (Rev: BCCB 3/99; BL 4/15/99; HBG 10/99; SLJ 3/99) [398.2]

11469 Cuyler, Margery. *Roadsigns: A Harey Race with a Tortoise* (PS–1). Illus. by Steve Haskamp. 2000, Winslow $15.95 (1-890817-23-6). 40pp. The Aesop fable of the race between the tortoise and the hare is cleverly retold using road signs and bright, cartoonlike illustrations. (Rev: BL 12/1/00; HBG 3/01; SLJ 9/00) [398.2]

11470 D'Aulaire, Ingri, and Edgar D'Aulaire. *D'Aulaire's Book of Greek Myths* (3–6). Illus. by authors. 1962, Dell paper $18.95 (0-440-40694-3). Full-color pictures highlight these brief stories, which are excellent for first readers in mythology. [398.2]

11471 Fisher, Leonard Everett. *Cyclops* (1–6). Illus. 1991, Holiday paper $5.95 (0-8234-1062-5). 32pp. The retelling of this classical tale inspires pity and terror in the reader. (Rev: BCCB 12/91; BL 1/1/91*; SLJ 1/92) [398.2]

11472 Fisher, Leonard Everett. *Theseus and the Minotaur* (3–6). Illus. by author. 1988, Holiday paper $5.95 (0-8234-0954-6). 32pp. The story of the birth of Theseus, his adventures, and his killing of the Minotaur. (Rev: BCCB 10/88; BL 10/15/88; SLJ 10/88) [398.2]

11473 Galloway, Priscilla. *Aleta and the Queen: A Tale of Ancient Greece* (4–7). Illus. 1995, Annick LB $29.95 (1-55037-400-1); paper $14.95 (1-55037-462-1). 158pp. Told from the standpoint of a 12-year-old girl, this novel traces the story of Penelope and the final weeks of her wait for Odysseus. (Rev: BL 1/1–15/96; SLJ 1/96)

11474 Galloway, Priscilla. *Daedalus and the Minotaur* (4–6). Illus. Series: Tales of Ancient Lands. 1997, Annick LB $27.95 (1-55037-459-1); paper $14.95 (1-55037-458-3). 112pp. This account explands and embellishes the story of Daedalus; his son, Icarus; and the king's monstrous son, Minotaur, who is held captive in a giant labyrinth. (Rev: BL 1/1–15/98; SLJ 2/98) [813.54]

11475 Gates, Doris. *A Fair Wind for Troy* (5–8). 1976, Puffin paper $4.99 (0-14-031718-X). 96pp. A retelling of legends connected with the Trojan War. [398.2]

11476 Gates, Doris. *Lord of the Sky: Zeus* (3–6). Illus. by Robert Handville. 1982, Puffin paper $4.99 (0-14-031532-2). 128pp. In the first of a series, the author has retold simply and directly myths in which Zeus plays a central part. [398.2]

11477 Geringer, Laura. *The Pomegranate Seeds: A Classic Greek Myth* (2–4). Illus. by Leonid Gore. 1995, Houghton $15.95 (0-395-68192-8). 48pp. Adapted from one of Hawthorne's *Tanglewood Tales,* this is the story of the kidnapping of Persephone and her eventual return to Demeter, her mother. (Rev: BL 2/1/96; SLJ 3/96) [398.21]

11478 Hawthorne, Nathaniel. *Wonder Book and Tanglewood Tales* (5–7). 1972, Ohio State Univ. Pr. $70.00 (0-8142-0158-X). 476pp. This is a highly original retelling of the Greek myths, originally published in 1853. [398.2]

11479 Homer. *The Odyssey* (3–5). Adapted by Adrian Mitchell. Illus. by Stuart Robertson. 2000, DK $14.95 (0-7894-5455-6). 64pp. A handsomely illustrated version of the Odyssey that covers all the major plot developments and the journeys of Odysseus. (Rev: SLJ 9/00) [398.2]

11480 Hovey, Kate. *Arachne Speaks* (4–6). Illus. by Blair Drawson. 2001, Simon & Schuster $17.95 (0-689-82901-9). A lyrical retelling of the Greek myth in which Athena caused a cruel metamorphosis when angered by the weaver Arachne. (Rev: BCCB 3/01; HB 1–2/01; SLJ 3/01) [398.2]

11481 Hutton, Warwick. *Odysseus and the Cyclops* (K–4). Illus. 1995, Simon & Schuster paper $15.00 (0-689-80036-3). 32pp. A retelling of the encounter between Odysseus and his men and the one-eyed monster. (Rev: BCCB 11/95; BL 10/1/95; SLJ 11/95) [398.2]

11482 Hutton, Warwick. *Perseus* (2–4). Illus. 1993, Macmillan $14.95 (0-689-50565-5). 32pp. A retelling of the myth of Perseus and the monsters he encounters. (Rev: BL 3/1/93; SLJ 6/93) [398.2]

11483 Hutton, Warwick. *Theseus and the Minotaur* (3–5). Illus. 1989, Macmillan paper $14.95 (0-689-50473-X). 32pp. A retelling of the Athenian hero's journey to Crete to slay the Minotaur. (Rev: BCCB 10/89; BL 11/1/89; HB 1–2/90; SLJ 10/89*) [398.2]

11484 Lasky, Kathryn. *Hercules: The Man, the Myth, the Hero* (3–5). Illus. by Mark Hess. 1997, Hyperion LB $16.49 (0-7868-2274-0). 32pp. In 15 double-page spreads in this large-format picture book, Hercules tells his own story. (Rev: BL 6/1–15/97; SLJ 7/97) [292.2]

11485 Low, Alice. *The Macmillan Book of Greek Gods and Heroes* (4–6). Illus. by Arvis Stewart. 1985, Macmillan LB $18.00 (0-02-761390-9). 192pp. Well-known myths and legends from ancient Greece in a large-format edition. (Rev: BCCB 11/85; BL 11/15/85; SLJ 1/86) [398.2]

11486 McCarty, Nick, reteller. *The Iliad* (4–8). Illus. by Victor G. Ambrus. 2000, Kingfisher $22.95 (0-7534-5330-4); paper $15.95 (0-7534-5321-5). 95pp. This account of the Trojan War uses an exciting text and action-packed illustrations. (Rev: SLJ 1/01) [398.2]

11487 McCaughrean, Geraldine. *Greek Gods and Goddesses* (4–7). Illus. 1998, Simon & Schuster $20.00 (0-689-82084-4). 112pp. This book, illustrated in a style like ancient Greek art, contains a lively retelling of a number of Greek myths, including the story of Hermes. (Rev: BL 11/15/98; HBG 3/99; SLJ 10/98) [292.13]

11488 McCaughrean, Geraldine. *Greek Myths* (4–6). Illus. by Emma C. Clark. 1993, Macmillan $20.00 (0-689-50583-3). 96pp. Sixteen epic stories of

heroes and monsters, gods and warriors. (Rev: BL 2/1/93*; SLJ 4/93) [883]

11489 McLean, Mollie, and Ann S. Wiseman. *Adventures of Greek Heroes* (4–6). Illus. by W. T. Mars. 1973, Houghton $18.00 (0-395-06913-0); paper $5.95 (0-685-42189-9). 192pp. Easily read version of myths involving such heroes as Jason, Hercules, and Theseus. [398.2]

11490 Malam, John. *Myths and Civilization of the Ancient Romans* (3–6). Illus. Series: Myths and Civilization. 2000, Bedrick $16.95 (0-87226-590-0). 45pp. After each of the myths that are covered here in double-page spreads, there is material on the history and culture of ancient Rome. (Rev: BL 3/1/00; HBG 10/00; SLJ 12/00) [292]

11491 Mark, Jan. *The Midas Touch* (PS–3). Illus. by Juan Wijngaard. 1999, Candlewick $16.99 (0-7636-0488-7). 32pp. A retelling of the myth of greedy King Midas and his gift of turning objects into gold, which became a horrifying curse. (Rev: BL 11/15/99; HBG 3/00; SLJ 11/99) [398.2]

11492 Mayer, Marianna. *Pegasus* (3–6). Illus. by Kinuko Craft. 1998, Morrow $16.00 (0-688-13382-7). 40pp. A retelling of the Greek myth about the winged horse Pegasus and how it helped Bellerophon kill Chimera the monster. (Rev: BL 3/15/98; HBG 10/98; SLJ 4/98) [398.2]

11493 Moore, Robin. *Hercules* (2–5). Illus. 1997, Simon & Schuster $14.00 (0-689-81228-0); paper $3.99 (0-689-81229-9). 80pp. An easily read paperback that tells of Hercules' exploits in short, nicely illustrated chapters. (Rev: BL 6/1–15/97; HBG 3/98; SLJ 7/97) [292.2]

11494 Morley, Jacqueline, reteller. *Greek Myths* (3–6). Illus. by Giovanni Caselli. 1998, Bedrick $22.50 (0-87226-560-9). 96pp. Beginning with the rise of the Titans and ending with Odysseus's wanderings, the myths in this book include those involving Prometheus, Arachne, Psyche, the Minotaur, and Apollo. (Rev: HBG 10/98; SLJ 7/98) [398.2]

11495 Myers, Christopher. *Wings* (PS–4). Illus. 2000, Scholastic $16.95 (0-590-03377-8). 40pp. In this modern retelling of the Icarus myth, a young boy who can fly nearly crashes, not because he flies too close to the sun but because repressive adults and bullying kids in the schoolyard try to break his spirit. (Rev: BCCB 12/00; BL 5/15/00; HBG 3/01; SLJ 10/00)

11496 Naden, Corinne J. *Jason and the Golden Fleece* (2–4). Illus. by Robert Baxter. 1980, Troll LB $18.60 (0-89375-360-2). 32pp. One of a series of retold myths. Others by the same author and publisher are: *Pegasus, the Winged Horse; Perseus and Medusa; Theseus and the Minotaur* (all 1980). [398.2]

11497 Nardo, Don. *Greek and Roman Mythology* (5–8). Series: World History. 1997, Lucent LB $17.96 (1-56006-308-4). 112pp. The author provides a background on classical mythology — where the myths came from and why they were an important part of each country's culture — and relates the most famous stories from ancient Greek and Roman times. (Rev: SLJ 5/98) [398.2]

11498 Nolan, Dennis. *Androcles and the Lion* (PS–3). Illus. 1997, Harcourt $15.00 (0-15-203355-6). 32pp. A bright retelling of the Roman story of the slave Androcles and how his life was saved by a lion he had helped years before. (Rev: BCCB 3/98; BL 10/15/97; HBG 3/98; SLJ 11/97) [398.2]

11499 Osborne, Mary Pope. *Favorite Greek Myths* (3–6). Illus. by Troy Howell. 1989, Scholastic paper $18.95 (0-590-41338-4). 96pp. This large-format book contains 13 of the best-known stories from classical mythology. (Rev: BL 8/89) [398.2]

11500 Oyibo, Papa. *Big Brother, Little Sister* (PS–3). Illus. by John Clementson. 2000, Barefoot $15.95 (1-84148-117-3). 40pp. The Aesop fable about the lion and the mouse is retold using an elephant instead of a lion. (Rev: BL 4/1/00; SLJ 8/00)

11501 Philip, Neil, reteller. *The Adventures of Odysseus* (3–6). Illus. by Peter Malone. 1997, Orchard $17.95 (0-531-30000-5). 72pp. A fine retelling of the epic journey home by Odysseus and his encounters with such creatures as Cyclops, Circe, and the Sirens. (Rev: SLJ 5/97*) [292.1]

11502 Richards, Jean. *The First Olympic Games: A Gruesome Greek Myth with a Happy Ending* (2–4). Illus. 2000, Millbrook LB $22.90 (0-7613-1311-7). 32pp. The story of Pelops, who was killed and eaten by his father, Tantalus, restored to life by the gods, and later created the first Olympic Games. (Rev: BCCB 11/00; BL 10/15/00; SLJ 11/00) [398.2]

11503 Richardson, I. M. *The Adventures of Eros and Psyche* (3–6). Illus. by Robert Baxter. 1983, Troll paper $3.95 (0-89375-862-0). 32pp. How Psyche is able to prove her love for Eros in this retelling of the Greek myth. Others by this author and publisher are: *The Adventures of Hercules; Demeter and Persephone: The Seasons of Time; Prometheus and the Story of Fire* (all 1983). [398.2]

11504 Riordan, James. *The Twelve Labors of Hercules* (4–6). Illus. 1997, Millbrook LB $22.40 (0-7613-0315-4). 64pp. Each of the 12 tasks performed by Hercules for King Eurystheus gets a separate chapter in the large-format book. (Rev: BL 1/1–15/98; SLJ 2/98) [398.2]

11505 Rockwell, Anne. *The Robber Baby: Stories from the Greek Myths* (1–4). Illus. 1994, Greenwillow LB $17.93 (0-688-09741-3). 80pp. Fifteen familiar stories from Greek mythology are retold with expressive illustrations. (Rev: BL 6/1–15/94; SLJ 6/94) [398.2]

11506 Rockwell, Anne, reteller. *Romulus and Remus* (1–2). Illus. by Anne Rockwell. Series: A Ready-to-Read Book. 1997, Simon & Schuster $15.00 (0-689-81291-4); paper $3.99 (0-689-81290-6). 40pp. An admirable retelling of the myth of the two brothers who were cared for by a wolf and later, when one stayed with the pack, the other founded the city of Rome. (Rev: HBG 3/98; SLJ 9/97) [292]

11507 Spinner, Stephanie. *Snake Hair: The Story of Medusa* (2–3). Illus. by Susan Swan. Series: All Aboard Reading. 1999, Penguin $13.89 (0-448-42049-X); paper $3.99 (0-448-41981-5). 32pp. This easy reader tells the story of Medusa, the beautiful girl turned Gorgon. (Rev: BL 12/1/99) [398.2]

11508 Stewig, John W. *King Midas* (K–3). Illus. by Omar Rayyan. 1999, Holiday $15.95 (0-8234-1423-X). 32pp. Filled with illustrations containing comic details, this is a fine retelling of the tale about the greedy king who turned his daughter into gold. (Rev: BCCB 3/99; BL 2/15/99; HBG 10/99; SLJ 3/99) [398.2]

11509 Strachan, Ian. *The Iliad* (5–8). Illus. 1997, Kingfisher $17.95 (0-7534-5107-7). 96pp. This large, handsome volume gives an exciting account of the main events in the siege and fall of Troy. (Rev: BL 1/1–15/98; HBG 3/98; SLJ 11/97) [292]

11510 Sutcliff, Rosemary. *Black Ships Before Troy: The Story of the Iliad* (5–8). Illus. by Alan Lee. 1993, Delacorte $24.95 (0-385-31069-2). 128pp. The story of the *Iliad* and the ten-year siege of Troy are retold by a master writer of historical fiction. (Rev: BCCB 1/94; BL 10/15/93) [883]

11511 Sutcliff, Rosemary. *The Wanderings of Odysseus: The Story of the Odyssey* (5–8). Illus. by Alan Lee. 1996, Delacorte $24.95 (0-385-32205-4). 120pp. An oversize volume that retells Homer's *Odyssey* and all the adventures of Odysseus on his homeward journey from the Trojan Wars. (Rev: BCCB 9/96; BL 9/1/96; HB 5–6/96; SLJ 6/96*) [883]

11512 Usher, Kerry. *Heroes, Gods and Emperors from Roman Mythology* (5–8). Illus. by John Sibbick. 1992, Bedrick LB $24.95 (0-87226-909-4). 132pp. The story of the Aeneid plus those of the Tarquino and Romulus and Remus are three of the legends retold here. [398.2]

11513 Vinge, Joan D. *The Random House Book of Greek Myths* (4–6). Illus. 1999, Random $25.00 (0-679-82377-8). 160pp. Fourteen well-known Greek myths are retold, with some alterations, including tales about Medea, Pandora, and Psyche. (Rev: BL 3/1/00; HBG 10/00; SLJ 4/00) [292.1]

11514 Williams, Marcia. *Greek Myths for Young Children* (1–6). Illus. by author. 1992, Candlewick $17.95 (1-56402-115-7). Eight famous Greek myths are retold in a pseudo comic-strip format. (Rev: BCCB 11/92; SLJ 10/92) [291.1]

11515 Williams, Marcia, reteller. *The Iliad and the Odyssey* (3–5). Illus. by Marcia Williams. 1996, Candlewick $17.99 (0-7636-0053-9). Using a comic strip format, the highlights of these two Greek epics are retold. (Rev: BCCB 2/97; HB 1–2/97; SLJ 5/97) [938]

11516 Woff, Richard. *Bright-Eyed Athena: Stories from Ancient Greece* (5–8). Illus. 1999, Getty Museum $12.95 (0-89236-558-7). 48pp. Using full-color illustrations from Greek sculpture and vase paintings, this book retells the important Greek myths involving Athena. (Rev: BL 11/15/99; HBG 3/00; SLJ 2/00) [398.2]

11517 Yolen, Jane. *Pegasus, the Flying Horse* (3–5). Illus. by Li Ming. 1998, Dutton $16.99 (0-525-65244-2). 40pp. The story of the rise and fall of a young Corinthian boy, Bellerophon, and his adventures on the winged horse Pegasus. (Rev: BL 12/15/98; HBG 3/99; SLJ 2/99) [396.3]

Scandinavian

11518 Climo, Shirley. *Stolen Thunder: A Norse Myth* (3–5). Illus. by Alexander Koshkin. 1994, Clarion $15.95 (0-395-64368-6). 32pp. In this Norse myth, Thor's magic hammer is stolen by Thrym, the Frost King, and he sends Loki to retrieve it. (Rev: BL 5/1/94; SLJ 7/94) [293.1]

11519 Osborne, Mary Pope. *Favorite Norse Myths* (4–6). Illus. by Troy Howell. 1996, Scholastic $17.95 (0-590-48046-4). 96pp. A masterful retelling of Norse myths, with a thorough glossary of names, places, events, and symbols connected with these tales. (Rev: BL 3/1/96; SLJ 4/96*) [293]

11520 Philip, Neil, reteller. *Odin's Family: Myths of the Vikings* (3–6). Illus. by Maryclare Foa. 1996, Orchard $19.95 (0-531-09531-2). 124pp. Fifteen Viking myths — including "Thor's Hammer" and "The Death of Balder" — are retold with vivid illustrations. (Rev: BCCB 10/96; SLJ 11/96*) [398.2]

Poetry

General

11521 *Absolutely Angels: Poems for Children and Other Believers* (PS–3). Ed. by Mary Lou Carney. Illus. by Viqui Maggio. 1998, Boyds Mills $14.95 (1-56397-708-7). A collection of poems, mostly by contemporary poets, about the role of angels as protectors and helpers. (Rev: BL 11/1/98; HBG 3/99; SLJ 11/98) [808.81]

11522 Adoff, Arnold. *All the Colors of the Race* (4–7). Illus. by John Steptoe. 1982, Lothrop LB $14.93 (0-688-00880-1). 56pp. Poems that deal with the many races of mankind.

11523 Adoff, Arnold. *Love Letters* (1–4). Illus. by Lisa Desimini. 1997, Scholastic $15.95 (0-590-48478-8). 32pp. All sorts and conditions of love are the subjects of this delightful work with outstanding illustrations. (Rev: BCCB 3/97; BL 1/1–15/97; SLJ 3/97*) [811]

11524 Adoff, Arnold. *Street Music: City Poems* (K–4). Illus. by Karen Barbour. 1995, HarperCollins LB $15.89 (0-06-021523-2). 32pp. Fourteen poems that deal realistically with city life, its noises, squalor, and beauty. (Rev: BCCB 3/95; BL 2/1/95; HB 5–6/95; SLJ 3/95*) [811]

11525 Adoff, Arnold. *Touch the Poem* (PS–3). Illus. by Lisa Desimini. 2000, Scholastic $16.95 (0-590-47970-9). 32pp. Common childhood experiences like walking on a beach or feeling the fuzz on a peach are explored in this collection of original poems illustrated with photographs. (Rev: BCCB 2/00; BL 3/15/00; HBG 10/00; SLJ 6/00) [811]

11526 Alarcon, Francisco X. *From the Bellybutton of the Moon and Other Summer Poems: Del Ombligo de la Luna y otros poemas de verano* (K–5). Illus. by Maya Christina Gonzalez. 1998, Children's Book Pr. $15.95 (0-89239-153-7). 32pp. A collection of 22 bilingual poems that celebrates the author's childhood in Mexico. (Rev: BL 10/15/98; HBG 3/99; SLJ 12/98) [811]

11527 Alarcon, Francisco X. *Laughing Tomatoes and Other Spring Poems/Jitomates Risueños y Otros Poemas de Primavera* (K–3). Illus. by Maya Christina Gonzalez. 1997, Children's Book Pr. $15.95 (0-89239-139-1). 32pp. A bilingual collection of short poems, many about California, by the Chicano poet Alarcón. (Rev: BCCB 6/97; BL 6/1–15/97; SLJ 5/97) [811]

11528 Anaya, Rudolfo A. *Elegy on the Death of Cesar Chavez* (4–7). Illus. 2000, Cinco Puntos $16.95 (0-938317-51-2). 32pp. This is an elegiac poem that celebrates the life, work, and struggle of the respected labor leader. (Rev: BL 12/15/00; HBG 3/01; SLJ 1/01) [811]

11529 Bagert, Brod. *Chicken Socks: And Other Contagious Poems* (2–5). Illus. by Tim Ellis. 1993, Boyds Mills $15.95 (1-56397-292-1). 32pp. A collection of 22 poems that depict, usually in a comic way, typical activities of children. (Rev: SLJ 3/94) [811]

11530 Bauer, Caroline Feller, ed. *Rainy Day: Stories and Poems* (3–5). Illus. by Michele Chessare. 1986, HarperCollins LB $15.89 (0-397-32105-8). 96pp. Poems and stories from mostly well-known children's poets such as John Ciardi and Langston Hughes. Also use: *Snowy Day: Stories and Poems* (1986). (Rev: BCCB 9/86; BL 7/86; SLJ 9/86)

11531 Baylor, Byrd. *The Way to Start a Day* (3–5). Illus. by Peter Parnall. 1978, Macmillan $16.00 (0-684-15651-2); paper $5.99 (0-689-71054-2). 32pp. A poetic tribute to the many ways people have greeted a new day.

11532 Bennett, Jill, ed. *A Cup of Starshine: Poems and Pictures for Young Children* (PS–1). Illus. by Graham Percy. 1991, Harcourt $16.95 (0-15-220982-4). 64pp. These include the traditional rhymes with modern verse and full-color drawings. (Rev: BL 10/15/91; SLJ 12/91) [811]

11533 Bennett, Jill, comp. *Seaside Poems* (PS–3). Illus. by Nick Sharratt. 1998, Oxford $11.95 (0-19-276173-0). Twelve poems by different writers depict seashore activities such as picnicking, swimming, building sandcastles, and looking for shells. (Rev: SLJ 1/99) [811]

11534 Bennett, Jill, ed. *Spooky Poems* (1–5). Illus. by Mary Rees. 1990, General Dist. Services $14.95 (0-7737-2350-1). 32pp. From a variety of poets comes a collection of scary poems about ghosts, monsters, and other supernatural beings. (Rev: BL 12/1/89; HB 1–2/90; SLJ 1/90) [811]

11535 Berry, James, ed. *Classic Poems to Read Aloud* (4–8). Illus. 1995, Kingfisher $18.95 (1-85697-987-3); paper $8.95 (0-7534-5069-0). 256pp. A fine collection of standard poems, chiefly English, that are arranged by theme. (Rev: BL 5/1/95; SLJ 5/95) [811]

11536 Blake, Quentin. *All Join In* (PS–2). Illus. 1991, Little, Brown $14.95 (0-316-09934-1). 32pp. The theme of cooperation is explored in six bright poems. (Rev: BCCB 5/91; BL 4/15/91; SLJ 7/91) [821]

11537 Bouchard, David. *If Sarah Will Take Me* (4–8). Illus. by Robb T. Dunfield. 1997, Orca $16.95 (1-55143-081-9). The author, who is paralyzed from the neck down, recalls his love of nature and his many inspiring experiences outdoors. (Rev: HBG 3/98; SLJ 8/97) [811]

11538 Brenner, Barbara, sel. *Voices: Poetry and Art from Around the World* (5–10). 2000, National Geographic $18.95 (0-7922-7071-1). 96pp. An excellent collection of world poetry presented in double-page spreads with striking photographs of sculptures, carvings, and modern ceramics. (Rev: HBG 3/01; SLJ 3/01) [811]

11539 Brown, Marc, ed. *Party Rhymes* (K–3). Illus. by Marc Brown. 1994, Puffin paper $4.99 (0-140-50318-8). 48pp. Vignettes filled with humorous touches including verses like "Farmer in the Dell." (Rev: HB 1–2/89)

11540 Brown, Margaret Wise. *Love Songs of the Little Bear* (PS–1). Illus. by Susan Jeffers. 2001, Hyperion LB $16.95 (0-7868-2445-X). 32pp. A collection of previously unpublished poetry by Brown that uses as a connective device illustrations of a plump young bear. (Rev: BL 3/15/01; SLJ 3/01) [811]

11541 Bryan, Ashley. *Sing to the Sun: Poems and Pictures* (K–8). Illus. 1996, HarperCollins paper $4.95 (0-064-43437-0). Short poems with a Caribbean lilt. (Rev: BCCB 10/92; BL 10/15/92; HB 3–4/93; SLJ 10/92) [811.54]

11542 Burkholder, Kelly. *Poetry* (2–5). Series: Artistic Adventures. 2001, Rourke LB $21.27 (1-57103-354-8). 24pp. This book explains the basic elements of poetry like rhythm, rhyme, and repetition, introduces different types of poems, and gives advice on how to write your own poetry. (Rev: SLJ 2/01) [811]

11543 Carlson, Lori M. *Sol a Sol* (2–5). Illus. by Emily Lisker. 1998, Holt $17.00 (0-8050-4373-X). A bilingual anthology of poems that describe the daily activities of a Hispanic family. (Rev: BCCB 5/98; BL 4/1/98; HB 5–6/98; HBG 10/98; SLJ 3/98) [808]

11544 Clarke, Gillian, comp. *The Whispering Room: Haunted Poems* (3–6). Illus. by Justin Todd. 1996, Kingfisher $15.95 (0-7534-5024-0). 72pp. An anthology of more than 50 poems about supernatural beings from both prominent and less well known poets. (Rev: BCCB 1/97; SLJ 12/96) [811]

11545 *Climb into My Lap: First Poems to Read Together* (PS–2). Ed. by Lee Bennett Hopkins. Illus. by Kathryn Brown. 1998, Simon & Schuster $19.95 (0-689-80715-5). 80pp. Traditional poems and new favorites are included in this collection of more than 50 poems for the very young arranged by such themes as bedtime poems and humorous pieces. (Rev: BL 11/15/98; HBG 3/99; SLJ 12/98) [811]

11546 Cooney, Barbara, reteller. *Chanticleer and the Fox* (1–4). Illus. by Barbara Cooney. 1958, HarperCollins LB $16.89 (0-690-18562-6); paper $3.95 (0-690-04318-X). 36pp. Chaucer's Nun's Priest Tale retold by the illustrator. Caldecott Medal winner, 1959.

11547 Cullinan, Bernice E., ed. *A Jar of Tiny Stars: Poems by NCTE Award-Winning Poets* (3–5). Illus. 1995, Boyds Mills $16.95 (1-56397-087-2). 94pp. A collection of more than 50 poems chosen by children from the works of the ten winners of the National Council of Teachers of English Award for Poetry for Children, including poems by Karla Kuskin, Myra Cohn Livingston, and Eve Merriam. (Rev: BCCB 2/96; BL 1/1–15/96; SLJ 2/96) [811.54]

11548 *Daddy Poems* (3–5). Ed. by John Micklos. Illus. 2000, Boyds Mills $15.95 (1-56397-735-4). 32pp. This anthology of poems about dads and how they interact with their children contains the work of both well-known and less-well-known poets. (Rev: BL 8/00; HBG 10/00; SLJ 10/00) [811]

11549 Dakos, Kalli. *Mrs. Cole on an Onion Roll and Other School Poems* (1–3). Illus. by JoAnn Adinolfi. 1995, Simon & Schuster paper $14.00 (0-02-725583-2). 40pp. A collection of 32 poems about the behavior and concerns of elementary school children. (Rev: BL 6/1–15/95; SLJ 8/95) [811]

11550 *Days Like This: A Collection of Small Poems* (PS–1). Ed. by Simon James. Illus. 2000, Candlewick $17.99 (0-7636-0812-2). 48pp. This anthology of 19 simple poems, accompanied by line-and-watercolor illustrations, explores the everyday life and experiences of children. (Rev: BCCB 7–8/00; BL 3/15/00; HB 5–6/00; HBG 10/00; SLJ 4/00) [811.008]

11551 De Regniers, Beatrice S., ed. *Sing a Song of Popcorn: Every Child's Book of Poems* (PS–6). Illus. by Marcia Brown. 1988, Scholastic $18.95 (0-590-43974-X). 160pp. A treasure from highly regarded poets, with exciting artwork. (Rev: BCCB 10/88; BL 8/88; SLJ 8/88)

11552 Dickinson, Emily. *A Brighter Garden* (4–6). Illus. by Tasha Tudor. 1990, Putnam $18.99 (0-399-21490-9). 64pp. Lovely paintings complement this edition of Dickinson's first volume of poetry. (Rev: BL 10/1/90; SLJ 10/90) [811]

11553 Dotlich, Rebecca. *Lemonade Sun and Other Summer Poems* (PS–3). Illus. by Jan S. Gilchrist.

1998, Boyds Mills paper $15.95 (1-56397-660-9). 32pp. This book of poems shows children in everyday situations and depicts their sense of wonder. (Rev: BL 2/15/98; HBG 10/98; SLJ 3/98) [811]

11554 Dunn, Opal. *Hippety-Hop Hippety-Hay: Growing with Rhymes from Birth to Age Three* (PS). Illus. by Sally Anne Lambert. 1999, Holt $16.95 (0-8050-6081-2). 46pp. A collection of rhymes and related finger plays arranged by age groups. (Rev: HBG 10/99; SLJ 7/99) [811]

11555 Dunning, Stephen, et al., eds. *Reflections on a Gift of Watermelon Pickle and Other Modern Verse* (6–8). Illus. 1967, Lothrop $20.00 (0-688-41231-9). 144pp. An attractive volume of 114 expressive poems by recognized modern poets, illustrated with striking photographs.

11556 Eccleshare, Julia, ed. *First Poems* (PS–3). Illus. by Selina Young. 1994, Bedrick $16.95 (0-87226-373-8). 64pp. A collection of happy, often humorous poems, including a number of old favorites and several by contemporary poets. (Rev: BL 7/94; SLJ 8/94) [821]

11557 *Edna St. Vincent Millay* (3–7). Ed. by Frances Schoonmaker. Illus. Series: Poetry for Young People. 2000, Sterling $14.95 (0-8069-5928-2). 48pp. A representative collection of Millay's poetry illustrated with evocative watercolors. (Rev: BL 3/15/00; HBG 10/00; SLJ 2/00) [811]

11558 Esbensen, Barbara J. *Who Shrank My Grandmother's House? Poems of Discovery* (1–3). Illus. by Eric Beddows. 1992, HarperCollins $15.00 (0-060-21827-4). 48pp. This book presents a celebration of everything in a collection of 23 poems. (Rev: BCCB 4/92; BL 6/1/92; HB 5–6/92; SLJ 4/92*) [811]

11559 Evans, Dilys, comp. *Fairies, Trolls and Goblins Galore: Poems About Fantastic Creatures* (1–4). Illus. by Jacqueline Rogers. 2000, Simon & Schuster $17.00 (0-689-82352-5). An anthology of 16 poems about imaginary creatures each illustrated with playful watercolors. (Rev: HBG 10/00; SLJ 3/00) [811]

11560 Ferris, Helen, ed. *Favorite Poems Old and New* (4–6). Illus. by Leonard Weisgard. 1957, Doubleday $24.95 (0-385-07696-7). 598pp. A book brimming with all kinds of poetry — lyrics, rhymes, doggerel, songs.

11561 Fisher, Aileen. *Sing of the Earth and Sky: Poems About Our Planet and the Wonders Beyond* (2–4). Illus. 2001, Boyds Mills $15.95 (1-56397-802-4). 48pp. A collection of short original poems that are divided into four subjects: earth, sun, moon, and stars. (Rev: BL 3/15/01) [811]

11562 Fleischman, Paul. *Big Talk: Poems for Four Voices* (4–7). Illus. 2000, Candlewick $14.99 (0-7636-0636-7). 48pp. This collection of spirited, evocative poems for four voices to read aloud covers a variety of topics. (Rev: BCCB 4/00; BL 6/1–15/00; HB 5–6/00; HBG 10/00; SLJ 6/00) [811]

11563 Fletcher, Ralph. *Buried Alive: The Elements of Love* (5–8). 1996, Simon & Schuster $14.00 (0-689-80593-4). 46pp. A series of free-verse poems explore various aspects of love — puppy and otherwise. (Rev: BCCB 6/96; BL 5/1/96; SLJ 5/96) [811]

11564 Fletcher, Ralph. *I Am Wings: Poems About Love* (5–7). Illus. by Joe Baker. 1994, Macmillan paper $14.00 (0-02-735395-8). 48pp. Thirty-three simple, short poems depict a boy's falling in and out of love. (Rev: BCCB 6/94; BL 3/15/94; HB 7–8/94; SLJ 6/94*) [811]

11565 Fletcher, Ralph. *Relatively Speaking: Poems About Family* (5–7). Illus. 1999, Orchard LB $15.99 (0-531-33141-5). 48pp. From an 11-year-old boy's point of view, these original poems explore relationships as family members go through periods of change. (Rev: BCCB 5/99; BL 7/99; HBG 10/99; SLJ 4/99) [811]

11566 Foster, John, comp. *First Verses* (PS–1). Illus. by Carol Thompson. 1998, Oxford $20.00 (0-19-276145-5). 94pp. This charming collection of poems includes counting, finger, and chanting rhymes. (Rev: HBG 10/98; SLJ 4/98) [811]

11567 Frank, Josette, ed. *Poems to Read to the Very Young* (PS). Illus. by Eloise Wilkin. 1982, Random paper $3.25 (0-394-89768-4). 48pp. A collection of short simple verses, many of them old favorites.

11568 Frost, Robert. *Stopping by Woods on a Snowy Evening* (K–4). Illus. by Susan Jeffers. 1978, Dutton $16.99 (0-525-40115-6). A richly illustrated version of Frost's most famous poem.

11569 Frost, Robert. *A Swinger of Birches: Poems of Robert Frost for Young People* (4–7). Illus. by Peter Koeppen. 1982, Stemmer $21.95 (0-916144-92-5); paper $14.95 (0-916144-93-3). 80pp. A collection of 38 poems suitable for young people.

11570 Frost, Robert. *You Come Too* (5–7). Illus. by Thomas W. Nason. 1959, Holt $18.00 (0-8050-0299-5). 96pp. A collection of some of the best-loved Frost poems illustrated with wood engravings.

11571 Gillooly, Eileen, ed. *Rudyard Kipling* (4–8). Illus. by Jim Sharpe. 2000, Sterling $14.95 (0-8069-4484-6). 48pp. This book contains complete poems or excerpts from 28 poems by this well-liked writer including "If" and "The Ballad of East and West." (Rev: HBG 3/01; SLJ 5/00) [821]

11572 Glaser, Isabel Joshlin, et al., eds. *Dreams of Glory: Poems Starring Girls* (2–5). Illus. 1995, Simon & Schuster $15.00 (0-689-31891-X). 48pp. A collection of 30 poems about girls, many of which tell about dreams of the future. (Rev: BL 11/15/95; SLJ 12/95) [811]

11573 Gold, Julie. *From a Distance* (1–4). Illus. by Jane Ray. 1999, Dutton $17.99 (0-525-45872-7). 32pp. This is an illustrated version of the celebrated antiwar poem. (Rev: BL 11/15/99; HBG 3/00; SLJ 12/99) [811.54]

11574 Goldstein, Bobbye S., ed. *Inner Chimes: Poems on Poetry* (2–6). Illus. by Jane Breskin Zalben. 1992, Boyds Mills LB $16.95 (1-56397-040-6). 24pp. This collection presents 20 poems that are inspirational, opening up a wealth of ideas and language in an entertaining manner. (Rev: BL 1/15/93; SLJ 10/92) [808.81]

11575 Goldstein, Bobbye S., comp. *Sweets and Treats: Dessert Poems* (K–3). Illus. by Kathy Couri.

Series: Hyperion Chapters. 1998, Hyperion LB $14.49 (0-7868-2354-2); paper $3.95 (0-7868-1280-X). 48pp. A collection of 21 poems divided into four sections: fruit; ice cream; cookies, candy, and cake; and snacks. (Rev: HBG 10/98; SLJ 9/98) [811]

11576 *Good Night, Sleep Tight: A Poem for Every Night of the Year* (PS–3). Ed. by Ivan Jones and Mal Jones. Illus. 2000, Scholastic $22.95 (0-439-18813-X). 256pp. A fine anthology of 366 (one for Leap Year) poems chiefly by English poets that cover different kinds of rhymes, situations, and moods. (Rev: BL 1/1–15/01) [811.08]

11577 Graham, Joan B. *Flicker Flash* (3–6). Illus. 1999, Houghton $15.95 (0-395-90501-X). 32pp. A collection of verses in geometric forms associated with light, among them a camera, a firefly, a lightbulb, and fireworks. (Rev: BL 1/1–15/00; HBG 3/00; SLJ 12/99*) [811]

11578 Graham, Joan B. *Splish Splash* (K–5). Illus. by Steve Scott. 1994, Ticknor $15.00 (0-395-70128-7). 32pp. Several whimsical poems about water in its various states, including hail and ice cubes. (Rev: BCCB 10/94; BL 9/1/94*; SLJ 8/94*) [813]

11579 Greenfield, Eloise. *Angels* (3–5). Illus. by Jan S. Gilchrist. 1998, Hyperion $14.95 (0-7868-0442-4). 32pp. A group of original poems that celebrate the real angels in a child's life — parents, siblings, stepparents, and friends. (Rev: BL 11/15/98; HBG 3/99; SLJ 1/99) [811]

11580 Greenfield, Eloise. *Under the Sunday Tree* (2–5). Illus. by Amos Ferguson. 1988, HarperCollins paper $10.95 (0-06-443257-2). 48pp. Poems of life in the Bahamas. (Rev: BCCB 12/88; HB 11–12/88)

11581 Grimes, Nikki. *Aneesa Lee and the Weaver's Gift* (3–6). Illus. by Ashley Bryan. 1999, Lothrop $16.00 (0-688-15997-4). A collection of 14 interrelated poems that deal with various aspects of the art and craft of weaving. (Rev: HBG 3/00; SLJ 12/99) [811]

11582 Grimes, Nikki. *A Dime a Dozen* (5–8). Illus. 1998, Dial $15.99 (0-8037-2227-3). 56pp. Through a series of original poems, the writer explores her childhood: its happy moments, its painful memories — including divorce, foster homes, and parents with drinking and gambling problems — and her search for herself as a teenager. (Rev: BL 12/1/98; HBG 3/99; SLJ 11/98) [811]

11583 Grimes, Nikki. *Hopscotch Love: A Family Treasury of Love Poems* (3–7). Illus. 1999, Lothrop LB $14.95 (0-688-15667-3). 40pp. A collection of original poems covering all aspects of love — from the teenage to the familial. (Rev: BL 2/15/99; HBG 10/99; SLJ 1/99) [811]

11584 Grimes, Nikki. *A Pocketful of Poems* (K–3). Illus. by Javaka Steptoe. 2001, Clarion $15.00 (0-618-93868-6). 32pp. Poems by a young African American girl named Tiana about urban topics — pigeons, baseball, the moon — are presented in double-page spreads, each traditional poem facing a haiku. (Rev: BL 2/15/01*) [811]

11585 Grimes, Nikki. *Shoe Magic* (2–5). Illus. by Terry Widener. 2000, Orchard LB $17.99 (0-531-33286-1). 32pp. In this collection of poems about different kinds of shoes, each shoe embodies a young person's pride in accomplishment and hope for the future. (Rev: BL 9/15/00; HBG 3/01; SLJ 10/00) [811]

11586 Gunning, Monica. *Under the Breadfruit Tree* (3–6). Illus. 1998, Boyds Mills $15.95 (1-56397-539-4). 48pp. These 38 poems describe the Caribbean peoples and their culture from the standpoint of a young Jamaican girl. (Rev: BL 2/15/98; HBG 10/98; SLJ 4/98) [811]

11587 Hall, Donald. *The Man Who Lived Alone* (4–7). Illus. 1998, Godine paper $11.95 (1-56792-050-0). 36pp. A narrative poem concerning a man who ran away from abuse to see the world and returns in later life.

11588 Hall, Donald, ed. *The Oxford Book of Children's Verse in America* (3–7). Illus. 1985, Oxford $35.00 (0-19-503539-9); paper $15.95 (0-19-506761-4). Poems adopted by or written for American children during certain periods. (Rev: BCCB 9/85; HB 9–10/85; SLJ 8/85)

11589 Harley, Avis. *Fly with Poetry: An ABC of Poetry* (3–5). Illus. by author. 2000, Boyds Mills $13.95 (1-56397-798-2). 48pp. A collection of 27 original short poems, generally one for each letter of the alphabet (Y leaves space to write one's own poem). (Rev: SLJ 9/00) [811]

11590 Harrison, David L. *The Boy Who Counted Stars* (K–3). Illus. by Betsy Lewin. 1994, Boyds Mills $14.95 (1-56397-125-9). 30pp. A collection of imaginative poems that deal with a variety of subjects and moods. (Rev: SLJ 11/94) [811]

11591 Harrison, David L. *The Purchase of Small Secrets* (3–5). Illus. by Meryl Henderson. 1998, Boyds Mills $14.95 (1-56397-054-6). 48pp. This introspective collection of poems touches upon some of the landmark occasions in a boy's journey to maturity, such as fistfights, flirting, and shooting a gun. (Rev: HBG 3/99; SLJ 11/98) [811]

11592 Harrison, David L. *A Thousand Cousins: Poems of Family Life* (2–4). Illus. by Betsy Lewin. 1996, Boyds Mills $14.95 (1-56397-131-3). 32pp. Short poems and cartoonlike drawings portray some of the humorous aspects of family life. (Rev: BL 1/1–15/96; SLJ 3/96) [811.54]

11593 Harrison, Michael, and Christopher Stuart-Clark, eds. *The Oxford Book of Story Poems* (4–7). Illus. 1990, Oxford $25.00 (0-19-276087-4). 176pp. A smorgasbord of narrative poems by both British and American poets in a large volume. (Rev: BL 2/1/91) [821]

11594 Harrison, Michael, and Christopher Stuart-Clark, comps. *The Oxford Treasury of Time Poems* (4–9). 1999, Oxford LB $25.00 (1-19-276175-7). 155pp. From John Milton and William Blake to W. H. Auden and Sylvia Plath, this anthology contains poetry and thoughts about time. (Rev: SLJ 7/99) [811]

11595 *Heart to Heart: New Poems Inspired by Twentieth-Century American Art* (5–10). Ed. by Jan

Greenberg. Illus. 2001, Abrams $19.95 (0-8109-4386-7). 80pp. This book contains specially commissioned poems from well-known writers to accompany some of the finest artworks of the 20th century. (Rev: BL 3/15/01*) [811]

11596 Hoberman, Mary Ann. *The Llama Who Had No Pajama* (PS–3). Illus. by Betty Fraser. 1998, Harcourt $20.00 (0-15-200111-5). 68pp. This collection of delightful poems mainly about childhood experiences and animals is illustrated with cheery pictures. (Rev: BL 4/15/98; HB 3–4/98; HBG 10/98; SLJ 4/98) [811]

11597 Hoberman, Mary Ann, ed. *My Song Is Beautiful: Poems and Pictures in Many Voices* (PS–3). Illus. 1994, Little, Brown $16.95 (0-316-36738-9). 32pp. An anthology of 14 poems that celebrate diversity in cultures and attitudes. (Rev: BCCB 4/94; BL 6/1–15/94; SLJ 6/94*) [808]

11598 Hopkins, Lee Bennett, ed. *April Bubbles Chocolate: An ABC of Poetry* (PS–1). Illus. by Barry Root. 1994, Simon & Schuster paper $14.00 (0-671-75911-6). 40pp. An enjoyable anthology of poems arranged from A to Z. (Rev: BCCB 6/94; BL 5/1/94; HB 7–8/94; SLJ 9/94) [811]

11599 Hopkins, Lee Bennett. *Been to Yesterdays* (4–7). Illus. 1995, Boyds Mills $14.95 (1-56397-467-3). 64pp. Through 28 simple but moving poems, the author chronicles the pleasures and pains of his middle years. (Rev: BL 1/1–15/96; SLJ 9/95*) [811.54]

11600 Hopkins, Lee Bennett, ed. *Good Books, Good Times* (K–3). Illus. by Harvey Stevenson. 1990, HarperCollins LB $16.89 (0-06-022528-9). 32pp. Fourteen short poems celebrate book reading. (Rev: BL 11/15/90; HB 1–2/91; SLJ 10/90*) [811]

11601 Hopkins, Lee Bennett, ed. *Hand in Hand* (4–8). Illus. 1994, Simon & Schuster $20.00 (0-671-73315-X). 144pp. An overview of the history of American poetry, with an interesting selection of poems arranged chronologically. (Rev: BCCB 1/95; BL 1/1/95; SLJ 12/94) [811]

11602 Hopkins, Lee Bennett. *Marvelous Math: A Book of Poems* (3–5). Illus. by Karen Barbour. 1997, Simon & Schuster paper $17.00 (0-689-80658-2). 31pp. A collection of simple poems by well-known writers that deal with math and numbers. (Rev: HBG 3/98; SLJ 10/97) [811]

11603 Hopkins, Lee Bennett, sel. *My America: A Poetry Atlas of the United States* (3–8). Illus. by Stephen Alcorn. 2000, Simon & Schuster $19.95 (0-689-81247-7). 83pp. Seven regions of the United states including Washington, D.C., are explored in this anthology of 51 poems by 40 different poets. (Rev: BCCB 10/00; HBG 3/01; SLJ 9/00) [811]

11604 Hopkins, Lee Bennett, ed. *School Supplies: A Book of Poems* (PS–1). Illus. by Renee Flower. 1996, Simon & Schuster paper $17.00 (0-689-80497-0). 37pp. Pencils, crayons, and books are some of the school supplies highlighted in 16 short poems. (Rev: BL 8/96; SLJ 11/96) [811]

11605 Hopkins, Lee Bennett, ed. *Song and Dance* (1–3). Illus. by Cheryl M. Taylor. 1997, Simon & Schuster paper $16.00 (0-689-80159-9). 32pp. A collection of 16 poems that celebrate the sounds of the language in verses that deal with songs and dancing. (Rev: BL 4/15/97; SLJ 6/97) [811]

11606 Hopkins, Lee Bennett, ed. *Surprises* (K–4). Illus. by Megan Lloyd. 1984, HarperCollins paper $3.95 (0-06-444105-9). 64pp. A collection of simple poems for beginning readers.

11607 Hopkins, Lee Bennett, et al., eds. *Blast Off! Poems About Space* (1–3). Illus. by Melissa Sweet. Series: I Can Read. 1995, HarperCollins LB $15.89 (0-06-024261-2). 48pp. An easily read book of poems about space and the wonders of the universe. (Rev: BCCB 4/95; BL 4/15/95; HB 7–8/95; SLJ 8/95) [811]

11608 Hubbell, Patricia. *City Kids* (PS–1). Illus. by Teresa Flavin. 2001, Marshall Cavendish $15.95 (0-7614-5079-3). 32pp. Simple poems and cheery pictures show kids engaged in such big-city activities as playing stickball, skipping rope, and stretching up like a skyscraper. (Rev: BL 3/1/01) [811]

11609 Hughes, Shirley. *Rhymes for Annie Rose* (PS–K). Illus. 1995, Lothrop $16.00 (0-688-14220-6). 48pp. In simple poems, daily occurrences in a young child's life are celebrated. (Rev: BCCB 11/95; BL 8/95; SLJ 9/95*) [821]

11610 Janeczko, Paul B. *The Place My Words Are Looking For: What Poets Say About and Through Their Work* (4–8). Illus. 1990, Macmillan paper $16.00 (0-02-747671-5). 128pp. A collection of some of the best contemporary poems. (Rev: BCCB 7–8/90; BL 5/1/90; HB 5–6/90*; SLJ 5/90) [811]

11611 Johnson, Dave, ed. *Movin': Teen Poets Take Voice* (5–10). Illus. by Chris Raschka. 2000, Orchard $15.95 (0-531-30258-X); paper $6.95 (0-531-07171-5). 52pp. An anthology of poems by teens who participated in New York Public Library workshops or submitted their work via the Web. (Rev: HBG 10/00; SLJ 5/00) [811]

11612 Johnston, Tony. *My Mexico/México Mío* (K–3). Illus. by F. John Sierra. 1996, Putnam $15.99 (0-399-22275-8). 36pp. Mexican scenes are presented in double-page spreads with 18 poems in both English and Spanish. (Rev: BCCB 7–8/96; HB 5–6/96; SLJ 4/96) [811]

11613 Johnston, Tony. *Once in the Country: Poems of a Farm* (K–3). Illus. by Thomas B. Allen. 1996, Putnam $15.95 (0-399-22644-3). 32pp. The joys of rural life are celebrated in this collection of 18 charming poems. (Rev: SLJ 12/96) [811]

11614 Joseph, Lynn. *Coconut Kind of Day: Island Poems* (K–2). Illus. by Sandra Speidel. 1990, Lothrop LB $13.88 (0-688-09120-2). 32pp. A portrait of a young black girl in the West Indies. (Rev: BCCB 1/91; BL 9/15/90; SLJ 11/90) [811]

11615 Katz, Bobbi. *We, the People: Poems* (5–8). Illus. by Nina Crews. 2000, Greenwillow LB $15.89 (0-688-16532-X). 102pp. The author has written a collection of 65 first-person poems placing herself in the shoes of individuals covering the entire span of American history. (Rev: HBG 3/01; SLJ 12/00) [811]

11616 Kennedy, X. J., and Dorothy M. Kennedy, eds. *Talking Like the Rain: A First Book of Poems*

(PS–3). Illus. by Jane Dyer. 1992, Little, Brown $19.95 (0-316-48889-5). 96pp. This is a cheerful collection of 100 well-illustrated poems in a variety of subjects and moods. (Rev: BCCB 7–8/92; BL 3/15/92; HB 7–8/92; SLJ 6/92) [821]

11617 Kipling, Rudyard. *Gunga Din* (5–8). Illus. by Robert Andrew Parker. 1987, Harcourt $12.95 (0-15-200456-4). 28pp. A vibrantly illustrated edition of the classic poem about the life of an Indian water carrier, Gunga Din. (Rev: BCCB 10/87; BL 11/1/87)

11618 *Knock at a Star: A Child's Introduction to Poetry.* Rev. ed. (3–6). Ed. by X. J. Kennedy and Dorothy M. Kennedy. Illus. 1999, Little, Brown $18.95 (0-316-48436-9). 178pp. An anthology of appealing verse, this book also explains such poetic devices as imagery, narrative, emotion, rhythm, wordplay, and parody. (Rev: BL 10/15/99; HBG 3/00; SLJ 10/99) [811.008]

11619 Kurtz, Jane. *River Friendly, River Wild* (PS–3). Illus. by Neil Brennan. 2000, Simon & Schuster $16.00 (0-689-82049-6). 40pp. This series of outstanding original poems traces the course of the Red River flood of 1997, the anguish it brought, and the poet's loss of her home and belongings. (Rev: BCCB 2/00; BL 2/1/00*; HB 3–4/00; HBG 10/00; SLJ 3/00) [811]

11620 Kuskin, Karla. *Dogs and Dragons, Trees and Dreams: A Collection of Poems* (3–6). Illus. by author. n.d., HarperCollins $7.00 (0-06-023543-8). 96pp. A welcome reissue of poems that had appeared previously in the author's works.

11621 Kuskin, Karla. *The Sky Is Always in the Sky* (PS–3). Illus. by Isabelle Dervaux. 1998, Harper-Collins LB $14.89 (0-06-027084-5). 48pp. A brilliant collection of poems culled from the author's many collections and illustrated in a folk-art style. (Rev: BL 5/15/98; HBG 10/98; SLJ 7/98) [811]

11622 Lansky, Bruce, ed. *No More Homework! No More Tests! Kids' Favorite Funny School Poems* (2–6). Illus. 1997, Meadowbrook Pr. LB $8.00 (0-671-57702-6). 80pp. Humorous, often outrageous, poems that deal with real and fantastic school situations. (Rev: BL 9/15/97) [811]

11623 Lesynski, Loris. *Dirty Dog Boogie* (2–5). Illus. by author. 1999, Annick LB $16.95 (1-55037-572-5); paper $6.95 (1-55037-573-3). 32pp. A joyous collection of poems that are filled with musical rhythms and quirky language. (Rev: HBG 10/99; SLJ 7/99) [811]

11624 Levy, Constance. *A Crack in the Clouds and Other Poems* (3–5). Illus. 1998, Simon & Schuster $15.00 (0-689-82204-9). 48pp. A collection of original short poems that celebrate and comment on ordinary occurrences and objects in life, such as spiderwebs, icicles, and fireworks. (Rev: BCCB 12/98; BL 1/1–15/99*; HBG 3/99; SLJ 12/98) [811]

11625 Levy, Constance. *When Whales Exhale and Other Poems* (3–5). Illus. 1996, Simon & Schuster $15.00 (0-689-80946-8). 42pp. A group of poems about the wonders of small things that are part of larger objects or events. (Rev: BL 12/15/96; SLJ 12/96) [811]

11626 Lewis, Claudia. *Long Ago in Oregon* (3–7). Illus. by Joel Fontaine. 1987, HarperCollins $11.95 (0-06-023839-9). 64pp. Short poems that recall the nostalgia of childhood in Oregon in the early 1900s. (Rev: BCCB 5/87; BL 7/87; SLJ 9/87)

11627 Lewis, J. Patrick. *The Bookworm's Feast: A Potluck of Poems* (3–6). Illus. by John O'Brien. 1999, Dial LB $15.89 (0-8037-1693-1). A tasty collection of poems of various styles. (Rev: BCCB 3/99; HBG 10/99; SLJ 3/99) [811]

11628 Lewis, J. Patrick. *A Burst of Firsts: Doers, Shakers, and Record Breakers* (2–4). Illus. by Brian Ajhar. 2001, Dial $15.99 (0-8037-2108-0). 40pp. This collection of imaginative original poems celebrates famous firsts, such as the first African American to win the Nobel prize. (Rev: BL 3/15/01) [811]

11629 Lewis, J. Patrick. *Doodle Dandies: Poems That Take Shape* (3–5). Illus. by Lisa Desimini. 1998, Simon & Schuster $16.00 (0-689-81075-X). 32pp. A collection of delightful, original poems that make a physical shape on the page. For example, a poem named "Dachshund" fills a dog-shaped illustration. (Rev: BCCB 9/98; BL 7/98; HBG 3/99; SLJ 8/98) [811]

11630 Liatsos, Sandra O. *Bicycle Riding: And Other Poems* (1–4). Illus. by Karen M. Dugan. 1997, Boyds Mills $15.95 (1-56397-235-2). A collection of 22 poems that deal with the everyday activities of children. (Rev: SLJ 5/97) [811]

11631 Lillegard, Dee. *Wake Up House! Rooms Full of Poems* (PS–K). Illus. by Don Carter. 2000, Knopf LB $17.99 (0-679-98351-1). 40pp. A collection of simple rhymes that explores the contents of a preschooler's house and ordinary occurrences there from dawn to dusk. (Rev: BCCB 2/00; BL 2/1/00; HBG 10/00; SLJ 2/00) [811]

11632 *Lives: Poems About Famous Americans* (3–6). Ed. by Lee Bennett Hopkins. Illus. 1999, HarperCollins $15.95 (0-06-027767-X). 40pp. Fourteen poems — 12 new to this collection — celebrate the lives of such famous Americans as Sacagawea, Thomas Edison, Eleanor Roosevelt, and Rosa Parks. (Rev: BL 3/15/99; HBG 10/99; SLJ 6/99) [811.008]

11633 Livingston, Myra Cohn. *Flights of Fancy and Other Poems* (3–5). 1994, Macmillan paper $13.95 (0-689-50613-9). 48pp. Some of the 40 short poems in this collection deal with airplanes, but most deal with flights of the imagination. (Rev: BCCB 1/95; BL 11/15/94; SLJ 12/94) [811]

11634 Livingston, Myra Cohn, ed. *I Am Writing a Poem About . . . a Game of Poetry* (4–6). 1997, Simon & Schuster $16.00 (0-689-81156-X). 72pp. A collection of poems that came from a master class taught by Myra Cohn Livingston. (Rev: BL 9/1/97; HBG 3/98; SLJ 10/97) [811]

11635 Livingston, Myra Cohn, ed. *I Like You, If You Like Me: Poems of Friendship* (4–8). 1987, Macmillan $16.00 (0-689-50408-X). 160pp. Ninety short poems on the theme of friendship, from many cultures and time periods. (Rev: BL 4/1/87; HB 5–6/87; SLJ 4/87)

11636 Livingston, Myra Cohn. *I Never Told and Other Poems* (3–6). 1992, Macmillan $12.95 (0-

689-50544-2). 44pp. Forty-two short poems highlight flight — in an airplane and in the imagination. (Rev: BCCB 4/92; BL 6/1/92; SLJ 4/92) [811]

11637 Livingston, Myra Cohn. *Remembering and Other Poems* (3–6). 1989, Macmillan LB $13.95 (0-689-50489-6). 64pp. Thoughts and emotions from a variety of childhood activities. (Rev: BCCB 1/90; BL 12/1/89; SLJ 12/89*) [811]

11638 Livingston, Myra Cohn, ed. *Roll Along: Poems on Wheels* (3–5). 1993, Macmillan $11.95 (0-689-50585-X). 72pp. An anthology of poems about wheels on various kinds of vehicles, from skateboards and bicycles to garbage trucks and trains. (Rev: BL 9/15/93; SLJ 8/93) [811]

11639 Longfellow, Henry Wadsworth. *The Children's Hour* (K–2). Illus. by Glenna Lang. 1993, Godine $17.95 (0-87923-971-9). 32pp. The classic poem is illustrated with paintings depicting Longfellow spending time with his children. (Rev: BL 11/15/93) [811]

11640 Longfellow, Henry Wadsworth. *The Children's Own Longfellow* (5–8). Illus. 1908, Houghton $20.00 (0-395-06889-4). 109pp. Eight selections from the best-known and best-loved of Longfellow's poems.

11641 Longfellow, Henry Wadsworth. *Hiawatha* (K–3). Illus. by Susan Jeffers. 1983, Dial $16.99 (0-8037-0013-X). 32pp. A beautifully illustrated version of sections of Longfellow's poem.

11642 Longfellow, Henry Wadsworth. *The Midnight Ride of Paul Revere* (3–5). Illus. by Jeffrey Thompson. 2000, National Geographic $16.95 (0-7922-7674-4). 32pp. Large, full-color pictures illustrate this edition of the complete text of Longfellow's tribute to a Revolutionary War hero. (Rev: BL 3/15/00; HBG 10/00; SLJ 5/00) [811]

11643 Longfellow, Henry Wadsworth. *Paul Revere's Ride* (2–4). Illus. by Nancy Winslow Parker. 1985, Morrow paper $4.95 (0-688-12387-2). 48pp. Soft illustrations relieve the suspense of this famous ride. (Rev: BCCB 5/85; BL 3/1/85; HB 5–6/85)

11644 Longfellow, Henry Wadsworth. *Paul Revere's Ride* (PS–3). Illus. by Ted Rand. 1990, Dutton $16.99 (0-525-44610-9). 40pp. The poem's essential drama is captured in a series of paintings. (Rev: BCCB 12/90; BL 9/15/90*; HB 1–2/91; SLJ 11/90*) [811]

11645 Lyne, Sandford, comp. *Ten-Second Rainshowers: Poems by Young People* (4–8). Illus. by Virginia Halstead. 1996, Simon & Schuster paper $16.00 (0-689-80113-0). 124pp. A variety of subjects — including nature, home, and family — are touched on in this collection of free verse written by 130 children from ages eight to 18. (Rev: SLJ 12/96) [811]

11646 Lyon, George E. *Book* (2–5). Illus. by Peter Catalanotto. 1999, DK $26.95 (0-7894-2560-2). A poetic description of a book that compares it to a house, a tree, a chest, and a farm. (Rev: BL 5/15/99; HBG 10/99; SLJ 6/99) [811]

11647 McCord, David. *All Day Long: Fifty Rhymes of the Never Was and Always Is* (4–7). Illus. by Henry B. Kane. 1975, Little, Brown paper $6.95 (0-316-55532-0). A collection of poems on a variety of

subjects, chiefly times that are important in childhood.

11648 McCord, David. *One at a Time: His Collected Poems for the Young* (3–8). Illus. by Henry B. Kane. 1986, Little, Brown $18.95 (0-316-55516-9). All seven of the poet's anthologies in one handsome volume.

11649 Mado, Michio. *The Magic Pocket* (PS–2). Illus. by Mitsumasa Anno. 1998, Simon & Schuster $16.00 (0-689-82137-9). 32pp. Fourteen charming poems by a prize-winning Japanese writer are included in this bilingual Japanese-English book. (Rev: BL 2/1/99; HB 9–10/98; HBG 3/99; SLJ 10/98) [895.615]

11650 *Maples in the Mist: Children's Poems from the Tang Dynasty* (K–5). Trans. by Minfong Ho. Illus. by Jean Tseng and Mou-Sien Tseng. 1996, Lothrop LB $14.93 (0-688-14723-2). 32pp. Sixteen rhymes from the Tang Dynasty in modern language, each accompanied by a watercolor. (Rev: BCCB 9/96; BL 10/1/96; SLJ 9/96) [895.1]

11651 Marzollo, Jean. *I Love You: A Rebus Poem* (PS). Illus. by Suse MacDonald. 2000, Scholastic paper $7.95 (0-590-37656-X). 40pp. A rebus puzzle book is used to present a series of simple poems about loving one another. (Rev: BL 12/15/99; HBG 10/00; SLJ 2/00) [811.54]

11652 Mavor, Salley, ed. *You and Me: Poems of Friendship* (PS–3). Illus. 1997, Orchard LB $17.99 (0-531-33045-1). 32pp. An anthology of 19 enjoyable poems that celebrate the joys and problems that come with friendships. (Rev: BL 7/97; HBG 3/98; SLJ 9/97) [811]

11653 Medina, Jane. *My Name Is Jorge: On Both Sides of the River* (3–7). Illus. by Fabricio Vandenbroeck. 1999, Boyds Mills $14.95 (1-56397-811-3). 48pp. An immigrant boy from Mexico describes his experiences in a series of 27 poems in English and Spanish. (Rev: HBG 3/00; SLJ 2/00) [811]

11654 Milne, A. A. *The World of Christopher Robin* (K–3). Illus. by E. H. Shepard. 1958, Dutton $21.99 (0-525-44448-3). 256pp. Original illustrations have been retained in this edition that combines the poems from *When We Were Very Young* and *Now We Are Six*.

11655 *Mommy Poems* (K–3). Ed. by John Micklos. Illus. by Lori McElrath-Eslick. 2001, Boyds Mills $15.95 (1-56397-849-0); paper $8.95 (1-56397-908-X). 32pp. An anthology of 18 poems about mothers by such writers as Gary Soto and Nikki Giovanni. (Rev: BL 3/15/01) [811]

11656 Moore, Lillian. *I Never Did That Before* (PS–K). Illus. by Lillian Hoban. 1995, Simon & Schuster $15.00 (0-689-31889-8). 32pp. Fourteen simple poems about the joys of such childhood accomplishments as learning to skip rope. (Rev: BL 11/1/95; SLJ 10/95) [811]

11657 Mora, Pat. *Confetti* (1–4). Illus. by Enrique O. Sanchez. 1996, Lee & Low $15.95 (1-880000-25-3). 32pp. A series of poems that mingle Spanish expressions with basic English. (Rev: BL 11/15/96; SLJ 11/96) [811]

11658 *More Spice than Sugar: Poems About Feisty Females* (4–7). Ed. by Lillian Morrison. Illus. 2001, Houghton $15.00 (0-618-06892-9). 80pp. This anthology of poems by many famous writers deals with women in three sections: women's identity, women in sports, and women's rights. (Rev: BL 3/15/01; SLJ 3/01) [811]

11659 Morninghouse, Sundaira. *Nightfeathers* (PS–K). Illus. by Jody Kim. 1990, Open Hand $9.95 (0-940880-27-X); paper $4.95 (0-940880-28-8). 32pp. In 24 short poems, a typical day in the life of an African American child is portrayed. (Rev: BL 6/1/90) [811]

11660 Moss, Jeff. *Bone Poems* (3–5). Illus. by Tom Leigh. 1997, Workman $14.95 (0-7611-0884-X). 78pp. A group of rhymes that explore facts about dinosaurs and make paleontology fun. (Rev: HBG 3/98; SLJ 12/97*) [811]

11661 Moss, Jeff. *The Butterfly Jar* (2–5). Illus. by Chris L. Demarest. 1989, Bantam $17.95 (0-553-05704-9). 128pp. Upbeat poetry, including the silly and the serious. (Rev: BL 2/1/90; SLJ 7/90) [811]

11662 *My First Oxford Book of Poems* (PS–4). Ed. by John Foster. Illus. 2000, Oxford $22.95 (0-19-276201-X). 96pp. About 100 poems are illustrated by different artists in this fine anthology that includes some old favorites by writers like Stevenson and Lear as well as a good selection of more contemporary works. (Rev: BL 9/15/00; HBG 10/00; SLJ 8/00) [811]

11663 Nye, Naomi S. *Come with Me: Poems for a Journey* (K–3). Illus. by Dan Yaccarino. 2000, Greenwillow LB $15.89 (0-688-15947-8). 40pp. From real trips to travels of the imagination, this collection of 16 original free-verse poems celebrates different kinds of journeys. (Rev: BCCB 10/00; BL 10/15/00; HB 9–10/00; HBG 3/01; SLJ 9/00) [811]

11664 *One Hundred Years of Poetry for Children* (5–7). Ed. by Michael Harrison and Christopher Stuart-Clark. Illus. 1999, Oxford $25.00 (0-19-276190-0). 195pp. Arranged by theme, this collection of 20th-century verse contains one poem from each of approximately 150 poets. (Rev: BL 9/1/99; HBG 3/00) [821.9]

11665 O'Neill, Mary. *Hailstones and Halibut Bones* (PS–3). Illus. by Leonard Weisgard. 1973, Double-day paper $8.95 (0-385-41078-6). Imaginative poems about color.

11666 *The Oxford Illustrated Book of American Children's Poems* (PS–4). Ed. by Donald Hall. Illus. 1999, Oxford $19.95 (0-19-512373-5). 93pp. From classics like *A Visit from St. Nicholas* to works by Robert Frost, Shel Silverstein, Nikki Giovanni, Karla Kuskin, and others, this is an attractive anthology, perfect for reading aloud. (Rev: BL 1/1–15/00; HBG 3/00; SLJ 1/00) [811]

11667 Paraskevas, Betty. *Junior Kroll* (2–4). Illus. by Michael Paraskevas. 1993, Harcourt $13.95 (0-15-241497-5). Fifteen poems about a mischievous boy and his adventures. (Rev: BCCB 5/93; SLJ 6/93) [822]

11668 Paul, Ann W. *All by Herself* (3–5). Illus. 1999, Harcourt $17.00 (0-15-201477-2). 32pp. A collection of 14 original poems celebrates the lives of such women as Rachel Carson, Pocahontas, Sacajawea, and Amelia Earhart. (Rev: BL 12/1/99; HBG 3/00; SLJ 1/00) [811]

11669 Philip, Neil, ed. *Songs Are Thoughts: Poems of the Inuit* (K–4). Illus. by Maryclare Foa. 1995, Orchard $15.95 (0-531-06893-5). 32pp. Short Inuit poems are featured in double-page spreads, each containing a poem and an illustration. (Rev: BCCB 5/95; BL 4/15/95; SLJ 4/95) [897]

11670 Philip, Neil, ed. *War and the Pity of War* (5–9). Illus. by Michael McCurdy. 1998, Clarion LB $20.00 (0-395-84982-9). 96pp. An anthology of antiwar poems by well-known and obscure poets, with striking illustrations. (Rev: HBG 10/99; SLJ 9/98) [811]

11671 *Poetry for Young People: Henry Wadsworth Longfellow* (4–6). Ed. by Frances Schoonmaker. Illus. 1999, Sterling $14.95 (0-8069-9417-7). 48pp. This collection offers 27 of Longfellow's poems including "The Children's Hour," "The Wreck of the Hesperus," and "Paul Revere's Ride." (Rev: BL 3/15/99; HBG 10/99; SLJ 3/99) [811]

11672 Pomerantz, Charlotte. *Halfway to Your House* (PS–1). Illus. by Gabrielle Vincent. 1993, Greenwillow LB $13.93 (0-688-11805-4). 32pp. The thoughts and feelings of different children at play are explored in watercolors and short poems. (Rev: BL 10/15/93) [811]

11673 Pomerantz, Charlotte. *If I Had a Paka: Poems in Eleven Languages* (PS–3). Illus. by Nancy Tafuri. 1993, Morrow paper $4.95 (0-688-12510-7). 32pp. In each of these poems, English is interspersed with one of 11 languages. A reissue. [811]

11674 Pooley, Sarah. *It's Raining, It's Pouring: A Book for Rainy Days* (PS–3). Illus. 1993, Greenwillow $18.00 (0-688-11803-8). 80pp. This book is filled with poems, songs, and ideas for all kinds of activities just perfect for a rainy day. (Rev: BL 5/1/93; SLJ 7/93) [808]

11675 Prelutsky, Jack. *The Gargoyle on the Roof* (2–6). Illus. by Peter Sis. 1999, Greenwillow LB $15.93 (0-688-16553-2). 40pp. A picture book for older children that contains imaginative poems about werewolves, goblins, vampires, trolls, and so on, with illustrations that catch the sinister mood of the poems. (Rev: BCCB 10/99; BL 10/1/99*; HBG 10/00; SLJ 10/99) [811]

11676 Prelutsky, Jack. *Monday's Troll* (4–6). Illus. by Peter Sis. 1996, Greenwillow $15.89 (0-688-14373-3). 40pp. Seventeen original poems that deal with supernatural beings like witches, trolls, wizards, and ogres. (Rev: BCCB 3/96; BL 4/15/96; HB 5–6/96; SLJ 4/96*) [811]

11677 Prelutsky, Jack. *Nightmares: Poems to Trouble Your Sleep* (5–8). Illus. by Arnold Lobel. 1976, Greenwillow $14.89 (0-688-84053-1). 38pp. Shuddery, macabre poems that will frighten but amuse a young audience. A sequel is: *The Headless Horseman Rides Tonight: More Poems to Trouble Your Sleep* (1980).

11678 Prelutsky, Jack. *A Pizza the Size of the Sun* (3–6). Illus. by James Stevenson. 1996, Greenwillow $17.93 (0-688-13236-7). 160pp. Humorous, imaginative light verses explore a variety of subjects. (Rev: BCCB 9/96; BL 9/15/96*; HB 9–10/96; SLJ 9/96*) [811]

11679 Prelutsky, Jack, ed. *The Random House Book of Poetry for Children* (2–6). Illus. by Arnold Lobel. 1983, Random LB $21.99 (0-394-95010-0). 248pp. Old standbys and new gems are included in this fine anthology of 572 poems.

11680 Ridlon, Marci. *Sun Through the Window: Poems for Children* (3–6). Illus. 1996, Boyds Mills paper $9.95 (1-56397-454-1). 64pp. A collection of 54 poems dealing with everyday experiences and emotions. (Rev: SLJ 10/96) [811]

11681 Robb, Laura, ed. *Music and Drum: Voices of War and Peace, Hope and Dream* (3–6). Illus. by Debra Lill. 1997, Putnam $16.95 (0-399-22024-0). 32pp. An anthology of war poems that are strikingly illustrated with photos reflecting the power and emotion of the poems. (Rev: BCCB 5/97; BL 4/1/97) [808]

11682 Rosen, Michael. *The Best of Michael Rosen* (3–5). Illus. by Quentin Blake. 1995, Wetlands paper $16.95 (1-57143-046-6). 136pp. Sixty-five insightful, often lighthearted poems by the popular English poet. (Rev: BL 2/1/96) [808.81]

11683 Rosen, Michael, sel. *Classic Poetry: An Illustrated Collection* (5–10). Illus. by Paul Howard. 1998, Candlewick $21.99 (1-56402-890-9). 159pp. A handsome chronological collection of representative poems from 38 poets including Shakespeare, Byron, Shelley, and Yeats, plus a generous selection of contemporary writers. (Rev: HBG 3/99; SLJ 5/99) [808.81]

11684 Rosen, Michael, ed. *Poems for the Very Young* (PS–2). Illus. by Bob Graham. 1993, Kingfisher $17.95 (1-85697-908-3). 80pp. A delightful collection of rhymes for young children, chiefly from American and British sources and illustrated with charming cartoonlike drawings. (Rev: BL 1/1/94*; SLJ 1/94) [821]

11685 Rosen, Michael J., ed. *Food Fight: Poets Join the Fight Against Hunger with Poems to Favorite Foods* (3–6). Illus. by Michael J. Rosen. 1996, Harcourt $17.00 (0-15-201065-3). 56pp. Thirty-five children's book writers share their impressions of food and eating in this delightful collection of poems. (Rev: BL 10/1/96; SLJ 4/97) [811]

11686 Rossetti, Christina. *Sing Song: A Nursery Rhyme Book* (K–3). Illus. by Arthur Hughes. 1969, Dover paper $4.95 (0-486-22107-5). 130pp. Many of the poems are about small creatures and familiar objects and have a singing quality that young children enjoy.

11687 *Running Lightly . . .: Poems for Young People* (4–9). Ed. by Tom Mullins. 1998, Mercier paper $12.95 (1-85342-193-9). 128pp. A collection of old songs and ballads, nonsense rhymes and lyrics, with a section of fine student pieces. (Rev: BL 5/15/98; SLJ 7/98) [808.8]

11688 *Salting the Ocean: 100 Poems by Young Poets* (4–12). Ed. by Naomi Shihab Nye. Illus. 2000, Greenwillow $16.95 (0-688-16193-6). 128pp.

This anthology of poetry by young people from grades one through 12 has been culled by the editor from her 25 years of teaching poetry in schools. (Rev: BL 3/15/00; HB 7–8/00; HBG 10/00; SLJ 7/00) [811]

11689 Sandburg, Carl. *Grassroots* (3–6). Illus. by Wendell Minor. 1998, Harcourt $18.00 (0-15-200082-8). 34pp. Fourteen poems by Sandburg that describe the Midwest are reprinted, with handsome framed pictures. (Rev: BCCB 6/98; BL 3/15/98; HBG 10/98; SLJ 6/98) [811]

11690 Sandburg, Carl. *The Sandburg Treasury: Prose and Poetry for Young People* (5–8). Illus. 1970, Harcourt $25.95 (0-15-270180-X). 480pp. Sandburg's whimsical stories, poetry, and portions of his autobiography.

11691 Schertle, Alice. *Keepers* (1–4). Illus. by Ted Rand. 1996, Lothrop LB $15.93 (0-688-11635-3). 32pp. A collection of original poems in which everyday objects become transformed through one's imagination. (Rev: BL 10/15/96; SLJ 12/96) [811]

11692 Schertle, Alice. *A Lucky Thing* (2–4). Illus. by Wendell Minor. 1999, Harcourt $17.00 (0-15-200541-2). 32pp. This outstanding picture book of poetry for older children contains interrelated simple poems — many about animals — about the world around them. (Rev: BCCB 6/99; BL 3/15/99*; HB 5–6/99; HBG 10/99; SLJ 6/99) [811]

11693 Schmidt, Gary D., ed. *Robert Frost* (5–7). Illus. by Henri Sorensen. Series: Poetry for Young People. 1994, Sterling $14.95 (0-8069-0633-2). 48pp. An anthology of 25 poems suitable for young people, with watercolor illustrations that picture the New England landscape that Frost loved. (Rev: BL 12/1/94; SLJ 2/95) [811]

11694 Service, Robert W. *The Cremation of Sam McGee* (5–8). Illus. by Ted Harrison. 1987, Greenwillow $18.00 (0-688-06903-7). 32pp. Poems for young readers who like a touch of the bizarre and macabre. (Rev: BL 4/15/87; HB 5–6/87; SLJ 3/87)

11695 Shields, Carol D. *Lunch Money and Other Poems About School* (1–3). Illus. by Paul Meisel. 1995, Dutton $15.99 (0-525-45345-8). 48pp. Daily events at school are celebrated in this charming group of poems. (Rev: BL 11/15/95; SLJ 1/96) [811]

11696 Siebert, Diane. *Heartland* (K–4). Illus. by Wendell Minor. 1989, HarperCollins paper $6.95 (0-06-443287-4). 32pp. A lyrical celebration of the Midwest. (Rev: BL 3/1/89; SLJ 5/89)

11697 Silverstein, Shel. *Falling Up* (3–6). Illus. 1996, HarperCollins LB $17.89 (0-06-024803-3). 176pp. More than 150 delightful original poems that amuse and amaze. (Rev: BCCB 6/96; BL 7/96*; HB 9–10/96; SLJ 7/96) [811]

11698 Silverstein, Shel. *Where the Sidewalk Ends* (3–6). Illus. by author. 1974, HarperCollins LB $17.89 (0-06-025668-0). 176pp. The author explores various facets and interests of children, with appropriate cartoonlike drawings. Also use: *A Light in the Attic* (1981).

11699 Simon, Francesca. *Toddler Time* (PS–K). Illus. by Susan Winter. 2000, Orchard $15.95 (0-531-30251-2). 40pp. The 17 poems in this original collection celebrate toddlers' accomplishments — everything from walking to riding bicycles. (Rev: BL 5/1/00; HBG 10/00; SLJ 5/00) [821]

11700 Simon, Seymour, ed. *Star Walk* (4–8). Illus. 1995, Morrow LB $14.93 (0-688-11887-7). 32pp. Simple poems and outstanding photographs create an impressive introduction to stars and outer space. (Rev: BL 3/1/95; SLJ 4/95) [811]

11701 Singer, Marilyn. *All We Needed to Say: Poems About School from Tanya and Sophie* (PS–3). Illus. by Lorna Clark. 1996, Simon & Schuster $15.00 (0-689-80667-1). 28pp. Two girls compare their school experiences in a series of short monologues. (Rev: BCCB 9/96; BL 8/96; SLJ 9/96) [811]

11702 Singer, Marilyn. *Family Reunion* (K–3). Illus. by R. W. Alley. 1994, Macmillan paper $14.95 (0-02-782883-2). 32pp. Fourteen poems that celebrate a family reunion, ending with Dad receiving photos of the proceedings. (Rev: BL 9/1/94; SLJ 11/94) [811]

11703 *A Small Child's Book of Cozy Poems* (PS). Ed. by Cyndy Szekeres. Illus. 1999, Scholastic $6.95 (0-590-38364-7). 32pp. From Mother Goose to nonsense verse, this is a sweet collection of rhymes for the very young. (Rev: BL 2/1/99; HBG 10/99; SLJ 4/99) [811.008]

11704 Smith, William J. *Here Is My Heart: Love Poems* (5–8). Illus. 1999, Little, Brown $12.95 (0-316-19765-3). 50pp. This is a delightful collection of short love poems, including some by the compiler. (Rev: BL 1/1–15/99; HBG 10/99; SLJ 1/99) [821.008]

11705 *Someone I Like: Poems About People* (3–5). Ed. by Judith Nicholls. Illus. 2000, Barefoot $16.95 (1-84148-004-5). 40pp. This anthology of 26 poems explores children's feelings for family members and friends. (Rev: BL 4/1/00; SLJ 7/00) [808.819]

11706 *Songs, Seas, and Green Peas: Poems for Anywhere* (K–4). Series: Poetry Parade. 2000, Heinemann LB $21.36 (1-57572-400-6). 32pp. A collection of poems by both well-known and obscure poets that contains no particular theme or subjects. Also use *Wishes, Wings, and Other Things: Poems for Anytime* (2000). (Rev: HBG 3/01; SLJ 2/01) [811]

11707 Soto, Gary. *Canto Familiar* (4–6). Illus. 1995, Harcourt $18.00 (0-15-200067-4). 88pp. Simple poems, many involving Mexican Americans, celebrate experiences at school, home, and in the street. A companion to *Neighborhood Odes* (1992). (Rev: BL 10/1/95; SLJ 12/95*) [811]

11708 Soto, Gary. *Neighborhood Odes* (4–6). Illus. by David Diaz. 1992, Harcourt $15.95 (0-15-256879-4). 80pp. Unrhymed verses celebrate such items in a Mexican-American neighborhood as pinatas, weddings, libraries, and tennis shoes. (Rev: BL 6/15/92; HB 5–6/92*; SLJ 5/92) [811]

11709 Spinelli, Eileen. *Tea Party Today: Poems to Sip and Savor* (1–3). Illus. by Karen M. Dugan. 1999, Boyds Mills $15.95 (1-56397-662-5). 32pp. Tea and teatime inspired this group of poems about

the ceremony and the emotions it evokes. (Rev: BL 4/1/99; HBG 10/99; SLJ 4/99) [811.54]

11710 Spinelli, Eileen. *Where Is the Night Train Going?* (PS–3). Illus. by Cyd Moore. 1996, Boyds Mills $14.95 (1-56397-171-2). 32pp. Everyday concerns and activities are portrayed in this group of well-illustrated, evocative poems. (Rev: BL 1/1–15/96; SLJ 4/96) [811]

11711 Stevenson, James. *Candy Corn* (2–5). Illus. 1999, Greenwillow $15.00 (0-688-15837-4). 56pp. Humorous recollections and details of ordinary life are the subjects of this delightful book of poems illustrated with ink-and-watercolor pictures. (Rev: BCCB 5/99; BL 3/15/99*; HB 7–8/99; HBG 10/99; SLJ 5/99) [811]

11712 Stevenson, James. *Cornflakes: Poems* (3–5). Illus. 2000, Greenwillow $15.95 (0-688-16718-7). 48pp. An eclectic collection of short verses on many subjects, illustrated with bright, clear, ink-and-watercolor pictures. (Rev: BL 3/15/00; HB 7–8/00; HBG 10/00; SLJ 6/00) [811]

11713 Stevenson, James. *Just Around the Corner* (2–5). Illus. 2001, Greenwillow LB $14.89 (0-06-029189-3). 56pp. The celebrated artist illustrates his own collection of simple poems that deal with the ordinary things of life — Christmas trees, umbrellas, and old diners, to name just a few. (Rev: BL 1/1–15/01; SLJ 3/01) [811]

11714 Stevenson, Robert Louis. *A Child's Garden of Verses* (K–4). Illus. by Tasha Tudor. 1988, Macmillan $13.95 (0-02-689093-3). 72pp. Verses known and loved by generations of young people, brilliantly illustrated.

11715 Stevenson, Robert Louis. *A Child's Garden of Verses* (K–4). Illus. 1989, Chronicle $17.95 (0-87701-608-9). 121pp. A handsome edition of the old favorite, using some 100 19th-century illustrations. (Rev: BL 11/1/89*; SLJ 2/90) [821]

11716 Stevenson, Robert Louis. *A Child's Garden of Verses* (PS). Illus. by Joanna Isles. 1994, Abrams $17.95 (0-8109-3196-6). 87pp. A freshly illustrated edition of this classic, published to commemorate the centenary of the author's death. (Rev: SLJ 10/94) [821]

11717 Stevenson, Robert Louis. *A Child's Garden of Verses* (PS–4). Illus. by Diane Goode. 1998, Morrow $18.00 (0-688-14584-1). 119pp. A handsome edition of these favorite childhood poems illustrated with attractive, appropriate illustrations. (Rev: HBG 3/99; SLJ 1/99) [821]

11718 Stevenson, Robert Louis. *My Shadow* (PS–K). Illus. by Penny Dale. 1999, Candlewick $12.99 (0-7636-0923-4). 24pp. A picture-book version of Stevenson's classic poem in which a child delights in the various forms his shadow takes. (Rev: BL 11/1/99; HBG 3/00) [821]

11719 Stevenson, Robert Louis. *Poetry for Young People: Robert Louis Stevenson* (3–5). Illus. Series: Poetry for Young People. 2000, Sterling $14.95 (0-8069-4956-2). 48pp. Chosen mainly from *A Child's Garden of Verses*, this is a representative collection of Stevenson's work for children preceded by a biographical note. (Rev: BL 3/15/00; HBG 10/00; SLJ 7/00) [821]

11720 Stevenson, Robert Louis. *Where Go the Boats?* (PS–3). Illus. by Max Grover. 1998, Harcourt $16.00 (0-15-201711-9). 32pp. Selections from Stevenson's *A Child's Garden of Verses,* are presented with accompanying brightly colored acrylic paintings. (Rev: BL 1/1–15/99; HBG 3/99; SLJ 4/99) [821]

11721 Strickland, Michael R. *Poems That Sing to You* (3–7). Illus. by Alan Leiner. 1993, Boyds Mills $14.95 (1-56397-178-X). 55pp. A collection of poems that suggest music and dancing, some from well-known writers and others from pop lyrics and age-old chants. (Rev: HB 11–12/93; SLJ 10/93) [811]

11722 Swann, Brian. *The House with No Door: African Riddle-Poems* (2–4). Illus. by Ashley Bryan. 1998, Harcourt $16.00 (0-15-200805-5). 32pp. Fourteen illustrated riddle-poems of two to 14 lines each, all originating in Africa, are presented in this picture book. (Rev: BCCB 2/99; BL 11/15/98; HBG 3/99; SLJ 5/99) [811]

11723 Swanson, Susan M. *Getting Used to the Dark: 26 Night Poems* (2–5). Illus. by Peter Catalanotto. Series: Richard Jackson Books. 1997, DK $14.95 (0-7894-2468-1). 45pp. The nature of night, darkness, and dreams is explored in this book of poetry. (Rev: HBG 3/98; SLJ 1/98) [811]

11724 Swenson, May. *The Complete Poems to Solve* (5–8). Illus. by Christy Hale. 1993, Macmillan LB $13.95 (0-02-788725-1). 128pp. From simple riddles to more complex questions, each of these poems contains a puzzle. (Rev: HB 3–4/93; SLJ 5/93) [811]

11725 Taberski, Sharon, ed. *Morning, Noon, and Night: Poems to Fill Your Day* (PS–3). Illus. by Nancy Doniger. 1996, Mondo $14.95 (1-57255-128-3). 32pp. The day's activities are traced in 29 poems by well-known writers. (Rev: BL 12/15/96; SLJ 5/96) [811]

11726 Turner, Ann. *Mississippi Mud: Three Prairie Journals* (4–8). Illus. by Robert J. Blake. 1997, HarperCollins LB $16.89 (0-06-024433-X). 48pp. Through a series of poems, one family's experiences are chronicled as they journey from Kentucky to Oregon in the 19th century. (Rev: BCCB 6/97; BL 4/15/97; SLJ 6/97*) [811]

11727 Turner, Ann. *Street Talk* (2–4). Illus. by Catherine Stock. 1988, Houghton paper $5.95 (0-395-61625-5). 47pp. A total of 29 original poems about everyday subjects like teachers and pizza. (Rev: BCCB 6/86; SLJ 9/86)

11728 *The 20th Century Children's Poetry Treasury* (3–5). Ed. by Jack Prelutsky. Illus. 1999, Random $19.95 (0-679-89314-8). 96pp. On each of the illustrated two-page spreads, there are four to six poems on a single theme, for a total of more than 200 poems by 137 poets. (Rev: BL 12/15/99; HBG 3/00; SLJ 12/99*) [811]

11729 *Very Best (Almost) Friends: Poems of Friendship* (2–4). Ed. by Paul B. Janeczko. Illus. by Christine Davenier. 1999, Candlewick $12.99 (0-7636-

0475-5). 40pp. A collection of 24 poems by well-known writers that explores friendships and other emotional spin-offs such as jealousy and loneliness. (Rev: BL 12/15/98; HB 11–12/98; HBG 10/99; SLJ 1/99) [811]

11730 Viorst, Judith. *If I Were in Charge of the World and Other Worries: Poems for Children and Their Parents* (5–8). Illus. by Lynne Cherry. 1981, Macmillan $16.95 (0-689-30863-9); paper $4.95 (0-689-70770-3). 64pp. Situations that vex are explored in these 41 poems.

11731 Wallace, Daisy, ed. *Ghost Poems* (4–7). Illus. by Tomie dePaola. 1979, Holiday paper $4.95 (0-8234-0849-3). 32pp. New and old poems to delight and frighten young readers.

11732 Wallace, Daisy, ed. *Witch Poems* (3–6). Illus. by Trina S. Hyman. 1976, Holiday LB $14.95 (0-8234-0281-9); paper $4.95 (0-8234-0850-7). 32pp. Eighteen poems chosen from several different sources on a wide variety of witches.

11733 Waters, Fiona, comp. *Dark as a Midnight Dream: Poetry Collection 2* (5–8). Illus. by Zara Slattery. 1999, Evans Brothers $24.95 (0-237-51845-7). 286pp. An extensive anthology of poetry arranged by subjects such as "Mythical Creatures" and "City Life" that features such writers as Robert Browning, William Shakespeare, William Butler Yeats, William Wordsworth, Langston Hughes, and Carl Sandburg. (Rev: SLJ 11/99) [811]

11734 Watson, Clyde. *Love's a Sweet* (K–2). Illus. by Wendy Watson. 1998, Viking $15.99 (0-670-83453-X). 32pp. Different kinds of love — from brotherly and parental to romantic — are expressed in these 25 original poems illustrated with drawing of bunnies, cats, dogs, and other animals. (Rev: BL 12/1/98; HBG 3/99; SLJ 12/98) [811]

11735 Whipple, Laura. *Eric Carle's Dragons Dragons and Other Creatures That Never Were* (2–6). Illus. by Eric Carle. 1991, Putnam $19.99 (0-399-22105-0). 69pp. This is a collection of poems about dragons and other mythological creatures illustrated by Eric Carle. (Rev: BCCB 12/91; BL 11/1/91; HB 11–12/91; SLJ 10/91) [811]

11736 Wilbur, Richard. *Runaway Opposites* (4–6). Illus. by Henrik Drescher. 1995, Harcourt $15.00 (0-15-258722-5). 32pp. An intriguing, involved book of poems that deal with synonyms and antonyms. (Rev: BCCB 4/95; BL 4/15/95; SLJ 5/95) [811]

11737 Willard, Nancy. *A Visit to William Blake's Inn: Poems for Innocent and Experienced Travelers* (2–5). Illus. by Alice Provensen and Martin Provensen. 1981, Harcourt $16.00 (0-15-293822-2); paper $7.00 (0-15-293823-0). 44pp. A collection of poems that won the Newbery Award, 1982.

11738 Willard, Nancy. *The Voyage of the Ludgate Hill: Travels with Robert Louis Stevenson* (1–4). Illus. by Alice Provensen and Martin Provensen. 1987, Harcourt $14.95 (0-15-294464-8). A poem told through the poet's eyes of his 1887 journey across the Atlantic. (Rev: BCCB 4/87; BL 6/1/87; SLJ 5/87)

11739 Wong, Janet S. *Night Garden* (3–6). Illus. 2000, Simon & Schuster $16.00 (0-689-82617-6).

32pp. This collection of 15 original poems explores the world of dreams and is illustrated with suitably near-surreal gouaches. (Rev: BCCB 1/00; BL 1/1–15/00; HBG 10/00; SLJ 3/00) [811.54]

11740 Wong, Janet S. *The Rainbow Hand: Poems About Mothers and Children* (5–8). Illus. 1999, Simon & Schuster $15.00 (0-689-82148-4). 32pp. This collection of 18 poems deals with maternal love — some from the mother's point of view and others from the child's. (Rev: BL 4/1/99; HBG 10/99; SLJ 4/99) [811]

11741 Wong, Janet S. *A Suitcase of Seaweed and Other Poems* (4–7). 1996, Simon & Schuster $15.00 (0-689-80788-0). 42pp. Personal poems that deal with the author's cultural backgrounds — Korean, Chinese, and American. (Rev: BCCB 4/96; BL 4/1/96; HB 7–8/96; SLJ 9/96) [811]

11742 Yolen, Jane. *O Jerusalem* (4–6). Illus. by John Thompson. 1996, Scholastic $15.95 (0-590-48426-5). A group of original poems that explore the importance of Jerusalem in Judaism, Christianity, and Islam. (Rev: BL 2/1/96*; SLJ 3/96*) [811]

11743 Yolen, Jane. *Sacred Places* (4–6). Illus. by David Shannon. 1996, Harcourt $16.00 (0-15-269953-8). 40pp. A worldwide collection of informational poems about the places sacred to various faiths. (Rev: BCCB 7–8/96; BL 10/1/96; HB 1–2/96; SLJ 3/96) [811]

11744 Yolen, Jane, ed. *Sky Scrape/City Scape: Poems of City Life* (1–4). Illus. by Ken Condon. 1996, Boyds Mills $15.95 (1-56397-179-8). 32pp. An anthology of 25 poems that deal with life in a big city. (Rev: BL 5/15/96*; SLJ 6/96) [808.81]

11745 Yolen, Jane, and Heidi E. Y. Stemple. *Dear Mother, Dear Daughter* (3–5). Illus. 2001, Boyds Mills $15.95 (1-56397-886-5). 32pp. Using simple verses this book consists of double-page spreads; on one side is a letter from a daughter to her mother, on the other the reply. (Rev: BL 3/15/01) [811]

11746 *Yummy! Eating Through a Day* (PS–3). Ed. by Lee Bennett Hopkins. Illus. 2000, Simon & Schuster $17.00 (0-689-81755-X). 32pp. Humorous poems introduce a number of different foods, their textures, and their tastes. (Rev: BL 6/1–15/00; HBG 3/01; SLJ 8/00) [811.008]

African American Poetry

11747 Adedjouma, Davida, ed. *The Palm of My Heart: Poetry by African American Children* (1–4). Illus. by Gregory Christie. 1996, Lee & Low $15.95 (1-880000-41-5). 32pp. Twenty poems by African American children about the beauty and joy of being black. (Rev: BCCB 12/96; BL 2/15/97; SLJ 1/97) [811]

11748 Berry, James. *Isn't My Name Magical? Sister and Brother Poems* (K–3). Illus. by Shelly Hehenberger. 1999, Simon & Schuster $16.00 (0-689-80013-4). 32pp. Told from differing points of view, this is a collection of 12 poems about the everyday experiences of an African American brother and sister. (Rev: BL 2/15/99; HBG 10/99; SLJ 3/99) [811]

11749 Brooks, Gwendolyn. *Bronzeville Boys and Girls* (2–5). Illus. by Ronni Solbert. 1956, HarperCollins LB $15.89 (0-06-020651-9). 48pp. Everyday experiences of African American children growing up in Chicago are revealed in these simple poems.

11750 Bryan, Ashley. *Ashley Bryan's ABC of African American Poetry* (PS–4). Illus. 1997, Simon & Schuster $16.00 (0-689-81209-4). 32pp. A collection of charming African American poetry using the alphabet as a framework. (Rev: BL 9/1/97; HBG 3/98; SLJ 9/97) [811]

11751 Clifton, Lucille. *Everett Anderson's Goodbye* (K–2). Illus. by Ann Grifalconi. 1983, Holt $16.95 (0-8050-0235-9); paper $5.95 (0-8050-0800-4). 32pp. Poems about a young African American boy.

11752 Clifton, Lucille. *Some of the Days of Everett Anderson* (K–2). Illus. by Evaline Ness. 1987, Holt paper $6.95 (0-8050-0289-8). 32pp. A 6-year-old African American boy has a poem for each day of the week — and two for Friday. Also use: *Everett Anderson's Nine Month Long* (1978).

11753 Clinton, Catherine. *I, Too, Sing America: Three Centuries of African American Poetry* (5–10). Illus. by Stephen Alcorn. 1998, Houghton $20.00 (0-395-89599-5). 128pp. An excellent, beautifully designed anthology of African American poetry from the 1700s to the present. (Rev: HBG 3/99; SLJ 11/98) [811]

11754 Dunbar, Paul Laurence. *Jump Back, Honey* (4–6). Illus. 1999, Hyperion $16.99 (0-7868-0464-5). 40pp. Some of America's leading book illustrators have contributed to make this collection of Dunbar's most famous poems an attractive and appealing book. (Rev: BCCB 1/00; BL 9/1/99; HB 9–10/99; HBG 3/00; SLJ 10/99) [811]

11755 Giovanni, Nikki. *Knoxville, Tennessee* (PS–3). Illus. by Larry Johnson. 1994, Scholastic $14.95 (0-590-47074-4). 32pp. Nikki Giovanni re-creates the summers she spent growing up in Knoxville and the simple pleasures she enjoyed. (Rev: BCCB 7–8/94; BL 2/15/94; HB 9–10/94; SLJ 4/94) [811]

11756 Giovanni, Nikki. *The Sun Is So Quiet* (K–2). Illus. by Ashley Bryan. 1996, Holt $14.95 (0-8050-4119-2). 32pp. Thirteen poems that depict everyday occurrences, with illustrations that feature African American children in many cultures. (Rev: BL 10/15/96; SLJ 1/97) [811]

11757 Greenfield, Eloise. *Honey, I Love, and Other Love Poems* (2–4). Illus. by Diane Dillon and Leo Dillon. 1978, HarperCollins $14.95 (0-690-01334-5); paper $5.95 (0-06-443097-9). 48pp. Sixteen poems on family love and friendship as experienced by an African American girl.

11758 Greenfield, Eloise. *Nathaniel Talking* (2–5). Illus. by Jan S. Gilchrist. 1988, Writers & Readers $12.95 (0-86316-200-2). 32pp. Simple poems on an African American's recollection of childhood. (Rev: BL 12/15/89; HB 9–10/90; SLJ 8/89) [811]

11759 Grimes, Nikki. *Meet Danitra Brown* (PS–3). Illus. by Floyd Cooper. 1994, Lothrop $16.00 (0-688-12073-3). 32pp. In a series of simple poems, the friendship between two African American children is explored. (Rev: BCCB 7–8/94; BL 2/15/94; HB 7–8/94; SLJ 5/94) [811]

11760 Grimes, Nikki. *My Man Blue* (2–5). Illus. by Jerome Lagarrigue. 1999, Dial $15.99 (0-8037-2326-1). 32pp. In a series of lyrical poems, Damon describes being a child in Harlem and his friendship for an older man, Blue, whose son was killed on the streets. (Rev: BL 10/15/99; HBG 10/99; SLJ 5/99) [811]

11761 Hudson, Wade, ed. *Pass It On: African-American Poetry for Children* (PS–3). Illus. by Floyd Cooper. 1993, Scholastic $15.95 (0-590-45770-5). 32pp. A fine anthology with contributions by such writers as Langston Hughes and Gwendolyn Brooks. (Rev: BL 1/15/93*) [811]

11762 *In Daddy's Arms I Am Tall: African Americans Celebrating Fathers* (3–5). Illus. by Javaka Steptoe. 1997, Lee & Low $15.95 (1-880000-31-8). 32pp. An impressively illustrated book of poems about African American fathers and their many roles. (Rev: BL 2/15/98*; HBG 3/98; SLJ 2/98) [811]

11763 Johnson, Angela. *The Other Side: Shorter Poems* (5–7). 1998, Orchard LB $16.99 (0-531-33114-8). 64pp. This African American poet gives us glimpses of her childhood in Alabama, her family life, and her views on such issues as Vietnam, racism, and the Black Panthers. (Rev: HB 11–12/98; HBG 3/99; SLJ 9/98) [811]

11764 Lewis, J. Patrick. *Freedom Like Sunlight: Praisesongs for Black Americans* (5–12). Illus. 2000, Creative Co. $17.95 (1-56846-163-1). 40pp. This collection of original poems pays tribute to such important African Americans as Sojourner Truth, Arthur Ashe, Rosa Parks, Marian Anderson, Malcolm X, and Langston Hughes. (Rev: BL 9/15/00*; HBG 3/01; SLJ 12/00) [811]

11765 Myers, Walter Dean. *Angel to Angel: A Mother's Gift of Love* (4–7). Illus. 1998, Harper-Collins LB $15.89 (0-06-027722-X). 40pp. This picture book of poems and old photos shows African American mothers and grandmothers in loving poses with their children. (Rev: BL 2/15/98; HBG 10/98; SLJ 6/98) [811]

11766 Nikola-Lisa, W. *Bein' with You This Way* (PS–2). Illus. by Michael Bryant. 1994, Lee & Low $15.95 (1-880000-05-9). 32pp. A rap poem led by an African American girl talks about racial tolerance. (Rev: BL 7/94; SLJ 7/94) [811]

11767 Shine, Deborah S., ed. *Make a Joyful Sound: Poems for Children by African-American Poets* (2–7). Illus. by Cornelius Van Wright and Ying-Hwa Hu. 1996, Scholastic $13.95 (0-590-67432-3). 107pp. More than 60 well-illustrated poems by 23 poets are found in this collection celebrating life in general and African American life in particular. (Rev: BL 6/1/91; SLJ 10/96) [811]

11768 Strickland, Dorothy S., and Michael R. Strickland, eds. *Families: Poems Celebrating the African American Experience* (K–3). Illus. by John Ward. 1994, Boyds Mills $14.95 (1-56397-288-3); paper $7.95 (1-56397-560-2). 32pp. Poems by such writers as Gwendolyn Brooks and Langston Hughes

are featured with large acrylic paintings. (Rev: BL 2/15/95; SLJ 10/94) [811]

11769 *Words with Wings: A Treasury of African-American Poetry and Art* (4–10). Ed. by Belinda Rochelle. Illus. 2001, HarperCollins LB $16.89 (0-06-029363-2). 48pp. An outstanding collection of 20 poems by such African American writers as Langston Hughes and Alice Walker with accompanying paintings by artists like Elizabeth Catlett and Romare Bearden. (Rev: BCCB 3/01; BL 12/15/00*; SLJ 2/01) [811.008]

Animals

11770 Albert, Burton. *Journey of the Nightly Jaguar* (3–6). Illus. by Robert Roth. 1996, Simon & Schuster $16.00 (0-689-31905-3). Watercolor illustrations enhance this poem about the daily activities of a jaguar and the Mayan culture. (Rev: HB 5–6/96; SLJ 6/96) [811]

11771 Andreae, Giles. *Rumble in the Jungle* (PS). Illus. by David Wojtowycz. 1997, Little Tiger $14.95 (1-888444-08-8). A collection of poems about the animals that a small group of ants encounter as they march through the jungle. (Rev: HBG 3/98; SLJ 11/97) [811]

11772 Baylor, Byrd. *Desert Voices* (3–6). Illus. by Peter Parnall. 1981, Macmillan $14.95 (0-684-16712-3); paper $6.99 (0-689-71691-5). 32pp. A series of poems written from the viewpoint of various desert creatures.

11773 Cole, William, ed. *An Arkful of Animals: Poems for the Very Young* (3–5). Illus. by Lynn Munsinger. 1992, Houghton paper $4.95 (0-395-61618-2). 128pp. A fine collection of humorous poems about animals.

11774 Cole, William, ed. *A Zooful of Animals* (K–4). Illus. by Lynn Munsinger. 1992, Houghton $17.95 (0-395-52278-1). 96pp. This large-size volume offers animal nonsense verse and appealing watercolors. (Rev: BCCB 7–8/92; BL 6/1/92; HB 7–8/92*; SLJ 9/92) [811]

11775 *Curious Cats: In Art and Poetry* (5–7). Ed. by William Lach. Illus. 1999, Simon & Schuster $16.00 (0-689-83055-6). 48pp. A fine collection of poems about cats, including the works of such authors as Langston Hughes, William Blake, and Kate Greenaway. (Rev: BL 12/15/99; HBG 3/00; SLJ 2/00) [808.81]

11776 De Vos, Philip. *Carnival of the Animals* (1–4). Illus. by Piet Grobler. 2000, Front Street $16.95 (1-886910-47-2). 38pp. Surreal paintings accompany clever verses to bring to life the Saint-Saens musical fantasy. (Rev: BL 8/00; HBG 10/00; SLJ 7/00) [821]

11777 Edwards, Richard. *Moon Frog: Animal Poems for Young Children* (PS–3). Illus. by Sarah Fox-Davies. 1993, Candlewick $16.95 (1-56402-116-5). 48pp. Lively poems describe the sounds and shapes of various animals. (Rev: BL 1/15/93; SLJ 4/93) [811]

11778 Eliot, T. S. *Growltiger's Last Stand: And Other Poems* (3–6). Illus. by Errol LeCain. 1987, Farrar paper $4.95 (0-374-42811-5). 32pp. Three poems excerpted from Old Possum's Book of Practical Cats and made popular by the musical *Cats*. (Rev: BL 12/1/87)

11779 Evans, Dilys, ed. *Weird Pet Poems* (PS–3). Illus. by Jacqueline Rogers. 1997, Simon & Schuster paper $16.00 (0-689-80734-1). 40pp. An anthology of 14 poems about pets, common and otherwise. (Rev: BL 9/15/97; HBG 3/98; SLJ 11/97) [811]

11780 Fleischman, Paul. *I Am Phoenix: Poems for Two Voices* (3–8). Illus. by Ken Nutt. 1985, Harper-Collins paper $5.95 (0-06-446092-4). 64pp. Poems about birds, designed to be read aloud by two voices; the focus is on the pleasure of sharing poetry. (Rev: BL 12/1/85; SLJ 11/85)

11781 Fleischman, Paul. *Joyful Noise: Poems for Two Voices* (3–6). Illus. by Eric Beddows. 1988, HarperCollins LB $14.89 (0-06-021853-3); paper $5.95 (0-06-446093-2). 64pp. Poems for reading aloud that explore the lives of insects. Newbery Medal winner, 1989. (Rev: BL 2/15/88; HB 5–6/88; SLJ 2/88)

11782 Florian, Douglas. *Beast Feast* (PS–3). Illus. 1994, Harcourt $16.00 (0-15-295178-4). 48pp. Twenty-one animals are featured, with a humorous poem for each. (Rev: BCCB 7–8/94; BL 2/15/94; SLJ 5/94*) [811]

11783 Florian, Douglas. *In the Swim* (1–4). Illus. 1997, Harcourt $16.00 (0-15-201307-5). 48pp. A collection of 21 original poems about freshwater and saltwater creatures. (Rev: BCCB 5/97; BL 3/15/97; HB 7–8/97; SLJ 5/97*) [811]

11784 Florian, Douglas. *Insectlopedia* (3–5). Illus. 1998, Harcourt $16.00 (0-15-201306-7). 56pp. A well-designed book of poems about insects and spiders. (Rev: BCCB 7–8/98; BL 3/15/98; SLJ 4/98) [811]

11785 Florian, Douglas. *Lizards, Frogs, and Polliwogs* (3–5). Illus. 2001, Harcourt $16.00 (0-15-202591-X). 48pp. Playful poetry and imaginative artwork are combined in this book of short original poems about a variety of reptiles and amphibians. (Rev: BL 3/15/01*) [811]

11786 Florian, Douglas. *Mammalabilia* (2–4). Illus. 2000, Harcourt $16.00 (0-15-202167-1). 48pp. Twenty-one short, clever rhymes and inventive illustrations examine various members of the animal kingdom. (Rev: BCCB 3/00; BL 3/15/00; HB 3–4/00; HBG 10/00; SLJ 4/00) [811]

11787 Florian, Douglas. *On the Wing* (3–5). Illus. 1996, Harcourt $16.00 (0-15-200497-1). 48pp. Twenty-one poems celebrate a wide variety of birds, from hummingbirds to vultures. (Rev: BCCB 4/96; BL 3/15/96; SLJ 6/96) [811]

11788 Frost, Robert. *The Runaway* (PS–2). Illus. by Glenna Lang. 1998, Godine $17.95 (1-56792-006-3). 32pp. Lovely illustrations accompany this poem about a colt's reaction to the first snowfall. (Rev: BL 3/1/99; HBG 3/99; SLJ 3/99) [811]

11789 George, Kristine O'Connell. *Little Dog Poems* (PS–K). Illus. by June Otani. 1999, Clarion $12.00 (0-395-82266-1). 40pp. Charming watercolors illustrate these simple, original poems about a little girl and her beloved dog. (Rev: BL 3/15/99; HB 3–4/99; HBG 10/99; SLJ 5/99) [811]

11790 Greenberg, David T. *Bugs!* (K–3). Illus. by Lynn Munsinger. 1997, Little, Brown $14.95 (0-316-32574-0). 32pp. In humorous verses, a number of insects and their distinctive characteristics are introduced. (Rev: BL 9/1/97; HBG 3/98; SLJ 9/97) [811]

11791 Hoberman, Mary Ann. *A Fine Fat Pig* (K–5). Illus. by Malcah Zeldis. 1991, HarperCollins $14.95 (0-06-022425-8). These 14 poems deal with animals, their characteristics, and habits. (Rev: HB 5–6/91; SLJ 4/91) [811]

11792 Hubbell, Patricia. *Earthmates* (K–4). Illus. by Jean Cassels. 2000, Marshall Cavendish $15.95 (0-7614-5062-9). 32pp. A collection of impressive poems about such animals as a lion, rat, frog, bat, and deer. (Rev: BL 3/15/00; HBG 10/00; SLJ 3/00) [811]

11793 Hulme, Joy N. *What If? Just Wondering Poems* (K–3). Illus. by Valeri Gorbachev. 1993, Boyds Mills $14.95 (1-56397-186-0). 32pp. In 29 poems, questions about animals and their behavior are answered. (Rev: SLJ 8/93) [811]

11794 Isaacs, Anne. *Cat Up a Tree* (3–6). Illus. by Stephen Mackey. 1998, Dutton $15.99 (0-525-45994-4). A collection of poems centering on a cat up a tree and featuring the points of view of several participants including a fire fighter and a passing balloonist. (Rev: BCCB 11/98; HBG 3/99; SLJ 11/98) [811]

11795 Johnston, Tony. *It's About Dogs* (2–4). 2000, Harcourt $16.00 (0-15-202022-5). 48pp. Many short, mostly free-verse poems typify the moods and behavior of various canines, domesticated and not. (Rev: BL 3/15/00; HBG 10/00; SLJ 6/00) [811]

11796 Levy, Constance. *I'm Going to Pet a Worm Today and Other Poems* (3–5). Illus. by Ronald Himler. 1991, Macmillan $14.00 (0-689-50535-3). 48pp. This book of original poems celebrates such creatures of nature as spiders, worms, and beetles. (Rev: BCCB 2/92*; BL 11/15/92; SLJ 10/91) [811]

11797 Lewis, J. Patrick. *A Hippopotamusn't and Other Animal Verses* (K–4). Illus. by Victoria Chess. 1994, Puffin paper $5.99 (0-14-055273-1). 40pp. Witty verse describing 35 animals. (Rev: BCCB 7–8/90; BL 5/1/90*; HB 5–6/90*; SLJ 5/90*) [811]

11798 Lewis, J. Patrick. *The Little Buggers* (K–4). Illus. by Victoria Chess. 1998, Dial LB $15.89 (0-8037-1770-9). 32pp. Twenty-four amusing, imaginative poems about insects and their activities. (Rev: BCCB 7–8/98; BL 8/98; HBG 10/98; SLJ 8/98) [811]

11799 Livingston, Myra Cohn, ed. *Cat Poems* (3–6). Illus. by Trina S. Hyman. 1987, Holiday LB $15.95 (0-8234-0631-8). 32pp. Poems that reflect the many moods of felines. (Rev: BCCB 6/87; BL 6/1/87; SLJ 5/87)

11800 Livingston, Myra Cohn, ed. *If the Owl Calls Again: A Collection of Owl Poems* (4–7). Illus. by

Antonio Frasconi. 1990, Macmillan $13.95 (0-689-50501-9). 128pp. A wide range of owl poems from various sources. (Rev: BCCB 1/91; BL 10/1/90; SLJ 1/91) [808.81]

11801 Livingston, Myra Cohn, ed. *If You Ever Meet a Whale* (1–4). Illus. by Leonard Everett Fisher. 1992, Holiday LB $14.95 (0-8234-0940-6). 32pp. Seventeen whale poems with full-color paintings. (Rev: BL 11/15/92) [811]

11802 McLoughland, Beverly. *A Hippo's a Heap and Other Animal Poems* (PS–3). Illus. by Laura Rader. 1993, Boyds Mills $14.95 (1-56397-017-1). 32pp. A collection of nonsense poems and chirpy illustrations. (Rev: BL 1/15/93; SLJ 3/93) [811]

11803 Nichol, Barbara. *Biscuits in the Cupboard* (K–4). Illus. by Philippe Beha. 1998, Stoddart $12.95 (0-7737-3025-7). 32pp. A delightful collection of poems about dogs, written entirely from their point of view. (Rev: SLJ 3/98) [808]

11804 Nichols, Grace. *Asana and the Animals* (PS–1). Illus. by Sarah Adams. 1997, Candlewick $16.99 (0-7636-0145-4). 32pp. A collection of 17 simple verses about all the animals that Asana likes, including a spider and a giraffe. (Rev: BL 6/1–15/97; SLJ 7/97) [811]

11805 O'Huigin, Sean. *Ghost Horse of the Mounties* (5–7). Illus. by Barry Moser. 1991, Godine $14.95 (0-87923-721-X). 72pp. A long poem about a black midsummer night in 1874 on the empty plains of the Northwest Territories in Canada. (Rev: BCCB 7–8/91; BL 5/1/91) [811]

11806 Polisar, Barry L. *Insect Soup: Bug Poems* (K–4). Illus. by David Clark. 1999, Rainbow Morning Music $14.95 (0-938663-22-4). Fifteen original poems about insects that are sometimes humorous, sometimes gross, and sometimes amazing. (Rev: SLJ 8/99) [811]

11807 Prelutsky, Jack, ed. *The Beauty of the Beast: Poems from the Animal Kingdom* (3–7). Illus. by Meilo So. 1997, Knopf $25.00 (0-679-87058-X). 101pp. A wonderful, beautifully illustrated collection of more than 200 animal poems by 20th-century writers whose works are arranged by animal genus. (Rev: BL 9/15/97; HBG 3/98; SLJ 1/98*) [811]

11808 Prelutsky, Jack. *The Dragons Are Singing Tonight* (K–4). Illus. by Peter Sis. 1993, Greenwillow $15.89 (0-688-12511-5). 40pp. These 17 poems all deal with the pastimes and problems that dragons face in their everyday life. (Rev: BL 9/1/93*; HB 9–10/93; SLJ 10/93*) [811]

11809 Prelutsky, Jack. *The Snopp on the Sidewalk and Other Poems* (3–6). Illus. by Byron Barton. 1977, Greenwillow LB $15.93 (0-688-84084-1). 32pp. Twelve wildly imaginative poems about strange imaginary beasts that bring to mind the Jabberwocky.

11810 Prelutsky, Jack. *Tyrannosaurus Was a Beast* (2–5). Illus. by Arnold Lobel. 1988, Morrow paper $4.95 (0-688-11569-1). 32pp. Poems and watercolor portraits bring dinosaurs to life. (Rev: BCCB 9/88; BL 8/88; HB 9–10/88)

11811 Schertle, Alice. *I Am the Cat* (2–4). Illus. by Mark Buehner. 1999, Lothrop LB $15.93 (0-688-13154-9). 40pp. All sorts of cats — nasty and nice — are featured in this book of original poems. (Rev: BL 4/1/99; HB 9–10/99; HBG 10/99; SLJ 6/99) [811]

11812 Sierra, Judy. *Antarctic Antics: A Book of Penguin Poems* (PS–2). Illus. by Jose Aruego and Ariane Dewey. 1998, Harcourt $16.00 (0-15-201006-8). 32pp. Thirteen poems of varying length and accompanying pictures describe the behavior and play of baby penguins in their Antarctic home. (Rev: BL 5/1/98; HBG 10/98; SLJ 5/98) [811]

11813 Singer, Marilyn. *Turtle in July* (K–3). Illus. by Jerry Pinkney. 1989, Macmillan paper $14.95 (0-02-782881-6). 32pp. This book contains animal poems arranged by season of the year. (Rev: BCCB 9/89*; BL 10/15/89*; HB 1–2/90; SLJ 11/89) [811]

11814 Spinelli, Eileen. *Song for the Whooping Crane* (PS–3). Illus. by Elsa Warnick. 2000, Eerdmans $16.00 (0-8028-5172-X). 32pp. A poem that celebrates the endangered whooping crane, its beauty, and its life cycle. (Rev: BL 10/1/00; HBG 3/01; SLJ 3/01) [811]

11815 Tiller, Ruth. *Cats Vanish Slowly* (K–3). Illus. by Laura L. Seeley. 1995, Peachtree $16.95 (1-56145-106-1). 32pp. Twelve poems about the cats (including B.P., for "bad penny") that are found on the farm of the author's grandmother. (Rev: BL 1/1–15/96; SLJ 1/96) [811]

11816 Whipple, Laura, ed. *Eric Carle's Animals Animals* (PS–3). Illus. by Eric Carle. 1989, Putnam $21.99 (0-399-21744-4). Eric Carle's collages illustrate various writers' poems, each dealing with an animal. (Rev: BCCB 10/89*; BL 9/1/89*; HB 11–12/89; SLJ 11/89) [811]

11817 Wise, William. *Dinosaurs Forever* (PS–3). Illus. by Lynn Munsinger. 2000, Dial $15.99 (0-8037-2114-5). 40pp. In a series of lighthearted illustrations and fun but informative poems, a stegosaurus tourist visits a dinosaur exhibit at the American Museum of Natural History in New York City. (Rev: BL 5/15/00; HBG 10/00; SLJ 7/00) [811]

11818 Yolen, Jane, ed. *Alphabestiary: Animal Poems from A to Z* (2–4). Illus. by Allan Eitzen. 1995, Boyds Mills $16.95 (1-56397-222-0). 64pp. A collection of animal poems, mostly nonsense verse. (Rev: BL 12/15/94; SLJ 4/95) [808]

11819 Yolen, Jane. *The Originals* (3–6). Illus. by Ted Lewin. 1998, Putnam $15.95 (0-399-23007-6). 32pp. In poetry and painting, this account celebrates animals that have hardly changed through time, like the red jungle fowl and the Exmoor pony. (Rev: BL 2/1/98; HBG 10/98; SLJ 3/98) [811]

11820 Yolen, Jane. *Sea Watch* (3–5). Illus. by Ted Lewin. 1996, Putnam $15.95 (0-399-22734-2). 32pp. Unusual sea creatures are pictured in watercolors and poetry. (Rev: BCCB 6/96; BL 6/1–15/96; SLJ 6/96) [811]

Haiku

11821 *In the Eyes of the Cat: Japanese Poetry for All Seasons* (PS–3). Trans. by Tze-si Huang. Illus. by Demi. 1994, Holt paper $6.95 (0-8050-3383-1). 80pp. These short Japanese poems, known as haiku, use words and images appreciated by young readers. (Rev: BCCB 5/92; BL 4/15/92; SLJ 5/92) [895.6]

11822 Lewis, J. Patrick. *Black Swan/White Crow* (K–4). Illus. by Christopher Manson. 1995, Simon & Schuster $15.00 (0-689-31899-5). 32pp. Thirteen haiku poems accompanied by dramatic woodcuts. (Rev: BL 10/15/95; SLJ 11/95) [811]

11823 Livingston, Myra Cohn. *Cricket Never Does: A Collection of Haiku and Tanka* (5–8). Illus. 1997, Simon & Schuster $15.00 (0-689-81123-3). 48pp. Seasonal changes are explored in more than 60 short haiku and tanka. (Rev: BL 3/1/97; SLJ 4/97) [811]

11824 Shannon, George. *Spring: A Haiku Story* (K–3). Illus. by Malcah Zeldis. 1996, Greenwillow $16.00 (0-688-13888-8). 32pp. Incidents that occur during a spring walk are depicted in 14 translated Japanese haiku. (Rev: BL 4/15/96; HB 3–4/96; SLJ 5/96) [895.6]

11825 *Stone Bench in an Empty Park* (5–12). Ed. by Paul B. Janeczko. Illus. 2000, Orchard LB $16.99 (0-531-33259-4). 40pp. An inspired collection of haiku from variety of poets illustrated with stunning black-and-white photographs. (Rev: BCCB 6/00; BL 3/15/00*; HB 3–4/00; HBG 10/00; SLJ 3/00) [811]

Holidays

11826 *Bright Star Shining: Poems for Christmas* (3–8). Ed. by Michael Harrison and Christopher Stuart-Clark. Illus. 1998, Eerdmans $15.00 (0-8028-5177-0). 48pp. Illustrated by three different artists, this is a fine collection of 32 Christmas poems. (Rev: BL 9/1/98; HBG 3/99) [808.81]

11827 Carlstrom, Nancy White. *Who Said Boo? Halloween Poems for the Very Young* (PS–1). Illus. by R. W. Alley. 1995, Simon & Schuster $14.00 (0-689-80308-7). 32pp. Scary poems that celebrate the mystery and menace of Halloween. (Rev: BL 9/15/95; SLJ 9/95) [811]

11828 Coatsworth, Elizabeth. *Song of the Camels: A Christmas Poem* (PS–3). Illus. by Anna Vojtech. 1997, North-South LB $15.88 (1-55858-812-4). 24pp. This is a Christmas poem narrated by the camels that carry the three kings to Bethlehem. (Rev: BL 11/15/97; HBG 3/98; SLJ 10/97) [811]

11829 Foster, John, comp. *Let's Celebrate: Festival Poems* (3–6). Illus. 1997, Oxford paper $11.95 (0-192-76085-8). 111pp. This collection of 85 poems celebrates a variety of holidays around the world. (Rev: SLJ 7/90) [811]

11830 Ghigna, Charles, and Debra Ghigna. *Christmas Is Coming* (PS–3). Illus. by Mary O'Keefe. 2000, Charlesbridge $15.95 (0-88106-113-1). 32pp.

A number of Christmas preparations, like selecting a tree and baking cookies, are depicted in these 27 original poems with expressive illustrations. (Rev: BL 9/1/00; HBG 3/01) [811]

11831 Harness, Cheryl. *Papa's Christmas Gift: Around the World on the Night Before Christmas* (1–3). Illus. 1995, Simon & Schuster paper $15.00 (0-689-80344-3). 32pp. In this poem, Christmas activities around the world are described on the night that "A Visit from Saint Nicholas" took place. (Rev: BL 9/15/95) [811]

11832 Hopkins, Lee Bennett, ed. *Hey-How for Halloween!* (3–6). Illus. by Janet McCaffery. 1974, Harcourt $12.95 (0-15-233900-0). 32pp. A varied and appealing selection of poems about happenings and creatures associated with Halloween.

11833 Horton, Joan. *Halloween Hoots and Howls* (2–5). Illus. 1999, Holt $15.95 (0-8050-5805-2). 32pp. A collection of amusing — sometimes wacky — poems about Halloween. (Rev: BCCB 9/99; BL 9/1/99; HBG 3/00; SLJ 10/99) [811]

11834 Lansky, Bruce, et al. *Happy Birthday to Me! Kids Pick the Funniest Birthday Poems* (2–5). Illus. by Jack Lindstrom. 1998, Meadowbrook Pr. $8.95 (0-671-57703-4). 27pp. Nine poets are represented in this joyous collection of 21 poems that celebrate birthdays. (Rev: SLJ 5/98) [811]

11835 Livingston, Myra Cohn, ed. *Celebrations* (1–4). Illus. by Leonard Everett Fisher. 1985, Holiday LB $16.95 (0-8234-0550-8); paper $6.95 (0-8234-0654-7). 32pp. A handsome book of verse illustrating 16 celebrations, such as Valentine's Day, birthdays, and Easter. (Rev: BCCB 4/85; BL 4/1/85; HB 5–6/85)

11836 Livingston, Myra Cohn, ed. *Christmas Poems* (PS–3). Illus. by Trina S. Hyman. 1984, Holiday LB $15.95 (0-8234-0508-7). 32pp. A collection of 18 poems, half of which were commissioned for the volume.

11837 Livingston, Myra Cohn, ed. *Poems for Jewish Holidays* (K–6). Illus. by Lloyd Bloom. 1986, Holiday LB $15.95 (0-8234-0606-7). 32pp. Poems that contain the essence of major Jewish holidays. (Rev: BCCB 2/87; BL 11/1/86; HB 1–2/87)

11838 Livingston, Myra Cohn, ed. *Valentine Poems* (3–6). Illus. 1987, Holiday LB $15.95 (0-8234-0587-7). 32pp. Sprightly poems from established names and modern ones, too. (Rev: BL 1/15/87; SLJ 12/86)

11839 Moore, Clement Clarke. *The Night Before Christmas* (PS–3). Illus. by Tomie dePaola. 1980, Holiday LB $16.95 (0-8234-0414-5); paper $6.95 (0-8234-0417-X). 32pp. A lovely edition of this popular and loved Christmas poem. Another edition is: Illus. by Anita Lobel (Knopf 1996).

11840 Moore, Clement Clarke. *The Night Before Christmas* (PS–1). Illus. by Cheryl Harness. 1990, Random $8.99 (0-394-82698-1). 40pp. A traditional treatment of the classic holiday poem. (Rev: BL 11/1/90; HB 11–12/90) [811]

11841 Moore, Clement Clarke. *The Night Before Christmas* (PS–3). Illus. by Ted Rand. 1995, North-South LB $16.88 (1-55858-466-8). 32pp. A large-format picture book with new illustrations for the classic poem, each using a double-page spread. (Rev: BL 10/15/95) [871]

11842 Moore, Clement Clarke. *The Night Before Christmas* (PS–3). Illus. by Ruth Sanderson. 1997, Little, Brown $13.95 (0-316-57963-7). 32pp. An old-fashioned version of this classic poem. (Rev: BL 9/15/97; HBG 3/98; SLJ 10/97) [811]

11843 Moore, Clement Clarke. *The Night Before Christmas* (PS–2). Illus. by Jan Brett. 1998, Putnam LB $16.99 (0-399-23190-0). This version of the classic Christmas poem contains illustrations of a Victorian house, an old-world Santa, and two stowaway elves. (Rev: HBG 3/99; SLJ 10/98) [811]

11844 Moore, Clement Clarke. *The Night Before Christmas* (PS–1). Ed. by Cooper Edens and Harold Darling. Illus. 1998, Chronicle $16.95 (0-8118-1712-1). 44pp. This new edition of the classic poem uses illustrations that originally appeared between 1890 and 1928. (Rev: BL 10/1/98; HBG 3/99; SLJ 10/98) [811]

11845 Moore, Clement Clarke. *The Night Before Christmas* (PS–2). Illus. by Tasha Tudor. 1999, Little, Brown $14.95 (0-316-85579-0). Wild and domestic animals on a Vermont farm form an important part of the illustrations in this version of the classic poem. (Rev: HBG 3/00; SLJ 10/99) [811]

11846 Moore, Clement Clarke. *The Night Before Christmas* (PS–3). Illus. by Bruce Whatley. 1999, HarperCollins LB $16.89 (0-06-028380-7). 40pp. The pictures in this attractive edition of the favorite poem depict events from the father's point of view. (Rev: BL 9/1/99*; HBG 3/00; SLJ 10/99) [811]

11847 Moore, Clement Clarke. *The Night Before Christmas: A Visit from St. Nicholas* (PS–1). Illus. by Max Grover. 1999, Harcourt $16.00 (0-15-201713-5). 32pp. In this version of the famous poem, the pictures are all of the present day, with automobiles on the streets and Christmas lights in the houses. (Rev: BL 9/1/99; HBG 3/00; SLJ 10/99) [811]

11848 Moore, Clement Clarke. *The Night Before Christmas: Or, a Visit of St. Nicholas* (PS–3). Illus. 1989, Putnam $17.95 (0-399-21614-6). 32pp. This handsomely produced edition of the famous poem was illustrated years ago by a now-forgotten artist. (Rev: BL 9/15/89) [811]

11849 Moore, Clement Clarke. *The Teddy Bears' Night Before Christmas* (PS–K). Illus. by Monica Stevenson. 1999, Scholastic $12.95 (0-590-03243-7). 40pp. Photographs of stuffed animals in snowy scenes illustrate this version of the classic rhyme. (Rev: BL 9/1/99; HBG 3/00; SLJ 10/99) [811]

11850 Prelutsky, Jack. *It's Thanksgiving* (PS–4). Illus. by Marylin Hafner. 1982, Greenwillow $15.89 (0-688-00442-3). 48pp. Twelve poems covering various aspects of Thanksgiving.

11851 Prelutsky, Jack. *It's Valentine's Day* (1–4). Illus. by Yossi Abolafia. 1985, Scholastic paper $2.50 (0-590-40979-4). 48pp. Bright, humorous poems in celebration of love and Valentine's Day.

11852 *A Small Treasury of Easter: Poems and Prayers* (K–4). Illus. by Susan Spellman. 1997, Boyds Mills $8.95 (1-56397-647-1). 32pp. An illustrated collection of secular and religious Easter poems, divided into two parts: "A Time to Play" and "A Time to Pray." (Rev: SLJ 7/97) [811]

11853 Thomas, Dylan. *A Child's Christmas in Wales* (5–8). Illus. by Trina S. Hyman. 1985, Holiday LB $16.95 (0-8234-0565-6). 48pp. A prose poem about the poet's childhood in a small Welsh village. Another edition is: Illus. by Edward Ardizzone (1980, Godine paper).

Humorous Poetry

11854 Ahlberg, Allan. *The Mysteries of Zigomar: Poems and Stories* (4–6). Illus. 1997, Candlewick $17.99 (0-7636-0352-X). 64pp. A collection of zany poems and stories sure to delight readers who enjoy the absurd and whimsical. (Rev: BL 12/1/97; HBG 3/98; SLJ 11/97) [828]

11855 Base, Graeme. *Lewis Carroll's Jabberwocky: A Book of Brillig Dioramas* (3–5). Illus. 1996, Abrams $19.95 (0-8109-3520-1). 14pp. Three-dimensional dinosaurs are used to illustrate Lewis Carroll's *Jabberwocky*. (Rev: BL 12/15/96) [811]

11856 Billings, John. *My Pet Crocodile and Other Slightly Outrageous Verse* (PS–3). Illus. by Janette Todd. 1993, Chokecherry $16.95 (1-884035-55-8). 128pp. Humorous poems on such subjects as bungee jumping, nose picking, and bubble gum. (Rev: BL 1/1/94) [811]

11857 Brewton, Sara, et al., eds. *Of Quarks, Quasars and Other Quirks: Quizzical Poems for the Supersonic Age* (5–8). Illus. by Quentin Blake. 1977, HarperCollins LB $13.89 (0-690-04885-8). 128pp. Contemporary poems that poke fun at such modern innovations as transplants and water beds.

11858 Brown, Calef. *Dutch Sneakers and Flea Keepers: 14 More Stories* (3–5). Illus. 2000, Houghton $15.00 (0-618-05183-X). 32pp. A collection of original poems that introduce the reader to several odd and eccentric characters, such as the Flea Keepers, who train fleas for cash. (Rev: BCCB 7–8/00; BL 4/1/00; HBG 10/00; SLJ 4/00) [811.54]

11859 Bush, Timothy. *Ferocious Girls, Steamroller Boys, and Other Poems in Between* (1–4). Illus. by author. 2000, Orchard LB $17.99 (0-531-33250-0). A funny book that uses seven poems to explore unusual boys and girls and their strange behavior. (Rev: HBG 10/00; SLJ 7/00) [811]

11860 Carroll, Lewis. *Jabberwocky* (1–4). Illus. by Graeme Base. 1989, Abrams $16.95 (0-8109-1150-7). 32pp. Carroll's nonsense poem is given a fresh treatment with illustrations picturing a medieval locale. (Rev: SLJ 8/89) [821]

11861 Carryl, Charles E. *The Walloping Window-Blind* (K–2). Illus. by Jim LaMarche. 1994, Lothrop $16.00 (0-688-12517-4). 24pp. A nonsense verse about a fantastic sea voyage illustrated in double-page spreads. (Rev: BL 5/1/94; SLJ 7/94) [811]

11862 Ciardi, John. *Doodle Soup* (3–6). Illus. by Merle Macht. 1992, Houghton paper $6.95 (0-395-61617-4). 64pp. The gentle wit of the poet shows up in these 38 tongue-in-cheek verses. (Rev: BCCB 10/85; BL 2/1/86; SLJ 1/86)

11863 Ciardi, John. *The Hopeful Trout and Other Limericks* (2–6). Illus. by Susan Meddaugh. 1992, Houghton paper $5.95 (0-395-61616-6). 52pp. Forty-one humorous limericks with wacky drawings. (Rev: BL 3/15/89; SLJ 3/89)

11864 Ciardi, John. *You Read to Me, I'll Read to You* (4–6). Illus. by Edward Gorey. 1987, Harper-Collins paper $7.95 (0-06-446060-6). 64pp. A collection of original verse for both adults and children.

11865 Cole, William, ed. *Poem Stew* (2–6). Illus. by Karen Ann Weinhaus. 1981, HarperCollins $7.66 (0-397-31963-0); paper $4.95 (0-06-440136-7). 96pp. A collection of 57 witty poems about food.

11866 Dakos, Kalli. *The Bug in Teacher's Coffee: And Other School Poems* (K–2). Illus. by Mike Reed. Series: An I Can Read Book. 1999, Harper-Collins LB $14.89 (0-06-027940-0). 38pp. For beginning readers, a book of humorous poetry with zany illustrations that use everyday objects found in a school. (Rev: HBG 3/00; SLJ 12/99) [811]

11867 Dakos, Kalli. *Don't Read This Book, Whatever You Do! More Poems About School* (2–4). Illus. by G. Brian Karas. 1993, Macmillan LB $15.00 (0-02-725582-4). 64pp. Classroom sketches in quick, easy lines. (Rev: BL 2/15/93; SLJ 4/93) [811]

11868 Duggan, Paul. *Two Skeletons on the Telephone: And Other Poems from Tough City* (3–6). Illus. by Daniel Sylvestre. 1999, Millbrook LB $20.40 (0-7613-1451-2). A humorous collection of original poems that feature such subjects as skeletons, werewolves, and vampires. (Rev: HBG 3/00; SLJ 11/99) [811]

11869 Fitch, Sheree. *If You Could Wear My Sneakers! A Book About Children's Rights* (K–3). Illus. by Darcia Labrosse. 1998, Firefly $14.95 (1-55209-275-5); paper $5.95 (1-55209-259-3). 32pp. Humorous poems about animals in ridiculous situations are used to interpret some of the articles in the United Nations Convention on the Rights of Children. (Rev: SLJ 3/99) [811]

11870 Florian, Douglas. *Bing Bang Boing* (4–6). Illus. 1994, Harcourt $16.00 (0-15-233770-9). 144pp. A lighthearted, imaginative collection of short, humorous verses. (Rev: BCCB 11/94; BL 12/1/94; SLJ 11/94) [811]

11871 Florian, Douglas. *Laugh-Eteria* (3–5). Illus. 1999, Harcourt $17.00 (0-15-202084-5). 158pp. A collection of 150 original, humorous poems that will appeal to a child's sometimes gross sense of humor. (Rev: BCCB 4/99; BL 3/15/99; HBG 10/99; SLJ 6/99) [811]

11872 Greenberg, David T. *Whatever Happened to Humpty Dumpty? And Other Surprising Sequels to Mother Goose Rhymes* (3–6). Illus. by S. D. Schindler. 1999, Little, Brown $14.95 (0-316-32767-0). An outrageous book of sequels to 20 Mother Goose rhymes in which, for example, Jack and Jill accidentally flush themselves down a toilet. (Rev: HBG 10/99; SLJ 8/99) [811]

11873 Greenfield, Eloise. *I Can Draw a Weeposaur and Other Dinosaurs* (K–3). Illus. by Jan S. Gilchrist. 2001, Greenwillow LB $14.89 (0-688-17635-6). 31pp. A group of poems about fanciful, imaginary dinosaurs along with drawings of them by the girl who dreamed them up. (Rev: SLJ 3/01) [811]

11874 Grimes, Nikki. *Is It Far to Zanzibar? Poems About Tanzania* (PS–3). Illus. by Betsy Lewin. 2000, Lothrop LB $15.89 (0-688-13158-1). 32pp. A series of rhyming, singsong verses that fancifully describe life in Tanzania. (Rev: BL 3/15/00; HBG 10/00; SLJ 5/00) [811]

11875 Hort, Lenny. *Tie Your Socks and Clap Your Feet: Mixed Up Poems* (K–3). Illus. by Stephen Kroninger. 2000, Simon & Schuster $16.00 (0-689-83195-1). 40pp. A collection of original nonsense verses that will delight young audiences. (Rev: BCCB 6/00*; BL 3/15/00; HBG 10/00; SLJ 4/00) [811.54]

11876 *Imagine That! Poems of Never-Was* (K–3). Ed. by Jack Prelutsky. Illus. by Kevin Hawkes. 1998, Knopf LB $19.99 (0-679-98206-X). 45pp. A collection of 50 humorous poems by such authors as Louis Carroll, Karla Kuskin, Jane Yolen, and John Ciardi. (Rev: BL 10/15/98; HBG 3/99; SLJ 11/98) [811]

11877 Kennedy, X. J. *Brats* (3–5). Illus. by James Watts. 1986, Macmillan $14.00 (0-689-50392-X). Short poems showing bratty kids getting their just desserts. (Rev: BCCB 7–8/86; BL 7/86; SLJ 8/86)

11878 Kennedy, X. J. *Fresh Brats* (3–5). Illus. by James Watts. 1990, Macmillan $14.00 (0-689-50499-3). 48pp. Short, snappy poems about bratty kids. (Rev: BCCB 3/90; BL 5/1/90*; HB 3–4/90; SLJ 7/90) [811]

11879 Kennedy, X. J. *Uncle Switch: Loony Limericks* (1–3). Illus. by John O'Brien. 1997, Simon & Schuster $15.00 (0-689-80967-0). 32pp. Twenty-two funny limericks involving the dimwitted Uncle Switch. (Rev: BCCB 4/97; BL 5/1/97; SLJ 4/97) [811]

11880 Korman, Gordon, and Bernice Korman. *The D-Poems of Jeremy Bloom: A Collection of Poems About School, Homework, and Life (Sort of)* (4–6). 1992, Scholastic paper $3.50 (0-590-44819-6). 98pp. The engaging and funny poems of rambunctious sixth-grader Jeremy Bloom. (Rev: BL 1/15/93; SLJ 2/93) [811]

11881 Lansky, Bruce, ed. *A Bad Case of the Giggles: Kids' Favorite Funny Poems* (2–5). Illus. by Stephen Carpenter. 1994, Meadowbrook Pr. $14.00 (0-88166-213-5). 132pp. A great collection of humorous poems that includes puns, tongue twisters, and parodies, many by well-known writers. (Rev: BL 11/15/94; SLJ 2/95) [811]

11882 Lansky, Bruce, ed. *Miles of Smiles: Kids Pick the Funniest Poems, Book 3* (2–6). Illus. by Stephen Carpenter. 1998, Meadowbrook Pr. $16.00 (0-88166-313-1). 115pp. A collection of 72 humorous poems some of them earthy in content and dealing with subjects such as underwear and bathroom humor. (Rev: HBG 3/99; SLJ 11/98) [811]

11883 Lear, Edward. *A Was Once an Apple Pie* (PS–2). Illus. by Julie Lacome. 1997, Candlewick paper $5.99 (0-7636-0103-9). 32pp. This book of nonsense verse is complemented by buoyant illustrations. (Rev: BL 1/15/92; SLJ 3/92) [821]

11884 Lear, Edward. *Complete Nonsense Book of Edward Lear* (4–6). Illus. by author. n.d., Dover paper $7.95 (0-486-20167-8). 287pp. Verse, prose, drawings, alphabets, and other amusing absurdities.

11885 Lear, Edward. *Daffy Down Dillies* (PS–3). Illus. by John O'Brien. 1992, Boyds Mills $14.95 (1-56397-007-4). 32pp. An edition that captures in drawings the irreverence that Lear's limericks demand. (Rev: BL 1/15/92; SLJ 3/92) [821]

11886 Lear, Edward. *Nonsense Songs* (K–3). Illus. by Bee Willey. 1997, Simon & Schuster $16.00 (0-689-81369-4). 40pp. Imaginative illustrations accompany four of Lear's most famous nonsense poems, including "The Owl and the Pussycat" and "The Jumblies." (Rev: BL 4/1/97; SLJ 6/97) [811]

11887 Lear, Edward. *The Owl and the Pussycat* (PS–1). Illus. by Jan Brett. 1991, Putnam $15.95 (0-399-21925-0). 32pp. Beautiful double-page spreads enhance the enchantment of this retelling. (Rev: BL 3/1/91*; SLJ 2/91*) [821]

11888 Lear, Edward. *Owl and the Pussycat* (PS–1). Illus. by Ian Beck. 1996, Simon & Schuster $13.00 (0-689-81032-6). 30pp. Full and double-page spreads are used to illustrate this classic poem. (Rev: BL 10/1/96; SLJ 12/96) [821]

11889 Lear, Edward. *The Owl and the Pussycat* (PS–2). Illus. by Louise Voce. 1997, Candlewick paper $5.99 (0-7636-0336-8). 32pp. Cartoon-style illustrations adorn this retelling of the classic Lear poem. (Rev: BL 1/1/91; SLJ 12/91) [821]

11890 Lear, Edward. *The Owl and the Pussycat* (PS–1). Illus. by James Marshall. 1998, Harper-Collins LB $15.89 (0-06-205011-7). 32pp. Fresh and funny artwork from James Marshall highlight this edition of the classic nonsense poem. (Rev: BL 2/1/99; HB 3–4/99; HBG 10/99; SLJ 12/98) [821]

11891 Lear, Edward. *The Quangle Wangle's Hat* (PS–1). Illus. by Janet Stevens. 1988, Harcourt $12.95 (0-15-264450-4); paper $6.00 (0-15-201478-0). 32pp. This classic nonsense poem is illustrated in sassy full color. (Rev: BL 10/1/88)

11892 Lee, Dennis. *The Ice Cream Store* (PS–3). Illus. by David McPhail. 1992, Scholastic $14.95 (0-590-45861-2). 64pp. A collection of sassy and bright poems, with occasional flashes of schoolyard humor. (Rev: BCCB 12/92; BL 11/15/92; SLJ 9/92*) [811]

11893 Lewis, J. Patrick. *Boshblobberbosh* (4–6). Illus. 1998, Harcourt $18.00 (0-15-201949-9). 40pp. Sixteen whimsical verses are included in this collection that pays tribute to Edward Lear, the English master of nonsense verse. (Rev: BCCB 12/98; BL 12/1/98; HBG 3/99; SLJ 11/98) [821]

11894 Lewis, J. Patrick. *Good Mousekeeping: And Other Animal Home Poems* (PS–3). Illus. by Lisa Desimini. 2001, Simon & Schuster $16.00 (0-689-

83161-7). 32pp. These original humorous poems speculate on the kinds of homes different animals might live in if they had their choice. (Rev: BL 3/15/01) [811]

11895 Lewis, J. Patrick. *The La-di-da Hare* (K–4). Illus. by Diana C. Bluthenthal. 1997, Simon & Schuster $16.00 (0-689-31925-8). In this nonsense rhyme, Honeypot Bear and Commodore Mouse journey to an island where they meet the La-di-da Hare. (Rev: SLJ 5/97) [811]

11896 Livingston, Myra Cohn, ed. *Lots of Limericks* (5–8). Illus. by Rebecca Perry. 1991, Simon & Schuster $16.00 (0-689-50531-0). 128pp. Nonsense limericks and wordplay abound in this collection. (Rev: BL 10/1/91; SLJ 1/92) [821]

11897 McNaughton, Colin. *Making Friends with Frankenstein: A Book of Monstrous Poems and Pictures* (2–4). Illus. 1994, Candlewick $19.99 (1-56402-308-7). 90pp. Nonsense verses that make fun of monsters and the macabre with puns, word play, and outrageous rhymes. (Rev: BCCB 4/94; BL 5/15/94*; HBG 3/01; SLJ 5/94) [821]

11898 McNaughton, Colin. *Who's Been Sleeping in My Porridge? A Book of Wacky Poems and Pictures* (K–3). Illus. by author. 1998, Candlewick $16.99 (0-7636-0106-3). 93pp. A collection of nonsense poems with slapstick illustrations that are bound to amuse grade-schoolers. (Rev: HBG 3/99; SLJ 10/98) [811]

11899 McNaughton, Colin. *Wish You Were Here (And I Wasn't): A Book of Poems and Pictures for Globe Trotters* (3–5). Illus. by author. 2000, Candlewick $16.99 (0-7636-0271-X). 60pp. A humorous collection of poems about traveling and visiting various places. (Rev: BCCB 5/00; HBG 10/00; SLJ 6/00) [811]

11900 Mahy, Margaret. *Bubble Trouble and Other Poems and Stories* (3–6). Illus. 1992, Macmillan LB $13.95 (0-689-50557-4). 70pp. Nonsense poems and stories made for reading aloud. (Rev: BL 12/1/92; SLJ 10/92) [828]

11901 Michelson, Richard. *Animals That Ought to Be: Poems About Imaginary Pets* (K–3). Illus. by Leonard Baskin. 1996, Simon & Schuster paper $16.00 (0-689-80635-3). 24pp. Poems about imaginary animals, like the Nightmare Scarer who protects one from under the bed. (Rev: BCCB 10/96; BL 10/15/96; HB 11–12/96; SLJ 9/96) [811]

11902 Morrison, Lillian. *I Scream, You Scream: A Feast of Food Rhymes* (3–5). Illus. 1997, August House $12.95 (0-87483-495-3). 96pp. Food is the subject of this humorous collection of rhymes, autograph-book verses, tongue twisters, and jokes. (Rev: BL 11/15/97; HBG 3/98; SLJ 11/97) [811]

11903 Opie, Iona, and Peter Opie, eds. *I Saw Esau: The Schoolchild's Pocket Book* (2–5). Illus. by Maurice Sendak. 1992, Candlewick $19.99 (1-56402-046-0). 160pp. Schoolyard folk rhymes that are absurd, fierce, vulgar, and compelling. (Rev: BCCB 5/92*; BL 4/15/92*; SLJ 6/92*) [811]

11904 Paraskevas, Betty. *Gracie Graves and the Kids from Room 402* (1–3). Illus. by Michael Paraskevas. 1995, Harcourt $15.00 (0-15-200321-

5). 40pp. A collection of 30 silly poems, each related to Miss Graves and her crazy classroom. (Rev: BL 12/1/95; SLJ 11/95) [811]

11905 Paraskevas, Betty. *Junior Kroll and Company* (K–3). Illus. by Michael Paraskevas. 1994, Harcourt $13.95 (0-15-292855-3). 40pp. A mischievous, shrewd toddler has a series of adventures, like learning to waltz with Cousin Blanche. (Rev: BL 4/15/94; SLJ 5/94) [811]

11906 *Poetry for Young People: Lewis Carroll* (3–5). Ed. by Edward Mendelson. Illus. 2001, Sterling $14.95 (0-8069-5541-4). 48pp. The poetry that is scattered throughout Lewis Carroll's books is collected here, including some of his nonsense creations like *Jabberwocky*. (Rev: BL 3/1/01; SLJ 3/01) [821]

11907 *A Poke in the I: A Collection of Concrete Poems* (3–8). Ed. by Paul B. Janeczko. Illus. by Chris Raschka. 2001, Candlewick $15.99 (0-7636-0661-8). 36pp. A collection of original humorous poems each of which takes a different shape on the page, for example, the poem about a popsicle is on a stick. (Rev: BL 3/15/01*) [811.008]

11908 Prelutsky, Jack, ed. *For Laughing Out Loud: Poems to Tickle Your Funnybone* (K–5). Illus. by Marjorie Priceman. 1991, Knopf LB $17.99 (0-394-92144-5). 32pp. Nonsense poems by different poets cover everything physical — food, animals, family members, and messiness, to name a few. (Rev: BL 5/1/91*; HB 7–8/91; SLJ 7/91*) [811]

11909 Prelutsky, Jack. *It's Raining Pigs and Noodles* (PS–3). Illus. by James Stevenson. 2000, Greenwillow LB $17.89 (0-06-029195-8). 160pp. There are more than 100 nonsense rhymes in this delightful collection; scribbly drawings carry on the humor. (Rev: BCCB 10/00; BL 11/1/00; HBG 3/01; SLJ 11/00) [811]

11910 Prelutsky, Jack. *The New Kid on the Block: Poems* (3–6). Illus. by James Stevenson. 1984, Greenwillow $17.89 (0-688-02272-3). 160pp. A collection of over 100 humorous poems by this prolific master.

11911 Prelutsky, Jack. *Ride a Purple Pelican* (PS–2). Illus. by Garth Williams. 1986, Greenwillow $17.95 (0-688-04031-4). 64pp. New verses that sound like old favorites. (Rev: BL 10/1/86; HB 1–2/87; SLJ 11/86)

11912 Prelutsky, Jack. *The Sheriff of Rottenshot* (2–4). Illus. by Victoria Chess. 1982, Greenwillow $14.93 (0-688-00198-X). 32pp. A collection of the author's humorous poetry, with many a well-turned rhyme.

11913 Prelutsky, Jack. *Something Big Has Been Here* (4–6). Illus. by James Stevenson. 1990, Greenwillow $17.95 (0-688-06434-5). 160pp. A bountiful collection of witty poems. (Rev: BCCB 12/90; BL 9/1/90*; HB 11–12/90*; SLJ 10/90*) [811]

11914 Rash, Andy. *The Robots Are Coming* (2–5). Illus. 2000, Scholastic $15.95 (0-439-06306-X). 40pp. This collection of 16 original poems includes as subjects an abominable snowman, a werewolf, and the Loch Ness Monster. (Rev: BCCB 12/00; BL 11/15/00; HBG 3/01; SLJ 11/00) [811]

11915 Sandburg, Carl. *Poems for Children Nowhere Near Old Enough to Vote* (PS–3). Illus. by Istvan Banyai. 1999, Knopf LB $16.99 (0-679-98990-0). 32pp. Playful poems, though now somewhat dated in tone, by the American master. (Rev: BL 9/1/99; HBG 10/99; SLJ 6/99) [811]

11916 Smith, William J. *Around My Room* (PS–K). Illus. by Erik Blegvad. 2000, Farrar $16.00 (0-374-30406-8). 32pp. A collection of original humorous poems, many of which are delightful nonsense rhymes. (Rev: BL 2/1/00; HB 3–4/00; HBG 10/00; SLJ 4/00) [811]

11917 Smith, William J. *Laughing Time: Collected Nonsense* (3–5). Illus. by Fernando Krahn. 1990, Farrar paper $3.50 (0-374-44315-7). 176pp. New poems have been added to this satisfyingly silly collection. Revision of the 1980 edition. (Rev: BL 2/15/90; SLJ 3/91) [811]

11918 Spilka, Arnold. *Bumples, Fumdidlers, and Jellybeans* (K–3). Illus. by author. 1996, Houghton $15.95 (0-395-74522-5). 31pp. The humorous, imaginative poetry in this collection is accompanied by appealing, childlike drawings. (Rev: SLJ 2/97) [811]

11919 Steig, Jeanne. *Consider the Lemming* (2–5). Illus. by William Steig. 1988, Farrar paper $3.50 (0-374-41361-4). 48pp. Poems that offer a lighthearted tour through the animal kingdom. (Rev: BCCB 10/88; HB 9–10/88; SLJ 9/88)

11920 Tripp, Wallace, ed. *A Great Big Ugly Man Came Up and Tied His Horse to Me: A Book of Nonsense Verse* (K–3). Illus. by Wallace Tripp. 1974, Little, Brown LB $14.95 (0-316-85280-5). 48pp. The hilarious drawings that accompany this selection of nonsense verses make this an especially entertaining book.

11921 Tripp, Wallace. *Rose's Are Red, Violet's Are Blue and Other Silly Poems* (3–6). Illus. 1999, Little, Brown $15.95 (0-316-85440-9). 32pp. A collection of humorous verse by writers from Edward Lear to Gertrude Stein. (Rev: BCCB 6/99; BL 3/15/99; HBG 10/99; SLJ 4/99) [811.008]

11922 Turner, Steve. *Dad, You're Not Funny and Other Poems* (3–5). Illus. by David Mostyn. 2000, Lion $16.95 (0-7459-4024-2). 96pp. A collection of humorous light verse from this well-known English writer. (Rev: SLJ 11/00) [821]

11923 Viorst, Judith. *Sad Underwear and Other Complications* (4–7). Illus. 1995, Atheneum $16.00 (0-689-31929-0). 78pp. A series of imaginative poems, some humorous, some contemplative. (Rev: BCCB 4/95; BL 4/1/95; SLJ 5/95) [811]

11924 Westcott, Nadine Bernard. *The Lady with the Alligator Purse* (PS–1). Illus. by author. 1988, Little, Brown paper $4.95 (0-316-93136-5). The lady with the alligator purse chooses pizza instead of penicillin in this jump-rope rhyme. (Rev: BL 3/15/88; HB 5–6/88)

11925 Westcott, Nadine Bernard, ed. *Never Take a Pig to Lunch and Other Poems About the Fun of Eating* (PS–3). Illus. 1994, Orchard $18.95 (0-531-06834-X). 64pp. A collection of poems — mostly humorous, many nonsensical — about the joy and crises caused by eating. (Rev: BCCB 6/94; BL 2/1/94; HB 5–6/94; SLJ 3/94*) [811]

11926 Wilbur, Richard. *The Disappearing Alphabet* (3–6). Illus. by David Diaz. 1998, Harcourt $16.00 (0-15-201470-5). 32pp. These alphabet poems by Pulitzer Prize-winning Wilbur demonstrate what would happen if the letters disappeared one-by-one to form words such as *quirrel* and *himpanzee*. (Rev: BCCB 12/98; BL 11/15/98; HB 9–10/98; HBG 3/99; SLJ 12/98) [811]

11927 Willard, Nancy. *The Moon and Riddles Diner and the Sunnyside Cafe* (K–3). Illus. by Chris Butler. 2001, Harcourt $17.00 (0-15-201941-3). 40pp. In this collection of fantasy poetry, Shoofly Sally and her dog travel through space and get involved with a variety of characters and objects when they visit the cosmic cafes run by the sun and the moon. (Rev: BL 3/15/01) [811.5]

11928 Yolen, Jane. *How Beastly! A Menagerie of Nonsense Poems* (K–3). Illus. by James Marshall. 1994, Boyds Mills $14.95 (1-56397-086-4). 48pp. Twenty-two rhymes, charmingly illustrated, about such creatures as the Edgehog, Pythong, and Crocodial. (Rev: BL 2/15/94) [811]

Native Americans

11929 Bruchac, Joseph, and Jonathan London. *Thirteen Moons on Turtle's Back: A Native American Year of Moons* (1–5). Illus. by Thomas Locker. 1992, Putnam $16.99 (0-399-22141-7). 32pp. For each of the 13 moon cycles in a year, this book contains a poem and an oil painting illustrating it. (Rev: BL 3/1/92; SLJ 7/92) [811.54]

11930 Field, Edward. *Magic Words* (3–5). Illus. by Stefano Vitale. 1998, Harcourt $17.00 (0-15-201498-5). 32pp. This book of original poems is based on the traditional songs and stories of the Netsilik Inuit and illustrated using oils on bark, wood, and stone. (Rev: BCCB 10/98; BL 10/15/98; HBG 3/99; SLJ 12/98) [811]

11931 Sneve, Virginia Driving Hawk, ed. *Dancing Teepees: Poems of American Indian Youth* (3–8). Illus. by Stephen Gammell. 1989, Holiday LB $16.95 (0-8234-0724-1); paper $8.95 (0-8234-0879-5). 32pp. A collection of traditional tribal prayers, songs, and short poems. (Rev: BCCB 5/89; BL 5/15/89; SLJ 6/89)

11932 Swann, Brian. *Touching the Distance: Native American Riddle-Poems* (3–6). Illus. by Maria Rendon. 1998, Harcourt $16.00 (0-15-200804-7). 32pp. This picture book, illustrated with collages, poses 14 riddle-poems from Native Americans, complete with answers and source notes. (Rev: BCCB 6/98; BL 5/15/98; HBG 10/98; SLJ 4/98) [811]

11933 *When the Rain Sings: Poems by Young Native Americans* (5–10). Illus. 1999, Simon & Schuster $16.00 (0-689-82283-9). 96pp. A collection of 37 poems from Native Americans ranging in age from seven to 17. (Rev: BL 12/1/99; HBG 3/00; SLJ 11/99) [811]

Nature and the Seasons

11934 Adoff, Arnold. *In for Winter, Out for Spring* (K–4). Illus. by Jerry Pinkney. 1991, Harcourt $14.95 (0-15-238637-8). 48pp. Big and small moments in the life of a young African American girl, with radiant illustrations. (Rev: BCCB 5/91; BL 2/1/91*; SLJ 4/91) [398.2]

11935 Alarcon, Francisco X. *Angels Ride Bikes and Other Fall Poems: Los Angeles Andan en Bicicleta y Otros Poems de Otono* (K–3). Illus. by Maya Christina Gonzalez. 1999, Children's Book Pr. $15.95 (0-89239-160-X). 32pp. Twenty poems written in English and Spanish tell about the fall season in Los Angeles. (Rev: BL 12/1/99; HBG 3/00; SLJ 10/99) [811.54]

11936 Alderson, Sue Ann. *Pond Seasons* (K–3). Illus. by Ann Blades. 1998, Douglas & McIntyre $15.95 (0-88899-283-1). 32pp. The four seasons, as seen at a pond where a variety of birds, plants, and animals coexist, are celebrated in a series of 14 short poems. (Rev: BL 6/1–15/98) [811.5]

11937 Asch, Frank. *Cactus Poems* (3–6). Illus. by Ted Levin. 1998, Harcourt $18.00 (0-15-200676-1). 48pp. A poet and a nature photographer combine talents to explore the desert and the animals and plants that live there. (Rev: BL 3/15/98; HBG 10/98; SLJ 6/98) [811]

11938 Asch, Frank. *Song of the North* (3–6). Illus. by Ted Levin. 1999, Harcourt $16.00 (0-15-201258-3). 32pp. A series of poems about the songs of various creatures of the north, such as the salmon, whale, walrus, puffin, and bear. (Rev: BL 4/1/99; HBG 10/99) [811]

11939 Baird, Audrey B. *Storm Coming!* (2–4). Illus. by Patrick O'Brien. 2001, Boyds Mills $15.95 (1-56397-887-3). 32pp. Twenty-two original poems explore the nature and effects of storms from many points of view. (Rev: BL 3/15/01) [811]

11940 Berry, James. *Rough Sketch Beginning* (3–6). Illus. by Robert Florczak. 1996, Harcourt $18.00 (0-15-200112-3). 32pp. A poem about the work of a landscape artist is accompanied by expressive drawings and a concluding painting of the outdoors. (Rev: BL 5/1/96; SLJ 5/96*) [821]

11941 Bishop, Rudine Sims, comp. *Wonders: The Best Children's Poems of Effie Lee Newsome* (K–3). Illus. by Lois Mailou Jones. 1999, Boyds Mills paper $8.95 (1-56397-825-3). 40pp. A collection of original nature poems by Effie Lee Newsome that were published 60 years ago and were long out of print. (Rev: BCCB 2/00; HBG 3/00; SLJ 4/00) [811]

11942 Brenner, Barbara, ed. *The Earth Is Painted Green: A Garden of Poems About Our Planet* (3–5). Illus. by S. D. Schindler. 1994, Scholastic $16.95 (0-590-45134-0). 96pp. An excellent collection of poetry about nature and the environment that includes many by contemporary poets but also old favorites like "Daffodils." (Rev: BL 1/15/94; SLJ 4/94) [808.81]

11943 Brown, Margaret Wise. *Under the Sun and the Moon and Other Poems* (K–2). Illus. by Tom Leonard. 1993, Hyperion LB $15.49 (1-56282-355-8). 32pp. Eighteen poems that deal with animals and nature. (Rev: SLJ 6/93) [811]

11944 Buchanan, Ken, and Debby Buchanan. *It Rained on the Desert Today* (2–4). Illus. by Libba Tracy. 1994, Northland LB $14.95 (0-87358-575-5). 32pp. A rainstorm in the desert is evoked in free verse and evocative watercolors. (Rev: BL 10/15/94; SLJ 8/94) [811]

11945 Carlstrom, Nancy White. *Midnight Dance of the Snowshoe Hare: Poems of Alaska* (K–4). Illus. by Ken Kuroi. 1998, Philomel $15.99 (0-399-22746-6). A series of lovely, seasonally arranged poems that introduce a variety of Alaskan animals. (Rev: HBG 10/98; SLJ 6/98) [811]

11946 Coleman, Mary Ann. *The Dreams of Hummingbirds: Poems from Nature* (4–6). Illus. by Robert Masheris. 1993, Whitman LB $14.95 (0-8075-1720-8). 32pp. A poetic nature hike through the changing seasons. (Rev: BCCB 4/93; BL 3/15/93; SLJ 6/93) [811]

11947 Cyrus, Kurt. *Oddhopper Opera: A Bug's Garden of Verses* (3–5). Illus. 2001, Harcourt $16.00 (0-15-202205-8). 32pp. A variety of garden creatures are featured in both the art and the poems in this original collection. (Rev: BL 3/15/01) [811]

11948 Fletcher, Ralph. *Ordinary Things: Poems from a Walk in Early Spring* (4–6). Illus. 1997, Simon & Schuster $16.00 (0-689-81035-0). 48pp. A fine collection of poems by Fletcher involving the thoughts and emotions that come with spring. (Rev: BL 4/15/97; SLJ 5/97*) [811]

11949 Florian, Douglas. *Winter Eyes* (K–4). Illus. 1999, Greenwillow $16.00 (0-688-16458-7). 48pp. A series of short, quiet poems that show the effects of winter on a small child. (Rev: BCCB 11/99; BL 11/1/99; HB 11–12/99; HBG 3/00; SLJ 9/99) [811.54]

11950 Frost, Robert. *Birches* (4–8). Illus. 1988, Holt paper $5.95 (0-8050-1316-4). 32pp. Frost's 1916 poem still entices new readers. (Rev: BL 10/1/88; SLJ 10/88)

11951 Geis, Jacqueline. *Where the Buffalo Roam* (PS–3). Illus. 1992, Ideals LB $14.00 (0-8249-8584-2). 32pp. With illustrations and verses to the familiar cowboy tune, the American Southwest is celebrated. (Rev: BL 11/15/92; SLJ 1/93) [811]

11952 George, Kristine O'Connell. *The Great Frog Race and Other Poems* (4–6). Illus. by Kate Kiesler. 1997, Clarion $15.00 (0-395-77607-4). 40pp. A richly atmospheric picture book that captures some of the outdoor activities of children, including watching captured frogs race. (Rev: BCCB 6/97; BL 3/15/97*; SLJ 4/97*) [811]

11953 George, Kristine O'Connell. *Old Elm Speaks: Tree Poems* (2–6). Illus. by Kate Kiesler. 1998, Clarion $15.00 (0-395-87611-7). 48pp. A collection of original poems that celebrates every wonderful aspect of trees. (Rev: BL 9/1/98*; HBG 3/99; SLJ 9/98) [811]

11954 George, Kristine O'Connell. *Toasting Marshmallows: Camping Poems* (2–6). Illus. 2001, Clarion $15.00 (0-395-04597-X). 32pp. A family's camping trip is the subject of this collection of original poems that express different moods and celebrate the wonders of the wilderness. (Rev: BL 3/15/01*) [811]

11955 Harrison, David L. *Wild Country* (4–6). Illus. 1999, Boyds Mills $14.95 (1-56397-784-2). 48pp. A collection of original nature poems that celebrates such natural wonders as butterflies, mountains, and forests. (Rev: BL 11/15/99; HBG 3/00; SLJ 12/99) [811]

11956 Hazeltine, Alice I., and Elva Smith, eds. *The Year Around: Poems for Children* (4–6). Illus. by Paula Hutchison. 1973, Ayer $18.95 (0-8369-6403-9). A collection of seasonal poems.

11957 Highwater, Jamake. *Songs for the Seasons* (PS–4). Illus. by Sandra Speidel. 1995, Lothrop LB $14.93 (0-688-10659-0). 32pp. A gentle look at the changes that occur with plants and animals during the cycle of the four seasons. (Rev: BL 4/15/95; SLJ 4/95) [811]

11958 Hines, Anna Grossnickle. *Pieces: A Year in Poems and Quilts* (K–4). Illus. 2001, Greenwillow LB $15.89 (0-688-16964-3). 32pp. Intricate quilting squares illustrate these poems that deal with each of the seasons. (Rev: BCCB 2/01; BL 1/1–15/01*; SLJ 3/01) [811]

11959 Hopkins, Lee Bennett, ed. *Small Talk: A Book of Short Poems* (2–4). Illus. by Susan Gaber. 1995, Harcourt $14.00 (0-15-276577-8). 48pp. Short poems by distinguished authors are arranged according to seasonal changes. (Rev: BCCB 5/95; BL 8/95; HB 5–6/95; SLJ 5/95*) [811]

11960 Hopkins, Lee Bennett. *Spectacular Science: A Book of Poems* (2–4). Illus. by Virginia Halstead. 1999, Simon & Schuster $17.00 (0-689-81283-3). 40pp. Fifteen poems on scientific topics including the wind, magnets, and insects. (Rev: BL 7/99; HBG 3/00; SLJ 9/99) [811.008]

11961 Hughes, Ted. *The Mermaid's Purse* (4–8). Illus. by Flora McDonnell. 2000, Knopf LB $17.99 (0-375-90569-3). 63pp. The 28 poems in this original collection deal with a variety of sea creatures. (Rev: BCCB 6/00; HB 9–10/00; HBG 10/00; SLJ 10/00) [821]

11962 Hundal, Nancy. *Prairie Summer* (3–5). Illus. 1999, Fitzhenry & Whiteside $16.95 (1-55041-403-8). 32pp. A poem, illustrated with impressionistic paintings, that depicts life on the prairie. (Rev: BL 11/1/99) [813.54]

11963 *Imaginary Gardens: American Poetry and Art for Young People* (3–7). Illus. by Charles Sullivan. 1989, Abrams $19.95 (0-8109-1130-2). 111pp. A number of garden poems are matched with beautiful color reproductions of famous paintings. (Rev: HB 1–2/90; SLJ 2/90) [811]

11964 Johnston, Tony. *An Old Shell: Poems of the Galapagos* (3–6). Illus. 1999, Farrar $15.00 (0-374-35648-3). 64pp. The 34 original poems in this collection chronicle the author's trip to the Galapagos

Islands. (Rev: BCCB 10/99; BL 12/1/99; SLJ 10/99) [811]

11965 Kennedy, Dorothy M., ed. *Make Things Fly: Poems About the Wind* (PS–3). Illus. by Sasha Meret. 1998, Simon & Schuster $16.00 (0-689-81544-1). 40pp. A collection of 27 rhythmic poems by such writers as Karla Kuskin, John Ciardi, and Christina Rossetti capture the various moods of the wind. Illustrated with thrilling brown-pencil drawings. (Rev: BL 4/1/98; HB 3–4/98; HBG 10/98; SLJ 5/98) [811.008]

11966 Levy, Constance. *A Tree Place and Other Poems* (3–5). Illus. 1994, Macmillan paper $15.00 (0-689-50599-X). 48pp. Forty short poems that show a keen observation of common phenomena in nature. (Rev: BCCB 3/94; BL 9/1/94; HB 5–6/94, 11–12/94; SLJ 4/94) [811]

11967 Lewis, J. Patrick. *Earth Verses and Water Rhymes* (2–5). Illus. by Robert Sabuda. 1991, Simon & Schuster LB $13.95 (0-689-31693-3). 128pp. The moods of the natural world are evoked with warm illustrations. (Rev: BCCB 1/92; BL 10/1/91; SLJ 9/91*) [811.54]

11968 Lewis, J. Patrick. *July Is a Mad Mosquito* (K–3). Illus. by Melanie Hall. 1994, Atheneum $14.95 (0-689-31813-8). 32pp. Each poem in this collection tells about the sights, sounds, and activities of a different month of the year. (Rev: BCCB 2/94; BL 7/94; SLJ 4/94) [811]

11969 Livingston, Myra Cohn. *A Circle of Seasons* (3–5). Illus. by Leonard Everett Fisher. 1982, Holiday paper $5.95 (0-8234-0656-3). 32pp. A group of poems that brings the seasons to life.

11970 Livingston, Myra Cohn. *Up in the Air* (3–5). Illus. by Leonard Everett Fisher. 1989, Holiday LB $14.95 (0-8234-0736-5). 32pp. A celebration of flight begins as an airliner takes off. (Rev: BCCB 5/89; BL 5/15/89)

11971 Merriam, Eve. *The Singing Green: New and Selected Poems for All Seasons* (3–7). Illus. by Kathleen C. Howell. 1992, Morrow $14.00 (0-688-11025-8). 112pp. The wordplay romps and frolics in this celebration of sun, trees, and the child in us all. (Rev: BCCB 2/93; BL 12/1/92; HB 1–2/93; SLJ 12/92) [811]

11972 Moore, Lillian. *Adam Mouse's Book of Poems* (2–5). Illus. by Kathleen G. McCord. 1992, Macmillan $12.95 (0-689-31765-4). 48pp. Poems from the natural world, written by a country mouse. (Rev: BCCB 3/93; BL 9/15/92; SLJ 10/92) [811]

11973 Moore, Lillian. *Poems Have Roots* (3–6). Illus. 1997, Simon & Schuster $15.00 (0-689-80029-0). 48pp. Seventeen short nature poems that explore the joy and wonder of land, sky, and water. (Rev: BL 9/1/97; HBG 3/98; SLJ 12/97) [811]

11974 Mora, Pat. *The Desert Is My Mother/El Desierto Es Mi Madre* (PS–3). Illus. by Daniel Lechon. 1994, Arte Publico $14.95 (1-55885-121-6). 32pp. In this bilingual book of poems, everyday life in the desert is seen through the eyes of a child. (Rev: BL 1/15/95) [811]

11975 Mora, Pat. *This Big Sky* (K–2). Illus. by Steve Jenkins. 1998, Scholastic $15.95 (0-590-37120-7).

32pp. Through poems and dynamic illustrations, the spirit and beauty of the American Southwest are captured. (Rev: BCCB 4/98; BL 2/15/98; HBG 10/98; SLJ 7/98) [811]

11976 Morrison, Lillian. *Whistling the Morning In* (4–6). Illus. by Joel Cook. 1992, Boyds Mills LB $16.95 (1-56397-035-X). 34pp. In spirited free verse, the quiet blessings of a new day are created. (Rev: BL 1/15/93; SLJ 1/93) [811]

11977 Olaleye, Isaac. *The Distant Talking Drum* (2–4). Illus. by Frane Lessac. 1995, Boyds Mills $15.95 (1-56397-095-3). 32pp. Through a series of short poems and colorful illustrations, the flora and fauna of the Nigerian rain forest are covered. (Rev: BL 1/1/95; HB 3–4/95; SLJ 2/95) [896]

11978 Paolilli, Paul, and Dan Brewer. *Silver Seeds* (K–2). Illus. by Lou Fancher and Steve Johnson. 2001, Viking $15.99 (0-670-88941-5). 32pp. In each of these 15 nature poems the first letters of each line spell out the name of the poem. (Rev: BL 12/15/00) [811.6]

11979 Prelutsky, Jack. *Dog Days: Rhymes Around the Year* (PS–K). Illus. by Dyanna Wolcott. 1999, Knopf LB $16.00 (0-375-80104-3). 32pp. In these 12 original poems, one for each month, a dog reveals his favorite activities in each season. (Rev: BL 11/1/99) [811]

11980 Rickey, Ann Heiskell. *Bugs and Critters I Have Known* (3–6). Illus. by Ardeane Heiskell Smith. 1998, Old Canyon $12.95 (0-9667834-1-7). 93pp. Illustrated with pen-and-ink drawings, this humorous collection of original poems deals mainly with insects. (Rev: SLJ 6/99) [811]

11981 Rogasky, Barbara. *Winter Poems* (3–6). Illus. by Trina S. Hyman. 1994, Scholastic $15.95 (0-590-42872-1). 40pp. An anthology of poems that deal with winter around the world and activities associated with it. (Rev: BCCB 1/95; BL 9/15/94; HB 11–12/94; SLJ 10/94*) [811]

11982 Sidman, Joyce. *Just Us Two: Poems About Animal Dads* (1–4). Illus. by Susan Swan. 2000, Millbrook LB $22.90 (0-7613-1563-2). Using double-page illustrations, this book of 11 original poems is about different fathers in the animal world. (Rev: HBG 3/01; SLJ 12/00) [811]

11983 Siebert, Diane. *Mojave* (4–6). Illus. by Wendell Minor. 1988, HarperCollins LB $15.89 (0-690-04569-7); paper $5.95 (0-06-443283-1). 32pp. A lyrical poem that describes the desert, its history, and the animals that live in it. (Rev: BCCB 4/88; BL 2/1/88)

11984 Singer, Marilyn. *Sky Words* (K–3). Illus. by Deborah Kogan Ray. 1994, Macmillan paper $14.95 (0-02-782882-4). 32pp. Fifteen poems about the sky and topics related to it are beautifully illustrated with multimedia artwork. (Rev: BL 2/15/94; HB 5–6/94; SLJ 5/94) [811]

11985 Smith, William J., and Carol Ra, comp. *The Sun Is Up: A Child's Year of Poems* (K–3). Illus. by Jane C. Wright. 1996, Boyds Mills $15.95 (1-56397-029-5). A poetic trip through the seasons by the two authors and several classic poets, like

Robert Louis Stevenson and Sara Teasdale. (Rev: SLJ 12/96) [811]

11986 Turner, Ann. *A Moon for Seasons* (3–6). Illus. by Robert Noreika. 1994, Macmillan paper $14.95 (0-02-789513-0). 40pp. Using a rural setting and double-page spreads with exciting watercolors, the seasons of the year are presented. (Rev: BL 3/1/94; SLJ 7/94) [811]

11987 Updike, John. *A Child's Calendar* (3–5). Illus. by Trina S. Hyman. 1999, Holiday $16.95 (0-8234-1445-0). 32pp. Updike has written a poem for each month, depicting seasonal activities of a multiracial family in rural New Hampshire. (Rev: BCCB 3/00; BL 9/1/99; HBG 3/00; SLJ 9/99) [811]

11988 Windham, Sophie. *The Mermaid and Other Sea Poems* (3–5). Illus. 1996, Scholastic $16.95 (0-590-20898-5). 32pp. Sea creatures from mermaids to fish are featured in 18 poems by well-known writers. (Rev: BL 2/1/96; SLJ 5/96) [821]

11989 Yolen, Jane. *Color Me a Rhyme: Nature Poems for Young People* (4–6). Illus. 2000, Boyds Mills $15.95 (1-56397-892-X). 32pp. Using related photos as illustrations, these poems each evoke a particular color in nature. (Rev: BL 10/15/00*; HBG 3/01; SLJ 12/00) [811.54]

11990 Yolen, Jane, ed. *Mother Earth, Father Sky* (5–8). Illus. 1995, Boyds Mills $15.95 (1-56397-414-2). 54pp. An anthology of 40 poems that celebrate the wonders of nature, chiefly from well-known English and American writers. (Rev: BL 2/1/96; SLJ 3/96) [808.81]

11991 Yolen, Jane, ed. *Once upon Ice* (3–6). Illus. by Jason Stemple. 1997, Boyds Mills $17.95 (1-56397-408-8). 32pp. A collection of poems from different writers, each of whom has reacted to photographs of ice formations. (Rev: BL 2/1/97; SLJ 3/97) [811]

11992 Yolen, Jane. *Snow, Snow: Winter Poems for Children* (2–5). Illus. by Jason Stemple. 1998, Boyds Mills $16.95 (1-56397-721-4). 32pp. Inspired by photographs of snow scenes, these original poems depict occurrences and express various moods involving winter landscapes and activities. (Rev: BCCB 10/98; BL 11/15/98; HBG 3/99; SLJ 12/98) [811.5]

11993 Yolen, Jane. *Water Music* (3–5). Photos by Jason Stemple. 1995, Boyds Mills $19.95 (1-56397-336-7). 40pp. Seventeen short poems that explore water and its various forms and uses. (Rev: BL 11/15/95; SLJ 11/95) [811]

Sports

11994 Adoff, Arnold. *The Basket Counts* (3–7). Illus. 2000, Simon & Schuster $17.00 (0-689-80108-4). 48pp. A collection of original poems about what it feels like to play basketball on neighborhood courts or with bedroom-door hoops and everything in between. (Rev: BCCB 3/00; BL 2/1/00; HBG 10/00; SLJ 2/00) [811]

11995 Burleigh, Robert. *Hoops* (4–8). Illus. by Stephen T. Johnson. 1997, Harcourt $16.00 (0-15-201450-0). 32pp. A poem that expresses the joy, exhilaration, and excitement of basketball, as seen from the player's point of view. (Rev: BL 11/15/97*; HBG 3/98; SLJ 11/97*) [811]

11996 Greenfield, Eloise. *For the Love of the Game: Michael Jordan and Me* (PS–4). Illus. by Jan S. Gilchrist. 1997, HarperCollins LB $15.89 (0-06-027299-6). 32pp. The basketball moves made by Michael Jordan are used as a metaphor for the game of life in this inspiring poem. (Rev: BCCB 3/97; BL 2/15/97; HB 3–4/97; SLJ 3/97) [811]

11997 Hopkins, Lee Bennett, ed. *Extra Innings: Baseball Poems* (4–6). Illus. by Scott Medlock. 1993, Harcourt $16.00 (0-15-226833-2). 48pp. Nineteen poems about baseball. (Rev: BL 3/15/93; SLJ 4/93) [811]

11998 Hopkins, Lee Bennett, ed. *Opening Days: Sports Poems* (3–6). Illus. by Scott Medlock. 1996, Harcourt $16.00 (0-15-200270-7). 48pp. There are 18 poems in this collection dealing with a variety of sports, each accompanied by a full-page painting. (Rev: BL 2/15/96; HB 5–6/96; SLJ 5/96) [811]

11999 Janeczko, Paul B. *That Sweet Diamond: Baseball Poems* (3–8). Illus. by Carole Katchen. 1998, Simon & Schuster $16.00 (0-689-80735-X). 40pp. A collection of poems that explores all aspects of baseball, including the refreshment stands and how to spit. (Rev: BCCB 7–8/98; BL 6/1–15/98; HBG 10/98; SLJ 4/98) [811]

12000 Korman, Gordon, and Bernice Korman. *The Last-Place Sports Poems of Jeremy Bloom: A Collection of Poems About Winning, Losing, and Being a Good Sport (Sometimes)* (3–6). 1996, Scholastic paper $3.99 (0-590-25516-9). 92pp. A book that explores the world of sports by using different kinds of poetry, from haiku to narrative verse. (Rev: SLJ 4/97) [811]

12001 Morrison, Lillian, ed. *At the Crack of the Bat* (4–6). Illus. by Steve Cieslawski. 1992, Little, Brown LB $15.49 (1-56282-177-6). 64pp. Full-color paintings add to the hero-loving glory of this all-American sport. (Rev: BCCB 5/92; BL 8/92; SLJ 6/92) [811]

12002 Morrison, Lillian, ed. *Slam Dunk: Poems About Basketball* (4–6). Illus. 1995, Hyperion LB $16.49 (0-7868-2042-X). 64pp. An anthology of 42 short poems about basketball, many by important writers like Walter Dean Myers and Jack Prelutsky. (Rev: BL 10/1/95; SLJ 11/95) [811]

12003 Smith, Charles R. *Rimshots: Basketball Pix, Rolls, and Rhythms* (4–7). Illus. 1999, Dutton $15.99 (0-525-46099-3). 32pp. A collection of rhythmical prose that often resembles rap verse and celebrates the excitement of basketball. (Rev: BCCB 5/99; BL 3/15/99; HBG 10/99; SLJ 2/99) [811]

12004 Smith, Charles R. *Short Takes: Fast-Break Basketball Poetry* (4–7). Illus. 2001, Dutton $17.99 (0-525-46454-9). 32pp. Young fans of basketball will enjoy this collection of original poems that capture the sights, sounds, and excitement of the game. (Rev: BCCB 2/01; BL 2/15/01; SLJ 3/01) [811]

12005 *Sports! Sports! Sports! A Poetry Collection* (1–3). Ed. by Lee Bennett Hopkins. Illus. by Brian Floca. 1999, HarperCollins LB $14.89 (0-06-027801-3). 48pp. The thrills and excitement of sports activities are captured in this collection of poems by several authors, including the editor. (Rev: BCCB 2/99; BL 4/1/99; HB 1–2/99; HBG 10/99; SLJ 3/99) [811]

12006 Thayer, Ernest Lawrence. *Casey at the Bat* (K–3). Illus. by Gerald Fitzgerald. 1995, Atheneum $15.00 (0-689-31945-2). 32pp. An entertaining version of the perennial favorite, with fresh, humorous drawings. (Rev: BL 4/15/95; SLJ 6/95) [811]

12007 Thayer, Ernest Lawrence. *Ernest L. Thayer's Casey at the Bat: A Ballad of the Republic Sung in the Year 1888* (K–3). Illus. by Christopher Bing. 2000, Handprint $17.95 (1-929766-00-9). 32pp. Fictional clippings and scratchboard engravings are used as illustrations to give an actual-event atmosphere to this poem about Casey's terrible defeat at bat. (Rev: BCCB 1/01*; BL 2/15/01; SLJ 1/01) [811.5]

12008 Troupe, Quincy. *Take It to the Hoop, Magic Johnson* (2–5). Illus. 2000, Hyperion $15.99 (0-7868-0510-2). 32pp. An exuberant picture book that not only celebrates the career of Magic Johnson but also the sport of basketball. (Rev: BCCB 1/01; BL 9/15/00; HBG 3/01; SLJ 12/00) [811.54]

Plays

General

12009 Adorjan, Carol, and Yuri Rasovsky. *WKID: Easy Radio Plays* (3–7). Illus. 1988, Whitman LB $10.95 (0-8075-9155-6). 80pp. Four scripts for radio plays for young people to act in and produce. (Rev: BL 10/1/88; SLJ 11/88)

12010 Alexander, Sue. *Small Plays for Special Days* (2–4). Illus. by Tom Huffman. 1988, Houghton paper $6.95 (0-89919-798-1). 64pp. Short two-character plays for many holidays.

12011 Bentley, Nancy, and Donna Guthrie. *Putting On a Play* (4–6). Illus. 1997, Millbrook LB $22.40 (0-7613-0011-2). 64pp. A guide to all aspects of playwriting and production, with practical tips for those on stage and behind the scenes. (Rev: BL 2/1/97; SLJ 3/97) [792]

12012 Boiko, Claire. *Children's Plays for Creative Actors: A Collection of Royalty-Free Plays for Boys and Girls* (3–6). 1985, Plays paper $16.95 (0-8238-0267-1). 384pp. Thirty-one playlets, comedies, holiday plays, and one-act plays.

12013 Bruchac, Joseph. *Pushing Up the Sky: Seven Native American Plays for Children* (2–6). Illus. 2000, Dial $17.99 (0-8037-2168-4). 96pp. Several folktales from Native American cultures are adapted into simple plays that are easily produced. (Rev: BCCB 2/00; BL 3/1/00; HBG 10/00; SLJ 3/00) [812]

12014 Burkholder, Kelly. *Plays* (2–5). Series: Artistic Adventures. 2001, Rourke LB $21.27 (1-57103-357-2). 24pp. Details on putting on a play are given including material on writing scripts, costumes, props, characters, and using voice and movement. (Rev: SLJ 2/01) [792]

12015 Butterfield, Moira. *Hansel and Gretel* (2–4). Photos by Trever Clifford. Illus. by Frances Cony. Series: Playtales. 1997, Heinemann $19.92 (1-57572-648-3). 24pp. Contains the script of a play based on this folktale plus direction on how to stage it, from casting and making props to the actual performance. Also use *Sleeping Beauty* (1997). (Rev: HBG 3/98; SLJ 2/98) [809]

12016 Butterfield, Moira. *Little Red Riding Hood* (2–4). Photos by Trever Clifford. Illus. by Frances Cony. Series: Playtales. 1997, Heinemann $19.92 (1-57572-650-5). 24pp. Provides a script based on this fairy tale, as well as a list of parts, directions for production of the play, and instructions for making costumes and sets. Also use *Puss-in-Boots* (1997). (Rev: HBG 3/98; SLJ 3/98) [809]

12017 Carlson, Lori M., ed. *You're On! Seven Plays in English and Spanish* (3–7). Illus. 1999, Morrow $17.00 (0-688-16237-1). 144pp. An anthology of seven varied-genre plays — each in English and Spanish — by noted Hispanic authors. (Rev: BCCB 9/99; BL 10/1/99; HBG 3/00; SLJ 10/99) [812.008]

12018 Dahl, Roald. *James and the Giant Peach: A Play* (3–5). 1983, Puffin paper $4.99 (0-14-031464-4). 128pp. A condensed version of the story about James, who has fantastic adventures.

12019 Fisher, Aileen. *Year-Round Programs for Young Players* (2–8). Illus. 1985, Plays paper $14.95 (0-8238-0266-3). 334pp. Twenty holidays and special occasions are covered in 100 skits, plays, poems, and recitations. (Rev: BL 2/1/86; SLJ 4/86)

12020 Fredericks, Anthony D. *Tadpole Tales and Other Totally Terrific Treats for Readers Theatre* (4–8). 1997, Libraries Unlimited paper $18.50 (1-56308-547-X). 139pp. A delightful collection of scripts for young performers that are spin-offs from folktales, fables, and nursery rhymes. (Rev: BL 3/1/98) [372.67]

12021 Gerke, Pamela. *Multicultural Plays for Children Grades K–3* (K–3). 1996, Smith & Kraus paper $19.95 (1-57525-005-5). 159pp. Ten entertaining plays, each of which deals with a different racial group. Also use volume 2 (1996), which contains ten plays for grades four to six. (Rev: BL 12/1/96; SLJ 9/96) [812]

12022 Jennings, Coleman A., and Aurand Harris, eds. *Plays Children Love, Volume II: A Treasury of*

Contemporary and Classic Plays for Children (5–8). Illus. by Susan Swan. 1988, St. Martin's $19.95 (0-312-01490-2). 512pp. A group of 20 plays requiring royalties based on such stories as Charlotte's Web, The Wizard of Oz, and The Wind in the Willows.

12023 Kamerman, Sylvia E., ed. *Christmas Play Favorites for Young People* (1–7). 1982, Plays paper $13.95 (0-8238-0257-4). Eighteen plays from the pages of *Plays* magazine.

12024 Kamerman, Sylvia E., ed. *Great American Events on Stage: 15 Plays to Celebrate America's Past* (5–8). 1996, Plays paper $16.95 (0-8238-0305-8). 231pp. A collection of 15 short plays on events in American history, mostly featuring such person-alities as Nathan Hale, Molly Pitcher, and Martin Luther King, Jr. (Rev: SLJ 5/97) [808]

12025 Kamerman, Sylvia E., ed. *Thirty Plays from Favorite Stories: Royalty-Free Dramatizations of Myths, Folktales, and Legends from Around the World* (2–4). 1997, Plays paper $15.95 (0-8238-0306-6). 291pp. Thirty short plays based loosely on folk-tales from around the world. (Rev: SLJ 12/97) [809]

12026 Kohl, MaryAnn F. *Making Make-Believe: Fun Props, Costumes, and Creative Play Ideas* (PS–4). 1999, Gryphon paper $14.95 (0-87659-198-5). 191pp. Using simple materials, this book sup-plies ideas for creating 138 different make-believe situations or plays. (Rev: SLJ 10/99) [809]

12027 McCullough, L. E. *"Now I Get It!" Vol. I: 12 Ten-Minute Classroom Drama Skits for Science, Math, Language, and Social Studies* (4–6). Series: Now I Get It! 2001, Smith & Kraus $11.95 (1-57525-161-2). 136pp. In addition to these 12 cur-riculum-related skits, there are before and after activities, discussion questions, and staging sugges-tions. Also use *"Now Get It Right!" Volume II* (2001). (Rev: BL 2/1/01) [812]

12028 McCullough, L. E. *Plays from Fairy Tales: Grades K–3* (1–3). 1998, Smith & Kraus $14.95 (1-57525-109-4). 192pp. Using well-known fairy tales as a basis, this collection of original plays includes recommendations for casting, costumes, sets, and related material. (Rev: BL 9/15/98; SLJ 8/98) [812]

12029 McCullough, L. E. *Plays from Mythology: Grades 4–6* (4–6). 1998, Smith & Kraus $14.95 (1-57525-110-8). 192pp. This is a collection of original plays based on important world myths such as the stories of Midas and Gilgamesh, with accompany-ing detailed notes and production tips. (Rev: BL 9/15/98; SLJ 7/98) [812]

12030 McCullough, L. E. *Plays of America from American Folklore for Children Grades K–6* (3–6). Series: Young Actors. 1996, Smith & Kraus paper $14.95 (1-57525-038-1). 161pp. A collection of 15 plays from American folklore and history that repre-sent many cultural backgrounds. (Rev: SLJ 8/96) [808.82]

12031 McCullough, L. E. *Plays of the Wild West* (3–7). 1997, Smith & Kraus paper $19.95 (1-57525-105-1). 224pp. Both serious and slapstick views of the Wild West are reflected in these 12 plays, most-ly musicals. A companion volume is *Plays of the*

Wild West: Grades K–3 (1997). (Rev: BL 11/1/97; SLJ 1/98) [812]

12032 MacDonald, Margaret Read. *The Skit Book: 101 Skits from Kids* (3–6). Illus. by Marie-Louise Scull. 1990, Shoe String LB $25.00 (0-208-02258-9); paper $18.00 (0-208-02283-X). 160pp. Funny, silly skits from kids that kids will like. (Rev: BL 6/1/90; SLJ 6/90) [812]

12033 Miller, Helen L. *Everyday Plays for Boys and Girls* (3–5). 1986, Plays paper $12.95 (0-8238-0274-4). 198pp. Fifteen one-act plays suitable for school performances. Also use: *Special Plays for Holidays* (1986). (Rev: BCCB 2/87; BL 11/15/86; SLJ 3/87)

12034 Miller, Helen L. *First Plays for Children* (3–7). 1985, Plays paper $12.95 (0-8238-0268-X). 295pp. A useful collection of nonroyalty plays.

12035 Nolan, Paul T. *Folk Tale Plays Round the World: A Collection of Royalty-Free, One-Act Plays About Lands Far and Near* (4–7). 1982, Plays paper $15.00 (0-8238-0253-1). Johnny Appleseed and Robin Hood are heroes featured in two of the 17 plays in this collection.

12036 Smith, Marisa, ed. *The Seattle Children's Theatre: Six Plays for Young Audiences* (5–8). Series: Young Actors. 1997, Smith & Kraus $14.95 (1-57525-008-X). 308pp. Six plays that contain young adolescents as characters, adapted from books like *Afternoon of the Elves* and *Anne of Green Gables*. (Rev: SLJ 6/97) [809]

12037 Soto, Gary. *Novio Boy: A Play* (5–8). 1997, Harcourt paper $7.00 (0-15-201531-0). 96pp. A play about Chicanos in which Rudy, a ninth-grader, asks an 11th-grade girl out on a date. (Rev: BL 4/15/97; SLJ 6/97) [812]

12038 Stevens, Chambers. *Magnificent Monologues for Kids* (4–8). 1999, Sandcastle paper $13.95 (1-883995-08-6). 71pp. A collection of 51 monologues — some best for girls, others for boys — represent-ing different situations and emotions. (Rev: BL 4/1/99; SLJ 8/99) [812]

12039 Trimble, Marcia. *Malinda Martha Meets Mariposa: A Star Is Born* (2–4). Illus. by John Lund. 1999, Images LB $15.95 (1-891577-57-3). 32pp. Malinda Martha conjures an unusual play pre-senting the four stages in the development of the Monarch butterfly with costumed children as cast members. (Rev: SLJ 9/99) [812]

12040 Vigil, Angel. *¡Teatro! Hispanic Plays for Young People* (4–8). Illus. 1996, Teacher Ideas paper $25.00 (1-56308-371-X). 220pp. This collec-tion contains 14 scripts that contain elements of the Hispanic traditions of the Southwest. (Rev: BL 3/1/97) [812]

12041 Willard, Nancy. *East of the Sun and West of the Moon: A Play* (3–5). Illus. by Barry Moser. 1989, Harcourt $14.95 (0-15-224750-5). 64pp. A Norse myth about a poor woodcutter in play form. (Rev: BCCB 4/89; BL 3/15/89)

12042 Winther, Barbara. *Plays from African Tales* (3–6). 1992, Plays paper $13.95 (0-8238-0296-5). 145pp. This book consists of a series of one-act plays based on folktales from all parts of Africa. (Rev: SLJ 9/92) [812.08]

12043 Winther, Barbara. *Plays from Hispanic Tales* (4–8). 1998, Plays paper $13.95 (0-8238-0307-4). 149pp. Tricksters, villains, princesses, ghosts, and talking animals are featured in these 11 royalty-free, one-act plays built on themes from Hispanic folklore. (Rev: SLJ 9/98) [812]

Shakespeare

12044 Birch, Beverley. *Shakespeare's Stories: Comedies* (5–8). Illus. 1988, Bedrick $12.95 (0-87226-191-3); paper $7.95 (0-87226-225-1). 126pp. Retelling Shakespeare's best-known comedies. (Rev: BL 2/15/89; SLJ 2/89)

12045 Birch, Beverley. *Shakespeare's Stories: Histories* (5–8). Illus. 1988, Bedrick paper $6.95 (0-87226-226-X). 126pp. Retelling the classic stories of Shakespeare. (Rev: BL 2/15/89; SLJ 2/89)

12046 Birch, Beverley. *Shakespeare's Stories: Tragedies* (5–8). Illus. 1988, Bedrick paper $6.95 (0-87226-227-8). 126pp. Retelling the great tragedies. (Rev: BL 2/15/89; SLJ 2/89)

12047 Burdett, Lois. *Hamlet for Kids* (2–4). Series: Shakespeare Can Be Fun! 2000, Firefly LB $19.95 (1-55209-522-3); paper $8.95 (1-55209-530-4). 64pp. A retelling of *Hamlet* in rhymed couplets with illustrations by the author's students, ages seven to 12. (Rev: HBG 3/01; SLJ 8/00) [822]

12048 Coville, Bruce. *William Shakespeare's Macbeth* (4–8). Illus. by Gary Kelley. 1997, Dial $16.89 (0-8037-1900-0). 48pp. Using a picture book format, the story of Macbeth is retold, with emphasis on the supernatural aspects. (Rev: BL 11/1/97; HBG 3/98; SLJ 12/97) [822.3]

12049 Coville, Bruce. *William Shakespeare's Romeo and Juliet* (4–6). 1999, Dial $16.99 (0-8037-2462-4). 40pp. A successful retelling of the Shakespearean tragedy with lushly romantic illustrations. (Rev: BL 12/1/99; HBG 3/00; SLJ 1/00) [822.3]

12050 Ganeri, Anita. *The Young Person's Guide to Shakespeare: With Performances on CD by the Royal Shakespeare Company* (4–9). 1999, Harcourt $25.00 (0-15-202101-9). 55pp. This heavily illustrated account covers both Shakespeare's life and plays with a CD of the most familiar speeches such as "To be or not to be." (Rev: SLJ 1/00) [822.3]

12051 Kahle, Peter V. T. *Shakespeare's The Tempest: A Prose Narrative* (5–8). Illus. by Barbara Nickerson. 1999, Seventy Fourth Street $22.95 (0-9655702-2-3). 96pp. An illustrated retelling of Shakespeare's play that uses much of its dialogue. (Rev: SLJ 1/00) [822.3]

12052 Nesbit, Edith. *The Best of Shakespeare* (4–6). Illus. 1997, Oxford $18.95 (0-19-511689-5). 128pp. E. Nesbit has retold the plots of ten of Shakespeare's most popular plays, illustrated with photos from English productions. (Rev: BL 10/15/97; HBG 3/98) [822.3]

12053 Shakespeare, William. *William Shakespeare* (5–7). Ed. by David Scott Kastan and Marina Kastan. Illus. Series: Poetry for Young People. 2000, Sterling $14.95 (0-8069-4344-0). 48pp. In a large format illustrated by paintings, this volume contains three sonnets and 23 short excerpts from the plays of William Shakespeare. (Rev: BL 1/1–15/01; HBG 3/01) [821]

12054 Williams, Marcia. *Bravo, Mr. William Shakespeare!* (5–8). Illus. 2000, Candlewick $16.99 (0-7636-1209-X). 40pp. Using an oversize, comic book format, this book summarizes seven plays (in each frame, the characters' words are Shakespeare's with a plot summary below) including *King Lear, Twelfth Night, As You Like It* , and *Richard the Third*. (Rev: BL 3/1/01; HBG 3/01; SLJ 12/00) [822.3]

12055 Williams, Marcia. *Tales from Shakespeare* (5–8). Illus. 1998, Candlewick $16.99 (0-7636-0441-0). Uses a comic-strip format where, below a prose summary of the action, actors proclaim their lines, and members of the audience comment on the action. Plays include *Hamlet, Romeo and Juliet, Macbeth,* and *Midsummer Night's Dream*. (Rev: BCCB 11/98; BL 11/1/98; HBG 3/99; SLJ 10/98) [741.5]

Biography

Adventurers and Explorers

Collective

12056 Collins, James L. *The Mountain Men* (4–6). Illus. 1996, Watts LB $22.00 (0-531-20229-1). 59pp. Brief biographies of mountain men like Jim Bridger and Kit Carson, all of whom explored the Far West. (Rev: BL 6/1–15/96; SLJ 7/96) [920]

12057 Fradin, Dennis B. *Explorers* (2–4). Illus. 1984, Children's LB $21.00 (0-516-01926-0). 48pp. Easy text and clear photos tell the story of explorations, from the earliest civilizations to the space program.

12058 Fritz, Jean. *Around the World in a Hundred Years: From Henry the Navigator to Magellan* (4–6). Illus. 1994, Putnam $18.99 (0-399-22527-7); paper $6.99 (0-698-11638-0). 128pp. A history of exploration and explorers, from 1421 to 1522, in a series of short biographies. (Rev: BCCB 6/94; BL 5/15/94; HB 7–8/94; SLJ 8/94) [920]

12059 Hacker, Carlotta. *Explorers* (3–6). Series: Women in Profile. 1998, Crabtree LB $21.28 (0-7787-0004-6); paper $8.95 (0-7787-0026-7). 48pp. Six famous female explorers are featured, with profiles on about a dozen more. (Rev: SLJ 9/98) [920]

12060 MacDonald, Fiona. *Exploring the World* (3–6). Illus. by Gerald Wood. Series: Voyages of Discovery. 1996, Bedrick $18.95 (0-87226-487-4). 48pp. With superb illustrations and many maps, this book tells of the voyages of Magellan and Drake. (Rev: SLJ 1/97) [920]

12061 McLoone, Margo. *Women Explorers of the Air: Harriet Quimby, Bessie Coleman, Amelia Earhart, Beryl Markham, Jacqueline Cochran* (3–6). Series: Capstone Short Biographies. 1999, Capstone $19.93 (0-7368-0310-6). 48pp. In a series of brief chapters with full-color illustrations, the achievements of five pioneering women aviators are highlighted. (Rev: BL 3/15/00) [920]

12062 McLoone, Margo. *Women Explorers of the Mountains: Nina Mazuchelli, Fanny Bullock Work-man, Mary Vaux Walcott, Gertrude Benham, Junko Tabei* (3–6). Illus. Series: Capstone Short Biographies. 1999, Capstone LB $19.93 (0-7368-0311-4). 48pp. This book profiles five adventurous female mountaineers and includes information on their achievements as well as maps and photos. (Rev: BL 3/1/00) [920]

12063 McLoone, Margo. *Women Explorers of the World: Isabella Bird Bishop, Florence Dixie, Nellie Bly, Gertrude Bel, Margaret Bourke-White* (3–6). Illus. Series: Capstone Short Biographies. 1999, Capstone LB $19.93 (0-7368-0313-0). 48pp. Brief biographies of five female explorers, including material on their accomplishments, influences, and family life, plus photos and maps. (Rev: BL 3/1/00) [920]

12064 Masters, Anthony. *Heroic Stories* (4–8). Illus. Series: Story Library. 1994, Kingfisher paper $6.95 (1-85697-983-0). 256pp. Various kinds of courage are explored in the lives of 23 people, including Charles Lindbergh and Anne Frank. (Rev: BL 3/1/95) [920]

12065 Maynard, Christopher. *Pirates! Raiders of the High Seas* (2–4). Illus. Series: Eyewitness Reader. 1998, DK $12.95 (0-7894-3768-6); paper $3.95 (0-7894-3443-1). 48pp. Double-page spreads are used to outline the lives and ways of a number of pirates, such as Henry Morgan, Billy the Kidd, and Blackbeard. (Rev: BL 3/1/99; HBG 10/99) [920]

12066 Rozakis, Laurie. *Dick Rutan and Jena Yeager: Flying Non-Stop Around the World* (3–4). Illus. by Jerry Harston. Series: Partners. 1994, Blackbirch LB $9.95 (1-56711-087-8). 47pp. The story of this pair of adventurers and their nonstop flight around the world. (Rev: SLJ 1/95) [920]

12067 Schraff, Anne. *American Heroes of Exploration and Flight* (5–7). Illus. Series: Collective Biographies. 1996, Enslow LB $20.95 (0-89490-619-4). 112pp. From the Wright Brothers, Lindbergh, and Earhart to Neil Armstrong and Sally Ride, this is a history of 12 Americans who dared the unknown. (Rev: BL 4/15/96; SLJ 5/96) [920]

12068 *Talking with Adventurers* (3–6). Ed. by Pat Cummings and Linda Cummings. Illus. 1998, National Geographic $19.95 (0-7922-7068-1). 96pp. In this book of profiles with accompanying photos, 12 adventurous scientists including an anthropologist and an ecologist answer questions about their lives and careers. (Rev: BL 11/15/98; HB 11–12/98; HBG 3/99; SLJ 11/98) [920]

12069 Twist, Clint. *Magellan and da Gama: To the Far East and Beyond* (4–7). Illus. Series: Beyond the Horizons. 1994, Raintree Steck-Vaughn LB $24.26 (0-8114-7254-X). 48pp. Describes the period in which these two explorers lived, as well as their voyages and accomplishments. (Rev: BL 8/94) [920]

12070 Weatherly, Myra. *Women Pirates: Eight Stories of Adventure* (4–7). Illus. 1998, Morgan Reynolds $20.95 (1-883846-24-2). 112pp. These stories of eight women pirates, including Grace O'Malley, Maria Cobham, and Rachel Wall, are enlivened by period prints and portraits plus good maps. (Rev: BCCB 4/98; BL 4/15/98; HBG 3/99) [920]

12071 Zaunders, Bo. *Crocodiles, Camels and Dugout Canoes: Eight Adventurous Episodes* (3–6). Illus. by Roxie Munro. 1998, Dutton $16.99 (0-525-45858-1). 32pp. Based on original sources, this work profiles the lives of eight amateur explorers including Shackleton and Saint-Exupery, and supplies details of their thrilling adventures. (Rev: BL 10/15/98; HB 1–2/99; HBG 3/99; SLJ 11/98) [920]

Individual

ARMSTRONG, NEIL

12072 Bredeson, Carmen. *Neil Armstrong: A Space Biography* (4–6). Series: Countdown to Space. 1998, Enslow LB $17.95 (0-89490-973-8). 48pp. A well-illustrated biography of the first human to walk on the moon. (Rev: BL 8/98; HBG 10/98; SLJ 7/98) [921]

12073 Brown, Don. *One Giant Leap: The Story of Neil Armstrong* (PS–2). Illus. 1998, Houghton $16.00 (0-395-88401-2). 32pp. A picture biography of Neil Armstrong in which the first half describes his childhood and the second his flight to the moon. (Rev: BL 8/98; HBG 3/99; SLJ 9/98) [921]

12074 Kramer, Barbara. *Neil Armstrong: The First Man on the Moon* (5–7). Illus. Series: People to Know. 1997, Enslow LB $20.95 (0-89490-828-6). 112pp. This biography covers Armstrong's public and private life, with details on his specialized training and many space missions. (Rev: HBG 3/98; SLJ 12/97) [921]

ARNER, LOUISE

12075 Anema, Durlynn. *Louise Arner Boyd: Arctic Explorer* (4–6). Illus. 2000, Morgan Reynolds $11.95 (1-883546-42-0). Louise Arner became fascinated with the far north in the early 20th century and financed several scientific expeditions to the Arctic in which she and her crews mapped previous-

ly uncharted regions and collected plant specimens. (Rev: BL 5/1/00) [921]

BAILEY, REX

12076 Greenberg, Keith E. *Test Pilot: Taking Chances in the Air* (4–7). Illus. Series: Risky Business. 1996, Blackbirch LB $16.95 (1-56711-158-0). 32pp. The story of Major Rex Bailey, who faces death in his many exploits as a test pilot. (Rev: BL 2/1/97) [921]

BALLARD, ROBERT

12077 Hill, Christine M. *Robert Ballard* (4–6). Series: People to Know. 1999, Enslow LB $19.95 (0-7660-1147-X). 128pp. An exciting, well-illustrated biography of the oceanographer who discovered the *Titanic*. (Rev: BL 1/1–15/00; HBG 3/00; SLJ 3/00) [921]

BLANCHARD, JEAN-PIERRE

12078 Wallner, Alexandra. *The First Air Voyage in the United States: The Story of Jean-Pierre Blanchard* (K–4). Illus. 1996, Holiday $15.95 (0-8234-1224-5). 32pp. The story of the man who participated in 1793 in the first air flight in the United States. (Rev: BCCB 5/96; BL 5/15/96; SLJ 6/96) [921]

BLUFORD, GUION

12079 Haskins, Jim, and Kathleen Benson. *Space Challenger: The Story of Guion Bluford* (4–7). Illus. 1984, Carolrhoda LB $23.93 (0-87614-259-5). 64pp. The story of the first African American man in space.

12080 Jeffrey, Laura S. *Guion Bluford: A Space Biography* (4–6). Illus. Series: Countdown to Space. 1998, Enslow LB $17.95 (0-89490-977-0). 48pp. A concise biography that tells about Bluford, the first African American to travel in space, his childhood, his training, and his personal qualities. (Rev: BL 8/98; HBG 10/98) [921]

BOONE, DANIEL

12081 Brandt, Keith. *Daniel Boone: Frontier Adventures* (3–5). Illus. by John Lawn. 1983, Troll LB $12.95 (0-89375-843-4); paper $3.95 (0-89375-844-2). 48pp. A readable account about the famous wilderness scout. [921]

12082 Kozar, Richard. *Daniel Boone and the Exploration of the Frontier* (4–6). Series: Explorers of New Worlds. 2000, Chelsea LB $16.95 (0-7910-5510-8). 63pp. Using a variety of illustrations and a crisp text, this book gives good information about Daniel Boone and the forces that inspired him to explore the frontier. (Rev: HBG 10/00; SLJ 7/00) [921]

12083 McCarthy, Pat. *Daniel Boone* (5–8). Series: Historical American Biographies. 2000, Enslow LB $19.95 (0-7660-1256-5). A well-organized and thoroughly documented biography of the legendary pioneer and hero of the American Revolution who died in 1820. (Rev: BL 1/1–15/00; HBG 10/00; SLJ 5/00) [921]

12084 Raphael, Elaine, and Don Bolognese. *Daniel Boone: Frontier Hero* (3–5). Series: Drawing America. 1996, Scholastic $14.95 (0-590-47900-8). An attractive book that presents the salient events in this frontiersman's life. (Rev: SLJ 3/96) [921]

12085 Sanford, William R., and Carl R. Green. *Daniel Boone: Wilderness Pioneer* (4–6). Illus. Series: Legendary Heroes of the Wild West. 1997, Enslow LB $16.95 (0-89490-674-7). 48pp. This short biography of the colorful frontiersman who promoted the settlement of Kentucky tries to separate fact from legend. (Rev: BL 3/15/97; SLJ 4/97) [921]

BOWDITCH, NATHANIEL

12086 Latham, Jean Lee. *Carry On, Mr. Bowditch* (6–8). Illus. by John O'Hara Cosgrove. 1955, Houghton $16.00 (0-395-06881-9); paper $6.95 (0-395-13713-6). 256pp. This fictionalized biography of the great American navigator is enlivened by fascinating material on sailing ships and the romance of old Salem. Newbery Medal winner, 1956.

BYRD, ADMIRAL

12087 Burleigh, Robert. *Black Whiteness: Admiral Byrd Alone in the Antarctic* (4–8). Illus. by Walter L. Krudop. 1998, Simon & Schuster $16.00 (0-689-81299-X). 40pp. An outstanding picture biography, with generous quotes from Byrd's diary that tell of his great endurance and his lonely vigil in a small underground structure in the Antarctic. (Rev: BL 1/1–15/98*; HB 3–4/98; HBG 10/98; SLJ 3/98) [921]

CARSON, KIT

12088 Sanford, William R., and Carl R. Green. *Kit Carson: Frontier Scout* (4–6). Illus. Series: Legendary Heroes of the Wild West. 1996, Enslow LB $16.95 (0-89490-650-X). 48pp. A lively biography of the frontier scout and mountain man, with details on how he survived in the wilderness. (Rev: SLJ 7/96) [921]

COCHRAN, JACQUELINE

12089 Smith, Elizabeth Simpson. *Coming Out Right: The Story of Jacqueline Cochran, the First Woman Aviator to Break the Sound Barrier* (5–8). Illus. 1991, Walker LB $15.85 (0-8027-6989-6). 114pp. From her impoverished childhood to her triumphs in the air and later, this is the story of a female aviation pioneer. (Rev: SLJ 5/91) [921]

COLEMAN, BESSIE

12090 Borden, Louise, and Mary Kay Kroeger. *Fly High! The Story of Bessie Coleman* (1–4). Illus. by Teresa Flavin. 2001, Simon & Schuster $16.00 (0-689-82457-2). 40pp. A highly illustrated, short biography of airplane pilot Bessie Coleman, who in 1921 became the first African American to get a pilot's license. (Rev: BCCB 2/01; BL 2/15/01; SLJ 1/01) [921]

12091 Fisher, Lillian M. *Brave Bessie: Flying Free* (4–7). Illus. 1995, Hendrick-Long $15.95 (0-

937460-94-X). 88pp. This biography tells of the struggles of Bessie Coleman, who became the first African American aviatrix in the United States. (Rev: BL 2/15/96; SLJ 2/96) [921]

12092 Hart, Philip S. *Up in the Air: The Story of Bessie Coleman* (4–6). Illus. 1996, Carolrhoda LB $23.93 (0-87614-949-2); paper $6.95 (0-87614-978-6). 80pp. Forced by restrictions at home to get her training in France in the 1920s, Coleman became the first African American female airplane pilot. (Rev: BL 8/96; SLJ 8/96) [921]

12093 Joseph, Lynn. *Fly, Bessie, Fly* (K–3). Illus. by Yvonne Buchanan. 1998, Simon & Schuster $16.00 (0-689-81339-2). A simple biography about the first female African American flier and her struggle for recognition. (Rev: HBG 3/99; SLJ 12/98) [921]

12094 Lindbergh, Reeve. *Nobody Owns the Sky* (PS–3). Illus. by Pamela Paparone. 1996, Candlewick $15.99 (1-56402-533-0). 32pp. A poem that commemorates the life of African American aviator Bessie Coleman. (Rev: BL 1/1–15/97; SLJ 11/96) [921]

COLUMBUS, CHRISTOPHER

12095 Adler, David A. *Christopher Columbus: Great Explorer* (3–5). Illus. by Lyle Miller. Series: First Biographies. 1991, Holiday LB $15.95 (0-8234-0895-7). 48pp. This account covers the entire life of Columbus, from his childhood through his last unhappy years. (Rev: SLJ 5/92) [921]

12096 Adler, David A. *A Picture Book of Christopher Columbus* (K–3). Illus. by John Wallner. Series: Picture Book Biographies. 1991, Holiday LB $16.95 (0-8234-0857-4); paper $6.95 (0-8234-0949-X). 32pp. The life of this famous explorer is described in simple text and many illustrations. (Rev: BL 6/1/91; SLJ 5/91) [921]

12097 Clare, John D., ed. *The Voyages of Christopher Columbus* (5–8). Illus. Series: Living History. 1992, Harcourt $16.95 (0-15-200507-2). 64pp. Using actors and backdrops of the period, this account reconstructs each of Columbus's New World voyages. (Rev: SLJ 11/92) [921]

12098 Columbus, Christopher. *The Log of Christopher Columbus' First Voyage to America in the Year 1492 as Copied Out in Brief by Bartholomew Las Casas* (4–6). Illus. by John O'Hara Cosgrove. 1989, Shoe String LB $17.00 (0-208-02247-3). 84pp. An abridged log giving day-to-day events of Columbus's sea journey. A reissue. [921]

12099 Fritz, Jean. *Where Do You Think You're Going, Christopher Columbus?* (3–5). Illus. by Margot Tomes. 1980, Putnam $13.95 (0-399-20723-6); paper $5.99 (0-698-11580-5). 80pp. A fresh, interesting account of Columbus and his voyages. [921]

12100 Pelta, Kathy. *Discovering Christopher Columbus: How History Is Invented* (5–7). Illus. 1991, Lerner LB $23.93 (0-8225-4899-2). 112pp. After telling what we do know about Columbus, the author examines how myths and legends about him have grown over the years. (Rev: BL 10/1/91) [921]

COUSTEAU, JACQUES

12101 DuTemple, Lesley A. *Jacques Cousteau* (4–6). Series: A&E Biography. 2000, Lerner LB $25.26 (0-8225-4979-4). 112pp. This is the story of the pioneering underwater adventurer and filmmaker who spent most of his life exploring the silent world beneath the sea. (Rev: BL 6/1–15/00; HBG 3/01) [921]

CROCKETT, DAVY

12102 Adler, David A. *A Picture Book of Davy Crockett* (K–3). Illus. by John Wallner. Series: Picture Book Biographies. 1996, Holiday $15.95 (0-8234-1212-1). 32pp. With simple, brief text and many illustrations, this is a beginning biography of a frontier hero. (Rev: BL 4/15/96; SLJ 5/96) [921]

12103 Sanford, William R., and Carl R. Green. *Davy Crockett: Defender of the Alamo* (4–6). Illus. Series: Legendary Heroes of the Wild West. 1996, Enslow LB $16.95 (0-89490-648-8). 48pp. A brief action-filled biography of Davy Crockett that tries to sort out fact from fiction. (Rev: BL 7/96; SLJ 7/96) [921]

12104 Santrey, Laurence. *Davy Crockett: Young Pioneer* (4–6). Illus. 1983, Troll paper $3.95 (0-89375-848-5). 48pp. All sorts of stories about Davy Crockett, one of the most interesting frontier scouts. [921]

DA GAMA, VASCO

12105 Kratoville, Betty Lou. *Vasco da Gama* (4–7). Series: Trade Route Explorers. 2000, High Noon paper $17.00 (1-57128-168-1). 44pp. The story of the famous explorer who rounded the Cape of Good Hope and visited India, told in a simple, interesting account. (Rev: SLJ 3/01) [921]

DAVIS, JAN

12106 Greenberg, Keith E. *Stunt Woman: Daredevil Specialist* (4–7). Illus. Series: Risky Business. 1996, Blackbirch LB $16.95 (1-56711-159-9). 32pp. The story of Jan Davis, who, for fun and profit, engages in such activities as jumping from airplanes. (Rev: BL 2/1/97; SLJ 1/97) [921]

EARHART, AMELIA

12107 Adler, David A. *A Picture Book of Amelia Earhart* (1–3). Illus. by Jeff Fisher. Series: Picture Book Biographies. 1998, Holiday $15.95 (0-8234-1315-2). 32pp. Single- and double-page illustrations are used in this interesting biography that highlights Amelia Earhart's unusual childhood. (Rev: BL 4/15/98; HBG 10/98; SLJ 4/98) [921]

12108 Bull, Angela. *Flying Ace: The Story of Amelia Earhart* (2–4). Illus. by Chris Forsey. Series: Eyewitness Reader. 2000, DK $12.95 (0-7894-5436-X); paper $3.95 (0-7894-5435-1). 48pp. An interesting biography for beginning readers that reveals many details of Earhart's life and speculates on the cause of her disappearance. (Rev: HBG 10/00; SLJ 7/00) [921]

12109 Chadwick, Roxane. *Amelia Earhart: Aviation Pioneer* (4–6). Illus. 1987, Lerner paper $4.95 (0-8225-9515-X). 56pp. The life of the young daredevil who lived to fly. (Rev: BCCB 6/87; BL 6/15/87; SLJ 8/87) [921]

12110 Davies, Kath. *Amelia Earhart Flies Around the World* (3–6). Illus. Series: Great 20th Century Expeditions. 1994, Dillon LB $16.95 (0-87518-531-2). 32pp. This is a lively biography that clearly summarizes Amelia Earhart's exciting and rebellious life. (Rev: SLJ 11/94) [921]

12111 Landsman, Susan. *What Happened to Amelia Earhart?* (3–5). Illus. 1991, Avon paper $3.50 (0-380-76221-8). 96pp. While giving background information on Amelia Earhart, this book focuses on her disappearance. (Rev: BL 9/15/91) [921]

12112 Langley, Andrew. *Amelia Earhart: The Pioneering Pilot* (2–4). Illus. Series: What's Their Story? 1998, Oxford LB $12.95 (0-19-521403-X). 32pp. Dramatic moments and heroic deeds in the life of Amelia Earhart are highlighted as well as details of her youthful adventures and independent spirit. (Rev: BL 8/98; HBG 10/98; SLJ 10/98) [921]

12113 Lauber, Patricia. *Lost Star: The Story of Amelia Earhart* (5–7). Illus. 1988, Scholastic paper $4.50 (0-590-41159-4). 96pp. A candid biography of the famed lost aviator. (Rev: BL 10/1/88; SLJ 12/88) [921]

12114 Parr, Jan. *Amelia Earhart: First Lady of Flight* (5–8). Illus. Series: Book Report Biographies. 1997, Watts LB $22.00 (0-531-11407-4). 112pp. A short, useful biography that tells about the public and private life of this adventurer who broke many records and helped open up the world of flight for women. (Rev: BL 11/15/97; HBG 3/98; SLJ 11/97) [921]

12115 Sabin, Francene. *Amelia Earhart: Adventure in the Sky* (3–5). Illus. by Karen Milone. 1983, Troll LB $17.25 (0-89375-839-6); paper $3.95 (0-89375-840-X). 48pp. A biography that shows this amazing woman's courage and endurance. [921]

12116 Szabo, Corinne. *Sky Pioneer: A Photobiography of Amelia Earhart* (4–8). Illus. 1997, National Geographic $16.00 (0-7922-3737-4). 64pp. A lavishly illustrated biography of Earhart that concentrates more on her accomplishments than her disappearance. (Rev: BL 2/15/97; SLJ 4/97) [921]

EXQUEMELIN

12117 Exquemelin, A. O. *Exquemelin and the Pirates of the Caribbean* (5–8). Ed. by Jane Shuter. Illus. Series: History Eyewitness. 1995, Raintree Steck-Vaughn LB $24.26 (0-8114-8282-0). 48pp. An edited version of the exciting journal of the 17th-century Frenchman who joined a pirate gang as a barber-surgeon. (Rev: BL 4/15/95) [921]

FREMONT, JOHN C.

12118 Sanford, William R., and Carl R. Green. *John C. Fremont: Soldier and Pathfinder* (4–6). Illus. Series: Legendary Heroes of the Wild West. 1996, Enslow LB $16.95 (0-89490-649-6). 48pp. A biography of the soldier and politician who also participated in many explorations that opened up the West, including California. (Rev: BL 7/96; SLJ 7/96) [921]

GRISSOM, GUS

12119 Bredeson, Carmen. *Gus Grissom: A Space Biography* (3–7). Illus. Series: Space Biography. 1998, Enslow LB $17.95 (0-89490-974-6). 48pp. Using large color pictures and a simple text, this book traces the exciting career of this space pioneer and his many contributions to the NASA space program. (Rev: BL 4/1/98; HBG 10/98; SLJ 5/98) [629.45]

HENSON, MATTHEW

12120 Ferris, Jeri. *Arctic Explorer: The Story of Matthew Henson* (3–6). Illus. 1989, Carolrhoda LB $24.50 (0-87614-370-2). 80pp. Robert Peary described his African American assistant as "a most nearly indispensable man." (Rev: BL 6/1/89; HB 7–8/89)

12121 Gaines, Ann Graham. *Matthew Henson and the North Pole Expedition* (4–6). Series: Journey to Freedom. 2000, Child's World LB $25.64 (1-56766-743-0). 40pp. The gripping story of the African American Arctic explorer and his role in the famous North Pole expedition. (Rev: BL 11/15/00; HBG 3/01; SLJ 3/01) [921]

HEYERDAHL, THOR

12122 Malam, John. *Thor Heyerdahl* (1–4). Series: Tell Me About. 1999, Carolrhoda LB $19.93 (1-57505-364-0). 24pp. A lively biography of the fearless voyager who set out in a balsa-wood raft, the *Kon Tiki*, to explore the Pacific Ocean. (Rev: HBG 10/99; SLJ 8/99) [921]

HILLARY, SIR EDMUND

12123 Coburn, Broughton. *Triumph on Everest: A Photobiography of Sir Edmund Hillary* (5–8). 2000, National Geographic $17.95 (0-7922-7114-9). 64pp. Using many quotes and excellent photographs, this work records the lifetime accomplishments of one of the first men to reach the top of Mount Everest. (Rev: BCCB 9/00; HBG 3/01; SLJ 10/00) [921]

12124 Stewart, Whitney. *Sir Edmund Hillary: To Everest and Beyond* (5–8). Photos by Anne B. Keiser. Illus. Series: Newsmakers. 1996, Lerner LB $25.26 (0-8225-4927-1). 128pp. The life of this famous mountain climber is presented with interesting details about his other interests, like bee keeping, conservation, and helping the Sherpa people. (Rev: SLJ 9/96) [921]

HUDSON, HENRY

12125 Goodman, Joan E. *Beyond the Sea of Ice: The Voyages of Henry Hudson* (3–6). Illus. Series: Great Explorers Books. 1999, Mikaya $19.95 (0-9650493-8-8). 48pp. This biography focuses on Hudson's four voyages of exploration. (Rev: BL 11/1/99; HBG 3/00; SLJ 3/00) [921]

JEMISON, MAE

12126 Burby, Liza N. *Mae Jemison: The First African American Woman Astronaut* (1–3). Series: Making Their Mark: Women in Science and Medicine. 1997, Rosen LB $13.95 (0-8239-5027-1).

24pp. A short, clearly written biography of this space pioneer for beginning readers. (Rev: SLJ 7/98) [921]

12127 Yannuzzi, Della A. *Mae Jemison: A Space Biography* (4–6). Illus. Series: Countdown to Space. 1998, Enslow LB $17.95 (0-89490-813-8). 48pp. As well as information about her youth, training, and personality, this book covers Mae Jemison's flight on the *Endeavor* in 1992, when she became the first African American woman to travel in space. (Rev: BL 8/98; HBG 10/98) [921]

KINGSLEY, MARY

12128 Brown, Don. *Uncommon Traveler: Mary Kingsley in Africa* (PS–3). Illus. 2000, Houghton $16.00 (0-618-00273-1). 32pp. A picture-book biography of the intrepid Englishwoman who twice journeyed alone to West Africa in the 19th century and later wrote and lectured about her experiences. (Rev: BCCB 7–8/00; BL 7/00*; HB 9–10/00; HBG 3/01; SLJ 9/00) [921]

LAW, RUTH

12129 Brown, Don. *Ruth Law Thrills a Nation* (1–3). Illus. 1993, Ticknor $15.00 (0-395-66404-7). 32pp. A simple biography about the woman flier who broke a nonstop cross-country record. (Rev: BL 8/93) [921]

LEATHERS, BLANCHE

12130 Gilliland, Judith Heide. *Steamboat! The Story of Captain Blanche Leathers* (2–4). Illus. by Holly Meade. 2000, DK $16.95 (0-7894-2585-8). 32pp. A well-written picture-book biography of Blanche Leathers who became America's first female steamboat captain and navigated the mighty Mississippi River for years. (Rev: BCCB 3/00; BL 3/15/00*; HB 3–4/00; HBG 10/00; SLJ 3/00) [921]

LEWIS AND CLARK

12131 Kroll, Steven. *Lewis and Clark: Explorers of the American West* (1–5). Illus. by Richard Williams. 1994, Holiday LB $16.95 (0-8234-1034-X). 32pp. An appealing picture book that dramatically describes the famous journey of Lewis and Clark. (Rev: BCCB 11/94; BL 11/1/94; SLJ 9/94) [921]

12132 Stein, R. Conrad. *Lewis and Clark* (3–5). Series: Cornerstones of Freedom. 1997, Children's LB $20.50 (0-516-20461-0). 32pp. A well-illustrated, attractive introduction to the famous Western expedition and the men who carried it out. (Rev: BL 12/15/97; HBG 3/98) [921]

12133 Streissguth, Thomas. *Lewis and Clark: Explorers of the Northwest* (4–9). Series: Historical American Biographies. 1998, Enslow LB $0.00 (0-7660-1016-3). The story of the two intrepid explorers who made their way overland to the Pacific Ocean. (Rev: BL 8/98) [921]

LINDBERGH, CHARLES

12134 Burleigh, Robert. *Flight: The Journey of Charles Lindbergh* (2–4). Illus. by Mike Wimmer. 1991, Putnam $16.99 (0-399-22272-3). 32pp. A picture book that uses Lindbergh's autobiography as a basis for the text. (Rev: BCCB 11/91; BL 9/1/91*; HB 11–12/91*; SLJ 10/91) [921]

LUCID, SHANNON

12135 Bredeson, Carmen. *Shannon Lucid* (4–6). Illus. 1998, Millbrook LB $20.90 (0-7613-0406-1). 48pp. A biography of America's most experienced astronaut who spent 188 days on *Mir* and later joked that she hadn't showered for six months. (Rev: BL 1/1–15/99; HBG 3/99; SLJ 1/99) [921]

MCAULIFFE, CHRISTA

12136 Jeffrey, Laura S. *Christa McAuliffe: A Space Biography* (4–6). Series: Countdown to Space. 1998, Enslow LB $17.95 (0-89490-976-2). The biography of the teacher who was to have been the first civilian in space. (Rev: BL 8/98; HBG 10/98; SLJ 9/98) [921]

12137 Naden, Corinne J., and Rose Blue. *Christa McAuliffe: Teacher in Space* (3–5). Illus. Series: Gateway Biographies. 1991, Millbrook LB $20.90 (1-56294-046-5). 48pp. Personal anecdotes about America's "first private citizen in space" are criss-crossed with space program information. (Rev: BL 1/1/92; SLJ 1/92) [921]

MACCREADY, PAUL B.

12138 Taylor, Richard L. *The First Human-Powered Flight: The Story of Paul B. MacCready and His Airplane, the Gossamer Condor* (4–8). Illus. Series: First Books. 1995, Watts LB $22.50 (0-531-20185-6). 63pp. After an introduction to the history of human-powered flight, this account focuses on MacCready's amazing flight in 1977. (Rev: SLJ 11/95) [921]

MCNAIR, RONALD

12139 Naden, Corinne J. *Ronald McNair* (5–7). Illus. Series: Black Americans of Achievement. 1991, Chelsea LB $19.95 (0-7910-1133-X). 109pp. The story of the second African American astronaut, who died in the Challenger disaster. (Rev: SLJ 3/91) [921]

MAGELLAN, FERDINAND

12140 Gallagher, Jim. *Ferdinand Magellan and the First Voyage Around the World* (4–6). Series: Explorers of New Worlds. 2000, Chelsea LB $16.95 (0-7910-5508-6). 63pp. With well-chosen illustrations and a lively text, this book re-creates the historic voyages of Magellan, the first man to circle the globe. (Rev: HBG 10/00; SLJ 7/00) [921]

12141 MacDonald, Fiona. *Magellan: A Voyage Around the World* (3–7). Illus. by Mark Bergin. Series: Expedition. 1998, Watts LB $20.00 (0-531-14454-2). 32pp. A biography focusing on Magellan's famous explorations and their lasting effects. (Rev: HBG 10/98; SLJ 7/98) [921]

MALLORY, GEORGE

12142 Salkeld, Audrey. *Mystery on Everest: A Photobiography of George Mallory* (5–8). Illus. Series: Photobiography. 2000, National Geographic $17.95 (0-7922-7222-6). 64pp. The life of the famous English mountain climber George Mallory, who died in 1924 in a climbing accident on Mount Everest, written by a member of the team that discovered his body in 1999. (Rev: BCCB 9/00; BL 11/1/00; HBG 3/01; SLJ 11/00) [921]

MARKHAM, BERYL

12143 Bowen, Andy Russell. *Flying Against the Wind: A Story About Beryl Markham* (3–6). Illus. 1998, Carolrhoda LB $14.95 (1-57505-081-1). 64pp. From her childhood in East Africa to her solo transatlantic flight in 1936, this is a thrilling biography of the English aviator. (Rev: BL 10/15/98; HBG 10/98; SLJ 8/98) [921]

O'GRADY, SCOTT

12144 O'Grady, Scott, and Michael French. *Basher Five-Two: The True Story of F-16 Fighter Pilot Captain Scott O'Grady* (5–8). Illus. 1997, Doubleday $16.95 (0-385-32300-X). 133pp. The true story of Scott O'Grady's survival ordeal after his F-16 fighter plane was shot down by the Serbs in Bosnia. (Rev: BCCB 7–8/97; HB 7–8/97; SLJ 7/97) [921]

O'MALLEY, GRANIA

12145 McCully, Emily Arnold. *The Pirate Queen* (1–3). Illus. 1995, Putnam $16.95 (0-399-22657-5). 32pp. The story of the Irish pirate queen Grania O'Malley, who was born in 1530 and later met England's Queen Elizabeth. (Rev: BCCB 10/95; BL 11/15/95; SLJ 11/95*) [921]

PEARY, ROBERT E.

12146 Charleston, Gordon. *Peary Reaches the North Pole* (4–6). Illus. Series: Great 20th Century Expeditions. 1993, Dillon LB $16.95 (0-87518-535-5). 32pp. Focuses on Peary's last expedition in 1910, in which he reached the North Pole. (Rev: BL 9/15/93; SLJ 9/93) [921]

PIKE, ZEBULON

12147 Sanford, William R., and Carl R. Green. *Zebulon Pike: Explorer of the Southwest* (4–6). Illus. Series: Legendary Heroes of the Wild West. 1996, Enslow LB $16.95 (0-89490-671-2). 48pp. The story of the Western explorer who, on one of his expeditions, traveled up the Arkansas River and sighted a peak later named after him. (Rev: BL 10/15/96; SLJ 9/96) [921]

POLO, MARCO

12148 MacDonald, Fiona. *Marco Polo: A Journey Through China* (3–7). Illus. by Mark Bergin. Series: Expedition. 1998, Watts LB $20.00 (0-531-14453-4). 32pp. This biography emphasizes Marco Polo's travels and their significance. (Rev: HBG 10/98; SLJ 7/98) [921]

PONCE DE LEON, JUAN

12149 Dolan, Sean. *Juan Ponce de Leon* (5–8). Illus. Series: Hispanics of Achievement. 1995,

Chelsea LB $19.95 (0-7910-2023-1). 112pp. The story of the conqueror and governor of Puerto Rico who also discovered Florida. (Rev: BL 10/15/95) [921]

12150 Harmon, Dan. *Juan Ponce de León and the Search for the Fountain of Youth* (4–6). Series: Explorers of New Worlds. 2000, Chelsea LB $16.95 (0-7910-5517-5). 63pp. As well as the life of Ponce de Leon and his exploits, this book gives good background information on the social and political forces that inspired him. (Rev: HBG 10/00; SLJ 7/00) [921]

POWELL, JOHN WESLEY

12151 Bruns, Roger A. *John Wesley Powell: Explorer of the Grand Canyon* (5–8). Illus. Series: Historical American Biographies. 1997, Enslow LB $20.95 (0-89490-783-2). 128pp. This biography tells about Powell's youth, education, and Civil War days, as well as his many expeditions and research activities. (Rev: SLJ 10/97) [921]

12152 Ross, Michael E. *Exploring the Earth with John Wesley Powell* (3–5). Series: Naturalist's Apprentice. 2000, Carolrhoda $19.93 (1-57505-254-7). 48pp. This biography of the noted explorer, geologist, and naturalist covers his important expeditions into the Grand Canyon and the Colorado plateau region. (Rev: BL 4/15/00; SLJ 8/00) [921]

QUIMBY, HARRIET

12153 Brown, Sterling. *First Lady of the Air: The Harriet Quimby Story* (4–6). 1997, Tudor $12.95 (0-936389-49-4); paper $7.95 (0-936389-53-2). 64pp.

A biography of a newspaper writer with a daredevil streak who became America's first licensed female pilot. (Rev: SLJ 4/98) [921]

RIDE, SALLY

12154 Kramer, Barbara. *Sally Ride: A Space Biography* (3–7). Illus. Series: Space Biography. 1998, Enslow LB $17.95 (0-89490-975-4). 48pp. For reluctant readers, this is a simple biography that highlights Sally Ride's best-known space missions and her other contributions to the U.S. space program as well as her decision to leave NASA and become a teacher. (Rev: BL 4/1/98; HBG 10/98; SLJ 5/98) [629.45]

SHACKLETON, SIR ERNEST

12155 Kostyal, K. M. *Trial by Ice: A Photobiography of Sir Ernest Shackleton* (4–8). Illus. 1999, National Geographic $17.95 (0-7922-7393-1). 64pp. A biography that details the life of Sir Ernest Shackleton, his 1915 Antarctic expedition, and the survival of the explorers aboard the *Endurance*. (Rev: BL 12/1/99; HBG 3/00; SLJ 3/00) [921]

YEAGER, CHUCK

12156 Stein, R. Conrad. *Chuck Yeager Breaks the Sound Barrier* (3–5). Illus. Series: Cornerstones of Freedom. 1997, Children's LB $20.50 (0-516-20294-4). 32pp. A well-organized, illustrated account of this historical aviation event that also gives details of Yeager's life, before and after breaking the sound barrier. (Rev: BL 6/1–15/97) [921]

Artists, Composers, Entertainers, and Writers

Collective

12157 Benedict, Kitty, and Karen Covington. *The Literary Crowd: Writers, Critics, Scholars, Wits* (5–9). Series: Remarkable Women: Past and Present. 2000, Raintree Steck-Vaughn LB $28.54 (0-8172-5732-2). 80pp. Profiles of 150 women writers and others associated with the literary world, including Virginia Woolf, Jane Austen, and Maya Angelou. (Rev: SLJ 8/00) [920]

12158 Bredeson, Carmen. *American Writers of the 20th Century* (5–8). Illus. 1996, Enslow LB $20.95 (0-89490-704-2). 104pp. Ten writers for adults, like Toni Morrison and F. Scott Fitzgerald, are profiled briefly. (Rev: BL 6/1–15/96; SLJ 9/96) [920]

12159 Covington, Karen. *Creators: Artists, Designers, Craftswomen* (5–9). Series: Remarkable Women: Past and Present. 2000, Raintree Steck-Vaughn LB $28.54 (0-8172-5725-X). 80pp. Mary Cassatt, Georgia O'Keefe, Frido Kahlo, and Beatrix Potter are four of the 150 female artists celebrated in this collective biography. (Rev: SLJ 8/00) [920]

12160 Datnow, Claire. *American Science Fiction and Fantasy Writers* (5–8). Illus. Series: Collective Biographies. 1999, Enslow LB $19.95 (0-7660-1090-2). 128pp. Science fiction and fantasy writers profiled in this book include Asimov, Heinlein, Bradbury, Anderson, Norton, L'Engle, and Le Guin. (Rev: BL 4/15/99) [920]

12161 Ehrlich, Amy, ed. *When I Was Your Age* (5–8). 1996, Candlewick $15.99 (1-56402-306-0). 160pp. Ten well-known writers — e.g., Avi, Susan Cooper, and Nicholasa Mohr — recall incidents from their childhood. (Rev: BCCB 4/96; BL 4/15/96; SLJ 8/96) [810.9]

12162 Ford, Carin T. *Legends of American Dance and Choreography* (5–7). Series: Collective Biographies. 2000, Enslow LB $19.95 (0-7660-1378-2). 128pp. This collective work presents ten short biographies of such dance luminaries as George Balan-

chine and Martha Graham. (Rev: BL 6/1–15/00; HBG 10/00) [920]

12163 Glubok, Shirley. *Great Lives: Painting* (5–8). 1994, Scribners $24.95 (0-684-19052-4). 256pp. Brief biographies of 23 artists, including five Americans: Homer, Whistler, Church, Cassatt, and O'Keeffe. Illustrated with reproductions and photos of the artists at work. (Rev: SLJ 7/94) [920]

12164 Hacker, Carlotta. *Great African Americans in Jazz* (3–5). Series: Outstanding African Americans. 1997, Crabtree LB $22.60 (0-86505-804-0); paper $8.95 (0-86505-818-0). 64pp. Seven portraits of great African American jazz musicians are given, among them Louis Armstrong, Duke Ellington, Billie Holiday, and Bessie Smith, plus seven other brief profiles. (Rev: BL 9/15/97) [920]

12165 Hacker, Carlotta. *Great African Americans in the Arts* (3–5). Series: Outstanding African Americans. 1997, Crabtree LB $22.60 (0-86505-807-5); paper $8.95 (0-86505-821-0). 64pp. Seven African Americans — e.g., Gordon Parks, Alvin Ailey, and Marion Anderson — are given lengthy coverage, with seven others introduced in shorter profiles. (Rev: BL 9/15/97; SLJ 12/97) [920]

12166 Hill, Christine M. *Ten Terrific Authors for Teens* (5–7). Series: Collective Biographies. 2000, Enslow LB $20.95 (0-7660-1380-4). 112pp. Among the authors profiled are Judy Blume, Virginia Hamilton, Julius Lester, Lois Lowry, Katherine Paterson, Gary Soto, and Lawrence Yep. (Rev: BL 9/15/00; SLJ 12/00) [920]

12167 Hudson, Wade, and Cheryl W. Hudson, comps. *In Praise of Our Fathers and Our Mothers: A Black Family Treasury by Outstanding Authors and Artists* (4–7). Illus. 1997, Just Us $29.95 (0-940975-59-9). 131pp. A collection of reminiscences of family life told by 40 African American writers and illustrators, e.g., Virginia Hamilton and Walter Dean Myers. (Rev: HB 3–4/97; SLJ 6/97) [920]

12168 Hunter, Shaun. *Visual and Performing Artists* (3–6). Series: Women in Profile. 1999, Crabtree LB $15.96 (0-7787-0035-6); paper $8.06 (0-7787-0013-

5). 48pp. This salute to women in show business features six profiles of important performing artists and brief entries for 15 more. (Rev: BL 9/15/99; SLJ 8/99) [920]

12169 Ishizuka, Kathy. *Asian American Authors* (5–9). Series: Collective Biographies. 2000, Enslow LB $20.95 (0-7660-1376-6). 128pp. Writers for children (including Laurence Yep) and for adults (Amy Tan) are included in this collective biography of ten Asian American writers. (Rev: SLJ 3/01) [920]

12170 Jackson, Nancy. *Photographers: History and Culture Through the Camera* (5–8). Illus. Series: American Profiles. 1997, Facts on File $19.95 (0-8160-3358-7). 134pp. Short biographies of eight famous photographers are given, including Matthew Brady, Alfred Stieglitz, Edward Steichen, and Gordon Parks. (Rev: SLJ 7/97) [920]

12171 Krull, Kathleen. *Lives of the Artists: Masterpieces, Messes (and What the Neighbors Thought)* (4–6). Illus. by Kathryn Hewitt. 1995, Harcourt $20.00 (0-15-200103-4). 96pp. Nineteen thumbnail sketches on such artists as van Gogh, O'Keeffe, and Warhol. (Rev: BCCB 11/95; BL 11/1/95; SLJ 10/95) [920]

12172 Krull, Kathleen. *Lives of the Musicians: Good Times, Bad Times (and What the Neighbors Thought)* (3–6). 1993, Harcourt $20.00 (0-15-248010-2). 96pp. This book contains lively biographies of 19 composers, including Bach, Beethoven, Chopin, Gershwin, and Joplin. (Rev: BCCB 4/93; BL 4/1/93*; SLJ 5/93*) [920]

12173 Krull, Kathleen. *Lives of the Writers: Comedies, Tragedies (and What the Neighbors Thought)* (3–6). Illus. by Kathryn Hewitt. 1994, Harcourt $20.00 (0-15-248009-9). 96pp. Twenty profiles of authors, some well known, like E. B. White and Shakespeare, and others more obscure. (Rev: BCCB 10/94; BL 9/15/94; SLJ 10/94*) [920]

12174 Marcus, Leonard S. *A Caldecott Celebration: Six Artists and Their Paths to the Caldecott Medal* (4–6). Illus. 1998, Walker LB $19.95 (0-8027-8658-8). 48pp. Six Caldecott-winning artists (one for each decade of the prize) introduce their prize-winning books and supply background information on each. The artists are Sendak, McCloskey, Marcia Brown, Steig, Van Allsburg, and Wiesner. (Rev: BL 11/15/98; HB 11–12/98; HBG 3/99; SLJ 12/98) [920]

12175 Marquez, Heron. *Latin Sensations* (5–9). 2001, Lerner LB $25.26 (0-8225-4993-X); paper $7.95 (0-8225-9695-4). 112pp. A collective biography that features profiles of Selena, Ricky Martin, Jennifer Lopez, Marc Anthony, and Enrique Iglesias. (Rev: SLJ 3/01) [920]

12176 Orgill, Roxane. *Shout, Sister, Shout! Ten Girl Singers Who Shaped a Century* (5–8). Illus. 2001, Simon & Schuster $18.00 (0-689-81991-9). 168pp. This collective biography presents profiles of ten important female singers, one from each decade of this past century: Bessie Smith, Sophie Tucker, Ma Rainey, Ethel Merman, Judy Garland, Anita O'Day, Joan Baez, Bette Midler, Madonna, and Lucinda Williams. (Rev: BL 1/1–15/01*) [921]

12177 Press, Skip. *Candice and Edgar Bergen* (4–8). Illus. Series: Star Families. 1995, Silver Burdett paper $7.95 (0-382-24940-2). 48pp. The story of a father and daughter who had vastly different talents, yet each became a star. (Rev: SLJ 9/95) [920]

12178 Press, Skip. *Natalie and Nat King Cole* (4–8). Illus. Series: Star Families. 1995, Silver Burdett LB $17.95 (0-89686-879-6); paper $4.95 (0-382-24942-9). 48pp. A short book that describes the upbringing and home life of Natalie Cole and her father's influence on her career. (Rev: SLJ 9/95) [920]

12179 Rediger, Pat. *Great African Americans in Entertainment* (4–6). Illus. Series: Outstanding African Americans. 1996, Crabtree LB $22.60 (0-86505-799-0); paper $8.95 (0-86505-813-X). 64pp. Bill Cosby, Spike Lee, and Whoopi Goldberg are three of the 13 African Americans profiled. (Rev: BL 9/15/96) [920]

12180 Rediger, Pat. *Great African Americans in Literature* (4–6). Illus. Series: Outstanding African Americans. 1996, Crabtree LB $22.60 (0-86505-802-4); paper $8.95 (0-86505-816-4). 64pp. Some of the 13 African Americans profiled are Maya Angelou, Toni Morrison, James Baldwin, and Alex Haley. (Rev: BL 9/15/96; SLJ 8/96) [920]

12181 Rediger, Pat. *Great African Americans in Music* (4–6). Illus. Series: Outstanding African Americans. 1996, Crabtree LB $22.60 (0-86505-800-8); paper $8.95 (0-86505-814-8). 64pp. Ray Charles, Nat King Cole, Ella Fitzgerald, and the rapper Hammer are profiled, along with nine others. (Rev: BL 9/15/96) [920]

12182 Sills, Leslie. *Inspirations: Stories About Women Artists* (5–7). Illus. 1989, Whitman LB $17.95 (0-8075-3649-0). 56pp. The stories of four talented women who followed their career dreams to success. (Rev: BCCB 1/89; BL 2/1/89; SLJ 1/89)

12183 Sills, Leslie. *Visions: Stories About Women Artists* (5–8). Illus. 1993, Whitman LB $18.95 (0-8075-8491-6). 58pp. The lives of four women artists — Cassatt, Saar, Carrington, and Frank — are covered in text and reproductions of their art. (Rev: BCCB 3/93; HB 7–8/93; SLJ 5/93) [920]

12184 Tate, Eleanora E. *African American Musicians* (4–7). Series: Black Stars. 2000, Wiley $22.95 (0-471-25356-1). 170pp. This collective biography highlights both past and present contributions to different kinds of music by several African Americans. (Rev: BL 7/00; HBG 3/01) [920]

12185 Ventura, Piero. *Great Composers* (5–8). 1989, Putnam $25.95 (0-399-21746-0). 124pp. Thumbnail profiles of the world's greatest composers are given in this large-format book. (Rev: SLJ 4/90) [920]

12186 Wilkinson, Brenda. *African American Women Writers* (4–7). Illus. Series: Black Stars. 1999, Wiley $22.95 (0-471-17580-3). 166pp. Arranged chronologically, this collective biography contains short profiles of more than 20 important female African American writers. (Rev: BL 2/15/00; HBG 10/00) [910]

Artists

ADAMS, ANSEL

12187 Dunlap, Julie. *Eye on the Wild: A Story About Ansel Adams* (3–6). Illus. Series: Creative Minds. 1995, Carolrhoda LB $21.27 (0-87614-944-1). 64pp. A brief biography about the great nature photographer Ansel Adams. (Rev: BL 10/15/95; SLJ 12/95) [921]

ARCIMBOLDO, GIUSEPPE

12188 Strand, Claudia. *Hello, Fruit Face! The Paintings of Giuseppe Arcimboldo* (3–5). Trans. by Michele A. Schons. Illus. 1999, Prestel $14.95 (3-7913-2084-X). 30pp. This is a well-illustrated biography of Arcimboldo, a 16th-century Italian artist who was noted for using everyday objects such as fruits and flowers and arranging them to present a human portrait. (Rev: BL 9/15/99; SLJ 1/00) [921]

AUDUBON, JOHN JAMES

12189 Kastner, Joseph. *John James Audubon* (5–8). Illus. Series: First Impressions. 1992, Abrams $19.95 (0-8109-1918-4). 92pp. A lively account of the adventurous life of Audubon, with many fine art reproductions. (Rev: HB 3–4/93; SLJ 12/92) [921]

12190 Roop, Peter, and Connie Roop, eds. *Capturing Nature* (5–7). Illus. by Rick Farley. 1993, Walker LB $17.85 (0-8027-8205-1). 48pp. Audubon's prints and original paintings and excerpts from his journals are combined to produce a stunning biography. (Rev: BCCB 12/93; BL 12/15/93; SLJ 1/94) [921]

BENTLEY, SNOWFLAKE

12191 Martin, Jacqueline B. *Snowflake Bentley* (K–3). Illus. by Mary Azarian. 1998, Houghton $16.00 (0-395-86162-4). 32pp. As a child Bentley was so obsessed with snow that he devoted his attention to photographing snow crystals and, now nicknamed Snowflake, gained a reputation as a nature photographer. (Rev: BCCB 12/98; BL 10/1/98*; HB 9–10/98; HBG 3/99; SLJ 9/98) [921]

BOURKE-WHITE, MARGARET

12192 Welch, Catherine A. *Margaret Bourke-White* (2–4). Illus. 1997, Carolrhoda LB $19.93 (0-87614-890-9). 56pp. The life of this outstanding photographer reveals the excitement and danger involved in her work. (Rev: BL 9/1/97; HBG 3/98; SLJ 8/97) [921]

12193 Welch, Catherine A. *Margaret Bourke-White: Racing with a Dream* (4–8). Illus. 1998, Carolrhoda LB $16.95 (1-57505-049-8). 104pp. A fine biography of the important photographer whose subjects included skyscrapers, the Depression, Buchenwald, and South African miners. (Rev: BL 10/1/98; HBG 3/99; SLJ 7/98) [921]

BRUEGEL, PIETER

12194 Malam, John. *Pieter Bruegel* (2–4). Series: Tell Me About. 1999, Carolrhoda LB $19.93 (1-57505-366-7). 24pp. The author explores Bruegel's life and times as well as his ideas and masterpieces. (Rev: HBG 10/99; SLJ 7/99) [921]

12195 Woodhouse, Jane. *Pieter Bruegel* (3–4). Series: The Life and Work Of. 2000, Heinemann LB $19.92 (1-57572-344-1). 32pp. This biography of the Flemish painter includes many examples of his paintings of earthy peasants and their surroundings. (Rev: BL 10/15/00; SLJ 2/01) [921]

CALDER, ALEXANDER

12196 Lipman, Jean, and Margaret Aspenwall. *Alexander Calder and His Magical Mobiles* (5–8). Illus. 1981, Hudson Hills $19.95 (0-933920-17-2). 96pp. An exciting biography of this controversial sculptor.

12197 Venezia, Mike. *Alexander Calder* (2–4). Series: Getting to Know. 1998, Children's LB $21.00 (0-516-26400-1). 32pp. An easy-to-read, well-illustrated biography of the American artist who was known for his mobiles. (Rev: BL 12/15/98) [921]

CARLE, ERIC

12198 Carle, Eric. *Flora and Tiger: 19 Very Short Stories from My Life* (4–8). Illus. 1997, Putnam $17.99 (0-399-23203-6). 57pp. An autobiography of the famous picture book artist who was born in Germany but who has lived in the United States since 1952. (Rev: BL 12/15/97; HBG 3/98; SLJ 2/98) [921]

CASSATT, MARY

12199 Brooks, Philip. *Mary Cassatt: An American in Paris* (4–7). Illus. Series: First Books. 1995, Watts LB $22.50 (0-531-20183-X). 64pp. A biography of the American artist who found fulfillment painting in Paris. (Rev: BL 10/1/95; HB 1–2/95; SLJ 10/95) [921]

12200 Giesecke, Ernestine. *Mary Cassatt* (3–5). Illus. Series: Life and Work Of. 1999, Heinemann LB $13.95 (1-57572-955-5). 32pp. This biography of the famous American artist who lived and worked in Paris is complemented by many examples of her work. (Rev: BL 2/1/00; SLJ 1/00) [921]

12201 Meyer, Susan E. *Mary Cassatt* (4–8). Illus. Series: First Impressions. 1991, Abrams $19.95 (0-8109-3154-0). 92pp. The story of the American artist who spent her most productive painting years in France. (Rev: SLJ 5/91) [921]

12202 Streissguth, Thomas. *Mary Cassatt* (4–8). Illus. Series: Trailblazer. 1999, Lerner $17.95 (1-57505-291-1). 112pp. Full-color illustrations enhance this biography of the American painter who was associated with the Impressionists and spent most of her adult life in France. (Rev: BL 5/1/99; HBG 10/99; SLJ 9/99) [921]

CATLIN, GEORGE

12203 Plain, Nancy. *The Man Who Painted Indians: George Catlin* (3–6). Series: Biographies. 1996, Benchmark LB $21.36 (0-7614-0486-4). 48pp. The story of the artist, born in 1796, who left his law career to live in the American wilderness and paint its people and places. (Rev: SLJ 2/97) [921]

CÉZANNE, PAUL

12204 Connolly, Sean. *Paul Cézanne* (3–4). Series: The Life and Work Of. 1999, Heinemann LB $13.95 (1-57572-957-1). 32pp. Covers the life and work of this famous Impressionist painter. (Rev: BL 2/15/00; SLJ 1/00) [921]

12205 Sellier, Marie. *Cézanne from A to Z* (4–8). Trans. from French by Claudia Zoe Bedrick. Illus. Series: Artists from A to Z. 1996, Bedrick LB $14.95 (0-87226-476-9). 59pp. An imaginative, well-executed account that covers the life and works of Cézanne. (Rev: SLJ 5/96) [921]

12206 Venezia, Mike. *Paul Cézanne* (4–6). Series: Getting to Know. 1998, Children's LB $21.00 (0-516-20762-8). Along with an easy-to-read text and full-color reproductions, this introduction to the life and art of Cézanne includes many amusing cartoon illustrations. (Rev: BL 8/98; HBG 10/98) [921]

CHAGALL, MARC

12207 Hopler, Brigitta. *Marc Chagall: Life Is a Dream* (4–7). Trans. by Catherine McCreadie. Illus. Series: Adventures in Art. 1999, Prestel $14.95 (3-7913-1986-8). 30pp. This biography of the surrealist painter not only relates the artist's life story but also encourages the reader to discover the meanings behind the images. (Rev: BL 2/1/99; SLJ 2/99) [921]

12208 Lemke, Elisabeth, and Thomas David. *Marc Chagall: What Colour Is Paradise?* (4–8). Illus. Series: Adventures in Art. 2001, Prestel $14.95 (3-7913-2393-8). 28pp. Using Chagall's biographical paintings as a focus, this innovative biography tells of his life, career, and work. (Rev: BL 1/1–15/01) [921]

12209 Venezia, Mike. *Marc Chagall* (2–4). Series: Getting to Know. 2000, Children's LB $22.00 (0-516-21055-6). 32pp. A biography of the innovative 20th-century painter told with an easy-to-read text, full-color reproductions, and amusing cartoons. (Rev: BL 5/15/00) [921]

CHANG, WAH MING

12210 Riley, Gail B. *Wah Ming Chang: Artist and Master of Special Effects* (4–8). Illus. Series: Multicultural Junior Biographies. 1995, Enslow LB $20.95 (0-89490-639-9). 112pp. A thorough, well-documented biography of this Chinese American, who has gained prominence in the field of special effects. (Rev: BL 2/15/96; SLJ 2/96) [921]

CLOSE, CHUCK

12211 Greenberg, Jan, and Sandra Jordan. *Chuck Close, Up Close* (3–6). Illus. 1998, DK $19.95 (0-7894-2486-X). 48pp. The inspiring story of the contemporary artist who suffered a learning disability as a youngster, became a famous artist, and had to start over after an attack of paralysis. (Rev: BCCB 5/98; HB 5–6/98*; HBG 10/98; SLJ 3/98*) [921]

DA VINCI, LEONARDO

12212 Connolly, Sean. *Leonardo da Vinci* (3–4). Series: The Life and Work Of. 1999, Heinemann LB $13.95 (1-57572-954-7). 32pp. This book explores the life and accomplishments of Leonardo da Vinci and tells how events influenced his masterpieces. (Rev: BL 2/15/00; SLJ 1/00) [921]

12213 Hart, Tony. *Leonardo da Vinci* (3–5). Illus. by Susan Hellard. Series: Famous Children. 1994, Barron's paper $6.95 (0-8120-1828-1). This biography focuses on the childhood of Leonardo and how his genius was shown at an early age. (Rev: SLJ 8/94) [921]

12214 Herbert, Janis. *Leonardo da Vinci for Kids: His Life and Ideas* (4–8). Illus. 1998, Chicago Review $16.95 (1-55652-298-3). 101pp. This biography of Leonardo da Vinci contains background information on history, art techniques, science, and philosophy. (Rev: BL 3/1/99; SLJ 4/99) [921]

12215 Kuhne, Heinz. *Leonardo da Vinci: Dreams, Schemes, and Flying Machines* (4–8). Illus. Series: Adventures in Art. 2000, Prestel $14.95 (3-7913-2166-8). 32pp. This well-illustrated biography covers da Vinci's accomplishments as a scientist, engineer, inventor, and artist. (Rev: BL 7/00) [921]

12216 Malam, John. *Leonardo da Vinci* (2–4). Series: Tell Me About. 1999, Carolrhoda LB $19.93 (1-57505-367-5). 24pp. A biography that gives details on da Vinci's life and accomplishments as well as material on the period in which he lived. (Rev: HBG 10/99; SLJ 7/99) [921]

12217 Mason, Antony. *Leonardo da Vinci* (4–8). Illus. 1994, Barron's $10.95 (0-8120-6460-7); paper $7.95 (0-8120-1997-0). 32pp. A brief biography that chronicles the achievements of this multifaceted genius and supplies pictures of some of his great triumphs. (Rev: BL 12/1/94) [921]

12218 Stanley, Diane. *Leonardo da Vinci* (3–7). Illus. 1996, Morrow $15.89 (0-688-10438-X). 48pp. Both the life of the artist and an introduction to the Italian Renaissance are contained in this beautifully illustrated book. (Rev: BCCB 9/96; BL 9/15/96*; SLJ 9/96*) [921]

12219 Venezia, Mike. *Da Vinci* (2–5). Illus. by author. Series: Getting to Know. 1989, Children's LB $22.00 (0-516-02275-X). 32pp. Using text, cartoons, and the artist's paintings, this is an introduction to the life and work of Leonardo da Vinci. (Rev: SLJ 3/90) [921]

DAY, TOM

12220 Lyons, Mary E. *Master of Mahogany: Tom Day, Free Black Cabinetmaker* (5–8). Illus. 1994, Scribners paper $15.95 (0-684-19675-1). 48pp. The story of a free black in the 18th century who excelled as a woodcarver in North Carolina. (Rev: BL 10/1/94; HB 11–12/94*; SLJ 10/94*) [921]

DEGAS, EDGAR

12221 Skira-Venturi, Rosabianca. *A Weekend with Degas* (3–8). Illus. Series: A Weekend With. 1992, Rizzoli $19.95 (0-8478-1439-4). 64pp. This account, told through the voice of the artist, introduces the reader to Degas, his art, and his life. (Rev: BL 8/92; HB 7–8/92; SLJ 6/92) [921]

12222 Venezia, Mike. *Edgar Degas* (2–4). Illus. Series: Getting to Know. 2000, Children's LB $22.50 (0-516-21593-0); paper $6.95 (0-516-27172-5). 32pp. An easy-to-read text, several reproductions, and humorous cartoons are used to introduce the life and works of this French master. (Rev: BL 9/15/00) [921]

DESJARLAIT, PATRICK

12223 Williams, Neva. *Patrick DesJarlait: Conversations with a Native American Artist* (5–7). Illus. 1994, Lerner LB $22.60 (0-8225-3151-8). 56pp. A beautifully illustrated biography of the Native American artist who worked at the Red Lake Indian Reservation in Minnesota. (Rev: BL 1/1/95; SLJ 1/95) [921]

DISNEY, WALT

12224 Cole, Michael D. *Walt Disney: Creator of Mickey Mouse* (4–7). Illus. Series: People to Know. 1996, Enslow LB $20.95 (0-89490-694-1). 112pp. A thoughtful biography of the great animator, perfectionist, and founder of an entertainment empire. (Rev: BL 6/1–15/96; SLJ 8/96) [921]

12225 Ford, Barbara. *Walt Disney* (4–8). Illus. 1989, Walker LB $16.85 (0-8027-6865-2). 160pp. The story of Disney's youth and his struggle to fulfill his dreams. (Rev: BL 5/15/89)

12226 Nardo, Don. *Walt Disney* (4–8). Series: The Importance Of. 2000, Lucent LB $18.96 (1-56006-605-9). A well-researched biography of Walt Disney that quotes from many original and secondary sources, documents facts, and gives an honest appraisal of his work. (Rev: BL 1/1–15/00; HBG 10/00) [921]

12227 Schroeder, Russell, ed. *Walt Disney: His Life in Pictures* (4–6). Illus. 1996, Disney LB $15.49 (0-7868-5043-4). 64pp. This pictorial biography of Walt Disney uses quotes from interviews, films, and articles. (Rev: BCCB 11/96; SLJ 10/96) [921]

12228 Selden, Bernice. *The Story of Walt Disney, Maker of Magical Worlds* (4–6). Illus. Series: Yearling Biographies. 1989, Dell paper $4.50 (0-440-40240-9). 92pp. A balanced account of the genius who established the art of animation in Hollywood. (Rev: BL 3/15/90; SLJ 4/90) [921]

12229 Simon, Charnan. *Walt Disney: Creator of Magical Worlds* (3–5). Series: Community Builders. 1999, Children's LB $23.00 (0-516-21198-6). 48pp. This biography of Walt Disney stresses his contributions to the economic and cultural life of the United States. (Rev: BL 11/15/99) [921]

EL GRECO

12230 Venezia, Mike. *El Greco* (2–4). Series: Getting to Know. 1997, Children's LB $22.00 (0-516-20586-2). 32pp. This appealing introduction to El Greco and his works contains several color reproductions plus the author's playful cartoons. (Rev: BL 10/15/97; HBG 3/98) [921]

EVANS, MINNIE

12231 Lyons, Mary E. *Painting Dreams: Minnie Evans, Visionary Artist* (5–7). Illus. 1996, Houghton $14.95 (0-395-72032-X). 48pp. The life of the deeply religious African American folk artist Millie Evans. (Rev: BCCB 9/96; BL 7/96; SLJ 7/96) [921]

FOREMAN, MICHAEL

12232 Foreman, Michael. *After the War Was Over* (4–8). Illus. 1996, Arcade $18.95 (1-55970-329-6). 95pp. A memoir by a British artist about growing up in an English coastal village after World War II. A sequel to *War Game* (1990). (Rev: BL 5/15/96) [921]

GEHRY, FRANK O.

12233 Greenberg, Jan, and Sandra Jordan. *Frank O. Gehry: Outside In* (4–7). 2000, DK $19.95 (0-7894-2677-3). 47pp. A stunning profile of this innovative architect who was responsible for the Guggenheim Museum in Bilbao, Spain, and the Experience Music Project in Seattle. (Rev: BCCB 10/00; HB 9–10/00; HBG 3/01; SLJ 9/00) [921]

GIOTTO

12234 Venezia, Mike. *Giotto* (2–4). Series: Getting to Know. 2000, Children's LB $22.00 (0-516-21592-9). 32pp. The story of the Florentine Renaissance artist and architect who influenced all of European painting is told in text, reproductions, and witty cartoons. (Rev: BL 5/15/00) [921]

GORMAN, R. C.

12235 Hermann, Spring. *R. C. Gorman: Navajo Artist* (4–8). Illus. Series: Multicultural Junior Biographies. 1995, Enslow LB $20.95 (0-89490-638-0). 104pp. The story of this contemporary Native American artist, who reflects his heritage in his work. (Rev: BL 2/15/96; SLJ 3/96) [921]

GOYA, FRANCISCO

12236 Schiaffino, Mariarosa. *Goya* (4–8). Illus. by Thomas Trojer and Claudia Saraceni. Series: Masters of Art. 2000, Bedrick $22.50 (0-87226-529-3). 64pp. Each of the double-page spreads in this attractive book is devoted to an aspect of Goya's life or work; for example, his contemporaries and his drawings of the bullfight. (Rev: HBG 10/00; SLJ 3/00) [921]

12237 Venezia, Mike. *Francisco Goya* (2–5). Illus. Series: Getting to Know. 1991, Children's LB $22.00 (0-516-02292-X). 32pp. This is an introduction to the life and work of the great Spanish portrait artist who was also a bitter social satirist. (Rev: BL 8/91; SLJ 12/91) [921]

12238 Waldron, Ann. *Francisco Goya* (5–8). Illus. Series: First Impressions. 1992, Abrams $19.95 (0-8109-3368-3). 92pp. Covers the stormy life of Goya and the many intrigues at court, along with many reproductions. (Rev: SLJ 12/92) [921]

HOMER, WINSLOW

12239 Beneduce, Ann Keay. *A Weekend with Winslow Homer* (3–8). Illus. Series: A Weekend With. 1993, Rizzoli $19.95 (0-8478-1622-2). 64pp. An introduction to the famous New England painter of landscapes and the sea, with an explanation of his importance and a sampling of his work. (Rev: BL 12/15/93; SLJ 11/93) [921]

HOUSTON, JAMES

12240 Houston, James. *Fire into Ice* (5–9). Illus. 1998, Tundra $15.95 (0-88776-459-2). 62pp. The author, who lived with and wrote about the Inuit, tells how he left the Arctic in the early 1960s and became a Steuben glass designer, incorporating his Inuit-influenced drawings into a new medium. (Rev: BL 4/15/99; HBG 3/99; SLJ 1/99) [921]

HUNTER, CLEMENTINE

12241 Lyons, Mary E., ed. *Talking with Tebe: Clementine Hunter, Memory Artist* (4–9). 1998, Houghton $16.00 (0-395-72031-1). 48pp. Using her own words from recorded interviews, this biography tells the story of the African American primitive painter who lived to be 101. (Rev: BCCB 1/99; HB 9–10/98; HBG 3/99; SLJ 9/98) [921]

JACKSON, WILLIAM HENRY

12242 Lawlor, Laurie. *Window on the West: The Frontier Photography of William Henry Jackson* (5–8). 1999, Holiday $18.95 (0-8234-1380-2). 132pp. In addition to tracing the life of this famous photographer who captured the life and spirit of frontier America, this account covers the history and development of the West and pioneer life. (Rev: HB 3–4/00; HBG 10/00; SLJ 3/00) [921]

KAHLO, FRIDA

12243 Frazier, Nancy. *Frida Kahlo: Mysterious Painter* (5–7). Illus. Series: Library of Famous Women. 1993, Rosen LB $17.95 (1-56711-012-6). 64pp. A biography of this enigmatic artist with examples of her work. (Rev: BL 2/15/93) [921]

12244 Garza, Hedda. *Frida Kahlo* (5–8). Illus. Series: Hispanics of Achievement. 1994, Chelsea LB $19.95 (0-7910-1698-6); paper $9.95 (0-7910-1699-4). 120pp. The life story of the famous and colorful Mexican artist and her many accomplishments. (Rev: BL 3/1/94) [921]

12245 Venezia, Mike. *Frida Kahlo* (2–4). Series: Getting to Know. 1999, Children's LB $22.00 (0-516-20975-2). 32pp. A brief biography of Kahlo that includes many reproductions of her works and some humorous cartoons about her by the author. (Rev: BL 9/15/99) [921]

KEATS, EZRA JACK

12246 Engel, Dean, and Florence B. Freedman. *Ezra Jack Keats: A Biography with Illustrations* (3–6). Illus. 1995, Silver Moon $24.95 (1-881889-65-3). 96pp. Using first-hand sources, including interviews, this is the story of the artist/author best

known for *The Snowy Day*. (Rev: BCCB 9/95; BL 4/15/95; HB 5–6/95, 9–10/95; SLJ 6/95) [921]

KLEE, PAUL

12247 Connolly, Sean. *Paul Klee* (3–4). Series: The Life and Work Of. 1999, Heinemann LB $13.95 (1-57572-952-0). 32pp. An illustrated introduction to the life and work of the Swiss abstract painter. (Rev: BL 2/15/00) [921]

12248 Venezia, Mike. *Paul Klee* (2–5). Illus. Series: Getting to Know. 1991, Children's LB $22.00 (0-516-02294-6). 32pp. An informal, simple biography of this Swiss artist, as well as many examples of his work and comments on his style. (Rev: BL 1/15/92) [921]

KLIMT, GUSTAV

12249 Wenzel, Angela. *Gustav Klimt: Silver, Gold, and Precious Stones* (4–8). Illus. Series: Adventures in Art. 2000, Prestel $14.95 (3-7913-2328-8). 32pp. The life of this Austrian artist is presented along with analysis of many of his paintings, including the famous *The Kiss*. (Rev: BL 7/00) [921]

KURELEK, WILLIAM

12250 Kurelek, William. *A Prairie Boy's Summer* (3–5). Illus. by author. 1975, Tundra paper $10.99 (0-88776-116-X). 48pp. Each of this Canadian artist's paintings depicts a farm activity, which the accompanying text describes in this companion piece to the author's earlier *A Prairie Boy's Winter* (1984).

LANGE, DOROTHEA

12251 Venezia, Mike. *Dorothea Lange* (2–4). Illus. Series: Getting to Know. 2000, Children's LB $22.50 (0-516-22026-8); paper $6.95 (0-516-27171-7). 32pp. A biography — enriched with amusing cartoons — of the famous American photographer noted mainly for her haunting pictures of migrant workers and victims of the Great Depression. (Rev: BL 9/15/00) [921]

LAWRENCE, JACOB

12252 Duggleby, John. *Story Painter: The Life of Jacob Lawrence* (5–8). Illus. 1998, Chronicle $16.95 (0-8118-2082-3). 64pp. Using 50 color reproductions, this biography of the great African American illustrator and painter tells how he moved to Harlem in the 1930s and developed his own techniques and style. (Rev: BCCB 1/99; BL 10/15/98; HB 3–4/99; HBG 3/99; SLJ 12/98) [921]

12253 Venezia, Mike. *Jacob Lawrence* (2–4). Illus. by author. Series: Getting to Know. 1999, Children's LB $22.00 (0-516-21012-2). 32pp. A fine introduction to the life and work of this contemporary African American artist that focuses on the aspects of his life that affected his art. (Rev: SLJ 5/00) [921]

LEWIN, TED

12254 Lewin, Ted. *Touch and Go: Travels of a Children's Book Illustrator* (4–6). Illus. 1999,

Lothrop $15.00 (0-688-14109-9). 80pp. The famous children's book illustrator tells how he has gathered material for his work from around the world and describes his adventures along the way. (Rev: BL 4/15/99) [921]

LIN, MAYA

12255 Ling, Bettina. *Maya Lin* (5–7). Illus. Series: Contemporary Asian Americans. 1997, Raintree Steck-Vaughn LB $25.69 (0-8172-3992-8). 48pp. A profile of the Asian American architect and an introduction to many of her projects, including the Vietnam War Memorial in Washington, D.C. (Rev: BL 5/1/97) [921]

12256 Malone, Mary. *Maya Lin: Architect and Artist* (4–6). Illus. Series: People to Know. 1995, Enslow LB $20.95 (0-89490-499-X). 112pp. The life story of the renowned architect best known for her Vietnam Veterans Memorial. (Rev: BL 4/15/95; SLJ 5/95) [921]

MARTINEZ, MARIA

12257 Morris, Juddi. *Tending the Fire: The Story of Maria Martinez* (5–8). 1997, Northland paper $6.95 (0-87358-654-9). 120pp. The life story of New Mexico's most famous potter, who was born in an Indian pueblo in 1887. (Rev: BL 12/1/97; HBG 3/98; SLJ 1/98) [921]

MATISSE, HENRI

12258 Venezia, Mike. *Henri Matisse* (2–4). Illus. Series: Getting to Know. 1997, Children's LB $22.00 (0-516-20311-8). 32pp. A light but realistic overview of Matisse and his work, with many color reproductions, clever cartoon illustrations, and an interesting story line. (Rev: BL 7/97) [921]

MICHELANGELO

12259 Hart, Tony. *Michelangelo* (3–5). Illus. by Susan Hellard. Series: Famous Children. 1994, Barron's paper $6.95 (0-8120-1827-3). An attractive biography that focuses on the boyhood of Michelangelo and how he revealed his genius as a young apprentice. (Rev: SLJ 8/94) [921]

12260 Pettit, Jayne. *Michelangelo: Genius of the Renaissance* (4–6). Series: Book Report Biographies. 1998, Watts LB $22.00 (0-531-11490-2). 128pp. An introduction to Michelangelo's personal and professional life with material on his importance as a sculptor, painter, and architect. (Rev: HBG 3/99; SLJ 1/99) [921]

12261 Stanley, Diane. *Michelangelo* (5–8). Illus. 2000, HarperCollins LB $15.98 (0-688-15086-1). 48pp. An intriguing biography of Michelangelo that also gives extensive coverage on the history of the Italian Renaissance. (Rev: BCCB 10/00; BL 8/00*; HBG 3/01; SLJ 8/00) [921]

12262 Tames, Richard. *Michelangelo Buonarroti* (3–4). Series: The Life and Work Of. 2000, Heinemann LB $19.92 (1-57572-343-3). 32pp. A brief biography of Michelangelo that gives examples of some of his finest works, including the Sistine Chapel. (Rev: BL 10/15/00; SLJ 2/01) [921]

MILLER, TOM

12263 Miller, Tom, and Camay C. Murphy. *Can a Coal Scuttle Fly?* (2–5). Illus. 1996, Maryland Historical Soc. $14.00 (0-938420-55-0). 32pp. Baltimore artist Tom Miller tells about his life and the great joy that can be found in art. (Rev: BL 10/15/96) [921]

MONET, CLAUDE

12264 Connolly, Sean. *Claude Monet* (3–4). Series: The Life and Work Of. 1999, Heinemann LB $13.95 (1-57572-956-3). 32pp. This is a simple introduction to the life and works of Monet, with photos showing him at different stages in his career. (Rev: BL 2/15/00; SLJ 1/00) [921]

12265 Koja, Stephan, and Katja Miksovsky. *Claude Monet: The Magician of Color* (3–7). Trans. by Andrea Belloli. Illus. Series: Adventures in Art. 1997, Prestel $14.95 (3-7913-1812-8). A straightforward biography of Monet that is enlivened by drawings, paintings, and photos. (Rev: SLJ 1/98) [921]

12266 Malam, John. *Claude Monet* (2–4). Series: Tell Me About. 1998, Carolrhoda LB $19.93 (1-57505-250-4). 24pp. Numerous color reproductions and a simple text are used to bring to life the artist Monet and his career. (Rev: HBG 3/99; SLJ 1/99) [921]

12267 Venezia, Mike. *Monet* (2–5). Illus. Series: Getting to Know. 1990, Children's LB $22.00 (0-516-02276-8). 32pp. Using many paintings by Monet, this book introduces the reader to Impressionism. (Rev: SLJ 11/90) [921]

MOORE, HENRY

12268 Connolly, Sean. *Henry Moore* (3–5). Illus. Series: Life and Work Of. 1999, Heinemann LB $13.95 (1-57572-953-9). 32pp. Color photos show examples of Moore's work while black-and-white photos document his life in this biography of the famous English sculptor. (Rev: BL 2/1/00; SLJ 1/00) [921]

12269 Gardner, Jane M. *Henry Moore: From Bones and Stones to Sketches and Sculptures* (2–4). Illus. 1993, Macmillan $15.95 (0-02-735812-7). 32pp. A simple biography told mainly through photographs of the great British 20th-century sculptor, Henry Moore. (Rev: BCCB 4/93; BL 4/15/93; HB 7–8/93; SLJ 6/93) [921]

MOSES, GRANDMA

12270 Oneal, Zibby. *Grandma Moses: Painter of Rural America* (5–7). Illus. by Donna Ruff. 1987, Puffin paper $4.99 (0-14-032220-5). 64pp. The story of Anna Mary Robertson, who became famous as Grandma Moses. (Rev: BCCB 10/86; BL 11/1/86; SLJ 10/86)

MOUNT, WILLIAM SIDNEY

12271 Howard, Nancy S. *William Sidney Mount: Painter of Rural America* (4–7). Illus. 1994, Sterling $14.95 (1-87192-275-4). 48pp. An interactive book that explores the work and paintings of the 19th-century American painter William Sidney Mount. (Rev: BL 1/15/95) [921]

NAST, THOMAS

12272 Pflueger, Lynda. *Thomas Nast: Political Cartoonist* (5–8). Series: Historical American Biographies. 2000, Enslow LB $19.95 (0-7660-1251-4). 128pp. An informative, entertaining, and well-written biography of this influential political cartoonist and critic. (Rev: BL 9/15/00; SLJ 11/00) [921]

12273 Shirley, David. *Thomas Nast* (4–6). Series: Book Report Biographies. 1998, Watts LB $21.50 (0-531-11372-8). 128pp. A biography of the 19th-century political cartoonist who was responsible for creating the Democratic donkey and the Republican elephant. (Rev: BL 5/15/98; HBG 10/98) [921]

OBATA, CHIURA

12274 Ross, Michael E. *Nature Art with Chiura Obata* (3–6). Series: Naturalist's Apprentice. 2000, Lerner $19.95 (1-57505-378-0). 48pp. From his childhood in Japan to his move to the U.S. in 1903 to his death in 1975, this is the story of the great painter who used Japanese painting techniques to depict the American landscape. (Rev: BCCB 3/00; BL 2/1/00; HBG 10/00; SLJ 4/00) [921]

O'KEEFFE, GEORGIA

12275 Brooks, Philip. *Georgia O'Keeffe: An Adventurous Spirit* (4–7). Illus. Series: First Books. 1995, Watts LB $22.50 (0-531-20182-1). 64pp. An insightful portrait of the American artist and her internal struggle to paint what, how, and where she chose. (Rev: BL 10/1/95; SLJ 10/95) [921]

12276 Lowery, Linda. *Georgia O'Keeffe* (2–4). Illus. 1996, Carolrhoda LB $19.93 (0-87614-860-7); paper $5.95 (0-87614-898-4). 48pp. A simple account of the life and work of this amazing painter of the Southwest. (Rev: BL 9/1/96; SLJ 8/96) [921]

12277 Winter, Jeanette. *My Name Is Georgia* (2–4). Illus. 1998, Harcourt $16.00 (0-15-201649-X). 48pp. Told from the artist's point of view, this is a quiet but intense look at the life and work of Georgia O'Keeffe. (Rev: BCCB 11/98; BL 10/15/98*; HB 9–10/98; HBG 3/99; SLJ 12/98) [921]

PEALE, CHARLES WILLSON

12278 Wilson, Janet. *The Ingenious Mr. Peale: Painter, Patriot and Man of Science* (5–8). Illus. 1996, Simon & Schuster $16.00 (0-689-31884-7). 122pp. A profile of the famous portrait painter of the colonial period, with details about his varied interests. (Rev: BCCB 6/96; BL 5/15/96; SLJ 6/96*) [921]

PEET, BILL

12279 Peet, Bill. *Bill Peet: An Autobiography* (2–5). Illus. 1989, Houghton $20.00 (0-395-50932-7). 192pp. The autobiography of the author/illustrator who worked at the Disney Studio for many years. (Rev: BL 7/89; HB 7–8/89*; SLJ 7/89) [921]

PICASSO, PABLO

12280 Hart, Tony. *Picasso* (3–5). Illus. by Susan Hellard. Series: Famous Children. 1994, Barron's paper $5.95 (0-8120-1826-5). Visually attractive, this biography limits its coverage to the childhood of Picasso, who was the son of rich, indulgent parents. (Rev: SLJ 8/94) [921]

12281 Lowery, Linda. *Pablo Picasso* (2–3). Illus. by Janice L. Porter. Series: On My Own Biographies. 1999, Lerner $19.93 (1-57505-331-4); paper $5.95 (1-57505-370-5). 48pp. An easy-to-read biography that touches on Picasso's different painting periods, his personal life, and his great originality. (Rev: BL 2/1/00; HBG 3/00; SLJ 2/00) [921]

12282 Meadows, Matthew. *Pablo Picasso* (5–7). Illus. Series: Art for Young People. 1996, Sterling $14.95 (0-8069-6160-0). 32pp. In double-page spreads, presents the life and work of this multitalented Spanish artist. (Rev: BL 2/1/97; HB 5–6/96; SLJ 3/97) [921]

12283 Pfleger, Susanne. *A Day with Picasso* (4–7). Series: Adventures in Art. 2000, Prestel $14.95 (3-7913-2165-X). 30pp. An introduction to the life and work of Picasso, including many full-color reproductions. (Rev: BL 2/15/00; SLJ 2/00) [921]

12284 Selfridge, John W. *Pablo Picasso* (5–8). Illus. Series: Hispanics of Achievement. 1993, Chelsea LB $19.95 (0-7910-1777-X). 120pp. A colorful biography of this great Spanish painter, who lived most of his life as a political exile in France. (Rev: BL 3/1/94) [921]

12285 Venezia, Mike. *Picasso* (PS–4). Illus. 1988, Children's LB $22.00 (0-516-02271-7); paper $6.95 (0-516-42271-5). 32pp. Amusing facts are tucked in with information about the artist and his work. (Rev: BL 10/1/88; SLJ 9/88)

PIPPIN, HORACE

12286 Lyons, Mary E. *Starting Home: The Story of Horace Pippin, Painter* (5–7). Illus. Series: African American Artists and Artisans. 1993, Scribners $15.95 (0-684-19534-8). 48pp. The story of this self-taught African American painter who depicted the horrors of World War I in his work. (Rev: BL 11/15/93; SLJ 2/94) [921]

POWERS, HARRIET

12287 Lyons, Mary E. *Stitching Stars: The Story Quilts of Harriet Powers* (5–7). Illus. Series: African American Artists and Artisans. 1993, Scribners $17.00 (0-684-19576-3). 48pp. After Emancipation, this former slave created two huge story quilts that hang today in the Smithsonian and Boston's Museum of Fine Arts. (Rev: BCCB 12/93; BL 11/15/93; SLJ 2/94) [921]

REMBRANDT VAN RIJN

12288 Bonafoux, Pascal. *A Weekend with Rembrandt* (3–8). Illus. Series: A Weekend With. 1992, Rizzoli $19.95 (0-8478-1441-6). 64pp. Lavish illustrations introduce Rembrandt, his training, technique, and creative style. (Rev: BL 8/92; HB 1–2/93; SLJ 6/92) [921]

12289 Venezia, Mike. *Rembrandt* (PS–4). Illus. 1988, Children's LB $22.00 (0-516-02272-5); paper $6.95 (0-516-42272-3). 32pp. Learning about art and great artists can be fun. (Rev: BL 10/1/88; SLJ 9/88)

REMINGTON, FREDERIC

12290 Giesecke, Ernestine. *Frederic Remington* (3–4). Series: The Life and Work Of. 1999, Heinemann LB $13.95 (1-57572-951-2). 32pp. This account of Remington's life and career as a painter, illustrator, and sculptor of the American West includes many illustrations of his works and photos of the artist and his world. (Rev: BL 2/15/00; SLJ 1/00) [921]

RENOIR, AUGUSTE

12291 Parsons, Tom. *Pierre Auguste Renoir* (5–7). Illus. Series: Art for Young People. 1996, Sterling $14.95 (0-8069-6162-7). 32pp. The life and work of this prolific French artist are examined in a series of double-page spreads. (Rev: BL 2/1/97; SLJ 3/97) [921]

12292 Venezia, Mike. *Pierre Auguste Renoir* (2–4). Illus. Series: Getting to Know. 1996, Children's LB $22.00 (0-516-02225-3). 32pp. This biography includes examples of Renoir's paintings and an introduction to Impressionism. (Rev: BL 9/15/96; SLJ 12/96) [921]

RIVERA, DIEGO

12293 Braun, Barbara. *A Weekend with Diego Rivera* (3–8). Illus. Series: A Weekend With. 1994, Rizzoli $19.95 (0-8478-1749-0). 64pp. A well-researched introduction to the life and work of this Mexican artist, best known as a muralist. (Rev: BL 9/15/94; SLJ 5/94) [921]

ROCKWELL, NORMAN

12294 Cohen, Joel H. *Norman Rockwell: America's Best-Loved Illustrator* (4–6). Illus. 1997, Watts LB $22.50 (0-531-20266-6). 64pp. Using 16 full-color reproductions, this book introduces the life of this all-American artist who lived in small towns in New England and painted their inhabitants. (Rev: BL 11/1/97; SLJ 8/97) [921]

12295 Gherman, Beverly. *Norman Rockwell: Storyteller with a Brush* (4–7). Illus. 2000, Simon & Schuster $19.95 (0-689-82001-1). 58pp. An appealing biography of this New England artist who reflected mid-20th-century American life and values in his many paintings. (Rev: BCCB 7–8/00; BL 2/15/00; HB 3–4/00; HBG 10/00; SLJ 2/00) [921]

12296 Venezia, Mike. *Norman Rockwell* (2–4). Series: Getting to Know. 2000, Children's LB $22.50 (0-516-21594-9). 32pp. The popular American artist is introduced with many full color reproductions, a lively text, and some amusing cartoons. (Rev: BL 1/1–15/01) [921]

RODIN, AUGUSTE

12297 Tames, Richard. *Auguste Rodin* (3–4). Series: The Life and Work Of. 2000, Heinemann LB $19.92 (1-57572-342-5). 32pp. This book chronicles the life and work of Rodin and includes material on the events that influenced his growth and development as an artist. (Rev: BL 10/15/00) [921]

ROUSSEAU, HENRI

12298 Pfleger, Susanne. *Henri Rousseau: A Jungle Expedition* (4–7). Trans. by Catherine McCreadie. Illus. Series: Adventures in Art. 1999, Prestel $14.95 (3-7913-1987-6). 28pp. The story of Henri Rousseau and the art that evolved from his visits to a botanical garden. (Rev: BL 2/1/99; SLJ 2/99) [921]

12299 Plazy, Gilles. *A Weekend with Rousseau* (3–8). Illus. Series: A Weekend With. 1993, Rizzoli $19.95 (0-8478-1717-2). 64pp. Using the format of a visit, the life and work of this great French primitive painter are presented. (Rev: BL 1/15/94; SLJ 11/93) [921]

RUSSELL, CHARLES

12300 Winter, Jeanette. *Cowboy Charlie: The Story of Charles M. Russell* (K–4). Illus. 1995, Harcourt $15.00 (0-15-200857-8). 32pp. Chronicles Russell's lifelong love of the West and his career immortalizing it in paintings. (Rev: BCCB 10/95; BL 11/1/95; SLJ 12/95) [921]

SCHULZ, CHARLES

12301 Woods, Mae. *Charles Schulz* (2–4). Series: Children's Authors. 2000, ABDO LB $13.95 (1-57765-425-0). 24pp. An attractive, brief biography of the creator of Peanuts and the gang. (Rev: HBG 3/01; SLJ 1/01) [921]

SIMMONS, PHILIP

12302 Lyons, Mary E. *Catching the Fire: Philip Simmons, Blacksmith* (3–6). Illus. 1997, Houghton $16.00 (0-395-72033-8). 48pp. A biography of a master craftsman and blacksmith, the African American Philip Simmons. (Rev: BL 9/1/97*; HB 9–10/97; HBG 3/98; SLJ 9/97) [921]

TOULOUSE-LAUTREC, HENRI DE

12303 Hart, Tony. *Toulouse-Lautrec* (3–5). Illus. by Susan Hellard. Series: Famous Children. 1994, Barron's paper $5.95 (0-8120-1825-7). This visually attractive biography is limited in scope to the childhood of Toulouse-Lautrec, when he suffered a crippling disease. (Rev: SLJ 8/94) [921]

TURNER, JOSEPH

12304 Woodhouse, Jane. *Joseph Turner* (3–4). Series: The Life and Work Of. 2000, Heinemann LB $19.92 (1-57572-345-X). 32pp. The life and works of this English painter noted chiefly for his luminous seascapes are covered in this brief, well-illustrated biography. (Rev: BL 10/15/00) [921]

VAN GOGH, VINCENT

12305 Connolly, Sean. *Vincent Van Gogh* (3–4). Series: The Life and Work Of. 1999, Heinemann LB $13.95 (1-57572-958-X). 32pp. A biography of

Vincent van Gogh, encompassing his work as well as the people and events that influenced him most. (Rev: BL 2/15/00) [921]

12306 Dionetti, Michelle. *Painting the Wind* (1–4). Illus. by Kevin Hawkes. 1996, Little, Brown $15.95 (0-316-18602-3). 32pp. Van Gogh's last tormented years in Arles, France, as seen through the eyes of his housekeeper's daughter. (Rev: BL 10/1/96; SLJ 10/96) [921]

12307 Lucas, Eileen. *Vincent van Gogh* (2–4). Illus. 1997, Carolrhoda LB $21.27 (1-57505-038-2). 56pp. A simple biography that captures the life and anxieties of the artist, with a good commentary on his work. (Rev: BCCB 9/96; BL 9/1/97; HBG 3/98; SLJ 9/97) [921]

12308 Malam, John. *Vincent van Gogh* (K–3). Series: Tell Me About. 1998, Carolrhoda LB $19.93 (1-57505-249-0). 24pp. This brief account that describes van Gogh's troubled life is illustrated with photographs and reproductions of his paintings. (Rev: HBG 3/99; SLJ 3/99) [921]

WARHOL, ANDY

12309 Venezia, Mike. *Andy Warhol* (2–4). Illus. Series: Getting to Know. 1996, Children's LB $22.00 (0-516-20053-4); paper $6.95 (0-516-26075-8). 32pp. An appealing introduction to this pop artist's life and work, with many fine art reproductions. (Rev: BL 12/15/96; HB 5–6/96) [921]

WEST, BENJAMIN

12310 Brenner, Barbara. *The Boy Who Loved to Draw: Benjamin West* (1–3). Illus. by Olivier Dunrea. 1999, Houghton $15.00 (0-395-85080-0). 48pp. A portrait of the colonial painter whose talent was so great that his parents sent him to Philadelphia to study with an artist at age nine. (Rev: BL 9/15/99; HB 9–10/99; HBG 3/00; SLJ 10/99) [921]

WILLIAMS, PAUL R.

12311 Hudson, Karen E. *The Will and the Way: Paul R. Williams, Architect* (5–7). Illus. 1994, Rizzoli $14.95 (0-8478-1780-6). 64pp. The story of this African American architect who, in his career from the 1920s to the 1970s, designed more than 3,000 buildings. (Rev: BL 2/15/94; SLJ 3/94) [921]

WOOD, GRANT

12312 Duggleby, John. *Artist in Overalls: The Life of Grant Wood* (5–7). Illus. 1996, Chronicle $15.95 (0-8118-1242-1). 48pp. The life of this American artist tells of his difficult struggle with poverty and his great attachment to the Midwest. (Rev: BCCB 6/96; BL 4/15/96; HB 7–8/96; SLJ 5/96) [921]

WOOD, MICHELE

12313 Igus, Toyomi. *Going Back Home: An Artist Returns to the South* (4–8). Illus. by Michele Wood. 1996, Children's Book Pr. $15.95 (0-89239-137-5). 32pp. The author tries to re-create the family history of the African American illustrator Michele Wood. (Rev: BCCB 12/96; BL 9/15/96; SLJ 7/97) [921]

WRIGHT, FRANK LLOYD

12314 Thorne-Thomsen, Kathleen. *Frank Lloyd Wright for Kids* (4–6). Illus. 1994, Chicago Review paper $14.95 (1-55652-207-X). 144pp. In addition to providing a life of this famous architect, this book contains many projects related to his work and a recipe for his favorite breakfast. (Rev: BL 4/15/94; SLJ 7/94) [921]

YANI, WANG

12315 Zhensun, Zheng. *A Young Painter: The Life and Paintings of Wang Yani — China's Extraordinary Young Artist* (5–8). Illus. 1991, Scholastic $17.95 (0-590-44906-0). 80pp. Teenager Wang Yani is hailed as a national treasure in China. (Rev: BCCB 9/91; BL 10/1/91*; SLJ 8/91) [921]

ZHANG, SONG NAN

12316 Zhang, Song Nan. *A Little Tiger in the Chinese Night: An Autobiography in Art* (5–8). Illus. 1993, Tundra $19.95 (0-88776-320-0). 48pp. The biography of a Chinese artist who endured many hardships before he was able to relocate in Montreal. (Rev: BCCB 3/94; BL 1/1/94*; SLJ 5/94) [921]

Composers

BACH, JOHANN SEBASTIAN

12317 Lynch, Wendy. *Bach* (K–3). Series: Lives and Times. 2000, Heinemann LB $13.95 (1-57572-214-3). 24pp. A brief account of the highlights of Bach's life illustrated with drawings and photographs. (Rev: SLJ 9/00) [921]

12318 Venezia, Mike. *Johann Sebastian Bach* (2–4). Series: Getting to Know. 1998, Children's LB $21.00 (0-516-20760-1). 32pp. A mix of historic prints and clever cartoon drawings help bring this prolific composer to life. (Rev: BL 5/15/98; HBG 10/98) [921]

12319 Winter, Jeanette. *Sebastian: A Book About Bach* (2–4). Illus. 1999, Harcourt $16.00 (0-15-200629-X). 40pp. A simple picture book that explores Bach's life, music, and times. (Rev: BCCB 5/99; BL 4/1/99*; HB 7–8/99; HBG 10/99; SLJ 4/99) [921]

BEETHOVEN, LUDWIG VAN

12320 Balcavage, Dynise. *Ludwig van Beethoven: Composer* (4–8). Illus. Series: Great Achievers: Lives of the Physically Challenged. 1997, Chelsea LB $19.95 (0-7910-2082-7). 119pp. A well-rounded biography of Beethoven that covers both his professional career and his personal life and problems. (Rev: SLJ 7/97) [921]

12321 Venezia, Mike. *Ludwig Van Beethoven* (2–4). Illus. Series: Getting to Know. 1996, Children's LB $22.00 (0-516-04542-3). 32pp. An informal portrait of Beethoven and an introduction to his music. (Rev: BL 9/15/96) [921]

BERLIN, IRVING

12322 Streissguth, Thomas. *Say It with Music: A Story About Irving Berlin* (3–5). Illus. 1994, Carolrhoda LB $14.95 (0-87614-810-0). 64pp. This biography of the great American songwriter concentrates on his first 30 years, from childhood in Russia to success on Broadway. (Rev: BL 5/1/94; SLJ 8/94) [921]

BERNSTEIN, LEONARD

12323 Hurwitz, Johanna. *Leonard Bernstein: A Passion for Music* (4–8). Illus. by Sonia O. Lisker. 1993, Jewish Publication Soc. $12.95 (0-8276-0501-3). 80pp. The career of this amazing conductor and composer who was also a gifted pianist and teacher. (Rev: BL 2/15/94; SLJ 12/93) [921]

12324 Venezia, Mike. *Leonard Bernstein* (2–4). Series: Getting to Know. 1997, Children's LB $22.00 (0-516-20492-0). 32pp. A brief profile of this great American composer, who also excelled as a conductor and pianist. (Rev: BL 10/15/97; HBG 3/98) [921]

CHOPIN, FREDERIC

12325 Dineen, Jacqueline. *Frederic Chopin* (K–3). Series: Tell Me About. 1998, Carolrhoda LB $19.93 (1-57505-248-2). 24pp. A short chapterless book on the life and accomplishments of the Polish pianist and composer who died prematurely of tuberculosis. (Rev: HBG 3/99; SLJ 3/99) [921]

GERSHWIN, GEORGE

12326 Mitchell, Barbara. *America, I Hear You: A Story About George Gershwin* (3–5). Illus. 1987, Carolrhoda LB $19.93 (0-87614-309-5). 64pp. The life, times, and career of one of America's great musicians. (Rev: BCCB 11/87; BL 10/1/87; SLJ 12/87)

12327 Reef, Catherine. *George Gershwin: American Composer* (5–8). Illus. Series: Masters of Music. 2000, Morgan Reynolds $19.95 (1-883846-58-7). 112pp. This biography traces the life one of America's great composers, giving insight into his personality, family, and times. (Rev: BL 2/15/00; HBG 10/00; SLJ 3/00) [921]

12328 Venezia, Mike. *George Gershwin* (2–4). Illus. by author. Series: Getting to Know. 1994, Children's LB $22.00 (0-516-04536-9). 32pp. A breezy retelling of the life and times of this multitalented American composer of both classical and popular music. (Rev: SLJ 4/95) [921]

12329 Vernon, Roland. *Introducing Gershwin* (5–7). Illus. 1996, Silver Burdett LB $18.95 (0-382-39161-6); paper $8.95 (0-382-39160-8). 32pp. This oversize volume with copious illustrations re-creates the life and times of George Gershwin. (Rev: BL 5/1/96; SLJ 9/96) [921]

JOPLIN, SCOTT

12330 Mitchell, Barbara. *Raggin': A Story About Scott Joplin* (3–5). Illus. 1987, Carolrhoda LB $21.27 (0-87614-310-9); paper $5.95 (0-87614-589-6). 64pp. The story of a great American musician whose genius was not recognized until after his death. (Rev: BL 10/1/87; SLJ 12/87)

12331 Sabir, C. Ogbu. *Scott Joplin: The King of Ragtime* (4–6). Series: Journey to Freedom. 2000, Child's World LB $25.64 (1-56766-746-5). 40pp. The story of the jazz pianist and composer known as the King of Ragtime. (Rev: BL 11/15/00; HBG 3/01; SLJ 1/01) [921]

MENDELSSOHN, FANNY

12332 Kamen, Gloria. *Hidden Music: The Life of Fanny Mendelssohn* (4–6). Illus. 1996, Simon & Schuster $15.00 (0-689-31714-X). 82pp. Fanny Mendelssohn, the sister of Felix, was also a talented musician and composer, but being a woman, she was denied the same opportunities as her brother. (Rev: BCCB 5/96; BL 3/15/96; HB 9–10/96) [921]

MOZART, WOLFGANG AMADEUS

12333 Downing, Julie. *Mozart Tonight* (2–4). Illus. 1991, Macmillan LB $15.95 (0-02-732881-3). 40pp. In picture-book format, the life of the young Mozart is presented. (Rev: BCCB 4/91; BL 4/15/91; SLJ 4/91) [921]

12334 Lynch, Wendy. *Mozart* (K–3). Series: Lives and Times. 2000, Heinemann LB $13.95 (1-57572-219-4). 24pp. After a brief biography of Mozart, there is a section on how young readers can learn more about him. (Rev: SLJ 9/00) [921]

12335 Malam, John. *Wolfgang Amadeus Mozart* (2–4). Series: Tell Me About. 1998, Carolrhoda LB $19.93 (1-57505-247-4). 24pp. Illustrations include period paintings of Mozart's family, musical scores, and outdoor scenes of Salzburg and Vienna, in this life of Mozart told simply for young readers. (Rev: HBG 3/99; SLJ 1/99) [921]

12336 Vernon, Roland. *Introducing Mozart* (5–7). Illus. 1996, Silver Burdett LB $18.95 (0-382-39159-4); paper $8.95 (0-382-39158-6). 32pp. The life and times of Mozart are covered in the oversize, heavily illustrated volume. (Rev: BL 5/1/96; SLJ 1/97) [921]

SCHUMANN, CLARA

12337 Allman, Barbara. *Her Piano Sang: A Story About Clara Schumann* (4–7). Illus. 1996, Carolrhoda LB $21.27 (1-57505-012-9). 64pp. The story of this groundbreaking composer and pianist who also championed her husband's music. (Rev: BL 1/1–15/97; SLJ 1/97) [921]

12338 Reich, Susanna. *Clara Schumann: Piano Virtuoso* (5–8). 1999, Houghton $18.00 (0-395-89119-1). 128pp. A thorough, well-researched biography of this amazing pianist and composer that tells of her life as a child prodigy, her marriage to Robert Schumann, and her life promoting his music after his death. (Rev: HB 3–4/99; HBG 10/99; SLJ 4/99*) [921]

STRAVINSKY, IGOR

12339 Venezia, Mike. *Igor Stravinsky* (2–4). Illus. Series: Getting to Know. 1996, Children's LB $22.00 (0-516-20054-2). 32pp. The life of this great

20th-century composer and his work are briefly presented, with many illustrations. (Rev: BCCB 7–8/96; BL 12/15/96) [921]

TCHAIKOVSKY, PETER

12340 Venezia, Mike. *Peter Tchaikovsky* (2–4). Illus. by author. Series: Getting to Know. 1994, Children's LB $22.00 (0-516-04537-7). 32pp. An introduction to the life, times, and music of this Russian composer, in a visually pleasing format. (Rev: SLJ 4/95) [921]

Entertainers

ABDUL, PAULA

12341 Ford, M. Thomas. *Paula Abdul: Straight Up* (3–6). Illus. Series: Taking Part. 1992, Macmillan LB $18.95 (0-87518-508-8). 72pp. The life story of the pop entertainer, who takes special interest in a young audience. (Rev: BL 11/15/92; SLJ 7/92) [921]

12342 Zannos, Susan. *Paula Abdul* (3–8). Illus. Series: Real-Life Reader Biographies. 1999, Mitchell Lane LB $15.95 (1-883845-74-2). 32pp. A brief biography of this choreographer and recording artist that recounts her many problems, including a struggle with bulimia and a series of failed marriages. (Rev: BL 6/1–15/99) [921]

AGUILERA, CHRISTINA

12343 Granados, Christine. *Christina Aguilera* (3–4). Series: Real-Life Reader Biographies. 2000, Mitchell Lane LB $15.95 (1-58415-044-0). 32pp. The story of the little girl with the big voice who started out as a member of the *New Mickey Mouse Club*. (Rev: BL 11/15/00) [921]

ANDERSON, MARIAN

12344 Ferris, Jeri. *What I Had Was Singing: The Story of Marian Anderson* (3–6). Illus. 1994, Carolrhoda LB $23.93 (0-87614-818-6); paper $6.95 (0-87614-634-5). 96pp. The story of this African American contralto's struggles and triumphs, including her appearances at the Lincoln Memorial in 1939 and the Metropolitan Opera in the 1950s. (Rev: BL 7/94) [921]

12345 Livingston, Myra Cohn. *Keep on Singing: A Ballad of Marian Anderson* (K–3). Illus. by Samuel Byrd. 1994, Holiday LB $15.95 (0-8234-1098-6). 32pp. In a narrative poem, the life and career of Marian Anderson is celebrated. (Rev: BL 11/1/94; SLJ 3/95) [921]

12346 McKissack, Patricia, and Fredrick McKissack. *Marian Anderson: A Great Singer* (2–4). Illus. Series: Great African Americans. 1991, Enslow LB $14.95 (0-89490-303-9). 32pp. A biography of the great American concert singer, the first African American to sing with the Metropolitan Opera in New York City. (Rev: SLJ 11/91) [921]

ARMSTRONG, LOUIS

12347 McKissack, Patricia, and Fredrick McKissack. *Louis Armstrong: Jazz Musician* (2–4). Illus. Series: Great African Americans. 1991, Enslow LB $14.95 (0-89490-307-1). 32pp. A simple biography of this well-loved American musician. (Rev: BL 1/1/92; SLJ 2/92) [921]

12348 Old, Wendie C. *Louis Armstrong: King of Jazz* (5–9). Series: African American Biographies. 1998, Enslow LB $19.95 (0-89490-997-5). 128pp. A biography of the legendary jazz trumpeter known as "Satchmo" who lived from 1900 to 1971. (Rev: BL 11/15/98) [921]

12349 Orgill, Roxane. *If I Only Had a Horn: Young Louis Armstrong* (K–8). Illus. by Leonard Jenkins. 1997, Houghton $16.00 (0-395-75919-6). 32pp. This lively retelling of key events in jazz musician Louis Armstrong's life is made exciting by the use of dynamic color paintings. (Rev: BL 11/1/97; HBG 3/98; SLJ 9/97) [921]

BALANCHINE, GEORGE

12350 Kristy, Davida. *George Balanchine: American Ballet Master* (5–8). Illus. Series: Biographies. 1996, Lerner LB $25.26 (0-8225-4951-4). 128pp. The story of the Russian émigré choreographer and how he changed the history of American ballet. (Rev: SLJ 8/96) [921]

BALL, LUCILLE

12351 Krohn, Katherine E. *Lucille Ball: Pioneer of Comedy* (4–6). Illus. Series: Achievers. 1992, Lerner LB $21.27 (0-8225-0543-6). 64pp. A biography that tries to capture the hilarity that was the "I Love Lucy" show. (Rev: BL 6/15/92; SLJ 7/92) [921]

BANKS, TYRA

12352 Levin, Pam. *Tyra Banks* (5–8). Illus. Series: Black Americans of Achievement. 1999, Chelsea $19.95 (0-7910-5195-1); paper $9.95 (0-7910-4964-7). 104pp. This is the story of an "ugly duckling" who was awkward and uncoordinated as a child but who later became a supermodel. (Rev: BL 2/15/00; HBG 3/00) [921]

BARNUM, P. T.

12353 Fleming, Alice. *P. T. Barnum: The World's Greatest Showman* (5–8). Illus. 1993, Walker LB $15.85 (0-8027-8235-3). 128pp. This biography of a master showman gives a rundown on his many careers before show business. (Rev: BL 1/15/94; SLJ 12/93) [921]

BARRYMORE, DREW

12354 Zannos, Susan. *Drew Barrymore* (3–4). Series: Real-Life Reader Biographies. 2000, Mitchell Lane LB $15.95 (1-58415-035-1). 32pp. The ups and downs in the career and life of the actress who starred in such films as *E. T.* as a child are touched on in this brief biography. (Rev: BL 11/15/00) [921]

BEATLES

12355 Venezia, Mike. *The Beatles* (2–4). Illus. Series: Getting to Know. 1997, Children's LB $22.00 (0-516-20310-X). 32pp. Color photos, humorous cartoons, and a clever text are used to re-create the fabulous careers of these boys from Liverpool. (Rev: BL 5/15/97) [920]

12356 Woog, Adam. *The Beatles* (4–8). Series: Importance Of. 1997, Lucent LB $17.96 (1-56006-088-3). 128pp. Outlines the lives and careers of these four Liverpool natives and their many achievements. (Rev: BL 10/15/97; SLJ 12/97) [921]

BLADES, RUBÉN

12357 Cruz, Barbara C. *Rubén Blades: Salsa Singer and Social Activist* (4–7). Illus. Series: Hispanic Biographies. 1997, Enslow LB $20.95 (0-89490-893-6). 128pp. A biography of this Panamanian entertainer who has become famous as a singer, actor, and activist. (Rev: HBG 3/98; SLJ 1/98) [921]

BRANDY (SINGER)

12358 Hayes, Donna. *Brandy* (3–4). Series: Real-Life Reader Biographies. 1999, Mitchell Lane LB $15.95 (1-883845-93-9). 32pp. A simple biography of this successful African American singer. (Rev: BL 10/15/99) [921]

12359 Newman, Michael. *Brandy* (5–8). Series: Galaxy of Superstars. 2000, Chelsea LB $17.95 (0-7910-5781-X). 64pp. A biography of the famous singer and star of *Moesha*. (Rev: BL 12/15/00) [921]

BROOKS, GARTH

12360 Howey, Paul. *Garth Brooks: Chart-Bustin' Country* (4–7). Illus. Series: Achievers Biographies. 1998, Lerner LB $14.95 (0-8225-2898-3). 64pp. Using interviews with Garth Brooks and his family plus many interesting photos, this biography tells of the country-western musician's slow rise to fame, his persistence, and his courage to explore forbidden topics in his songs. (Rev: BL 8/98; HBG 10/98) [921]

12361 Powell, Phelan. *Garth Brooks: Award-Winning Country Music Star* (4–7). Series: Real-Life Reader Biographies. 1999, Mitchell Lane LB $15.95 (1-58415-004-1). 32pp. A biography of the award-winning country music star and how he got there. (Rev: SLJ 1/00)

12362 Tallman, Edward. *Garth Brooks* (3–6). Illus. Series: Taking Part. 1993, Dillon LB $13.95 (0-87518-595-9). 64pp. The story of the country music superstar. (Rev: BL 10/15/93; SLJ 2/94) [921]

BULLOCK, SANDRA

12363 Hill, Anne E. *Sandra Bullock* (5–8). Series: People in the News. 2000, Lucent LB $19.96 (1-56006-711-X). 96pp. Quotes from Sandra Bullock and others expand this biography and explain how and why she has gained prominence as a Hollywood actress. (Rev: BL 9/15/00) [921]

12364 Zannos, Susan. *Sandra Bullock* (3–4). Series: Real-Life Reader Biographies. 2000, Mitchell Lane

LB $15.95 (1-58415-027-0). 32pp. A simple biography of the movie actress that stresses her hard work and determination. (Rev: BL 11/15/00; SLJ 1/01) [921]

CAREY, MARIAH

12365 Cole, Melanie. *Mariah Carey* (3–5). Series: Real-Life Reader Biographies. 1998, Mitchell Lane LB $15.95 (1-883845-51-3). 32pp. The life story of the little girl who wanted to be a rock star, who became famous right out of high school, and who married and divorced the man who discovered her. (Rev: BL 6/1–15/98; HBG 3/98) [921]

CARREY, JIM

12366 Wukovits, John F. *Jim Carrey* (4–8). Series: People in the News. 1999, Lucent LB $17.96 (1-56006-561-3). 112pp. From his boyhood in Canada to stardom in Hollywood, this biography reveals Carrey's efforts to become a multidimensional actor. (Rev: BL 8/99; HBG 3/00) [921]

CHAPLIN, CHARLIE

12367 Turk, Ruth. *Charlie Chaplin: Genius of the Silent Screen* (5–9). 2000, Lerner LB $25.26 (0-8225-4957-3). 112pp. A competent overview of this great movie maker's life from his childhood in England to his exile in Switzerland. (Rev: HBG 10/00; SLJ 4/00) [921]

CHARLES, RAY

12368 Turk, Ruth. *Ray Charles: Soul Man* (5–8). Illus. Series: Newsmakers. 1996, Lerner LB $25.26 (0-8225-4928-X). 112pp. This candid biography of the great blind entertainer gives compelling details about Ray Charles's childhood. (Rev: SLJ 8/96) [921]

COSBY, BILL

12369 Conord, Bruce W. *Bill Cosby: Family Man* (3–5). Series: Junior World Biographies. 1993, Chelsea LB $16.95 (0-7910-1761-3). 76pp. A biography of this famous actor and comedian. (Rev: SLJ 6/93) [921]

12370 Haskins, Jim. *Bill Cosby: America's Most Famous Father* (5–7). Illus. 1988, Walker LB $14.85 (0-8027-6786-9). 128pp. The childhood and career of this famous entertainer. (Rev: BL 6/1/88) [921]

12371 Schuman, Michael A. *Bill Cosby: Actor and Comedian* (4–6). Illus. Series: People to Know. 1995, Enslow LB $20.95 (0-89490-548-1). 128pp. The life of this multitalented African American entertainer is told in a highly readable style. (Rev: BL 9/15/95; SLJ 2/96) [921]

12372 Woods, Harold, and Geraldine Woods. *Bill Cosby: Making America Laugh and Learn* (4–7). Illus. 1988, Macmillan LB $13.95 (0-87518-240-2). 48pp. A biography of the outstanding African American comedian, educator, and humanitarian. [921]

DAMON, MATT

12373 Greene, Meg. *Matt Damon* (5–8). Series: Galaxy of Superstars. 2000, Chelsea LB $17.95 (0-7910-5779-8). 64pp. An entertaining biography of the actor who gained star status as the cowriter and lead actor in *Good Will Hunting*. (Rev: BL 12/15/00) [921]

DICAPRIO, LEONARDO

12374 Stauffer, Stacey. *Leonardo DiCaprio* (5–8). Illus. Series: Galaxy of Superstars. 1999, Chelsea $16.95 (0-7910-5151-X); paper $9.95 (0-7910-5326-1). 63pp. The story of this young actor's life gives special attention to his role in *Titanic*. (Rev: BL 4/15/99; HBG 10/99; SLJ 5/99) [921]

DION, CELINE

12375 Cole, Melanie. *Celine Dion* (3–6). Series: Real-Life Reader Biographies. 1998, Mitchell Lane LB $15.95 (1-883845-76-9). 32pp. This overview of the life of singer Celine Dion uses many quotes and sidebar facts. (Rev: SLJ 2/99) [921]

12376 Lutz, Norma Jean. *Celine Dion* (5–8). Series: Galaxy of Superstars. 2000, Chelsea LB $17.95 (0-7910-5777-1). 64pp. The story of the amazing career of this French Canadian singer and how she gained worldwide popularity. (Rev: BL 10/15/00) [921]

DUNCAN, ISADORA

12377 O'Connor, Barbara. *Barefoot Dancer: The Story of Isadora Duncan* (5–7). Illus. 1994, Carolrhoda LB $23.93 (0-87614-807-0). 96pp. The story of this eccentric individualist who influenced and liberated a generation of dancers. (Rev: BCCB 10/94; BL 7/94) [921]

DUNHAM, KATHERINE

12378 O'Connor, Barbara. *Katherine Dunham: Pioneer of Black Dance* (5–8). Illus. 2000, Carolrhoda LB $23.95 (1-57505-353-5). 104pp. A fine biography of the African American choreographer who used her study of anthropology to create works for her own dance company and for stage and screen productions. (Rev: BL 5/15/00; HBG 10/00; SLJ 7/00) [921]

ELLINGTON, DUKE

12379 Pinkney, Andrea D. *Duke Ellington: The Piano Prince and His Orchestra* (K–3). Illus. by Brian Pinkney. 1998, Hyperion LB $16.49 (0-7868-2150-7). 32pp. In a slangy text with wildly colored paintings, the life and work of Duke Ellington are celebrated in this outstanding picture book. (Rev: BCCB 7–8/98; BL 6/1–15/98*; HBG 10/98; SLJ 5/98) [921]

ESTEFAN, GLORIA

12380 Benson, Michael. *Gloria Estefan* (4–6). Series: A&E Biography. 2000, Lerner LB $25.26 (0-8225-4982-4). 112pp. A candid look at a singer who is also a devoted wife and mother, a humanitar-

ian, and an outstanding performer. (Rev: BL 6/1–15/00; HBG 10/00) [921]

12381 Boulais, Sue. *Gloria Estefan* (3–4). Series: Real-Life Reader Biographies. 1998, Mitchell Lane LB $15.95 (1-883845-62-9). 32pp. The story of this music star, born in Cuba, and the accident in 1990 that almost ended her career. (Rev: BL 10/15/98; HBG 10/98) [921]

12382 Gourse, Leslie. *Gloria Estefan: Pop Sensation* (4–6). Series: Book Report Biographies. 2000, Watts LB $22.00 (0-531-11569-0); paper $6.95 (0-531-16457-8). 112pp. The story of the Cuban-born singer who overcame a terrible injury to again rise to stardom. (Rev: BL 9/15/00) [921]

12383 Rodriguez, Janel. *Gloria Estefan* (4–8). Illus. Series: Contemporary Hispanic Americans. 1995, Raintree Steck-Vaughn LB $24.26 (0-8172-3982-0). 48pp. A fine biography of this Hispanic American entertainer, who has shown the power of music and of self-determination. (Rev: BL 3/15/96; SLJ 1/96) [921]

12384 Shirley, David. *Gloria Estefan* (4–7). Illus. Series: Hispanics of Achievement. 1994, Chelsea LB $15.95 (0-7910-2114-4); paper $6.95 (0-7910-2117-3). 80pp. A nicely illustrated biography of the Cuban-born rock star. (Rev: BL 11/15/94; SLJ 10/94) [921]

12385 Stefoff, Rebecca. *Gloria Estefan* (5–8). Illus. 1991, Chelsea LB $19.95 (0-7910-1244-1). 104pp. The story of the singer who broke her back in a 1990 bus accident and her eventual triumph. (Rev: BL 8/91) [921]

12386 Strazzabosco, Jeanne M. *Learning About Determination from the Life of Gloria Estefan* (2–5). Illus. Series: A Character Building Book. 1996, Rosen LB $15.93 (0-8239-2416-5). 24pp. The life story of this important entertainer, emphasizing that her success came from the determination to overcome obstacles. (Rev: BL 10/15/96; SLJ 12/96) [921]

FONDA, JANE

12387 Shorto, Russell. *Jane Fonda: Political Activist* (4–6). Series: New Directions. 1991, Millbrook LB $21.90 (1-56294-045-7); Houghton paper $5.70 (0-395-63564-0). 101pp. Covers Jane Fonda's public and private life, her acting career, and her devotion to a number of causes. (Rev: SLJ 10/91) [921]

GELLAR, SARAH MICHELLE

12388 Powell, Phelan. *Sarah Michelle Gellar* (3–4). Series: Real-Life Reader Biographies. 2000, Mitchell Lane LB $15.95 (1-58415-034-3). 32pp. This short biography tells the story of the popular star of *Buffy the Vampire Slayer*, who began acting at age 4. (Rev: BL 11/15/00) [921]

GOLDBERG, WHOOPI

12389 Adams, Mary A. *Whoopi Goldberg: From Street to Stardom* (4–6). Illus. Series: Taking Part. 1993, Macmillan LB $18.95 (0-87518-562-2). 64pp. An easily read biography of this talented comedian, actress, and talk-show hostess. (Rev: BL 5/1/93; SLJ 7/93) [921]

GRAHAM, MARTHA

12390 Freedman, Russell. *Martha Graham: A Dancer's Life* (4–9). 1998, Clarion $18.00 (0-395-74655-8). 175pp. A thorough, engaging biography of the dancer, company manager, and choreographer who changed the nature of modern dance. (Rev: BCCB 6/98; SLJ 5/98) [921]

12391 Pratt, Paula B. *Martha Graham* (4–8). Illus. Series: The Importance Of. 1995, Lucent LB $22.45 (1-56006-056-5). 112pp. The life of this amazing dancer, choreographer, and dance company founder. (Rev: BL 1/15/95; SLJ 1/95) [921]

12392 Probosz, Kathilyn S. *Martha Graham* (5–8). Illus. Series: People in Focus. 1995, Dillon paper $7.95 (0-382-24961-5). 184pp. A biography that tells of this dancer's many accomplishments while also giving details of her youth and the influences on her work. (Rev: SLJ 10/95) [921]

GRANT, AMY

12393 Italia, Bob. *Amy Grant: From Gospel to Pop* (4–6). Illus. Series: Leading Lady. 1992, ABDO LB $12.94 (1-56239-145-3). 32pp. An engaging biography with high-low interest. (Rev: BL 2/1/93; SLJ 4/93) [921]

HAMMER, M. C.

12394 Saylor-Marchant, Linda. *Hammer: 2 Legit 2 Quit* (3–6). Illus. Series: Taking Part. 1992, Macmillan LB $18.95 (0-87518-522-3). 64pp. The life of the popular African American rap musician and his struggle to succeed. (Rev: BL 1/15/93; SLJ 2/93) [921]

HANSON (MUSICAL GROUP)

12395 Powell, Phelan. *Hanson* (5–8). Series: Galaxy of Superstars. 1999, Chelsea $16.95 (0-7910-5148-X); paper $9.95 (0-7910-5325-3). 63pp. An attractive volume containing biographies of the three-brother singing group that hails from Tulsa, Oklahoma. (Rev: BL 4/15/98; HBG 10/99) [921]

HART, MELISSA JOAN

12396 Gaines, Ann Graham. *Melissa Joan Hart* (3–4). Series: Real-Life Reader Biographies. 2000, Mitchell Lane LB $15.95 (1-58415-036-X). 32pp. A simple profile of the TV actress best known for her roles as Clarissa and Sabrina. (Rev: BL 11/15/00) [921]

HENDRIX, JIMI

12397 Markel, Rita J. *Jimi Hendrix* (5–9). 2001, Lerner LB $25.26 (0-8225-4990-5); paper $7.95 (0-8225-9697-0). 112pp. A better-than-average account of the short life of this guitarist of the 1960s. (Rev: SLJ 3/01) [921]

HEWITT, JENNIFER LOVE

12398 Severs, Vesta-Nadine. *Jennifer Love Hewitt* (3–4). Series: Real-Life Reader Biographies. 2000,

Mitchell Lane LB $15.95 (1-58415-032-7). 32pp. The story of the popular actress who has been a professional since doing Barbie commercials for Mattel as a preteen. (Rev: BL 11/15/00) [921]

HILL, LAURYN

12399 Greene, Meg. *Lauryn Hill* (5–8). Series: Galaxy of Superstars. 1999, Chelsea $17.95 (0-7910-5495-0). 64pp. A biography of the music superstar who won five Grammy Awards for her breakout solo album. (Rev: BL 3/15/00; HBG 10/00) [921]

HINES, GREGORY

12400 De Angelis, Gina. *Gregory Hines* (4–7). Illus. Series: Black Americans of Achievement. 1999, Chelsea $19.95 (0-7910-5197-8); paper $9.95 (0-7910-5198-6). 99pp. Though he is known primarily as a dancer, this biography of Gregory Hines points out his many other talents, including acting. (Rev: BL 2/15/00; HBG 3/00) [921]

HOLMES, KATIE

12401 Boulais, Sue. *Katie Holmes* (3–4). Series: Real-Life Reader Biographies. 2000, Mitchell Lane LB $15.95 (1-58415-038-6). 32pp. A brief biography of the young actress who wisely completed high school before accepting the role in *Dawson's Creek* that made her famous. (Rev: BL 11/15/00) [921]

HOUDINI, HARRY

12402 Lalicki, Tom. *Spellbinder: The Life of Harry Houdini* (5–8). Illus. 2000, Holiday $18.95 (0-8234-1499-X). 88pp. A biography of Elrich Weiss, aka Harry Houdini, and his career as a magician and escape artist. (Rev: BCCB 3/01; BL 9/1/00; HBG 3/01; SLJ 9/00) [921]

12403 Woog, Adam. *Harry Houdini* (4–8). Illus. Series: The Importance Of. 1995, Lucent LB $18.96 (1-56006-053-0). 112pp. The story of the escape artist who amazed and baffled the world with his incredible stunts. (Rev: BL 1/15/95; SLJ 1/95) [921]

HOUSTON, WHITNEY

12404 Cox, Ted. *Whitney Houston* (5–8). Illus. Series: Black Americans of Achievement. 1998, Chelsea $19.95 (0-7910-4455-6); paper $8.95 (0-7910-4456-4). 102pp. A readable biography that tells of Whitney Houston growing up in New Jersey, the major influences in her life, her rise to fame, marriage, and philanthropic endeavors. (Rev: BL 8/98; HBG 10/98) [921]

HOWARD, RON

12405 Kramer, Barbara. *Ron Howard: Child Star and Hollywood Director* (5–9). Series: People to Know. 1998, Enslow LB $19.95 (0-89490-981-9). 112pp. From his days on *The Andy Griffith Show* when he was only six to his present work as a movie director, this is a workmanlike overview of the career of Ron Howard. (Rev: HBG 3/99; SLJ 3/99) [921]

IGLESIAS, ENRIQUE

12406 Granados, Christine. *Enrique Iglesias* (3–4). Series: Real-Life Reader Biographies. 2000, Mitchell Lane LB $15.95 (1-58415-045-9). 32pp. A profile of the son of singer Julio Iglesias and how he started out in show business as Enrique Martinez because he wanted to gain recognition based not his father's name but on his own ability. (Rev: BL 11/15/00) [921]

JACKSON, JANET

12407 Dyson, Cindy. *Janet Jackson* (4–7). Series: Black Americans of Achievement. 2000, Chelsea $19.95 (0-7910-5283-4). 109pp. The life story of the popular singer and the ups and downs of her career. (Rev: BL 6/1–15/00; HBG 10/00) [921]

JACKSON, MICHAEL

12408 Nicholson, Lois. *Michael Jackson* (4–8). Illus. Series: Black Americans of Achievement. 1994, Chelsea LB $19.95 (0-7910-1929-2); paper $9.95 (0-7910-1930-6). 104pp. A life of this popular singer that ends before the sexual abuse charges of 1993. (Rev: BL 10/15/94; SLJ 10/94) [921]

JACKSON, SAMUEL L.

12409 Dils, Tracey E. *Samuel L. Jackson* (4–7). Series: Black Americans of Achievement. 2000, Chelsea $19.95 (0-7910-5281-8). 104pp. The life story of the African American actor who has portrayed diverse characters in films including *Pulp Fiction* and *A Time to Kill*. (Rev: BL 6/1–15/00; HBG 10/00) [921]

LATIFAH, QUEEN

12410 Ruth, Amy. *Queen Latifah* (5–8). Series: A&E Biography. 2000, Lerner LB $19.96 (0-8225-4988-3). 112pp. The story of the female rap singer who used her positive attitudes, hard work, and determination to get ahead. (Rev: BL 3/1/01) [921]

LEE, BRUCE

12411 Tagliaferro, Linda. *Bruce Lee* (5–10). Series: A&E Biography. 2000, Lerner LB $25.26 (0-8225-4948-4); paper $7.95 (0-8225-9688-1). 112pp. This colorful biography of the famous action star is filled with information about him, his films, and his family. (Rev: HBG 10/00; SLJ 5/00) [921]

LEE, SPIKE

12412 McDaniel, Melissa. *Spike Lee: On His Own Terms* (5–8). Series: Book Report Biographies. 1998, Watts LB $22.00 (0-531-11460-0). 96pp. An objective portrait of this controversial director, writer, and promoter of motion pictures featuring black subjects. (Rev: HBG 3/99; SLJ 12/98) [921]

LENNON, JOHN

12413 Wright, David K. *John Lennon: The Beatles and Beyond* (4–6). Illus. Series: People to Know. 1996, Enslow LB $20.95 (0-89490-702-6). 112pp. The story of the famous Beatle, his rise to fame, his activities outside music, and his tragic death. (Rev: BL 10/15/96; SLJ 12/96) [921]

LOCKE, KEVIN

12414 Left Hand Bull, Jacqueline, and Suzanne Haldane. *Lakota Hoop Dancer* (3–6). Illus. 1999, Dutton $15.99 (0-525-45413-6). 32pp. A well-written narrative on the life of Kevin Locke, a Lakota Indian, who performs his hoop dance all over the world. (Rev: BCCB 7–8/99; BL 6/1–15/99; HBG 10/99; SLJ 6/99) [921]

LOPEZ, JENNIFER

12415 Hill, Anne E. *Jennifer Lopez* (5–8). Series: Galaxy of Superstars. 2000, Chelsea LB $17.95 (0-7910-5775-5). 64pp. This book chronicles the career of the young Latina star who is a fine singer and actress. (Rev: BL 10/15/00) [921]

12416 Menard, Valerie. *Jennifer Lopez* (3–4). Series: Real-Life Reader Biographies. 2000, Mitchell Lane LB $15.95 (1-58415-025-4). 32pp. This popular singer-actress got her big break when she played another young singer, Selena. (Rev: BL 11/15/00) [921]

LUCAS, GEORGE

12417 Rau, Dana Meachen, and Christopher Rau. *George Lucas: Creator of Star Wars* (5–8). Series: Book Report Biographies. 1999, Watts LB $22.00 (0-531-11457-0). 112pp. An entertaining look at the man who created *Star Wars*, with basic material about his life and work. (Rev: HBG 10/99; SLJ 7/99) [921]

12418 White, Dana. *George Lucas* (5–8). Series: A&E Biography. 1999, Lerner LB $18.95 (0-8225-4975-1); paper $7.95 (0-8225-9684-9). 128pp. This book covers the childhood and early career of this filmmaker but concentrates on his masterpiece, the creation of the *Star Wars* saga. (Rev: HBG 3/00; SLJ 3/00) [921]

MCGREGOR, EWAN

12419 Jones, Veda Boyd. *Ewan McGregor* (5–8). Series: Galaxy of Superstars. 1999, Chelsea $17.95 (0-7910-5501-9). 64pp. A well-illustrated biography of the Scottish-born actor in the *Star Wars* prequels. (Rev: BL 3/15/00; HBG 10/00) [921]

MARSALIS, WYNTON

12420 Ellis, Veronica F. *Wynton Marsalis* (4–6). Illus. Series: Contemporary African Americans. 1997, Raintree Steck-Vaughn LB $24.26 (0-8172-3998-X). 48pp. A fine biography of this Grammy award–winning musician who is equally at home with jazz and classical music. (Rev: BL 5/15/97; SLJ 2/98) [921]

12421 Gourse, Leslie. *Wynton Marsalis* (4–6). Series: Book Report Biographies. 1999, Watts LB $22.00 (0-531-11673-5). 112pp. Extensively illustrated with black-and-white photographs, this is an attractive biography of the black trumpeter whose versatility extends to both jazz and classical music. (Rev: BL 11/15/99; SLJ 4/00) [921]

MARTIN, RICKY

12422 Menard, Valerie. *Ricky Martin* (3–4). Series: Real-Life Reader Biographies. 1999, Mitchell Lane LB $15.95 (1-58415-059-9). 32pp. Black-and-white photos illustrate this easily read biography of the Puerto Rican singing sensation. (Rev: BL 11/15/99) [921]

MILANO, ALYSSA

12423 Bankston, John. *Alyssa Milano* (3–4). Series: Real-Life Reader Biographies. 2000, Mitchell Lane LB $15.95 (1-58415-040-8). 32pp. The life story of the young actress who grew up on TV's *Who's the Boss* and went on to star in *Charmed*. (Rev: BL 11/15/00) [921]

MONK, THELONIOUS

12424 Raschka, Chris. *Mysterious Thelonious* (3–7). Illus. 1997, Orchard LB $14.99 (0-531-33057-5). 32pp. In a lively mixture of color and motion, this book presents an unusual handling of an unusual subject, a tribute to jazz musician Thelonious Monk. (Rev: BL 11/1/97; HBG 3/98; SLJ 9/97*) [921]

NEW KIDS ON THE BLOCK

12425 McGibbon, Robin. *New Kids on the Block: The Whole Story* (5–8). Illus. 1990, Avon paper $6.95 (0-380-76344-3). 120pp. Stories about members of this band have been collected from a variety of sources, including the members themselves. (Rev: BL 10/1/90) [921]

NIMOY, LEONARD

12426 Micklos, John. *Leonard Nimoy: A Star's Trek* (3–6). Illus. 1988, Macmillan LB $13.95 (0-87518-376-X). 64pp. A simple biography of the man best known as Mr. Spock on "Star Trek." (Rev: BL 7/88; SLJ 10/88)

NORRIS, CHUCK

12427 Cole, Melanie. *Chuck Norris* (3–6). Series: Real-Life Reader Biographies. 1998, Mitchell Lane LB $15.95 (1-883845-91-2). 32pp. This action star of movies and television is a martial arts guru and claims Native American ancestry. (Rev: SLJ 2/99) [921]

NUREYEV, RUDOLF

12428 Maybarduk, Linda. *The Dancer Who Flew: A Memoir of Rudolf Nureyev* (5–9). Illus. 1999, Tundra $18.95 (0-88776-415-0). 188pp. The author, a friend and colleague of Nureyev, not only gives a straightforward biography of the dancer but also tells many backstage stories and introduces his most important roles. (Rev: BL 1/1–15/00; HBG 3/00; SLJ 2/00) [921]

OAKLEY, ANNIE

12429 Dadey, Debbie. *Shooting Star: Annie Oakley, the Legend* (K–3). Illus. by Scott Goto. 1997, Walker LB $16.85 (0-8027-8485-2). 32pp. Fact and fiction mingle in this tall tale about the famous

Western sharp shooter. (Rev: BCCB 6/97; BL 3/15/97; HB 5–6/97; SLJ 4/97*) [921]

12430 Flynn, Jean. *Annie Oakley: Legendary Sharpshooter* (4–9). Series: Historical American Biographies. 1998, Enslow LB $18.95 (0-7660-1012-0). Using a concise text, fact boxes, and a chronology, this is the story of the star attraction of Buffalo Bill's Wild West Show. (Rev: BL 8/98; SLJ 8/98) [921]

12431 Kunstler, James Howard. *Annie Oakley: The American Legend* (K–3). Illus. by Fred Warter. 1996, Simon & Schuster paper $19.95 (0-689-80605-1). The life of the female sharpshooter, of her partnership and marriage to Frank Butler, and her career with Buffalo Bill Cody's Wild West Show. (Rev: SLJ 8/96) [921]

12432 Spinner, Stephanie. *Little Sure Shot: The Story of Annie Oakley* (2–3). Illus. by Jose Miralles. 1993, Random paper $3.99 (0-679-83432-X). 48pp. An interesting portrait of Annie Oakley (real name, Phoebe Ann Moses) and her remarkable career as a markswoman. (Rev: BL 2/1/94; SLJ 2/94) [921]

O'DONNELL, ROSIE

12433 Granados, Christine. *Rosie O'Donnell* (3–4). Series: Real-Life Reader Biographies. 1999, Mitchell Lane LB $15.95 (1-883845-98-X). 32pp. The story of the comedienne, actress, and talk-show host who has used her success to give to others. (Rev: BL 10/15/99) [921]

12434 Kallen, Stuart A. *Rosie O'Donnell* (4–8). Illus. Series: People in the News. 1999, Lucent LB $17.96 (1-56006-546-X). 96pp. An interesting biography of the actress, comedienne, and talk-show host, covering her personal and her professional life. (Rev: BL 8/99; HBG 3/00) [910]

12435 Krohn, Katherine. *Rosie O'Donnell* (4–8). Series: A&E Biography. 1998, Lerner LB $25.26 (0-8225-4939-5). 112pp. Looks at O'Donnell's rise from stand-up comic to TV fame with glimpses of her personal life and the crushing effect of her mother's death when she was a child. (Rev: HBG 3/99; SLJ 2/99) [921]

12436 Meachum, Virginia. *Rosie O'Donnell* (4–6). Series: People to Know. 2000, Enslow LB $19.95 (0-7660-1148-8). 128pp. The life story of the comedian and talk-show host who is noted both for her show business career and for championing worthy causes. (Rev: BL 1/1–15/00; HBG 10/00) [921]

12437 Stone, Tanya L. *Rosie O'Donnell: America's Favorite Grown-up Kid* (4–7). Illus. 2000, Millbrook LB $22.90 (0-7613-1724-4). 48pp. A well-designed, chatty biography of the popular talk-show host and comedienne. (Rev: BL 12/15/00; HBG 3/01) [792.7]

OLMOS, EDWARD JAMES

12438 Carrillo, Louis. *Edward James Olmos* (4–8). Illus. Series: Contemporary Hispanic Americans. 1997, Raintree Steck-Vaughn LB $25.69 (0-8172-3989-8). 48pp. Along with a timeline and glossary, this account traces the life of this contemporary human rights activist and actor. (Rev: BL 4/15/97) [921]

12439 Martinez, Elizabeth Coonrod. *Edward James Olmos: Mexican American Actor* (3–5). Illus. 1994, Millbrook LB $19.90 (1-56294-410-X). 32pp. A biography of this acclaimed Hispanic American actor who has justifiably become a role model for young people. (Rev: BL 1/1/95; SLJ 1/95) [921]

OZAWA, SEIJI

12440 Tan, Sheri. *Seiji Ozawa* (5–7). Illus. Series: Contemporary Asian Americans. 1997, Raintree Steck-Vaughn LB $25.69 (0-8172-3993-6). 48pp. A profile of the Asian American musician who has been the chief conductor of the Boston Symphony for more than 20 years. (Rev: BL 5/1/97; SLJ 9/97) [921]

PAVLOVA, ANNA

12441 Levine, Ellen. *Anna Pavlova: Genius of the Dance* (5–7). 1995, Scholastic $14.95 (0-590-44304-6). 128pp. The life and career of this legendary ballerina, with coverage on the famous ballets in which she danced. (Rev: BCCB 5/95; BL 1/1/95; SLJ 4/95*) [921]

PICKETT, BILL

12442 Pinkney, Andrea D. *Bill Pickett: Rodeo-Ridin' Cowboy* (PS–3). Illus. by Brian Pinkney. 1996, Harcourt $16.00 (0-15-200100-X). 32pp. The story of Bill Pickett, African American rodeo superstar and superb horseman. (Rev: BCCB 11/96; BL 11/1/96; HB 11–12/96; SLJ 10/96) [921]

12443 Sanford, William R., and Carl R. Green. *Bill Pickett: African-American Rodeo Star* (4–6). Illus. Series: Legendary Heroes of the Wild West. 1997, Enslow LB $16.95 (0-89490-676-3). 48pp. This is a short biography of the colorful rodeo star who is considered one of the legends of the Wild West. (Rev: BL 3/15/97) [921]

PRESLEY, ELVIS

12444 Krohn, Katherine E. *Elvis Presley: The King* (5–7). Illus. 1994, Lerner LB $17.50 (0-8225-2877-0). 64pp. A somewhat sanitized biography of Elvis Presley that highlights important events in his career. (Rev: BL 7/94; SLJ 7/94) [921]

12445 Woog, Adam. *Elvis Presley* (4–8). Illus. Series: The Importance Of. 1997, Lucent LB $18.96 (1-56006-084-0). 112pp. The life of this great rocker and his lasting influence on popular music. (Rev: BL 1/1–15/97) [921]

PRICE, LEONTYNE

12446 McNair, Joseph. *Leontyne Price* (4–6). Series: Journey to Freedom. 2000, Child's World LB $25.64 (1-56766-720-1). 40pp. The life story of the famous opera star who rose from poverty to sing in all the major opera houses of the world. (Rev: BL 11/15/00; HBG 3/01) [921]

12447 Steins, Richard. *Leontyne Price: Opera Star* (4–6). Illus. Series: The Library of Famous Women. 1993, Blackbirch LB $17.95 (1-56711-009-6).

64pp. A candid view of the singer who, while thrilling millions, broke color barriers in the world of opera. (Rev: BL 6/1–15/93; SLJ 8/93) [921]

PRINZE, FREDDIE, JR.

12448 Wilson, Wayne. *Freddie Prinze, Jr.* (3–4). Series: Real-Life Reader Biographies. 2000, Mitchell Lane LB $15.95 (1-58415-063-7). 32pp. The story of the talented performer and actor whose famous father died before he could get to know him. (Rev: BL 11/15/00) [921]

QUINN, ANTHONY

12449 Amdur, Melissa. *Anthony Quinn* (5–8). Illus. Series: Hispanics of Achievement. 1993, Chelsea LB $19.95 (0-7910-1251-4). 104pp. The life of this Mexican American actor is told with many interesting asides concerning his career and black-and-white stills from his movies. (Rev: BL 9/15/93) [921]

REEVE, CHRISTOPHER

12450 Alter, Judith. *Christopher Reeve: Triumph Over Tragedy* (4–6). Series: Book Report Biographies. 2000, Watts LB $22.00 (0-531-11674-3). 112pp. The story of the motion picture actor who played Superman, his rise to stardom, his crippling equestrian accident, and his battle to recover. (Rev: BL 11/15/00) [921]

RIMES, LEANN

12451 Zymet, Cathy Alter. *LeAnn Rimes* (5–8). Series: Galaxy of Superstars. 1999, Chelsea $16.95 (0-7910-5152-8); paper $9.95 (0-7910-5327-X). 63pp. This book covers the rise to stardom and the career of this country-western singer who hails from Jackson, Mississippi. (Rev: BL 4/15/98; HBG 10/99) [921]

ROBERTS, JULIA

12452 Wilson, Wayne. *Julia Roberts* (3–4). Series: Real-Life Reader Biographies. 2000, Mitchell Lane LB $15.95 (1-58415-028-9). 32pp. A simple biography with plenty of pictures of the actress whose career took off after her performance in *Pretty Woman*. (Rev: BL 11/15/00; SLJ 1/01) [921]

ROBESON, PAUL

12453 McKissack, Patricia, and Fredrick McKissack. *Paul Robeson: A Voice to Remember* (2–4). Illus. by Michael D. Blegel. Series: Great African Americans. 1992, Enslow LB $14.95 (0-89490-310-1). 32pp. The story of the great singer and actor who spoke out against discrimination. (Rev: BL 9/15/92; SLJ 10/92) [921]

12454 Wright, David K. *Paul Robeson: Actor, Singer, Political Activist* (5–9). Illus. Series: African American Biographies. 1998, Enslow LB $19.95 (0-89490-944-4). 128pp. This book details Robeson's personal and professional life and the hardships he faced because of his race and beliefs. (Rev: BL 11/15/98) [921]

ROCK, CHRIS

12455 Blue, Rose, and Corinne J. Naden. *Chris Rock* (4–7). Series: Black Americans of Achievement. 2000, Chelsea $19.95 (0-7910-5277-X). 104pp. The story of the comedian and actor who began his career on *Saturday Night Live* and is noted for his acerbic wit. (Rev: BL 6/1–15/00; HBG 10/00) [921]

RODRIGUEZ, ROBERT

12456 Marvis, Barbara. *Robert Rodriguez* (3–5). Illus. Series: Real-Life Reader Biographies. 1998, Mitchell Lane LB $15.95 (1-883845-48-3). 24pp. Using a simple text, short chapters, and many black-and-white photographs, this is a biography of the well-known Hispanic American filmmaker Robert Rodriguez. (Rev: BL 6/1–15/98; HBG 3/98) [921]

ROGERS, WILL

12457 Bennett, Cathereen L. *Will Rogers: Quotable Cowboy* (4–6). Illus. 1995, Lerner LB $19.93 (0-8225-3155-0). 96pp. The exciting life of Will Rogers — noted actor, writer, humorist, and humanitarian. (Rev: BL 3/1/96; SLJ 12/95) [921]

12458 Dadey, Debbie. *Will Rogers: Larger than Life* (K–3). Illus. by Scott Goto. 1999, Walker LB $16.85 (0-8027-8682-0). 32pp. A picture-book introduction to the laconic, humble entertainer who displayed a unique sense of humor. (Rev: BL 4/1/99; HBG 10/99; SLJ 9/99) [921]

12459 Malone, Mary. *Will Rogers: Cowboy Philosopher* (4–7). Illus. Series: People to Know. 1996, Enslow LB $20.95 (0-89490-695-X). 128pp. A lively look at the life and accomplishments of this cowboy and show business idol. (Rev: BL 5/15/96; SLJ 6/96) [921]

RONSTADT, LINDA

12460 Amdur, Melissa. *Linda Ronstadt* (5–8). Illus. Series: Hispanics of Achievement. 1993, Chelsea LB $19.95 (0-7910-1781-8). 112pp. This biography of the popular singer focuses on her Mexican American heritage and how she became aware of it. (Rev: BL 9/15/93; SLJ 10/93) [921]

RUSSELL, KERI

12461 Hasday, Judy. *Keri Russell* (3–4). Series: Real-Life Reader Biographies. 2000, Mitchell Lane LB $15.95 (1-58415-033-5). 32pp. An easily read biography of the young actress who plays Felicity. (Rev: BL 11/15/00) [921]

RYDER, WINONA

12462 Menard, Valerie. *Winona Ryder* (3–4). Series: Real-Life Reader Biographies. 2000, Mitchell Lane LB $15.95 (1-58415-039-4). 32pp. A simple biography of the talented actress who appeared in 23 movies before her 30th birthday. (Rev: BL 11/15/00) [921]

SANDLER, ADAM

12463 Seldman, David. *Adam Sandler* (5–8). Series: Galaxy of Superstars. 2000, Chelsea LB $17.95 (0-7910-5773-9). 64pp. An entertaining biography of the actor and comedian who gained notoriety from his roles in *The Waterboy* and *Big Daddy*. (Rev: BL 12/15/00) [921]

SARALEGUI, CRISTINA

12464 Menard, Valerie. *Cristina Saralegui* (3–4). Illus. Series: Real-Life Reader Biographies. 1998, Mitchell Lane LB $15.95 (1-883845-60-2). 32pp. A Cuban refugee, Cristina is an Emmy Award-winning talk show host who is known as the Spanish-language Oprah Winfrey. (Rev: BL 10/15/98; HBG 10/98) [921]

SAVION

12465 Glover, Savion, and Bruce Weber. *Savion! My Life in Tap* (5–10). 2000, Morrow $19.95 (0-688-15629-0). 79pp. A fascinating autobiography of the young dancer and choreographer whose tap dancing includes rap and hip-hop in a wonderful combination that has entranced audiences. (Rev: BCCB 2/00; HBG 10/00; SLJ 3/00) [921]

SELENA (SINGER)

12466 Marvis, Barbara. *Selena* (3–5). Series: Real-Life Reader Biographies. 1998, Mitchell Lane LB $9.99 (1-883845-47-5). 32pp. An easily read biography of the rise to fame and the tragic death of the Texas-born Tejano singer Selena Perez. (Rev: BL 6/1–15/98; HBG 3/98) [921]

12467 Romero, Maritza. *Selena Perez: Queen of Tejano Music* (2–3). Series: Great Hispanics of Our Time. 1998, Rosen LB $13.95 (0-8239-5086-7). 24pp. Double-page spreads are used to tell the story of this popular Tejano singer and her tragic, premature death. (Rev: SLJ 9/98) [921]

SILVERSTONE, ALICIA

12468 Powell, Phelan. *Alicia Silverstone* (3–4). Series: Real-Life Reader Biographies. 2000, Mitchell Lane LB $15.95 (1-58415-037-8). 32pp. The life story of this popular young actress who began modeling at age 6 and had been in several movies by the time she turned 20. (Rev: BL 11/15/00) [921]

SMITS, JIMMY

12469 Cole, Melanie. *Jimmy Smits* (3–4). Illus. Series: Real-Life Reader Biographies. 1998, Mitchell Lane LB $15.95 (1-883845-59-9). 32pp. The story of the Latin American actor from New York who starred in such TV shows as *L.A. Law* and *NYPD Blue*. (Rev: BL 10/15/98; HBG 10/98) [921]

SPEARS, BRITNEY

12470 Gaines, Ann Graham. *Britney Spears* (3–4). Series: Real-Life Reader Biographies. 1999, Mitchell Lane LB $15.95 (1-58415-060-2). 32pp. This is a simple biography of the singer who is a former Mouseketeer and who once shared the stage with 'N Sync. (Rev: BL 11/15/99) [921]

12471 Lutz, Norma Jean. *Britney Spears* (5–8). Series: Galaxy of Superstars. 1999, Chelsea $17.95 (0-7910-5499-3). 64pp. A profile of the popular entertainer, telling how her childhood influenced her career path. (Rev: BL 3/15/00; HBG 10/00) [921]

SPICE GIRLS (MUSICAL GROUP)

12472 Shore, Nancy. *Spice Girls* (5–8). Series: Galaxy of Superstars. 1999, Chelsea $16.95 (0-7910-5149-8); paper $9.95 (0-7910-5328-8). 63pp. Biographies of members of the popular singing group that took first Britain and then the world by storm. (Rev: BL 4/15/98; HBG 10/99; SLJ 5/99) [921]

SPIELBERG, STEVEN

12473 Gottfried, Ted. *Steven Spielberg: From Reels to Riches* (4–6). Series: Book Report Biographies. 2000, Watts LB $22.00 (0-531-11672-7); paper $6.95 (0-531-16493-4). 112pp. From nerdy teenager to Hollywood's most successful filmmaker, this biography of Steven Spielberg also explores his techniques. (Rev: BL 9/15/00) [921]

12474 Meachum, Virginia. *Steven Spielberg: Hollywood Filmmaker* (4–6). Illus. Series: People to Know. 1996, Enslow LB $20.95 (0-89490-697-6). 112pp. The creator of such movie hits as *ET, Jaws,* and *Schindler's List,* is profiled in this easily read biography. (Rev: BL 8/96; SLJ 10/96) [921]

12475 Powers, Tom. *Steven Spielberg: Master Storyteller* (5–7). Illus. 1997, Lerner LB $25.26 (0-8225-4929-8). 128pp. A candid biography of this successful film maker, illustrated with stills from many of his most famous pictures, e.g., *Jaws* and *Schindler's List.* (Rev: BL 6/1–15/97) [921]

12476 Schoell, William. *Magic Man: The Life and Films of Steven Spielberg* (4–7). Illus. 1998, Tudor $18.95 (0-936389-57-5). 128pp. This biography of Spielberg concentrates on how he produces the astonishing special effects for his movies. (Rev: BL 5/15/98) [921]

TALLCHIEF, MARIA

12477 Tallchief, Maria, and Rosemary Wells. *Tallchief: America's Prima Ballerina* (3–5). 1999, Viking $15.99 (0-670-88756-0). 32pp. An autobiography of New York City Ballet's former star who began taking dance lessons while growing up on an Osage Indian reservation in Oklahoma. (Rev: BL 11/1/99*; HBG 3/00; SLJ 11/99) [921]

TWAIN, SHANIA

12478 Gallagher, Jim. *Shania Twain: Grammy Award-Winning Singer* (4–7). Series: Real-Life Reader Biographies. 1999, Mitchell Lane LB $15.95 (1-58415-000-9). 32pp. The story of the entertainer who was adopted into the Ojibwa tribe, began singing in bars at age 8, and went on to marry producer Mutt Lange. (Rev: SLJ 1/00) [921]

TYLER, LIV

12479 Boulais, Sue. *Liv Tyler* (3–4). Series: Real-Life Reader Biographies. 2000, Mitchell Lane LB $15.95 (1-58415-041-6). 32pp. This is the story of the talented model and actress who didn't learn until her teens that her father was Aerosmith's Steven Tyler. (Rev: BL 11/15/00) [921]

WASHINGTON, DENZEL

12480 Simmons, Alex. *Denzel Washington* (4–6). Illus. Series: Contemporary African Americans. 1997, Raintree Steck-Vaughn LB $25.69 (0-8172-3986-3). 48pp. In this biography of actor Denzel Washington, he claims that his mother and the Boys Club saved him from a life of crime. (Rev: BL 5/15/97; SLJ 2/98) [921]

WHITE, DIANA

12481 White, Diana. *Ballerina Dreams* (1–3). Illus. by Jacqueline Rogers. Series: Hello Reader! 1998, Scholastic paper $3.99 (0-590-37233-5). This easy chapter book is the autobiography of a ballerina with the New York City Ballet that contains a description of how she overcame many problems to achieve her goals. (Rev: SLJ 3/99) [921]

WILLIAMS, ROBIN

12482 Zannos, Susan. *Robin Williams* (3–4). Series: Real-Life Reader Biographies. 2000, Mitchell Lane LB $15.95 (1-58415-029-7). 32pp. From playing Mork the alien on TV to winning an Oscar for his film work, this is a brief biography of the famous comedian and actor. (Rev: BL 11/15/00) [921]

WILLIAMS, VANESSA

12483 Boulais, Sue. *Vanessa Williams* (3–8). Illus. Series: Real-Life Reader Biographies. 1999, Mitchell Lane LB $15.95 (1-883845-75-0). 32pp. In spite of losing her Miss America title because of a scandal in 1983, Williams bounced back and became a popular singer and entertainer. (Rev: BL 6/1–15/99) [921]

WINFREY, OPRAH

12484 Brooks, Philip. *Oprah Winfrey: A Voice for the People* (4–6). Series: Book Report Biographies. 1999, Watts LB $22.00 (0-531-11563-1). 112pp. A thorough biography that traces Oprah's rise to fame and the obstacles she confronted. (Rev: BL 10/15/99) [921]

12485 Otfinoski, Steven. *Oprah Winfrey: Television Star* (4–6). Illus. Series: Library of Famous Women. 1993, Blackbirch LB $17.95 (1-56711-015-0). 64pp. Accurately portrays the personal and public life of this influential superstar. (Rev: BL 11/15/93; SLJ 2/94) [921]

12486 Woods, Geraldine. *The Oprah Winfrey Story: Speaking Her Mind* (3–6). Series: Taking Part. 1991, Macmillan LB $13.95 (0-87518-463-4). 79pp. From dire poverty and abuse to talk show stardom, this is the story of Oprah Winfrey. (Rev: SLJ 3/92) [921]

Writers

AARDEMA, VERNA

12487 Aardema, Verna. *A Bookworm Who Hatched* (2–5). Illus. by Dede Smith. Series: Meet the Author. 1993, Richard C. Owen $14.95 (1-878450-39-5). 32pp. In this autobiographical account, the noted author reveals stories about her life, writing techniques, and how she interacts with her reading audience. (Rev: BL 9/1/93; HB 9–10/93) [921]

ADLER, DAVID A.

12488 Adler, David A. *My Writing Day* (3–5). Series: Meet the Author. 1999, Richard C. Owen LB $14.95 (1-57274-326-3). 32pp. The creator of the Cam Jansen mysteries tells a little about his life, writing career, and workday. (Rev: BL 9/15/99; HBG 3/00; SLJ 11/99) [921]

ALCOTT, LOUISA MAY

12489 Ruth, Amy. *Louisa May Alcott* (4–7). Series: A&E Biography. 1999, Lerner $25.26 (0-8225-4938-7). 128pp. A clear, readable life of the author who wrote from personal experience about family life at the time of the Civil War and later. (Rev: BL 3/15/00; HBG 3/99; SLJ 1/99) [921]

12490 Warrick, Karen Clemens. *Louisa May Alcott: Author of Little Women* (5–8). Series: Historical American Biographies. 2000, Enslow LB $18.95 (0-7660-1254-9). 128pp. Using many direct quotes from Alcott, along with fact boxes, maps, a chronology, and chapter notes, this is an interesting biography of the prolific writer from Pennsylvania. (Rev: BL 3/15/00; HBG 10/00) [921]

ANDERSEN, HANS CHRISTIAN

12491 Brust, Beth Wagner. *The Amazing Paper Cuttings of Hans Christian Andersen* (3–6). Illus. 1994, Ticknor $17.00 (0-395-66787-9). 80pp. The story of Hans Christian Andersen's life is told and illustrated with many examples of his famous paper cuttings. (Rev: BCCB 3/94; BL 3/1/94; HB 7–8/94; SLJ 3/94) [921]

12492 Burch, Joann J. *A Fairy-Tale Life: A Story About Hans Christian Andersen* (3–5). Illus. 1994, Carolrhoda LB $21.27 (0-87614-829-1). 64pp. A biography that concentrates on Andersen's childhood and his development as a writer. (Rev: BL 9/1/94) [921]

12493 Langley, Andrew. *Hans Christian Andersen: The Dreamer of Fairy Tales* (3–5). Series: What's Their Story? 1998, Oxford $12.95 (0-19-521435-8). 32pp. Vivid watercolors illustrate this simple, entertaining biography of the Danish fairy-tale writer. (Rev: BL 2/15/99; HBG 3/99; SLJ 1/99) [921]

ANGELOU, MAYA

12494 Cuffie, Terrasita A. *Maya Angelou* (4–8). Series: The Importance Of. 1999, Lucent LB $17.96 (1-56006-532-X). 80pp. A biography that traces Maya Angelou's life from her childhood exposure to poverty and bigotry in the rural South to her eventual fame as a writer. (Rev: BL 9/15/99) [921]

12495 Harper, Judith E. *Maya Angelou* (4–6). Series: Journey to Freedom. 1999, Child's World LB $16.95 (1-56766-570-5). 40pp. Stresses the important achievements and contributions of this contemporary African American writer. (Rev: BL 7/99; HBG 10/99; SLJ 7/99) [921]

12496 King, Sarah E. *Maya Angelou Greeting the Morning* (3–5). Illus. Series: Gateway Biographies. 1994, Millbrook LB $22.90 (1-56294-431-2). 48pp. The inspiring story of the great African American writer and the terrible difficulties she has overcome. (Rev: BL 8/94; SLJ 4/94) [921]

12497 Kite, L. Patricia. *Maya Angelou* (4–7). Series: A&E Biography. 1999, Lerner $25.26 (0-8225-4944-1). 112pp. Black-and-white photographs illustrate this biography of the woman who overcame great obstacles to become a leading African American author. (Rev: BL 3/15/00) [921]

12498 Raatma, Lucia. *Maya Angelou: Author and Documentary Filmmaker* (4–8). Series: Ferguson's Career Biographies. 2001, Ferguson LB $16.95 (0-89434-336-X). 127pp. As well as a life of Maya Angelou, this book includes information on how to become a writer, filmmaker, and director. (Rev: SLJ 2/01) [921]

12499 Spain, Valerie. *Meet Maya Angelou* (3–5). Illus. Series: Bullseye Biography. 1995, Knopf paper $3.99 (0-679-86542-X). 92pp. A short, simple biography that gives details of the personal and professional life of this great African American writer, with details taken from her autobiographical writings. (Rev: BL 2/15/95) [921]

ASCH, FRANK

12500 Asch, Frank. *One Man Show* (1–4). Photos by Jan Asch. Illus. Series: Meet the Author. 1997, Richard C. Owen $14.95 (1-57274-095-7). 32pp. In this autobiography, author Asch introduces himself and his family, interests, and writing techniques. (Rev: HBG 3/98; SLJ 9/97) [921]

ASIMOV, ISAAC

12501 Boerst, William J. *Isaac Asimov: Writer of the Future* (5–9). Illus. 1998, Morgan Reynolds $18.95 (1-883846-32-3). 112pp. An engaging biography of the amazingly prolific author and scientist who, as a young man, was considered a misfit. (Rev: BL 12/1/98) [921]

12502 Judson, Karen. *Isaac Asimov: Master of Science Fiction* (5–9). Illus. 1998, Enslow LB $19.95 (0-7660-1031-7). 112pp. A biography of Asimov that includes two chapters particularly helpful to researchers: his importance as a writer of science fiction and his work in other genres. (Rev: BL 12/1/98; HBG 3/99; SLJ 2/99) [921]

AVI

12503 Markham, Lois. *Avi* (5–7). Illus. 1996, Learning Works paper $6.95 (0-88160-280-9). 128pp. The life and writing techniques of Avi, a very successful writer of books for young people. (Rev: BL 4/1/96; SLJ 8/96) [921]

BALDWIN, JAMES

12504 Tackach, James. *James Baldwin* (4–8). Illus. Series: The Importance Of. 1997, Lucent LB $18.96 (1-56006-070-0). 95pp. Covers the life and accomplishments of this important African American writer. (Rev: BL 1/1–15/97) [921]

BATES, KATHERINE LEE

12505 Younger, Barbara. *Purple Mountain Majesties: The Story of Katherine Lee Bates and "America the Beautiful."* (3–5). Illus. by Stacey Schuett. 1998, Dutton $15.99 (0-525-45653-8). 40pp. The life story of Katherine Lee Bates and her transcontinental trip across the U.S. in 1893 that led to the writing of "America the Beautiful." (Rev: BCCB 10/98; BL 7/98; HBG 10/98; SLJ 8/98) [921]

BAUER, MARION DANE

12506 Bauer, Marion Dane. *A Writer's Story from Life to Fiction* (5–8). 1995, Clarion $14.95 (0-395-72094-X); paper $6.95 (0-395-75053-9). 133pp. This famous author explains how she has taken her own experiences and used them as the beginning of many of her books. (Rev: BL 9/15/95; SLJ 10/95) [921]

BROWN, HELEN GURLEY

12507 Falkof, Lucille. *Helen Gurley Brown: The Queen of Cosmopolitan* (5–8). Illus. Series: Wizards of Business. 1992, Garrett LB $17.26 (1-56074-013-2). 60pp. This life story of the magazine magnate includes excellent tips for aspiring entrepreneurs. (Rev: BL 6/15/92; SLJ 7/92) [921]

BROWN, MARGARET WISE

12508 Blos, Joan W. *The Days Before Now: An Autobiographical Note by Margaret Wise Brown* (K–3). Illus. by Thomas B. Allen. 1994, Simon & Schuster $15.00 (0-671-79628-3). 32pp. A picture book biography of the famous children's author using her own words to tell her story. (Rev: BCCB 1/95; BL 12/15/94; SLJ 3/95) [921]

BRUCHAC, JOSEPH

12509 Bruchac, Joseph. *Seeing the Circle* (3–5). Series: Meet the Author. 1999, Richard C. Owen LB $14.95 (1-57274-327-1). 32pp. Bruchac's account of his life includes his work as a children's author, focusing on Native American fiction and outstanding retellings of folklore and history. (Rev: BL 9/15/99; HBG 3/00; SLJ 11/99) [921]

BUCK, PEARL S.

12510 Mitchell, Barbara. *Between Two Worlds: A Story About Pearl Buck* (3–6). Illus. by Karen Ritz. 1988, Carolrhoda LB $21.27 (0-87614-332-X). 56pp. The life of this child of American missionaries in China, who grew up to become a famous novelist. (Rev: BL 3/1/89; SLJ 2/89) [921]

BUNTING, EVE

12511 Bunting, Eve. *Once Upon a Time* (2–5). Illus. 1995, Richard C. Owen $14.95 (1-878450-59-X). 32pp. An autobiography of the prolific writer of children's books, who spent her childhood in Ireland. (Rev: BCCB 7–8/95; BL 8/95; HB 7–8/95) [921]

BURNETT, FRANCES HODGSON

12512 Carpenter, Angelica S., and Jean Shirley. *Frances Hodgson Burnett: Beyond the Secret Garden* (4–8). Illus. 1990, Lerner LB $25.26 (0-8225-4905-0). 128pp. The story of the well-known English-born writer who came to America at the age of 15. (Rev: BCCB 12/90; BL 1/1/91; SLJ 3/91) [921]

BURROUGHS, EDGAR RICE

12513 Boerst, William J. *Edgar Rice Burroughs: Creator of Tarzan* (5–8). Illus. Series: World Writers. 2000, Morgan Reynolds LB $19.95 (1-883846-56-0). 112pp. A concise biography of the prolific author who created Tarzan and was a pioneer of the science fiction genre. (Rev: BL 7/00; HBG 3/01) [921]

BYARS, BETSY

12514 Byars, Betsy. *The Moon and I* (4–7). Illus. 1996, Morrow paper $4.95 (0-688-13704-0). 96pp. A memoir from this well-known children's author, which gives her the opportunity to tell how she likes both writing and snakes. (Rev: BCCB 3/92*; BL 5/15/92; SLJ 4/92) [921]

CATHER, WILLA

12515 Bedard, Michael. *The Divide* (K–4). Illus. by Emily Arnold McCully. 1997, Doubleday $16.95 (0-385-32124-4). 32pp. This partial biography tells about the move that Willa Cather made with her family when she was 9 to the plains of Nebraska in 1883 and the painful adjustment she had to make. (Rev: BL 10/1/97; HBG 3/98; SLJ 9/97) [921]

12516 Streissguth, Thomas. *Writer of the Plains: A Story About Willa Cather* (4–7). Illus. 1997, Carolrhoda LB $19.93 (1-57505-015-3). 64pp. A simple introduction to the works of Willa Cather and the places where she lived and wrote. (Rev: BL 6/1–15/97; SLJ 10/97) [921]

CERVANTES, MIGUEL DE

12517 Goldberg, Jake. *Miguel de Cervantes* (5–8). Illus. Series: Hispanics of Achievement. 1993, Chelsea LB $19.95 (0-7910-1238-7). 112pp. The biography of the creator of *Don Quixote*, whose life, including time spent as a slave in Algiers, also reads like a novel. (Rev: BL 9/15/93) [921]

CHERRY, LYNNE

12518 Cherry, Lynne. *Making a Difference in the World* (3–5). Series: Meet the Author. 2000, Richard C. Owen $14.95 (1-57274-373-5). 32pp. This noted author and illustrator of children's picture books talks about her life and how, when, and why she works. (Rev: BL 7/00; HBG 3/01; SLJ 12/00) [921]

COLE, JOANNA

12519 Cole, Joanna, and Wendy Saul. *On the Bus with Joanna Cole* (2–6). Illus. Series: Creative Sparks. 1996, Heinemann $16.95 (0-435-08131-4). 61pp. The creator of the Magic School Bus series talks about her life and writing. (Rev: HB 9–10/96; SLJ 6/96*) [921]

DAHL, ROALD

12520 Dahl, Roald. *Boy: Tales of Childhood* (5–8). Illus. 1984, Farrar $16.00 (0-374-37374-4); Puffin paper $5.99 (0-14-031890-9). 176pp. Beginning with a family history, the author recounts vignettes of memorable experiences in his childhood. [921]

12521 Powling, Chris. *Roald Dahl* (2–3). Series: Tell Me About. 1998, Carolrhoda $19.93 (1-57505-274-1). 24pp. Using many full-color photographs, this book traces the important events in Dahl's professional life, with emphasis on the use of imagination in writing. (Rev: BCCB 1/99; HBG 3/99; SLJ 1/99) [921]

12522 Shavick, Andrea. *Roald Dahl: The Champion Storyteller* (3–5). Illus. Series: What's Their Story? 1998, Oxford LB $12.95 (0-19-521432-3). 32pp. This biography of British author Roald Dahl emphasizes his writing career and includes excerpts from his autobiography. (Rev: BL 2/15/99; HBG 3/99; SLJ 1/99) [921]

D'ANGELO, PASCAL

12523 Murphy, Jim. *Pick and Shovel Poet: The Journeys of Pascal D'Angelo* (5–10). 2000, Clarion $20.00 (0-395-77610-4). 162pp. The story of the Italian American poet who also wrote an important autobiography about coming to the New World. (Rev: BCCB 12/00; HB 1–2/01; HBG 3/01; SLJ 1/01) [921]

DEPAOLA, TOMIE

12524 dePaola, Tomie. *Here We All Are: A 26 Fairmount Avenue Book* (2–5). Illus. 2000, Putnam $13.99 (0-399-23496-9). 80pp. A short chapter book that continues Tomie dePaola's *26 Fairmount Avenue* memoir when, as a 5-year-old, he gets a new baby sister. (Rev: BCCB 9/00; BL 5/1/00; HB 5–6/00; HBG 10/00; SLJ 6/00) [921]

12525 dePaola, Tomie. *On My Way* (2–4). Illus. 2001, Putnam $13.99 (0-399-23583-3). 32pp. A continuation of dePaola's remembrances of his childhood that includes a visit to the 1940 World's Fair. (Rev: BCCB 3/01; BL 12/15/00; SLJ 2/01)

12526 dePaola, Tomie. *26 Fairmount Avenue* (3–5). Illus. 1999, Putnam paper $13.99 (0-399-23246-X). 64pp. A charming memoir of his childhood by the famous children's writer. (Rev: BCCB 6/99; BL 8/99; HB 5–6/99; HBG 10/99; SLJ 6/99) [813]

DICKENS, CHARLES

12527 Ayer, Eleanor. *Charles Dickens* (4–8). Series: The Importance Of. 1998, Lucent LB $22.45 (1-56006-525-7). 96pp. This biography of Dickens includes an analysis of his most famous works and why they are important in English literature. (Rev: BL 5/15/98) [921]

12528 Collins, David R. *Tales for Hard Times: A Story About Charles Dickens* (4–8). Illus. by David Mataya. Series: Creative Minds. 1991, Carolrhoda LB $18.95 (0-87614-433-4). 64pp. The life of Charles Dickens, including his poverty-ridden childhood. (Rev: SLJ 3/91) [921]

12529 Stanley, Diane, and Peter Vennema. *Charles Dickens: The Man Who Had Great Expectations* (3–8). Illus. by Diane Stanley. 1993, Morrow $14.93 (0-688-09111-3). 48pp. A candid retelling of the author's life, which was often as dramatic as his novels. (Rev: BCCB 11/93; BL 9/1/93; HB 11–12/93; SLJ 8/93) [921]

DICKINSON, EMILY

12530 Steffens, Bradley. *Emily Dickinson* (5–10). Series: The Importance Of. 1997, Lucent LB $17.96 (1-56006-089-1). 96pp. This volume covers Dickinson's life and work and tries to re-create the character of this controversial poet. (Rev: SLJ 6/98) [921]

DORRIS, MICHAEL

12531 Weil, Ann. *Michael Dorris* (4–7). Illus. Series: Contemporary Native Americans. 1997, Raintree Steck-Vaughn LB $25.69 (0-8172-3994-4). 48pp. The life story of the late Native American writer and teacher and his crusade to fight alcohol abuse. (Rev: BL 6/1–15/97) [921]

DOYLE, SIR ARTHUR CONAN

12532 Adams, Cynthia. *The Mysterious Case of Sir Arthur Conan Doyle* (5–8). Illus. 1999, Morgan Reynolds $18.95 (1-883846-34-X). 112pp. This book traces the life of Sir Arthur Conan Doyle from his Scottish boyhood and failed medical practice to success as a writer and creator of Sherlock Holmes. (Rev: BL 3/1/99; SLJ 9/99) [921]

EHLERT, LOIS

12533 Ehlert, Lois. *Under My Nose* (3–5). Illus. 1996, Richard C. Owen $13.95 (1-57274-027-2). 32pp. A simple autobiography of this artist whose children's books are widely read. (Rev: BL 9/1/96; HB 9–10/96; SLJ 12/96) [921]

FAVERSHAM, CHARLES

12534 Gerrard, Roy. *The Favershams* (1–4). Illus. by author. 1983, Farrar paper $3.95 (0-374-42293-1). 32pp. Rhyming verses tell the story of the Favershams in Victorian England and Charles, the famous writer.

FITZGERALD, F. SCOTT

12535 Stewart, Gail B. *F. Scott Fitzgerald* (4–8). Series: The Importance Of. 1999, Lucent LB $17.96 (1-56006-541-9). 112pp. The story of the famous Jazz Age author whose enduring works reflect American life in his era. (Rev: BL 9/15/99) [921]

FRITZ, JEAN

12536 Fritz, Jean. *Homesick: My Own Story* (5–7). Illus. by Margot Tomes. 1982, Putnam $15.99 (0-399-20933-6); Dell paper $4.99 (0-440-43683-4). 160pp. Growing up in the troubled China of the 1920s. [921]

12537 Fritz, Jean. *Surprising Myself* (2–5). Illus. by Andrea F. Pfleger. Series: Meet the Author. 1993, Richard C. Owen $12.95 (1-878450-37-9). 32pp. As well as telling the reader about her life, Fritz explains how she does research for her many historical biographies. (Rev: BL 9/1/93; HB 9–10/93) [921]

GEISEL, THEODOR

12538 Lynch, Wendy. *Dr. Seuss* (1–4). Series: Lives and Times. 2000, Heinemann LB $13.95 (1-57572-216-X). 24pp. A simple biography of Theodor Geisel's alter ego with original drafts of artwork and many photographs. (Rev: HBG 3/01; SLJ 8/00) [921]

12539 Weidt, Maryann N. *Oh, the Places He Went: A Story About Dr. Seuss* (3–6). Illus. by Kerry Maguire. Series: Creative Minds Biographies. 1994, Carolrhoda LB $21.27 (0-87614-823-2); paper $5.95 (0-87614-627-2). 64pp. The life story of the famous children's author that tells of his many hardships and of some of his most important books. (Rev: BCCB 2/95; SLJ 1/95) [921]

12540 Woods, Mae. *Dr. Seuss* (2–4). Illus. Series: Children's Authors. 2000, ABDO $13.95 (1-57765-110-3). This book discusses the life and career on Theodor Geisel, better known as Dr. Seuss. (Rev: HBG 3/01; SLJ 1/01) [921]

GEORGE, JEAN CRAIGHEAD

12541 Cary, Alice. *Jean Craighead George* (4–6). Illus. 1996, Learning Works paper $6.95 (0-88160-283-3). 136pp. A lively re-creation of the life of this renowned nature writer and Newbery Award winner. (Rev: BL 11/15/96; SLJ 9/96) [921]

GOBLE, PAUL

12542 Goble, Paul. *Hau Kola Hello Friend* (2–4). Illus. by Gerry Perrin. Series: Meet the Author. 1994, Richard C. Owen $13.95 (1-878450-44-1). 32pp. This dedicated author, who has specialized in Native American folk material, tells about his life and writing. (Rev: BL 8/94; SLJ 8/94) [921]

GRISHAM, JOHN

12543 Weaver, Robyn M. *John Grisham* (5–8). Illus. Series: People in the News. 1999, Lucent LB $17.96 (1-56006-530-3). 80pp. An accessible, laudatory biography of the lawyer turned best-selling author. (Rev: BL 10/1/99; HBG 3/00) [921]

HANSBERRY, LORRAINE

12544 Scheader, Catherine. *Lorraine Hansberry: Playwright and Voice of Justice* (5–10). Series: African American Biographies. 1998, Enslow LB $19.95 (0-89490-945-2). 128pp. The story of the gifted playwright who was also a civil rights activist and a fighter for justice. (Rev: HBG 3/99; SLJ 11/98) [921]

12545 Tripp, Janet. *Lorraine Hansberry* (4–8). Series: Importance Of. 1997, Lucent LB $17.96 (1-56006-081-6). 112pp. Tells of the short life of this playwright and of her amazing achievements. (Rev: BL 10/15/97; SLJ 1/98) [921]

HELLER, RUTH

12546 Heller, Ruth. *Fine Lines* (3–5). Illus. 1996, Richard C. Owen $14.95 (1-878450-76-X). 32pp. In this autobiography, the author tells about her childhood, training, writing, and artwork. (Rev: BL 9/1/96; HB 9–10/96; SLJ 1/97) [921]

HENRY, MARGUERITE

12547 Collins, David R. *Write a Book for Me: The Story of Marguerite Henry* (4–6). Illus. 1999, Morgan Reynolds $18.95 (1-883846-39-0). 112pp. A straightforward biography of Marguerite Henry, the great writer of horse stories. (Rev: BL 3/15/99; SLJ 9/99) [921]

HERRERA, JUAN FELIPE

12548 Herrera, Juan Felipe. *Calling the Doves/El Canto de las Palomas* (3–6). Illus. by Elly Simmons. 1995, Children's Book Pr. $14.95 (0-89239-132-4). 32pp. In this bilingual autobiography, the Mexican American poet Juan Felipe Herrera describes his childhood in California as the son of migrant workers. (Rev: BCCB 12/95; BL 1/1–15/96; SLJ 12/95) [921]

HOPKINS, LEE BENNETT

12549 Hopkins, Lee Bennett. *The Writing Bug* (2–5). Illus. by Diane Rubinger. Series: Meet the Author. 1993, Richard C. Owen $14.95 (1-878450-38-7). 32pp. The acclaimed poet, author, and anthologist tells about his life and the experiences that inspire him to write. (Rev: BL 9/1/93; HB 9–10/93) [921]

HOWE, JAMES

12550 Howe, James. *Playing with Words* (1–4). Photos by Michael Craine. Series: Meet the Author. 1994, Richard C. Owen $12.95 (1-878450-40-9). 32pp. People who love this author's zany mysteries will enjoy reading about how he writes, gets his inspiration, and spends a typical day. (Rev: BL 8/94; SLJ 8/94) [921]

HUGHES, LANGSTON

12551 Cooper, Floyd. *Coming Home: From the Life of Langston Hughes* (3–6). Illus. 1994, Putnam $16.99 (0-399-22682-6). 32pp. A sensitive retelling of Langston Hughes's unhappy childhood and his search for a permanent home. (Rev: BCCB 1/95; BL 10/1/94; HB 9–10/94; SLJ 11/94) [921]

12552 McKissack, Patricia, and Fredrick McKissack. *Langston Hughes: Great American Poet* (2–4). Illus. by Michael D. Blegel. Series: Great African Americans. 1992, Enslow LB $14.95 (0-89490-315-2). 32pp. The sounds and language of

Harlem were incorporated into the poems of this African American writer. (Rev: BL 1/15/92; SLJ 1/93) [921]

HURSTON, ZORA NEALE

12553 Calvert, Roz. *Zora Neale Hurston* (5–8). Illus. Series: Black Americans of Achievement. 1993, Chelsea LB $16.95 (0-7910-1766-4). 80pp. A lively account of the life of the famous writer and folklorist. (Rev: BL 5/1/93; SLJ 6/93) [921]

12554 McKissack, Patricia, and Fredrick McKissack. *Zora Neale Hurston: Writer and Storyteller* (2–4). Illus. by Michael Bryant. Series: Great African Americans. 1992, Enslow LB $14.95 (0-89490-316-0). 32pp. Zora Hurston, anthropologist and storyteller, was an active writer during the Harlem Renaissance. (Rev: BL 10/15/92; SLJ 12/92) [921]

IRVING, WASHINGTON

12555 Collins, David R. *Washington Irving: Story-teller for a New Nation* (4–8). Illus. Series: World Writers. 2000, Morgan Reynolds $19.95 (1-883846-50-1). 112pp. This biography introduces the globe-trotting American writer and gives details of his work and personality. (Rev: BL 4/1/00; HBG 3/00) [921]

ISSA

12556 Gollub, Matthew. *Cool Melons Turn to Frogs! The Life and Poems of Issa* (3–5). Illus. by Kazuko Stone. 1998, Lee & Low $16.95 (1-880000-71-7). 32pp. Using lovely Japanese-like paintings and fine calligraphy, the life of Issa, the famous haiku poet is traced with many examples of his work. (Rev: BCCB 2/99; BL 12/1/98; HB 11–12/98; HBG 3/99; SLJ 11/98) [921]

JUANA DE LA GUZ, SISTER

12557 Martinez, Elizabeth Coonrod. *Sor Juana: A Trailblazing Thinker* (3–6). Illus. Series: Hispanic Heritage. 1994, Millbrook LB $19.90 (1-56294-406-1). 32pp. The story of the 17th-century Mexican-born poet who is considered the finest writer of Mexico's colonial period. (Rev: BL 6/1–15/94; SLJ 4/94) [921]

KING, STEPHEN

12558 Wilson, Suzan. *Stephen King* (4–6). Series: People to Know. 2000, Enslow LB $19.95 (0-7660-1233-6). 128pp. A well-documented, thorough account of the life of this former high-school teacher who became a best-selling writer of suspense and horror novels. (Rev: BL 1/1–15/00; HBG 10/00; SLJ 5/00) [921]

KIPLING, RUDYARD

12559 Kamen, Gloria. *Kipling: Storyteller of East and West* (3–5). Illus. 1985, Macmillan $15.00 (0-689-31195-8). 80pp. A lively biography centering on the writer's childhood and role as a father. (Rev: BCCB 3/86; BL 1/1/86; SLJ 2/86) [921]

KUSKIN, KARLA

12560 Kuskin, Karla. *Thoughts, Pictures, and Words* (2–5). Illus. Series: Meet the Author. 1995, Richard C. Owen $14.95 (1-878450-41-7). 32pp. This renowned writer discusses her prose, poetry, and illustrations, and discusses how she approaches writing. (Rev: BCCB 7–8/95; BL 8/95; HB 7–8/95; SLJ 9/95) [921]

LESTER, HELEN

12561 Lester, Helen. *Author: A True Story* (2–4). Illus. 1997, Houghton $11.00 (0-395-82744-2). 32pp. A delightful autobiography illustrated with her own cartoons. (Rev: BCCB 4/97; BL 3/15/97; HB 5–6/97; SLJ 5/97*) [921]

LOCKER, THOMAS

12562 Locker, Thomas. *The Man Who Paints* (3–5). Series: Meet the Author. 1999, Richard C. Owen LB $14.95 (1-57274-328-X). 32pp. An autobiography of the artist and author of children's books noted for such nature stories as *Where the River Begins* and *The Land of Grey Wolf*. (Rev: BL 9/15/99; HBG 3/00; SLJ 11/99) [921]

LONDON, JACK

12563 Lisandrelli, Elaine S. *Jack London* (4–6). Series: People to Know. 1999, Enslow LB $19.95 (0-7660-1144-5). 128pp. Part author and part adventurer, Jack London lived an action-packed but short life. This biography relates his story in an honest and balanced way. (Rev: BL 1/1–15/00; HBG 3/00) [921]

12564 Streissguth, Tom. *Jack London* (4–7). Series: A&E Biography. 2000, Lucent LB $25.26 (0-8225-4987-5). 112pp. The story of an adventurer and author who battled personal hardships and wrote eloquently about nature and survival. (Rev: BL 12/15/00; HBG 3/01; SLJ 3/01) [921]

LOWRY, LOIS

12565 Lowry, Lois. *Looking Back: A Book of Memories* (4–8). Illus. 1998, Houghton $16.00 (0-395-89543-X). 192pp. This autobiographical work centers around a series of photographs and the author's comments on each. (Rev: BL 11/1/98; HB 1–2/99; HBG 3/99; SLJ 9/98) [921]

12566 Markham, Lois. *Lois Lowry* (5–8). Illus. Series: Meet the Author. 1995, Learning Works paper $6.95 (0-88160-278-7). 128pp. This biography of the Newbery Award–winning author tells how she became a writer and what personal experiences can be found in her books. (Rev: SLJ 1/96) [921]

LYON, GEORGE ELLA

12567 Lyon, George E. *A Wordful Child* (3–5). Illus. 1996, Richard C. Owen $14.95 (1-57274-016-7). 32pp. The author tells about her life and the stories she heard as a child that influenced her work. (Rev: BL 9/1/96; HB 9–10/96; SLJ 1/97) [921]

MCKISSACK, PATRICIA

12568 McKissack, Patricia. *Can You Imagine?* (2–5). Illus. Series: Meet the Author. 1997, Richard C. Owen $14.95 (1-878450-61-1). 32pp. An autobiographical account of this fantasy writer in which she tells of the importance of imagination in her life. (Rev: BL 6/1–15/97; HBG 3/98; SLJ 9/97) [921]

MCPHAIL, DAVID

12569 McPhail, David. *In Flight with David McPhail* (2–6). Illus. by author. Series: Creative Sparks. 1996, Heinemann $15.95 (0-435-08132-2). 45pp. This famous artist talks about his life and the processes involved in illustrating a book. (Rev: HB 9–10/96; SLJ 6/96*) [921]

MAGEE, JOHN

12570 Granfield, Linda. *High Flight: A Story of World War II* (5–7). Illus. 1999, Tundra $15.95 (0-88776-469-X). 32pp. The moving story of John Magee, a young Canadian Air Force pilot who was killed in World War II and who is best known for writing the poem "High Flight." (Rev: BCCB 12/99; BL 1/1–15/00; HBG 3/00; SLJ 2/00) [921]

MAHY, MARGARET

12571 Mahy, Margaret. *My Mysterious World* (2–5). Illus. Series: Meet the Author. 1995, Richard C. Owen $13.95 (1-878450-58-1). 32pp. The New Zealand writer describes her many interests and how she approaches writing. (Rev: BCCB 7–8/95; BL 8/95; HB 7–8/95; SLJ 9/95) [921]

MARTÍ, JOSÉ J.

12572 West, Alan. *José Martí: Man of Poetry, Soldier of Freedom* (5–8). Illus. Series: Hispanic Heritage. 1994, Millbrook LB $19.90 (1-56294-408-8). 32pp. The life story of the famous 19th-century Cuban poet, with excerpts from his work in both Spanish and English. (Rev: SLJ 1/95) [921]

MARTIN, RAFE

12573 Martin, Rafe. *A Storyteller's Story* (3–6). Illus. by Jill Krementz. Series: Meet the Author. 1992, Owen $14.95 (0-913461-03-2). 32pp. The author takes readers to his home to meet family and friends. (Rev: BCCB 9/92; BL 8/92; SLJ 8/92) [921]

MORRISON, TONI

12574 Patrick-Wexler, Diane. *Toni Morrison* (4–6). Illus. Series: Contemporary African Americans. 1997, Raintree Steck-Vaughn LB $25.69 (0-8172-3987-1). 48pp. A fine biography of this influential writer, who has won both the Nobel and Pulitzer prizes. (Rev: BL 5/15/97; SLJ 2/98) [921]

PATERSON, KATHERINE

12575 Cary, Alice. *Katherine Paterson* (5–8). Illus. Series: Meet the Author. 1997, Learning Works paper $6.95 (0-88160-281-7). 136pp. A biography of the two-time Newbery winner, with many quotes from interviews and autobiographical essays. (Rev: BL 5/1/97; SLJ 7/97) [921]

PAULSEN, GARY

12576 Fine, Edith Hope. *Gary Paulsen: Author and Wilderness Adventurer* (5–8). Series: People to Know. 2000, Enslow LB $20.95 (0-7660-1146-1). 128pp. The story of an outdoorsman who turned many of his exciting adventures into stories for children and young adults. (Rev: BL 9/15/00; HBG 10/00; SLJ 9/00) [921]

12577 Paulsen, Gary. *Guts: The True Stories Behind Hatchet and the Brian Books* (5–10). 2001, Delacorte $16.95 (0-385-32650-5). 150pp. These six stories re-create childhood experiences of the author Gary Paulsen, who was born to alcoholic parents in 1939 and who spent much of his youth in the woods of Minnesota where he hunted and fished. (Rev: BL 2/15/01; SLJ 2/01) [813]

12578 Peters, Stephanie True. *Gary Paulsen* (4–8). Illus. 1999, Learning Works paper $6.95 (0-88160-324-4). 111pp. A straightforward biography of the outdoorsman and author that tells about his books, his interests, his alcoholism, and his continuing health problems. (Rev: BL 6/1–15/99; SLJ 6/99) [921]

POTTER, BEATRIX

12579 Collins, David R. *The Country Artist: A Story About Beatrix Potter* (3–5). Illus. by Karen Ritz. 1989, Carolrhoda LB $21.27 (0-87614-344-3); paper $5.95 (0-87614-509-8). 56pp. The story of the creator of Peter Rabbit and other famous creatures. (Rev: BL 5/1/89) [921]

12580 Johnson, Jane. *My Dear Noel: The Story of a Letter from Beatrix Potter* (PS–3). Illus. 1999, Dial LB $15.89 (0-8037-2051-3). 40pp. This is the story of the friendship between Beatrix Potter and the Moore family, told from the standpoint of the older Moore child, Noel. (Rev: BL 2/1/99; HBG 10/99; SLJ 3/99) [921]

12581 Malam, John. *Beatrix Potter* (1–4). Series: Tell Me About. 1998, Carolrhoda LB $19.93 (1-57505-275-X). 24pp. A brief biography of this writer and artist that covers the basics of her life and gives examples of her enchanting work. (Rev: BCCB 1/99; HBG 3/99; SLJ 2/99) [921]

12582 Wallner, Alexandra. *Beatrix Potter* (K–3). Illus. 1995, Holiday LB $16.95 (0-8234-1181-8). 32pp. A fascinating account of the life of this children's book author who was also an expert on mushrooms and an early conservationist. (Rev: BL 9/1/95; SLJ 10/95) [921]

PRINGLE, LAURENCE

12583 Pringle, Laurence. *Nature! Wild and Wonderful* (2–5). Illus. Series: Meet the Author. 1997, Richard C. Owen $14.95 (1-57274-071-X). 32pp. An autobiographical account of this writer of more than 80 books that tells how he became interested in nature study and in writing about it. (Rev: BL 6/1–15/97; HBG 3/98; SLJ 9/97) [921]

PYLE, ERNIE

12584 O'Connor, Barbara. *The Soldiers' Voice: The Story of Ernie Pyle* (4–7). Illus. 1996, Carolrhoda $23.93 (0-87614-942-5). 80pp. The story of the renowned World War II correspondent who died in the South Pacific while covering the war. (Rev: BCCB 10/96; BL 9/1/96; SLJ 8/96) [921]

ROWLING, J. K.

12585 Shapiro, Marc. *J. K. Rowling: The Wizard behind Harry Potter* (5–8). 2000, St. Martin's paper $4.99 (0-312-27224-3). The creator of Harry Potter is profiled, with material on university life, her year in Paris, and her struggle to keep writing. (Rev: BL 11/15/00; SLJ 12/00) [921]

RYLANT, CYNTHIA

12586 Rylant, Cynthia. *Best Wishes* (3–6). Illus. by Carlo Ontal. 1992, Owen $14.95 (1-878450-20-4). 32pp. The author takes her readers to her home in Ohio, then travels back to her childhood in West Virginia. (Rev: BCCB 9/92; BL 8/92; SLJ 8/92) [921]

SANDBURG, CARL

12587 Meltzer, Milton. *Carl Sandburg: A Biography* (5–10). Illus. 1999, Millbrook $29.90 (0-7613-1364-8). 144pp. The story of a literary giant who, in addition to his poetry, is noted for nonfiction works including a biography of Abraham Lincoln. (Rev: BL 12/15/99; HBG 10/00) [921]

12588 Mitchell, Barbara. *"Good Morning Mr. President": A Story About Carl Sandburg* (3–6). 1988, Carolrhoda LB $21.27 (0-87614-329-X). 56pp. The story of Sandburg's growing up and the experiences that were later reflected in his poetry. (Rev: BL 3/1/89; SLJ 2/89) [921]

SANDOZ, MARI

12589 Wilkerson, J. L. *Scribe of the Great Plains: Mari Sandoz* (3–5). Illus. 1999, Acorn $8.95 (0-9664470-0-X). 144pp. This biography of the author who wrote about the history of the Great Plains describes in detail her childhood struggle to survive the hardships of pioneer life. (Rev: BL 2/1/99; SLJ 3/99) [921]

SHAKESPEARE, WILLIAM

12590 Aliki. *William Shakespeare and the Globe* (4–7). Illus. 1999, HarperCollins LB $15.89 (0-06-027821-8). 48pp. Shakespeare and Elizabethan England come to life in this detailed picture book that uses many quotes from his plays and also tells of the recent rebuilding of the Globe theater. (Rev: BCCB 4/99; BL 6/1–15/99*; HB 5–6/99; HBG 10/99; SLJ 5/99) [921]

12591 Bender, Michael. *All the World's a Stage: A Pop-Up Biography of William Shakespeare* (4–6). Illus. 1999, Chronicle $14.95 (0-8118-1147-6). Using pop-ups, this biography relates the personal and professional sides of Shakespeare's life. (Rev: BL 12/15/99; SLJ 1/00) [921]

12592 Middleton, Haydn. *William Shakespeare: The Master Playwright* (3–5). Series: What's Their Story? 1998, Oxford $12.95 (0-19-521430-7). 32pp. Large type and color illustrations are used to tell the story of Shakespeare, who left his home in Stratford at 19 to journey to London where he became an actor, theater owner, and the greatest English playwright in history. (Rev: BL 2/15/99; HBG 3/99; SLJ 3/99) [921]

12593 Shellard, Dominic. *William Shakespeare* (5–10). Illus. Series: British Library Writers' Lives. 1999, Oxford LB $22.00 (0-19-521442-0). 120pp. This well-illustrated biography covers what little we know of Shakespeare's life and provides a good introduction to his plays. (Rev: BL 7/99) [921]

12594 Stanley, Diane, and Peter Vennema. *Bard of Avon: The Story of William Shakespeare* (3–8). Illus. by Diane Stanley. 1992, Morrow $16.95 (0-688-09108-3). 48pp. A handsome volume on the life of Shakespeare. (Rev: BCCB 12/92; BL 9/1/92*; HB 11–12/92*; SLJ 11/92) [921]

12595 Thrasher, Thomas. *The Importance of William Shakespeare* (4–8). Series: The Importance Of. 1998, Lucent LB $17.96 (1-56006-374-2). 108pp. This introduction to the life of Shakespeare also mentions some of his plays and explains why he is considered one of the world's great playwrights. (Rev: BL 12/15/98) [921]

SIMON, SEYMOUR

12596 Simon, Seymour. *From Paper Airplanes to Outer Space* (3–5). Series: Meet the Author. 2000, Richard C. Owen $14.95 (1-57274-374-3). 32pp. A noted writer of science books for young people talks about his life and how he writes. (Rev: BL 7/00; HBG 3/01; SLJ 12/00) [921]

SINGER, ISAAC BASHEVIS

12597 Singer, Isaac Bashevis. *A Day of Pleasure: Stories of a Boy Growing Up in Warsaw* (6–8). Illus. by Roman Vishniac. 1969, Farrar paper $7.95 (0-374-41696-6). 160pp. A Hasidic Jew's fond remembrances of the world in which he grew up. [921]

SPINELLI, JERRY

12598 Spinelli, Jerry. *Knots in My Yo-Yo String: The Autobiography of a Kid* (4–7). Illus. 1998, Knopf LB $15.99 (0-679-98791-6); paper $8.99 (0-679-88791-1). 160pp. A frank, delightful memoir of growing up in Norristown, Pennsylvania, during the 1950s by the renowned Newbery medal-winning writer of fiction for young people. (Rev: BCCB 7–8/98; BL 5/1/98; HBG 10/98; SLJ 6/98) [921]

STEVENSON, ROBERT LOUIS

12599 Carpenter, Angelica S., and Jean Shirley. *Robert Louis Stevenson: Finding Treasure Island* (5–8). Illus. 1997, Lerner LB $25.26 (0-8225-4955-7). 144pp. A lively narrative of this great writer, who was a disappointment to his family because he did not become a minister. (Rev: BL 11/15/97; HBG 3/98; SLJ 12/97) [921]

12600 Gherman, Beverly. *Robert Louis Stevenson: Teller of Tales* (5–8). Illus. 1996, Simon & Schuster $16.00 (0-689-31985-1). 136pp. The story of the author of *Treasure Island,* who though always in poor health lived a full, adventurous life. (Rev: BL 9/15/96; SLJ 2/97) [921]

STINE, R. L.

12601 Cohen, Joel H. *R. L. Stine* (5–8). Series: People in the News. 2000, Lucent LB $18.96 (1-56006-608-3). 96pp. This well-documented biography, illustrated with several black-and-white photographs, tells the story of an author who enjoys scaring his readers. (Rev: BL 6/1–15/00; HBG 10/00) [921]

12602 Stine, R. L., and Joe Arthur. *It Came From Ohio! My Life as a Writer* (4–6). Illus. 1997, Scholastic $9.95 (0-590-36674-2). 144pp. An autobiography of the creator of the hugely successful Fear Street and Goosebumps series. (Rev: BCCB 6/97; BL 8/97; HB 7–8/97; SLJ 7/97) [921]

STOWE, HARRIET BEECHER

12603 Bland, Celia. *Harriet Beecher Stowe: Antislavery Author* (3–5). Illus. Series: Junior World Biographies. 1993, Chelsea LB $16.95 (0-7910-1773-7). 79pp. The story of the renowned writer and her courageous stand against slavery. (Rev: SLJ 10/93) [921]

12604 Fritz, Jean. *Harriet Beecher Stowe and the Beecher Preachers* (5–8). Illus. 1994, Putnam $15.99 (0-399-22666-4). 144pp. In addition to covering *Uncle Tom's Cabin,* this biography gives a full account of Harriet Beecher's private life, marriage, and extended family. (Rev: BCCB 10/94; BL 8/94; HB 9–10/94; SLJ 9/94*) [921]

THOREAU, HENRY DAVID

12605 Burleigh, Robert. *A Man Named Thoreau* (4–6). Illus. 1985, Macmillan $15.00 (0-689-31122-2). 48pp. A profile of the 19th-century thinker in prose that makes him available to the younger grades. (Rev: BCCB 12/85; BL 3/15/86; SLJ 1/86) [921]

TOLKIEN, J. R. R.

12606 Neimark, Anne E. *Myth Maker: J. R. R. Tolkien* (4–6). Illus. by Brad Weinman. 1996, Harcourt $17.00 (0-15-298847-5). 111pp. A brief biography that covers the important events in the life of the writer who created Hobbits and other fantastic beings. (Rev: SLJ 10/96) [921]

TWAIN, MARK

12607 Collins, David R. *Mark T-W-A-I-N! A Story About Samuel Clemens* (3–5). Illus. by Vicky Carey. 1994, Carolrhoda LB $21.27 (0-87614-801-1). 64pp. Beginning with his boyhood in Hannibal, Missouri, through his many jobs as a youth, to his distinguished career as a writer, this is a lively biography of Clemens. (Rev: BL 3/1/94; SLJ 3/94) [921]

12608 Harness, Cheryl. *Mark Twain and the Queens of the Mississippi* (3–6). Illus. 1998, Simon &

Schuster $16.00 (0-689-81542-5). 40pp. An account of the colorful life of Mark Twain, this book also describes the Mississippi River and its steamboats. (Rev: BCCB 1/99; BL 1/1–15/99; HBG 3/99; SLJ 12/98) [921]

12609 Lasky, Kathryn. *A Brilliant Streak: The Making of Mark Twain* (4–7). Illus. by Barry Moser. 1998, Harcourt $18.00 (0-15-252110-0). 48pp. Using many quotes and anecdotes from the author's work, this nicely illustrated biography of Mark Twain concentrates on his first 30 years when he was a steamboat pilot, prospector, reporter, and budding writer. (Rev: BCCB 7–8/98; BL 4/1/98; HB 5–6/98; HBG 10/98; SLJ 4/98) [921]

12610 Pflueger, Lynda. *Mark Twain* (5–8). Series: Historical American Biographies. 1999, Enslow LB $19.95 (0-7660-1093-7). A balanced, well-documented biography that includes chapter notes, a bibliography, glossary, and some period black-and-white illustrations. (Rev: BL 1/1–15/00; HBG 3/00; SLJ 1/00) [921]

12611 Press, Skip. *Mark Twain* (4–8). Illus. 1994, Lucent LB $18.96 (1-56006-043-3). 112pp. A biography that reports on Clemens's intriguing personal and public lives and his prolific literary output. (Rev: BL 5/15/94; SLJ 4/94) [921]

12612 Ross, Stewart. *Mark Twain and Huckleberry Finn* (4–7). Illus. by Ronald Himler. 1999, Viking $16.99 (0-670-88181-3). 48pp. This picture book for older readers gives a candid look at the acclaimed author and supplies interesting details, such as his habit of smoking 40 cigars a day. (Rev: BL 3/1/99; HBG 10/99; SLJ 5/99) [921]

VERNE, JULES

12613 Streissguth, Thomas. *Science Fiction Pioneer: A Story About Jules Verne* (3–6). Illus. by Ralph L. Ramstad. 2000, Carolrhoda LB $21.27 (1-57505-440-X). 64pp. This biography traces the life and career of this novelist and how he used his interest and knowledge of science in his works. (Rev: HBG 3/01; SLJ 10/00) [921]

12614 Teeters, Peggy. *Jules Verne: The Man Who Invented Tomorrow* (5–7). Illus. 1993, Walker LB $14.85 (0-8027-8191-8). 128pp. The life of the famous writer of science fiction, including his childhood in France. (Rev: BL 3/15/93; SLJ 5/93) [921]

WALKER, ALICE

12615 Kramer, Barbara. *Alice Walker: Author of the Color Purple* (4–6). Illus. Series: People to Know. 1995, Enslow LB $20.95 (0-89490-620-8). 128pp. The life, struggles, and work of this celebrated African American writer are covered concisely in a conversational style. (Rev: BL 9/15/95; SLJ 11/95) [921]

WARNER, GERTRUDE C.

12616 Ellsworth, Mary Ellen. *Gertrude Chandler Warner and the Boxcar Children* (3–5). Illus. 1997, Albert Whitman LB $14.95 (0-8075-2837-4). 61pp. The life story of the author who created the Boxcar

Children and lived her entire life in Connecticut. (Rev: BL 8/97; HB 7–8/97; SLJ 7/97) [921]

WATSON, LYALL

12617 Watson, Lyall. *Warriors, Warthogs, and Wisdom: Growing Up in Africa* (4–7). Illus. 1997, Kingfisher $16.95 (0-7534-5066-6). 80pp. This well-known nature writer describes his childhood in the South African bush and how, at an early age, he learned to live off the land with his Zulu friend. (Rev: BL 10/1/97; HBG 3/98; SLJ 8/97) [921]

WELLS, H. G.

12618 Boerst, William J. *Time Machine: The Story of H. G. Wells* (5–8). Illus. Series: World Writers. 1999, Morgan Reynolds $19.95 (1-883846-40-4). 112pp. The story of the intriguing English author, including material on his childhood, romances, political views, and literary works. (Rev: BL 1/1–15/00; HBG 3/00) [921]

WHEATLEY, PHILLIS

12619 Salisbury, Cynthia. *Phillis Wheatley: Legendary African-American Poet* (5–8). Series: Historical American Biographies. 2001, Enslow LB $20.95 (0-7660-1394-4). The life story of the first important African American poet, who was brought to America as a slave and bought by a Quaker family who allowed her to develop her talents. (Rev: BL 3/1/01) [921]

12620 Sherrow, Victoria. *Phillis Wheatley: Poet* (4–7). Illus. Series: Junior World Biographies. 1992, Chelsea LB $16.95 (0-7910-1753-2). 80pp. The biography of the poet who is considered to be the first important African American writer. (Rev: BL 8/92; SLJ 8/92) [921]

12621 Weidt, Maryann N. *Revolutionary Poet: A Story About Phillis Wheatley* (3–6). Illus. Series: Creative Minds. 1997, Carolrhoda LB $21.27 (1-57505-037-4); paper $5.95 (1-57505-059-5). 64pp. The story of the poetry-writing slave girl who was the first African American to have a book published. (Rev: BL 2/15/98; HBG 3/98) [921]

WHITE, E. B.

12622 Collins, David R. *To the Point: A Story About E. B. White* (3–5). Illus. by Amy Johnson. 1989, Carolrhoda LB $21.27 (0-87614-345-1); paper $5.95 (0-87614-508-X). 56pp. The story of a writer who made a great impact on children's reading. (Rev: BL 5/1/89) [921]

WHITMAN, WALT

12623 Loewen, Nancy, ed. *Walt Whitman* (5–8). Illus. by Rob Day. 1994, Creative Ed. LB $23.95 (0-88682-608-X). 45pp. With generous quotes from *Leaves of Grass* and color photos, various vignettes from Whitman's life are retold. (Rev: SLJ 7/94*) [921]

WIESEL, ELIE

12624 Lazo, Caroline. *Elie Wiesel* (4–7). Illus. 1994, Dillon paper $7.95 (0-382-24715-9). 64pp. The story of the distinguished writer and spokesman on the Holocaust who won the Nobel Peace Prize in 1986. (Rev: BL 2/15/95; SLJ 7/95) [921]

12625 Pariser, Michael. *Elie Wiesel: Bearing Witness* (4–6). Illus. Series: Gateway Biographies. 1994, Millbrook LB $20.90 (1-56294-419-3). 48pp. A slim biography of the Nobel Prize winner, who at age 15 was sent to Auschwitz. (Rev: SLJ 4/95) [921]

WILDER, LAURA INGALLS

12626 Anderson, William. *Laura's Album: A Remembrance Scrapbook of Laura Ingalls Wilder* (3–6). Illus. 1998, HarperCollins $19.95 (0-06-027842-0). 80pp. This is a loving scrapbook of photos, early writings, letters, and drawings by the author of the Little House series. (Rev: BL 1/1–15/99; HBG 10/99) [921]

12627 Anderson, William. *Pioneer Girl: The Story of Laura Ingalls Wilder* (2–4). Illus. by Dan Andreasen. 1998, HarperCollins LB $15.89 (0-06-027244-9). This biography of the author covers the significant events in her life. (Rev: HBG 10/98; SLJ 3/98) [921]

12628 Giff, Patricia Reilly. *Laura Ingalls Wilder: Growing Up in the Little House* (3–6). Illus. by Eileen McKeating. 1988, Puffin paper $4.99 (0-14-032074-1). 64pp. Stories of growing up in the Big Woods of Wisconsin, long, long ago. (Rev: BCCB 9/87; BL 8/87; SLJ 4/87) [921]

12629 Wadsworth, Ginger. *Laura Ingalls Wilder: Storyteller of the Prairie* (4–6). Illus. 1997, Lerner LB $25.26 (0-8225-4950-6). 128pp. A solid, factual biography of the creator of the "Little House" books. (Rev: BL 3/1/97; HB 11–12/97; SLJ 4/97) [921]

12630 Wallner, Alexandra. *Laura Ingalls Wilder* (K–3). Illus. 1997, Holiday LB $16.95 (0-8234-1314-4). 32pp. A concise biography that traces Wilder's life from childhood to her emergence as a juvenile book author. (Rev: BL 10/1/97; HBG 3/98; SLJ 11/97) [921]

12631 Woods, Mae. *Laura Ingalls Wilder* (2–3). Series: Children's Authors. 2000, ABDO LB $13.95 (1-57765-113-8). 24pp. Eight double-page chapters cover Wilder's life from her birth in 1867 to her death in 1957. (Rev: HBG 3/01; SLJ 3/01) [921]

YOLEN, JANE

12632 Yolen, Jane. *A Letter from Phoenix Farm* (3–6). Illus. by Jason Stemple. 1992, Owen $14.95 (1-878450-36-0). 32pp. Spending a day with this writer of children's books. (Rev: BCCB 9/92; BL 8/92; SLJ 8/92) [921]

Contemporary and Historical Americans

Collective

12633 Aaseng, Nathan. *Business Builders in Oil* (5–8). Illus. 2000, Oliver LB $19.95 (1-881508-56-0). 160pp. Profiles of six individual oil businessmen and a set of partners, including John D. Rockefeller, Andrew Mellon, and J. Paul Getty. (Rev: BL 2/1/01) [920]

12634 Allen, Paula Gunn, and Patricia C. Smith. *As Long As the Rivers Flow: The Stories of Nine Native Americans* (5–8). Illus. 1996, Scholastic $15.95 (0-590-47869-9). 328pp. Profiles of nine Native Americans, including Geronimo, Will Rogers, and Maria Tallchief. (Rev: BL 12/1/96) [920]

12635 Altman, Susan. *Extraordinary Black Americans: From Colonial to Contemporary Times* (5–8). Illus. 1989, Children's LB $37.00 (0-516-00581-2). 240pp. A collection of 85 short biographies, valuable as a resource. (Rev: BL 6/15/89; SLJ 6/89) [920]

12636 Barber, James. *Presidents* (3–5). 2000, DK $15.95 (0-7894-5243-X). 64pp. An appealing, visually attractive account that profiles each of the presidents (before George W.) with material on the times in which each lived. (Rev: HBG 10/00; SLJ 7/00) [920]

12637 Blassingame, Wyatt. *The Look-It-Up Book of Presidents* (3–6). Illus. 1990, Random LB $14.99 (0-679-90353-4); paper $8.99 (0-679-80358-0). There is good coverage on each of our presidents and on their terms of office. [920]

12638 Blue, Rose, and Corinne J. Naden. *The White House Kids* (4–7). Illus. 1995, Millbrook LB $24.90 (1-56294-447-9). 96pp. An overview of the children of presidents who have called the White House their home. (Rev: BCCB 9/95; BL 6/1–15/95; SLJ 8/95) [920]

12639 Brooks, Philip. *Extraordinary Jewish Americans* (5–9). Series: Extraordinary People. 1998, Children's LB $37.00 (0-516-20609-5); paper $16.95 (0-516-26350-1). 288pp. In chronological order, this book presents brief biographical sketches of 60 prominent Jews from a wide variety of fields including science, business, sports, the arts, entertainment, and politics. (Rev: HBG 3/99; SLJ 10/98) [920]

12640 Burleigh, Robert. *Who Said That? Famous Americans Speak* (5–8). Illus. by David Catrow. 1997, Holt $16.95 (0-8050-4394-2). 45pp. Using quotes from 33 famous personalities, from Benjamin Franklin to Marilyn Monroe, brief profiles of the subjects are presented. (Rev: BL 3/1/97*; SLJ 5/97) [920]

12641 Calvert, Patricia. *Great Lives: The American Frontier* (4–8). Illus. 1997, Simon & Schuster $25.00 (0-689-80640-X). 400pp. A large book that contains profiles of 27 individuals who played a significant role in the opening up of the West. (Rev: BL 2/15/98; SLJ 1/98) [920]

12642 Cox, Clinton. *African American Teachers* (4–7). Series: Black Stars. 2000, Wiley $22.95 (0-471-24649-2). 172pp. A collection of short profiles of important African American teachers who have inspired their students and championed the cause of education. (Rev: BL 7/00; HBG 3/01) [920]

12643 Davidson, Sue. *Getting the Real Story: Nellie Bly and Ida B. Wells* (4–6). 1992, Seal Pr. paper $8.95 (1-878067-16-8). 152pp. The story of two gallant women news reporters, both of whom fought for justice and against corruption. (Rev: SLJ 7/92) [920]

12644 Davis, Burke. *Black Heroes of the American Revolution* (4–6). Illus. 1992, Harcourt paper $5.00 (0-15-208561-0). 80pp. A look at American blacks who performed key roles in the American Revolution. [920]

12645 Delisle, Jim. *Kidstories: Biographies of 20 Young People You'd Like to Know* (PS–3). Illus. 1991, Free Spirit paper $9.95 (0-915793-34-2). 168pp. This collection of short biographies tells about young people from different life-styles and locales. (Rev: BCCB 1/92; BL 12/15/91; SLJ 1/92) [920]

12646 Doherty, Kieran. *Explorers, Missionaries, and Trappers: Trailblazers of the West* (5–8). Series: Shaping America. 2000, Oliver LB $21.95 (1-881508-52-8). 176pp. Nine important pioneers of the American West are profiled including a Spanish conquistador, two Spanish priests, John Sutter, Marcus and Narcissa Whitman, and Brigham Young. (Rev: HBG 10/00; SLJ 5/00) [920]

12647 Drimmer, Frederick. *Incredible People: Five Stories of Extraordinary Lives* (4–7). Illus. 1997, Simon & Schuster $16.00 (0-689-31921-5). 192pp. The stories of five people who were considered outsiders, like seven-and-a-half-foot-tall Jack Earle and conjoined twins Daisy and Violet Hilton. (Rev: BCCB 7–8/97; BL 6/1–15/97; SLJ 5/97) [920]

12648 Dudley, Karen. *Great African Americans in Government* (3–5). Series: Outstanding African Americans. 1997, Crabtree LB $21.28 (0-86505-806-7); paper $8.95 (0-86505-820-2). 64pp. Indepth profiles of seven African Americans in government — e.g., Adam Clayton Powell, Colin Powell, and Shirley Chisholm — with seven shorter sketches that include Julian Bond and David Dinkins. (Rev: BL 9/15/97; SLJ 1/98) [920]

12649 Glass, Andrew. *Bad Guys* (4–6). Illus. 1998, Doubleday $16.95 (0-385-32310-7). Billy the Kid, Black Bart, Calamity Jane, and Wild Bill Hickok are only four of the large gallery of Wild West characters depicted here — most of them villainous. (Rev: BCCB 9/98; BL 10/15/98; HBG 3/99; SLJ 9/98) [920]

12650 Gormley, Beatrice. *First Ladies: Women Who Called the White House Home* (4–6). Illus. 1997, Scholastic paper $6.99 (0-590-25518-5). 96pp. A collection of short profiles of U.S. presidents' wives, from Martha Washington to Hillary Clinton. (Rev: BL 3/15/97) [920]

12651 Green, Carl R. *The Younger Brothers* (4–6). Illus. Series: Outlaws and Lawmen. 1995, Enslow LB $16.95 (0-89490-592-9). 48pp. The story of the interesting characters who were involved with Jesse James in the old West. (Rev: SLJ 9/95) [920]

12652 Green, Carl R., and William R. Sanford. *Confederate Generals of the Civil War* (5–8). Illus. Series: Collective Biographies. 1998, Enslow LB $18.95 (0-7660-1029-5). 112pp. After a brief introduction to the Civil War, this book highlights the careers of ten Southern generals and their contributions to the Confederate cause. (Rev: BL 8/98) [920]

12653 Green, Carl R., and William R. Sanford. *Union Generals of the Civil War* (5–8). Illus. 1998, Enslow LB $18.95 (0-7660-1028-7). 112pp. Using period photographs and prints plus a concise text, this book outlines the careers of ten Union generals and supplies background material on the Civil War, including charts and maps. (Rev: BL 8/98) [920]

12654 Hacker, Carlotta. *Great African Americans in History* (3–5). Illus. Series: Outstanding African Americans. 1997, Crabtree LB $22.60 (0-86505-805-9); paper $8.95 (0-86505-819-9). 64pp. Brief biographies of such historically important African Americans as Sojourner Truth, W. E. B. Du Bois,

and Booker T. Washington. (Rev: BL 9/15/97; SLJ 1/98) [920]

12655 Hansen, Joyce. *Women of Hope: African Americans Who Made a Difference* (5–12). Illus. 1998, Scholastic $16.95 (0-590-93973-4). 32pp. A large-size volume that celebrates the lives and accomplishments of 13 female African American leaders from various walks of life, including civil rights activists such as Fannie Lou Hamer and writers such as Maya Angelou. (Rev: BL 12/1/98; HBG 3/99; SLJ 10/98) [920]

12656 Harmon, Rod. *American Civil Rights Leaders* (5–7). Series: Collective Biographies. 2000, Enslow LB $20.95 (0-7660-1381-2). 104pp. This collective biography profiles ten individuals who are currently or once were active in the civil rights movement in the United States. (Rev: BL 12/15/00) [920]

12657 Harness, Cheryl. *Remember the Ladies: 100 Great American Women* (3–5). Illus. by author. 2001, HarperCollins LB $16.89 (0-688-17018-8). From colonial days to 2001, this book covers American history through profiles of 100 great women. (Rev: SLJ 2/01) [920]

12658 Harris, Laurie L., ed. *Biography for Beginners: Presidents of the United States* (3–6). Series: Biography for Beginners. 1998, Omnigraphics LB $50.00 (0-7808-0262-4). 467pp. A fine introduction to the lives and accomplishments of each of our presidents, ending with Clinton. (Rev: SLJ 11/98) [920]

12659 Haskins, Jim. *One More River to Cross: The Stories of Twelve Black Americans* (4–8). Illus. 1992, Scholastic $13.95 (0-590-42896-9). 160pp. Eight men and four women who defied the odds to achieve prominence in their fields are introduced, including Ralph Bunche, Shirley Chisholm, and Ron McNair. (Rev: BCCB 4/92; BL 2/1/92; SLJ 4/92) [920]

12660 Hudson, Wade, and Valerie Wesley Wilson. *Afro-Bets Book of Black Heroes from A to Z: An Introduction to Important Black Achievers* (4–7). Illus. 1988, Just Us paper $7.95 (0-940975-02-5). 64pp. Forty-nine African American men and women of outstanding accomplishment. (Rev: BL 1/1/89; SLJ 12/88) [920]

12661 Igus, Toyomi, ed. *Great Women in the Struggle* (3–6). Illus. Series: Book of Black Heroes. 1992, Just Us LB $17.95 (0-940975-27-0); paper $10.95 (0-940975-26-2). 107pp. More than 80 contemporary African American women are profiled. (Rev: SLJ 8/92) [920]

12662 Jeffrey, Laura S. *Great American Businesswomen* (4–7). Illus. 1996, Enslow LB $20.95 (0-89490-706-9). 112pp. Profiles of ten successful American businesswomen, e.g., Maggie L. Walker and Katherine Graham. (Rev: BL 9/1/96; SLJ 9/96) [920]

12663 Katz, William L. *Black People Who Made the Old West* (6–8). Illus. 1992, Africa World $35.00 (0-86543-363-1); paper $14.95 (0-86543-364-X). Sketches of 35 black explorers, pioneers, etc., who helped open up the West.

12664 Katz, William L., and Paula A. Franklin. *Proudly Red and Black: Stories of Native and African Americans* (4–7). Illus. 1993, Atheneum $15.00 (0-689-31801-4). 96pp. A collective biography of famous people of mixed Native American and African ancestry. (Rev: BL 12/1/93) [920]

12665 Ketchum, Liza. *Into a New Country: Eight Remarkable Women of the West* (5–9). 2000, Little, Brown $17.95 (0-316-49597-2). 135pp. This collection of eight biographies contains profiles of women connected with the western frontier, such as the Omaha Indian sisters Susette and Susan LaFlesche, Klondike Kate, a former slave named Biddy Mason, and a Chinese immigrant. (Rev: BCCB 10/00; SLJ 12/00) [920]

12666 King, David C. *First Facts About American Heroes* (3–6). Illus. 1995, Blackbirch LB $25.95 (1-56711-165-3). 112pp. The lives and accomplishments of 42 famous Americans are presented, each with a full-page photograph or painting and a single page of facts. (Rev: SLJ 2/96) [920]

12667 Knapp, Ron. *American Generals of World War II* (5–8). Series: Collective Biographies. 1998, Enslow LB $18.95 (0-7660-1024-4). 128pp. The ten U.S. generals profiled here are Henry Arnold, Omar Bradley, Dwight Eisenhower, Curtis LeMay, Douglas MacArthur, George Marshall, George Patton, Matthew Ridgway, Holland Smith, and Joseph Stilwell. (Rev: SLJ 9/98) [920]

12668 Kramer, Barbara. *Trailblazing American Women* (5–7). Series: Collective Biographies. 2000, Enslow LB $20.95 (0-7660-1377-4). 112pp. This collection of biographies profiles women who dared to branch out into new fields and break new ground. (Rev: BL 9/15/00; SLJ 12/00) [920]

12669 Krohn, Katherine. *Women of the Wild West* (4–6). Series: A&E Biography. 2000, Lerner LB $25.26 (0-8225-4980-8). 112pp. Among its several profiles, this book examines the lives of some infamous women of the Wild West: Calamity Jane, Belle Starr, Pearl Hart, and Annie Oakley. (Rev: BL 6/1–15/00; HBG 3/01) [920]

12670 Krull, Kathleen. *Lives of the Presidents: Fame, Shame (and What the Neighbors Thought)* (4–7). Illus. by Kathryn Hewitt. 1998, Harcourt $20.00 (0-15-200808-X). 96pp. This book is filled with trivia about each of the presidents and enough details of their everyday lives to humanize them. (Rev: BL 8/98; HB 11–12/98; HBG 3/99; SLJ 9/98) [920]

12671 Lindop, Edmund. *Dwight D. Eisenhower, John F. Kennedy, Lyndon B. Johnson* (4–7). Illus. Series: Presidents Who Dared. 1996, Twenty-First Century LB $18.90 (0-8050-3404-8). 64pp. The highlights of these three administrations are presented, preceded by an introduction to the American presidency. (Rev: BL 4/15/96; SLJ 6/96) [920]

12672 Lindop, Edmund. *George Washington, Thomas Jefferson, Andrew Jackson* (4–7). Illus. Series: Presidents Who Dared. 1995, Twenty-First Century LB $18.90 (0-8050-3401-3). 64pp. After a general introduction on the duties of the president, brief biographies of three are given, with emphasis on

their accomplishments in office. (Rev: BL 1/1–15/96; SLJ 11/95) [920]

12673 Lindop, Edmund. *James K. Polk, Abraham Lincoln, Theodore Roosevelt* (4–7). Illus. Series: Presidents Who Dared. 1995, Twenty-First Century LB $18.90 (0-8050-3402-1). 64pp. Highlights and evaluations of the presidencies of Polk, Lincoln, and Theodore Roosevelt. (Rev: BL 1/1–15/96; SLJ 11/95) [920]

12674 Lindop, Edmund. *Richard M. Nixon, Jimmy Carter, Ronald Reagan* (4–7). Illus. Series: Presidents Who Dared. 1996, Twenty-First Century LB $18.90 (0-8050-3405-6). 64pp. The office of the U.S. presidency is introduced, followed by important events and decisions involving these three presidents. (Rev: BL 4/15/96; SLJ 6/96) [920]

12675 Lindop, Edmund. *Woodrow Wilson, Franklin D. Roosevelt, Harry S. Truman* (4–7). Illus. Series: Presidents Who Dared. 1995, Twenty-First Century LB $18.90 (0-8050-3403-X). 64pp. After an overview of the presidency, this account briefly tells about the accomplishments of Wilson, FDR, and Truman. (Rev: BL 1/1–15/96; SLJ 11/95) [920]

12676 Lutz, Norma Jean. *Business and Industry* (5–8). Series: Female Firsts in Their Fields. 1999, Chelsea LB $16.95 (0-7910-5142-0). 64pp. The six women who are profiled in this book are Madam C. J. Walker, Katharine Graham, Mary Kay Ash, Martha Stewart, Oprah Winfrey, and Sherry Lansing. (Rev: HBG 10/99; SLJ 9/99) [920]

12677 McDonough, Yona Z. *Sisters in Strength: American Women Who Made a Difference* (3–5). 2000, Holt $17.95 (0-8050-6102-9). 48pp. A colorful, oversize volume that highlights the lives of such important American women as Pocahontas, Harriet Tubman, Susan B. Anthony, Amelia Earhart, and Eleanor Roosevelt. (Rev: BL 3/1/00; HBG 10/00; SLJ 4/00) [920]

12678 Marvis, Barbara. *Famous People of Asian Ancestry*, Vol. 4 (4–7). Illus. Series: Contemporary American Success Stories. 1994, Mitchell Lane paper $10.95 (1-883845-09-2). 96pp. A collective biography of Asian Americans, including actor Dustin Nguyen, novelist Amy Tan, and businessman Rocky Aoki. Also use volumes one through three (2nd ed., 1997). (Rev: BL 10/1/94; SLJ 11/94) [920]

12679 Marvis, Barbara. *Famous People of Hispanic Heritage*, Vol. 1 (4–7). Illus. Series: Contemporary American Success Stories. 1995, Mitchell Lane LB $21.95 (1-883845-21-1); paper $12.95 (1-883845-20-3). 96pp. This is the first of three volumes that give brief biographies of Hispanic Americans from all walks of life who have made significant contributions to our country. Also use volumes 2 through 10 (1995–1998). (Rev: BL 11/15/95; SLJ 1/96) [920]

12680 Mayberry, Jodine. *Business Leaders Who Built Financial Empires* (5–8). Illus. Series: 20 Events. 1995, Raintree Steck-Vaughn LB $24.26 (0-8114-4934-3). 48pp. The biographies of 19 financial wizards and entrepreneurs, beginning with Levi Strauss and Andrew Carnegie and ending with

Steven Jobs and Anita Roddick. (Rev: SLJ 7/95) [920]

12681 Meisner, James, and Amy Ruth. *American Revolutionaries and Founders of the Nation* (5–7). Series: Collective Biographies. 1999, Enslow LB $19.95 (0-7660-1115-1). 112pp. Ten brief biographies of prominent leaders of the American Revolution, each with a black-and-white portrait. (Rev: BL 9/15/99) [920]

12682 Morin, Isobel V. *Women Chosen for Public Office* (5–7). Illus. 1995, Oliver LB $18.95 (1-881508-20-X). 160pp. Nine biographies of women who are involved in the federal government from the superintendent of army nurses to Supreme Court justice Ruth Bader Ginsburg. (Rev: BL 5/1/95; SLJ 6/95) [920]

12683 Morris, Juddi. *At Home with the Presidents* (4–8). 1999, Wiley paper $12.95 (0-471-25300-6). 172pp. In three to five pages each, this account profiles the presidents of the United States from Washington through Clinton. (Rev: SLJ 3/00) [920]

12684 Munson, Sammye. *Today's Tejano Heroes* (5–8). Illus. 2000, Eakin $13.95 (1-57168-328-3). 80pp. In alphabetical order, this volume introduces 16 important 20th-century Mexican Americans who have contributed to the history and culture of Texas, including Vikki Carr, Attorney General Dan Morales, and federal judge Hilda Tagle. (Rev: BL 2/1/01) [920]

12685 Parker, Janice. *Great African Americans in Film* (3–5). Illus. Series: Outstanding African Americans. 1997, Crabtree LB $22.60 (0-86505-808-3); paper $8.95 (0-86505-822-9). 64pp. Among the 13 important African Americans highlighted here are Dorothy Dandridge, Richard Pryor, and Denzel Washington. (Rev: BL 9/15/97; SLJ 12/97) [920]

12686 Pascoe, Elaine. *First Facts About the Presidents* (4–8). Illus. Series: First Facts About. 1996, Blackbirch LB $25.95 (1-56711-167-X). 112pp. Divided into four historical periods, this book covers the major historical events of the time, introduces each of the presidents, and briefly describes his presidency. (Rev: SLJ 5/96) [920]

12687 Pelz, Ruth. *Black Heroes of the Wild West* (3–5). Illus. by Leandro Della Piana. 1989, Open Hand $12.95 (0-940880-25-3); paper $6.95 (0-940880-26-1). 56pp. The stories of five black men and four black women who contributed to the history of the Old West. (Rev: BL 6/1/90) [920]

12688 Pelz, Ruth. *Women of the Wild West: Biographies from Many Cultures* (3–5). Illus. 1995, Open Hand paper $6.95 (0-940880-50-4). 64pp. The biographies of eight women — e.g., Sacajawea and ex-slave Biddy Mason — who played important roles in the history of the American West. (Rev: BL 3/1/95) [921]

12689 Phillips, Louis. *Ask Me Anything About the Presidents* (5–8). Illus. by Valeria Costantino. 1992, Avon paper $4.50 (0-380-76426-1). 130pp. A collection of many unusual facts about various aspects of the U.S. presidency, in a question-and-answer format. (Rev: BL 4/15/92) [920]

12690 Pinkney, Andrea D. *Let It Shine: Stories of Black Women Freedom Fighters* (5–8). Illus. 2000, Harcourt $20.00 (0-15-201005-X). 120pp. This work contains chatty profiles of ten important African American women, including Sojourner Truth, Rosa Parks, and Shirley Chisholm. (Rev: BCCB 11/00; BL 11/15/00; HB 11–12/00; HBG 3/01; SLJ 10/00) [921]

12691 Potter, Joan, and Constance Claytor. *African Americans Who Were First* (4–8). Illus. 1997, Dutton $15.99 (0-525-65246-9). 128pp. A brief introduction to 65 African Americans who earned "firsts" in a variety of fields. (Rev: BL 9/1/97; HBG 3/98; SLJ 9/97) [920]

12692 Provensen, Alice. *My Fellow Americans: A Family Album* (4–6). Illus. 1995, Harcourt $19.95 (0-15-276642-1). 64pp. Hundreds of prominent Americans grouped by fields of accomplishment are pictured and identified. (Rev: BCCB 1/96; BL 12/1/95; SLJ 12/95*) [920]

12693 Rediger, Pat. *Great African Americans in Business* (4–6). Illus. Series: Outstanding African Americans. 1996, Crabtree LB $22.60 (0-86505-803-2); paper $8.95 (0-86505-817-2). 64pp. Such people as John H. Johnson and Oprah Winfrey are profiled. (Rev: BL 9/15/96; SLJ 8/96) [920]

12694 Rediger, Pat. *Great African Americans in Civil Rights* (4–6). Illus. Series: Outstanding African Americans. 1996, Crabtree LB $22.60 (0-86505-798-2); paper $8.95 (0-86505-812-1). 64pp. In short chapters, such civil rights leaders as Thurgood Marshall, Rosa Parks, and Jesse Jackson are introduced. (Rev: BL 9/15/96; SLJ 8/96) [920]

12695 Ringgold, Faith. *Dinner at Aunt Connie's House* (K–4). Illus. 1993, Hyperion LB $15.49 (1-56282-426-0). 32pp. Twelve African American women of importance, such as Rosa Parks and Fannie Lou Hamer, are introduced through portraits that two youngsters discover in their Aunt Connie's attic. (Rev: BL 9/15/93; SLJ 10/93) [920]

12696 Rubel, David. *Scholastic Encyclopedia of the Presidents and Their Times*. Rev. ed. (4–8). Illus. 1997, Scholastic $17.95 (0-590-49366-3). 232pp. This fine reference book not only introduces each of the presidents and his administration but also supplies material on other historical events, movements, and personalities. (Rev: SLJ 5/97) [920]

12697 St. George, Judith. *Dear Dr. Bell . . . Your Friend, Helen Keller* (5–7). Illus. 1992, Morrow paper $4.95 (0-688-12814-9). 172pp. A joint biography about the friendship between Alexander Graham Bell and Helen Keller. (Rev: BCCB 11–12/92 & 2/93; SLJ 12/92) [920]

12698 Thrasher, Thomas. *Gunfighters* (5–8). Series: History Makers. 2000, Lucent $27.45 (1-56006-570-2). 96pp. A fascinating collective biography that introduces the West of olden days and gives profiles of Wild Bill Hickok, Ben Thompson, Wyatt Earp, John Wesley Hardin, Billy the Kid, and Tom Horn. (Rev: HBG 10/00; SLJ 9/00) [920]

African Americans

ABERNATHY, DAVID

12699 Reef, Catherine. *Ralph David Abernathy* (5–8). Illus. Series: People in Focus. 1995, Dillon $18.95 (0-87518-653-X); paper $7.95 (0-382-24965-8). 167pp. A biography that describes this civil rights leader's youth and many accomplishments. (Rev: SLJ 10/95) [921]

ALLEN, RICHARD

12700 Klots, Steve. *Richard Allen* (5–8). Illus. Series: Black Americans of Achievement. 1990, Chelsea LB $19.95 (1-55546-570-6). 112pp. Born a slave in 1780, this convert to Christianity founded the first African American Methodist Church. (Rev: SLJ 2/91) [921]

BETHUNE, MARY MCLEOD

12701 Greenfield, Eloise. *Mary McLeod Bethune* (2–4). Illus. by Jerry Pinkney. 1994, HarperCollins paper $6.95 (0-06-446168-8). 40pp. Bethune was the only one of 17 children in her family to go to school. Through courage and hard work, she became an educator of national importance. [921]

12702 Kelso, Richard. *Building a Dream: Mary Bethune's School* (2–4). Illus. by Debbe Heller. Series: Stories of America. 1993, Raintree Steck-Vaughn LB $27.12 (0-8114-7217-5). 46pp. The story of Mary Bethune and how she realized her dream of building a school for poor African American children. (Rev: SLJ 7/93) [921]

12703 McKissack, Patricia, and Fredrick McKissack. *Mary McLeod Bethune: A Great Teacher* (2–4). Illus. Series: Great African Americans. 1991, Enslow LB $14.95 (0-89490-304-7). 32pp. The life and times of an extraordinary African American. (Rev: BL 1/1/92; SLJ 12/91) [921]

12704 Meltzer, Milton. *Mary McLeod Bethune: Voice of Black Hope* (4–7). Illus. 1988, Puffin paper $4.99 (0-14-032219-1). 64pp. An effective profile of the African American educator. (Rev: BCCB 5/87; BL 3/15/87; SLJ 3/87)

BROWN, AUNT CLARA

12705 Lowery, Linda. *Aunt Clara Brown: Official Pioneer* (2–4). Illus. by Janice L. Porter. Series: On My Own Biographies. 1999, Carolrhoda LB $14.95 (1-57505-045-5). 48pp. The inspiring story of a freed slave who used the wealth she accumulated in Colorado to help other freed blacks after the Civil War. (Rev: BCCB 12/99; HBG 3/00; SLJ 11/99*) [921]

CARMICHAEL, STOKELY

12706 Cwiklik, Robert. *Stokely Carmichael and Black Power* (4–6). Illus. Series: Gateway Civil Rights. 1993, Millbrook LB $20.90 (1-56294-276-X). 32pp. The life of the controversial civil rights leader who coined the term "black power." (Rev: BCCB 5/93; BL 8/93) [921]

CHISHOLM, SHIRLEY

12707 Pollack, Jill S. *Shirley Chisholm* (3–5). Illus. Series: First Books. 1994, Watts LB $22.00 (0-531-20168-6). 64pp. An interesting biography of this African American, with emphasis on her political career in Washington, D.C. (Rev: BL 1/15/95) [921]

DOUGLASS, FREDERICK

12708 Adler, David A. *A Picture Book of Frederick Douglass* (K–3). Illus. by Samuel Byrd. Series: Headliners. 1993, Holiday LB $16.95 (0-8234-1002-1). 32pp. A simple life story of the famous African American abolitionist who died in 1895. (Rev: BL 4/1/93; SLJ 8/93) [921]

12709 Bennett, Evelyn. *Frederick Douglass and the War Against Slavery* (3–5). Series: Gateway Civil Rights. 1993, Millbrook LB $20.90 (1-56294-341-3). 32pp. A brief biography of the man who began life as a slave and later became a presidential advisor. (Rev: BL 10/1/93; SLJ 10/93) [921]

12710 Girard, Linda Walvoord. *Young Frederick Douglass: The Slave Who Learned to Read* (3–5). Illus. by Colin Bootman. 1994, Albert Whitman LB $14.95 (0-8075-9463-6). 40pp. A brief biography based on Douglass's autobiography that is gripping in its use of dialogue and descriptions of inner feelings. (Rev: SLJ 11/94) [921]

12711 McKissack, Patricia, and Fredrick McKissack. *Frederick Douglass: Leader Against Slavery* (2–4). Illus. Series: Great African Americans. 1991, Enslow LB $14.95 (0-89490-306-3). 32pp. Fine documentary photographs highlight this biography. (Rev: BL 1/1/92; SLJ 2/92) [921]

12712 Marlowe, Sam. *Learning About Dedication from the Life of Frederick Douglass* (2–5). Illus. Series: Character Building Book. 1996, Rosen LB $15.93 (0-8239-2425-4). 24pp. Both slavery and the life of the man who fought against it are covered in this short book. (Rev: BL 10/15/96; SLJ 1/97) [921]

12713 Miller, William. *Frederick Douglass: The Last Day of Slavery* (2–4). Illus. by Cedric Lucas. 1995, Lee & Low $14.95 (1-880000-17-2). 32pp. A picture book biography of this freedom fighter who suffered the cruelty of slavery. (Rev: BL 3/15/95; SLJ 6/95) [921]

12714 Passaro, John. *Frederick Douglass* (4–6). Series: Journey to Freedom. 1999, Child's World LB $16.95 (1-56766-621-3). 32pp. The inspiring biography of the gifted African American who managed to escape slavery and become one of the earliest fighters for civil rights and freedom. (Rev: BL 10/15/99; HBG 3/00) [921]

12715 Santrey, Laurence. *Young Frederick Douglass: Fight for Freedom* (3–5). Illus. by Bert Dodson. 1983, Troll LB $17.25 (0-89375-857-4); paper $3.50 (0-89375-858-2). 48pp. The story of the slave who became a leader of the abolitionist movement. [921]

12716 Schomp, Virginia. *He Fought for Freedom: Frederick Douglass* (3–6). Illus. Series: Biographies. 1996, Benchmark LB $21.36 (0-7614-0488-0). 48pp. A brief but thorough account of the former slave who led the antislavery movement, with quotes from his autobiography. (Rev: HB 11–12/96; SLJ 2/97) [921]

DU BOIS, W. E. B.

12717 Cavan, Seamus. *W. E. B. Du Bois and Racial Relations* (3–5). Illus. Series: Gateway Civil Rights. 1993, Millbrook LB $20.90 (1-56294-288-3). 32pp. The story of the life and contributions of this great African American civil rights leader and author who died in 1963. (Rev: BL 10/1/93; SLJ 10/93) [921]

12718 Cryan-Hicks, Kathryn. *W. E. B. Du Bois: Crusader for Peace* (3–6). Illus. by David Huckins. 1991, Discovery $14.95 (1-878668-05-6); paper $7.95 (1-878668-09-9). 48pp. The life story of the writer and leader who devoted his life to rights for African Americans and world peace. (Rev: SLJ 10/91) [921]

12719 McDaniel, Melissa. *W. E. B. DuBois: Scholar and Civil Rights Activist* (4–6). Series: Book Report Biographies. 1999, Watts LB $22.00 (0-531-11433-3). 96pp. A story of the humanitarian and fighter against segregation who spent his life writing about and teaching his people. (Rev: BL 10/15/99) [921]

12720 Troy, Don. *W. E. B. Du Bois* (3–6). Series: Journey to Freedom. 1999, Child's World LB $16.95 (1-56766-555-1). 39pp. An attractive and clearly written biography of Du Bois that contains photos on each page, a timeline, and sources for further information. (Rev: BL 7/99; HBG 10/99; SLJ 7/99) [921]

FARMER, JAMES

12721 Jakoubek, Robert E. *James Farmer and the Freedom Rides* (3–5). Illus. Series: Gateway Civil Rights. 1994, Millbrook LB $20.90 (1-56294-381-2). 32pp. The story of the Freedom Riders and their leader, James Farmer, who dedicated his life to the struggle for civil rights. (Rev: BL 4/15/94; SLJ 6/94) [921]

FIELDS, MARY

12722 Miller, Robert H. *The Story of Stagecoach Mary Fields* (1–4). Illus. by Cheryl Hanna. 1995, Silver Burdett LB $14.95 (0-382-24390-0); paper $5.95 (0-382-24394-3). 32pp. In the late 1800s, Mary Fields, a freed slave, was the first African American woman letter carrier. (Rev: BL 4/15/95; SLJ 5/95) [921]

FLIPPER, HENRY O.

12723 Pfeifer, Kathryn B. *Henry O. Flipper* (4–8). Illus. Series: African American Soldiers. 1993, Twenty-First Century LB $17.90 (0-8050-2351-8). 80pp. The story of Henry Flipper, the first African American graduate of West Point, who lived from 1856 to 1940. (Rev: BL 2/15/94; SLJ 4/94) [921]

FORTUNE, AMOS

12724 Yates, Elizabeth. *Amos Fortune, Free Man* (6–8). Illus. by Nora S. Unwin. 1950, Puffin paper $4.99 (0-14-034158-7). 181pp. The simplicity and dignity of the human spirit and its triumph over degradation are movingly portrayed in this portrait

of a slave who bought his freedom. Newbery Medal winner, 1951.

HAMER, FANNIE LOU

12725 Colman, Penny. *Fannie Lou Hamer and the Fight for the Vote* (3–5). Illus. Series: Gateway Civil Rights. 1993, Millbrook LB $20.90 (1-56294-323-5). 32pp. A biography of the civil rights activist who fought for African American voter registration. (Rev: BL 10/1/93; SLJ 10/93) [921]

HILL, ANITA

12726 Italia, Bob. *Anita Hill: Speaking Out Against Harassment* (4–6). Illus. Series: Everyone Contributes. 1993, ABDO LB $12.94 (1-56239-259-X). 32pp. This biography concentrates on the Clarence Thomas hearings and Anita Hill's role in them. (Rev: BL 12/1/93; SLJ 1/94) [921]

JACKSON, JESSE

12727 Celsi, Teresa. *Jesse Jackson and Political Power* (4–6). Illus. Series: Gateway Civil Rights. 1991, Millbrook paper $4.95 (1-878-84170-X). 32pp. A short, basic biography that covers highlights of Jackson's life in text and both color and black-and-white illustrations. (Rev: BL 1/1/92; SLJ 1/92) [921]

12728 Meadows, James. *Jesse Jackson* (4–6). Series: Journey to Freedom. 2000, Child's World LB $25.64 (1-56766-742-2). 40pp. The story of a religious leader who has also become one of the most powerful civil rights activists in the country. (Rev: BL 11/15/00; HBG 3/01) [921]

12729 Steffens, Bradley, and Dan Wood. *Jesse Jackson* (5–8). Series: People in the News. 2000, Lucent LB $18.96 (1-56006-631-8). 126pp. This well-documented look at the life of the religious and civil rights leader gives interesting information on the events and people who influenced him. (Rev: BL 6/1–15/00; HBG 10/00) [921]

JACOBS, HARRIET

12730 Fleischner, Jennifer. *I Was Born a Slave: The Story of Harriet Jacobs* (4–7). Illus. 1997, Millbrook LB $24.90 (0-7613-0111-9). 96pp. An adaptation of the slave narrative that tells of the tragedies and triumphs of a plucky woman who finally escaped slavery. (Rev: BL 9/15/97; HBG 3/98; SLJ 1/98) [921]

JAMES, DANIEL

12731 Super, Neil. *Daniel "Chappie" James* (4–8). Series: African American Soldiers. 1992, Twenty-First Century LB $17.90 (0-8050-2138-8). 80pp. An inspiring story of the African American boy, growing up in Florida in the 1920s and 1930s, who would one day become a four-star general. (Rev: BL 12/15/92; SLJ 11/92) [921]

JORDAN, BARBARA

12732 McNair, Joseph. *Barbara Jordan: African American Politician* (4–6). Series: Journey to Freedom. 2000, Child's World LB $25.64 (1-56766-

741-4). 40pp. A biography of the noted politician who was Texas's first African American female senator and later served in Congress for six years. (Rev: BL 11/15/00; HBG 3/01) [921]

12733 Patrick-Wexler, Diane. *Barbara Jordan* (4–6). Illus. Series: Contemporary African Americans. 1995, Raintree Steck-Vaughn LB $25.69 (0-8172-3976-6). 48pp. The story of the famous African American congresswoman from childhood through her later career as an educator. (Rev: BL 2/15/96; SLJ 4/96) [921]

12734 Rhodes, Lisa R. *Barbara Jordan: Voice of Democracy* (5–8). Series: Book Report Biographies. 1998, Watts LB $22.00 (0-531-11450-3). 112pp. This biography of the famous African American legal expert and educator emphasizes her work in the investigation of the events in the Watergate scandal. (Rev: HBG 3/99; SLJ 2/99) [921]

KING, CORETTA SCOTT

12735 Klingel, Cynthia. *Coretta Scott King* (4–6). Illus. Series: Journey to Freedom. 1999, Child's World LB $16.95 (1-56766-567-5). 40pp. A life of Coretta Scott King, who gave up her singing career to follow in her husband's footsteps as a civil rights leader. (Rev: BL 5/1/99; HBG 10/99) [921]

12736 Medearis, Angela Shelf. *Dare to Dream: Coretta Scott King and the Civil Rights Movement* (3–5). Illus. by Anna Rich. 1994, Dutton $13.99 (0-525-67426-8). 64pp. A sensitive biography that uses Coretta Scott King's autobiography as its principal source. (Rev: BL 1/1/95; SLJ 2/95) [921]

12737 Rhodes, Lisa R. *Coretta Scott King* (5–8). Illus. Series: Black Americans of Achievement. 1998, Chelsea $19.95 (0-7910-4690-7); paper $8.95 (0-7910-4691-5). 143pp. This story of Coretta Scott King tells about her childhood, education, marriage, participation in the civil rights movement, and her work since her husband's assassination. (Rev: BL 8/98; HBG 10/98) [921]

12738 Wheeler, Jill C. *Coretta Scott King* (4–6). Illus. Series: Leading Ladies. 1992, ABDO LB $13.98 (1-56239-116-X). 32pp. The life of the civil rights leader, emphasizing her activities since her husband's death. (Rev: BL 2/1/93; SLJ 3/93) [921]

KING, MARTIN LUTHER, JR.

12739 Adler, David A. *A Picture Book of Martin Luther King, Jr.* (PS–2). Illus. by Robert Casilla. Series: Picture Book Biographies. 1989, Holiday LB $16.95 (0-8234-0770-5); paper $6.95 (0-8234-0847-7). 32pp. The life of the civil rights leader is presented in picture book format. (Rev: BCCB 2/90; BL 11/1/89; SLJ 9/89) [921]

12740 Bray, Rosemary L. *Martin Luther King* (2–4). Illus. by Malcah Zeldis. 1995, Greenwillow paper $5.95 (0-688-15219-8). 48pp. A large-format biography that supplies basic information with dramatic paintings on each page. (Rev: BL 2/15/95; HB 5–6/95; SLJ 2/95*) [921]

12741 Darby, Jean. *Martin Luther King, Jr.* (4–8). Illus. Series: Lerner Biographies. 1990, Lerner LB $25.26 (0-8225-4902-6). 144pp. An in-depth look at

King's life and the civil rights movement. (Rev: BL 7/90; SLJ 11/90) [921]

12742 Hakim, Rita. *Martin Luther King, Jr. and the March Toward Freedom* (4–6). Illus. Series: Gateway Civil Rights. 1991, Millbrook LB $20.90 (1-878841-13-0). 32pp. Good photographs add appeal to this basic short biography of the famed civil rights leader. (Rev: BL 1/1/92; SLJ 8/91) [921]

12743 Haskins, Jim. *I Have a Dream* (4–6). Illus. 1992, Millbrook LB $27.40 (1-56294-087-2). 112p. A well-researched biography, supported by excerpts from King's writings and speeches. (Rev: BL 2/15/93) [921]

12744 Haskins, Jim. *The Life and Death of Martin Luther King, Jr.* (5–7). Illus. 1992, Morrow paper $5.95 (0-688-11690-6). 176pp. Covering the life and career of the African American leader, with focus on the civil rights movement. [921]

12745 Lambert, Kathy K. *Martin Luther King, Jr.* (4–7). Illus. Series: Junior World Biographies. 1992, Chelsea LB $16.95 (0-7910-1759-1). 82pp. A well-designed biography using many photos to re-create the life of the great civil rights leader. (Rev: BL 11/1/92) [921]

12746 Lowery, Linda. *Martin Luther King Day* (2–4). Illus. by Hetty Mitchell. 1987, Carolrhoda LB $21.27 (0-87614-299-4); Lerner paper $5.95 (0-87614-468-7). 56pp. Origins of the holiday and high points of Dr. King's life. (Rev: BL 4/1/87; SLJ 6–7/87) [921]

12747 McKissack, Patricia, and Fredrick McKissack. *Martin Luther King, Jr.: Man of Peace* (2–4). Illus. Series: Great African Americans. 1991, Enslow LB $14.95 (0-89490-302-0). 32pp. An easily read biography of the leader whose dream was civil rights for all Americans. (Rev: SLJ 11/91) [921]

12748 Marzollo, Jean. *Happy Birthday, Martin Luther King* (PS–3). Illus. by Brian Pinkney. 1992, Scholastic $15.95 (0-590-44065-9). 32pp. The focus is on King's ability to bring people together in this simple biography. (Rev: BL 12/15/92; SLJ 3/93) [921]

12749 Milton, Joyce. *Marching to Freedom: The Story of Martin Luther King, Jr.* (5–7). Illus. 1987, Dell paper $3.99 (0-440-45433-6). 92pp. A biography of his life, from childhood to civil rights leader. (Rev: BL 6/15/87; SLJ 10/87)

12750 Murray, Peter. *Dreams: The Story of Martin Luther King, Jr.* (3–4). Illus. by Robin Lawrie. Series: Value Biographies. 1999, Child's World LB $14.95 (1-56766-223-4). 32pp. This biography of the famous civil rights leader covers his beliefs, education, marriage, and assassination. (Rev: HBG 10/99; SLJ 8/99) [921]

12751 Patrick, Diane. *Martin Luther King, Jr.* (4–8). Illus. 1990, Watts LB $21.00 (0-531-10892-9). 144pp. A colorful format helps to make this look at King's life accessible to middle-grade readers. (Rev: BL 7/90; SLJ 9/90) [921]

12752 Ringgold, Faith. *My Dream of Martin Luther King* (1–4). Illus. 1995, Crown $18.00 (0-517-59976-7). 32pp. Through the author's dream, key events in the life of Martin Luther King, Jr., are recalled in this picture book, which also explains the impact of his life on humanity. (Rev: BCCB 1/96; BL 2/15/96; SLJ 2/96) [921]

12753 Roop, Peter, and Connie Roop. *Martin Luther King, Jr.* (2–3). Series: Lives and Times. 1997, Heinemann $19.92 (1-57572-560-6). 24pp. A simple picture book biography that gives a very brief introduction to the life and contributions of Martin Luther King, Jr. (Rev: BL 3/15/98; HB 5–6/97; SLJ 6/98) [921]

12754 Schuman, Michael A. *Martin Luther King, Jr.: Leader for Civil Rights* (5–8). Illus. Series: African American Biographies. 1996, Enslow LB $20.95 (0-89490-687-9). 128pp. A straightforward biography that covers the main events of King's life. (Rev: SLJ 12/96) [921]

12755 Stein, R. Conrad. *The Assassination of Martin Luther King, Jr.* (3–5). Illus. Series: Cornerstones of Freedom. 1996, Children's LB $20.50 (0-516-20004-6). 32pp. After a brief introduction to the life and work of Martin Luther King, Jr., the assassination is described and its significance explored. (Rev: BL 12/15/96; SLJ 4/97) [921]

12756 Strazzabosco, Jeanne M. *Learning About Dignity from the Life of Martin Luther King, Jr.* (2–5). Illus. Series: A Character Building Book. 1996, Rosen $13.95 (0-8239-2415-7). 24pp. This brief biography describes King's many virtues, above all his innate dignity. (Rev: BL 10/15/96; SLJ 12/96) [921]

LOVE, NAT

12757 Miller, Robert, and Michael Bryant. *The Story of Nat Love* (K–3). Illus. 1994, Silver Burdett LB $14.95 (0-382-24389-7), paper $5.95 (0-382-24393-5). 32pp. A picture book biography of the cowboy of the Old West, Nat Love, who began his life as a slave. (Rev: BL 1/1/95; SLJ 1/95) [921]

MCCARTY, OSEOLA

12758 Coleman, Evelyn. *The Riches of Oseola McCarty* (3–7). Illus. 1998, Albert Whitman $14.95 (0-8075-6961-5). 48pp. This is the heartwarming story of the modest washerwoman who, at her death, gave her hard-earned fortune to the University of Mississippi for scholarships. (Rev: BCCB 3/99; BL 12/15/98; HB 1–2/99; HBG 3/99; SLJ 1/99) [921]

MALCOLM X

12759 Adoff, Arnold. *Malcolm X.* Rev. ed. (3–6). Illus. 2000, HarperCollins paper $4.25 (0-06-442118-X). 64pp. This clearly written biography reflects the intense drama of the African American leader's life and death. (Rev: BL 2/15/00) [921]

12760 Cwiklik, Robert. *Malcolm X and Black Pride* (4–6). Illus. Series: Gateway Civil Rights. 1991, Millbrook LB $20.90 (1-56294-042-2). 32pp. This clear overview of this important civil rights leader contains many excellent color and black-and-white photos. (Rev: BL 1/1/92; SLJ 4/92) [921]

12761 Myers, Walter Dean. *Malcolm X: A Fire Burning Brightly* (3–6). Illus. 2000, HarperCollins LB $15.89 (0-06-027708-4). 32pp. Using many quotes from Malcolm X, this biography focuses on the inner conflicts that plagued this amazing leader. (Rev: BCCB 4/00; BL 2/15/00; HB 5–6/00; HBG 10/00; SLJ 2/00) [921]

12762 Myers, Walter Dean. *Malcolm X: By Any Means Necessary* (5–8). Illus. 1993, Scholastic $13.95 (0-590-46484-1). 210pp. Malcolm X's life dealt with in four parts. (Rev: BCCB 3/93; SLJ 2/93) [921]

MARSHALL, THURGOOD

12763 Adler, David A. *A Picture Book of Thurgood Marshall* (3–4). Illus. by Robert Casilla. Series: Picture Book Biographies. 1997, Holiday LB $16.95 (0-8234-1308-X). 32pp. The life of this Supreme Court justice is well re-created in simple language that chronicles his battles against segregation and discrimination. (Rev: BL 11/15/97; HBG 3/98; SLJ 1/98) [921]

12764 Carpenter, Eric. *Young Thurgood Marshall: Fighter for Equality* (2–4). Illus. Series: Troll First Start. 1996, Troll paper $3.50 (0-8167-3771-1). 32pp. A beginning biography that stresses the childhood and early influences as well as the adult accomplishments of this Supreme Court justice. (Rev: BL 2/15/96) [921]

12765 Hitzeroth, Deborah, and Sharon Leon. *Thurgood Marshall* (4–8). Illus. Series: Importance Of. 1997, Lucent LB $18.96 (1-56006-061-1). 112pp. As well as tracing the career of this Supreme Court justice, this account pinpoints Marshall's lasting contributions to his country and his race. (Rev: BL 6/1–15/97; HBG 3/98; SLJ 9/97) [921]

12766 Kallen, Stuart A. *Thurgood Marshall: A Dream of Justice for All* (3–5). Illus. Series: I Have a Dream. 1993, ABDO LB $15.98 (1-56239-258-1). 40pp. The story of the first African American to serve on the Supreme Court and his contributions to the struggle for civil rights. (Rev: BL 2/1/94) [921]

12767 Kent, Deborah. *Thurgood Marshall and the Supreme Court* (3–5). Illus. Series: Cornerstones of Freedom. 1997, Children's LB $20.50 (0-516-20297-9). 32pp. The life story of this Supreme Court justice, who served from 1967 through 1991, and his struggle to bring equal rights to African Americans. (Rev: BL 6/1–15/97) [921]

12768 Prentzas, G. S. *Thurgood Marshall: Champion of Justice* (4–8). Illus. Series: Junior World Biographies. 1993, Chelsea LB $16.95 (0-7910-1769-9); paper $6.95 (0-7910-1969-1). 79pp. An interesting biography of Thurgood Marshall that touches on his civil rights work but focuses on his years as a Supreme Court justice. (Rev: SLJ 11/93) [921]

MASON, BIDDY

12769 Ferris, Jeri Chase. *With Open Hands: A Story About Biddy Mason* (4–6). Illus. by Ralph L. Ramstad. 1999, Carolrhoda LB $21.27 (1-57505-330-6). 64pp. The inspiring story of the woman, born a slave, who accompanied her Mormon master and his family to Utah where she later became a midwife, a wealthy landowner, and a philanthropist. (Rev: BL 2/1/99; HBG 10/99; SLJ 5/99) [921]

MATZELIGER, JAN

12770 Mitchell, Barbara. *Shoes for Everyone: A Story About Jan Matzeliger* (3–5). Illus. 1986, Carolrhoda LB $21.27 (0-87614-290-0); Lerner paper $5.95 (0-87614-473-3). 64pp. The life of the African American inventor who changed the industry with his shoe-lasting machine. (Rev: BCCB 7–8/86; BL 8/86; SLJ 9/86) [921]

MAYS, OSCEOLA

12771 *Osceola: Memories of a Sharecropper's Daughter* (3–7). Ed. by Alan Govenar. Illus. 2000, Hyperion LB $16.49 (0-7868-2357-7). 64pp. A powerful transcribed oral history of Osceola Mays, an African American woman now over 90 years old, and her life in East Texas under the yoke of segregation, prejudice, and discrimination. (Rev: BCCB 3/00; BL 2/15/00; HB 3–4/00; HBG 10/00; SLJ 5/00) [921]

MEREDITH, JAMES

12772 Elish, Dan. *James Meredith and School Desegregation* (3–5). Illus. Series: Gateway Civil Rights. 1994, Millbrook LB $20.90 (1-56294-379-0). 32pp. The biography of the young African American man who was a pioneer in integrating institutions of higher education in Mississippi. (Rev: BL 4/15/94; SLJ 5/94) [921]

PARKS, ROSA

12773 Adler, David A. *A Picture Book of Rosa Parks* (2–4). Illus. by Robert Casilla. Series: Picture Book Biographies. 1993, Holiday LB $16.95 (0-8234-1041-2). 30pp. The life story of the civil rights leader who refused to give up her bus seat to a white passenger. (Rev: BL 10/15/93; SLJ 12/93) [921]

12774 Benjamin, Anne. *Young Rosa Parks: Civil Rights Heroine* (2–4). Illus. Series: First Start Biography. 1996, Troll paper $3.50 (0-8167-3775-4). 32pp. Attractive color illustrations are included in this account of the life of a civil rights activist that emphasizes her childhood. (Rev: BL 2/15/96) [921]

12775 Celsi, Teresa. *Rosa Parks and the Montgomery Bus Boycott* (4–6). Illus. Series: Gateway Civil Rights. 1991, Millbrook LB $20.90 (1-878841-14-9). 32pp. In clear text and many color photos, the story of the Montgomery, Alabama, bus boycott is outlined in relation to its modest leader. (Rev: BL 1/1/92; SLJ 8/91) [921]

12776 Greenfield, Eloise. *Rosa Parks* (2–4). Illus. by Eric Marlow. 1996, HarperCollins LB $14.89 (0-06-027110-8); paper $4.25 (0-06-442025-6). 40pp. A convincing sketch of the woman whose brave stand precipitated the Montgomery bus strike and her ensuing involvement with the civil rights struggle. [921]

12777 Holland, Gini. *Rosa Parks* (2–4). Illus. by David Price. Series: First Biographies. 1997, Raintree Steck-Vaughn LB $24.26 (0-8172-4451-4). 32pp. A simple account of Rosa Parks's life, cover-

ing her childhood, civil rights work, imprisonment, and release. (Rev: SLJ 2/98) [921]

12778 Parks, Rosa, and Jim Haskins. *I Am Rosa Parks* (2–4). Illus. Series: Dial Easy-to-Read. 1997, Dial $13.99 (0-8037-1206-5). 48pp. An easy-to-read version of the civil rights leader's autobiography that retains its message and honesty. (Rev: BCCB 6/97; BL 5/1/97; HB 5–6/97; SLJ 5/97) [921]

12779 Ringgold, Faith. *If a Bus Could Talk: The Story of Rosa Parks* (K–4). Illus. 1999, Simon & Schuster $16.00 (0-689-81892-0). 32pp. A picture book biography that combines elements of fantasy with the true story of Rosa Parks, often called the mother of the Civil Rights movement. (Rev: BCCB 1/00; BL 1/1–15/00; HBG 3/00; SLJ 1/00) [921]

12780 Summer, L. S. *Rosa Parks* (4–6). Series: Journey to Freedom. 1999, Child's World LB $16.95 (1-56766-622-1). 32pp. A biography that pays tribute to the gallant African American who started an amazing chain of events in 1955 when she refused to give up her bus seat to a white person in Montgomery, Alabama. (Rev: BL 10/15/99; HBG 3/00) [921]

RANDOLPH, A. PHILIP

12781 Cwiklik, Robert. *A. Philip Randolph and the Labor Movement* (3–5). Series: Gateway Civil Rights. 1993, Millbrook LB $20.90 (1-56294-326-X). 32pp. The story of the African American who organized the sleeping-car porters into a union and later directed a march on Washington, D.C., in 1941, to protest unfair labor practices. (Rev: BL 10/1/93; SLJ 10/93) [921]

12782 Hanley, Sally. *A. Philip Randolph* (5–8). 1988, Chelsea LB $19.95 (1-55546-607-9); paper $9.95 (0-7910-0222-5). 112pp. Biography of the man who became a great labor leader and civil rights activist. (Rev: BL 10/1/88) [921]

RUSTIN, BAYARD

12783 Haskins, Jim. *Bayard Rustin: Behind the Scenes of the Civil Rights Movement* (5–8). Illus. 1997, Hyperion LB $15.49 (0-7868-2140-X). 128pp. The life of the great civil rights leader and 50 years in the struggle for equality are presented in this exciting biography. (Rev: BL 2/15/97*; SLJ 4/97) [921]

TAYLOR, MARSHALL B.

12784 Scioscia, Mary. *Bicycle Rider* (2–5). Illus. by Ed Young. 1983, HarperCollins paper $5.95 (0-06-443295-5). 48pp. The fictionalized biography of the African American man who at one time was the fastest bicyclist in the world.

TAYLOR, SUSIE KING

12785 Jordan, Denise. *Susie King Taylor: Destined to Be Free* (3–5). Illus. by Higgins Bond. 1994, Just Us paper $5.00 (0-940975-50-5). 42pp. The story of the freed slave who, after the Civil War, became a teacher of African American children and adults and wrote an account of her life. (Rev: SLJ 7/95) [921]

TERRELL, MARY CHURCH

12786 McKissack, Patricia, and Fredrick McKissack. *Mary Church Terrell: Leader for Equality* (2–4). Illus. by Ned Ostendorf. Series: Great African Americans. 1991, Enslow LB $14.95 (0-89490-305-5). 32pp. This educator and social reformer was the first president of the National Association of Colored Women. (Rev: SLJ 2/92) [921]

12787 Swain, Gwenyth. *Civil Rights Pioneer: A Story about Mary Church Terrell* (3–6). Illus. 1999, Lerner $21.27 (1-57505-355-1). 64pp. A straightforward biography of the well-educated African American woman who devoted her life to fighting for civil rights. (Rev: BL 1/1–15/00; HBG 3/00; SLJ 2/00) [921]

TITUBA

12788 Miller, William. *Tituba* (2–5). Illus. 2000, Harcourt $16.00 (0-15-201897-2). 32pp. Told in picture-book format, this is the fictional story of the slave Tituba, who was accused of witchcraft at the beginning of the Salem Witch Trials and sent to jail. (Rev: BCCB 11/00; BL 11/1/00; SLJ 12/00) [921]

TRUTH, SOJOURNER

12789 Adler, David A. *A Picture Book of Sojourner Truth* (2–4). Illus. by Gershom Griffith. Series: Picture Book Biographies. 1994, Holiday LB $16.95 (0-8234-1072-2). In an easily read format, the life and works of Sojourner Truth are introduced. (Rev: SLJ 6/94) [921]

12790 Ferris, Jeri. *Walking the Road to Freedom: A Story About Sojourner Truth* (3–6). Illus. 1988, Carolrhoda LB $21.27 (0-87614-318-4); Lerner paper $5.95 (0-87614-505-5). 64pp. The story of the woman born into slavery who vowed to travel the land singing of its evils. (Rev: BL 3/1/88; SLJ 3/88)

12791 Macht, Norman L. *Sojourner Truth* (4–7). Illus. Series: Junior World Biographies. 1992, Chelsea LB $16.95 (0-7910-1754-0). 80pp. The story of the freed slave who traveled through the North preaching emancipation and women's rights. (Rev: BL 10/1/92; SLJ 12/92) [921]

12792 McKissack, Patricia, and Fredrick McKissack. *Sojourner Truth: A Voice for Freedom* (2–4). Illus. by Michael D. Blegel. Series: Great African Americans. 1992, Enslow LB $14.95 (0-89490-313-6). 32pp. Through her life as a freed slave, Sojourner Truth traveled in the Northeast preaching against slavery. (Rev: BCCB 1/93; BL 11/15/92; HB 3–4/93; SLJ 1/93) [921]

12793 Rockwell, Anne. *Only Passing Through* (4–8). Illus. 2000, Knopf $16.95 (0-679-89186-2). 32pp. A moving picture-book biography of Sojourner Truth, who was a pioneer in the struggle for racial equality and devoted her life to the abolitionist movement. (Rev: BCCB 1/01; BL 11/15/00; HB 11–12/00; HBG 3/01; SLJ 12/00) [921]

12794 Soinale, Laura. *Sojourner Truth* (4–6). Series: Journey to Freedom. 1999, Child's World LB $16.95 (1-56766-623-X). 32pp. The story of the African American woman, born a slave in New York State and freed in 1827, who became an early abolitionist and inspiring orator. (Rev: BL 10/15/99; HBG 3/00) [921]

TUBMAN, HARRIET

12795 Adler, David A. *A Picture Book of Harriet Tubman* (2–4). Illus. by Samuel Byrd. Series: Picture Book Biographies. 1992, Holiday LB $16.95 (0-8234-0926-0). 32pp. Easy-to-read text describes the life of this famous American who helped slaves gain freedom. (Rev: BCCB 7–8/92; BL 6/15/92; SLJ 6/92) [921]

12796 Burns, Bree. *Harriet Tubman* (4–7). Illus. Series: Junior World Biographies. 1992, Chelsea LB $16.95 (0-7910-1751-6). 80pp. This is a straightforward account of the escaped slave who helped free more than 300 slaves via the Underground Railroad. (Rev: BL 10/1/92; SLJ 12/92) [921]

12797 Elish, Dan. *Harriet Tubman and the Underground Railroad* (4–6). Illus. Series: Gateway Civil Rights. 1993, Millbrook LB $20.90 (1-56294-273-5). 32pp. The story of the slave who led the organization that helped slaves escape via the Underground Railroad. (Rev: BL 8/93) [921]

12798 Ferris, Jeri. *Go Free or Die: A Story About Harriet Tubman* (3–6). Illus. 1988, Carolrhoda LB $21.27 (0-87614-317-6); Lerner paper $5.95 (0-87614-504-7). 64pp. The story of the former slave and her fight to rid the country of slavery. (Rev: BL 3/1/88; SLJ 3/88) [921]

12799 Kulling, Monica. *Escape North! The Story of Harriet Tubman* (2–4). Illus. by Teresa Flavin. Series: Step into Reading. 2000, Random $11.99 (0-375-90154-X). A book for beginning readers that tells the life story of Harriet Tubman and re-creates one of her journeys on the Underground Railroad. (Rev: BL 2/15/01) [921]

12800 Lawrence, Jacob. *Harriet and the Promised Land* (1–4). Illus. 1993, Simon & Schuster paper $18.00 (0-671-86673-7). 32pp. The story of Harriet Tubman, an escaped slave, who ventured into the South 19 times to help others escape. (Rev: BL 10/1/93*) [811]

12801 Mosher, Kiki. *Learning About Bravery from the Life of Harriet Tubman* (2–5). Illus. Series: A Character Building Book. 1996, Rosen LB $15.93 (0-8239-2424-6). 24pp. This short biography shows how the element of courage was paramount in the life of this leader of the Underground Railroad. (Rev: BL 10/15/96; SLJ 1/97) [921]

12802 Rowley, John. *Harriet Tubman* (2–3). Illus. Series: Lives and Times. 1997, Heinemann $19.92 (1-57572-558-4). 24pp. A simple picture book biography that talks about slavery and tells of the life, courage, and endurance of this leader on the Underground Railroad. (Rev: BL 3/15/98; SLJ 6/98) [921]

12803 Taylor, M. W. *Harriet Tubman* (5–8). Illus. Series: Black Americans of Achievement. 1990, Chelsea LB $19.95 (1-55546-612-5). 111pp. The story of the famous conductor on the Underground Railroad. (Rev: SLJ 1/91) [921]

12804 Troy, Don. *Harriet Ross Tubman* (4–6). Series: Journey to Freedom. 1999, Child's World

LB $16.95 (1-56766-568-3). 40pp. The life of a gallant, energetic former slave and abolitionist who is best remembered for her work with the Underground Railroad. (Rev: BL 7/99; HBG 10/99; SLJ 7/99) [921]

TURNER, NAT

12805 Hendrickson, Ann-Marie. *Nat Turner: Rebel Slave* (4–7). Illus. Series: Junior World Biographies. 1995, Chelsea LB $15.95 (0-7910-2386-9). 77pp. An attractive biography of this slave who led a revolution and became a symbol of heroism for his people. (Rev: BL 10/15/95) [921]

12806 Neshama, Rivvy. *Nat Turner and the Virginia Slave Revolt* (4–6). Series: Journey to Freedom. 2000, Child's World LB $25.64 (1-56766-744-9). 40pp. The story of the charismatic slave preacher who was hanged for his part in the slave revolt of 1831. (Rev: BL 11/15/00; HBG 3/01; SLJ 3/01) [921]

WALKER, MADAM C. J.

12807 Colman, Penny. *Madam C. J. Walker: Building a Business Empire* (3–6). Illus. 1994, Millbrook LB $20.90 (1-56294-338-3). 48pp. The success story of the African American woman who rose from extreme poverty to found a beauty preparation empire. (Rev: BL 6/1–15/94; SLJ 9/94) [921]

12808 Hobkirk, Lori. *Madam C. J. Walker* (4–6). Series: Journey to Freedom. 2000, Child's World LB $25.64 (1-56766-721-X). 40pp. The story of the African American entrepreneur who made a fortune in cosmetics. (Rev: BL 11/15/00; HBG 3/01) [921]

12809 Lasky, Kathryn. *Vision of Beauty: The Story of Sarah Breedlove Walker* (3–5). Illus. 2000, Candlewick $16.99 (0-7636-0253-1). 44pp. The inspiring story of a woman who was born into slavery and orphaned as a young child and her phenomenal success as an entrepreneur. (Rev: BCCB 9/00; BL 7/00*; HBG 10/00; SLJ 5/00) [921]

12810 McKissack, Patricia, and Fredrick McKissack. *Madam C. J. Walker: Self-Made Millionaire* (2–4). Illus. by Michael Bryant. Series: Great African Americans. 1992, Enslow LB $14.95 (0-89490-311-X). 32pp. The story of the woman who built a cosmetics empire and became the first self-made African American woman millionaire. (Rev: BL 10/15/92; SLJ 12/92) [921]

WALKER, MAGGIE

12811 Branch, Muriel M., and Dorothy M. Rice. *Pennies to Dollars: The Story of Maggie Lena Walker* (4–7). Illus. 1997, Linnet LB $17.95 (0-208-02453-0); paper $13.95 (0-208-02455-7). 128pp. Maggie Walker, the daughter of a former slave, helped African Americans through her financial schemes, including founding the Penny Savings Bank. (Rev: BL 11/1/97; SLJ 10/97) [921]

WASHINGTON, BOOKER T.

12812 Amper, Thomas. *Booker T. Washington* (2–5). Illus. 1998, Carolrhoda $18.60 (1-57505-094-3). 48pp. The inspiring story of the young Booker T.

Washington and his determination to receive an education in spite of his race and his extreme poverty. (Rev: BL 11/15/98; HBG 3/99; SLJ 11/98) [921]

12813 McKissack, Patricia, and Fredrick McKissack. *Booker T. Washington: Leader and Educator* (2–4). Illus. by Michael Bryant. Series: Great African Americans. 1992, Enslow LB $14.95 (0-89490-314-4). 32pp. This book tells how Booker T. Washington created a school for African Americans at Tuskegee Institute in Alabama. (Rev: BL 9/15/92; SLJ 10/92) [921]

12814 Troy, Don. *Booker T. Washington* (4–6). Illus. Series: Journey to Freedom. 1999, Child's World LB $16.95 (1-56766-556-X). 40pp. The story of the famous African American leader who was born a slave in Virginia and became a prominent educational and political leader. (Rev: BL 5/1/99; HBG 10/99) [921]

WATTS, J. C.

12815 Lutz, Norma Jean. *J. C. Watts* (4–7). Series: Black Americans of Achievement. 2000, Chelsea $19.95 (0-7910-5338-5). 110pp. The story of a former Oklahoma University football player who entered politics and was first elected to the House of Representatives in 1994. (Rev: BL 6/1–15/00; HBG 10/00) [921]

WELLS-BARNETT, IDA B.

12816 Fradin, Dennis B., and Judith B. Fradin. *Ida B. Wells: Mother of the Civil Rights Movement* (5–10). 2000, Clarion $18.00 (0-395-89898-6). 178pp. An inspiring biography of the African American who was born a slave and went on to become a school teacher, journalist, and an activist who fought for black women's right to vote and helped found the NAACP. (Rev: HB 5–6/00; HBG 10/00; SLJ 4/00*) [921]

12817 Freedman, Suzanne. *Ida B. Wells-Barnett and the Anti-Lynching Crusade* (3–5). Illus. Series: Gateway Civil Rights. 1994, Millbrook LB $20.90 (1-56294-377-4). 32pp. The biography of the African American journalist who fought for civil rights and justice in the South. (Rev: BL 4/15/94; SLJ 5/94) [921]

12818 McKissack, Patricia, and Fredrick McKissack. *Ida B. Wells-Barnett: A Voice Against Violence* (2–4). Illus. Series: Great African Americans. 1991, Enslow LB $14.95 (0-89490-301-2). 32pp. A simple biography of the founder of the NAACP. (Rev: SLJ 11/91) [921]

12819 Medearis, Angela Shelf. *Princess of the Press: The Story of Ida B. Wells-Barnett* (3–5). Illus. Series: Rainbow Biography. 1997, Dutton $14.99 (0-525-67493-4). 32pp. This daughter of slaves went on to become one of the founders of the NAACP and a co-owner of several African American journals. (Rev: BL 12/1/97; HBG 3/98; SLJ 12/97) [921]

12820 Welch, Catherine A. *Ida B. Wells-Barnett: Powerhouse with a Pen* (5–8). Illus. Series: Trailblazer Biography. 2000, Carolrhoda LB $23.95 (1-57505-352-7). 104pp. This book introduces Wells-Barnett, who was born a slave and became a powerful journalist and activist as well as a spokesperson for all African Americans. (Rev: BL 6/1–15/00; HBG 10/00; SLJ 7/00) [921]

WHITE, WALTER

12821 Jakoubek, Robert E. *Walter White and the Power of Organized Protest* (3–5). Illus. Series: Gateway Civil Rights. 1994, Millbrook LB $20.90 (1-56294-378-2). 32pp. Background material on the NAACP is given through the life story of one of its leaders, Walter White. (Rev: BL 4/15/94; SLJ 6/94) [921]

WOODSON, CARTER G.

12822 Haskins, Jim, and Kathleen Benson. *Carter G. Woodson: The Man Who Put "Black" in American History* (4–6). Illus. 2000, Millbrook LB $24.90 (0-7613-1264-1). 48pp. This biography examines the obstacles and triumphs experienced by the man who created the Association for the Study of Negro Life and History in 1915 and Negro History Week in 1926. (Rev: BL 4/1/00; HBG 10/00; SLJ 7/00) [921]

12823 McKissack, Patricia, and Fredrick McKissack. *Carter G. Woodson: The Father of Black History* (2–4). Illus. by Ned Ostendorf. Series: Great African Americans. 1991, Enslow LB $14.95 (0-89490-309-8). 32pp. This famous African American, who died in 1950, tried to educate people about the accomplishments of his people. (Rev: SLJ 2/92) [921]

Hispanic Americans

ANTONNETTY, EVELINA LOPEZ

12824 Mohr, Nicholasa. *All for the Better: A Story of El Barrio* (2–5). Illus. by Rudy Gutierrez. 1993, Raintree Steck-Vaughn LB $27.12 (0-8114-7220-5). 56pp. The story of Evelina Lopez Antonnetty and the difference she made in Spanish Harlem, New York. (Rev: BCCB 7–8/93; SLJ 5/93) [921]

CHAVEZ, CESAR

12825 Collins, David R. *Farmworker's Friend: The Story of Cesar Chavez* (3–5). Illus. 1996, Carolrhoda LB $23.93 (0-87614-982-4). 80pp. The story of this champion of poor farm workers is retold from a variety of original sources. (Rev: BL 12/15/96) [921]

12826 Conord, Bruce W. *Cesar Chavez: Union Leader* (4–7). Illus. Series: Junior World Biographies. 1993, Chelsea paper $4.95 (0-791-01999-3). 80pp. The life of the Mexican American who helped organize the farm workers of California is told in text and pictures. (Rev: BL 10/1/92; SLJ 12/92) [921]

12827 Zannos, Susan. *Cesar Chavez* (3–6). Series: Real-Life Reader Biographies. 1998, Mitchell Lane LB $15.95 (1-883845-71-8). 32pp. The life of this inspired Latino labor leader whose hard work and

accomplishments are still influential. (Rev: SLJ 2/99) [921]

CISNEROS, HENRY

12828 Martinez, Elizabeth Coonrod. *Henry Cisneros: Mexican-American Leader* (3–6). Illus. Series: Hispanic Heritage. 1993, Millbrook LB $19.90 (1-56294-368-5). 32pp. A biography of the Mexican American who was once a mayor and is still an important politician. (Rev: BL 11/15/93) [921]

DE LA RENTA, OSCAR

12829 Carrillo, Louis. *Oscar de la Renta* (4–8). Illus. Series: Contemporary Hispanic Americans. 1995, Raintree Steck-Vaughn LB $25.69 (0-8172-3980-4). 48pp. Focuses on the professional life of the renowned fashion designer. (Rev: BL 3/15/96; SLJ 1/96) [921]

GAC-ARTIGAS, ALEJANDRO

12830 Gac-Artigas, Alejandro. *Yo, Alejandro* (5–7). 2000, Ediciones Nuevo Espacio paper $11.95 (1-930879-21-0). 106pp. This is a collection of personal essays written by the author before his 12th birthday about his life in Puerto Rico, the state of Georgia, and later New York City. (Rev: BL 3/1/01) [921]

GALAN, NELY

12831 Rodriguez, Janel. *Nely Galan* (4–8). Illus. Series: Contemporary Hispanic Americans. 1997, Raintree Steck-Vaughn LB $25.69 (0-8172-3991-X). 48pp. The life of this contemporary Hispanic American who, as a Hollywood producer, is responsible for developing TV and video projects for other Hispanic Americans. (Rev: BL 4/15/97) [921]

HUERTA, DOLORES

12832 Perez, Frank. *Dolores Huerta* (4–8). Illus. Series: Contemporary Hispanic Americans. 1995, Raintree Steck-Vaughn LB $24.26 (0-8172-3981-2). 48pp. The accomplishments of Dolores Huerta, an organizer of farm workers, is highlighted in this informative biography. (Rev: BL 3/15/96) [921]

JULIA, RAUL

12833 Perez, Frank, and Ann Well. *Raul Julia* (4–8). Illus. Series: Contemporary Hispanic Americans. 1995, Raintree Steck-Vaughn LB $25.69 (0-8172-3984-7). 48pp. The story of the brilliant stage and film actor who gained fame in *The Addams Family* and on *Sesame Street*. (Rev: BL 3/15/96; SLJ 1/96) [921]

QUINTANILLA, GUADALUPE

12834 Wade, Mary D. *Guadalupe Quintanilla: Leader of the Hispanic Community* (4–8). Illus. Series: Multicultural Junior Biographies. 1995, Enslow LB $20.95 (0-89490-637-2). 104pp. An inspiring story of a woman who once was considered mentally disabled and now is a leader in her

Spanish American community. (Rev: BL 3/1/96; SLJ 2/96) [921]

RODRIGUEZ, LUIS

12835 Schwartz, Michael. *Luis Rodriguez* (4–8). Illus. Series: Contemporary Hispanic Americans. 1997, Raintree Steck-Vaughn LB $25.69 (0-8172-3990-1). 48pp. The life of this contemporary Hispanic American who went from gang leader and drug addict to writer, journalist, publisher, speaker, and youth activist. (Rev: BL 4/15/97; SLJ 6/97) [921]

Historical Figures and Important Contemporary Americans

ADAMS, SAMUEL

12836 Fradin, Dennis B. *Samuel Adams: The Father of American Independence* (5–9). Illus. 1998, Clarion $18.00 (0-395-82510-5). 182pp. An attractive biography of the amazing Sam Adams, whom Jefferson called "the Man of the Revolution." (Rev: BCCB 7–8/98; BL 7/98*) [921]

12837 Fritz, Jean. *Why Don't You Get a Horse, Sam Adams?* (3–5). Illus. by Trina S. Hyman. 1974, Putnam paper $5.99 (0-698-11416-7). 48pp. How Sam Adams was finally persuaded to ride a horse is told in this humorous re-creation of Revolutionary times.

ALBRIGHT, MADELEINE

12838 Blue, Rose, and Corinne J. Naden. *Madeleine Albright: U.S. Secretary of State* (3–5). Illus. 1998, Blackbirch LB $16.95 (1-56711-253-6). 64pp. The rise of this secretary of state is traced, along with a description of the job, the responsibilities, and its history. (Rev: BL 12/1/98; HBG 3/99) [921]

12839 Byman, Jeremy. *Madam Secretary: The Story of Madeleine Albright* (5–9). Series: Notable Americans. 1997, Morgan Reynolds $18.95 (1-883846-23-4). 96pp. An informative biography of the former secretary of state who, as a child, had to flee her native Czechoslovakia to escape the Nazis. (Rev: SLJ 4/98) [921]

12840 Freedman, Suzanne. *Madeleine Albright: She Speaks for America* (4–6). Illus. Series: Book Report Biographies. 1998, Watts LB $21.50 (0-531-11454-6). 112pp. This well-researched biography tells of Albright's childhood in Prague, London, and Denver, her marriage and family life, and her public positions as ambassador to the United Nations and her later work (to 1998) as secretary of state. (Rev: BL 4/15/98) [921]

12841 Maass, Robert. *UN Ambassador: A Behind-the-Scenes Look at Madeleine Albright's World* (3–5). Illus. 1995, Walker LB $17.85 (0-8027-8356-2). 48pp. A biography of Madeleine Albright, who, at the time of writing, was U.S. ambassador to the United Nations. (Rev: BL 11/15/95; SLJ 11/95) [921]

APPLESEED, JOHNNY

12842 Aliki. *The Story of Johnny Appleseed* (K–3). Illus. by author. 1971, Simon & Schuster paper $5.95 (0-671-66746-7). A picture story of the man who wandered through the Midwest spreading love and apple seeds.

12843 Demuth, Patricia. *Johnny Appleseed* (K–2). Illus. by Michael Montgomery. Series: All Aboard Reading. 1996, Grosset LB $13.89 (0-448-41131-8); paper $3.99 (0-448-41130-X). 32pp. An easy-to-read biography that covers the most appealing events in the life of Johnny Appleseed. (Rev: SLJ 4/97) [921]

12844 Hodges, Margaret. *The True Tale of Johnny Appleseed* (K–3). Illus. by Kimberly B. Root. 1997, Holiday LB $16.95 (0-8234-1282-2). 32pp. A biography that tells about John Chapman's childhood in Massachusetts and his relocation in the West, where he was noted for planting and caring for apple trees. (Rev: BL 7/97; SLJ 9/97) [921]

12845 Kellogg, Steven. *Johnny Appleseed* (2–4). Illus. by author. 1988, Morrow $16.89 (0-688-06418-3). 48pp. The story of the famed John Chapman, who traveled the country in the 1700s spreading good cheer and apple seeds. (Rev: BCCB 11/88; BL 9/1/88; SLJ 10/88)

12846 Lawlor, Laurie. *The Real Johnny Appleseed* (4–6). Illus. 1995, Albert Whitman LB $13.95 (0-8075-6909-7). 64pp. A well-researched biography of John Chapman, with details on his character and contributions to society. (Rev: BCCB 11/95; BL 9/1/95; SLJ 1/96) [921]

ARNOLD, BENEDICT

12847 King, David C. *Benedict Arnold and the American Revolution* (5–9). Series: Notorious Americans and Their Times. 1998, Blackbirch LB $18.95 (1-56711-221-8). 80pp. This biography of Benedict Arnold and his role in the American Revolution places his life in the context of the period in which he lived and the conflicts he faced. (Rev: BL 12/15/98; HBG 3/99) [921]

BANNAKY, MOLLY

12848 McGill, Alice. *Molly Bannaky* (PS–4). Illus. by Chris K. Soentpiet. 1999, Houghton $15.00 (0-395-72287-X). 32pp. This is the amazing story of white colonialist Molly Bannaky, who dared to buy and marry a slave and eventually became the grandmother of Benjamin Banneker, the famous African American astronomer and mathematician. (Rev: BCCB 10/99; BL 9/15/99; HBG 3/00; SLJ 10/99) [921]

BEAN, JUDGE ROY

12849 Green, Carl R., and William R. Sanford. *Judge Roy Bean* (4–6). Illus. Series: Outlaws and Lawmen. 1995, Enslow LB $16.95 (0-89490-591-0). 48pp. A biography of this colorful, many-sided character from the old Wild West. (Rev: SLJ 9/95) [921]

BEZOS, JEFF

12850 Sherman, Josepha. *Jeff Bezos: King of Amazon* (5–8). Illus. 2001, Twenty-First Century LB $21.90 (0-7613-1963-8). 80pp. Jeff Bezos, the genius behind Amazon.com, is introduced along with information on his struggle to found a book company on the Web. (Rev: BL 3/15/01) [921]

BILLY THE KID

12851 Bruns, Roger A. *Billy the Kid* (5–8). Series: Historical American Biographies. 2000, Enslow LB $19.95 (0-7660-1091-0). A well-researched and thoroughly documented biography of America's famous outlaw. (Rev: BL 1/1–15/00; HBG 10/00; SLJ 5/00) [921]

12852 Green, Carl R., and William R. Sanford. *Billy the Kid* (4–8). Illus. Series: Outlaws and Lawmen. 1992, Enslow LB $16.95 (0-89490-364-0). 48pp. The life story of the outlaw William H. Bonney, who lived from 1859 to 1881. (Rev: BL 7/92; SLJ 8/92) [921]

BOEING, WILLIAM

12853 Nelson, Sharlene, and Ted Nelson. *William Boeing: Builder of Planes* (3–5). Series: Community Builders. 1999, Children's LB $23.00 (0-516-20973-6). 48pp. A biography of the famous founder of an aircraft construction empire and his economic contributions to the United States. (Rev: BL 11/15/99) [921]

BOOTH, JOHN WILKES

12854 Otfinoski, Steven. *John Wilkes Booth and the Civil War* (5–9). Series: Notorious Americans and Their Times. 1998, Blackbirch LB $18.95 (1-56711-222-6). 80pp. A biography of John Wilkes Booth, born into a theatrical family, who turned political over the slavery issue and plotted to kill President Lincoln. (Rev: BL 12/15/98; HBG 3/99) [921]

BOWIE, JIM

12855 Gaines, Ann Graham. *Jim Bowie* (5–8). Series: Historical American Biographies. 2000, Enslow LB $19.95 (0-7660-1253-0). A well-documented biography of Jim Bowie, a hero of the revolution in Texas who was best known for fighting in the battle of the Alamo. (Rev: BL 1/1–15/00; HBG 10/00; SLJ 5/00) [921]

BRADFORD, WILLIAM

12856 Doherty, Kieran. *William Bradford: Rock of Plymouth* (5–9). 1999, Twenty-First Century LB $22.90 (0-7613-1304-4). 192pp. Using Bradford's own writings and other contemporary accounts as sources, this is an objective biography of the man who was the governor of the Plymouth Plantation. (Rev: HBG 3/00; SLJ 1/00) [921]

12857 Schmidt, Gary. *William Bradford: Plymouth's Faithful Pilgrim* (5–8). Illus. 1999, Eerdmans $15.00 (0-8028-5151-7); paper $8.00 (0-8028-5148-8). 256pp. The story of the famous Pilgrim

who helped found the Plymouth colony and who led it for many years. (Rev: BL 7/99) [921]

BRADLEY, BILL

12858 Andryszewski, Tricia. *Bill Bradley: Scholar, Athlete, Statesman* (4–6). Illus. Series: Gateway Biographies. 1999, Millbrook LB $21.90 (0-7613-1669-8); paper $8.95 (0-7613-1328-1). 48pp. Using material from Bill Bradley's autobiography, this account describes the life and struggles of the famous basketball star turned successful politician. (Rev: BL 11/15/99; HBG 3/00) [921]

BRADY, MATHEW

12859 Van Steenwyk, Elizabeth. *Mathew Brady: Civil War Photographer* (4–6). Illus. Series: First Books. 1997, Watts LB $22.50 (0-531-20264-X). 64pp. The life and work of the famous Civil War photographer are covered, with many reproductions of his pictures. (Rev: BL 9/1/97; HBG 3/98) [921]

BRECKENRIDGE, MARY

12860 Wells, Rosemary. *Mary on Horseback: Three Mountain Stories* (3–6). Illus. 1998, Dial LB $16.89 (0-8037-2155-2). 56pp. Using three different vignettes, the life of Mary Breckenridge is depicted, showing how she founded the Frontier Nursing Service, which has supplied medical service to rural Appalachian Kentucky since 1925. (Rev: BCCB 1/99; BL 9/1/98*; HBG 3/99; SLJ 10/98) [921]

BROWN, JOHN

12861 Collins, James L. *John Brown and the Fight Against Slavery* (4–6). Illus. Series: Gateway Civil Rights. 1991, Millbrook LB $20.90 (1-56294-043-0). 32pp. This volume gives an excellent overview of the life and accomplishments of this important leader in the Abolitionist movement. (Rev: BL 1/1/92; SLJ 1/92) [921]

12862 Streissguth, Thomas. *John Brown* (2–4). Illus. by Ralph L. Ramstad. Series: On My Own Biographies. 1999, Carolrhoda LB $14.95 (1-57505-334-9). 48pp. This is a fine life story of the abolitionist, his beliefs and actions, plus a good look at the dispute over slavery before the Civil War. (Rev: HBG 3/00; SLJ 11/99) [921]

BROWN, MOLLY

12863 Simon, Charnan. *Molly Brown: Sharing Her Good Fortune* (3–5). Series: Community Builders. 2000, Children's LB $23.50 (0-516-21606-6). 48pp. Although Molly Brown is known mainly as being "unsinkable," this account stresses her work as a humanitarian who supported many charities with her wealth. (Rev: BL 12/15/00) [921]

BURK, MARTHA JANE

12864 Sanford, William R., and Carl R. Green. *Calamity Jane* (4–6). Illus. Series: Legendary Heroes of the Wild West. 1996, Enslow LB $16.95 (0-89490-647-X). 48pp. The life of the legendary Western belle is presented with historical photos. (Rev: BL 7/96; SLJ 7/96) [921]

BUTCHER, SOLOMON

12865 Conrad, Pam. *Prairie Visions: The Life and Times of Solomon Butcher* (4–6). Illus. by Darryl S. Zudeck. 1994, HarperCollins paper $9.95 (0-064-46135-1). 85pp. Through the life of Solomon Butcher and his neighbors, life on the American frontier comes alive. (Rev: BCCB 4/91; BL 3/15/91; HB 5–6/91; SLJ 5/91) [921]

CAPONE, AL

12866 King, David C. *Al Capone and the Roaring Twenties* (5–9). Illus. Series: Notorious Americans and Their Times. 1998, Blackbirch $18.95 (1-56711-218-8). 80pp. In this biography of the gangster, the reader also gets information on the Jazz Age, the Ku Klux Klan, and other personalities of the time, such as Earhart and Lindbergh. (Rev: BL 12/15/98; HBG 3/99) [921]

CASSIDY, BUTCH

12867 Green, Carl R., and William R. Sanford. *Butch Cassidy* (4–8). Series: Outlaws and Lawmen. 1995, Enslow LB $16.95 (0-89490-587-2). 48pp. The Wild West is re-created in this brief account of the life of this colorful outlaw, whose death remains a mystery. (Rev: BL 6/1–15/95; SLJ 7/95) [921]

12868 Wukovits, John F. *Butch Cassidy* (4–7). Series: Legends of the West. 1997, Chelsea LB $15.95 (0-7910-3857-2). 64pp. This biography of Robert Leroy Parker, who is better known as Butch Cassidy, emphasizes the fact that he was a ruthless criminal and not the idealized character of the movies. (Rev: HBG 3/98; SLJ 4/98) [921]

CODY, BUFFALO BILL

12869 Sanford, William R., and Carl R. Green. *Buffalo Bill Cody: Showman of the Wild West* (4–6). Illus. Series: Legendary Heroes of the Wild West. 1996, Enslow LB $16.95 (0-89490-646-1). 48pp. The life of the Wild West hero in brief text and many black-and-white photos. (Rev: BL 7/96; SLJ 7/96) [921]

12870 Spies, Karen B. *Buffalo Bill Cody: Western Legend* (5–8). Series: Historical American Biographies. 1998, Enslow LB $20.95 (0-7660-1015-5). 128pp. An in-depth look at this legendary frontiersman and the Wild West show he later founded. (Rev: BL 3/15/98; SLJ 5/98) [921]

CUSTER, GEORGE ARMSTRONG

12871 Kent, Zachary. *George Armstrong Custer* (5–8). Series: Historical American Biographies. 2000, Enslow LB $19.95 (0-7660-1255-7). Using extensive chapter notes, a glossary, bibliography, and index, this is a well-documented and objective assessment of Custer's life and deeds. (Rev: BL 1/1–15/00; HBG 10/00) [921]

DAVIS, JEFFERSON

12872 Burch, Joann J. *Jefferson Davis: President of the Confederacy* (5–8). Series: Historical American Biographies. 1998, Enslow LB $19.95 (0-7660-1064-3). 128pp. Using personal documents and well-chosen illustrations, this lively biography describes Jefferson Davis's life as well as the causes and major events of the Civil War. (Rev: BL 10/15/98; SLJ 1/99) [921]

DOLE, BOB

12873 Lisandrelli, Elaine S. *Bob Dole, Legendary Senator* (4–6). Series: People to Know. 1997, Enslow LB $20.95 (0-89490-825-1). 128pp. An illustrated biography of this senator and unsuccessful presidential candidate. (Rev: BL 10/15/97; HBG 3/98) [921]

EARP, WYATT

12874 Green, Carl R., and William R. Sanford. *Wyatt Earp* (4–8). Illus. Series: Outlaws and Lawmen. 1992, Enslow LB $16.95 (0-89490-367-5). 48pp. With maps and authentic illustrations, this biography tells the story of the deputy marshal who tried to clean up Tombstone, Arizona. (Rev: BL 10/1/92; SLJ 11/92) [921]

EISNER, MICHAEL

12875 Tippins, Sherill. *Michael Eisner: Fun for Everyone* (5–8). Illus. Series: Wizards of Industry. 1992, Garrett LB $17.26 (1-56074-014-0). 64pp. The life of Walt Disney Productions' chief executive officer. (Rev: BL 6/15/92; SLJ 9/92) [921]

FARRAGUT, DAVID

12876 Shorto, Russell. *David Farragut and the Great Naval Blockade* (4–7). Illus. Series: The Story of the Civil War. 1991, Silver Burdett paper $7.95 (0-382-24050-2). 135pp. The story of the outstanding naval commander who closed the Gulf ports to Confederate blockade-running during the Civil War. (Rev: BL 9/1/91) [921]

FEINSTEIN, DIANNE

12877 McElroy, Lisa Tucker. *Meet My Grandmother: She's a United States Senator* (2–4). Series: Grandmothers at Work. 2000, Millbrook LB $22.90 (0-7613-1721-X). 32pp. Dianne Feinstein, once mayor of San Francisco and now a U.S. senator, as seen through the eyes of her 6-year-old granddaughter. (Rev: BL 3/15/00; HBG 10/00; SLJ 1/01) [921]

FRANKLIN, BENJAMIN

12878 Adler, David A. *A Picture Book of Benjamin Franklin* (K–3). Illus. by John Wallner and Alexandra Wallner. Series: Picture Book Biographies. 1990, Holiday LB $16.95 (0-8234-0792-6); paper $6.95 (0-8234-0882-5). 32pp. Glimpses of personality and family are interwoven in this simple biography. (Rev: BL 4/15/90; HB 5–6/90; SLJ 5/90) [921]

12879 Cousins, Margaret. *Ben Franklin of Old Philadelphia* (6–8). 1981, Random paper $5.99 (0-394-84928-0). 160pp. A well-rounded portrait of this major figure in American history.

12880 Foster, Leila M. *Benjamin Franklin: Founding Father and Inventor* (5–8). Illus. Series: Historical American Biographies. 1997, Enslow LB $20.95 (0-89490-784-0). 128pp. An admiring biography that describes Franklin's many talents — as a printer, businessman, scientist, inventor, and statesman. (Rev: SLJ 11/97) [921]

12881 Giblin, James Cross. *The Amazing Life of Benjamin Franklin* (4–6). Illus. 2000, Scholastic $17.95 (0-590-48534-2). 48pp. A picture-book biography of the amazing Benjamin Franklin, who excelled in a number of areas, including diplomacy, politics, science, writing, and inventing. (Rev: BCCB 2/00; BL 2/15/00*; HB 5–6/00; HBG 10/00; SLJ 3/00) [921]

12882 Greene, Carol. *Benjamin Franklin: A Man with Many Jobs* (2–3). Illus. 1988, Children's paper $4.95 (0-516-44202-3). 48pp. Introducing the important points in the life of this multitalented, multifaceted American. (Rev: BL 2/15/89; SLJ 4/89)

12883 Quackenbush, Robert. *Benjamin Franklin and His Friends* (2–3). Illus. 1991, Pippin $14.95 (0-945912-14-5). 40pp. A friend is described in each chapter, emphasizing the influence on Franklin's life. (Rev: BL 12/1/91; SLJ 11/91) [921]

12884 Riley, John. *Benjamin Franklin: A Photo Biography* (1–3). Series: First Biographies. 2000, Morgan Reynolds LB $15.95 (1-883846-64-1). 24pp. A very simple biography of Franklin for beginning readers that has a full-page illustration opposite each page of text. (Rev: HBG 10/00; SLJ 8/00) [921]

GALLAUDET, THOMAS

12885 Bowen, Andy Russell. *A World of Knowing: A Story About Thomas Hopkins Gallaudet* (3–5). Illus. Series: Creative Minds Biographies. 1995, Carolrhoda LB $21.27 (0-87614-871-2). 64pp. The story of the man who empathized with deaf persons and developed sign language to enable them to communicate with others. (Rev: BL 1/1–15/96; SLJ 1/96) [921]

GINSBURG, RUTH BADER

12886 Ayer, Eleanor. *Ruth Bader Ginsburg: Fire and Steel on the Supreme Court* (5–8). Illus. 1995, Dillon LB $22.00 (0-87518-651-3); paper $7.95 (0-382-24721-3). 128pp. A biography of the second woman Supreme Court justice, with emphasis on the many obstacles she had to overcome. (Rev: BL 5/15/95; SLJ 4/95) [921]

GLENN, JOHN

12887 Cole, Michael D. *John Glenn: Astronaut and Senator* (5–8). Series: People to Know. 2000, Enslow LB $20.95 (0-7660-1532-7). 128pp. A biography of the astronaut and politician with coverage on his two trips into space. (Rev: BL 9/15/00; HBG 3/01) [921]

12888 Kramer, Barbara. *John Glenn: A Space Biography* (4–6). Series: Countdown to Space. 1998, Lerner LB $17.95 (0-89490-964-9). 48pp. The story of the Marine Corps pilot who was the first American to orbit the earth and later became a distinguished statesman. (Rev: BL 8/98; HBG 10/98; SLJ 7/98) [921]

12889 Streissguth, Thomas. *John Glenn* (5–8). Series: A&E Biography. 1999, Lerner LB $18.95 (0-8225-4947-6); paper $7.95 (0-8225-9685-7). 112pp. This account of John Glenn's life includes childhood influences, his career with NASA, and his political life as a senator. (Rev: HBG 3/00; SLJ 3/00) [921]

12890 Vogt, Gregory L. *John Glenn's Return to Space* (4–7). Illus. 2000, Twenty-First Century LB $22.90 (0-7613-1614-0). 72pp. As well as describing John Glenn's two space flights on the *Mercury* capsule and later the *Discovery,* this biography gives information on astronauts' training and equipment. (Rev: BL 9/15/00; SLJ 1/01) [921]

GORE, AL

12891 Italia, Bob. *Al Gore: The Vice President of the United States* (4–6). Illus. Series: All the President's Men and Women. 1993, ABDO LB $14.98 (1-56239-253-0). 32pp. This biography of Gore covers his personality and interests, as well as his public life. (Rev: SLJ 3/94) [921]

12892 Jeffrey, Laura S. *Al Gore* (4–6). Series: People to Know. 1999, Enslow LB $19.95 (0-7660-1232-8). 112pp. Black-and-white photos accompany a well-documented text that tells of Al Gore's life up to, but not including, the 2000 election. (Rev: BL 1/1–15/00; HBG 10/00) [921]

12893 Stefoff, Rebecca. *Al Gore: Vice President* (3–5). Illus. Series: Gateway Biographies. 1994, Millbrook LB $20.90 (1-56294-433-9). 48pp. The life story of the vice president and his climb to high political office. (Rev: BL 8/94; SLJ 4/94) [921]

GRIMKE, SARAH AND ANGELINA

12894 McPherson, Stephanie S. *Sisters Against Slavery: A Story About Sarah and Angelina Grimke* (4–7). Illus. by Karen Ritz. Series: Creative Minds Biographies. 1999, Carolrhoda LB $15.95 (1-57505-361-6). 64pp. The story of the remarkable Grimke sisters from South Carolina who fought against slavery and later became suffragettes. (Rev: BCCB 1/00; HBG 3/00; SLJ 12/99) [921]

HAMILTON, ALEXANDER

12895 Whitelaw, Nancy. *More Perfect Union: The Story of Alexander Hamilton* (4–7). Illus. Series: Notable Americans. 1997, Morgan Reynolds LB $18.95 (1-883846-20-X). 112pp. This biography traces the dramatic story of Hamilton's life from his birth in Nevis (British West Indies) to his death after the duel with Aaron Burr. (Rev: BL 7/97; SLJ 10/97) [921]

HANCOCK, JOHN

12896 Fritz, Jean. *Will You Sign Here, John Hancock?* (3–5). Illus. by Trina S. Hyman. 1997, Putnam paper $5.99 (0-698-11440-X). 48pp. Under the sprightly title is a delightful, well-researched biography of this signer of the Declaration of Independence.

12897 Koslow, Philip. *John Hancock: A Signature Life* (4–6). Illus. Series: Book Report Biographies.

1998, Watts LB $21.50 (0-531-11429-5). 112pp. This biography of John Hancock tells of his role in signing the Declaration of Independence and his work in adopting the Constitution, plus supplying material on his youth, his success as a merchant, and his role in the American Revolution. (Rev: BL 4/15/98) [973.3]

HENRY, PATRICK

12898 Adler, David A. *A Picture Book of Patrick Henry* (K–3). Illus. by John Wallner and Alexandra Wallner. Series: Picture Book Biographies. 1995, Holiday LB $16.95 (0-8234-1187-7). 32pp. The story of the famous patriot who served five terms as governor of Virginia. (Rev: BL 9/15/95; SLJ 12/95) [921]

HERSHEY, MILTON S.

12899 Burford, Betty. *Chocolate by Hershey: A Story About Milton S. Hershey* (3–6). Illus. by Loren Chantland. Series: Creative Minds. 1994, Carolrhoda LB $21.27 (0-87614-830-5); paper $5.95 (0-87614-641-8). 64pp. An engrossing biography of the candy-making entrepreneur and his many philanthropies. (Rev: SLJ 1/95) [921]

HICKOK, WILD BILL

12900 Green, Carl R., and William R. Sanford. *Wild Bill Hickok* (4–8). Illus. Series: Outlaws and Lawmen. 1992, Enslow LB $16.95 (0-89490-366-5). 48pp. The life story of the famous frontier marshal in Kansas is retold in text and pictures. (Rev: BL 7/92; SLJ 8/92) [921]

HINE, LEWIS

12901 Freedman, Russell. *Kids at Work: Lewis Hine and the Crusade Against Child Labor* (5–8). Photos by Lewis Hine. 1994, Clarion $18.00 (0-395-58703-4). 104pp. This photo-essay describes child labor in the United States at the beginning of the century and how Lewis Hine fought for reforms. (Rev: BCCB 10/94; BL 8/94; HB 11–12/94; SLJ 9/94*) [921]

HOLLIDAY, DOC

12902 Green, Carl R., and William R. Sanford. *Doc Holliday* (4–8). Series: Outlaws and Lawmen. 1995, Enslow LB $16.95 (0-89490-589-9). 48pp. The life and exploits of this colorful character are reproduced with photos and maps. (Rev: BL 6/1–15/95) [921]

HOUSTON, SAM

12903 Fritz, Jean. *Make Way for Sam Houston* (4–7). Illus. by Elise Primavera. 1986, Putnam paper $7.95 (0-399-21304-X). 112pp. Houston, a larger-than-life Texan, lived a fascinating life well captured in this biography. (Rev: HB 5–6/86; SLJ 5/86)

12904 Wade, Mary D. *I Am Houston* (3–5). Illus. 1993, Colophon $14.95 (1-882539-05-2); paper $6.95 (1-882539-06-0). 64pp. The biography of the soldier and politician who has become one of Texas's favorite heroes. (Rev: BL 4/15/93) [921]

IACOCCA, LEE

12905 Collins, David R. *Lee Iacocca: Chrysler's Good Fortune* (5–8). Illus. Series: Wizards of Business. 1992, Garrett LB $17.26 (1-56074-017-5). 64pp. The life of Lee Iacocca, top manager in the auto industry, is retold in simple text and many photos. (Rev: BL 6/15/92; SLJ 7/92) [921]

JACKSON, STONEWALL

12906 Bennett, Barbara J. *Stonewall Jackson: Lee's Greatest Lieutenant* (4–7). Illus. Series: The History of the Civil War. 1990, Silver Burdett paper $7.95 (0-382-24048-0). 135pp. The story of the Confederate general who gained his nickname beause he stood "like a stone wall." (Rev: BL 9/1/91) [921]

12907 Pflueger, Lynda. *Stonewall Jackson: Confederate General* (5–8). Illus. 1997, Enslow LB $20.95 (0-89490-781-6). 128pp. This sympathetic biography of Jackson provides good material on his personal life and beliefs while quoting generously from firsthand sources. (Rev: BL 10/1/97) [921]

JAMES, JESSE

12908 Bruns, Roger A. *Jesse James: Legendary Outlaw* (5–8). Series: Historical American Biographies. 1998, Enslow LB $19.95 (0-7660-1055-4). 128pp. An interesting, illustrated biography of Jesse James that uses fact boxes, maps, a chronology, and chapter notes to highlight his exploits. (Rev: BL 10/15/98; SLJ 8/98) [921]

12909 Green, Carl R., and William R. Sanford. *Jesse James* (4–8). Illus. Series: Outlaws and Lawmen. 1992, Enslow LB $16.95 (0-89490-365-9). 48pp. In this easy-to-read text, the authentic as well as the legendary Jesse James is discussed. (Rev: BL 3/1/92; SLJ 5/92) [921]

12910 Wukovits, John F. *Jesse James* (5–8). Illus. Series: Legends of the West. 1996, Chelsea $16.95 (0-7910-3876-9). 60pp. An action-packed biography that tries to probe the complex nature of the famous Western outlaw. (Rev: SLJ 4/97) [921]

JOBS, STEVE

12911 Brashares, Ann. *Steve Jobs: Thinks Different* (5–8). Series: Techies. 2001, Twenty-First Century LB $21.90 (0-7613-1959-X). 80pp. The life story of the amazing creator of Apple computers and his phenomenal success as a businessman and entrepreneur. (Rev: BL 3/15/01) [921]

12912 Gaines, Ann Graham. *Steve Jobs* (3–4). Series: Real-Life Reader Biographies. 2000, Mitchell Lane LB $15.95 (1-58415-026-2). 32pp. The story of the founder of Apple computers who, after leaving the company he built, was brought back to rescue it from mismanagement. (Rev: BL 11/15/00) [921]

JONES, JOHN PAUL

12913 Brandt, Keith. *John Paul Jones: Hero of the Seas* (3–5). Illus. by Susan Swan. 1983, Troll LB $17.25 (0-89375-849-3); paper $3.95 (0-89375-850-7). 48pp. The U.S. naval hero is introduced in an account that does not ignore either his strengths or his weaknesses.

12914 Lutz, Norma Jean. *John Paul Jones: Father of the U.S. Navy* (3–6). Series: Revolutionary War Leaders. 2000, Chelsea LB $16.95 (0-7910-5359-8). 80pp. From his boyhood in Scotland to his death at age 45, this is the biography of a hero of the Revolutionary War. (Rev: HBG 10/00; SLJ 5/00) [921]

12915 Riley, John. *John Paul Jones: A Photo Biography* (1–3). Series: First Biographies. 2000, Morgan Reynolds LB $15.95 (1-883846-63-3). 24pp. A heavily illustrated simple biography for beginning readers of the Revolutionary War hero. (Rev: HBG 10/00; SLJ 8/00) [921]

KELLEY, FLORENCE

12916 Saller, Carol. *Florence Kelley* (2–4). Illus. by Ken Green. Series: On My Own Biographies. 1997, Carolrhoda LB $19.93 (1-57505-016-1). 48pp. The story of the labor leader and her fight against child labor. (Rev: BCCB 7–8/97; BL 6/1–15/97; SLJ 11/97) [921]

KELLOGG, W. K

12917 Epstein, Rachel. *W. K. Kellogg: Generous Genius* (3–5). Series: Community Builders. 2000, Children's LB $23.50 (0-516-21605-8). 48pp. This is the life story of the famous cereal entrepreneur and his work as a philanthropist. (Rev: BL 12/15/00) [921]

KENNEDY, JOHN F., JR.

12918 Landau, Elaine. *John F. Kennedy Jr.* (5–9). 2000, Twenty-First Century LB $26.90 (0-7613-1857-7). 128pp. Beginning with the tragic plane crash that ended his life, and moving back in time, this biography of JFK Jr. captures his personality and the aura that surrounded him. (Rev: HBG 3/01; SLJ 3/01) [921]

KENNEDY, ROBERT F.

12919 Harrison, Barbara, and Daniel Terris. *A Ripple of Hope: The Life of Robert F. Kennedy* (5–8). Illus. 1997, Dutton $16.99 (0-525-67506-X). 144pp. The story of the seventh of the Kennedy children, who grew up in the shadow of his older brothers but later found his own path to greatness. (Rev: BCCB 7–8/97; BL 6/1–15/97; HBG 3/98; SLJ 8/97) [921]

12920 Santella, Andrew. *The Assassination of Robert F. Kennedy* (3–5). Series: Cornerstones of Freedom. 1998, Children's LB $19.50 (0-516-20790-3). 32pp. A brief biography of Robert Kennedy that also examines the circumstances leading up to his assassination and its aftermath. (Rev: BL 5/15/98; HBG 10/98) [921]

KING, RICHARD

12921 Sanford, William R., and Carl R. Green. *Richard King: Texas Cattle Rancher* (4–6). Illus. Series: Legendary Heroes of the Wild West. 1997, Enslow LB $16.95 (0-89490-673-9). 48pp. This short biography of the colorful Texan tells how he was able to amass the land that became one of the

largest ranches in the world. (Rev: BL 3/15/97; SLJ 4/97) [921]

KOREMATSU, FRED

12922 Chin, Steven A. *When Justice Failed: The Fred Korematsu Story* (3–6). Illus. by David Tamura. 1993, Raintree Steck-Vaughn LB $28.55 (0-8114-7236-1). 105pp. The biography of the Japanese American whose rights were continually violated during World War II. (Rev: SLJ 7/93) [921]

LAUDER, ESTEE

12923 Epstein, Rachel. *Estee Lauder: Beauty Business Success* (4–6). Series: Book Report Biographies. 2000, Watts LB $22.00 (0-531-11705-7). 112pp. The story of the woman from Corona, Queens, who turned her uncle's cosmetic concoctions into a beauty empire. (Rev: BL 11/15/00) [921]

LAUREN, RALPH

12924 Canadeo, Anne. *Ralph Lauren: Master of Fashion* (5–8). Illus. Series: Wizards of Business. 1992, Garrett LB $17.26 (1-56074-021-3). 64pp. This book introduces one of the most influential fashion designers working today. (Rev: BL 6/15/92) [921]

LEE, ROBERT E.

12925 Adler, David A. *A Picture Book of Robert E. Lee* (3–4). Illus. by Alexandra Wallner and John Wallner. Series: Picture Book Biographies. 1994, Holiday LB $16.95 (0-8234-1111-7). Using a story format, this simple account covers the highlights of Lee's life and military career. (Rev: SLJ 5/94) [921]

12926 Dubowski, Cathy E. *Robert E. Lee: The Rise of the South* (4–7). Illus. Series: The History of the Civil War. 1990, Silver Burdett paper $7.95 (0-382-24051-0). 135pp. The life of the Confederate general who was a stirring commander and a man of great character. (Rev: BL 9/1/91) [921]

12927 Kerby, Mona. *Robert E. Lee: Southern Hero of the Civil War* (5–8). Illus. Series: Historical American Biographies. 1997, Enslow LB $20.95 (0-89490-782-4). 128pp. This thorough, sympathetic biography of Lee points out that he did not approve of slavery or the South's secession from the Union. (Rev: BL 10/1/97; SLJ 9/97) [921]

LILIUOKALANI, QUEEN

12928 Guzzetti, Paula. *The Last Hawaiian Queen: Liliuokalani* (3–5). Illus. Series: Biographies. 1996, Benchmark LB $21.36 (0-7614-0490-2). 48pp. A history of Hawaii with special emphasis on the life of its last queen, the fascinating Liliuokalani. (Rev: SLJ 3/97) [921]

LYON, MARY

12929 Rosen, Dorothy S. *A Fire in Her Bones: The Story of Mary Lyon* (5–7). Illus. 1995, Carolrhoda LB $23.93 (0-87614-840-2). 88pp. A biography of the woman who defied social barriers and founded

Mount Holyoke Female Seminary, now known as Mount Holyoke College. (Rev: BL 6/1–15/95; SLJ 4/95) [921]

MACARTHUR, DOUGLAS

12930 Darby, Jean. *Douglas MacArthur* (4–7). Illus. Series: Lerner Biographies. 1989, Lerner LB $25.26 (0-8225-4901-8). 112pp. This biography highlights the general's leadership during World War II and his later dismissal by Truman. (Rev: BL 11/15/89) [921]

12931 Finkelstein, Norman H. *The Emperor General: A Biography of Douglas MacArthur* (5–7). Illus. 1989, Macmillan LB $18.95 (0-87518-396-4). 128pp. The life of this famous five-star general of World War II. (Rev: BL 3/1/89; SLJ 4/89)

12932 Fox, Mary V. *Douglas MacArthur* (4–8). Series: The Importance Of. 1999, Lucent LB $17.96 (1-56006-545-1). 96pp. The story of one of the nation's most prominent generals, whose unorthodox actions made him a controversial figure. (Rev: BL 9/15/99) [921]

MCCAIN, JOHN

12933 Feinberg, Barbara S. *John McCain: Serving His Country* (4–7). Illus. Series: Gateway. 2000, Millbrook LB $22.90 (0-7613-1974-3). 48pp. A biography of the senator that tells about his youth and later political career but concentrates on his stint in the navy and his imprisonment during the Vietnam War. (Rev: BL 3/1/01) [921]

MCCARTHY, JOSEPH

12934 Sherrow, Victoria. *Joseph McCarthy and the Cold War* (5–9). Illus. Series: Notorious Americans and Their Times. 1998, Blackbirch $18.95 (1-56711-219-6). 80pp. The story of Washington's witch hunting under Joseph McCarthy includes good background information on the Cold War. (Rev: BL 12/15/98; HBG 3/99) [973.921]

MARIN, LUIS MUNOZ

12935 Bernier-Grand, Carmen T. *Poet and Politician of Puerto Rico: Don Luis Munoz Marin* (5–8). Illus. 1995, Orchard LB $16.99 (0-531-08737-9). 128pp. This story of the life of the man who helped make Puerto Rico a commonwealth also includes a history of the island. (Rev: BL 5/15/95; SLJ 4/95) [921]

12936 George, Linda, and Charles George. *Luis Munoz Marin: Father of Modern Puerto Rico* (3–5). Series: Community Builders. 1999, Children's LB $23.00 (0-516-21586-8). 48pp. An appealing and well-illustrated biography of the man who shaped the future of modern Puerto Rico. (Rev: BL 11/15/99) [921]

NEWTON, JOHN

12937 Haskins, Jim. *Amazing Grace: The Story Behind the Song* (5–7). Illus. 1992, Millbrook LB $20.90 (1-56294-117-8). 48pp. A profile of John Newton, the man behind one of the most popular of all songs. (Rev: BL 11/1/92) [921]

O'CONNOR, SANDRA DAY

12938 Deegan, Paul J. *Sandra Day O'Connor* (4–6). Illus. Series: Supreme Court Justices. 1992, ABDO LB $19.99 (1-56239-089-9). 40pp. This biography includes material on Judge O'Connor's position on various issues and quotes from her written opinions. (Rev: BL 6/1–15/93) [921]

12939 McElroy, Lisa Tucker. *Meet My Grandmother: She's a Supreme Court Justice* (2–4). Illus. Series: Grandmothers at Work. 1999, Millbrook LB $17.18 (0-7613-1566-7). 32pp. An affectionate portrait of a woman who is both a Supreme Court justice and a beloved grandmother. (Rev: BL 1/1–15/00; HBG 3/00; SLJ 12/99) [921]

12940 Macht, Norman L. *Sandra Day O'Connor: Supreme Court Justice* (4–7). Illus. Series: Junior World Biographies. 1992, Chelsea paper $9.95 (0-7910-0448-1). 80pp. In clear text with many photographs, this is a simple account of the first female Supreme Court Justice. (Rev: BL 8/92; SLJ 8/92) [921]

OLMSTED, FREDERICK LAW

12941 Dunlap, Julie. *Parks for the People: A Story About Frederick Law Olmsted* (3–6). Illus. by Susan F. Lieber. Series: Creative Minds Biographies. 1994, Carolrhoda LB $21.27 (0-87614-824-0). 63pp. The life story of America's first landscape architect, his masterpiece — Central Park in New York City — and how he tried to save Yosemite from commercial exploitation. (Rev: SLJ 2/95) [921]

12942 Wishinsky, Frieda. *The Man Who Made Parks: The Story of Parkbuilder Frederick Law Olmsted* (2–4). Illus. by Song Nan Zhang. 1999, Tundra $15.95 (0-88776-435-5). A short, illustrated biography of the man who created and designed some of the most beautiful parks in America, including Central Park in New York City. (Rev: BL 8/99; HBG 10/99; SLJ 10/99) [921]

PAINE, THOMAS

12943 McCarthy, Pat. *Thomas Paine: Revolutionary Patriot and Writer* (5–8). Series: Historical American Biographies. 2001, Enslow LB $20.95 (0-7660-1446-0). The story of the Revolutionary pamphleteer who influenced thought in both America and Europe. (Rev: BL 3/1/01) [921]

PATTON, GEORGE

12944 Peifer, Charles. *Soldier of Destiny: A Biography of George Patton* (4–7). Illus. 1988, Macmillan LB $13.95 (0-87518-395-6). 128pp. The life and times of the colorful general who commanded the Third Army in Europe during World War II. (Rev: BL 3/1/89)

PENN, WILLIAM

12945 Kroll, Steven. *William Penn: Founder of Pennsylvania* (3–5). Illus. 2000, Holiday $16.95 (0-8234-1439-6). 29pp. This picture book on the life of William Penn discusses his conversion to the Quaker faith and the land grant that was given him in the

New World. (Rev: BL 2/15/00; HBG 10/00; SLJ 4/00) [974.8]

PEROT, ROSS

12946 Italia, Bob. *Ross Perot: The Man Who Woke Up America* (4–6). Illus. Series: Everyone Contributes. 1993, ABDO LB $18.49 (1-56239-236-0). 40pp. The story of Perot's childhood and business success, with emphasis on his run for the presidency. (Rev: BL 12/1/93; SLJ 1/94) [921]

PINKERTON, ALLAN

12947 Green, Carl R., and William R. Sanford. *Allan Pinkerton* (4–8). Illus. Series: Outlaws and Lawmen. 1995, Enslow LB $16.95 (0-89490-590-2). 48pp. A simple biography that presents the highlights of the life of the creator of the famous detective agency. (Rev: BL 11/15/95) [921]

12948 Josephson, Judith P. *Allan Pinkerton: The Original Private Eye* (5–8). Illus. 1996, Lerner LB $17.21 (0-8225-2923-9). 128pp. The story of the famed criminal-catcher who founded the world-famous detective agency. (Rev: BL 10/15/96; SLJ 10/96) [921]

POWELL, COLIN

12949 Blue, Rose, and Corinne J. Naden. *Colin Powell: Straight to the Top* (3–5). Illus. Series: Gateway Biographies. 1997, Millbrook LB $20.90 (0-7613-0256-5). 48pp. A balanced biography of Colin Powell that focuses on his adult life and his stint as chairman of the Joint Chiefs of Staff. (Rev: BL 9/15/97; SLJ 1/98) [921]

12950 Finlayson, Reggie. *Colin Powell: People's Hero* (5–8). Illus. Series: Achievers Biographies. 1997, Lerner LB $21.27 (0-8225-2891-6). 64pp. From his birth in Harlem to his distinguished military career, this is a fine biography of Colin Powell. (Rev: SLJ 4/97) [921]

12951 Passaro, John. *Colin Powell* (4–6). Series: Journey to Freedom. 1999, Child's World LB $16.95 (1-56766-619-1). 32pp. The life story of the African American army officer who gained prominence during the Gulf War. (Rev: BL 10/15/99; HBG 3/00; SLJ 4/00) [921]

12952 Patrick-Wexler, Diane. *Colin Powell* (4–6). Illus. Series: Contemporary African Americans. 1995, Raintree Steck-Vaughn LB $25.69 (0-8172-3977-4). 48pp. A simple biography of the man who grew up in the Bronx and rose to be a four-star general and chairman of the Joint Chiefs of Staff. (Rev: BL 2/15/96; SLJ 1/96) [921]

12953 Reef, Kristensen. *Colin Powell* (4–8). Illus. Series: African American Soldiers. 1992, Twenty-First Century LB $17.90 (0-8050-2136-1). 80pp. This is a simple but comprehensive biography of the first African American to become chairman of the Joint Chiefs of Staff. (Rev: BL 11/15/92) [921]

12954 Senna, Carl. *Colin Powell: A Man of War and Peace* (4–8). Illus. 1992, Walker LB $16.85 (0-8027-8181-0). 192pp. The life of the general who became the first African American chairman of the Joint Chiefs of Staff. (Rev: BL 3/15/93) [921]

12955 Strazzabosco, Jeanne M. *Learning About Responsibility from the Life of Colin Powell* (2–4). Illus. Series: Character Building Book. 1996, Rosen LB $15.93 (0-8239-2414-9). 24pp. This biography emphasizes the many important responsibilities that Colin Powell faced in his various positions in the U.S. government. (Rev: SLJ 5/97) [921]

12956 Wukovits, John F. *Colin Powell* (5–8). Series: People in the News. 2000, Lucent LB $18.96 (1-56006-632-6). 112pp. This account of the African American military leader ends before he became part of the Bush administration, but it gives good coverage on his formative years and his early accomplishments. (Rev: BL 6/1–15/00; HBG 10/00) [921]

RENO, JANET

12957 Hamilton, John. *The Attorney General Through Janet Reno* (4–6). Illus. Series: All the President's Men and Women. 1993, ABDO LB $14.98 (1-56239-251-4). 32pp. The biography of Janet Reno also supplies material on the components of the Department of Justice. (Rev: SLJ 3/94) [921]

REVERE, PAUL

12958 Adler, David A. *A Picture Book of Paul Revere* (K–3). Illus. Series: Picture Book Biographies. 1995, Holiday LB $16.95 (0-8234-1144-3). 42pp. A simple biography of this Revolutionary War hero, with an emphasis on colorful illustrations. (Rev: BL 3/15/95; SLJ 4/95) [921]

12959 Sakurai, Gail. *Paul Revere* (3–5). Series: Cornerstones of Freedom. 1997, Children's LB $20.50 (0-516-20463-7). 32pp. The life of this early patriot is traced, with emphasis on his role during the Revolutionary War. (Rev: BL 12/15/97; HBG 3/98) [921]

ROCKEFELLER, JOHN D.

12960 Laughlin, Rosemary. *John D. Rockefeller: Oil Baron and Philanthropist* (5–8). Illus. Series: American Business Leaders. 2001, Morgan Reynolds $20.95 (1-883846-59-5). 128pp. A biography of the determined and skilled businessman who made Standard Oil the dominant company in the oil industry and who was later noted for his philanthropy. (Rev: BL 3/1/01) [921]

SEWARD, WILLIAM

12961 Kent, Zachary. *William Seward: The Mastermind of the Alaska Purchase* (5–8). Series: Historical American Biographies. 2001, Enslow LB $20.95 (0-7660-1391-X). The story of the man who was appointed secretary of state by Lincoln and who engineered the purchase of Alaska, an act that many called "Seward's folly." (Rev: BL 3/1/01) [921]

SHERBURNE, ANDREW

12962 Zeinert, Karen, ed. *The Memoirs of Andrew Sherburne: Patriot and Privateer of the American Revolution* (5–8). Illus. 1993, Shoe String LB $17.50 (0-208-02354-2). 96pp. An action-filled, first-person narrative about a colonialist who served in the navy during the American Revolution. (Rev: SLJ 7/93) [921]

SHERMAN, WILLIAM T.

12963 Whitelaw, Nancy. *William Tecumseh Sherman: Defender and Destroyer* (5–8). 1996, Morgan Reynolds LB $18.95 (1-883846-12-9). 112pp. Both the personal and public life of this Civil War general, who brought destruction to the South, is retold using many quotes. (Rev: BL 3/15/96; SLJ 6/96) [921]

SIEGEL, BUGSY

12964 Otfinoski, Steven. *Bugsy Siegel and the Postwar Boom* (5–9). Series: Notorious Americans and Their Times. 2000, Blackbirch LB $19.95 (1-56711-224-2). 112pp. The story of the gangster who began a life of crime while a boy in New York, continued in California, and helped create Las Vegas casinos in the 1940s. (Rev: HBG 3/01; SLJ 1/01) [921]

STARR, BELLE

12965 Naden, Corinne J., and Rose Blue. *Belle Starr and the Wild West* (5–9). Series: Notorious Americans and Their Times. 2000, Blackbirch LB $19.95 (1-56711-223-4). 112pp. A fascinating biography of the legendary female outlaw who died a violent death at age 51. (Rev: HBG 3/01; SLJ 1/01) [921]

STRAUSS, LEVI

12966 Weidt, Maryann N. *Mr. Blue Jeans: A Story About Levi Strauss* (3–5). Illus. 1990, Carolrhoda LB $21.27 (0-87614-421-0). 64pp. The story of the phenomenal blue jeans and of their phenomenal creator. (Rev: BL 12/1/90; SLJ 1/91) [921]

STUART, JEB

12967 Pflueger, Lynda. *Jeb Stuart: Confederate Cavalry General* (4–6). Series: Historical American Biographies. 1998, Enslow LB $18.95 (0-7660-1013-9). The life of the brilliant general who triumphed at the battle of Bull Run, Antietam, and Fredericksburg, but who committed a tactical error at Gettysburg. (Rev: BL 8/98; SLJ 8/98) [921]

WATTS, J. C., JR.

12968 De Capua, Sarah. *J.C. Watts, Jr. Character Counts* (3–5). Series: Community Builders. 1998, Children's LB $23.00 (0-516-21130-7). 48pp. The story of the former football player who became a U.S. congressman and introduced the American Community Renewal Act in 1995. (Rev: BL 1/1–15/99; HBG 3/99) [921]

YOUNG, BRIGHAM

12969 Sanford, William R., and Carl R. Green. *Brigham Young: Pioneer and Mormon Leader* (4–6). Illus. Series: Legendary Heroes of the Wild West. 1996, Enslow LB $16.95 (0-89490-672-0). 48pp. A simple account that chronicles the life and career of the great Mormon leader Brigham Young. (Rev: BL 10/15/96; SLJ 9/96) [921]

12970 Simon, Charnan. *Brigham Young: Mormon and Pioneer* (3–5). Illus. 1998, Children's LB $23.00 (0-516-20392-4). 48pp. The story of the great Mormon leader and the founding of the LDS church in Utah. (Rev: BL 1/1–15/99; HBG 3/99; SLJ 2/99) [921]

Native Americans

CRAZY HORSE, CHIEF

12971 Cunningham, Chet. *Chief Crazy Horse* (4–6). Series: A&E Biography. 2000, Lerner LB $25.26 (0-8225-4978-6). 112pp. This biography relates the life of the military leader of the Lakota Indians and tells how he became known for his bravery and ferocity in battle. (Rev: BL 6/1–15/00; HBG 3/01) [921]

GERONIMO

12972 Hermann, Spring. *Geronimo: Apache Freedom Fighter* (4–6). Illus. Series: Native American Biographies. 1997, Enslow LB $20.95 (0-89490-864-2). 128pp. The story of the great Apache chieftain who led his people first against the Mexicans and then against the Americans. (Rev: BL 4/15/97; SLJ 6/97) [921]

HARRIS, LA DONNA

12973 Schwartz, Michael. *La Donna Harris* (4–7). Illus. Series: Contemporary Native Americans. 1997, Raintree Steck-Vaughn LB $25.69 (0-8172-3995-2). 48pp. The life story and accomplishments of this Native American, who has openly championed her people's rights before the Senate. (Rev: BL 6/1–15/97) [921]

HIAWATHA

12974 Fradin, Dennis B. *Hiawatha: Messenger of Peace* (4–7). Illus. 1992, Macmillan $16.00 (0-689-50519-1). 48pp. Distinguishing between fact and fiction about the Iroquois leader is the premise of this book. (Rev: BL 9/15/92; HB 1–2/93; SLJ 7/92*) [921]

ISHI

12975 Kroeber, Theodora. *Ishi, Last of the Tribe* (5–7). Illus. by Ruth Robbins. 1973, Bantam paper $5.50 (0-553-24898-7). 224pp. A California Yahi, the last of his tribe, leaves his primitive life and enters the modern world.

MANKILLER, WILMA

12976 Glassman, Bruce. *Wilma Mankiller: Chief of the Cherokee Nation* (5–7). Illus. Series: Library of Famous Women. 1992, Blackbirch LB $17.95 (1-56711-032-0). 64pp. This is an inspiring biography of the amazing woman who led her Cherokee Indians through difficult crises. (Rev: BL 6/1/92; SLJ 4/92) [921]

12977 Lazo, Caroline. *Wilma Mankiller* (4–7). Illus. Series: Peacemakers. 1995, Silver Burdett paper $7.95 (0-382-24716-7). 64pp. The dramatic story of the woman who contributed to peace within the Native American community. (Rev: BL 7/95; SLJ 7/95) [921]

12978 Lowery, Linda. *Wilma Mankiller* (2–4). Illus. 1996, Carolrhoda LB $19.93 (0-87614-880-1); paper $5.95 (0-87614-953-0). 56pp. The great hardships that were faced by the Native American woman are the focus of this inspiring, simple biography. (Rev: BCCB 9/96; BL 9/1/96; SLJ 9/96) [921]

PARKER, ELY

12979 Van Steenwyk, Elizabeth. *Seneca Chief, Army General: A Story about Ely Parker* (4–6). Illus. by Karen Ritz. Series: Creative Minds Biographies. 2000, Carolrhoda LB $21.27 (1-57505-431-0). 64pp. The story of the Native American who was appointed by Ulysses Grant as Commissioner of Indian Affairs, the first Native American to hold that post. (Rev: HBG 3/01; SLJ 2/01) [921]

PHILIP (SACHEM OF THE WAMPANOAGS)

12980 Averill, Esther. *King Philip: The Indian Chief* (5–8). Illus. by Vera Belsky. 1993, Shoe String LB $20.00 (0-208-02357-7). 148pp. The story of the Wampanoag chief who befriended the Pilgrims and later waged war against the settlers. (Rev: BL 7/93) [921]

12981 Cwiklik, Robert. *King Philip and the War with the Colonists* (4–7). Illus. Series: Biography Series of American Indians. 1989, Silver Burdett LB $18.95 (0-382-09573-1); paper $7.95 (0-382-09762-9). 144pp. A biography of the Wampanoag Indian chief who led his people in the most important Indian War in New England. (Rev: BL 1/1/90) [921]

PICOTTE, SUSAN LAFLESCHE

12982 Ferris, Jeri. *Native American Doctor: The Story of Susan LaFlesche Picotte* (4–6). Illus. 1991, Carolrhoda LB $23.93 (0-87614-443-1). The story of the first Native American woman to earn a medical degree. (Rev: BCCB 12/91; BL 1/1/91; HB 1–2/92) [921]

12983 Wilkerson, J. L. *A Doctor to Her People: Dr. Susan LaFlesche Picotte* (4–6). Illus. 1999, Acorn paper $8.95 (0-9664470-2-6). 100pp. Many maps, drawings, and photographs enhance this biography of Susan LaFlesche Picotte, the first female Native American doctor. (Rev: BL 6/1–15/99; SLJ 12/99) [921]

POCAHONTAS

12984 Fritz, Jean. *The Double Life of Pocahontas* (4–7). Illus. 1987, Puffin paper $4.99 (0-14-032257-4). 128pp. A biography of the Native American woman now chiefly associated with Captain John Smith.

12985 Holler, Anne. *Pocahontas: Powhatan Peacemaker* (5–8). Illus. Series: North American Indians of Achievement. 1993, Chelsea $19.95 (0-7910-1705-2); paper $9.95 (0-7910-1952-7). 103pp. A brief biography of the woman who helped the English settlers survive at Jamestown. (Rev: SLJ 4/93) [921]

12986 Iannone, Catherine. *Pocahontas* (4–7). Illus. Series: Junior World Biographies. 1995, Chelsea LB $16.95 (0-7910-2496-2); paper $6.95 (0-7910-2497-0). 80pp. The fascinating story of the Native American who married a white man and was received by English royalty. (Rev: BL 10/15/95; SLJ 10/95) [921]

12987 Raphael, Elaine, and Don Bolognese. *Pocahontas: Princess of the River Tribes* (1–3). Illus. by authors. Series: Drawing America. 1993, Scholastic $12.95 (0-590-44371-2). Important episodes in the life of Pocahontas are retold in this brief picture book biography. (Rev: SLJ 10/93) [921]

SACAGAWEA

12988 Adler, David A. *A Picture Book of Sacagawea* (1–4). Illus. by Dan Brown. Series: Picture Book. 2000, Holiday $16.95 (0-8234-1485-X). 32pp. The important known facts about Sacagawea, from her birth to the silver dollar in her image, are recounted in this competent biography. (Rev: BL 6/1–15/00; HBG 10/00; SLJ 6/00) [921]

12989 Rowland, Della. *The Story of Sacajawea: Guide to Lewis and Clark* (4–6). Illus. by Richard Leonard. 1989, Dell paper $3.99 (0-440-40215-8). 96pp. In brief text, this account tells of the courage and daring of the Shoshone woman who guided Lewis and Clark. (Rev: BCCB 9/89; BL 12/15/89; SLJ 12/89) [921]

12990 St. George, Judith. *Sacagawea* (4–6). 1997, Putnam $16.99 (0-399-23161-7). 128pp. A sympathetic account of the life of this Shoshone Indian woman and her exciting adventures while helping in the Lewis and Clark expedition. (Rev: BL 8/97; HBG 3/98; SLJ 3/98) [921]

12991 Sanford, William R., and Carl R. Green. *Sacagawea: Native American Hero* (4–6). Illus. Series: Legendary Heroes of the Wild West. 1997, Enslow LB $16.95 (0-89490-675-5). 48pp. A short biography of the gallant Shoshone Indian woman who accompanied Lewis and Clark west during 1805–1806. (Rev: BL 3/15/97; SLJ 3/97) [921]

12992 White, Alana J. *Sacagawea: Westward with Lewis and Clark* (4–6). Illus. Series: Native American Biographies. 1997, Enslow LB $20.95 (0-89490-867-7). 128pp. A well-written account of this gallant woman's life. Also includes a further-reading list, chapter notes, and chronology. (Rev: BL 4/15/97; SLJ 8/97) [921]

SEQUOYAH

12993 Cwiklik, Robert. *Sequoyah and the Cherokee Alphabet* (4–7). Illus. Series: Biography Series of American Indians. 1989, Silver Burdett LB $12.95 (0-382-09570-7). 144pp. The story of the great Cherokee leader who was able to translate the language of his people to written form. (Rev: BL 1/1/90; SLJ 4/90) [921]

12994 Klausner, Janet. *Sequoyah's Gift: A Portrait of the Cherokee Leader* (4–7). Illus. 1993, Harper-Collins LB $15.89 (0-06-021236-5). 128pp. The life of this Cherokee leader is retold, with material on his invention of a written alphabet and his behavior during the Trail of Tears journey. (Rev: BL 9/1/93; HB 9–10/93; SLJ 11/93) [921]

SITTING BULL (SIOUX CHIEF)

12995 Black, Sheila. *Sitting Bull and the Battle of the Little Bighorn* (4–7). Illus. Series: Biography Series of American Indians. 1989, Silver Burdett LB $18.95 (0-382-09572-3); paper $7.95 (0-382-09761-0). 144pp. A biography of the Sioux leader who defeated Custer at the Little Bighorn. (Rev: BL 1/1/90; SLJ 4/90) [921]

12996 Schleichert, Elizabeth. *Sitting Bull: Sioux Leader* (4–6). Illus. Series: Native American Biographies. 1997, Enslow LB $20.95 (0-89490-868-5). 112pp. As well as describing the life of this great leader who fought to save the lands occupied by the Sioux, there is information on the life and culture of the Sioux. (Rev: BL 4/15/97; SLJ 6/97) [921]

SQUANTO

12997 Bulla, Clyde Robert. *Squanto, Friend of the Pilgrims* (3–6). Illus. by Peter Burchard. 1990, Scholastic paper $4.50 (0-590-44055-1). 112pp. The story of the first Native American to reach Europe.

12998 Kessel, Joyce K. *Squanto and the First Thanksgiving* (2–3). Illus. by Lisa Donze. 1983, Carolrhoda LB $21.27 (0-87614-199-8); paper $5.95 (0-87614-452-0). 48pp. An easily read story of a Native American sold into slavery but eventually freed close to the Plymouth Colony.

TECUMSEH (SHAWNEE CHIEF)

12999 Fleischer, Jane. *Tecumseh: Shawnee War Chief* (3–4). Illus. by Hal Frenck. 1979, Troll LB $15.85 (0-89375-153-7); paper $3.50 (0-89375-143-X). 48pp. A basic account of this chief and his fight to prevent a territorial takeover by the white settlers.

13000 Immell, Myra H., and William H. Immell. *Tecumseh* (4–8). Illus. Series: Importance Of. 1997, Lucent LB $17.96 (1-56006-087-5). 112pp. The story of the great Shawnee leader who tried to unify American Indians against white domination and who was killed during the War of 1812. (Rev: BL 5/15/97; HBG 3/98; SLJ 8/97) [921]

WINNEMUCCA, SARAH

13001 Morrow, Mary Frances. *Sarah Winnemucca* (3–5). Illus. by Ken Bronikowski. Series: American Indian Stories. 1990, Raintree Steck-Vaughn paper $4.95 (0-8114-4095-8). 32pp. The life story of the Paiute woman who stood for Native American rights and education. (Rev: SLJ 10/90) [921]

Presidents

ADAMS, JOHN

13002 Brill, Marlene T. *John Adams: Second President of the United States* (4–6). Illus. 1986, Children's LB $25.50 (0-516-01384-X). 100pp. A crisply written biography of the second U.S. president. (Rev: BL 3/15/87; SLJ 5/87)

13003 Welsbacher, Anne. *John Adams* (K–2). Series: United States Presidents. 1999, ABDO LB $13.95 (1-56239-738-9). 32pp. For beginning readers, this simple biography of John Adams gives an overview of his life and administration with a section on important facts and statistics. (Rev: HBG 10/99; SLJ 7/99) [921]

ADAMS, JOHN QUINCY

13004 Harness, Cheryl. *Young John Quincy* (3–5). Illus. 1994, Bradbury paper $15.95 (0-02-742644-0). 48pp. Through the childhood of John Quincy Adams, the reader is told about the Declaration of Independence, the American Revolution, and the amazing Adams family. (Rev: BL 3/1/94; SLJ 4/94) [921]

13005 Kent, Zachary. *John Quincy Adams: Sixth President of the United States* (4–7). Illus. 1987, Children's LB $25.50 (0-516-01386-6). 100pp. This son of the second president spent 50 years serving his country. (Rev: BL 10/15/87)

13006 Walker, Jane C. *John Quincy Adams* (4–6). Series: United States Presidents. 2000, Enslow LB $19.95 (0-7660-1161-5). 128pp. A well-organized profile of the man who was a Revolutionary War leader, vice president, and was elected president in 1824. (Rev: BL 10/15/00; HBG 3/01) [921]

ARTHUR, CHESTER A.

13007 Simon, Charnan. *Chester A. Arthur* (4–6). Illus. Series: Encyclopedia of Presidents. 1989, Children's LB $25.50 (0-516-01369-6). 100pp. The story of the honest, efficient president who reached office after Garfield's assassination. (Rev: BL 1/15/90) [921]

13008 Stevens, Rita. *Chester A. Arthur: 21st President of the United States* (5–7). Illus. 1989, Garrett LB $21.27 (0-944483-05-4). 122pp. Life story of a former Vermont teacher. (Rev: BL 5/1/89)

BUCHANAN, JAMES

13009 Brill, Marlene T. *James Buchanan: Fifteenth President of the United States* (4–7). Illus. 1988, Children's LB $25.50 (0-516-01358-0). 120pp. Biography of the man who was president just prior to the Civil War. (Rev: BL 3/15/89; SLJ 5/89)

BUSH, GEORGE

13010 Kent, Zachary. *George Bush: Forty-First President of the United States* (4–6). Illus. Series: Encyclopedia of Presidents. 1989, Children's LB $25.50 (0-516-01374-2). 100pp. A lively account of the life of the former president and of his wife, Barbara. (Rev: BL 1/15/90) [921]

13011 Spies, Karen B. *George Bush: Power of the President* (3–6). Illus. Series: Taking Part. 1991, Macmillan LB $18.95 (0-87518-487-1). 64pp. A profile of the former president, with references to Gorbachev and Iran-Contra. (Rev: BL 3/15/92; SLJ 3/92) [921]

13012 Stefoff, Rebecca. *George H. W. Bush: 41st President of the United States* (K–2). Illus. Series: Presidents of the United States. 1992, Garrett LB $21.27 (1-56074-033-7). 124pp. The political career of George Bush minus the last two years of his presidency. (Rev: BL 8/90) [921]

BUSH, GEORGE W.

13013 Cohen, Daniel. *George W. Bush: The Family Business* (4–6). Illus. 2000, Millbrook $21.90 (0-7613-1851-8). 48pp. This slim biography ends before the 2000 election that resulted in Bush winning the presidency, but gives valuable information about his youth and family. (Rev: BL 5/1/00; HBG 10/00) [921]

13014 Wukovits, John F. *George W. Bush* (5–8). Series: People in the News. 2000, Lucent LB $19.96 (1-56006-693-8). 96pp. Published before the 2000 election, this biography uses extensive quotes from Mr. Bush, his friends, and critics. (Rev: BL 9/15/00; HBG 3/01; SLJ 10/00) [921]

CARTER, JAMES E.

13015 George, Linda, and Charles George. *Jimmy Carter: Builder of Peace* (3–5). Series: Community Builders. 2000, Children's LB $23.50 (0-516-21601-5). 48pp. This account of the life of the former president focuses on his humanitarian work since leaving office. (Rev: BL 12/15/00) [921]

13016 Lazo, Caroline. *Jimmy Carter: On the Road to Peace* (4–7). Illus. 1996, Dillon LB $13.95 (0-382-39262-0); paper $7.95 (0-382-39263-9). 112pp. A biography of the president that also gives good coverage of his career since leaving office. (Rev: BL 8/96; SLJ 8/96) [921]

13017 Richman, Daniel A. *James E. Carter* (5–8). Series: Presidents of the United States. 1989, GEC LB $21.27 (0-944483-24-0). 121pp. The story of this former U.S. president, his political career, family, and present charitable activities. (Rev: SLJ 9/89) [921]

13018 Slavin, Ed. *Jimmy Carter* (4–8). Illus. 1989, Chelsea LB $19.95 (1-55546-828-4). 112pp. Introducing the 39th president of the United States. (Rev: BL 7/89)

13019 Smith, Betsy. *Jimmy Carter, President* (5–7). Illus. 1986, Walker LB $13.85 (0-8027-6652-8). 128pp. A profile of Jimmy Carter and his one-term presidency. (Rev: BL 2/15/87; SLJ 12/86)

13020 Wade, Linda R. *James Carter: Thirty-Ninth President of the United States* (4–6). Illus. Series: Encyclopedia of Presidents. 1989, Children's LB $25.50 (0-516-01372-6). 100pp. This account includes coverage on the early life, influences, and career of Jimmy Carter. (Rev: BL 1/15/90) [921]

CLEVELAND, GROVER

13021 Kent, Zachary. *Grover Cleveland: Twenty-Second and Twenty-Fourth President of the United States* (4–7). Illus. 1988, Children's LB $25.50 (0-516-01360-2). 100pp. Biography of the only president to serve two nonconsecutive terms. (Rev: BL 3/15/89)

CLINTON, BILL

13022 Cwiklik, Robert. *Bill Clinton: President of the 90's* (3–5). Illus. Series: Gateway Biographies. 1997, Millbrook LB $20.90 (0-7613-0129-1). 48pp. A readable biography that concentrates on Clinton's career as governor of Arkansas and his early years as president. (Rev: BL 9/15/97; SLJ 7/97) [921]

13023 Greenberg, Keith E. *Bill and Hillary: Working Together in the White House* (2–6). Illus. by Jerry Harston. Series: Partners. 1994, Blackbirch LB $9.95 (1-56711-067-3). 47pp. Deals with the cooperative and joint creative efforts that have made the Clintons the successful couple they are. (Rev: SLJ 7/94) [921]

13024 Landau, Elaine. *Bill Clinton and His Presidency* (4–6). Illus. 1997, Watts LB $22.00 (0-531-20295-X). 64pp. A concise biography with good coverage of the years Clinton has been in politics. (Rev: BL 9/15/97; SLJ 9/97) [921]

13025 Sherrow, Victoria. *Bill Clinton* (3–6). Illus. Series: Taking Part. 1993, Dillon LB $13.95 (0-87518-620-3). 72pp. A biography of the president that ends shortly after his first national election. (Rev: BL 10/15/93; SLJ 12/93) [921]

COOLIDGE, CALVIN

13026 Joseph, Paul. *Calvin Coolidge* (2–5). Illus. Series: United States Presidents. 1999, ABDO LB $13.95 (1-57765-237-1). 32pp. In this biography of Coolidge, there are chapters on youth, marriage, early career, presidential issues, and final years. (Rev: HBG 3/00; SLJ 12/99) [921]

13027 Kent, Zachary. *Calvin Coolidge: Thirtieth President of the United States* (4–7). Illus. 1988, Children's LB $25.50 (0-516-01362-9). 100pp. Biography of the man known as Silent Cal. (Rev: BL 3/15/89)

EISENHOWER, DWIGHT D.

13028 Darby, Jean. *Dwight D. Eisenhower: A Man Called Ike* (4–7). Illus. Series: Lerner Biographies. 1989, Lerner LB $25.26 (0-8225-4900-X). 112pp. The story of the World War II general who later became president of the United States. (Rev: BL 11/15/89) [921]

13029 Deitch, Kenneth, and Joanne B. Weisman. *Dwight D. Eisenhower: Man of Many Hats* (5–7). Illus. by Jay Connolly. 1990, Discovery LB $14.95 (1-878668-02-1). 48pp. Each stage of Eisenhower's multifaceted career is represented. (Rev: SLJ 2/91) [921]

13030 Ellis, Rafaela. *Dwight D. Eisenhower: 34th President of the United States* (5–7). Illus. 1989, Garrett LB $21.27 (0-944483-13-5). 122pp. Compact biography of the World War II hero and president. (Rev: BL 5/1/89)

13031 Hargrove, Jim. *Dwight D. Eisenhower: Thirty-Fourth President of the United States* (4–7). Illus. 1987, Children's LB $25.50 (0-516-01389-0). 100pp. The life of the World War II hero who became a loved president. (Rev: BL 12/15/87)

13032 Van Steenwyk, Elizabeth. *Dwight David Eisenhower, President* (5–8). Illus. 1987, Walker LB $13.85 (0-8027-6671-4). 128pp. The focus is on the career of this war-hero president. (Rev: BL 5/15/87) [921]

FILLMORE, MILLARD

13033 Casey, Jane C. *Millard Fillmore: Thirteenth President of the United States* (4–7). Illus. 1988, Children's LB $25.50 (0-516-01353-X). 100pp. A biography of a little-known president. (Rev: BL 8/88)

FORD, GERALD

13034 Sipiera, Paul P. *Gerald Ford: Thirty-Eighth President of the United States* (4–6). Illus. Series: Encyclopedia of Presidents. 1989, Children's LB $25.50 (0-516-01371-8). 100pp. The story of the man who succeeded Nixon and an account of the times in which he served. (Rev: BL 1/15/90) [921]

GARFIELD, JAMES A.

13035 Lillegard, Dee. *James A. Garfield* (4–7). Illus. 1988, Children's LB $25.50 (0-516-01394-7). 100pp. The life and career of the 20th U.S. president, who was assassinated. (Rev: BL 5/15/88; SLJ 6–7/88)

GRANT, ULYSSES S.

13036 Kent, Zachary. *Ulysses S. Grant* (4–7). Illus. Series: Encyclopedia of Presidents. 1989, Children's LB $25.50 (0-516-01364-5). 100pp. The troubled years of the Civil War and after are reflected in the life of Grant as soldier and statesman. (Rev: BL 7/89) [921]

13037 Rickarby, Laura A. *Ulysses S. Grant and the Strategy of Victory* (4–7). Illus. Series: The Story of the Civil War. 1991, Silver Burdett paper $7.95 (0-382-24053-7). 160pp. This book focuses mainly on Grant's role in the winning of the Civil War for the North. (Rev: BL 9/1/91) [921]

HARDING, WARREN G.

13038 Joseph, Paul. *Warren G. Harding* (2–5). Illus. Series: United States Presidents. 1999, ABDO LB $13.95 (1-57765-234-7). 32pp. In addition to Harding's life story, this account includes a section on little-known facts and two pages of vital statistics. (Rev: HBG 3/00; SLJ 12/99) [921]

13039 Wade, Linda R. *Warren G. Harding* (4–7). Illus. Series: Encyclopedia of Presidents. 1989, Children's LB $25.50 (0-516-01368-8). 100pp. The life of the president who served from 1921 to 1923 and died suddenly in San Francisco. (Rev: BL 7/89; SLJ 2/90) [921]

HARRISON, BENJAMIN

13040 Clinton, Susan. *Benjamin Harrison: Twenty-Third President of the United States* (4–6). Illus. Series: Encyclopedia of Presidents. 1989, Children's LB $25.50 (0-516-01370-X). 100pp. The story of the Republican president who defeated Cleveland through the electoral college process. (Rev: BL 1/15/90) [921]

HARRISON, WILLIAM H.

13041 Fitz-Gerald, Christine Maloney. *William Henry Harrison* (4–7). Illus. 1988, Children's LB $25.50 (0-516-01392-0). 100pp. The biography of the man who was president for 31 days. (Rev: BL 5/15/88; SLJ 6–7/88)

HAYES, RUTHERFORD B.

13042 Kent, Zachary. *Rutherford B. Hayes* (4–7). Illus. Series: Encyclopedia of Presidents. 1989, Children's LB $25.50 (0-516-01365-3). 100pp. The story of the president whose term ended the Reconstruction era. (Rev: BL 7/89; SLJ 2/90) [921]

HOOVER, HERBERT

13043 Clinton, Susan. *Herbert Hoover: Thirty-First President of the United States* (4–7). Illus. 1988, Children's LB $25.50 (0-516-01355-6). 100pp. Biography of the president associated with the Stock Market Crash of 1929. (Rev: BL 8/88)

13044 Holford, David M. *Herbert Hoover* (5–8). Series: United States Presidents. 1999, Enslow LB $19.95 (0-7660-1035-X). 128pp. An insightful look at the president who was orphaned as a child and gained a reputation for being rigid and insensitive. (Rev: SLJ 1/00) [921]

JACKSON, ANDREW

13045 Osinski, Alice. *Andrew Jackson: Seventh President of the United States* (4–7). Illus. 1987, Children's LB $25.50 (0-516-01387-4). 100pp. A frontier lawyer and backwoods judge, Jackson was a strong believer in the common people. (Rev: BL 10/15/87)

JEFFERSON, THOMAS

13046 Adler, David A. *A Picture Book of Thomas Jefferson* (K–3). Illus. by John Wallner and Alexandra Wallner. Series: Picture Book Biographies. 1990, Holiday LB $16.95 (0-8234-0791-8); paper $6.95 (0-8234-0881-7). 32pp. Basic facts and personal glimpses make up this simple biography of the third U.S. president. (Rev: BL 4/15/90; SLJ 5/90) [921]

13047 Barrett, Marvin. *Meet Thomas Jefferson* (2–4). Illus. by Pat Fogarty. 1967, Random paper $3.99 (0-394-81964-0). 72pp. A simple, informal story of the third president.

13048 Ferris, Jeri Chase. *Thomas Jefferson: Father of Liberty* (5–8). Illus. 1998, Carolrhoda $23.95 (1-57505-009-9). 111pp. This readable biography covers both the public and the private sides of Jefferson's life, with details on his personality and his family. (Rev: BL 3/1/99; HBG 3/99; SLJ 12/98) [921]

13049 Giblin, James Cross. *Thomas Jefferson: A Picture Book Biography* (4–6). Illus. by Michael Dooling. 1994, Scholastic $16.95 (0-590-44838-2). 48pp. This handsome, historically accurate biography of Thomas Jefferson covers his presidency and his accomplishments. (Rev: BCCB 10/94; BL 10/15/94; SLJ 9/94) [921]

13050 Hargrove, Jim. *Thomas Jefferson: Third President of the United States* (4–6). Illus. 1986, Children's LB $25.50 (0-516-01385-8). 100pp. A biography of the third U.S. president, a most creative, intelligent person. (Rev: BL 3/15/87; SLJ 5/87)

13051 Morris, Jeffrey. *The Jefferson Way* (5–8). Illus. Series: Great Presidential Decisions. 1994, Lerner LB $23.93 (0-8225-2926-2). 128pp. This book on Jefferson focuses on his terms as president, particularly the troubled second term. (Rev: BL 12/15/94; SLJ 12/94) [921]

13052 Old, Wendie C. *Thomas Jefferson* (4–6). Illus. Series: United States Presidents. 1997, Enslow LB $20.95 (0-89490-837-5). 112pp. This account of the life and presidency of Jefferson contains a number of reproductions of portraits and documents. (Rev: BL 2/1/98; HBG 3/98; SLJ 3/98) [921]

13053 Santella, Andrew. *Thomas Jefferson: Voice of Liberty* (3–5). Series: Community Builders. 1999, Children's LB $23.00 (0-516-21587-6). 48pp. The story of the third president of the United States, emphasizing his contributions to the intellectual and cultural life of this country. (Rev: BL 11/15/99) [921]

JOHNSON, ANDREW

13054 Kent, Zachary. *Andrew Johnson* (4–7). Illus. Series: Encyclopedia of Presidents. 1989, Children's LB $25.50 (0-516-01363-7). 100pp. The story of the post-Civil War president who narrowly escaped impeachment. (Rev: BL 7/89) [921]

13055 Stevens, Rita. *Andrew Johnson: 17th President of the United States* (5–7). Illus. 1989, Garrett LB $21.27 (0-944483-16-X). 122pp. Story of the man who became president on Lincoln's assassination. (Rev: BL 5/1/89)

JOHNSON, LYNDON B.

13056 Falkof, Lucille. *Lyndon B. Johnson: 36th President of the United States* (5–7). Illus. 1989, Garrett LB $21.27 (0-944483-20-8). 120pp. Life story of the man from Texas. (Rev: BL 5/1/89)

13057 Hargrove, Jim. *Lyndon B. Johnson* (4–7). Illus. 1988, Children's LB $25.50 (0-516-01396-3). 100pp. The life and times of the 36th president, who took office after the assassination of John F. Kennedy. (Rev: BL 5/15/88; SLJ 6/7/88)

KENNEDY, JOHN F.

13058 Adler, David A. *A Picture Book of John F. Kennedy* (2–4). Illus. by Robert Casilla. Series: Picture Book Biographies. 1991, Holiday LB $16.95 (0-8234-0884-1). A straightforward account in an attractive format that provides basic information about President John F. Kennedy. (Rev: SLJ 12/91) [921]

13059 Cole, Michael D. *John F. Kennedy: President of the New Frontier* (4–7). Illus. Series: People to Know. 1996, Enslow LB $20.95 (0-89490-693-3). 128pp. A profile of the life and accomplishments of this charismatic president. (Rev: BL 5/15/96; SLJ 6/96) [921]

13060 Donnelly, Judy. *Who Shot the President? The Death of John F. Kennedy* (3–4). Illus. 1989, Random paper $3.99 (0-394-89944-X). 48pp. An overview of the JFK presidency and assassination. (Rev: BL 3/1/89)

13061 Hampton, Wilborn. *Kennedy Assassinated! The World Mourns* (5–8). Illus. 1997, Candlewick $17.99 (1-56402-811-9). 96pp. A first-person account of the death of President Kennedy and of its devastating effects. (Rev: BL 9/15/97*; HBG 3/98; SLJ 10/97) [921]

13062 Kent, Zachary. *John F. Kennedy: Thirty-Fifth President of the United States* (4–7). Illus. 1987, Children's LB $25.50 (0-516-01390-4). 99pp. The life of the young idealized president who died by an assassin's bullet. (Rev: BL 12/15/87)

LINCOLN, ABRAHAM

13063 Adler, David A. *A Picture Book of Abraham Lincoln* (PS–3). Illus. by John Wallner and Alexandra Wallner. 1989, Holiday LB $16.95 (0-8234-0731-4); paper $6.95 (0-8234-0801-9). 32pp. The life of perhaps our most famous president told in a profusely illustrated format. (Rev: BL 6/1/89; SLJ 5/89)

13064 Bial, Raymond. *Where Lincoln Walked* (3–6). Illus. 1998, Walker $16.95 (0-8027-8630-8). 48pp. This unusual biography of Lincoln concentrates on the years before he became president and on the sight and people he knew at that time. (Rev: BL 3/1/98; HBG 10/98; SLJ 2/98) [921]

13065 Brenner, Martha. *Abe Lincoln's Hat* (1–3). Illus. by Donald Cook. 1994, Random paper $3.99 (0-679-84977-7). 48pp. A simple biography of Lincoln that makes him a believable person through the retelling of simple anecdotes. (Rev: BL 9/15/94; SLJ 11/94) [921]

13066 Freedman, Russell. *Lincoln: A Photobiography* (4–8). Illus. 1987, Houghton $18.00 (0-89919-380-3); paper $7.95 (0-395-51848-2). 160pp. A no-nonsense, unromanticized look at this beloved president. Newbery Medal winner, 1988. (Rev: BL 12/15/87; SLJ 12/87)

13067 Gross, Ruth Belov. *True Stories About Abraham Lincoln* (2–5). Illus. by Jill Kastner. 1991, Scholastic paper $2.50 (0-590-43879-4). 48pp. This is a collection of anecdotes about Lincoln. Originally published in 1973. (Rev: BCCB 3/90; BL 3/1/90; SLJ 4/90) [921]

13068 Hargrove, Jim. *Abraham Lincoln: Sixteenth President of the United States* (4–7). Illus. 1988, Children's LB $25.50 (0-516-01359-9). 100pp. Biography of the man forever associated with freedom. (Rev: BL 3/15/89; SLJ 5/89)

13069 Harness, Cheryl. *Abe Lincoln Goes to Washington, 1837–1865* (1–4). Illus. 1997, National Geographic $18.00 (0-7922-3736-6). 48pp. In this sequel to *Young Abe Lincoln* (1996), Lincoln's life from his arrival in Springfield, Illinois, to his assassination is covered. (Rev: BL 1/1–15/97; SLJ 3/97*) [921]

13070 Harness, Cheryl. *Young Abe Lincoln* (1–4). Illus. 1996, National Geographic $15.95 (0-7922-2713-1). 32pp. A picture book that traces Lincoln's early life until he leaves for Springfield, Illinois. (Rev: BL 9/1/96; SLJ 6/96) [921]

13071 Ito, Tom. *Abraham Lincoln* (5–8). Illus. Series: Mysterious Deaths. 1996, Lucent LB $22.45 (1-56006-259-2). 96pp. This book explores the various conspiracy theories that surround Lincoln's death. (Rev: SLJ 5/97) [921]

13072 January, Brendan. *The Assassination of Abraham Lincoln* (3–5). Series: Cornerstones of Freedom. 1998, Children's LB $19.50 (0-516-20947-7). 32pp. A simple account of the events leading up to the assassination in Ford's Theatre and of its aftermath. (Rev: BL 9/15/98; HBG 3/99) [921]

13073 Judson, Karen. *Abraham Lincoln* (4–6). Series: United States Presidents. 1998, Enslow LB $19.95 (0-89490-939-8). 128pp. Original source documents and a chronology are included in this insightful biography of a great president. (Rev: BL 12/15/98; HBG 3/99) [921]

13074 Mosher, Kiki. *Learning About Honesty from the Life of Abraham Lincoln* (2–5). Illus. Series: A Character Building Book. 1996, Rosen LB $13.95 (0-8239-2420-3). 24pp. A brief biography of Lincoln that emphasizes his belief in honesty and truth. (Rev: BL 10/15/96; SLJ 12/96) [921]

13075 Sandburg, Carl. *Abe Lincoln Grows Up* (6–8). Illus. by James Daugherty. 1975, Harcourt paper $7.00 (0-15-602615-5). 222pp. The classic account of Lincoln's boyhood based on Volume I of *The Prairie Years*.

13076 Stefoff, Rebecca. *Abraham Lincoln: 16th President of the United States* (5–7). Illus. 1989, Garrett LB $21.27 (0-944483-14-3). 122pp. A compact biography of a much respected and admired president. (Rev: BL 5/1/89)

13077 Sullivan, George. *Picturing Lincoln: Famous Photographs That Popularized the President* (5–8). Illus. 2000, Clarion $16.00 (0-395-91682-8). 88pp. Using five images of Lincoln taken between 1846 and 1864, this book gives historical and biographical information on each and tells how they have been used for posters, button, ribbons, postage stamps, and currency. (Rev: BL 2/1/01) [921]

13078 Turner, Ann. *Abe Lincoln Remembers* (1–3). Illus. by Wendell Minor. 2001, HarperCollins LB $15.89 (0-06-027578-2). 32pp. A free-verse fictional biography of Lincoln that covers the highlights of his life but concentrates on his accomplishments. (Rev: BCCB 2/01; BL 1/1–15/01; SLJ 2/01) [921]

13079 Van Steenwyk, Elizabeth. *When Abraham Talked to the Trees* (K–3). Illus. by Bill Farnsworth. 2000, Eerdmans $16.00 (0-8028-5191-6). 32pp. A picture book that tells of Lincoln's youth, his many outdoor activities, and the books he read. (Rev: BL 10/1/00; HBG 3/01; SLJ 12/00) [921]

MCKINLEY, WILLIAM

13080 Kent, Zachary. *William McKinley: Twenty-Fifth President of the United States* (4–7). Illus. 1988, Children's LB $25.50 (0-516-01361-0). 100pp. Biography of an assassinated president. (Rev: BL 3/15/89)

MADISON, JAMES

13081 Clinton, Susan. *James Madison: Fourth President of the United States* (4–6). Illus. 1986, Children's LB $25.50 (0-516-01382-3). 100pp. Depicting the important events in the life of the fourth U.S. president. (Rev: BL 3/15/87; SLJ 5/87)

13082 Fritz, Jean. *The Great Little Madison* (5–8). 1989, Putnam $15.95 (0-399-21768-1). 160pp. The story of the fourth president of the United States, James Madison, and of the people and events that surrounded his political career. (Rev: BCCB 10/89; HB 3–4/90*; SLJ 11/89) [921]

13083 Malone, Mary. *James Madison* (4–6). Illus. 1997, Enslow LB $20.95 (0-89490-834-0). 128pp. This interesting, well-researched biography of James Madison focuses on his presidency. (Rev: BL 9/15/97; HBG 3/98; SLJ 9/97) [921]

13084 Quackenbush, Robert. *James Madison and Dolley Madison and Their Times* (3–6). Illus. 1992, Pippin $14.95 (0-945912-18-8). 40pp. A fact-filled short biography of James and Dolley Madison with many interesting bits about their personal lives. (Rev: BL 1/15/93; SLJ 1/93) [921]

MONROE, JAMES

13085 Old, Wendie C. *James Monroe* (4–6). Series: United States Presidents. 1998, Enslow LB $19.95 (0-89490-941-X). 128pp. A biography of the fifth president, who is noted for drafting the doctrine that barred European intervention in the New World. (Rev: BL 12/15/98; HBG 3/99) [921]

13086 Welsbacher, Anne. *James Monroe* (K–2). Series: United States Presidents. 1999, ABDO LB $13.95 (1-56239-810-5). 32pp. A biography for beginning readers that gives basic facts about Monroe and the meaning of the doctrine that bears his name. (Rev: HBG 10/99; SLJ 7/99) [921]

NIXON, RICHARD M.

13087 Joseph, Paul. *Richard Nixon* (K–2). Series: United States Presidents. 1999, ABDO LB $13.95 (1-56239-746-X). 32pp. For beginning readers, this is an overview of Nixon's life and accomplishments with a double-page spread of important facts and statistics. (Rev: HBG 10/99; SLJ 7/99) [921]

13088 Lillegard, Dee. *Richard Nixon: Thirty-Seventh President of the United States* (4–7). Illus. 1988, Children's LB $25.50 (0-516-01356-4). 100pp. Ups and downs in the turbulent career of the 37th president. (Rev: BL 8/88; SLJ 10/88)

PIERCE, FRANKLIN

13089 Brown, Fern G. *Franklin Pierce* (5–8). Series: Presidents of the United States. 1989, GEC LB $21.27 (0-944483-25-9). 121pp. The story of

Pierce, his political life and presidency, plus material on his personal life. (Rev: SLJ 9/89) [921]

13090 Simon, Charnan. *Franklin Pierce: Fourteenth President of the United States* (4–7). Illus. 1988, Children's LB $25.50 (0-516-01357-2). 100pp. A biography of the New Hampshire lawyer elected president. (Rev: BL 3/15/89; SLJ 5/89)

POLK, JAMES K.

13091 Lillegard, Dee. *James K. Polk: Eleventh President of the United States* (4–7). Illus. 1988, Children's LB $25.50 (0-516-01351-3). 100pp. Includes chronological events in the life and career of the 11th president. (Rev: BL 8/88)

13092 Tibbitts, Alison Davis. *James K. Polk* (4–6). Series: United States Presidents. 1999, Enslow LB $19.95 (0-7660-1037-6). 128pp. The story of the 11th president of the United States, whose term encompassed the 1846–1848 war with Mexico, which brought California and New Mexico into the union. (Rev: BL 9/15/99; HBG 10/99) [921]

REAGAN, RONALD

13093 Kent, Zachary. *Ronald Reagan: Fortieth President of the United States* (4–6). Illus. Series: Encyclopedia of Presidents. 1989, Children's LB $25.50 (0-516-01373-4). 100pp. A dramatic account of the movie star who became a two-term president. (Rev: BL 1/15/90) [921]

13094 Robbins, Neal. *Ronald W. Reagan: 40th President of the United States* (K–2). Illus. Series: Presidents of the United States. 1990, Garrett LB $21.27 (0-944483-66-6). 124pp. The life of Ronald Reagan is presented. (Rev: BL 8/90) [921]

13095 Sullivan, George. *Ronald Reagan* (5–8). Illus. 1991, Simon & Schuster $14.98 (0-671-74537-9). 142pp. This revised edition adds new material on Reagan's second term. (Rev: BL 1/15/92) [921]

ROOSEVELT, FRANKLIN D.

13096 Freedman, Russell. *Franklin Delano Roosevelt* (5–8). Illus. 1990, Houghton $18.00 (0-89919-379-X). 200pp. A carefully researched and well-illustrated account of the man and the times. (Rev: HB 3–4/90; SLJ 12/90*) [921]

13097 Greenblatt, Miriam. *Franklin D. Roosevelt: 32nd President of the United States* (5–7). Illus. 1989, Garrett LB $21.27 (0-944483-06-2). 122pp. A biography of the man who guided the country through World War II. (Rev: BL 5/1/89)

13098 Morris, Jeffrey. *The FDR Way* (5–8). Illus. Series: Great Presidential Decisions. 1996, Lerner LB $23.93 (0-8225-2929-7). 136pp. In a straightforward style, this is an incisive analysis of the decisions, many of them painful, that FDR made and of their consequences. (Rev: BL 3/15/96) [921]

13099 Osinski, Alice. *Franklin D. Roosevelt* (4–7). Illus. 1988, Children's LB $25.50 (0-516-01395-5). 100pp. The life and career of the 32nd president, who led the nation through World War II. (Rev: BL 5/15/88; SLJ 6–7/88)

13100 Schuman, Michael A. *Franklin D. Roosevelt: The Four-Term President* (4–7). Illus. Series: People to Know. 1996, Enslow LB $20.95 (0-89490-696-8). 128pp. A thoughtful, serious biography of this great president, his important decisions, and his significance in history. (Rev: BL 6/1–15/96; SLJ 8/96) [921]

ROOSEVELT, THEODORE

13101 Fritz, Jean. *Bully for You, Teddy Roosevelt!* (5–8). Illus. by Mike Wimmer. 1991, Putnam $15.99 (0-399-21769-X). 103pp. An affectionate portrait of the president who considered himself a "true American." (Rev: BL 4/15/91; HB 7–8/91; SLJ 7/91) [921]

13102 Harness, Cheryl. *Young Teddy Roosevelt* (3–5). Illus. 1998, National Geographic $17.95 (0-7922-7094-0). 48pp. Illustrated with lavish watercolors, this picture-book biography tells of Roosevelt's sickly childhood and ends with him becoming president of the United States. (Rev: BCCB 4/98; BL 3/15/98; HBG 10/98) [921]

13103 Kent, Zachary. *Theodore Roosevelt: Twenty-Sixth President of the United States* (4–7). Illus. 1988, Children's LB $25.50 (0-516-01354-8). 100pp. The life and career of Teddy Roosevelt. (Rev: BL 8/88)

13104 Schuman, Michael A. *Theodore Roosevelt* (4–6). Illus. Series: United States Presidents. 1997, Enslow LB $20.95 (0-89490-836-7). 128pp. This well-illustrated account of the life and presidency of Theodore Roosevelt includes fascinating details of his very adventurous life. (Rev: BL 2/1/98; HBG 3/98; SLJ 2/98) [921]

TAFT, WILLIAM H.

13105 Casey, Jane C. *William Howard Taft* (4–7). Illus. Series: Encyclopedia of Presidents. 1989, Children's LB $25.50 (0-516-01366-1). 100pp. The story of the president who served from 1909 to 1913. (Rev: BL 7/89) [921]

TAYLOR, ZACHARY

13106 Collins, David R. *Zachary Taylor: 12th President of the United States* (5–7). Illus. 1989, Garrett LB $21.27 (0-944483-17-8). 121pp. Tells the life story of a military man elected president in 1848. (Rev: BL 5/1/89)

13107 Kent, Zachary. *Zachary Taylor: Twelfth President of the United States* (4–7). Illus. 1988, Children's LB $25.50 (0-516-01352-1). 100pp. A look at the life and career of the president in a young nation. (Rev: BL 8/88)

TRUMAN, HARRY S.

13108 Hargrove, Jim. *Harry S. Truman: Thirty-Third President of the United States* (4–7). Illus. 1987, Children's LB $25.50 (0-516-01388-2). 100pp. The life of the man who became president on FDR's death. (Rev: BL 12/15/87)

13109 Joseph, Paul. *Harry S. Truman* (2–5). Illus. Series: United States Presidents. 1999, ABDO LB $13.95 (1-56239-743-5). 32pp. A good biography of

Truman that also contains a section on trivia, a map, and two pages of vital statistics. (Rev: HBG 3/00; SLJ 12/99) [921]

TYLER, JOHN

13110 Lillegard, Dee. *John Tyler* (4–7). Illus. 1988, Children's LB $25.50 (0-516-01393-9). 100pp. The life and career of the tenth president. (Rev: BL 5/15/88)

VAN BUREN, MARTIN

13111 Ellis, Rafaela. *Martin Van Buren: 8th President of the United States* (5–7). Illus. 1989, Garrett LB $21.27 (0-944483-12-7). 120pp. The story of a New York governor who became president. (Rev: BL 5/1/89)

13112 Hargrove, Jim. *Martin Van Buren* (4–7). Illus. 1988, Children's LB $25.50 (0-516-01391-2). 100pp. Life during the administration of Van Buren, eighth U.S. president. (Rev: BL 5/15/88)

WASHINGTON, GEORGE

13113 Adler, David A. *A Picture Book of George Washington* (PS–3). Illus. by John Wallner and Alexandra Wallner. 1989, Holiday LB $16.95 (0-8234-0732-2); paper $6.95 (0-8234-0800-0). 32pp. A picture biography of America's first president for young readers. (Rev: BL 6/1/89; SLJ 5/89)

13114 Falkof, Lucille. *George Washington: 1st President of the United States* (5–7). Illus. 1989, Garrett LB $21.27 (0-944483-19-4). 120pp. A compact life story of the first president. (Rev: BL 5/1/89)

13115 Harness, Cheryl. *George Washington* (3–5). Illus. 2000, National Geographic $17.95 (0-7922-7096-7). 48pp. A heavily illustrated, large-format biography that covers the important events in Washington's life and describes his personality. (Rev: BL 3/1/00; HBG 10/00; SLJ 4/00) [921]

13116 Kent, Zachary. *George Washington: First President of the United States* (4–6). Illus. 1986, Children's LB $25.50 (0-516-01381-5). 100pp. The events in the life of the first U.S. president. (Rev: BL 3/15/87; SLJ 5/87)

13117 Morris, Jeffrey. *The Washington Way* (5–8). Illus. Series: Great Presidential Decisions. 1994, Lerner LB $23.93 (0-8225-2928-9). 128pp. This biography focuses on Washington's term of office as president and on his problems and accomplishments. (Rev: BL 12/15/94) [921]

13118 Mosher, Kiki. *Learning About Leadership from the Life of George Washington* (2–5). Illus. Series: A Character Building Book. 1996, Rosen LB $13.95 (0-8239-2421-1). 24pp. A brief biography of Washington that emphasizes his leadership qualities. (Rev: BL 10/15/96; SLJ 12/96) [921]

13119 Old, Wendie C. *George Washington* (5–8). Illus. 1997, Enslow LB $20.95 (0-89490-832-4). 128pp. Both Washington's personal and public lives are dealt with equally in this thoughtful biography. (Rev: BL 9/15/97; SLJ 12/97) [921]

13120 Rosenburg, John. *Young George Washington: The Making of a Hero* (6–8). Illus. 1997, Millbrook LB $22.40 (0-7613-0043-0). 128pp. The biography of Washington's life from his teens through his military career to age 27. (Rev: BL 2/15/97; SLJ 4/97) [921]

WILSON, WOODROW

13121 Collins, David R. *Woodrow Wilson: 28th President of the United States* (5–7). Illus. 1989, Garrett LB $21.27 (0-944483-18-6). 121pp. A compact biography of a Nobel Peace Prize–winning president. (Rev: BL 5/1/89)

13122 Osinski, Alice. *Woodrow Wilson* (4–7). Illus. Series: Encyclopedia of Presidents. 1989, Children's LB $25.50 (0-516-01367-X). 100pp. The life story of the president who saw this country through World War I. (Rev: BL 7/89) [921]

13123 Schraff, Anne. *Woodrow Wilson* (5–8). Series: United States Presidents. 1998, Enslow LB $18.95 (0-89490-936-3). 112pp. The story of the brilliant 28th president, his initial opposition to entering World War I, the defeat of his proposals concerning the League of Nations, and the stroke he suffered. (Rev: SLJ 9/98) [921]

First Ladies and Other Women

ADAMS, ABIGAIL

13124 Ferris, Jeri Chase. *Remember the Ladies: A Story About Abigail Adams* (3–5). Illus. by Ellen Beier. Series: Creative Minds Biographies. 2000, Carolrhoda LB $21.27 (1-57505-292-X). 64pp. A biography of this early first lady that relies heavily on original sources including the writings of Abigail Adams. (Rev: HBG 3/01; SLJ 1/01) [921]

13125 Wallner, Alexandra. *Abigail Adams* (K–3). Illus. 2001, Holiday $16.95 (0-8234-1442-6). 32pp. A picture book biography that examines the life of Abigail Adams, the wife of a president, the mother of another, and a champion of women's rights. (Rev: BL 3/15/01) [921]

ADAMS, LOUISA CATHERINE JOHNSON

13126 Heinrichs, Ann. *Louisa Catherine Johnson Adams* (4–6). Series: Encyclopedia of First Ladies. 1998, Children's LB $33.00 (0-516-20845-4). A biography of the wife of the sixth U.S. president, John Quincy Adams, that tells about her life, family, and accomplishments. (Rev: BL 8/98; HBG 3/99) [921]

ADDAMS, JANE

13127 Harvey, Bonnie Carman. *Jane Addams: Nobel Prize Winner and Founder of Hull House* (5–8). Illus. Series: Historic American Biographies. 1999, Enslow LB $19.95 (0-7660-1094-5). 128pp. This biography of the Nobel Peace Prize winner and founder of Hull House traces her life and her outstanding achievements as a social worker. (Rev: BL 11/1/99; HBG 3/00; SLJ 11/99) [921]

13128 McPherson, Stephanie S. *Peace and Bread: The Story of Jane Addams* (5–8). Illus. 1993, Carolrhoda LB $23.93 (0-87614-792-9). 96pp. A brief biography of the woman noted for her work with the poor people of Chicago. (Rev: BL 1/15/94; SLJ 2/94) [921]

13129 Wheeler, Leslie. *Jane Addams* (4–7). Illus. Series: Pioneers in Change. 1990, Silver Burdett LB $13.98 (0-382-09962-1); paper $6.95 (0-382-09968-0). 138pp. The story of the famous social worker who also worked for woman suffrage. (Rev: SLJ 4/91) [921]

ANTHONY, SUSAN B.

13130 Levin, Pamela. *Susan B. Anthony: Fighter for Women's Rights* (3–5). Illus. Series: Junior World Biographies. 1993, Chelsea LB $16.95 (0-7910-1762-1). 79pp. An informative, interesting biography of the great fighter for social causes, including women's right to vote. (Rev: SLJ 10/93) [921]

13131 Mosher, Kiki. *Learning About Fairness from the Life of Susan B. Anthony* (2–5). Illus. Series: A Character Building Book. 1996, Rosen LB $13.95 (0-8239-2422-X). 24pp. The spirit of fairness and justice is shown in the life of this leader for women's rights. (Rev: BL 10/15/96; SLJ 12/96) [921]

13132 Parker, Barbara Keevil. *Susan B. Anthony: Daring to Vote* (4–6). Illus. Series: Gateway Biographies. 1998, Millbrook LB $20.90 (0-7613-0358-8). 48pp. This interesting biography of this early abolitionist and fighter in the suffrage movement also contains brief biographies of other early feminists. (Rev: BL 6/1–15/98; HBG 10/98; SLJ 7/98) [921]

13133 Roop, Peter, and Connie Roop. *Susan B. Anthony* (2–3). Series: Lives and Times. 1997, Heinemann $21.36 (1-57572-563-0). 24pp. A simple picture book biography that gives a short introduction to the life and times of this fighter for women's rights. (Rev: BL 3/15/98) [921]

BAKER, S. JOSEPHINE

13134 Ptacek, Greg. *Champion for Children's Health: A Story About Dr. S. Josephine Baker* (3–5). Illus. by Lydia M. Anderson. 1994, Carolrhoda LB $21.27 (0-87614-806-2). 64pp. The story of the woman who pioneered public-health standards for children at the turn of the century. (Rev: BL 3/1/94; SLJ 3/94) [921]

BARTON, CLARA

13135 Rose, Mary Catherine. *Clara Barton: Soldier of Mercy* (3–5). Illus. 1991, Chelsea LB $16.95 (0-7910-1403-7). A simply written account of this courageous nurse who founded the Red Cross.

BLY, NELLIE

13136 Emerson, Kathy L. *Making Headlines: A Biography of Nellie Bly* (4–6). Illus. 1989, Macmillan LB $18.95 (0-87518-406-5). 112pp. The life of this journalist and outspoken reformer is presented. (Rev: BCCB 12/89; BL 7/89; SLJ 9/89) [921]

13137 Fredeen, Charles. *Nellie Bly: Daredevil Reporter* (5–9). Series: Lerner Biographies. 2000, Lerner LB $25.26 (0-8225-4956-5). 112pp. The story of the daring reporter who traveled around the world in 72 days and was a champion of the

women's suffrage movement. (Rev: HBG 10/00; SLJ 3/00) [921]

13138 Kendall, Martha E. *Nellie Bly: Reporter for the World* (3–5). Illus. Series: Gateway Biographies. 1992, Millbrook LB $21.90 (1-56294-061-9); paper $8.95 (0-395-64538-7). 48pp. The life story of the famous woman journalist whose real name was Elizabeth Seaman. (Rev: BL 8/92; SLJ 11/92) [921]

13139 Peck, Ira, and Nellie Bly. *Nellie Bly's Book: Around the World in 72 Days* (5–10). 1998, Twenty-First Century $26.90 (0-7613-0971-3). 128pp. An abridged version of *New York World* reporter Nellie Bly's entertaining account of her trip around the world during the 1880s and her many interesting observations of the world at that time. (Rev: HBG 10/99; SLJ 4/99) [921]

BRIDGMAN, LAURA DEWEY

13140 Hunter, Edith Fisher. *Child of the Silent Night* (3–5). Illus. 1963, Houghton $16.00 (0-395-06835-5). 128pp. The story of a blind-deaf child who paved the way for the successes of Helen Keller.

BUSH, BARBARA

13141 Spies, Karen B. *Barbara Bush: Helping America Read* (3–6). Illus. Series: Taking Part. 1991, Macmillan LB $18.95 (0-87518-488-X). 64pp. A look at the former First Lady, with some data on her interest in the literacy campaign. (Rev: BL 3/15/92; SLJ 3/92) [921]

CARTER, ROSALYNN

13142 Turk, Ruth. *Rosalynn Carter: Steel Magnolia* (4–6). Illus. Series: First Books. 1997, Watts $22.50 (0-531-20312-3). 64pp. From her childhood in Plains, Georgia, to the White House and her current interests, this is the story of Rosalynn Carter. (Rev: BL 12/1/97; HBG 3/98) [921]

CHILD, LYDIA MARIA

13143 Stux, Erica. *Writing for Freedom: A Story about Lydia Maria Child* (3–5). Illus. Series: Creative Minds Biographies. 2000, Carolrhoda $21.27 (1-57505-439-6). A biography of the poet who was also an abolitionist and courageously fought against slavery. (Rev: SLJ 1/01) [921]

CLINTON, HILLARY RODHAM

13144 Bach, Julie. *Hillary Rodham Clinton* (3–5). Illus. Series: Leading Ladies. 1993, ABDO LB $13.98 (1-56239-221-2). 32pp. An account of the First Lady's life, from childhood in a Chicago suburb to her arrival in Washington, D.C., for her husband's first term. (Rev: SLJ 3/94) [921]

13145 Guernsey, JoAnn B. *Hillary Rodham Clinton: A New Kind of First Lady* (4–7). Illus. 1993, Lerner LB $19.95 (0-8225-2875-4); paper $6.95 (0-8225-9650-4). 80pp. A behind-the-scenes biography of the First Lady that ends with her attempts to reform health care. (Rev: BL 11/1/93; SLJ 12/93) [921]

13146 LeVert, Suzanne. *Hillary Rodham Clinton: First Lady* (3–5). Illus. Series: Gateway Biographies. 1994, Millbrook LB $20.90 (1-56294-432-0); paper $8.95 (1-56294-726-5). 48pp. A biography of the First Lady that ends in 1993. (Rev: BL 7/94) [921]

13147 Sherrow, Victoria. *Hillary Rodham Clinton* (3–6). Illus. Series: Taking Part. 1993, Dillon LB $13.95 (0-87518-621-1). 64pp. A biography of the First Lady that focuses on her schooling and law career. (Rev: BL 10/15/93; SLJ 12/93) [921]

DE PASSE, SUZANNE

13148 Mussari, Mark. *Suzanne De Passe: Motown's Boss Lady* (5–8). Illus. Series: Wizards of Business. 1992, Garrett LB $17.26 (1-56074-026-4). 64pp. The story of the woman who helped make Motown the great name in the music industry. (Rev: BL 6/15/92) [921]

DOLE, ELIZABETH

13149 Lucas, Eileen. *Elizabeth Dole: A Leader in Washington* (4–6). Illus. Series: Gateway Biographies. 1998, Millbrook LB $20.90 (0-7613-0203-4). 48pp. This book takes the reader from Elizabeth Dole's childhood in North Carolina through her recent career in government and public service. (Rev: BL 6/1–15/98; HBG 10/98; SLJ 6/98) [921]

EDELMAN, MARIAN WRIGHT

13150 Burch, Joann J. *Marian Wright Edelman: Children's Champion* (4–6). Illus. Series: Gateway Biographies. 1994, Millbrook LB $20.90 (1-56294-457-6). 48pp. The engrossing life story of the founder of the Children's Defense Fund, who has devoted her life to protecting children's rights. (Rev: SLJ 2/95) [921]

13151 Old, Wendie C. *Marian Wright Edelman: Fighting for Children's Rights* (4–6). Illus. Series: People to Know. 1995, Enslow LB $20.95 (0-89490-623-2). 112pp. The story of this 20th-century American and her fight for the rights of children. (Rev: BL 10/15/95; SLJ 12/95) [921]

EDMONDS, EMMA

13152 Reit, Seymour. *Behind Rebel Lines: The Incredible Story of Emma Edmonds, Civil War Spy* (5–8). 1988, Harcourt $12.95 (0-15-200416-5); paper $6.00 (0-15-200424-6). 144pp. The remarkable Canadian-born spy who helped to defend the Union in the Civil War. (Rev: BL 3/1/88; SLJ 3/88)

13153 Stevens, Bryna. *Frank Thompson: Her Civil War Story* (5–7). Illus. 1992, Macmillan LB $14.00 (0-02-788185-7). 144pp. The life of Emma Edmonds, a Canadian woman who dressed as a man to join the U.S. Union Army. (Rev: BCCB 12/92; BL 12/15/92; HB 1–2/93; SLJ 10/92) [921]

FORD, BETTY

13154 Santow, Dan. *Elizabeth Bloomer Ford* (4–6). Series: Encyclopedia of First Ladies. 2000, Children's LB $33.00 (0-516-20641-9). 112pp. As well as describing Betty Ford's life and accomplish-

ments, this book tells of the social and political events that occurred during her husband's presidency. (Rev: BL 6/1–15/00) [921]

GORE, TIPPER

13155 Guernsey, JoAnn B. *Tipper Gore: Voice for the Voiceless* (4–6). Illus. 1994, Lerner LB $19.93 (0-8225-2876-2); paper $6.95 (0-8225-9651-2). 64pp. This biography of the vice president's wife reveals her to be an independent, determined woman who champions a number of worthy causes. (Rev: BL 9/15/94; SLJ 7/94) [921]

13156 Kramer, Barbara. *Tipper Gore* (4–7). Illus. Series: People to Know. 1999, Enslow LB $19.95 (0-7660-1142-9). 112pp. The story of the life of the former vice president's wife and her activities as a mother, professional photographer, and social issues advocate. (Rev: BL 8/99) [921]

GRANT, JULIA DENT

13157 Fitz-Gerald, Christine A. *Julia Dent Grant* (4–6). Series: Encyclopedia of First Ladies. 1998, Children's LB $33.00 (0-516-20696-6). 122pp. The life and contributions of this famous army wife and First Lady are detailed, with some background material on the Civil War and its aftermath. (Rev: BL 7/98; HBG 10/98; SLJ 7/98) [921]

HALE, CLARA

13158 Italia, Bob. *Clara Hale: Mother to Those Who Needed One* (3–5). Illus. Series: Everyone Contributes. 1993, ABDO LB $18.49 (1-56239-235-2). 32pp. The biography of the woman whose work with foster children has become a model for others. (Rev: BL 12/1/93) [921]

HOOVER, LOU

13159 Colbert, Nancy A. *Lou Hoover: The Duty to Serve* (5–8). Illus. 1997, Morgan Reynolds LB $18.95 (1-883846-22-6). 112pp. As well as being the wife of an unpopular president, Mrs. Hoover was also a most interesting person, who, among other accomplishments, was the first woman to get a degree in geology in this country. (Rev: BL 2/15/98; HBG 3/98; SLJ 3/98) [921]

HUTCHINSON, ANNE

13160 Ilgenfritz, Elizabeth. *Anne Hutchinson* (5–8). Illus. Series: American Women of Achievement. 1990, Chelsea LB $19.95 (1-55546-660-5). 111pp. The story of the woman in pre-Revolutionary days who stood trial to defend religious liberty. (Rev: SLJ 4/91) [921]

JONES, MOTHER

13161 Horton, Madelyn. *The Importance of Mother Jones* (4–8). Illus. Series: The Importance Of. 1996, Lucent LB $18.96 (1-56006-057-3). 95pp. The life of the legendary American labor organizer who was active in the United States before and after the turn of the century. (Rev: BL 5/15/96; SLJ 7/96) [921]

13162 Kraft, Betsy Harvey. *Mother Jones: One Woman's Fight for Labor* (5–8). Illus. 1995, Clarion

$16.95 (0-395-67163-9). 116pp. The story of the woman who became a leader in the American labor movement from 1870 to 1930. (Rev: BCCB 9/95; SLJ 7/95*) [921]

KARAN, DONNA

13163 Tippins, Sherill. *Donna Karan: Designing an American Dream* (5–8). Illus. Series: Wizards of Business. 1992, Garrett LB $17.26 (1-56074-019-1). 64pp. Along with the life story of one of America's top fashion designers is advice for those who wish to enter the field. (Rev: BL 6/15/92) [921]

KELLER, HELEN

13164 Adler, David A. *A Picture Book of Helen Keller* (2–4). Illus. by John Wallner and Alexandra Wallner. Series: Picture Book Biographies. 1990, Holiday LB $16.95 (0-8234-0818-3); paper $6.95 (0-8234-0950-3). 32pp. This account focuses on Keller's personality, stamina, and accomplishments. (Rev: BL 12/15/90; SLJ 11/90) [921]

13165 Dash, Joan. *The World at Her Fingertips: The Story of Helen Keller* (4–7). Illus. 2001, Scholastic $15.95 (0-590-90715-8). 223pp. A straightforward account of the girl who was left blind and deaf at 19 months and of her determination to be independent. (Rev: BCCB 3/01; BL 2/15/01) [921]

13166 Graff, Stewart, and Polly Graff. *Helen Keller: Toward the Light* (3–5). Illus. 1992, Chelsea LB $16.95 (0-7910-1412-6). 80pp. A simply written biography of the woman who overcame the handicaps of blindness and deafness.

LINCOLN, MARY TODD

13167 Hull, Mary E. *Mary Todd Lincoln* (5–8). Series: Historical American Biographies. 2000, Enslow LB $19.95 (0-7660-1252-2). This biography faithfully records the tragic life of Lincoln's widow, whose emotional health declined after the deaths of her son and her husband. (Rev: BL 1/1–15/00; HBG 10/00; SLJ 5/00) [921]

LOW, JULIETTE GORDON

13168 Brown, Fern G. *Daisy and the Girl Scouts: The Story of Juliette Gordon Low* (4–6). Illus. 1996, Albert Whitman LB $14.95 (0-8075-1440-3). 112pp. Juliette Gordon Low led a pampered young life but went on to found what became the Girl Scouts. (Rev: BL 5/1/96; SLJ 5/96) [921]

MADISON, DOLLEY

13169 Flanagan, Alice K. *Dolley Payne Todd Madison* (4–6). Illus. Series: Encyclopedia of First Ladies. 1998, Children's LB $33.00 (0-516-20642-7). 112pp. This is the story of the First Lady who showed good common sense and courage while enjoying her role as official hostess of the White House. (Rev: BL 7/98; HBG 10/98; SLJ 7/98) [921]

13170 Pflueger, Lynda. *Dolley Madison: Courageous First Lady* (5–8). Series: Historical American Biographies. 1999, Enslow LB $19.95 (0-7660-1092-9). 128pp. The story of the charming First Lady who added a new dimension to the role. (Rev: SLJ 1/99) [921]

NIXON, PATRICIA RYAN

13171 Feinberg, Barbara S. *Patricia Ryan Nixon* (4–6). Series: Encyclopedia of First Ladies. 1998, Children's LB $33.00 (0-516-20482-3). 122pp. Against the background of political events associated with President Nixon's career, this biography highlights First Lady Pat Nixon's accomplishments and devotion to her husband. (Rev: BL 7/98; HBG 10/98) [921]

ONASSIS, JACQUELINE KENNEDY

13172 Anderson, Catherine C. *Jackie Kennedy Onassis* (4–7). Illus. 1995, Lerner LB $21.27 (0-8225-2885-1); paper $6.95 (0-8225-9714-4). 88pp. An adoring biography of the former First Lady, who was a model of courage and dignity. (Rev: BL 2/1/96) [921]

13173 Santow, Dan. *Jacqueline Bouvier Kennedy Onassis* (4–6). Series: Encyclopedia of First Ladies. 1998, Children's LB $33.00 (0-516-20477-7). A biography of this glamorous First Lady that highlights her years in the White House. (Rev: BL 8/98; HBG 3/99) [921]

PALMER, CISSIE

13174 Alter, Judith. *Cissie Palmer: Putting Wealth to Work* (3–5). Illus. Series: Community Builders. 1998, Children's LB $23.00 (0-516-20972-8). 48pp. The story of little-known Cissie Palmer, a resident of Chicago, who was an early advocate for women's rights and used her money to create a display of women's accomplishments for the 1893 Columbian Exhibition. (Rev: BL 1/1–15/99; HBG 3/99; SLJ 2/99) [921]

POLK, SARAH CHILDRESS

13175 Sinnott, Susan. *Sarah Childress Polk, 1803–1891* (4–6). Illus. Series: Encyclopedia of First Ladies. 1998, Children's LB $33.00 (0-516-20601-X). 112pp. A well-illustrated account, using many period paintings and engravings, of the life of this First Lady who was noted for her graciousness and integrity. (Rev: BL 7/98; HBG 10/98) [921]

RICHARDS, ANN

13176 Siegel, Dorothy S. *Ann Richards: Politician, Feminist, Survivor* (4–7). Illus. Series: People to Know. 1996, Enslow LB $20.95 (0-89490-497-3). 112pp. In a conversational style, this biography covers the important events in the life of this Texas politician. (Rev: BL 5/15/96; SLJ 10/96) [921]

ROOSEVELT, EDITH

13177 Feinberg, Barbara S. *Edith Kermit Carow Roosevelt* (4–6). Series: Encyclopedia of First Ladies. 1999, Children's LB $33.00 (0-516-21001-7). 112pp. This is the biography of Theodore Roosevelt's second wife, who married him in 1886 and had five children. (Rev: BL 9/15/99) [921]

ROOSEVELT, ELEANOR

13178 Adler, David A. *A Picture Book of Eleanor Roosevelt* (K–3). Illus. by Robert Casilla. Series: Picture Book Biographies. 1991, Holiday LB $16.95 (0-8234-0856-6). 32pp. The life of this well-known First Lady is described in simple text and many illustrations. (Rev: BCCB 4/91; BL 6/1/91; SLJ 5/91) [921]

13179 Cooney, Barbara. *Eleanor* (K–3). Illus. 1996, Viking $15.99 (0-670-86159-6). 40pp. A picture book biography that supplies details on Eleanor Roosevelt's life, particularly her lonely childhood. (Rev: BCCB 11/96; BL 9/15/96*; HB 9–10/96; SLJ 9/96*) [921]

13180 Faber, Doris. *Eleanor Roosevelt: First Lady to the World* (5–7). Illus. by Donna Ruff. 1986, Puffin paper $4.99 (0-14-032103-9). 64pp. Eleanor Roosevelt's life before and after FDR is discussed. (Rev: BL 9/1/85; HB 9–10/85; SLJ 8/85)

13181 Gottfried, Ted. *Eleanor Roosevelt: First Lady of the Twentieth Century* (5–8). Illus. Series: Book Report Biographies. 1997, Watts LB $21.50 (0-531-11406-6). 112pp. A short, useful biography that traces Eleanor Roosevelt's life and her lasting achievements. (Rev: BCCB 7–8/97; BL 11/15/97; HBG 3/98; SLJ 12/97) [921]

13182 Kulling, Monica. *Eleanor Everywhere: The Life of Eleanor Roosevelt* (2–4). Illus. Series: Step into Reading. 1999, Random LB $11.99 (0-679-98996-X); paper $3.99 (0-679-88996-5). 32pp. An easily read, inspirational biography of the ugly duckling who married a president and became a much-admired world leader in her own right. (Rev: BL 4/15/99; HBG 10/99; SLJ 7/99) [921]

13183 Lazo, Caroline. *Eleanor Roosevelt* (4–7). Illus. Series: Peacemakers. 1993, Dillon $13.95 (0-87518-594-0). 64pp. A biography of the famous First Lady that focuses on her many lasting contributions, particularly in promoting world peace. (Rev: BL 12/15/93; SLJ 1/94) [921]

13184 Morey, Eileen. *Eleanor Roosevelt* (4–8). Series: Importance Of. 1997, Lucent LB $17.96 (1-56006-086-7). 96pp. The career of this famous First Lady and her many achievements fighting for world peace. (Rev: BCCB 7–8/97; BL 10/15/97; SLJ 12/97) [921]

13185 Weidt, Maryann N. *Stateswoman to the World: A Story About Eleanor Roosevelt* (4–6). Illus. by Lydia M. Anderson. 1991, Carolrhoda LB $21.27 (0-87614-663-9). 64pp. A frank biography of the First Lady so admired and respected throughout the world. (Rev: BL 12/15/91; SLJ 12/91) [921]

13186 Westervelt, Virginia Veeder. *Here Comes Eleanor: A New Biography of Eleanor Roosevelt for Young People* (5–7). Series: Avisson Young Adult. 1999, Avisson paper $16.00 (1-888105-33-X). 142pp. A clear account of the life of Eleanor Roosevelt that gives a fine assessment of her contributions. (Rev: SLJ 7/99) [921]

13187 Winget, Mary. *Eleanor Roosevelt* (5–8). Series: A&E Biography. 2000, Lerner LB $19.96 (0-8225-4985-9). 112pp. Growing up in a troubled but loving family, Eleanor Roosevelt showed that an ordinary woman can achieve greatness. (Rev: BL 3/1/01) [921]

ROSS, BETSY

13188 Miller, Susan Martins. *Betsy Ross: American Patriot* (3–6). Series: Revolutionary War Leaders. 2000, Chelsea LB $16.95 (0-7910-5360-1). 80pp. The story of the Quaker seamstress who went on to create the most recognized symbol of the United States. (Rev: HBG 10/00; SLJ 5/00) [921]

13189 St. George, Judith. *Betsy Ross: Patriot of Philadelphia* (3–6). Illus. 1997, Holt $15.95 (0-8050-5439-1). 118pp. A biography of Betsy Ross that tells of her childhood as a Quaker in Philadelphia as well as the meeting with George Washington that led to making our first flag. (Rev: BL 1/1–15/98; SLJ 2/98) [921]

13190 Wallner, Alexandra. *Betsy Ross* (K–3). Illus. 1994, Holiday LB $16.95 (0-8234-1071-4). 32pp. A biography of the famous seamstress who advised General Washington on the nature of the nation's first flag and ran the family business until her death in 1836. (Rev: BCCB 3/94; BL 2/15/94; SLJ 4/94) [921]

SAMPSON, DEBORAH

13191 McGovern, Ann. *The Secret Soldier: The Story of Deborah Sampson* (4–6). Illus. by Ann Grifalconi. 1987, Macmillan paper $4.50 (0-590-43052-1). 64pp. The story of the woman who disguised herself as a man and joined the Continental army. A reissue.

STANTON, ELIZABETH CADY

13192 Fritz, Jean. *You Want Women to Vote, Lizzie Stanton?* (4–7). Illus. 1995, Putnam $16.99 (0-399-22786-5). 96pp. An exciting, witty re-creation of the life of Elizabeth Cady Stanton, fighter for women's rights, including suffrage. (Rev: BCCB 10/95; BL 8/95*; SLJ 9/95*) [921]

13193 Loos, Pamela. *Elizabeth Cady Stanton* (5–8). Illus. Series: Women of Achievement. 2000, Chelsea $19.95 (0-7910-5293-1). 120pp. Drawing largely on Stanton's autobiography, this is the life story of the well-known suffragist of the 19th century. (Rev: BL 2/15/01) [921]

13194 Swain, Gwenyth. *The Road to Seneca Falls* (3–6). Illus. Series: Creative Minds. 1996, Carolrhoda LB $21.27 (0-87614-947-6); paper $5.95 (1-57505-025-0). 64pp. This biography of Elizabeth Cady Stanton chronicles the birth of the women's rights movement. (Rev: BL 2/15/97; SLJ 3/97) [921]

STEINEM, GLORIA

13195 Hoff, Mary. *Gloria Steinem: The Women's Movement* (4–6). Illus. Series: New Directions. 1991, Millbrook LB $21.90 (1-878841-19-X). 96pp. The life story of this journalist who questioned women's roles in modern society. (Rev: SLJ 4/91) [921]

13196 Lazo, Caroline. *Gloria Steinem: Feminist Extraordinaire* (5–7). Illus. Series: Lerner Biographies. 1998, Lerner LB $17.95 (0-8225-4934-4). 128pp. The story of Steinem, who overcame a troubled childhood to become a great humanitarian, writer, and leader of the feminist movement. (Rev: BL 7/98) [921]

STONE, LUCY

13197 McPherson, Stephanie S. *I Speak for the Women: A Story About Lucy Stone* (4–6). Illus. by Brian Liedahl. Series: Creative Minds. 1992, Carolrhoda LB $19.93 (0-87614-740-6). 64pp. The life of a dedicated abolitionist and champion of women's rights in 19th-century America. (Rev: BCCB 3/93; BL 3/15/93; SLJ 2/93) [921]

WASHINGTON, MARTHA

13198 McPherson, Stephanie S. *Martha Washington: First Lady* (4–6). Illus. Series: Historical American Biographies. 1998, Enslow LB $19.95 (0-7660-1017-1). 128pp. Using many period paintings and contemporary photos, this book traces the life of Martha Washington, her two marriages, and her private and public lives. (Rev: BL 1/1–15/99) [921]

13199 Simon, Charnan. *Martha Dandridge Curtis Washington* (4–6). Series: Encyclopedia of First Ladies. 2000, Children's LB $33.00 (0-516-20480-7). 112pp. The life and accomplishments of the first First Lady are covered, with material on the social and political history of her time. (Rev: BL 6/1–15/00) [921]

WASHINGTON, MARY BALL

13200 Fritz, Jean. *George Washington's Mother* (2–3). Illus. by DyAnne DiSalvo-Ryan. 1992, Putnam paper $3.95 (0-448-40384-6). 48pp. A simple biography of Mary Ball Washington, the mother of the first president. (Rev: BL 10/1/92; SLJ 10/92) [921]

Scientists, Inventors, and Naturalists

Collective

13201 Aaseng, Nathan. *Business Builders in Computers* (5–8). Illus. Series: Business Building. 2000, Oliver LB $19.95 (1-881508-57-9). 160pp. This book profiles six individuals and one set of partners who have dominated the computer world, including Thomas Watson, Jr., Bill Gates, Steve Jobs, and Steve Case. (Rev: BL 2/1/01) [920]

13202 Aaseng, Nathan. *Construction: Building the Impossible* (5–9). Illus. 2000, Oliver LB $19.95 (1-881508-59-5). 144pp. This book profiles eight famous builders — from Imhotep, who built the first stone pyramids in Egypt, to Frank Crowe, the visionary behind the Hoover Dam. (Rev: BL 5/1/00; HBG 10/00) [920]

13203 Archer, Jules. *To Save the Earth: The American Environmental Movement* (5–9). 1998, Viking $17.99 (0-670-87121-4). 198pp. A history of the environmentalist movement in this country is revealed in the biographies of four key individuals: John Muir, Rachel Carson, David McTaggart, and Dave Foreman. (Rev: HBG 3/99; SLJ 12/98) [920]

13204 Camp, Carole Ann. *American Astronomers: Searchers and Wonderers* (5–7). Illus. Series: Collective Biographies. 1996, Enslow LB $20.95 (0-89490-631-3). 104pp. Profiles with accompanying photos of nine important American astronomers, including Maria Mitchell, Edwin Hubble, and Carl Sagan. (Rev: BL 4/15/96; SLJ 5/96) [920]

13205 Clements, Gillian. *The Picture History of Great Inventors* (4–6). Illus. by author. 1994, Knopf $13.00 (0-679-84787-1). 77pp. A series of thumbnail sketches of some of the great inventors of the Western world and their inventions. (Rev: SLJ 7/94) [920]

13206 Cox, Clinton. *African American Healers* (4–7). Illus. Series: Black Stars. 1999, Wiley $22.95 (0-471-24650-6). 164pp. Using entries of two to three pages each, this work profiles more than 20 African Americans who have achieved prominence

in medicine and related areas. (Rev: BL 2/15/00; HBG 10/00) [910]

13207 De Angelis, Gina. *Science and Medicine* (5–8). Series: Female Firsts in Their Fields. 1999, Chelsea LB $16.95 (0-7910-5143-9). 64pp. The six women who are profiled in this standard account on medical achievements are Elizabeth Blackwell, Clara Barton, Marie Curie, Margaret Mead, Rachel Carson, and Antonia Novello. (Rev: HBG 10/99; SLJ 9/99) [920]

13208 Faber, Doris, and Harold Faber. *Nature and the Environment* (5–8). Series: Great Lives. 1991, Macmillan $22.95 (0-684-19047-8). 288pp. This book explores the lives of some of the great naturalists and conservationists. (Rev: BL 6/1/91; HB 7–8/91; SLJ 10/91) [920]

13209 Fradin, Dennis B. *"We Have Conquered Pain": The Discovery of Anesthesia* (5–8). Illus. 1996, Simon & Schuster paper $16.00 (0-689-50587-6). 145pp. The story of four 19th-century doctors, each of whom claimed to have developed anesthesia. (Rev: BCCB 6/96; BL 5/15/96; HB 9–10/96; SLJ 5/96) [920]

13210 Hacker, Carlotta. *Scientists* (3–6). Series: Women in Profile. 1998, Crabtree LB $21.28 (0-7787-0006-2); paper $8.95 (0-7787-0028-3). 48pp. This collection focuses on six female scientists, with about a dozen shorter sketches of others. (Rev: SLJ 9/98) [920]

13211 Harris, Laurie L., ed. *Biography Today: Profiles of People of Interest to Young Readers* (4–7). Illus. Series: Scientists and Inventors. 1996, Omnigraphics LB $38.00 (0-7808-0068-0). 194pp. Profiles of 14 important contemporaries like Carl Sagan and Jane Goodall with some lesser-known figures like geneticist and AIDS fighter Mathilde Krim. (Rev: SLJ 2/97) [920]

13212 Hunter, Shaun. *Leaders in Medicine* (3–6). Illus. Series: Women in Profile. 1999, Crabtree LB $15.96 (0-7787-0010-0); paper $8.06 (0-7787-0032-1). 48pp. Maria Montessori, Helen Taussig, and Elisabeth Kubler-Ross are among the women featured in this collective biography that contains six long profiles and 15 thumbnail sketches of famous women involved in medicine. (Rev: BL 9/15/99; SLJ 8/99) [920]

13213 Jones, Lynda. *Great Black Heroes: Five Brilliant Scientists* (2–3). Illus. by Ron Garnett. Series: Hello Reader! 2000, Scholastic paper $3.99 (0-590-48031-6). 48pp. This easy-to-read book profiles five African American scientists, among them Ernest Just, a marine biologist, and Percy Lavon Julian, a chemist. (Rev: BL 7/00; SLJ 8/00) [920]

13214 Keene, Ann T. *Earthkeepers: Observers and Protectors of Nature* (4–8). Illus. 1993, Oxford $35.00 (0-19-507867-5). 222pp. Profiles are given for more than 40 people throughout history who have worked to preserve the environment, beginning with the self-educated botanist John Bartram, who worked in the 1700s. (Rev: HB 11–12/93; SLJ 8/94*) [920]

13215 Kent, Jacqueline C. *Women in Medicine* (4–6). Series: Profiles. 1998, Oliver LB $16.95 (1-881508-46-3). 160pp. A collective biography of eight American women pioneers in medicine, including Elizabeth Blackwell, May Edward Chinn, and Dorothy Lavinia Brown. (Rev: SLJ 10/98) [920]

13216 Krensky, Stephen. *Four Against the Odds: The Struggle to Save Our Environment* (5–8). 1992, Scholastic paper $3.50 (0-590-44743-2). 112pp. The work of conservationists John Muir, Chico Mendes, Rachel Carson, and Lois Gibb is discussed. (Rev: BL 6/1/92; SLJ 10/92) [920]

13217 McClure, Judy. *Healers and Researchers: Physicians, Biologists, Social Scientists* (5–9). Series: Remarkable Women: Past and Present. 2000, Raintree Steck-Vaughn LB $28.54 (0-8172-5734-9). 80pp. This book profiles 150 women from the scientific community including Barbara McClintock, Anna Freud, Jocelyn Elders, and Sushila Nyir. (Rev: SLJ 8/00) [920]

13218 Mulcahy, Robert. *Medical Technology: Inventing the Instruments* (5–8). Illus. Series: Innovators. 1997, Oliver LB $19.95 (1-881508-34-X). 144pp. Seven short biographies of scientists who were responsible for such inventions as the X-ray, stethoscope, thermometer, and electrocardiograph. (Rev: BCCB 7–8/97; SLJ 7/97) [920]

13219 Pflaum, Rosalynd. *Marie Curie and Her Daughter Irene* (4–6). Illus. 1993, Lerner LB $25.26 (0-8225-4915-8). 144pp. A biography outlining the splendid teamwork of mother and daughter that resulted in three Nobel prizes. (Rev: SLJ 6/93) [920]

13220 Polking, Kirk. *Oceanographers and Explorers of the Sea* (5–8). Series: Collective Biographies. 1999, Enslow LB $19.95 (0-7660-1113-5). 128pp. Profiles are given of ten 20th-century American oceanographers including Robert Ballard, Eugenie Clark, and Sylvia Earle. (Rev: SLJ 9/99) [920]

13221 Stanley, Phyllis M. *American Environmental Heroes* (4–7). Illus. 1996, Enslow LB $20.95 (0-89490-630-5). 128pp. John Muir, Barry Commoner, Sylvia Earle, and seven other environmentalists are profiled. (Rev: BL 9/1/96; SLJ 7/96) [920]

13222 Sullivan, Otha Richard. *African American Inventors* (5–8). Illus. 1998, Wiley $19.95 (0-471-14804-0). 176pp. This book not only highlights the work of such well-known African American inventors as Benjamin Banneker and Madame C. J. Walker but also includes less familiar individuals such as John Moon, who developed floppy disks, and Dr. Charles Drew, whose research laid the basis for blood donation. (Rev: BL 7/98) [920]

13223 Weitzman, David. *Great Lives: Human Culture* (4–6). Illus. Series: Great Lives. 1994, Scribners $22.95 (0-684-19438-4). 294pp. An exhilarating collective biography of 27 archaeologists and anthropologists including Ruth Benedict, Franz Boas, Jane Goodall, and Zora Neale Hurston. (Rev: SLJ 4/95) [920]

13224 Wilkinson, Philip, and Michael Pollard. *Scientists Who Changed the World* (3–5). Illus. by Robert Ingpen. Series: Turning Points. 1994, Chelsea LB $19.95 (0-7910-2763-5). 93pp. Twenty brief biographies of scientists, including Galileo, Marie Curie, DNA decoders, and the first men on the moon. (Rev: BL 12/1/94) [920]

Individual

ANDREESSEN, MARC

13225 Ehrenhaft, Daniel. *Marc Andreessen: Web Warrior* (5–8). Illus. Series: The Techies. 2001, Twenty-First Century LB $21.90 (0-7613-1964-6). 80pp. This biography introduces Marc Andreessen, who coauthored the Web-browsing software Mosaic, cofounded the firm Netscape, and was a multimillionaire at age 24. (Rev: BL 3/15/01) [921]

ANDREWS, ROY CHAPMAN

13226 Bausum, Ann. *Dragon Bones and Dinosaur Eggs: A Photobiography of Explorer Roy Chapman Andrews* (5–8). Illus. 2000, National Geographic $17.95 (0-7922-7123-8). 48pp. A biography of the famous paleontologist who made several important dinosaur discoveries in central Asia and later became director of the American Museum of Natural History in New York City. (Rev: BCCB 5/00*; BL 3/15/00; HBG 10/00; SLJ 3/00) [921]

ANNING, MARY

13227 Anholt, Laurence. *Stone Girl, Bone Girl: The Story of Mary Anning* (K–3). Illus. by Sheila Moxley. 1999, Orchard $15.95 (0-531-30148-6). 32pp. The story of the 12-year-old British fossil hunter who discovered the skeleton of a huge sea creature, 165 million years old, in the limestone cliffs near Lyme Regis, Dorset. (Rev: BCCB 2/99; BL 2/1/99*; HBG 10/99; SLJ 5/99) [921]

13228 Atkins, Jeannine. *Mary Anning and the Sea Dragon* (K–4). Illus. by Michael Dooling. 1999, Farrar $16.00 (0-374-34840-5). 32pp. A picture book that tells of the exciting life of fossil hunter Mary Anning and her discoveries. (Rev: BL 9/1/99; HBG 3/00; SLJ 10/99) [560]

13229 Brighton, Catherine. *The Fossil Girl: Mary Anning's Dinosaur Discovery* (2–4). Illus. by author. 1999, Millbrook LB $21.40 (0-7613-1468-7). Born in 1799, Mary Anning was the amazing youngster who discovered and studied fossils, including an enormous creature embedded in rock that she found close to her English coastal home. (Rev: HBG 10/99; SLJ 5/99) [921]

13230 Brown, Don. *Rare Treasure: Mary Anning and Her Remarkable Discoveries* (K–3). Illus. 1999, Houghton $15.00 (0-395-92286-0). 32pp. This picture-book biography of Mary Anning's life emphasizes her fossil discoveries in England at the beginning of the 18th century. (Rev: BCCB 1/00; BL 11/15/99; HBG 10/99; SLJ 10/99) [921]

13231 Walker, Sally M. *Mary Anning: Fossil Hunter* (2–3). Series: On My Own. 2000, Carolrhoda LB $19.93 (1-57505-425-6). 48pp. Using many original documents as sources, this simple biography tells the life story of Mary Anning, who hunted for fossils on the cliffs of Lyme Regis in England. (Rev: BL 8/00; HBG 3/01; SLJ 12/00) [921]

BAIRD, JOHN LOGIE

13232 Reid, Struan. *John Logie Baird* (4–6). Series: Groundbreakers. 2000, Heinemann LB $25.64 (1-57572-372-7). 48pp. The ground-breaking inventor of television is featured in this biography that tells of his poor health and his many setbacks. (Rev: HBG 3/01; SLJ 3/01) [921]

BANNEKER, BENJAMIN

13233 Ferris, Jeri. *What Are You Figuring Now? A Story About Benjamin Banneker* (3–6). Illus. 1988, Lerner LB $21.27 (0-87614-331-1); Carolrhoda paper $5.95 (0-87614-521-7). 56pp. The life of this African American who was a math whiz. (Rev: BL 1/1/89; SLJ 2/89)

13234 Marupin, Melissa. *Benjamin Banneker* (4–6). Series: Journey to Freedom. 1999, Child's World LB $16.95 (1-56766-618-3). 32pp. The story of the famous 18th-century author and mathematician who produced the first scientific publication by an African American. (Rev: BL 10/15/99; HBG 3/00; SLJ 4/00) [921]

13235 Pinkney, Andrea D. *Dear Benjamin Banneker* (1–4). Illus. by Brian Pinkney. 1994, Harcourt $16.00 (0-15-200417-3). 32pp. Born into a family of freed slaves, Banneker became an important astronomer and corresponded with Thomas Jefferson. (Rev: BCCB 11/94; BL 9/15/94; SLJ 11/94) [921]

BELL, ALEXANDER GRAHAM

13236 Fisher, Leonard Everett. *Alexander Graham Bell* (3–5). Illus. 1999, Simon & Schuster $16.00 (0-689-81607-3). 32pp. Using an illustrated, large-book format, this account traces the life and accomplishments of the famous inventor. (Rev: BL 3/15/99; HB 7–8/99; HBG 10/99) [921]

13237 Lewis, Cynthia C. *Hello, Alexander Graham Bell Speaking* (4–7). Illus. Series: Taking Part. 1991, Macmillan LB $13.95 (0-87518-461-8). 64pp.

This inventor studied human speech and created one of the greatest means of communication, the telephone. (Rev: BL 9/1/91; SLJ 12/91) [921]

13238 MacLeod, Elizabeth. *Alexander Graham Bell: An Inventive Life* (4–6). Illus. 1999, Kids Can $12.95 (1-55074-456-9); paper $5.95 (1-55074-458-5). 32pp. A series of double-page spreads cover Bell's invention of the telephone, his experiments building airplanes, and summers spent with his family on Cape Breton Island. (Rev: BL 4/15/99; HBG 10/99; SLJ 5/99) [921]

13239 Matthews, Tom L. *Always Inventing: A Photobiography of Alexander Graham Bell* (3–6). Illus. 1999, National Geographic $16.99 (0-7922-7391-5). 64pp. A large-format book filled with period photographs tells about the inventor of the telephone and his many other interests and contributions. (Rev: BL 6/1–15/99; HB 7–8/99; HBG 10/99; SLJ 3/99) [921]

13240 Pollard, Michael. *Alexander Graham Bell: Father of Modern Communication* (5–7). Series: Giants of Science. 2000, Blackbirch LB $19.95 (1-56711-334-6). 64pp. Known primarily for the invention of the telephone, Bell also invented the first hydrofoil, an air-conditioning system, and an early fax machine. (Rev: BL 1/1–15/01; HBG 3/01) [921]

13241 Reid, Struan. *Alexander Graham Bell* (4–6). Series: Groundbreakers. 2000, Heinemann LB $25.64 (1-57572-366-2). 48pp. This biography of Bell covers the invention of the telephone plus other innovations he pioneered and his important work with the deaf. (Rev: SLJ 3/01) [921]

BLACKWELL, ELIZABETH

13242 Peck, Ira. *Elizabeth Blackwell: The First Woman Doctor* (4–5). Illus. 2000, Millbrook $21.90 (0-7613-1854-2). 48pp. This solid biography tells the story of the first woman to graduate from medical school in the United States and of her many accomplishments in her field. (Rev: BL 9/15/00) [921]

BURROUGHS, JOHN

13243 Wadsworth, Ginger. *John Burroughs: The Sage of Slabsides* (5–8). Illus. 1997, Clarion $16.95 (0-395-77830-1). 95pp. A biography of the American naturalist and essayist who lived in a cabin in the Catskill Mountains and wrote about his observations. (Rev: BCCB 5/97; BL 3/15/97; HB 7–8/97; SLJ 5/97) [921]

CARSON, RACHEL

13244 Harlan, Judith. *Sounding the Alarm: A Biography of Rachel Carson* (5–7). Illus. Series: People in Focus. 1989, Macmillan LB $13.95 (0-87518-407-3). 128pp. A good account of this founder of the modern ecology movement. (Rev: BL 10/1/89; SLJ 11/89) [921]

13245 Henricksson, John. *Rachel Carson: The Environmental Movement* (4–6). Illus. Series: New Directions. 1991, Millbrook paper $5.95 (1-56294-833-4). 96pp. A well-researched account of the life of the woman who opened up the topic of conservation. (Rev: SLJ 5/91) [921]

13246 Kudlinski, Kathleen V. *Rachel Carson: Pioneer of Ecology* (3–6). Illus. 1988, Puffin paper $4.99 (0-14-032242-6). 64pp. The life of the famous nature writer and environmentalist, born in 1907. (Rev: BL 3/15/88; SLJ 8/88) [921]

13247 Presnall, Judith J. *Rachel Carson* (4–8). Illus. Series: The Importance Of. 1995, Lucent LB $17.96 (1-56006-052-2). 96pp. The life of this innovative scientist whose writings, including *Silent Spring*, made the world aware of conservation and the erosion of our environment. (Rev: BL 1/15/95; SLJ 1/95) [921]

13248 Ransom, Candice. *Listening to Crickets: A Story About Rachel Carson* (3–5). Illus. by Shelly O. Haas. 1993, Carolrhoda LB $21.27 (0-87614-727-9). 64pp. Beginning with her childhood, this account traces the life of the woman who helped make millions aware of the destruction of their environment. (Rev: BL 5/15/93; SLJ 7/93) [921]

13249 Ring, Elizabeth. *Rachel Carson: Caring for the Earth* (3–5). Illus. Series: Eyewitness Juniors. 1992, Millbrook LB $19.90 (1-56294-056-2). 48pp. The story of the pioneer conservationist whose book Silent Spring influenced a whole generation. (Rev: BL 8/92; SLJ 11/92) [921]

13250 Wadsworth, Ginger. *Rachel Carson: Voice for the Earth* (5–7). Illus. Series: Lerner Biographies. 1992, Lerner LB $25.26 (0-8225-4907-7). 128pp. The life and work of the conservationist and author, best known for Silent Spring. (Rev: BL 6/1/92; HB 7–8/92; SLJ 7/92) [921]

CARVER, GEORGE WASHINGTON

13251 Adler, David A. *A Picture Book of George Washington Carver* (2–4). Illus. by Dan Brown. Series: Picture Book Biographies. 1999, Holiday $15.95 (0-8234-1429-9). A biography of this famous scientist with an emphasis on his private life and the racism he encountered. (Rev: BL 4/15/99; HBG 10/99; SLJ 5/99) [921]

13252 Benge, Janet, and Geoff Benge. *George Washington Carver, What Do You See?* (3–4). Illus. by Kennon James. Series: Another Great Achiever. 1997, Advance Publg. LB $14.95 (1-57537-102-2). 48pp. This biography stresses Carver's humanity, inventiveness, and deep religious faith. (Rev: SLJ 8/97) [921]

13253 Carey, Charles W. *George Washington Carver* (4–6). Series: Journey to Freedom. 1999, Child's World LB $16.95 (1-56766-569-1). 40pp. Using plenty of illustrations and interesting sidebars, this biography covers the life-shaping events of the great African American scientist. (Rev: BL 7/99; HBG 10/99; SLJ 7/99) [921]

13254 Carter, Andy, and Carol Saller. *George Washington Carver* (2–3). Series: On My Own. 2000, Carolrhoda LB $19.93 (1-57505-427-2); paper $5.95 (1-57505-458-2). 48pp. Born a slave near the end of the Civil War, Carver became famous for helping farmers grow better crops while sharing with them his love of nature. (Rev: BL 8/00; HBG 3/01) [921]

13255 McKissack, Patricia, and Fredrick McKissack. *George Washington Carver: The Peanut Scientist* (2–4). Illus. by Ned Ostendorf. Series: Great African Americans. 1991, Enslow LB $14.95 (0-89490-308-X). 32pp. More than the inventor of peanut butter, this scientist helped revive the economy of the South after the Civil War. (Rev: SLJ 2/92) [921]

13256 Mitchell, Barbara. *A Pocketful of Goobers: A Story About George Washington Carver* (3–5). Illus. 1986, Carolrhoda LB $21.27 (0-87614-292-7); Lerner paper $5.95 (0-87614-474-1). 64pp. An introductory biography partly fictionalized, with much information on Carver's research with peanuts. (Rev: BL 8/86; SLJ 9/86)

13257 Riley, John. *George Washington Carver: A Photo Biography* (1–3). Series: First Biographies. 2000, Morgan Reynolds LB $15.95 (1-883846-62-5). 24pp. With full-page pictures and a simple text this is a biography of the great African American scientist for beginning readers. (Rev: HBG 10/00; SLJ 8/00) [921]

CLARK, EUGENIE

13258 Butts, Ellen R., and Joyce R. Schwartz. *Eugenie Clark: Adventures of a Shark Scientist* (5–8). Illus. 2000, Linnet $19.50 (0-208-02440-9). 107pp. An interesting biography of a contemporary American scientist — an ichthyologist who has produced some startling research on sharks. (Rev: BCCB 2/00; BL 2/15/00; HBG 10/00; SLJ 7/00) [921]

13259 Ross, Michael. *Fish Watching with Eugenie Clark* (3–5). Series: Naturalist's Apprentice. 2000, Lerner LB $19.93 (1-57505-384-5). 48pp. This American scientist of Japanese ancestry has been fascinated by fish since childhood and has turned her interest into a groundbreaking scientific career. (Rev: BL 8/00; HBG 10/00; SLJ 7/00) [921]

CURIE, MARIE

13260 Birch, Beverley. *Marie Curie: Courageous Pioneer in the Study of Radioactivity* (5–7). Illus. Series: Giants of Science. 2000, Blackbirch LB $19.95 (1-56711-333-8). 64pp. This biography of Marie Curie covers her youth, the struggles to get an education, her marriage, and her scientific career and accomplishments. (Rev: BL 1/1–15/01; HBG 3/01) [921]

13261 Brandt, Keith. *Marie Curie: Brave Scientist* (3–5). Illus. by Karen Milone. 1983, Troll LB $17.25 (0-89375-855-8); paper $3.95 (0-89375-856-6). 48pp. An account that emphasizes the struggle before eventual success. [921]

13262 Fisher, Leonard Everett. *Marie Curie* (3–6). Illus. 1994, Macmillan paper $14.95 (0-02-735375-3). 32pp. This biography tells of Madame Curie's childhood and her struggle for recognition and the honors bestowed on her in later life. (Rev: BL 9/15/94; SLJ 10/94) [921]

13263 Poynter, Margaret. *Marie Curie: Discoverer of Radium* (4–7). Illus. Series: Great Minds of Science. 1994, Enslow LB $20.95 (0-89490-477-9). 128pp. The life and significance of this discoverer of radium are covered, with a chapter of suggested activities. (Rev: BL 1/1/95; SLJ 10/94) [921]

DARWIN, CHARLES

13264 Anderson, Margaret J. *Charles Darwin: Naturalist* (4–7). Illus. Series: Great Minds of Science. 1994, Enslow LB $20.95 (0-89490-476-0). 128pp. In addition to a biography of this controversial naturalist, there is a chapter on activities for the reader. (Rev: BL 1/1/95; SLJ 10/94) [921]

13265 Fullick, Ann. *Charles Darwin* (4–6). Series: Groundbreakers. 2000, Heinemann LB $25.64 (1-57572-368-9). 48pp. This biography of the scientist who formulated the theory of evolution concentrates on his five-year voyage on the *H.M.S. Beagle*. (Rev: SLJ 2/01) [921]

DOUGLAS, MARJORY STONEMAN

13266 Sawyer, Kem Knapp. *Marjory Stoneman Douglas: Guardian of the Everglades* (6–8). Illus. by Leslie Carow. 1993, Discovery LB $14.95 (1-878668-20-X). 72pp. The life story of the courageous woman who spent years fighting to preserve the Florida Everglades. (Rev: SLJ 12/93) [921]

EARLE, SYLVIA

13267 Baker, Beth. *Sylvia Earle: Guardian of the Sea* (4–7). Illus. Series: Lerner Biographies. 2000, Lerner LB $25.26 (0-8225-4961-1). 112pp. This is a thrilling biography of the famous underwater explorer and marine scientist who was one of the first humans to swim with whales. (Rev: BL 10/15/00; HBG 3/01; SLJ 11/00) [921]

EASTMAN, CHARLES

13268 Ross, Michael E. *Wildlife Watching with Charles Eastman* (4–6). Illus. by Laurie A. Caple. Series: Naturalist's Apprentice. 1997, Carolrhoda LB $14.95 (1-57505-004-8). 48pp. Charles Eastman, who was born in 1858 in the Dakota Nation, became a physician and later used his childhood experiences to teach children to love and respect nature. (Rev: BL 5/15/98; HBG 3/98; SLJ 3/98) [921]

EASTWOOD, ALICE

13269 Ross, Michael E. *Flower Watching with Alice Eastwood* (3–5). Illus. Series: Naturalist's Apprentice. 1997, Carolrhoda LB $19.93 (1-57505-005-6). 46pp. This account of the life of Alice Eastwood — an African American who became an expert on the wildflowers of the Rockies and the West Coast — also gives tips to the amateur flower watcher. (Rev: BL 3/1/98; HBG 3/98; SLJ 3/98) [921]

EDISON, THOMAS ALVA

13270 Dolan, Ellen M. *Thomas Alva Edison: Inventor* (5–8). Series: Historical American Biographies. 1998, Enslow LB $19.95 (0-7660-1014-7). Direct quotations, fact boxes, a chronology, and chapter notes make this an attractive life of the great inventor. (Rev: BL 8/98) [921]

13271 Middleton, Haydn. *Thomas Edison* (1–3). Series: What's Their Story? 1998, Oxford LB $12.95 (0-19-521401-3). Large type and attractive illustrations are used to convey the essential facts about Edison and his accomplishments. (Rev: BL 5/15/98; HBG 10/98; SLJ 8/98) [921]

13272 Mitchell, Barbara. *The Wizard of Sound: A Story About Thomas Edison* (4–6). Illus. by Hetty Mitchell. Series: Creative Minds. 1991, Carolrhoda LB $21.27 (0-87614-445-8). 64pp. The story of how a shy, inept youngster became the inventor of wonders. (Rev: SLJ 1/92) [921]

13273 Sabin, Louis. *Thomas Alva Edison: Young Inventor* (3–5). Illus. by George Ulrich. 1983, Troll LB $17.25 (0-89375-841-8); paper $3.95 (0-89375-842-6). 48pp. An account that concentrates on Edison's childhood. [921]

13274 Sproule, Anna. *Thomas Edison: The World's Greatest Inventor* (5–7). Series: Giants of Science. 2000, Blackbirch LB $19.95 (1-56711-331-1). 64pp. A prolific inventor, Edison not only worked on the electric light bulb but also the phonograph, the movie projector, and an early answering machine. (Rev: BL 1/1–15/01; HBG 3/01) [921]

EINSTEIN, ALBERT

13275 MacDonald, Fiona. *Albert Einstein: The Genius Behind the Theory of Relativity* (5–7). Illus. Series: Giants of Science. 2000, Blackbirch LB $19.95 (1-56711-330-3). 64pp. As well as his childhood, education, theories, personal life, and international awards, this biography of Albert Einstein assesses his lasting contributions to physics and mathematics. (Rev: BL 1/1–15/01; HBG 3/01) [921]

13276 McPherson, Stephanie S. *Ordinary Genius: The Story of Albert Einstein* (4–7). Illus. 1995, Carolrhoda LB $23.93 (0-87614-788-0). 96pp. Good historical background information is given on the life of Einstein plus a clear explanation of his discoveries. (Rev: BL 6/1–15/95; SLJ 9/95) [921]

13277 Reef, Catherine. *Albert Einstein: Scientist of the 20th Century* (4–7). Illus. Series: Taking Part. 1991, Macmillan LB $13.95 (0-87518-462-6). 64pp. Einstein gave the world a new way of looking at time, space, gravity, and the nature of light. (Rev: BL 9/1/91; SLJ 12/91) [921]

ERICSSON, JOHN

13278 Brophy, Ann. *John Ericsson: The Inventions of War* (4–7). Illus. Series: The History of the Civil War. 1990, Silver Burdett paper $7.95 (0-382-24052-9). 135pp. In clear text, this is the life story of the Swedish engineer who designed and constructed the Monitor. (Rev: BL 9/1/91) [921]

FARNSWORTH, PHILO

13279 McPherson, Stephanie S. *TV's Forgotten Hero: The Story of Philo Farnsworth* (4–7). Illus. 1996, Carolrhoda LB $23.93 (1-57505-017-X). 96pp. The biography of the genius who invented electronic television when he was only 14. (Rev: BL 2/1/97; SLJ 2/97) [921]

FORD, HENRY

13280 Gourley, Catherine. *Wheels of Time: A Biography of Henry Ford* (3–8). 1997, Millbrook LB $20.90 (0-7613-0214-X). 47pp. Archival illustrations add a new dimension to this biography of the pioneer automobile manufacturer, written with the cooperation of the Henry Ford Museum. (Rev: HBG 10/98; SLJ 6/98) [921]

13281 Middleton, Haydn. *Henry Ford* (1–3). Series: What's Their Story? 1998, Oxford LB $12.95 (0-19-521406-4). The inventor of the motor car comes to life in this well-written biography of a man who changed the modern world and became its richest citizen. (Rev: BL 5/15/98; HBG 10/98; SLJ 8/98) [921]

13282 Mitchell, Barbara. *We'll Race You, Henry: A Story About Henry Ford* (3–5). Illus. 1986, Carolrhoda LB $21.27 (0-87614-291-9); Lerner paper $5.95 (0-87614-471-7). 64pp. The focus is on race-car ventures in this partly fictionalized biography. (Rev: BL 8/86; SLJ 9/86) [921]

13283 Schaefer, Lola M. *Henry Ford* (K–2). Series: Famous People in Transportation. 2000, Capstone LB $13.25 (0-7368-0546-X). 24pp. For beginning readers, this is a biography of Henry Ford that uses double-page spreads to present important facts about his life and accomplishments. (Rev: HBG 10/00; SLJ 9/00) [921]

FOSSEY, DIAN

13284 Matthews, Tom L. *Light Shining Through the Mist: A Photobiography of Dian Fossey* (4–6). Illus. 1998, National Geographic $17.95 (0-7922-7300-1). 64pp. An illustrated book relating the life and work of Dian Fossey, founder of the Karisoke Research Center in Rwanda, who studied mountain gorillas and worked to prevent poachers from killing off this endangered species. (Rev: BL 9/15/98; HB 9–10/98; HBG 3/99; SLJ 9/98) [921]

13285 Schott, Jane A. *Dian Fossey and the Mountain Gorillas* (2–3). Series: On My Own Biographies. 2000, Carolrhoda LB $19.93 (1-57505-082-X). 48pp. The exciting story one of the foremost primate researchers of the 20th century, her groundbreaking work observing mountain gorillas in their native habitat, and her efforts to stop their poaching. (Rev: BL 6/1–15/00; HBG 10/00; SLJ 6/00) [921]

FULTON, ROBERT

13286 Bowen, Andy Russell. *A Head Full of Notions: A Story About Robert Fulton* (4–6). Illus. 1997, Carolrhoda LB $19.93 (0-87614-876-3); paper $5.95 (1-57505-026-9). 64pp. A brief biography of the life and times of the man who worked first on plans for a submarine and then on his famous steamboat. (Rev: BL 4/15/97; SLJ 3/97) [921]

13287 Flammang, James M. *Robert Fulton: Inventor and Steamboat Builder* (5–8). Illus. Series: Historical American Biographies. 1999, Enslow LB $19.95 (0-7660-1141-0). 128pp. Beginning with Fulton's 1807 demonstration of his steamboat, this biography moves back and forth in time to trace the complete career of this man who changed America's transportation history. (Rev: BL 11/1/99; HBG 3/00) [921]

GALDIKAS, BIRUTE

13288 Gallardo, Evelyn. *Among the Orangutans: The Birute Galdikas Story* (4–7). Illus. Series: Great Naturalists. 1993, Chronicle paper $7.95 (0-8118-0408-9). 48pp. The story of this important primate specialist who began studying orangutans in 1971. (Rev: BL 4/1/93; SLJ 6/93) [921]

GALILEO

13289 Fisher, Leonard Everett. *Galileo* (3–6). Illus. 1992, Macmillan LB $17.00 (0-02-735235-8). 32pp. A narrative that stresses Galileo's genius as a mathematician and physicist as well as his contributions to astronomy. (Rev: BL 6/1/92; HB 7–8/92; SLJ 6/92) [921]

13290 Hightower, Paul. *Galileo: Astronomer and Physicist* (4–7). Illus. Series: Great Minds of Science. 1997, Enslow LB $20.95 (0-89490-787-5). 128pp. This biography not only includes material on the life and accomplishments of this courageous scientist but also contains several activities that give an understanding of his work. (Rev: BL 6/1–15/97) [921]

13291 Mitton, Jacqueline. *Galileo* (1–3). Series: What's Their Story? 1998, Oxford LB $12.95 (0-19-521405-6). Told in simple, engaging prose, with splendid color illustrations, this biography reveals how Galileo's work changed our view of the universe. (Rev: BL 5/15/98; HBG 10/98; SLJ 8/98) [921]

13292 Sis, Peter. *Starry Messenger* (4–6). Illus. 1996, Farrar $16.00 (0-374-37191-1). 32pp. The world of Galileo and his amazing life and accomplishments are re-created in this unusual picture book. (Rev: BCCB 11/96; BL 10/15/96*; SLJ 10/96*) [921]

13293 White, Michael. *Galileo Galilei: Inventor, Astronomer, and Rebel* (5–8). Series: Giants of Science. 1999, Blackbirch LB $18.95 (1-56711-325-7). 64pp. The dramatic story of Galileo's life, his persecutions, accomplishments, and lasting contributions to science. (Rev: HBG 10/00; SLJ 2/00) [921]

GATES, BILL

13294 Dickinson, Joan D. *Bill Gates* (4–6). Series: People to Know. 1997, Enslow LB $20.95 (0-89490-824-3). 104pp. A brief, interesting biography of this billionaire computer giant. (Rev: BL 10/15/97; HBG 3/98; SLJ 12/97) [921]

13295 Lesinski, Jeanne. *Bill Gates* (4–6). Series: A&E Biography. 2000, Lerner LB $25.26 (0-8225-4949-2). 112pp. The story of the man whose name has become synonymous with computers, software, and wealth. (Rev: BL 6/1–15/00; HBG 3/01; SLJ 9/00) [921]

13296 Sherman, Josepha. *Bill Gates: Computer King* (4–6). Series: Gateway Biographies. 2000, Millbrook LB $22.90 (0-7613-1771-6). 48pp. This book successfully tells the story of Bill Gates's life and gives a history of Microsoft. (Rev: HBG 3/01; SLJ 11/00) [921]

13297 Wukovits, John F. *Bill Gates: Software King* (4–6). Series: Book Report Biographies. 2000, Watts LB $22.00 (0-531-11669-7). 128pp. This biography of the world's richest man touches on topics including the Microsoft empire, Windows, partnerships with NBC, and numerous charities. (Rev: BL 11/15/00) [921]

GODDARD, ROBERT

13298 Streissguth, Thomas. *Rocket Man: The Story of Robert Goddard* (5–7). Illus. Series: Trailblazer. 1995, Carolrhoda LB $23.93 (0-87614-863-1). 88pp. A history of rocketry, with emphasis on the life and accomplishments of Goddard. (Rev: BL 10/15/95; SLJ 9/95) [921]

GOODALL, JANE

13299 Fromer, Julie. *Jane Goodall: Living with the Chimps* (2–5). Illus. by Antonio Castro. Series: Earth Keepers. 1992, Twenty-First Century LB $14.95 (0-8050-2116-7). 72pp. An easily read biography of the zoologist who studied chimpanzee societies in Africa. (Rev: BL 5/1/92; SLJ 6/92) [921]

13300 Goodall, Jane. *My Life with the Chimpanzees* (3–6). Illus. 1992, Houghton paper $11.04 (0-395-61849-5). The famed zoologist talks about her life studying the chimps of Africa. (Rev: BCCB 5/88; BL 7/88; SLJ 4/88)

13301 Pettit, Jayne. *Jane Goodall: Pioneer Researcher* (5–8). Series: Book Report Biographies. 1999, Watts LB $22.00 (0-531-11522-4). 128pp. A solid biography illustrated with black-and-white photos of the daring woman who accomplished groundbreaking research involving chimpanzees. (Rev: SLJ 11/99) [921]

13302 Pratt, Paula B. *Jane Goodall* (4–8). Illus. Series: The Importance Of. 1997, Lucent LB $17.96 (1-56006-082-4). 112pp. The story of the great naturalist who studied and protected the primates of Africa. (Rev: BL 1/1–15/97) [921]

13303 Sean, J. A. *Jane Goodall: Naturalist* (4–6). Illus. Series: Library of Famous Women. 1993, Blackbirch LB $17.95 (1-56711-010-X). 64pp. An accurate, engrossing account of the life of this great naturalist, who produced landmark studies on apes and their society. (Rev: BL 11/15/93; SLJ 2/94) [921]

GUTENBERG, JOHANN

13304 Burch, Joann J. *Fine Print: A Story About Johann Gutenberg* (3–6). Illus. by Kent A. Aldrich. 1991, Carolrhoda LB $21.27 (0-87614-682-5). 64pp. An account of the man who changed world history by inventing the process of printing books from movable type. (Rev: BL 1/1/92; SLJ 3/92) [686.2]

13305 Fisher, Leonard Everett. *Gutenberg* (1–5). Illus. 1993, Macmillan $14.95 (0-02-735238-2). 32pp. This is a picture book about the life and accomplishments of the early printer Johann Gutenberg. (Rev: BL 6/1–15/93; SLJ 8/93) [921]

HAMILTON, ALICE

13306 McPherson, Stephanie S. *The Workers' Detective: A Story About Dr. Alice Hamilton* (3–6). Illus. by Janet Schulz. Series: Creative Minds. 1992, Carolrhoda LB $21.27 (0-87614-699-X). 64pp. Introducing the woman who studied the effects of lead and other lethal materials on workers' health and changed industrial medicine. (Rev: BL 1/15/93; SLJ 10/92) [921]

HARVEY, WILLIAM

13307 Yount, Lisa. *William Harvey: Discoverer of How Blood Circulates* (4–8). Illus. Series: Great Minds of Science. 1994, Enslow LB $20.95 (0-89490-481-7). 128pp. A biography of the 17th-century scientist that describes early theories about the blood system and the importance of Harvey's discoveries. (Rev: SLJ 2/95) [921]

HAWKING, STEPHEN

13308 Henderson, Harry. *Stephen Hawking* (4–8). Illus. Series: The Importance Of. 1995, Lucent LB $26.50 (1-56006-050-6). 96pp. A lively account of this amazing scientist's life, his physical handicaps, and the effects of his theories on modern thought. (Rev: BL 1/15/95) [921]

HUBBLE, EDWIN

13309 Datnow, Claire. *Edwin Hubble: Discoverer of Galaxies* (4–8). Illus. Series: Great Minds of Science. 1997, Enslow LB $20.95 (0-89490-934-7). 128pp. A biography of the great astronomer, noted for his amazing scientific abilities and quirky pretentions. (Rev: BL 12/1/97; HBG 3/98; SLJ 3/98) [921]

JONES, FREDERICK MCKINLEY

13310 Swanson, Gloria M., and Margaret V. Ott. *I've Got an Idea! The Story of Frederick McKinley Jones* (3–6). Illus. 1994, Lerner LB $18.60 (0-8225-3174-7); paper $7.95 (0-8225-9662-8). 112pp. Jones was an amazing African American inventor credited with devising refrigeration units for trucks and box office ticket machines. (Rev: BL 6/1–15/94; SLJ 7/94) [921]

KENNY, ELIZABETH

13311 Crofford, Emily. *Healing Warrior: A Story About Sister Elizabeth Kenny* (3–6). Illus. by Steve Michaels. Series: Creative Minds. 1989, Carolrhoda LB $21.27 (0-87614-382-6). 64pp. The story of the Australian nurse renowned for her revolutionary therapy and rehabilitation work with polio patients. (Rev: BL 2/15/90; SLJ 3/90) [921]

LAVOISIER, ANTOINE

13312 Yount, Lisa. *Antoine Lavoisier: Founder of Modern Chemistry* (4–7). Illus. Series: Great Minds of Science. 1997, Enslow LB $20.95 (0-89490-785-9). 128pp. In addition to providing an assessment of the life and works of Lavoisier, called the Father of Chemistry, this book includes several hands-on activities that depend on an understanding of his work. (Rev: BL 6/1–15/97) [921]

LEAKEY, LOUIS AND MARY

13313 Poynter, Margaret. *The Leakeys: Uncovering the Origins of Humankind* (5–8). Illus. Series: Great Minds of Science. 1997, Enslow LB $20.95 (0-89490-788-3). 128pp. The story of the famous husband-and-wife team of scientists, Louis and Mary Leakey, and how they expanded our knowledge of evolution. (Rev: BL 12/1/97; HBG 3/98; SLJ 12/97) [921]

LEEUWENHOEK, ANTONI VAN

13314 Yount, Lisa. *Antoni van Leeuwenhoek: First to See Microscopic Life* (4–7). Illus. Series: Great Minds of Science. 1996, Enslow LB $20.95 (0-89490-680-1). 128pp. A brief biography of the Dutch maker of microscopes, who was the first to closely examine bacteria and blood cells. (Rev: BL 10/15/96; SLJ 12/96) [921]

LEOPOLD, ALDO

13315 Lorbiecki, Marybeth. *Of Things Natural, Wild, and Free: A Story About Aldo Leopold* (4–7). Illus. 1993, Carolrhoda LB $21.27 (0-87614-797-X). 64pp. The story of a man who was a great hunter until he realized the importance of the balance in nature, and then turned a tract of farmland into a nature refuge. (Rev: BL 11/1/93; SLJ 11/93) [921]

LINNAEUS, CARL

13316 Anderson, Margaret J. *Carl Linnaeus: Father of Classification* (5–7). Illus. Series: Great Minds of Science. 1997, Enslow LB $20.95 (0-89490-786-7). 128pp. Discusses the personal life of Linnaeus, including his explorations in Lapland, but it focuses on the development of his important biological classification system. (Rev: BL 12/1/97; HBG 3/98; SLJ 9/97) [921]

LOVELACE, ADA KING

13317 Wade, Mary D. *Ada Byron Lovelace: The Lady and the Computer* (5–8). Illus. 1995, Silver Burdett LB $13.95 (0-87518-598-3); paper $7.95 (0-382-24717-5). 128pp. A biography of the poet Byron's amazing daughter, who was a distinguished mathematician and pioneer computer programmer. (Rev: BL 5/1/95) [921]

MAYO, WILLIAM AND CHARLES

13318 Crofford, Emily. *Frontier Surgeons: A Story About the Mayo Brothers* (3–6). Illus. by Karen Ritz. Series: Creative Minds Biographies. 1989, Carolrhoda LB $21.27 (0-87614-381-8); paper $5.95 (0-87614-553-5). 56pp. The fascinating story of the brothers, William and Charles, who started what became a world-class medical facility. (Rev: BL 2/15/90; SLJ 3/90) [921]

13319 Davis, Lucile. *The Mayo Brothers: Doctors to the World* (3–5). Series: Community Builders. 1998, Children's LB $23.00 (0-516-20965-5). 48pp. The story of the physician brothers William and

Charles Mayo, founders of the famed Mayo Clinic in Rochester, Minnesota. (Rev: BL 1/1–15/99; HBG 3/99) [921]

MEAD, MARGARET

13320 Pollard, Michael. *Margaret Mead: Bringing World Cultures Together* (5–8). Series: Giants of Science. 1999, Blackbirch LB $18.95 (1-56711-327-3). 64pp. This biography stresses the contribution Margaret Mead made to anthropology through her work in the South Pacific. (Rev: HBG 10/00; SLJ 2/00) [921]

13321 Ziesk, Edra. *Margaret Mead* (5–8). Illus. Series: American Women of Achievement. 1990, Chelsea LB $19.95 (1-55546-667-2). 109pp. A useful book covering the career and personal life of this unconventional anthropologist. (Rev: SLJ 9/90) [921]

MENDEL, GREGOR

13322 Klare, Roger. *Gregor Mendel: Father of Genetics* (5–7). Illus. Series: Great Minds of Science. 1997, Enslow LB $20.95 (0-89490-789-1). 128pp. The science of genetics is introduced through the life of Mendel and his experimentation with peas. (Rev: BL 12/1/97; HBG 3/98; SLJ 12/97) [921]

MENDES, CHICO

13323 Burch, Joann J. *Chico Mendes: Defender of the Rain Forest* (3–5). Illus. Series: Gateway Biographies. 1994, Millbrook LB $20.90 (1-56294-413-4). 48pp. The life story of the conservationist who has courageously tried to stop the destruction of the Amazon rain forest. (Rev: BL 8/94; SLJ 4/94) [921]

MITCHELL, MARIA

13324 McPherson, Stephanie S. *Rooftop Astronomer: A Story About Maria Mitchell* (4–6). 1990, Carolrhoda LB $21.27 (0-87614-410-5). 64pp. The woman who became the first professional female astronomer in the United States. (Rev: BCCB 11/90; BL 11/15/90; SLJ 1/91) [921]

MORGAN, ANN

13325 Ross, Michael E. *Pond Watching with Ann Morgan* (3–5). Series: Naturalist's Apprentice. 2000, Carolrhoda $19.93 (1-57505-385-3). 48pp. A biography about the expert on ponds that also serves as a field guide to pond ecology. (Rev: BL 4/15/00; HBG 10/00; SLJ 7/00) [921]

MORTON, J. STERLING

13326 Beaty, Sandy, and J. L. Wilkerson. *Champion of Arbor Day: J. Sterling Morton* (4–6). Series: The Great Heartlanders. 1999, Acorn paper $8.95 (0-9664470-1-8). 130pp. The story of the early conservationist who inspired Nebraskans to plant one million trees on the first Arbor Day in 1872. (Rev: SLJ 3/99) [921]

MOSS, CYNTHIA

13327 Pringle, Laurence. *Elephant Woman: Cynthia Moss Explores the World of Elephants* (3–6). Illus. 1997, Simon & Schuster $16.00 (0-689-80142-4). 48pp. Through this biography of Cynthia Moss, who has studied elephants in Kenya's Amboseli National Park for 25 years, the reader learns about the habits of elephants, why they are endangered, and how they can be saved. (Rev: BCCB 3/98; BL 11/15/97; HBG 3/98; SLJ 12/97*) [921]

MUIR, JOHN

13328 Ito, Tom. *The Importance of John Muir* (4–8). Illus. Series: The Importance Of. 1996, Lucent LB $22.45 (1-56006-054-9). 110pp. A short biography of the naturalist who pioneered the U.S. conservation movement. (Rev: BL 5/15/96) [921]

13329 Naden, Corinne J., and Rose Blue. *John Muir: Saving the Wilderness* (3–5). Illus. Series: Gateway Biographies. 1992, Millbrook LB $19.90 (1-56294-110-0). 48pp. The life and work of this well-known conservationist, especially his role in founding the national parks. (Rev: BL 5/1/92; SLJ 6/92)

13330 Wadsworth, Ginger. *John Muir: Wilderness Protector* (4–6). Illus. 1992, Lerner LB $23.93 (0-8225-4912-3). 144pp. From his childhood in Scotland to adulthood in California, this biography focuses on why Muir became a conservationist and his efforts in this area. (Rev: SLJ 9/92) [921]

MURRELL, MELVILLE

13331 Seymour, Tres. *Our Neighbor Is a Strange, Strange Man* (PS–3). Illus. by Walter L. Krudop. 1999, Orchard LB $16.99 (0-531-33107-5). 32pp. A picture-book story of Melville Murrell, who built the first human-powered airplane in 1876, years before the Wright brothers. (Rev: BCCB 2/99; BL 2/1/99; HBG 10/99; SLJ 3/99) [629.13]

NAVY, CARYN

13332 Verheyden-Hilliard, Mary Ellen. *Mathematician and Computer Scientist, Caryn Navy* (2–4). Illus. 1988, Equity paper $8.50 (0-932469-12-4). 32pp. Brief biography of a woman scientist who is blind. (Rev: BL 2/15/89; SLJ 1/89)

NEWTON, ISAAC

13333 Anderson, Margaret J. *Isaac Newton: The Greatest Scientist of All Time* (4–7). Illus. Series: Great Minds of Science. 1996, Enslow LB $20.95 (0-89490-681-X). 128pp. The life of the great English mathematician and physicist who formulated the laws of motion and gravity. (Rev: BL 10/15/96; SLJ 12/96) [921]

13334 White, Michael. *Isaac Newton: Discovering Laws That Govern the Universe* (5–8). Series: Giants of Science. 1999, Blackbirch LB $18.95 (1-56711-326-5). 64pp. A visually appealing biography of the great English mathematician who was the first scientist to be knighted. (Rev: HBG 10/00; SLJ 2/00) [921]

NICE, MARGARET MORSE

13335 Dunlap, Julie. *Birds in the Bushes: A Story About Margaret Morse Nice* (3–5). Illus. by Ralph L. Ramstad. Series: Creative Minds. 1996, Carolrhoda LB $19.93 (1-57505-006-4). 63pp. A biography of the noted American ornithologist and conservationist who died in 1974. (Rev: SLJ 10/96) [921]

13336 Ross, Michael E. *Bird Watching with Margaret Morse Nice* (4–6). Illus. by Laurie A. Caple. Series: Naturalist's Apprentice. 1997, Carolrhoda LB $19.93 (1-57505-002-1). 48pp. At the turn of the century, Margaret Morse Nice raised her family while pursuing her hobby of bird watching. (Rev: HBG 3/98; SLJ 3/98) [921]

PACHCIARZ, JUDITH

13337 Verheyden-Hilliard, Mary Ellen. *Scientist and Physician, Judith Pachciarz* (2–4). Illus. 1988, Equity paper $8.50 (0-932469-13-2). 32pp. The story of an M.D. and microbiologist who is deaf. (Rev: BL 2/15/89; SLJ 4/89) [921]

PASTEUR, LOUIS

13338 Fullick, Ann. *Louis Pasteur* (4–6). 2000, Heinemann LB $25.64 (1-57572-373-5). 48pp. As well as covering Pasteur's life, this book tells of the impact of his discoveries on medicine and science. (Rev: SLJ 2/01) [921]

13339 Sabin, Francene. *Louis Pasteur: Young Scientist* (3–5). Illus. by Susan Swan. 1983, Troll LB $17.25 (0-89375-853-1); paper $3.95 (0-89375-854-X). 48pp. A simple biography that concentrates on the boyhood of Pasteur. [921]

13340 Smith, Linda W. *Louis Pasteur: Disease Fighter* (4–8). Illus. Series: Great Minds of Science. 1997, Enslow LB $20.95 (0-89490-790-5). 128pp. The story of the "father of microbiology," who discovered pasteurization while working on a wine problem for Napoleon. (Rev: BL 12/1/97; HBG 3/98; SLJ 12/97) [921]

PLOTKIN, MARK

13341 Pascoe, Elaine, adapt. *Mysteries of the Rain Forest: 20th Century Medicine Man* (4–8). Illus. Series: New Explorers. 1997, Blackbirch LB $17.95 (1-56711-229-3). 48pp. Describes the work and findings of Mark Plotkin, an ethnobotanist, who has worked for years in the rain forest of the Amazon. (Rev: HBG 3/98; SLJ 2/98) [921]

RICHARDS, ELLEN

13342 Vare, Ethlie A. *Adventurous Spirit: A Story About Ellen Swallow Richards* (3–6). Illus. by Jennifer Hagerman. Series: Creative Minds. 1992, Carolrhoda LB $14.95 (0-87614-733-3). 64pp. The life of the first woman accepted at M.I.T. (Rev: BL 1/15/93) [921]

ROENTGEN, WILHELM

13343 Gherman, Beverly. *The Mysterious Rays of Dr. Roentgen* (2–5). Illus. by Stephen Marchesi. 1994, Atheneum LB $14.95 (0-689-31839-1). 32pp.

An engrossing biography of the man who discovered X-rays and won a Nobel Prize in 1901. (Rev: BCCB 10/94; BL 12/1/94; SLJ 9/94) [921]

ROOKS, JUNE

13344 Verheyden-Hilliard, Mary Ellen. *Scientist and Strategist, June Rooks* (2–4). Illus. 1988, Equity paper $8.50 (0-932469-14-0). 32pp. The story of June Rooks, an African American who battled poverty and polio to gain a degree in physics and a research analysis job in the navy. (Rev: BL 2/15/89; SLJ 1/89)

SAGAN, CARL

13345 Butts, Ellen R., and Joyce R. Schwarts. *Carl Sagan* (5–8). Series: A&E Biography. 2000, Lerner LB $25.26 (0-8225-4986-7). 112pp. The story of the great astronomer who interested millions in the study of the stars and the question of whether there is life elsewhere in our universe. (Rev: BL 10/15/00; HBG 3/01; SLJ 10/00) [921]

13346 Byman, Jeremy. *Carl Sagan: In Contact with the Cosmos* (5–8). Illus. Series: Great Scientists. 2000, Morgan Reynolds LB $19.95 (1-883846-55-2). 112pp. An informative biography of the scientist who popularized astronomy while maintaining a highly productive scholarly life. (Rev: BL 11/1/00; HBG 10/00; SLJ 8/00) [921]

STEARNER, PHYLLIS

13347 Verheyden-Hilliard, Mary Ellen. *Scientist and Activist, Phyllis Stearner* (2–4). Illus. 1988, Equity paper $8.50 (0-932469-15-9). 32pp. A biography of an expert in radiation biology who has cerebral palsy. (Rev: BL 2/15/89; SLJ 1/89) [921]

STRONG, MAURICE

13348 Westrup, Hugh. *Maurice Strong: Working for Planet Earth* (3–6). Illus. 1994, Millbrook LB $20.90 (1-56294-414-2). 48pp. A biography of the Canadian environmentalist who organized the Rio de Janeiro Earth Summit. (Rev: BL 12/1/94; SLJ 12/94) [921]

SWANSON, ANNE BARRETT

13349 Verheyden-Hilliard, Mary Ellen. *Scientist and Teacher, Anne Barrett Swanson* (2–4). Illus. 1988, Equity paper $8.50 (0-932469-16-7). 32pp. The story of a scientist who overcame a brittle bone condition that hampered her physical growth. (Rev: BL 2/15/89; SLJ 4/89) [921]

TOMBAUGH, CLYDE

13350 Wetterer, Margaret K. *Clyde Tombaugh and the Search for Planet X* (2–5). Illus. by Laurie A. Caple. 1996, Carolrhoda LB $21.27 (0-87614-893-3); paper $5.95 (0-87614-969-7). 56pp. The life story of Tombaugh, whose interest in astronomy led to the discovery of Pluto. (Rev: BL 12/15/96; SLJ 1/97) [921]

TURNER, HENRY

13351 Ross, Michael E. *Bug Watching with Charles Henry Turner* (3–5). Illus. Series: Naturalist's Ap-

prentice. 1997, Carolrhoda $19.93 (1-57505-003-X). 48pp. As well as providing many hints on bug watching, this book is a biography of the important African American zoologist who studied insects for many years. (Rev: BL 3/1/98; HBG 3/98; SLJ 3/98) [921]

WILLIAMS, DANIEL HALE

13352 Kaye, Judith. *The Life of Daniel Hale Williams* (5–8). Illus. Series: Pioneers in Health and Medicine. 1993, Twenty-First Century LB $13.95 (0-8050-2302-X). 80pp. The life story of the famous doctor who pioneered heart surgery and also helped open up the medical profession to African Americans. (Rev: SLJ 1/94) [921]

WOZNIAK, STEVE

13353 Gold, Rebecca. *Steve Wozniak: A Wizard Called Woz* (3–5). Illus. Series: Achievers. 1994, Lerner LB $21.27 (0-8225-2881-9). 72pp. The biography of the math whiz and multimillionaire who founded the Apple Computer Company. (Rev: BL 12/1/94) [921]

WRIGHT, WILBUR AND ORVILLE

13354 Krensky, Stephen. *Taking Flight: The Story of the Wright Brothers* (3–4). Illus. Series: Ready-to-Read. 2000, Simon & Schuster $15.00 (0-689-81225-6). 44pp. An easy reader that tells about the lives and accomplishments of the Wright brothers and quotes often from their letters. (Rev: BL 5/15/00; HBG 3/01; SLJ 8/00) [921]

13355 Old, Wendie C. *The Wright Brothers* (5–8). Series: Historical American Biographies. 2000, Enslow LB $19.95 (0-7660-1095-3). An accurate and objective biography of the heroes of Kitty Hawk, containing chapter notes, a bibliography, and a glossary. (Rev: BL 1/1–15/00; HBG 10/00; SLJ 7/00) [921]

13356 Reynolds, Quentin. *The Wright Brothers* (4–7). Illus. 1981, Random paper $5.99 (0-394-84700-8). 160pp. The lives of two mechanical geniuses. [921]

13357 Schaefer, Lola M. *The Wright Brothers* (K–2). 2000, Capstone LB $13.25 (0-7368-0549-4). 24pp. For beginning readers, this is an attractive biography of the Wright brothers, whose lives and accomplishments are presented in double-page spreads. (Rev: HBG 10/00; SLJ 9/00) [921]

13358 Sproule, Anna. *The Wright Brothers: The Birth of Modern Aviation* (5–8). Series: Giants of Science. 1999, Blackbirch LB $18.95 (1-56711-328-1). 64pp. This slim biography with an inviting format stresses the lasting contributions of the Wright brothers to world transportation. (Rev: HBG 10/00; SLJ 2/00) [921]

13359 Taylor, Richard L. *The First Flight: The Story of the Wright Brothers* (K–3). Illus. Series: First Books. 1990, Watts LB $21.00 (0-531-10891-0). 64pp. Explains the problems that the Wright brothers faced and the solutions they devised in making a functioning airplane. (Rev: BL 4/15/90; SLJ 10/90) [921]

Sports Figures

Collective

13360 Aaseng, Nathan. *Top 10 Basketball Scoring Small Forwards* (4–7). Series: Sports Top 10. 1999, Enslow LB $18.95 (0-7660-1152-6). 48pp. Each of these ten basketball forwards is covered by a two-page biography, a full-page picture, and a page of sports statistics. (Rev: BL 11/15/99; HBG 10/00) [920]

13361 Bjarkman, Peter C. *Top 10 Baseball Base Stealers* (3–6). Illus. Series: Sports Top 10. 1995, Enslow LB $18.95 (0-89490-609-7). 48pp. Short biographies of ten famous baseball players, past and present, known statistically as the top base stealers. (Rev: BL 9/15/95) [920]

13362 Bjarkman, Peter C. *Top 10 Basketball Slam Dunkers* (3–6). Illus. Series: Sports Top 10. 1995, Enslow LB $18.95 (0-89490-608-9). 48pp. Full-page photos and a two-page biography are given for each of these ten basketball stars. (Rev: BL 9/15/95) [920]

13363 Christopher, Andre. *Top 10 Men's Tennis Players* (4–7). Series: Sports Top 10. 1998, Enslow LB $17.95 (0-7600-1009-0). 48pp. Brief biographies of past and present tennis greats, with fact boxes, career statistics, and chapter notes. (Rev: BL 3/15/98) [920]

13364 Crisfield, Deborah. *Louisville Slugger Book of Great Hitters* (4–8). Series: Mountain Lion. 1998, Wiley paper $12.95 (0-471-19772-6). 186pp. This book contains 100 brief profiles of baseball's outstanding hitters, past and present. (Rev: SLJ 4/98) [920]

13365 Deane, Bill. *Top 10 Baseball Home Run Hitters* (4–7). Illus. Series: Sports Top 10. 1997, Enslow LB $18.95 (0-89490-804-9). 48pp. Ten brief biographies of baseball hitters, e.g., Hank Aaron, Mickey Mantle, Jimmie Foxx, and Frank Thomas. (Rev: BL 9/15/97; HBG 3/98) [920]

13366 Deane, Bill. *Top 10 Men's Baseball Hitters* (4–7). Series: Sports Top 10. 1998, Enslow LB $17.95 (0-7600-1007-4). 48pp. Brief biographies of

great past and present baseball hitters, with fact boxes, career statistics, and chapter notes. (Rev: BL 3/15/98) [920]

13367 Devaney, John. *Winners of the Heisman Trophy* (5–8). Illus. 1990, Walker LB $15.85 (0-8027-6907-1). 167pp. Profiles of 15 winners of this highest college football award. (Rev: SLJ 6/90) [920]

13368 Ditchfield, Christin. *Top 10 American Women's Olympic Gold Medalists* (4–7). Illus. Series: Sports Top 10. 2000, Enslow LB $18.95 (0-7660-1277-8). 48pp. Along with the profiles of ten female athletes, this book contains fact boxes, career statistics, and chapter notes. (Rev: BL 9/15/00) [920]

13369 Dolin, Nick, et al. *Basketball Stars* (4–8). Illus. 1997, Black Dog & Leventhal $24.98 (1-884822-61-4). 128pp. This oversize book contains 50 two-page profiles with statistics of today's star basketball players. (Rev: BL 8/97) [920]

13370 Donkin, Andrew. *Going for Gold!* (2–4). Series: Eyewitness Reader. 1999, DK $12.95 (0-7894-4765-7); paper $3.95 (0-7894-4764-9). 48pp. Tennis, swimming, and the shot put are three of the sports covered in this biography of six Olympians including Jesse Owen, Shelley Mann, Mamo Wolde, and Kerri Strug. (Rev: HBG 3/00; SLJ 2/00) [920]

13371 Golenbock, Peter. *Teammates* (1–3). Illus. by Paul Bacon. 1990, Harcourt $16.00 (0-15-200603-6). 32pp. Segregated life in the United States of the 1940s introduces the reader to the Negro Leagues. (Rev: BCCB 4/90; BL 4/1/90; HB 5–6/90; SLJ 6/90) [796.357]

13372 Green, Septima. *Top 10 Women Gymnasts* (4–7). Series: Sports Top 10. 1999, Enslow LB $18.95 (0-89490-809-X). 48pp. Each of these star gymnasts from the past and present gets a two-page biography, a page of important statistics, and a black-and-white photograph. (Rev: BL 11/15/99; HBG 10/00) [920]

13373 Harrington, Denis J. *Top 10 Women Tennis Players* (3–6). Illus. Series: Sports Top 10. 1995, Enslow LB $18.95 (0-89490-612-7). 48pp. Biographies of the top ten women tennis players of all time, with a photograph of each and accompanying statistics. (Rev: BL 7/95; SLJ 11/95) [921]

13374 Hunter, Shaun. *Great African Americans in the Olympics* (3–5). Series: Outstanding African Americans. 1997, Crabtree LB $22.60 (0-86505-809-1); paper $8.95 (0-86505-823-7). 64pp. In-depth profiles of seven African Americans — e.g., Gail Devers, George Foreman, Sugar Ray Leonard — and additional shorter profiles of six others. (Rev: BL 9/15/97) [920]

13375 Kaminsky, Marty. *Uncommon Champions: Fifteen Athletes Who Battled Back* (5–8). Illus. 2000, Boyds Mills $14.95 (1-56397-787-7). 147pp. Profiles of 15 athletes in several different sports who have conquered such mental and physical problems as blindness and drug addiction to achieve their goals. (Rev: BCCB 1/01; BL 11/1/00; HBG 3/01) [921]

13376 Kelly, J. *Superstars of Women's Basketball* (4–6). Series: Female Sports Stars. 1997, Chelsea LB $15.95 (0-7910-4389-4). 64pp. Five outstanding female basketball stars are featured in this book, which tells about each one's rise to fame. (Rev: SLJ 4/98) [920]

13377 Knapp, Ron. *Top 10 American Men Sprinters* (4–7). Series: Sports Top 10. 1999, Enslow LB $18.95 (0-7660-1074-0). 48pp. Profiles and photographs are given of ten important American male sprinters past and present. (Rev: BL 3/15/99; HBG 10/99) [920]

13378 Knapp, Ron. *Top 10 American Men's Olympic Gold Medalists* (4–7). Illus. Series: Sports Top 10. 2000, Enslow LB $18.95 (0-7660-1274-3). 48pp. This book of ten American male Olympic stars covers a number of sports, including track and field and diving. (Rev: BL 9/15/00; HBG 10/00) [920]

13379 Knapp, Ron. *Top 10 Basketball Centers* (3–6). Illus. Series: Sports Top 10. 1994, Enslow LB $18.95 (0-89490-515-5). 48pp. For each basketball star, there are about two pages of text and photographs. (Rev: BL 1/15/95; SLJ 6/95) [920]

13380 Knapp, Ron. *Top 10 Basketball Scorers* (3–6). Illus. Series: Sports Top 10. 1994, Enslow LB $18.95 (0-89490-516-3). 48pp. Ten short biographies of basketball's top scorers, past and present, with tables of comparative statistics. (Rev: BL 1/15/95; SLJ 6/95) [920]

13381 Knapp, Ron. *Top 10 Hockey Scorers* (3–6). Illus. Series: Sports Top 10. 1994, Enslow LB $18.95 (0-89490-517-1). 48pp. Statistics, a brief biography, and two photographs are given for each hockey player highlighted. (Rev: BL 1/15/95) [920]

13382 Knapp, Ron. *Top 10 NFL Super Bowl Most Valuable Players* (4–7). Series: Sports Top 10. 2000, Enslow LB $18.97 (0-7660-1273-5). 48pp. This book profiles ten of the past and present most valuable players in the National Football League's Super Bowl. (Rev: BL 12/15/00) [920]

13383 Kramer, S. A. *Baseball's Greatest Hitters* (2–4). Illus. Series: Step into Reading. 1995, Random paper $3.99 (0-679-85307-3). 48pp. Five great hitters — Honus Wagner, Ty Cobb, Babe Ruth, Ted Williams, and Hank Aaron — are introduced, each

with a simple biography and career statistics. (Rev: BL 7/95) [920]

13384 Kramer, S. A. *Baseball's Greatest Pitchers* (3–5). Illus. by Jim Campbell. 1992, Random paper $3.99 (0-679-82149-X). 48pp. Black-and-white photos and watercolor paintings add flavor to this collection of profiles of great pitchers. (Rev: BL 4/1/92; SLJ 7/92) [796.357]

13385 Kramer, S. A. *Wonder Women of Sports* (2–3). Illus. by Jim Campbell. Series: All Aboard Reading. 1997, Putnam LB $13.99 (0-448-41722-7); paper $3.95 (0-448-41589-5). 48pp. A beginning reader that profiles women athletes including Gail Devers, Dominique Moceanu, and Rebecca Lobo. (Rev: BL 2/1/98) [920]

13386 Krull, Kathleen. *Lives of the Athletes* (4–7). Illus. by Kathryn Hewitt. 1997, Harcourt $20.00 (0-15-200806-3). 96pp. A collective biography that describes the public and private lives of 20 famous athletes, including Johnny Weissmuller, Red Grange, Babe Didrikson Zaharias, Sonja Henie, and Bruce Lee. (Rev: BCCB 6/97; BL 3/15/97; HB 5–6/97; SLJ 5/97) [920]

13387 Kuhn, Betsy. *Top 10 Jockeys* (4–7). Series: Sports Top 10. 1999, Enslow LB $18.95 (0-7660-1130-5). 48pp. Important jockeys, both past and present, are featured with a short biography, a portrait, and a page of pertinent statistics. (Rev: BL 11/15/99; HBG 10/00) [920]

13388 Lace, William W. *Top 10 Football Quarterbacks* (3–6). Illus. Series: Sports Top 10. 1994, Enslow LB $18.95 (0-89490-518-X). 48pp. Star quarterbacks both past and present are highlighted in ten brief biographies, each with a photograph and a record of achievements. (Rev: BL 1/15/95) [920]

13389 Lace, William W. *Top 10 Football Rushers* (3–6). Illus. Series: Sports Top 10. 1994, Enslow LB $18.95 (0-89490-519-8). 48pp. Each of the ten featured stars gets a two-page biography, a photograph, and coverage of important statistics. (Rev: BL 1/15/95) [920]

13390 Molzahn, Arlene Bourgeois. *Top 10 American Women Sprinters* (4–7). Series: Sports Top 10. 1998, Enslow LB $18.95 (0-7660-1011-2). Fact boxes and photographs enhance ten short profiles of famous American female runners. (Rev: BL 8/98; HBG 10/99; SLJ 1/99) [920]

13391 Pietrusza, David. *Top 10 Baseball Managers* (4–7). Series: Sports Top 10. 1999, Enslow LB $18.95 (0-7660-1076-7). 48pp. This work gives brief profiles of ten famous past and present managers of American baseball teams. (Rev: BL 1/1–15/99; HBG 10/99) [920]

13392 Poynter, Margaret. *Top 10 American Women's Figure Skaters* (4–7). Series: Sports Top 10. 1998, Enslow LB $18.95 (0-7660-1075-9). This work offers brief profiles and photographs of ten female figure skaters. (Rev: BL 11/15/98; HBG 10/99) [920]

13393 Rappoport, Ken. *Guts and Glory: Making It in the NBA* (4–7). Illus. 1997, Walker LB $16.85 (0-8027-8431-3). 160pp. Ten short biographies of star players, like John Lucas and Isiah Thomas, who overcame obstacles to success in the NBA. (Rev: BL 8/97; SLJ 7/97) [920]

13394 Rappoport, Ken. *Top 10 Basketball Legends* (3–6). Illus. Series: Sports Top 10. 1995, Enslow LB $18.95 (0-89490-610-0). 48pp. Biographies of the top ten basketball players of the past, with statistics to prove the unique contribution of each. (Rev: BL 7/95; SLJ 11/95) [920]

13395 Rediger, Pat. *Great African Americans in Sports* (4–6). Illus. Series: Outstanding African Americans. 1996, Crabtree LB $22.60 (0-86505-801-6); paper $8.95 (0-86505-815-6). 64pp. Three of the 13 sports heroes profiled are Michael Jordan, Jackie Joyner-Kersee, and Carl Lewis. (Rev: BL 9/15/96) [920]

13396 Rennert, Richard S., ed. *Book of Firsts: Sports Heroes* (5–8). Illus. Series: Profiles of Great Black Americans. 1993, Chelsea LB $16.95 (0-7910-2055-X); paper $6.95 (0-7910-2056-8). 63pp. Contains profiles of these great African American athletes: Arthur Ashe, Chuck Cooper, Althea Gibson, Jesse Owens, Jackie Robinson, Jack Johnson, Frank Robinson, and Bill Russell. (Rev: SLJ 12/93) [920]

13397 Riley, Gail B. *Top 10 NASCAR Drivers* (3–4). Illus. Series: Sports Top 10. 1995, Enslow LB $18.95 (0-89490-611-9). 48pp. Ten of the top race car drivers are highlighted in these short biographies. (Rev: BL 9/15/95) [796.7]

13398 Rutledge, Rachel. *The Best of the Best in Figure Skating* (4–7). Series: Women of Sports. 1998, Millbrook LB $22.90 (0-7613-1302-8); paper $6.95 (0-7613-0444-4). 64pp. After a brief history of figure skating and mention of its women pioneers, this book devotes separate chapters to the sport's present-day female leaders. (Rev: BL 2/15/99; HBG 10/99) [920]

13399 Rutledge, Rachel. *The Best of the Best in Gymnastics* (5–8). Series: Women of Sports. 1999, Millbrook LB $22.90 (0-7613-1321-4); paper $6.95 (0-7613-0784-2). 64pp. After an overview of the history of gymnastics, there are profiles of eight important contemporary female gymnasts, five of whom are American. (Rev: HBG 10/99; SLJ 7/99) [920]

13400 Rutledge, Rachel. *The Best of the Best in Soccer* (4–7). Series: Women of Sports. 1998, Millbrook LB $22.90 (0-7613-1315-X); paper $6.95 (0-7613-0782-6). 64pp. A revised edition of the 1998 title, containing a brief history of women's soccer and profiles of the top women players of yesterday, today, and tomorrow. (Rev: BL 2/15/99; HBG 10/99) [920]

13401 Rutledge, Rachel. *The Best of the Best in Track and Field* (5–8). Series: Women of Sports. 1999, Millbrook LB $22.90 (0-7613-1300-1); paper $6.95 (0-7613-0446-0). 64pp. This book profiles eight female athletes from the United States and abroad, with material on their careers and off-the-field lives. (Rev: HBG 10/99; SLJ 7/99) [920]

13402 Savage, Jeff. *Home Run Kings* (4–6). Illus. 1999, Raintree Steck-Vaughn $22.83 (0-7398-0216-X); paper $6.95 (0-7398-0215-1). 48pp. Brief profiles are given of such home-run record setters as

Babe Ruth, Roger Maris, Mark McGwire, Sammy Sosa, Hank Aaron, Mickey Mantle, and Willie Mays plus lots of World Series action. (Rev: BL 5/15/99; HBG 10/99) [920]

13403 Savage, Jeff. *Top 10 Basketball Point Guards* (4–7). Series: Sports Top 10. 1997, Enslow LB $18.95 (0-89490-807-3). 48pp. Each of the athletes is presented in four pages containing a biography, statistics, and two photographs. Also use *Top ten Basketball Power Forwards* (1997). (Rev: BL 9/15/97) [920]

13404 Savage, Jeff. *Top 10 Football Sackers* (4–7). Series: Sports Top 10. 1997, Enslow LB $18.95 (0-89490-805-7). 48pp. Each of the ten football stars highlighted is covered in four pages that include a short biography, two photos, and a statistics table. (Rev: BL 9/15/97) [920]

13405 Savage, Jeff. *Top 10 Heisman Trophy Winners* (4–7). Series: Sports Top 10. 1999, Enslow LB $18.95 (0-7660-1072-4). 48pp. This work profiles ten winners of the trophy given each year to the most outstanding college football player in America. (Rev: BL 1/1–15/99; HBG 10/99) [920]

13406 Savage, Jeff. *Top 10 Physically Challenged Athletes* (4–7). Series: Sports Top 10. 2000, Enslow LB $18.95 (0-7660-1272-7). 48pp. Each of the ten short biographies in this book on physically handicapped athletes has an accompanying photo (usually in color) and a page of statistics. (Rev: BL 2/15/00; HBG 10/00; SLJ 10/00) [920]

13407 Savage, Jeff. *Top 10 Professional Football Coaches* (4–7). Series: Sports Top 10. 1998, Enslow LB $17.95 (0-7660-1006-6). 48pp. From professional football Hall of Famers George Halas and Curly Lambeau to the Miami Dolphins' Jimmy Johnson, this book profiles ten super coaches, with each given a two-page biography, photographs, and a career summary. (Rev: HBG 10/98; SLJ 9/98) [920]

13408 Schnakenberg, Robert E. *Teammates: Karl Malone and John Stockton* (5–7). Illus. 1998, Millbrook LB $20.90 (0-7613-0300-6). 96pp. A biography of two famous basketball stars from the Utah Jazz team who rely on each other to achieve their individual success. (Rev: BL 8/98; HBG 10/98; SLJ 5/98) [920]

13409 Schwabacher, Martin. *Superstars of Women's Tennis* (4–6). Illus. Series: Female Sports Stars. 1997, Chelsea LB $16.95 (0-7910-4393-2). 64pp. Profiles tennis greats Billie Jean King, Chris Evert, Martina Navratilova, Steffi Graff, and Monica Seles. (Rev: SLJ 8/97) [920]

13410 Sehnert, Chris W. *Top 10 Sluggers* (5–8). Illus. Series: Top 10 Champions. 1997, ABDO LB $23.54 (1-56239-797-4). 48pp. An overview of the careers of such notable hitters as Babe Ruth, Hank Aaron, and Roberto Clemente. (Rev: BL 1/1–15/98; HBG 3/98) [920]

13411 Smith, Pohla. *Superstars of Women's Figure Skating* (4–6). Illus. Series: Female Sports Stars. 1997, Chelsea LB $16.95 (0-7910-4392-4). 64pp. A clear easy reader that includes profiles of Sonja Henie, Peggy Fleming, Dorothy Hamill, Katarina

Witt, Kristi Yamaguchi, and Oksana Baiul. (Rev: SLJ 8/97) [920]

13412 Spiros, Dean. *Top 10 Hockey Goalies* (4–6). Series: Sports Top 10. 1998, Enslow $18.95 (0-7660-1010-4). Past and present star goalies are featured in ten short profiles. (Rev: BL 8/98; HBG 10/99) [921]

13413 Stewart, Mark, and Mike Kennedy. *Home Run Heroes: Mark McGwire and Sammy Sosa* (4–8). 1999, Millbrook LB $22.90 (0-7613-1559-4); paper $6.95 (0-7613-1045-2). 64pp. This book highlights the home-run battle of the 1998 baseball season and gives good profiles of both Sosa and McGwire. (Rev: HBG 10/99; SLJ 8/99) [920]

13414 Strudwick, Leslie. *Athletes* (3–6). Series: Women in Profile. 1999, Crabtree LB $15.96 (0-7787-0015-1); paper $8.06 (0-7787-0037-2). 48pp. Color photos and interesting information are included in this book that profiles six internationally known female athletes and briefly sketches an additional 12. (Rev: BL 9/15/99) [920]

13415 Sullivan, George. *Great Lives: Sports* (5–7). Illus. 1988, Macmillan $25.00 (0-684-18510-5). 288pp. Introducing 27 sports stars from all fields. (Rev: BL 1/1/89; HB 3–4/89)

13416 Sullivan, George. *Quarterbacks! Eighteen of Football's Greatest* (5–8). 1998, Simon & Schuster $18.00 (0-689-81334-1). 60pp. In two- to four-page entries, the author profiles 18 quarterbacks — current-day players such as Brett Favre and Troy Aikman and others from yesterday, such as Sammy Baugh and Sid Luckman. (Rev: HBG 3/99; SLJ 9/98) [920]

13417 Sullivan, George. *Sluggers!* (4–7). Illus. 1991, Macmillan $18.00 (0-689-31566-X). 74pp. Profiles of the careers of 27 of baseball's best hitters. (Rev: SLJ 1/92) [920]

13418 Sullivan, Michael J. *Top 10 Baseball Pitchers* (3–6). Illus. Series: Sports Top 10. 1994, Enslow LB $18.95 (0-89490-520-1). 48pp. Star pitchers from both the past and present are featured, each receiving a two-page biography and color photograph. (Rev: BL 1/15/95) [920]

13419 Thornley, Stew. *Top 10 Football Receivers* (3–6). Illus. Series: Sports Top 10. 1995, Enslow LB $18.95 (0-89490-607-0). 48pp. The position of receiver is highlighted in the biographies of ten of the greatest, past and present. (Rev: BL 7/95; SLJ 11/95) [920]

13420 Torres, John A. *Top 10 Basketball Three-Point Shooters* (4–7). Series: Sports Top 10. 1999, Enslow LB $18.95 (0-7660-1071-6). 48pp. A profile and a photograph of ten star basketball players make up this slender volume. (Rev: BL 1/1–15/99; HBG 10/99) [920]

13421 Torres, John A. *Top 10 NBA Finals Most Valuable Players* (4–7). Illus. Series: Sports Top 10. 2000, Enslow LB $18.95 (0-7660-1276-X). 48pp. Short profiles of these NBA players also include photos and some sports statistics. (Rev: BL 9/15/00; HBG 10/00) [920]

13422 Ungs, Tim. *Superstars of Men's Soccer* (3–5). Series: Male Sports Stars. 1998, Chelsea LB $15.95 (0-7910-4588-9). 64pp. After an introduction to soccer, this collective biography profiles Pele, Franz Beckenbauer, Johann Cruyff, and Diego Maradona. (Rev: HBG 3/99; SLJ 12/98) [920]

13423 Wickham, Martha. *Superstars of Women's Track and Field* (4–6). Series: Female Sports Stars. 1997, Chelsea LB $15.95 (0-7910-4394-0). 64pp. This book profiles five important female track-and-field stars, with details on their careers and a good selection of action photos. (Rev: SLJ 4/98) [920]

13424 Winter, Jonah. *Fair Ball! 14 Great Stars from Baseball's Negro Leagues* (3–5). Illus. 1999, Scholastic $15.95 (0-590-39464-9). 32pp. Using double-page spreads, this book profiles 14 great baseball players from the Negro Leagues, including Cool Papa Bell, Josh Gibson, and Satchel Paige. (Rev: BL 4/15/99; HBG 10/99; SLJ 3/99) [920]

13425 Young, Jeff C. *Top 10 Basketball Shot-Blockers* (4–7). Series: Sports Top 10. 2000, Enslow LB $18.95 (0-7660-1275-1). 48pp. For each of the basketball stars profiled, there is a full-page picture, a two-page biography, and a page of statistics. (Rev: BL 2/15/00; HBG 10/00) [920]

13426 Young, Ken. *Cy Young Award Winners* (4–6). Illus. 1994, Walker LB $15.85 (0-8027-8301-5). 160pp. Profiles of ten winners of the Cy Young Award for pitching, e.g., Whitey Ford, Sandy Koufax, Fernando Valenzuela, and Dwight Gooden. (Rev: BL 9/1/94; SLJ 8/94) [920]

Automobile Racing

EARNHARDT, DALE

13427 Steenkamer, Paul. *Dale Earnhardt: Star Race Car Driver* (4–6). Illus. Series: Sports Reports. 2000, Enslow LB $19.95 (0-7660-1335-9). 104pp. As well as a profile of Dale Earnhardt, this book has some action photos and gives a behind-the-scenes look at car racing. (Rev: BL 9/15/00; HBG 3/01) [921]

GORDON, JEFF

13428 Powell, Phelan. *Jeff Gordon* (3–4). Series: Real-Life Reader Biographies. 1999, Mitchell Lane LB $15.95 (1-58415-005-X). 32pp. A simple biography of the race-car driving star and his climb to fame. (Rev: BL 10/15/99) [921]

ST. JAMES, LYN

13429 Olney, Ross R. *Lyn St. James: Driven to Be First* (4–6). Illus. 1997, Lerner LB $22.60 (0-8225-2890-8); paper $5.95 (0-8225-9749-7). 64pp. The biography of one of the few women who has succeeded in the world of race-car driving. (Rev: BL 2/15/97; SLJ 3/97) [921]

Baseball

AARON, HANK

13430 Golenbock, Peter. *Hank Aaron: Brave in Every Way* (2–4). Illus. by Paul Lee. 2001, Harcourt $16.00 (0-15-202093-4). 32pp. Part of this stirring biography focuses on Hank Aaron's goal of breaking Babe Ruth's batting record and the controversy it caused because he was African American. (Rev: BL 2/15/01) [921]

13431 Tackach, James. *Hank Aaron* (4–6). Illus. Series: Baseball Legends. 1991, Chelsea LB $16.95 (0-7910-1165-8). 64pp. In addition to the life of baseball legend Aaron, this biography includes sections of statistics, a chronology, and numerous photographs. (Rev: BL 12/1/91) [921]

ABBOTT, JIM

13432 Johnson, Rick L. *Jim Abbott: Beating the Odds* (4–7). Illus. Series: Taking Part. 1991, Macmillan LB $13.95 (0-87518-459-6). 64pp. This account re-creates the life of the baseball pitcher who overcame a severe disability. (Rev: BL 9/1/91) [921]

13433 White, Ellen E. *Jim Abbott: Against All Odds* (3–5). Illus. Series: Scholastic Biography. 1990, Scholastic paper $2.99 (0-590-43503-5). 86pp. The amazing pitcher for the California Angels, who once pitched a no-hitter for the New York Yankees, who has only one hand. (Rev: SLJ 10/90) [921]

ALEXANDER, GROVER CLEVELAND

13434 Kavanagh, Jack. *Grover Cleveland Alexander* (4–6). Illus. Series: Baseball Legends. 1990, Chelsea LB $16.95 (0-7910-1166-6). 63pp. A fine profile of one of the greats of the baseball game. (Rev: BL 6/1/90) [921]

ALOMAR, ROBERTO

13435 Macht, Norman L. *Roberto Alomar* (4–8). Series: Latinos in Baseball. 1999, Mitchell Lane LB $18.95 (1-883845-84-X). 64pp. Using extensive interviews with Alomar, his family, friends, and colleagues, this biography of the famous Puerto Rican baseball player shows his strong self-discipline, work ethic, and close family ties. (Rev: HBG 10/99; SLJ 5/99) [921]

13436 Thornley, Stew. *Roberto Alomar: Star Second Baseman* (4–6). Series: Sports Reports. 1999, Enslow LB $19.95 (0-7660-1079-1). 104pp. Career statistics, action photos, and behind-the-scenes coverage are included in this biography of the famous second baseman. (Rev: BL 2/15/99; HBG 10/99) [921]

BENCH, JOHNNY

13437 Shannon, Mike. *Johnny Bench* (4–6). Illus. Series: Baseball Legends. 1990, Chelsea LB $16.95 (0-7910-1168-2). 64pp. Biographical data plus background statistics, a chronology, and many photos. (Rev: BL 10/1/90; SLJ 1/91) [921]

BONDS, BARRY

13438 Savage, Jeff. *Barry Bonds: Mr. Excitement* (4–8). Illus. Series: Sports Achievers. 1997, Lerner LB $22.60 (0-8225-2889-4). 64pp. The story of this fantastic baseball player who has won the Most Valuable Player award three times and who grew up

in the shadow of a famous father. (Rev: BL 4/15/97; SLJ 2/97) [921]

BONILLA, BOBBY

13439 Knapp, Ron. *Bobby Bonilla* (5–8). Illus. Series: Sports Great Books. 1993, Enslow LB $17.95 (0-89490-417-5). 64pp. Using easy-to-read prose and a number of action photos, this is a lively introduction to baseball star Bobby Bonilla. (Rev: BL 9/15/93) [921]

13440 Rappoport, Ken. *Bobby Bonilla* (5–8). Illus. 1993, Walker LB $15.85 (0-8027-8256-6). 144pp. A well-written sports biography on the New York Mets–Baltimore Orioles–Florida Marlins player. (Rev: SLJ 5/93) [921]

CANSECO, JOSÉ

13441 Aaseng, Nathan. *Jose Canseco: Baseball's Forty-Forty Man* (4–7). Illus. 1989, Lerner LB $21.27 (0-8225-0493-6); paper $4.95 (0-8225-9586-9). 56pp. The ups and downs of this sometimes controversial baseball star of the Oakland A's. (Rev: BCCB 9/89; BL 7/89; SLJ 8/89) [921]

CLEMENTE, ROBERTO

13442 Bjarkman, Peter C. *Roberto Clemente* (4–6). Illus. Series: Baseball Legends. 1991, Chelsea LB $16.95 (0-7910-1171-2). 64pp. The inspiring career of the Puerto Rican baseball legend. (Rev: BL 3/1/91) [921]

13443 Gilbert, Tom. *Roberto Clemente* (5–8). Illus. 1991, Chelsea LB $19.95 (0-7910-1240-9). 112pp. The life of the first Hispanic in the Baseball Hall of Fame. (Rev: BL 8/91) [921]

13444 Walker, Paul R. *Pride of Puerto Rico: The Life of Roberto Clemente* (4–7). 1988, Harcourt $14.00 (0-15-200562-5); paper $6.00 (0-15-263420-7). 132pp. The life of a baseball star and hero who died trying to help others. (Rev: BL 10/1/88; HB 9–10/88; SLJ 1/89) [921]

13445 West, Alan. *Roberto Clemente: Baseball Legend* (3–6). Illus. Series: Hispanic Heritage. 1993, Millbrook LB $20.90 (1-56294-367-7). 32pp. A biography of the Puerto Rican baseball superstar. (Rev: BL 11/15/93) [921]

COBB, TY

13446 Macht, Norman L. *Ty Cobb* (4–6). Illus. Series: Baseball Legends. 1992, Chelsea LB $15.95 (0-685-48322-3). 64pp. The life of this baseball great is recalled in a text that gives coverage of pivotal games, plus statistics and a chronology. (Rev: BL 4/1/93) [921]

DEAN, DIZZY

13447 Kavanagh, Jack. *Dizzy Dean* (4–6). Illus. Series: Baseball Legends. 1991, Chelsea LB $16.95 (0-7910-1173-9). 64pp. The story of the famous pitcher for the St. Louis Cardinals. (Rev: BL 2/1/91) [921]

DIMAGGIO, JOE

13448 Appel, Marty. *Joe DiMaggio* (4–6). Illus. Series: Baseball Legends. 1990, Chelsea LB $16.95

(0-7910-1164-X). 63pp. A biography of the ultimate baseball hero. (Rev: BL 6/1/90; SLJ 10/90) [921]

13449 Sanford, William R., and Carl R. Green. *Joe DiMaggio* (4–6). Illus. Series: Sports Immortals. 1993, Macmillan LB $16.95 (0-89686-738-2). 48pp. The biography of Joe DiMaggio, alias "The Yankee Clipper," who was given the Greatest Living Player Award in the 1969 Summer Olympics. (Rev: BL 4/15/93; SLJ 8/93) [921]

DOUTY, SHEILA CORNELL

13450 Douty, Sheila Cornell, and Judith Cohen. *You Can Be a Woman Softball Player* (3–6). Illus. 2000, Cascade Pass $13.95 (1-880599-47-3); paper $7.00 (1-880599-46-5). 40pp. This is the story of Sheila Douty, from her youth, when she was considered a "problem" child, to the 1996 Olympics, where she helped her team win a gold medal. (Rev: BL 7/00) [921]

FELLER, BOB

13451 Eckhouse, Morris. *Bob Feller* (4–6). Illus. Series: Baseball Legends. 1990, Chelsea LB $16.95 (0-7910-1174-7). 64pp. The life and career of the legendary baseball pitcher are re-created. (Rev: BL 10/1/90) [921]

GALARRAGA, ANDRES

13452 Boulais, Sue. *Andres Galarraga* (3–4). Series: Real-Life Reader Biographies. 1998, Mitchell Lane LB $15.95 (1-883845-61-0). 32pp. The story of a baseball hero from Caracas, Venezuela, his career in Atlanta, and his struggle with cancer. (Rev: BL 10/15/98; HBG 10/98; SLJ 12/98) [921]

GEHRIG, LOU

13453 Adler, David A. *Lou Gehrig: The Luckiest Man* (3–5). Illus. by Terry Widener. 1997, Harcourt $16.00 (0-15-200523-4). 32pp. An excellent biography of the "Iron Horse," the baseball legend who was a model of sportsmanship and courage. (Rev: BCCB 4/97; BL 5/15/97; HB 7–8/97, 9–10/97; SLJ 5/97) [921]

13454 Macht, Norman L. *Lou Gehrig* (4–6). Illus. Series: Baseball Legends. 1993, Chelsea LB $16.95 (0-7910-1176-3). 64pp. The story of this baseball great and gallant American is told with particular attention to his most important games. (Rev: BL 4/1/93) [921]

GIBSON, JOSH

13455 Mellage, Nanette. *Coming Home: A Story of Josh Gibson, Baseball's Greatest Home Run Hitter* (PS–3). Illus. by Cornelius Van Wright and Ying-Hwa Hu. 2001, Troll $15.95 (0-8167-7009-3). 32pp. An African American grandfather tells his grandson of the life of Josh Gibson, the star player of the Negro Leagues, and of the championship game he attended many years ago. (Rev: BL 3/1/01) [921]

GONZALEZ, JUAN

13456 Gutman, Bill. *Juan Gonzalez: Outstanding Outfielder* (4–6). Illus. Series: Sports World. 1995,

Millbrook LB $19.90 (1-56294-567-X). 48pp. A brief, well-illustrated biography of this baseball star. (Rev: BL 9/15/95; SLJ 1/96) [921]

GOODEN, DWIGHT

13457 Aaseng, Nathan. *Dwight Gooden: Strikeout King* (4–7). Illus. 1988, Lerner LB $21.27 (0-8225-0478-2). 56pp. The early stunning feats of "Dr. K," his drug problem and rehabilitation, and his fight to regain his form and reputation. (Rev: BL 8/88) [921]

GRIFFEY, KEN (FATHER AND SON)

13458 Gutman, Bill. *Ken Griffey, Sr., and Ken Griffey, Jr.* (4–6). Illus. Series: Millbrook Sports World. 1993, Millbrook LB $19.90 (1-56294-226-3). 48pp. An account of the father and son who made baseball history playing together for the Seattle Mariners. (Rev: BL 3/15/93) [921]

GRIFFEY, KEN, JR.

13459 Gutman, Bill. *Ken Griffey, Jr. Baseball's Best* (4–6). Series: Sports World. 1998, Millbrook LB $19.90 (0-7613-0415-0); paper $6.95 (0-7613-0381-2). 48pp. A lively biography that describes Griffey's life, character, and contributions to baseball. (Rev: BL 11/15/98; HBG 3/99) [921]

13460 Macnow, Glen. *Ken Griffey, Jr: Star Outfielder* (4–6). Series: Sports Reports. 1997, Enslow LB $20.95 (0-89490-802-2). 104pp. The life and career of this baseball star are covered, with action photos and behind-the-scenes coverage. (Rev: BL 2/15/98; HBG 3/98) [921]

HERSHISER, OREL

13461 Knapp, Ron. *Sports Great Orel Hershiser* (5–8). Illus. Series: Sports Great Books. 1993, Enslow LB $16.95 (0-89490-389-6). 64pp. This easily read biography of this current sports favorite re-creates Orel Hershiser's life and his most exciting sports moments. (Rev: BL 4/1/93) [921]

HORNSBY, ROGERS

13462 Kavanagh, Jack. *Rogers Hornsby* (4–6). Illus. Series: Baseball Legends. 1991, Chelsea LB $16.95 (0-7910-1178-X). 64pp. A well-illustrated biography of this baseball great. (Rev: BL 2/1/91) [921]

JACKSON, REGGIE

13463 Woods, Andrew. *Young Reggie Jackson: Hall of Fame Champion* (2–4). Illus. Series: Troll First Start. 1996, Troll paper $3.50 (0-8167-3763-0). 32pp. With emphasis on his early life, this is an easily read biography of this baseball legend. (Rev: BL 2/15/96) [921]

JETER, DEREK

13464 Stewart, Mark. *Derek Jeter: Substance and Style* (4–6). Series: Baseball's New Wave. 1999, Millbrook LB $19.90 (0-7613-1516-0). 48pp. This biography that ends with the 1998 season gives a good close-up view of the star shortstop of the New York Yankees. (Rev: HBG 3/00; SLJ 2/00) [921]

13465 Torres, John. *Derek Jeter* (3–4). Series: Real-Life Reader Biographies. 2000, Mitchell Lane LB $15.95 (1-58415-031-9). 32pp. A brief, attractive biography of the young star of the New York Yankees. (Rev: BL 11/15/00) [921]

JOHNSON, WALTER

13466 Kavanagh, Jack. *Walter Johnson* (4–8). Illus. Series: Baseball Legends. 1991, Chelsea LB $16.95 (0-7910-1179-8). 144pp. A biography of a baseball giant, including coverage of important games and many black-and-white photos. (Rev: BL 1/15/92) [921]

MCGWIRE, MARK

13467 Dougherty, Terri. *Mark McGwire* (2–4). Series: Jam Session. 1999, ABDO LB $14.95 (1-57765-349-1). 32pp. A heavily illustrated biography of the amazing batter that uses quotes from friends and family. (Rev: HBG 10/99; SLJ 8/99) [921]

13468 Thornley, Stew. *Mark McGwire: Star Home Run Hitter* (4–6). Series: Star Home Run Hitter. 1999, Enslow LB $19.95 (0-7660-1329-4). 104pp. The recent World Series hero is profiled in this readable biography containing pictures and background statistics. (Rev: BL 3/15/99; HBG 10/99; SLJ 7/99) [921]

MADDUX, GREG

13469 Christopher, Matt. *On the Mound with . . . Greg Maddux* (4–7). Illus. 1997, Little, Brown paper $4.95 (0-316-14191-7). 144pp. The life of the famous player with the Chicago Cubs and Atlanta Braves, who has been called the best pitcher in baseball. (Rev: BL 7/97) [921]

13470 Gutman, Bill. *Greg Maddux* (4–6). Series: Sports World. 1999, Millbrook LB $19.90 (0-7613-1454-7). 46pp. A simple biography that stresses Greg Maddux's many contributions to the Chicago Cubs and the Atlanta Braves. (Rev: BL 1/1–15/00; HBG 3/00) [921]

13471 Thornley, Stew. *Sports Great Greg Maddux* (5–8). Illus. Series: Sports Great Books. 1997, Enslow LB $17.95 (0-89490-873-1). 64pp. The life of this baseball great is traced, supplemented by career statistics and many action photos. (Rev: BL 2/15/97) [921]

MATHEWSON, CHRISTY

13472 Macht, Norman L. *Christy Mathewson* (4–6). Illus. Series: Baseball Legends. 1991, Chelsea LB $16.95 (0-7910-1182-8). 64pp. The life of the great pitcher, including important games in his career. (Rev: BL 9/15/91) [921]

MAYS, WILLIE

13473 Grabowski, John. *Willie Mays* (4–6). Illus. Series: Baseball Legends. 1990, Chelsea LB $16.95 (0-7910-1183-6). 63pp. A profile of one of baseball's greatest hitters. (Rev: BL 6/1/90) [921]

13474 Mandel, Peter. *Say Hey! A Song of Willie Mays* (K–3). Illus. by Don Tate. 2000, Hyperion LB $16.49 (0-7868-2417-4). 32pp. The basics of Willie

Mays's life are covered in this picture book that uses a sing-along text and computer-generated art. (Rev: BL 2/15/00; HBG 10/00; SLJ 8/00) [921]

PAIGE, SATCHEL

13475 Cline-Ransome, Lesa. *Satchel Paige* (2–4). Illus. by James E. Ransome. 2000, Simon & Schuster $16.00 (0-689-81151-9). 40pp. The mythic hero of baseball comes to life, with all his swagger and accomplishments, in this biography. (Rev: BCCB 2/00; BL 12/15/99*; HB 3–4/00; HBG 10/00; SLJ 3/00) [921]

13476 McKissack, Patricia, and Fredrick McKissack. *Satchel Paige: The Best Arm in Baseball* (2–4). Illus. by Michael D. Blegel. Series: Great African Americans. 1992, Enslow LB $14.95 (0-89490-317-9). 32pp. The life story of the Hall of Famer who was the first African American pitcher in the American League. (Rev: BL 10/15/92; SLJ 1/93) [921]

PALMEIRO, RAFAEL

13477 Marvis, Barbara. *Rafael Palmeiro* (3–5). Series: Real-Life Reader Biographies. 1998, Mitchell Lane LB $15.95 (1-883845-49-1). 32pp. Using short chapters, black-and-white photos, and a simple vocabulary, this is the story of Rafael Palmeiro, the Cuban refugee who became first baseman for the Texas Rangers. (Rev: BL 6/1–15/98; HBG 3/98) [921]

PUCKETT, KIRBY

13478 Puckett, Kirby, and Greg Brown. *Kirby Puckett: Be the Best You Can Be* (2–4). Illus. by Tim Houle. 1993, Waldman $14.95 (0-931674-20-4). A picture-book autobiography of the star of the Minnesota Twins, filled with advice on how to achieve one's potential. (Rev: BL 8/93; SLJ 2/94) [921]

RIPKEN, CAL, JR.

13479 Gutman, Bill. *Cal Ripken, Jr. Baseball's Iron Man* (4–6). Series: Sports World. 1998, Millbrook LB $19.90 (0-7613-0416-9); paper $6.95 (0-7613-0380-4). 48pp. A biography of baseball star Cal Ripken, Jr., emphasizing his determination and other positive character traits. (Rev: BL 11/15/98; HBG 3/99) [921]

13480 Macnow, Glen. *Sports Great Cal Ripken, Jr.* (5–8). Illus. Series: Sports Great Books. 1993, Enslow LB $17.95 (0-89490-387-X). 64pp. The life of this current baseball star is created in text and pictures that concentrate on the sports action that has made him famous. (Rev: BL 4/1/93) [921]

13481 Ripken, Cal, Jr., and Mike Bryan. *Cal Ripken Jr.: My Story* (3–7). Adapted by Dan Gutman. Illus. 1999, Dial $15.99 (0-8037-2348-2). 128pp. An autobiography of the Baltimore Orioles hero, stressing his strong sense of family and decency. (Rev: BL 6/1–15/99; HBG 10/99) [921]

13482 Ripken, Cal, Jr., and Mike Bryan. *Cal Ripken, Jr.: Play Ball!* (1–4). Adapted by Gail Herman. Illus. by Stan Silver. Series: Dial Easy-to-Read. 1999, Dial $13.99 (0-8037-2415-2). 48pp. A first-person account (adapted from the adult autobiography), in a beginning chapter book format, of the life of the Baltimore Orioles star who broke the record for playing the most games in a row. (Rev: HBG 10/99; SLJ 6/99) [921]

13483 Savage, Jeff. *Cal Ripken, Jr.: Star Shortstop* (4–6). Illus. Series: Sports Reports. 1994, Enslow LB $20.95 (0-89490-485-X). 104pp. A book about the star baseball player who gained fame as an all-star shortstop for the Baltimore Orioles. (Rev: SLJ 2/95) [921]

ROBINSON, BROOKS

13484 Wolff, Rick. *Brooks Robinson* (4–6). Illus. Series: Baseball Legends. 1990, Chelsea LB $16.95 (0-7910-1186-0). 64pp. This biography tells the life of Brooks Robinson and his most important games. (Rev: BL 10/1/90) [921]

ROBINSON, FRANK

13485 Macht, Norman L. *Frank Robinson* (4–6). Illus. Series: Baseball Legends. 1991, Chelsea LB $16.95 (0-7910-1187-9). 64pp. This account gives good coverage of Robinson's crucial games. (Rev: BL 2/1/91) [921]

ROBINSON, JACKIE

13486 Adler, David A. *Jackie Robinson: He Was the First* (3–5). Illus. by Robert Casilla. 1989, Holiday LB $15.95 (0-8234-0734-9). 48pp. A profile of the first African American player in the major leagues. (Rev: BL 7/89) [921]

13487 Adler, David A. *A Picture Book of Jackie Robinson* (K–3). Illus. by Robert Casilla. Series: Picture Book Biographies. 1994, Holiday LB $16.95 (0-8234-1122-2). 32pp. This simple biography of the baseball giant reads like a story for young children. (Rev: BL 11/15/94; SLJ 12/94) [921]

13488 Coombs, Karen Mueller. *Jackie Robinson: Baseball's Civil Rights Legend* (5–7). Illus. Series: African American Biographies. 1997, Enslow LB $20.95 (0-89490-690-9). 128pp. The story of the baseball great who stood up to racism in athletics. (Rev: BL 6/1–15/97) [921]

13489 Davidson, Margaret. *The Story of Jackie Robinson: Bravest Man in Baseball* (3–7). Illus. 1988, Dell paper $3.99 (0-440-40019-8). 92pp. The life of the man who broke the baseball color barrier. (Rev: BL 6/1/88; SLJ 5/88) [921]

13490 De Angelis, Gina. *Jackie Robinson: Overcoming Adversity* (5–8). Illus. Series: Overcoming Adversity. 2000, Chelsea $19.95 (0-7910-5897-2). 104pp. Using a highly readable text and black-and-white photos, this book gives a real picture of Robinson that touches on the reasons he felt extreme anger and his great determination to make a difference. (Rev: BL 2/15/01) [921]

13491 Denenberg, Barry. *Stealing Home: The Story of Jackie Robinson* (4–6). Illus. 1997, Scholastic paper $4.50 (0-590-42560-9). 116pp. A biography that balances Robinson's life and significance on and off the baseball diamond. (Rev: SLJ 1/91) [921]

13492 Dingle, Derek T. *First in the Field* (4–6). Illus. 1998, Hyperion LB $17.49 (0-7868-2289-9). 48pp. This book on the Brooklyn Dodgers star brings out some lesser-known aspects of his life, including his family in California and his career in the army. (Rev: BL 6/1–15/98; HBG 10/98; SLJ 5/98) [921]

13493 Grabowski, John. *Jackie Robinson* (4–6). Illus. Series: Baseball Legends. 1990, Chelsea LB $16.95 (0-7910-1188-7). 64pp. The life story of the pro baseball player who broke the color line. (Rev: BL 11/15/90) [921]

13494 O'Connor, Jim. *Jackie Robinson and the Story of All-Black Baseball* (3–5). Illus. by Jim Butcher. 1989, Random paper $3.99 (0-394-82456-3). 48pp. The story of Jackie Robinson and the Negro Leagues, preceding his entry into pro ball. (Rev: BCCB 9/89; BL 7/89) [921]

13495 Santella, Andrew. *Jackie Robinson Breaks the Color Line* (3–5). Illus. Series: Cornerstones of Freedom. 1996, Children's LB $20.50 (0-516-06637-4). 32pp. Discusses the career of Jackie Robinson and its significance in the history of baseball and for the civil rights movement. (Rev: BL 4/15/96; SLJ 11/96) [921]

RODRIGUEZ, ALEX

13496 Stewart, Mark. *Alex Rodriguez: Gunning for Greatness* (4–6). Series: Baseball's New Wave. 1999, Millbrook LB $19.90 (0-7613-1515-2). 48pp. An attractive biography with sidebars and plenty of photos on this superstar shortstop of the Seattle Mariners that ends with the 1998 season. (Rev: HBG 10/00; SLJ 2/00) [921]

RUTH, BABE

13497 Burleigh, Robert. *Home Run: The Story of Babe Ruth* (3–6). Illus. by Mike Wimmer. 1998, Harcourt $16.00 (0-15-200970-1). 32pp. A picture book for older readers that relates the life, career, character, and accomplishments of one of baseball's great heroes. (Rev: BCCB 9/98; BL 8/98; HBG 3/99; SLJ 8/98) [921]

13498 Macht, Norman L. *Babe Ruth* (4–6). Illus. Series: Baseball Legends. 1991, Chelsea LB $16.95 (0-7910-1189-5). 64pp. The life of the legendary left-handed pitcher, outfielder, and slugger is re-created. (Rev: BL 4/15/91) [921]

13499 Nicholson, Lois. *Babe Ruth: Sultan of Swat* (5–8). Illus. 1995, Goodwood $17.95 (0-9625427-1-7). 119pp. This well-written account of the famous slugger explains his lasting influence on baseball. (Rev: SLJ 7/95) [921]

13500 Sanford, William R., and Carl R. Green. *Babe Ruth* (4–6). Illus. Series: Sports Immortals. 1992, Macmillan LB $16.95 (0-89686-741-2). 48pp. Numerous photos enhance this bio of the great Yankee star for middle-grade readers. (Rev: BL 2/1/93; SLJ 1/93) [921]

RYAN, NOLAN

13501 Lace, William W. *Sports Great Nolan Ryan* (5–8). Illus. Series: Sports Great Books. 1993,

Enslow LB $17.95 (0-89490-394-2). 64pp. The life story and important games are covered in this biography of the exciting baseball star, Nolan Ryan. (Rev: BL 6/1–15/93) [921]

13502 Rappoport, Ken. *Nolan Ryan: The Ryan Express* (3–6). Illus. Series: Taking Part. 1992, Macmillan LB $18.95 (0-87518-524-X). 64pp. The life story of the amazing baseball player who has developed a large following. (Rev: BL 1/15/93) [921]

SNIDER, DUKE

13503 Bjarkman, Peter C. *Duke Snider* (4–6). Illus. Series: Baseball Legends. 1994, Chelsea LB $16.95 (0-7910-1190-9). 63pp. A biography of the superstar from the golden age of baseball. (Rev: BL 10/15/94) [921]

SOSA, SAMMY

13504 Dougherty, Terri. *Sammy Sosa* (2–4). Series: Jam Session. 1999, ABDO LB $14.95 (1-57765-348-3). 32pp. Using quotes from friends, family, and teammates, this simple, heavily illustrated biography presents the life and accomplishments of amazing batter Sammy Sosa. (Rev: HBG 10/99; SLJ 8/99) [921]

13505 Muskat, Carrie. *Sammy Sosa* (4–8). Series: Latinos in Baseball. 1999, Mitchell Lane LB $18.95 (1-883845-92-0). 64pp. This biography tells of Sosa's rise from extreme poverty, his ties to his homeland, the Dominican Republic, and his devotion to his game. (Rev: HBG 10/99; SLJ 5/99) [921]

STRAWBERRY, DARRYL

13506 Torres, John A., and Michael J. Sullivan. *Darryl Strawberry* (4–6). Illus. Series: Sports Great Books. 1990, Enslow LB $17.95 (0-89490-291-1). 64pp. The story of the fine but controversial baseball player, with good coverage of his childhood. (Rev: SLJ 11/90) [921]

THOMAS, FRANK

13507 Gutman, Bill. *Frank Thomas: Power Hitter* (4–6). Illus. Series: Sports World. 1996, Millbrook LB $19.90 (1-56294-569-6). 48pp. This biography of the baseball superstar tells about his life and his talent. (Rev: BL 5/15/96; SLJ 6/96) [921]

13508 Spiros, Dean. *Frank Thomas: Star First Baseman* (4–6). Illus. Series: Sports Reports. 1996, Enslow LB $20.95 (0-89490-659-3). 104pp. The life of this baseball hero is covered, with emphasis on key games and important career decisions. (Rev: BL 11/15/96) [921]

13509 Thornley, Stew. *Frank Thomas: Baseball's Big Hurt* (4–8). Series: Sports Achievers. 1997, Lerner $22.60 (0-8225-3651-X); paper $5.95 (0-8225-9759-4). 64pp. As well as being a big-time hitter in baseball, this star — nicknamed "The Big Hurt" — devotes much of his spare time to the fight against leukemia. (Rev: BL 1/1–15/98; HBG 3/98) [921]

YOUNG, CY

13510 Macht, Norman L. *Cy Young* (4–6). Illus. Series: Baseball Legends. 1991, Chelsea LB $15.95 (0-7910-1196-8). 144pp. The story of this legendary pitcher, with interesting background and team information. (Rev: BL 1/15/92) [921]

Basketball

ABDUL-JABBAR, KAREEM

13511 Sanford, William R., and Carl R. Green. *Kareem Abdul-Jabbar* (4–6). Illus. Series: Sports Immortals. 1993, Macmillan LB $11.95 (0-89686-737-4). 48pp. The life and career of Lew Alcindor, better known as Kareem Abdul-Jabbar, who was named the NBA Most Valuable Player six times. (Rev: BL 4/15/93; SLJ 8/93) [921]

BARKLEY, CHARLES

13512 Dolan, Sean. *Charles Barkley* (5–7). Illus. Series: Basketball Legends. 1996, Chelsea LB $16.95 (0-7910-2433-4). 62pp. The life of this basketball superstar, with details on his record on the court. (Rev: BL 7/96) [921]

13513 Knapp, Ron. *Charles Barkley: Star Forward* (4–6). Illus. Series: Sports Reports. 1996, Enslow LB $20.95 (0-89490-655-0). 104pp. A short biography of this basketball star, with career statistics and many action photos. (Rev: BL 8/96; SLJ 8/96) [921]

BIRD, LARRY

13514 Kavanagh, Jack. *Sports Great Larry Bird* (4–8). Illus. Series: Sports Great Books. 1992, Enslow LB $17.95 (0-89490-368-3). 64pp. The extraordinary story of the basketball player who drove his team, the Boston Celtics, to five NBA finals. (Rev: BL 7/92; SLJ 10/92) [921]

BRYANT, KOBE

13515 Savage, Jeff. *Kobe Bryant: Basketball Big Shot* (4–7). Illus. Series: Sports Biography. 2000, Lerner LB $22.60 (0-8225-3680-3). 64pp. A very readable, attractive biography of the new NBA sensation that ends with the 1999–2000 season. (Rev: BL 1/1–15/01) [921]

13516 Schnakenberg, Robert E. *Kobe Bryant* (4–6). Illus. Series: Basketball Legends. 1998, Chelsea $16.95 (0-7910-5005-X). 64pp. A detailed biography of the Lakers star who became the youngest man ever to play in an NBA game. (Rev: BL 3/1/99; HBG 10/99) [921]

13517 Stewart, Mark. *Kobe Bryant: Hard to the Hoop* (4–8). Series: Basketball's New Wave. 2000, Millbrook LB $20.90 (0-7613-1800-3). 48pp. The life story of this basketball star who was the son of an NBA player and who became the youngest player in league history to star in the All-Star Game. (Rev: HBG 10/00; SLJ 8/00) [921]

13518 Torres, John. *Kobe Bryant* (3–4). Series: Real-Life Reader Biographies. 2000, Mitchell Lane LB $15.95 (1-58415-030-0). 32pp. An easily read biography of the well-known basketball player who was a star before he graduated from high school. (Rev: BL 11/15/00) [921]

COOPER, CYNTHIA

13519 Schnakenberg, Robert E. *Cynthia Cooper* (5–9). Series: Women Who Win. 2000, Chelsea LB $17.95 (0-7910-5796-8). 64pp. A biography of this basketball star that focuses on her career and game-related information. (Rev: HBG 3/01; SLJ 2/01) [921]

DUNCAN, TIM

13520 Byman, Jeremy. *Tim Duncan* (4–8). Illus. Series: Great Athletes. 2000, Morgan Reynolds $19.95 (1-883846-43-9). 64pp. This biography about a basketball hero who has been playing professionally for only a short time focuses on his college years, his outstanding talent, and his determination. (Rev: BL 6/1–15/00; HBG 3/01) [921]

13521 Rappoport, Ken. *Tim Duncan: Star Forward* (5–8). Series: Sports Reports. 2000, Enslow LB $19.95 (0-7660-1334-0). 112pp. A look at one of basketball's star forwards, accompanied by statistics and action photos. (Rev: BL 10/15/00; HBG 3/01) [921]

13522 Stewart, Mark. *Tim Duncan: Tower of Power* (4–8). Series: Basketball's New Wave. 1999, Millbrook LB $19.90 (0-7613-1513-6). 48pp. Although this biography of basketball's rising star is brief, the information is ample and important topics are all covered. (Rev: HBG 10/00; SLJ 7/00) [921]

EWING, PATRICK

13523 Kavanagh, Jack. *Sports Great Patrick Ewing* (5–8). Illus. Series: Sports Great Books. 1992, Enslow LB $17.95 (0-89490-369-1). 64pp. An easily read, candid look at the basketball great from Jamaica. (Rev: BL 9/1/92) [921]

13524 Wiener, Paul. *Patrick Ewing* (4–6). Illus. Series: Basketball Legends. 1996, Chelsea LB $16.95 (0-7910-2434-2). 64pp. The story of this New York Knicks center and his quest for an NBA championship. (Rev: BL 7/96) [921]

HARDAWAY, ANFERNEE

13525 Gutman, Bill. *Anfernee Hardaway: Super Guard* (4–6). Illus. Series: Sports World. 1997, Millbrook LB $19.90 (0-7613-0062-7). 48pp. This basketball star's life story is given, with plenty of sports action and summary career statistics. (Rev: BL 4/15/97) [921]

13526 Rekela, George R. *Sports Great Anfernee Hardaway* (5–8). Illus. Series: Sports Great Books. 1996, Enslow LB $17.95 (0-89490-758-1). 64pp. An interesting biography illustrated with black-and-white photos of this basketball star. (Rev: BL 3/15/96) [921]

HILL, GRANT

13527 Christopher, Matt. *On the Court with . . . Grant Hill* (3–7). Illus. Series: Matt Christopher Sports Biography. 1996, Little, Brown paper $4.95 (0-316-13790-1). 144pp. A fine biography of this basketball hero whose rise to fame involved personal determination and courage. (Rev: BL 2/15/97; SLJ 6/97) [921]

13528 Gutman, Bill. *Grant Hill: Basketball's High Flier* (3–6). Illus. Series: Sports World. 1996, Millbrook LB $19.90 (0-7613-0038-4); paper $6.95 (0-7613-0133-X). 48pp. A brief biography that concentrates on Hill's basketball career, particularly at Duke University and with the Detroit Pistons. (Rev: SLJ 2/97) [921]

13529 Savage, Jeff. *Grant Hill: Humble Hotshot* (4–8). Illus. Series: Sports Achievers. 1997, Lerner LB $22.60 (0-8225-2893-2). 64pp. The story of the humble basketball star who has been a mainstay of the Detroit Pistons. (Rev: BL 4/15/97; SLJ 6/97) [921]

13530 Thornley, Stew. *Grant Hill: Star Forward* (4–6). Series: Sports Reports. 1999, Enslow LB $19.95 (0-7660-1078-3). 104pp. An in-depth look at the life and career of this basketball star, with many action photographs. (Rev: BL 2/15/99; HBG 10/99) [921]

HOWARD, JUWAN

13531 Savage, Jeff. *Sports Great Juwan Howard* (5–8). Series: Sports Great Books. 1998, Enslow LB $16.95 (0-7660-1065-1). 64pp. The Washington Wizards basketball star is profiled in this lively account, supplemented by many black-and-white photos. (Rev: BL 2/15/99; HBG 10/99) [921]

JOHNSON, MAGIC

13532 Greenberg, Keith E. *Magic Johnson: Champion with a Cause* (4–7). Illus. Series: Achievers. 1992, Lerner LB $22.60 (0-8225-0546-0). 64pp. The story of the gifted athlete for the L.A. Lakers, whose career was cut short when he discovered he was HIV-positive. (Rev: BL 8/92; SLJ 7/92) [921]

13533 Gutman, Bill. *Magic Johnson: Hero on and off the Court* (4–6). Illus. Series: Sports World. 1992, Millbrook paper $5.95 (1-56294-825-3). 48pp. This story of the life of the basketball superstar emphasizes that hard work and dedication lead to success. (Rev: BL 11/1/92; SLJ 12/92) [921]

13534 Haskins, Jim. *Sports Great Magic Johnson* (4–8). Illus. 1992, Enslow LB $17.95 (0-89490-348-9). 80pp. The story of the great "great" of the Los Angeles Lakers pro basketball team. (Rev: BL 6/15/89) [921]

JORDAN, MICHAEL

13535 Aaseng, Nathan. *Sports Great Michael Jordan* (5–8). Illus. Series: Sports Great Books. 1992, Enslow LB $17.95 (0-89490-370-5). 64pp. Michael Jordan's life, his successes as guard of the Chicago Bulls, and his commercials for TV are discussed in this easily read book. (Rev: BL 10/15/92) [921]

13536 Berger, Phil, and John Rolfe. *Michael Jordan* (4–7). Illus. 1990, Little, Brown paper $4.95 (0-316-09229-0). 124pp. This account covers Jordan's childhood and his career development. (Rev: BL 12/15/90; SLJ 4/91) [921]

13537 Christopher, Matt. *On the Court with . . . Michael Jordan* (3–7). Illus. Series: Matt Christopher Sports Biography. 1996, Little, Brown paper $4.95 (0-316-13792-8). 144pp. The life of this pro basketball legend whose self-determination and family support helped him rise to the top. (Rev: BL 2/15/97; SLJ 6/97) [921]

13538 Gutman, Bill. *Michael Jordan: A Biography* (5–8). 1995, Pocket paper $4.99 (0-671-51972-7). 133pp. This readable book contains good coverage on the formative years as well as the current accomplishments of this basketball hero. (Rev: SLJ 5/92) [921]

13539 Gutman, Bill. *Michael Jordan: Basketball Champ* (4–6). Illus. Series: Sports World. 1992, Houghton paper $4.80 (0-395-64545-X). The life and dedication to hard work of one of basketball's greatest stars. (Rev: BL 11/1/91; SLJ 12/92) [921]

13540 Rambeck, Richard. *Michael Jordan* (3–6). Series: Sports Superstars. 1999, Child's World LB $14.95 (1-56766-520-9). 23pp. A simple biography of the basketball superstar, suitable for reluctant readers because of its format and colorful photos. (Rev: BL 5/15/99; HBG 10/99) [921]

KEMP, SHAWN

13541 Thornley, Stew. *Shawn Kemp: Star Forward* (4–6). Series: Sports Reports. 1998, Enslow LB $20.95 (0-89490-929-0). 104pp. An account that stresses this fine basketball player's good character traits and strong athletic abilities. (Rev: BL 2/15/98; HBG 10/98) [921]

KIDD, JASON

13542 Gray, Valerie A. *Jason Kidd: Star Guard* (5–8). Series: Sports Reports. 2000, Enslow LB $19.95 (0-7660-1333-2). 112pp. The story of the basketball superstar with behind-the-scenes reporting on his life and career. (Rev: BL 10/15/00; HBG 10/00) [921]

13543 Torres, John A. *Sports Great Jason Kidd* (5–8). Series: Sports Great Books. 1998, Enslow LB $15.95 (0-7660-1001-5). 64pp. An action-filled biography of this basketball star, complete with career statistics and black-and-white photos of Kidd on the court. (Rev: BL 7/98; HBG 10/98) [921]

LESLIE, LISA

13544 Kelley, Brent. *Lisa Leslie* (5–9). Series: Women Who Win. 2000, Chelsea LB $17.95 (0-7910-5794-1). 64pp. This profile of a pioneer in the Women's National Basketball Association contains much game-related information. (Rev: HBG 3/01; SLJ 2/01) [921]

LIEBERMAN-CLINE, NANCY

13545 Greenberg, Doreen, and Michael Greenberg. *A Drive to Win: The Story of Nancy Lieberman-Cline* (4–8). Illus. by Phil Velikan. Series: Anything You Can Do — New Sports Heroes for Girls. 2000, Wish paper $9.95 (1-930546-40-8). 98pp. Based on personal interviews, this is an informative biography of the basketball star Lieberman-Cline. (Rev: SLJ 3/01) [921]

LOBO, REBECCA

13546 Rambeck, Richard. *Rebecca Lobo* (3–6). Illus. Series: Sports Superstars. 1999, Child's World

LB $14.95 (1-56766-524-1). 26pp. Using double-page spreads, this biography details Lobo's contributions to the University of Connecticut's basketball team, her part in the winning of the NCAA women's basketball tournament, and her role in the 1996 Olympics. (Rev: BL 5/15/99; HBG 10/99) [921]

LUCAS, JOHN

13547 Simmons, Alex. *John Lucas* (4–6). Illus. Series: Contemporary African Americans. 1995, Raintree Steck-Vaughn LB $25.69 (0-8172-3978-2). 48pp. An inspiring story of the man who conquered drug addiction and became the first African American coach of the San Antonio Spurs. (Rev: BL 2/15/96; SLJ 4/96) [921]

MALONE, KARL

13548 Rekela, George R. *Karl Malone: Star Forward* (4–6). Series: Sports Reports. 1998, Enslow LB $18.95 (0-89490-931-2). Plenty of action photographs and career statistics illustrate this biography of the Utah Jazz's great power forward. (Rev: BL 8/98; HBG 10/98) [921]

MILLER, REGGIE

13549 Thornley, Stew. *Sports Great Reggie Miller* (5–8). Illus. Series: Sports Great Books. 1996, Enslow LB $17.95 (0-89490-874-X). 64pp. The life of this basketball star is traced, with special emphasis on key games. (Rev: BL 9/15/96) [921]

MOURNING, ALONZO

13550 Fortunato, Frank. *Sports Great Alonzo Mourning* (5–8). Illus. Series: Sports Great Books. 1997, Enslow LB $17.95 (0-89490-875-8). 64pp. An easily read biography of this amazing basketball star. (Rev: BL 2/15/97) [921]

13551 Gutman, Bill. *Alonzo Mourning: Center of Attention* (4–6). Illus. Series: Sports World. 1997, Millbrook LB $19.90 (0-7613-0061-9). 48pp. This action-filled biography of the basketball star supplies good career statistics. (Rev: BL 4/15/97) [921]

MULLIN, CHRIS

13552 Morgan, Terri, and Shmuel Thaler. *Chris Mullin: Sure Shot* (4–8). Illus. Series: Sports Achievers. 1994, Lerner LB $10.13 (0-8225-2887-7). 64pp. The story of this amazing basketball star who overcame many obstacles, including alcoholism. (Rev: BL 1/1/95; SLJ 1/95) [921]

NUNEZ, TOMMY

13553 Boulais, Sue, and Barbara Marvis. *Tommy Nunez* (3–5). Illus. Series: Real-Life Reader Biographies. 1998, Mitchell Lane LB $15.95 (1-883845-52-1). 32pp. A simple biography that traces Nunez's life from the Phoenix barrio to a career as a referee in the National Basketball Association. (Rev: BL 6/1–15/98; HBG 3/98) [921]

OLAJUWON, HAKEEM

13554 Gutman, Bill. *Hakeem Olajuwon: Superstar Center* (4–6). Illus. Series: Sports World. 1995, Millbrook LB $19.90 (1-56294-568-8). 64pp. A fast-moving, well-illustrated biography of this basketball star. (Rev: BL 9/15/95; SLJ 1/96) [921]

13555 McMane, Fred. *Hakeem Olajuwon* (5–7). Series: Basketball Legends. 1997, Chelsea LB $16.95 (0-7910-4385-1). 64pp. The story of this basketball star of the Houston Rockets, his boyhood in Nigeria, and his role as part of the U.S. Olympic "Dream Team." (Rev: BL 9/15/97) [921]

13556 Torres, John A. *Hakeem Olajuwon: Star Center* (4–6). Series: Sports Reports. 1997, Enslow LB $20.95 (0-89490-803-0). 104pp. This biography of the star basketball player also contains career statistics, action photos, and chapter notes. (Rev: BL 11/15/97; HBG 3/98) [921]

O'NEAL, SHAQUILLE

13557 Macnow, Glen. *Shaquille O'Neal: Star Center* (4–6). Illus. Series: Sports Reports. 1996, Enslow LB $20.95 (0-89490-656-9). 104pp. An account of this pro basketball star, with career statistics and a behind-the-scenes look at his life and interests. (Rev: BL 11/15/96) [921]

13558 Sullivan, Michael J. *Sports Great Shaquille O'Neal* (5–8). Series: Sports Great Books. 1998, Enslow LB $16.95 (0-7660-1003-1). 64pp. The life and career of this well-known basketball star are covered in this easily read biography containing career statistics and many illustrations. (Rev: BL 2/15/99; HBG 10/99) [921]

13559 Tallman, Edward. *Shaquille O'Neal* (3–6). Illus. 1994, Silver Burdett $14.95 (0-87518-637-8). 72pp. The life of the NBA star who is also known as an actor and a rap artist. (Rev: BL 2/1/95) [921]

13560 Townsend, Brad. *Shaquille O'Neal: Center of Attention* (3–5). Illus. Series: Sports Achievers. 1994, Lerner LB $22.60 (0-8225-2879-7); paper $5.95 (0-8225-9655-5). 56pp. This life story tells about O'Neal's childhood, his school basketball career, and his first year in the NBA. (Rev: BL 5/15/94; SLJ 9/94) [921]

13561 Ungs, Tim. *Shaquille O'Neal* (5–7). Illus. Series: Basketball Legends. 1996, Chelsea LB $16.95 (0-7910-2437-7). 64pp. An interesting portrait of the unstoppable Lakers basketball superstar. (Rev: BL 7/96) [921]

PAYTON, GARY

13562 Bernstein, Ross. *Gary Payton: Star Guard* (4–6). Illus. Series: Sports Reports. 2000, Enslow LB $19.95 (0-7660-1330-8). 104pp. An in-depth look at this star basketball player, including his career statistics and some action photographs. (Rev: BL 9/15/00; HBG 10/00) [921]

PIPPEN, SCOTTIE

13563 Bjarkman, Peter C. *Sports Great Scottie Pippen* (5–8). Illus. Series: Sports Great Books. 1996, Enslow LB $17.95 (0-89490-755-7). 64pp. Action photos, career statistics, and an account of important

games are highlights of this basketball biography. (Rev: BL 9/15/96) [921]

13564 McMane, Fred. *Scottie Pippen* (5–7). Illus. Series: Basketball Legends. 1996, Chelsea LB $16.95 (0-7910-2498-9). 64pp. The life of this basketball star, highlighting his special abilities and his court record. (Rev: BL 7/96) [921]

13565 Pippen, Scottie, and Greg Brown. *Reach Higher* (4–7). 1997, Taylor $14.95 (0-87833-981-7). 40pp. The story of the famous Chicago Bulls basketball star, who came from a family of 12 and whose original sports were baseball and football. (Rev: BL 10/1/97) [921]

RICHMOND, MITCH

13566 Grody, Carl W. *Sports Great Mitch Richmond* (5–8). Series: Sports Great Books. 1998, Enslow LB $16.95 (0-7660-1070-8). 64pp. Using many black-and-white photos and a lively text, this book re-creates the life of the basketball great. (Rev: BL 2/15/99; HBG 10/99) [921]

ROBINSON, DAVID

13567 Aaseng, Nathan. *Sports Great David Robinson* (5–8). Illus. Series: Sports Great Books. 1992, Enslow LB $17.95 (0-89490-373-X). 64pp. This easily read biography highlights David Robinson of the San Antonio Spurs, the 1990 Rookie of the Year. (Rev: BL 10/15/92) [921]

13568 Bock, Hal. *David Robinson* (5–7). Series: Basketball Legends. 1997, Chelsea LB $16.95 (0-7910-4387-8). 64pp. The story of this star of the San Antonio Spurs, who was a brilliant student and an officer in the U.S. Navy before turning to professional sports. (Rev: BL 9/15/97) [921]

13569 Green, Carl R., and Roxanne Ford. *David Robinson* (4–8). Illus. Series: Sports Headliners. 1994, Silver Burdett LB $17.95 (0-89686-839-7); paper $7.95 (0-382-24808-2). 48pp. A slim biography of this basketball star, who gained fame during the 1987 Navy–Duke game. (Rev: BL 10/1/94) [921]

13570 Gutman, Bill. *David Robinson: NBA Super Center* (4–6). Illus. Series: Millbrook Sports World. 1993, Millbrook LB $19.90 (1-56294-228-X). 48pp. A brief biography about Robinson's contributions to basketball and his career with the San Antonio Spurs. (Rev: BL 3/15/93) [921]

13571 Macnow, Glen. *David Robinson: Star Center* (4–6). Illus. Series: Sports Reports. 1994, Enslow LB $20.95 (0-89490-483-3). 104pp. The life of this sports hero who gained fame as an all-pro center for the San Antonio Spurs. (Rev: SLJ 2/95) [921]

13572 Miller, Dawn M. *David Robinson: Backboard Admiral* (3–5). Illus. Series: The Achievers. 1991, Lerner LB $18.60 (0-8225-0494-4). 64pp. Story of the basketball star, including his Pan American and Olympic games. (Rev: SLJ 9/91) [921]

RODMAN, DENNIS

13573 Frank, Steven. *Dennis Rodman* (4–8). Series: Basketball Legends. 1997, Chelsea LB $15.95 (0-7910-4388-6). 64pp. A candid look at the bad boy of basketball, his troubled youth and current rebellious attitudes. (Rev: HBG 3/98; SLJ 4/98) [921]

13574 Thornley, Stew. *Sports Great Dennis Rodman* (5–8). Illus. Series: Sports Great Books. 1996, Enslow LB $17.95 (0-89490-759-X). 64pp. The life story of this controversial basketball star discusses his often outrageous behavior and his amazing accomplishments. (Rev: BL 31596) [921]

STEDING, KATY

13575 Gogol, Sara. *Katy Steding: Pro Basketball Pioneer* (3–6). Series: Sports Achievers. 1998, Lerner LB $19.93 (0-8225-3668-4); paper $5.95 (0-8225-9823-X). 64pp. A biography that focuses on the hardships Katy Steding faced before and after becoming the first woman to play professional basketball in America. (Rev: HBG 3/99; SLJ 12/98) [921]

STOCKTON, JOHN

13576 Aaseng, Nathan. *Sports Great John Stockton* (5–8). Illus. Series: Sports Great Books. 1995, Enslow LB $17.95 (0-89490-598-8). 64pp. A short biography of the basketball great John Stockton, with sports action and lively photographs. (Rev: BL 9/15/95) [921]

THOMAS, ISIAH

13577 Knapp, Ron. *Sports Great Isiah Thomas* (5–8). Illus. Series: Sports Great Books. 1992, Enslow LB $17.95 (0-89490-374-8). 64pp. Using a standard chronological approach and many photographs, this is an accurate, appealing biography of this great African American basketball player. (Rev: BL 9/1/92) [921]

VAN HORN, KEITH

13578 Kelley, Brent. *Keith Van Horn* (4–6). Illus. Series: Basketball Legends. 1998, Chelsea $16.95 (0-7910-5009-2). 64pp. This biography stressing team spirit traces the life and career of the New Jersey Nets player who helped his team reach the playoffs for the first time in four years. (Rev: BL 3/1/99; HBG 10/99) [921]

WEBBER, CHRIS

13579 Knapp, Ron. *Chris Webber: Star Forward* (4–6). Illus. Series: Sports Reports. 1997, Enslow LB $20.95 (0-89490-799-9). 104pp. Complete with career statistics and action photos, this is the story of the star basketball player and his rise to the top. (Rev: BL 8/97) [921]

WHITMORE, TAMIKA

13580 Anderson, Joan. *Rookie: Tamika Whitmore's First Year in the WNBA* (4–6). 2000, Penguin paper $7.99 (0-14-056740-2). 40pp. Excellent color photos introduce this basketball star and describe her first year with the New York Liberty team. (Rev: BL 7/00; SLJ 9/00) [921]

WILKINS, DOMINIQUE

13581 Bjarkman, Peter C. *Sports Great Dominique Wilkins* (5–8). Illus. Series: Sports Great Books. 1996, Enslow LB $17.95 (0-89490-754-9). 64pp. The story of this basketball star, with profiles of his most exciting games and career statistics. (Rev: BL 9/15/96) [921]

Boxing

ALI, MUHAMMAD

13582 Latimer, Clay. *Muhammad Ali* (4–6). Series: Journey to Freedom. 2000, Child's World LB $25.64 (1-56766-723-6). 40pp. The story of the great boxer and civil rights activist who became an inspiration around the world. (Rev: BL 11/15/00) [921]

CHAVEZ, JULIO CESAR

13583 Dolan, Terrance. *Julio Cesar Chavez* (5–8). Illus. Series: Hispanics of Achievement. 1994, Chelsea LB $19.95 (0-7910-2021-5). 128pp. A biography of the fighting boxer and his struggle to get to the top. (Rev: BL 9/15/94) [921]

DE LA HOYA, OSCAR

13584 Menard, Valerie. *Oscar De La Hoya* (3–4). Illus. Series: Real-Life Reader Biographies. 1998, Mitchell Lane LB $15.95 (1-883845-58-0). 24pp. The story of the amazing boxer whose father predicted he would be a champion after taking him to a gym at age six. (Rev: BL 10/15/98; HBG 10/98) [921]

13585 Torres, John A. *Sports Great Oscar De La Hoya* (5–8). Series: Sports Great Books. 1998, Enslow LB $16.95 (0-7660-1066-X). 64pp. A brief biography of the boxing sensation, with action photographs and career statistics. (Rev: BL 2/15/99; HBG 10/99) [921]

LOUIS, JOE

13586 Campbell, Jim. *Joe Louis* (4–8). Illus. Series: Importance Of. 1997, Lucent LB $12.50 (1-56006-085-9). 128pp. The fabulous life and career of the Brown Bomber are traced, with emphasis on his lasting contributions to boxing and his race. (Rev: BL 5/15/97; HBG 3/98) [921]

Figure Skating

BAIUL, OKSANA

13587 Baiul, Oksana. *Oksana: My Own Story* (4–6). Illus. 1997, Random $16.99 (0-679-88382-7). 46pp. An autobiography of the figure-skating champion who won the Olympic gold medal in 1994. (Rev: BL 5/1/97; SLJ 5/97) [921]

BOITANO, BRIAN

13588 Boitano, Brian, and Suzanne Harper. *Boitano's Edge: Inside the Real World of Figure Skat-*

ing (4–8). Illus. 1997, Simon & Schuster paper $25.00 (0-689-81915-3). 144pp. In this autobiography, Boitano tells about his life, the 1988 Olympics, his training program, touring, and his preparation for competitions. (Rev: BCCB 3/98; BL 2/15/98; SLJ 4/98) [921]

GORDEEVA, EKATARINA

13589 Gordeeva, Ekaterina, and Antonina W. Bouis. *A Letter for Daria* (3–5). 1998, Little, Brown $12.95 (0-316-32994-0). 83pp. This autobiography consists of nine short letters written by the gold medalist to her six-year-old daughter telling her about the life of a skater and the transition from a Russian to an American culture. (Rev: SLJ 7/98) [921]

13590 Shea, Pegi Deitz. *Ekatarina Gordeeva* (4–8). Series: Female Figure Skating Legends. 1999, Chelsea LB $16.95 (0-7910-5027-0). 64pp. Sports lovers will enjoy this look at the life of the famous skater before and after the death of her partner and husband, Sergei Grinkov. (Rev: SLJ 4/99) [921]

HAMILL, DOROTHY

13591 Sanford, William R., and Carl R. Green. *Dorothy Hamill* (4–6). Illus. Series: Sports Immortals. 1993, Macmillan LB $11.95 (0-89686-799-X). 48pp. The life and career of this remarkable ice skater is told in this slim volume filled with many black-and-white photos. (Rev: BL 10/1/93) [921]

KERRIGAN, NANCY

13592 Edelson, Paula. *Nancy Kerrigan* (4–6). Illus. 1998, Chelsea LB $16.95 (0-7910-5028-9). 64pp. The triumphs and tragedies of an Olympic medal winner are outlined in this biography. (Rev: BL 3/1/99) [921]

KWAN, MICHELLE

13593 James, Laura. *Michelle Kwan: Heart of a Champion* (4–8). Illus. 1997, Scholastic $14.95 (0-590-76340-7). 176pp. A highly personal account of this figure-skating champion's life and feelings that shows a maturity beyond her years. (Rev: BL 11/15/97; HBG 3/98; SLJ 11/97) [921]

LIPINSKI, TARA

13594 Gutman, Bill. *Tara Lipinski* (4–6). Series: Sports World. 1999, Millbrook LB $19.90 (0-7613-1456-3). 48pp. This biography of the prize-winning figure skater stresses her determination and talent as well as her accomplishments. (Rev: BL 1/1–15/00; HBG 3/00) [921]

13595 Rambeck, Richard. *Tara Lipinski* (3–6). Series: Sports Superstars. 1999, Child's World LB $14.95 (1-56766-525-5). 23pp. This biography of the diminutive American figure skater is suitable for reluctant readers because of the large number of photographs included and the brevity of the text. (Rev: BL 5/15/99) [921]

WITT, KATARINA

13596 Coffey, Wayne. *Katarina Witt* (4–7). Illus. 1992, Blackbirch LB $16.45 (1-56711-001-0). 64pp. This biography highlights the 1988 Olympic Games, where this figure skater became a star. (Rev: SLJ 11/92) [921]

13597 Kelly, Evelyn B. *Katarina Witt* (4–6). Illus. 1998, Chelsea LB $16.95 (0-7910-5026-2). 64pp. This biography of the Olympic ice skater describes her years growing up in East Germany and her determination, in spite of her age, to compete in the 1994 Olympics. (Rev: BL 3/1/99) [921]

YAMAGUCHI, KRISTI

13598 Donohue, Shiobhan. *Kristi Yamaguchi: Artist on Ice* (3–6). Illus. 1993, Lerner LB $21.27 (0-8225-0522-3). 64pp. A biography of the figure skater that stresses her dedication and hard work. (Rev: BL 2/15/94; SLJ 3/94) [921]

13599 Savage, Jeff. *Kristi Yamaguchi* (3–6). Illus. Series: Taking Part. 1993, Dillon LB $18.95 (0-87518-583-5). 64pp. A biography of the Japanese American ice skater and her triumph at the Olympic Games. (Rev: BL 10/15/93; SLJ 2/94) [921]

Football

AIKMAN, TROY

13600 Gutman, Bill. *Troy Aikman: Super Quarterback* (4–6). Illus. Series: Sports World. 1996, Millbrook LB $19.90 (1-56294-570-X). 48pp. A colorful biography that tells about the life, talent, and drive of this football hero. (Rev: BL 5/15/96; SLJ 6/96) [921]

13601 Macnow, Glen. *Sports Great Troy Aikman* (5–8). Illus. Series: Sports Great Books. 1995, Enslow LB $17.95 (0-89490-593-7). 64pp. The life story of the football great Troy Aikman, with good action photographs and sports statistics. (Rev: BL 9/15/95) [921]

13602 Spiros, Dean. *Troy Aikman: Star Quarterback* (4–6). Series: Sports Reports. 1997, Enslow LB $20.95 (0-89490-927-4). 104pp. An in-depth look at this star quarterback, with career statistics, action photos, and a behind-the-scenes look at this colorful player. (Rev: BL 12/15/97; HBG 3/98) [921]

BETTIS, JEROME

13603 Majewski, Stephen. *Sports Great Jerome Bettis* (5–8). Illus. Series: Sports Great Books. 1997, Enslow LB $17.95 (0-89490-872-3). 64pp. The great football hero Jerome Bettis is highlighted in this easily read biography. (Rev: BL 2/15/97) [921]

BRYANT, PAUL W.

13604 Smith, E. S. *Bear Bryant: Football's Winning Coach* (6–8). Illus. 1984, Walker $11.95 (0-8027-6526-2). 128pp. The story of one of the most famous coaches in football history. [921]

DAVIS, TERRELL

13605 Majewski, Stephen. *Terrell Davis: Star Running Back* (4–6). Illus. Series: Sports Reports. 2000, Enslow LB $19.95 (0-7660-1331-6). 104pp. Employing action photos, career statistics, and a clear text, this is a fine biography of this football star. (Rev: BL 9/15/00; HBG 3/01) [921]

13606 Stewart, Mark. *Terrell Davis: Toughing It Out* (4–8). Series: Football's New Wave. 1999, Millbrook LB $19.90 (0-7613-1514-4). 48pp. A brief biography of this football hero that uses color photographs and many fact boxes. (Rev: HBG 10/00; SLJ 7/00) [921]

ELWAY, JOHN

13607 Christopher, Matt. *In the Huddle with John Elway* (4–6). 1999, Little, Brown paper $4.50 (0-316-13355-8). 109pp. A lively biography with plenty of play-by-play action that tells the life story of John Elway up to 1998, when the quarterback won his first Super Bowl with the Denver Broncos. (Rev: SLJ 6/99) [921]

ESIASON, BOOMER

13608 Esiason, Boomer. *A Boy Named Boomer* (1–2). Illus. by Jacqueline Rogers. 1995, Scholastic paper $3.99 (0-590-52835-1). 46pp. Boomer Esiason, a former NFL quarterback, recalls several incidents from his childhood in this easy reader. (Rev: BL 1/1–15/96; SLJ 3/96) [921]

FAVRE, BRETT

13609 Gutman, Bill. *Brett Favre* (4–8). Illus. 1998, Pocket paper $3.99 (0-671-02077-3). 168pp. This biography of Favre, who became a Green Bay Packers' quarterback when he was only 22, covers his career and the course of pro football in the 1990s. (Rev: BL 12/1/98) [921]

13610 Gutman, Bill. *Brett Favre: Leader of the Pack* (3–6). Illus. Series: Sports World. 1998, Millbrook LB $19.90 (0-7613-0310-3); paper $6.95 (0-7613-0328-6). 48pp. A short, readable biography of Brett Favre, the Green Bay Packers' famous quarterback. (Rev: BL 8/98; HBG 10/98) [921]

13611 Mooney, Martin. *Brett Favre* (5–7). Illus. Series: Football Legends. 1997, Chelsea LB $16.95 (0-7910-4396-7). 64pp. The story of the famous quarterback who took the Green Bay Packers to victory in the 1997 Super Bowl. (Rev: BL 1/1–15/98; HBG 3/98) [921]

13612 Rekela, George R. *Brett Favre: Star Quarterback* (5–8). Series: Sports Reports. 2000, Enslow LB $19.95 (0-7660-1332-4). 112pp. A brief biography of one of football's star quarterbacks that provides good career statistics and behind-the-scenes reporting. (Rev: BL 10/15/00; HBG 10/00) [921]

13613 Savage, Jeff. *Sports Great Brett Favre* (5–8). Series: Sports Great Books. 1998, Enslow LB $17.95 (0-7660-1000-7). 64pp. An exciting biography of the star quarterback of the Green Bay Packers. (Rev: BL 3/15/98; HBG 10/98) [921]

JACKSON, BO

13614 Devaney, John. *Bo Jackson: A Star for All Seasons* (5–7). Illus. 1992, Walker LB $15.85 (0-802-78179-9). 110pp. Biography of the Kansas City Royals baseball star, who also played pro football for the Los Angeles Raiders. (Rev: BL 2/15/89; SLJ 1/89) [921]

13615 Gutman, Bill. *Bo Jackson: A Biography* (4–7). Illus. 1991, Pocket paper $2.99 (0-671-73363-X). 120pp. This account covers such topics as Jackson's winning the Heisman trophy and recent injuries. (Rev: BL 6/15/91) [921]

13616 Knapp, Ron. *Sports Great Bo Jackson* (5–8). Illus. Series: Sports Great Books. 1990, Enslow LB $17.95 (0-89490-281-4). 64pp. A standard biography that includes unexpected aspects of Jackson's personality. (Rev: BL 10/15/90; SLJ 3/91) [921]

KELLY, JIM

13617 Harrington, Denis J. *Sports Great Jim Kelly* (5–8). Illus. Series: Sports Great Books. 1996, Enslow LB $17.95 (0-89490-670-4). 64pp. A short, action-filled biography of this former star quarterback, complete with career statistics. (Rev: BL 3/15/96) [921]

MANNING, PEYTON

13618 Stewart, Mark. *Peyton Manning: Rising Son* (4–8). Series: Football's New Wave. 2000, Millbrook LB $19.90 (0-7613-1517-9). 48pp. An easily read account of the professional football player's life and family, including a father who also played in the NFL. (Rev: HBG 10/00; SLJ 1/01) [921]

MARINO, DAN

13619 Kennedy, Nick. *Dan Marino: Star Quarterback* (4–6). Series: Sports Reports. 1998, Enslow LB $19.95 (0-89490-933-9). Career statistics and action photos supplement this simple biography of the football great. (Rev: BL 8/98; HBG 10/99) [921]

MONTANA, JOE

13620 Kavanagh, Jack. *Sports Great Joe Montana* (4–8). Illus. Series: Sports Great Books. 1992, Enslow LB $17.95 (0-89490-371-3). 64pp. In simple text, this is the story of the quarterback who led his San Francisco 49ers to four Super Bowl championships. (Rev: BL 7/92; SLJ 10/92) [921]

13621 Raber, Thomas R. *Joe Montana: Comeback Quarterback* (4–6). Illus. 1989, Lerner LB $22.60 (0-8225-0486-3). 64pp. A career-oriented biography of the great pro quarterback. (Rev: BL 12/1/89; SLJ 1/90) [921]

MOSS, RANDY

13622 Stewart, Mark. *Randy Moss: First in Flight* (4–8). Illus. Series: Football's New Wave. 2000, Millbrook $19.90 (0-7613-1518-7). The story of the footballer who came from a poor, segregated West Virginia town, was arrested as a young man, but went on to attend college and play professional football. (Rev: HBG 10/00; SLJ 1/01) [921]

RICE, JERRY

13623 Dickey, Glenn. *Jerry Rice* (5–8). Illus. Series: Sports Great Books. 1993, Enslow LB $17.95 (0-89490-419-1). 64pp. A brief biography of the star football player who gained fame with the San Francisco 49ers. (Rev: BL 9/15/93) [921]

13624 Thornley, Stew. *Jerry Rice: Star Wide Receiver* (4–6). Series: Sports Reports. 1998, Enslow LB $20.95 (0-89490-928-2). 104pp. A biography of the football player for the San Francisco 49ers that tells about both his athletic abilities and his good character traits. (Rev: BL 2/15/98; HBG 10/98) [921]

SANDERS, BARRY

13625 Aaseng, Nathan. *Barry Sanders: Star Running Back* (4–7). Illus. Series: Sports Reports. 1994, Enslow LB $20.95 (0-89490-484-1). 104pp. This biography of the football star of the Detroit Lions contains many quotes about him from his associates. (Rev: SLJ 8/94) [921]

13626 Gutman, Bill. *Barry Sanders: Football's Rushing Champ* (4–6). Illus. Series: Millbrook Sports World. 1993, Millbrook LB $19.90 (1-56294-227-1). 48pp. The life and career of one of the stars of the Detroit Lions. (Rev: BL 3/15/93) [921]

13627 Knapp, Ron. *Barry Sanders* (5–8). Illus. Series: Sports Great Books. 1993, Enslow LB $17.95 (0-89490-418-3). 64pp. This brief biography of the star football player contains many action photos and a separate section on his career statistics. (Rev: BL 9/15/93) [921]

13628 Knapp, Ron. *Sports Great Barry Sanders* (5–8). Series: Sports Great Books. 1998, Enslow LB $16.95 (0-7660-1067-8). 64pp. The life and career of the football great are covered in this account that includes sport statistics and action photographs. (Rev: BL 2/15/99; HBG 10/99) [921]

SANDERS, DEION

13629 Savage, Jeff. *Deion Sanders: Star Athlete* (4–6). Illus. Series: Sports Reports. 1996, Enslow LB $20.95 (0-89490-652-6). 104pp. An in-depth look at this football hero, with black-and-white photos. (Rev: BL 4/15/96) [921]

SEAU, JUNIOR

13630 Morgan, Terri. *Junior Seau: High-Voltage Linebacker* (4–8). Illus. Series: Sports Achievers. 1996, Lerner $18.95 (0-8225-2896-7); paper $5.95 (0-8225-9746-2). 56pp. This biography traces Junior Seau's career in football and highlights his important games. (Rev: BL 12/15/96) [921]

13631 Savage, Jeff. *Junior Seau: Star Linebacker* (4–6). Illus. Series: Sports Reports. 1997, Enslow LB $20.95 (0-89490-800-6). 104pp. A biography of this famous football player, complete with career statistics and action photos. (Rev: BL 8/97) [921]

SMITH, EMMITT

13632 Grabowski, John. *Sports Great Emmitt Smith* (5–8). Series: Sports Great Books. 1998, Enslow LB $15.95 (0-7660-1002-3). 64pp. A high-interest biog-raphy of this football great, containing career statistics, photographs, and exciting game action. (Rev: BL 7/98; HBG 10/98) [921]

13633 Savage, Jeff. *Emmitt Smith: Star Running Back* (4–6). Illus. Series: Sports Reports. 1996, Enslow LB $20.95 (0-89490-653-4). 104pp. The professional life of one of the stars of the Dallas Cowboys is highlighted in this biography, which also covers Smith's childhood and character traits. (Rev: BL 4/15/96) [921]

13634 Thornley, Stew. *Emmitt Smith: Relentless Rusher* (4–8). Illus. Series: Sports Achievers. 1997, Lerner LB $22.60 (0-8225-2897-5). 64pp. This biography of the famous football star also contains career statistics and many action photos. (Rev: BL 4/15/97; SLJ 8/97) [921]

THOMAS, THURMAN

13635 Savage, Jeff. *Thurman Thomas: Star Running Back* (4–7). Illus. Series: Sports Reports. 1994, Enslow LB $20.95 (0-89490-445-0). 104pp. This life story of the football hero also contains action photos, fact boxes, and statistics. (Rev: SLJ 8/94) [921]

WALKER, HERSCHEL

13636 Benagh, Jim. *Sports Great Herschel Walker* (5–8). Illus. Series: Sports Great Books. 1990, Enslow LB $17.95 (0-89490-207-5). 64pp. This account tells how Walker grew up in Georgia and went on to a career in professional football. (Rev: BL 10/15/90; SLJ 3/91) [921]

YOUNG, STEVE

13637 Christopher, Matt. *In the Huddle with . . . Steve Young* (3–7). Illus. Series: Matt Christopher Sports Biography. 1996, Little, Brown paper $4.50 (0-316-13793-6). 144pp. A solid biography of this gridiron hero whose self-determination led to stardom. (Rev: BL 2/15/97; SLJ 2/97) [921]

13638 Gutman, Bill. *Steve Young: NFL Passing Wizard* (3–6). Illus. Series: Sports World. 1996, Millbrook LB $19.90 (1-56294-184-4); paper $6.95 (0-7613-0134-8). 48pp. An absorbing biography that describes Young's career at Brigham Young University, his short stint with the Tampa Bay Buccaneers, and his career as quarterback with the San Francisco 49ers. (Rev: SLJ 2/97) [921]

13639 Knapp, Ron. *Steve Young: Star Quarterback* (4–6). Illus. Series: Sports Reports. 1996, Enslow LB $20.95 (0-89490-654-2). 104pp. A profile of the San Francisco 49ers quarterback, his professional career, character traits, and outside interests. (Rev: BL 4/15/96) [921]

13640 Morgan, Terri, and Shmuel Thaler. *Steve Young: Complete Quarterback* (4–8). Illus. Series: Sports Achievers. 1995, Lerner LB $22.60 (0-8225-2886-X); paper $5.95 (0-8225-9716-0). 64pp. A short, easy-to-read biography of the star quarterback Steve Young, with a color photograph and career statistics. (Rev: BL 11/15/95) [921]

Tennis

AGASSI, ANDRE

13641 Knapp, Ron. *Andre Agassi: Star Tennis Player* (4–6). Illus. Series: Sports Reports. 1997, Enslow LB $20.95 (0-89490-798-0). 104pp. An in-depth look at the life and career of this amazing tennis star. (Rev: BL 8/97; SLJ 8/97) [921]

13642 Savage, Jeff. *Andre Agassi: Reaching the Top — Again* (4–8). Series: Sports Achievers. 1997, Lerner LB $22.60 (0-8225-2894-0); paper $5.95 (0-8225-9750-0). 64pp. A short, easily read biography of this volatile tennis star. (Rev: BL 1/1–15/98; HBG 3/98) [921]

ASHE, ARTHUR

13643 Dexter, Robin. *Young Arthur Ashe: Brave Champion* (2–4). Illus. by R. W. Alley. Series: First Start Biography. 1996, Troll paper $3.50 (0-8167-3773-8). 32pp. The life and death of this courageous tennis champion are dealt with in simple text and numerous color illustrations. (Rev: BL 2/15/96) [921]

13644 Lazo, Caroline. *Arthur Ashe* (4–7). Series: A&E Biography. 1999, Lerner $25.26 (0-8225-1932-8). 128pp. The inspiring story of this great African American tennis star and humanitarian is told in a clear, well-organized text with several black-and-white photos. (Rev: BL 3/15/00) [921]

13645 Wright, David K. *Arthur Ashe: Breaking the Color Barrier in Tennis* (4–7). Illus. Series: African American Biographies. 1996, Enslow LB $20.95 (0-89490-689-5). 128pp. The story of the groundbreaking tennis star and his battle with AIDS. (Rev: SLJ 10/96) [921]

CHANG, MICHAEL

13646 Ditchfield, Christin. *Sports Great Michael Chang* (5–8). Series: Sports Great Books. 1999, Enslow LB $16.95 (0-7660-1223-9). 62pp. A biography of this tennis phenomenon, with career statistics and plenty of action photographs. (Rev: BL 3/15/99; HBG 10/99) [921]

FERNANDEZ, MARY JOE

13647 Cole, Melanie. *Mary Joe Fernandez* (3–4). Series: Real-Life Reader Biographies. 1998, Mitchell Lane LB $15.95 (1-883845-63-7). 32pp. The story of the talented and charitable tennis star who turned pro at age 14 but continued with her education. (Rev: BL 10/15/98; HBG 10/98; SLJ 12/98) [921]

GARRISON, ZINA

13648 Porter, A. P. *Zina Garrison: Ace* (4–6). Series: Sports Achievers. 1992, Lerner LB $21.27 (0-8225-0499-5); paper $4.95 (0-8225-9596-6). 64pp. The life of the tennis star who became the first African American to play a singles final at famed Wimbledon, England. (Rev: BCCB 6/92; BL 12/15/92) [921]

HINGIS, MARTINA

13649 Rambeck, Richard. *Martina Hingis* (3–6). Series: Sports Superstars. 1999, Child's World LB $14.95 (1-56766-519-5). 23pp. A colorful, simple biography — that will appeal to reluctant readers — of the famous tennis star, with highlights from her career. (Rev: BL 5/15/99; HBG 10/99) [921]

KING, BILLIE JEAN

13650 Sanford, William R., and Carl R. Green. *Billie Jean King* (4–6). Illus. Series: Sports Immortals. 1993, Macmillan LB $16.95 (0-89686-781-1). 48pp. Illustrated with many black-and-white photos, this slim biography of tennis star Billie Jean King also contains several trivia questions. (Rev: BL 10/1/93) [921]

SAMPRAS, PETE

13651 Rambeck, Richard. *Pete Sampras* (2–5). Illus. 1996, Child's World LB $21.36 (1-56766-262-5). 23pp. A very brief biography, with more photos than text, about this tennis wonder. (Rev: SLJ 6/97) [921]

13652 Sherrow, Victoria. *Sports Great Pete Sampras* (5–8). Illus. Series: Sports Great Books. 1996, Enslow LB $17.95 (0-89490-756-5). 64pp. The story of this amazing tennis star, his accomplishments, and his career statistics, with a number of black-and-white photos. (Rev: BL 3/15/96) [921]

SELES, MONICA

13653 Rambeck, Richard. *Monica Seles* (2–5). Illus. 1996, Child's World LB $21.36 (1-56766-312-5). 23pp. A short biography of the tennis star, with coverage on her tragic stabbing and her comeback. (Rev: SLJ 6/97) [921]

WILLIAMS, VENUS

13654 Aronson, Virginia. *Venus Williams* (5–8). Illus. Series: Galaxy of Superstars. 1999, Chelsea $16.95 (0-7910-5153-6); paper $9.95 (0-7910-5329-6). 63pp. The story of this superstar of tennis, how her father trained her, and how he made her education more important than her tennis. (Rev: BL 4/15/99; HBG 10/99; SLJ 5/99) [921]

WILLIAMS, VENUS AND SERENA

13655 Fillon, Mike. *Young Superstars of Tennis: The Venus and Serena Williams Story* (4–8). Series: Avisson Young Adult. 1999, Avisson LB $19.95 (1-888105-43-7). 144pp. This biography of the Williams sisters tells about their childhood, the influence of their father, and their determination to get to the top in tennis. (Rev: SLJ 3/00) [921]

13656 Flynn, Gabriel. *Venus and Serena Williams* (3–5). Series: Sports Superstars. 1999, Child's World LB $14.95 (1-56766-664-7). 24pp. The story of the two tennis stars who are sisters and their family, their hard work and their dreams. (Rev: HBG 3/00; SLJ 2/00) [921]

13657 Stewart, Mark. *Venus and Serena Williams: Sisters in Arms* (4–7). Series: Tennis's New Wave. 2000, Millbrook LB $20.90 (0-7613-1803-8). 48pp.

A simple biography of the amazing tennis-playing sisters with good coverage of their early lives. (Rev: HBG 3/01; SLJ 3/01) [921]

Track and Field

DEVERS, GAIL

13658 Gutman, Bill. *Gail Devers* (3–6). Illus. Series: Overcoming the Odds. 1996, Raintree Steck-Vaughn LB $25.69 (0-8172-4122-1). 48pp. The story of this track star who was largely self-trained, her childhood in San Diego, and her participation in the 1993 World Championships. (Rev: SLJ 11/96) [921]

JONES, MARION

13659 Rutledge, Rachel. *Marion Jones: Fast and Fearless* (4–7). 2000, Millbrook LB $20.90 (0-7613-1870-4). 48pp. A biography of the track-and-field star of the 2000 Sydney Olympics that stresses her drive and tenacity. (Rev: HBG 3/01; SLJ 3/01) [921]

JOYNER, FLORENCE GRIFFITH

13660 Aaseng, Nathan. *Florence Griffith Joyner: Dazzling Olympian* (4–6). Illus. Series: Sports Achievers. 1989, Lerner LB $18.60 (0-8225-0495-2); paper $4.95 (0-8225-9587-7). 56pp. A profile of this gold medalist in the 1988 Summer Olympics. (Rev: BCCB 1/90; BL 12/15/89; SLJ 3/90) [921]

JOYNER-KERSEE, JACKIE

13661 Goldstein, Margaret J., and Jennifer Larson. *Jackie Joyner-Kersee: Superwoman* (3–5). Illus. Series: Sports Achievers. 1994, Lerner LB $22.60 (0-8225-0524-X); paper $5.95 (0-8225-9653-9). 56pp. The story of this famous track star's youth in Illinois, her training, and her Olympic successes. (Rev: BL 5/15/94; SLJ 9/94) [921]

13662 Green, Carl R. *Jackie Joyner-Kersee* (4–8). Illus. Series: Sports Headliners. 1994, Macmillan LB $17.95 (0-89686-838-9). 48pp. This biography of the African American track-and-field star highlights her winning the 1986 heptathlon at the Goodwill Games. (Rev: BL 10/1/94) [921]

LEWIS, CARL

13663 Aaseng, Nathan. *Carl Lewis: Legend Chaser* (4–8). Illus. 1985, Lerner LB $17.50 (0-8225-0496-0). 56pp. Childhood, college, and Olympic performances are covered in this biography, including both praise and criticism about Lewis's attempt at the long-jump record. (Rev: BCCB 11/85; BL 7/85; SLJ 8/85)

OWENS, JESSE

13664 Adler, David A. *A Picture Book of Jesse Owens* (K–3). Illus. by Robert Casilla. Series: Picture Book Biographies. 1992, Holiday LB $16.95 (0-8234-0966-X); paper $6.95 (0-8234-1066-8). 32pp. Relying heavily on illustrations to supply details, this is an introduction to the famous track-and-field star. (Rev: BL 11/15/92; SLJ 12/92) [921]

13665 McKissack, Patricia, and Fredrick McKissack. *Jesse Owens: Olympic Star* (2–4). Illus. by Michael D. Blegel. Series: Great African Americans. 1992, Enslow LB $14.95 (0-89490-312-8). 32pp. The story of the African American athlete whose four gold medals in the 1936 Olympics embarrassed Hitler. (Rev: BL 10/15/92; SLJ 1/93) [921]

13666 Nuwer, Hank. *The Legend of Jesse Owens* (5–9). Series: Impact Biographies. 1998, Watts LB $24.00 (0-531-11356-6). 176pp. The life of this legendary track-and-field star is covered in this well-balanced biography that also deals with the racial history of the period. (Rev: HBG 3/99; SLJ 1/99) [921]

13667 Rennert, Richard S. *Jesse Owens* (4–7). Illus. Series: Junior World Biographies. 1991, Chelsea LB $16.95 (0-7910-1570-X). 80pp. An attractive, well-illustrated account of this famous track-and-field star who embarrassed Hitler by winning four gold medals at the 1936 Olympic Games. (Rev: BL 9/1/91; SLJ 9/91) [921]

13668 Streissguth, Thomas. *Jesse Owens* (4–6). Illus. Series: A&E Biography. 1999, Lerner $25.26 (0-8225-4940-9). 112pp. A biography of the remarkable African American athlete who won four gold medals at the 1936 Summer Olympics in Berlin. (Rev: BL 2/15/00; HBG 3/00) [921]

13669 Sutcliffe, Jane. *Jesse Owens* (2–3). Series: On My Own. 2000, Carolrhoda LB $19.93 (1-57505-451-5); paper $5.95 (1-57505-487-6). 48pp. A simple biography of the athlete who overcame sickness, poverty, and discrimination to become a gold medal winner in Berlin in 1936. (Rev: BL 8/00) [921]

RUDOLPH, WILMA

13670 Krull, Kathleen. *Wilma Unlimited: How Wilma Rudolph Became the World's Fastest Woman* (2–5). Illus. by David Diaz. 1996, Harcourt $16.00 (0-15-201267-2). 48pp. A biography of the amazing Wilma Rudolph, who overcame incredible obstacles to become a track star. (Rev: BL 5/1/96*; HB 9–10/96; SLJ 6/96*) [921]

13671 Ruth, Amy. *Wilma Rudolph* (4–6). Series: A&E Biography. 2000, Lerner LB $25.26 (0-8225-4976-X). 112pp. The inspiring story of the African American athlete who overcame polio and won three gold medals in Olympic track-and-field events in 1960. (Rev: BL 6/1–15/00; HBG 10/00) [921]

13672 Sherrow, Victoria. *Wilma Rudolph* (2–3). Illus. by Larry Johnson. Series: On My Own Biographies. 2000, Lerner LB $19.93 (1-57505-246-6); paper $5.95 (1-57505-442-6). 48pp. The story of how a young girl whose legs were thin and crooked from polio grew up to win Olympic gold medals for running is told with simplicity and dignity. (Rev: BL 2/15/00; HBG 10/00; SLJ 2/00) [921]

13673 Sherrow, Victoria. *Wilma Rudolph: Olympic Champion* (4–6). Illus. Series: Junior World Biographies. 1995, Chelsea LB $16.95 (0-7910-2290-0). 79pp. The life of this great track star and of the poverty, bad health, and emotional challenges she faced and overcame in her desire to succeed. (Rev: BCCB 4/96; SLJ 8/95) [921]

THORPE, JIM

13674 Long, Barbara. *Jim Thorpe: Legendary Athlete* (5–7). Illus. Series: Native American Biographies. 1997, Enslow LB $20.95 (0-89490-865-0). 128pp. The story of the amazing Native American athlete whose career had tremendous highs and lows. (Rev: BL 6/1–15/97) [921]

13675 Santrey, Laurence. *Jim Thorpe: Young Athlete* (4–6). Illus. 1983, Troll LB $17.25 (0-89375-845-0); paper $3.95 (0-89375-846-9). 48pp. An account that details his heritage and his emerging athletic abilities.

Miscellaneous Sports

ARMSTRONG, LANCE

13676 Armstrong, Kristin. *Lance Armstrong: The Race of His Life* (2–3). Illus. Series: All Aboard Reading. 2000, Putnam $13.89 (0-448-42415-0); paper $3.90 (0-448-42407-X). 48pp. A book for beginning readers that tells about this famous cyclist, his many triumphs, and his battle with cancer — written by his wife. (Rev: BL 12/1/00; HBG 3/01) [921]

13677 Stewart, Mark. *Sweet Victory: Lance Armstrong's Incredible Journey: The Amazing Story of the Greatest Comeback in Sports* (4–8). 2000, Millbrook LB $23.90 (0-7613-1861-5). 64pp. The inspiring story of the man who won the Tour de France bicycle race despite struggles with cancer. (Rev: HBG 10/00; SLJ 8/00) [921]

BASS, TOM

13678 Wilkerson, J. L. *From Slave to World-Class Horseman: Tom Bass* (4–8). 2000, Acorn paper $9.95 (0-9664470-3-4). 135pp. A fast-paced narrative that tells of the man who was born a slave and later became such a renowned horseman that he performed for Queen Victoria. (Rev: SLJ 4/00) [921]

BLAIR, BONNIE

13679 Blair, Bonnie, and Greg Brown. *A Winning Edge* (3–5). Illus. 1996, Taylor $14.95 (0-87833-931-0). 40pp. The autobiography of the Olympic medal-winning speed skater, with insights into her life off the ice. (Rev: BL 5/15/96) [921]

13680 Breitenbucher, Cathy. *Bonnie Blair: Golden Streak* (4–8). Illus. Series: Sports Achievers. 1994, Lerner LB $21.27 (0-8225-2883-5). 64pp. A worthy biography of the U.S. speed skater and winner of many Olympic medals. (Rev: BL 1/1/95; SLJ 1/95) [921]

13681 Rambeck, Richard. *Bonnie Blair* (2–5). Illus. Series: Sports Superstars. 1995, Child's World LB $21.36 (1-56766-186-6). 23pp. A simple biography of this speed skater that focuses on her quiet determination and career accomplishments. (Rev: SLJ 4/96) [921]

BUTCHER, SUSAN

13682 Wadsworth, Ginger. *Susan Butcher: Sled Dog Racer* (4–7). Illus. Series: Sports Achievers. 1994, Lerner LB $18.60 (0-8225-2878-9). 63pp. This exciting biography brings to life the four-time Iditarod winner and the rigors and courage each race involved. (Rev: SLJ 6/94) [921]

DIMAS, TRENT

13683 Menard, Valerie, and Sue Boulais. *Trent Dimas* (3–5). Series: Real-Life Reader Biographies. 1998, Mitchell Lane LB $15.95 (1-883845-50-5). 32pp. The story of a young gymnast who saw his dreams come true when he took the gold medal in the 1992 Olympics. (Rev: BL 6/1–15/98; HBG 3/98; SLJ 4/98) [921]

EDERLE, GERTRUDE

13684 Adler, David A. *America's Champion Swimmer: Gertrude Ederle* (2–4). Illus. by Terry Widener. 2000, Harcourt $16.00 (0-15-201969-3). 32pp. A simple biography of the amazing athlete who was the first woman to swim across the English Channel. (Rev: BCCB 4/00; BL 3/15/00*; HB 5–6/00; HBG 10/00; SLJ 6/00) [921]

EL CHINO

13685 Say, Allen. *El Chino* (3–6). Illus. 1990, Houghton $16.00 (0-395-52023-1). 32pp. The first-person narrative of a Chinese American civil engineer who becomes a matador. (Rev: BCCB 9/90*; BL 9/1/90*; HB 1–2/91; SLJ 11/90) [921]

GRETZKY, WAYNE

13686 Christopher, Matt. *On the Ice with . . . Wayne Gretzky* (3–7). Illus. Series: Matt Christopher Sports Biography. 1996, Little, Brown paper $4.50 (0-316-13789-8). 144pp. The life story of this hockey superstar details both the highs and lows of his career. (Rev: BL 2/15/97) [921]

13687 Fortunato, Frank. *Wayne Gretzky: Star Center* (4–6). Series: Sports Reports. 1998, Enslow LB $20.95 (0-89490-930-4). 104pp. An in-depth look at the life and career of this amazing hockey player. (Rev: BL 2/15/98; HBG 10/98) [921]

13688 Rappoport, Ken. *Sports Great Wayne Gretzky* (5–8). Illus. Series: Sports Great Books. 1996, Enslow LB $17.95 (0-89490-757-3). 64pp. A brief biography of this hockey phenomenon, illustrated with black-and-white action photos. (Rev: BL 3/15/96) [921]

HAMM, MIA

13689 Rambeck, Richard. *Mia Hamm* (3–6). Series: Sports Superstars. 1999, Child's World LB $14.95 (1-56766-523-3). 23pp. A simple biography, good for reluctant readers, about the American Olympics soccer star and her sports career. (Rev: BL 5/15/99; HBG 10/99) [921]

13690 Rutledge, Rachel. *Mia Hamm: Striking Superstar* (3–6). Series: Soccer's New Wave. 2000, Millbrook LB $20.90 (0-7613-1802-X). 48pp. A fully rounded biography of the soccer star who was a member of the 1991 and 1999 Gold Medal World Cup Soccer teams. (Rev: HBG 10/00; SLJ 7/00) [921]

13691 Torres, John. *Mia Hamm* (3–4). Series: Real-Life Reader Biographies. 1999, Mitchell Lane LB $15.95 (1-883845-94-7). 32pp. An inspiring biography of this great female soccer player and how she succeeded through spirit and determination. (Rev: BL 10/15/99) [921]

HOGAN, HULK

13692 Zannos, Susan. *Hollywood Hulk Hogan: The Story of Terry Bollea* (3–4). Series: Real-Life Reader Biographies. 1999, Mitchell Lane LB $15.95 (1-58415-021-1). 32pp. A simple biography about this world-famous wrestler and how he devotes time and money to charities that help sick children. (Rev: BL 10/15/99) [921]

HULL, BRETT

13693 Goldstein, Margaret J. *Brett Hull: Hockey's Top Gun* (3–6). 1992, Lerner LB $22.60 (0-8225-0544-4); paper $4.95 (0-8225-9599-0). 48pp. A behind-the-scenes look at the St. Louis Blues' star scorer. (Rev: BCCB 7–8/92; SLJ 10/92) [921]

KRONE, JULIE

13694 Callahan, Dorothy. *Julie Krone: A Winning Jockey* (4–6). Illus. 1990, Macmillan LB $18.95 (0-87518-425-1). 64pp. A biography of the woman who became the leading female jockey at the age of 25. (Rev: BCCB 9/90; BL 7/90; SLJ 9/90) [921]

13695 Gutman, Bill. *Julie Krone* (3–6). Illus. Series: Overcoming the Odds. 1996, Raintree Steck-Vaughn LB $25.69 (0-8172-4121-3). 48pp. An absorbing biography of this female jockey, her participation in more than 16,000 races, and the 1993 accident that left her seriously injured. (Rev: SLJ 2/97) [921]

13696 Savage, Jeff. *Julie Krone, Unstoppable Jockey* (2–5). Illus. 1996, Lerner LB $22.60 (0-8225-2888-6). 56pp. The story of a top female jockey and her unique accomplishments. (Rev: BL 8/96; SLJ 9/96) [921]

LEMIEUX, MARIO

13697 Hughes, Morgan E. *Mario Lemieux: Beating the Odds* (4–6). Illus. Series: Sports Achievers. 1996, Lerner LB $22.60 (0-8225-2884-3); paper $5.95 (0-8225-9717-9). 64pp. A biography of the star hockey player, with a section on career statistics. (Rev: SLJ 9/96) [921]

LEMOND, GREG

13698 Porter, A. P. *Greg LeMond: Premier Cyclist* (4–7). Illus. Series: Sports Achievers. 1990, Lerner LB $21.27 (0-8225-0476-6). 64pp. Although he suffered severe injuries in a hunting accident, LeMond won the Tour de France bicycle race. (Rev: BL 6/15/90; SLJ 9/90) [921]

LINDROS, ERIC

13699 Rappoport, Ken. *Sports Great Eric Lindros* (5–8). Series: Sports Great Books. 1997, Enslow LB $17.95 (0-89490-871-5). 64pp. A biography of the famous hockey star that includes career statistics and several action photos. (Rev: BL 10/15/97) [921]

MESSIER, MARK

13700 Sullivan, Michael J. *Mark Messier: Star Center* (4–6). Series: Sports Reports. 1997, Enslow LB $20.95 (0-89490-801-4). 104pp. This biography of Messier contains career statistics, action photos, and a behind-the-scenes look at this hockey star. (Rev: BL 12/15/97; HBG 3/98) [921]

MILLER, SHANNON

13701 Miller, Shannon, and Nancy Ann Richardson. *Winning Every Day: Gold Medal Advice for a Happy, Healthy Life!* (5–9). Illus. 1998, Bantam paper $12.95 (0-553-09776-8). 144pp. The 1996 Olympic gold medal gymnast describes her life and training and offers tips on stress management, good sportsmanship, and a healthy lifestyle. (Rev: BL 6/1–15/98; SLJ 7/98) [921]

MOCEANU, DOMINIQUE

13702 Durrett, Deanne. *Dominique Moceanu* (5–8). Series: People in the News. 1999, Lucent LB $17.96 (1-56006-099-9). 111pp. This story of the Olympic champion gymnast concentrates on her coaching and her career rather than her personal life. (Rev: HBG 3/00; SLJ 8/99) [921]

13703 Quiner, Krista. *Dominique Moceanu: A Gymnastics Sensation* (4–7). Illus. 1997, Bradford paper $12.95 (0-9643460-3-6). 191pp. The story of the United States' youngest gold medal winner in gymnastics, with a special 24-page insert of photos. (Rev: SLJ 3/97) [921]

MONPLAISIR, SHARON

13704 Greenberg, Doreen, and Michael Greenberg. *Sword of a Champion: The Story of Sharon Monplaisir* (4–8). Illus. by Phil Velikan. Series: Anything You Can Do — New Sports Heroes for Girls. 2000, Wish paper $9.95 (1-930546-39-4). 81pp. The life story of the timid, shy high schooler who found her place in fencing via a coach who encouraged her to develop her natural talents. (Rev: SLJ 3/01) [796.8]

NASH, KEVIN

13705 Mudge, Jacqueline. *Kevin Nash* (4–7). Series: Pro Wrestling Legends. 2000, Chelsea LB $17.95 (0-7910-5828-X). 64pp. This is the biography of the wrestler known as "Diesel." Also use *The Story of the Wrestler They Call "Diamond" Dallas Page* (2000). (Rev: BL 10/15/00; HBG 3/01) [921]

PAK, SE RI

13706 Stewart, Mark. *Se Ri Pak: Driven to Win* (4–8). Series: Golf's New Wave. 2000, Millbrook LB $19.90 (0-7613-1519-5). 48pp. The story of the South Korean who won the Ladies Professional Golf Association Championship in 1998. (Rev: HBG 10/00; SLJ 8/00) [921]

PELE

13707 Arnold, Caroline. *Pele: The King of Soccer* (4–8). Illus. Series: First Books. 1992, Watts LB $22.00 (0-531-20077-9). 64pp. The career of one of the world's greatest soccer players is traced from early promise to superstar. (Rev: BL 10/1/92) [921]

REECE, GABRIELLE

13708 Morgan, Terri. *Gabrielle Reece: Volleyball's Model Athlete* (4–7). Illus. Series: Sports Achievers. 1999, Lerner $15.95 (0-8225-3667-6). 64pp. An accessible biography of the woman who is not only a volleyball champ but also a fashion model and TV personality. (Rev: BL 10/15/99; HBG 3/00) [921]

SIFFORD, CHARLIE

13709 Britt, Grant. *Charlie Sifford* (4–7). Illus. 1998, Morgan Reynolds LB $17.95 (1-883846-27-7). 64pp. This biography of the African American golfer stresses the problems he faced breaking the color barrier when he entered the sport after World War II. (Rev: BL 2/15/98; HBG 10/98; SLJ 7/98) [921]

VENTURA, JESSE

13710 Greenberg, Keith E. *Jesse Ventura* (5–8). Illus. Series: A&E Biography. 1999, Lerner $25.26 (0-8225-4977-8); paper $7.95 (0-8225-9680-6). 112pp. A look at this larger-than-life pop culture hero who has been an actor, a professional wrestler, a Navy SEAL, and the governor of Minnesota. (Rev: BL 3/1/00; HBG 3/00; SLJ 2/00) [921]

WOODS, TIGER

13711 Boyd, Aaron. *Tiger Woods* (5–7). Illus. 1997, Morgan Reynolds LB $17.95 (1-883846-19-6). 64pp. A brief, straightforward biography of this amazing golfer who was a prodigy. (Rev: BL 5/1/97; HBG 3/98; SLJ 8/97) [921]

13712 Christopher, Matt. *On the Course with . . . Tiger Woods* (3–5). Illus. 1998, Little, Brown paper $4.50 (0-316-13445-7). 128pp. A brief biography of Tiger Woods, including a short history of golf and its rules. (Rev: BL 7/98) [921]

13713 Collins, David R. *Tiger Woods: Golf Superstar* (K–3). Illus. by Larry Nolte. 1999, Pelican $14.95 (1-56554-321-1). This simple biography stresses the determination and hard work that made Tiger Woods the golf star that the world admires. (Rev: SLJ 6/99) [921]

13714 Collins, David R. *Tiger Woods, Golfing Champion* (5–8). Illus. by Larry Nolte. 1999, Pelican $14.95 (1-56554-322-X). 88pp. A chronologically arranged book ending in 1999 that reveals Tiger Woods's determination and love of the game. (Rev: SLJ 1/00) [921]

13715 Gutman, Bill. *Tiger Woods: Golf's Shining Young Star* (3–6). Illus. Series: Sports World. 1998, Millbrook LB $19.90 (0-7613-0309-X); paper $6.95 (0-7613-0329-4). 48pp. This biography of Tiger Woods stresses his family background, racial and age problems, and his career highlights. (Rev: BL 8/98; HBG 10/98) [921]

13716 Kramer, S. A. *Tiger Woods: Golf's Young Master* (2–4). Illus. 1998, Random LB $11.99 (0-679-98849-1); paper $3.99 (0-679-88849-7). 48pp. Using simple language, color photos, and large type, this book provides a good introduction to the life of Tiger Woods and his amazing career in golf. (Rev: BL 7/98) [921]

13717 Rambeck, Richard. *Tiger Woods* (3–6). Illus. Series: Sports Superstars. 1999, Child's World LB $14.95 (1-56766-407-5). 23pp. Double-page spreads tell about Tiger Woods's training, his move to professional status, and his breakthrough at the 1997 Masters Tournament. (Rev: BL 5/15/99) [921]

13718 Savage, Jeff. *Tiger Woods: King of the Course* (4–5). Illus. 1998, Lerner LB $14.95 (0-8225-3655-2). 64pp. Lavish color photographs illustrate this biography of Tiger Woods, which includes his family background, his training, style, and tournament action. (Rev: BL 7/98; HBG 10/98; SLJ 6/98) [921]

13719 Teague, Allison L. *Prince of the Fairway: The Tiger Woods Story* (4–7). Illus. 1997, Avisson LB $18.50 (1-888105-22-4). 106pp. A biography that emphasizes the wholesome behavioral traits of this golf phenomenon, the youngest professional player to win the Masters Tournament in Augusta, Georgia. (Rev: SLJ 10/97) [921]

ZAHARIAS, BABE DIDRIKSON

13720 Freedman, Russell. *Babe Didrikson Zaharias: The Making of a Champion* (5–12). Illus. 1999, Clarion $18.00 (0-395-63367-2). 192pp. Although this athlete was known to most for her golf career, this entertaining biography points out that Babe Didrikson Zaharias was also an Olympic athlete, a track star, leader of a woman's amateur basketball team, and entrepreneur. (Rev: BCCB 10/99; BL 7/99; HB 9–10/99; HBG 3/00; SLJ 7/99) [921]

13721 Sutcliffe, Jane. *Babe Didrikson Zaharias: All-around Athlete* (2–3). Series: On My Own Biographies. 2000, Carolrhoda LB $19.93 (1-57505-421-3). 48pp. A simple biography of one of the greatest athletes of the 20th century, winner of three medals in track and field at the 1932 Olympics. (Rev: BL 6/1–15/00; HBG 10/00; SLJ 6/00) [921]

13722 Wakeman, Nancy. *Babe Didrikson Zaharias: Driven to Win* (4–7). Illus. Series: Biography. 2000, Lerner $25.26 (0-8225-4917-4). 112pp. The account focuses on this sportswoman's professional career and her strong personality plus her accomplishments in track and field, basketball, and baseball. (Rev: BL 6/1–15/00; HBG 10/00) [921].

World Figures

Collective

13723 Aaseng, Nathan. *The Peace Seekers: The Nobel Peace Prize* (5–8). Illus. 1987, Lerner LB $18.60 (0-8225-0654-8); paper $5.95 (0-8225-9604-0). 80pp. Martin Luther King, Jr., and Lech Walesa are among those whose lives and works are introduced. (Rev: BL 2/1/88)

13724 Avakian, Monique. *Reformers: Activists, Educators, Religious Leaders* (5–9). Series: Remarkable Women: Past and Present. 2000, Raintree Steck-Vaughn LB $28.54 (0-8172-5733-0). 80pp. This book contains 150 profiles of woman who, throughout history and from many cultures, have fought for human rights, including Harriet Tubman, Mother Teresa, and Dolores Huerta. (Rev: SLJ 8/00) [920]

13725 Blue, Rose, and Corinne J. Naden. *People of Peace* (4–7). Illus. 1994, Millbrook LB $25.90 (1-56294-409-6). 80pp. Brief biographies of ten people in modern history who have made great sacrifices for world peace, including Mohandas Gandhi and Desmond Tutu. (Rev: BL 12/15/94; SLJ 2/95) [920]

13726 Gulatta, Charles. *Extraordinary Women in Politics* (5–9). Series: Extraordinary People. 1998, Children's LB $37.00 (0-516-20610-9). 288pp. From Cleopatra to Hillary Rodham Clinton, this book profiles 55 women who have been active in politics through the centuries. (Rev: HBG 3/99; SLJ 1/99) [920]

13727 Hacker, Carlotta. *Humanitarians* (3–6). Illus. Series: Women in Profile. 1999, Crabtree LB $15.96 (0-7787-0011-9); paper $8.06 (0-7787-0033-X). 48pp. Six major profiles and 15 brief biographies of female humanitarians, including Helen Keller and Mother Teresa, are included in this informative title. (Rev: BL 9/15/99; SLJ 8/99) [920]

13728 Hacker, Carlotta. *Nobel Prize Winners* (3–6). Illus. Series: Women in Profile. 1998, Crabtree LB $15.96 (0-7787-0007-0); paper $8.06 (0-7787-0029-1). 48pp. In addition to biographies of six female

Nobel Prize winners, including Barbara McClintock, Toni Morrison, Marie Curie, and Nadine Gordimer, this collection contains short profiles of dozens of other notables, such as Mother Teresa and Jane Addams. (Rev: BL 9/1/98; SLJ 9/98) [920]

13729 Hacker, Carlotta. *Rebels* (3–6). Series: Women in Profile. 1999, Crabtree LB $15.96 (0-7787-0014-3); paper $8.06 (0-7787-0036-4). 48pp. This work provides six major profiles and 15 brief sketches about women who, throughout history, have challenged the status quo. (Rev: BL 9/15/99; SLJ 8/99) [920]

13730 Hazell, Rebecca. *The Barefoot Book of Heroic Children* (4–7). Illus. 2000, Barefoot $19.95 (1-902283-23-6). 96pp. This book presents the lives of 12 heroic children from different times and places, among them Anne Frank, Fanny Mendelssohn, Annie Sullivan, and Iqbal Masih. (Rev: BL 4/15/00) [920]

13731 Hazell, Rebecca. *Heroes: Great Men Through the Ages* (4–6). Illus. 1997, Abbeville $19.95 (0-7892-0289-1). 80pp. From Socrates to Martin Luther King, Jr., this collection of 12 biographies of famous men also includes Shakespeare, Mozart, Leonardo da Vinci, and Jorge Luis Borges. (Rev: BL 7/97; HB 5–6/97; SLJ 6/97) [920]

13732 Krull, Kathleen. *Lives of Extraordinary Women: Rulers, Rebels (and What the Neighbors Thought)* (5–8). Illus. Series: Extraordinary Lives. 2000, Harcourt $20.00 (0-15-200807-1). 96pp. Short biographies of women who affected the course of history, from Cleopatra to contemporary Burma's Aung San Suu Kyi. (Rev: BCCB 9/00; BL 9/1/00; HB 11–12/00; HBG 3/01; SLJ 9/00) [920]

13733 Lace, William W. *Leaders and Generals* (5–10). Series: American War. 2000, Lucent LB $18.96 (1-56006-664-4). 112pp. This book contains eight profiles of about ten pages each of the following World War II leaders: Erwin Rommel, Georgi Zhukov, Erich von Manstein, Yamamoto Isoroku, Douglas MacArthur, Chester Nimitz, Dwight Eisenhower, and Bernard Law Montgomery. (Rev: HBG 10/00; SLJ 6/00) [920]

13734 Leon, Vicki. *Outrageous Women of Ancient Times* (4–7). Illus. 1997, Wiley paper $12.95 (0-471-17006-2). 128pp. Fifteen unusual women from ancient cultures in Europe, Asia, and Africa are profiled, including Cleopatra and Sappho. (Rev: BL 11/1/97; SLJ 12/97) [920]

13735 Leon, Vicki. *Outrageous Women of the Middle Ages* (4–7). Illus. 1998, Wiley paper $12.95 (0-471-17004-6). 128pp. Using everyday slang and colloquialisms, this collective biography profiles 14 "tough cookies" of the Middle Ages, including Eleanor of Aquitaine and others from Europe, North Africa, and the Middle and Far East. (Rev: BL 4/15/98; SLJ 8/98) [920]

13736 McLuskey, Krista. *Entrepreneurs* (3–6). Series: Women in Profile. 1999, Crabtree LB $15.96 (0-7787-0012-7); paper $8.06 (0-7787-0034-8). 48pp. Six female entrepreneurs, including Oprah Winfrey, are profiled here, with brief sketches of 15 more. (Rev: BL 9/15/99) [920]

13737 Marzollo, Jean. *My First Book of Biographies: Great Men and Women Every Child Should Know* (2–4). Illus. by Irene Trivas. 1994, Scholastic $14.95 (0-590-45014-X). 80pp. Brief profiles of 45 famous people whom youngsters have heard about, from Cleopatra to Beatrix Potter. (Rev: BL 12/1/94; SLJ 9/94) [920]

13738 Meltzer, Milton. *Ten Queens: Portraits of Women of Power* (5–8). Illus. by Bethanne Andersen. 1998, Dutton $24.99 (0-525-45643-0). 134pp. This handsomely illustrated book profiles ten queens, including Esther, Cleopatra, Eleanor of Aquitaine, Isabella of Spain, Elizabeth I, and Catherine the Great. (Rev: BCCB 7–8/98; BL 4/15/98*; HBG 3/99) [920]

13739 *1000 Makers of the Millennium: Men and Women Who Have Shaped the Last 1000 Years* (4–10). Series: DK Millennium. 1999, DK $19.95 (0-7894-4709-6). 256pp. This biographical dictionary gives basic information on 1,000 people famous in the past millennium from Brian Boru, an Irish leader born in 941, to test-tube baby Louise Brown born in 1978. (Rev: SLJ 3/00) [920]

13740 Parker, Janice. *Political Leaders* (3–6). Illus. 1998, Crabtree LB $15.96 (0-7787-0008-9); paper $8.95 (0-7787-0030-5). 48pp. As well as detailed sketches of Corazon Aquino, Benazir Bhutto, Indira Gandhi, Golda Meir, Margaret Thatcher, and Eva Peron, this book contains shorter profiles of other important female political leaders. (Rev: BL 9/1/98) [920]

13741 Pollard, Michael. *People Who Care* (4–6). Series: Pioneers in History. 1992, Garrett LB $19.93 (1-56074-035-3). 48pp. Nineteen individuals who devoted their lives to helping others are profiled in this book. People who participated in revolutions are covered in *Revolutionary Power* (1992) and great philosophers in *Thinkers* (1992). (Rev: SLJ 9/92) [920]

13742 Roehm, Michelle. *Girls Who Rocked the World 2: Heroines from Harriet Tubman to Mia Hamm* (4–6). Illus. by Jerry McCann. 2000, Beyond Words paper $8.95 (1-58270-025-7). 160pp. Pro-

files 30 outstanding women who hailed from many different countries, lived in various time periods, and accomplished advances in a number of fields. (Rev: SLJ 12/00) [920]

13743 Sullivan, George. *In the Line of Fire* (3–6). Illus. 1996, Scholastic paper $3.99 (0-590-48294-7). 118pp. From the American Revolution through World War II, the stories of eight female spies are retold. (Rev: BL 6/1–15/96) [920]

13744 Welden, Amelie. *Girls Who Rocked the World: Heroines from Sacagawea to Sheryl Swoopes* (4–7). 1998, Beyond Words paper $8.95 (1-885223-68-4). 120pp. A collection of short biographies of women who "have achieved something extraordinary while under the age of twenty." (Rev: BL 7/98; SLJ 7/98) [920]

13745 Wilkinson, Philip, and Jacqueline Dineen. *People Who Changed the World* (3–5). Illus. by Robert Ingpen. Series: Turning Points. 1994, Chelsea LB $19.95 (0-7910-2764-3). 93pp. Includes brief biographies of religious leaders, philosophers, and explorers like Pericles, Jesus Christ, Karl Marx, and Martin Luther King, Jr. Also use *Statesmen Who Changed the World* (1994). (Rev: BL 12/15/94) [920]

13746 Wilkinson, Philip, and Michael Pollard. *Generals Who Changed the World* (4–6). Illus. by Robert Ingpen. Series: Turning Points. 1994, Chelsea LB $19.95 (0-7910-2761-9). 93pp. A profile of 20 important military men and how their accomplishments changed the course of history. (Rev: SLJ 11/94) [920]

Individual

ALEXANDER THE GREAT

13747 Chrisp, Peter. *Alexander the Great: The Legend of a Warrior King* (3–5). Illus. 2000, DK $14.95 (0-7894-6166-8). 48pp. A fascinating look at the life of Alexander and the history of both Greece and the Persian Empire, using amazing illustrations and a clear text. (Rev: BL 1/1–15/01; SLJ 10/00) [921]

13748 Green, Robert. *Alexander the Great* (4–6). Illus. Series: First Books. 1996, Watts LB $22.50 (0-531-20230-5). 64pp. The life, conquests, and legacy of Alexander are well covered. (Rev: BL 7/96; SLJ 9/96) [921]

13749 Greenblatt, Miriam. *Alexander the Great and Ancient Greece* (5–8). Illus. Series: Rulers and Their Times. 1999, Marshall Cavendish LB $19.95 (0-7614-0913-0). 80pp. The first part of this biography introduces Alexander the Great and his accomplishments and the second tells about daily life in ancient Greece. (Rev: BL 1/1–15/00; HBG 10/00) [921]

13750 Langley, Andrew. *Alexander the Great: The Greatest Ruler of the Ancient World* (2–4). Illus. Series: What's Their Story? 1998, Oxford LB $12.95 (0-19-521402-1). 32pp. A concise biography of Alexander the Great, giving details of his family, education, conquests, and significance, and providing background information on the world he lived in. (Rev: BL 8/98; HBG 10/98; SLJ 9/98) [921]

13751 Stewart, Gail B. *Alexander the Great* (4–8). Illus. Series: The Importance Of. 1994, Lucent LB $17.96 (1-56006-047-6). 127pp. A brief biography of the conqueror whose great importance lay in introducing the East to Western culture. (Rev: BL 8/94; SLJ 7/94) [921]

ANNAN, KOFI

13752 Tessitore, John. *Kofi Annan: The Peacekeeper* (4–6). Series: Book Report Biographies. 2000, Watts LB $22.00 (0-531-11706-5). 96pp. This is the story of the secretary general of the United Nations who was born in Ghana. (Rev: BL 11/15/00) [921]

BHATT, ELA

13753 Sreenivasan, Jyotsna. *Ela Bhatt: Uniting Women in India* (5–8). Illus. Series: Women Changing the World. 2000, Feminist Pr. LB $19.95 (1-55861-229-7). 112pp. Inspired by Gandhi, this Indian lawyer founded an organization to help and protect the lives of her country's poorest women and organized a labor union for them. (Rev: BL 9/15/00; HBG 3/01) [921]

BOLIVAR, SIMON

13754 Adler, David A. *A Picture Book of Simon Bolivar* (3–5). Illus. by Robert Casilla. Series: Picture Book Biographies. 1992, Holiday LB $16.95 (0-8234-0927-9). 32pp. A biography of the "George Washington" of many South American nations. (Rev: BL 4/15/92; SLJ 7/92) [921]

13755 De Varona, Frank. *Simon Bolivar: Latin American Liberator* (3–6). Illus. Series: Hispanic Heritage. 1993, Millbrook LB $19.90 (1-56294-278-6). 32pp. Simon Bolivar, in spite of all odds, led much of South and Central America to overthrow Spanish rule. (Rev: BL 5/15/93; SLJ 7/93) [921]

BONETTA, SARAH FORBES

13756 Myers, Walter Dean. *At Her Majesty's Request: An African Princess in Victorian England* (5–8). Illus. 1999, Scholastic LB $15.95 (0-590-48669-1). The story of a 7-year-old African princess who was saved from becoming a sacrifice by an Englishman who sent her to England, where she became the special ward of Queen Victoria. (Rev: BCCB 2/99; BL 4/1/99; HBG 10/99; SLJ 1/99) [921]

BRAILLE, LOUIS

13757 Adler, David A. *A Picture Book of Louis Braille* (2–4). Illus. by John Wallner and Alexandra Wallner. Series: Picture Book Biographies. 1997, Holiday $16.95 (0-8234-1291-1). 34pp. For young readers, this is a simple, well-illustrated biography that also includes a page of the braille raised-dot alphabet and numbers. (Rev: BL 4/15/97; SLJ 6/97) [921]

13758 Bryant, Jennifer. *Louis Braille: Inventor* (5–7). Illus. 1994, Chelsea LB $19.95 (0-7910-

2077-0). 112pp. This well-researched biography of Braille tells about the horror of his own blindness as well as the development of the alphabet that allows blind people to read. (Rev: BL 7/94; SLJ 8/94) [921]

13759 Fradin, Dennis B. *Louis Braille: The Blind Boy Who Wanted to Read* (2–4). Illus. 1997, Silver Burdett LB $15.95 (0-382-39468-2); paper $5.95 (0-382-39469-0). 32pp. A picture-book biography of the amazing blind Frenchman who invented his famous reading system when he was only 15. (Rev: BL 5/1/97; SLJ 7/97) [921]

13760 Freedman, Russell. *Out of Darkness: The Story of Louis Braille* (4–8). Illus. 1997, Clarion $16.95 (0-395-77516-7). 81pp. The story of the blind Frenchman who, more than 170 years ago, invented a system of reading using raised dots. (Rev: BCCB 5/97; BL 3/1/97; HB 5–6/97; SLJ 3/97*) [921]

13761 O'Connor, Barbara. *The World at His Fingertips: A Story About Louis Braille* (3–5). Illus. by Rochelle Draper. Series: Creative Minds Biographies. 1997, Carolrhoda LB $21.27 (1-57505-052-8). 64pp. A fast-paced biography that reveals many interesting facts about this inventor of a writing system for the blind. (Rev: HBG 3/98; SLJ 10/97) [921]

13762 Woodhouse, Jayne. *Louis Braille* (2–3). Series: Lives and Times. 1997, Heinemann $19.92 (1-57572-559-2). 24pp. The life and contributions of this famous French blind man are told in this simple picture-book biography with a brief text. (Rev: BL 3/15/98) [921]

CAESAR, JULIUS

13763 Green, Robert. *Julius Caesar* (5–8). Illus. Series: First Books. 1996, Watts LB $22.50 (0-531-20241-0). 63pp. The story of Caesar's political and military careers, how he expanded the Roman Empire, and his lasting importance. (Rev: SLJ 2/97) [921]

13764 Nardo, Don. *Julius Caesar* (4–8). Illus. Series: The Importance Of. 1997, Lucent LB $16.95 (1-56006-083-2). 112pp. An introductory biography that stresses the lasting importance of this great leader, who expanded the Roman Empire significantly. (Rev: BL 1/1–15/97) [921]

CAROLINE, PRINCESS OF MONACO

13765 Wheeler, Jill C. *Princess Caroline of Monaco* (4–6). Illus. Series: Leading Ladies. 1992, ABDO LB $13.98 (1-56239-117-8). 32pp. A simple biography of the princess who is the daughter of the late Grace Kelly. (Rev: BL 2/1/93; SLJ 3/93) [921]

CHAMPOLLION, JEAN-FRANCOIS

13766 Rumford, James. *Seeker of Knowledge: The Man Who Deciphered Egyptian Hieroglyphs* (3–5). Illus. 2000, Houghton $15.00 (0-395-97934-X). 32pp. The story of Jean-Francois Champollion, who studied the Rosetta Stone and found the key to understanding Egyptian hieroglyphs. (Rev: BCCB 4/00; BL 4/15/00; HBG 10/00; SLJ 5/00) [493]

CHARLEMAGNE

13767 Biel, Timothy. *Charlemagne* (4–8). Illus. Series: Importance Of. 1997, Lucent LB $17.96 (1-56006-074-3). 127pp. The story of the king of the Franks, his empire, and his lasting importance in European history. (Rev: BL 6/1–15/97; HBG 3/98; SLJ 9/97) [921]

CHRISTOPHER, SAINT

13768 dePaola, Tomie. *Christopher: The Holy Giant* (K–3). Illus. 1994, Holiday LB $16.95 (0-8234-0862-0). 32pp. The story of Saint Christopher and how Jesus gave him that name for his good works. (Rev: BL 5/1/94; HB 5–6/94; SLJ 3/94*) [398.22]

CHURCHILL, WINSTON

13769 Driemen, J. E. *Winston Churchill: An Unbreakable Spirit* (5–8). Illus. Series: People in Focus. 1990, Macmillan LB $18.95 (0-87518-434-0). 128pp. A biography of this amazing statesman, leader, and writer. (Rev: SLJ 8/90) [921]

13770 Severance, John B. *Winston Churchill: Soldier, Statesman, Artist* (5–8). Illus. 1996, Clarion $17.95 (0-395-69853-7). 144pp. A well-organized, clearly written account of the life and works of Britain's great statesman. (Rev: BL 4/15/96; HB 7–8/96; SLJ 4/96*) [921]

CIARAN, SAINT

13771 Schmidt, Gary D. *Saint Ciaran: The Tale of a Saint of Ireland* (3–5). Illus. 2000, Eerdmans $18.00 (0-8028-5170-3). 40pp. The story of the gentle sixth-century Irish saint who, after journeying to Rome, went back to his home country to build a church. (Rev: BL 4/1/00; HBG 10/00; SLJ 8/00) [921]

CID, EL

13772 Koslow, Philip. *El Cid* (5–8). Illus. Series: Hispanics of Achievement. 1993, Chelsea LB $19.95 (0-7910-1239-5). 112pp. The story of Spain's national hero, who gained fame fighting the Moors. (Rev: BL 9/15/93) [921]

CLEOPATRA

13773 Green, Robert. *Cleopatra* (4–6). Illus. Series: First Books. 1996, Watts LB $22.50 (0-531-20231-3). 64pp. In a male-dominated world, this Egyptian queen wielded great power, but she lost her kingdom and life in a love affair with Mark Antony. (Rev: BL 7/96; SLJ 9/96) [921]

13774 Middleton, Haydn. *Cleopatra* (1–3). Series: What's Their Story? 1998, Oxford LB $12.95 (0-19-521404-8). In simple language with color illustrations, the author presents the story of Cleopatra, her dreams of restoring her country's glory, and the tragedy that ensued. (Rev: BL 5/15/98; HBG 10/98; SLJ 9/98) [921]

13775 Stanley, Diane, and Peter Vennema. *Cleopatra* (3–6). Illus. by Diane Stanley. 1994, Morrow $15.93 (0-688-10414-2). 48pp. With stunning illustrations, this biography covers Cleopatra's life from the time

she became Queen of Egypt until her death at 39. (Rev: BCCB 10/94; BL 9/15/94*; HB 11–12/94; SLJ 10/94) [921]

13776 Streissguth, Thomas. *Queen Cleopatra* (4–7). Series: A&E Biography. 2000, Lerner $25.26. (0-8225-4946-8). 112pp. The story of Cleopatra and her impact on world history. (Rev: BL 3/15/00; HBG 10/00; SLJ 5/00) [921]

DALAI LAMA

13777 Demi. *The Dalai Lama* (3–6). Illus. by author. 1998, Holt $17.95 (0-8050-5443-X). This biography of the contemporary, now-exiled, Dalai Lama also supplies details of his functions, mission, and responsibilities. (Rev: BCCB 4/98; HB 3–4/98; HBG 10/98; SLJ 3/98) [921]

13778 Stewart, Whitney. *The 14th Dalai Lama: Spiritual Leader of Tibet* (5–8). Illus. Series: Newsmakers. 1996, Lerner LB $25.26 (0-8225-4926-3). 128pp. As well as describing the life and spiritual beliefs of the 14th Dalai Lama, this account describes the political situation in Tibet at the time. (Rev: SLJ 6/96) [921]

DALOKAY, VEDAT

13779 Dalokay, Vedat. *Sister Shako and Kolo the Goat: Memories of My Childhood in Turkey* (5–7). Trans. by Guner Ener. 1994, Lothrop $14.00 (0-688-13271-5). 96pp. A memoir by the former mayor of Ankara about growing up Muslim in rural Turkey in the 1930s and of his friendship with an indomitable widow named Sister Shako. (Rev: BCCB 4/94; BL 5/1/94; SLJ 6/94) [921]

DAVID, KING OF ISRAEL

13780 Cohen, Barbara. *David: A Biography* (5–8). 1995, Clarion $15.95 (0-395-58702-6). 108pp. Recreates the events in the life of the biblical David, who began as a simple shepherd and ended as a warrior king. (Rev: BCCB 9/95; SLJ 7/95) [921]

DIANA, PRINCESS OF WALES

13781 Cerasini, Marc. *Diana: Queen of Hearts* (5–7). Illus. 1997, Random paper $4.99 (0-679-89214-1). 94pp. A breezy, easily read account of the life of this fairy-tale princess. (Rev: BL 12/1/97) [921]

13782 Licata, Renora. *Princess Diana: Royal Ambassador* (4–6). Illus. Series: The Library of Famous Women. 1993, Blackbirch LB $17.95 (1-56711-013-4). 64pp. Princess Diana comes alive in this account that covers her celebrity status and her public service work. (Rev: BL 6/1–15/93; SLJ 8/93) [921]

13783 Oleksy, Walter. *Princess Diana* (5–8). Series: People in the News. 2000, Lucent LB $18.96 (1-56006-579-6). 112pp. A well-documented life of this tragic, troubled princess that is illustrated with many black-and-white photographs. (Rev: BL 6/1–15/00; HBG 3/01) [921]

13784 Stone, Tanya L. *Diana: Princess of the People* (4–6). Series: Gateway Biographies. 1999, Millbrook LB $20.90 (0-7613-1262-5). 48pp. This book recounts the major events in Diana's life including her marriage to Charles and her bouts of depression and bulimia. (Rev: HBG 10/99; SLJ 8/99) [921]

13785 Whitelaw, Nancy. *Lady Diana Spencer: Princess of Wales* (4–7). Illus. 1998, Morgan Reynolds $20.95 (1-883846-35-8). 112pp. This is a readable, honest biography of Princess Diana, which deals realistically with her troubling behavior and her problems with Prince Charles. (Rev: BCCB 7–8/98; BL 8/98; HBG 10/98) [921]

13786 Wood, Richard. *Diana: The People's Princess* (4–7). Illus. 1998, Raintree Steck-Vaughn $24.98 (0-8172-3998-7); paper $7.95 (0-8172-7849-4). 48pp. A biography that includes bits of personal information about this multifaceted woman and details on the many causes she supported. (Rev: BL 7/98; HBG 10/98; SLJ 8/98) [921]

ELIZABETH I, QUEEN OF ENGLAND

13787 Green, Robert. *Queen Elizabeth I* (4–7). Illus. Series: First Books. 1997, Watts LB $22.50 (0-531-20302-6). 64pp. This account of the life of Elizabeth I also includes material on the religious conflicts of the day, her suitors, and the war with Spain. (Rev: BL 2/1/98; HBG 3/98; SLJ 1/98) [921]

13788 Stanley, Diane, and Peter Vennema. *Good Queen Bess: The Story of Elizabeth of England* (4–6). Illus. 1990, Macmillan LB $16.95 (0-02-786810-9). 40pp. An excellent biography of Elizabeth I, with emphasis on understanding the reasons for her actions in the context of the time. (Rev: BCCB 10/90; BL 9/1/90*; HB 1–2/91*; SLJ 12/90) [921]

13789 Thomas, Jane Resh. *Behind the Mask: The Life of Queen Elizabeth I* (5–8). Illus. 1998, Clarion $19.00 (0-395-69120-6). 196pp. A behind-the-scenes look at the long-lived queen, discussing her childhood, how she overcame opposition to become queen, and her subsequent manipulation of people, the court, and foreigners to attain greatness. (Rev: BL 12/15/98; HB 1–2/99; HBG 3/99) [921]

ELIZABETH II, QUEEN OF ENGLAND

13790 Green, Robert. *Queen Elizabeth II* (4–6). Illus. Series: First Books. 1997, Watts LB $32.50 (0-531-20303-4). 64pp. This account tells about Elizabeth's childhood during World War II, how she came to the throne, and changes that have occurred during her reign. (Rev: BL 12/1/97; HBG 3/98; SLJ 12/97) [921]

EQUIANO, OLAUDAH

13791 Cameron, Ann. *The Kidnapped Prince: The Life of Olaudah Equiano* (5–8). 1995, Knopf $16.00 (0-679-85619-6). 133pp. Adapted from his autobiography, this is the story of Olaudah Equiano, an African prince sold into slavery in the 18th century. (Rev: BCCB 4/95; BL 1/1/95; SLJ 2/95) [921]

ERIC THE RED

13792 Grant, Neil. *Eric the Red: The Viking Adventurer* (3–5). Series: What's Their Story? 1998, Oxford $12.95 (0-19-521431-5). 32pp. Color illus-

trations and simple writing tell the story of Eric the Red's daring explorations, his leadership, the voyages of his son, Leif, and the impact of Christianity on the Vikings. (Rev: BL 2/15/99; HBG 3/99; SLJ 12/98) [921]

FRANCIS OF ASSISI, SAINT

13793 dePaola, Tomie. *Francis: The Poor Man of Assisi* (4–7). Illus. by author. 1982, Holiday LB $18.95 (0-8234-0435-8); paper $9.95 (0-8234-0812-4). 48pp. A simple retelling of the life of St. Francis with fine pictures by dePaola.

13794 Mayo, Margaret. *Brother Sun, Sister Moon: The Life and Stories of St. Francis* (3–6). Illus. by Peter Malone. 2000, Little, Brown $16.95 (0-316-56466-4). 80pp. As well as telling the life story of Saint Francis of Assisi, this attractive volume contains eight stories about him, one of his poems, and accounts of his canonization and his influence on the Catholic religion. (Rev: BCCB 3/00; BL 3/1/00*; HB 5–6/00; HBG 10/00; SLJ 4/00) [921]

13795 Wildsmith, Brian. *Saint Francis* (1–3). Illus. 1996, Eerdmans $20.00 (0-8028-5123-1). 36pp. A large-size picture book that tells the story of St. Francis as a first-person narrative with a biographical note following the story. (Rev: BCCB 7–8/96; BL 1/1–15/96; SLJ 2/96) [921]

FRANK, ANNE

13796 Adler, David A. *A Picture Book of Anne Frank* (2–4). Illus. by Karen Ritz. 1993, Holiday LB $16.95 (0-8234-1003-X). 32pp. A simple biography for young readers. (Rev: BCCB 3/93; BL 3/1/93; SLJ 5/93) [921]

13797 Epstein, Rachel. *Anne Frank* (3–6). Illus. 1997, Watts $22.50 (0-531-20298-4). 64pp. A forthright and personal account of the life and death of this young Jewish girl, with quotes from her diary and from people who knew her. (Rev: BL 12/1/97; HBG 3/98; SLJ 11/97) [921]

13798 Frank, Anne. *Anne Frank: The Diary of a Young Girl* (5–8). 1967, Pocket paper $3.95 (0-685-05466-7). 312pp. A moving diary of a young Jewish girl hiding from the Nazis in World War II Amsterdam. [921]

13799 Gold, Alison L. *Memories of Anne Frank: Reflections of a Childhood Friend* (4–8). Illus. 1997, Scholastic $16.95 (0-590-90722-0). 160pp. Anne Frank's story as told through recollections of her best friend in Amsterdam, Hannah Goslar, a survivor of the Holocaust. (Rev: BL 9/1/97; HBG 3/98; SLJ 11/97) [921]

13800 Hurwitz, Johanna. *Anne Frank: Life in Hiding* (4–7). Illus. by Vera Rosenberry. 1989, Jewish Publication Soc. $13.95 (0-8276-0311-8). 64pp. Describes 25 months of hiding from the Nazis in the 1940s. (Rev: BL 4/15/89) [921]

GANDHI, MAHATMA

13801 Barraclough, John. *Mohandas Gandhi* (2–3). Illus. Series: Lives and Times. 1997, Heinemann $19.92 (1-57572-561-4). 24pp. A simple picture-book biography that tells of Gandhi's work in South

Africa and his struggle against British rule in India. (Rev: BL 3/15/98) [921]

13802 Fisher, Leonard Everett. *Gandhi* (5–7). Illus. 1995, Simon & Schuster paper $16.00 (0-689-80337-0). 32pp. In powerful black-and-white drawings and simple text, this is a handsome addition to the life of the Indian leader. (Rev: BL 10/1/95; SLJ 10/95) [921]

13803 Martin, Christopher. *Mohandas Gandhi* (4–7). Series: A&E Biography. 2000, Lucent LB $25.26 (0-8225-4984-0). 112pp. The story of the man who sought to unite and free his people not through violence by by prayer, civil disobedience, and communication. (Rev: BL 12/15/00; HBG 3/01) [921]

13804 Mitchell, Pratima. *Gandhi: The Father of Modern India* (3–5). Illus. Series: What's Their Story? 1998, Oxford LB $12.95 (0-19-521434-X). 32pp. A biography of Gandhi that stresses his peaceful efforts to persuade the British to leave India. (Rev: BL 2/15/99; HBG 3/99; SLJ 4/99) [921]

GEORGE III, KING OF ENGLAND

13805 Green, Robert. *King George III* (4–6). Series: First Books. 1997, Watts LB $22.50 (0-531-20333-6). 64pp. An objective account of the life of the troubled monarch whose policies toward his colonies caused the American Revolution. (Rev: BL 12/15/97; HBG 3/98; SLJ 12/97) [921]

HANNIBAL

13806 Green, Robert. *Hannibal* (5–8). Illus. Series: First Books. 1996, Watts LB $22.50 (0-531-20240-2). 63pp. Although some material is given on Hannibal's formative years, most of this account deals with his military career and the significance of his life. (Rev: SLJ 2/97) [921]

HATSHEPSUT

13807 Andronik, Catherine M. *Hatshepsut, His Majesty, Herself* (3–6). Illus. by Joseph Daniel Fiedler. 2001, Simon & Schuster $17.00 (0-689-82562-5). 40pp. An appealing picture-book biography of Egypt's only female pharaoh. (Rev: BCCB 3/01; SLJ 3/01) [921]

HENRY VIII, KING OF ENGLAND

13808 Green, Robert. *King Henry VIII* (4–6). Illus. Series: First Books. 1998, Watts LB $21.00 (0-531-20305-0). 64pp. A biography of the much-married Tudor king, sketching his life, his wives, and the world in which he lived. (Rev: BL 6/1–15/98; HBG 10/98) [921]

HEROD OF JUDEA

13809 Green, Robert. *Herod the Great* (4–6). Illus. Series: First Books. 1996, Watts LB $22.50 (0-531-20232-1). 64pp. The life of the notorious Roman ruler of Judea and the political and religious conditions during his life. (Rev: BL 7/96; SLJ 9/96) [921]

HITLER, ADOLF

13810 Ayer, Eleanor. *Adolf Hitler* (4–8). Illus. Series: The Importance Of. 1996, Lucent LB $18.96 (1-56006-072-7). 128pp. A biography of this dictator that discusses the impact of his life on Germany and the world. (Rev: BL 3/15/96; SLJ 1/96) [921]

JOAN OF ARC

13811 Bunson, Margaret, and Matthew Bunson. *St. Joan of Arc* (4–6). Illus. Series: Saints You Should Know. 1992, Sunday Visitor paper $5.95 (0-87973-558-9). 56pp. A clear, unsentimental portrait of the saint who lost her life trying to save her country. (Rev: BL 1/1/93) [921]

13812 Hodges, Margaret. *Joan of Arc: The Lily Maid* (2–4). Illus. by Robert Rayevsky. 1999, Holiday $16.95 (0-8234-1424-8). A simple, understandable account of the life of Joan of Arc and her devotion and bravery. (Rev: BL 11/1/99*; HBG 3/00; SLJ 9/99) [921]

13813 Poole, Josephine. *Joan of Arc* (K–3). Illus. by Angela Barrett. 1998, Knopf LB $19.99 (0-679-99041-0). 32pp. A lovely picture book that highlights the life of Joan of Arc, with emphasis on her courage and sense of purpose. (Rev: BCCB 9/98; BL 8/98*; HBG 3/99; SLJ 9/98) [921]

13814 Roberts, Jeremy. *Saint Joan of Arc* (4–6). Series: A&E Biography. 2000, Lerner LB $25.26 (0-8225-4981-6). 112pp. The story of a young woman whose honesty, devotion, and courage inspired an army, a king, and eventually a country to follow her. (Rev: BL 6/1–15/00; HBG 10/00) [921]

13815 Stanley, Diane. *Joan of Arc* (4–8). Illus. 1998, Morrow LB $15.93 (0-688-14330-X). 40pp. Using glorious illustrations, this picture book for older readers gives a detailed history of the life and times of Joan of Arc. (Rev: BCCB 9/98; BL 8/98*; HB 9–10/98*; HBG 3/99; SLJ 9/98) [921]

JOHN PAUL II, POPE

13816 Mohan, Claire J. *The Young Life of Pope John Paul II* (4–6). Illus. 1995, Young Sparrow $14.95 (0-943135-11-7); paper $7.95 (0-943135-12-5). 64pp. The story of Pope John Paul II when he was Karol Wojtyla growing up in Poland. (Rev: BL 9/1/95; SLJ 11/95) [921]

JUAREZ, BENITO

13817 De Varona, Frank. *Benito Juarez: President of Mexico* (3–6). Illus. Series: Hispanic Heritage. 1993, Millbrook LB $19.90 (1-56294-279-4). 32pp. The story of the rise to greatness of a native Indian who became president of Mexico. (Rev: BL 5/15/93; SLJ 7/93) [921]

13818 Palacios, Argentina. *Viva Mexico! A Story of Benito Juarez and Cinco de Mayo* (2–4). Illus. by Howard Berelson. 1993, Raintree Steck-Vaughn LB $25.69 (0-8114-7214-0). 32pp. For very young readers, this is a simple biography of the man often referred to as the architect of modern Mexico. (Rev: BL 5/15/93; SLJ 7/93) [921]

KA'IULANI, PRINCESS

13819 Linnea, Sharon. *Princess Ka'iulani: Hope of a Nation, Heart of a People* (5–8). Illus. 1999, Eerdmans $15.00 (0-8028-5145-2). 224pp. The story of the Hawaiian princess who tried to prevent the annexation of her country by the United States and of her untimely death at age 22. (Rev: BL 7/99) [921]

13820 Stanley, Fay. *The Last Princess: The Story of Princess Ka'iulani of Hawaii* (4–6). Illus. by Diane Stanley. 1991, Macmillan LB $18.00 (0-02-786785-4). 40pp. The ill-fated princess who never achieved her goal of being queen of Hawaii. (Rev: BL 3/15/91*) [921]

KHERDIAN, JERON

13821 Kherdian, Jeron. *The Road from Home: The Story of an Armenian Girl* (6–8). 1979, Greenwillow $15.89 (0-688-84205-4); Morrow paper $5.95 (0-688-14425-X). 256pp. A memoir of a survivor of the Turkish slaughter of Armenians. [921]

KOLBE, SAINT MAXIMILIAN

13822 Mohan, Claire J. *Saint Maximilian Kolbe: The Story of the Two Crowns* (4–8). Illus. 1999, Young Sparrow paper $8.95 (0-962-15003-7). 72pp. The story of a Polish Catholic monk who took the place of a fellow prisoner who was condemned to die at Auschwitz. (Rev: BL 2/1/00) [921]

KOLLEK, TEDDY

13823 Rabinovich, Abraham. *Teddy Kollek: Builder of Jerusalem* (5–8). Illus. 1996, Jewish Publication Soc. $14.95 (0-8276-0559-5); paper $9.95 (0-8276-0561-7). 124pp. The story of the former mayor of Jerusalem, who supervised the city's unification after the Six Days War in 1967. (Rev: BL 5/15/96) [921]

KOSSMAN, NINA

13824 Kossman, Nina. *Behind the Border* (5–7). 1994, Lothrop $14.00 (0-688-13494-7). 128pp. This book contains 12 episodes that tell about the author's childhood in Communist Russia before emigrating to the United States. (Rev: BCCB 10/94; BL 8/94; SLJ 10/94) [921]

LAFAYETTE, MARQUIS DE

13825 Fritz, Jean. *Why Not, Lafayette?* (5–8). Illus. 1999, Putnam $16.99 (0-399-23411-X). 96pp. Using many quotes and dry humor, this is a readable biography of General Lafayette, the French-born hero of the American Revolution. (Rev: BCCB 12/99; BL 9/15/99; HB 11–12/99; HBG 3/00; SLJ 12/99) [973.3]

L'OUVERTURE, TOUSSAINT

13826 Myers, Walter Dean. *Toussaint L'Ouverture: The Fight for Haiti's Freedom* (4–8). Illus. by Jacob Lawrence. 1996, Simon & Schuster paper $16.00 (0-689-80126-2). 32pp. Powerful paintings highlight this story of the liberator of the people of Haiti. (Rev: BCCB 1/97; BL 9/1/96; SLJ 11/96*) [921]

MANDELA, NELSON

13827 Connolly, Sean. *Nelson Mandela: An Unauthorized Biography* (5–7). 2000, Heinemann LB $24.22 (1-57572-225-9). 56pp. An appealing biography that contains good background material on South Africa, past and present. (Rev: SLJ 1/01) [921]

13828 Cooper, Floyd. *Mandela: From the Life of the South African Statesman* (2–4). Illus. 1996, Putnam $15.99 (0-399-22942-6). 40pp. A picture-book biography that focuses on Mandela's childhood and youth. (Rev: BL 9/15/96; SLJ 11/96*) [921]

13829 Finlayson, Reggie. *Nelson Mandela* (4–7). Illus. Series: A&E Biography. 1999, Lerner $25.26 (0-8225-4936-0). 112pp. The major strength of this biography of Mandela is the extensive coverage of his childhood and schooling. (Rev: BL 2/15/00; HBG 3/99; SLJ 2/99) [921]

13830 Holland, Gini. *Nelson Mandela* (2–4). Illus. by Mike White. Series: First Biographies. 1997, Raintree Steck-Vaughn LB $24.26 (0-8172-4454-9). 32pp. A simple retelling of Nelson Mandela's life from his childhood as the son of a black chieftain to his release from prison in 1990 and resumption of his political career. (Rev: SLJ 2/98) [921]

13831 Roberts, Jack L. *Nelson Mandela: Determined to Be Free* (2–4). Illus. Series: Gateway Biographies. 1995, Millbrook LB $20.90 (1-56294-558-0). 48pp. A short, direct biography illustrated by numerous photographs. (Rev: BL 5/1/95) [921]

13832 Strazzabosco, Jeanne M. *Learning About Forgiveness from the Life of Nelson Mandela* (2–5). Illus. Series: Character Building Book. 1996, Rosen LB $16.95 (0-8239-2413-0). 24pp. Covers, in a small-format book, the life of this South African hero and politician who fought successfully against apartheid. (Rev: BL 10/15/96; SLJ 11/96) [921]

MANJIRO

13833 Blumberg, Rhoda. *Shipwrecked! The True Adventures of a Japanese Boy* (5–9). Illus. 2001, HarperCollins $16.95 (0-688-17484-1). 80pp. The story of a shipwrecked Japanese boy who is adopted by an American sea captain and brought to Massachusetts for an education, where he became the first Japanese person to live in the United States. (Rev: BL 2/1/01*; SLJ 2/01) [921]

MARSHAL, WILLIAM

13834 Weatherly, Myra. *William Marshal: Medieval England's Greatest Knight* (5–8). Illus. 2001, Morgan Reynolds LB $20.95 (1-883846-48-X). 112pp. The story of the brave medieval English knight whose accomplishments numbered fighting in tournaments, traveling to the Holy Land, helping to draw up the Magna Carta, and serving as regent when Henry III was a child. (Rev: BCCB 3/01; BL 1/1–15/01; SLJ 3/01) [921]

MONTESSORI, MARIA

13835 O'Connor, Barbara. *Mammolina: A Story About Maria Montessori* (3–6). Illus. by Sara Campitelli. Series: Creative Minds. 1993, Carolrhoda LB $18.95 (0-87614-743-0). 64pp. Describes the life of the educational philosopher who developed revolutionary ideas on child development and their application in schools. (Rev: BCCB 4/93; BL 4/1/93; SLJ 4/93) [921]

13836 Shephard, Marie T. *Maria Montessori: Teacher of Teachers* (5–7). Illus. 1996, Lerner LB $25.26 (0-8225-4952-2). 128pp. A biography of the Italian educator and her unusual teaching methods for the young. (Rev: BL 8/96; SLJ 9/96) [921]

MORRIS, SAMUEL

13837 Jackson, Dave, and Neta Jackson. *Quest for the Lost Prince* (3–6). Illus. by Julian Jackson. Series: Trailblazer. 1996, Bethany paper $5.99 (1-55661-472-1). 144pp. The true story of an African prince, born in 1872, who became a Christian and came to the United States. (Rev: BL 10/1/96) [921]

MUGABE, ROBERT

13838 Worth, Richard. *Robert Mugabe of Zimbabwe* (5–8). Illus. Series: In Focus Biographies. 1990, Silver Burdett LB $13.95 (0-671-68987-8); paper $7.95 (0-671-70684-5). 111pp. Tells the story of Zimbabwe's first prime minister, along with a history of this emerging country. (Rev: SLJ 2/91) [921]

NAPOLEON BONAPARTE

13839 Carroll, Bob. *Napoleon Bonaparte* (4–8). Illus. Series: The Importance Of. 1994, Lucent LB $17.96 (1-56006-021-2). 112pp. From humble beginnings on the island of Corsica to becoming Emperor of the French and his final wartime defeat and exile, this is the story of Napoleon. (Rev: BL 5/15/94; SLJ 4/94) [921]

NIGHTINGALE, FLORENCE

13840 Adler, David A. *A Picture Book of Florence Nightingale* (K–3). Illus. by John Wallner. Series: Picture Book Biographies. 1992, Holiday LB $16.95 (0-8234-0965-1). 32pp. Through simple text and illustrations that supply details of time and place, the life of this gallant nurse is introduced. (Rev: BL 11/15/92; SLJ 10/92) [921]

13841 Gorrell, Gena K. *Heart and Soul: The Story of Florence Nightingale* (5–8). Illus. 2000, Tundra $18.95 (0-88776-494-0). 146pp. A readable biography of Florence Nightingale that details her drive and determination and how she became known as "the lady with the lamp." (Rev: BL 1/1–15/01; HB 1–2/01; HBG 3/01; SLJ 12/00) [921]

PATRICK, SAINT

13842 dePaola, Tomie. *Patrick: Patron Saint of Ireland* (PS–3). Illus. 1992, Holiday LB $16.95 (0-8234-0924-4). 32pp. Simple text and glowing pictures portray the life of Ireland's saint. (Rev: BCCB 4/92; BL 3/15/92; HB 9–10/92; SLJ 5/92) [921]

PETER THE GREAT

13843 Greenblatt, Miriam. *Peter the Great and Tsarist Russia* (5–8). Illus. Series: Rulers and Their Times. 1999, Marshall Cavendish LB $19.95 (0-7614-0914-9). 80pp. A biography of the czar who westernized Russia is followed by a section on daily life during his reign. (Rev: BL 1/1–15/00; HBG 10/00) [921]

PULASKI, CASIMIR

13844 Collins, David R. *Casimir Pulaski: Soldier on Horseback* (4–8). Illus. 1995, Pelican $14.95 (1-56554-082-4). 96pp. The stirring biography of the Polish patriot who organized Washington's cavalry during the American Revolutionary War. (Rev: BL 2/15/96) [921]

RAMPHELE, MAMPHELA

13845 Harlan, Judith. *Mamphela Ramphele: Challenging Apartheid in South Africa* (5–8). Illus. Series: Women Changing the World. 2000, Feminist Pr. LB $19.95 (1-55861-227-0). 112pp. This is the inspiring story of the black South African woman who fought racial segregation and injustice in her country and went on to be a doctor and educator. (Rev: BL 9/15/00; HBG 3/01) [921]

SAN MARTÍN, JOSÉ DE

13846 Fernandez, Jose B. *Jose de San Martin: Latin America's Quiet Hero* (3–6). Illus. Series: Hispanic Heritage. 1994, Millbrook LB $19.90 (1-56294-383-9). 32pp. The life story of the South American revolutionary who rivaled Bolívar in importance but who died in obscurity in Europe. (Rev: BL 6/1–15/94; SLJ 4/94) [921]

SASAKI, SADAKO

13847 Coerr, Eleanor. *Sadako and the Thousand Paper Cranes* (3–5). Illus. by Ronald Himler. 1977, Putnam $14.95 (0-399-20520-9); Dell paper $3.99 (0-440-47465-5). 64pp. The moving biography of a young Japanese girl who dies of leukemia that developed as a result of radiation sickness from the bombing of Hiroshima.

SAUTUOLA, MARIA DE

13848 Fradin, Dennis B. *Maria de Sautuola: The Bulls in the Cave* (3–5). Illus. Series: Remarkable Children. 1997, Silver Burdett LB $18.95 (0-382-39470-4); paper $5.95 (0-382-39471-2). 32pp. The story of the young Spanish girl who discovered the first known prehistoric cave paintings in 1879. (Rev: BL 6/1–15/97; HBG 3/98; SLJ 7/97) [921]

SCHINDLER, OSKAR

13849 Roberts, Jack L. *Oskar Schindler* (4–8). Illus. Series: The Importance Of. 1996, Lucent LB $17.96 (1-56006-079-4). 111pp. The story of one man's fight to save Jews from Nazi death camps during World War II. (Rev: BL 3/15/96; SLJ 1/96) [921]

SHAKA (ZULU CHIEF)

13850 Stanley, Diane, and Peter Vennema. *Shaka: King of the Zulus* (2–4). Illus. by Diane Stanley. 1988, Morrow LB $15.93 (0-688-07343-3). 40pp. The life story of a Zulu military genius who became king of his people in the 19th century. (Rev: BCCB 11/88; BL 11/1/88; HB 1–2/89)

SUGIHARA, CHIUNE

13851 Gold, Alison L. *A Special Fate: Chiune Sugihara: Hero of the Holocaust* (5–10). 2000, Scholastic $15.95 (0-590-39525-4). 176pp. The life story of the Japanese diplomat who saved thousands of Jewish lives during the Holocaust while he was stationed in Lithuania. (Rev: BCCB 5/00; HB 5–6/00; HBG 10/00; SLJ 5/00) [921]

TERESA, MOTHER

13852 Barraclough, John. *Mother Teresa* (2–3). Series: Lives and Times. 1997, Heinemann $19.92 (1-57572-562-2). 24pp. A simple picture-book biography that gives a very brief introduction to the life and contributions of Mother Teresa. (Rev: BL 3/15/98) [921]

13853 Giff, Patricia Reilly. *Mother Teresa: Sister to the Poor* (3–5). Illus. 1987, Puffin paper $4.99 (0-14-032225-6). 64pp. Beginning with her childhood in Macedonia, this is the story of the woman who has won the Nobel Peace Prize for her work to better thousands of lives. (Rev: BCCB 4/86; BL 8/86; SLJ 9/86) [921]

13854 Jacobs, William J. *Mother Teresa: Helping the Poor* (3–5). Illus. Series: Gateway Biographies. 1991, Millbrook LB $20.90 (1-56294-020-1). 48pp. An admiring portrait of this woman of compassion and peace, including an overview of her work with the poor. (Rev: BL 1/1/92; SLJ 1/92) [921]

13855 Johnson, Linda C. *Mother Teresa: Protector of the Sick* (5–8). Illus. Series: Library of Famous Women. 1991, Blackbirch LB $17.95 (1-56711-034-7). 64pp. Tracing Mother Teresa's life from her childhood in Yugoslavia to her renowned efforts to aid the sick around the world. (Rev: BL 3/15/93) [921]

13856 Mohan, Claire J. *The Young Life of Mother Teresa of Calcutta* (4–6). Illus. by Jane Robbins. 1996, Young Sparrow $14.95 (0-943135-26-5); paper $7.95 (0-943135-25-7). 64pp. This biography concentrates on Mother Teresa's life from when she was called to serve God at age 12 to her leaving the convent to go to Calcutta. (Rev: SLJ 1/97) [921]

13857 Morgan, Nina. *Mother Teresa: Saint of the Poor* (4–7). Illus. 1998, Raintree Steck-Vaughn $24.95 (0-8172-3997-9); paper $7.95 (0-8172-7848-6). 48pp. A biography of the nun whose work with the poor of India made her an international celebrity and earned her a Nobel Peace Prize. (Rev: BL 7/98; HBG 10/98; SLJ 7/98) [921]

13858 Pond, Mildred. *Mother Teresa: A Life of Charity* (4–7). Illus. Series: Junior World Biographies. 1992, Chelsea LB $15.95 (0-7910-1755-9). 80pp. The inspiring life story of the nun who has given her life to serve and help the poor, particularly in India. (Rev: BL 8/92; SLJ 7/92) [921]

13859 Tilton, Rafael. *Mother Teresa* (4–8). Series: The Importance Of. 2000, Lucent LB $18.96 (1-56006-656-6). This thoroughly researched account

describes the life of Mother Teresa and gives an honest appraisal of her importance. (Rev: BL 1/1–15/00) [921]

THATCHER, MARGARET

13860 Hughes, Libby. *Madam Prime Minister* (5–7). Illus. 1989, Macmillan LB $11.95 (0-87518-410-3). 144pp. This solid biography shows both the public and private sides of the former British prime minister. (Rev: BL 11/1/89*; SLJ 1/90) [921]

TUTANKHAMEN, KING

13861 Green, Robert. *Tutankhamun* (4–6). Illus. Series: First Books. 1996, Watts LB $22.50 (0-531-20233-X). 64pp. The opening of his tomb in the 20th century brought fame and importance to this little-known Egyptian monarch. (Rev: BL 7/96; SLJ 7/96) [921]

13862 Sabuda, Robert. *Tutankhamen's Gift* (K–4). Illus. 1994, Atheneum $17.00 (0-689-31818-9). 32pp. A fictionalized account of the boyhood of Tutankhamen and how he became pharaoh at an early age. (Rev: BL 4/15/94; SLJ 5/94) [921]

VICTORIA, QUEEN OF ENGLAND

13863 Green, Robert. *Queen Victoria* (4–6). Illus. Series: First Books. 1998, Watts LB $21.00 (0-531-20330-1). 64pp. This book on Queen Victoria discusses her childhood, education, and marriage and gives an assessment of her long reign and its significance. (Rev: BL 6/1–15/98; HBG 10/98; SLJ 6/98) [921]

VILLA, PANCHO

13864 Carroll, Bob. *Pancho Villa* (4–8). Illus. Series: The Importance Of. 1996, Lucent LB $16.95 (1-56006-069-7). 112pp. The story of this colorful fighter against tyranny and of his lasting influence on Mexico's history. (Rev: BL 3/15/96; SLJ 2/96) [921]

13865 O'Brien, Steven. *Pancho Villa* (5–8). Illus. Series: Hispanics of Achievement. 1994, Chelsea LB $19.95 (0-7910-1257-3). 112pp. The life and accomplishments of this Mexican freedom fighter. (Rev: BL 9/15/94) [921]

WALESA, LECH

13866 Lazo, Caroline. *Lech Walesa* (4–7). Illus. Series: Peacemakers. 1993, Dillon LB $13.95 (0-87518-525-8). 64pp. The story of the Polish Solidarity labor movement leader is told with generous quotes from Walesa's autobiography and speeches. (Rev: BL 12/15/93; SLJ 1/94) [921]

WALLENBERG, RAOUL

13867 Linnea, Sharon. *Raoul Wallenberg: The Man Who Stopped Death* (5–7). Illus. 1993, Jewish Publication Soc. paper $9.95 (0-8276-0448-3). 120pp. This Swedish architect saved thousands of Jews in Hungary from the Nazi Holocaust. (Rev: BL 6/1–15/93) [940]

WILLIAM THE CONQUEROR

13868 Green, Robert. *William the Conqueror* (4–6). Series: First Books. 1998, Watts LB $21.00 (0-531-20353-0). 64pp. This lively account of the Norman king who conquered England contains many period illustrations and photographs of historical sites. (Rev: BL 6/1–15/98; HBG 10/98) [921]

YELTSIN, BORIS

13869 Lambroza, Shlomo. *Boris Yeltsin* (5–8). Illus. Series: World Leaders. 1993, Rourke $19.93 (0-86625-482-X). 110pp. After describing recent events and the emergence of Russia from the Soviet Union, this biography outlines Yeltsin's life and accomplishments through 1993. (Rev: SLJ 12/93) [921]

The Arts and Language

Art and Architecture

General and Miscellaneous

13870 *A Is for Artist* (PS–1). Illus. 1997, Getty Museum $16.95 (0-89236-377-0). 60pp. Using an alphabetical approach, this book introduces 26 glorious paintings from the Getty Museum. (Rev: BL 10/15/97; HBG 3/98) [708.194]

13871 Alcraft, Rob. *Zoom City* (3–6). Illus. by Jonathan Adams. 1998, Heinemann LB $17.95 (1-57572-717-X). 32pp. Using strange camera angles and perspectives, this view of city life includes full-page photos of a traffic jam, underground life, a harbor, a skyscraper, parks, and a stadium. (Rev: HBG 10/99; SLJ 3/99) [725]

13872 Angelou, Maya. *My Painted House, My Friendly Chicken, and Me* (PS–3). Illus. by Margaret Courtney-Clarke. 1994, Crown $16.00 (0-517-59667-9). 36pp. The customs and beautifully decorated houses of the Ndebele people of South Africa are featured in this picture book. (Rev: BCCB 12/94; BL 10/1/94; SLJ 10/94*) [704]

13873 Baumbusch, Brigitte. *Animals Observed* (PS–3). Trans. from Italian by Erika Paoli. Series: Art for Children. 1999, Stewart, Tabori & Chang $9.95 (1-55670-970-6). 29pp. The works of artists both famous, like Picasso and Matisse, and unknown are used to show the animal world as reflected in art. Also use: *Looking at Nature* (1999). (Rev: HBG 10/00; SLJ 1/00) [701]

13874 Baumbusch, Brigitte. *Figuring Figures* (1–4). Trans. by Erika Paoli. Series: Art for Children. 1999, Stewart, Tabori & Chang $9.95 (1-55670-969-2). 29pp. From ancient to contemporary times and in a variety of media, this book focuses on how the human figure has been depicted in art. A companion volume is *The Many Faces of the Face* (1999). (Rev: HBG 10/00; SLJ 12/99) [709]

13875 Bigham, Julia. *The 60s: The Plastic Age* (5–7). Series: 20th Century Design. 2000, Gareth Stevens LB $22.60 (0-8368-2708-2). 32pp. A heavily illustrated title that looks at design and technology in the 1960s with coverage of fashion, art, household appliances, furniture, and architecture. (Rev: SLJ 3/01) [700]

13876 Björk, Christina. *Linnea in Monet's Garden* (1–4). Trans. by Joan Sandin. Illus. by Lena Anderson. 1987, Farrar $13.00 (9-129-58314-4). 56pp. Linnea, a young French girl, learns about flowers, the painter Monet, and Impressionism from her friend Mr. Bloom. (Rev: BL 12/1/87)

13877 Blanquet, Claire-Helene. *Miró: Earth and Sky* (5–7). Trans. from French by John Goodman. Illus. Series: Art for Children. 1994, Chelsea LB $16.95 (0-7910-2813-5). 59pp. Using a conversational style and some fictitious characters, the life and works of the famous 20th-century French painter Miró are introduced. (Rev: SLJ 12/94) [709]

13878 Blizzard, Gladys S. *Come Look with Me: Enjoying Art with Children* (1–4). Illus. 1991, Thomasson-Grant $13.95 (0-934738-76-9). 32pp. Readers are urged to examine 12 paintings of children by famous artists. (Rev: BCCB 5/91; BL 6/1/91) [750.1]

13879 Blizzard, Gladys S. *Come Look with Me: Exploring Landscape Art with Children* (1–4). Illus. 1992, Thomasson-Grant $13.95 (0-934738-95-5). 32pp. For primary-grade youngsters, this is an introduction to different styles of landscape painting as seen through the work of 12 important artists. (Rev: BL 3/1/92; HB 9–10/92) [758.1]

13880 Blizzard, Gladys S. *Come Look with Me: World of Play* (1–4). Illus. 1993, Thomasson-Grant $13.95 (1-56566-031-5). 32pp. This art appreciation book reproduces 11 paintings and one sculpture that depict various ways in which children play. (Rev: BL 9/1/93) [701.1]

13881 Bolton, Linda. *Cubism* (4–8). Illus. Series: Art Revolution. 2000, Bedrick $16.95 (0-87226-613-3). 32pp. Cubism is explained and its place in art history examined; rich, colorful layouts highlight examples of cubist art by many different artists. (Rev: BL 10/15/00; HBG 3/01; SLJ 1/01) [709.04]

13882 Bolton, Linda. *Impressionism* (4–5). Series: Art Revolution. 2000, NTC $16.95 (0-87226-611-7). 32pp. After a brief overview of Impressionism in art, there are separate sections on ten leading artists and their works. Also use *Surrealism* (2000). (Rev: HBG 3/01; SLJ 11/00) [701]

13883 Capek, Michael. *Artistic Trickery: The Tradition of Trompe l'Oeil Art* (5–8). Illus. 1995, Lerner LB $22.60 (0-8225-2064-8). 64pp. The art of creating images so perfect that the viewer thinks they are real is introduced, with many historical and contemporary examples. (Rev: BCCB 7–8/95; BL 6/1–15/95; SLJ 7/95) [758]

13884 Capek, Michael. *Murals: Cave, Cathedral, to Street* (5–8). Illus. 1996, Lerner LB $23.93 (0-8225-2065-6). 80pp. The history of mural painting from cave painting to such modern masters as Diego Rivera. (Rev: BL 6/1–15/96; SLJ 10/96) [751.7]

13885 Delafosse, Claude. *Animals* (PS–2). Illus. by Tony Ross. Series: First Discovery Art. 1995, Scholastic $11.95 (0-590-55202-3). 26pp. Youngsters are introduced to art through a series of laminated pages that alternate with transparencies and give the impression of change and motion. (Rev: BL 1/1–15/96; SLJ 1/96) [701]

13886 Delafosse, Claude. *Landscapes* (4–7). Illus. Series: First Discovery Art. 1996, Scholastic $11.95 (0-590-50216-6). 24pp. The art and techniques of landscape painting are introduced, with many examples from the masters in various historical periods. (Rev: BL 6/1–15/96; SLJ 7/96) [750]

13887 Delafosse, Claude. *Paintings* (4–7). Illus. Series: First Discovery Art. 1996, Scholastic $11.95 (0-590-55201-5). 28pp. A general introduction to painting, with many reproductions and lessons in art appreciation. (Rev: BL 6/1–15/96; SLJ 7/96) [750]

13888 Delafosse, Claude. *Portraits* (PS–2). Illus. by Tony Ross. Series: First Discovery Art. 1995, Scholastic $11.95 (0-590-55200-7). 26pp. Objects gain new dimensions when seen through transparencies in this introduction to art appreciation. (Rev: BL 1/1–15/96; SLJ 1/96) [701]

13889 Finley, Carol. *Aboriginal Art of Australia: Exploring Cultural Traditions* (5–9). Series: Art Around the World. 1999, Lerner LB $23.93 (0-8225-2076-1). 56pp. The author covers aboriginal art, aboriginal beliefs, and the contemporary works that reflect the Australian natives' struggle for equality. (Rev: HBG 3/00; SLJ 11/99) [701]

13890 Fisher, Leonard Everett. *Alphabet Art: Thirteen ABCs from Around the World* (5–8). Illus. 1984, Macmillan $16.95 (0-02-735230-7). 64pp. Thirteen alphabets — from Arabic to Tibetan — are pictured with their English equivalents.

13891 Gaff, Jackie. *1900–20: The Birth of Modernism* (5–7). Series: 20th Century Design. 2000, Gareth Stevens LB $22.60 (0-8368-2705-8). 32pp. This account traces developments in the worlds of art, design, and technology for the first 20 years of the past century. (Rev: SLJ 3/01) [708]

13892 Gibbons, Gail. *The Art Box* (PS–3). Illus. 1998, Holiday $16.95 (0-8234-1386-1). 32pp. In a series of brightly colored illustrations, the author displays the various tools and supplies that an artist uses. (Rev: BL 9/15/98; HBG 3/99; SLJ 12/98) [702]

13893 *Groom Your Room: Terrific Touches to Brighten Your Bedroom!* (3–8). Photos by Michael Walker and Fritz Geiger. Series: American Girl. 1997, Pleasant paper $7.95 (1-56247-531-2). 48pp. A beginning decorating book that also gives tips on cleaning and organizing possessions. (Rev: SLJ 3/98) [745]

13894 *The History of Printmaking* (3–6). Illus. Series: Voyages of Discovery. 1996, Scholastic $19.95 (0-590-47649-1). 48pp. Overlays and foldouts are used to present a history of prints and print images, including computer images. (Rev: BL 12/15/97) [769]

13895 Jockel, Nils. *Bruegel's Tower of Babel: The Builder with the Red Hat* (4–7). Illus. Series: Adventures in Art. 1998, Prestel $14.95 (3-7913-1941-8). 30pp. A detailed analysis of Pieter Bruegel's surreal masterpiece, using one of the characters in the painting to supply a point of view and an examination of the meaning of its contents. (Rev: BL 8/98; SLJ 8/98) [759.9493]

13896 Jones, Helen. *40s and 50s: War and Postwar Years* (5–7). Series: 20th Century Design. 2000, Gareth Stevens LB $22.60 (0-8368-2707-4). 32pp. Developments in art, design, and technology during and after World War II are chronicled in this heavily illustrated book. (Rev: SLJ 3/01) [708]

13897 Kalman, Bobbie. *The Victorian Home* (3–5). Illus. by Barbara Bedell. Series: Historic Communities. 1997, Crabtree LB $20.60 (0-86505-431-2); paper $7.95 (0-86505-461-4). 32pp. Examines 19th-century homes, their exteriors, interior rooms, and furnishings. (Rev: SLJ 7/97) [690]

13898 King, Penny, and Clare Roundhill. *Animals* (2–4). Illus. Series: Artists' Workshop. 1996, Crabtree LB $19.96 (0-86505-851-2); paper $8.95 (0-86505-861-X). 32pp. Readers learn how animals are depicted in art, examine six appropriate art works, and are given tips on how to create their own pictures. Also use *Landscapes, Portraits*, and *Stories* (all 1996). (Rev: SLJ 1/97) [709]

13899 King, Penny, and Clare Roundhill. *Myths and Legends* (3–6). Illus. by Lindy Norton. Series: Artists' Workshop. 1997, Crabtree LB $19.96 (0-86505-855-5); paper $8.95 (0-86505-865-2). 32pp. This book presents famous paintings from the 15th through the 20th century that depict mythological figures and scenes from around the world, as well as works on similar subjects by children. (Rev: HBG 3/98; SLJ 4/98) [750]

13900 King, Penny, and Clare Roundhill. *Sports and Games* (3–6). Illus. by Lindy Norton. Series: Artists' Workshop. 1997, Crabtree LB $19.96 (0-86505-854-7); paper $8.95 (0-86505-864-4). 32pp. Famous works of art from ancient times to the present are combined with children's art to show how various sports such as swimming, sailing, wrestling, and childhood games have been depicted. (Rev: HBG 3/98; SLJ 4/98) [750]

13901 Knapp, Ruthie, and Janice Lehmberg. *Impressionist Art* (5–9). Illus. Series: Off the Wall

Museum Guides. 1999, Davis paper $8.95 (0-87192-385-8). 72pp. This pocket-size guide supplies an overview of Impressionism and brief introductions to major artists, including Sisley and Monet. (Rev: BL 1/1–15/99) [709.03]

13902 Kutschbach, Doris. *The Blue Rider: The Yellow Cow Sees the World in Blue* (3–7). Trans. by Andrea Belloli. Illus. Series: Adventures in Art. 1997, Prestel $14.95 (3-7913-1811-X). 35pp. This art appreciation volume explores a group of painters — including Klee and Kandinsky — who freed color and form from reality. (Rev: SLJ 1/98) [709]

13903 Langley, Andrew. *Shakespeare's Theatre* (4–7). Illus. 1999, Oxford $17.95 (0-19-910565-0). 48pp. This work introduces Shakespeare and the Globe theatre of the early 1600s, also giving material on the restoration recently completed in London. (Rev: BL 7/99; HBG 3/00; SLJ 10/99) [792.09]

13904 Le Tord, Bijou. *A Blue Butterfly: A Story About Claude Monet* (K–3). Illus. 1995, Doubleday $16.95 (0-385-31102-8). 32pp. An account of how Monet painted, with illustrations that seem to be by the master himself. (Rev: BL 10/15/95; SLJ 11/95) [759.4]

13905 Loumaye, Jacqueline. *Chagall: My Sad and Joyous Village* (4–8). Trans. from French by John Goodman. Illus. by Veronique Boiry. Series: Art for Children. 1994, Chelsea LB $16.95 (0-7910-2807-0). 57pp. A youngster learns about Chagall and his paintings from a violinist who grew up in the artist's home town in Russia. (Rev: SLJ 8/94) [709]

13906 Loumaye, Jacqueline. *Degas: The Painted Gesture* (4–8). Trans. from French by John Goodman. Illus. by Nadine Massart. Series: Art for Children. 1994, Chelsea LB $16.95 (0-7910-2809-7). 57pp. Using a series of workshops for children at the Orsay Museum (Paris) as a focus, the life and works of Degas are introduced. (Rev: SLJ 8/94) [709]

13907 Loumaye, Jacqueline. *Van Gogh: The Touch of Yellow* (4–8). Trans. from French by John Goodman. Illus. by Claudine Roucha. Series: Art for Children. 1994, Chelsea LB $16.95 (0-7910-2817-8). 57pp. Two youngsters visit the museums in Amsterdam to learn about van Gogh, his tragic life, and his paintings. (Rev: SLJ 8/94) [709]

13908 Mallat, Kathy, and Bruce McMillan. *The Picture That Mom Drew* (2–4). Illus. 1997, Walker LB $15.85 (0-8027-8618-9). 24pp. Using "The House That Jack Built" as a framework, the materials and techniques used by an artist are introduced. (Rev: BL 1/1–15/97*; SLJ 4/97) [741.2]

13909 Manning, Mick, and Brita Granström. *Art School* (2–5). Illus. by authors. 1996, Kingfisher paper $9.95 (0-7534-5000-3). 47pp. Various art techniques are covered, as well as topics like scale, color theory, and light and shadow plus a number of art activities. (Rev: SLJ 12/96) [709]

13910 Merlo, Claudio. *The History of Art: From Ancient to Modern Times* (4–7). Trans. from Italian by Nathaniel Harris. Series: Masters of Art. 2000, Bedrick $29.95 (0-87226-531-5). 124pp. This ambitious volume, which tries to cover world art in all media in a single volume, is particularly valuable

for its color illustrations. (Rev: HBG 10/00; SLJ 4/00) [750]

13911 Micklethwait, Lucy. *A Child's Book of Art: Discover Great Paintings* (K–5). 1999, DK $16.95 (0-7894-4283-3). 31pp. Thirteen masterpieces by such painters as van Gogh, Bruegel, and Botticelli are introduced with thought-provoking questions that will facilitate appreciation. (Rev: BL 5/15/99; HBG 10/99; SLJ 6/99) [709]

13912 Micklethwait, Lucy. *A Child's Book of Art: Great Pictures, First Words* (1–4). Illus. 1993, DK $16.95 (1-56458-203-5). 64pp. Combines a word book with art appreciation by showing how common concepts like work and numbers are shown in great works of art. (Rev: BL 1/15/94; SLJ 2/94) [701]

13913 Micklethwait, Lucy. *A Child's Book of Play in Art* (PS–4). Illus. 1996, DK $16.95 (0-7894-1003-6). 45pp. Using a variety of paintings from many ages and places, this volume will help stimulate a child's interest in art. (Rev: BL 10/1/96*; SLJ 11/96*) [372.5]

13914 Micklethwait, Lucy. *Spot a Cat* (PS–2). Illus. 1995, DK $9.95 (0-7894-0144-4). 32pp. In this collection of paintings by famous artists, cats are featured, often where it is difficult to find them. A companion volume is *Spot a Dog* (1995). (Rev: BL 10/1/95; SLJ 2/96) [750]

13915 Milo, Francesco. *The Story of Architecture* (4–8). Illus. 2000, Bedrick $22.50 (0-87226-528-5). 64pp. The wealth of information on building materials, cultures, and trends in this book lend a historical perspective to the discussion of world architecture. It is colorfully illustrated with drawings, photos, and diagrams. (Rev: BL 6/1–15/00; HBG 10/00; SLJ 8/00) [720.9]

13916 Nilsen, Anna. *Art Fraud Detective* (4–6). Illus. 2000, Kingfisher $15.95 (0-7534-5308-8). 48pp. The reader becomes an art forgery detective in this oversize book that compares originals and forgeries of works by such artists as da Vinci, Picasso, and van Gogh. (Rev: BL 10/15/00; SLJ 12/00) [751.5]

13917 Pekarik, Andrew. *Painting: Behind the Scenes* (4–7). Illus. 1992, Hyperion LB $19.49 (1-56282-297-7). 64pp. Exploring the art of painting, including basic elements involved in each process. (Rev: BL 2/1/93; SLJ 2/93) [750]

13918 Platt, Richard. *Stephen Biesty's Incredible Cross-Sections* (4–7). 1992, Knopf $19.95 (0-679-81411-6). 48pp. Intricately drawn illustrations feature models of vehicles and buildings. (Rev: BL 9/1/92; HBG 3/00) [741.6]

13919 Richardson, Joy. *Inside the Museum: A Children's Guide to the Metropolitan Museum of Art* (4–7). Illus. 1993, Abrams paper $12.95 (0-8109-2561-3). 72pp. A guide to some of the treasures in the Metropolitan Museum of Art in New York City, with a peek behind the scenes. (Rev: BL 1/1/94; SLJ 2/94) [708.13]

13920 Richardson, Joy. *Looking at Faces in Art* (1–4). Series: How to Look at Art. 2000, Gareth Stevens LB $14.95 (0-8368-2624-8). 32pp. In a series of double-page spreads, famous paintings are examined with close-ups and questions and answers

697

to promote art appreciation. Also use *Showing Distance in Art* and *Using Shadows in Art* (both 2000). (Rev: HBG 10/00; SLJ 8/00) [709]

13921 Richardson, Joy. *Looking at Pictures: An Introduction to Art for Young People* (5–8). Illus. 1997, Abrams $19.95 (0-8109-4252-6). 80pp. A large-size volume that introduces art appreciation to middle-graders and describes different types of pictures and techniques. (Rev: BCCB 7–8/97; BL 4/15/97; SLJ 6/97*) [750]

13922 Richmond, Robin. *Children in Art: The Story in a Picture* (4–6). Illus. by author. 1992, Ideals LB $16.00 (0-8249-8588-5). 48pp. Children are introduced to art by the use of pictures with children as subjects. (Rev: BL 12/15/92; SLJ 2/93) [750]

13923 Roalf, Peggy. *Cats* (5–8). Illus. Series: Looking at Paintings. 1992, Hyperion paper $6.95 (1-56282-091-5). 48pp. This history of art shows how cats have been portrayed through the ages. Others in this series are: *Dancers; Families;* and *Seascapes* (all 1992). (Rev: SLJ 8/92) [709]

13924 Roalf, Peggy. *Dogs* (5–8). Illus. Series: Looking at Paintings. 1993, Hyperion paper $6.95 (1-56282-530-5). 48pp. Various ways that dogs have been represented in paintings are reproduced, with explanations, in this attractive book on art appreciation. (Rev: BL 2/15/94; SLJ 2/94) [758.3]

13925 Rohmer, Harriet, ed. *Just Like Me: Stories and Self-Portraits by Fourteen Artists* (3–6). Illus. 1997, Children's Book Pr. $15.95 (0-89239-149-9). 32pp. In double-page spreads, 14 artists, all of whom have produced books for children, talk about themselves and their inspirations. (Rev: BL 9/1/97; HBG 3/98; SLJ 12/97) [704.9]

13926 Scott, Elaine. *Funny Papers: Behind the Scenes of the Comics* (3–6). Photos by Margaret Miller. 1993, Morrow LB $14.93 (0-688-11576-4). 96pp. A richly illustrated history of comic strips, their different forms, and how they are created, sold, and distributed. (Rev: BCCB 1/94; BL 11/15/93; SLJ 11/93) [741.5]

13927 Sellier, Marie. *Matisse from A to Z* (3–7). Trans. from French by Claudia Zoe Bedrick. Illus. 1995, Bedrick LB $14.95 (0-87226-475-0). 59pp. The subjects used by Matisse in his paintings and events in his life feature in this unusual alphabet book containing many reproductions of his work. (Rev: SLJ 12/95) [759.4]

13928 Terzian, Alexandra M. *The Kids' Multicultural Art Book: Art and Craft Experiences from Around the World* (3–6). Illus. 1993, Williamson paper $12.95 (0-913589-72-1). 160pp. Using a walking tour across the continents as a framework, this book introduces the cultures of many areas in Africa, Asia, and Central America, with a section on the Indians of North America. (Rev: BL 9/1/93; SLJ 8/93) [745]

13929 Voss, Gisela. *Museum Colors* (PS–1). Illus. 1994, Museum of Fine Arts, Boston $14.00 (0-87846-369-0). 20pp. Works of art are used to point out different colors in this board book. Also use *Museum Numbers* and *Museum Shapes* (both 1994). (Rev: BL 5/1/94; SLJ 8/94) [701.8]

13930 Waters, Elizabeth, and Annie Harris. *Painting: A Young Artist's Guide* (4–8). Illus. Series: Young Artist. 1993, DK $14.95 (1-56458-348-1). 48pp. Concepts in art — like color, shape, texture, rhythm, and pattern — are explained through a series of color reproductions of famous paintings. (Rev: BL 1/15/94; SLJ 3/94) [751.4]

13931 Wellington, Monica. *Squeaking of Art: The Mice Go to the Museum* (PS–3). Illus. 2000, Dutton $15.99 (0-525-46165-5). 32pp. Seventy-seven of the world's greatest paintings are introduced in a delightful way as ten young mice visit an imaginary art museum. (Rev: BL 2/15/00; HBG 10/00; SLJ 5/00) [701.1]

13932 Wenzel, Angela. *Rene Magritte: Now You See It — Now You Don't* (4–7). Illus. Series: Adventures in Art. 1998, Prestel $14.95 (3-7913-1873-X). 30pp. An examination of some of the works of Belgian surrealist Rene Magritte. (Rev: BL 8/98; SLJ 8/98) [759.949]

13933 Wilkinson, Philip. *The Art Gallery: Faces: The Fascinating History of Faces in Art* (5–8). Series: Art Gallery. 2000, Bedrick $14.95 (0-87226-633-8). 48pp. From ancient to modern art, this book focuses on the depiction of the face in art with a special focus on ten self-portraits by such artists as da Vinci, Holbein, Velasquez, Vermeer, van Gogh, and Kahlo. (Rev: SLJ 12/00) [701]

13934 Wolfe, Gillian. *Oxford First Book of Art* (1–4). Illus. 1999, Oxford $18.95 (0-19-521556-7). 48pp. Excellent reproductions and a thoughtful text highlight this fine introduction to art for young people; paintings, drawings, sculpture, etc., are arranged by topic. (Rev: BCCB 1/00; BL 2/1/00; HBG 3/00; SLJ 12/99) [700]

Africa

13935 Finley, Carol. *The Art of African Masks: Exploring Cultural Traditions* (5–9). Series: Art Around the World. 1999, Lerner LB $23.93 (0-8225-2078-8). 64pp. This account on African mask making past and present focuses on the Western Sudan, the Guinea Coast, and Central Africa. (Rev: HBG 10/99; SLJ 11/99) [745.5]

13936 Stelzig, Christine. *Can You Spot the Leopard? African Masks* (3–6). Trans. from German by Fiona Elliot. Series: Adventures in Art. 1997, Prestel $14.95 (3-7913-1874-8). 28pp. An appealing book that pictures over 30 masks from different African peoples and explains where each came from, how it was made, and its significance. (Rev: SLJ 6/98) [750]

The Ancient World

13937 Angeletti, Roberta. *The Cave Painter of Lascaux* (1–3). Illus. by author. Series: A Journey Through Time. 1999, Oxford $16.95 (0-19-521558-3). 32pp. A "Homo sapiens" takes a child on a guided tour of the Lascaux caves and their amazing prehistoric paintings. (Rev: HBG 3/00; SLJ 3/00) [709]

13938 Avi-Yonah, Michael. *Piece by Piece! Mosaics of the Ancient World* (5–8). Illus. Series: Buried Worlds. 1993, Runestone LB $23.93 (0-8225-3204-2). 64pp. Using archaeological methods to determine facts, describes the creation of mosaics in various parts of the ancient world and how they differed among cultures. (Rev: BL 1/15/94; SLJ 3/94) [738.5]

13939 Gonen, Rivka. *Fired Up! Making Pottery in Ancient Times* (5–8). Illus. Series: Buried Worlds. 1993, Runestone LB $23.93 (0-8225-3202-6). 72pp. A heavily illustrated account that traces the manufacture, designs, and uses of pottery in various civilizations of the ancient world. (Rev: BL 1/15/94; SLJ 4/94) [738.3]

13940 Knapp, Ruthie, and Janice Lehmberg. *Egyptian Art* (5–9). Illus. Series: Off the Wall Museum Guides. 1999, Davis paper $8.95 (0-87192-384-X). 72pp. This pocket-size art appreciation book discusses mummies, sculpture, hieroglyphs, and other artifacts from Egyptian art. (Rev: BL 1/1–15/99) [709.32]

Native American Arts and Crafts

13941 Arnold, Caroline. *Stories in Stone: Rock Art Pictures by Early Americans* (4–6). Illus. by Richard Hewitt. 1996, Clarion $15.95 (0-395-72092-3). 48pp. Highlights of the rock art of Native Americans found in the Coso Range in California. (Rev: BL 12/15/96; SLJ 12/96) [709]

13942 Baylor, Byrd. *When Clay Sings* (2–5). Illus. by Tom Bahti. 1987, Macmillan $16.00 (0-684-18829-5); paper $5.99 (0-689-71106-9). 32pp. An exploration of the designs that originally appeared on the pottery of the Indians of the Southwest.

13943 Finley, Carol. *Art of the Far North: Inuit Sculpture, Drawing, and Printmaking* (4–6). Illus. Series: Art Around the World. 1998, Lerner LB $22.60 (0-8225-2075-3). 56pp. Inuit art from 1950 to the present is the focus of this heavily illustrated book containing a lengthy chapter on the influence of myths and legends. (Rev: BL 11/15/98; HBG 10/99; SLJ 1/99) [704.03]

13944 Keams, Geri. *Snail Girl Brings Water: A Navajo Story* (2–4). Illus. by Richard Ziehler-Martin. 1998, Rising Moon $15.95 (0-87358-662-X). 32pp. A retelling of the Navajo myth that relates how slow-moving Snail Girl was able to bring water to the Earth's surface. (Rev: BL 11/15/98; HBG 10/99; SLJ 5/99) [398.2]

13945 Presilla, Maricel E. *Mola: Cuna Life Stories and Art* (5–7). Illus. 1996, Holt $16.95 (0-8050-3801-9). 32pp. An examination of the life and art of the Cuna Indians, who live on islands off the coast of Panama. (Rev: BCCB 1/97; BL 10/1/96; SLJ 10/96) [305.48]

Middle Ages and the Renaissance

13946 Beckett, Wendy. *The Duke and the Peasant: Life in the Middle Ages* (4–6). Illus. Series: Adventures in Art. 1997, Prestel $14.95 (3-7913-1813-6). 30pp. The 12 calendar paintings from the Duc de Berry's *Book of Hours* are reproduced, with explanations of each and an introduction to the art of the Middle Ages. (Rev: BL 8/97; SLJ 10/97) [940.1]

13947 Macaulay, David. *Cathedral: The Story of Its Construction* (6–8). Illus. by author. 1973, Houghton $18.00 (0-395-17513-5). 80pp. Gothic architecture as seen through a detailed examination of the construction of an imaginary cathedral.

13948 Morrison, Taylor. *Antonio's Apprenticeship: Painting a Fresco in Renaissance Italy* (3–6). Illus. 1996, Holiday $15.95 (0-8234-1213-X). 32pp. A step-by-step description of how a fresco was created in 15th-century Florence as seen through the eyes of an apprentice. (Rev: BL 4/15/96; SLJ 5/96) [759.5]

13949 Perdrizet, Marie-Pierre. *The Cathedral Builders* (5–8). Trans. by Mary Beth Raycraft. Illus. by Eddy Krahenbuhl. Series: People of the Past. 1992, Millbrook LB $22.40 (1-56294-162-3). 64pp. This book introduces a Gothic cathedral and the people who built it. (Rev: SLJ 8/92) [726]

United States

13950 Bolton, Linda. *Pop Art* (4–8). Illus. Series: Art Revolution. 2000, Bedrick $16.95 (0-87226-614-1). 32pp. After explaining what pop art is and its historical context, this book presents a sampling of several artists' work to illustrate the style. (Rev: BL 10/15/00; HBG 3/01; SLJ 1/01) [709]

13951 Butler, Jerry. *A Drawing in the Sand: A Story of African American Art* (4–7). Illus. 1999, Zino $24.95 (1-55933-216-6). 64pp. This oversize book contains two narratives; the first is a history of African American art and artists, the second, an autobiography of Jerry Butler, the African American artist. (Rev: BL 2/15/99*) [704.03]

13952 Cummings, Pat, ed. *Talking with Artists*, Vol. 2 (3–7). Illus. 1995, Simon & Schuster $19.95 (0-689-80310-9). 96pp. Thirteen artists describe how they work and the media they use, with examples of their art work as children. Also use Volume One (1992). (Rev: BCCB 10/95; BL 9/1/95; HB 11–12/95; SLJ 10/95) [741.6]

13953 Cummings, Pat. *Talking with Artists*, Vol. 3 (4–8). Illus. Series: Talking with Artists. 1999, Clarion $20.00 (0-395-89132-9). 96pp. This is the third volume of interviews with children's artists and includes Peter Sis, Betsy Lewin, and Paul O. Zelinsky, with examples of their works. (Rev: BCCB 4/99; BL 3/15/99; HB 5–6/99; HBG 10/99; SLJ 4/99) [741.6]

13954 Emberley, Ed, et al. *Three: An Emberley Family Sketch Book* (3–4). Illus. 1998, Little, Brown $17.95 (0-316-23506-7). 64pp. This collection of stories, biographical material, and poetry celebrates the artistic genius of three members of the Emberley family — father Ed, daughter Rebecca, and son Michael. (Rev: BCCB 12/98; BL 8/98; HBG 3/99; SLJ 10/98) [808]

13955 Esterman, M. M. *A Fish That's a Box: Folk Art from the National Museum of American Art, Smithsonian Institution* (4–6). Illus. 1990, Great Ocean $12.95 (0-915556-21-9). 32pp. An eye-pleasing introduction to American folk art. (Rev: BCCB 2/91; BL 12/15/90; SLJ 3/91) [745]

13956 Gilbert, Alma, ed. *Maxfield Parrish: A Treasury of Art and Children's Literature* (3–6). Illus. 1995, Simon & Schuster $23.00 (0-689-80300-1). 88pp. A sampling of Maxfield Parrish's splendid illustrations for children's books, with the texts that inspired them. (Rev: BL 2/1/96; SLJ 11/95) [759.13]

13957 Goldstein, Ernest. *The Statue Abraham Lincoln: A Masterpiece by Daniel Chester French* (5–8). Series: Art Beyond Borders. 1998, Lerner LB $16.95 (0-8225-2067-2). 64pp. This book gives background information on both Lincoln and the sculptor Daniel Chester French, as well as details on how the statue in the Lincoln Memorial came to be. (Rev: SLJ 5/98)

13958 Howard, Nancy S. *Jacob Lawrence: American Scenes, American Struggles* (4–7). Illus. 1996, Davis $17.65 (0-87192-302-5). 48pp. The narrative paintings of this contemporary African American artist are featured, with several suggested follow-up activities. (Rev: BL 11/1/96) [759.13]

13959 Joyce, William. *The World of William Joyce Scrapbook* (4–7). Illus. 1997, HarperCollins $16.95 (0-06-027432-8). 48pp. A scrapbook collected by the author-artist that contains handwritten memoirs, sketches, finished artwork, and personal photos. (Rev: BL 1/1–15/98; HBG 10/98; SLJ 2/98) [813]

13960 Knapp, Ruthie, and Janice Lehmberg. *American Art* (5–9). Illus. Series: Off the Wall Museum Guides. 1999, Davis paper $8.95 (0-87192-386-6). 72pp. An informal pocket-size art appreciation book that features portraits from several centuries of American art, plus various artifacts and furniture. (Rev: BL 1/1–15/99) [709.73]

13961 Nikola-Lisa, W. *The Year with Grandma Moses* (2–5). Illus. 2000, Holt $20.00 (0-8050-6243-2). 32pp. The seasons as they are experienced in rural America are chronicled in 13 paintings by Grandma Moses; the narrative, some of it drawn from the artist's memoir, describes seasonal activities. (Rev: BCCB 11/00; BL 10/15/00; HBG 3/01; SLJ 10/00) [759.13]

13962 Porte, Barbara Ann. *Black Elephant with a Brown Ear (in Alabama)* (3–6). Illus. by Bill Traylor. 1996, Greenwillow $16.00 (0-688-14374-1). 48pp. Using ten of the primitive paintings of former slave Bill Traylor, the author weaves stories about each one. (Rev: BCCB 6/96; BL 5/15/96; SLJ 5/96) [813]

13963 Seltzer, Isadore. *The House I Live In: At Home in America* (2–5). Illus. by author. 1992, Macmillan $14.95 (0-02-781801-2). 32pp. Describes 12 American house designs, from log cabins to apartment buildings. (Rev: BCCB 4/92; BL 3/15/92; SLJ 5/92) [728]

13964 Thomson, Peggy, and Barbara Moore. *The Nine-Ton Cat: Behind the Scenes at an Art Museum* (4–8). Illus. 1997, Houghton $21.95 (0-395-81655-1); paper $14.95 (0-395-82683-7). 96pp. An inside look at the workings of the National Gallery in Washington, D.C., that gives descriptions of the work of a variety of personnel, from curators and conservators to gardeners. (Rev: BCCB 4/97; BL 3/15/97*; HB 5–6/97; SLJ 4/97) [708.153]

Communication

General and Miscellaneous

13965 Stewart, Alex. *Sending a Letter* (3–5). Illus. Series: Everyday History. 2000, Watts $20.00 (0-531-14547-6). 32pp. From messengers and smoke signals to E-mail and faxes, this is the story of long-distance communication through history. (Rev: BL 10/1/00) [383]

13966 Woods, Mary B., and Michael Woods. *Ancient Communication: From Grunts to Graffiti* (5–8). Series: Ancient Technologies. 2000, Runestone LB $25.26 (0-8225-2996-3). 88pp. Beginning with cave paintings and hieroglyphics and ending with modern alphabets and universal languages, this account of the history of communication emphasizes ancient cultures. (Rev: BL 9/15/00; HBG 3/01) [652]

Codes and Ciphers

13967 Mason, Adrienne. *Lu and Clancy's Secret Codes* (2–4). Illus. by Pat Cupples. Series: Lu and Clancy. 1999, Kids Can paper $5.95 (1-55074-553-0). 40pp. A Scotch terrier and a basset hound introduce a variety of secret codes involving backward writing, numerical codes, musical messages, pinprick codes, and crossword-puzzle codes. (Rev: SLJ 11/99) [652]

Flags

13968 Armbruster, Ann. *The American Flag* (4–6). Illus. 1991, Watts LB $22.00 (0-531-20045-0). 64pp. In addition to a history of the American flag, this illustrated account covers such subjects as the flag as a symbol, saluting, and modern flag manufacturing. (Rev: BL 1/1/92; SLJ 1/92) [929.9]

13969 Ayer, Eleanor. *Our Flag* (4–6). Illus. Series: I Know America. 1992, Millbrook paper $9.95 (1-878841-86-6). 48pp. This volume gives a colorfully illustrated introduction to the U.S. flag, its parts, and their meaning. (Rev: BL 5/15/92) [929.9]

13970 Brandt, Sue R. *State Flags* (3–5). Illus. Series: Our State Symbols. 1992, Watts LB $24.00 (0-531-20001-9). 64pp. Each state flag is pictured and its significance explained in brief text. (Rev: BL 2/1/93) [929.9]

13971 Haban, Rita D. *How Proudly They Wave: Flags of the Fifty States* (5–8). Illus. 1989, Lerner LB $23.95 (0-8225-1799-X). 111pp. Pictures and information on the background history of the state flags. (Rev: BL 12/15/89; SLJ 3/90) [929.9]

13972 Quiri, Patricia R. *The American Flag* (2–4). Illus. Series: True Books. 1998, Children's LB $21.00 (0-516-20617-6). 48pp. This story of the American flag includes material on Betsy Ross, the writing of "The Star-Spangled Banner," and how to honor the flag. (Rev: BL 8/98; HBG 10/98) [929.9]

13973 Radlauer, Ruth. *Honor the Flag: A Guide to Its Care and Display* (4–7). Illus. by J. J. Smith-Moore. 1992, Forest LB $14.95 (1-878363-61-1). 48pp. Lots of information about the American flag and its care. (Rev: BL 10/15/92) [929.92]

13974 Rollo, Vera F. *The American Flag* (3–6). Illus. by Alvin C. Jasper. 1990, Maryland $12.95 (0-917882-28-8). 78pp. The history of the U.S. flag plus myths that have grown up about its origins. (Rev: BL 6/1/90) [929.9]

13975 Ryan, Pam M. *The Flag We Love* (2–4). Illus. by Ralph Masiello. 1996, Charlesbridge $16.95 (0-88106-845-4). 32pp. The origins of the American flag, its history, and its uses are described in this colorful picture book. (Rev: BL 1/1–15/96; SLJ 5/96) [929.9]

13976 Spencer, Eve. *A Flag for Our Country* (K–3). Illus. by Mike Eagle. Series: Stories of America. 1993, Raintree Steck-Vaughn LB $25.69 (0-8114-7211-6). The story of how Betsy Ross made the first American flag. (Rev: SLJ 5/93) [929.9]

13977 Williams, Earl P. *What You Should Know About the American Flag* (4–8). Illus. 1989, Thomas Publns. paper $5.95 (0-939631-10-5). 68pp. A comprehensive guide to facts and legends, history and traditions concerning the U.S. flag. (Rev: BL 11/15/87)

Language and Languages

13978 Brook, Donna. *The Journey of English* (4–8). Illus. 1998, Clarion $17.00 (0-395-71211-4). 48pp. This richly illustrated volume describes the history of English, its changing composition, its spread, and the cultures around the world that use it. (Rev: BL 5/15/98; HBG 10/98; SLJ 7/98) [420]

13979 Burns, Peggy. *Writing* (3–5). Illus. Series: Stepping Through History. 1995, Raintree Steck-Vaughn LB $5.00 (1-56847-341-9). 32pp. A history of writing from ancient forms like hieroglyphics to the many languages of today. (Rev: BL 7/95) [411]

13980 Cooper, Kay. *Why Do You Speak as You Do? A Guide to World Languages* (5–8). Illus. by Brandon Kruse. 1992, Children's LB $14.85 (0-8027-8165-9). 66pp. A simple yet lively presentation of linguistics. (Rev: BCCB 2/93; BL 1/15/93) [400]

13981 Elya, Susan Middleton. *Say Hola to Spanish* (PS–4). Illus. by Loretta Lopez. 1996, Lee & Low $15.95 (1-880000-29-6). 32pp. More than 70 common Spanish words are introduced in delightful rhymes with pencil illustrations. (Rev: BL 5/1/96; SLJ 6/96) [468.1]

13982 Feder, Jane. *Table, Chair, Bear: A Book in Many Languages* (PS–2). Illus. 1997, Houghton paper $5.95 (0-395-85075-4). 32pp. The names of common objects in 13 different languages, including Korean, French, Spanish, and Chinese. (Rev: BL 3/1/95; HB 5–6/95; SLJ 3/95) [413]

13983 Johnson, Stephen T. *Alphabet City* (4–7). Illus. 1995, Viking $15.99 (0-670-85631-2). 32pp. A sophisticated alphabet book that consists of a series of paintings, each of which represents a letter. (Rev: BCCB 11/95; BL 1/1–15/96; HB 11–12/95; SLJ 1/96*) [421]

13984 Lee, Huy Voun. *At the Beach* (PS–3). Illus. 1994, Holt $16.95 (0-8050-2768-8). 32pp. Introduces ten Mandarin Chinese characters and the object each suggests. (Rev: BL 6/1–15/94; SLJ 7/94) [495.1]

13985 Lee, Huy Voun. *In the Park* (PS–3). Illus. 1998, Holt $15.95 (0-8050-4128-1). 32pp. Using scenes from a park visit as an inspiration, Xiao Ming's mother draws Chinese characters that illustrate objects from nature. (Rev: BL 7/98; HBG 10/98; SLJ 5/98)

13986 Lee, Huy Voun. *In the Snow* (PS–4). Illus. 1995, Holt $15.95 (0-8050-3172-3). 32pp. A Chinese mother writes ten Chinese characters in the snow in this introduction to simple Chinese writing for youngsters. (Rev: BL 10/15/95; SLJ 12/95)

13987 Samoyault, Tiphaine. *Alphabetical Order: How the Alphabet Began* (4–7). Illus. 1998, Viking $14.99 (0-670-87808-1). 32pp. This beautifully

designed book explains the history of the alphabet and traces the development of present-day languages, including braille. (Rev: BL 9/1/98; HBG 3/99; SLJ 11/98) [411.09]

13988 Wilson-Max, Ken. *Halala Means Welcome: A Book of Zulu Words* (PS–1). Illus. 1998, Hyperion $11.95 (0-7868-0414-9). 26pp. This bilingual book about friendship between a white boy and his black friend is set against the background of today's South Africa. (Rev: BL 8/98; HBG 3/99; SLJ 10/98) [496]

13989 Young, Ed. *Voices of the Heart* (4–8). Illus. 1997, Scholastic $18.95 (0-590-50199-2). 32pp. Twenty-six emotions and their corresponding modern Chinese characters are described. (Rev: BCCB 4/97; BL 4/15/97; HB 5–6/97; SLJ 6/97) [179]

Reading, Speaking, and Writing

Books, Printing, Libraries, and Schools

13990 Aliki. *How a Book Is Made* (K–3). Illus. by author. 1986, HarperCollins LB $17.49 (0-690-04498-4); paper $6.95 (0-06-446085-1). 32pp. Cat people play all the parts in this minimal text account of how picture books are made. (Rev: BCCB 11/86; BL 9/15/86; SLJ 9/86)

13991 Chapman, Gillian, and Pam Robson. *Making Shaped Books* (4–6). Illus. 1995, Millbrook LB $19.90 (1-56294-560-2). 32pp. Clear directions and many illustrations highlight this project book on how to create several books of different shapes. (Rev: BL 11/15/95; SLJ 12/95) [736]

13992 Cummins, Julie. *The Inside-Outside Book of Libraries* (1–4). Illus. by Roxie Munro. 1996, Dutton $15.99 (0-525-45608-2). 40pp. All sorts of libraries — big and small; public, school, and special — are visited in this introduction. (Rev: BCCB 10/96; BL 10/15/96; HB 9–10/96; SLJ 8/96*) [027]

13993 Falwell, Cathryn. *The Letter Jesters* (2–4). Illus. 1994, Ticknor $14.95 (0-395-66898-0). 48pp. Using the activities of two jesters as a framework, a number of different typefaces are introduced. (Rev: BCCB 12/94; BL 11/15/94; HB 11–12/94; SLJ 9/94) [686.224]

13994 Fowler, Allan. *The Dewey Decimal System* (3–5). Illus. 1996, Children's LB $22.00 (0-516-20132-8). 47pp. An explanation of the Dewey Decimal System, using clear text and many examples. (Rev: BL 2/1/97; SLJ 4/97) [025.4]

13995 Fowler, Allan. *The Library of Congress* (2–6). Illus. Series: True Books. 1996, Children's LB $22.00 (0-516-20137-9). 48pp. An information-packed account that describes the history, contents, and functions of the Library of Congress. (Rev: SLJ 2/97) [027]

13996 Ganeri, Anita. *The Story of Writing and Printing* (3–6). Illus. Series: Signs of the Times. 1997, Oxford LB $16.00 (0-19-521256-8). 30pp. In a series of double-page spreads, presents the story of writing in many cultures, as well as a history of printing up to desktop publishing. (Rev: BL 2/1/97; SLJ 2/97) [652]

13997 Gibbons, Gail. *Check It Out: The Book About Libraries* (K–3). Illus. 1985, Harcourt $16.00 (0-15-216400-6); paper $6.00 (0-15-216401-4). 32pp. An overview of what the library is and how it functions in picture-book format that is lively enough for older readers. (Rev: BCCB 9/85; BL 10/1/85; HB 11–12/85)

13998 Kehoe, Michael. *A Book Takes Root: The Making of a Picture Book* (4–7). Illus. 1993, Carolrhoda LB $22.60 (0-87614-756-2). 40pp. Covers the birth of a picture book from the first ideas to the finished product. (Rev: BL 8/93) [070]

13999 Knowlton, Jack. *Books and Libraries* (2–5). Illus. by Harriett Barton. 1991, HarperCollins LB $14.89 (0-06-021610-7). 48pp. The history of books and libraries is traced from cave paintings to the present. (Rev: BCCB 3/91; BL 4/1/91; SLJ 4/91) [002]

14000 Krensky, Stephen. *Breaking into Print: Before and After the Invention of the Printing Press* (2–5). Illus. by Bonnie Christensen. 1996, Little, Brown $15.95 (0-316-50376-2). 32pp. Beginning with the writing of manuscripts, this account traces the birth of printing and the contributions of Gutenberg. (Rev: BCCB 1/97; BL 10/15/96; SLJ 10/96*) [686.2]

14001 McInerney, Claire. *Find It! The Inside Story at Your Library* (4–6). Illus. by Harry Pulver. 1989, Lerner LB $15.93 (0-8225-2425-2). 56pp. An introduction to libraries and their uses, including computers. (Rev: BL 11/15/89; SLJ 1/90) [025]

14002 Madama, John. *Desktop Publishing: The Art of Communication* (5–8). Illus. Series: Media Workshop. 1993, Lerner LB $21.27 (0-8225-2303-5). 64pp. The history of desktop publishing, the equipment used, and the production of a newsletter. (Rev: SLJ 6/93) [686.2]

14003 *Oz: The Hundredth Anniversary Celebration* (4–8). Ed. by Peter Glassman. 2000, HarperCollins $24.95 (0-688-15915-X). 64pp. In this tribute to the children's classic, authors and illustrators — fans of the Oz books — pay homage in words and pictures. (Rev: BL 12/1/00; HBG 3/01; SLJ 11/00) [807]

14004 Pfeffer, Susan Beth. *Who Were They Really? The True Stories Behind Famous Characters* (3–6). Illus. 1999, Millbrook LB $22.40 (0-7613-0405-3). 72pp. This book explores the real people behind such fictional characters as Alice in Wonderland, the Lost Boys of Peter Pan, and Christopher Robin. (Rev: BL 12/15/99; HBG 10/00; SLJ 12/99) [820.9]

14005 Raatma, Lucia. *Libraries* (2–4). Series: True Books. 1998, Children's LB $21.00 (0-516-20672-9). 47pp. From the clay tablets of Mesopotamia to the specialized multimedia centers of today, this account traces the history and functions of the world's libraries. (Rev: HBG 10/98; SLJ 9/98) [027]

14006 *Scrawl! Writing in Ancient Times* (5–8). Illus. Series: Buried Worlds. 1994, Lerner LB $23.93 (0-8225-3209-3). 72pp. Using text, many illustrations, and sidebars, the development of writing in ancient civilizations is traced. (Rev: BL 1/15/95) [411.7]

14007 Senisi, Ellen B. *Reading Grows* (PS–K). Photos by author. 1999, Albert Whitman LB $15.95 (0-

8075-6898-8). Colorful photographs show children reacting to books, from babies looking at board books to older children reading alone or with others. (Rev: HBG 10/99; SLJ 8/99) [790.1]

14008 Steele, Philip. *Going to School* (3–5). Series: Everyday History. 2000, Watts LB $20.00 (0-531-14554-9). 32pp. This often-entertaining history of schools and schooling includes many interesting illustrations and activities. (Rev: BL 10/15/00; SLJ 1/01) [371]

14009 Stowell, Charlotte. *Step-by-Step Making Books* (4–6). Illus. Series: Step by Step. 1994, Kingfisher paper $6.95 (1-85697-518-5). 40pp. Provides the supplies needed and the basic procedures for creating a number of different books, including pop-ups and flap books. (Rev: BL 3/15/95) [741.6]

14010 Swain, Gwenyth. *Bookworks: Making Books by Hand* (4–7). Illus. 1995, Carolrhoda LB $22.60 (0-87614-858-5). 64pp. After a brief history of books and printing, this account gives directions for making paper and various kinds of books. (Rev: BL 7/95; SLJ 8/95*) [745.5]

14011 Warburton, Lois. *The Beginning of Writing* (5–8). Illus. 1991, Lucent LB $18.96 (1-56006-113-8). 112pp. The author traces pre-alphabetic communication through history and explains how our present-day alphabet evolved. [652.1]

Signs and Symbols

14012 Charlip, Remy, and Mary Beth Ancona. *Handtalk: An ABC of Finger Spelling and Sign Language* (3–6). Illus. by George Ancona. 1984, Simon & Schuster $15.95 (0-02-718130-8). 48pp. This is a beginning book on finger spelling and sign language.

14013 Gross, Ruth Belov. *You Don't Need Words! A Book About Ways People Talk Without Words* (1–4). Illus. by Susannah Ryan. 1991, Scholastic $14.95 (0-590-43897-2). 48pp. A demonstration of how people talk nonverbally. (Rev: BL 12/15/91; SLJ 1/92) [302]

14014 Gryski, Camilla. *Hands On, Thumbs Up: Secret Handshakes, Fingerprints, Sign Languages and More Handy Ways to Have Fun with Hands* (3–6). Illus. by Pat Cupples. 1991, Addison-Wesley paper $8.95 (0-201-56756-3). 112pp. All about the human hand — facts, trivia, superstitions, jokes, and more. (Rev: BL 12/15/91) [611.97]

14015 Klove, Lars. *I See a Sign* (PS–2). Photos by author. Series: Ready-to-Read. 1996, Simon & Schuster $14.00 (0-689-80800-3); paper $3.99 (0-689-80799-6). 32pp. This account pictures and explains a number of signs, like stop signs and railroad-crossing signs. (Rev: SLJ 9/96) [133]

14016 Kramer, Jackie, and Tali Ovadia. *You Can Learn Sign Language! More Than 300 Words in Pictures* (3–7). Illus. by John Smith. 2000, Troll paper $4.95 (0-8167-6336-4). 48pp. An easy-to-understand introduction to American Sign Language that presents both letters and numbers. (Rev: SLJ 7/00) [419]

14017 Miller, Mary Beth, and George Ancona. *Handtalk School* (PS–3). Illus. by George Ancona. 1991, Macmillan $14.95 (0-02-700912-2). At a school for the deaf, children use sign language as they prepare for Thanksgiving. (Rev: BCCB 11/91; SLJ 9/91)

14018 Rankin, Laura. *The Handmade Alphabet* (PS–6). Illus. 1991, Dial $16.99 (0-8037-0974-9). 32pp. Hands do the talking in this sign-language alphabet book. (Rev: BCCB 9/91; BL 8/91*; HB 11–12/91; SLJ 10/91*) [419]

14019 Wheeler, Cindy. *More Simple Signs* (1–4). Illus. 1998, Viking $14.99 (0-670-87477-9). 32pp. Simple words that children would use are translated into sign language using drawings that show the hand positions. (Rev: BL 1/1–15/98; HBG 10/98; SLJ 1/98) [419]

Words and Grammar

14020 Agee, Jon. *Elvis Lives! and Other Anagrams* (4–8). Illus. 2000, Farrar $15.00 (0-374-32127-2). 80pp. An entertaining introduction to anagrams — words or phases that can be rearranged to form new words or phrases — for children and adults. (Rev: BCCB 3/00; BL 2/1/00; HB 3–4/00; HBG 10/00; SLJ 4/00) [793.734]

14021 Agee, Jon. *So Many Dynamos! And Other Palindromes* (3–6). Illus. 1994, Farrar $13.31 (0-374-22473-0). 80pp. A collection of humorous, inventive palindromes illustrated by amusing cartoons. (Rev: BCCB 1/95; BL 12/15/94) [818]

14022 Agee, Jon. *Who Ordered the Jumbo Shrimp? And Other Oxymorons* (5–10). Illus. by author. 1998, HarperCollins $14.95 (0-06-205159-8). This is an amusing collection of oxymorons delightfully illustrated with drawings. (Rev: BCCB 12/98; HBG 3/99; SLJ 11/98) [428.1]

14023 Bailey, LaWanda. *Miss Myrtle Frag, the Grammar Nag* (5–9). Illus. by Brian Strassburg. 2000, Absey paper $13.95 (1-888842-19-9). 84pp. A clever book that explains key grammar rules through a series of witty letters from Miss Myrtle Frag. (Rev: SLJ 2/01) [415]

14024 Brown, Marc. *Arthur's Really Helpful Word Book* (PS–1). Illus. by author. 1997, Random LB $14.99 (0-679-98735-5). An entertaining word book that illustrates and identifies hundreds of common words. (Rev: SLJ 11/97) [400]

14025 Cleary, Brian P. *Hairy, Scary, Ordinary: What Is an Adjective?* (PS–3). Illus. by Jenya Prosmitsky. 2000, Lerner $12.95 (1-57505-401-9). 32pp. A playful rhyming text helps to explain what an adjective is and how it functions. (Rev: BL 6/1–15/00; HBG 10/00; SLJ 7/00) [428.2]

14026 Cleary, Brian P. *A Mink, a Fink, a Skating Rink: What Is a Noun?* (2–4). Illus. by Jenya Prosmitsky. Series: Words Are Categorical. 1999, Carolrhoda LB $12.95 (1-57505-402-7). Humorous rhymes and illustrations are used to introduce various kinds of nouns. (Rev: HBG 3/00; SLJ 11/99) [415]

14027 Dobkin, Bonnie. *Go-With Words* (1–2). Illus. by Tom Dunnington. Series: Rookie Readers. 1993, Children's LB $17.00 (0-516-02016-1). 32pp. An easy-to-read book that explores the concept of vocabulary and the value of words. (Rev: BL 3/1/94) [428.1]

14028 Gonzalez, Ralfka, and Ana Ruiz. *My First Book of Proverbs/Mi Primer Libro de Dichos* (2–5). Illus. by authors. 1995, Children's Book Pr. $15.95 (0-89239-134-0). A bilingual book of 27 Mexican dichos (proverbs) illustrated in bright, glowing colors. (Rev: SLJ 2/96) [398.9]

14029 Heller, Ruth. *Behind the Mask: A Book About Prepositions* (2–4). Illus. 1995, Putnam $17.99 (0-448-41123-7). 48pp. Using rhymes, a variety of prepositions are introduced and used. (Rev: BL 12/15/95) [428.2]

14030 Heller, Ruth. *Fantastic! Wow! and Unreal! A Book About Interjections and Conjunctions* (1–3). Illus. 1998, Putnam $16.99 (0-448-41862-2). 32pp. This book explains interjections and conjunctions, using vivid images in glowing colors and helpful examples. (Rev: BL 2/15/99; HBG 10/99; SLJ 3/99) [425]

14031 Heller, Ruth. *Kites Sail High: A Book About Verbs* (2–4). Illus. by author. 1988, Putnam LB $17.95 (0-448-10480-6); paper $6.99 (0-698-11389-6). 48pp. Romping through an explanation of verbs with various moods of verbs graphically illustrated. (Rev: BCCB 1/89)

14032 Heller, Ruth. *Many Luscious Lollipops* (1–4). Illus. by author. 1989, Putnam $17.99 (0-448-03151-5). In a series of rhymes, a variety of adjectives are introduced and identified. (Rev: BCCB 11/89; SLJ 1/90) [415]

14033 Heller, Ruth. *Merry-Go-Round: A Book About Nouns* (3–5). Illus. 1990, Putnam $17.99 (0-448-40085-5). 48pp. This picture book in verse explores the different types of nouns. (Rev: BCCB 1/91; BL 1/1/91; HB 1–2/91; SLJ 12/90) [425]

14034 Heller, Ruth. *Mine, All Mine: A Book About Pronouns* (2–5). Illus. 1997, Putnam $17.99 (0-448-41606-9). 48pp. Using large, colorful illustrations and a direct text, the world of pronouns and their uses is covered in an entertaining way. (Rev: BL 11/15/97; HB 3–4/98; HBG 3/98; SLJ 2/98*) [428.2]

14035 Heller, Ruth. *Up, Up and Away: A Book About Adverbs* (2–5). Illus. 1991, Putnam $17.99 (0-448-40249-1); paper $6.99 (0-698-11663-1). 32pp. In color drawings and catchy rhymes, Heller explains how adverbs answer precisely the questions of how, how often, when, and where. Also use by Heller: *A Cache of Jewels and Other Collective Nouns* (on collective nouns) and *Kites Sail High* (on verbs) (both 1998). (Rev: BCCB 1/92; BL 1/15/92; SLJ 2/92) [418]

14036 Hepworth, Cathi. *Bug Off! A Swarm of Insect Words* (3–6). Illus. 1998, Putnam $15.99 (0-399-22640-0). 32pp. Words that contain insect names (e.g., encroach, frisbee) are acted out by several bugs in a series of witty illustrations. (Rev: BCCB

9/98; BL 6/1–15/98*; HBG 10/98; SLJ 5/98) [428.1]

14037 Hill, Eric. *Spot's Big Book of Words* (PS). Illus. by author. 1988, Putnam $11.95 (0-399-21563-8). 28pp. Lovable Spot teaches young readers the words of their everyday world. (Rev: BL 10/1/88; SLJ 11/88)

14038 Juster, Norton. *As: A Surfeit of Similes* (2–5). Illus. by David Small. 1989, Morrow LB $15.93 (0-688-08140-1). 80pp. A long list of similes enter the conversation of two funny little men. (Rev: BCCB 5/89; BL 5/15/89; SLJ 4/89)

14039 Levey, Judith, ed. *The Macmillan Picture Wordbook* (PS–K). Illus. 1990, Simon & Schuster LB $8.95 (0-02-754641-1). 64pp. Several common words are introduced under broad headings. (Rev: BL 6/15/91)

14040 McKerns, Dorothy, and Leslie Motchkavitz. *The Kid's Guide to Good Grammar* (3–7). 1998, Lowell House paper $8.95 (1-56565-697-0). 96pp. An entertaining guide that combines information on grammar, spelling, parts of speech, common errors, and vocabulary, with related craft projects, puzzles, and games. (Rev: SLJ 4/99) [425]

14041 Riley, Jeni. *First Word Book* (PS). Illus. by Mandy Stanley. 2000, Kingfisher $12.95 (0-7534-5272-3). 47pp. This early vocabulary-building title uses simple drawings to introduce a number of common words. (Rev: HBG 3/01; SLJ 8/00) [423]

14042 Roberts, Michael. *Mumbo Jumbo: The Creepy ABC* (4–8). Illus. by author. 2000, Callaway $24.95 (0-935112-49-9). A scary alphabet book that features subjects like vampires, eyeball stew, quicksand, and bats. (Rev: HBG 3/01; SLJ 3/01) [428]

14043 Root, Betty. *My First Dictionary* (PS–2). Illus. by Jonathan Langley. Series: My First Reference. 1993, DK $17.95 (1-56458-277-9). 96pp. Definitions and illustrations are given for 1,000 words commonly used by children plus an appended collection of word games. (Rev: SLJ 1/94) [423]

14044 Scarry, Richard. *Richard Scarry's Best Word Book Ever* (PS–2). Illus. by author. 1963, Western $13.99 (0-307-15510-2). 72pp. A diverse, unorthodox picture dictionary for children who like lots of little pictures.

14045 Schneider, R. M. *Add It, Dip It, Fix It: A Book of Verbs* (PS–1). Illus. 1995, Houghton $13.95 (0-395-72771-5). 32pp. Action verbs arranged alphabetically are introduced by handsome collages. (Rev: BL 8/95; SLJ 9/95) [428]

14046 Shiffman, Lena. *My First Book of Words: 1,000 Words Every Child Should Know* (PS). Illus. by author. 1992, Scholastic $13.95 (0-590-45142-1). 62pp. Through a series of illustrations, many objects, actions, and emotions are identified in this basic word book. (Rev: SLJ 3/92)

14047 Terban, Marvin. *The Dove Dove: Funny Homograph Riddles* (4–7). Illus. by Tom Huffman. 1988, Houghton paper $7.95 (0-89919-810-4). 64pp. Making homographs less puzzling. Also use: *Mad As a Wet Hen! and Other Funny Idioms* (1987). (Rev: BL 1/1/89)

14048 Terban, Marvin. *Eight Ate: A Feast of Homonym Riddles* (2–3). Illus. by Giulio Maestro. 1982, Houghton paper $7.95 (0-89919-086-3). 64pp. A question-and-answer approach to introducing a variety of homonyms.

14049 Terban, Marvin. *Guppies in Tuxedos: Funny Eponyms* (3–6). Illus. by Giulio Maestro. 1988, Houghton paper $7.95 (0-89919-770-1). 64pp. Telling the story behind 100 eponyms arranged by categories. (Rev: BL 7/88; SLJ 8/88)

14050 Terban, Marvin. *In a Pickle and Other Funny Idioms* (3–6). Illus. by Giulio Maestro. 1983, Houghton paper $6.95 (0-89919-164-9). 64pp. Common idioms are explained, and their origins are given.

14051 Terban, Marvin. *Punching the Clock: Funny Action Idioms* (3–6). Illus. by Tom Huffman. 1990, Houghton paper $6.95 (0-89919-865-1). 64pp. Such expressions as "playing possum" and "batting a thousand" are among the nearly 100 explained and illustrated with amusing drawings. (Rev: BL 6/15/90; SLJ 7/90) [428.1]

14052 Terban, Marvin. *Too Hot to Hoot: Funny Palindrome Riddles* (3–6). Illus. by Giulio Maestro. 1985, Houghton paper $7.95 (0-89919-320-X). 64pp. A wordplay book exploring palindromes: words, phrases, sentences, and numbers that are the same read forward and backward. (Rev: BCCB 6/85; BL 5/15/85; SLJ 9/85)

14053 Terban, Marvin. *Your Foot's on My Feet! And Other Tricky Nouns* (3–5). Illus. by Giulio Maestro. 1986, Houghton paper $6.95 (0-89919-413-3). 64pp. A lively look at sometimes confusing singular and plural nouns. (Rev: BL 7/86; SLJ 9/86)

14054 *Tiny the Mouse Dictionary for 1-year-olds* (PS). Series: Tiny the Mouse. 1999, Sterling $4.95 (0-8069-5932-0). In this board book, a familiar object is pictured and on the verso four related items are also shown. There are also Tiny the Mouse Dictionaries for 2-, 3-, and 4-year-olds in this series. (Rev: SLJ 9/99)

14055 Treays, Rebecca, and Kate Needham, eds. *The Usborne Book of Everyday Words: A Picture Word Book* (PS–1). Photos by Howard Allman. Illus. by Jo Litchfield. Series: Everyday Words. 1999, EDC $12.95 (0-7460-2766-4). 47pp. This beginning word book with clever illustrations introduces more than 500 words. (Rev: HBG 3/00; SLJ 2/00) [422]

14056 Van Allsburg, Chris. *The Z Was Zapped: A Play in Twenty-Six Acts* (3–8). Illus. 1987, Houghton $17.95 (0-395-44612-0). 56pp. The 26 acts turn out to be a new way to introduce the alphabet. (Rev: BL 11/1/87; SLJ 11/87)

14057 Wilbur, Richard. *Opposites* (5–7). Illus. by author. 1991, Harcourt $11.95 (0-15-258720-9). 39pp. Through verses and cartoonlike illustrations, antonyms are given for a series of words.

14058 Wilbur, Richard. *The Pig in the Spigot* (3–5). Illus. 2000, Harcourt $16.00 (0-15-202019-5). 48pp. An amusing book about words that cleverly introduces long words that contain shorter ones, like "nausea" and "sea" or "location" and "cat." (Rev:

BL 11/15/00; HB 9–10/00; HBG 3/01; SLJ 12/00) [428.1]

14059 Wildsmith, Brian. *Brian Wildsmith's Amazing World of Words* (K–4). Illus. by author. 1997, Millbrook LB $23.90 (0-7613-0045-7). Many environments — like jungles, playgrounds, and farms — are pictured, with labels for each of the objects. (Rev: SLJ 5/97) [401]

14060 Williams, Sam. *The Baby's Word Book* (PS). Illus. by author. 1999, Greenwillow $9.95 (0-688-16834-5). A book of basic words for toddlers covering topics like clothing, body parts, basic verbs and adjectives, animals, nature, and outdoor activities. (Rev: SLJ 1/00) [428.1]

14061 Wittels, Harriet, and Joan Greisman. *A First Thesaurus* (4–6). Illus. 1985, Western paper $8.99 (0-307-15835-7). 144pp. Simple entry words are in boldface with synonyms and antonyms for more than 2,000 words. (Rev: BL 11/1/85; SLJ 2/86)

14062 Young, Selina. *My Favorite Word Book: Words and Pictures for the Very Young* (PS–1). Illus. 1999, Doubleday $17.95 (0-385-32683-1). 80pp. This entertaining book introduces 500 common words found in such locales as a house, school, town, farm, and playground. (Rev: BL 1/1–15/00; HBG 3/00; SLJ 1/00) [428.1]

14063 Ziefert, Harriet. *Baby Buggy, Buggy Baby* (PS–2). Illus. by Richard Brown. Series: Word Play Flap Book. 1997, Houghton $10.95 (0-395-85161-0). Using flaps, this word book shows how phrases change meaning if one reverses the word order. Homonyms are introduced in *Night, Knight* (1997). (Rev: BCCB 4/97; SLJ 7/97)

Writing and Speaking

14064 Asher, Sandy. *Where Do You Get Your Ideas? Helping Young Writers Begin* (5–7). Illus. 1987, Walker LB $13.85 (0-8027-6691-9). 96pp. Keeping a journal and other interesting ideas for would-be journalists. (Rev: BCCB 12/87; BL 9/15/87; SLJ 9/87)

14065 *Author Talk* (4–6). Ed. by Leonard S. Marcus. Illus. 2000, Simon & Schuster $22.00 (0-689-81383-X). 112pp. After each brief biography there is a question-and-answer session with these 15 popular authors of children's books, including Judy Blume, Bruce Brooks, E. L. Konigsburg, Lois Lowry, Gary Paulsen, and Laurence Yep. (Rev: BL 6/1–15/00; HB 7–8/00; HBG 3/01; SLJ 8/00) [810.9]

14066 Bailly, Sharon. *Pass It On!* (3–5). Illus. 1995, Millbrook LB $23.40 (1-56294-588-2). 64pp. Hints on how to perk up the writing and sending of notes, including secret codes. (Rev: BL 2/1/96; SLJ 2/96) [652]

14067 Bedard, Michael. *Glass Town* (3–5). Illus. by Laura Fernandez and Rick Jacobson. 1997, Simon & Schuster $16.00 (0-689-81185-3). 40pp. An unusual picture book that explores the secret world of the Brontë children, their fantasies, and their vast output of children's stories. (Rev: BL 8/97; HBG 3/98; SLJ 10/97) [652]

14068 Bentley, Nancy, and Donna Guthrie. *Writing Mysteries, Movies, Monster Stories, and More* (5–8). Illus. 2001, Millbrook LB $23.90 (0-7613-1452-0). 80pp. This book gives solid information on all kinds of fictional writing, including novels, short stories, fantasy, science fiction, humor, and even movie scripts. (Rev: BL 3/15/01) [808]

14069 Betz, Adrienne, comp. *Scholastic Treasury of Quotations for Children* (4–8). 1998, Scholastic $16.95 (0-590-27146-6). 254pp. From Socrates to Bill Clinton, this is a useful compendium of quotations arranged under 75 subjects. (Rev: SLJ 2/99) [080]

14070 Bruchac, Joseph. *Tell Me a Tale* (4–8). 1997, Harcourt $16.00 (0-15-201221-4). 144pp. A master storyteller reveals tricks of the trade, tells where to find stories, and explores their origins and effects, with many examples from various cultures. (Rev: BL 3/15/97; SLJ 8/97) [808.5]

14071 Burkholder, Kelly. *Pen Pals* (2–5). Series: Artistic Adventures. 2001, Rourke LB $21.27 (1-57103-353-X). 24pp. This title tells how and why one wants to communicate with others through regular mail and e-mail, with a section on safety tips involving the computer. (Rev: SLJ 2/01) [808]

14072 Burkholder, Kelly. *Stories* (2–5). Series: Artistic Adventures. 2001, Rourke LB $21.27 (1-57103-356-4). 24pp. This book introduces different types of writing — descriptive, persuasive, expository, and narrative — with ideas on expressing oneself through writing plus material on editing and revising. (Rev: SLJ 2/01) [808]

14073 Burns, Peggy. *News* (3–5). Illus. Series: Stepping Through History. 1995, Thomson Learning LB $5.00 (1-56847-342-7). 32pp. A history of journalism and the distribution of news from ancient times to the present. (Rev: BL 7/95) [070.4]

14074 Christelow, Eileen. *What Do Authors Do?* (3–5). Illus. 1995, Clarion $15.00 (0-395-71124-X). 32pp. Using cartoonlike drawings, the process of writing a book is traced using the experiences of two imaginary authors. (Rev: BCCB 11/95; BL 9/15/95; HB 11–12/95; SLJ 12/95*) [808.06]

14075 Cibula, Matt. *How to Be the Greatest Writer in the World* (4–8). Illus. by Brian Strassburg. 1999, Zino $11.95 (1-55933-276-X). 92pp. A spiral-bound book that presents 88 interesting and engaging exercises to help youngsters who feel they have nothing to write about. (Rev: SLJ 2/00) [808]

14076 Curry, Barbara K., and James Michael Brodie. *Sweet Words So Brave: The Story of African American Literature* (5–8). Illus. by Jerry Butler. 1996, Zino $24.95 (1-55933-179-8). 64pp. An outline of African American literature, from slave narratives to the great writers of today — e.g., Nikki Giovanni and Toni Morrison. (Rev: BL 2/15/97*; SLJ 4/97) [810.9]

14077 Detz, Joan. *You Mean I Have to Stand Up and Say Something?* (4–8). Illus. 1986, Macmillan LB $13.95 (0-689-31221-0). 96pp. A chatty guide to effective speaking before an audience. (Rev: BCCB 2/87; BL 2/1/87)

14078 Dubrovin, Vivian. *Storytelling Adventures: Stories Kids Can Tell* (4–7). Illus. by Bobbi Shupe. 1997, Storycraft paper $14.95 (0-9638339-2-8). 64pp. This book not only includes a selection of stories to tell but also suggests appropriate props to use, with directions on how to make them. (Rev: SLJ 5/97) [808.5]

14079 Dubrovin, Vivian. *Storytelling for the Fun of It* (4–8). Illus. by Bobbi Shupe. 1994, Storycraft paper $16.95 (0-9638339-0-1). 160pp. This useful guide is divided into three parts that give general information, where and what kinds of stories to tell, and how to learn and perform them. (Rev: SLJ 4/94) [808.5]

14080 Feller, Ron, and Marsha Feller. *Fanciful Faces and Handbound Books: Fairy Tales* (3–6). Illus. by Kathryn K. Hastings. 1989, Arts Factory paper $9.95 (0-9615873-1-8). 72pp. How to make fairy tale figures and write stories about them. (Rev: BL 7/89) [808]

14081 Fletcher, Ralph. *How Writers Work: Finding a Process That Works for You* (4–8). 2000, Harper-Trophy paper $4.95 (0-380-79702-X). 114pp. Using a conversational style, the author explains the process of writing with material on brainstorming, rough drafts, revising, proofreading, and publishing. (Rev: SLJ 12/00) [808]

14082 Gibbons, Gail. *Deadline! From News to Newspaper* (K–3). 1987, HarperCollins LB $15.89 (0-690-04602-2). 32pp. With a small-town newspaper as a backdrop, readers can follow the workings of the press. (Rev: BL 6/15/87; HB 5–6/87; SLJ 6–7/87)

14083 Goldstein, Peggy. *Long Is a Dragon: Chinese Writing for Children* (2–5). Illus. 1991, China Books $17.95 (1-881896-01-3). 32pp. This introduction to Chinese writing gives a brief history and 75 simple characters, including the numbers 1 to 12. (Rev: BCCB 5/91; BL 6/1/91; SLJ 7/91) [495.1]

14084 Gourley, Catherine. *Media Wizards: A Behind-the-Scenes Look at Media Manipulations* (5–9). 1999, Twenty-First Century LB $24.90 (0-7613-0967-5). 128pp. An informative account of how the media can manipulate the truth. (Rev: HBG 3/00; SLJ 2/00) [380.3]

14085 Graham, Paula W. *Speaking of Journals: Children's Book Writers Talk About Their Diaries, Notebooks and Sketchbooks* (5–8). Illus. 1999, Boyds Mills paper $14.95 (1-56397-741-9). 226pp. A book that discusses the how-tos and the rewards of keeping a personal journal, and features interviews with 27 writers including Jim Arnosky, Pam Conrad, and Jean George. (Rev: BL 3/1/99; SLJ 5/99) [818]

14086 Guthrie, Donna, and Nancy Bentley. *The Young Journalist's Book: How to Write and Produce Your Own Newspaper* (4–7). Illus. 1998, Millbrook LB $23.40 (0-7613-0360-X). 64pp. The authors explain what a journalist does and, in addition to explaining the parts of a newspaper, tells how to start one. (Rev: BL 3/1/99; HBG 3/99; SLJ 12/98) [070.1]

14087 Guthrie, Donna, et al. *The Young Author's Do-It-Yourself Book* (3–4). Illus. 1994, Millbrook LB $21.90 (1-56294-350-2). 64pp. This simple guide on how to make a book explains each stage from writing the manuscript to binding the finished product. (Rev: BL 4/15/94; SLJ 4/94) [070.5]

14088 Hamilton, Martha, and Mitch Weiss. *Stories in My Pocket: Tales Kids Can Tell* (4–7). Illus. 1997, Fulcrum paper $15.95 (1-55591-957-X). 184pp. This handbook of storytelling for young storytellers includes 30 tales to begin with. (Rev: BL 1/1–15/97) [372.6]

14089 Heiligman, Deborah. *The New York Public Library Kid's Guide to Research* (5–8). Illus. by David Cain. 1998, Scholastic $14.95 (0-590-30715-0). 134pp. A fine introduction to research techniques including material on taking notes, using print and nonprint resources, conducting interviews and surveys, searching the Internet, and locating toll-free numbers. (Rev: HBG 3/99; SLJ 2/99) [808.023]

14090 Hulme, Joy N., and Donna Guthrie. *How to Write, Recite, and Delight in All Kinds of Poetry* (3–6). 1996, Millbrook LB $24.90 (1-56294-576-9). 96pp. Using examples of poetry written by grade school children, this book introduces different types of poetry and gives help in writing and reciting poems. (Rev: SLJ 12/96) [811]

14091 James, Elizabeth, and Carol Barkin. *How to Write Super School Reports*. Rev. ed. (4–9). Series: A School Survival Guide Book. 1998, Lothrop $15.00 (0-688-16132-4). 90pp. This research guide takes readers through the steps involved in writing a research paper with material on choosing a topic, finding facts, using a library, organizing notes, and putting the report together. (Rev: HBG 3/99; SLJ 2/99) [808.023]

14092 James, Elizabeth, and Carol Barkin. *How to Write Terrific Book Reports*. Rev. ed. (3–5). Series: A School Survival Guide Book. 1998, Lothrop $15.00 (0-688-16131-6). 80pp. A step-by-step guide to writing good book reports that gives several examples of reports and makes suggestions on how to avoid common pitfalls. (Rev: HBG 3/99; SLJ 1/99) [808]

14093 James, Elizabeth, and Carol Barkin. *How to Write Your Best Book Report* (4–6). Illus. by Roy Doty. 1998, Lothrop paper $4.95 (0-688-16140-5). 80pp. A chatty account of dos and don'ts that can make book report writing seem almost painless. (Rev: BL 11/15/86)

14094 Janeczko, Paul B. *How to Write Poetry* (4–8). Series: ScholasticGuides. 1999, Scholastic LB $12.95 (0-590-10077-7). 128pp. An enthusiastic, clearly written how-to manual that uses many examples from well-known poems. (Rev: BL 3/15/99; HBG 10/99; SLJ 7/99) [808.1]

14095 Janeczko, Paul B. *Poetry from A to Z: A Guide for Young Writers* (5–7). Illus. 1994, Bradbury paper $16.00 (0-02-747672-3). 176pp. Poets speak about their work and give examples, but the core of this book is the author's encouraging tips to youngsters who might give poetry writing a try. (Rev: BCCB 3/95; BL 12/15/94) [808.1]

14096 Kenny, Chantal Lacourciere. *The Kids Can Press French and English Phrase Book* (1–4). Illus. by Linda Hendry. 1999, Kids Can $12.95 (1-55074-477-1). 40pp. The daily life of an 8-year-old girl is illustrated with drawings and the actions are described in both French and English phrases. A companion book is *The Kids Can Press Spanish and English Phrase Book* (1999). (Rev: SLJ 10/99) [407]

14097 Leedy, Loreen. *Messages in the Mailbox: How to Write a Letter* (2–4). Illus. 1991, Holiday LB $16.95 (0-8234-0889-2). 32pp. In this cheery guide, an alligator teacher shows the class of children and animals how to write a letter. (Rev: BCCB 12/91; BL 1/1/91; SLJ 9/91*) [295.4]

14098 Lewis, Amanda. *Writing: A Fact and Fun Book* (4–6). Illus. by Heather Collins. 1992, Kids Can paper $8.95 (1-55074-052-0). 96pp. A lively book packed with information on all aspects of writing. (Rev: BL 1/15/93; SLJ 1/93) [411]

14099 McGuinness, Diane. *My First Phonics Book* (K–3). Series: My First. 1999, DK $16.95 (0-7894-4737-1). 48pp. Riddles and a whimsical text introduce 42 sounds including vowels, consonants, and blends. (Rev: HBG 3/00; SLJ 1/00) [410]

14100 *New Moon: Writing: How to Express Yourself with Passion and Practice* (5–9). Series: New Moon. 2000, Crown LB $16.99 (0-517-88588-3); paper $9.99 (0-517-88587-5). 96pp. This practical guide to writing and being published contains interviews with such writers as Karen Cushman, Nikki Giovanni, and Madeleine L'Engle. (Rev: SLJ 2/00) [372.6]

14101 Nixon, Joan Lowery. *If You Were a Writer* (3–5). Illus. by Bruce Degen. 1988, Macmillan LB $15.00 (0-02-768210-2). 32pp. A re-creation of what goes on in a writer's mind, as Melia thinks she might like to be like her writer-mother. (Rev: BL 10/1/88; SLJ 11/88)

14102 Otfinoski, Steven. *Speaking Up, Speaking Out: A Kid's Guide to Making Speeches, Oral Reports, and Conversation* (5–8). Illus. 1996, Millbrook LB $23.90 (1-56294-345-6). 96pp. All kinds of public-speaking situations are introduced, with suggestions on how to be a success at each. (Rev: BL 1/1–15/97; SLJ 1/97) [808.5]

14103 Pellowski, Anne. *The Storytelling Handbook* (4–6). Illus. 1995, Simon & Schuster paper $16.00 (0-689-80311-7). 122pp. A fine practical guide for the young storyteller, with several good stories as examples. (Rev: BL 2/1/96; SLJ 12/95) [372.64]

14104 *Quotations for Kids* (5–10). Ed. by J. A. Senn. Illus. 1999, Millbrook LB $37.90 (0-7613-0267-0). 256pp. A fascinating collection of humorously illustrated quotes from children's literature, the Bible, historical documents, folklore, speeches, and other sources, with subject and author indexes. (Rev: BL 3/1/99*; SLJ 4/99) [082]

14105 *Scholastic Explains Reading Homework: Everything Children (and Parents) Need to Survive 2nd and 3rd Grade* (2–3). Series: Scholastic

Explains Homework. 1998, Scholastic $14.95 (0-590-39755-9); paper $6.95 (0-590-39758-3). 64pp. Using a variety of learning approaches, this book helps primary-grade students develop reading comprehension. (Rev: SLJ 12/98) [372.4]

14106 *Scholastic Explains Writing Homework: Everything Children (and Parents) Need to Survive 2nd and 3rd Grade* (2–3). Series: Scholastic Explains Homework. 1998, Scholastic $14.95 (0-590-39756-7); paper $6.95 (0-590-39759-1). 64pp. This book helps children and parents understand such writing concepts as characters, reviews, and basic grammar. (Rev: SLJ 12/98) [808]

14107 Seuling, Barbara. *To Be a Writer: A Guide for Young People Who Want to Write and Publish* (4–8). Illus. 1997, Twenty-First Century LB $20.40 (0-8050-4692-5). 128pp. A well-organized how-to book that gives good advice to budding writers, including how to outline a book and define characters. (Rev: BL 6/1–15/97; SLJ 8/97) [808]

14108 Stevens, Carla. *A Book of Your Own: Keeping a Diary or Journal* (5–8). 1993, Clarion $16.00 (0-89919-256-4). 94pp. A useful manual on how to keep a journal, with tips on writing expressively, along with samples from diaries by notables like Anne Frank. (Rev: BL 1/15/94; SLJ 11/93) [808]

14109 Stevens, Janet. *From Pictures to Words: A Book About Making a Book* (2–4). Illus. 1995, Holiday LB $16.95 (0-8234-1154-0). 42pp. This manual for youngsters who want to create their own picture books deals with such topics as setting, plot, and characterization. (Rev: BCCB 6/95; BL 4/15/95; SLJ 7/95*) [741.6]

14110 Terban, Marvin. *Checking Your Grammar* (5–8). Series: Scholastic Guides. 1993, Scholastic $10.95 (0-590-49454-6). 144pp. An attractive, witty guide to effective writing of all sorts of letters, book reports, essays, and reviews. (Rev: BL 10/1/93; SLJ 2/94) [428.2]

14111 Terban, Marvin. *It Figures! Fun Figures of Speech* (4–6). Illus. by Giulio Maestro. 1993, Clarion $13.95 (0-395-61584-4); paper $6.95 (0-395-66591-4). 62pp. Six figures of speech — including similes, alliteration, hyperbole, and personification — are explained, with examples from literature and folklore plus exercises on their use. (Rev: BL 12/1/93; SLJ 11/93) [808]

14112 Terban, Marvin. *Punctuation Power: Punctuation and How to Use It* (4–9). Illus. by Eric Brace. 2000, Scholastic LB $12.95 (0-590-38673-5). 96pp. After a description of each punctuation mark and its uses, this account covers topics like bibliographies, quotations, play scripts, and sentences, and the kinds of punctuation they require. (Rev: SLJ 7/00) [410]

14113 *To Swim in Our Own Pond: A Book of Vietnamese Proverbs* (3–6). Trans. from Vietnamese by Ngoc-Dung Tran. Illus. by Xuan-Quang Dang. 1998, Shen's $15.95 (1-885008-08-2). This collection of 22 Vietnamese proverbs also contains the best Western equivalents plus a series of delightful paintings. (Rev: SLJ 3/99) [398]

14114 Vinton, Ken. *Alphabet Antics: Hundreds of Activities to Challenge and Enrich Letter Learners*

of All Ages (5–8). Illus. by author. 1996, Free Spirit paper $19.95 (0-915793-98-9). 135pp. For each letter of the alphabet, there is a history, how it appears in different alphabets, important words that begin with that letter, a quotation from someone whose name starts with it, and a number of interesting related projects. (Rev: SLJ 1/97) [411]

14115 *When I Was Your Age: Original Stories About Growing Up*, Vol. 2 (5–9). Ed. by Amy Ehrlich. Illus. 1999, Candlewick $16.99 (0-7636-0407-0). 192pp. Ten well-known writers for young people, including Norma Fox Mazer and Paul Fleischman, tell of their childhood experiences and how key incidents affected their writing. (Rev: BCCB 6/99; BL 4/15/99*; SLJ 7/99) [810.9]

14116 Wilson-Max, Ken. *Furaha Means Happy: A Book of Swahili Words* (PS–3). Illus. 2000, Hyperion $12.99 (0-7868-0552-8). 32pp. A little girl on a day's excursion with her family introduces some common words in Swahili along with their English

translations. (Rev: BL 6/1–15/00; HBG 10/00; SLJ 10/00) [496]

14117 Young, Sue. *Writing with Style* (4–6). Series: Scholastic Guides. 1997, Scholastic paper $12.95 (0-590-50977-2). 144pp. A guide for the novice writer, with chapters on planning, presenting, and publishing one's work. (Rev: BL 3/1/97; SLJ 5/97) [372.6]

14118 Zeman, Anne, and Kate Kelly. *Everything You Need to Know About American History Homework: A Desk Reference for Students and Parents* (4–6). Illus. Series: Scholastic Homework Reference. 1994, Scholastic $18.95 (0-590-49362-0). 136pp. This book helps youngsters understand concepts in American history and how to apply them while doing homework assignments. Also use *Everything You Need to Know About Math Homework* and *Everything You Need to Know About Science Homework* (both 1994). (Rev: SLJ 1/95) [372.13]

Music

General

14119 Ardley, Neil. *A Young Person's Guide to Music* (5–8). Illus. 1995, DK $24.95 (0-7894-0313-7). 80pp. With an accompanying CD, this book introduces instruments of the orchestra and supplies a concise history of classical music. (Rev: BL 12/15/95; SLJ 1/96) [780]

14120 Ayazi-Hashjin, Sherry. *Rap and Hip Hop: The Voice of a Generation* (4–7). Illus. Series: Library of African American Arts and Culture. 1999, Rosen LB $17.95 (0-8239-1855-6). 62pp. This account traces the history of rap and hip hop music from their origins in spirituals, jazz, blues, and storytelling traditions; it also gives some information on musicians. (Rev: BL 2/15/00; SLJ 1/00) [782.4]

14121 Brunning, Bob. *Heavy Metal* (5–8). Series: Sound Trackers. 2000, Bedrick $15.95 (0-87226-580-3). 32pp. This work contains profiles of such bands as Black Sabbath, Cream, Guns N' Roses, Iron Maiden, Kiss, and Metallica. For biographies of stars like Madonna and Prince use the companion volume *Pop* (1999). (Rev: HBG 10/00; SLJ 3/00) [781]

14122 Brunning, Bob. *1960s Pop* (5–9). Series: Sound Trackers. 1999, Bedrick $15.95 (0-87226-576-5). 32pp. After a brief history of pop music in the 1960s, this account profiles dozens of individuals and groups that were prominent during that time. Also use *1970s Pop* (1999). (Rev: HBG 3/00; SLJ 11/99) [780]

14123 Brunning, Bob. *Rock 'n' Roll* (5–9). Series: Sound Trackers. 1999, Bedrick $15.95 (0-87226-575-7). 32pp. This book gives a two-page history of rock music and biographies of a few paragraphs each for about a dozen prominent artists including Elvis Presley and Chuck Berry. A similar format is used in *Reggae* (1999). (Rev: HBG 3/00; SLJ 11/99) [780]

14124 *Carnival of the Animals: By Saint-Saens.* (PS–2). Illus. by Sue Williams. 1999, Holt $19.95 (0-8050-6180-0). 45pp. This book gives a one-page

explanation of each part of this piece by Saint-Saens; the accompanying CD contains the music. (Rev: SLJ 1/00) [780]

14125 *Chatter with the Angels: An Illustrated Songbook for Children* (2–6). Ed. by Linda A. Richer and Anita Stoltzfus Breckbill. Illus. 2000, GIA $29.95 (1-57999-082-7). 90pp. An outstanding songbook containing 90 selections of Christian music from different countries and cultures that are printed with piano and guitar arrangements. (Rev: BL 10/1/00; HBG 3/01) [782.25]

14126 Elmer, Howard. *Blues: Its Birth and Growth* (4–7). Series: The Library of African American Arts and Culture. 1999, Rosen LB $17.95 (0-8239-1853-X). 64pp. This title traces the history of the blues, its origins, and its influence on American society as well as on the development of jazz and rock 'n' roll. (Rev: SLJ 8/99) [781]

14127 Englander, Roger. *Opera! What's All the Screaming About?* (6–8). Illus. 1983, Walker $12.95 (0-8027-6491-6). 192pp. A history of opera and an explanation of the different parts of an opera.

14128 Gatti, Anne, reteller. *The Magic Flute* (4–7). Illus. by Peter Malone. 1997, Chronicle $17.95 (0-8118-1003-8). An elegant retelling of the Mozart opera, with each scene given a full-color painting and a page of text. The accompanying CD has 16 selections coded to each page. (Rev: SLJ 1/98*) [782.1]

14129 George-Warren, Holly. *Shake, Rattle and Roll: The Founders of Rock and Roll* (4–7). 2001, Houghton $15.00 (0-618-05540-1). 32pp. After an informative introduction on the history of rock and roll, there is a series of one-page biographies of famous personalities. (Rev: BL 3/1/01) [781.66]

14130 Geras, Adele. *The Random House Book of Opera Stories* (4–6). Illus. 1998, Random $29.99 (0-679-99315-0). 127pp. This oversize book tells the stories of eight important operas, including *The Magic Flute, Carmen, Aida,* and *Cinderella.* (Rev: BL 10/15/98; HBG 3/99; SLJ 10/98) [782.1]

14131 Husain, Shahrukh. *The Barefoot Book of Stories from the Opera* (4–6). Illus. 1999, Barefoot

$19.95 (1-902283-28-7). 80pp. The plots of seven operas that would appeal to children because of their familiar stories (e.g., *La Cenerentola, Hansel and Gretel, The Magic Flute*) are retold with many illustrations. (Rev: BL 11/1/99; SLJ 10/99) [782.1]

14132 Igus, Toyomi. *I See the Rhythm* (5–8). Illus. by Michele Wood. 1998, Children's Book Pr. $15.95 (0-89239-151-0). 32pp. Using a timeline and a succinct text, this title traces African American contributions to such musical forms as the blues, big band, jazz, bebop, gospel, and rock. (Rev: BCCB 7–8/98; BL 2/15/98) [780]

14133 Lee, Jeanne. *Jam! The Story of Jazz Music* (4–7). Illus. Series: Library of African American Arts and Culture. 1999, Rosen LB $17.95 (0-8239-1852-1). 62pp. This book tells about the African American musicians who were responsible for the early development of jazz and blues. (Rev: BL 2/15/00; SLJ 1/00) [781.65]

14134 Malam, John. *Song and Dance* (3–5). Series: Everyday History. 2000, Watts LB $20.00 (0-531-14587-5). 32pp. A basic history of music and dance and how they developed through the years. (Rev: BL 10/15/00) [782]

14135 Medearis, Angela Shelf, and Michael R. Medearis. *Music* (5–7). Illus. Series: African American Arts. 1997, Twenty-First Century LB $16.98 (0-8050-4482-5). 64pp. This book on African Americans and music covers those African instruments, chants, and rhythms that evolved into ragtime, blues, jazz, soul, and rock. (Rev: BL 7/97; SLJ 7/97) [780]

14136 Price, Leontyne, reteller. *Aida* (4–8). Illus. by Leo Dillon and Diane Dillon. 1990, Harcourt $19.00 (0-15-200405-X). The story of one of the grandest of operas retold by one of opera's grandest divas. (Rev: BCCB 10/90; HB 3–4/91; SLJ 11/90*) [782.1]

14137 Rowe, Julian. *Music* (4–7). Illus. Series: Science Encounters. 1997, Rigby $22.79 (1-57572-091-4). 32pp. This book shows how scientific principles are used in music, musical instruments, hearing, and recording devices. (Rev: SLJ 10/97) [780]

14138 Weatherford, Carole Boston. *The Sound that Jazz Makes* (2–4). Illus. 2000, Walker LB $17.85 (0-8027-8721-5). 32pp. Beginning in Africa, this account traces the history of jazz and its different forms using a series of illustrations and four-line lyric-like captions. (Rev: BCCB 5/00; BL 8/00; HBG 10/00; SLJ 7/00) [781.65]

Ballads and Folk Songs

14139 Axelrod, Alan, ed. *Songs of the Wild West* (3–6). Illus. 1991, Simon & Schuster paper $19.95 (0-671-74775-4). 128pp. Through paintings and songs, this volume tells of the American West. (Rev: BL 12/15/91; SLJ 1/92*) [784.7]

14140 Berger, Melvin. *The Story of Folk Music* (6–8). Illus. 1976, Phillips LB $29.95 (0-87599-215-3). How and why American folk music evolved, with biographical information on singers from Woody Guthrie to John Denver.

14141 Bryan, Ashley, ed. *All Night, All Day: A Child's First Book of African-American Spirituals* (PS–3). Illus. by Ashley Bryan. 1991, Macmillan $16.00 (0-689-31662-3). 48pp. Contains 20 African American spirituals, with musical notations for each. (Rev: BCCB 7–8/91; BL 10/1/91; HB 7–8/91*; SLJ 5/91) [783.6]

14142 Bullock, Kathleen. *She'll Be Comin' Round the Mountain* (PS–4). Illus. 1993, Simon & Schuster paper $14.00 (0-671-79153-2). 32pp. An exuberant version of this folk song, with humorous paintings filled with amazing details. (Rev: BL 9/1/93; SLJ 12/93) [811]

14143 Catalano, Dominic. *Frog Went A-Courting: A Musical Play in Six Acts* (PS–1). Illus. 1998, Boyds Mills $14.95 (1-56397-637-4). 32pp. This charming adaptation of the folk song includes stunning paintings and charcoal drawings. (Rev: BL 10/15/98; HBG 3/99; SLJ 10/98) [782.42]

14144 Clarke, Gus. *E I E I O: The Story of Old MacDonald Who Had a Farm* (PS–K). Illus. 1993, Lothrop $14.00 (0-688-12215-9). 32pp. With cartoonlike illustrations, this is an old favorite folk song with a surprise ending. (Rev: BL 5/1/93) [782.42]

14145 Cohn, Amy L., ed. *From Sea to Shining Sea: A Treasury of American Folklore and Folk Songs* (PS–8). Illus. 1993, Scholastic $29.95 (0-590-42868-3). 416pp. A rich, vibrant collection of more than 140 folk songs and tales, illustrated by 15 distinguished artists, many of them Caldecott winners. (Rev: BCCB 1/94; BL 9/15/93*; HB 11–12/93; SLJ 11/93*) [810.8]

14146 Collins, Judy. *My Father* (3–6). Illus. by Jane Dyer. 1997, Little, Brown paper $4.95 (0-316-15238-2). 32pp. A picture-book treatment of the nostalgic song of the 1960s sung by folksinger Collins. (Rev: BL 11/1/89; SLJ 10/89) [784]

14147 Cony, Frances, and Iain Smyth. *Old Mac-Donald Had a Farm* (PS–K). Illus. 1999, Orchard $9.95 (0-531-30129-X). A pop-up version of the familiar song, with chickens moving their heads in time to the music. (Rev: BL 12/15/99; SLJ 6/99) [784.4]

14148 Cooper, Floyd. *Cumbayah* (PS–3). Illus. 1998, Morrow $16.00 (0-688-13543-9). 32pp. The illustrations that accompany this folk song show a multiracial group enjoying themselves. (Rev: BL 2/15/98; HBG 10/98; SLJ 5/98) [782.42]

14149 Engvick, William. *Lullabies and Night Songs* (K–3). Illus. by Maurice Sendak. 1965, Harper-Collins $26.00 (0-06-021820-7). A collection of the poet's verses and those of others set to music by Alec Wilder.

14150 Fox, Dan, ed. *Go in and out the Window: An Illustrated Song Book for Young People* (1–8). Illus. 1987, Holt $25.95 (0-8050-0628-1). 144pp. Sixty-one favorite songs — from "Amazing Grace" to "Yankee Doodle" — listed alphabetically and well illustrated. (Rev: BL 12/15/87)

14151 Gammell, Stephen. *Once Upon MacDonald's Farm* (PS–3). Illus. 2000, Simon & Schuster $15.00 (0-689-82885-3). 32pp. This humorous version of the old song has MacDonald trying to farm with an elephant, a baboon, and a lion. (Rev: BL 5/15/00; HBG 10/00) [784.4]

14152 Granfield, Linda. *Amazing Grace: The Story of the Hymn* (4–8). Illus. by Janet Wilson. 1997, Tundra $15.95 (0-88776-389-8). This account tells about the life of John Newton; his rejection of slavery, even though he once transported slaves; and his later ministry, when he wrote hymns like "Amazing Grace." (Rev: SLJ 8/97) [264]

14153 Guthrie, Woody. *Howdi Do* (PS–K). Illus. by Vladimir Radunsky. 2000, Candlewick $12.99 (0-7636-1261-8). 24pp. This 1960s folk song of rhyming couplets expressing various greetings is illustrated with a series of clever collages. (Rev: BCCB 9/00; BL 3/15/99; HBG 10/00; SLJ 6/00) [782.42]

14154 Guthrie, Woody. *This Land Is Your Land* (3–6). Illus. by Kathy Jakobsen. 1998, Little, Brown $14.95 (0-316-39215-4). 32pp. This beautiful picture book depicts a variety of people singing the folk song inspired by the Great Depression. (Rev: BCCB 11/98; BL 8/98*; HB 11–12/98; HBG 3/99; SLJ 8/98) [782.4216]

14155 *Hush, Little Baby: A Folk Song* (PS–K). Illus. by Marla Frazee. 1999, Harcourt $15.00 (0-15-201429-2). 40pp. The Appalachian folk song about a small girl who suggests that her father buy all sorts of gifts, including a mockingbird, to keep her baby sibling quiet. (Rev: BCCB 12/99; BL 11/15/99; HB 11–12/99; HBG 3/00; SLJ 10/99) [792.42]

14156 Johnson, James W. *Lift Every Voice and Sing: A Pictorial Tribute to the Negro National Anthem* (3–6). Illus. 2001, Hyperion LB $15.99 (0-7868-2542-1). 32pp. Using 22 black-and-white photographs, this book celebrates the 100th birthday of the song that many have called the Negro national anthem. (Rev: BL 2/15/01; SLJ 1/01) [782.4]

14257 Johnson, James W. *Lift Every Voice and Sing* (PS–8). Illus. by Elizabeth Catlett. 1993, Walker LB $15.85 (0-8027-8251-5). 36pp. Dramatic linecut prints highlight the song known as the African American national anthem. (Rev: BCCB 4/93; BL 2/15/93*; SLJ 3/93) [782.42]

14158 Johnson, James W. *Lift Ev'ry Voice and Sing* (PS–4). Illus. by Jan S. Gilchrist. 1995, Scholastic $14.95 (0-590-46982-7). 32pp. Using the lyrics of this beautiful anthem as a framework, the history and culture of African Americans are traced in touching illustrations. (Rev: BL 2/15/95*; SLJ 2/95) [782]

14159 Karas, G. Brian. *I Know an Old Lady* (PS–1). Illus. 1995, Scholastic $14.95 (0-590-46575-9). 32pp. An uproarious version of the traditional cumulative nonsense rhyme. (Rev: BCCB 2/95; BL 1/15/95*; SLJ 3/95) [782]

14160 Kovalski, Maryann. *Take Me Out to the Ballgame* (PS–2). Illus. 1993, Scholastic $14.95 (0-590-45638-5). 32pp. Jenny and Joanna go to the ball game with their wacky and fun-loving grandmother. (Rev: BL 1/15/93; SLJ 4/93) [811]

14161 Kroll, Steven. *By the Dawn's Early Light: The Story of the Star Spangled Banner* (2–4). Illus. by Dan Andreasen. 1994, Scholastic $15.95 (0-590-

45054-9). 40pp. The circumstances of writing our national anthem are re-created, along with a history of the Battle of Baltimore, in this handsomely illustrated book. (Rev: BL 12/15/93; SLJ 3/94) [349.73]

14162 Krull, Kathleen, ed. *Gonna Sing My Head Off!* (2–8). Illus. by Allen Garns. 1995, Knopf paper $13.95 (0-679-87232-9). 146pp. A collection of 62 contemporary and traditional singing favorites. (Rev: BCCB 10/92*; BL 10/15/92*; HB 3–4/93; SLJ 10/92*) [784.7]

14163 Langstaff, John. *Frog Went A-Courtin'* (K–3). Illus. by Feodor Rojankovsky. 1955, Harcourt $14.95 (0-15-230214-X); paper $7.00 (0-15-633900-5). 32pp. A rollicking folk song with matching illustrations. Caldecott Medal winner, 1956.

14164 Langstaff, Nancy, and John Langstaff. *Sally Go Round the Moon* (K–4). Illus. by Jan Pienkowski. 1986, Revels paper $14.95 (0-9640836-3-9). 127pp. A collection of folk songs and singing games originally published in 1970.

14165 Leodhas, Sorche Nic. *Always Room for One More* (K–3). Illus. by Nonny Hogrogian. 1965, Holt $14.95 (0-8050-0331-2); paper $5.95 (0-8050-0330-4). 32pp. From the Scottish folk song about Machie MacLachlan, who had so many people into his house that it burst. Caldecott Medal winner, 1966.

14166 Lishak, Anthony. *Row Your Boat: A Pop-Up and Push-Tab Book* (PS–K). Illus. 1999, DK $14.95 (0-7894-3489-X). In this interactive book, the old folk song gets new life as a mouse and his friends engage in a variety of activities. (Rev: BL 12/15/99; SLJ 8/99) [782.42]

14167 McGill, Alice. *In the Hollow of Your Hand: Slave Lullabies* (5–7). Illus. 2000, Houghton $18.00 (0-395-85755-4). 40pp. Family life in the days of slavery is revealed in this moving collection of 13 folk lullabies; a CD of the songs is also included. (Rev: BCCB 1/01; BL 11/15/00; HBG 3/01; SLJ 12/00) [811.008]

14168 McNeil, Keith, and Rusty McNeil. *Colonial and Revolution Songbook: With Historical Commentary* (4–7). 1996, WEM Records paper $11.95 (1-878360-08-6). 71pp. This songbook contains 39 traditional songs from the 17th century through the War of 1812, with brief historical comments for each. (Rev: SLJ 12/96) [973]

14169 Mallett, David. *Inch by Inch: The Garden Song* (PS–1). Illus. by Ora Eitan. 1995, HarperCollins $14.95 (0-06-024303-1). 32pp. This folk song describes all of the work and activities necessary to make a garden grow. (Rev: BCCB 7–8/95; BL 5/15/95; HB 11–12/95; SLJ 8/95) [781.62]

14170 Mattox, Cheryl W., ed. *Shake It to the One That You Love the Best: Play Songs and Lullabies from Black Musical Traditions* (PS–6). Illus. by Varnette P. Honeywood. 1990, Warren-Mattox paper $9.95 (0-9623381-0-9). 56pp. Music and lyrics for 16 songs and ten lullabies. (Rev: BL 12/1/90*) [781.62]

14171 *Old MacDonald Had a Farm* (PS–1). Illus. by Carol Jones. 1989, Houghton $13.95 (0-395-49212-2). Detailed watercolors on one page and the words to the old song on the opposite. (Rev: BL 5/1/89) [784.4]

14172 *Old MacDonald Had a Farm* (PS–2). Illus. by Holly Berry. 1994, North-South LB $14.88 (1-55858-282-7). 26pp. A delightful rendition of the traditional song, with all of the barnyard animals playing musical instruments. (Rev: BL 6/1–15/94; SLJ 6/94) [782]

14173 Priceman, Marjorie. *Froggie Went A-Courting: An Old Tale with a New Twist* (PS–3). Illus. 2000, Little, Brown $14.95 (0-316-71227-2). 32pp. In this updated version of the traditional Scottish folk song, Froggie goes a-courting via taxicab in the Upper West Side of Manhattan. (Rev: BCCB 5/00; BL 4/1/00; HBG 10/00; SLJ 6/00) [782.4]

14174 Raschka, Chris. *Simple Gifts: A Shaker Hymn* (PS–4). Illus. 1998, Holt $15.95 (0-8050-5143-0). 32pp. A brilliantly original treatment of the old Shaker hymn, with dynamic illustrations. (Rev: BCCB 5/98; BL 3/1/98*; HB 3–4/98; HBG 10/98; SLJ 4/98) [294]

14175 *Rock-a-Bye Baby: Lullabies for Bedtime* (PS–2). Illus. by Margaret Walty. 1998, Barefoot $14.95 (1-902283-03-1). 40pp. This is a charming collection of 16 bedtime songs including "Twinkle, Twinkle, Little Star." (Rev: BL 12/15/98; SLJ 1/99) [781.5]

14176 Rogers, Sally. *Earthsong* (PS–1). Illus. by Melissa Mathis. 1998, Dutton $16.99 (0-525-45873-5). 32pp. A reworking of the traditional song "Over in the Meadow" in which 11 endangered animals from around the world are introduced. (Rev: BCCB 5/98; BL 3/1/98; SLJ 3/98) [782]

14177 Rounds, Glen, ed. *I Know an Old Lady Who Swallowed a Fly* (PS–3). Illus. by Glen Rounds. 1990, Holiday LB $16.95 (0-8234-0814-0). 32pp. This humorous folk song is cleverly illustrated with mottled colors. (Rev: BCCB 9/90; BL 5/15/90; SLJ 8/90) [782]

14178 Schwartz, Amy. *Old MacDonald* (PS–1). Illus. 1999, Scholastic $15.95 (0-590-46189-3). 32pp. Double-page spreads and wonderful paintings breathe new life into this humorous traditional song. (Rev: BL 5/15/99; HB 3–4/99; HBG 10/99; SLJ 6/99) [782.42162]

14179 Silverman, Jerry. *Children's Songs* (4–6). Illus. 1993, Chelsea paper $9.95 (0-7910-1847-4). 64pp. This collection of 31 African American songs includes church songs, slave songs, and folk songs. (Rev: BL 2/15/94; SLJ 12/93) [782]

14180 Silverman, Jerry. *Singing Our Way West: Songs and Stories of America's Westward Expansion* (4–6). Illus. 1998, Millbrook LB $27.40 (0-7613-0417-7). 96pp. Twelve stories and folk songs associated with specific events in the settling of the West, including the railroad, the Erie Canal, and the Chisholm and Oregon Trails. (Rev: BL 12/1/98; HBG 3/99; SLJ 6/99) [782.4]

14181 Siomades, Lorianne. *The Itsy Bitsy Spider* (PS). Illus. 1999, Boyds Mills $9.95 (1-56397-727-3). 24pp. The spider, in this version of the catchy rhyme and song, carries an umbrella and waves a flashlight. (Rev: BL 3/1/99; HBG 10/99; SLJ 4/99)

14182 Sloat, Teri. *There Was an Old Lady Who Swallowed a Trout!* (PS–1). Illus. by Reynold Ruffins. 1998, Holt $15.95 (0-8050-4294-6). 32pp. Set in the Pacific Northwest, this variation on the popular cumulative rhyme has the old lady swallowing a trout, salmon, otter, seal, porpoise, walrus, and even a whale. (Rev: BL 11/15/98*; HBG 3/99; SLJ 11/98) [782]

14183 Souhami, Jessica. *Old MacDonald* (PS–K). Illus. 1996, Orchard $11.95 (0-531-09493-6). 24pp. Old MacDonald uses a variety of vehicles to transport all of the animals he has on his farm. (Rev: BL 4/1/96; HB 5–6/96; SLJ 5/96) [784.4]

14184 *This Old Man* (PS–1). Illus. by Carol Jones. 1990, Houghton $15.00 (0-395-54699-0). An attractively designed edition of this well-loved children's song. (Rev: SLJ 1/91) [784.7]

14185 Trapani, Iza. *The Itsy Bitsy Spider* (K–1). Illus. 1993, Whispering Coyote $16.95 (1-879085-77-1). 32pp. Building on the popular song, this book continues the adventures of the tiny spider. (Rev: BL 3/1/93)

14186 Trapani, Iza. *Row Row Row Your Boat* (PS–1). Illus. by author. 1999, Whispering Coyote $15.95 (1-58089-022-9). The traditional song is reprinted with additional verses and pictures that depict a bear family on a boat excursion. (Rev: HBG 3/00; SLJ 11/99) [782]

14187 Wallner, Alexandra. *The Farmer in the Dell* (PS). Illus. 1998, Holiday $15.95 (0-8234-1382-9). 32pp. An illustrated version of this favorite children's song, including the music and complete lyrics. (Rev: BL 9/1/98; HBG 3/99; SLJ 11/98) [782.4216]

14188 Weeks, Sarah. *Crocodile Smile* (PS–2). Illus. by Lois Ehlert. 1994, HarperCollins $15.95 (0-06-022867-9). 48pp. Charming songs that are sung by animals that are either extinct, like the dinosaur, or endangered, like the Komodo dragon. Includes audio cassette. (Rev: BL 12/1/94; SLJ 11/94*) [782]

14189 Weiss, Nicki. *If You're Happy and You Know It: Eighteen Story Songs Set to Pictures* (PS–2). Illus. 1987, Greenwillow $17.00 (0-688-06444-2). 40pp. Songs familiar to preschoolers and early elementary audiences "set to pictures." (Rev: BL 9/15/87; SLJ 11/87)

14190 Wells, Rosemary. *Old MacDonald* (PS). Illus. by author. Series: Bunny Reads Back. 1998, Scholastic $4.95 (0-590-76985-5). A board-book version of the traditional song, featuring a rabbit in overalls as Old MacDonald. (Rev: HBG 10/98; SLJ 10/98) [782]

14191 Westcott, Nadine Bernard. *I Know an Old Lady Who Swallowed a Fly* (2–4). Illus. by author. 1980, Little, Brown paper $6.95 (0-316-93127-6). 32pp. A newly illustrated edition of this outrageously funny song.

14192 Westcott, Nadine Bernard. *I've Been Working on the Railroad* (PS–1). Illus. 1996, Hyperion LB $14.49 (0-7868-2041-1). 32pp. This familiar folk song is seen through the eyes of a small boy who, with his dog, have adventures on a train. (Rev: BL 4/1/96; SLJ 6/96) [782]

14193 *Yankee Doodle* (PS–3). Illus. by Steven Kellogg. 1996, Simon & Schuster paper $5.99 (0-689-80726-0). 32pp. In a large format, the words of this song are illustrated, with background notes on its origin. (Rev: BL 7/96) [782]

14194 Yolen, Jane, ed. *Jane Yolen's Songs of Summer* (K–2). Illus. by Cyd Moore. 1993, Boyds Mills $12.95 (1-56397-110-0). 32pp. Of the 16 songs included in this collection with their lyrics and music, 13 are folk songs from a number of countries, including the United States. (Rev: BL 6/1–15/93; SLJ 8/93) [782.42]

14195 Yolen, Jane, and Adam Stemple. *Jane Yolen's Old MacDonald Songbook* (PS–1). Illus. by Rosekrans Hoffman. 1994, Boyds Mills $16.95 (1-56397-281-6). 96pp. A spirited collection of 43 songs featuring animals on the farm. (Rev: BL 11/15/94; SLJ 10/94) [784.6]

14196 Ziefert, Harriet. *Sleepy-O!* (PS–2). Illus. by Laura Rader. 1997, Houghton $15.00 (0-395-87369-X). 32pp. A song that explains what to do with a baby who won't go to sleep at a barn dance. (Rev: BL 9/1/97; HBG 3/98; SLJ 1/98) [782.4]

Holidays

14197 Delacre, Lulu. *Las Navidades: Popular Christmas Songs from Latin America* (K–4). Illus. 1990, Scholastic $13.95 (0-590-43548-5). 32pp. Christmas traditions of Latin America through seasonal songs. (Rev: BL 11/15/90) [782.42]

14198 *Elvis Presley's the First Noel* (K–3). Illus. by Bruce Whatley. 1999, HarperCollins $12.95 (0-06-028126-X). A visual interpretation of the Christmas carol plus a CD of Elvis Presley singing it. (Rev: HBG 3/00; SLJ 10/99) [782]

14199 Fine, Howard. *A Piggie Christmas* (K–3). Illus. 2000, Hyperion $15.99 (0-7868-0587-0). 32pp. A jolly book, illustrated with drawings of pigs in happy moods, that presents five Christmas carols, among them "Jingle Bells," "Deck the Halls," and "The Twelve Days of Christmas." (Rev: BL 9/1/00; HBG 3/01) [782.42]

14200 *The First Noel: A Child's Book of Christmas Carols to Play and Sing* (4–8). Ed. by Nicholas Turpin and Marie Greenwood. Illus. 1998, DK $12.95 (0-7894-3483-0). 32pp. Thirteen Christmas carols, with words and music for piano, voice, and guitar, are presented in a picture-book format including illustrations of historical paintings. (Rev: BL 11/1/98; HBG 3/99) [782.28]

14201 *The Glorious Christmas Songbook* (3–7). Illus. 1999, Chronicle $18.95 (0-8118-2204-4). 77pp. A collection of traditional and modern Christmas carols and songs, with charming period illustrations and a few bars of the music. (Rev: BL 9/1/99; HBG 3/00) [782.42172]

14202 Granfield, Linda. *Silent Night: The Song from Heaven* (2–4). Illus. by Nelly Hofer and Ernst Hofer. 1997, Tundra $15.95 (0-88776-395-2). The story of the writing and first performance of this hymn, as experienced by two children who are help-

ing in the church in Obendorf, Austria, where it was written in 1818. (Rev: HBG 3/98; SLJ 10/97)

14203 Keats, Ezra Jack, illus. *The Little Drummer Boy* (2–4). 1987, Macmillan paper $4.95 (0-689-71158-1). 32pp. The lyrics of this popular Christmas song are well illustrated.

14204 Knight, Hilary. *Hilary Knight's the Twelve Days of Christmas* (K–3). Illus. by author. 1987, Macmillan paper $4.95 (0-689-71150-6). 34pp. The traditional folk song with animals as participants.

14205 Langstaff, John, ed. *What a Morning! The Christmas Story in Black Spirituals* (2–7). Illus. by Ashley Bryan. 1987, Macmillan $14.95 (0-689-50422-5). 32pp. Five black spirituals that celebrate the Christmas story are joyously presented. (Rev: BCCB 12/87; BL 9/1/87)

14206 Long, Sylvia. *Deck the Hall* (PS–1). Illus. 2000, Candlewick $12.95 (0-8118-2821-2). 32pp. An illustrated version of the lovely Christmas carol featuring a rabbit family engaging in holiday activities. (Rev: BL 9/1/00; HBG 3/01) [782.42]

14207 McCullough, L. E. *Stories of the Songs of Christmas* (3–5). Illus. by Irene Kelly. 1997, Smith & Kraus paper $8.95 (1-57525-116-7). 149pp. Background material on such Christmas carols and songs as "Silent Night," "Jingle Bells," and "The Twelve Days of Christmas." (Rev: SLJ 10/97) [782]

14208 McGinley, Sharon. *The Friendly Beasts* (PS–K). Illus. 2000, Greenwillow $15.95 (0-688-17421-3). 24pp. This joyful picture book illustrates the text of the carol "The Friendly Beasts," which describes the roles played by several different animals during the Nativity. (Rev: BCCB 11/00; BL 9/15/00) [782.28]

14209 Mohr, Joseph. *Silent Night, Holy Night* (PS–3). Illus. by Maja Dusikova. 1999, North-South LB $15.88 (0-7358-1153-9). 32pp. Illustrations and text are used to tell the story of this famous carol and of the events it describes. (Rev: BL 9/1/99; HBG 3/00; SLJ 10/99) [782.281]

14210 *On Christmas Day in the Morning: A Traditional Carol* (PS–2). Illus. by Melissa Sweet. 1999, Candlewick $15.95 (0-7636-0375-9). 32pp. An illustrated edition of this traditional English Christmas folk song in which animals perform special chores on Christmas morn. (Rev: BL 11/1/99; HBG 3/00; SLJ 10/99) [782.42]

14211 Riley, Linnea. *The 12 Days of Christmas* (PS–2). Illus. 1995, Simon & Schuster $15.00 (0-689-80275-7). 32pp. A version of the Christmas carol in which a young lord tries to impress his beloved by giving her some unusual gifts. (Rev: BL 9/15/95; SLJ 10/95*) [782.42]

14212 Sabuda, Robert. *The Twelve Days of Christmas: A Pop-up Celebration* (K–4). Illus. 1996, Simon & Schuster paper $19.95 (0-689-80865-8). 12pp. A delightful pop-up version of the popular Christmas carol. (Rev: BCCB 9/96; BL 9/1/96*; HB 11–12/96) [782]

14213 Stevens, Jan R. *Twelve Lizards Leaping: A New Twelve Days of Christmas* (PS–3). Illus. by Christine Mau. 1999, Rising Moon $14.95 (0-87358-744-8). A southwestern version of the standard Christmas carol with music, lyrics, and vivid paintings. (Rev: HBG 3/00; SLJ 10/99) [782]

14214 *The Twelve Days of Christmas* (PS–3). Illus. by John O'Brien. 1993, Boyds Mills $14.95 (1-56397-142-9). 32pp. In this version of the Christmas carol, a gentleman is the receiver of 12 days of unusual gifts. (Rev: BL 9/15/93) [783]

14215 *The Twelve Days of Christmas* (PS–3). Illus. by Vladimir Vagin. 1999, HarperCollins LB $15.89 (0-06-028399-8). 32pp. A finely illustrated version of this carol that evokes allusions to both Russian folklore and New England landscapes. (Rev: BL 1/1–15/00; HBG 3/00) [782.42]

14216 *The Twelve Days of Christmas: A Song Rebus* (PS–3). Illus. by Emily Bolam. 1997, Simon & Schuster $16.00 (0-689-81101-2). 32pp. A happy version of the traditional Christmas carol using a rebus format. (Rev: BL 9/1/97; HBG 3/98; SLJ 10/97) [782.42]

14217 Tyrrell, Frances. *Woodland Christmas: Twelve Days of Christmas in the North Woods* (PS–2). Illus. 1996, Scholastic $15.95 (0-590-86367-3). 32pp. Woodland creatures portray the "true love's" gifts on each of the 12 days of Christmas. (Rev: BL 9/1/96) [782]

Musical Instruments

14218 Corbett, Sara. *Shake, Rattle, and Strum* (3–7). Illus. Series: A World of Difference. 1995, Children's LB $21.00 (0-516-08194-2). 32pp. The world of musical instruments is explored, with examples from various cultures and explanations of how they related to the traditions and customs of each land. (Rev: BL 7/95) [784.19]

14219 Davis, Wendy. *From Metal to Music* (PS–2). Illus. Series: Changes. 1997, Children's LB $24.00 (0-516-20707-5). 32pp. Explains how horns are made, from mining the ore to producing sheets of metal and to the attachment of valves and testing the final product. (Rev: BL 10/15/97) [788.9]

14220 Drew, Helen. *My First Music Book* (2–5). Illus. 1993, DK $12.95 (1-56458-215-9). 48pp. For young readers, this book describes and gives instructions on how to make a number of musical instruments with common household objects. (Rev: BL 6/1–15/93; SLJ 8/93) [784]

14221 Ganeri, Anita. *The Young Person's Guide to the Orchestra: Benjamin Britten's Composition on CD* (4–6). Illus. 1996, Harcourt $25.00 (0-15-201304-0). 64pp. The text explains and illustrates the various instruments of the orchestra, with an accompanying CD of Britten's music. (Rev: BL 10/1/96; SLJ 10/96) [784.2]

14222 Harris, Pamela K. *Clarinets* (K–3). Series: Music Makers. 2000, Child's World LB $22.79 (1-56766-679-5). 24pp. This is a simple, illustrated introduction to clarinets, their types, and their place in the orchestra. Also use *Drums* and *Trumpets* (both 2000). (Rev: SLJ 1/01) [784]

14223 Hayes, Ann. *Meet the Marching Smithereens* (K–3). Illus. by Karmen Thompson. 1995, Harcourt

$15.00 (0-15-253158-0). 32pp. Several musical instruments are introduced through a description of an animal marching band called the Smithereens. (Rev: BCCB 6/95; BL 7/95; SLJ 5/95) [784.3]

14224 Hayes, Ann. *Meet the Orchestra* (4–7). Illus. by Karmen Thompson. 1991, Harcourt $16.00 (0-15-200526-9). 32pp. Animals in evening dress introduce young readers to the orchestra. (Rev: BCCB 3/91; BL 4/15/91; SLJ 5/91) [784.19]

14225 Koscielniak, Bruce. *The Story of the Incredible Orchestra* (K–4). Illus. 2000, Houghton $15.00 (0-395-96052-5). 40pp. This account traces the growth of the orchestra and the development of modern musical instruments and also comments on the work of several composers. (Rev: BCCB 6/00; BL 4/15/00; HBG 10/00; SLJ 6/00) [784.2]

14226 Miles, J. C. *First Book of the Keyboard* (5–8). Illus. by Kim Blundell. Series: First Music. 1993, EDC paper $10.95 (0-7460-0962-3). 64pp. A beginner's guide to the electronic keyboard. (Rev: SLJ 7/93) [786]

14227 Moss, Lloyd. *Zin! Zin! Zin! A Violin* (1–3). Illus. by Marjorie Priceman. 1995, Simon & Schuster $16.00 (0-671-88239-2). 28pp. Ten instruments of the orchestra are introduced in rhyming couplets. (Rev: BL 5/15/95; SLJ 5/95*)

14228 Rubin, Mark. *The Orchestra* (2–4). Illus. by Alan Daniel. 1992, Firefly paper $8.95 (0-920668-99-2). After a general introduction to music, this book introduces each of the instruments of the orchestra. (Rev: SLJ 6/92) [781.91]

14229 Sabbeth, Alex. *Rubber-Band Banjos and a Java Jive Bass: Projects and Activities on the Science of Music and Sound* (4–7). Illus. 1997, Wiley paper $12.95 (0-471-15675-2). 112pp. Describes the basic elements of music while giving directions for making a variety of homemade instruments. (Rev: BL 3/15/97; SLJ 6/97) [781]

14230 Thyacott, Louise. *Musical Instruments* (5–7). Illus. Series: Traditions Around the World. 1995, Thomson Learning LB $24.26 (1-56847-228-5). 48pp. A continent-by-continent survey of the many kinds of musical instruments found in various cultures. (Rev: BCCB 11/94; BL 9/15/95) [784.3]

14231 Woods, Samuel G. *Guitars: From Start to Finish* (3–5). Illus. Series: Made in the USA. 1999, Blackbirch LB $16.95 (1-56711-392-3). 32pp. This account focuses on the manufacture of guitars and supplies a guided tour of the Martin Guitar Company in Nazareth, Pennsylvania. (Rev: BL 12/1/99; HBG 3/00; SLJ 3/00) [787.87]

National Anthems and Patriotic Songs

14232 Bates, Katherine L. *America the Beautiful* (K–4). Illus. by Neil Waldman. 1993, Macmillan $16.00 (0-689-31861-8). 32pp. An effective picture book illustrating the first verse of "America the Beautiful." (Rev: BL 7/93) [811]

14233 St. Pierre, Stephanie. *Our National Anthem* (4–6). Illus. Series: I Know America. 1992, Millbrook LB $20.90 (1-56294-106-2). 48pp. A heavily illustrated history of the U.S. national song. (Rev: BL 5/15/92; SLJ 7/92) [782.42]

Singing Games and Songs

14234 Amery, Heather, comp. *The Usborne Children's Songbook* (PS–3). Illus. by Stephen Cartwright. 1998, Usborne paper $10.95 (0-7460-2981-0). 64pp. A collection of 35 traditional songs (e.g., "Twinkle, twinkle, little star") with musical arrangements and chords for a variety of different instruments. (Rev: SLJ 2/99) [782]

14235 Carle, Eric. *Today Is Monday* (PS–K). Illus. 1992, Putnam $15.95 (0-399-21966-8). 32pp. A picture book that bursts with food, animals, and energy, and also includes music and lyrics, so everyone can sing along. (Rev: BL 1/1/93*; SLJ 4/93) [782]

14236 Delacre, Lulu, ed. *Arroz con Leche: Popular Songs and Rhymes from Latin America* (PS–1). Trans. by Elena Paz. Illus. by Lulu Delacre. 1989, Scholastic paper $4.99 (0-590-41886-6). A bilingual collection of folk rhymes, chants, and fingerplays. (Rev: BCCB 5/89)

14237 Dylan, Bob. *Man Gave Names to All the Animals* (PS–2). Illus. by Scott Menchin. 1999, Harcourt $16.00 (0-15-202005-5). 32pp. The lyrics to Dylan's song are illustrated with imaginative mixed-media techniques, including collage and black ink. (Rev: BL 12/15/99; HBG 3/00; SLJ 1/00) [782.42164]

14238 Emberley, Barbara. *Drummer Hoff* (K–3). Illus. by Ed Emberley. 1967, Simon & Schuster $16.00 (0-671-66248-1); paper $5.95 (0-671-66245-X). 32pp. The classic song about the assembling of a cannon. Caldecott Medal winner, 1968.

14239 Farjeon, Eleanor. *Morning Has Broken* (PS–3). Illus. by Tim Ladwig. 1996, Eerdmans $15.00 (0-8028-5127-4); paper $7.50 (0-8028-5132-0). 32pp. An illustrated version of the hymn that was once recorded by Cat Stevens. (Rev: BL 10/1/96; SLJ 12/96) [782]

14240 *For Our Children: A Book to Benefit the Pediatric AIDS Foundation* (PS–3). Illus. 1991, Disney LB $16.89 (1-56282-112-1). 72pp. An album of 20 songs by Carol King, Little Richard, and other artists. (Rev: BL 10/1/91; SLJ 10/91) [782.42]

14241 Garcia, Jerry, and David Grisman. *There Ain't No Bugs on Me* (PS). Illus. by Bruce Whatley. 1999, HarperCollins $15.95 (0-06-028142-1). 40pp. A cheerful rendition of the popular song, with a tape to accompany the words. (Rev: BL 8/99; SLJ 7/99) [782.4]

14242 Gershwin, George, et al. *Summertime: From Porgy and Bess* (PS–3). Illus. by Mike Wimmer. 1999, Simon & Schuster $16.95 (0-689-80719-8). 32pp. A picture book that illustrates the haunting lyrics to this song from *Porgy and Bess*. (Rev: BL 8/99; HBG 3/00; SLJ 10/99) [782.1]

14243 Girl Scouts of the U.S.A. *Sing Together: Girl Scout Songbook* (4–8). Illus. 1973, Girl Scouts of the U.S.A. $8.25 (0-88441-309-8). 192pp. More than 140 songs of all types.

14244 Hart, Jane, ed. *Singing Bee! A Collection of Favorite Children's Songs* (PS–3). Illus. by Anita Lobel. 1989, Lothrop $22.95 (0-688-41975-5). 160pp. A collection of 125 simple songs with piano and guitar arrangements.

14245 Hoberman, Mary Ann. *The Eensy-Weensy Spider* (PS–1). Illus. by Nadine Bernard Westcott. 2000, Little, Brown $12.95 (0-316-36330-8). 32pp. The traditional song is expanded in a delightful way to include many adventures for Eensy-Weensy beyond the drainpipe. (Rev: BCCB 3/00; BL 3/1/00; HBG 10/00; SLJ 4/00) [782.4]

14246 Hort, Lenny. *The Seals on the Bus* (PS–1). Illus. by G. Brian Karas. 2000, Holt $15.95 (0-8050-5952-0). 32pp. This variation on the song "The Wheels on the Bus" tells of a series of wild animals who find their way onto a city bus. (Rev: BCCB 5/00; BL 4/1/00; HB 5–6/00; HBG 10/00; SLJ 5/00) [782.4]

14247 Hudson, Wade, and Cheryl W. Hudson. *How Sweet the Sound: African-American Songs for Children* (PS–3). Illus. by Floyd Cooper. 1995, Scholastic $15.95 (0-590-48030-8). 48pp. A collection of the words of African American songs, from spirituals and work songs to jazz and the works of Stevie Wonder. (Rev: BL 9/15/95; SLJ 11/95) [844]

14248 Judd, Naomi. *Naomi Judd's Guardian Angels* (K–2). Illus. 2000, HarperCollins $15.95 (0-06-027208-2). 40pp. Using as its text the words of a song by Naomi Judd, this picture book with accompanying CD pays tribute to grandparents. (Rev: BL 7/00; HBG 10/00; SLJ 10/00) [782]

14249 Kennedy, Jimmy. *The Teddy Bears' Picnic* (PS–1). Illus. by Michael Hague. 1995, Holt paper $6.95 (0-8050-5349-2). 32pp. A large format and drawings complement this popular song about teddy bears gathering for a picnic. (Rev: BL 4/15/92; SLJ 6/92) [782]

14250 Kovalski, Maryann. *The Wheels on the Bus* (PS–2). Illus. by author. 1987, Little, Brown paper $4.95 (0-316-50259-6). 32pp. Grandmother takes her lookalike granddaughters shopping and teaches them a silly song while waiting for the bus. (Rev: BL 12/15/87; SLJ 11/87)

14251 MacDonald, Margaret Read, and Winifred Jaeger. *The Round Book: Rounds Kids Love to Sing* (4–6). Illus. 1999, Linnet $22.50 (0-208-02441-7); paper $16.50 (0-208-02472-7). 124pp. A paperback containing 80 songs designed to be sung as rounds. (Rev: BL 9/1/99; HBG 10/99; SLJ 7/99) [782.42]

14252 Miller, J. Philip, and Sheppard M. Greene. *We All Sing with the Same Voice* (PS–K). Illus. by Paul Meisel. 2001, HarperCollins $15.95 (0-06-027475-1). This book-and-CD set features the Sesame Street song about understanding one another's cultures and the similarities of children all over the world. (Rev: SLJ 2/01) [784]

14253 Moreillon, Judi. *Sing Down the Rain* (2–5). Illus. by Michael Chiago. 1997, Kiva $14.95 (1-

885772-07-6). This choral reading in eight parts celebrates the Saguaro Wine Ceremony of the Tohono O'odham tribe of the Sonoran desert. (Rev: SLJ 1/98) [811]

14254 Near, Holly. *The Great Peace March* (4–6). Illus. by Lisa Desimini. 1993, Holt $15.95 (0-8050-1941-3). 32pp. Lyrics to the title song about the Great Peace March for Nuclear Disarmament in 1986. (Rev: BCCB 4/93; BL 3/1/93; SLJ 5/93) [782]

14255 Raffi. *Rise and Shine* (PS–2). Illus. by Eugenie Fernandes. 1996, Crown $16.00 (0-517-70939-2). 32pp. The excitement of facing a new day is conveyed in this song by Raffi. (Rev: BL 1/1–15/97; SLJ 1/97) [782.42]

14256 *Sing Through the Day: Eighty Songs for Children* (4–6). Ed. by Marlys Swinger. Illus. 1999, Plough $24.00 (0-87486-971-4). 112pp. This collection of 80 children's songs from America and around the world is accompanied by a CD of 56 of the songs. (Rev: BL 9/15/99; HBG 3/00) [724.329]

14257 Sullivan, Arthur. *I Have a Song to Sing, O! An Introduction to the Songs of Gilbert and Sullivan* (4–8). Ed. by John Langstaff. Illus. by Emma C. Clark. 1994, Macmillan $17.95 (0-689-50591-4). 80pp. Sixteen famous songs from Gilbert and Sullivan's operettas are handsomely presented with arrangements for both piano and guitar. (Rev: BL 12/1/94; SLJ 10/94) [782]

14258 Trapani, Iza, reteller. *How Much Is That Doggie in the Window?* (PS–3). Score and lyrics by Bob Merrill. Illus. by Iza Trapani. 1997, Whispering Coyote $15.95 (1-879085-74-7). This expanded version of the once-popular song tells about a little boy who wants a spotted puppy in a pet shop but can't afford to buy it. (Rev: HBG 3/98; SLJ 3/98) [782]

14259 Weiss, George D., and Bob Thiele. *What a Wonderful World* (PS–3). Illus. by Ashley Bryan. 1995, Simon & Schuster LB $16.00 (0-689-80087-8). 32pp. Children use a puppet stage to introduce this song. (Rev: BL 5/15/95; SLJ 5/95)

14260 *Who Built the Ark?* (PS–1). Illus. by Pamela Paparone. 1994, Simon & Schuster $15.00 (0-671-87129-3). 32pp. An illustrated version of the African American spiritual about the building of Noah's Ark and bringing the animals into it. (Rev: BL 7/94; SLJ 6/94) [782]

14261 Zelinsky, Paul O., adapt. *The Wheels on the Bus* (PS–1). Illus. 1990, Dutton paper $16.99 (0-525-44644-3). A pop-up edition with pull tabs of the familiar song. (Rev: BCCB 10/90; SLJ 10/90) [784]

14262 Zelinsky, Paul O. *The Wheels on the Bus* (PS–K). Illus. 2000, Dutton $16.99 (0-525-46506-5). The tenth-anniversary edition of this classic becomes an interactive book with wheels going round and windows sliding up and down. (Rev: BL 12/1/00) [784]

Performing Arts

Circuses, Fairs, and Parades

14263 Alter, Judith. *Amusement Parks, Roller Coasters, Ferris Wheels, and Cotton Candy* (4–6). Illus. 1997, Watts $22.50 (0-531-20304-2). 64pp. The author traces the history of amusement parks, starting with the Columbian Exposition of 1893, and then describes some current favorites, like Coney Island and Disney World. (Rev: BL 12/15/97; HBG 3/98) [791.06]

14264 Alter, Judith. *Beauty Pageants: Tiaras, Roses, and Runways* (4–8). Illus. 1997, Watts LB $22.50 (0-531-20253-4). 64pp. After introducing various kinds of pageants, this book describes in detail the Miss America pageant, its history and organization. (Rev: BL 12/1/97; SLJ 9/97) [791.6]

14265 Alter, Judith. *Meet Me at the Fair: County, State, and World's Fairs and Expositions* (3–5). Series: First Books. 1997, Watts LB $21.00 (0-531-20307-7). 64pp. A thorough history of fairs — how they evolved and how the local, county, and state versions developed — plus material on international expositions. (Rev: HBG 3/98; SLJ 4/98) [394]

14266 Alter, Judith. *Wild West Shows: Rough Riders and Sure Shots* (4–7). Illus. 1997, Watts LB $22.50 (0-531-20274-7). 63pp. A brief photo-essay that covers the history of the Wild West show, with a special focus on the contributions of Buffalo Bill to this form of entertainment. (Rev: BL 10/1/97; SLJ 8/97) [791.8]

14267 Cook, Nick. *Roller Coasters; or, I Had So Much Fun, I Almost Puked* (4–7). Illus. 1998, Carolrhoda LB $16.95 (1-57505-071-4). 56pp. This intriguing book describes the excitement of a roller-coaster ride and discusses the history, types, construction, and safety features of various roller coasters. (Rev: BCCB 6/98; BL 4/15/98; HBG 10/98) [791]

14268 Davenport, Meg, and Lisa V. Werenko. *Circus! A Pop-Up Adventure* (PS–1). Illus. 1998, Simon $18.95 (0-689-82093-3). These pop-ups introduce all the stars and animals associated with the big top. (Rev: BL 1/1–15/99; SLJ 1/99) [791.3]

14269 Granfield, Linda. *Circus: An Album* (4–8). Illus. 1998, DK $19.95 (0-7894-2453-3). 96pp. Following a history of the circus from ancient times to the present, this title describes famous people connected with the circus and gives details on its problems and scandals. (Rev: BCCB 4/98; BL 3/1/98; HBG 10/98; SLJ 3/98*) [791.3]

14270 Presnall, Judith J. *Circuses: Under the Big Top* (4–7). Illus. Series: First Books. 1996, Watts LB $22.50 (0-531-20235-6). 63pp. A history of circuses from ancient times to today with material on star performers. (Rev: SLJ 3/97) [791.3]

Dance

14271 Ancona, George. *Let's Dance!* (PS–4). Illus. 1998, Morrow $16.00 (0-688-16211-8). 40pp. Native dances from around the world are presented in a simple text and sharp, colorful photographs. (Rev: BL 9/1/98; HBG 3/99; SLJ 11/98) [793.3]

14272 Barber, Antonia. *Shoes of Satin, Ribbons of Silk: Tales from the Ballet* (4–6). Illus. 1995, Kingfisher $18.95 (1-85697-693-2). 96pp. In dramatic retellings, the stories of nine ballets (several less well known) are presented. (Rev: BL 11/15/95; SLJ 1/96) [792.8]

14273 Bell, Anthea. *Swan Lake: A Traditional Folktale* (2–4). Illus. by Chihiro Iwasaki. 1991, Picture Book paper $15.95 (0-88708-028-6). 28pp. Picture book version of the Swan Lake ballet. (Rev: BL 12/1/86; SLJ 12/86) [792.8]

14274 Berger, Melvin. *The World of Dance* (6–8). Illus. 1978, Phillips $29.95 (0-87599-221-8). An overview of the subject that begins in prehistoric times and ends with today's social dancing and ballet.

14275 Bowes, Deborah. *The Ballet Book: The Young Performer's Guide to Classical Dance* (4–6). Illus. 1999, Firefly $19.95 (1-55209-352-2); paper

$12.95 (1-55209-353-0). 144pp. A detailed practice guide for the serious ballet student that includes material on movements and positions, finding a good teacher, and staying healthy. (Rev: BL 11/15/99; HBG 3/00; SLJ 11/99) [798.8]

14276 Bussell, Darcey. *Ballet* (3–8). Series: Super-guides. 2000, DK $9.95 (0-7894-5429-7). 64pp. Written with the cooperation of the Royal Ballet School and illustrated with photos of its young dancers, this is a fine introduction to ballet, with a step-by-step guide to basic positions and steps as well as a glossary of dance terms. (Rev: BL 6/1–15/00; HBG 10/00) [792.8]

14277 Bussell, Darcey, and Patricia Linton. *The Young Dancer* (3–6). Illus. 1994, DK $15.95 (1-56458-468-2). 64pp. Two ballet practitioners explain the basic steps and movements and provide a history of ballet and its traditions. (Rev: BL 9/1/94; SLJ 8/94) [792.8]

14278 Castle, Kate. *Ballet* (4–6). Illus. 1996, Kingfisher $16.95 (0-7534-5001-1). 64pp. A well-illustrated introduction to the world of ballet, with material on the composer, choreographer, designer, famous dancers, and stories of well-known ballets. (Rev: SLJ 12/96) [792.8]

14279 Castle, Kate. *My Ballet Book* (3–6). Illus. 1998, DK $15.95 (0-7894-3432-6). 61pp. This introduction to the world of ballet presents, in large double-page spreads, basic positions, costuming, history, careers, and important dancers and choreographers. (Rev: BL 11/15/98; HBG 3/99; SLJ 2/99) [792.8]

14280 Elliott, Donald. *Frogs and Ballet* (4–6). Illus. by Clinton Arrowood. 1979, Harvard Common paper $8.95 (0-87645-119-9). Familiar ballet steps and how they are woven into the classical ballet.

14281 Ephron, Amy, reteller. *Swan Lake* (4–9). Photos by Nancy Ellison. 2000, Abrams $19.95 (0-8109-4192-9). A straightforward retelling of the ballet story using stunning full-page, color photographs. (Rev: HBG 10/00; SLJ 7/00) [792]

14282 Feldman, Jane. *I Am a Dancer* (4–7). Photos by author. Series: Young Dreamers. 1999, Random $14.99 (0-679-88665-6). An attractive photo-essay about 12-year-old Eva Lipman, who is a student at the School of American Ballet in New York City. (Rev: HBG 10/99; SLJ 8/99) [792.8]

14283 Fonteyn, Margot. *Coppelia* (K–3). Illus. by Steve Johnson and Lou Fancher. 1998, Harcourt $17.00 (0-15-200428-9). 40pp. In this retelling of the ballet story based on a tale by E. T. A. Hoffman, Franz falls in love with the doll Coppelia and his girlfriend Swanhilda assumes the doll's identity to secure his love. (Rev: BCCB 1/99; BL 10/15/98*; HBG 3/99; SLJ 12/98)

14284 Friedman, Lise. *First Lessons in Ballet* (3–5). Illus. 1999, Workman $14.95 (0-7611-1804-7); paper $8.95 (0-7611-1352-5). 64pp. Illustrated with photographs, this book for beginning ballet students explains techniques, positions, exercises, and more. (Rev: BL 2/15/00; SLJ 4/00) [792.8]

14285 Ganeri, Anita. *The Young Person's Guide to the Ballet* (4–6). Illus. 1998, Harcourt $25.00 (0-15-

201184-6). 64pp. A broad introduction to the world of ballet, including a CD of famous ballet music. (Rev: BL 11/1/98; SLJ 9/98) [792.8]

14286 Grau, Andrea. *Dance* (4–9). Series: Eyewitness Books. 1998, Knopf LB $20.00 (0-679-99316-9). 64pp. A stunning introduction to the world of dance, including ballet. (Rev: BL 8/98; HBG 3/99; SLJ 1/99) [792]

14287 Greaves, Margaret. *Stories from the Ballet* (3–5). Illus. by Lisa Kopper. 1999, Star Bright $17.95 (1-887734-73-2). 69pp. Simple retellings of the stories of eight classical ballets including *Giselle, Swan Lake, The Nutcracker*, and *The Firebird*. (Rev: SLJ 2/00) [792.8]

14288 Hayden, Melissa, ed. *The Nutcracker Ballet* (K–4). Illus. by Stephen T. Johnson. 1992, Andrews & McMeel $14.95 (0-8362-4501-6). 32pp. This retelling is based on Balanchine's version of the ballet. (Rev: BL 2/1/93) [792]

14289 Horosko, Marian. *Sleeping Beauty: The Ballet Story* (3–6). Illus. by Todd L. W. Doney. 1994, Atheneum $14.95 (0-689-31885-5). 32pp. A scene-by-scene description of the Petipa-choreographed ballet, with noteworthy explanations and lush illustrations. (Rev: BL 1/1/95; SLJ 11/94) [792.8]

14290 Jessel, Camilla. *Ballet School* (3–5). Illus. 2000, Viking $15.99 (0-670-88628-9). 64pp. A behind-the-scenes look at London's Royal Ballet School and the daily life of its pupils. (Rev: BL 1/1–15/00; HBG 10/00; SLJ 2/00) [792.802]

14291 Johnson, Anne E. *Jazz Tap: From African Drums to American Feet* (4–7). Series: The Library of African American Arts and Culture. 1999, Rosen LB $17.95 (0-8239-1856-4). 64pp. This book traces the history of jazz tap from a variety of African dances to its emergence in the 1920s and its later development in night clubs, on Broadway, and in movies. (Rev: SLJ 1/00) [793.3]

14292 Jones, Bill T., and Susan Kuklin. *Dance* (1–4). Illus. 1998, Hyperion LB $14.45 (0-7868-2307-0). 32pp. An unusual picture book that introduces the world and feelings of dancer/choreographer Bill T. Jones. (Rev: BCCB 1/99; BL 11/15/98; HB 1–2/99; HBG 3/99; SLJ 12/98) [792.8]

14293 McCaughrean, Geraldine. *The Nutcracker* (PS–4). Illus. by Nicki Palin. 1999, Oxford $16.95 (0-19-279969-X). A simple, shortened retelling of the story of the *Nutcracker* ballet. (Rev: HBG 10/00; SLJ 10/99) [792]

14294 McCaughrean, Geraldine. *The Random House Book of Stories from the Ballet* (4–6). Illus. 1995, Random $20.00 (0-679-87125-X). 112pp. A delightful retelling of ten stories of full-length ballets like *Cinderella* and *The Sleeping Beauty*. (Rev: BL 10/1/95; SLJ 12/95) [792.8]

14295 Medearis, Angela Shelf, and Michael R. Medearis. *Dance* (5–7). Illus. Series: African American Arts. 1997, Twenty-First Century $20.40 (0-8050-4481-7). 64pp. The contributions of African Americans to dance is covered, including their roles in jazz, tap, and modern dance. (Rev: BL 7/97; SLJ 7/97) [793.3]

14296 Newman, Barbara. *The Illustrated Book of Ballet Stories* (4–6). Illus. 1997, DK $15.95 (0-7894-2225-5). 64pp. This book not only gives the stories of five popular ballets, but also explains the dance elements that are found in each. (Rev: BL 12/15/97) [792.8]

14297 Riordan, James. *Favorite Stories of the Ballet* (4–6). Illus. by Victor G. Ambrus. 1993, Checkerboard $14.95 (1-56288-252-X). These ballet stories include *The Nutcracker, Swan Lake, Sleeping Beauty,* and *Cinderella.*

14298 *Step-by-Step Ballet Class: The Official Illustrated Guide* (4–6). Illus. 1994, Contemporary paper $14.95 (0-8092-3499-8). 144pp. This guide developed by the Royal Academy of Dancing in England gives material for various levels of development, including positions, movements, and advice on appearance. (Rev: BL 12/1/94) [792.8]

14299 Tythacott, Louise. *Dance* (5–7). Illus. Series: Traditions Around the World. 1995, Thomson Learning LB $24.26 (1-56847-275-7). 48pp. The ways people dance around the world and the reasons they do are presented with many color photos. (Rev: BL 6/1–15/95; SLJ 9/95) [793.3]

14300 Vagin, Vladimir. *The Nutcracker Ballet* (K–3). Illus. 1995, Scholastic $14.95 (0-590-47220-8). 32pp. All the characters in the *Nutcracker,* including Clara and Herr Drosselmeier, come to life in this retelling of the ballet story with effective, detailed illustrations. (Rev: BL 9/15/95)

14301 Varriale, Jim. *Kids Dance: The Students of Ballet Tech* (4–6). Illus. 1999, Dutton $15.99 (0-525-45536-1). 32pp. The story of Ballet Tech — the first public school in America to train ballet dancers. (Rev: BCCB 1/00; BL 9/15/99; HB 11–12/99; HBG 3/00; SLJ 12/99) [792.8]

14302 Wilkes, Angela. *The Best Book of Ballet* (1–4). Series: The Best Book Of. 2000, Kingfisher $12.95 (0-7534-5275-8). 32pp. A fine introduction to ballet that includes material on history, famous ballets, a ballet class, basic positions and steps, and what professional dancers do. (Rev: HBG 3/01; SLJ 7/00) [792.8]

Marionettes and Puppets

14303 Buetter, Barbara MacDonald. *Simple Puppets from Everyday Materials* (PS–3). Illus. by Barbara M. Buetter and George Buetter. 1997, Sterling $19.95 (1-895569-05-2). 80pp. Features easy-to-make puppets like a dragon, frog, and Humpty Dumpty, using readily available materials. (Rev: SLJ 3/97) [745.592]

14304 Doney, Meryl. *Puppets* (4–6). Illus. Series: World Crafts. 1996, Watts LB $21.00 (0-531-14399-6). 32pp. An impressive number of puppets are introduced from different cultures, with full instructions on how to make them. (Rev: SLJ 7/96) [745.5]

14305 Lade, Roger. *The Most Excellent Book of How to Be a Puppeteer* (3–5). Illus. Series: Most Excellent Book Of. 1996, Millbrook $6.95 (0-7613-0505-X). 32pp. This how-to book tells how to make

puppets and how to use them to give a brilliant performance. (Rev: BL 10/15/96; SLJ 2/97) [791.5]

14306 Renfro, Nancy. *Puppet Show Made Easy!* (3–6). Illus. 1984, Renfro $18.95 (0-931044-13-8). 96pp. Creating puppets and how to stage a show.

14307 Supraner, Robyn, and Lauren Supraner. *Plenty of Puppets to Make* (1–3). Illus. by Renzo Barto. 1981, Troll LB $16.65 (0-89375-432-3); paper $3.95 (0-89375-433-1). 48pp. A book about 11 easy-to-make puppets.

14308 Wallace, Mary. *I Can Make Puppets* (2–5). Photos by author. 1994, Greey de Pencier Bks. $14.95 (1-895688-24-8); paper $6.95 (1-895688-20-5). 32pp. Directions for making different puppets and marionettes are given using everyday materials. (Rev: SLJ 12/94) [745]

Motion Pictures, Radio, and Television

14309 Gleasner, Diana C. *The Movies (Inventions That Changed Our Lives)* (4–6). Illus. 1983, Walker LB $8.85 (0-8027-6483-5). A history of moviemaking.

14310 Hautzig, Esther. *On the Air: Behind the Scenes at a TV Newscast* (4–6). Illus. by David Hautzig. 1991, Macmillan $15.95 (0-02-743361-7). 48pp. A straightforward look at the workings of a TV newscast, with background information and job descriptions. (Rev: BCCB 3/92; BL 2/1/92; SLJ 2/92) [070.1]

14311 *The History of Moviemaking* (3–6). Illus. 1995, Scholastic $19.95 (0-590-47645-9). 47pp. A history of film is enlivened by transparencies, flaps, and other interactive devices. (Rev: BL 2/1/96; SLJ 5/96) [791]

14312 Hitzeroth, Deborah, and Sharon Heerboth. *Movies: The World on Film* (5–8). Illus. Series: Encyclopedia of Discovery and Invention. 1992, Lucent LB $18.96 (1-56006-210-X). 96pp. A brief history of movies and their effects on society. (Rev: SLJ 4/92) [791]

14313 Krauss, Ronnie. *Take a Look, It's in a Book: How Television Is Made at Reading Rainbow* (2–4). Illus. by Christopher Hornsby. 1997, Walker LB $16.85 (0-8027-8489-5). 32pp. A behind-the-scenes look at the television program *Reading Rainbow* and how it is put together. (Rev: BL 3/1/97; SLJ 6/97*) [791.45]

14314 Lund, Kristin. *Star Wars, Episode I: Incredible Locations* (3–6). Illus. 2000, DK $19.95 (0-7894-6692-9). 48pp. A visual treat that uses fold-out pages to present drawings and scenes from the movie *The Phantom Menace.* (Rev: BL 1/1–15/01; HBG 3/01) [791.43]

14315 Miller, Marilyn. *Behind the Scenes at the TV News Studio* (PS–3). Illus. Series: Behind the Scenes. 1996, Raintree Steck-Vaughn LB $21.40 (0-8172-4089-6). 32pp. A fascinating inside look at the inner workings of a TV news studio. (Rev: BL 4/15/96; SLJ 12/96) [070.1]

14316 Reynolds, David West. *Star Wars: Incredible Cross-Sections* (4–8). Illus. 1998, DK $19.95 (1-7894-3480-6). 32pp. This large-format book includes cross sections of the TIE fighter, the X-wing fighter, the AT-AT, the Millennium Falcon, Jabba's sail barge, and the Death Star. (Rev: BL 12/15/98) [791.43]

14317 Reynolds, David West. *Star Wars: The Visual Dictionary* (4–8). Illus. 1998, DK $19.95 (0-7894-3481-4). 64pp. Using a large-format dictionary approach, the people, creatures, and droids of the Star Wars saga are presented. Includes large photos of the characters and many stills from the movies. (Rev: BL 12/15/98; HBG 3/99; SLJ 2/99) [791.43]

14318 Reynolds, David West. *Star Wars Episode I: Incredible Cross-sections: The Definitive Guide to the Craft of Star Wars Episode I* (4–8). Illus. by Hans Jenssen and Richard Chasemore. 1999, DK $19.95 (0-7894-3962-X). 32pp. An excellent guidebook that features cross-sections of vehicles and spacecraft featured in *Star Wars: Episode I*. (Rev: HBG 3/00; SLJ 12/99) [791]

14319 Reynolds, David West. *Star Wars Episode I: The Visual Dictionary* (4–8). Illus. 1999, DK $19.95 (0-7894-4701-0). 64pp. In this large-format book, a follow-up to *Star Wars: The Visual Dictionary,* the author, an archaeologist, reports on creatures and events in *Episode 1,* using movie stills and posed photos to explain the galaxy's history, technology, anthropology, and politics. (Rev: BL 8/99) [791.43]

Theater and Play Production

14320 Bany-Winters, Lisa. *On Stage: Theater Games and Activities for Kids* (4–7). Illus. 1997, Chicago Review paper $14.95 (1-55652-324-6). 160pp. This book provides a number of theater games involving improvisation, creating characters, using and becoming objects, and ideas for pantomime and puppetry. (Rev: BL 2/1/98; SLJ 3/98) [327.12]

14321 Bany-Winters, Lisa. *Show Time! Music, Dance, and Drama Activities for Kids* (3–6). Illus. by Fran Lee. 2000, Chicago Review paper $14.95 (1-55652-361-0). 189pp. Using short chapters, this covers musical theater from Shakespeare to Sondheim with added activities like games, scenes for experimentation, and short scripts to stage. (Rev: SLJ 8/00) [327.12]

14322 Caruso, Sandra, and Susan Kosoff. *The Young Actor's Book of Improvisation: Dramatic Situations Based on Literature: Ages 7–11* (2–6). 1998, Heinemann paper $19.95 (0-325-00048-4). 164pp. Describes hundreds of books, such as *Shiloh,* from which readers can create scenes and dramatic monologues. (Rev: BL 9/15/98) [792]

14323 Malam, John. *Theater: From First Rehearsal to Opening Night* (3–5). Illus. Series: Building Works. 2000, Bedrick $16.95 (0-87226-588-9). 32pp. This guided tour of a theater includes the box office, orchestra pit, and dressing rooms plus a brief history of theaters. (Rev: BL 7/00; HBG 10/00; SLJ 11/00) [792]

14324 Morley, Jacqueline. *Shakespeare's Theater* (4–6). Illus. Series: Inside Story. 1995, Bedrick LB $18.95 (0-87226-309-6). 48pp. Details on Shakespeare's Globe Theatre and performances that took place there are preceded by a brief history of European theater. (Rev: BL 4/15/95) [792]

14325 Slaight, Craig, and Jack Sharrar, eds. *Great Scenes and Monologues for Children* (5–8). Series: Young Actors. 1993, Smith & Kraus paper $11.95 (1-880399-15-6). 172pp. A collection of scenes and monologues from children's stories and fairy tales, and from adult plays like Thornton Wilder's *The Skin of Our Teeth.* (Rev: BL 10/1/93; SLJ 11/93) [808.82]

History and Geography

History and Geography in General

Miscellaneous

14326 Aaseng, Nathan. *You Are the Explorer* (4–8). Illus. Series: Great Decision. 2000, Oliver LB $18.95 (1-881508-55-2). 160pp. In this interactive book about famous explorers, the reader is asked to make decisions similar to those made by real explorers such as Columbus, Cortes, Champlain, and Robert Scott. (Rev: BL 5/1/00; HBG 10/00) [910]

14327 Ajmera, Maya K., and John D. Ivanko. *To Be a Kid* (PS–1). Illus. 1999, Charlesbridge $15.95 (0-88106-841-1). 32pp. Children from around the world share a community of interests involving play, families, schools, animals, and friends. (Rev: BL 2/1/99; HBG 10/99; SLJ 4/99) [305.23]

14328 Ajmera, Maya K., and Anna R. Versola. *Children from Australia to Zimbabwe: A Photographic Journey Around the World* (3–6). Illus. 1997, Charlesbridge $18.95 (0-88106-999-X). 64pp. A photographic journey around the globe that introduces 25 countries and gives basic fact about each. (Rev: BL 1/1–15/98; HBG 3/98; SLJ 7/97) [305.23]

14329 *Atlas of Countries* (1–3). Illus. by Donald Grant. Series: First Discovery Atlases. 1996, Scholastic $12.95 (0-590-58282-8). This atlas explains maps and globes, landforms, the earth's evolution and rotation, while also supplying maps of the world's countries. (Rev: SLJ 9/96) [912]

14330 Bell, Neill. *The Book of Where: Or How to Be Naturally Geographic* (4–7). Illus. by Richard Wilson. 1982, Little, Brown paper $12.95 (0-316-08831-5). 140pp. A collection of activities that make one aware of the study of geography.

14331 Bramwell, Martyn. *Central and South America* (4–6). Illus. Series: World in Maps. 2000, Carolrhoda $23.93 (0-8225-2912-2). 48pp. This collection of maps of all the countries in Central and South America also covers population, government, languages, currency, size, and capitals. (Rev: BL 10/15/00; SLJ 1/01) [917.28]

14332 Burger, Leslie, and Debra L. Rahm. *Sister Cities in a World of Difference* (4–8). Illus. 1996, Lerner LB $22.60 (0-8225-2697-2). 93pp. The pairing of cities internationally and its many positive results are introduced. (Rev: BL 9/1/96; SLJ 9/96) [303.48]

14333 Chiarelli, Brunetto. *The Atlas of World Cultures* (4–6). Illus. by Paola Ravaglia. 1997, Bedrick $19.95 (0-87226-499-8). 61pp. Arranged by geographical area, this book examines various peoples and their religion, language, food, dress, and arts. (Rev: SLJ 10/97) [910]

14334 Claybourne, Anna, and Caroline Young. *The Usborne Book of Treasure Hunting* (4–7). Illus. 1999, Usborne paper $14.95 (0-7460-3445-8). 79pp. In a series of short chapters, this book covers famous treasures that were buried underground, lost at sea, or existed in ancient times — with coverage of such subjects as the clay soldiers in Huang Di's tomb and the restoration of the Tudor ship *Mary Rose*. (Rev: BL 4/1/99) [622.19]

14335 Collard, Sneed B. *1,000 Years Ago on Planet Earth* (3–6). Illus. 1999, Houghton $15.00 (0-395-90866-3). 32pp. Double-page spreads describe what was happening in the year 1000 in various civilizations around the world. (Rev: BL 8/99; HBG 3/00; SLJ 9/99) [909]

14336 Demarco, Neil. *The Children's Atlas of World History* (4–7). 2000, Bedrick $19.95 (0-87226-603-6). 96pp. Double-page spreads introduce a series of maps and explanatory text that cover the history of the world. (Rev: HBG 10/00; SLJ 8/00) [910]

14337 *Dorling Kindersley Children's Atlas* (4–8). Ed. by Elizabeth Wyse and Caroline Lucas. Illus. 2000, DK $24.95 (0-7894-5845-4). 176pp. An excellent all-purpose atlas that includes material on history, climate, vegetation, population, and more. (Rev: BL 10/15/00) [912]

14338 Gallimard Jeunesse, and Donald Grant. *Atlas of Islands* (PS–2). Series: First Discovery. 1999, Scholastic $12.95 (0-439-04402-2). 24pp. This simple book explains what islands are and covers other basic geographical terms. (Rev: BL 10/15/99; HBG 3/00) [551.4]

14339 Gold, John C. *Environments of the Western Hemisphere* (5–8). Illus. Series: Comparing Continents. 1997, Twenty-First Century $21.40 (0-8050-5601-7). 96pp. Compares the climates of South, North, and Central America and shows how these affect the environment and the way people live and work. (Rev: BL 2/1/98; SLJ 3/98) [363.7]

14340 Halley, Ned. *Disasters* (3–6). Illus. 1999, Kingfisher $15.95 (0-7534-5221-9). 64pp. Disasters in history such as earthquakes, tornadoes, famine, volcanoes, and the sinking of the *Titanic* are covered in this well-illustrated book. (Rev: BL 10/15/99; HBG 3/00; SLJ 12/99) [363.34]

14341 Hollyer, Beatrice. *Wake Up, World! A Day in the Life of Children Around the World* (K–3). Illus. 1999, Holt $16.95 (0-8050-6293-9). A boy in Siberia and a girl in northern Brazil are two of the eight children from around the world in this introductory book on different environments. (Rev: BL 9/15/99; HBG 3/00; SLJ 12/99) [306.09]

14342 Kent, Peter. *Go to Jail! A Look at Prisons Through the Ages* (3–5). Illus. by author. 1998, Millbrook LB $20.90 (0-7613-0402-9). 29pp. Double-page drawings showing cutaway views help to describe prisons and prison practices worldwide from 1534 to 1943. (Rev: HBG 10/98; SLJ 2/99) [365]

14343 Kindersley, Barnabas, and Anabel Kindersley. *Children Just Like Me: A Unique Celebration of Children Around the World* (3–6). Illus. 1995, DK $19.95 (0-7894-0201-7). 79pp. An attractive book that views children around the world, arranged by continents. (Rev: BCCB 2/95; SLJ 1/96) [305]

14344 Knowlton, Jack. *Geography from A to Z: A Picture Glossary* (2–5). Illus. by Harriett Barton. 1988, HarperCollins $16.95 (0-690-04616-2); paper $6.95 (0-06-446099-1). 48pp. Each entry describes the earth's physical geography. (Rev: BL 11/1/88)

14345 Llewellyn, Claire. *Our Planet Earth* (K–3). Illus. Series: Scholastic First Encyclopedia. 1997, Scholastic paper $14.95 (0-590-87929-4). 77pp. An introductory book on the Earth's origins, physical geography, and the life forms that inhabit our planet. (Rev: SLJ 2/98) [910]

14346 Love, Ann, and Jane Drake. *The Kids Guide to the Millennium* (3–6). Illus. 1998, Kids Can $12.95 (1-55074-556-5); paper $7.95 (1-55074-436-4). 64pp. This book explains the meaning of the millennium and provides ideas for a variety of millennium-related activities and crafts. (Rev: BCCB 11/98; BL 7/98; HBG 10/98; SLJ 8/98) [909]

14347 MacDonald, Fiona. *A Child's Eye View of History* (3–6). 1998, Simon & Schuster $16.95 (0-689-81378-3). 61pp. Using both topical and chronological approaches, this book gives an interesting overview of world history in a series of double-page spreads. (Rev: HBG 10/98; SLJ 7/98) [910]

14348 Maisner, Heather. *The Magic Globe: An Around-the-World Adventure Game* (4–6). Illus. by Alan Baron. 1995, Candlewick $12.95 (1-56402-

445-8). 29pp. A game book that takes the reader through a number of countries where they get a glimpse of the culture and geography of each. A companion volume is *The Magic Hourglass: A Time-Travel Adventure Game* (1995). (Rev: SLJ 9/95) [910]

14349 Matthews, Rupert. *Cooking a Meal* (3–5). Illus. Series: Everyday History. 2000, Watts $20.00 (0-531-14545-X); paper $6.95 (0-531-15399-1). 32pp. This work traces the history of food preparation from mammoth hunters and ancient farmers to today's fast food chains. (Rev: BL 10/1/00; SLJ 6/00) [224]

14350 Mellett, Peter. *Pyramids* (3–6). Illus. Series: Young Scientist Concepts and Projects. 1999, Gareth Stevens LB $16.95 (0-8368-2267-6). 64pp. After a general introduction to pyramids, this book focuses on the pyramids of Egypt, with interesting related projects. (Rev: BL 4/15/99) [909]

14351 Millard, Anne. *A Street Through Time* (3–6). Illus. by Steve Noon. 1998, DK $16.95 (0-7894-3426-1). 32pp. An outline of world history as seen in the development of a street, from being part of a prehistoric hunters' camp to becoming a bustling, big-city thoroughfare. (Rev: BL 1/1–15/99; HB 1–2/99; HBG 3/99; SLJ 12/98) [936]

14352 Parker, Steve, and Sally Morgan. *Ultimate Atlas of Almost Everything* (4–6). 1999, Sterling $24.95 (0-8069-7759-0). 117pp. An atlas that contains information on the earth, wildlife, people, and places. (Rev: HBG 3/00; SLJ 2/00) [900]

14353 Pascoe, Elaine, and Deborah Kops. *Scholastic Kid's Almanac for the 21st Century* (4–7). Illus. by Bob Italiano and David C. Bell. 1999, Scholastic $18.95 (0-590-30723-1); paper $12.95 (0-590-30724-X). 352pp. An almanac that covers subjects including aerospace, animals, chemistry, computers, energy, geography, plants, religion, and sports. (Rev: SLJ 2/00) [900]

14354 Petersen, David. *North America* (2–4). Illus. Series: True Books. 1998, Children's LB $21.00 (0-516-20768-7). 48pp. Excellent maps, satellite photos, and drawings are used to highlight the topographical features, animals and plants, and the native peoples of North America. (Rev: BL 1/1–15/99; HBG 3/99) [970]

14355 Reid, Struan. *Cultures and Civilizations* (5–8). Illus. Series: Silk and Spice Routes. 1994, Silver Burdett LB $19.95 (0-02-726315-0). 48pp. In a handsome, oversize book with stunning illustrations, the many historic cultures that thrived along the ancient trade route to the East are introduced. (Rev: BL 12/15/94; SLJ 12/94) [909]

14356 Sammis, Fran. *Measurements* (2–5). 1997, Marshall Cavendish LB $22.79 (0-7614-0539-9). 32pp. Explains how geographical distances are measured and how these systems began. (Rev: BL 2/15/98; HBG 3/98) [910]

14357 Siegel, Alice, and Margo McLoone. *The Blackbirch Kid's Almanac of Geography* (4–7). 2000, Blackbirch LB $39.95 (1-56711-300-1). 336pp. A good browsing book that contains information on such topics as natural and man-made wonders, countries, currencies, events, weather, languages, foods, and culture. (Rev: HBG 3/01; SLJ 2/01) [910]

14358 Steele, Philip. *Clothes and Crafts in Victorian Times* (4–6). Series: Clothing and Crafts in History. 2000, Gareth Stevens LB $21.27 (0-8368-2738-4). 32pp. Nineteenth-century crafts including handmade woolens, lace embroidery, wood carvings, and pottery are described; projects include making a Victorian valentine and a Punch and Judy puppet. (Rev: BL 1/1–15/01) [940]

14359 Stienecker, David L. *The World* (2–5). Series: Discovering Geography. 1997, Marshall Cavendish LB $22.79 (0-7614-0543-7). 32pp. The geography of the world is introduced, with material on land formations, climate, and various environments. (Rev: BL 2/15/98; HBG 3/98) [910]

14360 Wood, Robert W. *Easy Geography Activities* (3–6). Illus. by John D. Wood. 1991, TAB $16.95 (0-8306-2493-7); paper $9.95 (0-8306-2492-9). 141pp. Helping to understand the principles and vocabulary of geography through such activities as reading road maps, making a compass, and understanding continental drift. (Rev: BL 2/1/92) [910]

Maps and Globes

14361 Baicker-McKee, Carol. *Mapped Out! The Search for Snookums* (4–6). Illus. by Traci O. Covey. 1997, Gibbs Smith $19.95 (0-87905-788-2). 32pp. Using map-reading skills and other references techniques, the reader is able to find the "petnapper" of a rare iguana. (Rev: SLJ 1/98) [912]

14362 Berger, Melvin, and Gilda Berger. *The Whole World in Your Hands: Looking at Maps* (2–3). Illus. by Robert Quackenbush. Series: Discovery Readers. 1993, Ideals paper $4.50 (0-8249-8609-1). 48pp. This book for beginning readers introduces maps from simple to complex. (Rev: BCCB 4/93; BL 7/93) [912]

14363 Bramwell, Martyn. *How Maps Are Made* (5–8). Illus. Series: Maps and Mapmakers. 1998, Lerner LB $22.60 (0-8225-2920-3). 48pp. The difficulties in representing the globe on a flat surface are explored, plus details on how maps are made — both by hand and by computer — and on the use of aerial photography in mapmaking. (Rev: BL 3/15/99; HBG 3/99; SLJ 2/99) [526]

14364 Bramwell, Martyn. *Mapping Our World* (5–8). Series: Maps and Mapmakers. 1998, Lerner LB $22.60 (0-8225-2924-6). 48pp. A history of how the world was pictured by ancient mapmakers and the tools they used, in contrast to today's techniques. (Rev: BL 3/15/99; SLJ 2/99) [912]

14365 Bramwell, Martyn. *Mapping the Seas and Airways* (5–8). Series: Maps and Mapmakers. 1998, Lerner LB $22.60 (0-8225-2921-1). 48pp. This volume deals with special kinds of maps prepared and used by oceanographers and by airline cartographers. (Rev: BL 3/15/99; HBG 3/99) [912]

14366 Bramwell, Martyn. *Maps in Everyday Life* (5–8). Illus. Series: Maps and Mapmakers. 1998, Lerner LB $22.60 (0-8225-2923-8). 48pp. This book explores how different maps are used for different purposes. (Rev: BL 3/15/99; HBG 3/99) [912]

14367 Ganeri, Anita. *The Story of Maps and Navigation* (3–6). Series: Signs of the Times. 1998, Oxford LB $16.00 (0-19-521410-2). 32pp. A history of maps and navigational devices is given, with brief coverage on their uses during the age of exploration. (Rev: BL 3/15/98; SLJ 5/98) [912]

14368 Johnson, Sylvia A. *Mapping the World* (4–7). Illus. 1999, Simon & Schuster $16.00 (0-689-81813-0). 32pp. A history of maps and mapmaking from Ptolemy in ancient Greece to the satellite and computer images of today. (Rev: BCCB 11/99; BL 12/1/99; HBG 3/00; SLJ 12/99*) [912]

14369 Knowlton, Jack. *Maps and Globes* (2–4). Illus. 1985, HarperCollins paper $6.95 (0-06-446049-5). 48pp. This is a clear introduction to maps and globes and how to read them. (Rev: BCCB 3/86; BL 12/15/85)

14370 Smith, A. G. *Where Am I? The Story of Maps and Navigation* (4–8). Illus. 1997, Stoddart paper $13.95 (0-7737-5836-4). 96pp. Each of the important discoveries and innovations involved in the history of mapmaking are explained. (Rev: BL 9/1/97) [910]

14371 Stienecker, David L. *Maps* (2–5). Series: Discovering Geography. 1997, Marshall Cavendish LB $22.79 (0-7614-0538-0). 32pp. The evolution of maps is traced, and basic map-reading skills are introduced. (Rev: BL 2/15/98; HBG 3/98; SLJ 4/98) [912]

14372 Sweeney, Joan. *Me on the Map* (K–3). Illus. by Annette Cable. 1996, Crown $12.00 (0-517-70095-6). 32pp. The concept of maps is introduced, from a floor plan of a room to a representation of the earth. (Rev: BL 4/1/96; SLJ 6/96) [912]

Paleontology and Dinosaurs

14373 Aliki. *Digging Up Dinosaurs* (2–4). Illus. by author. 1989, HarperCollins LB $15.89 (0-690-04716-9); paper $4.95 (0-06-445078-3). 32pp. This book answers the question "How do dinosaurs get into museums?"

14374 Aliki. *Dinosaur Bones* (PS–3). Illus. by author. 1988, HarperCollins paper $4.95 (0-06-445077-5). 32pp. In this book, her fourth on dinosaurs, Aliki discusses the discovery of fossils and the many theories that emerged about their meaning. (Rev: BCCB 1/88; BL 2/1/88; SLJ 4/88)

14375 Aliki. *Fossils Tell of Long Ago* (2–4). Illus. Series: Let's-Read-and-Find-Out. 1990, HarperCollins LB $15.89 (0-690-04829-7); paper $4.95 (0-06-445093-7). 32pp. A handsome revision of the original 1972 title with full-color artwork. (Rev: BL 4/15/90; SLJ 7/90) [560]

14376 Aliki. *My Visit to the Dinosaurs* (PS–3). Illus. by author. 1985, HarperCollins LB $15.89 (0-690-04423-2); paper $4.95 (0-06-445020-1). 32pp. Revision of the 1969 book, including new material. Also use: *Dinosaurs Are Different* (1985). (Rev: BCCB 10/85; BL 9/15/85; SLJ 1/86)

14377 Arnold, Caroline. *Dinosaur Mountain: Graveyard of the Past* (4–7). Illus. 1990, Ticknor $16.00 (0-89919-693-4). A visit to the Dinosaur National Monument quarry in Utah. (Rev: BL 5/15/89)

14378 Arnold, Caroline. *Dinosaurs All Around: An Artist's View of the Prehistoric World* (3–6). Photos by Richard Hewett. 1993, Houghton $14.95 (0-395-62363-4). 48pp. This book concentrates on the art of creating dinosaur models from miniature and life-sized ones. (Rev: BCCB 4/93; BL 4/15/93; HB 7–8/93; SLJ 5/93) [567.9]

14379 Arnold, Caroline. *Giant Shark: Megalodon, Prehistoric Super Predator* (4–6). Illus. 2000, Clarion $15.00 (0-395-91419-1). 32pp. This book introduces the megalodon, an extinct giant shark, and explains how paleontologists have determined its characteristics and how it behaved. (Rev: BL 11/1/00; HBG 3/01; SLJ 11/00) [567]

14380 Asimov, Isaac. *Death from Space: What Killed the Dinosaurs?* (3–5). Illus. Series: Isaac Asimov's New Library of the Universe. 1994, Gareth Stevens LB $21.27 (0-8368-1129-1). 32pp. Explores the theory that dinosaurs became extinct because of a cosmic collision. (Rev: BL 2/15/95) [567.9]

14381 Barton, Byron. *Dinosaurs, Dinosaurs* (PS–1). Illus. 1989, HarperCollins LB $15.89 (0-690-04768-1); paper $5.95 (0-06-443298-X). 40pp. Dinosaur characteristics in splashy colors. (Rev: BL 3/15/89; HB 5–6/89; SLJ 4/89)

14382 Benton, Michael. *Dinosaur and Other Prehistoric Animal Factfinder* (3–6). Illus. 1992, Kingfisher paper $14.95 (1-85697-802-8). 256pp. A quick reference source about prehistoric life, including profiles of dinosaurs and other animals. (Rev: BL 12/15/92) [560]

14383 Benton, Michael. *Dinosaurs* (3–6). Illus. 1998, Kingfisher $15.95 (0-7534-5131-X). 64pp. An easy-to-read account of the rise and fall of the dinosaurs, explaining why they became extinct. (Rev: BL 11/15/98; HBG 3/99; SLJ 11/98) [567.9]

14384 Berger, Melvin. *Mighty Dinosaurs* (4–8). Illus. 1990, Avon paper $2.95 (0-380-76052-5). 128pp. Covers various kinds of dinosaurs and includes the latest research on their extinction. (Rev: BL 12/15/90) [567.9]

14385 Berger, Melvin, and Gilda Berger. *Did Dinosaurs Live in Your Backyard? Questions And Answers About Dinosaurs* (3–5). Series: Question and Answer. 1999, Scholastic $12.95 (0-590-13078-1); paper $5.95 (0-590-08568-3). 148pp. Using questions that children would ask about dinosaurs, this well-organized account supplies succinct answers and useful illustrations. (Rev: BL 11/15/99; HBG 3/00; SLJ 12/99) [567.9]

14386 Bishop, Nic. *Digging for Bird-Dinosaurs: An Expedition to Madagascar* (4–6). Illus. Series: Scientists in the Field. 2000, Houghton $16.00 (0-395-96056-8). 48pp. Shifting from Madagascar to a lab in New York, this account traces the work of paleontologist Cathy Forster, who is investigating the link between birds and dinosaurs. (Rev: BCCB 5/00; BL 4/15/00*; HB 5–6/00; HBG 10/00; SLJ 5/00) [567.9]

14387 Bishop, Roma. *My First Pop-up Book of Prehistoric Animals* (K–3). Illus. 1994, Simon & Schuster $12.95 (0-671-86556-7). An engaging text and a series of pop-ups introduce the world of the dinosaur to primary graders. (Rev: BL 11/15/94) [560]

14388 Branley, Franklyn M. *What Happened to the Dinosaurs?* (1–3). Illus. by Marc Simont. 1989, HarperCollins LB $15.89 (0-690-04749-5). 32pp. A good discussion of what might have happened to cause the end of the dinosaurs. (Rev: BL 9/1/89; HB 11–12/89; SLJ 10/89) [567.9]

14389 Brett-Surman, Michael, and Thomas R. Holtz, Jr. *James Gurney: The World of Dinosaurs* (5–8). Illus. by James Gurney. 1998, GWP $19.95 (0-86713-046-6). 48pp. This story of the 15 dinosaur stamps designed for the U.S. Postal Service includes a description of each of the beasts. (Rev: SLJ 9/98) [567.9]

14390 Burton, Jane, and Kim Taylor. *The Nature and Science of Fossils* (3–6). Series: Exploring the Science of Nature. 1999, Gareth Stevens LB $14.95 (0-8368-2183-1). 32pp. A well-illustrated introduction to paleontology that explains where and how fossils were formed. A section is devoted to projects and activities using simple materials. (Rev: BL 7/99; SLJ 1/00) [560]

14391 Cohen, Daniel. *Pteranodon* (3–4). Series: Discovering Dinosaurs. 2000, Bridgestone LB $17.26 (0-7368-0617-2). 24pp. A basic title that introduces this prehistoric animal. Also use *Stegosaurus* (2000). (Rev: HBG 3/01; SLJ 1/01) [567.9]

14392 Cole, Joanna. *The Magic School Bus in the Time of the Dinosaurs* (K–4). Illus. by Bruce Degen. 1994, Scholastic $15.95 (0-590-44688-6). 46pp. Through time travel, Ms. Frizzle takes her students to various geological periods when dinosaurs lived in this fact-filled book about prehistoric life. (Rev: BCCB 10/94; BL 8/94; HB 11–12/94; SLJ 9/94) [567.9]

14393 Cooley, Brian, and Mary Ann Wilson. *Make-a-Saurus: My Life with Raptors and Other Dinosaurs* (4–8). Photos by Gary Campbell. 2000, Annick $24.95 (1-55037-645-4); paper $14.95 (1-55037-644-6). 58pp. A two-part book giving a step-by step description of how museum-quality models of dinosaurs are made using the latest discoveries in paleontology, followed by an exploration of how these techniques can be adapted so the reader can make models at home. (Rev: HBG 3/01; SLJ 9/00) [567.9]

14394 Currie, Philip J., and Colleayn O. Mastin. *The Newest and Coolest Dinosaurs* (4–8). Illus. by Jan Sovak. 1998, Grasshopper $18.95 (1-895910-41-2). 30pp. Using double-page spreads, this volume supplies factual information on newly identified dinosaurs and their discoveries. (Rev: SLJ 1/99) [567.9]

14395 Cutts, David. *More About Dinosaurs* (K–2). Illus. by Greg Wenzel. 1982, Troll LB $17.25 (0-89375-668-7); paper $3.50 (0-89375-669-5). 32pp. A simple introduction to this fascinating subject for primary grades.

14396 Dal Sasso, Cristiano. *Animals: Origins and Evolution* (4–8). Illus. Series: Beginnings — Origins and Evolution. 1995, Raintree Steck-Vaughn LB $24.26 (0-8114-3333-1). 48pp. This well-illustrated account traces the development of animals from bacteria to the invertebrates and then fish, amphibians, reptiles, birds, and mammals. (Rev: BL 5/1/95; SLJ 6/95) [591]

14397 De Magalhaes, Roberto Carvalho. *Prehistory* (4–6). Series: Art and Civilization. 2000, Bedrick $16.95 (0-87226-615-X). 36pp. Using illustrations of many artifacts, this book explains daily life and culture during prehistoric times. (Rev: HBG 3/01; SLJ 1/01) [930.1]

14398 Dingus, Lowell. *What Color Is That Dinosaur? Questions, Answers, and Mysteries* (4–6). Illus. by Stephen C. Quinn. 1994, Millbrook LB $23.90 (1-56294-365-0). 79pp. Unusual facts about dinosaurs, including their color, are covered in this fascinating volume. (Rev: SLJ 7/94) [567.9]

14399 Dingus, Lowell, and Luis Chiappe. *The Tiniest Giants: Discovering Dinosaur Eggs* (4–6). Illus. 1999, Doubleday $27.95 (0-385-32642-4). 42pp. The authors describe their 1997 expedition to Patagonia where they found thousands of fossilized dinosaur eggs. (Rev: BCCB 7–8/99; BL 6/1–15/99; HBG 10/99; SLJ 6/99) [567.9]

14400 Dingus, Lowell, and Mark A. Norell. *Searching for Velociraptor* (4–6). Illus. 1996, HarperCollins LB $15.89 (0-06-025894-2). 32pp. A first-person account of discovering raptor fossils in Mongolia. (Rev: BL 9/1/96; SLJ 2/97) [567.9]

14401 *Dinosaurs* (1–3). Illus. by James Prunier and Henri Galeron. Series: First Discovery. 1993, Scholastic $12.95 (0-590-46358-6). With cutaway illustrations and transparencies, different dinosaurs and their anatomy are shown. (Rev: SLJ 8/93) [567.9]

14402 *Dinosaurs* (3–6). Ed. by Paul Willis. Illus. Series: Pathfinders. 1999, Reader's Digest $16.99 (1-57584-288-2). 64pp. Two-page spreads introduce the world of dinosaurs, when and where they lived, when they died, and the study of fossils. (Rev: BL 8/99) [567.9]

14403 Dixon, Dougal. *Be a Dinosaur Detective* (1–4). Illus. 1988, Lerner paper $6.95 (0-8225-9538-9). 32pp. The author explains how all evidence for dinosaurs is deduced from fossils. (Rev: BL 5/1/88; SLJ 8/88)

14404 Dixon, Dougal. *Dougal Dixon's Amazing Dinosaurs* (3–6). Illus. 2000, Boyds Mills $17.95 (1-56397-773-7). 128pp. An attractive, informative field book that introduces groups of dinosaurs and offers solid information on their physical makeup, habits, and special characteristics. (Rev: BL 3/15/00; HBG 10/00; SLJ 5/00) [567.9]

14405 Dixon, Dougal. *Dougal Dixon's Dinosaurs.* Rev. ed. (4–8). 1998, Boyds Mills $19.95 (1-56397-722-2). 160pp. This revision of the 1993 edition introduces about 30 different dinosaurs in double-page spreads. (Rev: HBG 10/98; SLJ 6/98) [567.9]

14406 Dixon, Dougal. *Questions and Answers About Dinosaurs* (3–6). Illus. Series: Questions and Answers About. 1995, Kingfisher paper $7.95 (1-

85697-553-3). 40pp. In a question-and-answer format, basic information about dinosaurs is covered, as well as some unusual facts such as "Which were the deadliest?" (Rev: SLJ 4/95) [567.9]

14407 Dixon, Dougal. *The Search for Dinosaurs* (4–7). Illus. Series: Digging Up the Past. 1995, Thomson Learning LB $24.26 (1-56847-396-6). 48pp. A history of the various discoveries that paleontologists have made about dinosaurs and other prehistoric beasts. (Rev: SLJ 2/96) [567.9]

14408 Dodson, Peter. *An Alphabet of Dinosaurs* (2–4). Illus. by Wayne D. Barlowe. 1995, Scholastic $16.95 (0-590-46486-8). 64pp. Twenty-six kinds of dinosaurs are introduced in text and drawings in this unusual alphabet book. (Rev: BL 1/15/95; SLJ 3/95*) [567.9]

14409 Eastman, David. *Story of Dinosaurs* (K–2). Illus. by Joel Snyder. 1997, Troll paper $3.50 (0-89375-649-0). Simple material presented in short sentences with many illustrations.

14410 Facklam, Margery. *Tracking Dinosaurs in the Gobi* (5–8). Illus. 1997, Twenty-First Century $21.40 (0-8050-5165-1). 96pp. The story of the paleontologist Roy Chapman Andrews and his amazing dinosaur finds in the Gobi Desert beginning in the 1920s. (Rev: BL 2/1/98; SLJ 2/98*) [567.9]

14411 Fisher, Enid. *The Great Dinosaur Record Book* (3–5). Illus. by Richard Grant. Series: World of Dinosaurs. 1998, Gareth Stevens LB $14.95 (0-8368-2176-9). 32pp. Large colorful illustrations are used in this book that tells about the record holders (biggest, fastest, etc.) of the dinosaur world. (Rev: HBG 10/99; SLJ 2/99) [567.9]

14412 Fisher, Enid. *They Lived with the Dinosaurs* (4–6). Illus. by Richard Grant. Series: World of Dinosaurs. 1999, Gareth Stevens LB $14.95 (0-8368-2292-7). 32pp. This book covers a multitude of living creatures including insects, turtles, mammals, and plants that lived at the time of dinosaurs. Also use *True-Life Monsters of the Prehistoric Seas* (1999) and *True-Life Monsters of the Prehistoric Skies* (both 1999). (Rev: SLJ 8/99) [567.9]

14413 Floca, Brian. *Dinosaurs at the Ends of the Earth: The Story of the Central Asiatic Expeditions* (3–5). Illus. 2000, DK $15.95 (0-7894-2539-4). 32pp. A description of the 1922 expeditions to Mongolia made by Roy Chapman Andrews, Walter Granger, and George Olsen and the fabulous dinosaur fossils they found. (Rev: BCCB 3/00; BL 2/15/00; HB 3–4/00; HBG 10/00; SLJ 6/00) [508]

14414 Fowler, Allan. *It Could Still Be a Dinosaur* (1–2). Illus. Series: Rookie Readers. 1993, Children's LB $19.00 (0-516-06002-3). 32pp. For beginning readers, this is a very simple book about dinosaurs. (Rev: BL 3/1/94) [567.9]

14415 Gallant, Jonathan R. *The Tales Fossils Tell* (5–7). 2000, Benchmark LB $19.95 (0-7614-1153-4). 80pp. This introduction to paleontology explains how the importance of fossils was only clearly understood after the ideas of evolution and extinction were accepted. (Rev: SLJ 2/01) [560]

14416 Gallant, Roy A. *Fossils* (3–5). Illus. Series: Kaleidoscope. 2000, Marshall Cavendish $15.95 (0-

7614-1041-4). 48pp. Beginning with basic information on fossils that shows, for example, how a dying fish can become a fossil, this book goes on to more complex subjects related to paleontology. (Rev: BL 2/1/01; HBG 3/01; SLJ 3/01) [560]

14417 Gibbons, Gail. *Dinosaurs* (2–4). Illus. 1987, Holiday LB $16.95 (0-8234-0657-1); paper $6.95 (0-8234-0708-X). 32pp. Giant reptiles explained in simple terms for the young set. (Rev: BL 12/15/87; SLJ 11/87)

14418 Gibbons, Gail. *Prehistoric Animals* (K–2). Illus. 1988, Holiday LB $16.95 (0-8234-0707-1). 32pp. A brief overview of a subject that fascinates young readers. (Rev: BL 9/1/88; SLJ 10/88)

14419 Giblin, James Cross. *The Mystery of the Mammoth Bones* (4–8). Illus. 1999, HarperCollins $14.95 (0-06-027493-X). 128pp. A biography of the paleontologist Charles Willson Peale that also tells the story of the mastodon (or mammoth) bones Peale uncovered, assembled, and displayed. (Rev: BL 1/1–15/99; HB 9–10/99; HBG 10/99; SLJ 4/99) [560.9]

14420 Gillette, J. Lynett. *Dinosaur Ghosts: The Mystery of Coelophysis* (3–5). Illus. by Douglas Henderson. 1997, Dial $15.99 (0-8037-1721-0). 32pp. The author, a paleontologist, explains the mystery of the mass grave of tiny dinosaur skeletons found at Ghost Ranch, New Mexico. (Rev: BCCB 7–8/97; BL 4/1/97; HB 7–8/97; SLJ 4/97*) [567.9]

14421 Granger, Judith. *Amazing World of Dinosaurs* (1–3). Illus. by Pamela Baldwin Ford. 1982, Troll LB $17.25 (0-89375-562-1); paper $3.50 (0-89375-563-X). 32pp. This book describes many plant and meat-eating dinosaurs.

14422 Green, Tamara. *Cretaceous Dinosaur World* (3–5). Illus. by Richard Grant. Series: World of Dinosaurs. 1998, Gareth Stevens LB $14.95 (0-8368-2173-4). 32pp. This colorful account of the last age of the dinosaurs also gives material on plants and other animals of the period. (Rev: HBG 10/99; SLJ 2/99) [567.9]

14423 Green, Tamara. *Dinosaur Babies* (4–6). Illus. by Richard Grant. Series: World of Dinosaurs. 1999, Gareth Stevens LB $14.95 (0-8368-2290-0). 32pp. This book introduces baby dinosaurs of various kinds and explains their care and feeding. Also use *Great Dinosaur Hunters* (1999). (Rev: SLJ 8/99) [567.9]

14424 Green, Tamara. *Jurassic Dinosaur World* (3–5). Illus. by Richard Grant. Series: World of Dinosaurs. 1998, Gareth Stevens LB $14.95 (0-8368-2174-2). 32pp. This review of the Jurassic period that was characterized by large dinosaurs also includes material on the first birds and mammals and the vegetation of the time. (Rev: HBG 10/99; SLJ 2/99) [567.9]

14425 Halls, Kelly M. *Dino-Trekking: The Ultimate Dinosaur Lover's Travel Guide* (4–8). Illus. by Rick Spears. 1996, Wiley paper $14.95 (0-471-11498-7). 199pp. This dinosaur directory describes sites, museums, and theme parks in the United States and Canada. (Rev: SLJ 3/96) [567.9]

14426 Harrison, Carol. *Dinosaurs Everywhere!* (PS–2). Illus. by Richard Courtney. 1998, Scholastic

$12.95 (0-590-00089-6). 40pp. An introduction to various kinds of dinosaurs, their habits, appearance, size, and behavior — all in a big, beautiful picture book. (Rev: BL 11/15/98; HBG 3/99; SLJ 1/99) [567.9]

14427 Hincks, Joseph. *Dinosaur Dictionary* (4–6). 1999, Rourke LB $24.95 (0-86593-586-6). 96pp. A highly readable, well-illustrated dictionary that presents two or three short paragraphs about each dinosaur. (Rev: SLJ 2/00) [567.9]

14428 Johnston, Marianne. *From the Dinosaurs of the Past to the Birds of the Present* (3–5). Illus. Series: Prehistoric Animals and Their Modern-Day Relatives. 2000, Rosen LB $18.60 (0-8239-5204-5). 24pp. This account points out the structural similarities between dinosaurs and birds and tells why scientists think they are related. (Rev: BL 12/1/00) [567]

14429 Kelsey, Elin. *Finding Out About Dinosaurs* (3–5). Illus. 2000, Owl $19.95 (1-895688-97-3); paper $9.95 (1-895688-98-1). 40pp. Questions about dinosaurs are asked on each double-page spread, and the answers reveal how paleontologists work and what they have learned about these prehistoric animals. (Rev: BL 12/1/00; HBG 3/01; SLJ 10/00) [567.9]

14430 Kittinger, Jo S. *Stories in Stone: The World of Animal Fossils* (4–6). Illus. Series: Earth and Sky Science. 1998, Watts LB $21.00 (0-531-20384-0). 64pp. About 500 million years are covered in this book that discusses all forms of animal fossils, including dinosaurs, from trilobites to mammals. (Rev: BL 2/1/99; HBG 3/99; SLJ 4/99) [560]

14431 Krueger, Richard. *The Dinosaurs* (2–5). Illus. Series: Prehistoric North America. 1996, Millbrook LB $21.90 (1-56294-548-3). 48pp. With plenty of color illustrations, this chatty overview tells about North American dinosaurs. (Rev: BL 5/15/96; SLJ 4/96) [567.9]

14432 Lambert, David. *DK Guide to Dinosaurs: A Thrilling Journey Through Prehistoric Times* (2–7). 2000, DK $19.95 (0-7894-5237-5). 64pp. An appealing oversize volume that portrays a number of different dinosaurs in their natural habitats. (Rev: BCCB 9/00; HBG 10/00; SLJ 7/00) [567.9]

14433 Lauber, Patricia. *Dinosaurs Walked Here: And Other Stories Fossils Tell* (3–5). Illus. 1987, Macmillan LB $16.95 (0-02-754510-5); paper $5.95 (0-689-71603-6). 64pp. More about fossils and what they tell us than about dinosaurs. (Rev: BCCB 9/87; BL 9/1/87; SLJ 9/87)

14434 Lauber, Patricia. *How Dinosaurs Came to Be* (4–6). Illus. 1996, Simon & Schuster $17.00 (0-689-80531-4). 48pp. The ancestors of dinosaurs are described in this account that traces the evolution of these giant reptiles. (Rev: BL 4/15/96; SLJ 5/96) [567.9]

14435 Lauber, Patricia. *Living with Dinosaurs* (3–6). Illus. by Douglas Henderson. 1991, Macmillan $16.95 (0-02-754521-0). 49pp. Re-creating what life was like in Montana 75 million years ago. (Rev: BL 3/1/91*; HB 5–6/91; SLJ 5/91*) [567.9]

14436 Lessem, Don. *Dinosaur Worlds: New Dinosaurs, New Discoveries* (5–8). Illus. 1996, Boyds Mills $19.95 (1-56397-597-1). 192pp. The reader visits various dinosaur digs worldwide in a review of what we know about these amazing creatures. (Rev: BL 11/15/96; SLJ 12/96*) [567.9]

14437 Lessem, Don. *Ornithomimids: The Fastest Dinosaur* (3–6). Illus. Series: Special Dinosaurs. 1996, Carolrhoda LB $19.95 (0-87614-813-5). 40pp. How the remains of these speedy dinosaurs were discovered and how our knowledge of them was collected highlight this well-illustrated volume. (Rev: BL 2/15/96; SLJ 4/96) [567.9]

14438 Lessem, Don. *Seismosaurus: The Longest Dinosaur* (3–5). Illus. by Donna Braginetz. Series: Special Dinosaurs. 1996, Carolrhoda LB $19.95 (0-87614-987-5). 40pp. This account introduces the seismosaurus and its characteristics and explains how we have determined these facts from fossils. (Rev: SLJ 9/96) [567.9]

14439 Lessem, Don. *Supergiants! The Biggest Dinosaurs* (4–6). Illus. by David Peters. 1997, Little, Brown $14.95 (0-316-52118-3). 32pp. Current information about gigantic dinosaurs is given in this well-organized book, which includes the latest theories and discoveries concerning them. (Rev: HBG 3/98; SLJ 9/97) [567.9]

14440 Lessem, Don. *Troodon: The Smartest Dinosaur* (3–6). Illus. Series: Special Dinosaurs. 1996, Carolrhoda LB $14.96 (0-87614-798-8). 40pp. The role of paleontologists in piecing together bits of information about this dinosaur is covered, along with information on its appearance, habits, and intelligence. (Rev: BL 2/15/96; SLJ 4/96) [567.9]

14441 Lindsay, William. *DK Great Dinosaur Atlas* (3–7). Illus. 1999, DK $19.95 (0-7894-4728-2). 64pp. An oversize book that uses collage-like spreads of maps, richly detailed illustrations, text, and sidebars to explain dinosaur facts and where dinosaurs lived all around the world. (Rev: BL 2/15/00; HBG 10/00; SLJ 3/00) [567.9]

14442 Llamas, Andreu. *The Era of the Dinosaurs* (4–8). Illus. by Luis Rizo. Series: Development of the Earth. 1996, Chelsea LB $15.95 (0-7910-3452-6). 32pp. Various kinds of dinosaurs are introduced in this account that emphasizes their evolution. Also use *The First Amphibians* (1996). (Rev: SLJ 7/96) [567.9]

14443 MacLeod, Elizabeth. *Dinosaurs: The Fastest, the Fiercest, the Most Amazing* (3–5). Illus. by Gordon Sauve. 1995, Viking $11.99 (0-670-86026-3). A Guinness-type book that explores record holders in the world of the dinosaur. (Rev: SLJ 8/95) [567.9]

14444 McMullan, Kate. *Dinosaur Hunters* (2–4). Illus. by John R. Jones. 1989, Random paper $3.99 (0-394-81150-X). 46pp. An easy reader on how fossils are found and studied, with coverage on new theories about dinosaurs. (Rev: BCCB 12/89; SLJ 9/89) [567.9]

14445 Mannetti, William. *Dinosaurs in Your Backyard* (5–7). Illus. by author. 1982, Macmillan $15.00 (0-689-30906-6). 160pp. The latest discoveries and theories concerning dinosaurs and their history are incorporated into this account.

14446 Markle, Sandra. *Outside and Inside Dinosaurs* (3–5). Illus. 2000, Simon & Schuster $16.00 (0-689-82300-2). 40pp. This is a rundown of what scientists know about dinosaurs, their behavior, and their internal and external structures. (Rev: BL 12/1/00; HB 9–10/00; HBG 3/01; SLJ 11/00) [567.9]

14447 Maynard, Christopher. *The Best Book of Dinosaurs* (3–5). 1998, Kingfisher $10.95 (0-7534-5116-6). 33pp. A clearly written, lavishly illustrated introduction to several groups of dinosaurs, focusing on specific traits of about 20 of them. (Rev: HBG 10/98; SLJ 7/98) [567.9]

14448 Milner, Angela, ed. *Dinosaurs* (4–6). Illus. Series: Nature Company Discoveries. 1995, Time Life $16.00 (0-7835-4765-X). 64pp. A brief introduction to the world of dinosaurs, with colorful illustrations and an eight-page foldout. (Rev: BL 1/1–15/96; SLJ 1/96) [567.9]

14449 Moody, Richard. *Over 65 Million Years Ago: Before the Dinosaurs Died* (4–6). Illus. Series: History Detective. 1992, Macmillan LB $16.95 (0-02-767270-0). 32pp. How paleontologists have found out about dinosaurs and a summary of how they lived. (Rev: SLJ 12/92) [567.92]

14450 Most, Bernard. *Dinosaur Cousins?* (1–3). Illus. by author. 1987, Harcourt paper $6.00 (0-15-223498-5). 40pp. Musing about whether a rhinoceros, for instance, could be a dinosaur's cousin leads to facts about prehistoric animals. (Rev: BL 2/15/87; SLJ 5/85)

14451 Most, Bernard. *Dinosaur Questions* (PS–2). Illus. 1995, Harcourt $16.00 (0-15-292885-5). 40pp. Common questions about dinosaurs are answered, with many asides to test the reader. (Rev: BL 10/1/95; SLJ 2/96) [567.9]

14452 Most, Bernard. *How Big Were the Dinosaurs?* (PS–2). Illus. 1994, Harcourt $16.00 (0-15-236800-0). 32pp. The size of 20 different dinosaurs is shown by comparisons with everyday modern objects, like a school bus or a bowling alley. (Rev: BL 3/1/94; SLJ 4/94) [567.9]

14453 Most, Bernard. *Where to Look for a Dinosaur* (1–4). Illus. 1993, Harcourt $12.95 (0-15-295616-6). 32pp. An actual geographical guidebook pinpointing the remains of more than 25 beasts. (Rev: BL 2/15/93; SLJ 6/93) [567.9]

14454 Munro, Margaret. *The Story of Life on Earth* (3–5). Illus. 2000, Douglas & McIntyre $19.95 (0-88899-401-X). 32pp. This informative introduction to the evolution of life on Earth uses double-page spreads to illustrate the flora and fauna of different geological periods. (Rev: BL 11/1/00; HBG 3/01; SLJ 12/00) [560]

14455 Norell, Mark A., and Lowell Dingus. *A Nest of Dinosaurs: The Story of the Oviraptor* (5–8). 1999, Random $17.95 (0-385-32558-4). 48pp. As well as introducing oviraptors (perhaps the ancestors of chickens) and how they lived, this account covers paleontology in general. (Rev: BL 12/1/99; HBG 3/00; SLJ 11/99) [567]

14456 Norman, David, and Angela Milner. *Dinosaur* (4–8). Illus. Series: Eyewitness Books. 1989, Knopf LB $20.99 (0-394-92253-0). 64pp. Rich illustrations highlight various dinosaurs, with details on structure and habits. (Rev: BL 10/15/89; SLJ 1/90) [567.9]

14457 O'Brien, Patrick. *Gigantic! How Big Were the Dinosaurs?* (K–2). Illus. 1999, Holt $15.95 (0-8050-5738-2). 32pp. Modern objects such as cars, monster trucks, and fire engines are used to explain the comparative size of various dinosaurs in practical terms. (Rev: BL 6/1–15/99; HBG 10/99; SLJ 4/99) [567.9]

14458 Osborne, Will, and Mary Pope Osborne. *Dinosaurs: A Nonfiction Companion to Dinosaurs Before Dark* (2–4). Illus. by Sal Murdocca. Series: Magic Tree House Research Guide. 2000, Random LB $11.99 (0-375-90296-1); paper $4.99 (0-375-80296-7). 119pp. Using a time-travel format involving two children, this book discusses the kinds of dinosaurs, their characteristics, misconceptions about them, and the other creatures that lived at the same time. (Rev: HBG 3/01; SLJ 11/00) [567.9]

14459 Parish, Peggy. *Dinosaur Time* (K–2). Illus. by Arnold Lobel. 1974, HarperCollins LB $15.89 (0-06-024654-5); paper $3.95 (0-06-444037-0). 32pp. Eleven dinosaurs are introduced in this book for the beginning reader.

14460 Parker, Steve, and Jane Parker. *Collecting Fossils: Hold Prehistory in the Palm of Your Hand* (5–8). Illus. 1998, Sterling $14.95 (0-8069-9762-1). 80pp. After a discussion of how fossils are formed, this work introduces different types of fossils, explains important terms, and tells how to collect and organize them. (Rev: BL 6/1–15/98) [560]

14461 Pascoe, Elaine, adapt. *New Dinosaurs: Skeletons in the Sand* (4–6). Illus. Series: New Explorers. 1997, Blackbirch LB $17.95 (1-56711-231-5). 48pp. An account of the hardships and eventual success of a group of paleontologists who went to the Sahara in 1993 to find evidence of new dinosaurs. (Rev: HBG 3/98; SLJ 2/98) [567.9]

14462 Patent, Dorothy Hinshaw. *In Search of Maiasaurs* (4–7). Series: Frozen in Time. 1998, Benchmark LB $18.95 (0-7614-0787-1). 64pp. This book on dinosaurs describes the recent find of a huge bed of bones and Jack Horner's work to retrieve the fossils and learn from them. (Rev: HBG 10/99; SLJ 3/99) [567.9]

14463 Pope, Joyce. *Fossil Detective* (3–6). Illus. by Chris Forsey. Series: Nature Club. 1993, Troll LB $17.25 (0-8167-2781-3); paper $4.95 (0-8167-2782-1). 31pp. This introduction to paleontology as a hobby contains material on what fossils are, how they were formed, and how young people can collect them. (Rev: SLJ 3/94) [560]

14464 Press, Judy. *The Kids' Natural History Book: Making Dinos, Fossils, Mammoths and More* (3–5). Illus. Series: Kids Can! 2000, Williamson $12.95 (1-885593-24-4). 144pp. A discussion of the animal classification system and how scientists have discovered and organized information about animals, with many related craft projects. (Rev: BL 12/15/00; SLJ 1/01) [745.5]

14465 Pringle, Laurence. *Dinosaurs! Strange and Wonderful* (K–3). Illus. by Carol Heyer. 1995, Boyds Mills $15.95 (1-878093-16-9). 32pp. With a brief text and striking illustrations, 11 dinosaurs are described. (Rev: BL 3/15/95; SLJ 3/95) [567.9]

14466 Relf, Patricia. *A Dinosaur Named Sue: The Story of the Colossal Fossil* (3–6). Illus. 2000, Scholastic $15.95 (0-439-09985-4). 64pp. This is the story of the largest and most complete Tyrannosaurus rex skeleton ever found, how it was transported from South Dakota to the Field Museum in Chicago, and what life was like when Sue was alive. (Rev: BL 12/1/00; HBG 3/01; SLJ 1/01) [567.912]

14467 Royston, Angela. *Dinosaurs* (PS–2). Illus. by Jane Cradock-Watson and Dave Hopkins. Series: Eye Openers. 1991, Macmillan paper $8.99 (0-689-71518-8). 24pp. Many of the most important kinds of dinosaurs are introduced. (Rev: BL 9/15/91; SLJ 1/92) [567.9]

14468 Ryder, Joanne. *Tyrannosaurus Time* (K–4). Illus. by Michael Rothman. 1999, Morrow $16.00 (0-688-13682-6). 32pp. A vivid re-creation of a day in the life of a Tyrannosaurus rex and a memorable depiction of prehistoric life in a picture-book format. (Rev: BL 9/1/99; HBG 3/00; SLJ 9/99) [567.9]

14469 Schlein, Miriam. *Discovering Dinosaur Babies* (2–4). Illus. by Margaret Colbert. 1991, Macmillan LB $14.95 (0-02-778091-0). 40pp. Explaining what is known about dinosaur babies and how mothers cared for them. (Rev: BL 3/1/91; SLJ 7/91) [567.9]

14470 Senior, Kathryn. *Dinosaurs and Other Prehistoric Creatures* (3–8). Illus. by Carolyn Scrace. Series: X-Ray Picture Books. 1995, Watts LB $24.00 (0-531-14352-X). 48pp. In this general introduction to dinosaurs, two of the many topics discussed are survival techniques and reproduction. (Rev: SLJ 12/95) [567.9]

14471 Simon, Seymour. *New Questions and Answers About Dinosaurs* (2–5). Illus. by Jennifer Dewey. 1990, Morrow $15.93 (0-688-08196-7). 48pp. Using a question-and-answer approach, covers interesting facts and figures about dinosaurs. (Rev: BCCB 5/90; BL 2/15/90; HB 7–8/90; SLJ 5/90) [567.9]

14472 Simpson, Judith. *Mighty Dinosaurs* (2–4). Illus. Series: Nature Company Young Discoveries. 1996, Time Life $10.00 (0-7835-4837-0). 32pp. Some of the most noteworthy dinosaurs are pictured and described in this brief introduction. (Rev: BL 12/15/96) [567.9]

14473 Sloan, Christopher. *Feathered Dinosaurs* (3–6). Illus. 2000, National Geographic $17.95 (0-7922-7219-6). 64pp. Using recent paleontological discoveries as its starting point, this book explores what feathered dinosaurs, the distant ancestors of modern birds, might have looked like. (Rev: BL 11/1/00; HBG 3/01; SLJ 11/00) [567.9]

14474 Tanaka, Shelley. *Graveyards of the Dinosaurs: What It's Like to Discover Prehistoric Creatures* (4–7). Illus. 1998, Hyperion $16.95 (0-7868-0375-4). 48pp. This introduction to paleontology introduces readers to key paleontologists and the major dinosaur bone sites around the world. (Rev: BL 9/1/98; HBG 10/98; SLJ 7/98) [567.9]

14475 Taylor, Barbara. *The Really Deadly and Dangerous Dinosaur: And Other Monsters of the Prehistoric World* (PS–4). Illus. Series: The Really Horrible Guides. 1997, DK $9.95 (0-7894-2051-1). This account explores the various ways — like teeth, claws, horns, and stingers — that prehistoric animals defended themselves. (Rev: HBG 3/98; SLJ 12/97) [567.79]

14476 Thompson, Sharon E. *Death Trap: The Story of the La Brea Tar Pits* (4–8). Illus. 1995, Lerner LB $23.95 (0-8225-2851-7). 72pp. A history of the 40,000-year-old tar pits in Los Angeles and of the many species of prehistoric animals that were trapped in them. (Rev: BL 6/1–15/95; SLJ 5/95) [560]

14477 Unwin, David. *The New Book of Dinosaurs* (3–6). Illus. 1997, Millbrook LB $23.90 (0-7613-0568-8); paper $9.95 (0-7613-0589-0). 32pp. Computer-generated illustrations bring different dinosaurs alive, with lucid accompanying text. (Rev: BL 9/15/97; SLJ 9/97) [567.9]

14478 VanCleave, Janice. *Dinosaurs for Every Kid: Easy Activities That Make Learning Science Fun* (4–7). Illus. Series: Science for Every Kid. 1994, Wiley $29.95 (0-471-30813-7); paper $10.95 (0-471-30812-9). 224pp. With accompanying activities, this book explores the world of dinosaurs and how paleontology has discovered, through fossils, how they lived. (Rev: BL 4/1/94; SLJ 7/94) [567.9]

14479 Westrup, Hugh. *The Mammals* (3–5). Illus. Series: Prehistoric North America. 1996, Millbrook LB $21.90 (1-56294-546-7). 48pp. The woolly mammoth and saber-toothed tiger are two of the prehistoric mammals described in words and pictures. (Rev: BL 5/15/96; SLJ 4/96) [569]

14480 Whitfield, Philip. *Macmillan Children's Guide to Dinosaurs and Other Prehistoric Animals* (3–6). Illus. 1992, Macmillan LB $19.95 (0-02-762362-9). 96pp. A handsome guide to prehistoric animal life. (Rev: BL 10/15/92; SLJ 12/92) [567.9]

14481 Wilkes, Angela. *The Big Book of Dinosaurs: A First Book for Young Children* (PS–2). Illus. 1994, DK $14.95 (1-56458-718-5). 32pp. An oversize book that contains double-page spreads introducing a wide variety of dinosaurs, including some that are little known. (Rev: BL 11/15/94; SLJ 1/95) [567.9]

14482 Worth, Bonnie. *Oh Say Can You Say Dinosaur? All About Dinosaurs* (K–3). Illus. by Steve Haefele. Series: The Cat in the Hat's Learning Library. 1999, Random LB $11.99 (0-679-99114-X). 45pp. Several of Dr. Seuss's characters introduce different dinosaurs and their physical traits using illustrations and rhyming couplets. (Rev: SLJ 9/99) [567.9]

14483 Zallinger, Peter. *Dinosaurs and Other Archosaurs* (4–6). Illus. 1986, Random LB $15.99 (0-394-94421-6). 96pp. A solid overview of these fascinating creatures, era by era, group by group. (Rev: BL 9/1/86; HBG 3/00)

14484 Zallinger, Peter. *Prehistoric Animals* (1–3). Illus. by author. 1981, Random paper $3.25 (0-394-83737-1). A brief guide to prehistoric animals — chiefly dinosaurs — and their habits.

14485 Zimmerman, Howard. *Dinosaurs! The Biggest Baddest Strangest Fastest* (2–5). Illus. 2000, Simon & Schuster $17.95 (0-689-83276-1). 64pp. An oversize volume that is particularly noteworthy for its excellent illustrations of all sorts of dinosaurs. (Rev: BL 9/1/00; HBG 10/00; SLJ 5/00) [567.9]

14486 Zoehfeld, Kathleen W. *Dinosaur Babies* (K–3). Illus. by Lucia Washburn. Series: Let's-Read-and-Find-Out. 1999, HarperCollins LB $15.89 (0-06-027142-6); paper $4.95 (0-06-445162-3). 40pp. This simple science book explains the wonders of paleontology and how scientists use fossils to find out about dinosaurs. (Rev: BL 11/15/99; HBG 3/00; SLJ 9/99) [567.9]

14487 Zoehfeld, Kathleen W. *Terrible Tyrannosaurs* (PS–2). Illus. by Lucia Washburn. 2001, HarperCollins LB $15.89 (0-06-027934-6); paper $4.95 (0-06-445181-X). 40pp. This book highlights the most familiar and most feared dinosaur and tells what we know about it from science. (Rev: BL 2/1/01) [567.912]

Anthropology and Prehistoric Life

14488 *Atlas of People* (PS–2). Illus. Series: First Discovery. 1996, Scholastic $12.95 (0-590-58281-X). 24pp. A basic introduction to the various races of humankind, with attractive visuals. (Rev: BL 10/15/96; SLJ 2/97) [305.8]

14489 Buell, Janet. *Bog Bodies* (5–8). Illus. Series: Time Travelers. 1997, Twenty-First Century $20.40 (0-8050-5164-3). 64pp. This account tells of the discovery of Lindow Man, a Celtic man preserved by an English bog, with details on his life and information on how scientists use carbon dating, X-rays, and other forensic techniques. (Rev: BL 2/1/98; SLJ 3/98) [599.9]

14490 Buell, Janet. *Greenland Mummies* (5–8). Series: Time Travelers. 1998, Twenty-First Century LB $23.40 (0-7613-3004-6). 63pp. The recent discovery of mummified human corpses in Greenland produced studies that reveal how the Inuit people lived in the far north 500 years ago. (Rev: SLJ 10/98) [930.1]

14491 Buell, Janet. *Ice Maiden of the Andes* (5–8). Illus. Series: Time Travelers. 1997, Twenty-First Century $20.40 (0-8050-5185-6). 64pp. The story of the discovery of the frozen body of a young Inca girl who died 500 years ago and of how forensic methods like DNA testing have revealed details of Inca society, its religion, and gender roles. (Rev: BL 2/1/98; SLJ 3/98) [985]

14492 Childress, Diana. *Prehistoric People of North America* (3–5). Illus. Series: Junior Library of American Indians. 1996, Chelsea $16.95 (0-7910-2481-4); paper $9.95 (0-7910-2482-2). 80pp. The story of the people who inhabited America in prehistoric times, with material on how they survived. (Rev: BL 11/15/96; SLJ 12/96) [970.01]

14493 Corbishley, Mike. *What Do We Know About Prehistoric People?* (4–7). Illus. Series: What Do We Know About. 1996, Bedrick LB $18.95 (0-87226-383-5). 40pp. Using double-page spreads, this book explores the known facts about human prehistoric life around the world. (Rev: BL 6/1–15/96) [930.1]

14494 Deem, James M. *Bodies from the Bog* (5–8). Illus. 1998, Houghton $16.00 (0-395-85784-8). 48pp. With striking color and black-and-white photographs, this is a riveting book about the various humans from past European cultures who were mummified in bogs and discovered centuries later. (Rev: BCCB 6/98; BL 5/15/98; HBG 10/98; SLJ 4/98) [569.9]

14495 Denny, Sidney, and Ernest L. Schusky. *The Ancient Splendor of Prehistoric Cahokia* (4–8). Illus. 1997, Ozark $12.95 (1-56763-271-8); paper $3.45 (1-56763-272-6). 41pp. Using the findings from the Cahokia Mounds in southern Illinois as a beginning, the author re-creates the life and culture of these prehistoric American Indians. (Rev: BL 5/1/97) [977.3]

14496 Facchini, Fiorenzo. *Humans: Origins and Evolution* (4–8). Illus. Series: Beginnings — Origins and Evolution. 1995, Raintree Steck-Vaughn LB $24.26 (0-8114-3336-6). 48pp. Theories and facts involving human evolution are presented in a straightforward way, with extensive art work and diagrams. (Rev: BL 4/15/95; SLJ 6/95) [573.2]

14497 Gallant, Roy A. *Early Humans* (5–8). Series: The Story of Science. 1999, Benchmark LB $19.95 (0-7614-0960-2). 80pp. Neanderthals, Homo erectus, and early hominids are covered in this work on human evolution and important anthropological finds. (Rev: HBG 3/00; SLJ 3/00) [573.2]

14498 Gamlin, Linda. *Evolution* (3–6). Illus. Series: Eyewitness Science. 1993, DK $15.95 (1-56458-233-7). 64pp. A very attractive book that begins with early theories about life, continues through the work of Darwin and Mendel, and ends with a discussion about DNA and its implications for the future. (Rev: SLJ 9/93) [575]

14499 Garassino, Alessandro. *Life: Origins and Evolution* (4–8). Illus. Series: Beginnings — Origins and Evolution. 1995, Raintree Steck-Vaughn LB $24.26 (0-8114-3335-8). 48pp. Discusses the structure of plant and animal cells plus how organisms evolve and are classified. (Rev: BL 5/1/95) [575]

14500 Getz, David. *Frozen Man* (4–6). Illus. 1994, Holt $14.95 (0-8050-3261-4). 68pp. An account of the discovery of the Copper Age man frozen in the Italian Alps, how his age was determined, and the facts that could be deduced from examining the body. (Rev: BCCB 1/95; BL 11/15/94; SLJ 12/94) [937.3]

14501 Guiberson, Brenda Z. *Mummy Mysteries: Tales from North America* (4–7). Illus. by author. Series: A Redfeather Chapter Book. 1998, Holt $15.95 (0-8050-5369-7). 74pp. Reading like a mystery story, this book focuses on mummies found in North America, how and where they were found, and the information they reveal. (Rev: BCCB 2/99; HBG 3/99; SLJ 12/98) [937]

14502 Hodge, Susie. *Prehistoric Art* (3–6). Series: Art in History. 1997, Heinemann LB $13.95 (1-57572-553-3). 32pp. This book focuses on the materials and methods used by prehistoric people to create art objects in such areas as the Pacific, Africa, and North and South America. (Rev: SLJ 4/98) [930]

14503 Lauber, Patricia. *Painters of the Caves* (4–8). Illus. 1998, National Geographic $17.95 (0-7922-7095-9). 48pp. Drawing upon fossil finds and the paintings in the Chauvet cave in southeastern France, the author brilliantly re-creates life during the Stone Age. (Rev: BL 4/15/98*; HBG 10/98; SLJ 3/98*) [799.01]

14504 Lindsay, William. *Prehistoric Life* (4–8). Illus. Series: Eyewitness Books. 1994, Knopf LB $20.99 (0-679-96001-5). 64pp. Prehistoric life is described, as well as the process of evolution and the methods used by anthropologists. (Rev: BL 10/15/94; SLJ 8/94) [560]

14505 McCutcheon, Marc. *The Beast in You! Activities and Questions to Explore Evolution* (4–8). Illus. by Michael Kline. Series: A Kaleidoscope Kids Book. 1999, Williamson paper $10.95 (1-885593-36-8). 96pp. In a humorous, creative presentation, the author shows the similarities between humans and other animals and introduces the topic of evolution, our early ancestors, and their development. (Rev: SLJ 3/00) [575]

14506 MacDonald, Fiona. *The Stone Age News* (4–7). Illus. 1998, Candlewick $16.99 (0-7636-0451-8). 32pp. This oversize volume uses a newspaper format to highlight the Stone Age, including the end of the Neanderthal period. (Rev: BL 5/15/98; HBG 3/99; SLJ 6/98) [930.1]

14507 McGowen, Tom. *Giant Stones and Earth Mounds* (4–8). Illus. 2000, Millbrook LB $24.90 (0-7613-1372-9). 80pp. A history of the New Stone Age of about 9,000 years ago and the constructions that still exist in the United States today from that period. (Rev: BL 10/1/00; SLJ 10/00) [930.1]

14508 Martell, Hazel M. *Over 6,000 Years Ago: In the Stone Age* (3–6). Illus. by Chris Rothero. 1992, Macmillan LB $20.00 (0-02-762429-3). 32pp. A look at life in the Stone Age, with watercolor drawings and photos. (Rev: BL 9/15/92; SLJ 12/92) [930.12]

14509 Patent, Dorothy Hinshaw. *Mystery of the Lascaux Cave* (4–7). Series: Frozen in Time. 1998, Benchmark LB $18.95 (0-7614-0784-7). 64pp. As well as displaying these remarkable cave paintings, this book covers what is known or surmised about the prehistoric people who produced these artistic wonders. (Rev: HBG 10/99; SLJ 3/99) [930.12]

14510 Patent, Dorothy Hinshaw. *Secrets of the Ice Man* (4–7). Series: Frozen in Time. 1998, Benchmark LB $18.95 (0-7614-0782-0). 72pp. The author discusses life during the Ice Age with material from recent discoveries. (Rev: HBG 10/99; SLJ 3/99) [937]

14511 Perham, Molly, and Julian Rowe. *People* (4–6). Illus. Series: Mapworlds. 1996, Watts LB $20.00 (0-531-14362-7). 32pp. The important races of the world and their homelands are identified in an atlaslike format with many illustrations. (Rev: BL 10/15/96; SLJ 1/97) [306]

14512 Pickering, Robert. *The People* (3–5). Illus. Series: Prehistoric North America. 1996, Millbrook LB $21.90 (1-56294-550-5). 48pp. An account of the people who lived in prehistoric North America, with details on how they lived. (Rev: BL 5/15/96; SLJ 4/96) [973.01]

14513 Place, Robin. *Bodies from the Past* (4–7). Illus. Series: Digging Up the Past. 1995, Thomson Learning LB $22.78 (1-56847-397-4). 48pp. Explores the preserved remains of people around the world from burial sites in China and mummies in peat bogs to the Ice Man recently discovered in the Alps. (Rev: SLJ 2/96) [567.9]

14514 Ruiz, Andres L. *Evolution* (3–5). Illus. Series: Cycles of Life. 1997, Sterling $13.95 (0-8069-9329-4). 32pp. A step-by-step explanation of evolution, beginning with single-cell organisms and ending with the appearance of humans. (Rev: SLJ 6/97) [575]

14515 Tanaka, Shelley. *Discovering the Iceman: What Was It Like to Find a 5,300-Year-Old Mummy?* (4–7). Illus. 1997, Hyperion $16.95 (0-7868-0284-7). 48pp. The story of discovering the 5,300-year-old Iceman in the Swiss Alps in 1991 and his importance to science. (Rev: BCCB 5/97; BL 4/15/97; SLJ 6/97) [937]

14516 Unwin, David. *Prehistoric Life* (5–8). Illus. Series: Mysteries Of. 1996, Millbrook LB $22.90 (0-7613-0535-1). 40pp. In addition to discussing dinosaurs, this book gives a history of the evolution of both animals and humans. (Rev: SLJ 1/97) [575]

14517 Wilcox, Charlotte. *Mummies, Bones, and Body Parts* (4–7). Illus. 2000, Lerner $22.60 (1-57505-486-8). 64pp. The study of human remains is covered, including material on how death is treated in various cultures, embalming practices, and the work of archaeologists and anthropologists. (Rev: BCCB 9/00; BL 9/1/00; SLJ 10/00) [393]

14518 Wood, Marion. *The World of Native Americans* (2–5). Illus. 1998, Bedrick LB $19.95 (0-87226-280-4). 48pp. Traces the journey to North America of prehistoric people from across the Bering Strait, tells where they settled, and describes the eight cultural groups of American Indians. (Rev: BL 3/15/98; HBG 10/98) [970]

Archaeology

14519 Avi-Yonah, Michael. *Dig This! How Archaeologists Uncover Our Past* (5–8). Illus. Series: Buried Worlds. 1993, Lerner LB $23.93 (0-8225-3200-X). 96pp. As well as explaining what archaeologists do, this book gives a history of the profession, a glimpse at their techniques, and a look at some ancient civilizations. (Rev: BL 1/15/94; SLJ 2/94) [930.1]

14520 Barber, Nicola. *The Search for Lost Cities* (4–6). Illus. Series: Treasure Hunters. 1997, Raintree Steck-Vaughn LB $27.12 (0-8172-4840-4). 46pp. Using double-page spreads for each site, this account covers such places as Troy, Knossos, Pompeii, and Angkor Wat. (Rev: BL 11/15/97; HBG 3/98; SLJ 1/98) [909]

14521 Barber, Nicola, and Anita Ganeri. *The Search for Sunken Treasure* (4–6). Series: Treasure Hunters. 1997, Raintree Steck-Vaughn LB $27.12 (0-8172-4838-2). 46pp. This overview covers such topics as the lost treasures in sunken ships and the sacred well of Chichén Itzá, with additional material on how ancient artifacts have been recovered and what they tell us about other times. (Rev: BL 11/15/97; HBG 3/98) [930]

14522 Caselli, Giovanni. *In Search of Knossos: The Quest for the Minotaur's Labyrinth* (4–6). Illus. by author. Series: In Search Of. 2000, Bedrick $18.95 (0-87226-544-7). 44pp. This account explores the Minoan civilization on ancient Crete, tells the legend of the Minotaur, and covers the work of several archaeologists including Sir Arthur Evans. (Rev: HBG 10/00; SLJ 6/00) [931]

14523 Caselli, Giovanni. *In Search of Troy* (4–7). Illus. Series: In Search Of. 1999, Bedrick $18.95 (0-87226-542-0). 48pp. Each of the two-page spreads in this book focuses on different aspects of Heinrich Schliemann's quest to find the city of Troy and on the archaeological discoveries he made. (Rev: BL 10/15/99; HBG 3/00; SLJ 8/99) [939]

14524 Corbishley, Mike. *How Do We Know Where People Came From?* (5–8). Illus. Series: How Do We Know. 1995, Raintree Steck-Vaughn LB $22.80 (0-8114-3880-5). 41pp. The rudiments of archaeology are introduced, with discussion of such topics as Stonehenge, the Great Wall of China, and Easter Island. (Rev: SLJ 1/96) [930]

14525 Donnelly, Judy. *True-Life Treasure Hunts* (2–4). Illus. by Thomas La Padula. 1993, Random paper $3.99 (0-679-83980-1). 48pp. True stories of finding hidden treasure in all sorts of places, like sunken ships. (Rev: BL 4/1/94) [930.1]

14526 Duke, Kate. *Archaeologists Dig for Clues* (1–4). Series: Let's-Read-and-Find-Out. 1997, HarperCollins LB $15.89 (0-06-027057-8). 32pp. Archaeologist Sophie describes how her colleagues collect information and analyze their findings. (Rev: BL 12/1/96; SLJ 2/97*) [930]

14527 Ganeri, Anita. *The Search for Tombs* (4–6). Illus. Series: Treasure Hunters. 1997, Raintree Steck-Vaughn LB $27.12 (0-8172-4839-0). 46pp. This fascinating account covers such burial places as the Egyptian pyramids, the royal tombs of China, and the Roman catacombs. (Rev: BL 11/15/97; HBG 3/98; SLJ 2/98) [393]

14528 Goldenstern, Joyce. *Lost Cities* (3–6). Illus. Series: Weird and Wacky Science. 1996, Enslow LB $18.95 (0-89490-615-1). 48pp. The history and rediscovery of such lost cities as Troy, Machu Picchu, Mohenjo-daro, and Herculaneum are covered. (Rev: SLJ 6/96) [930]

14529 Holub, Joan. *How to Find Lost Treasure in All 50 States and Canada, Too!* (4–6). Illus. by author. 2000, Simon & Schuster paper $4.99 (0-689-82643-5). 182pp. There is a story of lost or buried treasure for every state and four for Canada, ranging from Inca gold to outlaw spoils. (Rev: SLJ 8/00) [930]

14530 Hoobler, Dorothy. *Lost Civilizations* (5–7). Illus. by Thomas Hoobler. 1992, Walker LB $15.85 (0-8027-8153-5). 176pp. Interesting discussion of Stonehenge, the Mound Builders, and other lost ancient civilizations. (Rev: BL 5/1/92; SLJ 9/92) [930]

14531 Jameson, W. C. *Buried Treasures of the Atlantic Coast: Legends of Sunken Pirate Treasures, Mysterious Caches, and Jinxed Ships* (4–8). Series: Buried Treasure. 1997, August House paper $11.95 (0-87483-484-8). 192pp. Describes how buried treasures were acquired and lost and the modern attempts to retrieve them. Also use *Buried Treasures of New England* (1997). (Rev: SLJ 10/97) [910.4]

14532 Kent, Peter. *A Slice Through a City* (4–8). Illus. by author. 1996, Millbrook LB $23.90 (0-7613-0039-2). 29pp. This introduction to archaeology shows cutaway views of a European city from the Stone Age to the present. (Rev: SLJ 3/97) [930]

14533 Knapp, Ron. *Mummies* (3–6). Illus. Series: Weird and Wacky Science. 1996, Enslow LB $18.95 (0-89490-618-6). 48pp. Describes how bodies have been preserved in different cultures and situations, ending with the recent discovery of the Ice Man in the Alps. (Rev: SLJ 6/96) [930]

14534 Knight, Margy B. *Talking Walls* (3–5). Illus. by Anne S. O'Brien. 1992, Tilbury $17.95 (0-88448-102-6). 40pp. Prehistoric paintings on walls in Australia and notable walls from six continents introduce children to the world and its many cultures. (Rev: BL 8/92*; SLJ 9/92) [900]

14535 Lauber, Patricia. *Tales Mummies Tell* (5–8). Illus. 1985, HarperCollins LB $17.89 (0-690-04389-9). 128pp. How people and animals were mummified and what mummies can tell scientists. (Rev: BCCB 7/85; HB 5–6/85; SLJ 8/85)

14536 McGowen, Tom. *Adventures in Archaeology* (4–8). Series: Scientific American Sourcebooks. 1997, Twenty-First Century LB $18.98 (0-8050-4688-7). 95pp. An overview of the methods and tools of the archaeologist with particular attention paid to important sites in Egypt, Greece, and Italy. (Rev: SLJ 5/98) [930]

14537 Patent, Dorothy Hinshaw. *Treasures of the Spanish Main* (4–7). Series: Frozen in Time. 1999, Benchmark LB $18.95 (0-7614-0786-3). 64pp. This book describes the sinking of Spanish galleons near the Florida Keys in the 1600s and how their excavation has brought us amazing information about life and culture in the New World at that time. (Rev: HBG 10/00; SLJ 3/00) [910.4]

14538 Reid, Struan. *The Children's Atlas of Lost Treasures* (4–7). Illus. Series: Children's Atlases. 1997, Millbrook LB $27.40 (0-7613-0219-0); paper $14.95 (0-7613-0240-9). 96pp. Using a double-page spread for each site, this book supplies a survey of the world-famous discoveries of treasures that began as religious offerings, pirate booty, and items lost in war or by natural disasters. (Rev: HBG 3/98; SLJ 3/98) [930.1]

14539 Schultz, Ron. *Looking Inside Sunken Treasure* (4–6). Illus. by Nick Gadbois and Peter Aschwanden. Series: X-Ray Vision. 1993, John Muir paper $6.95 (1-56261-074-0). 43pp. This oversized paperback describes the world of underwater archaeology. (Rev: SLJ 8/93) [930.1]

14540 Smith, K. C. *Exploring for Shipwrecks* (5–7). Series: Shipwrecks. 2000, Watts LB $24.00 (0-531-20377-8). 64pp. This book explains and explores the world of underwater archaeology, the techniques and training involved, and gives many examples from specific shipwreck studies. (Rev: BL 10/15/00) [930.1]

14541 Smith, K. C. *Shipwrecks of the Explorers* (5–7). Illus. Series: Watts Library: Shipwrecks. 2000, Watts $24.00 (0-531-20378-6); paper $8.95 (0-531-16485-3). 64pp. This look at underwater archaeology tells how scientists locate shipwrecks and what the ships reveal about the explorers who sailed in them. There are also descriptions of famous voyages like those of Columbus and Amundsen. (Rev: BL 10/15/00) [910.4]

14542 *Sunk! Exploring Underwater Archaeology* (5–8). Illus. Series: Buried Worlds. 1994, Lerner LB $23.93 (0-8225-3205-0). 72pp. An introduction to underwater archaeology that explains the methods of examining artifacts to re-create the past. (Rev: BL 10/15/94; SLJ 9/94) [930.1]

World History

General

14543 Adams, Simon, et al. *Junior Chronicle of the 20th Century: Month-by-Month History of Our Amazing Century* (5–8). Illus. 1997, DK $39.95 (0-7894-2033-3). 336pp. A collection of articles, photos, and other illustrations that cover the important events of the 20th century, with double-page spreads and a month-by-month arrangement. (Rev: SLJ 1/98) [909.82]

14544 Barber, Nicola. *The Search for Gold* (4–6). Series: Treasure Hunters. 1997, Raintree Steck-Vaughn LB $27.12 (0-8172-4837-4). 46pp. This overview covers such topics as the Spanish destruction of the Aztec and Inca cultures, the African gold trade, and the California Gold Rush. (Rev: BL 11/15/97; HBG 3/98) [900]

14545 *Children's History of the 20th Century* (4–8). Series: DK Millennium. 1999, DK $29.95 (0-7894-4722-3). 344pp. A year-by-year account of important events, illustrated with period photos and color pictures of people, places, works of art, and artifacts. (Rev: BL 11/15/99; SLJ 2/00) [909.8]

14546 Chisholm, Jane. *The Usborne Book of World History Dates: The Key Events in History* (4–8). 1998, EDC paper $22.95 (0-7460-2318-9). 194pp. Double-page spreads present a panorama of world history covering such topics as the ancient world, the Dark Ages, the Vikings, the British in India, and the Cold War. (Rev: SLJ 5/99) [910]

14547 Cooper, Kay. *Who Put the Cannon in the Courthouse Square?* (5–8). Illus. 1984, Walker LB $11.85 (0-8027-6561-0). Advice on how to become a local historian. (Rev: BL 7/85; SLJ 9/85)

14548 Funston, Sylvia. *Mummies* (5–7). Illus. by Joe Weissmann. Series: Strange Science. 2000, Owl $19.95 (1-894379-03-9); paper $9.95 (1-894379-04-7). 40pp. All kinds of mummified human remains are discussed, from those in ancient Egypt to the 1999 discovery of George Mallory's body on Mount Everest. (Rev: HBG 3/01; SLJ 11/00) [909]

14549 Garwood, Val. *The World of the Pirate* (3–6). Illus. 1998, Bedrick LB $19.95 (0-87226-281-2). 48pp. The lives of pirates are explored through history, with material on famous pirates and topics like their food and weapons. (Rev: BL 2/1/98; HBG 10/98; SLJ 1/98) [910.4]

14550 Gelber, Carol. *Masks Tell Stories* (5–7). Illus. Series: Beyond Museum Walls. 1993, Millbrook LB $23.90 (1-56294-224-7). 62pp. Explores the nature, meaning, and uses of masks in different cultures at various times. (Rev: BL 8/93) [391]

14551 Gibbons, Gail. *Pirates: Robbers of the High Seas* (2–4). Illus. 1993, Little, Brown $15.95 (0-316-30975-3). 32pp. A fascinating account that recreates the world of pirates, their swashbuckling fights, and their hidden treasures. (Rev: BCCB 9/93; BL 11/15/93; SLJ 10/93) [910.5]

14552 Gold, Susan D. *Governments of the Western Hemisphere* (5–8). Illus. Series: Comparing Continents. 1997, Twenty-First Century $21.40 (0-8050-5602-5). 96pp. Examines the struggle for independence in the United States, Canada, Mexico, Central America, and South America and the different directions each area moved toward once independence was achieved. (Rev: BL 2/1/98; SLJ 3/98) [320.3]

14553 Griffey, Harriet. *Secrets of the Mummies* (2–5). Series: Eyewitness Reader. 1998, DK $12.95 (0-7894-3764-3); paper $3.95 (0-7894-3442-3). 48pp. All kinds of mummies — from ancient Egypt to the Sicilian catacomb filled with 6,000 bodies — are covered in this effectively illustrated, intriguing book. (Rev: HBG 3/99; SLJ 1/99) [930]

14554 Harness, Cheryl. *Ghosts of the Twentieth Century* (3–5). Illus. 2000, Simon & Schuster $17.00 (0-689-82118-2). 48pp. With the ghost of Albert Einstein as a guide, a young boy time-travels to each of the decades of the 20th century and reviews significant events. (Rev: BL 11/15/99; HBG 10/00; SLJ 2/00) [909.82]

14555 Harris, Nicholas. *The Incredible Journey to the Beginning of Time* (4–7). Illus. by Andrea Ricciardi di Gaudesi and Alessandro Rabatti. 1998, Bedrick $18.95 (0-87226-293-6). 32pp. Beginning with the present and working backward, this book recounts world history in various locations and times as far back as ten billion years ago. (Rev: HBG 3/99; SLJ 3/99) [900]

14556 Horrell, Sarah. *The History of Emigration from Eastern Europe* (4–8). Series: Origins. 1998, Watts LB $20.00 (0-531-14449-6). 32pp. Seven short chapters cover emigration from Eastern Europe from the 17th century to the present and its impact on such areas as North America, Western Europe, and Israel. (Rev: HBG 10/98; SLJ 9/98) [940]

14557 Jackson, Ellen. *Turn of the Century* (3–5). Illus. by Jan Davey Ellis. 1998, Charlesbridge LB $15.95 (0-88106-369-X). 32pp. This book outlines life at the turn of each century from A.D. 1000 to the present, as seen through the eyes of a child in Great Britain and later in America. (Rev: BL 7/98*; HBG 3/99; SLJ 9/98) [305.2]

14558 Kallen, Stuart A. *Life Among the Pirates* (5–10). Series: The Way People Live. 1998, Lucent LB $17.96 (1-56006-393-9). 96pp. A fascinating history of world piracy with an emphasis on the "Golden Age" from 1519 until the 1720s. (Rev: SLJ 3/99) [910.4]

14559 Kent, Peter. *Fabulous Feasts* (3–5). Illus. by author. 1999, Millbrook LB $21.40 (0-7613-1415-6). 30pp. A lighthearted glance at special meals served at various times and places in history. (Rev: HBG 10/99; SLJ 8/99) [900]

14560 Knight, Margy B. *Talking Walls: The Stories Continue* (3–7). Illus. by Anne S. O'Brien. 1996, Tilbury $17.95 (0-88448-164-6). Double-page spreads are used to introduce some famous walls, like the dikes in the Netherlands, Hadrian's Wall, the Belfast Peace Lines, and prayer-wheel walls in India and Tibet. (Rev: SLJ 10/96) [900]

14561 Lichtenheld, Tom. *Everything I Know About Pirates: A Collection of Made-up Facts, Educated Guesses and Silly Pictures About Bad Guys of the High Seas* (PS–2). Illus. 2000, Simon & Schuster $16.00 (0-689-82625-7). 40pp. Mixed in with factual material about pirates, this fanciful book also makes some guesses about their lifestyles. (Rev: BCCB 4/00; BL 5/15/00; HBG 10/00; SLJ 5/00) [910.4]

14562 *Life: Our Century in Pictures for Young People* (5–12). Ed. by Richard B. Stolley. Illus. 2000, Little, Brown LB $25.45 (0-316-81577-2). 225pp. Adapted from an adult coffee-table book, this survey of the past century is divided into nine chronological, heavily illustrated chapters with contributions from many children's writers including Lois Lowry and Robert Cormier. (Rev: BL 12/15/00) [909.82]

14563 Maynard, Christopher. *The History News: Revolution* (4–7). Illus. 1999, Candlewick $16.99 (0-7636-0491-7). 32pp. Using a tabloid-newspaper format, this book covers four revolutions: the American, French, Russian, and Chinese. (Rev: BL 12/15/99; HBG 3/00; SLJ 10/99) [909]

14564 Meltzer, Milton. *Witches and Witch-Hunts: A History of Persecution* (5–9). 1999, Scholastic $16.95 (0-590-48517-2). 128pp. This is a record of scapegoating through history on the basis of gender, religion, or politics, beginning with witches in the Middle Ages and continuing through the 20th century to Hitler's Germany and Senator McCarthy's hearings. (Rev: BCCB 10/99; BL 11/1/99; HB 11–12/99; HBG 3/00) [303]

14565 Morgan, Kate. *The Story of Things* (3–5). Illus. by Joyce A. Zarins. 1991, Walker LB $15.85 (0-8027-6919-5). 32pp. A history of civilization in a slim volume that will attract a child's interest. (Rev: BL 6/15/91; SLJ 7/91) [523.4]

14566 Pirotta, Saviour. *Pirates and Treasure* (4–5). Illus. Series: Remarkable World. 1995, Thomson Learning LB $24.26 (1-56847-366-4). 47pp. A history of piracy from the days of the Phoenicians onward, with full-color art reproductions, maps, and many sidebars. (Rev: SLJ 1/96) [910.4]

14567 Platt, Richard. *In the Beginning: The Nearly Complete History of Almost Everything* (3–7). Illus. 1995, DK $19.95 (0-7894-0206-8). 76pp. A basic history of the world from the big bang theory to the present in a lavishly illustrated volume. (Rev: BL 12/1/95; SLJ 1/96) [909]

14568 Platt, Richard. *Pirate* (4–8). Illus. Series: Eyewitness Books. 1995, Knopf $19.00 (0-679-87255-8). 64pp. A history of piracy, with profiles of some of the major buccaneers of the past, in an account that separates truth from myth. (Rev: BL 8/95; SLJ 8/95) [364.1]

14569 Ross, Stewart. *Conquerors and Explorers* (5–7). Illus. Series: Fact or Fiction. 1996, Millbrook LB $24.90 (0-7613-0532-7). 48pp. The subtitle of this work is "The Greed, Cunning, and Bravery of the Travelers and Plunderers Who Opened Up the World." (Rev: BL 10/15/96; SLJ 4/97) [910]

14570 Ross, Stewart. *Oxford Children's Book of the 20th Century: A Concise Guide to a Century of Contrast and Change* (4–10). 1999, Oxford LB $18.95 (0-19-521488-9). 48pp. Double-page spreads cover events, people, and places important in the 20th century under such topics as "Getting and Spending" and "The Fight Against Racism." (Rev: HBG 10/99; SLJ 7/99) [909.8]

14571 Steele, Philip. *Pirates* (3–5). Illus. 1997, Kingfisher $16.95 (0-7534-5052-6). 64pp. A chronologically arranged history of piracy from Roman times through the Vikings to modern high-jackings. (Rev: HBG 3/98; SLJ 5/97) [910]

14572 Stienecker, David L. *Countries* (2–5). Series: Discovering Geography. 1997, Marshall Cavendish LB $22.79 (0-7614-0542-9). 32pp. Basic geographical concepts are explored in a question-and-answer format. (Rev: BL 2/15/98; HBG 3/98) [910]

14573 Weitzman, David. *My Backyard History Book* (4–7). Illus. by James Robertson. 1975, Little, Brown paper $13.95 (0-316-92902-6). 128pp. A guide to re-creating history that occurred close to home by interviewing, for example, family and friends.

14574 Williams, Brian. *The Modern World: From the French Revolution to the Computer Age* (5–8). Illus. by James Field. Series: Timelink. 1994, Bedrick LB $18.95 (0-87226-312-6). 64pp. An overview of the 200 years of world history that outlines major events, with useful timelines and maps. (Rev: SLJ 1/95) [909]

14575 Williams, Brian, and Brenda Williams. *The Age of Discovery: From the Renaissance to American Independence* (5–8). Illus. by James Field. Series: Timelink. 1994, Bedrick LB $18.95 (0-87226-311-8). 64pp. An overview of world history from the Renaissance through the American Revolution presented in 50-year segments. (Rev: SLJ 1/95) [909]

14576 Wilson, Janet. *Imagine That!* (4–8). Illus. by author. 2000, Stoddart $14.95 (0-7737-3221-7). In the form of a reminiscence by 100-year-old Auntie Violet, this is a brief history of the past century, with major events highlighted. (Rev: SLJ 11/00) [909]

Ancient History

General and Miscellaneous

14577 Adams, Simon. *Visual Timeline of the 20th Century* (5–8). Illus. 1996, DK $15.95 (0-7894-0997-6). 48pp. Important events in the 20th century are described in chronological order. (Rev: BL 12/1/96; SLJ 1/97) [909.8]

14578 Ash, Russell. *Great Wonders of the World* (4–7). Illus. by Richard Bonson. Series: Eyewitness Books. 2000, DK $19.95 (0-7894-6505-1). 64pp. The seven wonders of the ancient world are presented with material comparing them to other ancient and modern technological marvels. (Rev: SLJ 9/00) [930]

14579 Avikian, Monique. *The Mejii Restoration and the Rise of Modern Japan* (5–8). Illus. Series: Turning Points. 1991, Silver Burdett LB $14.95 (0-382-24132-0); paper $7.95 (0-382-24139-8). 64pp. The major factors that led to Japan's economic superiority are discussed. (Rev: BL 3/15/92) [952.03]

14580 Burrell, Roy. *Oxford First Ancient History* (4–7). Illus. 1994, Oxford $37.95 (0-19-521058-1). 320pp. A survey of ancient civilizations, particularly those of the Mediterranean but also including the Chinese and Assyrians. (Rev: BL 7/94) [930]

14581 Carlson, Laurie. *Classical Kids: An Activity Guide to Life in Ancient Greece and Rome* (4–6). Illus. by Fran Lee. 1998, Chicago Review paper $14.95 (1-55652-290-8). 186pp. After background information on these two civilizations, there are many projects under such categories as eating, dressing up, and the arts. (Rev: SLJ 1/99) [930]

14582 De Angelis, Therese. *Wonders of the Ancient World* (5–8). Illus. Series: Costume, Tradition, and Culture: Reflecting on the Past. 1998, Chelsea LB $16.95 (0-7910-5170-6). 64pp. This work features, in double-page spreads, such wonders as the Great Pyramids, Easter Island, and Stonehenge. (Rev: BL 3/15/99; HBG 10/99) [930]

14583 Greene, Jacqueline D. *Slavery in Ancient Egypt and Mesopotamia* (4–7). Series: Watts Library: History of Slavery. 2000, Watts LB $24.00 (0-531-11692-1). 64pp. This unusual book covers the earliest forms of slavery, how the pharaohs used

slaves to construct the pyramids, and the place of slavery in Hebrew society. (Rev: BL 3/1/01; SLJ 3/01) [930]

14584 Greene, Jacqueline D. *Slavery in Ancient Greece and Rome* (4–7). Series: Watts Library: History of Slavery. 2000, Watts LB $24.00 (0-531-11693-X). 64pp. Topics covered include the treatment of slaves in Greece and Rome, how they thrived in Greece's democracy, the slave fire brigades, battles of slave gladiators, and the attitudes toward slavery in the early Christian church. (Rev: BL 3/1/01; SLJ 3/01) [930]

14585 Gregory, Tony. *The Dark Ages* (4–7). Illus. 1993, Facts on File $21.95 (0-8160-2787-0). 78pp. Beginning with human evolution, this account traces the history of early settlements to about 200 B.C. (Rev: SLJ 7/93) [938]

14586 Jessop, Joanne. *The X-Ray Picture Book of Big Buildings of the Ancient World* (2–6). Illus. 1994, Watts LB $25.00 (0-531-14286-8). 48pp. This handsomely illustrated book shows cutaway views of such structures as the Great Pyramid, the Parthenon, the Coliseum, Notre Dame, Mont St. Michel, and the Taj Mahal. (Rev: BL 6/1–15/94; SLJ 7/94) [720]

14587 Lye, Keith. *The World Today* (4–6). Illus. 1986, Facts on File $15.95 (0-8160-1072-2). 64pp. This large-size volume gives an overview of communication and transportation links. (Rev: BL 8/86)

14588 MacDonald, Fiona. *Women in a Changing World: 1945–2000* (4–6). Series: The Other Half of History. 2001, Bedrick $17.95 (0-87226-572-2). 48pp. Traces the position of women in the United States and England from the 1950s to the present. This book is preceded by *Women in Peace and War: 1900–1950* (2001). (Rev: SLJ 3/01) [909]

14589 MacDonald, Fiona. *Women in 19th-Century Europe* (4–8). Series: The Other Half of History. 1999, Bedrick $17.95 (0-87226-565-X). 48pp. Describes women's progress and contributions in 19th-century Europe and gives biographies of famous women of the time. (Rev: HBG 3/00; SLJ 11/99) [940.2]

14590 Martell, Hazel M. *The Kingfisher Book of the Ancient World: From the Ice Age to the Fall of Rome* (4–8). Illus. 1995, Kingfisher $24.95 (1-85697-565-7). 160pp. Presents ancient civilizations from 11 areas, like the Americas, Africa, and the Mediterranean. (Rev: BL 2/1/96; SLJ 1/96) [930]

14591 Nardo, Don. *Greek and Roman Science* (5–8). Series: World History. 1997, Lucent LB $17.96 (1-56006-317-3). 128pp. A concise account that outlines the contributions of the Greeks and Romans in such scientific fields as math, medicine, astronomy, and the development of writing. (Rev: SLJ 5/98) [930]

14592 Nardo, Don. *Greek and Roman Sport* (5–10). Series: World History. 1999, Lucent LB $17.96 (1-56006-436-6). 112pp. A very detailed account, using many quotes from classical sources, that gives a realistic picture of the place of sports in both ancient Greece and Rome, the different events, and the rewards and hardships of participants. (Rev: SLJ 8/99) [930]

14593 Odijk, Pamela. *The Phoenicians* (4–7). Illus. Series: Ancient World. 1989, Silver Burdett LB $14.95 (0-382-09891-9). 48pp. The ancient traders of the Mediterranean Sea are introduced. (Rev: BL 1/15/90; SLJ 5/90) [939.44]

14594 Smith, K. C. *Ancient Shipwrecks* (5–7). Series: Shipwrecks. 2000, Watts LB $24.00 (0-531-20381-6). 64pp. From the Bronze Age through the Roman Empire, this volume explores the fascinating stories behind ancient wrecks found in the Mediterranean and explored by archaeologists. (Rev: BL 10/15/00) [930]

14595 Steins, Richard. *The Postwar Years: The Cold War and the Atomic Age (1950–1959)* (5–8). Series: First Person America. 1994, Twenty-First Century LB $18.90 (0-8050-2587-1). 64pp. Coverage of the 1950s includes first-person material on the Cold War, the Korean conflict, and developments on the home front. (Rev: SLJ 12/94) [940.55]

14596 Waldman, Neil. *Masada* (4–6). Illus. 1998, Morrow $16.00 (0-688-14481-0). 64pp. The story of the Masada fortress, built in the first century B.C. and captured by the Romans in 72–73 A.D. Rather than surrender, the Jewish defenders committed suicide. (Rev: BCCB 10/98; BL 10/1/98; HBG 3/99; SLJ 11/98) [933]

14597 Wilkinson, Philip, and Jacqueline Dineen. *The Mediterranean* (4–7). Illus. by Robert Ingpen. Series: Mysterious Places. 1994, Chelsea LB $19.95 (0-7910-2751-1). 92pp. Ten sites around the Mediterranean are investigated, including Knossos, Rhodes, Delphi, Mistra, the Topkapi Palace, and Hagia Sophia. (Rev: BL 1/15/94; SLJ 5/94) [930.3]

14598 Woods, Michael, and Mary Woods. *Ancient Agriculture: From Foraging to Farming* (5–8). Series: Ancient Technologies. 2000, Runestone $25.26 (0-8225-2995-5). 88pp. Beginning with prehistoric food-gathering peoples, this book traces the history of plant cultivation and agriculture through each of the great ancient civilizations. (Rev: BL 8/00; HBG 10/00; SLJ 6/00) [630]

14599 Woods, Michael, and Mary Woods. *Ancient Machines from Wedges to Waterwheels* (5–8). Series: Ancient Technologies. 1999, Lerner $25.26 (0-8225-2994-7). 88pp. This heavily illustrated account describes the important machines that came into being from ancient history to the fall of the Western Roman Empire. (Rev: BL 1/1–15/00; HBG 10/00; SLJ 6/00) [936]

14600 Woods, Michael, and Mary B. Woods. *Ancient Medicine: From Sorcery to Surgery* (5–8). Illus. Series: Ancient Technologies. 2000, Lerner $25.26 (0-8225-2992-0). 88pp. Medical practices in ancient times and cultures — the Stone Age, ancient Egypt, and early Hindu cultures, for example — are discussed in this volume. (Rev: BL 1/1–15/00; HBG 10/00) [610]

14601 Woods, Michael, and Mary B. Woods. *Ancient Transportation: From Camels to Canals* (5–8). Illus. Series: Ancient Technologies. 2000, Lerner $25.26 (0-8225-2993-9). 88pp. This book covers such topics related to early transportation as the first bridges and roads, early skis and sleds, primitive wagons, and the beginnings of maps. (Rev: BL 1/1–15/00; HBG 10/00; SLJ 6/00) [629.04]

Egypt and Mesopotamia

14602 Alcraft, Rob. *Valley of the Kings* (5–7). Series: Visiting the Past. 1999, Heinemann LB $16.95 (1-57572-860-5). 32pp. This account uses double-page spreads to cover topics like the history, landscape, beliefs, and daily life of the ancient Egyptians. (Rev: SLJ 3/00) [932]

14603 Aliki. *Mummies Made in Egypt* (3–5). Illus. by author. 1979, HarperCollins LB $15.89 (0-690-03859-3); paper $6.95 (0-06-446011-8). 32pp. The burial practices and beliefs of the ancient Egyptians are explored in text and handsome illustrations.

14604 Anderson, Scoular. *A Puzzling Day in the Land of the Pharaohs* (3–8). Illus. by author. 1996, Candlewick $14.99 (1-56402-877-1). A picture puzzle book that features different aspects of life in ancient Egypt in double-page spreads. (Rev: SLJ 10/96) [932]

14605 Angeletti, Roberta. *Nefertari, Princess of Egypt* (3–5). Illus. by author. Series: A Journey Through Time. 1999, Oxford $16.95 (0-19-521507-9). 29pp. In this picture book Anna time-travels to ancient Egypt and learns about the gods and goddesses and a little about the general culture. (Rev: HBG 3/00; SLJ 9/99) [299]

14606 Bailey, Linda. *Adventures in Ancient Egypt* (2–5). Illus. Series: Good Times Travel Agency. 2000, Kids Can $14.95 (1-55074-546-8); paper $7.95 (1-55074-548-4). 48pp. Using an old travel guide, three children are transported to Egypt in 2500 B.C. where they become acquainted with the sights and sites as well as becoming involved in a series of adventures. (Rev: BL 1/1–15/01; HBG 3/01; SLJ 12/00) [932]

14607 Balkwill, Richard. *Clothes and Crafts in Ancient Egypt* (4–6). Series: Clothing and Crafts in History. 2000, Gareth Stevens LB $21.27 (0-8368-2733-3). 32pp. As well as coverage on ancient Egyptian painting, pottery, carving, clothes, and jewelry, this book gives step-by-step instructions for several craft projects including making a snake game and fashioning a clay pot. (Rev: BL 1/1–15/01) [932]

14608 Barker, Henry. *Egyptian Gods and Goddesses* (1–3). Illus. by Jeff Crosby. Series: All Aboard Reading. 1999, Grosset LB $13.89 (0-448-42029-5); paper $3.99 (0-448-42081-3). This beginning reader introduces the religion of the ancient Egyptians, their fascination with death, and such gods and goddesses as Horus, Re, Osiris, and Isis. (Rev: SLJ 2/00) [932]

14609 Berger, Melvin, and Gilda Berger. *Mummies of the Pharaohs: Exploring the Valley of the Kings* (4–7). Illus. 2001, National Geographic $17.95 (0-7922-7223-4). 64pp. Beginning with King Tut's tomb and continuing through other sites, this book uses stunning photos and a clear text to describe workings of archaeological digs that are studying Egypt's past. (Rev: BL 2/1/01) [932]

14610 Broida, Marian. *Ancient Egyptians and Their Neighbors: An Activity Guide* (4–8). Illus. 1999, Chicago Review paper $16.95 (1-55652-360-2). 208pp. The lives and times of the ancient Egyptians, Nubians, Hittites, and Mesopotamians are examined using text and a series of 40 fascinating projects. (Rev: BL 3/15/00; SLJ 2/00) [939]

14611 Caselli, Giovanni. *In Search of Tutankhamun: The Discovery of a King's Tomb* (4–7). Series: In Search Of. 1999, Bedrick $18.95 (0-87226-543-9). 48pp. As well as supplying information on King Tut's tomb, this heavily illustrated book supplies good general material on the culture and history of the ancient Egyptian civilization. (Rev: BL 10/15/99; HBG 3/00; SLJ 8/99) [932]

14612 Chapman, Gillian. *The Egyptians* (4–8). Series: Crafts from the Past. 1997, Heinemann LB $14.95 (1-57572-556-8). 37pp. This book contains many appealing and inventive projects related to the life and culture of the ancient Egyptians. (Rev: SLJ 4/98) [932]

14613 Clare, John D., ed. *Pyramids of Ancient Egypt* (4–6). Illus. Series: Living History. 1992, Harcourt $16.95 (0-15-200509-9). 64pp. Besides telling about the building of the Pyramids, this book uses human models to describe the daily life of the ancient Egyptians. (Rev: SLJ 10/92) [932]

14614 Clarke, Sue. *The Tombs of the Pharaohs: A Three-Dimensional Discovery* (2–5). Illus. 1994, Hyperion $16.95 (1-56282-485-6). 10pp. In this interactive book shaped like a pyramid, pop-ups and flaps are used to introduce topics involving ancient Egypt. (Rev: BL 11/15/94) [932]

14615 Cooper, Roscoe. *The Great Pyramid: An Interactive Book* (PS–K). Illus. by Carolyn Croll. 1998, Troll $18.95 (0-8167-4390-8). This pyramid-shaped book, with many pop-ups, traces the building of King Khufu's pyramid from the beginning to his mummification. (Rev: BL 1/1–15/99) [932]

14616 Crosher, Judith. *Ancient Egypt* (4–6). Illus. Series: See Through History. 1993, Viking $19.99 (0-670-84755-0). 48pp. A visually interesting introduction to the history and accomplishments of the ancient Egyptians. (Rev: BL 4/15/93; SLJ 8/93) [932]

14617 Crosher, Judith. *Technology in the Time of Ancient Egypt* (4–8). Series: Technology in the Time Of. 1998, Raintree Steck-Vaughn LB $25.69 (0-8172-4875-7). 48pp. Each double-page spread presents another aspect of technology in ancient Egypt in such areas as food production, transportation, and building. (Rev: HBG 10/98; SLJ 3/99) [932]

14618 David, Rosalie. *Growing Up in Ancient Egypt* (3–5). Illus. by Angus McBride. Series: Growing Up In. 1993, Troll paper $4.95 (0-8167-2718-X). 32pp. Everyday life in the different social classes of ancient Egypt is covered, with a focus on children and their upbringing. (Rev: BL 1/15/94) [932]

14619 Day, Nancy. *Your Travel Guide to Ancient Egypt* (4–8). Series: Passport to History. 2000, Runestone LB $26.60 (0-8225-3075-9). 96pp. Written in the style of a modern-day travel guide, this book on ancient Egypt covers such subjects as sites

to see, food, clothing, religious beliefs, politics, and daily life. (Rev: BL 11/15/00; HBG 3/01) [932]

14620 Deem, James M. *How to Make a Mummy Talk* (4–7). Illus. 1995, Houghton $14.95 (0-395-62427-4). 192pp. All kinds of mummies are introduced, with background history of the times in which they were created. (Rev: BCCB 10/95; BL 9/15/95; SLJ 9/95) [393]

14621 Delafosse, Claude, and Philippe Biard. *Pyramids* (PS–2). Illus. by authors. Series: First Discovery. 1995, Scholastic $12.95 (0-590-42786-5). Describes how the pyramids of Egypt were built, as well as mummification and the seven wonders of the ancient world. (Rev: SLJ 3/96) [932]

14622 Dobson, Mary. *Mouldy Mummies* (3–6). Series: Smelly Old History. 1998, Oxford paper $7.95 (0-19-910495-6). 32pp. Through cartoons and scratch-and-sniff patches, readers experience such stenches as moldy mummies, a dung pile, and a pharaoh's stinky feet. (Rev: SLJ 4/99) [932]

14623 Donoughue, Carol. *The Mystery of the Hieroglyphs: The Story of the Rosetta Stone and the Race to Decipher Egyptian Hieroglyphs* (3–6). Illus. 1999, Oxford LB $18.95 (0-19-521553-2). 48pp. This book tells how the Rosetta Stone was discovered, discusses its significance, describes how Egyptians wrote, and provides a lesson in reading hieroglyphs. (Rev: BL 12/1/99; HBG 3/00; SLJ 10/99) [493.1]

14624 Fisher, Leonard Everett. *The Gods and Goddesses of Ancient Egypt* (3–5). Illus. 1997, Holiday LB $16.95 (0-8234-1286-5). 32pp. With accompanying stories, this book introduces 13 Egyptian deities, including Horus and Osiris. (Rev: BL 12/1/97; HBG 3/98; SLJ 11/97) [299]

14625 Frank, John. *The Tomb of the Boy King* (K–3). Illus. by Tom Pohrt. 2001, Farrar $16.00 (0-374-37674-3). 32pp. Using free verse, the author first tells about the boy king, Tutankhamen, and then describes the expedition that discovered his tomb and the wonders that were found inside. (Rev: BL 3/1/01) [932.014]

14626 Giblin, James Cross. *The Riddle of the Rosetta Stone: Key to Ancient Egypt* (5–7). Illus. 1990, HarperCollins LB $15.89 (0-690-04799-1). 96pp. Beginning with the British museum, where the Rosetta Stone is now, this is an explanation of its importance. (Rev: BCCB 11/90; BL 9/15/90*; HB 11–12/90; SLJ 9/90) [493]

14627 Grant, Neil, ed. *The Egyptians* (4–6). Illus. Series: Spotlights. 1996, Oxford paper $11.95 (0-19-521239-8). 46pp. Double-page spreads are used to introduce such topics about ancient Egypt as its history, culture, social life, religion, and political organization. (Rev: SLJ 9/96) [932]

14628 Harris, Nathaniel. *Mummies* (4–7). Illus. Series: A Very Peculiar History. 1995, Watts LB $23.00 (0-531-14354-6). 48pp. This account explores the process of mummification and embalming of bodies from ancient Egypt through the ages. (Rev: BL 6/1–15/95; SLJ 7/95) [393.3]

14629 Hart, Avery, and Paul Mantell. *Pyramids! 50 Hands-on Activities to Experience Ancient Egypt*

(3–5). Illus. Series: Kaleidoscope Kids. 1997, Williamson paper $10.95 (1-885593-10-4). 96pp. Some of the craft projects that explore the culture of ancient Egypt are building model pyramids, writing messages in hieroglyphics, and preparing clothes, food, and games for an Egyptian costume party. (Rev: BL 11/15/97) [932]

14630 Hart, George, ed. *Ancient Egypt* (4–6). Illus. Series: Nature Company Discoveries. 1995, Time Life $16.00 (0-7835-4763-3). 64pp. A handsomely designed book with a brief text that introduces the history and accomplishments of the people of ancient Egypt. (Rev: BL 1/1–15/96; SLJ 1/96) [932]

14631 Hodge, Susie. *Ancient Egyptian Art* (3–6). Series: Art in History. 1997, Heinemann LB $13.95 (1-57572-550-9). 32pp. This book presents the art of ancient Egypt as a reflection of its culture in such areas as religion and science. (Rev: HBG 3/98; SLJ 4/98) [932]

14632 Honan, Linda. *Spend the Day in Ancient Egypt: Projects and Activities That Bring the Past to Life* (3–6). Illus. by Ellen Kosmer. 1999, Wiley paper $12.95 (0-471-29006-8). 116pp. Craft projects and other activities are used to introduce the culture and everyday of the ancient Egyptians. (Rev: SLJ 1/00) [932]

14633 James, Louise. *How We Know About the Egyptians* (3–6). Series: How We Know About. 1998, Bedrick $0.00 (0-87226-236-6). 32pp. Using double-page spreads, this work focuses on ancient Egypt and explains the detective-like work of archaeologists and others who have increased our knowledge of this civilization. (Rev: BL 5/15/98) [932]

14634 Katan, Norma Jean, and Barbara Mintz. *Hieroglyphics: The Writing of Ancient Egypt* (4–6). Illus. 1981, Macmillan $16.00 (0-689-50176-5). 96pp. A fine introduction that includes material on the Rosetta Stone and how to draw and decipher hieroglyphics.

14635 Landau, Elaine. *The Assyrians* (4–6). Series: Cradle of Civilization. 1997, Millbrook LB $21.40 (0-7613-0217-4). 64pp. This overview of the Assyrian civilization stresses its history, rulers, and lasting contributions. (Rev: BL 1/1–15/98; HBG 3/98; SLJ 3/98) [932]

14636 Landau, Elaine. *The Babylonians* (4–6). Illus. Series: Cradle of Civilization. 1997, Millbrook LB $21.40 (0-7613-0216-6). 64pp. The history, religion, and contributions of this early civilization that invented the wheel and was the first to establish laws and government. (Rev: BL 1/1–15/98; HBG 3/98; SLJ 3/98) [935]

14637 Landau, Elaine. *The Curse of Tutankhamen* (4–6). Illus. Series: Mysteries of Science. 1996, Millbrook LB $20.90 (0-7613-0014-7). 48pp. The story of the discovery of King Tut's tomb and of the curse that supposedly plagued the archaeologists that were involved. (Rev: BL 10/15/96; SLJ 11/96) [931]

14638 Landau, Elaine. *The Sumerians* (4–6). Illus. Series: Cradle of Civilization. 1997, Millbrook LB $21.40 (0-7613-0215-8). 64pp. An overview of the Sumerians, their rulers and gods, and their contribu-

tions to science, government, and the arts. (Rev: BL 1/1–15/98; HBG 3/98; SLJ 3/98) [935]

14639 Macaulay, David. *Pyramid* (5–8). Illus. by author. 1975, Houghton $18.00 (0-395-21407-6). 80pp. The engineering and architectural feats of the Egyptians are explored with detailed drawings.

14640 MacDonald, Fiona. *Women in Ancient Egypt* (4–7). Series: The Other Half of History. 1999, Bedrick $17.95 (0-87226-567-6). 48pp. A colorful account that uses double-page spreads to describe the status of women in ancient Egypt and detail their contributions and occupations. (Rev: HBG 3/00; SLJ 2/00) [932]

14641 Malam, John. *Ancient Egypt* (5–8). Series: Remains to Be Seen. 1998, Evans Brothers $19.95 (0-237-51839-2). 47pp. This introduction to ancient Egypt is organized in double-page spreads and is noteworthy for its many sidebars, charts, and illustrations. (Rev: SLJ 9/98) [932]

14642 Malam, John. *Mesopotamia and the Fertile Crescent: 10,000 to 539 B.C.* (5–8). Series: Looking Back. 1999, Raintree Steck-Vaughn LB $25.69 (0-8172-5434-X). 32pp. The story of the ancient civilizations that grew up in the rich area around the Tigris and Euphrates rivers. (Rev: BL 5/15/99; SLJ 7/99) [930]

14643 Mann, Elizabeth. *The Great Pyramid* (4–7). Illus. Series: Wonders of the World. 1996, Mikaya $19.95 (0-9650493-1-0). 48pp. The building of this architectural marvel is told graphically, with details on the society of ancient Egypt. (Rev: BL 2/1/97; SLJ 6/97*) [932]

14644 Marston, Elsa. *The Ancient Egyptians* (5–8). Illus. Series: Cultures of the Past. 1995, Benchmark LB $28.50 (0-7614-0073-7). 80pp. A history of ancient Egypt that tells how the people lived and gives information on the various dynasties and the Egyptian religion. (Rev: SLJ 6/96) [932]

14645 Martell, Hazel M. *The Great Pyramid* (3–5). Illus. Series: Great Buildings. 1997, Raintree Steck-Vaughn LB $27.12 (0-8172-4918-4). 48pp. This title answers questions concerning why, when, where, and how the Great Pyramid in Egypt was built. (Rev: BL 11/15/97; HBG 3/98) [932]

14646 Millard, Anne. *The World of the Pharaoh* (4–6). Illus. by Louis R. Galante. Series: The World Of. 1998, Bedrick $19.95 (0-87226-292-8). 48pp. This book describes how ancient Egypt was ruled, with material on the power of the pharaohs, priests, viziers, and members of the royal family. (Rev: HBG 3/99; SLJ 1/99) [932]

14647 Milton, Joyce. *Mummies* (2–3). Illus. by Susan Swan. 1996, Putnam paper $3.99 (0-448-41325-6). 48pp. The purpose and process of mummification are explained, with special reference to ancient Egypt. (Rev: BL 11/15/96; SLJ 6/97) [932]

14648 Montavon, Jay. *The Curse of King Tut's Tomb* (3–5). Illus. 1991, Avon paper $3.50 (0-380-76220-X). 96pp. Tells about King Tut and the discovery of his tomb, but focuses on the supposed curse that was associated with its opening. (Rev: BL 9/15/91) [932]

14649 Morley, Jacqueline. *An Egyptian Pyramid* (4–6). Illus. by Mark Bergin and John James. Series: Inside Story. 1991, Bedrick $18.95 (0-87226-346-0). 32pp. This work explains how pyramids were built and their purposes and parts. (Rev: BL 11/15/91; SLJ 12/91) [932]

14650 Morley, Jacqueline. *How Would You Survive as an Ancient Egyptian?* (4–7). Illus. Series: How Would You Survive? 1995, Watts LB $25.00 (0-531-14345-7). 48pp. Everyday life in Egypt of 1500 B.C. is covered, with material on the preparation of mummies, crops harvested, and the types of food eaten. (Rev: BL 6/1–15/95; SLJ 8/95) [932]

14651 Morley, Jacqueline. *The Living Tomb* (3–6). Illus. Series: Magnifications. 2000, Bedrick $18.95 (0-87226-651-6). 48pp. Information on early Egyptian temples, tombs, and mummification is presented on double-page spreads; enlargements of parts of illustrations are used effectively. (Rev: BL 10/15/00; HBG 3/01; SLJ 1/01) [932]

14652 Morris, Neil. *Ancient Egypt* (4–6). Illus. 2000, Bedrick $16.95 (0-87226-617-6). The daily life, culture, buildings, and accomplishments of the ancient Egyptians are covered in this attractive volume. (Rev: HBG 3/01; SLJ 1/01) [932]

14653 Morris, Neil. *The Atlas of Ancient Egypt* (4–8). Series: Atlas. 2000, Bedrick $19.95 (0-87226-610-9). 59pp. Using many illustrations as well as maps, this is an attractive, colorful account of ancient Egypt that covers history, people, culture, lifestyles, and geography. (Rev: HBG 3/01; SLJ 3/01) [932]

14654 Moscovitch, Arlene. *Egypt, the Culture* (4–6). Series: Lands, Peoples, and Cultures. 2000, Crabtree LB $15.45 (0-86505-234-4); paper $7.16 (0-86505-314-6). 32pp. This book deals with the culture of ancient Egypt, the accomplishments of its people and their religious beliefs. (Rev: SLJ 7/00) [932]

14655 Moss, Carol. *Science in Ancient Mesopotamia* (4–6). Illus. Series: Science of the Past. 1998, Watts LB $24.00 (0-531-20364-6). 64pp. This work outlines the amazing contributions made to world science by the ancient Mesopotamians and the impact these findings have on the world today. (Rev: BL 12/1/98; HBG 3/99; SLJ 11/98) [509.35]

14656 Odijk, Pamela. *The Egyptians* (4–7). Illus. Series: Ancient World. 1989, Silver Burdett LB $14.95 (0-382-09886-2). 48pp. An introduction to the history of ancient Egypt. (Rev: BL 1/15/90; SLJ 5/90) [932]

14657 Odijk, Pamela. *The Sumerians* (4–7). Illus. Series: Ancient World. 1990, Silver Burdett LB $14.95 (0-382-09892-7). 48pp. History and contributions of the Sumerians in the Fertile Crescent. (Rev: BL 11/1/90; SLJ 1/91) [935.01]

14658 Payne, Elizabeth. *The Pharaohs of Ancient Egypt* (6–8). Illus. 1981, Random paper $5.99 (0-394-84699-0). 42pp. A fascinating study of this important period in Egyptian history.

14659 Perl, Lila. *Mummies, Tombs, and Treasure: Secrets of Ancient Egypt* (5–7). Illus. 1987, Houghton $16.00 (0-89919-407-9). 128pp. An inviting look at the fascinating preservation techniques of the early Egyptians. (Rev: BCCB 6/87; BL 6/15/87; SLJ 8/87)

14660 Putnam, James. *Pyramid* (4–6). Illus. Series: Eyewitness Books. 1994, Knopf LB $20.99 (0-679-96170-4). 63pp. Using color photos, the author introduces pyramids in many countries, including Egypt, Mexico, and Nubia. (Rev: SLJ 12/94) [932]

14661 Quie, Sarah. *The Myths and Civilization of the Ancient Egyptians* (4–8). Illus. by Ivan Stalio and Francesca D'Ottavi. Series: Myths and Civilization. 1999, Bedrick LB $16.95 (0-87226-282-0). 44pp. Each of the important myths of ancient Egypt is presented, followed by an extensive section on related topics involving the culture, history, and accomplishments of the Egyptians. (Rev: HBG 10/99; SLJ 3/99) [932]

14662 Rees, Rosemary. *The Ancient Egyptians* (3–4). Illus. Series: Understanding People in the Past. 1997, Heinemann $22.79 (0-431-07789-4). 64pp. Photos of museum artifacts plus maps, diagrams, and drawings are used liberally to introduce such topics about the ancient Egyptians as their pharaohs, gods, history, pyramids, and mummies. (Rev: SLJ 9/97) [932]

14663 Russmann, Edna R. *Nubian Kingdoms* (5–7). Series: African Civilizations. 1999, Watts LB $22.00 (0-531-20283-6). 64pp. Although somewhat dry in its presentation, this account offers interesting information on the culture and people of ancient Nubia, a state to the south of Egypt. (Rev: HBG 10/99; SLJ 8/99) [932]

14664 Shuter, Jane. *Ancient Egypt* (4–6). Series: History Beneath Your Feet. 1999, Raintree Steck-Vaughn LB $25.69 (0-8172-5751-9). 48pp. This work on ancient Egypt covers topics including burials, pyramids, mummies, hieroglyphs, temples, tombs, and towns plus coverage on how archaeologists have accumulated these facts. (Rev: HBG 10/00; SLJ 3/00) [932]

14665 Shuter, Jane. *The Ancient Egyptians* (3–5). Series: History Starts Here! 2000, Raintree Steck-Vaughn LB $22.83 (0-7398-1351-X). 32pp. This overview of ancient Egypt includes material on history, culture, daily life, structures, and religion. (Rev: HBG 10/00; SLJ 7/00) [932]

14666 Shuter, Jane. *Egypt* (5–10). Illus. Series: Ancient World. 1998, Raintree Steck-Vaughn LB $27.12 (0-8172-5058-1). 64pp. Ancient Egypt's mysterious hieroglyphs, treasure-filled tombs, puzzling pyramid construction, and embalming techniques as well as its history, politics, ideas, religion, art, architecture, science, and everyday life are covered in this introductory volume. (Rev: BL 1/1–15/99; HBG 3/99; SLJ 3/99) [932]

14667 Steedman, Scott. *The Egyptian News* (4–6). Illus. 1997, Candlewick $15.99 (1-56402-873-9). 32pp. Using a modern newspaper format, this book describes life in ancient Egypt and covers topics like the pyramids, mummies, and pharaohs. (Rev: BL 7/97; SLJ 9/97) [932]

14668 Steedman, Scott. *Egyptian Town* (4–6). Illus. Series: Metropolis. 1998, Watts LB $24.00 (0-531-14466-6). 48pp. A heavily illustrated volume that provides information on everyday life in ancient Egypt, focusing on such topics as food, climate, buildings, sports, and shopping. (Rev: BL 4/15/98; HBG 10/98) [932]

14669 Steele, Philip. *The Best Book of Mummies* (3–6). Series: The Best Book Of. 1998, Kingfisher $10.95 (0-7534-5132-8). 33pp. This book of ancient Egypt gives a step-by-step glimpse at the process of mummification and also includes Egyptian tomb descriptions. (Rev: HBG 3/99; SLJ 10/98) [932]

14670 Steele, Philip. *The Egyptians and the Valley of the Kings* (4–6). Illus. Series: Hidden Worlds. 1994, Dillon $16.95 (0-87518-539-8). 32pp. Some of the topics covered are mummification, hieroglyphics, the Rosetta Stone, and archaeological findings. (Rev: SLJ 12/94) [932]

14671 Tagholm, Sally. *Ancient Egypt: A Guide to Egypt in the Time of the Pharaohs* (4–7). Series: Sightseers. 1999, Kingfisher $8.95 (0-7534-5182-4). 31pp. In the form of a tourist guide to ancient Egypt, this book tells the traveler what to wear, see, eat, and buy. (Rev: HBG 10/99; SLJ 8/99) [932]

14672 Trumble, Kelly. *Cat Mummies* (3–6). Illus. 1996, Clarion $15.95 (0-395-68707-1). 50pp. An introduction to the place of cats in ancient Egypt and to the process of mummification. (Rev: BCCB 10/96; BL 9/15/96; SLJ 8/96) [932]

14673 Woods, Geraldine. *Science in Ancient Egypt* (4–7). Series: Science of the Past. 1998, Watts LB $24.00 (0-531-20341-7). 64pp. The many contributions to science by the ancient Egyptians, including architecture, astronomy, and mathematics, are outlined in this richly illustrated volume. (Rev: BL 6/1–15/98; HBG 10/98; SLJ 6/98) [509]

Greece

14674 Chapman, Gillian. *The Greeks* (4–7). Series: Crafts from the Past. 1998, Heinemann LB $16.95 (1-57572-733-1). 39pp. Double-page spreads each outline a project inspired by an art object, i.e. a Greek vase yields papier-mâché pottery. (Rev: SLJ 2/99) [938]

14675 Chrisp, Peter. *The Parthenon* (3–5). Illus. Series: Great Buildings. 1997, Raintree Steck-Vaughn LB $27.12 (0-8172-4917-6). 48pp. The original architecture and appearance of the Parthenon is covered, as well as later history, when it became a Christian temple and a Muslim mosque. (Rev: BL 11/15/97; HBG 3/98) [938]

14676 Clare, John D., ed. *Ancient Greece* (3–6). Illus. Series: Living History. 1994, Harcourt $16.95 (0-15-200516-1). 64pp. An overview of the history of ancient Greece, with emphasis on its heritage and contributions to world civilization. (Rev: BL 4/15/94; SLJ 4/94) [938]

14677 Day, Nancy. *Your Travel Guide to Ancient Greece* (4–8). Illus. Series: Passport to History. 2000, Runestone $26.60 (0-8225-3076-7). 96pp. An outstanding introduction to ancient Greece arranged in the format of a guided tour and covering topics including geography, history, customs, and places to

visit in an exciting, interesting way. (Rev: BL 10/15/00*; HBG 3/01; SLJ 2/01) [938]

14678 Descamps-Lequime, Sophie, and Denise Vernerey. *The Ancient Greeks: In the Land of the Gods* (5–8). Trans. by Mary K. LaRose. Illus. by Annie-Claude Martin. Series: People of the Past. 1992, Millbrook LB $22.90 (1-56294-069-4). 64pp. A glimpse into the lives of the ancient Greeks, including the way people dressed and kept their homes. (Rev: SLJ 8/92) [932]

14679 Dobson, Mary. *Greek Grime* (4–6). Illus. by author. Series: Smelly Old History. 1998, Oxford paper $7.95 (0-19-910493-X). 32pp. Using some scratch-and-sniff panels, this account offers a breezy introduction to everyday life in Ancient Greece including its hygienic habits. (Rev: SLJ 1/99) [938]

14680 Freeman, Charles, ed. *The Ancient Greeks* (4–6). Illus. Series: Spotlights. 1996, Oxford $11.95 (0-19-521238-X). 46pp. Traces the history of ancient Greece, tells about its religion and the pantheon of gods, and supplies generous quotes from original sources. (Rev: SLJ 9/96) [938]

14681 Gay, Kathlyn. *Science in Ancient Greece* (4–6). Illus. Series: Science of the Past. 1998, Watts LB $24.00 (0-531-20357-3). 64pp. This work discusses the theories and accomplishments of such important Greek astronomers, philosophers, and mathematicians as Ptolemy, Aristotle, and Hippocrates. (Rev: BL 12/1/98; HBG 3/99; SLJ 11/98) [509]

14682 Hart, Avery, and Paul Mantell. *Ancient Greece! 40 Hands-On Activities to Experience This Wonderous Age* (4–7). Illus. 1999, Williamson paper $10.95 (1-885593-25-2). 96pp. A concise text and several craft projects introduce us to the world of ancient Greece, its geography, history, people, culture, and lasting contributions. (Rev: BL 9/15/99; SLJ 8/99) [938]

14683 Hicks, Peter. *Ancient Greece* (4–6). Series: History Beneath Your Feet. 1999, Raintree Steck-Vaughn LB $25.69 (0-8172-5750-0). 48pp. Using pictures of artifacts, buildings, and monuments, this account uses double-page spreads to describe the work of archaeologists and what we know, from them, about life in ancient Greece. (Rev: HBG 10/00; SLJ 3/00) [938]

14684 Hodge, Susie. *Ancient Greek Art* (4–8). Series: Art in History. 1997, Heinemann LB $19.92 (1-57572-551-7). 32pp. This slim but well-illustrated book discusses the contributions of ancient Greeks to mosaics, pottery, architecture, and sculpture. (Rev: HBG 3/98; SLJ 5/98) [938]

14685 Hull, Robert. *Greece* (5–10). Series: The Ancient World. 1998, Raintree Steck-Vaughn LB $27.12 (0-8172-5055-7). 64pp. This brief introduction to ancient Greece touches on its religion and mythology, its great philosophers, important historical events, and its contributions to world culture. (Rev: BL 1/1–15/99; HBG 3/99) [938]

14686 Hutton, Warwick. *The Trojan Horse* (1–4). Illus. 1992, Macmillan paper $16.00 (0-689-50542-6). 32pp. The old story of the Trojan horse is told, this time from the viewpoint of ordinary people. (Rev: BCCB 4/92; BL 3/1/92*; HB 5–6/92*; SLJ 4/92*) [398.2]

14687 James, Louise. *How We Know About the Greeks* (3–6). Series: How We Know About. 1998, Bedrick $17.95 (0-87226-537-4). 32pp. Using double-page spreads, this book explores ancient Greek civilization and explains how archaeologists work in the field. (Rev: BL 5/15/98; HBG 10/98; SLJ 8/98) [938]

14688 Little, Emily. *The Trojan Horse: How the Greeks Won the War* (2–4). Illus. by Mike Eagle. 1988, Random paper $3.99 (0-394-89674-2). 48pp. A lesson in ancient history in this account of the Trojan horse. (Rev: BCCB 1/89; BL 3/1/89; SLJ 2/89) [398.2]

14689 Loverance, Rowena, and Tim Wood. *Ancient Greece* (4–6). Illus. Series: See Through History. 1993, Viking $19.99 (0-670-84754-2). 48pp. An overview in text and interesting illustrations of the life, history, and culture of the ancient Greeks. (Rev: BL 4/15/93; SLJ 8/93) [938]

14690 MacDonald, Fiona. *A Greek Temple* (4–6). Illus. Series: Inside Story. 1992, Bedrick $18.95 (0-87226-361-4). 48pp. In pictures and text, this is the story of the jewel of the Acropolis: the Parthenon. (Rev: BL 11/1/92; SLJ 1/93) [938.3]

14691 MacDonald, Fiona. *I Wonder Why Greeks Built Temples and Other Questions About Ancient Greece* (2–4). Illus. Series: I Wonder Why. 1997, Kingfisher $9.95 (0-7534-5056-9). 32pp. Each double-page spread in this book answers two or three basic questions about the ancient Greeks, how they lived, and their accomplishments. (Rev: HBG 3/98; SLJ 9/97) [938]

14692 MacDonald, Fiona. *Women in Ancient Greece* (4–7). Series: The Other Half of History. 1999, Bedrick $17.95 (0-87226-568-4). 48pp. The status of women in ancient Greece and their occupations and contributions are discussed in this colorful account. (Rev: HBG 3/00; SLJ 2/00) [938]

14693 Malam, John. *Exploring Ancient Greece* (5–8). Series: Remains to Be Seen. 1999, Evans Brothers $19.95 (0-237-51994-1). 47pp. Particularly noteworthy in this basic account of the history of ancient Greece are the stunning photos of temples, theaters, artifacts, and landscapes. (Rev: SLJ 1/00) [938]

14694 Malam, John. *Gods and Goddesses* (4–7). Series: Ancient Greece. 2000, Bedrick LB $18.95 (0-87226-598-6). 48pp. This book identifies and describes each of the major gods and goddesses of ancient Greece and retells the myths in which they are characters. (Rev: BL 1/1–15/01; HBG 10/00; SLJ 8/00) [938]

14695 Malam, John. *Greek Town* (4–6). Series: Metropolis. 1999, Watts LB $25.00 (0-531-14529-8). 48pp. A colorful introduction to ancient Greek civilization that takes readers on a visit to a town where they see important landmarks, learn what to eat and drink, and find out how the people live. (Rev: BL 10/15/99; SLJ 12/99) [938]

14696 Martell, Hazel M. *The Myths and Civilization of the Ancient Greeks* (4–8). Illus. by Ivan Stalio

and Francesca D'Ottavi. Series: Myths and Civilization. 1999, Bedrick LB $16.95 (0-87226-283-9). 43pp. A handsome volume in which myths are presented as well as related material on the culture, crafts, everyday life, and artifacts of ancient Greece. (Rev: HBG 10/99; SLJ 3/99) [932]

14697 Odijk, Pamela. *The Greeks* (4–7). Illus. Series: Ancient World. 1989, Silver Burdett LB $17.95 (0-382-09884-6). 48pp. An oversize book that covers history, art, architecture, clothing, and other aspects of ancient Greece. (Rev: BL 1/15/90; SLJ 5/90) [938]

14698 Pipe, Jim. *Trojan Horse* (3–5). Illus. by Roger Hutchins and Donald Hartley. Series: Mystery History. 1997, Millbrook LB $23.90 (0-7613-0614-5). 32pp. Using games, puzzles, and hidden pictures, this simple account introduces the causes of the Trojan War, the people involved, and the ruse that ended it. (Rev: HBG 3/98; SLJ 4/98) [938]

14699 Rees, Rosemary. *The Ancient Greeks* (3–4). Illus. Series: Understanding People in the Past. 1997, Heinemann $24.22 (0-431-07790-8). 64pp. Photos of museum artifacts plus maps, diagrams, and drawings are used liberally to introduce such topics about the ancient Greeks as their history, accomplishments, buildings, Olympic games, theater, family life, and trade. (Rev: SLJ 9/97) [938]

14700 Ross, Stewart. *Daily Life* (4–7). Illus. Series: Ancient Greece. 2000, Bedrick LB $18.95 (0-87226-599-4). 48pp. An attractive volume that explores daily life in ancient Greece with coverage of topics including food, dress, eating habits, war, and religion. (Rev: BL 1/1–15/01; HBG 10/00) [938]

14701 Ross, Stewart. *Greek Theatre* (4–7). Series: Ancient Greece. 2000, Bedrick LB $18.95 (0-87226-597-8). 48pp. This book describes ancient Greek theaters and their parts and introduces the major playwrights and their works. (Rev: BL 1/1–15/01; HBG 10/00; SLJ 9/00) [938]

14702 Shuter, Jane. *The Acropolis* (5–7). Series: Visiting the Past. 1999, Heinemann LB $16.95 (1-57572-855-9). 32pp. As well as describing the main buildings found in ancient Greece, this account uses double-page spreads to introduce the daily life and culture of the Athenians. (Rev: SLJ 3/00) [938]

14703 Shuter, Jane. *Builders, Traders and Craftsmen* (4–5). Series: Ancient Greece. 1999, Heinemann LB $14.95 (1-57572-736-6). 32pp. This book covers the builders in ancient Greece who worked on the Parthenon, the craftsmen who made clothing, statues, and pottery, and the merchants who traded goods for grain. (Rev: HBG 10/99; SLJ 7/99) [938]

14704 Shuter, Jane. *Cities and Citizens* (4–5). Series: Ancient Greece. 1999, Heinemann LB $14.95 (1-57572-738-2). 32pp. This book on ancient Greece describes city-states and the interests and social life of citizens including theater, acting, and sports. (Rev: HBG 10/99; SLJ 7/99) [938]

14705 Shuter, Jane. *Discoveries, Inventions and Ideas* (2–5). Series: Ancient Greece. 1999, Heinemann LB $14.95 (1-57572-739-0). 32pp. Following a map and timeline, this book covers many Greek innovations such as the development of libraries, advances in medicine, and progress in mapmaking. (Rev: HBG 10/99; SLJ 7/99) [938]

14706 Shuter, Jane. *Farmers and Fighters* (2–5). Series: Ancient Greece. 1999, Heinemann LB $14.95 (1-57572-737-4). 32pp. A heavily illustrated book that describes various aspects of warfare and the weapons used plus an account of farming methods, tools, and food preparation. (Rev: HBG 10/99; SLJ 7/99) [938]

14707 Steele, Philip. *Clothes and Crafts in Ancient Greece* (4–6). Series: Clothing and Crafts in History. 2000, Gareth Stevens LB $21.27 (0-8368-2734-1). 32pp. This book describes such crafts as pottery, metalwork, architecture, temple decorations, paintings, and textiles as well as outlining projects including creating a soldier's shield and making a painting for a palace wall. (Rev: BL 1/1–15/01) [938]

14708 Tyler, Deborah. *The Greeks and Troy* (4–7). Illus. Series: Hidden Worlds. 1993, Dillon $13.95 (0-87518-537-1). 32pp. The story of the Trojan War is retold, along with a tour of the ruins of Troy and a re-creation of what it once was. (Rev: BL 12/1/93) [938]

14709 Woodford, Susan. *The Parthenon* (6–8). Illus. 1981, Cambridge Univ. Pr. paper $13.95 (0-521-22629-5). 48pp. The history and structure of the Parthenon and a description of the religion of ancient Greece.

Rome

14710 Andrews, Ian. *Pompeii* (4–6). Illus. 1978, Cambridge Univ. Pr. paper $13.95 (0-521-20973-0). 48pp. A description of the city of Pompeii and of its destruction.

14711 Angeletti, Roberta. *Vulca the Etruscan* (3–5). Illus. by author. Series: A Journey Through Time. 1999, Oxford $16.95 (0-19-521506-0). 27pp. Robbie and his dog travel to ancient times where he meets an Etruscan near the Necropolis and learns a little about the history and culture of this time. (Rev: HBG 3/00; SLJ 9/99) [937]

14712 Ash, Rhiannon. *Roman Colosseum* (3–5). Illus. by Mike Bell, et al. Series: Mystery History. 1997, Millbrook LB $23.90 (0-7613-0613-7). 32pp. Games, puzzles, hidden pictures, and a simple text are used to introduce the Colosseum in Rome and the activities it housed. (Rev: HBG 3/98; SLJ 4/98) [937]

14713 Burrell, Roy. *The Romans* (5–7). Illus. by Peter Connolly. 1998, Oxford paper $14.95 (0-199-17102-5). 112pp. A brief overview of Rome's history from its legendary beginnings to the Barbarian invasions. (Rev: SLJ 1/92) [937]

14714 Chapman, Gillian. *The Romans* (4–7). Series: Crafts from the Past. 1998, Heinemann LB $16.95 (1-57572-734-X). 39pp. Using double-page spreads, this work describes Roman culture while outlining several craft projects inspired by art objects, places, or people. (Rev: HBG 10/99; SLJ 2/99) [937]

14715 Chrisp, Peter. *The Colosseum* (3–5). Illus. Series: Great Buildings. 1997, Raintree Steck-Vaughn LB $27.12 (0-8172-4916-8). 48pp. The history of the Colosseum, its construction, and its uses through the centuries is detailed in this nicely illustrated title. (Rev: BL 11/15/97; HBG 3/98) [937]

14716 Clare, John D., ed. *Classical Rome* (3–6). Illus. Series: Living History. 1993, Harcourt $16.95 (0-15-200513-7). 64pp. With informative text and photos showing people in period costume, this is a good introduction to ancient Rome. (Rev: BL 2/15/93) [937.06]

14717 Corbishley, Mike. *Growing Up in Ancient Rome* (3–5). Illus. by Christine Molan. Series: Growing Up In. 1993, Troll paper $4.95 (0-8167-2722-8). 32pp. The social life and customs of ancient Rome are covered, with a particular focus on the life-style of children. (Rev: BL 1/15/94) [937]

14718 Ganeri, Anita. *The Ancient Romans* (3–5). Series: History Starts Here! 2000, Raintree Steck-Vaughn LB $22.83 (0-7398-1349-8). 32pp. A brief overview that introduces ancient Rome, its daily life, culture, social structure, history, and fall. (Rev: HBG 10/00; SLJ 7/00) [937]

14719 Ganeri, Anita. *How Would You Survive as an Ancient Roman?* (4–7). Illus. Series: How Would You Survive? 1995, Watts LB $25.00 (0-531-14349-X). 48pp. Typical entertainment, education, and religious beliefs in ancient Rome are covered, with sidebars on the proper way to appear before a court of law or how to become a Vestal Virgin. (Rev: BL 6/1–15/95; SLJ 8/95) [937]

14720 Guittard, Charles. *The Romans: Life in the Empire* (4–6). Trans. by Mary K. LaRose. Illus. by Annie-Claude Martin. Series: People of the Past. 1992, Millbrook LB $22.40 (1-56294-200-X). 64pp. This account presents an overview of how life was lived in the Roman Empire and gives information on such topics as history, culture, and religion. (Rev: BL 10/15/92) [937]

14721 Haywood, John, ed. *The Romans* (4–6). Illus. Series: Spotlights. 1996, Oxford paper $11.95 (0-19-521240-1). 46pp. This attractive introduction to the history and political organization of ancient Rome also includes material on its cultural and social life. (Rev: SLJ 9/96) [937]

14722 Hodge, Susie. *Ancient Roman Art* (4–8). Series: Art in History. 1997, Heinemann LB $19.92 (1-57572-552-5). 32pp. This slim but well-illustrated volume outlines Roman contributions to architecture, sculpture, pottery, and mosaics. (Rev: SLJ 5/98) [937.6]

14723 Humphrey, Kathryn L. *Pompeii: Nightmare at Midday* (4–6). Illus. 1995, Houghton $9.28 (0-395-73265-4). 64pp. The destruction caused by the eruption of Mount Vesuvius in A.D. 79. (Rev: BL 4/15/90) [937]

14724 James, Louise. *The Romans* (3–6). Illus. Series: How We Know About. 1997, Bedrick LB $17.95 (0-87226-534-X). 32pp. Using both contemporary photos and many reconstructions, this book describes how people lived in ancient Rome, along with material on how archaeologists have determined these facts. (Rev: BL 12/15/97; HBG 3/98; SLJ 10/97) [937.6]

14725 Johnson, Stephen. *A Roman Fort* (3–6). Illus. Series: Magnifications. 2000, Bedrick $18.95 (0-87226-650-8). 48pp. This introduction to Roman forts uses close-up pictures to describe a fort's layout, barracks, lifestyle, amusements, religion, and hygiene. (Rev: BL 10/15/00; HBG 3/01; SLJ 1/01) [355.7]

14726 Langley, Andrew, and Philip De Souza. *The Roman News* (4–7). Illus. 1996, Candlewick $15.99 (0-7636-0055-5). 32pp. Using the format of a tabloid newspaper, this book highlights the history of ancient Rome. (Rev: BL 10/1/96; SLJ 1/97) [937]

14727 Macaulay, David. *City: A Story of Roman Planning and Construction* (6–8). Illus. by author. 1983, Houghton $18.00 (0-395-19492-X); paper $8.95 (0-395-34922-2). 112pp. The imaginary Roman city of Verbonia is constructed through accurate and finely detailed drawings.

14728 MacDonald, Fiona. *I Wonder Why Romans Wore Togas and Other Questions About Ancient Rome* (2–4). Illus. Series: I Wonder Why. 1997, Kingfisher $9.95 (0-7534-5057-7). 32pp. Each double-page spread in this book answers two or three basic questions about the ancient Romans, how they lived, their empire, and their accomplishments. (Rev: HBG 3/98; SLJ 9/97) [937]

14729 MacDonald, Fiona. *The Roman Colosseum* (4–6). Illus. Series: Inside Story. 1997, Bedrick LB $18.95 (0-87226-275-8). 48pp. In a series of double-page spreads, the world of ancient Rome is introduced, focusing on the structure and functions of the Colosseum. (Rev: BL 2/15/97) [937]

14730 MacDonald, Fiona. *Women in Ancient Rome* (4–8). Series: The Other Half of History. 2000, NTC $17.95 (0-87226-570-6). 48pp. Topics about women in ancient Rome include their roles at home and at work, their health and beauty, and famous individuals. (Rev: HBG 3/01; SLJ 9/00) [937]

14731 Mann, Elizabeth. *The Roman Colosseum* (4–7). Illus. Series: Wonders of the World. 1998, Mikaya $19.95 (0-9650493-3-7). 48pp. An oversize book that is crammed with factual material on the Colosseum in Rome. (Rev: BL 12/15/98; SLJ 2/99) [937]

14732 Martell, Hazel M. *Roman Town* (4–6). Illus. Series: Metropolis. 1998, Watts LB $24.00 (0-531-14467-4). 48pp. Using cutaways, aerial views, and dozens of other illustrations, this fascinating account describes everyday Roman life — its climate, sports, food, shopping, etc. (Rev: BL 4/15/98; HBG 10/98) [937]

14733 Morley, Jacqueline. *A Roman Villa* (4–6). Illus. by John James. Series: Inside Story. 1992, Bedrick LB $18.95 (0-87226-360-6). 48pp. Through many double-page spreads and cutaway drawings, the interiors and exteriors of Roman villas are explored. (Rev: BL 12/15/92; SLJ 1/93) [937]

14734 Nardo, Don. *The Age of Augustus* (5–8). Series: World History. 1996, Lucent LB $17.96 (1-56006-306-8). 112pp. The rise of Augustus Caesar

is chronicled with material on his political and military career and his effects on the Roman Empire. (Rev: SLJ 2/97) [937]

14735 Ochoa, George. *The Assassination of Julius Caesar* (5–8). Series: Turning Points. 1991, Silver Burdett LB $14.95 (0-382-24130-4). 64pp. The events that led to the assassination of Julius Caesar in Rome. (Rev: BL 3/15/92) [937]

14736 Odijk, Pamela. *The Romans* (4–7). Illus. Series: Ancient World. 1989, Silver Burdett LB $17.95 (0-382-09885-4). 48pp. An oversize book about the ancient Romans and their way of life. (Rev: BL 1/15/90; SLJ 5/90) [937]

14737 Patent, Dorothy Hinshaw. *Lost City of Pompeii* (4–7). Series: Frozen in Time. 1999, Benchmark LB $18.95 (0-7614-0785-5). 64pp. The story of the ancient city of Pompeii, its destruction, and how its excavation has given us a wealth of information about ancient Rome. (Rev: HBG 10/00; SLJ 3/00) [937]

14738 Petrén, Birgitta, and Elisabetta Putini. *Why Are You Calling Me a Barbarian?* (2–5). Trans. from Italian by Mary Becker. Illus. by Lara Artone and Monica Barsotti. 1999, Getty Museum paper $17.95 (0-89236-559-5). 59pp. Set in the time of the Romans, a slave girl and the son of a Scandinavian merchant compare their lives and lifestyles in this colorful introduction to life in the ancient Roman Empire from a non-Roman point of view. (Rev: SLJ 4/00) [937]

14739 Pickels, Dwayne E. *Roman Myths, Heroes, and Legends* (5–8). Series: Costume, Tradition, and Culture: Reflecting on the Past. 1998, Chelsea LB $16.95 (0-7910-5164-1). 64pp. Historic collectors' cards illustrate this introduction to Roman culture — its gods and goddesses, its heroes and their stories. (Rev: BL 3/15/99; HBG 10/99) [937]

14740 Rees, Rosemary. *The Ancient Romans* (3–6). Series: Understanding People in the Past. 1999, Heinemann LB $15.95 (1-57572-890-7). 64pp. Double-page spreads with illustrations of historical sites, artifacts, art, and maps help the reader envision the daily life and contributions of the ancient Romans. (Rev: BL 6/1–15/99) [937]

14741 Ridd, Stephen, ed. *Julius Caesar in Gaul and Britain* (5–8). Illus. Series: History Eyewitness. 1995, Raintree Steck-Vaughn LB $24.26 (0-8114-8283-9). 48pp. An edited version of Caesar's fascinating accounts of the Gallic Wars, with pictures and maps. (Rev: BL 4/15/95; SLJ 5/95) [937]

14742 Roberts, Paul C., ed. *Ancient Rome* (4–6). Series: Nature Company Discoveries. 1997, Time Life $16.00 (0-7835-4909-1). 64pp. Using a series of double-page spreads, the culture and history of ancient Rome are covered, with outstanding illustrations. (Rev: BL 9/15/97; HBG 3/98; SLJ 12/97) [937]

14743 Sheehan, Sean. *Ancient Rome* (4–6). Series: History Beneath Your Feet. 1999, Raintree Steck-Vaughn LB $25.69 (0-8172-5752-7). 48pp. This account, which focuses on the ruins of Pompeii, re-creates the daily life of the Romans and describes how archaeologists have gathered this information. (Rev: HBG 10/00; SLJ 3/00) [937]

14744 Sheehan, Sean, and Pat Levy. *Rome* (5–10). Series: The Ancient World. 1998, Raintree Steck-Vaughn LB $27.12 (0-8172-5057-3). 64pp. A brief history of Rome and the Roman Empire, including its culture, buildings, amusements, and emperors. (Rev: BL 1/1–15/99; HBG 3/99; SLJ 3/99) [937]

14745 Snedden, Robert. *Technology in the Time of Ancient Rome* (4–8). Series: Technology in the Time Of. 1998, Raintree Steck-Vaughn LB $25.69 (0-8172-4876-5). 48pp. Each double-page spread introduces a different aspect of Roman accomplishments in such areas as transportation, building, food production, weaving, and metalwork. (Rev: HBG 10/98; SLJ 3/99) [937]

14746 Steele, Philip. *Clothes and Crafts in Roman Times* (4–6). Illus. Series: Clothing and Crafts in History. 2000, Gareth Stevens $21.27 (0-8368-2737-6). 32pp. After a brief introduction to Roman history, this book introduces Roman artisans and gives directions for craft projects including making a dolphin brooch, a mosaic, an actor's mask, and small clay statues. (Rev: BL 1/1–15/01) [745]

14747 Steele, Philip. *Food and Feasts in Ancient Rome* (4–8). Illus. Series: Food and Feasts. 1994, New Discovery LB $17.95 (0-02-726321-5). 32pp. A description of food and food preparation in ancient Rome and how it differed among the classes, as well as a selection of tasty recipes. (Rev: BCCB 10/94; SLJ 12/94) [937]

14748 Stroud, Jonathan. *Ancient Rome: A Guide to the Glory of Imperial Rome* (4–7). Series: Sightseers. 2000, Kingfisher $8.95 (0-7534-5235-9). 30pp. This book on ancient Rome is presented like a handbook for tourists with material on topics like accommodations, shopping, key sites, etc. (Rev: HBG 3/01; SLJ 9/00) [937]

14749 Tanaka, Shelley. *The Buried City of Pompeii* (4–7). Illus. Series: I Was There. 1997, Hyperion $16.95 (0-7868-0285-5). 48pp. The facts concerning the destruction of the city of Pompeii are told through the fictionalized account of one of its victims. (Rev: BL 12/1/97; HBG 3/98; SLJ 3/98)

14750 Watkins, Richard. *Gladiator* (4–7). Illus. 1997, Houghton $17.00 (0-395-82656-X). 64pp. This attractive book surveys the gladiators of ancient Rome, their training, their performances, and their fights. (Rev: BL 11/1/97*; HBG 3/98; SLJ 10/97*) [796.8]

14751 Whittock, Martyn. *The Roman Empire* (4–6). Illus. Series: Biographical History. 1996, Bedrick $17.95 (0-87226-118-2). 64pp. A history of the Roman Empire, its expansion, and life in the republic are given, with many short biographies and excerpts from both primary and secondary sources. (Rev: SLJ 9/96) [937]

Middle Ages

14752 Aliki. *A Medieval Feast* (2–6). Illus. by author. 1983, HarperCollins LB $15.89 (0-690-

04246-9); paper $6.95 (0-06-446050-9). 32pp. A visit from the king provides the occasion for a well-described feast.

14753 *Castles* (PS–3). Illus. Series: First Discovery. 1993, Scholastic $12.95 (0-590-46377-2). 30pp. A highly visual introduction to castles that supplies basic information with an interactive approach. (Rev: BL 10/1/93; SLJ 8/93) [940.1]

14754 Child, John, et al. *The Crusades* (4–6). Illus. Series: Biographical History. 1996, Bedrick $17.77 (0-87226-119-0). 64pp. Describes the nature and the causes of the various Crusades and covers important events, battles, and people. (Rev: SLJ 9/96) [940.1]

14755 Clare, John D. *Fourteenth-Century Towns* (3–6). Illus. Series: Living History. 1993, Harcourt $16.95 (0-15-200515-3). 64pp. Life in a medieval town is portrayed with double-page spreads and informative text. (Rev: BL 2/15/923) [307]

14756 Clare, John D., ed. *Knights in Armor* (3–6). Illus. 1992, Harcourt $17.00 (0-15-200508-0). 64pp. Photos of people in period costume help bring to life this historical era. (Rev: BL 12/1/92; SLJ 11/92) [940]

14757 Clements, Gillian. *The Truth About Castles* (2–5). Illus. 1990, Carolrhoda LB $15.95 (0-87614-401-6). 40pp. Humorous cartoon-style drawings and text show castles and their structure. (Rev: SLJ 10/90) [725]

14758 Corbishley, Mike. *The Medieval World* (5–7). Illus. Series: Timelink. 1993, Bedrick LB $18.95 (0-87226-362-2). 64pp. Using a chronological approach, this book covers the years 450 through 1500 in Europe, Asia, Africa, and the Americas. (Rev: SLJ 8/93) [940.1]

14759 Corzine, Phyllis. *The Black Death* (5–8). Series: World History. 1996, Lucent LB $17.96 (1-56006-299-1). 112pp. Traces the spread of the bubonic plague from Asia and its effects in Europe, including the breakdown of feudalism. (Rev: SLJ 2/97) [940.1]

14760 Dawson, Imogen. *Clothes and Crafts in the Middle Ages* (4–6). Illus. Series: Clothing and Crafts in History. 2000, Gareth Stevens $21.27 (0-8368-2736-8). 32pp. After a brief history of the Middle Ages, craftsmen and their materials are introduced with projects including making medieval clothing, jewelry, a pilgrim's badge, and an illuminated manuscript. (Rev: BL 1/1–15/01) [745]

14761 Dawson, Imogen. *Food and Feasts in the Middle Ages* (4–8). Illus. Series: Food and Feasts. 1994, New Discovery LB $17.95 (0-02-726324-X). 32pp. This account re-creates the culinary aspects of the Middle Ages, with material on farming, dishes, and town and city fare plus several recipes and many attractive illustrations. (Rev: BCCB 10/94; SLJ 12/94) [940.1]

14762 Dunn, John M. *Life During the Black Death* (5–9). Series: The Way People Live. 2000, Lucent LB $18.96 (1-56006-542-7). 96pp. This account traces the spread of the Black Death from Mongolia in 1320 to Western Europe and its lasting effects on history, society, and culture. (Rev: HBG 10/00; SLJ 6/00) [940]

14763 Gibbons, Gail. *Knights in Shining Armor* (PS–3). Illus. 1995, Little, Brown $15.95 (0-316-30948-6). 32pp. A picture book about knights, tournaments, chivalry, and armor, with brief introductions to such famous knights as St. George. (Rev: BL 11/1/95; SLJ 10/95) [394]

14764 Gravett, Christopher. *The World of the Medieval Knight* (4–6). Illus. 1997, Bedrick LB $19.95 (0-87226-277-4). 64pp. Various aspects of knighthood — from armor and jousting to castle life and the Crusades — are presented. (Rev: BL 1/1–15/97; SLJ 3/97) [940.1]

14765 Hart, Avery, and Paul Mantell. *Knights and Castles: 50 Hands-On Activities to Experience the Middle Ages* (3–6). Illus. 1998, Williamson paper $10.95 (1-885593-17-1). 96pp. Directions for making a catapult, a castle, and a knight's helmet are three of the projects in this craft book that also supplies good information about life in the Middle Ages. (Rev: BL 11/15/98; SLJ 2/99) [940.1]

14766 Hinds, Kathryn. *The Castle* (5–8). Series: Life in the Middle Ages. 2000, Marshall Cavendish LB $19.95 (0-7614-1007-4). 80pp. A book that explores the construction and parts of the medieval castle as well as the lifestyles of those who lived in them, from kings and knights to humble servants. (Rev: BL 3/1/01; HBG 3/01; SLJ 3/01) [940]

14767 Hinds, Kathryn. *The Church* (5–8). Series: Life in the Middle Ages. 2000, Marshall Cavendish LB $19.95 (0-7614-1008-2). 80pp. Explains the role of the church and the clergy in medieval life as well as giving examples of church construction. (Rev: BL 3/1/01; HBG 3/01; SLJ 3/01) [940]

14768 Hinds, Kathryn. *The City* (5–8). Illus. Series: Life in the Middle Ages. 2000, Marshall Cavendish LB $19.95 (0-7614-1005-8). 80pp. A beautifully designed book that tells about daily life in medieval cities and their functions as centers of learning, commerce, worship, construction, and recreation as well as disease and disaster. (Rev: BL 2/15/01; HBG 3/01; SLJ 3/01) [940.1]

14769 Hinds, Kathryn. *The Countryside* (5–8). Illus. Series: Life in the Middle Ages. 2000, Marshall Cavendish LB $19.95 (0-7614-1006-6). 80pp. The author explains manorialism — a primary social structure in rural areas during the Middle Ages — and describes a medieval village, its residents, and their work and pastimes. (Rev: BL 2/15/01; HBG 3/01; SLJ 3/01) [940.1]

14770 Howarth, Sarah. *The Middle Ages* (4–8). Illus. Series: See Through History. 1993, Viking $19.99 (0-670-85098-5). 48pp. In a series of heavily illustrated double-page spreads, various topics related to the Middle Ages are presented, including social structure, food, clothing, and dwellings. (Rev: BL 12/15/93; SLJ 2/94) [940.1]

14771 Howarth, Sarah. *What Do We Know About the Middle Ages?* (4–7). Illus. Series: What Do We Know About. 1996, Bedrick LB $18.95 (0-87226-384-3). 40pp. The way people lived in the Middle Ages in Western Europe is described in a series of double-page spreads. (Rev: BL 6/1–15/96) [940.1]

14772 Howe, John. *Knights* (3–6). Illus. 1995, Orchard $18.95 (0-531-09456-1). 16pp. Aspects of the Middle Ages — like castles, armor, and the Crusades — come alive in this pop-up book. (Rev: BL 2/1/96) [940]

14773 Jordan, William Chester, ed. *The Middle Ages: A Watts Guide for Children* (4–7). 2000, Watts LB $32.00 (0-531-11715-4); paper $19.95 (0-531-16488-8). 112pp. A basic guide to life in the Middle Ages with entries on major events, important places, and significant people arranged in alphabetical order. (Rev: SLJ 7/00) [940]

14774 Langley, Andrew. *Castle at War: The Story of a Siege* (4–8). Series: Discoveries. 1998, DK paper $14.95 (0-7894-3418-0). 48pp. Using a fictional siege as background, this book presents various aspects of this military tactic and its participants through well-illustrated double-page spreads that place a special focus on the training, gear, and weapons of soldiers and the strategies used. (Rev: HBG 3/99; SLJ 4/99) [940.1]

14775 Langley, Andrew. *Medieval Life* (4–8). Illus. Series: Eyewitness Books. 1996, Knopf $20.99 (0-679-98077-6). 63pp. This book takes one behind the scenes of life in a castle during the Middle Ages, explaining and illustrating its parts and how people lived within its walls. (Rev: BL 6/1–15/96; SLJ 7/96) [940.1]

14776 Macaulay, David. *Castle* (5–8). Illus. by author. 1977, Houghton $18.00 (0-395-25784-0); paper $8.95 (0-395-32920-5). 80pp. Another of the author's brilliant, detailed works, this one on the planning and building of a Welsh castle.

14777 MacDonald, Fiona. *A Medieval Castle* (4–6). Illus. by Mark Bergin. Series: Inside Story. 1990, Bedrick LB $18.95 (0-87226-340-1). 48pp. An oversize volume that surveys the development of castles and highlights life in the Middle Ages. (Rev: BL 3/1/91; SLJ 6/91) [940.1]

14778 MacDonald, Fiona. *Medieval Cathedral* (3–6). Illus. by John James. Series: Inside Story. 1991, Bedrick $18.95 (0-87226-350-9). 48pp. This book explains in many pictures how cathedrals were built in the Middle Ages, their various parts and the roles they played in medieval civilization. (Rev: BL 12/1/91; SLJ 12/91) [726.6]

14779 MacDonald, Fiona. *The Middle Ages* (4–6). Illus. 1993, Facts on File $19.95 (0-8160-2788-9). 80pp. Double-page spreads feature topics of the Middle Ages — feudalism, food and family, houses, family life, and so on. (Rev: BL 8/85; SLJ 9/85)

14780 MacDonald, Fiona. *Women in Medieval Times* (4–8). Series: The Other Half of History. 2000, NTC $17.95 (0-87226-569-2). 48pp. Using a topical arrangement this book discusses the role of women in medieval times in the castle, in the workplace, and at court. (Rev: HBG 3/01; SLJ 9/00) [940]

14781 McNeill, Sarah. *The Middle Ages* (3–6). Illus. Series: Spotlights. 1998, Oxford $10.95 (0-19-521394-7). 46pp. An eye-catching account of the Middle Ages, tracing important events, culture, and social conditions. (Rev: BL 12/1/98; SLJ 10/98) [909.07]

14782 Morgan, Gwyneth. *Life in a Medieval Village* (5–7). Illus. by author. 1991, HarperCollins paper $14.00 (0-06-092046-7). A story of activities in a medieval village and of the church's importance in life in the Middle Ages.

14783 Nicolle, David. *Medieval Knights* (4–8). Series: See Through History. 1997, Viking $19.99 (0-670-87463-9). 48pp. An introduction to knights, their functions, weapons, quests, and accomplishments. (Rev: BL 10/15/97; HBG 3/98; SLJ 1/98) [940]

14784 Nikola-Lisa, W. *Till Year's Good End: A Calendar of Medieval Labors* (1–4). Illus. by Christopher Manson. 1997, Simon & Schuster $16.00 (0-689-80020-7). 32pp. This book provides a fresh look at the Middle Ages by observing the chores performed in a year by the peasant class. (Rev: BL 10/15/97; HBG 3/98; SLJ 12/97) [942.02]

14785 Osband, Gillian. *Castles* (4–6). Illus. by Robert Andrew. 1991, Orchard $18.95 (0-531-05949-9). 16pp. Impressive and informative pop-ups add to the appeal of this book. (Rev: BL 9/15/91) [728.8]

14786 Pernoud, Regine. *A Day with a Noble-woman* (4–6). Trans. by Dominique Clift. Illus. Series: A Day With. 1997, Runestone LB $22.60 (0-8225-1916-X). 48pp. Traces a typical day in the life of Blanche of Champagne, a French noblewoman of the Middle Ages. (Rev: BL 1/1–15/98; HBG 3/98; SLJ 2/98) [944]

14787 Pernoud, Regine. *A Day with a Stonecutter* (3–6). Illus. 1997, Runestone LB $22.60 (0-8225-1913-5). 48pp. Includes both an introduction to medieval society and a case study of a stonecutter who is working on a project for an abbey. (Rev: BL 11/1/97; HBG 3/98; SLJ 1/98) [731.4]

14788 Pipe, Jim. *Medieval Castle* (4–6). Illus. Series: Mystery History. 1996, Millbrook LB $23.90 (0-7613-0495-9). 31pp. Games, brainteasers, and jokes are combined with good factual material to make an entertaining introduction to the parts of a castle and its surrounding land. (Rev: SLJ 7/97) [940.1]

14789 Platt, Richard. *Castles* (4–7). Illus. by Stephen Biesty. Series: Cross-Sections. 1994, DK $16.95 (1-56458-467-4). 32pp. Detailed drawings depict the parts of a 14th-century castle and supply details on the everyday life of its inhabitants, from knights to the lowliest worker. (Rev: BL 11/1/94; SLJ 10/94) [940.1]

14790 Ross, Stewart. *Knights* (5–7). Illus. Series: Fact or Fiction. 1996, Millbrook LB $24.90 (0-7613-0453-3). 48pp. In double-page spreads with many illustrations, facts are separated from fiction about knights from King Arthur's time to soldiers of the U.S. Cavalry. (Rev: BL 3/15/96; SLJ 6/96) [940.1]

14791 Scarry, Huck. *Looking into the Middle Ages* (3–6). Illus. 1985, HarperCollins $12.50 (0-06-025224-3). 12pp. This 12-page pop-up book literally allows readers to look into the Middle Ages —

into castles, cathedrals, jousting tournaments. (Rev: BCCB 6/85; BL 9/15/85)

14792 Shuter, Jane. *The Middle Ages* (3–6). Series: History Opens Windows. 1999, Heinemann LB $14.95 (1-57572-886-9). 32pp. This useful account of the medieval period uses double-page spreads and many illustrations to bring the social forces and events of this period to life. (Rev: SLJ 2/00) [940.1]

14793 Steele, Philip. *Castles* (5–7). Illus. 1995, Kingfisher $16.95 (1-85697-547-9). 64pp. In this oversized, well-designed book, castles, jousting, armor, and feast days are described. (Rev: BL 8/95; SLJ 4/95) [940.1]

14794 Steele, Philip. *Knights* (3–6). Illus. 1998, Kingfisher $15.95 (0-7534-5154-9). 64pp. Chivalry, heraldry, tournaments, daily life, and famous knights of fiction are a few of the topics handled in a series of double-page spreads on knighthood in the Middle Ages. (Rev: BL 11/15/98; HBG 3/99) [940.1]

14795 Tanaka, Shelley. *In the Time of Knights: The Real-Life Story of History's Greatest Knight* (4–7). Illus. by Greg Ruhl. Series: I Was There. 2000, Hyperion $16.99 (0-7868-0651-6). 48pp. This fictionalized account of the life of William Marshal, who became a famous knight during the 12th century, also gives a great deal of information on life during the Middle Ages. (Rev: BCCB 2/01; SLJ 3/01) [921]

14796 Yue, Charlotte, and David Yue. *Armor* (4–7). Illus. 1994, Houghton $16.00 (0-395-68101-4). 90pp. Describes the origin, use, and types of armor in the Middle Ages in Europe as well as in other cultures. (Rev: BL 11/15/94; SLJ 12/94) [355.8]

Renaissance

14797 Day, Nancy. *Your Travel Guide to Renaissance Europe* (4–8). Series: Passport to History. 2000, Lerner LB $26.60 (0-8225-3080-5). 96pp. This book uses a travel guide format to introduce the reader to the life and people of Europe from 1350 to 1550 with coverage of culture, style, inventions, religious beliefs, and scientific discoveries. (Rev: BL 3/1/01) [940.2]

14798 Giudici, Vittorio. *The Sistine Chapel: Its History and Masterpieces* (5–10). Illus. 2000, Bedrick $16.95 (0-87226-638-9). 48pp. After extensive material on the popes involved, the Renaissance artists who worked on the chapel, and a brief history of the Vatican, this book becomes a painting-by-painting tour of its art collection. (Rev: BL 11/1/00; SLJ 3/01) [726.55]

14799 Halliwell, Sarah, ed. *The Renaissance: Artists and Writers* (5–8). Series: Who and When? 1997, Raintree Steck-Vaughn LB $28.55 (0-8172-4725-4). 96pp. This introduction to 13 artists and three writers of the Renaissance relies heavily of Giorgi Vasari and his eyewitness book about Renaissance art. (Rev: SLJ 1/98) [940.2]

14800 January, Brendan. *Science in the Renaissance* (4–7). Illus. Series: Science of the Past. 1999, Watts

LB $24.00 (0-531-11526-7). 64pp. Covers the reawakening of science during the Renaissance in such areas as astronomy, medicine, physics, anatomy, and geometry and perspective in art. (Rev: BL 3/15/99; HBG 10/99) [509.4]

14801 Langley, Andrew. *Renaissance* (4–9). Photos by Andy Crawford. Series: Eyewitness Books. 1999, Knopf LB $20.99 (0-375-90136-1). 59pp. A concise account, illustrated with photographs, that describes such aspects of the Renaissance as city-states, trade, art, architecture, and religion. (Rev: HBG 3/00; SLJ 9/99) [909.07]

14802 Morley, Jacqueline. *A Renaissance Town* (4–6). Illus. Series: Inside Story. 1997, Bedrick LB $18.95 (0-87226-276-6). 48pp. This richly illustrated book focuses on Florence during the Renaissance, with material on government, social life, customs, art, and the economy. (Rev: BL 2/15/97) [945]

14803 Prum, Deborah Mazzotta. *Rats, Bulls, and Flying Machines: A History of Renaissance and Reformation* (4–8). Illus. Series: Core Chronicles. 1999, Core Knowledge $21.95 (1-890517-19-4); paper $11.95 (1-890517-18-6). 106pp. A handsome volume that gives a basic history of the Renaissance and Reformation and highlights the accomplishments of people such as the Medici family, Machiavelli, Michelangelo, Cervantes, Shakespeare, and Gutenberg. (Rev: BL 12/15/99) [909.08]

14804 Shuter, Jane. *The Renaissance* (3–6). Series: History Opens Windows. 1999, Heinemann LB $14.95 (1-57572-887-7). 32pp. The people, events, and social forces that produced the Renaissance are described in text and pictures. (Rev: SLJ 2/00) [940.2]

14805 Wood, Tim. *The Renaissance* (4–8). Illus. Series: See Through History. 1993, Viking $19.99 (0-670-85149-3). 48pp. Various topics related to the Renaissance — including city states, trade with the East, and the position of women — are covered in a series of double-page spreads. (Rev: BL 12/15/93; SLJ 2/94) [940.2]

World War I

14806 Clare, John D., ed. *First World War* (5–8). Illus. Series: Living History. 1995, Gulliver $16.95 (0-15-200087-9). 64pp. Excellent visuals and a vivid text are used in this history of World War I. (Rev: SLJ 6/95) [940.53]

14807 Dolan, Edward F. *America in World War I* (5–8). Illus. 1996, Millbrook LB $27.40 (1-56294-522-X). 96pp. A large-format book that introduces background material on World War I and specific information on the role the United States played in it. (Rev: BL 6/1–15/96; SLJ 5/96) [940.3]

14808 Gay, Kathlyn, and Martin Gay. *World War I* (5–8). Illus. Series: Voices from the Past. 1995, Twenty-First Century LB $18.90 (0-8050-2848-X). 64pp. The causes, major battles, and effects of World War I are covered, with many excerpts from

personal accounts. (Rev: BL 12/15/95; SLJ 2/96) [940.3]

World War II

14809 Abells, Chana Byers. *The Children We Remember* (2–5). Illus. 1986, Greenwillow $15.93 (0-688-06372-1). 48pp. A compelling photographic remembrance of the horror of the Holocaust, intended for a young audience. (Rev: BCCB 10/86; BL 10/1/86; HB 11–12/86)

14810 Adams, Simon. *World War II* (4–8). Illus. 2000, DK $15.95 (0-7894-3298-2). 64pp. Each double-page spread presents a different aspect of World War II, such as the Battle of Britain, military equipment, women at work, and conditions inside the Soviet Union. (Rev: BL 11/1/00) [940.53]

14811 Adler, David A. *Child of the Warsaw Ghetto* (3–6). Illus. by Karen Ritz. 1995, Holiday LB $15.95 (0-8234-1160-5). 32pp. The story of the Warsaw Ghetto during World War II as seen through the eyes of a survivor. (Rev: BCCB 5/95; BL 4/1/95; SLJ 7/95) [943.8]

14812 Adler, David A. *Hiding from the Nazis* (3–5). Illus. by Karen Ritz. 1997, Holiday LB $15.95 (0-8234-1288-1). 32pp. This picture book for older children tells how Lore, a young Jewish girl, is hidden and cared for by a Dutch family during World War II. (Rev: BL 11/1/97; HBG 3/98; SLJ 2/98) [940.53]

14813 Adler, David A. *Hilde and Eli: Children of the Holocaust* (3–5). Illus. by Karen Ritz. 1994, Holiday $16.95 (0-8234-1091-9). 32pp. A picture book that tells the true stories of two Jewish children who were killed in the Holocaust. (Rev: BCCB 11/94; BL 9/15/94; SLJ 12/94) [940.54]

14814 Adler, David A. *We Remember the Holocaust* (4–7). 1995, Holt paper $14.00 (0-8050-3715-2). 147pp. Through interview excerpts, the terrible days of the Holocaust are remembered. (Rev: SLJ 12/89) [940.54]

14815 Anflick, Charles. *Resistance: Teen Partisan and Resisters Who Fought Nazi Tyranny* (5–9). Series: Teen Witnesses to the Holocaust. 1999, Rosen LB $17.95 (0-8239-2847-0). 64pp. This volume celebrates the teenagers who fought against the Nazis in ghettos, concentration camps, inside Germany, and in the lands that the Nazis conquered. (Rev: BL 4/15/98) [940.54]

14816 Auerbacher, Inge. *I Am a Star: Child of the Holocaust* (5–7). Illus. 1993, Puffin paper $5.99 (0-14-036401-3). 80pp. The memoirs of a former child survivor of the Terezin concentration camp in Czechoslovakia. (Rev: BCCB 7–8/87; BL 6/1/87; SLJ 4/87)

14817 Axelrod, Toby. *In the Camps: Teens Who Survived the Nazi Concentration Camps* (5–9). Series: Teen Witnesses to the Holocaust. 1999, Rosen LB $17.95 (0-8239-2844-6). 64pp. These are the stories of teenagers who survived the death camps, their despair and sadness, and the hope they maintained despite the horror around them. (Rev: BL 7/99) [940.54]

14818 Axelrod, Toby. *Rescuers Defying the Nazis: Non-Jewish Teens Who Rescued Jews* (5–9). Series: Teen Witnesses to the Holocaust. 1999, Rosen LB $17.95 (0-8239-2848-9). 64pp. The inspiring true stories of teenagers during World War II who risked their lives to save Jews from the Holocaust. (Rev: BL 7/99; SLJ 8/99) [940.54]

14819 Ayer, Eleanor. *In the Ghettos: Teens Who Survived the Ghettos of the Holocaust* (5–9). Series: Teen Witnesses to the Holocaust. 1999, Rosen LB $17.95 (0-8239-2845-4). 64pp. This book relates the harrowing stories of courageous teenagers who survived life in the ghettos of Lodz, Theresienstadt, and Warsaw. (Rev: BL 7/99; SLJ 8/99) [940.54]

14820 Ballard, Robert D. *Exploring the Bismarck* (5–8). Illus. 1991, Scholastic $15.95 (0-590-44268-6). 64pp. This is an account of the history and rediscovery of the German battleship *Bismarck*, which was sunk more than 50 years ago. (Rev: BL 1/1/91; SLJ 8/91) [943]

14821 Black, Wallace B., and Jean F. Blashfield. *America Prepares for War* (5–7). Illus. Series: World War II 50th Anniversary. 1991, Macmillan LB $12.95 (0-89686-554-1). 48pp. The U.S. entry into World War II, with numerous photos. (Rev: BL 6/15/91; SLJ 9/91) [940.53]

14822 Black, Wallace B., and Jean F. Blashfield. *Bataan and Corregidor* (5–7). Illus. Series: World War II 50th Anniversary. 1991, Macmillan LB $12.95 (0-89686-557-6). 48pp. Using documentary photos, this book examines the major events in the struggle over the Philippines in World War II. (Rev: BL 12/1/91; SLJ 2/92) [940.54]

14823 Black, Wallace B., and Jean F. Blashfield. *Battle of Britain* (5–7). Illus. Series: World War II 50th Anniversary. 1991, Macmillan LB $12.95 (0-89686-553-3). 48pp. The story of Britain's valiant stand against the German power. Also use: *Blitzkrieg* (1991). (Rev: BL 6/15/91; SLJ 9/91) [940.53]

14824 Black, Wallace B., and Jean F. Blashfield. *Battle of the Atlantic* (5–7). Illus. Series: World War II 50th Anniversary. 1991, Macmillan LB $12.95 (0-89686-558-4). 48pp. The war in the Atlantic Ocean during World War II, when the Allies tried to keep the seas open for the movement of troops and supplies, is retold in text and pictures. (Rev: BL 12/1/91; SLJ 2/92) [940.54]

14825 Black, Wallace B., and Jean F. Blashfield. *Battle of the Bulge* (5–7). Illus. Series: World War II 50th Anniversary. 1993, Macmillan LB $15.95 (0-89686-568-1). 48pp. This account describes Hitler's desperate offensive and his gamble to split the Allied army in two. (Rev: BL 4/15/93) [940.54]

14826 Black, Wallace B., and Jean F. Blashfield. *Bombing Fortress Europe* (5–7). Illus. Series: World War II 50th Anniversary. 1992, Macmillan LB $12.95 (0-89686-562-2). 48pp. The thrilling, heroic exploits of British and American airmen and their war over the skies of Europe are retold in this illustrated account. (Rev: BL 8/92; SLJ 1/93) [940.54]

14827 Black, Wallace B., and Jean F. Blashfield. *D-Day* (5–7). Illus. Series: World War II 50th Anniversary. 1992, Macmillan LB $12.95 (0-89686-566-5). 48pp. The fateful day when the Allied forces invaded France during World War II. (Rev: BL 2/1/93; SLJ 4/93) [940.54]

14828 Black, Wallace B., and Jean F. Blashfield. *Desert Warfare* (5–7). Illus. Series: World War II 50th Anniversary. 1992, Macmillan LB $12.95 (0-89686-561-4). 48pp. This account chronicles the Allied campaigns in North Africa against the desert forces of the Germans and Italians. (Rev: BL 8/92; SLJ 1/93) [940.54]

14829 Black, Wallace B., and Jean F. Blashfield. *Flattops at War* (5–7). Illus. Series: World War II 50th Anniversary. 1991, Macmillan LB $12.95 (0-89686-559-2). 48pp. The use of aircraft carriers in the Pacific area of combat is described in this account. (Rev: BL 12/1/91) [940.54]

14830 Black, Wallace B., and Jean F. Blashfield. *Guadalcanal* (5–7). Illus. Series: World War II 50th Anniversary. 1992, Macmillan LB $12.95 (0-89686-560-6). 48pp. The war in the South Pacific, as revealed in the battle of Guadalcanal during 1942–1943, is retold in text and pictures. (Rev: BL 8/92; SLJ 1/93) [940.54]

14831 Black, Wallace B., and Jean F. Blashfield. *Hiroshima and the Atomic Bomb* (5–7). Illus. Series: World War II 50th Anniversary. 1993, Macmillan LB $12.95 (0-89686-571-1). 48pp. This is a chronicle of President Truman's decision to drop the atomic bomb on Hiroshima and Nagasaki and the results of that decision. (Rev: BL 4/15/93; SLJ 10/93) [940.54]

14832 Black, Wallace B., and Jean F. Blashfield. *Invasion of Italy* (5–7). Illus. Series: World War II 50th Anniversary. 1992, Macmillan LB $12.95 (0-89686-565-7). 48pp. This book describes the campaign by the Allied forces to liberate Italy from the Axis. (Rev: BL 2/1/93; SLJ 4/93) [940.54]

14833 Black, Wallace B., and Jean F. Blashfield. *Island Hopping in the Pacific* (5–7). Illus. Series: World War II 50th Anniversary. 1992, Macmillan LB $12.95 (0-89686-567-3). 48pp. The campaign to retake Pacific islands from the Japanese is described in brief text and many photos. (Rev: BL 2/1/93; SLJ 4/93) [940.54]

14834 Black, Wallace B., and Jean F. Blashfield. *Iwo Jima and Okinawa* (5–7). Illus. Series: World War II 50th Anniversary. 1993, Macmillan LB $12.95 (0-89686-569-X). 48pp. The story of the savage battles that the Allies faced while taking these two islands from the Japanese during World War II. (Rev: BL 4/15/93; SLJ 10/93) [940.54]

14835 Black, Wallace B., and Jean F. Blashfield. *Jungle Warfare* (5–7). Illus. Series: World War II 50th Anniversary. 1992, Macmillan LB $12.95 (0-89686-563-0). 48pp. This generously illustrated account re-creates the World War II campaigns waged in the jungle of southeastern Asia. (Rev: BL 8/92; SLJ 1/93) [940.54]

14836 Black, Wallace B., and Jean F. Blashfield. *Pearl Harbor!* (5–7). Illus. Series: World War II

50th Anniversary. 1991, Macmillan LB $12.95 (0-89686-555-X). 48pp. The Japanese surprise attack that shocked the United States into World War II. (Rev: BL 6/15/91; SLJ 9/91) [940.53]

14837 Black, Wallace B., and Jean F. Blashfield. *Russia at War* (5–7). Illus. Series: World War II 50th Anniversary. 1991, Macmillan LB $12.95 (0-89686-556-8). 48pp. Describes the role played by Russia in World War II and how they stopped the Germans in spite of terrible losses, with many documentary photographs. (Rev: BL 12/1/91; SLJ 2/92) [940.54]

14838 Black, Wallace B., and Jean F. Blashfield. *Victory in Europe* (5–7). Illus. Series: World War II 50th Anniversary. 1993, Macmillan LB $12.95 (0-89686-570-3). 48pp. This account outlines the events that led to the Allied victory in Europe including the Russian advance and the fall of Berlin. (Rev: BL 4/15/93) [940.54]

14839 Black, Wallace B., and Jean F. Blashfield. *War Behind the Lines* (5–7). Illus. Series: World War II 50th Anniversary. 1992, Macmillan LB $12.95 (0-89686-564-9). 48pp. This book tells about the many gallant underground movements that tried to undermine the Fascist powers from within. (Rev: BL 2/1/93; SLJ 4/93) [940.54]

14840 Chaikin, Miriam. *A Nightmare in History: The Holocaust 1933–1945* (4–6). Illus. 1992, Houghton paper $10.00 (0-395-61580-1). 128pp. From the history of Judaism, the author traces the horror of the Holocaust. (Rev: BL 12/15/87)

14841 Coerr, Eleanor. *Sadako* (1–5). Illus. by Ed Young. 1993, Putnam $17.99 (0-399-21771-1). 40pp. A picture-book version of the story of a young Japanese girl dying of leukemia as a result of the bombing of Hiroshima. (Rev: BCCB 12/93; BL 11/1/93*; SLJ 12/93*) [362.1]

14842 Cretzmeyer, Stacy. *Your Name Is Renée: Ruth Kapp Hartz's Story as a Hidden Child in Nazi-Occupied France* (5–8). 1999, Oxford $17.95 (0-19-513259-9). 240pp. The story of a German Jewish family living in France during the Holocaust, how they survived, and how young Ruth hid in an orphanage run by Catholic nuns. (Rev: BCCB 7–8/99; SLJ 8/99) [940.54]

14843 Cross, Robin. *Children and War* (4–7). Illus. Series: World War II. 1994, Thomson Learning LB $24.26 (1-56847-180-7). 48pp. True case histories of children in various circumstances during World War II, including in a gulag, the resistance movement, and a death camp. (Rev: BL 12/15/94; SLJ 2/95) [940.53]

14844 Daily, Robert. *The Code Talkers: American Indians in World War II* (4–8). Illus. Series: First Books. 1995, Watts LB $22.50 (0-531-20190-2). 63pp. Describes the roles that Native Americans played in World War II, both as soldiers and as translators. (Rev: SLJ 10/95) [940.54]

14845 Davis, Gary. *Submarine Wahoo* (3–5). Illus. Series: Those Daring Machines. 1995, Macmillan paper $5.95 (0-382-24753-1). 48pp. A brief account of the exploits of the World War II submarine that distinguished itself in the Pacific campaign. (Rev: BL 2/15/95) [940.54]

14846 Devaney, John. *America Goes to War: 1941* (5–8). Illus. 1991, Walker LB $17.85 (0-8027-6980-2). 192pp. Almost daily notations cover events of the times in 1941. (Rev: BL 10/1/91) [940.53]

14847 Dolan, Edward F. *America in World War II: 1943* (5–8). Illus. Series: America in World War II. 1991, Millbrook paper $6.95 (1-878-84181-5). 64pp. The events of 1943 as they related to the United States and World War II are retold in text and many full-color illustrations. (Rev: BL 4/1/92; SLJ 5/92) [940.54]

14848 Drogues, Valerie. *Battleship Missouri* (3–5). Illus. Series: Those Daring Machines. 1995, Macmillan LB $17.95 (0-89686-825-7). 48pp. A short, well-illustrated description of the battleship *Missouri* and its amazing record during World War II. (Rev: BL 2/15/95) [359.3]

14849 Drucker, Olga L. *Kindertransport* (5–8). 1995, Holt paper $7.95 (0-8050-4251-2). 146pp. A true account of a Jewish girl sent from Germany to live in England until she could join her parents in New York City in 1945. (Rev: BCCB 1/93; SLJ 11/92) [940.54]

14850 Dvorson, Alexa. *The Hitler Youth: Marching Toward Madness* (5–9). Illus. Series: Teen Witnesses to the Holocaust. 1999, Rosen LB $17.95 (0-8239-2783-0). 64pp. This volume describes how thousands of German boys and girls joined the Hitler Youth, why they were seduced into obeying the Nazis, and how their dreams were eventually shattered. (Rev: BL 4/15/99) [943.086]

14851 Fox, Anne L., and Eva Abraham-Podietz. *Ten Thousand Children: True Stories Told by Children Who Escaped the Holocaust on the Kindertransport* (5–8). Illus. 1998, Behrman paper $12.95 (0-87441-648-5). 128pp. The moving stories of 21 survivors who were part of the rescue operation known as the Kindertransport that took 10,000 Jewish children from Nazi-occupied Europe to freedom during late 1938 and 1939. (Rev: BL 1/1–15/99) [940.53]

14852 Gay, Kathlyn, and Martin Gay. *World War II* (5–8). Illus. Series: Voices from the Past. 1995, Twenty-First Century LB $18.90 (0-8050-2849-8). 64pp. World War II is covered, from causes to consequences, with quotes from many original sources. (Rev: BL 12/15/95; SLJ 2/96) [940.53]

14853 Giddens, Sandra. *Escape: Teens Who Escaped the Holocaust to Freedom* (5–9). Series: Teen Witnesses to the Holocaust. 1999, Rosen LB $17.95 (0-8239-2843-8). 64pp. This volume focuses on the ordeals of four Jewish teens who were able to elude the Nazis during the Holocaust. (Rev: BL 4/15/98) [940.54]

14854 Gourley, Catherine. *Welcome to Molly's World, 1944: Growing Up in World War Two America* (3–6). Illus. Series: American Girls Collection. 1999, Pleasant $14.95 (1-56247-773-0). 58pp. This book focuses on the human side of World War II, employing material on a USO canteen, blackouts in the U.S., rationing, air raids in England, and V-E Day. (Rev: BL 1/1–15/00; HBG 3/00) [940.53]

14855 Green, Robert. *"Vive La France": The French Resistance During World War II* (5–8).

Illus. Series: First Books. 1995, Watts LB $22.50 (0-531-20192-9). 63pp. The story of the role played by the French underground during World War II. (Rev: SLJ 10/95) [940.54]

14856 Grossman, Mendel. *My Secret Camera: Life in the Lodz Ghetto* (4–8). Illus. 2000, Harcourt $16.00 (0-15-202306-2). 32pp. Using a hidden camera, a young Jewish man recorded life in the Lodz ghetto in Poland; he later died during a forced march in 1945. Sixteen of his photos are reproduced here with a brief text. (Rev: BCCB 5/00; BL 4/1/00; HB 5–6/00; HBG 10/00; SLJ 5/00) [940.53]

14857 Hopkinson, Deborah. *Pearl Harbor* (4–6). Illus. Series: Places in American History. 1991, Macmillan LB $14.95 (0-87518-475-8). 72pp. A visual and narrative introduction to this well-known site of World War II. (Rev: BL 2/15/92; SLJ 4/92) [940.54]

14858 Kaplan, William, and Shelley Tanaka. *One More Border: The True Story of One Family's Escape from War-Torn Europe* (3–5). Illus. by Stephen Taylor. 1998, Douglas & McIntyre $18.95 (0-88899-332-3). 60pp. The true story of a Lithuanian Jewish family who escaped their homeland in 1939 and journeyed to a new life in Ontario, Canada. (Rev: BCCB 1/99; BL 9/1/98; HBG 3/99; SLJ 12/98) [940.5]

14859 King, David C. *World War II Days: Discover the Past with Exciting Projects, Games, Activities, and Recipes* (4–6). Illus. by Cheryl K. Noll. Series: American Kids in History. 2000, Wiley paper $12.95 (0-471-37101-7). 100pp. Interspersed with material on the home front during World War II are easy-to-perform projects such as making a victory garden, a flashlight, a periscope, a crystal radio, and a wind vane. (Rev: SLJ 2/01) [940.54]

14860 Kodama, Tatsuharu. *Shin's Tricycle* (5–8). Trans. by Kazuko Hokumen-Jones. Illus. by Noriyuki Ando. 1995, Walker LB $16.85 (0-8027-8376-7). 32pp. A father recalls the life of his young son, who was killed in the bombing of Hiroshima. (Rev: BCCB 12/95; BL 9/1/95*; SLJ 12/95) [940.54]

14861 Kuhn, Betsy. *Angels of Mercy* (5–8). Illus. 1999, Simon & Schuster $18.00 (0-689-82044-5). 128pp. A series of narratives on courage and bravery give us a fascinating look at the contributions of nurses in World War II. (Rev: BCCB 12/99; BL 10/15/99; HBG 3/00) [940.54]

14862 Kustanowitz, Esther. *The Hidden Children of the Holocaust: Teens Who Hid from the Nazis* (5–9). Series: Teen Witnesses to the Holocaust. 1999, Rosen LB $17.95 (0-8239-2562-5). 64pp. Many first-person narratives are used in this account of teenage Jews who hid in homes, barns, and forests during World War II, and of others who disguised themselves as non-Jews to escape the Nazis. (Rev: BL 7/99; SLJ 8/99) [940.54]

14863 Lawson, Don, and Wendy Barish. *The French Resistance* (5–7). 1984, Simon & Schuster LB $8.00 (0-671-50832-6). 192pp. A description of a spy network that existed during World War II.

14864 Lawton, Clive. *The Story of the Holocaust* (5–8). Illus. 2000, Watts LB $25.00 (0-531-14524-

7). 48pp. A graphically illustrated account of the rise of anti-Semitism in Germany, a trend that culminated in the horror of the concentration camps. (Rev: BL 7/00) [940.53]

14865 Levine, Ellen. *Darkness Over Denmark: The Danish Resistance and the Rescue of the Jews* (5–8). 2000, Holiday $18.95 (0-8234-1447-7). 164pp. This is a straightforward history that uses many first-person accounts to relate the remarkable efforts of the Danish people to save their Jewish citizens during World War II. (Rev: HB 9–10/00; HBG 10/00; SLJ 8/00) [940.54]

14866 McGowen, Tom. *The Battle for Iwo Jima* (4–6). Illus. Series: Cornerstones of Freedom. 1999, Children's LB $19.50 (0-516-21141-2). 32pp. Describes the U.S. Marines' invasion and battle on the volcanic island of Iwo Jima in March 1945. (Rev: BL 5/15/99; HBG 10/99) [940.54]

14867 McGowen, Tom. *Germany's Lightning War: Panzer Divisions of World War II* (5–8). Series: Military Might. 1999, Twenty-First Century LB $23.90 (0-7613-1511-X). 64pp. After a general history of tank warfare, this account focuses on the German's Panzer tank divisions and the part they played in World War II. (Rev: HBG 3/00; SLJ 9/99) [940.54]

14868 McGowen, Tom. *"Go for Broke": Japanese Americans in World War II* (5–8). Illus. Series: First Books. 1995, Watts LB $22.50 (0-531-20195-3). 63pp. An attractive, accessible presentation that describes the fate of Japanese Americans during World War II. (Rev: SLJ 10/95) [940.54]

14869 McGowen, Tom. *Sink the Bismarck: Germany's Super-Battleship of World War II* (5–8). Series: Military Might. 1999, Twenty-First Century LB $23.90 (0-7613-1510-1). 64pp. A history of German sea power during World War II and the many (eventually successful) British efforts to sink the *Bismarck*. (Rev: HBG 3/00; SLJ 9/99) [940.54]

14870 Maruki, Toshi. *Hiroshima No Pika* (3–6). Illus. by author. 1982, Lothrop $16.00 (0-688-01297-3). 48pp. The story of a seven-year-old girl and the bombing of Hiroshima in 1945.

14871 Marx, Trish. *Echoes of World War II* (5–8). Illus. 1994, Lerner LB $19.95 (0-8225-4898-4). 96pp. The true stories of six children around the world whose lives were changed dramatically by World War II. (Rev: BCCB 5/94; BL 9/15/94; SLJ 5/94) [940.53]

14872 Milman, Barbara. *Light in the Shadows* (5–8). Illus. 1997, Jonathan David paper $14.95 (0-8246-0401-6). 82pp. This account tells the stories of five Holocaust survivors illustrated with powerful woodcut prints. (Rev: BL 11/15/97) [940.53]

14873 Mochizuki, Ken. *Passage to Freedom: The Sugihara Story* (3–5). Illus. by Dom Lee. 1997, Lee & Low $15.95 (1-880000-49-0). 32pp. The story of Chiune Sugihara, the Japanese consul in Lithuania, and how he issued visas during the Holocaust that enabled Polish Jews to escape. (Rev: BL 5/15/97; HB 11–12/97; HBG 3/98; SLJ 7/97) [940.53]

14874 Nicholson, Dorinda M. *Pearl Harbor Child: A Child's View of Pearl Harbor — from Attack to*

Peace (5–8). Illus. 1998, Woodson House paper $9.95 (1-892858-00-2). 84pp. This photo-essay describes a child's experience during the Japanese bombing of Pearl Harbor, the temporary evacuation, and everyday life growing up in Hawaii during World War II. (Rev: BL 1/1–15/99) [996.9]

14875 Pettit, Jayne. *A Time to Fight Back: True Stories of Wartime Resistance* (5–8). 1996, Houghton $14.95 (0-395-76504-8). 176pp. Eight true stories about courageous acts involving young people during World War II. (Rev: BCCB 3/96; BL 4/1/96; SLJ 4/96) [940.53]

14876 Pfeifer, Kathryn B. *The 761st Tank Battalion* (5–8). Illus. Series: African American Soldiers. 1994, Twenty-First Century LB $17.90 (0-8050-3057-3). 80pp. An account of the achievements of members of the African American soldiers of the 761st Tank Battalion in World War II. (Rev: BL 9/1/94; SLJ 11/94) [940.54]

14877 Pringle, Laurence. *One Room School* (1–4). Illus. by Barbara Garrison. 1998, Boyds Mills $15.95 (1-56397-583-1). This is a memoir by the noted author in which he remembers the year 1944, when he was attending a one-room school and collecting scrap metal for the war effort. (Rev: BCCB 4/98; BL 3/1/98; HBG 10/98; SLJ 4/98) [371]

14878 Rubin, Susan G. *Fireflies in the Dark: The Story of Friedl Dicker-Brandeis and the Children of Terezin* (5–10). Illus. 2000, Holiday $18.95 (0-8234-1461-2). 48pp. A heartbreaking picture book that reproduces some of the artwork and writings of the children imprisoned at the Terezin concentration camp, where only 100 of 15,000 children survived. (Rev: BCCB 11/00; BL 7/00*; HB 9–10/00; HBG 10/00; SLJ 8/00) [940.53]

14879 Simon, Charnan. *Hollywood at War: The Motion Picture Industry and World War II* (4–8). Illus. Series: First Books. 1995, Watts LB $22.50 (0-531-20193-7). 63pp. Chronicles the role of the movie industry during World War II in supplying propaganda and entertainment. (Rev: SLJ 10/95) [940.54]

14880 Sinnott, Susan. *Doing Our Part: American Women on the Home Front During World War II* (4–8). Illus. Series: First Books. 1995, Watts LB $22.50 (0-531-20198-8). 63pp. The role of women at home and in defense industries during World War II is covered in this interesting account. (Rev: SLJ 10/95) [940.54]

14881 Sinnott, Susan. *Our Burden of Shame: Japanese-American Internment During World War II* (5–8). Illus. Series: First Books. 1995, Watts LB $22.50 (0-531-20194-5). 63pp. The story of the heartbreaking internment of Japanese Americans during World War II is told in this easily understood, well-illustrated volume. (Rev: SLJ 10/95) [940.54]

14882 Stalcup, Ann. *On the Home Front: Growing Up in Wartime England* (4–6). Illus. 1998, Linnet $19.50 (0-208-02482-4). 103pp. Important English children's writers, including Nina Bawden and Robert Westall, share their memories of growing up in wartime England. (Rev: BCCB 9/98; BL 10/15/98; HBG 10/98) [940.54]

14883 Stein, R. Conrad. *World War II in Europe: "America Goes to War."* (5–7). Illus. Series: American War. 1994, Enslow LB $20.95 (0-89490-525-2). 128pp. An unbiased account of the European theater of war during World War II, with emphasis on American participation. (Rev: BL 10/15/94; SLJ 1/95) [940.54]

14884 Stein, R. Conrad. *World War II in the Pacific: Remember Pearl Harbor* (5–7). Illus. Series: American War. 1994, Enslow LB $20.95 (0-89490-524-4). 128pp. A well-organized, concise account of the Pacific war from the attack on Pearl Harbor to V-J Day that describes key battles and important personnel. (Rev: BL 7/94; SLJ 7/94) [940.54]

14885 Steins, Richard. *The Allies Against the Axis: World War II (1940–1950)* (5–8). Series: First Person America. 1994, Twenty-First Century LB $18.90 (0-8050-2586-3). 64pp. The story of World War II and early postwar conditions are covered, with generous use of primary sources. (Rev: SLJ 12/94) [940.54]

14886 Talbott, Hudson. *Forging Freedom* (4–7). Illus. 2000, Putnam $15.99 (0-399-23434-9). 64pp. This is the story of Jaap Penraat, a young architectural student in Amsterdam during the Nazi occupation who saved hundreds of Jews from deportation by forging papers and smuggling them out of the city. (Rev: BCCB 11/00; BL 7/00; HB 1–2/01; HBG 3/01; SLJ 11/00) [940.53]

14887 Taylor, Theodore. *Air Raid — Pearl Harbor: The Story of December 7, 1941* (5–8). 1991, Harcourt paper $6.00 (0-15-201655-4). 179pp. A fine account of why the attack occurred and the effects that were felt around the world. A revised edition. (Rev: SLJ 12/91) [940.54]

14888 Tito, E. Tina. *Liberation: Teens in the Concentration Camps and the Teen Soldiers Who Liberated Them* (5–9). Illus. Series: Teen Witnesses to the Holocaust. 1999, Rosen LB $17.95 (0-8239-2846-2). 64pp. A harrowing account in which two teenage Nazi camp survivors and two American soldiers who were also teenagers during World War II tell their respective stories. (Rev: BL 4/15/99) [940.53]

14889 Warren, Andrea. *Surviving Hitler: A Boy in the Nazi Death Camps* (5–10). Illus. 2001, HarperCollins LB $16.89 (0-06-029218-0). 160pp. The true story of Jack Mandelbaum who as a teenager survived three years in Nazi death camps through a combination of luck, courage, and friendship. (Rev: BCCB 3/01; BL 1/1–15/01; SLJ 3/01) [940.53]

14890 *Weapons of War* (5–9). Series: American War. 2000, Lucent LB $18.96 (1-56006-584-2). 112pp. This book covers the weaponry, tank combat, U-boat activities, fighter planes, aircraft carriers, and some of the better-known campaigns of World War II. (Rev: HBG 10/00; SLJ 7/00) [940.54]

14891 Welch, Catherine A. *Children of the Relocation Camps* (3–6). Series: Picture the American Past. 2000, Carolrhoda $16.95 (1-57505-350-0). 48pp. The story of the relocation of thousands of

Japanese Americans after Pearl Harbor, how the children reacted, and how they built new lives within the camps. (Rev: BL 6/1–15/00; HBG 10/00; SLJ 10/00) [940.54]

14892 Whitman, Sylvia. *Children of the World War II Home Front* (2-5). Series: Picture the American Past. 2001, Carolrhoda $22.60 (1-57505-484-1). 48pp. A fact-filled text and interesting photographs portray the impact of the war on children in America and their efforts to support the troops.

14893 Whitman, Sylvia. *Uncle Sam Wants You!* (5–7). Illus. 1993, Lerner LB $22.60 (0-8225-1728-0). 80pp. This work describes the experiences of the many men and women who served in the various armed forces during World War II. (Rev: BL 5/1/93) [940.54]

14894 Whitman, Sylvia. *V Is for Victory: The American Home Front During World War II* (4–7). Illus. 1993, Lerner LB $22.60 (0-8225-1727-2). 80pp. Rosie the Riveter, ration stamps, and the relocation of Japanese Americans are among the topics covered in this look at the United States in another time. (Rev: BL 2/15/93) [973.9]

14895 Wills, Charles A. *Pearl Harbor* (5–7). Illus. Series: Turning Points. 1991, Silver Burdett LB $14.95 (0-382-24125-8); paper $7.95 (0-382-24119-3). 64pp. The "Day of Infamy" that brought America into World War II is re-created through text and pictures. (Rev: BL 1/15/92) [940.54]

14896 Wukovits, John F. *Life as a POW* (5–9). Series: American War. 2000, Lucent LB $18.96 (1-56006-665-2). 112pp. This book describes the treatment of World War II prisoners of war by the Germans and Japanese, the emotional upheavals involved, and the transition to freedom after release. (Rev: HBG 10/00; SLJ 7/00) [940.54]

14897 Wukovits, John F. *Life of an American Soldier in Europe* (5–10). Series: American War. 2000, Lucent LB $18.96 (1-56006-666-0). 112pp. As well as giving a history of World War II and the major battles involving Americans, this account tells about U.S. army personnel, their training, daily life, and living conditions. (Rev: HBG 10/00; SLJ 6/00) [940.54]

14898 Younkin, Paula. *V-2 Rockets* (3–5). Illus. Series: Those Daring Machines. 1995, Silver Burdett paper $5.95 (0-614-09467-4). 48pp. The history of the development of the *V-2* rocket by Germany, its use against the British in World War II, and the career of its developer, Wernher von Braun. (Rev: BL 2/15/95) [940.54]

Geographical Regions

Africa

General

14899 Ayo, Yvonne. *Africa* (4–8). Illus. Series: Eyewitness Books. 1995, Knopf LB $20.99 (0-674-97334-6). 64pp. This introduces the continent of Africa, with its amazing diversity of people, places, wildlife, and cultures. (Rev: BL 12/15/95) [960]

14900 Chambers, Catherine. *Africa* (4–7). Illus. Series: Origins. 1997, Watts LB $21.00 (0-531-14416-X). 32pp. The story of emigration from Africa, the slave trade, and the conditions that African Americans have faced through history on their arrival in the United States. (Rev: BL 4/15/97; SLJ 7/97) [960]

14901 Golding, Vivien. *Traditions from Africa* (3–6). Illus. Series: Cultural Journeys. 1999, Raintree Steck-Vaughn $25.69 (0-8172-8382-3). 48pp. This photo-essay gives a quick view of some of the cultural characteristics of various African regions. (Rev: BL 5/15/99) [306]

14902 Halliburton, Warren J. *African Industries* (4–6). Illus. Series: Africa Today. 1993, Macmillan LB $17.95 (0-89686-672-6). 48pp. Since colonialism, Africans have tried to develop such industries as agriculture, fishing, and mining. (Rev: BL 4/15/93) [338]

14903 Halliburton, Warren J. *African Landscapes* (4–6). Illus. Series: Africa Today. 1993, Silver Burdett LB $17.95 (0-89686-673-4). 48pp. From tropical forests to freezing mountain tops and arid deserts, this book describes the African landscape and geography. (Rev: BL 4/15/93) [916]

14904 Halliburton, Warren J. *Africa's Struggle for Independence* (4–6). Illus. Series: Africa Today. 1992, Macmillan LB $13.95 (0-89686-679-3). 48pp. An overview of the people and kingdoms of Africa, slave trade, colonial invasion, and the fight of individual nations for freedom. (Rev: BCCB 2/93; BL 3/1/93; SLJ 2/93) [960]

14905 Halliburton, Warren J. *Africa's Struggle to Survive* (4–6). Illus. 1993, Macmillan LB $17.95 (0-89686-675-0). 48pp. This book describes the natural disasters and forces of nature dictating the lives of the people of Africa. (Rev: BL 4/15/93) [960]

14906 Halliburton, Warren J. *Celebrations of African Heritage* (4–6). Illus. Series: Africa Today. 1992, Macmillan LB $13.95 (0-89686-676-9). 48pp. This book describes African holidays and celebrations and tells how some of these have been brought to America. (Rev: BL 2/15/93; SLJ 2/93) [394.2]

14907 Haskins, Jim, and Kathleen Benson. *African Beginnings* (3–7). Illus. by Floyd Cooper. 1998, Lothrop $18.00 (0-688-10256-5). 48pp. Eleven ancient African cultures, including the Egyptian, are described, beginning with Nubia around 3800 B.C. (Rev: BL 2/15/98; HBG 10/98; SLJ 6/98) [960]

14908 Ibazebo, Isimeme. *Exploration into Africa* (4–6). Illus. Series: Exploration. 1994, New Discovery paper $7.95 (0-382-24732-9). 48pp. An account of the foreign influences in the history of Africa, including the slave trade, and how these have changed its history. (Rev: SLJ 5/95) [960]

14909 Knight, Margy B., and Mark Melnicove. *Africa Is Not a Country* (1–3). Illus. by Anne S. O'Brien. 2000, Millbrook $24.90 (0-7613-1266-8). 40pp. This book celebrates the diversity of the African continent by portraying children from various countries and supplying a vignette about each of them. (Rev: BL 11/15/00; HBG 3/01; SLJ 1/01) [960]

14910 Martell, Hazel M. *Exploring Africa* (4–8). Illus. by Gerald Wood. Series: Voyages of Discovery. 1998, Bedrick LB $18.95 (0-87226-490-4). 48pp. After discussing early trade routes in northern Africa, this work describes the European exploratory expeditions that led to the colonization and exploitation of the land. (Rev: HBG 10/98; SLJ 4/98) [960]

14911 Pollard, Michael. *The Nile* (4–6). Series: Great Rivers. 1997, Benchmark LB $21.36 (0-7614-0503-8). 45pp. The story of the Nile, the lands through which it flows, its flooding, and its place in history. (Rev: HBG 3/98; SLJ 5/98) [960]

14912 Rich, Susan, et al. *Africa South of the Sahara: Understanding Geography and History Through Art* (5–9). Series: Artisans Around the World. 1999, Raintree Steck-Vaughn LB $25.69 (0-7398-0118-X). 48pp. After a brief overview of the history and geography of southern Africa, this book presents a colorful introduction to such crafts as beadwork from Kenya, a carved wooden mask from Congo, and a wire toy from South Africa. Most will require adult help or supervision. (Rev: HBG 3/00; SLJ 1/00) [960]

14913 Sheehan, Sean. *Great African Kingdoms* (5–10). Series: The Ancient World. 1998, Raintree Steck-Vaughn LB $27.12 (0-8172-5124-3). 64pp. This coverage of the great African kingdoms includes the spectacular palace of Great Zimbabwe, the majestic sculptures of Benin, and the Zulu empire's struggle for survival. (Rev: BL 1/1–15/99; HBG 3/99) [960]

Central and Eastern Africa

14914 Arnold, Helen. *Kenya* (1–3). Illus. Series: Postcards From. 1996, Raintree Steck-Vaughn LB $21.40 (0-8172-4024-1). 32pp. An overview of Kenya as portrayed in 13 postcards that describe the capital city, markets, parks, transportation, customs, and important sights. (Rev: SLJ 3/97) [967.62]

14915 Ayodo, Awuor. *Luo* (4–7). Illus. Series: Heritage Library of African Peoples. 1995, Rosen LB $17.95 (0-8239-1758-4). 64pp. A portrait of the culture, history, and society of the Luo people, who lived on the shores of Lake Victoria in Kenya. (Rev: BL 3/1/96) [967.8]

14916 Bangura, Abdul Karim. *Kipsigis* (5–8). Illus. Series: Heritage Library of African Peoples. 1994, Rosen LB $17.95 (0-8239-1765-7). 64pp. An attractive title that deals with the history and present status of the Kipsigis people of Kenya. (Rev: SLJ 5/95) [967.62]

14917 Baroin, Catherine. *Tubu: The Teda and the Daza* (5–7). Illus. Series: Heritage Library of African Peoples. 1997, Rosen LB $15.95 (0-8239-2000-3). 64pp. The history and contemporary life of these African peoples who now live in Central Africa, including Chad, Libya, Niger, and the Sudan. (Rev: BL 4/15/97) [967.43]

14918 Berg, Elizabeth. *Ethiopia* (2–4). Series: Festivals of the World. 1999, Gareth Stevens LB $15.95 (0-8368-2032-0). 32pp. This account describes Ethiopia's secular and religious holidays and gives instructions for creating the crafts and foods associated with these festivals. (Rev: BL 12/15/99; HBG 10/00) [963]

14919 Blauer, Ettagale, and Jason Lauré. *Uganda* (5–8). Illus. Series: Enchantment of the World. 1997, Children's LB $32.00 (0-516-20306-1). 128pp. This introduction to Uganda covers such topics as geography, climate, plants and animals, history, religion, culture, and daily life. (Rev: BL 7/97; HBG 3/98) [967.61]

14920 Burnham, Philip. *Gbaya* (5–7). Illus. Series: Heritage Library of African Peoples. 1997, Rosen LB $17.95 (0-8239-1995-1). 64pp. Covers the contemporary culture and the significant history of the Gbaya people, who live in Cameroon, Central African Republic, Congo, and Zaire. (Rev: BL 4/15/97) [967]

14921 Cobb, Vicki. *This Place Is Wild: East Africa* (3–5). Illus. Series: Imagine Living Here. 1998, Walker LB $16.85 (0-8027-8633-2). 32pp. This slim book explores the uniqueness of East Africa, describes its unusual animal and plant life, and introduces the reader to the Masai people. (Rev: BL 4/1/98; HBG 10/98; SLJ 5/98) [599]

14922 Corona, Laurel. *Ethiopia* (5–8). Series: Modern Nations of the World. 2000, Lucent LB $19.96 (1-56006-823-X). 128pp. An attractive, well-organized introduction to Ethiopia that gives its history, geography, and culture plus national statistics, a chronology, and bibliographies. (Rev: BL 3/1/01) [963]

14923 Corona, Laurel. *Kenya* (5–8). Illus. Series: Modern Nations of the World. 1999, Lucent LB $18.96 (1-56006-590-7). 127pp. A profile of this poor African country that is a study in contrasts and cultures, with material on such subjects as geography, economics, people, and current problems. (Rev: BL 2/15/00; HBG 10/00) [967.62]

14924 Deer, Victoria. *Kenya* (4–6). Series: Countries of the World. 1999, Gareth Stevens LB $19.95 (0-8368-2311-7). 96pp. An excellent introduction to Kenya with material on history, geography, government, unique customs, language, food, and current conditions. (Rev: BL 12/15/99; HBG 10/00) [967.6]

14925 Diouf, Sylviane. *Kings and Queens of Central Africa* (4–7). Series: Watts Library: Africa — Kings and Queens. 2000, Watts LB $24.00 (0-531-20372-7). 64pp. This book on the political and social evolution of central Africa describes some of its important royalty including the 15th-century Afonso and Bolongongo, the legendary Bakuba king, with a final chapter on the region today. (Rev: BL 3/1/01) [960]

14926 Diouf, Sylviane. *Kings and Queens of East Africa* (4–7). Illus. Series: Watts Library: Africa — Kings and Queens. 2000, Watts LB $24.00 (0-531-20373-5). 64pp. This book gives biographical information about royalty in East Africa and through these sketches re-creates the history of this part of Africa. (Rev: BL 2/15/01) [967.6]

14927 *Ethiopia in Pictures* (5–8). Illus. 1994, Lerner LB $21.27 (0-8225-1836-8). 64pp. Land, history and government, culture, education, religion, education, and health are covered. (Rev: BL 2/1/89)

14928 Fox, Mary V. *Somalia* (5–8). Illus. Series: Enchantment of the World. 1996, Children's LB $32.00 (0-516-20019-4). 127pp. An introduction to the land and people of this Muslim republic, which occupies the eastern horn of Africa. (Rev: BL 1/1–15/97) [967.73]

14929 Gish, Steven. *Ethiopia* (4–7). Illus. Series: Cultures of the World. 1996, Marshall Cavendish LB $35.64 (0-7614-0276-4). 128pp. After general

760

background information on Ethiopia, such topics as lifestyles, religion, and language are discussed. (Rev: BL 8/96; SLJ 8/96) [963]

14930 Greenberg, Keith E. *Rwanda: Fierce Clashes in Central Africa* (1–4). Photos by John Isaac. Series: Children in Crisis. 1996, Blackbirch LB $16.95 (1-56711-185-8). 30pp. A harrowing eyewitness account in text and photos of the effects of the war in Rwanda on the lives of children in the refugee camps. (Rev: SLJ 6/97) [967]

14931 Holtzman, Jon. *Samburu* (5–8). Illus. Series: Heritage Library of African Peoples. 1995, Rosen LB $17.95 (0-8239-1759-2). 64pp. A detailed account of the culture, history, and life-styles of these Kenyan people. (Rev: SLJ 5/95) [967.62]

14932 Jones, Schuyler. *Pygmies of Central Africa* (5–8). Illus. 1989, Rourke LB $16.67 (0-86625-268-1). 48pp. A vivid look into the lives of these fascinating people. (Rev: BL 5/15/89)

14933 Kairi, Wambui. *Kenya* (2–4). Series: We Come From. 2000, Raintree Steck-Vaughn LB $22.83 (0-8172-5512-5). 32pp. A young native guide gives basic facts about Kenya, explains how to cook some delicious dishes, and makes simple toys. (Rev: BL 4/15/00; HBG 10/00) [967.62]

14934 *Kenya in Pictures* (5–8). Illus. 1997, Lerner LB $21.27 (0-8225-1830-9). 64pp. Information on all aspects of life in this African country, including extensive coverage of its history. (Rev: BL 4/15/88; SLJ 11/88)

14935 Klyce, Katherine P., and Virginia O. McLean. *Kenya, Jambo!* (2–5). Illus. 1989, Redbird $21.95 (0-9606046-4-2). 36pp. In photos and simple text, a ten-year-old girl tells of her family's vacation in Kenya. (Rev: BL 12/1/89) [916]

14936 Kurtz, Jane. *Ethiopia: The Roof of Africa* (5–8). Illus. Series: Discovering Our Heritage. 1991, Macmillan LB $14.95 (0-87518-483-9). 128pp. Beginning with a map and two pages of basic facts, this account gives an introduction to the land, people, and modern problems of Ethiopia. (Rev: BL 2/1/92; SLJ 5/92) [963]

14937 Lindblad, Lisa. *The Serengeti Migration: Africa's Animals on the Move* (3–7). Photos by Sven-Olof Lindblad. 1994, Hyperion $15.95 (1-56282-668-9). 40pp. A short text and stunning photos describe the annual migration of zebras and wildebeests through Tanzania and Kenya. (Rev: BCCB 5/94; BL 7/94*; SLJ 5/94) [599.73]

14938 McCollum, Sean. *Kenya* (3–5). Illus. Series: Globe-Trotters Club. 1999, Carolrhoda LB $22.60 (1-57505-105-2). 48pp. This book introduces Kenya, with material on its history, geography, religion, people, culture, and population. (Rev: BL 9/15/99; HBG 10/99) [967.62]

14939 McCollum, Sean. *Kenya* (1–3). Illus. Series: A Ticket To. 1999, Carolrhoda LB $22.60 (1-57505-130-3). 48pp. A basic introduction to this African nation that includes many color photographs. (Rev: BL 9/15/99; HBG 10/99) [967.62]

14940 *Malawi in Pictures* (5–8). Illus. 1989, Lerner LB $21.27 (0-8225-1842-2). 64pp. An overview of

climate, history, geography, culture, education, and other aspects of life. (Rev: BL 2/1/89)

14941 Ng'weno, Fleur. *Kenya* (4–7). Illus. Series: Focus On. 1992, Trafalgar $22.95 (0-237-60194-X). 32pp. Discusses Kenya's history, peoples, and lifestyles. (Rev: SLJ 8/92) [967.6]

14942 Njoku, Onwuka N. *Mbundu* (5–7). Illus. Series: Heritage Library of African Peoples. 1997, Rosen LB $17.95 (0-8239-2004-6). 64pp. An introduction to the history and contemporary culture of this people of the African republic of Zaire. (Rev: BL 4/15/97) [9678.3]

14943 Nnoromele, Salome. *Somalia* (5–8). Series: Modern Nations of the World. 2000, Lucent LB $18.96 (1-56006-396-3). 112pp. An introduction to this east African country with material on its history and geography and a large section on daily life. (Rev: BL 5/15/00; HBG 10/00) [967.73]

14944 Okeke, Chika. *Kongo* (5–7). Illus. 1997, Rosen LB $15.95 (0-8239-2001-1). 64pp. The Kongo people of Angola, Congo, and Zaire in central Africa are featured, with material on their history and contemporary culture. (Rev: BL 4/15/97) [967]

14945 Parris, Ronald. *Rendille* (5–8). Illus. Series: Heritage Library of African Peoples. 1994, Rosen LB $17.95 (0-8239-1763-0). 64pp. With extensive use of black-and-white and color photos, introduces the history and customs of the Rendille people of Kenya. (Rev: SLJ 5/95) [967.62]

14946 Pateman, Robert. *Kenya* (4–7). Illus. Series: Cultures of the World. 1993, Marshall Cavendish LB $35.64 (1-85435-572-4). 128pp. The background story of Kenya is revealed through color photos and a text that also covers present concerns. (Rev: BL 8/93) [967.62]

14947 Sayre, April Pulley. *If You Should Hear a Honey Guide* (K–3). Illus. by S. D. Schindler. 1995, Houghton $14.95 (0-395-71545-8). 32pp. An imaginative guide to the animals and plants that are found in the savanna region of Kenya. (Rev: BL 9/1/95; HB 11–12/95; SLJ 10/95*) [598.7]

14948 Stewart, Judy. *A Family in Sudan* (4–6). Illus. 1988, Lerner LB $18.60 (0-8225-1682-9). 32pp. Customs, work, and play are covered in this look at life in this African land. (Rev: BL 8/88)

14949 *Sudan in Pictures* (5–8). Illus. 1990, Lerner LB $21.27 (0-8225-1839-2). 64pp. An overview of history, culture, geography, economy, education, and health. (Rev: BL 2/1/89)

14950 Swinimer, Ciarunji C. *Pokot* (5–8). Illus. Series: Heritage Library of African Peoples. 1994, Rosen LB $17.95 (0-8239-1756-8). 64pp. Using a good balance of text and visuals, this account describes the history, culture, and present status of the Pokot people of Kenya. (Rev: SLJ 5/95) [967.62]

14951 *Tanzania in Pictures* (5–8). Illus. 1989, Lerner LB $21.27 (0-8225-1838-4). 64pp. Part of the Visual Geography series, contains information on history, geography, economy, religion, and culture. (Rev: BL 2/1/89)

14952 Wangari, Esther. *Ameru* (5–8). Illus. Series: Heritage Library of American Peoples. 1995, Rosen

LB $15.95 (0-8239-1766-5). 64pp. A history and description of the culture of the Ameru people of Kenya and the humiliation of being conquered by the British. (Rev: SLJ 11/95) [967.62]

14953 Wilkes, Sybella. *One Day We Had to Run!* (5–8). Illus. 1995, Millbrook LB $20.90 (1-56294-557-2). 61pp. A moving document that was produced from interviews with three young African children who were in a refugee camp in Kenya. (Rev: SLJ 12/95) [967.62]

14954 Zeleza, Tiyambe. *Maasai* (5–8). Illus. Series: Heritage Library of African Peoples. 1994, Rosen LB $15.95 (0-8239-1757-6). 64pp. An introduction to these people of Kenya and Tanzania, their culture, customs, and history. (Rev: SLJ 5/95) [967.62]

14955 Zeleza, Tiyambe. *Mijikenda* (5–8). Illus. Series: Heritage Library of American Peoples. 1995, Rosen LB $15.95 (0-8239-1767-3). 64pp. The history and present-day lifestyle of this group that lives in Kenya and is made up of nine peoples. (Rev: SLJ 11/95) [967.62]

Northern Africa

14956 Blauer, Ettagale, and Jason Lauré. *Morocco* (4–7). Series: Enchantment of the World. 1999, Children's LB $32.00 (0-516-20961-2). 144pp. In this fine introduction to Morocco topics include history, government, economics, people, religion, culture, and the arts. (Rev: BL 9/15/99) [964]

14957 Fox, Mary V. *Tunisia* (5–8). Illus. Series: Enchantment of the World. 1990, Children's LB $32.00 (0-516-02724-7). 128pp. Introduces this North African country. (Rev: BL 1/1/91) [961.1]

14958 Hermes, Jules. *The Children of Morocco* (3–6). Illus. 1995, Carolrhoda LB $23.93 (0-87614-857-7); paper $7.95 (0-87614-899-2). 48pp. Features children from various Moroccan settings, such as cities like Casablanca and nomadic desert settlements. (Rev: BL 5/1/95; SLJ 7/95) [964]

14959 Kagda, Falaq. *Algeria* (4–7). Illus. Series: Cultures of the World. 1997, Marshall Cavendish LB $35.64 (0-7614-0680-8). 128pp. This book on Algeria emphasizes the people and how they live. (Rev: BL 8/97) [965]

14960 *Libya in Pictures* (5–8). Illus. Series: Visual Geography. 1996, Lerner LB $21.27 (0-8225-1907-0). 64pp. Introduces this North African country's geography, history, and people, with many illustrations. (Rev: BL 11/15/96) [961.2]

14961 Malcolm, Peter. *Libya* (4–7). Illus. 1993, Marshall Cavendish LB $35.64 (1-85435-573-2). 128pp. Well-chosen photos and readable text give good background information as well as material on present problems. (Rev: BL 8/93) [961.2]

14962 Mann, Kenny. *Egypt, Kush, Aksum: Northeast Africa* (4–6). Illus. Series: African Kingdoms of the Past. 1997, Dillon LB $19.95 (0-87518-655-6); paper $7.95 (0-382-39657-X). 105pp. Describes these famous ancient African civilizations as well as northeast Africa today. Also use *Zenj, Buganda: East Africa*. (Rev: SLJ 9/97) [967]

14963 Raskin, Lawrie, and Debora Pearson. *52 Days by Camel: My Sahara Adventure* (4–7). Illus. 1998, Annick LB $24.95 (1-55037-519-9); paper $14.95 (1-55037-518-0). 88pp. A first-person account of a journey in and around the Sahara Desert, with details on Moroccan life and culture. (Rev: BL 6/1–15/98; SLJ 7/98) [966]

14964 Stewart, Judy. *A Family in Morocco* (2–4). Illus. 1986, Lerner LB $18.60 (0-8225-1664-0). 32pp. Basic geography and the facts of daily living, focusing on one child in a family. (Rev: BL 5/15/86; SLJ 10/86)

Southern Africa

14965 Biesele, Megan, and Kxao Royal. *San* (5–7). Series: Heritage Library of African Peoples. 1997, Rosen LB $15.95 (0-8239-1997-8). 63pp. The San people of Botswana, Namibia, and South Africa are featured in this account that tells of their rich tradition and their struggle for freedom. (Rev: BL 9/15/97) [968.06]

14966 Blauer, Ettagale, and Jason Lauré. *Madagascar* (4–7). Series: Enchantment of the World. 2000, Children's LB $33.00 (0-516-21634-1). 144pp. Madagascar, the island nation off the coast of Africa, is introduced. Topics addressed include its land and people, wildlife, history, traditions, daily life, and economy. (Rev: BL 12/15/00) [969]

14967 Blauer, Ettagale, and Jason Lauré. *South Africa* (5–10). Series: Enchantment of the World. 1998, Children's LB $32.00 (0-516-20606-0). 144pp. An introduction to South Africa that gives good coverage of the struggle of black Africans for freedom and the problems facing the population today. (Rev: HBG 3/99; SLJ 11/98) [968]

14968 Blauer, Ettagale, and Jason Lauré. *Swaziland* (5–8). Illus. Series: Enchantment of the World. 1996, Children's LB $32.00 (0-516-20020-8). 128pp. This landlocked kingdom north of South Africa is introduced, with material on its physical features, history, and economy. (Rev: BL 1/1–15/97) [968.87]

14969 Bolaane, Maitseo, and Part T. Mgadla. *Batswana* (5–7). Series: Heritage Library of African Peoples. 1997, Rosen LB $15.95 (0-8239-2008-9). 64pp. Discusses the Batswana people, who live in Botswana and South Africa, with material on their history, culture, and present status. (Rev: BL 1/1–15/98) [968]

14970 Brandenburg, Jim. *Sand and Fog: Adventures in Southern Africa* (5–8). Illus. 1994, Walker LB $17.85 (0-8027-8233-7). 44pp. A stunning photo-essay about the wildlife found in Namibia in southwest Africa. (Rev: BCCB 5/94; BL 3/1/94*; HB 5–6/94; SLJ 5/94) [968.1]

14971 Brownlie, Alison. *South Africa* (2–4). Illus. Series: We Come From. 2000, Raintree Steck-Vaughn $22.83 (0-8172-5221-5). 32pp. Readers are introduced to South Africa, the homeland of this book's 7-year-old narrator, including its geography, food, weather, work, schools, and other topics. (Rev: BL 4/15/00; HBG 10/00; SLJ 10/00) [968]

14972 Corona, Laurel. *South Africa* (5–8). Series: Modern Nations of the World. 2000, Lucent LB $18.96 (1-56006-601-6). 112pp. A fact-filled account that is particularly strong on South Africa's history, life today, and famous personalities. (Rev: BL 2/15/00; HBG 10/00) [968]

14973 Dawson, Zoe. *South Africa* (K–3). Illus. Series: Postcards From. 1995, Raintree Steck-Vaughn LB $22.83 (0-8172-4015-2). 32pp. In double-page spreads, points of interest in South Africa are described. (Rev: SLJ 3/96) [968]

14974 Diouf, Sylviane. *Kings and Queens of Southern Africa* (4–7). Illus. Series: Watts Library: Africa — Kings and Queens. 2000, Watts LB $24.00 (0-531-20374-3). 64pp. Through the lives of Shaka the Zulu king, Moshoeshoe of the Sotho kingdom, and others, the reader gets a good history of this region before and during the colonial period. (Rev: BL 2/15/01) [968]

14975 Ellis, Royston, and John R. Jones. *Madagascar* (2–4). Series: Festivals of the World. 1999, Gareth Stevens LB $14.95 (0-8368-2023-1). 32pp. A few craft projects and recipes accompany this description of Madagascar's unique holidays — both religious and secular. (Rev: BL 4/15/98) [969.1]

14976 Flint, David. *South Africa* (5–8). Illus. Series: Modern Industrial World. 1996, Raintree Steck-Vaughn $24.26 (0-8172-4554-5). 48pp. The present economic status of South Africa is studied through personal narratives and case studies. (Rev: BL 2/15/97) [968]

14977 Green, Jen. *A Family from South Africa* (3–5). Illus. Series: Families Around the World. 1997, Raintree Steck-Vaughn LB $25.69 (0-8172-4902-8). 32pp. Everyday life in South Africa is covered through the daily activities of a hard-working family at home and at school. (Rev: BL 2/1/98; HBG 3/98; SLJ 6/98) [306.85]

14978 Green, Rebecca L. *Merina* (5–7). Illus. Series: Heritage Library of African Peoples. 1997, Rosen LB $17.95 (0-8239-1991-9). 64pp. This account tells of the life, past and present, of this African tribal group that lives on the island of Madagascar. (Rev: BL 4/15/97) [969.1]

14979 Halvorsen, Lisa. *Letters Home from Zimbabwe* (2–5). Series: Letters Home From. 2000, Blackbirch LB $16.95 (1-56711-412-1). 32pp. Formatted as letters from a child visiting Zimbabwe to a friend back home, this book gives basic information on the country with postcard-like illustrations. (Rev: HBG 3/01; SLJ 11/00) [968.91]

14980 Heale, Jay. *South Africa* (2–3). Illus. Series: Festivals of the World. 1998, Gareth Stevens LB $18.60 (0-8368-2007-X). 32pp. Lists the principal holidays in South Africa, details the main ones, and provides a section on crafts. (Rev: BL 5/15/98; HBG 10/98; SLJ 10/98) [394.2]

14981 Heinrichs, Ann. *South Africa* (2–4). Illus. Series: True Books. 1997, Children's LB $22.00 (0-516-20340-1). 48pp. South Africa is introduced, with material on its history, geography, economy, and peoples. (Rev: BL 9/15/97) [968]

14982 Inserra, Rose, and Susan Powell. *The Kalahari* (5–8). Illus. Series: Ends of the Earth. 1997, Heinemann $25.45 (0-431-06932-8). 48pp. An introduction to the desert region of southern Botswana, eastern Namibia, and western South Africa. (Rev: SLJ 11/97) [968]

14983 Kaschula, Russel. *Xhosa* (5–7). Series: Heritage Library of African Peoples. 1997, Rosen LB $17.95 (0-8239-2013-5). 64pp. The Xhosa people of South Africa are introduced with stunning photos and coverage of their past as well as present culture and lifestyles. (Rev: BL 1/1–15/98) [968]

14984 Lauré, Jason. *Angola* (5–8). Illus. Series: Enchantment of the World. 1990, Children's LB $32.00 (0-516-02721-2). 128pp. The troubled history of Angola is given, and geography and key people are introduced. (Rev: BL 1/1/91) [967.3]

14985 Lauré, Jason. *Botswana* (5–8). Illus. Series: Enchantment of the World. 1993, Children's LB $32.00 (0-516-02616-X). 128pp. An introduction to this republic in southern Africa, which gained independence in 1964 and is famous for its gold and wildlife preserves. (Rev: BL 11/1/93; SLJ 4/94) [968.83]

14986 Lauré, Jason. *Namibia* (5–8). Illus. Series: Enchantment of the World. 1993, Children's LB $32.00 (0-516-02615-1). 128pp. The story of this African nation — formerly South-West Africa — and its history and present problems. (Rev: BL 8/93) [968.81]

14987 Lauré, Jason. *Zambia* (4–6). Illus. Series: Enchantment of the World. 1989, Children's LB $32.00 (0-516-02716-6). 128pp. The land and people of Zambia are covered with special material in a ten-page section of important facts. (Rev: BL 1/1/90) [941.5]

14988 Lauré, Jason. *Zimbabwe* (4–7). Illus. 1989, Children's LB $32.00 (0-516-02704-2). 128pp. The history, culture, people, and customs of this African land. (Rev: BL 8/88)

14989 Leigh, Nila K. *Learning to Swim in Swaziland: A Child's-Eye View of a Southern African Country* (2–4). Illus. 1993, Scholastic $15.95 (0-590-45938-4). 48pp. Nila's first-person account of her year in Swaziland. (Rev: BCCB 3/93; BL 1/15/93; SLJ 5/93) [968.8]

14990 McKee, Tim. *No More Strangers Now: Young Voices from a New South Africa* (5–10). Photos by Anne Blackshaw. 1998, DK $19.95 (0-7894-2524-6). 107pp. Twelve South African teenagers from varied backgrounds describe conditions under apartheid and the impact it had on their lives. (Rev: HB 9–10/98; HBG 3/99; SLJ 12/98) [968]

14991 *Madagascar in Pictures* (5–8). Illus. 1988, Lerner LB $21.27 (0-8225-1841-4). 64pp. Covers geography, history, culture, economics, religion, and health. (Rev: BL 2/1/89)

14992 Ngwane, Zolani. *Zulu* (5–7). Series: Heritage Library of African Peoples. 1997, Rosen LB $15.95 (0-8239-2014-3). 64pp. Introduces the past history and culture of the Zulus of South Africa. Also use *Sukuma* and *Luba* (both 1997). (Rev: BL 9/15/97) [968.06]

14993 Nwaezeigwe, Nwankwo T. *Ngoni* (5–7). Illus. Series: Heritage Library of African Peoples. 1997, Rosen LB $17.95 (0-8239-2006-2). 64pp. Describes the history, traditions, and struggle for freedom of this African group in Malawi. (Rev: BL 4/15/97) [968.97]

14994 Oluikpe, Benson O. *Swazi* (5–7). Illus. Series: Heritage Library of African Peoples. 1997, Rosen LB $15.95 (0-8239-2012-7). 64pp. The Swazi people live in Swaziland and South Africa, and this book describes their history, traditions, and struggles for freedom. (Rev: BL 4/15/97; SLJ 12/97) [968]

14995 Oluonye, Mary N. *Madagascar* (1–3). Series: Globe-Trotters Club. 2000, Carolrhoda LB $22.60 (1-57505-120-6). 48pp. From the monsoons to the comfortable dry season, this is a simple introduction to the island off the coast of Africa that is known as "a World Apart." (Rev: BL 5/15/00; HBG 10/00) [969]

14996 Oluonye, Mary N. *South Africa* (3–5). Series: Globe-Trotters Club. 1999, Carolrhoda $22.60 (1-57505-116-8). 48pp. Double-page spreads cover standard topics on South Africa and are enhanced with sidebars containing activities and unusual bits of information. (Rev: BL 9/15/99; HBG 3/00; SLJ 3/00) [968]

14997 Oluonye, Mary N. *South Africa* (1–3). Series: A Ticket To. 1999, Carolrhoda LB $22.60 (1-57505-141-9). 48pp. Following a large map of the country, this first look at South Africa introduces the land and its people, using easy-to-understand language and many color pictures. (Rev: BL 9/15/99; HBG 3/00; SLJ 3/00) [968]

14998 Rosemarin, Ike. *South Africa* (4–7). Illus. Series: Cultures of the World. 1993, Marshall Cavendish LB $35.64 (1-85435-575-9). 128pp. Historical and modern concerns are covered in this look at South Africa. (Rev: BL 8/93) [968]

14999 Ryan, Patrick. *South Africa* (K–3). Series: Faces and Places. 1997, Child's World LB $22.79 (1-56766-373-7). 32pp. Using double-page spreads, this work introduces South Africa — the land and its people, plants and animals, history, society, and modern life. (Rev: SLJ 6/98) [968]

15000 Schneider, Elizabeth Ann. *Ndebele* (5–7). Illus. Series: Heritage Library of African Peoples. 1997, Rosen LB $17.95 (0-8239-2009-7). 64pp. Topics covered about the Ndebele people of South Africa include environment, history, religion, social organization, politics, and customs. (Rev: BL 4/15/97) [968]

15001 *South Africa in Pictures* (5–8). Illus. 1996, Lerner LB $21.27 (0-8225-1835-X). 64pp. Focusing on climate, geography, wildlife, and the history of this troubled country. (Rev: BL 8/88)

15002 Stark, Al. *Zimbabwe: A Treasure of Africa* (4–7). Illus. 1986, Macmillan $19.95 (0-87518-308-5). 160pp. The colorful history, culture, wildlife, geography, and diversity of the people of Zimbabwe are detailed. (Rev: BL 6/15/86; SLJ 5/86)

15003 Stein, R. Conrad. *Cape Town* (5–8). Illus. Series: Cities of the World. 1998, Children's LB $26.00 (0-516-20781-4). 64pp. A photo-essay showing this modern, multicultural, multiracial South African capital, with its rich diversity of people at work, at school, and at play. (Rev: BL 12/15/98; HBG 3/99) [968.7]

15004 Udechukwu, Ada. *Herero* (5–7). Illus. Series: Heritage Library of African Peoples. 1996, Rosen LB $17.95 (0-8239-2003-8). 64pp. The history, customs, and culture of the Herero people are described. (Rev: BL 3/15/96; SLJ 6/96) [968.8]

15005 Van Wyk, Gary N. *Basotho* (5–7). Illus. Series: Heritage Library of African Peoples. 1996, Rosen LB $15.95 (0-8239-2005-4). 63pp. Describes the Basotho people, who live in Lesotho and South Africa, with material on their history, religion, social organization, and customs. (Rev: BL 11/15/96; SLJ 3/97) [968]

15006 Van Wyk, Gary N., and Robert Johnson. *Shona* (5–7). Series: Heritage Library of African Peoples. 1997, Rosen LB $15.95 (0-8239-2011-9). 64pp. The Shona people of Zimbabwe are presented in outstanding photos, with a text that covers their past, their culture, and their present living conditions and problems. (Rev: BL 1/1–15/98) [968]

15007 *Zimbabwe in Pictures* (5–8). Illus. 1997, Lerner LB $21.27 (0-8225-1825-2). 64pp. Many photos highlight this overview of Zimbabwe's history, climate, wildlife, and culture. (Rev: BL 4/15/88) [968]

Western Africa

15008 Adeeb, Hassan, and Bonnetta Adeeb. *Nigeria: One Nation, Many Cultures* (4–8). Illus. Series: Exploring Cultures of the World. 1995, Benchmark LB $27.07 (0-7614-0190-3). 64pp. Opening with an account of a legendary figure, this book continues with an introduction to Nigeria that emphasizes its culture and how the people live. (Rev: SLJ 6/96) [966.9]

15009 Adeleke, Tunde. *Songhay* (5–7). Illus. Series: Heritage Library of African Peoples. 1996, Rosen LB $15.95 (0-8239-1986-2). 63pp. Both historical information and material on contemporary life are given in this account of the African people who live chiefly in Mali, Niger, and Benin. (Rev: BL 11/15/96) [960]

15010 Ahiagble, Gilbert Bobbo, and Louise Meyer. *Master Weaver from Ghana* (3–5). Photos by Nestor Hernandez. 1998, Open Hand $18.00 (0-940880-61-X). 32pp. Daily life in Ghana is explored in this book about a master weaver, Ahiagble, his techniques, craft, and the culture he represents. (Rev: SLJ 3/99) [966.7]

15011 Anda, Michael O. *Yoruba* (5–7). Illus. Series: Heritage Library of African Peoples. 1996, Rosen LB $15.95 (0-8239-1988-9). 64pp. Looks at the environment, history, religion, social organization, politics, customs, and culture of the Yoruba people. (Rev: BL 3/15/96; SLJ 6/96) [960]

15012 Azuonye, Chukwuma. *Edo: The Bini People of the Benin Kingdom* (5–7). Illus. Series: Heritage Library of African Peoples. 1996, Rosen LB $17.95

(0-8239-1985-4). 64pp. In this discussion of the Edo people of Nigeria, such topics as history, religion, customs, and culture are covered. (Rev: BL 3/15/96) [966.9]

15013 Beaton, Margaret. *Senegal* (5–8). Illus. Series: Enchantment of the World. 1997, Children's LB $32.00 (0-516-20304-5). 128pp. An introduction to this West African nation, its people, and its cities, including the capital, Dakar. (Rev: BL 7/97; HBG 3/98) [916.63]

15014 Berg, Elizabeth. *Nigeria* (2–4). Series: Festivals of the World. 1998, Gareth Stevens LB $14.95 (0-8368-2017-7). 32pp. A few suitable crafts and recipes accompany this introduction to the land and people of Nigeria, with emphasis on their special holidays and how they are celebrated. (Rev: BL 12/15/98; HBG 10/99) [966.8]

15015 Blauer, Ettagale, and Jason Lauré. *Ghana* (4–7). Series: Enchantment of the World. 1999, Children's LB $32.00 (0-516-20962-0). 144pp. A geographical and cultural exploration of the African nation of Ghana, once a center of the slave trade. (Rev: BL 12/15/99) [966.7]

15016 Boateng, Faustine Ama. *Asante* (5–7). Illus. Series: Heritage Library of African Peoples. 1996, Rosen LB $17.95 (0-8239-1975-7). 63pp. This African people living in present-day Ghana is described — its history, traditions, and lifestyle. (Rev: BL 11/15/96; SLJ 3/97) [966.7]

15017 Brace, Steve. *Ghana* (4–8). Illus. Series: Economically Developing Countries. 1995, Thomson Learning LB $24.26 (1-56847-242-0). 48pp. Rich and poor rural and urban families are introduced in this attractive book on Ghana, its past, and its present. (Rev: SLJ 7/95) [966.7]

15018 Brook, Larry. *Daily Life in Ancient and Modern Timbuktu* (5–7). Illus. 1999, Lerner LB $23.93 (0-8225-3215-8). 64pp. A fascinating look at this ancient West African city that was once a center of commerce and learning. (Rev: BL 9/1/99; HBG 10/99; SLJ 7/99) [966.23]

15019 Brownlie, Alison. *Nigeria* (2–4). Series: We Come From. 2000, Raintree Steck-Vaughn LB $22.83 (0-8172-5513-3). 32pp. Using a native child as a guide, this introduction to Nigeria gives basic information on the country plus such specialized coverage as a trip to local markets, making a fish stew, a game of hide and seek, and several recipes. (Rev: BL 4/15/00; HBG 10/00; SLJ 10/00) [966.9]

15020 Brownlie, Alison. *West Africa* (3–5). Series: Foods and Festivals. 1999, Raintree Steck-Vaughn LB $22.83 (0-8172-5552-4). 32pp. Recipes for festival dishes enhance this account of life in West Africa as seen through its various holidays. (Rev: BL 5/15/99; HBG 10/99; SLJ 7/99) [966]

15021 Chambers, Catherine. *West African States: 15th Century to the Colonial Era* (5–8). Series: Looking Back. 1999, Raintree Steck-Vaughn LB $25.69 (0-8172-5427-7). 63pp. A brief overview of the history and culture of the great empires of West Africa and how they disappeared with the arrival of the Europeans. (Rev: BL 5/15/99) [966.2]

15022 Chicoine, Stephen D. *A Liberian Family* (3–5). Photos by Stephen Chicoine. Series: Journey Between Two Worlds. 1997, Lerner LB $22.60 (0-8225-3411-8); paper $8.95 (0-8225-0975-6). 64pp. Explains why a family was forced to leave Liberia to escape persecution. Also gives a history of this land and its people. (Rev: HBG 3/98; SLJ 2/98) [966]

15023 Chocolate, Deborah M. *Kente Colors* (PS–3). Illus. by John Ward. 1996, Walker LB $16.85 (0-8027-8389-9). 32pp. The history and traditions of kente cloth of Ghana are told, along with a description of its meaning and colors. (Rev: BL 2/15/96; SLJ 6/96) [391]

15024 *Cote d'Ivoire (Ivory Coast) in Pictures* (5–8). Illus. 1988, Lerner LB $21.27 (0-8225-1828-7). 64pp. Covering all aspects of life in this overview, with pictorial emphasis and coverage on possible future developments. (Rev: BL 4/15/88; SLJ 11/88)

15025 Diouf, Sylviane. *Kings and Queens of West Africa* (4–7). Series: Watts Library: Africa — Kings and Queens. 2000, Watts LB $24.00 (0-531-20375-1). 64pp. Some of the royal figures covered in this historical survey of West Africa are Emperor Mansa Musa of Mali and Nsate Yalla Mbodj, queen of the Walo of Senegal. (Rev: BL 3/1/01) [960]

15026 *Ghana in Pictures* (5–8). Illus. 1988, Lerner LB $21.27 (0-8225-1829-5). 64pp. Photos, maps, and charts enhance this overview. (Rev: BL 8/88)

15027 Goodsmith, Lauren. *The Children of Mauritania: Days in the Desert and by the River Shore* (3–6). Illus. Series: World's Children. 1994, Carolrhoda LB $23.93 (0-87614-782-1). 56pp. The lives of two children growing up in Mauritania in northwest Africa are described, as well as their different environments, one from a desert and the other from a river valley. (Rev: BCCB 4/94; BL 2/1/94) [966.1]

15028 Hathaway, Jim. *Cameroon in Pictures* (5–8). Illus. Series: Visual Geography. 1992, Lerner LB $21.27 (0-8225-1857-0). 64pp. With numerous charts, maps, and photos, the country of Cameroon is introduced. (Rev: BL 9/15/89) [967]

15029 Hetfield, Jamie. *The Yoruba of West Africa* (PS–2). Illus. Series: Celebrating the Peoples and Civilizations of Africa. 1996, Rosen LB $13.95 (0-8239-2332-0). 24pp. A simple introduction to the Yoruba people of West Africa, with material on their culture, food, rituals, and lifestyle. (Rev: SLJ 11/96) [966.9]

15030 Koslow, Philip. *Dahomey: The Warrior Kings* (5–8). Illus. Series: The Kingdoms of Africa. 1996, Chelsea LB $18.95 (0-7910-3137-3); paper $8.95 (0-7910-3138-1). 63pp. A history of the West African kingdom that flourished in the 17th and 18th centuries and how the slave trade affected it. (Rev: SLJ 12/96) [960]

15031 Kummer, Patricia K. *Cote d'Ivoire* (5–8). Illus. Series: Enchantment of the World. 1996, Children's LB $32.00 (0-516-02641-0). 124pp. An introduction to the small French-speaking African republic Ivory Coast, which gained its freedom in 1960 and is now known as Cote d'Ivoire. (Rev: BL 7/96) [966.68]

15032 Kushner, Nina. *The Democratic Republic of the Congo* (4–6). Series: Countries of the World. 2000, Gareth Stevens LB $26.60 (0-8368-2330-3). 96pp. Details the history of this African republic once controlled by the French, along with material on geography, government, lifestyles, food, economy, and current problems. (Rev: BL 3/15/01) [967]

15033 Levy, Patricia. *Nigeria* (4–7). Illus. Series: Cultures of the World. 1993, Marshall Cavendish LB $35.64 (1-85435-574-0). 128pp. Information on history, geography, lifestyles, people, and culture. (Rev: BL 8/93) [966.9]

15034 *Liberia in Pictures* (5–8). Illus. 1996, Lerner LB $21.27 (0-8225-1837-6). 64pp. Covers climate, geography, wildlife, vegetation, and natural resources. (Rev: BL 8/88)

15035 MacDonald, Fiona. *Ancient African Town* (4–7). Illus. by Gerald Wood. Series: Metropolis. 1998, Watts LB $24.00 (0-531-14480-1). 45pp. Using a well-written text and colorful drawings, this work describes life in a 17th-century African community based on Benin City of the Edo empire in present-day Nigeria. (Rev: HBG 3/99; SLJ 1/99) [966.9]

15036 Mack-Williams, Kibibi V. *Mossi* (5–7). Illus. Series: Heritage Library of African Peoples. 1996, Rosen LB $17.95 (0-8239-1984-6). 64pp. The history, social organization, and culture of the Mossi people of West Africa are described. (Rev: BL 3/15/96) [966.25]

15037 Mann, Kenny. *Ghana, Mali, Songhay: The Western Sudan* (4–8). Illus. Series: African Kingdoms of the Past. 1996, Silver Burdett $19.95 (0-87518-656-4); paper $7.95 (0-382-39176-4). 108pp. After retelling a heroic African folktale, this account describes the once powerful empires of Ghana, Mali, and Songhay. (Rev: SLJ 9/96) [967]

15038 *Nigeria in Pictures* (5–8). Illus. 1995, Lerner LB $21.27 (0-8225-1826-0). 64pp. A visual focus on this African land. (Rev: BL 8/88)

15039 Nnoromele, Salome. *Life Among the Ibo Women of Nigeria* (4–7). Illus. 1998, Lucent LB $17.96 (1-56006-344-0). 96pp. A beautifully written account of women's role in Nigeria's Ibo society, tracing the country's history, social structure, and changes brought about by contacts with Western culture. (Rev: BL 9/1/98) [305.48]

15040 Nwanunobi, C. O. *Malinke* (5–7). Illus. Series: Heritage Library of African Peoples. 1996, Rosen LB $15.95 (0-8239-1979-X). 63pp. Features the culture, history, and contemporary lifeways of the Malinke people, now living along the western coast of Africa. (Rev: BL 11/15/96) [966.23]

15041 Nwanunobi, C. O. *Soninke* (5–7). Illus. Series: Heritage Library of African Peoples. 1996, Rosen LB $17.95 (0-8239-1978-1). 63pp. This African people — found in such countries as Ghana, Mali, Nigeria, and Senegal — is discussed, with material on its history, customs, and present living conditions. (Rev: BL 11/15/96) [966]

15042 Ogbaa, Kalu. *Igbo* (5–8). Illus. Series: Heritage Library of American Peoples. 1995, Rosen LB $15.95 (0-8239-1977-3). 64pp. An introduction to the Igbo people, who are one of the three most important ethnic groups in Nigeria. (Rev: SLJ 11/95) [966.9]

15043 Onyefulu, Ifeoma. *Ogbo: Sharing Life in an African Village* (1–5). Illus. 1996, Harcourt $15.00 (0-15-200498-X). 32pp. In a Nigerian village, people in the same age group, called ogbo, work together for the good of the community. (Rev: BCCB 4/96; BL 4/15/96; HB 9–10/96; SLJ 4/96*) [306]

15044 Parris, Ronald. *Hausa* (5–7). Illus. Series: Heritage Library of African Peoples. 1996, Rosen LB $17.95 (0-8239-1983-8). 63pp. The Hausa people of Niger and Nigeria are discussed, with material on history and contemporary life. (Rev: BL 11/15/96) [966]

15045 Peffer-Engels, John. *The Benin Kingdom of West Africa* (K–2). Illus. Series: Celebrating the Peoples and Civilizations of Africa. 1996, Rosen LB $13.95 (0-8239-2334-7). 24pp. This account describes the Benin kingdom, the Edo people, how many were enslaved and taken to the United States, and their present culture and lifestyle. (Rev: SLJ 1/97) [966.9]

15046 Sallah, Tijan M. *Wolof* (5–7). Illus. Series: Heritage Library of African Peoples. 1996, Rosen LB $17.95 (0-8239-1987-0). 64pp. Using maps, many color illustrations, and text, the Wolof people of Africa are introduced. (Rev: BL 3/15/96; SLJ 7/96) [966.3]

15047 *Senegal in Pictures* (5–8). Illus. 1989, Lerner LB $21.27 (0-8225-1827-9). 64pp. A look at the geography, history, culture, and economics of Senegal. (Rev: BL 4/15/89; SLJ 11/88)

15048 Sheehan, Patricia. *Côte d'Ivoire* (5–8). 1999, Marshall Cavendish LB $24.95 (0-7614-0980-7). 128pp. The Ivory Coast is presented with coverage of its geography, history, government, economy, and social and cultural life. (Rev: HBG 10/00; SLJ 4/00) [966.68]

15049 Tenquist, Alasdair. *Nigeria* (5–8). Illus. Series: Economically Developing Countries. 1996, Raintree Steck-Vaughn LB $24.26 (0-8172-4527-8). 48pp. This introduction to Nigeria emphasizes present-day government and economic conditions. (Rev: BL 3/1/97; SLJ 9/97) [330]

15050 Zimmermann, Robert. *The Gambia* (5–8). Illus. Series: Enchantment of the World. 1994, Children's LB $32.00 (0-516-02625-9). 128pp. This tiny West African country is introduced in text and color photos that cover all major topics related to this new nation. (Rev: BL 12/15/94; SLJ 4/95) [966.51]

Asia

General

15051 Sayre, April Pulley. *Asia* (5–8). Illus. Series: Seven Continents. 1999, Twenty-First Century LB $23.40 (0-7613-1368-0). 64pp. Using maps, photos, and sidebars, this concise work discusses Asia — its people, geography and geology, climate and oceans, flora and fauna. (Rev: BL 8/99; HBG 3/00) [915]

15052 Wilkinson, Philip, and Michael Pollard. *The Magical East* (4–7). Illus. by Robert Ingpen. Series: Mysterious Places. 1994, Chelsea LB $19.95 (0-7910-2754-6). 92pp. An oversize volume that highlights several places and cities of importance in the history of the Orient. (Rev: BL 1/15/94; SLJ 4/94) [930.1]

China

15053 Baldwin, Robert F. *Daily Life in Ancient and Modern Beijing* (4–7). Illus. by Ray Webb. Series: Cities Through Time. 1999, Runestone LB $23.93 (0-8225-3214-X). 64pp. Topics introduced in this contrast between Beijing past and present include the arts, religion, school, history, and daily life. (Rev: HBG 10/99; SLJ 7/99) [951]

15054 Beshore, George. *Science in Ancient China* (4–7). Series: Science of the Past. 1998, Watts LB $24.00 (0-531-11334-5). 64pp. Photographs of period artifacts, documents, and artworks illustrate this exploration of ancient China's important scientific contributions. (Rev: BL 6/1–15/98; HBG 10/98; SLJ 8/98) [509]

15055 *China in Pictures* (5–8). Illus. 1994, Lerner LB $21.27 (0-8225-1859-7). 64pp. Covers history and government, cities, minerals, vegetation, and wildlife. (Rev: BL 5/1/89)

15056 Dawson, Zoe. *China* (K–3). Illus. Series: Postcards From. 1995, Raintree Steck-Vaughn LB $22.83 (0-8172-4007-1). 32pp. Using different postcards as a focus, this account describes salient features of China. (Rev: SLJ 3/96) [951]

15057 Dramer, Kim. *China* (3–6). Illus. Series: Games People Play! 1997, Children's LB $23.50 (0-516-20308-8). 64pp. After an introduction to China, this book discusses a number of recreational pursuits, including those practiced at festivals and those that are universally popular, like kite flying, chess, and several sports. (Rev: BL 10/15/97) [790]

15058 Dramer, Kim. *People's Republic of China* (4–7). Series: Enchantment of the World. 1999, Children's LB $32.00 (0-516-21077-7). 144pp. A revision of a standard source on China, including its history, government, people, languages, culture, and current conditions. (Rev: BL 9/15/99) [951]

15059 Ferroa, Peggy. *China* (4–7). Illus. Series: Cultures of the World. 1991, Marshall Cavendish LB $35.64 (1-85435-399-3). 128pp. Unusual facts highlight this look at China, with emphasis on culture. (Rev: BL 2/15/92; SLJ 3/92) [951]

15060 Field, Catherine. *China* (4–8). Illus. Series: Nations of the World. 2000, Raintree Steck-Vaughn LB $31.40 (0-8172-5781-0). 128pp. This is a fine introduction to China's past and present that supplies even more interesting information through the use of sidebars. (Rev: BL 10/15/00; HBG 10/00) [951.21]

15061 Flint, David. *China* (2–4). Series: On the Map. 1994, Raintree Steck-Vaughn LB $22.83 (0-8114-3421-4). 32pp. Alternating a page of color photos with a page of text, such topics as China's geography, education, industry, and family life are covered. (Rev: BL 2/1/94; SLJ 7/94) [951]

15062 Goh, Sui Noi. *China* (4–8). Series: Countries of the World. 1998, Gareth Stevens LB $18.95 (0-8368-2124-6). 96pp. As well as general coverage on the history, geography, and people of China, this volume discusses Confucius, women in society, the Silk Road, and Tiananmen Square. (Rev: BL 12/15/98; HBG 10/99; SLJ 6/99) [951]

15063 Goh, Sui Noi, and Lim Bee Ling. *Welcome to China* (2–4). Series: Welcome to My Country. 1999, Gareth Stevens LB $16.95 (0-8368-2395-8). 48pp. With an illustration on each page, this introduction to China covers such topics as geography, history, government, everyday life, language, and food. (Rev: SLJ 3/00) [951]

15064 Gresko, Marcia S. *Letters Home from China* (3–5). Illus. Series: Letters Home From. 1999, Blackbirch LB $16.95 (1-56711-400-8). 32pp. Written from the viewpoint of a young tourist, this book of letters introduces China, its land, people, and history. (Rev: BL 11/15/99; HBG 3/00; SLJ 1/00) [915.104]

15065 Harkonen, Reijo. *The Children of China* (4–6). Illus. by Matti Pitkanen. Series: The World's Children. 1990, Carolrhoda LB $23.93 (0-87614-394-X). 40pp. A travelogue narrative with striking color photos. (Rev: BL 6/15/90; SLJ 9/90) [951]

15066 Harvey, Miles. *Look What Came from China* (2–5). Series: Look What Came From. 1998, Watts LB $20.00 (0-531-11495-3). 32pp. A colorful introduction to China's contribution to world culture in areas such as inventions, sports, food, holidays, and customs. (Rev: HBG 3/99; SLJ 12/98) [951]

15067 Haskins, Jim. *Count Your Way Through China* (3–5). Illus. 1987, Carolrhoda LB $19.93 (0-87614-302-8); Lerner paper $5.95 (0-87614-486-5). 24pp. Concepts about China are introduced with the use of numbers 1 through 10. (Rev: BL 10/15/87; SLJ 9/87)

15068 Heinrichs, Ann. *China* (2–4). Illus. Series: True Books. 1997, Children's LB $22.00 (0-516-20329-0). 48pp. This introduction to China includes material on the land, people, history, and culture. (Rev: BL 9/15/97; SLJ 11/97) [951]

15069 Kent, Deborah. *Beijing* (3–6). Illus. Series: Cities of the World. 1996, Children's LB $26.50 (0-516-20023-2). 64pp. A history of Beijing, photos of its famous landmarks, and details on how its residents live are covered in this well-illustrated account. (Rev: BL 1/1–15/97) [951]

15070 Lazo, Caroline. *The Terra Cotta Army of Emperor Qin* (5–8). Illus. 1993, Macmillan LB $14.95 (0-02-754631-4). 80pp. The story of the 7,500 terra-cotta figures that guard the tomb of China's first emperor. (Rev: BL 7/93; SLJ 8/93) [931]

15071 McLenighan, Valjean. *China: A History to 1949* (5–8). Illus. 1983, Children's LB $32.00 (0-516-02754-9). 128pp. China from its earliest days to the founding of the People's Republic in 1949.

15072 McMahon, Patricia. *Six Words, Many Turtles, and Three Days in Hong Kong* (4–6). Illus. 1997,

Houghton $16.00 (0-395-68621-0). 64pp. A photo-essay about middle-class life in modern Hong Kong. (Rev: BL 7/97; HBG 3/98; SLJ 12/97) [306.85]

15073 Mamdani, Shelby. *Traditions from China* (3–6). Series: Cultural Journeys. 1999, Raintree Steck-Vaughn LB $25.69 (0-8172-5383-1). 48pp. This introduction to the culture of China also includes some Chinese folktales and craft projects such as making dumplings, designing an opera mask, and building a kite. (Rev: BL 5/15/99; HBG 10/99; SLJ 8/99) [951]

15074 Mann, Elizabeth. *The Great Wall* (4–6). Illus. Series: Wonders of the World. 1997, Mikaya $18.95 (0-9650493-2-9). 48pp. The story of the building of this great structure, with a special focus on the history of the period of its construction. (Rev: BL 1/1–15/98; SLJ 12/97) [951]

15075 Martell, Hazel M. *The Ancient Chinese* (4–6). Illus. Series: World of the Past. 1993, Macmillan LB $14.95 (0-02-730653-4). 64pp. A history of early China with emphasis on culture and accomplishments. (Rev: BL 8/93) [951]

15076 Odijk, Pamela. *The Chinese* (4–7). Illus. Series: Ancient World. 1991, Silver Burdett LB $14.95 (0-382-09894-3). 47pp. Brief, informative, and eye-catching treatment of the Chinese, including their influences on medicine and architecture. (Rev: BL 1/15/92) [951]

15077 Patent, Dorothy Hinshaw. *The Incredible Story of China's Buried Warriors* (4–7). Series: Frozen in Time. 1999, Benchmark LB $18.95 (0-7614-0783-9). 64pp. This book explores the mystery of the creation of China's buried warriors, the thousands of terracotta statues that belonged to the first Emperor of China and were uncovered in 1974. (Rev: HBG 10/00; SLJ 3/00) [951]

15078 Pollard, Michael. *The Yangtze* (5–7). Series: Great Rivers. 1997, Benchmark LB $14.95 (0-7614-0505-4). 45pp. Covers historical and geographical aspects of the Yangtze River and discusses current dam-building projects. (Rev: HBG 3/98; SLJ 4/98) [951]

15079 Prior, Katherine. *The History of Emigration from China and Southeast Asia* (4–7). Series: Origins. 1997, Watts LB $21.00 (0-531-14442-9). 32pp. Outlines the political, social, and economic conditions in China that led to people leaving during different periods in its history, as well as material on where they went and their reception. (Rev: BL 12/15/97; HBG 3/98; SLJ 2/98) [951]

15080 Roop, Peter, and Connie Roop. *China* (1–3). Series: A Visit To. 1998, Heinemann LB $19.92 (1-57572-123-6). 32pp. An introduction to China in double-page spreads covering the land, its history and geography, culture, language, and transportation. (Rev: SLJ 7/98) [951]

15081 Shemie, Bonnie. *Houses of China* (4–7). Illus. Series: Native Dwellings. 1996, Tundra $13.95 (0-88776-369-3). 24pp. The various cultures of China, past and present, are introduced through an examination of ten traditional houses. (Rev: SLJ 2/97) [951]

15082 Shui, Amy, and Stuart Thompson. *China* (3–5). Illus. Series: Foods and Festivals. 1999, Raintree Steck-Vaughn $22.83 (0-8172-5757-8). 32pp. A few suitable recipes accompany descriptions of such Chinese festivals as New Year's, the Dragon-Boat festival, and the Moon festival. (Rev: BL 5/15/99; HBG 10/99) [394.1]

15083 Simpson, Judith, ed. *Ancient China* (4–6). Illus. Series: Nature Company Discoveries. 1996, Time Life $16.00 (0-8094-9248-2). 64pp. A special feature of this introduction to the history, people, and culture of ancient China is an eight-page foldout featuring an exciting scene from history. (Rev: BL 6/1–15/96; SLJ 7/96) [931]

15084 Steele, Philip. *Journey Through China* (3–5). Illus. by Martin Camm. Series: Journey Around the World. 1990, Troll LB $18.60 (0-8167-2112-2); paper $4.95 (0-8167-2113-0). 32pp. From its northern desert wastelands to lush southern countryside, the culture, history, and geography of China are explored. (Rev: BL 5/15/91; SLJ 5/91) [951]

15085 Stepanchuk, Carol. *Red Eggs and Dragon Boats: Celebrating Chinese Festivals* (3–6). Illus. 1994, Pacific View $16.95 (1-881896-08-0). 48pp. Five traditional Chinese festivals, including the Dragon Boat Festival and Moon Festival, are introduced, with details on customs and traditions plus recipes for food. (Rev: BL 3/15/94; SLJ 4/94) [394]

15086 Tao, Wang. *Exploration into China* (4–7). Illus. Series: Exploration. 1996, Dillon LB $23.00 (0-02-718087-5); paper $7.95 (0-382-39185-3). 48pp. The story of Chinese history until the opening up of the country by Europeans is given, with a brief overview of its recent history and contemporary life. (Rev: BL 8/96) [951]

15087 Teague, Ken. *Growing Up in Ancient China* (3–5). Illus. Series: Growing Up In. 1993, Troll paper $4.95 (0-8167-2716-3). 32pp. An introduction to life in ancient China, with information on history, customs, schooling, food, clothing, and daily activities. (Rev: BL 1/15/94) [931]

15088 Waterlow, Julia. *China* (4–7). Illus. Series: Country Insights. 1997, Raintree Steck-Vaughn LB $27.12 (0-8172-4787-4). 48pp. Compares the social conditions — home life, employment, schooling, and recreation — in a large city and a rural village in China. (Rev: BL 7/97; SLJ 8/97) [951]

15089 Waterlow, Julia. *China* (2–4). Series: We Come From. 1999, Raintree Steck-Vaughn LB $22.83 (0-8172-5219-3). 32pp. As well as a little information on Chinese home life, schools, and daily activities, this short book discusses geography and weather and gives a single recipe. (Rev: HBG 3/00; SLJ 3/00) [951]

15090 Waterlow, Julia. *A Family from China* (3–5). Series: Families Around the World. 1998, Raintree Steck-Vaughn LB $15.98 (0-8172-4912-5). 32pp. This colorful and well-illustrated book introduces a Chinese family and describes life in contemporary China. (Rev: BL 11/15/98; HBG 3/99) [951]

15091 Williams, Suzanne. *Made in China: Ideas and Inventions from Ancient China* (4–6). Illus. 1997, Pacific View LB $19.95 (1-881896-14-5).

48pp. Covers such topics as papermaking, medicine, and inventions as they were developed in ancient China. (Rev: BL 2/1/97; SLJ 7/97) [931]

15092 Zhang, Song Nan. *The Children of China* (3–6). Illus. 1996, Tundra $17.95 (0-88776-363-4). 32pp. Children of nomadic minorities in China (e.g., Mongolians) are highlighted in this well-illustrated account. (Rev: BL 2/1/96) [759.11]

15093 Zhang, Song Nan. *Cowboy on the Steppes* (4–7). Illus. 1997, Tundra $15.95 (0-88776-410-X). 32pp. The true story of an 18-year-old Chinese boy and the first eight months he spent living in the steppes of Mongolia, where he has been sent during the Cultural Revolution to herd sheep. (Rev: BL 2/15/98; HBG 3/98; SLJ 2/98) [951.7]

India

15094 Arora Lal, Sunandini. *India* (4–5). Series: Countries of the World. 1999, Gareth Stevens LB $18.95 (0-8368-2262-5). 95pp. A colorful introduction to India, covering its geography, history, government, culture, and current problems. (Rev: BL 9/15/99; SLJ 10/99) [954]

15095 Cumming, David. *The Ganges Delta and Its People* (5–8). Illus. Series: People and Places. 1994, Thomson Learning LB $24.26 (1-56847-168-8). 48pp. An introduction to the Ganges delta, the people who live there, the economy it supports, and the tragedy of its frequent flooding. (Rev: BL 10/15/94) [954]

15096 Cumming, David. *India* (4–7). Illus. Series: Our Country. 1998, Raintree Steck-Vaughn $27.12 (0-8172-4797-1). 48pp. Several young inhabitants introduce India and describe life, customs, food, and their homes. (Rev: BL 12/1/89; HBG 10/98; SLJ 3/92) [954]

15097 Cumming, David. *India* (2–4). Series: We Come From. 1999, Raintree Steck-Vaughn LB $22.83 (0-8172-5213-4). 32pp. A short book that gives an introduction to daily life in India plus some material on cities, weather, land features, and a recipe. (Rev: HBG 3/00; SLJ 3/00) [954]

15098 Das, Prodeepta. *I Is for India* (2–5). Photos by author. 1996, Silver Pr. LB $14.95 (0-382-39278-7). Using an alphabet book format, this account describes India and its geography, culture, religions, and peoples. (Rev: SLJ 11/96) [954]

15099 Dhanjal, Beryl. *Amritsar* (3–6). Illus. Series: Holy Cities. 1994, Dillon LB $21.00 (0-87518-571-1). 46pp. A colorful introduction to the holy city of Amritsar in northern India and to the religion of Sikhism. (Rev: SLJ 8/94) [915.404]

15100 Ganeri, Anita. *Exploration into India* (4–6). Illus. Series: Exploration. 1994, New Discovery $19.95 (0-02-718082-4); paper $7.95 (0-382-24733-7). 48pp. A history of India and its people that focuses on the outside individuals and empires that were influences through exploration and exploitation. (Rev: SLJ 5/95) [954]

15101 Goodwin, William. *India* (5–8). Series: Modern Nations of the World. 2000, Lucent LB $18.96 (1-56006-598-2). 112pp. An admirable introduction

to India that gives material on the land and its past but concentrates on today's population, living conditions, and problems. (Rev: BL 3/15/00; HBG 10/00) [954]

15102 Gresko, Marcia S. *India* (3–5). Series: Letters Home From. 1999, Blackbirch LB $16.95 (1-56711-403-2). 32pp. Basic material on India's land, history, people, religion, and cities is given in a series of letters addressed home by a young American traveler. (Rev: BL 2/15/00; HBG 3/00) [954]

15103 Haskins, Jim. *Count Your Way Through India* (3–5). Illus. by Liz B. Dodson. Series: Count Your Way. 1990, Carolrhoda LB $19.93 (0-87614-414-8). 24pp. Using a numbers approach, this book introduces the culture, climate, and people of India. (Rev: BL 4/1/91) [954]

15104 Hermes, Jules. *The Children of India* (3–6). Illus. Series: World's Children. 1994, Carolrhoda LB $23.93 (0-87614-759-7). 48pp. A brief look at the diversity of children and their cultures in the vast subcontinent of India. (Rev: BCCB 4/94; BL 2/1/94) [305.23]

15105 Hirst, Mike. *A Flavor of India* (3–5). Series: Foods and Festivals. 1999, Raintree Steck-Vaughn LB $22.83 (0-8172-5551-6). 32pp. Various festivals and holidays observed in India are discussed, with four simple recipes for the dishes associated with them. (Rev: BL 5/15/99; HBG 10/99) [954]

15106 Howard, Dale E. *India* (4–6). Illus. Series: Games People Play! 1996, Children's LB $23.00 (0-516-04437-0). 64pp. This book describes the recreational pursuits of the Indian people, including soccer, cricket, and sports and games that originated in the Indian subcontinent. (Rev: SLJ 11/96) [954]

15107 *India in Pictures* (5–8). Illus. 1995, Lerner LB $21.27 (0-8225-1852-X). 64pp. Basic coverage of people, religion, history, government, vegetation, and wildlife. (Rev: BL 5/1/89)

15108 Lewin, Ted. *Sacred River* (2–4). Illus. 1995, Clarion $14.95 (0-395-69846-4). 32pp. In a series of beautiful watercolors and brief text, the holy city of Benares (Varanasi) and its dominating force, the River Ganges, are introduced. (Rev: BL 6/1–15/95; SLJ 8/95) [954.1]

15109 McNair, Sylvia. *India* (5–8). Illus. Series: Enchantment of the World. 1991, Children's LB $32.00 (0-516-02719-0). 128pp. Such topics as civilization, ethnic groups, and history are treated in this lively introduction to India. (Rev: SLJ 5/91) [954]

15110 Mamdani, Shelby. *Traditions from India* (3–6). Illus. Series: Cultural Journeys. 1999, Raintree Steck-Vaughn $25.69 (0-8172-5385-8). 48pp. This photo-essay on India introduces us to the culture and customs of that colorful country. (Rev: BL 5/15/99; HBG 10/99; SLJ 8/99) [954]

15111 Moorcroft, Christine. *The Taj Mahal* (4–7). Illus. Series: Great Buildings. 1997, Raintree Steck-Vaughn $27.12 (0-8172-4920-6). 48pp. The story of the Moghul emperor who planned this building as a mausoleum for his wife is also a tale filled with treachery and murder. (Rev: BL 2/1/98; HBG 3/98; SLJ 7/98) [726]

15112 Pollard, Michael. *The Ganges* (5–7). Series: Great Rivers. 1997, Benchmark LB $14.95 (0-7614-0504-6). 45pp. This work describes the course of the Ganges from the Himalayas to its muddy delta, covers its history, and touches on the poverty and pollution that is found around it today. (Rev: HBG 3/98; SLJ 4/98) [954]

15113 Prior, Katherine. *Indian Subcontinent* (4–7). Illus. Series: Origins. 1997, Watts LB $21.00 (0-531-14418-6). 32pp. Describes the conditions in India, Pakistan, and Bangladesh that led to emigration, where their people went, and their reception in such countries as the United States and Great Britain. (Rev: BL 4/15/97; SLJ 7/97) [304.8]

15114 Srinivasan, Rodbika. *India* (5–8). Illus. Series: Cultures of the World. 1990, Marshall Cavendish LB $35.64 (1-85435-298-9). 128pp. Covers the land, peoples, cultural diversity, and current concerns of India. (Rev: BL 3/1/91) [954]

15115 Stewart, Melissa. *Science in Ancient India* (4–8). Series: Science of the Past. 1999, Watts LB $24.00 (0-531-11626-3). 64pp. Using a chronological approach beginning with the ancient cities of Mohenjo-daro and Harappa (both now in Pakistan), this account traces the growth of science in India with material on medicine, mathematics, astronomy, and physics. (Rev: HBG 10/99; SLJ 6/99) [954]

Japan

15116 Baines, John. *Japan* (3–5). Illus. Series: Country Facts Files. 1994, Raintree Steck-Vaughn LB $27.12 (0-8114-1847-2). 45pp. Contemporary Japan is introduced under such headings as landscape, climate, trade, and daily life. (Rev: SLJ 10/94) [952]

15117 Blumberg, Rhoda. *Commodore Perry in the Land of the Shogun* (5–8). Illus. 1985, Lothrop $17.00 (0-688-03723-2). 128pp. Japan was a mysterious country when Perry arrived in 1853 to open its harbors to American ships. (Rev: BL 11/1/85; SLJ 10/85)

15118 Bornoff, Nick. *Japan* (4–7). Illus. Series: Country Insights. 1997, Raintree Steck-Vaughn LB $27.12 (0-8172-4786-6). 48pp. This description of modern life in the city of Okazaki and in the village of Narai compares home life, employment, schooling, and recreation. (Rev: BL 7/97; SLJ 8/97) [952]

15119 Cobb, Vicki. *This Place Is Crowded: Japan* (3–5). Illus. by Barbara Lavallee. Series: Imagine Living Here. 1992, Walker LB $15.85 (0-8027-8146-2). 32pp. The focus is on the concept of space in this book that provides basic information about living in a highly populated nation of islands. (Rev: BL 9/1/92; SLJ 8/92) [952.04]

15120 Dawson, Zoe. *Japan* (K–3). Illus. Series: Postcards From. 1995, Raintree Steck-Vaughn LB $21.40 (0-8172-4011-X). 32pp. Points of interest in Japan are described through a series of postcards. (Rev: SLJ 3/96) [952]

15121 Galvin, Irene F. *Japan: A Modern Land with Ancient Roots* (4–6). Illus. Series: Exploring Cultures of the World. 1996, Benchmark LB $27.07 (0-

7614-0188-1). 64pp. This introduction to Japan includes good background information plus coverage on the arts, religion, sports, and traditions. (Rev: SLJ 6/96) [952]

15122 Gresko, Marcia S. *Letters Home from Japan* (3–5). Series: Letters Home From. 2000, Blackbirch LB $16.95 (1-56711-409-1). 32pp. Using a chatty, letter-from-a-friend format, this book covers the basic facts about Japan and its people. (Rev: BL 5/15/00; HBG 10/00) [952]

15123 Hamanaka, Sheila, and Ayano Ohmi. *In Search of the Spirit: The Living National Treasures of Japan* (3–6). Illus. 1999, Morrow LB $15.93 (0-688-14608-2). 48pp. Profiles of six Japanese master craftsmen — a kimono painter, a basket weaver, a puppeteer, a sword maker, a Noh actor, and a potter. (Rev: BCCB 4/99; BL 3/1/99; HBG 10/99; SLJ 5/99) [700]

15124 Harvey, Miles. *Look What Came from Japan* (2–5). Series: Look What Came From. 1999, Watts LB $20.00 (0-531-11500-3). 31pp. Large color photos accompany this breezy account of the culture and products of Japan including toys and crafts. (Rev: HBG 10/99; SLJ 7/99) [952]

15125 Haskins, Jim. *Count Your Way Through Japan* (3–5). Illus. 1987, Carolrhoda LB $19.93 (0-87614-301-X); paper $5.95 (0-87614-485-7). 24pp. "Two chopsticks" and other numbers help to introduce the culture of Japan. (Rev: BL 10/15/87; SLJ 9/87)

15126 Heinrichs, Ann. *Japan* (4–6). Series: True Books. 1997, Children's LB $22.00 (0-516-20336-3). 48pp. This simple, colorful photo-essay includes material on Japanese geography, history, culture, and how the people live. (Rev: BL 9/15/97; SLJ 11/97) [952]

15127 Heinrichs, Ann. *Japan* (4–6). Series: Enchantment of the World. 1998, Children's LB $32.00 (0-516-20649-4). 143pp. This completely new edition of a standard work includes material on Japanese culture, cities, nature, history, government, and people. (Rev: SLJ 2/99) [952]

15128 *Japan in Pictures* (5–8). Illus. Series: Visual Geography. 1994, Lerner LB $21.27 (0-8225-1861-9). 64pp. The land and people of Japan are profiled, with many illustrations. (Rev: BL 9/15/89; SLJ 5/90) [952]

15129 Kent, Deborah. *Tokyo* (3–6). Illus. 1996, Children's LB $26.50 (0-516-00354-2). 64pp. An introduction in text and many pictures to the principal sights of the capital of Japan. (Rev: BL 11/1/96; SLJ 10/96) [952]

15130 Littlefield, Holly. *Colors of Japan* (3–4). Illus. by Helen Byers. 1997, Carolrhoda $19.93 (0-87614-885-2); paper $5.95 (1-57505-215-6). 24pp. A picture book that uses different colors to explore various aspects of Japanese culture. (Rev: HBG 3/98; SLJ 1/98) [952]

15131 MacDonald, Fiona. *A Samurai Castle* (4–6). Illus. Series: Inside Story. 1995, Bedrick LB $18.95 (0-87226-381-9). 48pp. This account supplies details of the Samurai culture of the 17th century, with material on daily life and activities and detailed illustrations of a Samurai castle. (Rev: BL 1/1–15/96; SLJ 3/96) [952]

15132 MacMillan, Dianne M. *Japanese Children's Day and the Obon Festival* (3–5). Series: Best Holiday. 1997, Enslow LB $18.95 (0-89490-818-9). 48pp. The origins of these closely related Japanese holidays are described, with material on how they are celebrated. (Rev: BL 12/15/97; HBG 3/98; SLJ 8/97) [952]

15133 Metcalf, Florence E. *A Peek at Japan: A Lighthearted Look at Japan's Language and Culture* (3–6). Illus. by Tomoko. 1992, Metco paper $14.95 (0-9631684-3-6). 136pp. After a section on Japanese language and vocabulary, this book deals with Japan's culture, games, origami, and unusual facts. (Rev: SLJ 7/92) [952]

15134 Netzley, Patricia D. *Japan* (5–8). Series: Modern Nations of the World. 1999, Lucent LB $18.96 (1-56006-599-0). 112pp. Background historic and geographic information is given in this introduction to Japan, but the emphasis is on modern history, the people today, and current living conditions and problems. (Rev: BL 2/15/00; HBG 10/00) [952]

15135 Odijk, Pamela. *The Japanese* (4–7). Illus. Series: Ancient World. 1991, Silver Burdett LB $14.95 (0-382-09898-6). 47pp. This brief, informative volume includes sections on famous figures and places. (Rev: BL 1/15/92) [952]

15136 Pilbeam, Mavis. *Japan Under the Shoguns, 1185–1868* (5–8). Illus. Series: Looking Back. 1999, Raintree Steck-Vaughn LB $25.69 (0-8172-5431-5). 63pp. A handsome book that traces Japanese history during the age of the shoguns, 1185 to 1868. (Rev: BL 5/15/99) [952]

15137 Say, Allen. *Tea with Milk* (4–8). Illus. 1999, Houghton $17.00 (0-395-90495-1). 32pp. A picture book about the author's mother, who was forced by her father to leave her California home and return to the family's original home in Japan. (Rev: BL 3/15/99*; HB 7–8/99; HBG 10/99; SLJ 5/99) [952]

15138 Schemenauer, Elma. *Japan* (2–3). Illus. Series: Faces and Places. 1997, Child's World LB $22.79 (1-56766-371-0). 32pp. A simple introduction to Japan, with many color photos and basic information on geography, history, people, and customs. (Rev: BL 2/1/98) [952]

15139 Tames, Richard. *Exploration into Japan* (5–7). Illus. Series: Exploration. 1996, Dillon LB $19.95 (0-02-751390-4); paper $7.95 (0-382-39186-1). 48pp. A brief history of Japan is given, including the effects of early Western influences. (Rev: BL 8/96) [952]

15140 Tames, Richard. *Journey Through Japan* (3–5). Illus. by Martin Camm. Series: Journey Around the World. 1990, Troll LB $18.60 (0-8167-2114-9); paper $4.95 (0-8167-2115-7). 32pp. Japan is explored, including its crowded cities, natural beauty, ceremonies, and modern technological advances. (Rev: BL 5/15/91; SLJ 5/91) [952]

15141 Tyler, Deborah. *Japan* (3–5). Illus. Series: Discovering. 1993, Crestwood LB $17.95 (0-89686-773-0). 32pp. A brief introduction to modern Japan

that stresses its distinctive culture and modern accomplishments. (Rev: BL 2/1/94) [952]

15142 Whyte, Harlinah. *Japan* (4–6). Series: Countries of the World. 1998, Gareth Stevens LB $25.26 (0-8368-2126-2). 96pp. This introduction to Japan's history and geography covers such topics as lifestyle, food, customs, government, and relations with Canada and the U.S. (Rev: BL 12/15/98; HBG 10/99; SLJ 6/99) [952]

15143 Zurlo, Tony. *Japan: Superpower of the Pacific* (5–8). Illus. Series: Discovering Our Heritage. 1991, Macmillan LB $19.95 (0-87518-480-4). 128pp. Following a section of basic facts, this book concentrates on modern history and the problems of this island kingdom. (Rev: BL 2/1/92; SLJ 4/92) [952]

Other Asian Lands

15144 *Afghanistan in Pictures* (5–8). Illus. 1997, Lerner LB $21.27 (0-8225-1849-X). 64pp. Includes sections on vegetation and wildlife, minerals, cities, history, and government. (Rev: BL 5/1/89)

15145 Ali, Sharifah Enayat. *Afghanistan* (4–7). Illus. Series: Cultures of the World. 1995, Marshall Cavendish LB $35.64 (0-7614-0177-6). 128pp. After general background information, this account focuses on the arts, leisure activities, and festivals of the people of Afghanistan. (Rev: BL 1/1–15/96; SLJ 4/96) [958.1]

15146 Ansary, Mir T. *Afghanistan: Fighting for Freedom* (5–8). Illus. Series: Discovering Our Heritage. 1991, Macmillan LB $14.95 (0-87518-482-0). 128pp. In text and pictures, this account gives some background information, but concentrates on modern Afghanistan. (Rev: BL 2/1/92; SLJ 3/92) [958.1]

15147 Bennett, Gay. *A Family in Sri Lanka* (3–6). Illus. 1985, Lerner LB $18.60 (0-8225-1661-6). 32pp. The focus is on one family member in this look at the everyday life of a family in this small nation. (Rev: BL 11/15/85)

15148 Brace, Steve. *Bangladesh* (4–8). Illus. Series: Economically Developing Countries. 1995, Thomson Learning LB $24.26 (1-56847-243-9). 48pp. An overview of life in Bangladesh told in a simple, large-print text and many color photos. (Rev: SLJ 7/95) [954.9]

15149 Brill, Marlene T. *Mongolia* (5–8). Illus. Series: Enchantment of the World. 1992, Children's LB $32.00 (0-516-02605-4). 128pp. This little-known and isolated Asian country is introduced with material on its history, people, and geography. (Rev: BL 6/1/92) [951.7]

15150 Brown, Marion M. *Singapore* (4–6). Illus. Series: Enchantment of the World. 1989, Children's LB $32.00 (0-516-02715-8). 128pp. In this introduction, topics covered include geography, history, key attractions, and important people. (Rev: BL 1/1/90; SLJ 4/90) [959.57]

15151 Burbank, Jon. *Nepal* (4–7). Illus. Series: Cultures of the World. 1991, Marshall Cavendish LB $35.64 (1-85435-401-9). 128pp. The emphasis is on culture as well as the basics of geography, history, government, and people. (Rev: BL 2/15/92) [954.96]

15152 *Cambodia in Pictures* (5–8). Illus. Series: Visual Geography. 1996, Lerner LB $21.27 (0-8225-1905-4). 64pp. Cambodia is introduced, with accurate text and many photos, maps, and charts. (Rev: BL 11/15/96) [959.6]

15153 Cha, Dia. *Dia's Story Cloth* (3–5). Illus. by Chue Cha and Nhia Thao Cha. 1996, Lee & Low $15.95 (1-880000-34-2). 32pp. The story of the author's family, who fled first from Laos and then from Thailand to settle in the United States. (Rev: BCCB 7–8/96; BL 6/1–15/96; SLJ 7/96) [973]

15154 Clifford, Mary Louise. *The Land and People of Afghanistan* (5–7). Illus. 1989, HarperCollins LB $14.00 (0-397-32339-5). 240pp. An introduction to past life in this central Asian country. A reissue.

15155 Cromie, Alice. *Taiwan* (5–8). Illus. Series: Enchantment of the World. 1994, Children's LB $32.00 (0-516-02627-5). 128pp. In an attractive format with many color photos, this Asian nation is introduced, with material on such topics as history, government, people, and economy. (Rev: BL 12/15/94) [951.24]

15156 Fisher, Frederick. *Indonesia* (4–6). Series: Countries of the World. 2000, Gareth Stevens LB $19.95 (0-8368-2317-6). 96pp. Colored illustrations and maps, a glossary, and a clear text make this is a fine introduction to Indonesia and its people. (Rev: BL 6/1–15/00; HBG 10/00; SLJ 12/00) [959.8]

15157 Foster, Leila M. *Afghanistan* (5–8). Illus. Series: Enchantment of the World. 1996, Children's LB $32.00 (0-516-20017-8). 127pp. This introduction to the troubled land torn by civil war emphasizes its history, geography, and people. (Rev: BL 1/1–15/97) [958.1]

15158 Garland, Sherry. *Vietnam: Rebuilding a Nation* (4–6). Illus. 1990, Macmillan $19.95 (0-87518-422-7). 127pp. This overview of Vietnam describes landscape, people, history, and culture. (Rev: BL 4/1/90*) [959.7]

15159 Gogol, Sara. *A Mien Family* (4–7). Illus. Series: Journey Between Two Worlds. 1996, Lerner LB $21.50 (0-8225-3407-X); paper $8.95 (0-8225-9745-4). 64pp. The story of a refugee family from the mountainous area of Laos and their journey to the United States. (Rev: BL 11/15/96; SLJ 1/97) [306.85]

15160 Goodman, Jim. *Thailand* (4–6). Illus. Series: Cultures of the World. 1991, Marshall Cavendish LB $35.64 (1-85435-402-7). 128pp. This account stresses both the history and the culture of Thailand as well as the contemporary problems it is facing. (Rev: BL 3/15/92) [959.3]

15161 Goodman, Susan. *Chopsticks for My Noodle Soup: Eliza's Life in Malaysia* (1–3). Illus. by Michael Doolittle. 2000, Millbrook LB $21.40 (0-7613-1552-7). 32pp. A kindergartner from Connecticut visits a Malaysian village with her parents and comments on its daily life and customs in an account illustrated with her father's photographs. (Rev: BL 3/15/00; HBG 10/00; SLJ 5/00) [959.5]

15162 Goom, Bridget. *A Family in Singapore* (3–4). Illus. 1986, Lerner LB $18.60 (0-8225-1663-2). 32pp. With the focus on one child in one family, readers discover what life is like in Singapore. (Rev: BL 5/15/86; SLJ 10/86)

15163 Hansen, Ole Steen. *Vietnam* (5–8). Illus. Series: Economically Developing Countries. 1996, Raintree Steck-Vaughn LB $24.26 (0-8172-4526-X). 48pp. This introduction to Vietnam includes background information and material on its emerging economy. (Rev: BL 3/1/97) [959.7]

15164 Heinrichs, Ann. *Nepal* (5–8). Illus. Series: Enchantment of the World. 1996, Children's LB $29.70 (0-516-02642-0). 123pp. Using color photos on each page, this attractive book introduces the history, geography, and people of Nepal. (Rev: BL 7/96) [954.96]

15165 Heinrichs, Ann. *Tibet* (5–8). Illus. Series: Enchantment of the World. 1996, Children's LB $32.00 (0-516-20155-7). 160pp. An introduction to the history, land, and people of this country, now under the occupation of China. (Rev: BL 1/1–15/97) [951]

15166 Ho, Siow Yen. *South Korea* (2–4). Illus. Series: Festivals of the World. 1998, Gareth Stevens LB $14.95 (0-8368-2019-3). 32pp. Although this book focuses on national holidays, including Buddha's Birthday, Tan-O Day, and Sokchonje Rites, and describes a number of related craft projects, it also provides background information on South Korea. (Rev: BL 12/15/98; HBG 10/99) [394.26]

15167 Huynh, Quang Nhuong. *Water Buffalo Days* (4–6). Illus. 1997, HarperCollins LB $13.00 (0-06-024958-7). 128pp. This is a story of growing up in rural Vietnam in the late 1940s and of a family's water buffalo, Tank. (Rev: BL 11/15/97; SLJ 2/98*) [636.2]

15168 Jacobs, Judy. *Indonesia: A Nation of Islands* (4–8). Illus. Series: Discovering Our Heritage. 1990, Macmillan LB $14.95 (0-87518-423-5). 127pp. History and geography of the major Indonesian islands. (Rev: SLJ 9/90) [959.8]

15169 Jung, Sung-Hoon. *South Korea* (5–8). Illus. Series: Economically Developing Countries. 1997, Raintree Steck-Vaughn LB $24.26 (0-8172-4530-8). 48pp. This overview of current economic conditions in South Korea describes the country's success with electronic exports and provides case studies of family-run companies. (Rev: BL 5/15/97) [951.95]

15170 Kagda, Falaq. *Hong Kong* (5–8). Series: Cultures of the World. 1998, Marshall Cavendish LB $34.21 (0-7614-0692-1). 128pp. An attractive book that introduces us to Hong Kong's history and geography, its people, and their culture and lifestyles. (Rev: HBG 3/98; SLJ 6/98) [951]

15171 Kalman, Bobbie. *Vietnam: The Culture* (3–5). Illus. Series: Lands, Peoples, and Cultures. 1996, Crabtree LB $20.60 (0-86505-225-5); paper $7.95 (0-86505-305-7). 32pp. With many color illustrations, this account discusses such topics as Vietnamese arts, festivals, processions, food, and games. (Rev: BL 8/96; SLJ 11/96) [959.7]

15172 Kalman, Bobbie. *Vietnam: The Land* (3–5). Illus. Series: Lands, Peoples, and Cultures. 1996, Crabtree LB $20.60 (0-86505-223-9); paper $7.95 (0-86505-303-0). 32pp. The geography of Vietnam is introduced with sections on farming, cities, and famous monuments. (Rev: BL 8/96; SLJ 11/96) [959.7]

15173 Kalman, Bobbie. *Vietnam: The People* (3–5). Illus. Series: Lands, Peoples, and Cultures. 1996, Crabtree LB $20.60 (0-86505-224-7); paper $7.95 (0-86505-304-9). 32pp. Covers everyday life and compares life in the country and in the city. (Rev: BL 8/96; SLJ 11/96) [959.7]

15174 Karkonen, Reijo. *The Children of Nepal* (4–6). Illus. by Matti Pitkanen. Series: World's Children. 1990, Carolrhoda LB $23.93 (0-87614-395-8). 40pp. Comments on life in Nepal, with striking color photos. (Rev: BL 6/15/90; SLJ 8/90) [954.96]

15175 Khng, Pauline. *Myanmar* (4–6). Series: Countries of the World. 2000, Gareth Stevens LB $19.95 (0-8368-2320-6). 96pp. This introduction to Myanmar (formerly Burma) includes coverage of such topics as history, geography, people, form of government, current concerns, and relations with Canada and the U.S. (Rev: BL 6/1–15/00; HBG 10/00; SLJ 12/00) [954.9]

15176 Kilborne, Sarah S. *Leaving Vietnam: The True Story of Tuan Ngo* (2–4). Illus. by Melissa Sweet. Series: Ready-to-Read. 1999, Simon & Schuster $15.00 (0-689-80798-8). 48pp. Told in the first person and in the present tense, this is the true story of young Tuan Ngo and his father, who flee Vietnam and, through a series of harrowing experiences, finally reach the U.S. (Rev: BL 3/15/99*; HBG 10/99; SLJ 6/99) [959.704]

15177 Koh, Frances M. *Korean Holidays and Festivals* (2–5). Illus. by Liz B. Dodson. 1990, East-West LB $15.00 (0-9606090-5-9). 32pp. Nine holidays and cultural festivals that are celebrated in South Korea are described. (Rev: BL 3/1/91; SLJ 6/91) [394.25]

15178 *Laos in Pictures* (5–8). Illus. Series: Visual Geography. 1996, Lerner LB $21.27 (0-8225-1906-2). 64pp. The past and present of Laos are introduced using a simple text and many illustrations, including maps and charts. (Rev: BL 11/15/96) [959.4]

15179 Lauré, Jason. *Bangladesh* (5–8). Illus. Series: Enchantment of the World. 1992, Children's LB $32.00 (0-516-02609-7). 126pp. The history, culture, and economic problems of this crowded Asian land are covered. (Rev: BL 11/15/92; SLJ 1/93) [954.92]

15180 Layton, Lesley. *Singapore* (5–8). Illus. Series: Cultures of the World. 1990, Marshall Cavendish LB $35.64 (1-85435-295-4). 128pp. As well as history and economy, this introduction to Singapore includes coverage on lifestyles and current problems. (Rev: BL 3/1/91; SLJ 6/91) [959.57]

15181 Levy, Patricia. *Tibet* (4–7). Illus. Series: Cultures of the World. 1996, Marshall Cavendish LB $35.64 (0-7614-0277-2). 128pp. Tibet is introduced

with general background information, followed by material on its people and their culture, festivals, and food. (Rev: BL 8/96; SLJ 9/96) [951.1]

15182 Lorbiecki, Marybeth. *Children of Vietnam* (4–7). Photos by Paul P. Rome. Series: The World's Children. 1997, Carolrhoda LB $23.93 (1-57505-034-X). 45pp. Beginning in the north and working south, this photo-essay describes the people of Vietnam and the lives of their children. (Rev: HBG 3/98; SLJ 2/98) [959.7]

15183 McNair, Sylvia. *Indonesia* (5–8). Illus. Series: Enchantment of the World. 1993, Children's LB $33.00 (0-516-02618-6). 128pp. Introduces the history, geography, and peoples of this vast country, the world's largest island group. (Rev: BL 11/1/93; SLJ 3/94) [959.8]

15184 McNair, Sylvia. *Korea* (4–6). Illus. 1986, Children's LB $32.00 (0-516-02771-9). 127pp. Geography, culture, economy, and history are featured, as well as tourist sights. (Rev: BL 8/15/86; SLJ 10/86)

15185 *Malaysia in Pictures* (5–8). Illus. 1997, Lerner LB $21.27 (0-8225-1854-6). 64pp. Basic coverage from people to the land in this Visual Geography addition. (Rev: BL 5/1/89)

15186 Mirpuri, Gouri. *Indonesia* (5–8). Illus. Series: Cultures of the World. 1990, Marshall Cavendish LB $35.64 (1-85435-294-6). 128pp. Present-day problems and concerns of Indonesia are covered, as well as information on history and geography. (Rev: BL 3/1/91) [959.8]

15187 Moiz, Azra. *Taiwan* (4–7). Illus. Series: Cultures of the World. 1995, Marshall Cavendish LB $35.64 (0-7614-0180-6). 128pp. The accomplishments, lifestyle, and religious festivals of the people of Taiwan are covered, along with its history and geography. (Rev: BL 1/1–15/96; SLJ 9/96) [957.24]

15188 Munan, Heidi. *Malaysia* (5–8). Illus. Series: Cultures of the World. 1990, Marshall Cavendish LB $35.64 (1-85435-296-2). 128pp. Cultural diversity and lifestyles of the people are two topics covered in this introduction to Malaysia. (Rev: BL 3/1/91) [959.5]

15189 O'Connor, Karen. *Vietnam* (3–5). Series: Globe-Trotters Club. 1999, Carolrhoda LB $22.60 (1-57505-117-6). 48pp. Sidebars and stunning color photos bring to life the land and people of Vietnam in an entertaining and instructive manner. (Rev: BL 11/15/99; HBG 3/00; SLJ 2/00) [959.7]

15190 O'Connor, Karen. *Vietnam* (1–3). Series: A Ticket To. 1999, Carolrhoda LB $22.60 (1-57505-142-7). 48pp. This first look at Vietnam introduces the land, people, culture, customs, and famous sights with a simple, large-type text, color photos, and well-organized topics. (Rev: BL 11/15/99; HBG 3/00; SLJ 2/00) [959.7]

15191 *Pakistan in Pictures* (5–8). Illus. Series: Visual Geography. 1996, Lerner LB $21.27 (0-8225-1850-3). 64pp. Photos, charts, and maps help to introduce the country of Pakistan. (Rev: BL 9/15/89) [954.9]

15192 Pang, Guek-Cheng. *Mongolia* (5–8). Series: Cultures of the World. 1999, Marshall Cavendish

LB $24.95 (0-7614-0954-8). 128pp. A clear, well-illustrated introduction to this remote land that includes good background information as well as coverage of modern life. (Rev: HBG 10/99; SLJ 10/99) [957]

15193 Park, Frances, and Ginger Park. *My Freedom Trip* (K–4). Illus. by Debra R. Jenkins. 1998, Boyds Mills $15.95 (1-56397-468-1). 32pp. A true story about the authors' mother, Soo, and her escape with her father from North Korea on the eve of the Korean War, leaving behind a mother she would never see again. (Rev: BL 9/1/98; HBG 3/99; SLJ 1/99) [951.93]

15194 Ramulshah, Mano. *Pakistan* (3–8). Illus. 1992, Viking $22.95 (0-237-60193-1). 32pp. Famous landmarks, social and political life, and history are discussed. (Rev: SLJ 8/92) [954]

15195 Reynolds, Jan. *Himalaya: Vanishing Cultures* (3–5). Illus. Series: Vanishing Cultures. 1991, Harcourt $17.00 (0-15-234465-9). 32pp. A photo-essay in the National Geographic style about people whose way of life is disappearing. (Rev: BCCB 11/91; BL 9/1/91; SLJ 10/91) [954.96]

15196 Reynolds, Jan. *Mongolia* (3–5). Photos by author. Series: Vanishing Cultures. 1994, Harcourt $16.95 (0-15-255312-6); paper $8.95 (0-15-255313-4). A handsome photo-essay about the land and the nomadic people of Mongolia. (Rev: SLJ 4/94) [951]

15197 Roop, Peter, and Connie Roop. *Vietnam* (1–3). Series: A Visit To. 1998, Heinemann LB $19.92 (1-57572-120-1). 32pp. Introduces us to the land and people of Vietnam, showing how they live, work, and celebrate their festivals. (Rev: SLJ 7/98) [959.7]

15198 Rowell, Jonathan. *Malaysia* (5–8). Illus. Series: Economically Developing Countries. 1997, Raintree Steck-Vaughn LB $24.26 (0-8172-4531-6). 48pp. The growth and development of Malaysia are traced, with material on its new technology ventures. Also use in this series *Peru* and *Mexico* (both 1996). (Rev: BL 5/15/97) [959.505]

15199 Ryan, Patrick. *South Korea* (2–5). Series: Faces and Places. 1999, Child's World LB $15.95 (1-56766-517-9). 32pp. A brief overview that introduces South Korea and covers topics including the land, history, customs, daily life, and holidays. (Rev: HBG 10/99; SLJ 8/99) [951.95]

15200 Schmidt, Jeremy, and Ted Wood. *Two Lands, One Heart: An American Boy's Journey to His Mother's Vietnam* (3–5). Illus. 1995, Walker LB $18.85 (0-8027-8358-9). 48pp. A young boy is introduced to the culture and life of contemporary Vietnam when he visits his mother's homeland. (Rev: BCCB 6/95; BL 5/1/95; SLJ 4/95) [915.97]

15201 Schwabach, Karen. *Thailand: Land of Smiles* (5–8). Illus. Series: Discovering Our Heritage. 1991, Macmillan LB $19.95 (0-87518-454-5). 128pp. Explores the land and people of Thailand, with a chapter on the immigrants who have come to the United States. (Rev: BL 4/1/91; SLJ 7/91) [959.3]

15202 Scoones, Simon. *A Family from Vietnam* (3–5). Series: Families Around the World. 1998, Raintree Steck-Vaughn LB $15.98 (0-8172-4908-7).

32pp. This book describes the life of a typical family and presents a concise introduction to Vietnam. (Rev: BL 11/15/98; HBG 3/99) [959.7]

15203 Sheehan, Sean. *Cambodia* (4–7). Illus. Series: Cultures of the World. 1996, Marshall Cavendish LB $35.64 (0-7614-0281-0). 128pp. The troubled land of Cambodia is introduced, with emphasis on its people, their lifestyles, and culture. (Rev: BL 8/96; SLJ 9/96) [959]

15204 Sheehan, Sean. *Pakistan* (5–8). Illus. Series: Cultures of the World. 1993, Marshall Cavendish LB $35.64 (1-85435-583-X). 128pp. This informative account describes the history and culture of Pakistan, with coverage of its economy and how its people live. (Rev: SLJ 2/94) [954.9]

15205 Smith, Roland, and Michael J. Schmidt. *In the Forest with the Elephants* (4–7). 1998, Harcourt paper $9.00 (0-15-201290-7). A photo-essay that takes a look at the timber elephants of Myanmar, their *oozies* or trainers, and the logging industry that keeps them busy. (Rev: HBG 10/98; SLJ 4/98) [954]

15206 *South Korea in Pictures* (5–7). Series: Visual Geography. 1997, Lerner LB $21.27 (0-8225-1868-6). 64pp. Introduction to South Korea that focuses on its politics and economy. (Rev: SLJ 5/90) [951.9]

15207 *Thailand in Pictures* (5–8). Illus. Series: Visual Geography. 1994, Lerner LB $21.27 (0-8225-1866-X). 64pp. Thailand is presented in this well-illustrated account. (Rev: BL 9/15/89; SLJ 5/90) [959.3]

15208 Thomson, Ruth, and Neil Thomson. *A Family in Thailand* (4–6). Illus. 1988, Lerner LB $18.60 (0-8225-1684-5). 32pp. Thai children point out the characteristics of life in their country. (Rev: BL 8/88)

15209 Tull, Mary, et al. *Northern Asia* (4–7). Illus. Series: Artisans Around the World. 1990, Raintree Steck-Vaughn LB $25.69 (0-7398-0119-8). 48pp. This book introduces Mongolia and its neighbors, with descriptions of arts and crafts and many projects. (Rev: BL 10/15/99; HBG 3/00; SLJ 1/00) [745.5]

15210 *Vietnam in Pictures* (5–8). Illus. Series: Visual Geography. 1994, Lerner LB $21.27 (0-8225-1909-7). 64pp. This well-illustrated account of Vietnam covers its history, geography, people, government, and economy. (Rev: BL 11/1/94) [915.97]

15211 Wanasundera, Nanda P. *Sri Lanka* (4–7). Illus. Series: Cultures of the World. 1991, Marshall Cavendish LB $213.86 (1-85435-397-7). 128pp. The history, geography, and culture of Sri Lanka are introduced with an emphasis on contemporary problems. (Rev: BL 2/15/92) [954.93]

15212 Whyte, Harlinah. *Thailand* (2–4). Series: Festivals of the World. 1998, Gareth Stevens LB $18.60 (0-8368-2009-6). 32pp. Discusses the major holidays celebrated in Thailand and provides some related craft projects, recipes, and general information about the country. (Rev: BL 5/15/98; HBG 10/98) [959.3]

15213 Whyte, Mariam. *Bangladesh* (5–9). Series: Cultures of the World. 1998, Marshall Cavendish

LB $24.95 (0-7614-0869-X). 128pp. A sympathetic account that gives information on the rich history of this area, its geography, peoples, and problems with material on Emperor Asoka, the writer Tagore, and the Muslim religion. (Rev: HBG 10/99; SLJ 6/99) [954.9]

15214 Willis, Karen. *Vietnam* (5–8). Illus. Series: Modern Nations of the World. 2000, Lucent LB $19.96 (1-56006-635-0). 126pp. A thorough history of Vietnam, this work also focuses on progress after the war and daily life in modern Vietnam. (Rev: BL 9/15/00; HBG 3/01) [959.7]

15215 Withington, William A. *Southeast Asia* (5–8). Illus. 1988, Gateway $16.95 (0-934291-32-2). 160pp. Sections on lifestyle, land and climate, history and government, festivals, sports, arts, and crafts. (Rev: BL 12/1/88)

15216 Wright, David K. *Brunei* (5–8). Illus. Series: Enchantment of the World. 1991, Children's LB $32.00 (0-516-02602-X). 128pp. The country of Brunei is introduced with many photographs covering its geography, history, and culture. (Rev: BL 2/1/92) [959.55]

15217 Wright, David K. *Burma* (5–8). Illus. Series: Enchantment of the World. 1991, Children's LB $32.00 (0-516-02725-5). 128pp. The land and people of Myanmar (Burma), together with its culture and history, are covered in this colorful introduction. (Rev: BL 8/91; SLJ 9/91) [788.9]

15218 Wright, David K. *Vietnam* (4–7). Illus. 1989, Children's LB $32.00 (0-516-02712-3). 128pp. Standard information is highlighted by color illustrations and war coverage. (Rev: BL 8/89; SLJ 1/90) [959.7]

15219 Yu, Ling. *Taiwan in Pictures* (5–8). Illus. Series: Visual Geography. 1997, Lerner LB $21.27 (0-8225-1865-1). 64pp. The history and geography of Taiwan are introduced, with coverage on cities, culture, religion, and economy. (Rev: BL 9/15/89) [915.1]

15220 Yusufali, Jabeen. *Pakistan: An Islamic Treasure* (4–8). Illus. Series: Discovering Our Heritage. 1990, Macmillan LB $14.95 (0-87518-433-2). 128pp. This book covers the country of Pakistan from its foundation in 1947 to the present, with coverage on economy, geography, and more. (Rev: BL 7/90; SLJ 8/90) [954.91]

15221 Zimmermann, Robert. *Sri Lanka* (5–8). Illus. Series: Enchantment of the World. 1992, Children's LB $32.00 (0-516-02606-2). 128pp. In addition to background information on the history and geography of Sri Lanka, this book provides material on its current problems. (Rev: BL 6/1/92) [954.93]

Australia and the Pacific Islands

15222 Arnold, Caroline. *Easter Island: Giant Stone Statues Tell of a Rich and Tragic Past* (4–7). Illus. 2000, Clarion $15.00 (0-395-87609-5). 48pp. This chronological history of Easter Island tells how the stone statues got there and what they mean. (Rev:

BCCB 4/00; BL 3/15/00; HB 5–6/00; HBG 10/00; SLJ 4/00) [996.1]

15223 Arnold, Caroline. *A Walk on the Great Barrier Reef* (4–7). Illus. 1988, Lerner LB $23.93 (0-87614-285-4). 48pp. Exploring one of the great natural wonders of the world. (Rev: BL 7/88; SLJ 8/88)

15224 Berendes, Mary. *Australia* (2–5). Series: Faces and Places. 1999, Child's World LB $15.95 (1-56766-513-6). 32pp. A serviceable introduction to Australia that covers such topics as the land, animals and plants, history, cities, food, and daily life. (Rev: HBG 10/99; SLJ 8/99) [994]

15225 Browne, Rollo. *An Aboriginal Family* (3–6). Illus. 1985, Lerner LB $18.60 (0-8225-1655-1). 32pp. A taste of aboriginal culture is highlighted with color photos. (Rev: BCCB 6/85; BL 6/15/85; SLJ 10/85)

15226 Coffey, Maria, and Debora Pearson. *Jungle Islands: My South Sea Adventure* (4–6). Illus. 2000, Annick LB $26.95 (1-55037-597-0); paper $14.95 (1-55037-596-2). 88pp. The waters, land, people, and history of the Solomon Islands are presented in vibrant photos and an interesting narrative. (Rev: BL 1/1–15/01; HBG 3/01; SLJ 12/00) [919.59]

15227 Cooper, Rod, and Emilie Cooper. *Journey Through Australia* (3–5). Illus. Series: Journey Around the World. 1994, Troll LB $18.60 (0-8167-2757-0). 32pp. This brief tour of Australia introduces its most important regions and cities. (Rev: SLJ 8/94) [919.4]

15228 Darian-Smith, Kate. *Exploration into Australia* (5–7). Illus. Series: Exploration. 1996, Dillon LB $15.95 (0-02-718088-3); paper $7.95 (0-382-39227-2). 48pp. Descriptions are given of the prehistory of Australia and the changes made after European exploration. (Rev: BL 8/96; SLJ 9/96) [994]

15229 Darian-Smith, Kate, and David Lowe. *The Australian Outback and Its People* (4–7). Illus. Series: People and Places. 1995, Thomson Learning LB $24.26 (1-56847-337-0). 48pp. A well-organized guide to the Australian outback, its exploration and history, flora and fauna, mining, environmental issues, and people. (Rev: SLJ 7/95) [994]

15230 Ercelawn, Ayesha. *New Zealand* (4–6). Series: Countries of the World. 2000, Gareth Stevens LB $26.60 (0-8368-2332-X). 96pp. As well as the geography, history, system of government, and lifestyles of New Zealand, this book covers the country's unique customs and its current concerns. (Rev: BL 3/15/01) [992]

15231 Fox, Mary V. *New Zealand* (5–8). Illus. Series: Enchantment of the World. 1991, Children's LB $32.00 (0-516-02728-X). 128pp. This island country is introduced in text and pictures that cover geography, history, the people, and key attractions. (Rev: BL 10/1/91) [992]

15232 Franklin, Sharon, et al. *Southwest Pacific* (4–7). Series: Artisans Around the World. 1999, Raintree Steck-Vaughn LB $25.69 (0-7398-0120-1). 48pp. The influence of traditions and geography is shown in this survey of folk art from Australia, New

Guinea, New Zealand, and Indonesia, with directions for projects such as a Maori woven band and a batik wall hanging. (Rev: BL 10/15/99; HBG 3/00; SLJ 1/00) [994]

15233 Gonzalez, Joaquin L. *The Philippines* (4–6). Series: Countries of the World. 2000, Gareth Stevens LB $26.60 (0-8368-2334-6). 96pp. The Philippine Islands are introduced with material on the geography, history, government, lifestyle, language, food, unique customs, and current issues. (Rev: BL 3/15/01) [959.9]

15234 Griffith, Jonathan. *New Zealand* (2–4). Series: Festivals of the World. 1999, Gareth Stevens LB $15.95 (0-8368-2033-9). 32pp. An introduction to the major festivals celebrated in New Zealand, this account also describes Maori culture and traditions, takes the reader to sheep-shearing competitions, and gives directions for creating one's own celebration. (Rev: BL 12/15/99; HBG 10/00) [993.1]

15235 Griffiths, Diana. *Australia* (2–4). Series: Festivals of the World. 1999, Gareth Stevens LB $14.95 (0-8368-2021-5). 32pp. Introduces the land and people of Australia, describes their main holidays, and offers craft projects and tasty recipes for these celebrations. (Rev: BL 4/15/98; SLJ 8/99) [919.4]

15236 Grupper, Jonathan. *Destination: Australia* (4–6). Illus. 2000, National Geographic $16.95 (0-7922-7165-3). 32pp. This stunningly illustrated introduction to Australia covers many subjects but concentrates on its unusual animals. (Rev: BL 6/1–15/00; HBG 10/00; SLJ 5/00) [591]

15237 Hermes, Jules. *The Children of Micronesia* (4–6). Illus. Series: World's Children. 1994, Carolrhoda LB $23.93 (0-87614-819-4). 48pp. A look at growing up in these South Pacific islands, including the Caroline, Gilbert, and Marshall island groups. (Rev: BCCB 9/94; BL 9/15/94) [996.5]

15238 Keyworth, Valerie. *New Zealand: Land of the Long White Cloud* (4–7). Illus. Series: Discovering Our Heritage. 1990, Macmillan LB $14.95 (0-87518-414-6). 111pp. New Zealand is introduced with information on people, history, culture, and geography. (Rev: SLJ 1/91) [993.1]

15239 Kinkade, Sheila. *Children of the Philippines* (3–6). Illus. Series: World's Children. 1996, Carolrhoda LB $23.93 (0-87614-993-X). 48pp. Through the stories of children, the history, geography, and culture of the Philippines are covered. (Rev: BL 12/1/96; SLJ 12/96) [959.9]

15240 Krasno, Rena. *Kneeling Carabao and Dancing Giants: Celebrating Filipino Festivals* (4–6). Illus. by Ileana C. Lee. 1997, Pacific View $19.95 (1-881896-15-3). 48pp. Contains information on Filipino festivals, customs, folktales, games, and activities. (Rev: BL 12/1/97; HBG 3/98) [394]

15241 Lepthien, Emilie U. *The Philippines* (4–7). 1986, Children's LB $32.00 (0-516-02782-4). 128pp. These islands are introduced through a discussion of their history, geography, and culture.

15242 Lowe, David, and Andrea Shimmen. *Australia* (5–8). Illus. Series: Modern Industrial World. 1996, Raintree Steck-Vaughn LB $24.26 (0-8172-

4553-7). 48pp. The present economic status, living standards, educational system, and industry in Australia are covered. (Rev: BL 2/15/97) [919.4]

15243 McCollum, Sean. *Australia* (3–5). Series: Globe-Trotters Club. 1999, Carolrhoda $22.60 (1-57505-104-4). 48pp. Each of the colorful two-page spreads covers a different topic about Australia, including the people, major sights, and unusual animals. (Rev: BL 9/15/99; HBG 10/99; SLJ 11/99) [994]

15244 McCollum, Sean. *Australia* (1–3). Series: A Ticket To. 1999, Carolrhoda LB $22.60 (1-57505-129-X). 48pp. For beginning readers, this is a first look at Australia, its people, chief attractions, and landscape. (Rev: BL 9/15/99; HBG 10/99; SLJ 11/99) [994]

15245 Macdonald, Robert. *Islands of the Pacific Rim and Their People* (5–8). Illus. Series: People and Places. 1994, Thomson Learning LB $24.26 (1-56847-167-X). 48pp. An overview of the islands of the Pacific Ocean and their people, different environments, and economies. (Rev: BL 10/15/94; SLJ 10/94) [990]

15246 Meisel, Jacqueline D. *Australia: The Land Down Under* (3–5). Illus. Series: Exploring Cultures of the World. 1997, Marshall Cavendish LB $27.07 (0-7614-0139-3). 64pp. A description of various aspects of life in Australia, with material on the range of races and lifestyles. (Rev: BL 7/97; SLJ 4/98) [994]

15247 Mendoza, Lunita. *Philippines* (2–4). Series: Festivals of the World. 1999, Gareth Stevens LB $14.95 (0-8368-2025-8). 32pp. Contemporary photographs and a simple text introduce the Philippines, the people, and the holidays they celebrate, plus step-by-step craft projects and some tasty recipes. (Rev: BL 4/15/98) [959.9]

15248 NgCheong-Lum, Roseline. *Tahiti* (4–7). Illus. Series: Cultures of the World. 1997, Marshall Cavendish LB $35.64 (0-7614-0682-4). 128pp. Background material on history and geography is given, with information on how Tahitians live today. (Rev: BL 8/97; HBG 3/98) [919.62]

15249 Nile, Richard. *Australian Aborigines* (4–7). Illus. Series: Threatened Cultures. 1993, Raintree Steck-Vaughn LB $24.26 (0-8114-2303-4). 48pp. The aboriginal culture of Australia is presented. (Rev: BL 8/93; SLJ 8/93) [305]

15250 North, Peter. *Australia* (4–6). Series: Countries of the World. 1998, Gareth Stevens LB $25.26 (0-8368-2122-X). 96pp. This broad introduction to Australia covers its history, geography, government, and culture. (Rev: BL 12/15/98; HBG 10/99; SLJ 2/99) [994]

15251 North, Peter, and Susan McKay. *Welcome to Australia* (2–4). Series: Welcome to My Country. 1999, Gareth Stevens LB $16.95 (0-8368-2393-1). 48pp. An attractive introduction to Australia with material on its geography, history, government, people, recreation, and food. (Rev: HBG 10/00; SLJ 1/00) [994]

15252 Oleksy, Walter. *The Philippines* (4–7). Series: Enchantment of the World. 2000, Children's

LB $32.00 (0-516-21010-6). 144pp. These South Pacific islands are presented with coverage of history, geography, economy, the people, current problems, culture, and recreation. (Rev: BL 7/00) [959.9]

15253 Rajendra, Vijeya, and Sundran Rajendra. *Australia* (4–7). Illus. Series: Cultures of the World. 1991, Marshall Cavendish LB $35.64 (1-85435-400-0). 128pp. Beyond the basics, this volume highlights contemporary problems and concerns in the Land Down Under. (Rev: BL 2/15/92; SLJ 3/92) [994]

15254 Sullivan, Margaret. *The Philippines: Pacific Crossroads* (4–8). Illus. Series: Discovering Our Heritage. 1993, Macmillan LB $14.95 (0-87518-548-7). 127pp. A history with emphasis on relations with the United States and current developments. (Rev: SLJ 8/93) [959.9]

15255 Tope, Lily R. *Philippines* (4–7). Illus. Series: Cultures of the World. 1991, Marshall Cavendish LB $35.64 (1-85435-403-5). 128pp. With emphasis on contemporary problems and concerns, the land and culture of the Philippines are introduced in text and well-chosen color photographs. (Rev: BL 2/15/92) [959.9]

15256 Wilson, Barbara K. *Acacia Terrace* (2–4). Illus. by David Fielding. 1990, Scholastic $13.95 (0-590-42885-3). 40pp. This is the story of an Australian family's fortunes and misfortunes through the years. (Rev: BL 2/15/90) [994.4]

Europe

General and Miscellaneous

15257 Bramwell, Martyn. *Europe* (4–6). Illus. Series: World in Maps. 2000, Carolrhoda $23.93 (0-8225-2913-0). 48pp. Portrays the countries of Europe in a series of maps and accompanying text that supply information on such topics as population, government, geography, cities, and notable physical features. (Rev: BL 10/15/00; SLJ 1/01) [940]

15258 Sheehan, Sean. *Malta* (5–9). Series: Cultures of the World. 2000, Marshall Cavendish LB $24.95 (0-7614-0993-9). 128pp. This work covers the culture, geography, and history of Malta with material on such subjects as government, economy, people, lifestyles, and leisure. (Rev: HBG 10/00; SLJ 11/00) [945]

Central and Eastern Europe

15259 Andryszewski, Tricia. *Kosovo: The Splintering of Yugoslavia* (5–8). Illus. Series: Headliners. 2000, Millbrook LB $23.40 (0-7613-1750-3). 64pp. Introduced by refugees' accounts of the horror in Kosovo, this book traces the origins of ethnic conflicts in Yugoslavia, with a concentration on events of the past ten years. (Rev: BL 6/1–15/00; HBG 10/00) [949.7]

15260 Baralt, Luis A. *Turkey* (5–8). Illus. Series: Enchantment of the World. 1997, Children's LB

$32.00 (0-516-20305-3). 128pp. A visually attractive book that covers such topics as Turkey's population, natural resources, historic landmarks, and people. (Rev: BL 8/97; HBG 3/98) [915.61]

15261 Burke, Patrick. *Eastern Europe* (3–6). Illus. Series: Country Facts Files. 1997, Raintree Steck-Vaughn LB $27.12 (0-8172-4628-2). 45pp. An overview of current governmental, economic, and social conditions in the Czech Republic, Slovakia, Bulgaria, Romania, Poland, and Hungary. (Rev: BL 7/97; SLJ 8/97) [947]

15262 Carran, Betty B. *Romania* (4–7). Illus. 1988, Children's LB $32.00 (0-516-02703-4). 124pp. Coverage includes geography, culture, history, and politics. (Rev: BL 8/88)

15263 Corona, Laurel. *Poland* (5–8). Illus. Series: Modern Nations of the World. 2000, Lucent LB $19.96 (1-56006-600-8). 126pp. A good history of Poland that also covers Polish achievements and daily life. (Rev: BL 9/15/00; HBG 3/01) [943.8]

15264 *Cyprus in Pictures* (5–8). Illus. Series: Visual Geography. 1992, Lerner LB $21.27 (0-8225-1910-0). 64pp. In addition to describing the history and geography of this rugged island, efforts to reunite its Turkish and Greek zones are described. (Rev: BL 2/1/93) [956.45]

15265 *Czech Republic in Pictures* (5–8). Illus. Series: Visual Geography. 1995, Lerner LB $21.27 (0-8225-1879-1). 64pp. Text, pictures, charts, and maps provide a basic introduction to the new Czech Republic. (Rev: BL 8/95) [943.7]

15266 Feinstein, Steve. *Turkey in Pictures* (5–8). Illus. 1989, Lerner LB $21.27 (0-8225-1831-7). 64pp. Lots of visual coverage in this overview. (Rev: BL 8/88)

15267 Fox, Mary V. *Cyprus* (5–8). Illus. Series: Enchantment of the World. 1993, Children's LB $32.00 (0-516-02617-8). 128pp. An introduction to this Mediterranean island, its troubled history, and its present division between Turkey and Greece. (Rev: BL 11/1/93; SLJ 3/94) [956.93]

15268 Gabrielpillai, Matilda. *Bosnia and Herzegovina* (4–6). Series: Countries of the World. 2000, Gareth Stevens LB $26.60 (0-8368-2329-X). 96pp. Describes the history, government, geography, and current concerns of this troubled area, once part of Yugoslavia. (Rev: BL 3/15/01) [949.703]

15269 Ganeri, Anita. *I Remember Bosnia* (3–6). Illus. Series: Why We Left. 1995, Raintree Steck-Vaughn LB $22.83 (0-8114-5607-2). 32pp. An introduction to Bosnia that gives good background material and an explanation of the recent political and military problems. (Rev: BCCB 3/95; SLJ 6/95) [949.702]

15270 Greenberg, Keith E. *Bosnia: Civil War in Europe* (3–5). Photos by John Isaac. Series: Children in Crisis. 1996, Blackbirch LB $16.95 (1-56711-186-6). 31pp. The hardships faced by children in Bosnia because of the civil war are re-created through first-person accounts and many photos. (Rev: SLJ 12/96) [949.6]

15271 Hintz, Martin. *Switzerland* (4–6). Illus. 1986, Children's LB $32.00 (0-516-02790-5). 128pp.

Standard, useful information highlighted by color photos. (Rev: BL 4/1/87; SLJ 5/87)

15272 Humphreys, Rob. *Czech Republic* (4–7). Illus. Series: Country Insights. 1998, Raintree Steck-Vaughn LB $24.97 (0-8172-4795-5). 48pp. Discusses developments in the Czech Republic since the fall of Communism and contrasts city/village life. (Rev: BL 5/1/98; HBG 10/98) [943.71]

15273 *Hungary in Pictures* (5–8). Illus. Series: Visual Geography. 1993, Lerner LB $21.27 (0-8225-1883-X). 64pp. With concise text and extensive photographs, the past and present of Hungary are introduced. (Rev: BL 12/1/93; SLJ 12/93) [943.9]

15274 Kagda, Sakina. *Lithuania* (4–7). Illus. Series: Cultures of the World. 1997, Marshall Cavendish LB $35.64 (0-7614-0681-6). 128pp. The story of this small republic, once part of the Soviet Union, and of its distinctive culture, traditions, and customs. (Rev: BL 8/97; SLJ 10/97) [947.93]

15275 Levy, Patricia. *Switzerland* (4–6). Illus. Series: Cultures of the World. 1994, Marshall Cavendish LB $35.64 (1-85435-591-0). 128pp. This attractive introduction to Switzerland includes material on lifestyles, economy, geography, arts, and leisure. (Rev: SLJ 7/94) [949.4]

15276 McCollum, Sean. *Poland* (1–3). Series: A Ticket To. 1999, Carolrhoda LB $22.60 (1-57505-131-1). 48pp. Easy-to-understand language and a large map enhance this beginning account of the land, people, and main cultural features of Poland. (Rev: BL 9/15/99; HBG 3/00; SLJ 1/00) [943.8]

15277 McCollum, Sean. *Poland* (3–5). Series: Globe-Trotters Club. 1999, Carolrhoda LB $16.95 (1-57505-106-0). 48pp. After a brief history, this book focuses on modern life covering topics including religion, food, education, and family life. (Rev: BL 9/15/99; HBG 3/00; SLJ 2/00) [943.8]

15278 McKay, Susan. *Switzerland* (2–4). Series: Festivals of the World. 1999, Gareth Stevens LB $14.95 (0-8368-2027-4). 32pp. Switzerland's uniqueness is stressed in this description of its chief holidays, with craft projects and recipes to help readers celebrate. (Rev: BL 4/15/98; SLJ 8/99) [949.4]

15279 Marx, Trish. *One Boy from Kosovo* (3–6). Illus. 2000, HarperCollins LB $15.89 (0-688-17733-6). 32pp. Using a case study of an Albanian family in Kosovo and their son Edi, the author discusses the conflict in Kosovo, its causes, its course, and its consequences. (Rev: BL 6/1–15/00; HB 7–8/00; HBG 10/00; SLJ 6/00) [305.9]

15280 Milivojevic, JoAnn. *Serbia* (4–7). Series: Enchantment of the World. 1999, Children's LB $32.00 (0-516-21196-X). 144pp. This introduction to the country that was once a part of Yugoslavia discusses past and present problems as well as the land and its people. (Rev: BL 9/15/99) [949.7]

15281 Nollen, Tim. *Czech Republic* (2–4). Series: Festivals of the World. 1999, Gareth Stevens LB $15.95 (0-8368-2031-2). 32pp. This description of Czech festivals such as the *slavnost* and the Burning of the Witches also includes instructions for staging

one's own *slavnost*. (Rev: BL 12/15/99; HBG 10/00) [943.7]

15282 O'Shea, Maria. *Turkey* (2–4). Series: Festivals of the World. 1999, Gareth Stevens LB $15.95 (0-8368-2037-1). 32pp. This book introduces the land and people of Turkey through their national holidays, such as the Festival of Sacrifice and the Kirkpinar wrestling competition. Instructions for crafts and related foods are included. (Rev: BL 12/15/99; HBG 10/00) [956.1]

15283 Pfeiffer, Christine. *Poland: Land of Freedom Fighters* (5–8). Illus. 1991, Macmillan LB $19.95 (0-87518-464-2). 144pp. An introduction to the land and people of Poland and of their migration to the United States.

15284 Ricchiardi, Sherry. *Bosnia: The Struggle for Peace* (5–8). Illus. 1996, Millbrook LB $23.40 (0-7613-0031-7). 64pp. An account that emphasizes the recent history (through 1995) of Bosnia. (Rev: BL 7/96; SLJ 7/96) [949]

15285 *Romania in Pictures* (5–8). Illus. Series: Visual Geography. 1993, Lerner LB $21.27 (0-8225-1894-5). 64pp. In addition to background material on history and geography, this account gives a good picture of contemporary life in Romania. (Rev: BL 9/1/93) [949.8]

15286 Ryan, Patrick. *Poland* (3–5). Illus. Series: Faces and Places. 2000, Child's World LB $25.64 (1-56766-716-3). 32pp. A general introduction to Poland that uses double-page spreads to cover such topics as geography, history, animals, people, food, and holidays. (Rev: BL 3/1/01; HBG 3/01) [943.8]

15287 Schrepfer, Margaret. *Switzerland: The Summit of Europe* (4–7). Illus. Series: Discovering Our Heritage. 1989, Macmillan LB $19.95 (0-87518-405-7). 142pp. Four ethnic groups plus Switzerland's ancient and modern history are covered in this introduction. (Rev: BL 7/89; SLJ 10/89) [949.4]

15288 Sheehan, Sean. *Austria* (4–7). Illus. Series: Cultures of the World. 1992, Marshall Cavendish LB $35.64 (1-85435-454-X). 128pp. This introduction to Austria covers its history, lifestyles of the people, and contemporary problems. (Rev: BL 10/15/92) [943.6]

15289 Sheehan, Sean. *Turkey* (4–7). Illus. Series: Cultures of the World. 1993, Marshall Cavendish LB $35.64 (1-85435-576-7). 128pp. This introduction to Turkey covers history, culture, economics, and present-day concerns. (Rev: BL 8/93) [956.1]

15290 *Slovakia in Pictures* (5–8). Illus. Series: Visual Geography. 1995, Lerner LB $21.27 (0-8225-1912-7). 64pp. Coverage on this newly formed nation is enhanced by many recent photos, maps, charts, and a clear text. (Rev: BL 11/15/95) [942.7305]

15291 Stein, R. Conrad. *Austria* (4–7). Series: Enchantment of the World. 2000, Children's LB $33.00 (0-516-21049-1). 144pp. A thorough introduction to Austria with material on such subjects as history, the land, government, people, culture, cities, and daily life. (Rev: BL 1/1–15/01) [943.6]

15292 Steins, Richard. *Hungary: Crossroads of Europe* (3–5). Illus. Series: Exploring Cultures of the World. 1997, Marshall Cavendish LB $27.07 (0-7614-0141-5). 64pp. Current conditions in Hungary are covered, along with good background information about its people, culture, and history. (Rev: BL 7/97; SLJ 1/98) [943.9]

15293 *Switzerland in Pictures* (5–8). Illus. Series: Visual Geography. 1996, Lerner LB $21.27 (0-8225-1895-3). 64pp. With a generous number of color pictures, this account traces the history and geography of Switzerland, with emphasis on the present day and its people. (Rev: BL 9/15/96; SLJ 8/96) [949.4]

15294 Waterlow, Julia. *A Family from Bosnia* (3–5). Illus. 1997, Raintree Steck-Vaughn LB $25.69 (0-8172-4901-X). 32pp. A moving account of a family in Bosnia and the incredible hardships they endured during the war with Serbia. (Rev: BL 12/15/97; HBG 3/98) [949.703]

15295 Zwierzynska-Coldicott, Aldona Maria. *Poland* (2–4). Series: Festivals of the World. 1998, Gareth Stevens LB $14.95 (0-8368-2018-5). 32pp. Discusses Poland and its people, with emphasis on its unique holidays, crafts, and food. (Rev: BL 12/15/98; HBG 10/99) [947]

France

15296 Arnold, Helen. *France* (1–3). Illus. Series: Postcards From. 1995, Raintree Steck-Vaughn LB $21.40 (0-8172-4004-7). 32pp. France is introduced through a series of postcards written by fictitious children. (Rev: SLJ 2/96) [944]

15297 Bader, Philip. *France* (3–5). Series: Dropping In On. 2001, Rourke LB $25.27 (1-55916-280-5). 32pp. A brief tour of France in a hot-air balloon — with stops at interesting places — that includes material on landmarks, the people, food, and growing up. (Rev: SLJ 1/01) [944]

15298 Benedict, Kitty. *The Fall of the Bastille* (5–8). Series: Turning Points. 1991, Silver Burdett LB $14.95 (0-382-24129-0); paper $8.95 (0-382-24135-5). 64pp. The major factors that led to the establishment of a new France are chronicled. (Rev: BL 3/15/92) [944.04]

15299 Boast, Clare. *France* (2–4). Series: Next Stop. 1998, Heinemann LB $19.92 (1-57572-565-7). 32pp. A lively introduction to France that covers its history, geography, and people. (Rev: SLJ 6/98) [944]

15300 Butler, Daphne. *France* (2–4). Illus. Series: On the Map. 1993, Raintree Steck-Vaughn LB $22.83 (0-8114-3675-6). 32pp. An overview of life in France, with coverage of geogrphy, industry, customs, and landmarks. (Rev: BL 9/1/93) [944]

15301 Dunford, Mick. *France* (5–8). Illus. Series: Modern Industrial World. 1994, Thomson Learning LB $24.26 (1-56847-263-3). 48pp. An introduction to modern France that gives information about government, people, economic conditions, and recent history. (Rev: BL 1/15/95) [944]

15302 Fisher, Teresa. *France* (3–6). Series: Foods and Festivals. 1999, Raintree Steck-Vaughn LB $22.83 (0-8172-5550-8). 32pp. This book gives an overview of the celebrations and holidays of France, with material on related food crops and special dishes plus many simple recipes. (Rev: HBG 10/99; SLJ 7/99) [944]

15303 Fisher, Teresa. *France* (2–4). Series: We Come From. 1999, Raintree Steck-Vaughn LB $22.83 (0-8172-5212-6). 32pp. This book gives a little information on daily life in France, plus some coverage of its geography, cities, and weather, and a recipe. (Rev: HBG 3/00; SLJ 3/00) [944]

15304 Fisher, Teresa. *France: City and Village Life* (4–7). Illus. Series: Country Insights. 1997, Raintree Steck-Vaughn LB $27.12 (0-8172-4788-2). 48pp. A specific city and village are used to compare and contrast two lifestyles in contemporary France. (Rev: SLJ 8/97) [944]

15305 Gamgee, John. *Journey Through France* (K–3). Illus. Series: Journey Around the World. 1994, Troll LB $18.60 (0-8167-2759-7). 32pp. An introduction to contemporary life in France using color photos and a brief text. (Rev: SLJ 9/94) [914.4]

15306 Gilbert, Adrian. *The French Revolution* (4–6). Series: Revolution! 1995, Thomson Learning LB $24.26 (1-56847-390-7). 48pp. Beginning with the execution of Louis XVI in 1793, this account moves back in time to trace the history of the French Revolution. (Rev: SLJ 2/96) [944]

15307 Gofen, Ethel C. *France* (4–7). Illus. Series: Cultures of the World. 1992, Marshall Cavendish LB $35.64 (1-85435-449-3). 128pp. This account provides information on the history, culture, and people of France and discusses the current problems and concerns. (Rev: BL 10/15/92) [944]

15308 Harvey, Miles. *Look What Came from France* (2–5). Series: Look What Came From. 1999, Watts LB $20.00 (0-531-11501-1). 32pp. A breezy account that looks at the culture and products of France with a focus on food and kitchen products. (Rev: HBG 10/99; SLJ 7/99) [944]

15309 Haskins, Jim, and Kathleen Benson. *Count Your Way Through France* (2–4). Illus. by Andrea Shine. Series: Count Your Way. 1996, Carolrhoda LB $19.93 (0-87614-874-7); paper $5.95 (0-87614-972-7). 24pp. Using the numbers 1 through 10, each page contains useful information about the history, traditions, and people of France. (Rev: BL 9/15/96; SLJ 8/96) [944]

15310 Hoban, Sarah. *Daily Life in Ancient and Modern Paris* (4–7). Illus. 2000, Runestone $17.95 (0-8225-3222-0). 64pp. This well-illustrated history of Paris is divided chronologically into seven sections, beginning with early Paris and working through the Middle Ages to World War II and the Paris of today. (Rev: BL 2/1/01; HBG 3/01; SLJ 2/01) [944]

15311 Ingham, Richard. *France* (4–8). Illus. 2000, Raintree Steck-Vaughn LB $31.40 (0-8172-5782-9). 128pp. A fine introduction to France — its past, its present, and its people — that is particularly noteworthy for its use of graphics. (Rev: BL 10/15/00; HBG 10/00) [944]

15312 McKay, Susan. *France* (2–4). Series: Festivals of the World. 1998, Gareth Stevens LB $18.60 (0-8368-2003-7). 32pp. Bastille Day is only one of several French national holidays discussed in this colorful book containing craft projects and recipes. (Rev: BL 5/15/98; HBG 10/98; SLJ 6/98) [944]

15313 Nardo, Don. *France* (4–7). Series: Enchantment of the World. 2000, Children's LB $32.00 (0-516-21052-1). 144pp. This attractively formatted and illustrated new edition gives solid information about France, its land, and its people. (Rev: BL 7/00) [944]

15314 NgCheong-Lum, Roseline. *France* (5–7). Series: Countries of the World. 1999, Gareth Stevens LB $18.95 (0-8368-2260-9). 96pp. A wide range of topics including history, government, people, customs, and geography are covered in this colorful introduction to France. (Rev: BL 9/15/99; SLJ 8/99) [944]

15315 Pluckrose, Henry. *France* (PS–2). Series: Picture a Country. 1998, Watts LB $18.00 (0-531-11503-8). 30pp. For the primary grades, this is a simple introduction to France that briefly covers topics such as the land and people, food, customs, cities, sports, and festivals. (Rev: HBG 10/99; SLJ 2/99) [944]

15316 Powell, Jillian. *A History of France Through Art* (5–8). Illus. Series: History Through Art. 1996, Thomson Learning LB $24.26 (1-56847-441-5). 48pp. In 21 double-page spreads, the history of France is re-created through text and art reproductions. (Rev: BL 3/1/96; SLJ 2/96) [944]

15317 Shuter, Jane, ed. *Helen Williams and the French Revolution* (5–8). Illus. Series: History Eyewitness. 1996, Raintree Steck-Vaughn LB $24.26 (0-8114-8287-1). 48pp. An abridged firsthand account describes the causes and the course of the French Revolution. (Rev: BL 5/15/96; SLJ 6/96) [944.04]

15318 Stein, R. Conrad. *Paris* (3–6). Illus. Series: Cities of the World. 1996, Children's LB $26.50 (0-516-20026-7). 64pp. The City of Light is introduced, with material on its history, people, culture, and present status. (Rev: BL 1/1–15/97) [944]

15319 Sturges, Jo. *France* (3–5). Illus. Series: Discovering. 1993, Crestwood LB $13.95 (0-89686-778-1). 32pp. This brief review of French life covers geography, history, holidays, food, entertainment, and landmarks. (Rev: BL 2/1/94; SLJ 12/93) [944]

15320 Wright, Rachel. *Paris 1789: A Guide to Paris on the Eve of the Revolution* (4–7). Series: Sightseers. 1999, Kingfisher $8.95 (0-7534-5183-2). 31pp. Using the format of a tourist guide, this book tells you what to see, eat, wear, and buy in the Paris of the late 18th century. (Rev: HBG 10/99; SLJ 8/99) [944]

Germany

15321 Ayer, Eleanor. *Germany: In the Heartland of Europe* (4–6). Illus. Series: Exploring Cultures of the World. 1996, Benchmark LB $27.07 (0-7614-0189-X). 64pp. Good background material on Germany is presented, with special emphasis on the arts, sports, leisure, holidays, and festivals. (Rev: SLJ 6/96) [943]

15322 Fuller, Barbara. *Germany* (4–7). Illus. Series: Cultures of the World. 1992, Marshall Cavendish LB $35.64 (1-85435-530-9). 128pp. In addition to the usual information on the history and geography of Germany, this account stresses how the people live and their traditions. (Rev: BL 1/1/93) [943]

15323 *Germany in Pictures* (5–8). Illus. Series: Visual Geography. 1994, Lerner LB $21.27 (0-8225-1873-2). 64pp. The new Germany is introduced with a basic text and copious illustrations, including maps, charts, and attractive photos. (Rev: BL 1/15/95) [943]

15324 Hargrove, Jim. *Germany* (5–8). Illus. Series: Enchantment of the World. 1991, Children's LB $32.00 (0-516-02601-1). 128pp. German geography, people, culture, and history through reunification are covered in text and pictures. (Rev: BL 2/1/92) [943]

15325 Haskins, Jim. *Count Your Way Through Germany* (2–4). Illus. by Helen Byers. Series: Count Your Way. 1990, Carolrhoda LB $19.93 (0-87614-407-5). The reader is introduced to Germany through numbers. (Rev: SLJ 8/90) [943]

15326 Lord, Richard. *Germany* (3–5). Illus. Series: Festivals of the World. 1997, Gareth Stevens LB $21.27 (0-8368-1682-X). 32pp. Such German festivals as St. Martin's Day, Karneval, St. Nikolaus Day and Christmas, Oktoberfest, and Walpurgis Night are introduced and described. (Rev: SLJ 1/98) [943]

15327 Lord, Richard. *Germany* (4–5). Series: Countries of the World. 1999, Gareth Stevens LB $18.95 (0-8368-2261-7). 95pp. Vivid color photos and an up-to-date text are used in this comprehensive introduction to Germany. (Rev: BL 9/15/99) [943]

15328 Mirable, Lisa. *The Berlin Wall* (5–8). Series: Turning Points. 1991, Silver Burdett LB $14.95 (0-382-24133-9); paper $8.95 (0-382-24140-1). 64pp. How the fall of the Berlin Wall dramatically changed German history. (Rev: BL 3/15/92) [943.1]

15329 Peters, Sonja. *A Family from Germany* (3–5). Series: Families Around the World. 1997, Raintree Steck-Vaughn $25.69 (0-8172-4905-2). 32pp. Introduces the Pfitzner family of Cologne and such everyday activities as a swimming lesson, a carnival parade, and the beginnings of a Lenten observance. (Rev: BL 2/15/98; HBG 3/98) [943]

15330 Pollard, Michael. *The Rhine* (5–8). Illus. Series: Great Rivers. 1997, Benchmark LB $22.79 (0-7614-0500-3). 45pp. The history of the Rhine is told, with material on legends, canals, tributaries, tourism, habitats, and current ecological problems. (Rev: HBG 3/98; SLJ 3/98) [943]

15331 Shuter, Jane, ed. *Christabel Bielenberg and Nazi Germany* (5–8). Illus. Series: History Eyewitness. 1996, Raintree Steck-Vaughn LB $24.26 (0-8114-8285-5). 48pp. Using a first-person narrative as a framework, this account traces the growth, flowering, and defeat of Nazism in Germany. (Rev: BL 5/15/96; SLJ 6/96) [943]

15332 Steele, Philip. *Germany* (3–5). Illus. Series: Discovering. 1993, Crestwood LB $13.95 (0-89686-777-3). 32pp. A brief introduction to modern Germany, with good background material on its culture and reunification. (Rev: BL 2/1/94; SLJ 2/94) [943]

15333 Stein, R. Conrad. *Berlin* (3–6). Series: Cities of the World. 1997, Children's LB $26.50 (0-516-20582-X). 64pp. Describes present-day Berlin, Germany, its landmarks, people, geography, and history, including the division during the Communist period. (Rev: BL 1/1–15/98; HBG 3/98) [943]

Great Britain and Ireland

15334 Arnold, Caroline. *Stone Age Farmers Beside the Sea: Scotland's Prehistoric Village of Skara Brae* (4–7). Illus. by Arthur P. Arnold. 1997, Clarion $15.95 (0-395-77601-5). 48pp. A stunning volume that introduces the ruins of the village of Skara Brae on Scotland's Orkney Islands, which was inhabited between 3100 and 2500 B.C. (Rev: BCCB 4/97; BL 4/15/97; SLJ 7/97) [936.1]

15335 Ashby, Ruth. *Elizabethan England* (5–8). Series: Cultures of the Past. 1998, Benchmark LB $19.95 (0-7614-0269-1). 80pp. Stresses the cultural aspects of Elizabethan England, with material on the art and literature of the period plus coverage of daily life, religion, and major personalities. (Rev: HBG 10/99; SLJ 2/99) [942]

15336 Bell, Rachael. *Ireland* (1–3). Series: A Visit To. 1999, Heinemann LB $13.95 (1-57572-847-8). 32pp. Double-page spreads present information on Ireland's geography, landmarks, homes, work, food, schools, and celebrations. (Rev: HBG 10/99; SLJ 10/99) [941.5]

15337 Blashfield, Jean F. *England* (4–7). Illus. Series: Enchantment of the World. 1997, Children's $33.00 (0-516-20471-8). 144pp. This fine introduction to England gives material on its history, politics, the royal family, religion, and daily life. (Rev: BL 2/1/98; HBG 10/98) [942]

15338 Burgan, Michael. *England* (2–4). Series: True Books. 1999, Children's LB $21.00 (0-516-21187-0). 47pp. An attractive introduction to England with a text that covers such topics as history, geography, climate, people, and culture. (Rev: HBG 10/99; SLJ 10/99) [942]

15339 Buscher, Sarah, and Bettina Ling. *Mairead Corrigan and Betty Williams: Making Peace in Northern Ireland* (5–8). Illus. 1999, Feminist Pr. LB $19.95 (1-55861-200-9); paper $9.95 (1-55861-201-7). 112pp. The story of the two women in Northern Ireland who won the Nobel Peace Prize for their efforts to help end the civil strife in their country. (Rev: BL 3/15/00) [941]

15340 Corona, Laurel. *Scotland* (5–8). Series: Modern Nations of the World. 2000, Lucent LB $19.96 (1-56006-703-9). 128pp. The history, geography, and culture of Scotland are discussed along with material on daily life in modern Scotland. (Rev: BL 3/1/01) [941]

15341 Dumas, Philippe. *A Farm* (3–6). Illus. 1999, Creative Co. $29.95 (1-56846-169-0). 42pp. The inner workings of a 19th-century English farm are revealed in this oversize book containing extraordinary illustrations. (Rev: BL 12/1/99) [630.42]

15342 Ferris, Julie. *Shakespeare's London: A Guide to Elizabethan London* (2–5). Illus. 2000, Kingfisher $8.95 (0-7534-5234-0). 32pp. Written as a modern travel book, this guide to Elizabethan London lists tourist attractions, transportation, clothing, food, commerce, and accommodations. (Rev: BL 4/15/00; HBG 3/01) [942.1]

15343 Fisher, Leonard Everett. *The Tower of London* (4–6). Illus. by author. 1987, Macmillan paper $15.95 (0-02-735370-2). 32pp. Thirteen stories tell the bloody history of the Tower of London. (Rev: BCCB 11/87; BL 10/15/87)

15344 Flint, David. *Great Britain* (5–8). Illus. Series: Modern Industrial World. 1996, Raintree Steck-Vaughn LB $24.26 (0-8172-4555-3). 48pp. Modern Great Britain is the focus of this volume, which concentrates on the economy and industrial development. (Rev: BL 2/15/97) [330.941]

15345 Flint, David. *The United Kingdom* (3–6). Illus. Series: Country Facts Files. 1994, Raintree Steck-Vaughn LB $27.12 (0-8114-1849-9). 48pp. A fact-filled introduction to the United Kingdom, with coverage of such topics as its economy, daily life, climate, and traditions. (Rev: BL 9/1/94; SLJ 7/94) [941]

15346 Fradin, Dennis B. *The Republic of Ireland* (4–7). Illus. 1984, Children's LB $32.00 (0-516-02767-0). 128pp. An introduction to this country that touches briefly on many subjects.

15347 Fuller, Barbara. *Britain* (4–6). Illus. Series: Cultures of the World. 1994, Marshall Cavendish LB $35.64 (1-85435-587-2). 128pp. This fact-filled, heavily illustrated account gives a good overview of life in Great Britain today. (Rev: SLJ 7/94) [941.06]

15348 Gresko, Marcia S. *Letters Home from Scotland* (3–5). Series: Letters Home From. 2000, Blackbirch LB $16.95 (1-56711-408-3). 32pp. With postcard-style color illustrations and a chatty text, this first-person account introduces important topics about Scotland, such as the land, people, cities, food, and daily life. (Rev: BL 5/15/00; HBG 10/00) [941.106]

15349 Griffith, Jonathan. *Scotland* (2–4). Series: Festivals of the World. 1999, Gareth Stevens LB $15.95 (0-8368-2034-7). 32pp. A description of Scotland's holidays — both secular and religious — is accompanied by a section on related crafts and recipes. (Rev: BL 12/15/99; HBG 10/00) [941.1]

15350 Haskins, Jim, and Kathleen Benson. *Count Your Way Through Ireland* (2–4). Illus. by Beth Wright. Series: Count Your Way. 1996, Carolrhoda LB $19.93 (0-87614-872-0); paper $5.95 (0-87614-974-3). 24pp. After a brief introduction, each double-page spread, numbered from 1 to 10, gives interesting facts about Ireland. (Rev: BL 9/15/96; SLJ 8/96) [941.5]

15351 Hirst, Mike. *The History of Emigration from Scotland* (4–7). Series: Origins. 1997, Watts LB $21.00 (0-531-14441-0). 32pp. Details on the political, social, and economic conditions in Scotland through various periods in its history that led to emigration to the United States and other lands. (Rev: BL 12/15/97; HBG 3/98; SLJ 2/98) [941.106]

15352 *Ireland in Pictures* (5–8). Illus. 1997, Lerner LB $21.27 (0-8225-1878-3). 64pp. Contemporary Ireland is highlighted in this illustrated account. (Rev: BL 12/1/90) [941.5]

15353 January, Brendan. *Ireland* (2–4). Series: True Books. 1999, Children's LB $21.00 (0-516-21186-2). 47pp. A large-print text and many color illustrations introduce the history, geography, people, climate, and culture of Ireland. (Rev: HBG 10/99; SLJ 10/99) [941]

15354 Kent, Deborah. *Dublin* (3–6). Illus. Series: Cities of the World. 1997, Children's LB $26.50 (0-516-20302-9). 64pp. This introduction to the Irish capital introduces its history, people, and famous sights. (Rev: BL 8/97) [941.8]

15355 Killeen, Richard. *The Easter Rising* (4–6). Illus. Series: Revolution! 1995, Thomson Learning LB $24.26 (1-56847-391-5). 48pp. Presents, in a well-paced text, the story of the 1916 Irish Easter Rebellion, during which the Fenians fought for independence from British rule. (Rev: SLJ 2/96) [941.508]

15356 Levy, Patricia. *Ireland* (4–7). Illus. Series: Cultures of the World. 1993, Marshall Cavendish LB $35.64 (1-85435-580-5). 128pp. An account that traces the role of women in Irish history to the present day. (Rev: SLJ 2/94) [941]

15357 Lister, Maree, and Marti Sevier. *England* (4–6). Illus. 1998, Gareth Stevens LB $25.26 (0-8368-2125-4). 96pp. Introduces readers to England's rich historical, geographical, and cultural background, touching on a variety of topics, such as Robin Hood, Stonehenge, and the university cities of Oxford and Cambridge. (Rev: BL 12/15/98; HBG 10/99; SLJ 2/99) [942]

15358 Lister, Maree, and Marti Sevier. *Welcome to England* (2–4). Series: Welcome to My Country. 1999, Gareth Stevens LB $16.95 (0-8368-2396-6). 48pp. England is introduced with separate chapters on land, history, government and economy, people, language, arts, leisure, and food. (Rev: HBG 10/00; SLJ 1/00) [942]

15359 McKay, Patricia. *Ireland* (2–4). Series: Festivals of the World. 1998, Gareth Stevens LB $18.60 (0-8368-2004-5). 32pp. A brief introduction to the land and people of Ireland is followed by a discussion of why and how such holidays as St. Patrick's Day are celebrated. A few background craft projects and recipes are included. (Rev: BL 5/15/98; HBG 10/98; SLJ 8/98) [941.5]

15360 McMahon, Patricia. *One Belfast Boy* (4–6). Illus. 1999, Houghton $16.00 (0-395-68620-2). 64pp. This photo-essay tells about the daily life of an Irish Catholic boy growing up in violence-torn Northern Ireland. (Rev: BCCB 7–8/99; BL 3/15/99; HBG 10/99; SLJ 5/99) [941]

15361 Martell, Hazel M. *The Celts* (5–8). Illus. Series: See Through History. 1996, Viking $19.99 (0-670-86558-3). 48pp. A visually attractive, fact-filled look at the Celts and how they lived, with interior shots of their homes, fortresses, and burial sites. (Rev: SLJ 3/96) [299]

15362 *Northern Ireland in Pictures* (3–5). Illus. Series: Visual Geography. 1991, Lerner LB $21.27 (0-8225-1898-8). 64pp. Using photos, maps, charts, and a concise text, the land and history of this troubled country are covered. (Rev: BL 2/15/92) [941.6]

15363 Prior, Katherine. *Ireland* (4–7). Illus. Series: Origins. 1997, Watts LB $20.00 (0-531-14415-1). 32pp. Tells of the conditions in Ireland that led to emigration, where the Irish went, and their reception in Great Britain, the United States, and elsewhere. (Rev: BL 4/15/97) [941.5]

15364 Shuter, Jane. *Carisbrooke Castle* (4–6). Series: Visiting the Past. 1999, Heinemann LB $16.95 (1-57572-857-5). 32pp. This book covers the history of this stronghold on the Isle of Wight, including the construction of the castle after the Norman conquest, its uses through the centuries, and its restoration in 1896. (Rev: SLJ 3/00) [942]

15365 Smith, Nigel. *The Houses of Parliament* (4–7). Illus. Series: Great Buildings. 1997, Raintree Steck-Vaughn LB $27.12 (0-8172-4921-4). 48pp. As well as giving a history of the British Houses of Parliament, this book tells about the British form of government. (Rev: BL 2/1/98; HBG 3/98) [725]

15366 Spencer, Shannon. *Ireland* (4–6). Series: Countries of the World. 2000, Gareth Stevens LB $19.95 (0-8368-2318-4). 96pp. A fine, colorful introduction that includes the standard coverage plus material on such topics as folklore, food, and unique customs. (Rev: BL 6/1–15/00; HBG 10/00) [941.7]

15367 Sproule, Anna. *Great Britain: The Land and Its People* (4–6). Illus. 1991, Silver Burdett LB $14.95 (0-382-24243-2). 48pp. An overview of history, people, religion, and industry is highlighted by numerous illustrations. (Rev: 11/15/87)

15368 Sutherland, Dorothy B. *Wales* (4–6). Illus. 1987, Children's LB $32.00 (0-516-02794-8). 128pp. Color photos help to explain the history, geography, and culture of Wales. (Rev: BL 10/15/87)

15369 *Wales in Pictures* (5–8). Illus. 1994, Lerner LB $21.27 (0-8225-1877-5). 64pp. Wales is introduced and material is given on history and current conditions. (Rev: BL 12/1/90) [942.9]

Greece and Italy

15370 Allard, Denise. *Greece* (K–2). Illus. Series: Postcards From. 1996, Raintree Steck-Vaughn LB $22.83 (0-8172-4022-5). 32pp. Using a postcard format, this book supplies a brief overview of the geography, culture, and sights of Greece. (Rev: SLJ 2/97) [938]

15371 Barghusen, Joan. *Daily Life in Ancient and Modern Rome* (3–6). Illus. by Ray Webb. Series: Cities Through Time. 1999, Runestone LB $17.95 (0-8225-3213-1). 64pp. Daily life and the culture of ancient and modern Rome are covered in double-page spreads illustrated with original drawings and photographs. (Rev: HBG 10/99; SLJ 6/99) [945]

15372 Blashfield, Jean F. *Italy* (4–7). Series: Enchantment of the World. 1999, Children's LB $32.00 (0-516-20960-4). 144pp. The topics covered in this book about Italy range from history, geography, and government to mythology, culture, daily life, and sports. (Rev: BL 1/1–15/00) [945]

15373 Britton, Tamara L. *Greece* (2–4). Series: Countries. 2000, ABDO LB $14.95 (1-57765-385-8). 40pp. A workable introduction to Greece with a focus on modern times. (Rev: SLJ 3/01) [949.5]

15374 Butler, Daphne. *Italy* (2–4). Illus. 1992, Raintree Steck-Vaughn LB $22.83 (0-8114-3677-2). 32pp. A broad overview of Italy, described in terms of topography and lifestyle. (Rev: BL 3/15/93) [945]

15375 Clark, Colin. *Journey Through Italy* (K–3). Illus. Series: Journey Around the World. 1994, Troll LB $13.95 (0-8167-2763-5). 32pp. A look at present-day life in Italy in a brief text and many color photographs. (Rev: SLJ 9/94) [914.5]

15376 Dubois, Jill. *Greece* (4–7). Illus. Series: Cultures of the World. 1992, Marshall Cavendish LB $35.64 (1-85435-450-7). 128pp. This book supplies an introduction to Greece with emphasis on its culture and lifestyles. (Rev: BL 10/15/92) [949.5]

15377 Ferro, Jennifer. *Italian Foods and Culture* (3–5). Series: Festive Foods and Celebrations. 1999, Rourke LB $19.45 (1-57103-302-5). 48pp. Saint Joseph's Day, Christmas, and the Festival of Santa Rosalia are three of the Italian celebrations that are covered in this book that also contains recipes. (Rev: SLJ 2/00) [945]

15378 Foster, Leila M. *Italy* (5–9). Series: Modern Nations of the World. 1998, Lucent LB $17.96 (1-56006-481-1). 112pp. A fine introduction to Italy's past and present with an overview of its amazing history, modern popular culture, achievements, daily life, and geography. (Rev: SLJ 5/99) [945]

15379 Frank, Nicole, and Josephine Sander Hausam. *Welcome to Italy* (2–4). Illus. Series: Welcome to My Country. 2000, Gareth Stevens $22.60 (0-8368-2510-1). Full-page illustrations on every page and a simple text are used to introduce modern Italy and its people to young readers. (Rev: SLJ 1/01) [945]

15380 Frank, Nicole, and Yeoh Hong Nam. *Welcome to Greece* (2–4). Series: Welcome to My Country. 2000, Gareth Stevens LB $22.60 (0-8368-2509-8). 48pp. A simple introduction to Greece and its people with many color illustrations. (Rev: SLJ 1/01) [949.5]

15381 *Greece in Pictures* (5–8). Illus. Series: Visual Geography. 1996, Lerner LB $19.95 (0-8225-1882-1). 64pp. Through photographs, maps, charts, and concise text, the land and people of Greece are introduced. (Rev: BL 10/1/92) [949.5]

15382 Gresko, Marcia S. *Letters Home from Greece* (3–5). Illus. 1999, Blackbirch LB $16.95 (1-56711-406-7). 32pp. Through a series of letters, the land, people, and history of Greece are seen from the standpoint of a young tourist. (Rev: BL 11/15/99; HBG 3/00; SLJ 1/00) [914.950]

15383 Harvey, Miles. *Look What Came from Italy* (2–5). Series: Look What Came From. 1998, Watts

LB $20.00 (0-531-11497-X). 32pp. The contributions of Italians in such areas as food, fashion, culture, invention, and customs are described in double-page spreads. (Rev: HBG 3/99; SLJ 12/98) [945]

15384 Haskins, Jim. *Count Your Way Through Italy* (2–4). Illus. by Beth Wright. Series: Count Your Way. 1990, Carolrhoda LB $19.93 (0-87614-406-7). Introduces the geography and culture of Italy through numbers. (Rev: SLJ 8/90) [945]

15385 Haskins, Jim, and Kathleen Benson. *Count Your Way Through Greece* (2–4). Illus. by Janice L. Porter. Series: Count Your Way. 1996, Carolrhoda LB $19.93 (0-87614-875-5); paper $5.95 (0-87614-973-5). 24pp. Greece is introduced in a counting book that goes from 1 to 10. (Rev: BL 9/15/96; SLJ 8/96) [949.5]

15386 Hausam, Josephine Sanders. *Italy* (4–6). Series: Countries of the World. 1999, Gareth Stevens LB $19.95 (0-8368-2310-9). 96pp. A broad introduction to Italy — its history and geography, its language and lifestyle, its government and culture. (Rev: BL 12/15/99; HBG 10/00; SLJ 1/00) [945]

15387 Nardo, Don. *Greece* (5–8). Series: Modern Nations of the World. 2000, Lucent LB $18.96 (1-56006-587-7). 128pp. Although there is coverage of ancient Greece, this account stresses modern history, the people today, and current living conditions and problems. (Rev: BL 2/15/00; HBG 10/00) [949.5]

15388 Pirotta, Saviour. *Rome* (4–6). Illus. Series: Holy Cities. 1993, Dillon LB $17.95 (0-87518-570-3). 46pp. This account focuses on Rome as the center of the pagan religion during the ancient empire and its evolution into the heart of the largest Christian denomination in the world. (Rev: BL 9/15/93; SLJ 8/93) [263]

15389 Riehecky, Janet. *Greece* (1–3). Series: Countries of the World. 2000, Bridgestone LB $17.26 (0-7368-0628-8). 24pp. Full-page photos and current information are the highlights of this basic introduction to Greece. (Rev: HBG 3/01; SLJ 3/01) [949.5]

15390 Sioras, Efstathia. *Greece* (2–4). Series: Festivals of the World. 1998, Gareth Stevens LB $14.95 (0-8368-2014-2). 32pp. This description of Greek traditions and holidays includes an introduction to the land and people and some related recipes and craft projects. (Rev: BL 12/15/98; HBG 10/99) [949.5]

15391 Stein, R. Conrad. *Athens* (3–6). Illus. Series: Cities of the World. 1997, Children's LB $26.50 (0-516-20300-2). 64pp. A heavily illustrated account that describes Athens, gives a brief history, tells about its famous landmarks, and introduces its people. (Rev: BL 8/97) [949.5]

15392 Stein, R. Conrad. *Greece* (4–7). Illus. 1988, Children's LB $32.00 (0-516-02759-X). 128pp. Photos and maps highlight this overview of an ancient land. (Rev: BL 5/15/88)

15393 Stein, R. Conrad. *Rome* (3–6). Series: Cities of the World. 1997, Children's LB $26.50 (0-516-20465-3). 64pp. This account gives a basic history of Rome and its current status, with additional material on important sights, the people, and present-day problems. (Rev: BL 1/1–15/98; HBG 3/98) [945]

15394 Winter, Jane K. *Italy* (5–8). Illus. Series: Cultures of the World. 1992, Marshall Cavendish LB $35.64 (1-85435-453-1). 128pp. Gives geographic and historical information about Italy and tells about its people and their concerns. (Rev: BL 10/15/92) [945]

15395 Yeoh, Hong Nam. *Greece* (4–6). Series: Countries of the World. 1999, Gareth Stevens LB $19.95 (0-8368-2309-5). 96pp. A look at life in present-day Greece that also examines its past. (Rev: BL 12/15/99; HBG 10/00; SLJ 1/00) [949.5]

15396 Zinovieff, Sofka. *Greece* (4–7). Illus. Series: Origins. 1997, Watts LB $21.00 (0-531-14417-8). 32pp. Studies the conditions in Greece at various times in history that led to emigration to the United States and Canada, and the experiences of these immigrants. (Rev: BL 4/15/97) [949.5]

Low Countries

15397 Burgan, Michael. *Belgium* (4–7). Series: Enchantment of the World. 2000, Children's LB $32.00 (0-516-21006-8). 144pp. This new edition of a standard title contains up-to-date material on such topics as geography and climate, plants and animals, people and culture, the arts, and sports. (Rev: BL 7/00) [949.3]

15398 Hintz, Martin. *The Netherlands* (4–7). Series: Enchantment of the World. 1999, Children's LB $32.00 (0-516-21053-X). 144pp. An up-to-date, well-illustrated, and comprehensive introduction to the Netherlands. (Rev: BL 12/15/99) [949.2]

15399 Kent, Deborah. *Amsterdam* (3–6). Illus. Series: Cities of the World. 1997, Children's LB $26.50 (0-516-20299-5). 64pp. In this introduction to Amsterdam, readers are given a tour of the city, told about its history, and given a picture of its people. (Rev: BL 8/97; SLJ 2/98) [949.2]

15400 Pateman, Robert. *Belgium* (4–7). Illus. Series: Cultures of the World. 1995, Marshall Cavendish LB $35.64 (0-7614-0176-8). 128pp. After a brief introduction to the history and geography of Belgium, this book focuses on the populace, how they live, and their major contributions to the world. (Rev: BL 1/1–15/96; SLJ 9/96) [949.3]

15401 Sheehan, Patricia. *Luxembourg* (4–7). Illus. Series: Cultures of the World. 1997, Marshall Cavendish LB $35.64 (0-7614-0685-9). 128pp. Includes information on this tiny European country's history, culture, and lifestyles. (Rev: BL 8/97) [914.935]

15402 Van Fenema, Joyce. *Netherlands* (2–4). Illus. Series: Festivals of the World. 1998, Gareth Stevens LB $14.95 (0-8368-2016-9). 32pp. Introduces Netherlands festivals such as Sinterklaas, Carnaval, and Queensday, along with basic facts about the country and a few related craft projects. (Rev: BL 12/15/98; HBG 10/99) [394.26]

Russia and the Former Soviet States

15403 *Armenia* (5–8). Illus. Series: Then and Now. 1993, Lerner LB $23.93 (0-8225-2806-1). 64pp. A source of background information on this ancient western Asian territory, a former USSR state. (Rev: SLJ 3/93) [947]

15404 Arnold, Helen. *Russia* (1–3). Illus. Series: Postcards From. 1995, Raintree Steck-Vaughn LB $22.83 (0-8172-4006-3). 32pp. In this quick overview of Russia, such topics as food, shopping, transportation, money, and language are covered. (Rev: SLJ 2/96) [947]

15405 Bassis, Volodymyr. *Ukraine* (2–4). Series: Festivals of the World. 1998, Gareth Stevens LB $18.60 (0-8368-2010-X). 32pp. A colorful look at the people and customs of the Ukraine as seen through their holidays, with related crafts and recipes included. (Rev: BL 5/15/98; HBG 10/98; SLJ 6/98) [947]

15406 Bassis, Volodymyr. *Ukraine* (4–7). Illus. Series: Cultures of the World. 1997, Marshall Cavendish LB $35.64 (0-7614-0684-0). 128pp. An introduction to this former Soviet state, with emphasis on current history and culture. (Rev: BL 8/97; SLJ 10/97) [947.7]

15407 *Belarus* (5–8). Illus. 1993, Lerner LB $23.93 (0-8225-2811-8). 56pp. This is a portrait of the former Soviet Republic, sometimes called "White Russia," situated between Poland and the Russian federation. (Rev: BL 5/15/93) [947]

15408 Boast, Clare. *Russia* (2–4). Series: Next Stop. 1998, Heinemann LB $19.92 (1-57572-569-X). 32pp. A general introduction to Russia, its history, geography, people, and current living standards. (Rev: SLJ 6/98) [947]

15409 Brewster, Hugh. *Anastasia's Album* (5–8). Illus. 1996, Hyperion $17.95 (0-7868-0292-8). 64pp. The story of the young daughter of the last of the Romanov czars. (Rev: BCCB 1/97; BL 10/1/96; SLJ 12/96*) [947.08]

15410 Carrion, Esther. *The Empire of the Czars* (4–7). Illus. Series: World Heritage. 1994, Children's LB $15.00 (0-516-08319-0). 34pp. An overview of Russian history from early times to the breakup of the Soviet Union, with special material on Russia's famous sights, such as Red Square, the Kremlin, and St. Petersburg. (Rev: SLJ 5/95) [947.07]

15411 Cumming, David. *Russia* (5–8). Illus. Series: Modern Industrial World. 1994, Thomson Learning LB $24.26 (1-56847-240-4). 48pp. An introduction to Russia that stresses current conditions and the economic upheaval that the breakup of the USSR has caused. (Rev: BL 1/15/95; SLJ 3/95) [947]

15412 Dhilawala, Sakina. *Armenia* (4–7). Illus. Series: Cultures of the World. 1997, Marshall Cavendish LB $35.64 (0-7614-0683-2). 128pp. An introduction to this troubled land that describes how its people live, their lifestyles, and culture. (Rev: BL 8/97; HBG 3/98) [945.56]

15413 Flint, David. *The Baltic States: Estonia, Latvia, Lithuania* (4–6). Illus. Series: Former Soviet

States. 1992, Millbrook LB $21.90 (1-56294-310-3). 32pp. A brief look at the geography, history, and outlook for these former Soviet states. (Rev: BL 1/15/93; SLJ 1/93) [947.4]

15414 Flint, David. *The Russian Federation* (4–6). Illus. Series: Former Soviet States. 1992, Millbrook LB $21.90 (1-56294-305-7). 32pp. Examines this area, which contains more than half of the population of the former USSR, and its current problems. (Rev: BL 1/15/93; SLJ 1/93) [947]

15415 *Georgia: Then and Now* (5–8). Illus. Series: Then and Now. 1994, Lerner LB $23.93 (0-8225-2807-X). 56pp. This former Soviet Republic is introduced, and such topics as topography, ethnic makeup, history, economy, and future challenges are discussed. (Rev: BL 2/1/94; SLJ 3/94) [947.95]

15416 Gosnell, Kelvin. *Belarus, Ukraine, and Moldova* (4–6). Illus. Series: Former Soviet States. 1992, Millbrook LB $21.90 (1-56294-306-5). 32pp. This account highlights the vast Ukraine, the breadbasket of the region, plus two smaller lands. (Rev: BL 1/15/93; SLJ 1/93) [947]

15417 Gresko, Marcia S. *Letters Home from Russia* (3–5). Series: Letters Home From. 2000, Blackbirch LB $16.95 (1-56711-411-3). 32pp. A first-person account that introduces Russia and presents such topics as the history, land, and people from a child's point of view. (Rev: BL 5/15/00; HBG 10/00; SLJ 6/00) [947]

15418 Harvey, Miles. *The Fall of the Soviet Union* (3–6). Illus. Series: Cornerstones of Freedom. 1995, Children's LB $20.50 (0-516-06694-3). 30pp. A highly readable text that begins with the revolution in 1917 and ends with Gorbachev's resignation in December 1991. (Rev: SLJ 8/95) [947]

15419 Harvey, Miles. *Look What Came from Russia* (2–5). Series: Look What Came From. 1999, Watts LB $20.00 (0-531-11499-6). 32pp. Russian culture and products — from food and fashion to sports and games — are introduced with a simple text, pictures, and a single recipe. (Rev: HBG 10/99; SLJ 7/99) [947]

15420 Haskins, Jim. *Count Your Way Through Russia* (3–5). Illus. 1987, Carolrhoda LB $19.93 (0-87614-303-6); paper $5.95 (0-87614-488-1). Snowshoes and folk dancers are two of the concepts used with numbers to highlight Russian culture. (Rev: BL 10/15/87; SLJ 9/87)

15421 *Kazakhstan* (5–8). Illus. Series: Then and Now. 1993, Lerner LB $23.93 (0-8225-2815-0). 56pp. This book introduces the second-largest republic of the former USSR and supplies details on climate, geography, history, and the life of the people. (Rev: BL 9/1/93; SLJ 9/93) [958.45]

15422 Kent, Deborah. *Moscow* (3–6). Series: Cities of the World. 2000, Children's LB $26.00 (0-516-21193-5). 64pp. A broad account of Moscow — its history, geography, tourist attractions, and social problems. (Rev: BL 7/00; SLJ 6/00) [947]

15423 Kent, Deborah. *St. Petersburg* (3–6). Series: Cities of the World. 1997, Children's LB $26.50 (0-516-20467-X). 64pp. This introduction to St. Petersburg, Russia, covers its history from the days of

Peter the Great, its landmarks (e.g., the Hermitage), and its current urban problems. (Rev: BL 3/15/98; HBG 10/98) [947]

15424 Lychack, William. *Russia* (4–7). Illus. Series: Games People Play! 1996, Children's LB $23.50 (0-516-04441-9). 64pp. Gives some historical information about the country but primarily explores the leisure activities of Russians, including their sports, famous athletes, and Olympic Games contributions. (Rev: SLJ 5/97) [947]

15425 *Moldova* (5–8). Illus. Series: Then and Now. 1993, Lerner LB $23.93 (0-8225-2809-6). 64pp. Background data on this young nation. (Rev: SLJ 3/93) [947]

15426 Murrell, Kathleen Berton. *Russia* (4–8). Illus. Series: Eyewitness Books. 1998, Knopf LB $20.99 (0-679-99118-2). 60pp. A broad introduction to Russia — its diverse people and culture, its history and geography, and its contributions to science and architecture. (Rev: BL 7/98; HBG 10/98; SLJ 8/98) [947]

15427 Nadel, Laurie. *The Kremlin Coup* (5–8). Illus. Series: Headliners. 1992, Millbrook LB $23.40 (1-56294-170-4). 64pp. The story of the coup by Communist hard-liners that began on August 19, 1991, and almost returned the Communists to power in the former USSR. (Rev: BL 12/1/92) [947]

15428 Resnick, Abraham. *The Commonwealth of Independent States: Russia and the Other Republics* (5–8). Illus. Series: Enchantment of the World. 1993, Children's LB $32.00 (0-516-02613-5). 144pp. Following a description of the fall of Communism, this title introduces the geography, history, society, and economies of each of the independent republics. (Rev: SLJ 9/93) [947]

15429 Rice, Terence M. G. *Russia* (4–5). Series: Countries of the World. 1999, Gareth Stevens LB $18.95 (0-8368-2263-3). 95pp. Vivid color photos and an up-to-date text introduce the land and people of Russia; special sections on unique customs and current issues are included. (Rev: BL 9/15/99; SLJ 8/99) [947]

15430 Roberts, Elizabeth. *Georgia, Armenia, and Azerbaijan* (4–6). Illus. Series: Former Soviet States. 1992, Millbrook LB $21.90 (1-56294-309-X). 32pp. This account highlights the politically tumultuous Caucasian states and explores the unrest between Azerbaijan and Armenia. (Rev: BL 1/15/93; SLJ 1/93) [947.9]

15431 Sallnow, John, and Tatyana Saiko. *Russia* (3–6). Illus. Series: Country Facts Files. 1997, Raintree Steck-Vaughn LB $27.12 (0-8172-4625-8). 45pp. Russia's journey from communism to capitalism is traced, with information on current economic and social conditions. (Rev: BL 7/97; SLJ 8/97) [947]

15432 Schomp, Virginia. *Russia: New Freedoms, New Challenges* (4–6). Illus. Series: Exploring Cultures of the World. 1996, Benchmark LB $27.07 (0-7614-0186-5). 64pp. As well as providing background information on Russia, this account stresses current conditions, with an emphasis on culture and the arts. (Rev: SLJ 6/96) [947]

15433 Sheehan, Patricia. *Moldova* (5–9). Series: Cultures of the World. 2000, Marshall Cavendish LB $24.95 (0-7614-0997-1). 128pp. This book on the former Soviet republic that borders on the Ukraine covers such topics as culture, land, people, history, resources, and government. (Rev: HBG 10/00; SLJ 11/00) [947]

15434 *Tajikistan* (5–8). Illus. Series: Then and Now. 1993, Lerner LB $23.93 (0-8225-2816-9). 56pp. An introduction to the land and people of this remote former Soviet republic located north of Afghanistan. (Rev: BL 10/15/93; SLJ 11/93) [958.6]

15435 Thomas, Paul. *The Central Asian States* (4–6). Illus. Series: Former Soviet States. 1992, Millbrook LB $21.90 (1-56294-307-3). 32pp. The four southern states of the former USSR are examined. (Rev: BL 1/15/93; SLJ 1/93) [977.3]

15436 *Ukraine* (5–8). Illus. Series: Then and Now. 1993, Lerner LB $22.95 (0-8225-2808-8). 64pp. A former USSR state is introduced. (Rev: BCCB 3/93; SLJ 3/93) [947]

15437 *Uzbekistan* (5–8). Illus. 1993, Lerner LB $23.93 (0-8225-2812-6). 56pp. This area in west-central Asia with Tashkent as its capital is highlighted with information on its possible future as a new republic. (Rev: BL 5/15/93) [958.7]

Scandinavia, Iceland, Greenland, and Finland

15438 Blashfield, Jean F. *Norway* (4–7). Series: Enchantment of the World. 2000, Children's LB $33.00 (0-516-20651-6). 144pp. An introduction to Norway that covers such subjects as geography and climate, history and government, mythology and culture, and people and economy. (Rev: BL 7/00) [948.1]

15439 Carlsson, Bo Kage. *Sweden* (5–8). Illus. Series: Modern Industrial World. 1995, Thomson Learning LB $24.26 (1-56847-436-9). 48pp. This account focuses on modern Sweden, its industries, economy, resources, and people. (Rev: BL 12/15/95) [949.4]

15440 Clare, John D., ed. *The Vikings* (3–6). Illus. 1992, Harcourt $16.95 (0-15-200512-9). 64pp. Period costumes and period settings help to dramatize this historical era. (Rev: BL 12/1/92; SLJ 11/92) [948]

15441 Corona, Laurel. *Norway* (5–8). Series: Modern Nations of the World. 2000, Lucent LB $19.96 (1-56006-647-4). 128pp. Norway is introduced with coverage on history, geography, and culture plus material on everyday modern life. (Rev: BL 3/1/01) [948.1]

15442 *Denmark in Pictures* (5–8). Illus. Series: Visual Geography. 1997, Lerner LB $21.27 (0-8225-1880-5). 64pp. In photos, maps, charts, and concise text, the land of Denmark and its people are introduced. (Rev: BL 4/1/91; SLJ 7/91) [948]

15443 Dobson, Mary. *Vile Vikings* (4–6). Illus. by author. Series: Smelly Old History. 1998, Oxford paper $7.95 (0-19-910494-8). 32pp. The everyday life of the Vikings and their hygienic habits are cov-

ered in this book that includes several scratch-and-sniff panels. (Rev: SLJ 1/99) [948]

15444 DuTemple, Lesley A. *Sweden* (5–8). Series: Modern Nations of the World. 2000, Lucent LB $18.96 (1-56006-588-5). 112pp. A general introduction to Sweden that includes its history and geography but stresses today's living conditions and the people's lifestyles. (Rev: BL 3/15/00; HBG 10/00) [948.5]

15445 *Finland in Pictures* (5–8). Illus. Series: Visual Geography. 1995, Lerner LB $21.27 (0-8225-1881-3). 64pp. This well-illustrated account introduces Finland and describes its people, history, geography, and government. (Rev: BL 12/15/91) [948.97]

15446 Franklin, Sharon, et al. *Scandinavia* (4–7). Series: Artisans Around the World. 1999, Raintree Steck-Vaughn LB $25.69 (0-7398-0122-8). 48pp. This book, which contains many hands-on activities, surveys Scandinavian crafts and shows how geography has influenced this area's artisans. (Rev: BL 10/15/99; HBG 3/00; SLJ 1/00) [948]

15447 Gan, Delice. *Sweden* (4–7). Illus. Series: Cultures of the World. 1992, Marshall Cavendish LB $35.64 (1-85435-452-3). 128pp. This introduction to Sweden gives special coverage on the people and their lifestyles. (Rev: BL 10/15/92) [948.5]

15448 Grant, Neil. *The Vikings* (3–6). Illus. Series: Spotlights. 1998, Oxford $10.95 (0-19-521393-9). 46pp. Traces the history of the Vikings and covers their culture, customs, and contributions. (Rev: BL 12/1/98; SLJ 10/98) [948]

15449 Hansen, Ole Steen. *Denmark* (4–7). Series: Country Insights. 1998, Raintree Steck-Vaughn LB $24.97 (0-8172-4794-7). 48pp. This book provides a broad description of the country — its lifestyle, culture, and traditions — and contrasts Denmark's rural and urban environments. (Rev: BL 6/1–15/98; HBG 10/98) [948]

15450 Hintz, Martin. *Norway* (4–6). Illus. 1982, Children's LB $32.00 (0-516-02780-8). 128pp. The land and the people of Norway are introduced in text and pictures.

15451 *Iceland in Pictures* (5–8). Illus. Series: Visual Geography. 1996, Lerner LB $21.27 (0-8225-1892-9). 64pp. The history, government, people, and economy of the northern republic of Iceland are covered in words and pictures. (Rev: BL 8/91) [949.12]

15452 James, Louise. *The Vikings* (3–6). Illus. Series: How We Know About. 1997, Bedrick LB $17.95 (0-87226-535-8). 32pp. Using both contemporary photos and many reconstructions, the everyday life of the Vikings is described, with information on how archaeologists determined these facts. (Rev: BL 12/15/97; HBG 3/98; SLJ 10/97) [948.022]

15453 Janeway, Elizabeth. *The Vikings* (4–6). 1964, Random paper $4.99 (0-394-84885-3). 160pp. A basic introduction to the Vikings, their explorations, exploits, and contributions.

15454 Kagda, Sakina. *Norway* (4–7). Illus. Series: Cultures of the World. 1995, Marshall Cavendish LB $35.64 (0-7614-0181-4). 128pp. After general information on Norway's geography and history, this account concentrates on the Norwegian people, how they live, and their artistic accomplishments. (Rev: BL 1/1–15/96; SLJ 9/96) [948.1]

15455 Kopka, Deborah. *Norway* (1–3). Series: Globe-Trotters Club. 2000, Carolrhoda LB $22.60 (1-57505-123-0). 48pp. Double-page spreads with stunning photographs introduce the land and people of Norway, with material on the Vikings, fjords, and skiing. (Rev: BL 10/15/00; HBG 3/01) [948.1]

15456 Lee, Tan Chung. *Finland* (4–7). Illus. Series: Cultures of the World. 1996, Marshall Cavendish LB $35.64 (0-7614-0280-2). 128pp. The small country of Finland with its thousands of lakes is introduced, with emphasis on the people and how they live. (Rev: BL 8/96; SLJ 7/96) [984.97]

15457 Lee, Tan Chung. *Finland* (2–4). Series: Festivals of the World. 1998, Gareth Stevens LB $14.95 (0-8368-2013-4). 32pp. Introduces the festivals and traditions of Finland, with some coverage on the land, people, and related craft projects. (Rev: BL 12/15/98; HBG 10/99) [984.97]

15458 Lepthien, Emilie U. *Iceland* (4–6). Illus. 1987, Children's LB $32.00 (0-516-02775-1). 128pp. Life in Iceland is portrayed in straight text and color photos and maps. (Rev: BL 10/15/87)

15459 Martell, Hazel M. *The Vikings and Jorvik* (4–7). Illus. Series: Hidden Worlds. 1993, Dillon LB $13.95 (0-87518-541-X). 32pp. A detailed account of how the Vikings lived, based on sound archaeological research. (Rev: BL 10/15/93; SLJ 8/93) [942.8]

15460 Mason, Antony. *Viking Times* (4–7). Illus. by Michael Welply. Series: If You Were There. 1997, Simon & Schuster paper $16.95 (0-689-81198-5). 29pp. Using many illustrations, a timeline, and a pictorial map, this account describes the homeland of the Vikings, and their wars, explorations, trade, Christianization. (Rev: HBG 3/98; SLJ 12/97) [948]

15461 Meichun, Zhong. *Finland* (4–6). Series: Countries of the World. 2000, Gareth Stevens LB $26.60 (0-8368-2331-1). 96pp. The history of this northern nation is given plus material on its land and people, the economy, unique customs, current concerns, and relations with the United States and Canada. (Rev: BL 3/15/01) [984.97]

15462 Morley, Jacqueline. *How Would You Survive as a Viking?* (4–7). Illus. Series: How Would You Survive? 1995, Watts LB $25.00 (0-531-14344-9). 48pp. The way Vikings lived in A.D. 1000 is discussed, with information on such topics as their food, forms of worship, and how they settled disputes. (Rev: BL 6/1–15/95; SLJ 8/95) [948]

15463 Morley, Jacqueline. *Viking Town* (4–6). Series: Metropolis. 1999, Watts LB $25.00 (0-531-14530-1). 48pp. A visit to a fictional Viking town teaches the reader about the everyday life of the people, their customs, way of life, food, lodging, and language. (Rev: BL 10/15/99; SLJ 12/99) [948]

15464 Odijk, Pamela. *The Vikings* (4–7). Illus. Series: Ancient World. 1990, Silver Burdett LB $17.95 (0-382-09893-5). 48pp. The exploits, explo-

rations, and contributions of the Vikings. (Rev: BL 7/90; SLJ 8/90) [936]

15465 Pitkanen, Matti A. *The Grandchildren of the Vikings* (3–6). Illus. Series: World's Children. 1996, Carolrhoda LB $23.93 (0-87614-889-5). 47pp. A photo-essay that explores family life in five areas settled by the Vikings, including the Faeroe Islands, Iceland, Gotland, Aland, and Lofoten. (Rev: SLJ 2/97) [949]

15466 Rabe, Monica. *Sweden* (2–4). Series: Festivals of the World. 1998, Gareth Stevens LB $18.60 (0-8368-2008-8). 32pp. This work introduces the Swedes, describes their distinctive holidays, and provides some related crafts. (Rev: BL 5/15/98; HBG 10/98; SLJ 8/98) [949.4]

15467 *Sweden in Pictures* (5–8). Illus. 1993, Lerner LB $21.27 (0-8225-1872-4). 64pp. Gives the background geography and history of Sweden, along with contemporary material. (Rev: BL 12/1/90) [948.5]

15468 Tweddle, Dominic. *Growing Up in Viking Times* (3–5). Illus. by Angus McBride. Series: Growing Up In. 1993, Troll paper $4.95 (0-8167-2726-0). 32pp. The upbringing of Viking children is the focus of this account that also describes everyday life in a Viking community. (Rev: BL 1/15/94) [948]

15469 Wilcox, Jonathan. *Iceland* (4–7). Illus. Series: Cultures of the World. 1996, Marshall Cavendish LB $35.64 (0-7614-0279-9). 128pp. This remote island republic is introduced, and such topics as history, geography, the people, and culture are covered with many color photos. (Rev: BL 8/96; SLJ 7/96) [949.12]

15470 Wright, Rachel. *The Viking News* (4–7). Illus. 1998, Candlewick $16.99 (0-7636-0450-X). 32pp. Using a newspaper format, headlines such as "Eric the Red Discovers Greenland" begin features stories in this description of the Vikings. (Rev: BL 5/15/98; HBG 3/99; SLJ 6/98) [948]

Spain and Portugal

15471 Berendes, Mary. *Spain* (2–5). Series: Faces and Places. 1999, Child's World LB $15.95 (1-56766-518-7). 32pp. A brief overview of Spain and its people with material on history, geography, traditions, food, pastimes, and schools. (Rev: HBG 10/99; SLJ 8/99) [946]

15472 Champion, Neil. *Portugal* (5–8). Illus. Series: Modern Industrial World. 1995, Thomson Learning LB $24.26 (1-56847-435-0). 48pp. Modern Portugal is highlighted in text and pictures, with coverage of its economy, industries, and resources. (Rev: BL 12/15/95) [946.904]

15473 Chicoine, Stephen D. *Spain: Bridge Between Continents* (3–5). Illus. Series: Exploring Cultures of the World. 1997, Marshall Cavendish LB $27.07 (0-7614-0143-1). 64pp. This introduction to Spain covers geography, history, the people, family life, the arts, festivals, and recreation. (Rev: BL 7/97; SLJ 1/98) [946]

15474 Grabowski, John F. *Spain* (5–8). Series: Modern Nations of the World. 1999, Lucent LB $18.96 (1-56006-602-4). 112pp. This fact-filled introduction to Spain emphasizes both history and current life and contains black-and-white photos and interesting sidebars. (Rev: BL 2/15/00; HBG 10/00) [946]

15475 Grinsted, Katherine. *Spain* (4–6). Series: Countries of the World. 1999, Gareth Stevens LB $19.95 (0-8368-2312-5). 96pp. A broad introduction to Spain that focuses on both its past and its present. (Rev: BL 12/15/99; HBG 10/00) [946]

15476 Heale, Jay. *Portugal* (5–8). Illus. Series: Cultures of the World. 1995, Marshall Cavendish LB $35.64 (0-7614-0169-5). 128pp. Present-day conditions in Portugal are emphasized in this account, which also covers history, geography, and culture. (Rev: SLJ 11/95) [914.9]

15477 Humble, Richard, and Mark Bergin. *A 16th Century Galleon* (4–6). Illus. Series: Inside Story. 1995, Bedrick LB $18.95 (0-87226-372-X). 48pp. A richly illustrated volume that begins with the construction of the galleon from massive tree trunks and continues through its launching and techniques of ocean navigation. (Rev: BL 8/95) [623.8]

15478 Kohen, Elizabeth. *Spain* (4–7). Illus. Series: Cultures of the World. 1992, Marshall Cavendish LB $35.64 (1-85435-451-5). 128pp. With text, photos, maps, and fact sheets, the land and people of Spain are introduced. (Rev: BL 10/15/92) [946]

15479 Leahy, Philippa. *Spain* (3–5). Illus. Series: Discovering. 1993, Crestwood LB $17.95 (0-89686-772-2). 32pp. An introduction to Spain that covers geography, history, landmarks, language, customs, food, and entertainment. (Rev: BL 2/1/94; SLJ 11/93) [946]

15480 McKay, Susan. *Spain* (2–4). Series: Festivals of the World. 1999, Gareth Stevens LB $14.95 (0-8368-2035-5). 32pp. A brief introduction to Spain and its people, focusing on the major festivals and holidays celebrated there and accompanied by a few craft projects and recipes. (Rev: BL 4/15/98) [946]

15481 Millar, Heather. *Spain in the Age of Exploration* (5–8). Series: Cultures of the Past. 1998, Benchmark LB $19.95 (0-7614-0303-5). 80pp. This book covers Spanish history from the time of Columbus to about 1700, with an emphasis on art and literature plus material on daily life and major personalities. (Rev: HBG 10/99; SLJ 2/99) [946]

15482 Miller, Arthur. *Spain* (4–6). Illus. 1989, Chelsea LB $16.95 (1-55546-795-4). 112pp. Culture, history, geography, and daily lifestyles are covered in this introduction. (Rev: BL 4/1/89; SLJ 5/89)

15483 *Portugal in Pictures* (5–8). Illus. Series: Visual Geography. 1996, Lerner LB $21.27 (0-8225-1886-4). 64pp. Current conditions and problems in Portugal are introduced as well as the standard material on history, geography, and social conditions. (Rev: BL 12/15/97) [946.9]

15484 Selby, Anna. *Spain* (4–7). Illus. Series: Country Facts Files. 1994, Raintree Steck-Vaughn LB $27.12 (0-8114-1848-0). 45pp. A well-illustrated

introduction to Spain, with coverage of such subjects as current social conditions, the economy, food and farming, and the environment. (Rev: SLJ 7/94) [946]

15485 *Spain in Pictures* (5–8). Illus. Series: Visual Geography. 1995, Lerner LB $21.27 (0-8225-1887-2). 64pp. Modern Spain is the focus of this introduction, which relies heavily on photos, charts, and maps. (Rev: BL 11/15/95) [914.6]

The Middle East

General

15486 Beshore, George. *Science in Early Islamic Culture* (4–7). Illus. Series: Science of the Past. 1998, Watts LB $24.00 (0-531-20355-7). 64pp. This book traces the many contributions to science made by the early Muslims, including mathematics, alchemy, astronomy, and medicine. (Rev: BL 6/1–15/98; HBG 10/98; SLJ 8/98) [509]

15487 Bratman, Fred. *War in the Persian Gulf* (4–6). Series: Headliners. 1991, Millbrook paper $6.95 (1-878-84161-0). 64pp. This book gives a brief, introductory account of the Persian Gulf War, with historical background material on the region and the rise of Saddam Hussein. (Rev: SLJ 12/91) [956]

15488 Foster, Leila M. *The Story of the Persian Gulf War* (3–5). Illus. Series: America at War. 1991, Children's LB $20.50 (0-516-04762-0). 32pp. With simple text and many photos, the story of the desert war is presented in a straightforward manner. (Rev: BL 3/1/92) [956.704]

15489 Gay, Kathlyn, and Martin Gay. *Persian Gulf War* (5–8). Illus. Series: Voices from the Past. 1996, Twenty-First Century LB $18.90 (0-8050-4102-8). 63pp. A clearly written, objective overview of the Gulf War that gives material on the recent history of Iraq and Saddam Hussein's rise to power. (Rev: SLJ 2/97) [956.704]

15490 King, John. *Bedouin* (4–6). Illus. Series: Threatened Cultures. 1992, Raintree Steck-Vaughn LB $24.26 (0-8114-2304-2). 48pp. This book presents the life and culture of the nomadic Bedouins. (Rev: BCCB 7–8/93; BL 8/93; SLJ 9/93) [961]

15491 Long, Cathryn J. *The Middle East in Search of Peace*. Rev. ed. (4–7). Illus. Series: Headliners. 1996, Millbrook LB $23.40 (0-7613-0105-4). 64pp. An objective account of the conflict between Arabs and Jews in the Middle East, with good historical information and a description of various peace plans. (Rev: SLJ 1/97) [956]

15492 MacDonald, Fiona. *A 16th Century Mosque* (4–6). Illus. Series: Inside Story. 1995, Bedrick $18.95 (0-87226-310-X). 48pp. After a discussion of the fundamentals of the Muslim faith, this account graphically covers the construction of the Sulemaniye mosque in Constantinople in 1557. (Rev: BL 4/15/95) [297]

15493 Nardo, Don. *The War Against Iraq* (5–8). Series: American War. 2000, Lucent LB $19.96 (1-56006-715-2). 112pp. An nonjudgmental account of the Gulf War that includes a good final chapter on the results of the war. (Rev: SLJ 3/01) [956.704]

15494 Whitcraft, Melissa. *The Tigris and Euphrates Rivers* (4–8). Series: Watts Library. 1999, Watts LB $24.00 (0-531-11741-3). 64pp. Describes the historical importance of these rivers and their ancient civilizations and traces their course today through Turkey, Iraq, and Syria. (Rev: BL 1/1–15/00; SLJ 2/00) [956]

Egypt

15495 Arnold, Helen. *Egypt* (K–2). Illus. Series: Postcards From. 1996, Raintree Steck-Vaughn LB $21.40 (0-8172-4017-9). 32pp. The geography, culture, and sights of Egypt are covered in this book that uses a series of postcards as its focus. (Rev: SLJ 2/97) [962]

15496 Bennett, Olivia. *A Family in Egypt* (3–6). Illus. 1985, Lerner LB $18.60 (0-8225-1652-7). 32pp. Color photos highlight the life of a family in this Middle East land. (Rev: BL 6/15/85; SLJ 10/85)

15497 Deady, Kathleen W. *Egypt* (1–3). Series: Countries of the World. 2000, Bridgestone LB $17.26 (0-7368-0626-1). 24pp. A very basic introduction to Egypt that contains current facts and full-page photos. (Rev: HBG 3/01; SLJ 3/01) [962]

15498 Feinstein, Steve. *Egypt in Pictures* (5–8). Illus. 1992, Lerner LB $21.27 (0-8225-1840-6). 64pp. Covers all areas of life in this Middle East land. (Rev: BL 2/1/89)

15499 Flint, David. *Egypt* (2–4). Illus. Series: On the Map. 1993, Raintree Steck-Vaughn LB $22.83 (0-8114-3420-6). 32pp. Using many color photos, this account covers briefly such topics related to Egypt as geography, religion, history, and landmarks. (Rev: BL 2/1/94) [954.9]

15500 Frank, Nicole, and Susan L. Wilson. *Welcome to Egypt* (2–4). Series: Welcome to My Country. 2000, Gareth Stevens LB $22.60 (0-8368-2494-6). 48pp. Brilliantly colored photos on each page are the highlight of this brief introduction to Egypt past and present and the way people live today. (Rev: HBG 10/00; SLJ 3/01) [962]

15501 Gresko, Marcia S. *Letters Home from Egypt* (3–5). Series: Letters Home From. 1999, Blackbirch LB $16.95 (1-56711-401-6). 32pp. A series of letters written home by a young traveler present basic facts about Egypt and its people, land, cities, food, and daily life. (Rev: BL 2/15/00; HBG 3/00; SLJ 2/00) [962]

15502 Harkonen, Reijo. *The Children of Egypt* (4–6). Illus. by Matti Pitkanen. Series: The World's Children. 1991, Carolrhoda LB $23.93 (0-87614-396-6). 40pp. In this profile, two of the children highlighted guide tourists to the pyramids, and another is a brickmaker. (Rev: BL 6/1/91) [962]

15503 Harvey, Miles. *Look What Came from Egypt* (2–5). Series: Look What Came From. 1998, Watts LB $20.00 (0-531-11498-8). 32pp. Discusses Egyptian contributions, past and present, to such areas as inventions, sports, culture, and food. (Rev: HBG 3/99; SLJ 12/98) [962]

15504 Heinrichs, Ann. *Egypt* (4–7). Illus. Series: Enchantment of the World. 1997, Children's LB $33.00 (0-516-20470-X). 144pp. This fine introduction to Egypt gives substantial information on ancient and modern history, with coverage on religion, daily life, politics and relations with Israel. (Rev: BL 2/1/98; HBG 10/98; SLJ 5/98) [962]

15505 Kallen, Stuart A. *Egypt* (4–8). Series: Modern Nations of the World. 1999, Lucent LB $17.96 (1-56006-535-4). 111pp. Sidebars are used for specialized topics in this overview that is particularly strong on the history of Egypt. (Rev: HBG 3/00; SLJ 10/99) [962]

15506 King, David C. *Egypt: Ancient Traditions, Modern Hopes* (3–5). Illus. Series: Exploring Cultures of the World. 1997, Marshall Cavendish LB $27.07 (0-7614-0142-3). 64pp. Describes various aspects of life in modern Egypt, with comparisons and contrasts made to past conditions. (Rev: BL 7/97; SLJ 1/98) [932]

15507 Loveridge, Emma. *Egypt* (3–6). Illus. Series: Country Facts Files. 1997, Raintree Steck-Vaughn LB $27.12 (0-8172-4626-6). 45pp. An overview of current conditions in Egypt, with details on tourism, the growing educational system, and the lifestyles of the people. (Rev: BL 7/97; SLJ 9/97) [962]

15508 Moscovitch, Arlene. *Egypt, the Land* (4–6). Series: Lands, Peoples, and Cultures. 2000, Crabtree LB $15.45 (0-86505-232-8); paper $7.16 (0-86505-312-X). 32pp. This book concentrates on the use of land and water in modern Egypt and the growth of cities like Cairo and Alexandria. Also use in the same series *Egypt, the People* (2000). (Rev: SLJ 7/00) [962]

15509 Pateman, Robert. *Egypt* (4–7). Illus. Series: Cultures of the World. 1992, Marshall Cavendish LB $35.64 (1-85435-535-X). 128pp. Egypt past and present is introduced in this account that stresses how the people live. (Rev: BL 1/1/93) [962]

15510 Pluckrose, Henry. *Egypt* (PS–2). Series: Picture a Country. 1998, Watts LB $18.00 (0-531-11506-2). 30pp. For the primary grades, this is a simple introduction to Egypt with material on the land, people, economy, food, sports, and festivals. (Rev: HBG 10/99; SLJ 2/99) [962]

15511 Roop, Peter, and Connie Roop. *Egypt* (2–4). Series: A Visit To. 1998, Heinemann LB $19.92 (1-57572-122-8). 32pp. An attractive introduction to modern Egypt, covering its geography, history, cities, people, and culture. (Rev: SLJ 9/98) [967]

15512 Stein, R. Conrad. *Cairo* (3–6). Illus. Series: Cities of the World. 1996, Children's LB $26.50 (0-516-20024-0). 64pp. Cairo's history and geography are covered, as well as famous sites, festivals, and the people's lifestyle. (Rev: BL 1/1–15/97) [962]

15513 Streissguth, Thomas. *Egypt* (3–5). Series: Globe-Trotters Club. 1999, Carolrhoda $16.95 (1-57505-110-9). 48pp. Two-page spreads present a variety of topics related to Egypt, including its geography, history, the people, religion, schools, food, and government. (Rev: BL 9/15/99; HBG 3/00; SLJ 12/99) [962]

15514 Streissguth, Thomas. *Egypt* (1–3). Series: A Ticket To. 1999, Carolrhoda LB $22.60 (1-57505-135-4). 48pp. This heavily illustrated first look at Egypt covers the land, its people, and its main ethnic and cultural features. (Rev: BL 9/15/99; HBG 3/00; SLJ 12/99) [962]

15515 Tenquist, Alasdair. *Egypt* (5–7). Illus. Series: Economically Developing Countries. 1995, Thomson Learning LB $24.26 (1-56847-385-0). 48pp. A look at present-day conditions in Egypt and its concerns and problems. (Rev: SLJ 2/96) [962]

15516 Wilson, Susan. *Egypt* (4–5). Series: Countries of the World. 1999, Gareth Stevens LB $18.95 (0-8368-2259-5). 95pp. Geography, history, lifestyle, art, food, and government are some of the topics covered in this introduction to Egypt, which also discusses current problems. (Rev: BL 9/15/99; SLJ 10/99) [962]

Israel

15517 Dubois, Jill. *Israel* (4–7). Illus. Series: Cultures of the World. 1992, Marshall Cavendish LB $35.64 (1-85435-531-7). 128pp. This introduction to Israel emphasizes its culture and the lifestyles of the people. (Rev: BL 1/1/93) [956.94]

15518 Dué, Andrea. *The Atlas of the Bible Lands: History, Daily Life and Traditions* (4–9). Illus. by Paola Ravaglia and Matteo Chesi. Series: Atlas. 1999, Bedrick $19.95 (0-87226-559-5). 62pp. This atlas (with abundant text) traces the history of the Holy Land from prehistory through today's Israeli-Arab conflict. (Rev: HBG 10/99; SLJ 3/99) [956.94]

15519 Feinstein, Steve. *Israel in Pictures* (5–8). Illus. 1992, Lerner LB $21.27 (0-8225-1833-3). 64pp. An overview of geography, climate, wildlife, and vegetation with photos, maps, and charts. (Rev: BL 8/88)

15520 Fisher, Frederick. *Israel* (4–6). Series: Countries of the World. 2000, Gareth Stevens LB $19.95 (0-8368-2319-2). 96pp. This well-illustrated guide to Israel covers its geography, history, government, current problems, language, food, and relations with Canada and the United States. (Rev: BL 6/1–15/00; HBG 10/00) [956.94]

15521 Gresko, Marcia S. *Letters Home from Israel* (3–5). Series: Letters Home From. 1999, Blackbirch LB $16.95 (1-56711-404-0). 32pp. Basic facts about Israel — its land, people, daily life, and history — are given in a series of letters written by a young traveler, illustrated with postcard-style photographs. (Rev: BL 2/15/00; HBG 3/00; SLJ 2/00) [956.94]

15522 Haskins, Jim. *Count Your Way Through Israel* (2–4). Illus. by Rick Handson. Series: Count Your Way. 1990, Carolrhoda LB $19.93 (0-87614-415-6). Using the format of counting from 1 to 10 in Hebrew, the land and people of Israel are introduced. (Rev: SLJ 2/91) [956.94]

15523 Hintz, Martin, and Stephen Hintz. *Israel* (4–7). Series: Enchantment of the World. 1999, Children's LB $32.00 (0-516-21108-0). 144pp. This attractive account provides current information on many topics related to Israel, including history,

geography, people, religion, and problems. (Rev: BL 9/15/99) [956.94]

15524 Kuskin, Karla. *Jerusalem, Shining Still* (3–5). Illus. by David Frampton. 1987, HarperCollins paper $5.50 (0-06-443243-2). 32pp. The history of Jerusalem is briefly told in lyrical prose and touches of verse. (Rev: BL 10/1/87; HB 11–12/87; SLJ 11/87)

15525 Odijk, Pamela. *The Israelites* (4–7). Illus. Series: Ancient World. 1990, Silver Burdett LB $17.95 (0-382-09888-9). 48pp. Covers the early history of the Jewish people, from their origins in Canaan through the Diaspora. (Rev: BL 7/90; SLJ 8/90) [956.94]

15526 Paris, Alan. *Jerusalem 3000: Kids Discover the City of Gold!* (4–6). Illus. by Peter Gandolfi. 1995, Pitspopany $16.95 (0-943706-59-9). 47pp. This fine introduction to Jerusalem includes material on its history as determined by archaeological research. (Rev: SLJ 12/95) [956.94]

15527 Patterson, Jose. *Israel* (3–6). Illus. Series: Country Facts Files. 1997, Raintree Steck-Vaughn LB $27.12 (0-8172-4627-4). 45pp. This account covers modern-day Israel and its political and economic status, resources, and people. (Rev: BL 7/97) [956.94]

15528 Pirotta, Saviour. *Jerusalem* (4–6). Illus. Series: Holy Cities. 1993, Dillon LB $17.95 (0-87518-569-X). 46pp. An oversize volume that introduces Jerusalem, its buildings, holy sites, and the facts and legends surrounding them. (Rev: BL 9/15/93; SLJ 8/93) [956.94]

15529 Scharfstein, Sol. *Understanding Israel* (5–7). Illus. 1994, KTAV paper $14.95 (0-88125-428-2). 144pp. A heavily illustrated introduction to Israel that covers history, religion, government, culture, and current concerns. (Rev: SLJ 10/94) [956.94]

15530 Silverman, Maida. *Israel: The Founding of a Modern Nation* (4–7). Illus. 1998, Dial LB $15.00 (0-8034-2136-6). 112pp. This account covers 3,000 years of Jewish history, with emphasis on recent centuries, and includes a timeline showing Israel's history from 1948 to 1998. (Rev: BL 5/1/98) [956.94]

15531 Taitz, Emily, and Sondra Henry. *Israel: A Sacred Land* (5–7). Illus. 1988, Macmillan LB $19.95 (0-87518-364-6). 160pp. The focus is on everyday life in this Middle East land. (Rev: BL 2/15/88)

15532 Waldman, Neil. *The Golden City: Jerusalem's 3,000 Years* (4–6). Illus. 1995, Simon & Schuster $15.00 (0-689-80080-0). 32pp. Beginning with Moses, this account traces the important events in the history of Jerusalem during its 3,000-year existence. (Rev: BL 9/1/95; SLJ 11/95) [965.94]

15533 Wolf, Bernard. *If I Forget Thee, O Jerusalem* (4–7). Illus. 1998, Dutton $17.99 (0-525-45738-0). 64pp. Presents an illustrated history of Jerusalem and describes its importance to three religions — Judaism, Christianity, and Islam. (Rev: BCCB 11/98; BL 10/1/98; HBG 3/99; SLJ 9/98) [956.94]

Other Middle Eastern Lands

15534 Anderson, Laurie Halse. *Saudi Arabia* (1–3). Series: Globe-Trotters Club. 2000, Lerner LB $22.60 (1-57505-121-4). 48pp. An introduction to this country on the Arabian Peninsula that tells about its landmarks, ethnic groups, oil riches, ancient traditions, and modern conveniences. (Rev: BL 12/15/00; HBG 3/01; SLJ 1/01) [953]

15535 Augustin, Byron, and Rebecca A. Augustin. *Qatar* (5–8). Illus. Series: Enchantment of the World. 1997, Children's LB $32.00 (0-516-20303-7). 128pp. An introduction to the small oil-producing country on the Persian Gulf that describes its history under British rule and how the people now live. (Rev: BL 7/97; HBG 3/98) [953.63]

15536 Bader, Philip. *Iran* (3–5). Illus. Series: Dropping In On. 2001, Rourke $25.27 (1-55916-285-6). This brief tour of Iran via hot-air balloon includes material on geography, famous sights, and the people. (Rev: SLJ 1/01) [955]

15537 Bernards, Neal. *The Palestinian Conflict: Identifying Propaganda Techniques* (4–7). Illus. 1990, Greenhaven LB $16.20 (0-89908-602-0). 32pp. Such skills as distinguishing between fact and fiction and detecting bias are stressed in this book. (Rev: BL 6/15/91) [956.04]

15538 Dutton, Roderic. *An Arab Family* (3–6). Illus. 1985, Lerner LB $18.60 (0-8225-1660-8). 32pp. The author focuses mainly on one family member to give fascinating details of life, noting how the discovery of oil has influenced daily activities. (Rev: BL 11/15/85)

15539 Foster, Leila M. *Jordan* (5–8). Illus. Series: Enchantment of the World. 1991, Children's LB $32.00 (0-516-02603-8). 128pp. An introduction in text and pictures to the geography, history, culture, and important people of Jordan. (Rev: BL 2/1/92) [956.95]

15540 Foster, Leila M. *Kuwait* (5–10). Series: Enchantment of the World. 1998, Children's LB $32.00 (0-516-20604-4). 143pp. An introduction to Kuwait for older readers, with extensive coverage of the Gulf War. (Rev: SLJ 11/98) [956]

15541 Foster, Leila M. *Oman* (4–7). Series: Enchantment of the World. 1999, Children's LB $32.00 (0-516-20964-7). 144pp. A fine introduction to this oil-producing country, covering topics such as history, geography, government, religion, and the economy. (Rev: BL 9/15/99) [956]

15542 Foster, Leila M. *Saudi Arabia* (5–8). Illus. Series: Enchantment of the World. 1993, Children's LB $32.00 (0-516-02611-9). 128pp. This oil-rich country is introduced with material on history, geography, culture, and religion. (Rev: BL 8/93; SLJ 8/93) [953.8]

15543 Foster, Merrell L. *Iraq* (4–9). Series: Enchantment of the World. 1997, Children's $33.00 (0-516-20584-6). 144pp. As well as standard information about Iraq, this account gives a brief history of Mesopotamia, tells about Islam's influence on the people, and introduces the exploits of Saddam Hussein. (Rev: HBG 3/99; SLJ 4/99) [953]

15544 Fox, Mary V. *Bahrain* (3–8). Illus. Series: Enchantment of the World. 1992, Children's LB $32.00 (0-516-02608-9). 126pp. This is an introduction to the tiny island sheikdom in the Persian Gulf. (Rev: BL 11/15/92; SLJ 1/93) [953.63]

15545 Fox, Mary V. *Iran* (5–8). Illus. Series: Enchantment of the World. 1991, Children's LB $32.00 (0-516-02727-1). 128pp. The history of the country once known as Persia is covered along with present-day conditions and brief biographies of famous people. (Rev: BL 10/1/91) [955]

15546 Gresko, Marcia S. *Israel* (1–3). Series: Globe-Trotters Club. 2000, Carolrhoda LB $22.60 (1-57505-118-4). 48pp. From the rocky Negev Desert to the Sea of Galilee, the state of Israel is brought to life in this account that introduces the country through double-page spreads on a variety of subjects. (Rev: BL 5/15/00; HBG 3/01) [956.94]

15547 Haskins, Jim. *Count Your Way Through the Arab World* (3–5). Illus. 1987, Carolrhoda LB $19.93 (0-87614-304-4); Lerner paper $5.95 (0-87614-487-3). 24pp. "Muslims pray to Mecca 5 times a day" and other numbers help to introduce the culture of the Arab world. (Rev: BL 10/15/87; SLJ 9/87)

15548 Hassig, Susan M. *Iraq* (4–7). Illus. Series: Cultures of the World. 1992, Marshall Cavendish LB $35.64 (1-85435-533-3). 128pp. This introduction stresses the lifestyles of the people, their religion, and culture. (Rev: BL 1/1/93) [956.7]

15549 Hestler, Anna. *Yemen* (5–8). Series: Cultures of the World. 1999, Marshall Cavendish LB $24.95 (0-7614-0956-4). 128pp. A fine introduction to this country on the Gulf of Aden with good background information and an overview of modern life. (Rev: HBG 10/99; SLJ 10/99) [956]

15550 *Iran in Pictures* (5–8). Illus. 1992, Lerner LB $21.27 (0-8225-1848-1). 64pp. Basic coverage in the Visual Geography series on this Middle East land much in the news. (Rev: BL 5/1/89)

15551 Janin, Hunt. *Saudi Arabia* (4–7). Illus. Series: Cultures of the World. 1992, Marshall Cavendish LB $35.64 (1-85435-532-5). 128pp. The history, geography, economy, language, and people are discussed in this book about Saudi Arabia. (Rev: BL 1/1/93) [953.8]

15552 *Jordan in Pictures* (5–8). Illus. 1992, Lerner LB $21.27 (0-8225-1834-1). 64pp. Young readers learn what life is like in this Middle East land. (Rev: BL 2/1/89; SLJ 2/89)

15553 King, John. *A Family from Iraq* (3–5). Illus. Series: Families Around the World. 1997, Raintree Steck-Vaughn $25.69 (0-8172-4904-4). 32pp. Chronicles the daily activities of a single family in Iraq, as well as the differences between the older and younger generations. (Rev: BL 2/1/98; HBG 3/98; SLJ 2/98) [306.85]

15554 *Lebanon in Pictures* (5–8). Illus. 1992, Lerner LB $21.27 (0-8225-1832-5). 64pp. A country torn apart by strife is the focus of this Visual Geography edition. (Rev: BL 2/1/89)

15555 Marston, Elsa. *Lebanon: New Light in an Ancient Land* (5–8). Illus. Series: Discovering Our

Heritage. 1994, Dillon LB $19.95 (0-87518-584-3). 124pp. A well-organized, readable introduction to the history, geography, and people of Lebanon, together with material on the impact of Lebanese immigration on the United States. (Rev: SLJ 7/94) [956]

15556 Moktefi, Mokhtar. *The Arabs in the Golden Age* (4–6). Illus. by Veronique Ageorges. 1992, Millbrook LB $22.40 (1-56294-201-8). 64pp. This book takes the reader back to the 8th through mid-13th centuries. (Rev: BL 10/15/92) [909]

15557 O'Shea, Maria. *Saudi Arabia* (2–4). Series: Festivals of the World. 1999, Gareth Stevens LB $15.95 (0-8368-2026-6). 32pp. The major holidays celebrated in Saudi Arabia are highlighted, including *eid*, a hajj pilgrimage to the holy city of Mecca, and the ways Muslims observe the founding of Islam. (Rev: BL 12/15/99; HBG 10/00) [953.8]

15558 Rajendra, Vijeya, and Gisela Kaplan. *Iran* (4–7). Illus. Series: Cultures of the World. 1992, Marshall Cavendish LB $35.64 (1-85435-534-1). 128pp. As well as standard introductory information about Iran, this book tells about how the people live and what the country's present problems are. (Rev: BL 1/1/93) [955]

15559 Schemenauer, Elma. *Iran* (3–5). Illus. Series: Faces and Places. 2000, Child's World LB $25.64 (1-56766-738-4). 32pp. An introduction to Iran that covers topics including geography, history, people, customs, pastimes, and religion as well as material on politics past and present. (Rev: BL 3/1/01; HBG 3/01) [955]

15560 Stein, R. Conrad. *The Iran Hostage Crisis* (3–5). Illus. Series: Cornerstones of Freedom. 1994, Children's LB $18.70 (0-516-06681-1). 32pp. This international incident that brought humiliation to the United States and helped cause the fall of a president are vividly re-created. (Rev: BL 1/15/95; SLJ 4/95) [955.05]

15561 *Yemen in Pictures* (5–8). Illus. Series: Visual Geography. 1993, Lerner LB $21.27 (0-8225-1911-9). 64pp. This Middle Eastern republic on the Gulf of Aden is introduced, with concise text and extensive photographs and maps. (Rev: BL 12/1/93; SLJ 12/93) [953.3]

North and South America (Excluding the United States)

North and South America

15562 Bramwell, Martyn. *North America and the Caribbean* (4–6). Series: World in Maps. 2000, Lerner LB $23.93 (0-8225-2911-4). 48pp. A comprehensive and well-illustrated treatment of all the countries that make up North America, from Canada to Mexico and the Caribbean islands. (Rev: BL 10/15/00) [970]

15563 Woods, Geraldine. *Science of the Early Americas* (4–7). Illus. Series: Science of the Past. 1999, Watts LB $24.00 (0-531-11524-0). 64pp. A survey of the scientific knowledge accrued by the

early inhabitants of North and South America in such fields as medicine, mathematics, engineering, astronomy, and agriculture. (Rev: BL 3/15/99; HBG 10/99; SLJ 6/99) [509.7]

Canada

15564 Barlas, Bob, and Norman Tompsett. *Canada* (4–6). Series: Countries of the World. 1998, Gareth Stevens LB $25.26 (0-8368-2123-8). 96pp. An introduction to Canada that includes material on history, government, people, economy, language, art, and lifestyles. (Rev: BL 12/15/98; HBG 10/99; SLJ 2/99) [971]

15565 Barlas, Bob, and Norman Tompsett. *Welcome to Canada* (2–4). Series: Welcome to My Country. 1999, Gareth Stevens LB $16.95 (0-8368-2394-X). 48pp. An overview that contain separate chapters on Canada's history, government and economy, people, language, arts, leisure, and food. (Rev: HBG 10/00; SLJ 1/00) [971.9]

15566 Beattie, Owen, and John Geiger. *Buried in Ice: The Mystery of a Lost Arctic Expedition* (4–7). Illus. by Janet Wilson. Series: Time Quest. 1993, Scholastic paper $6.95 (0-590-43849-2). 64pp. The story of Sir John Franklin's unsuccessful 1845 expedition from England to find the Northwest Passage. (Rev: BCCB 3/92; BL 4/1/92; SLJ 4/92*) [919.804]

15567 Bowers, Vivien. *Wow Canada! Exploring This Land from Coast to Coast to Coast* (4–6). Illus. 2000, Firefly $29.95 (1-895688-93-0); paper $19.95 (1-895688-94-9). 160pp. A family travels across Canada visiting important sites and gathering material on the land and its people in this relaxed travelogue. (Rev: BL 2/15/00; HBG 10/00; SLJ 4/00) [917.104]

15568 Campbell, Kumari. *Prince Edward Island* (3–6). Illus. Series: Hello Canada. 1996, Lerner LB $19.93 (0-8225-2762-6). 72pp. This volume highlights Canada's island province, its inhabitants, history, famous people, and economy. (Rev: BL 4/15/96) [971.7]

15569 *Canada in Pictures* (4–6). Series: Visual Geography. 1993, Lerner LB $21.27 (0-8225-1870-8). 64pp. In four separate sections that explore the land, the history and government, the people, and the economy, the basic facts about Canada and Canadians are presented. (Rev: SLJ 2/90) [971]

15570 *Christmas in Canada: Christmas Around the World from World Book* (4–6). Illus. 1994, World Book $18.50 (0-7166-0894-4). 80pp. An overview of how several ethnic groups in Canada spend their Christmas, with asides about special rituals and traditions. (Rev: BL 12/15/94) [394.26]

15571 Cooper, Michael. *Klondike Fever: The Famous Gold Rush of 1898* (5–8). Illus. 1990, Houghton paper $6.95 (0-395-54784-9). 80pp. The events that turned a remote part of the Yukon into a three-ring circus of gold-hungry prospectors. (Rev: BCCB 1/90; BL 11/15/89; HB 1–2/90) [971.9]

15572 Daitch, Richard W. *Northwest Territories* (3–6). Illus. Series: Hello Canada. 1996, Lerner

$19.93 (0-8225-2761-8). 72pp. A remote northern part of Canada is featured in this book, with material on its people, history, government, and economy. (Rev: BL 4/15/96) [971.9]

15573 Ekoomiak, Normee. *Arctic Memories* (3–5). Illus. 1990, Holt paper $5.95 (0-8050-2347-X). 32pp. Memories of an Inuit artist who was raised in the James Bay area of Arctic Quebec. (Rev: BCCB 3/90; BL 3/1/90; HB 5–6/90; SLJ 4/90) [998]

15574 Gibbons, Gail. *The Great St. Lawrence Seaway* (2–5). Illus. 1992, Morrow $17.95 (0-688-06984-3). 40pp. This book shows the progress of a ship as it carries iron from the Atlantic coast through the great seaway toward the Great Lakes. (Rev: BCCB 3/92; BL 3/15/92; SLJ 4/92) [386]

15575 Grabowski, John F. *Canada* (5–8). Illus. 1998, Lucent LB $22.45 (1-56006-520-6). 112pp. A fine introduction to Canada, with material on its history, politics, the separatist movement, principal cities, culture, and industries. (Rev: BL 6/1–15/98) [971]

15576 Greenwood, Barbara. *A Pioneer Sampler: The Daily Life of a Pioneer Family in 1840* (4–6). Illus. 1995, Ticknor $18.95 (0-395-71540-7). 240pp. Everyday life of a Canadian pioneer family is described, with accompanying projects and activities, such as how to make ink. (Rev: BCCB 5/95; BL 4/1/95; HB 5–6/95; SLJ 4/95) [971.3]

15577 Gresko, Marcia S. *Letters Home from Canada* (3–5). Series: Letters Home From. 2000, Blackbirch LB $16.95 (1-56711-410-5). 32pp. Using full-color photos on every page and a letter format, this book covers basic topics about Canada, including the land, people, cities, wildlife, and history. (Rev: BL 5/15/00; HBG 10/00) [971]

15578 Hamilton, Janice. *Canada* (3–5). Illus. Series: Globe-Trotters Club. 1999, Carolrhoda LB $22.60 (1-57505-108-7). 48pp. A fine introduction to Canada for young readers that includes material on history, geography, culture, religion, and present-day conditions. (Rev: BL 9/15/99; HBG 10/99) [971]

15579 Hamilton, Janice. *Canada* (1–3). Illus. Series: A Ticket To. 1999, Carolrhoda LB $22.60 (1-57505-133-8). 48pp. A basic, well-illustrated introduction to Canada, the land and its people. (Rev: BL 9/15/99; HBG 10/99) [971]

15580 Hamilton, Janice. *Quebec* (3–6). Illus. Series: Hello Canada. 1996, Lerner LB $19.93 (0-8225-2766-9). 72pp. This Canadian province, currently divided about its political future, is featured, with material on its heritage, geography, and economy. (Rev: BL 4/15/96) [971.4]

15581 Hancock, Lyn. *Nunavut* (3–6). Illus. Series: Hello Canada. 1995, Lerner LB $19.93 (0-8225-2758-8). 76pp. Basic information is given on this Canadian territory founded in 1993 from the eastern part of the Northwest Territories. (Rev: BL 12/15/95) [971.9]

15582 Harrison, Ted. *O Canada* (2–5). Illus. 1993, Ticknor $14.95 (0-395-66075-0). 32pp. A brief province-by-province tour of Canada, with paintings by the author. (Rev: BCCB 9/93; BL 10/15/93; SLJ 8/93) [971]

15583 Jackson, Lawrence. *Newfoundland and Labrador* (3–6). Illus. Series: Hello Canada. 1995, Lerner LB $19.93 (0-8225-2757-X). 72pp. A slim volume that presents a guided tour of these regions of Canada, with coverage on history, economic development, principal cities, and important residents, past and present. (Rev: BL 12/15/95) [971.8]

15584 Kalman, Bobbie. *Canada: The Culture* (3–5). Illus. Series: Lands, Peoples, and Cultures. 1993, Crabtree LB $20.60 (0-86505-219-0); paper $7.95 (0-86505-299-9). 32pp. Canadian culture is explored in such areas as television, music, film, art, theater, dance, and sports. (Rev: BL 2/1/94) [971]

15585 Kalman, Bobbie. *Canada: The Land* (3–5). Illus. Series: Lands, Peoples, and Cultures. 1993, Crabtree LB $20.60 (0-86505-217-4); paper $7.95 (0-86505-297-2). 32pp. Topics include Canada's provinces and territories, natural resources, industry, agriculture, transportation, wildlife, and national parks. (Rev: BL 2/1/94) [971]

15586 Kalman, Bobbie. *Canada: The People* (3–5). Illus. 1993, Crabtree LB $20.60 (0-86505-218-2); paper $7.95 (0-86505-298-0). 32pp. The multicultural nature of the Canadian people is stressed in this portrait that also covers problems in the English-French relationship. (Rev: BL 2/1/94) [306]

15587 Kalman, Bobbie. *Canada Celebrates Multiculturalism* (3–5). Illus. Series: Lands, Peoples, and Cultures. 1993, Crabtree LB $20.60 (0-86505-220-4); paper $7.95 (0-86505-300-6). 32pp. Some topics covered are the beginnings of multiculturalism in Canada, religious and heritage days, cross-cultural festivals, and the traditions of various ethnic groups. (Rev: BL 2/1/94) [971]

15588 Lourie, Peter. *Yukon River: An Adventure to the Gold Fields of the Klondike* (3–6). Illus. 1992, Boyds Mills LB $15.95 (1-878093-90-8). 48pp. Following the route of prospectors in the 1890s, this book takes the reader on a trip down the Yukon by canoe. (Rev: BCCB 10/92; BL 10/1/92; SLJ 10/92) [917.98]

15589 Marx, David F. *Canada* (1–2). Illus. Series: Rookie Readers. 2000, Children's LB $19.00 (0-516-21550-7); paper $6.95 (0-516-27083-4). 32pp. This book for beginning readers gives a quick introduction to Canada, its history, people, and languages. (Rev: BL 12/1/00) [971]

15590 Richardson, Gillian. *Saskatchewan* (3–6). Illus. Series: Hello Canada. 1995, Lerner LB $19.93 (0-8225-2760-X). 72pp. This introduction to Canada's midwestern province and bread basket includes material on history, geography, resources, and famous people. (Rev: BL 12/15/95) [971.24]

15591 Rogers, Barbara Radcliffe, and Stillman D. Rogers. *Canada* (4–7). Series: Enchantment of the World. 2000, Children's LB $33.00 (0-516-21076-9). 144pp. This fine introduction to Canada, its land and its people, also contains coverage of its history, economy, plants and animals, languages, sports, and the arts. (Rev: BL 1/1–15/01) [971]

15592 Rogers, Barbara Radcliffe, and Stillman D. Rogers. *Toronto* (3–6). Series: Cities of the World. 2000, Children's LB $26.50 (0-516-22034-9). 64pp.

Good travel-guide information, pictures, maps, and a discussion of how the city is solving its social problems make this an excellent introduction to Toronto. (Rev: BL 12/15/00) [971]

15593 Rogers, Stillman D. *Montreal* (3–6). Series: Cities of the World. 2000, Children's LB $26.00 (0-516-21637-6). 64pp. This interesting guidebook covers the history of Montreal, its landmarks, people, languages, and problems. (Rev: BL 7/00) [971.4]

15594 Shepherd, Donna Walsh. *The Klondike Gold Rush* (3–6). Series: A First Book. 1998, Watts LB $22.00 (0-531-20360-3). 64pp. The daily life of Klondike gold miners is outlined along with a history of this gold rush and the many lives it changed. (Rev: HBG 3/99; SLJ 1/99) [971.9]

15595 Shepherd, Jennifer. *Canada* (4–7). Illus. 1988, Children's LB $32.00 (0-516-02757-3). 128pp. Geography, history, climate, and people are discusssed in this look at the northern U.S. neighbor. (Rev: BL 5/15/88; SLJ 8/88)

15596 Tames, Richard. *Journey Through Canada* (3–5). Illus. by Martin Camm. Series: Journey Around the World. 1990, Troll LB $18.60 (0-8167-2110-6); paper $4.95 (0-8167-2111-4). 32pp. This book explores the majestic scenery, history, and bilingual culture of Canada. (Rev: BL 5/15/91) [971]

15597 Thompson, Alexa. *Nova Scotia* (3–6). Illus. Series: Hello Canada. 1995, Lerner LB $19.93 (0-8225-2759-6). 76pp. History, geography, and the economy are covered, with material on the various peoples and cultures represented in Nova Scotia. (Rev: BL 12/15/95; SLJ 3/96) [971.6]

15598 Yates, Sarah. *Alberta* (3–6). Illus. Series: Hello Canada. 1995, Lerner LB $19.93 (0-8225-2763-4). 76pp. A colorful, slim volume that crams many facts about this western Canadian province, its culture, history, geography, and resources into a few attractive pages. (Rev: BL 12/15/95; SLJ 3/96) [971.23]

Mexico

15599 Ancona, George. *Charro* (4–8). Illus. 1999, Harcourt $18.00 (0-15-201047-5); paper $9.00 (0-15-201046-7). 48pp. A handsome photo-essay that focuses on Mexican cowboys, called *charros*, and *la charreada*, a rodeolike competition where they display their skills. (Rev: BCCB 5/99; BL 5/15/99; HBG 10/99; SLJ 6/99) [972]

15600 Ancona, George. *Pablo Remembers: The Fiesta of the Day of the Dead* (3–6). Illus. 1993, Lothrop $16.95 (0-688-11249-8). 48pp. The customs and traditions surrounding the three-day Mexican celebration, the Fiesta of the Day of the Dead, are described in this photo-essay. A Spanish-language edition is also available. (Rev: BCCB 12/93; BL 2/1/94; SLJ 12/93) [393.9]

15601 Ancona, George. *The Pinata Maker/El Piñatero* (1–3). Illus. 1994, Harcourt $17.00 (0-15-261875-9); paper $9.00 (0-15-200060-7). 40pp. Many Mexican crafts, like the piñata and puppet making, are highlighted when a group of children visit an aged craftsman in this dual-language book. (Rev: BL 2/15/94; HB 7–8/94; SLJ 4/94) [745]

15602 Arnold, Helen. *Mexico* (1–3). Illus. Series: Postcards From. 1995, Raintree Steck-Vaughn LB $22.83 (0-8172-4012-8). 32pp. A quick overview of Mexico is given through a series of postcards written by fictitious children. (Rev: SLJ 2/96) [972]

15603 Baquedano, Elizabeth. *Aztec, Inca and Maya* (4–8). Illus. Series: Eyewitness Books. 1993, Knopf LB $20.99 (0-679-93883-4). 64pp. An overview of the history of these Indian civilizations of the Americas, their cultures, and their fate at the hands of the invading Spaniards. (Rev: BL 10/1/93; SLJ 12/93) [972]

15604 Berendes, Mary. *Mexico* (K–3). Illus. Series: Faces and Places. 1997, Child's World LB $22.79 (1-56766-372-9). 32pp. Concisely describes the land, plants, animals, history, and culture of Mexico. (Rev: SLJ 2/98) [972]

15605 Bulmer-Thomas, Barbara. *Journey Through Mexico* (3–5). Illus. by Martin Camm. Series: Journey Around the World. 1990, Troll paper $4.95 (0-8167-2117-3). 32pp. Mexico, a mix of Native American traditions and the culture of the conquistadores, is introduced in colorful photos and text. (Rev: BL 5/15/91) [972]

15606 Burr, Claudia, et al. *Broken Shields* (4–8). Illus. 1997, Douglas & McIntyre $15.95 (0-88899-303-X); paper $6.95 (0-88899-304-8). 32pp. From firsthand eyewitness accounts, this is the story of the betrayal of Montezuma at the hands of the Spanish conqueror Cortez. (Rev: BL 12/1/97; HB 11–12/97; HBG 3/98; SLJ 1/98) [972]

15607 Burr, Claudia, et al. *Cinco de Mayo: Yesterday and Today* (3–5). Illus. 1999, Douglas & McIntyre $15.95 (0-88899-355-2). 32pp. Translated from Spanish, this book gives the origins of the national holiday and describes how it is celebrated. (Rev: BL 10/1/99; SLJ 9/99) [972]

15608 Burr, Claudia, et al. *When the Viceroy Came* (3–5). Illus. 1999, Groundwood $15.95 (0-88899-354-4). 33pp. Told from a young boy's point of view, this slice of Mexican history relates how the new Spanish viceroy came to Mexico in 1702. (Rev: BL 8/99; SLJ 8/99) [972]

15609 Chapman, Gillian. *The Aztecs* (4–8). Series: Crafts from the Past. 1997, Heinemann LB $14.95 (1-57572-555-X). 37pp. This book is short on information about the Aztecs, but it does contain a number of intriguing craft projects related to their life and culture. (Rev: SLJ 4/98) [972]

15610 Chrisp, Peter. *The Aztecs* (4–6). Series: History Beneath Your Feet. 1999, Raintree Steck-Vaughn LB $25.69 (0-8172-5753-5). 48pp. Using authentic drawings and paintings, this account presents the daily life of the Aztecs and how archaeologists have gathered this information. (Rev: HBG 10/00; SLJ 3/00) [972]

15611 Conlon, Laura. *People of Mexico* (2–4). Illus. Series: South of the Border. 1994, Rourke LB $15.93 (1-55916-052-7). 24pp. Introduces the various peoples of Mexico and where they live in a simple text with many attractive color photos. Also use in this series *Products of Mexico, Visiting Mexico,* and *Wonders of Mexico* (all 1994). (Rev: SLJ 2/95) [972]

15612 Cory, Steve. *Daily Life in Ancient and Modern Mexico City* (3–6). Illus. by Ray Webb. Series: Cities Through Time. 1999, Runestone LB $17.95 (0-8225-3212-3). 64pp. Daily life in Mexico City during the time of the Aztecs and the Spanish conquest is presented, followed by information on the city today. (Rev: HBG 10/99; SLJ 6/99) [972]

15613 Dawson, Imogen. *Clothes and Crafts in Ancient Aztec Times* (4–6). Series: Clothing and Crafts in History. 2000, Gareth Stevens LB $21.27 (0-8368-2735-X). 32pp. Covers Aztec crafts such as stoneworking, pottery, basketmaking, metalwork, weaving, and textiles, as well as outlining several projects including face painting and making an Aztec headband. (Rev: BL 1/1–15/01) [972]

15614 Flint, David. *Mexico* (2–4). Illus. Series: On the Map. 1993, Raintree Steck-Vaughn LB $22.83 (0-8114-3419-2). 32pp. Such topics as geography, history, customs, lifestyles, and landmarks are covered in this well-illustrated introduction to Mexico. (Rev: BL 2/1/94) [972]

15615 Franklin, Sharon, et al. *Mexico and Central America* (4–7). Illus. Series: Artisans Around the World. 1999, Raintree Steck-Vaughn LB $25.69 (0-7398-0121-X). 48pp. This craft book, with related projects, describes the folk art of each of the countries in Central America and Mexico. (Rev: BL 10/15/99; HBG 3/00; SLJ 1/00) [745.5]

15616 Furlong, Kate A. *Mexico* (2–4). Series: Countries. 2000, ABDO LB $14.95 (1-57765-390-4). 40pp. An adequate, brief introduction to Mexico that contains excellent photographs, a timeline, and a recipe. (Rev: SLJ 3/01) [972]

15617 Harvey, Miles. *Look What Came from Mexico* (2–5). Series: Look What Came From. 1998, Watts LB $20.00 (0-531-11496-1). 32pp. An introduction to Mexico and its culture. (Rev: HBG 3/99; SLJ 12/98) [972]

15618 Heinrichs, Ann. *Mexico* (4–6). Series: True Books. 1997, Children's LB $22.00 (0-516-20337-1). 48pp. Basic materials on Mexico — history, geography, culture, and the people — is covered in this attractive title with many bright photos and a map. (Rev: BL 9/15/97; HBG 3/98; SLJ 11/97) [972]

15619 Higginson, Mel. *Wildlife of Mexico* (2–4). Illus. Series: South of the Border. 1994, Rourke LB $15.93 (1-55916-055-1). 24pp. The flora and fauna of Mexico are introduced in a heavily illustrated volume with an easy-to-read text. (Rev: SLJ 2/95) [972]

15620 Hull, Robert. *The Aztecs* (5–10). Series: The Ancient World. 1998, Raintree Steck-Vaughn LB $27.12 (0-8172-5056-5). 64pp. This history of the Aztecs and their culture tells about their great pyramids, feathered headdresses, gods, human sacrifices, and the coming of the Spanish. (Rev: BL 1/1–15/99; HBG 3/99) [972]

15621 Illsley, Linda. *Mexico* (3–5). Series: Foods and Festivals. 1999, Raintree Steck-Vaughn LB $22.83 (0-8172-5553-2). 32pp. An overview of festivals celebrated in Mexico, the special foods associated with each, and four simple recipes to prepare authentic Mexican holiday food. (Rev: BL 5/15/99; HBG 10/99; SLJ 7/99) [972]

15622 Jermyn, Leslie. *Mexico* (4–6). Series: Countries of the World. 1998, Gareth Stevens LB $25.26 (0-8368-2127-0). 96pp. Provides an introduction to Mexico's history, geography, and people, and discusses its unique customs, current problems, and relations with the U.S. and Canada. (Rev: BL 12/15/98; HBG 10/99; SLJ 2/99) [972]

15623 Jermyn, Leslie, and Fiona Conboy. *Welcome to Mexico* (2–4). Series: Welcome to My Country. 1999, Gareth Stevens LB $16.95 (0-8368-2398-2). 48pp. A heavily illustrated introduction to Mexico with coverage of the land and its people, history, daily life, food, and government. (Rev: HBG 10/00; SLJ 3/00) [972]

15624 Kalman, Bobbie. *Mexico: The Culture* (3–5). Illus. Series: Lands, Peoples, and Cultures. 1993, Crabtree LB $20.60 (0-86505-216-6); paper $7.95 (0-86505-296-4). 32pp. Topics covered include arts, crafts, music, dance, literature, legends, cooking, leisure pursuits, and Spanish influences in the Mayan and Aztec cultures. (Rev: BL 2/1/94) [917.2]

15625 Kalman, Bobbie. *Mexico: The Land* (3–5). Illus. Series: Lands, Peoples, and Cultures. 1993, Crabtree LB $20.60 (0-86505-214-X); paper $7.95 (0-86505-294-8). 32pp. Mexican geography and resources are covered, along with a discussion of Mexico's regions, transportation, industries, wildlife, and conservation. (Rev: BL 2/1/94) [917.2]

15626 Kalman, Bobbie. *Mexico: The People* (3–5). Illus. 1993, Crabtree LB $20.60 (0-86505-215-8); paper $7.95 (0-86505-295-6). 32pp. The various contrasts among the peoples of Mexico — rich and poor, urban and rural — are covered, along with general material on religion, social conditions, and the position of women. (Rev: BL 2/1/94) [972]

15627 Kent, Deborah. *Mexico: Rich in Spirit and Tradition* (4–8). Illus. Series: Exploring Cultures of the World. 1995, Benchmark LB $27.07 (0-7614-0187-3). 64pp. In addition to basic information on Mexico, this account gives coverage on religion, holidays, festivals, sports, foods, and education. (Rev: SLJ 6/96) [972]

15628 Lasky, Kathryn. *Days of the Dead* (3–6). Illus. by Christopher G. Knight. 1994, Hyperion LB $16.49 (0-7868-2018-7). 48pp. Through the story of a single Mexican family, the customs and significance of the Days of the Dead are revealed. (Rev: BCCB 10/94; BL 10/15/94; SLJ 10/94) [394.2]

15629 Laufer, Peter. *Made in Mexico* (K–4). Illus. by Susan L. Roth. 2000, National Geographic $16.95 (0-7922-7118-1). A beautifully illustrated book that describes the guitar-making business that flourishes in the remote village of Paracho in Mexico. (Rev: HBG 10/00; SLJ 4/00) [972]

15630 Lewis, Thomas P. *Hill of Fire* (1–3). Illus. by Joan Sandin. 1971, HarperCollins LB $15.89 (0-06-

023804-6); paper $3.95 (0-06-444040-0). 64pp. The eruption of the volcano Paricutin and its effect on the lives of the people.

15631 Libura, Krystyna, et al. *What the Aztecs Told Me* (4–8). Illus. 1997, Douglas & McIntyre $15.95 (0-88899-305-6); paper $6.95 (0-88899-306-4). 32pp. Based on an original 12-volume work written in the 16th century, this book describes the Aztec people from observation and eyewitness accounts. (Rev: BL 12/1/97; HB 11–12/97; HBG 3/98; SLJ 12/97) [973]

15632 MacDonald, Fiona. *How Would You Survive as an Aztec?* (4–7). Illus. Series: How Would You Survive? 1995, Watts LB $25.00 (0-531-14348-1). 48pp. Food, clothing, and everyday life in an Aztec community are covered in a series of double-page spreads. (Rev: BL 6/1–15/95) [972]

15633 MacMillan, Dianne M. *Mexican Independence Day and Cinco de Mayo* (3–5). Series: Best Holiday. 1997, Enslow LB $18.95 (0-89490-816-2). 48pp. The history of Mexico is interwoven in the description of these related holidays, with material on how they are celebrated. (Rev: BL 12/15/97; HBG 3/98; SLJ 8/97) [972]

15634 Marquez, Heron. *Destination Veracruz* (5–8). Series: Port Cities of North America. 1998, Lerner LB $23.93 (0-8225-2791-X). 72pp. Covers the history of this port city and gives extensive material on present-day Veracruz and its importance. (Rev: HBG 3/99; SLJ 3/99) [972]

15635 Mason, Antony. *Aztec Times* (4–7). Illus. by Michael White. Series: If You Were There. 1997, Simon & Schuster paper $16.95 (0-689-81199-3). 29pp. Using many illustrations, a timeline, and a pictorial map, this account describes the origins of this civilization, its daily life, customs, and the arrival the Spaniards. (Rev: HBG 3/98; SLJ 12/97) [972]

15636 Mathews, Sally S. *The Sad Night: The Story of an Aztec Victory and a Spanish Loss* (3–5). Illus. 1994, Clarion $16.95 (0-395-63035-5). 39pp. A picture book that introduces the Aztecs, their cities, and the dramatic confrontation between Montezuma and Cortés. (Rev: BL 7/94; SLJ 6/94) [972]

15637 *Mexico in Pictures* (4–7). Illus. 1994, Lerner LB $21.27 (0-8225-1801-5). 64pp. An introduction to our south-of-the-border neighbor. (Rev: BL 8/87)

15638 Milord, Susan. *Mexico! 50 Activities to Experience Mexico Past and Present* (3–7). Series: A Kaleidoscope Kids Book. 1999, Williamson paper $10.95 (1-885593-22-8). 96pp. The author presents a survey of Mexican history and culture from ancient history through the Spanish conquest to the present day, followed by craft projects that include a piñata, a skull for Day of the Dead, and recipes for salsa, tortillas, and hot chocolate. (Rev: SLJ 5/99) [972]

15639 Odijk, Pamela. *The Aztecs* (4–7). Illus. Series: Ancient World. 1990, Silver Burdett LB $14.95 (0-382-09887-0). 48pp. A well-illustrated account of the rise and fall of the ancient Mexican civilization. (Rev: BL 7/90; SLJ 8/90) [972]

15640 Olawsky, Lynn A. *Colors of Mexico* (2–5). Illus. by Janice L. Porter. Series: Colors of the World. 1997, Carolrhoda LB $20.76 (0-87614-886-0); paper $5.95 (1-57505-216-4). 24pp. Ten different colors are used to introduce facts about Mexico, its history, geography, traditions, and people. (Rev: HBG 3/98; SLJ 10/97) [972]

15641 Presilla, Maricel E., and Gloria Soto. *Life Around the Lake* (4–6). Illus. 1996, Holt $16.95 (0-8050-3800-0). 30pp. Life around Lake Patzcuaro in central Mexico is reflected in the embroidery of the native women. (Rev: BCCB 6/96; BL 4/1/96; SLJ 6/96) [972]

15642 Rees, Rosemary. *The Aztecs* (3–6). Illus. Series: Understanding People in the Past. 1999, Heinemann LB $15.95 (1-57572-888-5). 64pp. Topics such as Aztec history, culture, floating gardens, food, feasts, and sports are covered in a series of double-page spreads. (Rev: BL 6/1–15/99) [972]

15643 Reilly, Mary J. *Mexico* (5–8). Illus. Series: Cultures of the World. 1991, Marshall Cavendish LB $35.64 (1-85435-385-3). 128pp. This account emphasizes the geography, history, economy, and lifestyles of the Mexican people. (Rev: BL 4/1/91) [972]

15644 Rummel, Jack. *Mexico*. Rev. ed. (4–7). Series: Major World Nations. 1998, Chelsea LB $19.95 (0-7910-4763-6). 128pp. This guide supplies a fine introduction to Mexico, the land and the people, with good coverage on current problems. (Rev: HBG 3/99; SLJ 12/98) [972]

15645 Shepherd, Donna Walsh. *The Aztecs* (4–6). Illus. 1992, Watts paper $6.95 (0-531-15634-6). 64pp. Covers the history, culture, and society of the ancient Aztec civilization of Mexico and its fate under the Spanish conquerers. (Rev: BL 6/15/92; SLJ 8/92) [972]

15646 Staub, Frank. *The Children of the Sierra Madre* (3–6). Illus. Series: The World's Children. 1996, Carolrhoda LB $14.96 (0-87614-943-4); paper $7.95 (0-87614-967-0). 48pp. The young people of the Sierra Madre and their social conditions are discussed, with additional historical information. (Rev: BL 10/1/96; SLJ 8/96) [972]

15647 Staub, Frank. *Children of Yucatan* (3–6). Illus. Series: The World's Children. 1996, Carolrhoda LB $23.93 (0-87614-984-0). 48pp. The daily activities and social conditions of children in this remote part of Mexico are featured, along with good background information. (Rev: BCCB 11/96; BL 10/1/96; SLJ 10/96) [972]

15648 Steele, Philip. *The Aztec News* (4–6). Illus. 1997, Candlewick $15.99 (0-7636-0115-2). 32pp. Using a newspaper format, this account covers a number of topics related to Aztecs and their history, including farming, recreation, religion, and the practice of human sacrifice. (Rev: BL 7/97; SLJ 9/97) [972.01]

15649 Stein, R. Conrad. *The Aztec Empire* (5–8). Illus. Series: Cultures of the Past. 1995, Benchmark LB $28.50 (0-7614-0072-9). 80pp. As well as telling the history of the Aztecs, this attractive, well-written account describes their everyday life and religion. (Rev: SLJ 6/96) [972]

15650 Stein, R. Conrad. *Mexico* (4–7). Series: Enchantment of the World. 1998, Children's LB $32.00 (0-516-20650-8). 144pp. As well as the history, geography, and economy of Mexico, this account covers modern culture, holidays, the arts, and religion. (Rev: HBG 3/99; SLJ 1/99) [972]

15651 Stein, R. Conrad. *Mexico City* (3–6). Illus. Series: Cities of the World. 1996, Children's LB $26.50 (0-516-00352-6). 64pp. History, religion, and the principal sights are covered in this introduction to Mexico City. (Rev: BL 11/1/96; SLJ 9/96) [972]

15652 Tanaka, Shelley. *Lost Temple of the Aztecs: What It Was Like When the Spaniards Invaded Mexico* (4–7). Illus. by Greg Ruhl. Series: An I Was There Book. 1998, Hyperion $16.95 (0-7868-0441-6). 48pp. A readable text that centers on the Great Temple of Tenochtitlan and details the life of the Aztecs from the arrival of the Spaniards until the capital city's destruction in 1521. (Rev: BCCB 1/99; HBG 3/99; SLJ 2/99) [972]

15653 Wolf, Bernard. *Beneath the Stone: A Mexican Zapotec Tale* (4–6). Illus. 1994, Orchard LB $17.99 (0-531-08685-2). 48pp. In photos and text, several months in the life of a Zapotec Indian family in Mexico are followed, with descriptions of their holidays and family business. (Rev: BL 3/15/94; SLJ 8/94) [972]

15654 Wood, Marion. *Growing Up in Aztec Times* (3–5). Illus. by Richard Hook. Series: Growing Up In. 1993, Troll paper $4.95 (0-8167-2724-4). 32pp. Describes Aztec community life and their beliefs, customs, and rituals, with details on the education of children. (Rev: BL 1/15/94) [972]

15655 Wood, Tim. *The Aztecs* (4–6). Illus. Series: See Through History. 1992, Viking $19.99 (0-670-84492-6). 48pp. Enhanced by overlays, this is a well-designed look at an amazing culture. (Rev: BL 10/15/92; SLJ 1/93) [972.018]

Other Central American Lands

15656 Adams, Faith. *El Salvador: Beauty Among the Ashes* (4–6). Illus. 1986, Macmillan $14.95 (0-87518-309-3). 136pp. Basic facts on geography, culture, and history are combined with a sensitive look at the lives of Salvadorans today. (Rev: BCCB 2/86; BL 3/1/86; SLJ 3/86)

15657 Adams, Faith. *Nicaragua: Struggling with Change* (5–8). Illus. 1987, Macmillan LB $14.95 (0-87518-340-9). 152pp. A balanced telling of a troubled Central American country's story. (Rev: BL 5/15/87; SLJ 8/87)

15658 Amado, Elisa. *Barrilete: A Kite for the Day of the Dead* (2–3). Illus. by Joya Hairs. 1999, Douglas & McIntyre $15.95 (0-88899-366-8). 32pp. Photographs illustrate this story of a young Guatemalan village boy and his efforts to prepare and fly a kite as part of the celebration of the Day of the Dead. (Rev: BL 2/1/00; SLJ 1/00) [796.15]

15659 Brill, Marlene T., and Harry R. Targ. *Guatemala* (5–8). Illus. Series: Enchantment of the World. 1993, Children's LB $33.00 (0-516-02614-3). 128pp. This introduction to Guatemala covers history, geography, people, and culture. (Rev: BL 8/93) [972.8]

15660 *Costa Rica in Pictures* (4–7). Illus. 1997, Lerner LB $21.27 (0-8225-1805-8). 64pp. Separate chapters on land, people, government, history, and economy, plus numerous illustrations and revised text. (Rev: BL 8/87)

15661 Day, Nancy. *Your Travel Guide to Ancient Mayan Civilization* (4–8). Series: Passport to History. 2000, Lerner LB $26.60 (0-8225-3077-5). 96pp. Using the format of a modern-day travel guide, this book explores the ancient Mayan cities of Uzmal, Tikal, Copan, and others to discover the lifestyles of the Maya, their food, clothes, religion, discoveries, and behavior. (Rev: BL 3/1/01) [972]

15662 Fisher, Frederick. *Costa Rica* (2–4). Series: Festivals of the World. 1999, Gareth Stevens LB $15.95 (0-8368-2022-3). 32pp. Lists the holidays celebrated in Costa Rica, profiles the main ones, and provides related crafts and recipes. (Rev: BL 12/15/99; HBG 10/00) [972.86]

15663 Franklin, Kristine L., and Nancy McGirr, eds. *Out of the Dump: Writings and Photographs by Children from Guatemala* (4–8). Illus. 1996, Lothrop LB $18.93 (0-688-13924-8). 56pp. A photographic essay that focuses on the poor children who exist by scavenging in the garbage dump of Guatemala City. (Rev: BCCB 3/96; BL 3/15/96*; SLJ 4/96*) [861]

15664 Gaines, Ann Graham. *The Panama Canal in American History* (4–8). Illus. Series: American History. 1998, Enslow $19.95 (0-7660-1216-6). 128pp. This is a thorough account of the construction of the canal and the difficulties encountered. An explanation of the mechanics of the locks is also included. (Rev: BL 3/1/99; HBG 10/99) [972.87]

15665 Garcia, Guy. *Spirit of the Maya: A Boy Explores His People's Mysterious Past* (4–6). Illus. 1995, Walker LB $17.85 (0-8027-8380-5). 48pp. A young Mayan boy discovers his heritage when he explores the ruins at Palenque and learns of the boy-king Pacal, who is buried there. (Rev: BCCB 12/95; BL 10/1/95; SLJ 1/96) [972]

15666 Greene, Jacqueline D. *The Maya* (3–5). Illus. Series: First Books. 1992, Watts LB $22.50 (0-531-20067-1). 64pp. This account explores the daily life of the Central American civilization that survived for thousands of years. (Rev: BL 6/15/92; SLJ 8/92) [972.81]

15667 *Guatemala in Pictures* (4–7). Illus. 1997, Lerner LB $21.27 (0-8225-1803-1). 64pp. Photos and revised text highlight this review of the land, history, people, and culture. (Rev: BL 8/87)

15668 Hassig, Susan M. *Panama* (4–7). Illus. Series: Cultures of the World. 1996, Marshall Cavendish LB $35.64 (0-7614-0278-0). 128pp. The troubled history of Panama is covered, with material on geography and the lifestyle and culture of its people. (Rev: BL 8/96) [972.87]

15669 Haverstock, Nathan A. *Nicaragua in Pictures* (5–8). Illus. 1993, Lerner LB $21.27 (0-8225-1817-1). 64pp. A visit to this controversial country is highlighted by color photos and clear text. (Rev: BL 10/15/87)

15670 Hermes, Jules. *Children of Guatemala* (2–4). Photos by author. Series: World's Children. 1997, Carolrhoda LB $23.93 (0-87614-994-8). 48pp. Children from different classes and districts are introduced in this book describing life in Guatemala. (Rev: HBG 3/98; SLJ 3/98) [917.28]

15671 *Honduras in Pictures* (4–7). Illus. 1994, Lerner LB $21.27 (0-8225-1804-X). 64pp. Chapters focus on history, culture, education, people, geography, and lifestyles. (Rev: BL 8/87)

15672 Lindop, Edmund. *Panama and the United States: Divided by the Canal* (5–8). Illus. 1997, Twenty-First Century LB $21.40 (0-8050-4768-9). 128pp. An account that traces U.S.–Panama relations, from the building of the canal to the present. (Rev: BL 8/97; SLJ 7/97) [327.73]

15673 McGaffey, Leta. *Honduras* (5–9). Series: Cultures of the World. 1999, Marshall Cavendish LB $24.95 (0-7614-0955-6). 128pp. After background material on the history and geography of Honduras, this book focuses on modern times and such topics as the economy, population, religion, holidays, and recreation. (Rev: HBG 10/99; SLJ 11/99) [972.8]

15674 McKissack, Patricia. *The Maya* (1–3). Illus. 1985, Children's LB $21.00 (0-516-01270-3); paper $5.50 (0-516-41270-1). 45pp. A simple introduction to the lifestyle of the Mayan people for beginning readers. (Rev: BL 3/1/86; SLJ 4/86)

15675 McNeese, Tim. *The Panama Canal* (5–8). Illus. Series: Building History. 1997, Lucent LB $19.96 (1-56006-425-0). 96pp. A description of the building of the Panama Canal that also supplies valuable insights into the economic and social conditions of the times. (Rev: BL 8/97; HBG 3/98; SLJ 7/97) [386]

15676 Malone, Michael. *A Guatemalan Family* (4–7). Illus. Series: Journey Between Two Worlds. 1996, Lerner paper $8.95 (0-8225-9742-X). 64pp. The story of a refugee family from Guatemala and of its resettlement in the United States. (Rev: BL 11/15/96; SLJ 1/97) [975.9]

15677 Mann, Elizabeth. *The Panama Canal* (4–6). Illus. Series: Wonders of the World. 1998, Mikaya $19.95 (0-9650493-4-5). 48pp. The story of the construction of the Panama Canal from the failed French attempt by Ferdinand de Lesseps to the American success and opening in 1914. (Rev: BL 2/1/99; SLJ 12/98) [972.87]

15678 Markun, Patricia M. *It's Panama's Canal!* (5–9). Illus. 1999, Linnet LB $22.50 (0-208-02499-9). 103pp. This account gives a good background history of the canal plus current information on Panama's control of the zone and its plans for successful management. (Rev: BL 1/1–15/00; HBG 3/00) [972.87]

15679 Morrison, Marion. *Belize* (5–8). Illus. Series: Enchantment of the World. 1996, Children's LB

$32.00 (0-516-02639-9). 124pp. An introduction to the small Central American nation, formerly called British Honduras. (Rev: BL 7/96) [972.82]

15680 Odijk, Pamela. *The Mayas* (4–7). Illus. Series: Ancient World. 1990, Silver Burdett LB $17.95 (0-382-09890-0). 48pp. The history and accomplishments of the Mayas are covered in this illustrated account. (Rev: BL 11/1/90; SLJ 1/91) [972.81]

15681 *Panama in Pictures* (4–7). Illus. 1996, Lerner LB $21.27 (0-8225-1818-X). 64pp. The life and culture, history, and geography of the people of Panama. (Rev: BL 8/87)

15682 Parker, Nancy W. *Locks, Crocs, and Skeeters: The Story of the Panama Canal* (3–5). Illus. 1996, Greenwillow $16.00 (0-688-12241-8). 32pp. A history of the Isthmus of Panama, with details of the dangers and triumphs connected with the building of the canal. (Rev: BCCB 6/96; BL 5/15/96; SLJ 4/96) [972.87]

15683 Sherrow, Victoria. *The Maya Indians* (3–5). Illus. Series: Junior Library of American Indians. 1993, Chelsea LB $16.95 (0-7910-1666-8). 80pp. An account of the Mayan culture, principally of the Yucatan area of Mexico and Guatemala, its destruction by the Spaniards, and the present status of the descendants. (Rev: BL 2/15/94; SLJ 2/94) [973.81]

15684 Silverstone, Michael. *Rigoberta Menchu: Defending Human Rights in Guatemala* (5–8). Illus. 1999, Feminist Pr. LB $19.95 (1-55861-198-3); paper $9.95 (1-55861-199-1). 112pp. In addition to a biography of Nobel Peace Prize winner Rigoberta Menchu, this account presents Guatemala, its civil war, and the efforts to end it. (Rev: BL 3/15/00) [972.81]

15685 Sola, Michele. *Angela Weaves a Dream* (4–6). Illus. by Jeffrey J. Foxx. 1997, Hyperion LB $17.49 (0-7868-2060-8). 48pp. Present-day Mayan culture is introduced, as well as their art of weaving clothes and other articles using the same techniques as those of their ancestors. (Rev: BCCB 6/97; BL 4/15/97; SLJ 7/97) [746.1]

15686 Staub, Frank. *Children of Belize* (3–6). Series: The World's Children. 1997, Carolrhoda $23.93 (1-57505-039-0). 45pp. The reader meets a variety of children from this small Central American country with a unique history and a population of remarkable diversity. (Rev: BL 3/15/98; SLJ 3/98) [972.82]

15687 Vazquez, Ana Maria B. *Panama* (5–8). Illus. Series: Enchantment of the World. 1991, Children's LB $32.00 (0-516-02604-6). 128pp. In addition to historical and geographic information, this book discusses the canal and its troubled present. (Rev: BL 2/1/92) [972.87]

15688 Waterlow, Julia. *A Family from Guatemala* (3–5). Series: Families Around the World. 1997, Raintree Steck-Vaughn $25.69 (0-8172-4903-6). 32pp. The everyday activities of the Calabay family of Guatemala are described, including Vicente's project of weaving a blanket, the sale of which will be the family's sole source of income. (Rev: BL 2/15/98; HBG 3/98; SLJ 3/98) [972.81]

15689 West, Tracey. *Costa Rica* (3–5). Series: Globe-Trotters Club. 1999, Carolrhoda $22.60 (1-57505-109-5). 48pp. The land of Costa Rica is given a colorful introduction in this informal treatment, which covers the basic topics, with an emphasis on contemporary life. (Rev: BL 9/15/99; HBG 3/00; SLJ 2/00) [972.8]

15690 West, Tracey. *Costa Rica* (1–3). Series: A Ticket To. 1999, Carolrhoda LB $22.60 (1-57505-134-6). 48pp. This beginning glimpse of Costa Rica introduces the country's landscape and its main ethnic and cultural features, using plenty of pictures and a simple text. (Rev: BL 9/15/99; HBG 3/00; SLJ 1/00) [972]

15691 Winkelman, Barbara Gaines. *The Panama Canal* (4–6). Illus. Series: Cornerstones of Freedom. 1999, Children's LB $19.50 (0-516-21142-0). 32pp. An attractive account of how the Panama Canal was built, the political struggle to maintain U.S. dominance, and the transfer of ownership in 1999. (Rev: BL 5/15/99; HBG 10/99; SLJ 8/99) [972.87]

Puerto Rico and Other Caribbean Islands

15692 Ada, Alma F. *Under the Royal Palms: A Childhood in Cuba* (3–6). Illus. 1998, Simon & Schuster $15.00 (0-689-80631-0). 96pp. The story of a little girl growing up in a small town in Cuba is presented in a series of short vignettes. (Rev: BL 11/15/98; HBG 3/99; SLJ 12/98) [813]

15693 Ancona, George. *Cuban Kids* (3–5). Illus. 2000, Marshall Cavendish $15.95 (0-7614-5077-7). 40pp. This photo-essay gives a fine picture of contemporary Cuba as seen through the eyes and actions of the country's children at work and at play. (Rev: BL 12/15/00; HBG 3/01; SLJ 1/01) [972.91]

15694 Barlas, Bob. *Jamaica* (2–4). Series: Festivals of the World. 1998, Gareth Stevens LB $18.60 (0-8368-2005-3). 32pp. Introduces the people and culture of Jamaica, describes their most important holidays, and provides related recipes and craft ideas. (Rev: BL 5/15/98; HBG 10/98; SLJ 9/98) [975.9]

15695 Belafonte, Harry, and Lord Burgess. *Island in the Sun* (PS–2). Illus. by Alex Ayliffe. 1999, Dial $15.99 (0-8037-2387-3). 32pp. A lyrical introduction to Jamaica, its people, plants, and animals. (Rev: BL 8/99; HBG 10/99; SLJ 7/99) [782.4]

15696 Capek, Michael. *Jamaica* (3–5). Series: Globe-Trotters Club. 1999, Carolrhoda $16.95 (1-57505-112-5). 48pp. Using two-page spreads, this breezy account provides a broad introduction to Jamaica, with many colorful photos, fact boxes, and sidebars. (Rev: BL 9/15/99; HBG 3/00) [972.92]

15697 Capek, Michael. *Jamaica* (1–3). Series: A Ticket To. 1999, Carolrhoda LB $22.60 (1-57505-137-0). 48pp. Color photos and a simple, concise text enhance this first look at Jamaica, which gives basic information about the people and their land. (Rev: BL 9/15/99; HBG 3/00) [972.92]

15698 Cramer, Mark. *Cuba* (4–6). Series: Countries of the World. 2000, Gareth Stevens LB $19.95 (0-8368-2316-8). 96pp. This colorful introduction to Cuba tells about its history, geography, people, current conditions, and relations with the United States and Canada. (Rev: BL 6/1–15/00; HBG 10/00) [972.9]

15699 Dash, Paul. *Traditions from the Caribbean* (3–6). Series: Cultural Journeys. 1999, Raintree Steck-Vaughn LB $25.69 (0-8172-5384-X). 48pp. This introduction to Caribbean island life includes cultural folktales and such projects as making an island fruit salad, creating a Carnival costume, and constructing a drum set. (Rev: BL 5/15/99; HBG 10/99) [972]

15700 Davis, Lucile. *Puerto Rico* (5–8). Series: America the Beautiful. 2000, Children's LB $33.00 (0-516-21042-4). 144pp. This introduction to Puerto Rico contains information on the island's history, geography, economy, people, culture, and current concerns. (Rev: BL 5/15/00) [972.95]

15701 Ellis, Royston. *Trinidad* (2–4). Series: Festivals of the World. 1999, Gareth Stevens LB $15.95 (0-8368-2036-3). 32pp. Color photos and a simple text are used to describe the main holidays in Trinidad, how they are celebrated, plus crafts and cooking associated with each. (Rev: BL 12/15/99; HBG 10/00) [972.98]

15702 Feeney, Kathy. *Puerto Rico Facts and Symbols* (1–4). Series: States and Their Symbols. 2000, Capstone LB $15.93 (0-7368-0644-X). 24pp. Double-page spreads present illustrations followed by descriptions of pertinent facts including Puerto Rico's flag, flower, animal, seal, and bird. (Rev: BL 3/1/01) [972.9]

15703 Greenberg, Keith E. *A Haitian Family* (4–7). Illus. Series: Journey Between Two Worlds. 1998, Lerner LB $22.60 (0-8225-3410-X). 56pp. The story of the Beaubrun family, the political oppression they suffered in Haiti, and their eventual journey to freedom in the United States. (Rev: BL 3/1/98; HBG 10/98) [305.9]

15704 *Haiti in Pictures* (4–7). Illus. 1995, Lerner LB $21.27 (0-8225-1816-3). 64pp. Life in Haiti is pictured, with chapters on the people, history, government, and flora and fauna. (Rev: BCCB 9/87; BL 8/87)

15705 Haverstock, Nathan A. *Cuba in Pictures* (5–8). Illus. 1997, Lerner LB $21.27 (0-8225-1811-2). 64pp. A look at America's island neighbor, with color photos. Also use: *Dominican Republic in Pictures* (1997). (Rev: BL 10/15/87)

15706 Illsley, Linda. *The Caribbean* (3–5). Illus. Series: Foods and Festivals. 1999, Raintree Steck-Vaughn $22.83 (0-8172-5758-6). 32pp. Because the Caribbean Islands contain a diverse population, the festivals vary from Hindu and Christian holidays to the special children's carnival in Trinidad and Tobago. (Rev: BL 5/15/99; HBG 10/99) [394.1]

15707 *Jamaica in Pictures* (5–8). Illus. 1997, Lerner LB $21.27 (0-8225-1814-7). 64pp. Color photos highlight this visit to a popular and beautiful island. (Rev: BL 10/15/87)

15708 Kent, Deborah. *Puerto Rico* (4–6). Illus. Series: America the Beautiful. 1991, Children's LB

$28.00 (0-516-00498-0). 144pp. In a fine combination of text and graphics, the history, geography, and culture of Puerto Rico are introduced. (Rev: BL 1/15/92) [972.95]

15709 Marquez, Heron. *Destination San Juan* (5–8). Series: Port Cities of North America. 1998, Lerner LB $23.93 (0-8225-2792-8). 80pp. A matter-of-fact introduction to San Juan that describes the city, people, economy, and port activities. (Rev: HBG 3/99; SLJ 3/99) [972.95]

15710 Milivojevic, JoAnn. *Puerto Rico* (1–3). Series: Globe-Trotters Club. 2000, Carolrhoda LB $22.60 (1-57505-119-2). 48pp. A simple look at the land and people of Puerto Rico, including natural wonders and such attractions as the Arecibo Observatory, home of the world's largest telescope. (Rev: BL 5/15/00; HBG 10/00; SLJ 9/00) [972.95]

15711 Milivojevic, JoAnn. *Puerto Rico* (2–3). Series: A Ticket To. 2000, Lerner LB $22.60 (1-57505-144-3). 48pp. A simple introduction to Puerto Rico that covers basic history, geography, and society. (Rev: HBG 10/00; SLJ 9/00) [972.9]

15712 Morrison, Marion. *Cuba* (4–7). Illus. Series: Country Insights. 1998, Raintree Steck-Vaughn LB $24.97 (0-8172-4796-3). 48pp. An introduction to contemporary life in Cuba, showing the contrast between life in a big city (Havana) and in a country village. (Rev: BL 5/1/98; HBG 10/98) [972.91]

15713 Morrison, Marion. *Cuba* (5–9). Illus. Series: Enchantment of the World. 1999, Children's $32.00 (0-516-21051-3). 144pp. A fine, colorful introduction to Cuba past and present, with material on climate, industry, government, daily life, social customs, and religions. (Rev: BL 12/15/99) [972.91]

15714 NgCheong-Lum, Roseline. *Haiti* (2–4). Series: Festivals of the World. 1999, Gareth Stevens LB $15.95 (0-8368-2015-0). 32pp. The people and land of Haiti are introduced through a description of their main holidays, festivals, and voodoo religion, plus sections on related crafts and food. (Rev: BL 12/15/99; HBG 10/00) [972.94]

15715 *Puerto Rico in Pictures* (4–7). Illus. 1995, Lerner LB $21.27 (0-8225-1821-X). 64pp. Life and history, culture and geography are introduced. (Rev: BL 8/87)

15716 Rogers, Barbara Radcliffe, and Lure Rogers. *The Dominican Republic* (4–7). Series: Enchantment of the World. 1999, Children's LB $32.00 (0-516-21125-0). 144pp. An introduction to the Dominican Republic with coverage of such topics as history, climate, geography, people, religion, culture, daily life, and landmarks. (Rev: BL 12/15/99) [972.93]

15717 Sheehan, Sean. *Jamaica* (5–8). Illus. Series: Cultures of the World. 1993, Marshall Cavendish LB $35.64 (1-85435-581-3). 128pp. This informative account describes many facets of Jamaican life, including history, religion, and reggae music. (Rev: SLJ 2/94) [972.92]

15718 Staub, Frank. *Children of Cuba* (3–6). Illus. Series: World's Children. 1996, Carolrhoda LB $23.93 (0-87614-989-1). 48pp. Interesting background information on Cuba is introduced through

the experiences of several children. (Rev: BL 12/1/96; SLJ 2/97) [972.91]

15719 Staub, Frank. *Children of Dominica* (4–6). Illus. Series: World's Children. 1998, Lerner $22.60 (1-57505-217-2). 48pp. This book introduces the people of Dominica, part of the Lesser Antilles, and tells how they live, their history, and the role of children in their culture. (Rev: BL 4/1/99; SLJ 3/99) [972.9841]

15720 Telemaque, Eleanor Wong. *Haiti Through Its Holidays* (4–5). Illus. by Earl Hill. 1980, Blyden Pr. $8.50 (0-685-00779-0). 64pp. An introduction to Haiti through its holidays and customs surrounding them.

15721 Wolf, Bernard. *Cuba: After the Revolution* (3–6). Illus. 1999, Dutton $16.99 (0-525-46058-6). 48pp. An account that focuses on the city of Havana, Cuba's present economy and society, and a look at the daily life of an artist and his family. (Rev: BCCB 1/00; BL 9/1/99; HBG 3/00; SLJ 10/99) [972.91]

South America

15722 *Argentina in Pictures* (5–8). Illus. 1994, Lerner LB $21.27 (0-8225-1807-4). 64pp. Overview of climate, wildlife, cities, vegetation, and mineral resources. (Rev: BL 4/15/88; SLJ 5/88)

15723 Beirne, Barbara. *Children of the Ecuadorean Highlands* (3–6). Illus. Series: The World's Children. 1996, Carolrhoda LB $23.93 (1-57505-000-5). 48pp. Historical and geographical materials are included in this story about young people in Equador. (Rev: BL 10/1/96; SLJ 11/96) [972]

15724 *Bolivia in Pictures* (5–8). Illus. 1993, Lerner LB $21.27 (0-8225-1808-2). 64pp. Color photos add to the appeal of this overview of a South American land. (Rev: BL 10/15/87)

15725 Brill, Marlene T. *Guyana* (5–8). Illus. Series: Enchantment of the World. 1994, Children's LB $32.00 (0-516-02626-7). 127pp. With color photos on each page, this account introduces Guyana and supplies material on its geography, history, peoples, culture, and resources. (Rev: BL 12/15/94) [988.1]

15726 Carpenter, Mark L. *Brazil: An Awakening Giant* (5–7). Illus. 1988, Macmillan $14.95 (0-87518-366-2). 128pp. A wide range of information is included, with the focus on everyday life. (Rev: BL 2/15/88)

15727 *Colombia in Pictures* (5–8). Illus. 1996, Lerner LB $21.27 (0-8225-1810-4). 64pp. Many photos highlight this visit to a South American nation. (Rev: BL 10/15/87)

15728 Corona, Laurel. *Brazil* (5–8). Series: Modern Nations of the World. 1999, Lucent LB $18.96 (1-56006-621-0). 128pp. A lively account of Brazil's history, geography, famous people, and conditions today. (Rev: BL 2/15/00; HBG 10/00) [981]

15729 Dubois, Jill. *Colombia* (5–8). Illus. Series: Cultures of the World. 1991, Marshall Cavendish LB $35.64 (1-85435-384-5). 128pp. Background information on Colombia is given as well as coverage on contemporary concerns. (Rev: BL 4/1/91) [986.1]

15730 *Ecuador in Pictures* (4–7). Illus. 1994, Lerner LB $21.27 (0-8225-1813-9). 64pp. Illustrations, many in color, highlight basic facts about this country. (Rev: BL 1/1/88)

15731 Falconer, Kieran. *Peru* (4–7). Illus. Series: Cultures of the World. 1995, Marshall Cavendish LB $35.64 (0-7614-0179-2). 128pp. The focus of this book is on the people of Peru, their lifestyles, artistic endeavors, religion, and leisure activities. (Rev: BL 1/1–15/96; SLJ 4/96) [985]

15732 Ferro, Jennifer. *Brazilian Foods and Culture* (3–5). Series: Festive Foods and Celebrations. 1999, Rourke LB $19.45 (1-57103-301-7). 48pp. Information on Brazilian history and culture are featured along with a number of recipes and explanations for such celebrations as Carnival, Iemanj, and Saint John's Day. (Rev: SLJ 2/00) [981]

15733 Foley, Erin. *Ecuador* (5–8). Illus. Series: Cultures of the World. 1995, Marshall Cavendish LB $35.64 (0-7614-0173-3). 128pp. This book supplies good background material on Ecuador but is strongest in describing contemporary conditions. (Rev: SLJ 11/95) [980]

15734 Frank, Nicole. *Argentina* (4–6). Series: Countries of the World. 2000, Gareth Stevens LB $19.95 (0-8368-2315-X). 96pp. A well-illustrated guide to Argentina that includes coverage of the land, economy, history, government, people, customs, and relations with United States and Canada. (Rev: BL 6/1–15/00; HBG 10/00) [982]

15735 Furlong, Arlene. *Argentina* (2–4). Series: Festivals of the World. 1999, Gareth Stevens LB $15.95 (0-8368-2030-4). 32pp. This account describes the people and the land but emphasizes Argentina's main holidays and provides related craft projects and recipes. (Rev: BL 12/15/99; HBG 10/00) [982]

15736 Getz, David. *Frozen Girl* (4–6). Illus. 1998, Holt $15.95 (0-8050-5153-8). 70pp. Pencil illustrations and a well-written text enhance this description of the Inca girl frozen for 500 years in the Andes. (Rev: BL 5/15/98; HBG 10/98; SLJ 6/98) [985]

15737 Gofen, Ethel C. *Cultures of the World: Argentina* (5–8). Illus. Series: Cultures of the World. 1991, Marshall Cavendish LB $213.86 (1-85435-380-2). 128pp. This book provides standard information on history and geography and tells about the contemporary lifestyles of the people. (Rev: BL 4/1/91) [962]

15738 Gresko, Marcia S. *Brazil* (3–5). Series: Letters Home From. 1999, Blackbirch LB $16.95 (1-56711-407-5). 32pp. A series of letters written by a young traveler, illustrated in color, presents basic information about Brazil. (Rev: BL 2/15/00; HBG 3/00; SLJ 2/00) [981]

15739 *Guyana in Pictures* (5–8). Illus. 1997, Lerner LB $21.27 (0-8225-1815-5). 64pp. History, climate, wildlife, and major cities are covered in this overview. (Rev: BL 4/15/88)

15740 Haskins, Jim, and Kathleen Benson. *Count Your Way Through Brazil* (2–4). Illus. by Liz B. Dodson. Series: Count Your Way. 1996, Carolrhoda LB $19.93 (0-87614-873-9); paper $5.95 (0-87614-971-9). 24pp. Facts about Brazil are introduced in a counting book that goes from 1 to 10. (Rev: BL 9/15/96; SLJ 8/96) [981]

15741 Haverstock, Nathan A. *Brazil in Pictures* (4–7). Illus. 1997, Lerner LB $21.27 (0-8225-1802-3). 64pp. Current data on the political scene, plus chapters on history, people, and culture in this revised text. Also use: *Chile in Pictures* (1988). (Rev: BL 8/87)

15742 Haverstock, Nathan A. *Paraguay in Pictures* (5–8). Illus. 1995, Lerner LB $21.27 (0-8225-1819-8). 64pp. This overview of Paraguay includes its history to 1987 and possible future developments. (Rev: BL 4/15/88)

15743 Heinrichs, Ann. *Brazil* (4–6). Series: True Books. 1997, Children's LB $22.00 (0-516-20328-2). 48pp. Short chapters on Brazil cover such topics as land, people, history, homes, and culture. (Rev: BL 9/15/97; HBG 3/98) [981]

15744 Heinrichs, Ann. *Venezuela* (4–6). Series: True Books. 1997, Children's LB $22.00 (0-516-20344-4). 48pp. Venezuela is introduced with a simple text, many color photos, and a map. (Rev: BL 9/15/97; HBG 3/98) [987]

15745 Hermes, Jules. *The Children of Bolivia* (3–5). Illus. Series: World's Children. 1996, Carolrhoda LB $23.93 (0-87614-935-2). 47pp. By focusing on children in the country and in cities, the two distinct native cultures of Bolivia are explored. (Rev: SLJ 5/96) [984]

15746 Hintz, Martin. *Chile* (4–6). Illus. 1985, Children's LB $32.00 (0-516-02755-7). 128pp. Covers basic aspects of life in this South American land.

15747 Jermyn, Leslie. *Brazil* (4–5). Series: Countries of the World. 1999, Gareth Stevens LB $18.95 (0-8368-2258-7). 95pp. Basic information on the land and its people is supplemented with special sections on unique customs and current problems. (Rev: BL 9/15/99; SLJ 8/99) [981]

15748 Jermyn, Leslie. *Colombia* (4–6). Series: Countries of the World. 1999, Gareth Stevens LB $19.95 (0-8368-2308-7). 96pp. A basic introduction to Colombia that also delves into current problems, lifestyles, language, and culture. (Rev: BL 12/15/99; HBG 10/00) [986]

15749 Jermyn, Leslie. *Paraguay* (5–8). 1999, Marshall Cavendish LB $24.95 (0-7614-0979-3). 128pp. This book about Paraguay covers history, geography, government, and economy as well as such social and cultural topics as religion, the arts, food, and recreation. (Rev: HBG 10/00; SLJ 4/00) [989]

15750 Jermyn, Leslie. *Peru* (2–3). Illus. Series: Festivals of the World. 1998, Gareth Stevens LB $18.60 (0-8368-2006-1). 32pp. Color photos and a simple text are used to describe Peru's religious holidays and those with Inca origins. (Rev: BL 5/15/98; HBG 10/98; SLJ 9/98) [394.2]

15751 Jones, Helga. *Venezuela* (1–3). Series: Globe-Trotters Club. 2000, Carolrhoda LB $22.60 (1-

57505-122-2). 48pp. Some of the topics covered in this simple introduction to Venezuela are the land, people, culture, rain forests, and Angel Falls, the highest waterfall in the world. (Rev: BL 5/15/00; HBG 10/00) [987]

15752 Kendall, Sarita. *The Incas* (5–6). Illus. Series: World of the Past. 1992, Macmillan LB $17.95 (0-02-750160-4). 64pp. A history of the Incas before, during, and after the Spanish conquest. (Rev: SLJ 11/92) [940.54]

15753 Kent, Deborah. *Rio de Janeiro* (3–6). Illus. Series: Cities of the World. 1996, Children's LB $26.50 (0-516-00353-4). 64pp. The great energy of this Brazilian city is captured in this simple introduction that includes material on history, population, famous sights, religion, holidays, and ethnic blending. (Rev: SLJ 9/96) [981]

15754 Lehtinen, Ritva, and Karl E. Nurmi. *The Grandchildren of the Incas* (4–6). Illus. by Matti Pitkanen. Series: The World's Children. 1991, Carolrhoda LB $23.93 (0-87614-397-4). 40pp. Some children herd sheep while others work in the city in this profile of young Incan descendants. (Rev: BL 6/1/91) [980]

15755 Lepthien, Emilie U. *Peru* (5–8). Illus. Series: Enchantment of the World. 1992, Children's LB $32.00 (0-516-02610-0). 128pp. With many photos and clear text, this volume introduces Peru and gives summary materials in separate minifacts sections. (Rev: BL 2/1/93) [985]

15756 Lewington, Anna. *What Do We Know About the Amazonian Indians?* (4–6). Illus. by Ian Thompson. Series: What Do We Know About. 1993, Bedrick LB $18.95 (0-87226-367-3); paper $8.95 (0-87226-262-6). 43pp. Double-page spreads are used to introduce the history, lives, and cultures of the Indians of the Amazon River. (Rev: SLJ 3/94) [981.1]

15757 Lichtenberg, Andre. *Brazil* (2–4). Illus. 2000, Raintree Steck-Vaughn $22.83 (0-8172-5514-1). 32pp. A young Brazilian boy introduces the reader to his homeland, its geography, food, customs, schools, and everyday life. (Rev: BL 4/15/00; HBG 10/00) [981]

15758 Lourie, Peter. *Lost Treasure of the Inca* (4–7). Illus. 1999, Boyds Mills $18.95 (1-56397-743-5). 48pp. A thrilling narrative of a modern search for the gold supposedly hidden by the Incas in the Ecuadorian mountains. (Rev: BCCB 11/99; BL 10/15/99; HBG 3/00; SLJ 11/99) [986.6]

15759 MacDonald, Fiona. *Inca Town* (4–7). Illus. by Mark Bergin. Series: Metropolis. 1998, Watts LB $24.00 (0-531-14481-X). 45pp. Double-page spreads, a well-organized text, and colorful drawings present life in an Inca town in the 15th century. (Rev: SLJ 1/99) [985]

15760 McNair, Sylvia. *Chile* (4–7). Series: Enchantment of the World. 2000, Children's LB $32.00 (0-516-21007-6). 144pp. This attractive new edition of an old title includes material on Chile's land and people, history and government, economics and landmarks, daily life, and sports. (Rev: BL 7/00) [983]

15761 Mann, Elizabeth. *Machu Picchu* (3–5). Illus. Series: Wonders of the World. 2000, Mikaya $19.95 (0-9650493-9-6). 48pp. Beginning with the discovery of Machu Picchu in 1911, this book goes back to trace its construction and history. (Rev: BL 7/00*; HBG 10/00; SLJ 6/00) [985]

15762 Markham, Lois. *Colombia: The Gateway to South America* (3–5). Illus. Series: Exploring Cultures of the World. 1997, Marshall Cavendish LB $27.07 (0-7614-0140-7). 64pp. The past and present are contrasted in this account that gives good background information about Colombia plus material on its culture and the arts. (Rev: BL 7/97; SLJ 4/98) [986.1]

15763 Martell, Hazel M. *Civilizations of Peru, Before 1535* (5–8). Illus. Series: Looking Back. 1999, Raintree Steck-Vaughn LB $25.69 (0-8172-5428-5). 63pp. This book covers the history and culture of the Inca empire that stretched far beyond the boundaries of Peru. (Rev: BL 5/15/99; SLJ 7/99) [985]

15764 Morrison, Marion. *Brazil* (4–7). Illus. Series: Country Insights. 1997, Raintree Steck-Vaughn LB $27.12 (0-8172-4785-8). 48pp. Compares the home life, employment, schooling, and recreation in a large city and in a small village in Brazil. (Rev: BL 7/97; SLJ 8/97) [918.1]

15765 Morrison, Marion. *Colombia* (4–7). Series: Enchantment of the World. 1999, Children's LB $32.00 (0-516-21106-4). 144pp. A revision of a standard introduction to this South American country that covers such topics as history, government, people, economy, and current issues. (Rev: BL 9/15/99; HBG 3/00) [986.1]

15766 Morrison, Marion. *Ecuador* (4–7). Series: Enchantment of the World. 2000, Children's LB $33.00 (0-516-21544-2). 144pp. This book examines the geography and climate of Ecuador, its history, government, language, economy, and people. (Rev: BL 1/1–15/01) [986]

15767 Morrison, Marion. *Indians of the Andes* (4–6). Illus. 1987, Rourke LB $16.67 (0-86625-260-6). 48pp. With attractive design and numerous color photos, the Indians of the Andes are introduced to young readers. (Rev: BL 1/15/88)

15768 Morrison, Marion. *Paraguay* (5–8). Illus. Series: Enchantment of the World. 1993, Children's LB $32.00 (0-516-02619-4). 128pp. The history, geography, and people of Paraguay are covered, along with its economy, traditions, and landmarks. (Rev: BL 11/1/93; SLJ 3/94) [989.2]

15769 Morrison, Marion. *Peru* (4–7). Series: Enchantment of the World. 2000, Children's LB $33.00 (0-516-21545-0). 144pp. History, geography and climate, daily life and ancient civilizations, cities, culture, and traditions are some of the topics covered in this attractive introduction to Peru. (Rev: BL 7/00) [985]

15770 Morrison, Marion. *Uruguay* (5–8). Illus. Series: Enchantment of the World. 1992, Children's LB $32.00 (0-516-02607-0). 128pp. Introduces Uruguay, the small South American republic that was once part of Argentina. (Rev: BL 6/1/92) [989.5]

15771 Morrison, Marion. *Venezuela* (5–8). Illus. Series: Enchantment of the World. 1989, Children's LB $32.00 (0-516-02711-5). 128pp. Economy, geography, history, and people are some of the topics covered. (Rev: BL 8/89; SLJ 2/90) [987]

15772 Myers, Lynne B., and Christopher A. Myers. *Galapagos: Islands of Change* (4–7). Illus. 1995, Hyperion LB $17.49 (0-7868-2061-6). 48pp. The formation of these islands and the evolution of life on them are covered in text and amazing photographs. (Rev: BL 12/15/95; SLJ 11/95) [508]

15773 Nesbitt, Kris. *My Amazon River Day* (2–5). Illus. 2000, Shedd Aquarium $23.95 (0-9701035-0-6). 48pp. This book chronicles everyday life on the banks of the Amazon River in Peru for Patricia, her family, and her friends. (Rev: BL 10/15/00) [577.098]

15774 Odijk, Pamela. *The Incas* (4–7). Illus. Series: Ancient World. 1990, Silver Burdett LB $14.95 (0-382-09889-7). 48pp. In addition to a history of the civilization that prospered in Peru, there is a timeline, glossary, and list of famous names. (Rev: BL 7/90; SLJ 8/90) [985]

15775 Pateman, Robert. *Bolivia* (4–7). Illus. Series: Cultures of the World. 1995, Marshall Cavendish LB $35.64 (0-7614-0178-4). 128pp. The people of Bolivia, how they live, and their traditions are some of the topics covered in this general introduction. (Rev: BL 1/1–15/96; SLJ 4/96) [984]

15776 *Peru in Pictures* (5–8). Illus. 1997, Lerner LB $21.27 (0-8225-1820-1). 64pp. Young readers visit this South American land, highlighted by color photos. (Rev: BL 10/15/87)

15777 Petersen, David. *South America* (2–4). Illus. 1998, Children's LB $21.00 (0-516-20769-5). 48pp. Topographical features, climate, animals and plants, and the native peoples are covered in this overview of South America that uses maps, satellite photos, and other illustrations. (Rev: BL 1/1–15/99; HBG 3/99) [968]

15778 Pollard, Michael. *The Amazon* (4–6). Series: Great Rivers. 1997, Benchmark LB $21.36 (0-7614-0501-1). 45pp. The story of the river that rises in the Andes of Peru and flows for almost 4,000 miles to the Atlantic. (Rev: HBG 3/98; SLJ 5/98) [981]

15779 Rawlins, Carol B. *The Orinoco River* (4–7). Illus. Series: World of Water. 1999, Watts LB $24.00 (0-531-11740-5). 64pp. An introduction to this important Venezuelan river, with material on its history and current status and the areas through which it passes. (Rev: BL 1/1–15/00) [987.06]

15780 Rees, Rosemary. *The Incas* (3–6). Illus. 1999, Heinemann LB $15.95 (1-57572-889-3). 64pp. In addition to giving a general history of the Incas, their culture and contributions, this book describes their calendar, family life, and the Spanish conquest. (Rev: BL 6/1–15/99) [985]

15781 Reinhard, Johan. *Discovering the Inca Ice Maiden: My Adventures on Ampato* (5–8). Illus. 1998, National Geographic $17.95 (0-7922-7142-4). 48pp. This well-illustrated book contains a reconstruction of the life and death of the Inca Ice Maiden by the anthropologist who discovered her. (Rev: BCCB 5/98; BL 5/15/98; HBG 10/98) [985]

15782 Reynolds, Jan. *Amazon Basin* (3–6). Illus. Series: Vanishing Cultures. 1993, Harcourt paper $10.00 (0-15-202832-3). 32pp. Examines the daily life of the Indians who live in the Amazon rain forest and explains why their culture is endangered. (Rev: BCCB 11/93; BL 12/1/93; SLJ 10/93) [306]

15783 Richard, Christopher. *Brazil* (5–8). Illus. Series: Cultures of the World. 1991, Marshall Cavendish LB $35.64 (1-85435-382-9). 128pp. Brazil is introduced with information on such topics as history, economics, people, and modern problems. (Rev: BL 4/1/91) [981]

15784 Roraff, Susan. *Chile* (2–4). Series: Festivals of the World. 1998, Gareth Stevens LB $14.95 (0-8368-2012-6). 32pp. An introduction to the land and people of Chile, describing its unique traditions and holidays, and giving step-by-step instructions for some related craft projects and recipes. (Rev: BL 12/15/98; HBG 10/99) [983]

15785 St. John, Jetty. *A Family in Chile* (2–4). Illus. 1986, Lerner LB $18.60 (0-8225-1667-5). 32pp. Focusing on one child in a Chilean family, the reader learns of life in this South American land. (Rev: BL 5/15/86; SLJ 10/86)

15786 Sayer, Chloe. *The Incas* (5–10). Illus. Series: Ancient World. 1998, Raintree Steck-Vaughn LB $27.12 (0-8172-5125-1). 64pp. An in-depth look at the life of the Incas, from their beautiful gold ornaments to their unique form of record keeping and their impressive citadels and forts. (Rev: BL 1/1–15/99; HBG 3/99) [985]

15787 Siy, Alexandra. *The Waorani: People of the Ecuadoran Rain Forest* (4–7). Illus. Series: Global Villages. 1993, Macmillan LB $17.95 (0-87518-550-9). 80pp. Presents the history, culture, and prospects for the future of these people. (Rev: SLJ 8/93) [980]

15788 Steele, Philip. *The Incas and Machu Picchu* (4–7). Illus. Series: Hidden Worlds. 1993, Dillon LB $13.95 (0-87518-536-3). 32pp. A history of the Inca people and a tour of their ruined fortress city in Peru are included in this fascinating account. (Rev: BL 12/1/93) [985.37]

15789 *Venezuela in Pictures* (4–7). Illus. 1993, Lerner LB $21.27 (0-8225-1824-4). 64pp. The land, people, and government of this oil-rich country are explored in maps, text, and photos. (Rev: BL 1/1/88)

15790 Winter, Jane K. *Chile* (5–8). Illus. Series: Cultures of the World. 1991, Marshall Cavendish LB $35.64 (1-85435-383-7). 128pp. The geography, history, government, and economy of Chile are some of the topics covered in this fine introduction. (Rev: BL 4/1/91) [983]

15791 Winter, Jane K. *Venezuela* (5–8). Illus. Series: Cultures of the World. 1991, Marshall Cavendish LB $35.64 (1-85435-386-1). 128pp. In detailed text and color photographs, the land and people of Venezuela are introduced and coverage is given on contemporary problems and concerns. (Rev: BL 4/1/91) [987]

Polar Regions

15792 Aldis, Rodney. *Polar Lands* (5–8). Illus. Series: Ecology Watch. 1992, Macmillan LB $13.95 (0-87518-494-4). 46pp. After describing the polar regions and the life that exists there, this account emphasizes the need for conservation. (Rev: BL 11/1/92) [574]

15793 Alexander, Bryan, and Cherry Alexander. *An Eskimo Family* (3–6). Illus. 1985, Lerner LB $18.60 (0-8225-1656-X). 32pp. Young readers get a taste of life in the far north in this look at an Eskimo family. (Rev: BL 6/15/85; SLJ 10/85)

15794 Alexander, Bryan, and Cherry Alexander. *What Do We Know About the Inuit?* (3–6). Illus. Series: What Do We Know About. 1995, Bedrick LB $18.95 (0-87226-380-0). 45pp. An attractive volume that supplies very basic information about the Inuit people and how they live. (Rev: SLJ 1/96) [979.8]

15795 Armstrong, Jennifer. *Spirit of Endurance* (4–8). Illus. 2000, Crown $16.95 (0-517-80091-8). 32pp. An oversize book that tells the incredible survival story of Shackleton in the Antarctic. (Rev: BCCB 10/00; BL 9/15/00; HBG 3/01; SLJ 10/00) [919.8]

15796 Billings, Henry. *Antarctica* (5–8). Illus. Series: Enchantment of the World. 1994, Children's LB $32.00 (0-516-02624-0). 127pp. With color photos on each page, this account covers the history and geography of the Antarctic region, with material on plant and animal life. (Rev: BL 12/15/94) [998.2]

15797 Cordoba, Yasmine A. *Igloo* (3–5). Illus. by Kimberly L. Dawson Kurnizki. Series: Native American Homes. 2001, Rourke LB $25.27 (1-55916-277-5). 32pp. Using well-chosen photos and a good text, this book explains the construction of the igloo, its uses, and its place in the culture of the Inuit. (Rev: SLJ 3/01) [979.8]

15798 Curlee, Lynn. *Into the Ice: The Story of Arctic Exploration* (4–6). Illus. by author. 1998, Houghton $16.00 (0-395-83013-3). 40pp. Attractive acrylic paintings are used to illustrate this history of Arctic exploration, emphasizing the motivation behind the fearless explorers who venture into this cold, hostile environment. (Rev: BCCB 6/98; BL 4/1/98; HB 5–6/98; HBG 10/98; SLJ 5/98) [998]

15799 Darling, Kathy. *Arctic Babies* (K–3). Illus. by Tara Darling. 1996, Walker LB $16.85 (0-8027-8414-3). 32pp. Using full-color photos of each animal, the author introduces a variety of babies from a lynx kitten to a baby beluga whale. (Rev: BL 4/15/96; SLJ 4/96) [591.9]

15800 Dewey, Jennifer O. *Antarctic Journal: Four Months at the Bottom of the World* (4–6). Illus. 2001, HarperCollins LB $16.89 (0-06-028587-7). 64pp. A travel diary kept by the award-winning author and illustrator when she spent four months at Palmer Station on Anvers Island in Antarctica. (Rev: BCCB 2/01; BL 2/15/01; SLJ 3/01) [919.8]

15801 Dunphy, Madeleine. *Here Is the Arctic Winter* (K–4). Illus. by Alan J. Robinson. 1993, Hyperi-

on $14.95 (1-562-82336-1). A look at the land and the animals that survive the long Arctic night of winter. (Rev: SLJ 5/93) [998]

15802 Esbensen, Barbara J. *The Night Rainbow* (1–4). Illus. by Helen K. Davie. 2000, Orchard LB $17.99 (0-531-33244-6). 32pp. A poetic picture book that discusses the Northern Lights and the many images from different folk traditions that are associated with this phenomenon. (Rev: BL 3/1/00; HBG 10/00; SLJ 4/00) [538.768]

15803 Forman, Michael H. *Arctic Tundra* (K–3). Illus. Series: Habitats. 1997, Children's LB $24.00 (0-516-20710-5). 31pp. The Arctic and its animals, birds, plants, and insects are introduced in a fine combination of photos, illustrations, and a clear text. (Rev: SLJ 9/97) [575.5]

15804 Green, Jen. *Exploring the Polar Regions* (4–8). Illus. by David Antram. Series: Voyages of Discovery. 1998, Bedrick LB $18.95 (0-87226-489-0). 48pp. After an introduction to the polar regions, this book covers the exploration of these areas from the days of Eric the Red in A.D. 998 through 1993. (Rev: HBG 10/98; SLJ 4/98) [998]

15805 Grupper, Jonathan. *Destination: Polar Regions* (K–3). 1999, National Geographic $15.95 (0-7922-7143-2). 32pp. This oversize, lavishly illustrated title introduces the land and life of the polar regions with an emphasis on the Arctic. (Rev: HBG 3/00; SLJ 11/99) [508]

15806 Hooper, Meredith. *Antarctic Journal: The Hidden Worlds of Antarctica's Animals* (5–7). Illus. by Lucia deLeiris. 2001, National Geographic $16.95 (0-7922-7188-2). An exciting account of a summer the author spent at Palmer Station in the Antarctic and the wildlife there. (Rev: SLJ 3/01) [988]

15807 Hoyt-Goldsmith, Diane. *Arctic Hunter* (3–6). 1992, Holiday LB $16.95 (0-8234-0972-4). 32pp. Ten-year-old Reggie and his family travel to their camp north of the Arctic Circle to add to their food supply. (Rev: BL 12/15/92; HB 1–2/93; SLJ 11/92*) [979.8]

15808 Johnson, Rebecca L. *Braving the Frozen Frontier: Women Working in Antarctica* (3–6). Illus. 1997, Lerner LB $23.95 (0-8225-2855-X). 112pp. A profile of positions open to women in Antarctica including those of doctor, cartographer, biologist, and bulldozer driver. (Rev: BCCB 3/97; BL 2/15/97; SLJ 3/97*) [919.8]

15809 Johnson, Rebecca L. *A Walk in the Tundra* (2–4). Illus. Series: Biomes of North America. 2000, Carolrhoda LB $23.93 (1-57505-157-5). 48pp. A lively account that uses maps, pictures, and text to describe the climate, flora and fauna, and the people of the tundra regions of North America. (Rev: BL 10/15/00; HBG 3/01; SLJ 12/00) [577.5]

15810 Kaplan, Elizabeth. *Tundra* (4–6). Illus. Series: Biomes of the World. 1995, Marshall Cavendish LB $25.64 (0-7614-0080-X). 64pp. Material is given on the location of this frigid biome and the life it supports. (Rev: BL 12/15/95; SLJ 3/96) [551.4]

15811 Kendall, Russ. *Eskimo Boy: Life in an Inupiaq Eskimo Village* (2–4). Illus. 1992, Scholastic

$15.95 (0-590-43695-3). 40pp. An informal photo-essay that focuses on seven-year-old Norman Kokeok, who lives on the remote Alaskan island of Shishmaref. (Rev: BCCB 2/92; BL 1/15/92; SLJ 4/92) [979.8]

15812 Kimmel, Elizabeth C. *Ice Story: Shackleton's Lost Expedition* (4–7). Illus. 1999, Clarion $18.00 (0-395-91524-4). 120pp. A fine, accurate, and engrossing description of Shackleton's Imperial Transatlantic Expedition to the Antarctic — one of the great survival stories of all time. (Rev: BL 4/1/99; HBG 10/99; SLJ 4/99) [910.9]

15813 Lambert, David. *Polar Regions* (5–8). Illus. 1988, Silver Burdett LB $12.95 (0-382-09502-2). 48pp. Striking color photos, plus maps and diagrams highlight this description of the world's polar regions. (Rev: BL 4/1/88)

15814 Lassieur, Allison. *The Inuit* (2–4). Illus. Series: Native Peoples. 2000, Bridgestone LB $15.93 (0-7368-0498-6). 24pp. Such topics as history, housing, government, culture, and daily life are covered in this simple introduction to the Inuit people. (Rev: BL 10/1/00; HBG 10/00; SLJ 12/00) [971.9]

15815 Lewin, Ted. *The Reindeer People* (3–5). Illus. 1994, Macmillan paper $14.95 (0-02-757390-7). 40pp. The story of the Sami people of Lapland, their environment, and their culture are told in text and splendid paintings. (Rev: BL 10/1/94; SLJ 2/95) [948.97]

15816 Love, Ann, and Jane Drake. *The Kids Book of the Far North* (2–4). Illus. 2000, Kids Can $15.95 (1-55074-563-8). 48pp. Topics covered in this introduction to the Arctic include climate and landscape, natural resources, exploration and settlement, and the life, past and present, of the native people. (Rev: BL 9/15/00; SLJ 1/01) [909]

15817 Lynch, Wayne. *Arctic Alphabet: Exploring the North from A to Z* (3–5). Illus. 1999, Firefly $19.95 (1-55209-336-0); paper $6.95 (1-55209-334-4). 32pp. Using an alphabetical arrangement, the author/photographer introduces Arctic wildlife as well as the aurora borealis, glaciers, hibernation, and the Inuit. (Rev: BL 2/1/00; HBG 3/00; SLJ 2/00) [577]

15818 McCurdy, Michael. *Trapped by the Ice: Shackleton's Amazing Antarctic Adventure* (3–5). Illus. 1997, Walker LB $17.85 (0-8027-8439-9). 40pp. The breathtaking account of Shackleton's six-month ordeal living on the ice after his ship sank in the Arctic. (Rev: BL 9/15/97; HBG 3/98; SLJ 10/97) [919.9804]

15819 McMillan, Bruce. *Summer Ice: Life Along the Antarctic Peninsula* (4–6). Illus. 1995, Houghton $16.00 (0-395-66561-2). 48pp. A photo-essay that describes the geography and the plants and animals that live on the Antarctic Peninsula. (Rev: BL 11/1/95; SLJ 9/95) [508]

15820 Markle, Sandra. *Pioneering Frozen Worlds* (3–6). Illus. 1996, Simon & Schuster $17.00 (0-689-31824-3). 48pp. The frozen worlds of the polar regions and current research taking place in these areas are described, with several suggested experi-ments. (Rev: BCCB 2/96; BL 5/1/96; SLJ 5/96) [919.8]

15821 Markle, Sandra. *Super Cool Science: South Pole Stations Past, Present, and Future* (3–5). Illus. 1998, Walker LB $17.85 (0-8027-8471-2). 32pp. After describing the first research station at the South Pole built in 1956, the author describes the present facilities and their uses, with coverage on plans for a newer, larger station in the future. (Rev: BL 3/15/98; HBG 10/98; SLJ 4/98) [507]

15822 Martin, Jacqueline B. *The Lamp, the Ice, and the Boat Called Fish* (2–4). Illus. 2000, Houghton $15.00 (0-618-00341-X). 48pp. The story of the personnel aboard a research boat named Fish and how they survived with the help of some natives after they were trapped in the ice during an Arctic expedition. (Rev: BCCB 2/01; BL 3/1/01) [919.804]

15823 Newman, Shirlee P. *The Inuits* (4–6). Illus. Series: First Books. 1993, Watts LB $22.00 (0-531-20073-6). 64pp. A vivid account of Inuit, or Eskimo, life that supplies information on their homes, food, clothing, family life, and social structure. (Rev: BL 12/1/93) [973]

15824 Oberman, Sheldon. *The Shaman's Nephew: A Life in the Far North* (4–8). Illus. 2000, Stoddart $18.95 (0-7737-3200-4). 56pp. This first-person narrative explores Inuit art and culture as experienced by Tookoome, an Inuit artist, who reflects on the daily life, beliefs, and myths of his people as presented in his work. (Rev: BL 6/1–15/00) [971.9]

15825 Osinski, Alice. *The Eskimo: The Inuit and Yupik People* (1–3). Illus. 1985, Children's LB $21.00 (0-516-01267-3); paper $5.50 (0-516-41267-1). 45pp. Beginning readers are introduced to the land and peoples of the far north. (Rev: BL 3/1/86; SLJ 4/86)

15826 Penny, Malcolm. *The Polar Seas* (4–6). Illus. Series: Seas and Oceans. 1997, Raintree Steck-Vaughn LB $27.12 (0-8172-4513-8). 48pp. An overview of the history and importance of the polar seas, as well as the dangers that tourism and the search for natural resources now pose. (Rev: BL 7/97) [551.46]

15827 Pipes, Rose. *Tundra and Cold Deserts* (2–4). Series: World Habitats. 1998, Raintree Steck-Vaughn LB $15.98 (0-8172-5010-7). 32pp. The world's tundra areas are introduced along with their physical characteristics, wildlife, climate, and uses. (Rev: BL 3/15/99; HBG 3/99) [574.5]

15828 Poncet, Sally. *Antarctic Encounter: Destination South Georgia* (5–7). Illus. 1995, Simon & Schuster paper $17.00 (0-02-774905-3). 48pp. A photo-essay on the bird population of the islands of the Antarctic plus details on the everyday life of the author and her family in this difficult environment. (Rev: BCCB 9/95; BL 6/1–15/95; SLJ 9/95) [508.95]

15829 Reynolds, Jan. *Frozen Land* (3–6). Illus. Series: Vanishing Cultures. 1993, Harcourt $16.95 (0-15-238787-0); paper $8.95 (0-15-238788-9). 32pp. An Inuit family of caribou hunters is introduced and their daily life described, with material on why their culture is endangered. (Rev: BCCB 11/93; BL 12/1/93; SLJ 2/94) [306]

15830 Rootes, David. *The Arctic* (3–6). Illus. Series: Endangered People and Places. 1996, Lerner LB $22.60 (0-8225-2776-6). 48pp. A glimpse of the Arctic region and the people who live in this hostile environment. (Rev: BL 11/15/96; SLJ 1/97) [333.73]

15831 Sayre, April Pulley. *Antarctica* (5–8). Illus. Series: Seven Continents. 1998, Twenty-First Century LB $23.40 (0-7613-3227-8). 64pp. Many color photos and maps add to this introduction to the land, ice, plants, animals, and research facilities of Antarctica. (Rev: BL 2/1/99; HBG 10/99; SLJ 4/99) [919.8]

15832 Sayre, April Pulley. *Tundra* (4–7). Illus. Series: Exploring Earth's Biomes. 1994, Twenty-First Century LB $18.90 (0-8050-2829-3). 64pp. The treeless plains found in the northern Arctic are described, along with details of the flora and fauna found there. (Rev: BL 1/15/95; SLJ 2/95) [574]

15833 Shemie, Bonnie. *Houses of Snow, Skin and Bones* (3–6). Illus. 1989, Tundra $13.95 (0-88776-240-9). 24pp. Covers a variety of dwellings used by people of the extreme north. (Rev: BCCB 12/89; BL 12/15/89; SLJ 4/90) [392.36]

15834 Shepherd, Donna Walsh. *Tundra* (4–6). Illus. 1996, Watts LB $22.50 (0-531-20249-6). 62pp. The climate, life forms, and people of the Arctic tundra are introduced. (Rev: BL 2/1/97; SLJ 4/97) [574.5]

15835 Steele, Philip. *Tundra* (3–5). Illus. Series: Geography Detectives. 1997, Carolrhoda LB $19.93 (1-57505-040-4). 32pp. The treeless plains of the Arctic and parts of Antarctica are introduced, with material on the people who live there and how these areas have changed through the centuries. (Rev: BL 8/97; SLJ 1/98) [574.5]

15836 Steger, Will, and Jon Bowermaster. *Over the Top of the World: Explorer Will Steger's Trek Across the Arctic* (4–7). Illus. 1997, Scholastic $17.95 (0-590-84860-7). 64pp. Describes the grueling, dangerous adventures involved in a present-day journey across the Arctic Ocean. (Rev: BCCB 2/97; BL 4/15/97; SLJ 4/97*) [919.804]

15837 Steltzer, Ulli. *Building an Igloo* (4–6). Illus. 1995, Holt $15.95 (0-8050-3753-5). 32pp. Black-and-white photographs are used to show how an Inuit father and son build an igloo out of snow. (Rev: BL 9/15/95*; SLJ 12/95) [693]

15838 Stewart, Gail B. *In the Polar Regions* (4–6). Illus. Series: Living Spaces. 1989, Rourke LB $21.27 (0-86592-108-3). 32pp. How people adjust to living in polar regions. (Rev: BL 11/1/89) [919.8]

15839 Taylor, Barbara. *Arctic and Antarctic* (4–8). Illus. Series: Eyewitness Books. 1995, Knopf $19.00 (0-679-87257-4). 64pp. A profile of the two polar regions that contrasts the environments and introduces their plant and animal life. (Rev: BL 8/95; SLJ 9/95) [508.311]

15840 Tessendorf, K. C. *Over the Edge: Flying with the Arctic Heroes* (4–8). Illus. 1998, Simon & Schuster $17.00 (0-689-31804-9). 128pp. Beginning with Salomon Andree's ill-fated helium-balloon expedition to the North Pole, this chronicle includes other aerialists such as Roald Amundsen and Richard Byrd who also accepted the challenge. (Rev: BL 12/15/98; HB 11–12/98) [910]

15841 Theodorou, Rod. *From the Arctic to Antarctica* (2–4). Series: Amazing Journeys. 2000, Heinemann LB $15.95 (1-57572-485-5). 32pp. Both the Arctic and Antarctic regions are described in this brief overview that also introduces plant and animal life. (Rev: HBG 3/01; SLJ 7/00) [998]

15842 Turnbull, Andy. *By Truck to the North* (4–6). Illus. 1998, Annick LB $24.95 (1-55037-551-2). 88pp. This book describes in text, photos, and sidebars, the author's often harrowing journey in an 18-wheeler from Vancouver to the Arctic Circle, with many asides on history, weather, and animal life. (Rev: BL 1/1–15/99; SLJ 1/99) [971.9]

15843 Wadsworth, Ginger. *Tundra Discoveries* (PS–3). Illus. by John Carrozza. 1999, Charlesbridge LB $15.95 (0-88106-875-6); paper $6.95 (0-88106-876-4). 32pp. Each double-page spread chronicles a different month in the Arctic tundra and describes the changes in both animals and plants. (Rev: BL 9/1/99; HBG 3/00; SLJ 8/99) [591.75]

15844 Wallace, Mary. *The Inuksuk Book* (4–6). Illus. 1999, Firefly LB $19.95 (1-895688-90-6). 64pp. The daily life of the Inuit are described in this illustrated account that emphasizes *inuksuk,* the stone structures these people build for a variety of reasons. (Rev: BL 9/1/99; HBG 10/99; SLJ 6/99) [306]

15845 Wheeler, Sara. *Greetings from Antarctica* (1–5). Photos by author. 1999, Bedrick $15.95 (0-87226-295-2). 45pp. An attractive, lively introduction to Antarctica with coverage of geography, geology, ecology, history, and climate. (Rev: HBG 3/00; SLJ 8/99) [998.2]

15846 Winckler, Suzanne. *Our Endangered Planet: Antarctica* (4–7). Illus. Series: Our Endangered Planet. 1992, Lerner LB $22.60 (0-8225-2506-2). 72pp. Introduces the continent of Antarctica, including current environmental concerns. (Rev: BL 5/15/92) [918.8]

15847 Yolen, Jane. *Welcome to the Ice House* (PS–3). Illus. by Laura Regan. 1998, Putnam $15.99 (0-399-23011-4). 32pp. Using illustrations that portray the bleak Arctic landscapes, the poet introduces various animals that live in this inhospitable climate. (Rev: BL 2/15/98; HBG 10/98; SLJ 3/98*) [591.7586]

15848 Yue, Charlotte, and David Yue. *The Igloo* (3–6). Illus. 1988, Houghton $16.00 (0-395-44613-9); paper $6.95 (0-395-62986-1). 128pp. Describes the construction and function of igloos. (Rev: BCCB 1/89; BL 9/1/88; SLJ 12/88)

United States

General

15849 Ayer, Eleanor. *Our National Monuments* (4–6). Illus. Series: I Know America. 1992, Millbrook LB $20.90 (1-56294-078-3). 48pp. The most important of our national monuments are highlighted and their history explained in this well-illustrated account. (Rev: BL 9/1/92; SLJ 10/92) [973]

15850 Brandt, Sue R. *State Trees* (3–5). Illus. Series: Our State Symbols. 1992, Watts LB $24.00 (0-531-20000-0). 64pp. This book pictures and describes each of the states' and Puerto Rico's designated trees. (Rev: BL 2/1/93) [582]

15851 Johnson, Linda C. *Our National Symbols* (4–6). Illus. Series: I Know America. 1992, Millbrook LB $20.90 (1-56294-108-9). 48pp. American symbols — historical and current, such as yellow ribbons during the Persian Gulf War — are discussed. (Rev: BL 5/15/92; SLJ 7/93) [929.9]

15852 Landau, Elaine. *State Birds* (3–6). Illus. Series: Our State Symbols. 1992, Watts LB $24.00 (0-531-20058-2). 64pp. For each of the states and for Puerto Rico, the state bird is pictured and described. (Rev: BL 2/1/93) [582]

15853 Landau, Elaine. *State Flowers* (3–6). Illus. Series: Our State Symbols. 1992, Watts LB $24.00 (0-531-20059-0). 64pp. State flowers for each state and for Puerto Rico are pictured and described. (Rev: BL 2/1/93) [582]

15854 Locker, Thomas. *Home: A Journey Through America* (4–6). Illus. 1998, Harcourt $16.00 (0-15-201473-X). 32pp. Using excerpts from poems, letters, and novels, plus outstanding full-page oil paintings, this book celebrates the beauty of various American landscapes. (Rev: BL 11/1/98; HBG 3/99; SLJ 10/98) [810.8]

15855 MacDonald, Fiona. *Women in 19th-Century America* (4–8). Series: The Other Half of History. 1999, Bedrick $17.95 (0-87226-566-8). 48pp. A very brief account of the history of women and their progress during the 19th century with information on some important individuals. (Rev: HBG 3/00; SLJ 11/99) [973.6]

15856 Saller, Carol. *Working Children* (3–6). Illus. Series: Picture the American Past. 1998, Carolrhoda LB $22.60 (1-57505-276-8). 48pp. This work supplies a history of child labor, particularly in this country, and efforts to stop it. (Rev: BL 3/1/99; HBG 3/99; SLJ 1/99) [331.3]

15857 Stone, Tanya L. *America's Top 10 National Monuments* (3–6). Illus. Series: America's Top 10. 1997, Blackbirch LB $16.95 (1-56711-194-7). 24pp. Presidential memorials in Washington, D.C., and the Mesa Verde National Park are some of the monuments introduced in a series of two-page spreads. (Rev: HBG 3/98; SLJ 1/98) [973]

15858 West, Delno C., and Jean M. West. *Uncle Sam and Old Glory: Symbols of America* (2–5). Illus. 2000, Simon & Schuster $17.00 (0-689-82043-7). 40pp. From the bald eagle and the Liberty Bell to Smokey the Bear, this is a history of 15 symbols, their origins, and meanings. (Rev: BCCB 1/00; BL 12/15/99; HBG 10/00; SLJ 1/00) [929.9]

General History and Geography

15859 Andryszewski, Tricia. *Step by Step Along the Appalachian Trail* (4–6). Illus. Series: Step by Step. 1998, Twenty-First Century LB $23.90 (0-7613-

0273-5). 80pp. With geological and historical background material, this account introduces the famous route that stretches from Georgia to Maine. (Rev: BL 3/1/99; HBG 10/99; SLJ 4/99) [796.5]

15860 Baines, John. *The United States* (4–8). Illus. Series: Country Facts Files. 1994, Raintree Steck-Vaughn LB $27.12 (0-8114-1857-X). 45pp. In a series of double-page spreads, basic information about the United States is given, including geography, economy, population, industry, education, government, and environment. (Rev: SLJ 7/94) [973]

15861 Beckett, Harry. *Lake Erie* (3–5). Series: Great Lakes of North America. 1999, Rourke LB $17.45 (0-86593-527-0). 32pp. This book introduces the history of Lake Erie as well as its geography and industries. (Rev: SLJ 2/00) [973]

15862 Beckett, Harry. *Lake Superior* (3–5). Series: Great Lakes of North America. 1999, Rourke LB $17.45 (0-86593-528-9). 32pp. Maps, graphs, and photographs illustrate this introduction to Lake Superior, its history, geography, and commercial value. (Rev: SLJ 2/00) [973]

15863 Beckett, Harry. *Waterways to the Great Lakes* (3–5). Series: Great Lakes of North America. 1999, Rourke LB $17.45 (0-86593-529-7). 32pp. This book discusses how the Great Lakes were formed, the fur trade, the lock system, and current environmental problems. (Rev: SLJ 2/00) [973]

15864 Berg, Elizabeth. *USA* (4–6). Series: Countries of the World. 1999, Gareth Stevens LB $19.95 (0-8368-2313-3). 96pp. This introduction to the geography and history of the U.S. gives additional information on government, lifestyles, art, food, and unique holidays and customs. (Rev: BL 12/15/99; HBG 10/00; SLJ 1/00) [973]

15865 Berg, Elizabeth. *USA* (2–4). Series: Festivals of the World. 1999, Gareth Stevens LB $15.95 (0-8368-2028-2). 32pp. After listing both secular and religious holidays celebrated in the United States, the most important are described and related craft projects and recipes supplied. (Rev: BL 12/15/99; HBG 10/00) [973]

15866 Bial, Raymond. *One-Room School* (3–6). Illus. 1999, Houghton $15.00 (0-395-90514-1). 48pp. This photo-essay gives a history of the rural one-room schoolhouse in America from the 1700s through the 1950s. (Rev: BCCB 10/99; BL 11/1/99; HBG 3/00; SLJ 10/99) [370]

15867 Brownell, Barbara. *Spin's Really Wild U.S.A. Tour* (K–4). Illus. 1996, National Geographic paper $7.95 (0-7922-3422-7). An introduction to the geography of the United States that highlights the flora, fauna, and land formations, conducted by Spin from the National Geographic TV series. (Rev: SLJ 6/96) [910]

15868 Butler, Daphne. *U.S.A.* (2–4). Illus. 1992, Raintree Steck-Vaughn LB $23.83 (0-8114-3676-4). 32pp. Color photos aid in a broad overview of the United States, described in terms of topography and lifestyle. (Rev: BL 3/15/93) [973]

15869 Clinton, Catherine. *The Black Soldier: 1492 to the Present* (5–8). Illus. 2000, Houghton $17.00 (0-395-67722-X). 128pp. This history of African

Americans in the army begins with colonial slaves who were given muskets to fight the Indians and continues through each of America's wars to the present with emphasis on the slow progress toward equality in the ranks. (Rev: BCCB 10/00; BL 9/15/00; HBG 3/01) [355]

15870 Collier, Christopher, and James Lincoln Collier. *A Century of Immigration, 1820–1924* (5–8). Series: Drama of American History. 1999, Marshall Cavendish LB $20.95 (0-7614-0821-5). 91pp. A compelling account that focuses on 100 years of migration to this country, with material on where the immigrants came from, why they emigrated, where they settled, and the problems of assimilation. (Rev: BL 2/15/00; HBG 10/00; SLJ 3/00) [973]

15871 Collier, Christopher, and James Lincoln Collier. *The Rise of the Cities* (5–8). Illus. Series: The Drama of American History. 2001, Marshall Cavendish LB $20.95 (0-7614-1051-1). 96pp. This book traces the development of American cities from 1820 through 1920 and traces the problems involved and the growing prominence of cities in American life. (Rev: BL 3/15/01) [973]

15872 Collins, Mary. *The Industrial Revolution* (4–6). Series: Cornerstones of Freedom. 2000, Children's LB $20.00 (0-516-21596-5). 32pp. A highly readable, accurate account tracing the changes that transformed America into a manufacturing and industrial nation. (Rev: BL 5/15/00) [973]

15873 Colman, Penny. *Girls: A History of Growing Up Female in America* (5–8). Illus. 2000, Scholastic $18.95 (0-590-37129-0). 192pp. Using diaries, memoirs, letters, magazine articles, and other sources, the author presents a history of girls in America from the first females to cross the Bering Strait to the present day. (Rev: BCCB 2/00; BL 2/1/00; HBG 10/00; SLJ 3/00) [305.23]

15874 Colman, Penny. *Strike! The Bitter Struggle of American Workers from Colonial Times to the Present* (4–6). Illus. 1995, Millbrook LB $23.40 (1-56294-459-2). 80pp. A history of labor relations from the first strike in 1677 to the present. (Rev: BL 11/15/95; SLJ 1/96) [331.89]

15875 Draper, Charla L. *Cooking on Nineteenth Century Whaling Ships* (4–7). Series: Exploring History Through Simple Recipes. 2000, Capstone LB $22.60 (0-7368-0602-4). 32pp. As well as learning about life on a whaling ship, this book provides a series of simple recipes. (Rev: BL 3/1/01) [974.8]

15876 Fischer, Maureen M. *Nineteenth Century Lumber Camp Cooking* (4–7). Series: Exploring History Through Simple Recipes. 2000, Capstone LB $22.60 (0-7368-0604-0). 32pp. After describing life in a lumber camp of over a hundred years ago, this book supplies some authentic recipes. (Rev: BL 3/1/01) [973.8]

15877 Foster, Genevieve, and Joanna Foster. *George Washington's World*. Rev. ed. (5–8). Illus. 1997, Beautiful Feet paper $15.95 (0-9643803-4-X). 357pp. A new edition of this 50-year-old book that re-creates what was happening in the world during Washington's life, now with expanded coverage on minorities. (Rev: SLJ 3/98) [909]

15878 Frank, Nicole, and Elizabeth Berg. *Welcome to the USA* (2–4). Illus. Series: Welcome to My Country. 2000, Gareth Stevens $22.60 (0-8368-2513-6). With color pictures on each page and a simple text, this is a basic introduction to the United States, its geography, and its people. (Rev: SLJ 1/01) [973]

15879 Gold, Susan D. *Land Pacts* (5–8). Illus. 1997, Twenty-First Century LB $21.40 (0-8050-4810-3). 128pp. Covers the many international agreements that resulted in the acquisition of land, as in the Louisiana and Alaska purchases. (Rev: BL 5/15/97; SLJ 6/97) [973.5]

15880 Hakim, Joy. *Sourcebook: Documents that Shaped the American Nation* (5–8). Series: A History of Us. 1999, Oxford LB $18.95 (0-19-512773-0); paper $12.95 (0-19-512774-9). 204pp. This, the final volume of the outstanding A History of Us series, consists of the complete texts of 94 essential documents in American history, with a commentary on each. (Rev: BL 12/15/99) [973]

15881 Harness, Cheryl. *Ghosts of the White House* (2–5). Illus. 1998, Simon & Schuster paper $16.00 (0-689-80872-0). 48pp. Sara takes her own tour of the White House, with the ghosts of dead presidents acting as her guides. (Rev: BCCB 3/98; BL 3/1/98; HBG 10/98; SLJ 4/98) [973]

15882 Hatt, Christine. *Slavery: From Africa to the Americas* (5–8). 1998, Bedrick $19.95 (0-87226-552-8). 63pp. A broad overview of slavery in America that covers slave ships, plantation life, abolitionism, the Civil War, and Reconstruction. (Rev: HBG 10/98; SLJ 5/98) [973]

15883 Holling, Holling C. *Paddle-to-the-Sea* (3–6). Illus. by author. 1980, Houghton $20.00 (0-395-15082-5); paper $10.00 (0-395-29203-4). From Ontario to the Atlantic in a toy canoe, in this classic juvenile tale.

15884 Hoobler, Dorothy, and Thomas Hoobler. *Real American Girls Tell Their Own Stories* (4–7). Illus. 1999, Simon & Schuster $15.00 (0-689-82083-6). 112pp. Excerpts from personal diaries and autobiographies are used to introduce a number of young American girls from colonial times to the 1950s. (Rev: BCCB 12/99; BL 10/15/99; HBG 3/00; SLJ 12/99) [305.23]

15885 Jones, Rebecca C. *The President Has Been Shot! True Stories of the Attacks on Ten U.S. Presidents* (4–7). Illus. 1996, Dutton $15.99 (0-525-45333-4). 144pp. In chronological order, ten attacks on U.S. presidents are presented in a very readable account. (Rev: BCCB 9/96; BL 7/96; SLJ 9/96) [364.1]

15886 Kalman, Bobbie, and Greg Nickles. *Spanish Missions* (4–7). Illus. Series: Historic Communities. 1996, Crabtree LB $20.60 (0-86505-436-3); paper $7.95 (0-86505-466-5). 32pp. In double-page spreads, this book covers the building of the mission in the southern United States and of its functions: teaching Christianity, educating children, and supplying housing and food. (Rev: SLJ 4/97) [973]

15887 King, David C. *First Facts About U.S. History* (4–7). Illus. 1996, Blackbirch LB $25.95 (1-

56711-168-8). 112pp. In well-illustrated, double-page spreads, major events in U.S. history are covered. (Rev: BL 7/96; SLJ 7/96) [973]

15888 Kroll, Steven. *Ellis Island: Doorway to Freedom* (3–5). Illus. by Karen Ritz. 1995, Holiday LB $16.95 (0-8234-1192-3). 32pp. This history, beginning with colonial times, concentrates on the period when Ellis Island's immigration center processed millions of immigrants. (Rev: BL 11/15/95; SLJ 1/96) [325.73]

15889 Krull, Kathleen. *Wish You Were Here: Emily's Guide to the 50 States* (3–5). Illus. by Amy Schwartz. 1997, Doubleday $19.95 (0-385-31146-X). 118pp. After a description of a quick trip around the 50 states, this book supplies basic information on each. (Rev: BCCB 5/97; BL 6/1–15/97; SLJ 6/97) [917.3]

15890 Leedy, Loreen. *Celebrate the 50 States!* (1–3). Illus. 1999, Holiday $16.95 (0-8234-1431-0). 32pp. Each page in this simple geography book introduces two states and gives basic information such as capitals, state symbols, and bits of state lore. (Rev: BL 9/1/99; HBG 3/00; SLJ 9/99) [973]

15891 Lourie, Peter. *Mississippi River* (3–5). Illus. 2000, Boyds Mills $17.95 (1-56397-756-7). 48pp. While describing his trip on the Mississippi from Minnesota to Louisiana, the author gives facts about the waterway and the life that surrounds it. (Rev: BCCB 10/00; BL 10/1/00; HBG 3/01; SLJ 10/00) [976.81]

15892 Lourie, Peter. *Rio Grande: From the Rocky Mountains to the Gulf of Mexico* (4–6). Illus. 1999, Boyds Mills $17.95 (1-56397-706-0). 46pp. In dramatic prose and stunning photos, the course of the Rio Grande and its place in American history are covered. (Rev: BCCB 4/99; BL 2/15/99; HBG 10/99; SLJ 6/99) [917.3]

15893 Meltzer, Milton. *There Comes a Time: The Struggle for Civil Rights* (5–10). Series: Landmark Books. 2001, Random LB $18.99 (0-375-90407-7). 193pp. From the beginning of slavery in this country to the present day, this account tells of the civil rights movement in the United States with an emphasis on the 1950s and 1960s. (Rev: SLJ 1/01) [973]

15894 Miller, Marilyn. *Words That Built a Nation: A Young Person's Collection of Historic American Documents* (4–8). Illus. 1999, Scholastic $18.95 (0-590-29881-X). 176pp. A collection of 37 documents important in American history — from the Mayflower Compact and the Declaration of Independence to Hillary Rodham Clinton's address to the United Nations Conference on Women and Malcolm X's "The Ballot or the Bullet" speech. (Rev: BL 10/15/99; HBG 3/00; SLJ 2/00) [973]

15895 Miller, Millie, and Cyndi Nelson. *The United States of America: A State-by-State Guide* (3–6). Illus. 1999, Scholastic $14.95 (0-590-04374-9). 64pp. A state-by-state guide to the U.S. and Puerto Rico that supplies basic information, including a map and population figures for each. (Rev: BL 11/15/99; HBG 3/00; SLJ 12/99) [973]

15896 Newman, Shirlee P. *Slavery in the United States* (4–7). Series: Watts Library: History of Slav-

ery. 2000, Watts LB $24.00 (0-531-11695-6). 64pp. This account covers the shameful American record concerning slavery with coverage from the African slave trade through plantation life, the Underground Railroad, and abolitionists to the Civil War and emancipation. (Rev: BL 3/1/01) [973]

15897 Perl, Lila. *It Happened in America: True Stories from the Fifty States* (4–6). Illus. by Ib Ohlsson. 1992, Holt $24.95 (0-8050-1719-4). 288pp. Fifty true accounts in alphabetical (by state) order showing how exciting history can be. (Rev: BL 1/15/93; SLJ 3/93) [973]

15898 Rawlins, Carol B. *The Colorado River* (4–8). Series: Watts Library. 1999, Watts LB $24.00 (0-531-11738-3). 64pp. With full-color photographs and maps that complement the text, this book traces the famous Rocky Mountain waterway from north-central Colorado through the Southwest into the Gulf of California and covers its history and uses. (Rev: BL 1/1–15/00; SLJ 2/00) [973]

15899 Roop, Peter, and Connie Roop. *A Farm Album* (2–3). Series: Long Ago and Today. 1998, Heinemann LB $13.95 (1-57572-601-7). 24pp. Pairing old illustrations with modern photographs, this work compares life on a farm today with that of 100 years ago. (Rev: BL 12/15/98) [973]

15900 Roop, Peter, and Connie Roop. *A Home Album* (2–3). Series: Long Ago and Today. 1998, Heinemann LB $13.95 (1-57572-602-5). 24pp. American home life today and 100 years ago are compared through a simple text and contrasting photographs. (Rev: BL 12/15/98) [973]

15901 Rubel, David. *Scholastic Atlas of the United States* (3–5). 2000, Scholastic $19.95 (0-590-72562-9). 144pp. Arranged by region and then by state, this atlas also contains a text that gives good background on each state plus maps that indicate principal towns, highways, natural resources, national parks, etc. (Rev: HBG 3/01; SLJ 2/01) [917.3]

15902 Sandak, Cass R. *The United States* (5–8). Illus. Series: Modern Industrial World. 1996, Raintree Steck-Vaughn LB $24.26 (0-8172-4556-1). 48pp. Examines the present economic and industrial situation in the United States, with additional information on education, living standards, and related subjects. (Rev: BL 2/15/97) [973]

15903 Sanders, Nancy I. *A Kid's Guide to African American History: More Than 70 Activities* (4–6). Illus. 2000, Chicago Review paper $14.95 (1-55652-417-X). 242pp. Along with a history of African Americans from slavery through the civil rights movement and hopes for the future, there are more than 70 activities and crafts including recipes, making a bead necklace, constructing a star-watching chart, and crafts about Kwanzaa. (Rev: BL 2/15/01) [973]

15904 Siebert, Diane. *Mississippi* (3–5). Illus. 2001, HarperCollins LB $16.89 (0-688-16446-3). 40pp. This volume uses free-verse to describe the history associated with the Mississippi River as well as its course from its beginnings in the north to its mouth on the Gulf of Mexico. (Rev: BL 3/15/01) [976.2]

15905 Stienecker, David L. *States* (2–5). Illus. Series: Discovering Geography. 1997, Marshall Cavendish LB $22.79 (0-7614-0541-0). 32pp. Using a question-and-answer approach, this book teaches youngsters how to read maps that show topics such as terrain, weather, landmarks, population, capitals and products. (Rev: BL 2/1/98; HBG 3/98) [917.3]

15906 Straub, Deborah G., ed. *African American Voices* (5–8). Illus. 1996, Gale $70.00 (0-8103-9497-9). 320pp. This is a collection of excerpts from important speeches delivered by a vast array of African Americans, past and present. (Rev: SLJ 2/97) [973]

15907 Sullivan, Charles, ed. *Children of Promise: African-American Literature and Art for Young People* (4–8). Illus. 1991, Abrams $24.95 (0-8109-3170-2). 126pp. Through poems, songs, literary excerpts, and illustrations, the history of African Americans is traced. (Rev: SLJ 1/92) [973]

15908 Telford, Carole, and Rod Theodorou. *Down a River* (2–6). Illus. by Stephen Lings and Jane Pickering. Series: Amazing Journeys. 1997, Heinemann LB $13.95 (1-57572-153-8). 32pp. This journey of the entire length of the Mississippi and Missouri rivers supplies maps, illustrations and a description of the plants and animals that live in this ecosystem. (Rev: SLJ 5/98) [917.3]

15909 Tesar, Jenny. *America's Top 10 National Parks* (3–6). Illus. Series: America's Top 10. 1997, Blackbirch LB $16.95 (1-56711-190-4). 24pp. The most frequently visited national parks are described with good historical information. Also use *America's Top ten Rivers* (1997). (Rev: HBG 3/98; SLJ 1/98) [917.3]

15910 Travis, George. *State Facts* (3–5). Series: The Rourke Guide to State Symbols. 1999, Rourke LB $19.45 (1-57103-297-5). 48pp. Basic information about each state is given including nicknames, size, number of counties, and bordering states, plus colorful topographical maps. (Rev: SLJ 2/00) [973]

15911 *United States in Pictures* (5–8). Illus. Series: Visual Geography. 1995, Lerner LB $21.27 (0-8225-1896-1). 64pp. An attractive, basic introduction to the geography, history, and people of the United States. (Rev: BL 8/95) [973]

15912 Van Zandt, Eleanor. *A History of the United States Through Art* (5–8). Illus. Series: History Through Art. 1996, Thomson Learning LB $5.00 (1-56847-443-1). 48pp. American history is covered in 21 double-page spreads that feature text and famous artworks. (Rev: BL 3/1/96; SLJ 2/96) [973]

15913 Wacker, Grant. *Religion in Nineteenth Century America* (5–8). Series: Religion in American Life. 2000, Oxford $22.00 (0-19-511021-8). 183pp. This is the story of how religion in America affected such 19th-century events as the westward movement, the Civil War, and immigration, with additional coverage of the careers of such people as Sojourner Truth and Mary Baker Eddy. (Rev: BL 6/1–15/00; HBG 10/00) [973]

15914 Warren, Andrea. *Orphan Train Rider: One Boy's True Story* (4–6). Illus. 1996, Houghton $16.00 (0-395-69822-7). 80pp. Although it focuses

on one child's experiences on the orphan train in 1926, this account also covers the entire history of the phenomenon from 1850 to 1930. (Rev: BCCB 9/96; BL 7/96; HB 9–10/96; SLJ 8/96*) [362.7]

15915 Webb, Marcus. *The United States* (5–8). Series: Modern Nations of the World. 2000, Lucent LB $18.96 (1-56006-663-6). 112pp. A mature look at the past and present United States with an extended section on modern culture. (Rev: BL 5/15/00; HBG 10/00) [973]

15916 Weber, Michael. *Our National Parks* (4–6). Illus. Series: I Know America. 1994, Millbrook LB $21.90 (1-56294-438-X). 48pp. Three parks in each of four areas of the country are introduced with material on their histories and attractions. (Rev: SLJ 6/94) [917]

Historical Periods

NATIVE AMERICANS

15917 Abbink, Emily. *Colors of the Navajo* (2–4). Illus. by Janice L. Porter. Series: Colors of the World. 1998, Carolrhoda LB $19.93 (1-57505-207-5); paper $5.95 (1-57505-269-5). 24pp. Ten different colors are used to tie together this book about Navajo life, culture, arts, and traditions. (Rev: SLJ 12/98) [973]

15918 Adams, McCrea. *Tipi* (3–5). Illus. by Kimberly L. Dawson Kurnizki. Series: Native American Homes. 2001, Rourke LB $25.27 (1-55916-275-9). 32pp. This volume discusses Native American tipis and how, why, where, and by whom they were built. (Rev: SLJ 3/01) [973]

15919 Ancona, George. *Powwow* (3–6). Illus. 1993, Harcourt $17.00 (0-15-263268-9); paper $9.00 (0-15-263269-7). 48pp. Colorful photos and sprightly text capture the flavor of the largest powwow held in the United States at Crow Fair. (Rev: BCCB 5/93; BL 3/15/93; HB 5–6/93*; SLJ 4/93*) [394.2]

15920 Andryszewski, Tricia. *The Seminoles: People of the Southeast* (3–6). Illus. Series: Native Americans. 1995, Millbrook LB $21.90 (1-56294-530-0). 64pp. As well as giving a history of the Seminoles, this account tells about their culture and traditions and includes a recipe, a legend, and instructions for the Seminole pole-ball game. (Rev: SLJ 1/96) [973]

15921 Arnold, Caroline. *The Ancient Cliff Dwellers of Mesa Verde* (4–7). Illus. by Richard Hewett. 1992, Houghton $16.00 (0-395-56241-4). 64pp. This is the fascinating story of the Anasazi of southwestern Colorado, who made their homes in the cliffs of steep canyons and later abandoned them. (Rev: BL 5/1/92; SLJ 7/92*) [978.8]

15922 Baylor, Byrd. *The Desert Is Theirs* (2–4). Illus. by Peter Parnall. 1987, Macmillan $16.00 (0-684-14266-X); paper $5.95 (0-689-71105-0). 32pp. Through colorful, strong pictures and a lyric text, the life of the Papago Indians and their reverence for the desert are revealed.

15923 Bealer, Alex W. *Only the Names Remain: The Cherokees and the Trail of Tears* (4–6). Illus. by William Sauts Bock. 1996, Little, Brown paper $5.95 (0-316-08519-7). A history of the Cherokees, with emphasis on their tragic exile west of the Mississippi River in 1839.

15924 Beres, Cynthia Breslin. *Longhouse* (3–5). Illus. by Kimberly L. Dawson Kurnizki. 2001, Rourke LB $25.27 (1-55916-247-3). 32pp. This book describes the building and uses of the Native American longhouses and the part they played in the culture. (Rev: SLJ 3/01) [973]

15925 Bial, Raymond. *The Apache* (5–8). Series: Lifeways. 2000, Benchmark LB $22.95 (0-7614-0939-4). 128pp. Presents the dramatic, often tragic history of the Apache Indians, with biographies of leaders such as Geronimo and a description of the social and cultural life of these nomadic people. (Rev: BL 11/15/00; HBG 3/01; SLJ 3/01) [973]

15926 Bial, Raymond. *The Cheyenne* (5–8). Series: Lifeways. 2000, Benchmark LB $22.95 (0-7614-0938-6). 128pp. Part of the Great Plains Indian group, the Cheyenne's daily life, religious beliefs, social system, and history are introduced in this book. (Rev: BL 11/15/00; HBG 3/01; SLJ 3/01) [973]

15927 Bial, Raymond. *The Comanche* (4–8). Series: Lifeways. 1999, Benchmark LB $22.95 (0-7614-0864-9). 127pp. This impressive volume gives an accurate picture of the social and political life of the Comanche from their early history to the present day. (Rev: BL 3/15/00; HBG 10/00; SLJ 3/00) [973]

15928 Bial, Raymond. *The Haida* (5–8). Series: Lifeways. 2000, Benchmark LB $22.95 (0-7614-0937-8). 128pp. This book describes these Native Americans of the Northwest and introduces their artistic and carving skills, their social system, beliefs, history, and daily life. (Rev: BL 11/15/00; HBG 3/01; SLJ 3/01) [973]

15929 Bial, Raymond. *The Huron* (5–8). Series: Lifeways. 2000, Benchmark LB $22.95 (0-7614-0940-8). 128pp. Color pictures and clear text describe this Indian group's past and present and give details of their daily life, religion, and rituals. (Rev: BL 11/15/00; HBG 3/01; SLJ 3/01) [973]

15930 Bial, Raymond. *The Ojibwe* (5–8). Illus. Series: Lifeways. 1999, Marshall Cavendish LB $22.95 (0-7614-0863-0). 127pp. Topics covered in this introduction to the Ojibwe nation include history, traditions, beliefs, and the nation today. (Rev: BL 3/1/00; HBG 10/00; SLJ 3/00) [977]

15931 Bial, Raymond. *The Pueblo* (5–8). Illus. Series: Lifeways. 1999, Marshall Cavendish LB $22.95 (0-7614-0861-4). 127pp. Good photos and a lucid text combine to produce a fine introduction to the Pueblo Indians, their history, culture, traditions, present status, and notable members of the nation. (Rev: BL 3/1/00; HBG 10/00; SLJ 3/00) [978.9]

15932 Bial, Raymond. *The Seminole* (4–8). Series: Lifeways. 1999, Benchmark LB $22.95 (0-7614-0862-2). 127pp. Topics covered in this account of the Seminole Indians include history, daily life, religious beliefs, sacred rituals, and attitudes toward themselves. (Rev: BL 3/15/00; HBG 10/00; SLJ 3/00) [973]

15933 *A Braid of Lives: Native American Childhood* (4–8). Ed. by Neil Philip. Illus. 2000, Clarion

$20.00 (0-395-64528-X). 80pp. Twenty vignettes of one or two pages in length give a many-faceted picture of growing up Native American in different parts of the county. (Rev: BL 10/1/00) [973]

15934 Braine, Susan. *Drumbeat . . . Heartbeat: A Celebration of the Powwow* (4–6). Photos by author. Series: We Are Still Here: Native Americans Today. 1995, Lerner LB $21.27 (0-8225-2656-5); paper $6.95 (0-8225-9711-X). 48pp. An introduction to powwows that explains their history, where they are held, and what they mean to Native Americans today. (Rev: SLJ 9/95) [973]

15935 Brody, J. J. *A Day with a Mimbres* (4–6). Illus. by Giorgio Bacchin. Series: A Day With. 1999, Runestone LB $22.60 (0-8225-1917-8). 48pp. This book explores the history and daily life of this ancient Native American group who lived in the Southwest. (Rev: HBG 10/99; SLJ 10/99) [973]

15936 Bruchac, Joseph. *The Trail of Tears* (2–4). Illus. by Diana Magnuson. Series: Step into Reading. 1999, Random LB $11.99 (0-679-99052-6); paper $3.99 (0-679-89052-1). 48pp. An easy reader that movingly tells the story of the Cherokees and the bitter 1,200-mile forced journey from Georgia to Oklahoma between 1838 and 1839. (Rev: BL 12/1/99) [973]

15937 Burks, Brian. *Walks Alone* (5–8). 1998, Harcourt $16.00 (0-15-201612-0). 115pp. A harrowing story about a young Apache heroine, Walks Alone, and her struggle for survival in the America of the 1870s. (Rev: BCCB 5/98; HBG 10/98; SLJ 4/98)

15938 Claro, Nicole. *The Cherokee Indians* (3–5). Illus. Series: Indians of North America. 1991, Chelsea LB $16.95 (0-7910-1652-8). 80pp. The concentration is on the history of the Cherokee since their contact with Europeans. (Rev: BL 10/15/91) [973]

15939 Collins, David R., and Kris Bergren. *Ishi: The Last of His People* (5–8). Illus. 2000, Morgan Reynolds $19.95 (1-883846-54-4). 96pp. Believed to be a survivor of the lost Yahi tribe, this is the story of Ishi, the ill-clad and half-starved man who emerged from the wilderness in California in 1911. (Rev: BL 12/1/00; HBG 10/00) [979.4004]

15940 Cooper, Michael L. *Indian School: Teaching the White Man's Way* (5–10). Illus. 1999, Clarion $15.00 (0-395-92084-1). 103pp. A moving photo-essay about Native American children and how they have been removed from their homes and uprooted from their culture to attend Indian boarding schools in an effort to "civilize" them. (Rev: BL 12/1/99; HBG 3/00; SLJ 2/00) [370]

15941 Cory, Steven. *Pueblo Indian* (5–8). Illus. by Richard Erickson. Series: American Pastfinder. 1996, Lerner LB $21.95 (0-8225-2976-9). 48pp. Color illustrations and maps accompany this account of the Pueblo Indians and the incredible cities that they built. (Rev: BL 7/96) [973]

15942 Costabel, Eva D. *The Early People of Florida* (4–6). Illus. 1993, Smithmark $3.98 (0-831-72339-4). 34pp. The life of the indigenous peoples of Florida from prehistoric times to 1845. (Rev: BL 2/15/93; SLJ 3/93) [975.9]

15943 Crum, Robert. *Eagle Drum: On the Powwow Trail with a Young Grass Dancer* (4–7). Illus. 1994, Four Winds paper $16.95 (0-02-725515-8). 48pp. The preparation and execution of a powwow dance is told through the eyes of a nine-year-old Kalispel Indian in Montana. (Rev: BL 10/1/94; SLJ 12/94) [394.3]

15944 Delgado, James P. *Native American Shipwrecks* (5–7). Illus. Series: Watts Library: Shipwrecks. 2000, Watts $24.00 (0-531-20379-4); paper $8.95 (0-531-16473-X). 64pp. This book covers the boats that Native Americans made, their uses and voyages, the culture of these peoples, and how underwater archaeologists have explored their wrecks. (Rev: BL 10/15/00) [623.8]

15945 Duvall, Jill D. *The Cayuga* (1–3). Illus. Series: New True Books. 1991, Children's LB $21.00 (0-516-01123-5). 48pp. This book supplies basic introductory material on the Cayuga Indians in simple text and photos, some in color. (Rev: BL 3/1/92) [973]

15946 Duvall, Jill D. *The Mohawk* (1–3). Illus. Series: New True Books. 1991, Children's LB $21.00 (0-516-01115-4). 48pp. In short chapters and large print, the history, customs, and social life of the Mohawk Indians are introduced. (Rev: BL 12/15/91; SLJ 1/92) [973]

15947 Fisher, Leonard Everett. *Anasazi* (4–6). Illus. 1997, Simon & Schuster $16.00 (0-689-80737-6). 32pp. The Anasazi Indian tribe of the Southwest is introduced, with information on their homes, agriculture, and artwork. (Rev: BL 11/1/97; HBG 3/98; SLJ 12/97) [973]

15948 Fitzpatrick, Marie-Louise. *The Long March: The Choctaw's Gift to Irish Famine Relief* (4–7). Illus. 1998, Beyond Words $14.95 (1-885223-71-4). 32pp. Tells the story of how the Choctaws helped the Irish during the famine of 1847 and provides flashbacks to the horrors of the 500-mile Long March in which half of their people died. (Rev: BL 7/98; HBG 10/98; SLJ 6/98) [973]

15949 Fowler, Verna. *The Menominee* (4–7). Series: Indian Nations. 2000, Raintree Steck-Vaughn LB $25.69 (0-8172-5458-7). 48pp. Opening with a folk tale, this book describes the Menominee Indians, their life and culture, and how they were overrun in the 19th century and pushed onto a reservation in northern Wisconsin. (Rev: BL 3/15/01) [973]

15950 Fradin, Dennis B. *The Cheyenne* (2–4). Illus. 1988, Children's paper $5.50 (0-516-41211-6). 48pp. History of this Native American tribe called "the people." (Rev: BL 8/88; SLJ 11/88)

15951 Fradin, Dennis B. *The Shoshoni* (2–3). Illus. 1989, Children's LB $21.00 (0-516-01156-1); paper $5.50 (0-516-41156-X). 48pp. The story of this Native American tribe of the Pacific Northwest. (Rev: BL 5/15/89)

15952 Frantz, Jennifer. *Totem Poles* (2–3). Illus. by Allan Eitzen. Series: All Aboard Reading. 2001, Grosset $13.89 (0-448-42476-2); paper $3.99 (0-448-42423-1). 48pp. This book for beginning readers describes the history of the totem pole of the

Pacific Northwest, the people who carved them, and the carving process. (Rev: BL 2/15/01) [971.1]

15953 Freedman, Russell. *Buffalo Hunt* (4–6). Illus. 1988, Holiday LB $21.95 (0-8234-0702-0). 52pp. How the Plains Indians worshiped and depended on the buffalo. (Rev: BCCB 10/88; BL 10/1/88; SLJ 10/88)

15954 Freedman, Russell. *An Indian Winter* (4–8). Illus. by Karl Bodmer. 1992, Holiday $21.95 (0-8234-0930-9). 88pp. A fascinating re-creation of the winter of 1833-34 that the German prince Maximilian and a Swiss artist spent with the Indians in North Dakota. (Rev: HB 7–8/92; SLJ 6/92) [970]

15955 Fulkerston, Chuck. *The Shawnee* (4–6). Illus. by Katherine Ace. Series: Native American People. 1992, Rourke LB $21.27 (0-86625-392-0). 32pp. This account emphasizes the history of the Shawnee and presents material on their everyday life and religion. (Rev: BL 12/15/92) [973]

15956 Gallimard Jeunesse, et al. *Native Americans* (PS–2). Series: First Discovery. 1998, Scholastic $11.95 (0-590-38153-9). 24pp. Using sturdy plastic pages, overlays, and colorful illustrations, this introduction to Native Americans emphasizes the part they have played in U.S. history. (Rev: BL 9/15/98; HBG 10/98) [973]

15957 Gold, Susan D. *Indian Treaties* (5–8). Illus. 1997, Twenty-First Century LB $21.40 (0-8050-4813-8). 128pp. Tells of the many settlements and treaties that robbed the Native Americans of their lands. (Rev: BL 5/15/97; SLJ 6/97) [973]

15958 Goodman, Susan E. *Stones, Bones, and Petroglyphs: Digging into Southwest Archaeology* (4–6). Illus. 1998, Simon & Schuster $17.00 (0-689-81121-7). 48pp. A group of eighth-graders visits the Southwest's Four Corners area and explores the mystery surrounding the Pueblo Indians who lived there for nearly 1,000 years. (Rev: BL 6/1–15/98; HB 3–4/98; HBG 10/98; SLJ 4/98) [978.8]

15959 Gorsline, Marie, and Douglas Gorsline. *North American Indians* (5–8). Illus. by Douglas Gorsline. 1978, Random paper $3.25 (0-394-83702-9). Major tribes are identified and briefly described.

15960 Gravelle, Karen. *Growing Up Where the Partridge Drums Its Wings: A Mohawk Childhood* (4–6). Illus. 1997, Watts LB $24.00 (0-531-11453-8). 64pp. This account focuses on Chantelle Francis and her cousin David Francis and their youth on a Mohawk reservation that bridges Canada and the United States. (Rev: BL 1/1–15/98; HBG 3/98; SLJ 3/98) [971.4]

15961 Greene, Jacqueline D. *Powwow: A Good Day to Dance* (4–6). Illus. 1998, Watts LB $22.00 (0-531-20337-9). 64pp. Ten-year-old Little Man and his family participate in the annual Wampanoag powwow in eastern Massachusetts where they celebrate their culture with family and friends. (Rev: BL 1/1–15/99; HBG 3/99; SLJ 2/99) [394]

15962 Griffin, Lana T. *The Navajo* (4–7). Illus. Series: Indian Nations. 1999, Raintree Steck-Vaughn LB $25.69 (0-8172-5463-3). 48pp. This book describes the history of the Navajo, their everyday life, customs, and tribal government, and includes two Navajo creation stories. (Rev: BL 2/15/00; HBG 10/00; SLJ 4/00) [979.1]

15963 Gunderson, Mary. *American Indian Cooking Before 1500* (4–7). Series: Exploring History Through Simple Recipes. 2000, Capstone LB $22.60 (0-7368-0605-9). 32pp. This book describes the everyday life of Native Americans before Europeans arrived and gives a few simple recipes. (Rev: BL 3/1/01) [973]

15964 Haderer, Kurt. *Journey to Native Americans* (2–5). Illus. 1999, Prestel $14.95 (3-7913-2083-1). 30pp. This is a report on Native Americans as studied by German prince Maximilian of Wied and Swiss painter Karl Bodmer in the 1830s. (Rev: BL 11/1/99; SLJ 1/00) [978]

15965 Hahn, Elizabeth. *The Creek* (4–6). Illus. by Katherine Ace. Series: Native American People. 1992, Rourke LB $21.27 (0-86625-393-9). 32pp. History is emphasized in this book that features the point of view of the Native Americans. (Rev: BL 12/15/92) [976]

15966 Hahn, Elizabeth. *The Pawnee* (4–6). Illus. by Katherine Ace. Series: Native American People. 1992, Rourke LB $21.27 (0-86625-391-2). 32pp. Everyday life of the Pawnee, their religion, history, and present-day status are covered in this illustrated account. (Rev: BL 12/15/92) [973]

15967 Hakim, Joy. *The First Americans.* 2nd ed. (5–8). Series: A History of Us. 1999, Oxford LB $18.95 (0-19-512751-X); paper $12.95 (0-19-512752-8). 177pp. The first volume in this outstanding series traces the history of America from prehistory through the coming of the Europeans, with emphasis on the development of Native American culture. (Rev: BL 12/15/99) [973.1]

15968 Haluska, Vicki. *The Arapaho Indians* (3–5). Illus. Series: Junior Library of American Indians. 1993, Chelsea LB $16.95 (0-7910-1657-9). 80pp. Coverage is given on both the past and the present of this Indian group, with special material on their arts and crafts. (Rev: BL 5/15/93) [973]

15969 Hazen-Hammond, Susan. *Thunder Bear and Ko: The Buffalo Nation and Nambe Pueblo* (3–5). Illus. 1999, Dutton $16.99 (0-525-46013-6). 48pp. Through the eyes of 8-year-old Thunder Bear, the reader explores the culture of the Pueblo Indians and their fight to save a sacred buffalo slated to be killed for sport. (Rev: BCCB 5/99; BL 3/1/99; HBG 10/99; SLJ 3/99) [978.9]

15970 Hoyt-Goldsmith, Diane. *Apache Rodeo* (3–5). Photos by Lawrence Migdale. 1995, Holiday LB $15.95 (0-8234-1164-8). 32pp. The current lifestyles and traditions of the Apache people are revealed through the eyes of young Felicita. (Rev: BCCB 2/95; BL 2/1/95; SLJ 6/95) [973]

15971 Hoyt-Goldsmith, Diane. *Buffalo Days* (3–7). Illus. by Lawrence Migdale. 1997, Holiday LB $16.95 (0-8234-1327-6). 32pp. By focusing on ten-year-old Clarence Three Irons, Jr., the reader is introduced to the Crow Indians of the present and their heritage, which includes celebrating Buffalo Days. (Rev: BL 11/1/97*; HBG 3/98; SLJ 12/97*) [973]

15972 Hoyt-Goldsmith, Diane. *Potlatch: A Tsimshian Celebration* (4–6). Illus. 1997, Holiday LB $16.95 (0-8234-1290-3). 32pp. A 13-year-old boy explains the meaning of potlatch for the Tsimshian tribe in Alaska and describes the many rituals and activities it involves. (Rev: BL 5/1/97; SLJ 6/97) [394.2]

15973 Hoyt-Goldsmith, Diane. *Pueblo Storyteller* (3–5). Illus. by Lawrence Migdale. 1991, Holiday LB $16.95 (0-8234-0864-7). 32pp. A present-day account of how a Pueblo family in New Mexico lives. (Rev: BCCB 4/91; BL 3/5/91; SLJ 5/91) [978.9]

15974 Hucko, Bruce. *A Rainbow at Night: The World in Words and Pictures by Navajo Children* (4–6). Illus. 1997, Chronicle $14.95 (0-8118-1294-4). 44pp. Twenty-three Navajo children, ages 5–13, talk about their daily activities, families, culture, and myths. (Rev: BL 3/15/97; SLJ 3/97*) [973]

15975 Hunter, Sally M. *Four Seasons of Corn: A Winnebago Tradition* (3–6). Illus. 1997, Lerner LB $21.27 (0-8225-2658-1); paper $6.95 (0-8225-9741-1). 40pp. The daily life of a boy who assimilates his Anglo-American heritage, along with the traditional activities of his Winnebago people. (Rev: BL 2/1/97; SLJ 3/97) [394.2]

15976 Isaacs, Sally Senzell. *Life in a Hopi Village* (1–3). Series: Picture the Past. 2000, Heinemann $21.36 (1-57572-314-X). A well-organized, visually attractive account that describes daily life in a Hopi village and covers such topics as food, clothing, shelter, and care of children. (Rev: HBG 3/01; SLJ 11/00) [973]

15977 Jemison, Mary. *The Diary of Mary Jemison: Captured by the Indians* (3–6). Ed. by Connie Roop and Peter Roop. Illus. Series: My Own Words. 2000, Marshall Cavendish LB $16.95 (0-7614-1010-4). 64pp. Based on the account published in 1824, this short, nicely illustrated book tells, in a first-person narrative, how Mary Jemison was captured by Indians at age 12 and describes her life with these Native Americans. (Rev: BL 2/15/01; HBG 3/01; SLJ 3/01) [974.7]

15978 Kalman, Bobbie. *Celebrating the Powwow* (2–4). Illus. Series: Crabapples. 1997, Crabtree LB $19.96 (0-86505-640-4); paper $5.95 (0-86505-740-0). 32pp. Using a number of quality photos, this account describes powwows and their various components. (Rev: SLJ 1/98) [973]

15979 Kavasch, E. Barrie. *The Seminoles* (4–7). Illus. Series: Indian Nations. 1999, Raintree Steck-Vaughn LB $25.69 (0-8172-5464-1). 48pp. This account gives a history of the Seminole Indians, with material on their society, customs, festivals, government, present-day conditions, and one of their creation myths. (Rev: BL 2/15/00; HBG 10/00; SLJ 4/00) [975.9]

15980 Keegan, Marcia. *Pueblo Girls: Growing Up in Two Worlds* (3–6). Photos by author. 1999, Clear Light $14.95 (1-57416-020-6). A brief look at how two girls of the San Ildefonso Pueblo in New Mexico are growing up and learning about two cultures, religions, and languages, first their Native American one and secondly that of modern America. (Rev: HBG 3/00; SLJ 10/99) [973]

15981 King, Sandra. *Shannon: An Ojibway Dancer* (4–7). Illus. by Catherine Whipple. 1993, Lerner $19.95 (0-8225-2752-2); paper $6.95 (0-8225-9643-1). 48pp. Thirteen-year-old Shannon Anderson, an Ojibway girl, prepares for the summer powwow and her part in the shawl dance. (Rev: BCCB 1/94; BL 1/15/94; SLJ 2/94) [394]

15982 Krull, Kathleen. *One Nation, Many Tribes: How Kids Live in Milwaukee's Indian Community* (3–7). Illus. Series: A World of My Own. 1995, Dutton $15.99 (0-526-67440-3). 48pp. The story of the daily life and activities of Native American children who are growing up in a community in Milwaukee, Wisconsin. (Rev: BCCB 2/95; BL 2/15/95; SLJ 3/95) [977.5]

15983 Landau, Elaine. *The Ottawa* (4–6). Illus. Series: First Books. 1996, Watts LB $22.00 (0-531-20226-7). 64pp. A description of the history, life, and ways of the Great Lakes Ottawa people. (Rev: BL 8/96; SLJ 1/97) [977]

15984 La Pierre, Yvette. *Native American Rock Art: Messages from the Past* (4–8). Illus. 1994, Thomasson-Grant $16.95 (1-56566-064-1). 48pp. Different types and techniques of Native American rock art are discussed, with additional information on the cultures that produced this phenomenon. (Rev: BL 12/1/94; SLJ 11/94) [709]

15985 Lavender, David. *Mother Earth, Father Sky: Pueblo Indians of the American Southwest* (5–8). Illus. 1998, Holiday $16.95 (0-8234-1365-9). 117pp. After introducing the geographical area of the Southwest known as Four Corners — where Arizona, New Mexico, Colorado, and Utah meet — this book traces the history and culture of the Pueblo Indians who live there. (Rev: BL 9/1/98; HBG 10/99) [978]

15986 Lee, Georgia. *A Day with a Chumash* (4–6). Illus. by Giorgio Bacchin. Series: A Day With. 1999, Runestone LB $22.60 (0-8225-1918-6). 48pp. Based on archaeological and anthropological findings, this account traces the history and lifestyles of this ancient people of California. (Rev: HBG 10/99; SLJ 10/99) [973]

15987 Lee, Martin. *The Seminoles* (4–6). Illus. 1989, Watts LB $22.00 (0-531-10752-3); paper $5.95 (0-531-15604-4). 64pp. The formation of the Seminole tribe is covered, including how they were forced into the swamps. (Rev: BL 10/1/89; SLJ 3/90) [975]

15988 Lepthien, Emilie U. *The Cherokee* (1–3). Illus. 1985, Children's LB $21.00 (0-516-01938-4); paper $5.50 (0-516-41938-2). 48pp. Insights into Native American customs and history for the young reader. (Rev: BL 12/1/85; SLJ 3/86)

15989 Lepthien, Emilie U. *The Choctaw* (2–4). Illus. 1988, Children's LB $21.00 (0-516-01240-1); paper $5.50 (0-516-41240-X). 48pp. History and culture of these Native Americans. (Rev: BL 5/1/88; SLJ 10/88)

15990 Limberland, Dennis, and Mary Em Parrilli. *The Cheyenne* (4–7). Series: Indian Nations. 2000, Raintree Steck-Vaughn LB $25.69 (0-8172-5469-2). 48pp. This history of the Cheyenne Indians begins with a folk tale and goes on to describe their lifestyles before and after being sent to reservations in Oklahoma and Montana. (Rev: BL 3/15/01) [973]

15991 Liptak, Karen. *North American Indian Survival Skills* (4–6). Illus. Series: First Books. 1990, Watts LB $22.00 (0-531-10870-8). 64pp. An intriguing introduction to survival skills used by various North American tribes. (Rev: BCCB 12/90; BL 2/1/91) [613.6]

15992 Lucas, Eileen. *The Cherokees: People of the Southeast* (5–8). Illus. Series: Native Americans. 1993, Millbrook LB $21.90 (1-56294-312-X). 64pp. Following a map showing where the Cherokee lived, there are four chapters covering their origins, culture, interactions with whites, and the people today. (Rev: SLJ 1/94) [973]

15993 McCarthy, Cathy. *The Ojibwa* (4–7). Series: Indian Nations. 2000, Raintree Steck-Vaughn LB $25.69 (0-8172-5460-9). 48pp. A history of the Ojibwa Indians that includes material on the daily life and traditions of this group that now lives in Minnesota, Wisconsin, and central Canada. (Rev: BL 3/15/01) [973]

15994 McCurdy, Michael. *An Algonquian Year: The Year According to the Full Moon* (4–6). Illus. 2000, Houghton $15.00 (0-618-00705-9). 32pp. Starting with the full moon in January and progressing through a year of full moons, this handsome book traces the daily activities, shelter, and food of the Algonquian Indians of New England as the seasons change. (Rev: BL 11/1/00; HBG 3/01; SLJ 12/00) [973]

15995 McDaniel, Melissa. *The Sac and Fox Indians* (3–5). Illus. Series: Junior Library of American Indians. 1995, Chelsea LB $16.95 (0-7910-1670-6); paper $9.95 (0-7910-2034-7). 80pp. This account tells of these Wisconsin-based Indians, their near annihilation by the French, and their part in the Black Hawk War. (Rev: BL 1/1–15/96) [977]

15996 McGovern, Ann. *If You Lived with the Sioux Indians* (2–4). Illus. by Robert Levering. 1992, Scholastic paper $5.99 (0-590-45162-6). Using a question-and-answer technique, the author gives a great deal of information about the daily life of the Sioux and their relationship with white people.

15997 McLerran, Alice. *The Ghost Dance* (3–6). Illus. by Paul Morin. 1995, Clarion $15.95 (0-395-63168-8). The story of the hardships inflicted on Native Americans by whites and of the Ghost Dance, which was believed would magically rid their land of these intruders. (Rev: BCCB 11/95; SLJ 11/95*) [973]

15998 McLester, L. Gordon, and Elisabeth Towers. *The Oneida* (4–7). Series: Indian Nations. 2000, Raintree Steck-Vaughn LB $25.69 (0-8172-5457-9). 48pp. The Oneida left their New York lands for Wisconsin and Canada. Beginning with a folk tale, this account describes their past and present with some indication of what the future holds. (Rev: BL 3/15/01) [973]

15999 Margolin, Malcolm, and Yolanda Montijo, eds. *Native Ways: California Indian Stories and Memories* (5–8). Illus. 1996, Heyday paper $8.95 (0-930588-73-8). 128pp. Reminiscences and stories reflect California Indian culture, both past and present. (Rev: BL 7/96) [979.4]

16000 Martell, Hazel M. *Native Americans and Mesa Verde* (4–7). Illus. Series: Hidden Worlds. 1993, Dillon LB $16.95 (0-87518-540-1). 32pp. The history of the Pueblo Indians, their amazing cliff dwellings, and the Mesa Verde National Park. (Rev: BL 10/15/93; SLJ 8/93) [948.8]

16001 May, Robin. *Plains Indians of North America* (4–6). Illus. 1987, Rourke LB $16.67 (0-86625-258-4). 48pp. Lifestyle and customs of the Plains Indians are described in this well-illustrated introduction to these indigenous people, part of the Original Peoples series. (Rev: BL 1/15/88)

16002 Mayfield, Thomas Jefferson. *Adopted by Indians: A True Story* (5–8). Ed. by Malcolm Margolin. Illus. 1997, Heyday paper $10.95 (0-930588-93-2). 144pp. This is an adaption of the memoirs of a white man who lived with the Choinumne Indians in California for ten years, beginning in 1850 when he was eight. (Rev: BL 3/1/98) [979.4]

16003 Meli, Franco. *A Day with a Cheyenne* (4–6). Illus. by Giorgio Bacchin. Series: A Day With. 1999, Runestone LB $16.95 (0-8225-1920-8). 48pp. An account of the Cheyenne Indians that gives background historical information and then describes the daily life of a hunter and his son in the late 1800s. (Rev: HBG 3/00; SLJ 6/00) [973]

16004 Mercredi, Morningstar. *Fort Chipewyan Homecoming: A Journey to Native Canada* (3–6). Photos by Darren McNally. 1997, Lerner LB $21.27 (0-8225-2659-X); paper $6.95 (0-8225-9731-4). 48pp. Twelve-year-old Matthew visits relatives at Fort Chipewyan in Alberta, Canada, and learns a great deal about his Native American heritage. (Rev: SLJ 9/97) [973]

16005 Meyers, Madeleine, ed. *Cherokee Nation: Life Before the Tears* (4–8). Series: Perspectives on History. 1994, Discovery paper $6.95 (1-878668-26-9). 60pp. A history of the Cherokees that emphasizes the leadership of Sequoyah and the life of the tribe before their forced displacement. (Rev: BL 8/94) [970.3]

16006 Miller, Jay. *American Indian Families* (3–5). Illus. Series: True Books. 1996, Children's LB $22.00 (0-516-20133-6). 47pp. Discusses family structure and importance in various Native American tribes. (Rev: SLJ 8/97) [973]

16007 Miller, Jay. *American Indian Festivals* (2–3). Illus. Series: True Books. 1996, Children's LB $22.00 (0-516-20134-4). 47pp. Presents various festivals of Native Americans, like rain dances and thanksgiving celebrations. (Rev: BL 3/1/97; SLJ 8/97) [394.2]

16008 Miller, Jay. *American Indian Foods* (2–3). Illus. Series: True Books. 1996, Children's LB $22.00 (0-516-20135-2). 47pp. The foods eaten by different Native American groups are described by region. (Rev: BL 3/1/97; SLJ 8/97) [641.59]

16009 Miller, Jay. *American Indian Games* (2–3). Illus. Series: True Books. 1996, Children's LB $22.00 (0-516-20136-0). 47pp. With a color photograph on each page and brief text, this title presents the games Native Americans played in the past, like canoe racing and lacrosse, and how they compare with today's interests. (Rev: BL 3/15/97) [394]

16010 Miller, Jay. *Native Americans* (2–4). Illus. Series: New True Books. 1993, Children's LB $21.00 (0-516-01192-8). 48pp. Using large type and many illustrations, this is an attractive, brief introduction to the Indians of North America and their cultures. (Rev: BL 7/94) [973]

16011 Mooney, Martin. *The Comanche Indians* (4–7). Illus. Series: Junior Library of American Indians. 1993, Chelsea LB $16.95 (0-7910-1653-6). 71pp. A historical account of the Comanches from about 1700 to the present. (Rev: SLJ 4/93) [970]

16012 Myers, Arthur. *The Cheyenne* (4–6). Illus. Series: First Books. 1992, Watts paper $6.95 (0-531-15636-2). 64pp. In addition to a description of social organization and customs of the Cheyenne, this book tells of their history, including the Battle of Little Bighorn. (Rev: BL 6/15/92) [970.004]

16013 Naranjo, Tito E. *A Day with a Pueblo* (4–6). Illus. by Giorgio Bacchin. Series: A Day With. 1999, Runestone LB $16.95 (0-8225-1919-4). 48pp. Historical information is given about the Pueblo Indians followed by an account of an elder today and his daily activities at Taos Pueblo. (Rev: HBG 3/00; SLJ 6/00) [973]

16014 Newman, Shirlee P. *The Creek* (4–6). Illus. Series: Indians of the Americas. 1996, Watts LB $22.50 (0-531-20236-4); paper $6.95 (0-531-15809-8). 62pp. The history of the Creek (Muskogee) people, who were moved from southeastern United States to Oklahoma. (Rev: BL 12/15/96) [975]

16015 O'Neill, Laurie A. *Wounded Knee: The Death of a Dream* (4–6). Illus. Series: Spotlight on American History. 1993, Millbrook LB $21.90 (1-56294-253-0). 64pp. The battle of Wounded Knee, in which a large number of Sioux Indians were massacred, is re-created as a dark chapter in American history. (Rev: BL 6/1–15/93; SLJ 5/93) [973.8]

16016 Osinski, Alice. *The Chippewa* (2–4). Illus. 1987, Children's LB $21.00 (0-516-01230-4); paper $5.50 (0-516-41230-2). 48pp. History, customs, religious beliefs, and the difficulties faced by today's Native Americans. (Rev: BCCB 11/87; BL 11/1/87)

16017 Osinski, Alice. *The Navajo* (2–4). Illus. 1987, Children's LB $21.00 (0-516-01236-3); paper $5.50 (0-516-41236-1). 45pp. Navajo customs and traditions, history, and religious beliefs. (Rev: BCCB 11/87; BL 11/1/87)

16018 Osinski, Alice. *The Nez Perce* (3–5). Illus. 1988, Children's LB $21.00 (0-516-01154-5); paper $5.50 (0-516-41154-3). 48pp. Introducing this tribe of Northwest Indians. (Rev: BL 2/15/89)

16019 Osinski, Alice. *The Sioux* (1–4). Illus. 1984, Children's LB $21.00 (0-516-01929-5); paper $5.50 (0-516-41929-3). 48pp. Brief history of the Sioux, or Dakota, Indians of the Great Plains and material on their customs and social organization.

16020 Pasqua, Sandra M. *The Navajo Nation* (2–4). Illus. 2000, Bridgestone LB $15.93 (0-7368-0499-4). 24pp. This introduction to the largest group of

Native Americans in the U.S. briefly covers their history, culture, government, and daily life. (Rev: BL 10/1/00; HBG 10/00; SLJ 12/00) [979.1]

16021 Pennington, Daniel. *Itse Selu: Cherokee Harvest Festival* (K–3). Illus. by Don Stewart. 1994, Charlesbridge paper $6.95 (0-88106-850-0). 32pp. Little Wolf and his Cherokee family celebrate the Green Corn Festival with rituals and feasting to acknowledge the ripening of the corn. (Rev: BL 5/15/94; SLJ 7/94) [394.2]

16022 Peters, Russell. *Clambake: A Wampanoag Tradition* (3–5). Illus. by John Madama. Series: We Are Still Here: Native Americans Today. 1992, Lerner LB $21.27 (0-8225-2651-4); paper $6.95 (0-8225-9621-0). 48pp. Origins and present-day observations of the traditional ceremony that we know as a clambake. (Rev: BCCB 11/92; SLJ 12/92) [973]

16023 Philip, Neil, ed. *In a Sacred Manner I Live: Native American Wisdom* (4–8). Illus. 1997, Clarion $20.00 (0-395-84981-0). 93pp. More than 30 Native American leaders — including Geronimo and Cochise — are quoted on topics related to the conduct of life. (Rev: BL 7/97; HBG 3/98; SLJ 12/97) [973]

16024 Powell, Suzanne. *The Pueblos* (4–7). Illus. Series: First Books. 1993, Watts LB $22.00 (0-531-20068-X); paper $6.95 (0-531-15703-2). 64pp. Covers the history and present status of the Pueblos and their ability to survive the harsh weather and terrain of the American Southwest. (Rev: BL 2/15/94) [978.9]

16025 Press, Petra. *Indians of the Northwest: Traditions, History, Legends, and Life* (4–6). Illus. Series: Native Americans. 2000, Gareth Stevens LB $17.95 (0-8368-2647-7). 64pp. This account describes the land where many Indian peoples lived for thousands of years and their many earthworks, including the Great Serpent Mound in Ohio. (Rev: BL 5/15/00; HBG 10/00) [979]

16026 Rasmussen, R. Kent. *Pueblo* (3–5). Illus. by Kimberly L. Dawson Kurnizki. 2001, Rourke LB $25.27 (1-55916-249-X). 32pp. The amazing clay-based homes and villages of the Pueblo Indians are highlighted in this account that explains how they were built, their parts, and their many uses. (Rev: SLJ 3/01) [973]

16027 Regguinti, Gordon. *The Sacred Harvest: Ojibway Wild Rice Gathering* (4–8). Illus. by Dale Kakkak. Series: We Are Still Here: Native Americans Today. 1992, Lerner LB $21.27 (0-8225-2650-6). 48pp. The past and present of the ceremony of the harvest by the Ojibways in Minnesota. (Rev: SLJ 12/92) [973]

16028 Remington, Gwen. *The Sioux* (5–9). Series: Indigenous Peoples of North America. 1999, Lucent LB $18.96 (1-56006-615-6). 112pp. A thorough discussion of the history of the Sioux tribe, their origins, and their traditions and culture, with good coverage of conflicts like Wounded Knee, their forced assimilation, and their style of life since 1920. (Rev: SLJ 3/00) [973.1]

16029 Rendon, Marcie R. *Powwow Summer: A Family Celebrates the Circle of Life* (3–6). Illus. 1996, Lerner LB $22.60 (0-87614-986-7); paper

$7.95 (0-57505-011-0). 48pp. The Downwind family, which includes ten children (five of them in foster care), spend the summer attending many powwows in northern Minnesota. (Rev: BL 7/96; SLJ 10/96) [394]

16030 Roessel, Monty. *Kinaalda: A Navajo Girl Grows Up* (4–7). Illus. 1993, Lerner LB $21.27 (0-8225-2655-7); paper $6.95 (0-8225-9641-5). 48pp. Celinda McKelvey, a Navajo girl, returns to the reservation to participate in her Kinaalda, the coming-of-age ceremony. (Rev: BCCB 1/94; BL 1/15/94; SLJ 2/94) [392.1]

16031 Roessel, Monty. *Songs from the Loom: A Navajo Girl Learns to Weave* (3–6). Illus. 1995, Lerner LB $21.27 (0-8225-2657-3); paper $6.95 (0-8225-9712-8). 48pp. A photo-essay about weaving the Navajo way that reveals information about the culture and way of life of these people. (Rev: BL 9/15/95; SLJ 11/95) [746.1]

16032 Rose, LaVera. *Grandchildren of the Lakota* (4–6). Illus. Series: World's Children. 1998, Carolrhoda $22.60 (1-57505-279-2). 48pp. An introduction to the Lakota Indians, their history, how they live, and their current struggles with the U.S. government. (Rev: BL 4/1/99; HBG 3/99; SLJ 12/98) [305.23]

16033 Sattler, Helen R. *The Earliest Americans* (5–7). Illus. by Jean Day Zallinger. 1993, Houghton $16.95 (0-395-54996-5). 128pp. This account of early human life in North America also discusses the controversy about the origin of the first hunters to arrive here. (Rev: BCCB 6/93; BL 5/1/93; SLJ 6/93*) [970.1]

16034 Schwabacher, Martin. *The Huron Indians* (3–5). Illus. Series: The Junior Library of American Indians. 1995, Chelsea $16.95 (0-7910-2489-X); paper $8.95 (0-7910-2033-9). 80pp. An introduction to the history and culture of the Huron peoples, with material on how they preserve their traditions today. (Rev: BL 7/95) [392.2]

16035 Sewall, Marcia. *People of the Breaking Day* (3–6). Illus. 1990, Macmillan $17.00 (0-689-31407-8). 48pp. An in-depth account of the life-style of the Wampanoag Indians, who were living in Massachusetts when the Pilgrims arrived. (Rev: BL 10/1/90; HB 1–2/91; SLJ 1/91) [305.8]

16036 Shemie, Bonnie. *Houses of Adobe: Native Dwellings: The Southwest* (3–5). Illus. Series: Native Dwellings. 1995, Tundra $13.95 (0-88776-330-8); paper $6.99 (0-88776-353-7). 24pp. Various dwellings built by Indians of the Southwest — like pit houses and cliff homes — are described in double-page spreads with detailed drawings. (Rev: BL 9/1/95) [392]

16037 Shemie, Bonnie. *Houses of Bark: Tipi, Wigwam and Longhouse* (3–6). Illus. 1990, Tundra $13.95 (0-88776-246-8). 24pp. The lives of Native Americans in and around their traditional homes. (Rev: BL 1/1/91) [970]

16038 Shemie, Bonnie. *Mounds of Earth and Shell* (3–6). Illus. Series: Native Dwellings. 1993, Tundra $13.95 (0-88776-318-9). 24pp. Explores the mound-building Indians of North America, where the mounds are located, and why they were built. (Rev: BL 1/1/94) [393.1]

16039 Sherrow, Victoria. *The Iroquois Indians* (3–5). Series: Junior Library of American Indians. 1993, Chelsea LB $16.95 (0-7910-1655-2). 82pp. History and culture of Iroquis arts and crafts. Includes an eight-page photo-essay. (Rev: BL 11/1/92) [973]

16040 Shuter, Jane. *Mesa Verde* (4–6). Series: Visiting the Past. 1999, Heinemann LB $16.95 (1-57572-858-3). 32pp. This work introduces the homes and lifestyle of the ancient Pueblo Indians (A.D. 500 to 1292), with coverage of their clothing, beliefs, trade, farming, and tools. (Rev: SLJ 3/00) [973.1]

16041 Siegel, Beatrice. *Indians of the Northeast Woodlands* (4–8). Illus. by William Sauts Bock. 1991, Walker LB $14.85 (0-8027-8157-8). 96pp. In question-and-answer format — following the original 1972 edition — this volume contains much information on Native Americans in New England. (Rev: BL 11/15/92) [973]

16042 Sita, Lisa. *Indians of the Great Plains: Traditions, History, Legends, and Life* (4–6). Series: The Native Americans. 2000, Gareth Stevens LB $17.95 (0-8368-2645-0). 64pp. Topics covered in this introduction to such tribes as the Pawnee, Blackfoot, Cheyenne, Sioux, and Cree include history, society, government, and cultural traditions. (Rev: BL 5/15/00; HBG 10/00) [973]

16043 Sita, Lisa. *Indians of the Southwest: Traditions, History, Legends, and Life* (4–6). Illus. Series: Native Americans. 2000, Gareth Stevens LB $17.95 (0-8368-2648-5). 64pp. This account traces the history of the many Native American nations that still live in the Southwest today. (Rev: BL 5/15/00; HBG 10/00) [970.4]

16044 Siy, Alexandra. *The Eeyou: People of Eastern James Bay* (4–7). Illus. Series: Global Villages. 1993, Macmillan $17.95 (0-87518-549-5). 80pp. Introduces the Indian culture of the Eeyou, a people with their own writing system. (Rev: BCCB 7–8; SLJ 8/93) [970]

16045 Sneve, Virginia Driving Hawk. *The Apaches* (3–6). Illus. by Ronald Himler. Series: First Americans. 1997, Holiday LB $16.95 (0-8234-1287-3). 32pp. An overview of the six tribes that make up the Apache nation, accompanied by handsome illustrations. (Rev: BL 4/1/97; SLJ 7/97) [973]

16046 Sneve, Virginia Driving Hawk. *The Cherokees* (3–6). Illus. by Ronald Himler. Series: First Americans. 1996, Holiday $16.95 (0-8234-1214-8). 32pp. The story of this large, important Indian group, its culture, and its present status. (Rev: BCCB 5/96; BL 2/15/96; HB 5–6/96; SLJ 4/96) [973]

16047 Sneve, Virginia Driving Hawk. *The Cheyennes* (K–4). Illus. Series: First Americans. 1996, Holiday LB $16.95 (0-8234-1250-4). 32pp. The story of the Cheyenne, their history, customs, and how the white man affected their lives. (Rev: BL 9/15/96; SLJ 2/97) [970]

16048 Sneve, Virginia Driving Hawk. *The Hopis* (3–5). Illus. by Ronald Himler. Series: First Americans. 1995, Holiday LB $16.95 (0-8234-1194-X).

32pp. Details are given of the religion, social structure, history, and lifestyle of the Hopi, along with a creation myth. (Rev: SLJ 10/95) [973]

16049 Sneve, Virginia Driving Hawk. *The Iroquois* (K–4). Illus. by Ronald Himler. Series: A First American Book. 1995, Holiday LB $16.95 (0-8234-1163-X). 32pp. Provides a history of the Iroquois, as well as their beliefs, way of life, religion, and current situation. (Rev: BL 6/1–15/95; SLJ 7/95) [973]

16050 Sneve, Virginia Driving Hawk. *The Navajos* (K–3). Illus. by Ronald Himler. Series: First Americans. 1993, Holiday LB $16.95 (0-8234-1039-0). 32pp. After a creation story, the Navajos are introduced with details given on their daily life, society, relations with other Indian groups, and their fortune after the white man came. (Rev: BCCB 10/93; BL 12/15/93; SLJ 10/93) [973]

16051 Sneve, Virginia Driving Hawk. *The Nez Perce* (K–3). Illus. by Ronald Himler. Series: First Americans. 1994, Holiday LB $16.95 (0-8234-1090-0). 32pp. Beginning with a creation myth, this account continues with an exploration of the daily life and history of the Nez Perce. (Rev: BL 10/1/94) [973]

16052 Sneve, Virginia Driving Hawk. *The Seminoles: A First Americans Book* (3–5). Illus. by Ronald Himler. 1994, Holiday LB $16.95 (0-8234-1112-5). 32pp. Discusses many aspects of the Seminole history and culture, including the career of Osceola, the Seminole Wars, and their living conditions today. (Rev: BCCB 7–8/94; SLJ 4/94) [973]

16053 Sneve, Virginia Driving Hawk. *The Sioux* (K–3). Illus. by Ronald Himler. Series: First Americans. 1993, Holiday LB $15.95 (0-8234-1017-X). 32pp. The history of the Sioux Indians is given, with information on their social structure, daily life, ceremonies, and contemporary condition. (Rev: BCCB 10/93; BL 12/15/93; SLJ 10/93) [973]

16054 Sonneborn, Liz. *The Cheyenne Indians* (3–5). Illus. Series: Junior Library of American Indians. 1991, Chelsea LB $16.95 (0-7910-1654-4). 80pp. The history and culture of the Cheyenne are covered in simple text, historic photos, maps, and an eight-page color section on arts and crafts. (Rev: BL 3/1/92) [973.04973]

16055 Sonneborn, Liz. *The New York Public Library Amazing Native American History: A Book of Answers for Kids* (5–8). 1999, Wiley paper $12.95 (0-471-33204-6). 169pp. Organized by regions and using a question-and-answer approach, this is a fine overview of the history of Native Americans, ending with a chapter on contemporary conditions. (Rev: BL 5/1/00) [970.004]

16056 Steedman, Scott. *How Would You Survive as an American Indian?* (4–7). Illus. Series: How Would You Survive? 1996, Watts LB $25.00 (0-531-14383-X). 48pp. The life of the Plains Indians is described, with material on hunting, meals, shelter, and festivals. (Rev: BL 5/15/96) [978]

16057 Steele, Philip. *Little Bighorn* (5–8). Illus. by Richard Hook. Series: Great Battles and Sieges. 1992, Macmillan $17.95 (0-02-786885-0). 32pp. How General George Custer was defeated by

Cheyenne and Sioux Indians in 1876. (Rev: BL 10/1/92; SLJ 2/93) [973.8]

16058 Stein, R. Conrad. *The Battle of the Little Bighorn* (3–5). Illus. Series: Cornerstones of Freedom. 1997, Children's LB $20.50 (0-516-20296-0). 32pp. The fascinating, well-illustrated account of the battle on June 25, 1876, in which Custer was defeated by the combined forces of the Sioux and Cheyenne warriors. (Rev: BL 6/1–15/97) [973.8]

16059 Stein, R. Conrad. *The Trail of Tears* (3–5). Illus. Series: Cornerstones of Freedom. 1993, Children's LB $20.50 (0-516-06666-8). 32pp. The tragic story of the removal of the Cherokee Indian tribe from their native lands in 1838. (Rev: BL 8/93) [975]

16060 Sundling, Charles W. *Native Americans of the Frontier* (4–6). Illus. Series: Frontier Land. 2000, ABDO $15.95 (1-57765-042-5). 32pp. A simple text and many illustrations are used in this accessible account of the daily life of the American Plains Indians during the 19th century. (Rev: BL 10/15/00; HBG 10/00; SLJ 6/00) [978]

16061 Swentzell, Rina. *Children of Clay: A Family of Pueblo Potters* (3–5). Illus. by Bill Steen. 1992, Lerner LB $21.27 (0-8225-2654-9). 40pp. The family of Gia Rose of Santa Clara Pueblo takes the reader through the ancient process of pottery making. (Rev: BCCB 3/93; BL 1/15/93; SLJ 2/92) [978.9]

16062 Terry, Michael Bad Hand. *Daily Life in a Plains Indian Village: 1868* (3–6). Illus. 1999, Clarion $20.00 (0-395-94542-9). 48pp. This book gives a detailed description of the daily life — including housing, food, clothing, government, and games — of the Northern Cheyenne Indians in 1868, before the Europeans forced them onto reservations. (Rev: BL 2/15/00; HBG 3/00; SLJ 9/99) [978]

16063 Thomas, David Hurst, and Lorann Pendleton, eds. *Native Americans* (4–6). Illus. Series: Nature Company Discoveries. 1995, Time Life $16.00 (0-7835-4759-5). 64pp. This overview of Native Americans and their history and geography contains an eight-page foldout depicting a buffalo hunt. (Rev: BL 1/1–15/96; SLJ 1/96) [970.004]

16064 Tomcheck, Ann Heinrichs. *The Hopi* (2–4). Illus. 1987, Children's LB $21.00 (0-516-01234-7); paper $5.50 (0-516-41234-5). 48pp. A look at the Hopi, their customs and history, religious beliefs, and difficulties in today's world. (Rev: BCCB 11/87; BL 11/1/87)

16065 Viola, Herman J. *It Is a Good Day to Die: Indian Eyewitnesses Tell the Story of the Battle of the Little Bighorn* (5–8). Illus. 1998, Crown LB $19.99 (0-517-70913-9). 128pp. Taken from first-person accounts of Native Americans, this is the authentic story of the 1876 Battle of Little Bighorn, which ended in General Custer's defeat. (Rev: BCCB 9/98; BL 9/1/98; HB 9–10/98; HBG 10/98; SLJ 7/98) [973.8]

16066 Waldman, Neil. *Wounded Knee* (5–9). Illus. 2001, Simon & Schuster $18.00 (0-689-82559-5). 64pp. This balanced account traces the clash of values, misunderstandings, and lack of cultural knowledge that led to the bloody conflict at Wounded

Knee where, in 1890, the U.S. Army killed many Sioux Indians. (Rev: BL 3/15/01) [973.8]

16067 White Deer of Autumn. *The Native American Book of Knowledge* (5–8). Illus. by Shonto Begay. 1992, Beyond Words paper $5.95 (0-941831-42-6). 88pp. A description of Native American hero figures before Columbus is part of the information in this native view of history and life-styles. (Rev: BL 10/15/92) [970]

16068 White Deer of Autumn. *The Native American Book of Life* (5–8). Illus. by Shonto Begay. 1992, Beyond Words paper $5.95 (0-941831-43-4). 88pp. In this look at life-styles from the Native American point of view, the focus is on child rearing. (Rev: BL 10/15/92) [970]

16069 Wittstock, Laura W. *Ininatig's Gift of Sugar: Traditional Native Sugarmaking* (3–5). Illus. by Dale Kakkak. Series: We Are Still Here: Native Americans Today. 1993, Lerner LB $21.27 (0-8225-2653-0); paper $6.95 (0-8225-9642-3). 48pp. Describes the traditional way of making maple sugar and syrup by Minnesota Indians. (Rev: BL 9/1/93; HB 11–12/93) [338.1]

16070 Wolfson, Evelyn. *Growing Up Indian* (5–7). Illus. 1986, Walker LB $11.85 (0-8027-6644-7). 96pp. What it was like to grow up Indian in traditional American culture before the influence of the white race. (Rev: BL 1/15/87; SLJ 3/87)

16071 Wood, Leigh. *The Crow Indians* (3–5). Illus. Series: Junior Library of American Indians. 1993, Chelsea LB $16.95 (0-7910-1661-7). 80pp. This account tells about the past, present, and culture of the Crow Indians who now live in southeastern Montana. (Rev: BL 5/15/93) [973]

16072 Wood, Ted, and Wanbli Numpa Afraid of Hawk. *A Boy Becomes a Man at Wounded Knee* (4–6). Illus. 1992, Walker LB $16.85 (0-8027-8175-6). 42pp. An eight-year-old Lakota boy wants to participate in his ancestor's journey to Wounded Knee. (Rev: BCCB 12/92; BL 9/1/92; SLJ 11/92) [973.8]

16073 Young, Robert. *A Personal Tour of Mesa Verde* (4–7). Illus. Series: How It Was. 1999, Lerner LB $23.93 (0-8225-3577-7). 64pp. This book gives a special glimpse into the lives of the Native Americans known as the Puebloans, how they lived, and the culture they developed. (Rev: BL 6/1–15/99; HBG 10/99; SLJ 7/99) [978.8]

16074 Yue, Charlotte, and David Yue. *The Wigwam and the Longhouse* (4–9). Illus. by authors. 2000, Houghton $15.00 (0-395-84169-0). 118pp. A well-balanced account that describes the life and history of several tribes of Native Americans from the eastern woodlands. (Rev: HB 7–8/00; HBG 10/00; SLJ 10/00) [973]

DISCOVERY AND EXPLORATION

16075 Asikinack, Bill, and Kate Scarborough. *Exploration into North America* (5–7). Illus. Series: Exploration. 1996, Dillon LB $19.95 (0-02-718086-7); paper $7.95 (0-382-39228-0). 48pp. This account tells the history of North America from prehistory to European exploration and settlement. (Rev: BL 8/96; SLJ 9/96) [970]

16076 Bowen, Andy Russell. *The Back of Beyond: A Story About Lewis and Clark* (3–5). Illus. 1997, Carolrhoda LB $21.27 (1-57505-010-2). 64pp. A gripping account of the journey that took Lewis and Clark to the mouth of the Columbia River in 1805. (Rev: BL 9/1/97; HB 11–12/97; SLJ 3/98) [917.804]

16077 Brenner, Barbara. *If You Were There in 1492* (3–6). Illus. 1991, Macmillan LB $15.00 (0-02-712321-9). 112pp. A time-travel trip back to the year of the explorer's famous voyage. (Rev: BL 9/1/91; HB 1–2/92; SLJ 11/91)

16078 Craig, Claire. *Explorers and Traders* (4–6). Illus. Series: Nature Company Discoveries. 1996, Time Life $16.00 (0-8094-9373-X). 64pp. The roles played by explorers and traders in the opening up of the U.S. are traced, with many illustrations and an eight-page foldout. (Rev: BL 9/15/96) [948]

16079 Dyson, John. *Westward with Columbus* (4–6). Illus. by Peter Christopher. 1991, Scholastic paper $6.95 (0-590-43847-6). 64pp. A fictionalized account of the 1492 voyage, theorizing that Columbus used a secret map. (Rev: BL 11/15/91; SLJ 11/91) [910.4]

16080 Gunderson, Mary. *Cooking on the Lewis and Clark Expedition* (3–6). 2000, Capstone LB $22.60 (0-7368-0354-8). 32pp. As well as historical material on the Lewis and Clark expedition, this book contains a number of modern recipes for food that might have been eaten on this memorable journey. (Rev: HBG 10/00; SLJ 12/00) [978]

16081 Hirschfelder, Arlene B. *Photo Odyssey: Solomon Carvalho's Remarkable Western Adventure, 1853–54* (5–9). 2000, Clarion $18.00 (0-395-89123-X). 118pp. The story of the last westward journey of John C. Fremont as seen through the eyes of a painter/photographer who was a member of this 1853 expedition. (Rev: BCCB 9/00; HBG 10/00; SLJ 8/00*) [978]

16082 Johnstone, Michael. *The History News: Explorers* (4–7). Illus. Series: History News. 1997, Candlewick $15.99 (0-7636-0314-7). 32pp. Famous explorers and their discoveries are covered using a newspaper format that even includes advertisements and letters to the editor, like one from Columbus telling about reaching an island close to Japan. (Rev: BL 2/1/98; HBG 3/98; SLJ 1/98) [910.92]

16083 Krensky, Stephen. *Christopher Columbus* (1–2). Illus. by Norman Green. 1991, Random paper $3.99 (0-679-80369-6). 32pp. This is an easy-reading book that tells about Columbus's first voyage to America. (Rev: BL 12/1/91; SLJ 12/91) [970.01]

16084 Krensky, Stephen. *Who Really Discovered America?* (4–6). Illus. 1991, Scholastic paper $2.50 (0-590-40854-2). 64pp. A parade of discoverers who came to North or South America are uncovered in the attempt to answer this intriguing question. (Rev: BL 1/15/88; SLJ 4/88) [970.01]

16085 Lasky, Kathryn. *The Journal of Augustus Pelletier: The Lewis and Clark Expedition* (4–6). Series: My Name Is America. 2000, Scholastic (0-590-68489-2). 172pp. Fourteen-year-old Augustus

Pelletier, half French and half Omaha Indian, relates his adventures into unknown territory.

16086 McGrath, Patrick. *The Lewis and Clark Expedition* (5–8). Illus. 1986, Silver Burdett LB $17.95 (0-382-06828-9); paper $7.95 (0-382-09899-4). 64pp. A straightforward account illustrated with maps, photographs, paintings, and diary entries. (Rev: BCCB 6/86)

16087 Maurer, Richard. *The Wild Colorado: The True Adventures of Fred Dellenbaugh, Age 17, on the Second Powell Expedition into the Grand Canyon* (5–9). 1999, Crown LB $19.99 (0-517-70946-5). 120pp. This is an account of the 16-month journey down the Colorado River by Major John Wesley Powell in 1869 as experienced by a young man who documented the voyage in pictures and maps. (Rev: HBG 3/00; SLJ 8/99) [976]

16088 Morley, Jacqueline. *Across America: The Story of Lewis and Clark* (4–5). Illus. by David Antram. Series: Expedition. 1998, Watts LB $21.00 (0-531-14455-0). 32pp. Double-page spreads portray different segments of the Lewis and Clark adventure and reveal interesting facts about the period. (Rev: HBG 3/99; SLJ 2/99) [917.8]

16089 Quiri, Patricia R. *The Lewis and Clark Expedition* (3–6). Series: We the People. 2000, Compass Point LB $15.95 (0-7565-0044-3). 48pp. A profusely illustrated, readable account of the Lewis and Clark expedition that makes for a good introductory overview. (Rev: SLJ 2/01) [917.8]

16090 Roop, Peter, and Connie Roop, eds. *Off the Map: The Journals of Lewis and Clark* (4–6). Illus. by Tim Tanner. 1993, Walker LB $15.85 (0-8027-8208-6). 40pp. Excerpts from the journals and diaries of Lewis and Clark are used to present a vivid picture of their amazing explorations. (Rev: BL 9/1/93; SLJ 6/93) [917.8]

16091 Schanzer, Rosalyn. *How We Crossed the West: The Adventures of Lewis and Clark* (3–5). Illus. 1997, National Geographic $18.00 (0-7922-3738-2). 48pp. A richly illustrated volume that deals with the expedition of Lewis and Clark as taken from their journals. (Rev: BL 9/15/97; HBG 3/98; SLJ 10/97*) [917.8]

16092 Stefoff, Rebecca. *Exploring the New World* (4–7). Illus. Series: North American Historical Atlases. 2000, Benchmark $16.95 (0-7614-1056-2). Using historical maps and reproductions, the important explorers and their accomplishments are covered in this slim, attractive volume. (Rev: HBG 3/01; SLJ 1/01) [970.01]

16093 Stefoff, Rebecca. *Lewis and Clark* (4–7). Illus. 1992, Chelsea LB $16.95 (0-7910-1750-8). 80pp. A simple text and pictures of the Lewis and Clark expedition that helped open up the West. (Rev: BL 7/92) [978.02]

16094 Steins, Richard. *Exploration and Settlement* (5–8). Illus. Series: Making of America. 2000, Raintree Steck-Vaughn $19.98 (0-8172-5700-4). 96pp. This account begins with prehistoric migrations to North America and continues with European explorers, including the Spanish, English, French, and

Dutch. (Rev: BL 5/1/00; HBG 10/00; SLJ 9/00) [970.01]

16095 West, Delno C., and Jean M. West. *Braving the North Atlantic: The Vikings, the Cabots, and Jacques Cartier Voyage to America* (4–6). Illus. 1996, Simon & Schuster $16.00 (0-689-31822-7). 82pp. From St. Brendan and Erik the Red to Henry Hudson, this is a history of the early explorers of North America. (Rev: BCCB 9/96; BL 12/15/96; SLJ 12/96) [970.01]

COLONIAL PERIOD

16096 Appelbaum, Diana. *Giants in the Land* (2–4). Illus. by Michael McCurdy. 1993, Houghton $17.00 (0-395-64720-7). 32pp. An ecological story concerning the forests of giant white pines in New England that were destroyed to build ships for the British in the 18th century. (Rev: BCCB 9/93; BL 10/1/93*; SLJ 11/93*) [634.9]

16097 Barrett, Tracy. *Growing Up in Colonial America* (4–6). Illus. 1995, Millbrook LB $23.40 (1-56294-578-5). 96pp. Colonial settlements in the North and South are contrasted in their theories and practices of child rearing. (Rev: BL 12/15/95; SLJ 12/95) [973]

16098 Brown, Gene. *Discovery and Settlement: Europe Meets the New World (1490–1700)* (5–7). Series: First Person America. 1993, Twenty-First Century LB $18.90 (0-8050-2574-X). 64pp. Using excerpts from original documents, this book covers the exploration of the United States, the Puritans, and the role of Native Americans, African Americans, and women in early colonial days. (Rev: SLJ 3/94) [973.2]

16099 Butler, Jon. *Religion in Colonial America* (5–8). Series: Religion in American Life. 2000, Oxford $22.00 (0-19-511998-3). 154pp. This book describes the mix of Catholics, Jews, Africans, Native Americans, Puritans, and various Protestant faiths that coexisted during colonial times. (Rev: BL 6/1–15/00; HBG 10/00) [973.2]

16100 Carlson, Laurie. *Colonial Kids: An Activity Guide to Life in the New World* (4–6). Illus. 1997, Chicago Review paper $12.95 (1-55652-322-X). 160pp. Along with facts about colonial America, this book gives directions for many related projects and activities, like tying sailors' knots, steaming clams, dyeing a shirt, and stitching a sampler. (Rev: BL 2/15/98; SLJ 3/98) [973.2]

16101 Cobb, Mary. *A Sampler View of Colonial Life: With Projects Kids Can Make* (3–5). Illus. 1999, Millbrook LB $23.90 (0-7613-0372-3). 64pp. This book discusses many of the home crafts of colonial times, with an emphasis on samplers and crafts projects that the reader can make. (Rev: BL 10/15/99; HBG 3/00; SLJ 1/00) [746.44]

16102 Collier, Christopher, and James Lincoln Collier. *Clash of Cultures, Prehistory–1638* (5–8). Series: Drama of American History. 1998, Marshall Cavendish LB $19.95 (0-7614-0436-8). 96pp. This is a well-illustrated examination of the culture clash between Native Americans and Europeans in the

years before and during the formation of the colonies. (Rev: BL 4/15/98*; HBG 10/98) [970]

16103 Collier, Christopher, and James Lincoln Collier. *The French and Indian War* (5–8). Illus. Series: Drama of American History. 1998, Marshall Cavendish LB $29.93 (0-7614-0439-2). 96pp. A nicely illustrated book providing a broad perspective on the French and Indian War, and noting the conflict's importance on both sides of the Atlantic. (Rev: BL 4/15/98*; HBG 10/98) [973.2]

16104 Collier, Christopher, and James Lincoln Collier. *The Paradox of Jamestown: 1585–1700* (5–8). Illus. Series: Drama of American History. 1998, Marshall Cavendish LB $29.93 (0-7614-0437-6). 96pp. Describes how Jamestown gave democratic freedom to its residents through its elected legislature, while introducing the first African slaves into the colonies. (Rev: BL 4/15/98*; HBG 10/98) [975.5]

16105 Collier, Christopher, and James Lincoln Collier. *Pilgrims and Puritans: 1620–1676* (5–8). Illus. Series: Drama of American History. 1997, Marshall Cavendish LB $29.93 (0-7614-0438-4). 96pp. This volume describes the routes the Pilgrims and Puritans took to America, their beliefs and practices, and how present-day American life continues to be influenced by them. (Rev: BL 4/15/98*; HBG 10/98) [974.4]

16106 Corwin, Judith Hoffman. *Colonial American Crafts: The Home* (3–5). Illus. Series: Colonial American Crafts. 1989, Watts LB $23.00 (0-531-10713-2). 48pp. This book gives an overview of home life in colonial times with instructions for such projects as a sampler, a friendship pillow, and paper dolls. Another in this series is: *Colonial American Crafts: The School* (1989). (Rev: BL 1/15/90; SLJ 3/90) [745.5]

16107 Daugherty, James. *The Landing of the Pilgrims* (5–7). Illus. by author. 1981, Random paper $5.99 (0-394-84697-4). 160pp. Based on his own writings, this is the story of the Pilgrims from the standpoint of William Bradford.

16108 Day, Nancy. *Your Travel Guide to Colonial America* (4–8). Series: Passport to History. 2000, Lerner LB $26.60 (0-8225-3079-1). 96pp. Using a modern-day guidebook format, this account time-travels the reader to colonial times with glimpses of the *Mayflower* and visits to such colonies as Jamestown, Virginia, and Plymouth, Massachusetts. (Rev: BL 3/1/01) [973.2]

16109 Dean, Ruth, and Melissa Thomson. *Life in the American Colonies* (4–8). Illus. Series: The Way People Live. 1999, Lucent LB $17.96 (1-56006-376-9). 96pp. Topics in this discussion of the American colonies include life in cities and on frontier farms, immigration and slavery, science and culture, and other aspects of everyday existence. (Rev: BL 5/1/99; SLJ 7/99) [973.2]

16110 Doherty, Kieran. *Puritans, Pilgrims, and Merchants: Founders of the Northeastern Colonies* (4–8). Illus. 1999, Oliver $21.95 (1-881508-50-1). 176pp. A history of each of the northeastern colonies is supplemented with brief biographies of such people as William Bradford, John Winthrop,

Peter Stuyvesant, Anne Hutchinson, and William Penn. (Rev: BL 8/99; HBG 3/00) [974]

16111 Doherty, Kieran. *Soldiers, Cavaliers, and Planters: Settlers of the Southeastern Colonies* (4–8). Illus. 1999, Oliver $21.95 (1-881508-51-X). 176pp. Each of the southeastern colonies is featured, with brief biographies of such people as Sir Walter Raleigh, Captain John Smith, and James Oglethorpe. (Rev: BL 8/99; HBG 3/00) [975]

16112 Dosier, Susan. *Colonial Cooking* (4–7). Illus. Series: Exploring History Through Simple Recipes. 2000, Capstone LB $22.60 (0-7368-0352-1). 32pp. This work covers the home life of the colonialists in the north, with material on kitchens, celebrations, food, and some recipes. (Rev: BL 8/00; HBG 10/00) [394.1]

16113 Dunnahoo, Terry. *Boston's Freedom Trail* (4–7). Illus. Series: Places in American History. 1994, Dillon LB $22.00 (0-87518-623-8); paper $7.95 (0-382-24762-0). 72pp. An explanation of the historical events of the colonial period that are commemorated in the famous Boston walking tour. (Rev: BL 1/1/95; SLJ 3/95) [917.4]

16114 Egger-Bovet, Howard, and Marlene Smith-Baranzini. *US Kids History: Book of the American Colonies* (5–7). Illus. Series: Brown Paper School. 1996, Little, Brown paper $14.95 (0-316-22201-1). 96pp. In an informal writing style with plenty of drawings and activities, the American colonial period is introduced. (Rev: BL 8/96; SLJ 8/96) [973.2]

16115 Fisher, Leonard Everett. *The Hatters* (4–6). Illus. Series: Colonial Craftsmen. 2000, Marshall Cavendish LB $14.95 (0-7614-1146-1). 48pp. This book supplies a glimpse into the hat trade of the 17th and 18th centuries with material on how different hats were made, worn, and marketed. Also use *The Potters* (2000). (Rev: BL 3/15/01) [646.5]

16116 Fisher, Leonard Everett. *The Papermakers* (4–6). Series: Colonial Craftsmen. 2000, Marshall Cavendish LB $14.95 (0-7614-1147-X). 48pp. A reissue of this beautifully illustrated work that describes the process of manufacturing, selling, and using paper during colonial times. Also use from the same series *The Tanners* (2000). (Rev: BL 3/15/01) [973.2]

16117 Foley, Sheila, ed. *Faith Unfurled: The Pilgrims' Quest for Freedom* (4–8). Series: Perspectives on History. 1993, Discovery paper $6.95 (1-878668-24-2). 64pp. Through the diaries, journals, and letters of many people, the story of the journey to the New World by the Pilgrims and their difficulties forming a new colony is retold. (Rev: BL 11/15/93) [974.4]

16118 Fradin, Dennis B. *The Connecticut Colony* (5–8). Illus. Series: The Thirteen Colonies. 1990, Children's LB $32.00 (0-516-00393-3). 160pp. In large print, this is an appealing look at the Connecticut colony. (Rev: BL 8/90) [974.6]

16119 Fradin, Dennis B. *The Georgia Colony* (4–7). Illus. Series: The Thirteen Colonies. 1989, Children's LB $32.00 (0-516-00392-5). 160pp. This account traces the history of Georgia from prehistory to ratification of the Constitution. (Rev: BL 1/15/90) [975]

16120 Fradin, Dennis B. *The Maryland Colony* (5–8). Illus. Series: The Thirteen Colonies. 1990, Children's LB $32.00 (0-516-00394-1). 160pp. The history of the Maryland colony from its first settlers to statehood. (Rev: BL 1/1/91) [975.2]

16121 Fradin, Dennis B. *The New Hampshire Colony* (4–7). Illus. 1988, Children's LB $32.00 (0-516-00388-7). 190pp. The history of the first of the original 13 colonies to form its own government. (Rev: BL 5/15/88)

16122 Fradin, Dennis B. *The New Jersey Colony* (5–8). Illus. Series: The Thirteen Colonies. 1991, Children's LB $32.00 (0-516-00395-X). 156pp. Life in colonial New Jersey is discussed in this account that ends with the eventual gaining of statehood. (Rev: BL 8/91; SLJ 10/91) [974]

16123 Fradin, Dennis B. *The New York Colony* (4–7). Illus. 1988, Children's LB $32.00 (0-516-00389-5). 160pp. Tracing the development of New York, beginning in the 1300s with the Algonquian and Iroquois Indian tribes. (Rev: BL 10/1/88)

16124 Fradin, Dennis B. *The Pennsylvania Colony* (4–7). Illus. 1988, Children's LB $32.00 (0-516-00390-9). 160pp. A history of the Keystone state from the early 1600s. (Rev: BL 3/15/89; SLJ 4/89)

16125 Fradin, Dennis B. *The Rhode Island Colony* (4–7). Illus. Series: The Thirteen Colonies. 1989, Children's LB $32.00 (0-516-00391-7). 160pp. This is an introduction to the smallest U.S. state — Rhode Island. (Rev: BL 8/89; SLJ 11/89) [974.5]

16126 Fradin, Dennis B. *The South Carolina Colony* (5–8). Illus. Series: The Thirteen Colonies. 1992, Children's LB $32.00 (0-516-00397-6). 160pp. This illustrated account tells the story of South Carolina from the first settlements to statehood. (Rev: BL 9/1/92) [975.7]

16127 Fradin, Dennis B. *The Virginia Colony* (4–6). Illus. 1986, Children's LB $32.00 (0-516-00387-9). 160pp. A thorough introduction to one of the 13 original colonies. (Rev: BL 4/1/87)

16128 Goor, Ron, and Nancy Goor. *Williamsburg: Cradle of the Revolution* (4–6). Illus. 1994, Atheneum $15.95 (0-689-31795-6). 90pp. Describes the people, buildings, and history of Williamsburg, Virginia, immediately before the American Revolution. (Rev: BL 1/15/95; SLJ 6/95) [975.5]

16129 Gourley, Catherine. *Welcome to Felicity's World, 1774* (3–6). Illus. 1999, Pleasant $14.95 (1-56247-768-4). 58pp. Using double-page spreads, this book covers everyday life in Colonial Williamsburg in the 1770s, with material on such topics as the plantation village, slave laws, women, and epidemics. (Rev: BCCB 9/99; BL 9/1/99; HBG 3/00; SLJ 10/99) [973.2]

16130 Hakim, Joy. *From Colonies to Country.* 2nd ed (5–8). Series: A History of Us. 1999, Oxford LB $18.95 (0-19-512755-2); paper $12.95 (0-19-512756-0). 208pp. The colonial period and Revolutionary War are covered in this outstanding account that uses many quotes, profiles of personalities, and vivid details. (Rev: BL 12/15/99) [973.2]

16131 Hakim, Joy. *Making Thirteen Colonies.* 2d ed. (5–8). Illus. Series: A History of Us. 1999,

Oxford $18.95 (0-19-512753-6). 160pp. This excellent history of the colonial period is a reissue of the 1993 volume with some revisions and new illustrations. (Rev: BL 12/15/99) [973.2]

16132 Hale, Anna W. *The Mayflower People: Triumphs and Tragedies* (5–8). Illus. 1995, Harbinger $15.95 (1-57140-002-8); paper $9.95 (1-57140-003-6). 96pp. The story of the Pilgrims from their departure at Southampton, England, in 1620 to the death of Squanto in 1622. (Rev: BL 1/1–15/96) [974.4]

16133 Howarth, Sarah. *Colonial People* (4–8). Illus. Series: People and Places. 1994, Millbrook LB $21.90 (1-56294-512-2). 48pp. Various trades and professions that were important in American colonial days are described. (Rev: BL 5/15/95; SLJ 3/95) [973]

16134 Howarth, Sarah. *Colonial Places* (4–8). Illus. Series: People and Places. 1994, Millbrook LB $21.90 (1-56294-513-0). 48pp. Highlights various places of importance in everyday colonial life, like the meeting house and the church. (Rev: BL 5/15/95; SLJ 3/95) [973]

16135 Hubbard-Brown, Janet. *The Secret of Roanoke Island* (4–7). Illus. 1991, Avon paper $3.50 (0-380-76223-4). 96pp. An intriguing look at this bit of history in colonial times. (Rev: BL 12/15/91) [975.63]

16136 Ichord, Loretta Frances. *Hasty Pudding, Johnnycakes, and Other Good Stuff: Cooking in Colonial America* (3–6). Illus. 1998, Millbrook LB $22.40 (0-7613-0369-3). 64pp. Topics related to colonial life and early Thanksgivings are covered, with background information on colonial cooking and step-by-step recipes (the original and updated versions). (Rev: BL 1/1–15/99; HBG 3/99; SLJ 2/99) [641.5973]

16137 Isaacs, Sally Senzell. *Life in a Colonial Town* (1–3). Series: Picture the Past. 2000, Heinemann LB $21.36 (1-57572-312-3). This well-organized account covers such topics as communication, houses, occupations, education, clothing, and food. Similar coverage for colonial cities is given in *Life in America's First Cities* (2000). (Rev: HBG 3/01; SLJ 11/00) [973.2]

16138 Jackson, Shirley. *The Witchcraft of Salem Village* (4–7). Illus. 1963, Random paper $5.99 (0-394-89176-7). An account of the witch-hunting hysteria that hit Salem Village.

16139 January, Brendan. *The Jamestown Colony* (3–6). Series: We the People. 2000, Compass Point LB $15.95 (0-7565-0043-5). 48pp. A heavily illustrated account of the Jamestown colony that is simple in appearance and format. (Rev: SLJ 2/01) [973.2]

16140 January, Brendan. *Science in Colonial America* (4–8). Series: Science of the Past. 1999, Watts LB $24.00 (0-531-11525-9). 64pp. An attractive title that surveys the progress of science in colonial times with material on such contributors as Cotton Mather, Thomas Jefferson, David Rittenhouse, and Ben Franklin. (Rev: HBG 10/99; SLJ 6/99) [973.2]

16141 Kallen, Stuart A. *The Salem Witch Trials* (5–8). Series: World History. 1999, Lucent LB $17.96 (1-56006-544-3). 96pp. After a general history of witch-hunting, this book describes the Salem

trials and quotes extensively from firsthand accounts and trial notes. (Rev: SLJ 9/99) [973.2]

16142 Kalman, Bobbie. *Colonial Crafts* (3–6). Illus. by Antoinette DeBiasi. Series: Historic Communities. 1992, Crabtree LB $20.60 (0-86505-490-8); paper $7.95 (0-86505-510-6). 32pp. This book introduces crafts from colonial America through those found in the many reconstructed craft shops in Williamsburg, Virginia. Two others in this series dealing with colonial life are: *A Colonial Town: Williamsburg* and *Tools and Gadgets* (both 1992). (Rev: SLJ 7/92) [973.2]

16143 Kalman, Bobbie. *Colonial Life* (3–6). Illus. Series: Historic Communities. 1992, Crabtree LB $20.60 (0-86505-491-6); paper $7.95 (0-86505-511-4). 32pp. Using many illustrations and simple text, this book describes how people lived during the colonial period in U.S. history. (Rev: BL 11/1/92) [973.2]

16144 Kent, Deborah. *African-Americans in the Thirteen Colonies* (3–5). Illus. Series: Cornerstones of Freedom. 1996, Children's LB $20.50 (0-516-06631-5). 32pp. Using many photographs, this is a simple overview of the part played by African Americans during the formative years of the colonial period. (Rev: BL 4/15/96; SLJ 11/96) [973]

16145 Kent, Deborah. *In Colonial New England* (4–8). Series: How We Lived. 1999, Benchmark LB $18.95 (0-7614-0905-X). 72pp. Topics such as home life, childhood, religion, problems, and amusements are covered for the colonial period in New England. Companion volumes are *In the Middle Colonies* and *In the Southern Colonies* (1999). (Rev: HBG 10/00; SLJ 2/00) [973.2]

16146 Kent, Deborah. *Salem, Massachusetts* (4–6). Illus. Series: Places in American History. 1995, Silver Burdett LB $14.95 (0-87518-648-3). 72pp. The place of Salem in the country's history, with special emphasis on the witch trials during the colonial period. (Rev: BL 2/15/96; SLJ 1/96) [133.4]

16147 Kent, Zachary. *Williamsburg* (3–5). Illus. Series: Cornerstones of Freedom. 1992, Children's LB $20.50 (0-516-04854-6). 32pp. This account includes both the history of the former capital of Virginia and its present restoration. (Rev: BL 6/1/92; SLJ 9/92) [975.5]

16148 King, David C. *Colonial Days: Discover the Past with Fun Projects, Games, Activities, and Recipes* (3–6). Illus. 1998, Wiley paper $12.95 (0-471-16168-3). 128pp. Focusing on a year in the lives of a fictional colonial family, this book outlines 40 projects, including making a sundial, dyeing yarn, and dipping candles. (Rev: BL 2/1/98; SLJ 6/98) [973]

16149 Knight, James E. *Blue Feather's Vision: The Dawn of Colonial America* (4–6). Illus. by George Guzzi. 1982, Troll paper $3.50 (0-89375-723-3). 32pp. The first volume of a ten-volume set on colonial America. Followed by: *Boston Tea Party: Rebellion in the Colonies; The Farm: Life in Colonial Pennsylvania; Jamestown: New World Adventure; Journey to Monticello: Traveling in Colonial Times; Sailing to America: Colonists at Sea* (all 1982); and four other titles.

16150 Krensky, Stephen. *Witch Hunt: It Happened in Salem Village* (2–4). Illus. by James Watling. 1989, Random paper $3.99 (0-394-81923-3). 48pp. An easily read account of the 1692 witch trials that took the lives of 19 women. (Rev: BCCB 7–8/90; SLJ 8/89) [345.744]

16151 Kroll, Steven. *The Boston Tea Party* (3–6). Illus. by Peter M. Fiore. 1998, Holiday $16.95 (0-8234-1316-0). 32pp. A mature picture book in which the events leading up to and during the Boston Tea Party are described, with an afterword on its consequences. (Rev: BL 9/15/98; HBG 10/98; SLJ 12/98) [973.3]

16152 Kurelek, William, and Margaret S. Engelhart. *They Sought a New World* (3–7). Illus. 1985, Tundra paper $9.95 (0-88776-213-1). 48pp. The story of European immigration to North America. (Rev: BCCB 1/86; BL 12/15/85; SLJ 2/86)

16153 Loeper, John J. *Going to School in 1776* (3–6). Illus. 1973, Macmillan $16.00 (0-689-30089-1). 112pp. An interesting account of education and childhood activities in colonial America.

16154 McDonald, Megan. *Shadows in the Glasshouse* (4–6). Illus. by Paul Bachem and Laszlo Kubinyi. Series: History Mysteries. 2000, Pleasant $9.95 (1-58485-093-0); paper $5.95 (1-58485-092-2). 163pp. Set in Jamestown in 1621, this is the story of an indentured servant named Mary and her involvement in a mystery concerning someone who is sabotaging the glassblowing shop where she works. (Rev: SLJ 2/01)

16155 McGovern, Ann. *If You Lived in Colonial Times* (2–4). Illus. 1992, Scholastic paper $5.99 (0-590-45160-X). A re-creation of incidents and situations that could have occurred in the colonial period.

16156 McGovern, Ann. *If You Sailed on the Mayflower* (3–4). Illus. by Anna Devito. 1991, Scholastic paper $5.99 (0-590-45161-8). 80pp. In a question-and-answer format, information is given on the historic voyage and the settlement in New England.

16157 Maestro, Betsy. *The New Americans: Colonial Times, 1620–1689* (2–5). Illus. by Giulio Maestro. Series: American Story. 1998, Lothrop LB $15.93 (0-688-13449-1). 48pp. Describes the various European immigrants to the United States during the colonial period and tells why they came and where they settled. (Rev: BCCB 5/98; BL 4/1/98; SLJ 3/98) [973.2]

16158 Maestro, Betsy. *Struggle for a Continent: The French and Indian Wars, 1689–1763* (3–6). Illus. Series: American Story. 2000, HarperCollins LB $15.89 (0-688-13451-3). 48pp. This picture book tells of the series of wars that pitted the French and Algonquins against the English and the Iroquois. (Rev: BL 1/1–15/01; HBG 3/01; SLJ 9/00) [973.2]

16159 Marrin, Albert. *Struggle for a Continent: The French and Indian Wars, 1690–1760* (5–8). Illus. 1987, Macmillan LB $15.95 (0-689-31313-6). 232pp. History comes to life in this story of the events leading to the French and Indian wars and their contribution to independence for the colonists. (Rev: BL 1/15/88)

16160 Masoff, Joy. *Colonial Times, 1600–1700* (4–7). Series: Chronicle of America. 2000, Scholastic $15.95 (0-439-05107-X). 48pp. As well as describing why the colonists came to America, this work covers life aboard ships crossing the Atlantic and the challenges these people faced on arrival in the New World. (Rev: BCCB 9/00; HBG 3/01; SLJ 10/00) [973.2]

16161 Ochoa, George. *The Fall of Quebec and the French and Indian War* (5–7). Illus. Series: Turning Points. 1990, Silver Burdett LB $17.95 (0-382-09954-0); paper $7.95 (0-382-09950-8). 64pp. Illustrated account of the French and Indian Wars and the importance of the defeat of Montcalm and the taking of Quebec under Wolfe. (Rev: BL 3/1/91) [973.2]

16162 O'Neill, Laurie A. *The Boston Tea Party* (4–6). Illus. 1996, Millbrook LB $21.90 (0-7613-0006-6). 64pp. The causes and effects of the Boston Tea Party are presented, as well as the battles of Lexington and Concord. (Rev: BL 1/1–15/97; SLJ 3/97) [973.3]

16163 Penner, Lucille R. *Eating the Plates: A Pilgrim Book of Food and Manners* (3–5). Illus. 1991, Macmillan LB $16.00 (0-02-770901-9). 128pp. The focus is on food and other aspects of life at the Plymouth colony and aboard the Mayflower. (Rev: BCCB 9/91; BL 9/1/91; SLJ 3/92) [394.1]

16164 Roach, Marilynne K. *In the Days of the Salem Witchcraft Trials* (4–6). Illus. 1996, Houghton $15.00 (0-395-69704-2). 96pp. After a discussion of the Salem witchcraft trials, this account focuses on the way people lived in this period and what they believed. (Rev: BCCB 6/96; BL 5/15/96; SLJ 7/96) [133.4]

16165 Roop, Connie, and Peter Roop, eds. *Pilgrim Voices: Our First Year in the New World* (4–7). Illus. 1995, Walker LB $17.85 (0-8027-8315-5). 48pp. Using first-person sources, the experiences of the Pilgrims from their sea journey to the first Thanksgiving are re-created. (Rev: BL 2/1/96; SLJ 1/96) [974.4]

16166 Sakurai, Gail. *The Jamestown Colony* (3–5). Illus. 1997, Children's LB $20.50 (0-516-20295-2). 32pp. The story of the first permanent English settlement in America and its almost total destruction during Bacon's Rebellion in 1676. (Rev: BL 6/1–15/97) [975.5]

16167 Sakurai, Gail. *The Thirteen Colonies* (4–6). Series: Cornerstones of Freedom. 2000, Children's LB $20.00 (0-516-21603-1). 32pp. A basic introduction to the colonial period with a brief history of each of the colonies and how they were founded. (Rev: BL 5/15/00) [973.2]

16168 San Souci, Robert D. *N. C. Wyeth's Pilgrims* (2–5). Illus. by N. C. Wyeth. 1991, Chronicle $14.95 (0-87701-806-5). 40pp. A clear text and stunning reproductions of Wyeth murals combine in a beautiful volume. (Rev: BL 11/15/91; SLJ 10/91) [974.4]

16169 Sewall, Marcia. *The Pilgrims of Plimoth* (3–6). Illus. 1986, Macmillan $15.95 (0-689-31250-4). 48pp. A first-person account of the landing of the Pilgrims and the first years at Plymouth. (Rev: BL 9/15/86; HB 11–12/86; SLJ 11/86)

16170 Sewall, Marcia. *Thunder from the Clear Sky* (3–6). Illus. 1995, Simon & Schuster $17.00 (0-689-31775-1). 56pp. The story of the Pilgrims' relations with Wampanoag Indians in 1675, as told from both points of view. (Rev: BCCB 10/95; BL 11/15/95; SLJ 10/95) [973.2]

16171 Sherrow, Victoria. *Huskings, Quiltings, and Barn Raisings: Work-Play Parties in Early America* (4–7). Illus. by Laura LoTurco. 1992, Walker LB $14.85 (0-8027-8188-8). 78pp. How people in early America helped each other with difficult tasks, such as clearing land and raising barns. (Rev: BL 1/15/93) [973.2]

16172 Smith, Carter, ed. *The Arts and Sciences: A Sourcebook on Colonial America* (5–8). Illus. Series: American Albums from the Collections of the Library of Congress. 1991, Millbrook LB $25.90 (1-56294-037-6). 96pp. Through many well-captioned illustrations and brief text, this sourcebook traces cultural and scientific life during the U.S. colonial period. (Rev: BL 1/1/92) [973.2]

16173 Smith, Carter, ed. *Daily Life: A Sourcebook on Colonial America* (5–8). Series: American Albums from the Collections of the Library of Congress. 1991, Millbrook LB $25.90 (1-56294-038-4). 96pp. The everyday life and social customs of the colonists are covered in this sourcebook, with an emphasis on original prints, engravings, and other illustrations. (Rev: BL 1/1/92) [973.2]

16174 Smith, Carter. *The Jamestown Colony* (5–7). Illus. Series: Turning Points. 1991, Silver Burdett LB $14.95 (0-382-24121-5); paper $7.95 (0-382-24116-9). 64pp. An introduction in text and excellent illustrations to the ill-fated early colony in Virginia. (Rev: BL 1/15/92) [975.5]

16175 Steen, Sandra, and Susan Steen. *Colonial Williamsburg* (4–7). Illus. 1993, Macmillan LB $14.95 (0-87518-546-0). 72pp. The historic town of Williamsburg, the birthplace of the Bill of Rights, has been restored to its colonial state through John D. Rockefeller's generosity. (Rev: BL 5/15/93; SLJ 6/93) [975.5]

16176 Stefoff, Rebecca. *The Colonies* (4–7). Series: North American Historical Atlases. 2000, Benchmark LB $16.95 (0-7614-1057-0). 48pp. A slim, clearly written account that gives a history of the American colonies, important places, and outstanding people. (Rev: HBG 3/01; SLJ 1/01) [973.2]

16177 Stein, R. Conrad. *The Boston Tea Party* (3–5). Illus. Series: Cornerstones of Freedom. 1996, Children's LB $20.50 (0-516-20005-4). 32pp. After a brief introduction to life in colonial America, the events surrounding the Boston Tea Party and their historical significance are described. (Rev: BL 12/15/96; SLJ 5/97) [973.3]

16178 Steins, Richard. *Colonial America* (5–8). Series: Making of America. 2000, Raintree Steck-Vaughn LB $28.55 (0-8172-5701-2). 96pp. A brief history of the colonies from 1607 to 1763 with details of their founding, composition, and history. (Rev: HBG 10/00; SLJ 8/00) [973.2]

16179 Stevens, Bernardine S. *Colonial American Craftspeople* (5–8). Illus. Series: Colonial America.

1993, Watts LB $23.00 (0-531-12536-X). 112pp. The workings of the apprenticeship system are explored, with a discussion of such crafts as woodworking, paper making, printing, and metalworking. (Rev: BL 1/1/94; SLJ 2/94) [680]

16180 Terkel, Susan N. *Colonial American Medicine* (5–8). Illus. Series: Colonial America. 1993, Watts LB $23.00 (0-531-12539-4). 112pp. The practice of medicine in colonial America is explored, with material on physicians, barbers, midwives, and astrologers. (Rev: BL 1/1/94; SLJ 11/93) [362.1]

16181 Warner, John F. *Colonial American Home Life* (5–8). Illus. Series: Colonial America. 1993, Watts LB $23.00 (0-531-12541-6). 112pp. Topics covered in this book about colonial home life include the kinds of houses people lived in and their clothing, food, work, and schools. (Rev: BL 1/1/94; SLJ 2/94) [973.2]

16182 Washington, George. *George-isms* (5–10). 2000, Atheneum $7.95 (0-689-84082-9). 80pp. This is a collection of the rules of behavior copied out by George Washington as a teenager and includes dos and don'ts in such areas as dress, table manners, and polite conversation. (Rev: BL 10/15/00; HBG 3/01; SLJ 8/00) [973.4]

16183 Waters, Kate. *On the Mayflower: Voyage of the Ship's Apprentice and a Passenger Girl* (3–5). Illus. 1996, Scholastic $16.95 (0-590-67308-4). 40pp. A young ship's apprentice on the *Mayflower* tells the story of the historic crossing, with photographs taken during the voyage of *Mayflower II*. (Rev: BL 10/1/96; SLJ 10/96) [973.2]

16184 Waters, Kate. *Sara Morton's Day: A Day in the Life of a Pilgrim Girl* (4–6). Illus. by Russ Kendall. 1989, Scholastic paper $16.95 (0-590-42634-6). 32pp. A typical day in the life of a girl in the Plymouth plantation of 1627. (Rev: BCCB 1/90; BL 10/1/89; SLJ 11/89) [974.4]

16185 Waters, Kate. *Tapenum's Day: A Wampanoag Indian Boy in Pilgrim Times* (3–5). Illus. by Russ Kendall. 1996, Scholastic $16.95 (0-590-20237-5). 40pp. Re-enactment photos of the Plimoth Plantation site in Massachusetts enhance this account of a Wampanoag Indian boy in the 1620s. (Rev: BCCB 3/96; BL 5/1/96; HB 5–6/96; SLJ 5/96) [974.4]

16186 Wilmore, Kathy. *A Day in the Life of a Colonial Innkeeper* (3–5). Illus. Series: Library of Living and Working in Colonial Times. 2000, Rosen $18.60 (0-8239-5430-7). 24pp. In this picture of life at an inn in colonial times, innkeepers Mr. and Mrs. Watkins go about their daily chores — cooking, minding the horses in the stable, cleaning the rooms, and so forth. (Rev: BL 10/15/00) [973.2]

16187 Wilmore, Kathy. *A Day in the Life of a Colonial Wigmaker* (3–5). Illus. Series: Library of Living and Working in Colonial Times. 2000, Rosen $18.60 (0-8239-5426-9). 24pp. Set in a colonial American wig shop, this account shows how Mr. Hawkins and his staff of wig makers accomplish such tasks as making scull caps, sewing hair onto them, and powdering the finished wigs. (Rev: BL 10/15/00) [973.3]

16188 Wroble, Lisa A. *Kids in Colonial Times* (1–3). Series: Kids Throughout History. 1997, Rosen LB $13.95 (0-8239-5118-9). 24pp. An introduction to daily life and customs in the New England colonies. (Rev: SLJ 4/98) [973.2]

REVOLUTIONARY PERIOD

16189 Amstel, Marsha. *Sybil Ludington's Midnight Ride* (2–4). Illus. by Ellen Beier. 2000, Carolrhoda LB $21.27 (1-57505-211-3); paper $5.95 (1-57505-456-6). 48pp. A readable account of 16-year-old Sybil Ludington's exciting midnight ride to spread the word that the British were attacking Danbury, Connecticut. (Rev: HBG 10/00; SLJ 6/00) [973.3]

16190 Brenner, Barbara. *If You Were There in 1776* (4–8). Illus. 1994, Bradbury paper $17.00 (0-02-712322-7). 112pp. The year 1776 is explored, with particular emphasis on the everyday life of young people in the colonies. (Rev: BCCB 6/94; BL 5/15/94; SLJ 6/94) [973.3]

16191 Collier, Christopher, and James Lincoln Collier. *The American Revolution, 1763–1783* (5–8). Series: Drama of American History. 1998, Marshall Cavendish LB $19.95 (0-7614-0440-6). 94pp. Using period illustrations, this basic history of the American Revolution describes the colonialists and the major battles and important figures of the war. (Rev: BL 4/15/98*; HBG 10/98) [973.3]

16192 Collier, Christopher, and James Lincoln Collier. *Creating the Constitution, 1787* (5–8). Illus. Series: Drama of American History. 1998, Marshall Cavendish LB $19.95 (0-7914-0776-6). 89pp. This history of the U.S. Constitution describes the background and importance of the document and the compromises made to ensure ratification. (Rev: BL 2/15/99) [970.00497]

16193 Cox, Clinton. *Come All You Brave Soldiers: Blacks in the Revolutionary War* (5–7). Illus. 1999, Scholastic $15.95 (0-590-47576-2). 208pp. An exciting account of the role played by 5,000 African Americans who served as soldiers, sailors, and spies during the American Revolution. (Rev: BL 2/15/99; HBG 10/99) [973.3]

16194 Dolan, Edward F. *The American Revolution: How We Fought the War of Independence* (5–8). Illus. 1995, Millbrook LB $27.40 (1-56294-521-1). 112pp. An outline of the American Revolution that covers key events and profiles all the familiar historical figures. (Rev: BL 12/15/95; SLJ 1/96) [973.3]

16195 Ferrie, Richard. *The World Turned Upside Down: George Washington and the Battle of Yorktown* (5–9). Illus. 1999, Holiday $18.95 (0-8234-1402-7). 168pp. A lavishly illustrated account of the battle that was the turning point in the Revolution, with details on strategies, personalities, and period warfare. (Rev: BL 9/1/99; HBG 3/00) [973.3]

16196 Freedman, Russell. *Give Me Liberty! The Story of the Declaration of Independence* (4–7). Illus. 2000, Holiday $24.95 (0-8234-1448-5). 90pp. Beginning with the Boston Tea Party, this stirring account introduces characters including Patrick Henry and Paul Revere, events such as the battles at

Lexington and Concord, and ends with the Continental Congress and the drawing up of the Declaration of Independence. (Rev: BCCB 10/00; BL 10/1/00*; HB 1–2/01; HBG 3/01; SLJ 10/00) [973.3]

16197 Gay, Kathlyn, and Martin Gay. *Revolutionary War* (5–8). Illus. Series: Voices from the Past. 1995, Twenty-First Century LB $18.90 (0-8050-2844-7). 64pp. Eyewitness accounts are used extensively in this account that covers the causes, key events, and results of the Revolutionary War. (Rev: BL 12/15/95; SLJ 3/96) [973.7]

16198 Harper, Judith E. *African Americans and the Revolutionary War* (4–6). Series: Journey to Freedom. 2000, Child's World $25.64 (1-56766-745-7). 40pp. This account traces the contributions of African Americans in the struggle for freedom against the English. (Rev: BL 11/15/00; HBG 3/01; SLJ 3/01) [973.3]

16199 Hughes, Libby. *Valley Forge* (4–6). Illus. Series: Places in American History. 1993, Macmillan LB $18.95 (0-87518-547-9). 72pp. The story of Valley Forge, Pennsylvania, and the terrible winter during the American Revolutionary War when more than 3,000 of General Washington's troops died. (Rev: BL 4/15/93; SLJ 7/93) [973]

16200 Kent, Deborah. *The American Revolution: "Give Me Liberty, or Give Me Death!"* (5–7). Illus. Series: American War. 1994, Enslow LB $20.95 (0-89490-521-X). 128pp. A succinct history of the Revolution that uses many firsthand quotations and period illustrations and maps. (Rev: BL 7/94; SLJ 7/94) [973.3]

16201 King, David. *Lexington and Concord* (4–8). Illus. Series: Battlefields Across America. 1997, Twenty-First Century $23.40 (0-8050-5225-9). 64pp. A straightforward account that gives good background material before describing the battles and the sites as they are today. (Rev: SLJ 1/98) [973.3]

16202 Kirby, Philippa. *Glorious Days, Dreadful Days: The Battle of Bunker Hill* (4–6). Illus. by John Edens. Series: Stories of America. 1993, Raintree Steck-Vaughn LB $28.55 (0-8114-7226-4). 88pp. Describes the Battle of Bunker Hill and its significance to the Revolution. (Rev: HB 11–12/97; SLJ 9/93) [973.3]

16203 Lunn, Janet. *Charlotte* (4–6). Illus. by Brian Deines. 1998, Tundra $15.95 (0-88776-383-9). 32pp. Based on fact, this picture book for older readers tells the story of Charlotte who, as a child living in New York City during Revolutionary times, is forced to accompany her Loyalist aunt and uncle to Nova Scotia as punishment for disobeying her father. (Rev: BCCB 9/98; BL 8/98; HBG 10/98; SLJ 9/98) [974.7]

16204 Marrin, Albert. *The War for Independence: The Story of the American Revolution* (5–8). 1988, Macmillan $19.00 (0-689-31390-X). 288pp. Historical fact woven into the story of the eight-year war for independence. (Rev: BCCB 4/88; BL 7/88)

16205 Martin, Joseph Plumb. *A Revolutionary War Soldier* (3–6). Series: In My Own Words. 2000,

Marshall Cavendish LB $16.95 (0-7614-1014-7). 64pp. Sly humor is present in diary excerpts that bring to life stirring moments in America's war for independence. (Rev: BL 3/1/01; HBG 3/01; SLJ 3/01) [973.3]

16206 Masoff, Joy. *American Revolution: 1700–1800* (4–7). Series: Chronicle of America. 2000, Scholastic $15.95 (0-439-05109-6). 48pp. A successful basic introduction to the American Revolution. (Rev: BCCB 9/00; HBG 3/01; SLJ 10/00) [973.3]

16207 Murphy, Jim. *A Young Patriot: The American Revolution as Experienced by One Boy* (5–8). Illus. 1996, Clarion $16.00 (0-395-60523-7). 101pp. The American Revolution as seen through the eyes of a 15-year-old volunteer. (Rev: BCCB 6/96; BL 6/1–15/96*; HB 9–10/96; SLJ 6/96*) [973.3]

16208 Nordstrom, Judy. *Concord and Lexington* (4–6). Illus. Series: Places in American History. 1993, Macmillan LB $14.95 (0-87518-567-3). 72pp. The history and monuments of these two historic towns are covered, plus their place in the history of the Revolution. (Rev: BL 4/15/93; SLJ 7/93) [973.3]

16209 Peacock, Louise. *Crossing the Delaware: A History in Many Voices* (4–6). Illus. by Walter L. Krudop. 1998, Simon & Schuster $17.00 (0-689-80994-8). 48pp. Using several points of view, this retelling of Washington's historic crossing of the Delaware River presents the facts — and their significance to different people. (Rev: BCCB 9/98; BL 11/15/98; HBG 3/99; SLJ 10/98) [973.3]

16210 Penner, Lucille R. *The Liberty Tree: The Beginning of the American Revolution* (2–4). Illus. by David Wenzel. Series: Picture Landmark Books. 1998, Random $14.00 (0-679-83482-6). 39pp. Focusing on the actual Liberty Tree, an elm in Boston, this account covers the events leading to the American Revolution, such as the Stamp Act of 1765, the Boston Massacre, Paul Revere's ride, and the first shot at Lexington. (Rev: HBG 3/99; SLJ 9/98) [973.3]

16211 Quiri, Patricia R. *The Declaration of Independence* (3–4). Illus. Series: True Books. 1998, Children's LB $21.00 (0-516-20664-8). 48pp. After outlining the colonists' grievances, this account discusses the drafting of the Declaration of Independence and its final congressional approval. (Rev: BL 2/1/99; HBG 3/99) [973.3]

16212 Rappaport, Doreen. *The Boston Coffee Party* (1–3). Illus. by Emily Arnold McCully. 1988, HarperCollins paper $3.95 (0-06-444141-5). 64pp. Angry women force a greedy merchant to turn over coffee in this true Revolutionary War incident. (Rev: BL 4/1/88; HB 9–10/88; SLJ 5/88)

16213 Schleifer, Jay. *Our Declaration of Independence* (4–6). Illus. Series: I Know America. 1992, Millbrook LB $20.90 (1-56294-205-0). 48pp. A well-illustrated history of the writing of the Declaration of Independence and its significance. (Rev: BL 9/1/92; SLJ 10/92) [973.3]

16214 Silox-Jarrett, Diane. *Heroines of the American Revolution: America's Founding Mothers* (4–6). Illus. 1998, Green Angel $19.95 (0-9658065-

2-0). 94pp. Profiles of 25 important women who championed the colonists' cause during the American Revolution. (Rev: BL 2/15/98) [973.3]

16215 Stefoff, Rebecca. *Revolutionary War* (4–7). Illus. Series: North American Historical Atlases. 2000, Benchmark $16.95 (0-7614-1058-9). Using historical maps and reproductions plus a clear text, this is a basic account of the American Revolution. (Rev: HBG 3/01; SLJ 1/01) [973.3]

16216 Stein, R. Conrad. *Valley Forge* (3–5). Illus. Series: Cornerstones of Freedom. 1994, Children's LB $20.50 (0-516-06683-8). 32pp. The crucial battle that determined the future of the American Revolution is retold with many illustrations and maps. (Rev: BL 1/15/95; SLJ 3/95) [973.7]

16217 Steins, Richard. *A Nation Is Born: Rebellion and Independence in America (1700–1820)* (5–8). Illus. Series: First Person America. 1993, Twenty-First Century LB $18.90 (0-8050-2582-0). 64pp. The events preceding and during the American Revolution are covered with extensive first-person narratives, connecting text, and copious illustrations. (Rev: BL 2/1/94; SLJ 2/94) [973.3]

16218 Weber, Michael. *The American Revolution* (5–8). Series: Making of America. 2000, Raintree Steck-Vaughn $28.54 (0-8172-5702-0). 96pp. A fine overview of the American Revolution from the French and Indian War to the creation of the United States. (Rev: BL 7/00; HBG 10/00; SLJ 8/00) [973.3]

16219 Weber, Michael. *Yorktown* (4–7). Illus. Series: Battlefields Across America. 1997, Twenty-First Century $23.40 (0-8050-5226-7). 63pp. Background material on the Revolutionary War is given, along with details of the battle and the present-day condition of its site. (Rev: SLJ 1/98) [973.3]

16220 Wilbur, C. Keith. *Revolutionary Medicine 1700–1800* (4–8). Illus. 1997, Chelsea $19.95 (0-7910-4532-3). 96pp. In a large-book format, this account gives a great deal of information about medicine in 18th-century America. (Rev: BL 6/1–15/97; SLJ 7/97) [973.3]

16221 Wilbur, C. Keith. *The Revolutionary Soldier 1775–1783* (4–8). Illus. 1997, Chelsea LB $19.95 (0-7910-4533-1). 96pp. Topics covered in this book about the Continental Army include clothing, weapons, camp life, food, hospitals, and leisure activities. (Rev: BL 6/1–15/97; SLJ 7/97) [973.3]

16222 Wister, Sally. *A Colonial Quaker Girl: The Diary of Sally Wister, 1777–1778* (4–6). Series: Diaries, Letters, and Memoirs. 2000, Capstone LB $22.60 (0-7368-0349-1). 32pp. This diary of a young girl, kept during the Revolution, reflects everyday family life during this period. (Rev: BL 10/15/00; SLJ 9/00) [973.3]

16223 Young, Robert. *The Real Patriots of the American Revolution* (4–6). Illus. Series: Both Sides. 1997, Dillon LB $18.95 (0-87518-612-2). 72pp. The points of view of Revolutionists, Loyalists, and the British are represented in this account of the causes and important events of the American Revolution. (Rev: BL 9/15/97) [973.3]

16224 Zeinert, Karen. *Those Remarkable Women of the American Revolution* (5–8). Illus. 1996, Millbrook LB $27.40 (1-56294-657-9). 96pp. A fascinating account of the various roles women played in the American Revolution, from fighting and spying to fund raising. (Rev: BL 12/1/96; SLJ 3/97) [973.3]

THE YOUNG NATION, 1789–1861

16225 Baldwin, Robert F. *New England Whaler* (5–8). Illus. by Richard Erickson. Series: American Pastfinder. 1996, Lerner LB $21.50 (0-8225-2978-5). 48pp. Life on a 19th-century whaling ship is detailed, with many maps and color photos. (Rev: BL 7/96; SLJ 6/96) [638.2]

16226 Bentley, Judith. *"Dear Friend" : Thomas Garrett and William Still, Collaborators on the Underground Railroad* (5–8). Illus. 1997, Dutton $15.99 (0-525-65156-X). 119pp. A white Quaker, Thomas Garrett, and a freed slave, William Still, work together in the Underground Railroad to smuggle slaves to freedom. (Rev: BCCB 2/97; BL 2/15/97; SLJ 6/97) [973.7]

16227 Bial, Raymond. *The Strength of These Arms: Life in the Slave Quarters* (3–6). Illus. 1997, Houghton $15.00 (0-395-77394-6). 48pp. Using photos extensively, this account re-creates the conditions of life during the days of slavery, both in the mansion house and in the slave quarters. (Rev: BL 9/15/97; HBG 3/98; SLJ 11/97) [975]

16228 Bial, Raymond. *The Underground Railroad* (4–7). Illus. 1995, Houghton $16.00 (0-395-69937-1). 48pp. This photo-essay re-creates the places involved in the Underground Railroad and the heroism of the people involved. (Rev: BCCB 3/95; BL 4/1/95; HB 7–8/95; SLJ 4/95) [973.7]

16229 Blumberg, Rhoda. *What's the Deal? Jefferson, Napoleon, and the Louisiana Purchase* (5–9). Illus. 1998, National Geographic $18.95 (0-7922-7013-4). 144pp. A dramatic retelling of the events surrounding the Louisiana Purchase, the people involved, the greed and double-dealing it induced, and what would have happened had Napoleon refused to sell it. (Rev: BL 11/1/98*; HB 11–12/98; HBG 3/99) [973.4]

16230 Bredeson, Carmen. *The Battle of the Alamo: The Fight for Texas Territory* (5–8). Series: Spotlight on American History. 1996, Millbrook LB $21.90 (0-7613-0019-8). 64pp. A well-organized account that describes important events and people involved in the fall of the Alamo, with quotes from original sources and many art reproductions. (Rev: SLJ 4/97) [976.4]

16231 Chambers, Veronica. *Amistad Rising: A Story of Freedom* (3–6). Illus. by Paul Lee. 1998, Harcourt $16.00 (0-15-201803-4). 40pp. A partly fictionalized account of the Amistad mutiny that focuses on Cinque and his restlessness. (Rev: BCCB 5/98; BL 2/15/98; HBG 10/98; SLJ 4/98) [326]

16232 Collier, Christopher, and James Lincoln Collier. *Andrew Jackson's America, 1824–1850* (5–8). Illus. Series: Drama of American History. 1998, Marshall Cavendish LB $19.95 (0-7614-0779-0). 89pp. This account traces American history over an eventful 26 years that encompassed great change, from the Industrial Revolution to the Trail of Tears. (Rev: BL 2/15/99; HBG 10/99) [973.5]

16233 Collier, Christopher, and James Lincoln Collier. *Building a New Nation, 1789–1801* (5–8). Illus. Series: Drama of American History. 1998, Marshall Cavendish LB $19.95 (0-7614-0776-6). 89pp. An account of how the Federalists began to use the Constitution as a blueprint for guiding the young nation. (Rev: BL 2/15/99) [973.4]

16234 Collier, Christopher, and James Lincoln Collier. *Hispanic America, Texas and the Mexican War, 1835–1850* (5–8). Illus. Series: Drama of American History. 1998, Marshall Cavendish LB $19.95 (0-7614-0780-4). 89pp. This account covers the history of Europeans in the Southwest, the Hispanic culture in the region, the doctrine of Manifest Destiny, the Mexican War, and the settling of California. (Rev: BL 2/15/99; HBG 10/99; SLJ 4/99) [979]

16235 Collier, Christopher, and James Lincoln Collier. *The Jeffersonian Republicans, 1800–1823: The Louisiana Purchase and the War of 1812* (5–8). Illus. Series: Drama of American History. 1998, Marshall Cavendish LB $19.95 (0-7614-0778-2). 87pp. This lively account describes 23 eventful years in our history that include the Louisiana Purchase, the Lewis and Clark expedition, and the War of 1812. (Rev: BL 2/15/99; HBG 10/99; SLJ 4/99) [973.4]

16236 Collier, Christopher, and James Lincoln Collier. *Slavery and the Coming of the Civil War, 1831–1861* (5–8). Illus. 1999, Marshall Cavendish LB $20.95 (0-7614-0817-7). 87pp. A reliable, interesting account the traces the history of slavery in the United States, with an emphasis on the events leading up to the Civil War. (Rev: BL 2/15/00; HBG 10/00; SLJ 3/00) [973.7]

16237 Doherty, Craig A., and Katherine M. Doherty. *The Erie Canal* (4–7). Illus. Series: Building America. 1996, Blackbirch LB $17.95 (1-56711-112-2). 48pp. Photos and maps are used effectively in this introduction to the Erie Canal, an engineering marvel. (Rev: BL 2/15/97; SLJ 2/97) [386]

16238 Donaldson, Joan. *A Pebble and a Pen* (5–8). 2000, Holiday $15.95 (0-8234-1500-7). 176pp. In 1853, to avoid an arranged marriage, 14-year-old Matty runs away to study penmanship at Mr. Spencer's famous Ohio school. (Rev: BCCB 12/00; BL 1/1–15/01; SLJ 12/00)

16239 Erickson, Paul. *Daily Life on a Southern Plantation 1853* (4–7). 1998, Lodestar $16.99 (0-525-67547-7). 48pp. Gives an hour-by-hour tour of a Southern plantation in Louisiana in 1853, revealing how both the landowners and the slaves lived. (Rev: HBG 10/98; SLJ 12/98) [973.5]

16240 Fleischner, Jennifer. *The Dred Scott Case: Testing the Right to Live Free* (4–6). Illus. 1997, Millbrook LB $21.90 (0-7613-0005-8). 64pp. An account of the life of the slave Dred Scott and the historic court case in 1857 against his owner, John Sanford. (Rev: BL 5/1/97; SLJ 4/97) [342.73]

16241 Forten, Charlotte. *A Free Black Girl Before the Civil War: The Diary of Charlotte Forten, 1854*

(4–8). Ed. by Kerry Graves. Illus. Series: Diaries, Letters, and Memoirs. 2000, Capstone LB $22.60 (0-7368-0345-9). 32pp. This first-person account based on actual sources describes, in diary format, the life of a 16-year-old African American girl living in Massachusetts before the Civil War and her participation in the antislavery movement. (Rev: BL 10/15/00; HBG 10/00; SLJ 9/00) [974.4]

16242 Fradin, Dennis B. *Bound for the North Star: True Stories of Fugitive Slaves* (5–9). 2000, Clarion $20.00 (0-395-97017-2). 206pp. This is a gripping narrative that tells the true stories of 12 runaway slaves, including Harriet Tubman, who successfully escaped to the North and freedom. (Rev: HB 1–2/01; HBG 3/01; SLJ 11/00) [973.6]

16243 Garland, Sherry. *Voices of the Alamo* (3–6). 2000, Scholastic $16.95 (0-590-98833-6). 40pp. Using a series of first-person narratives, this picture book describes the siege of the Alamo as well as covering the origins of the conflict and its aftermath. (Rev: BL 2/15/00; HBG 10/00; SLJ 6/00) [976.4]

16244 Gay, Kathlyn, and Martin Gay. *War of 1812* (5–8). Illus. Series: Voices from the Past. 1995, Twenty-First Century LB $18.90 (0-8050-2846-3). 64pp. Accounts taken from letters, memoirs, and official reports highlight this well-illustrated history of the War of 1812 and its consequences. (Rev: BL 12/15/95; SLJ 3/96) [973.5]

16245 Goodman, Susan E. *Ultimate Field Trip 4* (3–6). Series: Ultimate Field Trip. 2000, Simon & Schuster $17.00 (0-689-83045-9). 56pp. This volume tells of a week spent by a group of American students living as 19th-century children in the Kings Landing Historical Settlement in Canada, where they learn about the various trades and everyday life in those days. (Rev: BCCB 9/00; BL 5/15/00; SLJ 5/00) [973.5]

16246 Greene, Meg. *Slave Young, Slave Long: The American Slave Experience* (5–8). Illus. Series: People's History. 1999, Lerner LB $16.95 (0-8225-1739-6). 88pp. Using a direct style and illustrations on every page, this account traces the history of slavery in America. (Rev: BL 4/1/99; HBG 10/99; SLJ 10/99) [973]

16247 Guccione, Leslie D. *Come Morning* (4–7). 1995, Carolrhoda LB $21.27 (0-87614-892-5). 120pp. A young boy takes over his father's duties as a conductor on the Underground Railroad. (Rev: BCCB 1/96; HB 11–12/95; SLJ 11/95)

16248 Gunderson, Mary. *Southern Plantation Cooking* (4–7). Illus. 2000, Capstone LB $22.60 (0-7368-0357-2). 32pp. This book explores life on Southern plantations during the days of slavery with emphasis on the importance of food and food preparation. A few representative recipes are provided. (Rev: BL 8/00; HBG 10/00) [394.1]

16249 Hakim, Joy. *Liberty for All? 2nd ed* (5–8). Series: A History of Us. 1999, Oxford LB $18.95 (0-19-512759-5); paper $12.95 (0-19-512760-9). 204pp. An excellent account of American history from 1800 to the outbreak of the Civil War, with emphasis on the slave economy and events leading up to the war. (Rev: BL 12/15/99) [973.5]

16250 Harness, Cheryl. *The Amazing Impossible Erie Canal* (3–5). Illus. 1995, Simon & Schuster paper $17.99 (0-02-742641-6). 42pp. This history of the Erie Canal concentrates on the festivities during its opening in 1825. (Rev: BCCB 6/95; BL 5/15/95; SLJ 8/95) [977.1]

16251 Haskins, Jim, and Kathleen Benson. *Bound for America: The Forced Migration of Africans to the New World* (4–9). Illus. by Floyd Cooper. Series: From African Beginnings. 1999, Lothrop LB $17.93 (0-688-10259-X). 48pp. This stirring account traces the fate of African slaves from capture, imprisonment, and branding to the brutal conditions on slave ships and finally to the survivors' arrival in the New World. (Rev: BCCB 3/99; BL 12/15/98; HBG 10/99) [382]

16252 Hull, Mary E. *Shays' Rebellion and the Constitution in American History* (5–10). Series: In American History. 2000, Enslow LB $19.95 (0-7660-1418-5). 112pp. Photos and reproductions of documents are used to bring to life this rebellion against the Massachusetts government in 1787. (Rev: HBG 10/00; SLJ 6/00) [973.4]

16253 Isaacs, Sally Senzell. *Life on a Southern Plantation* (1–3). Series: Picture the Past. 2000, Heinemann $21.36 (1-57572-316-6). A well-organized account that uses double-page spreads to describe life on a southern plantation before the Civil War with coverage of the lives of both the planters and the slaves. (Rev: HBG 3/01; SLJ 11/00) [973.6]

16254 Jacobs, William J. *War with Mexico* (4–6). Illus. Series: Spotlight on American History. 1993, Millbrook LB $21.90 (1-56294-366-9). 64pp. The events of the 1846–1848 war with Mexico are reported, with an objective account of its causes and results. (Rev: BL 12/15/93; SLJ 1/94) [973.6]

16255 January, Brendan. *John Brown's Raid on Harpers Ferry* (4–6). Series: Cornerstones of Freedom. 2000, Children's LB $20.00 (0-516-21144-7). 32pp. The story of the raid in 1859 on Harpers Ferry, West Virginia, led by abolitionist John Brown, who was later captured and executed. (Rev: BL 5/15/00) [973.6]

16256 January, Brendan. *The Lincoln-Douglas Debates* (3–5). Series: Cornerstones of Freedom. 1998, Children's LB $19.50 (0-516-20844-6). 32pp. The series of influential debates in 1858 are bought to life with a simple, direct text and useful photographs and prints. (Rev: BL 5/15/98; HBG 10/98) [973.6]

16257 Jurmain, Suzanne. *Freedom's Sons: The True Story of the Amistad Mutiny* (5–8). Illus. 1998, Lothrop $15.00 (0-688-11072-X). 128pp. Told with true storytelling skill, this fascinating chapter in American history is re-created brilliantly, with a special focus on the nobility of Cinque and his men. (Rev: BCCB 5/98; BL 2/15/98; HBG 10/98; SLJ 4/98) [326]

16258 Kallen, Stuart A. *Life on the Underground Railroad* (5–8). Series: The Way People Live. 2000,

Lucent LB $18.96 (1-56006-667-9). 96pp. After a brief history of slavery in America, this account covers the organization of and people involved in the Underground Railroad, the journeys made on it, and its impact on future history. (Rev: HBG 10/00; SLJ 5/00) [973.6]

16259 Kalman, Bobbie. *The General Store* (3–5). Illus. Series: Historic Communities. 1997, Crabtree LB $20.60 (0-86505-432-0); paper $7.95 (0-86505-462-2). 32pp. Using photos of reconstructions in such places as Old Sturbridge Village, this account describes the importance, contents, and workings of the general store in 18th- and 19th-century America. (Rev: SLJ 7/97) [381]

16260 Kalman, Bobbie. *Life on a Plantation* (3–6). Illus. Series: Historic Communities. 1997, Crabtree LB $20.60 (0-86505-435-5); paper $7.95 (0-86505-465-7). 32pp. Daily life on the plantation for both the owners and their slaves is covered, with details about working in the fields and the roles and duties of various workers. (Rev: BL 7/97) [975]

16261 Macaulay, David. *Mill* (5–8). Illus. by author. 1983, Houghton $18.00 (0-395-34830-7); paper $8.95 (0-395-52019-3). 128pp. The construction of an early 19th-century spinning mill in Rhode Island.

16262 McKissack, Patricia, and Fredrick McKissack. *Christmas in the Big House, Christmas in the Quarters* (4–6). Illus. by John Thompson. 1994, Scholastic $17.95 (0-590-43027-0). 80pp. This book describes life on a Virginia plantation in 1859 and includes social life and master-slave relations plus material on how Christmas was celebrated. (Rev: BCCB 10/94; BL 8/94; SLJ 10/94*) [975]

16263 McKissack, Patricia, and Fredrick McKissack. *Rebels Against Slavery: American Slave Revolts* (5–8). Illus. 1996, Scholastic $14.95 (0-590-45735-7). 176pp. The careers of such leaders of slave revolts as Nat Turner, Toussaint-Louverture, Cinque, and Harriet Tubman are covered in this informative book illustrated with photos. (Rev: BCCB 6/96; BL 2/15/96; SLJ 3/96) [970.00496]

16264 McNeese, Tim. *America's Early Canals* (4–6). Illus. Series: America on the Move. 1993, Macmillan LB $11.95 (0-89686-730-7). 48pp. An introduction to canals famous in American history, such as the Potomac Canal and the Erie Canal, with discussion of the builders and how the canals were built. (Rev: BL 11/15/93) [386]

16265 Miller, Marilyn. *The Transcontinental Railroad* (5–8). Illus. 1987, Silver Burdett paper $7.95 (0-382-09912-5). 64pp. The great event that linked East and West by rail is portrayed with numerous illustrations. (Rev: BL 7/87; SLJ 9/87)

16266 Myers, Walter Dean. *Amistad: A Long Road to Freedom* (5–8). Illus. 1998, Dutton $16.99 (0-525-45970-7). 96pp. The fascinating story of the 1839 mutiny and its consequences told with a skillful narrative that emphasizes the courage, strength, and dignity of the mutineers. (Rev: BCCB 5/98; BL 2/15/98; HBG 10/98) [326]

16267 Newman, Shirlee P. *The African Slave Trade* (4–7). Illus. Series: Watts Library: History of Slavery. 2000, Watts LB $24.00 (0-531-11694-8). 64pp.

From the brutality of capture through the unimaginable horrors of the Middle Passage and the humiliation of slave life, to the Emancipation Proclamation and slavery's lasting effects, this is a riveting narrative. (Rev: BL 2/15/01; SLJ 3/01) [380.1]

16268 Nofi, Albert A. *The Underground Railroad and the Civil War* (4–8). Series: Untold History of the Civil War. 2000, Chelsea $17.95 (0-7910-5434-9). 64pp. A history of the dangers, devotion, excitement, and daring involved in this collaborative system that was developed to help fugitive Southern slaves reach freedom in the North or in Canada. (Rev: BL 5/15/00; HBG 10/00; SLJ 6/00) [973.7]

16269 Pelta, Kathy. *Eastern Trails: From Footpaths to Turnpikes* (4–6). Series: American Trails. 1997, Raintree Steck-Vaughn LB $39.75 (0-8172-4071-3). 96pp. Focusing on trails, footpaths, and emerging roads, this account traces the opening up of the American East to settlers and explorers. Also use *Trails to the West: Beyond the Mississippi* (1997). (Rev: BL 10/15/97; HBG 3/98) [973.6]

16270 Richards, Caroline Cowles. *A 19th Century Schoolgirl: The Diary of Caroline Cowles Richards, 1852–1855* (4–8). Ed. by Kerry Graves. Illus. Series: Diaries, Letters, and Memoirs. 2000, Capstone LB $22.60 (0-7368-0342-4). 32pp. This diary of a young girl living in western New York state in the early 1850s describes her daily life, schooling, and her reaction to the women's rights movement. (Rev: BL 10/15/00; HBG 10/00; SLJ 9/00) [974.7]

16271 Sakurai, Gail. *The Louisiana Purchase* (3–5). Series: Cornerstones of Freedom. 1998, Children's LB $19.50 (0-516-20791-1). 32pp. A dramatic account of the land purchase in 1803 that added almost a million square miles to the United States. (Rev: BL 5/15/98; HBG 10/98) [973.5]

16272 Santella, Andrew. *The Battle of the Alamo* (3–5). Illus. Series: Cornerstones of Freedom. 1997, Children's LB $20.50 (0-516-20293-6). 32pp. The history of the San Antonio, Texas, chapel and the famous siege there in which Davy Crockett and Jim Bowie were killed. (Rev: BL 6/1–15/97) [976.4]

16273 Shuter, Jane, ed. *Charles Ball and American Slavery* (5–8). Illus. Series: History Eyewitness. 1995, Raintree Steck-Vaughn LB $24.26 (0-8114-8281-2). 48pp. This autobiographical account in simplified language brings the horrors of slavery to life, with period prints and maps. (Rev: BL 4/15/95; SLJ 5/95) [975]

16274 Silverstein, Herma. *The Alamo* (4–6). Illus. Series: Places in American History. 1992, Macmillan LB $14.95 (0-87518-502-9). 72pp. A visual and narrative introduction to the historical site in San Antonio that was besieged by Mexican forces. (Rev: BL 9/1/92; SLJ 8/92) [976]

16275 Simonds, Christopher. *Samuel Slater's Mill and the Industrial Revolution* (5–7). Illus. Series: Turning Points. 1990, Silver Burdett LB $17.95 (0-382-09951-6); paper $7.95 (0-382-09947-8). 64pp. Describes how the pioneer in the cotton textile industry reproduced English machinery and how the Industrial Revolution began in this country. (Rev: BL 3/1/91) [338]

16276 Smith, Carter, ed. *The Founding Presidents: A Sourcebook on the U.S. Presidency* (5–8). Illus. Series: American Albums. 1993, Millbrook LB $25.90 (1-56294-357-X). 96pp. A visually oriented review of the personal and political lives of the presidents from Washington through James Monroe. (Rev: BL 12/1/93) [973]

16277 Smith, Carter, ed. *Presidents of a Young Republic: A Sourcebook on the U.S. Presidency* (5–8). Illus. Series: American Albums. 1993, Millbrook LB $25.90 (1-56294-359-6). 96pp. A well-illustrated account that traces U.S. history from the presidency of John Quincy Adams through James Buchanan. (Rev: BL 12/1/93; SLJ 4/94) [973.5]

16278 Smith-Baranzini, Marlene, and Howard Egger-Bovet. *Brown Paper School USKids History: Book of the New American Nation* (5–7). Illus. 1995, Little, Brown paper $14.95 (0-316-22206-2). 96pp. From George Washington to the building of the Erie Canal, key issues and people in American history are introduced. (Rev: BL 8/95; SLJ 8/95) [973.5]

16279 Stefoff, Rebecca. *The War of 1812* (4–7). Illus. Series: North American Historical Atlases. 2000, Benchmark $16.95 (0-7614-1060-0). A clearly written text plus historical maps and reproductions are used to give an easy-to-read account of the War of 1812. (Rev: HBG 3/01; SLJ 1/01) [973.8]

16280 Toynton, Evelyn. *Growing Up in America: 1830 to 1860* (4–6). Illus. 1995, Millbrook LB $24.90 (1-56294-453-3). 96pp. Describes the life of pre-Civil War children from five social groups, including Native Americans, slaves, and farmers. (Rev: BL 4/15/95; SLJ 4/95) [973.5]

16281 Turner, Glennette Tilley. *The Underground Railroad in Illinois* (5–8). Illus. 2001, Newman Educational Publg. $16.95 (0-938990-05-5). 320pp. Using a question-and-answer format, this book focuses on the Underground Railroad in Illinois, the historical period, the problems, people who worked on the effort, and the many heroic deeds. (Rev: BL 2/15/01) [973.7]

16282 Weber, Michael. *The Young Republic* (5–8). Illus. Series: Making of America. 2000, Raintree Steck-Vaughn $19.98 (0-8172-5703-9). 94pp. This well-illustrated account begins in the 1780s with the creation of the federal system, the ratification of the Constitution, and the inauguration of Washington as president in 1789. (Rev: BL 5/1/00; HBG 10/00; SLJ 9/00) [973]

16283 Wells, Rosemary. *Streets of Gold* (2–5). Illus. by Dan Andreasen. 1999, Dial $16.99 (0-8037-2149-8). 40pp. This picture book for older readers is the biography of a Russian Jewish girl who leaves the old country for a new life in America. (Rev: BCCB 7–8/99; BL 5/1/99; HBG 3/00; SLJ 6/99) [973]

PIONEER LIFE AND WESTWARD EXPANSION

16284 Alter, Judith. *The Santa Fe Trail* (3–5). Series: Cornerstones of Freedom. 1998, Children's LB $19.50 (0-516-21145-5). 32pp. A well-illustrat-ed account of the western trail that stretched from Missouri to Santa Fe. (Rev: BL 9/15/98; HBG 3/99) [978.8]

16285 Altman, Linda Jacobs. *The California Gold Rush in American History* (4–8). Illus. Series: In American History. 1997, Enslow LB $20.95 (0-89490-878-2). 128pp. After a brief history of the California Gold Rush, this book covers topics such as frontier injustice, racial discrimination, and the place of women. (Rev: HBG 3/98; SLJ 3/98) [979.4]

16286 Ammon, Richard. *Conestoga Wagons* (2–5). Illus. 2000, Holiday $16.95 (0-8234-1475-2). 32pp. This illustrated account gives the history of the vehicles used for long-distance hauling between 1750 and 1850 and discusses their construction, parts, uses, and the people who drove them. (Rev: BCCB 9/00; BL 10/1/00; HBG 3/01; SLJ 9/00) [388.3]

16287 Anderson, Joan. *Spanish Pioneers of the Southwest* (3–6). Illus. 1989, Dutton paper $16.00 (0-525-67546-9). 64pp. A photo-essay of life in mid-18th-century New Mexico. (Rev: BCCB 4/89; BL 4/15/89; SLJ 5/89)

16288 Anderson, Peter. *The Pony Express* (3–5). Illus. Series: Cornerstones of Freedom. 1996, Children's LB $20.00 (0-516-20002-X). 32pp. A brief history of the Pony Express, the men involved in its operation, and its contributions to the opening of the American West. (Rev: BL 11/15/96) [383]

16289 Bial, Raymond. *Frontier Home* (3–6). Illus. 1993, Houghton $17.00 (0-395-64046-6). 40pp. A description of the exteriors and contents of frontier homes, with many quotes from original sources. (Rev: BCCB 10/93; BL 11/1/93; SLJ 9/93) [978]

16290 Bial, Raymond. *Ghost Towns of the American West* (3–5). Illus. 2001, Houghton $16.00 (0-618-06557-1). Several western ghost towns are presented, with pictures of how they looked then and look today and details of why they were abandoned. (Rev: BCCB 2/01; BL 1/1–15/01; SLJ 2/01) [978]

16291 Blackwood, Gary L. *Life on the Oregon Trail* (5–8). Series: The Way People Live. 1999, Lucent LB $17.96 (1-56006-540-0). 111pp. Using many excerpts from diaries, this is a thorough, appealing account of life on the Oregon Trail, which took pioneers from Missouri to the Pacific Ocean. (Rev: HBG 3/00; SLJ 8/99) [978]

16292 Blashfield, Jean F. *The California Gold Rush* (3–6). Series: We the People. 2000, Compass Point LB $15.95 (0-7565-0041-9). 48pp. A straightforward account of why and how people traveled to California during the Gold Rush and of the lasting effects this migration had on western history. (Rev: SLJ 3/01) [979.4]

16293 Blashfield, Jean F. *The Oregon Trail* (3–6). 2000, Compass Point LB $15.95 (0-7565-0045-1). 48pp. This book explains the building of the Oregon Trail, its uses, and travel conditions along it. Also use: *The Santa Fe Trail* (2000). (Rev: SLJ 3/01) [978]

16294 Calabro, Marian. *The Perilous Journey of the Donner Party* (5–8). Illus. 1999, Clarion $20.00 (0-395-86610-3). 192pp. The story of the ill-fated Donner Party and their horrifying end on their way to California, as seen through the eyes of 12-year-old Virginia Reed. (Rev: BL 4/1/99*; HB 5–6/99) [979.4]

16295 Carlson, Laurie. *Westward Ho! An Activity Guide to the Wild West* (4–6). 1996, Chicago Review paper $12.95 (1-55652-271-1). 160pp. Clear directions accompany this introduction to 50 activities — like hooking rugs or keeping a trapper's journal — associated with the westward movement. (Rev: BL 10/1/96; SLJ 12/96) [978]

16296 Cobb, Mary. *The Quilt-Block History of Pioneer Days: With Projects Kids Can Make* (3–6). Illus. 1995, Millbrook LB $23.90 (1-56294-485-1). 64pp. A history of America's Western pioneers as seen through the patterns in their quilts plus a number of related craft projects, such as making bookmarks. (Rev: BL 4/15/95; SLJ 6/95) [746.9]

16297 Collier, Christopher, and James Lincoln Collier. *Indians, Cowboys, and Farmers: And the Battle for the Great Plains* (5–8). Series: The Drama of American History. 2001, Marshall Cavendish LB $20.95 (0-7614-1052-X). The excellently written and illustrated account covers the history of the Great Plains from the end of the Civil War to 1910, by which time the Native Americans had been scattered and the ranchers and farmers had reached a truce. (Rev: BL 3/15/01) [973.8]

16298 De Angelis, Gina. *The Black Cowboys* (4–8). Illus. Series: African American Achievers. 1997, Chelsea LB $19.95 (0-7910-2589-6); paper $9.95 (0-7910-2590-X). 64pp. As well as telling how African Americans helped open up the West, this book describes the contributions of black cowboys in the latter half of the 1800s and gives profiles of some, such as Nat Love and Bill Pickett. (Rev: BL 2/15/98; HBG 3/98) [978]

16299 De Angelis, Gina. *The Wild West* (5–8). Series: Costume, Tradition, and Culture: Reflecting on the Past. 1998, Chelsea LB $16.95 (0-7910-5169-2). 64pp. Illustrated with historical collectors' cards, this account relates the legends and stories of the Wild West — its explorers, lawmen, outlaws, and Native Americans. (Rev: BL 3/15/99; HBG 10/99) [978]

16300 Delgado, James P. *Shipwrecks from the Westward Movement* (5–7). Series: Shipwrecks. 2000, Watts LB $24.00 (0-531-20380-8). 64pp. A discussion and exploration of the shipwrecks — from small canoes to steam-powered riverboats — that occurred as European settlers moved across America. (Rev: BL 10/15/00) [978]

16301 Dolan, Edward F. *Beyond the Frontier: The Story of the Trails West* (4–8). Series: Great Journeys. 1999, Benchmark LB $21.95 (0-7614-0969-6). 112pp. As well as describing life on the Santa Fe, Oregon, and California trails, and the sea routes taken west, this account covers such specific topics as the Donner party and life in western settlements. (Rev: HBG 3/00; SLJ 2/00) [978]

16302 Emsden, Katharine. *Voices from the West: Life Along the Trail* (4–8). Series: Perspectives on History. 1993, Discovery paper $6.95 (1-878668-18-8). 60pp. Through excerpts from diaries, journals, and letters, the hardships and everyday life of pioneers along the Oregon and Santa Fe trails are re-created. (Rev: BL 11/15/93) [978]

16303 Fisher, Leonard Everett. *The Oregon Trail* (4–6). Illus. 1990, Holiday LB $18.95 (0-8234-0833-7). 64pp. A clear, readable account of the westward expansion in the 1800s. (Rev: BCCB 1/91; BL 12/15/90; HB 3–4/91; SLJ 1/91) [979.5]

16304 Fradin, Dennis B. *Pioneers* (2–4). Illus. 1984, Children's LB $21.00 (0-516-01927-9). 48pp. The story of the brave people who opened up the American West. (Rev: BL 3/1/85; SLJ 4/85)

16305 Freedman, Russell. *Children of the Wild West* (5–8). Illus. 1983, Houghton $18.00 (0-89919-143-6); paper $6.95 (0-395-54785-7). 128pp. The life of children on the frontier told in text and old photos.

16306 Freedman, Russell. *Cowboys of the Wild West* (5–8). Illus. 1990, Houghton paper $9.95 (0-395-54800-4). 128pp. Text and excellent historical photographs describe these romantic figures. (Rev: BCCB 12/85; HB 3–4/86)

16307 Gibbons, Gail. *Yippee-Yay! A Book About Cowboys and Cowgirls* (1–4). Illus. by author. 1998, Little, Brown $14.95 (0-316-30944-3). Focusing on a period of 30 years after the Civil War, this account describes the life and gear of a cowboy, with strongest coverage on the roundup. (Rev: BL 4/15/98; HBG 10/98; SLJ 3/98) [978]

16308 Gillespie, Sarah. *A Pioneer Farm Girl: The Diary of Sarah Gillespie, 1877–1878* (4–6). Series: Diaries, Letters, and Memoirs. 2000, Capstone LB $22.60 (0-7368-0347-5). 32pp. Told in diary entries, this is the true story of everyday life on a pioneer farm after the Civil War as experienced by a young girl. (Rev: BL 10/15/00; HBG 10/00; SLJ 9/00) [978]

16309 Gorsline, Marie, and Douglas Gorsline. *Cowboys* (3–4). Illus. by Douglas Gorsline. 1980, Random paper $3.25 (0-394-83935-8). 32pp. An amazing amount of information is included in this slim text.

16310 Granfield, Linda. *Cowboy: An Album* (5–7). Illus. 1994, Ticknor $18.95 (0-395-68430-7). 96pp. The history of the cowboy, legends about him, and his daily life are covered, with material on cowboys from minority groups. (Rev: BCCB 3/94; BL 2/1/94; SLJ 1/94*) [636.2]

16311 Green, Carl R., and William R. Sanford. *The Dalton Gang* (4–8). Illus. Series: Outlaws and Lawmen. 1995, Enslow LB $16.95 (0-89490-588-0). 48pp. The story of the gang of outlaws who roamed the West during pioneer days. (Rev: BL 11/15/95) [978]

16312 Gunderson, Mary. *Oregon Trail Cooking* (4–7). Series: Exploring History Through Simple Recipes. 2000, Capstone LB $22.60 (0-7368-0355-6). 32pp. This book tells about journeys on the Oregon Trail, the lifestyles of the pioneers, the foods they ate, and some of the recipes that they used.

Also use *Cowboy Cooking* (2000). (Rev: BL 8/00; HBG 10/00; SLJ 12/00) [973.5]

16313 Hakim, Joy. *The New Nation.* 2nd ed. (5–8). Series: A History of Us. 1999, Oxford LB $18.95 (0-19-512757-9); paper $12.95 (0-19-512758-7). 192pp. Political and social developments, including territorial expansion and pioneer life, are covered in this excellent history of America from 1789 through 1850. (Rev: BL 12/15/99) [973.5]

16314 Harness, Cheryl. *They're Off! The Story of the Pony Express* (3–5). Illus. 1996, Simon & Schuster $16.00 (0-689-80523-3). 28pp. A vivid account of the origin of the Pony Express prior to the Civil War and the typical life of a rider. (Rev: BL 11/15/96; SLJ 12/96) [383]

16315 Hatt, Christine. *The American West: Native Americans, Pioneers and Settlers* (4–7). Series: History in Writing. 1999, Bedrick $19.95 (0-87226-290-1). 62pp. A broad overview of frontier life in America with material on such topics as the Louisiana Purchase, Indian relocations, the Gold Rush, and a settler's daily life. (Rev: HBG 3/00; SLJ 5/99) [978]

16316 Hester, Sallie. *A Covered Wagon Girl: The Diary of Sallie Hester, 1849–1850* (4–6). Series: Diaries, Letters, and Memoirs. 2000, Capstone LB $22.60 (0-7368-0344-0). 32pp. Diary entries by a young pioneer girl reveal everyday life on the American frontier. (Rev: BL 10/15/00; HBG 10/00; SLJ 9/00) [978]

16317 Isaacs, Sally Senzell. *Life on a Pioneer Homestead* (1–3). Series: Picture the Past. 2000, Heinemann LB $21.36 (1-57572-313-1). Using double-page spreads, this well-organized account covers such basic topics as pioneer food, clothing, and rearing of children. Also use from this series *Life on the Oregon Trail* (2000). (Rev: HBG 3/01; SLJ 11/00) [978]

16318 Johmann, Carol A., and Elizabeth J. Rieth. *Going West! Journey on a Wagon Train to Settle a Frontier Town* (3–6). Illus. by Michael Kline. Series: Kaleidoscope Kids. 2000, Williamson paper $10.95 (1-885593-38-4). 96pp. As well as information on wagon trains, this book gives good background history involving the opening up of the West and outlines projects that use the crafts and skills of the pioneers. (Rev: SLJ 1/01) [978]

16319 Kallen, Stuart A. *Life on the American Frontier* (5–8). Series: The Way People Live. 1998, Lucent LB $17.96 (1-56006-366-1). 108pp. Thematically arranged chapters offer material on everyday life on the American frontier and on such groups as the trailblazers, the mountain men, the miners, the railroad men, the sodbusters, and the cattlemen. (Rev: SLJ 1/99) [973.5]

16320 Kalman, Bobbie. *Bandannas, Chaps, and Ten-Gallon Hats* (3–6). Series: Life in the Old West. 1999, Crabtree LB $14.37 (0-7787-0073-9); paper $7.16 (0-7787-0105-0). 32pp. An interesting but somewhat disorganized account on the part played by cowboys in the opening up of the West. (Rev: SLJ 9/99) [978]

16321 Kalman, Bobbie. *The Gristmill* (3–6). Illus. Series: Historic Communities. 1991, Crabtree LB $20.60 (0-86505-486-X); paper $7.95 (0-86505-506-8). 32pp. Text and pictures show the construction and operation of the mill as well as the skills of the millers. (Rev: BL 7/91) [664]

16322 Kalman, Bobbie. *Home Crafts* (3–6). Illus. Series: Historic Communities. 1991, Crabtree LB $20.60 (0-86505-485-1); paper $7.95 (0-86505-505-X). 32pp. How early settlers produced wool and other cloth and made quilts, soap, leather goods, and other necessities. (Rev: BL 7/91) [745.5]

16323 Kalman, Bobbie. *In the Barn* (3–6). Illus. Series: Historic Communities. 1997, Crabtree LB $20.60 (0-86505-433-9); paper $7.95 (0-86505-463-0). 32pp. Shows how the barn was the center of activity on a settler's farm and supplies details on its design, barn raising, and all the seasonal activities it housed. (Rev: BL 7/97) [631.2]

16324 Kalman, Bobbie. *The Kitchen* (3–6). Illus. Series: Historic Communities. 1991, Crabtree LB $20.60 (0-86505-484-3); paper $7.95 (0-86505-504-1). 32pp. The kitchen and its utensils as they existed in pioneer times are pictured and described. (Rev: BL 7/91) [643.3]

16325 Kalman, Bobbie. *A One-Room School* (3–5). Illus. Series: Historic Communities. 1994, Crabtree LB $20.60 (0-86505-497-5); paper $7.95 (0-86505-517-3). 32pp. Through pictures and text, the physical plan of a one-room school is presented, with material on supplies, routines, expected conduct, and school rules. (Rev: SLJ 9/94) [371.7]

16326 Kalman, Bobbie. *Settler Sayings* (3–5). Illus. Series: Historic Communities. 1994, Crabtree LB $20.60 (0-86505-498-3); paper $7.95 (0-86505-518-1). 32pp. In a conversational text, sayings popular with settlers are described under such headings as the kitchen and the farm. (Rev: SLJ 7/94) [973.8]

16327 Kalman, Bobbie. *Visiting a Village* (3–6). Illus. Series: Historic Communities. 1991, Crabtree $20.60 (0-86505-487-8); paper $7.95 (0-86505-507-6). 32pp. Life in a frontier village is described in this well-illustrated account. (Rev: BL 7/91) [971]

16328 Kalman, Bobbie. *Who Settled the West?* (3–6). Series: Life in the Old West. 1999, Crabtree LB $14.37 (0-7787-0075-5); paper $7.16 (0-7787-0107-7). 32pp. An eclectic collection of material about the various groups of pioneers who settled in the West. Also use *Boomtowns of the West.* (Rev: SLJ 9/99) [978]

16329 Kalman, Bobbie, and Kate Calder. *The Life of a Miner* (3–6). Series: Life in the Old West. 1999, Crabtree LB $14.97 (0-7787-0077-1); paper $7.16 (0-7787-0109-3). 32pp. This well-researched title traces the development of the mining industry in the mid-1800s and takes the reader underground to show how miners worked. (Rev: SLJ 5/00) [973.6]

16330 Kalman, Bobbie, and Kate Calder. *Women of the West* (3–6). 1999, Crabtree LB $14.97 (0-7787-0080-1); paper $7.16 (0-7787-0112-3). 32pp. Traces the roles of both white and Native American women in the history of the old West with material on daily life and hardships. (Rev: SLJ 5/00) [973.6]

16331 Kalman, Bobbie, and Tammy Everts. *Customs and Traditions* (3–5). Illus. Series: Historic Communities. 1994, Crabtree LB $20.60 (0-86505-495-9); paper $7.95 (0-86505-515-7). 32pp. Various customs and traditions from the days of the settlers are described and their origins traced in this heavily illustrated volume. (Rev: SLJ 7/94) [973.8]

16332 Kalman, Bobbie, and David Schimpky. *Fort Life* (3–5). Illus. Series: Historic Communities. 1994, Crabtree LB $20.60 (0-86505-496-7); paper $7.95 (0-86505-516-5). 32pp. This book describes life in a fort, with details on early American defenses and the daily life of soldiers. (Rev: SLJ 9/94) [978]

16333 Ketchum, Liza. *The Gold Rush* (5–8). Illus. 1996, Little, Brown paper $12.95 (0-316-49047-4). 128pp. An overview of the Gold Rush in California and its effects on the development of the West, based on the PBS series. (Rev: BL 8/96; SLJ 10/96) [979.4]

16334 King, David C. *Pioneer Days: Discover the Past with Fun Projects, Games, Activities, and Recipes* (3–6). Illus. by Bobbie Moore. Series: American Kids in History. 1997, Wiley paper $12.95 (0-471-16169-1). 118pp. In chapters arranged by season, the daily life of pioneers is re-created through an assortment of history, culture, crafts, and stories. (Rev: SLJ 2/98) [973.5]

16335 Klausmeier, Robert. *Cowboy* (4–7). Illus. Series: American Pastfinder. 1996, Lerner LB $21.50 (0-8225-2975-0). 48pp. This account focuses on the huge cattle drives and the men who led them in the years following the Civil War. (Rev: BL 3/1/96; SLJ 3/96) [636.2]

16336 Knight, Amelia S. *The Way West: Journal of a Pioneer Woman* (2–5). Illus. by Michael McCurdy. 1993, Simon & Schuster paper $16.00 (0-671-72375-8). 32pp. Using parts of a pioneer woman's story of life on the trail from Iowa to Oregon in 1853, this book presents, with stunning woodcuts, a realistic picture of life on the frontier. (Rev: BL 11/15/93; HB 9–10/93; SLJ 9/93) [917.8]

16337 Krehbiel, Randy. *Little Bighorn* (4–8). Illus. Series: Battlefields Across America. 1997, Twenty-First Century $23.40 (0-8050-5236-4). 64pp. After good background material, this account describes the battle and tells about the site as it is today. (Rev: SLJ 1/98) [973.8]

16338 Krensky, Stephen. *Striking It Rich: The Story of the California Gold Rush* (2–3). Illus. by Anna DiVito. 1996, Simon & Schuster $15.00 (0-689-80804-6); paper $3.99 (0-689-80803-8). 48pp. A very simple retelling of the excitement and pain involved in the California Gold Rush. (Rev: BCCB 11/96; BL 9/15/96; SLJ 2/97) [979.4]

16339 La Pierre, Yvette. *Welcome to Josefina's World, 1824* (3–6). Series: The American Girls Collection. 1999, Pleasant $14.95 (1-56247-769-2). 58pp. With excellent illustrations and good historical information, this book uses a series of double-page spreads to introduce life on the American Southwest frontier in 1824 as experienced by a young girl. (Rev: BL 1/1–15/00; HBG 3/00) [973.4]

16340 Leeper, David R. *The Diary of David R. Leeper: Rush for Gold* (3–6). Ed. by Connie Roop and Peter Roop. Illus. Series: My Own Words. 2000, Marshall Cavendish LB $16.95 (0-7614-1011-2). 64pp. This book, taken from Leeper's memoirs published in 1894, tells how he crossed the country by wagon train and his life as a prospector for gold in California. (Rev: BL 2/15/01; HBG 3/01; SLJ 3/01) [979.4]

16341 Loeper, John J. *Meet the Drakes on the Kentucky Frontier* (3–5). Series: Early American Family. 1998, Marshall Cavendish LB $25.64 (0-7614-0845-2). 64pp. Based on fact, this account depicts the life of the Drake family, who moved to the unsettled Kentucky frontier in 1781. (Rev: HBG 10/99; SLJ 4/99) [973.3]

16342 Loeper, John J. *Meet the Wards on the Oregon Trail* (3–5). Series: Early American Family. 1998, Marshall Cavendish LB $25.64 (0-7614-0844-4). 64pp. Using many authentic details, this is an exciting re-creation of a family's everyday experiences as they travel on the Oregon Trail in the 1850s. (Rev: HBG 10/99; SLJ 4/99) [973.6]

16343 Miller, Brandon M. *Buffalo Gals: Women of the Old West* (4–7). Illus. 1995, Lerner LB $22.60 (0-8225-1730-2). 88pp. A realistic portrait of the hardships faced by women pioneers during the 19th century on the Western frontier. (Rev: BCCB 7–8/95; BL 5/1/95; SLJ 6/95*) [978]

16344 Monceaux, Morgan, and Ruth Katcher. *My Heroes, My People: African Americans and Native Americans in the West* (3–6). Illus. 1999, Farrar $18.00 (0-374-30770-9). 64pp. This book traces the role played by African Americans, Native Americans, and people of mixed race in the opening of the American West. (Rev: BCCB 1/00; BL 11/1/99; HBG 3/00) [978]

16345 Morley, Jacqueline. *How Would You Survive in the American West?* (4–7). Illus. Series: How Would You Survive? 1996, Watts LB $25.00 (0-531-14382-1). 48pp. Information about supplies and shelter are given in this imaginary journey through the American West, with encounters with Native Americans, buffalo, and various obstacles. (Rev: BL 5/15/96) [978]

16346 Nelson, Sharlene, and Ted Nelson. *Bull Whackers to Whistle Punks: Logging in the Old West* (4–6). Illus. 1996, Watts LB $22.50 (0-531-20228-3). 63pp. The early days of logging in the West, with descriptions of each of the jobs and the tools used. (Rev: BL 8/96; SLJ 7/96) [634.6]

16347 Nirgiotis, Nicholas. *West by Waterway: Rivers and U.S. Expansion* (4–6). Illus. 1995, Watts LB $22.50 (0-531-20188-0). 64pp. A history of the opening up of the West that emphasizes the roles played by boats and inland waterways. (Rev: BL 9/1/95) [386]

16348 Patent, Dorothy Hinshaw. *Homesteading: Settling America's Heartland* (2–5). Photos by William Munoz. 1998, Walker $16.95 (0-8027-8664-2). 32pp. Building a sod house, farming, housekeeping, schooling, and amusements are some of the subjects in this account of homesteading on the American frontier. (Rev: BL 11/1/98; HBG 10/99; SLJ 10/98) [978]

16349 Patent, Dorothy Hinshaw. *West by Covered Wagon: Retracing the Pioneer Trails* (3–6). Illus. by William Munoz. 1995, Walker LB $16.85 (0-8027-8378-3). 32pp. A modern covered-wagon trip is compared to the original journeys accomplished by pioneers as they opened up the West. (Rev: BCCB 11/95; BL 11/1/95; SLJ 10/95*) [978]

16350 Paul, Ann W. *The Seasons Sewn: A Year in Patchwork* (4–6). Illus. by Michael McCurdy. 1996, Harcourt $16.00 (0-15-276918-8). 40pp. Various squares on historical patchwork quilts reflect life on the American frontier in the late 19th century. (Rev: BCCB 5/96; BL 4/1/96; SLJ 5/96) [746.46]

16351 Pelta, Kathy. *Cattle Trails: "Git Along Little Dogies."* (4–6). Illus. Series: American Trails. 1997, Raintree Steck-Vaughn LB $28.55 (0-8172-4073-X). 96pp. A thorough discussion of the cattle drives that were a part of Western history from 1850 to 1890. (Rev: BL 7/97; SLJ 12/97) [978]

16352 Pelta, Kathy. *The Royal Roads: Spanish Trails in North America* (4–6). Illus. Series: American Trails. 1997, Raintree Steck-Vaughn LB $28.55 (0-8172-4074-8). 96pp. The story of Spanish trails in California, Florida, New Mexico, and Texas, and the people who traveled them looking for material or spiritual gains. (Rev: BL 7/97; SLJ 12/97) [970.01]

16353 Reef, Catherine. *Buffalo Soldiers* (4–6). Illus. 1993, Twenty-First Century LB $22.90 (0-8050-2372-0). 80pp. The story of the African American regiments that helped protect settlers during the westward movement. (Rev: BL 8/93) [978]

16354 Ritchie, David. *Frontier Life* (5–7). Illus. Series: Life in America 100 Years Ago. 1995, Chelsea $19.95 (0-7910-2842-9). 104pp. A concise overview of life on the American frontier that does not gloss over the harsh and often violent aspects. (Rev: SLJ 1/96) [973.5]

16355 Roop, Peter, and Connie Roop. *Westward, Ho, Ho, Ho!* (3–5). Illus. 1996, Millbrook LB $21.90 (0-7613-0020-1). 40pp. This book mixes a history of the American West with appropriate riddles and cartoons. (Rev: BL 12/15/96; SLJ 1/97) [978]

16356 Ross, Stewart. *Cowboys* (5–7). Illus. Series: Fact or Fiction. 1995, Millbrook LB $24.90 (1-56294-618-8). 48pp. The life of cowboys during the late 1800s is covered, with information that tries to separate fact from fable. (Rev: BL 7/95; SLJ 5/95) [978.02]

16357 Russell, Marion. *Along the Santa Fe Trail: Marion Russell's Own Story* (3–5). Adapted by Ginger Wadsworth. Illus. by James Watling. 1993, Albert Whitman LB $16.95 (0-8075-0295-2). 32pp. In a reworking of a memoir of pioneer life, the experiences of a seven-year-old traveling in a wagon train on the Santa Fe Trail are recalled. (Rev: BL 1/15/94; SLJ 12/93) [917.8]

16358 Sakurai, Gail. *Asian-Americans in the Old West* (4–6). Series: Cornerstones of Freedom. 2000, Children's LB $20.00 (0-516-21152-8). 32pp. A history of Asian Americans' contributions to the opening up of the West — how they helped to build the railroads and how they were shamelessly exploited. (Rev: BL 5/15/00) [978]

16359 Sandler, Martin W. *Vaqueros: America's First Cowboys* (3–8). 2001, Holt $18.00 (0-8050-6019-7). 117pp. A interesting account that traces the role of the *vaquero* — the Hispanic cowboy — in the opening up of the West and in the history of ranch development in the U.S. (Rev: HB 1–2/01; SLJ 1/01) [978]

16360 Sanford, William R. *The Chisholm Trail in American History* (4–6). Series: In American History. 2000, Enslow LB $19.95 (0-7660-1345-6). 112pp. This book traces the history of the Chisholm Trail, the daily life of the cowboys who used it, and its eventual demise. (Rev: HBG 3/01; SLJ 12/00) [978]

16361 Santella, Andrew. *The Chisholm Trail* (3–5). Series: Cornerstones of Freedom. 1997, Children's LB $20.50 (0-516-20393-2). 32pp. The history of the cattle trail from San Antonio, Texas, to Abilene, Kansas, with information on its lasting importance. (Rev: BL 12/15/97; HBG 3/98) [973.6]

16362 Savage, Jeff. *Cowboys and Cow Towns of the Wild West* (4–7). Illus. Series: Trailblazers of the Wild West. 1995, Enslow LB $16.95 (0-89490-603-8). 48pp. Through the experiences of a single cowboy, the reader learns about his equipment, dangers, leisure time, cattle drives, and roundups. (Rev: SLJ 2/96) [978]

16363 Savage, Jeff. *Gunfighters of the Wild West* (3–5). Illus. Series: Trailblazers of the Wild West. 1995, Enslow LB $16.95 (0-89490-600-3). 48pp. This book briefly covers the lives and exploits of such gunslingers as Doc Holliday, the Earps, John Fisher King, Billy the Kid, the Jameses, the Daltons, and the Wild Bunch. (Rev: SLJ 1/96) [973.5]

16364 Savage, Jeff. *Pioneering Women of the Wild West* (3–5). Illus. Series: Trailblazers of the Wild West. 1995, Enslow LB $16.95 (0-89490-604-6). 48pp. The struggles and hardships of women in the Wild West are covered, with particular mention of such famous characters as Calamity Jane and Carrie Nation. (Rev: SLJ 1/96) [973.5]

16365 Schanzer, Rosalyn. *Gold Fever! Tales from the California Gold Rush* (3–5). Illus. 1999, National Geographic $17.95 (0-7922-7303-6). 48pp. Beginning with the discovery of gold nuggets at Sutter's Mill in 1847, this story of the California Gold Rush is told through diaries and original writings. (Rev: BCCB 6/99; BL 4/15/99; HBG 10/99; SLJ 4/99) [979.4]

16366 Schlissel, Lillian. *Black Frontiers: A History of African-American Heroes in the Old West* (3–6). Illus. 1995, Simon & Schuster $18.00 (0-689-80285-4). 80pp. Through the experiences of a cross-section of African Americans — homesteaders, cowboys, mountain men, and some that defy classification — the history of the American West comes to life. (Rev: BCCB 1/96; BL 1/1–15/96; SLJ 12/95) [978]

16367 Schroeder, Lisa Golden. *California Gold Rush Cooking* (4–7). Series: Exploring History Through Simple Recipes. 2000, Capstone LB $22.60 (0-7368-0603-2). 32pp. This book discusses the California Gold Rush and everyday life of the period with details of the kinds of food eaten and some simple recipes. (Rev: BL 3/1/01) [979.4]

16368 Sherrow, Victoria. *Life During the Gold Rush* (5–9). Series: The Way People Live. 1998, Lucent LB $17.96 (1-56006-382-3). 96pp. This story of the California Gold Rush, from Sutter's Mill to the advent of huge companies, gives good information on the daily life of the forty-niners. (Rev: SLJ 12/98) [979.5]

16369 Shuter, Jane, ed. *Francis Parkman and the Plains Indians* (5–8). Illus. Series: History Eyewitness. 1995, Raintree Steck-Vaughn LB $24.26 (0-8114-8280-4). 48pp. An edited and abridged version of Parkman's autobiographical writing about the opening up of the West and the Oregon Trail. (Rev: BL 4/15/95) [978]

16370 Shuter, Jane, ed. *Sarah Royce and the American West* (5–8). Illus. Series: History Eyewitness. 1996, Raintree Steck-Vaughn LB $24.26 (0-8114-8286-3). 48pp. Pioneer life on the American frontier is described, based on the firsthand account of Sarah Royce. (Rev: BL 5/15/96; SLJ 6/96) [978]

16371 Sinnott, Susan. *Welcome to Kirsten's World, 1854: Growing Up in Pioneer America* (3–6). Illus. Series: American Girls Collection. 1999, Pleasant $14.95 (1-56247-770-6). 58pp. As seen through the eyes of a family of Swedish immigrants, this account describes frontier life in the Minnesota Territory in the 1840s. (Rev: BL 1/1–15/00; HBG 3/00) [978]

16372 Stanley, Jerry. *Frontier Merchants: Lionel and Barron Jacobs and the Jewish Pioneers Who Settled the West* (5–10). 1998, Crown LB $20.99 (0-517-80020-9). 100pp. This fascinating biography of the Jacobs brothers, who set up a successful business venture in Tucson in 1867, illustrates business development in pioneer communities and the role of Jewish immigrants in building the economic foundation of the West. (Rev: HBG 3/99; SLJ 3/99) [973.8]

16373 Steedman, Scott. *A Frontier Fort on the Oregon Trail* (4–6). Illus. Series: Inside Story. 1994, Bedrick $18.95 (0-87226-371-1); paper $10.95 (0-87226-264-2). 48pp. An examination of both the exterior and interior of a frontier fort, with details on its construction and everyday life in it. (Rev: BL 10/15/94; SLJ 9/94) [978]

16374 Stefoff, Rebecca. *Children of the Westward Trail* (4–7). Illus. 1996, Millbrook LB $23.40 (1-56294-582-3). 96pp. An account of the westward movement that relies heavily on first-person accounts. (Rev: BL 5/15/96; SLJ 7/96) [917.804]

16375 Stefoff, Rebecca. *First Frontier* (4–7). Series: North American Historical Atlases. 2000, Benchmark LB $16.95 (0-7614-1059-7). 48pp. This book presents an illustrated view of the western expansion and its effects on Native Americans, frontiers-

men, speculators, and soldiers. (Rev: HBG 3/01; SLJ 1/01) [978]

16376 Stein, R. Conrad. *The California Gold Rush* (3–6). Illus. Series: Cornerstones of Freedom. 1995, Children's LB $20.50 (0-516-06691-9). 30pp. A brief review of the salient facts in the California Gold Rush, beginning at Sutter's sawmill in 1848. (Rev: SLJ 7/95) [979.5]

16377 Stein, R. Conrad. *In the Spanish West* (4–8). Series: How We Lived. 1999, Benchmark LB $18.95 (0-7614-0906-8). 72pp. This well-balanced account describes the American West under Spanish control and influence with material on history, social life, agriculture, and home life. (Rev: HBG 10/00; SLJ 3/00) [978]

16378 Stein, R. Conrad. *On the Old Western Frontier* (4–8). Series: How We Lived. 1999, Benchmark LB $18.95 (0-7614-0909-2). 72pp. An interesting book that gives an overview of the history and living conditions on the American frontier with material on everyday life, farming and ranching, social life, religion, Native Americans, and slaves. (Rev: HBG 10/00; SLJ 3/00) [978]

16379 Sundling, Charles W. *Cowboys of the Frontier* (4–6). Illus. Series: Frontier Land. 2000, ABDO $15.95 (1-57765-045-X). 32pp. An accessible text that describes the daily life of hardworking cattle drivers, with emphasis on the second half of the 19th century. (Rev: BL 10/15/00; HBG 10/00; SLJ 7/00) [978]

16380 Sundling, Charles W. *Explorers of the Frontier* (4–6). Series: Frontier Land. 2000, ABDO LB $15.95 (1-57765-044-1). 32pp. Using many easy-to-read maps and a fact-filled text, this book traces the exploits of the explorers who opened up the West. A companion volume is *Mountain Men of the Frontier* (2000). (Rev: BL 10/15/00; HBG 10/00) [978]

16381 Sundling, Charles W. *Pioneers of the Frontier* (4–6). Series: Frontier Land. 2000, ABDO LB $15.95 (1-57765-047-6). 32pp. The day-to-day struggles of the early pioneers of the West are re-created in text and pictures. Also use *Women of the Frontier* (2000). (Rev: BL 10/15/00; HBG 10/00) [978]

16382 Toht, David W. *Sodbuster* (3–6). Illus. by Richard Erickson. Series: American Pastfinder. 1996, Lerner LB $21.50 (0-8225-2977-7). 48pp. In double-page chapters, the life of early pioneers is described, with many quotes from original sources. (Rev: SLJ 3/96) [973.6]

16383 Van Steenwyk, Elizabeth. *The California Gold Rush: West with the Forty-Niners* (3–7). Illus. Series: First Books. 1991, Watts LB $21.00 (0-531-20032-9). 64pp. A vivid retelling of a fascinating chapter in America's past, from Sutter's arrival in California in 1839 to glimpses of such pioneers as Levi Strauss and Mark Hopkins. (Rev: BL 1/1/92; SLJ 12/91) [979.4]

16384 Warren, Andrea. *Pioneer Girl: Growing Up on the Prairie* (3–6). 1998, Morrow $15.00 (0-688-15438-7). 96pp. Based on the memoirs of Grace McCance Snyder, this is the true story of a homesteading family in Nebraska during the late 1800s.

(Rev: BCCB 12/98; BL 10/1/98; HB 11–12/98; HBG 3/99; SLJ 11/98) [978.2]

16385 Winslow, Mimi. *Loggers and Railroad Workers* (5–8). Illus. Series: Settling the West. 1995, Twenty-First Century LB $20.40 (0-8050-2997-4). 96pp. The story of the men and machines who settled in the West, cleared the wilderness, and built the railroads that opened the way for agriculture and industry. (Rev: SLJ 9/95) [973.8]

16386 Worcester, Don. *Cowboy with a Camera, Erwin E. Smith: Cowboy Photographer* (3–5). 1999, Amon Carter Museum $18.95 (0-88360-091-9). 48pp. With photos from the turn of the last century, this book chronicles the life and work of cowboys, including roping, wrangling, and bronco busting. (Rev: BCCB 2/99; BL 1/1–15/99; HBG 10/99) [636.2]

THE CIVIL WAR

16387 Beller, Susan P. *Billy Yank and Johnny Reb: Soldiering in the Civil War* (5–8). Illus. 2000, Twenty-First Century $26.90 (0-7613-1869-0). 96pp. Solid, interesting information is provided in this illustrated account that describes the everyday life of soldiers on both sides of the Civil War. (Rev: BL 10/15/00; HBG 3/01; SLJ 12/00) [973.7]

16388 Beller, Susan P. *The Confederate Ladies of Richmond* (5–8). Illus. 1999, Twenty-First Century LB $25.90 (0-7613-1470-9). 96pp. The Civil War seen through the eyes and activities of the upperclass women of Richmond, the capital of the Confederacy. (Rev: BCCB 1/00; BL 12/15/99; HBG 3/00) [973.7]

16389 Black, Wallace B. *Blockade Runners and Ironclads: Naval Action in the Civil War* (3–5). Illus. Series: First Books. 1997, Watts $22.50 (0-531-20272-0). 64pp. Introduces naval operations during the Civil War, with material on battles, strategies, shipbuilding, and prominent military personnel. (Rev: BL 2/1/98; HBG 3/98) [973.7]

16390 Black, Wallace B. *Slaves to Soldiers: African-American Fighting Men in the Civil War* (4–6). Series: First Books. 1998, Watts LB $21.00 (0-531-20252-6). 63pp. This story of the African Americans who served during the Civil War discusses the campaigns in which they participated. (Rev: HBG 10/98; SLJ 10/98) [973.7]

16391 Blashfield, Jean F. *Horse Soldiers: Cavalry in the Civil War* (4–6). 1998, Watts LB $22.00 (0-531-20300-X). A history of the the Union and Confederate cavalries, their officers, and their roles in the Civil War. (Rev: BL 8/98; HBG 10/98; SLJ 8/98) [793.7]

16392 Blashfield, Jean F. *Mines and Minie Balls* (4–6). Illus. Series: First Books. 1997, Watts LB $22.50 (0-531-20273-9). 64pp. Discusses Union and Confederate weapons at the beginning of the Civil War and shows how they became more deadly and sophisticated as the war went on. (Rev: BL 1/1–15/98; HBG 3/98) [973.7]

16393 Blashfield, Jean F. *Women at the Front: Their Changing Roles in the Civil War* (4–6). Illus. Series: First Books. 1997, Watts LB $22.50 (0-531-20275-5). 64pp. An introduction to the roles of female nurses, spies, soldiers, and camp followers during the Civil War, with material on women on the home front. (Rev: BL 1/1–15/98; HBG 3/98) [973.7]

16394 Brooks, Victor. *African Americans in the Civil War* (4–8). Illus. Series: Untold History of the Civil War. 2000, Chelsea $17.95 (0-7910-5435-7). 64pp. This book describes African American soldiers' roles in the Civil War, on both the Confederate and Union sides. (Rev: BL 5/15/00; HBG 10/00; SLJ 6/00) [355.7]

16395 Brooks, Victor. *Civil War Forts* (4–8). Illus. Series: Untold History of the Civil War. 2000, Chelsea $17.95 (0-7910-5438-1). 64pp. Describes the important roles played by such forts as Fort Sumter and Fort Wagner in South Carolina, Fort Fischer in North Carolina, Fort Henry and Fort Donelson in Tennessee, and the city of Vicksburg, Mississippi. (Rev: BL 5/15/00; HBG 10/00; SLJ 7/00) [973.7]

16396 Brooks, Victor. *Secret Weapons in the Civil War* (4–8). Series: Untold History of the Civil War. 2000, Chelsea $17.95 (0-7910-5433-0). 64pp. Covers such secret weapons and maneuvers as underwater transportation, advanced artillery, communications devices, and explosive materials. (Rev: BL 5/15/00; HBG 10/00; SLJ 7/00) [973.7]

16397 Carey, Charles W. *The Emancipation Proclamation* (4–6). Series: Journey to Freedom. 1999, Child's World LB $16.95 (1-56766-620-5). 32pp. Sepia-toned illustrations enhance this account of the end of slavery, the document's importance in African American history, and the civil war that resulted. (Rev: BL 10/15/99; HBG 3/00) [973.7]

16398 Clinton, Catherine. *Scholastic Encyclopedia of the Civil War* (4–7). Illus. 1999, Scholastic $18.95 (0-590-37227-0). 112pp. Using many black-and-white illustrations, this narrative gives a good chronological introduction to the Civil War, with interesting supplementary information. (Rev: BL 1/1–15/00; HBG 3/00; SLJ 5/00) [973.7]

16399 Collier, Christopher, and James Lincoln Collier. *The Civil War, 1860–1865* (5–8). Series: Drama of American History. 1999, Marshall Cavendish LB $20.95 (0-7614-0818-5). 95pp. A dramatic, accurate account that covers causes, leaders, battles, effects, and the immediate aftermath of the Civil War. (Rev: BL 2/15/00; HBG 10/00; SLJ 3/00) [973.7]

16400 Damon, Duane. *When This Cruel War Is Over* (5–8). Illus. 1996, Lerner LB $22.60 (0-8225-1731-0). 88pp. Behind-the-scenes of Civil War battlefields and the social conditions on the home front are covered. (Rev: BL 8/96; SLJ 8/96*) [973.7]

16401 Day, Nancy. *Your Travel Guide to Civil War America* (4–8). Series: Passport to History. 2000, Lerner LB $26.60 (0-8225-3078-3). 96pp. Using the format of a guide book, this account takes the reader back to the Civil War with coverage on topics including food, civil and military clothing, Lincoln's office, Gettysburg, and various battlefields. (Rev: BL 3/1/01) [073.7]

16402 Dolan, Edward F. *The American Civil War: A House Divided* (5–8). Illus. 1997, Millbrook LB $28.90 (0-7613-0255-7). 112pp. A chronologically arranged, well-organized account of the Civil War, beginning with the shots fired at Fort Sumter. (Rev: BL 3/1/98; HBG 3/98; SLJ 3/98) [973.7]

16403 Dosier, Susan. *Civil War Cooking: The Confederacy* (4–7). Series: Exploring History Through Simple Recipes. 2000, Capstone LB $22.60 (0-7368-0350-5). 32pp. As well as simple, authentic recipes of Civil War times, this book tells of customs, family roles, and everyday life during this period. Also use *Civil War Cooking: The Union* (2000). (Rev: BL 8/00; HBG 10/00) [973.7]

16404 Egger-Bovet, Howard, and Marlene Smith-Baranzini. *Book of the American Civil War* (5–7). Illus. by D. J. Simison. Series: Brown Paper School. 1998, Little, Brown $21.95 (0-316-22239-9); paper $12.95 (0-316-22243-7). 95pp. Facts, photographs, illustrations, stories and appealing activities are combined in this overview of the Civil War. (Rev: SLJ 12/98) [973.7]

16405 Feinberg, Barbara S. *Abraham Lincoln's Gettysburg Address: Four Score and More . . .* (4–8). Illus. 2000, Twenty-First Century LB $24.40 (0-7613-1410-8). 80pp. Illustrated with period photographs, this well-researched volume reveals surprising facts about the Gettysburg Address and its delivery. (Rev: BL 11/15/00) [973.7]

16406 Fleischman, Paul. *Bull Run* (5–8). 1993, HarperCollins LB $14.89 (0-06-021447-3). 102pp. An innovative account of the first great battle of the Civil War. (Rev: BCCB 3/93; BL 5-6/93) [973.7]

16407 Fraser, Mary Ann. *Vicksburg: The Battle That Won the Civil War* (4–8). Illus. 1999, Holt $16.95 (0-8050-6106-1). 100pp. The focus of this book is the Battle of Vicksburg, the events surrounding it, the participants, and its importance. (Rev: BCCB 1/00; BL 3/1/00; HBG 3/00; SLJ 3/00) [973.7]

16408 Fritz, Jean. *Just a Few Words, Mr. Lincoln: The Story of the Gettysburg Address* (1–3). Illus. by Charles Robinson. 1993, Putnam paper $3.99 (0-448-40170-3). 48pp. An easy-to-read book that tells the background of the Gettysburg Address and explains its importance. (Rev: BL 10/1/93; SLJ 10/93) [973.7]

16409 Gay, Kathlyn, and Martin Gay. *Civil War* (5–8). Illus. Series: Voices from the Past. 1995, Twenty-First Century LB $18.90 (0-8050-2845-5). 64pp. An introduction to the causes, events, and consequences of the Civil War that relies on eyewitness accounts. (Rev: BL 12/15/95; SLJ 2/96) [973.7]

16410 Hakim, Joy. *Liberty for All?* (5–8). Illus. Series: History of U.S. 1994, Oxford $14.95 (0-19-507753-9); paper $10.95 (0-19-507754-7). 192pp. This lively history of the Civil War is written in an engaging style, with many illustrations and personal asides. (Rev: SLJ 7/94) [973.7]

16411 Hakim, Joy. *War, Terrible War*. 2d ed. (5–8). Illus. Series: A History of Us. 1999, Oxford $18.95 (0-19-512761-7). 160pp. This excellent history of

the Civil War is basically a reissue of the 1994 edition with a few minor revisions and changes in illustrations. (Rev: BL 12/15/99) [973.7]

16412 Haskins, Jim. *Black, Blue, and Gray: African Americans in the Civil War* (5–8). Illus. 1998, Simon & Schuster paper $16.00 (0-689-80655-8). 160pp. A concise and rewarding picture of the role of African Americans before, during, and after the Civil War. (Rev: BL 2/15/98; HBG 10/98; SLJ 3/98*) [973.7]

16413 Haskins, Jim. *The Day Fort Sumter Was Fired On: A Photo History of the Civil War* (5–8). Illus. 1995, Scholastic paper $6.95 (0-590-46397-7). 96pp. A short, well-illustrated history of the Civil War, with coverage of the roles of women and African Americans. (Rev: BL 7/95) [973.7]

16414 Herbert, Janis. *The Civil War for Kids: A History with 21 Activities* (4–8). Illus. 1999, Chicago Review paper $14.95 (1-55652-355-6). 166pp. As well as supplying information about leaders, battles, daily life, and the contributions of women and African Americans, this book on the Civil War includes activities such as reenactments of battles, most of which are geared toward groups. (Rev: SLJ 12/99) [973.7]

16415 January, Brendan. *The Emancipation Proclamation* (3–5). Series: Cornerstones of Freedom. 1997, Children's LB $20.50 (0-516-20394-0). 32pp. The story of the events leading up to the Emancipation Proclamation, its contents, and its lasting consequences. (Rev: BL 12/15/97; HBG 3/98) [973.7]

16416 January, Brendan. *Fort Sumter* (3–5). Series: Cornerstones of Freedom. 1997, Children's LB $20.50 (0-516-20395-9). 32pp. The events leading up to the firing of the first shot in the Civil War are covered, as well as the immediate and lasting results. (Rev: BL 12/15/97; HBG 3/98) [973.7]

16417 Kantor, MacKinlay. *Gettysburg* (5–8). Illus. 1963, Random paper $5.99 (0-394-89181-3). This explains how Gettysburg became the site of the bloodiest Civil War battle; a vivid re-creation of the struggle.

16418 Kent, Zachary. *The Civil War: "A House Divided."* (5–7). Illus. Series: American War. 1994, Enslow LB $20.95 (0-89490-522-8). 128pp. Using many original quotes, period illustrations, and maps, this account gives a concise history of the Civil War. (Rev: BL 7/94; SLJ 9/94) [973.7]

16419 King, Wilma. *Children of the Emancipation* (2–5). Illus. Series: Picture the American Past. 2000, Carolrhoda $22.60 (1-57505-396-9). 48pp. This book covers the years 1860 through 1890 and examines the lives of children born as slaves, and how they fared before the Emancipation Proclamation, during the Civil War, and also during Reconstruction. (Rev: BL 6/1–15/00; HBG 10/00; SLJ 7/00) [973.7]

16420 Lincoln, Abraham. *The Gettysburg Address* (4–6). Illus. by Michael McCurdy. 1995, Houghton $14.95 (0-395-69824-3). 32pp. An illustrated edition of the address, with pictures that show the audience and the thoughts they might have had. (Rev: BL 10/15/95; HB 11–12/95; SLJ 9/95*) [973.7]

16421 Morrison, Taylor. *Civil War Artist* (5–7). Illus. 1999, Houghton $15.00 (0-395-91426-4). 32pp. Explains the long and complex process involved in transmitting drawings of Civil War scenes from the field to the public via a newspaper. (Rev: BL 4/15/99; HBG 3/00; SLJ 5/99) [070.4]

16422 Nofi, Albert A. *Spies in the Civil War* (5–8). Series: Untold History of the Civil War. 2000, Chelsea LB $17.95 (0-7910-5427-6). 64pp. In this account readers meet famous (including Allan Pinkerton and Belle Boyd) and lesser-known spies of the Civil War. (Rev: HBG 10/00; SLJ 7/00) [973.7]

16423 Ransom, Candice. *Children of the Civil War* (3–6). Series: Picture the American Past. 1998, Carolrhoda LB $19.93 (0-57505-241-5). 48pp. This book, divided into three parts — before, during, and after the Civil War — uses photos to show children in such roles as soldiers, slaves, servants, prisoners, and orphans. (Rev: SLJ 1/99) [973.7]

16424 Reef, Catherine. *Civil War Soldiers* (4–6). Illus. 1993, Twenty-First Century LB $17.90 (0-8050-2371-2). 80pp. The part that African American soldiers played in preserving the Union. (Rev: BL 8/93) [973.7]

16425 Reef, Catherine. *Gettysburg* (4–6). Illus. Series: Places in American History. 1992, Macmillan LB $18.95 (0-87518-503-7). 72pp. After background material on the Battle of Gettysburg, this account introduces the national military park of today. (Rev: BL 9/1/92; SLJ 8/92) [973]

16426 Roberts, Russell. *Lincoln and the Abolition of Slavery* (5–12). Series: American War. 1999, Lucent LB $18.96 (1-56006-580-X). 112pp. This gripping, fully documented account describes the events leading to the Civil War and Lincoln's role in these events. (Rev: BL 1/1–15/00; HBG 10/00) [973.7]

16427 Savage, Douglas J. *Ironclads and Blockades in the Civil War* (4–8). Series: Untold History of the Civil War. 2000, Chelsea $17.95 (0-7910-5429-2). 64pp. A clear text and period illustrations introduce the huge ships used in the Union and Confederate navies and their efforts to block different ports during the Civil War. (Rev: BL 7/00; HBG 10/00; SLJ 9/00) [973.7]

16428 Savage, Douglas J. *Prison Camps in the Civil War* (4–8). Series: Untold History of the Civil War. 2000, Chelsea $17.95 (0-7910-5428-4). 64pp. This account describes the prisoner-of-war camps on both sides during the Civil War, the appalling conditions in them, and the acts of heroism that sometimes occurred. (Rev: BL 7/00; HBG 10/00; SLJ 9/00) [973.7]

16429 Savage, Douglas J. *Women in the Civil War* (4–8). Series: Untold History of the Civil War. 2000, Chelsea $17.95 (0-7910-5436-5). 64pp. This book describes the roles played by women in the Civil War as nurses, suppliers of support services, and crusaders for issues including suffrage and abolition. (Rev: BL 7/00; HBG 10/00; SLJ 9/00) [973.7]

16430 Sinnott, Susan. *Charley Waters Goes to Gettysburg* (3–5). Illus. 2000, Millbrook LB $22.90 (0-7613-1567-5). 48pp. Told from the point of view of an 8-year-old boy who is visiting the Gettysburg battlefield with his parents, this book gives information on the battle and its reenactments. (Rev: BL 3/15/00; HBG 10/00; SLJ 6/00) [973.7]

16431 Sinnott, Susan. *Welcome to Addy's World, 1864* (3–6). Series: The American Girls Collection. 1999, Pleasant $14.95 (1-56237-771-4). 58pp. Addy was born a slave and lived on a Southern plantation until age nine. Through her eyes, life during the last year of the Civil War is re-created in a series of double-page spreads that explore slavery and other social and political topics of the time. (Rev: BL 1/1–15/00) [973.7]

16432 Smith, Carter, ed. *Behind the Lines: A Sourcebook on the Civil War* (5–8). Illus. Series: American Albums from the Collections of the Library of Congress. 1993, Millbrook LB $25.90 (1-56294-265-4). 96pp. A visual sourcebook describing life on the home front and in the army camps. (Rev: BL 3/1/93) [973.7]

16433 Smith, Carter, ed. *1863: The Crucial Year: A Sourcebook on the Civil War* (5–8). Illus. Series: American Albums from the Collections of the Library of Congress. 1993, Millbrook LB $25.90 (1-56294-263-8). 96pp. Events of 1863, including the Emancipation Proclamation and the battles of Vicksburg and Gettysburg. (Rev: BL 3/1/93) [973.7]

16434 Smith, Carter, ed. *The First Battles: A Sourcebook on the Civil War* (5–8). Illus. Series: American Albums from the Collections of the Library of Congress. 1993, Millbrook LB $25.90 (1-56294-262-X). 96pp. From the battle of Fort Sumter to the battle of Fredericksburg at the end of 1862. (Rev: BL 3/1/93) [973.7]

16435 Somerlott, Robert. *The Lincoln Assassination in American History* (5–8). Series: In American History. 1998, Enslow LB $18.95 (0-89490-886-3). 128pp. Using primary sources, the author has created a gripping story of the causes of the assassination, the shooting itself, and its aftermath. (Rev: SLJ 6/98) [973.7]

16436 Stanchak, John. *Civil War* (5–8). Illus. Series: Eyewitness Books. 2000, DK $15.95 (0-7894-6302-4). 64pp. This highly visual treatment presents topics related to the Civil War such as causes, battles, slavery, states' rights, weapons, and uniforms in a series of double-page spreads. (Rev: BL 1/1–15/01; HBG 3/01; SLJ 12/00) [973.7]

16437 Steins, Richard. *The Nation Divides: The Civil War (1820–1880)* (5–8). Illus. Series: First Person America. 1993, Twenty-First Century LB $18.90 (0-8050-2583-9). 64pp. Excerpts from eyewitness accounts and extensive illustrations are used to re-create the causes, events, and aftermath of the Civil War. (Rev: BL 2/1/94; SLJ 2/94) [973.7]

16438 Steins, Richard. *Shiloh* (4–7). Illus. Series: Battlefields Across America. 1997, Twenty-First Century $23.40 (0-8050-5229-1). 63pp. Background information on the Civil War is followed by a description of this battle and the site as it is today. (Rev: SLJ 1/98) [973.7]

16439 Sullivan, George. *The Civil War at Sea* (5–8). Illus. 2001, Twenty-First Century LB $26.40 (0-7613-1553-5). 64pp. This book tells of the struggle between the Union and Confederate forces in American bays, harbor, and rivers with material on famous ships and their commanders, important battles, and the daily life of the sailors. (Rev: BL 2/1/01) [973.7]

16440 Sullivan, George. *Portraits of War: Civil War Photographers and Their Work* (5–9). Illus. 1998, Twenty-First Century LB $24.40 (0-7613-3019-4). 80pp. Having already written a book about Civil War photographer Mathew Brady, the author now focuses on other Civil War photographers, giving many examples of their work. (Rev: BL 11/15/98; HBG 3/99) [973.7]

16441 Taylor, Maureen. *Through the Eyes of Your Ancestors* (5–9). Illus. 1999, Houghton $16.00 (0-395-86980-3). 96pp. A detailed, well-documented retelling of the first assassination of a U.S. president and its world-shaking results. (Rev: BCCB 5/99; BL 3/1/99; HB 5–6/99; HBG 10/99; SLJ 5/99) [929.1]

16442 Yancey, Diane. *Leaders of the North and South* (5–12). Series: American War. 1999, Lucent LB $18.96 (1-56006-497-8). 128pp. Military and political leaders on both sides of the Civil War are profiled with an objective evaluation of their relative importance. (Rev: BL 1/1–15/00; HBG 10/00) [973.7]

16443 Yancey, Diane. *Strategic Battles* (5–12). Series: American War. 1999, Lucent LB $18.86 (1-56006-496-X). 128pp. The key battles of the Civil War are covered in chronological order with maps and other illustrations. (Rev: BL 1/1–15/00; HBG 10/00) [973.7]

RECONSTRUCTION TO THE KOREAN WAR, 1865–1950

16444 Altman, Linda Jacobs. *The Pullman Strike of 1894: Turning Point for American Labor* (4–6). Illus. Series: Spotlight on American History. 1994, Millbrook LB $21.90 (1-56294-346-4). 64pp. This strike caused by wage cuts and firing of union representatives, considered a landmark in the history of the American labor movement, is well re-created with good illustrations. (Rev: BL 9/15/94; SLJ 4/94) [331.89]

16445 Andrews, Jan. *Pa's Harvest* (3–7). Illus. 2000, Douglas & McIntyre $12.95 (0-88899-405-2). 40pp. Small, framed pictures in sepia tones illustrate this remembrance of the Great Depression and the hardship it brought to one family. (Rev: BL 12/15/00; SLJ 2/01) [813]

16446 Arnold, Caroline. *Children of the Settlement Houses* (4–7). Illus. Series: Picture the American Past. 1998, Carolrhoda $19.93 (1-57505-242-3). 48pp. Using historical photos and a simple text, this book introduces the turn-of-the-century settlement house, where the poor and new immigrants found shelter and a place to learn, explore the arts, and

develop a sense of belonging. (Rev: BL 9/15/98; HBG 3/99; SLJ 1/99) [362.5]

16447 Axelrod-Contrada, Joan. *The Lizzie Borden "Axe Murder" Trial: A Headline Court Case* (5–9). Series: Headline Court Cases. 2000, Enslow LB $20.95 (0-7660-1422-3). 128pp. A well-documented account of the famous 1892 trial, the events that led up to it, and its aftermath. (Rev: HBG 3/01; SLJ 1/01) [973.8]

16448 Bartoletti, Susan Campbell. *Growing Up in Coal Country* (5–8). Illus. 1996, Houghton $16.95 (0-395-77847-6). 127pp. The life of child laborers in the coal mines of Pennsylvania 100 years ago is covered in this photo-essay. (Rev: BCCB 2/97; BL 12/1/96*; SLJ 2/97*) [331.3]

16449 Bartoletti, Susan Campbell. *Kids on Strike!* (5–8). Illus. 1999, Houghton $20.00 (0-395-88892-1). 208pp. This book chronicles the history of child labor in America during the 19th and early 20th centuries and features such personalities as William Randolph Hearst, Pauline Newman, and Mother Jones. (Rev: HBG 3/00; SLJ 12/99*) [973.8]

16450 Blackman, Cally. *The 20s and 30s: Flappers and Vamps* (5–10). Series: 20th Century Fashion. 2000, Gareth Stevens LB $15.95 (0-8368-2599-3). 32pp. Social history is combined with fashion and design in this account of the 1920s and 1930s that is illustrated with period photos and magazine covers. (Rev: HBG 10/00; SLJ 6/00) [973.9]

16451 Blake, Arthur. *The Scopes Trial: Defending the Right to Teach* (4–7). Illus. Series: Spotlight on American History. 1994, Millbrook LB $21.90 (1-56294-407-X). 64pp. The story of the Great Monkey Trial of 1925 and its significance for American education. (Rev: BL 10/15/94; SLJ 10/94) [344.73]

16452 Brown, Gene. *The Struggle to Grow: Expansionism and Industrialization (1880–1913)* (5–8). Illus. Series: First Person America. 1993, Twenty-First Century LB $18.90 (0-8050-2584-7). 64pp. Excerpts from original sources and period illustrations are used to create a history of the period 1880–1913 that touches on frontier life, politics, industry, and immigration. (Rev: BL 2/1/94; SLJ 3/94) [973.8]

16453 Cohen, Daniel. *Prohibition: America Makes Alcohol Illegal* (4–6). Illus. Series: Spotlight on American History. 1995, Millbrook LB $21.90 (1-56294-529-7). 64pp. A history of America's attitude toward alcohol, from the rise of the temperance movement through the repeal of Prohibition. (Rev: BL 11/1/95; SLJ 11/95) [363.4]

16454 Collier, Christopher, and James Lincoln Collier. *Progressivism, the Great Depression, and the New Deal* (5–8). Illus. Series: The Drama of American History. 2001, Marshall Cavendish LB $20.95 (0-7614-1054-6). 96pp. A highly readable account that covers such topics as the stock market crash, the reformation of business practices, the Great Depression, and the social policies of the New Deal. (Rev: BL 3/15/01) [973.91]

16455 Collier, Christopher, and James Lincoln Collier. *Reconstruction and the Rise of Jim Crow, 1864–1896* (5–8). Series: Drama of American History. 1999, Marshall Cavendish LB $20.95 (0-7614-0819-3). 89pp. A clear, objective account of the problems facing the country after the Civil War and how they were resolved. (Rev: BL 2/15/00; HBG 10/00; SLJ 3/00) [973.8]

16456 Collier, Christopher, and James Lincoln Collier. *The Rise of Industry, 1860–1900* (5–8). Illus. Series: Drama of American History. 1999, Marshall Cavendish LB $20.95 (0-7614-0820-7). 89pp. A readable account of 40 years of industrialism and its effect on the United States. (Rev: BL 2/15/00; HBG 10/00; SLJ 3/00) [338.0973]

16457 Collier, Christopher, and James Lincoln Collier. *The United States Enters the World Stage: From the Alaska Purchase Through World War I* (5–8). Series: The Drama of American History. 2001, Marshall Cavendish LB $20.95 (0-7614-1053-8). Covering the years 1867 through 1918, this well-illustrated account traces America's emergence as a world power. (Rev: BL 3/15/01) [973.9]

16458 Collins, Mary. *The Spanish-American War* (3–5). Series: Cornerstones of Freedom. 1998, Children's LB $19.50 (0-516-20759-8). 32pp. A concise, illustrated story of the 1898–99 war that made Puerto Rico, Guam, and the Philippines American possessions. (Rev: BL 5/15/98; HBG 10/98) [973.8]

16459 Coombs, Karen Mueller. *Children of the Dust Days* (3–6). Illus. Series: Picture the American Past. 2000, Carolrhoda LB $22.60 (1-57505-360-8). 48pp. A mainly illustrated account of the hardships associated with the Dust Bowl and the journeys of many displaced farmers to California. (Rev: BL 4/1/00; HBG 10/00; SLJ 6/00) [978]

16460 Cryan-Hicks, Kathryn, ed. *Pride and Promise: The Harlem Renaissance* (4–8). Illus. Series: Perspectives on History. 1994, Discovery paper $6.95 (1-878668-30-7). 52pp. The story of the great 20th-century artistic awakening in New York's Harlem and of its many leaders, like Langston Hughes. (Rev: BL 8/94) [305]

16461 Duden, Jane. *1940s* (3–7). Illus. 1989, Macmillan LB $16.95 (0-89686-475-8). 48pp. The eventful decade of the 1940s, which included World War II and adjustments to a peacetime economy, is covered in this well-illustrated book. (Rev: SLJ 4/90) [973.9]

16462 Feinberg, Barbara S. *Black Tuesday: The Stock Market Crash of 1929* (4–7). Illus. Series: Spotlight on American History. 1995, Millbrook LB $21.90 (1-56294-574-2). 64pp. The causes and consequences of the great stock market crash of 1929 are interestingly retold with many photographs and illustrations. (Rev: BL 10/15/95) [338.5]

16463 Freedman, Russell. *Immigrant Kids* (3–7). Illus. 1995, Puffin paper $5.99 (0-140-37594-5). 64pp. An account of the immigration to the United States from 1880 to 1920.

16464 Fremon, David K. *The Jim Crow Laws and Racism in American History* (5–9). 2000, Enslow LB $20.95 (0-7660-1297-2). 128pp. This is a history of racism in America from the end of the Civil War to the death of Martin Luther King, Jr., in 1968. (Rev: HBG 3/01; SLJ 12/00) [973]

16465 Gay, Kathlyn, and Martin Gay. *Spanish-American War* (5–8). Illus. Series: Voices from the Past. 1995, Twenty-First Century LB $18.90 (0-8050-2847-1). 64pp. This coverage of the Spanish-American War uses excerpts from letters, memoirs, and official reports to cover the causes, battles, and results. (Rev: BL 12/15/95; SLJ 3/96) [973.8]

16466 Gourley, Catherine. *Good Girl Work: Factories, Sweatshops, and How Women Changed Their Role in the American Workforce* (4–8). 1999, Millbrook LB $23.40 (0-7613-0951-9). 96pp. A history of female labor in U.S. factories during the late 19th and early 20th centuries with material on the terrible working conditions and the gradual changes that took place. (Rev: SLJ 8/99) [973.8]

16467 Gourley, Catherine. *Welcome to Samantha's World, 1904* (3–6). Series: The American Girls Collection. 1999, Pleasant $14.95 (1-56247-772-2). 58pp. Using double-page spreads, this book introduces social and cultural life in America at the beginning of the 20th century. (Rev: BL 1/1–15/00; HBG 3/00) [973.9]

16468 Hakim, Joy. *An Age of Extremes*. 2nd ed (5–8). Series: A History of Us. 1999, Oxford LB $18.95 (0-19-512765-X); paper $12.95 (0-19-512766-8). 205pp. A thorough and accurate history of the United States' coming of age after Reconstruction — from 1870 through World War I. (Rev: BL 12/15/99) [973.8]

16469 Hakim, Joy. *Reconstruction and Reform*. 2nd ed. (5–8). Series: A History of Us. 1999, Oxford LB $18.95 (0-19-512763-3); paper $12.95 (0-19-512764-1). 192pp. The years immediately following the Civil War (1865–1896) are covered in this outstanding history that uses many quotes, anecdotes, and excellent illustrations. (Rev: BL 12/15/99) [973.8]

16470 Hakim, Joy. *War, Peace, and All That Jazz*. 2nd ed (5–8). Series: A History of Us. 1999, Oxford LB $18.95 (0-19-512767-6); paper $12.95 (0-19-512768-4). 206pp. Political, social, and cultural events and developments are traced in this fascinating account of life in the United States between the world wars and through World War II, with coverage of the Jazz Age, the Great Depression, and the war itself. (Rev: BL 12/15/99) [973.9]

16471 Isaacs, Sally Senzell. *America in the Time of Franklin Delano Roosevelt: The Story of Our Nation from Coast to Coast, from 1929 to 1948* (4–8). Series: America in the Time Of. 1999, Heinemann LB $16.95 (1-57572-761-7). 48pp. Using the life of Roosevelt as a framework, this account describes life in America during the Great Depression and World War II. (Rev: SLJ 5/00) [973.9]

16472 Isaacs, Sally Senzell. *America in the Time of Susan B. Anthony: The Story of Our Nation from Coast to Coast, from 1845 to 1928* (4–8). 1999, Heinemann LB $16.95 (1-57572-763-3). 48pp. Using the life of Susan B. Anthony as a framework, this work covers topics including woman's suffrage, poverty, and World War I. (Rev: SLJ 5/00) [973.9]

16473 January, Brendan. *Reconstruction* (4–6). Illus. Series: Cornerstones of Freedom. 1999, Children's LB $19.50 (0-516-21143-9). 32pp. This attractive account tells of the Reconstruction period, the legislative changes after the Civil War, and the disillusionment of the freed slaves. (Rev: BL 5/15/99; HBG 10/99) [973.8]

16474 Jernegan, Laura. *A Whaling Captain's Daughter: The Diary of Laura Jernegan, 1868–1871* (4–6). Series: Diaries, Letters, and Memoirs. 2000, Capstone LB $22.60 (0-7368-0319-1). Excerpts from a young girl's diary introduce the reader to life ashore and aboard a whaling ship immediately after the Civil War. (Rev: BL 10/15/00; SLJ 9/00) [973.8]

16475 Kalman, Bobbie. *19th Century Girls and Women* (3–5). Illus. 1997, Crabtree LB $20.60 (0-86505-434-7); paper $7.95 (0-86505-464-9). 32pp. A realistic portrait of the life women led in both the working and wealthy classes, with details on home life, chores, health hazards, and stifling clothing. (Rev: BL 7/97; SLJ 8/97) [305.4]

16476 Kalman, Bobbie, and Tammy Everts. *A Child's Day* (3–5). Illus. by Antoinette DeBiasi. Series: Historic Communities. 1994, Crabtree LB $20.60 (0-86505-494-0); paper $7.95 (0-86505-514-9). 32pp. A day in the life of settlers' children is shown through such activities as doing chores, playing games, going to school, and visiting a fair. (Rev: SLJ 9/94) [978]

16477 King, David C. *Victorian Days: Discover the Past with Fun Projects, Games, Activities, and Recipes* (4–6). Illus. by Cheryl K. Noll. Series: American Kids in History. 2000, Wiley paper $12.95 (0-471-33122-8). 96pp. Through an interesting text and more than 30 activities like making paper flowers and shadow puppets and following some delicious recipes, young readers can re-create life in New York in the year 1893. (Rev: SLJ 4/00) [973.8]

16478 Mee, Sue. *1900–20: Linen and Lace* (5–10). Series: 20th Century Fashion. 2000, Gareth Stevens LB $15.95 (0-8368-2598-5). 32pp. The fashion and design of the first two decades of the last century are pictured and described in this book that also contains a great deal of social history. (Rev: HBG 10/00; SLJ 6/00) [973.9]

16479 Meltzer, Milton. *Driven from the Land: The Story of the Dust Bowl* (4–8). Series: Great Journeys. 1999, Benchmark LB $21.95 (0-7614-0968-8). 111pp. Traces the development of the Dust Bowl, its effects on the land and the people, and how many were forced to leave their farms and seek a new life elsewhere. (Rev: HBG 3/00; SLJ 2/00) [973.9]

16480 Murphy, Jim. *Blizzard! The Storm that Changed America* (5–9). Illus. 2000, Scholastic $18.95 (0-590-67309-2). 136pp. A brilliant narrative about the great storm that hit the Northeast on March 10, 1888, and brought 31 inches of snow and 800 deaths in New York City alone. (Rev: BL 2/15/01*; HB 1–2/01; HBG 3/01; SLJ 12/00) [974.7]

16481 Nobisso, Josephine. *John Blair and the Great Hinckley Fire* (1–4). Illus. by Ted Rose. 2000, Houghton $15.00 (0-618-01560-4). This is the story of the African American railway porter who was the hero of the forest fire that killed more than 400 people in Minnesota in 1894. (Rev: BCCB 10/00; HBG 3/01; SLJ 12/00) [973.9]

16482 Sherrow, Victoria. *The Triangle Factory Fire* (4–6). Illus. Series: Spotlight on American History. 1995, Millbrook LB $21.90 (1-56294-572-6). 64pp. The story of the terrible fire that exposed the shameful labor exploitation in this country and led to needed reforms. (Rev: BL 12/15/95; SLJ 3/96) [363.37]

16483 Simonds, Patricia. *The Founding of the AFL and the Rise of Organized Labor* (5–7). Illus. Series: Turning Points. 1991, Silver Burdett LB $21.00 (0-382-24123-1); paper $7.95 (0-382-24118-5). 64pp. The inspiring story of the beginning of the labor movement in the United States and its impact on American history and society. (Rev: BL 1/15/92) [331.88]

16484 Smith, Carter, ed. *Presidents of a Growing Country: A Sourcebook on the U.S. Presidency* (5–8). Illus. Series: American Albums. 1993, Millbrook LB $25.90 (1-56294-358-8). 96pp. Through extensive use of pictorials, a thorough timeline, and concise text, this attractive book traces the presidency from Hayes through McKinley. (Rev: BL 12/1/93; SLJ 4/94) [973.8]

16485 Smith, Carter, ed. *Presidents of a World Power: A Sourcebook on the U.S. Presidency* (5–8). Illus. Series: American Albums. 1993, Millbrook LB $25.90 (1-56294-361-8). 96pp. Presidents from Teddy Roosevelt through Franklin Roosevelt are covered with many excellent illustrations, an overview chapter, good captions, and an extensive timeline. (Rev: BL 12/1/93; SLJ 4/94) [973.91]

16486 Spedden, Daisy C. S. *Polar the Titanic Bear* (3–5). Illus. by Laurie McGaw. 1994, Little, Brown $17.95 (0-316-80625-0). 64pp. The true story of a toy bear, his many owners, and his rescue from the Titanic. (Rev: BCCB 12/94; BL 12/1/94*; SLJ 1/95) [910.91]

16487 Splear, Elise Lee. *Growing Seasons* (3–5). Illus. 2000, Putnam $16.99 (0-399-23460-8). 40pp. This nonfiction book of remembrances paints a vivid picture of growing up in America about 100 years ago. (Rev: BCCB 7–8/00; BL 5/15/00; HBG 10/00; SLJ 7/00) [973.8]

16488 Stanley, Jerry. *Children of the Dust Bowl: The True Story of the School at Weedpatch Camp* (4–8). Illus. 1992, Crown LB $15.99 (0-517-58782-3). 50pp. A vivid account, with compelling photos, of youngsters in this troubled time. (Rev: BCCB 10/92; BL 9/1/92*; HB 1–2/93*) [371.96]

16489 Stein, R. Conrad. *The Great Depression* (3–5). Illus. Series: Cornerstones of Freedom. 1993, Children's LB $20.50 (0-516-06668-4). 32pp. The story of the causes and effects of this great economic tragedy, its toll in human suffering, and the gradual recovery. (Rev: BL 2/1/94; SLJ 3/94) [973.91]

16490 Stein, R. Conrad. *The Roaring Twenties* (3–6). Illus. Series: Cornerstones of Freedom. 1994, Children's LB $20.50 (0-516-06675-7). 31pp. Period photos and ads bring authenticity to this account of life in the days of flappers, Prohibition, and speakeasies. (Rev: SLJ 7/94) [973.9]

16491 Stewart, Gail B. *1900s* (5–8). Illus. Series: Timelines. 1990, Macmillan LB $16.95 (0-89686-471-5). 48pp. Events and trivia of the decade, with many illustrations. Also use: *1910s; 1920s; 1930s* (all 1989). (Rev: SLJ 6/90) [973.9]

16492 Uschan, Michael V. *The 1940s* (5–10). Series: A Cultural History of the United States Through the Decades. 1998, Lucent LB $17.96 (1-56510-554-0). 128pp. World War II, its effects on American life, and its aftermath dominate this history of the United States during the 1940s that also covers the arts, slang, and scientific accomplishments. (Rev: SLJ 1/99) [973.9]

16493 Weber, Valerie, and Valerie Baker. *Traveling in Grandma's Day* (3–4). 2000, Carolrhoda LB $21.2 (1-57505-326-8). 32pp. A nostalgic look at traveling in the 1930s and 1940s told through first-person narratives and plenty of photographs. Also use *School in Grandma's Day, Shopping in Grandma's Day,* and *Food in Grandma's Day* (all 2000). (Rev: HBG 10/00; SLJ 6/00) [973.9]

16494 Wetterer, Margaret K., and Charles M. Wetterer. *The Snow Walker* (2–4). Illus. 1996, Carolrhoda LB $18.60 (0-87614-891-7); paper $5.95 (0-87614-959-X). 48pp. During the terrible blizzard of 1888, Milton Daub unselfishly helped his neighbors in the Bronx by delivering needed supplies. (Rev: BCCB 12/96; BL 2/15/96; SLJ 3/96) [973.9]

16495 Whitman, Sylvia. *Immigrant Children: Late 1800s to Early 1900s* (3–5). Series: Picture the American Past. 2000, Carolrhoda LB $22.60 (1-57505-395-0). 48pp. This book describes the lives of immigrant children who arrived in this country, many to work in mines, factories, or farms but all trying to get ahead. (Rev: HBG 10/00; SLJ 7/00) [973.9]

16496 Wroble, Lisa A. *Kids During the Great Depression* (3–5). Series: Kids Throughout History. 1999, Rosen LB $11.95 (0-8239-5255-X). 24pp. This book tells of the events preceding the Depression, its effects on people and particularly children, and the gradual recovery before World War II. (Rev: SLJ 11/99) [973.9]

THE 1950S TO THE PRESENT

16497 Bridges, Ruby. *Through My Eyes* (3–8). Illus. 1999, Scholastic $16.95 (0-590-18923-9). 64pp. A first-person account by Ruby Bridges who, at age six, became the first African American student to attend a formerly segregated school in New Orleans. (Rev: BCCB 1/00*; BL 11/15/99*; HBG 3/00; SLJ 12/99*) [379.2]

16498 Cole, Michael D. *The L.A. Riots: Rage in the City of Angels* (5–9). Illus. 1999, Enslow LB $18.95 (0-7660-1219-0). 48pp. This book describes the police beating of Rodney King in Los Angeles and the subsequent riots — the worst in U.S. history. (Rev: BL 2/1/99; HBG 10/99; SLJ 6/99) [979.4]

16499 Coles, Robert. *The Story of Ruby Bridges* (K–4). Illus. by George Ford. 1995, Scholastic $13.95 (0-590-43967-7). 32pp. A re-creation of the trauma faced by a young African American girl who is the first to integrate an all-white school in New Orleans in 1960. (Rev: BCCB 3/95; BL 1/15/95; SLJ 3/95)

16500 Duden, Jane. *1950s* (3–7). 1989, Macmillan LB $20.00 (0-89686-476-6). 48pp. Events and people associated with this eventful decade come to life in this book that is divided by years. It is continued in *1960s* and *1970s* (both 1989). (Rev: SLJ 4/90) [973.9]

16501 Erlbach, Arlene. *Kent State* (3–5). Series: Cornerstones of Freedom. 1998, Children's LB $19.50 (0-516-20787-3). 32pp. Focusing on the 1970 riot at Kent State University, during which four protesters were killed, this book also examines the anti-Vietnam War movement. (Rev: BL 5/15/98; HBG 10/98) [973.9]

16502 Feinstein, Stephen. *The 1980s: From Ronald Reagan to MTV* (4–7). Series: Decades of the 20th Century. 2000, Enslow LB $17.95 (0-7660-1424-X). 64pp. Presents the 1980s' major events, important people, and developments in such areas as politics, science, the arts, and sports. (Rev: BL 10/15/00; HBG 10/00; SLJ 12/00) [973.9]

16503 Feinstein, Stephen. *The 1970s: From Watergate to Disco* (4–7). Series: Decades of the 20th Century. 2000, Enslow LB $17.95 (0-7660-1425-8). 64pp. This book covers the people and events of the 1970s along with developments in such areas as politics, science, and sports. (Rev: BL 10/15/00; HBG 3/01; SLJ 12/00) [973.9]

16504 Feinstein, Stephen. *The 1960s: From the Vietnam War to Flower Power* (4–7). Illus. Series: Decades of the 20th Century. 2000, Enslow LB $17.95 (0-7660-1426-6). 64pp. An account of America's turbulent 1960s that includes lifestyles, politics, fashion, fads, and entertainment. (Rev: BL 10/15/00; HBG 3/01; SLJ 12/00) [973.92]

16505 Finkelstein, Norman H. *The Way Things Never Were: The Truth About the "Good Old Days."* (5–10). Illus. 1999, Simon & Schuster $16.00 (0-689-81412-7). 112pp. The 1950s and 1960s are revisited in this social history that describes a time of Cold War jitters, unsafe automobiles, poor diet, and less-comfortable old age. (Rev: BCCB 9/99; BL 9/1/99; HBG 3/00; SLJ 7/99) [973.92]

16506 Gay, Kathlyn, and Martin Gay. *Korean War* (6–8). Illus. Series: Voices from the Past. 1996, Twenty-First Century LB $18.90 (0-8050-4100-1). 64pp. A discussion of the often forgotten Korean War — its causes, the battles, and the people involved. (Rev: BL 11/15/96; SLJ 12/96) [951.904]

16507 Gay, Kathlyn, and Martin Gay. *Vietnam War* (6–8). Illus. Series: Voices from the Past. 1996, Twenty-First Century LB $18.90 (0-8050-4101-X). 64pp. An objective overview of the Vietnam War, illustrated with many black-and-white photos. (Rev: BL 11/15/96; SLJ 12/96) [959.704]

16508 Grant, R. G. *The Seventies* (4–7). Series: A Look at Life In. 2000, Raintree Steck-Vaughn LB $22.60 (0-7398-1340-4). 48pp. After the major news events of the 1970s, this book describes important developments in science, the arts, and popular culture. Also use *The Sixties* (2000). (Rev: HBG 10/00; SLJ 9/00) [973.9]

16509 Hakim, Joy. *All the People.* 2nd ed. (5–8). Series: A History of Us. 1999, Oxford LB $18.95 (0-19-512769-2); paper $12.95 (0-19-512770-6). 235pp. An outstanding history of the political and social events, trends, and developments in the United States from the end of World War II through 1998. (Rev: BL 12/15/99) [973.9]

16510 Haskins, Jim. *The Day Martin Luther King, Jr., Was Shot: A Photo History of the Civil Rights Movement* (4–8). Illus. 1992, Scholastic paper $5.99 (0-590-43661-9). 96pp. Despite its title, this is a photo history of the civil rights struggle from slavery to the present. (Rev: BL 2/1/92; SLJ 5/92) [323.4]

16511 Isaacs, Sally Senzell. *America in the Time of Martin Luther King Jr.: The Story of Our Nation from Coast to Coast, from 1948 to 1976* (4–8). Series: America in the Time Of. 1999, Heinemann LB $16.95 (1-57572-780-3). 48pp. As well as describing the accomplishment of Martin Luther King, Jr., this account traces important developments during his time including the 1960s peace movement, the Vietnam War, space travel, and the Watergate scandal. (Rev: SLJ 5/00) [973.9]

16512 Kallen, Stuart A. *The 1950s* (5–8). Illus. Series: Cultural History of the United States. 1998, Lucent LB $17.96 (1-56006-555-9). 127pp. Readable text and many photos are used to survey the contrasting political and cultural trends, events, and movements of the 1950s in the United States and to examine what life was like for young people at that time. (Rev: BL 1/1–15/99) [973.921]

16513 Kent, Deborah. *The Vietnam War: "What Are We Fighting For?"* (5–7). Illus. Series: American War. 1994, Enslow LB $20.95 (0-89490-527-9). 128pp. An objective overview of this war, its causes, progression, and results. (Rev: BL 10/15/94; SLJ 11/94) [959.704]

16514 Kent, Zachary. *The Persian Gulf War: "The Mother of All Battles"* (5–7). Illus. 1994, Enslow LB $20.95 (0-89490-528-7). 128pp. The story of the 1991 Gulf War, its causes and effects, told with striking action photos. (Rev: BL 4/15/95; SLJ 2/95) [956.7]

16515 Lomas, Clare. *The 80s and 90s: Power Dressing to Sportswear* (5–10). Series: 20th Century Fashion. 2000, Gareth Stevens LB $15.95 (0-8368-2603-5). 32pp. Power dressing, androgyny, sportswear, and grunge characterize the world of fashion during the 1980s and 1990s in this book that covers both design and social history. (Rev: HBG 10/00; SLJ 6/00) [973.9]

16516 Powe-Temperley, Kitty. *The 60s: Mods and Hippies* (5–10). Series: 20th Century Fashion. 2000, Gareth Stevens LB $15.95 (0-8368-2601-9). 32pp. Mods, hippies, miniskirts, Eastern influences, and art as fashion are covered in this overview of clothing fads of the 1960s, along with background information. (Rev: HBG 10/00; SLJ 6/00) [973.9]

16517 Reynolds, Helen. *The 40s and 50s: Utility to New Look* (5–10). Series: 20th Century Fashion. 2000, Gareth Stevens LB $15.95 (0-8368-2600-0). 32pp. Using a lively style and many period illustrations, this book highlights the world of fashion and design during and after World War II and gives some background social history. (Rev: HBG 10/00; SLJ 6/00) [973.9]

16518 Ruffin, Frances E. *Martin Luther King, Jr., and the March on Washington* (1–3). Illus. by Stephen Marchesi. Series: All Aboard Reading. 2001, Grosset LB $13.89 (0-448-42424-X); paper $3.99 (0-448-42421-5). 48pp. This book describes the 1963 March on Washington, the events leading up to it, the civil rights movement, and the "I Have a Dream" speech. (Rev: BL 2/15/01) [973.9]

16519 Smith, Carter. *The Korean War* (4–7). Illus. Series: Turning Points. 1990, Silver Burdett LB $17.95 (0-382-09953-2); paper $7.95 (0-382-09949-4). 64pp. Covers the causes and events of the Korean War, as well as its significance in American history. (Rev: BL 3/1/91; SLJ 5/91) [951]

16520 Smith, Carter, ed. *Presidents in a Time of Change: A Sourcebook on the U.S. Presidency* (5–8). Illus. Series: American Albums. 1993, Millbrook LB $25.90 (1-56294-362-6). 96pp. A heavily illustrated, attractive review of the presidency from Truman to Clinton. (Rev: BL 12/1/93; SLJ 4/94) [973.92]

16521 Stein, R. Conrad. *The Korean War: "The Forgotten War"* (5–7). Illus. 1994, Enslow LB $20.95 (0-89490-526-0). 128pp. This well-organized account of the Korean War presents a balanced picture of the war and includes personal observations. (Rev: BL 4/15/95; SLJ 2/95) [951]

16522 Summer, L. S. *The March on Washington* (4–6). Series: Journey to Freedom. 2000, Child's World LB $25.64 (1-56766-718-X). 40pp. The story of the August 28, 1963, march on Washington to support President Kennedy's civil rights legislation, during which Martin Luther King Jr. gave his "I Have a Dream" speech. (Rev: BL 11/15/00; HBG 3/01; SLJ 1/01) [973.9]

16523 Turck, Mary C. *The Civil Rights Movement for Kids: A History with 21 Activities* (4–8). 2000, Chicago Review paper $14.95 (1-55652-370-X). 189pp. The story of the civil rights movement with coverage of key events and personalities plus a number of related activities. (Rev: SLJ 10/00) [973.9]

16524 Wade, Linda R. *Montgomery: Launching the Civil Rights Movement* (4–6). Illus. Series: Doors to America's Past. 1992, Rourke LB $22.60 (0-86592-465-1). 48pp. The city of Montgomery, Alabama, is introduced, together with historical information, its role in the civil rights movement, and its present status. (Rev: BL 5/1/92) [305.890]

16525 Westerfeld, Scott. *Watergate* (5–7). Illus. Series: Turning Points. 1991, Silver Burdett paper $7.95 (0-382-24120-7). 64pp. An objective account in text and pictures of the Watergate break-in during Nixon's presidency and its consequences. (Rev: BL 1/15/92) [364.1]

16526 Zeinert, Karen. *The Valiant Women of the Vietnam War* (5–8). Illus. 2000, Millbrook LB $28.40 (0-7613-1268-4). 96pp. Provides a good overview of the Vietnam War and highlights the contributions of women at home and abroad during this conflict. (Rev: BL 4/1/00; HBG 10/00; SLJ 5/00) [959.704]

Regions

MIDWEST

16527 Anderson, Kathy P. *Illinois* (3–6). Illus. Series: Hello USA. 1993, Lerner LB $19.93 (0-8225-2723-5). 72pp. Presents the history and geography of this state, and includes biographies of famous native sons and daughters. (Rev: BL 1/15/93) [977.3]

16528 Armbruster, Ann. *Lake Huron* (2–4). Illus. Series: A True Book. 1996, Children's LB $22.00 (0-516-20012-7). 48pp. An overview of the formation of this lake and the early Indians who lived around it plus additional history and its current importance. Also use *Lake Michigan* and *Lake Superior* (both 1996). (Rev: SLJ 3/97) [917.709]

16529 Armbruster, Ann. *Lake Ontario* (2–4). Illus. Series: A True Book. 1996, Children's LB $22.00 (0-516-20014-3). 48pp. A history of Lake Ontario, the role it has played in Canadian-American history, and its importance today. Also use *St. Lawrence Seaway* (1996). (Rev: SLJ 4/97) [917.704]

16530 Aylesworth, Thomas G., and Virginia L. Aylesworth. *Eastern Great Lakes: Indiana, Michigan, Ohio* (4–7). Illus. Series: State Reports. 1995, Chelsea $19.95 (0-7910-3409-7). 64pp. Information is given for each of the three states covered, including major cities, history, geography, climate, and important cities. (Rev: BL 3/15/92) [977]

16531 Badt, Karin Luisa. *The Mississippi Flood of 1993* (3–5). Illus. Series: Cornerstones of Freedom. 1994, Children's LB $20.50 (0-516-06680-3). 32pp. The causes and effects of this major modern disaster are traced with eyewitness reports. (Rev: BL 1/15/95) [977.033]

16532 Baldwin, Guy. *Oklahoma* (4–8). Series: Celebrate the States. 2000, Marshall Cavendish LB $24.95 (0-7614-1061-9). 144pp. The beauties and hidden treasures of Oklahoma are covered in this colorful introduction to the state, its past, its present, and its people. (Rev: BL 12/15/00) [976.6]

16533 Bjorkland, Ruth. *Kansas* (4–8). Series: Celebrate the States. 2000, Marshall Cavendish LB $24.95 (0-7614-0646-8). 143pp. A broad introduction to Kansas — its geography and history, its government and people, its songs and folktales, and a few of its recipes. (Rev: BL 6/1–15/00; HBG 10/00) [978.1]

16534 Blashfield, Jean F. *Wisconsin* (5–8). Series: America the Beautiful. 1998, Children's LB $32.00 (0-516-20640-0). 144pp. This book supplies important facts about Wisconsin such as its history, places, economy, and famous people. (Rev: BL 1/1–15/99; SLJ 4/99) [977.5]

16535 Brandenburg, Jim. *An American Safari: Adventures on the North American Prairie* (4–6). Illus. 1995, Walker LB $17.85 (0-8027-8320-1). 48pp. This American photographer describes in words and pictures the western prairies and the animals that live there. (Rev: BCCB 6/95; BL 4/15/95; SLJ 8/95) [508.73]

16536 Bratvold, Gretchen. *Wisconsin* (3–6). Illus. Series: Hello USA. 1991, Lerner LB $19.93 (0-8225-2700-6). 72pp. An introduction to the dairy state, with full-color photos. (Rev: BL 4/15/91; SLJ 7/91) [977.5]

16537 Brill, Marlene T. *Illinois* (4–8). Illus. Series: Celebrate the States. 1996, Marshall Cavendish LB $35.64 (0-7614-0113-X). 144pp. Maps, diagrams, and photos enliven this introduction to Illinois that gives good coverage of history, geography, and social conditions. (Rev: BL 2/1/97; SLJ 2/97) [913.73]

16538 Brill, Marlene T. *Indiana* (4–8). Illus. Series: Celebrate the States. 1997, Marshall Cavendish LB $35.64 (0-7614-0147-4). 144pp. An introduction to this Midwest state that covers such topics as agriculture, industries, and famous natives, as well as its history and geography. (Rev: BL 7/97; SLJ 8/97) [977.2]

16539 Brown, Dottie. *Ohio* (3–6). Illus. Series: Hello USA. 1992, Lerner LB $19.93 (0-8225-2725-1). 72pp. Ohio, the nation's seventh-largest state, is described from the days of the Indians and settlers until today. (Rev: BL 11/15/92) [977.1]

16540 Butler, Dori Hillestad. *M Is for Minnesota* (3–5). Illus. by Janice L. Porter. 1998, Univ. of Minnesota $16.95 (0-8166-3041-0). 32pp. Using an A through Z approach, this picture book covers basic facts about Minnesota. (Rev: BL 1/1–15/99; HBG 3/99; SLJ 3/99) [977.6]

16541 Carlson, Jeffrey D. *A Historical Album of Minnesota* (5–8). Illus. Series: Historical Album. 1993, Millbrook LB $23.40 (1-56294-006-6). 64pp. A heavily illustrated volume that traces the history of Minnesota from Native American communities through exploration and settlement to present-day concerns. (Rev: SLJ 10/93) [977.6]

16542 Curlee, Lynn. *Rushmore* (4–6). Illus. 1999, Scholastic $17.95 (0-590-22573-1). 49pp. A thorough examination of the creation of this monument in South Dakota, designed by Gutzon Borglum and completed by his son in 1941. (Rev: BCCB 3/99; BL 3/1/99; HB 3–4/99; HBG 10/99; SLJ 3/99) [730]

16543 Deady, Kathleen W. *Kansas Facts and Symbols* (1–4). Series: States and Their Symbols. 2000, Capstone LB $15.93 (0-7368-0638-5). 24pp. As well as state symbols, this book gives a map, a page of fast facts, and a list of places to visit. (Rev: BL 3/1/01) [978.1]

16544 Doherty, Craig A., and Katherine M. Doherty. *The Gateway Arch* (3–6). Illus. Series: Building America. 1995, Blackbirch LB $17.95 (1-56711-105-X). 48pp. A description of the construction and parts of this St. Louis landmark. (Rev: BL 9/15/95; SLJ 7/95) [725]

16545 Doherty, Craig A., and Katherine M. Doherty. *Mount Rushmore* (3–6). Illus. Series: Build America. 1995, Blackbirch LB $17.95 (1-56711-108-4). 48pp. The story of the planning through the execution of the four gigantic heads on Mount Rushmore and the controversy concerning taking the land from the Sioux. (Rev: BL 9/15/95; SLJ 7/95) [730]

16546 Doherty, Craig A., and Katherine M. Doherty. *The Sears Tower* (3–6). Illus. Series: Building America. 1995, Blackbirch LB $17.95 (1-56711-109-2). 48pp. The story of the design and construction of the world's tallest building and of some of the wonders found inside. (Rev: BL 9/15/95; SLJ 7/95) [725]

16547 Feeney, Kathy. *South Dakota Facts and Symbols* (1–4). Series: States and Their Symbols. 2000, Capstone LB $15.93 (0-7368-0646-6). 24pp. This short book uses double-page spreads to introduce South Dakota's major symbols including the state flower, flag, animal, tree, and seal. (Rev: BL 3/1/01) [978.3]

16548 Ford, Barbara. *Saint Louis* (3–5). Illus. Series: Downtown America. 1989, Macmillan LB $13.95 (0-87518-402-2). 64pp. This introduction includes history, geography, and places to visit. (Rev: BL 8/89; SLJ 11/89) [977.8]

16549 Fradin, Dennis B. *Illinois* (2–5). Illus. Series: From Sea to Shining Sea. 1991, Children's LB $27.00 (0-516-03813-3). 64pp. Many full-color photos add to the attractive coverage of this midwestern state. (Rev: BL 2/1/92) [977.3]

16550 Fradin, Dennis B. *Iowa* (3–5). Illus. Series: From Sea to Shining Sea. 1993, Children's LB $27.00 (0-516-03815-X). 64pp. This midwestern state is examined, with material on its history, geography, people, industries, and famous residents. (Rev: BL 11/1/93) [922.7]

16551 Fradin, Dennis B. *Michigan* (3–5). Illus. Series: From Sea to Shining Sea. 1992, Children's LB $27.00 (0-516-03822-2). 64pp. In addition to material on history and geography, this simple introduction includes a two-page Fact Sheet summary. (Rev: BL 5/1/92) [977.4]

16552 Fradin, Dennis B. *Missouri* (3–5). Illus. Series: From Sea to Shining Sea. 1994, Children's LB $27.00 (0-516-03825-7). 64pp. Some of the topics covered are Missouri's geography, history, and industries, plus a gallery of famous residents. (Rev: BL 8/94) [977.8]

16553 Fradin, Dennis B. *Ohio* (3–5). Illus. Series: From Sea to Shining Sea. 1993, Children's LB $27.00 (0-516-03835-4). 64pp. Ohio is covered through such topics as geography, history, industries, and cities. (Rev: BL 7/93) [977.1]

16554 Fredeen, Charles. *Kansas* (3–6). Illus. Series: Hello USA. 1992, Lerner LB $19.93 (0-8225-2716-2). 72pp. With excellent color illustrations, this account covers the state of Kansas and includes information on history, geography, and social and economic conditions. (Rev: BL 6/1/92) [978.1]

16555 Gibson, Karen Bush. *North Dakota Facts and Symbols* (1–4). Series: States and Their Symbols.

2000, Capstone LB $15.93 (0-7368-0642-3). 24pp. The flag, flower, seal, tree, bird, and animal that are the state symbols of North Dakota are presented in photographs and text. (Rev: BL 3/1/01) [978.4]

16556 Gibson, Karen Bush. *Oklahoma Facts and Symbols* (1–4). Series: States and Their Symbols. 2000, Capstone LB $15.93 (0-7368-0643-1). 24pp. A page of state facts and another of places to visit are included in this book that focuses on Oklahoma's state symbols, such as its flag, flower, seal, tree, and animal. (Rev: BL 3/1/01) [976.6]

16557 Heinrichs, Ann. *Indiana* (5–8). Series: America the Beautiful. 2000, Children's LB $32.00 (0-516-21038-6). 144pp. Topics covered in this excellent introduction to Indiana include geography, history, government, economy, people, and places. (Rev: BL 5/15/00) [977]

16558 Heinrichs, Ann. *Ohio* (5–8). Series: America the Beautiful. 1999, Children's LB $32.00 (0-516-20995-7). 144pp. Clear writing plus many color illustrations and maps are used to cover a wide range of topics about Ohio, including history, geography, famous residents, cities, economy, and government. (Rev: BL 11/15/99) [977.1]

16559 Hintz, Martin. *Iowa* (5–8). Series: America the Beautiful. 2000, Children's LB $32.00 (0-516-21070-X). 144pp. This introduction to Iowa includes such topics as its history, government, celebrities, and sports teams. (Rev: BL 5/15/00) [977.8]

16560 Hintz, Martin. *Michigan* (4–6). Series: America the Beautiful. 1998, Children's LB $32.00 (0-516-20636-2). 144pp. A colorful introduction to Michigan, using many maps, photos, and sidebars. (Rev: BL 10/15/98; HBG 3/99) [977.4]

16561 Hintz, Martin. *Minnesota* (5–8). Series: America the Beautiful. 2000, Children's LB $32.00 (0-516-21040-8). 144pp. This revision of the standard work on Minnesota gives expanded coverage and includes a timeline, fact sheets, and extensive lists of outside resources. (Rev: BL 5/15/00) [977.6]

16562 Hintz, Martin. *Missouri* (5–8). Series: America the Beautiful. 1999, Children's LB $32.00 (0-516-20836-5). 144pp. This colorful introduction to Missouri covers such topics as geography, history, government, economy, famous personalities, people, and culture. (Rev: BL 11/15/99) [977.8]

16563 Hintz, Martin. *North Dakota* (5–8). Series: America the Beautiful. 2000, Children's LB $33.00 (0-516-21072-6). 144pp. An introduction to North Dakota that includes the economy, land, people, history, state symbols, and sports teams. (Rev: BL 11/15/00) [978.4]

16564 Jameson, W. C. *Buried Treasures of the Great Plains* (5–8). Series: Buried Treasure. 1997, August House paper $11.95 (0-87483-486-4). 192pp. After a general introduction to the area, provides three to seven stories per state about buried treasure in Kansas, Nebraska, North Dakota, Oklahoma, South Dakota, and Texas. (Rev: SLJ 7/97) [977]

16565 Kent, Deborah. *Iowa* (4–6). Illus. Series: America the Beautiful. 1991, Children's LB $29.40

(0-516-00461-1). 144pp. In addition to geography, history, and economics, this state profile includes special fact sections and a list of important people. (Rev: BL 7/91; SLJ 9/91) [977.8]

16566 Kule, Elaine. *Iowa Facts and Symbols* (1–4). Series: States and Their Symbols. 2000, Capstone LB $15.93 (0-7368-0637-7). 24pp. The state symbols of Iowa including its flower, flag, tree, bird, seal, and animal are presented in double-page spreads with a photo opposite a few lines of explanatory text. (Rev: BL 3/1/01) [977.7]

16567 LaDoux, Rita C. *Iowa* (3–6). Illus. Series: Hello USA. 1992, Lerner LB $19.93 (0-8225-2724-3). 72pp. This introduction to Iowa gives capsule biographies, a timeline, fact sheets, and chapters on topics like history and geography. (Rev: BL 9/1/92) [977.7]

16568 LaDoux, Rita C. *Missouri* (3–6). Illus. Series: Hello USA. 1991, Lerner LB $19.93 (0-8225-2710-3). 72pp. With timelines, capsule biographies, many fact sheets, and the usual information, the state of Missouri is introduced. (Rev: BL 12/1/91) [977.8]

16569 LaDoux, Rita C. *Oklahoma* (3–6). Illus. Series: Hello USA. 1992, Lerner LB $19.93 (0-8225-2717-0). 72pp. Oklahoma is introduced with topics that include famous inhabitants, timelines, and fact sheets. (Rev: BL 6/1/92) [976.6]

16570 Lepthien, Emilie U. *South Dakota* (4–6). Illus. Series: America the Beautiful. 1991, Children's LB $28.00 (0-516-00487-5). 144pp. In addition to basic information, this account supplies various maps, a tour of the state, and profiles of important people. (Rev: BL 6/1/91) [978.3]

16571 Masters, Nancy Robinson. *Kansas* (5–8). Series: America the Beautiful. 1999, Children's LB $32.00 (0-516-20993-0). 144pp. An introduction to Kansas that covers its history and government, geography and people, tourism and state symbols, culture, and celebrities. (Rev: BL 12/15/9) [978.1]

16572 Murphy, Jim. *The Great Fire* (5–8). Illus. 1995, Scholastic $16.95 (0-590-47267-4). 144pp. A dramatic re-creation of the catastrophic Chicago fire of 1871 that left 100,000 people homeless. (Rev: BCCB 5/95; BL 6/1–15/95*; HB 5–6/95, 9–10/95; SLJ 7/95*) [977.3]

16573 Pfeiffer, Christine. *Chicago* (3–6). Illus. 1989, Macmillan LB $17.95 (0-87518-385-9). 60pp. History and modern life in the great midwestern metropolis. (Rev: BL 3/15/89; SLJ 3/89)

16574 Pollard, Michael. *The Mississippi* (5–8). Illus. Series: Great Rivers. 1997, Benchmark LB $22.79 (0-7614-0502-X). 45pp. The history of this great river and its influence on American history are covered, with descriptive photos, maps, and diagrams. (Rev: HBG 3/98; SLJ 3/98) [917.7]

16575 Porter, A. P. *Minnesota* (3–6). Illus. Series: Hello USA. 1992, Lerner LB $19.93 (0-8225-2718-9). 72pp. Fact sheets, timelines, and biographies of famous native sons and daughters are included in this introduction to Minnesota. (Rev: BL 6/1/92) [977.6]

16576 Porter, A. P. *Nebraska* (3–6). Illus. Series: Hello USA. 1991, Lerner LB $19.93 (0-8225-2708-

1). 72pp. With information on the environment as well as on topics like population, industries, symbols, history, and geography, Nebraska is given good coverage. (Rev: BL 12/1/91) [978.2]

16577 Reedy, Jerry. *Oklahoma* (5–8). Series: America the Beautiful. 1998, Children's LB $32.00 (0-516-20639-7). 144pp. Basic material on Oklahoma is supplemented with a special reference section that includes key statistics, important dates, famous people, and maps. (Rev: BL 1/1–15/99; SLJ 2/99) [976.6]

16578 Ross, Jim, and Paul Myers, eds. *Dear Oklahoma City, Get Well Soon* (3–6). Illus. 1996, Walker LB $17.85 (0-8027-8437-2). 48pp. A sampling of the letters and drawings sent by children to victims of the 1995 bombing of the Oklahoma City Federal Building. (Rev: BCCB 6/96; BL 5/15/96; SLJ 5/96) [976.6]

16579 Santella, Andrew. *Illinois* (5–8). Illus. Series: America the Beautiful. 1998, Children's LB $32.00 (0-516-20633-8). 144pp. This comprehensive account of Illinois includes its history and geography, principal cities and important landmarks, and culture and people. (Rev: BL 1/1–15/99) [977.3]

16580 Santella, Andrew. *Mount Rushmore* (4–6). Series: Cornerstones of Freedom. 1999, Children's LB $19.50 (0-516-21140-4). 32pp. Conceived in 1923, this famous landmark with its carved busts of four U.S. presidents, took from 1927 to 1941 to complete. (Rev: BL 5/15/99; HBG 10/99; SLJ 8/99) [978.3]

16581 Schwabacher, Martin. *Minnesota* (4–7). Series: Celebrate the States. 1999, Benchmark LB $24.95 (0-7614-0658-1). 144pp. Minnesota is introduced in six chapters that cover history, geography, government and economy, people, achievements, and landmarks. (Rev: HBG 10/99; SLJ 10/99) [977.6]

16582 Sherrow, Victoria. *The Oklahoma City Bombing: Terror in the Heartland* (4–8). Illus. Series: American Disasters. 1998, Enslow LB $18.95 (0-7660-1061-9). 48pp. Using many first-person descriptions, this account of the Oklahoma City bombing ends with the sentencing of Timothy McVeigh and Terry Nichols. (Rev: BL 1/1–15/99; HBG 3/99; SLJ 3/99) [364.16]

16583 Sirvaitis, Karen. *Michigan* (3–5). Illus. Series: Hello USA. 1994, Lerner LB $19.93 (0-8225-2722-7). 72pp. With photos on every page, this account supplies a brief trip around Michigan plus historical information and material on resources, cities, and people. (Rev: BL 4/15/94) [977.4]

16584 Stein, R. Conrad. *Chicago* (3–6). Illus. Series: Cities of the World. 1997, Children's LB $26.50 (0-516-20301-0). 64pp. A heavily illustrated account that describes Chicago, gives a brief history, and provides a tour of famous landmarks. (Rev: BL 8/97; SLJ 2/98) [977.3]

16585 Stein, R. Conrad. *Minnesota* (4–6). Illus. Series: America the Beautiful. 1990, Children's LB $28.00 (0-516-00469-7). 144pp. Historical and geographical coverage, plus a tour of important sites. (Rev: BL 1/1/91) [977.6]

16586 Stewart, Gail B. *Chicago* (3–6). Illus. Series: Great Cities of the U.S.A. 1989, Rourke LB $23.93 (0-86592-538-0). 48pp. Describes the history and development of this important Great Lakes port. (Rev: BL 1/1/90) [917]

16587 Sturman, Susan. *Kansas City* (3–5). Illus. Series: Downtown America. 1990, Macmillan LB $13.95 (0-87518-432-4). 60pp. The history of Kansas City, Missouri, is covered, with data on sights and cultural life. (Rev: BL 6/1/90) [977.8]

16588 Verba, Joan M. *North Dakota* (2–6). Illus. Series: Hello USA. 1992, Lerner LB $19.93 (0-8225-2746-4). 72pp. This guide to the Flickertail State includes coverage of history, geography, and famous North Dakotans. (Rev: BL 12/15/92) [978.4]

16589 Wade, Linda R. *Badlands: Beauty Carved from Nature* (4–6). Illus. Series: Doors to America's Past. 1992, Rourke LB $22.60 (0-86592-471-6). 48pp. The history and present importance of Badlands National Park in South Dakota are told in text and illustrations. (Rev: BL 5/1/92; SLJ 1/92) [508.73]

16590 Wade, Linda R. *Hannibal: Mark Twain's Boyhood Home* (4–7). Series: Doors to America's Past. 1991, Rourke LB $22.60 (0-86592-466-X). 48pp. After describing Hannibal as it was in Twain's time, this account describes the city as it is today. (Rev: BL 5/1/92; SLJ 3/92) [977]

16591 Wills, Charles A. *A Historical Album of Illinois* (4–8). Illus. Series: Historical Album. 1994, Millbrook LB $23.40 (1-56294-482-7). 64pp. A brief history of Illinois that touches on the most important events from before the white man to the 1990s. (Rev: SLJ 3/95) [977.3]

16592 Wills, Charles A. *A Historical Album of Michigan* (4–7). Illus. Series: Historical Album. 1996, Millbrook LB $23.40 (0-7613-0036-8); paper $7.95 (0-7613-0126-7). 64pp. Using many archival prints, drawings, photographs, and ample text, the history of Michigan is told. (Rev: BL 10/15/96) [977]

16593 Wills, Charles A. *A Historical Album of Ohio* (4–7). Illus. Series: Historical Album. 1996, Millbrook LB $23.40 (1-56294-593-9); paper $6.95 (0-7613-0086-4). 64pp. The history of Ohio is traced from prehistoric times to the present. (Rev: BL 7/96; SLJ 7/96) [977.1]

16594 Zimmerman, Chanda K. *Detroit* (3–5). Illus. Series: Downtown America. 1989, Macmillan LB $13.95 (0-87518-409-X). 64pp. Physical features and the history of Detroit are covered. (Rev: BL 8/89; SLJ 11/89) [977.4]

MOUNTAIN STATES

16595 Anderson, Peter. *A Grand Canyon Journey: Tracing Time in Stone* (4–6). Illus. Series: First Books. 1997, Watts LB $22.50 (0-531-20259-3). 64pp. This tour down the Grand Canyon tells how ancient history has helped shape this terrain and gives information on the origins and geology of each rock layer. (Rev: BL 5/15/97; SLJ 8/97) [917.91]

16596 Ayer, Eleanor. *Colorado* (4–8). Illus. Series: Celebrate the States. 1997, Marshall Cavendish LB $35.64 (0-7614-0148-2). 144pp. An introduction to the mountain state, with information on its history, geography, and people. (Rev: BL 7/97; SLJ 8/97) [978.8]

16597 Ayres, Becky. *Salt Lake City* (3–5). Illus. Series: Downtown America. 1990, Macmillan LB $17.95 (0-87518-436-7). 60pp. Introduces Salt Lake City, its sights, sounds, and history. (Rev: BL 2/1/91) [979.2]

16598 Blashfield, Jean F. *Arizona* (5–8). Series: America the Beautiful. 2000, Children's LB $33.00 (0-516-21068-8). 144pp. This excellent guide to Arizona covers all the basic topics about the southwestern state. (Rev: BL 9/15/00) [979.1]

16599 Blashfield, Jean F. *Colorado* (5–8). Series: America the Beautiful. 1999, Children's LB $32.00 (0-516-20684-2). 144pp. A solid introduction to Colorado that contains the standard historical and geographical information plus state symbols, a government chart, about a dozen maps, and a historical timeline. (Rev: BL 11/15/99; HBG 10/99; SLJ 10/99) [978.8]

16600 Bledsoe, Sara. *Colorado* (3–6). Illus. Series: Hello USA. 1993, Lerner LB $19.93 (0-8225-2750-2). 72pp. A small volume that covers Colorado's history, geography, people, industries, and landmarks. (Rev: BL 12/1/93) [978.8]

16601 Doherty, Craig A., and Katherine M. Doherty. *Hoover Dam* (3–6). Illus. Series: Building America. 1995, Blackbirch LB $17.95 (1-56711-107-6). 48pp. Traces the construction of the Hoover Dam on the Colorado River, from its conception through its completion in 1936 to its present importance. (Rev: BL 9/15/95; SLJ 7/95) [627]

16602 Dubois, Muriel. *Wyoming: Facts and Symbols* (1–4). Series: The States and Their Symbols. 2000, Capstone LB $15.93 (0-7368-0529-X). 24pp. After a few easily read pages of basic facts about Wyoming, this account covers in double-page spreads such topics as the state seal, flag, flower, bird, and animal. (Rev: BL 6/1–15/00; HBG 10/00) [972.95]

16603 Feeney, Kathy. *Utah: Facts and Symbols* (1–4). Illus. Series: States and Their Symbols. 2000, Capstone LB $15.93 (0-7368-0526-5). 24pp. This introduction to Utah uses a basic fact sheet followed by information on its state symbols. (Rev: BL 6/1–15/00; HBG 10/00; SLJ 10/00) [979.2]

16604 Filbin, Dan. *Arizona* (3–6). Illus. Series: Hello USA. 1991, Lerner LB $19.93 (0-8225-2705-7). 72pp. This account covers all aspects of this southwestern state and includes many color photos. (Rev: BL 4/15/91; SLJ 6/91) [979.1]

16605 Foster, Lynne. *Exploring the Grand Canyon: Adventures of Yesterday and Today* (3–6). Illus. by Margaret Sanfilippo. 1990, Grand Canyon Natural History Assn. paper $15.95 (0-938216-33-3). 150pp. This work gives a history of the Grand Canyon, the kinds of people who have been involved with it, and tips for the first-time visitor. (Rev: BL 9/1/90) [917]

16606 Fradin, Dennis B. *Arizona* (3–5). Illus. Series: From Sea to Shining Sea. 1993, Children's LB $27.00 (0-516-03803-6). 64pp. This account takes the reader on a trip around Arizona, as well as covering its basic history and geography. (Rev: BL 11/1/93; SLJ 1/94) [979.1]

16607 Fradin, Dennis B. *Colorado* (3–5). Illus. Series: From Sea to Shining Sea. 1993, Children's LB $27.00 (0-516-03806-0). 64pp. Maps, diagrams, and color photos on each page enliven this introduction to Colorado, its history, geography, landmarks, and people. (Rev: BL 11/1/93; SLJ 1/94) [978.8]

16608 Fradin, Dennis B. *Montana* (3–5). Illus. Series: From Sea to Shining Sea. 1992, Children's LB $27.00 (0-516-03826-5). 64pp. With many color photos, this introduction to Montana includes material on people, industries, and principal cities. (Rev: BL 5/1/92) [978.6]

16609 Fradin, Dennis B. *Utah* (3–5). Illus. Series: From Sea to Shining Sea. 1993, Children's LB $27.00 (0-516-03844-3). 64pp. Coverage includes history, geography, people, and famous places. (Rev: BL 7/93) [979.2]

16610 Fradin, Dennis B., and Judith B. Fradin. *Wyoming* (3–5). Illus. Series: From Sea to Shining Sea. 1994, Children's LB $27.00 (0-516-03850-8). 64pp. An attractive presentation of the geography, history, and people of Wyoming, with maps, glossary, reference section, and thorough index. (Rev: BL 8/94) [978.7]

16611 Fraser, Mary Ann. *In Search of the Grand Canyon: Down the Colorado with John Wesley Powell* (4–6). Illus. 1995, Holt $14.95 (0-8050-3495-1). 69pp. The story of Powell and his amazing exploration of the Colorado River and the Grand Canyon in spite of many disasters. (Rev: BL 7/95; SLJ 7/95*) [979.1]

16612 Frisch, Carlienne. *Wyoming* (3–6). Illus. Series: Hello USA. 1994, Lerner LB $19.93 (0-8225-2736-7). 72pp. The famous sights and attractions of Wyoming are covered, along with its history, development, and people. (Rev: BL 4/15/94; SLJ 7/94) [978.7]

16613 George, Charles, and Linda George. *Idaho* (5–8). Series: America the Beautiful. 2000, Children's LB $33.00 (0-516-21037-8). 144pp. A fine introduction to Idaho that includes such topics as geography, history, government, landmarks, people, recreation, and culture. (Rev: BL 9/15/00) [978]

16614 George, Charles, and Linda George. *Montana* (5–8). Series: America the Beautiful. 2000, Children's LB $33.00 (0-516-21092-0). 144pp. A broad introduction to the state of Montana, including its history and geography, cities and landmarks, people, and economy. (Rev: BL 11/15/00) [978.6]

16615 Gibson, Karen Bush. *Nevada Facts and Symbols* (1–4). Series: States and Their Symbols. 2000, Capstone LB $15.93 (0-7368-0641-5). 24pp. Following a page of important state facts, this book uses color photos and a brief text to present Nevada's official symbols. (Rev: BL 3/1/01) [979.3]

16616 Halvorsen, Lisa. *Letters Home from Grand Canyon* (3–6). Series: Letters Home from Our National Parks. 2000, Blackbirch LB $16.95 (1-56711-463-6). 32pp. An interesting, first-person account of a visit to the Grand Canyon with material on land formations, animals, plants, and sights. Also use *Letters Home from Yosemite* (2000). (Rev: BL 5/15/00; HBG 10/00; SLJ 8/00) [979.1]

16617 Halvorsen, Lisa. *Letters Home from Zion* (2–5). Series: Letters Home From. 2000, Blackbirch LB $16.95 (1-56711-464-4). 32pp. Taking the format of letters to a friend back home, this book describes Zion National Park in Utah with its red cliffs and deep canyons. (Rev: HBG 3/01; SLJ 11/00) [979.2]

16618 Heinrichs, Ann. *Arizona* (4–6). Illus. Series: America the Beautiful. 1991, Children's LB $28.00 (0-516-00449-2). 144pp. This introduction to Arizona includes a chronology, maps, and biographies of important people. (Rev: BL 7/91) [979.1]

16619 Heinrichs, Ann. *Montana* (4–6). Illus. Series: America the Beautiful. 1991, Children's LB $28.00 (0-516-00472-7). 144pp. After an introduction to Montana, there is a special reference section that contains key facts. (Rev: BL 7/91) [978.8]

16620 Kent, Deborah. *Utah* (5–8). Series: America the Beautiful. 2000, Children's LB $32.00 (0-516-21045-9). 144pp. A guide to this mountain state, covering all the basic topics plus information on sports, religion, celebrities, and the Indian tribes that lived there. (Rev: BL 5/15/00) [979.2]

16621 Kent, Deborah. *Wyoming* (5–8). Series: America the Beautiful. 2000, Children's LB $33.00 (0-516-21075-0). 144pp. An introduction to Wyoming, including its geography, history, government, economy, people, sports, and celebrities. (Rev: BL 9/15/00) [978.7]

16622 Kule, Elaine. *Idaho Facts and Symbols* (1–4). Series: States and Their Symbols. 2000, Capstone LB $15.93 (0-7368-0636-9). 24pp. This book presents a few basic facts about Idaho followed by double-page spreads that illustrate and describe this state's flag, bird, flower, seal, animal, and tree. (Rev: BL 3/1/01) [979.6]

16623 LaDoux, Rita C. *Montana* (3–6). Illus. Series: Hello USA. 1992, Lerner LB $19.93 (0-8225-2714-6). 72pp. In addition to standard introductory material, coverage includes timelines about Montana and biographies of famous residents. (Rev: BL 5/15/92; SLJ 7/92) [978.6]

16624 Lauber, Patricia. *Summer of Fire: Yellowstone 1988* (3–5). Illus. 1991, Orchard $19.95 (0-531-05943-X). 64pp. Striking photos dramatize the fires of 1988 and their aftermath in Yellowstone National Park. (Rev: BCCB 10/91; BL 9/1/91; HB 9–10/91*; SLJ 9/91) [581.5]

16625 Lillegard, Dee, and Wayne Stoker. *Nevada* (4–6). Illus. Series: America the Beautiful. 1990, Children's LB $28.00 (0-516-00474-3). 144pp. This introduction includes history, geography, life today, and statistics. (Rev: BL 1/1/91) [979.3]

16626 McCarthy, Betty. *Utah* (5–7). Illus. Series: America the Beautiful. 1989, Children's LB $28.00 (0-516-00490-5). 144pp. The story of Utah is told in pictures and text covering such topics as economy, history, geography, and recreation. (Rev: BL 1/1/90) [979.2]

16627 McDaniel, Melissa. *Arizona* (4–8). Series: Celebrate the States. 2000, Marshall Cavendish LB $24.95 (0-7614-0647-6). 139pp. This introduction to Arizona discusses its land, history, economy, festivals, cultural diversity, and landmarks. (Rev: BL 6/1–15/00; HBG 10/00; SLJ 9/00) [979.1]

16628 Meister, Cari. *Grand Canyon* (2–4). Series: Going Places. 2000, ABDO LB $13.95 (1-57765-024-7). 24pp. This well-organized introduction to the Grand Canyon describes the geological formations and supplies material on the plants, animals, and interesting sights in the area. (Rev: HBG 10/00; SLJ 1/01) [917.91]

16629 Meister, Cari. *Yellowstone National Park* (2–4). Illus. Series: Going Places. 2000, ABDO $13.95 (1-57765-026-3). This tour of Yellowstone National Park includes material on history, its things to see and do, and the plants and animals. (Rev: HBG 10/00; SLJ 1/01) [917.8]

16630 Minor, Wendell. *Grand Canyon: Exploring a Natural Wonder* (3–6). Illus. 1998, Scholastic $16.95 (0-590-47968-7). 40pp. The author describes, in paintings and text, the sights he saw and the animal and plant life he observed during a 12-day trip to the Grand Canyon. (Rev: BL 9/15/98; HBG 3/99; SLJ 8/98) [741]

16631 Petersen, David. *Bryce Canyon National Park* (2–3). Illus. Series: True Books. 1996, Children's LB $22.00 (0-516-20048-8). 48pp. A well-illustrated introduction to this national park and its amazing rock formations. Also use *Death Valley National Park* (1996). (Rev: SLJ 5/97) [917.91]

16632 Petersen, David. *Dinosaur National Monument* (2–4). Illus. Series: New True Books. 1995, Children's LB $21.00 (0-516-01074-3). 48pp. A description in text and pictures of the Dinosaur National Monument in Colorado and Utah and its historical importance. (Rev: BL 7/95; SLJ 8/95) [978.8]

16633 Petersen, David. *Grand Canyon National Park* (1–3). Illus. Series: New True Books. 1992, Children's LB $21.00 (0-516-02197-4). 48pp. In stunning color photos and simple text, the Grand Canyon National Park in Arizona is described. (Rev: BL 2/1/93) [917.91]

16634 Petersen, David. *Rocky Mountain National Park* (2–4). Illus. Series: New True Books. 1993, Children's LB $21.00 (0-516-01196-0). 48pp. This attractive book introduces this Colorado national park with simple text and many photos. (Rev: BL 7/94) [978.8]

16635 Petersen, David. *Yellowstone National Park* (1–3). Illus. Series: New True Books. 1992, Children's LB $19.00 (0-516-01148-0). 48pp. The story of the oldest national park, famous for its scenery, wildlife, and geysers. (Rev: BL 9/1/92; SLJ 3/93) [917.8]

16636 Powell, John Wesley. *Conquering the Grand Canyon* (3–6). Series: In My Own Words. 2000, Marshall Cavendish LB $16.95 (0-7614-1013-9). 64pp. These excerpts from the writings of John Wesley Powell describe how he felt as the first white man to view the natural wonders of the Grand Canyon. (Rev: BL 3/1/01; HBG 3/01) [978]

16637 Sirvaitis, Karen. *Utah* (3–6). Illus. Series: Hello USA. 1991, Lerner LB $19.93 (0-8225-2707-3). 72pp. This introduction to Utah features color illustrations on each page, facts-at-a-glance sections, and a historical timeline. (Rev: BL 8/91; SLJ 2/92) [979.2]

16638 Spies, Karen B. *Denver* (3–5). Illus. 1988, Macmillan LB $17.95 (0-87518-386-7). 60pp. Living in Denver as described by a resident. (Rev: BL 1/15/89; SLJ 3/89)

16639 Staub, Frank. *Yellowstone's Cycle of Fire* (3–6). Illus. Series: Earth Watch. 1994, Carolrhoda LB $19.95 (0-87614-778-3). 48pp. The cycle of forest fires and later renewal in Yellowstone Park is described, with major coverage of the huge fire of 1988. (Rev: BL 2/1/94; SLJ 6/94) [574.5]

16640 Stefoff, Rebecca. *Idaho* (4–8). Series: Celebrate the States. 2000, Benchmark LB $14.95 (0-7614-0663-8). Interesting charts, graphs, and maps are used to illustrate such topics as the people, land, history, and culture of Idaho. (Rev: BL 1/1–15/00; HBG 10/00) [978.8]

16641 Stefoff, Rebecca. *Utah* (4–8). Series: Celebrate the States. 2000, Marshall Cavendish LB $24.95 (0-7614-1064-3). 144pp. Utah's unique characteristics and places are highlighted in this account that also covers the state's history, geography, and government. (Rev: BL 12/15/00; HBG 3/01; SLJ 2/01) [979.2]

16642 Stein, R. Conrad. *Nevada* (5–8). Series: America the Beautiful. 2000, Children's LB $32.00 (0-516-21041-6). 144pp. A good introduction to Nevada's history and geography, economy, culture, people, sights, and entertainment. (Rev: BL 5/15/00) [979.3]

16643 Vieira, Linda. *Grand Canyon: A Trail Through Time* (3–5). Illus. by Christopher Canyon. 1997, Walker $15.95 (0-8027-8625-1). 32pp. A mule trail is the focus of this description of the Grand Canyon, with material on the formation of this wonder and of the various layers of rock that are visible. (Rev: BL 2/1/98; HBG 3/98) [917.91]

16644 Wills, Charles A. *A Historical Album of Colorado* (4–7). Illus. Series: Historical Album. 1996, Millbrook LB $23.40 (1-56294-592-0); paper $6.95 (1-56294-858-X). 64pp. Using many old engravings and photographs, the history of Colorado is traced, beginning with its Native American population. (Rev: BL 7/96; SLJ 7/96) [978.8]

NORTHEAST

16645 Adams, Barbara J. *New York City* (3–5). Illus. 1988, Macmillan LB $13.95 (0-87518-384-0). 60pp. Explaining the unique character of this city in words and pictures. (Rev: BL 1/15/89; SLJ 5/89)

16646 Ashabranner, Brent. *Badge of Valor: The National Law Enforcement Officers Memorial* (5–8). Illus. 2000, Twenty-First Century LB $24.90 (0-7613-1522-5). 64pp. This history of the memorial, from the original proposal in the 1970s to its opening in 1991, also discusses what it stands for and reveals the heroic deeds of some important law officers. (Rev: BL 10/1/00; HBG 3/01; SLJ 1/01) [363.2]

16647 Ashabranner, Brent. *A Date with Destiny: The Women in Military Service for America Memorial* (5–8). Illus. 2000, Twenty-First Century LB $23.90 (0-7613-1472-5). 64pp. This book tells the story of the memorial outside Arlington National Cemetery that honors American women in the military and retells some of the stories of these servicewomen. (Rev: BL 2/1/00; HBG 10/00) [355.1]

16648 Ashabranner, Brent. *No Better Hope: What the Lincoln Memorial Means to America* (4–8). Illus. Series: Great American Memorials. 2001, Twenty-First Century LB $24.90 (0-7613-1523-3). 64pp. As well as telling about Lincoln and his importance to the country, this volume describes the building of the memorial and the important events that have occurred on the site. (Rev: BL 3/1/01) [975.3]

16649 Ashabranner, Brent. *Their Names to Live: What the Vietnam Veterans Memorial Means to America* (5–8). Photos by Jennifer Ashabranner. 1998, Twenty-First Century LB $23.90 (0-7613-3235-9). 64pp. As well as describing the conception, construction, and dedication of the Vietnam Veterans Memorial, the author profiles four young men whose names are on the monument. (Rev: BL 3/1/99; HBG 10/99; SLJ 3/99) [975.3]

16650 Avakian, Monique. *A Historical Album of Massachusetts* (4–8). Illus. Series: Historical Album. 1994, Millbrook LB $23.40 (1-56294-481-9). 64pp. A history of Massachusetts that begins with the Native American culture and ends with the 1900s, including basic material on major events and personalities. (Rev: SLJ 2/95) [974.4]

16651 Avakian, Monique, and Carter Smith, III. *A Historical Album of New York* (5–8). Illus. Series: Historical Album. 1993, Millbrook LB $23.40 (1-56294-005-8). 64pp. An overview of New York State history from Native Americans settlements to the present day, using extensive archival illustrations. (Rev: SLJ 10/93) [974.7]

16652 Aylesworth, Thomas G., and Virginia L. Aylesworth. *Upper Atlantic: New Jersey, New York* (3–8). Illus. 1995, Chelsea LB $19.95 (0-7910-3399-6); paper $9.95 (0-7910-3417-8). 64pp. Encyclopedia-like coverage of New York and New Jersey. (Rev: BL 9/1/87; SLJ 11/87)

16653 Balcer, Bernadette, and Fran O'Byrne-Pelham. *Philadelphia* (3–6). Illus. 1989, Macmillan LB $17.95 (0-87518-388-3). 60pp. All aspects of the old city's history, as well as modern living, are discussed. (Rev: BL 3/15/89; SLJ 3/89)

16654 Benson, Laura Lee. *Washington, D.C.: A Scrapbook* (2–6). Illus. by Iris Van Rynbach. 1999, Charlesbridge LB $15.95 (0-88106-064-X); paper $6.95 (0-88106-063-1). A young African American student records a class trip to Washington, D.C., where he uses the subway line and visits such landmarks as the White House and the National Zoo. (Rev: HBG 3/00; SLJ 11/99) [975.3]

16655 Blashfield, Jean F. *Delaware* (5–8). Series: America the Beautiful. 2000, Children's LB $33.00 (0-516-21090-4). 144pp. Delaware's geography and history are explored in this attractive volume, which also discusses its culture, people, and lifestyle. (Rev: BL 11/15/00) [975.1]

16656 Brill, Marlene T. *Building the Capital City* (3–5). Illus. Series: Cornerstones of Freedom. 1996, Children's LB $20.50 (0-516-06633-1). 32pp. The story of the planning, building, and growth of Washington, D.C., through the years. (Rev: BL 7/96; SLJ 8/96) [975.3]

16657 Brooks, Philip. *The United States Holocaust Memorial Museum* (3–5). Illus. Series: Cornerstones of Freedom. 1996, Children's LB $20.50 (0-516-20007-0). 32pp. The story of this Washington, D.C., landmark, its design, its contents, and the tragic events that it commemorates. (Rev: BL 11/15/96) [940.53]

16658 Brown, Dottie. *Delaware* (3–6). Illus. Series: Hello USA. 1994, Lerner LB $19.93 (0-8225-2733-2). 72pp. A compact book that introduces Delaware's history, geography, resources, and famous people. (Rev: BL 4/15/94) [975.1]

16659 Brown, Dottie. *New Hampshire* (3–6). Illus. Series: Hello USA. 1993, Lerner LB $19.93 (0-8225-2730-8). 72pp. A brief, colorful introduction to New Hampshire that takes the reader on a tour of the state, covers its history, tells how the people live, and gives biographies of famous residents. (Rev: BL 12/1/93) [974.2]

16660 Climo, Shirley. *City! Washington, D.C.* (4–6). 1991, Macmillan LB $16.95 (0-02-719036-6). 64pp. An upbeat look at the nation's capital. (Rev: BL 8/91; SLJ 9/91) [917.5304]

16661 Collins, Mary. *The Smithsonian Institution* (4–6). Series: Cornerstones of Freedom. 1999, Children's LB $20.00 (0-516-21168-4). 32pp. The history of the Smithson grant to the nation, the founding of the institution, and the nature and range of its present collections and buildings are covered in this well-illustrated account. (Rev: BL 10/15/99) [975.33]

16662 Curlee, Lynn. *Liberty* (3–8). Illus. by author. 2000, Simon & Schuster $18.00 (0-689-82823-3). 41pp. This slim volume presents, in picture-book format, a history of the Statue of Liberty with material on its construction, its recent restoration, and what it symbolizes. (Rev: BCCB 5/00; HB 5–6/00; HBG 10/00; SLJ 5/00) [974.7]

16663 Cytron, Barry. *Fire! The Library Is Burning* (4–7). Illus. 1988, Lerner LB $15.93 (0-8225-0525-8). 56pp. How workers and volunteers helped to restore the Jewish Theological Seminary in New York City when it was nearly destroyed by fire. (Rev: BL 7/88; SLJ 9/88)

16664 Dean, Julia. *A Year on Monhegan Island* (3–6). Illus. 1995, Ticknor $14.95 (0-395-66476-4). 48pp. A photo-essay that describes the seasons and the activities of the residents of this small island off the coast of Maine. (Rev: BCCB 3/95; BL 4/15/95; SLJ 4/95) [974.1]

16665 Doherty, Craig A., and Katherine M. Doherty. *The Empire State Building* (4–7). 1997, Blackbirch LB $17.95 (1-56711-116-5). 48pp. The story of the planning and construction of this skyscraper, with material on its functions today. (Rev: BL 10/15/97; HBG 3/98; SLJ 1/98) [917.47]

16666 Doherty, Craig A., and Katherine M. Doherty. *The Statue of Liberty* (3–6). Illus. Series: Building America. 1996, Blackbirch LB $17.95 (1-56711-111-4). 48pp. The Statue of Liberty, from the original idea to the finished sculpture. (Rev: BL 11/15/96; SLJ 1/97) [974.7]

16667 Doherty, Craig A., and Katherine M. Doherty. *The Washington Monument* (3–6). Illus. Series: Building America. 1995, Blackbirch LB $17.95 (1-56711-110-6). 48pp. The story of this Washington, D.C., landmark from the original idea, through its phases of construction, to its present use as a tourist attraction. (Rev: BL 9/15/95; SLJ 7/95) [975.3]

16668 Dubois, Muriel L. *New Hampshire: Facts and Symbols* (1–4). Illus. Series: States and Their Symbols. 2000, Capstone LB $15.93 (0-7368-0524-9). 24pp. A colorfully illustrated guide to New Hampshire that supplements basic facts with information on the state seal, motto, flag, bird, tree, flower, and animal. (Rev: BL 6/1–15/00; HBG 10/00) [974.2]

16669 Elish, Dan. *Vermont* (4–8). Illus. Series: Celebrate the States. 1997, Marshall Cavendish LB $35.64 (0-7614-0146-6). 144pp. An introduction to this New England state that covers such topics as famous sights, history, and how the people live. (Rev: BL 7/97; SLJ 8/97) [974.3]

16670 Elish, Dan. *Washington, D.C.* (5–8). Series: Celebrate the States. 1998, Benchmark LB $22.95 (0-7614-0423-6). 144pp. An attractive introduction to the people and government of the U.S. capital with material on parks, landmarks, history, economics, and racial problems. (Rev: HBG 10/98; SLJ 1/99) [975.3]

16671 Engfer, LeeAnne. *Maine* (3–6). Illus. Series: Hello USA. 1991, Lerner LB $19.93 (0-8225-2701-4). 72pp. With many illustrations, this is a solid introduction to the New England state Maine. (Rev: BL 4/15/91; SLJ 6/91) [974.1]

16672 Fazio, Wende. *Times Square* (4–6). Series: Cornerstones of Freedom. 1999, Children's LB $20.00 (0-516-21184-6); paper $5.95 (0-516-26530-X). 32pp. The history of this famous crossroad in New York City, its changes throughout history, and current efforts to revitalize it. (Rev: BL 10/15/99) [974.7]

16673 Feeney, Kathy. *Rhode Island Facts and Symbols* (1–4). Series: States and Their Symbols. 2000, Capstone LB $15.93 (0-7368-0645-8). 24pp. After a few basic facts about Rhode Island, most of this book's contents are devoted to photos and brief explanations of the state's flag, flower, seal, animal, and other symbols. (Rev: BL 3/1/01) [974.5]

16674 Feeney, Kathy. *Vermont Facts and Symbols* (1–4). Series: States and Their Symbols. 2000, Capstone LB $15.93 (0-7368-0647-4). 24pp. After a page of basic facts about Vermont, this book introduces, through photos and text, such state symbols as its flag, seal, flower, animal, tree, and bird. (Rev: BL 3/1/01) [974.3]

16675 Feeney, Kathy. *Washington, D.C. Facts and Symbols* (3–4). Series: States and Their Symbols. 2000, Capstone LB $15.93 (0-7368-0527-3). 24pp. A brief account of Washington, D.C., that includes material on the District's symbols including its seal and motto, bird, tree, flower, the national mall, and places to visit. (Rev: HBG 10/00; SLJ 10/00) [975.3]

16676 Feinberg, Barbara S. *The Changing White House* (4–6). Series: Cornerstones of Freedom. 2000, Children's LB $20.50 (0-516-21651-1); paper $5.95 (0-516-27164-4). 32pp. This well-illustrated book covers the history of the White House and how it has changed through the years — both physically and functionally. (Rev: BL 9/15/00) [975.3]

16677 Fradin, Dennis B. *Maine* (3–5). Illus. Series: From Sea to Shining Sea. 1994, Children's LB $27.00 (0-516-03819-2). 64pp. In addition to providing standard geographical and historical information, this well-illustrated book contains a checklist of important information about Maine, a timeline, maps, and a glossary. (Rev: BL 8/94) [974.1]

16678 Fradin, Dennis B. *Massachusetts* (2–5). Illus. Series: From Sea to Shining Sea. 1991, Children's LB $27.00 (0-516-03821-4). 64pp. An attractive, informative package covering this New England state. (Rev: BL 2/1/92; SLJ 3/92) [974.4]

16679 Fradin, Dennis B. *New Hampshire* (3–5). Illus. Series: From Sea to Shining Sea. 1992, Children's LB $27.00 (0-516-03829-X). 64pp. This introduction to New Hampshire tells about its geography, early history, present status, and state symbols. (Rev: BL 1/15/93) [974.2]

16680 Fradin, Dennis B. *New Jersey* (3–5). Illus. Series: From Sea to Shining Sea. 1993, Children's LB $27.00 (0-516-03830-3). 64pp. A tour of the Garden State is included in this good introduction. (Rev: BL 7/93) [974.9]

16681 Fradin, Dennis B. *New York* (3–5). Illus. Series: From Sea to Shining Sea. 1993, Children's LB $27.00 (0-516-03832-X). 64pp. This account takes one on a tour of the state, highlighting landmarks and geography, with material on history, industries, and famous New Yorkers. (Rev: BL 11/1/93; SLJ 2/94) [974.7]

16682 Fradin, Dennis B. *Pennsylvania* (3–5). Illus. Series: From Sea to Shining Sea. 1994, Children's LB $27.00 (0-516-03838-9). 64pp. An attractive portrait of the past and present of Pennsylvania, with coverage of the people and how they work and play. (Rev: BL 8/94) [974.8]

16683 Fradin, Dennis B. *Vermont* (3–5). Illus. Series: From Sea to Shining Sea. 1993, Children's LB $27.00 (0-516-03845-1). 64pp. Many photographs and simple text introduce the New England state of Vermont. (Rev: BL 7/93) [974.3]

16684 Fradin, Dennis B. *Washington, D.C.* (3–5). Illus. Series: From Sea to Shining Sea. 1992, Children's LB $27.00 (0-516-03851-6). 64pp. This introduction to the nation's capital includes a fact summary and a guide to major monuments. (Rev: BL 5/1/92; SLJ 8/92) [975.3]

16685 Fredeen, Charles. *New Jersey* (3–6). Illus. Series: Hello USA. 1993, Lerner LB $19.93 (0-8225-2732-4). 72pp. The Garden State is introduced with color illustrations and informative text. (Rev: BL 7/93; SLJ 8/93) [974.9]

16686 Gibbons, Gail. *From Path to Highway: The Story of the Boston Post Road* (2–4). Illus. 1986, HarperCollins LB $14.89 (0-690-04514-X). 32pp. A picture-book history of the road used by early travelers and today's citizens when traveling between Boston and New York. (Rev: BCCB 6/86; BL 6/15/86; SLJ 9/86)

16687 Gleman, Amy. *Connecticut* (3–6). Illus. 1991, Lerner LB $19.93 (0-8225-2709-X). 72pp. In text and pictures, this book covers history, economics, and interesting features and includes a timeline, maps, and charts. (Rev: BL 10/15/91) [974.6]

16688 Guzzetti, Paula. *The White House* (4–6). Illus. Series: Places in American History. 1995, Silver Burdett LB $14.95 (0-87518-650-5). 72pp. A tour of the White House and its history, with brief asides on some of its inhabitants and their effects on the building. (Rev: BL 2/15/96; SLJ 1/96) [975.3]

16689 Haas, Jessie. *Fire! My Parents' Story* (4–6). Illus. 1998, Greenwillow $15.00 (0-688-15203-1). 72pp. Told from the standpoint of an eight-year-old girl, this is the true story of how a fire destroyed a Vermont farm and how the family eventually rebuilt and returned to their property. (Rev: BCCB 3/98; BL 5/1/98; HBG 10/98; SLJ 5/98) [974.3]

16690 Hansen, Joyce, and Gary McGowan. *Breaking Ground, Breaking Silence: The Story of New York's African Burial Ground* (5–9). 1998, Holt $16.95 (0-8050-5012-4). 118pp. The story of the archaeologists' find in New York City — the African Burial Ground — that reveals the part that African Americans have played in the history of New York City, dating back to the Dutch settlers. (Rev: HBG 10/98; SLJ 5/98) [974.7]

16691 Heinrichs, Ann. *Pennsylvania* (5–8). Series: America the Beautiful. 2000, Children's LB $32.00 (0-516-20692-3). 144pp. A basic introduction to Pennsylvania that also covers such topics as state symbols, sports teams, and regional food. (Rev: BL 5/15/00) [975]

16692 Heinrichs, Ann. *Rhode Island* (4–6). Illus. Series: America the Beautiful. 1990, Children's LB $28.00 (0-516-00485-9). 144pp. This profile of tiny Rhode Island includes a chronology and map section. (Rev: BL 7/90) [974]

16693 Herda, D. J. *Environmental America: The Northeastern States* (4–7). Illus. Series: American Scene. 1991, Millbrook LB $22.40 (1-878841-06-8). 64pp. This volume discusses the condition of the environment and presents information on such topics as water and land pollution in the northeastern states. (Rev: BL 8/91; SLJ 7/91) [639.9]

16694 Herda, D. J. *Ethnic America: The Northeastern States* (5–7). Illus. Series: American Scene. 1991, Millbrook LB $22.40 (1-56294-014-7). 64pp. In this heavily illustrated account, the ethnic make-

up, including Native Americans, is described and the accomplishments detailed. (Rev: BL 2/1/92; SLJ 2/92) [572.973]

16695 High, Linda O. *Under New York* (PS–3). Illus. by Robert Rayevsky. 2001, Holiday $16.95 (0-8234-1551-1). 32pp. A richly illustrated picture book that takes the reader underground in New York City to a world of pipes, power lines, trains, and tunnels. (Rev: BL 3/1/01) [974.7]

16696 Holland, Gini. *The Empire State Building* (3–5). Illus. Series: Great Buildings. 1997, Raintree Steck-Vaughn LB $27.12 (0-8172-4919-2). 48pp. This account supplies details of the planning and construction of this landmark building and of its present uses. (Rev: BL 11/15/97; HBG 3/98) [917.347]

16697 Jacobs, William J. *Ellis Island* (4–6). Illus. 1990, Macmillan $17.00 (0-684-19171-7). 40pp. A well-written introduction to Ellis Island in the you-are-there style. (Rev: BCCB 5/90; BL 4/15/90; SLJ 6/90) [304.8]

16698 Jakobsen, Kathy. *My New York* (K–4). Illus. 1993, Little, Brown $16.95 (0-316-45653-5). 34pp. A young New Yorker writes to a friend describing all the wonders of New York City, including some that tourists often miss. (Rev: BL 9/1/93*; HB 11–12/93; SLJ 12/93*) [974.7]

16699 January, Brendan. *The National Mall* (4–6). Illus. Series: Cornerstones of Freedom. 2000, Children's LB $20.50 (0-516-21616-3); paper $5.95 (0-516-27167-9). 32pp. This heavily illustrated book takes the reader on a tour of the National Mall giving background material on each building. (Rev: BL 9/15/00) [975.3]

16700 Johnston, Joyce. *Washington, D.C.* (3–6). Illus. Series: Hello USA. 1994, Lerner LB $19.93 (0-8225-2751-0). 72pp. This brief introduction to Washington, D.C., tells about its history, local government, landmarks, and daily life. (Rev: BL 2/1/94) [975.3]

16701 Kent, Deborah. *Boston* (3–8). Series: Cities of the World. 1998, Children's LB $26.00 (0-516-20591-9). 64pp. Both historic and contemporary Boston are introduced in this attractive, heavily illustrated volume that contains information on landmarks, neighborhoods, and important events. (Rev: HBG 10/98; SLJ 1/99) [974.4]

16702 Kent, Deborah. *Delaware* (4–6). Illus. Series: America the Beautiful. 1991, Children's LB $28.00 (0-516-00454-9). 144pp. Material on history, geography, and economy, plus a tour of the state. (Rev: BL 6/1/91) [975.1]

16703 Kent, Deborah. *The Lincoln Memorial* (3–5). Illus. Series: Cornerstones of Freedom. 1996, Children's LB $20.50 (0-516-20006-2). 30pp. An account of the design and building of the Lincoln Memorial in 1922 and of the many controversies that surrounded its construction. (Rev: SLJ 2/97) [917.5]

16704 Kent, Deborah. *Maine* (5–8). Series: America the Beautiful. 1999, Children's LB $32.00 (0-516-20994-9). 144pp. A standard account of the history, geography, and people of Maine, with additional information on state symbols, famous personalities, annual events, and weather. (Rev: BL 11/15/99) [974.1]

16705 Kent, Deborah. *New York City* (3–6). Illus. Series: Cities of the World. 1996, Children's LB $26.50 (0-516-20025-9). 64pp. After a history and geography of New York City, such topics as famous buildings, leisure time activities, and cultural institutions are covered. (Rev: BL 1/1–15/97) [974.7]

16706 Krementz, Jill. *A Visit to Washington, D.C.* (K–3). Illus. by author. 1987, Scholastic paper $5.95 (0-590-40583-7). 48pp. A six-year-old tells of his home town, the nation's capital city. (Rev: BL 5/15/87; HB 7–8/87; SLJ 5/87)

16707 Kule, Elaine. *Delaware Facts and Symbols* (1–4). Series: States and Their Symbols. 2000, Capstone LB $15.93 (0-7368-0635-0). 24pp. The flag, seal, bird, tree, flower, and animal that are the symbols of Delaware are presented in double-page spreads that consist of a full-page photograph opposite a few lines of simple text. (Rev: BL 3/1/01) [975.1]

16708 Lawlor, Veronica. *I Was Dreaming to Come to America* (3–5). Illus. 1995, Viking $15.99 (0-670-86164-2). 40pp. A small picture book that draws on the experiences of some of the 12 million people who passed through Ellis Island. (Rev: BL 6/1–15/95; HB 7–8/95; SLJ 6/95) [304.8]

16709 LeVert, Suzanne. *Massachusetts* (4–8). Series: Celebrate the States. 2000, Benchmark LB $14.95 (0-7614-0666-2). A fine introduction to the people and places of the Bay State that also includes recipes, folktales, and songs. (Rev: BL 1/1–15/00; HBG 10/00; SLJ 5/00) [974.4]

16710 Locker, Thomas. *In Blue Mountains: An Artist's Return to America's First Wilderness* (4–8). Illus. by author. 2000, Bell Pond $18.00 (0-88010-471-6). This is a personal tour of New York's Hudson Valley with lyrical paintings and prose by the author-artist. (Rev: SLJ 11/00) [974.7]

16711 Loewen, Nancy. *Philadelphia* (3–6). Illus. Series: Great Cities of the U.S.A. 1989, Rourke LB $23.93 (0-86592-542-9). 48pp. The Pennsylvania "City of Brotherly Love" is profiled. (Rev: BL 1/1/90) [917]

16712 Loewen, Nancy. *Washington, D.C.* (3–6). Illus. Series: Great Cities of the U.S.A. 1989, Rourke LB $23.93 (0-86592-544-5). 48pp. The nation's capital is introduced, with strong historical material. (Rev: BL 1/1/90) [917]

16713 Lourie, Peter. *Erie Canal: Canoeing America's Great Waterway* (5–8). Illus. 1997, Boyds Mills $17.95 (1-56397-669-2). 48pp. This colorful book about a journey along the Erie Canal also supplies historical facts about its construction and uses. (Rev: BL 7/97; HBG 3/98; SLJ 9/97) [974.7]

16714 McNair, Sylvia. *Connecticut* (5–8). Series: America the Beautiful. 1999, Children's LB $32.00 (0-516-20832-2). 144pp. Color photographs and about a dozen maps are included in this survey of Connecticut that covers history, geography, economy, famous sights, recreation, and state symbols. (Rev: BL 11/15/99) [974.6]

16715 McNair, Sylvia. *Massachusetts* (5–8). Series: America the Beautiful. 1998, Children's LB $32.00 (0-516-20635-4). 144pp. With a special reference section and a fine use of graphics, this book introduces the Bay State's history, geography, and important people. (Rev: BL 1/1–15/99; HBG 3/99) [974.4]

16716 McNair, Sylvia. *New Hampshire* (4–6). Illus. Series: America the Beautiful. 1991, Children's LB $28.00 (0-516-00475-1). 144pp. Topics such as history, geography, industry, and famous residents are covered. (Rev: BL 1/15/92) [972.95]

16717 McNair, Sylvia. *Rhode Island* (5–8). Series: America the Beautiful. 2000, Children's LB $33.00 (0-516-21043-2). 144pp. An accessible fund of knowledge is contained in this book on Rhode Island that gives well-organized, basic information on this tiny state, its past, its present, and its people. (Rev: BL 5/15/00) [974.5]

16718 McNair, Sylvia. *Vermont* (4–6). Illus. Series: America the Beautiful. 1991, Children's LB $28.00 (0-516-00491-3). 144pp. This New England state is profiled with material on geography, history, government, important sights, and interesting residents. (Rev: BL 1/15/92; SLJ 2/92) [974.3]

16719 Miller, Natalie. *The Statue of Liberty* (3–5). Illus. Series: Cornerstones of Freedom. 1992, Children's LB $20.50 (0-516-06655-2). 32pp. The story of the building of the Statue of Liberty and the place it has taken in American history. (Rev: BL 1/1/93; SLJ 1/93) [974.7]

16720 Monke, Ingrid. *Boston* (3–6). Illus. 1989, Macmillan LB $13.95 (0-87518-382-4). 60pp. History and modern living in the famous old city. (Rev: BL 3/15/89; SLJ 3/89)

16721 Morgane, Wendy. *New Jersey* (4–8). Series: Celebrate the States. 2000, Benchmark LB $14.95 (0-7614-0673-5). This excellent introduction to New Jersey covers its history, land, government, economy, unique characteristics, and famous residents. (Rev: BL 1/1–15/00; HBG 10/00) [974.9]

16722 *The North Atlantic Coast* (5–8). Ed. by Sara St. Antoine. Illus. Series: Stories from Where We Live. 2000, Milkweed $19.95 (1-57131-627-2). 280pp. This anthology presents stories, essays, folktales, journal entries, songs, and poems related to the north coast of the Atlantic Ocean from Newfoundland to Delaware. (Rev: BL 1/1–15/01) [974]

16723 Pascoe, Elaine. *The Brooklyn Bridge* (4–6). Illus. Series: Building America. 1999, Blackbirch LB $17.95 (1-56711-173-4). 48pp. The story of the Brooklyn Bridge from the first proposals in 1811 to 1983 when it celebrated its 100th birthday. (Rev: BL 12/1/99; HBG 3/00; SLJ 2/00) [624]

16724 Peduzzi, Kelli. *Shaping a President: Sculpting for the Roosevelt Memorial* (3–6). Illus. 1997, Millbrook LB $22.40 (0-7613-0207-7); paper $9.95 (0-7613-0325-1). 48pp. This photo-essay tells of the work of the sculptor Neil Estrin, who sculpted figures of Franklin, Eleanor, and their dog Fala, for the Roosevelt Memorial in Washington, D.C. (Rev: BL 12/1/97; HBG 3/98; SLJ 3/98) [730]

16725 Peters, Stephen. *Pennsylvania* (4–7). Series: Celebrate the States. 2000, Marshall Cavendish $35.64 (0-7614-0644-1). 144pp. An overview of the history, geography, and culture of Pennsylvania with additional material on state symbols, industry, the people, and the economy. (Rev: BL 6/1–15/00; SLJ 9/00) [974.8]

16726 Phillips, Anne. *The Franklin Delano Roosevelt Memorial* (4–6). Series: Cornerstones of Freedom. 2000, Children's LB $20.50 (0-516-21598-1); paper $5.95 (0-516-27165-2). 32pp. This is a guide to the newest national monument in Washington, D.C., including material on F.D.R. and his importance. (Rev: BL 9/15/00) [975.3]

16727 Quiri, Patricia R. *Ellis Island* (2–4). Series: True Books. 1998, Children's LB $21.00 (0-516-20622-2). 47pp. This account covers the history and purposes of Ellis Island and is enhanced by many archival and contemporary photographs. (Rev: HBG 10/98; SLJ 9/98) [974.7]

16728 Quiri, Patricia R. *The White House* (4–6). Illus. 1996, Watts LB $22.00 (0-531-20221-6). 63pp. A history of the White House is given, with a description of the exterior design and rooms inside. (Rev: BL 6/1–15/96; SLJ 8/96) [975.3]

16729 Rebman, Renee C. *Life on Ellis Island* (5–8). Series: The Way People Live. 1999, Lucent LB $18.96 (1-56006-533-8). 95pp. With extensive use of firsthand accounts, this book relates the purpose of Ellis Island, the processing of immigrants, and the joys and hardships involved. (Rev: HBG 10/00; SLJ 1/00) [325.1]

16730 Reef, Catherine. *The Lincoln Memorial* (3–6). Illus. Series: Places in American History. 1994, Dillon $14.95 (0-87518-624-6). 71pp. This guide to one of Washington's landmark buildings also touches on the importance of Lincoln, as well as supplying details on the planning and construction of the monument. (Rev: SLJ 8/94) [975.3]

16731 Reef, Catherine. *Washington, D.C.* (3–6). Illus. Series: Downtown America. 1989, Macmillan LB $13.95 (0-87518-411-1). 72pp. This introduction includes a "Fast Facts" section, maps, and a timeline. (Rev: BL 1/1/90; SLJ 4/90) [975.3]

16732 Sakurai, Gail. *The Liberty Bell* (3–5). Illus. Series: Cornerstones of Freedom. 1996, Children's LB $20.50 (0-516-06634-X). 32pp. The story of the Liberty Bell from its casting to its final resting place in Philadelphia. (Rev: BL 7/96; SLJ 8/96) [974.8]

16733 Sakurai, Gail. *The Library of Congress* (3–5). Series: Cornerstones of Freedom. 1998, Children's LB $19.50 (0-516-20940-X). 32pp. The story of how an institution originally meant only for members of Congress, and once destroyed by the British, became our national library. (Rev: BL 9/15/98; HBG 3/99) [975.3]

16734 Sanders, Mark. *The White House* (3–6). Series: American Government Today. 2000, Raintree Steck-Vaughn LB $22.83 (0-7398-1791-4). 48pp. An account that gives a history of the White House, its construction and renovations, plus details on its rooms and offices. (Rev: HBG 10/00; SLJ 8/00) [975]

16735 Schnurnberger, Lynn. *Kids Love New York! The A-to-Z Resource Book* (4–8). Illus. 1990, Congdon & Weed paper $133.65 (0-312-92415-1). 224pp. A group of suggestions for various activities in New York City.

16736 Schomp, Virginia. *New York* (4–8). Illus. Series: Celebrate the States. 1996, Marshall Cavendish LB $22.95 (1-7614-0108-3). 144pp. The Empire State is introduced, with information on history, geography, people, landmarks, and distinguished New Yorkers. (Rev: BL 2/15/97) [917.47]

16737 Schuman, Michael. *Delaware* (4–8). Series: Celebrate the States. 2000, Marshall Cavendish LB $24.95 (0-7614-0645-X). 139pp. Beginning with quotes about Delaware and its people, this account covers the basic topics plus information on folklore, food, and festivals. (Rev: BL 6/1–15/00; HBG 10/00) [975.1]

16738 Sherrow, Victoria. *The World Trade Center Bombing: Terror in the Towers* (4–8). Series: American Disasters. 1998, Enslow LB $18.95 (0-7660-1056-2). 48pp. An illustrated discussion of the events and individuals leading up to the World Trade Center bombing. (Rev: BL 1/1–15/99; HBG 3/99; SLJ 3/99) [363.2]

16739 Steen, Sandra, and Susan Steen. *Independence Hall* (3–6). Illus. Series: Places in American History. 1994, Dillon LB $14.95 (0-87518-603-3). 71pp. This introduction to Philadelphia's famous landmark tells about its construction, historical importance, and present status, with material on the State House and the Liberty Bell. (Rev: SLJ 8/94) [974.8]

16740 Stein, R. Conrad. *Ellis Island* (3–5). Illus. Series: Cornerstones of Freedom. 1992, Children's LB $20.50 (0-516-06653-6). 32pp. The history of the island that served as the best-known immigration station, plus material on its present function as a museum. (Rev: BL 6/1/92; SLJ 9/92) [325.1]

16741 Stein, R. Conrad. *New Hampshire* (5–8). Series: America the Beautiful. 2000, Children's LB $33.00 (0-516-21071-8). 144pp. A basic introduction to New Hampshire, including its people, history, geography, economy, government, and state symbols. (Rev: BL 11/15/00) [974.2]

16742 Stein, R. Conrad. *New Jersey* (5–8). Series: America the Beautiful. 1998, Children's LB $32.00 (0-516-20637-0). 144pp. Full-color graphics and a clear text highlight this introduction to New Jersey's history, geography, economy, people, and culture. (Rev: BL 1/1–15/99) [974.9]

16743 Stein, R. Conrad. *Washington, D.C.* (5–8). Series: America the Beautiful. 1999, Children's LB $32.00 (0-516-21046-7). 144pp. The District of Columbia is covered in text, color photos, sidebars, maps, and a timeline, with material on its history, local government, people, economy, sights, and related subjects. (Rev: BL 12/15/99) [975.3]

16744 Steins, Richard. *Our National Capital* (4–6). Illus. Series: I Know America. 1994, Millbrook LB $21.90 (1-56294-439-8). 48pp. Important government buildings, historical monuments, and other Washington, D.C., attractions are introduced, with some general background information. (Rev: SLJ 6/94) [917.53]

16745 Stewart, Gail B. *New York* (3–6). Illus. Series: Great Cities of the U.S.A. 1989, Rourke LB $23.93 (0-86592-541-0). 48pp. Good historical background information is included in this profile. (Rev: BL 1/1/90) [917]

16746 Sullivan, George. *How the White House Really Works* (5–8). Illus. 1990, Scholastic paper $3.95 (0-590-43403-9). Home, office, museum, and tourist attraction — how the White House operates. (Rev: BCCB 5/89; BL 5/15/89; HB 7–8/89)

16747 Swain, Gwenyth. *Pennsylvania* (3–5). Illus. Series: Hello USA. 1994, Lerner LB $19.93 (0-8225-2727-8). 72pp. After an introductory trip around Pennsylvania, this concise book covers its history, attractions, environment, and famous people. (Rev: BL 4/15/94; SLJ 8/94) [974.8]

16748 Tagliaferro, Linda. *Destination New York* (4–8). Series: Port Cities of North America. 1998, Lerner LB $22.60 (0-8225-2793-6). 80pp. New York City's history, economy, and daily life are covered, with emphasis on its importance as a port city. (Rev: HBG 3/99; SLJ 1/99) [974.7]

16749 Thomas, Pamela. *Brooklyn Pops Up* (3–10). Illus. 2000, Simon & Schuster $19.95 (0-689-84019-5). This pop-up book takes you on a tour of this borough of New York City, including visits to Coney Island and the Brooklyn Museum. (Rev: BL 12/1/00; HBG 3/01) [917.47]

16750 Thompson, Kathleen. *New York* (4–6). Illus. Series: Portrait of America. 1996, Raintree Steck-Vaughn LB $22.83 (0-8114-7377-5). 48pp. The unique aspects of life in New York State are covered in this account that also deals with its history, economy, culture, and what the future might bring. (Rev: SLJ 8/96) [917.47]

16751 Thompson, Kathleen. *Pennsylvania* (4–6). Illus. Series: Portrait of America. 1996, Raintree Steck-Vaughn LB $25.69 (0-8114-7383-X). 48pp. The history, economy, culture, and the future are covered in this introduction to Pennsylvania, based on the "Portrait of America" TV series. (Rev: SLJ 8/96) [917.48]

16752 Topper, Frank, and Charles A. Wills. *A Historical Album of New Jersey* (3–5). Illus. Series: Historical Album. 1995, Millbrook LB $23.40 (1-56294-505-X). 64pp. Beginning with the Native American culture and ending with the present day, the most important events and people in New Jersey history are touched on in a rapid overview. (Rev: SLJ 7/95) [974.9]

16753 Warner, J. F. *Rhode Island* (3–6). Illus. Series: Hello USA. 1993, Lerner LB $19.93 (0-8225-2731-6). 72pp. In excellent color illustrations and informative text, Rhode Island and its history, geography, cities, and social and economic life are covered. (Rev: BL 1/15/93) [974]

16754 Welsbacher, Anne. *New York* (3–4). Series: Checkerboard Geography Series. 1999, ABDO LB $14.95 (1-56239-891-1). 32pp. By focusing on the people, history, and geography of New York State, this simple book introduces the different regions

and supplies such unusual facts as how Uncle Sam originated. (Rev: HBG 10/99; SLJ 8/99) [974.7]

16755 Whitcraft, Melissa. *The Hudson River* (4–7). Illus. Series: World of Water. 1999, Watts LB $24.00 (0-531-11739-1). 64pp. A handsome volume that traces the history of New York State's most important river and how it currently affects people's lives. (Rev: BL 1/1–15/00) [974.7]

16756 Wills, Charles A. *A Historical Album of Pennsylvania* (4–7). Illus. Series: Historical Album. 1996, Millbrook LB $23.40 (1-56294-595-5); paper $6.95 (1-56294-853-9). 64pp. Beginning with a little geography and coverage of the native population, this account traces the history of Pennsylvania to the present. (Rev: BL 7/96; SLJ 7/96) [974.8]

16757 Yolen, Jane. *House, House* (3–6). Illus. 1998, Marshall Cavendish $15.95 (0-7614-5013-0). 32pp. Life in Hatfield, Massachusetts, in 1900 and 2000 is contrasted in a series of then-and-now photographs and explanatory text. (Rev: BL 5/15/98; HBG 10/98; SLJ 6/98) [974.4]

PACIFIC STATES

16758 Abbink, Emily. *Missions of the Monterey Bay Area* (4–7). Series: California Missions. 1996, Lerner LB $23.93 (0-8225-1928-3). 80pp. Covers the history of the missions at San Carlos Borromeo de Carmelo, San Juan Bautista, and Santa Cruz. (Rev: BL 2/15/97) [979.4]

16759 Altman, Linda Jacobs. *California* (4–8). Illus. Series: Celebrate the States. 1996, Marshall Cavendish LB $35.64 (0-7614-0111-3). 144pp. This introduction to California includes chapters on its history, geography, people, achievements, and landmarks. (Rev: BL 2/1/97; SLJ 2/97) [979.4]

16760 Ancona, George. *Barrio: Jose's Neighborhood* (3–6). Illus. 1998, Harcourt $18.00 (0-15-201049-1). 48pp. A year in the life of San Francisco's Mission District as experienced by a Mexican American boy who loves to participate in all the festivities and activities of the community. (Rev: BL 12/1/98; HBG 3/99; SLJ 12/98) [979.4]

16761 Andryszewski, Tricia. *Step by Step Along the Pacific Crest Trail* (4–6). Illus. 1998, Twenty-First Century LB $23.90 (0-7613-0274-3). 80pp. A discussion of the famous trail that stretches from California through Oregon and Washington into British Columbia, with geological, historical, geographical, and biological information. (Rev: BL 3/1/99; HBG 10/99; SLJ 4/99) [796.51]

16762 Aylesworth, Thomas G., and Virginia L. Aylesworth. *The Pacific: California, Hawaii* (3–8). Illus. 1995, Chelsea LB $19.95 (0-7910-3407-0); paper $9.95 (0-7910-3425-9). 64pp. People and places are included in this study of the West. (Rev: BL 11/1/87; SLJ 11/95)

16763 Behrens, June. *Missions of the Central Coast* (4–7). Series: California Missions. 1996, Lerner LB $23.93 (0-8225-1930-5). 80pp. The missions at Santa Barbara, Santa Ines, and La Purisima Concepción are discussed, with material on their history and importance. (Rev: BL 2/15/97) [979.4]

16764 Bratvold, Gretchen. *Oregon* (3–6). Illus. Series: Hello USA. 1991, Lerner LB $19.93 (0-8225-2704-9). 72pp. Topics include geography; history; and social, economic, and environmental concerns, with full-color photos. (Rev: BL 4/15/91; SLJ 6/91) [979.5]

16765 Bredeson, Carmen. *Fire in Oakland, California: Billion-Dollar Blaze* (4–8). Series: American Disasters. 1999, Enslow LB $18.95 (0-7660-1220-4). 48pp. A high-interest book that tells of the terrible fire in Oakland and the massive destruction it caused. (Rev: BL 10/15/99; HBG 3/00) [976.8]

16766 Brower, Pauline. *Missions of the Inland Valleys* (4–7). Series: California Missions. 1996, Lerner LB $23.93 (0-8225-1929-1). 80pp. Examines four missions, including San Luis Obispo and San Miguel Arcangel, with material on their early history and their impact on the existing cultures. (Rev: BL 2/15/97) [979.4]

16767 Brown, Tricia. *Children of the Midnight Sun: Young Native Voices of Alaska* (4–7). Illus. 1998, Graphic Arts Center $16.95 (0-88240-500-4). 48pp. This illustrated book gives a fine introduction to various aspects of the Alaskan environment, describing the lives of eight preteens from different regions and ethnic backgrounds. (Rev: BL 7/98; HBG 10/98; SLJ 9/98) [979.8]

16768 Brown, Tricia. *The City by the Bay: A Magical Journey Around San Francisco* (K–3). Illus. by Elisa Kleven. 1993, Chronicle $14.95 (0-8118-0233-7). 32pp. Using an entertaining series of collages, this simple guidebook introduces the famous sights of San Francisco, including Chinatown, the Golden Gate Bridge, and cable cars. (Rev: BL 9/1/93) [917.94]

16769 Cohen, Daniel. *The Alaska Purchase* (4–7). Illus. Series: Spotlight on American History. 1996, Millbrook LB $21.90 (1-56294-528-9). 64pp. The story of the purchase of Alaska from Russia and how it has affected the history of the United States. (Rev: BL 3/15/96; SLJ 5/96) [979.8]

16770 Corral, Kimberly, and Hannah Corral. *A Child's Glacier Bay* (4–8). Illus. 1998, Graphic Arts Center $15.95 (0-88240-503-9). 32pp. This photo-essay describes the three-week camping adventure of the Corral family in Alaska's Glacier Bay Park. (Rev: BL 7/98; HBG 10/98; SLJ 8/98) [978.6]

16771 Doherty, Craig A., and Katherine M. Doherty. *The Golden Gate Bridge* (3–6). Illus. Series: Building America. 1995, Blackbirch LB $17.95 (1-56711-106-8). 48pp. From concept to completion, this is a thorough, engrossing description of the Golden Gate Bridge in San Francisco. (Rev: BL 9/15/95; SLJ 7/95) [624]

16772 Dubois, Muriel. *Alaska: Facts and Symbols* (1–4). Series: The States and Their Symbols. 2000, Capstone LB $15.93 (0-7368-0522-2). 24pp. An easily read introduction to Alaska that covers its history, geography, and major state symbols. (Rev: BL 6/1–15/00; HBG 10/00; SLJ 10/00) [979.8]

16773 Feeney, Stephanie. *Hawaii Is a Rainbow* (2–6). Illus. 1985, Univ. of Hawaii Pr. $12.95 (0-8248-1007-4). 64pp. Color photos present the peo-

ple and land of Hawaii as they present the colors of the rainbow. (Rev: BL 2/1/85; SLJ 1/86)

16774 Fradin, Dennis B. *Alaska* (3–5). Illus. Series: From Sea to Shining Sea. 1993, Children's LB $27.00 (0-516-03802-8). 64pp. With color photos on each page, this attractive account supplies basic information about Alaska, its past and present, and unusual facts that make it unique. (Rev: BL 3/1/94) [979.8]

16775 Fradin, Dennis B. *California* (3–5). Illus. Series: From Sea to Shining Sea. 1992, Children's LB $27.00 (0-516-03805-2). 64pp. History, geography, famous names, and a chronology are presented in this introduction to California. (Rev: BL 2/1/93; SLJ 4/93) [976.8]

16776 Fradin, Dennis B. *Hawaii* (3–5). Illus. Series: From Sea to Shining Sea. 1994, Children's LB $27.00 (0-516-03811-7). 64pp. Among the topics covered in this introduction to Hawaii are its natural wonders, economy, history, and people. (Rev: BL 8/94; SLJ 11/94) [996.9]

16777 Fradin, Dennis B., and Judith B. Fradin. *Oregon* (3–5). Illus. Series: From Sea to Shining Sea. 1995, Children's LB $27.00 (0-516-03837-0). 64pp. This guide to the Beaver State presents Oregon's geography, history, climate, wildlife, history, and people. (Rev: SLJ 8/95) [917.95]

16778 Fraser, Mary Ann. *A Mission for the People: The Story of La Purisima* (4–8). Illus. 1998, Holt $15.95 (0-8050-5050-7). 38pp. Using the Spanish mission of La Purisima as an example in miniature of early California history, this account describes life among the natives before and after the arrival of Spanish missionaries. (Rev: BL 5/1/98; HBG 10/98; SLJ 4/98) [979.4]

16779 Fremon, David K. *The Alaska Purchase in American History* (5–8). Series: In American History. 1999, Enslow LB $19.95 (0-7660-1138-0). 128pp. This account covers both the purchase of Alaska in 1867 and an early history of the Native Americans who lived there. (Rev: HBG 3/00; SLJ 3/00) [979.8]

16780 George, Linda. *Alcatraz* (3–5). Series: Cornerstones of Freedom. 1998, Children's LB $19.50 (0-516-20949-3). 32pp. A well-illustrated account of life in the island prison that became a national monument. (Rev: BL 9/15/98; HBG 3/99) [979.4]

16781 Goldberg, Jake. *Hawaii* (5–8). Series: Celebrate the States. 1998, Benchmark LB $22.95 (0-7614-0203-9). 144pp. Using fine illustrations, fact boxes, graphs, and maps, this attractive book gives an excellent introduction to Hawaii, with the added bonus of a recipe and two songs. (Rev: HBG 10/98; SLJ 1/99) [996.9]

16782 Grabowski, John, and Patricia Grabowski. *The Northwest: Alaska, Idaho, Oregon, Washington* (3–6). Series: State Reports. 1995, Chelsea LB $19.95 (0-7910-3406-2); paper $9.95 (0-7910-3424-0). 64pp. History, geography, state symbols, capitals, principal cities, and places to visit are some of the topics covered in this introduction to these four states. (Rev: SLJ 9/92) [978]

16783 Haddock, Patricia. *San Francisco* (3–6). Illus. 1989, Macmillan LB $17.95 (0-87518-383-2). 60pp. A close-up look at life in one of America's favorite cities. (Rev: BL 3/15/89)

16784 Halvorsen, Lisa. *Letters Home from Yosemite* (3–5). Series: Letters Home From. 2000, Blackbirch LB $16.95 (1-56711-462-8). 32pp. Using a letter format and captioned snapshots, this first-person account describes Yosemite National Park's attractions, history, wildlife, and conservation efforts. (Rev: BL 5/15/00; HBG 10/00; SLJ 8/00) [979.4]

16785 Harder, Dan, and Lawrence Migdale. *A Child's California* (2–4). Illus. 2000, Graphic Arts $15.95 (1-55868-520-0). 48pp. This introduction to California covers topics of particular interest to children and emphasizes the state's diversity and contrasts. (Rev: BL 2/1/01; SLJ 1/01) [917.94]

16786 Heinrichs, Ann. *California* (5–8). Series: America the Beautiful. 1998, Children's LB $32.00 (0-516-20631-1). 144pp. A fine introduction to California's history, geography, economy, arts, and recreation. (Rev: BL 1/1–15/99; HBG 3/99; SLJ 2/99) [979.4]

16787 Herda, D. J. *Environmental America: The Northwestern States* (4–7). Illus. Series: American Scene. 1991, Millbrook LB $22.40 (1-878841-10-6). 64pp. This account presents information on such topics as pollution, waste, logging, and the general condition of the environment in Idaho, Montana, Oregon, Washington, and Wyoming. (Rev: BL 8/91; SLJ 7/91) [639.9]

16788 Hintz, Martin. *Hawaii* (5–8). Series: America the Beautiful. 1999, Children's LB $32.00 (0-516-20686-9). 144pp. An introduction to Hawaii — its land and people, its government and economy, its state symbols and famous sights. (Rev: BL 11/15/99; HBG 10/99) [996.9]

16789 Ingram, W. Scott. *Oregon* (5–8). Series: America the Beautiful. 2000, Children's LB $32.00 (0-516-20996-5). 144pp. An attractive guide to Oregon that is packed with facts about its history, geography, population, economy, culture, cities, and recreation. (Rev: BL 5/15/00) [979.5]

16790 Jaskol, Julie, and Brian Lewis. *City of Angels* (3–6). Illus. 1999, Dutton $16.99 (0-525-46214-7). 48pp. A delightful introduction to 20 Los Angeles neighborhoods and their interesting sights. (Rev: BL 12/1/99; HBG 3/00; SLJ 12/99) [979.4]

16791 Johnston, Joyce. *Alaska* (3–6). Illus. Series: Hello USA. 1994, Lerner LB $19.93 (0-8225-2735-9). 72pp. This introduction to Alaska features a trip around the state, historical information, and material on the life-styles of its people. (Rev: BL 4/15/94; SLJ 8/94) [979.8]

16792 Jones, Charlotte F. *Yukon Gold: The Story of the Klondike Gold Rush* (4–8). 1999, Holiday $18.95 (0-8234-1403-5). 99pp. A solid presentation of the Alaska/Yukon gold rush that is enlivened by black-and white photos and intriguing asides and anecdotes. (Rev: BCCB 6/99; HB 7–8/99; HBG 10/99; SLJ 5/99) [979.8]

16793 Kent, Deborah. *San Francisco* (3–6). Series: Cities of the World. 1997, Children's $26.50 (0-

516-20466-1). 64pp. An introduction to San Francisco that covers its history, communities, landmarks, maps, and a discussion of the city's problems. (Rev: BL 3/15/98; HBG 10/98) [917.9]

16794 Kimmel, Elizabeth C. *Balto and the Great Race* (3–5). Illus. 1999, Random LB $11.99 (0-679-99198-0); paper $3.99 (0-679-89198-6). 112pp. The true story set of a dog team, led by a Siberian husky, that delivered medicine to sick children in Alaska in 1925. (Rev: BL 10/15/99; HBG 10/00; SLJ 3/00) [636.73]

16795 Lemke, Nancy. *Missions of the Southern Coast* (4–7). Illus. Series: California Missions. 1996, Lerner LB $23.93 (0-8225-1925-9). 80pp. The three missions described here are San Diego de Alcala, San Luis Rey de Francia, and San Juan Capistrano. (Rev: BL 9/15/96; SLJ 8/96) [979.4]

16796 Loewen, Nancy. *Seattle* (3–6). Illus. Series: Great Cities of the U.S.A. 1989, Rourke LB $23.93 (0-86592-545-3). 48pp. Information on history, climate, people, and so forth is given on the Washington port of Seattle. (Rev: BL 1/1/90) [917]

16797 McMillan, Bruce. *Salmon Summer* (K–3). Illus. 1998, Houghton $16.00 (0-395-84544-0). 32pp. An outstanding photo-essay about 9-year-old Alex, an Aleut boy, and his summer at his family's salmon fishing camp. (Rev: BCCB 5/98; BL 4/1/98; HB 5–6/98; HBG 10/98; SLJ 5/98) [639.2]

16798 MacMillan, Dianne. *Destination Los Angeles* (4–6). Illus. Series: Port Cities of North America. 1998, Lerner LB $23.93 (0-8225-2786-3). 80pp. Describes Los Angeles and its history but concentrates on the harbor, trade, and the cargo shipped in and out. (Rev: HBG 10/98; SLJ 3/98) [917.94]

16799 MacMillan, Dianne. *Missions of the Los Angeles Area* (4–7). Illus. Series: California Missions. 1996, Lerner LB $23.93 (0-8225-1927-5). 80pp. This volume gives a description and history of three missions: San Gabriel Arcangel, San Fernando Rey de España, and San Buenaventura. (Rev: BL 9/15/96; SLJ 8/96) [979.4]

16800 Markle, Sandra. *After the Spill: The Exxon Valdez Disaster Then and Now* (3–5). Illus. 1999, Walker $15.95 (0-8027-8610-3). 32pp. A photo-essay that describes the oil spill and events through mid-1999 involving the cleanup. (Rev: BL 8/99; HBG 10/99; SLJ 9/99) [363.738]

16801 Miller, Debbie S. *Disappearing Lake: Nature's Magic in Denali National Park* (K–3). Illus. by Jon Van Zyle. 1997, Walker $15.95 (0-8027-8474-7). 32pp. The story of an area in Alaska's Denali National Park, which is transformed annually into a lake and then, as the waters recede, into a flowering meadow. (Rev: BCCB 2/97; BL 3/15/97; SLJ 4/97*) [508.798]

16802 Miller, Debbie S. *River of Life* (K–3). Illus. by Jon Van Zyle. 2000, Clarion $15.00 (0-395-96790-2). 32pp. Realistic oil paintings are used to illustrate this book that describes a year in the life of an Alaskan river and the wildlife surrounding it. (Rev: BL 3/15/00; HBG 10/00; SLJ 7/00) [577.6]

16803 Oberle, Joseph. *Anchorage* (3–5). Illus. Series: Downtown America. 1990, Macmillan LB

$17.95 (0-87518-420-0). 60pp. The sights and sounds of Anchorage are captured, along with the city's colorful history and people. (Rev: BL 6/1/90; SLJ 11/90) [979]

16804 O'Connor, Karen. *San Diego* (3–5). Illus. Series: Downtown America. 1990, Macmillan LB $17.95 (0-87518-439-1). 60pp. In color photos and brief text, the city of San Diego, California, is introduced. (Rev: BL 2/1/91) [974.94]

16805 Oliver, Marilyn Tower. *Alcatraz Prison in American History* (4–8). Series: In American History. 1998, Enslow LB $19.95 (0-89490-990-8). 128pp. The history of Alcatraz Island from its early days as a fort and lighthouse through its time as a federal prison to its present status as a tourist-attraction status. (Rev: HBG 3/99; SLJ 1/99) [976.8]

16806 Pelta, Kathy. *California* (3–5). Illus. Series: Hello USA. 1994, Lerner LB $19.93 (0-8225-2738-3). 72pp. This small book is crammed with basic information about California, including its history, famous attractions, and important residents. (Rev: BL 4/15/94) [979.4]

16807 Penisten, John. *Honolulu* (3–6). Illus. Series: Downtown America. 1989, Macmillan LB $12.95 (0-87518-416-2). 72pp. Included in this introduction are maps, a timeline, and lists of places to visit. (Rev: BL 1/1/90; SLJ 5/90) [996.9]

16808 Powell, E. Sandy. *Washington* (3–6). Illus. Series: Hello USA. 1993, Lerner LB $19.93 (0-8225-2726-X). 72pp. A visually attractive book that includes fact sheets, timelines, and capsule biographies. (Rev: BL 3/15/93; SLJ 8/93) [979.7]

16809 Pratt, Helen Jay. *The Hawaiians: An Island People* (6–8). Illus. 1991, Tuttle paper $9.95 (0-8048-1709-X). 210pp. An account of early Hawaii and its inhabitants, with emphasis on folk customs.

16810 Rice, Oliver D. *Lone Woman of Ghalas-Hat* (5–7). Illus. by Charles Zafuto. 1993, California Weekly LB $13.00 (0-936778-52-0); paper $6.00 (0-936778-51-2). 32pp. The true story of the Indian woman who lived alone on a California island for 18 years. This was the basis of Island of the Blue Dolphins. A reissue. [979.7]

16811 Seibold, J. Otto, and Vivian Walsh. *Going to the Getty: A Book About the Getty Center in Los Angeles* (4–7). Illus. 1997, Getty Museum $16.95 (0-89236-493-9). 32pp. This introduction to the Getty Museum in Los Angeles is a patchwork of impressions, photographs, drawings, and reproductions of artworks. (Rev: BL 2/15/98; HBG 10/98) [708]

16812 Senungetuk, Vivian. *Wise Words of Paul Tiulana: An Inupiat Alaskan's Life* (5–8). Illus. 1998, Watts LB $22.00 (0-531-11448-1). 80pp. The story of Paul Tiulana's life and the culture of the natives who have lived for centuries on a tiny island in the Bering Sea between Siberia and Alaska. (Rev: BL 1/1–15/99; HBG 10/99; SLJ 2/99) [979.8]

16813 Sherrow, Victoria. *The Exxon Valdez: Tragic Oil Spill* (4–8). Series: American Disasters. 1998, Enslow LB $18.95 (0-7660-1058-9). 48pp. The dramatic story of the Exxon Valdez oil spill and the legacy of environmental damage it bequeathed to the Alaskan coast and its wildlife. (Rev: BL 1/1–15/99; HBG 3/99; SLJ 3/99) [979.8]

16814 Sherrow, Victoria. *San Francisco Earthquake, 1989: Death and Destruction* (4–8). Illus. Series: American Disasters. 1998, Enslow LB $18.95 (0-7660-1060-0). 48pp. This account of the San Francisco earthquake uses many eyewitness reports to emphasize the human-interest facets of this tragedy. (Rev: BL 1/1–15/99; HBG 3/99; SLJ 6/99) [363.34]

16815 Snelson, Karin. *Seattle* (3–5). Illus. Series: Downtown America. 1992, Macmillan LB $13.95 (0-87518-509-6). 64pp. This introduction to Seattle includes its history, ethnic life, and places to visit. (Rev: BL 6/1/92) [979.7]

16816 Staub, Frank. *Children of Hawaii* (4–6). Series: The World's Children. 1999, Carolrhoda $16.95 (1-57505-253-9). 48pp. Through enticing photographs of Hawaiian children, the reader learns about the history, geography, and culture of the 50th U.S. state. (Rev: BL 7/99; HBG 10/99) [996.9]

16817 Staub, Frank. *Children of the Tlingit* (3–6). Illus. Series: The World's Children. 1999, Carolrhoda LB $21.27 (1-57505-333-0). 48pp. A look at the daily life of several children who belong to the Tlingit people of southeastern Alaska. (Rev: BL 6/1–15/99; HBG 10/99; SLJ 10/99) [979.8]

16818 Stefoff, Rebecca. *Oregon* (4–8). Illus. Series: Celebrate the States. 1997, Marshall Cavendish LB $35.64 (0-7614-0145-8). 140pp. Life in this Pacific state is covered, along with topics like its history, famous sights, cities, and industries. (Rev: BL 7/97; SLJ 7/97) [917.95]

16819 Stein, R. Conrad. *Oregon* (4–6). Illus. Series: America the Beautiful. 1989, Children's LB $28.00 (0-516-00483-2). 144pp. The Pacific state of Oregon is highlighted, covering history, geography, famous people, and important sites. (Rev: BL 7/89) [979.5]

16820 Stein, R. Conrad. *Seattle* (3–6). Series: Cities of the World. 1999, Children's LB $26.00 (0-516-20782-2). 64pp. Using maps, sidebars, and glossy pictures, this book introduces Seattle with material on its history, landmarks, people, climate, and lifestyle. (Rev: HBG 10/99; SLJ 9/99) [979.7]

16821 Stein, R. Conrad. *Washington* (4–6). Illus. Series: America the Beautiful. 1991, Children's LB $28.00 (0-516-00493-X). 144pp. A fine balance of text and pictures presents the geography, history, government, and famous sites. (Rev: BL 1/15/92) [972.95]

16822 Stewart, Gail B. *Los Angeles* (3–6). Illus. Series: Great Cities of the U.S.A. 1989, Rourke LB $23.93 (0-86592-540-2). 48pp. The sprawling Southern California "City of the Angels" is introduced. (Rev: BL 1/1/90) [917]

16823 Van Steenwyk, Elizabeth. *The California Missions* (4–6). Illus. Series: First Books. 1995, Watts LB $22.50 (0-531-20187-2). 63pp. A description of the 21 coastal missions founded in California and their history, functions, and workings. (Rev: SLJ 11/95) [979.4]

16824 White, Tekla N. *Missions of the San Francisco Bay Area* (4–7). Illus. Series: California Missions. 1996, Lerner LB $23.93 (0-8225-1926-7). 80pp. The history of five Spanish missions in the San Francisco Bay Area, including Santa Clara de Asis and San Rafael Arcangel. (Rev: BL 9/15/96; SLJ 8/96) [979.4]

16825 Wills, Charles A. *A Historical Album of California* (4–8). Illus. Series: Historical Album. 1994, Millbrook LB $23.40 (1-56294-479-7). 64pp. A slim volume that covers the basic history of California, with material on major events and important personalities. (Rev: SLJ 3/95) [979.4]

16826 Wills, Charles A. *A Historical Album of Oregon* (4–7). Illus. 1995, Millbrook LB $23.40 (1-56294-594-7). 64pp. A history of Oregon from prehistoric times to the present is outlined with many illustrations, some in color. (Rev: BL 12/15/95; SLJ 1/96) [979.5]

16827 Young, Robert. *A Personal Tour of La Purisima* (4–7). Series: How It Was. 1999, Lerner LB $17.95 (0-8225-3576-9). 64pp. A you-are-there visit to La Purisima — one of the 21 missions built by the Spanish in California — where the reader experiences life in the mission as it was in 1820. (Rev: BL 6/1–15/99; HBG 10/99) [979.4]

SOUTH

16828 Altman, Linda Jacobs. *Arkansas* (4–8). Series: Celebrate the States. 2000, Benchmark LB $14.95 (0-7614-0672-7). An broad introduction to the culture, land, government, history, and unique characteristics of Arkansas, with emphasis on its inhabitants. (Rev: BL 1/1–15/00; HBG 10/00) [976.7]

16829 Aylesworth, Thomas G., and Virginia L. Aylesworth. *The Southeast: Georgia, Kentucky, Tennessee* (3–8). Illus. 1995, Chelsea LB $19.95 (0-7910-3411-9); paper $8.95 (0-7910-3429-1). 64pp. An inviting look at this region, with color photos and map. (Rev: BL 11/1/87; SLJ 11/87)

16830 Barrett, Tracy. *Kentucky* (4–7). Series: Celebrate the States. 1999, Benchmark LB $24.95 (0-7614-0657-3). 144pp. An attractive, concise introduction to Kentucky that covers geography, history, government and economy, people, achievements, and landmarks. (Rev: HBG 10/99; SLJ 10/99) [976.9]

16831 Barrett, Tracy. *Virginia* (4–8). Illus. Series: Celebrate the States. 1996, Marshall Cavendish LB $35.64 (0-7614-0110-5). 144pp. This introduction to Virginia covers such topics as history, culture, famous sites, and important Virginians. (Rev: BL 2/15/97) [975.5]

16832 Bial, Raymond. *Cajun Home* (4–7). Illus. 1998, Houghton $16.00 (0-395-86095-4). 48pp. This is the story of the people who left France to find freedom in Canada, only to be transported to Louisiana where they settled in the backwood swamp areas. (Rev: BL 3/15/98; HB 5–6/98; HBG 10/98; SLJ 5/98) [976.3]

16833 Bial, Raymond. *Mist over the Mountains: Appalachia and Its People* (4–7). Illus. 1997, Houghton $14.95 (0-395-73569-6). 48pp. The people and culture of Appalachia are introduced, including history, agriculture, and folk arts. (Rev: BCCB 6/97; BL 3/1/97; SLJ 5/97) [975]

16834 Blashfield, Jean F. *Virginia* (5–8). Series: America the Beautiful. 1999, Children's LB $32.00 (0-516-20831-4). 144pp. A solid account of the land and people of Virginia, with full-color maps, sidebars, a timeline, and a discussion of its state symbols. (Rev: BL 11/15/99) [975.5]

16835 Brown, Dottie. *Kentucky* (3–6). Illus. Series: Hello USA. 1992, Lerner LB $19.93 (0-8225-2715-4). 72pp. The visual beauty of the Bluegrass State is captured in text and pictures in this introductory volume. (Rev: BL 5/15/92; SLJ 7/92) [976.9]

16836 Burgan, Michael. *Maryland* (5–8). Series: America the Beautiful. 1999, Children's LB $32.00 (0-516-21039-4). 144pp. History and government, economy and population, famous sights, and annual events are only a few of the topics covered in this fine introduction to Maryland. (Rev: BL 11/15/99) [975]

16837 Chang, Perry. *Florida* (5–8). Series: Celebrate the States. 1998, Benchmark LB $22.95 (0-7614-0420-1). 144pp. An attractive general introduction to Florida that includes fact boxes and information on famous people and state economics and government. (Rev: HBG 10/98; SLJ 1/99) [975.9]

16838 Cocke, William. *A Historical Album of Virginia* (4–7). Illus. 1995, Millbrook LB $23.40 (1-56294-596-3). 64pp. Beginning with Native Americans and ending with the present, this history of Virginia uses many period paintings and prints as illustrations. (Rev: BL 12/15/95; SLJ 1/96) [975.5]

16839 Cole, Michael D. *The Siege at Waco: Deadly Inferno* (5–9). Illus. 1999, Enslow LB $18.95 (0-7660-1218-2). 48pp. The story of the disaster that ended the 51-day siege at Waco and resulted in the deaths of cult leader David Koresh and 73 of his followers. (Rev: BL 2/15/99; HBG 10/99) [976.4]

16840 Collins, Mary. *Mount Vernon* (3–5). Series: Cornerstones of Freedom. 1998, Children's LB $19.50 (0-516-20939-6). 32pp. The story of George Washington's legendary home in Virginia that became a national shrine in 1853. (Rev: BL 9/15/98; HBG 3/99) [973]

16841 Davis, Lucile. *Alabama* (4–10). Series: America the Beautiful. 1999, Children's LB $32.00 (0-516-20683-4). 144pp. A well-organized, appealing introduction to Alabama, the land, its history, the people, and contemporary life. (Rev: HBG 3/00; SLJ 1/00) [976.1]

16842 Deady, Kathleen W. *Kentucky Facts and Symbols* (1–4). Series: States and Their Symbols. 2000, Capstone LB $15.93 (0-7368-0639-3). 24pp. A beginner's book that displays and describes Kentucky's state flag, seal, bird, tree, flower, and animal. (Rev: BL 3/1/01) [976.9]

16843 DiPiazza, Domenica. *Arkansas* (3–6). Illus. Series: Hello USA. 1994, Lerner LB $19.93 (0-8225-2742-1). 72pp. A brief introduction to Arkansas that covers salient facts, history, industries, people, unique features, and famous residents. (Rev: BL 9/15/94) [976.7]

16844 Dubois, Muriel. *Maryland: Facts and Symbols* (1–4). Series: The States and Their Symbols. 2000, Capstone LB $15.93 (0-7368-0523-0). 24pp. An attractive and useful book that presents important social studies material on geography and history in addition to coverage of Maryland's state symbols. (Rev: BL 6/1–15/00; HBG 10/00) [975]

16845 Fazio, Wende. *West Virginia* (5–8). Series: America the Beautiful. 2000, Children's LB $32.00 (0-516-21074-2). 144pp. As well as the standard information on history, geography, and the people, this colorful introduction covers topics such as state symbols and famous West Virginians. (Rev: BL 5/15/00) [975.5]

16846 Feeney, Kathy. *Tennessee: Facts and Symbols* (1–4). Illus. Series: States and Their Symbols. 2000, Capstone LB $15.93 (0-7368-0525-7). 24pp. This basic account of Tennessee also includes a map and its state symbols. (Rev: BL 6/1–15/00; HBG 10/00) [976]

16847 Feeney, Kathy. *West Virginia: Facts and Symbols* (1–4). Series: The States and Their Symbols. 2000, Capstone LB $15.93 (0-7368-0528-1). 24pp. An easily read, basic introduction to West Virginia that also includes its state symbols. (Rev: BL 6/1–15/00; HBG 10/00) [975.4]

16848 Fischer, Marsha. *Miami* (3–5). Illus. Series: Downtown America. 1990, Macmillan LB $13.95 (0-87518-428-6). 60pp. This introduction to Miami includes a map, a historical timeline, and places to visit. (Rev: BL 6/1/90) [975.9]

16849 Fisher, Leonard Everett. *Monticello* (4–7). Illus. by author. 1988, Holiday LB $18.95 (0-8234-0688-1). 64pp. Touring the famous home of the third president. (Rev: BCCB 6/88; BL 6/1/88; SLJ 6–7/88)

16850 Fradin, Dennis B. *Alabama* (3–5). Illus. Series: From Sea to Shining Sea. 1993, Children's LB $27.00 (0-516-03801-X). 64pp. A good introduction to this southern state. (Rev: BL 7/93) [976.1]

16851 Fradin, Dennis B. *Georgia* (3–5). Illus. Series: From Sea to Shining Sea. 1991, Children's LB $27.00 (0-516-03810-9). 64pp. A simple, attractive look at geography, early history, and current status of this southern state. (Rev: BL 2/1/92) [975.8]

16852 Fradin, Dennis B. *Kentucky* (3–5). Illus. Series: From Sea to Shining Sea. 1993, Children's LB $27.00 (0-516-03817-6). 64pp. A fine introduction to the Bluegrass State. (Rev: BL 7/93) [976.9]

16853 Fradin, Dennis B. *North Carolina* (3–5). Illus. Series: From Sea to Shining Sea. 1992, Children's LB $27.00 (0-516-03833-8). 64pp. This introduction to North Carolina includes history, geography, and a trip through the state. (Rev: BL 5/1/92) [917.5604]

16854 Fradin, Dennis B. *Tennessee* (3–5). Illus. Series: From Sea to Shining Sea. 1992, Children's LB $27.00 (0-516-03842-7). 64pp. Tennessee is introduced with coverage of geography, history,

people, and their work. (Rev: BL 2/1/93; SLJ 4/93) [976.8]

16855 Fradin, Dennis B. *Virginia* (3–5). Illus. Series: From Sea to Shining Sea. 1992, Children's LB $27.00 (0-516-03846-X). 64pp. This introduction to Virginia includes standard information on history and geography and an imaginary trip through the state. (Rev: BL 2/1/93) [975.5]

16856 Fradin, Dennis B., and Judith B. Fradin. *Arkansas* (3–5). Illus. Series: From Sea to Shining Sea. 1994, Children's LB $27.00 (0-516-03804-4). 64pp. A nicely illustrated introduction to Arkansas past and present, with information on natural resources, its cities, and its people. (Rev: BL 8/94) [976.7]

16857 Fredeen, Charles. *South Carolina* (3–6). Illus. Series: Hello USA. 1992, Lerner LB $19.93 (0-8225-2712-X). 72pp. Timelines and simple biographies add to the appeal of this introduction to South Carolina. (Rev: BL 5/15/92; SLJ 10/92) [975.2]

16858 George, Jean Craighead. *Everglades* (2–4). Illus. by Wendell Minor. 1995, HarperCollins LB $15.89 (0-06-021229-2). 32pp. A storyteller explains to five children the origins and characteristics of the Everglades and the destruction that humans have caused to this ecosystem. (Rev: BCCB 7–8/95; BL 6/1–15/95; SLJ 6/95*) [975.9]

16859 Gibson, Karen Bush. *Mississippi Facts and Symbols* (1–4). Series: States and Their Symbols. 2000, Capstone LB $15.93 (0-7368-0640-7). 24pp. Color photos and brief text introduce Mississippi's state flower, flag, seal, animal, tree, and other symbols. (Rev: BL 3/1/01) [976.2]

16860 Gravelle, Karen. *Growing Up in a Holler in the Mountains: An Appalachian Childhood* (4–6). Illus. Series: Growing Up in America. 1997, Watts LB $24.00 (0-531-11452-X). 64pp. This account focuses on the unique aspects of growing up in the Appalachian mountains by focusing on the childhood of Joseph Ratliff in Kentucky. (Rev: BL 1/1–15/98; HBG 3/98; SLJ 3/98) [974]

16861 Gravelle, Karen, and Sylviane Diouf. *Growing Up in Crawfish Country: A Cajun Childhood* (3–6). Illus. Series: Growing Up in America. 1998, Watts LB $24.00 (0-531-11535-6). 64pp. Cajun culture, including food, music, and architecture, is described through the eyes of children in the Bayou country. (Rev: BL 12/1/98; HBG 3/99; SLJ 1/99) [976.3]

16862 Heinrichs, Ann. *Arkansas* (4–6). Illus. Series: America the Beautiful. 1989, Children's LB $28.00 (0-516-00450-6). 144pp. In addition to standard information, this book includes a 30-page reference section. (Rev: BL 7/89) [974.1]

16863 Heinrichs, Ann. *Florida* (4–6). Series: America the Beautiful. 1998, Children's LB $32.00 (0-516-20632-X). 144pp. Fact bars, numerous maps, and plenty of color photos are used to introduce the growing state of Florida. (Rev: BL 10/15/98; SLJ 1/99) [975.9]

16864 Herda, D. J. *Environmental America: The South Central States* (4–7). Illus. Series: American Scene. 1991, Millbrook LB $22.40 (1-878841-09-

2). 64pp. This account discusses the general state of the environment and presents information on animal species, pollution, waste, and urban sprawl for ten states, including Georgia, Kansas, Missouri, and Texas. (Rev: BL 8/91; SLJ 7/91) [639.9]

16865 Hintz, Martin. *Louisiana* (5–8). Series: America the Beautiful. 1998, Children's LB $32.00 (0-516-20634-6). 144pp. Clear writing and clever use of graphics provide a wealth of information on Louisiana, past and present. (Rev: BL 1/1–15/99; SLJ 2/99) [975.6]

16866 Hintz, Martin, and Stephen Hintz. *North Carolina* (5–8). Illus. Series: America the Beautiful. 1998, Children's LB $32.00 (0-516-20638-9). 144pp. A revised edition of a comprehensive introduction to North Carolina's history and geography, natural resources and industry, people and landmarks. (Rev: BL 1/1–15/99; SLJ 4/99) [975.6]

16867 Hoffman, Nancy. *South Carolina* (4–8). Series: Celebrate the States. 2000, Marshall Cavendish LB $24.95 (0-7614-1065-1). 144pp. An interesting introduction to South Carolina, with material on its land and waterways, history, government, economy, landmarks, and success stories. (Rev: BL 12/15/00; HBG 3/01) [975.7]

16868 Johnston, Joyce. *Maryland* (3–6). Illus. Series: Hello USA. 1992, Lerner LB $19.93 (0-8225-2713-8). 72pp. In this overview on Maryland, there are chapters on history and geography, as well as social and economic conditions. (Rev: BL 5/15/92; SLJ 10/92) [975]

16869 Kule, Elaine. *Arkansas Facts and Symbols* (1–4). Series: States and Their Symbols. 2000, Capstone LB $15.93 (0-7368-0634-2). 24pp. A page of basic facts about Arkansas and another page of places to visit are included in this book whose main body consists of pictures and text describing such state symbols as the flag, seal, tree, flower, and bird. (Rev: BL 3/1/01) [976.7]

16870 LaDoux, Rita C. *Georgia* (3–6). Illus. Series: Hello USA. 1991, Lerner LB $19.93 (0-8225-2703-0). 72pp. Geography, economics, history, and the environment are some of the topics covered in this look at a southern state. (Rev: BL 4/15/91; SLJ 6/91) [975.8]

16871 LaDoux, Rita C. *Louisiana* (3–6). Illus. Series: Hello USA. 1993, Lerner LB $19.93 (0-8225-2740-5). 72pp. An introduction to Louisiana with data on famous native sons and daughters. (Rev: BL 7/93) [976]

16872 LeVert, Suzanne. *Louisiana* (4–8). Illus. Series: Celebrate the States. 1997, Marshall Cavendish LB $35.64 (0-7614-0112-1). 144pp. The unique aspects of life in this southern state are stressed in this introduction that also covers standard background material. (Rev: BL 7/97; SLJ 7/97) [976.3]

16873 Loewen, Nancy. *Atlanta* (3–6). Illus. Series: Great Cities of the U.S.A. 1989, Rourke LB $23.93 (0-86592-543-7). 48pp. The history of Georgia's capital is given plus material on sights, climate, and people. (Rev: BL 1/1/90) [917]

16874 Lynch, Amy. *Nashville* (3–5). Illus. Series: Downtown America. 1990, Macmillan LB $17.95 (0-87518-453-7). 60pp. The sights and people of the nation's country music capital are introduced. (Rev: BL 2/1/91) [976.8]

16875 Morgan, Cheryl Koenig. *The Everglades* (3–5). Illus. 1990, Troll paper $3.95 (0-8167-1734-6). 32pp. A description of the Everglades with emphasis on ecology. (Rev: SLJ 8/90) [975.9]

16876 Nichols, Joan Kane. *New Orleans* (3–5). Illus. Series: Downtown America. 1989, Macmillan LB $13.95 (0-87518-403-0). 64pp. History, neighborhoods, and unique features of New Orleans are covered. (Rev: BL 8/89; SLJ 1/90) [976.3]

16877 Odinoski, Steve. *Georgia* (4–8). Series: Celebrate the States. 2000, Marshall Cavendish LB $24.95 (0-7614-1062-7). 144pp. An informative, attractive introduction to Georgia with material on its land, history, people, social issues, and hidden treasures. (Rev: BL 12/15/00; HBG 3/01; SLJ 2/01) [975.8]

16878 Petersen, David. *Great Smoky Mountains National Park* (1–3). Illus. Series: New True Books. 1993, Children's LB $21.00 (0-516-01332-7). 48pp. This national park in the Great Smokies is introduced, along with special sights. (Rev: BL 8/93) [976.8]

16879 Rauth, Leslie. *Maryland* (5–9). Series: Celebrate the States. 1999, Benchmark LB $24.95 (0-7614-0671-9). 144pp. This book explores Maryland with material on topics including land and waterways, government, economy, festivals, people, and hidden treasures. (Rev: BL 1/1–15/00; HBG 10/00; SLJ 5/00) [975.2]

16880 Ready, Anna. *Mississippi* (3–6). Illus. Series: Hello USA. 1993, Lerner LB $19.93 (0-8225-2743-X). 72pp. Such topics as geography, culture, history, and economics are covered in this introduction. (Rev: BL 7/93) [976.2]

16881 Reef, Catherine. *Arlington National Cemetery* (4–6). Illus. Series: Places in American History. 1991, Macmillan $18.95 (0-87518-471-5). 72pp. The history and development of this cemetery known as "America's greatest national shrine." (Rev: BL 2/15/92; SLJ 3/92) [975.5]

16882 Reef, Catherine. *Monticello* (4–6). Illus. Series: Places in American History. 1991, Macmillan LB $14.95 (0-87518-472-3). 72pp. Through pictures and text, the fascinating home of President Thomas Jefferson is introduced. (Rev: BL 2/15/92) [973.4]

16883 Reef, Catherine. *Mount Vernon* (4–6). Illus. Series: Places in American History. 1992, Macmillan LB $18.95 (0-87518-474-X). 72pp. This account not only introduces the home of this first president, but also tells about the life of George Washington. (Rev: BL 9/1/92) [973]

16884 Richards, Norman. *Monticello*. Rev. ed. (2–5). Illus. Series: Cornerstones of Freedom. 1995, Children's LB $20.50 (0-516-06695-1). 30pp. The construction and furnishing of Monticello are described, as well as their relation to events in Jefferson's life. (Rev: SLJ 9/95) [917.5]

16885 Schulz, Andrea. *North Carolina* (3–6). Illus. Series: Hello USA. 1994, Lerner LB $19.93 (0-8225-2744-8). 72pp. A colorful introduction to North Carolina's history, geography, landmarks, and life-styles. (Rev: BL 2/1/94) [975.6]

16886 Shirley, David. *Alabama* (4–8). Series: Celebrate the States. 2000, Marshall Cavendish LB $24.95 (0-7614-0648-4). 141pp. An introduction to Alabama that covers its land and waterways, its history, government, and economy, and its culture and success stories. (Rev: BL 6/1–15/00; HBG 10/00) [976.1]

16887 Sirvaitis, Karen. *Florida* (3–5). Illus. Series: Hello USA. 1994, Lerner LB $19.93 (0-8225-2728-6). 72pp. With photos on every page, this compact book contains basic background information about Florida, including its history, famous sights, and important residents. (Rev: BL 4/15/94) [973]

16888 Sirvaitis, Karen. *Tennessee* (3–6). Illus. Series: Hello USA. 1991, Lerner LB $19.93 (0-8225-2711-1). 72pp. This book covers the geography, history, and socioeconomic conditions, along with timelines and biographies of famous residents. (Rev: BL 12/1/91) [976.8]

16889 Sirvaitis, Karen. *Virginia* (3–6). Illus. Series: Hello USA. 1991, Lerner LB $19.93 (0-8225-2702-2). 72pp. With full-color photos, this is a good, fact-filled introduction to Virginia. (Rev: BL 4/15/91; SLJ 6/91) [975.5]

16890 Smith, Adam, and Katherine S. Smith. *A Historical Album of Kentucky* (4–7). Illus. Series: Historical Album. 1995, Millbrook LB $23.40 (1-56294-507-6). 64pp. A clear, lavishly illustrated account of Kentucky's history from prehistory to the present, with accompanying fact sheets and a rundown on state symbols. (Rev: SLJ 6/95) [976.9]

16891 Snow, Pegeen. *Atlanta* (3–6). Illus. 1989, Macmillan LB $13.95 (0-87518-389-1). 60pp. History and modern life in this growing southern city. (Rev: BL 3/15/89; SLJ 5/89)

16892 Stein, R. Conrad. *South Carolina* (5–8). Series: America the Beautiful. 1999, Children's LB $32.00 (0-516-20997-3). 144pp. A comprehensive and well-illustrated introduction to South Carolina — its history and geography, its government and economy, its people and important places. (Rev: BL 11/15/99) [975.2]

16893 Stein, R. Conrad. *West Virginia* (4–6). Illus. Series: America the Beautiful. 1990, Children's LB $28.00 (0-516-00494-8). 144pp. The small state of West Virginia is introduced with coverage on government, history, economy, and geography. (Rev: BL 1/1/91) [975.4]

16894 Wade, Linda R. *St. Augustine: America's Oldest City* (3–5). Illus. Series: Doors to America's Past. 1991, Rourke LB $22.60 (0-86592-468-6). 48pp. This book traces the history of St. Augustine, Florida, to the present. (Rev: BL 5/1/92; SLJ 1/92) [975.9]

16895 Weatherford, Carole Boston. *Sink or Swim: African-American Lifesavers of the Outer Banks* (4–8). Illus. 1999, Coastal Carolina $15.95 (1-928556-01-9); paper $12.95 (1-928556-03-5). 80pp. A history of the African Americans who participated in lifesaving efforts on the Outer Banks of North Carolina, known as "the graveyard of the Atlantic." (Rev: BL 12/15/99) [363.28]

16896 Wills, Charles A. *Alabama* (4–7). Illus. Series: Historical Album. 1995, Millbrook LB $23.40 (1-56294-591-2). 64pp. Using many period paintings and engravings, this account traces the history of Alabama from prehistoric days to today, with a special section on important facts. (Rev: BL 12/15/95; SLJ 1/96) [976.1]

16897 Wills, Charles A. *A Historical Album of Florida* (4–8). Illus. Series: Historical Album. 1994, Millbrook LB $23.40 (1-56294-480-0). 64pp. This compressed history of Florida deals with major events from prehistory through the 1990s. (Rev: SLJ 2/95) [975.9]

16898 Wills, Charles A. *A Historical Album of Georgia* (4–7). Illus. Series: Historical Album. 1996, Millbrook LB $23.40 (0-7613-0035-X); paper $7.95 (0-7613-0125-9). 64pp. With many period illustrations, some in color, and a simple text, the history and geography of Georgia are presented. (Rev: BL 12/15/96) [975.8]

16899 Young, Robert. *A Personal Tour of Monticello* (4–7). Illus. Series: How It Was. 1999, Lerner LB $23.93 (0-8225-3575-0). 64pp. Through the eyes of Jefferson, his daughter, and one of his slaves, the reader is introduced to the home of the third president of the United States. (Rev: BL 6/1–15/99; HBG 10/99; SLJ 7/99) [975.5]

SOUTHWEST

16900 Anderson, Joan. *Cowboys* (4–6). Illus. by George Ancona. 1996, Scholastic $16.95 (0-590-48424-9). 48pp. All of the Eby family, including their young sons and hired cowboys, work during the spring roundup. (Rev: BL 3/15/96*; HB 5–6/96; SLJ 3/96*) [978]

16901 Aylesworth, Thomas G., and Virginia L. Aylesworth. *The Southwest: Colorado, New Mexico, Texas* (3–6). Illus. 1995, Chelsea LB $19.95 (0-7910-3412-7); paper $9.95 (0-7910-3430-5). 64pp. An easy-to-use study of three southwestern states. (Rev: BL 8/88; SLJ 11/88)

16902 Bredeson, Carmen. *The Spindletop Gusher: The Story of the Texas Oil Boom* (4–7). Illus. Series: Spotlight on American History. 1996, Millbrook LB $21.90 (1-56294-916-0). 64pp. A discussion of the Texas oil boom, its effects on the state and its economy, and the present status of the oil industry. (Rev: BL 3/15/96) [338.4]

16903 Bredeson, Carmen. *Texas* (4–8). Illus. Series: Celebrate the States. 1996, Marshall Cavendish LB $35.64 (0-7614-0109-1). 144pp. Basic information about Texas is presented in an attractive format with many color photos, maps, and diagrams. (Rev: BL 2/15/97) [976.4]

16904 Early, Theresa S. *New Mexico* (3–6). Illus. Series: Hello USA. 1993, Lerner LB $19.93 (0-8225-2748-0). 72pp. An introduction to New Mexico that includes geography, history, and social and economic conditions. (Rev: BL 7/93; SLJ 8/93) [978.9]

16905 Fradin, Dennis B. *Texas* (3–5). Illus. Series: From Sea to Shining Sea. 1992, Children's LB $27.00 (0-516-03843-5). 64pp. A chronology of Texas history and a state map are included in this account. (Rev: BL 2/1/93; SLJ 4/93) [976.4]

16906 Fradin, Judith B., and Dennis B. Fradin. *New Mexico* (3–5). Illus. Series: From Sea to Shining Sea. 1993, Children's LB $27.00 (0-516-03831-1). 64pp. Includes material on such topics as the land, people, history, important sights, and economy. (Rev: BL 11/1/93) [978.9]

16907 Garza, Carmen Lomas, and Harriet Rohmer. *Magic Windows: Ventanas Magicas* (3–7). Illus. 1999, Children's Book Pr. $15.95 (0-89239-157-X). 32pp. This bilingual book introduces Mexican American culture and lifestyle through an examination of *papel picado* (cut-paper art). Also see *Making Magic Windows.* (Rev: BL 5/1/99; HBG 10/99; SLJ 7/99) [745.54]

16908 Heinrichs, Ann. *Texas* (5–8). Series: America the Beautiful. 1999, Children's LB $32.00 (0-516-20998-1). 144pp. Photos and maps illustrate this account of Texas — its history and geography, economy and government, people and resources. (Rev: BL 11/15/99) [976.4]

16909 Herda, D. J. *Environmental America: The Southwestern States* (4–7). Illus. Series: American Scene. 1991, Millbrook LB $22.40 (1-878841-11-4). 64pp. This account, which discusses the state of the environment and how it can be changed for the better, covers Arizona, California, Colorado, Nevada, New Mexico, and Utah. (Rev: BL 8/91; SLJ 7/91) [639.9]

16910 Herda, D. J. *Ethnic America: The Southwestern States* (5–7). Illus. Series: American Scene. 1991, Millbrook LB $22.40 (1-56294-019-8). 64pp. The waves of immigration, including Hispanic, into the southwestern states, including California and Hawaii, are covered in text and many excellent photos. (Rev: BL 2/1/92; SLJ 3/92) [572.973]

16911 Kent, Deborah. *Dallas* (3–6). Series: Cities of the World. 2000, Children's LB $26.50 (0-516-21678-3). 64pp. A good travel guide to Dallas that also describes its urban problems and efforts to solve them. (Rev: BL 12/15/00) [976.4]

16912 Kent, Deborah. *New Mexico* (4–10). Series: America the Beautiful. 1999, Children's LB $32.00 (0-516-20690-7). 144pp. New Mexico is introduced with material on the land, its people, history, and current conditions in this fine revision of an earlier edition. (Rev: HBG 3/00; SLJ 1/00) [978.9]

16913 Lee, Sally. *San Antonio* (4–7). Illus. Series: Downtown America. 1992, Macmillan LB $17.95 (0-87518-510-X). 63pp. This introduction to San Antonio covers history, people, festivals, and interesting landmarks like the Alamo, the river walk, and Spanish missions. (Rev: BL 4/15/92; SLJ 5/92) [976]

16914 Peifer, Charles. *Houston* (3–5). Illus. 1988, Macmillan $17.95 (0-87518-387-5). 60pp. A look at life in this big Texas city. (Rev: BL 1/15/89; SLJ 5/89)

16915 Stewart, Gail B. *Houston* (3–6). Illus. Series: Great Cities of the U.S.A. 1989, Rourke LB $23.93 (0-86592-539-9). 48pp. Named after Sam Houston, this Texas city is introduced through text and pictures. (Rev: BL 1/1/90) [917]

16916 Tweit, Susan J. *Meet the Wild Southwest: Land of Hoodoos and Gila Monsters* (4–8). Illus. 1996, Alaska Northwest paper $14.95 (0-88240-468-7). 124pp. An impressive collection of facts and curiosities about the natural history of our Southwest, with many appendixes that supply more-traditional information. (Rev: BL 3/1/96) [508.79]

16917 Wills, Charles A. *A Historical Album of Texas* (4–7). Illus. Series: Historical Album. 1995, Millbrook LB $23.40 (1-56294-504-1). 64pp. This account of the history of Texas from earliest times to today is also particularly noteworthy for its many illustrations. (Rev: SLJ 6/95) [976.4]

Social Institutions and Issues

Business and Economics

16918 Berger, Melvin, and Gilda Berger. *Round and Round the Money Goes: What Money Is and How We Use It* (1–3). Illus. by Jane McCreary. Series: Discovery Readers. 1993, Ideals paper $4.50 (0-8249-8598-2). 48pp. Many topics about money are briefly introduced in this beginner's account, including the forms money takes, why it is necessary, world monetary units, and how banks work. (Rev: SLJ 12/93) [332]

16919 Burns, Peggy. *The Mail* (3–5). Illus. Series: Stepping Through History. 1995, Thomson Learning LB $19.92 (1-56847-249-8). 32pp. A broad history of mail service, beginning with the ancient Persians and including material on today's computerized mail sorting and the hobby of stamp collecting. (Rev: BL 4/15/95; SLJ 6/95) [383]

16920 Burns, Peggy. *Money* (3–5). Illus. Series: Stepping Through History. 1995, Thomson Learning LB $5.00 (1-56847-248-X). 32pp. As well as a history of coins and paper money, this account tells of the development of banks, credit cards, and foreign exchange. (Rev: BL 4/15/95; SLJ 6/95) [332.4]

16921 Caes, Charles J. *The Young Zillionaire's Guide to the Stock Market* (5–8). Series: Be a Zillionaire. 2000, Rosen Central LB $17.95 (0-8239-3265-6). 48pp. Basic information on the inner workings of the stock market is presented with many examples from the corporate world. (Rev: SLJ 3/01) [332.6]

16922 Green, Meg. *The Young Zillionaire's Guide to Investments and Savings* (5–8). Series: Be a Zillionaire. 2000, Rosen Central LB $17.95 (0-8239-3261-3). 48pp. A guide to the investment markets and methods of saving with good use of examples and case studies. (Rev: SLJ 3/01) [338.5]

16923 Hall, Margaret. *Credit Cards and Checks* (3–5). Illus. Series: Earning, Saving, Spending. 2000, Heinemann $14.95 (1-57572-232-1). 32pp. Using double-page spreads, this colorful book describes what checks and credit cards are, how they are used, and how they can become a substitute for money. (Rev: BL 10/15/00) [332.76]

16924 Hall, Margaret. *Money* (3–5). Illus. Series: Earning, Saving, Spending. 2000, Heinemann $14.95 (1-57572-233-X). 32pp. This history of coins and paper money also discusses their value and uses and how people earn and spend money. (Rev: BL 10/15/00) [332.4]

16925 Karlitz, Gail, and Debbie Honig. *Growing Money: A Complete Investing Guide for Kids* (4–8). Illus. by Stephen Lewis. 1999, Price Stern Sloan paper $6.99 (0-8431-7481-1). 120pp. A fine introduction to the world of investing including material on reading a financial page, recording income, types of interest, and risk tolerance. (Rev: SLJ 9/99) [332.6]

16926 Maestro, Betsy. *The Story of Money* (2–4). Illus. by Giulio Maestro. 1993, Houghton $17.00 (0-395-56242-2). 48pp. The story of the ancient Sumerians who invented the idea of making money. (Rev: BCCB 3/93; BL 3/1/93; SLJ 4/93) [332.4]

16927 Parker, Nancy W. *Money, Money, Money* (3–6). Illus. 1995, HarperCollins LB $16.89 (0-06-023412-1). 32pp. An explanation of what is on the front and back of our paper currency from $1 to $100,000, with interesting facts about the presidents pictured. (Rev: BCCB 7–8/95; BL 6/1–15/95*; SLJ 6/95) [769.5]

16928 Seidman, David. *The Young Zillionaire's Guide to Supply and Demand* (5–7). Series: Be a Zillionaire. 2000, Rosen Central LB $17.95 (0-8239-3264-8). 48pp. The basic principles of supply and demand are explained, with information on how they are influenced by producers and consumers and how they help create economic conditions. (Rev: SLJ 2/01) [330]

16929 *Sold! The Origins of Money and Trade* (5–8). Illus. Series: Buried Worlds. 1994, Runestone LB $23.93 (0-8225-3206-9). 64pp. Explains the world origins of commerce and money, with coverage on how the earliest coins were made in the West and how other cultures developed unique forms of currency. (Rev: BL 9/15/94; SLJ 9/94) [737.4]

16930 Wilson, Antoine. *The Young Zillionaire's Guide to Distributing Goods and Services* (5–7). Series: Be a Zillionaire. 2000, Rosen Central LB $17.95 (0-8239-3259-1). 48pp. This book explains how goods and services are distributed, the importance of retailing and wholesaling, how transportation affects prices and availability, and how the Internet might change these conditions. (Rev: SLJ 2/01) [330]

16931 Young, Robert. *Money* (3–6). Illus. Series: Household History. 1998, Carolrhoda LB $16.95 (1-57505-070-6). 48pp. A breezy account of the history of money in its various forms, including counterfeiting, credit, and even some magic tricks with coins and bills. (Rev: BL 9/1/98; HBG 10/98; SLJ 7/98) [332.4]

Consumerism

16932 Bendick, Jeanne, and Robert Bendick. *Markets: From Barter to Bar Codes* (3–5). Illus. 1997, Watts LB $22.00 (0-531-20263-1). 64pp. Illustrates the history of trade in the Western world by viewing a number of different markets. (Rev: BL 9/1/97; SLJ 1/98) [380.1]

16933 Burns, Peggy. *Stores and Markets* (3–5). Illus. Series: Stepping Through History. 1995, Thomson Learning LB $5.00 (1-56847-344-3). 32pp. A history of the distribution of goods from ancient markets and bazaars to today's shopping malls. (Rev: BL 7/95) [381]

16934 Dunn, John. *Advertising* (5–8). Illus. Series: Overview. 1997, Lucent LB $17.96 (1-56006-182-0). 112pp. As well as a history of advertising, this well-organized book tells about present practices, markets, and media. (Rev: BL 5/15/97; SLJ 7/97) [659.1]

16935 Miller, Marilyn. *Behind the Scenes at the Shopping Mall* (PS–3). Illus. Series: Behind the Scenes. 1996, Raintree Steck-Vaughn LB $21.40 (0-8172-4088-8). 32pp. Using many leading questions and cartoon–style illustrations, this book provides an inside look at the activities that make a shopping mall work. (Rev: BL 4/15/96; SLJ 12/96) [381]

16936 Schmitt, Lois. *Smart Spending: A Consumer's Guide* (5–8). 1989, Macmillan $13.95 (0-684-19035-4). 112pp. A no-nonsense text incorporating teen-oriented case studies. (Rev: BL 5/1/89)

16937 Yardley, Thompson. *Buy Now, Pay Later: Smart Shopping Counts* (2–3). Illus. by author. Series: Lighter Look. 1992, Millbrook LB $20.90 (1-56294-149-6). 39pp. In an entertaining format, facts about smart shopping and recycling are given. (Rev: SLJ 6/92) [640.73]

Money-Making Ideas and Budgeting

16938 Barkin, Carol, and Elizabeth James. *The New Complete Babysitter's Handbook* (5–7). Illus. 1995, Clarion $16.95 (0-395-66557-4); paper $7.95 (0-

395-66558-2). 164pp. A fine manual that covers such topics as first aid, ways to amuse children, and how to get jobs baby sitting. (Rev: BL 5/1/95; SLJ 6/95) [649.1]

16939 Bernstein, Daryl. *Better Than a Lemonade Stand! Small Business Ideas for Kids* (4–8). Illus. by Rob Husberg. 1992, Beyond Words paper $7.95 (0-941831-75-2). 170pp. How to start 51 small businesses is the focus of this book by a 15-year-old entrepreneur. (Rev: BL 10/1/92; SLJ 1/93) [650.1]

16940 Byers, Patricia, and Julia Preston. *The Kids' Money Book* (2–6). Illus. 1983, Liberty paper $4.95 (0-89709-041-1). A number of ways kids can make money.

16941 Drew, Bonnie, and Noel Drew. *Fast Cash for Kids* (4–7). Illus. 1995, Career Pr. paper $13.99 (1-564-14154-3). 168pp. Many ideas for ways of making money. (Rev: BL 6/15/87)

16942 Godfrey, Neale S. *Neale S. Godfrey's Ultimate Kids' Money Book* (5–8). Illus. by Randy Verougstraete. 1998, Simon & Schuster $18.00 (0-689-81717-7). 128pp. Using cartoons, diagrams, and photos, this work explains the history and uses of money and then gives tips on how to make it, spend it, and budget it wisely. (Rev: BL 11/1/98*; HBG 3/99; SLJ 2/99) [332.024]

16943 Hall, Margaret. *Your Allowance* (3–5). Illus. Series: Earning, Saving, Spending. 2000, Heinemann $14.95 (1-57572-234-8). 32pp. This book looks seriously at budgeting one's allowance, at good consumer practices, savings accounts, and gifts to charity. (Rev: BL 10/15/00) [332.024]

16944 Halperin, Wendy A. *Once upon a Company: A True Story* (1–5). Illus. 1998, Orchard LB $17.99 (0-531-33089-3). 40pp. A winningly illustrated picture book about the three Halperin children who raised money for their college fund by creating and selling Christmas wreaths and, in the summer, opening a food stand. (Rev: BCCB 9/98; BL 9/1/98*; HBG 3/99; SLJ 9/98) [658]

16945 Nathan, Amy. *The Kids' Allowance Book* (4–7). Illus. 1998, Walker $15.95 (0-8027-8651-0). 96pp. A total of 166 students, ages 9–14, explore the pros and cons of allowances and money management. (Rev: BCCB 6/98; BL 7/98; HBG 10/98; SLJ 10/98) [332.02]

16946 *New Moon: Money: How to Get It, Spend It, and Save It* (4–8). Series: New Moon. 2000, Crown LB $16.99 (0-517-88586-7); paper $9.99 (0-517-88585-9). 86pp. Using a number of interviews and quotes, this book by nine girls ages 10 to 14 describes ways to make money and how to manage it wisely. (Rev: SLJ 4/00) [650.1]

16947 Weintraub, Aileen. *Everything You Need to Know About Being a Baby-sitter: A Teen's Guide to Responsible Child Care* (5–8). 2000, Rosen LB $17.95 (0-8239-3085-8). 64pp. This book covers all facets of baby-sitting from preparation, responsibilities, and safety precautions to employment opportunities. (Rev: SLJ 7/00) [649]

16948 Zakarin, Debra M. *The Ultimate Baby-Sitter's Handbook: So You Wanna Make Tons of Money?* (4–8). Illus. 1997, Price Stern Sloan paper

$4.99 (0-8431-7936-8). 128pp. A practical, easily read guide to baby sitting and setting up a business. (Rev: BL 9/15/97; SLJ 12/97) [649]

Retail Stores and Other Workplaces

16949 Jaspersohn, William. *Cookies* (4–6). Illus. 1993, Macmillan LB $14.95 (0-02-747822-X). 48pp. A photo-essay that uses a Famous Amos cookie factory in Georgia. (Rev: BCCB 4/93; BL 3/1/93; SLJ 5/93) [664]

16950 Sirimarco, Elizabeth. *At the Bank* (PS–2). Photos by David M. Budd. Series: Field Trips. 1999, Child's World LB $14.95 (1-56766-572-1). 32pp. This photo-essay describes a bank and some of the transactions that take place there. (Rev: HBG 3/00; SLJ 2/00) [332.1]

16951 Waters, Alice, et al. *Fanny at Chez Panisse* (4–6). Illus. by Ann Arnold. 1992, HarperCollins $23.00 (0-06-016896-X). 134pp. Young Fanny tells of life in her mother's popular restaurant. (Rev: BL 2/1/93) [647]

Ecology and Environment

General

16952 Allen, Judy, ed. *Anthology for the Earth* (4–6). Illus. 1998, Candlewick $21.99 (0-7636-0301-5). 96pp. This beautifully illustrated anthology of great writing by authors such as Thomas Hardy, John Muir, and Willa Cather explores the earth's ecology and its fragile nature. (Rev: BCCB 4/98; BL 4/1/98; SLJ 4/98) [574.5]

16953 Butterfield, Moira. *Richard Orr's Nature Cross-Sections* (4–6). Illus. by Richard Orr. 1995, DK $17.95 (0-7894-0147-9). 30pp. Includes cross-sections of ecosystems, such as a rain forest, and structures, such as a beehive. (Rev: BL 12/1/95; SLJ 1/96) [574.5]

16954 Chandler, Gary, and Kevin Graham. *Kids Who Make a Difference* (4–8). Illus. Series: Making a Better World. 1996, Twenty-First Century LB $16.98 (0-8050-4625-9). 64pp. Describes various community projects in which young people have played a significant role. (Rev: BL 12/1/96; SLJ 4/97) [363.7]

16955 Crenson, Victoria. *Bay Shore Park: The Death and Life of an Amusement Park* (3–5). Illus. 1995, W.H. Freeman paper $16.95 (0-7167-6580-2). 32pp. This fascinating nature book describes how nature gradually reclaimed the area after an amusement park on upper Chesapeake Bay was closed. (Rev: BL 7/95; SLJ 8/95) [752]

16956 Gates, Richard. *Conservation* (1–4). Illus. 1982, Children's LB $21.00 (0-516-01618-0). 48pp. A simple but informative introduction intended for the primary grades.

16957 Hill, Lee S. *Parks Are to Share* (1–3). Series: Building Blocks Books. 1997, Carolrhoda $21.27 (1-57505-068-4). 32pp. This book explores all kinds of parks and their care and uses, from Yosemite National Park to Central Park in New York City. (Rev: BL 3/15/98; HBG 3/98) [363.6]

16958 Holmes, Anita. *I Can Save the Earth: A Kid's Handbook for Keeping Earth Healthy and Green*

(4–6). Illus. by David Neuhaus. 1993, Simon & Schuster LB $13.98 (0-671-74544-1); paper $7.95 (0-671-74545-X). 96pp. A practical guide that offers many suggestions on ways for young people to actively help in conservation. (Rev: SLJ 7/93) [320.5]

16959 Javna, John. *50 Simple Things Kids Can Do to Save the Earth* (3–6). Illus. by Michele Montez. 1990, Andrews & McMeel paper $6.95 (0-8362-2301-2). 156pp. This book shows how small changes can help to save the environment. (Rev: BL 6/15/90; SLJ 9/90) [333.7]

16960 Levine, Shar, and Allison Grafton. *Projects for a Healthy Planet: Simple Environmental Experiments for Kids* (3–7). Illus. by Terry Chui. 1992, Wiley paper $10.95 (0-471-55484-1). 64pp. A worthy addition to the many ecology books on the market. (Rev: BL 8/92; SLJ 8/92) [628]

16961 Lowery, Linda, and Marybeth Lorbiecki. *Earthwise at Home* (3–5). Illus. by David Mataya. 1993, Carolrhoda LB $19.95 (0-87614-730-9). 48pp. This book gives tips on how to recycle, reuse, and preserve materials at home. Others in this series are: *Earthwise at Play* and *Earthwise at School* (both 1993). (Rev: SLJ 5/93) [320]

16962 Mattson, Mark. *Scholastic Environmental Atlas of the United States* (3–6). Illus. 1993, Scholastic $14.95 (0-590-49354-X). 80pp. In this atlas, natural resources and ecological threats like water pollution and toxic dumps are pictured globally. (Rev: BL 10/15/93; SLJ 4/94) [333.7]

16963 Penny, Malcolm. *Our Environment* (2–3). Series: Talking About. 1999, Raintree Steck-Vaughn LB $15.98 (0-8172-5889-2). 32pp. A simple format and many illustrations enhance this beginner's book on conservation and environmental protection, using such everyday examples as littering. (Rev: BL 2/15/00; HBG 10/00) [333.75]

16964 Pringle, Laurence. *The Environmental Movement: From Its Roots to the Challenges of a New Century* (5–8). Illus. 2000, HarperCollins $15.95 (0-688-15626-6). 144pp. This is a fine history of environmentalism in America, beginning with the conflicts between Native Americans and early settlers concerning natural resources and ending with current issues. (Rev: BL 4/1/00; HBG 10/00; SLJ 6/00) [363.7]

16965 Pringle, Laurence. *Fire in the Forest: A Cycle of Growth and Renewal* (4–6). Illus. by Bob Marstall. 1995, Simon & Schuster $16.00 (0-689-80394-X). 32pp. Discusses the effects of forest fires and the cycle of renewal involving plants and animals that follows. (Rev: BL 12/1/95; SLJ 12/95) [574.5]

16966 Reed-Jones, Carol. *The Tree in the Ancient Forest* (K–3). Illus. by Christopher Canyon. 1995, Dawn $16.95 (1-883220-32-7); paper $7.95 (1-883220-31-9). 32pp. The food cycle of interdependence that involves both plants and animals and a 300-year-old fir tree is the subject of this stunning picture book. (Rev: BL 7/95; SLJ 9/95) [574]

16967 Scott, Michael. *Ecology* (5–8). Illus. Series: Young Oxford. 1996, Oxford LB $30.00 (0-19-521166-9). 166pp. An attractive introduction to the world of ecology, adaptation, conservation, and species diversity. (Rev: BL 3/1/96; SLJ 3/96) [574.5]

16968 Seibert, Patricia. *Toad Overload: A True Tale of Nature Knocked Off Balance in Australia* (K–3). Illus. by Jan Davey Ellis. 1996, Millbrook LB $21.90 (1-56294-613-7). 32pp. The balance of nature in Australia is upset when large toads are imported to eat marauding beetles. (Rev: BCCB 2/96; BL 2/15/96; SLJ 4/96) [597.8]

16969 VanCleave, Janice. *Janice VanCleave's Ecology for Every Kid* (4–7). Illus. 1996, Wiley paper $10.95 (0-471-10086-2). 240pp. Clear instructions and many diagrams introduce a series of experiments that highlight environmental issues. (Rev: BL 3/1/96; SLJ 4/96) [574.5]

16970 Whitman, Sylvia. *This Land Is Your Land: The American Conservation Movement* (5–7). Illus. 1994, Lerner LB $22.60 (0-8225-1729-9). 88pp. A history of the conservation movement from its beginnings in 1870 when there were efforts to save Yellowstone and ending with today's major problems such as oil spills and trash disposal. (Rev: BL 12/15/94; HB 3–4/94; SLJ 12/94) [363.7]

Cities

16971 Jestadt, Peter, and Karen Millyard. *City at Night* (3–5). Photos by Peter Jestadt. 1998, Annick LB $18.95 (1-55037-549-0); paper $8.95 (1-55037-548-2). 47pp. This book describes in pictures and text what happens in a big city after dark, on the streets, in buildings, at airports, hospitals, radio stations, etc. (Rev: SLJ 2/99) [307.76]

16972 Parker, Philip. *Global Cities* (4–6). Illus. Series: Project Eco-City. 1995, Thomson Learning LB $7.95 (1-56847-286-2). 48pp. This account concentrates on the ecology and balance of nature found in large cities. (Rev: BL 6/1–15/95) [307.76]

16973 Sammis, Fran. *Cities and Towns* (2–5). Illus. Series: Discovering Geography. 1997, Marshall Cavendish LB $22.79 (0-7614-0540-2). 32pp. Using a question-and-answer approach, this account introduces cities and towns and outlines projects in map making, including finding houses along a newspaper route or stores in a mall. (Rev: BL 2/1/98; HBG 3/98; SLJ 4/98) [307.76]

Garbage and Waste Recycling

16974 Burton, Jane, and Kim Taylor. *The Nature and Science of Waste* (3–6). Series: Exploring the Science of Nature. 1999, Gareth Stevens LB $14.95 (0-8368-2186-6). 32pp. Different kinds of waste and their disposal techniques and problems are discussed in this well-illustrated account that includes a special activities section. (Rev: BL 7/99; SLJ 1/00) [363.7]

16975 Chandler, Gary, and Kevin Graham. *Recycling* (4–8). Illus. Series: Making a Better World. 1996, Twenty-First Century LB $20.40 (0-8050-4622-4). 64pp. Reports on various recycling endeavors and their beneficial results. (Rev: BL 12/1/96; SLJ 4/97) [363.73]

16976 Coombs, Karen Mueller. *Flush! Treating Wastewater* (3–6). Illus. 1995, Carolrhoda LB $22.60 (0-87614-879-8). 56pp. A history of sanitation through the centuries is given, plus a description of present-day water purification systems. (Rev: BCCB 1/96; BL 12/1/95; SLJ 12/95) [628.3]

16977 *50 Simple Things Kids Can Do to Recycle* (4–7). Illus. 1994, EarthWorks paper $6.95 (1-879682-00-1). 144pp. A collection of projects and activities that can help recycling efforts at home, at school, and in the community. (Rev: BL 7/94; SLJ 8/94) [363.7]

16978 Hall, Eleanor J. *Garbage* (5–8). Illus. Series: Overview. 1997, Lucent LB $22.45 (1-56006-188-X). 96pp. A history of how we have handled waste disposal, and current ecological and environmental approaches, including recycling. (Rev: BL 8/97; HBG 3/98) [363.73]

16979 Heilman, Joan R. *Tons of Trash: Why You Should Recycle and What Happens When You Do* (3–5). 1992, Avon paper $3.50 (0-380-76379-6). 80pp. This lively tour of processing plants shows how garbage is recycled. (Rev: BL 4/15/92) [363.72]

16980 Jacobs, Francine. *Follow That Trash! All About Recycling* (K–3). Illus. by Mavis Smith. Series: All Aboard Reading. 1996, Grosset paper $3.95 (0-448-41314-0). 47pp. Discusses landfills, garbage burning, pollution, composting, and what happens at a recycling plant. (Rev: SLJ 3/97) [628.4]

16981 Kalbacken, Joan, and Emilie U. Lepthien. *Recycling* (2–4). Illus. Series: New True Books. 1991, Children's LB $21.00 (0-516-01118-9). 48pp. This book tells why recycling is necessary, describes various types, and tells how effective each type is. (Rev: BL 7/91; SLJ 10/91) [363.72]

16982 Maass, Robert. *Garbage* (PS–2). Illus. 2000, Holt $16.95 (0-8050-5951-2). 32pp. A photo-essay about garbage that shows how it is created, collected, and disposed of. (Rev: BL 5/1/00; HBG 10/00; SLJ 5/00) [363.72]

16983 Parker, Steve. *Waste, Recycling and Re-Use* (4–6). Illus. Series: Protecting Our Planet. 1998, Raintree Steck-Vaughn LB $25.68 (0-8172-4940-0). 48pp. This book gives a realistic picture of the various types of waste, the problems of waste disposal, and how each consumer can help. (Rev: BL 7/98; HBG 10/98) [363.7]

16984 Ring, Elizabeth. *What Rot! Nature's Mighty Recycler* (3–5). Illus. 1996, Millbrook LB $23.40 (1-56294-671-4). 32pp. Numerous photos and a lively text describe how nature provides organisms and processes to decompose materials naturally. (Rev: BL 2/15/96; SLJ 4/96) [574.2]

16985 Seltzer, Meyer. *Here Comes the Recycling Truck!* (PS–3). Illus. 1992, Whitman LB $14.95 (0-8075-3235-5). 32pp. Follow the garbage truck — not to the dump, but to the recycling center! (Rev: BL 5/1/92; SLJ 5/92) [363.7]

16986 Snodgrass, Mary Ellen. *Solid Waste* (4–6). Illus. Series: Environmental Awareness. 1991, Bancroft-Sage LB $14.95 (0-944280-28-5). 48pp. The techniques and problems of waste removal and recycling, with many color illustrations. Also use: *Water Pollution* (1991). (Rev: BL 2/15/92) [363.73]

16987 Tesar, Jenny. *The Waste Crisis* (5–8). Illus. 1991, Facts on File $19.95 (0-8160-2491-X). 112pp. This well-illustrated account describes types of waste, the current crisis in disposal, and possible solutions. (Rev: BL 11/15/91) [363.72]

16988 Wilcox, Charlotte. *Trash!* (3–5). Illus. 1988, Carolrhoda LB $16.95 (0-87614-311-7); Lerner paper $5.95 (0-87614-511-X). 40pp. What happens to garbage after it's collected. (Rev: BL 12/1/88; HB 1–2/89; SLJ 1/89)

Pollution

16989 Baines, John. *Keeping the Air Clean* (4–6). Illus. Series: Protecting Our Planet. 1998, Raintree Steck-Vaughn LB $25.68 (0-8172-4936-2). 48pp. Air pollution and its natural and man-made sources are discussed, with suggestions for controlling this problem. (Rev: BL 7/98; HBG 10/98) [363.739]

16990 Berger, Melvin. *Oil Spill!* (K–3). Illus. by Paul Mirocha. 1994, HarperCollins paper $4.95 (0-06-445121-6). 32pp. After a description of the *Exxon Valdez* catastrophe, general material on oil spills is presented, including their causes, effects, and how they can be prevented. (Rev: BL 6/1–15/94) [363.73]

16991 Chandler, Gary, and Kevin Graham. *Protecting Our Air, Land, and Water* (4–8). Illus. Series: Making a Better World. 1996, Twenty-First Century LB $20.40 (0-8050-4624-0). 64pp. Such methods of protecting our natural resources as purifying and conserving water and reducing air pollution are described. (Rev: BL 12/15/96; SLJ 1/97) [363.7]

16992 Cherry, Lynne. *A River Ran Wild* (1–3). Illus. 1992, Harcourt $16.00 (0-15-200542-0). 40pp. Tracing the environmental history and present status of the Nashua River, which runs through New Hampshire and Massachusetts. (Rev: BL 3/15/92; HB 5–6/92; SLJ 5/92) [974.4]

16993 Cole, Joanna. *The Magic School Bus: At the Water Works* (2–5). Illus. by Bruce Degen. 1995, Scholastic $14.95 (0-614-03341-1); paper $4.99 (0-590-40360-5). 40pp. Scientific fun with Ms. Frizzle, the world's strangest teacher and an unflappable naturalist. (Rev: BL 11/15/86; SLJ 1/87)

16994 Collinson, Alan. *Pollution* (5–8). Illus. Series: Repairing the Damage. 1992, Macmillan LB $17.96 (0-02-722995-5). 46pp. In this well-organized book, complete with many charts and diagrams, the various kinds of pollution are introduced. (Rev: BL 9/15/92) [363.73]

16995 Dudley, William. *The Environment: Distinguishing Between Fact and Opinion* (4–7). Illus. Series: Opposing Viewpoints Juniors. 1991, Greenwillow LB $16.20 (0-89908-603-9). 32pp. Various viewpoints are presented on topics such as whether there is an environmental crisis and how serious acid rain is. (Rev: BL 6/15/91) [363.7]

16996 Gutnik, Martin J. *Experiments That Explore Acid Rain* (5–8). Illus. by Sharon L. Holm. Series: Investigate! 1992, Millbrook LB $21.40 (1-56294-115-1). 72pp. After an introduction to acid rain, experiments are outlined with clear instructions and simple drawings. (Rev: BL 2/1/92) [628.5]

16997 Hoff, Mary, and Mary M. Rodgers. *Our Endangered Planet: Groundwater* (4–7). Illus. Series: Our Endangered Planet. 1991, Lerner LB $22.60 (0-8225-2500-3). 64pp. A discussion of the supply, access, uses, and pollution of groundwater around the world. (Rev: BL 6/15/91; SLJ 5/91) [333.91]

16998 Johnson, Rebecca L. *Investigating the Ozone Hole* (5–8). Illus. 1994, Lerner LB $23.95 (0-8225-1574-1). 112pp. Using interviews, documents, and firsthand research, the author charts the development and possible consequences of an ozone hole above the Antarctic. (Rev: BL 3/1/94) [551.5]

16999 Morgan, Sally. *Acid Rain* (3–5). Series: Earth Watch. 1999, Watts LB $20.25 (0-531-14567-0). 32pp. After explaining the water cycle, this book examines the problem of acid rain, its causes, and possible solutions. (Rev: SLJ 3/00) [363.73]

17000 Morgan, Sally. *The Ozone Hole* (3–5). Series: Earth Watch. 1999, Watts LB $20.25 (0-531-14569-7). 32pp. This book discusses the different layers of the earth's atmosphere, the ozone levels, problems, and possible solutions. (Rev: SLJ 3/00) [363.73]

17001 O'Neill, Mary. *Air Scare* (4–7). Illus. by John Bindon. Series: SOS Planet Earth. 1991, Troll paper $5.95 (0-8167-2083-5). 32pp. An oversize book that deals with the important environmental issue of air pollution. (Rev: BL 6/15/91) [363]

17002 Pringle, Laurence. *Oil Spills: Damage, Recovery, and Prevention* (3–8). Illus. 1993, Morrow LB $14.93 (0-688-09861-4). 64pp. In addition to describing the importance of petroleum, the author tells of the thousands of annual oil spills, the incredible damage they cause, and how more preventive measures must be taken. (Rev: BL 9/15/93) [363]

17003 Pringle, Laurence. *Vanishing Ozone: Protecting Earth from Ultraviolet Radiation* (4–8). Illus. Series: Save-the-Earth Books. 1995, Morrow LB $15.93 (0-688-04158-2). 64pp. The exciting but disturbing story of the thinning ozone layer and the conflicts it is producing among governments, environmentalists, and industry. (Rev: SLJ 9/95*) [363.73]

17004 Snodgrass, Mary Ellen. *Acid Rain* (4–6). Illus. Series: Environmental Awareness. 1991, Bancroft-Sage LB $14.95 (0-944280-30-7). 48pp. Basic, up-to-date information on acid rain. Also use: *Toxic Waste* (1991). (Rev: BL 2/15/92) [363.73]

17005 Snodgrass, Mary Ellen. *Air Pollution* (4–6). Illus. Series: Environmental Awareness. 1991, Bancroft-Sage LB $14.95 (0-944280-31-5). 48pp. Using color photos, diagrams, and straightforward information, the problems of air pollution are introduced, along with possible solutions. Also use: *Land Pollution* (1991). (Rev: BL 2/15/92) [363.73]

17006 Stille, Darlene R. *The Ozone Hole* (1–3). Illus. Series: New True Books. 1991, Children's LB $21.00 (0-516-01117-0). 48pp. After a brief explanation of the ozone layer, tells how recent air pollution has changed it and how this trend can be reversed. (Rev: BL 9/1/91; SLJ 11/91) [363.73]

17007 Stille, Darlene R. *Water Pollution* (1–3). Illus. 1990, Children's LB $21.00 (0-516-01190-1). 48pp. Full-color photos and readable text explain water pollution to the young. (Rev: BL 10/1/90; SLJ 10/90) [363.73]

17008 Zipko, Stephen J. *Toxic Threat: How Hazardous Substances Poison Our Lives* (5–7). Illus. by Malle N. Whitaker. 1990, Simon & Schuster paper $5.95 (0-671-69331-X). 249pp. Many environmental pollutants, including radon and PCBs, are introduced. (Rev: SLJ 8/90) [363.7]

Population

17009 Bernards, Neal. *Population: Detecting Bias* (5–7). Illus. Series: Opposing Viewpoints Juniors. 1992, Greenhaven LB $21.00 (0-89908-622-5). 36pp. Pro and con viewpoints are presented about such topics as family planning and the problems of overpopulation. (Rev: BL 1/15/93) [304.6]

17010 Winckler, Suzanne, and Mary M. Rodgers. *Our Endangered Planet: Population Growth* (4–7). Illus. Series: Our Endangered Planet. 1991, Lerner LB $22.60 (0-8225-2502-X). 64pp. A discussion of the effects that rapid population growth has had on the environment. (Rev: BL 6/15/91; SLJ 5/91) [304.6]

Government and Politics

Courts and the Law

17011 Beaudry, Jo, and Lynne Ketchum. *Carla Goes to Court* (3–6). Illus. 1983, Human Sciences $16.95 (0-89885-088-6); paper $10.95 (0-89885-354-0). 32pp. The court process is explored through Carla's experience after she witnesses a burglary.

17012 Deegan, Paul J. *Supreme Court Book* (4–6). Illus. Series: Supreme Court Justices. 1992, ABDO LB $19.99 (1-56239-097-X). 50pp. This account explains the various functions of the court and how they have changed from George Washington's time to the present. (Rev: BL 6/1–15/93) [347]

17013 Goldish, Meish. *Our Supreme Court* (4–6). Illus. Series: I Know America. 1994, Millbrook LB $21.90 (1-56294-445-2). 48pp. An introduction to the Supreme Court that gives its history, composition, and a few historic decisions. (Rev: BL 11/15/94; SLJ 1/95) [347.73]

17014 Reef, Catherine. *The Supreme Court* (4–7). Illus. Series: Places in American History. 1994, Dillon paper $7.95 (0-382-24722-1). 72pp. An introduction to the Supreme Court, its powers, composition, and landmark decisions. (Rev: BL 1/1/95) [347.73]

17015 Stein, R. Conrad. *Powers of the Supreme Court*. Rev. ed. (3–5). Illus. Series: Cornerstones of Freedom. 1995, Children's LB $20.50 (0-516-06697-8). 30pp. The composition of the Supreme Court, as well as its powers and history, are covered through a discussion of landmark cases. (Rev: SLJ 8/95) [347]

United Nations and International Affairs

17016 Bradley, Catherine. *Freedom of Movement* (5–8). Illus. Series: What Do We Mean by Human Rights? 1998, Watts LB $22.00 (0-531-14447-X).
48pp. A lavishly illustrated account that uses double-page spreads to explore such subjects as nationalism, immigration, refugees, and asylum. (Rev: BL 4/1/98; HBG 10/98) [323]

17017 Burger, Leslie, and Debra L. Rahm. *Red Cross/Red Crescent: When Help Can't Wait* (5–7). Illus. 1996, Lerner $22.60 (0-8225-2698-0). 80pp. The story of the Red Cross and the role it plays in helping people today. (Rev: BL 1/1–15/97; SLJ 1/97) [361.7]

17018 Burger, Leslie, and Debra L. Rahm. *United Nations High Commission for Refugees: Making a Difference in Our World* (5–7). Illus. 1996, Lerner LB $22.60 (0-8225-2699-9). 80pp. Describes the plight of refugees worldwide and the aid that this UN agency gives. (Rev: BL 12/15/96; SLJ 1/97) [362.87]

17019 Castle, Caroline. *For Every Child: The UN Convention on the Rights of the Child in Words and Pictures* (1–4). Illus. 2001, Penguin $16.99 (0-8037-2650-3). 40pp. Based on the principles adopted by the United Nations, this book presents 14 rights of children each with a painting by a distinguished artist. (Rev: BL 2/1/01; SLJ 3/01) [346.01]

17020 Giesecke, Ernestine. *Governments Around the World* (3–5). Series: Kids' Guide. 2000, Heinemann $21.36 (1-57572-511-8). 32pp. This book explains different kinds of governments — democracies, communist and socialist states, monarchies, and other systems. (Rev: HBG 3/01; SLJ 10/00) [320]

17021 Grant, R. G. *Genocide* (5–10). Illus. Series: Talking Points. 1999, Raintree Steck-Vaughn LB $27.11 (0-8172-5314-9). 64pp. This book covers the Holocaust in World War II as well as more recent massacres in Cambodia, Rwanda, and Bosnia, and probes such questions as who is guilty in genocide — the person who pulls the trigger or those who plan and organize it, and what about the bystander? (Rev: BL 9/1/99) [304.6]

17022 Newman, Shirlee P. *Child Slavery in Modern Times* (4–7). Illus. Series: Watts Library: History of

Slavery. 2000, Watts LB $24.00 (0-531-11696-4). 64pp. From Europe to Asia and Africa, this book explores the deplorable lives of servitude forced on child laborers and slaves, and how some have escaped. (Rev: BL 2/15/01; SLJ 3/01) [306.3]

17023 O'Connor, Maureen. *Equal Rights* (5–8). Illus. Series: What Do We Mean by Human Rights? 1998, Watts LB $22.00 (0-531-14448-8). 48pp. Uses an illustrated, double-page format to explore subjects such as racism, freedom, and various types of prejudice. (Rev: BL 4/1/98) [323]

17024 Spies, Karen B. *Isolation vs. Intervention: Is America the World's Police Force?* (4–6). Illus. Series: Issues of Our Time. 1995, Twenty-First Century LB $18.90 (0-8050-3880-9). 64pp. Objectively presents arguments, pro and con, concerning involvement in the political and economic problems of other countries. (Rev: SLJ 2/96) [327.73]

17025 Stearman, Kaye. *Homelessness.* (5–10). Illus. Series: Talking Points. 1999, Raintree Steck-Vaughn LB $27.11 (0-8172-5312-2). 64pp. A worldwide view of homelessness, its causes — including eviction, natural disasters, and war — plus a discussion of international efforts to combat it. (Rev: BL 9/1/99) [363.5]

United States

Civil Rights

17026 Bradley, David, and Shelley Fisher Fishkin, eds. *The Encyclopedia of Civil Rights in America* (5–10). 1997, Sharpe Reference $299.00 (0-7656-8000-9). This three-volume set contains 683 alphabetically arranged articles that explore the history, meaning, and application of civil rights issues in the United States. (Rev: SLJ 5/98) [323]

17027 Brill, Marlene T. *Let Women Vote!* (4–6). Illus. Series: Spotlight on American History. 1995, Millbrook LB $15.90 (0-56294-589-0). 64pp. The history of the struggle to gain the vote for U.S. women and of the key personalities involved. (Rev: BL 12/15/95; SLJ 1/96) [324.6]

17028 Burns, Marilyn. *I Am Not a Short Adult: Getting Good at Being a Kid* (5–7). Illus. by Martha Weston. 1977, Little, Brown paper $12.95 (0-316-11746-3). Many facets of childhood are discussed, including children's legal status and institutions that affect them.

17029 Colbert, Jan, and Ann M. Harms, eds. *Dear Dr. King: Letters from Today's Children to Dr. Martin Luther King, Jr* (4–7). Illus. 1998, Hyperion $14.95 (0-7868-0417-3). 64pp. This is a selection of letters written by white and black Memphis school children to Dr. King telling him about themselves and how conditions have changed since his death. (Rev: BCCB 5/98; BL 2/15/98; HBG 10/98; SLJ 5/98) [323]

17030 Edelman, Marian Wright. *Stand for Children* (5–8). Illus. by Adrienne Yorinks. 1998, Hyperion LB $16.49 (0-7868-2310-0). 32pp. A picture book for older readers in which collages, photos, and excerpts from the author's speech at a rally are used

to illuminate the rights of children and how they can be protected. (Rev: BL 7/98; HBG 10/98; SLJ 8/98) [305.2]

17031 Greenberg, Keith E. *Adolescent Rights: Are Young People Equal Under the Law?* (5–8). Illus. Series: Issues of Our Time. 1995, Twenty-First Century LB $18.90 (0-8050-3877-9). 64pp. This unbiased account of the controversial subject encourages readers to form their own conclusions. (Rev: SLJ 9/95) [323]

17032 Harvey, Miles. *Women's Voting Rights* (3–5). Illus. Series: Cornerstones of Freedom. 1996, Children's LB $20.50 (0-516-20003-8). 32pp. With illustrations on each page (many in color), this account traces the history of women's suffrage and the important people who were active in the movement. (Rev: BL 12/15/96; SLJ 2/97) [324.6]

17033 Haskins, Jim. *Freedom Rides: Journey for Justice* (5–7). Illus. 1995, Hyperion LB $15.49 (0-7868-2037-3). 128pp. This account focuses on a single dramatic aspect of the civil rights movement: the integration of buses and trains. (Rev: BL 1/1/95; SLJ 4/95) [323.1]

17034 Hirst, Mike. *Freedom of Belief* (4–8). Illus. Series: What Do We Mean by Human Rights? 1997, Watts LB $22.50 (0-531-14435-6). 48pp. An information-packed overview of religious and political freedom and the people who fought and sometimes died for it. (Rev: BL 1/1–15/98; HBG 3/98) [323.44]

17035 Jacobs, William J. *Great Lives: Human Rights* (5–8). Illus. 1990, Macmillan $24.00 (0-684-19036-2). 272pp. Profiles of 30 historical figures "united in a commitment to individual rights." (Rev: BL 7/90) [920]

17036 Johnston, Norma. *Remember the Ladies: The First Women's Rights Convention* (4–6). Illus. 1995, Scholastic paper $3.50 (0-590-47086-8). 169pp. The story of the 1848 Women's Rights Convention in Seneca Falls, New York, includes biographies of its leaders, like Elizabeth Cady Stanton and Lucretia Mott. (Rev: BL 5/1/95) [323.34]

17037 Kelso, Richard. *Walking for Freedom: The Montgomery Bus Boycott* (3–5). Illus. by Michael Newton. 1993, Raintree Steck-Vaughn LB $27.12 (0-8114-7218-3). 52pp. The events and personalities associated with the Montgomery bus boycott are noted. (Rev: SLJ 8/93) [323.4]

17038 Kent, Deborah. *The Disability Rights Movement* (3–5). Illus. Series: Cornerstones of Freedom. 1996, Children's LB $20.50 (0-516-06632-3). 32pp. The story of the growth of the movement that preserves and protects the civil rights of people with disabilities. (Rev: BL 7/96) [323.3]

17039 King, David C. *Freedom of Assembly* (4–6). Illus. Series: Land of the Free. 1997, Millbrook LB $19.90 (0-7613-0064-3). 48pp. This book covers this basic civil right and its many applications in the courts, including those involving militia movements and hate groups. Also use *The Right to Speak Out* (1997). (Rev: BL 5/15/97; SLJ 10/97) [342.73]

17040 King, Martin Luther, Jr. *I Have a Dream* (4–8). Illus. 1997, Scholastic $16.95 (0-590-20516-1). 40pp. The full text of Dr. King's speech is reprinted, with illustrations by 15 important African American artists. (Rev: BL 2/15/98*; HBG 3/98; SLJ 11/97) [305]

17041 Lucas, Eileen. *Civil Rights: The Long Struggle* (5–8). Illus. Series: Issues in Focus. 1996, Enslow LB $19.95 (0-89490-729-8). 112pp. After a discussion of the first ten amendments to the U.S. Constitution, this account focuses on the civil rights struggles of African Americans. (Rev: SLJ 12/96) [323]

17042 Lucas, Eileen. *Cracking the Wall: The Struggles of the Little Rock Nine* (3–5). Illus. 1998, Carolrhoda $21.27 (0-87614-990-5). 48pp. A simple narrative that tells of the desegregation of Central High School in Little Rock, Arkansas, and gives background information on the 1953 Supreme Court decision. (Rev: BCCB 3/98; BL 2/15/98; HBG 10/98; SLJ 6/98) [379.2]

17043 Luthringer, Chelsea. *So What Is Citizenship Anyway?* (5–8). Series: A Student's Guide to American Civics. 1999, Rosen Central LB $17.95 (0-8239-3097-1). 48pp. Describes and defines the roles and responsibilities of citizens in a democracy and encourages young people to become active in political and social affairs and issues. (Rev: HBG 10/00; SLJ 3/00) [323.6]

17044 Malaspina, Ann. *Children's Rights* (5–8). Series: Overview. 1998, Lucent LB $22.45 (1-56006-175-8). Shows how children's and adults' rights have sometimes been in conflict and how the rights of children are gradually being defined through the courts. (Rev: BL 8/98) [323.4]

17045 Meyers, Madeleine, ed. *Forward into Light: The Struggle for Woman's Suffrage* (4–8). Illus. Series: Perspectives on History. 1994, Discovery paper $6.95 (1-878668-25-0). 64pp. The story of how women fought to get the vote in this country and of their most influential leaders. (Rev: BL 8/94) [324.6]

17046 O'Neill, Laurie A. *Little Rock: The Desegregation of Central High* (4–7). Illus. Series: Spotlight on American History. 1994, Millbrook LB $21.90 (1-56294-354-5). 64pp. A moving re-creation of the painful integration of the public school in Little Rock, Arkansas, its background, and the aftermath. (Rev: BCCB 11/94; BL 10/15/94; SLJ 10/94) [373.76]

17047 Pacoe, Elaine. *The Right to Vote* (4–6). Illus. Series: Land of the Free. 1997, Millbrook LB $19.90 (0-7613-0066-X). 48pp. Explores the principles behind the right to vote and how it was gradually awarded to all citizens. (Rev: BL 5/15/97; SLJ 5/97) [324.6]

17048 Parks, Rosa, and Gregory J. Reed. *Dear Mrs. Parks: A Dialogue with Today's Youth* (4–6). 1996, Lee & Low $16.95 (1-880000-45-8). 112pp. A collection of letters sent to Rosa Parks and the answers this amazing civil rights leader sent back. (Rev: BL 12/1/96; SLJ 12/96) [323]

17049 Quiri, Patricia R. *The Bill of Rights* (3–4). Illus. Series: True Books. 1998, Children's LB $21.00 (0-516-20661-3). 48pp. An examination of the Bill of Rights, a discussion of the difficulties

encountered in writing the document, and paraphrases of each of its ten amendments. (Rev: BL 2/1/99; HBG 3/99) [323]

17050 Sherrow, Victoria. *Freedom of Worship* (4–6). Illus. Series: Land of the Free. 1997, Millbrook LB $19.90 (0-7613-0065-1). 48pp. As well as discussing the right to worship as one pleases, this account covers the religious right, religious intolerance, school prayer, and cults. (Rev: BL 5/15/97; SLJ 5/97) [323.44]

17051 Sullivan, George. *The Day the Women Got the Vote: A Photo History of the Women's Rights Movement* (5–8). Illus. 1994, Scholastic paper $6.95 (0-590-47560-6). 96pp. The women's rights movement from the early suffragists to the feminist movement that started in the 1960s. (Rev: BL 6/1–15/94; SLJ 7/94) [323.34]

17052 Tillage, Leon W. *Leon's Story* (4–8). Illus. by Susan L. Roth. 1997, Farrar $14.00 (0-374-34379-9). 112pp. An autobiographical account of growing up black and poor in the segregated South and of participating in the civil rights movement. (Rev: BL 10/1/97*; HB 11–12/97; HBG 3/98; SLJ 12/97) [975.6]

17053 Wilson, Reginald. *Think About Our Rights: Civil Liberties and the United States* (5–8). Illus. 1991, Walker LB $15.85 (0-8027-8127-6); paper $9.95 (0-8027-7371-0). 128pp. The focus is on such civil rights questions as integration, affirmative action, and women's rights. (Rev: SLJ 1/92) [323.4]

Constitution

17054 Dudley, William. *The U.S. Constitution: Locating the Author's Main Idea* (4–7). Illus. Series: Opposing Viewpoints Juniors. 1991, Greenwillow LB $16.20 (0-89908-601-2). 32pp. Various viewpoints are expressed on such topics as how important the Constitution is and whether it should be revised. (Rev: BL 6/15/91) [347]

17055 Feinberg, Barbara S. *Constitutional Amendments* (4–6). Illus. Series: Inside Government. 1996, Twenty-First Century LB $15.98 (0-8050-4619-4). 80pp. This account tells how constitutional amendments come to be and the meaning of each that is currently in effect. (Rev: BL 9/15/96; SLJ 12/96) [342.73]

17056 Fritz, Jean. *Shh! We're Writing the Constitution* (3–5). Illus. by Tomie dePaola. 1987, Putnam paper $8.95 (0-399-21404-6). 64pp. Lots of details make it clear that writing the Constitution was no easy task. (Rev: BCCB 6–7/87; BL 6/1/87; SLJ 8/87)

17057 Johnson, Linda C. *Our Constitution* (4–6). Illus. Series: I Know America. 1992, Millbrook LB $20.90 (1-56294-090-2). 48pp. This history of our Constitution includes an explanation of its important parts. (Rev: BL 9/1/92; SLJ 10/92) [342.73]

17058 Krull, Kathleen. *A Kids' Guide to America's Bill of Rights: Curfews, Censorship, and the 100-Pound Giant* (5–8). Illus. 1999, Avon $16.00 (0-380-97497-5). 224pp. After a description of the first ten amendments, this book details famous court cases and what each amendment means to young people. (Rev: BL 12/1/99; HBG 3/00) [342.73]

17059 Levy, Elizabeth. *If You Were There When They Signed the Constitution* (2–4). Illus. 1992, Scholastic paper $5.99 (0-590-45159-6). 80pp. All about the delegates and the U.S. Constitution. (Rev: BL 9/15/87; SLJ 11/87)

17060 Maestro, Betsy, and Giulio Maestro. *A More Perfect Union: The Story of Our Constitution* (2–4). Illus. 1987, Lothrop LB $15.93 (0-688-06840-5); Morrow paper $7.95 (0-688-10192-5). 48pp. The U.S. Constitution is explained for young readers. (Rev: BCCB 10/87; BL 9/1/87; SLJ 9/87)

17061 Stein, R. Conrad. *The Bill of Rights* (3–5). Illus. Series: Cornerstones of Freedom. 1992, Children's LB $20.50 (0-516-04853-8). 32pp. The story of how the various amendments known as the Bill of Rights became part of the U.S. Constitution. (Rev: BL 6/1/92) [347.73]

Crime and Criminals

17062 Ballinger, Erich. *Detective Dictionary: A Handbook for Aspiring Sleuths* (4–8). Illus. 1994, Lerner LB $19.95 (0-8225-0721-8). 144pp. An unusual A-to-Z book that looks at various techniques used in crime detection. (Rev: BL 9/15/94) [363.2]

17063 Barden, Renardo. *Gangs* (5–8). Series: Facts About. 1990, Rourke LB $17.95 (0-865-93073-2). 47pp. An examination of street gangs, their composition, and their frequent links with drugs. (Rev: SLJ 2/90) [394.3]

17064 Bowers, Vivien. *Crime Science* (3–6). Illus. 1997, Owl paper $10.95 (1-895688-69-8). 64pp. Using three case histories that test the reader's powers of detection, this title is a fine introduction to forensic science. (Rev: BL 12/1/97) [363.2]

17065 Dickson, Louise. *Lu and Clancy's Crime Science* (2–4). Illus. by Pat Cupples. Series: Lu and Clancy. 1999, Kids Can paper $5.95 (1-55074-552-2). 40pp. While solving a mystery about missing pups, a Scotch terrier and a basset hound teach readers about observational skills, how to take finger and lip prints, how to analyze footprints and teeth prints, and how to perform other procedures in criminal science. (Rev: SLJ 11/99) [364]

17066 Grabowski, John F. *The Death Penalty* (5–8). Series: Overview Series. 1999, Lucent LB $17.96 (1-56006-371-8). 96pp. A fair, unbiased review of the history, pro and con arguments, and present status of the death penalty in America. (Rev: BL 8/99) [364.6]

17067 Graham, Ian. *Crime-Fighting* (5–8). Illus. Series: Science Spotlight. 1995, Raintree Steck-Vaughn LB $24.26 (0-8114-3840-6). 46pp. A discussion of scientific methods used in analyzing evidence at crime scenes, such as DNA testing. (Rev: SLJ 7/95) [364]

17068 Graham, Ian. *Fakes and Forgeries* (5–8). Illus. Series: Science Spotlight. 1995, Raintree Steck-Vaughn LB $24.26 (0-8114-3843-0). 46pp. Examines famous scandals in history involving such

fakes as the Loch Ness monster, counterfeit money, and the forged Hitler diaries. (Rev: SLJ 7/95) [364]

17069 Greenberg, Keith E. *Out of the Gang* (5–8). Illus. 1992, Lerner LB $19.93 (0-8225-2553-4). 40pp. A realistic portrait of what gang life is like, revealed by a man who escaped it and a boy who stayed out of it. (Rev: BCCB 6/92; BL 6/15/92; SLJ 9/92) [364.1]

17070 Hjelmeland, Andy. *Prisons: Inside the Big House* (4–8). Illus. Series: Pro/Con. 1996, Lerner LB $25.26 (0-8225-2607-7). 112pp. Different viewpoints on the purposes and functions of prisons in today's society are presented in this objective account. (Rev: BL 8/96; SLJ 9/96) [365]

17071 Jackson, Donna M. *The Bone Detectives: How Forensic Anthropologists Solve Crimes and Uncover Mysteries of the Dead* (5–7). Illus. 1996, Little, Brown $16.95 (0-316-82935-8). 48pp. Explores the role of forensic anthropologists in solving crimes, including murder. (Rev: BCCB 4/96; BL 4/1/96; HB 5–6/96; SLJ 5/96*) [363.2]

17072 Jones, Charlotte F. *Fingerprints and Talking Bones: How Real Life Crimes Are Solved* (5–8). Illus. 1997, Delacorte $16.95 (0-385-32299-2). 111pp. A clear, concise account of what forensic science means and how it has been applied in real cases. (Rev: BCCB 6/97; BL 6/1–15/97; SLJ 8/97) [363.2]

17073 Lane, Brian. *Investigation of Murder* (4–6). Illus. Series: Crimebusters. 1996, Millbrook LB $20.90 (0-7613-0527-0). 32pp. A fictitious murder is used as the framework for this discussion of the work of police and forensic experts. (Rev: BL 1/1–15/97; SLJ 1/97) [363.2]

17074 Larsen, Anita. *Psychic Sleuths* (5–7). 1994, Macmillan LB $14.95 (0-02-751645-8). 112pp. Pros and cons concerning the use of psychics in solving crimes are discussed, with many case studies. (Rev: BL 10/1/94; SLJ 11/94) [363.2]

17075 Oliver, Marilyn Tower. *Gangs: Trouble in the Streets* (4–8). Illus. 1995, Enslow LB $19.95 (0-89490-492-2). 128pp. A history of gangs since the 19th century plus coverage of the various types and activities of gangs that exist today. (Rev: BL 8/95) [364.1]

17076 Oxlade, Chris. *Crime Detection* (3–5). Illus. Series: Science Encounters. 1997, Rigby $22.79 (1-57572-090-6). 32pp. An introduction to detective work that covers forensic science, security, fingerprints, and how evidence is chemically treated. (Rev: SLJ 11/97) [364]

17077 Platt, Richard. *Spy* (4–7). Illus. 1996, Knopf LB $20.99 (0-679-98123-7). 64pp. All aspects of spying, including equipment and techniques, are described, along with profiles of famous spies. (Rev: BL 12/1/96; SLJ 6/97) [327.12]

17078 Powell, Jillian. *Drug Trafficking* (4–6). Illus. Series: Crimebusters. 1997, Millbrook LB $20.90 (0-7613-0555-6). 32pp. Using a fabricated crime as a focus, this book describes the many avenues of drug trafficking in the United States and how various agencies are combating it. (Rev: BL 6/1–15/97) [364.1]

17079 Rainis, Kenneth G. *Crime-Solving Science Projects: Forensic Science Experiments* (5–9). 2000, Enslow LB $20.95 (0-7660-1289-1). 128pp. After defining forensic science, this book contains experiments and projects involving such areas as fingerprints, inks, writing samples, fibers, forgeries, and blood evidence. (Rev: SLJ 2/01) [363.2]

17080 Roden, Katie. *Solving International Crime* (4–6). Illus. Series: Crimebusters. 1996, Millbrook LB $20.90 (0-7613-0528-9). 32pp. Drug trafficking, terrorism, and crime rings are discussed in this book on international crime-fighting efforts. (Rev: BL 1/1–15/97; SLJ 1/97) [363.2]

17081 Roden, Katie. *Terrorism* (4–6). Illus. Series: Crimebusters. 1997, Millbrook LB $20.90 (0-7613-0556-4). 32pp. Using many text boxes, photos, diagrams, file folder formats, and a fabricated crime to set the stage, this book studies the causes and effects of terrorism. (Rev: BL 6/1–15/97; SLJ 9/97) [363.2]

17082 Ross, Stewart. *Bandits and Outlaws* (5–7). Illus. Series: Fact or Fiction. 1995, Millbrook LB $24.90 (1-56294-649-8). 48pp. The jacket of this book says, "The truth about outlaws, highwaymen, smugglers, and robbers from the bandit gangs of ancient China to the desperadoes of today." (Rev: BL 11/15/95; SLJ 1/96) [364.1]

17083 Ross, Stewart. *Spies and Traitors* (5–7). Illus. Series: Fact or Fiction. 1995, Millbrook paper $24.90 (1-56294-648-X). 48pp. A history of the people who have placed themselves above their country in the dangerous game of espionage and betrayal. (Rev: BL 11/15/95; SLJ 3/96) [355.3]

17084 Salak, John. *Violent Crime: Is It Out of Control?* (6–8). Illus. Series: Issues of Our Time. 1995, Twenty-First Century LB $18.90 (0-8050-4239-3). 64pp. An honest presentation of why violent crimes are committed more frequently and how young people are becoming increasingly involved in them. (Rev: BL 2/1/96; SLJ 2/96) [364.1]

17085 Stewart, Gail B. *Gangs* (5–8). Illus. Series: The Other America. 1996, Lucent LB $17.96 (1-56006-340-8). 96pp. This account describes past and present gangs, discusses causes for their formation, tells about their characteristics, and profiles several members. (Rev: SLJ 3/97) [394.3]

17086 Szumski, Bonnie, and Neal Bernards. *Prisons: Detecting Bias* (4–7). Illus. Series: Opposing Viewpoints Juniors. 1991, Greenhaven LB $16.20 (0-89908-604-7). 32pp. Can prisons rehabilitate and how do they affect criminals are two of several issues explored. (Rev: BL 6/15/91) [365]

17087 Tipp, Stacey L. *Causes of Crime: Distinguishing Between Fact and Opinion* (5–7). Illus. Series: Opposing Viewpoints Juniors. 1991, Greenhaven LB $16.20 (0-89908-615-2). 32pp. A variety of opinions concerning the causes of crime are presented in an objective way to make the reader evaluate the validity of each. (Rev: BL 5/15/92) [364]

17088 Trapani, Margi. *Working Together Against Gang Violence* (4–8). Illus. Series: Library of Social Activism. 1996, Rosen LB $16.95 (0-8239-2260-X). 64pp. Covers gangs, their makeup, purposes,

activities, and, most important, how to avoid them and their violence. (Rev: SLJ 2/97) [364.1]

17089 Wiese, Jim. *Detective Science: 40 Crime-Solving, Case-Breaking, Crook-Catching Activities for Kids* (4–7). 1996, Wiley paper $12.95 (0-471-11980-6). 128pp. Presents 40 experiments and activities that illustrate techniques in forensic science related to observing, collecting, and analyzing evidence. (Rev: BL 4/15/96; SLJ 6/96) [363.2]

17090 Williams, Stanley, and Barbara Cottman Becnel. *Gangs and Drugs* (3–5). Illus. Series: Tookie Speaks Out Against Gang Violence. 1996, Rosen LB $13.95 (0-8239-2348-7). 24pp. A former gang leader and current prison inmate, Tookie Williams tells about the part drugs play in the gang scene. (Rev: BL 2/15/97) [364.1]

17091 Winkleman, Katherine K. *Police Patrol* (PS–3). Illus. by John S. Winkleman. 1996, Walker LB $16.85 (0-8027-8454-2). 32pp. Activities in a police station and the duties of police are described in words and photos. (Rev: BCCB 1/97; BL 1/1–15/97; SLJ 12/96) [363.2]

17092 Yaffe, Rebecca M., and Lonnie F. Hoade. *When a Parent Goes to Jail: A Comprehensive Guide for Counseling Children of Incarcerated Parents* (3–5). Illus. by Barbara S. Moody. 2000, Rayve $49.95 (1-877810-08-8). 45pp. This book about adults in trouble with the law goes through the incarceration process from arrest to sentencing. (Rev: SLJ 12/00) [363.2]

Elections and Political Parties

17093 Audryszewski, Tricia. *The Reform Party* (5–8). Series: Headliners. 2000, Millbrook LB $23.90 (0-7613-1906-9). 64pp. This book describes the formation of the Reform Party and highlights the work of Ross Perot, Pat Buchanan, and Jesse Ventura. (Rev: BL 8/00; SLJ 1/01) [324.273]

17094 Bernards, Neal. *Elections: Locating the Author's Main Idea* (5–7). Illus. Series: Opposing Viewpoints Juniors. 1992, Greenhaven LB $16.20 (1-56510-022-0). 36pp. Eight pro and con viewpoints examine America's election process. (Rev: BL 1/15/93) [324]

17095 Brown, Gene. *The 1992 Election* (5–8). Illus. Series: Headliners. 1993, Millbrook LB $23.40 (1-56294-080-5). 64pp. This book presents the issues, the campaigns, and the result of the 1992 presidential election. (Rev: BL 4/1/93; SLJ 7/93) [324]

17096 Henry, Christopher. *Presidential Conventions* (4–6). Illus. Series: First Books. 1996, Watts LB $22.00 (0-531-20219-4). 62pp. Discusses the purpose of political party conventions and their place in the election process. (Rev: BL 9/1/96; SLJ 10/96) [324.6]

17097 Lindop, Edmund. *Political Parties* (4–6). Illus. Series: Inside Government. 1996, Twenty-First Century LB $18.90 (0-8050-4618-6). 64pp. The origin of political parties and the role they play in elections and the government. (Rev: BL 9/15/96; SLJ 12/96) [324.273]

17098 Lutz, Norma Jean. *The History of Third Parties* (4–6). Series: Your Government: How It Works. 2000, Chelsea LB $17.95 (0-7910-5541-8). 64pp. The Abolitionists, Liberty Party, Southern Democrats, Nativists, Prohibitionists, Socialists, and Reform Party are a few of the American third parties discussed here. (Rev: HBG 10/00; SLJ 8/00) [324.273]

17099 Majure, Janet. *Elections* (5–8). Illus. Series: Overview. 1996, Lucent LB $22.45 (1-56006-174-X). 112pp. After a general history of elections, this account explains present-day procedures and practices. (Rev: BL 7/96) [324.7]

17100 Morin, Isobel V. *Politics, American Style: Political Parties in American History* (5–8). 1999, Twenty-First Century LB $22.40 (0-7613-1267-6). 144pp. A history of political parties in America, how they originated, evolved, and are influenced by events and personalities. (Rev: HBG 3/00; SLJ 1/00) [324.273]

17101 Robb, Don. *Hail to the Chief: The American Presidency* (3–5). Illus. by Alan Witschonke. 2000, Charlesbridge LB $16.95 (0-88106-392-4); paper $7.95 (0-88106-939-2). 31pp. In 14 double-page spreads, the office of the presidency is introduced with material on duties, responsibilities and powers plus coverage of some men who have held the office and changed its character. (Rev: HBG 3/01; SLJ 3/01) [353.03]

17102 Spies, Karen B. *Our Presidency* (4–6). Illus. Series: I Know America. 1994, Millbrook LB $20.90 (1-56294-444-4). 48pp. Provides a basic history of the office of the presidency, an explanation of the president's duties and responsibilities, and a rundown of those who have served. (Rev: BL 11/15/94; SLJ 12/94) [353.03]

17103 Steins, Richard. *Our Elections* (4–6). Illus. 1994, Millbrook LB $20.90 (1-56294-446-0). 48pp. The process of being elected to office (primarily at the national level) is outlined in text, pictures, and diagrams. (Rev: BL 11/15/94; SLJ 12/94) [324.6]

Federal Government and Agencies

17104 Bay, Ann Phillips. *The Kid's Guide to the Smithsonian* (4–6). Illus. by Steven Rotblatt. 1996, Smithsonian Institution $26.95 (1-56098-734-0); paper $15.95 (1-56098-693-X). 160pp. A handy guide to historical information on many of the treasures of the Smithsonian. (Rev: BL 9/1/96) [069]

17105 Berger, Melvin, and Gilda Berger. *Where Does the Mail Go? A Book About the Postal System* (K–3). Illus. by Geoffrey Brittingham. Series: Discovery Readers. 1994, Ideals paper $4.50 (1-57102-006-3). 48pp. Explores the U.S. Postal Service by tracing a letter from posting to delivery. (Rev: SLJ 9/94) [353]

17106 Bolick, Nancy O. *Mail Call! The History of the U.S. Postal Service* (4–6). Illus. Series: First Books. 1995, Watts LB $22.50 (0-531-20170-8). 64pp. From colonial days to the present, this is a chronological survey of the history of the U.S. Postal Service. (Rev: BL 2/15/95; SLJ 6/95) [383]

17107 Feinberg, Barbara S. *The Cabinet* (4–6). Illus. Series: Inside Government. 1995, Twenty-First Century LB $18.90 (0-8050-3421-8). 64pp. The history and changing composition of the cabinet are traced, with an explanation of each member's duties. (Rev: BL 9/1/95; SLJ 10/95) [353.04]

17108 Feinberg, Barbara S. *Electing the President* (4–6). Illus. Series: Inside Government. 1995, Twenty-First Century LB $18.90 (0-8050-3422-6). 64pp. A brief history of presidential elections is given, with an outline of the development of the various parties. (Rev: BL 9/1/95) [324.6]

17109 Feinberg, Barbara S. *The National Government* (4–8). Illus. Series: First Books. 1993, Watts LB $22.00 (0-531-20155-4). 64pp. After an introduction to the federal government, this book explains the functions of each department and how they work together. (Rev: SLJ 1/94) [336.73]

17110 Feinberg, Barbara S. *Term Limits for Congress?* (4–6). Illus. Series: Inside Government. 1996, Twenty-First Century LB $18.90 (0-8050-4099-4). 64pp. A clear and concise overview of the arguments for and against congressional term limits. (Rev: BL 5/15/96; SLJ 8/96) [328.73]

17111 Gibbons, Gail. *The Post Office Book: Mail and How It Moves* (K–3). Illus. by author. 1982, HarperCollins LB $14.89 (0-690-04199-3); paper $5.95 (0-06-446029-0). 32pp. A simple description of how the post office works.

17112 Giesecke, Ernestine. *National Government* (3–5). Series: Kids' Guide. 2000, Heinemann $21.36 (1-57572-510-X). 32pp. A simple explanation of the three branches of government in the U.S. and the duties and responsibilities of each. (Rev: HBG 3/01; SLJ 10/00) [320]

17113 Greenberg, Judith E. *Young People's Letters to the President* (4–6). Series: In Their Own Voices. 1998, Watts LB $22.00 (0-531-11435-X). An anthology of 23 letters sent to presidents from Lincoln to Clinton that also includes six replies. (Rev: HBG 3/99; SLJ 4/99) [973]

17114 Henry, Christopher. *The Electoral College* (4–6). Illus. Series: First Books. 1996, Watts LB $22.00 (0-531-20218-6). 63pp. Introduces the electoral college, its origins, composition, and functions. (Rev: BL 9/1/96; SLJ 10/96) [324.6]

17115 Kassinger, Ruth. *U.S. Census: A Mirror of America* (5–8). Illus. 1999, Raintree Steck-Vaughn LB $25.69 (0-7398-1217-3). 80pp. Written before the 2000 census began, this book describes the history of the census and the methods used to count Americans. (Rev: BL 12/15/99; HBG 3/00) [304]

17116 McCave, Marta E. *Counting Heads, and More: The Work of the U.S. Census Bureau* (3–5). Illus. 1998, Twenty-First Century LB $22.40 (0-7613-3017-8). 64pp. An introduction to the U.S. Census Bureau, with information on its history, organization, functions, and the day-to-day work of its employees. (Rev: BL 12/15/98) [352.7]

17117 Maestro, Betsy. *The Voice of the People: American Democracy in Action* (3–5). Illus. by Giulio Maestro. 1996, Lothrop LB $15.93 (0-688-10679-X). 48pp. The election process and the three branches of government are two of the topics covered in this overview of our government. (Rev: BCCB 5/96; BL 4/1/96; SLJ 6/96) [324.973]

17118 Patrick, Diane. *The Executive Branch* (4–6). Illus. Series: First Books. 1995, Watts LB $22.00 (0-531-20179-1). 64pp. An introduction to the executive wing, the cabinet, and the duties of the U.S. president. (Rev: BL 3/1/95) [353]

17119 Ricciuti, Edward R. *Wildlife Special Agent: Protecting Endangered Species* (3–5). Illus. Series: Risky Business. 1996, Blackbirch LB $16.95 (1-56711-160-2). 32pp. A look at the exciting work of the people involved in the Law Enforcement Division of the U.S. Fish and Wildlife Service and how it helps protect endangered species. (Rev: SLJ 2/97) [363.11]

17120 St. George, Judith. *So You Want to Be President?* (3–5). Illus. by David Small. 2000, Putnam $17.99 (0-399-23407-1). 56pp. A delightful, lively compendium of facts about the presidency and the presidents covering such topics as favorite sports, appearance, pets, musical abilities, ages, and personalities. (Rev: BCCB 7–8/00; BL 7/00*; HB 7–8/00; HBG 3/01; SLJ 8/00) [324.6]

17121 Sandak, Cass R. *Congressional Committees* (4–6). Illus. Series: Inside Government. 1995, Twenty-First Century LB $18.90 (0-8050-3425-0). 64pp. The purposes, structure, and functions of congressional committees are covered in this illustrated account. (Rev: BL 12/15/95) [328.73]

17122 Sandak, Cass R. *Lobbying* (4–6). Illus. Series: Inside Government. 1995, Twenty-First Century LB $18.90 (0-8050-3424-2). 64pp. An objective account that discusses the history, purposes, and results of lobbying in the U.S. Congress. (Rev: BL 12/15/95; SLJ 1/96) [324]

17123 Sandak, Cass R. *The National Debt* (4–6). Illus. Series: Inside Government. 1996, Twenty-First Century LB $18.90 (0-8050-3423-4). 64pp. The origins and causes of the national debt are covered, with options for the future. (Rev: BCCB 3/96; BL 5/15/96; SLJ 8/96) [336.3]

17124 Santella, Andrew. *Impeachment* (4–6). Illus. Series: Cornerstones of Freedom. 2000, Children's LB $20.50 (0-516-21677-5); paper $5.95 (0-516-27166-0). 32pp. This work explains the process of impeachment and describes its history through President Clinton. (Rev: BL 9/15/00) [336.73]

17125 Shea, Pegi Deitz. *The Impeachment Process* (4–6). Series: Your Government: How It Works. 2000, Chelsea LB $17.95 (0-7910-5538-8). 64pp. Beginning with the Watergate and Clinton scandals, this account traces the impeachment process and why the Constitution was written as it was. (Rev: HBG 10/00; SLJ 8/00) [320]

17126 Stier, Catherine. *If I Were President* (1–3). Illus. by DyAnne DiSalvo-Ryan. 1999, Whitman $14.95 (0-8075-3541-9). An easy picture book that explains in simple terms what the duties of the president are — including tossing the first pitch of the baseball season. (Rev: BL 10/1/99; HBG 3/00; SLJ 10/99) [352.23]

17127 Sullivan, George. *Presidents at Play* (4–6). Illus. 1995, Walker LB $16.85 (0-8027-8334-1). 176pp. An unusual side of U.S. presidents is explored: the sports and other recreational activities they engaged in. (Rev: BL 1/1/95; SLJ 2/95) [973]

17128 Weber, Michael. *Our Congress* (4–6). Illus. Series: I Know America. 1994, Millbrook LB $13.90 (1-56294-443-6). 48pp. Provides a history of Congress, its composition, and its duties. (Rev: BL 11/15/94; SLJ 1/95) [328.73]

State Government and Agencies

17129 Feinberg, Barbara S. *State Governments* (4–8). Illus. Series: First Books. 1993, Watts LB $22.00 (0-531-20154-6). 64pp. Introduces the various parts of a state government, explains how each works, and stresses the need for cooperation among the components. (Rev: SLJ 1/94) [320]

17130 Giesecke, Ernestine. *State Government* (3–5). Series: Kids' Guide. 2000, Heinemann $21.36 (1-57572-513-4). 32pp. An appealing, simple account that discusses the structure of state governments in the U.S. and the responsibilities involved. (Rev: HBG 3/01; SLJ 10/00) [320]

Municipal Government and Agencies

17131 Giesecke, Ernestine. *Local Government* (3–5). Series: Kids' Guide. 2000, Heinemann $21.36 (1-57572-512-6). 32pp. The functions of city, country, and school district governments are explained with material on duties and responsibilities. (Rev: HBG 3/01; SLJ 10/00) [320.8]

Social Problems and Solutions

17132 Brimner, Larry. *A Migrant Family* (4–8). Illus. 1992, Lerner LB $19.93 (0-8225-2554-2). 40pp. The daily life of 12-year-old Juan and his Mexican-American family is captured in this photo-essay. (Rev: BCCB 10/92; BL 9/15/92) [305.5]

17133 Cann, Kate. *Living in the World* (5–8). Illus. by Derek Matthews. Series: Life Education. 1997, Watts LB $19.00 (0-531-14430-5). 32pp. A book that explores group interactions, including racism, prejudice, and social activism. (Rev: HBG 3/98; SLJ 1/98) [305.8]

17134 Dee, Catherine. *The Girls' Guide to Life: How to Take Charge of the Issues That Affect You* (5–8). Illus. 1997, Little, Brown paper $14.95 (0-316-17952-3). 160pp. Such concerns as self-esteem, political awareness, cultural stereotypes, and sexual harassment are introduced through first-person narratives, poetry, and advice. (Rev: BCCB 7–8/97; BL 7/97; HB 7–8/97, 11–12/97) [305.42]

17135 de Ruiz, Dana C., and Richard Larios. *La Causa: The Migrant Farmworkers' Story* (4–7). Illus. by Rudy Gutierrez. 1992, Raintree Steck-Vaughn LB $28.55 (0-8114-7231-0). 92pp. The story of the founding of the United Farm Workers highlights the work of Cesar Chavez and Dolores Huerta. (Rev: BL 6/1–15/93) [331]

17136 Fleming, Robert. *Rescuing a Neighborhood: The Bedford-Stuyvesant Volunteer Ambulance Corps* (4–8). Illus. 1995, Walker LB $16.85 (0-8027-8330-9). 48pp. The story of how two determined, dedicated men organized emergency response services in their inner-city neighborhood. (Rev: BL 5/1/95; SLJ 9/95) [362]

17137 Gedatus, Gus. *Violence in Public Places* (5–8). Series: Perspectives on Violence. 2000, Capstone LB $22.60 (0-7368-0428-5). 64pp. This examines violence in public places from hate crimes to road rage. Also use in the same series *Violence in the Media* (2000). (Rev: HBG 10/00; SLJ 8/00) [362]

17138 Goldentyer, Debra. *Street Violence* (4–8). Series: Preteen Pressures. 1998, Raintree Steck-Vaughn LB $24.97 (0-8172-5028-X). 48pp. This book discusses street violence and gang issues and shows how young people can protect themselves from both. (Rev: BL 5/15/98; HBG 10/98; SLJ 6/98) [364]

17139 Goodman, Alan. *Nickelodeon's The Big Help Book: 365 Ways You Can Make a Difference by Volunteering!* (4–6). 1994, Pocket paper $3.99 (0-671-51927-1). 134pp. Various kinds of community service projects are described, with hints on how to organize and activate them. (Rev: BL 11/15/94) [302.14]

17140 Green, Jen. *Dealing with Racism* (2–4). Photos by Roger Vlitos. Illus. by Chris O'Neill. Series: How Do I Feel About. 1998, Millbrook LB $19.90 (0-7613-0810-5). 24pp. Using the words of children, this book defines racism, gives examples, and makes suggestions on how to stop it. (Rev: HBG 10/98; SLJ 7/98) [305.8]

17141 Green, Jen. *Racism* (2–3). Series: Talking About. 1999, Raintree Steck-Vaughn LB $15.98 (0-7398-1375-7). 32pp. In this simple, attractive book, several examples of racism are given, with ways of dealing with them and tips on how to get along in a multicultural society. (Rev: BL 2/15/00; HBG 10/00; SLJ 7/00) [305.42]

17142 Hauser, Pierre. *Illegal Aliens* (5–8). Illus. Series: Immigrant Experience. 1996, Chelsea LB $19.95 (0-7910-3363-5). 142pp. A history of the attitudes toward immigration is given, followed by a discussion of illegal aliens, where they come from, and the government's policy toward them. (Rev: SLJ 2/97) [932]

17143 Hoyt-Goldsmith, Diane. *Migrant Worker: A Boy from the Rio Grande Valley* (4–7). Illus. 1996, Holiday $15.95 (0-8234-1225-3). 32pp. A photo-essay about the grim living conditions endured by an 11-year-old Mexican American migrant worker. (Rev: BCCB 3/96; BL 3/1/96; SLJ 5/96) [331.5]

17144 Hubbard, Jim. *Lives Turned Upside Down: Homeless Children in Their Own Words and Photographs* (4–7). Illus. 1996, Simon & Schuster paper $17.00 (0-689-80649-3). 40pp. This work contains first-person accounts of four youngsters who come from homeless families. (Rev: BCCB 1/97; BL 11/15/96; SLJ 12/96) [362.7]

17145 Hull, Mary. *Ethnic Violence* (5–8). Illus. Series: Overview. 1997, Lucent LB $17.96 (1-56006-184-7). 112pp. Gives a history of racial prejudice that has led to violence and tells about decisions and policies that currently guide our behavior and attitudes toward this problem. (Rev: BL 8/97; SLJ 9/97) [305.8]

17146 Hurwitz, Eugene, and Sue Hurwitz. *Working Together Against Homelessness* (4–6). Illus. Series: Library of Social Activism. 1995, Rosen LB $16.95 (0-8239-1772-X). 64pp. A history of homelessness both nationally and globally, its present frequency, and possible solutions. (Rev: BL 2/15/95; SLJ 12/94) [362.5]

17147 Karnes, Frances A., and Suzanne M. Bean. *Girls and Young Women Leading the Way: 20 True Stories About Leadership* (5–8). Illus. 1993, Free Spirit paper $12.95 (0-915793-52-0). 160pp. Contains case histories of 20 girls who changed their communities by starting projects like collecting food for the homeless or starting a recycling program. (Rev: SLJ 12/93) [307.1]

17148 Katella-Cofrancesco, Kathy. *Children's Causes* (4–6). Illus. Series: Celebrity Activist. 1998, Twenty-First Century LB $23.40 (0-7613-3013-5). 64pp. Each chapter in this book examines the contributions made by a celebrity to a cause involving children. (Rev: BL 8/98; HBG 10/98) [361.7]

17149 Katella-Cofrancesco, Kathy. *Economic Causes* (4–6). Illus. Series: Celebrity Activist. 1998, Twenty-First Century LB $23.40 (0-7613-3014-3). 64pp. Focuses on how celebrities, including Sharon Stone (Planet Hope) and former President Carter (Habitat for Humanity), support causes involving poverty and related problems. (Rev: BL 8/98; HBG 10/98) [361.7]

17150 Lewis, Barbara A. *The Kid's Guide to Service Projects: Over 500 Service Ideas for Young People Who Want to Make a Difference* (4–7). 1995, Free Spirit Pr. paper $12.95 (0-915793-82-2). 175pp. After an introduction on how to organize and conduct service projects, this book gives details on 500 ideas from running errands for seniors to working for voter registration. (Rev: SLJ 7/95) [307]

17151 McGuire, Leslie. *Victims* (5–7). Series: Women Today. 1991, Rourke LB $17.95 (0-86593-120-8). 64pp. This disturbing book tells the story of several women who have been subjected to physical and emotional violence. (Rev: SLJ 2/92) [305]

17152 Nichelason, Margery G. *Homeless or Hopeless?* (5–8). Illus. Series: Pro/Con. 1994, Lerner LB $25.26 (0-8225-2606-9). 112pp. The causes of homelessness and the plight of those affected are described in this account, which views all sides of this problem. (Rev: BL 6/1–15/94; SLJ 7/94) [362.5]

17153 O'Neill, Terry. *The Homeless: Distinguishing Between Fact and Opinion* (4–7). Illus. Series: Opposing Viewpoints Juniors. 1991, Greenwillow LB $16.20 (0-89908-605-5). 32pp. Homelessness is explored, with different points of view on how serious the problem is and who is to blame. (Rev: BL 6/15/91) [362.5]

17154 Rozakis, Laurie. *Homelessness: Can We Solve the Problem?* (5–8). Illus. Series: Issues of Our Time. 1995, Twenty-First Century LB $18.90 (0-8050-3878-7). 64pp. A history of homelessness is given, with various opinions and possible solutions. (Rev: SLJ 9/95) [362.5]

17155 Siegel, Danny. *Tell Me a Mitzvah: Little and Big Ways to Repair the World* (3–6). Illus. by Judith Friedman. 1993, Kar-Ben paper $7.95 (0-929371-78-X). 64pp. Profiles of 12 people who have made the world a better place by performing mitzvahs, or good deeds. (Rev: SLJ 3/94) [307.1]

17156 Steins, Richard. *Censorship: How Does It Conflict with Freedom?* (5–8). Illus. Series: Issues of Our Time. 1995, Twenty-First Century LB $18.90 (0-8050-3879-5). 64pp. A clearly written introduction to censorship, its history, and the various positions possible toward it. (Rev: SLJ 9/95) [363.3]

17157 Tipp, Stacey L. *Child Abuse: Detecting Bias* (5–7). Series: Opposing Viewpoints Juniors. 1991, Greenhaven LB $13.96 (0-89908-611-X). 32pp. Four different issues involving child abuse (e.g.,

whether abusers should be sent to prison) are presented from various points of view. (Rev: BL 5/15/92; SLJ 3/92) [362.7]

17158 Walker, Richard. *A Right to Die?* (4–8). Illus. Series: Viewpoints. 1997, Watts LB $22.50 (0-531-14413-5). 32pp. This objective account traces traditional views of death, tells how medicine is prolonging life, and discusses topics like suicide, euthanasia, and life support systems and the controversy surrounding each. (Rev: SLJ 5/97) [306.88]

17159 Wolf, Bernard. *Homeless* (2–4). Illus. 1995, Orchard LB $17.99 (0-531-08736-0). 46pp. The plight of a homeless family caught up in the New York City welfare system is the subject of this affecting picture book. (Rev: BCCB 3/95; BL 2/15/95; HB 5–6/95; SLJ 4/95) [362.5]

17160 Worth, Richard. *Poverty* (5–8). Illus. Series: Overview. 1997, Lucent LB $22.45 (1-56006-192-8). 96pp. A carefully researched title that gives a history of poverty in America, changing attitudes toward it, and current policies and practices. (Rev: BL 8/97; SLJ 9/97) [362.5]

Religion and Holidays

General and Miscellaneous

17161 Ammon, Richard. *An Amish Wedding* (K–3). Illus. by Pamela Patrick. 1998, Simon & Schuster $17.00 (0-689-81677-4). 32pp. This picture book details the preparations for an Amish wedding, the customs associated with it, and the ceremony itself. (Rev: BL 10/1/98; HBG 3/99; SLJ 12/98) [392.5]

17162 Ammon, Richard. *An Amish Year* (3–5). Illus. 2000, Simon & Schuster $16.95 (0-689-82622-2). 40pp. Using the cycle of seasons as a framework, this book explains Amish life as experienced by Anna, a fourth-grader. (Rev: BL 1/1–15/00; HBG 10/00; SLJ 2/00) [291]

17163 Armstrong, Carole. *Lives and Legends of the Saints: With Paintings from the Great Art Museums of the World* (4–7). Illus. 1995, Simon & Schuster $17.00 (0-689-80277-3). 45pp. An introduction to the lives of 20 of the most important saints, with illustrations from the world's great paintings. (Rev: BL 9/1/95*; HB 11–12/95; SLJ 12/95) [270]

17164 Barnes, Trevor. *The Kingfisher Book of Religions: Festivals, Ceremonies, and Beliefs from Around the World* (4–9). 1999, Kingfisher $22.95 (0-7534-5199-9). 160pp. Short chapters and many attractive photographs and reproductions are used to introduce an array of religions and their customs with emphasis on Judaism, Christianity, and Islam. (Rev: HBG 10/00; SLJ 1/00) [200]

17165 Bial, Raymond. *Amish Home* (3–6). Illus. by author. 1993, Houghton $17.00 (0-395-59504-5). 40pp. A haunting photo-essay of Amish life without the Amish themselves because their religious doctrine forbids portraiture. (Rev: BCCB 5/93; BL 2/15/93; SLJ 5/93) [973.08]

17166 Bial, Raymond. *Shaker Home* (3–6). Illus. 1994, Houghton $15.95 (0-395-64047-4). 35pp. The Shaker way of life is explored in text and color photos that touch on their beliefs, activities, clothing, crafts, and humanitarian activities. (Rev: BCCB 3/94; BL 2/1/94*; HB 5–6/94; SLJ 3/94) [289.8]

17167 Birdseye, Debbie H., and Tom Birdseye. *What I Believe: Kids Talk About Faith* (4–7). 1996, Holiday $15.95 (0-8234-1268-7). 32pp. Children from six faiths explain what their religion means to them. (Rev: BL 12/15/96; SLJ 2/97) [200]

17168 Bolick, Nancy O., and Sallie G. Randolph. *Shaker Inventions* (4–6). Illus. by Melissa Francisco. 1990, Walker LB $14.85 (0-8027-6934-9). 96pp. A rundown on many inventions by the Shakers, and a general introduction to their way of life. (Rev: SLJ 9/90) [289]

17169 Bolick, Nancy O., and Sallie G. Randolph. *Shaker Villages* (4–8). Illus. by Laura LoTurco. 1993, Walker LB $13.85 (0-8027-8210-8). 79pp. A history of the Shaker movement. (Rev: SLJ 6/93) [289]

17170 Borchard, Therese. *Taste and See: The Goodness of the Lord* (PS–K). Illus. by Phyllis V. Saroff. 2000, Paulist Pr. $9.95 (0-8091-6665-8). 32pp. With images that use the five senses, children are made to feel that God is everywhere and in all living things. (Rev: BL 10/1/00; HBG 3/01) [231]

17171 Brown, Alan, and Andrew Langley. *What I Believe: A Young Person's Guide to the Religions of the World* (4–7). Illus. 1999, Millbrook LB $23.90 (0-7613-1501-2). 64pp. This book supplies a brief overview of eight religions: Judaism, Christianity, Islam, Hinduism, Buddhism, Taoism, Shintoism, and Sikhism. (Rev: BL 10/1/99; HBG 3/00; SLJ 2/00) [291]

17172 Carlstrom, Nancy White. *Does God Know How to Tie Shoes?* (PS–K). Illus. by Lori McElrath-Eslick. 1993, Eerdmans $15.00 (0-8028-5074-X). 32pp. A child questions her parents about the nature of God, and the answers are correlated with passages from the Bible. (Rev: BL 12/1/93; SLJ 3/94)

17173 Chalfonte, Jessica. *I Am Muslim* (1–4). Illus. Series: Religions of the World. 1996, Rosen LB $15.93 (0-8239-2375-4). 24pp. An introduction to the Muslim religion and the world of Islam as seen through the eyes of Ahmet, a boy living in Detroit. (Rev: SLJ 2/97) [297]

17174 *The Children's Book of Faith* (4–6). Ed. by William J. Bennett. Illus. by Michael Hague. 2000, Doubleday $24.95 (0-385-32771-4). 112pp. A collection of poems, Bible stories, proverbs, short stories, and pieces of nonfiction that have a moral purpose chiefly from a Christian point of view. (Rev: BL 10/1/00; HBG 3/01; SLJ 12/00) [248]

17175 Demi. *Buddha* (4–6). Illus. 1996, Holt $18.95 (0-8050-4203-2). 32pp. In this picture book for older children, the story of Buddha's life and teachings is effectively retold. (Rev: BCCB 6/96; BL 4/1/96; HB 9–10/96; SLJ 6/96) [294.3]

17176 Demi. *Buddha Stories* (3–6). Illus. 1997, Holt $16.95 (0-8050-4886-3). 32pp. Ten of the author's favorite Buddha stories, or jakatas, are elegantly retold with excellent illustrations. (Rev: BCCB 4/97; BL 2/15/97; SLJ 6/97) [294.3]

17177 Dhanjal, Beryl. *What Do We Know About Sikhism?* (3–6). Illus. Series: What Do We Know About. 1997, Bedrick LB $18.95 (0-87226-387-8). 45pp. The history of Sikhism is covered, along with material on its founder, Guru Nanak; the ten succeeding Gurus; the Sikh Holy Book; and the Golden Temple at Amritsar. (Rev: SLJ 3/97) [294.6]

17178 Dillon, Leo, and Diane Dillon. *To Every Thing There Is a Season: Verses from Ecclesiastes* (4–7). Illus. 1998, Scholastic $15.95 (0-590-47887-7). 40pp. Using verses from Ecclesiastes such as "A time to be born and a time to die," the artists have created a stunning picture book on the cycle of life. (Rev: BCCB 11/98; BL 10/1/98*; HB 9–10/98; HBG 3/99; SLJ 9/98) [223]

17179 Faber, Doris. *The Amish* (3–5). Illus. by Michael Erkel. 1990, Doubleday $17.95 (0-385-44518-0). An enlightening look at the people, who live plainly, in harmony with nature. (Rev: BL 1/15/91) [973.08]

17180 Fine, Doreen. *What Do We Know About Judaism?* (3–6). Illus. by Celia Hart. Series: What Do We Know About. 1996, Bedrick LB $18.95 (0-87226-386-X). 45pp. An introduction to Judaism and the Jewish way of life that includes material on Orthodox, Reform, and Conservative Jews. (Rev: SLJ 2/97) [296]

17181 Fisher, James T. *Catholics in America* (5–9). Illus. Series: Religion in American Life. 2000, Oxford $22.00 (0-19-511179-6). 176pp. This account traces the history of Roman Catholicism in America, its adherents, their role in public affairs, and debates over topics such as abortion. (Rev: BL 6/1–15/00; HBG 3/01) [282]

17182 Fisher, Leonard Everett. *To Bigotry No Sanction: The Story of the Oldest Synagogue in America* (5–8). Illus. 1999, Holiday $16.95 (0-8234-1401-9). 64pp. Beginning with the expulsion of the Jews from Spain in 1492, the author traces the history of Jews in America, including the 1763 building — with George Washington's blessing — of the Touro Synagogue. (Rev: BCCB 4/99; BL 2/1/99; HBG 10/99; SLJ 3/99) [296]

17183 Fitch, Florence Mary. *A Book About God* (PS–3). Illus. by Henri Sorensen. 1999, Lothrop LB $15.93 (0-688-16129-4). 24pp. A new edition of a book originally published in 1953 that tries to explain the nature of God and how this spirit is found everywhere. (Rev: BL 4/1/99; HBG 10/99; SLJ 5/99) [231]

17184 Ganeri, Anita. *Growing Up: From Child to Adult* (4–6). Series: Life Times. 1999, Bedrick LB $15.95 (0-87226-287-1). 32pp. This book describes rites of passage from child to adult as practiced in six major religions, including Buddhism, Christianity, Judaism, and Hinduism. (Rev: BL 5/15/99; SLJ 3/99) [291]

17185 Ganeri, Anita. *Out of the Ark: Stories from the World's Religions* (4–7). Illus. by Jackie Morris. 1996, Harcourt $18.00 (0-15-200943-4). 96pp. Traditional tales from seven of the world's major religions are retold in this thematically arranged book. (Rev: BCCB 4/96; SLJ 4/96) [200]

17186 Ganeri, Anita. *What Do We Know About Buddhism?* (4–7). Illus. Series: What Do We Know About. 1997, Bedrick LB $18.95 (0-87226-389-4). 45pp. Using double-page spreads, basic facts about Buddha's life and teachings are covered, with information on Buddhist beliefs, sacred texts, festivals, and the art and folk literature connected with this religion. (Rev: HBG 3/98; SLJ 10/97) [294]

17187 Ganeri, Anita. *What Do We Know About Hinduism?* (3–6). Illus. by Celia Hart. Series: What Do We Know About. 1996, Bedrick LB $18.76 (0-87226-385-1). 45pp. In this introduction to Hinduism, topics like reincarnation, gods and goddesses, the Sacred Scriptures, types of worship, and yoga are presented. (Rev: SLJ 2/97) [294.5]

17188 Gellman, Marc, and Thomas Hartman. *How Do You Spell God? Answers to the Big Questions from Around the World* (5–8). Illus. by Joseph A. Smith. 1995, Morrow $16.95 (0-688-13041-0). 224pp. A priest and a rabbi have written this introduction to the world's most important religions: Judaism, Christianity, Islam, Buddhism, and Hinduism. (Rev: BCCB 7–8/95; BL 6/1–15/95; SLJ 5/95) [200]

17189 Gold, Susan D. *Religions of the Western Hemisphere* (5–8). Illus. Series: Comparing Continents. 1997, Twenty-First Century $21.40 (0-8050-5603-3). 96pp. Explores the history and influence of religions, beliefs, and customs on life in the United States, Canada, and Latin America, with material on the roles of religious leaders in the government, economy, and everyday life. (Rev: BL 2/1/98; SLJ 3/98) [200]

17190 Goodnough, David. *Cult Awareness: A Hot Issue* (5–8). Series: Hot Issues. 2000, Enslow LB $19.95 (0-7660-1196-8). 64pp. This book explains the nature of cults and how they differ as well as giving information on many groups including Jehovah's Witnesses, Unification Church, Hare Krishna, Shakers, Mormons, and Church of Scientology. (Rev: HBG 10/00; SLJ 6/00) [291.9]

17191 Grimes, Nikki. *At Break of Day* (PS–3). Illus. by Paul Morin. 1999, Eerdmans $17.00 (0-8028-5104-5). 32pp. In this version of the creation story, God and his Son work together to produce the universe and its wonders. (Rev: BL 10/1/99; HBG 3/00; SLJ 1/00)

17192 Husain, Shahrukh. *What Do We Know About Islam?* (4–7). Illus. Series: What Do We Know About. 1997, Bedrick LB $18.95 (0-87226-388-6). 45pp. Covers the major aspects of Islam, including its history, the lifestyles of its believers, holidays like Ramadan, dietary obligations, and the Haj pilgrimage to Mecca. (Rev: SLJ 5/97) [297]

17193 Jaffe, Nina. *The Mysterious Visitor: Stories of the Prophet Elijah* (4–6). Illus. 1997, Scholastic $19.95 (0-590-48422-2). 112pp. Eight Jewish stories that involve the prophet Elijah are retold. (Rev: BCCB 6/97; BL 5/1/97; HBG 3/98; SLJ 6/97*) [222]

17194 John Paul II, Pope. *For the Children: Words of Love and Inspiration from His Holiness John Paul II* (4–7). Illus. 2000, Scholastic $16.95 (0-439-14902-9). 32pp. Letters and speeches by Pope John Paul II and photos of children from around the world are used to illustrate inspirational messages about such subjects as hope, faith, and school. (Rev: BL 3/1/00; HBG 10/00; SLJ 3/00) [248.8]

17195 Kanitkar, V. P. *Hinduism* (4–6). Illus. 1986, Dufour paper $21.00 (1-871402-09-3). History, major tenets, and an explanation of holidays and festivals. (Rev: BL 12/15/86)

17196 Kaur-Singh, Kanwaljit. *Sikh Gurdwara* (1–3). Series: Places of Worship. 2000, Gareth Stevens LB $15.95 (0-8368-2610-8). 32pp. This book explores the gurdwara, where Sikhs worship God and show respect for the Guru Granth Sahib, and also tells about the the basic beliefs and practices of the Sikh faith. (Rev: BL 6/1–15/00; HBG 10/00) [294.6]

17197 Kenna, Kathleen. *A People Apart* (PS–3). Illus. by Andrew Stawicki. 1995, Houghton $18.00 (0-395-67344-5). 64pp. A photo-essay about the Mennonites that supplies important information on their history, customs, and beliefs. (Rev: BCCB 1/96; BL 11/1/95*; SLJ 12/95*) [289.7]

17198 Krishnaswami, Uma. *The Broken Tusk: Stories of the Hindu God Ganesha* (4–6). Illus. 1996, Linnet LB $21.50 (0-208-02442-5). 98pp. A collection of folktales about the elephant-headed Hindu god Ganesha, the god of good beginnings. (Rev: BCCB 10/96; BL 10/1/96; SLJ 7/97) [294.5]

17199 Kroll, Virginia. *I Wanted to Know All About God* (PS–1). Illus. by Debra R. Jenkins. 1994, Eerdmans $15.00 (0-8028-5078-2). 32pp. A book about the nature of God that emphasizes human relationships and the wonders of nature. (Rev: BL 2/15/94; SLJ 8/94) [231.2]

17200 Krull, Kathleen, ed. *Songs of Praise* (PS–1). Illus. by Kathryn Hewitt. 1989, Harcourt paper $5.95 (0-15-277109-3). 32pp. A collection of 15 hymns. (Rev: BCCB 9/88; BL 11/15/88)

17201 Kushner, Lawrence, and Karen Kushner. *Because Nothing Looks Like God* (PS–2). Illus. by Dawn Majewski. 2001, Jewish Lights $16.95 (1-58023-092-X). 32pp. The concept of God is explored in this picture book filled with paintings of

nature scenes. (Rev: BL 1/1–15/01; SLJ 2/01) [291.2]

17202 Langley, Myrtle. *Religion* (4–7). Illus. Series: Eyewitness Books. 1996, Knopf $20.99 (0-679-98123-3). 59pp. Each double-page spread introduces a different religion, including those of ancient Egypt and Greece as well as Hinduism, Buddhism, Confucianism, Taoism, Sikhism, Judaism, Christianity, and Islam. (Rev: SLJ 12/96) [291]

17203 Lindbergh, Reeve. *The Circle of Days* (PS–3). Illus. by Cathie Felstead. 1998, Candlewick $15.99 (0-7637-0357-0). 32pp. This adaptation of the writings of St. Francis of Assisi translates the cycle of creation, life, and death in nature into simple, flowing prose and detailed illustrations. (Rev: BL 4/1/98*) [242]

17204 Lucas, Daryl J. *The Baker Bible Dictionary for Kids* (3–6). Illus. 1997, Baker Book House $19.99 (0-8010-4345-X). 503pp. More than 2,000 words found in the Bible are simply and clearly explained. (Rev: SLJ 11/97) [222]

17205 McFarlane, Marilyn. *Sacred Myths: Stories of World Religions* (4–7). 1996, Sibyl $26.95 (0-9638327-7-8). 110pp. A collection of myths from a number of religions, including Judaism, Christianity, Islam, and Hinduism. (Rev: BL 10/1/96; SLJ 1/97) [291.1]

17206 Maestro, Betsy. *The Story of Religion* (4–7). Illus. by Giulio Maestro. 1996, Clarion $15.95 (0-395-62364-2). 46pp. Traces the history of religion from the beliefs of primitive peoples to the development of such modern religions as Islam and Christianity. (Rev: BL 10/1/96; SLJ 9/96*) [291]

17207 Moehn, Heather. *World Holidays: A Watts Guide for Children* (3–6). Illus. 2000, Watts LB $32.00 (0-531-11714-6); paper $19.95 (0-531-16490-X). 128pp. The origins and methods of celebrating more than 100 world holidays, both religious and secular, are included in this illustrated book. (Rev: BL 9/1/00; SLJ 7/00) [394.26]

17208 Mulvihill, Margaret. *The Treasury of Saints and Martyrs* (5–7). Illus. 1999, Viking $19.99 (0-670-88789-7). 80pp. A handsome, oversize book about the lives of 40 saints from the beginning of Christianity to the present day. (Rev: BL 10/1/99; HBG 10/00; SLJ 3/00) [270.029]

17209 Nomura, Noriko S. *I Am Shinto* (K–3). Illus. Series: Religions of the World. 1996, Rosen LB $15.93 (0-8239-2380-0). 24pp. In double-page spreads, various aspects of the Shinto religion are introduced, including Dami spirits, shrines, and purification rituals. (Rev: SLJ 11/96) [299]

17210 Osborne, Mary Pope. *One World, Many Religions: The Ways We Worship* (4–7). Illus. 1996, Knopf $26.99 (0-679-93930-X). 86pp. Six of the world's major religions are introduced in an account that emphasizes their similarities. (Rev: BCCB 1/97; BL 10/1/96; SLJ 11/96) [291]

17211 Paterson, Katherine. *Who Am I?* (4–6). 1992, Lerner paper $8.00 (0-8028-5072-3). 96pp. This book asks such questions as "Where do I belong?" and "Where in the world is God?" (Rev: BL 12/15/92) [248.8]

17212 Pilling, Ann. *A Kingfisher Treasury of Bible Stories, Poems, and Prayers for Bedtime* (3–6). Illus. 2000, Kingfisher $18.95 (0-7534-5329-0). 96pp. Poetry, songs, and Bible stories from the Old and New Testaments are included in this anthology aimed at Christian children. (Rev: BL 10/1/00) [242]

17213 Raimondo, Lois. *The Little Lama of Tibet* (K–4). Illus. 1994, Scholastic $15.95 (0-590-46167-2). 40pp. This photo-essay deals with the everyday life of Ling Rinpoche, a six-year-old high lama in the Tibetan Buddhist religion. (Rev: BCCB 1/94; BL 1/1/94; HB 9–10/94; SLJ 3/94) [294.3]

17214 Rushton, Lucy. *Birth Customs* (4–6). Illus. Series: Religions. 1993, Thomson Learning LB $19.92 (1-56847-030-4). 32pp. This book examines the rituals and customs associated with birth as found in many of the world's religions. A companion volume is: *Death Customs* (1993). (Rev: BL 6/1–15/93; SLJ 7/93) [291.2]

17215 Sasso, Sandy Eisenberg. *God in Between* (PS–3). Illus. by Sally Sweetland. 1998, Jewish Lights $16.95 (1-879045-86-9). 32pp. Two townspeople are disappointed when their journey to find God ends unsuccessfully — until they realize that God is found while reaching out to others in need. (Rev: BL 10/15/98; HBG 10/98; SLJ 9/98) [211]

17216 Serrano, Francisco. *Our Lady of Guadalupe* (2–4). Illus. by Felipe Davalos. 1998, Groundwood $16.95 (0-88899-335-8). This pop-up book tells about the appearance of the Virgin Mary to a simple Mexican peasant. (Rev: BL 1/1–15/99) [282]

17217 Sevastiades, Philemon D. *I Am Eastern Orthodox* (1–4). Illus. Series: Religions of the World. 1996, Rosen LB $16.95 (0-8239-2377-0). 24pp. The unique qualities of this church are covered through the story of Anastasia and her brother, who is the priest of her church in Chicago. (Rev: SLJ 2/97) [291]

17218 Sevastiades, Philemon D. *I Am Protestant* (1–4). Illus. Series: Religions of the World. 1996, Rosen LB $15.93 (0-8239-2378-9). 24pp. Focusing on Yvonne, a Southern African American girl who is an Evangelical Protestant, this and other branches of Protestantism and their beliefs are covered. (Rev: SLJ 2/97) [280]

17219 Sevastiades, Philemon D. *I Am Roman Catholic* (K–3). Illus. Series: Religions of the World. 1996, Rosen LB $17.26 (0-8239-2376-2). 24pp. Such Roman Catholic institutions, beliefs, and rituals as the Trinity, the Pope, baptism, Mass, confession, communion, and confirmation are discussed. (Rev: SLJ 11/96) [282]

17220 Sita, Lisa. *Worlds of Belief: Religion and Spirituality* (5–8). Illus. Series: Our Human Family. 1995, Blackbirch LB $22.45 (1-56711-125-4). 80pp. An overview of world religions and religious practices in a book divided into five broad geographic areas. (Rev: SLJ 1/96) [210]

17221 Stanton, Sue. *Child's Guide to the Mass* (PS–3). Illus. by H. M. Alan. 2001, Paulist Pr. $9.95 (0-8091-6682-8). 32pp. Using a lighthearted approach, this book explains the parts of the Roman Catholic Mass and what each means. (Rev: BL 3/15/01) [264]

17222 *Stories Told by Mother Teresa* (2–4). Ed. by Edward Le Joly and Jaya Chaliha. Illus. by Allan Drummond. 2000, Element Books $15.95 (1-90261-865-3). 32pp. These 11 moving stories derived from the personal experiences of Mother Teresa describe acts of sacrifice, faith, and devotion by ordinary people. (Rev: BL 3/15/00; HBG 10/00) [271.97]

17223 Sturges, Philemon. *Sacred Places* (4–6). Illus. 2000, Putnam $16.99 (0-399-23317-2). 40pp. This general introduction to religion describes different places of worship including a pagoda, mosque, synagogue, church, and Hindu temple. (Rev: BCCB 12/00; BL 10/1/00; HBG 3/01; SLJ 12/00) [291.3]

17224 Sugarman, Joan G., and Grace R. Freeman. *Inside the Synagogue* (K–3). Illus. 1984, UAHC paper $7.00 (0-8074-0268-0). In text and photos, the Jewish house of worship is introduced. (Rev: SLJ 3/85)

17225 Tompert, Ann. *Saint Nicholas* (2–4). Illus. 2000, Boyds Mills $15.95 (1-56397-844-X). 32pp. A retelling of the legends surrounding St. Nicholas and the attributes that made him one of the most beloved of all saints. (Rev: BCCB 10/00; BL 10/1/00; HBG 3/01) [398.2]

17226 Vishaka. *Our Most Dear Friend: Bhagavad-gita for Children* (K–3). Illus. 1996, Torchlight $14.95 (1-887089-04-7). 30pp. A reworking of this sacred book of the Hindus in which Lord Krishna explains that every living thing has a soul. (Rev: BL 10/1/96) [294.5]

17227 Walters, Julie. *God Is Like . . . Three Parables for Children* (PS–2). Illus. by Thea Kliros. 2000, WaterBrook $12.95 (1-57856-246-5). Metaphorical concepts of God, Jesus, and the Holy Spirit — "God is a rock," for example — are presented in three short stories. (Rev: SLJ 9/00) [200]

17228 Weiss, Bernard P. *I Am Jewish* (1–4). Illus. Series: Religions of the World. 1996, Rosen LB $13.95 (0-8239-2349-5). 24pp. This explanation of Judaism shows the links between the religion, Jewish history, and the country of Israel. (Rev: SLJ 2/97) [296]

17229 Westridge Young Writers Workshop. *Kids Explore America's Jewish Heritage* (4–7). Illus. Series: Kids Explore. 1996, John Muir paper $9.95 (1-56261-274-3). 147pp. This book explores various aspects of Jewish life, from participation in American historical events to material on special holidays, the arts, folktales, foods, and crafts. (Rev: SLJ 11/96) [305.5]

17230 Wilcox, Charlotte. *Mummies and Their Mysteries* (5–7). Illus. 1993, Carolrhoda LB $23.93 (0-87614-767-8). 64pp. An account of how throughout history many civilizations and religions have attempted to preserve bodies. (Rev: BCCB 7–8/93*; BL 6/1–15/93*) [393.3]

17231 Wood, Angela. *Buddhist Temple* (1–3). Series: Places of Worship. 2000, Gareth Stevens LB $15.95 (0-8368-2605-1). 32pp. A description of a Buddhist temple and an explanation of the basic beliefs and practices of this Eastern religion. (Rev: BL 6/1–15/00; HBG 10/00) [294.3]

17232 Wood, Angela. *Christian Church* (1–3). Illus. Series: Places of Worship. 2000, Gareth Stevens LB $15.95 (0-8368-2606-X). 32pp. This book introduces Christian churches and describes the structure and contents of many. (Rev: BL 6/1–15/00; HBG 10/00) [262]

17233 Wood, Angela. *Hindu Mandir* (1–3). Series: Places of Worship. 2000, Gareth Stevens LB $15.95 (0-8368-2607-8). 32pp. This book introduces the reader to the beliefs and practices of Hinduism and describes home shrines and the parts of a Hindu mandir. (Rev: BL 6/1–15/00; HBG 10/00) [294.5]

17234 Wood, Angela. *Jewish Synagogue* (1–3). Illus. 2000, Gareth Stevens LB $15.95 (0-8368-2608-6). 32pp. An introduction to a synagogue, with information about rabbis, the Torah scrolls, and other important aspects. (Rev: BL 6/1–15/00; HBG 10/00; SLJ 8/00) [296.6]

17235 Wood, Angela. *Judaism* (5–8). Illus. Series: World Religions. 1995, Thomson Learning LB $24.26 (1-56847-376-1). 48pp. A history of Judaism, with color photos and a clear, understandable text. (Rev: BL 9/1/95; SLJ 11/95) [296]

17236 Wood, Angela. *Muslim Mosque* (1–3). Illus. 2000, Gareth Stevens LB $15.95 (0-8368-2609-4). 32pp. A typical mosque is presented, with material on its functions and on the Koran. (Rev: BL 6/1–15/00; HBG 10/00; SLJ 8/00) [297.3]

Bible Stories

17237 Aaseng, Rolfe E. *Augsburg Story Bible* (4–8). Illus. by Annegert Fuchshuber. 1992, Augsburg LB $19.99 (0-8066-2607-0). 270pp. This copiously illustrated version of the Bible is only slightly abridged. (Rev: SLJ 7/92) [222]

17238 Anderson, Joel. *Jonah's Trash . . . God's Treasure* (K–2). Photos by David Bailey. Illus. by Joel Anderson and Abe Goolsby. 1998, Tommy Nelson $12.99 (0-8499-5825-3). 28pp. This rhyming story about Jonah is cleverly illustrated with collages made from found objects such as pretzels, pipe cleaners, and dried peas. (Rev: SLJ 12/98) [220.9]

17239 Auld, Mary. *Daniel in the Lions' Den* (3–4). Illus. Series: Bible Stories. 1999, Watts LB $20.25 (0-531-14514-X). 32pp. This retelling of the Old Testament tale also provides historical and biblical background. (Rev: BL 10/1/99; SLJ 12/99) [224]

17240 Auld, Mary. *David and Goliath* (3–4). Illus. Series: Bible Stories. 2000, Watts LB $20.50 (0-531-14522-0); paper $7.95 (0-531-15393-2). 32pp. Using both narration and dialogue, this is a dramatic recreation of the David vs. Goliath story. Also use from the same series *Jacob and Esau* and *Noah's Ark* (both 2000). (Rev: BL 1/1–15/01; SLJ 1/01) [222]

17241 Auld, Mary, reteller. *Exodus from Egypt* (K–3). Illus. by Diana Mayo. Series: Bible Stories. 2000, Watts LB $20.50 (0-531-14585-9); paper $7.95 (0-531-15437-8). 31pp. This book tells the story of Moses from his arrival before the Pharaoh with Aaron to the escape of the Israelites through the Red Sea. Also use *Jacob and Esau* (2000). (Rev: SLJ 1/01) [224]

17242 Auld, Mary. *Moses in the Bulrushes* (3–4). Illus. Series: Bible Stories. 1999, Watts LB $20.25 (0-531-14516-6). 32pp. After explaining how the Israelites became slaves in Egypt, this account describes the life of Moses until his conversion. (Rev: BL 10/1/99; SLJ 12/99) [224]

17243 Auld, Mary. *The Story of Jonah* (K–3). Illus. by Diana Mayo. Series: Bible Stories. 1999, Watts LB $20.25 (0-531-14517-4). 31pp. Using simple language and an attractive format, this retelling of the Bible story about Jonah follows the original closely. (Rev: SLJ 12/99) [224]

17244 Barner, Bob. *To Everything* (K–2). Illus. by author. 1998, Chronicle $14.95 (0-8118-2086-6). Stylized illustrations are used to present ten familiar verses from Ecclesiastes about time's cycle. (Rev: HBG 3/99; SLJ 11/98) [222]

17245 Beaude, Pierre-Marie. *The Book of Creation* (2–8). Trans. by Andrew Clements. Illus. by Georges Lemoine. 1991, Picture Book paper $16.95 (0-88708-141-X). 48pp. The Creation story as it might have been handed down through oral tradition. (Rev: BCCB 7–8/91; BL 7/91; SLJ 7/91) [222]

17246 Bible. *And It Was Good* (PS–2). Illus. by Harold H. Nofziger. 1993, Herald Pr. $12.99 (0-8361-3634-9). The Creation story is reproduced with brightly colored collages and a text from the New Revised Standard Version of the Bible. (Rev: SLJ 12/93) [222]

17247 Bible. *The Ark* (PS–2). Illus. by Arthur Geisert. 1988, Houghton $18.00 (0-395-43078-X). 48pp. A richly detailed account that includes both well-known and unusual animals. (Rev: HB 11–12/89)

17248 Bible. *The Lord Is My Shepherd* (3–7). Illus. by Tasha Tudor. 1989, Putnam $12.99 (0-399-20756-2). 32pp. An illustrated edition of the Twenty-third Psalm.

17249 Bogot, Howard I., and Mary K. Bogot, retellers. *Seven Animal Stories for Children* (K–3). Illus. by Harry Araten. 1997, Pitspopany $16.95 (0-943706-40-8); paper $9.95 (0-943706-41-6). 45pp. A collection of Bible stories and Jewish folktales that tell about such people as Noah, Solomon, David, and Jonah. (Rev: HBG 3/98; SLJ 12/97) [226]

17250 Boroson, Martin. *Becoming Me* (K–3). Illus. by Christopher Gilvan-Cartwright. 2000, Skylight Paths $16.95 (1-893361-11-X). 32pp. The Bible creation story as told from the standpoint of God. (Rev: BL 7/00; SLJ 10/00) [291.2]

17251 Boss, Sarah Jane. *Mary's Story* (3–5). Illus. by Helen Cann. 1999, Barefoot $16.95 (1-901223-44-2). 48pp. Using biblical sources as well as folk traditions, this book re-creates the life of Mary, the mother of Jesus. (Rev: BL 10/1/99; SLJ 10/99) [224]

17252 Brunelli, Roberto. *A Family Treasury of Bible Stories: One for Each Week of the Year* (4–8).

Illus. by Mikhail Fiodorov. 1997, Abrams $24.95 (0-8109-1248-7). 124pp. A collection of 52 briefly told stories (one for each week) from the Old and New Testaments. (Rev: BL 10/1/97; SLJ 2/98) [220.9]

17253 Chaikin, Miriam. *Clouds of Glory: Legends and Stories about Bible Times* (4–8). Illus. by David Frampton. 1998, Clarion $19.00 (0-395-74654-X). 118pp. Illustrated with charming woodcuts, this collection of stories mixes Bible accounts with Jewish parallel legends (midrashim) to create an unusual retelling of Genesis tales. (Rev: BL 4/1/98; HBG 10/98; SLJ 4/98) [296.1]

17254 Chaikin, Miriam, adapt. *Exodus* (3–5). Illus. by Charles Mikolaycak. 1987, Holiday LB $14.95 (0-8234-0607-5). 32pp. The story of the Israelites' flight out of Egypt. (Rev: BCCB 5/87; BL 5/15/87; HB 5–6/87)

17255 Chaikin, Miriam. *Joshua in the Promised Land* (4–8). Illus. by David Frampton. 1990, Houghton paper $7.95 (0-395-54797-0). The story of Moses' success and the Israelites' journey to the Holy Land.

17256 Clements, Andrew. *Noah and the Ark and the Animals* (PS–2). Illus. 1992, Scholastic paper $4.95 (0-590-44457-3). 28pp. Subdued watercolors enhance this retelling.

17257 Cooper, Ilene. *The Dead Sea Scrolls* (5–8). Illus. by John Thompson. 1997, Morrow $15.00 (0-688-14300-8). 64pp. This account tells about the discovery of the Dead Sea Scrolls, their content, and archaeological importance. (Rev: BCCB 5/97; BL 3/1/97; HB 9–10/97; SLJ 6/97) [296.1]

17258 Cousins, Lucy. *Noah's Ark* (PS). Illus. 1993, Candlewick $14.99 (1-56402-213-7). 40pp. A simple, direct retelling of the Bible story of Noah and the ark. (Rev: BL 10/1/93; HB 11–12/93; SLJ 9/93) [222]

17259 dePaola, Tomie. *Mary: The Mother of Jesus* (K–3). Illus. 1995, Holiday LB $16.95 (0-8234-1018-8). 32pp. This account combines stories from the Bible with popular legends to create a life of Mary. (Rev: BCCB 11/95; BL 9/1/95; SLJ 12/95) [232.91]

17260 dePaola, Tomie. *The Miracles of Jesus* (3–6). Illus. by author. 1987, Holiday LB $16.95 (0-8234-0635-0). 32pp. These one-page adaptations from the New Testament include the 12 miracles of Jesus. (Rev: BL 11/1/87; SLJ 10/87)

17261 dePaola, Tomie. *The Parables of Jesus* (3–6). Illus. by author. 1987, Holiday LB $16.95 (0-8234-0636-9). 32pp. Seven retellings of the parables of Jesus, such as "The Good Samaritan" and "The Mustard Seed." (Rev: BL 11/1/87; SLJ 10/87)

17262 dePaola, Tomie. *Tomie dePaola's Book of Bible Stories* (K–3). Illus. 1990, Putnam $24.99 (0-399-21690-1). 128pp. A collection of stories from the Old and New Testaments. (Rev: BCCB 11/90; BL 10/15/90; SLJ 12/90*) [220]

17263 De Regniers, Beatrice S. *David and Goliath* (1–3). Illus. by Scott Cameron. 1996, Orchard LB $16.99 (0-531-08796-4). 32pp. The story of the shepherd boy David and his deadly confrontation with Goliath. (Rev: BL 3/15/96; SLJ 3/96) [222]

17264 Devon, Paddie. *The Grumpy Shepherd* (PS–2). Illus. 1995, Abingdon paper $7.00 (0-687-00129-3). 32pp. A grumpy shepherd named Joram changes his attitude when he meets Jesus. (Rev: BL 12/1/95)

17265 Douglas, Kirk. *Kirk Douglas's Young Heroes of the Bible* (2–4). Illus. 1999, Simon & Schuster $15.00 (0-689-81491-7). 134pp. Old Testament stories about young Abraham, Rebecca, Miriam, Joseph, and David are retold in colloquial English. (Rev: BL 10/1/99; HBG 3/00; SLJ 1/00) [221.9]

17266 Downey, Lynn. *This Is the Earth That God Made* (PS–1). Illus. by Benrei Huang. 2000, Augsburg $8.99 (0-8066-3960-1). In this good-natured look at the Creation, images such as mountains, fountains, seas, winds, animals, and bees gradually appear, ending with a human family giving thanks. (Rev: SLJ 9/00) [224]

17267 Figley, Marty R. *Noah's Wife* (K–3). Illus. by Anita Riggio. 1998, Eerdmans $15.00 (0-8028-5107-X); paper $7.50 (0-8028-5133-9). 32pp. The Bible story of the creation of the ark is retold from the standpoint of Noah's faithful, understanding wife. (Rev: BCCB 5/98; BL 4/1/98; HBG 10/98) [222]

17268 Fisher, Leonard Everett. *David and Goliath* (K–3). Illus. 1993, Holiday LB $15.95 (0-8234-0997-X). 32pp. An expertly illustrated retelling of the Bible story of the brave lad who saved the land of the Israelites. (Rev: BL 5/1/93*; SLJ 6/93) [222]

17269 Fisher, Leonard Everett. *Moses* (PS–4). Illus. 1995, Holiday LB $15.95 (0-8234-1149-4). 32pp. The life of Moses and the salvation of the Jewish people are portrayed in double-page spreads. (Rev: BCCB 5/95; BL 5/15/95; SLJ 5/95) [222]

17270 Gauch, Patricia L. *Noah* (K–3). Illus. by Jonathan Green. 1994, Putnam $14.95 (0-399-22548-X). 32pp. This is a straightforward retelling of the Noah story showing his courage and leadership. (Rev: BCCB 6/94; BL 3/1/94; HB 7–8/94; SLJ 4/94) [222]

17271 Geisert, Arthur. *After the Flood* (PS–3). Illus. 1994, Houghton $16.95 (0-395-66611-2). 32pp. Shows what happens after the flood when the ship is overturned to serve as a shelter and the business of repopulating the earth begins. (Rev: BCCB 2/94; BL 3/1/94; HB 7–8/94; SLJ 4/94) [222]

17272 Gellman, Marc. *Does God Have a Big Toe? Stories About Stories in the Bible* (4–6). Illus. by Oscar de Mejo. 1989, HarperCollins $16.00 (0-060-22432-0); paper $7.95 (0-064-40453-6). 96pp. A look at familiar tales in the Bible through new eyes. (Rev: BL 10/15/89; HB 3–4/90; SLJ 12/89) [221]

17273 Gellman, Marc. *God's Mailbox: More Stories About Stories in the Bible* (4–7). Illus. by Debbie Tilley. 1996, Morrow $15.00 (0-688-13169-7). 92pp. Some stories retold from the Bible, including the Creation, Garden of Eden, Jacob's ladder, the Exodus, and Moses receiving the Ten Commandments. (Rev: BCCB 5/96; SLJ 3/96) [222]

17274 Gerstein, Mordicai. *Jonah and the Two Great Fish* (PS–3). Illus. 1997, Simon & Schuster $16.00

(0-689-81373-2). 32pp. The story of Jonah, who is swallowed by a fish, is expanded through the use of Jewish legends. (Rev: BL 10/1/97; HBG 3/98; SLJ 8/97*) [224]

17275 Gerstein, Mordicai. *Noah and the Great Flood* (K–4). Illus. 1999, Simon & Schuster $16.00 (0-689-81371-6). 32pp. The inspiring biblical story — enriched with some Jewish legends — of Noah and his family and their voyage in the ark. (Rev: BCCB 2/99; BL 1/1–15/99; HB 3–4/99; HBG 10/99; SLJ 4/99) [222]

17276 Goldin, Barbara D. *Journeys with Elijah: Eight Tales of the Prophet* (4–7). Illus. by Jerry Pinkney. 1999, Harcourt $20.00 (0-15-200445-9). 96pp. Eight tales depict the prophet Elijah in his many roles as teacher, miracle worker, and mysterious stranger. (Rev: BCCB 4/99; BL 4/15/99; HB 3–4/99; HBG 10/99; SLJ 6/99) [222]

17277 Goodhart, Pippa. *Noah Makes a Boat* (PS–2). Illus. by Bernard Lodge. 1997, Houghton $15.00 (0-395-86957-9). 32pp. A picture book that humanizes the story of Noah building the ark and of the flood that covered the earth. (Rev: BL 10/1/97; HB 9–10/97; HBG 3/98; SLJ 9/97) [222]

17278 Graham, Lorenz. *How God Fix Jonah* (3–5). Illus. 2000, Boyds Mills $17.95 (1-56397-698-6). 156pp. This collection of biblical-story poems contains tales from both the Testaments told from a West African native's viewpoint. (Rev: BL 10/1/00; SLJ 12/00) [220.9]

17279 Greenberg, Blu, and Linda Tarry. *King Solomon and the Queen of Sheba* (2–5). Illus. by Avi Katz. 1997, Pitspopany $16.95 (0-943706-90-4). 48pp. The biblically based story of the Ethiopian queen, her love for the wise, Jewish king, Solomon, and their child. (Rev: SLJ 5/98)

17280 Greenfield, Karen R. *Sister Yessa's Story* (2–5). Illus. by Claire Ewart. 1992, HarperCollins $15.00 (0-06-020278-5). As she walks through the woods, Yessa gathers animals for her brother's ark. (Rev: SLJ 8/92)

17281 Grindley, Sally, and Jan Barger. *Bible Stories for the Young* (PS–2). Illus. 1998, Little Tiger $16.95 (1-888444-42-8). 96pp. Twenty well-known stories from the Old and New Testaments are presented in language and pictures suitable for a young audience. (Rev: BCCB 2/99; BL 10/1/98; HBG 10/99; SLJ 10/98) [220.9]

17282 Hastings, Selina. *The Children's Illustrated Bible* (4–7). Illus. 1994, DK $22.95 (1-56458-472-0). 320pp. Several stories from both testaments of the Bible are retold, with some background material on history and geographical settings. (Rev: BL 6/1–15/94) [220.9]

17283 Hayward, Linda. *Baby Moses* (K–1). Illus. by Barb Henry. 1989, Random paper $3.99 (0-394-89410-3). 32pp. For beginning readers, the story of how Moses was saved in a basket of bulrushes. (Rev: BL 6/1/89; SLJ 12/89) [222]

17284 Hickman, Martha W. *And God Created Squash: How the World Began* (PS–3). Illus. by Giuliano Ferri. 1993, Whitman LB $15.95 (0-8075-

0340-1). 32pp. This is a fanciful retelling of the Creation story. (Rev: BL 3/15/93; SLJ 5/93)

17285 Hoffman, Mary, reteller. *A First Bible Story Book* (K–2). Illus. by Julie Downing. 1998, DK $12.95 (0-7894-1555-0). 80pp. A basic Bible storybook that contains easy-to-read narratives from both the Old and New Testaments. (Rev: HBG 10/99; SLJ 2/99) [221.9]

17286 Hoffman, Mary. *Parables: Stories Jesus Told* (PS–3). Illus. by Jackie Morris. 2000, Penguin $16.99 (0-8037-2560-4). 32pp. A distinguished retelling of seven of the parables of Jesus, with thoughtful introductions and interpretations. (Rev: BL 10/1/00*; HBG 3/01; SLJ 11/00) [226.8]

17287 Hutton, Warwick, adapt. *Moses in the Bulrushes* (PS–1). Illus. by Warwick Hutton. 1992, Simon & Schuster paper $4.95 (0-689-71553-6). 32pp. The story of the infant Moses, doomed to death by the pharaoh and saved by the pharaoh's daughter. (Rev: BL 7/86; HB 5–6/86; SLJ 5/86)

17288 Janisch, Heinz. *Noah's Ark* (PS–3). Trans. by Rosemary Lanning. Illus. by Lisbeth Zwerger. 1997, North-South LB $16.95 (1-55858-785-3). 28pp. The story of Noah and the ark is embellished with such details as animals carrying umbrellas and the unicorn being left out in the rain. (Rev: BL 10/1/97; HB 3–4/98; HBG 3/98; SLJ 11/97)

17289 *Jesus of Nazareth: A Life of Christ Through Pictures* (5–7). Illus. 1994, Simon & Schuster $16.00 (0-671-88651-7). 37pp. The life of Jesus Christ, with words from the King James Bible and illustrations from Washington's National Gallery. (Rev: BL 1/1/95; SLJ 3/95) [232]

17290 Johnson, James W. *The Creation* (K–4). Illus. by James E. Ransome. 1994, Holiday LB $16.95 (0-8234-1069-2). 32pp. The story of the first seven days of the world is told in the paintings and a poem by a famous African American writer. (Rev: BL 4/15/94; HB 9–10/94; SLJ 5/94*) [811]

17291 Jonas, Ann. *Aardvarks, Disembark!* (PS). Illus. 1990, Greenwillow $15.93 (0-688-07207-0). 40pp. Happy rhymes and songs with appealing design. (Rev: BCCB 11/90; BL 11/15/90; HB 11–12/90*; SLJ 10/90*) [222]

17292 Kassirer, Sue. *Joseph and His Coat of Many Colors* (1–2). Illus. by Danuta Jarecka. 1997, Simon & Schuster paper $15.00 (0-689-81227-2). 32pp. An easily read version of the Bible story of Joseph and his brothers. (Rev: BL 8/97; HBG 3/98; SLJ 10/97) [222]

17293 Kessler, Brad. *Moses in Egypt* (1–3). Illus. by Phil Huling. 1997, Simon & Schuster paper $22.00 (0-689-80226-9). This picture book traces Moses from his birth and upbringing as an Egyptian prince to the flight from Egypt with his people. (Rev: SLJ 12/97) [222]

17294 Kimmel, Eric A. *Be Not Far from Me: The Oldest Love Story: Legends from the Bible* (4–8). Illus. by David Diaz. 1998, Simon & Schuster $25.00 (0-689-81088-1). 256pp. Beginning with Abraham and ending with Daniel, this book tells about various heroes and heroines from the Bible, using both biblical texts and Jewish folklore. Illustrated by Caldecott winner David Diaz. (Rev: BCCB 5/98; BL 4/1/98; SLJ 6/98) [221.9]

17295 Langstaff, John, ed. *Climbing Jacob's Ladder: Heroes of the Bible in African-American Spirituals* (K–6). Illus. by Ashley Bryan. 1991, Macmillan $14.95 (0-689-50494-2). Nine heroes from the Bible, including Noah, are introduced through spirituals. (Rev: BL 1/15/92; HB 1–2/92; SLJ 1/92) [222]

17296 Lester, Julius. *When the Beginning Began: Stories About God, the Creatures, and Us* (4–9). 1999, Harcourt $17.00 (0-15-201138-9). Using parts of Genesis and creation stories from Jewish legends, this wondrous retelling adds thought-provoking human interest to the stories that end with Adam and Eve. (Rev: BL 4/15/99*; SLJ 5/99) [296.1]

17297 Le Tord, Bijou. *God's Little Seeds: A Book of Parables* (PS–1). Illus. 1998, Eerdmans $15.00 (0-8028-5169-X). 32pp. This book contains a retelling of Jesus' parables nicely illustrated with gentle, happy, framed paintings. (Rev: BL 9/1/98; HBG 10/98; SLJ 7/98) [232.9]

17298 Le Tord, Bijou. *Noah's Tree* (PS–2). Illus. 1999, HarperCollins LB $15.89 (0-06-028527-3). 40pp. Noah is hoping to pass on his lovely forest to his sons but God instructs him to cut down the trees and make an ark. (Rev: BL 10/15/99; HBG 3/00; SLJ 12/99)

17299 Le Tord, Bijou, ed. *Sing a New Song: A Book of Psalms* (PS–3). Illus. 1997, Eerdmans $15.00 (0-8028-5139-8). 32pp. Verses taken from the Psalms, with matching illustrations, reveal the wonders of nature. (Rev: BL 12/15/96; SLJ 3/97) [223]

17300 Lucado, Max. *Small Gifts in God's Hands* (K–3). Illus. by Cheri Bladholm. 2000, Nelson/Tommy Nelson $14.99 (0-8499-5842-3). 32pp. A poor boy offers Jesus his humble bread and fishes, and from these He feeds the multitude. (Rev: BL 2/1/01) [224]

17301 McCaughrean, Geraldine. *God's Kingdom* (4–7). Illus. 2000, Simon & Schuster $20.00 (0-689-82488-2). 128pp. This is a fine retelling of the major stories in the New Testament, including some of the parables of Jesus. (Rev: BL 1/1–15/00; HBG 10/00; SLJ 4/00) [226]

17302 McCaughrean, Geraldine. *God's People: Stories from the Old Testament* (4–7). Illus. 1997, Simon & Schuster $19.95 (0-689-81366-X). 128pp. A brilliant retelling of the major stories found in the Old Testament. (Rev: BL 3/1/98*; HBG 3/98; SLJ 3/98) [221.9]

17303 Mark, Jan. *The Tale of Tobias* (K–3). Illus. by Rachel Merriman. 1996, Candlewick $15.99 (1-56402-692-2). A story from the Apocrypha about Tobias and how he sets out on a journey with his dog to get help for his blind father. (Rev: BCCB 12/96; SLJ 10/96) [222]

17304 Martin, Bill, Jr., and Michael Sampson. *Adam, Adam, What Do You See?* (PS–K). Illus. by Cathie Felstead. 2000, Tommy Nelson $14.99 (0-8499-7614-6). This book introduces a number of biblical characters including Jesus with queries about what each one sees. (Rev: SLJ 12/00) [224]

17305 Matthews, Caitlin. *The Blessing Seed: A Creation Myth for the New Millennium* (1–5). Illus. by Alison Dexter. 1998, Barefoot $14.95 (1-901223-28-0). 32pp. An enthralling new version of the world's beginnings, using the Judeo-Christian creation story as a basis, supplemented with mystical interpretations. (Rev: BL 10/15/98; SLJ 9/98) [291.2]

17306 Mayer, Marianna. *The Twelve Apostles: Their Lives and Acts* (5–8). Illus. 2000, Penguin $16.99 (0-8037-2533-7). 32pp. Using a variety of sources, the author introduces each of the 12 apostles, with text and reproductions of classical art. (Rev: BCCB 9/00; BL 10/1/00; HBG 3/01; SLJ 10/00) [270.1]

17307 Mayer, Marianna. *Young Jesus of Nazareth* (2–4). Illus. 1999, Morrow LB $15.93 (0-688-16728-4). 32pp. From the Nativity to the Sermon on the Mount, this is a retelling of stories about the youthful Jesus. (Rev: BCCB 11/99; BL 10/1/99; HBG 3/00; SLJ 12/99) [232.92]

17308 Mayer, Marianna. *Young Mary of Nazareth* (3–5). Illus. 1998, Morrow LB $15.93 (0-688-14062-9). 40pp. Drawing from the writings of saints, other sacred scripts, and her own imagination, the author has re-created the early life of Mary, mother of Jesus. (Rev: BL 10/1/98; HBG 3/99; SLJ 9/98) [232.91]

17309 Metaxas, Eric, reteller. *David and Goliath* (2–5). Illus. by Douglas Fraser. 1996, Simon & Schuster paper $10.95 (0-689-80604-3). A dramatic retelling of the exciting Bible story that begins with Saul being made king of the Israelites. (Rev: SLJ 1/97) [222]

17310 Monte, Richard. *The Flood Tales* (3–6). Illus. 2000, Pavilion $22.95 (1-86205-211-5). 96pp. A lively retelling of the flood story, with humor and contemporary references to topics such as global warming and pollution. (Rev: BL 10/1/00) [222.11]

17311 Nerlove, Miriam. *The Ten Commandments: For Jewish Children* (PS–1). Illus. 1999, Whitman $14.95 (0-8075-7770-7). 32pp. In a series of double-page spreads, each of the Ten Commandments is presented and explained. (Rev: BL 10/1/99; HBG 3/00; SLJ 12/99) [296.3]

17312 Oberman, Sheldon. *The Wisdom Bird: A Tale of Solomon and Sheba* (K–4). Illus. by Neil Waldman. 2000, Boyds Mills $15.95 (1-56397-816-4). 32pp. Drawing on many sources, including the Bible, African folklore, and Jewish tales, this is the story of Sheba's request that Solomon build her a palace out of bird's beaks. (Rev: BCCB 10/00; BL 10/1/00; HBG 3/01; SLJ 10/00)

17313 Osborne, Mary Pope. *The Life of Jesus in Masterpieces of Art* (4–7). Illus. 1998, Viking $17.99 (0-670-87313-6). 48pp. A clear, beautiful narrative links reproductions depicting the life of Christ by Renaissance painters including Botticelli and Hieronymus Bosch. (Rev: BL 10/1/98*; HBG 10/99; SLJ 1/99) [704.9]

17314 Paterson, John, and Katherine Paterson. *Images of God* (5–8). Illus. by Alexander Koshkin. 1998, Clarion $20.00 (0-395-70734-X). 79pp. Using biblical texts, parables, and Bible stories, the authors demonstrate the various descriptions and roles attributed to God. (Rev: BL 5/1/98; HBG 10/98; SLJ 4/98) [231]

17315 Paterson, Katherine. *The Angel and the Donkey* (1–4). Illus. by Alexander Koshkin. 1996, Clarion $15.95 (0-395-68969-4). 34pp. Based on passages in the Hebrew Bible, this is the story of Pethor, a soothsayer, and his encounter with Moses. (Rev: BCCB 4/96; BL 3/1/96; SLJ 3/96) [222]

17316 *Psalm Twenty-Three* (PS–3). Illus. by Tim Ladwig. 1997, Eerdmans $16.00 (0-8028-5160-6); paper $8.00 (0-8028-5163-0). 32pp. This version of the famous psalm pictures two African American children growing up in a bleak, urban neighborhood. (Rev: BL 10/1/97; HBG 3/98) [123.2]

17317 Ross, Lillian H. *Daughters of Eve: Strong Women of the Bible* (5–7). Illus. 2000, Barefoot $19.99 (1-902283-82-1). 96pp. Fictionalized accounts that expand on the material given in the Bible and Apocrypha about 12 strong women and their deeds. (Rev: BL 10/1/00; SLJ 11/00) [220.9]

17318 Sanderson, Ruth. *Tapestries: Stories of Women in the Bible* (3–5). Illus. 1998, Little, Brown $15.95 (0-316-77093-0). 32pp. Many of the most famous women of the Old and New Testaments are profiled in brief biographies. (Rev: BL 10/1/98; HBG 3/99; SLJ 9/98) [220.9]

17319 Santore, Charles. *A Stowaway on Noah's Ark* (K–3). Illus. 2000, Random LB $17.99 (0-679-98820-3). 34pp. Little Achbar, a mouse, was not one of the two chosen by Noah, so he decides to becomes a stowaway. (Rev: BL 10/1/00; HBG 3/01; SLJ 10/00)

17320 Sasso, Sandy Eisenberg. *But God Remembered: Stories of Women from Creation to the Promised Land* (3–6). Illus. by Bethanne Andersen. 1995, Jewish Lights $16.95 (1-879045-43-5). 32pp. In this picture book, the stories of several almost-forgotten women in the Old Testament are retold. (Rev: BL 9/1/95*; SLJ 12/95) [221.9]

17321 Schmidt, Gary D. *The Blessing of the Lord: Stories from the Old and New Testaments* (3–7). Illus. 1997, Eerdmans $20.00 (0-8028-3789-1). 160pp. Realistic details add authenticity to this enjoyable retelling of stories from both the Old and New Testaments. (Rev: BL 11/1/97; HBG 3/98; SLJ 10/97) [220.9]

17322 Sobel, Ileene Smith. *Moses and the Angels* (4–6). Illus. 1999, Delacorte $16.95 (0-385-32612-2). 80pp. Many sources are used, including the Bible, to tell the story of Moses. (Rev: BCCB 2/99; BL 3/1/99; HBG 10/99; SLJ 7/99) [296.1]

17323 Spier, Peter, reteller. *Noah's Ark* (PS–K). Illus. by Peter Spier. 1977, Dell paper $7.99 (0-440-40693-5). 44pp. Vital, humorous, detailed pictures present a panorama of the animals and their voyage in the ark. Caldecott Medal winner, 1978.

17324 *Stories from the Old Testament: With Masterwork Paintings Inspired by the Stories* (4–6). Illus. 1996, Simon & Schuster $18.00 (0-689-80955-7). 45pp. Seventeen Old Testament stories with texts from the St. James Bible are illustrated with paintings by such old masters as Rubens and Rembrandt. (Rev: BL 10/1/96; SLJ 10/96) [221.5]

17325 Topek, Susan Remick. *Ten Good Rules* (PS–K). Illus. by Rosalyn Schanzer. 1992, Kar-Ben paper $5.95 (0-929371-28-3). In modern language, the Ten Commandments and their meanings are presented in an attractive concept book. (Rev: SLJ 7/92) [222]

17326 *The 23rd Psalm* (PS–1). Illus. by Michael Hague. 1999, Holt $14.95 (0-8050-3820-5). 24pp. The 23rd psalm is presented with a set of charming illustrations involving children and God as a shepherd. (Rev: BL 10/1/99; HBG 3/00; SLJ 9/99) [223]

17327 Wiesel, Elie. *King Solomon and His Magic Ring* (3–5). Illus. 1999, Greenwillow $16.00 (0-688-16959-7). An informal retelling of the stories surrounding wise King Solomon, using the Old Testament, the Talmud, and Midrash as sources. (Rev: BL 10/1/99; HBG 10/00; SLJ 9/99) [222]

17328 Wildsmith, Brian. *Exodus* (3–5). Illus. 1999, Eerdmans $20.00 (0-8028-5175-4). 36pp. A lushly illustrated and detailed life of Moses, from his beginnings in Egypt to his arrival in the promised land. (Rev: BL 2/15/99; HBG 10/99; SLJ 1/99) [222]

17329 Wildsmith, Brian. *Jesus* (PS–3). Illus. 2000, Eerdmans $20.00 (0-8028-5212-2). 32pp. Using quotes from the four gospels, the illustrator covers the important incidents in the life of Jesus beginning with the Nativity story and ending with Jesus' death and resurrection. (Rev: BCCB 1/01; BL 2/1/01) [224]

17330 Wildsmith, Brian. *Joseph* (K–4). Illus. 1997, Eerdmans $20.00 (0-8028-5161-4). 40pp. A handsome, well-told version of the biblical story of Joseph. (Rev: BL 2/1/98; HBG 3/98) [222]

17331 *Words of Gold: A Treasury of Bible Poetry and Wisdom* (4–6). Ed. by Lois Rock. Illus. 2000, Eerdmans $18.00 (0-8028-5199-1). 48pp. Using 22 double-page spreads, this book contains passages from the Old and New Testaments covering the story of the Jewish people from Abraham to Revelations. (Rev: BL 4/1/00; HBG 10/00; SLJ 9/00) [220.9]

17332 Ziefert, Harriet. *First He Made the Sun* (PS–1). Illus. by Todd McKie. 2000, Putnam $15.99 (0-399-23199-4). 32pp. A retelling of the biblical creation story in rhyme and simple illustrations. (Rev: BL 4/15/00; HBG 10/00; SLJ 5/00) [224]

Holidays and Holy Days

General and Miscellaneous

17333 Ancona, George. *Carnaval* (3–6). Illus. 1999, Harcourt $18.00 (0-15-201793-3); paper $9.00 (0-15-201792-5). 48pp. A photo-essay describing the celebration of the pre-Lenten "carnaval" in the northeastern Brazilian town of Olinda. (Rev: BL 11/15/99; HBG 3/00; SLJ 2/00) [394.26]

17334 Ancona, George. *Fiesta U.S.A.* (3–6). Illus. 1995, Dutton $16.99 (0-525-67498-5). 48pp. Various Latin American festivals — like Three Kings'

Day and the Day of the Dead — are pictured as they are celebrated in various parts of the United States. (Rev: BL 10/1/95; HB 11–12/95; SLJ 9/95) [394.2]

17335 Ansary, Mir T. *Columbus Day* (K–2). Series: Holiday Histories. 1998, Heinemann LB $13.95 (1-57572-702-1). 32pp. Though somewhat oversimplified, this is a history of Columbus Day and the celebration of the discovery of America. (Rev: SLJ 2/99) [394]

17336 Ansary, Mir T. *Labor Day* (2–3). Illus. Series: Holiday Histories. 1998, Heinemann LB $13.95 (1-57572-703-X). 32pp. This holiday book explains how workers banded together to fight poor working conditions and how, in time, this national holiday was born. (Rev: BL 1/1–15/99; SLJ 2/99) [394.264]

17337 Ansary, Mir T. *Martin Luther King Jr. Day* (2–3). Series: Holiday Histories. 1998, Heinemann LB $13.95 (1-57572-873-7). 32pp. This easy reader examines the history of Martin Luther King Day, tells how it is celebrated, and why it is important. (Rev: BL 12/15/98) [394.2]

17338 Ansary, Mir T. *Memorial Day* (2–3). Series: Holiday Histories. 1998, Heinemann LB $13.95 (1-57572-874-5). 32pp. Gives the history of Memorial Day, explaining how and why we celebrate it. (Rev: BL 12/15/98) [394.2]

17339 Ansary, Mir T. *Veterans Day* (2–3). Illus. Series: Holiday Histories. 1998, Heinemann LB $13.95 (1-57572-876-1). 32pp. A discussion of Veterans Day — its origins, history, and its growing importance after World Wars I and II. (Rev: BL 1/1–15/99) [394.264]

17340 Barrett, Anna Pearl. *Juneteenth: Celebrating Freedom in Texas* (3–6). Illus. by Gary Laronde. 1999, Eakin $12.95 (1-57168-180-9). 80pp. This book tells how the author and her family celebrated in 1945 the 80th Juneteenth, the holiday that celebrates the emancipation of African Americans from slavery. (Rev: SLJ 8/99)

17341 Barth, Edna. *Shamrocks, Harps and Shillelaghs: The Story of St. Patrick's Day Symbols* (3–5). Illus. by Ursula Arndt. 1982, Houghton paper $5.95 (0-89919-038-3). 96pp. Customs and symbols associated with St. Patrick's Day, with the origin of each explained.

17342 Behrens, June. *Gung Hay Fat Choy: Happy New Year* (2–4). Illus. 1982, Children's paper $4.95 (0-516-48842-2). A description of the Chinese New Year and how it is celebrated.

17343 Bernhard, Emery. *Happy New Year!* (3–5). Illus. by Durga Bernhard. 1996, Dutton $15.99 (0-525-67532-9). 32pp. From ancient to modern times, celebrations and rituals connected with the New Year are presented. (Rev: BCCB 10/96; BL 9/1/96; SLJ 9/96) [394.2]

17344 Brady, April A. *Kwanzaa Karamu: Cooking and Crafts for a Kwanzaa Feast* (4–6). Illus. 1995, Carolrhoda LB $21.27 (0-87614-842-9); paper $6.95 (0-87614-633-7). 64pp. Following a general introduction to Kwanzaa, this book introduces crafts and gives 18 recipes for appropriate food. (Rev: BL 4/15/95) [641.59]

17345 Branch, Muriel M. *Juneteenth: Freedom Day* (5–8). Photos by Willis Branch. 1998, Cobblehill $15.99 (0-525-65222-1). 54pp. Describes the history and customs of the African American holiday Juneteenth. (Rev: HBG 10/98; SLJ 10/98) [394.2]

17346 Brown, Tricia. *Chinese New Year* (3–5). Illus. 1997, Holt paper $6.95 (0-8050-5544-4). 48pp. A description of this centuries-old spring holiday that families celebrate in different ways. (Rev: BL 12/1/87; SLJ 12/87)

17347 Campbell, Louisa. *A World of Holidays! Family Festivities All Over the World!* (3–5). Illus. by Michael Bryant. Series: Family Ties. 1993, Silver Moon LB $14.95 (1-881889-08-4). 60pp. Using a ficticious framework, five holidays from such places as Pakistan, Japan, and Namibia are introduced. (Rev: SLJ 2/94) [394.2]

17348 Chambers, Catherine. *Carnival* (4–6). Illus. Series: World of Holidays. 1998, Raintree Steck-Vaughn LB $22.11 (0-8172-4613-4). 32pp. Reveals the African influences that have shaped the pre-Lenten celebration of Carnival and provides suitable activities such as recipes and mask-making. (Rev: BL 5/1/98; HBG 10/98) [394.25]

17349 Chambers, Catherine. *Chinese New Year* (3–5). Illus. Series: World of Holidays. 1997, Raintree Steck-Vaughn LB $25.69 (0-8172-4605-3). 31pp. With many color photos and several craft ideas, this book supplies background information on this spring celebration of good fortune and success and the rituals that surround it. (Rev: BL 6/1–15/97) [394.261]

17350 Chandler, Clare. *Harvest Celebrations* (2–4). Illus. Series: Festivals. 1998, Millbrook LB $20.90 (0-7613-0964-0). 32pp. This book outlines the best-known and most popular harvest celebrations around the world. (Rev: BL 3/1/99; HBG 3/99; SLJ 4/99) [394.264]

17351 Cook, Deanna F. *FamilyFun's Parties: 100 Party Plans for Birthdays, Holidays, and Every Day* (3–8). 1999, Hyperion $24.95 (0-7868-6454-0). 223pp. This spiral-bound book gives thorough details on planning and holding different kinds of holiday-related parties. Fifty children's birthday parties are outlined. (Rev: SLJ 9/99) [394.2]

17352 Erlbach, Arlene. *Happy Birthday, Everywhere!* (3–5). Illus. 1997, Millbrook LB $23.90 (0-7613-0007-4). 48pp. With accompanying food and craft projects, this book describes birthday celebrations around the world. (Rev: BL 12/1/97; HBG 3/98; SLJ 2/98) [394.2]

17353 Erlbach, Arlene. *Happy New Year, Everywhere!* (K–3). Illus. by Sharon L. Holm. 2000, Millbrook LB $23.90 (0-7613-1707-4). 48pp. Lavish double-page spreads introduce New Year celebrations in 20 countries, including Belgium, Haiti, Iran, and Israel. (Rev: BL 11/1/00; HBG 3/01; SLJ 12/00) [394.261]

17354 Fradin, Dennis B. *Columbus Day* (2–4). Illus. Series: Best Holiday Books. 1990, Enslow LB $18.95 (0-89490-233-4). 48pp. Highlights of the explorer's life and his four voyages. (Rev: BL 5/1/90) [970.01]

17355 Freeman, Dorothy R. *St. Patrick's Day* (3–5). Illus. Series: Best Holiday Books. 1992, Enslow LB $18.95 (0-89490-383-7). 48pp. This easily read account describes the origins of St. Patrick's Day and how it is celebrated. (Rev: BL 10/1/92) [394.2]

17356 Freeman, Dorothy R., and Dianne M. Mac-Millan. *Kwanzaa* (3–5). Illus. Series: Best Holiday Books. 1992, Enslow LB $18.95 (0-89490-381-0). 48pp. A full treatment of this African American holiday. (Rev: BL 10/1/92) [394.2]

17357 Ganeri, Anita. *Journey's End: Death and Mourning* (4–6). Illus. 1999, Bedrick LB $15.95 (0-87226-289-8). 32pp. This book looks at death rituals in six major religions: Hinduism, Buddhism, Sikhism, Islam, Judaism, and Christianity. (Rev: BL 5/15/99; HBG 10/99; SLJ 3/99) [291.3]

17358 Ganeri, Anita. *New Beginnings: Celebrating Birth* (4–6). Series: Life Times. 1999, Bedrick LB $15.95 (0-87226-286-3). 32pp. Rites and rituals associated with birth and early childhood are outlined in six religions: Buddhism, Christianity, Hinduism, Judaism, Islam, and Sikhism. (Rev: BL 5/15/99; HBG 10/99; SLJ 3/99) [291]

17359 Ganeri, Anita. *Wedding Days: Celebrations of Marriage* (4–6). Illus. 1999, Bedrick LB $15.95 (0-87226-288-X). 32pp. Covers marriage and marriage customs in six religions: Hinduism, Buddhism, Sikhism, Islam, Judaism, and Christianity. (Rev: BL 5/15/99; SLJ 3/99) [291.3]

17360 Gardner, Robert. *Celebrating Earth Day: A Sourcebook of Activities and Experiments* (5–8). Illus. 1992, Millbrook LB $22.40 (1-56294-070-8). 96pp. A discussion, with experiments, of such global problems as conservation and overpopulation. (Rev: BL 12/1/92) [333.7]

17361 Gelber, Carol. *Love and Marriage Around the World* (5–7). 1998, Millbrook LB $21.40 (0-7613-0102-X). 72pp. From courtship to the wedding, this book introduces marriage customs from around the world and among different ethnic groups. (Rev: BCCB 7–8/98; HBG 10/98; SLJ 6/98) [392]

17362 Gibbons, Gail. *St. Patrick's Day* (2–4). Illus. 1994, Holiday LB $16.95 (0-8234-1119-2). 32pp. As well as telling the story of St. Patrick's life, this simple account describes how we celebrate his day and the symbols connected with it. (Rev: BCCB 2/94; BL 2/1/94; SLJ 4/94) [394.2]

17363 Giblin, James Cross. *Fireworks, Picnics, and Flags: The Story of Fourth of July Symbols* (3–6). Illus. by Ursula Arndt. 1983, Houghton paper $8.95 (0-89919-174-6). 96pp. A history of the Fourth of July holiday and how it was and is celebrated. (Rev: BCCB 7–8/92; BL 7/92; SLJ 3/92) [394]

17364 Graham-Barber, Lynda. *Doodle Dandy! The Complete Book of Independence Day Words* (4–7). Illus. by Betsy Lewin. 1992, Macmillan LB $13.95 (0-02-736675-8). 128pp. Thirty-four words and phrases that reflect our history and government and explain how they came to be. (Rev: BCCB 7–8/92; BL 7/92; SLJ 3/92) [394]

17365 Grier, Ella. *Seven Days of Kwanzaa: A Holiday Step Book* (PS–2). Illus. by John Ward. 1997, Viking paper $10.99 (0-670-87327-6). Double-page spreads are used for each of the seven days of Kwanzaa in this book about the rituals and symbols connected with this harvest festival. (Rev: HBG 3/98; SLJ 10/97) [394.26]

17366 Harris, Zoe, and Suzanne Williams. *Pinatas and Smiling Skeletons* (4–8). Illus. by Yolanda Garfias Woo. 1998, Pacific View $19.95 (1-881896-19-6). 48pp. This book introduces six festivals celebrated in Mexico: the Feast of the Virgin of Guadalupe, Christmas, Carnaval, Corpus Christi, Independence Day, and the Day of the Dead. (Rev: BL 3/15/99; HBG 3/99; SLJ 3/99) [394.26972]

17367 Hoyt-Goldsmith, Diane. *Celebrating Chinese New Year* (3–5). Illus. 1998, Holiday $16.95 (0-8234-1393-4). 32pp. A richly illustrated book that traces the activities of a Chinese American family in San Francisco as they prepare for and participate in Chinese New Year. (Rev: BL 12/1/98; HBG 3/99; SLJ 2/99) [394.261]

17368 Hoyt-Goldsmith, Diane. *Celebrating Kwanzaa* (4–6). Illus. by Lawrence Migdale. 1993, Holiday LB $16.95 (0-8234-1048-X). 32pp. A photo-essay about a Chicago family's celebration of Kwanzaa that explains the origins and meanings of the Seven Principles. (Rev: BCCB 11/93; BL 10/1/93*) [394.2]

17369 Hoyt-Goldsmith, Diane. *Mardi Gras: A Cajun Country Celebration* (4–6). Illus. 1995, Holiday LB $15.95 (0-8234-1184-2). 32pp. A story of the rituals of Mardi Gras plus a history of the Cajun people and even a recipe for gumbo. (Rev: BL 10/1/95; SLJ 11/95) [394.2]

17370 Jackson, Ellen. *The Autumn Equinox: Celebrating the Harvest* (2–5). Illus. by Jan Davey Ellis. 2000, Millbrook LB $22.90 (0-7613-1354-0). Harvest festivals, past and present, from around the world are described with attractive craft projects, games, and recipes. (Rev: HBG 3/01; SLJ 11/00) [394.3]

17371 Jackson, Ellen. *Here Come the Brides* (3–5). Illus. by Carol Heyer. 1998, Walker LB $16.85 (0-8027-8469-0). 32pp. Brides, wedding customs, symbols, and attire are a few of the topics covered in this overview of wedding practices in different cultures. (Rev: BL 5/1/98; HBG 10/98; SLJ 4/98) [392.5]

17372 Johnson, Dolores. *The Children's Book of Kwanzaa: A Guide to Celebrating the Holiday* (4–7). Illus. 1996, Simon & Schuster $16.00 (0-689-80864-X). 159pp. This account discusses African American history and the origins of Kwanzaa, its meaning, and its rituals. (Rev: BCCB 11/96; BL 9/1/96) [394.2]

17373 Jones, Amy Robin. *Kwanzaa* (4–6). Series: Journey to Freedom. 2000, Child's World LB $25.64 (1-56766-719-8). 40pp. Sepia-toned pictures and a lively text present the origins, festivities, and customs of Kwanzaa. (Rev: BL 11/15/00) [394.2]

17374 Jones, Lynda. *Kids Around the World Celebrate! The Best Feasts and Festivals from Many Lands* (3–6). Illus. by Michelle Nidenoff. Series: Kids Around the World. 1999, Wiley paper $12.95 (0-471-34527-X). 124pp. Each chapter covers the customs of different cultures organized by themes, like giving thanks and celebrating New Year; for each there are a number of hands-on activities. (Rev: SLJ 2/00) [394.3]

17375 Kadodwala, Dilip. *Divali* (4–6). Illus. Series: World of Holidays. 1998, Raintree Steck-Vaughn LB $22.11 (0-8172-4616-9). 32pp. Discusses the origins, methods of celebrating, and the many gods and goddesses involved in the Hindu holiday of Diwali. (Rev: BL 5/1/98; HBG 10/98) [294.5]

17376 Kadodwala, Dilip. *Holi* (3–5). Illus. Series: World of Holidays. 1997, Raintree Steck-Vaughn LB $25.69 (0-8172-4610-X). 31pp. A description of this joyous Hindu spring festival and how it is observed. (Rev: BL 6/1–15/97) [294.5]

17377 Kerven, Rosalind. *Id-ul-Fitr* (3–5). Illus. Series: World of Holidays. 1997, Raintree Steck-Vaughn LB $25.69 (0-8172-4609-6). 31pp. After giving a brief introduction to Islam, describes the celebration that marks the end of the sacred month of Ramadan. (Rev: BL 6/1–15/97) [297]

17378 Kindersley, Barnabas, and Anabel Kindersley. *Celebrations!* (2–6). Illus. Series: Children Just Like Me. 1997, DK $17.95 (0-7894-2027-9). 63pp. Using double-page spreads, a number of holidays from around the world are featured, such as Christmas in Germany and Diwali in India. (Rev: HBG 3/98; SLJ 1/98) [394.2]

17379 King, Elizabeth. *Quinceanera: Celebrando los quince* (4–9). Trans. by Dolores M. Koch. Photos by author. 1998, Dutton $15.99 (0-525-45844-1). 40pp. Using dramatic photographs, this book in Spanish tells of the Hispanic American celebration of quinceanera, a coming-of-age fiesta for young girls. (Rev: HBG 3/99; SLJ 12/98) [394.2]

17380 King, Elizabeth. *Quinceanera: Celebrating Fifteen* (5–8). Illus. 1998, Dutton $15.99 (0-525-45638-4). 40pp. This photo-essay traces the everyday life of two beautiful young Latin American women about to turn 15, as they prepare for quinceanera, a coming-of-age ritual. (Rev: BCCB 10/98; BL 8/98; HBG 3/99; SLJ 12/98) [395.2]

17381 Krasno, Rena. *Floating Lanterns and Golden Shrines: Celebrating Japanese Festivals* (3–5). Illus. by Toru Sugita. 2000, Pacific View $19.95 (1-881896-21-8). 49pp. Important celebrations for both Japanese and Japanese Americans are covered in this attractive book. (Rev: HBG 10/00; SLJ 6/00) [394.2]

17382 Liestman, Vicki. *Columbus Day* (2–3). Illus. by Rick Hanson. Series: On My Own. 1991, Carolrhoda LB $21.27 (0-87614-444-X). 56pp. The history of this holiday, plus the life of the explorer, illustrated with colorful paintings. (Rev: BCCB 10/91; BL 9/1/91; SLJ 9/91) [970.01]

17383 Livingston, Myra Cohn. *Festivals* (K–3). Illus. by Leonard Everett Fisher. 1996, Holiday $16.95 (0-8234-1217-2). 32pp. Fourteen of the world's festivals, both common and obscure, are introduced in poetry and paintings. (Rev: BCCB 5/96; BL 5/1/96; SLJ 7/96) [811]

17384 Luenn, Nancy. *Celebrations of Light: A Year of Holidays around the World* (3–5). Illus. 1998,

Simon & Schuster $16.00 (0-689-31986-X). 32pp. Describes 12 festivals of light, including Christmas, Hanukkah, Buddha's Birthday, and the Swedish Luciadagen. (Rev: BL 9/15/98; HBG 3/99; SLJ 12/98) [394.2]

17385 MacMillan, Dianne M. *Diwali: Hindu Festival of Lights* (3–5). Illus. Series: Best Holiday. 1997, Enslow LB $18.95 (0-89490-817-0). 48pp. Introduces the Hindu festival Diwali and explains how it is celebrated. (Rev: BL 7/97; SLJ 8/97) [294.5]

17386 MacMillan, Dianne M. *Mardi Gras* (3–5). Series: Best Holiday. 1997, Enslow LB $18.95 (0-89490-819-7). 48pp. Gives a description and history of this holiday with religious roots, with details on how it is celebrated around the world, particularly in New Orleans. (Rev: BL 12/15/97; HBG 3/98; SLJ 8/97) [394.2]

17387 MacMillan, Dianne M. *Martin Luther King, Jr. Day* (3–5). Illus. Series: Best Holiday Books. 1992, Enslow LB $18.95 (0-89490-382-9). 48pp. This easy-to-read book describes how Martin Luther King, Jr. Day originated and how it is celebrated in schools and towns. (Rev: BL 10/1/92; SLJ 1/93) [323]

17388 MacMillan, Dianne M. *Presidents Day* (3–5). Illus. Series: Best Holiday. 1997, Enslow LB $18.95 (0-89490-820-0). 48pp. An introduction to the day on which Americans pay tribute to their presidents and a discussion of the ways in which it is celebrated. (Rev: BL 7/97) [973.4]

17389 Marchant, Kerena. *Id-Ul-Fitr* (3–5). Series: Festivals. 1998, Millbrook LB $20.90 (0-7613-0963-2). 32pp. An explanation of this Muslim festival is followed by colorful descriptions of how it is celebrated around the world. (Rev: HBG 3/99; SLJ 4/99) [297]

17390 Martinet, Jeanne, comp. *The Year You Were Born, 1986* (2–6). Illus. by Judy Lanfredi. Series: Day-By-Day Record Of. 1993, Tambourine paper $7.95 (0-688-11968-9). This book, like the others in the series, gives facts and assorted trivia for each day of the featured year. (Rev: SLJ 2/94) [793.21]

17391 Merrick, Patrick. *Fourth of July Fireworks* (2–3). Series: Holiday Symbols. 1999, Child's World LB $15.95 (1-56766-640-X). 32pp. After explaining Fourth of July celebrations, this book gives a history of fireworks, plus material on how they are made and used. (Rev: HBG 3/00; SLJ 1/00) [394.2]

17392 Most, Bernard. *Happy Holidaysaurus!* (K–3). Illus. 1992, Harcourt $13.95 (0-15-233386-X). 32pp. Contains a parade of dinosaurs that illustrate a year of holidays. (Rev: BL 3/15/92; SLJ 6/92) [394.2]

17393 Penner, Lucille R. *Celebration: The Story of American Holidays* (3–5). Illus. by Ib Ohlsson. 1993, Macmillan LB $15.95 (0-02-770903-5). 79pp. A discussion of the origins of and celebrations associated with 13 important American holidays, e.g., Columbus Day, Veterans Day, Martin Luther King Day, Halloween, and New Year's Day. (Rev: SLJ 11/93) [394.2]

17394 Perl, Lila. *Pinatas and Paper Flowers: Holidays of the Americas in English and Spanish* (4–8). Illus. by Victoria de Larrea. 1985, Houghton paper $7.95 (0-89919-155-X). 91pp. Eight Hispanic holidays are highlighted in this bilingual volume.

17395 Porter, A. P. *Kwanzaa* (2–4). Illus. by Janice L. Porter. 1991, Carolrhoda LB $21.27 (0-87614-668-X). 56pp. African Americans celebrate their rich history and culture by observing Kwanzaa. (Rev: BCCB 12/91; BL 12/1/91) [394.2]

17396 Ross, Kathy. *The Best Birthday Parties Ever! A Kid's Do-It-Yourself Guide* (2–5). Illus. by Sharon L. Holm. 1999, Millbrook LB $23.90 (0-7613-1410-5). 78pp. This do-it-yourself guide to great birthday parties includes instructions on invitations, hats, decorations, cakes, favors, and games. (Rev: HBG 3/00; SLJ 11/99) [394.2]

17397 Schaefer, Lola M. *Chinese New Year* (PS–2). Series: Holidays and Celebrations. 2000, Capstone LB $13.25 (0-7368-0660-1). 24pp. A simple beginning reader that introduces the traditions and meaning behind the Chinese New Year. (Rev: HBG 3/01; SLJ 12/00) [394.2]

17398 Schaefer, Lola M. *Cinco de Mayo* (PS–2). Series: Holidays and Celebrations. 2000, Capstone LB $13.25 (0-7368-0661-X). 24pp. The traditions and customs surrounding the Mexican Independence Day are outlined in this simple book for beginning readers. (Rev: HBG 3/01; SLJ 12/00) [394.2]

17399 Scott, Geoffrey. *Labor Day* (1–4). Illus. by Cherie R. Wyman. 1982, Carolrhoda LB $17.50 (0-87614-178-5). 48pp. A simple book about the first Labor Day.

17400 Sita, Lisa. *Coming of Age* (2–5). Series: World Celebrations and Ceremonies. 1998, Blackbirch LB $15.95 (1-56711-276-5). 24pp. Presenting facts and maps about each country highlighted, this account describes the ceremonies associated with the rites of passage that lead to adulthood in ten countries on six continents. (Rev: HBG 3/99; SLJ 4/99) [612]

17401 Spirn, Michele. *Birth* (2–5). Series: World Celebrations and Ceremonies. 1998, Blackbirch LB $15.95 (1-56711-277-3). 24pp. Outlines the rituals and traditions surrounding the birth of a child in 15 countries in six continents. (Rev: HBG 3/99; SLJ 4/99) [392]

17402 Spirn, Michele. *New Year* (3–5). Series: World Celebrations and Ceremonies. 1998, Blackbirch LB $14.95 (1-56711-249-8). 24pp. Introduces New Year's celebrations in Brazil, China, England, India, Israel, Mexico, Nigeria, Puerto Rico, Russia, and the United States. (Rev: HBG 3/99; SLJ 1/99) [394]

17403 Thompson, Jan. *Christian Festivals* (3–6). Illus. Series: Celebrate! 1997, Heinemann $19.92 (0-431-06961-1). 48pp. Familiar Christian holidays like Christmas, Lent, Ascension Day, and Easter are explained through the experiences of three children. (Rev: BL 8/97; SLJ 12/97) [263]

17404 Viesti, Joe, and Diane Hall. *Celebrate! In South Asia* (2–5). Illus. 1996, Lothrop LB $15.93 (0-688-13775-X). 32pp. Nine holidays as celebrated on the Indian subcontinent are introduced. (Rev: BCCB 10/96; BL 9/1/96; SLJ 9/96) [394.2]

17405 Viesti, Joe, and Diane Hall. *Celebrate! In Southeast Asia* (2–5). Illus. 1996, Lothrop LB $15.93 (0-688-13489-0). 32pp. Such countries as Vietnam, Thailand, Malaysia, and the Philippines are represented in this explanation of nine celebrations. (Rev: BCCB 10/96; BL 9/1/96; SLJ 9/96) [394.2]

17406 Viesti, Joe, and Diane Hall. *Celebrate! In Central America* (3–5). Illus. Series: Celebrate! 1997, Lothrop LB $15.93 (0-688-15162-0). 32pp. Describes holidays that are celebrated in various Central American countries, from Guatemala to Panama. (Rev: BL 9/15/97; HBG 3/98; SLJ 8/97) [394]

17407 Wilcox, Jane. *Why Do We Celebrate That?* (4–6). Illus. Series: Why Do We? 1996, Watts LB $20.00 (0-531-14393-7). 31pp. This book looks at various cultures, their holidays and festivals, and how they observe birthdays, weddings, and funeral rites. (Rev: SLJ 8/97) [394.2]

17408 Wilson, Sule Greg C. *Kwanzaa! Africa Lives in a New World Festival* (4–7). Series: The Library of African American Arts and Culture. 1999, Rosen LB $17.95 (0-8239-1857-2). 64pp. This book begins with a history of slavery and the civil rights movement, then explains the origins and meaning of Kwanzaa. (Rev: SLJ 10/99) [641.59]

Christmas

17409 Bible. *The Nativity* (PS–3). Illus. by Julie Vivas. 1988, Harcourt $13.95 (0-15-200535-8). 34pp. A retelling using Bible verses and earthy, sometimes humorous illustrations. A reissue. (Rev: HB 11–12/88)

17410 Chambers, Catherine. *Christmas* (3–5). Illus. Series: World of Holidays. 1997, Raintree Steck-Vaughn LB $25.69 (0-8172-4608-8). 31pp. This book explains the origins of Christmas and how it is observed around the world, along with decorating ideas and some craft projects. (Rev: BL 6/1–15/97) [394.2]

17411 *Christmas in Colonial and Early America* (4–7). Illus. 1996, World Book $15.95 (0-7166-0875-8). 80pp. The evolution of Christmas celebrations is traced through more than 100 years of American history to the end of the 19th century. (Rev: BL 11/1/96) [394.26]

17412 *Christmas in Greece* (5–10). Illus. Series: Christmas Around the World. 2000, World Book $19.00 (0-7166-0859-6). 80pp. This account focuses on the religious practices of the Greek Orthodox Church at Christmastime, which begins with a long fasting period. (Rev: BL 9/1/00) [398.2]

17413 *Christmas in Switzerland* (4–6). Illus. 1995, World Book $18.50 (0-7166-0895-2). 80pp. This book introduces Swiss customs and traditional activities surrounding Christmas. (Rev: BL 9/15/95) [394.26]

17414 *Christmas Soul: African American Holiday Memories* (PS–4). Ed. by Allison Samuels. Illus. by Michele Wood. 2000, Hyperion $17.99 (0-7868-0521-8). 48pp. A number of African American celebrities, including Debbie Allen, Whitney Houston, and Aretha Franklin, recall family gatherings and gift exchanges. (Rev: BL 9/15/00) [394.2]

17415 *The First Christmas* (3–7). Illus. 1992, Simon & Schuster paper $17.00 (0-671-79364-0). 30pp. This Christmas story, in the words of Isaiah, St. Matthew, and St. Luke, is illustrated with the work of such artists as Botticelli and Fra Filippo Lippi. (Rev: BL 11/1/92) [226]

17416 Foreman, Michael. *Michael Foreman's Christmas Treasury* (3–6). 2000, Pavilion $22.95 (1-86205-197-6). 124pp. A delightful collection of songs, stories, poems, and carols. (Rev: BL 12/1/00) [394.26]

17417 French, Vivian. *The Story of Christmas* (PS–2). Illus. by Jane Chapman. 1999, Candlewick paper $3.99 (0-7636-0762-2). A joyful introduction to the Nativity story that begins with the angel Gabriel's appearance to Mary and ends with the visits of the shepherds and wise men. (Rev: SLJ 10/99) [224]

17418 Graham, Ruth B. *One Wintry Night* (4–6). Illus. by Richard J. Watson. 1995, Baker $12.97 (0-8010-3848-0). 72pp. A woman tells an injured mountain boy the story of the importance of Christmas after she rescues him from a snowstorm. (Rev: BL 9/1/95)

17419 Graham-Barber, Lynda. *Ho Ho Ho! The Complete Book of Christmas Words* (4–6). Illus. by Betsy Lewin. 1993, Bradbury $16.00 (0-02-736933-1). 128pp. A collection of words associated with Christmas, with their definitions and derivations. (Rev: BL 10/1/93) [394.2]

17420 Hickman, Martha W. *A Baby Born in Bethlehem* (K–5). Illus. by Giuliano Ferri. 1999, Albert Whitman $15.95 (0-8075-5522-3). 32pp. Simplified biblical verses tell the story of Jesus' birth and the visits by the shepherds and the magi. (Rev: BCCB 11/99; BL 9/1/99; HBG 3/00; SLJ 10/99) [232]

17421 Hoyt-Goldsmith, Diane. *Las Posadas: An Hispanic Christmas Celebration* (3–6). Illus. 1999, Holiday $16.95 (0-8234-1449-3). 32pp. Using a Hispanic American family as a focus, this book explains the nine-night celebration known as Las Posadas, which tells the story of Mary and Joseph's journey to Bethlehem and the birth of Jesus. (Rev: BL 10/1/99; HBG 3/00; SLJ 10/99) [394.266]

17422 Jeffers, H. Paul. *Legends of Santa Claus* (4–7). Series: A&E Biography. 2000, Lucent LB $25.26 (0-8225-4983-2). 112pp. This book recounts the tales, legends, and myths about Santa Claus and sorts the truth from the fiction. (Rev: BL 12/15/00; HBG 3/01) [394.2]

17423 Kelley, Emily. *Christmas Around the World* (2–4). Illus. 1986, Carolrhoda LB $21.27 (0-87614-249-8); Lerner paper $5.95 (0-87614-453-9). 48pp. Traditions and celebrations around the world in simple language. (Rev: BCCB 9/86; BL 7/86)

17424 Kennedy, Pamela. *A Christmas Celebration: Traditions and Customs from Around the World* (3–6). Illus. 1992, Ideals LB $12.00 (0-8249-8587-7). 32pp. The author presents international customs and those that are particular to certain cultures and emphasizes the whole season of Christmas rather than one day. (Rev: BL 11/1/92) [394.2]

17425 Kurelek, William. *A Northern Nativity: Christmas Dreams of a Prairie Boy* (1–3). Illus. by author. 1976, Tundra paper $9.95 (0-88776-099-6). Twenty paintings of the Holy Family transferred to various locales, accompanied by a lyrical text.

17426 Lankford, Mary D. *Christmas Around the World* (2–5). Illus. 1995, Morrow $15.93 (0-688-12167-5). 48pp. An examination of Christmas traditions in 12 countries. (Rev: BL 9/15/95) [394.2]

17427 Maccarone, Grace. *A Child Was Born: A First Nativity Book* (PS–K). Illus. by Sam Williams. 2000, Scholastic $10.95 (0-439-18296-4). 32pp. Expressive watercolors are the highlight of this retelling of the Nativity story in rhyming verse. (Rev: BCCB 10/00; BL 9/1/00; HBG 3/01) [232.92]

17428 Ouwendijk, George. *Santas of the World* (3–6). Series: Looking Into the Past: People, Places, and Customs. 1998, Chelsea LB $16.95 (0-7910-4678-8). 64pp. A overview of the Santa Claus legend is followed by an examination of Christmas gift-giving customs in 24 countries and regions. (Rev: HBG 10/98; SLJ 10/98) [394.26]

17429 Pingry, Patricia A. *Joseph's Story* (1–3). Illus. by George Hinke. 1998, Ideals $16.95 (0-8249-4092-X). The traditional stories surrounding the birth of Jesus are retold from the standpoint of Joseph, Mary's husband. (Rev: SLJ 10/98) [394.2]

17430 Rollins, Charlemae H., ed. *Christmas Gif': An Anthology of Christmas Poems, Songs, and Stories* (5–8). Illus. by Ashley Bryan. 1993, Morrow $14.00 (0-688-11667-1). 128pp. An anthology first published 30 years ago that contains songs and stories about Christmas and about African Americans from slavery days. (Rev: BL 7/93) [810.8]

17431 Roop, Peter, and Connie Roop. *Let's Celebrate Christmas* (3–5). Illus. 1997, Millbrook LB $19.90 (0-7613-0115-1); paper $5.95 (0-7613-0283-2). 32pp. As well as a history of the customs surrounding Christmas, this book contains crafts, puzzles, and riddles. (Rev: BL 9/1/97; HBG 3/98; SLJ 10/97) [394]

17432 *A Small Treasury of Christmas: Poems and Prayers* (1–3). Illus. by Susan Spellman. 1997, Boyds Mills $8.95 (1-56397-680-3). 32pp. A collection of 26 poems and prayers dealing with Christmas. (Rev: HBG 3/98; SLJ 10/97) [811]

Easter

17433 Barth, Edna. *Lilies, Rabbits and Painted Eggs: The Story of the Easter Symbols* (3–6). Illus. by Ursula Arndt. 1981, Houghton paper $6.95 (0-395-30550-0). The pagan and Christian origins of many of the celebrations associated with Easter.

17434 Chambers, Catherine. *Easter* (4–6). Series: A World of Holidays. 1998, Raintree Steck-Vaughn

LB $22.11 (0-8172-4615-0). 32pp. Tells the story of Easter and Christ's resurrection, and covers the secular aspects of this spring celebration, such as Easter eggs, bunnies, and baskets. (Rev: BL 6/1–15/98; HBG 10/98) [394.2]

17435 *The Easter Story: According to the Gospels of Matthew, Luke and John* (3–6). Illus. by Gennady Spirin. 1999, Holt $19.95 (0-8050-5052-3). 32pp. Using verses from the books of Matthew, Luke, and John in the King James version of the Bible, this account traces the events leading to Easter. (Rev: BL 3/15/99; HBG 10/99; SLJ 3/99) [232.9]

17436 Kennedy, Pamela. *An Easter Celebration: Traditions and Customs from Around the World* (4–6). Illus. 1991, Ideals $10.95 (0-8249-8506-0). 32pp. Color photos and historical drawings add to this handy volume on Easter celebrations. (Rev: BL 3/15/91) [394.2]

17437 Merrick, Patrick. *Easter Bunnies* (2–3). Series: Holiday Symbols. 1999, Child's World LB $15.95 (1-56766-639-6). 32pp. This account tells how rabbits became associated with Easter and also discusses several traditions connected to the holiday. (Rev: HBG 3/00; SLJ 1/00) [394.2]

17438 *Michael Hague's Family Easter Treasury* (3–5). Ed. by Michael Hague. Illus. 1999, Holt $19.95 (0-8050-3819-1). 134pp. Thirty-two poetry and prose selections explore the holiday of Easter and spring celebrations. (Rev: BL 3/15/99; HBG 10/99; SLJ 3/99) [808.8]

17439 Stalcup, Ann. *Ukrainian Egg Decoration: A Holiday Tradition* (3–5). Series: Crafts of the World. 1999, Rosen $19.33 (0-8239-5335-1). 24pp. This photo-essay covers the history and lore of the Ukrainian tradition of creating beautifully patterned eggs at Easter. Also features one craft project. (Rev: SLJ 4/99) [394.2]

17440 Thompson, Lauren. *Love One Another: The Story of Easter* (1–3). Illus. by Elizabeth Uyehara. 2000, Scholastic $15.95 (0-590-31830-6). 32pp. This story of the crucifixion of Jesus, from his arrival in Jerusalem to the Last Supper and the Resurrection, stresses the message of love and forgiveness. (Rev: BL 2/1/00; HBG 10/00; SLJ 3/00) [232.9]

17441 Winthrop, Elizabeth, adapt. *He Is Risen: The Easter Story* (4–7). Illus. by Charles Mikolaycak. 1985, Holiday LB $16.95 (0-8234-0547-8). 32pp. The Easter story taken from parts of the King James version of the Bible and dramatically illustrated. (Rev: BCCB 4/85; HB 7–8/85; SLJ 4/85)

Halloween

17442 Bull, Jane. *The Halloween Book: 50 Creepy Crafts for a Hair-Raising Halloween* (2–5). Photos by Andy Crawford. 2000, DK $12.95 (0-7894-6655-4). 48pp. This book includes crafts, costumes, food, and party ideas for Halloween in an attractive, well-illustrated format. (Rev: HBG 3/01; SLJ 9/00) [745.5]

17443 Chambers, Catherine. *All Saints, All Souls, and Halloween* (3–5). Illus. Series: World of Holi-

days. 1997, Raintree Steck-Vaughn LB $25.69 (0-8172-4606-1). 31pp. An explanation of the origins of this holiday as an observance for the spirits of the dead, customs associated with it, and a number of craft activities. (Rev: BL 6/1–15/97) [394.2]

17444 Gibbons, Gail. *Halloween* (PS–1). Illus. by author. 1984, Holiday LB $16.95 (0-8234-0524-9); paper $6.95 (0-8234-0577-X). 32pp. Halloween history and traditions are explained in this simple picture book.

17445 Limburg, Peter R. *Weird! The Complete Book of Halloween Words* (4–7). Illus. by Betsy Lewin. 1989, Macmillan LB $13.95 (0-02-759050-X). 128pp. This book defines 41 words and expressions, such as trick or treat, associated with Halloween. (Rev: BL 9/1/89; SLJ 9/89) [394]

17446 Roop, Peter, and Connie Roop. *Let's Celebrate Halloween* (3–5). Illus. 1997, Millbrook LB $19.90 (0-7613-0113-5); paper $5.95 (0-7613-0284-0). 32pp. Includes a number of crafts, like making a haunted house and different masks, as well as a history of Halloween and its significance. (Rev: BL 9/1/97; HBG 3/98; SLJ 8/97) [745.5]

17447 Stevens, Kathryn. *Halloween Jack-o'-Lanterns* (2–3). Series: Holiday Symbols. 1999, Child's World LB $15.95 (1-56766-641-8). 32pp. This book gives a history of Halloween and jack-o'-lanterns in a clear, well-organized text. (Rev: HBG 3/00; SLJ 1/00) [394.2]

17448 Trumbauer, Lisa. *Computer Fun Halloween* (2–5). Illus. by Sydney Wright. Series: Click It! 1999, Millbrook LB $21.90 (0-7613-1560-8). 32pp. These projects involving a computer and a paint program give directions on how to make decorations, masks and costumes, party invitations, place cards, and more. (Rev: HBG 3/00; SLJ 2/00) [745.5]

17449 Wolff, Ferida, and Dolores Kozielski. *Halloween Fun for Everyone* (1–6). Illus. by Judy Lanfredi. 1997, Morrow paper $7.95 (0-688-15257-0). 79pp. After a history of Halloween, this book gives directions on how to make costumes, games, decorations, and holiday food. (Rev: SLJ 1/98) [745.5]

Jewish Holy Days and Celebrations

17450 Adler, David A. *The Kids' Catalog of Jewish Holidays* (4–7). Illus. 1996, Jewish Publication Soc. paper $14.95 (0-8276-0581-1). 244pp. Thirteen major and several minor Jewish holidays are introduced, along with activities, songs, and recipes. (Rev: BL 12/15/96; SLJ 3/97) [296.4]

17451 Berger, Gilda. *Celebrate! Stories of the Jewish Holidays* (3–5). Illus. 1998, Scholastic $17.95 (0-590-93503-8). 128pp. Eight different Jewish holidays, including Shabbat, Rosh Hashanah, Yom Kippur, and Hanukkah are introduced and explained, with suggested activities and crafts for each. (Rev: BL 10/1/98; HBG 3/99; SLJ 2/99) [296.4]

17452 Brinn, Ruth Esrig. *Jewish Holiday Crafts for Little Hands* (PS–4). Illus. by Katherine J. Kahn. 1993, Kar-Ben paper $10.95 (9-929371-47-X). 127pp. Using 11 different Jewish holidays as a focus, this unique craft book gives an average of a dozen simple projects for each. (Rev: SLJ 10/93) [296.4]

17453 Burns, Marilyn. *The Hanukkah Book* (4–7). Illus. by Martha Weston. 1991, Avon paper $3.99 (0-380-71520-1). 128pp. Not only the history and traditions of this day but also attitudes Jewish children have about Christmas are discussed.

17454 Burstein, Chaya M. *The Jewish Kids Catalog* (3–7). Illus. by author. 1983, Jewish Publication Soc. paper $14.95 (0-8276-0215-4). 224pp. An introduction to Jewish holidays, traditions, and crafts.

17455 Chaikin, Miriam. *Menorahs, Mezuzas, and Other Jewish Symbols* (5–8). Illus. by Erika Weihs. 1990, Houghton $17.00 (0-89919-856-2). 102pp. Exploring some of the symbols of the Jewish faith. (Rev: BL 1/1/91; HB 5–6/91; SLJ 1/91) [296.4]

17456 Clark, Anne, et al. *Hanukkah* (4–6). Series: A World of Holidays. 1998, Raintree Steck-Vaughn LB $22.11 (0-8172-4614-2). 32pp. Tells the story of Hanukkah, its traditions, symbols, and heroes, such as Judah Maccabee and others who faced incredible odds. (Rev: BL 6/1–15/98; HBG 10/98) [296.4]

17457 Cohn, Janice. *The Christmas Menorahs: How a Town Fought Hate* (3–5). Illus. 1995, Albert Whitman LB $16.95 (0-8075-1152-8). 40pp. The true story about the people of Billings, Montana, who put menorahs in their windows to fight bigotry. (Rev: BL 9/15/95) [305]

17458 Cone, Molly. *The Story of Shabbat* (2–5). Illus. 2000, HarperCollins LB $15.89 (0-06-027945-1). 40pp. A discussion of the weekly Jewish holiday — its history, customs, and such practices as abstaining from work and studying the Torah. (Rev: BL 4/1/00; HBG 10/00; SLJ 8/00) [296.4]

17459 Corwin, Judith Hoffman. *Jewish Holiday Fun* (4–6). Illus. by author. 1987, Silver Burdett paper $5.95 (0-671-60127-X). 64pp. All sorts of ways to celebrate plus an explanation of the meaning of each holiday in this reissued book.

17460 Drucker, Malka. *The Family Treasury of Jewish Holidays* (4–6). Illus. 1994, Little, Brown $24.95 (0-316-19343-7). 180pp. Organized around the Jewish calendar, this collection of fact and fiction introduces the holidays, including the weekly Shabbat. (Rev: BL 11/15/94; SLJ 11/94) [296.4]

17461 Ferro, Jennifer. *Jewish Foods and Culture* (3–5). Series: Festive Foods and Celebrations. 1999, Rourke LB $19.45 (1-57103-303-3). 48pp. Bar and bat mitzvahs, Passover, and Purim are three facets of Jewish life that are featured, along with recipes, in this book that also discusses Jewish history and culture. (Rev: SLJ 2/00) [296.4]

17462 Fishman, Cathy G. *On Hanukkah* (K–3). Illus. by Melanie Hall. 1998, Simon & Schuster $16.00 (0-689-80643-4). 40pp. A young narrator describes the historical background of Hanukkah and how her family observes each night of this eight-day Jewish holiday. (Rev: BL 9/1/98; HBG 3/99; SLJ 10/98) [296.4]

17463 Fishman, Cathy G. *On Purim* (PS–1). Illus. by Melanie Hall. 2000, Simon & Schuster $16.00

(0-689-82392-4). 40pp. The story of gallant Queen Esther is retold along with ways in which the holiday of Purim is observed. (Rev: BL 12/15/99; HBG 10/00; SLJ 2/00) [296.4]

17464 Fishman, Cathy G. *On Rosh Hashanah and Yom Kippur* (4–7). Illus. by Melanie Hall. 1997, Simon & Schuster $16.00 (0-689-80526-8). 40pp. Explores and explains the traditions associated with Jewish High Holidays, with particular emphasis of Rosh Hashanah. (Rev: BL 10/1/97; HBG 3/98; SLJ 10/97) [296.4]

17465 Freedland, Sara. *Hanukkah! A Three-Dimensional Celebration* (3–5). Illus. by Sue Clark. 1999, Candlewick $18.99 (0-7636-0890-4). Using three-dimensional illustrations, this book covers the history of Hanukkah and provides recipes and games. (Rev: BL 12/15/99; HBG 3/00) [296.4]

17466 Gerstein, Mordicai. *Queen Esther, the Morning Star* (1–3). Illus. 2000, Simon & Schuster $16.00 (0-689-81372-4). 32pp. The biblical tale of Queen Esther and its evolution into the holiday called Purim. (Rev: BCCB 2/00; BL 12/15/99; HBG 10/00; SLJ 4/00) [222]

17467 Goldin, Barbara D. *The Passover Journey: A Seder Companion* (4–8). Illus. by Neil Waldman. 1994, Viking $15.99 (0-670-82421-6). 64pp. Rabbinical stories and excerpts from Exodus are used to re-create the traditions of the Jewish holiday Passover in this attractively illustrated book. (Rev: BCCB 4/94; BL 3/1/94*; HB 5–6/94; SLJ 2/94) [269.4]

17468 Goldin, Barbara D. *Ten Holiday Jewish Children's Stories* (K–3). Illus. by Jeffrey Allon. 2000, Pitspopany $16.95 (0-943706-47-5); paper $9.95 (0-943706-48-3). 48pp. A lively collection of ten stories, each of which stems from a tradition or practice associated with a Jewish holiday. (Rev: BL 10/1/00)

17469 Groner, Judye, and Madeline Wikler. *All About Passover* (2–4). Illus. by Kinny Kreiswirth. 2000, Kar-Ben paper $5.95 (1-58013-060-7). 32pp. A concise guide to this holiday, with a summary of the Passover story, details on suitable preparations, including cooking the seder meal, and a description of the seder itself. (Rev: BL 10/1/00) [296.4]

17470 Groner, Judye, and Madeline Wikler. *All About Sukkot* (1–5). Illus. by Kinny Kreiswirth. 1998, Kar-Ben paper $4.95 (1-58013-018-6). 32pp. This book gives information on the origins and history of this Jewish festival, on how it is celebrated and the connection between Sukkot and Thanksgiving, and provides suitable prayers, a story, and some poems. (Rev: SLJ 3/99) [296.4]

17471 *A Hanukkah Treasury* (5–8). Ed. by Eric A. Kimmel. Illus. 1998, Holt $19.95 (0-8050-5293-3). 99pp. A diverse collection of Hanukkah stories, songs, poems, and activities, including making a menorah, playing dreidel games, and cooking special foods associated with the holiday. (Rev: BL 12/1/98; HBG 3/99; SLJ 10/98) [296.4]

17472 Hildebrandt, Ziporah. *This Is Our Seder* (PS–2). Illus. by Robin Roraback. 1999, Holiday $15.95 (0-8234-1436-1). 32pp. Wonderful illustrations and a simple text introduce each of the items associated with a Passover seder. (Rev: BL 3/1/99; HBG 10/99; SLJ 4/99) [296.4]

17473 Hoyt-Goldsmith, Diane. *Celebrating Hanukkah* (3–6). Illus. by Lawrence Migdale. 1996, Holiday $16.95 (0-8234-1252-0). 32pp. A photo-essay about Hanukkah and how it is celebrated in the United States. (Rev: BCCB 11/96; BL 9/1/96) [296.4]

17474 Hoyt-Goldsmith, Diane. *Celebrating Passover* (2–5). Illus. 2000, Holiday $16.95 (0-8234-1420-5). 32pp. A 9-year-old boy explains the origins of Passover and how he and his extended family celebrate it. (Rev: BL 5/1/00; HBG 10/00; SLJ 6/00) [296.4]

17475 Jaffe, Nina. *The Uninvited Guest and Other Jewish Holiday Tales* (4–6). Illus. by Elivia. 1993, Scholastic $16.95 (0-590-44653-3). 80pp. Seven Jewish holidays, including Rosh Hashanah, Yom Kippur, and Passover, are highlighted in these delightful folktales. (Rev: BL 11/15/93; SLJ 2/94) [296.4]

17476 Kimmelman, Leslie. *Dance, Sing, Remember* (PS–1). Illus. by Ora Eitan. 2000, HarperCollins LB $18.89 (0-06-027726-2). 48pp. A distinguished introduction to 12 Jewish holy days, beginning with Rosh Hashanah and ending with Shabbat, each with stories, traditions, and history. (Rev: BL 10/1/00*; HBG 3/01; SLJ 10/00) [296.4]

17477 Kolatch, Alfred J. *The Jewish Child's First Book of Why* (PS–4). Illus. by Harry Araten. 1992, Jonathan David $14.95 (0-8246-0354-0). 32pp. Fifteen questions and answers dealing mainly with Jewish holidays. (Rev: BL 4/15/92) [296.4]

17478 Manushkin, Fran. *Miriam's Cup: A Passover Story* (2–4). Illus. by Bob Dacey. 1998, Scholastic $15.95 (0-590-67720-9). 32pp. An account of the origins of Passover in ancient Egypt and of the role played by Miriam, Moses' sister. (Rev: BL 2/1/98; HBG 10/98; SLJ 2/98) [222]

17479 Musleah, Rahel. *Why on This Night? A Passover Haggadah for Family Celebration* (3–6). Illus. by Louise August. 2000, Simon & Schuster $24.95 (0-689-81356-2). 112pp. Using linocuts and poetic explanations, the author and illustrator introduce the seder, home service, and festive meal that begin Passover, with additional folk stories and a brief play. (Rev: BL 1/1–15/00*; HB 3–4/00; HBG 10/00; SLJ 2/00) [296.4]

17480 Musleah, Rahel, and Michael Klayman. *Sharing Blessings: Children's Stories for Exploring the Spirit of the Jewish Holidays* (3–5). Illus. 1997, Jewish Lights $18.95 (1-879045-71-0). 64pp. Through the observances of a single family, all the major Jewish holidays are introduced and explained. (Rev: BL 10/1/97; HBG 3/98; SLJ 9/97) [296.4]

17481 Podwal, Mark. *The Menorah Story* (1–4). Illus. by author. 1998, Greenwillow LB $14.93 (0-688-15759-9). This account of the menorah's role in Jewish religion includes stories about Moses and Judah Maccabee. (Rev: HBG 3/99; SLJ 10/98) [296.4]

17482 Rose, David, and Gill Rose. *Passover* (3–5). Illus. Series: World of Holidays. 1997, Raintree Steck-Vaughn LB $25.69 (0-8172-4607-X). 31pp. This book explains the origins of Passover and the Seder that accompanies it, along with many activities and craft projects. (Rev: BL 6/1–15/97) [296.4]

17483 Ross, Kathy. *Crafts for Hanukkah* (2–4). Illus. 1996, Millbrook LB $21.90 (1-56294-919-5); paper $6.95 (0-7613-0078-3). 48pp. Outlines crafts associated with Hanukkah, like making dreidels and menorahs. (Rev: BL 9/1/96) [745.594]

17484 Rush, Barbara, and Cherie Karo Schwartz. *The Kids' Catalog of Passover: A Worldwide Celebration of Stories, Songs, Customs, Crafts, Food, and Fun* (K–5). 2000, Jewish Publication Soc. paper $15.95 (0-8276-0687-7). 223pp. A mixed bag of songs, stories, riddles, recipes, crafts, and other activities related to Passover plus background information on the holiday and how it is observed around the world. (Rev: SLJ 7/00) [296.4]

17485 Scharfstein, Sol. *Understanding Jewish Holidays and Customs: Historical and Contemporary* (4–7). Illus. 1999, KTAV $27.50 (0-88125-634-X); paper $18.95 (0-88125-626-9). 186pp. From ancient Jewish traditions to the present day, this book describes the history, customs, and teaching of Judaism. (Rev: BL 10/1/99; HBG 3/00; SLJ 2/00) [296.4]

17486 Schecter, Ellen. *The Family Haggadah* (3–6). Illus. 1999, Viking $13.99 (0-670-88341-7). 80pp. For use by both parents and children, this guide to a Passover seder has instructions for table settings, a version of the service, and some traditional prayers and music. (Rev: BCCB 3/99; BL 5/15/99; SLJ 6/99) [296.4]

17487 Siegel, Bruce H. *The Magic of Kol Nidre: A Yom Kippur Story* (1–4). Illus. by Shelly O. Haas. 1998, Kar-Ben $16.95 (1-58013-003-8); paper $6.95 (1-58013-002-X). The meanings behind Kol Nidre, the opening prayer of the Yom Kippur eve service, are explored in this book illustrated with realistic watercolors. (Rev: HBG 3/99; SLJ 3/99) [296.4]

17488 Techner, David, and Judith Hirt-Manheimer. *A Candle for Grandpa* (K–3). Illus. by Joel Iskowitz. 1993, UAHC $11.95 (0-8074-0507-8). Using the first anniversary of the death of a boy's grandfather as a focus, this book presents Jewish funeral practices. (Rev: SLJ 10/93) [296.4]

17489 Wood, Angela. *Jewish Festivals* (4–6). Illus. Series: Celebrate! 1997, Heinemann $22.79 (0-431-06962-X). 48pp. A boy in Jerusalem and a girl in Chicago explain how their families celebrate a number of Jewish holidays and holy days. (Rev: SLJ 12/97) [221.6]

17490 Yolen, Jane. *Milk and Honey: A Year of Jewish Holidays* (4–6). Illus. by Louise August. 1996, Putnam $21.99 (0-399-22652-4). 80pp. Eight of the most important holidays in the Jewish calendar are discussed, with accompanying folktales, poems, or other forms of literature. (Rev: BCCB 11/96; BL 10/1/96; SLJ 12/96) [296.4]

Thanksgiving

17491 Bruchac, Joseph. *Squanto's Journey: The Story of the First Thanksgiving* (4–8). Illus. by Greg Shed. 2000, Harcourt $16.00 (0-15-201817-4). 32pp. A picture book for older readers about the Pilgrims, the first Thanksgiving, and the important role played by the Paluxet Indian Squanto in helping the colony survive. (Rev: BL 9/1/00; HBG 3/01; SLJ 11/00) [394.2]

17492 Conaway, Judith. *Happy Thanksgiving! Things to Make and Do* (2–4). Illus. 1986, Troll LB $16.65 (0-8167-0668-9); paper $3.95 (0-8167-0669-7). 48pp. A Pilgrim belt buckle, a miniature Mayflower, and a mobile are some of the easy-to-do projects in this book. (Rev: BL 12/1/86)

17493 Corwin, Judith Hoffman. *Harvest Festivals Around the World* (4–6). Illus. 1995, Messner LB $6.95 (0-671-87240-0). 48pp. Fifteen projects, like mask and doll making, that celebrate harvests and thanksgiving globally. (Rev: BL 2/1/96; SLJ 5/96) [394.2]

17494 Corwin, Judith Hoffman. *Thanksgiving Fun* (2–4). Illus. 1984, Silver Burdett paper $5.95 (0-671-50849-0). 64pp. A number of Thanksgiving projects are outlined, including a big dinner.

17495 Fink, Deborah F. *It's a Family Thanksgiving! A Celebration of an American Tradition for Children and Their Families* (K–4). Illus. by Kinny Kreiswirth. 2000, Harmony Hearth paper $9.95 (0-9678871-0-0). 32pp. History, foods, and traditions are covered in this book about Thanksgiving that also contains recipes and craft projects. (Rev: BL 9/15/00) [394.2]

17496 George, Jean Craighead. *The First Thanksgiving* (3–5). Illus. by Thomas Locker. 1993, Putnam $15.95 (0-399-21991-9). 32pp. Text and dramatic pictures complement this sturdy retelling of the first Thanksgiving. (Rev: BL 7/93; SLJ 7/93) [394.2]

17497 Gibbons, Gail. *Thanksgiving Day* (PS–2). Illus. by author. 1983, Holiday LB $16.95 (0-8234-0489-7); paper $6.95 (0-8234-0576-1). 32pp. A very simple introduction to Thanksgiving Day.

17498 Graham-Barber, Lynda. *Gobble! The Complete Book of Thanksgiving Words* (4–6). Illus. by Betsy Lewin. 1993, Avon paper $3.99 (0-380-71963-0). 128pp. In readable fashion, all the words associated with this holiday are featured. (Rev: BL 1/1/91; SLJ 11/91) [394.2]

17499 Greenwood, Barbara. *A Pioneer Thanksgiving: A Story of Harvest Celebrations in 1841* (3–6). Illus. by Heather Collins. 1999, Kids Can $12.95 (1-55074-744-4); paper $5.95 (1-55074-574-3). 48pp. This book about a family's Thanksgiving celebration in 1841 includes recipes, craft projects, and games. (Rev: BCCB 11/99; BL 9/1/99; HBG 3/00; SLJ 9/99) [394]

17500 Hayward, Linda. *The First Thanksgiving* (1–3). Illus. by James Watling. Series: Step into Reading. 1990, Random LB $11.99 (0-679-90218-X); paper $3.99 (0-679-80218-5). 48pp. This easy-to-read book tells about the journey of the Pilgrims

and of their first colony. (Rev: BCCB 11/90; BL 12/1/90) [394.2]

17501 MacMillan, Dianne M. *Thanksgiving Day* (3–5). Illus. Series: Best Holiday. 1997, Enslow LB $18.95 (0-89490-822-7). 48pp. The origins of this holiday are traced, with discussion of the ways in which it is celebrated. (Rev: BL 7/97; SLJ 8/97) [394.2]

17502 Markham, Lois. *Harvest* (3–5). Series: World Celebrations and Ceremonies. 1998, Blackbirch LB $14.95 (1-56711-275-7). 23pp. Harvest festivals are described in such countries as Brazil, China, England, India, Israel, Mexico, and the United States. (Rev: HBG 3/99; SLJ 1/99) [394.2]

17503 Miller, Marilyn. *Thanksgiving* (4–6). Series: A World of Holidays. 1998, Raintree Steck-Vaughn LB $22.11 (0-8172-4612-6). 32pp. This book discusses America's Thanksgiving Day and compares it with similar harvest festivals in such countries as the Czech Republic and Sierra Leone. (Rev: BL 6/1–15/98; HBG 10/98) [394.2]

Valentine's Day

17504 Brownrigg, Sheri. *Hearts and Crafts* (4–7). Illus. 1995, Tricycle Pr. paper $9.95 (1-883672-28-7). 96pp. Clear instructions on how to complete a variety of Valentine's Day projects, including making necklaces and candles. (Rev: BL 3/1/96; SLJ 3/96) [745.5]

17505 Bulla, Clyde Robert. *The Story of Valentine's Day* (3–5). Illus. by Susan Estelle Kwas. 1999, HarperCollins LB $14.89 (0-06-027884-6). 40pp. This well-illustrated volume discusses the origins of Valentine's Day, shows how it is celebrated, and presents a few related projects. (Rev: BL 2/1/99; HBG 10/99; SLJ 6/99) [394.2618]

17506 Fradin, Dennis B. *Valentine's Day* (3–5). Illus. 1990, Enslow LB $18.95 (0-89490-237-7). 48pp. A look at how this holiday has been celebrated over the years. (Rev: BL 8/90; SLJ 2/91) [394.2]

17507 Gibbons, Gail. *Valentine's Day* (PS–1). Illus. by author. 1986, Holiday LB $16.95 (0-8234-0572-9); paper $6.95 (0-8234-0764-0). 32pp. History, meaning, and customs of Valentine's Day with simple drawings in bright colors. (Rev: BCCB 2/86; BL 12/15/85)

17508 Graham-Barber, Lynda. *Mushy! The Complete Book of Valentine Words* (4–8). Illus. by Betsy Lewin. 1993, Avon paper $3.50 (0-380-71650-X). 122pp. An explanation of the words, symbols, and customs concerning Valentine's Day. (Rev: BCCB 3/91; BL 2/15/91; SLJ 5/91) [394.2]

17509 Kessel, Joyce K. *Valentine's Day* (2–4). Illus. by Karen Ritz. 1981, Carolrhoda LB $21.27 (0-87614-166-1); Lerner paper $5.95 (0-87614-502-0). 48pp. An easily read account of the origins of this holiday and the traditions surrounding it.

17510 Sabuda, Robert. *Saint Valentine* (K–4). Illus. 1992, Macmillan $16.95 (0-689-31762-X). 32pp. Mosaiclike illustrations accompany the story of the gentle Christian physician and priest who lived in

Rome during the Christian persecutions. (Rev: BL 11/15/92; SLJ 11/92) [270.1]

Prayers

17511 Batchelor, Mary, ed. *Children's Prayers: From Around the World* (4–7). Illus. 1995, Augsburg $13.99 (0-8066-2830-8). 93pp. Two hundred prayers for children from many sources worldwide, with some for special holidays and holy days. (Rev: BL 9/1/95) [242]

17512 Baynes, Pauline, ed. *Thanks Be to God: Prayers from Around the World* (PS–3). Illus. by Pauline Baynes. 1990, Macmillan paper $9.95 (0-02-708541-4). 32pp. This is a collection of prayers and thanksgiving. (Rev: BCCB 4/90; BL 3/15/90*; SLJ 5/90) [291.4]

17513 Beckett, Wendy. *A Child's Book of Prayer in Art* (3–6). Illus. 1995, DK $14.95 (1-56458-875-0). 32pp. Using the work of 15 artists, from Michelangelo to Millet, the editor shows how the act of praying has been represented in art. (Rev: BL 9/1/95*; SLJ 8/95) [242]

17514 Bernos de Gasztold, Carmen. *Prayers from the Ark* (4–7). Trans. by Rumer Godden. Illus. by Barry Moser. 1995, Puffin paper $5.99 (0-140-54585-9). 32pp. A poem written during World War II by a woman who is now a nun. (Rev: BCCB 12/92; BL 9/1/92; HB 11–12/92) [841]

17515 Bible. *Give Us This Day: The Lord's Prayer* (PS–4). Illus. by Tasha Tudor. 1989, Putnam $12.95 (0-399-21442-9). Children in New England a century ago highlight the lovely paintings that illustrate the words of this Christian prayer. (Rev: BL 2/1/88)

17516 Brown, Susan Taylor. *Can I Pray with My Eyes Open?* (K–3). Illus. by Garin Baker. 1999, Hyperion LB $16.49 (0-7868-2273-2). 32pp. This book with a rhyming text is about how and when to pray. (Rev: BL 10/1/99; HBG 10/00; SLJ 12/99) [291.4]

17517 *The Children's Book of Poems, Prayers and Meditations* (4–6). Ed. by Liz Attenborough. Illus. 1998, Element Books $19.95 (1-90188-185-7). 128pp. From St. Francis of Assisi to Bob Dylan and Maya Angelou, this is a fine collection of meditative poems dealing with such topics as the nature of time and brotherly love. (Rev: BL 12/15/98; HBG 3/99; SLJ 1/99) [808.81]

17518 *A Child's Book of Prayers* (PS–2). Illus. by Michael Hague. 1985, Holt $14.95 (0-8050-0211-1). 32pp. Twenty familiar prayers and devotions, lovingly illustrated. (Rev: BL 3/1/86; SLJ 3/86)

17519 Cuthbert, Susan, comp. *The Classic Treasury of Children's Prayers* (K–5). Illus. by Alison Jay. 2000, Augsburg $19.99 (0-8066-4070-7). 223pp. A well-chosen collection of prayers with an emphasis on Christian ones that deal with such subjects as animals, seasons, festivals, forgiveness, virtues, and blessings. (Rev: SLJ 3/01) [242]

17520 Dearborn, Sabrina, ed. *A Child's Book of Blessings* (3–6). Illus. 1999, Barefoot $16.95 (1-84148-010-X). 40pp. A collection of simple bless-

ings from various world cultures and religions. (Rev: BL 10/1/99; SLJ 2/00) [291.43]

17521 *A Family Treasury of Prayers* (5–7). Illus. 1996, Simon & Schuster $16.00 (0-689-80956-5). 93pp. Classic art works illustrate this lovely collection of prayers from famous sources. (Rev: BL 10/1/96; SLJ 10/96) [242]

17522 Field, Rachel. *Prayer for a Child* (1–3). Illus. by Elizabeth Orton Jones. 1968, Macmillan LB $14.00 (0-02-735190-4); paper $5.99 (0-02-043070-1). 32pp. A prayer bespeaking the faith, hope, and love of little children. Caldecott Medal winner, 1945.

17523 Groner, Judye, and Madeline Wikler. *Thank You, God! A Jewish Child's Book of Prayers* (PS–2). Illus. by Shelly O. Haas. 1994, Kar-Ben $16.95 (0-929371-65-8). 32pp. A series of blessings and prayers involving Jewish traditions, written in Hebrew letters with an English translation. (Rev: BL 3/15/94; SLJ 4/94) [296.7]

17524 Hopkins, Lee Bennett, sel. *All God's Children: A Book of Prayers* (K–2). Illus. by Amanda Schaffer. 1998, Harcourt $15.00 (0-15-201499-3). 48pp. A collection of 22 short prayers that are both moving and easy to understand. (Rev: BL 4/1/98; HBG 10/98; SLJ 3/98) [242]

17525 *I Imagine Angels: Poems and Prayers for Parents and Children* (4–8). Ed. by William Lach. Illus. 2000, Simon & Schuster $16.00 (0-689-84080-2). 48pp. Handsomely reproduced pictures illustrate this collection of prayers and thoughtful poems from many sources, including the Bible. (Rev: BL 10/1/00; SLJ 1/01) [808.81]

17526 *In Every Tiny Grain of Sand: A Child's Book of Prayers and Praise* (3–6). Ed. by Reeve Lindbergh. Illus. 2000, Candlewick $21.99 (0-7636-0176-4). 80pp. A marvelous collection of 77 poems and prayers drawn from many cultures, including Native American, Jewish, Muslim, Buddhist, African, and Celtic sources. (Rev: BCCB 12/00; BL 11/1/00*; HBG 3/01; SLJ 12/00) [291.4]

17527 Knowlton, Laurie L. *God Be in My Heart: Poems and Prayers for Children* (K–3). Illus. 1999, Boyds Mills $9.95 (1-56397-646-3). 32pp. A charming collection of 11 Christian prayers — some from history and others written by the author. (Rev: BL 4/1/99; HBG 10/99; SLJ 4/99) [291.4]

17528 Ladwig, Tim. *The Lord's Prayer* (PS–4). 2000, Eerdmans $17.00 (0-8028-5180-0). 32pp. Full-page paintings are used with the text of the Lord's Prayer to tell the story of an African American father and daughter who help an elderly neighbor. (Rev: BCCB 12/00; BL 10/1/00; SLJ 1/01) [226.9]

17529 O'Keefe, Susan Heyboer. *Angel Prayers: Prayers for All Children* (PS–1). Illus. by Sophia Suzan. 1999, Boyds Mills $15.95 (1-56397-683-8). A warm, gentle collection of prayers addressed to God and angels, plus several blessings. (Rev: HBG 3/00; SLJ 12/99) [242]

17530 Owens, Mary Beth. *Be Blest* (K–3). Illus. 1999, Simon & Schuster $16.00 (0-689-80546-2). 40pp. Celtic prayers and blessings are given for each month of the year in this exquisitely illustrated book. (Rev: BCCB 11/99; BL 12/1/99; HBG 10/00; SLJ 1/00) [291.4]

17531 Rylant, Cynthia. *Bless Us All: A Child's Yearbook of Blessings* (PS–K). Illus. 1998, Simon & Schuster $14.00 (0-689-82370-3). 32pp. This book features 12 rhymed blessings — one for each month — each illustrated with childlike paintings. (Rev: BCCB 2/99; BL 11/1/98; HBG 3/99; SLJ 12/98) [291.4]

17532 Rylant, Cynthia. *Give Me Grace: A Child's Daybook of Prayers* (PS–K). Illus. 1999, Simon & Schuster $12.00 (0-689-82293-6). 32pp. A simple book of seven prayers, one for each day of the week. (Rev: BL 10/1/99; HBG 3/00; SLJ 12/99) [291.4]

17533 *A Small Child's Book of Prayers* (PS–1). Ed. by Cyndy Szekeres. Illus. 1999, Scholastic $6.95 (0-590-38363-9). 32pp. A fine collection of prayers that also includes poems about God and nature. (Rev: BL 2/1/99; HBG 10/99; SLJ 4/99) [242]

17534 Staub, Leslie. *Bless This House: A Bedtime Prayer for the Whole World* (PS). Illus. 2000, Harcourt $16.00 (0-15-201984-7). 32pp. A bedtime prayer that asks for blessings on all living creatures. (Rev: BL 10/1/00; HBG 3/01; SLJ 1/01) [242]

17535 Trist, Glenda, comp. *A Child's Book of Prayers: New and Traditional Prayers for Children* (PS–1). 1999, DK $12.95 (0-7894-3976-X). 48pp. A Christian-oriented book of devotions that includes Bible quotations, traditional favorites, and some simple prayers written for children. (Rev: HBG 10/99; SLJ 1/00) [242]

17536 Wheeler, Susan. *Holly Pond Hill: A Child's Book of Prayers* (PS–K). Illus. 2000, Dutton $9.99 (0-525-46187-6). 22pp. This charming board book includes six famous prayers and two selections from the Bible. (Rev: BL 3/15/00) [242]

17537 Willard, Nancy. *The Good-Night Blessing Book* (K–3). Illus. 1996, Scholastic $15.95 (0-590-62393-1). 32pp. This is a good-night prayer illustrated with the author's photographs. (Rev: BL 10/1/96; SLJ 10/96) [811]

Social Groups

Ethnic Groups

17538 Alexander, Anita, and Susan Payne. *Gingersnaps: Daily Affirmations for African American Children and Families* (3–6). Illus. by Nancy Doniger. 1998, Hyperion paper $8.95 (0-7868-1306-7). Using the themes of racial and cultural pride, this book gives daily affirmations grouped under topics including family, school, and feelings. (Rev: SLJ 1/99) [155.8]

17539 Aliotta, Jerome J. *The Puerto Ricans* (5–8). Illus. Series: Land of Immigrants. 1995, Chelsea LB $19.95 (0-7910-3360-0). 110pp. A history of Puerto Rico and its people plus coverage on their traditions and contributions. (Rev: BL 10/15/95) [305]

17540 Archibald, Erika F. *A Sudanese Family* (4–7). Illus. Series: Journey Between Two Worlds. 1997, Lerner paper $8.95 (0-8225-9753-5). 56pp. Introduces Dei Jock Dei and his family, who left Sudan to escape religious persecution and, through the help of a church, settled in Atlanta, Georgia. (Rev: BL 6/1–15/97; SLJ 7/97) [975.8]

17541 Ashabranner, Brent. *The New African Americans* (5–9). Illus. 1999, Linnet LB $21.00 (0-208-02420-4). 105pp. After a brief history of early African immigration and slavery, this account focuses on present-day immigrants — where they come from and their reception in the United States. (Rev: BCCB 12/99; BL 10/15/99; HB 11–12/99; HBG 3/00) [304.87]

17542 Bandon, Alexandra. *Asian Indian Americans* (5–8). Illus. Series: Footsteps to America. 1995, New Discovery LB $22.00 (0-02-768144-0). 111pp. An account of the conditions that have caused emigration from India and a description of life in the United States for the immigrants. (Rev: SLJ 8/95) [973]

17543 Bandon, Alexandra. *Dominican Americans* (5–8). Illus. Series: Footsteps to America. 1995, New Discovery $22.00 (0-02-768152-1). 111pp. A readable account of why many residents of the Dominican Republic left their country to come to the United States and the conditions they found. (Rev: SLJ 8/95) [973]

17544 Bandon, Alexandra. *West Indian Americans* (5–8). Illus. Series: Footsteps to America. 1994, New Discovery LB $18.95 (0-02-768148-3). 111pp. Describes why some West Indians left their islands to come to the United States, their reception, and their present lifestyles and contributions to their new nation. (Rev: SLJ 12/94) [304.8]

17545 Berg, Lois Anne. *An Eritrean Family* (4–7). Illus. Series: Journey Between Two Worlds. 1997, Lerner LB $22.60 (0-8225-3405-3); paper $8.95 (0-8225-9755-1). 64pp. The story of the Kiklu family, which fled Eritrea in eastern Africa in 1978, spent ten years in a refugee camp, and resettled in Minnesota. (Rev: BL 6/1–15/97; SLJ 8/97) [304.895]

17546 Berger, Melvin, and Gilda Berger. *Where Did Your Family Come From? A Book About Immigrants* (2–3). Illus. by Robert Quackenbush. Series: Discovery Readers. 1993, Ideals paper $4.50 (0-8249-8610-5). 48pp. A simple text about the waves of immigration to the United States. (Rev: BCCB 4/93; BL 7/93; SLJ 6/93) [325.73]

17547 Bierman, Carol, and Barbara Hehner. *Journey to Ellis Island: How My Father Came to America* (2–5). Illus. by Laurie McGaw. 1998, Hyperion $17.95 (0-7868-0377-0). 48pp. Based on real-life experiences, this is the story of 11-year-old Yehuda Weinstein and his detention on Ellis Island because of an injured arm. (Rev: SLJ 5/99) [304.8]

17548 Birdseye, Debbie H., and Tom Birdseye. *Under Our Skin: Kids Talk About Race* (3–7). Illus. 1997, Holiday LB $15.95 (0-8234-1325-X). 32pp. Six American middle-schoolers from various racial backgrounds talk about their pride in their culture and their feelings of belonging to the human race. (Rev: BL 12/15/97; HBG 3/98; SLJ 4/98) [305.8]

17549 Catalano, Julie. *The Mexican Americans* (5–8). Illus. Series: Immigrant Experience. 1995, Chelsea LB $19.95 (0-7910-3359-7); paper $9.95 (0-7910-3381-3). 100pp. This book traces the reasons for leaving Mexico, the immigrants' reception in the United States, and their contributions and achievements. (Rev: BL 11/15/95; SLJ 1/96) [973]

17550 Cavan, Seamus. *The Irish-American Experience* (5–7). Illus. Series: Coming to America. 1993, Millbrook LB $22.40 (1-56294-218-2). 64pp. Beginning with the potato famine that forced millions of Irish to come to America, this is the story of the rise of Irish Americans to positions of prominence. (Rev: BCCB 4/93; BL 6/1–15/93) [973]

17551 Cole, Melanie, et al. *Famous People of Hispanic Heritage* (4–7). Series: Contemporary American Success Stories. 1997, Mitchell Lane LB $21.95 (1-883845-44-0); paper $12.95 (1-883845-43-2). 96pp. This useful series, now in nine volumes, profiles famous Hispanics, past and present, from around the world. (Rev: BL 3/15/98; HBG 3/98) [920]

17552 Cooper, Martha, and Ginger Gordon. *Anthony Reynoso: Born to Rope* (2–4). Illus. 1996, Clarion $14.95 (0-395-71690-X). 32pp. A young Mexican American displays many skills from his native culture, like roping and riding. (Rev: BL 3/15/96; HB 7–8/96; SLJ 6/96) [791.8]

17553 Daley, William. *The Chinese Americans* (5–8). Illus. 1995, Chelsea LB $19.95 (0-7910-3357-0); paper $9.95 (0-7910-3379-1). 112pp. The background and culture of this group are explained, as well as its adjustment to life in America. (Rev: BL 1/1/88)

17554 Di Franco, J. Philip. *The Italian Americans* (5–8). Illus. 1995, Chelsea LB $19.95 (0-791-03353-8); paper $9.95 (0-7910-3375-9). 112pp. A heavily illustrated discussion of the culture that Italian immigrants left behind and their contributions to American life. (Rev: BL 1/1/88)

17555 Emsden, Katharine, ed. *Coming to America: A New Life in a New Land* (4–8). Series: Perspectives on History. 1993, Discovery paper $6.95 (1-878668-23-4). 64pp. People from many countries tell of their experiences as immigrants through quotes from their diaries, journals, and letters. (Rev: BL 11/15/93) [325.73]

17556 Feelings, Tom. *Tommy Traveler in the World of Black History* (3–8). Illus. 1991, Writers & Readers $13.95 (0-86316-202-9). 48pp. This classic comic strip is about a young African American boy who witnesses highlights in the history of his race. (Rev: BL 9/15/91) [741]

17557 Gabor, A. *Polish Americans* (4–6). Illus. Series: Cultures of America. 1995, Marshall Cavendish $19.95 (1-7614-0154-7). 80pp. After a description of life in Poland, this account describes the history of Polish Americans and various aspects of their culture. (Rev: BL 7/95) [305.89]

17558 Galicich, Anne. *The German Americans* (5–8). Illus. Series: Immigrant Experience. 1995, Chelsea LB $19.95 (0-7910-3362-7); paper $9.95 (0-7910-3384-8). 120pp. From the reasons for their leaving Germany and their initial reception in the United States to the present, this account traces the history of German Americans. (Rev: BL 4/1/89) [973]

17559 George, Linda, and Charles George. *Civil Rights Marches* (4–6). Series: Cornerstones of Freedom. 1999, Children's LB $20.00 (0-516-21183-8). 32pp. This account re-creates the important civil rights marches of the past 40 years, with material on their leaders and their consequences. (Rev: BL 10/15/99) [973]

17560 Gernand, Renee. *The Cuban Americans* (5–8). Illus. 1995, Chelsea LB $19.95 (0-791-03354-6); paper $9.95 (0-791-03376-7). 112pp. The contributions of Cuban Americans and reasons why they came to America. (Rev: BL 2/1/89)

17561 Goldish, Meish. *Immigration: How Should It Be Controlled?* (4–6). Illus. Series: Issues of Our Time. 1994, Twenty-First Century LB $18.90 (0-8050-3182-0). 64pp. Contains historical information about immigration plus material on citizenship laws, illegal aliens, and the pros and cons of allowing more immigrants into the United States. (Rev: SLJ 7/94) [304.8]

17562 Greenfield, Eloise, and Lessie Jones Little. *Childtimes: A Three-Generation Memoir* (5–8). Illus. by Jerry Pinkney. 1979, HarperCollins LB $15.89 (0-690-03875-5); paper $8.95 (0-06-446134-3). 160pp. The childhood of three generations of African American women.

17563 Hamanaka, Sheila. *The Journey: Japanese Americans, Racism and Renewal* (4–7). Illus. by author. 1990, Orchard LB $20.99 (0-531-08449-3). 39pp. With brief text, this book is a series of paintings from a large mural that describes the Japanese American experience, including internment during World War II. (Rev: HB 5–6/90; SLJ 5/90) [940.54]

17564 *Honoring Our Ancestors: Stories and Pictures by Fourteen Artists* (3–6). Ed. by Harriet Rohmer. Illus. 1999, Children's Book Pr. $15.95 (0-89239-158-8). 32pp. A diverse group of artists from various ethnic groups honor family members and describe how they succeeded in America. (Rev: BCCB 3/99; BL 2/1/99; HBG 10/99; SLJ 6/99) [759.13]

17565 Hoobler, Dorothy, and Thomas Hoobler. *The Italian American Family Album* (5–8). Illus. 1994, Oxford $19.95 (0-19-509124-8). 127pp. Using many primary sources, this book covers such topics as life in Italy, coming to the United States, working, forming a new life, and becoming Italian Americans. (Rev: SLJ 7/94) [973]

17566 Horton, Casey. *The Jews* (4–8). Series: We Came to North America. 2000, Crabtree LB $15.96 (0-7787-0187-5); paper $8.06 (0-7787-0201-4). 32pp. As well as discussing the reasons why Jews left Europe, this account describes the trip across the Atlantic, reception in America, and the many contributions to the United States. (Rev: SLJ 10/00) [973]

17567 Hoyt-Goldsmith, Diane. *Hoang Anh: A Vietnamese-American Boy* (3–5). Illus. by Lawrence Migdale. Series: Cornerstones of Freedom. 1992, Holiday LB $16.95 (0-8234-0948-1). 32pp. Color photos and a first-person narrative describe the life of a Vietnamese boy living in California. (Rev:

BCCB 4/92; BL 4/15/92; HB 5–6/92; SLJ 4/92) [378.1]

17568 Israel, Fred L. *The Amish* (5–8). Illus. Series: Immigrant Experience. 1996, Chelsea LB $19.95 (0-7910-3368-6). 100pp. The story of this conservative division of the Mennonites, why they settled in the United States, and their contributions to the nation. (Rev: BL 7/96; SLJ 10/96) [305.6]

17569 Kitano, Harry. *The Japanese Americans*. 2nd ed. (5–8). Photos by Richard Hewett. Series: Land of Immigrants. 1995, Chelsea LB $19.95 (0-7910-3358-9); paper $9.95 (0-7910-3380-5). 92pp. The story of Japanese Americans and their history, traditions, and contributions to American life and culture. (Rev: BL 10/15/95) [305]

17570 Knight, Margy B. *Who Belongs Here? An American Story* (4–7). Illus. by Anne S. O'Brien. 1993, Tilbury $16.95 (0-88448-110-7). 40pp. The story of ten-year-old Nari, who survived the killing fields of Cambodia and found a new life in the United States. (Rev: BL 3/1/94; SLJ 10/93) [305.895]

17571 Kroll, Virginia. *With Love, to Earth's Endangered Peoples* (3–6). Illus. by Roberta Collier-Morales. 1998, Dawn $17.95 (1-883220-83-1); paper $8.95 (1-883220-82-3). This book deals with such endangered peoples as the Australian aborigine, the Inuit, the Toda of India, and the Ainu of Japan. (Rev: HBG 3/99; SLJ 12/98) [910]

17572 Kuropas, Myron B. *Ukrainians in America* (5–7). Illus. Series: In America. 1996, Lerner LB $5.95 (0-8225-1043-X). 80pp. The story of Ukrainian immigrants to the United States, their cultural traditions, and their contributions to American life. (Rev: BL 3/15/96; SLJ 3/96) [973]

17573 Leder, Jane M. *A Russian Jewish Family* (4–7). Illus. Series: Journey Between Two Worlds. 1996, Lerner LB $22.60 (0-8225-3401-0); paper $8.95 (0-8225-9744-6). 56pp. Describes the living conditions experienced by a Jewish family in Russia and in their new American home. (Rev: BL 11/1/96; SLJ 11/96) [977.3]

17574 Lester, Julius. *To Be a Slave* (5–8). Illus. by Tom Feelings. 1968, Dial $16.99 (0-8037-8955-6); Scholastic paper $4.50 (0-590-42460-2). Through the words of slaves themselves, the reader is helped to realize what it was like to be a slave in America.

17575 Levine, Ellen. *If Your Name Was Changed at Ellis Island* (3–5). Illus. by Wayne Parmenter. 1993, Scholastic $15.95 (0-590-46134-6). 80pp. Informative and lively case histories highlight the stories of the millions who passed through Ellis Island for a new life in America. (Rev: BCCB 4/93; BL 3/1/93; SLJ 3/93) [325.1]

17576 Lomas Garza, Carmen. *Family Pictures/ Cuadros de Familia* (3–7). Illus. 1990, Children's Book Pr. $15.95 (0-89239-050-6); paper $7.95 (0-89239-108-1). 32pp. A Mexican American artist shares memories of her childhood in Texas. (Rev: BCCB 10/90; BL 6/1/90; SLJ 11/90*) [306]

17577 McGill, Allyson. *The Swedish Americans* (5–8). Series: Immigrant Experience. 1997, Chelsea $19.95 (0-7910-4551-X); paper $9.95 (0-7910-4552-8). 107pp. Explains why Swedes have emi-

grated from their homeland, their reception in the United States, and their contributions to the nation. (Rev: BL 10/15/97) [322.4]

17578 Maestro, Betsy. *Coming to America: The Story of Immigration* (K–3). Illus. by Susannah Ryan. 1996, Scholastic $15.95 (0-590-44151-5). 40pp. A picture-book introduction to what the many waves of immigrants have meant to the United States. (Rev: BCCB 2/96; BL 2/1/96; SLJ 5/96) [304]

17579 Magocsi, Paul R. *The Russian Americans* (5–8). Illus. Series: Immigrant Experience. 1995, Chelsea LB $19.95 (0-7910-3367-8). 110pp. Coverage includes reasons for leaving Russia, customs and traditions, contributions to their new nation, and famous Russian Americans. (Rev: BL 11/15/95; SLJ 1/96) [973]

17580 Martinez, Elizabeth Coonrod. *The Mexican-American Experience* (5–7). Illus. Series: Coming to America. 1995, Millbrook LB $22.40 (1-56294-515-7). 64pp. Conditions in Mexico that produce a flow of immigrants are discussed, with information on the contributions of Mexican Americans and brief biographies of famous Mexican Americans. (Rev: BL 6/1–15/95) [973]

17581 Meier, Gisela. *Minorities* (5–7). Series: Women Today. 1991, Rourke LB $17.95 (0-86593-124-0). 64pp. An account that explores the financial status of women in minority groups. (Rev: SLJ 2/92) [305.42]

17582 Mendez, Adriana. *Cubans in America* (5–7). Illus. Series: In America. 1994, Lerner LB $19.93 (0-8225-1953-4). 80pp. An account that describes why Cubans left their homeland, where they live in the United States, their lifestyles, and their contributions to society. (Rev: BL 8/94; SLJ 8/94) [973]

17583 Muggamin, Howard. *The Jewish Americans* (5–8). Illus. Series: Immigrant Experience. 1995, Chelsea LB $19.95 (0-7910-3365-1); paper $9.95 (0-7910-3387-2). 126pp. This account describes the lands from which many Jewish Americans came and their religion, customs, family life, food, and contributions. (Rev: BL 11/15/95) [973]

17584 Murphy, Nora. *A Hmong Family* (4–7). Illus. Series: Journey Between Two Worlds. 1997, Lerner LB $22.60 (0-8225-3406-1); paper $8.95 (0-8225-9756-X). 64pp. After fleeing Laos in 1975 to escape the Communists, this family spent time in a refugee camp in Thailand before settling in Minneapolis, Minnesota. (Rev: BL 6/1–15/97; SLJ 8/97) [305.895]

17585 Ochoa, George. *The New York Public Library Amazing Hispanic American History: A Book of Answers for Kids* (4–9). Illus. 1998, Wiley paper $12.95 (0-471-19204-X). 192pp. Using a question-and-answer format, this work explores such topics as Hispanic American identity and history, cultural groups, accomplishments, and immigrant experiences. (Rev: BL 12/1/98) [973]

17586 O'Connor, Karen. *Dan Thuy's New Life in America* (4–8). Illus. 1992, Lerner LB $19.93 (0-8225-2555-0). 40pp. A photo-essay of a 13-year-old Vietnamese girl and her family, newly arrived in San Diego. (Rev: BL 9/15/92; SLJ 9/92) [325]

17587 O'Connor, Karen. *A Kurdish Family* (4–7). Illus. Series: Journey Between Two Worlds. 1996, Lerner LB $22.60 (0-8225-3402-9); paper $8.95 (0-8225-9743-8). 56pp. Describes the living conditions endured by a Kurdish family in their homeland and their new life in the United States. (Rev: BCCB 12/96; BL 11/1/96; SLJ 11/96) [305.891]

17588 Press, Petra. *Puerto Ricans* (4–6). Illus. Series: Cultures of America. 1996, Marshall Cavendish LB $19.95 (0-7614-0160-0). 80pp. A nicely illustrated description of the island of Puerto Rico details the customs, traditions, and contributions of its people. (Rev: BL 5/15/96) [973]

17589 Reimers, David M. *A Land of Immigrants* (5–8). Illus. Series: Immigrant Experience. 1995, Chelsea LB $19.95 (0-7910-3361-9). 120pp. An overview of how the waves of immigration developed and determined the nature of the United States and its culture. (Rev: BL 10/15/95; SLJ 12/95) [304.8]

17590 Sawyers, June S. *Famous Firsts of Scottish-Americans* (4–8). Illus. 1997, Pelican $13.95 (1-56554-122-7). 160pp. Biographies of 30 Americans of Scottish descent, including Neil Armstrong, Alexander Calder, Herman Melville, and Patrick Henry. (Rev: BL 6/1–15/97) [973]

17591 Schanzer, Rosalyn. *Escaping to America: A True Story* (K–4). Illus. by author. 2000, HarperCollins LB $15.89 (0-688-16990-2). This book tells how and why the author's Jewish grandparents left Poland in 1921 and describes their journey and arrival in America. (Rev: BL 8/00; HBG 3/01; SLJ 9/00) [973]

17592 Schouweiler, Thomas. *Germans in America* (5–7). Illus. Series: In America. 1994, Lerner LB $19.93 (0-8225-0245-3). 72pp. The causes and results of German immigration to the United States are outlined, with good coverage of their contributions and important figures. (Rev: BL 1/15/95; SLJ 12/94) [973]

17593 Shalant, Phyllis. *Look What We've Brought You from Vietnam: Crafts, Games, Recipes, Stories, and Other Cultural Activities from New Americans* (3–6). Illus. 1988, Simon & Schuster paper $6.95 (0-671-65978-2). 48pp. Activities to foster an appreciation of Vietnamese culture. (Rev: BL 9/1/88)

17594 Silverman, Robin L. *A Bosnian Family* (4–7). Illus. Series: Journey Between Two Worlds. 1997, Lerner LB $22.60 (0-8225-3404-5); paper $8.95 (0-8225-9754-3). 64pp. The story of Velma Dusper, her homeland of Bosnia, and her journey with her family to freedom and a new home in North Dakota. (Rev: BL 6/1–15/97; SLJ 7/97) [304.8]

17595 Stanek, Muriel. *We Came from Vietnam* (4–6). Illus. 1985, Whitman LB $11.95 (0-8075-8699-4). 48pp. Photos and text focus on the Nguyen family from Vietnam, now settled in Chicago. (Rev: BCCB 11/85; BL 11/1/85)

17596 Strom, Yale. *Quilted Landscape: Conversations with Young Immigrants* (5–8). Illus. 1996, Simon & Schuster paper $18.00 (0-689-80074-6). 80pp. Young immigrants from 15 countries tell about their homelands and the lives they now lead in the United States. (Rev: BCCB 2/97; BL 10/15/96; SLJ 12/96) [305.8]

17597 Watts, J. F. *The Irish Americans* (5–8). Illus. Series: Immigrant Experience. 1995, Chelsea LB $19.95 (0-7910-3366-X); paper $9.95 (0-7910-3388-0). 110pp. A history of the Irish Americans, how and why they came to the United States, their history here, and their contributions. (Rev: BL 10/15/95) [973]

17598 *We Are All Related: A Celebration of Our Cultural Heritage* (3–6). Illus. 1997, Orca paper $15.95 (0-9680479-0-4). 64pp. Reproduces the collages created by students at a Vancouver, B.C., elementary school during a yearlong arts program that focused on intercultural and intergenerational studies. (Rev: BL 8/97) [704]

17599 Weitzman, Elizabeth. *I Am Jewish American* (K–3). Series: Our American Family. 1998, Rosen LB $13.95 (0-8239-5006-9). 24pp. A young girl living in Chicago describes her feelings about her family and the Jewish American community of which she is a part. (Rev: SLJ 9/98) [973]

17600 Wu, Dana Ying-Hul, and Jeffrey Dao-Sheng Tung. *The Chinese-American Experience* (5–7). Illus. Series: Coming to America. 1993, Millbrook LB $22.40 (1-56294-271-9). 64pp. The story of Chinese immigration to the United States, from exploitation, prejudice, and discrimination to gradual acceptance. (Rev: BL 6/1–15/93) [973]

Personal Development

Behavior

General

17601 Aaron, Jane. *When I'm Afraid* (PS–K). Illus. Series: Language of Parenting Guide. 1998, Golden Bks. $15.00 (0-307-44057-5). 36pp. A first-person account that explains in pictures and text what it is like to feel various fears such as getting lost or visiting the doctor. A booklet is included to help parents handle a child's fears. (Rev: BL 8/98; SLJ 11/98) [152.4]

17602 Aaron, Jane. *When I'm Angry* (PS–K). Illus. Series: Language of Parenting Guide. 1998, Golden Bks. $15.00 (0-307-44019-2). 36pp. The nature of anger, its causes, expressions, and cures, is covered from a child's point of view, with an accompanying parents' booklet containing advice on handling a child's emotions. (Rev: BL 8/98; SLJ 11/98) [152.4]

17603 Arredia, Joni. *Sex, Boys and You: Be Your Own Best Girlfriend* (5–9). 1998, Perc paper $15.95 (0-9653203-2-4). 181pp. A guidance book that gives good advice on how to look and feel good, and how to develop healthy relationships with boys. (Rev: SLJ 10/98) [305.23]

17604 Berger, Terry. *I Have Feelings* (1–5). Illus. 1971, Human Sciences $18.95 (0-87705-021-X); paper $10.95 (0-89885-342-7). 32pp. Text and photos show children that their feelings and emotions — good and bad — are natural.

17605 Erlbach, Arlene. *Worth the Risk: True Stories About Risk Takers, Plus How You Can Be One, Too* (5–9). Illus. 1999, Free Spirit paper $12.95 (1-57542-051-1). 127pp. These are 20 case studies of teenagers who took risks, from defying the dominant cliques in school to entering a burning house to save siblings. (Rev: BL 5/1/99) [158]

17606 Fleischman, Paul, ed. *Cannibal in the Mirror* (5–10). Photos by John Whalen. 2000, Twenty-First Century LB $23.90 (0-7613-0968-3). 64pp. This thought-provoking book takes 27 quotations that describe barbarous behavior of primitive societies and pairs each with a telling photograph of similar behavior in modern American society. (Rev: HBG 10/00; SLJ 4/00) [150]

17607 Frost, Helen. *Feeling Angry* (PS–1). Series: Emotions. 2000, Capstone LB $13.25 (0-7368-0668-7). 24pp. Nine full-color photos and nine short sentences are used to illustrate anger. Others in the series are *Feeling Happy* and *Feeling Scared* (both 2000). (Rev: HBG 3/01; SLJ 1/01) [152.4]

17608 Funston, Sylvia. *The Book of You: The Science and Fun of Why You Look, Feel, and Act the Way You Do* (3–6). Photos by Gilbert Duclos. Illus. by Susanna Denti. 2000, HarperTrophy paper $8.95 (0-688-17751-4). 48pp. An amusing read on pop psychology that covers topics including DNA, fingerprints, body language, and palm reading. (Rev: SLJ 7/00) [155.2]

17609 Gardner, Richard A. *The Girls and Boys Book About Good and Bad Behavior* (3–6). Illus. by Al Lowenheim. 1990, Creative Therapeutics paper $17.00 (0-933812-21-3). 221pp. This book talks about ethics and values. (Rev: SLJ 12/90) [155.5]

17610 Greenberg, Judith E. *A Girl's Guide to Growing Up: Making the Right Choices* (5–8). Illus. 2000, Watts $25.00 (0-531-11592-5). 144pp. Lots of personal stories are quoted in this guidance book for preteen and teenage girls dealing with such subjects as school, risky behaviors, dating, sex, self-esteem, eating disorders, and cliques. (Rev: BL 2/15/01) [305.23]

17611 Hovanec, Erin M. *Get Involved! A Girl's Guide to Volunteering* (5–8). Series: Girls' Guides. 1999, Rosen Central LB $17.95 (0-8239-2985-X). 48pp. Two case studies of successful volunteers are given in this account that explains where to volunteer, how to approach organizations, and how to determine one's interests. (Rev: HBG 10/00; SLJ 1/00) [361]

17612 Hubbard, Woodleigh Marx. *All That You Are* (K–3). Illus. 2000, Putnam $12.99 (0-399-23364-4). 32pp. Various qualities that make a child special, such as loyalty and confidence, are pictured in this book about admirable human characteristics. (Rev: BL 3/1/00; HBG 3/01; SLJ 4/00) [158]

17613 Inwald, Robin. *Cap It Off with a Smile: A Guide for Making Friends* (K–3). Illus. by author. 1994, Hilson Pr. $16.95 (1-885738-00-5). This book offers practical tips to young people on how they can make friends. (Rev: SLJ 12/94) [158]

17614 James, Elizabeth, and Carol Barkin. *How to Be School Smart: Secrets of Successful Schoolwork* (4–6). Illus. 1988, Morrow $15.00 (0-688-16130-8); Lothrop paper $4.95 (0-688-16139-1). Getting better grades is made easier in this easily read practical guide. (Rev: BL 3/15/88; HBG 3/99; SLJ 5/88)

17615 Johnson, Julie. *Being Angry* (1–3). Illus. by Chris O'Neill. Series: How Do I Feel About. 1999, Millbrook LB $19.90 (0-7613-0910-1). 24pp. Photographs and drawings are used to explore the emotion of anger as experienced by five children in different situations. (Rev: BL 9/15/99; HBG 10/99; SLJ 12/99) [152.4]

17616 Johnston, Marianne. *Dealing with Anger* (2–4). Illus. Series: Conflict Resolution Library. 1996, Rosen LB $13.95 (0-8239-2325-8). 24pp. This simple introduction to anger defines it, explains its different forms, and tells how to handle it. (Rev: SLJ 9/96) [152.4]

17617 Kalb, Jonah, and David Viscott. *What Every Kid Should Know* (4–6). Illus. 1976, Houghton paper $7.95 (0-395-62983-7). 128pp. An introduction to the study of how people behave toward each other.

17618 Kincher, Jonni. *Psychology for Kids II: 40 Fun Experiments That Help You Learn About Others* (4–6). Illus. 1995, Free Spirit paper $17.95 (0-915793-83-0). 157pp. This second volume supplies more activities and projects to help explore the world of human behavior. (Rev: BL 7/95) [155.2]

17619 Landau, Elaine. *Wild Children: Growing Up Without Human Contact* (4–6). Series: A First Book. 1998, Watts LB $22.00 (0-531-20256-9). 64pp. This book describes the phenomenon — in fact and fiction — of children who have been raised without human contact. Details are provided on four important cases from the past and present. (Rev: HBG 10/98; SLJ 7/98) [612]

17620 Lankford, Mary D. *Quinceañera: A Latina's Journey to Womanhood* (4–7). Photos by Jesse Herrera. 1994, Millbrook LB $20.90 (1-56294-363-4). 47pp. Using the story of a 15-year-old Mexican American girl as a focus, this account describes the rite of passage to womanhood in the Latina culture. (Rev: SLJ 4/94) [305.23]

17621 Lewis, Barbara A. *The Kid's Guide to Social Action: How to Solve the Social Problems You Choose — and Turn Creative Thinking into Positive Action*. Rev. ed. (4–8). 1998, Free Spirit paper $16.95 (1-57542-038-4). 211pp. From cleaning up toxic waste to helping youth-rights groups, this book describes how young people can become involved in social causes and provides many case histories. (Rev: SLJ 1/99) [361.6]

17622 Lewis, Barbara S. *Being Your Best: Character Building for Kids 7–10* (4–6). Illus. 1999, Free Spirit paper $14.95 (1-57542-063-5). 148pp. A child-centered book that presents ten positive character traits and suggests practical ways and activi-

ties to develop and strengthen them. (Rev: BL 5/15/00) [155.2]

17623 Nathan, Amy. *Surviving Homework: Tips from Teens* (4–6). Illus. 1997, Millbrook LB $23.90 (1-56294-185-2). 80pp. Using answers on questionnaires given to middle and high school kids as a focus, this book supplies many useful study tips and suggestions on how to organize one's time. (Rev: BL 6/1–15/97; SLJ 7/97) [372.12]

17624 Payne, Lauren M. *We Can Get Along: A Child's Book of Choices* (PS–2). Illus. by Claudia Rohling. 1997, Free Spirit paper $9.95 (1-57542-013-9). 36pp. A simple guide on getting along with others and how to be aware of other people's feelings. (Rev: BL 8/97; SLJ 4/97) [302]

17625 Peacock, Judith. *Anger Management* (5–8). Illus. Series: Perspectives on Mental Health. 2000, Capstone LB $22.60 (0-7368-0433-1). 64pp. A discussion of anger, its various types, its causes, its effects on the body and on others, and how and when to control it. (Rev: BL 8/00; HBG 10/00) [152.4]

17626 Pendleton, Scott. *The Ultimate Guide to Student Contests, Grades K–6* (4–6). 1998, Walker paper $14.95 (0-8027-7513-6). 208pp. A directory of organizations that sponsor student competitions or reward outstanding student work, arranged by subject. (Rev: BL 3/15/98; SLJ 9/98) [370]

17627 Pickering, Marianne. *Lessons for Life: Education and Learning* (5–8). Illus. Series: Our Human Family. 1995, Blackbirch LB $22.45 (1-56711-127-0). 80pp. The content and organization of public education are examined around the world in this book divided into five broad geographical areas. (Rev: SLJ 1/96) [370]

17628 Robson, Pam. *Body Language* (2–5). Illus. Series: Hello Out There. 1997, Watts LB $20.00 (0-531-14468-2). 32pp. As well as giving good advice on reading the body signals of others, this book includes examples from the animal kingdom and a number of suggested activities. (Rev: BL 1/1–15/98; HBG 3/98; SLJ 3/98) [153.6]

17629 Romain, Trevor. *How to Do Homework Without Throwing Up* (3–6). Illus. by author. 1997, Free Spirit paper $8.95 (1-57542-011-2). 67pp. Using humorous text and drawings, this work supplies a positive approach to homework with many tips on how to do it efficiently. (Rev:*SLJ 5/97) [371.3]

17630 Sanders, Pete, and Steve Myers. *Feeling Violent* (3–6). Illus. by Mike Lacey. Series: What Do You Know About. 1997, Millbrook LB $20.90 (0-7613-0700-1). 32pp. This book explores violence, its different forms, its causes, and how to handle it. (Rev: HBG 10/98; SLJ 4/98) [616.8]

17631 Schneider, Meg. *Help! My Teacher Hates Me* (5–8). Illus. 1994, Workman paper $7.95 (1-56305-492-2). 160pp. A book of practical advice on how to weather the problems of getting along in school. (Rev: BL 3/15/95) [371.8]

17632 Sheindlin, Judy. *Win or Lose by How You Choose!* (2–6). Illus. by Bob Tore. 2000, HarperCollins LB $14.89 (0-06-028474-9). Television's Judge Judy offers questions and answers on issues involving character and value judgments. (Rev: HBG 10/00; SLJ 6/00) [305.2]

17633 Swain, Gwenyth. *Smiling* (PS–1). Illus. Series: Small Worlds. 1999, Carolrhoda $14.95 (1-57505-256-3). 24pp. Children from around the world, including China, Australia, Sudan, and Mexico, display a variety of smiles in this happy book about childhood. (Rev: BL 6/1–15/99; HBG 10/99; SLJ 6/99) [153.6]

Etiquette

17634 Best, Alyse. *Miss Best's Etiquette for Young People: Manners for Real People in Today's World* (3–7). Illus. 1991, PEP paper $9.95 (0-945033-02-8). 137pp. Advice is given to young people on proper behavior for both formal and informal social events. (Rev: BL 9/15/91) [395]

17635 Holyoke, Nancy. *Oops! The Manners Guide for Girls* (3–7). Illus. by Debbie Tilley. Series: American Girl. 1997, Pleasant paper $7.95 (1-56247-530-4). 116pp. An amusing book of manners aimed at girls that covers almost any situation. (Rev: SLJ 3/98) [393]

17636 James, Elizabeth, and Carol Barkin. *Social Smarts: Manners for Today's Kids* (4–7). Illus. 1996, Clarion $15.00 (0-395-66585-X); paper $6.95 (0-395-81312-3). 103pp. Table manners and responsible, appropriate public behavior are two topics covered. (Rev: BL 9/1/96; SLJ 9/96) [395]

17637 Kirtland, Mark. *Why Do We Do That?* (4–6). Illus. Series: Why Do We? 1996, Watts LB $20.00 (0-531-14394-5). 31pp. Using cross-cultural and historical approaches, this book explores etiquette and protocol around the world. (Rev: SLJ 8/97) [395]

17638 Lauber, Patricia. *What You Never Knew About Fingers, Forks, and Chopsticks* (2–5). Illus. by John Manders. 1999, Simon & Schuster $16.00 (0-689-80479-2). 40pp. An amusing, fascinating look at manners and eating utensils, from the Stone Age to the present. (Rev: BCCB 12/99; BL 9/1/99*; HBG 3/00; SLJ 9/99) [394.1]

17639 Smith, Mavis. *Mind Your Manners, Ben Bunny: A Lift-the-Flap Book About Table Manners* (PS–K). Illus. by author. 1998, Scholastic $8.95 (0-590-06844-X). This book uses flaps and advice from a crow to teach Ben Bunny and two friends proper table manners. (Rev: HBG 3/99; SLJ 7/98) [395]

17640 Stewart, Marjabelle Young, and Ann Buchwald. *What to Do When and Why* (4–7). 1988, Luce $14.95 (0-88331-105-4). An easily read introduction to the basics of good manners and behavior.

Family Relationships

17641 Aldape, Virginia Totorica. *David, Donny, and Darren: A Book About Identical Triplets* (2–4). Illus. Series: Meeting the Challenge. 1997, Lerner LB $21.27 (0-8225-2584-4). 40pp. Using a first-person narrative, this is the story of an identical

triplet and how his life is different from those of average kids. (Rev: BL 3/15/98; HBG 3/98) [306.875]

17642 Berman, Claire. *"What Am I Doing in a Step-Family?"* (3–6). Illus. by Dick Wilson. 1982, Carol Publg. $12.00 (0-8184-0325-X). A somewhat superficial view of stepfamilies and the adjustments necessary in these situations.

17643 Bode, Janet. *For Better, For Worse: A Guide to Surviving Divorce for Preteens and Their Families* (5–8). Illus. 2001, Simon & Schuster $16.00 (0-689-81945-5). 162pp. Using extensive interviews with preteens, this is a practical guide to handling divorce. Half of the book is for preteens, the other half for parents. (Rev: BCCB 2/01; BL 1/1–15/01; SLJ 2/01) [306.89]

17644 Brown, Laurie Krasny, and Marc Brown. *Dinosaurs Divorce: A Guide for Changing Families* (PS–3). Illus. by Marc Brown. 1988, Little, Brown $15.95 (0-316-11248-8); paper $7.95 (0-316-10996-7). 32pp. These green, somewhat crocodilian dinosaurs demonstrate all the feelings and problems children encounter with divorce in the family. (Rev: SLJ 10/86)

17645 Charlish, Anne. *Divorce* (5–10). Series: Talking Points. 1999, Raintree Steck-Vaughn $27.11 (0-8172-5310-6). 64pp. This book discusses the causes of divorce, its legal aspects, and the difficult adjustments that must be made. (Rev: BL 8/99) [306.89]

17646 Cole, Joanna. *The New Baby at Your House.* Rev. ed. (PS–1). Illus. by Margaret Miller. 1998, Morrow $15.93 (0-688-13898-5). 48pp. A revision of the standard account on adjustments that are made in a family when a new baby arrives. (Rev: BL 3/1/98; HBG 10/98; SLJ 4/98) [306.875]

17647 Cole, Julia. *My Parents' Divorce* (K–4). Illus. by Chris O'Neill. Series: How Do I Feel About. 1998, Millbrook LB $19.90 (0-7613-0869-5). 24pp. This self-help book describes divorce, the way children react to it, the problems it raises, and suggestions for solving them. (Rev: HBG 3/99; SLJ 1/99) [306.89]

17648 Cooper, Kay. *Where Did You Get Those Eyes? A Guide to Discovering Your Family History* (5–7). Illus. by Anthony Accardo. 1988, Walker LB $14.85 (0-8027-6803-2). A helpful guide for researching the family tree. (Rev: BCCB 11/88; BL 1/15/89; SLJ 2/89)

17649 Currie, Stephen. *Adoption* (5–8). Illus. Series: Overview. 1997, Lucent LB $22.45 (1-56006-183-9). 96pp. A well-illustrated account of the history of adoption and present-day practices, procedures, and problems. (Rev: BL 5/15/97; SLJ 4/97) [362.7]

17650 Douglas, Ann. *The Family Tree Detective: Cracking the Case of Your Family's Story* (4–8). Illus. by Stephen MacEachern. 1999, Owl $19.95 (1-895688-88-4); paper $9.95 (1-895688-89-2). 48pp. In 16 brief chapters, this book gives thorough coverage to the steps, techniques, and methodology used in conducting successful genealogical research. (Rev: SLJ 6/99) [305.5]

17651 Drescher, Joan. *Your Family, My Family* (K–3). Illus. by author. 1980, Walker LB $13.85 (0-8027-6383-9). 32pp. All kinds of family arrangements, such as single parents and working mothers, are described.

17652 Gardner, Richard A. *Boys and Girls Book About Divorce* (5–8). Illus. 1992, Bantam paper $6.50 (0-553-27619-0). 160pp. A self-help book written for adolescents trying to cope with parental marriage problems.

17653 Gellman, Marc. *"Always Wear Clean Underwear!" and Other Ways Parents Say "I Love You."* (4–7). 1997, Morrow $14.95 (0-688-14492-6). 128pp. Some kids think that the expressions featured in this book are parental nagging, but the message really is that parents care. (Rev: BL 10/1/97; HBG 3/98; SLJ 11/97) [306.874]

17654 Girard, Linda Walvoord. *We Adopted You, Benjamin Koo* (3–5). Illus. by Linda Shute. 1989, Whitman LB $14.95 (0-8075-8694-3); paper $6.95 (0-8075-8695-1). 32pp. Nine-year-old Benjamin tells how he was adopted from a Korean orphanage. (Rev: BCCB 5/89; BL 5/1/89; SLJ 6/89)

17655 Goldentyer, Debra. *Child Abuse* (4–8). Series: Preteen Pressures. 1998, Raintree Steck-Vaughn LB $24.97 (0-8172-5032-8). 48pp. This work describes the types, causes, and effects of child abuse and supplies material on how to change an abusive situation. (Rev: BL 5/15/98; HBG 10/98) [362.7]

17656 Goldentyer, Debra. *Divorce* (4–8). Series: Preteen Pressures. 1998, Raintree Steck-Vaughn LB $24.97 (0-8172-5030-1). 48pp. This work discusses the reasons for divorce, the legal aspects, its effect on children, remarriage, and relationships with new family members. (Rev: BL 5/15/98; HBG 10/98; SLJ 6/98) [306.8]

17657 Green, Jen. *Our New Baby* (K–4). Illus. by Chris O'Neill. Series: How Do I Feel About. 1998, Millbrook LB $19.90 (0-7613-0871-7). 24pp. A self-help book that describes the concerns when a new sibling arrives, cites questions that should be addressed, and gives suggestions for solving problems that may arise. (Rev: HBG 3/99; SLJ 1/99) [306]

17658 Greenberg, Keith E. *Zack's Story: Growing Up with Same-Sex Parents* (5–7). Illus. Series: Meeting the Challenge. 1996, Lerner $21.27 (0-8225-2581-X). 32pp. A true account of 11-year-old Zack, who is growing up with his lesbian mother and her lover, whom he has grown to regard as a second mother. (Rev: BL 10/15/96; SLJ 3/97) [306]

17659 Havelin, Kate. *Family Violence: My Parents Hurt Each Other!* (4–10). 1999, Capstone LB $16.95 (0-7368-0286-X). 64pp. Examines causes and forms of domestic violence and offers coping strategies. (Rev: SLJ 5/00) [364.3]

17660 Holyoke, Nancy. *Help! A Girl's Guide to Divorce and Stepfamilies* (3–6). Illus. 1999, Pleasant paper $8.95 (1-56247-749-8). 128pp. An upbeat account about divorce and stepfamilies, including topics such as fear, guilt, anger, money, violence, and parents' dating. (Rev: BL 2/1/00; SLJ 11/99) [306.89]

17661 Isler, Claudia. *Caught in the Middle: A Teen Guide to Custody* (5–8). Series: The Divorce Resource. 2000, Rosen LB $17.95 (0-8239-3109-9). 64pp. This book about divorce uses many actual case histories to explore such questions as what happens to the children when parents divorce and whether grandparents get visitation rights. (Rev: SLJ 6/00) [306.8]

17662 Johnson, Julie. *My Stepfamily* (2–4). Series: How Do I Feel About. 1998, Millbrook LB $19.90 (0-7613-0868-7). 24pp. Four children explain their feelings about being part of a stepfamily and how they have dealt with various situations. (Rev: HBG 10/99; SLJ 4/99) [646.7]

17663 Kandel, Bethany. *Trevor's Story: Growing Up Biracial* (2–4). Illus. Series: Meeting the Challenge. 1997, Lerner LB $21.27 (0-8225-2583-6). 40pp. A first-person narrative in which a boy talks about the racism he has had to face growing up with a white mother and an African American father. (Rev: BL 3/15/98; HBG 3/98) [362.1]

17664 Koh, Frances M. *Adopted from Asia: How It Feels to Grow Up in America* (5–8). 1993, East-West $16.95 (0-9606090-6-7). 95pp. Using interviews, the author has gathered stories, impressions, and opinions from 11 young people who were born in Korea and adopted by Caucasian Americans. (Rev: BL 2/15/94) [306.874]

17665 Krementz, Jill. *How It Feels to Be Adopted* (5–8). Illus. 1988, Knopf paper $15.00 (0-394-75853-6). Interviews with 19 young people, ages eight to 16, on how it feels to be adopted.

17666 Krementz, Jill. *How It Feels When Parents Divorce* (4–8). Illus. 1988, Knopf paper $15.00 (0-394-75855-2). Boys and girls, ages eight to 16, share their experiences with divorced parents.

17667 Krohn, Katherine. *Everything You Need to Know About Birth Order* (5–9). Series: Need to Know Library. 2000, Rosen LB $17.95 (0-8239-3228-1). 64pp. An interesting book that looks at a number of theories about how birth order affects people. (Rev: SLJ 12/00) [306.85]

17668 Landau, Elaine. *Sibling Rivalry: Brothers and Sisters at Odds* (3–6). Illus. 1994, Millbrook LB $19.90 (1-56294-328-6). 64pp. Factors that influence sibling rivalry, such as family size, gender, and divorce, are discussed, with tips on how to understand and lessen the problem. (Rev: BL 5/1/94; SLJ 4/94) [306]

17669 Leibowitz, Julie. *Finding Your Place: A Teen Guide to Life in a Blended Family* (5–8). 2000, Rosen LB $17.95 (0-8239-3114-5). 64pp. This book explores possible problems and solutions for members of blended families. (Rev: SLJ 6/00) [645.7]

17670 LeShan, Eda. *When Grownups Drive You Crazy* (4–7). 1988, Macmillan paper $14.00 (0-02-756340-5). 128pp. A book that tries to bridge the gap of misunderstanding between children and their parents. (Rev: BL 4/15/88; HB 7–8/88; SLJ 6–7/88)

17671 Lindsay, Jeanne W. *Do I Have a Daddy? A Story About a Single-Parent Child* (PS–2). Illus. by Jami Moffett. 2000, Morning Glory $14.95 (1-885356-62-5); paper $7.95 (1-885356-63-3). 48pp. A single mother reassures her son that, although he does not have a father, his uncle and grandfather will be there to help him. (Rev: BL 5/15/00; HBG 10/00; SLJ 7/00) [306.85]

17672 Miner, Chalise. *Rain Forest Girl: More Than an Adoption Story* (3–6). Photos by Phil Miner. 1998, Mitchell Lane LB $16.95 (1-883845-65-3); paper $12.95 (1-883845-81-5). 48pp. This book relates a young Brazilian girl's adoptive process — a transaction that took two years to complete. (Rev: HBG 3/99; SLJ 9/98) [362.7]

17673 Morris, Ann. *Families* (PS–1). Illus. 2000, HarperCollins LB $15.89 (0-688-17199-0). 32pp. Different kinds of families around the world are introduced in this photo-essay that uses very little text. (Rev: BL 5/15/00; HBG 10/00; SLJ 5/00) [306.85]

17674 Perl, Lila. *The Great Ancestor Hunt: The Fun of Finding Out Who You Are* (5–8). Illus. 1989, Houghton $16.00 (0-89919-745-0). 104pp. A how-to book for amateur genealogists. (Rev: BCCB 12/89; BL 11/1/89; SLJ 12/89) [929.1]

17675 Powell, Jillian. *Adoption* (2–3). Series: Talking About. 1999, Raintree Steck-Vaughn LB $15.98 (0-8172-5890-6). 32pp. Stories with happy endings enhance this simple account of adoptions — their meaning, reasons, and effects on children's feelings. (Rev: BL 2/15/00; HBG 10/00) [362.7]

17676 Powell, Jillian. *Family Breakup* (1–3). Photos by Martyn F. Chillmaid. Series: Talking About. 1999, Raintree Steck-Vaughn LB $22.83 (0-8172-5542-7). 32pp. Covers children's concerns when a family is breaking up — why this happens, what becomes of the children, who one can talk to, and what a stepfamily is. (Rev: HBG 10/99; SLJ 7/99) [306.8]

17677 Rogers, Fred. *Let's Talk About It: Divorce* (PS–2). Illus. by Jim Judkis. 1996, Putnam $16.99 (0-399-22449-1). 32pp. A photo-essay that explores the effects of divorce on three families. (Rev: BL 5/15/96; SLJ 4/96) [306.89]

17678 Rogers, Fred. *Let's Talk About It: Stepfamilies* (K–3). Illus. by Jim Judkis. Series: Let's Talk. 1997, Putnam $15.99 (0-399-23144-7); paper $7.95 (0-399-23145-5). 32pp. A simple narrative illustrated with photos that explores the practical and emotional situations involved in stepfamily living. (Rev: BL 10/15/97; HBG 3/98; SLJ 10/97) [646.7]

17679 Rosenberg, Maxine B. *Living with a Single Parent* (4–7). 1992, Macmillan $14.95 (0-02-777915-7). 160pp. In interview format, this topic is presented through the opinions of youngsters from eight to 13. (Rev: BCCB 2/93; BL 11/15/92; SLJ 12/92) [306.85]

17680 Rotner, Shelley, and Sheila M. Kelly. *About Twins* (PS–1). Illus. by Shelley Rotner. 1999, DK $16.95 (0-7894-2556-4). 32pp. This exploration of twinhood emphasizes that although twins may look alike they often don't feel the same. (Rev: BCCB 4/99; BL 6/1–15/99; HBG 10/99; SLJ 4/99) [306.875]

17681 Rotner, Shelley, and Sheila M. Kelly. *Lots of Dads* (PS–1). Illus. 1997, Dial $12.89 (0-8037-2089-0). 24pp. A photo-essay about all kinds of fathers and how each has a different way of expressing himself. (Rev: BL 8/97; SLJ 12/97) [306]

17682 Sanders, Pete, and Steve Myers. *Divorce and Separation* (4–8). Illus. by Mike Lacey. Series: What Do You Know About. 1997, Millbrook LB $20.90 (0-7613-0574-2). 32pp. An introduction to separation and divorce, with an emphasis on tips to help youngsters adjust and cope. (Rev: SLJ 10/97) [346]

17683 Schwartz, Perry. *Carolyn's Story: A Book About an Adopted Girl* (5–7). Illus. Series: Meeting the Challenge. 1996, Lerner $21.27 (0-8225-2580-1). 40pp. Using fictional case histories, various aspects of adoption are explored. (Rev: BL 10/15/96; SLJ 4/97) [362.7]

17684 Scott, Elaine. *Twins!* (PS–3). Illus. by Margaret Miller. 1998, Simon & Schuster $16.00 (0-689-80347-8). 40pp. A photo-essay that discusses twins — fraternal and identical — and covers such subjects as behavior problems and the pros and cons of dressing alike. (Rev: BL 5/15/98; HBG 10/98; SLJ 7/98) [306.87]

17685 Simon, Norma. *All Kinds of Families* (4–6). Illus. by Joe Lasker. 1976, Whitman LB $14.95 (0-8075-0282-0). 40pp. Explores various kinds of families and their problems.

17686 Stein, Sara Bonnett. *On Divorce* (2–4). Illus. 1979, Walker $10.95 (0-8027-6344-8); paper $4.95 (0-8027-7226-9). Photographs and text cover this subject in an elementary fashion.

17687 Stein, Sara Bonnett. *That New Baby* (1–3). Illus. Series: Open Family. 1979, Walker $12.95 (0-8027-6175-5); paper $8.95 (0-8027-7227-7). 48pp. A very helpful book in getting youngsters to accept a new member in the family.

17688 Swan-Jackson, Alys, and Lynn Rosenfield. *When Your Parents Split Up . . .: How to Keep Yourself Together* (5–9). Illus. by Andy Cooke. Series: Plugged In. 1999, Price Stern Sloan paper $4.99 (0-8431-7451-X). 90pp. This book contains information on how to handle parental separation and divorce and provides additional material on custody law, single parents, and stepfamilies. (Rev: SLJ 10/99) [306.8]

17689 Thomas, Pat. *My Family's Changing* (PS–2). Illus. by Lesley Harker. 1999, Barron's paper $5.95 (0-7641-0995-2). 32pp. A beginning book about divorce and how it affects different members of the family. (Rev: BL 5/15/99; SLJ 6/99) [306.89]

17690 Wasson, Valentina P. *The Chosen Baby* (PS–K). Illus. by Glo Coalson. 1977, HarperCollins $15.00 (0-397-31738-7). 48pp. A later edition of an excellent book on adoption.

17691 Weitzman, Elizabeth. *Let's Talk About Foster Homes* (K–2). Illus. Series: Let's Talk. 1996, Rosen LB $15.93 (0-8239-2310-X). 24pp. After defining what a foster home is, this title explains why some children are placed in one and the adjustments that they must make. Other family problems are explored in *Let's Talk About Staying in a Shelter, Let's Talk About When a Parent Dies*, and *Let's Talk About Your Parents' Divorce* (all 1996). (Rev: SLJ 12/96) [362.7]

17692 Wolfman, Ira. *Do People Grow on Family Trees? Genealogy for Kids and Other Beginners*

(5–8). Illus. by Michael Klein. 1991, Workman paper $10.95 (0-89480-348-4). 179pp. The purposes of genealogy are discussed and information is given on how to trace family history. (Rev: SLJ 1/92) [929]

Personal Problems and Relationships

17693 Adams, Lisa K. *Dealing with Teasing* (K–4). Series: Conflict Resolution Library. 1997, Rosen LB $13.95 (0-8239-5070-0). 24pp. This book explains the different kinds of teasing — from the innocent to the harmful — and how to cope when teasing gets out of hand. (Rev: SLJ 4/98) [152.4]

17694 Brody, Janis. *Your Body: The Girls' Guide* (5–10). 2000, St. Martin's paper $4.99 (0-312-97563-5). 256pp. This book on puberty and body changes covers such subjects as self-image, menstruation, sexuality, sports participation, nutrition, eating disorders, substance abuse, and counseling. (Rev: SLJ 10/00) [612]

17695 Brown, Laurie Krasny. *When Dinosaurs Die: A Guide to Understanding Death* (K–3). Illus. by Marc Brown. 1996, Little, Brown $14.95 (0-316-10917-7). 32pp. A beginner's book about death and its meaning. (Rev: BCCB 3/96; BL 4/1/96; HB 9–10/96; SLJ 4/96) [155.9]

17696 *Camy Baker's Body Electric: 30 Cool Rules for a Brand-New You* (5–7). Series: Camy Baker. 1999, Bantam paper $3.99 (0-553-48658-6). 170pp. This is a practical guide to surviving the problems of early adolescence. Also use *Camy Baker's It Must be Love: 15 Cool Rules for Choosing a Better Boyfriend* (1999). (Rev: SLJ 6/99) [362]

17697 *Camy Baker's Love You Like a Sister: 30 Cool Rules for Making and Being a Better Best Friend* (4–6). 1998, Bantam paper $3.99 (0-553-48656-X). 165pp. This book on friendship gives useful, practical tips for making and keeping friends. (Rev: SLJ 2/99) [302]

17698 Cohen-Posey, Kate. *How to Handle Bullies, Teasers and Other Meanies: A Book That Takes the Nuisance out of Name Calling and Other Nonsense* (4–7). 1995, Rainbow paper $8.95 (1-56825-029-0). 91pp. A practical book that offers useful suggestions on how to handle bullies. (Rev: BCCB 12/95; BL 11/15/95) [646.7]

17699 Cordes, Helen. *Girl Power in the Classroom: A Book about Girls, Their Fears, and Their Future* (5–8). Illus. 2000, Lerner LB $25.26 (0-8225-2693-X). 112pp. This book of personal guidance for girls describes how to conquer fears and cope with difficult situations at school. (Rev: BL 5/15/00; HBG 10/00; SLJ 5/00) [373.1822]

17700 Cordes, Helen. *Girl Power in the Mirror: A Book about Girls, Their Bodies, and Themselves* (5–8). Illus. 2000, Lerner LB $25.26 (0-8225-2691-3). 112pp. This book for girls explains proper attitudes about appearance and gives coping strategies concerning pressures about one's looks. (Rev: BL 5/15/00; HBG 10/00; SLJ 5/00) [306.4]

17701 Dee, Catherine, ed. *The Girls' Book of Wisdom: Empowering, Inspirational Quotes from Over 400 Fabulous Females* (5–8). Illus. by Lou M. Pollack. 1999, Little, Brown paper $8.95 (0-316-17956-6). 192pp. A collection of quotes from more than 400 famous women grouped by such subjects as "Friends," "Happiness," and "Leadership." (Rev: SLJ 12/99) [305.23]

17702 Fisher, Enid. *Emotional Ups and Downs* (4–6). Series: Good Health Guides. 1998, Gareth Stevens LB $14.95 (0-8368-2179-3). 32pp. A heavily illustrated account that covers such topics as handling emotions such as shyness and anger; dealing with bullies, death of a loved one, and divorce; and coping with difficult family situations and with problems involving personal relationships. (Rev: HBG 10/99; SLJ 6/99) [362]

17703 Gellman, Marc, and Thomas Hartman. *Lost and Found: A Kid's Book for Living Through Loss* (4–6). Illus. 1999, Morrow $15.00 (0-688-15752-1). 144pp. A rabbi and a Roman Catholic priest discuss the concept of loss, from losing a toy or an absent friend to divorce or the death of a loved one. (Rev: BL 5/15/99; HBG 10/99; SLJ 6/99) [248.8]

17704 Girard, Linda Walvoord. *Who Is a Stranger and What Should I Do?* (2–5). Illus. by Helen Cogancherry. 1985, Whitman LB $13.95 (0-8075-9014-2); paper $5.95 (0-8075-9016-9). 32pp. Dealing with strangers in different situations, emphasizing that sometimes the best thing to do is to run away. (Rev: BCCB 3/85; BL 4/1/85; SLJ 9/85)

17705 Greenberg, Keith E. *Family Abuse: Why Do People Hurt Each Other?* (3–6). Illus. 1994, Twenty-First Century LB $18.90 (0-8050-3183-9). 64pp. An easily read book that explores physical, emotional, and sexual abuse of children as well as neglect and abuse of spouses, the elderly, and the disabled. (Rev: SLJ 9/94) [362.7]

17706 Gurian, Michael. *From Boys to Men: All about Adolescence and You* (5–7). Illus. by Brian Floca. Series: Plugged In. 1999, Price Stern Sloan LB $13.89 (0-8431-7474-9); paper $4.99 (0-8431-7483-8). 86pp. Using a conversational tone, the author covers preteen emotional and physical changes and discusses topics including friendship, social and sexual relationships, peer pressure, and keeping healthy as they relate to boys. (Rev: SLJ 7/99) [605.23]

17707 Halperin, Wendy A. *Love Is . . .* (PS–3). Illus. 2001, Simon & Schuster $16.00 (0-689-82980-9). 32pp. Different kinds of love are explored in this unusually beautiful picture book. (Rev: BL 1/1–15/01*; SLJ 2/01) [242]

17708 Havelin, Kate. *Child Abuse: Why Do My Parents Hit Me?* (4–10). Series: Perspectives on Relationships. 1999, Capstone LB $16.95 (0-7368-0287-8). 64pp. This book defines the forms of child abuse, explains its causes and characteristics, and offers advice on handling it. (Rev: SLJ 5/00) [362.7]

17709 Heegaard, Mary E. *Coping with Death and Grief* (4–6). 1990, Lerner LB $19.93 (0-8225-0043-4). 64pp. This account helps children understand how the grieving process promotes emotional growth. (Rev: BL 11/1/90; SLJ 11/90) [155.6]

17710 Hyde, Margaret O. *Know About Abuse* (5–7). Illus. 1992, Walker LB $14.85 (0-8027-8177-2). 93pp. Various kinds of abuse in the home are described and information on how to get help is given. (Rev: SLJ 9/92) [362.7]

17711 Johnson, Julie. *Bullies and Gangs* (2–4). Photos by Roger Vlitos. Illus. by Chris O'Neill. Series: How Do I Feel About. 1998, Millbrook LB $19.90 (0-7613-0807-5). 24pp. This work describes how and why bullies behave the way they do and how to cope with them. (Rev: HBG 10/98; SLJ 7/98) [646.7]

17712 Johnston, Marianne. *Dealing with Bullying* (K–3). Illus. Series: Conflict Resolution Library. 1996, Rosen LB $15.93 (0-8239-2374-6). 24pp. A helpful book that helps young people understand bullies and offers techniques for self-protection. (Rev: SLJ 1/97) [155.5]

17713 Johnston, Marianne. *Let's Talk About Being Shy* (4–8). Illus. Series: Let's Talk. 1996, Rosen LB $15.93 (0-8239-2304-5). 24pp. The causes and possible cures of shyness are covered in this straightforward discussion. Also use *Let's Talk About Being Afraid* (1996). (Rev: BL 3/15/97) [155.4]

17714 Kent, Susan. *Let's Talk About Needing Extra Help at School* (3–5). Series: Let's Talk. 2000, Rosen LB $17.26 (0-8239-5422-6). 24pp. Using actual cases and realistic photos, this book explores the many reasons why kids might need extra help at school and what they can do about it. (Rev: SLJ 2/01) [371.2]

17715 Klebanoff, Susan, and Ellen Luborsky. *Ups and Downs: How to Beat the Blues and Teen Depression* (5–9). Illus. by Andy Cooke. Series: Plugged In. 1999, Price Stern Sloan paper $4.99 (0-8431-7450-1). 90pp. This account tells how to distinguish between bad moods and depression and gives tips on how to help oneself or get outside help when necessary. (Rev: SLJ 10/99) [616.85]

17716 Krementz, Jill. *How It Feels When a Parent Dies* (4–7). Illus. 1988, Knopf paper $15.00 (0-394-75854-4). 128pp. Eighteen experiences of parental death are recounted.

17717 LeShan, Eda. *Learning to Say Good-bye: When a Parent Dies* (5–7). Illus. by Paul Giovanopoulos. 1976, Avon paper $8.00 (0-380-40105-3). 96pp. A sympathetic explanation of the many reactions children have to death.

17718 Levete, Sarah. *Being Jealous* (1–3). Illus. by Chris O'Neill. Series: How Do I Feel About. 1999, Millbrook LB $19.90 (0-7613-0911-X). 24pp. The experiences of five youngsters in the same class are used to explore the concept of jealousy. (Rev: BL 9/15/99; HBG 10/99; SLJ 12/99) [152.4]

17719 Lound, Karen. *Girl Power in the Family: A Book About Girls, Their Rights, and Their Voice* (5–10). Series: Girl Power. 2000, Lerner LB $25.26 (0-8225-2692-1). 80pp. A book that explores the problems of growing up female today with material on gender roles, biases, and relationships. (Rev: HBG 10/00; SLJ 6/00) [303.6]

17720 Middleton, Don. *Dealing with Competitiveness* (2–4). Series: Conflict Resolution Library. 1999, Rosen $17.26 (0-8239-5267-3). 24pp. An attractive introduction to this difficult subject that uses fictional anecdotes to explain the nature of competitiveness and its problems and solutions. Also use (from the same series and author) *Dealing with Secrets* (1998). (Rev: SLJ 4/99) [155]

17721 Monson-Burton, Marianne, comp. *Girls Know Best 2: Tips On Life and Fun Stuff to Do!* (5–8). Series: Girl Power. 1998, Beyond Words paper $8.95 (1-885223-84-6). 152pp. Girls ages ten to 16 give hundreds of tips, bits of advice, and projects concerning adolescent problems both serious and trivial. (Rev: SLJ 1/99) [155]

17722 *New Moon on Friendship: How to Make, Keep, and Grow Your Friendships* (3–7). Illus. 1999, Crown $16.99 (0-517-88581-6). 96pp. How to be a friend and stay one, how to solve friendship problems, and how to have fun with friends are among the topics in this book. (Rev: BL 8/99; SLJ 9/99) [158.2]

17723 Peacock, Judith. *Depression* (5–8). Illus. Series: Perspectives on Mental Health. 2000, Capstone LB $22.60 (0-7368-0435-8). 64pp. The causes and effects of mental depression are introduced, with material on how to handle it and its effects on the human body. (Rev: BL 8/00; HBG 10/00) [616.85]

17724 Polland, Barbara K. *We Can Work it Out: Conflict Resolution for Children* (K–3). Illus. by Craig DeRoy. 2000, Tricycle Pr. $13.95 (1-58246-031-0). 64pp. This book poses questions about various kinds of behavioral problems (e.g., teasing, poor sportsmanship) and enables children to solve these problems through self-direction. (Rev: BL 1/1–15/01) [303.6]

17725 Powell, Jillian. *Talking About Bullying* (2–3). Illus. Series: Talking About. 1999, Raintree Steck-Vaughn LB $22.83 (0-8172-5535-4). 32pp. This book explains to young children why kids become bullies and how to cope with them. (Rev: BL 7/99; HBG 10/99; SLJ 7/99) [371.58]

17726 Roehm, Michelle, comp. *Girls Know Best: Advice for Girls from Girls on Just About Everything!* (5–8). Illus. 1997, Beyond Words paper $8.95 (1-885223-63-3). 160pp. Clear, direct advice is given on such problems as embarrassing situations, staying healthy, participation in activities, and such family issues as divorce and illness. (Rev: SLJ 12/97) [362]

17727 Romain, Trevor. *Bullies Are a Pain in the Brain* (3–7). Illus. by author. 1997, Free Spirit paper $9.95 (1-57542-023-6). 105pp. Explains why bullies act the way they do, types of bullying, and ways to cope with it. (Rev: SLJ 2/98) [371.5]

17728 Romain, Trevor. *Cliques, Phonies, and Other Baloney* (3–8). Illus. by author. 1998, Free Spirit Publg. paper $9.95 (1-57542-045-7). 136pp. This book deals with social groups centered around friendships (many false and destructive) and suggests ways to form and hold solid friendships. (Rev: SLJ 4/99) [177]

17729 Ross, Dave. *A Book of Friends* (PS–3). Illus. by Laura Rader. 1999, HarperCollins LB $12.89 (0-06-028362-9). This simple picture book shows in words and pictures how to be a good friend. (Rev: HBG 10/99; SLJ 7/99) [177]

17730 Sanders, Pete. *Bullying* (4–7). Illus. Series: What Do You Know About. 1996, Millbrook LB $20.90 (0-7613-0537-8). 32pp. The causes of people being bullies are explored, with tips on how to handle them. (Rev: SLJ 3/97) [155.5]

17731 Scott, Elaine. *Friends!* (K–3). Illus. by Margaret Miller. 2000, Simon & Schuster $16.00 (0-689-82105-0). 40pp. Using posed photographs, this book explores the different components that make up a friendship. (Rev: BL 5/15/00; HBG 10/00; SLJ 5/00) [177.62]

17732 Simon, Norma. *The Saddest Time* (K–3). Illus. by Jacqueline Rogers. 1986, Whitman LB $13.95 (0-8075-7203-9); paper $5.95 (0-8075-7204-7). 40pp. Three stories talk to children about death — of an uncle, a child accident victim, and a grandparent. (Rev: BCCB 4/86; BL 4/15/86; SLJ 8/86)

17733 Spelman, Cornelia Maude. *Your Body Belongs to You* (K–3). Illus. by Teri Weidner. 1997, Albert Whitman LB $13.95 (0-8075-9474-1). 24pp. An introduction to child sexual abuse, with a special section of advice for parents. (Rev: BL 9/1/97; HBG 3/98; SLJ 9/97) [613.6]

17734 Sprung, Barbara. *Stress* (4–8). Illus. Series: Preteen Pressures. 1998, Raintree Steck-Vaughn LB $24.97 (0-8172-5033-6). 48pp. A concise, practical account of the types and causes of stress in young people and how to manage it. (Rev: BL 4/15/98; HBG 10/98; SLJ 6/98) [155.4]

17735 Wachter, Oralee. *No More Secrets for Me* (3–5). Illus. by Jane Aaron. 1984, Little, Brown paper $8.95 (0-316-91491-6). Four stories about sexual abuse of young people.

17736 Waldman, Jackie. *Teens with the Courage to Give: Young People Who Triumphed Over Tragedy and Volunteered to Make a Difference* (4–10). 2000, Conari paper $15.95 (1-57324-504-6). 240pp. A compelling set of narratives in which 30 teens describe how they conquered various personal problems, such as loss of a limb or drug addiction, and went on to help others solve their problems. (Rev: BL 4/1/00) [179]

17737 Weston, Carol. *Private and Personal: Questions and Answers for Girls Only* (5–7). 2000, HarperCollins $9.95 (0-380-81025-5). 272pp. Using categories such as family, friendship, boyfriends, and growing up, this book consists of letters requesting advice and the author's responses to these letters. (Rev: BL 5/1/00; SLJ 7/00) [158]

Careers

General and Miscellaneous

17738 Bauld, Jane Scoggins. *We Need Librarians* (PS–1). Series: Helpers in Our Schools. 2000, Capstone LB $13.25 (0-7368-0531-1). 24pp. The many roles of school librarians are discussed in this beginning reader. (Rev: HBG 10/00; SLJ 10/00) [027]

17739 Bauld, Jane Scoggins. *We Need Principals* (PS–1). Series: Helpers in Our Schools. 2000, Capstone LB $13.25 (0-7368-0532-X). 24pp. For beginning readers, this is a book about school principals and what they do. (Rev: HBG 10/00; SLJ 10/00) [371]

17740 Bourgeois, Paulette. *Postal Workers* (PS–2). Illus. by Kim LaFave. 1999, Kids Can $12.95 (1-55074-504-2). 32pp. This work introduces the many types of postal workers — from those who work in the post office to mail carriers. (Rev: BL 7/99; HBG 10/99; SLJ 7/99) [383.4973]

17741 Cody, Tod. *The Cowboy's Handbook: How to Become a Hero of the Wild West* (4–6). Illus. 1996, Cobblehill $12.99 (0-525-65210-8). 29pp. The life of the modern cowboy is introduced, including gear, life on the trail, and the chuck wagon. Some craft projects are included. (Rev: BCCB 3/96; SLJ 6/96) [979.1]

17742 Dubois, Muriel L. *I Like Sports* (1–3). Series: What Can I Be? 2000, Bridgestone LB $17.26 (0-7368-0633-4). 24pp. A beginning career book that talks about sports broadcasters, referees, coaches, and players and gives instructions on how to make a racket-and-ball game. (Rev: HBG 3/01; SLJ 2/01) [796]

17743 Duvall, Jill D. *Chef Ki Is Serving Dinner!* (1–2). Illus. Series: Our Neighborhood. 1997, Children's LB $19.50 (0-516-20313-4). 32pp. In a photojournalistic style, readers are introduced to a chef who cooks Oriental food. Also use *Mr. Duvall Reports the News* and *Ms. Moja Makes Beautiful Clothes* (both 1997). (Rev: BL 8/97) [641.59519]

17744 Ermitage, Kathleen. *Recreation Director* (2–4). Series: Workers You Know. 2000, Raintree Steck-Vaughn LB $25.59 (0-8172-5593-1). 32pp. A children's recreation director describes a typical work day, which includes coordinating special events, encouraging parent involvement, and making curriculum content a part of everyday fun. (Rev: HBG 10/00; SLJ 11/00) [363.6]

17745 Fannon, Cecilia. *Leaders* (5–7). Series: Women Today. 1991, Rourke LB $17.95 (0-86593-118-6). 64pp. This book focuses on the lives of 24 women who have succeeded in business, education, science, and medicine. (Rev: SLJ 2/92) [650.1]

17746 Flanagan, Alice K. *A Day in Court with Mrs. Trinh* (1–2). Series: Our Neighborhood. 1997, Children's LB $19.50 (0-516-20008-9). 32pp. This career book describes the legal profession through the day-to-day activities of a real-life lawyer. (Rev: BL 12/15/97; SLJ 1/98) [340]

17747 Flanagan, Alice K. *Exploring Parks with Ranger Dockett* (1–2). Series: Our Neighborhood. 1997, Children's LB $19.50 (0-516-20496-3). 32pp. The work of National Park Service personnel is highlighted in this account that features a real member of the force, Ranger Dockett. (Rev: BL 12/15/97) [363.6]

17748 Flanagan, Alice K. *Raising Cows on the Koebel's Farm* (PS–1). Series: Our Neighborhood. 1999, Children's LB $19.50 (0-516-21133-1). 32pp. A simple, direct text and many illustrations tell this story of life on a cattle farm. (Rev: BL 7/99; HBG 10/99; SLJ 9/99) [631.2]

17749 Flanagan, Alice K. *The Zieglers and Their Apple Orchard* (PS–1). Series: Our Neighborhood. 1999, Children's LB $19.50 (0-516-21134-X). 32pp. A simple text and pictures introduce the work, duties, and lifestyle of a couple who operate an apple orchard. (Rev: BL 7/99; HBG 10/99) [631.2]

17750 Gibson, Karen Bush. *Child Care Workers* (K–3). Series: Community Helpers. 2000, Bridgestone LB $17.26 (0-7368-0622-9). 24pp. A solid introduction to various people who are involved in child care. (Rev: HBG 3/01; SLJ 2/01) [649]

17751 Greenberg, Keith E. *Window Washer: At Work Above the Clouds* (2–5). Illus. Series: Risky Business. 1995, Blackbirch LB $16.95 (1-56711-154-8). 32pp. The dangers involved and the safety measures required are stressed in this career book about two men who wash windows at the World Trade Center in New York City. (Rev: SLJ 8/95) [646.2]

17752 *I Want to Be a Chef* (4–6). Series: I Want to Be. 1999, Harcourt $17.00 (0-15-201864-6); paper $9.00 (0-15-201936-7). 48pp. A photo-essay that describes various careers in food preparation from head chef to dishwasher. (Rev: HBG 10/99; SLJ 4/99*) [641.5]

17753 Johnson, Neil. *All in a Day's Work: Twelve Americans Talk About Their Jobs* (5–7). Illus. 1989, Little, Brown $14.95 (0-316-46957-2). 89pp. People in various occupations — such as farmer, musician, and judge — show that work can be fun. (Rev: BCCB 2/90; BL 1/15/90; HB 3–4/90) [331.7]

17754 Lee, Barbara. *Working in Sports and Recreation* (4–8). Illus. Series: Exploring Careers. 1996, Lerner LB $23.93 (0-8225-1762-0). 112pp. Twelve people involved in careers related to sports and recreation talk candidly about their professions. (Rev: BL 2/15/97) [796]

17755 L'Hommedieu, Arthur J. *Working at a Museum* (1–3). Photos by Judith Angel. Series: Working Here. 1998, Children's LB $23.00 (0-516-20748-2). 32pp. Brief text and pictures show various workers at the Brooklyn Children's Museum and what they do. (Rev: HBG 3/99; SLJ 3/99) [562]

17756 Maynard, Christopher. *Jobs People Do* (PS–1). Illus. 1997, DK $12.95 (0-7894-1492-9). 32pp. This large-size book focuses on the world of work and includes children dressed as a fire fighter, dancer, surgeon, lawyer, mail carrier, pilot, etc. (Rev: BL 6/1–15/97) [331.7]

17757 Maze, Stephanie. *I Want to Be an Environmentalist* (3–6). Series: I Want to Be. 2000, Harcourt $18.00 (0-15-201862-X); paper $9.00 (0-15-201939-1). 48pp. Featuring many attractive color photos, this book describes various careers in conservation and environmental control. (Rev: BL 8/00; HBG 3/01; SLJ 1/01) [363.7]

17758 Maze, Stephanie, and Catherine O. Grace. *I Want to Be an Astronaut* (3–5). Illus. Series: I Want to Be. 1997, Harcourt $16.00 (0-15-201300-8). 48pp. A career book that describes the duties of an astronaut, the educational requirements, and how to get involved in the field. (Rev: BCCB 5/97; BL 4/15/97; HB 5–6/97; SLJ 4/97) [629.45]

17759 Pasternak, Ceel, and Linda Thornburg. *Cool Careers for Girls in Food* (5–10). Series: Cool Careers for Girls. 2000, Impact $19.95 (1-57023-127-3); paper $12.95 (1-57023-120-6). 128pp. The 11 women featured in this book are involved in various aspects of the food industry such as cheese making, baking, wine making, selling health food, and cooking for the military. (Rev: SLJ 2/00) [641]

17760 Pasternak, Ceel, and Linda Thornburg. *Cool Careers for Girls in Sports* (5–10). Series: Cool Careers for Girls. 1999, Impact $19.95 (1-57023-107-9); paper $12.95 (1-57023-104-4). 120pp. A golf pro, basketball player, ski instructor, sports broadcaster, trainer, sports psychologist, and athletic director are some of the ten women profiled in this overview of careers for women in sports. (Rev: SLJ 7/99) [796]

17761 Reeves, Diane Lindsey. *Career Ideas for Kids Who Like Math* (4–8). Illus. by Nancy Bond. 2000, Facts on File $18.95 (0-8160-4095-8). 186pp. Presents an amazing array of careers available for the mathematically inclined, arranged alphabetically with good solid information on each. (Rev: HBG 10/00; SLJ 9/00) [510]

17762 Reeves, Diane Lindsey, and Peter Kent. *Career Ideas for Kids Who Like Sports* (5–9). Illus. by Nancy Bond. Series: Career Ideas for Kids. 1998, Facts on File $18.95 (0-8160-3684-5); paper $12.95 (0-8160-3690-X). 167pp. After some general material on how to choose a career, this book highlights different careers involving sports, with material on necessary skills, opportunities, duties, and a report from someone in the field. (Rev: SLJ 6/99) [796]

17763 Roberts, Robin. *Careers for Women Who Love Sports* (4–6). Illus. Series: Get in the Game. 2000, Millbrook LB $21.90 (0-7613-1282-X). 48pp. Eight women discuss their jobs in sports as coach, official, journalist, athletic trainer, agent, marketing specialist, nutritionist, and sportscaster. (Rev: BL 9/1/00) [796.023]

17764 Schomp, Virginia. *If You Were a Farmer* (3–4). Series: If You Were A. 2000, Benchmark LB $15.95 (0-7614-1001-5). 32pp. The daily routines of a farmer and the equipment used are included in this simple career book. (Rev: BL 11/15/00; HBG 3/01; SLJ 3/01) [631]

17765 Schomp, Virginia. *If You Were a Teacher* (1–3). Series: If You Were A. 1999, Benchmark LB $15.95 (0-7614-0916-5). 32pp. After a brief history of teaching, there is coverage of various kinds of teachers in this attractive book. (Rev: HBG 10/00; SLJ 3/00) [371.7]

17766 Schomp, Virginia. *If You Were an Astronaut* (3–4). Series: If You Were A. 1997, Marshall Cavendish LB $22.79 (0-7614-0618-2). 32pp. Covers the education, training, and duties of astronauts. (Rev: BL 2/15/98; HBG 3/98; SLJ 2/98) [629]

17767 Stockdale, Linda. *ABC Career Book for Girls/El Libro de Carreras para Niñas* (K–3). Illus. by John Schafer. 1996, Columbia Univ. Pr. paper $9.95 (1-884830-00-5). 31pp. Using the letters of the alphabet, this book describes a wide range of occupations in English and Spanish. (Rev: SLJ 2/97) [331.7]

17768 Weiss, Ellen. *Odd Jobs: The Wackiest Jobs You've Never Heard Of!* (4–8). Photos by Damon Ross. 2000, Simon & Schuster paper $8.99 (0-689-82934-5). 64pp. Describes such unusual occupations as roller-coaster designer, comedy writer, movie sound-effects producer, food stylist, and storm chaser. (Rev: SLJ 7/00) [331.7]

Arts and Entertainment

17769 Aaseng, Nathan. *Wildshots: The World of the Wildlife Photographer* (5–8). Illus. 2001, Millbrook LB $27.90 (0-7613-1551-9). 80pp. This account describes the work of a wildlife photographer and tells exciting stories about unusual encounters. (Rev: BL 3/1/01*; SLJ 3/01) [778.9]

17770 Christelow, Eileen. *What Do Illustrators Do?* (2–4). Illus. 1999, Clarion $15.00 (0-395-90230-4). 40pp. Showing two illustrators — both working on a version of *Jack and the Beanstalk* — this book explores the illustration process and its finished product. (Rev: BCCB 5/99; BL 3/1/99; HB 5–6/99; HBG 10/99; SLJ 11/99) [741.6]

17771 Dubois, Muriel L. *I Like Music* (1–3). 2000, Bridgestone LB $17.26 (0-7368-0632-6). 24pp. Opposite each full-page photo, there is a description of a music-related occupation such as composer, conductor, sound engineer, or disc jockey. (Rev: HBG 3/01; SLJ 2/01) [780]

17772 Duvall, Jill D. *Meet Rory Hohenstein, a Professional Dancer* (1–2). Illus. Series: Our Neighborhood. 1997, Children's LB $19.50 (0-516-20312-6). 32pp. This is a photo-essay with simple text on the life, training, and problems faced by a young male professional dancer. (Rev: BL 5/15/97; SLJ 7/97) [792.8]

17773 Flanagan, Alice K. *Mrs. Scott's Beautiful Art* (PS–1). Series: Our Neighborhood. 1999, Children's LB $19.50 (0-516-21135-8). 32pp. A photo-filled account and a simple text introduce a woman who works with fabrics and weaving. (Rev: BL 7/99; HBG 10/99) [746.1]

17774 Greenberg, Keith E. *Photojournalist: In the Middle of Disaster* (2–4). Illus. Series: Risky Business. 1995, Blackbirch LB $16.95 (1-56711-157-2). 32pp. In this career book, the work of photojournalist John Isaac — a native of India and an official photographer for the United Nations — is highlighted. (Rev: SLJ 2/96) [770]

17775 Lee, Barbara. *Working in Music* (4–8). Illus. Series: Exploring Careers. 1996, Lerner $23.93 (0-8225-1761-2). 112pp. Such careers as composing, performing, and violin making are covered in this book profiling 12 people who work in the music field. (Rev: BL 2/15/97; SLJ 2/97) [780]

17776 Lyon, George E. *A Sign* (K–4). Illus. by Chris K. Soentpiet. 1998, Orchard $15.95 (0-531-30073-0). 32pp. As a child, the author wanted to pursue many different careers, but finally she decided that the best one would be writing. (Rev: BL 2/15/98; HBG 10/98; SLJ 3/98) [813]

17777 Maze, Stephanie. *I Want to Be a Dancer* (4–6). Illus. Series: I Want to Be. 1997, Harcourt $16.00 (0-15-201299-0). 48pp. Careers in dance are examined, with information on education, training, the history of dance, famous people, and special terms. (Rev: BL 2/1/98; HBG 3/98; SLJ 12/97) [792.8]

17778 Nathan, Amy. *The Young Musician's Survival Guide: Tips from Teens and Pros* (5–8). 2000, Oxford LB $18.95 (0-19-512611-4); paper $9.95 (0-19-512612-2). 126pp. A thorough study of how to break into the music world, with information on working with music teachers, conductors, and peers, and tips on practicing, choosing an instrument, and handling fears and frustrations. (Rev: HBG 10/00; SLJ 6/00) [780]

17779 Reeves, Diane Lindsey. *Career Ideas for Kids Who Like Art* (5–9). Illus. by Nancy Bond. Series: Career Ideas for Kids. 1998, Facts on File $18.95 (0-8160-3681-0); paper $12.95 (0-8160-3687-X). 168pp. An upbeat book that explores a variety of art-related careers, including many peripheral ones such as chef, animator, and photojournalist. (Rev: SLJ 10/98) [331.7]

17780 Reeves, Diane Lindsey. *Career Ideas for Kids Who Like Talking* (5–9). Illus. by Nancy Bond. Series: Career Ideas for Kids. 1998, Facts on File $18.95 (0-8160-3683-7); paper $12.95 (0-8160-3689-6). 154pp. This book explains various careers in communication, such as publicist and broadcaster, with practical advice on how to investigate each. (Rev: SLJ 10/98) [331.7]

17781 Reeves, Diane Lindsey. *Career Ideas for Kids Who Like Writing* (5–9). Illus. by Nancy Bond. Series: Career Ideas for Kids. 1998, Facts on File $18.95 (0-8160-3685-3); paper $12.95 (0-8160-3691-8). 166pp. From talk show producer to advertising copywriter, this book introduces 15 writing careers with an exercise to see if each one is suitable for the reader, resource listings including Internet sites, and a profile of someone working in the field. (Rev: SLJ 3/99) [808]

17782 Schomp, Virginia. *If You Were a Ballet Dancer* (3–4). Illus. Series: If You Were A. 1997, Marshall Cavendish LB $22.79 (0-7614-0616-6). 32pp. This introduction to a career in ballet tells about practicing, performing, styles of dance, costumes, and terminology. (Rev: BL 2/15/98; HBG 3/98; SLJ 2/98) [792.8]

17783 Schomp, Virginia. *If You Were a Musician* (3–4). Series: If You Were A. 2000, Benchmark LB $15.95 (0-7614-1002-3). 32pp. Using color photos and a simple text, this career book covers a typical day in the life of a musician. (Rev: BL 11/15/00; HBG 3/01; SLJ 3/01) [780]

17784 Vitkus-Weeks, Jessica. *Television* (4–8). Illus. Series: Now Hiring. 1994, Crestwood LB $14.95 (0-89686-783-8). 48pp. Using real people as case histories, this book describes such TV careers as grip, camera operator, production assistant, costume designer, and actor. (Rev: SLJ 8/94) [621.388]

Engineering, Technology, and Trades

17785 Brown, Angela McHaney. *Carpenter* (2–4). Series: Workers You Know. 2000, Raintree Steck-Vaughn LB $25.59 (0-8172-5596-6). 32pp. Explains what a carpenter does by following him through one of his projects. (Rev: HBG 10/00; SLJ 11/00) [694]

17786 Brown, Marty. *Webmaster* (4–8). Series: Coolcareers.com. 2000, Rosen Central LB $17.95

(0-8239-3111-0). 44pp. This volume describes a Web page, types of networks, servers, browsers, and protocols and introduces some careers in Web-related areas. (Rev: SLJ 6/00) [004]

17787 Flanagan, Alice K. *Mr. Paul and Mr. Luecke Build Communities* (1–2). Series: Our Neighborhood. 1999, Children's LB $19.50 (0-516-21131-5). 32pp. Two careers in building and construction are explored in a heavily illustrated book with minimal text. (Rev: BL 10/15/99) [624]

17788 McGinty, Alice B. *Software Designer* (4–8). Series: Coolcareers.com. 2000, Rosen Central LB $17.95 (0-8239-3149-8). 48pp. This book explains what a software engineer does, the skills required, education needed, and future prospects. (Rev: SLJ 6/00) [004]

17789 Maze, Stephanie. *I Want to Be an Engineer* (4–6). Illus. Series: I Want to Be. 1997, Harcourt $16.00 (0-15-201298-2). 48pp. Engineering and its various branches are introduced, along with the education and training necessary, terms used, and famous engineers. (Rev: BL 2/1/98; HBG 3/98; SLJ 12/97) [620]

17790 Mazor, Barry. *Multimedia and New Media Developer* (4–8). Series: Coolcareers.com. 2000, Rosen Central LB $17.95 (0-8239-3102-1). 45pp. This work explains the nature of multimedia careers, the training and skills necessary, and the job opportunities. (Rev: SLJ 6/00) [004]

17791 O'Donnell, Annie. *Computer Animator* (4–8). Series: Coolcareers.com. 2000, Rosen Central LB $17.95 (0-8239-3101-3). 44pp. This book gives a brief history of animation and explains how it is used today, the specialized roles of animators, educational requirements, and the future of the industry. (Rev: SLJ 6/00) [004]

17792 Oleksy, Walter. *Video Game Designer* (4–8). Series: Coolcareers.com. 2000, Rosen Central LB $17.95 (0-8239-3117-X). 47pp. This account explains how video games work and how they are designed, with material on the careers involved and the qualifications necessary. (Rev: SLJ 6/00) [794.8]

17793 Oleksy, Walter. *Web Page Designer* (4–8). Series: Coolcareers.com. 2000, Rosen Central LB $17.95 (0-8239-3112-9). 47pp. This well-illustrated account, which features case studies of several teenagers, gives information on Web page construction, what a designer does, the training required, and the job outlook. (Rev: SLJ 6/00) [004]

17794 Pasternak, Ceel, and Linda Thornburg. *Cool Careers for Girls in Computers* (5–8). 1999, Impact $19.95 (1-57023-106-0); paper $12.95 (1-57023-103-6). 121pp. This book introduces ten women of various ages and ethnic backgrounds who have been successful in different aspects of the computer industry. (Rev: SLJ 4/00) [004]

17795 Pasternak, Ceel, and Linda Thornburg. *Cool Careers for Girls in Engineering* (5–8). Series: Cool Careers for Girls. 1999, Impact $19.95 (1-57023-126-5); paper $12.95 (1-57023-119-2). 132pp. Examines engineering specializations — such as computer, biomedical, civil, and agricultural — and

the opportunities for women in these fields. (Rev: SLJ 1/00) [620]

17796 Reeves, Diane Lindsey, and Peter Kent. *Career Ideas for Kids Who Like Computers* (5–9). Illus. by Nancy Bond. Series: Career Ideas for Kids. 1998, Facts on File $18.95 (0-8160-3682-9); paper $12.95 (0-8160-3688-8). 167pp. After material on how to choose a career path based on interests, this account describes several jobs involving computers, the skills needed, and opportunities available, and gives a profile of a person in each area. (Rev: SLJ 6/99) [004]

17797 Schomp, Virginia. *If You Were a Construction Worker* (3–4). Illus. Series: If You Were A. 1997, Marshall Cavendish LB $22.79 (0-7614-0617-4). 32pp. This title describes the different jobs involved in a construction project, the various kinds of buildings these people work on, and some of the world's great structures, such as the Empire State Building and the pyramids. (Rev: BL 2/15/98; HBG 3/98) [624]

Health and Medicine

17798 Flanagan, Alice K. *Ask Nurse Pfaff, She'll Help You!* (1–2). Series: Our Neighborhood. 1997, Children's LB $19.50 (0-516-20495-5). 32pp. The life story of a nurse is given in this simple book that tells about nurses and their contributions to a community. (Rev: BL 12/15/97) [610]

17799 Flanagan, Alice K. *Dr. Kanner, Dentist with a Smile* (1–2). Series: Our Neighborhood. 1997, Children's LB $20.00 (0-516-20493-9). 32pp. What dentists do and their contributions to a community are covered in this book highlighting the work of an actual dentist, Dr. Kanner. (Rev: BL 12/15/97; SLJ 1/98) [617]

17800 Gibson, Karen Bush. *Emergency Medical Technicians* (K–3). Series: Community Helpers. 2000, Bridgestone LB $17.26 (0-7368-0623-7). 24pp. A solid introduction to emergency medical technicians, their work, training, and rewards. (Rev: HBG 3/01; SLJ 2/01) [610]

17801 Lee, Barbara. *Working in Health Care and Wellness* (4–8). Illus. Series: Exploring Careers. 1996, Lerner LB $23.93 (0-8225-1760-4). 112pp. Profiles 12 people who are in health care professions, including the pros and cons of each career. (Rev: BL 2/15/97) [610.69]

17802 Liebman, Dan. *I Want to Be a Doctor* (PS–1). Illus. Series: I Want to Be. 2000, Firefly LB $14.95 (1-55209-463-4); paper $3.99 (1-55209-461-8). 24pp. Using a simple text and many full-color photos, this book introduces the medical profession. (Rev: BL 9/15/00; HBG 10/00; SLJ 9/00) [610]

17803 Moses, Amy. *Doctors Help People* (PS–2). Illus. Series: Career Books. 1996, Child's World LB $21.36 (1-56766-304-4). 32pp. A career book that describes what doctors do, particularly when they care for children. (Rev: SLJ 3/97) [610]

17804 Pasternak, Ceel, and Linda Thornburg. *Cool Careers for Girls in Health* (5–9). Series: Cool

Careers for Girls. 1999, Impact $19.95 (1-57023-125-7); paper $12.95 (1-57023-118-4). 160pp. This book describes health-related careers for girls — as doctors, nurses, dentists, personal trainers, medical technologists, physical therapists, and dietitians. (Rev: SLJ 10/99) [610]

17805 Schomp, Virginia. *If You Were a Doctor* (3–4). Series: If You Were A. 2000, Benchmark LB $15.95 (0-7614-1000-7). 32pp. Full-color photographs and an easy text are used to describe the daily routines of a doctor. (Rev: BL 11/15/00; HBG 3/01) [610]

Police and Fire Fighters

17806 Beil, Karen M. *Fire in Their Eyes: Wildfires and the People Who Fight Them* (5–7). Illus. 1999, Harcourt $18.00 (0-15-201043-2). 64pp. Excellent photographs and text tell the story of smoke jumpers and the tools, methods, and training they receive for their exciting but dangerous job. (Rev: BCCB 4/99; BL 5/1/99; HB 3–4/99; HBG 10/99; SLJ 7/99) [363.37]

17807 Bourgeois, Paulette. *Police Officers* (PS–2). Illus. by Kim LaFave. Series: My Neighborhood. 1999, Kids Can $12.95 (1-55074-502-6). 32pp. This picture book explains the basic duties of neighborhood police officers. (Rev: BL 7/99; HBG 10/99; SLJ 7/99) [363.2]

17808 Flanagan, Alice K. *Ms. Murphy Fights Fires* (1–2). Series: Our Neighborhood. 1997, Children's LB $20.00 (0-516-20494-7). 32pp. A modern fire fighter is the focus of this book, which describes what these people do and their contributions to a neighborhood. (Rev: BL 12/15/97; SLJ 1/98) [363.77]

17809 Fortney, Mary T. *Fire Station Number 4: The Daily Life of Firefighters* (2–4). Illus. 1998, Carolrhoda LB $22.60 (1-57505-089-7). 48pp. Using the fire station at Livermore, a suburb of San Francisco, as home base, this photo-essay clearly details the day-to-day activities in a fire station and the duties and responsibilities of typical fire fighters. (Rev: BL 10/1/98; HBG 3/99; SLJ 1/99) [363.37]

17810 Gorrell, Gena K. *Catching Fire: The Story of Firefighting* (4–6). Illus. 1999, Tundra $16.95 (0-88776-430-4). 144pp. After giving a history of fire fighting, this account describes different kinds of fires and the methods used to combat them. (Rev: BCCB 5/99; BL 6/1–15/99) [363.37]

17811 Greenberg, Keith E. *Bomb Squad Officer: Expert with Explosives* (2–4). Illus. Series: Risky Business. 1995, Blackbirch LB $16.95 (1-56711-155-6). 32pp. A career book, set in New Jersey, that explains the work of the men who remove and dismantle or detonate suspicious objects. (Rev: SLJ 2/96) [363]

17812 Greenberg, Keith E. *Smokejumper: Firefighter from the Sky* (2–5). Illus. Series: Risky Business. 1995, Blackbirch LB $16.95 (1-56711-153-X). 32pp. This career book gives details on the training and skills needed to become a smoke jumper — a

person who parachutes into wildfires. (Rev: SLJ 8/95) [634.9]

17813 Greene, Carol. *Firefighters Fight Fires* (2–4). Illus. Series: Career Books. 1996, Child's World LB $21.36 (1-56766-301-X). 32pp. In this career book, readers accompany fire fighters to a blazing house where they rescue a cat. (Rev: SLJ 4/97) [363]

17814 Greene, Carol. *Police Officers Protect People* (PS–2). Illus. Series: Career Books. 1996, Child's World LB $21.36 (1-56766-311-7). 32pp. This career book shows many of the jobs that police officers do like coping with an accident and helping to find a missing child. (Rev: SLJ 3/97) [363]

17815 Liebman, Dan. *I Want to Be a Police Officer* (PS–1). Illus. Series: I Want to Be. 2000, Firefly LB $14.95 (1-55209-467-7); paper $3.99 (1-55209-465-0). 24pp. Full-color photographs and a brief text introduce police officers and what they do. (Rev: BL 6/1–15/00; SLJ 9/00) [363.2]

17816 Maass, Robert. *Fire Fighters* (2–3). Illus. 1989, Scholastic paper $4.99 (0-590-41460-7). 32pp. Photos of fire fighters in training, relaxing, and working a fire. (Rev: BCCB 2/89; BL 4/1/89)

17817 Masoff, Joy. *Fire!* (3–7). Illus. 1998, Scholastic $16.95 (0-590-97872-1). 48pp. The facts about and excitement of fire fighting are covered in this fast-paced book filled with pictures, sidebars, and extensive captions. (Rev: BCCB 4/98; BL 2/1/98; HB 3–4/98; HBG 10/98; SLJ 3/98) [363.37]

17818 Maze, Stephanie. *I Want to Be a Firefighter* (4–6). Illus. Series: I Want to Be. 1999, Harcourt $18.00 (0-15-201865-4); paper $9.00 (0-15-201937-5). 47pp. Urban, wild land, and international fire fighting are included in this fine career guide that covers many aspects of the job and famous people in the field. (Rev: HB 11–12/99; HBG 3/00; SLJ 12/99) [363]

17819 Royston, Angela. *Fire Fighters* (1–3). Illus. Series: Eyewitness Reader. 1998, DK paper $3.95 (0-7894-2960-8). 32pp. Using photographs and a simple text, this easy reader describes a house fire and the role of fire fighters in controlling it. (Rev: BL 7/98) [628.9]

17820 Ruth, Maria Mudd. *Firefighting: Behind the Scenes* (3–5). Illus. 1998, Houghton $17.00 (0-395-70129-5). 64pp. This book discusses the tools, training, and procedures of today's fire fighters and various specializations such as dispatcher and pump operator. (Rev: BL 10/15/98; HB 9–10/98; HBG 3/99; SLJ 9/98) [628.9]

17821 Schomp, Virginia. *If You Were a Firefighter* (3–4). Series: If You Were A. 1997, Marshall Cavendish LB $22.79 (0-7614-0615-8). 32pp. In this simple career book, the training and responsibilities of fire fighters are introduced. (Rev: BL 2/15/98; HBG 3/98) [363]

17822 Schomp, Virginia. *If You Were a Police Officer* (3–4). Series: If You Were A. 1997, Marshall Cavendish LB $22.79 (0-7614-0614-X). 32pp. The everyday activities of a police officer are described in this simple career book. (Rev: BL 2/15/98; HBG 3/98) [363]

17823 Winkleman, Katherine K. *Firehouse* (2–4). Illus. by John S. Winkleman. 1994, Walker $15.85 (0-8027-8317-1). 32pp. Facts about firehouses, past and present, and how they operate are presented in this fascinating behind-the-scenes look. (Rev: BCCB 10/94; BL 10/1/94; SLJ 1/95) [363.37]

Science

17824 Duvall, Jill D. *Who Keeps the Water Clean? Ms. Schindler!* (1–2). Illus. Series: Our Neighborhood. 1997, Children's LB $20.00 (0-516-20315-0). 32pp. This unusual book looks at the life and career of a worker in a water treatment plant. (Rev: BL 5/15/97; SLJ 7/97) [628.1]

17825 Ghez, Andrea Mia, and Judith Cohen. *You Can Be a Woman Astronomer* (3–5). Illus. by David Katz. 1995, Cascade Pass paper $6.00 (1-880599-17-1). 38pp. A career book in which the author tells how she became a scientist and of the excitement and wonder of using telescopes and other tools of the astronomer. (Rev: SLJ 1/96) [520]

17826 Greenberg, Keith E. *Marine Biologist: Swimming with the Sharks* (2–4). Illus. Series: Risky Business. 1995, Blackbirch LB $16.95 (1-56711-156-4). 32pp. A career book that focuses on the work of marine biologist Sonny Gruber, who has studied sharks for the past 30 years. (Rev: SLJ 2/96) [574.92]

17827 Higginson, Mel. *Scientists Who Study Ancient Temples and Tombs* (1–2). Illus. Series: Scientists. 1994, Rourke LB $10.95 (0-86593-376-6). 24pp. A simple introduction to archaeologists, what they do, the education necessary, and some of their important discoveries. (Rev: SLJ 2/95) [930]

17828 Higginson, Mel. *Scientists Who Study Fossils* (1–2). Illus. Series: Scientists. 1994, Rourke LB $10.95 (0-86593-375-8). 24pp. This basic book describes what paleontologists do, what sort of education and training they require, and some of their important accomplishments. (Rev: SLJ 2/95) [560]

17829 Higginson, Mel. *Scientists Who Study Ocean Life* (1–2). Illus. Series: Scientists. 1994, Rourke LB $10.95 (0-86593-371-5). 24pp. Describes the science of oceanography, as well as the training required and discoveries of these scientists who study the oceans. (Rev: SLJ 2/95) [551.46]

17830 Higginson, Mel. *Scientists Who Study the Earth* (1–2). Illus. Series: Scientists. 1994, Rourke LB $10.95 (0-86593-372-3). 24pp. A basic introduction to the work that geologists do and how they prepare for it. (Rev: SLJ 2/95) [557]

17831 Higginson, Mel. *Scientists Who Study Wild Animals* (1–2). Illus. Series: Scientists. 1994, Rourke LB $10.95 (0-86593-374-X). 24pp. Careers in animal biology are introduced briefly, with a description of the education and training necessary. (Rev: SLJ 2/95) [591]

17832 Lehn, Barbara. *What Is a Scientist?* (K–2). 1998, Millbrook $19.90 (0-7613-1272-2). 32pp. Outlines the various steps in the scientific method — designing experiments, making observations, and

so forth — and introduces the work of different kinds of scientists. (Rev: HBG 3/99; SLJ 4/99) [500]

17833 McElroy, Lisa Tucker. *Meet My Grandmother: She's a Deep Sea Explorer* (2–4). Series: Grandmothers at Work. 2000, Millbrook LB $22.90 (0-7613-1720-1). 32pp. A young boy introduces his grandmother, Sylvia Earle, who regularly swims with sharks as she explores the ocean's depths. (Rev: BL 9/15/00; HBG 3/01; SLJ 1/01) [551.46]

17834 Paige, David. *A Day in the Life of a Marine Biologist* (4–6). Illus. 1981, Troll paper $3.95 (0-89375-447-1). 32pp. Colorful pictures and brief text are used to describe the daily tasks of a marine biologist. [551.46]

17835 Reeves, Diane Lindsey. *Career Ideas for Kids Who Like Science* (5–9). Illus. by Nancy Bond. Series: Career Ideas for Kids. 1998, Facts on File $18.95 (0-8160-3680-2); paper $12.95 (0-8060-3686-1). 165pp. This book provides an aptitude test and then describes 15 science-related careers, providing information on educational requirements, working conditions, activities, etc. (Rev: SLJ 9/98) [500]

Transportation

17836 Flanagan, Alice K. *Flying an Agricultural Plane with Mr. Miller* (PS–1). Series: Our Neighborhood. 1999, Children's LB $19.50 (0-516-21132-3). 32pp. The various duties of an agricultural airplane pilot, such as crop spraying, are covered in this photo-filled book with a simple text. (Rev: BL 7/99; HBG 10/99) [629.13]

17837 Jaspersohn, William. *A Week in the Life of an Airline Pilot* (4–8). Illus. 1991, Little, Brown $14.95 (0-316-45822-8). 96pp. A close-up look at the duties and lives of members of an airline crew. (Rev: BL 3/15/91; HB 5–6/91; SLJ 5/91) [629.132]

17838 Robinson, Fay. *Pilots Fly Planes* (2–4). Illus. Series: Career Books. 1996, Child's World LB $21.36 (1-56766-308-7). 32pp. A career book that shows both male and female pilots going through a typical day of preparation and flight. (Rev: SLJ 4/97) [629.13]

17839 Royston, Angela. *Truck Trouble* (1–3). Illus. Series: Eyewitness Reader. 1998, DK paper $3.95 (0-7894-2958-6). 32pp. This easy reader describes the problems — a flat tire and a rainstorm — encountered by a truck driver who is making a special delivery to a children's hospital. (Rev: BL 7/98) [629.2]

17840 Schomp, Virginia. *If You Were a Pilot* (1–3). Series: If You Were A. 1999, Benchmark LB $15.95 (0-7614-0919-X). 32pp. A brief, attractive introduction to what a pilot does, plus a discussion of different kinds of planes. (Rev: HBG 10/00; SLJ 3/00) [629.132]

17841 Schomp, Virginia. *If You Were a Truck Driver* (3–4). Series: If You Were A. 2000, Benchmark LB $15.95 (0-7614-1003-1). 32pp. Covers the daily life of a truck driver, with information on the care and handling of trucks. (Rev: BL 11/15/00; HBG 3/01) [629.24]

Veterinarians

17842 Bryant, Jennifer. *Jane Sayler: Veterinarian* (3–5). Illus. Series: Working Moms. 1991, Children's LB $21.27 (0-516-07378-8). 40pp. Combining the jobs of mother and animal doctor is the focus of this career book. (Rev: BL 6/15/91; SLJ 6/91) [636]

17843 Davis, Wendy. *Working at a Marine Institute* (1–3). Series: Working Here. 1998, Children's LB $23.00 (0-516-21223-0). 32pp. Different workers at the Marine Resources Development Foundation in Key Largo, Florida, are introduced with a description of their jobs and a picture of each. (Rev: HBG 3/99; SLJ 3/99) [636]

17844 Ermitage, Kathleen. *Veterinarian* (2–4). Series: Workers You Know. 2000, Raintree Steck-Vaughn LB $25.59 (0-8172-5592-3). 32pp. Describes a day in the life of a vet, including routine diagnoses, emergency procedures, and follow-up activities. (Rev: HBG 10/00; SLJ 11/00) [636.089]

17845 Flanagan, Alice K. *Dr. Friedman Helps Animals* (1–2). Series: Our Neighborhood. 1999, Children's LB $19.50 (0-516-21138-2). 32pp. Colorful illustrations and large-type text introduce the reader to veterinary medicine, through the daily experiences of a female vet. (Rev: BL 10/15/99) [636]

17846 Greene, Carol. *Veterinarians Help Animals* (2–4). Illus. Series: Career Books. 1996, Child's World LB $21.36 (1-56766-310-9). 32pp. In this career book, veterinarians care for a number of animals, mainly cats and dogs. (Rev: SLJ 4/97) [636]

17847 Horenstein, Henry. *My Mom's a Vet* (4–6). Illus. 1994, Candlewick $17.95 (1-56402-234-X); paper $7.99 (1-56402-922-0). 64pp. In this photo-essay, young Darcie describes a week in which she helps her mother, a veterinarian. (Rev: BCCB 3/94; BL 5/1/94; HB 5–6/94; SLJ 6/94) [636.089]

17848 Hurwitz, Jane. *Choosing a Career in Animal Care* (4–8). Illus. Series: World of Work. 1996, Rosen LB $15.95 (0-8239-2268-5). 64pp. Various careers in working with animals are described, along with the education required, desirable personality traits, and ways to break into the field. (Rev: SLJ 8/97) [371.7]

17849 Jacobs, Shannon K. *Healers of the Wild: People Who Care for Injured and Orphaned Wildlife* (4–7). Illus. 1998, Coyote Moon paper $19.95 (0-9661070-0-4). 212pp. The process of helping orphaned, injured, or displaced wildlife is covered thoroughly under three operational headings: rescue, rehabilitation, and release. (Rev: BL 10/1/98) [339.946]

17850 Knight, Bertram T. *Working at a Zoo* (1–3). Photos by Tom Stack and Therisa Stack. Series: Working Here. 1998, Children's LB $23.00 (0-516-20751-2). 32pp. Various workers at the zoo in Miami are introduced with descriptions of their jobs and how they keep the animals healthy and happy. (Rev: HBG 3/99; SLJ 3/99) [590]

17851 Lauber, Patricia. *The Tiger Has a Toothache: Helping Animals at the Zoo* (1–4). Illus. by Mary Morgan. 1999, National Geographic $15.95 (0-7922-3441-3). 32pp. An informative book about the work of zookeepers and veterinarians as they treat sick and injured birds and animals. (Rev: BCCB 12/99; BL 11/1/99; HBG 3/00; SLJ 12/99) [636.089]

17852 Lee, Barbara. *Working with Animals* (4–8). Illus. Series: Exploring Careers. 1996, Lerner LB $23.93 (0-8225-1759-0). 112pp. Profiles of 12 careers involving animals, such as veterinarian, animal shelter worker, or pet sitter. (Rev: BL 2/15/97) [591]

17853 Liebman, Dan. *I Want to Be a Vet* (PS–1). Illus. Series: I Want to Be. 2000, Firefly LB $14.95 (1-55209-471-5); paper $3.99 (1-55209-469-3). 24pp. A very simple introduction to what veterinarians do and how they are prepared for their jobs. (Rev: BL 9/15/00; HBG 10/00; SLJ 2/01) [636]

17854 Maze, Stephanie, and Catherine O. Grace. *I Want to Be a Veterinarian* (3–5). Illus. Series: I Want to Be. 1997, Harcourt $16.00 (0-15-201296-6). 48pp. Describes the responsibilities of a veterinarian, educational requirements for the profession, and how to make a start toward getting into the field. (Rev: BCCB 5/97; BL 4/15/97; HB 5–6/97; SLJ 4/97) [636]

17855 Pasternak, Ceel. *Cool Careers for Girls with Animals* (5–8). Series: Cool Careers for Girls. 1998, Impact $19.95 (1-57023-108-7); paper $12.95 (1-57023-105-2). This book covers such careers as a veterinarian, pet sitter, bird handler, animal trainer, and horse-farm owner. (Rev: SLJ 4/99) [371.7]

17856 Schomp, Virginia. *If You Were a Veterinarian* (3–4). Series: If You Were A. 1997, Marshall Cavendish LB $22.79 (0-7614-0613-1). 32pp. In this simple career book, the everyday activities of a veterinarian are described, with some information on the educational background necessary. (Rev: BL 2/15/98; HBG 3/98; SLJ 2/98) [636]

Health and the Human Body

Aging and Death

17857 Helmer, Diana Star. *Let's Talk About When Someone You Know Is in a Nursing Home* (PS–2). Photos by Seth Dinnerman. Series: Let's Talk. 1999, Rosen LB $11.95 (0-8239-5190-1). 24pp. A simply written account that answers questions that children might have about nursing homes, including how to be comfortable when visiting. (Rev: SLJ 12/99) [362]

17858 Hyde, Margaret O., and Lawrence E. Hyde. *Meeting Death* (5–8). 1989, Walker LB $15.85 (0-8027-6874-1). 144pp. Demystifying death for children while acknowledging that it is the central mystery of our lives. (Rev: BL 1/1/90) [306.9]

17859 Johnston, Marianne. *Let's Talk About Going to a Funeral* (1–4). Series: Let's Talk. 1998, Rosen LB $13.95 (0-8239-5038-7). 24pp. This book describes what happens before, during, and after a funeral and discusses grieving, the cemetery, the grave, and cremation. (Rev: SLJ 7/98) [393]

17860 Sprung, Barbara. *Death* (4–8). Series: Preteen Pressures. 1998, Raintree Steck-Vaughn LB $24.97 (0-8172-5029-8). 48pp. This book supplies information on topics such as terminal illness, sudden death, and suicide, as well as customs of remembrance and the grieving process. (Rev: BL 5/15/98; HBG 10/98) [304.6]

Alcohol, Drugs, and Smoking

17861 Bryant-Mole, Karen. *Drugs* (2–3). Series: Talking About. 1999, Raintree Steck-Vaughn LB $15.98 (0-8172-5887-6). 32pp. Large pages, large type, big color photos, and short sentences introduce, from a child's point of view, drugs and their use and misuse. (Rev: BL 2/15/00; HBG 10/00; SLJ 5/00) [362.29]

17862 Clayton, Lawrence. *Alcohol Drug Dangers* (4–7). Illus. Series: Drug Dangers. 1999, Enslow LB $19.95 (0-7660-1159-3). 64pp. Using real-life case histories, this book describes the effects of alcohol on the body and mind. (Rev: BL 8/99; HBG 10/99) [362.292]

17863 Clayton, Lawrence. *Diet Pill Drug Dangers* (5–9). Series: Drug Dangers. 1999, Enslow LB $19.95 (0-7660-1158-5). 64pp. Beginning with a case history of a young person's abuse of diet pills, this account uses other real-life stories to explore the nature of these drugs and their possible dangers. (Rev: HBG 10/99; SLJ 9/99) [616]

17864 Green, Jen. *Alcohol* (2–3). Series: Talking About. 1999, Raintree Steck-Vaughn LB $15.98 (0-8172-5888-4). 32pp. A simple but colorfully illustrated introduction to alcohol — what it is and how it affects the human body. (Rev: BL 2/15/00; HBG 10/00) [613.8]

17865 Grosshandler-Smith, Janet. *Working Together Against Drinking and Driving* (4–8). Illus. Series: Library of Social Activism. 1996, Rosen LB $16.95 (0-8239-2259-6). 64pp. A book that gives advice on how to avoid alcohol and how one can be involved in the crusade against drinking and driving. (Rev: SLJ 2/97) [616.86]

17866 Hanan, Jessica. *When Someone You Love Is Addicted* (5–9). Series: The Drug Abuse Prevention Library. 1999, Rosen LB $17.95 (0-8239-2831-4). 64pp. A short book that begins with teenage case histories and then discusses treatments for young people with drug problems. (Rev: SLJ 7/99) [362.2]

17867 Harris, Jacqueline L. *Drugs and Disease* (5–8). Illus. Series: Bodies in Crisis. 1993, Twenty-First Century LB $18.90 (0-8050-2602-9). 64pp. Introduces various drugs and their role in fighting diseases in a simple, well-illustrated format. (Rev: BL 1/15/94; SLJ 1/94) [616.86]

17868 Haughton, Emma. *Alcohol* (5–10). Series: Talking Points. 1999, Raintree Steck-Vaughn $27.11 (0-8172-5317-1). 64pp. A candid look at the use and abuse of alcohol and its physical and emotional effects. (Rev: BL 8/99) [613.8]

17869 Haughton, Emma. *A Right to Smoke?* (3–6). Illus. Series: Viewpoints. 1997, Watts LB $22.50 (0-531-14412-7). 32pp. The controversy concerning cigarette advertising and special taxes is covered, along with facts on the effects of smoking. (Rev: BL 6/1–15/97; SLJ 5/97) [362.29]

17870 Hirschfelder, Arlene. *Kick Butts! A Kid's Action Guide to a Tobacco-Free America* (5–8). Illus. 1998, Silver Burdett LB $19.95 (0-382-39632-4); paper $9.95 (0-382-39633-2). 160pp. This account outlines the history of smoking in the United States, traces the activities of antismoking activists, and chronicles the connections between smoking and health problems. (Rev: BL 6/1–15/98; HBG 10/98; SLJ 7/98) [613.8]

17871 Hyde, Margaret O. *Know About Drugs.* 4th ed (5–8). 1995, Walker LB $15.85 (0-8027-8395-3). 93pp. An introduction to drugs and their effects, including marijuana, alcohol, PCP, inhalants, crack/cocaine, heroin, and nicotine. (Rev: BL 7/90; SLJ 3/96) [362.2]

17872 Hyde, Margaret O. *Know About Smoking.* Rev. ed. (5–8). Illus. 1995, Walker LB $14.85 (0-8027-8400-3). 100pp. After a history of tobacco and nicotine, this book describes their effects on the body, addiction prevention, and the role of advertising in smoking. (Rev: BL 7/90; SLJ 9/95) [362.2]

17873 Hyde, Margaret O., and John F. Setaro. *Alcohol 101: An Overview for Teens* (5–10). 1999, Twenty-First Century LB $23.90 (0-7613-1274-9). 128pp. Kinds of alcohol and their effects are described, with material on alcoholism and binge drinking. (Rev: HBG 3/00; SLJ 3/00) [613.8]

17874 Kreiner, Anna. *Let's Talk About Drug Abuse* (1–4). Illus. Series: Let's Talk. 1996, Rosen LB $13.95 (0-8239-2302-9). 24pp. Various kinds of drugs and their effects on the human body are introduced. (Rev: BL 3/1/97; SLJ 12/96) [362.29]

17875 Landau, Elaine. *Hooked: Talking About Addiction* (5–7). Illus. 1995, Millbrook LB $21.90 (1-56294-469-X). 64pp. This account defines addiction broadly — from use of alcohol and drugs to various forms of compulsive behavior — and gives suggestions for recovery. (Rev: BL 1/1–15/96; SLJ 1/96) [362.29]

17876 Lawler, Jennifer. *Drug Testing in Schools: A Pro/Con Issue* (5–8). Series: Hot Issues. 2000, Enslow LB $19.95 (0-7660-1367-7). 64pp. The pros and cons of drug testing in schools are presented in an unbiased manner with sections on methods of drug testing, policies of various organizations, and the opinions of students, teachers, and parents. (Rev: HBG 3/01; SLJ 12/00) [362.29]

17877 Littell, Mary Ann. *Heroin Drug Dangers* (5–8). Series: Drug Dangers. 1999, Enslow LB $19.95 (0-7660-1156-9). 64pp. A short, well-illustrated book that describes the physiological effects of heroin, the dangers of its use, and how to resist its temptations. (Rev: BL 9/15/99; HBG 3/00) [362.2]

17878 McGuire, Paula. *Alcohol* (4–8). Illus. Series: Preteen Pressures. 1998, Raintree Steck-Vaughn LB $24.97 (0-8172-5026-3). 48pp. Topics discussed in this practical account include peer pressure to drink, the physical effects of alcohol, underage drinking, alcoholic parents, and ways to seek help. (Rev: BL 4/15/98; HBG 10/98) [362.29]

17879 Marr, John S. *Breath of Air and a Breath of Smoke* (4–6). Illus. 1971, Evans $4.95 (0-87131-038-4). 48pp. After a description of the respiratory system, there is a description of the effects of smoking on the body.

17880 Monroe, Judy. *Inhalant Drug Dangers* (4–7). Illus. 1999, Enslow LB $19.95 (0-7660-1153-4). 64pp. Using case histories — such as the story of Ian, who is addicted to inhaling fabric protector — this slim volume tells of the effects and dangers of inhalants. (Rev: BL 8/99; HBG 10/99; SLJ 9/99) [362.29]

17881 Monroe, Judy. *Steroid Drug Dangers* (5–8). Illus. Series: Drug Dangers. 1999, Enslow LB $19.95 (0-7660-1154-2). 64pp. Case histories, facts, and statistics introduce the reader to steroid drugs — their legal and illegal uses, their effects and dangers, and the organizations that promote safe usage. (Rev: BL 9/15/99; HBG 3/00) [362.29]

17882 Murdico, Suzanne J. *Drug Abuse* (4–8). Series: Preteen Pressures. 1998, Raintree Steck-Vaughn LB $24.97 (0-8172-5027-1). 48pp. This work discusses drug abuse, with emphasis on healthy alternatives and solutions to typical drug-related problems faced by many young people. (Rev: BL 5/15/98; HBG 10/98) [362.2]

17883 Pietrusza, David. *Smoking* (4–7). Illus. Series: Overview. 1997, Lucent LB $18.96 (1-56006-186-3). 112pp. This well-organized account gives a history of smoking, tells about its effects on the human body, and contains information on smokers' rights and lawsuits against tobacco companies. (Rev: BL 8/97; SLJ 7/97) [362.29]

17884 Pringle, Laurence. *Smoking: A Risky Business* (3–7). Illus. 1996, Morrow $16.00 (0-688-13039-9). 128pp. A history of smoking and its effects, with tips on how to quit when you're hooked. (Rev: BL 12/1/96; SLJ 1/97) [362.29]

17885 Robbins, Paul R. *Crack and Cocaine Drug Dangers* (5–8). Series: Drug Dangers. 1999, Enslow LB $19.95 (0-7660-1155-0). 64pp. Charts, photographs, fact boxes, and a succinct text are used to discuss crack cocaine, its effects, and how to avoid its use. (Rev: BL 9/15/99; HBG 3/00) [362.2]

17886 Salak, John. *Drugs in Society: Are They Our Suicide Pill?* (5–8). Illus. Series: Issues of Our Time. 1993, Twenty-First Century LB $18.90 (0-8050-2572-3). 64pp. A slim, easily read account that describes the history of drug abuse, its unfortunate byproducts, and important cases involving such people as Manuel Noriega. (Rev: SLJ 2/94) [616]

17887 Sanders, Pete. *Smoking* (4–7). Illus. Series: What Do You Know About. 1996, Millbrook LB $20.90 (0-7613-0536-X). 32pp. Covers the effects of smoking and ways in which youngsters can avoid getting hooked. (Rev: SLJ 3/97) [362.2]

17888 Sanders, Pete, and Steve Myers. *Drinking Alcohol* (4–8). Illus. by Mike Lacey. Series: What Do You Know About. 1997, Millbrook LB $20.90 (0-7613-0573-4). 32pp. An introduction to alcohol use, with material on its dangerous effects on the body and behavior. (Rev: SLJ 10/97) [362.29]

17889 Schleifer, Jay. *Methamphetamine: Speed Kills* (5–9). Series: The Drug Abuse Prevention Library. 1999, Rosen LB $17.95 (0-8239-2512-9). 64pp. After a few teen case studies involving speed, this book explains its composition, effects, and dangers. (Rev: SLJ 7/99) [362.2]

17890 Somdahl, Gary L. *Marijuana Drug Dangers* (5–8). Series: Drug Dangers. 1999, Enslow LB $19.95 (0-7660-1214-X). 64pp. After introducing marijuana and its effects, this account covers its misuse and abuse and ways to resist it. (Rev: BL 11/15/99; HBG 3/00) [362.29]

17891 Steffens, Bradley. *Addiction: Distinguishing Between Fact and Opinion* (5–7). Illus. Series: Opposing Viewpoints Juniors. 1994, Greenhaven LB $16.20 (1-56510-094-8). 36pp. Critical thinking is encouraged by having the reader study a variety of attitudes and opinions about addiction. (Rev: BL 1/1/94) [362.29]

17892 Steins, Richard. *Alcohol Abuse: Is This Danger on the Rise?* (5–8). Illus. Series: Issues of Our Time. 1995, Twenty-First Century LB $18.90 (0-8050-3882-5). 64pp. After defining what an alcoholic is, this account describes the physical effects of alcohol and the emotional problems alcoholism causes within families. (Rev: SLJ 2/96) [613.8]

17893 Super, Gretchen. *Drugs and Our World* (K–3). Illus. by Blanche Sims. 1991, Troll paper $3.95 (0-8167-2365-6). 48pp. For young children, this and the two other titles in the series, *What Are Drugs?* and *You Can Say "NO" to Drugs* (both 1995), explain what harmful drugs are and how to avoid them. (Rev: SLJ 11/90) [616]

17894 Taylor, Clark. *The House That Crack Built* (3–8). Illus. by Jan T. Dicks. 1992, Chronicle paper $6.95 (0-8118-0123-3). 36pp. An old children's rhyme is turned into a dark verse, with a relentless rap beat, about drugs. (Rev: BL 4/15/92; SLJ 6/92) [362.29]

17895 Washburne, Carolyn K. *Drug Abuse* (5–8). Illus. Series: Overview. 1996, Lucent LB $18.96 (1-56006-169-3). 112pp. A carefully researched account that gives important background information on drug abuse and present-day practices and problems. (Rev: BL 1/1–15/96) [362.29]

17896 Wax, Wendy. *Say No and Know Why: Kids Learn About Drugs* (4–7). Illus. by Toby McAfee. 1992, Walker LB $13.85 (0-8027-8141-1). 80pp. A serious look at drug problems as a sixth-grade class in the Bronx, New York, gets a visit from a local nurse and an assistant district attorney. (Rev: BL 1/15/93; SLJ 10/92) [362.29]

17897 Weitzman, Elizabeth. *Let's Talk About Smoking* (4–8). Illus. Series: Let's Talk. 1996, Rosen LB $13.95 (0-8239-2307-X). 24pp. This book explains why people smoke, its effects, and ways to avoid

starting, with tips on how to give up. (Rev: BL 3/15/97; SLJ 1/97) [362.29]

Bionics and Transplants

17898 Beecroft, Simon. *Super Humans: A Beginner's Guide to Bionics* (5–7). Illus. by Ian Thompson and Stephen Sweet. Series: Future Files. 1998, Millbrook LB $22.40 (0-7613-0621-8); paper $8.95 (0-7613-0636-6). 32pp. This work explores such futuristic topics as cloning humans, gene manipulation, electronic body parts, and life extension. (Rev: HBG 10/98; SLJ 10/98) [617.9]

Disabilities, Physical and Mental

17899 Abeel, Samantha. *What Once Was White* (5–8). Illus. by Charles R. Murphy. 1993, Village Pr. $19.95 (0-941653-13-7). The author is a 13-year-old learning-disabled student who can't tell time but writes sensitive interpretations of a group of watercolor paintings. (Rev: SLJ 9/93*) [618.62]

17900 Alexander, Sally H. *Do You Remember the Color Blue? And Other Questions Kids Ask About Blindness* (5–8). Illus. 2000, Viking $15.99 (0-670-88043-4). 80pp. The writer, a blind person, tells about her daily life — how she tells time and works with her guide dog and how she and others have reacted to her disability. (Rev: BCCB 3/00; BL 3/15/00; HBG 10/00; SLJ 4/00) [305.9]

17901 Aseltine, Lorraine, et al. *I'm Deaf and It's Okay* (3–5). Illus. by Helen Cogancherry. 1986, Whitman LB $13.95 (0-8075-3472-2). 40pp. A boy copes with the frustrations of deafness. (Rev: BL 5/15/86; SLJ 8/86)

17902 Brown, Fern G. *Special Olympics* (4–7). Illus. 1992, Watts LB $22.00 (0-531-20062-0). 64pp. The history of the Special Olympics, which began in 1963. (Rev: BCCB 5/92; BL 6/1/92; SLJ 7/92) [796]

17903 Dwight, Laura. *We Can Do It!* (PS–3). Illus. 1992, Checkerboard $7.95 (1-56288-301-1). 36pp. Children with various disabilities are shown at home, at play, at school. (Rev: BL 1/15/93) [305]

17904 Dwyer, Kathleen M. *What Do You Mean I Have a Learning Disability?* (3–6). 1991, Walker LB $15.85 (0-8027-8103-9). 48pp. Feelings of inferiority are related in this story of a ten-year-old boy who fails in school. (Rev: BCCB 9/91; BL 9/1/91; SLJ 11/91) [371.9]

17905 Dwyer, Kathleen M. *What Do You Mean I Have Attention Deficit Disorder?* (4–6). Illus. 1996, Walker LB $15.85 (0-8027-8393-7). 128pp. Patrick doesn't know why he can't pay attention in school until he is diagnosed as having ADD. (Rev: BCCB 9/96; BL 8/96; SLJ 8/96) [618.92]

17906 Emmert, Michelle. *I'm the Big Sister Now* (3–5). Illus. by Gail Owens. 1989, Whitman LB $14.95 (0-8075-3458-7). 32pp. The younger sister of a child severely handicapped with cerebral palsy explains what life is like for them and their special love for each other. (Rev: BL 1/1/90; SLJ 12/89) [618.92]

17907 Fisher, Gary L., and Rhoda Cummings. *The Survival Guide for Kids with LD (Learning Differences)* (5–8). 1990, Free Spirit paper $9.95 (0-915793-18-0). 98pp. A supportive book aimed directly at kids with learning problems. (Rev: BL 7/90; SLJ 6/90) [371.9]

17908 Giacobello, John. *Everything You Need to Know About Anxiety and Panic Attacks* (5–9). Series: Need to Know Library. 2000, Rosen LB $17.95 (0-8239-3219-2). 64pp. This book explains anxiety attacks' causes, symptoms, and treatments in a reassuring tone. (Rev: SLJ 1/01) [616]

17909 Gold, Susan D. *Attention Deficit Disorder* (4–8). Series: Health Watch. 2000, Enslow LB $18.95 (0-7660-1657-9). 48pp. This account focuses on one boy from childhood to college and how he coped with attention deficit disorder. Several young people are profiled in the companion volume *Bipolar Disorder and Depression* (2000). (Rev: SLJ 2/01) [618.92]

17910 Gordon, Melanie Apel. *Let's Talk About Dyslexia* (2–4). Series: Let's Talk. 1999, Rosen LB $13.95 (0-8239-5199-5). 24pp. This book describes problems with reading and gives several examples of reading difficulties. (Rev: SLJ 3/99) [371.92]

17911 Gregson, Susan R. *Stress Management: Managing and Reducing Stress* (5–8). Series: Perspectives on Mental Health. 2000, Capstone LB $22.60 (0-7368-0432-3). 64pp. This book discusses the causes of stress, explains its positive and negative effects on the body and mind, and outlines strategies for reducing and managing it. (Rev: HBG 10/00; SLJ 8/00) [152.4]

17912 Hall, David E. *Living with Learning Disabilities: A Guide for Students* (5–8). 1993, Lerner LB $19.93 (0-8225-0036-1). 64pp. This book explains what learning disabilities are, what causes them, how they can be detected, and today's techniques for treatment. (Rev: BL 1/1/94; SLJ 4/94) [371.9]

17913 Haughton, Emma. *Living with Deafness* (3–5). 1999, Raintree Steck-Vaughn LB $22.83 (0-8172-5742-X). 32pp. Full-color illustrations are used to introduce people coping with deafness and cover topics including the anatomy of the ear, types of hearing loss and their causes, sign language, finger spelling, and lip reading. (Rev: HBG 10/00; SLJ 4/00) [617.8]

17914 Heelan, Jamee Riggio. *The Making of My Special Hand: Madison's Story* (PS–3). Photos by author. Illus. by Nicola Simmonds. 2000, Peachtree $14.95 (1-56145-186-X). Described the process of making a prosthesis for a girl who was born with one hand, from taking a plaster cast to connecting the electrode and battery and giving occupational therapy. (Rev: BL 4/1/00; HBG 3/01; SLJ 9/00) [617.5]

17915 Heelan, Jamee Riggio. *Rolling Along: The Story of Taylor and His Wheelchair* (PS–4). Illus. by Nicola Simmonds. 2000, Peachtree $14.95 (1-56145-219-X). 32pp. The true story of Taylor, who

was born with cerebral palsy and uses a wheelchair. (Rev: BL 9/1/00; HBG 3/01; SLJ 12/00) [616.6]

17916 Kent, Susan. *Let's Talk About Stuttering* (3–5). Series: Let's Talk. 2000, Rosen LB $17.26 (0-8239-5423-4). 24pp. As well as explaining what causes stuttering and who is most likely to stutter, this book tells how to deal with teasing and how to get help. (Rev: SLJ 2/01) [616.85]

17917 Landau, Elaine. *Blindness* (4–7). Illus. Series: Understanding Illness. 1994, Twenty-First Century LB $18.90 (0-8050-2992-3). 64pp. Both the emotional and scientific aspects of blindness are covered, with an excellent chapter on prevention. (Rev: BL 12/15/94; SLJ 2/95) [617.7]

17918 Landau, Elaine. *Deafness* (4–7). Illus. Series: Understanding Illness. 1994, Twenty-First Century LB $18.90 (0-8050-2993-1). 64pp. Beginning with the story of a deaf child, this book explores the causes of deafness, the scientific and emotional factors involved, treatments, and problems in adjusting. (Rev: BL 12/15/94; SLJ 2/95) [617.8]

17919 Landau, Elaine. *Living with Albinism* (4–6). Illus. Series: First Books. 1998, Watts LB $22.00 (0-531-20296-8). 64pp. The story of Ariel, an 11-year-old whose skin is very pale and who has white hair and light blue eyes, provides a basis for this exploration of albinism. (Rev: BL 11/15/98; HBG 10/98; SLJ 8/98) [616.5]

17920 Lauren, Jill. *Succeeding with LD: 20 True Stories About Real People with LD* (5–8). Illus. 1997, Free Spirit paper $14.95 (1-57542-012-0). 160pp. Case histories of 20 people, ages ten to 61, who have overcome various learning difficulties. (Rev: BL 6/1–15/97; SLJ 7/97) [371.92]

17921 McCarthy-Tucker, Sherri. *Coping with Special-Needs Classmates* (5–8). 1993, Rosen LB $18.95 (0-8239-1598-0). 115pp. First-person accounts describe physical, mental, and emotional problems faced by some young people. (Rev: SLJ 8/93) [616]

17922 MacKinnon, Christy. *Silent Observer* (K–4). Illus. 1993, Gallaudet Univ. $15.95 (1-56368-022-X). 48pp. The journal of a young deaf girl growing up in Nova Scotia at the end of the 19th century and her experiences at a boarding school. (Rev: BL 1/15/94; SLJ 3/94) [362.4]

17923 McMahon, Patricia. *Dancing Wheels* (3–7). Illus. 2000, Houghton $16.00 (0-395-88889-1). 48pp. Founded by a woman born with spina bifida, the Dancing Wheels project teaches people to "dance" from their wheelchairs. (Rev: BL 10/1/00; HBG 3/01; SLJ 11/00) [792.8]

17924 McNey, Martha. *Leslie's Story: A Book About a Girl with Mental Retardation* (3–5). Illus. 1996, Lerner LB $21.27 (0-8225-2576-3). 32pp. The lifestyle and limitations of a mentally retarded girl are explained. (Rev: BL 7/96; SLJ 9/96) [362.3]

17925 Meyer, Donald, ed. *Views from Our Shoes: Growing Up with a Brother or Sister with Special Needs* (4–6). Illus. 1997, Woodbine paper $14.95 (0-933149-98-0). 106pp. Using the words of 45 youngsters ages four to 18 as a focus, this book tells what it is like living with a sibling who has a physical or mental disability. (Rev: BL 1/1–15/98; SLJ 4/98) [362.1]

17926 Moragne, Wendy. *Dyslexia* (5–8). Illus. Series: Medical Library. 1997, Millbrook LB $23.90 (0-7613-0206-9). 96pp. Using interviews with a number of dyslexic teenagers, this book describes the symptoms, treatments, and emotional problems involved with dyslexia. (Rev: SLJ 3/97) [617.7]

17927 Nemiroff, Marc A., and Jane Annunziata. *Help Is on the Way: A Child's Book about ADD* (K–3). Illus. by Margaret Scott. 1998, Magination $19.95 (1-55798-505-7). 60pp. A picture book for children who suffer from attention deficit disorder, with material on its symptoms, the emotions it causes, and treatments that are available. (Rev: SLJ 9/98) [371.9]

17928 Powell, Jillian. *Talking About Disability* (2–3). Illus. Series: Talking About. 1999, Raintree Steck-Vaughn LB $22.83 (0-8172-5537-0). 32pp. Large pages, big type, and color photographs introduce children to physical and mental disabilities. (Rev: BL 7/99; HBG 10/99) [362.4]

17929 Powers, Mary Ellen. *Our Teacher's in a Wheelchair* (PS–1). Illus. by author. 1986, Whitman LB $13.95 (0-8075-6240-8). 32pp. Photo-essay showing how a young teacher manages a classroom in a day-care center even though he is in a wheelchair. (Rev: BL 11/15/86; SLJ 12/86)

17930 Roby, Cynthia. *When Learning Is Tough: Kids Talk About Their Learning Disabilities* (4–6). Illus. by Elena Dorfman. 1994, Albert Whitman LB $13.95 (0-8075-8892-X). 32pp. Eight youngsters talk about their learning problems and their accomplishments and dreams for the future. (Rev: BL 6/1–15/94; SLJ 9/94) [371.9]

17931 Rogers, Fred. *Let's Talk About It: Extraordinary Friends* (PS–4). Illus. by Jim Judkis. Series: Let's Talk. 2000, Putnam $15.99 (0-399-23146-3). 32pp. This book introduces young children to the world of physical disabilities and gives commonsense advice on how to treat people with handicaps. (Rev: BL 1/1–15/00; HB 3–4/00; HBG 10/00; SLJ 2/00) [362.4]

17932 Rosenberg, Marsha Sarah. *Everything You Need to Know When a Brother or Sister Is Autistic* (5–9). Series: Need to Know Library. 2000, Rosen LB $17.95 (0-8239-3123-4). 64pp. Autism is defined and described, with material on its diagnosis and treatment plus coverage of how this condition can affect other members of the family. (Rev: SLJ 8/00) [616.8]

17933 Rotner, Shelley, and Sheila Kelly. *The A.D.D. Book for Kids* (K–3). Illus. 2000, Millbrook LB $22.90 (0-7613-1722-8). 32pp. This photo-essay describes attention deficit disorder and its various symptoms and coping mechanisms. (Rev: BL 4/15/00; HBG 10/00; SLJ 7/00) [618.9]

17934 Stein, Sara Bonnett. *About Handicaps* (2–3). Illus. 1974, Walker $14.95 (0-8027-6174-7); paper $8.95 (0-8027-7225-0). 48pp. A book about learning to accept people who have physical handicaps.

17935 Westcott, Patsy. *Living with Blindness* (3–5). 1999, Raintree Steck-Vaughn LB $22.83 (0-8172-5741-1). 32pp. This book shows how blind people go about their daily lives and informs the reader about how the eye functions, kinds of visual impairment, and the causes of cataracts, glaucoma, and other conditions. (Rev: HBG 10/00; SLJ 4/00) [617.7]

Disease and Illness

17936 Aldape, Virginia Totorica. *Nicole's Story: A Book About a Girl with Juvenile Rheumatoid Arthritis* (3–5). Illus. 1996, Lerner LB $21.27 (0-8225-2578-X). 40pp. The case history of a young girl who has rheumatoid arthritis. (Rev: BL 7/96; SLJ 9/96) [362.1]

17937 Arnold, Lynda. *My Mommy Has AIDS* (PS–3). Illus. by Rosemont School of the Holy Child Students. 1998, Dream $18.95 (1-892073-01-3). 32pp. This story about a boy and his sick mother is a first-person narrative describing AIDS, how to avoid infection, and current treatments. (Rev: SLJ 5/99) [616.97]

17938 Bee, Peta. *Living with Asthma* (3–5). Illus. Series: Living With. 1999, Raintree Steck-Vaughn $22.83 (0-8172-5568-0). 32pp. This work discusses the causes and nature of asthma, various medications and treatments, and gives advice on how friends and family can help. (Rev: BL 8/99; HBG 10/99) [618.92]

17939 Berger, Melvin. *Germs Make Me Sick!* Rev. ed (K–3). Illus. by Marylin Hafner. Series: Let's-Read-and-Find-Out. 1995, HarperCollins LB $15.89 (0-06-024250-7); paper $4.95 (0-06445-154-2). 32pp. In this easily read book, germs and viruses and their effects on the human body are introduced. (Rev: BL 10/1/95; SLJ 3/96) [616.9]

17940 Blake, Claire, et al. *The Paper Chain* (PS–2). Illus. by Kathy Parkinson. 1998, Health paper $8.95 (0-929173-28-7). 30pp. As seen through the eyes of Marcus and Ben, this book deals with breast cancer and what happens when their mother undergoes surgery, chemotherapy, and radiation. (Rev: SLJ 6/98) [616.99]

17941 Bode, Janet. *Food Fight: A Guide to Eating Disorders for Pre-teens and Their Parents* (5–7). 1997, Simon & Schuster paper $16.00 (0-689-80272-2). 144pp. A clearly written account of the physical, psychological, and social aspects of anorexia and bulimia, plus practical suggestions for help. (Rev: BL 6/1–15/97; HB 1–2/97; SLJ 8/97*) [618.92]

17942 Bowman-Kruhm, Mary. *Everything You Need to Know About Down Syndrome* (4–7). Series: Need to Know Library. 2000, Rosen LB $17.95 (0-8239-2949-3). 63pp. Describes the causes, symptoms, and treatment of Down syndrome, and looks at the education and family life of individuals with this condition. (Rev: HBG 10/00; SLJ 3/00) [362.1]

17943 Brimner, Larry. *The Names Project: The AIDS Quilt* (4–6). Series: Cornerstones of Freedom.

1999, Children's LB $20.00 (0-516-20999-X). 32pp. The story of the AIDS epidemic, with special attention to the AIDS quilt and its significance. (Rev: BL 10/15/99) [616.97]

17944 Bryan, Jenny. *Living with Diabetes* (3–5). Illus. 1999, Raintree Steck-Vaughn $22.83 (0-8172-5575-3). 32pp. An introduction to diabetes, with material on its causes, effects, treatments, and control. (Rev: BL 8/99; HBG 10/99) [618.92]

17945 Bryan, Jenny. *What's Wrong with Me? What Happens When You're Sick, and Ways to Stay Healthy* (2–4). Illus. 1995, Thomson Learning LB $5.00 (1-56847-199-8). 32pp. In this book about illnesses, double-page spreads reveal possible causes and treatments for various symptoms. (Rev: BL 3/15/95) [616]

17946 Caffey, Donna. *Yikes — Lice!* (PS–4). Illus. by Patrick Girouard. 1998, Whitman $13.95 (0-8075-9374-5). 32pp. Uses rhymed couplets and cartoon illustrations to introduce head lice and their control. (Rev: BCCB 6/98; BL 4/15/98; HBG 10/98; SLJ 5/98) [616.5]

17947 Carson, Mary Kay. *Epilepsy* (4–8). Series: Diseases and People. 1998, Enslow LB $18.95 (0-7660-1049-X). 112pp. Traces the history of epilepsy and gives details on symptoms, diagnosis, and current treatments. (Rev: SLJ 9/98) [616.8]

17948 Carter, Alden R. *Stretching Ourselves: Kids with Cerebral Palsy* (2–4). 2000, Albert Whitman $14.95 (0-8075-7637-9). 32pp. Using case studies of three children, this book explores cerebral palsy — a disease that affects the control of muscles — and discusses how it is currently being treated. (Rev: BL 3/15/00; HBG 10/00; SLJ 5/00) [362.1]

17949 Carter, Alden R., and Siri M. Carter. *I'm Tougher Than Asthma!* (PS–2). Illus. 1996, Albert Whitman LB $14.95 (0-8075-3474-9). 32pp. In photos and text, the author explores the world of Siri, who suffers from asthma. (Rev: BL 3/1/96; SLJ 8/96) [616.2]

17950 Cefrey, Holly. *Coping with Cancer* (5–10). Series: Coping. 2000, Rosen LB $18.95 (0-8239-2849-7). 138pp. As well as discussing how cancer develops in various parts of the body, this book gives self-help advice for anyone who is diagnosed with the disease. (Rev: SLJ 12/00) [616.99]

17951 Connelly, John P., and Leonard Berlow. *You're Too Sweet: A Guide for the Young Diabetic* (4–6). Illus. 1968, Astor-Honor $14.95 (0-8392-1173-2). The cause and treatment of diabetes from the standpoint of a nine-year-old boy.

17952 Demuth, Patricia. *Achoo! All About Colds* (1–2). Illus. by Maggie Smith. 1997, Putnam $13.99 (0-448-41348-5); paper $3.95 (0-448-41347-7). 48pp. An easy reader that tells about colds, how they happen, and the treatments for them, using a fictional case history as a framework. (Rev: BL 8/97; SLJ 12/97) [616.2]

17953 Donnelly, Karen. *Everything You Need to Know About Lyme Disease* (5–8). Illus. Series: Need to Know Library. 2000, Rosen LB $17.95 (0-8239-3216-8). 64pp. This book explains how Lyme disease was discovered, how it is transmitted, its

symptoms, and its treatments. (Rev: BL 12/1/00) [616.9]

17954 Facklam, Howard, and Margery Facklam. *Viruses* (4–7). Illus. Series: Invaders. 1994, Twenty-First Century $18.90 (0-8050-2856-0). 64pp. The composition of viruses and their various types, including HIV, are introduced. (Rev: BL 1/1/95; SLJ 3/95) [576.62]

17955 Fassler, David, and Kelly McQueen. *What's a Virus, Anyway? The Kids' Book About AIDS* (K–4). 1993, Waterfront $10.95 (0-914525-14-X). 67pp. This book describes what AIDS is through an explanation of what a virus is and how some viruses attack our immune system. A reissue. (Rev: BL 6/1/90) [616]

17956 Forbes, Anna. *Kids with AIDS* (2–5). Illus. Series: AIDS Awareness Library. 1996, Rosen LB $13.95 (0-8239-2372-X). 24pp. Essential facts about AIDS are presented simply, with a focus on living with the disease and that being with AIDS- or HIV-infected individuals need not involve a health risk. (Rev: SLJ 1/97) [616.97]

17957 Forbes, Anna. *When Someone You Know Has AIDS* (3–5). Illus. Series: The AIDS Awareness Library. 1996, Rosen LB $13.95 (0-8239-2369-X). 24pp. A simple introduction to AIDS that covers its causes, effects, and treatments. Also use *Where Did AIDS Come From?* (1996). (Rev: SLJ 12/96) [616.97]

17958 Getz, David. *Purple Death: The Mysterious Flu of 1918* (3–5). Illus. 2000, Holt $16.00 (0-8050-5751-X). 86pp. This account describes the deadliest six months in human history — the 1918 flu epidemic that infected 2 billion people. (Rev: BCCB 12/00; BL 12/1/00; HBG 3/01; SLJ 2/01) [614.5]

17959 Gold, Susan D. *Alzheimer's Disease* (4–7). Illus. Series: Health Watch. 1995, Silver Burdett LB $15.95 (0-89686-857-5). 48pp. Using a case study as the focus, this account introduces Alzheimer's disease, its treatment, and current research. (Rev: BL 5/15/96; SLJ 1/96) [362.1]

17960 Goodnough, David. *Eating Disorders: A Hot Issue* (5–8). Series: Hot Issues. 1999, Enslow LB $19.95 (0-7660-1336-7). 64pp. This is a clear introduction to anorexia nervosa, bulimia, and binge eating with material and case studies on symptoms, causes, and consequences but little coverage of prevention and treatment. (Rev: HBG 3/00; SLJ 1/00) [618.92]

17961 Gordon, Melanie Apel. *Let's Talk About Head Lice* (2–4). Series: Let's Talk. 1999, Rosen LB $13.95 (1-56838-276-6). 24pp. The habits of head lice are covered plus material on how they are transmitted and how to get rid of them. (Rev: SLJ 3/99) [595.7]

17962 Greenberg, Keith E. *Disease Detective: Solving Deadly Mysteries* (4–7). Series: Risky Business. 1997, Blackbirch LB $16.95 (1-56711-162-9). 32pp. Profiles the many services performed by scientists in their quest to find cures for diseases. (Rev: BL 10/15/97; HBG 3/98; SLJ 1/98) [616]

17963 Gutman, Bill. *Harmful to Your Health* (5–8). Illus. Series: Focus on Safety. 1996, Twenty-First

Century LB $20.40 (0-8050-4144-3). 80pp. Health hazards of AIDS, steroids, drugs, and sexual abuse are covered in a straightforward manner. (Rev: BL 2/1/97; SLJ 2/97) [616.86]

17964 Harris, Jacqueline L. *Communicable Diseases* (5–8). 1993, Twenty-First Century LB $18.90 (0-8050-2599-5). 64pp. Various contagious diseases are covered, with material on how they are spread and treated. (Rev: BL 1/15/94; SLJ 1/94) [616.9]

17965 Harris, Jacqueline L. *Hereditary Diseases* (5–8). Illus. Series: Bodies in Crisis. 1993, Twenty-First Century LB $18.90 (0-8050-2603-7). 64pp. Diagnosis, effects, treatments, and possible cures are discussed in relation to hereditary diseases. (Rev: BL 1/15/94; SLJ 1/94) [616]

17966 Huegel, Kelly. *Young People and Chronic Illness: True Stories, Help, and Hope* (5–9). 1998, Free Spirit paper $14.95 (1-57542-041-4). 199pp. This book highlights ten case histories of young people with such medical problems as hemophilia, diabetes, epilepsy, asthma, cancer, heart problems, and lupus. (Rev: SLJ 10/98) [362.1]

17967 Hyde, Margaret O., and Elizabeth Forsyth. *The Disease Book: A Kid's Guide* (5–8). Illus. 1997, Walker LB $17.85 (0-8027-8498-4). 160pp. An overview of the causes, symptoms, and treatments of more than 100 physical and mental diseases. (Rev: BL 9/15/97; HBG 3/98; SLJ 11/97) [616]

17968 Hyde, Margaret O., and Elizabeth Forsyth. *Know About AIDS* (4–8). Illus. Series: Know About. 1994, Walker LB $14.85 (0-8027-8346-5). 100pp. Advances in research and current status are covered in this revised edition. (Rev: BL 7/90; SLJ 7/90) [616.97]

17969 Hyde, Margaret O., and Elizabeth Forsyth. *Know About Mental Illness* (5–8). Illus. 1996, Walker LB $15.85 (0-8027-8429-1). 144pp. In an anecdotal manner, several mental illnesses and their treatments are discussed. (Rev: BL 9/1/96; SLJ 7/96) [616.89]

17970 Hyde, Margaret O., and Elizabeth Forsyth. *Living with Asthma* (4–6). Illus. 1995, Walker LB $15.85 (0-8027-8287-6). 96pp. The physical and emotional aspects of asthma are introduced, with several case histories of people who cope with this condition. (Rev: BL 6/1–15/95; SLJ 7/95) [362]

17971 Katz, Bobbi. *Germs! Germs! Germs!* (1–2). Illus. by Steve Bjorkman. Series: Beginning Reader: Science. 1996, Scholastic $3.99 (0-590-67295-9). 40pp. The contributions and havoc caused by germs are revealed from their point of view. (Rev: BL 2/1/97) [616]

17972 Katz, Bobbi. *Lots of Lice* (1–3). Illus. by Steve Bjorkman. Series: Hello Reader! 1998, Scholastic paper $3.99 (0-590-10834-4). 40pp. A funny and informative book for beginning readers that tells about lice, how one gets them, and what to do about them — as told from the standpoint of one of the lice. (Rev: BL 11/1/98; SLJ 2/99) [613]

17973 Kehret, Peg. *Small Steps: The Year I Got Polio* (3–5). 1996, Albert Whitman LB $14.95 (0-8075-7457-0). 179pp. The author describes seven months in her life when, at age 12, she was stricken with polio. (Rev: BCCB 11/96; BL 11/1/96; SLJ 11/96*) [362.1]

17974 Lampton, Christopher. *Epidemic* (4–6). Illus. Series: Disaster! 1992, Millbrook LB $19.90 (1-56294-126-7). 64pp. The causes and effects of epidemics are covered, plus the possibility of predicting them. (Rev: BL 4/1/92; SLJ 8/92) [614.4]

17975 Landau, Elaine. *Allergies* (4–7). Illus. Series: Understanding Illness. 1994, Twenty-First Century LB $18.90 (0-8050-2989-3). 64pp. After a case history that explores allergies in personal terms, an objective presentation is given of their causes, effects, and treatment. (Rev: BL 12/15/94; SLJ 2/95) [616.97]

17976 Landau, Elaine. *Cancer* (4–7). Illus. Series: Understanding Illness. 1994, Twenty-First Century LB $18.90 (0-8050-2990-7). 64pp. This book explains the many types of cancer, their causes, present-day treatments, and possible developments in the future. (Rev: BL 12/15/95; SLJ 2/95) [616.99]

17977 Landau, Elaine. *Diabetes* (4–7). Illus. Series: Understanding Illness. 1994, Twenty-First Century LB $18.90 (0-8050-2988-5). 64pp. Causes of diabetes, prevention, and treatment are covered, with case studies to describe how people adjust. (Rev: BL 12/15/94; SLJ 2/95) [616.4]

17978 Landau, Elaine. *Epilepsy* (4–7). Illus. Series: Understanding Illness. 1994, Twenty-First Century LB $18.90 (0-8050-2991-5). 64pp. Following the story of a youngster who has epilepsy, this account describes the disorder, its emotional and medical aspects, and treatments. (Rev: BL 12/15/94; SLJ 2/95) [616.8]

17979 Landau, Elaine. *Parkinson's Disease* (5–8). Series: Venture Books. 1999, Watts LB $24.00 (0-531-11423-6). 112pp. A well-organized overview that explains the various motor, emotional, and speech symptoms of Parkinson's, plus material on the different treatments available and why some are controversial. (Rev: SLJ 6/99) [616]

17980 Lassieur, Allison. *Head Lice* (3–5). Illus. Series: My Health. 2000, Watts LB $22.50 (0-531-11624-7); paper $6.95 (0-531-16450-0). 48pp. Using amazing photos taken with microscopes, this account introduces head lice, their physical characteristics, how they are transmitted, and how to get rid of them. (Rev: BL 6/1–15/00) [616.5]

17981 Leigh, Vanora. *Mental Illness* (5–10). Series: Talking Points. 1999, Raintree Steck-Vaughn $27.11 (0-8172-5311-4). 64pp. This book defines mental illness, gives examples, and discusses causes, treatments, and how to stay mentally healthy. (Rev: BL 8/99) [362.2]

17982 McGuire, Paula. *AIDS* (4–8). Series: Preteen Pressures. 1998, Raintree Steck-Vaughn LB $24.97 (0-8172-5025-5). 48pp. Straight facts and current statistics are given on AIDS, including methods of prevention and stories of people with HIV/AIDS, such as Magic Johnson and the late Ryan White. (Rev: BL 5/15/98; HBG 10/98) [616,97]

17983 Manning, Karen. *AIDS: Can This Epidemic Be Stopped?* (6–8). Illus. Series: Issues of Our Time. 1995, Twenty-First Century LB $18.90 (0-

8050-4240-7). 64pp. A frank, objective account of how AIDS is transmitted and present treatment strategies. (Rev: BL 2/1/96; SLJ 2/96) [616.97]

17984 Marx, Trish, and Dorita Beh-Eger. *I Heal: The Children of Chernobyl in Cuba* (3–6). Illus. 1996, Lerner LB $21.27 (0-8225-4897-6). 48pp. This book contains the story of two young victims of the Chernobyl nuclear disaster and of their medical treatment in Cuba. (Rev: BCCB 12/96; BL 12/1/96; SLJ 10/96) [618.92]

17985 Massari, Francesca. *Everything You Need to Know About Cancer* (5–9). Series: Need to Know Library. 2000, Rosen LB $17.95 (0-8239-3164-1). 64pp. This book defines what cancer is and looks at its causes, prevention, symptoms, diagnosis, and treatment. (Rev: HBG 10/00; SLJ 8/00) [616.99]

17986 Moehn, Heather. *Everything You Need to Know When Someone You Know Has Leukemia* (5–10). Series: Need to Know Library. 2000, Rosen $23.95 (0-8239-3121-8). 64pp. The basic facts about leukemia are covered with material on its various types and treatments, possible causes, and the emotional aspects of the illness. (Rev: SLJ 9/00) [616.99]

17987 Moragne, Wendy. *Allergies* (5–8). Series: Twenty-First Century Medical Library. 1999, Twenty-First Century LB $23.90 (0-7613-1359-1). 128pp. After general material on allergies, their causes and treatment, this account describes specific allergies involving food, skin, rhinitis, drugs, and insects. (Rev: HBG 3/00; SLJ 3/00) [616.97]

17988 Peacock, Carol Antoinette. *Sugar Was My Best Food: Diabetes and Me* (3–6). Illus. 1998, Albert Whitman $12.95 (0-8075-7646-8). 55pp. An 11-year-old boy describes his daily experiences in coping with diabetes, which he has had since age nine. (Rev: BL 8/98; HBG 10/98; SLJ 6/98) [362.1]

17989 Peacock, Judith. *Bipolar Disorder: A Roller Coaster of Emotions* (5–8). Series: Perspectives on Mental Health. 2000, Capstone LB $22.60 (0-7368-0434-X). 64pp. Manic depression is defined with material on its various types and how it is diagnosed and treated in both youngsters and adults. (Rev: HBG 10/00; SLJ 8/00) [616.85]

17990 Pimm, Paul. *Living with Cerebral Palsy* (3–5). Series: Living With. 1999, Raintree Steck-Vaughn LB $22.83 (0-8172-5744-6). 32pp. Using double-page spreads, this book introduces cerebral palsy, describes how it affects people, its treatment, and the daily lives of those who have it. (Rev: HBG 10/00; SLJ 4/00) [616]

17991 Pincus, Dion. *Everything You Need to Know About Cerebral Palsy* (4–7). Series: Need to Know Library. 2000, Rosen LB $17.95 (0-8239-2960-4). 64pp. The causes and characteristics of cerebral palsy are discussed with material on the treatments and the daily life of those affected. (Rev: HBG 10/00; SLJ 3/00) [618.92]

17992 Pirner, Connie W. *Even Little Kids Get Diabetes* (PS–2). Illus. by Nadine Bernard Westcott. 1991, Whitman LB $13.95 (0-8075-2158-2). 24pp. A young girl tells of her life with diabetes. (Rev: BL 3/1/91; SLJ 4/91) [616.4]

17993 Rowan, Kate. *I Know How We Fight Germs* (K–2). Illus. by Katharine McEwen. 1999, Candlewick paper $9.99 (0-7636-0503-4). 32pp. When Sam sneezes on Mom, she takes the opportunity to tell him about germs, disease, white and red blood cells, and platelets. (Rev: BL 12/15/98; HBG 10/99; SLJ 1/99) [616.07]

17994 Sanders, Pete, and Steve Myers. *Anorexia and Bulimia* (4–8). Illus. by Mike Lacy and Liz Sawyer. Series: What Do You Know About. 1999, Millbrook LB $21.90 (0-7613-0914-4). 32pp. Using an actual case study as a beginning, this book explores the causes, effects, and treatment of these eating disorders and covers the behavioral patterns of those afflicted. (Rev: HBG 10/99; SLJ 10/99) [618.92]

17995 Sanders, Pete, and Steve Myers. *Dyslexia* (4–8). Illus. by Mike Lacy and Liz Sawyer. Series: What Do You Know About. 1999, Millbrook LB $21.90 (0-7613-0915-2). 32pp. Using a case study, this book explores one boy's problems with dyslexia, its causes, symptoms, and treatment. (Rev: HBG 10/99; SLJ 10/99) [617.7]

17996 Schwartz, Robert H., and Peter M. G. Deane. *Coping with Allergies* (4–7). Series: Coping. 1999, Rosen $17.95 (0-8239-2511-0). 160pp. After a run-down of the types and causes of allergies, this account describes their physical and emotional impact and current treatments. (Rev: BL 2/15/00) [616.97]

17997 Shein, Lori. *AIDS* (5–8). Series: Overview. 1998, Lucent LB $18.95 (1-56006-193-6). A concise overview of the AIDS epidemic, the attempts to treat and restrict the spread of the disease, and the controversies surrounding it. (Rev: BL 8/98) [616.99]

17998 Silverstein, Alvin, et al. *Allergies* (3–5). Series: My Health. 1999, Watts LB $22.50 (0-531-11581-X). 48pp. This simple work with entertaining drawings and photos explains, from a child's point of view, what allergies are, the different kinds, and how they can be treated. (Rev: BL 10/15/99; HBG 3/00; SLJ 12/99) [616]

17999 Silverstein, Alvin, et al. *Common Colds* (3–5). Illus. Series: My Health. 1999, Watts LB $22.50 (0-531-11579-8). 48pp. This book explains the symptoms of the common cold, how people catch and pass colds along, and how they are treated. (Rev: BL 10/15/99; HBG 3/00) [616.2]

18000 Silverstein, Alvin, et al. *Lyme Disease* (4–7). Illus. 2000, Watts LB $24.00 (0-531-11751-0); paper $8.95 (0-531-16531-0). 64pp. This book introduces Lyme disease, its symptoms, history, the tick that carries it, prevention, and treatments. (Rev: BL 10/15/00) [616.9]

18001 Silverstein, Alvin, et al. *Sickle Cell Anemia* (4–8). Illus. Series: Diseases and People. 1997, Enslow LB $20.95 (0-89490-711-5). 112pp. The symptoms, treatment, and screening of this hereditary disorder are explained in a clear, well-organized text. (Rev: SLJ 2/97) [616]

18002 Silverstein, Alvin, et al. *Sore Throats and Tonsillitis* (3–5). Series: My Health. 2000, Watts LB

$22.50 (0-531-11640-9). 48pp. Photos, medical information, and amusing cartoons are used to describe throat problems — their causes and cures. (Rev: BL 11/15/00) [616.3]

18003 Simpson, Carolyn. *Coping with Asthma* (4–7). 1995, Rosen LB $17.95 (0-8239-2069-0). 140pp. After discussing the respiratory system and the causes of asthma, this book deals with how to treat it. (Rev: BL 9/15/95) [616.2]

18004 Simpson, Carolyn. *Everything You Need to Know About Asthma* (5–9). Series: Need to Know Library. 1998, Rosen LB $16.95 (0-8239-2567-6). 64pp. This book discusses the symptoms, diagnosis, and treatment of asthma. (Rev: SLJ 10/98) [616.2]

18005 Smart, Paul. *Everything You Need to Know About Mononucleosis* (5–9). Series: Need to Know Library. 1998, Rosen LB $16.95 (0-8239-2550-1). 64pp. This book details the symptoms of mononucleosis, provides case studies, and stresses the need for rest as a treatment for the disease. (Rev: SLJ 10/98) [616]

18006 Stewart, Gail B. *Diabetes* (5–8). Series: Overview Series. 1999, Lucent LB $17.96 (1-56006-527-3). 95pp. Readers learn what causes diabetes, how it affects people, and how it is treated — with emphasis on proper nutrition and medication to control the disease. (Rev: BL 8/99; SLJ 8/99) [616.4]

18007 Strauss, Peggy Guthart. *Relieve the Squeeze* (5–7). Illus. 2000, Viking $14.99 (0-670-89330-7). 48pp. This book about asthma explains what it is, what triggers it, kinds of medication, and how to cope with it. (Rev: BL 1/1–15/01; HBG 3/01; SLJ 1/01) [616.2]

18008 Susman, Edward. *Multiple Sclerosis* (4–7). Series: Diseases and People. 1999, Enslow LB $19.95 (0-7660-1185-2). 128pp. A description of this debilitating disease that attacks the nervous system. (Rev: HBG 3/00; SLJ 2/00) [616]

18009 Tsubakiyama, Margaret. *Lice Are Lousy! All About Headlice* (3–5). Illus. 1999, Millbrook $19.90 (0-7613-1316-8). 32pp. A breezy but fact-filled introduction to head lice, their habits, how you get them, and how to get rid of them. (Rev: BL 8/99; HBG 10/99; SLJ 9/99) [616.5]

18010 Veggeberg, Scott. *Lyme Disease* (4–8). Series: Diseases and People. 1998, Enslow LB $18.95 (0-7660-1052-X). 104pp. Describes the symptoms of Lyme disease, discusses how it is diagnosed and treated, and emphasizes the importance of prevention. (Rev: HBG 10/98; SLJ 9/98) [616]

18011 Ward, Brian. *Epidemic* (4–7). Illus. Series: Eyewitness Books. 2000, DK $15.95 (0-7894-6296-6). 64pp. This book covers the nature of epidemics, their causes, how they are spread and contained, and gives examples from history. (Rev: BL 12/1/00) [614.4]

18012 Weiss, Jonathan H. *Breathe Easy: Young People's Guide to Asthma* (4–7). Illus. 1994, Magination paper $9.95 (0-945354-62-2). 64pp. An account that describes the causes of asthma, what

happens during an attack, and how to manage this condition. (Rev: BL 2/15/95) [618.92]

18013 Weitzman, Elizabeth. *Let's Talk About When Someone You Love Has Alzheimer's Disease* (1–4). Illus. Series: Let's Talk. 1996, Rosen LB $15.93 (0-8239-2306-1). 24pp. A discussion of the nature of Alzheimer's disease, the changes it causes, and how to adjust to it. (Rev: BL 3/1/97; SLJ 8/96) [618.97]

18014 Westcott, Patsy. *Living with Epilepsy* (3–5). Series: Living With. 1999, Raintree Steck-Vaughn LB $22.83 (0-8172-5570-2). 32pp. This book introduces epilepsy and explains the causes, different kinds of seizures, and treatment options. (Rev: BL 8/99; HBG 10/99) [616.8]

18015 Westcott, Patsy. *Living with Leukemia* (3–5). Series: Living With. 1999, Raintree Steck-Vaughn LB $22.83 (0-8172-5743-8). 32pp. Case histories of three youngsters with leukemia are presented along with information on this kind of cancer, its treatment, and how it changes one's everyday life. (Rev: HBG 10/00; SLJ 4/00) [616.9]

18016 Wiener, Lori S., et al. *Be a Friend: Children Who Live with HIV Speak* (1–4). Illus. 1994, Albert Whitman LB $14.95 (0-8075-0590-0). 40pp. The nature of AIDS is made dramatically clear through the voices of several youthful sufferers and their families. (Rev: BCCB 4/94; BL 3/15/94; SLJ 4/94) [362.1]

18017 Yount, Lisa. *Cancer* (5–8). Series: Overview. 1999, Lucent LB $17.96 (1-56006-363-7). 111pp. This book defines cancer in its various forms and discusses the different treatments available. (Rev: BL 9/15/99; HBG 3/00) [616.994]

18018 Zonderman, Jon, and Laurel Shader. *Environmental Diseases* (5–8). Illus. 1993, Twenty-First Century LB $18.90 (0-8050-2600-2). 64pp. This well-illustrated account deals with the causes of and treatment for such diseases as poison ivy, Lyme disease, and hypothermia. Also use *Nutritional Diseases* (1994). (Rev: BL 7/94; SLJ 4/94) [616.9]

Doctors and Medicine

18019 Casanellas, Antonio. *Great Discoveries and Inventions That Improved Human Health* (3–5). Illus. 2000, Gareth Stevens $21.27 (0-8368-2585-3). Using double-page spreads this book discusses such inventions as radioisotopes, DNA, and genetic engineering. (Rev: SLJ 1/01) [610]

18020 Gates, Phil. *The History News: Medicine* (4–7). Illus. Series: History News. 1997, Candlewick $15.99 (0-7636-0316-3). 32pp. The history of doctors and medicine is covered using a newspaper format that even includes "advertisements" (one announces leeches for sale) and letters. (Rev: BL 2/1/98; HBG 3/98; SLJ 1/98) [610.9]

18021 Ichord, Loretta Frances. *Toothworms and Spider Juice: An Illustrated History of Dentistry* (5–8). Illus. 2000, Millbrook LB $22.40 (0-7613-1465-2). 96pp. A history of dentistry that reveals many of the barbaric treatments of the past and how superstition and ignorance gradually gave way to modern practices. (Rev: BCCB 2/00; BL 2/15/00; HBG 10/00; SLJ 2/00) [617.6]

18022 Innes, Brian. *Mysterious Healing* (4–7). Series: Unsolved Mysteries. 1999, Raintree Steck-Vaughn LB $16.98 (0-8172-5489-7). 48pp. This is a very balanced account of some of the unusual healing methods used today, including acupuncture, yoga, light therapy, and some forms of telepathy. (Rev: BL 5/15/99; HBG 10/99; SLJ 9/99) [610]

18023 Jacobs, Lee. *The Orthopedist* (3–5). Illus. Series: Doctors in Action. 1998, Blackbirch LB $14.95 (1-56711-236-6). 24pp. Using many color photos and a reassuring text, this book gives a candid look at what specialists in muscle and bone deformities do — especially when they work with children. (Rev: BL 12/15/98; HBG 3/99) [616.7]

18024 Miller, Brandon M. *Just What the Doctor Ordered: The History of American Medicine* (5–8). Illus. Series: People's History. 1997, Lerner LB $22.60 (0-8225-1737-X). 88pp. A history of American medicine from the extensive use of plants and herbs to the development of laser surgery. (Rev: SLJ 5/97*) [610.9]

18025 Parker, Steve. *Medicine* (4–6). Illus. Series: Eyewitness Science. 1995, DK $15.95 (1-56458-882-3). 64pp. In this history of medicine from ancient times to the future, such topics as modern drugs, diagnostic techniques, medical instruments, and fads are introduced. (Rev: SLJ 10/95) [610]

18026 Powledge, Fred. *Pharmacy in the Forest: How Medicines Are Found in the Natural World* (4–6). Illus. 1998, Simon & Schuster $17.00 (0-689-80863-1). 48pp. This work provides a brief historical background on modern medicines, how many of them have come from forest plants, and how they are used to fight disease. (Rev: BL 8/98; HBG 10/98; SLJ 6/98) [615]

18027 Snedden, Robert. *Medical Ethics: Changing Attitudes 1900–2000* (4–7). 1999, Raintree Steck-Vaughn LB $27.11 (0-8172-5893-0). 64pp. Beginning with Hippocrates, this book gives a history of bioethics and follows with coverage of topics including reproductive rights, euthanasia, organ donation, psychiatry, eugenics, and cloning. (Rev: HBG 10/00; SLJ 5/00) [616]

18028 Storring, Rod. *A Doctor's Life: A Visual History of Doctors and Nurses Through the Ages* (3–6). Illus. 1998, Dutton $17.99 (0-525-67577-9). 48pp. From Roman times to the present, this oversize book profiles 22 figures who represent the progress of medical advances. (Rev: BL 1/1–15/99; HBG 3/99; SLJ 12/98) [610.9]

18029 Van Steenwyk, Elizabeth. *Frontier Fever: The Silly, Superstitious — and Sometimes Sensible — Medicine of the Pioneers* (5–8). Illus. 1995, Walker LB $16.85 (0-8027-8403-8). 160pp. A history of medicine in the United States from colonial times through the 19th century, including information on the training of caregivers. (Rev: BL 7/95; SLJ 12/95) [610]

18030 Ward, Sally G. *The Anesthesiologist* (3–5). Series: Doctors in Action. 1998, Blackbirch LB $14.95 (1-56711-233-1). 24pp. A behind-the-scenes

look at these medical specialists, with coverage on the problems and procedures they face each day. (Rev: BL 12/15/98; HBG 3/99) [610]

18031 Winkler, Kathy. *Radiology* (3–6). Illus. Series: Inventors and Inventions. 1996, Marshall Cavendish LB $25.64 (0-7614-0075-3). 63pp. Provides short profiles of the leaders, past and present, in the field of radiology, with details on how this scientific breakthrough is changing our lives. (Rev: BL 7/96; SLJ 9/96) [616.07]

18032 Wolfson, Evelyn. *From the Earth to Beyond the Sky: Native American Medicine* (4–8). Illus. 1993, Houghton $16.00 (0-395-55009-2). 86pp. This book explains herbal medicine, the plants used, and how Native Americans' relationship with nature played a role in the development of their medical treatments. (Rev: BCCB 1/94; BL 12/15/93; SLJ 12/93) [615.8]

18033 Woods, Samuel. *The Pediatrician* (3–5). Illus. Series: Doctors in Action. 1998, Blackbirch LB $14.95 (1-56711-237-4). 24pp. Introduces the branch of medicine that deals with children and their health problems, and provides many examples of good patient-doctor relationships. (Rev: BL 12/15/98; HBG 3/99) [618.92]

Genetics

18034 Bornstein, Sandy. *What Makes You What You Are: A First Look at Genetics* (5–8). Illus. by Frank Cecala. 1989, Silver Burdett paper $6.95 (0-671-68650-X). 115pp. This book affords a fine introduction to cell structure, dominant and recessive traits, and heredity. (Rev: SLJ 1/90) [573.2]

18035 Jefferis, David. *Cloning: Frontiers of Genetic Engineering* (5–7). Series: Megatech. 1999, Crabtree LB $14.37 (0-7787-0048-8); paper $8.06 (0-7787-0058-5). 32pp. This account discusses the history of genetic discoveries and theories, cell reproduction, and the present and possible future of genetic engineering with plants, animals, and humans. (Rev: SLJ 9/99) [174.957]

18036 Wells, Donna. *Biotechnology* (3–6). Illus. Series: Inventors and Inventions. 1996, Marshall Cavendish LB $25.64 (0-7614-0046-X). 63pp. Cell structure, DNA, and ways of altering genetic make-up are discussed, with short profiles of past and current leaders in the field. (Rev: BL 7/96; SLJ 9/96) [660]

Hospitals

18037 Brink, Benjamin. *David's Story: A Book About Surgery* (3–5). Illus. 1996, Lerner LB $21.27 (0-8225-2577-1). 32pp. A step-by-step account of a boy undergoing surgery. (Rev: BL 12/1/96; SLJ 10/96) [617.5]

18038 Dooley, Virginia. *Tubes In My Ears: My Trip to the Hospital* (PS–1). Illus. by Miriam Katin. 1996, Mondo paper $4.95 (1-57255-118-6). 32pp.

The experiences of a young boy when he goes to a hospital for the first time to treat an ear infection. (Rev: BL 5/1/96; SLJ 6/96) [362.1]

18039 Howe, James. *The Hospital Book*. Rev. ed. (2–6). Illus. by Mal Warshaw. 1994, Morrow $16.00 (0-688-12731-2). 96pp. This book filled with photos explains hospital procedures to young patients and tries to lessen any fears they might have about hospitals. (Rev: BL 4/1/94; HB 7–8/94) [362.1]

18040 Johnston, Marianne. *Let's Talk About Going to the Hospital* (1–4). Series: Let's Talk. 1998, Rosen LB $13.95 (0-8239-5036-0). 24pp. Two-page sections cover such hospital-related topics as admission, meals, IV tubes, blood tests, anesthesia, and surgery. (Rev: SLJ 4/98) [362.1]

18041 Masoff, Joy. *Emergency* (4–6). Illus. 1999, Scholastic $16.95 (0-590-97898-5). 56pp. Double-page spreads and many color photos enliven this account of the life and work of emergency medical personnel — from EMTs to emergency room staff. (Rev: BCCB 2/99; BL 1/1–15/99; HB 3–4/99; HBG 10/99; SLJ 8/99) [616.02]

18042 Miller, Marilyn. *Behind the Scenes at the Hospital* (PS–3). Illus. 1996, Raintree Steck-Vaughn LB $21.40 (0-8172-4087-X). 32pp. The workers and activities that make hospitals function are introduced in a simple question-and-answer format. (Rev: BL 4/15/96; SLJ 12/96) [362.1]

18043 Rosenberg, Maxine B. *Mommy's in the Hospital Having a Baby* (PS–1). Illus. by Robert Maass. 1997, Clarion $15.00 (0-395-71813-9). 29pp. Questions are answered about what happens in a hospital when mommy is having a baby, including "How do I behave on visits?" (Rev: BL 4/1/97; SLJ 5/97) [618.4]

18044 Stein, Sara Bonnett. *A Hospital Story* (1–3). Illus. 1984, Walker paper $8.95 (0-8027-7222-6). A fine introduction to hospitals and what a hospital stay involves.

The Human Body

General

18045 Aliki. *My Feet* (PS–1). Illus. Series: Let's-Read-and-Find-Out. 1990, HarperCollins LB $16.89 (0-690-04815-7). 32pp. Children are asked to consider the uniqueness of their feet. (Rev: BL 10/1/90; HB 11–12/90; SLJ 11/90) [612]

18046 Aliki. *My Hands* (1–3). Illus. by author. 1990, HarperCollins LB $15.89 (0-690-04880-7); paper $4.95 (0-06-445096-1). 32pp. The structure and uses of our hands are presented.

18047 Allison, Linda. *Blood and Guts: A Working Guide to Your Own Little Insides* (5–8). 1976, Little, Brown paper $13.95 (0-316-03443-6). An off-putting title but a fine explanation of the functions of the human body.

18048 Balkwill, Fran. *Cells Are Us* (4–5). Illus. by Mic Rolph. 1993, Carolrhoda LB $19.93 (0-87614-762-7). 32pp. This book introduces the many types of cells found in the human body. Other related

books by the same author are: *Cell Wars* and *DNA Is Here to Stay* (both 1993). (Rev: SLJ 4/93) [611]

18049 Berger, Melvin. *Why I Sneeze, Shiver, Hiccup, and Yawn*. Rev. ed. (K–2). Illus. by Paul Meisel. Series: Let's-Read-and-Find-Out. 2000, HarperCollins LB $15.89 (0-06-028143-X); paper $4.95 (0-06-445193-3). 33pp. A simple science book that offers basic explanations about automatic reflexes, their causes and purposes, as well as ways to test these reflexes. (Rev: HBG 10/00; SLJ 3/00) [612]

18050 Berger, Melvin, and Gilda Berger. *Why Don't Haircuts Hurt? Questions and Answers About the Human Body* (3–5). Series: Question and Answer. 1999, Scholastic $12.95 (0-590-13079-X); paper $5.95 (0-590-08569-1). 48pp. Using questions that children might ask about the human body, this account supplies concise, well-organized answers, which are illustrated with many original paintings. (Rev: BL 11/15/99; HBG 3/00; SLJ 12/99) [612]

18051 Bruun, Ruth Dowling, and Bertel Bruun. *The Human Body* (4–7). Illus. by Patricia J. Wynne. 1982, Random LB $15.99 (0-394-94424-0); paper $12.99 (0-394-84424-6). 96pp. A simple account that concentrates on parts of the body and its systems.

18052 Cole, Joanna. *The Magic School Bus: Inside the Human Body* (2–5). Illus. by Bruce Degen. 1989, Scholastic $15.95 (0-590-41426-7); paper $4.99 (0-590-41427-5). Ms. Frizzle's class goes on a guided tour of the human body. (Rev: BCCB 4/89; BL 4/15/89; HB 5–6/89)

18053 Cole, Joanna. *Your Insides* (PS–1). Illus. by Paul Meisel. 1998, Putnam paper $9.99 (0-698-11675-5). Clear overlays help to explain the workings of the human body for the young reader. (Rev: BL 12/1/92) [612]

18054 Crelinstein, Jeffrey. *To the Limit* (5–8). Illus. Series: Wide World. 1992, Harcourt $17.95 (0-15-200616-8). 64pp. The effects of exercise on the human body are explored in this book containing amazing photographs. (Rev: SLJ 10/92) [932]

18055 Darling, Kathy. *There's a Zoo on You!* (3–5). Illus. 2000, Millbrook LB $24.90 (0-7613-1357-5). 48pp. The supermagnified photographs in this book are of the bacteria, fungi, and other organisms that live in or on the human body. (Rev: BL 11/1/00; HBG 10/00; SLJ 7/00) [579]

18056 Day, Trevor. *The Random House Book of 1001 Questions and Answers About the Human Body* (5–8). Illus. Series: 1001 Questions and Answers. 1994, Random $15.00 (0-679-85432-0). 128pp. A profusely illustrated question-and-answer book that combines up-to-date information on a wide range of fascinating subjects with an attractive format. (Rev: BL 12/1/94; SLJ 7/94) [612]

18057 *First Questions and Answers About the Human Body: What Is a Bellybutton?* (PS–1). Illus. Series: Library of First Questions and Answers. 1993, Time Life $16.95 (0-7835-0854-9). 47pp. Using a question-and-answer format, this book supplies basic information about bodily functions. (Rev: SLJ 3/94) [612]

18058 Fowler, Allan. *Arms and Legs and Other Limbs* (1–2). Series: Rookie Readers. 1999, Children's LB $18.50 (0-516-20809-8). 32pp. This small book, with many pictures and large print, introduces arms and legs as found in various animals, including humans. (Rev: BL 7/99; HBG 10/99) [612]

18059 Ganeri, Anita. *Inside the Body* (4–7). Illus. by Giuliano Fornari. 1996, DK $16.95 (0-7894-0999-2). 12pp. When tabs are lifted, various parts of the human body are revealed. (Rev: BL 12/15/96; SLJ 8/96) [612]

18060 Gardner, Robert. *Science Projects About the Human Body* (5–7). 1992, Enslow LB $20.95 (0-89490-443-4). 104pp. Simple experiments and activities are used to illustrate various areas of the human body, like the senses, bones, teeth, and hair. (Rev: SLJ 11/93) [612]

18061 Hawcock, David. *The Amazing Pop-Up Pull-Out Body in a Book* (2–4). Illus. 1997, DK $19.95 (0-7894-2052-X). 9pp. Unfolding pages in this book brings out a full-length 3-D skeleton, accompanied by facts about the human body. (Rev: BL 12/15/97) [612]

18062 Hindley, Judy. *Eyes, Nose, Fingers, and Toes: A First Book All About You* (PS). Illus. by Brita Granström. 1999, Candlewick $15.99 (0-7636-0440-2). 32pp. A delightful activity book for toddlers that points out parts of the body. (Rev: BL 6/1–15/99*; HBG 10/99; SLJ 7/99) [612]

18063 Janulewicz, Mike. *Yikes! Your Body, Up Close* (3–5). Illus. 1997, Simon & Schuster paper $15.00 (0-689-81520-4). 32pp. Close-ups of such parts of the body as skin and red blood cells. (Rev: BL 9/1/97; HBG 3/98; SLJ 12/97) [611]

18064 Kroll, Virginia. *Hands!* (PS–1). Illus. by Cathryn Falwell. 1997, Boyds Mills $7.95 (1-56397-051-1). 32pp. In this unusual picture book, hands are seen fulfilling a variety of tasks. (Rev: BL 9/15/97; HBG 3/98; SLJ 12/97) [612]

18065 Landau, Elaine. *Joined at Birth: The Lives of Conjoined Twins* (4–7). Illus. Series: A First Book. 1997, Watts LB $22.50 (0-531-20331-X). 64pp. This book explains the phenomenon of conjoining and gives several famous examples of these twins. (Rev: BL 9/15/97; SLJ 8/97) [616.043]

18066 Landau, Elaine. *Short Stature: From Folklore to Fact* (4–7). Illus. Series: A First Book. 1997, Watts LB $22.50 (0-531-20265-8). 64pp. After giving good historical information, this account explains dwarfism and gives several case histories. (Rev: BL 9/15/97; SLJ 8/97) [573.8]

18067 Landau, Elaine. *Standing Tall: Unusually Tall People* (4–7). Series: A First Book. 1997, Watts LB $22.50 (0-531-20257-7). 64pp. This introduction to tall people gives a history of society's attitudes toward them and coverage on the challenges that they must face even today. (Rev: BL 9/15/97; SLJ 7/97) [612]

18068 Ontario Science Centre Staff. *Sportsworks* (4–8). Illus. by Pat Cupples. 1989, Addison-Wesley paper $9.95 (0-201-15296-7). 96pp. Discusses the human body in relation to sports, with a number of

experiments and activities. (Rev: BL 6/15/89; SLJ 7/89) [611]

18069 Parker, Steve. *The Body Atlas: A Pictorial Guide to the Human Body* (3–6). Illus. by Giuliano Fornari. 1993, DK $19.95 (1-56458-224-8). 64pp. This atlas of the human body pictures bones, organs, and muscles from head to toe. (Rev: BL 6/1–15/93; SLJ 7/93) [611]

18070 Parker, Steve. *The Human Body* (3–6). Illus. Series: What If. 1995, Millbrook LB $19.90 (1-56294-914-4); paper $7.95 (1-56294-949-7). 32pp. A series of hypothetical questions like "What if we had no skin?" are used to explore the human body and its parts. (Rev: SLJ 1/96) [612]

18071 Perols, Sylvaine. *The Human Body* (PS–1). Trans. from French by Jennifer Riggs. Illus. by author. Series: First Discovery. 1996, Scholastic $12.95 (0-590-73876-3). With the uses of transparencies, the skeleton and different systems and organs of the human body are introduced. (Rev: BL 10/15/96; SLJ 2/97) [612]

18072 Phifer, Kate Gilbert. *Tall and Small: A Book About Height* (4–6). Illus. 1987, Walker LB $12.85 (0-8027-6685-4). 96pp. Lots of data about growth patterns, plus how to chart growth. (Rev: BCCB 4/87; BL 7/87; SLJ 8/87)

18073 Platt, Richard. *Stephen Biesty's Incredible Body* (5–9). Illus. 1998, DK $19.95 (0-7894-3424-5). 32pp. A breezy account that uses a large format, cutaways, foldouts, visual jokes, and lots of text to complete a tour of the inner workings of Stephen Biesty's body. (Rev: BL 12/1/98; HBG 3/99; SLJ 1/99) [611]

18074 Pringle, Laurence. *Everybody Has a Bellybutton* (PS–3). Illus. by Clare Wood. 1997, Boyds Mills $14.95 (1-56397-009-0). 32pp. A simple account of the growth of a fetus from a single cell to the birth of a baby. (Rev: BL 9/15/97; HBG 3/98; SLJ 10/97) [612]

18075 Rice, Chris, and Melanie Rice. *My First Body Book* (2–4). Illus. 1995, DK $16.95 (1-56458-893-9). 32pp. Excellent illustrations highlight this beginner's book on the human body, with separate sections on each of the senses. (Rev: BL 11/1/95; SLJ 3/96) [612]

18076 Rowan, Kate. *I Know How My Cells Make Me Grow* (PS–2). Illus. by Katharine McEwen. Series: Sam's Science. 1999, Candlewick $9.99 (0-7636-0502-6). 29pp. Using a fictional format, a mother explains to her son about cells in the boy's bones, muscles, and skin, and how they are responsible for his growth. (Rev: HBG 3/00; SLJ 8/99) [612]

18077 Rowan, Pete. *Big Head* (5–7). Illus. 1998, Knopf $20.00 (0-679-89018-1). 44pp. This book discusses all the organs housed in the head, including the eyes and ears, with emphasis placed on the brain and its functions. (Rev: BCCB 1/99; BL 10/1/98; HBG 3/99; SLJ 9/98) [612.8]

18078 Saunderson, Jane. *Heart and Lungs* (3–6). Illus. by Andrew Farmer and Robina Green. Series: You and Your Body. 1992, Troll LB $18.60 (0-8167-2096-7); paper $4.95 (0-8167-2097-5). 32pp.

Explores both the respiratory and the circulatory systems and explains how they work. (Rev: BL 5/15/92; SLJ 10/92) [612.1]

18079 Stangl, Jean. *What Makes You Cough* (3–5). Series: My Health. 2000, Watts LB $22.50 (0-531-20382-4). 48pp. The full title of this book is *What Makes You Cough, Sneeze, Burp, Hiccup, Yawn, Blink, Sweat, and Shiver?* (Rev: BL 11/15/00) [612]

18080 Suzuki, David, and Barbara Hehner. *Looking at the Body* (3–6). Illus. Series: Looking At. 1991, Stoddart $24.95 (0-471-54752-2); paper $9.95 (0-471-54052-8). 96pp. A brief introduction to the human body, with a few accompanying activities to explain its parts and their functions. (Rev: SLJ 5/92) [611]

18081 Sweeney, Joan. *Me and My Amazing Body* (PS–4). Illus. by Annette Cable. 1999, Crown LB $14.99 (0-517-80054-3). 32pp. Starting with her skin and working inward, a little girl talks about her body and its systems. (Rev: BL 8/99; HBG 3/00; SLJ 2/00) [611]

18082 VanCleave, Janice. *The Human Body for Every Kid: Easy Activities That Make Learning Science Fun* (5–7). Illus. Series: Science for Every Kid. 1995, Wiley $29.95 (0-471-02413-9); paper $12.95 (0-471-02408-2). 240pp. The various systems in the human body are introduced and decribed, with many projects and experiments. (Rev: BL 4/15/95; SLJ 5/95) [612]

18083 VanCleave, Janice. *Janice VanCleave's Play and Find Out About the Human Body: Easy Experiments for Young Children* (PS–1). Illus. Series: Play and Find Out. 1998, Wiley $24.95 (0-471-12934-8); paper $12.95 (0-471-12935-6). 122pp. Using questions such as "Where does the food I eat go?" a series of simple experiments are presented that explore the human body and its functions. (Rev: BL 12/1/98; SLJ 8/98) [612]

18084 Walker, Richard. *The Kingfisher First Human Body Encyclopedia* (3–5). 1999, Kingfisher $16.95 (0-7534-5177-8). 112pp. Using a topical arrangement, this book offers an outstanding look at the inside and outside of the human body. (Rev: HBG 3/00; SLJ 11/99) [612]

18085 Wiese, Jim. *Head to Toe Science: Over 40 Eye-Popping, Spine-Tingling, Heart-Pounding Activities That Teach Kids* (4–8). Illus. 2000, Wiley paper $12.95 (0-471-33203-8). 120pp. A collection of experiments and projects that is arranged by body systems (e.g., nervous, digestive), accompanied by good instructions and scientific explanations. (Rev: BL 7/00; SLJ 7/00) [612]

Circulatory System

18086 Ballard, Carol. *The Heart and Circulatory System* (5–8). Illus. Series: Human Body. 1997, Raintree Steck-Vaughn LB $27.12 (0-8172-4800-5). 48pp. Topics discussed in this nicely illustrated volume include how blood is made, how it is pumped through the body, and how the heart and circulation system work together. (Rev: BL 6/1–15/97; SLJ 8/97) [612.1]

18087 Bryan, Jenny. *The Pulse of Life: The Circulatory System* (4–6). Illus. Series: Body Talk. 1993, Dillon LB $18.95 (0-87518-566-5). 48pp. A clear, concise introduction to the circulatory system and an explanation of current concerns and research. (Rev: SLJ 10/93) [612]

18088 Parker, Steve. *Blood* (4–6). Series: Look at Your Body. 1997, Millbrook LB $20.90 (0-7613-0611-0). 32pp. The composition of blood, its uses, and the circulatory system are introduced in this visually appealing, clearly written book. (Rev: BL 1/1–15/98; HBG 3/98; SLJ 4/98) [612]

18089 Parramon, Merce. *How Our Blood Circulates* (5–7). Illus. by Marcel Socias. Series: Invisible World. 1994, Chelsea LB $15.95 (0-7910-2127-0). 31pp. Double-page spreads introduce the circulatory system and discuss such topics as blood cells, clotting, the heart and its functions, and the lymphatic system. (Rev: SLJ 8/94) [612]

18090 Sandeman, Anna. *Blood* (1–3). Illus. Series: Body Books. 1996, Millbrook LB $18.90 (0-7613-0477-0). 32pp. An introduction to the composition and function of blood and the circulatory system, with clearly labeled artwork. (Rev: BL 4/15/96; SLJ 4/96) [612.1]

18091 Showers, Paul. *Hear Your Heart* (2–5). Illus. by Holly Keller. Series: Let's-Read-and-Find-Out. 2001, HarperCollins LB $15.89 (0-06-025411-4); paper $4.95 (0-06-445139-9). 32pp. An amusing introduction to the human heart accompanied by activities such as making a stethoscope, taking a pulse, and listening to heartbeats. (Rev: BL 1/1–15/01) [612.1]

18092 Silverstein, Alvin, et al. *The Circulatory System* (5–8). Illus. Series: Human Body Systems. 1994, Twenty-First Century LB $20.40 (0-8050-2833-1). 96pp. After a general introduction to circulation systems in plants and animals, the human system is introduced. (Rev: BL 3/15/95; SLJ 4/95) [612.1]

18093 Simon, Seymour. *The Heart: Our Circulatory System* (3–6). Illus. 1996, Morrow $15.93 (0-688-11408-3). 32pp. An excellent introduction to the circulatory system, with illustrations on each page. (Rev: BCCB 10/96; BL 7/96*; HB 9–10/96; SLJ 8/96) [612.1]

18094 Stille, Darlene R. *The Circulatory System* (2–4). Illus. Series: True Books. 1997, Children's LB $22.00 (0-516-20438-6). 48pp. This account tells how the heart works, what blood does, the flow of blood through the body, and how to keep the heart healthy. (Rev: BL 12/1/97; HBG 3/98; SLJ 2/98) [612.1]

Digestive and Excretory Systems

18095 Ballard, Carol. *The Stomach and Digestive System* (5–8). Illus. Series: Human Body. 1997, Raintree Steck-Vaughn LB $25.69 (0-8172-4801-3). 48pp. Topics discussed in this nicely illustrated volume include the digestive organs, how they work together, how food is tasted, and where nutrients are stored. (Rev: BL 6/1–15/97; SLJ 8/97) [612.3]

18096 Bryan, Jenny. *Digestion: The Digestive System* (4–6). Illus. Series: Body Talk. 1993, Dillon LB $13.95 (0-87518-564-0). 48pp. A clear, informative text and large captioned illustrations tell about the digestive system and related topics. (Rev: SLJ 10/93) [612]

18097 Burgess, Jan. *Food and Digestion* (5–8). Illus. 1988, Silver Burdett LB $12.95 (0-382-09704-1). 48pp. Advice for staying healthy in this addition to the How Our Bodies Work series. (Rev: BL 4/15/89)

18098 Cho, Shinta. *The Gas We Pass: The Story of Farts* (PS–2). Trans. by Amanda Mayer Stinchecum. Illus. 1994, Kane/Miller $11.95 (0-916291-52-9). 28pp. This book tells about the causes, production, and effects of farts in a variety of animals, mainly humans. (Rev: BL 10/1/94; SLJ 11/94) [612.3]

18099 Haduch, Bill. *Food Rules! The Stuff You Munch, Its Crunch, Its Punch, and Why You Sometimes Lose Your Lunch* (4–7). Illus. 2001, Dutton $19.99 (0-525-46419-0). 112pp. An amusing book about food and the digestive process that also gives nutritional information, historical material, and humorous facts. (Rev: BL 3/15/01) [613.]

18100 Holub, Joan. *I Have a Weird Brother Who Digested a Fly* (K–3). Illus. by Patrick Girouard. 1999, Albert Whitman LB $13.95 (0-8075-3506-0). A whimsical tour of the digestive system that follows a fly from ingestion to elimination. (Rev: HBG 3/00; SLJ 12/99) [612.3]

18101 Lambourne, Mike. *Down the Hatch: Find Out About Your Food* (2–3). Illus. by Thompson Yardley. Series: Lighter Look. 1992, Millbrook LB $20.90 (1-56294-150-X). 39pp. In simple text and cartoonlike illustrations, the story of food and nutrition is presented. (Rev: SLJ 6/92) [641]

18102 Maynard, Jacqui. *I Know Where My Food Goes* (K–2). Illus. by Katharine McEwen. Series: Sam's Science. 1999, Candlewick $9.99 (0-7636-0505-0). 29pp. In this British import, a little boy asks questions about digestion and his mother explains the process clearly. (Rev: HBG 10/99; SLJ 1/99) [612]

18103 Parker, Steve. *Digestion* (4–6). Series: Look at Your Body. 1997, Millbrook LB $20.90 (0-7613-0603-X). 32pp. An introductory account of the process of digestion with details about each of the organs involved. (Rev: BL 11/15/97; HBG 3/98) [612]

18104 Sandeman, Anna. *Eating* (1–2). Illus. Series: Body Books. 1995, Millbrook LB $18.90 (1-56294-945-4). 32pp. Different organs of the body involved in eating and digestion are introduced in this simple book that also touches on nutrition and energy from food. (Rev: BL 12/15/95; SLJ 2/96) [612.3]

18105 Showers, Paul. *What Happens to a Hamburger* (1–3). Illus. by Anne Rockwell. 1985, HarperCollins LB $14.89 (0-690-04427-5); paper $4.95 (0-06-445013-9). 32pp. This revision of the 1970 text that introduced the digestive system reflects current views on nutrition. (Rev: BL 6/1/85; SLJ 8/85)

18106 Silverstein, Alvin, et al. *The Digestive System* (5–8). Illus. Series: Human Body Systems. 1994, Twenty-First Century LB $20.40 (0-8050-2832-3). 96pp. Beginning with food assimilation in plants and animals, this account focuses on the human digestive system. (Rev: BL 3/15/95; SLJ 3/95) [612.3]

18107 Silverstein, Alvin, et al. *The Excretory System* (5–8). Illus. Series: Human Body Systems. 1994, Twenty-First Century LB $20.40 (0-8050-2834-X). 96pp. Waste elimination in nature is discussed, with emphasis on this function in the human body. (Rev: BL 3/15/95; SLJ 3/95) [612.6]

18108 Stille, Darlene R. *The Digestive System* (2–4). Illus. Series: True Books. 1997, Children's LB $22.00 (0-516-20439-4). 47pp. Explains the process of digestion and the organs involved, with special coverage on topics like ulcers, diet, and the importance of cleanliness. (Rev: HBG 3/98; SLJ 2/98) [612]

Nervous System

18109 Ballard, Carol. *How Do We Think?* (3–5). Series: How Your Body Works. 1998, Raintree Steck-Vaughn LB $22.11 (0-8172-4740-8). 32pp. This book includes material on learning, memory, information processing, and message transmittal and provides activities on mental reactions and memory testing. (Rev: BL 5/15/98; HBG 10/98; SLJ 7/98) [612.8]

18110 Barmeier, Jim. *The Brain* (5–8). Illus. Series: Overview. 1996, Lucent LB $17.96 (1-56006-107-3). 128pp. Many kinds of graphics, including cartoons and photos, illustrate this description of the brain, its functions, and how we have learned about it. (Rev: BL 3/15/96; SLJ 7/96) [612.8]

18111 Innes, Brian. *Powers of the Mind* (4–7). Series: Unsolved Mysteries. 1999, Raintree Steck-Vaughn LB $16.98 (0-8172-5488-9). 48pp. A balanced account that explores the powers of the brain in such controversial areas as moving objects, planting thoughts, and predicting events. (Rev: BL 5/15/99; HBG 10/99) [612.8]

18112 Lambert, Mark. *The Brain and Nervous System* (5–7). Illus. 1988, Silver Burdett LB $19.00 (0-382-09703-3). 48pp. Diagrams and photos highlight this description. (Rev: BL 4/1/89)

18113 Mathers, Douglas. *Brain* (3–6). Illus. by Andrew Farmer and Robina Green. Series: You and Your Body. 1992, Troll LB $18.60 (0-8167-2090-8). 32pp. Topics include how the brain passes messages, how people think, and what happens when we sleep. (Rev: BL 5/15/92; SLJ 10/92) [712.8]

18114 Parker, Steve. *Brain and Nerves* (4–6). Illus. by Ian Thompson. Series: Look at Your Body. 1998, Millbrook LB $20.90 (0-7613-0812-1). 31pp. This explanation of the nervous system covers the brain, spinal cord, and nerves, with additional material on such topics as memory, headaches, and meningitis. (Rev: HBG 10/98; SLJ 10/98) [612]

18115 Parker, Steve. *The Brain and Nervous System* (5–8). Illus. Series: Human Body. 1997, Raintree

Steck-Vaughn LB $27.12 (0-8172-4802-1). 48pp. Double-page spreads introduce such topics about the nervous system as parts of the brain and their function, what brain waves are, and the nature of sleep and dreams. (Rev: BL 6/1–15/97; SLJ 8/97) [612.8]

18116 Parker, Steve. *Brain Surgery for Beginners: And Other Major Operations for Minors* (4–7). Illus. 1995, Millbrook LB $21.90 (1-56294-604-8); paper $8.95 (1-56294-895-4). 64pp. After a brief introduction to the human body, this account focuses on the brain, its composition, and its functions. (Rev: BL 5/1/95; SLJ 7/95) [612]

18117 Sandeman, Anna. *Brain* (1–2). Illus. Series: Body Books. 1996, Millbrook LB $18.90 (0-7613-0490-8). 32pp. With a simple text and full-color photos and diagrams, the brain is explored and explanations are given on how it works. (Rev: BL 10/15/96; SLJ 1/97) [612]

18118 Showers, Paul. *Sleep Is for Everyone* (PS–1). Illus. by Wendy Watson. Series: Let's-Read-and-Find-Out. 1997, HarperCollins LB $14.89 (0-06-025393-2). 32pp. This simple science book explains what sleep is, why it is necessary, and what happens if we do without it. (Rev: BL 8/97; SLJ 8/97) [612.8]

18119 Silverstein, Alvin, et al. *The Nervous System* (5–8). Illus. Series: Human Body Systems. 1994, Twenty-First Century LB $20.40 (0-8050-2835-8). 96pp. The human nervous system and how it functions and can malfunction are described, with information on the systems of other animals. (Rev: BL 3/15/95; SLJ 5/95) [612.8]

18120 Simon, Seymour. *The Brain: Our Nervous System* (3–6). Illus. 1997, Morrow $15.89 (0-688-14641-4). 32pp. The anatomy and functions of the nervous system and brain are carefully explained and illustrated with photos and diagrams. (Rev: BL 8/97; HB 9–10/97; HBG 3/98; SLJ 8/97) [612.8]

18121 Smith, Kathie Billingslea, and Victoria Crenson. *Thinking* (1–3). Illus. 1988, Troll LB $15.85 (0-8167-1016-3). 24pp. How the brain works is the focus of this simple introduction. (Rev: BL 3/15/88)

18122 Stille, Darlene R. *The Nervous System* (3–5). Illus. 1997, Children's LB $22.00 (0-516-20445-9). 48pp. In this introduction to the nervous system, the brain, nerve cells, and muscles are featured, with information on how they interact. (Rev: BL 2/15/98; HBG 3/98) [612.8]

Respiratory System

18123 Bryan, Jenny. *Breathing: The Respiratory System* (4–6). Illus. Series: Body Talk. 1993, Dillon LB $18.95 (0-87518-563-0). 48pp. Large captioned photos are used to explain what happens when we breathe plus giving information on health problems associated with the respiratory system. (Rev: SLJ 10/93) [612]

18124 Lambert, Mark. *The Lungs and Breathing* (5–7). Illus. 1988, Silver Burdett LB $12.95 (0-382-09701-7). Profusely illustrated addition to the How Our Bodies Work series. (Rev: BL 4/15/89)

18125 Parker, Steve. *Lungs* (4–6). Illus. Series: Look at Your Body. 1996, Millbrook LB $20.90 (0-7613-0530-0). 32pp. A well-organized, clearly illustrated description of lungs and their functions. (Rev: BL 11/1/96) [612.2]

18126 Parker, Steve. *The Lungs and Respiratory System* (5–7). Illus. Series: Human Body. 1997, Raintree Steck-Vaughn LB $27.12 (0-8172-4803-X). 48pp. This nicely illustrated volume examines the organs used in breathing, tells how the respiratory system works, and explains what happens when it fails. (Rev: BL 6/1–15/97; SLJ 8/97) [612.6]

18127 Silverstein, Alvin, et al. *The Respiratory System* (5–8). Illus. Series: Human Body Systems. 1994, Twenty-First Century LB $20.40 (0-8050-2831-5). 96pp. The purpose and process of breathing are discussed generally, with text and pictures focusing on the human respiratory system. (Rev: BL 3/15/95; SLJ 4/95) [612.2]

18128 Stille, Darlene R. *The Respiratory System* (2–4). Illus. Series: True Books. 1997, Children's LB $22.00 (0-516-20448-3). 47pp. Explains the process of respiration and the role of the lungs, with additional material on topics like asthma, tuberculosis, lung cancer, and emphysema. (Rev: HBG 3/98; SLJ 2/98) [612]

Senses

18129 Aliki. *My Five Senses* (PS–1). Illus. by author. 1989, HarperCollins paper $4.95 (0-06-445083-X). 32pp. A young boy finds that he is learning about the world through the marvels of his five senses. (Rev: SLJ 1/90) [152.1]

18130 Ardley, Neil. *The Science Book of the Senses* (3–6). Illus. Series: Science Books. 1992, Harcourt $9.95 (0-15-200614-1). 28pp. Simple experiments for each of the five senses, with clear directions and attractive illustrations. (Rev: BL 3/15/92; HB 9–10/92) [612]

18131 Ballard, Carol. *How Do Our Ears Hear?* (3–5). Illus. Series: How Your Body Works. 1998, Raintree Steck-Vaughn LB $22.11 (0-8172-4737-8). 32pp. Using attractive double-page spreads, this book explains the anatomy of the ear, its role in hearing and balance, and methods for coping with a hearing loss. (Rev: BL 4/15/98; HBG 10/98) [612.8]

18132 Ballard, Carol. *How Do Our Eyes See?* (3–5). Illus. Series: How Your Body Works. 1998, Raintree Steck-Vaughn LB $22.11 (0-8172-4736-X). 32pp. Double-page spreads and clearly labeled diagrams introduce the structure and functions of the eyes along with material on optical illusions, optometry, and vision problems. (Rev: BL 4/15/98; HBG 10/98) [612.8]

18133 Ballard, Carol. *How Do We Feel and Touch?* (3–5). Series: How Your Body Works. 1998, Raintree Steck-Vaughn LB $22.11 (0-8172-4739-4). 32pp. Informative photos and drawings help explain the sense of touch, with added activities such as creating a "feely" box and using a test to determine different degrees of sensitivity. (Rev: BL 5/15/98; HBG 10/98) [612.8]

18134 Ballard, Carol. *How Do We Taste and Smell?* (3–5). Series: How Your Body Works. 1998, Raintree Steck-Vaughn LB $22.11 (0-8172-4738-6). 32pp. Good explanations, fine diagrams and photos, and a few related activities are used to explain how we are able to smell and taste. (Rev: BL 5/15/98; HBG 10/98; SLJ 7/98) [612.8]

18135 Bryan, Jenny. *Smell, Taste and Touch: The Sensory Systems* (4–6). Illus. Series: Body Talk. 1994, Dillon LB $13.95 (0-87518-590-8). 48pp. An illustrated introduction to three of the senses and how they function. Also use *Sound and Vision* (1994). (Rev: SLJ 8/94) [612.8]

18136 Byles, Monica. *Experiment with Senses* (2–5). Illus. Series: Science Experiments. 1994, Lerner LB $19.93 (0-8225-2455-4). 32pp. Fifteen experiments explain the senses, how they operate, and how they send messages to the brain. (Rev: BL 3/1/94; SLJ 4/94) [612.8]

18137 Cobb, Vicki. *Follow Your Nose: Discover Your Sense of Smell* (3–5). Illus. Series: Five Senses. 2000, Millbrook LB $21.90 (0-7613-1521-7). 32pp. This book blends facts and humor in an exploration of the sense of smell and also offers suggestions for easy experiments. (Rev: BL 11/15/00; HBG 3/01) [612.8]

18138 Cobb, Vicki. *Your Tongue Can Tell: Discover Your Sense of Taste* (3–5). Illus. Series: Five Senses. 2000, Millbrook LB $21.90 (0-7613-1473-3). 32pp. As well as giving an entertaining introduction to the sense of taste, this book supplies many ideas for activities and simple projects. (Rev: BL 11/15/00; HBG 3/01) [612.8]

18139 Cole, Joanna. *The Magic School Bus Explores the Senses* (2–4). Illus. by Bruce Degen. 1999, Scholastic $15.95 (0-590-44697-5). 48pp. The Magic School Bus travels with its passengers through an eye, an ear, a nose, and a mouth as it explores the human senses. (Rev: BL 2/15/99; HB 7–8/99; HBG 10/99; SLJ 2/99) [612.8]

18140 Cole, Joanna. *You Can't Smell a Flower with Your Ear! All About Your Five Senses* (1–3). Illus. by Mavis Smith. 1994, Putnam paper $3.99 (0-448-40469-9). 48pp. Using everyday experiences as examples, the five senses are introduced in this easy-to-read book. (Rev: BL 1/1/95) [612.8]

18141 Fowler, Allan. *Knowing About Noses* (1–2). Series: Rookie Readers. 1999, Children's LB $18.50 (0-516-20810-1). 32pp. This attractive beginning science book explains the functions of noses and explores the sense of smell. (Rev: BL 7/99; HBG 10/99) [612.8]

18142 Hewitt, Sally. *The Five Senses* (K–3). Series: It's Science! 1999, Children's LB $20.00 (0-516-21179-X). 30pp. A very basic introduction to the senses with a few simple activities included. (Rev: SLJ 5/99) [612]

18143 Isadora, Rachael. *I See* (PS). Illus. by Rachel Isadora. 1985, Greenwillow $14.89 (0-688-04060-8). 32pp. A little girl sees objects — her ball, her teddy bear. (Rev: BCCB 6/85; BL 3/15/85; SLJ 4/85)

18144 Isadora, Rachael. *I Touch* (PS). Illus. by Rachel Isadora. 1991, Greenwillow paper $6.95 (0-

688-10524-6). 32pp. "I touch my bear, he's soft" says this book that calls attention to tactile sensations. (Rev: BL 11/15/85; SLJ 2/86)

18145 Jedrosa, Aleksander. *Eyes* (3–6). Illus. by Andrew Farmer and Robina Green. Series: You and Your Body. 1992, Troll LB $18.60 (0-8167-2094-0); paper $4.95 (0-8167-2095-9). 32pp. Basic information about the eye is introduced in an appealing format. (Rev: BL 5/15/92) [612.8]

18146 Litchfield, Ada B. *A Button in Her Ear* (1–3). Illus. by Eleanor Mill. 1976, Whitman LB $14.95 (0-8075-0987-6). 32pp. A simple introduction to hearing problems and correctional devices such as the hearing aid.

18147 Martin, Paul D. *Messengers to the Brain: Our Fantastic Five Senses* (4–6). Illus. 1984, National Geographic LB $12.50 (0-87044-504-9). 104pp. A well-illustrated explanation of how the organs of the human body send messages to the brain, which acts as a message center.

18148 Mathers, Douglas. *Ears* (3–6). Illus. by Andrew Farmer and Robina Green. Series: You and Your Body. 1992, Troll LB $18.60 (0-8167-2092-4); paper $3.95 (0-8167-2093-2). 32pp. Explores the structures and functions of the outer, middle, and inner ear. (Rev: BL 5/15/92) [612.8]

18149 Murphy, Mary. *You Smell: And Taste and Feel and See and Hear* (PS–1). Illus. 1997, DK $9.95 (0-7894-2471-1). 32pp. Using a curious young dog in drawings, this book introduces the five senses to a young audience. (Rev: BL 12/1/97; HBG 3/98; SLJ 1/98) [612]

18150 O'Brien-Palmer, Michelle. *Sense-Abilities: Fun Ways to Explore the Senses: Activities for Children 4 to 8* (PS–2). Illus. by Fran Lee. 1998, Chicago Review paper $12.95 (1-55652-327-1). 166pp. With a single chapter devoted to each of the senses, this activity book contains facts and experiments that explore various sensory experiences. (Rev: SLJ 1/99) [612.8]

18151 Parker, Steve. *Senses* (4–6). Series: Look at Your Body. 1997, Millbrook LB $20.90 (0-7613-0602-1). 32pp. In this visually appealing, clearly written book, the five senses are introduced and explored, with interesting accompanying activities. (Rev: BL 1/1–15/98; HBG 3/98) [612]

18152 Parramon, J. M., and J. J. Puig. *Hearing* (PS–1). Illus. by Maria Rius. 1985, Barron's paper $6.95 (0-8120-3563-1). 32pp. An easy introduction to the sense of hearing. (Rev: BL 9/1/85)

18153 Parramon, J. M., and J. J. Puig. *Sight* (PS–1). Illus. by Maria Rius. 1985, Barron's paper $6.95 (0-8120-3564-X). 32pp. The sense of sight is explained to young readers. (Rev: BL 9/1/85; SLJ 11/85)

18154 Parramon, J. M., and J. J. Puig. *Smell* (PS–1). Illus. by Maria Rius. 1985, Barron's paper $6.95 (0-8120-3565-8). 32pp. An easy explanation of the sense of smell. (Rev: BL 9/1/85)

18155 Parramon, J. M., and J. J. Puig. *Taste* (PS–1). Illus. by Maria Rius. 1985, Barron's paper $6.95 (0-8120-3566-6). 32pp. Easy reading about the sense of taste. (Rev: BL 9/1/85)

18156 Parramon, J. M., and J. J. Puig. *Touch* (PS–1). Illus. by Maria Rius. 1985, Barron's paper $6.95 (0-8120-3567-4). 32pp. An easy-to-read explanation of the sense of touch. (Rev: BL 9/1/85)

18157 Pringle, Laurence. *Hearing* (3–6). Illus. Series: Explore Your Senses. 1999, Marshall Cavendish LB $15.95 (0-7614-0735-9). 32pp. Using a large format and clear diagrams, this book discusses the structure of the ear, how it operates, possible malfunctions, and how to preserve hearing. (Rev: BL 2/1/00; HBG 10/00; SLJ 3/00) [612.8]

18158 Pringle, Laurence. *Smell* (3–6). Series: Explore Your Senses. 1999, Marshall Cavendish LB $15.95 (0-7614-0737-5). 32pp. A clear text, diagrams, and photographs are used to explain how the sense of smell works, problems that can occur, and the differences between animals and humans. (Rev: BL 2/15/00; HBG 10/00; SLJ 3/00) [612]

18159 Pringle, Laurence. *Taste* (3–6). Illus. Series: Explore Your Senses. 1999, Marshall Cavendish LB $15.95 (0-7614-0736-7). 32pp. The structure of the tongue, taste buds, taste cells, and the relationship between smell and taste are some of the subjects covered in this large-format book. (Rev: BL 2/1/00; HBG 10/00; SLJ 3/00) [612.8]

18160 Pringle, Laurence. *Touch* (3–6). Series: Explore Your Senses. 1999, Marshall Cavendish LB $15.95 (0-7614-0738-3). 32pp. A fresh look at the sense of touch that uses many color diagrams, photos, and an accessible text. (Rev: BL 2/15/00; HBG 10/00) [612]

18161 Sandeman, Anna. *Senses* (1–2). Illus. Series: Body Books. 1995, Millbrook LB $18.90 (1-56294-944-6). 32pp. Body organs that are involved with the senses, like eyes, are discussed in this simple introduction that also mentions such topics as color blindness and the ears' role in balance. (Rev: BL 12/15/95; SLJ 2/96) [612.8]

18162 Showers, Paul. *Look at Your Eyes* (PS–2). Illus. by True Kelley. Series: Let's-Read-and-Find-Out. 1992, HarperCollins LB $15.89 (0-06-020189-4). 32pp. A little boy looks in the bathroom mirror and begins to think about his eyes. (Rev: BL 1/1/93) [612.8]

18163 Suhr, Mandy. *Taste* (PS–1). Illus. by Mike Gordon. Series: I'm Alive. 1994, Carolrhoda LB $19.93 (0-87614-836-4). 32pp. Why and how we taste is covered in a nontechnical way, with simple activities and projects to amplify the text. From the same series, also use *Touch* (1994). (Rev: SLJ 12/94) [152.1]

18164 Suzuki, David, and Barbara Hehner. *Looking at Senses* (3–6). Illus. Series: Looking At. 1991, Stoddart $24.95 (0-471-54751-4); paper $9.95 (0-471-54048-X). 96pp. Each of the senses is highlighted, with a series of projects to explain each. (Rev: SLJ 5/92) [612]

Skeletal-Muscular System

18165 Balestrino, Philip. *The Skeleton Inside You* (2–4). Illus. by True Kelley. 1989, HarperCollins paper $4.95 (0-06-445087-2). 32pp. Color illustra-tions help to explain the body's structure. (Rev: BL 6/15/89)

18166 Ballard, Carol. *How Do We Move?* (3–5). Series: How Your Body Works. 1998, Raintree Steck-Vaughn LB $22.11 (0-8172-4741-6). 32pp. This book explains how the skeletal and muscular systems work and includes activities such as creating a model of a muscle. (Rev: BL 5/15/98; HBG 10/98) [612]

18167 Ballard, Carol. *The Skeleton and Muscular System* (5–8). Illus. Series: Human Body. 1997, Raintree Steck-Vaughn $27.12 (0-8172-4805-6). 48pp. This well-organized book introduces in text and pictures such topics as muscles and how they work, joint diseases, bones, and skeletal diseases. (Rev: SLJ 2/98) [612]

18168 Barner, Bob. *Dem Bones* (K–3). Illus. 1996, Chronicle $14.95 (0-8118-0827-0). 32pp. The human skeleton is introduced by using the words of the old song "Dem Dry Bones." (Rev: BL 12/1/96; SLJ 11/96) [611]

18169 Bryan, Jenny. *Movement: The Muscular and Skeletal System* (4–6). Illus. Series: Body Talk. 1993, Dillon LB $18.95 (0-87518-565-7). 48pp. This clear introduction to muscles and bones also discusses such topics as running, weightlessness, joint replacement, genetic engineering, and artificial limbs. (Rev: SLJ 10/93) [612]

18170 Dineen, Jacqueline. *The Skeleton and Movement* (5–7). Illus. 1988, Silver Burdett $12.95 (0-382-09702-5). An explanation of human body movement. (Rev: BL 4/15/89)

18171 Parker, Steve. *Skeleton* (4–6). Illus. Series: Look at Your Body. 1996, Millbrook LB $20.90 (0-7613-0529-7). 32pp. The human skeleton, its composition, and its uses are covered, with extensive, unusual illustrations like X-rays and CAT scans. (Rev: BL 11/1/96) [611]

18172 Saunderson, Jane. *Muscles and Bones* (3–6). Illus. by Robina Green. Series: Your and Your Body. 1992, Troll LB $18.60 (0-8167-2088-6); paper $3.95 (0-8167-2089-4). 32pp. The structure and function of human muscles in a well-designed book. (Rev: BL 5/15/92) [612.7]

18173 Silverstein, Alvin, et al. *The Muscular System* (5–8). Illus. Series: Human Body Systems. 1994, Twenty-First Century LB $21.90 (0-8050-2836-6). 96pp. Full-color diagrams, drawings, and photographs highlight this survey of the human muscular system. (Rev: BL 3/15/95; SLJ 5/95) [612.7]

18174 Silverstein, Alvin, et al. *The Skeletal System* (5–8). Illus. Series: Human Body Systems. 1994, Twenty-First Century LB $21.40 (0-8050-2837-4). 96pp. The purpose and nature of the human skeleton, its maintenance and repair, and the composition of bones are three topics discussed. (Rev: BL 3/15/95) [612.7]

18175 Simon, Seymour. *Bones: Our Skeletal System* (3–6). Illus. 1998, Morrow LB $15.93 (0-688-14645-7). 32pp. This book describes the human skeleton and explains the structure of bones, their important groups, how they connect, and how they move. (Rev: BCCB 9/98; BL 9/1/98; HBG 3/99; SLJ 12/98) [612.7]

18176 Simon, Seymour. *Muscles: Our Muscular System* (3–6). Illus. 1998, Morrow LB $15.93 (0-688-14643-0). 32pp. This work describes the different types of muscles — including voluntary, involuntary, and cardiac — and where each is found and how each functions. (Rev: BCCB 9/98; BL 9/1/98; HB 11–12/98; HBG 3/99; SLJ 12/98) [612.7]

Skin and Hair

18177 Badt, Karin Luisa. *Hair There and Everywhere* (3–7). Illus. Series: A World of Difference. 1994, Children's LB $21.00 (0-516-08187-X). 32pp. A cross-cultural look at hair, its variant types and different styles. (Rev: BL 1/1/95; SLJ 1/95) [391.5]

18178 Kinch, Michael P. *Warts* (3–5). Illus. Series: My Health. 2000, Watts LB $22.50 (0-531-11625-5); paper $6.95 (0-531-16453-5). 48pp. Different kinds of warts are discussed, with material and activities related to how they are transmitted, how they grow, and how they can be eliminated. (Rev: BL 6/1–15/00) [616.5]

18179 Sandeman, Anna. *Skin, Teeth, and Hair* (1–2). Illus. Series: Body Books. 1996, Millbrook LB $18.90 (0-7613-0489-4). 32pp. For beginning readers, this colorful account explains the composition and use in the human body of skin, teeth, and hair. (Rev: BL 10/15/96; SLJ 1/97) [612]

18180 Showers, Paul. *Your Skin and Mine* (PS–3). Illus. by Kathleen Kuchera. Series: Let's-Read-and-Find-Out. 1991, HarperCollins paper $5.95 (0-06-445102-X). 32pp. A look at skin, with simple experiments to show skin reactions. (Rev: BL 10/15/91; SLJ 8/91) [612.7]

18181 Silverstein, Alvin, et al. *Cuts, Scrapes, Scabs, Scars* (3–5). Series: My Health. 1999, Watts LB $22.50 (0-531-11582-8). 48pp. Using colored medical illustrations, photos, and amusing cartoons, this book describes various skin injuries and how the body heals itself and produces new skin. (Rev: BL 10/15/99; HBG 3/00) [612.7]

18182 Silverstein, Alvin, et al. *Is That a Rash?* (3–5). Illus. Series: My Health. 2000, Watts LB $22.50 (0-531-11637-9); paper $6.95 (0-531-16451-9). 48pp. With many suggested activities and excellent color photos, this account introduces skin problems — their causes and treatments. (Rev: BL 6/1–15/00) [616.5]

18183 Yagyu, Genichiro. *All About Scabs* (K–3). Trans. by Amanda Mayer Stinchecum. Illus. 1998, Kane/Miller $11.95 (0-916291-82-0). 28pp. This attention-getting book tells what a scab is, how it is formed, its uses, and what eventually happens to it. (Rev: BL 1/1–15/99; HBG 3/99; SLJ 2/99) [617.1]

Teeth

18184 Keller, Laurie. *Open Wide: Tooth School Inside* (2–4). Illus. 2000, Holt $16.95 (0-8050-6192-

4). 32pp. A fun book that explores the different kinds of teeth, dental care, and the causes of tooth decay. (Rev: BCCB 9/00; BL 5/1/00; HB 5–6/00; HBG 10/00; SLJ 5/00) [617.6]

18185 Lee, Jordan. *Coping with Braces and Other Orthodontic Work* (4–9). Series: Coping. 1998, Rosen LB $16.95 (0-8239-2721-0). 95pp. A book about braces, their purposes, and the problems they can cause. (Rev: SLJ 11/98) [612.3]

18186 McGinty, Alice B. *Staying Healthy: Dental Care* (K–3). Series: The Library of Healthy Living. 1998, Rosen LB $15.95 (0-8239-5139-1). 24pp. A fine introduction to teeth that covers such topics as different types of teeth, parts of a tooth, dental hygiene, and problems such as decay and cavities. (Rev: SLJ 9/98) [612.3]

18187 Rockwell, Harlow. *My Dentist* (1–2). Illus. 1975, Morrow paper $4.95 (0-688-07040-X). 32pp. A matter-of-fact, informative book about dentists and the instruments they use.

18188 Rowan, Kate. *I Know Why I Brush My Teeth* (PS–2). Illus. by Katharine McEwen. Series: Sam's Science. 1999, Candlewick $9.99 (0-7636-0504-2). 29pp. A beginner's book in which a mother explains to her son about the composition and parts of teeth as well as the basics of good dental care. (Rev: HBG 3/00; SLJ 8/99) [612.3]

18189 Showers, Paul. *How Many Teeth?* (PS–2). Illus. by True Kelley. Series: Let's-Read-and-Find-Out. 1991, HarperCollins paper $4.95 (0-06-445098-8). 32pp. A full-color, funny, informative book showing a multiracial classroom. (Rev: BL 6/15/91; SLJ 10/91) [612.3]

18190 Silverstein, Alvin, et al. *Tooth Decay and Cavities* (3–5). Illus. Series: My Health. 1999, Watts LB $22.50 (0-531-11580-1). 48pp. Discusses the structure and functions of teeth, how decay occurs, and how it can be prevented. (Rev: BL 10/15/99; HBG 3/00; SLJ 12/99) [617.6]

Hygiene, Physical Fitness, and Nutrition

18191 Colman, Penny. *Toilets, Bathtubs, Sinks, and Sewers: A History of the Bathroom* (5–8). Illus. 1994, Atheneum $16.00 (0-689-31894-4). 96pp. A fascinating look at sanitation systems and personal hygiene from ancient times to the present. (Rev: BCCB 2/95; BL 1/1/95; SLJ 3/95) [643]

18192 Frost, Helen. *Drinking Water* (K–2). 2000, Capstone LB $13.25 (0-7368-0534-6). 24pp. This book explains simply why drinking water is a necessary part of one's diet. (Rev: HBG 10/00; SLJ 10/00) [613.2]

18193 Frost, Helen. *Eating Right* (K–2). Series: Food Guide Pyramid. 2000, Capstone LB $13.25 (0-7368-0535-4). 24pp. A very simple introduction to nutrition and the food pyramid. (Rev: HBG 10/00; SLJ 10/00) [613.2]

18194 Glibbery, Caroline. *Join the Total Fitness Gang* (4–6). Series: Good Health Guides. 1998,

Gareth Stevens LB $14.95 (0-8368-2181-5). 32pp. In this guide to good health, topics covered include personal hygiene, weight control, sleep habits, dental and eye care, first aid, and drugs and smoking. (Rev: HBG 10/99; SLJ 6/99) [613]

18195 Green, Tamara. *Exercise Is Fun!* (4–6). Series: Good Health Guides. 1998, Gareth Stevens LB $14.95 (0-8368-2180-7). 32pp. Many illustrations are included in this beginner's guide to exercise that includes material on yoga, breathing and posture exercises, dancing, jumping rope, and jogging. (Rev: HBG 10/99; SLJ 6/99) [613.7]

18196 Hammerslough, Jane. *Everything You Need to Know About Skin Care* (4–8). Illus. Series: Everything You Need to Know About. 1994, Rosen LB $17.95 (0-8239-1686-3). 64pp. This book tells about skin structure, skin types, blemishes, acne, sunburn, warts, freckles, athlete's foot and other skin disorders, with information on skin care products. (Rev: SLJ 9/94) [616.5]

18197 Kerr, Daisy. *Keeping Clean: A Very Peculiar History* (4–7). Illus. 1995, Watts LB $23.00 (0-531-14353-8). 48pp. A history of sanitation from the ancient world to the present plus a discussion of how sanitation procedures differ in various cultures. (Rev: BCCB 6/95; BL 6/1–15/95) [613]

18198 Luby, Thia. *Children's Book of Yoga: Games and Exercises Mimic Plants and Animals and Objects* (PS–7). 1998, Clear Light $14.95 (1-57416-003-6). 112pp. Brief, clear instructions are used to introduce yoga exercises — from the very easy to the more complex. (Rev: SLJ 10/98) [181.45]

18199 Lukes, Bonnie L. *How to Be a Reasonably Thin Teenage Girl: Without Starving, Losing Your Friends or Running Away from Home* (5–8). Illus. 1986, Macmillan $15.00 (0-689-31269-5). 96pp. Sensible advice from an "ex-fatty" directed toward the young teenager. (Rev: BCCB 10/86; BL 1/1/87)

18200 Mainland, Pauline. *A Yoga Parade of Animals: A First Fun Picture Book of Yoga* (2–6). Photos by Katie Vandyck. Illus. by Chris Perry. 1998, Element Books $15.95 (1-90188-165-2). This book shows children how they can assume the shapes and positions of various animals and supplies information about yoga and its history. (Rev: HBG 3/99; SLJ 11/98) [613.7]

18201 Parker, Steve. *Professor Protein's Fitness, Health, Hygiene and Relaxation Tonic* (4–6). Illus. by Rob Shone. 1996, Millbrook LB $23.90 (0-7613-0494-0). 48pp. A witty presentation of material about fitness, health, and hygiene, with accompanying humorous cartoons. (Rev: SLJ 1/97) [613]

18202 Parsons, Alexandra. *Fit for Life* (3–6). Illus. by John Shackell and Stuart Harrison. Series: Life Education. 1996, Watts LB $19.00 (0-531-14372-4). 32pp. A beginner's guide to nutrition, hygiene, and exercise, with coverage of the effects of drugs, smoking, and alcohol. (Rev: SLJ 10/96) [613.2]

18203 Powell, Jillian. *Exercise and Your Health* (2–5). Illus. Series: Health Matters. 1997, Raintree Steck-Vaughn LB $25.69 (0-8172-4927-3). 32pp. Explains how exercise affects good health and gives tips on types of exercises, warming-up and cooling

activities, proper dress, and ways to design a personalized program. (Rev: HBG 3/98; SLJ 2/98) [613.7]

18204 Powell, Jillian. *Food and Your Health* (2–5). Illus. Series: Health Matters. 1997, Raintree Steck-Vaughn LB $25.69 (0-8172-4925-7). 32pp. Explains how food is digested, what constitutes good nutrition, problem foods, and data on proper body weight. (Rev: HBG 3/98; SLJ 2/98) [613.2]

18205 Rockwell, Lizzy. *Good Enough to Eat: A Kid's Guide to Food and Nutrition* (K–4). Illus. 1999, HarperCollins $14.95 (0-06-027434-4). 40pp. A nutritional guide for preschoolers that tells them about food groups, good eating habits, and how proper nutrition can keep them healthy and growing. (Rev: BL 1/1–15/99; HBG 10/99; SLJ 1/99) [613.2]

18206 Royston, Angela. *Eat Well* (K–2). Series: Safe and Sound. 1999, Heinemann LB $13.95 (1-57572-982-2). 32pp. This basic book on nutrition explains the food pyramid and the nutrients that are essential for good health. Exercise is given a similar treatment in the author's *A Healthy Body* (1999). (Rev: SLJ 1/00) [613]

18207 Savage, Jeff. *Aerobics* (4–6). Illus. Series: Working Out. 1995, Silver Burdett LB $17.95 (0-89686-853-2); paper $7.95 (0-382-24945-3). 48pp. This book describes the nature and benefits of aerobic exercise, how to get started, and how to develop a routine. (Rev: SLJ 10/95) [613.7]

18208 Savage, Jeff. *Fundamental Strength Training* (5–9). Photos by Jimmy Clarke. Series: Fundamental Sports. 1998, Lerner LB $22.60 (0-8225-3461-4). 64pp. This beginner's manual discusses weight machines, training without weights, and various exercises for developing specific parts of the body. (Rev: HBG 10/99; SLJ 2/99) [613.7]

18209 Serafin, Kim. *Everything You Need to Know About Being a Vegetarian* (5–8). Series: Need to Know Library. 1999, Rosen LB $17.95 (0-8239-2951-5). 64pp. This book explains vegetarianism and its various varieties, the reasons why people become vegetarians, the nature of their diets, social problems involved, and names celebrities who are vegetarians. (Rev: SLJ 1/00) [613.2]

18210 Silverstein, Alvin, et al. *Eat Your Vegetables! Drink Your Milk!* (3–5). Series: My Health. 2000, Watts LB $22.50 (0-531-11635-2); paper $6.95 (0-531-16507-8). 48pp. This is a beginner's guide to nutrition and the part played by foods in maintaining a healthy body. (Rev: BL 9/15/00) [613]

18211 Stewart, Alex. *Keeping Clean* (2–4). Illus. 2000, Watts $20.00 (0-531-14546-8). A heavily illustrated history of personal hygiene and bathing techniques including care of hair and teeth through the ages. (Rev: BL 10/15/00; SLJ 6/00) [391]

18212 VanCleave, Janice. *Janice VanCleave's Food and Nutrition for Every Kid: Easy Activities That Make Learning Science Fun* (4–8). Illus. by Laurel Aiello. Series: Science for Every Kid. 1999, Wiley $27.95 (0-471-17666-4); paper $12.95 (0-471-17665-6). 256pp. Provides explanations and activities for such subjects as food groups, vitamins and minerals, food energy, and nutrition labels. (Rev: SLJ 8/99) [641.1]

18213 Weiss, Stefanie Iris. *Everything You Need to Know About Being a Vegan* (5–8). Series: Need to Know Library. 1999, Rosen LB $17.95 (0-8239-2958-2). 64pp. This book discusses vegans, people who do not eat or use animal products (usually for religious reasons), their lifestyles, diets, and possible social problems. (Rev: SLJ 1/00) [613.2]

Safety and Accidents

18214 Boelts, Maribeth. *A Kid's Guide to Staying Safe Around Water* (K–3). Series: The Kids' Library of Personal Safety. 1997, Rosen LB $13.95 (0-8239-5078-6). 24pp. This simple book on water safety presents basic rules for situations in a pool, lake, or ocean, plus coverage on swimming lessons, sunscreen, and what to do if someone is in trouble. (Rev: SLJ 4/98) [613.7]

18215 Boelts, Maribeth, and Darwin Boelts. *Kids to the Rescue! First Aid Techniques for Kids* (3–6). Illus. by Marina Megale. 1992, Parenting Pr. LB $20.00 (0-943990-83-1). 72pp. This book helps children react properly to 14 different medical emergencies and includes directions for appropriate actions in each case. (Rev: SLJ 9/92) [616.04]

18216 Chaiet, Donna, and Francine Russell. *The Safe Zone: A Kid's Guide to Personal Safety* (4–7). Illus. 1998, Morrow $15.00 (0-688-15307-0); paper $4.95 (0-688-16091-3). 160pp. Through a number of real-life situations, this book shows kids how to handle unpleasant social problems such as bullying at home, school, and in the community. (Rev: BL 4/1/98; HBG 10/98) [613.6]

18217 Gutman, Bill. *Be Aware of Danger* (5–8). Illus. Series: Focus on Safety. 1996, Twenty-First Century LB $24.95 (0-8050-4142-7). 80pp. Situations that could be dangerous to young people are highlighted, with preventive measures outlined. (Rev: BL 2/1/97; SLJ 2/97) [613.6]

18218 Gutman, Bill. *Hazards at Home* (4–8). Illus. Series: Focus on Safety. 1996, Twenty-First Century LB $20.40 (0-8050-4141-9). 80pp. This account stresses safety at home and how to avoid accidents, with information on first-aid procedures. (Rev: SLJ 9/96) [363.1]

18219 Gutman, Bill. *Recreation Can Be Risky* (4–8). Illus. Series: Focus on Safety. 1996, Holt LB $20.40 (0-8050-4143-5). 80pp. Using a number of sports as examples, the author gives tips on how to play safe-

ly and avoid accidents. (Rev: BL 7/96; SLJ 9/96) [790]

18220 Loewen, Nancy. *Emergencies* (1–4). Illus. by Penny Dann. 1996, Child's World LB $18.50 (1-56766-259-5). 24pp. Anthropomorphic animals are used to illustrate safety measures and emergency first aid. Also use *School Safety* (1996). (Rev: SLJ 3/97) [617.1]

18221 MacGregor, Cynthia. *Ten Steps to Staying Safe* (2–4). Illus. Series: Abduction Prevention Library. 1998, Rosen LB $11.95 (0-8239-5248-7). 24pp. This book focuses on the inherent dangers of being with strangers and how to protect oneself in these situations. (Rev: BL 2/1/99) [613.6]

18222 MacGregor, Cynthia. *What to Do If You Get Lost* (2–4). Illus. Series: Abduction Prevention Library. 1998, Rosen LB $11.95 (0-8239-5250-9). 24pp. This is a practical guide for children who get separated from familiar places and people, telling how they can get help. (Rev: BL 2/1/99) [613.6]

18223 Mattern, Joanne. *Safety at School* (K–3). Series: Safety First. 1999, ABDO LB $13.95 (1-57765-070-0). 24pp. This book tells youngsters how to stay safe at school. Also use *Safety in Public Places* (1999). (Rev: HBG 3/00; SLJ 1/00) [613.6]

18224 Mattern, Joanne. *Safety on the Go* (K–3). Series: Safety First. 1999, ABDO LB $13.95 (1-57765-075-1). 24pp. This account tells children how to remain safe while using public transportation. Also use *Safety in the Water* and *Safety on Your Bicycle* (both 1999). (Rev: HBG 3/00; SLJ 1/00) [613.6]

18225 *Now I Know Better: Kids Tell About Safety* (4–6). Illus. 1996, Millbrook LB $21.90 (0-7613-0109-7); paper $7.95 (0-7613-0149-6). 96pp. This book on safety features true accounts from children whose lives have been changed by accidents. (Rev: BL 10/15/96; SLJ 2/97) [613.6]

18226 Silverstein, Alvin, et al. *Staying Safe* (3–5). Series: My Health. 2000, Watts LB $22.50 (0-531-11639-5). 48pp. This is an amusing, accurate look at accidents and their prevention, along with tips on safety. (Rev: BL 11/15/00) [613.6]

Sleep and Dreams

18227 Silverstein, Alvin, et al. *Sleep* (3–5). Illus. 2000, Watts LB $22.50 (0-531-11636-0); paper $6.95 (0-531-16452-7). 48pp. An exploration of the nature of sleep and the causes and meanings of dreams, with several interesting related activities. (Rev: BL 6/1–15/00) [616.5]

Sex Education and Reproduction

Babies

18228 Davis, Jennifer. *Before You Were Born* (PS–2). Illus. by Laura Cornell. 1998, Workman $10.95 (0-7611-1200-6). 24pp. The nine months of prenatal development are chronicled in a simple text with thumbnail drawings and told from a pregnant woman's point of view. (Rev: HBG 3/99; SLJ 9/98) [612]

18229 Dilley, Becki, and Keith Dilley. *Sixty Fingers, Sixty Toes: See How the Dilley Sextuplets Grow* (PS). Photos by E. Anthony Valainis. 1998, Walker $15.95 (0-8027-8613-8). 32pp. In a series of photographs, the life and activities of the Dilley sextuplets are covered from infancy through age four. (Rev: HBG 10/98; SLJ 7/98) [305]

18230 Douglas, Ann. *Baby Science: How Babies Really Work!* (PS–2). Illus. by Helene Desputeaux. 1998, Firefly $17.95 (1-895688-83-3). 32pp. The behavioral habits of babies during the first year of life are explored in this colorful picture book. (Rev: BL 1/1–15/99; SLJ 12/98) [305.232]

18231 Gentieu, Penny. *Grow! Babies!* (PS). Illus. 2000, Crown $12.95 (0-517-80029-2). 24pp. A baby's development during the first 12 months of life is traced in photographs of 19 babies taken at various intervals during a one-year period. (Rev: BL 6/1–15/00; HBG 10/00; SLJ 5/00) [155.42]

18232 Nanao, Jun. *Contemplating Your Bellybutton* (PS–K). Trans. by Amanda Mayer Stinchecum. Illus. by Tomoko Hasegawa. 1995, Kane/Miller $11.95 (0-916291-60-X). 32pp. Young Tettchan is told how he got his belly button and the purpose it serves. (Rev: BL 1/1–15/96; SLJ 12/95) [611.95]

18233 Stein, Sara Bonnett. *Oh, Baby!* (PS–1). Illus. by Holly Anne Shelowitz. 1993, Walker LB $15.85 (0-8027-8262-0). 32pp. Using a series of baby pictures, physical and mental developments during the first year of a child's life are outlined. (Rev: BL 3/1/94*; SLJ 12/93*) [305]

18234 Thomas, Shelley M. *A Baby's Coming to Your House!* (PS–1). Illus. by Eric Futran. 2001, Albert Whitman $15.95 (0-8075-0502-1). 32pp. Using funny family pictures as illustrations, this book explains to youngsters the changes that take place when a new baby enters the house — like the appearance of high chairs and messy diapers. (Rev: BL 3/15/01) [305.2]

18235 Wilkes, Angela. *See How I Grow* (PS–1). Illus. 1994, DK $13.95 (1-56458-464-X). 32pp. This is the story of a baby's first 18 months of life, told in photo-essay format. (Rev: BL 5/1/94; SLJ 8/94) [612.6]

Reproduction

18236 Audry, Andrew C., and Steven Schepp. *How Babies Are Made* (K–3). Illus. 1984, Little, Brown paper $12.95 (0-316-04227-7). 80pp. Explaining intercourse, pregnancy, and birth — using flowers, animals, and humans.

18237 Cole, Babette. *Mommy Laid an Egg!* (K–3). Illus. 1993, Chronicle $13.95 (0-8118-0350-3). 30pp. After parents try to explain where babies come from, the children tell them the truth. (Rev: BL 7/93) [649]

18238 Cole, Joanna. *How You Were Born* (PS–3). Illus. by Margaret Miller. 1993, Morrow paper $5.95 (0-688-12061-X). 48pp. Fetal development is tracked in text and color pictures, plus tips are given on how to use this book with children. (Rev: BL 6/1–15/93; SLJ 4/93*) [612]

18239 Douglas, Ann. *Before You Were Born: The Inside Story!* (PS–4). Photos by Gilbert Duclos. Illus. by Eugenie Fernandes. 2000, Owl $18.95 (1-894379-01-2); paper $6.95 (1-894379-02-0). 32pp. This book, illustrated with drawings, depicts the prenatal life of a baby with information on such topics as movement, sight, and food. (Rev: HBG 3/01; SLJ 10/00) [618.4]

18240 Girard, Linda Walvoord. *You Were Born on Your Very First Birthday* (PS). Illus. by Christa Kieffer. 1983, Whitman paper $5.95 (0-8075-9456-3). 32pp. A simple introduction to pregnancy and birth.

18241 Landau, Elaine. *Multiple Births* (4–6). Illus. Series: First Books. 1998, Watts LB $22.00 (0-531-20309-3). 64pp. Beginning with the Dionne quintuplets born in Canada during the 1930s, this book uses many examples and scientific explanations to explore and discuss the phenomenon of multiple births in humans. (Rev: BL 11/15/98; HBG 10/98) [618.2]

18242 Overend, Jenni. *Welcome with Love* (1–3). Illus. by Julie Vivas. 2000, Kane/Miller $15.95 (0-916291-96-0). 32pp. A direct, graphic treatment of childbirth showing the members of a close family participating in a home delivery. (Rev: BCCB 6/00; BL 3/15/00; HBG 10/00; SLJ 4/00) [618.4]

18243 Parker, Steve. *The Reproductive System* (5–8). Illus. Series: Human Body. 1997, Raintree Steck-Vaughn LB $27.12 (0-8172-4806-4). 48pp. A well-organized, straightforward account that covers male and female anatomy, genes, fertility problems, contraception, STDs, and human development from conception to adolescence. (Rev: SLJ 2/98) [613.9]

18244 Royston, Angela. *Where Do Babies Come From? A Delightful First Look at How Life Begins* (PS–1). Illus. 1996, DK $9.95 (0-7894-0579-2). 37pp. This simple introduction to reproduction uses the sunflower, ducks, cats, and humans as examples and uses schematic drawings superimposed on photos to show fetuses. (Rev: SLJ 8/96) [613.9]

18245 Sandeman, Anna. *Babies* (2–4). Illus. Series: Body Books. 1996, Millbrook LB $18.90 (0-7613-0478-9). 31pp. Clear information is given on conception, pregnancy, childbirth, and the growth of babies. (Rev: SLJ 6/96) [613.9]

18246 Schnitter, Jane T. *Let Me Explain: A Story About Donor Insemination* (2–4). Illus. by Joanne Bowring. 1995, Perspectives $14.00 (0-944934-12-9). 32pp. A young girl tells how much she adores her father and also explains that she was the product of artificial insemination. (Rev: SLJ 7/95) [618]

18247 Silverstein, Alvin, et al. *The Reproductive System* (5–8). Illus. Series: Human Body Systems. 1994, Twenty-First Century LB $20.40 (0-8050-2838-2). 96pp. Reproduction in the plant and animal world is introduced, with the focus on the human system and body parts. (Rev: BL 3/15/95; SLJ 5/95) [612.6]

18248 Taylor, Nicole. *Baby* (3–5). Illus. Series: Images. 1994, Creative Ed. LB $25.30 (0-88682-595-4). The process of conception is described in text and photos, along with a month-by-month depiction of fetal development and pictures of a birth. (Rev: SLJ 12/94) [306]

Sex Education and Puberty

18249 Blackstone, Margaret, and Elissa Haden Guest. *Girl Stuff: A Survival Guide to Growing Up* (5–7). Illus. 2000, Harcourt $14.95 (0-15-201830-1); paper $8.95 (0-15-202644-4). 144pp. Coverage of such topics as puberty, physical changes, sex,

birth control, and sexually transmitted diseases helps girls learn about becoming young women. (Rev: BL 5/15/00; HBG 10/00; SLJ 6/00) [613]

18250 Bourgeois, Paulette, and Martin Wolfish. *Changes in You and Me: A Book About Puberty, Mostly for Boys* (4–7). Illus. 1994, Andrews & McMeel $14.95 (0-8362-2814-6). 64pp. A straightforward account about the changes, problems, and challenges associated with puberty. A companion volume is *Changes . . . for Girls* (1994). (Rev: BL 2/1/95; SLJ 3/95) [612]

18251 Brewer, Janet Neff. *In God's Image* (PS–K). Illus. 1998, Bridge Resources $14.95 (1-57895-055-4). 32pp. Using a Christian framework that stresses God's love, this book on sex education explains to the very young how babies grow inside mothers, the differences between a boy's and a girl's body, what "bad" touching is about, and how to cope with various emotions. (Rev: BL 10/1/98) [241]

18252 Brown, Laurie Krasny. *What's the Big Secret? Talking About Sex with Girls and Boys* (2–4). Illus. by Marc Brown. 1997, Little, Brown $15.95 (0-316-10915-0). 32pp. This picture book on sex education discusses sexuality, gender roles, reproduction, and the issue of privacy. (Rev: BL 10/1/97; HBG 3/98; SLJ 3/98) [613]

18253 Cole, Babette. *Hair in Funny Places* (3–5). Illus. 2000, Hyperion $15.99 (0-7868-0590-0). 32pp. A simple introduction to puberty and the changes Mr. and Mrs. Hormone produce in the body, with coverage of menstruation and ejaculation. (Rev: BL 7/00; HBG 10/00; SLJ 7/00) [612]

18254 Cole, Joanna. *Asking About Sex and Growing Up: A Question-and-Answer Book for Boys and Girls* (4–6). Illus. by Alan Tiegreen. 1988, Morrow $16.00 (0-688-06927-4); paper $4.95 (0-688-06928-2). 96pp. Answers questions about sex and physical changes that occur as one grows up. (Rev: BCCB 6/88; BL 6/15/88; SLJ 8/88)

18255 Girard, Linda Walvoord. *My Body Is Private* (PS–3). Illus. by Rodney Pate. 1984, Whitman LB $13.95 (0-8075-5320-4); paper $5.95 (0-8075-5319-0). 32pp. A girl of seven or eight talks about unwarranted touching of one's body by another in this lesson on prevention of sexual abuse.

18256 Gordon, Sol, and Judith Gordon. *A Better Safe Than Sorry Book: A Family Guide for Sexual Assault Prevention* (PS–1). Illus. 1992, Prometheus paper $10.00 (0-87975-768-X). A book that approaches the subjects of sexual abuse and threats from strangers in a nonscary manner. (Rev: BL 11/15/85)

18257 Gordon, Sol, and Judith Gordon. *Did the Sun Shine Before You Were Born? A Sex Education Primer* (PS–3). Illus. 1974, Okpaku $12.00 (0-89388-179-1); Prometheus paper $9.95 (0-879-75723-X). A self-styled sex education manual for the very young.

18258 Gravelle, Karen, and Nick Castro. *What's Going on Down There? Answers to Questions Boys Find Hard to Ask* (5–10). Illus. by Robert Leighton. 1998, Walker paper $8.95 (0-8027-7540-3). 128pp. This boys' guide to puberty covers such topics as physical changes, sexual intercourse, peer pressure, and pregnancy and birth. (Rev: HB 1–2/99; HBG 3/99; SLJ 12/98) [613]

18259 Gravelle, Karen, and Jennifer Gravelle. *The Period Book: Everything You Don't Want to Ask (but Need to Know)* (4–6). Illus. 1996, Walker $15.95 (0-8027-8420-8); paper $8.95 (0-8027-7478-4). 128pp. A chatty guide to menstruation that also describes reproductive anatomy and the many changes that occur during puberty. (Rev: BCCB 7–8/96; BL 3/15/96; SLJ 3/96) [612.6]

18260 Harris, Robie H. *It's Perfectly Normal: A Book About Changing Bodies, Growing Up, Sex, and Sexual Health* (4–7). Illus. by Michael Emberley. 1994, Candlewick $19.99 (1-56402-199-8). 96pp. A frank discussion with candid illustrations are contained in this discussion of the changes, problems, and choices that puberty brings. (Rev: BCCB 10/94; BL 9/15/94*; SLJ 12/94*) [613]

18261 Harris, Robie H. *It's So Amazing: A Book about Eggs, Sperm, Birth, Babies, and Families* (2–5). Illus. by Michael Emberley. 1999, Candlewick $21.99 (0-7636-0051-2). 80pp. An outstanding book that explains human reproduction and birth in straightforward prose and bold, colorful illustrations. (Rev: BCCB 2/00; BL 1/1–15/00*; HBG 3/00; SLJ 2/00) [612.6]

18262 Johnson, Eric W. *People, Love, Sex, and Families: Answers to Questions That Preteens Ask* (5–8). Illus. 1985, Walker LB $14.85 (0-8027-6605-6). 144pp. Based on the results of a survey of 1,000 preteens, this book covers a broad range of topics, from sexual abuse to venereal disease to divorce and incest. (Rev: BL 3/15/86)

18263 Jukes, Mavis. *Growing Up: It's a Girl Thing: Straight Talk about First Bras, First Periods, and Your Changing Body* (4–6). Illus. 1998, Knopf LB $16.99 (0-679-99027-5); paper $10.00 (0-679-89027-0). 96pp. Using personal stories as a framework, this book talks about a girl's anatomy, menstruation, and related topics, and includes an excellent section on bras. (Rev: BL 11/1/98; SLJ 11/98) [616.6]

18264 Kleven, Sandy. *The Right Touch: A Read-Aloud Story to Help Prevent Child Sexual Abuse* (PS–3). Illus. by Jody Bergsma. 1998, Illumination

Arts $15.95 (0-935699-10-4). 32pp. This book instructs children on how to deal with unwanted and inappropriate touching. (Rev: SLJ 7/98) [306]

18265 Loulan, JoAnn, and Bonnie Worthen. *Period: A Girl's Guide to Menstruation with a Parent's Guide*. Rev. ed. (5–7). Illus. 2001, Book Peddlers $15.95 (0-916773-97-3); paper $9.95 (0-916773-96-5). 96pp. This practical guide to menstruation is arranged by such questions as "What do I do when I get my first period?" and "What kind of exercise can I do?" (Rev: BL 2/1/01) [612.6]

18266 Marsh, Carole. *AIDS to Zits: A "Sextionary" for Kids* (3–7). 1987, Gallopade $29.95 (1-55609-263-6); paper $19.95 (1-55609-210-5). 28pp. This dictionary contains definitions of about 100 words related to sexuality. (Rev: BL 12/1/89) [613.951]

18267 Mosatche, Harriet S., and Karen Unger. *Too Old for This, Too Young for That! Your Survival Guide for the Middle-School Years* (5–8). Illus. 2000, Free Spirit paper $14.95 (1-57542-067-8). 200pp. This guide to the early years of puberty contains material on self-esteem, family relationships, friendships, and activities; also included is a lengthy section on bodily changes and such events as the onset of menstruation, erections, and ejaculation. (Rev: BL 7/00; SLJ 9/00) [646.7]

18268 Nardo, Don. *Teen Sexuality* (5–8). Illus. Series: Overview. 1997, Lucent LB $17.96 (1-56006-189-8). Traces the changing attitudes toward sex and what are considered acceptable practices according to present standards. In this series are also *Suicide, Drugs and Sports*, and *Homeless Children* (all 1997). (Rev: BL 3/15/97) [362.29]

18269 Rozakis, Laurie. *Teen Pregnancy: Why Are Kids Having Babies?* (5–8). Illus. Series: Issues of Our Time. 1993, Twenty-First Century LB $18.90 (0-8050-2569-3). 64pp. A slim, easily read account that explains birth control and deplores the fact that teens do not have access to information about it. (Rev: SLJ 2/94) [612.6]

18270 Westheimer, Ruth. *Dr. Ruth Talks to Kids: Where You Came From, How Your Body Changes, and What Sex Is All About* (5–8). Illus. by Diane De Groat. 1993, Macmillan LB $14.00 (0-02-792532-3). 96pp. A chatty, frank discussion of growing up. (Rev: BCCB 7–8/93; SLJ 6/93) [306.7]

Physical and Applied Sciences

General Science

Miscellaneous

18271 Aaseng, Nathan. *Yearbooks in Science: 1930–1939* (5–8). Illus. Series: Yearbooks in Science. 1995, Twenty-First Century LB $20.40 (0-8050-3433-1). 80pp. An overview of the accomplishments in science in the 1930s arranged by such divisions as physics and chemistry. (Rev: BL 12/1/95; SLJ 1/96) [609]

18272 Aaseng, Nathan. *Yearbooks in Science: 1940–1949* (5–8). Illus. Series: Yearbooks in Science. 1995, Twenty-First Century LB $20.40 (0-8050-3434-X). 80pp. An important decade in scientific discovery is chronicled, with emphasis on the impact of these advances on society. (Rev: BL 1/1–15/96; SLJ 5/96) [609]

18273 Angliss, Sarah. *Future World: A Beginner's Guide to Life on Earth in the 21st Century* (4–6). Series: Future Files. 1998, Millbrook LB $22.40 (0-7613-0821-0); paper $8.95 (0-7613-0740-0). 32pp. A book that looks 50 to 250 years into the future with coverage of such topics as energy resources, housing, and technological advances. (Rev: HBG 10/99; SLJ 4/99) [500]

18274 Ash, Russell. *Incredible Comparisons* (4–8). Illus. 1996, DK $19.95 (0-7894-1009-5). 64pp. Such concepts in nature as speed and weight are discussed in this fascinating book of comparisons. (Rev: BL 12/1/96*; SLJ 3/97) [031.02]

18275 Beres, Samantha. *101 Things Every Kid Should Know About Science* (4–7). Illus. 1998, Lowell House $14.95 (1-56565-956-2); paper $9.95 (1-56565-916-3). 96pp. This information-packed book supplies basic scientific facts organized under headings such as chemistry, physics, biology, and geography. (Rev: BL 10/15/98; SLJ 12/98) [500]

18276 Ehrlich, Robert. *What If? Mind-Boggling Science Questions for Kids* (4–6). Illus. 1998, Wiley paper $12.95 (0-471-17608-7). 192pp. Chapters on such subjects as time, the earth, and the planets pro-

vide explanations for intriguing science puzzlers. (Rev: BL 6/1–15/98; SLJ 10/98) [500]

18277 Ganeri, Anita, and Chris Oxlade. *The Kingfisher First Science Encyclopedia* (2–4). Illus. 1997, Kingfisher $16.95 (0-7534-5089-5). 112pp. This alphabetically arranged book covers about 75 topics in science, such as color, calculators, television, and physics. (Rev: SLJ 11/97) [500]

18278 Gates, Phil. *Nature Got There First* (5–8). Illus. 1995, Kingfisher $17.95 (1-85697-587-8). 80pp. Using lessons from nature, modern technology has developed such innovations as cameras, safety helmets, and armored cars. (Rev: BL 10/1/95; SLJ 2/96) [508]

18279 Gutfreund, Geraldine M. *Yearbooks in Science: 1970–1979* (5–8). Illus. Series: Yearbooks in Science. 1995, Twenty-First Century LB $20.40 (0-8050-3437-4). 80pp. A decade of new scientific concepts and inventions is discussed, with profiles of the scientists behind them. (Rev: BL 1/1–15/96; SLJ 5/96) [609]

18280 Hickman, Pamela. *The Night Book: Exploring Nature After Dark with Activities, Experiments and Information* (3–6). Illus. 1999, Kids Can $12.95 (1-55074-318-X); paper $6.95 (1-55074-306-6). 48pp. This is a collection of activities exploring the night world, including starlight, stargazing, night vision, and such nocturnal creatures as owls and fireflies. (Rev: BL 2/15/99; HBG 10/99; SLJ 8/99) [591.5]

18281 *Inside Out: The Best of National Geographic Diagrams and Cutaways* (5–10). Illus. 1998, National Geographic $25.00 (0-7922-7371-0). 128pp. A collection of 60 illustrations from the magazine's past 75 years, with drawings, cross sections, and cutaways of such subjects as a prairie dog town, Chernobyl's ruined core, and a beluga whale's sound-producing mechanism. (Rev: BL 10/15/98) [686.2]

18282 Kramer, Stephen. *How to Think Like a Scientist: Answering Questions by the Scientific Method* (3–5). Illus. 1987, HarperCollins LB $15.89 (0-690-

04565-4). 48pp. An intriguing account of the ways in which questions are asked, and how scientists try to make sure they are answered correctly. (Rev: BCCB 1/87; BL 5/15/87; SLJ 5/87)

18283 McGowen, Tom. *The Beginnings of Science* (5–8). Illus. 1998, Twenty-First Century LB $25.90 (0-7613-3016-X). 80pp. Beginning with primitive people and their use of magic, fire, counting, writing, and astronomy, this book traces the history of science up to the 16th century. (Rev: BL 12/1/98; HBG 3/99) [509]

18284 McGowen, Tom. *Yearbooks in Science: 1900–1919* (5–8). Illus. Series: Yearbooks in Science. 1995, Twenty-First Century LB $20.40 (0-8050-3431-5). 80pp. Science landmarks for 1900–1919 are chronicled in a series of articles dealing with different fields. (Rev: BL 12/1/95; SLJ 1/96) [609]

18285 McGowen, Tom. *Yearbooks in Science: 1960–1969* (5–8). Illus. Series: Yearbooks in Science. 1996, Twenty-First Century LB $20.40 (0-8050-3436-6). 80pp. Developments in the history of science and technology during the 1960s are covered in an exciting step-by-step approach. (Rev: BL 1/1–15/96; SLJ 5/96) [609]

18286 Martin, Paul D. *Science: It's Changing Your World* (5–8). Illus. 1985, National Geographic LB $12.50 (0-87044-521-9). 104pp. An overview of the science field today, crediting computers and lasers with the vast growth of scientific information. (Rev: BL 9/15/85; SLJ 10/85)

18287 Myers, Jack. *On the Trail of the Komodo Dragon: And Other Explorations of Science in Action* (3–6). Illus. 1999, Boyds Mills $17.95 (1-56397-761-3). 63pp. A collection of 11 "Science Reporting" columns from *Highlights for Children* that explore unusual topics, such as how horses sleep and why cats can often fall safely. (Rev: BL 2/15/99; HBG 10/99; SLJ 4/99) [591]

18288 Newton, David E. *Yearbooks in Science: 1920–1929* (5–8). Illus. Series: Yearbooks in Science. 1995, Twenty-First Century LB $20.40 (0-8050-3432-3). 80pp. The 1920s in science is surveyed, with chapters devoted to each breakthrough. (Rev: BL 12/1/95; SLJ 1/96) [609]

18289 Rice, David L. *Lifetimes* (3–6). Illus. 1997, Dawn $16.95 (1-883220-58-0); paper $7.95 (1-883220-59-9). 32pp. Various activities are interspersed with facts about a number of animals, plants, and astronomical bodies. (Rev: BL 6/1–15/97; SLJ 2/98) [574.3]

18290 *Science and Technology: The World of Modern Science* (3–6). Illus. Series: Children's Reference. 1993, Oxford $40.00 (0-19-910143-4). 160pp. Using an encyclopedic arrangement, this work covers many topics in the physical sciences under headings like science and materials, space, energy, transport, and information technologies. (Rev: SLJ 1/94) [500]

18291 Silverstein, Herma. *Yearbooks in Science: 1990 and Beyond* (5–8). Illus. Series: Yearbooks in Science. 1995, Twenty-First Century LB $20.40 (0-8050-3439-0). 80pp. The final volume in this series not only traces recent developments in science and technology but also presents the challenges of the future. (Rev: BL 1/1–15/96) [609]

18292 Simon, Seymour. *The Dinosaur Is the Biggest Animal That Ever Lived: And Other Wrong Ideas You Thought Were True* (3–5). Illus. by Giulio Maestro. 1984, HarperCollins paper $5.95 (0-06-446053-3). 64pp. Twenty-nine popularly believed science myths are exposed.

18293 Simon, Seymour. *Out of Sight: Pictures of Hidden Worlds* (3–6). Illus. 2000, North-South $15.88 (1-58717-012-4). 48pp. A book of unusual pictures of phenomena — such as the operation of the human heart, Jupiter's red spot, and a racing bullet — that can only be seen using scientific instruments. (Rev: BL 10/1/00; HBG 3/01; SLJ 11/00) [612.8]

18294 Stein, Sara Bonnett. *The Science Book* (4–8). Illus. by author. 1980, Workman paper $9.95 (0-89480-120-1). 288pp. A whole-earth approach to strange and fascinating science facts.

18295 Wilkes, Angela. *Your World: A First Encyclopedia* (K–2). 1999, Kingfisher $24.95 (0-7534-5217-0). 320pp. Questions and answers are given on such topics as the universe, the environment, prehistoric life, plants, animals, the human body, people, and places. (Rev: HBG 3/00; SLJ 2/00) [030]

18296 Wollard, Kathy. *How Come?* (5–8). Illus. 1993, Workman paper $12.95 (1-56305-324-1). 300pp. Includes questions and answers to a number of common scientific questions, like "Do parrots understand what they say?" (Rev: BL 5/1/94) [500]

18297 Wollard, Kathy. *How Come Planet Earth?* (4–7). Illus. by Debra Solomon. 1999, Workman paper $12.95 (0-7611-1239-1). 332pp. This book contains 125 science questions asked by children involving subjects such as warts, dust, cholesterol, and volcanoes. (Rev: SLJ 5/00) [500]

Experiments and Projects

18298 *The Ben Franklin Book of Easy and Incredible Experiments* (4–6). Illus. 1995, Wiley $29.95 (0-471-07639-2); paper $12.95 (0-471-07638-4). 144pp. From the Franklin Institute Museum in Philadelphia comes a book of experiments involving weather, music, paper, electricity, light, and sound. (Rev: BL 9/15/95; SLJ 4/96) [507.8]

18299 *The Big Book of Nature Projects* (4–6). Illus. 1997, Thames & Hudson paper $16.95 (0-500-01773-5). 128pp. An attractive large-format paperback that introduces a wide variety of nature projects for both indoors and outdoors with easy instructions. (Rev: BL 7/97; SLJ 1/98) [507.8]

18300 Bleifeld, Maurice. *Experimenting with a Microscope* (5–8). Illus. 1988, Watts LB $22.50 (0-531-10580-6). 128pp. Step-by-step explanation of how to use a compound microscope. (Rev: BL 1/15/89; SLJ 2/89)

18301 Bonnet, Bob, and Dan Keen. *Science Fair Projects: Chemistry* (4–6). Illus. by Frances Zweifel. 2000, Sterling $17.95 (0-8069-7771-X). 95pp. A book of 47 experiments and projects including growing crystals, testing acids and bases, and separating liquids by density. (Rev: SLJ 1/01) [509]

18302 Brynie, Faith Hickman. *Six-Minute Nature Experiments* (3–6). Illus. by Kim Whittingham. 1999, Sterling $17.95 (0-8069-9827-X). 80pp. The 39 simple experiments and projects in this book explore topics including weight, water, temperature, sound, motion, and the sun. (Rev: SLJ 10/99) [507]

18303 Carrow, Robert. *Put a Fan in Your Hat! Inventions, Contraptions, and Gadgets Kids Can Build* (5–8). Illus. by Rick Brown. 1997, McGraw-Hill paper $14.95 (0-07-011658-X). 139pp. A book of useful science projects, including making a natural battery, building a motor, and creating a hat with a cooling fan. (Rev: SLJ 5/97) [507]

18304 Chapman, Gillian, and Pam Robson. *Exploring Time* (3–5). Illus. 1995, Millbrook LB $19.90 (1-56294-559-9). 32pp. Fourteen projects of varying difficulty related to time, such as creating a timeline and a sundial. (Rev: BL 11/1/95; SLJ 3/96) [529]

18305 Cobb, Vicki. *Science Experiments You Can Eat* (5–7). Illus. by Peter Lippman. 1994, HarperCollins $14.89 (0-060-23551-9). 128pp. Experiments illustrating principles of chemistry and physics utilize edible ingredients. Also use: *More Science Experiments You Can Eat* (1979).

18306 Cobb, Vicki, and Kathy Darling. *Bet You Can't! Science Impossibilities to Fool You* (5–8). Illus. by Martha Weston. 1983, Avon paper $4.50 (0-380-54502-0). 128pp. Sixty different tricks and experiments involving such scientific subjects as fluids and energy. Also use: *Bet You Can! Science Possibilities to Fool You* (1983).

18307 Cobb, Vicki, and Kathy Darling. *Don't Try This at Home! Science Fun for Kids on the Go* (4–6). Illus. 1998, Morrow $15.00 (0-688-14856-5). 128pp. An appealing book of science experiments best carried out in such locales as playgrounds, beaches, parks, airplanes, and public buildings. (Rev: BCCB 4/98; BL 4/1/98; HBG 10/98; SLJ 7/98) [507.8]

18308 Cobb, Vicki, and Kathy Darling. *Wanna Bet? Science Challenges to Fool You* (3–6). Illus. by Meredith Johnson. 1993, Lothrop $15.00 (0-688-11213-7). 128pp. This book of experiments and projects for young people covers such areas as physics, chemistry, mathematics, physiology, and electricity. (Rev: BL 5/1/93; SLJ 8/93) [793]

18309 Cobb, Vicki, and Kathy Darling. *You Gotta Try This!* (3–6). Illus. 1999, Morrow $15.00 (0-688-15740-8). 144pp. Projects such as making cubical hard-boiled eggs and using a balloon to create power illustrate basic scientific concepts. (Rev: BCCB 5/99; BL 8/99; HBG 3/00; SLJ 8/99) [507.8]

18310 Coulter, George, and Shirley Coulter. *Science in Art* (3–4). Illus. Series: Science Projects. 1995, Rourke LB $23.93 (0-86625-519-2). 32pp. Six science activities are included in this volume, each of which explores some aspect of art, color, or artists' materials. Companion volumes are *Science in Food* and *Science in History* (both 1995). (Rev: SLJ 1/96) [507]

18311 Falk, John H., et al. *Bubble Monster: And Other Science Fun* (PS–3). Illus. by Charles C. Somerville. 1996, Chicago Review paper $17.95 (1-55652-301-7). 168pp. Five scientific areas — patterns, matter, communication, the human body, and technology — are covered in a series of activities that require some adult help. (Rev: SLJ 4/97) [507]

18312 Friedhoffer, Robert. *Science Lab in a Supermarket* (5–9). Illus. 1998, Watts LB $24.00 (0-531-11335-3). 96pp. A book of projects that explores the chemical ingredients in many supermarket items and the processes involved in their production, such as the manufacture of pasta. (Rev: BL 12/1/98; HBG 3/99; SLJ 12/98) [540]

18313 Gardner, Robert. *Kitchen Chemistry: Science Experiments to Do at Home* (4–8). Illus. 1989, Silver Burdett paper $4.95 (0-671-67576-1). 136pp. Simple experiments that can be performed in the kitchen with everyday equipment and supplies.

18314 Gardner, Robert. *Projects in Space Science* (4–8). Illus. 1988, Silver Burdett paper $5.95 (0-671-65993-6). 136pp. Science projects involving space travel and astronomy. (Rev: BL 1/15/89; SLJ 2/89)

18315 Gardner, Robert. *Science Around the House* (4–6). Illus. 1989, Silver Burdett paper $4.95 (0-671-68139-7). 136pp. Simple experiments using everyday objects are detailed in this reissued project book.

18316 Gibson, Gary. *Making Shapes* (3–5). Photos by Roger Vlitos. Illus. by Tony Kenyon. Series: Science for Fun. 1995, Millbrook LB $20.90 (1-56294-631-5). 32pp. In double-page spreads, experiments in shape making and shifting are described, as well as how they illustrate various principles of science. (Rev: SLJ 3/96) [507]

18317 Gibson, Gary. *Making Things Change* (3–5). Illus. Series: Science for Fun. 1995, Millbrook LB $20.90 (1-56294-645-5). 32pp. Double-page spreads are used to introduce a series of experiments and projects that illustrate how objects and materials can change their forms and structures. (Rev: BL 12/15/95) [507.8]

18318 Hartzog, John Daniel. *Everyday Science Experiments in the Kitchen* (PS–3). Series: Science Suprises. 2000, Rosen $19.33 (0-8239-5456-0). 24pp. Eight simple experiments are outlined from using lemon juice to shine a penny to creating a celery straw. (Rev: SLJ 9/00) [509]

18319 Hauser, Jill F. *Science Play! Beginning Discoveries for 2- to 6-Year-Olds* (PS–K). Illus. by Michael Kline. Series: Little Hands Books. 1998, Williamson paper $12.95 (1-885593-20-1). 135pp. Basic science concepts are taught in this book for preschoolers that contains 65 simple activities. (Rev: SLJ 1/99) [507.8]

18320 Herbert, Don. *Mr. Wizard's Experiments for Young Scientists* (5–8). Illus. by Don Noonan. 1991, Doubleday paper $10.95 (0-385-26585-9). 187pp. Directions for 13 science experiments that can be done easily with equipment found in the home.

18321 Herbert, Don. *Mr. Wizard's Supermarket Science* (4–7). Illus. by Roy McKie. 1980, Random

$10.00 (0-394-83800-9). 96pp. More than 100 projects using supermarket items.

18322 Hirschfeld, Robert, and Nancy White. *The Kids' Science Book: Creative Experiences for Hands-on Fun* (2–5). Illus. by Loretta Braren. Series: Kids Can! 1995, Williamson paper $12.95 (0-913589-88-8). 157pp. An interesting collection of games, experiments, and activities that illustrate various principles of science and are fun to perform. (Rev: SLJ 12/95) [507]

18323 Johnson, Kipchak. *Worm's Eye View: Make Your Own Wildlife Refuge* (3–8). Illus. Series: Lighter Look. 1991, Millbrook LB $20.90 (1-878841-30-0). 40pp. After exploring the wildlife found in a patch of vacant ground, the author suggests various projects for encouraging it. (Rev: SLJ 8/91) [507]

18324 Kramer, Alan. *How to Make a Chemical Volcano and Other Mysterious Experiments* (4–7). Illus. by Paul Harvey. 1991, Watts paper $6.95 (0-531-15610-9). 111pp. Thirty experiments for "detectives of chemistry" by a 13-year-old student. (Rev: BCCB 2/90; BL 12/15/89; SLJ 3/90) [532]

18325 Levine, Shar, and Leslie Johnstone. *Everyday Science: Fun and Easy Projects for Making Practical Things* (4–6). Illus. by Ed Shems. 1995, Wiley paper $9.95 (0-471-11014-0). 97pp. The science behind everyday objects is explored in this book of 25 simple projects under such headings as Light and Optics, Heat, Earth Science, Electricity, and Chemistry. (Rev: SLJ 8/95) [507]

18326 Levine, Shar, and Leslie Johnstone. *Science Around the World: Travel Through Time and Space with Fun Experiments and Projects* (3–6). Illus. by Laurel Aiello. 1996, Wiley paper $10.95 (0-471-11916-4). 84pp. This project book presents activities from ten countries around the world, including making paper and creating a sand timer. (Rev: SLJ 7/96) [507]

18327 Levine, Shar, and Leslie Johnstone. *Silly Science: Strange and Startling Projects to Amaze Your Family and Friends* (4–6). Illus. by Ed Shems. 1995, Wiley paper $9.95 (0-471-11013-2). 91pp. Twenty-eight seemingly foolish experiments using common materials illustrate important scientific principles and processes. (Rev: SLJ 8/95) [507]

18328 Manning, Mick, and Brita Granström. *Science School* (2–4). Illus. by authors. 1998, Kingfisher paper $8.95 (0-7534-5097-6). 47pp. A simple experiment book that contains 50 activities on such subjects as matter, heat, air, water, forces, light, sound, and electricity. (Rev: SLJ 3/99) [507]

18329 Markle, Sandra. *Creepy, Spooky Science* (3–7). Illus. by Cecile Schoberle. 1996, Hyperion LB $15.49 (0-7868-2178-7); paper $4.95 (0-7868-1088-2). 72pp. Easy-to-perform experiments and projects are presented using scary titles like "Whip Up Some Blood" and "Bewitch an Egg." (Rev: SLJ 10/96) [507]

18330 Markle, Sandra. *Exploring Autumn: A Season of Science Activities, Puzzlers, and Games* (4–7). Illus. Series: Exploring Seasons. 1991, Avon paper $3.50 (0-380-71910-X). 160pp. Science, history,

myth, quizzes, and more combined in this book on seasonal activities in the classroom and home. (Rev: BL 1/1/91; SLJ 1/92) [574.5]

18331 Markle, Sandra. *Icky, Squishy Science* (3–7). Illus. by Cecile Schoberle. 1996, Hyperion paper $3.95 (0-7868-1087-4). 70pp. This breezy book of science activities is geared to a youngster's interests and fascination with things unusual and humorous. (Rev: SLJ 8/96) [507]

18332 Markle, Sandra. *Science to the Rescue* (4–7). Illus. 1994, Atheneum $15.95 (0-689-31783-2). 48pp. Explains the scientific method and shows how science has found solutions to many problems. (Rev: BL 3/15/94; SLJ 4/94) [507.8]

18333 Markle, Sandra. *Super Science Secrets: Exploring Nature Through Games, Puzzles and Activities* (1–3). Illus. 1997, Longstreet $14.95 (1-56352-396-5). 36pp. Scientific topics like evaporation, static electricity, and animal defenses are examined, with follow-up questions and simple experiments. (Rev: HBG 3/98; SLJ 9/97) [507]

18334 Mason, Adrienne. *Living Things* (K–4). Series: Starting with Science. 1998, Kids Can LB $10.95 (1-55074-343-0). 32pp. Basic science concepts about life are examined, using 13 simple experiments such as "worm farming," "hairy egg heads," and "baking beasts." (Rev: BL 5/15/98; HBG 10/98; SLJ 5/98) [507.8]

18335 Muller, Eric. *While You're Waiting for the Food to Come* (4–6). Illus. 1999, Orchard $15.95 (0-531-30199-0); paper $8.95 (0-531-07144-8). 96pp. An appealing experiment book that contains simple projects, arranged like a menu, designed to be performed where food is served. (Rev: BCCB 9/99; BL 1/1–15/00; HBG 3/00; SLJ 10/99) [507]

18336 Murphy, Pat, et al. *The Science Explorer Out and About: Fantastic Science Experiments Your Family Can Do Anywhere!* (3–8). Illus. by Jason Gorski. Series: Exploratorium Science-at-Home Book. 1997, Holt paper $12.95 (0-8050-4537-6). 127pp. A wide variety of science experiments are outlined, many that can be performed alone and others that require adult help. (Rev: SLJ 2/98) [507]

18337 Murray, Peter. *Silly Science Tricks (with Professor Solomon Snickerdoodle)* (2–4). Illus. by Anastasia Mitchell. 1993, Child's World LB $21.36 (0-89565-976-X). 32pp. Seven science tricks in one eye-catching book. (Rev: BL 3/15/93) [507.8]

18338 Nye, Bill. *Bill Nye the Science Guy's Big Blast of Science* (5–8). Illus. 1993, Addison-Wesley paper $15.00 (0-201-60864-2). 172pp. Several topics, including matter, heat, light, electricity, magnetism, weather, and space, are introduced in this quick tour of the world of science. (Rev: BL 2/15/94) [507.8]

18339 Ontario Science Centre Staff. *Scienceworks: 65 Experiments That Introduce the Fun and Wonder of Science* (4–6). Illus. 1986, Addison-Wesley paper $11.95 (0-201-16780-8). Emphasizing that science can be fun, this book includes numerous experiments, many of them easily mastered puzzles or tricks.

18340 Parker, Steve. *Shocking, Slimy, Stinky, Shiny Science Experiments* (3–5). Illus. 1999, Sterling $19.95 (0-8069-6295-X). 96pp. Using carefully laid-out steps and sharp photographs, this book provides 73 simple experiments covering basic concepts in light, electricity, and the properties of common household objects. (Rev: BL 5/15/99; HBG 10/99; SLJ 4/99) [507.8]

18341 Potter, Jean. *Science in Seconds with Toys: Over 100 Experiments You Can Do in Ten Minutes or Less* (2–5). 1998, Wiley paper $12.95 (0-471-17900-0). 131pp. Each page contains a separate easy-to-perform activity that answers a question involving a simple scientific principle. (Rev: SLJ 4/98) [507.8]

18342 Press, H. J. *Giant Book of Science Experiments* (3–6). 1998, Sterling paper $14.95 (0-8069-8139-3). 352pp. This collection of experiments contains 325 simple activities, each outlined on a single page and most using easy-to-find materials. (Rev: SLJ 7/98) [507]

18343 Richards, Jon. *The Science Factory* (4–6). Photos by Roger Vlitos. Illus. by Ian Thompson and Ian Moores. 2000, Millbrook paper $16.95 (0-7613-0832-6). 224pp. An excellent collection of experiments that covers such subjects as simple machines, weather, electricity, air, and flight. (Rev: SLJ 12/00) [509]

18344 Richards, Roy. *101 Science Surprises: Exciting Experiments with Everyday Materials* (3–5). Illus. 1993, Sterling $17.95 (0-8069-8822-3). 104pp. The activities and experiments presented in this book represent various branches of science and vary in difficulty. (Rev: BL 9/1/93; SLJ 6/93) [507.8]

18345 Richards, Roy. *101 Science Tricks: Fun Experiments with Everyday Materials* (4–8). Illus. by Alex Pang. 1992, Sterling $16.95 (0-8069-8388-4). 104pp. Interesting, easy-to-do science and math activities, with emphasis on understanding the principles behind the tricks. (Rev: BL 2/1/92; SLJ 1/92) [507.8]

18346 Ross, Michael E. *Sandbox Scientist: Real Science Activities for Little Kids* (PS–2). Illus. by Mary Anne Lloyd. 1995, Chicago Review paper $12.95 (1-55652-248-7). 206pp. Simple experiments and activities introduce young children to the principles involving such components as light and water. (Rev: BL 2/1/96) [372.3]

18347 *Science Fairs: Ideas and Activities* (4–8). 1998, World Book $15.00 (0-7166-4498-3); paper $10.00 (0-7166-4497-5). 80pp. Research methodology and hints on project development are included along with outlines of projects in areas such as space, earth science, geology, botany, machines, and structures. (Rev: SLJ 1/99) [507.8]

18348 Simon, Seymour. *How to Be an Ocean Scientist in Your Own Home* (4–7). Illus. by David A. Carter. 1988, Macmillan LB $14.89 (0-397-32292-5). 144pp. Twenty-four experiments and projects mostly using salt and water. (Rev: BCCB 11/88)

18349 Sobey, Ed. *Car Smarts: Activities for Kids on the Open Road* (4–6). 1997, McGraw-Hill paper $9.95 (0-07-059597-6). 106pp. A clever collection of activities for kids traveling by car, such as designing a license plate, reading maps, finding directions, and formulating a weather prediction. (Rev: SLJ 4/98) [507]

18350 Sobey, Ed. *Wrapper Rockets and Trombone Straws: Science at Every Meal* (4–7). Illus. 1996, McGraw-Hill paper $14.95 (0-07-021745-9). 137pp. Using tableware like glasses, straws, and napkins, a number of simple tricks and experiments are introduced. (Rev: BL 3/1/97; SLJ 6/97) [500]

18351 Supraner, Robyn. *Science Secrets* (1–3). Illus. by Renzo Barto. 1981, Troll LB $16.65 (0-89375-426-9). 48pp. Science principles like magnetism and gravity are simply explained.

18352 Tocci, Salvatore. *Science Fair Success in the Hardware Store* (5–8). Series: Science Fair Success. 2000, Enslow LB $19.95 (0-7660-1287-5). 128pp. A group of science fair projects that use materials and objects found in a hardware store, with clear explanations of the scientific principles behind each project. (Rev: BL 4/15/00; HBG 10/00) [507]

18353 Tocci, Salvatore. *Science Fair Success Using Supermarket Products* (5–8). Series: Science Fair Success. 2000, Enslow LB $19.95 (0-7660-1288-3). 128pp. Using common items found in a supermarket, this work outlines a number of excellent science projects that demonstrate important scientific principles. (Rev: BL 4/15/00; HBG 10/00) [507]

18354 UNESCO. *700 Science Experiments for Everyone* (5–8). Illus. 1964, Doubleday $18.95 (0-385-05275-8). 252pp. An excellent collection of experiments, noted for its number of entries and breadth of coverage.

18355 VanCleave, Janice. *Janice VanCleave's Animals* (4–6). Illus. Series: Spectacular Science Projects. 1992, Wiley paper $10.95 (0-471-55052-3). 84pp. This book contains many easy-to-follow projects involving animals. (Rev: BL 1/1/93; SLJ 2/93) [591]

18356 VanCleave, Janice. *Janice VanCleave's Biology for Every Kid: 101 Easy Experiments That Really Work* (4–7). Illus. 1989, Wiley paper $11.95 (0-471-50381-9). 224pp. This book outlines simple experiments that use readily available equipment and supplies. (Rev: BL 2/15/90) [574]

18357 VanCleave, Janice. *Janice VanCleave's Earth Science for Every Kid: 101 Easy Experiments That Really Work* (3–6). Illus. 1991, Wiley $29.95 (0-471-54389-6); paper $12.95 (0-471-53010-7). 231pp. In this book of interesting experiments, such topics as erosion, rocks, weather, and the oceans are introduced. [551]

18358 VanCleave, Janice. *Janice VanCleave's Guide to More of the Best Science Fair Projects* (4–8). 2000, Wiley paper $14.95 (0-471-32627-5). 156pp. After general information about the scientific method, research, and presentation, this book outlines about 50 projects in the areas of astronomy, biology, earth science, engineering, physical science, and mathematics. (Rev: SLJ 5/00) [509]

18359 VanCleave, Janice. *Janice VanCleave's Guide to the Best Science Fair Projects* (3–6). Illus.

1997, Wiley paper $14.95 (0-471-14802-4). 144pp. An excellent experiment book that covers 50 science projects in the life and physical sciences, astronomy, mathematics, and engineering. (Rev: BL 3/15/97; SLJ 4/97) [507.8]

18360 VanCleave, Janice. *Janice VanCleave's Play and Find Out About Nature: Easy Experiments for Young Children* (3–5). Illus. 1997, Wiley $29.95 (0-471-12939-9); paper $12.95 (0-471-12940-2). 128pp. Fifty models and activities using common household materials are outlined to help parents and others introduce the natural world to children. (Rev: BL 6/1–15/97; SLJ 7/97) [574]

18361 VanCleave, Janice. *Janice VanCleave's Play and Find Out About Science: Easy Experiments for Young Children* (2–4). Illus. 1996, Wiley paper $12.95 (0-471-12941-0). 128pp. Topics like sound, magnets, and electricity are explored through more than 50 easy experiments and activities. (Rev: BL 10/15/96; SLJ 10/96) [530]

18362 VanCleave, Janice. *Janice VanCleave's 203 Icy, Freezing, Frosty, Cool and Wild Experiments* (4–7). 1999, Wiley paper $12.95 (0-471-25223-9). 122pp. An excellent book filled with easily performed experiments in such areas as biology, chemistry, earth science, and physics. (Rev: SLJ 4/00) [507.8]

18363 VanCleave, Janice. *Janice VanCleave's 202 Oozing, Bubbling, Dripping and Bouncing Experiments* (4–6). Illus. 1996, Wiley paper $12.95 (0-471-14025-2). 120pp. Fun and learning are combined in these experiments that investigate astronomy, biology, chemistry, earth science, and physics. (Rev: SLJ 2/97) [507]

18364 Vecchione, Glen. *100 First Prize Make It Yourself Science Fair Projects* (4–10). 1998, Sterling $21.95 (0-8069-0703-7). 192pp. Ranging from the simple to the complex, the experiments in this collection include such standards as a lava-flow volcano and a bottled tornado plus more difficult ones like testing hydrodynamic hull designs. (Rev: SLJ 4/99) [509]

18365 Voth, Danna. *Kidsource: Science Fair Handbook* (4–6). Illus. 1998, Lowell House paper $9.95 (1-56565-514-1). 112pp. A thorough overview of how to tackle a science project, from choosing a topic to presenting the results. (Rev: BL 2/15/99; SLJ 5/99) [507.8]

18366 Walpole, Brenda. *175 Science Experiments to Amuse and Amaze Your Friends* (2–6). Illus. 1988, Random paper $14.99 (0-394-89991-1). 176pp. Science fair ideas — tricks, experiments, and things to make. (Rev: BL 12/1/88; SLJ 1/89)

18367 Webster, Vera. *Plant Experiments* (1–4). Illus. 1982, Children's LB $21.00 (0-516-01638-5). 48pp. A manual of simple experiments with plants. Also use: *Science Experiments* (1982).

18368 Wiese, Jim. *Magic Science: 50 Jaw-Dropping, Mind-Boggling, Head-Scratching Activities for Kids* (4–6). Illus. 1998, Wiley paper $12.95 (0-471-18239-7). 128pp. The author explains the science behind 50 magic tricks, which are divided into six categories: matter, reactions, water, air, force and energy, and electricity and magnetism. (Rev: BL 5/15/98) [507.8]

18369 Wiese, Jim. *Rocket Science: 50 Flying, Floating, Flipping, Spinning Gadgets Kids Create Themselves* (3–6). Illus. 1995, Wiley paper $12.95 (0-471-11357-3). 128pp. Principles related to physics, electricity, optics, acoustics, and other branches of science are explored in a number of interesting projects and experiments. (Rev: BL 12/1/95; SLJ 3/96) [507.8]

18370 Willow, Diane, and Emily Curran. *Science Sensations* (3–5). Illus. by Lady McCrady. Series: Boston Children's Museum Activity Books. 1990, Addison-Wesley paper $11.00 (0-201-07189-4). 95pp. A simple child-tested experiment book using everyday objects. (Rev: SLJ 6/90) [507]

18371 Wyatt, Valerie. *The Science Book for Girls and Other Intelligent Beings* (3–5). Illus. by Pat Cupples. 1997, Kids Can paper $8.95 (1-55074-113-6). 80pp. Introduces various science experiments from different branches of science, as well as several female scientists, like Mary Leakey and Sally Ride. (Rev: SLJ 10/97) [509]

18372 Wyler, Rose. *Science Fun with Peanuts and Popcorn* (2–4). Illus. 1986, Simon & Schuster paper $4.95 (0-671-62452-0). 48pp. Simple experiments that explain scientific principles. Also use: *Science Fun with Mud and Dirt* (1986). (Rev: BL 7/86; SLJ 11/86)

18373 Wyler, Rose. *Science Fun with Toy Boats and Planes* (2–4). Illus. 1986, Simon & Schuster paper $4.95 (0-671-62453-9). 48pp. Experiments that explain the forces that move these vehicles. Also use: *Science Fun with Toy Cars and Trucks* (1988). (Rev: BL 7/86; SLJ 10/86)

18374 Young, Jay. *The Art of Science* (5–8). Illus. 1999, Candlewick $27.99 (0-7636-0754-1). This interactive book contains removable pieces that demonstrate scientific phenomena, including a magnetic pendulum and wave sculpture. (Rev: BL 12/15/99; SLJ 4/00) [507]

Astronomy

General

18375 Asimov, Isaac. *Cosmic Debris: The Asteroids* (3–5). Illus. Series: Isaac Asimov's New Library of the Universe. 1994, Gareth Stevens LB $21.27 (0-8368-1130-5). 32pp. This account explains what asteroids are, theories of their formation, how some have become planetary moons, and their possible uses as the mines of the future. (Rev: BL 2/15/95) [523.4]

18376 Asimov, Isaac. *Mysteries of Deep Space: Black Holes, Pulsars, and Quasars* (3–5). Illus. Series: Isaac Asimov's New Library of the Universe. 1994, Gareth Stevens LB $21.27 (0-8368-1133-X). 32pp. Outer space is explored in this account of celestial energy, collapsing stars, types of black holes, pulsars, and quasars. (Rev: BL 2/15/95; SLJ 2/95) [523.8]

18377 Asimov, Isaac, and Francis Reddy. *Astronomy in Ancient Times* (3–4). Illus. Series: Isaac Asimov's New Library of the Universe. 1995, Gareth Stevens LB $21.27 (0-8368-1191-7). 32pp. A breezy, easy-to-read introduction to the history of astronomy from the ancient Greeks to Galileo. (Rev: SLJ 4/95) [523]

18378 Becklake, Sue. *All About Space* (2–5). Series: Scholastic First Encyclopedia. 1999, Scholastic $14.95 (0-590-10471-3). 77pp. This book crams an amazing amount of important information about space into a few pages with coverage of such topics as the solar system, telescopes, stars, space travel, space exploration, and space programs. (Rev: SLJ 6/99) [528]

18379 Bendick, Jeanne. *The Universe: Think Big!* (2–4). Illus. by Lynne Willey and Mike Roffe. Series: Early Bird Astronomy. 1991, Millbrook LB $19.90 (1-878841-01-7). 32pp. Theories and facts about galaxies and the universe are presented in an easy-to-read fashion with many illustrations. (Rev: BL 9/1/91; SLJ 8/91) [523.1]

18380 Berger, Melvin, and Gilda Berger. *Do Stars Have Points? Questions and Answers About Stars and Planets* (3–5). Illus. Series: Question and Answer. 1999, Scholastic $12.95 (0-590-13080-3); paper $5.95 (0-590-08570-5). 48pp. Using a question-and-answer format, this book covers important facts in astronomy involving the solar system and the universe. (Rev: BL 11/1/99; HBG 3/00; SLJ 2/00) [523]

18381 Bonnet, Bob, and Dan Keen. *Science Fair Projects: Flight, Space and Astronomy* (4–6). Illus. by Frances Zweifel. 1997, Sterling $17.95 (0-8069-9450-9). 95pp. A collection of 53 clever astronomy-related experiments that vary considerably in difficulty and in the nature of the equipment involved. (Rev: SLJ 2/98) [520]

18382 Bortz, Fred. *Martian Fossils on Earth? The Story of Meteorite ALH 84001* (4–6). Illus. 1997, Millbrook LB $21.40 (0-7613-0270-0). 64pp. The story of the meteorite discovered in Antarctica that hints at the fact that life might have once existed on Mars and the massive scientific investigation that it has caused. (Rev: BCCB 4/98; BL 1/1–15/98; HBG 10/98; SLJ 3/98) [523.5]

18383 Cole, Michael D. *Hubble Space Telescope: Exploring the Universe* (4–7). Illus. Series: Countdown to Space. 1999, Enslow $18.95 (0-7660-1120-8). 48pp. This close-up look at the Hubble space telescope covers its parts, uses, problems, and photos that the telescope has sent back to earth. (Rev: BL 2/1/99; HBG 10/99) [522]

18384 Couper, Heather, and Nigel Henbest. *Big Bang* (5–8). Illus. 1997, DK $16.95 (0-7894-1484-8). 45pp. Explains, in double-page spreads, the big-bang theory and its implications for the future. (Rev: BL 6/1–15/97; SLJ 8/97) [523.1]

18385 Couper, Heather, and Nigel Henbest. *The Space Atlas* (5–8). Illus. by Luciano Corbella. 1992, Harcourt $19.00 (0-15-200598-6). 64pp. An oversize book that gives a guided tour of the solar system and outer space through maps, paintings, photos, and charts. (Rev: SLJ 5/92) [523]

18386 Croswell, Ken. *See the Stars* (4–8). Illus. 2000, Boyds Mills $16.95 (1-56397-757-5). 32pp. Twelve constellations are introduced in double-page spreads, with material on where and when to look for them. (Rev: BL 11/1/00; HBG 3/01; SLJ 10/00) [523]

18387 Delafosse, Claude, et al. *Hidden World: Space* (PS–2). Series: First Discovery. 2000, Scholastic $12.95 (0-439-14826-X). 24pp. For the very young, this is a colorful, well-illustrated introduction to space and what it means. (Rev: BL 8/00) [523]

18388 Dyer, Alan. *Space* (4–7). Series: Reader's Digest Pathfinders. 1999, Reader's Digest $16.99 (1-57584-291-2). 64pp. Using a total of 25 double-page spreads and lavish illustrations, this book is divided into three sections that discuss space exploration, the solar system, and the universe. (Rev: HBG 3/00; SLJ 2/00) [523]

18389 Ford, Harry. *The Young Astronomer* (4–8). Illus. 1998, DK $15.95 (0-7894-2061-9). 40pp. Using many fine illustrations and a series of interesting projects, this volume provides a basic introduction to astronomy and tells young people how to explore the worlds found in the sky. (Rev: BL 4/15/98; HBG 10/98) [520]

18390 Fradin, Dennis B. *Astronomy* (1–4). Illus. 1983, Children's LB $21.00 (0-516-01673-3). 48pp. The science is introduced in a simple text, many photographs, and a glossary of terms.

18391 Fradin, Dennis B. *Searching for Alien Life: Is Anyone Out There?* (5–7). Illus. 1997, Twenty-First Century $20.40 (0-8050-4573-2). 80pp. A history of space travel is followed by an account of attempts to contact life in space and of recent discoveries. (Rev: SLJ 1/98) [523]

18392 *Galaxies* (3–6). Illus. Series: Window on the Universe. 1994, Barron's $12.95 (0-8120-6367-8). 32pp. In a series of double-page spreads and full-color illustrations, galaxies are introduced, with special coverage of the Milky Way. (Rev: BL 4/15/94; SLJ 5/94) [523.1]

18393 Gallan, Roy. *Comets, Asteroids, and Meteorites* (2–4). Series: Kaleidoscope. 2000, Marshall Cavendish LB $15.95 (0-7614-1034-1). 48pp. An up-to-date account that combines good visuals with an exciting text in this examination of these visitors from space. (Rev: BL 1/1–15/01) [523]

18394 Gallant, Roy A. *The Life Stories of Stars* (5–7). Series: Story of Science. 2000, Benchmark LB $19.95 (0-7614-1152-6). 80pp. This is a history of astronomy with coverage of how our attitudes about the heavens have changed over the years as well as our methods of studying the sky. (Rev: SLJ 2/01) [523]

18395 Hirst, Robin, and Sally Hirst. *My Place in Space* (3–4). Illus. by Roland Harvey. 1992, Orchard paper $6.95 (0-531-07030-1). 40pp. A sky show from earth to solar system to the outer reaches of the universe. (Rev: BCCB 3/90; BL 4/1/90; HB 5–6/91; SLJ 4/90) [520]

18396 Jobb, Jamie. *The Night Sky Book* (5–8). Illus. by Linda Bennett. 1977, Little, Brown paper $12.95 (0-316-46552-6). A primer for novice stargazers.

18397 Kallen, Stuart A. *Exploring the Origins of the Universe* (4–8). Series: Secrets of Space. 1997, Twenty-First Century LB $20.40 (0-8050-4478-7). 64pp. This account tells in simple terms the various major theories about how the universe was created, including creation stories and the big bang theory. (Rev: BL 9/15/97; SLJ 6/97) [523]

18398 Maynard, Christopher. *The Young Scientist Book of Stars and Planets* (4–7). Illus. 1978, EDC LB $14.95 (0-88110-313-6); paper $6.95 (0-86020-094-9). 32pp. Attractive illustrations and plentiful experiments and projects add to this book's appeal.

18399 Mechler, Gary. *National Audubon Society First Field Guide: Night Sky* (4–6). Series: First Field Guide. 1999, Scholastic $17.95 (0-590-64085-2); paper $11.95 (0-590-64086-0). 160pp. This atlas to the night sky identifies and gives information on the most common stars and constellations. (Rev: BL 10/15/99) [523]

18400 Miles, Lisa, and Alastair Smith. *The Usborne Complete Book of Astronomy and Space* (3–4). Illus. by Gary Bines and Peter Bull. 1998, EDC paper $14.95 (0-7460-3104-1). 96pp. A clear introduction to astronomy and famous astronomers, plus tips for stargazers and sky photographers. (Rev: SLJ 1/99) [523]

18401 Miotto, Enrico. *The Universe: Origins and Evolution* (4–5). Illus. Series: Beginnings — Origins and Evolution. 1995, Raintree Steck-Vaughn LB $24.26 (0-8114-3334-X). 48pp. From the Big Bang to the possible Big Crunch, the evolution of the universe is explained, along with a basic history of astronomy. (Rev: BL 4/15/95) [523]

18402 Mitton, Simon, and Jacqueline Mitton. *The Young Oxford Book of Astronomy* (5–8). Illus. Series: Young Oxford. 1998, Oxford paper $16.95 (0-19-521445-5). 160pp. A well-written, lavishly illustrated introduction to astronomy with large fact boxes used for special insights into this topic. (Rev: BL 3/15/96; SLJ 6/96) [520]

18403 Moche, Dinah L. *Astronomy Today: Planets, Stars, Space Exploration* (5–8). Illus. by Harry McNaught. 1982, Random $12.99 (0-394-84423-8). 96pp. A survey of astronomy and space exploration.

18404 Moeschl, Richard. *Exploring the Sky: 100 Projects for Beginning Astronomers* (5–8). Illus. 1992, Chicago Review paper $16.95 (1-55652-160-X). 320pp. Many ideas for experiments and observations in an information-packed book. (Rev: BL 5/1/89)

18405 Muirden, James. *Seeing Stars: The Night Sky* (3–5). Series: SuperSmarts. 1998, Candlewick $11.99 (0-7636-0373-2); paper $4.99 (0-7636-0647-2). 24pp. A look at the night sky that includes information on galaxies and gravity, comets and meteors, supernovas and constellations. (Rev: BL 10/15/98; HBG 3/99; SLJ 1/99) [523]

18406 Newton, David E. *Black Holes and Supernovae* (4–8). Illus. Series: Secrets of Space. 1997, Twenty-First Century LB $20.40 (0-8050-4477-9). 64pp. A richly illustrated volume that explores theories about black holes and tells the facts concerning them as well as supernovas. (Rev: BL 7/97; SLJ 6/97) [523.8]

18407 Oxlade, Chris. *The Mystery of Black Holes* (4–6). Series: Can Science Solve? 1999, Heinemann LB $15.95 (1-57572-808-7). 32pp. Using a dynamic format, this book supplies a brief overview of theories concerning the existence of black holes. (Rev: SLJ 1/00) [523]

18408 Pearce, Q. L. *The Stargazer's Guide to the Galaxy* (4–8). Illus. by Mary Ann Fraser. 1991, Tor paper $4.99 (0-812-59423-1). 60pp. In this introduction to star gazing in the Northern Hemisphere, material covered includes a look at the night sky in each of the four seasons. (Rev: SLJ 12/91) [523]

18409 Petty, Kate. *The Sun Is a Star: And Other Amazing Facts About the Universe* (1–3). Illus. by Francis Phillips and Ian Thompson. Series: I Didn't Know That. 1997, Millbrook LB $19.90 (0-7613-0567-X). 32pp. As well as introducing the sun, this book describes other parts of the solar system, black holes, the Milky Way, and other parts of the universe. (Rev: SLJ 9/97) [523]

18410 Rabe, Tish. *There's No Place Like Space: All About Our Solar System* (K–3). Illus. by Aristides Ruiz. Series: The Cat in the Hat's Learning Library. 1999, Random LB $11.99 (0-679-99115-8). 44pp. Using rhyming couplets and cartoon-like illustrations, this is a basic introduction to space and the solar system. (Rev: HBG 10/00; SLJ 3/00) [523]

18411 Redfern, Martin. *The Kingfisher Young People's Book of Space* (4–6). 1998, Kingfisher $19.95 (0-7534-5136-0). 95pp. This work contains a short history of astronomy, a tour of the universe with material on galaxies and the solar system, a rundown on space exploration, and a list of questions about space still to be answered. (Rev: HBG 3/99; SLJ 2/99) [523]

18412 Rockwell, Anne. *Our Stars* (PS–4). Illus. 1999, Harcourt $13.00 (0-15-201868-9). 24pp. A stylish picture book that introduces a young audience to the stars, planets, comets, and meteors. (Rev: BL 3/1/99; HBG 10/99; SLJ 5/99) [523.8]

18413 Schultz, Ron. *Looking Inside Telescopes and the Night Sky* (4–6). Illus. by Nick Gadbois and Peter Aschwanden. Series: X-Ray Vision. 1993, John Muir paper $9.95 (1-56261-072-4). 43pp. A rundown of the main optical and radio telescopes as they are today and those proposed for the future. (Rev: SLJ 8/93) [523]

18414 Scott, Elaine. *Close Encounters* (4–7). Illus. 1998, Hyperion LB $17.49 (0-7868-2120-5). 64pp. With stunning photos and a concise text, this book not only describes the information provided by the Hubble space telescope but also gives a brief history of astronomy and the development of the telescope. (Rev: BL 5/15/98; HBG 10/98; SLJ 5/98) [523]

18415 Shepherd, Donna Walsh. *Auroras: Light Shows in the Night Sky* (4–6). Illus. Series: First Books. 1995, Watts LB $22.50 (0-531-20181-3); paper $5.95 (0-531-15766-0). 63pp. Provides a definition of auroras plus coverage of where they are found and how they occur. (Rev: SLJ 11/95) [998]

18416 Simon, Seymour. *The Universe* (3–6). 1998, Morrow LB $15.93 (0-688-15302-X). In a series of double-page spreads, this book introduces topics related to the universe, including nebulas, galaxies, the Big Bang, quasars, stars, and planets. (Rev: HBG 3/99; SLJ 5/98) [523]

18417 Sipiera, Diane M., and Paul P. Sipiera. *The Hubble Space Telescope* (2–4). Illus. Series: True Books. 1997, Children's LB $22.00 (0-516-20442-4). 48pp. As well as describing the Hubble Space Telescope and its uses, this account tells about space explorations that are unsafe for both humans and telescopes. (Rev: BL 12/1/97; HBG 3/98) [522]

18418 Steele, Philip. *Astronomy* (4–8). Illus. Series: Pocket Facts. 1991, Macmillan LB $10.95 (0-89686-586-X). 32pp. A concise introduction to astronomy, complemented by color photos and drawings. (Rev: BL 3/15/92) [520]

18419 Stott, Carole. *Out of This World: Exploring the Universe* (3–5). Series: SuperSmarts. 1998, Candlewick $11.99 (0-7636-0372-4); paper $4.99 (0-7636-0646-4). 24pp. A look at outer space that discusses black holes, astronauts, space exploration, and a planned space base on the planet Mars. (Rev: BL 10/15/98; HBG 3/99; SLJ 1/99) [523]

18420 Sweeney, Joan. *Me and My Place in Space* (PS–2). Illus. by Annette Cable. 1998, Crown LB $14.99 (0-517-70969-4). A tour guide dons a spacesuit and takes the young reader on a tour of the solar system, the Milky Way, and beyond. (Rev: HBG 3/99; SLJ 1/99) [523]

18421 Verdet, Jean-Pierre. *The Universe* (PS–2). Illus. Series: First Discovery. 1997, Scholastic $11.95 (0-590-96212-4). 24pp. From the endless cosmos to exploding stars and a view of our blazing sun, this brilliantly illustrated book introduces the universe. (Rev: BL 2/1/98; HBG 3/98) [520]

18422 *The Visual Dictionary of the Universe* (4–8). Illus. Series: Eyewitness Books. 1993, DK $18.95 (1-56458-335-X). 64pp. Pictures astral bodies from massive galaxies to comets and meteorites plus various telescopes, space exploration equipment, and lunar vehicles. (Rev: BL 12/15/93; SLJ 2/94) [520]

18423 Vogt, Gregory L. *Deep Space Astronomy* (5–8). Illus. 1999, Twenty-First Century LB $23.90 (0-7613-1369-9). 80pp. This look beyond our own star system covers such topics as the development of space-based detectors, information-gathering techniques, and recent discoveries. (Rev: BL 1/1–15/00; HBG 3/00; SLJ 2/00) [520]

18424 Wiese, Jim. *Cosmic Science: Over 40 Gravity-Defying, Earth-Orbiting, Space-Cruising Activities for Kids* (4–6). Illus. 1997, Wiley paper $12.95 (0-471-15852-6). 128pp. Principles of astronomy and space technology are explored through a series of engaging projects with common materials that involve topics like gravity, orbits, planets, and space travel. (Rev: BL 7/97; SLJ 7/97) [929.4]

18425 Wyler, Rose. *The Starry Sky* (K–4). Illus. by Steven J. Petruccio. Series: Outdoor Science. 1989, Simon & Schuster paper $4.95 (0-671-66349-6). 48pp. This book introduces such topics as the earth's rotation, planets, stars, and the phases of the moon. (Rev: SLJ 9/89) [523]

Earth

18426 Alessandrello, Anna. *The Earth: Origins and Evolution* (4–8). Illus. Series: Beginnings — Origins and Evolution. 1995, Raintree Steck-Vaughn LB $24.26 (0-8114-3331-5). 48pp. An oversized book that discusses with lavish illustrations the theories concerning the formation of the earth, its structure and composition, and ways in which it is changing. (Rev: BL 4/15/95; SLJ 6/95) [550]

18427 Baker, Wendy, and Andrew Haslam. *Earth* (3–6). Illus. Series: Make It Work! 1993, Macmillan $12.95 (0-689-71662-1). 48pp. Basic concepts about the earth are explained and activities and experiments are provided. (Rev: SLJ 4/93) [551]

18428 Branley, Franklyn M. *What Makes Day and Night?* (1–3). Illus. by Arthur Dorros. 1986, HarperCollins paper $4.95 (0-06-445050-3). 32pp. A clear, simple explanation of the rotation of the earth. (Rev: BL 3/15/86; SLJ 9/86)

18429 Brimner, Larry. *Earth* (2–5). Illus. Series: True Books. 1998, Children's LB $21.00 (0-516-20620-6). 48pp. Using a chronological approach, this book describes what we have found out about our planet, its composition, layers, and its rotational calendar. (Rev: BL 12/1/98; HBG 3/99) [550]

18430 Gallant, Roy A. *Earth's Place in Space* (5–8). Series: The Story of Science. 1999, Benchmark LB $19.95 (0-7614-0963-7). 80pp. Using a chronological approach, this account traces our knowledge of the earth and its place in the solar system and space. (Rev: HBG 3/00; SLJ 2/00) [525]

18431 Kerrod, Robin. *Planet Earth* (4–6). Series: Planet Library. 2000, Lerner LB $21.27 (0-8225-3902-0). 32pp. This book discusses the earth's formation, its journey through space, its drifting continents, its waters and weather, and its many forms of life. (Rev: BL 10/15/00; HBG 3/01) [525]

18432 Lauber, Patricia. *How We Learned the Earth Is Round* (K–4). Illus. by Megan Lloyd. 1990, HarperCollins LB $14.89 (0-690-04862-9). 32pp. Showing how perceptions of the earth's shape changed through the years and how it was finally determined. (Rev: BCCB 12/90; BL 10/15/90; HB 11–12/90; SLJ 10/90) [525.1]

18433 Lauber, Patricia. *Seeing Earth from Space* (3–8). Illus. 1990, Orchard LB $22.99 (0-531-08502-3). 80pp. In a series of photographs taken from the moon and beyond, secrets of the earth are revealed. (Rev: BCCB 9/90; BL 8/90; HB 3–4/91; SLJ 8/90) [525]

18434 Nicolson, Cynthia P. *The Earth* (2–5). Illus. Series: Starting with Space. 1997, Kids Can $14.95 (1-55074-314-7). 40pp. Appropriate folktales and projects are included, along with information about the earth and night and day. (Rev: BL 9/1/97; SLJ 9/97) [525]

18435 *Our Planet: Earth* (3–6). Illus. Series: Window on the Universe. 1994, Barron's $12.95 (0-

8120-6368-6). 32pp. Traces the origins of the planet, its present composition, and the ways in which it is still changing. (Rev: BL 4/15/94; SLJ 5/94) [525]

18436 Patent, Dorothy Hinshaw. *Shaping the Earth* (4–7). Illus. 2000, Clarion $18.00 (0-395-85691-4). 88pp. The evolution of the earth is traced in this compelling book that describes how the surface has changed and continues to change, with coverage of plate tectonics, ice ages, natural disasters, and descriptions of its natural wonders. (Rev: BL 3/15/00; HBG 10/00; SLJ 4/00) [550]

18437 Riley, Peter D. *Earth* (4–5). Series: Cycles in Science. 1998, Heinemann LB $21.36 (1-57572-620-3). 32pp. This colorfully illustrated book looks at the earth's major cycles, including orbits, rotations, seasons, time zones, and the sun's life. (Rev: SLJ 7/98) [525]

18438 Ross, Michael E. *Earth Cycles* (1–3). Illus. by Gustav Moore. 2001, Millbrook $22.40 (0-7613-1815-1). 32pp. The earth's rotation pattern is described with material on the reasons for night and day and the causes of seasons, plus why the moon appears to change shape during a lunar month. (Rev: BL 1/1–15/01) [525]

18439 Vogt, Gregory L. *Earth* (2–4). Illus. Series: Gateway Solar System. 1996, Millbrook LB $19.90 (1-56294-602-1). 32pp. A beginning introduction to the planet, its composition, and its place in the solar system. (Rev: BL 4/15/96; SLJ 5/96) [550]

Moon

18440 Asimov, Isaac. *The Moon* (3–5). Illus. Series: Isaac Asimov's New Library of the Universe. 1994, Gareth Stevens LB $21.27 (0-8368-1131-3). 32pp. Explores theories of the origin of the moon, its phases and composition, moon landings, and possible colonies. (Rev: BL 2/15/95) [523.3]

18441 Bourgeois, Paulette. *The Moon* (3–4). Illus. by Bill Slavin. Series: Starting with Space. 1997, Kids Can $12.95 (1-55074-157-8). 40pp. This introduction to the moon includes material on its features, phases, and tides, important lunar landings, and legends about the moon from around the world. (Rev: SLJ 9/97) [523.3]

18442 Branley, Franklyn M. *What the Moon Is Like* (1–3). Illus. by True Kelley. Series: Let's-Read-and-Find-Out. 2000, HarperCollins LB $15.89 (0-06-027993-1). 40pp. An updated version of this standard title that includes important new material about the moon and its composition. (Rev: BL 6/1–15/00; HBG 10/00; SLJ 7/00) [559.9]

18443 Bredeson, Carmen. *The Moon* (3–5). Illus. Series: First Books. 1998, Watts LB $21.00 (0-531-20308-5). 64pp. In this fine introduction to the moon, topics covered include its composition, lunar exploration, moon rocks, superstitions and legends concerning the moon, and the effect of the moon on the earth. (Rev: BL 5/1/98; HBG 10/98) [523.3]

18444 Fowler, Allan. *So That's How the Moon Changes Shape!* (1–2). Illus. Series: Rookie Readers. 1991, Children's LB $19.00 (0-516-04917-8).

32pp. The phases of the moon are introduced in minimal text and many color photographs. (Rev: BL 4/1/92) [523.3]

18445 Gardner, Robert. *Science Project Ideas About the Moon* (4–7). Illus. Series: Science Project Ideas. 1997, Enslow LB $19.95 (0-89490-844-8). 96pp. After giving basic information about the moon, this book outlines projects involving ways of observing the moon and how to make models to show its movements. (Rev: BL 12/1/97; HBG 3/98) [523.3]

18446 Gibbons, Gail. *The Moon Book* (2–4). Illus. 1997, Holiday LB $16.95 (0-8234-1297-0). 32pp. An introductory description of the moon, its orbit and phases, its place in eclipses, and its effects of the earth's oceans. (Rev: BCCB 7–8/97; BL 5/1/97; SLJ 4/97) [523.3]

18447 Graham, Ian. *The Best Book of the Moon* (2–5). Series: The Best Book Of. 1999, Kingfisher $10.95 (0-7534-5174-3). 31pp. A fine introduction to the moon with material on its composition, exploration including the *Apollo* and recent *Prospector* missions, and lunar and solar eclipses. (Rev: HBG 10/99; SLJ 5/99) [523.3]

18448 Kerrod, Robin. *The Moon* (4–6). Series: Planet Library. 2000, Lerner LB $21.27 (0-8225-3900-4). 32pp. The moon's formation, history, orbit, and makeup are covered, plus material on the moon landing. (Rev: BL 10/15/00; HBG 3/01; SLJ 11/00) [523.3]

18449 Krupp, E. C. *The Moon and You* (3–6). Illus. by Robin R. Krupp. 1993, Macmillan LB $15.00 (0-02-751142-1). 48pp. In picture-book format, this account covers all the basic facts about the moon, including its formation, phases, and exploration. (Rev: BL 11/1/93; SLJ 2/94) [523.3]

18450 Lassieur, Allison. *The Moon* (2–4). Series: True Books. 2000, Children's LB $22.00 (0-516-22001-2). 48pp. A well-illustrated introduction to our moon, the myths that surround it, its composition and exploration, and the effect it has on life on earth. (Rev: BL 3/1/01) [523.3]

18451 *Our Satellite: The Moon* (3–6). Illus. Series: Window on the Universe. 1994, Barron's $12.95 (0-8120-6369-4). 32pp. In double-page spreads, features of the moon are explained, such as lunar eclipses and the appearance of the moon's far side. (Rev: BL 4/15/94; SLJ 5/94) [523.3]

18452 Rosen, Sidney. *Where Does the Moon Go?* (2–4). Illus. 1992, Carolrhoda LB $19.95 (0-87614-685-X). 40pp. In excellent photos, clever illustrations, and simple text, the moon and its phases are introduced. (Rev: SLJ 11/92) [523.3]

18453 Simon, Seymour. *The Moon* (3–6). Illus. 1984, Macmillan LB $16.00 (0-02-782840-9). 32pp. A simple description of the moon and its effect on earth.

18454 Siy, Alexandra. *Footprints on the Moon* (3–5). Illus. 2001, Charlesbridge $16.95 (1-57091-408-7). 32pp. This heavily illustrated book covers human fascination with the moon throughout history and then focuses on Project Apollo and the moon landings. (Rev: BL 2/1/01; SLJ 2/01) [629.45]

Planets

18455 Asimov, Isaac. *The Red Planet: Mars* (3–5). Illus. Series: Isaac Asimov's New Library of the Universe. 1994, Gareth Stevens LB $21.27 (0-8368-1132-1). 32pp. This richly illustrated account concentrates on the findings of the Mars probes from 1962 through 1992 and speculates on possible futuristic colonies. (Rev: BL 2/15/95) [523.4]

18456 Bendick, Jeanne. *The Planets: Neighbors in Space* (2–4). Illus. by Mike Roffe. Series: Early Bird Astronomy. 1991, Millbrook LB $19.90 (1-878841-03-3). 32pp. The planets are introduced in a simple, basic text and full-color artwork. (Rev: BL 9/1/91; SLJ 8/91) [523.4]

18457 Berger, Melvin. *Discovering Jupiter: The Amazing Collision in Space* (3–6). Illus. by Tom Leonard. 1995, Scholastic paper $4.95 (0-590-48824-4). 55pp. After covering the general facts we know about Jupiter, this account tells of the Comet Shoemaker-Levy 9 and its crash into the planet. (Rev: SLJ 3/96) [523.4]

18458 Branley, Franklyn M. *The Planets in Our Solar System* (K–2). Illus. by Kevin O'Malley. Series: Let's-Read-and-Find-Out. 1998, HarperCollins LB $15.89 (0-06-027770-X); paper $4.95 (0-06-445178-X). 31pp. The planets of our solar system are described — their similarities, differences, and distinctive characteristics. (Rev: HBG 10/98; SLJ 6/98) [523.4]

18459 Brimner, Larry. *Jupiter* (2–5). Series: True Books. 1999, Children's LB $21.00 (0-516-21153-6). 48pp. An attractive introduction to the largest planet of the solar system, what we know about it, and the space probes that have added to our knowledge. (Rev: BL 7/99; HBG 10/99; SLJ 9/99) [523.4]

18460 Brimner, Larry. *Mars* (2–4). Series: True Books. 1998, Children's LB $21.00 (0-516-20618-4). 48pp. This richly illustrated account reports on recent findings about the Red Planet. (Rev: BL 9/15/98; HBG 3/99) [523.4]

18461 Brimner, Larry. *Mercury* (2–4). Series: True Books. 1998, Children's LB $21.00 (0-516-20619-2). 48pp. A colorful introduction to Mercury, the planet closest to the sun. (Rev: BL 9/15/98; HBG 3/99) [523.4]

18462 Brimner, Larry. *Neptune* (2–5). Series: True Books. 1999, Children's LB $21.00 (0-516-21157-9). 48pp. An interesting overview of the distant planet Neptune, from its discovery in 1846 to the present day. (Rev: BL 7/99; HBG 10/99) [523.4]

18463 Brimner, Larry. *Pluto* (2–5). Series: True Books. 1999, Children's LB $21.00 (0-516-21155-2). 48pp. This attractive, well-illustrated book takes the reader on a tour of Pluto, the outermost known planet of our solar system. (Rev: BL 7/99; HBG 10/99) [523.4]

18464 Brimner, Larry. *Saturn* (2–5). Series: True Books. 1999, Children's LB $21.00 (0-516-21154-4). 48pp. Using recently discovered data and pictures, this is a solid introduction to Saturn, the sixth planet from the sun, which is noted for the broad flat rings circling it. (Rev: BL 7/99; HBG 10/99; SLJ 9/99) [523.4]

18465 Brimner, Larry. *Uranus* (2–5). Series: True Books. 1999, Children's LB $21.00 (0-516-21156-0). 48pp. An interesting, heavily illustrated account that introduces Uranus and describes recent findings about this planet, discovered in 1781, which is one of the most distant in the solar system. (Rev: BL 7/99; HBG 10/99) [523.4]

18466 Brimner, Larry. *Venus* (2–5). Illus. Series: True Books. 1998, Children's LB $21.00 (0-516-21158-7). 48pp. This book summarizes what we know about the planet Venus, its composition, structure, rotation patterns, and distance from the sun. (Rev: BL 12/1/98) [523.42]

18467 Cole, Michael D. *Living on Mars: Mission to the Red Planet* (4–6). Illus. Series: Countdown to Space. 1999, Enslow LB $18.95 (0-7660-1121-6). 48pp. This book covers our findings thus far from the exploration of Mars and discusses the possibility of visiting and colonizing this planet in the future. (Rev: BL 12/1/98; HBG 10/99; SLJ 4/99) [919.9]

18468 Fowler, Allan. *The Sun's Family of Planets* (1–2). Illus. Series: Rookie Readers. 1992, Children's LB $19.00 (0-516-06004-X); paper $4.95 (0-516-46004-8). 32pp. The planets are introduced in full-color photos and minimal text. This simple book is also available in an oversized "Big Book" edition. (Rev: BL 12/15/92) [523.4]

18469 Fradin, Dennis B. *Is There Life on Mars?* (5–9). 1999, Simon & Schuster $19.95 (0-689-82048-8). 136pp. This fascinating account gives a history of attitudes and beliefs about Mars as well as a full account of what we actually know about the Red Planet and a rundown of recent discoveries. (Rev: BCCB 1/00; HBG 3/00; SLJ 1/00) [523.4]

18470 Fradin, Dennis B. *The Planet Hunters: The Search for Other Worlds* (5–8). Illus. 1997, Simon & Schuster paper $19.95 (0-689-81323-6). 160pp. This well-researched book traces how we discovered each of the planets and how we were made aware that the earth is also a planet. (Rev: BL 12/1/97*; HBG 3/98; SLJ 1/98) [523.4]

18471 Gallant, Roy A. *Planets* (2–4). Illus. Series: Kaleidoscope. 2000, Marshall Cavendish LB $15.95 (0-7614-1033-3). 48pp. With colorful illustrations, each of the planets of our solar system is introduced with a brief descriptive text. (Rev: BL 1/1–15/01) [523.4]

18472 Getz, David. *Life on Mars* (3–5). Illus. Series: Redfeather. 1997, Holt $14.95 (0-8050-3708-X). 70pp. A simple description of a trip to Mars and what the reader would find there. (Rev: BL 5/15/97; SLJ 6/97) [574]

18473 Gibbons, Gail. *The Planets* (K–3). Illus. 1993, Holiday LB $16.95 (0-8234-1040-4). 32pp. In a well-illustrated format, this is a good introduction to the planets of our solar system. (Rev: BL 12/15/93; SLJ 10/93) [523.4]

18474 Harris, Nicholas. *The Incredible Journey to the Planets: Close Encounters with Our Neighbors in Space* (4–6). Illus. by Sebastian Quigley and Gary Hincks. 1999, Bedrick $18.95 (0-87226-600-1). 32pp. A tour of the planets that allows readers to see planets from different directions by using die-cut holes in the pages. (Rev: HBG 3/00; SLJ 10/99) [523]

18475 Kelch, Joseph W. *Millions of Miles to Mars: A Journey to the Red Planet* (4–6). Illus. by Connell P. Byrne. 1995, Messner $18.95 (0-671-88249-X); paper $9.95 (0-671-88250-3). 121pp. A make-believe journey to the Red Planet reveals what we know and do not know about Mars. (Rev: SLJ 9/95) [523.4]

18476 Kerrod, Robin. *Jupiter* (4–6). Illus. Series: Planet Library. 2000, Lerner $21.27 (0-8225-3907-1). 32pp. Jupiter, the largest of the planets, is presented in text and pictures with material on its formation, makeup, atmosphere, and the space probes that have gathered information about it. Two others in this series are *Mars* and *Mercury and Venus*. (Rev: BL 10/15/00; HBG 3/01) [523.45]

18477 Kerrod, Robin. *Saturn* (4–6). Series: Planet Library. 2000, Lerner LB $21.27 (0-8225-3909-8). 32pp. Breathtaking photographs and a clear text introduce Saturn, the planet of swirling clouds, bright rings, and 18 moons. (Rev: BL 10/15/00; HBG 3/01; SLJ 1/01) [523.4]

18478 Kerrod, Robin. *Uranus, Neptune, and Pluto* (4–6). Series: Planet Library. 2000, Lerner LB $21.27 (0-8225-3908-X). 32pp. An exploration of the planets on the edge of our solar system, beginning with the ringed gas giants, Uranus and Neptune, and ending with mysterious Pluto. (Rev: BL 10/15/00; HBG 3/01; SLJ 1/01) [513.4]

18479 Landau, Elaine. *Jupiter* (5–7). Series: Watts Library. 1999, Watts LB $24.00 (0-531-20387-5). 63pp. This is an update of the fine earlier book, with material on the Ulysses and Galileo probes. (Rev: SLJ 2/00) [523.4]

18480 Landau, Elaine. *Mars* (5–7). Series: Watts Library. 1999, Watts LB $24.00 (0-531-20388-3). 63pp. This updated version of an earlier title is a fine introduction to the planet Mars with new material on the *Pathfinder* landing that launched little *Sojourner* in 1993. (Rev: SLJ 2/00) [523.4]

18481 Landau, Elaine. *Neptune* (4–6). Illus. Series: First Books. 1991, Watts LB $22.00 (0-531-20014-0). 64pp. Using information from the 1989 *Voyager II* mission, this account introduces this distant planet and its surrounding moons. (Rev: BL 6/15/91; SLJ 8/91) [523.4]

18482 Landau, Elaine. *Saturn* (4–6). Series: Watts Library. 1999, Watts LB $24.00 (0-531-20389-1). 63pp. This revision of the 1991 volume includes recent material gathered by the Hubble Space Telescope and a report on the current Cassini/Huygens probe. (Rev: SLJ 11/99) [523.4]

18483 Moore, Patrick. *The Planets* (K–3). Illus. Series: Starry Sky. 1995, Millbrook LB $18.90 (1-56294-624-2). 24pp. The size and makeup of the planets are discussed in this beginning astronomy book that also looks at the possibility of interplanetary travel. (Rev: SLJ 7/95) [523.4]

18484 Nicolson, Cynthia P. *The Planets* (2–5). Series: Starting with Space. 1998, Kids Can $12.95

(1-55074-512-3). Using a question-and-answer format and NASA mission photos, this concise book introduces the planets to a young audience. (Rev: BL 8/98; HBG 3/99; SLJ 10/98) [523.4]

18485 Ride, Sally, and Tam O'Shaughnessy. *The Mystery of Mars* (2–5). Illus. 1999, Crown $17.95 (0-517-70971-6). 48pp. An excellent introduction to the Red Planet that gives information on the various space probes and is illustrated with stunning visuals. (Rev: BL 1/1–15/00; HB 3–4/00; HBG 3/00; SLJ 3/00) [523.43]

18486 Schraff, Anne. *Are We Moving to Mars?* (3–4). Illus. by Michael Carroll. 1996, John Muir paper $6.95 (1-56261-310-3). 32pp. This account answers the question "What would living on Mars be like?" (Rev: SLJ 2/97) [523.4]

18487 Shepherd, Donna Walsh. *Uranus* (4–6). Illus. Series: First Books. 1994, Watts LB $22.00 (0-531-20167-8). 64pp. From its discovery in 1787 to present-day findings, this book looks at the seventh planet in our solar system. (Rev: BL 10/15/94) [523.4]

18488 Simon, Seymour. *Destination: Jupiter*. Rev. ed. (3–5). Illus. 1998, Morrow $16.00 (0-688-15620-7). 32pp. This update of the 1985 edition includes information on the findings of the Hubble space telescope, material on the *Galileo* space probe, and basic information about the planet. (Rev: BL 4/15/98; HBG 10/98; SLJ 5/98) [523.45]

18489 Simon, Seymour. *Destination: Mars* (3–5). Illus. 2000, HarperCollins LB $15.89 (0-688-15771-8). 32pp. This new edition of the well-received 1987 book now contains pictures from the Orbiter camera, the Hubble space telescope, and the *Pathfinder* lander. (Rev: BL 5/1/00; HB 7–8/00; HBG 10/00) [523.43]

18490 Simon, Seymour. *Jupiter* (2–4). Illus. 1988, Morrow paper $5.95 (0-688-08403-6). 32pp. A detailed look at Jupiter, enhanced by photographs taken mostly from unmanned spacecraft. (Rev: BCCB 12/85; BL 9/15/85; SLJ 10/85)

18491 Simon, Seymour. *Mars* (2–5). Illus. 1987, Morrow paper $6.95 (0-688-09928-9). 32pp. Lucid text and spectacular photos highlight this detailed study of the Red Planet. (Rev: BL 10/15/87; HB 11–12/87; SLJ 12/87)

18492 Simon, Seymour. *Neptune* (4–8). Illus. 1991, Morrow $17.93 (0-688-09632-8). 32pp. The voyage of *Voyager II* as it swept past Neptune provided scientists with more information on this planet than they had ever had. (Rev: BCCB 4/91; BL 2/15/91; HB 5–6/91; SLJ 4/91) [523.4]

18493 Simon, Seymour. *Saturn* (2–4). Illus. 1985, Morrow $15.93 (0-688-05799-3); paper $6.95 (0-688-08404-4). 32pp. Lots of information about Saturn and its rings, enhanced with color photographs. (Rev: BL 9/15/85; HB 1–2/86; SLJ 10/85)

18494 Simon, Seymour. *Uranus* (2–5). Illus. 1987, Morrow paper $6.95 (0-688-09929-7). 32pp. Descriptions and photos of its five moons highlight this look at Uranus, which was not recognized as a planet until 1781. (Rev: BL 10/15/87; HB 11–12/87; SLJ 12/87)

18495 Skurzynski, Gloria. *Discover Mars* (4–6). 1998, National Geographic $17.95 (0-7922-7099-1). 44pp. An overview of what we know about Mars, a rundown on space probes in the area, and plenty of illustrations — some in 3–D that require special glasses, which are provided. (Rev: SLJ 11/98) [523.4]

18496 Vogt, Gregory L. *Jupiter* (3–4). Series: Galaxy. 2000, Capstone LB $15.93 (0-7368-0512-5). 24pp. This book and the others listed cover basic facts and material on atmospheres, rings, physical features, and moons. Others are *Neptune*, *Pluto*, and *Uranus* (all 2000). (Rev: HBG 10/00; SLJ 9/00) [523.4]

18497 Vogt, Gregory L. *Mars* (3–6). Illus. Series: Gateway Solar System. 1994, Millbrook LB $19.90 (1-56294-392-8). 31pp. Color and black-and-white photos and drawings highlight this introduction to Mars and its geography. Also use *Pluto* (1994). (Rev: BL 7/94; SLJ 5/94) [523.4]

18498 Vogt, Gregory L. *Mercury* (3–6). Illus. Series: Gateway Solar System. 1994, Millbrook LB $19.90 (1-56294-390-1). 32pp. A useful introduction to the planet Mercury that includes material on Project Mariner and its findings. (Rev: BL 7/94; SLJ 5/94) [523.4]

18499 Vogt, Gregory L. *Neptune* (3–5). Illus. Series: Gateway Solar System. 1993, Millbrook LB $19.90 (1-56294-331-6). 32pp. An overview of the composition, atmosphere, and satellites of the planet next-to-last from our sun. (Rev: SLJ 11/93) [523.2]

18500 Vogt, Gregory L. *Pluto* (2–4). Illus. Series: Gateway Solar System. 1994, Millbrook LB $19.90 (1-56294-393-6). 32pp. This introduction to Pluto describes its origins plus a history of what we know about it and things we should find out in the future. Also use *Venus* (1994). (Rev: BL 7/94; SLJ 5/94) [523.1]

18501 Vogt, Gregory L. *Saturn* (3–5). Illus. Series: Gateway Solar System. 1993, Millbrook LB $19.90 (1-56294-332-4). 32pp. This introduction to Saturn includes material on its cloud layers, magnetic field, and thousands of rings. (Rev: SLJ 11/93) [523.2]

18502 Vogt, Gregory L. *Uranus* (3–5). Illus. Series: Gateway Solar System. 1993, Millbrook LB $19.90 (1-56294-330-8). 32pp. Sharp, full-color illustrations and a brief text introduce the salient features of Uranus, including its moons, rings, and atmosphere. (Rev: SLJ 11/93) [523.2]

Solar System

18503 Aronson, Billy. *Meteors: The Truth Behind Shooting Stars* (4–6). Illus. 1996, Watts LB $22.50 (0-531-20242-9). 63pp. A useful manual that explains the differences between meteors, meteorites, and meteoroids, with general information on their composition and when they can be seen. (Rev: BL 2/15/97; SLJ 3/97) [523.5]

18504 Asimov, Isaac. *How Did We Find Out About Comets?* (5–7). Illus. 1975, Walker LB $10.85 (0-8027-6204-2). 64pp. The history of comets, their nature, and their effects on people are covered in this overview.

18505 Bendick, Jeanne. *Comets and Meteors: Visitors from Space* (2–4). Illus. by Mike Roffe. Series: Early Bird Astronomy. 1991, Millbrook LB $19.90 (1-56294-001-5). 32pp. This introduction to comets and meteors is enlivened with many full-color illustrations. (Rev: BL 11/15/91) [523.6]

18506 Bendick, Jeanne. *Moons and Rings* (2–4). Illus. by Mike Roffe. Series: Early Bird Astronomy. 1991, Millbrook LB $19.90 (1-56294-000-7). 32pp. The concept of satellites is explained and examples are shown within our solar system. (Rev: BL 11/15/91) [523.3]

18507 Bonar, Samantha. *Asteroids* (4–6). Series: Watts Library. 1999, Watts LB $24.00 (0-531-20367-0). 63pp. This book describes the various kinds of rocky debris that are found in the solar system and the possible problems they can cause. (Rev: SLJ 11/99) [523]

18508 Bonar, Samantha. *Comets* (3–5). Series: First Books. 1998, Watts LB $22.00 (0-531-20301-8). 63pp. A history of what we know about comets from the ancient Greeks to Halley, with material on their composition, frequency, and where and how they can be seen. (Rev: HBG 10/98; SLJ 6/98) [523.5]

18509 Branley, Franklyn M. *The Sun and the Solar System* (4–6). Illus. Series: Secrets of Space. 1996, Twenty-First Century LB $20.40 (0-8050-4475-2). 80pp. Traces the origin of the solar system and the place of the earth and its moon within it. (Rev: BL 12/15/96; SLJ 1/97) [523.2]

18510 Cole, Joanna. *The Magic School Bus Lost in the Solar System* (3–5). Illus. by Bruce Degen. 1990, Scholastic $15.95 (0-590-41428-3). 40pp. Basic facts about the cosmos are revealed in this fantasy. (Rev: BCCB 10/90; BL 11/15/90; HB 1–2/91; SLJ 8/90*) [523.4]

18511 Dickinson, Terence. *Other Worlds: A Beginner's Guide to Planets and Moons* (4–8). Illus. 1995, Firefly LB $19.95 (1-895565-71-5); paper $9.95 (1-895565-70-7). 64pp. An entertaining introduction to the solar system, the planets, and the most important moons. (Rev: BL 11/15/95; SLJ 1/96) [523.4]

18512 Dussling, Jennifer. *Planets* (1–3). Illus. by Denise Ortakales. Series: All Aboard Reading. 2000, Putnam LB $13.89 (0-448-42416-9); paper $3.99 (0-448-42406-1). 48pp. A simple science book that introduces the solar system and makes many difficult concepts easy to grasp. (Rev: BL 12/1/00) [523.4]

18513 Gustafson, John. *Planets, Moons and Meteors: The Young Stargazer's Guide to the Galaxy* (4–8). Illus. 1992, Simon & Schuster LB $12.95 (0-671-72534-3); paper $6.95 (0-671-72535-1). 64pp. Studying the solar system by observing the moon, planets, and meteors, plus basic information on the planets. (Rev: BL 11/1/92) [523]

18514 Hansen, Rosanna, and Robert A. Bell. *My First Book About Space* (3–6). Illus. 1985, Simon & Schuster $13.00 (0-671-60262-4). The solar system

is explained, including each planet, discussed in terms of appearance, atmosphere, orbit, and revolutions. (Rev: BCCB 7–8/86; BL 12/1/85; SLJ 2/86)

18515 Harris, Alan, and Paul Weissman. *The Great Voyager Adventure: A Guided Tour Through the Solar System* (4–8). Illus. 1990, Simon & Schuster LB $16.95 (0-671-72538-6). 80pp. An introduction to the missions and discoveries of the Voyager spacecraft. (Rev: BL 2/1/91; SLJ 2/91) [523.4]

18516 Kerrod, Robin. *Asteroids, Comets, and Meteors* (4–6). Series: Planet Library. 2000, Lerner LB $21.27 (0-8225-3905-5). 32pp. This book explores the smallest members of the solar system and tells how they were formed, how they shaped the surface of the planets and moons, and how they sometimes light up our sky. (Rev: BL 10/15/00; HBG 3/01) [523.4]

18517 Kerrod, Robin. *The Solar System* (4–6). Illus. Series: Planet Library. 2000, Lerner $21.27 (0-8225-3903-9). 32pp. A discussion on the formation of the sun, the planets, their moons, and the asteroid belt is followed by additional coverage of topics such as orbiting stars, space exploration, and the search for extraterrestrial life. (Rev: BL 10/15/00; HBG 3/01; SLJ 11/00) [523.3]

18518 Kraske, Robert. *Asteroids: Invaders from Space* (5–7). Illus. 1995, Simon & Schuster $15.00 (0-689-31860-X). 90pp. A history of these cosmic wanderers, their formation, and the results, positive and negative, when they collide with earth. (Rev: BCCB 11/95; BL 7/95; SLJ 9/95) [523.4]

18519 Leedy, Loreen. *Postcards from Pluto: A Tour of the Solar System* (1–3). Illus. 1993, Holiday LB $16.95 (0-8234-1000-5). 32pp. A group of children are introduced to the solar system via a spaceship tour conducted by a robot, Dr. Quasar. (Rev: BL 10/15/93; SLJ 10/93) [523.2]

18520 Marsh, Carole. *Asteroids, Comets, and Meteors* (4–6). Illus. Series: Secrets of Space. 1996, Twenty-First Century LB $20.40 (0-8050-4473-6). 64pp. The history of our knowledge of these bodies from outer space is traced, with descriptions of the nature of each. (Rev: BL 12/15/96; SLJ 1/97) [523.4]

18521 Moore, Patrick. *Comets and Shooting Stars* (K–3). Illus. Series: Starry Sky. 1995, Millbrook LB $18.90 (1-56294-625-0). 24pp. An attractive beginning astronomy book that describes the composition and orbits of comets and shooting stars. (Rev: SLJ 7/95) [523.5]

18522 Moore, Patrick. *The Sun and Moon* (K–3). Illus. Series: Starry Sky. 1995, Millbrook LB $18.90 (1-56294-622-6). 24pp. A description of the sun and moon is given, with an explanation of their movements and eclipses. (Rev: SLJ 7/95) [523]

18523 Poynter, Margaret. *Killer Asteroids* (3–6). Illus. Series: Weird and Wacky Science. 1996, Enslow LB $18.95 (0-89490-616-X). 48pp. Violent clashes involving asteroids and the earth are described, along with coverage of the recent encounter of a comet with Jupiter. (Rev: SLJ 5/96) [551.3]

18524 Rau, Dana Meachen. *The Solar System* (2–3). 2000, Compass Point LB $14.95 (0-7565-0036-2). 32pp. After discussing the sun, the author conducts a quick tour of the solar system including meteors, comets, and moons. (Rev: SLJ 2/01) [523.4]

18525 Rosen, Sidney. *Can You Catch a Falling Star?* (2–4). Illus. by Dean Lindberg. Series: A Question of Science. 1996, Carolrhoda LB $19.95 (0-87614-882-8). 40pp. A simple question-and-answer book that examines meteors, what happens when they fall to earth, and where and when to look for meteorite showers. (Rev: SLJ 4/96) [523.5]

18526 Rosen, Sidney. *Can You Hitch a Ride on a Comet?* (1–3). Illus. by Dean Lindberg. Series: A Question of Science. 1993, Carolrhoda LB $19.95 (0-87614-773-2). 40pp. Using a question-and-answer format, all sorts of information is given about comets, including their formation, discovery, and tracking. (Rev: BL 10/15/93) [525.6]

18527 Simon, Seymour. *Comets, Meteors, and Asteroids* (3–5). Illus. 1994, Morrow LB $14.93 (0-688-12710-X). 32pp. These three space bodies are described, with material on their composition and differences. (Rev: BL 9/15/94; SLJ 8/94) [523.6]

18528 Simon, Seymour. *Our Solar System* (2–6). Illus. 1992, Morrow $19.93 (0-688-09993-9). 72pp. A quick tour of the solar system, with many of NASA's striking photos. (Rev: BL 10/15/92; HB 11–12/92; SLJ 10/92) [523.2]

18529 Sipiera, Paul P. *Comets and Meteor Showers* (2–4). Illus. Series: True Books. 1997, Children's LB $22.00 (0-516-20330-4). 48pp. Large print and clear diagrams highlight this description of comets and the way they have been regarded through history. (Rev: BL 9/15/97) [523.6]

18530 Sipiera, Paul P. *The Solar System* (2–4). Illus. Series: True Books. 1997, Children's $22.00 (0-516-20339-8). 48pp. A brief informative introduction to the solar system, with excellent graphics and a large-print text. (Rev: BL 9/15/97) [523.2]

18531 Spangenburg, Ray, and Diane Moser. *Exploring the Reaches of the Solar System* (5–8). Illus. 1990, Facts on File $22.95 (0-8160-1850-2). 109pp. An overview of the solar system. (Rev: SLJ 12/90) [523.4]

18532 Theodorou, Rod. *Across the Solar System* (2–4). Series: Amazing Journeys. 2000, Heinemann LB $15.95 (1-57572-486-3). 32pp. In this journey into outer space there are double-page spreads with information on each planet including distance from the sun, size, and length of a day and year. (Rev: HBG 3/01; SLJ 7/00) [523.4]

18533 VanCleave, Janice. *Janice VanCleave's Solar System: Mind-Boggling Experiments You Can Turn into Science Fair Projects* (4–6). Illus. by Laurel Aiello. Series: Spectacular Science Projects. 2000, Wiley paper $10.95 (0-471-32204-0). 90pp. Twenty interesting experiments involving the solar system are outlined with material on how to turn them into science projects. (Rev: SLJ 6/00) [523.4]

18534 Vogt, Gregory L. *Asteroids, Comets, and Meteors* (2–4). Illus. Series: Gateway Solar System. 1996, Millbrook LB $19.90 (1-56294-601-3). 32pp.

A beginning introduction to these celestial bodies and their characteristics. (Rev: BL 4/15/96; SLJ 5/96) [523.6]

18535 Vogt, Gregory L. *The Solar System: Facts and Exploration* (5–8). Illus. Series: Scientific American Sourcebooks. 1995, Twenty-First Century LB $22.40 (0-8050-3249-5). 96pp. As well as describing the planets, moons, and small astral bodies, this account gives a history of the space program. (Rev: BL 12/1/95; SLJ 11/95) [523.2]

18536 Wilsdon, Christina. *The Solar System: An A–Z Guide* (4–7). 2000, Watts LB $26.00 (0-531-11710-3). 96pp. An alphabetically arranged book that covers many aspect of the solar system including planets, space probes and missions, famous personalities, and such phenomena as greenhouse effect and solar wind. (Rev: SLJ 7/00) [523.4]

Stars

18537 Apfel, Necia H. *Orion, the Hunter* (3–6). Illus. 1995, Clarion $16.95 (0-395-68962-7). 48pp. The constellation Orion and its separate nebulae are introduced, described, and pictured. (Rev: BL 12/1/95; SLJ 11/95) [523.8]

18538 Bendick, Jeanne. *The Stars: Lights in the Night Sky* (2–4). Illus. by Chris Forsey. Series: Early Bird Astronomy. 1991, Millbrook LB $19.90 (1-878841-00-9). 32pp. Ideas and theories about stars and their formation are presented in a clear and simple text and with many diagrams. (Rev: BL 9/1/91; SLJ 8/91) [523.8]

18539 Berger, Melvin, and Gilda Berger. *Where Are the Stars During the Day? A Book About Stars* (3–5). Illus. by Blanche Sims. Series: Discovery Readers. 1993, Ideals paper $4.50 (0-8249-8607-5). 48pp. An easy-to-read book that introduces the stars, sun, and constellations. (Rev: BCCB 4/93; SLJ 5/93) [523]

18540 Branley, Franklyn M. *The Big Dipper* (K–2). Illus. by Ed Emberley. 1991, HarperCollins paper $4.95 (0-06-445100-3). 32pp. An introduction to the composition, mythology, and location of the Big and Little Dippers.

18541 Branley, Franklyn M. *The Sky Is Full of Stars* (2–4). Illus. by Felicia Bond. 1981, HarperCollins paper $4.95 (0-06-445002-3). 40pp. A simple introduction to constellations and star watching.

18542 Branley, Franklyn M. *Star Guide* (4–6). Illus. by Ellen Eagle. 1997, Macmillan paper $9.10 (0-028-62019-4). 64pp. An exploration of what stars are made of, how they change, and how they are formed. (Rev: BL 8/87; SLJ 9/87)

18543 Clay, Rebecca. *Stars and Galaxies* (4–8). Series: Secrets of Space. 1997, Twenty-First Century LB $22.40 (0-8050-4476-0). 64pp. This account describes the birth and death of stars and gives a description of galaxies and their composition. (Rev: BL 9/15/97; SLJ 6/97) [523.8]

18544 Dussling, Jennifer. *Stars* (PS–2). Illus. by Mavis Smith. Series: All Aboard Reading. 1996, Grosset LB $13.99 (0-448-41149-0); paper $3.99

(0-448-41148-2). 32pp. A beginning reader that introduces stars and constellations. (Rev: SLJ 8/96) [523.8]

18545 Gallant, Roy. *Stars* (2–4). Series: Kaleidoscope. 2000, Marshall Cavendish LB $15.95 (0-7614-1036-8). 48pp. This book introduces stars, how they are born and die, and their constellations. (Rev: BL 1/1–15/01) [523]

18546 Gibbons, Gail. *Stargazers* (1–3). Illus. 1992, Holiday LB $16.95 (0-8234-0983-X). 32pp. With full-color artwork, the author explains what stars are and how we look at them. (Rev: BCCB 1/93; BL 10/15/92; SLJ 10/92) [520]

18547 Gustafson, John. *Stars, Clusters and Galaxies* (5–8). Illus. Series: Young Stargazer's Guide to the Galaxy. 1993, Simon & Schuster LB $18.95 (0-671-72536-X); paper $6.95 (0-671-72537-8). 64pp. Information about stars, clusters, nebulae, and galaxies, plus tips on effective stargazing. (Rev: BL 7/93; SLJ 6/93) [523.8]

18548 Levy, David H., ed. *Stars and Planets* (4–6). Illus. Series: Nature Company Discoveries. 1996, Time Life $16.00 (0-8094-9246-6). 64pp. Stars and planets are introduced with handsome illustrations and a brief text plus an unusual final eight-page foldout. (Rev: BL 6/1–15/96) [523.2]

18549 Mitton, Jacqueline. *Zoo in the Sky: A Book of Animal Constellations* (K–3). Illus. by Christina Balit. 1998, National Geographic $17.95 (0-7922-7069-X). 32pp. This attractive introduction to the animal constellations uses sparkling silver stars to outline each of them in the night sky. (Rev: BL 11/1/98; HBG 3/99; SLJ 12/98) [523.8]

18550 Moore, Patrick. *The Stars* (K–3). Illus. Series: Starry Sky. 1995, Millbrook LB $18.90 (1-56294-623-4). 24pp. A beginning astronomy book that describes the birth and death of stars and the composition of the Milky Way and other galaxies. (Rev: SLJ 7/95) [523.8]

18551 Nicolson, Cynthia P. *The Stars* (4–6). 1998, Kids Can $12.95 (1-55074-524-7). The stars are introduced in a question-and-answer format with good photographs and a glossary of terms. (Rev: BL 8/98; HBG 3/99; SLJ 10/98) [523.8]

18552 Rey, H. A. *Find the Constellations* (5–7). Illus. 1976, Houghton $20.00 (0-395-24509-5); paper $9.95 (0-395-24418-8). 80pp. Through clear text and illustrations, the reader is helped to recognize stars and constellations in the northern United States. Also use: *The Stars: A New Way to See Them* (1973).

18553 Rosen, Sidney. *Where's the Big Dipper?* (2–4). Illus. by Dean Lindberg. Series: A Question of Science. 1996, Carolrhoda $14.95 (0-87614-883-6). 40pp. In a question-and-answer format, this book supplies a simple introduction to deep space, with a focus on the Big Dipper. (Rev: SLJ 4/96) [523]

18554 Santrey, Laurence. *Discovering the Stars* (1–3). Illus. by James Watling. 1982, Troll LB $17.25 (0-89375-568-0); paper $3.50 (0-89375-569-9). 32pp. A simple book that tells about galaxies, constellations, and other astral bodies.

18555 Simon, Seymour. *Galaxies* (2–5). Illus. 1988, Morrow paper $6.95 (0-688-10992-6). 32pp. Engrossing photographs highlight this look at galaxies. (Rev: BCCB 4/88; BL 3/1/88; SLJ 5/88)

18556 Simon, Seymour. *The Stars* (3–5). Illus. 1986, Morrow $16.93 (0-688-05856-6); paper $6.95 (0-688-09237-3). 32pp. Large photos and diagrams highlight the story of the life cycles of stars, giving a sense of their great numbers and relationship to earth. (Rev: BCCB 10/86; BL 9/1/86; SLJ 12/86)

18557 Sipiera, Diane M., and Paul P. Sipiera. *Constellations* (2–4). Series: True Books. 1997, Children's LB $22.00 (0-516-20331-2). 48pp. A simple, basic introduction to constellations in a highly accessible format. Also use *Black Holes, Galaxies, and Stars* (all 1997). (Rev: BL 9/15/97) [523]

Sun and the Seasons

18558 Bendick, Jeanne. *The Sun: Our Very Own Star* (2–4). Illus. by Mike Roffe. Series: Early Bird Astronomy. 1991, Millbrook LB $19.90 (1-878841-02-5). Astronomy is presented in simple terms and with colorful illustrations. (Rev: BL 9/1/91; SLJ 8/91) [523.4]

18559 Bourgeois, Paulette. *The Sun* (2–5). Illus. Series: Starting with Space. 1997, Kids Can $12.95 (1-55074-158-6). 40pp. As well as providing information about the sun, stars, and the seasons, this work contains folktales and projects. (Rev: BL 9/1/97; SLJ 9/97) [523.7]

18560 Branley, Franklyn M. *The Sun: Our Nearest Star* (1–3). Illus. by Don Madden. 1988, HarperCollins LB $14.89 (0-690-04678-2). 32pp. An easily read book about the sun and its importance in our lives. Update of 1962 edition.

18561 Branley, Franklyn M. *Sunshine Makes the Seasons* (3–4). Illus. by Giulio Maestro. 1988, HarperCollins paper $4.95 (0-06-445019-8). 32pp. A very simple account that explains the seasons by exploring the relationship of the sun to the earth and its orbit. Update of 1974 edition.

18562 Burton, Jane, and Kim Taylor. *The Nature and Science of Autumn* (3–6). Series: Exploring the Science of Nature. 1999, Gareth Stevens LB $15.95 (0-8368-2190-4). 32pp. This book explains the causes of autumn, its weather, and the animal and plant changes that occur during this season. A special activities section is included. Also use *The Nature and Science of Spring, The Nature and Science of Summer,* and *The Nature and Science of Winter* (all 1999). (Rev: BL 12/15/99; HBG 10/00) [525]

18563 Fowler, Allan. *How Do You Know It's Fall?* (1–2). Illus. Series: Rookie Readers. 1992, Children's LB $19.00 (0-516-04922-4). 32pp. For beginning readers, the season of autumn is introduced in many color photos and brief text. (Rev: BL 6/15/92) [508]

18564 Fowler, Allan. *How Do You Know It's Summer?* (1–2). Illus. Series: Rookie Readers. 1992, Children's LB $19.00 (0-516-04923-2). 32pp. Summer and its characteristics are introduced in many color illustrations and minimal text. (Rev: BL 6/15/92) [508]

18565 Fowler, Allan. *The Sun Is Always Shining Somewhere* (1–2). Illus. Series: Rookie Readers. 1991, Children's LB $19.00 (0-516-04906-2). 32pp. This simple introduction to astronomy tells about the sun and the earth's rotation around it. (Rev: BL 8/91) [523.7]

18566 George, Michael. *The Sun* (3–8). Illus. 1997, Child's World LB $17.95 (1-567-66385-0). 40pp. This account covers the structure and activity of the sun as well as its effects on the earth. (Rev: BL 12/15/91; SLJ 7/92) [523.7]

18567 Gibbons, Gail. *Sun Up, Sun Down* (1–3). Illus. by author. 1983, Harcourt $16.00 (0-15-282781-1); paper $6.00 (0-15-282782-X). 32pp. An introductory account of the sun and its effects on earth.

18568 Jackson, Ellen. *The Winter Solstice* (2–4). Illus. 1994, Millbrook LB $23.40 (1-56294-400-2). 32pp. The customs and beliefs surrounding the winter solstice are explored in many cultures, e.g., the ancient Britons, Romans, and Peruvians. (Rev: BL 2/15/94; SLJ 4/94) [394.2]

18569 Kerrod, Robin. *The Sun* (4–6). Series: Planet Library. 2000, Lerner LB $21.27 (0-8225-3901-2). 32pp. This work explains how the sun was formed, its role in the solar system, in the galaxy, and beyond, and what the future holds. (Rev: BL 10/15/00; HBG 3/01; SLJ 1/01) [523.7]

18570 Lassieur, Allison. *The Sun* (2–4). Series: True Books. 2000, Children's LB $22.00 (0-516-22002-0). 48pp. This book explains the functions of the sun, its composition, and its importance in our lives. (Rev: BL 10/15/00) [523.7]

18571 Markle, Sandra. *Exploring Winter* (3–6). Illus. by author. 1984, Avon paper $2.99 (0-380-71321-7). 160pp. Science and recreation are mixed in this book about winter and activities that are associated with it.

18572 Simon, Seymour. *Spring Across America* (3–5). Illus. 1996, Hyperion LB $16.49 (0-7868-2056-X). 32pp. A book about spring as it develops in various sections of our country. A sequel to *Autumn Across America* (1993) and *Winter Across America* (1994). (Rev: BL 3/1/96; SLJ 4/96) [508.73]

18573 Simon, Seymour. *The Sun* (3–5). Illus. 1986, Morrow paper $5.95 (0-688-09236-5). 32pp. A look at the structure and atmosphere of this "middle-size" star. (Rev: BCCB 10/86; BL 9/1/86; SLJ 12/86)

18574 Vogt, Gregory L. *The Sun* (2–4). Illus. Series: Gateway Solar System. 1996, Millbrook LB $19.90 (1-56294-600-5). 32pp. An introduction to the star of our solar system and its life-sustaining force. (Rev: BL 4/15/96; SLJ 7/96) [523.7]

18575 *Why Do Seasons Change?* (PS–3). Illus. Series: Why. 1997, DK $9.95 (0-7894-1529-1). 24pp. Using a question-and-answer format, the rotation of the earth is explained and each season is described. (Rev: BL 8/97) [529]

Biological Sciences

General

18576 Arnosky, Jim. *Crinkleroot's Nature Almanac* (PS–3). Illus. 1999, Simon & Schuster $16.00 (0-689-80534-9). 64pp. A tour through the seasons, with nature lore, material on habitats, animal tracks, quizzes, and picture puzzles. (Rev: BL 9/1/99; HBG 3/00; SLJ 10/99) [508]

18577 Biesiot, Elizabeth. *Natural Treasures Field Guide for Kids* (3–6). Illus. 1996, Roberts Rinehart paper $12.95 (1-57098-082-9). 64pp. A paperback that explains the lives of wild animals by examining such evidence as paw prints, nests, and night sounds. (Rev: BL 9/1/96; SLJ 7/96) [591]

18578 Björk, Christina. *Linnea's Almanac* (3–5). Trans. by Joan Sandin. Illus. by Lena Anderson. 1989, R&S $13.00 (91-29-59176-7). 60pp. Twelve months of nature lore and activities. (Rev: BL 2/15/90; SLJ 4/90) [508]

18579 Brimner, Larry. *Unusual Friendships: Symbiosis in the Animal World* (4–6). Illus. 1993, Watts LB $22.50 (0-531-20106-6). 64pp. This book presents the various plant and animal relationships in nature in which the host, the guest, or both benefit. (Rev: BL 8/93) [591]

18580 Burnie, David. *How Nature Works* (3–8). Illus. 1991, Reader's Digest $24.00 (0-89577-391-0). 190pp. Well-organized science topics give young readers solid explanations at their fingertips. (Rev: BL 11/15/91*; SLJ 12/91*) [508]

18581 Burton, Jane, and Kim Taylor. *The Nature and Science of Survival* (3–6). Series: Exploring the Science of Nature. 2001, Gareth Stevens LB $21.27 (0-8368-2211-0). 32pp. This book, which contains a projects and activities section, shows how various animals and plants adapt and survive. (Rev: BL 3/15/01) [574]

18582 Busch, Phyllis S. *Backyard Safaris: 52 Year-Round Science Adventures* (4–6). Illus. 1995, Simon & Schuster $16.00 (0-689-80302-8). 142pp. Fifty-two activities that span the four seasons and involve simple nature study projects. (Rev: BL 8/95) [508]

18583 Doris, Ellen. *Woods, Ponds, and Fields* (4–7). Illus. Series: Real Kids Real Science. 1994, Thames & Hudson $16.95 (0-500-19006-2). 64pp. A book that gives background essays as well as step-by-step directions for nature study projects in all seasons. (Rev: BL 9/1/94) [508]

18584 Graham-Barber, Lynda. *Toad or Frog, Swamp or Bog? A Big Book of Nature's Confusables* (K–5). Illus. by Alec Gillman. 1994, Four Winds paper $16.00 (0-02-736931-5). 48pp. Twenty sets of common science misunderstandings (e.g., the difference between an alligator and a crocodile) are explained. (Rev: BL 8/94; SLJ 7/94) [508]

18585 Huber, Carey. *Nature Explorer: A Step-by-Step Guide* (3–6). Illus. 1990, Troll LB $15.85 (0-8167-1953-5); paper $3.95 (0-8167-1954-3). 64pp. Through walks and hikes, this book explains how one can become a student of nature. (Rev: SLJ 4/91) [574]

18586 Kalman, Bobbie, and Jacqueline Langille. *What Are Food Chains and Webs?* (3–5). Series: Science of Living Things. 1998, Crabtree LB $14.37 (0-86505-876-8); paper $5.36 (0-86505-888-1). 32pp. This book uses clear photographs, illustrations, charts, and short chapters to describe food chains and explain their various levels and types. A game is included to enhance the learning process. (Rev: SLJ 11/98) [574.5]

18587 Kalman, Bobbie, and Jacqueline Langille. *What Is a Life Cycle?* (3–5). Series: Science of Living Things. 1998, Crabtree LB $14.37 (0-86505-874-1); paper $5.36 (0-86505-886-5). 32pp. Using many visuals and a concise text, this book traces life cycles from birth to adulthood of a number of plants and animals, including humans. (Rev: SLJ 11/98) [508]

18588 Lang, Susan. *Nature in Your Backyard: Simple Activities for Children* (2–4). Illus. 1995, Millbrook LB $22.90 (1-56294-451-7). 48pp. Easy activities and experiments that illustrate the princi-

966

ples of science and nature using the backyard as a laboratory. (Rev: BL 5/1/95; SLJ 7/95) [508]

18589 Lang, Susan S., et al. *More Nature in Your Backyard: Simple Activities for Children* (2–4). Illus. 1998, Millbrook LB $22.90 (0-7613-0308-1). 48pp. Uses readily available materials to sharpen one's observational skills and learn more about insects, spiders, birds, plants, and spores. (Rev: BL 9/15/98; HBG 10/98; SLJ 8/98) [507.8]

18590 Lauber, Patricia. *Who Eats What? Food Chains and Food Webs* (K–3). Illus. by Holly Keller. Series: Let's-Read-and-Find-Out. 1995, HarperCollins LB $15.89 (0-06-022982-9); paper $4.95 (0-06-445130-5). 32pp. Food webs and chains as they exist both on land and in the water are explained, with such activities as how to create a food chain for everyday foods like milk. (Rev: BCCB 5/95; BL 5/1/95) [574.5]

18591 Leslie, Clare W. *Nature All Year Long* (2–5). Illus. 1991, Greenwillow $18.00 (0-688-09183-0). 56pp. Describing the plant and animal life in one habitat during the year. (Rev: BCCB 9/91; BL 12/15/91; SLJ 12/91) [508]

18592 Lobb, Janice. *Dig and Sow! How Do Plants Grow? Experiments in the Backyard* (K–2). Illus. by Peter Utton and Ann Savage. Series: At Home with Science. 2000, Kingfisher $10.95 (0-7534-5245-6). 32pp. Plants and animals associated with backyards and ponds are introduced in easy, short chapters with activities and a final quiz. (Rev: HBG 3/01; SLJ 8/00) [574]

18593 Martin, Linda. *Watch Them Grow* (PS–1). Illus. 1994, DK $14.95 (1-56458-458-5). 45pp. This book chronicles the early development of plants, animals that hatch from eggs, and animals that are born alive. (Rev: BL 6/1–15/94; SLJ 8/94) [574]

18594 *Our Environment* (4–8). Series: Time-Life Student Library. 1999, Time Life $24.95 (0-7835-1358-5). 128pp. Using double-page spreads, this gives an overview of plants and animals that inhabit our planet, with material on such subjects as the food chain, symbiosis, and climate. (Rev: SLJ 5/00) [574]

18595 Quinlan, Susan. *The Case of the Mummified Pigs and Other Mysteries in Nature* (4–6). Illus. 1995, Boyds Mills $15.95 (1-878093-82-7). 128pp. Fourteen mysteries of science are explored, e.g., why the monarch butterfly is so brightly colored. (Rev: BCCB 3/95; BL 1/1/95; HB 5–6/95; SLJ 3/95) [508]

18596 Rockwell, Anne. *Growing Like Me* (PS–K). Illus. by Holly Keller. 2001, Harcourt $14.00 (0-15-202202-3). 24pp. This simple book about change and development in the plant and animal world shows an organism on one page and what it becomes on the next (e.g., a caterpillar and then a butterfly). (Rev: BL 3/1/01) [571.8]

18597 Russo, Monica. *Watching Nature: A Beginner's Field Guide* (3–6). Photos by Kevin Byron. 1998, Sterling $19.95 (0-8069-9515-7). 96pp. This is a splendid guide to nature watching, with material on identifying animals and plants, equipment to use, techniques to follow, and the best places for watching. (Rev: SLJ 12/98) [574]

18598 Schmid, Eleonore. *The Living Earth* (1–3). Illus. 1994, North-South LB $14.88 (1-55858-299-1). 26pp. An introduction to the varied flora and fauna found on the earth and below its surface. (Rev: BL 2/15/95; SLJ 12/94) [574.5]

18599 Silverstein, Alvin, and Virginia Silverstein. *Symbiosis* (5–9). Series: Science Concepts. 1998, Twenty-First Century LB $23.40 (0-7613-3001-1). 64pp. The concept of cooperation in nature for mutual benefit is explored, with explanations of various forms of symbiotic partnerships including the relationships humans have with animals, plants, fungi, and microorganisms. (Rev: HBG 3/99; SLJ 2/99) [574.5]

18600 Smith, Miranda. *Living Earth* (3–8). Illus. Series: Eyewitness Books. 1996, DK $29.95 (0-7894-0644-6). 192pp. All kinds of plants and animals are introduced, with material on how they adapt to various climatic and geographical conditions. (Rev: SLJ 10/96) [574]

Animal Life

General

18601 Aaseng, Nathan. *Poisonous Creatures* (4–7). Illus. Series: Scientific American Sourcebooks. 1997, Twenty-First Century $25.90 (0-8050-4690-9). 96pp. This book looks at a number of poisonous creatures, including mollusks, spiders, snakes, and insects, with many divisions into subspecies. (Rev: BL 2/1/98; SLJ 8/98) [591.6]

18602 Arnold, Caroline. *Australian Animals* (1–3). 2000, HarperCollins LB $15.89 (0-688-16767-5). 48pp. Seventeen Australian animals are introduced in four sections that represent individual biomes. (Rev: HBG 3/01; SLJ 10/00) [591]

18603 Arnold, Caroline. *South American Animals* (2–4). Illus. 1999, Morrow $16.00 (0-688-15564-2). 48pp. Double-page spreads introduce 17 South American creatures from forests, mountains, grasslands, and coastal areas. (Rev: BL 7/99; HBG 10/99; SLJ 9/99) [591.98]

18604 Arnold, Tim. *Natural History from A to Z: A Terrestrial Sampler* (4–6). Illus. 1991, Macmillan LB $15.95 (0-689-50467-5). 61pp. Discusses one scientific topic for each letter of the alphabet. (Rev: BL 10/1/91) [591]

18605 *Atlas of Animals* (PS–2). Illus. Series: First Discovery. 1996, Scholastic $12.95 (0-590-58280-1). 24pp. Using a highly visual approach, this short book discusses the animals found in the basic regions of the world. (Rev: BL 10/15/96) [591]

18606 Baillie, Marilyn. *Side by Side: Animals Who Help Each Other* (K–4). Illus. by Romi Caron. Series: Amazing Things Animals Do. 1997, Owl $17.95 (1-895688-56-6); paper $6.95 (1-895688-57-4). 32pp. A simple exploration of symbiotic relationships in nature, like the petrel bird that lives with the tuatara lizard to their mutual benefit. (Rev: BL 5/15/97; SLJ 7/97) [591.52]

18607 Bateman, Robert, and Rick Archbold. *Safari* (3–7). Illus. 1998, Little, Brown $17.95 (0-316-

08265-1). 32pp. Through the illustrations of nature artist Bateman, this book introduces and discusses such African animals as elephants, leopards, and gorillas. (Rev: BL 11/15/98; HBG 3/99; SLJ 10/98) [599]

18608 Bial, Raymond. *A Handful of Dirt* (3–5). Photos by author. 2000, Walker $16.95 (0-8027-8698-7). 32pp. This set of photographs with accompanying text examines life found underground from invertebrates to the mammals and reptiles that burrow into the earth. (Rev: BCCB 5/00; HBG 10/00; SLJ 4/00) [591]

18609 Bloyd, Sunni. *Animal Rights* (5–7). 1991, Lucent LB $22.45 (1-56006-114-6). 128pp. This book discusses animal rights, covering such areas as laboratory animals, farm creatures, hunting, and fur-bearing animals. (Rev: SLJ 8/91) [346]

18610 Bowen, Betsy. *Tracks in the Wild* (K–3). Illus. by author. 1998, Houghton $16.00 (0-395-92067-1). A beautifully illustrated book in which the author introduces the many animals from mice to moose that are found around her northern Minnesota home. (Rev: HBG 3/99; SLJ 10/98) [574]

18611 Burnie, David. *Mammals* (4–6). Illus. Series: Eyewitness Explorers. 1993, DK $9.95 (1-56458-228-0). 64pp. This book gives examples of various mammals and includes brief information on characteristics and habitats. (Rev: BL 3/1/93) [973.7]

18612 Cassie, Brian. *Say It Again* (1–3). Illus. by David Mooney. 2000, Charlesbridge LB $16.95 (0-88106-341-X); paper $6.95 (0-88106-342-8). This unusual animal book features, in picture and text, 12 creatures whose names involve a repetitive sound, such as a killy-killy and a caracara. (Rev: HBG 10/00; SLJ 3/00) [591]

18613 Chermayeff, Ivan. *Furry Facts* (PS–1). Illus. by author. 1994, Gulliver $10.95 (0-15-230425-8). A heavily illustrated introduction to a number of mammals, each of which is given a double-page spread. Also use *Fishy Facts* (1994). (Rev: SLJ 6/94) [591]

18614 Cobb, Allan B. *Super Science Projects About Animals and Their Habitats* (4–8). Series: Psyched for Science. 2000, Rosen Central $23.95 (0-8239-3175-7). 48pp. Six hand-on activities are introduced to help children observe animals and to study their adjustments to climate, habitat, and food. (Rev: SLJ 9/00) [591]

18615 Cohen, Daniel. *Phantom Animals* (4–5). 1993, Pocket paper $2.99 (0-671-75930-2). 111pp. A collection of true material about ghostly animals. (Rev: SLJ 7/91) [133]

18616 Creagh, Carson. *Things with Wings* (2–4). Illus. Series: Nature Company Young Discoveries. 1996, Time Life $10.00 (0-7835-4838-9). 32pp. A variety of creatures with wings are pictured in a series of double-page spreads. (Rev: BL 12/15/96; SLJ 12/96) [591]

18617 Davis, Lee. *The Lifesize Animal Opposites Book* (PS–K). Illus. 1994, DK $12.95 (1-56458-720-7). 32pp. Using large photos of animals, this nature book explores the concept of simple oppo-

sites, like big and little. (Rev: BL 12/1/94; SLJ 4/95) [591]

18618 Day, Trevor. *Youch!* (3–5). Illus. 2000, Simon & Schuster $16.00 (0-689-83416-0). 32pp. The "real-life monsters" that this book introduces in stunning photographs include poisonous frogs, snakes, and spiders; carnivorous fish; and stinging insects. (Rev: BL 11/1/00; HBG 3/01; SLJ 10/00) [591.6]

18619 *Do Bears Give Bear Hugs? First Questions and Answers About Animals* (PS–1). Series: Library of First Questions and Answers. 1994, Time Life $14.95 (0-7835-0870-0). 47pp. A fun book that explores some common questions about animals. (Rev: SLJ 8/94) [591]

18620 Elliott, Leslee. *Mind-Blowing Mammals* (3–6). Illus. Series: Amazing Animals. 1995, Sterling $12.95 (0-8069-1270-7); paper $9.95 (0-8069-1271-5). 64pp. Introduces some amazing mammals with full-color photos on each page. (Rev: SLJ 4/95) [591]

18621 Emory, Jerry. *Nightprowlers: Everyday Creatures Under Every Night Sky* (4–6). Illus. 1994, Harcourt paper $14.95 (0-15-200694-X). 48pp. After an explanation of the day/night cycle, there are sections on the phases of the moon, the senses of nighttime animals, and an introduction to such creatures as owls and bats. (Rev: BL 11/15/94) [591.5]

18622 Facklam, Howard, and Margery Facklam. *Parasites* (4–7). Illus. Series: Invaders. 1994, Twenty-First Century LB $21.90 (0-8050-2858-7). 64pp. Various kinds of parasites, like leeches and tapeworms, are highlighted. (Rev: BL 1/1/95; SLJ 3/95) [574.5]

18623 Fleisher, Paul. *Life Cycles of a Dozen Diverse Creatures* (4–8). Illus. 1996, Millbrook LB $24.90 (0 7613-0000-7). 80pp. The life cycles of 12 animals — including the oyster, honeybee, penguin, butterfly, and sea horse — are covered, with many color illustrations. (Rev: BL 12/1/96*; SLJ 1/97) [591.3]

18624 Fowler, Allan. *Animals Under the Ground* (1–3). Series: Rookie Readers. 1997, Children's $19.00 (0-516-20427-0). 32pp. An easy-to-read science book that introduces basic material about such animals as moles. (Rev: BL 12/15/97; HBG 3/98) [591]

18625 Ganeri, Anita. *The Hunt for Food* (1–5). Illus. Series: Life Cycle. 1997, Millbrook LB $21.40 (0-7613-0304-9). 32pp. This book deals with animals in a meadow and their feeding habits throughout the four seasons. (Rev: BL 12/1/97; HBG 3/98; SLJ 1/98) [577.4]

18626 George, Jean Craighead. *Morning, Noon, and Night* (PS–3). Illus. by Wendell Minor. 1999, HarperCollins LB $15.89 (0-06-023629-9). 32pp. An easy reader about a full day from Maine to California and the activities of such animals as antelopes, lizards, and cardinals. (Rev: HBG 10/99; SLJ 4/99) [591]

18627 Goodman, Susan E. *Animal Rescue: The Best Job There Is* (2–4). Series: Ready-to-Read. 2000, Simon & Schuster $15.00 (0-689-81794-0). 48pp.

This book about John Walsh of the World Society for the Protection of Animals tells about three of his animal rescue missions around the world in an easy-to-read format. (Rev: HBG 10/00; SLJ 3/00) [591]

18628 Guiberson, Brenda Z. *Exotic Species: Invaders in Paradise* (4–6). Illus. 1999, Twenty-First Century LB $23.90 (0-7613-1319-2). 80pp. Using examples including starlings, kudzu, and zebra mussels, this account reveals the disastrous results that occur when a foreign species is introduced into a different ecosystem. (Rev: BL 7/99; HBG 3/00; SLJ 9/99) [577]

18629 Gunzl, Christiane. *Cave Life* (3–6). Illus. by Frank Greenaway. Series: Look Closer. 1993, DK $9.95 (1-56458-212-4). 32pp. Animal and plant life in caves are introduced with stunning double-page spreads. (Rev: BL 8/93; SLJ 8/93) [574]

18630 Halfmann, Janet. *Life in a Garden* (5–7). Photos by David Liebman. 2000, Creative Co. LB $15.95 (1-58341-072-4). This book explores such life forms found in a garden as fungi, beetles, slugs, snails, and aphids. (Rev: SLJ 8/00) [635]

18631 Halliburton, Warren J. *African Wildlife* (4–6). Illus. Series: Africa Today. 1992, Macmillan LB $13.95 (0-89686-674-2). 48pp. Color photos complement this look at four areas — savanna, forest, wetlands, and desert — of wildlife habitat in Africa. (Rev: BL 3/1/93) [591]

18632 Hanly, Sheila. *The Big Book of Animals* (PS–2). Illus. 1997, DK $14.95 (0-7894-1485-6). 48pp. In a book arranged by habitat, more than 300 familiar or little-known animals are introduced and pictured. (Rev: BL 7/97; HBG 3/98) [590]

18633 Hanna, Jack, and Rick A. Prebeg. *Jungle Jack Hanna's Safari Adventure* (3–5). Illus. 1996, Scholastic $12.95 (0-590-67322-X). 44pp. The animals of Kenya and Uganda are introduced in this handsomely illustrated account. (Rev: BL 10/15/96; SLJ 11/96) [591.96]

18634 Heller, Ruth. *"Galápagos" Means "Tortoises."* (3–5). Illus. by author. 2000, Sierra Club $14.95 (0-87156-917-5). 41pp. The animals and birds of the Galapagos Islands are described in this book of rhymes and accompanying realistic paintings. (Rev: SLJ 3/01) [985]

18635 Himmelman, John. *A Pill Bug's Life* (K–2). Illus. by author. Series: Nature Upclose. 1999, Children's LB $24.00 (0-516-21165-X). The life cycle of a pill bug (actually a crustacean) is covered in a simple text and amazing close-up paintings. (Rev: SLJ 3/00) [632]

18636 Hodgkins, Fran. *Animals Among Us: Living with Suburban Wildlife* (5–8). Illus. 2000, Linnet $19.50 (0-208-02478-6). 116pp. This book discusses the behavior and lifestyles of animals such as deer, coyotes, bears, skunks, and bats that live in suburbs, close to their original haunts. (Rev: BL 6/1–15/00; HB 7–8/00; HBG 10/00) [591.7]

18637 Jackson, Donna M. *The Wildlife Detectives: How Forensic Scientists Fight Crimes Against Nature* (3–7). Illus. 2000, Houghton $16.00 (0-395-86976-5). 48pp. This book introduces the forensic scientists who track down criminals who harm wild

animals. (Rev: BL 4/1/00; HBG 10/00; SLJ 7/00) [363.28]

18638 James, Barbara. *Animal Rights* (5–10). Series: Talking Points. 1999, Raintree Steck-Vaughn $27.11 (0-8172-5317-3). 64pp. Various aspects of the animal rights controversy are explored in an objective, straightforward manner. (Rev: BL 8/99) [179.3]

18639 Jenkins, Martin. *Wings, Stings and Wriggly Things* (3–5). Illus. Series: SuperSmarts. 1996, Candlewick $11.99 (0-7636-0036-9). 24pp. Double-page spreads are used to introduce such creatures as butterflies, worms, bees, and snails. (Rev: BL 12/1/96; SLJ 2/97) [595.7]

18640 Jenkins, Steve. *Biggest, Strongest, Fastest* (PS–3). Illus. 1995, Ticknor $14.95 (0-395-69701-8). 32pp. Double-page collages illustrate some of the animal kingdom's record holders. (Rev: BCCB 6/95; BL 2/1/95*; HB 7–8/95; SLJ 5/95*) [591]

18641 Kitchen, Bert. *When Hunger Calls* (2–4). Illus. 1994, Candlewick $15.95 (1-56402-316-8). 32pp. The eating habits of 12 creatures, including a vulture and a gazelle-eating python. (Rev: BL 9/1/94; SLJ 12/94) [591.5]

18642 Kite, L. Patricia. *Blood-Feeding Bugs and Beasts* (4–6). Illus. 1996, Millbrook LB $21.90 (1-56294-599-8). 48pp. Fifteen bloodsuckers are described, including mosquitoes, bed bugs, lice, ticks, assassin bugs, vampire moths, tsetse flies, and bats. (Rev: SLJ 6/96) [591]

18643 Knapp, Ron. *Bloodsuckers* (3–6). Illus. Series: Weird and Wacky Science. 1996, Enslow LB $18.95 (0-89490-614-3). 48pp. An interesting look at such creatures as vampire bats, leeches, fleas, lice, mosquitoes, and lampreys. (Rev: SLJ 6/96) [591]

18644 Kneidel, Sally. *Slugs, Bugs, and Salamanders: Discovering Animals in Your Garden* (5–7). Illus. by Anna-Maria L. Crum. 1997, Fulcrum paper $15.95 (1-55591-313-X). 120pp. As well as introducing backyard insects and other small creatures, this account gives a number of tips on growing healthy flowers and vegetables. (Rev: SLJ 10/97) [595.7]

18645 Krupinski, Loretta. *Into the Woods: A Woodland Scrapbook* (PS–2). Illus. by author. 1997, HarperCollins LB $15.89 (0-06-026444-6). 31pp. Using a scrapbook approach, this charming picture book introduces the flora and fauna of a forest, retells three American Indian legends, and has a section on weather. (Rev: SLJ 5/97) [591]

18646 Lauber, Patricia. *Fur, Feathers, and Flippers: How Animals Live Where They Do* (4–8). Illus. 1994, Scholastic paper $4.95 (0-590-45072-7). 48pp. Using various habitats such as the grasslands of East Africa as examples, this photo-essay describes how animals have adapted to their different environments. (Rev: BL 12/1/94*; SLJ 12/94) [591.5]

18647 Lesinski, Jeanne M. *Exotic Invaders: Killer Bees, Fire Ants, and Other Alien Species Are Infesting America!* (4–6). Illus. 1996, Walker LB $17.85 (0-8027-8391-0). 49pp. In separate chapters, five pests — sea lampreys, fire ants, zebra mussels, starlings, and African honeybees — are featured, with a description of the harm they do. (Rev: SLJ 5/96) [591]

18648 Maynard, Christopher. *Micromonsters: Life Under the Microscope* (3–5). Illus. Series: Eyewitness Reader. 1999, DK LB $12.95 (0-7894-4757-6); paper $3.95 (0-7894-4756-8). 48pp. Tapeworms, fleas, and lice are among the monsters introduced in this book illustrated with magnifications of microscope photographs. (Rev: BL 12/15/99; HBG 3/00) [595]

18649 Moser, Madeline. *Ever Heard of an Aardwolf? A Miscellany of Uncommon Animals* (K–3). Illus. by Barry Moser. 1996, Harcourt $16.00 (0-15-200474-2). 40pp. Unusual animals are introduced in a picture-book format. (Rev: BL 9/15/96; SLJ 10/96) [599]

18650 Most, Bernard. *Catbirds and Dogfish* (1–3). Illus. 1995, Harcourt $13.00 (0-15-292844-8); paper $6.00 (0-15-200779-2). 32pp. Animals named after other animals, such as the dogfish, are the subject of this nature book. (Rev: BL 4/1/95; SLJ 7/95) [591]

18651 Palazzo, Tony. *The Biggest and the Littlest Animals* (4–7). Illus. by author. 1973, Lion LB $13.95 (0-87460-225-4). 40pp. Many ways of comparing animals, including size and mobility, are explored.

18652 Paul, Tessa. *In Fields and Meadows* (2–5). Illus. Series: Animal Trackers. 1997, Crabtree LB $20.60 (0-86505-585-8); paper $7.95 (0-86505-593-9). 32pp. Using evidence like footprints, teeth marks, holes, nests, and hair or fur, about a dozen creatures that live in fields and meadows are described. (Rev: HBG 3/98; SLJ 10/97) [591]

18653 Pearce, Q. L. *Piranhas and Other Wonders of the Jungle* (3–6). Illus. by Mary Ann Fraser. Series: Amazing Science. 1990, Simon & Schuster paper $5.95 (0-671-70690-X). 64pp. Sketches of animals found in the jungle, such as driver ants and vampire bats. (Rev: SLJ 2/91) [591]

18654 Perham, Molly, and Julian Rowe. *Wildlife* (4–6). Illus. Series: Mapworlds. 1997, Watts LB $20.00 (0-531-14388-0). 32pp. Using an atlaslike format, this work shows where a variety of animals, birds, and insects are found in the world, with details on their habits and habitats. (Rev: BL 4/15/97) [591.9]

18655 Pope, Joyce. *Living Fossils: Animals Unchanged by Time* (3–6). Illus. by Stella Stilwell and Helen Ward. Series: Curious Creatures. 1992, Raintree Steck-Vaughn LB $5.00 (0-8114-3151-7). 46pp. Many examples of animals that exist in prehistoric form, from dragonflies to horseshoe crabs, are explored in this volume. A companion volume is *Two Lives: Metamorphosis in the Natural World* (1992). (Rev: SLJ 5/92) [591]

18656 Powell, Jillian. *Animal Rights* (2–3). Series: Talking About. 1999, Raintree Steck-Vaughn LB $15.98 (0-7398-1374-9). 32pp. This simple account shows how society's use of animals can conflict with the animals' needs and how this dilemma can be tackled. (Rev: BL 2/15/00; HBG 10/00) [346]

18657 Presnall, Judith J. *Animals That Glow* (5–7). Illus. Series: First Books. 1993, Watts LB $22.50 (0-531-20071-X). 64pp. From fireflies to tiny sea creatures, this book covers the amazing phenomenon of bioluminescence. (Rev: BL 5/15/93; SLJ 6/93) [591]

18658 Pringle, Laurence. *Animal Monsters: The Truth About Scary Creatures* (4–6). Illus. 1997, Marshall Cavendish $15.95 (0-7614-5003-3). 64pp. The truth about such feared animals as alligators, killer bees, and tarantulas — and why they are not as dangerous as many believe. (Rev: BL 9/1/97; HBG 3/98; SLJ 10/97) [591]

18659 Renne. *Animal Males and Females* (1–3). Trans. by Alison Taurel. Illus. by author. 2000, Gareth Stevens LB $21.27 (0-8368-2712-0). 38pp. Using stunning photographs, the differences between the males and females of a species are vividly presented. (Rev: SLJ 2/01) [591]

18660 Rochford, Dierdre. *Rights for Animals?* (4–8). Illus. Series: Viewpoints. 1997, Watts LB $22.50 (0-531-14414-3). 32pp. After a discussion of the many uses of animals today, this account focuses on their role in cosmetic and pharmaceutical testing, blood sports, and hunting, with additional material on endangered animals and zoos. (Rev: SLJ 5/97) [179.3]

18661 Roop, Connie, and Peter Roop. *Walk on the Wild Side!* (4–8). Illus. by Anne Canevari Green. 1997, Millbrook LB $21.40 (0-7613-0021-X). 40pp. Short introductions to 14 animals and their habitats, complete with jokes, riddles, and humorous illustrations. (Rev: SLJ 6/97) [591]

18662 Ross, Michael E. *Rolypolyology* (4–6). Illus. Series: Backyard Creatures. 1996, Carolrhoda LB $19.95 (0-87614-862-3). 48pp. Several common backyard creatures and their habits are described with interesting accompanying activities. (Rev: BL 3/15/96; SLJ 7/96) [595.3]

18663 Ruiz, Andres L. *Metamorphosis* (3–5). Illus. by Francisco Arredondo. Series: Cycles of Life. 1997, Sterling $12.95 (0-8069-9325-1). 32pp. In double-page spreads, explains how some creatures transform themselves into another life form, such as tadpoles becoming frogs. (Rev: SLJ 6/97) [591]

18664 Sateren, Shelley Swanson. *The Humane Societies: A Voice for the Animals* (4–6). Illus. 1996, Silver Burdett LB $14.95 (0-87518-622-X); paper $7.95 (0-382-39309-0). 80pp. Introduces animal rights groups and humane societies and the work they do, including prevention of cruelty to animals and ways of controlling pet populations. (Rev: SLJ 11/96) [179.3]

18665 Sayre, April Pulley. *Put On Some Antlers and Walk Like a Moose* (4–6). Illus. 1997, Twenty-First Century $20.40 (0-8050-5182-1). 80pp. Outlines the many techniques of observation used by scientists to study animals. (Rev: BL 12/1/97; SLJ 2/98*) [590]

18666 Schubert, Ingrid, and Dieter Schubert. *Amazing Animals* (1–3). Trans. from Dutch by Leigh Sauerwein. 1995, Front Street $15.95 (1-886910-05-7). Using catchy rhymes and pleasant illustrations, this book shows how common animals live, reproduce, and deal with danger. (Rev: SLJ 1/96) [591]

18667 Shedd, Warner. *The Kids' Wildlife Book: Exploring Animal Worlds Through Indoor/Outdoor Experiences* (2–6). Illus. by Loretta Braren. Series: Kids Can! 1994, Williamson paper $12.95 (0-913589-77-2). 156pp. This book of projects and experiments features common mammals, amphibians, and birds of Canada and the United States. (Rev: SLJ 8/94) [591]

18668 Silver, Donald M. *Extinction Is Forever* (2–3). Illus. by Patricia J. Wynne. 1995, Simon & Schuster $19.95 (0-671-86769-5); paper $7.95 (0-671-86770-9). 48pp. Beginning with the end of dinosaurs during the Ice Ages and ending with the present, this account traces the reasons why various species have become extinct. (Rev: SLJ 2/96) [575.7]

18669 Silverstein, Alvin, et al. *Vertebrates* (3–6). Illus. Series: Kingdoms of Life. 1996, Twenty-First Century LB $21.40 (0-8050-3517-6). 64pp. Vertebrates — animals with enclosed spinal cords — are introduced, with many color photos. (Rev: BL 6/1–15/96) [596]

18670 Simon, Seymour. *Animals Nobody Loves* (4–6). Illus. 2001, North-South $15.95 (1-58717-079-5). 48pp. Profiles 20 animals, including the vulture, rat, shark, hyena, and wasp. (Rev: BL 3/1/01) [591.6]

18671 Simon, Seymour. *Ride the Wind: Airborne Journeys of Animals and Plants* (3–5). Illus. by Elsa Warnick. 1997, Harcourt $15.00 (0-15-292887-1). 40pp. Highlights nature's air travelers, including the Arctic tern, albatross, snow goose, monarch butterfly, and various seeds. (Rev: BL 4/1/97; SLJ 5/97) [591.52]

18672 Singer, Marilyn. *A Wasp Is Not a Bee* (2–4). Illus. by Patrick O'Brien. 1995, Holt $15.95 (0-8050-2820-X). 32pp. This book distinguishes between 14 seemingly similar pairs of animals, like a bat and a bird, and a crocodile and an alligator. (Rev: BL 10/15/95; SLJ 1/96) [595]

18673 Squire, Ann. *101 Questions and Answers About Backyard Wildlife* (3–6). Illus. 1996, Walker LB $16.85 (0-8027-8458-5). 128pp. Birds, bats, and snails are three common creatures explored in a question-and-answer format. (Rev: BL 12/1/96; SLJ 1/97) [591]

18674 Steele, Philip. *Vampire Bats and Other Creatures of the Night* (3–5). Illus. Series: Young Observer. 1995, Kingfisher paper $7.95 (1-85697-575-4). 40pp. An overview of nocturnal animal life that also explains why these creatures live by a reversed time schedule. (Rev: SLJ 1/96) [591]

18675 Stewart, Melissa. *Life Without Light* (5–8). Illus. 1999, Watts LB $24.00 (0-531-11529-1). 128pp. This book explores the world of nature that exists without sun, including creatures discovered during research on hydrothermal vents, caves, aquifers, and rocks. (Rev: BL 7/99) [577]

18676 Whyman, Kate. *The Animal Kingdom* (5–8). Illus. 1999, Raintree Steck-Vaughn LB $25.69 (0-8172-5885-X). 48pp. A valuable account that intro-

duces animal classification basics through text, sidebars, diagrams, and many eye-catching color photographs. (Rev: BL 2/1/00) [596]

18677 Woods, Geraldine. *Animal Experimentation and Testing: A Pro/Con Issue* (5–8). Series: Hot Issues. 1999, Enslow LB $19.95 (0-7660-1191-7). 64pp. The controversial subject of using animals in experiments is discussed with a history of the problem, arguments for and against, and a summary of important actions taken by government and individual groups. (Rev: HBG 3/00; SLJ 3/00) [179.3]

Amphibians and Reptiles

GENERAL AND MISCELLANEOUS

18678 Behler, John L. *National Audubon Society First Field Guide: Reptiles* (4–6). Series: First Field Guide. 1999, National Audubon Society paper $11.95 (0-590-05487-2). 16pp. This field guide first discusses the nature of reptiles and then introduces, in color pictures and text, the most common ones found in North America. (Rev: BL 3/15/99; SLJ 7/99) [597.9]

18679 Brenner, Barbara, and Bernice Chardiet. *Where's That Reptile?* (2–4). Illus. Series: Hide and Seek. 1993, Scholastic $10.95 (0-590-45212-6). 32pp. An interactive book that introduces a variety of reptiles to primary-age children. (Rev: BL 10/15/93; SLJ 1/94) [597.9]

18680 Burns, Diane L. *Frogs, Toads and Turtles* (3–6). Illus. 1997, NorthWord paper $6.95 (1-55971-593-6). 48pp. A paperback field guide that introduces the world of 30 amphibians, with coverage of their habitats, food, and appearance. (Rev: BL 8/97) [597.8]

18681 Cassie, Brian. *National Audubon Society First Field Guide: Amphibians* (4–6). Series: First Field Guide. 1999, Scholastic $17.95 (0-590-63982-X); paper $11.95 (0-590-64008-9). 160pp. This field guide, with more than 450 full-color illustrations, introduces 50 easily found amphibians, with material on their characteristics and habitats. (Rev: BL 10/15/99) [597.5]

18682 Chermayeff, Ivan. *Scaly Facts* (PS–1). Illus. 1995, Harcourt $11.00 (0-15-200109-3). 32pp. Reptiles are introduced through brief, simple text and dynamic illustrations. (Rev: BL 4/1/95; SLJ 7/95) [597.9]

18683 Creagh, Carson, ed. *Reptiles* (4–6). Illus. Series: Nature Company Discoveries. 1996, Time Life $16.00 (0-8094-9247-4). 64pp. The world of reptiles is introduced with many colorful illustrations, brief text, and a special foldout section. (Rev: BL 6/1–15/96) [597.96]

18684 Fridell, Ron. *Amphibians in Danger: A Worldwide Warning* (5–9). 1999, Watts LB $22.50 (0-531-11373-5). 96pp. This book identifies the amphibians that are in danger, explains the reasons why, and outlines various efforts to save them. (Rev: SLJ 8/99) [597.9]

18685 Gove, Doris. *Red-Spotted Newt* (3–6). Illus. by Beverly Duncan. 1994, Atheneum $14.95 (0-689-31697-6). 28pp. Using effective watercolor illustrations, this book portrays the life cycle of a red-spotted newt from egg to embryo, larva, eft, and finally to an adult ready to lay her own eggs. (Rev: BL 12/1/94; SLJ 12/94) [597.5]

18686 Kalman, Bobbie, and Jacqueline Langille. *What Is an Amphibian?* (2–5). Series: Science of Living Things. 1999, Crabtree LB $14.97 (0-86505-934-9); paper $5.36 (0-86505-952-7). 32pp. Amphibians and their general characteristics, habits, and habitats are covered plus material on some specific members of the group in this lavishly illustrated book. (Rev: SLJ 3/00) [597.8]

18687 Lamprell, Klay. *Scaly Things* (2–4). Illus. Series: Nature Company Young Discoveries. 1996, Time Life $10.00 (0-7835-4842-7). 32pp. A pictorially beautiful introduction to creatures whose exteriors are scaly. (Rev: BL 12/15/96) [597.9]

18688 Maruska, Edward J. *Salamanders* (3–5). Illus. Series: Naturebooks. 1996, Child's World LB $22.79 (1-56766-273-0). 32pp. Salamanders are introduced in a series of full-page color photos that face each page of text. (Rev: BL 12/15/96) [597.6]

18689 Miller, Sara S. *Salamanders: Secret Silent Lives* (3–5). Series: Animals in Order. 1999, Watts LB $23.00 (0-531-11568-2). 48pp. This book discusses the amphibian class known as salamanders and gives a pictorial glimpse into their types, lives, structure, habits, and homes. (Rev: BL 12/15/99; HBG 3/00) [597.6]

18690 Miller, Sara S. *Snakes and Lizards: What They Have in Common* (3–5). Series: Animals in Order. 2000, Watts LB $23.00 (0-531-16448-9). 48pp. A brief introduction to animal classification is followed by a description of reptiles, with many examples in text and pictures. (Rev: BL 4/15/00) [597.9]

18691 Pipe, Jim. *The Giant Book of Snakes and Slithery Creatures* (3–8). Illus. 1998, Millbrook LB $25.90 (0-7613-0804-0). 32pp. This richly illustrated, oversize volume contains details about snakes, lizards, and amphibians. (Rev: BL 8/98; HBG 10/98; SLJ 12/98) [597.9]

18692 Savage, Stephen. *Amphibians* (2–4). Series: What's the Difference. 2000, Raintree Steck-Vaughn LB $25.69 (0-7398-1359-5). 32pp. This book introduces a number of amphibians that live on water, land, or both. (Rev: BL 10/15/00; HBG 3/01) [597.6]

18693 Savage, Stephen. *Reptiles* (2–4). Series: What's the Difference. 2000, Raintree Steck-Vaughn LB $25.69 (0-7398-1358-7). 32pp. This book explores the similarities and differences in the class known as reptiles and introduces such creatures as crocodiles, rattlesnakes, and tortoises. (Rev: BL 10/15/00; HBG 3/01; SLJ 1/01) [597.96]

18694 Sill, Cathryn. *About Reptiles: A Guide for Children* (PS–2). Illus. by John Sill. 1999, Peachtree $14.95 (1-56145-183-5). 40pp. This introduction to reptiles in general and snakes in particular is aimed at young children and has a colorful, realistic painting on one page followed by brief text on the facing page. (Rev: BL 6/1–15/99; HBG 10/99; SLJ 7/99) [597.9]

18695 Souza, D. M. *Shy Salamanders* (3–5). Illus. Series: Creatures All Around Us. 1995, Carolrhoda LB $22.60 (0-87614-826-7). 40pp. The life cycle of the salamander and its structure, food, and habitats are topics covered with beautiful illustrations. (Rev: BL 4/15/95; SLJ 9/95) [597.6]

18696 Theodorou, Rod. *Amphibians* (2–4). Series: Animal Babies. 1999, Heinemann LB $14.95 (1-57572-950-4). 32pp. The babies of about half a dozen species of amphibians are presented, with material on their anatomy, life cycles, and habits. (Rev: SLJ 4/00) [597.6]

18697 Winner, Cherie. *Salamanders* (3–6). Illus. Series: Nature Watch. 1993, Carolrhoda LB $23.93 (0-87614-757-0). 48pp. Various kinds of salamanders are introduced, with material given on life cycle, habits, and endangered status. (Rev: BL 8/93) [597.6]

ALLIGATORS AND CROCODILES

18698 Bare, Colleen S. *Never Kiss an Alligator!* (2–4). Illus. 1994, Puffin paper $4.99 (0-140-55257-X). 32pp. Sharp color photos highlight this close-up look at the alligator. (Rev: BCCB 9/89; BL 9/1/89; SLJ 8/89) [597.98]

18699 Clarke, Ginjer L. *Baby Alligator* (1–3). Illus. by Neecy Twinem. 2000, Putnam $13.89 (0-448-41851-7); paper $3.99 (0-448-42095-3). 48pp. For beginning readers, this is a simple introduction to alligators that traces the life cycle from hatching from an egg in the spring to waiting out the winter in a dark tunnel. (Rev: BL 7/00; HBG 10/00) [597.98]

18700 Deeble, Mark, and Victoria Stone. *The Crocodile Family Book* (2–5). Illus. Series: Animal Families. 1994, North-South LB $16.88 (1-55858-264-9). 50pp. Crocodiles from the Serengeti National Park are featured in this superbly illustrated book that describes their life, anatomy, and hunting methods. (Rev: BL 11/15/94; SLJ 11/94) [597.98]

18701 Dow, Lesley. *Alligators and Crocodiles* (5–8). Illus. 1990, Facts on File $17.95 (0-8160-2273-9). 68pp. This oversize book illustrates various species of alligators and crocodiles. (Rev: BL 11/15/90; SLJ 5/91) [598.98]

18702 Fitzgerald, Patrick J. *Croc and Gator Attacks* (4–7). Series: Animal Attack! 2000, Children's LB $19.00 (0-516-23314-9); paper $6.95 (0-516-23514-1). 48pp. Aimed at the reluctant reader, this book tells true stories of attacks by crocodiles and alligators and gives information about these species and their behavior. (Rev: SLJ 2/01) [597.98]

18703 Jango-Cohen, Judith. *Crocodiles* (5–8). Series: AnimalWays. 2000, Marshall Cavendish LB $19.95 (0-7614-1136-4). 112pp. This book examines the habitat, range, classification, evolution, anatomy, behavior, and endangered status of the crocodile. (Rev: BL 1/1–15/01; HBG 3/01) [597.98]

18704 Markle, Sandra. *Outside and Inside Alligators* (2–5). Illus. 1998, Simon & Schuster $16.00 (0-689-81457-7). 40pp. Discusses the alligator's anatomy, habits, and habitats. (Rev: BL 12/1/98; HBG 3/99; SLJ 11/98) [597.98]

18705 Muñoz, William. *Waiting Alligators* (PS–2). Series: Pull Ahead Books. 1999, Lerner LB $15.95 (0-8225-3615-3). 32pp. Using interactive material, this simple science book introduces alligators and includes many photos, a map, a body diagram, glossary, and index. (Rev: BL 8/99; HBG 10/99) [597.98]

18706 Patent, Dorothy Hinshaw. *The American Alligator* (4–6). Photos by William Munoz. 1994, Clarion $15.95 (0-395-63392-3). 77pp. Generous use of color photos enhances this book on the life cycle of the alligator. (Rev: BL 12/15/94) [597.98]

18707 Perry, Phyllis J. *The Crocodilians: Reminders of the Age of Dinosaurs* (4–6). Illus. Series: First Books. 1997, Watts LB $22.50 (0-531-20254-2). 64pp. Although the dinosaurs are gone, their descendants — the alligator, gavial, caiman, and crocodile — are still here, and this book describes them and how they live. (Rev: BL 8/97; SLJ 8/97) [597.98]

18708 Robinson, Claire. *Crocodiles* (2–3). Illus. Series: In the Wild. 1997, Heinemann $19.92 (1-57572-133-3). 24pp. A simple introduction to crocodiles that tells how they live, communicate, find food, and raise their young. (Rev: BL 2/1/98; SLJ 4/98) [597.98]

18709 Simon, Seymour. *Crocodiles and Alligators* (3–6). Illus. 1999, HarperCollins LB $15.89 (0-06-027474-3). 32pp. Basic information about alligators and crocodiles is given, including their history, differences, habitats, food, reproduction, and endangered status. (Rev: BL 4/1/99; HBG 10/99; SLJ 6/99) [597.98]

18710 Souza, D. M. *Roaring Reptiles: A Book About Crocodilians* (3–5). Illus. Series: Creatures All Around Us. 1992, Carolrhoda LB $19.95 (0-87614-710-4). 40pp. Close-up photographs and lively text introduce the types of crocodilians found in North America. (Rev: BL 10/1/92; SLJ 12/92) [597.98]

18711 Staub, Frank. *Alligators* (2–4). Photos by author. Illus. Series: Early Bird Nature Books. 1995, Lerner LB $22.60 (0-8225-3007-4). 48pp. Discusses the appearance and habits of alligators, as well as the role they play in their environment. (Rev: SLJ 8/95) [597.6]

18712 Stoops, Erik D., and Debbie L. Stone. *Alligators and Crocodiles* (4–7). Illus. 1995, Sterling $16.95 (0-8069-0422-4). 80pp. Using a question-and-answer format, this book introduces the structure and habits of many alligators and crocodiles. (Rev: BL 1/1/95; SLJ 3/95) [597.98]

FROGS AND TOADS

18713 Back, Christine. *Tadpole and Frog* (1–3). Illus. 1986, Silver Burdett LB $15.95 (0-382-09285-6); paper $3.95 (0-382-24021-9). 24pp. A basic science book in full color explaining the reproductive cycle of the frog. (Rev: BL 1/1/87)

18714 Berman, Ruth. *Climbing Tree Frogs* (PS–2). Series: Pull Ahead Books. 1998, Lerner LB $21.27 (0-8225-3605-6). 32pp. This unusual branch of the frog family is introduced with a series of thoughtful

questions, color photos, maps, and simple text. (Rev: BL 2/15/99; HBG 3/99; SLJ 6/99) [597.8]

18715 Brown, Ruth. *Toad* (PS–1). Illus. 1997, Dutton $15.99 (0-525-45757-7). 32pp. Pond life and a single toad's activities are introduced in this picture book with amazing watercolors. (Rev: BCCB 3/97; BL 1/1–15/97*; SLJ 3/97) [597.8]

18716 Chinery, Michael. *Frog* (3–5). Illus. by Martin Camm. Series: Life Story. 1990, Troll LB $17.25 (0-8167-2102-5); paper $4.95 (0-8167-2103-3). 32pp. The life cycle of the frog is revealed through detailed text, color photographs, and other illustrations. (Rev: BL 4/1/91) [597.8]

18717 Cowley, Joy. *Red-Eyed Tree Frog* (PS–K). Illus. by Nic Bishop. 1999, Scholastic $16.95 (0-590-87175-7). 32pp. In this stunning work, the feeding habits of several animals in a rain forest in Central America are described from a tree frog's point of view. (Rev: BCCB 3/99; BL 5/15/99*; HB 3–4/99; HBG 10/99; SLJ 3/99) [597.8]

18718 Delafosse, Claude. *Frogs* (PS–2). Illus. Series: First Discovery. 1997, Scholastic $12.95 (0-590-93782-0). 24pp. With a highly visual approach, this book introduces frogs using excellent drawings and a brief text. (Rev: BL 2/15/97) [597.8]

18719 Dell'Oro, Suzanne Paul. *Hiding Toads* (PS–2). Series: Pull Ahead Books. 1999, Lerner $21.27 (0-8225-3626-9); paper $6.95 (0-8225-3630-7). 32pp. Using questions and plenty of close-up photos to produce interest, this simple science book introduces the behavior and physical characteristics of toads and provides a map that shows where they live. (Rev: BL 12/15/99; HBG 3/00) [597.8]

18720 Dewey, Jennifer O. *Poison Dart Frogs* (K–3). Illus. 1998, Boyds Mills $15.95 (1-56397-655-2). This introduction to the many kinds of poison dart frogs of Latin American rain forests explains how they release a poison through their skin that is used by hunters on blowpipe darts. (Rev: BCCB 4/98; BL 3/1/98; HB 3–4/98; HBG 10/98; SLJ 4/98) [597.8]

18721 Fowler, Allan. *Frogs and Toads and Tadpoles Too!* (1–2). Illus. Series: Rookie Readers. 1992, Children's LB $19.00 (0-516-04925-9). 32pp. In minimal text and many color photos, the life cycle of frogs and toads is introduced. (Rev: BL 6/15/92) [597.8]

18722 Gibbons, Gail. *Frogs* (K–3). Illus. 1993, Holiday LB $16.95 (0-8234-1052-8). 32pp. Colorful water scenes and a simple text depict frogs in all stages of development from spawn to maturity. (Rev: BL 10/15/93; SLJ 12/93) [597.8]

18723 Glaser, Linda. *Fabulous Frogs* (PS–1). Illus. by Loretta Krupinski. 1999, Millbrook LB $21.90 (0-7613-0424-X). An enjoyable picture book that presents the life of a frog from mating to birth and growth, plus material on such varieties as the leopard frog, spring peeper, and bullfrog. (Rev: HBG 10/99; SLJ 5/99) [597.8]

18724 Greenberg, Dan. *Frogs* (5–8). Series: AnimalWays. 2000, Marshall Cavendish LB $19.95 (0-7614-1138-0). 112pp. As well as chapters devoted to the amazing variety of frogs, this book discusses their anatomy, habits, and survival skills. (Rev: BL 1/1–15/01; HBG 3/01) [597.8]

18725 Hawes, Judy. *Why Frogs Are Wet* (K–3). Illus. by Mary Ann Fraser. Series: Let's-Read-and-Find-Out. 2000, HarperCollins LB $15.89 (0-06-028162-6); paper $4.95 (0-06-445195-X). 40pp. The physical characteristics, life cycle, evolution, and behavior of frogs are introduced in this revision of the 1968 title. (Rev: BL 9/15/00; HBG 3/01) [597.8]

18726 Hickman, Pamela. *A New Frog: My First Look at the Life Cycle of an Amphibian* (PS–2). Illus. by Heather Collins. Series: My First Look At. 1999, Kids Can $6.95 (1-55074-615-4). 20pp. A beginning science book that explains the life cycle of a frog, using rhymes, factual text, and watercolor paintings. (Rev: BL 6/1–15/99; HBG 10/99; SLJ 8/99) [571.8]

18727 Himmelman, John. *A Wood Frog's Life* (K–2). Illus. Series: Nature Upclose. 1998, Children's LB $24.00 (0-516-21178-1). 32pp. Beginning with a frog laying its eggs, this illustrated book traces its life cycle until it, too, is able to produce eggs. (Rev: BL 12/1/98; HBG 3/99) [597]

18728 Johnson, Sylvia A. *Tree Frogs* (4–6). Illus. 1986, Lerner LB $22.60 (0-8225-1467-2). 48pp. A look at the characteristics, environment, breeding, and life cycles of the tree frog. (Rev: BL 10/1/86; SLJ 11/86)

18729 Mara, William P. *The Fragile Frog* (3–6). Illus. 1996, Albert Whitman LB $16.95 (0-8075-2580-4). 48pp. A description is given of the life cycle of this tiny frog, whose existence is now threatened. (Rev: BL 11/1/96; SLJ 11/96) [597.8]

18730 Merrick, Patrick. *Toads* (PS–3). Series: Naturebooks. 1999, Child's World LB $15.95 (1-56766-502-0). 32pp. More than a dozen full-page color photographs, with a few lines of simple text for each, introduce the toad, its life cycle, habitats, habits, and physical characteristics. (Rev: BL 6/1–15/99; HBG 10/99) [597.8]

18731 Miller, Sara S. *Frogs and Toads: The Leggy Leapers* (3–5). Series: Animals in Order. 2000, Watts LB $23.00 (0-531-11632-8). 48pp. A brief introduction to animal classification is followed by a description of frogs and toads, their similarities, differences, and life cycles. (Rev: BL 10/15/00) [597.8]

18732 Netherton, John. *Red-Eyed Tree Frogs* (2–3). Series: Early Bird Nature Books. 2000, Lerner LB $22.60 (0-8225-3037-6). 48pp. An introduction to these colorful rain forest amphibians — with their orange feet, lime green skin, blue stripes, and big red eyes. (Rev: BL 7/00; HBG 3/01) [597.8]

18733 Pascoe, Elaine. *Tadpoles* (3–6). Photos by Dwight Kuhn. Series: Nature Close-up. 1996, Blackbirch LB $18.95 (1-56711-179-3). 48pp. A frog book that concentrates on the growth and development of tadpoles, using excellent color photos. (Rev: SLJ 10/96) [597.8]

18734 Patent, Dorothy Hinshaw. *Flashy Fantastic Rain Forest Frogs* (K–3). Illus. by Kendahl J. Jubb. 1997, Walker $15.95 (0-8027-8615-4). 32pp. Rain

forest frogs, their characteristics, habits, and habitats are introduced in this attractive picture book. (Rev: BCCB 3/97; BL 2/1/97; SLJ 3/97) [597.8]

18735 Pfeffer, Wendy. *From Tadpole to Frog* (PS–1). Illus. by Holly Keller. Series: Let's-Read-and-Find-Out. 1994, HarperCollins paper $4.95 (0-06-445123-2). 32pp. This simple science book shows one year in the life cycle of a frog, beginning with the end of its hibernation in the spring. (Rev: BL 8/94; HB 7–8/94; SLJ 11/94) [597.8]

18736 Robinson, Fay. *Fantastic Frogs* (1–2). Illus. by Jean Cassels. Series: Hello Reader! 2000, Scholastic paper $3.99 (0-590-52269-8). 32pp. Different varieties of frogs like brown, green, and jungle frogs are introduced in this beginning reader with material on their looks and behavior. (Rev: BL 2/15/01) [597.8]

18737 Royston, Angela. *Life Cycle of a Frog* (2–3). Illus. Series: Life Cycle. 1998, Heinemann $13.95 (1-57572-613-0). 32pp. Using a color photograph and a continuing timeline on each page, the development of a frog is traced from egg to full-grown adult, who, in turn, produces eggs. (Rev: BL 4/15/98; SLJ 7/98) [597.8]

18738 Souza, D. M. *Frogs, Frogs Everywhere* (3–5). Illus. Series: Creatures All Around Us. 1995, Carolrhoda LB $22.60 (0-87614-825-9). 40pp. Physical and behavioral characteristics of frogs are attractively presented, along with various species and habitats. (Rev: BL 4/15/95; SLJ 9/95) [597.8]

18739 Starosta, Paul. *The Frog: Natural Acrobat* (3–6). Photos by author. Series: Animal Close-Ups. 1996, Charlesbridge paper $6.95 (0-88106-437-8). 27pp. A simple account with plenty of photos that tells about the various species, habitats, life cycles, and behavior of frogs. (Rev: SLJ 1/97) [597.8]

18740 Tagholm, Sally. *The Frog* (2–3). Illus. by Bert Kitchen. Series: Animal Lives. 2000, Kingfisher $9.95 (0-7534-5215-4). 32pp. After a series of pictures depicting the daily activities of a frog and its mating procedures, this account focuses on the development of an egg to adulthood. (Rev: BL 5/15/00; HBG 3/01; SLJ 8/00) [597.8]

18741 Wallace, Karen. *Tale of a Tadpole* (PS–2). Series: Eyewitness Reader. 1998, DK $3.95 (0-7894-3437-7); paper $12.95 (0-7894-3761-9). 32pp. The growth cycle of a frog from egg to mature adult is traced in a spare text with well-chosen photographs. (Rev: HBG 3/99; SLJ 4/99) [597.8]

18742 White, William. *All About the Frog* (4–8). Illus. 1992, Sterling $14.95 (0-8069-8274-8). 72pp. History, anatomy, reproduction, food, and other aspects of this amphibian are covered, with many illustrations. (Rev: BL 7/92) [597.8]

LIZARDS

18743 Darling, Kathy. *Chameleons: On Location* (3–6). Illus. by Tara Darling. 1997, Lothrop LB $15.93 (0-688-12538-7). 40pp. An introduction to chameleons in their natural habitat in Madagascar that tells about their lives, habits, diets, and mating. (Rev: BCCB 5/97; BL 4/1/97; SLJ 4/97) [597.95]

18744 Darling, Kathy. *Komodo Dragon: On Location* (4–6). Illus. by Tara Darling. Series: On Location. 1997, Lothrop LB $16.89 (0-688-13777-6). 40pp. Color photographs enliven the description of this reptile, its habits, and its habitat on Komodo Island. (Rev: BCCB 5/97; BL 2/15/97; SLJ 4/97) [597.95]

18745 Jenkins, Martin. *Chameleons Are Cool* (1–3). Illus. by Sue Shields. 1998, Candlewick $15.99 (0-7636-0144-6). 29pp. A good introduction to chameleons that describes their unusual characteristics, habits, and behavior. (Rev: HBG 10/98; SLJ 6/98) [597.95]

18746 Schafer, Susan. *The Komodo Dragon* (3–5). Illus. Series: Remarkable Animals. 1992, Macmillan LB $13.95 (0-87518-504-5). 60pp. Evolution, adaptation, habitat and behavior are covered, as well as why this animal is in danger of extinction. (Rev: BL 11/1/92; SLJ 10/92) [597.95]

18747 Schnieper, Claudia. *Chameleons* (3–6). Illus. by Max Meier. Series: Nature Watch. 1989, Carolrhoda LB $19.95 (0-87614-341-9). 48pp. Introduces the life cycle, physical characteristics, and habits of chameleons. (Rev: BL 9/15/89; HB 11–12/89; SLJ 10/89) [597.95]

18748 Schnieper, Claudia. *Lizards* (3–6). Illus. by Max Meier. Series: Nature Watch. 1990, Carolrhoda LB $19.95 (0-87614-405-9). 48pp. Characteristics and reproductive patterns are covered, with color photos. (Rev: BCCB 10/90; BL 6/15/90; SLJ 9/90) [597.95]

18749 Sherrow, Victoria. *The Gecko* (4–6). Illus. 1990, Macmillan LB $13.95 (0-87518-441-3). 60pp. Color photos highlight this introduction to the gecko. (Rev: BL 1/1/90; SLJ 2/91) [597.95]

18750 Souza, D. M. *Catch Me If You Can: A Book About Lizards* (3–5). Illus. Series: Creatures All Around Us. 1992, Carolrhoda LB $22.60 (0-87614-713-9). 40pp. From race runners to gila monsters, this book describes lizards found in the United States. (Rev: BL 10/1/92; SLJ 12/92) [597.95]

18751 Stefoff, Rebecca. *Chameleon* (2–4). Illus. Series: From the Living Things. 1996, Marshall Cavendish LB $22.79 (0-7614-0118-0). 32pp. The African chameleon, its life history, and its habits are presented in brief text and colorful photos. (Rev: BL 2/1/97; SLJ 3/97) [597.95]

18752 Twinem, Neecy. *Changing Colors* (PS–3). Illus. by author. Series: Animal Clues Board Books. 1996, Charlesbridge $4.95 (0-88106-941-8). A puzzle book that gives clues through close-up pictures of parts of a chameleon, finally revealing the whole animal. (Rev: SLJ 12/96) [597.6]

SNAKES

18753 Arnosky, Jim. *All About Rattlesnakes* (3–5). Illus. 1997, Scholastic $15.95 (0-590-46794-8). 32pp. This account is filled with information about snakes, from their physical structure to how they behave, with special material on rattlesnakes. (Rev: BL 12/1/97; HB 9–10/97; HBG 3/98; SLJ 10/97) [597.96]

18754 Berman, Ruth. *Buzzing Rattlesnakes* (PS–2). Series: Pull Ahead Books. 1998, Lerner LB $21.27 (0-8225-3603-X). 32pp. An innovative book that uses questions to introduce the topic of rattlesnakes, their homes, food, and habits. (Rev: BL 2/15/99; HBG 3/99; SLJ 1/99) [597.96]

18755 Broekel, Ray. *Snakes* (1–4). Illus. 1982, Children's LB $21.00 (0-516-01649-0); paper $5.50 (0-516-41649-9). 48pp. An introduction to snakes for the primary grades.

18756 Chinery, Michael. *Snake* (3–5). Illus. by Denys Ovenden. Series: Life Story. 1990, Troll LB $17.25 (0-8167-2106-8); paper $4.95 (0-8167-2107-6). 32pp. The life of the corn snake is featured in this colorfully illustrated account. (Rev: BL 4/1/91) [597.96]

18757 Demuth, Patricia. *Snakes* (1–3). Illus. by Judith Moffatt. 1993, Putnam paper $3.99 (0-448-40513-X). 48pp. An introduction to snakes, their habits, size, and food. (Rev: BL 7/93; SLJ 7/93) [597.66]

18758 Dewey, Jennifer O. *Rattlesnake Dance: True Tales, Mysteries, and Rattlesnake Ceremonies* (3–6). Illus. 1997, Boyds Mills $17.95 (1-56397-247-6). 48pp. An oversize book that tells about the author's many encounters with rattlesnakes and pit vipers. (Rev: BCCB 3/97; BL 3/15/97; HB 3–4/97; SLJ 4/97) [597.96]

18759 Gove, Doris. *A Water Snake's Year* (3–5). Illus. by Beverly Duncan. 1991, Macmillan $13.95 (0-689-31597-X). 40pp. This book describes a year in the life of a female snake in the Great Smoky Mountains. (Rev: BL 10/15/91; SLJ 10/91) [597.96]

18760 Johnson, Sylvia A. *Snakes* (4–6). Illus. 1986, Lerner paper $5.95 (0-8225-9503-6). 48pp. Diagrams help explain the way snakes move; also includes behavior, breeding, life cycles, and environment. (Rev: BL 10/1/86; SLJ 11/86)

18761 Lauber, Patricia. *Snakes Are Hunters* (PS–2). Illus. by Holly Keller. 1988, HarperCollins LB $14.89 (0-690-04630-8); paper $4.95 (0-06-445091-0). 32pp. Focusing on how snakes hunt and devour their food, this is a well-organized introduction to these often misunderstood creatures. (Rev: BL 2/1/88; HB 7–8/88; SLJ 9/88)

18762 Lavies, Bianca. *A Gathering of Garter Snakes* (3–6). Illus. 1993, Dutton $15.99 (0-525-45099-8). 32pp. The annual life cycle of garter snakes is described, from awakening after hibernation, through migration, hunting, mating, and shedding skins, and back to hibernation. (Rev: BCCB 2/94; BL 12/1/93; SLJ 2/94*) [597.96]

18763 Ling, Mary, and Mary Atkinson. *The Snake Book* (4–6). Illus. 1997, DK $12.95 (0-7894-1526-7). 32pp. A fascinating book that introduces 12 varieties of snakes, with a four-panel foldout of a python. (Rev: BCCB 5/97; BL 7/97; SLJ 9/97) [597.96]

18764 Llewellyn, Claire. *Some Snakes Spit Poison and Other Amazing Facts About Snakes* (2–4). Illus. Series: I Didn't Know That. 1997, Millbrook LB $19.90 (0-7613-0561-0). 32pp. Strange facts about unusual snakes and their behavior are given along with basic facts about the life span, food, and reproduction of snakes. (Rev: HBG 3/98; SLJ 10/97) [597.96]

18765 McDonald, Mary Ann. *Anacondas* (PS–3). Series: Naturebooks. 1999, Child's World LB $15.95 (1-56766-494-6). 32pp. The habits, habitats, physical characteristics, and life cycle of these giant snakes are covered in this oversize book with over a dozen full-page color photographs. (Rev: BL 6/1–15/99; HBG 10/99) [597.96]

18766 McDonald, Mary Ann. *Boas* (3–5). Illus. Series: Naturebooks. 1996, Child's World LB $22.79 (1-56766-212-9). 32pp. This account features in text and photos the large snake that crushes its prey. (Rev: BL 12/15/96) [597.96]

18767 McDonald, Mary Ann. *Cobras* (3–5). Illus. Series: Naturebooks. 1996, Child's World LB $22.79 (1-56766-265-X). 32pp. The exotic world of the cobra is explored through full-page illustrations and large-print text. (Rev: BL 12/15/96) [597.96]

18768 McDonald, Mary Ann. *Garter Snakes* (PS–3). Illus. Series: Naturebooks. 1999, Child's World LB $22.79 (1-56766-500-4). 32pp. A book that features the physical characteristics, habitats, and habits of these common small snakes. (Rev: BL 6/1–15/99; HBG 10/99) [597.96]

18769 Markle, Sandra. *Outside and Inside Snakes* (3–6). Illus. Series: Outside and Inside. 1995, Simon & Schuster paper $5.99 (0-689-81998-6). 40pp. The text clearly presents material on the anatomy and behavior of snakes, with amazing color photographs. (Rev: BCCB 5/95; BL 7/95; HB 7–8/95; SLJ 6/95*) [597.96]

18770 Montgomery, Sy. *The Snake Scientist* (4–6). Illus. 1999, Houghton $16.00 (0-395-87169-7). 48pp. Oregon zoologist Bob Mason and his studies of the red-sided garter snake are the focus of this account. (Rev: BCCB 4/99; BL 2/15/99*; HB 7–8/99; HBG 10/99; SLJ 5/99) [597.96]

18771 Parsons, Alexandra. *Amazing Snakes* (1–4). Illus. Series: Eyewitness Juniors. 1990, Knopf LB $11.99 (0-679-90225-2). 32pp. A general introduction to snakes, with pictures and text on individual species and locomotion. (Rev: BL 8/90) [597.96]

18772 Patent, Dorothy Hinshaw. *Slinky Scaly Slithery Snakes* (K–3). Illus. by Kendahl J. Jubb. 2000, Walker LB $17.85 (0-8027-8744-4). 32pp. This colorful introduction to snakes explains how they move, their body parts, where they live, and how they can eat animals larger than themselves. (Rev: BL 12/1/00; HBG 3/01; SLJ 3/01) [597.96]

18773 Patton, Don. *Pythons* (2–4). Illus. Series: Naturebooks: Animals. 1995, Child's World LB $22.79 (1-56766-180-7). 32pp. Amazing full-page photos highlight this introduction to pythons, their structure, and how they live. (Rev: BL 11/15/95; SLJ 4/96) [597.96]

18774 Penner, Lucille R. *S-S-Snakes!* (1–2). Illus. by Peter Barrett. Series: Step into Reading. 1994, Random LB $9.99 (0-679-94777-9); paper $3.99 (0-679-84777-4). 32pp. An easy-to-read book about snakes, their structure, and their habits. (Rev: BL 1/1/95; SLJ 2/95) [597.96]

18775 Robinson, Fay. *Great Snakes!* (2–3). Illus. by Jean Day Zallinger. 1996, Scholastic paper $3.99 (0-590-26243-2). 32pp. In an easily read format, this counting book introduces various snakes. (Rev: BL 11/15/96) [597.96]

18776 Schnieper, Claudia. *Snakes: Silent Hunters* (3–5). Illus. Series: Nature Watch. 1995, Carolrhoda LB $23.93 (0-87614-881-X); paper $7.95 (0-87614-952-2). 48pp. An introduction to snakes organized under such headings as physical characteristics, reproduction, hunting, and self-defense. (Rev: BL 10/1/95; SLJ 12/95) [597.96]

TURTLES AND TORTOISES

18777 Arnosky, Jim. *All About Turtles* (1–3). Illus. Series: All About. 2000, Scholastic $15.95 (0-590-48149-5). 32pp. This brief, well-illustrated account introduces turtles and touches on such topics as how and where they live, their shells, feeding habits, and reproductive cycle. (Rev: BL 2/1/00; HBG 10/00; SLJ 4/00) [597.92]

18778 Bair, Diane, and Pamela Wright. *Sea Turtle Watching* (2–5). Series: Wildlife Watching. 1999, Capstone $19.93 (0-7368-0323-8). 48pp. A description of sea turtles, their habits, and habitats that also provides special tips for successful turtle watching. (Rev: BL 2/15/00) [597.92]

18779 Baskin-Salzberg, Anita, and Allen Salzberg. *Turtles* (3–7). Illus. 1996, Watts LB $22.50 (0-531-20220-8). 64pp. From tiny bog turtles to giant sea turtles, many species are presented, along with their habitats and life-styles. (Rev: BL 9/1/96) [597.92]

18780 Berger, Melvin. *Look Out for Turtles!* (1–4). Illus. by Megan Lloyd. 1992, HarperCollins LB $15.89 (0-06-022540-8). 32pp. Information on all kinds and sizes of turtles and how their shells are so useful for their survival. (Rev: BL 1/1/93; SLJ 3/93) [597.92]

18781 Fowler, Allan. *Turtles Take Their Time* (1–2). Illus. Series: Rookie Readers. 1992, Children's LB $19.00 (0-516-06005-8). 32pp. For young children, turtles are introduced with a large color photo on each page and very brief text. (Rev: BL 12/15/92) [597.92]

18782 Gibbons, Gail. *Sea Turtles* (2–4). Illus. 1995, Holiday LB $16.95 (0-8234-1191-5). 32pp. This account covers the anatomy, life cycle, diet, and habitat of the sea turtle and how it differs from other members of its reptile family. (Rev: BL 10/1/95; SLJ 10/95) [597.92]

18783 Guiberson, Brenda Z. *Into the Sea* (2–4). Illus. by Alix Berenzy. 1996, Holt $16.95 (0-8050-2263-5). 28pp. The life of a sea turtle from being hatched to becoming an egg-laying adult. (Rev: BCCB 9/96; BL 9/15/96; HB 11–12/96; SLJ 9/96*) [597.92]

18784 Holling, Holling C. *Minn of the Mississippi* (4–6). Illus. by author. 1951, Houghton $20.00 (0-395-17578-X); paper $11.95 (0-395-27399-4). A snapping turtle's trip down the Mississippi.

18785 Lasky, Kathryn. *Interrupted Journey* (3–6). Illus. 2001, Candlewick $16.99 (0-7636-0635-9). 32pp. Beginning with a boy and his mother finding an injured Kemp's ridley turtle, this outstanding photo-essay explores the endangered animal — its life cycle, hazards it faces, and the miracle of its survival. (Rev: BL 12/1/00*) [639.9]

18786 Lepthien, Emilie U. *Sea Turtles* (3–4). Illus. Series: True Books. 1996, Children's LB $22.00 (0-516-20161-1). 48pp. An introduction to sea turtles that covers their environment, physiology, feeding, mating, nesting, and current endangered status. (Rev: SLJ 6/97) [597.92]

18787 Martin-James, Kathleen. *Sturdy Turtles* (PS–2). Series: Pull Ahead Books. 1999, Lerner $21.27 (0-8225-3627-7); paper $6.95 (0-8225-3631-5). 32pp. This book uses provocative questions, outstanding photos, and simple text to describe turtles, their habits, and habitats. (Rev: BL 12/15/99; HBG 3/00) [597.92]

18788 Patton, Don. *Sea Turtles* (3–5). Illus. Series: Naturebooks: Animals. 1995, Child's World LB $22.79 (1-56766-188-2). 32pp. Both land and sea turtles are introduced, with information on their life cycles, habits, and food. (Rev: BCCB 11/95; BL 11/15/95; SLJ 4/96) [597.92]

18789 Sayre, April Pulley. *Turtle, Turtle, Watch Out!* (PS–2). Illus. by Lee Christiansen. 2000, Orchard LB $17.99 (0-531-33285-3). 32pp. A lovely nature book with some fictional touches that covers the life cycle of a sea turtle and how a boy protected one turtle's eggs so they could hatch. (Rev: BL 8/00; HBG 3/01; SLJ 10/00) [597.92]

18790 Schafer, Susan. *The Galapagos Tortoise* (3–5). Illus. Series: Remarkable Animals. 1992, Macmillan LB $18.95 (0-87518-544-4). 64pp. With text, pictures, and maps, the story of the endangered Galapagos tortoise is told with information on habitat and behavior. (Rev: BL 12/1/92; SLJ 3/93) [597.92]

18791 Schafer, Susan. *Turtles* (2–5). Series: Perfect Pets. 1998, Benchmark LB $15.95 (0-7614-0796-0). 31pp. This book deals with turtles as pets and gives material on physical characteristics, behavior patterns, and tips on caring and raising them. (Rev: HBG 10/99; SLJ 5/99) [597.92]

18792 Souza, D. M. *What's Under That Shell? A Book About Turtles* (3–5). Illus. Series: Creatures All Around Us. 1992, Carolrhoda LB $19.95 (0-87614-712-0). 40pp. Various varieties of turtles and tortoises are introduced in color photographs and a lively text. (Rev: BL 10/1/92; SLJ 12/92) [597.92]

18793 Ziter, Cary B. *When Turtles Come to Town* (3–6). 1989, Watts LB $22.50 (0-531-10691-8). 64pp. This book focuses on protecting the eggs of the sea turtle along the Florida coast. (Rev: BL 4/1/89)

Animal Behavior and Anatomy

GENERAL

18794 Apperley, Dawn. *Animal Moves: A Pull-Tab Book* (PS). Illus. by author. 1999, Little, Brown $9.95 (0-316-04902-6). A tab book that explores animal locomotion through picturing creatures that hop, waddle, wiggle, snap, stretch, and scratch. Also use *Animal Noises* (1999). (Rev: SLJ 9/99) [591]

18795 Arnold, Caroline. *Mealtime for Zoo Animals* (PS–3). Illus. by Richard Hewett. Series: Zoo Animals. 1999, Carolrhoda LB $15.95 (1-57505-286-5). 32pp. Unusual color photographs and a simple text show a variety of zoo animals and how and what they eat. (Rev: BL 6/1–15/99; HBG 10/99) [636.088]

18796 Arnold, Caroline. *Noisytime for Zoo Animals* (PS–3). Illus. by Richard Hewett. Series: Zoo Animals. 1999, Carolrhoda LB $15.95 (1-57505-289-X). 32pp. All sorts of noises made by zoo animals are portrayed in lively photographs and a simple text. (Rev: BL 6/1–15/99; HBG 10/99) [636.088]

18797 Arnold, Caroline. *Playtime for Zoo Animals* (PS–3). Series: Zoo Animals. 1999, Carolrhoda LB $15.95 (1-57505-287-3); paper $9.95 (1-57505-391-8). 32pp. A very simple text identifies 15 zoo animals shown at play in full-page illustrations, and stresses similarities between human and animal behavior. (Rev: BL 6/1–15/99; HBG 10/99) [591.51]

18798 Arnold, Caroline. *Sleepytime for Zoo Animals* (PS–3). Series: Zoo Animals. 1999, Carolrhoda LB $15.95 (1-57505-290-3); paper $9.95 (1-57505-393-4). 32pp. The sleeping habits of zoo animals are shown in full-page color photos and a brief text. (Rev: BL 6/1–15/99; HBG 10/99; SLJ 8/99) [591]

18799 Arnold, Caroline. *Splashtime for Zoo Animals* (PS–3). Series: Zoo Animals. 1999, Carolrhoda LB $15.95 (1-57505-288-1); paper $9.95 (1-57505-394-2). 32pp. A simple, engaging text and full-page color photos of zoo animals show that animals bathe in ways often similar to their human counterparts. (Rev: BL 6/1–15/99; HBG 10/99; SLJ 8/99) [591]

18800 Arnosky, Jim. *Crinkleroot's Book of Animal Tracking* (2–5). Illus. 1989, Macmillan $14.95 (0-02-705851-4). 48pp. In this remake of the 1979 edition, the folksy hero leads a trek through the woods. (Rev: BL 4/15/89)

18801 Bancroft, Henrietta, and Richard G. Van Gelder. *Animals in Winter* (PS–1). Illus. by Helen K. Davie. Series: Let's-Read-and-Find-Out. 1997, HarperCollins LB $15.89 (0-06-027158-2). 32pp. An easily read title that describes how some animals prepare for winter and how others don't. (Rev: BL 12/1/96; SLJ 3/97) [591.54]

18802 Barre, Michel. *Animal Senses* (3–6). Series: Animal Survival. 1998, Gareth Stevens LB $19.93 (0-8368-2078-9). 48pp. This well-organized account explains how animals use their senses on land, in the sea, and in the air. (Rev: HBG 10/98; SLJ 7/98) [591]

18803 Challoner, Jack. *Wet and Dry* (K–4). Illus. Series: Start-Up Science. 1996, Raintree Steck-Vaughn LB $24.26 (0-8172-4322-4). 32pp. Using both text and experiments, discusses the different habitats of water and land and the creatures that exist in/on them. (Rev: SLJ 2/97) [530]

18804 Crump, Donald J., ed. *How Animals Behave: A New Look at Wildlife* (5–7). Illus. 1984, National Geographic LB $12.50 (0-87044-505-7). 104pp. How animals obtain food, court, raise their young, and protect themselves.

18805 Crump, Donald J., ed. *Secrets of Animal Survival* (4–8). Illus. 1983, National Geographic LB $12.50 (0-87044-431-X). 104pp. The survival tactics of animals in five geographical environments are discussed.

18806 Daly, Catherine. *Whiskers* (1–2). Illus. by Tom Leonard. Series: Road to Reading. 2000, Golden Bks. $10.99 (0-307-46214-5); paper $3.99 (0-307-26214-6). 32pp. Using walruses, seals, mice, mole rats, and cats as examples, this easy reader tells how animals use whiskers in many ways, including for protection, navigation, and finding food. (Rev: BL 12/1/00) [591]

18807 Dossenbach, Monika, and Hans D. Dossenbach. *EyeOpeners! All About Animal Vision* (3–5). Illus. 1998, Blackbirch LB $16.95 (1-56711-216-1). 32pp. Describes the characteristics and functions of vision in various animals. (Rev: BL 12/1/98; HBG 3/99; SLJ 3/99) [573.8]

18808 Facklam, Margery. *Bugs for Lunch* (PS–3). Illus. by Sylvia Long. 1999, Charlesbridge LB $15.95 (0-88106-271-5); paper $6.95 (0-88106-272-3). 32pp. This work highlights the creatures that eat insects, including bats, bears, aardvarks, rainbow trout, praying mantises, and Venus's-flytraps. (Rev: BL 2/1/99; HBG 10/99; SLJ 3/99) [591.5]

18809 Flegg, Jim. *Animal Movement* (4–7). Illus. by David Hosking. Series: Wild World. 1991, Millbrook $17.90 (1-878137-21-2). 32pp. Various ways animals move and at what speeds are discussed in this well-illustrated book. (Rev: BL 1/1/91; SLJ 2/92) [591.18]

18810 Flegg, Jim, et al. *Animal Hunters* (4–7). Illus. Series: Wild World. 1991, Millbrook $17.90 (1-878137-04-2). 32pp. This account describes the hunting techniques of sharks, piranhas, the parasitic wasp, and others. (Rev: BL 7/91; SLJ 7/91) [591.51]

18811 Fowler, Allan. *Animals on the Move* (1–2). Series: Rookie Readers. 2000, Children's LB $19.00 (0-516-21589-2). 32pp. This is a simple introduction to animal and bird migration that explains why and where they go. (Rev: BL 4/15/00) [591]

18812 Fowler, Allan. *How Animals See Things* (1–2). Series: Rookie Readers. 1998, Children's LB $18.50 (0-516-20797-0). 32pp. Minimal text and full-page color photographs are used to explain sight in animals. (Rev: BL 9/15/98; HBG 10/99) [591]

18813 Fraser, Mary Ann. *Where Are the Night Animals?* (PS–1). Illus. Series: Let's-Read-and-Find-Out. 1999, HarperCollins LB $15.89 (0-06-027718-1). 32pp. Several nocturnal animals are introduced, including the coyote, skunk, harvest mouse, barn owl, opossum, raccoon, bat, and tree frog. (Rev: BL 2/15/99; HBG 10/99; SLJ 1/99) [591.5]

18814 Fredericks, Anthony D. *Cannibal Animals: Animals That Eat Their Own Kind* (5–7). Illus. Series: Watts Library: Animals. 1999, Watts LB $24.00 (0-531-11701-4). 64pp. A book that focuses on such animals as the female praying mantis, sharks, gerbils, and Tyrannosaurus rex, and how

they have been accused of cannibalism. (Rev: BL 12/1/99; SLJ 12/99) [591.5]

18815 Funston, Sylvia. *Animal Feelings* (3–5). Illus. by Pat Stephens. Series: The Secret Life of Animals. 1998, Owl $19.95 (1-895688-82-5); paper $9.95 (1-895688-81-7). 48pp. An investigation of emotions in both wild and domestic animals is included in this book that also emphasizes that animals should be treated with compassion and respect. (Rev: SLJ 3/99) [591]

18816 Funston, Sylvia. *Animal Smarts* (4–6). Illus. 1997, Firefly $19.95 (1-895688-66-3); paper $9.95 (1-895688-67-1). 48pp. Explores the levels of intelligence in various mammals, birds, and insects, with material on how they think, solve problems, and understand human language. (Rev: BL 2/1/98; SLJ 4/98) [591.5]

18817 Gardner, Robert, and David Webster. *Science Project Ideas About Animal Behavior* (4–7). Series: Science Project Ideas. 1997, Enslow LB $19.95 (0-89490-842-1). 96pp. A fascinating project book that outlines techniques and easily followed activities to study animal behavior. (Rev: BL 12/15/97; HBG 3/98; SLJ 2/98) [591]

18818 Goodman, Susan E. *Unseen Rainbows, Silent Songs: The World Beyond Human Senses* (2–4). Illus. by Beverly Duncan. 1995, Simon & Schuster $16.00 (0-689-31892-8). 40pp. The senses of various animals are explored and compared to the senses found in humans. (Rev: BL 9/15/95; SLJ 9/95) [591.1]

18819 Greenaway, Theresa. *Paws and Claws* (3–5). Illus. by Ann Savage, et al. Series: Head to Tail. 1995, Raintree Steck-Vaughn LB $5.00 (0-8114-8266-9). 39pp. An appealing introduction to various kinds of animal feet and their uses for movement, digging, climbing, etc. (Rev: SLJ 5/95) [591]

18820 Hartley, Karen, and Chris Macro. *Hearing in Living Things* (K–2). Series: Sense Series. 2000, Heinemann LB $13.95 (1-57572-246-1). 32pp. An overview that explains hearing in animals and uses as examples such animals as bats, frogs, insects, owls, elephants, and humans. Also use *Tasting in Living Things* (2000). (Rev: HBG 3/01; SLJ 8/00) [591]

18821 Hickman, Pamela. *Animal Senses: How Animals See, Hear, Taste, Smell and Feel* (3–5). Illus. 1998, Kids Can $10.95 (1-55074-423-2). 40pp. In double-page spreads with text and accompanying activities, this book explores the senses of such animals as frogs, bats, butterflies, and deer. (Rev: BL 5/15/98; HBG 10/98; SLJ 5/98) [573.8]

18822 Hickman, Pamela. *Animals Eating* (3–5). Illus. 2001, Kids Can $10.95 (1-55074-577-8); paper $5.95 (1-55074-579-4). 40pp. After a general discussion of animal mouths, tongues, and teeth, this book explains how various animals eat and drink. It also gives a number of interesting simple activities. (Rev: BL 3/15/01) [591.5]

18823 Hickman, Pamela. *Animals in Motion: How Animals Swim, Jump, Slither and Glide* (3–5). Illus. 2000, Kids Can $10.95 (1-55074-573-5); paper $5.95 (1-55074-575-1). 40pp. This book on animal locomotion classifies animals by how they move — running, hopping, slipping, swimming, and climbing, for example. (Rev: BL 5/1/00; HBG 10/00; SLJ 9/00) [573.7]

18824 Hirschi, Ron. *When Morning Comes* (1–4). Photos by Thomas D. Mangelsen. 2000, Boyds Mills $15.95 (1-56397-767-2). Using striking photographs, this book on nature study shows various forms of wildlife in the morning. A companion volume is *When Night Comes* (2000). (Rev: BL 10/15/00; HBG 3/01; SLJ 12/00) [508]

18825 Hirschi, Ron. *When Night Comes* (1–3). Illus. by Thomas D. Mangelsen. 2000, Boyds Mills $15.95 (1-56397-766-4). 32pp. The activities of such animals as otters, raccoons, and coyotes at night are described in excellent photos and a simple text. (Rev: BL 10/15/00; HBG 3/01; SLJ 12/00) [591.5]

18826 Kajikawa, Kimiko. *Sweet Dreams: How Animals Sleep* (PS–1). Illus. 1999, Holt $15.95 (0-8050-5890-7). Animals including a chipmunk, flamingo, bear, and bat are pictured and described while asleep. (Rev: BL 4/1/99; HBG 10/99; SLJ 4/99) [591.5]

18827 Kalman, Bobbie. *How Do Animals Adapt?* (1–3). Series: Science of Living Things. 2000, Crabtree LB $14.97 (0-86505-980-2); paper $5.36 (0-86505-957-8). 32pp. This beginning science book on animal adaptations includes camouflage, hibernation, and migration. (Rev: SLJ 11/00) [591]

18828 Kerrod, Robin, et al. *Pets and Farm Animals* (2–8). Illus. Series: Encyclopedia of the Animal World. 1990, Facts on File $17.95 (0-8160-1969-X). 96pp. This book describes the body structure of such animals as cats, dogs, donkeys, and horses. (Rev: BL 7/90) [636]

18829 Llewellyn, Claire. *The Big Book of Bones: An Introduction to Skeletons* (3–6). Illus. 1998, Bedrick $17.95 (0-87226-546-3). 48pp. Using frequent examples from the animal world and a description of the human skeleton's functions, this book explains how bones work. (Rev: BL 9/1/98; HBG 10/98; SLJ 7/98) [611]

18830 MacDonald, Suse. *Peck Slither and Slide* (PS–1). Illus. 1997, Harcourt $15.00 (0-15-200079-8). 48pp. The ways that animals move and travel are illustrated, and the words that describe their motions — for example, *wade* and *slither* — are explained. (Rev: BL 4/1/97; SLJ 4/97) [591]

18831 McGrath, Susan. *The Amazing Things Animals Do* (4–7). Illus. 1989, National Geographic $8.95 (0-87044-709-2). 96pp. Unusual animal behavior is shown in such areas as communication, motion, raising young, and survival. (Rev: SLJ 2/90) [591.5]

18832 Manning, Mick, and Brita Granström. *My Body, Your Body* (PS–2). Illus. by authors. Series: Wonderwise. 1997, Watts LB $21.00 (0-531-14486-0). 31pp. An easy science book that explains various parts of human anatomy and compares each with similar parts of animals' bodies. (Rev: HBG 3/98; SLJ 6/98) [591]

18833 Masson, Jeffrey Moussaieff. *Dogs Have the Strangest Friends: And Other True Stories of Animal Feelings* (4–6). Illus. 2000, Dutton $19.99 (0-525-45745-3). 128pp. This book explores animals' emotions, particularly those involved in caring for others, such as the story of the elephant that helped a trapped baby hippo. (Rev: BCCB 6/00; BL 4/1/00; HB 5–6/00; HBG 10/00; SLJ 8/00) [591.5]

18834 Matero, Robert. *Animals Asleep* (3–6). Illus. 2000, Millbrook LB $25.90 (0-7613-1652-3). 80pp. Covers the sleep and rest habits of humans and animals, including bears, woodchucks, bats, hummingbirds, lobsters, and frogs. (Rev: BL 11/1/00; HBG 3/01; SLJ 2/01) [579.5]

18835 Morgan, Sally. *Animals and Their World* (1–4). Illus. Series: Young Discoverers. 1996, Kingfisher LB $13.90 (0-7534-5035-6); paper $6.95 (0-7534-5034-8). 32pp. Various animals and their environments are briefly introduced, with many illustrations. (Rev: BL 12/1/96) [591.1]

18836 Moses, Brian. *Winking, Blinking, Wiggling, and Waggling* (2–3). Illus. Series: Eyewitness Reader. 2000, DK $12.95 (0-7894-5414-9); paper $3.95 (0-7894-5413-0). 32pp. This book for beginning readers describes fascinating facts about animals that have unusual eyes and ears. (Rev: BL 4/15/00; HBG 10/00; SLJ 8/00) [573.8]

18837 Mullin, Rita Thievon. *Who's for Dinner? Predators and Prey* (3–6). Illus. by Anders Wengren. Series: Animal Planet. 1998, Crown LB $16.99 (0-517-80005-5); paper $9.99 (0-517-80004-7). 64pp. A far-reaching view of animal hunters of various species and their victims. (Rev: SLJ 6/98) [591.51]

18838 Myers, Jack. *What Happened to the Mammoths? And Other Explorations of Science in Action* (4–6). Illus. 2000, Boyds Mills $17.95 (1-56397-801-6). 64pp. A collection of articles from *Highlights for Children* magazine that explores such aspects of animal behavior as the seal's ability to dive and the cat's purr. (Rev: BL 3/1/00; HBG 10/00; SLJ 6/00) [591]

18839 Nail, Jim. *Whose Tracks Are These? A Clue Book of Familiar Forest Animals* (PS–3). Illus. by Hyla Skudder. 1994, Roberts Rinehart $13.95 (1-879373-89-0). Presents six guessing games in which readers are challenged to identify various common forest creatures through their tracks and a description of their habits. (Rev: SLJ 9/94) [591]

18840 Pearce, Q. L. *Great Predators of the Land* (3–5). Illus. by Ed Yakovetic. 1999, Tor paper $12.95 (0-312-85981-3). 57pp. A mostly pictorial presentation that deals with various methods used to capture prey and highlights animals including tigers and eagles. Also use *Great Predators of the Sea* (1999). (Rev: SLJ 3/00) [591]

18841 Pipe, Jim. *The Giant Book of Creatures of the Night* (3–5). Illus. 1998, Millbrook LB $25.90 (0-7613-0858-X). 32pp. An entertaining, oversize book with copious illustrations and lots of information about night creatures, including various insects as well as birds and animals. (Rev: BL 12/15/98; HBG 3/99) [591.5]

18842 Renne. *Animals Trails and Tracks* (1–3). Trans. by Alison Taurel. Illus. by author. Series: Animals Up Close. 2000, Gareth Stevens LB $21.27 (0-8368-2713-9). 38pp. A brief text and many full-color pictures are used to introduce different animals and their tracks. (Rev: SLJ 2/01) [591]

18843 Riha, Susanne. *Animal Journeys: Life Cycles and Migrations* (4–6). Illus. by author. Series: Animals in the Wild. 1999, Blackbirch LB $16.95 (1-56711-426-1). 30pp. This colorful book describes the life cycle and migration patterns of both land and water animals. (Rev: HBG 3/00; SLJ 4/00) [591.52]

18844 Riha, Susanne. *Animals at Rest: Sleeping Patterns and Habitats* (4–6). Illus. by author. Series: Animals in the Wild. 1999, Blackbirch LB $16.95 (1-56711-425-3). 30pp. This book covers sleeping and resting patterns in a number of birds, fish, and mammals. (Rev: HBG 3/00; SLJ 4/00) [154.6]

18845 Riley, Linda C. *Elephants Swim* (PS–1). Illus. by Steve Jenkins. 1995, Houghton $14.95 (0-395-73654-4). 40pp. This picture book shows how a variety of animals react to water. (Rev: BL 9/1/95*; HB 9–10/95; SLJ 9/95) [591.1]

18846 Royston, Angela. *Night-time Animals* (PS). Illus. by Dave King. Series: Eye Openers. 1992, Macmillan paper $7.95 (0-689-71646-X). 22pp. Each double-page spread contains a large photo of a nocturnal animal plus other illustrations and some text. (Rev: BL 10/15/92; SLJ 2/93) [595.7]

18847 Savage, Stephen. *Skin* (2–4). Illus. Series: Adaptation for Survival. 1995, Thomson Learning LB $5.00 (1-56847-353-2). 32pp. Describes the skin covering on a variety of animals, including humans and other mammals, reptiles, birds, fish, and shellfish. (Rev: SLJ 3/96) [591]

18848 Sayre, April Pulley. *Home at Last: A Song of Migration* (PS–4). Illus. by Alix Berenzy. 1998, Holt $15.95 (0-8050-5154-6). Fish, birds, butterflies, whales, lobsters, and other animals are used to explain and explore the mystery of animal migration. (Rev: BL 12/1/98; HBG 3/99; SLJ 12/98) [591.56]

18849 Sayre, April Pulley. *Splish! Splash! Animal Baths* (PS–1). Illus. 2000, Millbrook LB $21.90 (0-7613-1821-6). 32pp. Lots of photos and a spare text are used to introduce unusual grooming techniques in the animal kingdom, such as chimpanzees picking fleas off each other. (Rev: BL 4/1/00; HBG 10/00; SLJ 5/00) [591.56]

18850 Settel, Joanne. *Exploding Ants: Amazing Facts About How Animals Adapt* (5–7). Illus. 1999, Simon & Schuster $16.00 (0-689-81739-8). 40pp. This is an engrossing collection of animal oddities, such as the cuckoo that uses other birds' nests and the African frog that can drop its eyeballs into its mouth. (Rev: BCCB 3/99; BL 4/15/99; HBG 10/99; SLJ 4/99) [591.5]

18851 Simon, Seymour. *They Swim the Seas: The Mystery of Animal Migration* (3–5). Illus. 1998, Harcourt $16.00 (0-15-292888-X). 40pp. Describes the migration of marine plants and animals — from the microscopic plankton to the 4,000-mile journey of the gray whale. (Rev: BL 9/15/98; HBG 3/99; SLJ 10/98) [578.77]

18852 Simon, Seymour. *They Walk the Earth: The Extraordinary Travels of Animals on Land* (3–5). Illus. 2000, Harcourt $17.00 (0-15-292889-8). 40pp. This picture book uses a poetic text and detailed paintings to explore the migrations of such animals as the caribou, lemming, polar bear, elephant, and bison. (Rev: BL 3/15/00; HBG 10/00; SLJ 6/00) [599.156]

18853 Singer, Marilyn. *Bottoms Up!* (3–6). Illus. by Patrick O'Brien. 1998, Holt $14.95 (0-8050-4246-6). 32pp. A book about the behinds of animals and humans, their various uses, and variations in color, size and structure. (Rev: BL 3/15/98; HBG 10/98; SLJ 7/98) [591.5]

18854 Singer, Marilyn. *Prairie Dogs Kiss and Lobsters Wave: How Animals Say Hello* (2–4). Illus. 1998, Holt $15.95 (0-8050-3703-9). An informal look at how animals greet each other, including bears circling, zebras chewing, and elephants touching. (Rev: BL 12/1/98; HBG 3/99; SLJ 12/98) [591.59]

18855 Stockdale, Susan. *Nature's Paintbrush: The Patterns and Colors Around You* (K–2). Illus. 1999, Simon & Schuster $15.00 (0-689-81081-4). 32pp. With a series of clear color drawings, the author shows how animals use their coloration for a variety of purposes — hiding, escaping, reproducing, and repelling enemies. (Rev: BL 7/99; HBG 10/99; SLJ 6/99) [578.4]

18856 Sussman, Susan, and Robert James. *Lies (People Believe) About Animals* (3–6). Illus. 1987, Whitman LB $13.95 (0-8075-4530-9). 48pp. A snake's skin is not wet and slimy; this is typical of the fascinating science facts included here. (Rev: BCCB 7–8/87; BL 8/87; SLJ 11/87)

18857 Swanson, Diane. *Animals Eat the Weirdest Things* (3–6). Illus. 1998, Holt $16.95 (0-8050-5846-X). 64pp. The eating habits of animals, from carrion scavenging and cannibalism to sucking blood and chewing wood, are covered in this fascinating book on animal behavior. (Rev: BL 1/1–15/99; HBG 3/99; SLJ 1/99) [591.5]

18858 Swanson, Diane. *Feet That Suck and Feed* (2–4). Illus. Series: Up Close. 2000, Greystone $9.95 (1-55054-767-4); paper $5.95 (1-55054-769-0). 32pp. Excellent close-up photos are used to show a number of animal feet that are used to absorb food. (Rev: BL 10/15/00) [573.9]

18859 Swanson, Diane. *Noses That Plow and Poke* (2–4). Series: Up Close. 2000, Greystone $9.95 (1-55054-715-1). 30pp. A colorful, well-organized book that examines noses on a number of animals and their uses beyond breathing. (Rev: SLJ 4/00) [591]

18860 Swanson, Diane. *Tails That Talk and Fly* (2–4). Series: Up Close. 2000, Greystone $9.95 (1-55054-717-8). 30pp. This book presents a variety of animal tails and explains their many uses in a well-organized book with good photos and captions. (Rev: SLJ 4/00) [591]

18861 Swanson, Diane. *Teeth That Stab and Grind* (2–4). Illus. Series: Up Close. 2000, Greystone $9.95 (1-55054-768-2); paper $5.95 (1-55054-770-4). 32pp. Teeth that are used for protection and processing food are shown in a series of close-up photographs that picture. (Rev: BL 10/15/00; SLJ 11/00) [573.3]

18862 Swinburne, Stephen R. *Safe, Warm, and Snug* (PS–2). Illus. by Jose Aruego and Ariane Dewey. 1999, Harcourt $16.00 (0-15-201734-8). 40pp. A book that highlights in illustrations and rhyming couplets how a number of animals protect and nurture their young. (Rev: BL 6/1–15/99; HBG 10/99; SLJ 6/99) [591.56]

18863 Walker, Niki, and Bobbie Kalman. *How Do Animals Move?* (1–3). Series: Science of Living Things. 2000, Crabtree LB $14.97 (0-86505-981-0); paper $5.36 (0-86505-958-6). 32pp. Using pictures and a very simple text, this book introduces such forms of animal locomotion as swimming, running, flying, and jumping. (Rev: SLJ 11/00) [591]

18864 Wells, Robert E. *What's Faster Than a Speeding Cheetah?* (K–4). Illus. 1997, Albert Whitman LB $14.95 (0-8075-2280-5); paper $6.95 (0-8075-2281-3). 32pp. The author explores the concept of speed in the animal kingdom by focusing on the cheetah, the fastest animal. (Rev: BL 10/1/97; HBG 3/98; SLJ 1/98) [531]

18865 Ziefert, Harriet. *A Polar Bear Can Swim: What Animals Can and Cannot Do* (1–2). Illus. by Emily Bolam. 1998, Viking LB $13.89 (0-670-88056-6). 32pp. A book for beginning readers in which simple science facts about animals are presented in charming lists of what various animals can and cannot do, such as swim or sleep upside down. (Rev: BL 11/1/98; HBG 3/99; SLJ 1/99) [590]

BABIES

18866 Arnold, Caroline. *Mother and Baby Zoo Animals* (PS–3). Series: Zoo Animals. 1999, Carolrhoda LB $15.95 (1-57505-285-7); paper $9.95 (1-57505-390-X). 32pp. Similarities between human and animal behavior are stressed in this delightful book that introduces several zoo animals and how they care for their young. (Rev: BL 6/1–15/99; HBG 10/99) [591.3]

18867 *Baby* (PS–1). Illus. Series: What's Inside? 1992, DK $8.95 (1-56458-004-0). 24pp. With diagrams that peel back, the internal parts of animal babies are revealed. (Rev: BL 4/15/92) [591.3]

18868 Baillie, Marilyn. *Little Wonders: Animal Babies and Their Families* (K–3). Illus. by Romi Caron. 1995, Owl $14.95 (1-895688-37-X); paper $5.95 (1-895688-31-0). 32pp. The child-rearing habits of 12 animal species around the world are covered in this attractive picture book. (Rev: SLJ 12/95) [591]

18869 Bauer, Marion Dane. *If You Were Born a Kitten* (PS–3). Illus. by JoEllen M. Stammen. 1997, Simon & Schuster paper $16.00 (0-689-80111-4). 32pp. Each double-page spread shows a different animal — like a cat, sea horse, or porcupine —

along with a picture of its newborn. (Rev: BL 10/15/97; HBG 3/98; SLJ 11/97*) [591.3]

18870 Carlson, Kit. *Bringing Up Baby: Wild Animal Families* (3–6). Illus. by Anders Wenngren. Series: Animal Planet. 1998, Crown LB $16.99 (0-517-80008-X); paper $9.99 (0-517-80007-1). 64pp. A good browsing book for the middle grades that tells how various animals raise their young. (Rev: SLJ 6/98) [591.3]

18871 Collard, Sneed B. *Animal Dads* (PS–2). Illus. by Steve Jenkins. 1997, Houghton $15.95 (0-395-83621-2). 32pp. The role of fathers in the animal kingdom is presented in large type and beautiful collages. (Rev: BCCB 5/97; BL 5/15/97; SLJ 6/97*) [591.56]

18872 Craig, Claire. *Animal Babies* (2–4). Illus. Series: Nature Company Young Discoveries. 1996, Time Life $10.00 (0-7835-4839-7). 32pp. Double-page spreads and a brief text are used to introduce the young of various species. (Rev: BL 12/15/96) [591.3]

18873 Darling, Kathy. *Desert Babies* (3–5). Illus. by Tara Darling. 1997, Walker LB $16.85 (0-8027-8480-1). 32pp. An introduction to deserts, with a focus on the young animals found there, their size, food, enemies, and world location. (Rev: BCCB 3/97; BL 4/1/97; SLJ 3/97) [591.909]

18874 Dewey, Jennifer O. *Faces Only a Mother Could Love* (K–3). Illus. 1996, Boyds Mills $14.95 (1-56397-046-5). 32pp. Baby pictures of such unusual creatures as hognose snakes, sloths, and giant anteaters are highlighted in this unique picture book. (Rev: BCCB 2/96; BL 1/1–15/96; SLJ 2/96) [591.3]

18875 Dewey, Jennifer O. *Family Ties: Raising Wild Babies* (4–6). Illus. 1998, Marshall Cavendish $15.95 (0-7614-5037-8). 80pp. Using case histories involving five different animals, these accounts demonstrate the strong — often fierce — drive to protect the family. (Rev: BL 10/1/98; HBG 3/99; SLJ 10/98) [591.5]

18876 Flegg, Jim. *Animal Families* (4–7). Illus. by David Hosking. Series: Wild World. 1991, Millbrook $17.90 (1-878137-20-4). 32pp. In pictures and text, this book shows the various ways animals take care of their young. (Rev: BL 1/1/91) [591.51]

18877 Helman, Andrea. *Northwest Animal Babies* (PS–1). Illus. by Art Wolfe. 1998, Sasquatch $15.95 (1-57061-144-0). 32pp. Close-up photographs are used with a simple text to introduce the offspring of 26 Pacific Northwest animals such as red fox kits and salmon fry. (Rev: BL 9/15/98; HBG 3/99; SLJ 12/98) [591.3]

18878 Maynard, Christopher. *Amazing Animal Babies* (1–4). Illus. Series: Eyewitness Juniors. 1993, Knopf paper $9.99 (0-679-83924-0). 32pp. The infancy of a number of animals is pictured and described in a simple text. (Rev: BL 9/15/93) [591.3]

18879 Priddy, Roger. *Baby's Book of Animals* (PS). 1993, DK $9.95 (1-56458-278-7). 21pp. An album of photos that contains pictures of 70 animals and their babies. (Rev: SLJ 4/94) [591]

18880 Ryan, Pam M. *A Pinky Is a Baby Mouse* (K–3). Illus. by Diane De Groat. 1997, Hyperion LB $15.49 (0-7868-2190-6). 32pp. Using rhyming verse, this book introduces the young of several animals and names them. (Rev: BL 6/1–15/97; SLJ 7/97) [591]

18881 Wallace, Karen. *Wild Baby Animals* (K–3). Illus. Series: Eyewitness Reader. 2000, DK $12.95 (0-7894-5420-3); paper $3.95 (0-7894-5419-X). 32pp. Beginning readers will enjoy this book on various animal babies, their body parts, behavior, protection, and diet. (Rev: BL 7/00; HBG 10/00) [591.3]

CAMOUFLAGE

18882 Eugene, Toni. *Hide and Seek* (2–4). Illus. 1999, National Geographic $16.00 (0-7922-7102-5). This pop-up book shows how animals use camouflage to protect themselves. (Rev: BL 12/15/99) [591.57]

18883 Fowler, Allan. *Hard-to-See Animals* (1–2). Series: Rookie Readers. 1997, Children's LB $19.00 (0-516-20548-X). 32pp. This book introduces animal camouflage, with striking photos and minimal text, suitable for beginning readers. (Rev: BL 11/15/97; HBG 3/98; SLJ 10/97) [591]

18884 Holmes, Anita. *Can You Find Us?* (1–2). Illus. 2000, Benchmark $14.95 (0-7614-1108-9). 32pp. A beginner reader that explores animal camouflage and challenges children to find small animals hidden in their surroundings. (Rev: BL 12/1/00; HBG 3/01; SLJ 2/01) [591.47]

18885 Llewellyn, Claire. *Disguises and Surprises* (3–5). Illus. Series: SuperSmarts. 1996, Candlewick $11.99 (0-7636-0037-7). 24pp. A wide range of creatures are used to explore the topic of camouflage in nature. (Rev: BL 12/1/96; SLJ 2/97) [591.59]

18886 McDonnell, Janet. *Animal Camouflage* (K–2). Illus. Series: Animal Behavior. 1997, Child's World LB $22.79 (1-56766-400-8). 32pp. The ways that animals can conceal their identities through protective coloration, body shapes, or unusual behavior are covered in text and pictures. (Rev: SLJ 2/98) [591]

18887 Otto, Carolyn. *What Color Is Camouflage?* (K–4). Illus. by Megan Lloyd. 1996, HarperCollins LB $14.89 (0-06-027099-3). 32pp. How animal coloration is used to provide safety is explored in a series of pictures containing hidden animal life. (Rev: BL 11/1/96; SLJ 12/96) [591.57]

18888 Patent, Dorothy Hinshaw. *Bold and Bright: Black-and-White Animals* (K–3). Illus. by Kendahl J. Jubb. 1998, Walker LB $16.85 (0-8027-8673-1). 32pp. This work presents a number of black-and-white animals, such as the skunk and the penguin, and shows how this coloration has helped them survive. (Rev: BL 9/1/98; HBG 3/99; SLJ 10/98) [591.42]

18889 Perry, Phyllis J. *Hide and Seek: Creatures in Camouflage* (3–5). Illus. Series: First Books. 1997, Watts $22.50 (0-531-20306-9). 63pp. Describes animal camouflage in various groups of animals, including mammals, birds, insects, reptiles, and ocean life. (Rev: HBG 3/98; SLJ 2/98) [591]

18890 Tildes, Phyllis L. *Animals in Camouflage* (PS–3). Illus. 2000, Charlesbridge $16.95 (0-88106-120-4); paper $6.95 (0-88106-134-4). 32pp. An effective picture book that shows through double-page spreads how such animals as the polar bear, crab spider, and great horned owl blend into their surroundings. (Rev: BL 1/1–15/00; HBG 10/00; SLJ 4/00) [591.47]

COMMUNICATION

18891 Bailey, Gerald. *Talking to Animals: How Animals Really Communicate!* (4–8). Illus. by John W. Taylor. 1999, Element Books paper $4.95 (1-901881-97-0). 127pp. After describing how his dog communicates with him, the author goes on to discuss such animals as wolves, cats, horses, dolphins, whales, chimpanzees, and gorillas. (Rev: SLJ 7/99) [591.1]

18892 Flegg, Jim, et al. *Animal Communication* (4–7). Illus. by David Hosking. Series: Wild World. 1991, Millbrook $17.90 (1-878137-23-9). 32pp. This account shows how animals communicate with one another through sounds and actions. (Rev: BL 1/1/91) [591.59]

18893 Kalman, Bobbie. *How Animals Communicate* (2–4). Illus. Series: Crabapples. 1996, Crabtree LB $19.96 (0-86505-635-8); paper $5.95 (0-86505-735-4). 32pp. Discusses sound, scent, touch, color, and movement in such animals as elephants, giraffes, and honeybees. (Rev: SLJ 6/97) [591]

18894 McDonnell, Janet. *Animal Communication* (K–2). Illus. Series: Animal Behavior. 1997, Child's World LB $22.79 (1-56766-401-6). 32pp. The ways that animals communicate through sounds and movements are explored in this simple science book. (Rev: SLJ 2/98) [591.59]

DEFENSES

18895 Barre, Michel. *How Animals Protect Themselves* (3–6). Series: Animal Survival. 1998, Gareth Stevens LB $19.93 (0-8368-2080-0). 48pp. Animal protection is discussed in this well-organized book that explains defenses, camouflage, and how homes are used for safety. (Rev: HBG 10/98; SLJ 7/98) [591.47]

18896 Bennett, Paul. *Escaping from Enemies* (1–4). Illus. Series: Nature's Secrets. 1995, Thomson Learning LB $21.40 (1-56847-358-3). 32pp. Describes how animals defend themselves by fighting, running, or resorting to trickery. (Rev: SLJ 8/95) [591]

18897 Fredericks, Anthony D. *Animal Sharpshooters* (5–7). Illus. Series: Watts Library: Animals. 1999, Watts LB $24.00 (0-531-11700-6). 64pp. This book focuses on the strange adaptations some animals have made to protect themselves and to find food. (Rev: BL 12/1/99; SLJ 12/99) [591.47]

18898 Jenkins, Steve. *What Do You Do When Something Wants to Eat You?* (PS–3). Illus. 1997, Houghton $16.00 (0-395-82514-8). 32pp. In this thrilling science book illustrated with paper collages, 14 different animals employ unusual tricks of nature to escape their predators. (Rev: BL 12/1/97; HBG 3/98; SLJ 11/97) [591.47]

18899 Kaner, Etta. *Animal Defenses: How Animals Protect Themselves* (2–5). Illus. by Pat Stephens. 1999, Kids Can $10.95 (1-55074-419-4). 40pp. Each section of this book is devoted to a particular type of defense, with several animals used as examples. (Rev: BL 4/15/99; HBG 10/99; SLJ 6/99) [591.47]

18900 Perry, Phyllis J. *Armor to Venom: Animal Defenses* (3–5). Illus. Series: First Books. 1997, Watts $22.50 (0-531-20299-2). 63pp. This book explores animal defenses and survival mechanisms, from camouflage to venom production. (Rev: HBG 3/98; SLJ 12/97) [591]

18901 Sowler, Sandie. *Amazing Armored Animals* (1–4). Illus. Series: Eyewitness Juniors. 1992, Knopf paper $6.95 (0-679-82767-6). 32pp. After a general section on armored animals, such individual species as armadillos are pictured in double-page spreads. (Rev: BL 8/92; SLJ 8/92) [591.57]

HIBERNATION

18902 Berger, Melvin, and Gilda Berger. *What Do Animals Do in Winter? How Animals Survive the Cold* (2–4). Illus. Series: Discovery Readers. 1995, Ideals paper $4.50 (1-57102-041-1). 48pp. Such winter survival tactics as hibernation and migration are presented with many examples. (Rev: BL 12/1/95; SLJ 2/96) [591.54]

18903 Facklam, Margery. *Do Not Disturb: The Mysteries of Animal Hibernation and Sleep* (3–5). Illus. by Pamela Johnson. 1989, Little, Brown $15.95 (0-316-27379-1). 48pp. Explaining the mysterious biological processes of hibernation and long winter sleep. (Rev: BL 3/1/89; SLJ 3/89)

18904 Seuling, Barbara. *Winter Lullaby* (PS–1). Illus. by Greg Newbold. 1998, Harcourt $16.00 (0-15-201403-9). 32pp. Poetic language and colorful acrylic paintings are used to tell where such animals as bees, ducks, and mice spend the winter. (Rev: BL 9/1/98; HBG 3/99; SLJ 9/98) [591.54]

HOMES

18905 Arnosky, Jim. *Crinkleroot's Guide to Knowing Animal Habitats* (PS–4). Illus. 1997, Simon & Schuster $14.00 (0-689-80583-7). 32pp. In double-page spreads and a chatty text, several habitats — such as wetlands, grasslands, and cornfields — and the animals that live there are introduced. (Rev: BL 6/1–15/97; SLJ 6/97) [591.5]

18906 Crump, Donald J., ed. *Animal Architects* (3–8). Illus. 1987, National Geographic LB $12.50 (0-87044-617-7). 104pp. Chapters on animal builders are divided according to techniques — mound builders, weavers, excavators, and so on. (Rev: BL 12/15/87)

18907 Flegg, Jim, et al. *Animal Builders* (4–7). Illus. Series: Wild World. 1991, Millbrook $17.90 (1-878137-05-0). 32pp. This book shows the different types of housing that all sorts of animals build and live in. (Rev: BL 7/91; SLJ 7/91) [591.564]

18908 Forsyth, Adrian. *The Architecture of Animals: The Equinox Guide to Wildlife Structures* (5–8). 1989, Camden House paper $9.95 (0-920656-08-0). 72pp. The relationship between the homes animals build and how animal behavior influences home design and location is explored in this fascinating book. (Rev: SLJ 5/90) [591.5]

18909 Kitchen, Bert. *And So They Build* (3–5). Illus. 1993, Candlewick $15.95 (1-56402-217-X). 32pp. Twelve different animals, like swallows and harvest mice, and the amazing structures they build are described in text and detailed paintings. (Rev: BL 1/1/94) [591.56]

18910 Miranda, Anne. *Does a Mouse Have a House?* (PS). Illus. by author. 1994, Bradbury paper $14.95 (0-02-767251-4). The homes of 17 different insects and other animals are introduced in rhyming couplets and striking collages. (Rev: SLJ 12/94) [591.5]

18911 Robinson, W. Wright. *How Mammals Build Their Amazing Homes* (5–8). Illus. by Carlyn Iverson. Series: Animal Architects. 1999, Blackbirch LB $19.95 (1-56711-381-8). 64pp. After defining what a mammal is, this account shows the homes of animals including beavers, chimpanzees, squirrels, prairie dogs, and moles, and describes how they are constructed. (Rev: HBG 3/00; SLJ 5/00) [591.56]

18912 Ryan, Pam M. *Armadillos Sleep in Dugouts: And Other Places Animals Live* (K–2). Illus. by Diane De Groat. 1997, Hyperion LB $14.89 (0-7868-2222-8). About 30 animal homes, from a beaver lodge to a woody thicket for deer, are described in text and pictures in this simple science book. (Rev: HBG 3/98; SLJ 12/97) [591]

18913 Taylor, Barbara. *Animal Hide and Seek* (2–4). Illus. by John Francis. 1998, DK $15.95 (0-7894-3435-0). 48pp. This oversize book uses page flaps to reveal a variety of animals and explain their different habitats. (Rev: BL 12/15/98; HBG 3/99) [590]

18914 Taylor, Barbara. *Animal Homes* (4–6). Illus. Series: Inside Guides. 1996, DK $15.95 (0-7894-1012-5). 44pp. A heavily illustrated book that introduces various animal dwellings, including nests, burrows, cocoons, and compost heaps. (Rev: SLJ 11/96) [591.56]

18915 Terreson, Jeffrey. *Animal Homes* (3–5). Illus. 1998, National Geographic $16.00 (0-7922-7075-4). Using amazing paper engineering, this interactive book looks at various animals and their homes. (Rev: BL 1/1–15/99; HBG 10/98) [591.56]

18916 Zoehfeld, Kathleen W. *What Lives in a Shell?* (PS–1). Illus. by Helen K. Davie. Series: Let's-Read-and-Find-Out. 1994, HarperCollins paper $4.95 (0-06-445124-0). 32pp. A simple science book that introduces such creatures as snails, turtles, crabs, and oysters, that use their shells as homes. (Rev: BL 8/94; HB 11–12/94; SLJ 9/94) [591.4]

REPRODUCTION

18917 Burton, Robert. *Egg* (K–3). Illus. by Jane Burton and Kim Taylor. 1994, DK $14.95 (1-56458-460-7). 45pp. After tracing the development of a chicken embryo, this book describes 27 animals, mostly birds, that hatch from eggs. (Rev: BL 4/1/94; SLJ 6/94) [591.3]

18918 Collard, Sneed B. *Making Animal Babies* (1–4). Illus. by Steve Jenkins. 2000, Houghton $16.00 (0-395-95317-0). 32pp. This beginning science book explains how animals reproduce — from budding and splitting to sexual reproduction — and provides material on the strategies used to mate. (Rev: BCCB 9/00; BL 5/1/00; HBG 10/00; SLJ 7/00) [571.8]

18919 *Look Who's Hatching!* (PS–1). Series: World Wildlife Fund. 1998, Cedco $12.95 (0-7683-2043-7). A variety of animals that hatch from eggs are introduced with verbal clues and lifting of flaps to see pictures of the creatures. (Rev: HBG 3/99; SLJ 1/99) [591.3]

18920 Seddon, Tony. *Animal Parenting* (5–8). Illus. Series: Nature Watch. 1989, Facts on File $15.95 (0-8160-1654-2). 61pp. Mating, birth, and parenting are covered, from the primitive to the most complex forms of life. (Rev: SLJ 2/90) [591.56]

Animal Species

GENERAL AND MISCELLANEOUS

18921 Ancona, George. *The Golden Lion Tamarin Comes Home* (3–5). Illus. 1994, Macmillan paper $15.95 (0-02-700905-X). 40pp. This account describes how the National Zoo in Washington, D.C. prepares small Brazilian monkeys to return to their natural habitat. (Rev: BL 12/1/94; SLJ 2/95) [639.9]

18922 Arnold, Caroline. *Zebra* (3–7). Illus. 1993, Morrow paper $5.95 (0-688-12273-6). 48pp. Characteristics and behavior of zebras just like Punda, who lives in an animal park in New Jersey. (Rev: BL 9/1/87; SLJ 9/87)

18923 Arnosky, Jim. *Raccoons and Ripe Corn* (PS–1). Illus. by author. 1991, Morrow paper $4.95 (0-688-10489-4). 32pp. An autumn night with mother and baby raccoon eating corn in the field. (Rev: BL 9/1/87; SLJ 9/87)

18924 Arthur, Alex. *Shell* (4–8). Illus. Series: Eyewitness Books. 1989, Knopf LB $20.99 (0-394-92256-5). 64pp. All kinds of shelled creatures are highlighted, including mollusks, crustaceans, turtles, and tortoises. (Rev: BL 9/15/89; SLJ 8/89) [594]

18925 Berman, Ruth. *American Bison* (3–6). Illus. by Cheryl Walsh Bellville. Series: Nature Watch. 1992, Carolrhoda LB $23.93 (0-87614-697-3). 48pp. The lifestyle, habitat, and current status of the American buffalo is covered in text and pictures. (Rev: BL 8/92; SLJ 10/82) [599.73]

18926 Brett, Jessica. *Animals on the Go* (1–2). Illus. by Richard Cowdrey. Series: Green Light. 2000, Harcourt $10.95 (0-15-202584-7); paper $3.95 (0-15-202590-1). 20pp. A beginning reader that introduces five speedy animals — wild horses, ostriches, rabbits, bobcats, and cheetahs. (Rev: BL 2/15/00; HBG 10/00; SLJ 8/00) [590]

18927 Brimner, Larry. *Polar Mammals* (3–4). Illus. Series: A True Book. 1996, Children's LB $22.00 (0-516-20042-9). 48pp. An introduction to the Arc-

tic biome, followed by general information on the many different mammals that live there. (Rev: SLJ 4/97) [590]

18928 Browne, Philippa-Alys. *A Gaggle of Geese: The Collective Names of the Animal Kingdom* (PS–2). Illus. by author. 1996, Simon & Schuster $15.00 (0-689-80761-9). In this imaginative picture book, the collective names of 26 animals are given. (Rev: HB 5–6/96; SLJ 3/96) [591]

18929 Butterfield, Moira. *Fast, Strong, and Striped: What Am I?* (PS–3). Illus. by Wayne Ford. Series: What Am I? 1997, Raintree Steck-Vaughn LB $22.83 (0-8172-4583-9); paper $5.95 (0-8172-7229-1). 32pp. Using double-page spreads, clues are given about an animal by introducing its physical characteristics, habitat, and diet and then identifying it. Also use *Brown, Fierce, and Furry: What Am I?* (1997). (Rev: SLJ 7/97) [591]

18930 Cooper, Ann. *In the Forest* (1–3). Illus. by Dorothy Emerling. Series: Wild Wonders. 1996, Roberts Rinehart paper $7.95 (0-916278-71-9). An intriguing look at woodland animals that contains life-size paw prints, a treasure map of the forest floor, and a look at animal life on each forest level. (Rev: SLJ 8/96) [591]

18931 Craig, Claire. *Incredible Creatures* (2–4). Illus. Series: Nature Company Young Discoveries. 1997, Time Life $10.00 (0-7835-4840-0). 32pp. Some of nature's oddities are introduced in double-page spreads with a simple text. (Rev: BL 2/15/97) [591]

18932 Creagh, Carson. *Mammals* (4–6). Illus. Series: Nature Company Discoveries. 1996, Time Life $16.00 (0-8094-9372-1). 64pp. A wide range of mammals are introduced in text and illustrations, with an eight-page foldout. (Rev: BL 9/15/96) [599]

18933 Crump, Donald J., ed. *Amazing Animals of Australia* (5–8). Illus. 1985, National Geographic LB $12.50 (0-87044-520-0). 104pp. Creatures of the rain forest, ocean, outback, and Tasmania are highlighted with color photos. (Rev: BL 6/1/85)

18934 Delafosse, Claude. *Under the Ground: Hidden World* (PS–2). Series: First Discovery. 1999, Scholastic $12.95 (0-590-43813-1). 24pp. For young children, this colorful, well-illustrated account introduces underground animals such as moles and worms. (Rev: BL 6/1–15/99; SLJ 7/99) [591]

18935 Dossenbach, Hans D. *Beware! We Are Poisonous: How Animals Defend Themselves* (4–6). Illus. 1998, Blackbirch LB $16.95 (1-56711-215-3). 40pp. Many poisonous animals are discussed including some that are relatively harmless, such as the tarantula, and others that mimic poisonous ones to avoid predators. (Rev: BL 12/1/98; HBG 3/99) [591.6]

18936 Everts, Tammy, and Bobbie Kalman. *Really Weird Animals* (2–5). Illus. Series: Crabapples. 1995, Crabtree LB $19.96 (0-86505-627-7); paper $5.95 (0-86505-727-3). 32pp. A brief introduction to 13 strange animals, including the armadillo, tarsier, hagfish, and the smelliest animal in the world, the zorilla. (Rev: SLJ 6/96) [591]

18937 Fontanel, Beatrice. *Monsters: The World's Most Incredible Animals* (3–6). Illus. 2000, Bedrick $19.95 (0-87226-605-2). 94pp. Strange animals such as a transparent frog and a mole with a tentacled snout are highlighted in this beautifully illustrated volume that includes descriptions of their appearance, movement, and reproduction. (Rev: BL 12/1/00; HBG 3/01) [596]

18938 Fowler, Allan. *The Biggest Animal on Land* (PS–3). Illus. Series: Rookie Readers. 1996, Children's LB $19.00 (0-516-06050-3). 31pp. This easy-to-read science book describes some of the world's largest animals, like the elephant, and includes full-color pictures of each. (Rev: SLJ 8/96) [591]

18939 Fowler, Allan. *It Could Still Be a Mammal* (1–2). Illus. Series: Rookie Readers. 1990, Children's LB $19.00 (0-516-04903-8). 32pp. The nature of mammals and some examples are covered in this easily read science book. (Rev: BL 2/1/91) [599]

18940 Fowler, Allan. *Raccoons* (1–2). Series: Rookie Readers. 2000, Children's LB $19.00 (0-516-21590-6). 32pp. A basic introduction to raccoons, their behavior, and appearance, with full-color photos on one page and six or seven lines of simple text on the facing page. (Rev: BL 4/15/00) [599.74]

18941 Fredericks, Anthony D. *Zebras* (2–3). Series: Early Bird Nature Books. 2000, Lerner LB $22.60 (0-8225-3043-0). 48pp. A fact-filled text and amazing color photos explore how zebras live and grow in their native Africa or in zoos around the world. (Rev: BL 7/00; HBG 3/01) [599.72]

18942 Gibbons, Gail. *Pigs* (PS–2). Illus. 1999, Holiday $16.95 (0-8234-1441-8). This book introduces various breeds of pigs, their physical characteristics, their history and habits, and common myths about them. (Rev: BL 3/15/99; HBG 10/99; SLJ 5/99) [636.4]

18943 Grassy, John, and Chuck Keene. *National Audubon Society First Field Guide: Mammals* (4–8). Series: Audubon Society First Field Guide. 1998, Scholastic $17.95 (0-590-05471-6). 160pp. A book that supplies identification information on a variety of mammals with color photos, a basic text, maps, and drawings of the animal's tracks. (Rev: SLJ 4/99) [599]

18944 Hare, Tony. *Animal Fact-File: Head-to-Tail Profiles of More Than 90 Mammals* (4–8). 1999, Facts on File $35.00 (0-8160-3921-6); paper $18.95 (0-8160-4016-8). 191pp. From aardvarks to wombats, this is an alphabetical guide to more than 90 mammals with details including classification, size, coloration, and habits. (Rev: SLJ 9/99) [599]

18945 Harman, Amanda. *Rhinoceroses* (3–5). Illus. Series: Endangered! 1996, Benchmark LB $22.79 (0-7614-0290-X). 32pp. The ferocious rhinoceros is described, with material on its habits, habitats, and why it is on the endangered list. (Rev: SLJ 2/97) [599.72]

18946 Hoban, Tana. *A Children's Zoo* (PS). Illus. 1985, Greenwillow $16.89 (0-688-05204-5). 24pp. Appealing portraits of 11 common zoo animals. (Rev: BCCB 10/85; BL 9/1/85; SLJ 10/85)

18947 Johnson, Sylvia A. *Ferrets* (3–6). Illus. 1997, Carolrhoda LB $23.93 (1-57505-014-5). 48pp. Several types of wild and domestic ferrets and their cousins, including otters and skunks, are introduced, with a concentration on efforts to save the black-footed ferret. (Rev: BL 7/97; HBG 3/98; SLJ 8/97) [636]

18948 Kalbacken, Joan. *Badgers* (3–4). Illus. Series: A True Book. 1996, Children's LB $22.00 (0-516-20157-3). 48pp. In text and photos, the badger is introduced, with material on its physical characteristics, life-style, breeding, and survival. (Rev: SLJ 4/97) [599.74]

18949 LaBonte, Gail. *The Llama* (4–6). Illus. 1989, Macmillan $13.95 (0-87518-393-X). 60pp. Introducing this gentle-natured member of the camel family. (Rev: BL 3/1/89)

18950 Lee, Sandra. *Anteaters* (PS–3). Series: Naturebooks. 1999, Child's World LB $15.95 (1-56766-498-9). 32pp. Using a brief text that faces a full-page color photo, this book introduces the anteater, with material on its home, physical characteristics, life cycle, and habits. (Rev: BL 6/1–15/99; HBG 10/99) [599]

18951 Lee, Sandra. *Skunks* (PS–3). Series: Naturebooks. 1999, Child's World LB $15.95 (1-56766-503-9). 32pp. A colorful introduction to the skunk — its appearance, habitats, food, habits, and life cycle. (Rev: BL 6/1–15/99; HBG 10/99) [599.74]

18952 Lepthien, Emilie U. *Llamas* (3–4). Illus. Series: True Books. 1996, Children's LB $22.00 (0-516-20160-3). 48pp. An introduction to llamas and their relatives that tells about body structure, wool, and habits. (Rev: SLJ 6/97) [599.7]

18953 Lepthien, Emilie U. *Skunks* (2–4). Illus. Series: New True Books. 1993, Children's LB $21.00 (0-516-01197-9). 48pp. Using a simple text, large type, and many attractive illustrations, skunks and their world are introduced. (Rev: BL 7/94) [599.74]

18954 Merrick, Patrick. *Raccoons* (PS–3). Series: Naturebooks. 1999, Child's World LB $15.95 (1-56766-504-7). 32pp. The life cycle of the raccoon, its physical characteristics, homes, food, and habits are touched on in this attractive account that uses many full-page color illustrations. (Rev: BL 6/1–15/99; HBG 10/99) [591]

18955 Midge, Tiffany. *Buffalo* (PS–3). Illus. by Diana Magnuson. Series: Animal Lore and Legend. 1995, Scholastic $4.95 (0-590-22489-1). 32pp. The food, habitats, and behavior of buffalo are described, along with three Indian folktales about them. (Rev: SLJ 3/96) [591.52]

18956 Miller, Sara S. *Horses and Rhinos: What They Have in Common* (3–5). Series: Animals in Order. 1999, Watts LB $23.00 (0-531-11586-0). 48pp. After a general introduction to animal classification, this beautifully illustrated book discusses horses and rhinos — how they are considered alike and how they differ. (Rev: BL 12/15/99; HBG 3/00) [591]

18957 Mostue, Trude. *Wild About Animals: A Book of Beastly Behaviour* (4–6). 2000, Madcap $24.95 (0-233-99684-2). 112pp. A total of 26 mammals — some familiar, like the elephant, and others not so, like the hyrax — are introduced with four-page descriptions of each animal, its habits, and habitats. (Rev: SLJ 1/01) [591]

18958 Nelson, Kristin L. *Clever Raccoons* (PS–2). Series: Pull Ahead Books. 2000, Lerner LB $21.27 (0-8225-3763-X); paper $6.95 (0-8225-3644-7). 32pp. This simple science book covers raccoons — their homes, when they are active, and how they use their paws. (Rev: BL 9/15/00; HBG 3/01) [599.32]

18959 Nicholson, Darrel. *Wild Boars* (2–4). Illus. 1987, Carolrhoda LB $23.93 (0-87614-308-7). 48pp. Full-color photos highlight the habits and characteristics of the boar, introduced in the United States 100 years ago. (Rev: BCCB 9/87; BL 7/87; SLJ 9/87)

18960 Parsons, Alexandra. *Amazing Mammals* (1–4). Illus. by Jerry Young. Series: Eyewitness Juniors. 1990, Knopf LB $11.99 (0-679-90224-4); paper $9.99 (0-679-80224-X). 32pp. Good introductions to mammals and how they care for their young. (Rev: BL 8/90) [599]

18961 Patton, Don. *Armadillos* (2–4). Illus. Series: Naturebooks: Animals. 1995, Child's World LB $22.79 (1-56766-182-3). 32pp. Color photos on each page and a simple text highlight this introduction to armadillos, their structure, and habitats. (Rev: BL 11/15/95; SLJ 4/96) [599.3]

18962 Pearce, Q. L. *Armadillos and Other Unusual Animals* (4–6). Illus. by Mary Ann Fraser. Series: Amazing Science. 1989, Simon & Schuster paper $5.95 (0-671-68645-3). 64pp. Unusual animals and their habits are introduced in this well-organized volume. (Rev: SLJ 4/90) [599]

18963 Pembleton, Seliesa. *The Armadillo* (2–5). Illus. Series: Amazing Animals. 1992, Macmillan LB $13.95 (0-87518-507-X). 60pp. The story of the armed mammal, the armadillo, telling where and how it lives and why it is presently endangered. (Rev: BL 11/1/92; SLJ 10/92) [599.3]

18964 *Polar Animals* (PS–2). Illus. by Paul Hess. 1996, De Agostini $6.95 (1-899883-36-3). Humorous rhymes accompany paintings that describe eight animals from the polar regions. (Rev: SLJ 12/96) [591]

18965 Ransford, Sandy. *The Otter* (K–3). Illus. by Bert Kitchen. Series: Animal Lives. 1999, Kingfisher $9.95 (0-7534-5176-X). 32pp. Using a story format, this charming book traces the life of a female otter as she hunts, mates, and raises her young. (Rev: HBG 10/99; SLJ 8/99) [599]

18966 Robbins, Ken. *Thunder on the Plains: The Story of the American Buffalo* (3–5). Illus. 2001, Simon & Schuster $16.00 (0-689-83025-4). 32pp. An introduction to the American buffalo, its place in American history, and why its population went from 50 million to near extinction. (Rev: BL 12/1/00; SLJ 3/01) [599.64]

18967 Rothaus, Don P. *Warthogs* (2–4). Illus. Series: Naturebooks: Animals. 1995, Child's World LB $22.79 (1-56766-185-8). 32pp. Important facts about warthogs are presented in a clear, large-print text and full-page color photos. (Rev: BL 11/15/95) [599.73]

18968 Ryder, Nora L. *In the Wild* (PS–1). Illus. 1995, Holt $15.95 (0-8050-1775-5). 20pp. Flaps are used to depict parts of animals' bodies in this guessing game to determine each creatures' identity. (Rev: BL 12/15/97; SLJ 5/97) [591]

18969 Savage, Stephen. *Mammals* (2–4). Illus. Series: What's the Difference. 2000, Raintree Steck-Vaughn $25.69 (0-7398-1354-4). 32pp. This book reveals common characteristics and differences among mammals and discusses habitats, babies, food, and locomotion. (Rev: BL 10/15/00; HBG 3/01) [599]

18970 Schlaepfer, Gloria G., and Mary Lou Samuelson. *The African Rhinos* (3–5). Illus. Series: Remarkable Animals. 1992, Macmillan LB $18.95 (0-87518-505-3). 60pp. Full-color photos help tell the story of this great animal and why it is in danger of extinction. (Rev: BL 11/1/92; SLJ 10/92) [599]

18971 Seidensticker, John, and Susan Lumpkin, eds. *Dangerous Animals* (4–6). Illus. Series: Nature Company Discoveries. 1995, Time Life $16.00 (0-7835-4762-5). 64pp. A number of ferocious animals are introduced in stunning pictures and brief text, with an eye-catching eight-page foldout. (Rev: BL 1/1–15/96; SLJ 1/96) [591]

18972 Sherrow, Victoria. *The Porcupine* (4–6). Illus. Series: Remarkable Animals. 1991, Macmillan LB $18.95 (0-87518-442-1). 60pp. The life cycle and habits of the porcupine are explored in colorful photographs and informative text. (Rev: BL 8/91; SLJ 1/92) [599.32]

18973 Short, Joan, et al. *Platypus* (3–4). Illus. by Andrew Wichlinski. 1997, Mondo paper $4.95 (1-57255-195-X). 22pp. There is coverage on the anatomy, habits, and habitat of this unusual animal, with a cross-section drawing of its underground burrow. (Rev: SLJ 8/97) [599]

18974 Sill, Cathryn. *About Mammals: A Guide for Children* (1–2). Illus. by John Sill. 1997, Peachtree $14.95 (1-56145-141-X). 32pp. In this very simple volume with full-color paintings, several mammals and their habits are introduced to young children. (Rev: BL 6/1–15/97; SLJ 6/97) [500]

18975 Silverstein, Alvin, et al. *The Black-Footed Ferret* (4–7). Illus. Series: Endangered in America. 1995, Millbrook LB $22.40 (1-56294-552-1). 64pp. An introduction to this endangered species and efforts being made to ensure its survival. (Rev: BL 10/15/95; SLJ 1/96) [333.95]

18976 Squire, Ann O. *Anteaters, Sloths, and Armadillos* (3–5). Series: Animals in Order. 1999, Watts LB $22.00 (0-531-11515-1). 48pp. After a general introduction to animal classification, this book discusses three oddities of the animal world. (Rev: BL 8/99; HBG 10/99) [591]

18977 Staub, Frank. *Mountain Goats* (2–5). Photos by author. Series: Early Bird Nature Books. 1994, Lerner LB $22.60 (0-8225-3000-7). 48pp. A simple text and excellent photos are used to introduce mountain goats of the American Northwest. (Rev: SLJ 8/94) [599]

18978 Stewart, Melissa. *Mammals* (2–3). Series: True Books. 2001, Children's LB $22.00 (0-516-22035-7). 48pp. Common characteristics of mammals are pointed out in this simple book that shows many different mammals and covers similarities as well as differences. (Rev: BL 3/15/01) [599]

18979 Stone, Lynn M. *Back from the Edge: The American Bison* (4–6). Series: Animal Odysseys. 1991, Rourke LB $16.95 (0-86593-101-1). 48pp. The history of the American buffalo and the conservation efforts to prevent its extinction. Also use from this series: *The Wildebeest's Great Migration* (1991). (Rev: SLJ 3/92) [591.52]

18980 Stuart, Dee. *The Astonishing Armadillo* (3–6). Illus. Series: Nature Watch. 1993, Carolrhoda LB $23.93 (0-87614-769-4). 48pp. The amazing armadillo is featured in text and sharp color photos. (Rev: BL 8/93) [599.3]

18981 Swan, Erin Pembrey. *Land Predators of North America* (2–4). Series: Animals in Order. 1999, Watts LB $22.00 (0-531-11451-1). 47pp. After an examination of animal classification, a number of land predators are introduced with material on lifestyles, appearance, homes, and food. (Rev: HBG 10/99; SLJ 5/99) [599]

18982 Taylor, Barbara. *Oxford First Book of Animals* (K–2). 2000, Oxford $18.95 (0-19-521687-3). 48pp. A first book that uses double-page spreads to answer basic questions about types of animals, where they live, behaviors, and animal babies. (Rev: SLJ 2/01) [591]

18983 Thornhill, Jan. *Before and After: A Book of Nature Timescapes* (PS–3). Illus. 1997, National Geographic $16.00 (0-7922-7093-2). 32pp. Using different habitats, this book pictures a variety of animals and plants using a single dramatic incident, like the charge of a lioness, to show before-and-after situations. (Rev: BL 10/1/97; HBG 3/98; SLJ 9/97) [577]

18984 Toda, Kyoko. *Animal Faces* (PS). Trans. from Japanese by Amanda Mayer Stinchecum. Photos by Akira Satoh. 1996, Kane/Miller $16.95 (0-916291-62-6). 53pp. This book shows how animal faces differ, even within a particular species. (Rev: SLJ 11/96) [591]

18985 Walker, Sally M. *Hippos* (4–6). Illus. Series: Nature Watch. 1998, Carolrhoda LB $14.95 (1-57505-078-1). 48pp. Two types of hippos are introduced, with material on physical characteristics, life cycles, habits, communication, and habitats. (Rev: BL 5/1/98; HBG 10/98; SLJ 4/98) [599.63]

18986 Walker, Sally M. *Rhinos* (4–6). Illus. 1996, Carolrhoda LB $23.93 (1-57505-008-0). 48pp. An introduction to rhinos that stresses their present near extinction and conservation efforts. (Rev: BL 12/1/96; SLJ 12/96*) [599.72]

18987 Webber, Desiree Morrison. *The Buffalo Train Ride* (4–7). Illus. by Sandy Shropshire. 1999, Eakin $14.95 (1-57168-275-9). 91pp. This is a history of the American buffalo, how it was hunted to near extinction, and the modern efforts to make sure it

survives, with special attention to the work of William Hornaday. (Rev: HBG 3/00; SLJ 3/00) [591.52]

18988 Whayne, Susanne S. *Night Creatures* (3–6). Illus. by Steven Schindler. 1993, Simon & Schuster paper $15.00 (0-671-73395-8). 45pp. Five nocturnal animals are introduced and described. (Rev: BL 7/93; SLJ 7/93) [591]

APE FAMILY

18989 Ashby, Ruth. *The Orangutan* (4–6). Illus. Series: Remarkable Animals. 1994, Dillon LB $18.95 (0-87518-600-9). 60pp. As well as a description of the orangutan and its environment, this account discusses conservation efforts being undertaken to save this endangered species. (Rev: SLJ 8/94) [599.88]

18990 Darling, Kathy. *Lemurs on Location* (3–5). Illus. Series: On Location. 1998, Lothrop $16.00 (0-688-12539-5). 32pp. Three species of Madagascar lemurs are introduced in text and color illustrations, with material on their physical characteristics, habits, diet, and social organization. (Rev: BL 4/15/98; HBG 3/99; SLJ 5/98) [599.8]

18991 Darling, Tara, and Kathy Darling. *How to Babysit an Orangutan* (2–4). Illus. 1996, Walker LB $16.85 (0-8027-8467-4). 32pp. The description of the activities and functions of Camp Leakey on Borneo, where orphaned orangutans are cared for. (Rev: BL 12/15/96; HB 11–12/96; SLJ 10/96) [599.88]

18992 Fleisher, Paul. *Gorillas* (5–8). Illus. Series: AnimalWays. 2000, Marshall Cavendish $19.95 (0-7614-1140-2). 104pp. Color photos and clear text introduce gorillas, their scientific classification, physical and behavioral characteristics, and relationship to humans. (Rev: BL 1/1–15/01; HBG 3/01) [599.884]

18993 Gallimard Jeunesse. *Monkeys and Apes* (PS–2). Series: First Discovery. 1999, Scholastic $12.95 (0-590-87610-4). 24pp. Using many color photos and a brief text, this colorful book introduces different members of the ape family and explains their differences. (Rev: BL 6/1–15/99; HBG 10/99; SLJ 8/99) [599.88]

18994 Gelman, Rita G. *Monkeys and Apes of the World* (2–5). Illus. 1990, Watts LB $24.00 (0-531-10749-3). 64pp. Apes and monkeys are compared and contrasted in this well-illustrated study. (Rev: BL 7/90; SLJ 8/90) [599.8]

18995 Goodall, Jane. *The Chimpanzee Family Book* (4–6). Illus. 1997, North-South paper $8.95 (1-558-58803-5). 72pp. Illustrated with photographs, this is an affectionate portrayal of a family of chimps. (Rev: BL 7/89; HB 7–8/89; SLJ 6/89) [599.88]

18996 Goodall, Jane. *With Love* (4–6). Illus. by Alan Marks. 1998, Noth/South LB $15.88 (1-55858-912-0). 44pp. This book contains a handful of true stories about chimpanzees and their lives as members of a large family community. (Rev: BL 4/15/98*; HBG 3/99) [599.885]

18997 Hansard, Peter. *I Like Monkeys Because . . .* (PS–1). Illus. by Patricia Casey. Series: Read and Wonder. 1993, Candlewick $14.95 (1-56402-196-

3). 32pp. A simple introduction to apes and monkeys around the world. (Rev: BL 10/15/93; SLJ 10/93) [599.8]

18998 Harman, Amanda. *South American Monkeys* (4–6). Illus. Series: Endangered! 1996, Benchmark LB $22.79 (0-7614-0218-7). 32pp. The monkeys of South America are introduced, with material on how they differ from their African counterparts and why they are endangered. (Rev: SLJ 8/96) [599.88]

18999 Horton, Casey. *Apes* (3–6). Illus. Series: Endangered! 1996, Benchmark LB $22.79 (0-7614-0212-8). 32pp. Several species of great and lesser apes are introduced, with material on habitats, physical traits, behavior, and endangered status. (Rev: SLJ 3/96) [599.88]

19000 Kalman, Bobbie, and Heather Levigne. *What Is a Primate?* (3–5). Illus. by Barbara Bedell. Series: Science of Living Things. 1999, Crabtree LB $14.37 (0-86505-922-5); paper $5.36 (0-86505-950-0). 32pp. Double-page spreads are used to introduce primates of different species like gorillas, gibbons, orangutans, chimpanzees, and bonobos. (Rev: SLJ 12/99) [599.8]

19001 Lasky, Kathryn. *Shadows in the Dawn: The Lemurs of Madagascar* (4–6). Illus. 1998, Harcourt $18.00 (0-15-200258-8). 64pp. Using splendid photographs, the author introduces the lemur, its habits, environment, social structure, and remarkable similarities to humans. (Rev: BL 4/1/98; HBG 3/99; SLJ 7/98) [599.8]

19002 Lewin, Ted, and Betsy Lewin. *Gorilla Walk* (4–6). Illus. 1999, Lothrop LB $15.93 (0-688-16510-9). 48pp. An oversize book that describes the authors' 1997 trip to Uganda where they studied the mountain gorilla and its habitat. (Rev: BL 8/99; HBG 3/00; SLJ 9/99) [599.884]

19003 McDonald, Mary Ann. *Chimpanzees* (PS–3). Series: Naturebooks. 1999, Child's World LB $15.95 (1-56766-497-0). 32pp. This oversize book, with 15 full-page color photographs, introduces the chimpanzee and gives basic information on topics such as appearance, habits, homes, food, and life cycle. (Rev: BL 6/1–15/99; HBG 10/99) [599.885]

19004 McDonald, Mary Ann. *Lemurs* (PS–3). Illus. Series: Naturebooks. 1999, Child's World LB $22.79 (1-56766-495-4). 32pp. Lemurs, the tree-dwelling small primates of Madagascar and Comoro are described, with pictures and text discussions of their appearance, habits, lifestyles, and food. (Rev: BL 6/1–15/99; HBG 10/99) [599.8]

19005 Martin, Patricia A. *Chimpanzees* (3–5). Series: True Books. 2000, Children's LB $21.50 (0-516-24013-3). 48pp. Large text and color photos introduce chimpanzees, their habits, food, and homes. (Rev: BL 5/15/00) [599.88]

19006 Martin, Patricia A. *Gorillas* (3–5). Series: True Books. 2000, Children's LB $21.50 (0-516-21570-1). 48pp. Colorful photographs illustrate this book on gorillas, their physical characteristics, habitats, and endangered status. (Rev: BL 5/15/00) [599.8]

19007 Martin, Patricia A. *Lemurs, Lorises, and Other Lower Primates* (3–5). Series: True Books.

2000, Children's LB $21.50 (0-516-21575-2). 48pp. The lemur of Madagascar and the tailless loris are two of the lower primates presented in this colorful account. (Rev: BL 5/15/00) [599.8]

19008 Martin, Patricia A. *Monkeys of Asia and Africa* (3–5). Series: True Books. 2000, Children's LB $21.50 (0-516-21573-6). 48pp. Large type, simple text, and full-color photos are used to introduce these monkeys from Asia and Africa. Also use *Monkeys of Central and South America* (2000). (Rev: BL 5/15/00) [599.88]

19009 Martin, Patricia A. *Orangutans* (3–5). Series: True Books. 2000, Children's LB $21.50 (0-516-21571-X). 48pp. This is a simple introduction to these tree-living primates native to Borneo and Sumatra. (Rev: BL 5/15/00) [599.8]

19010 Milton, Joyce. *Gorillas: Gentle Giants of the Forest* (1–3). Illus. by Bryn Barnard. Series: Step into Reading. 1997, Random paper $3.99 (0-679-87284-1). 48pp. This easy-to-read account introduces gorillas, where they live, what they eat, and how they move. (Rev: BL 5/1/97; SLJ 8/97) [598.98]

19011 Patterson, Francine. *Koko-Love! Conversations with a Signing Gorilla* (3–5). Illus. 1999, Dutton $14.99 (0-525-46319-4). 32pp. This slim, colorful volume tells the story of Koko, the gorilla who can "speak" through sign language. (Rev: BL 11/1/99; HBG 3/00; SLJ 12/99) [599.8]

19012 Powzyk, Joyce. *In Search of Lemurs: My Days and Nights in a Madagascar Rain Forest* (4–7). Illus. 1998, National Geographic $17.95 (0-7922-7072-X). 48pp. The author describes and illustrates her journey into the wilds of Madagascar and the many animals, plants, and birds she encountered, culminating in the elusive lemur. (Rev: BL 9/15/98; HBG 3/99; SLJ 10/98) [599.8]

19013 Redmond, Ian. *Gorilla* (4–8). Illus. Series: Eyewitness Books. 1995, Knopf $20.99 (0-679-97332-X). 64pp. Illustrations highlight this introduction to the life, personality, and environment of the gorilla. (Rev: BL 12/15/95; SLJ 1/96) [599.8]

19014 Robinson, Claire. *Chimpanzees* (2–3). Illus. Series: In the Wild. 1997, Heinemann $21.36 (1-57572-136-8). 24pp. A simple introduction to chimpanzees with close-up views of family life, information on how apes use tools, and material about their endangered status. (Rev: BL 2/1/98) [599.885]

19015 Saign, Geoffrey. *The Great Apes* (3–5). Illus. Series: First Books. 1998, Watts LB $21.00 (0-531-20361-1). 64pp. Introduces gorillas, chimpanzees, bonobos, and orangutans, noting their similarities to humans and describing the status of conservation efforts. (Rev: BL 5/15/98; HBG 10/98) [599.8]

19016 Simon, Seymour. *Gorillas* (3–5). Illus. 2000, HarperCollins LB $15.89 (0-06-023036-3). 32pp. This book about gorillas covers the three subspecies, anatomy, family groups, feeding habits, and care of the young. (Rev: BL 10/15/00; HBG 3/01; SLJ 10/00) [599.884]

19017 Stone, Lynn M. *Baboons* (1–3). Illus. Series: Monkey Discovery Library. 1991, Rourke LB $10.95 (0-86593-067-8). 24pp. A brief introduction to baboons: physical traits, behavior, and habitats.

Also use: *Chimpanzees; Gorillas;* and *Snow Monkeys* (all 1990). (Rev: SLJ 6/91) [599.8]

BATS

19018 Ackerman, Diane. *Bats: Shadows in the Night* (4–6). Illus. 1997, Crown $18.00 (0-517-70919-8). 32pp. The author reports on her bat-watching experiences in the Big Bend National Park in Texas and of the amazing observations she made concerning these unusual creatures. (Rev: BL 10/1/97; HBG 3/98; SLJ 10/97*) [599.4]

19019 Arnold, Caroline. *Bat* (3–6). Illus. by Richard Hewett. 1996, Morrow $15.89 (0-688-13727-X). 48pp. The structure, behavior, habitats, and mythology of bats are covered. (Rev: BCCB 10/96; BL 8/96; SLJ 9/96) [599.4]

19020 Bair, Diane, and Pamela Wright. *Bat Watching* (2–5). Series: Wildlife Watching. 1999, Capstone $19.93 (0-7638-0318-1). 48pp. An introduction to bats, their habits, habitats, and practical advice on how, when, and where to observe them. (Rev: BL 2/15/00) [599.4]

19021 Berger, Melvin, and Gilda Berger. *Screech! A Book About Bats* (2–3). Illus. Series: Hello Reader! 2000, Scholastic paper $3.99 (0-439-20164-0). 40pp. This easy-to-read introduction to bats tells about their colonies, behavior, many varieties, and habitats. (Rev: BL 2/15/01) [599.4]

19022 Berman, Ruth. *Squeaking Bats* (PS–2). Series: Pull Ahead Books. 1998, Lerner LB $21.27 (0-8225-3602-1). 32pp. An interactive text, color photos, and a body diagram are used to explore the fascinating world of bats. (Rev: BL 2/15/99; HBG 3/99; SLJ 1/99) [599.4]

19023 Earle, Ann. *Zipping, Zapping, Zooming Bats* (2–3). Illus. by Henry Cole. 1995, HarperCollins LB $15.89 (0-06-023480-6). 32pp. Coverage is given on various types of bats and their body structure, senses, eating habits, and homes. (Rev: BCCB 2/96; BL 8/95; SLJ 8/95) [599.4]

19024 Gibbons, Gail. *Bats* (K–3). Illus. 1999, Holiday $16.95 (0-8234-1457-4). 32pp. An introduction to bats that discusses their physical characteristics, habits, food, and lifestyle. (Rev: BL 9/1/99; HBG 3/00; SLJ 1/00) [599.4]

19025 Glaser, Linda. *Beautiful Bats* (PS–K). Illus. by Sharon L. Holm. 1997, Millbrook LB $21.40 (0-7613-0254-9). Basic information about bats is given in the body of this simple science book, with six pages of additional details at the back of the book. (Rev: HBG 3/98; SLJ 12/97) [599.4]

19026 Greenaway, Frank. *Amazing Bats* (1–4). Illus. by Jerry Young. Series: Eyewitness Juniors. 1991, Knopf LB $11.99 (0-679-91518-4); paper $9.99 (0-679-81518-X). 32pp. In amazing photos spread over two pages, the world of bats and their habits is introduced. (Rev: BL 10/1/91) [599.4]

19027 Haffner, Marianne, and Hans-Peter B. Stutz. *Bats! Amazing and Mysterious Creatures of the Night* (3–4). Illus. 1998, Blackbirch LB $16.95 (1-56711-214-5). 40pp. Using text and well-captioned photos, this account describes the anatomy, habits, and habitats of several species of bats, with empha-

sis on the mouse-eared variety. (Rev: BL 12/1/98; HBG 3/99) [599.4]

19028 Johnson, Sylvia A. *Bats* (4–7). Illus. 1985, Lerner LB $22.60 (0-8225-1461-3); paper $5.95 (0-8225-9500-1). 48pp. Characteristics and behavior patterns of this flying mammal. (Rev: BCCB 3/86; BL 4/15/86; SLJ 2/86)

19029 McNulty, Faith. *When I Lived with Bats* (1–4). Illus. by Lena Shiffman. Series: Hello Reader! 1999, Scholastic paper $3.99 (0-590-04980-1). Basic information about bats is given by an author who studied them while living one summer in a house filled with them. (Rev: HB 7–8/99; HBG 10/99; SLJ 8/99) [599.4]

19030 Maestro, Betsy. *Bats: Night Fliers* (K–3). Illus. by Giulio Maestro. 1994, Scholastic $15.95 (0-590-46150-8). 32pp. An attractive picture book that exposes the myths concerning this night flier and replaces them with the truth. (Rev: SLJ 12/94) [599.4]

19031 Markle, Sandra. *Outside and Inside Bats* (4–6). Illus. 1997, Simon & Schuster $16.00 (0-689-81165-9). 40pp. A straightforward examination of bats that covers topics like their anatomy, physiology, senses, and habits. (Rev: BL 10/1/97; HBG 3/98; SLJ 11/97) [599.8]

19032 Milton, Joyce. *Bats: Creatures of the Night* (1–3). Illus. by Judith Moffatt. 1993, Putnam paper $3.95 (0-448-40193-2). 48pp. Simple vocabulary and short sentences are used to convey basic information about bats and their habits. (Rev: BL 12/1/93; SLJ 2/94) [599.4]

19033 Penny, Malcolm. *How Bats "See" in the Dark* (3–5). Illus. Series: Nature's Mysteries. 1996, Benchmark LB $22.79 (0-7614-0455-4). 32pp. The facts about bats are interestingly presented with details on how we uncovered their secrets and what questions remain unanswered. (Rev: SLJ 2/97) [599.4]

19034 Perry, Phyllis J. *Bats: The Amazing Upside-Downers* (3–6). Illus. Series: First Books. 1998, Watts LB $21.00 (0-531-20342-5). 64pp. This introduction to the world of bats describes varieties, how they live, feed, raise their young, and contribute to the world's ecology. (Rev: BL 5/1/98; HBG 3/98) [599.4]

19035 Pringle, Laurence. *Bats! Strange and Wonderful* (3–5). 2000, Boyds Mills $15.95 (1-56397-327-8). 32pp. This book gives basic information about various types of bats and their habitats and lifestyles, and exposes popular myths about these misunderstood mammals. (Rev: BCCB 4/00; BL 3/15/00; HBG 10/00; SLJ 6/00) [599.4]

19036 Ruff, Sue, and Don E. Wilson. *Bats* (5–8). Series: AnimalWays. 2000, Marshall Cavendish LB $19.95 (0-7614-1137-2). 112pp. Some of the topics that are covered include anatomy, habits, range, classification, habitats, evolution, and survival skills. (Rev: BL 1/1–15/01; HBG 3/01) [599.4]

19037 Stuart, Dee. *Bats: Mysterious Flyers of the Night* (3–6). Illus. Series: Nature Watch. 1994, Carolrhoda LB $27.75 (0-87614-814-3). 48pp. With outstanding photographs, this is a fine introduction to bats and their habits, food, and habitats. (Rev: BL 9/15/94; SLJ 10/94) [599.4]

BEARS

19038 Berger, Melvin. *Growl! A Book About Bears* (1–3). Series: Hello Reader! 1999, Scholastic paper $3.99 (0-590-63266-3). A useful book for beginning readers that introduces bears, their homes, habits, and life cycles. (Rev: SLJ 7/99) [599.74]

19039 Berman, Ruth. *Fishing Bears* (PS–2). Series: Pull Ahead Books. 1998, Lerner LB $21.27 (0-8225-3601-3). 32pp. For beginning readers, this introduction to bears, their habits, and habitats uses color photographs, questions and answers, and an easy-to-read text. (Rev: BL 2/15/99; HBG 3/99; SLJ 1/99) [599.74]

19040 Crewe, Sabrina. *The Bear* (K–3). Illus. by Robert Morton. Series: Life Cycle. 1996, Raintree Steck-Vaughn LB $21.40 (0-8172-4367-4). 32pp. Double-page spreads are used to present material on the black bear, its anatomy, behavior, and habitats. (Rev: SLJ 4/97) [599.74]

19041 Down, Mike. *Bear* (3–5). Illus. Series: Life Story. 1993, Troll $17.25 (0-8167-2765-1); paper $4.95 (0-8167-2766-X). 32pp. Bears and their life cycle are introduced in this short, well-illustrated book. (Rev: BL 2/1/94) [599.74]

19042 DuTemple, Lesley A. *Polar Bears* (2–3). Series: Early Bird Nature Books. 1998, Lerner LB $22.60 (0-8225-3025-2). 48pp. An easily read, extremely attractive introduction to polar bears that covers their life cycle and habitats. (Rev: BL 3/15/98; HBG 10/98; SLJ 7/98) [599.74]

19043 Fair, Jeff. *Black Bears: Black Bear Magic for Kids* (2–4). 1991, Stevens LB $22.60 (0-8368-0760-X). 48pp. This introduction to black bears and their behavior includes special material on hibernation. (Rev: BL 6/1/92; SLJ 7/92) [599.74]

19044 Fertl, Dagmar, et al. *Bears* (4–6). Illus. 2001, Sterling $17.95 (0-8069-6541-X). 80pp. This overview of bears presents a wealth of information on such topics as habitat, physical characteristics, eating, mating, defenses, and sleeping behavior. (Rev: BL 2/1/01) [599.78]

19045 Fitzgerald, Patrick J. *Bear Attacks* (4–7). Series: Animal Attack! 2000, Children's LB $19.00 (0-516-23312-2); paper $6.95 (0-516-23512-5). 48pp. Along with reasons why bears attack people and animals, this account describes their habitats, preferred food, and survival techniques. (Rev: SLJ 3/01) [599.7]

19046 Fraggalosch, Audrey. *Great Grizzly Wilderness: A Story of the Pacific Rain Forest* (K–3). Illus. by Donald G. Eberhart. Series: Habitats. 2000, Soundprints $15.95 (1-56899-838-4). This highly pictorial account traces one year in the lives of a British Columbia grizzly bear and her cubs. (Rev: HBG 3/01; SLJ 1/01) [599.7]

19047 Gilks, Helen. *Bears* (2–5). Illus. by Andrew Bale. 1993, Ticknor $15.95 (0-395-66899-9). 32pp. Besides giving basic information about bears and where they live, this account introduces eight different types. (Rev: BL 7/93; SLJ 8/93) [599.72]

19048 Hodge, Deborah. *Bears: Polar Bears, Black Bears and Grizzly Bears* (K–3). Illus. by Pat Stephens. Series: Wildlife. 1997, Kids Can $10.95 (1-55074-269-8). 32pp. Discusses bears' food, habitats, hibernation, and life cycle. (Rev: BL 9/15/97; SLJ 9/97) [599.78]

19049 Horton, Casey. *Bears* (3–5). Illus. Series: Endangered! 1996, Benchmark LB $22.79 (0-7614-0211-X). 32pp. Different species of bears are introduced, with their habitats, physical traits, behavior, and endangered status. (Rev: SLJ 3/96) [599.74]

19050 Kulling, Monica. *Bears: Life in the Wild* (2–3). Illus. Series: Road to Reading. 1998, Golden Bks. paper $3.99 (0-307-26303-7). 32pp. In a book for beginning readers, several different species of bears are introduced with material on what they eat and how they hibernate and behave. (Rev: BL 3/15/99) [599.78]

19051 Leeson, Tom, and Pat Leeson. *Black Bear* (2–4). Series: Wild Bears! 2000, Blackbirch LB $16.95 (1-56711-343-5). 24pp. This book describes the black bear — its habitat, survival techniques, reproduction, and interaction with humans. (Rev: BL 12/15/00; HBG 3/01) [599.7]

19052 Lepthien, Emilie U. *Grizzlies* (3–4). Illus. Series: A True Book. 1996, Children's LB $22.00 (0-516-20159-X). 48pp. Many photos and a large typeface are used in this book introducing grizzly bears, their characteristics and habitats. (Rev: SLJ 4/97) [599.74]

19053 Lepthien, Emilie U. *Polar Bears* (1–3). Illus. Series: New True Books. 1991, Children's LB $21.00 (0-516-01127-8); paper $5.50 (0-516-41127-6). 48pp. Through brief, readable text and many color photos, the characteristics and habitats of the polar bear are explored. (Rev: BL 2/1/92; SLJ 2/92) [599.74]

19054 McDonald, Mary Ann. *Grizzlies* (3–5). Illus. Series: Naturebooks. 1996, Child's World LB $22.79 (1-56766-213-7). 32pp. This fierce North American bear is highlighted in full-page pictures and large-print text. (Rev: BL 12/15/96) [599.74]

19055 Markle, Sandra. *Growing Up Wild: Bears* (2–4). Illus. 2000, Simon & Schuster $16.00 (0-689-81888-2). 32pp. Stunning photos introduce different kinds of bears, their young, their habitats, and their habits. (Rev: BL 5/15/00; HBG 10/00; SLJ 5/00) [599.78]

19056 Merrick, Patrick. *Bears* (3–5). Series: Naturebooks: Animals. 1999, Child's World LB $15.95 (1-56766-585-3). 32pp. Habits, hibernation, physical structure, and care of their cubs are some of the topics about bears covered in outstanding photographs and a simple text. (Rev: BL 10/15/99; HBG 3/00) [599.74]

19057 Miller, Debbie S. *A Polar Bear Journey* (K–4). Illus. by Jon Van Zyle. 1997, Little, Brown $15.95 (0-316-57244-6). 32pp. Dramatic paintings add to the impact of this picture book about the life cycle of polar bears, as seen through the experiences of a single bear and her cubs. (Rev: BL 12/15/97; HBG 3/98; SLJ 10/97) [599.74]

19058 Milton, Joyce. *Bears Are Curious* (PS–1). Illus. by Christopher Santoro. Series: Step into Reading. 1998, Random LB $11.99 (0-679-95301-9); paper $3.99 (0-679-85301-4). 32pp. Different types of bears are introduced with coverage on their habits, size, and life cycle, in this easy-to-read account. (Rev: SLJ 3/99) [599.74]

19059 Patent, Dorothy Hinshaw. *Great Ice Bear: The Polar Bear and the Eskimo* (3–5). Illus. 1999, Morrow LB $15.93 (0-688-13768-7). 48pp. An appealing account of the characteristics, habits, and habitats of the polar bear. (Rev: BL 12/1/99; HBG 3/00; SLJ 10/99) [599.786]

19060 Patent, Dorothy Hinshaw. *Looking at Bears* (2–5). Photos by William Munoz. 1994, Holiday LB $15.95 (0-8234-1139-7). 40pp. An attractive book on bears that covers such subjects as classification, behavior, food, reproduction, hibernation, and evolution. (Rev: BL 12/1/94; SLJ 1/95) [599.74]

19061 Patent, Dorothy Hinshaw. *Polar Bears* (3–6). Series: Nature Watch. 2000, Carolrhoda $22.60 (1-57505-020-X). 48pp. The biggest and strongest animal of the arctic, the polar bear is the subject of this simple science book that contains outstanding color photographs. (Rev: BL 3/15/00; HBG 10/00; SLJ 7/00) [599.78]

19062 Penny, Malcolm. *Polar Bear* (2–4). Series: Natural World. 2000, Raintree Steck-Vaughn LB $25.69 (0-7398-1060-X). 48pp. This fine introduction to the polar bear, with clear photos and a good layout, covers topics including appearance, life cycle, mating, food, and habits. (Rev: HBG 10/00; SLJ 7/00) [599.7]

19063 Pfeffer, Wendy. *Polar Bears* (K–3). Illus. 1996, Dillon LB $14.95 (0-382-39327-9); paper $5.95 (0-382-39326-0). 32pp. An account of the first two years of a polar bear's life, with material on its habitat. (Rev: BCCB 10/96; BL 8/96; SLJ 9/96) [599]

19064 Ring, Susan. *Polar Babies* (1). Illus. by Lisa McCue. Series: Step into Reading. 2000, Random $13.99 (0-679-99387-8); paper $3.99 (0-679-89387-3). 32pp. In this book for beginning readers, polar bears are introduced in a short, simple narrative that follows a mother and her two cubs through a day's activities. (Rev: BL 2/15/01) [599.786]

19065 Robinson, Claire. *Bears* (2–3). Series: In the Wild. 1997, Heinemann $21.36 (1-57572-134-1). 24pp. In this simple introduction to bears, such topics as food, care of cubs, and communication are covered. (Rev: BL 2/15/98) [599.74]

19066 Silverstein, Alvin, et al. *The Grizzly Bear* (3–6). Illus. Series: Endangered in America. 1998, Millbrook LB $22.40 (0-7613-0265-4). 64pp. This book describes the life cycle, physical characteristics, and habits of the grizzly and why it is now considered an endangered animal. (Rev: BL 9/1/98; HBG 10/98) [639.97]

19067 Stone, Jason, and Jody Stone. *Grizzly Bear* (2–4). Illus. 2000, Blackbirch $16.95 (1-56711-342-7). 24pp. Striking photos and a straightforward text are used to introduce grizzly bears, their physical characteristics, habits, hibernation, food, and habitats. (Rev: BL 12/15/00; HBG 3/01) [599.784]

19068 Stone, Jason, and Judy Stone. *Polar Bear* (2–4). Series: Wild Bears! 2000, Blackbirch LB $16.95 (1-56711-344-3). 24pp. This stunningly illustrated book describes the physical characteristics and homes of the polar bear, its food, mating, care of young, and interaction with humans. (Rev: BL 12/15/00; HBG 3/01) [599.7]

19069 Stone, Lynn M. *Grizzlies* (3–6). Illus. Series: Nature Watch. 1993, Carolrhoda LB $23.93 (0-87614-800-3). 48pp. Outstanding color photos and clear text are used to introduce grizzlies, their habitats, food, and family life. (Rev: BL 1/15/94; SLJ 2/94) [599.74]

19070 Swinburne, Stephen R. *Moon in Bear's Eyes* (PS–3). Illus. by Crista Forest. 1998, Millbrook LB $20.40 (0-7613-0059-7). 32pp. An attractive book that describes the daily life of a grizzly bear family in Yellowstone National Park, with material on their life cycle, social structure, habits, and their endangered status. (Rev: BL 5/1/98; HBG 10/98; SLJ 8/98) [599.784]

19071 Tracqui, Valerie. *The Brown Bear: Giant of the Mountains* (3–5). Illus. Series: Animal Close-Ups. 1998, Charlesbridge paper $6.95 (0-88106-439-4). 32pp. Introduces brown bears and discusses their habitats, characteristics, habits, and life cycles. (Rev: BL 5/15/98) [599.74]

19072 Wallace, Karen. *Bears in the Forest* (1–3). Illus. by Barbara Firth. Series: Read and Wonder. 1994, Candlewick $14.95 (1-56402-336-2). 32pp. Many facts are covered in this novel about two bear cubs that are cared for by their mother from birth through their second summer. (Rev: BL 11/1/94) [599.74]

BIG CATS

19073 Arnold, Caroline. *Bobcats* (2–3). Series: Early Bird Nature Books. 1998, Lerner LB $22.60 (0-8225-3021-X). 48pp. A very attractive introduction to the world of the bobcat and its life cycle. (Rev: BL 3/15/98; HBG 10/98; SLJ 3/98) [599.74]

19074 Arnold, Caroline. *Lion* (3–6). Photos by Richard Hewett. 1995, Morrow LB $15.93 (0-688-12693-6). 48pp. The physical features of lions are discussed, with material on their habitats, behavior, and family life. (Rev: BL 9/15/95; SLJ 12/95) [599.74]

19075 Ball, Jacqueline A., and Kit Carlson. *The Leopard Son: A True Story* (3–5). Illus. 1996, McGraw-Hill $14.95 (0-07-016061-9). 32pp. The animals and vegetation of the Serengeti are seen through the eyes of a young leopard. (Rev: BL 11/1/96; SLJ 1/97) [599.74]

19076 Barfuss, Matto H. *My Cheetah Family* (4–6). Trans. by Amy Gelman. Illus. by author. 1999, Carolrhoda LB $17.95 (1-57505-377-2). 48pp. This photo-essay chronicles the life of a female cheetah and her cubs on the Serengeti Plain. (Rev: HBG 3/00; SLJ 12/99) [599.74]

19077 Barrett, Jalma. *Bobcat* (3–5). Series: Wildcats of North America. 1998, Blackbirch LB $14.95 (1-

56711-257-9). 24pp. Excellent photographs and an appealing, simple text are used to introduce the North American bobcat, its habits, and habitats. (Rev: BL 12/15/98; HBG 3/99; SLJ 11/98) [599.74]

19078 Barrett, Jalma. *Cougar* (3–5). Illus. Series: Wildcats of North America. 1998, Blackbirch LB $14.95 (1-56711-258-7). 24pp. A discussion of the cougar — also known as the panther, puma, or mountain lion — that includes material on its life cycle and physical features. (Rev: BL 12/1/98; HBG 3/99) [599.73]

19079 Barrett, Jalma. *Feral Cat* (3–5). Series: Wildcats of North America. 1998, Blackbirch LB $14.95 (1-56711-260-9). 24pp. The world of the feral cat is explored in photographs and an appealing text. (Rev: BL 12/15/98; HBG 3/99; SLJ 11/98) [599.74]

19080 Barrett, Jalma. *Lynx* (3–5). Illus. Series: Wildcats of North America. 1998, Blackbirch LB $14.95 (1-56711-259-5). 24pp. Introduces the lynx, with material on its habits, habitats, and physical features. (Rev: BL 12/1/98; HBG 3/99; SLJ 11/98) [599.75]

19081 Chancellor, Deborah. *Tiger Tales: And Big Cat Stories* (2–4). Illus. by Peter Dennis. Series: Eyewitness Reader. 2000, DK $12.95 (0-7894-5424-6); paper $3.95 (0-7894-5423-8). 48pp. A beginning reader that features lions, tigers, and other big cats and incidents in which they clash with humans. (Rev: HBG 10/00; SLJ 7/00) [599.74]

19082 Costello, Emily. *Realm of the Panther: A Story of South Florida's Forests* (K–3). Illus. by Wes Siegrist. Series: Habitats. 2000, Soundprints $15.95 (1-56899-847-3). A richly illustrated account that focuses on a pair of yearling panthers in the Big Cypress National Preserve in Florida. (Rev: HBG 3/01; SLJ 1/01) [599.74]

19083 Darling, Kathy. *Lions* (3–6). Series: Nature Watch. 2000, Carolrhoda $22.60 (1-57505-404-3). 48pp. The unique life of the lion is described in this simple book that contains a wealth of attention-getting color photographs. (Rev: BL 3/15/00; HBG 10/00) [599.74]

19084 Delano, Marfe Ferguson. *Tigers* (PS). Series: Animal Safari. 1999, National Geographic $5.95 (0-7922-7107-6). Stunning color photos are combined with minimal information in this introduction to tigers. (Rev: SLJ 9/99) [599.74]

19085 Dupont, Philippe, and Valerie Tracqui. *The Cheetah: Animal Close-Ups* (2–4). Illus. 1992, Charlesbridge paper $6.95 (0-88106-425-4). 28pp. A large-format paperback with excellent color photos that focus on the animal's family life. (Rev: BL 2/1/93) [599]

19086 DuTemple, Lesley A. *Tigers* (2–4). Photos by Lynn M. Stone. Series: Early Bird Nature Books. 1996, Lerner LB $22.60 (0-8225-3010-4). 48pp. Beginning readers will find this an interesting introduction to tigers, their characteristics, and their endangered status. (Rev: SLJ 9/96) [599.74]

19087 Gallimard Jeunesse, et al. *Lions* (PS–2). Series: First Discovery. 2000, Scholastic $12.95 (0-439-14824-3). 24pp. A beginner's look at lions in a heavily illustrated book that presents their physical

characteristics, homes, and family life. (Rev: BL 8/00) [599.74]

19088 Harman, Amanda. *Leopards* (3–5). Illus. Series: Endangered! 1996, Benchmark LB $22.79 (0-7614-0223-3). 32pp. Introduces the three species of leopards and their characteristics and describes the circumstances that have caused them to be placed on the endangered list. (Rev: SLJ 8/96) [599.74]

19089 Harman, Amanda. *Tigers* (4–6). Illus. Series: Endangered! 1996, Benchmark LB $22.79 (0-7614-0215-2). 32pp. The world of the tiger is introduced, with material on its hunting skills, habitats, parenting habits, and endangered status. (Rev: SLJ 4/96) [599.74]

19090 Higgins, Maria Mihalik. *Cats: From Tigers to Tabbies* (3–6). Illus. by Anders Wenngren. Series: Animal Planet. 1998, Crown LB $16.99 (0-517-80003-9); paper $9.99 (0-517-80002-0). 64pp. Using color photographs, this book introduces a number of members of the cat family — both wild and domestic. (Rev: SLJ 6/98) [599]

19091 Hodge, Deborah. *Wild Cats: Cougars, Bobcats and Lynx* (K–3). Illus. by Nancy Gray Ogle. Series: Wildlife. 1997, Kids Can $10.95 (1-55074-267-1). 32pp. Double-page spreads cover such topics about these big cats as their homes, food, habits, and relations with humans. (Rev: BL 9/15/97; SLJ 9/97) [599.75]

19092 Hofer, Angelika. *The Lion Family Book* (3–5). Trans. by Patricia Crampton. Illus. 1988, Picture Book paper $15.95 (0-88708-070-7). 52pp. An overview of the lives of a family of lions. (Rev: BL 1/15/89; HB 1–2/89; SLJ 11/88)

19093 Hopcraft, Xan, and Carol C. Hopcraft. *How It Was with Dooms: A True Story from Africa* (2–4). Illus. 1997, Simon & Schuster $19.95 (0-689-81091-1). 64pp. A scrapbook of pictures about Dooms, the beloved pet cheetah of the Hopcraft family. (Rev: BCCB 6/97; BL 5/15/97; SLJ 4/97) [599.74]

19094 Jordan, Billy. *Lion* (3–5). Illus. Series: Natural World. 1999, Raintree Steck-Vaughn $25.69 (0-7398-1057-X). 48pp. This book, illustrated with many stunning photographs, introduces the lion and how it lives. (Rev: BL 10/15/99; HBG 3/00) [599.757]

19095 London, Jonathan. *Panther: Shadow of the Swamp* (1–3). Illus. by Paul Morin. 2000, Candlewick $15.99 (1-56402-623-X). Oil paintings and free verse illustrate a panther's daily activities, looking for food for her cubs. (Rev: BL 1/1–15/01; HBG 3/01; SLJ 1/01) [599.74]

19096 Lumpkin, Susan. *Small Cats* (5–8). Illus. 1993, Facts on File $17.95 (0-8160-2848-6). 68pp. A handsome oversized volume about the smaller wild cats, with many photos and charts. (Rev: BL 2/15/93) [599.74]

19097 McDonald, Mary Ann. *Leopards* (1–3). Illus. 1996, Child's World LB $22.79 (1-56766-211-0). 30pp. Large print and color photos give basic information about leopards. (Rev: SLJ 4/96) [599.74]

19098 MacMillan, Dianne M. *Cheetahs* (3–5). Illus. Series: Nature Watch. 1998, Carolrhoda $23.93 (1-

57505-044-7). 48pp. An attractive title that introduces the cheetah and tells about its anatomy, habitats, behavior, and its endangered status. (Rev: BL 2/15/98; HBG 10/98) [599.74]

19099 Middleton, Don. *Jaguars* (2–4). Illus. Series: Big Cats. 1998, Rosen $17.27 (0-8239-5210-X). 24pp. A simple, easy-to-read introduction to jaguars that describes their characteristics, habits, and danger of extinction. (Rev: BL 2/1/99) [599.75]

19100 Middleton, Don. *Tigers* (2–4). Illus. Series: Big Cats. 1998, Rosen $17.27 (0-8239-5213-4). 24pp. The appearance, behavior, and mating habits of tigers are introduced along with a discussion of their endangered status. (Rev: BL 2/1/99) [599.756]

19101 Milton, Joyce. *Big Cats* (1–3). Illus. by Silvia Duran. Series: All Aboard Reading. 1994, Putnam paper $3.95 (0-448-40564-4). 48pp. An easy-to-read book that introduces such big cats as leopards, tigers, lions, jaguars, cougars, and cheetahs. (Rev: BCCB 4/95; BL 1/1/95; HB 3–4/94; SLJ 2/95) [599.74]

19102 Montgomery, Sy. *The Man-Eating Tigers of Sundarbans* (4–7). Illus. 2001, Houghton $16.00 (0-618-07704-9). 64pp. This oversize volume introduces the savage tigers found in the Sundarbans Tiger Reserve on the border between India and Bangladesh and gives details on their behavior, food, and physical characteristics. (Rev: BCCB 2/01; BL 3/1/01*; SLJ 3/01) [599.756]

19103 Morrison, Taylor. *Cheetah* (PS–2). Illus. 1998, Holt $15.95 (0-8050-5121-X). 32pp. Information about this endangered species, including physical characteristics, habits, and survival skills, is given through text and pictures that depict a day in the life of Duma, a mother cheetah, and her three cubs. (Rev: BL 5/15/98; HBG 10/98; SLJ 4/98) [599.7]

19104 Perry, Phyllis J. *The Snow Cats* (4–6). Illus. Series: First Books. 1997, Watts LB $22.50 (0-531-20267-4). 64pp. Describes the anatomy and characteristics of such winter cats as the Siberian tiger, lynx, bobcat, cougar, and snow leopard. (Rev: BL 8/97; SLJ 8/97) [599.74]

19105 Potter, Keith R. *Cat Nap: A Wild Romp with the Big Cats* (2–4). Illus. by Keith R. Potter and Jana Leo. Series: Doodlezoo. 1999, Chronicle $12.95 (0-8118-2069-6). 43pp. A breezy, entertaining look at cheetahs, lions, and Bengal tigers, with material on size, coloration, behavior, hunting, and eating, plus short quips in cartoon form. (Rev: HBG 10/99; SLJ 7/99) [599.74]

19106 Robinson, Claire. *Lions* (2–3). Series: In the Wild. 1997, Heinemann $18.50 (1-57572-132-5). 24pp. A heavily illustrated introduction to lions that uses double-page spreads to cover such topics as behavior, food, habitats, and care of young. (Rev: BL 2/15/98) [599.74]

19107 Saign, Geoffrey. *The African Cats* (3–5). Illus. Series: First Books. 1999, Watts LB $22.00 (0-531-20365-4). 64pp. After general information about the evolution of African cats, this well-illustrated volume highlights ten cats, including the lion,

leopard, cheetah, and the tiny sand cat. (Rev: BL 5/15/99; HBG 10/99) [599.75]

19108 Schneider, Jost. *Lynx* (4–7). Illus. 1994, Carolrhoda LB $23.93 (0-87614-844-5). 48pp. The life cycle, habits, and behavior of the lynx are described. (Rev: BL 1/15/95; SLJ 3/95) [599.74]

19109 Silverstein, Alvin, et al. *The Florida Panther* (4–7). Illus. Series: Endangered in America. 1997, Millbrook LB $22.40 (0-7613-0049-X). 64pp. Explains why the Florida panther has become endangered, with material on its life cycle and behavior and the efforts being made to save it. (Rev: BL 3/15/97; SLJ 6/97) [599.74]

19110 Simon, Seymour. *Big Cats* (K–3). 1991, HarperCollins LB $16.89 (0-06-021647-6). 40pp. The life and characteristics of big cats all over the world, with large color photos. (Rev: BCCB 6/91; BL 5/1/91; SLJ 5/91) [599.74]

19111 Smith, Roland. *Cats in the Zoo* (4–6). Photos by William Munoz. Series: New Zoo. 1994, Millbrook LB $21.90 (1-56294-319-7). 64pp. Describes what happens to big cats after their capture and tells of their lives in a modern zoo. (Rev: BL 10/1/94; SLJ 10/94) [599.74]

19112 Stone, Lynn M. *Cougars* (2–3). Series: Early Bird Nature Books. 1997, Lerner LB $22.60 (0-8225-3013-9). 48pp. These large cats, noted for their speed and ferocity, are introduced with stunning photos and a simple text. (Rev: BL 9/15/97; SLJ 10/97) [599.74]

19113 Stone, Lynn M. *Cougars* (3–6). Illus. Series: Nature Watch. 1999, Carolrhoda LB $22.60 (1-57505-050-1). 48pp. Topics discussed in this colorful volume include the cougar's structure, habitats, reproduction, hunting, and relations with humans. (Rev: BL 9/1/99; HBG 10/99) [599.75]

19114 Taylor, Bonnie Highsmith. *Ezra: A Mountain Lion* (3–5). Illus. Series: Cover-to-Cover Books. 2000, Perfection Learning $14.95 (0-7807-9313-7); paper $8.95 (0-7891-5166-9). 56pp. The reader learns through text and color photos about the life cycle of a mountain lion named Ezra. (Rev: BL 2/1/01) [599.75]

19115 Thapar, Valmik. *Tiger* (3–5). Illus. Series: Natural World. 1999, Raintree Steck-Vaughn $25.69 (0-7398-1055-3). 48pp. This book introduces the tiger, labels the parts of its body, and explains how it lives. (Rev: BL 10/15/99; HBG 3/00) [599.766]

19116 Thompson, Sharon E. *Built for Speed: The Extraordinary, Enigmatic Cheetah* (5–8). Illus. 1998, Lerner LB $17.95 (0-8225-2854-1). 88pp. The habits and lifestyle of this endangered animal are introduced, using full-color illustrations. (Rev: BL 6/1–15/98; HBG 10/98) [599.75]

COYOTES, FOXES, AND WOLVES

19117 Berman, Ruth. *Watchful Wolves* (PS–2). Illus. by William Munoz. Series: Pull Again Books. 1998, Lerner LB $21.27 (0-8225-3600-5). 32pp. Questions with answers and colorful photos are used to explore the world of wolves with material on their habits, habitats, and social behavior. (Rev: BL 2/1/99; HBG 3/99; SLJ 1/99) [599.773]

19118 Brandenburg, Jim. *To the Top of the World: Adventures with Arctic Wolves* (5–7). Illus. 1993, Walker LB $17.85 (0-8027-8220-5). 44pp. Amazing color photographs highlight this account of a photographer's experiences living near a pack of Arctic wolves. (Rev: BCCB 11/93; BL 1/1/94*; SLJ 12/93*) [599.74]

19119 George, Michael. *Wolves* (3–5). Series: Naturebooks: Animals. 1999, Child's World LB $15.95 (1-56766-584-5). 32pp. The world of the wolf is introduced in 15 full-page, full-color illustrations and a concise, simple text. (Rev: BL 10/15/99; HBG 3/00; SLJ 2/00) [599.74]

19120 Gibbons, Gail. *Wolves* (2–4). Illus. 1994, Holiday LB $16.95 (0-8234-1127-3). 32pp. The habitat, life cycle, and habits of the gray (timber) wolf are explored in large color drawings and a detailed text. (Rev: BL 9/15/94; SLJ 9/94) [599.74]

19121 Havard, Christian. *The Fox: Playful Prowler* (PS–3). Illus. Series: Animal Close-Ups. 1995, Charlesbridge paper $6.95 (0-88106-434-3). 28pp. Using clear, colorful photos and a simple text, this is an attractive introduction to foxes and their lifestyle. (Rev: BL 4/15/95) [599.74]

19122 Heinz, Brian J. *The Wolves* (K–3). Illus. by Bernie Fuchs. 1996, Dial LB $15.89 (0-8037-1636-9). 32pp. The life of wolves and the activities of the pack are chronicled in this entertaining picture book. (Rev: BL 9/15/96*; SLJ 10/96) [599.74]

19123 Hodge, Deborah. *Wild Dogs: Wolves, Coyotes and Foxes* (K–3). Series: Wildlife. 1997, Kids Can $10.95 (1-55074-360-0). 32pp. Effective illustrations highlight these double-page spreads introducing these "wild dogs" and their lives, food, habits, and sleep. (Rev: BL 9/15/97; SLJ 11/97) [599.74]

19124 Horton, Casey. *Wolves* (3–5). Illus. Series: Endangered! 1996, Benchmark LB $22.79 (0-7614-0213-6). 32pp. Different species of wolves are discussed, with material on habitats, physical traits, behavior, and endangered status. (Rev: SLJ 3/96) [599.74]

19125 Howker, Janni. *Walk with a Wolf* (PS–3). Illus. by Sarah Fox-Davies. 1998, Candlewick $15.99 (0-7636-0319-8). 32pp. An eloquent picture book that introduces the life of a wolf in the Far North, with scenes that deal with hunting, family life, training the pups, and resting. (Rev: BL 3/15/98; HBG 10/98; SLJ 4/98) [599.74]

19126 Johnson, Sylvia A., and Alice Aamodt. *Wolf Pack: Tracking Wolves in the Wild* (5–8). Illus. 1985, Lerner paper $6.95 (0-8225-9526-5). 96pp. Fascinating details of the lives of these animals that travel in packs and share hunting, raising the young, and protection. (Rev: BCCB 12/85; BL 2/1/86; SLJ 1/86)

19127 Lepthien, Emilie U. *Coyotes* (1–3). Illus. Series: New True Books. 1993, Children's LB $21.00 (0-516-01331-9). 48pp. This distant cousin of the dog is introduced in simple text and attractive photos. (Rev: BL 8/93) [333.9]

19128 Lepthien, Emilie U. *Wolves* (1–3). Illus. Series: New True Books. 1991, Children's LB $21.00 (0-516-01129-4). 48pp. The habits and habitats of wolves are discussed in this easily read, well-illustrated volume. (Rev: BL 2/1/92) [962]

19129 Lepthien, Emilie U., and Joan Kalbacken. *Foxes* (2–4). Illus. Series: New True Books. 1993, Children's LB $21.00 (0-516-01191-X). 48pp. For primary graders, this is a simple introduction to foxes and their habits and homes. (Rev: BL 7/94) [599.74]

19130 Ling, Mary. *Amazing Wolves, Dogs, and Foxes* (1–4). Illus. by Jerry Young. 1991, Knopf LB $11.99 (0-679-91521-4); paper $9.99 (0-679-81521-X). 32pp. The wolf family and relatives are pictured in double-page spreads. (Rev: BL 10/1/91) [598.29]

19131 Ling, Mary. *Fox* (PS–1). Illus. by Jane Burton. Series: See How They Grow. 1992, DK $9.95 (1-56458-114-4). 24pp. A glimpse of natural history with the aid of color photos. (Rev: BL 11/1/92; HB 1–2/93; SLJ 2/93) [599]

19132 Mason, Cherie. *Wild Fox* (3–5). Illus. by JoEllen M. Stammen. 1993, Down East $15.95 (0-89272-319-X). 32pp. This picture book tells about the author's encounter with a lame red fox. (Rev: BL 6/1–15/93; SLJ 8/93*) [599.7]

19133 Mitchell, Hayley R. *The Wolf* (5–8). Series: Endangered Animals and Habitats. 1998, Lucent LB $17.96 (1-56006-252-5). 96pp. Describes wolves' characteristics, behavior, their endangerment, and methods used to save them. (Rev: SLJ 11/98) [599.74]

19134 Murdico, Suzanne J. *Coyote Attacks* (4–7). 2000, Children's LB $19.00 (0-516-23313-0); paper $6.95 (0-516-23513-3). 48pp. As well as covering the causes of coyote attacks on animals and humans, this account gives basic information on coyotes, their habitat, survival techniques, behavior, and preferred food. (Rev: SLJ 3/01) [599.74]

19135 Parker, Barbara Keevil. *North American Wolves* (4–6). Illus. Series: Nature Watch. 1998, Carolrhoda LB $21.27 (1-57505-095-1). 48pp. A superior account that describes the North American wolf's physical characteristics, habitat, social behavior, hunting habits, family care, and means of communication. (Rev: BL 12/1/98; HBG 3/99; SLJ 11/98) [599.773]

19136 Patent, Dorothy Hinshaw. *Gray Wolf, Red Wolf* (4–7). Illus. by William Munoz. 1990, Houghton $16.00 (0-89919-863-5). 64pp. Two native species of North American wolf are covered. (Rev: BL 12/1/90; HB 1–2/91) [777.74]

19137 Perry, Phyllis J. *Crafty Canines* (3–5). Illus. 1999, Watts LB $24.00 (0-531-11680-8). 64pp. An introduction to the physical characteristics, behavior, and habitats of North American coyotes, foxes, and wolves. (Rev: BL 11/1/99; HBG 3/00) [599.77]

19138 Samuelson, Mary Lou, and Gloria G. Schlaepfer. *The Coyote* (3–5). Illus. Series: Remarkable Animals. 1993, Dillon LB $13.95 (0-87518-560-6). 60pp. An introduction to this renegade of the dog family, its habits, anatomy, and family life. (Rev: BL 11/1/93) [599.74]

19139 Silverstein, Alvin, et al. *The Red Wolf* (4–8). Illus. Series: Endangered Species. 1994, Millbrook LB $22.40 (1-56294-416-9). 48pp. The story of the red wolf, once thought to have become extinct in the United States, and the recent efforts to reintroduce it in North Carolina. (Rev: BL 4/15/95) [333.95]

19140 Smith, Roland. *Journey of the Red Wolf* (4–8). Illus. 1996, Dutton $16.99 (0-525-65162-4). 60pp. What caused the near extinction of the red wolf and efforts to preserve the species are covered in this fascinating account. (Rev: BCCB 2/96; BL 5/1/96; SLJ 5/96) [599.7]

19141 Stoops, Erik D., and Dagmar Fertl. *Wolves and Their Relatives* (3–6). Illus. 1997, Sterling $16.95 (0-8069-0926-9). 80pp. Different wolves from around the world are featured in this account, with material on their eating habits, self-defense, and reproduction. (Rev: BL 11/1/97; HBG 3/98; SLJ 12/97) [599.74]

19142 Swinburne, Stephen R. *Coyote: North America's Dog* (4–6). Illus. 1999, Boyds Mills $15.95 (1-56397-765-6). 32pp. The author, a veteran park ranger who knows these animals well, describes the coyote and supplies details on the animals' life and habits. (Rev: BL 10/15/99; HBG 3/00; SLJ 11/99) [599.77]

19143 Swinburne, Stephen R. *Once a Wolf: How Wildlife Biologists Fought to Bring Back the Gray Wolf* (5–8). Illus. 1999, Houghton $16.00 (0-395-89827-7). 48pp. An account of the 25-year struggle to bring the gray wolf back to Yellowstone Park and of the controversy surrounding this effort. (Rev: BCCB 7–8/99; BL 3/1/99; HB 7–8/99; HBG 10/99; SLJ 5/99) [333.95]

19144 Wallace, Karen. *Red Fox* (PS–1). Illus. by Peter Melnyczuk. Series: Read and Wonder. 1994, Candlewick $14.95 (1-56402-422-9). 32pp. A story that introduces a red fox and his hunting habits. (Rev: BL 12/1/94) [599.74]

19145 Weide, Bruce, and Patricia Tucker. *There's a Wolf in the Classroom!* (3–5). Illus. 1995, Carolrhoda LB $22.60 (0-87614-939-5). 56pp. After a general introduction to gray wolves, this book gives details on raising Koani, from cub to an adult wolf that can be taken into classrooms. (Rev: BCCB 12/95; BL 9/1/95; SLJ 10/95) [599.74]

19146 Winner, Cherie. *Coyotes* (3–6). Illus. Series: Nature Watch. 1995, Carolrhoda LB $23.93 (0-87614-938-7). 48pp. With color photos on each page and an interesting text, the world of the coyote is introduced, with material on its habitats, family life, and place in America's folklore. (Rev: BL 10/15/95) [599.74]

DEER FAMILY

19147 Arnold, Caroline. *Tule Elk* (3–6). Illus. by Richard Hewett. Series: Nature Watch. 1989, Carolrhoda LB $19.95 (0-87614-343-5). 48pp. This account is highlighted with data on structure, habits, and preservation techniques on this nearly extinct species of elk. (Rev: BL 9/15/89; HB 11–12/89; SLJ 9/89) [599.73]

19148 Bair, Diane, and Pamela Wright. *Deer Watching* (2–5). Illus. Series: Wildlife Watching. 1999, Capstone $19.93 (0-7368-0321-1). 48pp. As well as material on how, when, and where to observe deer, this book explains some of the behavioral characteristics of this animal. (Rev: BL 2/15/00) [599.65]

19149 Berendes, Mary. *Deer* (3–5). Series: Naturebooks: Animals. 1999, Child's World LB $15.95 (1-56766-586-1). 32pp. Using a question-and-answer approach and large color photographs, deer are introduced with material on such topics as food, habitat, and breeding. (Rev: BL 10/15/99; HBG 3/00; SLJ 2/00) [599.73]

19150 DuTemple, Lesley A. *North American Moose* (3–6). Series: Nature Watch. 2000, Carolrhoda LB $22.60 (1-57505-426-4). 48pp. An introduction to these gentle giants of the north, how and where they live, and their life cycle. (Rev: BL 5/15/00) [599.73]

19151 Guiberson, Brenda Z. *Teddy Roosevelt's Elk* (2–4). Illus. by Patrick O'Brien. 1997, Holt paper $15.95 (0-8050-4296-2). 32pp. A book that combines information about Teddy Roosevelt, the elk named after him, and national parks. (Rev: BL 9/15/97; HBG 3/98; SLJ 10/97) [599.65]

19152 Hodge, Deborah. *Deer, Moose, Elk and Caribou* (3–5). Illus. Series: Wildlife. 1998, Kids Can $10.95 (1-55074-435-6). 32pp. Using colorful pictures, diagrams, and sidebars, this work introduces the moose, its habitats, life cycle, survival techniques, and reproductive process. (Rev: BL 1/1–15/99; HBG 3/99; SLJ 2/99) [599.65]

19153 Kalbacken, Joan. *White-Tailed Deer* (1–3). Illus. Series: New True Books. 1992, Children's LB $21.00 (0-516-01138-3). 48pp. In short chapters with many illustrations, the white-tailed deer and its habits and habitats are introduced. (Rev: BL 5/1/92) [599.73]

19154 McDonald, Mary Ann. *Reindeer* (PS–3). Series: Naturebooks. 1999, Child's World LB $15.95 (1-56766-491-1). 32pp. An introduction to the reindeer, where and how it lives, its life cycle, and its habits, using more than a dozen full-page color illustrations that face a simple text. (Rev: BL 6/1–15/99; HBG 10/99; SLJ 9/99) [599.73]

19155 Market, Jenny. *Moose* (3–5). Series: Naturebooks: Animals. 1999, Child's World LB $15.95 (1-56766-583-7). 32pp. In this oversize book, more than a dozen full-page, color photographs are used with a concise text facing each to introduce the moose and its living habits. (Rev: BL 10/15/99; HBG 3/00) [599.73]

19156 Miller, Debbie S. *A Caribou Journey* (2–4). Illus. by Jon Van Zyle. 1994, Little, Brown $15.95 (0-316-57380-9). 32pp. This picture book explores the characteristics and habits of caribou in this story of a caribou and her calf. (Rev: BL 9/15/94; SLJ 10/94*) [599.73]

19157 Patent, Dorothy Hinshaw. *Deer and Elk* (4–6). Photos by William Munoz. 1994, Clarion $15.95 (0-395-52003-7). 78pp. The deer family and its branches are described, with coverage of mating, caring for young, overpopulation, hunting, and harvesting. (Rev: BL 5/1/94; HB 7–8/94; SLJ 6/94) [599.73]

19158 Swan, Erin Pembrey. *Camels and Pigs: What They Have in Common* (3–5). Series: Animals in Order. 1999, Watts LB $23.00 (0-531-11585-2). 47pp. This title deals with 14 specific animals from the Artiodactyla, or "even-toed," order, which includes camels, llamas, deer, and pigs. (Rev: SLJ 11/99) [599]

19159 Wolpert, Tom. *Whitetail Magic for Kids* (2–4). Illus. Series: Animal Magic for Kids. 1991, Stevens LB $22.60 (0-8368-0661-1). 48pp. The whitetail deer and its habits and habitats are introduced in text and illustrations. (Rev: BL 4/15/91) [599.73]

ELEPHANTS

19160 Blakeman, Sarah. *Elephant* (3–5). Illus. Series: Life Story. 1993, Troll LB $17.25 (0-8167-2769-4). 32pp. A nicely illustrated brief account that traces the life cycle of an elephant. (Rev: BL 2/1/94) [599.6]

19161 Blumberg, Rhoda. *Jumbo* (2–4). Illus. by Jonathan Hunt. 1992, Smithmark $4.98 (0-765-10075-4). The story of the famous African elephant whose name has become our word for "huge." (Rev: BCCB 1/93; BL 11/1/92; SLJ 10/92) [791]

19162 Dorros, Arthur. *Elephant Families* (2–3). Illus. Series: Let's-Read-and-Find-Out. 1994, HarperCollins paper $4.95 (0-06-445122-4). 32pp. The African elephant and its family structure are introduced. (Rev: BL 9/15/94; SLJ 7/94) [599.6]

19163 Douglas-Hamilton, Oria. *The Elephant Family Book* (3–5). Illus. 1996, North-South paper $8.95 (1-558-58549-4). 60pp. A beautifully illustrated book about this endangered species. (Rev: BL 1/1/91; HB 9–10/90; SLJ 4/91) [599.6]

19164 Harman, Amanda. *Elephants* (3–5). Illus. Series: Endangered! 1996, Benchmark LB $22.79 (0-7614-0221-7). 32pp. After an introduction to the two species of elephants and their characteristics, this book describes why they are considered endangered. (Rev: SLJ 8/96) [599.6]

19165 Lewin, Ted, and Betsy Lewin. *Elephant Quest* (4–9). Illus. by authors. 2000, HarperCollins $15.95 (0-688-14111-0); paper $15.89 (0-688-14112-9). 47pp. This account of the flora and fauna of Botswana's Moremi Reserve also describes the author's search for elephants. (Rev: HB 1–2/01; HBG 3/01; SLJ 9/00) [599.67]

19166 MacMillan, Dianne M. *Elephants: Our Last Land Giants* (3–6). Illus. Series: Nature Watch. 1993, Lerner LB $19.95 (0-87614-770-8). 48pp. A well-organized look at the animal's physical, social, and behavioral characteristics, with excellent full-color photos. (Rev: BL 1/15/94; SLJ 2/94) [599.6]

19167 Moss, Cynthia. *Little Big Ears: The Story of Ely* (K–3). Illus. by Martyn Colbeck. 1996, Simon & Schuster paper $17.00 (0-689-80031-2). 32pp. The true story of Ely, the elephant that triumphed over a birth defect. (Rev: BCCB 2/97; BL 1/1–15/97; SLJ 3/97) [599.6]

19168 Overbeck, Cynthia. *Elephants* (4–7). Illus. 1981, Lerner LB $22.60 (0-8225-1452-4). 48pp.

Elephants and their life cycle and habitats are discussed in this well-illustrated volume.

19169 Robinson, Claire. *Elephants* (2–3). Series: In the Wild. 1997, Heinemann $21.36 (1-57572-135-X). 24pp. A heavily illustrated introduction to elephants that covers topics like how they move, find food, and raise their young. (Rev: BL 2/15/98) [599.6]

19170 Schmidt, Jeremy. *In the Village of the Elephants* (3–6). Illus. by Ted Wood. 1994, Walker LB $16.85 (0-8027-8227-2). 32pp. This book focuses on an elephant keeper who works with other mahouts and their elephants in a wildlife sanctuary in India. (Rev: BCCB 3/94; BL 4/15/94; SLJ 5/94) [636]

19171 Schwabacher, Martin. *Elephants* (4–6). Illus. 2000, Marshall Cavendish LB $15.95 (0-7614-1168-2). 32pp. A useful volume that describes the physical structure of the elephant and gives coverage on its habitats, behavior, mating habits, life cycle, and food. (Rev: BL 3/15/01; HBG 3/01) [599.67]

19172 Smith, Roland. *African Elephants* (2–4). Photos by Gerry Ellis. Illus. Series: Early Bird Nature Books. 1995, Lerner LB $22.60 (0-8225-3006-6). 48pp. Beginning with a map of Africa, this account describes the African elephant, its habits and habitats, and why it is scarce and valuable. (Rev: SLJ 8/95) [599.6]

19173 Travers, Will. *Elephant* (3–5). Series: Natural World. 1999, Raintree Steck-Vaughn $25.69 (0-7398-1056-1). 48pp. Through amazing photos and brief text, this book traces the life cycle of the elephant from its first steps in the African savanna through learning essential skills to finally taking its place as an adult in the herd. (Rev: BL 10/15/99; HBG 3/00) [599.6]

GIRAFFES

19174 *Giraffe* (PS–1). Photos by Peter Anderson. Illus. Series: See How They Grow. 1993, DK $9.95 (1-56458-311-2). 24pp. In very simple text and outstanding color photos, this brief account traces the life of a giraffe from birth to adulthood. (Rev: BL 11/1/93) [599.73]

19175 Lepthien, Emilie U. *Giraffes* (3–4). Illus. Series: True Books. 1996, Children's LB $22.00 (0-516-20158-1). 48pp. This introduction to giraffes includes coverage on its physiology, habitat, food, and lifestyle. (Rev: SLJ 6/97) [599.7]

MARSUPIALS

19176 Burt, Denise. *Kangaroos* (3–6). Series: Nature Watch. 2000, Carolrhoda $22.60 (1-57505-388-8). 48pp. This attractive volume uses a number of color photos to introduce the kangaroo, its physical characteristics, habits, and homes. (Rev: BL 3/15/00; HBG 10/00) [599.2]

19177 Burt, Denise. *Koalas* (3–6). Illus. Series: Nature Watch. 1999, Carolrhoda $22.60 (1-57505-380-2). 48pp. Colorful photographs and clear text introduce koalas, their food, physical characteristics, lifestyles, habitats, and mating habits. (Rev: BL 12/15/99; HBG 3/00) [599.2]

19178 Kalman, Bobbie, and Heather Levigne. *What Is a Marsupial?* (1–3). Series: Science of Living Things. 2000, Crabtree LB $14.97 (0-86505-978-0); paper $5.36 (0-86505-955-1). 32pp. This beginning science book introduces in text and pictures such marsupials as the kangaroo, koala, and opossum. (Rev: SLJ 11/00) [599.1]

19179 Markle, Sandra. *Outside and Inside Kangaroos* (3–6). Illus. Series: Outside and Inside. 1999, Simon & Schuster $16.00 (0-689-81456-9). 40pp. A thorough introduction to kangaroos that includes material on their diet, behavior, physical characteristics, habitats, and life cycles. (Rev: BL 1/1–15/00; HB 11–12/99; HBG 3/00; SLJ 12/99) [599.2]

19180 Royston, Angela. *Life Cycle of a Kangaroo* (PS–3). Series: Life Cycle. 1998, Heinemann LB $13.95 (1-57572-615-7). 32pp. Using a color photo and four lines of text per page, this book introduces the kangaroo and its life cycle. (Rev: BL 5/15/98; SLJ 6/98) [599]

19181 Sotzek, Hannelore, and Bobbie Kalman. *A Koala Is Not a Bear!* (1–3). Illus. by Barbara Bedell. Series: Crabapples. 1997, Crabtree LB $19.96 (0-86505-639-0); paper $5.95 (0-86505-739-7). 32pp. After distinguishing between this marsupial and bears, this book introduces their subspecies and traits and habits. (Rev: SLJ 9/97) [599.1]

19182 Swan, Erin Pembrey. *Kangaroos and Koalas: What They Have in Common* (3–5). Series: Animals in Order. 2000, Watts LB $23.00 (0-531-11593-3). 48pp. After describing how animals are classified, this book concentrates on marsupials and features the two most famous members of this group — the kangaroo and the koala. (Rev: BL 4/15/00) [599.1]

19183 Tesar, Jenny. *What on Earth Is a Quokka?* (3–4). Illus. Series: What on Earth? 1996, Blackbirch LB $17.95 (1-56711-104-1). 32pp. Describes the characteristics and habitat of this cat-sized Australian marsupial. (Rev: SLJ 3/97) [599.1]

19184 Twinem, Neecy. *High in the Trees* (PS–3). Illus. by author. Series: Animal Clues Board Books. 1996, Charlesbridge $4.95 (0-88106-940-X). Close-up pictures of parts of an animal are revealed to be those of a koala in this picture puzzle book. (Rev: SLJ 12/96) [599.74]

PANDAS

19185 Dudley, Karen. *Giant Pandas* (3–6). Illus. Series: Untamed World. 1997, Raintree Steck-Vaughn LB $28.95 (0-8172-4566-9). 64pp. This presentation includes material on the panda's classification, life span, behavior, and endangered status, plus the myths and legends that surround this animal. (Rev: SLJ 8/97) [599.74]

19186 Fowler, Allan. *Giant Pandas: Gifts from China* (1–2). Illus. Series: Rookie Readers. 1995, Children's LB $19.00 (0-516-06031-7). 32pp. The life of the giant panda is explored, with information about its habitats, food, and endangered-species status. (Rev: BL 7/95) [599.74]

19187 Jiguang, Xin, and Markus Kappeler. *The Giant Panda* (5–7). Trans. by Noel Simon. Illus. 1984, China Books paper $9.95 (0-8351-1388-4). 118pp. China's giant panda is introduced in its natural habitat. (Rev: BL 12/15/86; HB 1–2/87; SLJ 12/86)

19188 Lee, Sandra. *Giant Pandas* (K–3). Illus. Series: Naturebooks. 1994, Child's World LB $22.79 (1-56766-009-6). 30pp. With stunning photos, the giant panda is introduced, with coverage on anatomy, habitat, food, and its endangered-species status. (Rev: SLJ 6/94) [599.74]

19189 Leeson, Tom, and Pat Leeson. *Panda* (2–4). Illus. Series: Wild Bears! 2000, Blackbirch $16.95 (1-56711-341-9). 24pp. Using a direct text and quality photos, this book covers topics related to pandas, such as the world population, physical characteristics, behavior, diet, and endangered status. (Rev: BL 12/15/00; HBG 3/01) [599.789]

19190 Penny, Malcolm. *Giant Panda* (2–4). Series: Natural World. 2000, Raintree Steck-Vaughn LB $25.69 (0-7398-1063-4). 48pp. Clear photos and a good layout distinguish this book about the giant panda, its habitat, mating, diet, and endangered status. (Rev: HBG 10/00; SLJ 7/00) [599.74]

19191 Wong, Ovid K. *Giant Pandas* (2–4). Illus. 1988, Children's LB $21.00 (0-516-01241-X). 48pp. A look at the animals called China's "national treasure." (Rev: BL 5/1/88)

RODENTS

19192 Bastian, Lois Brunner. *Chipmunk Family* (3–5). Illus. Series: Wildlife Conservation Society Books. 2000, Watts LB $22.50 (0-531-11683-2). 48pp. Photographed in the author's backyard in New Jersey, this is a stunning book that focuses on a mother chipmunk and how she raises her brood. (Rev: BL 2/15/01) [599.36]

19193 Bernhard, Emery. *Prairie Dogs* (1–4). Illus. by Durga Bernhard. 1997, Harcourt $15.00 (0-15-201286-9). 40pp. With text and double-page watercolors, this handsome book introduces the prairie dog, its home and habits, and the symbiotic relationship it has with large grazing animals. (Rev: BL 12/1/97; HB 11–12/97; HBG 3/98; SLJ 12/97) [599.32]

19194 Crewe, Sabrina. *The Prairie Dog* (K–2). Illus. by Graham Allen. Series: Life Cycle. 1996, Raintree Steck-Vaughn LB $24.26 (0-8172-4365-8). 32pp. Discusses the life cycle of the prairie dog, including a cross-section of a burrow and information on similar rodents. (Rev: SLJ 3/97) [599.32]

19195 Fowler, Allan. *Of Mice and Rats* (1–2). Series: Rookie Readers. 1998, Children's LB $18.50 (0-516-20800-4). 32pp. These rodents are introduced through full-page illustrations and minimal text. (Rev: BL 9/15/98; HBG 10/99) [599.32]

19196 Gallagher, Kristin Ellersbusch. *Cottontail Rabbits* (PS–2). Series: Pull Ahead Books. 2000, Lerner LB $21.27 (0-8225-3617-X); paper $6.95 (0-8225-3623-4). 32pp. Using many questions built into the text, this attractive easy reader introduces the cottontail rabbit, its physical characteristics, habits, food, and habitats. (Rev: BL 8/00; HBG 3/01) [599.32]

19197 Hodge, Deborah. *Beavers* (3–5). Illus. Series: Wildlife. 1998, Kids Can $10.95 (1-55074-429-1). 32pp. As well as the habitats, appearance, survival techniques, and life cycle of the beaver, this work discusses the animal's incredible building skills. (Rev: BL 1/1–15/99; HBG 3/99; SLJ 2/99) [599.37]

19198 Jarrow, Gail, and Paul Sherman. *Naked Mole-Rats* (4–7). Illus. Series: Nature Watch. 1996, Carolrhoda LB $23.93 (0-87614-995-6). 48pp. An informative introduction to the naked mole-rat, a most unusual animal that seems to copy habits from a variety of other species. (Rev: SLJ 10/96) [599.32]

19199 Kalman, Bobbie, and Jacqueline Langille. *What Is a Rodent?* (2–5). Series: Science of Living Things. 1999, Crabtree LB $14.97 (0-86505-923-3); paper $5.36 (0-86505-951-9). 32pp. Excellent photos and an informative text introduce rodents, their characteristics, and habitat, as well as giving information on specific members of the group. (Rev: SLJ 3/00) [599.32]

19200 Martin-James, Kathleen. *Building Beavers* (PS–2). Series: Pull Ahead Books. 1999, Lerner $21.27 (0-8225-3628-5); paper $6.95 (0-8225-3632-3). 32pp. This introduction to the physical characteristics and habits of the beaver includes a map activity, a body diagram, and many close-up color photos. (Rev: BL 12/15/99; HBG 3/00; SLJ 3/00) [599.32]

19201 Miller, Sara S. *Rodents: From Mice to Muskrats* (3–5). Illus. Series: Animals in Order. 1998, Watts LB $22.00 (0-531-11488-0). 48pp. Using a scientific classification, this book describes, in photos and text, 14 species of rodents, their various habitats, and ways to observe these creatures. (Rev: BL 9/15/98; HBG 3/99) [599.35]

19202 Murray, Peter. *Porcupines* (K–3). Illus. Series: Naturebooks. 1994, Child's World LB $22.79 (1-56766-019-3). 30pp. The anatomy, life cycle, and habits of this unusual rodent are presented in a simple text and color photographs. (Rev: SLJ 5/94) [599.32]

19203 Patent, Dorothy Hinshaw. *Prairie Dogs* (3–6). Illus. by William Munoz. 1993, Clarion $16.00 (0-395-56572-3). 63pp. The varieties, habits, features, and habitats of prairie dogs are described, with coverage of their plight today because of land development. (Rev: BCCB 9/93; BL 10/1/93; SLJ 9/93) [599.32]

19204 Powell, Sandy. *Rats* (2–4). Illus. 1994, Lerner LB $22.60 (0-8225-3003-1). 48pp. The characteristics, habits, and life cycle of various species of rats are described. (Rev: BL 1/1/95) [599.32]

19205 Ricciuti, Edward R. *What on Earth Is a Capybara?* (3–5). Illus. Series: What on Earth? 1995, Blackbirch LB $17.95 (1-56711-097-5). 32pp. The habitat, characteristics, and behavior of this unusual rodent are described in pictures and text. (Rev: SLJ 11/95) [636.3]

19206 Ring, Elizabeth. *Lucky Mouse* (2–4). Illus. by Dwight Kuhn. 1995, Millbrook LB $21.40 (1-56294-344-8). 32pp. The life cycle, structure,

habits, and enemies of a wild deer mouse are presented with full-color illustrations. (Rev: BL 12/1/95; SLJ 1/96) [599.32]

19207 Rounds, Glen. *Beaver* (PS–2). Illus. by author. 1999, Holiday $15.95 (0-8234-1440-X). With text and drawings, this book shows many beaver activities including tree cutting, bark eating, and dam building. (Rev: BCCB 6/99; HB 5–6/99; HBG 10/99; SLJ 7/99*) [599.32]

19208 Sharth, Sharon. *Rabbits* (3–5). Series: Naturebooks: Animals. 1999, Child's World LB $15.95 (1-56766-587-X). 32pp. Rabbits, wild and tame, are pictured in handsome color photos and a simple text that covers their appearance, life cycle, homes, and food. (Rev: BL 10/15/99; HBG 3/00) [599.32]

19209 Souza, D. M. *What's a Lemming?* (4–5). Series: Creatures All Around Us. 1998, Carolrhoda $22.60 (1-57505-088-9). 40pp. This book on the tiny rodents found in subarctic regions tells of their appearance, mating, life cycle, habits, and food. (Rev: HBG 3/99; SLJ 1/99) [599.32]

19210 Staub, Frank. *Prairie Dogs* (2–3). Series: Early Bird Nature Books. 1998, Lerner $22.60 (0-8225-3038-4). 48pp. This work introduces the prairie dog, its habitat, and its unique burrows. (Rev: BL 10/15/98; HBG 3/99; SLJ 1/99) [599.32]

19211 Tagholm, Sally. *The Rabbit* (2–3). Illus. by Bert Kitchen. Series: Animal Lives. 2000, Kingfisher $9.95 (0-7534-5214-6). 32pp. After a description of the daily routines of a rabbit and its mating habits, this account details the building of a nest by the female, the birth of little rabbits, and their care until adulthood. (Rev: BL 5/15/00; HBG 3/01; SLJ 8/00) [599.32]

19212 Zuchora-Walske, Christine. *Peeking Prairie Dogs* (PS–2). Series: Pull Ahead Books. 1999, Lerner $21.27 (0-8225-3616-1); paper $6.95 (0-8225-3622-6). 32pp. The prairie dog's physical characteristics, habitats, and habits are introduced in a simple text with a color picture on each page. (Rev: BL 12/15/99; HBG 3/00; SLJ 3/00) [599.32]

Birds

GENERAL AND MISCELLANEOUS

19213 Arnold, Caroline. *House Sparrows Everywhere* (3–6). Illus. Series: Nature Watch. 1992, Carolrhoda LB $23.93 (0-87614-696-5). 48pp. Gives details on the house sparrow's life cycle, how it was introduced into the United States, and how its population has grown. (Rev: BL 7/92) [598.8]

19214 Arnold, Caroline. *Ostriches and Other Flightless Birds* (3–6). Illus. by Richard Hewett. Series: Nature Watch. 1990, Carolrhoda LB $23.93 (0-87614-377-X). 48pp. Smooth text and sharp photos tell of the amazing ostrich and other flightless birds. (Rev: BL 3/1/90; SLJ 7/90) [598.5]

19215 Arnosky, Jim. *All About Turkeys* (1–4). Illus. Series: All About. 1998, Scholastic $15.95 (0-590-48147-9). 32pp. Using double-page spreads, this book introduces wild turkeys, their bodies, habitats, behavior, and food. (Rev: BL 10/15/98; HBG 3/99; SLJ 11/98) [598.6]

19216 Arnosky, Jim. *Crinkleroot's 25 Birds Every Child Should Know* (PS–3). Illus. 1993, Bradbury LB $15.00 (0-02-705859-X). 32pp. In this junior field guide, 25 common birds are identified and depicted in engaging watercolor drawings. (Rev: BL 9/1/93; SLJ 9/93) [598]

19217 Bailey, Jill, and David Burnie. *Birds* (4–6). Illus. Series: Eyewitness Explorers. 1997, DK paper $5.95 (0-7894-2212-3). 64pp. This book includes general information on avian biology and behavior. (Rev: BL 2/1/93; SLJ 8/92) [598]

19218 Berman, Ruth. *Peacocks* (2–5). Photos by Richard Hewett. Series: Early Bird Nature Books. 1996, Lerner LB $22.60 (0-8225-3009-0). 47pp. A clear, succinct text and full-color photographs are used to introduce the members of the peafowl family. (Rev: SLJ 5/96) [598]

19219 *Birds* (PS–3). Illus. by Rene Mettler. Series: First Discovery. 1993, Scholastic $12.95 (0-590-46367-5). 29pp. Includes basic information about birds — including their beaks, claws, nests, feathers, and food — in a series of transparencies in a spiral-bound book. (Rev: BL 10/1/93; SLJ 8/93) [598.2]

19220 Bishop, Nic. *The Secrets of Animal Flight* (3–6). Illus. 1997, Houghton $16.00 (0-395-77848-4). 32pp. An explanation of why birds fly is followed by a discussion of how they do it, different types of wings, and various modes of flight. (Rev: BCCB 6/97; BL 3/15/97; HB 5–6/97; SLJ 4/97*) [591.9]

19221 Chermayeff, Ivan. *Feathery Facts* (PS–1). Illus. 1995, Harcourt $11.00 (0-15-200110-7). 32pp. Short, simple text and attractive illustrations are used to introduce the world of birds. (Rev: BL 4/1/95; SLJ 7/95) [598]

19222 Demuth, Patricia. *Cradles in the Trees: The Story of Bird Nests* (1–3). Illus. by Suzanne Barnes. 1994, Macmillan LB $14.95 (0-02-728466-2). 32pp. Describes and pictures a number of different bird nests and the way in which each meets the special needs of a species. (Rev: BL 9/15/94; SLJ 11/94) [598.2]

19223 Doris, Ellen. *Ornithology* (4–7). Illus. Series: Real Kids Real Science. 1994, Thames & Hudson $16.95 (0-500-19008-9). 64pp. An excellent manual on how to study birds in their natural habitats, with accompanying activities for all seasons. (Rev: BL 9/1/94) [598]

19224 DuTemple, Lesley A. *North American Cranes* (3–6). Illus. Series: Nature Watch. 1999, Carolrhoda $15.95 (1-57505-302-0). 48pp. Includes material on the physical characteristics and life cycles of the sandhill crane and the whooping crane. (Rev: BL 5/1/99; HBG 10/99; SLJ 4/99) [598.3]

19225 Flanagan, Alice K. *Desert Birds* (2–4). Illus. Series: New True Books. 1996, Children's LB $21.00 (0-516-01087-5). 48pp. Using rich illustrations and an easy-to-read text, deserts are introduced, with special focus on the various bird species found in them. (Rev: BL 6/1–15/96; SLJ 8/96) [598.29]

19226 Flanagan, Alice K. *Night Birds* (2–4). Illus. Series: New True Books. 1996, Children's LB $21.00 (0-516-01089-1). 48pp. Various species of nocturnal birds are introduced, with special emphasis on how they live and hunt. (Rev: BL 6/1–15/96; SLJ 8/96) [598.251]

19227 Flanagan, Alice K. *Songbirds* (2–4). Illus. Series: New True Books. 1996, Children's LB $21.00 (0-516-01095-6). 48pp. A number of birds noted for their songs are described and pictured in this easily read science book. (Rev: BL 6/1–15/96; SLJ 12/96) [598.8]

19228 Fowler, Allan. *The Chicken or the Egg?* (1–2). Illus. Series: Rookie Readers. 1993, Children's LB $19.00 (0-516-06008-2). 31pp. This small-format book with large print and color photos on each page traces the development of an egg and the hatching of a chick. (Rev: BL 9/1/93; SLJ 9/93) [636.5]

19229 Fowler, Allan. *These Birds Can't Fly* (1–2). Series: Rookie Readers. 1998, Children's LB $18.50 (0-516-20798-9). 32pp. Color photographs and a few lines of text introduce penguins and other flightless birds. (Rev: BL 9/15/98; HBG 10/99) [598.2]

19230 Friedman, Judi. *Operation Siberian Crane: The Story Behind the International Effort to Save an Amazing Bird* (4–7). 1992, Macmillan LB $13.95 (0-87518-515-0). 96pp. Ron Sauey and George Archibald founded the International Crane Foundation and concentrated on the most endangered species. (Rev: BL 1/15/93; SLJ 1/93*) [639.9]

19231 Gans, Roma. *How Do Birds Find Their Way?* (PS–3). Illus. by Paul Mirocha. Series: Let's-Read-and-Find-Out. 1996, HarperCollins LB $15.89 (0-06-020225-4); paper $4.95 (0-06-445150-X). 32pp. Various kinds of birds that migrate are introduced and the mysteries connected with their semiannual flights are explored. (Rev: BL 2/1/96; SLJ 4/96) [598.2]

19232 Garelick, May. *What Makes a Bird a Bird?* (K–3). Illus. 1995, Mondo paper $4.95 (1-57255-008-2). 32pp. In a series of questions and answers, the distinctive characteristics of birds are enumerated. (Rev: BL 8/95) [598.2]

19233 Harrison, George H. *Backyard Bird Watching for Kids* (2–5). Illus. 1997, Willow Creek $14.95 (1-57223-089-4). 64pp. Describes the joys of bird watching and introduces 20 popular backyard birds, with material on their calls, food, and habitats. (Rev: BL 12/1/97) [598]

19234 Hickman, Pamela. *Starting with Nature Bird Book* (2–4). Illus. by Heather Collins. Series: Starting with Nature. 2000, Kids Can $12.95 (1-55074-471-2); paper $5.95 (1-55074-810-6). 32pp. An introduction to birds that gives basic material on species, homes, migration, songs, and banding as well as advice to bird watchers and a series of activities including making a birdhouse. (Rev: HBG 10/00; SLJ 7/00) [598]

19235 Hickman, Pamela M. *Birdwise* (4–8). Illus. by Judie Shore. 1989, Addison-Wesley paper $11.00 (0-201-51757-4). 96pp. This introduction to birds discusses anatomy, habits, habitats, and family life. (Rev: BL 10/15/89; SLJ 3/90) [598]

19236 Himmelman, John. *A Hummingbird's Life* (K–2). Series: Nature Upclose. 2000, Children's LB $24.00 (0-516-21166-8). 32pp. Original, full-page watercolor paintings are used to introduce the hummingbird, its characteristics, and its life cycle. (Rev: BL 10/15/00) [598]

19237 Hirschi, Ron. *What Is a Bird?* (PS–3). Illus. 1987, Walker LB $11.85 (0-8027-6721-4). 31pp. Birds in flight, leaping, dancing, and sleeping are depicted and identified. Also use: *Where Do Birds Live?* (1987). (Rev: BL 2/1/88)

19238 Horton, Casey. *Parrots* (3–6). Illus. Series: Endangered! 1996, Benchmark LB $22.79 (0-7614-0222-5). 32pp. This account focuses on eight species of parrots from around the world and why they are endangered. (Rev: SLJ 9/96) [598.71]

19239 Jenkins, Priscilla B. *A Nest Full of Eggs* (1–3). Illus. by Lizzy Rockwell. 1995, Harper-Collins LB $15.89 (0-06-023442-3). 32pp. By observing a pair of robins build a nest and raise a family, two youngsters learn about birds and their habits. (Rev: BCCB 7–8/95; BL 6/1–15/95; SLJ 8/95) [598.8]

19240 Johnson, Jinny. *Simon & Schuster Children's Guide to Birds* (4–7). Illus. 1996, Simon & Schuster paper $19.95 (0-689-80199-8). 96pp. After each of the major types of birds is described, one bird from each group is highlighted. (Rev: BL 5/15/96) [676.2]

19241 Johnson, Sylvia A. *Albatrosses of Midway Island* (3–6). Illus. by Frans Lanting. 1990, Carolrhoda LB $22.60 (0-87614-391-5). 48pp. Amazing facts and statistics about the wondrous albatross. (Rev: BL 3/1/90; SLJ 7/90) [598.4]

19242 Klein, Tom. *Loon Magic for Kids* (2–4). Illus. 1990, NorthWord paper $6.95 (1-55971-121-3). 48pp. This colorful account includes information on the behavior and life cycle of the loon. (Rev: BL 6/1/90; SLJ 3/91) [598.4]

19243 Kuchalla, Susan. *Birds* (K–3). Illus. by Gary Britt. 1982, Troll paper $3.50 (0-89375-657-1). 32pp. A simple introduction with a few short sentences and many illustrations.

19244 Latimer, Jonathan P., and Karen Stray Nolting. *Backyard Birds* (3–6). Series: Peterson Field Guides for Young Naturalists. 1999, Houghton $15.00 (0-395-95210-7); paper $5.95 (0-395-92276-3). 48pp. After a general introduction to birds and observation techniques, this account, illustrated with drawings and photos, uses about 20 double-page spreads to present common backyard birds with coverage of such topics as size, appearance, food, habitats, and special features. (Rev: BL 6/1–15/99; SLJ 8/99) [598]

19245 Latimer, Jonathan P., and Karen Stray Nolting. *Bizarre Birds* (3–6). Series: Peterson Field Guides for Young Naturalists. 1999, Houghton $15.00 (0-395-95213-1); paper $5.95 (0-395-92279-8). 48pp. Using double-page spreads, this field guide describes and pictures a number of birds that are unusual for their appearance, habits, mating ritu-

als, habitats, or other considerations. (Rev: BL 6/1–15/99; SLJ 8/99) [598]

19246 Latimer, Jonathan P., and Karen Stray Nolting. *Shorebirds* (3–6). Illus. Series: Peterson Field Guides for Young Naturalists. 1999, Houghton $15.00 (0-395-95212-3); paper $5.95 (0-395-92278-X). 48pp. A wide variety of shore birds that live near fresh water as well as oceans and the Gulf of Mexico are described in a series of colorful double-page spreads. (Rev: BL 6/1–15/99; SLJ 8/99) [598.3]

19247 Llamas, Andreu. *Birds Conquer the Sky* (4–8). Illus. by Miriam Ferrón and Miguel Ferrón. Series: Development of the Earth. 1996, Chelsea LB $15.95 (0-7910-3455-0). 32pp. A science book that explains the evolution of birds from prehistoric land birds onward and defines their characteristics. (Rev: SLJ 7/96) [598]

19248 London, Jonathan. *Gone Again Ptarmigan* (K–3). Illus. by Jon Van Zyle. 2001, National Geographic $16.95 (0-7922-7561-6). 32pp. The life cycle of the Arctic ptarmigan is covered in this picture book that shows how its feathers change color to offer camouflage in both winter and summer. (Rev: BL 1/1–15/01) [598.6]

19249 Lynne, Cherry. *Flute's Journey: The Life of a Wood Thrush* (K–3). Illus. 1997, Harcourt $15.00 (0-15-292853-7). 40pp. The story of a single wood thrush's journey from Maryland to a Central American rain forest and back. (Rev: BCCB 5/97; BL 4/1/97; SLJ 7/97) [599.8]

19250 McDonald, Mary Ann. *Doves* (3–5). Series: Naturebooks: Animals. 1999, Child's World LB $15.95 (1-56766-593-4). 32pp. Doves are introduced in a question-and-answer text and outstanding color photographs that cover such topics as nests, food, and habits. (Rev: BL 10/15/99; HBG 3/00; SLJ 5/00) [598]

19251 McDonald, Mary Ann. *Jays* (3–5). Series: Naturebooks: Animals. 1999, Child's World LB $15.95 (1-56766-591-8). 32pp. Using 15 full-page color photos and a simple text, the habits, habitats, and physical characteristics of different kinds of jays are introduced. (Rev: BL 10/15/99; HBG 3/00) [598]

19252 McDonald, Mary Ann. *Toucans* (PS–3). Series: Naturebooks. 1999, Child's World LB $15.95 (1-56766-496-2). 32pp. Using a question-and-answer approach, basic information about these colorful tropical birds is given with stunning full-page color illustrations and a simple text. (Rev: BL 6/1–15/99; HBG 10/99) [598]

19253 McDonald, Mary Ann. *Woodpeckers* (3–5). Illus. Series: Naturebooks. 1996, Child's World LB $22.79 (1-56766-218-8). 32pp. These birds with chisel-like bills that drill into wood are pictured in full-page illustrations with simple text. (Rev: BL 12/15/96) [598.7]

19254 McMillan, Bruce. *A Beach for the Birds* (4–6). Illus. 1993, Houghton $16.00 (0-395-64050-4). 32pp. This book introduces the sea swallow and discusses its life cycle, behavior, and habitats. Information is also given on its endangered status. (Rev: BCCB 6/93; BL 4/1/93; SLJ 4/93) [598.3]

19255 McMillan, Bruce. *Wild Flamingos* (3–5). Illus. 1997, Houghton $15.00 (0-395-84545-9). 32pp. Introduces the flamingos of Bonaire in the Caribbean using clear text and spectacular photos. (Rev: BL 7/97; HB 9–10/97; HBG 3/98; SLJ 8/97*) [598.3]

19256 McNulty, Faith. *Peeping in the Shell: A Whooping Crane Is Hatched* (2–4). Illus. by Irene Brady. 1986, HarperCollins $11.95 (0-06-024134-9). 64pp. The process of hatching a whooping crane egg, with a personal narrative. (Rev: BCCB 10/86; BL 1/1/87; SLJ 12/86)

19257 Mania, Cathy, and Robert Mania. *Woodpecker in the Backyard* (3–5). Series: Wildlife Conservation Society Books. 2000, Watts LB $22.50 (0-531-11799-5). 48pp. A heavily illustrated book that describes the physical characteristics of the woodpecker and gives material on its habits, lifestyle, food, and homes. (Rev: BL 3/15/01) [598]

19258 Markle, Sandra. *Outside and Inside Birds* (2–4). Illus. 1994, Bradbury paper $15.95 (0-02-762312-2). 40pp. The anatomy of various birds is described and pictured in color photos on every page. (Rev: BCCB 11/94; BL 11/1/94; SLJ 11/94) [598]

19259 Maynard, Thane. *Ostriches* (3–5). Illus. Series: Naturebooks. 1996, Child's World LB $22.79 (1-56766-274-9). 32pp. This swift-footed, flightless bird is featured in a series of color illustrations and simple text. (Rev: BL 12/15/96; SLJ 5/97) [598.5]

19260 Mazzola, Frank, Jr. *Counting Is for the Birds* (K–3). Illus. 1997, Charlesbridge $16.95 (0-88106-951-5); paper $6.95 (0-88106-950-7). 32pp. Different birds and their characteristics are introduced in this counting book that progresses in pairs to 20. (Rev: BL 4/15/97; SLJ 5/97) [598]

19261 Merrick, Patrick. *Cardinals* (3–5). Series: Naturebooks: Animals. 1999, Child's World LB $15.95 (1-56766-592-6). 32pp. Handsome full-page photos facing eight to ten lines of simple text are used to introduce the cardinal, its home, habits, food, and life cycle. (Rev: BL 10/15/99; HBG 3/00; SLJ 5/00) [598]

19262 Merrick, Patrick. *Loons* (K–3). Series: Naturebooks. 1999, Child's World LB $15.95 (1-56766-595-0). 32pp. Covers the loon's life cycle from egg to maturity, with information on its appearance, habits and habitats. (Rev: HBG 3/00; SLJ 5/00) [598]

19263 Miller, Sara S. *Perching Birds of North America* (2–4). Series: Animals in Order. 1999, Watts LB $22.00 (0-531-11520-8). 47pp. This book explains animal classification and then introduces a group of perching birds, their characteristics, appearance, habits, and habitats. (Rev: HBG 10/99; SLJ 5/99) [598]

19264 Murray, Peter. *Parrots* (3–4). Illus. Series: Naturebooks. 1993, Child's World LB $22.79 (1-56766-015-0). 30pp. Basic information about parrots is given, including material on their physical

characteristics, behavior, and adaptations. (Rev: SLJ 4/94) [598.71]

19265 Parsons, Alexandra. *Amazing Birds* (1–4). Illus. by Jerry Young. Series: Eyewitness Juniors. 1990, Knopf paper $9.99 (0-679-80223-1). 32pp. After a general introduction to birds, this book has large double-page spreads of a single species plus smaller photos and charts. (Rev: BL 8/90) [598]

19266 Patent, Dorothy Hinshaw. *Pigeons* (3–6). Illus. 1997, Clarion $16.00 (0-395-69848-0). 78pp. An introduction to pigeons that covers their history, homes, uses, and intelligence. (Rev: BL 9/1/97; HBG 3/98; SLJ 10/97) [598.6]

19267 Patent, Dorothy Hinshaw. *Wild Turkeys* (2–3). Series: Early Bird Nature Books. 1999, Lerner LB $16.95 (0-8225-3026-0). 48pp. A well-written, handsomely illustrated guide to the life cycle, habits, and physical characteristics of wild turkeys. (Rev: BL 8/99; HBG 10/99; SLJ 5/99) [598]

19268 Pembleton, Seliesa. *The Pileated Woodpecker* (3–5). Illus. 1989, Macmillan LB $13.95 (0-87518-392-1). 60pp. A report on the physical characteristics and life cyle of this large woodpecker. (Rev: BL 2/1/89; SLJ 4/89)

19269 Pfeffer, Wendy. *Mute Swans* (PS–3). Illus. Series: Creatures in White. 1996, Silver Pr. LB $14.95 (0-382-39325-2). Using two-page spreads, the reader follows two swans through nest building, protecting the eggs, raising their young, and migrating. (Rev: SLJ 2/97) [598.4]

19270 Powell, Jillian. *Eggs* (3–5). Illus. Series: Everyone Eats. 1997, Raintree Steck-Vaughn LB $25.69 (0-8172-4759-9). 32pp. This book introduces eggs — their sizes, from caviar to ostrich; the construction, production, and nutritional value of chickens' eggs; rituals connected with eggs; and two recipes. (Rev: SLJ 8/97) [598.6]

19271 Quinlan, Susan E. *Puffins* (3–5). Illus. 1999, Lerner LB $22.60 (1-57505-090-0). 48pp. Three species of puffins are introduced, with material on their life cycles, habits, and habitats. (Rev: BL 1/1–15/99; HBG 10/99; SLJ 2/99) [598.3]

19272 Rauzon, Mark. *Hummingbirds* (4–6). Illus. Series: First Books. 1997, Watts LB $22.50 (0-531-20260-7). 63pp. Describes the anatomy and characteristics of the smallest and most active bird and introduces various species, such as the rufous, sword-billed, and ruby-throated hummingbird. (Rev: BL 8/97; SLJ 8/97) [598.8]

19273 Rauzon, Mark. *Parrots* (4–6). Illus. 1996, Watts LB $22.50 (0-531-20244-5). 62pp. Types of parrots, their mating and nesting habits, and their life cycles are discussed. (Rev: BL 1/1–15/97; SLJ 4/97) [598.7]

19274 Rauzon, Mark. *Seabirds* (4–6). Illus. 1996, Watts LB $22.00 (0-531-20246-1). 64pp. Various seabirds and how each lives, raises nestlings, and gathers food are covered, with material on endangered species. (Rev: BL 1/1–15/97; SLJ 4/97) [598.29]

19275 Rauzon, Mark. *Vultures* (4–6). Illus. Series: First Books. 1997, Watts LB $22.50 (0-531-20271-2). 63pp. Discusses the important role these scavengers play and describes various species, such as the condor, lammergeier, and Egyptian vulture. (Rev: BL 8/97) [598.9]

19276 Ricciuti, Edward R. *Birds* (4–6). Illus. Series: Our Living World. 1993, Blackbirch LB $19.95 (1-56711-038-X). 64pp. This introduction covers general topics related to birds. (Rev: SLJ 8/93) [598]

19277 Robinson, Fay. *Singing Robins* (PS–2). Series: Pull Ahead Books. 2000, Lerner $21.27 (0-8225-3641-2). 32pp. With four lines of simple text and a color photo on each page, this book tells of the bird with the beautiful orange breast feathers and the pretty blue eggs. (Rev: BL 5/15/00; HBG 10/00) [598.8]

19278 Roop, Peter, and Connie Roop. *Seasons of the Crane* (2–6). Illus. 1989, Walker LB $15.85 (0-8027-6860-1). 48pp. With outstanding photos and lucid text, the migratory habits of this endangered bird are described. (Rev: BL 8/89; SLJ 9/89) [598.31]

19279 Royston, Angela. *Birds* (PS). Illus. by Dave King. Series: Eye Openers. 1992, Macmillan $7.95 (0-689-71644-3). 22pp. In eight double-page spreads, each containing a large photo and small illustrations, various birds are introduced. (Rev: BL 10/15/92; SLJ 2/93) [598]

19280 Savage, Stephen. *Birds* (2–4). Illus. Series: What's the Difference. 2000, Raintree Steck-Vaughn $25.69 (0-7398-1356-0). 32pp. A most attractive volume that presents a number of different birds and explains their common characteristics, along with material on their nests, food, and how they care for their young. (Rev: BL 10/15/00; HBG 3/01) [598]

19281 Sharth, Sharon. *Finches* (3–5). Series: Naturebooks: Animals. 1999, Child's World LB $15.95 (1-56766-594-2). 32pp. Various types of finches are shown in amazing color photos with a text that explains their different varieties, nests, food, and habits. (Rev: BL 10/15/99; HBG 3/00) [598]

19282 Sill, Cathryn. *About Birds: A Guide for Children* (3–6). Illus. by John Sill. 1991, Peachtree $14.95 (1-56145-028-6). 40pp. This very simple introduction to birds describes common species and their characteristics. (Rev: BL 12/15/91; SLJ 2/92*) [598]

19283 Smith, Roland. *Vultures* (2–3). Series: Early Bird Nature Books. 1998, Lerner LB $22.60 (0-8225-3011-2). 48pp. A sympathetic, easily read introduction to the world of the vulture, including the ways they find and eat their food, their life cycle, and habitats. (Rev: BL 3/15/98; HBG 10/98; SLJ 3/98) [598]

19284 Spaulding, Dean T. *Feeding Our Feathered Friends* (4–6). Series: Birder's Bookshelf. 1997, Lerner LB $19.93 (0-8225-3175-5). 56pp. This book covers many aspects of backyard bird feeding, like how to build bird feeders, where and when to hang them, their contents, and how to keep squirrels away. (Rev: BL 3/15/98; HBG 3/98; SLJ 4/98) [598]

19285 Spaulding, Dean T. *Housing Our Feathered Friends* (4–6). Illus. Series: Birder's Bookshelf.

1997, Lerner LB $19.93 (0-8225-3176-3). 56pp. As well as supplying information on nests and other conveniences birds use as homes, this book gives directions on how to make a number of birdhouses. Also use: *Protecting Our Feathered Friends* (1997). (Rev: BL 10/15/97; HBG 3/98; SLJ 9/97) [690]

19286 Spaulding, Dean T. *Watching Our Feathered Friends* (4–6). Series: Birder's Bookshelf. 1997, Lerner LB $19.93 (0-8225-3177-1). 56pp. This book introduces the hobby of bird watching, with material on its history, how to use a field guide, the best times and places for birding, and the necessary equipment. (Rev: BL 3/15/98; HBG 3/98) [598]

19287 Stewart, Melissa. *Birds* (2–3). Series: True Books. 2001, Children's LB $22.00 (0-516-22039-X). 48pp. This beginning look at birds includes basic material on their structure, how they fly, their homes, and how they care for their young. (Rev: BL 3/15/01) [598]

19288 Stone, Lynn M. *Sandhill Cranes* (2–3). Series: Early Bird Nature Books. 1998, Lerner LB $22.60 (0-8225-3027-9). 48pp. This easily read, beautifully illustrated account introduces the sand hill crane and its life cycle, with material on its habitat, food, and enemies. (Rev: BL 3/15/98; HBG 10/98; SLJ 7/98) [597]

19289 Swinburne, Stephen R. *Unbeatable Beaks* (PS–3). Illus. by Joan Paley. 1999, Holt $15.95 (0-8050-4802-2). Using colorful collages and a singsong verse, this book introduces 39 birds each with a distinctive beak and also includes a quiz to match the birds with their beaks. (Rev: BCCB 11/99; HBG 3/00; SLJ 11/99) [598]

19290 Tesar, Jenny. *What on Earth Is a Bustard?* (3–5). Illus. Series: What on Earth? 1996, Blackbirch LB $17.95 (1-56711-102-5). 32pp. Examines the world of the bustard, a ground-dwelling bird found in grasslands on several continents. (Rev: SLJ 2/97) [598]

19291 Voeller, Edward. *The Red-Crowned Crane* (3–6). Illus. 1989, Macmillan LB $13.95 (0-87518-417-0). 60pp. A book about the amazing Japanese red-crowned crane and a retelling of the folktale it inspired, The Grateful Crane. (Rev: BL 12/15/89; SLJ 3/90) [598.31]

19292 Wechsler, Doug. *Bizarre Birds* (3–5). Illus. 1999, Boyds Mills $17.95 (1-56397-760-5). 48pp. This description of birds with unique habits — such as strange food preferences — offers scientific explanations for their behavior. (Rev: BL 1/1–15/00; HBG 3/00; SLJ 11/99) [598]

19293 Weidensaul, Scott. *National Audubon Society First Field Guide to Birds* (4–6). Illus. 1998, Scholastic $17.95 (0-590-05446-5); paper $10.95 (0-590-05482-1). 160pp. This field guide consisting of two-page spreads on 50 of the most common North American birds also provides basic facts about birds in general. (Rev: BL 8/98; SLJ 10/98) [598]

19294 Welsbacher, Anne. *Flying Brown Pelicans* (K–2). Photos by John Netherton. Series: Pull Ahead Books. 1999, Lerner LB $15.95 (0-8225-3613-7). 32pp. A colorful introduction to pelicans that includes material on appearance, habits, habitats, a map, and a physiological diagram. (Rev: HBG 10/99; SLJ 5/99) [598]

19295 Welsbacher, Anne. *Wading Birds* (K–2). Photos by John Netherton. Series: Pull Ahead Books. 1999, Lerner LB $15.95 (0-8225-3614-5). 32pp. This book focuses on herons as wading birds and describes their physical characteristics, food, where they live, and how they bring up their young. (Rev: HBG 10/99; SLJ 5/99) [598]

19296 Wildsmith, Brian. *Birds by Brian Wildsmith* (K–4). Illus. by author. 1967, Oxford paper $9.95 (0-19-272117-8). Excellent illustrations of common birds.

19297 Williams, Nick. *How Birds Fly* (3–5). Illus. Series: Nature's Mysteries. 1996, Benchmark LB $22.79 (0-7614-0454-6). 32pp. The flight of birds is explained through an investigation of the internal and external design of their bodies in this book that gives many different examples and descriptions to amplify the text. (Rev: SLJ 2/97) [598]

19298 Willis, Nancy C. *The Robins in Your Backyard* (K–3). Illus. 1996, Cucumber Island Storytellers $15.95 (1-887813-21-7). 32pp. The life of robins is covered, with material on mating habits and nest building. (Rev: BCCB 6/97; BL 1/1–15/97; SLJ 7/97) [598.8]

19299 Winner, Cherie. *Woodpeckers* (3–6). Series: Nature Watch. 2000, Carolrhoda LB $23.93 (1-57505-445-0). 48pp. This colorful introduction to the varieties of woodpeckers explains why they tap holes in wood. (Rev: BL 7/00) [598]

19300 Zeaman, John. *Birds: From Forest to Family Room* (4–6). Series: Before They Were Pets. 1999, Watts LB $24.00 (0-531-20351-4). 64pp. The author describes the physical and psychological changes that occurred as certain birds became pets. (Rev: BL 6/1–15/99; HBG 10/99) [598]

19301 Zim, Herbert S., and Ira N. Gabrielson. *Birds* (5–8). Illus. 1991, Western paper $21.27 (0-307-64053-1). A guide to the most commonly seen birds, with accompanying illustrations and basic materials.

BEHAVIOR

19302 Back, Christine, and Jens Olesen. *Chicken and Egg* (1–3). Illus. 1986, Silver Burdett LB $15.95 (0-382-09284-8); paper $3.95 (0-382-09959-1). Basic science explaining how the reproductive cycle operates. (Rev: BL 1/1/87)

19303 Bash, Barbara. *Urban Roosts: Where Birds Nest in the City* (3–5). Illus. 1992, Little, Brown paper $6.95 (0-316-08312-7). 32pp. This unusual nature study shows that wildlife can thrive in an urban setting. (Rev: BCCB 3/91; BL 1/1/91*; HB 1–2/91; SLJ 11/90*) [598]

19304 Johnson, Sylvia A. *Inside an Egg* (5–8). Illus. 1982, Lerner LB $22.60 (0-8225-1472-9); paper $5.95 (0-8225-9522-2). 48pp. The chicken egg, from fertilization to hatching.

19305 Johnson, Sylvia A. *Songbirds: The Language of Song* (3–6). Series: Nature Watch. 2000, Carolrhoda LB $23.70 (1-57505-483-3). 48pp. This book

introduces a number of songbirds and describes their songs. (Rev: BL 3/1/01) [598]

19306 Selsam, Millicent E. *Egg to Chick* (K–3). Illus. by Barbara Wolff. 1970, HarperCollins paper $3.95 (0-06-444113-X). 64pp. A concise guide to how an egg develops.

19307 Stevens, Ann Shepard. *Strange Nests* (2–5). Illus. by Jennifer Owings Dewey. 1998, Millbrook LB $20.40 (0-7613-0413-4). 31pp. Covers the nests and building habits of 11 common North American birds, including robins, swallows, eagles, wrens, house sparrows, Baltimore orioles, and crows. (Rev: HBG 10/99; SLJ 7/99) [598]

DUCKS, GEESE, AND SWANS

19308 Beaty, Dave. *Waterfowl* (3–6). Illus. Series: Naturebooks. 1993, Child's World LB $22.79 (1-56766-006-1). 32pp. Various kinds of waterfowl are introduced in large color photos facing each page of text. (Rev: BCCB 6/96; BL 3/1/94) [598.4]

19309 Goldin, Augusta. *Ducks Don't Get Wet* (PS–2). Illus. Series: Let's-Read-and-Find-Out. 1999, HarperCollins LB $15.89 (0-06-027882-X); paper $4.95 (0-06-445187-9). 32pp. Explains why ducks don't get wet in water and introduces several types of wild ducks, their habits, diet, migration, and habitats. (Rev: BL 8/99*; HBG 10/99; SLJ 6/99) [598.4]

19310 Hickman, Pamela. *A New Duck: My First Look at the Life Cycle of a Bird* (PS–K). Illus. by Heather Collins. Series: My First Look At. 1999, Kids Can $6.95 (1-55074-613-8). The nesting habits of a pair of mallards and the hatching and growth of their ducklings are covered in attractive pictures and simple text. (Rev: HBG 10/99; SLJ 8/99) [598.4]

19311 Horton, Tom. *Swanfall: Journey of the Tundra Swans* (4–6). Illus. by David Harp. 1991, Walker LB $16.85 (0-8027-8107-1). 48pp. All about migration and the life of a swan family for one year. (Rev: BCCB 2/92; BL 12/15/91) [598.4]

19312 Kalas, Sybille. *The Goose Family Book* (2–4). Illus. by author. 1986, Picture Book paper $15.95 (0-88708-019-7). 53pp. A family of goslings from hatching to adulthood. (Rev: BL 6/15/86; HB 7–8/86; SLJ 11/86)

19313 Loomis, Jennifer A. *A Duck in a Tree* (K–3). Illus. 1996, Stemmer $18.95 (0-88045-136-X). 40pp. A year in the lives of two wood ducks includes raising a family and migrating to Florida. (Rev: BL 2/1/97) [598.4]

19314 Miller, Sara S. *Waterfowl: From Swans to Screamers* (3–5). Series: Animals in Order. 1999, Watts LB $23.00 (0-531-11584-4). 48pp. After a discussion of animal classification, water birds are introduced and several are pictured and described. (Rev: BL 12/15/99; HBG 3/00) [598.4]

19315 Savage, Stephen. *Duck* (K–2). Illus. by Stephen Lings. Series: Observing Nature. 1995, Thomson Learning LB $21.20 (1-56847-328-1). 32pp. Using double-page spreads, very basic information is given on the life cycle of the mallard duck. (Rev: SLJ 10/95) [598.4]

19316 Selsam, Millicent E., and Joyce Hunt. *A First Look at Ducks, Geese, and Swans* (1–3). Illus. by Harriett Springer. Series: A First Look At. 1990, Walker LB $12.85 (0-8027-6976-4). 32pp. Features and species are covered in this introduction. Also use: *A First Look at Bats* (1991). (Rev: BL 12/1/90; SLJ 2/92) [598.2]

19317 Stone, Lynn M. *Swans* (2–3). Series: Early Bird Nature Books. 1997, Lerner LB $22.60 (0-8225-3019-8). 48pp. A well-written introduction for beginners to these handsome birds, with a simple text and many color photos. (Rev: BL 9/15/97; SLJ 10/97) [598.4]

19318 Wallace, Karen. *Duckling Days* (1). Illus. Series: Eyewitness Reader. 1999, DK $12.95 (0-7894-3995-6); paper $3.95 (0-7894-3994-8). 32pp. Six ducks hatch from mother duck's eggs, one of them a loner in this easily read book. (Rev: BL 5/15/99; HBG 10/99) [598.4]

EAGLES, HAWKS, AND OTHER BIRDS OF PREY

19319 Arnold, Caroline. *Saving the Peregrine Falcon* (4–6). Illus. 1985, Lerner paper $7.95 (0-87614-523-3). 48pp. Once threatened because its eggs were weakened by the pesticide DDT, the peregrine falcon can now be seen in American cities. The story of their comeback. (Rev: BCCB 3/85; BL 4/1/85; SLJ 3/85)

19320 Bair, Diane, and Pamela Wright. *Eagle Watching* (2–5). Series: Wildlife Watching. 1999, Capstone $19.93 (0-7368-0322-X). 48pp. An introduction to the world of the eagle, with special information on how to observe these birds. (Rev: BL 2/15/00) [598.9]

19321 Bernhard, Emery. *Eagles: Lions of the Sky* (PS–3). Illus. by Durga Bernhard. 1994, Holiday LB $15.95 (0-8234-1105-2). 32pp. Many aspects of the life of eagles, including mating, eating, flying, hunting, and parenting, are discussed in this richly illustrated book. (Rev: BL 2/1/94; HB 5–6/94; SLJ 5/94) [598.9]

19322 Collard, Sneed B. *Birds of Prey: A Look at Daytime Raptors* (4–7). Illus. 1999, Watts LB $24.00 (0-531-20363-8). 64pp. Eagles, hawks, ospreys, falcons, and vultures of North America are introduced with material on the appearance and habits of each. (Rev: BL 10/15/99; HBG 3/00) [598.9]

19323 Craighead, Charles. *The Eagle and the River* (2–4). Photos by Tom Mangelsen. 1994, Macmillan paper $16.00 (0-02-762265-7). 32pp. Stunning photographs provide an eagle's-eye view of the Snake River in Wyoming as the bird goes hunting. (Rev: BL 9/15/94; SLJ 12/94*) [591.5]

19324 Gibbons, Gail. *Soaring with the Wind: The Bald Eagle* (3–5). Illus. 1998, Morrow $16.00 (0-688-13730-X). 32pp. Excellent full-color illustrations dominate this account of the bald eagle, its characteristics, behavior, life cycle, struggle for survival, and its emergence as a national symbol. (Rev: BL 4/15/98; HBG 3/99; SLJ 4/98) [598.9]

19325 Gieck, Charlene. *Bald Eagles: Bald Eagle Magic for Kids* (2–4). 1991, Stevens LB $22.60 (0-8368-0761-8). 48pp. This book tells about the historical significance of this bird and discusses its life cycle and habits. (Rev: BL 6/1/92; SLJ 7/92) [598]

19326 Grambo, Rebecca L. *Eagles* (5–8). Illus. Series: WorldLife Library. 1999, Voyageur paper $16.95 (0-89658-363-5). 72pp. This beautifully illustrated book describes the legends and lore surrounding eagles, their physical characteristics, behavior, habitats, and different species. (Rev: BL 8/99) [598.9]

19327 Hodge, Deborah. *Eagles* (2–5). Illus. Series: Kids Can! 2000, Kids Can $10.95 (1-55074-715-0); paper $5.95 (1-55074-717-7). 32pp. After a general look at eagles around the world, this account focuses on two American breeds and gives information on their habitats, food, physical characteristics, flight, behavior, and young. (Rev: BL 11/1/00; HBG 3/01) [598.9]

19328 Horton, Casey. *Eagles* (4–6). Illus. Series: Endangered! 1996, Benchmark LB $22.79 (0-7614-0214-4). 32pp. The endangered eagle is presented, with individual chapters on eight species. (Rev: SLJ 4/96) [598.9]

19329 Jenkins, Priscilla B. *Falcons Nest on Skyscrapers* (K–3). Illus. by Megan Lloyd. Series: Let's-Read-and-Find-Out. 1996, HarperCollins paper $4.95 (0-06-445149-6). 32pp. The story of Scarlett, the first peregrine falcon raised in captivity, is used to introduce a species that recently faced extinction. (Rev: BL 8/96; SLJ 7/96) [598.9]

19330 Lang, Aubrey. *Eagles* (4–6). Illus. by Wayne Lynch. 1995, Little, Brown paper $7.95 (0-316-51383-0). 64pp. An attractive, well-organized look at these fascinating birds. (Rev: BCCB 2/91; BL 1/1/91; HB 3–4/91) [598.9]

19331 Latimer, Jonathan P., and Karen Stray Nolting. *Birds of Prey* (3–6). Illus. Series: Peterson Field Guides for Young Naturalists. 1999, Houghton $15.00 (0-395-95211-5); paper $5.95 (0-395-92277-1). 48pp. A general introduction to birds of prey is followed by 20 double-page spreads that introduce the appearance and habits of such birds as eagles, hawks, falcons, and owls. (Rev: BL 6/1–15/99; SLJ 8/99) [598.9]

19332 Merrick, Patrick. *Eagles* (3–5). Series: Naturebooks: Animals. 1999, Child's World LB $15.95 (1-56766-588-8). 32pp. Outstanding color photographs accompanied by a few lines of text each are used to introduce eagles, their habitats, physical characteristics, and habits. (Rev: BL 10/15/99; HBG 3/00) [598.8]

19333 Morrison, Gordon. *Bald Eagle* (PS–4). Illus. 1998, Houghton $16.00 (0-395-87328-2). 32pp. Using watercolor paintings that trace the life cycle of two bald eagles, from hatching to producing an egg of their own, this is a fine introduction to these majestic birds of prey. (Rev: BL 6/1–15/98; HBG 3/99; SLJ 5/98) [598.9]

19334 Olsen, Glenda P. *Birds of Prey* (3–6). Illus. Series: Naturebooks. 1993, Child's World LB $22.79 (1-56766-059-2). 32pp. In this introductory account, each double-page spread contains a color picture and descriptive text on such birds as eagles, hawks, and falcons. (Rev: BL 3/1/94) [598.9]

19335 Parry-Jones, Jemima. *Amazing Birds of Prey* (1–4). Illus. by Mike Dunning. Series: Eyewitness Juniors. 1992, Knopf LB $11.99 (0-679-92771-9); paper $9.99 (0-679-82771-4). 32pp. Following a brief explanation of a bird of prey, several double-page spreads show various species. (Rev: BL 11/1/92; SLJ 5/93) [598.9]

19336 Patent, Dorothy Hinshaw. *The Bald Eagle Returns* (4–8). Illus. 2000, Clarion $15.00 (0-395-91416-7). 68pp. This book not only discusses the successful efforts to save the bald eagle but also gives material on its anatomy, habitats, mating, and behavior. (Rev: BCCB 1/01; BL 10/15/00; SLJ 11/00) [598.9]

19337 Patent, Dorothy Hinshaw. *Eagles of America* (4–6). Photos by William Munoz. 1995, Holiday $15.95 (0-8234-1198-2). 40pp. Bald and golden eagles are described, with information on their habits and endangered status. (Rev: BL 3/1/96; SLJ 2/96) [598.9]

19338 Patent, Dorothy Hinshaw. *Where the Bald Eagles Gather* (4–7). Illus. by William Munoz. 1990, Houghton paper $5.95 (0-395-52598-5). 64pp. A description of the United States' national bird, its habits, and behavior.

19339 Priebe, Mac. *The Peregrine Falcon* (2–5). Illus. by Jennifer Priebe. 1999, Mindfull $15.95 (0-9669551-9-6). 32pp. This environmental success story tells how the peregrine falcon was saved from extinction by the banning of the pesticide DDT. (Rev: SLJ 4/00) [598.9]

19340 Rauzon, Mark. *Golden Eagles of Devil Mountain* (3–5). Series: Wildlife Conservation Society Books. 2000, Watts LB $22.50 (0-531-11787-1). 48pp. The golden eagle is introduced, with material on its anatomy, behavioral patterns, life cycle, and habitat. (Rev: BL 3/15/01) [598.9]

19341 Silverstein, Alvin, et al. *The California Condor* (3–6). Illus. Series: Endangered in America. 1998, Millbrook LB $22.40 (0-7613-0264-6). 64pp. In addition to a description of the characteristics and habits of the California condor, this book explains why the species has declined in number and outlines efforts to save it. (Rev: BL 9/1/98; HBG 10/98) [639.97]

19342 Silverstein, Alvin, et al. *The Peregrine Falcon* (4–7). Illus. Series: Endangered in America. 1995, Millbrook LB $22.40 (1-56294-417-7). 64pp. The story of how the peregrine falcon became an endangered species, its life cycle, and efforts to restore the population. (Rev: BL 6/1–15/95) [598.9]

19343 Stone, Lynn M. *Eagles* (2–4). Illus. Series: Bird Discovery Library. 1989, Rourke LB $14.60 (0-86592-321-3). 24pp. A brief overview of the life cycle and habitats of the eagle. Also use: *Pelicans* (1989). (Rev: BL 4/1/89; SLJ 11/89) [598]

19344 Stone, Lynn M. *Vultures* (3–6). Illus. Series: Nature Watch. 1993, Carolrhoda LB $19.95 (0-87614-768-6). 48pp. The life cycle of the vulture is

covered, and material is given on its habitat and food. (Rev: BL 8/93; SLJ 8/93*) [598.9]

19345 Swinburne, Stephen R. *In Good Hands: Behind the Scenes at a Center for Orphaned and Injured Birds* (3–6). Illus. 1998, Sierra Club $16.95 (0-87156-397-5). 32pp. A behind-the-scenes visit to the Vermont Raptor Center where orphaned or injured birds of prey, such as owls and eagles, are cared for. (Rev: BL 7/98; HBG 3/99; SLJ 8/98) [639.9]

GULLS AND OTHER SEA BIRDS

19346 Arnosky, Jim. *Watching Water Birds* (1–4). Illus. 1997, National Geographic $16.00 (0-7922-7073-8). 32pp. An informal introduction to such diving birds as loons, grebes, mallards, wood ducks, Canada geese, gulls, and herons. (Rev: BL 10/1/97; HBG 3/98; SLJ 10/97*) [598.179]

19347 Flanagan, Alice K. *Seabirds* (2–4). Illus. Series: New True Books. 1996, Children's LB $21.00 (0-516-01088-3). 48pp. Using color photos and a simple text, this account introduces various marine birds, their special habitats, and how they live. (Rev: BL 6/1–15/96; SLJ 8/96) [589.29]

19348 Gibbons, Gail. *Gulls . . . Gulls . . . Gulls* (3–5). Illus. 1997, Holiday LB $15.95 (0-8234-1323-3). 32pp. Brief text and watercolor pictures are used to explore the world of the gull, its structure, diet, habits, mating behavior, and migration. (Rev: BL 9/1/97; HBG 3/98; SLJ 9/97) [598.3]

19349 Holling, Holling C. *Seabird* (4–6). 1978, Houghton $20.00 (0-395-18230-1); paper $10.00 (0-395-26681-5). A gull accompanies a whaling expedition.

19350 Kress, Stephen W., and Pete Salmansohn. *Project Puffin: How We Brought Puffins Back to Egg Rock* (3–6). Illus. 1997, Tilbury $16.95 (0-88448-170-0). 40pp. A first-person narrative about the project starting in 1973 that had as a goal bringing puffins back to Eastern Egg Rock off the Maine coast. (Rev: BCCB 7–8/97; BL 8/97) [636.9]

19351 McMillan, Bruce. *Nights of the Pufflings* (2–4). Illus. 1995, Houghton $15.00 (0-395-70810-9). 32pp. On an island off the coast of Iceland, children help young puffins succeed in their first flight. (Rev: BCCB 3/95; BL 3/15/95; SLJ 3/95*) [598.3]

19352 Miller, Sara S. *Shorebirds: From Stilts to Sanderlings* (3–5). Illus. Series: Animals in Order. 2000, Watts LB $23.00 (0-531-11596-8); paper $6.95 (0-531-16498-5). 48pp. Introductory material on animal classification is followed by an overview of shorebirds, their varieties, habits, structure, and care of young. (Rev: BL 9/15/00) [598.29]

19353 O'Connor, Karen. *The Herring Gull* (3–5). Illus. Series: Amazing Animals. 1992, Macmillan $18.95 (0-87518-506-1). 60pp. This introduction to the herring gull discusses its evolution, habitat, behavior, and the reasons why it is endangered. (Rev: BL 11/1/92) [598]

19354 Patent, Dorothy Hinshaw. *Ospreys* (4–7). Illus. by William Munoz. 1993, Houghton $14.95 (0-395-63391-5). 64pp. Covers topics that are related to the osprey, such as feeding habits, body structure, nesting patterns, and life cycle. (Rev: BL 6/1–15/93) [598]

19355 Staub, Frank. *Herons* (2–5). Illus. Series: Early Bird. 1997, Lerner LB $22.60 (0-8225-3017-1). 48pp. Text and wonderful photos introduce a variety of heron species and their behavior and habitats. (Rev: BL 7/97; SLJ 8/97) [598.3]

19356 Taylor, Kenny. *Puffins* (5–9). Series: World-Life Library. 1999, Voyageur $16.95 (0-89658-419-4). 72pp. Outstanding photographs and conservation awareness are highlights of this introduction to puffins, their characteristics, habitats, and habits. (Rev: BL 8/99) [598.3]

OWLS

19357 Arnosky, Jim. *All About Owls* (K–3). Illus. Series: All About. 1995, Scholastic $15.95 (0-590-46790-5). 32pp. The physical features of owls and their habits are discussed, with an introduction to some common species. (Rev: BL 9/1/95; SLJ 10/95*) [598.9]

19358 Browne, Vee. *Owl* (PS–3). Illus. by Diana Magnuson. Series: Animal Lore and Legend. 1995, Scholastic paper $4.95 (0-590-22488-3). 32pp. Factual information is given about owls on their characteristics, habitats, species, and food, as well as three folktales. (Rev: SLJ 3/96) [598.9]

19359 Epple, Wolfgang. *Barn Owls* (3–6). Illus. by Manfred Rogl. Series: Nature Watch. 1992, Carolrhoda LB $23.93 (0-87614-742-2). 48pp. This informative book looks at the life cycle, habitat, and feeding habits of the barn owl. (Rev: BCCB 1/93*; BL 10/1/92; SLJ 1/93) [598.97]

19360 Esbensen, Barbara J. *Tiger with Wings: The Great Horned Owl* (3–5). Illus. by Mary B. Brown. 1991, Orchard $16.95 (0-531-05940-5); paper $5.95 (0-531-07071-9). 32pp. This deadly hunter, with stripes and a catlike face, is known as a tiger with wings. (Rev: BL 9/1/91; HB 9–10/91; SLJ 8/91*) [598.97]

19361 Jarvis, Kila, and Denver W. Holt. *Owls: Whoo Are They?* (3–5). Illus. 1996, Mountain paper $12.00 (0-87842-336-2). 64pp. This introduction to owls includes descriptions of the 19 species found in North America. (Rev: BL 8/96; SLJ 12/96) [598.9]

19362 Ling, Mary. *Owl* (PS–1). Illus. by Kim Taylor. Series: See How They Grow. 1992, DK $19.95 (1-56458-115-2). 24pp. In a brief text written from the owl's viewpoint and many photographs, the first months of an owl's life are shown. (Rev: BL 11/1/92; HB 1–2/93; SLJ 3/93) [598]

19363 Miller, Sara S. *Owls: The Silent Hunters* (3–5). Series: Animals in Order. 2000, Watts LB $23.00 (0-531-11595-X). 48pp. This book describes how animals are classified and then tells about different kinds of owls, their physical characteristics, food, habits, and habitats. (Rev: BL 10/15/00) [598.9]

19364 Sattler, Helen R. *The Book of North American Owls* (3–6). Illus. 1995, Clarion $17.00 (0-395-60524-5). 64pp. After a general introduction to owls, their habits, and habitats, there is a rundown

on 21 species. (Rev: BCCB 5/95; BL 4/15/95; HB 5–6/95; SLJ 5/95) [598]

19365 Silverstein, Alvin, et al. *The Spotted Owl* (4–8). Illus. Series: Endangered Species. 1994, Millbrook LB $22.40 (1-56294-415-0). 48pp. The story of the spotted owl, its endangered status, efforts to protect it, and the conflicts with the timber industry. (Rev: BL 4/15/95) [333.95]

19366 Stefoff, Rebecca. *Owl* (K–3). Series: Living Things. 1997, Marshall Cavendish LB $22.79 (0-7614-0443-0). 32pp. This simple introduction to the owl contains short bits of basic information and many colorful photos. (Rev: BL 2/15/98; HBG 3/98) [598.9]

19367 Tagholm, Sally. *The Barn Owl* (K–3). Illus. by Bert Kitchen. Series: Animal Lives. 1999, Kingfisher LB $9.95 (0-7534-5171-9). 32pp. The first part of this richly illustrated book describes the first year of life of a barn owl; the second part gives facts about this bird, including its endangered status. (Rev: BL 5/15/99; HBG 10/99; SLJ 6/99) [598.9]

PENGUINS

19368 Bonners, Susan. *A Penguin Year* (K–4). Illus. by author. 1981, Delacorte $9.43 (0-440-00170-6). 48pp. An introduction to the lifestyle of penguins of the South Pole.

19369 Cousteau Society. *Penguins* (PS–3). Illus. 1992, Simon & Schuster $3.95 (0-671-77058-6). 20pp. The Gentoo penguin is introduced in simple text and color photos. (Rev: BL 5/1/92; SLJ 7/92) [598.4]

19370 Fontanel, Beatrice. *The Penguin: A Funny Bird* (2–4). Illus. by Andre Fatras. 1992, Charlesbridge paper $6.95 (0-88106-426-2). 28pp. The growth, development, and behavior of this "funny bird" are presented in color photos and large format. (Rev: BL 2/1/93) [598]

19371 Gibbons, Gail. *Penguins!* (2–4). Illus. 1998, Holiday $16.95 (0-8234-1388-8). With pen-and-ink and watercolor paintings, the author introduces different species of penguins and describes their characteristics, food, habits, and enemies. (Rev: BL 11/1/98; HBG 3/99; SLJ 11/98) [598.47]

19372 Jenkins, Martin. *The Emperor's Egg* (PS–1). Illus. by Jane Chapman. 1999, Candlewick $16.99 (0-7636-0557-3). 32pp. A simple introduction to the emperor penguin that stresses the role played by the father in hatching the egg. (Rev: BCCB 1/00; BL 1/1–15/00; HBG 3/00; SLJ 12/99) [598.42]

19373 Johnson, Sylvia A. *Penguins* (4–7). Illus. 1981, Lerner LB $22.60 (0-8225-1453-2). 48pp. Handsome photographs enliven the text of this introduction to penguins and their habitats.

19374 Kalman, Bobbie. *Penguins* (2–4). Illus. Series: Crabapples. 1995, Crabtree LB $19.96 (0-86505-624-2); paper $5.95 (0-86505-724-9). 32pp. Color photos and text are used to give basic facts about the habits, anatomy, food, and enemies of penguins. (Rev: SLJ 5/96) [598.4]

19375 Lepthien, Emilie U. *Penguins* (1–4). Illus. 1983, Children's paper $5.50 (0-516-41683-9).

48pp. This account is distinguished by a simple text and fine color photographs.

19376 Ling, Mary. *Penguin* (3–5). Photos by Nell Fletcher. Illus. Series: See How They Grow. 1993, DK $9.95 (1-56458-312-0). 24pp. This first-person account uses a simple text and stunning color photos to trace the life of a penguin from birth to having a chick of its own. (Rev: BL 11/1/93) [598]

19377 Lynch, Wayne. *Penguins!* (4–7). Illus. 1999, Firefly LB $19.95 (1-55209-421-9); paper $9.95 (1-55209-424-3). 64pp. An appealing book that introduces penguins and their various species with coverage on their evolution, food, life cycle, habits, and habitats. (Rev: BCCB 12/99; BL 9/15/99; HBG 3/00) [598.47]

19378 McMillan, Bruce. *Penguins at Home: Gentoos of Antarctica* (3–6). Illus. 1993, Houghton $17.00 (0-395-66560-4). 32pp. A photo-essay on the Gentoo penguins of Antarctica that describes their anatomy, behavior, and mating cycle. (Rev: BCCB 9/93; BL 11/15/93; SLJ 12/93) [598]

19379 McMillan, Bruce. *Puffins Climb, Penguins Rhyme* (PS–1). Illus. 1995, Harcourt $16.00 (0-15-200362-2). 32pp. A rhyming text is used to describe various activities of penguins and puffins. (Rev: BL 4/1/95; SLJ 5/95) [598.3]

19380 Market, Jenny. *Penguins* (PS–3). Series: Naturebooks. 1999, Child's World LB $15.95 (1-56766-490-3). 32pp. Using a question-and-answer approach, this book provides basic material on penguins including types, habits, habitats, food, and life cycle in a basic text and full-page color photographs. (Rev: BL 6/1–15/99; HBG 10/99) [598.4]

19381 Patent, Dorothy Hinshaw. *Looking at Penguins* (3–5). Illus. by Graham Robertson. 1993, Holiday LB $16.95 (0-8234-1037-4). 40pp. Various kinds of penguins are introduced, with material on their world habitats and on the endangered emperor penguin. (Rev: BL 1/1/94; SLJ 1/94*) [598]

19382 *Penguins* (PS–2). Series: First Discovery. 1996, Scholastic $12.95 (0-590-73877-1). 24pp. Using interactive techniques and interesting visuals, answers basic questions about penguins, such as where they live. (Rev: BL 10/15/96) [598.441]

19383 Robinson, Claire. *Penguin* (3–5). Illus. Series: Life Story. 1993, Troll paper $4.95 (0-8167-2772-4). 32pp. The habits and habitats of penguins are covered in this brief, illustrated volume. (Rev: BL 2/1/94) [594.4]

19384 Robinson, Claire. *Penguins* (2–3). Series: In the Wild. 1997, Heinemann $18.50 (1-57572-137-6). 24pp. A heavily illustrated introduction to penguins that uses double-page spreads to cover such topics as behavior, food, habitats, and care of young. (Rev: BL 2/15/98; SLJ 4/98) [598.4]

19385 Schlein, Miriam. *What's a Penguin Doing in a Place Like This?* (3–5). Illus. 1997, Millbrook LB $23.90 (0-7613-0003-1). 48pp. A guide to 17 species of penguins, arranged by habitat. (Rev: BL 6/1–15/97; SLJ 7/97) [598.4]

19386 Stefoff, Rebecca. *Penguin* (K–3). Series: Living Things. 1997, Marshall Cavendish LB $22.79 (0-7614-0446-5). 32pp. Using double-page spreads

and many color photos, the habits, homes, and behavior of penguins are introduced very simply. (Rev: BL 2/15/98; HBG 3/98) [598.4]

19387 Stone, Lynn M. *Penguins* (2–4). Series: Bird Discovery Library. 1989, Rourke LB $14.60 (0-86592-325-6). 24pp. Introduces penguins, with brief text, color photos, and a glossary on the effects of pollution on penguins. Also use: *Vultures* (1989). (Rev: SLJ 11/89) [598.4]

19388 Stone, Lynn M. *Penguins* (2–4). Illus. Series: Early Bird Nature Books. 1998, Lerner LB $22.60 (0-8225-3022-8). 48pp. Questions are used throughout this book to explain important facts about penguins, their habits, family life, and homes. (Rev: BL 12/1/98; HBG 3/99) [598.47]

19389 Webb, Sophie. *My Season with Penguins: An Antarctic Journal* (4–8). Illus. by author. 2000, Houghton $15.00 (0-395-92291-7). 48pp. Journal entries plus effective drawings show the joys and tribulations of a two-month stay in the Antarctic studying penguins and their behavior. (Rev: HB 11–12/00; HBG 3/01; SLJ 12/00) [598]

Conservation of Endangered Species

19390 Arnosky, Jim. *Arnosky's Ark* (1–3). Illus. 1999, National Geographic $15.95 (0-7922-7112-2). 32pp. This beginner's picture book about conservation presents 13 animals that are currently or were formerly endangered. (Rev: BL 11/15/99; HBG 3/00; SLJ 9/99) [590]

19391 Chandler, Gary, and Kevin Graham. *Guardians of Wildlife* (4–8). Illus. Series: Making a Better World. 1996, Twenty-First Century LB $20.40 (0-8050-4626-7). 64pp. Solutions to overhunting, poaching, and overfishing are explored, as well as new wildlife management techniques. (Rev: BL 12/15/96; SLJ 4/97) [639.9]

19392 Cohen, Daniel. *The Modern Ark* (4–8). Illus. 1995, Putnam $15.95 (0-399-22442-4). 128pp. An account of modern efforts to save such species as the red wolf, California condor, panda, and cheetah. (Rev: BL 12/1/95; SLJ 2/96) [333.95]

19393 Dobson, David. *Can We Save Them? Endangered Species of North America* (4–5). Illus. by James M. Needham. 1997, Charlesbridge $16.95 (0-88106-823-3); paper $6.95 (0-88106-822-5). 32pp. Features 12 North American species of endangered wildlife, including Florida panthers, tree snails, gray bats, peregrine falcons, and wildflowers. (Rev: BL 4/1/97; SLJ 7/97) [591.52]

19394 Few, Roger. *Macmillan Children's Guide to Endangered Animals* (5–8). Illus. 1993, Macmillan LB $17.95 (0-02-734545-9). 96pp. Using a geographical approach, this account profiles the world's endangered animals in pictures and descriptive text. (Rev: BL 10/1/93; SLJ 12/93) [592.52]

19395 Fowler, Allan. *It Could Still Be Endangered* (K–2). Illus. Series: Rookie Readers. 2000, Children's $19.00 (0-516-21208-7). 32pp. Full-page colors photos introduce the concept of endangerment and introduce several animals large and small that are on the endangered list. (Rev: BL 1/1–15/01) [333.95]

19396 Galan, Mark. *There's Still Time: The Success of the Endangered Species Act* (2–5). Illus. 1997, National Geographic $15.00 (0-7922-7092-4). 40pp. A heartening account of the animals that have been saved from extinction as a result of the Endangered Species Act. (Rev: BL 12/15/97; SLJ 10/97) [333.95]

19397 Gutfreund, Geraldine M. *Vanishing Animal Neighbors* (4–6). Illus. 1993, Watts LB $22.00 (0-531-20060-4). 64pp. Five different endangered species are introduced, with a discussion of why they are decreasing and what their loss can mean. (Rev: BL 7/93; SLJ 6/93) [591]

19398 Hoff, Mary, and Mary M. Rodgers. *Life on Land* (4–7). Illus. Series: Our Endangered Planet. 1992, Lerner LB $22.60 (0-8225-2507-0). 72pp. This account covers such topics as the interdependence of all living things, pollution, and necessary food sources. (Rev: BL 1/15/93; SLJ 2/93) [333]

19399 Irvine, Georgeanne. *Protecting Endangered Species at the San Diego Zoo* (3–5). Illus. 1990, Simon & Schuster paper $14.95 (0-671-68776-X). 48pp. The efforts made to preserve endangered animals at the zoo. (Rev: BL 11/15/90; HB 11–12/90; SLJ 12/90) [636.08]

19400 Kessler, Cristina. *All the King's Animals* (3–6). Illus. 1995, Boyds Mills $17.95 (1-56397-364-2). 64pp. The story of the conservationist Ted Reilly and the wildlife preserve he started in Swaziland to help endangered species. (Rev: BL 10/15/95; SLJ 12/95) [591]

19401 Lessum, Don. *Dinosaurs to Dodos: An Encyclopedia of Extinct Animals* (4–7). Illus. 1999, Scholastic $16.95 (0-590-31684-2). 112pp. Moving through 12 time periods, this book describes each period and how geological changes caused the extinction of certain species and the creation of new ones. (Rev: BL 11/1/99; HBG 3/00; SLJ 11/99) [560]

19402 Lovett, Sarah. *Extremely Weird Endangered Species* (3–6). Illus. by Mary Sundstrom and Sally Blakemore. Series: Extremely Weird. 1997, Davidson LB $21.27 (1-884756-26-3); John Muir paper $5.95 (0-56261-280-8). 48pp. This colorful book introduces such unusual endangered species as manatees, bats, guans, rhinos, and condors. (Rev: SLJ 7/92) [574]

19403 McClung, Robert M. *Lost Wild America: The Story of Our Extinct and Vanishing Wildlife. Rev. ed* (5–8). Illus. by Bob Hines. 1993, Shoe String LB $29.50 (0-208-02359-3). 272pp. Describes America's past and present wildlife management and gives a rundown on extinct and endangered animals. (Rev: BL 1/1/94; SLJ 2/94*) [591.5]

19404 Mallory, Kenneth. *A Home by the Sea: Protecting Coastal Wildlife* (5–8). Illus. Series: New England Aquarium. 1998, Harcourt $18.00 (0-15-200043-7); paper $9.00 (0-15-201802-6). 64pp. This book, outlining efforts to save and protect coastal wildlife in New Zealand, discusses various species of dolphins, blue penguins, and other marine animals. (Rev: BL 9/1/98; HBG 3/99; SLJ 9/98) [333.95]

19405 Markle, Sandra, and William Markle. *Gone Forever! An Alphabet of Extinct Animals* (1–3). Illus. by Felipe Davalos. 1998, Simon & Schuster $16.00 (0-689-31961-4). 40pp. This is both an alphabet book and a list of important extinct animals, their characteristics, and the reasons for their extinction. (Rev: BL 6/1–15/98; HBG 10/98; SLJ 5/98) [591]

19406 Nirgiotis, Nicholas, and Theodore Nigiortis. *No More Dodos: How Zoos Help Endangered Wildlife* (5–8). Illus. 1996, Lerner $23.95 (0-8225-2856-8). 112pp. An introduction to the many organizations that are trying to protect and preserve endangered wildlife worldwide. (Rev: BCCB 2/97; BL 2/15/97*; SLJ 2/97) [639.9]

19407 O'Neill, Mary. *Nature in Danger* (4–7). Illus. by John Bindon. Series: SOS Planet Earth. 1991, Troll paper $5.95 (0-8167-2286-2). 32pp. Background information and history lead into the problem of animals in danger. (Rev: BL 6/15/91) [333.7]

19408 Paladino, Catherine. *One Good Apple: Growing Our Food for the Sake of the Earth* (4–6). Illus. 1999, Houghton $15.00 (0-395-85009-6). 32pp. A passionate plea to stop the use of agricultural pesticides, with material on their history, the harm they do, and the alternatives. (Rev: BCCB 7–8/99; BL 4/1/99; HBG 10/99; SLJ 4/99) [363.738]

19409 Sayre, April Pulley. *Endangered Birds of North America* (4–6). Illus. Series: Scientific American Sourcebooks. 1997, Twenty-First Century $25.90 (0-8050-4549-X). 96pp. After giving some general facts about birds, the author devotes one chapter to each of five endangered species. (Rev: BL 12/1/97; SLJ 1/98) [333.95]

19410 Sherrow, Victoria. *Endangered Mammals of North America* (5–8). Illus. Series: Scientific American Sourcebooks. 1995, Twenty-First Century LB $22.40 (0-8050-3253-3). 96pp. A general introduction to the causes of endangered species, like pollution, followed by specific mammals affected, like the bowhead whale and the red wolf. (Rev: BL 12/1/95; SLJ 1/96) [599]

19411 Stone, Lynn M. *Endangered Animals* (1–3). Illus. 1984, Children's LB $21.00 (0-516-01724-1); paper $5.50 (0-516-41724-X). 48pp. Explores why some species become endangered and what can be done about it.

19412 Stuart, Gene S. *Wildlife Alert: The Struggle to Survive* (3–6). Illus. 1980, National Geographic LB $12.00 (0-87044-323-2). 104pp. This book outlines the steps being taken to help endangered animals around the world.

19413 Taylor, Dave. *Endangered Forest Animals* (3–5). Illus. Series: Endangered Animals. 1992, Crabtree LB $19.96 (0-86505-529-7); paper $7.95 (0-86505-539-4). 32pp. In this heavily illustrated book, several endangered animals and forest ecology are highlighted. (Rev: BL 11/15/92) [591]

19414 Taylor, Dave. *Endangered Grassland Animals* (3–5). Series: Endangered Animals. 1992, Crabtree LB $19.96 (0-86505-528-9); paper $7.95 (0-86505-538-6). 32pp. Animals of the African, Australian, and North American grasslands are introduced, with many full-color photos. (Rev: BL 12/15/92) [591]

19415 Taylor, Dave. *Endangered Wetland Animals* (3–5). Illus. Series: Endangered Animals. 1992, Crabtree LB $19.96 (0-86505-530-0); paper $7.95 (0-86505-540-8). 32pp. Wetlands are described, and several wetlands animals currently considered endangered are pictured. Also use *Endangered Mountain Animals* (1992). (Rev: BL 11/15/92; SLJ 11/92) [591]

19416 Thomas, Peggy. *Big Cat Conservation* (5–8). Illus. Series: Science of Saving Animals. 2000, Twenty-First Century LB $23.90 (0-7613-3231-6). 64pp. This book focuses on seven species, including panthers, cheetahs, and tigers, and discusses wildlife conservation programs, challenges, and successes. (Rev: BL 6/1–15/00; HBG 10/00; SLJ 7/00) [333.95]

19417 Thomas, Peggy. *Bird Alert* (5–8). Series: The Science of Saving Animals. 2000, Twenty-First Century LB $23.90 (0-7613-1457-1). 64pp. This book discusses conservation programs designed to save endangered bird species and tells how youngsters can get involved in saving birds. (Rev: BL 10/15/00; SLJ 12/00) [591.52]

19418 Thomas, Peggy. *Marine Mammal Preservation* (5–8). Series: The Science of Saving Animals. 2000, Twenty-First Century LB $23.90 (0-7613-1458-X). 64pp. Focuses on endangered marine mammals and describes a wide range of conservation programs. (Rev: BL 10/15/00; SLJ 1/01) [574.92]

19419 Thomas, Peggy. *Reptile Rescue* (5–8). Illus. Series: Science of Saving Animals. 2000, Twenty-First Century LB $23.90 (0-7613-3232-4). 64pp. A description of various conservation programs and how they operate in relation to several reptile species, including tortoises, crocodiles, and snakes. (Rev: BL 6/1–15/00; HBG 10/00; SLJ 7/00) [333.95]

19420 Turbak, Gary. *Mountain Animals in Danger* (1–4). Illus. by Lawrence Ormsby. 1994, Northland LB $14.95 (0-87358-573-9). 32pp. Introduces ten endangered species, like the gray wolf, bald eagle, and spotted owl. (Rev: BL 2/1/95; SLJ 2/95) [599]

19421 Turbak, Gary. *Ocean Animals in Danger* (1–4). Illus. by Lawrence Ormsby. 1994, Northland LB $14.95 (0-87358-574-7). 32pp. Ten endangered marine animals are introduced, including sea otters, fur seals, sockeye salmon, brown pelicans, and manatees. (Rev: BL 11/15/94; SLJ 2/95) [574.92]

19422 Vergoth, Karin, and Christopher Lampton. *Endangered Species*. Rev. ed. (5–7). Illus. 1999, Watts LB $26.00 (0-531-11480-5). 112pp. A valuable overview of the subject that updates the 1988 edition with good, comprehensive lists of endangered species. (Rev: BL 2/1/00) [578.68]

Insects and Arachnids

GENERAL AND MISCELLANEOUS

19423 Anderson, Margaret J. *Bizarre Insects* (3–6). Illus. Series: Weird and Wacky Science. 1996, Enslow LB $19.95 (0-89490-613-5). 48pp. Fascinating facts and lots of pictures highlight this

account of unusual insects and their habits. (Rev: SLJ 6/96) [595.7]

19424 Bailey, Jill. *Mosquito* (1–3). Illus. by Alan Male. Series: Bug Books. 1998, Heinemann LB $19.92 (1-57572-663-7). 32pp. Large photos of mosquitoes accompanied by short paragraphs of text introduce such subjects as mating, physical structure, life cycle, and diet. (Rev: HBG 10/99; SLJ 1/99) [595.77]

19425 Barner, Bob. *Bugs! Bugs! Bugs!* (PS–1). Illus. 1999, Chronicle $12.95 (0-8118-2238-9). 32pp. A rhyming text and bold color illustrations effectively introduce the world of bugs. (Rev: BL 7/99; SLJ 8/99) [595.7]

19426 Berger, Melvin. *Buzz! A Book About Insects* (1–2). Illus. 2000, Scholastic $3.99 (0-439-08748-1). 40pp. This easy-to-read science book uses color photographs to introduce various insects, explain their physical characteristics, and show the changes from caterpillar to butterfly. (Rev: BL 10/1/00) [595.7]

19427 Berger, Melvin. *Chirping Crickets* (2–3). Illus. by Megan Lloyd. 1998, HarperCollins LB $15.89 (0-06-024962-5). 32pp. A well-rounded introduction to crickets that includes information on anatomy, life cycle, habits, habitats, and why and how they make a chirping sound. (Rev: BL 5/1/98; HBG 10/98; SLJ 7/98) [595]

19428 Berger, Melvin. *Killer Bugs* (4–8). Illus. 1990, Avon paper $3.50 (0-380-76036-3). 88pp. This account explores the world of killer bees, fire ants, and other such bugs. (Rev: BL 12/15/90) [595.7]

19429 Berger, Melvin, and Gilda Berger. *How Do Flies Walk Upside Down? Questions and Answers About Insects* (3–5). Illus. Series: Question and Answer. 1999, Scholastic $12.95 (0-590-13082-X); paper $5.95 (0-590-08572-1). 48pp. An attractive book that describes the characteristics of insects in a question-and-answer format. (Rev: BL 11/1/99; HBG 3/00; SLJ 12/99) [595.7]

19430 Brenner, Barbara, and Bernice Chardiet. *Where's That Insect?* (2–4). Illus. by Carol Schwartz. 1995, Scholastic paper $4.99 (0-590-45211-8). 32pp. Simple facts are presented about 14 kinds of insects. (Rev: BL 8/93; SLJ 3/93) [595.7]

19431 Brimner, Larry. *Cockroaches* (3–5). Series: True Books. 1999, Children's LB $21.50 (0-516-21159-5). 48pp. This squarish book with large print and many captioned photographs gives basic information about the cockroach, its structure, habits, life cycle, and habitats. (Rev: BL 11/15/99) [595.7]

19432 Brimner, Larry. *Flies* (3–5). Series: True Books. 1999, Children's LB $21.50 (0-516-21161-7). 48pp. Different kinds of flies are introduced with material on their structure, life cycles, habits, food, and habitats. (Rev: BL 11/15/99) [595.7]

19433 Brimner, Larry. *Praying Mantises* (3–5). Series: True Books. 1999, Children's LB $21.50 (0-516-21163-3). 48pp. This carnivorous insect — named because the position of its forelegs suggests hands in prayer — is introduced in a large-type text and numerous captioned photos. (Rev: BL 11/15/99) [959.7]

19434 Dallinger, Jane. *Grasshoppers* (4–7). Illus. 1981, Lerner paper $5.95 (0-8225-9568-0). 48pp. The life cycle of grasshoppers, well illustrated.

19435 Dewey, Jennifer O. *Bedbugs in Our House: True Tales of Insect, Bug, and Spider Discovery* (4–6). Illus. 1997, Marshall Cavendish $14.95 (0-7614-5006-8). 64pp. Using personal encounters with insects as a focus, the author presents details about all sorts of creatures, including fireflies, locusts, and spiders. (Rev: BL 1/1–15/98; HBG 10/98) [595.7]

19436 Doris, Ellen. *Entomology* (4–6). Illus. by Len Rubenstein. 1993, Thames & Hudson $16.95 (0-500-19004-6). 64pp. In this project book, the classification of insects is covered, along with their habitats and metamorphosis and ideas for field trips and collecting specimens. (Rev: BL 10/1/93; SLJ 9/93) [595.7]

19437 Dussling, Jennifer. *Bugs! Bugs! Bugs!* (2–4). Series: Eyewitness Reader. 1998, DK $12.95 (0-7894-3762-7); paper $3.95 (0-7894-3438-5). 32pp. Using lavish illustrations, a chatty text, information boxes, and fact pages, this book introduces a variety of insects, their physical characteristics, habits, food, and life cycles. (Rev: HBG 3/99; SLJ 1/99) [595.7]

19438 Else, George, et al., eds. *Insects and Spiders* (4–6). Series: Nature Company Discoveries. 1997, Time Life $16.00 (0-7835-4881-8). 64pp. Using a series of double-page spreads, several insects and spiders are introduced, with material on their structure and habits given through a brief text and outstanding illustrations. (Rev: BL 9/15/97; HBG 3/98) [595]

19439 Facklam, Howard, and Margery Facklam. *Insects* (4–7). Illus. Series: Invaders. 1994, Twenty-First Century LB $18.90 (0-8050-2859-5). 64pp. The characteristics and types of insects are introduced, with material on some of the more exotic ones. (Rev: BL 1/1/95; SLJ 3/95) [595]

19440 Facklam, Margery. *The Big Bug Book* (1–3). Illus. by Paul Facklam. 1994, Little, Brown $16.95 (0-316-27389-9). 32pp. Thirteen large insects, such as a walking stick and Goliath beetle, are introduced in pictures and text. (Rev: BL 4/1/94*; SLJ 6/94*) [595.7]

19441 Fischer-Nagel, Heiderose, and Andreas Fischer-Nagel. *The Housefly* (3–6). Illus. Series: Nature Watch. 1990, Carolrhoda LB $19.95 (0-87614-374-5). 48pp. A well-organized text with many details about the housefly. (Rev: BL 6/15/90; SLJ 9/90) [595.7]

19442 Fowler, Allan. *It's a Good Thing There Are Insects* (1–2). Illus. Series: Rookie Readers. 1990, Children's LB $19.00 (0-516-04905-4). 32pp. Insects and their characteristics are introduced in this beginner's science book. (Rev: BL 2/1/91) [595.7]

19443 Froman, Nan. *What's That Bug?* (4–6). Illus. 2001, Little, Brown $16.95 (0-316-29692-9). 32pp. An informal but informative introduction to nine

insect orders, complete with descriptions, characteristics, and habitats for each. (Rev: BL 3/1/01) [595.7]

19444 Goldsen, Louise. *The Ladybug and Other Insects* (PS–2). Illus. by Sylvaine Perols. Series: First Discovery. 1991, Scholastic $12.95 (0-590-45235-5). Through painted overlays, the transformation of a larva to a ladybug is depicted, and information is given on the habits and habitats of this and other insects. (Rev: SLJ 6/92) [595.7]

19445 Green, Jen. *Insects* (3–6). Series: Young Scientist Concepts and Projects. 1999, Gareth Stevens LB $16.95 (0-8368-2266-8). 64pp. This illustrated book of easy-to-do projects — including how to make an ant colony — introduces children to the secret world of insects. (Rev: BL 4/15/98) [595.7]

19446 Hartley, Karen, et al. *Centipede* (K–3). Series: Heinemann First Library. 1999, Heinemann LB $13.95 (1-57572-796-X). 32pp. Using color photos and a brief text, this book introduces a variety of centipedes and explains locomotion and how and where they live. (Rev: BL 6/1–15/99; HBG 10/99) [595.7]

19447 Hartley, Karen, et al. *Cockroach* (K–3). Series: Heinemann First Library. 1999, Heinemann LB $13.95 (1-57572-797-8). 32pp. Through amazing color photos and a simple text, the cockroach is introduced, with material on types, food, habitats, and life cycle. (Rev: BL 6/1–15/99; HBG 10/99) [595.7]

19448 Hartley, Karen, et al. *Fly* (1–4). Illus. Series: Bug Books. 2000, Heinemann LB $19.92 (1-57572-548-7). 32pp. Traces the life cycle of the fly, with illustrations and text that also cover its habitats and food. (Rev: BL 7/00) [595.77]

19449 Hartley, Karen, et al. *Grasshopper* (K–3). Illus. Series: Heinemann First Library. 1999, Heinemann LB $13.95 (1-57572-798-6). 32pp. A large labeled drawing of a grasshopper's body is accompanied by descriptions in pictures and text of its life cycle, habits, habitats, and unique characteristics. (Rev: BL 6/1–15/99; HBG 10/99) [595]

19450 Hartley, Karen, et al. *Head Louse* (1–4). Illus. Series: Bug Books. 2000, Heinemann LB $19.92 (1-57572-549-5). 32pp. Close-up photos are used to introduce the life cycle of the head louse, its food, and habits. (Rev: BL 7/00) [616.5]

19451 Hartley, Karen, et al. *Termite* (K–3). Series: Heinemann First Library. 1999, Heinemann LB $13.95 (1-57572-800-1). 32pp. The termite is introduced in stunning photographs and a simple text that gives basic information about varieties, habits, habitats, and their destructive behavior. (Rev: BL 6/1–15/99; HBG 10/99) [595.7]

19452 Hawes, Judy. *Fireflies in the Night* (PS–3). Illus. by Ellen Alexander. Series: Let's-Read-and-Find-Out. 1991, HarperCollins $13.95 (0-06-022484-3); paper $4.95 (0-06-445101-1). 32pp. Full-color illustrations help to explain the world of fireflies. A remake of the original 1963 edition. (Rev: BL 11/15/91; SLJ 3/92) [595.76]

19453 Hickman, Pamela. *Bug Book* (3–5). Illus. Series: Starting with Nature. 1999, Kids Can $12.95

(1-55074-475-5). 32pp. Using double-page spreads and fact boxes, this is an attractive introduction to insects including beetles, moths, termites, and butterflies. (Rev: BL 2/1/99; HBG 10/99) [595.7]

19454 Holmes, Anita. *Insect Detector* (1–2). Illus. Series: We Can Read About — Nature! 2000, Benchmark $14.95 (0-7614-1110-0). 32pp. A beginning reader that defines the characteristics of an insect and asks if particular creatures such as a scorpion or a spider would meet these criteria. (Rev: BL 12/1/00; HBG 3/01; SLJ 2/01) [595.7]

19455 Johnson, Jinny. *Children's Guide to Insects and Spiders* (3–5). Illus. 1997, Simon & Schuster $19.95 (0-689-81163-2). 64pp. Using a large format, the author identifies and describes families of insects and spiders and furnishes drawings and photos of body parts and stages of life cycles. (Rev: BL 5/1/97; SLJ 11/97) [595.7]

19456 Johnson, Sylvia A. *Fireflies* (4–6). 1986, Lerner LB $22.60 (0-8225-1485-0). 48pp. Life cycle, breeding, environment, and characteristics of the firefly. (Rev: BL 10/1/86; SLJ 11/86)

19457 Johnson, Sylvia A. *Water Insects* (3–6). Illus. by Modoki Masuda. 1989, Lerner LB $22.60 (0-8225-1489-3). 48pp. Various kinds of aquatic insects are pictured and described. (Rev: BL 2/15/90; SLJ 4/90) [595]

19458 Kneidel, Sally. *Pet Bugs: A Kid's Guide to Catching and Keeping Touchable Insects* (4–6). Illus. 1994, Wiley paper $12.95 (0-471-31188-X). 117pp. Describes 25 insects; how they live, eat, and reproduce; and how they can be kept as specimens. (Rev: BL 7/94; SLJ 9/94) [638]

19459 Lavies, Bianca. *Backyard Hunter: The Praying Mantis* (K–3). Illus. 1995, Puffin paper $4.99 (0-14-055494-7). 32pp. The stages in this insect's life are described with striking photos. (Rev: BL 3/15/90*; SLJ 6/90) [595.7]

19460 Lavies, Bianca. *Compost Critters* (3–5). Illus. 1993, Dutton $15.99 (0-525-44763-6). 32pp. Amazing photos and simple text introduce such organisms as mites, various bugs, and snails in compost piles. (Rev: BCCB 6/93; BL 7/93*; SLJ 7/93*) [591]

19461 Llewellyn, Claire. *The Best Book of Bugs* (3–5). 1998, Kingfisher $10.95 (0-7534-5118-2). 33pp. A lavishly illustrated book that introduces insects and spiders and describes more than 20 different species, including information on the life cycles of honeybees, dragonflies, and butterflies. (Rev: HBG 10/98; SLJ 7/98) [595.7]

19462 Llewellyn, Claire. *Some Bugs Glow in the Dark: And Other Amazing Facts About Insects* (1–3). Illus. by Mike Taylor, et al. Series: I Didn't Know That. 1997, Millbrook LB $19.90 (0-7613-0562-9). 32pp. As well as explaining what insects are, this book covers amazing facts about their speed, size, weight, metamorphosis, and unusual behavior. (Rev: SLJ 9/97) [595.7]

19463 McDonald, Mary Ann. *Grasshoppers* (PS–3). Series: Naturebooks. 1999, Child's World LB $15.95 (1-56766-505-5). 32pp. The life cycle of the grasshopper, its physical characteristics, habitats, habits, and food are some of the subjects briefly covered in this basic introduction that contains more than a dozen stunning full-page illustrations. (Rev: BL 6/1–15/99; HBG 10/99) [595.7]

19464 McLaughlin, Molly. *Dragonflies* (2–6). Illus. 1988, Walker LB $15.85 (0-8027-6847-4). 48pp. The life cycle of dragonflies plus information on different varieties are provided with outstanding photographs. (Rev: BCCB 10/89; BL 8/89*; SLJ 9/89) [595.7]

19465 Markle, Sandra. *Creepy, Crawly Baby Bugs* (3–5). Illus. 1996, Walker LB $16.85 (0-8027-8444-5). 32pp. The growth cycle of insects is explored, with emphasis on each infant stage. (Rev: BL 11/15/96; SLJ 4/97*) [595.7]

19466 Merrick, Patrick. *Ticks* (2–4). Illus. Series: Creepy Crawlers. 1997, Child's World LB $22.79 (1-56766-384-2). 32pp. Different kinds of ticks are presented, with material on their life cycle, method of locomotion, habitat, food, and defense mechanisms. Also use *Walkingsticks* (1997). (Rev: SLJ 3/98) [595.4]

19467 Miller, Sara S. *Flies: From Flower Flies to Mosquitoes* (3–5). Illus. Series: Animals in Order. 1998, Watts LB $22.00 (0-531-11486-4). 48pp. After an explanation of the classification of living things, this book profiles 14 different flies commonly found in America and gives details on the life cycle, habits, physical characteristics, and behavior of each. (Rev: BL 1/1–15/99; HBG 3/99; SLJ 12/98) [595.77]

19468 Miller, Sara S. *True Bugs: When Is a Bug Really a Bug?* (3–5). Illus. Series: Animals in Order. 1998, Watts LB $22.00 (0-531-11479-1). 48pp. The classification of animals is explained, followed by a profile of 14 common insects with material on their physical characteristics, behavior, and life cycles. (Rev: BL 1/1–15/99; HBG 3/99) [595.7]

19469 Mound, Laurence. *Amazing Insects* (1–4). Illus. Series: Eyewitness Juniors. 1993, Knopf paper $9.99 (0-679-83925-9). 32pp. The world of insects is introduced through a series of unusual color photos and a simple text. (Rev: BL 9/15/93; SLJ 10/93) [595.7]

19470 Murawski, Darlyne A. *Bug Faces* (K–4). Illus. 2000, National Geographic $16.95 (0-7922-7557-8). 32pp. Huge, sometimes scary photographs in gorgeous color show close-up views of such creatures as a spider, cockroach, bumblebee, deer fly, and weevil. (Rev: BL 11/15/00; HBG 3/01; SLJ 11/00) [595.7]

19471 Nathan, Emma. *What Do You Call a Group of Butterflies? And Other Insect Groups* (3–5). Illus. 2000, Blackbirch LB $15.95 (1-56711-359-1). 24pp. This simple science book uses questions and answers to give basic facts about insects and to reveal each one's group name, such as a colony of ants. (Rev: BL 12/1/00; HBG 3/01) [595.7]

19472 Oppenheim, Joanne. *Have You Seen Bugs?* (K–3). Illus. by Ron Broda. 1998, Scholastic $15.95 (0-590-05963-7). 32pp. A series of charming verses and paper sculptures introduce moths, bees, spiders, and several insects, and describe their life cycles and characteristics. (Rev: BL 4/1/98; HBG 10/98; SLJ 9/98) [595.7]

19473 Parker, Janice. *Cockroaches, Cocoons, and Honeycombs: The Science of Insects* (3–5). Series: Science@Work. 1999, Raintree Steck-Vaughn LB $25.69 (0-7398-0135-X). 48pp. This book about insects presents interesting facts, diagrams, and lots of appended information, along with material on careers related to the study of insects. (Rev: SLJ 3/00) [595.7]

19474 Parker, Janice. *The Science of Insects* (2–5). Series: Living Science. 1999, Gareth Stevens LB $14.95 (0-8368-2466-0). 32pp. In double-page spreads, different types of insects are introduced, with material on their life cycles and habitats. (Rev: HBG 10/00; SLJ 1/00) [595.7]

19475 Parker, Nancy W., and Joan Richards Wright. *Bugs* (K–3). Illus. by Nancy Winslow Parker. 1987, Morrow paper $4.95 (0-688-08296-3). A picture-book format provides solid facts on bugs — including 16 common insects. (Rev: BL 11/1/87; SLJ 10/87)

19476 Pascoe, Elaine. *Crickets and Grasshoppers* (4–7). Series: Nature Close-up. 1998, Blackbirch LB $16.95 (1-56711-176-9). 48pp. Easy projects introduce youngsters to these insects in this book illustrated with color photographs. (Rev: BL 9/15/98; HBG 3/99) [595.7]

19477 Pascoe, Elaine. *Flies* (4–7). Series: Nature Close-up. 2000, Blackbirch LB $18.95 (1-56711-149-1). 48pp. This introduction to flies uses stunning photographs and text to describe their body parts, life cycle, and how to observe them; a few focused experiments are also included. (Rev: BL 4/15/00; HBG 3/01; SLJ 9/00) [595.7]

19478 Penner, Lucille R. *Monster Bugs* (1–3). Illus. by Pamela Johnson. Series: Step into Reading. 1996, Random LB $11.99 (0-679-96974-8); paper $3.99 (0-679-86974-3). 44pp. An easy-to-read introduction to large insects in a series of double-page spreads. (Rev: BCCB 5/96; SLJ 9/96) [595.7]

19479 Pipe, Jim. *The Giant Book of Bugs and Creepy Crawlies* (3–8). Illus. 1998, Millbrook LB $25.90 (0-7613-0716-8). 32pp. Both common and exotic insects and spiders are presented in this oversize book with eye-catching pictures and fascinating text. (Rev: BL 8/98) [595.7]

19480 Rabe, Tish. *On Beyond Bugs! All About Insects* (K–3). Series: The Cat in the Hat's Learning Library. 1999, Random LB $11.99 (0-679-97303-6). 45pp. A beginning reader that contains basic facts about insects in rhyming couplets. (Rev: HBG 10/00; SLJ 3/00) [595.7]

19481 Robertson, Matthew. *Insects and Spiders* (4–8). Illus. Series: Pathfinders. 2000, Reader's Digest $16.99 (1-57584-375-7). 64pp. This oversize, attractive volume uses double-page spreads to introduce various insects and spiders, their physical characteristics, habits, and habitats. (Rev: BL 9/15/00; HBG 3/01; SLJ 2/01) [595.7]

19482 Robinson, W. Wright. *How Insects Build Their Amazing Homes* (5–8). Illus. by Carlyn Iverson. Series: Animal Architects. 1999, Blackbirch

LB $19.95 (1-56711-375-3). 64pp. After defining what an insect is, this book shows how termites, wasps, ants, and bees construct their houses and nests. (Rev: HBG 3/00; SLJ 5/00) [595.7]

19483 Ross, Michael E. *Cricketology* (4–6). Illus. Series: Backyard Buddies. 1996, Carolrhoda LB $19.95 (0-87614-985-9). 48pp. The classification, life cycle, and habits of crickets are discussed in this science activity book. (Rev: BL 7/96; SLJ 8/96) [595.7]

19484 Royston, Angela. *Insects and Crawly Creatures* (PS). Illus. by Jerry Young. Series: Eye Openers. 1992, Macmillan $8.99 (0-689-71645-1). 22pp. Various insects and crawling animals are introduced to preschoolers through brief text and large photos. (Rev: BL 10/15/92; SLJ 3/93) [595.7]

19485 Savage, Stephen. *Insects* (2–4). Series: What's the Difference. 2000, Raintree Steck-Vaughn LB $25.69 (0-7398-1355-2). 32pp. This book points out similar characteristics among insects — such as the three parts of their bodies — but also shows how they can differ in size, color, and shape. (Rev: BL 10/15/00; HBG 3/01; SLJ 1/01) [595.7]

19486 Schaffer, Donna. *Pillbugs* (2–4). Illus. Series: Life Cycle. 1999, Capstone LB $14.00 (0-7368-0212-6). 24pp. This book introduces pillbugs (also known as rolypolies or wood lice) and explains their structure, habits, habitats, and reproductive cycle. (Rev: BL 7/99) [595.3]

19487 Schaffer, Donna. *Silkworms* (2–4). Illus. Series: Life Cycle. 1999, Capstone LB $14.00 (0-7368-0213-4). 24pp. Covers the life story of the silkworm, with material on how the cocoons are used to produce silk thread. (Rev: BL 7/99) [595.78]

19488 Selsam, Millicent E., and Ron Goor. *Backyard Insects* (K–3). Illus. 1988, Scholastic paper $4.99 (0-590-42256-1). 40pp. How backyard insects camouflage themselves for protection.

19489 Sill, Cathryn. *About Insects: A Guide for Children* (PS–2). Illus. by John Sill. Series: About Books. 2000, Peachtree $14.95 (1-56145-207-6). 48pp. Naturalistic paintings present several insects and their characteristics. (Rev: BL 2/1/00; HBG 10/00; SLJ 7/00) [595.7]

19490 Souza, D. M. *Insects Around the House* (3–5). Illus. Series: Creatures All Around Us. 1991, Carolrhoda LB $22.60 (0-87614-438-5). 40pp. Describes household insects, from termites under the front steps to caterpillars in the carpet. Also use: *Insects in the Garden* (1991). (Rev: BL 4/15/91; SLJ 7/91) [595.7]

19491 Souza, D. M. *What Bit Me?* (3–5). Illus. Series: Creatures All Around Us. 1991, Carolrhoda LB $22.60 (0-87614-440-7). 40pp. In pictures and text, this book introduces creatures that can bite and sting, such as water bugs, ticks, and mosquitoes. (Rev: BL 4/15/91; SLJ 7/91) [595.7]

19492 Stewart, Melissa. *Insects* (2–3). Series: True Books. 2001, Children's LB $22.00 (0-516-22040-3). 48pp. Introduces the basic characteristics of all insects and then introduces specific insects and explains how they live. (Rev: BL 3/15/01) [595.7]

19493 Telford, Carole, and Rod Theodorou. *Through a Termite City* (3–5). Series: Amazing Journeys. 1997, Heinemann LB $13.95 (1-57572-155-4). 32pp. Organized like a journey, this trek through a termite mound in Africa reveals details on termite life, food, and society. (Rev: SLJ 4/98) [595.7]

19494 Theodorou, Rod. *Insects* (2–4). Series: Animal Babies. 1999, Heinemann LB $14.95 (1-57572-880-X). 32pp. Several insect species are introduced with material on their characteristics, habits, habitats, and life cycles. (Rev: SLJ 4/00) [595.7]

19495 VanCleave, Janice. *Bugs C* (PS–2). Series: Play and Find Out. 1999, Wiley $29.95 (0-471-17664-8). 121pp. A series of entertaining experiments and projects that explores such topics as life cycles, movement, communication, feeding, and camouflage. (Rev: HBG 10/99; SLJ 4/99) [595.7]

19496 VanCleave, Janice. *Janice VanCleave's Insects and Spiders: Mind-Boggling Experiments You Can Turn into Science Fair Projects* (3–5). Illus. by Doris Ettlinger. Series: Spectacular Science Projects. 1998, Wiley paper $10.95 (0-471-16396-1). 92pp. Divided into 20 chapters arranged by specific questions about insects and spiders, each supplying a step-by-step activity to answer the question, with variations on that project and ways of turning it into a science fair entry. (Rev: SLJ 6/98) [595]

19497 Van Dyck, Sara. *Insect Wars* (4–6). Illus. Series: First Books. 1997, Watts LB $22.50 (0-531-20261-5). 64pp. Shows how farmers, restaurant owners, and theme park operators are using beneficial insects to destroy harmful ones, rather than relying on pesticides. (Rev: BL 5/15/97; SLJ 8/97) [632]

19498 Wangberg, James K. *Do Bees Sneeze? And Other Questions Kids Ask About Insects* (4–6). Illus. 1997, Fulcrum paper $17.95 (1-55591-963-4). 194pp. A noted entomologist answers 200 questions about insects that were actually asked him by children, like "Do bugs have emotions?" (Rev: BL 1/1–15/98; SLJ 4/98) [595.7]

19499 Whayne, Susanne S. *The World of Insects* (PS–3). Illus. by Ebet Dudley. 1990, Simon & Schuster paper $9.95 (0-671-69018-3). 48pp. A large-format book for browsing, with color paintings on every page. (Rev: BL 1/1/91) [595.7]

19500 Wilsdon, Christina. *National Audubon Society First Field Guide to Insects* (4–6). Series: First Field Guide. 1998, Scholastic $17.95 (0-590-05447-3). More than 50 of the most easily found species of insects are introduced in this field guide that contains over 450 color illustrations. (Rev: BL 8/98; SLJ 10/98) [595]

19501 *The World in Your Backyard: And Other Stories of Insects and Spiders* (3–5). Illus. 1990, Zaner-Bloser $10.95 (0-88309-132-1). 63pp. Eighteen articles and stories from *Highlights for Children* magazine. (Rev: SLJ 6/90) [595.7]

19502 Zakowski, Connie. *The Insect Book: A Basic Guide to the Collection and Care of Common Insects for Young Children* (3–5). Illus. 1996, Rainbow paper $8.95 (1-56825-037-1). 64pp. A practical

beginner's guide to collecting, caring for, and studying insects. (Rev: BL 12/1/96; SLJ 5/97) [595.7]

19503 Ziefert, Harriet. *Bugs, Beetles, and Butterflies* (PS–1). Illus. by Lisa Flather. Series: A Viking Easy-to-Read Book. 1998, Viking $13.89 (0-670-88055-8). 32pp. A very basic introduction to insects that is attractively illustrated but short on substantive facts. (Rev: HBG 3/99; SLJ 1/99) [595]

19504 Zim, Herbert S., and Clarence Cottam. *Insects* (4–7). Illus. 1991, Western paper $21.27 (0-307-64055-8). A guide to familiar American insects.

19505 Zuchora-Walske, Christine. *Leaping Grasshoppers* (PS–2). Series: Pull Ahead Books. 2000, Lerner $21.27 (0-8225-3634-X). 32pp. This simple, colorful introduction to grasshoppers explains the reasons why they hop: to find food, to avoid predators, and to find mates. (Rev: BL 5/15/00; HBG 10/00) [595.7]

ANTS

19506 Berman, Ruth. *Ants* (2–3). Illus. Series: Early Bird Nature Books. 1996, Lerner LB $22.60 (0-8225-3012-0). 48pp. The formica ant and its community are described in this introduction to the ant world. (Rev: BL 8/96; SLJ 7/96) [595.78]

19507 Brenner, Barbara. *Thinking About Ants* (2–3). Illus. by Carol Schwartz. 1997, Mondo $15.95 (1-57255-210-7). 32pp. In a readable style, 11 types of ants are introduced, with material on their bodies, colors, diet, colonies, and enemies. (Rev: BL 6/1–15/97; SLJ 10/97) [595.79]

19508 Chinery, Michael. *Ant* (3–5). Illus. by Nichola Armstrong. Series: Life Story. 1997, Troll paper $4.95 (0-8167-2099-1). 32pp. Life in an anthill is introduced in this informative text with color photographs. (Rev: BL 4/1/91) [595.79]

19509 Demuth, Patricia. *Those Amazing Ants* (PS–2). Illus. by S. D. Schindler. 1994, Macmillan paper $14.95 (0-02-728467-0). 32pp. Fascinating facts are given concerning the food, homes, society, and breeding of ants. (Rev: BL 10/1/94; SLJ 10/94) [595.79]

19510 Dorros, Arthur. *Ant Cities* (K–2). Illus. by author. 1987, HarperCollins LB $15.89 (0-690-04570-0); paper $4.95 (0-06-445079-1). 32pp. A simplified explanation of the ant world: jobs of worker ants, operation of the ant hill, social divisions of the ant colony. (Rev: BCCB 3/87; BL 2/15/87; SLJ 8/87)

19511 Overbeck, Cynthia. *Ants* (3–5). Illus. 1982, Lerner LB $22.60 (0-8225-1468-0); paper $5.95 (0-8225-9525-7). 48pp. A description of the parts of an ant's body, plus an introduction to their complex society.

19512 Pascoe, Elaine. *Ants* (4–7). Series: Nature Close-up. 1998, Blackbirch LB $16.95 (1-56711-183-1). 48pp. Using outstanding photographs, this book introduces ants and a series of projects designed to teach more about these creatures. (Rev: BL 9/15/98; HBG 3/99; SLJ 3/99) [595.78]

19513 Sabin, Francene. *Amazing World of Ants* (1–3). Illus. by Eulala Conner. 1982, Troll paper

$3.50 (0-89375-559-1). 32pp. An examination of an ant colony, its inhabitants, and construction.

19514 Stefoff, Rebecca. *Ant* (K–3). Series: Living Things. 1997, Marshall Cavendish LB $22.79 (0-7614-0447-3). 32pp. A colorful introduction to the world of ants that describes colonies, homes and food. (Rev: BL 2/15/98; HBG 3/98; SLJ 3/98) [595.79]

BEES AND WASPS

19515 Brimner, Larry. *Bees* (3–5). Series: True Books. 1999, Children's LB $21.50 (0-516-21160-9). 48pp. The structure, varieties, behavior, social nature, and uses of bees are presented in a book with large print and plenty of captioned photographs. (Rev: BL 11/15/99) [595.79]

19516 Chinery, Michael. *How Bees Make Honey* (3–5). Illus. Series: Nature's Mysteries. 1996, Benchmark LB $22.79 (0-7614-0453-8). 32pp. In this introduction to bees, such topics as a bee's anatomy, life cycle, enemies, nectar gathering, and honey production are covered. (Rev: SLJ 2/97) [595.79]

19517 Cole, Joanna. *The Magic School Bus Inside a Beehive* (3–5). Illus. by Bruce Degen. 1996, Scholastic $15.95 (0-590-44684-3). 48pp. Mrs. Frizzle's school bus becomes a beehive in this exploration of the anatomy, activities, and social structure of bees. (Rev: BCCB 10/96; BL 9/1/96; HB 11–12/96; SLJ 10/96) [585.79]

19518 Crewe, Sabrina. *The Bee* (K–3). Illus. by Stuart Lafford. Series: Life Cycle. 1996, Raintree Steck-Vaughn LB $21.40 (0-8172-4362-3). 32pp. Honey bees are introduced in a number of double-page spreads that cover such topics as anatomy, characteristics, and social life. (Rev: SLJ 4/97) [595.79]

19519 Davis, Kathleen, and Dave Mayes. *Killer Bees* (3–5). Illus. Series: Remarkable Animals. 1993, Dillon LB $18.95 (0-87518-582-7). 60pp. This well-illustrated account explains where these Africanized honeybees come from, their habits, and the damage they can cause. (Rev: BL 11/1/93) [599.79]

19520 Delafosse, Claude. *Bees* (PS–2). Illus. Series: First Discovery. 1997, Scholastic $12.95 (0-590-93780-4). 24pp. Basic information about bees and their colonies is given concisely in this interactive book with overlays. (Rev: BL 2/15/97) [595.79]

19521 Fischer-Nagel, Heiderose, and Andreas Fischer-Nagel. *Life of the Honeybee* (2–5). Illus. 1986, Carolrhoda paper $7.95 (0-87614-470-9). 48pp. A simply written science book showing the work of three kinds of bees. (Rev: BCCB 4/86; BL 4/15/86; SLJ 2/86)

19522 Flanagan, Alice K. *Learning About Bees from Mr. Krebs* (1–2). Series: Our Neighborhood. 1999, Children's LB $19.50 (0-516-21136-6). 32pp. The daily work of a beekeeper is explored through color photos and a simple text. (Rev: BL 10/15/99) [595.79]

19523 Gibbons, Gail. *The Honey Makers* (1–4). Illus. 1997, Morrow $15.93 (0-688-11387-7). 32pp.

An informative picture book that introduces honeybees and their society. (Rev: BCCB 4/97; BL 3/15/97; SLJ 5/97) [595.79]

19524 Johnson, Sylvia A. *Wasps* (4–6). Illus. 1984, Lerner LB $22.60 (0-8225-1460-5). 48pp. A year in the life of a wasp is presented in a clear text and fascinating illustrations.

19525 Micucci, Charles. *The Life and Times of the Honeybee* (3–5). Illus. 1995, Ticknor $15.00 (0-395-65968-X). 32pp. Detailed drawings on double-page spreads introduce the anatomy, habits, and behavior of honeybees. (Rev: BCCB 7–8/95; BL 2/1/95*; SLJ 4/95*) [595.79]

19526 Ross, Edward S. *Yellowjackets* (3–6). Illus. Series: Naturebooks. 1993, Child's World LB $22.79 (1-56766-017-7). 32pp. This species of wasp, its life cycle, and its habits are featured in this attractive picture book with stunning full-page color illustrations. (Rev: BL 3/1/94; SLJ 5/94) [596.79]

19527 Watts, Barrie. *Honeybee* (PS–3). Illus. Series: Stopwatch. 1990, Silver Burdett LB $15.95 (0-382-24011-1). 25pp. The life of the honeybee, beginning with newly laid eggs, is revealed in clear photos and text. (Rev: BL 6/15/90) [595]

BEETLES

19528 Allen, Judy. *Are You a Ladybug?* (PS–1). Illus. by Tudor Humphries. Series: Backyard Books. 2000, Kingfisher $9.95 (0-7534-5241-3). 32pp. A beginner's book that explains in text and pictures what a ladybug is, what it eats, and how it grows from egg to first flight. (Rev: BL 5/15/00; HBG 3/01; SLJ 9/00) [595.76]

19529 Chrustowski, Rick. *Bright Beetle* (PS–2). Illus. 2000, Holt $15.95 (0-8050-6058-8). 32pp. The life cycle of the ladybug, its habits, and physical characteristics are covered in this good introduction for beginning scientists. (Rev: BL 6/1–15/00; HBG 10/00; SLJ 5/00) [595.76]

19530 Fischer-Nagel, Heiderose, and Andreas Fischer-Nagel. *Life of the Ladybug* (2–5). Illus. 1986, Carolrhoda LB $22.60 (0-87614-240-4). 48pp. The life cycle of the ladybug with full-color, informative photographs. (Rev: BCCB 3/86; BL 5/15/86; SLJ 4/86)

19531 Hartley, Karen, and Chris Macro. *Ladybug* (1–3). Illus. by Alan Male. Series: Bug Books. 1998, Heinemann LB $19.92 (1-57572-662-9). 32pp. Double-page spreads, each with a large photo of a ladybug, introduce such topics as structure, behavior, enemies, food, and life cycle. (Rev: HBG 10/99; SLJ 1/99) [595.7]

19532 Himmelman, John. *A Ladybug's Life* (PS–2). Illus. by author. Series: Nature Upclose. 1998, Children's LB $24.00 (0-516-20819-5). For beginning readers, an introduction to ladybugs that gives brief information about their life cycle and habits. (Rev: HBG 10/98; SLJ 7/98) [595.7]

19533 Johnson, Sylvia A. *Beetles* (4–7). Illus. 1982, Lerner LB $22.60 (0-8225-1476-1). 48pp. Color photography highlights this account that concentrates on the scarab beetle.

19534 Johnson, Sylvia A. *Ladybugs* (5–8). Illus. by Yuko Sato. 1983, Lerner LB $22.60 (0-8225-1481-8). 48pp. A description of the ladybug, its habits, behavior, and uses.

19535 Mason, Adrienne. *Mealworms: Raise Them, Watch Them, See Them Change* (3–5). Illus. 1998, Kids Can $10.95 (1-55074-448-8). 24pp. Gives the life story of mealworms (the larval stage of the darkling beetle) and tips on how to raise and observe them. (Rev: BL 6/1–15/98; HBG 10/98; SLJ 9/98) [638.5]

19536 Murray, Peter. *Beetles* (3–6). Illus. Series: Naturebooks. 1993, Child's World LB $22.79 (1-56766-000-2). 32pp. Each double-page spread introduces a different beetle in this attractive book with simple, large-type text and color photos. (Rev: BL 3/1/94) [595.76]

19537 Pascoe, Elaine. *Beetle* (4–7). Series: Nature Close-up. 2000, Blackbirch LB $18.95 (1-56711-175-0). 48pp. Outstanding photographs grace this simple introduction to beetles that discusses their anatomy, habits, and food. (Rev: BL 4/15/00; HBG 3/01; SLJ 9/00) [595.76]

19538 Ross, Michael E. *Ladybugology* (3–5). Photos by Brian Grogan. Illus. by Darren Erickson. Series: Backyard Buddies. 1998, Carolrhoda $19.93 (1-57505-051-X). 48pp. This introduction to ladybugs describes their structure and habits and outlines a number of activities that involve capturing and observing them. (Rev: BL 7/98; HBG 10/98; SLJ 3/98) [595.7]

CATERPILLARS, BUTTERFLIES, AND MOTHS

19539 Allen, Judy. *Are You a Butterfly?* (PS–1). Illus. by Tudor Humphries. Series: Backyard Books. 2000, Kingfisher $9.95 (0-7534-5240-5). 32pp. By allowing the child to imagine that he or she is the insect discussed, this simple book goes through the stages of growth from egg and caterpillar to chrysalis and butterfly. (Rev: BL 10/15/00) [544.2]

19540 Bair, Diane, and Pamela Wright. *Butterfly Watching* (2–5). Series: Wildlife Watching. 1999, Capstone $19.93 (0-7368-0320-3). 48pp. As well as giving good basic information about butterflies, this book is a practical guide to butterfly watching with plenty of tips for the amateur naturalist. (Rev: BL 2/15/00) [595.78]

19541 Beaty, Dave. *Moths and Butterflies* (3–6). Illus. Series: Naturebooks. 1993, Child's World LB $22.79 (1-56766-001-0). 32pp. Large color photos face each page of text in this attractive introduction to butterflies and moths. (Rev: BL 3/1/94) [595.78]

19542 Brimner, Larry. *Butterflies and Moths* (3–5). Series: True Books. 1999, Children's LB $21.50 (0-516-21162-5). 48pp. Butterflies and moths are introduced in this book that discusses life cycles, varieties, structure, habitats, and behavior in a simple text with splendid photos. (Rev: BL 11/15/99) [595.78]

19543 Cassie, Brian, and Jerry Pallotta. *The Butterfly Alphabet Book* (PS–2). Illus. by Mark Astrella. 1995, Charlesbridge paper $6.95 (0-88106-894-2).

From an Apollo butterfly to a Zephyr Metalmark, this alphabet book features amazing butterflies with descriptions of their characteristics. (Rev: SLJ 12/95) [595.78]

19544 Chinery, Michael. *Butterfly* (3–5). Illus. by Helen Senior. Series: Life Story. 1990, Troll LB $17.25 (0-8167-2100-9); paper $4.95 (0-8167-2101-7). 32pp. A butterfly's life and its transformations are revealed in this book with color photographs. (Rev: BL 4/1/91) [595.789]

19545 Delafosse, Claude. *Butterflies* (PS–2). Illus. Series: First Discovery. 1997, Scholastic $12.95 (0-590-93781-2). 24pp. The life cycle of butterflies and their movements are pictured in this beginning book with impressive pictures. (Rev: BL 2/15/97) [595.78]

19546 Ehlert, Lois. *Waiting for Wings* (PS–1). Illus. 2001, Harcourt $17.00 (0-15-202608-8). 38pp. Using a short rhyming text and glowing illustrations, this book covers the life cycle of the butterfly, with information on physical characteristics, diet, and behavior. (Rev: BL 3/1/01*) [595.78]

19547 Feltwell, John. *Butterflies and Moths* (4–6). Illus. Series: Eyewitness Explorers. 1993, DK $9.95 (1-56458-227-2). 64pp. Different kinds of butterflies and moths are pictured in colorful double-page spreads and brief text. (Rev: BL 3/1/93) [595.79]

19548 Fischer-Nagel, Heiderose, and Andreas Fischer-Nagel. *Life of the Butterfly* (4–6). Illus. 1987, Lerner paper $7.95 (0-87614-484-9). 48pp. Clear, readable text and color photos detail the life of a peacock butterfly. (Rev: BL 4/1/87; SLJ 5/87)

19549 French, Vivian. *Caterpillar Caterpillar* (PS–3). Illus. by Charlotte Voake. 1993, Candlewick $14.95 (1-56402-206-4). 32pp. From her observations and answers supplied by her grandmother, a young girl learns about the caterpillars she sees in the garden. (Rev: BL 10/15/93; SLJ 12/93) [595.78]

19550 Gibbons, Gail. *Monarch Butterfly* (1–3). Illus. 1989, Holiday LB $16.95 (0-8234-0773-X). 32pp. The basic life cycle of the monarch butterfly from egg to adult. (Rev: BCCB 12/89; BL 11/1/89; HB 11–12/89; SLJ 12/89) [595.78]

19551 Glaser, Linda. *Magnificent Monarchs* (K–3). Illus. by Gay Holland. 2000, Millbrook LB $21.40 (0-7613-1700-7). This is a very attractive work on monarch butterflies and their amazing lives and migrations. (Rev: SLJ 1/01) [595.78]

19552 Hamilton, Kersten. *The Butterfly Book: A Kid's Guide to Attracting, Raising, and Keeping Butterflies* (3–6). Illus. 1997, John Muir paper $8.95 (1-56261-309-X). 40pp. Introduces 20 species of butterflies and how to attract and keep them, as well as describing their life cycle, anatomy, and habits. (Rev: BL 7/97) [595.78]

19553 Hariton, Anca. *Butterfly Story* (2–4). Illus. 1995, Dutton $15.99 (0-525-45212-5). 32pp. The five-week process of turning a caterpillar into a butterfly is described in words and pictures. (Rev: BL 1/15/95; SLJ 4/95) [595.78]

19554 Hartley, Karen, et al. *Caterpillar* (K–3). Series: Heinemann First Library. 1999, Heinemann

LB $13.95 (1-57572-795-1). 32pp. Different kinds of caterpillars are introduced, with material on lifestyles and habitats, richly illustrated with full-page color photographs that accompany a simple text. (Rev: BL 6/1–15/99; HBG 10/99) [595.78]

19555 Heiligman, Deborah. *From Caterpillar to Butterfly* (PS–1). Illus. by Bari Weissman. Series: Let's-Read-and-Find-Out. 1996, HarperCollins LB $15.89 (0-06-024268-X); paper $4.95 (0-06-445129-1). 31pp. Using a classroom setting, this book shows children watching the miracle of the metamorphosis from caterpillar to butterfly. (Rev: SLJ 8/96) [595.78]

19556 Himmelman, John. *A Luna Moth's Life* (PS–2). Illus. by author. Series: Nature Upclose. 1998, Children's LB $24.00 (0-516-20821-7). The life cycle of the luna moth and details on its habits are presented in this book for beginning readers. (Rev: HBG 10/98; SLJ 7/98) [595.78]

19557 Himmelman, John. *A Monarch Butterfly's Life* (K–2). Illus. by author. Series: Nature Upclose. 1999, Children's LB $24.00 (0-516-21147-1). The life of the monarch butterfly is traced in simple sentences and many close-up paintings including material on its amazing migration. (Rev: SLJ 3/00) [595.78]

19558 Lasky, Kathryn. *Monarchs* (4–6). Illus. by Christopher G. Knight. 1993, Harcourt paper $11.00 (0-15-255297-9). 64pp. The life cycle of the monarch butterfly is presented with details of its mammoth migration. Also tells how communities have helped preserve this species. (Rev: BCCB 11/93; BL 11/15/93; HB 11–12/93; SLJ 9/93*) [595.78]

19559 Lavies, Bianca. *Monarch Butterflies: Mysterious Travelers* (4–7). Illus. 1992, Dutton $15.99 (0-525-44905-1). 32pp. A secluded forest in Mexico's Sierra Madres is the winter home of these beautiful butterflies that summer in the eastern United States and Canada. (Rev: BL 1/15/93; SLJ 4/93*) [595.78]

19560 Lepthien, Emilie U. *Monarch Butterflies* (1–3). Illus. Series: New True Books. 1989, Children's LB $21.00 (0-516-01165-0). 48pp. This species is presented in simple, concise text with many color photos. (Rev: BL 9/1/89) [595.78]

19561 Ling, Mary. *Butterfly* (PS–1). Illus. by Kim Taylor. Series: See How They Grow. 1992, DK $9.95 (1-56458-112-8). 24pp. Excellent color photos help to give children a glimpse of natural history. (Rev: BL 11/1/92; HB 1–2/93; SLJ 12/92) [595.789]

19562 Merrick, Patrick. *Caterpillars* (2–4). Illus. Series: Creepy Crawlers. 1997, Child's World LB $22.79 (1-56766-380-X). 32pp. Describes various kinds of caterpillars, how they move, their habitats, diets, and enemies, with material on their complete life cycle. (Rev: SLJ 3/98) [595.78]

19563 Neye, Emily. *Butterflies* (1–2). Illus. by Ron Broda. Series: All Aboard Reading. 2000, Putnam LB $13.89 (0-448-42280-8); paper $3.99 (0-448-41966-1). 32pp. This easy-to-read book introduces butterflies and discusses their life cycle, physical characteristics, camouflage, migration, and the dif-

ference between butterflies and moths. (Rev: BL 2/15/01; HBG 3/01) [595.78]

19564 Pascoe, Elaine. *Butterflies and Moths* (3–6). Photos by Dwight Kuhn. Illus. Series: Nature Close-up. 1996, Blackbirch LB $18.95 (1-56711-180-7). 48pp. After a general introduction to butterflies and moths, this book shows how they can be caught, housed, fed, and observed. (Rev: SLJ 4/97) [595.78]

19565 Pringle, Laurence. *An Extraordinary Life: The Story of a Monarch Butterfly* (3–6). Illus. by Bob Marstall. 1997, Orchard LB $19.99 (0-531-33002-8). 32pp. The life cycle of a single monarch butterfly and its migration from Massachusetts to Mexico. (Rev: BCCB 5/97; BL 3/15/97*; HB 5–6/97; SLJ 5/97) [595.78]

19566 Ring, Elizabeth. *Night Flier* (1–3). Photos by Dwight Kuhn. 1994, Millbrook LB $21.90 (1-56294-467-3). 32pp. The life cycle of the cecropia moth is chronicled from its hatching. (Rev: BL 10/1/94; SLJ 12/94) [595.78]

19567 Rosenblatt, Lynn. *Monarch Magic! Butterfly Activities and Nature Discoveries* (3–6). Illus. Series: Good Times! 1998, Williamson paper $12.95 (1-885593-23-6). 96pp. This work covers many topics involving the monarch butterfly, including physical characteristics, feeding habits, habitats, and migratory patterns plus material on how to raise them and protect them from extinction. (Rev: BL 12/1/98; SLJ 4/99) [595.78]

19568 Ross, Michael E. *Caterpillarology* (3–5). Photos by Brian Grogan. Illus. by Darren Erickson. Series: Backyard Buddies. 1998, Carolrhoda LB $19.93 (1-57505-055-2). 48pp. A great deal of scientific information is presented about caterpillars in an entertaining way, with experiments and instructions on how to capture and release them. (Rev: BL 7/98; HBG 10/98; SLJ 3/98) [595.78]

19569 Sabin, Louis. *Amazing World of Butterflies and Moths* (1–3). Illus. by Jean Helmer. 1982, Troll paper $3.50 (0-89375-561-3). 32pp. A simple account for young readers with brief text and many illustrations.

19570 Wilner, Yvonne. *Butterflies Fly* (2–5). Illus. by Karen Lloyd-Jones. 2001, Charlesbridge LB $16.95 (1-57091-446-X). 32pp. A poetic text with large illustrations shows butterflies of the world in their natural habitats. (Rev: BL 2/15/01; SLJ 2/01) [595.78]

SPIDERS AND SCORPIONS

19571 Allen, Judy. *Are You a Spider?* (PS–1). Illus. by Tudor Humphries. Series: Backyard Books. 2000, Kingfisher $9.95 (0-7534-5243-X). 32pp. The reader becomes a newly hatched spider and learns how to spin threads, make webs, and watch out for dangers such as birds. (Rev: BL 10/15/00) [595.4]

19572 Back, Christine. *Spider's Web* (1–3). Illus. 1986, Silver Burdett paper $3.95 (0-382-24020-0). 25pp. How the garden spider spins its web and uses it as a food trap. (Rev: BL 1/1/87)

19573 Bailey, Jill. *How Spiders Make Their Webs* (3–5). Illus. Series: Nature's Mysteries. 1996, Benchmark LB $22.79 (0-7614-0456-2). 32pp.

Using a large number of illustrations, this account describes a variety of spider constructions and how they are made. (Rev: SLJ 2/97) [595.4]

19574 Berman, Ruth. *Spinning Spiders* (PS–2). Illus. by David T. Roberts. Series: Pull Ahead Books. 1998, Lerner LB $21.27 (0-8225-3604-8). 32pp. Using questions within the text, this book introduces spiders and their habits along with information on the differences between spiders and insects, spider webs, egg sacs, and spiderlings. (Rev: BL 2/1/99; HBG 3/99; SLJ 6/99) [595.4]

19575 Chinery, Michael. *Spider* (3–5). Illus. by Alan Male. Series: Life Story. 1990, Troll paper $4.95 (0-8167-2109-2). 32pp. The life of the common spider is introduced in detailed text and unusual photos. (Rev: BL 4/1/91) [595.4]

19576 Clyne, Densey. *Spotlight on Spiders* (4–6). Illus. Series: Small Worlds. 1996, Allen & Unwin paper $6.95 (1-86373-862-2). 32pp. Australian spiders, their habits and structure, are described in this colorful import. (Rev: SLJ 7/96) [595.4]

19577 Dallinger, Jane. *Spiders* (4–7). Illus. 1981, Lerner LB $22.60 (0-8225-1456-7); paper $5.95 (0-8225-9534-6). 48pp. Excellent color photographs complement the text.

19578 Facklam, Margery. *Spiders and Their Web Sites* (5–8). Illus. by Alan Male. 2001, Little, Brown $15.95 (0-316-27329-5). 32pp. This book takes a look at 12 kinds of spiders, with material on webs, lifestyles, and reproduction. (Rev: BL 3/15/01) [595.4]

19579 Fowler, Allan. *Spiders Are Not Insects* (PS–3). Illus. Series: Rookie Readers. 1996, Children's LB $19.00 (0-516-06054-6). 31pp. A beginning reader that introduces spiders and features such species as the tarantula, bird spider, and the black widow. (Rev: SLJ 8/96) [595.4]

19580 Gibbons, Gail. *Spiders* (1–2). Illus. 1993, Holiday LB $16.95 (0-8234-1006-4). 32pp. An introductory account with stunning drawings of spiders, plus their structure, behavior, and important species. (Rev: BL 4/15/93; SLJ 7/93) [595.4]

19581 Glaser, Linda. *Spectacular Spiders* (K–2). Illus. by Gay Holland. 1998, Millbrook LB $21.40 (0-7613-0353-7). 32pp. A young girl explains the habits and behavior of garden spiders, including their diet and how they spin webs. (Rev: BL 1/1–15/99; HBG 3/99; SLJ 3/99) [595.4]

19582 Hartley, Karen, et al. *Spider* (K–3). Series: Heinemann First Library. 1999, Heinemann LB $13.95 (1-57572-799-4). 32pp. Different kinds of spiders are pictured in full-color photos with textual material on habits, physical characteristics, and life cycles. (Rev: BL 6/1–15/99; HBG 10/99) [595.4]

19583 Himmelman, John. *A House Spider's Life* (K–2). Illus. by author. Series: Nature Upclose. 1999, Children's LB $24.00 (0-516-21185-4). Using realistic paintings (one per page), this simple account traces the life cycle of the common spider. (Rev: SLJ 3/00) [595.4]

19584 Kalman, Bobbie. *Web Weavers and Other Spiders* (2–5). Illus. Series: Crabapples. 1997, Crabtree LB $19.96 (0-86505-632-3); paper $5.95 (0-

86505-732-X). 32pp. A description of how spiders live is given, with material on physical characteristics, web building, defenses, and mating behavior. (Rev: BL 7/97; SLJ 7/97) [595.4]

19585 Lassieur, Allison. *Scorpions: The Sneaky Stingers* (3–5). Illus. Series: Animals in Order. 2000, Watts LB $23.00 (0-531-11651-4); paper $6.95 (0-531-16497-7). 48pp. After a general introduction to animal classification, this book describes scorpions, their structure, where they live, and their habits. (Rev: BL 9/15/00) [595.7]

19586 Llewellyn, Claire. *Spiders Have Fangs: And Other Amazing Facts About Arachnids* (1–3). Illus. by Mike Taylor and Jo Moore. Series: I Didn't Know That. 1997, Millbrook LB $19.90 (0-7613-0610-2). 32pp. A fascination book that reveals little-known facts about spiders and other arachnids. (Rev: SLJ 3/98) [595.4]

19587 Markle, Sandra. *Outside and Inside Spiders* (4–6). Illus. 1994, Bradbury LB $17.00 (0-02-762314-9). 40pp. The spider's anatomy is described, along with material on mating, habitats, and behavior. (Rev: BL 4/1/94; HB 5–6/94; SLJ 6/94) [595.4]

19588 Murray, Peter. *Scorpions* (3–5). Illus. Series: Naturebooks. 1996, Child's World LB $22.79 (1-56766-217-X). 32pp. This book features in color photos and simple text this spiderlike creature with a sting in its tail. (Rev: BL 12/15/96) [595.4]

19589 Murray, Peter. *Tarantulas* (3–6). Illus. Series: Naturebooks. 1993, Child's World LB $22.79 (1-56766-060-6). 32pp. Amazing full-page photos highlight this simple introduction to tarantulas, how they live, and how they gather food. (Rev: BL 3/1/94) [595.4]

19590 Parsons, Alexandra. *Amazing Spiders* (1–4). Illus. Series: Eyewitness Juniors. 1990, Knopf LB $11.99 (0-679-90226-0). 32pp. After the nature of spiders is discussed, various kinds are introduced. (Rev: BL 8/90) [595.4]

19591 Podendorf, Illa. *Spiders* (1–4). Illus. 1982, Children's LB $21.00 (0-516-01653-9); paper $5.50 (0-516-41653-7). 48pp. Color photographs and a well-organized text are highlights of this simple introduction.

19592 Pringle, Laurence. *Scorpion Man: Exploring the World of Scorpions* (4–7). Illus. 1994, Scribners paper $15.95 (0-684-19560-7). 48pp. A profile of the world of scorpions, with material on the life of a man who studied them, Gary Polis. (Rev: BL 1/15/95; SLJ 3/95) [595.4]

19593 Ross, Michael E. *Spiderology* (3–6). Illus. 2000, Carolrhoda LB $19.93 (1-57505-387-X); paper $6.95 (1-57505-438-8). 48pp. After describing how to collect and observe spiders humanely, this book suggests a number of activities to learn more about them. (Rev: BL 5/15/00; HBG 10/00; SLJ 7/00) [595.4]

19594 Schnieper, Claudia. *Amazing Spiders* (3–6). Illus. by Max Meier. 1989, Carolrhoda LB $23.93 (0-87614-342-7). 48pp. In often startling photos and a clear text, spiders are introduced. (Rev: BL 9/15/89; HB 11–12/89; SLJ 8/89) [595.4]

19595 Souza, D. M. *Eight Legs* (3–5). Illus. Series: Creatures All Around Us. 1991, Carolrhoda LB $22.60 (0-87614-441-5). 40pp. Close-up photographs and clear explanations introduce spiders, scorpions, and other crawling creatures with eight legs. (Rev: BL 4/15/91; SLJ 7/91) [595.4]

19596 Squire, Ann O. *Spiders of North America* (3–5). Series: Animals in Order. 2000, Watts LB $23.00 (0-531-11516-X). 48pp. This book explains the animal classification system and then goes on to describe arachnids and introduce different varieties of spiders and their behavior. (Rev: BL 4/15/00) [595.4]

19597 Storad, Conrad J. *Tarantulas* (2–3). Series: Early Bird Nature Books. 1998, Lerner LB $22.60 (0-8225-3024-4). 48pp. This easily read, beautifully illustrated account introduces the tarantula, its life cycle, and its feeding habits. (Rev: BL 3/15/98; HBG 10/98; SLJ 7/98) [595.4]

19598 Winer, Yvonne. *Spiders Spin Webs* (PS–3). Illus. by Karen Lloyd-Jones. 1998, Charlesbridge $15.95 (0-88106-983-3); paper $6.95 (0-88106-984-1). 32pp. This visually exciting field guide introduces 15 types of spiders and their characteristics. (Rev: BL 7/98; HBG 3/99; SLJ 11/98) [595.4]

Land Invertebrates

19599 Aaseng, Nathan. *Invertebrates* (5–8). Illus. 1993, Watts LB $25.00 (0-531-12550-5). 112pp. Describes the varieties of life forms without backbones, including insects, and how they have diversified through the ages. (Rev: BL 3/15/94; SLJ 3/94) [592]

19600 Allen, Judy. *Are You a Snail?* (PS–1). Illus. by Tudor Humphries. Series: Backyard Books. 2000, Kingfisher $9.95 (0-7534-5242-1). 32pp. An introduction to snails that discusses their appearance, food, and how they grow from egg to adult. (Rev: BL 5/15/00; HBG 3/01; SLJ 9/00) [594]

19601 Barrow, Lloyd H. *Science Fair Projects Investigating Earthworms* (5–8). Series: Science Fair Success. 2000, Enslow LB $19.95 (0-7660-1291-3). 104pp. This book contains a fascinating number of experiments involving earthworms, with very explicit directions and explanations of the scientific principles behind each project. (Rev: BL 4/15/00; HBG 10/00) [595.1]

19602 Buholzer, Theres. *Life of the Snail* (2–5). Illus. 1987, Carolrhoda LB $22.60 (0-87614-246-3). 48pp. Close-up photos highlight the story of this small, fascinating animal. (Rev: BL 3/15/87; SLJ 6–7/87)

19603 Dell'Oro, Suzanne Paul. *Tunneling Earthworms* (PS–2). Series: Pull Ahead Books. 2000, Lerner LB $21.27 (0-8225-3762-1). 32pp. A lavishly illustrated book that introduces the earthworm, its anatomy, food, and how it is able to move through earth. (Rev: BL 3/1/01) [595]

19604 Doris, Ellen. *Meet the Arthropods* (4–7). 1996, Thames & Hudson $16.95 (0-500-19010-0). 64pp. Such arthropods as the horseshoe crab, potato

beetle, and praying mantis are introduced with photographs and activities. (Rev: BL 10/15/96) [595.2]

19605 Fowler, Allan. *A Snail's Pace* (1–2). Illus. Series: Rookie Readers. 1999, Children's LB $18.50 (0-516-20812-8). 32pp. This introduction to snails and slugs features large type, many color pictures, and a small format. (Rev: BL 7/99; HBG 10/99) [594]

19606 Fredericks, Anthony D. *Slugs* (2–3). Series: Early Bird Nature Books. 2000, Lerner LB $22.60 (0-8225-3041-4). 48pp. A beginning science book that describes, in pictures and text, what a slug looks like, where it lives, how it reproduces, and how it survives in spite of predators. (Rev: BL 5/15/00; HBG 10/00) [595]

19607 Glaser, Linda. *Wonderful Worms* (PS–2). Illus. by Loretta Krupinski. 1992, Millbrook LB $21.90 (1-56294-062-7). 32pp. A close peek at the wriggly world of earthworms. (Rev: BL 1/15/93; SLJ 3/93) [595]

19608 Hartley, Karen, and Chris Macro. *Snail* (1–3). Illus. by Alan Male. Series: Bug Books. 1998, Heinemann LB $19.92 (1-57572-664-5). 32pp. Large color photos of snails and short paragraphs of text are used to explain the physical structure, behavior, food, and life cycle of the snail. (Rev: HBG 10/99; SLJ 1/99) [594.3]

19609 Himmelman, John. *An Earthworm's Life* (K–2). Series: Nature Upclose. 2000, Children's LB $24.00 (0-516-21164-1). 32pp. Original watercolor paintings are used to illustrate this simple introduction to earthworms, their habits, where they live, and their life cycle. (Rev: BL 10/15/00) [595]

19610 Himmelman, John. *A Slug's Life* (PS–2). Illus. by author. Series: Nature Upclose. 1998, Children's LB $24.00 (0-516-20822-5). Using many photographs, this introduction to the life cycle of the slug and its activities is intended for beginning readers. (Rev: HBG 10/98; SLJ 7/98) [594]

19611 Johnson, Sylvia A. *Silkworms* (4–7). Illus. 1982, Lerner paper $5.95 (0-8225-9557-5). 48pp. The life cycle of the silkworm, told in text and striking color pictures.

19612 Johnson, Sylvia A. *Snails* (4–6). Illus. 1982, Lerner LB $22.60 (0-8225-1475-3). 48pp. The structure, habits, and life cycle of a snail.

19613 McLaughlin, Molly. *Earthworms, Dirt, and Rotten Leaves: An Exploration in Ecology* (4–6). Illus. 1986, Avon paper $3.50 (0-380-71074-9). 96pp. Activities that lead to an understanding of the behavior and appearance of earthworms. (Rev: BCCB 2/87; BL 2/1/87; SLJ 3/87)

19614 Merrick, Patrick. *Earthworms* (K–3). Series: Naturebooks. 1999, Child's World LB $15.95 (1-56766-501-2). 32pp. Physical characteristics of the earthworm, its habitat, usefulness, habits, food, and life cycle are presented in amazing color photographs and a brief text. (Rev: BL 6/1–15/99; HBG 10/99) [595.1]

19615 Murray, Peter. *Snails* (2–4). Illus. Series: Creepy Crawlers. 1997, Child's World LB $22.79 (1-56766-382-6). 32pp. The physical and behavioral characteristics of snails are presented, with additional material on diet, habitats, movements, and enemies. (Rev: SLJ 3/98) [594.3]

19616 Pascoe, Elaine. *Earthworms* (4–7). Illus. Series: Nature Close-up. 1996, Blackbirch LB $18.95 (1-56711-177-7). 48pp. An account of the anatomy of earthworms and how they live, as well as how to collect and care for them. (Rev: BL 12/1/96) [595.1]

19617 Pascoe, Elaine. *Snails and Slugs* (4–7). Series: Nature Close-up. 1998, Blackbirch LB $16.95 (1-56711-181-5). 48pp. Outstanding photographs, an interesting text, and several easy-to-do projects highlight this introduction to snails and slugs. (Rev: BL 9/15/98; HBG 3/99) [594.3]

19618 Ross, Michael E. *Millipedeology* (3–6). Illus. Series: Backyard Buddies. 2000, Carolrhoda LB $19.93 (1-57505-398-5); paper $6.95 (1-57505-436-1). 48pp. This book shows how to collect and humanely study millipedes, with experiments that can be performed to learn more about them. (Rev: BL 5/15/00; HBG 10/00; SLJ 7/00) [595.6]

19619 Ross, Michael E. *Snailology* (4–6). Illus. Series: Backyard Buddies. 1996, Carolrhoda LB $19.95 (0-87614-894-1). 48pp. Various types of snails are introduced, with material on their classification, physical structure, and habits. (Rev: BL 7/96; SLJ 8/96) [594]

19620 Ross, Michael E. *Wormology* (4–6). Illus. 1996, Carolrhoda LB $14.95 (0-87614-937-9). 48pp. Worms and their classification, structure, and habits are introduced, with several activities and experiments. (Rev: BL 3/15/96; SLJ 7/96) [595.1]

19621 Silverstein, Alvin, et al. *Invertebrates* (3–6). Illus. Series: Kingdoms of Life. 1996, Twenty-First Century LB $20.40 (0-8050-3518-4). 64pp. Animals without backbones are discussed in a brief text with many color photographs. (Rev: BL 6/1–15/96) [592]

Marine and Freshwater Life

GENERAL AND MISCELLANEOUS

19622 Armstrong, Pam. *Young Explorer's Guide to Undersea Life* (3–5). Illus. 1996, Monterey Bay $16.95 (1-878244-10-8). 64pp. Some plants and about 20 animals that live in or around the sea are described. (Rev: BL 9/15/96; SLJ 9/96) [574.92]

19623 Batten, Mary. *The Winking, Blinking Sea: All About Bioluminescence* (3–5). 2000, Millbrook LB $20.90 (0-7613-1550-0). Large photos of 11 bioluminescent sea creatures are presented opposite a paragraph or two of descriptive text. (Rev: BCCB 6/00; HBG 10/00; SLJ 7/00) [591.92]

19624 Berger, Melvin. *Dive! A Book of Deep-Sea Creatures* (1–2). Illus. Series: Hello Reader! 2000, Scholastic $3.99 (0-439-08747-3). 40pp. This easy reader introduces the marine life found on the ocean floor, with color photographs mostly at a close range. (Rev: BL 10/1/00) [591.77]

19625 Berger, Melvin, and Gilda Berger. *Do Whales Have Belly Buttons? Questions and Answers About Whales and Dolphins* (3–5). Series: Question and Answer. 1999, Scholastic $12.95 (0-590-13081-1); paper $5.95 (0-590-08571-3). l48pp. Simple ques-

tions related to whales and dolphins are asked and answered in a clear and precise way in this book illustrated with dramatic, often beautiful, paintings. (Rev: BL 11/15/99; HBG 3/00; SLJ 12/99) [599.5]

19626 Cerullo, Mary. *Sea Soup: Phytoplankton* (4–7). Illus. 1999, Tilbury $16.95 (0-88448-208-1). 40pp. An introduction to the microscopic world of tiny plants known as phytoplankton and their contributions to life on this planet. (Rev: BL 3/15/00; SLJ 5/00) [578.77]

19627 Cooney, Helen. *Underwater Animals* (2–4). Illus. Series: Nature Company Young Discoveries. 1997, Time Life $10.00 (0-7835-4841-9). 32pp. In a series of double-page spreads and impressive illustrations, a number of marine animals are introduced in a simple text. (Rev: BL 2/15/97) [591.92]

19628 Darling, Kathy. *Seashore Babies* (3–5). Illus. by Tara Darling. 1997, Walker LB $16.85 (0-8027-8477-1). 32pp. Seashores are introduced, with details of the young of the creatures found there and their lives and enemies. (Rev: BL 4/1/97; SLJ 3/97) [591.3]

19629 Delafosse, Claude. *Under the Sea: Hidden World* (PS–2). Series: First Discovery. 1999, Scholastic $12.95 (0-590-10992-8). 24pp. This beginning science book explores life in the ocean depths through many color pictures and a simple text. (Rev: BL 6/1–15/99; SLJ 7/99) [591]

19630 Demuth, Patricia. *Way Down Deep: Strange Ocean Creatures* (1–3). Illus. by Jim Deal. Series: All Aboard Reading. 1995, Putnam paper $3.99 (0-448-40851-1). 48pp. This easy-to-read science book introduces youngsters to the amazing creatures found at the bottom of the ocean. (Rev: BL 1/1–15/96; SLJ 6/96) [551.46]

19631 Earle, Sylvia A. *Dive! My Adventures in the Deep Frontier* (3–7). Illus. 1999, National Geographic $18.95 (0-7922-7144-0). 64pp. This photo-essay contains a spectacular view of underwater life as experienced by the author, an eminent marine biologist. (Rev: BCCB 6/99; BL 2/15/99*; HBG 10/99; SLJ 3/99) [627]

19632 Earle, Sylvia A. *Sea Critters* (1–4). Illus. by Wolcott Henry. 2000, National Geographic $16.95 (0-7922-7181-5). 32pp. Color photos and a lyrical text are used to introduce such unusual sea creatures as Christmas-tree worms, sea squirts, sponges, and moray eels. (Rev: BL 11/1/00; HBG 3/01; SLJ 9/00) [591.92]

19633 Feeney, Stephanie, and Ann Fielding. *Sand to Sea: Marine Life of Hawaii* (2–4). Illus. by Ed Robinson. 1989, Univ. of Hawaii Pr. $13.95 (0-8248-1180-1). 64pp. A look at the fascinating sea life in Hawaii. (Rev: BL 11/1/89) [574]

19634 Gowell, Elizabeth T. *Whales and Dolphins: What They Have in Common* (3–5). Series: Animals in Order. 2000, Watts LB $23.00 (0-531-20396-4). 48pp. After material on animal classification, this book explains how dolphins and whales are related and goes on to present their individual characteristics. (Rev: BL 4/15/00; SLJ 7/00) [591.9]

19635 Grupper, Jonathan. *Destination: Deep Sea* (1–4). 2000, National Geographic $16.95 (0-7922-

7693-0). 31pp. A beautiful collection of photographs and informative text present many sea creatures, from the inhabitants of coral reefs to dolphins, whales, and sea otters. (Rev: BL 10/15/00; HBG 3/01; SLJ 9/00) [591.92]

19636 Halfmann, Janet. *Life in the Sea* (5–7). Series: LifeViews. 2000, Creative Co. LB $22.60 (1-58341-074-0). 25pp. All life in the sea is discussed with a focus on the tiniest — plankton, algae, sea spiders, coral, and worms. (Rev: SLJ 8/00) [591.92]

19637 Johnson, Jinny. *Simon and Schuster Children's Guide to Sea Creatures* (4–7). 1998, Simon & Schuster $19.95 (0-689-81534-4). 80pp. This book contains broad coverage of the invertebrates, birds, mammals, and fish found in various parts of the oceans and their shores. (Rev: HBG 10/98; SLJ 5/98) [591]

19638 Kalman, Bobbie. *AB Sea* (K–3). Illus. Series: Crabapples. 1995, Crabtree LB $19.96 (0-86505-625-0); paper $5.95 (0-86505-725-7). 32pp. An alphabet book that uses full-color pictures of marine life to illustrate the ABCs. (Rev: SLJ 4/96) [574.92]

19639 Kalman, Bobbie, and Heather Levigne. *What Is a Whale?* (2–4). Series: Science of Living Things. 1999, Crabtree LB $14.97 (0-86505-935-7); paper $5.36 (0-86505-953-5). 32pp. This introduction to whales, dolphins, and other cetaceans is well illustrated and informative. (Rev: SLJ 4/00) [599]

19640 Kite, Patricia. *Down in the Sea: The Sea Slug* (2–4). Illus. 1994, Albert Whitman LB $14.95 (0-8075-1717-8). 32pp. In photos and easily read text, the life, appearance, and habits of the sea slug are explored. (Rev: BL 5/15/94; SLJ 5/94) [594]

19641 Kovacs, Deborah, and Kate Madin. *Beneath Blue Waters: Meetings with Remarkable Deep-Sea Creatures* (5–8). Illus. 1996, Viking $16.99 (0-670-85653-3). 64pp. Text and color photos are used to explore marine life one mile below the ocean's surface. (Rev: BL 12/1/96I; SLJ 1/97) [591.92]

19642 Pallotta, Jerry. *The Freshwater Alphabet Book* (1–4). Illus. by David Biedrzycki. 1996, Charlesbridge $15.95 (0-88106-901-9). Freshwater fish and crustaceans are used, along with a mythical monster or two, in this nicely illustrated alphabet book. (Rev: SLJ 4/96) [597]

19643 Perry, Phyllis J. *Freshwater Giants* (3–5). Illus. 1999, Watts LB $24.00 (0-531-11681-6). 64pp. For each "giant," such as the hippopotamus, dolphin, and manatee, details are given on its characteristics, behavior, and habitat. (Rev: BL 11/1/99; HBG 3/00) [599.176]

19644 Podendorf, Illa. *Animals of Sea and Shore* (1–4). Illus. 1982, Children's LB $21.00 (0-516-01615-6); paper $5.50 (0-516-41615-4). 48pp. A fine introduction to marine life for primary grades.

19645 Rothaus, Don P. *Moray Eels* (3–5). Illus. Series: Naturebooks: Animals. 1995, Child's World LB $22.79 (1-56766-187-4). 32pp. The mysterious moray eel is discussed, with information on habitats, structure, habits, and diet. (Rev: BL 11/15/95; SLJ 4/96) [597]

19646 Savage, Stephen. *Animals of the Oceans* (2–6). Illus. Series: Animals by Habitat. 1997, Raintree Steck-Vaughn LB $22.83 (0-8172-4753-X). 32pp. Readers are taken on a tour of vast underwater habitats and encounter such animals as the moray eel, green turtle, and sea anemone. (Rev: BL 5/15/97; SLJ 8/97) [591.9]

19647 Sheather, Allan. *Neptune's Nursery* (2–3). Illus. by Kim Michelle Toft. 2000, Charlesbridge LB $16.95 (1-57091-391-9); paper $6.95 (1-57091-392-7). 32pp. A rhyming text and stunning paintings introduce a number of marine animals and their young. (Rev: BL 12/15/00; HBG 3/01; SLJ 10/00) [591.77]

19648 Sibbald, Jean H. *Strange Eating Habits of Sea Creatures* (4–8). Illus. 1987, Macmillan LB $13.95 (0-87518-349-2). 112pp. Eating habits of numerous creatures of the sea are divided into techniques — grazers, gulpers, poisoners, and so on. (Rev: BL 12/1/86; SLJ 2/87)

19649 Souza, D. M. *Sea Snakes* (2–3). Illus. Series: Creatures All Around Us. 1998, Carolrhoda LB $19.93 (1-57505-263-6). 40pp. An illustrated study of the habits, life cycles, and reproductive behavior of sea snakes and sea kraits, including a fact summary and glossary. (Rev: BL 12/1/98; HBG 3/99; SLJ 3/99) [597.96]

19650 Taylor, Barbara. *The Really Sinister Savage Shark: And Other Creatures of the Deep* (PS–4). Illus. Series: The Really Horrible Guides. 1997, DK $9.95 (0-7894-2050-3). This account explores the various ways — such as poisonous stings, electric shocks, and pointed tusks — in which sea creatures defend themselves. (Rev: HBG 3/98; SLJ 12/97) [574]

19651 Taylor, Leighton. *Creeps from the Deep* (4–8). Illus. 1997, Chronicle $13.95 (0-8118-1297-9). 48pp. In startling color photos and a fascinating text, this title examines the strange creatures that live in the deepest regions of the ocean. (Rev: BL 12/15/97; HBG 3/98; SLJ 4/98) [578.77]

19652 Treat, Rose. *The Seaweed Book: How to Find and Have Fun with Seaweed* (4–7). Illus. 1995, Star Bright paper $5.95 (1-887724-00-7). 32pp. The identification, collection, and preservation of various kinds of seaweed. (Rev: BL 2/1/96) [589.45]

19653 Worth, Bonnie. *Wish for a Fish: All About Sea Creatures* (K–3). Illus. by Aristides Ruiz. Series: The Cat in the Hat's Learning Library. 1999, Random LB $11.99 (0-679-99116-6). 37pp. In a deep-sea submarine Dr. Seuss's characters explore five different undersea zones and introduce the creatures found in each. (Rev: SLJ 9/99) [597]

CORALS AND JELLYFISH

19654 Buttfield, Helen. *The Secret Life of Fishes: From Angels to Zebras on the Coral Reef* (5–8). Illus. by author. 2000, Abrams $19.95 (0-8109-3933-9). 72pp. As well as introducing the fish found on coral reefs, this handsome book talks about the reef itself and other creatures found there such as the octopus and sea star. (Rev: SLJ 7/00) [574.9]

19655 Cerullo, Mary. *Coral Reef: A City That Never Sleeps* (5–8). Illus. 1996, Dutton $17.99 (0-525-65193-4). 58pp. Exceptional photographs highlight the account of coral reefs and the life they support. (Rev: BL 3/1/96; SLJ 1/96*) [574.9]

19656 Collard, Sneed B. *Lizard Island: Science and Scientists on Australia's Great Barrier Reef* (5–7). Illus. 2000, Watts $26.00 (0-531-11719-7). 144pp. Introduces the work being undertaken at Lizard Island Research Station in Australia and describes the mysteries of reefs that they hope to solve. (Rev: BL 2/1/01) [577.7]

19657 Dunphy, Madeleine. *Here Is the Coral Reef* (K–2). Illus. by Tom Leonard. 1998, Hyperion LB $15.49 (0-7868-2135-3). 32pp. Using a variation on "The House That Jack Built" as a framework for its text, this brightly illustrated picture book introduces the varied creatures that live on Australia's Great Barrier Reef. (Rev: BCCB 6/98; BL 4/1/98; HBG 10/98; SLJ 5/98) [577.7]

19658 Earle, Sylvia A. *Hello, Fish! Visiting the Coral Reef* (PS–4). Photos by Wolcott Henry. 1999, National Geographic $15.95 (0-7922-7103-3). Stunning photography is featured in a series of double-page spreads that introduce 12 fish that live in the waters around coral reefs. (Rev: BCCB 6/99; HBG 10/99; SLJ 3/99) [574]

19659 Fleisher, Paul. *Coral Reef* (3–5). Series: Webs of Life. 1997, Marshall Cavendish LB $22.79 (0-7614-0432-5). 40pp. This look at life in a coral reef explains how they are formed and the kinds of life found within them. (Rev: BL 2/15/98; HBG 3/98; SLJ 4/98) [574.9]

19660 George, Twig C. *Jellies: The Life of Jellyfish* (K–3). Illus. 2000, Millbrook LB $21.90 (0-7613-1659-0). 32pp. Handsome photographs introduce jellyfish, their many varieties, special features, and beauty. (Rev: BL 5/1/00; HBG 10/00; SLJ 8/00) [593.5]

19661 Johnson, Rebecca L. *The Great Barrier Reef: A Living Laboratory* (5–8). Illus. 1991, Lerner LB $23.93 (0-8225-1596-2). 96pp. This account describes the formation and inhabitants of the Great Barrier Reef from an investigative scientist's point of view. (Rev: BL 5/15/92; SLJ 7/92) [574.92]

19662 Kalman, Bobbie. *Life in the Coral Reef* (2–5). Illus. Series: Crabapples. 1997, Crabtree LB $19.96 (0-86505-629-3); paper $5.95 (0-86505-729-X). 32pp. A description of how coral reefs are formed, their interdependence with other animals and plants, and methods used to save them. (Rev: BL 7/97) [574.5]

19663 Kite, Patricia. *Down in the Sea: The Jellyfish* (1–3). Illus. Series: Down by the Sea. 1993, Whitman LB $14.95 (0-8075-1712-7). 32pp. Color photos highlight this introduction to the fascinating jellyfish. (Rev: BL 3/15/93; SLJ 3/93) [593.7]

19664 Landau, Elaine. *Jellyfish* (3–5). Illus. Series: True Books. 1999, Children's LB $21.00 (0-516-20676-1). 48pp. With plenty of captioned photographs, this work describes the structure, variety, and unique features of jellyfish. (Rev: BL 6/1–15/99; HBG 10/99) [593.5]

19665 Pringle, Laurence. *Coral Reefs: Earth's Undersea Treasures* (4–6). Illus. 1995, Simon & Schuster $16.00 (0-689-80286-2). 45pp. A pictorial account that displays the diversity of life on a coral reef, its uses to humankind, and the dangers of destruction. (Rev: BL 10/15/95; HB 11–12/95; SLJ 10/95) [574.5]

19666 Sayre, April Pulley. *Coral Reef* (4–7). Illus. Series: Exploring Earth's Biomes. 1996, Twenty-First Century LB $20.40 (0-8050-4087-0). 80pp. An accurate, interesting explanation of the composition of coral reefs and description of the life forms they support. (Rev: BL 10/15/96; HB 3–4/96; SLJ 1/97) [574.9]

19667 Siy, Alexandra. *The Great Astrolabe Reef* (5–8). Illus. Series: Circle of Life. 1992, Macmillan $14.95 (0-87518-499-5). 80pp. Color photos help to tell the story of this delicate coral ecosystem. (Rev: BL 9/1/92; SLJ 11/92) [574.5]

19668 Taylor, Barbara. *Coral Reef* (3–6). Illus. Series: Look Closer. 1992, DK $9.95 (1-879431-92-0). 32pp. In a series of double-page spreads with brief captions, the origins and composition of coral reefs are explained. (Rev: BL 6/1/92; HB 7–8/92; SLJ 6/92) [591.9]

19669 Telford, Carole, and Rod Theodorou. *Inside a Coral Reef* (2–6). Illus. by Stephen Lings and Jane Pickering. Series: Amazing Journeys. 1997, Heinemann LB $13.95 (1-57572-154-6). 32pp. Using a journey format with maps and other illustrations, this account introduces readers to the Great Barrier Reef and its flora and fauna. (Rev: SLJ 5/98) [574.9]

19670 Wood, Jenny. *Coral Reefs: Hidden Colonies of the Sea* (3–5). Illus. Series: Wonderworks of Nature. 1991, Stevens LB $22.60 (0-8368-0630-1). 32pp. Three types of reefs are explored — coral, fringe, and barrier — with material on where they can be found and how coral live on them. (Rev: SLJ 9/92) [574.84]

19671 Wu, Norbert. *A City Under the Sea: Life in a Coral Reef* (3–6). Illus. 1996, Simon & Schuster $16.00 (0-689-31896-0). 32pp. A fascinating glimpse of the life surrounding a coral reef. (Rev: BL 6/1–15/96; SLJ 3/96) [574]

CRUSTACEANS

19672 Cerullo, Mary. *Lobsters: Gangsters of the Sea* (4–6). Photos by Jeffrey L. Rotman. 1994, Dutton $16.99 (0-525-65153-5). 64pp. A photo-essay about the life cycle of lobsters and what happens when they are caught by lobster trappers. (Rev: BL 3/1/94; HB 1–2/94; SLJ 3/94) [595.3]

19673 Day, Nancy. *The Horseshoe Crab* (3–5). Illus. Series: Remarkable Animals. 1992, Macmillan $13.95 (0-87518-545-2). 60pp. The evolution of the horseshoe crab is given, plus material on its structure, habitats, and behavior. (Rev: BL 12/1/92; SLJ 3/93) [595.3]

19674 Fowler, Allan. *Shellfish Aren't Fish* (1–2). Series: Rookie Readers. 1998, Children's LB $18.50 (0-516-20802-0). 32pp. An interesting introduction to shrimps, crabs, and other crustaceans. (Rev: BL 9/15/98; HBG 10/99) [595.3]

19675 Grimm, Phyllis W. *Crayfish* (2–3). Series: Early Bird Nature Books. 2000, Lerner LB $22.60 (0-8225-3030-9). 48pp. A look at this unusual sea creature that has eight legs, two large claws, four antennae, and many mouth parts. (Rev: BL 10/15/00; HBG 3/01; SLJ 2/01) [595.3]

19676 Holling, Holling C. *Pagoo* (4–6). Illus. 1957, Houghton $20.00 (0-395-06826-6); paper $10.00 (0-395-53964-1). 96pp. Life cycle of the hermit crab.

19677 Johnson, Sylvia A. *Crabs* (4–6). Illus. 1982, Lerner LB $22.60 (0-8225-1471-0). 48pp. A look at the structure and life cycle of various crabs.

19678 Kite, Patricia. *Down in the Sea: The Crab* (2–4). Illus. 1994, Albert Whitman LB $14.95 (0-8075-1709-7). 32pp. Photographs and simple text introduce the crab, with interesting material on how they communicate. (Rev: BL 6/1–15/94; SLJ 5/94) [595.3]

19679 Ricciuti, Edward R. *Crustaceans* (5–7). Illus. Series: Our Living World. 1994, Blackbirch LB $19.95 (1-56711-046-0). 64pp. Introduces crabs, lobsters, and other crustaceans, and tells about their unique characteristics, senses, metabolisms, and life cycles. (Rev: BL 12/1/94) [595.3]

19680 Stefoff, Rebecca. *Crab* (K–3). Series: Living Things. 1997, Marshall Cavendish LB $22.79 (0-7614-0444-9). 32pp. Using double-page spreads, the crab is introduced, with material on its structure, habits, and food. (Rev: BL 2/15/98; HBG 3/98) [595.3]

DOLPHINS AND PORPOISES

19681 Cerullo, Mary. *Dolphins: What They Can Teach Us* (4–6). Photos by Jeffrey L. Rotman. 1999, Dutton $16.99 (0-525-65263-9). 42pp. This account concentrates on the behavior of dolphins and the research centers where these popular animals are studied. (Rev: BCCB 2/99; HBG 10/99; SLJ 3/99) [599.5]

19682 Dudzinski, Kathleen. *Meeting Dolphins: My Adventures in the Sea* (3–6). Illus. 2000, National Geographic $17.95 (0-7922-7129-7). 64pp. Using her own experiences and scientific research, the author introduces the reader to dolphins, their appearance, behavior, and life cycle. (Rev: BL 5/15/00; HBG 10/00; SLJ 7/00) [599.53]

19683 Fowler, Allan. *Friendly Dolphins* (1–2). Series: Rookie Readers. 1997, Children's LB $19.00 (0-516-20428-9). 32pp. Introduces dolphins, with striking photos and minimal text suitable for beginning readers. (Rev: BL 11/15/97; HBG 3/98; SLJ 10/97) [599.5]

19684 Grover, Wayne. *Dolphin Adventure: A True Story* (3–5). Illus. by Jim Fowler. 1990, Greenwillow $16.00 (0-688-09442-2). 48pp. An encounter with wild dolphins off the Florida coast. (Rev: BL 9/15/90; SLJ 12/90) [599.5]

19685 Hatherly, Janelle, and Delia Nicholls. *Dolphins and Porpoises* (5–8). Illus. 1990, Facts on File $17.95 (0-8160-2272-0). 68pp. The habitats, eating habits, and reproduction of these favorite animals are covered along with other topics. (Rev: BL 11/15/90; SLJ 5/91) [599.5]

19686 Horton, Casey. *Dolphins* (3–5). Illus. Series: Endangered! 1996, Benchmark LB $22.79 (0-7614-0216-0). 32pp. A basic introduction to dolphins, their characteristics, habitats, and structure is given through text and full-color photos. (Rev: SLJ 3/96) [599.5]

19687 Morris, Robert A. *Dolphin* (K–3). Illus. by Mamoru Funai. 1975, HarperCollins $6.93 (0-06-024337-6). 64pp. A simple account of the first five months of this lovable sea mammal.

19688 Read, Andrew. *Porpoises* (5–8). Illus. Series: WorldLife Library. 1999, Voyageur paper $16.95 (0-89658-420-8). 72pp. With many color illustrations and large print, this book introduces porpoises, their characteristics, behavior, habitats, and how humans study them. (Rev: BL 8/99) [599.53]

19689 Samuels, Amy. *Follow That Fin! Studying Dolphin Behavior* (4–6). Illus. Series: Turnstone Ocean Pilot. 1999, Raintree Steck-Vaughn LB $25.69 (0-7398-1230-0). 48pp. Using many photographs, the author, a biologist, describes the bottlenose dolphin, its behavior and characteristics, recent research, and how scientists collect this information. (Rev: BL 3/1/00; HBG 10/00) [559.53]

19690 Schomp, Virginia. *The Bottlenose Dolphin* (3–5). Illus. 1994, Silver Burdett LB $13.95 (0-87518-605-X). 60pp. Fact and mythology mingle in this account of the dolphin, its life cycle, and its habitats. (Rev: BL 3/1/95) [599.5]

19691 Stoops, Erik D., et al. *Dolphins* (3–5). Illus. 1997, Sterling $17.95 (0-8069-0568-9). 80pp. An attractive volume that introduces dolphins, their unique characteristics, eating habits, reproduction, and self-defense. (Rev: BL 5/1/97; SLJ 7/97) [599.5]

19692 Sweeney, Diane, and Michelle Reddy. *Dolphin Babies: Making a Splash* (4–6). Photos by Jeff Smith. Illus. by Jim Corey. 1998, Roberts Rinehart paper $14.95 (1-57098-194-9). 64pp. Using remarkable photos and a brief text, this book chronicles the pregnancy of four dolphins and the subsequent births at the Dolphin Learning Center in Hawaii. (Rev: SLJ 9/98) [599.5]

19693 Walker, Sally M. *Dolphins* (3–6). Illus. Series: Nature Watch. 1999, Carolrhoda LB $22.60 (1-57505-221-0). 48pp. This attractive introduction to dolphins includes material on their physical characteristics, communication, behavior, life cycle, and relations with people. (Rev: BL 9/1/99; HBG 10/99) [599.53]

FISH

19694 Arnold, Caroline. *Shockers of the Sea and Other Electrical Animals* (1–3). Illus. by Crista Forest. 1999, Charlesbridge $15.95 (0-88106-873-X); paper $6.95 (0-88106-874-8). 32pp. Covers electric fish and how they use this attribute for purposes such as getting food, defense, and communication. (Rev: BL 10/15/99; HBG 3/00; SLJ 1/00) [597]

19695 Arnosky, Jim. *Crinkleroot's 25 Fish Every Child Should Know* (PS–3). Illus. 1993, Bradbury LB $12.95 (0-02-705844-1). 32pp. A picture-book field guide that introduces with paintings and brief text 25 common species of fish. (Rev: BL 9/1/93; SLJ 9/93) [597]

19696 Bailey, Jill. *How Fish Swim* (3–5). Illus. by Colin Newman. Series: Nature's Mysteries. 1996, Benchmark LB $22.79 (0-7614-0451-1). 32pp. This work covers how fish and other aquatic animals move and the different anatomical specializations that make locomotion possible. (Rev: SLJ 2/97) [597]

19697 Berendes, Mary. *Piranhas* (PS–3). Series: Naturebooks. 1999, Child's World LB $15.95 (1-56766-493-8). 32pp. Amazing full-page photographs opposite one or two short paragraphs of text are used to introduce these savage marine creatures. (Rev: BL 6/1–15/99; HBG 10/99; SLJ 9/99) [597]

19698 Broekel, Ray. *Dangerous Fish* (1–4). Illus. 1982, Children's LB $21.00 (0-516-01635-0); paper $5.50 (0-516-41635-9). An introduction to some of the less friendly members of the fish family.

19699 Cole, Joanna. *A Fish Hatches* (3–5). Illus. 1978, Morrow $14.89 (0-688-32153-4). 40pp. The story of a trout, from egg to fully grown fish, in text and photographs.

19700 Crewe, Sabrina. *The Salmon* (K–2). Illus. by Colin Newman. Series: Life Cycle. 1996, Raintree Steck-Vaughn LB $24.26 (0-8172-4371-2). 32pp. The story of the salmon from the hatching of the egg to adulthood, with coverage on the migrations to and from the ocean. (Rev: SLJ 3/97) [597.55]

19701 Eastman, David. *What Is a Fish?* (K–3). Illus. by Lynn Sweat. 1982, Troll LB $17.25 (0-89375-660-1); paper $3.50 (0-89375-661-X). 32pp. A simple account that shows various kinds of fish.

19702 Gallimard Jeunesse. *Fish* (PS–2). Illus. Series: First Discovery. 1998, Scholastic $11.95 (0-590-38155-5). 24pp. Using overlays and colorful illustrations, this book introduces several types of fish and describes how fish breathe, reproduce, eat, and protect themselves. (Rev: BL 9/15/98; HBG 10/98) [579]

19703 Grossman, Susan. *Piranhas* (4–6). Illus. Series: Remarkable Animals. 1994, Dillon LB $13.95 (0-87518-593-2). 60pp. An introduction to piranhas that points out their value to fisherman and that the harm they do to humans is exaggerated. (Rev: SLJ 8/94) [597]

19704 Hirschi, Ron. *Salmon* (3–6). Series: Nature Watch. 2000, Carolrhoda LB $23.93 (1-57505-482-5). 48pp. Amazing photos and a clear text describe how salmon change from egg to fry to grown fish that then complete the cycle by making a journey upstream to reproduce. (Rev: BL 10/15/00) [597.55]

19705 Jango-Cohen, Judith. *Clinging Sea Horses* (PS–2). Series: Pull Ahead Books. 2000, Lerner LB $21.27 (0-8225-3764-8); paper $6.95 (0-8225-3767-2). 32pp. Stunning underwater photos bring to life this unique fish whose young grow in a pouch on the father's body. (Rev: BL 8/00; HBG 3/01; SLJ 1/01) [597]

19706 Landau, Elaine. *Angelfish* (3–5). Series: A True Book. 1999, Children's LB $21.00 (0-516-20660-5). 48pp. A brief introduction to angelfish and their appearance and life cycle, along with instructions for caring for them in an aquarium. (Rev: BL 8/99; HBG 10/99) [597]

19707 Landau, Elaine. *Electric Fish* (3–5). Series: A True Book. 1999, Children's LB $21.00 (0-513-20660-4). 48pp. With stunning photos and a simple text, this account introduces fish that produce electricity and explains the causes and effects of this phenomenon. (Rev: BL 8/99) [597]

19708 Landau, Elaine. *Piranhas* (3–5). Series: True Books. 1999, Children's LB $21.00 (0-516-20673-7). 48pp. Using a square format, large type, and plenty of captioned photographs, this account introduces the piranha, its physical characteristics, habits, and why it is dreaded. (Rev: BL 6/1–15/99; HBG 10/99; SLJ 8/99) [597]

19709 Landau, Elaine. *Sea Horses* (3–5). Series: True Books. 1999, Children's LB $21.00 (0-516-20675-3). 48pp. The fascinating sea horse and its habits, habitats, and life cycle are introduced in this square-shaped book that contains many excellent color illustrations. (Rev: BL 6/1–15/99; HBG 10/99; SLJ 8/99) [597]

19710 Landau, Elaine. *Siamese Fighting Fish* (3–5). Illus. Series: True Books. 1999, Children's LB $21.00 (0-516-20678-8). 48pp. Describes the varieties of Siamese fighting fish with a number of color photographs and a brief text. (Rev: BL 6/1–15/99; HBG 10/99; SLJ 8/99) [639.3]

19711 Perry, Phyllis J. *Sea Stars and Dragons* (3–5). Illus. Series: First Books. 1996, Watts LB $22.00 (0-531-20223-2). 63pp. A concise text introduces the life and habits of the sea star and sea horse. (Rev: SLJ 8/96) [591.92]

19712 Ricciuti, Edward R. *What on Earth Is a Pout?* (3–5). Illus. Series: What on Earth? 1996, Blackbirch LB $17.95 (1-56711-103-3). 32pp. An introduction to the pout, a bottom-dwelling fish of the Atlantic, covering its appearance, lifestyle, and habits. (Rev: SLJ 2/97) [597]

19713 Royston, Angela. *Life Cycle of a Salmon* (PS–3). Series: Life Cycle. 2000, Heinemann LB $19.92 (1-57572-212-7). 32pp. From egg to adult, this book explains the life cycle of a salmon, using a simple text and full-color photos on each page. (Rev: BL 5/15/00; HBG 3/01) [597.55]

19714 Savage, Stephen. *Fish* (2–4). Series: What's the Difference. 2000, Raintree Steck-Vaughn LB $25.69 (0-7398-1357-9). 32pp. Fish can be as different as a goldfish and a shark, but this book points out their common features (e.g., gills) as well as salient differences. (Rev: BL 10/15/00; HBG 3/01) [597]

19715 Stefoff, Rebecca. *Sea Horse* (2–4). Illus. Series: From the Living Things. 1996, Marshall Cavendish LB $22.79 (0-7614-0116-4). 32pp. Various kinds of sea horses are described, along with their habits and life cycles. (Rev: BL 2/1/97; SLJ 3/97) [597]

19716 Stewart, Melissa. *Fishes* (2–3). Series: True Books. 2001, Children's LB $22.00 (0-516-22038-1). 48pp. This book looks at a number of kinds of fish and points out similarities as well as differences. (Rev: BL 3/15/01) [597]

19717 Walker, Sally M. *Sea Horses* (3–6). Illus. Series: Nature Watch. 1999, Lerner $16.95 (1-57505-317-9). 48pp. The sea horse is introduced with many color photographs and material on its physical characteristics, bonding rituals, classification, and the mythology surrounding these small animals. (Rev: BL 5/1/99; HBG 10/99; SLJ 11/99) [597]

19718 Zim, Herbert S., and Hurst H. Shoemaker. *Fishes* (5–8). Illus. by James G. Irving. 1991, Western paper $21.27 (0-307-64059-0). 160pp. This is a basic guide to both fresh and saltwater species.

MOLLUSKS, SPONGES, AND STARFISH

19719 Esbensen, Barbara J. *Sponges Are Skeletons* (1–4). Illus. by Holly Keller. Series: Let's-Read-and-Find-Out. 1993, HarperCollins LB $15.89 (0-06-021037-0). 32pp. This account tells about the original bath sponges and how they originated on the ocean floor. (Rev: BL 12/1/93; HBG 10/98; SLJ 2/94) [593.4]

19720 Fowler, Allan. *Star of the Sea* (1–2). Series: Rookie Readers. 2000, Children's LB $19.00 (0-516-21214-1). 32pp. Using a full-page picture opposite six or seven lines of simple text, this beginning science book introduces starfish, explains their physical characteristics, and describes their food and habitats. (Rev: BL 4/15/00) [593.9]

19721 Hurd, Edith Thacher. *Starfish* (1–3). Illus. by Robin Brickman. Series: Let's-Read-and-Find-Out. 2000, HarperCollins LB $15.89 (0-06-028357-2). 40pp. Attractive new illustrations are included in this revision of the standard introduction to starfish and their characteristics and habitats. (Rev: BL 6/1–15/00; HBG 10/00; SLJ 6/00) [593.9]

OCTOPUS

19722 Cerullo, Mary. *The Octopus: Phantom of the Sea* (4–8). Illus. 1997, Dutton $16.99 (0-525-65199-3). 64pp. The life cycle of this mysterious sea creature is described, with illustrations of its anatomy and of its relatives, such as the squid. (Rev: BCCB 2/97; BL 2/1/97; SLJ 12/97*) [594]

19723 Hirschi, Ron. *Octopuses* (3–6). Series: Nature Watch. 2000, Carolrhoda $22.60 (1-57505-386-1). 48pp. An informative text about the octopus, its daily life, and how it uses its eight arms for swimming, eating, catching prey, and even tasting food. (Rev: BL 3/15/00; HBG 10/00; SLJ 7/00) [594]

19724 Kite, Patricia. *Down in the Sea: The Octopus* (1–3). Illus. Series: Down by the Sea. 1993, Whitman LB $14.95 (0-8075-1715-1). 32pp. Color photos highlight this introduction to the feared and fascinating octopus. (Rev: BL 3/15/93; SLJ 3/93) [594.56]

19725 Souza, D. M. *Sea Creatures with Many Arms* (2–3). Illus. Series: Creatures All Around Us. 1998, Carolrhoda LB $19.93 (1-57505-262-8). 40pp. The life cycle, habits, and reproduction of squid, octopuses, cuttlefish, and chambered nautiluses are introduced through color photos and clear captions. (Rev: BL 12/1/98; HBG 3/99; SLJ 3/99) [594]

19726 Stefoff, Rebecca. *Octopus* (K–3). Illus. Series: Living Things. 1996, Marshall Cavendish LB $22.79 (0-7614-0119-9). 32pp. This colorful introduction to the octopus uses short bits of information and many illustrations on double-page spreads. Also use in this series *Starfish, Giant Turtle,* and *Praying Mantis.* (Rev: BL 3/15/97; SLJ 3/97) [597.92]

19727 Wallace, Karen. *Gentle Giant Octopus* (K–2). Illus. by Mike Bostock. 1998, Candlewick $15.99 (0-7636-0318-X). 32pp. Watercolors enliven this introduction to the giant octopus and the care she takes with her eggs until they are hatched. (Rev: BL 11/15/98; HB 11–12/98; HBG 3/99; SLJ 12/98) [594]

19728 Zuchora-Walske, Christine. *Giant Octopuses* (PS–2). Series: Pull Ahead Books. 1999, Lerner $21.27 (0-8225-3633-1); paper $6.95 (0-8225-3637-4). 32pp. The physical characteristics and habits of the octopus are covered with a brief text and a color photo on each page plus a body diagram, map, glossary, and simple index. (Rev: BL 12/15/99; HBG 3/00) [594.56]

SEA MAMMALS

19729 Boyle, Doe. *Otter on His Own: The Story of a Sea Otter* (K–3). Illus. by Lisa Bonforte. Series: Smithsonian Oceanic Collection. 1995, Soundprints $15.95 (1-56899-129-0). 30pp. Describes the childhood of a sea otter and how, for several months, the mother shares her meals with him until he can dive for his own food. (Rev: SLJ 6/95) [599.74]

19730 Cossi, Olga. *Harp Seals* (3–6). Illus. 1991, Carolrhoda LB $23.93 (0-87614-437-7). 48pp. The life cycle, migratory patterns, and behavior of the Arctic harp seal are described. (Rev: BCCB 4/91; BL 5/5/91; SLJ 6/91) [599.74]

19731 Cousteau Society. *Seals* (PS–3). Illus. 1992, Simon & Schuster paper $4.95 (0-671-77061-6). 24pp. Introducing the harp seal to a young audience with minimal text and color photographs. (Rev: BL 5/1/92; SLJ 7/92) [599.74]

19732 Darling, Kathy. *Walrus: On Location* (1–4). Illus. by Tara Darling. Series: On Location. 1991, Lothrop $14.95 (0-688-09032-Y). 40pp. Watching the walrus who come to shore every year on Round Island off the coast of Alaska. (Rev: BL 8/91; SLJ 12/91) [599.74]

19733 Delano, Marfe Ferguson. *Sea Otters* (PS). Series: Animal Safari. 1999, National Geographic $5.95 (0-7922-7108-4). A sturdy board book that supplies minimal information but many color photos introducing sea otters. (Rev: SLJ 9/99) [599.74]

19734 Grace, Eric S. *Seals* (4–6). Illus. by Fred Bruemmer. Series: Sierra Club Wildlife Library. 1994, Little, Brown paper $7.95 (0-316-32291-1). 62pp. This slim, oversized volume supplies an attractive, well-organized introduction to seals and their cousins, sea lions and walruses. (Rev: BL 1/15/92; SLJ 2/92*) [599.74]

19735 Harman, Amanda. *Manatees and Dugongs* (3–5). Illus. Series: Endangered! 1996, Benchmark LB $22.79 (0-7614-0294-2). 32pp. These endangered sea creatures are described in text and pictures, with material on their habitats, lifestyles, and how they can be helped. (Rev: SLJ 2/97) [599.5]

19736 Hurd, Edith Thacher. *The Song of the Sea Otter* (4–6). Illus. by Jennifer Dewey. 1989, Sierra Club paper $5.95 (0-316-38323-6). 40pp. In a harbor on the Pacific coast, a baby sea otter explores his world. A reissue.

19737 Jenkins, Priscilla B. *A Safe Home for Manatees* (PS–3). Illus. by Martin Classen. Series: Let's-Read-and-Find-Out. 1997, HarperCollins LB $14.89 (0-06-027150-7); paper $4.95 (0-06-445164-X). 32pp. An introduction to Florida's sea cows, or manatees, their habits, why they are facing extinction, and the efforts being made to save them. (Rev: BL 12/1/97; HBG 3/98; SLJ 10/97) [599.5]

19738 Johnson, Sylvia A. *Elephant Seals* (3–6). Illus. 1989, Lerner LB $22.60 (0-8225-1487-7). 48pp. The story of these animals, hunted almost to extinction, along the California and Mexico coasts. (Rev: BL 3/1/89)

19739 Lepthien, Emilie U. *Manatees* (1–3). Illus. Series: New True Books. 1991, Children's LB $21.00 (0-516-01114-6). 48pp. This elusive, now endangered aquatic mammal is introduced in simple text and many color photographs. (Rev: BL 8/91) [599.52]

19740 Lepthien, Emilie U. *Walruses* (3–4). Illus. Series: True Books. 1996, Children's LB $22.00 (0-516-20162-X). 48pp. Introduces the walrus and its life at sea, anatomy, food, child rearing, and habits. (Rev: SLJ 6/97) [599.7]

19741 Matthews, Downs. *Harp Seal Pups* (3–5). Illus. by Dan Guravich. 1997, Simon & Schuster paper $17.00 (0-689-80014-2). 32pp. The life of a harp seal pup and her fight for survival against her enemies are covered in text and appealing photos. (Rev: BL 1/1–15/97; SLJ 2/97) [599.74]

19742 Meeker, Clare Hodgson. *Lootas, Little Wave Eater: An Orphaned Sea Otter's Story* (3–5). Photos by C. J. Casson. 1999, Sasquatch paper $12.95 (1-57061-164-5). 43pp. Describes the early life of a young sea otter and how she was rescued after a boating accident and raised in the Seattle Aquarium. (Rev: SLJ 1/00) [599.74]

19743 Rinard, Judith E. *Amazing Animals of the Sea* (5–8). Illus. 1981, National Geographic LB $12.50 (0-87044-387-9). 104pp. Whales, dolphins, sea otters, sea lions, seals, manatees, and other marine mammals are described.

19744 Sibbald, Jean H. *The Manatee* (4–7). Illus. 1990, Macmillan LB $13.95 (0-87518-429-4). 60pp. The life of this gentle sea mammal is examined, along with material on how its survival is threatened by humans. (Rev: BL 6/15/90; SLJ 8/90) [599.5]

19745 Silverstein, Alvin, et al. *The Manatee* (4–7). Illus. Series: Endangered in America. 1995, Millbrook LB $23.90 (1-56294-551-3). 64pp. A profile of this sea creature, its lifestyle and habits, and how it became an endangered species. (Rev: BL 10/15/95; SLJ 1/96) [599.5]

19746 Silverstein, Alvin, et al. *The Sea Otter* (4–7). Illus. Series: Endangered in America. 1995, Millbrook LB $22.40 (1-56294-418-5). 64pp. The sea otter's habits and life cycle are covered, with details on how the fur trade, oil spills, and other environmental disasters have made it an endangered species. (Rev: BL 6/1–15/95; SLJ 7/95) [599.74]

19747 Staub, Frank. *Manatees* (2–3). Series: Early Bird Nature Books. 1998, Lerner $22.60 (0-8225-3023-6). 48pp. Good illustrations and simple text are used to introduce this endangered sea mammal. (Rev: BL 10/15/98; HBG 3/99; SLJ 1/99) [599.5]

19748 Staub, Frank. *Sea Lions* (2–3). Series: Early Bird Nature Books. 2000, Lerner LB $22.60 (0-8225-3018-X). 48pp. This simple introduction to the California sea lion covers its habitat, appearance, behavior, and the dangers it faces. (Rev: BL 5/15/00; HBG 10/00) [599]

19749 Swanson, Diane. *Otters* (2–4). Series: Welcome to the World of Animals. 1998, Gareth Stevens LB $14.95 (0-8368-2214-5). 32pp. A slim volume that offers information on the homes, diet, communication, and lifestyles of both sea and river otters. (Rev: HBG 10/99; SLJ 5/99) [599.74]

19750 Walker, Sally M. *Manatees* (3–6). Illus. Series: Nature Watch. 1999, Carolrhoda $22.60 (1-57505-299-7). 48pp. Amazing photographs are used to illustrate this introduction to the manatee, its physical characteristics, lifestyle, habits, and habitats. (Rev: BL 12/15/99; HBG 3/00) [599.55]

SHARKS

19751 Berger, Melvin. *Chomp! A Book About Sharks* (1–3). Series: Hello Reader! 1999, Scholastic paper $3.99 (0-590-52298-1). Lots of introductory information about sharks is given in this book for beginning readers. (Rev: SLJ 7/99) [597.31]

19752 Cerullo, Mary. *The Truth About Great White Sharks* (4–7). Illus. 2000, Chronicle $14.95 (0-8118-2467-5). 48pp. A fascinating account with excellent underwater photos that explores such topics about sharks as physical characteristics, behavior, feeding habits, and the difficulty of studying them. (Rev: BL 4/1/00; SLJ 7/00) [597.3]

19753 Cole, Joanna. *Hungry, Hungry Sharks* (1–3). Illus. by Patricia J. Wynne. 1986, Random paper $3.99 (0-394-87471-4). 48pp. Different kinds of sharks are explained in simple terms. (Rev: BL 8/86)

19754 Coupe, Sheena. *Sharks* (5–7). Illus. Series: Great Creatures of the World. 1990, Facts on File $17.95 (0-8160-2270-4). 72pp. Many kinds of sharks are identified and pictured with information on their structures, habits, and methods of attack. (Rev: BL 4/1/90; SLJ 7/90) [597]

19755 Del Prado, Dana. *Terror Below! True Shark Stories* (2–3). Illus. by Stephen Marchesi. Series: All Aboard Reading. 1997, Grosset paper $3.99 (0-448-41124-5). 47pp. Three true stories about encounters with sharks in which the victims lived to tell their stories. (Rev: SLJ 10/97) [597.31]

19756 Dubowski, Cathy E. *Shark Attack!* (2–4). Series: Eyewitness Reader. 1998, DK $12.95 (0-7894-3763-5); paper $3.95 (0-7894-3440-7). 48pp. As well as a description of several shark attacks, this book covers scientific research on these attacks, introduces several shark species, and talks about overfishing and indiscriminate hunting. (Rev: HBG 3/99; SLJ 1/99) [597.31]

19757 Fowler, Allan. *The Best Way to See a Shark* (1–2). Illus. Series: Rookie Readers. 1995, Children's LB $19.00 (0-516-06032-5). 32pp. In a small format, this colorful book introduces sharks and their bodies, types, and habits. (Rev: BL 7/95) [596.31]

19758 Gibbons, Gail. *Sharks* (2–4). Illus. 1992, Holiday LB $16.95 (0-8234-0960-0). For the primary level, this account presents basic general facts as well as specific data on 12 common sharks. (Rev: BL 5/1/92; SLJ 7/92) [597.31]

19759 Gourley, Catherine. *Sharks! True Stories and Legends* (4–7). Illus. 1996, Millbrook LB $27.40 (0-7613-0001-5). 96pp. Both fact and fiction involving sharks are presented in this informal, readable account. (Rev: BCCB 1/97; BL 10/15/96; SLJ 12/96) [597]

19760 Grace, Eric S. *Sharks* (5–8). Series: Wildlife Library. 2000, Sierra Club $14.95 (0-87156-926-4). 48pp. This book explains sharks' evolution, physiology, behavior, and reproduction. (Rev: SLJ 1/01) [597.31]

19761 Harman, Amanda. *Sharks* (4–6). Illus. Series: Endangered! 1996, Benchmark LB $15.95 (0-7614-0220-9). 32pp. This account concentrates on three kinds of sharks — the great white, the whale, and the basking — and tells about the differences in their anatomies and why they are endangered. (Rev: SLJ 8/96) [597]

19762 Johnston, Marianne. *Sharks Past and Present* (3–5). Illus. 2000, Rosen LB $18.60 (0-8239-5206-1). 24pp. The shark's anatomy is discussed, as well as its 400-million-year history and why it has changed so little during that time. (Rev: BL 12/1/00) [567.3]

19763 Llewellyn, Claire. *The Best Book of Sharks* (3–5). Illus. by Ray Grinaway and Roger Stewart. Series: The Best Book Of. 1999, Kingfisher $12.95 (0-7534-5173-5). 31pp. A book about sharks that contains information on body structure, teeth, species, life cycle, and shark attacks. (Rev: HBG 3/00; SLJ 2/00) [597]

19764 Maestro, Betsy. *A Sea Full of Sharks* (3–6). Illus. by Giulio Maestro. 1997, Scholastic paper $5.99 (0-590-43101-3). 32pp. An informative look at this feared but fascinating creature. (Rev: BL 1/1/91; SLJ 10/90) [597.31]

19765 Markle, Sandra. *Outside and Inside Sharks* (3–5). Illus. Series: Outside and Inside. 1996, Simon & Schuster $16.00 (0-689-80348-6). 40pp. The exterior structure and inside anatomy of sharks are described. (Rev: BCCB 7–8/96; BL 6/1–15/96; HB 5–6/96; SLJ 3/96) [597]

19766 Maynard, Christopher. *Informania: Sharks* (4–7). Illus. 1997, Candlewick $14.99 (0-7636-0328-7). 92pp. A spiral-bound book that attractively presents basic material about sharks in a series of different formats, including a foldout model. (Rev: HBG 3/98; SLJ 1/98) [597.31]

19767 Parker, Steve. *Sharks* (3–5). Illus. Series: What If. 1996, Millbrook LB $19.90 (0-7613-0456-8); paper $6.95 (0-7613-0471-1). 32pp. Using questions and answers, various characteristics of sharks are highlighted. (Rev: SLJ 6/96) [597.13]

19768 Simon, Seymour. *Sharks* (2–4). Illus. 1995, HarperCollins LB $15.89 (0-06-023032-0). 32pp. Basic information about sharks, including life cycles, anatomy, and habits, is given with full-color illustrations. (Rev: BL 10/15/95; HB 11–12/95; SLJ 9/95) [597]

19769 Ward, Nathalie. *Do Sharks Ever . . .?* (3–4). Illus. by Tessa Morgan. 1999, Down East paper $9.95 (0-89272-438-2). Using a question-and-answer format, this book covers topics related to sharks including physical characteristics, species, life cycle, food, and mating. (Rev: SLJ 2/00) [597.31]

19770 Zoehfeld, Kathleen W. *Great White Shark: Ruler of the Sea* (PS–3). Illus. by Steven J. Petruccio. Series: Smithsonian Oceanic Collection. 1995, Soundprints $15.95 (1-56899-122-3). 31pp. The life cycle of a great white shark, the Ruler of the Sea, which grows to 20 feet in length in adulthood. (Rev: SLJ 6/95) [597]

SHELLS

19771 Burton, Jane, and Kim Taylor. *The Nature and Science of Shells* (3–6). Series: Exploring the Science of Nature. 1999, Gareth Stevens LB $14.95 (0-8368-2185-8). 32pp. The composition of shells, different varieties, their uses, and location are some of the topics discussed in this volume that contains a special activity and project section. (Rev: BL 7/99; SLJ 1/00) [594]

19772 Cassie, Brian. *Shells* (4–6). Series: National Audubon Society First Field Guides. 2000, Scholastic $17.95 (0-590-64233-2); paper $8.95 (0-590-64258-8). 160pp. With more than 450 color photographs, this attractive volume focuses on about 50 of the most easily found shells and their characteristics. (Rev: BL 8/00; SLJ 1/01) [591]

19773 Lember, Barbara Hirsch. *The Shell Book* (K–3). Photos by author. 1997, Houghton $17.00 (0-395-72030-3). 32pp. Two-page layouts are used to introduce and describe several seashells that are found along the North American coastline. (Rev: SLJ 4/97) [594]

WHALES

19774 Arnold, Caroline. *Killer Whale* (3–5). Illus. by Richard Hewett. 1994, Morrow $14.93 (0-688-12030-X). 48pp. Using the facilities of Sea World in California, the anatomy and behavior of killer whales are examined in the wild and in captivity. (Rev: BL 9/15/94; HB 11–12/94; SLJ 10/94) [599.5]

19775 Arnold, Caroline, and Richard Hewett. *Baby Whale Rescue: The True Story of J. J.* (2–4). Illus. 1999, Troll $15.95 (0-8167-4961-2). 32pp. This real-life adventure tells how J. J., a baby gray whale, was rescued and brought back to health at Sea World in California. (Rev: BL 3/1/99; SLJ 3/99) [599.5]

19776 Bair, Diane, and Pamela Wright. *Whale Watching* (2–5). Series: Wildlife Watching. 1999, Capstone $19.93 (0-7368-0325-4). 48pp. After a general introduction to whales, the different types, and their habits, this book explains how and where whales can be seen in their natural habitats. (Rev: BL 2/15/00) [599.5]

19777 Berendes, Mary. *Beluga Whales* (PS–3). Series: Naturebooks. 1999, Child's World LB $15.95 (1-56766-489-X). 32pp. An oversize book that uses a question-and-answer approach to give basic information about beluga whales through a simple text and stunning, full-page photographs. (Rev: BL 6/1–15/99; HBG 10/99; SLJ 9/99) [599.5]

19778 Carrick, Carol. *Whaling Days* (3–6). Illus. by David Frampton. 1993, Houghton $15.95 (0-395-50948-3). 40pp. With an emphasis on conservation, this is a history of whaling, from ancient times to the present. (Rev: BCCB 7–8/93; BL 5/1/93*; HB 5–6/93; SLJ 5/93*) [639.2]

19779 Carwardine, Mark. *Killer Whale* (3–5). Series: Natural World. 1999, Raintree Steck-Vaughn $25.69 (0-7398-1058-8). 48pp. Illustrated with brilliant color photos, this book describes the life cycle of the killer whale from being a 400-pound baby, to learning to hunt with other members of the pod, and finally reaching maturity. (Rev: BL 10/15/99; HBG 3/00) [599.5]

19780 Chrisp, Peter. *The Whalers* (4–6). Illus. 1995, Thomson Learning LB $24.26 (1-56847-421-0). 48pp. A history of whaling from ancient to modern times, with information on present-day efforts to protect whales. (Rev: BL 2/15/96; SLJ 3/96) [639.2]

19781 Collard, Sneed B. *A Whale Biologist at Work* (3–5). Illus. Series: Wildlife Conservation Society Books. 2000, Watts LB $22.50 (0-531-11786-3). 48pp. This book focuses on a marine biologist's observations of humpback and blue whales off the Pacific coast of North America. (Rev: BL 2/15/01; SLJ 3/01) [578.77]

19782 Davies, Nicola. *Big Blue Whale* (PS–1). Illus. by Nick Maland. 1997, Candlewick $15.99 (1-56402-895-X). 28pp. Using a picture-book format, the characteristics, habits, and behavior of the blue whale are explored. (Rev: BL 9/1/97; HB 5–6/97; SLJ 7/97) [599.5]

19783 Delafosse, Claude, and Ute Fuhr. *Whales* (PS–3). Illus. Series: First Discovery. 1993, Scholastic $12.95 (0-590-47130-9). 24pp. This interactive, highly visual beginner's book introduces whales, how and where they live, and what they eat. (Rev: BL 11/15/93; HB 3–4/93; SLJ 4/94) [599.5]

19784 Dow, Lesley. *Whales* (5–7). Illus. Series: Great Creatures of the World. 1990, Facts on File $17.95 (0-8160-2271-2). 68pp. Different types of

whales are identified and material is given on habits and structure. (Rev: BL 4/1/90; SLJ 7/90) [599.5]

19785 DuTemple, Lesley A. *Whales* (2–3). Illus. Series: Early Bird Nature Books. 1996, Lerner LB $22.60 (0-8225-3008-2). 48pp. Several kinds of whales are introduced, with descriptions of their appearance and behavior. (Rev: BL 8/96; SLJ 7/96) [599.5]

19786 Esbensen, Barbara J. *Baby Whales Drink Milk* (PS–1). Illus. by Lambert Davis. Series: Let's-Read-and-Find-Out. 1994, HarperCollins paper $4.95 (0-06-445119-4). 32pp. This book explains why whales are not fish and in so doing covers the characteristics of mammals. (Rev: BL 2/15/94; SLJ 3/94) [599.5]

19787 Fowler, Allan. *The Biggest Animal Ever* (1–2). Illus. Series: Rookie Readers. 1992, Children's paper $4.95 (0-516-46001-3). 32pp. With many color photos and sparse text, whales are introduced to very young readers. (Rev: BL 12/15/92; SLJ 2/93) [599.5]

19788 Gibbons, Gail. *Whales* (PS–1). Illus. 1991, Holiday LB $16.95 (0-8234-0900-7). 32pp. The world of the fascinating whale, with good photos. (Rev: BL 10/15/91; HB 11–12/91; SLJ 12/91) [599.5]

19789 Greenberg, Dan. *Whales* (4–6). Illus. Series: Animals Animals. 2000, Marshall Cavendish LB $15.95 (0-7614-1167-4). 32pp. A useful book that introduces several types of whales and supplies information on their habitats, mating habits, structure, and behavior. (Rev: BL 3/15/01; HBG 3/01) [599.5]

19790 Harman, Amanda. *Whales* (4–6). Illus. Series: Endangered! 1996, Benchmark LB $22.79 (0-7614-0219-5). 32pp. Different species of whales are introduced, with coverage on why they have been hunted to near extinction and the efforts being made to save them. (Rev: SLJ 8/96) [599.5]

19791 Hodge, Deborah. *Whales: Killer Whales, Blue Whales and More* (K–3). Series: Wildlife. 1997, Kids Can $14.95 (1-55074-356-2). 32pp. In a series of double-page spreads, various whales are introduced, with material on food, habitats, and mobility. (Rev: BL 9/15/97; SLJ 11/97) [599.5]

19792 Hopkins, Ellen. *Orcas: High Seas Supermen* (3–7). Illus. 2000, Perfection Learning $13.95 (0-7807-9670-5); paper $8.95 (0-7891-5258-4). 56pp. For reluctant readers, this attractive book introduces different species of whales, their habitats, food, and methods of communication. (Rev: BL 11/1/00) [599.5]

19793 Kelsey, Elin. *Finding Out About Whales* (3–8). Illus. Series: Science Explorers. 1998, Owl $19.95 (1-895688-79-5); paper $9.95 (1-895688-80-9). 40pp. This account focuses on what we know and how we found out about five different species of whales: blue, humpback, gray, beluga, and killer. (Rev: BL 3/1/99; SLJ 3/99) [595.5]

19794 Kurth, Linda Moore. *Keiko's Story: A Killer Whale Goes Home* (4–6). 2000, Millbrook $23.90 (0-7613-1500-4). 72pp. An informative, enjoyable read about Keiko, the killer whale who played in the movie *Free Willy* and the efforts to return him to the wild. (Rev: HBG 10/00; SLJ 9/00) [595.5]

19795 McMillan, Bruce. *Going on a Whale Watch* (PS–3). Illus. 1993, Scholastic $19.95 (0-590-72826-1). 40pp. Readers go on a whale watch and watch two children watching the whales. (Rev: BL 10/15/92; SLJ 4/93) [599.5]

19796 McNulty, Faith. *How Whales Walked into the Sea* (2–4). Illus. by Ted Rand. 1999, Scholastic $16.95 (0-590-89830-2). 32pp. The evolution of whales from land to sea mammals is traced, with a survey of several kinds of modern whales. (Rev: BL 1/1–15/99; HB 3–4/99; HBG 10/99; SLJ 2/99) [599.5]

19797 Matero, Robert. *The Birth of a Humpback Whale* (5–8). Illus. 1996, Simon & Schuster $16.00 (0-689-31931-2). 53pp. A narrative with pencil drawings that covers the birth of a humpbacked whale and its journey from Hawaii to Alaska. (Rev: BL 4/1/96; SLJ 6/96) [599.5]

19798 Posell, Elsa. *Whales and Other Sea Mammals* (1–4). Illus. 1982, Children's paper $5.50 (0-516-41663-4). A description of these sea animals in large type and many color illustrations.

19799 Short, Joan, and Bettina Bird. *Whales* (3–5). Illus. by Deborah Savin. 1997, Mondo paper $4.95 (1-57255-190-9). 31pp. Colorful illustrations are used to cover such particulars about whales as anatomy, swimming, breathing, feeding, and communication. (Rev: SLJ 9/97) [599.5]

19800 Skerry, Brian. *A Whale on Her Own: The True Story of Wilma the Beluga Whale* (3–4). Photos by author. 2000, Blackbirch LB $18.95 (1-56711-431-8). 32pp. This true story tells of the friendly relationship that developed between a diver and a beluga whale in Chedabucto Bay, Nova Scotia. (Rev: HBG 10/00; SLJ 10/00) [595.5]

19801 Smyth, Karen C. *Crystal: The Story of a Real Baby Whale* (3–6). Illus. 1986, Down East paper $10.95 (0-89272-327-0). 96pp. The first year in the life of a humpback whale. (Rev: BL 8/86; SLJ 4/87)

19802 Stonehouse, Bernard. *Whales: A Visual Introduction to Whales, Dolphins, and Porpoises* (4–6). Illus. Series: Animal Watch. 1998, Facts on File LB $16.95 (0-8160-3922-4). 48pp. Maps, photos, paintings, and double-page spreads are used to introduce readers to the world of cetaceans. (Rev: BL 12/1/98) [599.5]

19803 Stoops, Erik D., et al. *Whales* (3–6). Illus. 1995, Sterling $17.95 (0-8069-0566-2). 80pp. Using a question-and-answer format, this book provides basic facts about whales, including why they don't drown. (Rev: BL 12/1/95; SLJ 1/96) [599.5]

19804 Wolpert, Tom. *Whale Magic for Kids* (2–4). Illus. Series: Animal Magic for Kids. 1991, Stevens LB $22.60 (0-8368-0660-3). 48pp. Through text and full-color photographs, whales, with their varieties and habits, are introduced. (Rev: BL 4/15/91) [599.5]

Microscopes and Microbiology

19805 Facklam, Howard, and Margery Facklam. *Bacteria* (4–7). Illus. Series: Invaders. 1994, Twenty-First Century LB $18.90 (0-8050-2857-9). 64pp. A concise explanation of bacteria and their composition and functions. (Rev: BL 1/1/95; SLJ 3/95) [589.9]

19806 Levine, Shar, and Leslie Johnstone. *Fun with Your Microscope* (4–6). Illus. 1998, Sterling $19.95 (0-8069-9945-4). 80pp. Introduces readers to microscopes and slide making and presents 36 different experiments that explore animal life, plants, food, bacteria, and common household items. (Rev: BL 11/15/98; SLJ 12/98) [502]

19807 Levine, Shar, and Leslie Johnstone. *The Microscope Book* (5–8). Illus. by David Sovka. 1997, Sterling $19.95 (0-8069-4898-1); paper $10.95 (0-8069-4899-X). 80pp. An excellent introduction to microscopes, with material on parts of the microscope, lenses, how to focus and produce slides, and tips on keeping a journal. (Rev: SLJ 7/97) [502]

19808 Loewer, Peter. *Pond Water Zoo: An Introduction to Microscopic Life* (5–8). Illus. 1996, Simon & Schuster $16.00 (0-689-31736-0). 86pp. Various life forms found in a drop of pond water are revealed by the microscope. (Rev: BCCB 12/96; BL 9/15/96; SLJ 2/97) [576]

19809 Rogers, Kirsteen. *The Usborne Complete Book of the Microscope* (4–8). Illus. by Kim Lane and Gary Bines. 1999, EDC paper $14.95 (0-7460-3106-8). 96pp. Various kinds of microscopes and microscopy techniques are presented in double-page spreads that explore objects and organisms that can't be seen without a microscope. (Rev: SLJ 7/99) [502]

19810 Selsam, Millicent E. *Greg's Microscope* (K–3). Illus. by Arnold Lobel. 1963, HarperCollins paper $3.95 (0-06-444144-X). 64pp. Greg and his parents observe small household items through a microscope.

19811 Silverstein, Alvin, et al. *Monerans and Protists* (3–6). Illus. Series: Kingdoms of Life. 1996, Twenty-First Century LB $21.40 (0-8050-3521-4). 64pp. The authors explain scientific classification and include information on viruses, bacteria, protozoa, and algae. (Rev: BL 6/1–15/96; SLJ 7/96) [576]

19812 Snedden, Robert. *Yuck! A Big Book of Little Horrors* (2–5). Illus. 1996, Simon & Schuster $15.00 (0-689-80676-0). 32pp. Everyday materials like hair and food particles are magnified to look like horrifying objects. (Rev: BCCB 6/96; BL 6/1–15/96; SLJ 5/96) [778.31]

19813 Stwertka, Eve, and Albert Stwertka. *Microscope: How to Use It and Enjoy It* (5–7). Illus. 1989, Simon & Schuster LB $11.95 (0-671-63705-3); paper $4.95 (0-671-67060-3). An instructive introduction to the use of the microscope. (Rev: BL 3/1/89; SLJ 4/89)

Oceanography

GENERAL

19814 Chambers, Catherine. *Oceans and Seas* (3–5). Series: Mapping Earthforms. 2000, Heinemann LB $14.95 (1-57572-526-6). 32pp. A basic overview that describes the characteristics of oceans and seas, life within them, and how environmental factors like global warming affect them. (Rev: HBG 3/01; SLJ 8/00) [551.46]

19815 Cobb, Allan B. *Super Science Projects About Oceans* (4–7). Series: Psyched for Science. 2000, Rosen Central LB $17.95 (0-8239-3174-9). 48pp. Although the format is unattractive, this book contains six fine experiments that explore concepts involving the ocean. (Rev: SLJ 7/00) [551.46]

19816 Cole, Joanna. *The Magic School Bus on the Ocean Floor* (3–5). Illus. by Bruce Degen. 1992, Scholastic $15.95 (0-590-41430-5). 48pp. Miss Frizzle's class takes a class trip down to the ocean floor to study the animals and plants that live there. (Rev: BCCB 12/92; BL 6/15/92; SLJ 8/92*) [591.92]

19817 Ganeri, Anita. *I Wonder Why the Sea Is Salty: And Other Questions About the Oceans* (PS–2). Illus. by Tony Kenyon, et al. Series: I Wonder Why. 1995, Kingfisher $11.95 (1-85697-549-5); paper $6.95 (0-85697-664-5). 32pp. Amazing and commonplace facts about marine life are presented in a question-and-answer format with entertaining drawings. (Rev: SLJ 7/95) [551.46]

19818 Gibbons, Gail. *Exploring the Deep, Dark Sea* (3–5). Illus. 1999, Little, Brown $14.95 (0-316-30945-1). 32pp. This book describes in pictures and text each level or zone on the way to the ocean's bottom, with additional material on the history of deep sea diving. (Rev: BCCB 4/99; BL 4/1/99; HB 3–4/99; HBG 10/99; SLJ 6/99) [551.46]

19819 Gowell, Elizabeth T. *Fountains of Life: The Story of Deep-Sea Vents* (4–6). Illus. Series: First Books. 1998, Watts LB $22.00 (0-531-20369-7). 64pp. This book explores the undersea phenomenon of hydrothermal vents, how they are created, their discovery and exploration, and the ecosystems they support. (Rev: BL 8/98; HBG 10/98; SLJ 1/99) [577.7]

19820 Gowell, Elizabeth T. *Life in the Deep Sea* (4–6). Series: First Books. 1999, Watts LB $22.00 (0-531-20391-3). 63pp. A well-organized book that described the habitats and life forms at three ocean levels: photic, twilight, and deep. (Rev: HBG 10/99; SLJ 9/99) [551.46]

19821 Heinrichs, Susan. *The Atlantic Ocean* (2–4). Illus. 1986, Children's LB $21.00 (0-516-01289-4). 48pp. An introduction to the Atlantic — shorelines, currents, flora and fauna. (Rev: BL 5/1/87)

19822 Hoff, Mary, and Mary M. Rodgers. *Our Endangered Planet: Oceans* (4–6). Illus. Series: Our Endangered Planet. 1992, Lerner LB $22.60 (0-8225-2505-4); paper $8.95 (0-8225-9628-8). 72pp. This volume gives a good overview of oceans and the major environmental concerns they present. (Rev: BL 5/15/92; SLJ 7/92) [551.46]

19823 Kraske, Robert. *The Voyager's Stone* (4–6). Illus. 1995, Orchard LB $16.99 (0-531-08740-9). 96pp. The framework of a message in a bottle cast into the sea is used to introduce oceanography, currents, and sea life. (Rev: BCCB 3/95; BL 3/1/95; SLJ 3/95) [551.46]

19824 Lambert, David. *The Kingfisher Young People's Book of Oceans* (4–6). Illus. 1997, Kingfisher $21.95 (0-7534-5098-4). 95pp. A colorful look at oceans and marine biology is given in a series of double-page spreads. (Rev: HBG 3/98; SLJ 3/98) [551.46]

19825 Lambert, David. *The Mediterranean Sea* (4–6). Illus. Series: Seas and Oceans. 1997, Raintree Steck-Vaughn LB $24.26 (0-8172-4512-X). 48pp. Describes the role of the Mediterranean throughout history, its features and formations, and the plant and animal life it supports. (Rev: BL 7/97) [551.46]

19826 Lambert, David. *The Pacific Ocean* (4–6). Illus. Series: Seas and Oceans. 1996, Raintree Steck-Vaughn LB $27.12 (0-8172-4507-3). 48pp. Ocean life, currents, the formation of islands, and pollution are a few of the topics discussed in this introduction to the Pacific Ocean. (Rev: BL 1/1–15/97) [551.46]

19827 Lambert, David. *Seas and Oceans* (5–8). Illus. 1988, Silver Burdett LB $16.95 (0-382-09503-0). 48pp. Covers waves, tides, currents, underwater exploration, and ocean life. (Rev: BL 4/1/88)

19828 MacQuitty, Miranda. *Ocean* (4–8). Illus. Series: Eyewitness Books. 1995, Knopf LB $20.99 (0-679-97331-1). 64pp. Illustrations highlight the world's oceans. (Rev: BL 12/15/95) [551.46]

19829 Markle, Sandra. *Down, Down, Down in the Ocean* (3–5). Illus. by Bob Marstall. 1999, Walker LB $17.85 (0-8027-8655-3). 32pp. This is a dramatic journey through the different levels of life in the ocean told in double-page spreads. (Rev: HBG 3/00; SLJ 11/99) [551.46]

19830 Morgan, Nina. *The Caribbean and the Gulf of Mexico* (4–6). Illus. Series: Seas and Oceans. 1996, Raintree Steck-Vaughn LB $27.12 (0-8172-4508-1). 48pp. For these two bodies of water, material is presented on such topics as ocean life, shipping, tourism, currents, and people. (Rev: BL 1/1–15/97) [917.29]

19831 Morgan, Nina. *The North Sea and the Baltic Sea* (4–6). Illus. Series: Seas and Oceans. 1996, Raintree Steck-Vaughn LB $27.12 (0-8172-4510-3). 48pp. These two European bodies of water are introduced, with coverage on their importance, history, shipping routes, and plant and animal life. (Rev: BL 1/1–15/97) [551.46]

19832 Nye, Bill. *Bill Nye the Science Guy's Big Blue Ocean* (3–6). Illus. 1999, Hyperion LB $16.49 (0-7868-5063-9). 48pp. Oceans and the science of oceanography are introduced with material on marine animals and plants, currents, tides, and present-day methods of exploration. (Rev: BL 9/15/99; HBG 3/00; SLJ 10/99) [551.46]

19833 Penny, Malcolm. *The Indian Ocean* (4–6). Illus. Series: Seas and Oceans. 1997, Raintree Steck-Vaughn LB $24.26 (0-8172-4514-6). 48pp. The history of the world's third-largest ocean, the migration and exploration paths that people took from Europe to Asia, and the marine life it supports. (Rev: BL 7/97) [551.46]

19834 Ricciuti, Edward R. *Ocean* (4–6). Illus. Series: Biomes of the World. 1995, Marshall Cavendish LB $25.64 (0-7614-0079-6). 64pp. With clear explanations and full-color photos, the world's ocean environment and its animal and plant life are introduced. (Rev: BL 12/15/95) [551.46]

19835 Robinson, W. Wright. *Incredible Facts About the Ocean: The Land Below, the Life Within, vol. 2* (4–8). Illus. 1987, Macmillan LB $13.95 (0-87518-358-1). 120pp. Maps, diagrams, color photos, and glossary add to this detailed explanation. (Rev: BL 11/1/87; SLJ 10/87)

19836 Sabin, Louis. *Wonders of the Sea* (1–3). Illus. by Bert Dodson. 1982, Troll paper $3.50 (0-89375-579-6). 32pp. An easy-to-read account for primary grades that covers basic topics.

19837 Sauvain, Philip. *Oceans* (3–5). Illus. Series: Geography Detectives. 1997, Carolrhoda LB $19.93 (1-57505-043-9). 32pp. This account identifies and describes the world's oceans, explains the saltwater ecosystem, and explores coastlines, the ocean floor, tides, and marine plant and animal life. (Rev: BL 8/97; SLJ 1/98) [551.46]

19838 Sayre, April Pulley. *Ocean* (4–7). Illus. Series: Exploring Earth's Biomes. 1996, Twenty-First Century LB $20.40 (0-8050-4084-6). 80pp. An introduction to the nature and composition of oceans and the animal and plant life that they support. (Rev: BL 10/15/96; SLJ 1/97) [551.46]

19839 Stille, Darlene R. *Oceans* (2–4). Series: True Books. 1999, Children's LB $21.50 (0-516-21510-8). 48pp. Oceans and the life found in them are introduced briefly in this book that is heavily illustrated with color photos. (Rev: BL 10/15/99) [591.92]

19840 Talbot, Frank H., ed. *Under the Sea* (4–6). Illus. Series: Nature Company Discoveries. 1995, Time Life $16.00 (0-7835-4760-9). 64pp. Marine life, both plant and animal, is introduced in this handsome book with lavish illustrations and an eight-page foldout section. (Rev: BL 1/1–15/96; SLJ 1/96) [551.46]

19841 Taylor, Leighton. *The Atlantic Ocean* (4–7). Series: Life in the Sea. 1999, Blackbirch LB $17.95 (1-56711-246-3). 48pp. In 20 short chapters, this book introduces the Atlantic Ocean and life forms found in it at various levels. (Rev: HBG 3/00; SLJ 2/00) [551.46]

19842 Taylor, Leighton. *The Mediterranean Sea* (4–7). Series: Life in the Sea. 1999, Blackbirch LB $17.95 (1-56711-247-1). 48pp. This account introduces the Mediterranean Sea, its geography, life forms, uses, and pollution. (Rev: HBG 3/00; SLJ 2/00) [551.46]

19843 Tesar, Jenny. *Threatened Oceans* (5–8). Illus. 1991, Facts on File LB $19.95 (0-8160-2494-4). 112pp. Explains the decline of the world's large bodies of water. (Rev: SLJ 1/92) [551.46]

19844 Twist, Clint. *Seas and Oceans* (5–8). Illus. Series: Ecology Watch. 1991, Macmillan LB $21.00

(0-87518-491-X). 45pp. Ethical issues are discussed in this attractive, oversize volume dealing with problems of the earth's seas and oceans. (Rev: BL 3/1/92) [333.95]

19845 VanCleave, Janice. *Janice VanCleave's Oceans for Every Kid: Easy Activities That Make Learning Science Fun* (5–7). Illus. Series: Science for Every Kid. 1996, Wiley paper $12.95 (0-471-12453-2). 256pp. This book gives good background information about oceans plus a number of entertaining and instructive projects and activities. (Rev: BL 4/15/96; SLJ 5/96) [551.46]

19846 Waterlow, Julia. *The Atlantic Ocean* (4–6). Illus. Series: Seas and Oceans. 1996, Raintree Steck-Vaughn LB $27.12 (0-8172-4509-X). 48pp. Such topics as geography, currents, history, and economic and recreational importance are covered in relation to the Atlantic Ocean. (Rev: BL 1/1–15/97) [551.46]

19847 Waterlow, Julia. *The Red Sea and the Arabian Gulf* (4–6). Illus. Series: Seas and Oceans. 1997, Raintree Steck-Vaughn LB $27.12 (0-8172-4515-4). 48pp. An overview of the history and importance of these bodies of water, with information on the coral reefs and animals of the Red Sea and oil reserves of the Arabian Gulf. (Rev: BL 7/97) [551.46]

COMMERCIAL FISHING

19848 Love, Ann, and Jane Drake. *Fishing* (2–4). Illus. by Pat Cupples. Series: America at Work. 1999, Kids Can $12.95 (1-55074-457-7). 31pp. This book introduces the fishing industry on both coasts by visiting a fish farm, taking a voyage on a trawler, and studying the life cycles and habitats of various fish. (Rev: HBG 3/00; SLJ 11/99) [639]

CURRENTS, TIDES, AND WAVES

19849 Heiligman, Deborah. *The Mysterious Ocean Highway: Benjamin Franklin and the Gulf Stream* (4–7). Illus. Series: Turnstone Ocean Pilot. 1999, Raintree Steck-Vaughn LB $25.69 (0-7398-1226-2). 48pp. Beginning with Benjamin Franklin's discoveries about the Gulf Stream, this book traces what we know about this ocean current and how it affects our lives. (Rev: BL 10/15/99; HBG 10/00) [551.47]

19850 Lampton, Christopher. *Tidal Wave* (4–6). Illus. Series: Disaster! 1992, Houghton paper $5.70 (0-395-62464-9). 40pp. This explanation of the causes and effects of tidal waves includes many color photos and detailed descriptions of important tidal-wave disasters of the past. (Rev: BL 3/15/92) [363.3]

19851 *Why Are There Waves?* (PS–3). Illus. Series: Why. 1997, DK $9.95 (0-7894-1531-3). 24pp. Using a question-and-answer format, the text covers basic science material related to oceans and lakes. (Rev: BL 8/97; SLJ 8/97) [553.7]

19852 Zubrowski, Bernie. *Making Waves: Finding Out About Rhythmic Motion* (4–8). Illus. Series: Boston Children's Museum Activity Books. 1994, Morrow $14.93 (0-688-11787-2). 96pp. Step-by-step instructions are given for creating a wave machine, plus activities to observe waves in various media. (Rev: BL 7/94; SLJ 8/94) [532]

SEASHORES AND TIDAL POOLS

19853 Bair, Diane, and Pamela Wright. *Tide Pool Life Watching* (2–5). Illus. Series: Wildlife Watching. 1999, Capstone $19.93 (0-7368-0324-6). 48pp. As well as introducing the flora and fauna in tidal pools, this book explains how and when to observe these life forms in their natural habitat. (Rev: BL 2/15/00) [591.769]

19854 Bendick, Jeanne. *Exploring an Ocean Tide Pool* (3–5). Illus. by Todd Telander. 1994, Holt paper $7.95 (0-8050-3273-8). 56pp. Includes basic information about a tide pool's plants and animals, with full-color photos and black-and-white diagrams and drawings. (Rev: BL 8/92; SLJ 11/92) [574]

19855 Bredeson, Carmen. *Tide Pools* (3–6). Illus. Series: First Books. 1999, Watts LB $22.00 (0-531-20368-9). 64pp. A discussion of tide pools, how they are formed, and the plant and animal life found there. (Rev: BL 5/1/99; HBG 10/99) [577.69]

19856 Cohat, Elisabeth. *The Seashore* (PS–2). Illus. by Pierre de Hugo. Series: First Discovery. 1995, Scholastic $12.95 (0-590-20303-7). A spiral-bound book with transparencies that show the many organisms found in tidal pools. (Rev: SLJ 9/95) [591]

19857 Cooper, Ann. *Along the Seashore* (3–5). Illus. Series: Wild Wonders. 1997, Roberts Rinehart paper $9.95 (1-57098-121-2). 46pp. A little book that introduces animals associated with seas and seashores: the seal, cormorant, hermit crab, raccoon, osprey, sea star, dolphin, gull, and sea trout. (Rev: BL 7/97; SLJ 8/97) [577.7]

19858 Fleisher, Paul. *Tide Pool* (3–5). Illus. Series: Webs of Life. 1997, Marshall Cavendish LB $22.79 (0-7614-0431-7). 40pp. This wet-and-dry environment is introduced, along with the animals and plants that thrive under conditions where flooding occurs twice a day. (Rev: BL 2/15/98; HBG 3/98; SLJ 4/98) [574.5]

19859 Giesecke, Ernestine. *Seashore Plants* (K–3). Illus. Series: Heinemann First Library. 1999, Heinemann $13.95 (1-57572-828-1). 32pp. Ten plants, six from sandy shores such as sea oats and eelgrass and four from rocky shores including kelp and rock weed, are introduced in full-page photos and a brief text. (Rev: BL 6/1–15/99; SLJ 8/99) [581.769]

19860 Goodman, Susan E. *Ultimate Field Trip 3: Wading into Marine Biology* (3–5). Illus. 1999, Simon & Schuster $17.00 (0-689-81963-3). 48pp. A report on a field trip in which Boston-area middle schoolers explore the seashore wonders along Maine's Cobscook Bay. (Rev: BL 4/15/99; HBG 10/99; SLJ 6/99) [577.69]

19861 Hunter, Anne. *What's in the Tide Pool?* (K–2). Illus. 2000, Houghton $4.95 (0-618-01510-8). 32pp. Ten animals that live in tidal pools, such as the sea anemone, herring gull, hermit crab, and barnacle, are introduced in this little book. (Rev: BL 9/15/00; HBG 3/01) [578.769]

19862 Malnig, Anita. *Where the Waves Break: Life at the Edge of the Sea* (3–5). Illus. 1985, Carolrhoda LB $19.93 (0-87614-226-9); Lerner paper $7.95 (0-87614-477-6). 48pp. An introduction to life at the sea's edge, including descriptions of starfish, brittle stars, snails, and seaweed. (Rev: BL 6/1/85; HB 9–10/85; SLJ 5/85)

19863 Parker, Steve. *Seashore* (4–6). Illus. by Dave King. 1989, Knopf LB $20.99 (0-394-92254-9). 64pp. Life on a seashore is introduced with handsome, well-captioned illustrations. (Rev: BL 10/15/89; SLJ 1/90) [591]

19864 Paul, Tessa. *By the Seashore* (2–5). Illus. Series: Animal Trackers. 1997, Crabtree $20.60 (0-86505-587-4); paper $7.95 (0-86505-595-5). 32pp. Ten creatures found at the seashore are introduced and identified by the evidence they leave behind, like prints, holes, nests, and hair or fur. (Rev: HBG 3/98; SLJ 10/97) [591]

19865 Pipes, Rose. *Coasts and Shores* (2–4). Series: World Habitats. 1998, Raintree Steck-Vaughn LB $15.98 (0-8172-5008-5). 32pp. This book describes the physical features of coastal regions with material on climates, wildlife, human interaction, and the need for protection. (Rev: BL 3/15/99; HBG 3/99) [591]

19866 Sayre, April Pulley. *Seashore* (4–7). Illus. Series: Exploring Earth's Biomes. 1996, Twenty-First Century $20.40 (0-8050-4085-4). 80pp. The composition of seashores and the life that they support are covered in this nicely illustrated account. (Rev: BL 10/15/96; SLJ 1/97) [574.5]

19867 Silverstein, Alvin, and Virginia Silverstein. *Life in a Tidal Pool* (4–6). Illus. by Pamela Carroll and Walter Carroll. 1990, Little, Brown $14.95 (0-316-79120-2). 60pp. The tidal pool habitat is explored. (Rev: SLJ 10/90) [574]

19868 Stolz, Mary. *Night of Ghosts and Hermits: Nocturnal Life on the Seashore* (3–5). Illus. 1985, Harcourt $12.95 (0-15-257333-X). 48pp. After three brothers play on the beach during the day, high drama takes place at night with the emergence of marine life. (Rev: BL 10/1/85; SLJ 1/86)

19869 Taylor, Barbara. *Shoreline* (3–6). Illus. by Frank Greenaway. Series: Look Closer. 1993, DK $9.95 (1-56458-213-2). 32pp. The plants and animals found along the seashores are introduced. (Rev: BL 8/93; SLJ 8/93) [674]

19870 Theodorou, Rod. *Along the Seashore* (2–4). Series: Amazing Journeys. 2000, Heinemann LB $15.95 (1-57572-483-9). 32pp. This brief overview of seashores focuses on several specific plants and animals found there. (Rev: HBG 3/01; SLJ 7/00) [591]

19871 Wright-Frierson, Virginia. *An Island Scrapbook: Dawn to Dusk on a Barrier Island* (2–5). Illus. 1998, Simon & Schuster $16.00 (0-689-81563-8). 40pp. The author and her young daughter have recorded in text and drawings the flora and fauna of a barrier island off the coast of Virginia. (Rev: BL 8/98; HBG 3/99; SLJ 8/98) [508.75]

19872 Zim, Herbert S., and Lester Ingle. *Seashores* (5–8). Illus. 1991, Western paper $21.27 (0-307-64496-0). 160pp. This is a guide to animals and plants found along the beaches.

UNDERWATER EXPLORATION

19873 Ballard, Robert D. *Exploring the Titanic* (4–8). Illus. by Ken Marschall. 1988, Scholastic $15.95 (0-590-41953-6). A compelling description of the undersea search for the ocean liner, for young readers. (Rev: BCCB 10/88; HB 5–6/89; SLJ 11/88)

19874 Gennings, Sara. *The Atocha Treasure* (4–7). Illus. 1988, Rourke LB $22.60 (0-86592-874-6). 32pp. The 20-year search for two Spanish treasure ships lost off the Florida Keys in 1622. (Rev: BL 12/1/88; SLJ 12/88)

19875 Gibbons, Gail. *Sunken Treasure* (2–5). Illus. 1988, HarperCollins LB $15.89 (0-690-04736-3); paper $6.95 (0-06-446097-5). 32pp. Searching for the cargo of the Atocha, a Spanish galleon sunk off Florida in 1622. (Rev: BCCB 10/88; BL 10/15/88; HB 9–10/88)

19876 Harris, Nicholas. *The Incredible Journey to the Depths of the Ocean: An Epic Voyage from the Seashore to the Bottom of the Deepest Trench* (4–6). Illus. 2000, Bedrick $18.95 (0-87226-601-X). 32pp. Using double-page spreads, this book starts with a seashore and coral reef and moves down through six depths to the deepest ocean floor. (Rev: BL 3/15/01; HBG 3/01) [551.46]

19877 Kovacs, Deborah. *Dive to the Deep Ocean: Voyages of Exploration and Discovery* (5–9). Illus. Series: Turnstone Ocean Explorer. 1999, Raintree Steck-Vaughn $18.98 (0-7398-1234-3). 64pp. This is a brief, illustrated account that describes the various machines used to explore the ocean floor, how they operate, and what they have found. (Rev: BL 10/15/99; HBG 3/00; SLJ 4/00) [623.8]

19878 Kovacs, Deborah. *Off to Sea: An Inside Look at a Research Cruise* (4–6). Illus. Series: Turnstone Ocean Pilot. 1999, Raintree Steck-Vaughn LB $25.69 (0-7398-1228-9). 48pp. A firsthand account of an expedition to explore hydrothermal ocean floor vents, with descriptions of findings, equipment, routines, and the responsibilities of various crew members. (Rev: BL 3/1/00; HBG 10/00; SLJ 4/00) [551.46]

19879 Rawlinson, Jonathan. *Discovering the Titanic* (4–7). Illus. 1988, Rourke LB $22.60 (0-86592-873-8). 32pp. The successful search for the ship sunk 70 years before on its maiden voyage. (Rev: BL 12/1/88; SLJ 12/88)

19880 Sullivan, George. *To the Bottom of the Sea: The Exploration of Exotic Life, the Titanic, and Other Secrets of the Oceans* (4–6). Illus. 1999, Twenty-First Century LB $24.90 (0-7613-0352-9). 80pp. A history of underwater exploration with fascinating information on contemporary accomplishments and discoveries such as locating the *Titanic*. (Rev: BL 10/1/99; HBG 3/00; SLJ 10/99) [551.46]

19881 Young, Karen Romano. *Arctic Investigations: Exploring the Frozen Ocean* (4–6). Series: Turnstone Ocean Pilot. 2000, Raintree Steck-Vaughn LB $25.69 (0-7398-1232-7). 48pp. An exciting book filled with excellent illustrations about an underwater quest, in the world's most brutal climate, to find krill — the tiny, shrimplike crea-

tures at the bottom of the food chain. (Rev: BL 12/15/00; HBG 10/00; SLJ 4/00) [551.46]

Pets

GENERAL AND MISCELLANEOUS

19882 Altman, Linda Jacobs. *Parrots* (4–6). Illus. Series: Perfect Pets. 2000, Marshall Cavendish LB $15.95 (0-7614-1102-X). 32pp. Full-color photographs and accessible text introduce parrots, their physical characteristics, and how to care for them. (Rev: BL 3/15/01; HBG 3/01) [636.6]

19883 Chrystie, Frances N. *Pets: A Comprehensive Handbook for Kids*. 4th ed. (4–6). Illus. 1995, Little, Brown paper $8.95 (0-316-14281-6). 261pp. A new edition of this basic work on a variety of pets and how to care for them. (Rev: BL 5/15/95; SLJ 7/95) [636]

19884 Curran, Wanda L. *Your Guinea Pig: A Kid's Guide to Raising and Showing* (4–6). Illus. 1995, Storey paper $14.95 (0-88266-889-7). 160pp. Topics in this book on how to keep guinea pigs as pets include selecting, feeding, mating, and showing. (Rev: BL 9/1/95) [636]

19885 Engfer, LeeAnne. *My Pet Hamster and Gerbils* (2–4). Photos by Andy King. Series: All About Pets. 1998, Lerner LB $22.60 (0-8225-2261-6); paper $7.95 (0-8225-9794-2). 64pp. Real-life situations are used to give details of the selection, care, and feeding of hamsters and gerbils. (Rev: BL 4/1/98; HBG 10/98; SLJ 3/98) [636]

19886 Engfer, LeeAnne. *My Pet Lizards* (3–6). Photos by Andy King. Series: All About Pets. 1999, Lerner LB $16.95 (0-8225-2263-2). 64pp. An unusual book that deals with lizards as pets with material on how to acquire them, care for them, feed them, handle them, and detect health problems. (Rev: HBG 10/99; SLJ 8/99) [597.95]

19887 Evans, Mark. *Guinea Pigs* (3–6). Illus. Series: ASPCA Pet Care Guides for Kids. 1992, DK $10.95 (1-56458-125-X). 48pp. The physical characteristics of guinea pigs are described, plus tips are given on how to choose one and care for it as a pet. (Rev: BL 4/1/93; SLJ 2/93) [636]

19888 Evans, Mark. *Hamster* (3–6). Illus. Series: ASPCA Pet Care Guides for Kids. 1993, DK $10.95 (1-56458-223-X). 45pp. Discusses the care and feeding of hamsters and how to keep them as happy pets. (Rev: BL 8/93) [636]

19889 Evans, Mark. *Rabbit* (3–5). Illus. Series: ASPCA Pet Care Guides for Kids. 1992, DK $10.95 (1-56458-128-4). 46pp. This book offers a wide variety of data for the brand-new pet owner. (Rev: BL 12/15/92) [636]

19890 Gelman, Amy. *My Pet Ferrets* (2–5). Photos by Andy King. Series: All About Pets. 2000, Lerner LB $22.60 (0-8225-2264-0). 64pp. The care and feeding of ferrets are covered in this book that also gives details on grooming, bathing, and even litter-box training. (Rev: BL 1/1–15/01; HBG 3/01; SLJ 11/00) [636]

19891 Gibbons, Gail. *Rabbits, Rabbits and More Rabbits!* (K–3). Illus. 2000, Holiday $16.95 (0-

8234-1486-8). 32pp. Simple text and colored drawings introduce different types of rabbits, their physical characteristics, habits, behavior, and how to care for them. (Rev: BCCB 3/00; BL 1/1–15/00; HBG 10/00; SLJ 3/00) [636.9]

19892 Gutman, Bill. *Adopting Pets: How to Choose Your New Best Friend* (3–6). Illus. by Anne Canevari Green. Series: Pet Friends. 2001, Millbrook LB $22.90 (0-7613-1863-1). 64pp. This book gives special tips on choosing a pet with attention to topics such as the kind of home and food it will need and the attention required. (Rev: BCCB 3/01; BL 3/1/01) [636]

19893 Gutman, Bill. *Becoming Best Friends with Your Hamster, Guinea Pig, or Rabbit* (3–6). Illus. 1997, Millbrook LB $21.90 (0-7613-0201-8). 64pp. Practical advice on the care of these pets, with tips on how to make their lives comfortable. (Rev: BCCB 6/97; BL 8/97; SLJ 7/97) [636]

19894 Gutman, Bill. *Becoming Best Friends with Your Iguana, Snake, or Turtle* (3–6). Illus. by Anne Canevari Green. Series: Pet Friends. 2001, Millbrook LB $22.90 (0-7613-1862-3). 64pp. Explains the special needs of reptiles that are kept as pets. (Rev: BL 3/1/01) [636]

19895 Gutman, Bill. *Becoming Your Bird's Best Friend* (3–6). Illus. 1996, Millbrook LB $21.90 (1-56294-662-5). 64pp. Various species of birds are described, as well as information on how to care for them as pets. (Rev: BL 12/1/96; SLJ 11/96) [636.9]

19896 Hansen, Elvig. *Guinea Pig* (3–6). Illus. 1992, Carolrhoda LB $23.93 (0-87614-681-7). 48pp. Charming, informative photos explore the life and care of guinea pigs. (Rev: BL 6/15/92; SLJ 8/92) [636]

19897 Hinds, Kathryn. *Hamsters and Gerbils* (4–6). Illus. Series: Perfect Pets. 2000, Marshall Cavendish LB $15.95 (0-7614-1104-6). 32pp. Gives tips on housing, feeding, training, and keeping these pets safe. (Rev: BL 3/15/01; SLJ 3/01) [636]

19898 Hinds, Kathryn. *Rabbits* (2–5). Series: Perfect Pets. 1998, Benchmark LB $15.95 (0-7614-0793-6). 32pp. The physical characteristics of rabbits, how they live, and tips on caring for them are given in this simple book with color photos. (Rev: HBG 10/99; SLJ 5/99) [636.932]

19899 King-Smith, Dick. *Dick King-Smith's Animal Friends: Thirty-One True Life Stories* (3–5). Illus. by Anita Jeram. 1996, Candlewick $19.99 (1-56402-960-3). 96pp. The famous English writer of children's books recalls some of the interesting pets he has had. (Rev: BL 12/1/96; SLJ 12/96) [591]

19900 King-Smith, Dick. *I Love Guinea Pigs* (PS–3). Illus. by Anita Jeram. 1995, Candlewick $15.99 (1-56402-389-3). 32pp. Three of the topics explored about guinea pigs are their habits, physical features, and history. (Rev: BCCB 4/95; BL 3/15/95; SLJ 5/95) [636]

19901 Miller, Michaela. *Guinea Pigs* (K–2). Series: Pets. 1997, Heinemann LB $18.50 (1-57572-575-4). 24pp. A simple introduction to guinea pigs, their care and feeding, and how to treat them as pets. (Rev: SLJ 4/98) [636]

19902 Petty, Kate. *Rabbits* (1–3). Illus. Series: First Pets. 1993, Barron's paper $4.95 (0-8120-1473-1). 24pp. This manual explains the characteristics, habits, and care of rabbits. (Rev: BL 10/1/89; SLJ 4/90) [636.932]

19903 Royston, Angela. *Life Cycle of a Guinea Pig* (PS–3). Series: Life Cycle. 1998, Heinemann LB $13.95 (1-57572-614-9). 32pp. With a color photo and four or five lines of text per page, this book explains the life cycle of the guinea pig and gives a timeline to help identify stages of development. (Rev: BL 5/15/98; SLJ 6/98) [636]

19904 Schafer, Susan. *Lizards* (4–6). Series: Perfect Pets. 2000, Marshall Cavendish LB $15.95 (0-7614-1103-8). 32pp. History, folklore, and practical tips are included in this introduction to the care, feeding, and raising of pet lizards. (Rev: BL 3/15/01; HBG 3/01) [595.95]

19905 Silverstein, Alvin, et al. *A Pet or Not?* (3–6). Illus. Series: What a Pet! 1999, Twenty-First Century LB $21.40 (0-7613-3230-8). 48pp. This book looks as some exotic animals that could be unusual pets such as the pig, coatimundi, and armadillo. (Rev: BCCB 9/99; BL 8/99; HBG 3/00; SLJ 10/99) [636.008]

19906 Silverstein, Alvin, et al. *Snakes and Such* (3–6). Illus. Series: What a Pet! 1999, Twenty-First Century LB $21.40 (0-7613-3229-4). 48pp. In pictures and text, this book explore the idea that such reptiles and amphibians as chameleons, geckos, iguanas, as well as frogs and toads, can be kept as pets. (Rev: BL 8/99; HBG 3/00; SLJ 10/99) [639.3]

19907 Silverstein, Alvin, and Virginia Silverstein. *Pocket Pets* (4–7). Series: What a Pet! 2000, Twenty-First Century LB $21.90 (0-7613-1370-2). 48pp. In pictures and text the hamster, gerbil, guinea pig, rabbit, chinchilla, and flying squirrel are introduced, with material on cost, food, housing, and nurture. (Rev: BCCB 4/00; HBG 10/00; SLJ 5/00) [636]

19908 Simon, Seymour. *Pets in a Jar: Collecting and Caring for Small Wild Animals* (4–6). Illus. by Betty Fraser. 1979, Puffin paper $6.99 (0-14-049186-4). How to catch and care for such small wild creatures as snails, toads, and ants.

19909 Squire, Ann. *101 Questions and Answers About Pets and People* (4–6). Illus. 1988, Macmillan $13.95 (0-02-786580-0). 96pp. Common questions on a range of topics, such as relationships, behavior, physiology. (Rev: BL 11/1/88; SLJ 2/89)

19910 Watts, Barrie. *Hamster* (1–3). Illus. 1986, Silver Burdett LB $15.95 (0-382-09281-3); paper $3.95 (0-382-09957-5). 28pp. Well-organized, basic scientific information, with full-color photos. (Rev: BL 1/1/87)

19911 Wexler, Jerome. *Pet Gerbils* (2–5). Illus. 1990, Whitman LB $15.95 (0-8075-6523-7). 48pp. Raising these rodents, with intriguing photos. (Rev: BCCB 11/90; BL 9/15/90; SLJ 11/90) [636]

19912 Wexler, Jerome. *Pet Hamsters* (3–6). Illus. 1992, Whitman LB $15.95 (0-8075-6525-3). 48pp. Personal advice from a hamster raiser on the care and handling of these pets. (Rev: BCCB 2/93; BL 2/15/93; SLJ 2/93) [636]

19913 Zeaman, John. *Exotic Pets: From Alligators to Zebra Fish* (4–6). Series: Before They Were Pets. 1999, Watts LB $24.00 (0-531-20352-2). 64pp. The author discusses unusual pets and the problems of domesticating animals that are essentially wild. (Rev: BL 6/1–15/99; HBG 10/99; SLJ 6/99) [636]

19914 Zeaman, John. *From Pests to Pets: How Small Animals Became Our Friends* (4–6). Illus. 1998, Watts LB $24.00 (0-531-20350-6). 64pp. Such small mammals as ferrets, mice, and rabbits are introduced, with material on their evolution and their relationship with humans. (Rev: BL 12/1/98; HBG 3/99) [636.9]

CATS

19915 Arnold, Caroline. *Cats: In from the Wild* (4–7). Photos by Richard Hewett. 1993, Carolrhoda LB $19.95 (0-87614-692-2). 48pp. Domestic and wild cats are highlighted with comparisons and contrasts. (Rev: BL 8/93) [636.8]

19916 Bonners, Susan. *Why Does the Cat Do That?* (2–4). Illus. 1998, Holt $15.95 (0-8050-4377-2). 32pp. Asked to take care of a neighbor's cat, a boy sets out to learn what he can about these interesting animals and why they behave as they do. (Rev: BL 12/1/98; HBG 3/99; SLJ 1/99) [599.75]

19917 Engfer, LeeAnne. *My Pet Cats* (2–4). Photos by Andy King. Series: All About Pets. 1998, Lerner LB $22.60 (0-8225-2258-6); paper $7.95 (0-8225-9793-4). 64pp. Tips on cat selection and care are found in this book that focuses on a girl who adopts two cats from a shelter and raises them to adulthood. (Rev: BL 4/1/98; HBG 10/98; SLJ 3/98) [636.8]

19918 Evans, Mark. *Kitten* (3–6). Illus. Series: Pet Care Guides for Kids. 1992, DK $10.95 (1-56458-126-8). 48pp. The structure and behavior patterns of cats are described, with tips on how to choose a kitten and care for it. (Rev: BL 4/1/93; SLJ 2/93) [636.8]

19919 Fowler, Allan. *It Could Still Be a Cat* (1–2). Illus. Series: Rookie Readers. 1993, Children's LB $19.00 (0-516-06015-5). 32pp. The cat family is introduced in this easy-to-read book for beginners. (Rev: BL 3/1/94) [636.8]

19920 George, Jean Craighead. *How to Talk to Your Cat* (2–4). Illus. by Paul Meisel. 2000, HarperCollins LB $9.89 (0-06-027969-9). 40pp. After a history of the domestication of cats, this account tells how and what they communicate with humans. (Rev: BCCB 4/00; BL 12/15/99; HB 3–4/00; HBG 10/00; SLJ 2/00) [636.8]

19921 Gibbons, Gail. *Cats* (PS–2). Illus. by author. 1996, Holiday LB $16.95 (0-8234-1253-9). Watercolor illustrations are used to introduce a number of breeds of cats, their characteristics, and behavior. (Rev: SLJ 12/96) [636.8]

19922 Gutman, Bill. *Becoming Your Cat's Best Friend* (3–6). Illus. Series: Pet Friends. 1997, Millbrook LB $21.90 (0-7613-0200-X). 64pp. This book expresses the cat's point of view and gives advice on how to make the pet and its owner happy with

the relationship. (Rev: BCCB 6/97; BL 8/97; SLJ 7/97) [636.8]

19923 Hinds, Kathryn. *Cats* (2–5). Series: Perfect Pets. 1998, Benchmark LB $15.95 (0-7614-0794-4). 31pp. As well as a history of cats and their role in mythology, this simple book describes their physical characteristics and how to take care of them. (Rev: HBG 10/99; SLJ 5/99) [636.8]

19924 Holub, Joan. *Why Do Cats Meow?* (1–2). Illus. Series: Easy-to-Read. 2001, Dial $13.99 (0-8037-2503-5); paper $3.99 (0-14-056788-7). 48pp. This informative, easy-to-read book, with many photos and cartoons, discusses behavioral traits of cats and provides material on breeds and their characteristics. (Rev: BCCB 2/01; BL 2/15/01) [636.8]

19925 Jessel, Camilla. *The Kitten Book* (1–4). Illus. 1994, Candlewick paper $4.99 (1-56402-278-1). 32pp. The record, in marvelous photographs, of the birth process for a Burmese cat. (Rev: BL 2/1/92; SLJ 4/92) [636.8]

19926 Lauber, Patricia. *The True-or-False Book of Cats* (2–4). Illus. 1998, National Geographic $15.95 (0-7922-3440-5). 32pp. Cat behavior is explored through the answers to 15 true-or-false statements like "Cats have nine lives." (Rev: BL 2/15/98; HBG 10/98) [636.8]

19927 Meadows, Graham. *Cats* (PS–2). Photos by author. Series: Animals Are Not Like Us. 1999, Gareth Stevens LB $13.95 (0-8368-2251-X). 24pp. Very basic information about cats — material on their senses, communication, and appearance, for example — is given with comparisons to humans. (Rev: HBG 10/99; SLJ 7/99) [636.8]

19928 Overbeck, Cynthia. *Cats* (4–6). Illus. by Shin Yoshino. 1983, Lerner LB $22.60 (0-8225-1480-X). 48pp. This work concentrates on domestic cats and their habits and appearance.

19929 Quasha, Jennifer. *The Manx: The Cat with No Tail* (2–4). Illus. Series: Kids Can! 2000, Rosen LB $18.60 (0-8239-5512-5). 24pp. Many color close-ups are used to present the Manx cat, its characteristics, habits, and the myth about how it lost its tail. (Rev: BL 10/15/00) [636.8]

19930 Quasha, Jennifer. *Shorthaired Cats in America* (2–4). Illus. 2000, Rosen LB $18.60 (0-8239-5513-3). 24pp. This is a general book about cats that covers American attitudes toward them, their history from the Mayflower to today, their part in the Salem witch trials, and similar material. (Rev: BL 10/15/00) [636.8]

19931 Rosen, Michael J., ed. *Purr . . . Children's Book Illustrators Brag About Their Cats* (2–5). Illus. 1996, Harcourt $18.00 (0-15-200837-3). 48pp. Paintings and text illustrate the moods and activities of a variety of cats. (Rev: BL 4/1/96; SLJ 5/96) [636.8]

19932 Scott, Carey. *Kittens* (K–5). Illus. 1997, DK $12.95 (0-7894-2132-1). 37pp. Beautiful photos are featured in this book about kittens and how to choose and care for one as a pet. (Rev: HBG 3/98; SLJ 2/98) [636.8]

19933 Selsam, Millicent E. *How Kittens Grow* (1–2). Illus. by Esther Bubley. 1992, Scholastic paper $3.25 (0-590-44784-X). Photographs and simply written text describe the stages in a kitten's growth.

19934 Tildes, Phyllis L. *Calico's Cousins: Cats from Around the World* (K–3). Illus. 1999, Charlesbridge LB $15.95 (0-88106-648-6); paper $6.95 (0-88106-649-4). 32pp. General information about different breeds of cats is given in this book that features beautiful watercolor art. (Rev: BL 2/1/99; HBG 10/99; SLJ 3/99) [636.8]

19935 Zeaman, John. *Why the Cat Chose Us* (4–6). Illus. Series: Before They Were Pets. 1998, Watts LB $24.00 (0-531-11458-9). 64pp. With color photographs and a lucid text, this book traces the history of the domestic cat and how the various breeds evolved. (Rev: BL 4/1/98; HBG 10/98; SLJ 5/98) [636.8]

DOGS

19936 Altman, Linda Jacobs. *Big Dogs* (4–6). Series: Perfect Pets. 2000, Marshall Cavendish LB $15.95 (0-7614-1101-1). 32pp. Filled with historical and factual material, this book introduces several breeds of large dogs and gives tips for raising and caring for them. (Rev: BL 3/15/01; HBG 3/01) [636.7]

19937 Altman, Linda Jacobs. *Small Dogs* (2–5). Series: Perfect Pets. 1998, Benchmark LB $15.95 (0-7614-0795-2). 32pp. Young dog lovers will enjoy this simple introduction to dogs that gives some history plus behavioral traits and tips on caring for them. (Rev: HBG 10/99; SLJ 5/99) [636.7]

19938 Arnold, Caroline. *A Guide Dog Puppy Grows Up* (3–5). Photos by Richard Hewett. 1991, Harcourt $16.95 (0-15-232657-X); paper $7.00 (0-15-201557-4). 48pp. The life and training of a golden retriever named Honey. (Rev: BCCB 3/91; BL 4/15/91; HB 5–6/91; SLJ 5/91) [362.4]

19939 Bare, Colleen S. *Sammy, Dog Detective* (K–3). Illus. 1998, Dutton $15.99 (0-525-65253-1). 32pp. A photo-essay about the life and work of a police dog, Sammy, who is part of the K-9 team in Modesto, California. (Rev: BCCB 3/98; BL 1/1–15/98; HBG 10/98; SLJ 1/98) [363.2]

19940 Calmenson, Stephanie. *Rosie: A Visiting Dog's Story* (PS–3). Illus. by Justin Sutcliffe. 1994, Houghton $16.00 (0-395-65477-7). 48pp. The true story of the dog Rosie, who is being trained to be a visiting dog to help those who are sad or lonely. (Rev: BL 4/15/94; HB 7–8/94; SLJ 4/94) [636.7]

19941 Calmenson, Stephanie. *Shaggy, Waggy Dogs (and Others)* (K–3). Illus. by Justin Sutcliffe. 1998, Clarion $15.00 (0-395-77605-8). 48pp. Twenty canine breeds are introduced in a series of four-line poems and clear color photographs. (Rev: BL 5/1/98; HBG 10/98; SLJ 7/98) [636.7]

19942 Clutton-Brock, Juliet. *Dog* (4–8). Illus. Series: Eyewitness Books. 1991, Knopf LB $20.99 (0-679-91459-5). 64pp. The anatomical features of dogs and their different types and outstanding characteristics are covered in this heavily illustrated book. (Rev: BL 12/1/91) [599.74]

19943 *The Complete Dog Book for Kids* (3–6). Illus. 1996, Macmillan $34.95 (0-87605-458-0); paper $22.95 (0-87605-460-2). 274pp. This publication of the American Kennel Club is an excellent handbook on the various breeds of dogs and how to choose, care for, and train a dog. (Rev: BL 1/1–15/97) [636.7]

19944 Darling, Kathy. *ABC Dogs* (PS–3). Illus. by Tara Darling. 1997, Walker LB $16.85 (0-8027-8635-9). 32pp. This ABC book introduces various breeds of dogs and shows them in photographs, both as puppies and as adults. (Rev: BL 10/15/97; HBG 3/98; SLJ 10/97) [636.7]

19945 Evans, Mark. *Puppy* (3–5). Illus. Series: ASPCA Pet Care Guides for Kids. 1992, DK $10.95 (1-56458-127-6). Intended for the child who is a brand-new pet owner, this book offers much information and full-color photos. (Rev: BL 12/15/91) [636.7]

19946 Feldman, Heather. *The Story of the Golden Retriever* (2–4). Illus. Series: Dogs Throughout History. 2000, Rosen $18.60 (0-8239-5514-1). 24pp. This history of the golden retriever also describes its physical characteristics and its roles in rescue missions and as a guide dog. (Rev: BL 10/15/00) [636.752]

19947 Gallimard Jeunesse. *Dogs* (PS–2). Series: First Discovery. 1999, Scholastic $12.95 (0-590-87608-2). 24pp. A heavily illustrated, simple introduction to dogs, their characteristics, and some of the important breeds. (Rev: BL 6/1–15/99; HBG 10/99) [636.7]

19948 George, Jean Craighead. *How to Talk to Your Dog* (2–4). Illus. by Sue Truesdell. 2000, HarperCollins LB $9.89 (0-06-027093-4). 40pp. Jean Craighead George teaches us what dogs are trying to tell us — and how to communicate back — as well as giving a history of how dogs were domesticated. (Rev: BCCB 4/00; BL 12/15/99; HBG 10/00; SLJ 2/00) [636.7]

19949 Gibbons, Gail. *Dogs* (K–2). Illus. by author. 1996, Holiday LB $16.95 (0-8234-1226-1). An easy-to-read overview of dogs and their history, breeds, and anatomy. (Rev: BCCB 5/96; HB 5–6/96; SLJ 9/96) [636.7]

19950 Gutman, Bill. *Becoming Your Dog's Best Friend* (3–6). Illus. 1996, Millbrook LB $21.90 (1-56294-661-7). 64pp. In addition to providing information about caring for and training dogs, several breeds are introduced. (Rev: BL 12/1/96; SLJ 11/96) [636.7]

19951 Holub, Joan. *Why Do Dogs Bark?* (1–2). Illus. Series: Easy-to-Read. 2001, Dial $13.99 (0-8037-2504-3). 48pp. This beginning reader discusses dogs' behavior and describes some of their heroic deeds. (Rev: BCCB 2/01; BL 2/15/01) [636.7]

19952 Jessel, Camilla. *The Puppy Book* (1–4). Illus. 1994, Candlewick paper $4.99 (1-56402-279-X). 32pp. Saffy, a Labrador retriever, is about to give birth, captured in marvelous photographs. (Rev: BL 2/1/92; SLJ 7/92) [636.7]

19953 Jones, Robert F. *Jake: A Labrador Puppy at Work and Play* (3–5). Illus. 1992, Farrar $15.00 (0-

374-33655-5). 32pp. At the age of eight weeks, Jake goes to a family to begin his training as a hunting dog. (Rev: BCCB 1/92; BL 11/1/92; SLJ 12/92) [636.7]

19954 Kehret, Peg. *Shelter Dogs: Amazing Stories of Adopted Strays* (3–5). Illus. 1999, Albert Whitman $14.95 (0-8075-7334-5). 134pp. A collection of eight true stories about shelter dogs that went on to great things — starring on TV, for example. (Rev: BCCB 4/99; BL 5/1/99; HBG 10/99; SLJ 10/99) [636.7]

19955 King-Smith, Dick. *Puppy Love* (PS–1). Illus. by Anita Jeram. 1997, Candlewick $15.99 (0-7636-0116-0). 32pp. Charmingly illustrated with water-color-and-ink drawings, this book tells about the many wonderful dogs that Dick King-Smith has as pets. (Rev: BL 12/15/97; HBG 3/98; SLJ 11/97) [636.7]

19956 Meadows, Graham. *Dogs* (PS–2). Photos by author. Series: Animals Are Not Like Us. 1999, Gareth Stevens LB $13.95 (0-8368-2252-8). 24pp. Very basic information about dogs — material on their senses, communication, and appearance, for example — is given with comparisons with humans. (Rev: HBG 10/99; SLJ 7/99) [636.7]

19957 Moore, Eva. *Buddy: The First Seeing Eye Dog* (2–3). Illus. by Don Bolognese. 1996, Scholastic paper $3.99 (0-590-26585-7). 48pp. In simple prose, this book traces the beginning of the Seeing Eye movement in the 1930s. (Rev: BL 11/15/96) [392.4]

19958 Mulvany, Martha. *The Story of the Boxer* (2–4). Illus. Series: Dogs Throughout History. 2000, Rosen $18.60 (0-8239-5519-2). 24pp. This history of the boxer also describes its physical characteristics and its reputation for loyalty and courage. (Rev: BL 10/15/00) [636.73]

19959 O'Neill, Amanda. *Dogs* (3–5). 1999, Kingfisher $15.95 (0-7534-5175-1). 63pp. This oversize introduction to dogs covers such topics as physical features, evolution, history, breeds, behavior, and care. (Rev: HBG 10/99; SLJ 7/99) [636.7]

19960 Otto, Carolyn. *Our Puppies Are Growing* (1). Illus. by Mary Morgan. Series: Let's-Read-and-Find-Out. 1998, HarperCollins LB $15.89 (0-06-027272-4); paper $4.95 (0-06-445169-0). 32pp. In this book for beginning readers, the experiences of a preschooler whose dog has five puppies help readers learn about the dog's pregnancy, the birth process, and the care of the newborn puppies. (Rev: BL 11/1/98; HBG 3/99; SLJ 7/99) [636.7]

19961 Patent, Dorothy Hinshaw. *Dogs: The Wolf Within* (3–6). Illus. by William Munoz. 1993, Carolrhoda LB $19.95 (0-87614-691-4); paper $7.95 (0-87614-604-3). 48pp. This book describes the relationship between the habits of the domesticated dog and its distant ancestor, the wolf. (Rev: BCCB 7–8/93; BL 6/1–15/93) [599]

19962 Petersen-Fleming, Judy, and Bill Fleming. *Puppy Care and Critters, Too!* (1–3). Illus. by Debra Reingold-Reiss. 1994, Morrow $15.00 (0-688-12563-8). 40pp. This manual focuses on raising, feeding, and caring for a puppy, with material

on other kinds of pets. (Rev: BL 4/1/94; SLJ 6/94) [636.7]

19963 Pinkwater, Jill, and Daniel Pinkwater. *Superpuppy* (4–6). Illus. 1977, Houghton paper $9.95 (0-89919-084-7). 208pp. All one needs to know about choosing and rearing the "best possible" dog.

19964 *Puppies* (3–6). Illus. 1997, DK $12.95 (0-7894-2133-X). 37pp. Using double-page spreads, several breeds of dogs are introduced, with good tips for their proper care. (Rev: BL 10/15/97; HBG 3/98; SLJ 2/98) [636.7]

19965 Rock, Maxine. *Totally Fun Things to Do with Your Dog* (3–6). Illus. 1998, Wiley paper $12.95 (0-471-19754-X). 128pp. An informative manual for young dog owners on training, suitable activities, and building bonds of trust and friendship between owner and dog. (Rev: BL 6/1–15/98) [636.7]

19966 Rosenthal, Lisa. *A Dog's Best Friend: An Activity Book for Kids and Their Dogs* (4–7). Illus. by Bonnie Matthews. 1999, Chicago Review paper $12.95 (1-55652-362-9). 181pp. This book that gives hints on how to choose a dog and care for a puppy offers 60 projects related to these subjects including crafts, recipes, and games. (Rev: SLJ 1/00) [636.7]

19967 Rossiter, Nan P. *Rugby and Rosie* (1–3). Illus. by author. 1997, Dutton $14.99 (0-525-45484-5). Background information about guide dogs is given in this story about a young boy who keeps a puppy for a year before it leaves to be trained as a guide dog. (Rev: BCCB 3/97; SLJ 2/97) [636.7]

19968 Royston, Angela. *Life Cycle of a Dog* (PS–3). Series: Life Cycle. 2000, Heinemann LB $19.92 (1-57572-209-7). 32pp. This book describes a dog's life cycle with a simple text and color photos on each page. (Rev: BL 5/15/00; HBG 3/01) [636.7]

19969 Selsam, Millicent E. *How Puppies Grow* (1–2). Illus. 1990, Scholastic paper $2.99 (0-590-42736-9). 32pp. The stages in a puppy's life — from birth through walking, seeing, eating, and playing — described in excellent photographs and simple text.

19970 Selsam, Millicent E., and Joyce Hunt. *A First Look at Dogs* (1–3). Illus. by Harriett Springer. 1981, Walker LB $9.85 (0-8027-6421-5). 32pp. A history of dogs and an introduction to present breeds.

19971 Silverstein, Alvin, and Virginia Silverstein. *Different Dogs* (4–7). Series: What a Pet! 2000, Twenty-First Century LB $21.90 (0-7613-1371-0). 48pp. Several different breeds of dogs are introduced in pictures and text plus information on cost, food, housing, and training. (Rev: HBG 10/00; SLJ 5/00) [636.7]

19972 Silverstein, Alvin, and Virginia Silverstein. *Dogs: All About Them* (5–8). Illus. 1986, Lothrop $16.00 (0-688-04805-6). 256pp. Coverage on history, anatomy, and breeds. (Rev: BCCB 11/86; SLJ 9/86)

19973 Singer, Marilyn. *A Dog's Gotta Do What a Dog's Gotta Do* (3–6). Illus. 2000, Holt $16.00 (0-8050-6074-X). 86pp. This book on working dogs includes material on their roles as defenders, herders, detectives, rescuers, and entertainers. (Rev: BCCB 11/00; BL 11/15/00; HBG 3/01; SLJ 2/01) [636.7]

19974 Squire, Ann. *Understanding Man's Best Friend: Why Dogs Look and Act the Way They Do* (5–7). 1991, Macmillan LB $14.95 (0-02-786590-8). 128pp. A history and analysis of dog breeds and behavior. (Rev: BCCB 7–8/91; BL 6/15/91; SLJ 9/91) [636.7]

19975 Storer, Pat. *Your Puppy, Your Dog: A Kid's Guide to Raising a Happy, Healthy Dog* (4–6). Illus. 1997, Storey paper $14.95 (0-88266-959-1). 172pp. Chapters in this complete dog care manual cover such subjects as feeding, walking, playing, grooming, and toilet needs. (Rev: BL 12/15/97) [636.7]

19976 Temple, Bob. *Chihuahuas* (3–5). Series: Dogs. 2000, ABDO LB $13.95 (1-57765-419-6). 24pp. This heavily illustrated book covers the history of this breed, its structure, habits, and required care and feeding. Also use from the same series: *Pugs*, *Scottish Terriers*, and *Shih Tzus* (all 2000). (Rev: BL 3/15/01; HBG 3/01) [636.7]

19977 Temple, Bob. *Jack Russell Terriers* (3–5). Illus. Series: Dogs. 2000, ABDO $13.95 (1-57765-424-2). 24pp. This book introduces terriers, their physical characteristics, habits, how to care for them, and their special needs. Similar material is found in *Siberian Huskies* (2000). (Rev: BL 3/15/01; HBG 3/01) [636.755]

19978 White, Nancy. *Why Do Dogs Do That?* (2–4). Illus. by Gioia Fiammenghi. 1995, Scholastic paper $4.99 (0-590-26597-0). 32pp. Through answers to 24 simple questions, such common canine behavior as tail wagging is explained. (Rev: BL 2/15/96) [599]

19979 Zeaman, John. *How the Wolf Became the Dog* (4–6). Illus. Series: Before They Were Pets. 1998, Watts LB $24.00 (0-531-11459-7). 64pp. This book explains how dogs evolved from wolves tamed by prehistoric people and how the various breeds of dogs developed. (Rev: BL 4/1/98; HBG 10/98; SLJ 5/98) [599.773]

FISH

19980 Coleman, Lori. *My Pet Fish* (3–6). Illus. Series: All About Pets. 1998, Lerner LB $16.95 (0-8225-2262-4). 64pp. This book supplies basic information on aquariums, the equipment involved, and the problems of maintenance. (Rev: BL 9/1/98; HBG 10/98) [639.34]

19981 Evans, Mark. *Fish* (3–6). Illus. Series: Pet Care Guides for Kids. 1993, DK $10.95 (1-56458-222-1). 45pp. The setting up of an aquarium is discussed as well as various kinds of fish and their care. (Rev: BL 8/93) [636.6]

19982 Pfeffer, Wendy. *What's It Like to Be a Fish?* (1–3). Illus. by Holly Keller. 1996, HarperCollins LB $15.89 (0-06-024429-1); paper $4.95 (0-06-445151-8). 32pp. In this easily read science book, the structure and habits of goldfish are described, with hints on caring for them as pets. (Rev: BL 3/15/96; HB 7–8/96; SLJ 4/96) [597]

HORSES AND PONIES

19983 Ancona, George. *Man and Mustang* (3–6). Illus. 1992, Macmillan LB $15.95 (0-02-700802-9). 48pp. Black-and-white photos help to tell the story of how the Bureau of Land Management manages the growing population of wild mustangs. (Rev: BCCB 4/92; BL 3/15/92; HB 7–8/92; SLJ 4/92) [636.1]

19984 Budd, Jackie. *The Best Book of Ponies* (2–3). Series: The Best Book Of. 1999, Kingfisher $10.95 (0-7534-5172-7). 32pp. A beginning chapter book with attractive double-page spreads on such topics as horses and ponies of the world, bridles and bits, learning to ride, and going to a show. (Rev: HBG 10/99; SLJ 7/99) [636.1]

19985 Budd, Jackie. *Horse and Pony Breeds* (4–8). Series: The Complete Guides to Horses and Ponies. 1998, Gareth Stevens LB $21.27 (0-8368-2046-0). 64pp. Each type of horse is profiled with action photos, fact boxes, checklists, and a clear text. (Rev: HBG 10/98; SLJ 7/98) [636.1]

19986 Budd, Jackie. *Horse and Pony Care* (4–8). Series: The Complete Guides to Horses and Ponies. 1998, Gareth Stevens LB $21.27 (0-8368-2047-9). 64pp. This book discusses such topics related to horse and pony care as feeding, stables, grooming, shoeing, and common ailments. (Rev: HBG 10/98; SLJ 7/98) [636.1]

19987 Budd, Jackie. *Horses* (3–8). Illus. 1995, Kingfisher $15.95 (1-85697-566-5). 64pp. Drawings and text cover such subjects related to horses as anatomy, breeds, care, and grooming. (Rev: BL 10/1/95; SLJ 12/95) [636.1]

19988 Budd, Jackie. *Learning to Ride Horses and Ponies* (4–8). Series: The Complete Guides to Horses and Ponies. 1998, Gareth Stevens LB $21.27 (0-8368-2045-2). 64pp. This book supplies basic information that prospective young riders need to know including gear, types of lessons, and attitudes. (Rev: HBG 10/98; SLJ 7/98) [636.1]

19989 Budiansky, Stephen. *The World According to Horses: How They Run, See, and Think* (4–8). Illus. 2000, Holt $16.95 (0-8050-6054-5). 101pp. This book explores horses' behavior — such as their sight and thinking powers — and goes on to explain how this knowledge was gained through observation and experiments. (Rev: BCCB 5/00; BL 3/1/00; HB 5–6/00; HBG 10/00; SLJ 7/00) [636.1]

19990 Cole, Joanna. *Riding Silver Star* (K–3). Illus. by Margaret Miller. 1996, Morrow $14.93 (0-688-13896-9). 48pp. A nonfiction account of how young Abby cares for her horse, Silver Star, and of the activities they share. (Rev: BCCB 3/96; BL 4/1/96; HB 5–6/96; SLJ 5/96) [798.2]

19991 Farley, Walter. *Man O' War* (4–6). Illus. 1983, Random paper $4.99 (0-394-86015-2). 352pp. The story of the famous racehorse.

19992 Fowler, Allan. *Horses, Horses, Horses* (1–2). Illus. Series: Rookie Readers. 1992, Children's LB $19.00 (0-516-04921-6). 32pp. With a minimum of text and lots of pictures, this account introduces various kinds of horses and tells how they help people. (Rev: BL 7/92) [636.1]

19993 Henderson, Carolyn. *Horse and Pony Breeds* (3–6). Series: DK Riding Club. 1999, DK LB $12.95 (0-7894-4268-X). 48pp. Numerous color photos and extensive captions introduce young horse enthusiasts to the various breeds and their characteristics. (Rev: BL 8/99; HBG 10/99) [636.1]

19994 Henderson, Carolyn. *Horse and Pony Care* (3–6). Illus. Series: DK Riding Club. 1999, DK LB $12.95 (0-7894-4270-1). 48pp. Tips on how to care for a horse or pony include material on handling, health, and feeding. (Rev: BL 8/99; HBG 10/99) [636.1]

19995 Henderson, Carolyn. *Horse and Pony Shows and Events* (3–6). Series: DK Riding Club. 1999, DK LB $12.95 (0-7894-4266-3). 48pp. A heavily illustrated step-by-step guide to preparing for and entering various types of horse shows. (Rev: BL 8/99; HBG 10/99) [636.1]

19996 Henry, Marguerite. *Album of Horses* (5–8). Illus. by Wesley Dennis. 1951, Macmillan paper $11.99 (0-689-71709-1). 112pp. A beautifully illustrated guide to 20 breeds of horses.

19997 Isenbart, Hans-Heinrich. *Birth of a Foal* (2–5). Illus. 1986, Carolrhoda LB $22.60 (0-87614-239-0). 48pp. Complemented by color photos, the phases of fetal development and the birth process are detailed. (Rev: BL 4/1/86; HB 5–6/86; SLJ 3/86)

19998 Jauck, Andrea. *Assateague: Island of the Wild Ponies* (2–4). Illus. 1997, Sierra Club paper $7.95 (0-939365-59-6). 32pp. A color photo-essay to interest horse fans. (Rev: BCCB 5/93; BL 3/15/93; SLJ 6/93) [599.72]

19999 Kalas, Sybille. *The Wild Horse Family Book* (2–4). Trans. by Patricia Crampton. Illus. 1990, Picture Book paper $15.95 (0-88708-110-X). 52pp. In photos and text, the life and habits of the wild horses of Iceland are explored. (Rev: BL 3/1/90; SLJ 5/90) [636.1]

20000 LaBonte, Gail. *The Miniature Horse* (3–5). Illus. 1990, Macmillan LB $13.95 (0-87518-424-3). 60pp. The origin of these tiny horses, some no more than 25 inches tall. (Rev: BCCB 4/90; BL 4/1/90; SLJ 7/90) [636.1]

20001 Lauber, Patricia. *The True-or-False Book of Horses* (2–3). Illus. by Rosalyn Schanzer. 2000, HarperCollins LB $16.99 (0-688-16920-1). 32pp. Using a question-and-answer format, this book covers topics about horses including their physical characteristics, behavior, and history. (Rev: BL 4/15/00; HBG 10/00; SLJ 6/00) [636.1]

20002 Ling, Mary. *Foal* (PS–1). Illus. by Gordon Clayton. Series: See How They Grow. 1992, DK $9.95 (1-56458-113-6). 24pp. This simple picture book shows the development of a horse from birth through the first months. (Rev: BL 11/1/92; HB 1–2/93) [559.72]

20003 McMillan, Bruce. *My Horse of the North* (K–3). Illus. 1997, Scholastic $15.95 (0-590-97205-7). 32pp. Three Icelandic youngsters tell about the horses that were originally brought there by the Vikings. (Rev: BL 9/1/97; HB 9–10/97; HBG 3/98; SLJ 9/97) [636.3]

20004 Meadows, Graham. *Horses* (PS–2). Photos by author. Series: Animals Are Not Like Us. 1999, Gareth Stevens LB $13.95 (0-8368-2253-6). 24pp. This is a very simple introduction to horses, their appearance, senses, and behavior, with some comparisons with humans. (Rev: HBG 10/99; SLJ 7/99) [636.1]

20005 Meltzer, Milton. *Hold Your Horses! A Feedbag Full of Fact and Fable* (4–8). Illus. 1995, HarperCollins LB $15.89 (0-06-024478-X). 160pp. The place of horses in history is explored in this account that tells about horses in art, war, sports, and work. (Rev: BCCB 12/95; BL 11/15/95; SLJ 12/95*) [636.1]

20006 Parker, Jane. *The Fantastic Book of Horses* (4–6). Illus. Series: Fantastic Book Of. 1997, Millbrook LB $22.40 (0-7613-0566-1). 40pp. The care, uses, and breeds of horses are introduced in this copiously illustrated book with foldout sections. (Rev: SLJ 8/97) [636.1]

20007 Patent, Dorothy Hinshaw. *Horses* (3–5). Illus. by William Munoz. 1994, Carolrhoda LB $19.93 (0-87614-766-X). 48pp. This excellent introduction to the world of horses includes material on their history, types, behavior, and current uses. (Rev: BCCB 3/94; BL 4/1/94; SLJ 3/94) [636.1]

20008 Patent, Dorothy Hinshaw. *Where the Wild Horses Roam* (PS–2). Illus. by William Munoz. 1989, Houghton $15.95 (0-89919-507-5). 72pp. The history of wild horses that roam the West and the problems they cause. (Rev: BL 7/89; HB 9–10/89; SLJ 8/89) [639.9]

20009 Peterson, Cris. *Horsepower: The Wonder of Draft Horses* (K–4). Photos by Alvis Upitis. 1997, Boyds Mills $16.95 (1-56397-626-9). A photo-essay that introduces the history, physical characteristics, and functions of the draft horse, with special coverage on Belgians, Percherons, and Clydesdales. (Rev: BCCB 4/97; SLJ 4/97) [636.1]

20010 Petty, Kate. *Horse Heroes* (2–4). Illus. Series: Eyewitness Reader. 1999, DK $12.95 (0-7894-4001-6); paper $3.95 (0-7894-4000-8). 48pp. This is an exciting collection of true stories about amazing horses including Roy Rogers' Trigger, the Royal Lipizzaners, and Paddy of Buckingham Palace fame. (Rev: BL 7/99; HBG 10/99) [636.1]

20011 Posell, Elsa. *Horses* (2–3). Illus. 1981, Children's LB $21.00 (0-516-01623-7); paper $5.50 (0-516-41623-5). 48pp. Color photographs and simple text are used in this introductory volume.

20012 Price, Steven D. *The Kids' Book of the American Quarter Horse* (3–5). Illus. 2000, Lyons Pr. paper $19.95 (1-55821-975-7). 159pp. As well as telling how to choose, care for, and ride quarter horses, this account tells their history and explains the functions of the American Quarter Horse Association. (Rev: BL 2/1/00) [636.1]

20013 Pritchard, Louise. *My Pony Book* (3–7). Photos by Bob Langrish. 1998, DK $15.95 (0-7894-2810-5). 61pp. This book describes such pony breeds as the Shetland and Connemara and supplies information on their physical characteristics, history, and behavior. (Rev: HBG 10/98; SLJ 7/98) [636.1]

20014 Ryden, Hope. *Wild Horses I Have Known* (4–7). Illus. 1999, Clarion $18.00 (0-395-77520-5). 88pp. The author's spectacular photographs of wild horses highlight this account of these creatures of the West and their amazing behavior. (Rev: BCCB 4/99; BL 4/15/99; HB 3–4/99; HBG 10/99; SLJ 4/99) [599.665]

20015 Silverstein, Alvin, et al. *The Mustang* (4–7). Illus. Series: Endangered in America. 1997, Millbrook LB $22.40 (0-7613-0048-1). 64pp. Examines the life cycle and behavior of the mustang, the reasons it has become endangered, and the techniques employed to ensure survival. (Rev: BL 3/15/97; SLJ 6/97) [599.72]

20016 Stefoff, Rebecca. *Horses* (5–8). Illus. Series: AnimalWays. 2000, Marshall Cavendish $19.95 (0-7614-1139-9). 112pp. A well-illustrated account that describes the physical and behavioral characteristics of horses, their place in the classification system, and their relationships with humans. (Rev: BL 1/1–15/01) [599.884]

20017 van der Linde, Laurel. *From Mustangs to Movie Stars: Five True Horse Legends of Our Time* (4–7). Illus. 1995, Millbrook LB $23.40 (1-56294-456-8). 71pp. Biographies of five famous horses are recounted, from the racer Native Dancer to Cass Olé, who was the star of the film *The Black Stallion*. (Rev: BCCB 12/95; SLJ 12/95) [636.1]

20018 *The Visual Dictionary of the Horse* (5–8). Illus. Series: Eyewitness Visual Dictionaries. 1994, DK $18.95 (1-56458-504-2). 64pp. This pictorial study includes information on anatomy, breeds, grooming, racing, jumping, and equipment. (Rev: BCCB 7–8/94; SLJ 7/94) [636]

20019 Zeaman, John. *Climbing onto the Horse's Back* (4–6). Illus. Series: Before They Were Pets. 1998, Watts LB $24.00 (0-531-20349-2). 64pp. This book explains the evolution of the horse, its changing role in human history, and the important breeds that are present today. (Rev: BL 12/1/98; HBG 3/99; SLJ 3/99) [636.1]

Zoos and Marine Aquariums

20020 Aliki. *My Visit to the Aquarium* (K–3). Illus. 1993, HarperCollins LB $15.89 (0-06-021459-7). 40pp. Facts about fish are given as a boy tours an aquarium and examines various species. (Rev: BL 10/15/93; SLJ 1/94*) [597]

20021 Aliki. *My Visit to the Zoo* (PS–2). Illus. 1997, HarperCollins LB $15.89 (0-06-024943-9). 40pp. A young girl acts as guide in a zoo and introduces the purposes of zoos as well as many of the animals that are kept there. (Rev: BL 7/97; HB 9–10/97; HBG 3/98; SLJ 10/97) [590]

20022 Altman, Joyce. *Dear Bronx Zoo* (3–6). Illus. by Sue Goldberg. 1992, Avon paper $3.50 (0-380-71649-6). 102pp. The answers to questions most frequently asked by Bronx Zoo visitors. (Rev: BL 1/1/91; SLJ 3/91) [590.74]

20023 Altman, Joyce. *Lunch at the Zoo: What Zoo Animals Eat and Why* (3–6). Illus. 2001, Holt $16.00 (0-8050-6070-7). 88pp. This outstanding science book goes behind the scenes at a zoo to show the care and medical expertise that goes into preparing and feeding the different animals. (Rev: BCCB 2/01; BL 12/1/00*; SLJ 2/01) [636]

20024 Gerstenfeld, Sheldon L. *Zoo Clues: Making the Most of Your Visit to the Zoo* (4–6). Illus. by Eldon C. Doty. 1993, Puffin paper $4.99 (0-140-32813-0). 113pp. This is a survey of 28 different groups of animals that are found in zoos. (Rev: SLJ 7/91) [590.74]

20025 Hanna, Jack. *Jungle Jack Hanna's What Zookeepers Do* (2–3). Illus. by Rick A. Prebeg. Series: Hello Reader! 1998, Scholastic paper $3.99 (0-590-67324-6). 48pp. A fascinating subject and dramatic photos make this easy-to-read book a popular one on zookeepers and their duties, such as feeding the tigers and caring for newly hatched eagle chicks. (Rev: BL 11/1/98) [636.088]

20026 McMillan, Bruce. *The Baby Zoo* (1–6). 1995, Scholastic paper $3.95 (0-590-44635-5). 40pp. A survey of 16 baby animals in two American zoos. (Rev: HB 3–4/92; SLJ 5/92) [599]

20027 Nagda, Ann Whitehead, and Cindy Bickel. *Tiger Math* (3–6). Illus. 2000, Holt $16.00 (0-8050-6248-3). 30pp. This account traces the growth and maturation of a Siberian tiger cub who was cared for at the Denver Zoo after his mother died when he was only ten weeks old. (Rev: BCCB 9/00; BL 10/1/00; HBG 3/01; SLJ 10/00) [511]

20028 Patent, Dorothy Hinshaw. *Back to the Wild* (4–6). Photos by William Munoz. 1997, Harcourt $18.00 (0-15-200280-4). 69pp. This account shows how present-day zoos are helping save endangered animals and gives four case studies where tamarins, red wolves, lemurs, and the black-footed ferret have been rescued. (Rev: SLJ 4/97) [590]

20029 Pfeffer, Wendy. *Popcorn Park Zoo: A Haven with a Heart* (3–6). Illus. by J. Gerard Smith. 1992, Simon & Schuster paper $16.95 (0-671-74589-1). 64pp. A unique zoo in New Jersey that cares for animals that are sick, old, hurt, abused, or unwanted. (Rev: BL 6/1/92; SLJ 7/92) [590]

20030 Rinard, Judith E. *Zoos Without Cages* (5–8). Illus. 1981, National Geographic LB $12.50 (0-87044-340-2). 104pp. An examination of zoos where the enclosures are like natural habitats.

20031 Yancey, Diane. *Zoos* (5–8). Illus. Series: Overview. 1995, Lucent LB $16.95 (1-56006-163-4). 128pp. A history of zoos explaining present-day practices and the controversy that surrounds them. (Rev: BL 6/1–15/95; SLJ 3/95) [590]

Botany

General and Miscellaneous

20032 Greenaway, Theresa. *The Plant Kingdom* (5–8). Illus. 1999, Raintree Steck-Vaughn LB $25.69 (0-8172-5886-8). 48pp. Using diagrams, sidebars, and color photos, this account introduces the basics of plant classification while also covering such topics as photosynthesis and plant reproduction. (Rev: BL 2/1/00) [580]

20033 Silverstein, Alvin, and Virginia Silverstein. *Photosynthesis* (5–9). Series: Science Concepts. 1998, Twenty-First Century LB $23.40 (0-7613-3000-3). 63pp. Photosynthesis is explained, with a history of the discoveries about the process and material on related issues including acid rain and the greenhouse effect. (Rev: HBG 3/99; SLJ 2/99) [581.1]

Flowers

20034 *Flowers* (PS–3). Illus. Series: First Discovery. 1993, Scholastic $11.95 (0-590-46383-7). 30pp. In this interactive book, various kinds of flowers and their parts are introduced. (Rev: BL 10/1/93; SLJ 8/93) [582.13]

20035 Holmes, Anita. *Flowers and Friends* (K–2). Series: We Can Read About — Science! 2000, Benchmark LB $14.95 (0-7614-1113-5). 32pp. An easy-to-read book that describes the process of pollination through the perception of various creatures. (Rev: HBG 3/01; SLJ 2/01) [582]

20036 Hood, Susan. *National Audubon Society First Field Guide to Wildflowers* (4–6). Illus. Series: First Field Guide. 1998, Scholastic $17.95 (0-590-05464-3); paper $10.95 (0-590-05486-4). 160pp. A general introduction to wildflowers — their names, their habitats — followed by descriptions of 50 common North American species. (Rev: BL 8/98; SLJ 8/98) [582.13]

20037 Johnson, Sylvia A. *Morning Glories* (4–7). Illus. 1985, Lerner LB $22.60 (0-8225-1462-1). 48pp. Color photographs display the stages of this plant's development. (Rev: BCCB 3/86; BL 4/15/86; SLJ 4/86)

20038 Johnson, Sylvia A. *Roses Red, Violets Blue: Why Flowers Have Colors* (5–8). Illus. by Yuko Sato. 1991, Lerner LB $23.95 (0-8225-1594-6). 64pp. An explanation of the role color plays in the lives of plants. (Rev: BCCB 12/91; BL 12/1/91) [582.13]

20039 Murray, Peter. *Roses* (3–5). Illus. Series: Nature Books. 1995, Child's World LB $22.79 (1-56766-192-0). 32pp. The beauty and variety of roses are highlighted in stunning full-page photographs and large-type text. (Rev: BL 12/15/95) [583]

20040 Ryden, Hope. *Wildflowers Around the Year* (4–6). Illus. 2001, Clarion $17.00 (0-395-85814-3). 48pp. A handsome book on wildflowers that gives details on characteristics, uses in food or medicine, and fertilization. (Rev: BL 3/1/01) [582.13]

20041 Winner, Cherie. *The Sunflower Family* (4–7). Illus. 1996, Carolrhoda LB $23.93 (1-57505-007-2); paper $7.95 (1-57505-029-3). 48pp. Growth patterns, structures, and reproduction are topics covered in this account of the sunflower family, including thistles, daisies, and asters. (Rev: BL 10/1/96; SLJ 10/96) [583]

20042 Zim, Herbert S., and Alexander C. Martin. *Flowers* (5–8). Illus. 1991, Western paper $21.27 (0-307-64054-X). 160pp. An identification guide that describes many species in words and pictures.

Foods and Farming

GENERAL

20043 Lampton, Christopher. *Famine* (4–6). Illus. Series: Disaster Book. 1994, Millbrook LB $19.90 (1-56294-317-0). 48pp. The causes and effects of famines are covered, with information on some historic disasters. (Rev: BL 6/1–15/94; SLJ 4/94) [363.8]

20044 Morgan, Sally. *Flowers, Trees, and Fruits* (1–4). Illus. Series: Young Discoverers. 1996, Kingfisher paper $6.95 (0-7534-5032-1). 32pp. In addition to general information about plants, this account suggests many simple activities. (Rev: BL 12/1/96) [581]

20045 Solheim, James. *It's Disgusting — and We Ate It! True Food Facts from Around the World — and Throughout History!* (4–6). Illus. by Eric Brace. 1998, Simon & Schuster $16.00 (0-689-80675-2). 48pp. With zany illustrations and some poems and recipes, this book explores food trivia and uncovers little-known facts such as the use of seaweed in ice cream. (Rev: BCCB 4/98; BL 4/1/98; HBG 10/98; SLJ 6/98) [641.3]

FARMS, RANCHES, AND FARM ANIMALS

20046 Anderson, Joan. *The American Family Farm* (4–6). Illus. by George Ancona. 1989, Harcourt $18.95 (0-15-203025-5). 96pp. A photo tour of a dairy farm. (Rev: BCCB 11/89; BL 11/15/89; SLJ 10/89*) [630.973]

20047 Artley, Bob. *Once Upon a Farm* (4–9). Illus. by author. 2000, Pelican $21.95 (1-56554-753-5). 127pp. Fine watercolors accompany a readable look at the seasons as experienced by the author while growing up on a farm in Iowa. (Rev: SLJ 12/00) [630]

20048 Bell, Rachael. *Cows* (K–3). Series: Farm Animals. 2000, Heinemann LB $13.95 (1-57572-529-0). 32pp. Using double-page spreads, this book introduces cows and their uses as a source of meat and milk. Also use *Pigs* (2000). (Rev: HBG 3/01; SLJ 7/00) [630]

20049 Bial, Raymond. *Portrait of a Farm Family* (4–7). Illus. 1995, Houghton $15.95 (0-395-69936-3). 48pp. A behind-the-scenes look at a dairy farm in Illinois that gives details on day-to-day operations and problems. (Rev: BCCB 10/95; BL 9/1/95*; HB 11–12/95; SLJ 12/95) [338.1]

20050 Damerow, Gail. *Your Chickens: A Kid's Guide to Raising and Showing* (4–7). Illus. 1993, Storey paper $14.95 (0-88266-823-4). 160pp. A straightforward, practical guide on raising prize-winning chickens that is both thorough and filled with information. (Rev: BL 5/15/94; SLJ 1/94) [636.5]

20051 Damerow, Gail. *Your Goats: A Kid's Guide to Raising and Showing* (4–7). Illus. 1993, Storey paper $16.95 (0-88266-825-0). 176pp. This is a complete guide to raising, breeding, and showing goats, with many useful tips and helpful illustrations. (Rev: BL 5/15/94; SLJ 1/94) [636.3]

20052 Drake, Jane, and Ann Love. *Farming* (3–4). Illus. by Pat Cupples. Series: America at Work. 1998, Kids Can $12.95 (1-55074-451-8). 31pp. Factual information about a vegetable farm and a cattle ranch, including chores, processes, and equipment, is introduced by fictional children who live on these farms and ranches. (Rev: HBG 3/99; SLJ 12/98) [630]

20053 Fowler, Allan. *If It Weren't for Farmers* (1–2). Illus. Series: Rookie Readers. 1993, Children's LB $19.00 (0-516-06009-0). 32pp. For beginning readers, this is an introduction to what farmers do and how various foods are grown. (Rev: BL 3/1/94) [630]

20054 Fowler, Allan. *Thanks to Cows* (1–2). Illus. Series: Rookie Readers. 1992, Children's LB $19.00 (0-516-04924-0). 32pp. With large color photos and simple text, this book introduces cattle and their importance. (Rev: BL 6/15/92) [636.2]

20055 Fowler, Allan. *Woolly Sheep and Hungry Goats* (1–2). Illus. Series: Rookie Readers. 1993, Children's Book Pr. LB $19.00 (0-516-06014-7). 32pp. Sheep and goats and their habits are introduced with a simple text, color pictures on each page, and a small format. (Rev: BL 9/1/93; SLJ 9/93) [636.3]

20056 Geisert, Bonnie, and Arthur Geisert. *Haystack* (K–3). Illus. 1995, Houghton $15.95 (0-395-69722-0). 32pp. The story of how haystacks are made and of their uses on farms. (Rev: BCCB 10/95; BL 9/15/95; HB 11–12/95; SLJ 9/95) [633.2]

20057 Gibbons, Gail. *Farming* (PS–2). Illus. by author. 1988, Holiday LB $16.95 (0-8234-0682-2); paper $6.95 (0-8234-0797-7). 32pp. Farm landscapes through the seasons. (Rev: BL 6/1/88; SLJ 8/88)

20058 Graff, Nancy P. *The Strength of the Hills: A Portrait of a Family Farm* (4–6). Illus. by Richard Howard. 1989, Little, Brown $14.95 (0-316-32277-6). 80pp. This account highlights life on a family dairy farm in Vermont. (Rev: BL 11/15/89; SLJ 4/90*) [338.1]

20059 Halley, Ned. *Farm* (4–8). Illus. Series: Eyewitness Books. 1996, Knopf $20.99 (0-679-98078-4). 63pp. This book takes one behind the scenes at a farm, explaining with many illustrations its inner workings and the problems and rewards involved in managing one. (Rev: BL 6/1–15/96; SLJ 7/96) [630]

20060 Hill, Lee S. *Farms Feed the World* (1–3). Series: Building Blocks Books. 1997, Carolrhoda LB $21.27 (1-57505-075-7). 32pp. This book takes the reader on a visit to many kinds of farms around the world, from a wheat field in Montana to a rice paddy in Indonesia. (Rev: BL 3/15/98; HBG 3/98) [630]

20061 Jacobsen, Karen. *Farm Animals* (4–6). Illus. by author. 1981, Children's LB $21.00 (0-516-01619-9). 48pp. Large typeface is used in this simple introduction with many color photographs.

20062 Kalman, Bobbie. *Hooray for Sheep Farming!* (K–3). Series: Hooray for Farming! 1997, Crabtree LB $19.96 (0-86505-655-2); paper $7.95 (0-86505-669-2). 32pp. This book describes the habits and physical structure of sheep, different kinds of wool, and the everyday routines on a sheep farm. (Rev: HBG 3/98; SLJ 4/98) [630]

20063 Miller, Sara S. *Chickens* (2–3). Series: True Books. 2000, Children's LB $22.00 (0-516-21576-0). 32pp. A simple introduction to chickens that describes their anatomy, uses, homes, and habits. (Rev: BL 1/1–15/01) [636.5]

20064 Miller, Sara S. *Cows* (2–3). Illus. Series: True Books. 2000, Children's LB $22.00 (0-516-21577-9). 48pp. Covers dairy cows and their domestication as well as giving information on dairy products and life on a dairy farm. (Rev: BL 1/1–15/01) [636.3]

20065 Miller, Sara S. *Goats* (2–3). Series: True Books. 2000, Children's LB $22.00 (0-516-21578-7). 32pp. A look at the life cycle of the goat, its habits, and its uses. (Rev: BL 1/1–15/01) [636.3]

20066 Miller, Sara S. *Pigs* (2–3). Series: True Books. 2000, Children's LB $22.00 (0-516-21579-5). 32pp. Using colorful pictures and a minimum of text, this farm animal is introduced with material on its anatomy, habits, and uses. (Rev: BL 1/1–15/01) [636.3]

20067 Miller, Sara S. *Sheep* (2–3). Illus. Series: True Books. 2000, Children's LB $22.00 (0-516-21580-9). 48pp. This book introduces sheep and sheep farming with material on the animal's use both for food and for wool. (Rev: BL 1/1–15/01) [636.3]

20068 Olney, Ross R. *The Farm Combine* (4–8). Illus. 1984, Walker LB $10.85 (0-8027-6568-8). 64pp. The development of the reaper and thrasher is discussed, with information on today's combine harvester.

20069 Peterson, Cris. *Century Farm: One Hundred Years on a Family Farm* (2–4). Illus. 1999, Boyds Mills $16.95 (1-56397-710-9). 32pp. Traces the changes in farm life over a century and includes material on the machinery used, the tasks performed, and the different farm animals. (Rev: BCCB 3/99; BL 3/1/99; HBG 10/99; SLJ 4/99) [636.2]

20070 Peterson, Cris. *Extra Cheese, Please! Mozzarella's Journey from Cow to Pizza* (PS–2). Illus. by Alvis Upitis. 1994, Boyds Mills $15.95 (1-56397-177-1). 30pp. Dairy farms and the treatment of dairy cattle are described in this explanation of how cheese is made. (Rev: BL 3/15/94; SLJ 4/94) [637.219]

20071 Rogers, Hal. *Milking Machines* (PS–K). Series: Farm Machines at Work. 2000, Child's World LB $21.36 (1-56766-753-8). 24pp. Color pictures and a brief text introduce milking machines, their parts, and their uses. Also use from the same series: *Combines*, *Plows*, and *Tractors* (all 2000). (Rev: BL 1/1–15/01; SLJ 1/01) [621]

20072 Smith, E. Boyd. *The Farm Book* (2–5). Illus. by author. 1982, Houghton paper $8.95 (0-395-

54951-5). 64pp. A picture book that details many activities associated with farm life.

20073 Wallace, Karen. *My Hen Is Dancing* (PS–1). Illus. by Anita Jeram. 1994, Candlewick $14.95 (1-56402-303-6). 32pp. The anatomy and habits of a chicken are explained simply with color drawings and large type. (Rev: BL 5/1/94; SLJ 7/94) [636.5]

20074 Willard, Nancy. *Cracked Corn and Snow Ice Cream* (4–6). Illus. 1997, Harcourt $18.00 (0-15-227250-X). 64pp. Farm life and the families of the author and illustrator are highlighted in this book that ushers in each season and month with photos, poems, and a list of important dates and festivals. (Rev: BL 11/1/97; HBG 3/98; SLJ 10/97) [031.02]

20075 Wolfman, Judy. *Life on a Pig Farm* (3–5). Illus. 1998, Carolrhoda $22.60 (1-57505-237-7). 48pp. This photo-essay describes life on a pig farm, as experienced by three sisters. (Rev: BL 10/15/98; HBG 3/99; SLJ 3/99) [636.4]

FOODS

20076 Back, Christine. *Bean and Plant* (1–3). Illus. 1986, Silver Burdett LB $15.95 (0-382-09286-4); paper $3.95 (0-382-24014-6). 25pp. A basic science book in full color telling how beans grow. (Rev: BL 1/1/87)

20077 Badt, Karin Luisa. *Pass the Bread!* (3–7). Illus. Series: A World of Difference. 1995, Children's LB $20.30 (0-516-08191-8). 32pp. Different kinds of bread found around the world are highlighted, as well as their methods of production and how they are related to their various cultures. (Rev: BL 7/95; SLJ 12/95) [394.1]

20078 Bryant-Mole, Karen. *Food* (PS–3). Illus. Series: Picture This! 1997, Rigby $18.50 (1-57572-150-3). 24pp. Various kinds of food are introduced, cooking methods are discussed, and the principles of good nutrition are mentioned. (Rev: BL 10/15/97; SLJ 12/97) [641.3]

20079 Burns, Diane L. *Cranberries: Fruit of the Bogs* (3–5). Illus. by Cheryl Walsh Bellville. 1994, Carolrhoda LB $22.60 (0-87614-822-4). 48pp. A book about cranberry growing and activities during and after harvesting. (Rev: BL 12/1/94; SLJ 3/95) [633.76]

20080 Burns, Diane L. *Sugaring Season: Making Maple Syrup* (1–5). Illus. 1990, Carolrhoda $22.60 (0-87614-420-2); paper $5.95 (0-87614-554-3). 32pp. Crisp photos and good diagrams help to explain the maple syrup process. (Rev: BL 11/1/90; SLJ 12/90) [664]

20081 Chandler, Gary, and Kevin Graham. *Natural Foods and Products* (4–8). Illus. Series: Making a Better World. 1996, Twenty-First Century LB $20.40 (0-8050-4623-2). 64pp. This work discusses genetically engineered foods, safe eco-friendly methods of growing crops, and companies that engage in safe practices. (Rev: BL 12/15/96; SLJ 1/97) [333.76]

20082 Charles, Oz. *How Does Soda Get into the Bottle?* (2–4). Illus. 1996, Silver Burdett paper $4.95 (0-382-24375-7). 32pp. A brief photo-essay

on this manufacturing process that takes the reader into a bottling plant. (Rev: BL 4/15/88)

20083 Charlip, Remy. *Peanut Butter Party: Including the History, Uses, and Future of Peanut Butter* (K–4). Illus. by author. 1999, Tricycle Pr. $14.95 (1-883672-69-4). Peanut butter is celebrated in a book that covers its history and outlines such activities as recipes for foods with peanut butter, edible arts and crafts, riddles, games, a one-act play on the subject, and a series of clever illustrations. (Rev: BCCB 7–8/99; HBG 10/99; SLJ 6/99) [641.3]

20084 Cooper, Jason. *Beef* (1–3). Series: Farm to Market. 1997, Rourke LB $14.60 (0-86625-617-2). 24pp. This book describes how North American beef cattle are raised, slaughtered, processed, and marketed. (Rev: SLJ 6/98) [641]

20085 Cooper, Jason. *Dairy Products* (1–3). Series: Farm to Market. 1997, Rourke LB $14.60 (0-86625-619-9). 24pp. After a description of how dairy cattle are raised, this book covers their products, how they are processed, and how they are marketed. (Rev: SLJ 6/98) [637]

20086 Cooper, Jason. *Poultry* (1–3). Series: Farm to Market. 1997, Rourke LB $14.60 (0-86625-618-0). 24pp. This book shows how different types of poultry are raised, processed, and marketed. (Rev: SLJ 6/98) [598]

20087 D'Amico, Joan, and Karen Eich Drummond. *The Science Chef: 100 Fun Food Experiments and Recipes for Kids* (4–6). Illus. 1994, Wiley paper $12.95 (0-471-31045-X). 192pp. Simple experiments introduce various properties of foods and give youngsters a chance to be cooks. (Rev: BL 11/1/94; SLJ 12/94) [641.3]

20088 dePaola, Tomie. *The Popcorn Book* (1–3). Illus. 1978, Holiday LB $15.95 (0-8234-0314-9); paper $6.95 (0-8234-0533-8). 32pp. While Tony makes a plate of popcorn, Tiny relates interesting facts about this delicious food.

20089 Egan, Robert. *From Wheat to Pasta* (PS–2). Series: Changes. 1997, Children's LB $24.00 (0-516-20709-1). 32pp. Beginning with a wheat farm and the production of flour, this account tells about the origins of pasta and explains its different shapes. (Rev: BL 10/15/97; SLJ 9/97) [664.755]

20090 Erdosh, George. *The African American Kitchen: Food for Body and Soul* (4–7). Series: The Library of African American Arts and Culture. 1999, Rosen LB $17.95 (0-8239-1850-5). 64pp. Traces the origins and evolution of "soul food" in American culture and includes a number of recipes. (Rev: SLJ 8/99) [394.1]

20091 Erlbach, Arlene. *Soda Pop* (3–6). Illus. 1994, Lerner LB $19.93 (0-8225-2386-8). 48pp. Tells about the origins, history, and manufacture of soda pop, with recipes for making various kinds at home. Also use *Peanut Butter* (1994). (Rev: BL 5/1/94) [663]

20092 Frost, Helen. *The Grain Group* (K–2). Series: Food Guide Pyramid. 2000, Capstone LB $13.25 (0-7368-0538-9). 24pp. This text for beginning readers introduces different grains and explains their importance in the food pyramid. (Rev: HBG 10/00; SLJ 10/00) [633.1]

20093 Gelman, Rita G. *Rice Is Life* (1–4). Illus. by Yangsook Choi. 2000, Holt $15.95 (0-8050-5719-6). 32pp. In original poems and nonfiction vignettes, the author tells of the importance of rice in the life and culture of the Balinese. (Rev: BL 5/15/00; HBG 10/00; SLJ 6/00) [633.1]

20094 Gibbons, Gail. *The Milk Makers* (1–4). Illus. 1985, Macmillan LB $16.00 (0-02-736640-5); paper $5.99 (0-689-71116-6). 32pp. Young readers learn all about cows and how milk is produced and distributed. (Rev: BCCB 5/85; BL 4/15/85; SLJ 4/85)

20095 Harbison, Elizabeth M. *Loaves of Fun: A History of Bread with Activities and Recipes from Around the World* (3–6). Illus. 1997, Chicago Review paper $12.95 (1-55652-311-4). 91pp. A history of bread from ancient times to the present day, with several activities and 24 recipes. (Rev: BL 5/1/97; SLJ 9/97) [641.8]

20096 Hartzog, John Daniel. *Everyday Science Experiments with Food* (PS–3). 2000, Rosen $19.33 (0-8239-5460-9). 24pp. The eight projects outlined in this simple science book include recipes for making butter and homemade soda. (Rev: SLJ 9/00) [641.3]

20097 Hausherr, Rosmarie. *What Food Is This?* (1–3). Illus. 1994, Scholastic $14.95 (0-590-46583-X). 40pp. Questions about common foods we eat are answered in simple text and luscious photos. (Rev: BCCB 5/94; BL 4/15/94; SLJ 5/94) [641.3]

20098 Hughes, Meredith S. *Cool as a Cucumber, Hot as a Pepper* (5–8). Illus. Series: Plants We Eat. 1999, Lerner LB $18.95 (0-8225-2832-0). 88pp. Cucumbers, peppers, and other foods are discussed in pictures and text with a history of each and some recipes. (Rev: BL 7/99; HBG 10/99; SLJ 8/99) [635]

20099 Hughes, Meredith S. *Flavor Foods: Spices and Herbs* (5–8). Series: Plants We Eat. 2000, Lerner LB $25.26 (0-8225-2835-5). 88pp. This book explains how roots, leaves, flowers, seeds, fruit, and bark of some plants are transformed in the seasonings that flavor so many dishes. (Rev: BL 7/00; HBG 10/00) [633.8]

20100 Hughes, Meredith S. *Glorious Grasses* (5–8). Series: Plants We Eat. 1999, Lerner $18.95 (0-8225-2831-2). 88pp. A description of the history, cultivation, processing, and dietary importance of wheat, rice, corn, millet, barley, oats, and rye, plus recipes and activities. (Rev: BL 7/99; HBG 10/99; SLJ 8/99) [633.1]

20101 Jaspersohn, William. *Ice Cream* (3–5). Illus. 1988, Macmillan LB $14.95 (0-02-747821-1). 48pp. How ice cream is made at the Ben and Jerry's ice cream plant in Vermont. (Rev: BL 11/1/88; SLJ 12/88)

20102 Johnson, Sylvia A. *Wheat* (4–6). Illus. by Masaharu Susuki. 1990, Lerner LB $21.50 (0-8225-1490-7). 48pp. The life cycle of the wheat plant is described, with material on harvesting and processing. (Rev: BL 4/15/90; SLJ 8/90) [633.1]

20103 Jones, Charlotte F. *Eat Your Words: A Fascinating Look at the Language of Food* (4–7). Illus. 1999, Delacorte $16.95 (0-385-32575-4). 87pp. Interesting facts and trivia about food are given here, such as the origin of terms like couch potato, eating humble pie, and sandwich. (Rev: BCCB 9/99; BL 4/15/99; HBG 10/99; SLJ 7/99) [641]

20104 Keller, Stella. *Ice Cream* (PS). Illus. by John Holm. Series: Real Readers. 1989, Raintree Steck-Vaughn LB $21.40 (0-8172-3523-X). 32pp. This easily read account describes the history of ice cream. (Rev: BL 2/1/90) [637.4]

20105 King, Hazel. *Milk and Yogurt* (3–5). Series: Food in Focus. 1998, Heinemann LB $15.95 (1-57572-657-2). 32pp. This work gives a history of milk and yogurt, plus material on their processing, nutritional value, nutrients, and related experiments and recipes. (Rev: SLJ 2/99) [636.2]

20106 Knight, Bertram T. *From Cow to Ice Cream* (PS–2). Illus. Series: Changes. 1997, Children's LB $24.00 (0-516-20706-7). 32pp. This book explains how ice cream is made, including the cow's role, pasteurization, the ice cream factory, the sugar refinery, and flavorings. (Rev: BL 10/15/97; SLJ 9/97) [637]

20107 Landau, Elaine. *Wheat* (2–4). Series: True Books. 1999, Children's LB $21.50 (0-516-21029-7). 48pp. Where wheat is grown, its appearance, uses, and nutritional value are topics covered in this colorful introduction. (Rev: BL 10/15/99) [633.1]

20108 Lasky, Kathryn. *Sugaring Time* (4–7). Illus. 1998, Center for Applied Research paper $4.95 (0-87628-350-4). 64pp. Through photos and text, the process of maple sugar production in New England is described.

20109 Llewellyn, Claire. *Chocolate* (K–2). Series: What's for Lunch? 1998, Children's LB $20.00 (0-516-20837-3). 32pp. A clear, simple look at chocolate, how it is made, its uses, and how it is eaten. (Rev: BL 6/1–15/98; HBG 10/98) [641.3]

20110 Llewellyn, Claire. *Milk* (K–2). Series: What's for Lunch? 1998, Children's LB $20.00 (0-516-20840-3). 32pp. The production of milk, how it is processed, and how it is used are topics covered in this simple account illustrated with many color photographs. (Rev: BL 6/1–15/98; HBG 10/98) [637]

20111 Llewellyn, Claire. *Peanuts* (K–2). Series: What's for Lunch? 1998, Children's LB $20.00 (0-516-20839-X). 32pp. This heavily illustrated account describes how peanuts are grown, harvested, and consumed. (Rev: BL 6/1–15/98; HBG 10/98; SLJ 9/98) [641.3]

20112 Llewellyn, Claire. *What's for Lunch? Bread* (K–2). Series: What's for Lunch? 1999, Children's LB $20.50 (0-516-21546-9). 32pp. Different kinds of breads, how and where they are made, their composition, and food value are topics introduced in this simple book. (Rev: BL 10/15/99) [641.8]

20113 Llewellyn, Claire. *What's for Lunch? Eggs* (K–2). Series: What's for Lunch? 1999, Children's LB $20.50 (0-516-21547-7). 32pp. Where eggs come from, how they are cooked, and their nutritional value are discussed in this book using two-page spreads each consisting of a color photo and a few lines of large-type text. (Rev: BL 10/15/99) [641]

20114 Mandell, Muriel. *Simple Kitchen Experiments: Learning Science with Everyday Foods* (4–6). Illus. 1994, Sterling paper $4.95 (0-8069-8415-5). 128pp. The kitchen becomes a chemistry lab in this book of simple experiments and projects, such as degassing beans. (Rev: BL 5/1/94; SLJ 8/93) [641.3]

20115 Martino, Teresa. *Pizza!* (PS). Illus. by Brigid Faranda. Series: Real Readers. 1989, Raintree Steck-Vaughn LB $21.40 (0-8172-3533-7). 32pp. This easy-to-read account describes the development of pizza from its beginnings 1,000 years ago. (Rev: BL 2/1/90) [641.8]

20116 Meltzer, Milton. *Food* (4–8). Illus. 1998, Millbrook LB $23.90 (0-7613-0354-5). 96pp. A fascinating account that traces food history and shows the relationship between food and how we live. (Rev: BL 1/1–15/99; HBG 3/99; SLJ 1/99) [641.3]

20117 Micucci, Charles. *The Life and Times of the Peanut* (1–4). Illus. 1997, Houghton $16.00 (0-395-72289-6). 32pp. A lively combination of words and pictures that describe the peanut, where it is grown, and its many uses. (Rev: BCCB 5/97; BL 5/1/97*; SLJ 5/97) [641.3]

20118 Nottridge, Rhoda. *Sugars* (3–6). Illus. Series: Food Facts. 1993, Carolrhoda LB $19.93 (0-87614-796-1). 32pp. Covers such topics as the various forms of sugars, the ways they are made, and their uses, with some simple recipes and activities. (Rev: SLJ 10/93) [613.2]

20119 Paulsen, Gary. *The Tortilla Factory* (1–4). Illus. by Ruth W. Paulsen. 1995, Harcourt $16.00 (0-15-292876-6). 32pp. Simple text and paintings show how kernels of corn become flour and eventually tortillas. (Rev: BL 6/1–15/95; HB 7–8/95; SLJ 7/95) [641.8]

20120 Peters, Celeste A. *Peppers, Popcorn, and Pizza: The Science of Food* (3–5). Series: Science@Work. 1999, Raintree Steck-Vaughn LB $25.69 (0-7398-0136-8). 48pp. This account illustrates how food is related to everyday life through technology, careers, society, and the environment. (Rev: SLJ 3/00) [641]

20121 Peterson, Cris. *Harvest Year* (1–3). Illus. by Alvis Upitis. 1996, Boyds Mills $15.95 (1-56397-571-8). 28pp. Using a month-by-month arrangement, various crops grown in the United States are highlighted. (Rev: BL 9/15/96; SLJ 11/96) [641]

20122 Powell, Jillian. *Milk* (3–5). Illus. Series: Everyone Eats. 1997, Raintree Steck-Vaughn LB $25.69 (0-8172-4766-1). 32pp. This book introduces milk from different animals, but it focuses on the production, uses, and nutritional value of cow's milk. (Rev: SLJ 8/97) [636.2]

20123 Powell, Jillian. *Pasta* (1–4). Illus. Series: Everyone Eats. 1997, Raintree Steck-Vaughn LB $25.69 (0-8172-4760-2). 32pp. A tour of a pasta-producing facility and a guide to the various shapes of pasta highlight this account, which includes a few tasty recipes. (Rev: SLJ 7/97) [664]

20124 Ridgewell, Jenny. *Fruit and Vegetables* (3–5). Series: Food in Focus. 1998, Heinemann LB $15.95 (1-57572-656-4). 32pp. A history of fruits and vegetables is given with material on their cultivation, food value, and processing as well as recipes and a few experiments. (Rev: SLJ 2/99) [634]

20125 Ripley, Catherine. *Why Does Popcorn Pop? and Other Kitchen Questions* (PS–3). Illus. by Scot Ritchie. Series: Question and Answer Storybook. 1997, Owl $17.95 (1-895688-70-1); paper $6.95 (1-895688-71-X). 32pp. Everyday questions about food are posed, with answers on the same page, in this delightfully illustrated book. (Rev: BL 12/1/97; SLJ 2/98) [500]

20126 Robson, Pam. *Honey* (K–2). Illus. Series: What's for Lunch? 1998, Children's LB $20.00 (0-516-20825-X). 32pp. How bees make honey, how it is gathered and processed, and how it is consumed are some of the topics covered in this book illustrated with color photographs. (Rev: BL 6/1–15/98; HBG 10/98) [638]

20127 Robson, Pam. *Rice* (K–2). Series: What's for Lunch? 1998, Children's LB $20.00 (0-516-20824-1). 32pp. A clearly illustrated book that tells how rice is planted, cultivated, and harvested, and its usefulness as a food. (Rev: BL 6/1–15/98; HBG 10/98) [633.1]

20128 Tate, Lindsey. *Teatime with Emma Buttersnap* (K–4). Illus. by Linda Bronson. 1998, Holt $16.95 (0-8050-5476-6). During the course of preparations for a tea party given by Emma Buttersnap and her Aunt Pru, the reader learns about the origins, varieties, and importance of tea. (Rev: BL 11/1/98; HBG 3/99; SLJ 12/98) [641.5]

20129 Thomson, Peggy. *Siggy's Spaghetti Works* (1–3). Illus. by Gloria Kamen. 1993, Morrow $13.93 (0-688-11374-5). 32pp. During a tour of a spaghetti factory, seven kids learn how pasta is made. (Rev: BL 10/1/93; SLJ 1/94) [664]

20130 Thomson, Ruth. *Rice* (3–5). Illus. by Prodeepta Das. Series: Threads. 1990, Garrett LB $15.93 (0-944483-71-2). 26pp. The story of rice, from its growth in paddies to its uses in many cultures. (Rev: BL 2/1/91; SLJ 5/91) [633.1]

20131 Ventura, Piero. *Food: Its Evolution Through the Ages* (4–8). Illus. by author. 1994, Houghton $16.95 (0-395-66790-9). 64pp. A history of food, food preparation, and methods of preservation are presented in a well-organized, visually attractive way. (Rev: SLJ 11/94) [664]

20132 Wardlaw, Lee. *Bubblemania* (4–8). 1997, Simon & Schuster paper $4.99 (0-689-81719-3). 176pp. Provides a thorough history of chewing gum and describes how gum is made, marketed, and distributed. (Rev: BL 10/1/97; SLJ 1/98) [641.3]

20133 Wardlaw, Lee. *We All Scream for Ice Cream: The Scoop on America's Favorite Dessert* (4–7). Illus. by Sandra Forrest. 2000, HarperTrophy paper $4.95 (0-380-80250-3). 216pp. A history of this frozen dessert from ancient times to the present with a concentration on modern times and such variations as Eskimo pies and the Good Humor business. (Rev: SLJ 11/00) [637]

20134 Watts, Barrie. *Tomato* (PS–3). Illus. 1990, Silver Burdett LB $15.95 (0-382-24008-1). 25pp. The growth of a tomato plant is shown above and below ground. (Rev: BL 6/15/90; SLJ 9/90) [635]

20135 *What Makes Popcorn Pop? First Questions and Answers About Food* (K–2). Series: Library of First Questions and Answers. 1994, Time Life $14.95 (0-7835-0862-X). 47pp. Cartoonlike illustrations help answer such questions about food as how potato chips are made and why Swiss cheese has holes. (Rev: SLJ 8/94) [641]

20136 Woods, Samuel G. *Chocolate: From Start to Finish* (3–5). Photos by Gale Zucker. Series: Made in the USA. 1999, Blackbirch LB $16.95 (1-56711-391-5). 32pp. An attractive book that takes the reader to a chocolate factory in Pennsylvania where they see the manufacturing process from raw material to finished product. (Rev: HBG 3/00; SLJ 2/00) [633.7]

20137 Young, Robert. *The Chewing Gum Book* (3–5). Illus. 1989, Macmillan LB $12.95 (0-87518-401-4). 72pp. Some related topics include history, production, ingredients, and effects on health. (Rev: BL 9/1/89; SLJ 11/89) [664]

20138 Zubrowski, Bernie. *Soda Science: Designing and Testing Soft Drinks* (5–8). Illus. 1997, Morrow $14.93 (0-688-13917-5). 96pp. More than 50 experiments explore the properties of soft drinks and give directions for producing and bottling one's own product. (Rev: BL 8/97; SLJ 10/97) [641.8]

FRUITS

20139 Coldrey, Jennifer. *Strawberry* (K–3). Illus. 1989, Silver Burdett LB $15.95 (0-382-09801-3). 25pp. This simple account traces the development of the strawberry and describes how the use of runners creates new plants. (Rev: SLJ 1/90) [582]

20140 Davies, Kay, and Wendy Oldfield. *My Apple* (PS–1). Illus. by Fiona Pragoff. Series: First Step Science. 1994, Gareth Stevens LB $21.27 (0-8368-1114-3). 32pp. Introduces the characteristics of an apple, its parts, and its uses. Also use *My Drum* (1994). (Rev: BL 2/15/95) [634]

20141 Farmer, Jacqueline. *Bananas!* (2–4). Illus. by Page Eastburn O'Rourke. 1999, Charlesbridge LB $15.95 (0-88106-114-X); paper $6.95 (0-88106-115-8). Plenty of information about bananas is given in this book, including how and where they grow, their varieties, how they are shipped and stored, and their nutritional value, plus simple recipes. (Rev: HBG 3/00; SLJ 3/00) [634]

20142 Frost, Helen. *The Fruit Group* (K–2). Series: Food Guide Pyramid. 2000, Capstone LB $13.25 (0-7368-0537-0). 24pp. This easy-to-read guide to good health through eating properly introduces the fruit group and gives examples. (Rev: HBG 10/00; SLJ 10/00) [634]

20143 Gibbons, Gail. *Apples* (2–3). Illus. 2000, Holiday $16.95 (0-8234-1497-3). 32pp. This introduction to apples includes information on their history, varieties, parts, and development from blossom to fruit. (Rev: BL 8/00; HBG 3/01; SLJ 9/00) [634]

20144 Goldsen, Louise. *Fruit* (PS–2). Illus. by P. M. Valet. Series: First Discovery. 1991, Scholastic paper $12.95 (0-590-45233-9). Through the use of overlays, several kinds of fruit are depicted in various stages, such as the ripening of an apple. (Rev: SLJ 6/92) [641]

20145 Hughes, Meredith S. *Tall and Tasty: Fruit Trees* (5–8). Series: Plants We Eat. 2000, Lerner LB $25.26 (0-8225-2837-1). 80pp. This book explores the world of apples, peaches, mangoes, and other fruits that grow on trees and explains each one's life cycle, and how the fruit has migrated during its history. (Rev: BL 4/15/00; HBG 10/00) [641.3]

20146 Hughes, Meredith S. *Yes, We Have Bananas: Fruits from Shrubs and Vines* (5–8). Series: Plants We Eat. 1999, Lerner LB $22.26 (0-8225-2836-3). 80pp. A fascinating introduction to bananas, pineapples, grapes, berries, and melons with material on how and where they grow, their cultivation and marketing, plus fun recipes and activities. (Rev: BL 11/15/99; HBG 3/00; SLJ 3/00) [641]

20147 Johnson, Sylvia A. *Apple Trees* (5–8). Illus. by Hiro Koike. 1983, Lerner LB $22.60 (0-8225-1479-6). 48pp. The story of the apple tree and seed and fruit formation.

20148 Landau, Elaine. *Apples* (2–4). Illus. Series: True Books. 1999, Children's LB $21.50 (0-516-21024-6). 48pp. This book gives a history of apples, shows how they grow, introduces different species, and supplies a few simple recipes. (Rev: BL 10/15/99) [634]

20149 Landau, Elaine. *Bananas* (2–4). Series: True Books. 2000, Children's paper $6.95 (0-516-26574-1). 48pp. Color photos and a simple text are used to introduce bananas, where they are grown, and their nutritional value. (Rev: BL 10/15/99) [641]

20150 Lember, Barbara Hirsch. *A Book of Fruit* (PS–K). Illus. 1994, Ticknor $14.95 (0-395-66989-8). 32pp. Expressive photographs are used to introduce 14 fruits and where they grow. (Rev: BCCB 2/95; BL 7/94; SLJ 9/94) [634]

20151 Llewellyn, Claire. *What's for Lunch? Oranges* (K–2). Series: What's for Lunch? 1999, Children's LB $20.50 (0-516-21548-5). 32pp. The growth of oranges, their appearance, uses, and food value are discussed in this simple book with many color photos and concise text. (Rev: BL 10/15/99) [641.3]

20152 McMillan, Bruce. *Apples, How They Grow* (3–7). Illus. 1979, Houghton $18.00 (0-395-27806-6). 48pp. A well-presented work on the life cycle and uses of the apple, as revealed in a series of captioned photographs.

20153 Maestro, Betsy. *How Do Apples Grow?* (5–8). Illus. by Giulio Maestro. Series: Let's-Read-and-Find-Out. 1992, HarperCollins LB $15.89 (0-06-020056-1). 32pp. The development of the apple from bud to fruit. (Rev: BL 12/15/91; HB 1–2/92; SLJ 2/92) [582]

20154 Powell, Jillian. *Fruit* (1–4). Illus. Series: Everyone Eats. 1997, Raintree Steck-Vaughn LB $25.69 (0-8172-4765-3). 32pp. Describes how fruit are grown, and some of the varieties, legends, and traditional customs surrounding them, with a few tasty recipes. (Rev: SLJ 7/97) [634]

20155 Robinson, Fay. *We Love Fruit!* (1–2). Illus. Series: Rookie Readers. 1992, Children's LB $19.00 (0-516-06006-6). 32pp. Various kinds of fruit are pictured in color photos and identified in a simple text. An oversized edition of this title is available. (Rev: BL 12/15/92; SLJ 2/93) [641.3]

20156 Robson, Pam. *Banana* (K–2). Series: What's for Lunch? 1998, Children's LB $20.00 (0-516-20826-8). 32pp. This simple reader tells how bananas are grown, harvested, and used. (Rev: BL 6/1–15/98; HBG 10/98) [634]

20157 Watts, Barrie. *Apple Tree* (PS–2). Illus. 1987, Silver Burdett LB $15.95 (0-382-09436-0). 24pp. Photos help to show the annual cycle of an apple tree. (Rev: BL 11/15/87)

20158 *Why Are Pineapples Prickly?* (PS–3). Illus. Series: Why. 1997, DK $9.95 (0-7894-1530-5). 24pp. Using a question-and-answer format, this account discusses various plants and their characteristics. (Rev: BL 8/97; SLJ 8/97) [641.3]

NUTRITION

20159 Inglis, Jane. *Fiber* (4–6). Illus. Series: Food Facts. 1993, Carolrhoda LB $19.93 (0-87614-793-7). 32pp. This nutrition book focuses on the natural fiber the body needs and how to obtain it. (Rev: BL 11/15/93; SLJ 10/93) [613.2]

20160 Inglis, Jane. *Proteins* (3–6). Illus. Series: Food Facts. 1993, Carolrhoda LB $19.93 (0-87614-780-5). 32pp. After introducing proteins' structure and uses, this book outlines simple experiments and recipes. (Rev: SLJ 10/93) [574.19]

20161 Kalbacken, Joan. *The Food Pyramid* (2–4). Illus. Series: True Books. 1998, Children's LB $21.00 (0-516-20756-3). 48pp. This book explains the various levels of the food pyramid and its use in meal planning. (Rev: BL 7/98; HBG 10/98; SLJ 8/98) [613.2]

20162 Kalbacken, Joan. *Food Safety* (2–4). Illus. Series: True Books. 1998, Children's LB $21.00 (0-516-20757-1). 48pp. This book describes various food-borne illnesses, such as salmonella and trichinosis, and shows how proper food preparation can prevent these illnesses. (Rev: BL 7/98; HBG 10/98) [615.9]

20163 Kalbacken, Joan. *Vitamins and Minerals* (2–4). Illus. Series: True Books. 1998, Children's LB $21.00 (0-516-20758-X). 48pp. This book describes vitamins and minerals, their nutritional importance, and the various foods in which they are found. (Rev: BL 7/98; HBG 10/98; SLJ 8/98) [613.2]

20164 Leedy, Loreen. *The Edible Pyramid: Good Eating Every Day* (K–2). Illus. 1994, Holiday LB $16.95 (0-8234-1126-5). 30pp. A waiter in a restaurant introduces the nutritional pyramid that the U.S. Department of Agriculture has developed. (Rev: BCCB 2/95; BL 11/15/94; SLJ 4/95) [613.2]

20165 Nottridge, Rhoda. *Additives* (4–6). Illus. Series: Food Facts. 1993, Carolrhoda LB $19.93 (0-87614-794-5). 32pp. The value of such food additives as preservatives and flavorings is discussed, with an analysis of their possible harmful effects. (Rev: BL 11/15/93; SLJ 10/93) [664]

20166 Nottridge, Rhoda. *Fats* (4–6). Illus. Series: Food Facts. 1993, Lerner LB $19.93 (0-87614-779-1). 32pp. Introduces saturated and unsaturated fats and tells how much should be consumed in the daily diet. (Rev: BL 11/15/93; SLJ 10/93) [613.2]

20167 Nottridge, Rhoda. *Vitamins* (3–6). Illus. Series: Food Facts. 1993, Carolrhoda LB $19.93 (0-87614-795-3). 32pp. This book introduces the classification of vitamins, where they are found, their properties and uses, and some experiments and recipes connected with vitamins. (Rev: SLJ 10/93) [613.2]

20168 Silverstein, Alvin, et al. *Fats* (4–7). Illus. by Anne Canevari Green. Series: Food Power. 1992, Millbrook LB $20.90 (1-56294-208-5). 48pp. With full-color drawings and much boxed information, the various kinds of fats and their roles in one's diet are explored. (Rev: BL 11/15/92; SLJ 1/93) [612.3]

VEGETABLES

20169 Aliki. *Corn Is Maize: The Gift of the Indians* (2–4). Illus. by author. 1976, HarperCollins LB $15.89 (0-690-00975-5); paper $4.95 (0-06-445026-0). 40pp. A simply written, comprehensive treatment of corn, its origins, how it is husbanded and harvested, and its many uses.

20170 Bial, Raymond. *Corn Belt Harvest* (4–6). Illus. 1991, Houghton $17.00 (0-395-56234-1). 48pp. A photo-essay about how corn is grown and harvested. (Rev: BCCB 1/92; BL 12/15/91; SLJ 2/92) [633.1]

20171 Cook, Deanna F. *Kids' Pumpkin Projects* (3–6). Illus. 1998, Williamson paper $9.95 (1-885593-21-X). 104pp. Discusses the planting and cultivating of pumpkins and contains craft and cooking ideas arranged by the seasons. (Rev: BL 10/15/98; SLJ 9/98) [745.5]

20172 De Bourgoing, Pascale, and Gallimard Jeunesse. *Vegetables in the Garden* (PS–3). Illus. by Gilbert Houbre. Series: First Discovery. 1994, Scholastic $11.95 (0-590-48326-7). 24pp. In this well-illustrated interactive book, small children learn about gardens and different kinds of vegetables and how they grow. (Rev: BL 11/15/94) [635]

20173 Fowler, Allan. *Corn — On and Off the Cob* (1–2). Illus. Series: Rookie Readers. 1994, Children's LB $19.00 (0-516-06027-9). 32pp. An easily read science book about different kinds of corn and their uses. (Rev: BL 4/15/95) [633.1]

20174 Fowler, Allan. *Taking Root* (1–2). Series: Rookie Readers. 2000, Children's LB $19.00 (0-516-21591-4). 32pp. This simple science book introduces taproots that we eat including carrots, beets, and radishes. (Rev: BL 4/15/00) [641.6]

20175 Gibbons, Gail. *The Pumpkin Book* (K–3). Illus. 1999, Holiday $16.95 (0-8234-1465-5). 32pp. After a discussion of how pumpkins grow and reproduce, the author explains their roles in Halloween and Thanksgiving celebrations and gives some craft projects. (Rev: BL 9/1/99; HBG 3/00; SLJ 9/99) [635]

20176 Hughes, Meredith S. *Spill the Beans and Pass the Peanuts: Legumes* (5–8). Series: Plants We Eat. 1999, Lerner LB $22.26 (0-8225-2834-7). 80pp. Peas and beans are two of the legumes introduced in this book that explains, in an entertaining way, their origins, how they grow, their appearance, and nutritional value, plus giving the occasional recipe or activity. (Rev: BL 10/15/99; HBG 3/00; SLJ 12/99) [641.6]

20177 Hughes, Meredith S. *Stinky and Stringy* (5–8). Series: Plants We Eat. 1999, Lerner $18.95 (0-8225-2833-9). 88pp. This introduction to stem and bulb vegetables is a delightful mixture of information on the origins of each plant, how it is grown and processed, how it is eaten around the world, plus cross sections of plants, sidebars, recipes, and activities. (Rev: BL 7/99; HBG 10/99; SLJ 8/99) [635]

20178 Hughes, Meredith S., and E. Thomas Hughes. *Buried Treasure: Roots and Tubers* (4–7). Series: Plants We Eat. 1998, Lerner LB $26.60 (0-8225-2830-4). 96pp. Covering such vegetables as potatoes, sweet potatoes, carrots, turnips, beets, and radishes, this account describes the origin, history, cultivation, and importance of each. (Rev: HBG 3/99; SLJ 4/99) [635]

20179 Kudlinski, Kathleen V. *Popcorn Plants* (2–3). Series: Early Bird Nature Books. 1998, Lerner $22.60 (0-8225-3014-7). 48pp. The life cycle of the popcorn plant is traced in excellent photos and simple text. (Rev: BL 10/15/98; HBG 3/99; SLJ 1/99) [633.1]

20180 Landau, Elaine. *Corn* (2–4). Illus. 1999, Children's LB $21.50 (0-516-21026-2). 48pp. A history of corn is accompanied by descriptions of different species and how they grow plus a few simple tasty recipes. (Rev: BL 10/15/99) [633.1]

20181 Levenson, George. *Pumpkin Circle: The Story of a Garden* (PS–3). Illus. 1999, Tricycle Pr. $14.95 (1-58246-004-3). 40pp. This book, illustrated with excellent photographs, traces the life cycle of a pumpkin from seed to a mature plant that produces more seeds. (Rev: BL 10/15/99; HB 11–12/99; HBG 3/00; SLJ 10/99) [635]

20182 Llewellyn, Claire. *Potatoes* (K–2). Series: What's for Lunch? 1998, Children's LB $20.00 (0-516-20838-1). 32pp. This book identifies the parts of a potato, how it is grown and harvested, and how it is processed, and describes various cooking methods. (Rev: BL 6/1–15/98; HBG 10/98; SLJ 9/98) [641.3]

20183 Llewellyn, Claire. *What's for Lunch? Peas* (K–2). Series: What's for Lunch? 1999, Children's LB $20.50 (0-516-21549-3). 32pp. Each double-page spread contains a picture and simple text in this book that tells about varieties of peas, where and how they are grown, their uses, and nutritional value. (Rev: BL 10/15/99) [635]

20184 Robinson, Fay. *Vegetables, Vegetables!* (1–2). Illus. Series: Rookie Readers. 1994, Children's LB $19.00 (0-516-06030-9). 32pp. An easily

read book that introduces various vegetables and shows ways in which they are prepared as food. (Rev: BL 4/15/95) [635]

20185 Robson, Pam. *Corn* (K–2). Illus. Series: What's for Lunch? 1998, Children's LB $20.00 (0-516-20823-3). 32pp. Uses color photographs and simple text to introduce corn, its physical characteristics, its varieties, how it is grown, and how it is prepared. (Rev: BL 6/1–15/98; HBG 10/98) [635]

20186 Watts, Barrie. *Potato* (1–3). Illus. 1988, Silver Burdett LB $15.95 (0-382-09527-8); paper $3.95 (0-382-24018-9). How a potato grows and is harvested. (Rev: BL 10/1/88; SLJ 10/88)

Fungi

20187 Frazer, Simon. *The Mushroom Hunt* (1–4). Illus. by Penny Dale. Series: Read and Wonder. 1995, Candlewick $14.95 (1-56402-500-4). 32pp. Facts and lore about the much-misunderstood mushroom are entertainingly presented. (Rev: BL 7/95; SLJ 7/95) [589.2]

20188 Murray, Peter. *Mushrooms* (3–5). Illus. Series: Naturebooks: Plants. 1995, Child's World LB $22.79 (1-56766-193-9). 32pp. Edible and poisonous mushrooms are discussed, with information on how and where mushrooms grow and reproduce. (Rev: BL 12/1/95) [589.2]

20189 Pascoe, Elaine. *Slime, Molds, and Fungus* (4–7). Series: Nature Close-up. 1998, Blackbirch LB $16.95 (1-56711-182-3). 48pp. Stunning photographs, good background information, and a number of interesting projects help introduce the world of fungi. (Rev: BL 9/15/98; HBG 3/99; SLJ 3/99) [589.2]

20190 Royston, Angela. *Life Cycle of a Mushroom* (PS–3). Series: Life Cycle. 2000, Heinemann LB $19.92 (1-57572-210-0). 32pp. Using a color photo and four or five lines of text on each page, this book describes different mushrooms and gives their basic life cycle. (Rev: BL 5/15/00; HBG 3/01) [589.2]

20191 Silverstein, Alvin, et al. *Fungi* (3–6). Illus. Series: Kingdoms of Life. 1996, Twenty-First Century LB $21.40 (0-8050-3520-6). 64pp. All kinds of fungi and molds are pictured, with brief text. (Rev: BL 6/1–15/96) [589.2]

20192 Tesar, Jenny. *Fungi* (5–7). Illus. Series: Our Living World. 1994, Blackbirch LB $19.45 (1-56711-044-4). 64pp. A volume that explains what a fungus is, how the various types reproduce and grow, their unique characteristics, and how they fit into food webs and chains. (Rev: BL 12/1/94) [589.2]

Leaves and Trees

20193 Arnosky, Jim. *Crinkleroot's Guide to Knowing the Trees* (2–4). Illus. 1992, Macmillan $15.00 (0-02-705855-7). 40pp. Crinkleroot the woodsman guides young readers through the wilderness, teaching nature along the way. (Rev: BL 2/1/92; SLJ 3/92) [582.1]

20194 Brandt, Keith. *Discovering Trees* (1–3). Illus. by Christine Willis Nigoghossian. 1982, Troll LB $17.25 (0-89375-566-4); paper $3.50 (0-89375-567-2). 32pp. How a tree is born and how it grows.

20195 Burnie, David. *Tree* (4–8). Illus. 1988, Knopf LB $20.99 (0-394-99617-8). 64pp. This photo-essay covers different leaves, needles, and scales. (Rev: BL 12/1/88; SLJ 12/88)

20196 Cassie, Brian. *National Audubon Society First Field Guide: Trees* (4–6). Series: First Field Guide. 1999, National Audubon Society paper $11.95 (0-590-05490-2). 16pp. The parts of a tree are introduced and several common trees of North America and their leaves are identified, pictured, and discussed. (Rev: BL 3/15/99; SLJ 7/99) [582.16]

20197 Dorros, Arthur. *A Tree Is Growing* (2–4). Illus. by S. D. Schindler. 1997, Scholastic $15.95 (0-590-45300-9). 32pp. In double-page spreads, various types of trees and leaves are introduced, with material on how trees grow. (Rev: BCCB 6/97; BL 2/1/97; SLJ 3/97) [582.16]

20198 Fischer-Nagel, Heiderose, and Andreas Fischer-Nagel. *Fir Trees* (3–6). Illus. Series: Nature Watch. 1989, Carolrhoda LB $19.93 (0-87614-340-0). 48pp. The development and growth of the conifers. (Rev: BL 10/15/89; SLJ 1/90) [585.2]

20199 Fleisher, Paul. *Oak Tree* (3–5). Illus. Series: Webs of Life. 1997, Marshall Cavendish LB $22.79 (0-7614-0434-1). 40pp. Describes an Eastern deciduous forest and the plant and animal life that surrounds an oak tree. (Rev: BL 2/15/98; HBG 3/98) [583]

20200 Fowler, Allan. *It Could Still Be a Tree* (1–2). Illus. Series: Rookie Readers. 1990, Children's LB $19.00 (0-516-04904-6). 32pp. With simple text and many photos, the characteristics of trees are introduced. (Rev: BL 2/1/91) [582.12]

20201 Gardner, Robert. *Science Project Ideas About Trees* (4–7). Illus. Series: Science Project Ideas. 1997, Enslow LB $19.95 (0-89490-846-4). 96pp. The parts of trees and their functions are described, with activities involving leaves, seeds, flowers, roots, and twigs. (Rev: BL 12/1/97; HBG 3/98; SLJ 2/98) [582.16]

20202 Henderson, Douglas. *Dinosaur Tree* (2–4). Illus. 1994, Bradbury paper $16.00 (0-02-743547-4). 32pp. The story of a 500-year-old tree that is now in the Petrified Forest National Park. (Rev: BL 1/1/95; SLJ 2/95*) [560]

20203 Hickman, Pamela. *Tree Book* (3–5). Illus. 1999, Kids Can $12.95 (1-55074-485-2). 32pp. An introduction to trees, how they grow and reproduce, and their parts, plus a few related activities and projects. (Rev: BL 2/1/99; HBG 10/99) [582.16]

20204 Holmes, Bonnie. *Quaking Aspen* (2–4). Series: Nature Watch. 1999, Carolrhoda $16.95 (1-57505-351-9). 48pp. This illustrated book about the aspen tree includes material on its location, characteristics, ecology, and possible future endangerments. (Rev: BL 10/1/99; HBG 3/00) [583]

20205 Jennings, Terry. *Wood* (3–5). Illus. by Ed Barber. Series: Threads. 1991, Garrett LB $15.93 (1-56074-002-7). 28pp. Various types of wood

products are pictured with facts on how they are produced and used. (Rev: BL 11/15/91) [674]

20206 Johnson, Sylvia A. *How Leaves Change* (3–5). Illus. 1986, Lerner LB $22.60 (0-8225-1483-4); paper $5.95 (0-8225-9513-3). 48pp. Explains how and why leaves change color in the fall. (Rev: BCCB 4/87; BL 1/15/87; SLJ 3/87)

20207 Jorgensen, Lisa. *Grand Trees of America: Our State and Champion Trees* (4–7). Illus. 1992, Roberts paper $8.95 (1-879373-15-7). 120pp. This book describes the official tree of each state and introduces the National Register of Big Trees. (Rev: BL 2/15/93) [582.16]

20208 Kittinger, Jo S. *Dead Log Alive!* (4–7). Illus. Series: A First Book. 1996, Watts LB $22.50 (0-531-20237-2). 63pp. A description of the animals, insects, birds, and fungi that live in or on dead trees. (Rev: SLJ 5/97) [586.16]

20209 Lauber, Patricia. *Be a Friend to Trees* (2–4). Illus. by Holly Keller. Series: Let's-Read-and-Find-Out. 1994, HarperCollins LB $15.89 (0-06-021529-1). 32pp. The many uses of trees — such as providing homes for birds and supplying wood for construction — are outlined, with material on trees' structure, parts, and how their leaves make food. (Rev: BCCB 1/94; BL 6/1–15/94; SLJ 3/94) [582.16]

20210 Maestro, Betsy. *Why Do Leaves Change Color?* (K–4). Illus. by Loretta Krupinski. Series: Let's-Read-and-Find-Out. 1994, HarperCollins LB $15.89 (0-06-022874-1). 32pp. This book explains the process that causes leaf color change in the autumn and why leaves fall from the trees. (Rev: BCCB 11/94; BL 11/15/94; SLJ 7/95) [582.16]

20211 Miller, Cameron, and Dominique Falla. *Woodlore* (3–5). Illus. 1995, Ticknor $14.95 (0-395-72034-6). 32pp. Various kinds of wood and their uses are explored in text and full-color illustrations. (Rev: BCCB 3/95; BL 3/1/95; SLJ 3/95) [674.8]

20212 Morrison, Gordon. *Oak Tree* (4–6). Illus. 2000, Houghton $16.00 (0-395-95644-7). 32pp. A year in the life of an oak tree is described in this appealing account that uses a picture-book format. (Rev: BL 3/1/00; HBG 10/00; SLJ 6/00) [583]

20213 Murray, Peter. *Redwoods* (3–5). Illus. Series: Naturebooks: Plants. 1996, Child's World LB $22.79 (1-56766-216-1). 32pp. The majestic redwoods, how they grow, and the characteristics of a single tree are highlighted in this colorful book. (Rev: BL 1/1–15/97) [585]

20214 Patent, Dorothy Hinshaw. *Apple Trees* (2–3). Series: Early Bird Nature Books. 1998, Lerner LB $22.60 (0-8225-3020-1). 48pp. An easily read introduction to the apple tree and its life cycle, told in a simple text with attractive color photographs. (Rev: BL 3/15/98; HBG 10/98; SLJ 4/98) [582.16]

20215 Pfeffer, Wendy. *A Log's Life* (K–3). Illus. by Robin Brickman. 1997, Simon & Schuster paper $16.00 (0-689-80636-1). 32pp. The life cycle of an oak tree and its many roles in the forest ecology. (Rev: BL 9/15/97; HBG 3/98; SLJ 9/97) [574.5]

20216 Robbins, Ken. *Autumn Leaves* (PS–2). Illus. 1998, Scholastic $15.95 (0-590-29879-8). 32pp. Using full-color photographs, a variety of autumn leaves are pictured and identified. (Rev: BCCB 1/99; BL 8/98; HBG 3/99; SLJ 9/98) [581.4]

20217 Royston, Angela. *Life Cycle of an Oak Tree* (PS–3). Series: Life Cycle. 2000, Heinemann LB $19.92 (1-57572-211-9). 32pp. From acorn to giant oak, this book describes the life cycle of an oak tree using a few lines of text and a color photo on each page. (Rev: BL 5/15/00; HBG 3/01) [583]

20218 Tesar, Jenny. *Shrinking Forests* (5–8). Illus. Series: Our Fragile Earth. 1991, Facts on File $19.95 (0-8160-2492-8). 112pp. A worldwide survey of the decline of forests. (Rev: SLJ 1/92) [582.16]

20219 Vieira, Linda. *The Ever-Living Tree: The Life and Times of a Coast Redwood* (2–5). Illus. by Christopher Canyon. 1994, Walker LB $15.85 (0-8027-8278-7). 32pp. The life of a 2,000-year-old redwood, with details of some important events that occurred during its life. (Rev: BL 3/1/94; SLJ 5/94) [584]

20220 Wadsworth, Ginger. *Giant Sequoia Trees* (2–4). Photos by Frank Staub. Series: Early Bird Nature Books. 1995, Lerner LB $22.60 (0-8225-3001-5). 48pp. A photo-essay about the world's largest tree, the sequoia, with details on its parts, environment, and life cycle. (Rev: SLJ 10/95) [582]

20221 Zim, Herbert S., and Alexander C. Martin. *Trees* (5–8). Illus. 1991, Western paper $21.27 (0-307-64056-6). 160pp. A small, handy volume packed with information and color illustrations that help identify our most important trees.

Plants

20222 Aaseng, Nathan. *Meat-Eating Plants* (3–6). Illus. Series: Weird and Wacky Science. 1996, Enslow LB $18.95 (0-89490-617-8). 48pp. Such plants as bladderworts, sundews, pitcher plants, and Venus's-flytraps are described, along with their methods of obtaining food. (Rev: SLJ 5/96) [581.5]

20223 Ardley, Neil. *The Science Book of Things That Grow* (3–6). Illus. Series: Science Books. 1991, Harcourt $9.95 (0-15-200586-2). 29pp. With everyday equipment and step-by-step procedures, the process of plant growth is explained. (Rev: BL 10/15/91) [581]

20224 *Atlas of Plants* (1–3). Illus. by Sylvaine Perols. Series: First Discovery Atlases. 1996, Scholastic $11.95 (0-590-58113-9). Using extensive captions and maps, this atlas tells where plants come from. (Rev: SLJ 9/96) [581.5]

20225 Baker, Wendy, and Andrew Haslam. *Plants* (3–6). Illus. Series: Make It Work! 1993, Macmillan $12.95 (0-689-71664-8). 48pp. Such concepts as photosynthesis are introduced and activities and experiments are provided. (Rev: SLJ 4/93) [581]

20226 Bash, Barbara. *Desert Giant: The World of the Saguaro Cactus* (3–6). Illus. 1989, Little, Brown paper $5.95 (0-685-33583-6). 32pp. The Tohono O'odham Indians — the Desert People — gather the fruit of the saguaro in a centuries-old harvest ritual. (Rev: BL 3/15/89; HB 3–4/89)

20227 Batten, Mary. *Hungry Plants* (1–4). Illus. by Paul Mirocha. Series: Road to Reading. 2000, Golden Bks. $10.99 (0-307-46401-6); paper $3.99 (0-307-26401-7). 48pp. This book on carnivorous plants such as the Venus's-flytrap, sundew, pitcher plant, and bladderwort describes their structure and behavior. (Rev: BL 5/15/00) [583]

20228 Bocknek, Jonathan. *The Science of Plants* (2–5). Series: Living Science. 1999, Gareth Stevens LB $14.95 (0-8368-2467-9). 32pp. Different kinds of plants are presented in double-page spreads with activities and coverage on their life cycles, habitats, and products. (Rev: HBG 10/00; SLJ 1/00) [581]

20229 Byles, Monica. *Experiment with Plants* (2–5). Illus. Series: Experiment With. 1994, Lerner LB $19.93 (0-8225-2456-2). 32pp. Various types of plants, parts of plants, their uses, and how they grow are covered in this book filled with simple experiments. (Rev: BL 3/1/94; SLJ 5/94) [537]

20230 Carolin, Roger, ed. *Incredible Plants* (4–6). Illus. Series: Nature Company Discoveries. 1997, Time Life $16.00 (0-7835-4799-4). 64pp. A fine introduction to plants, their various forms and uses, and different growing areas. (Rev: BL 6/1–15/97; SLJ 7/97) [581]

20231 Coil, Suzanne M. *Poisonous Plants* (3–6). Illus. Series: First Books. 1992, Watts paper $6.95 (0-531-15647-8). 64pp. An attractive format with lots of information about these plants and with many illustrations. (Rev: BL 5/15/91; SLJ 7/91) [582]

20232 Dowden, Anne O. *The Clover and the Bee: A Book of Pollination* (5–8). Illus. 1990, Harper-Collins LB $17.89 (0-690-04679-0). 90pp. A beautifully illustrated book with much information on plant pollination. (Rev: BCCB 6/90; SLJ 7/90*) [647]

20233 Dowden, Anne O. *Poisons in Our Path: Plants That Harm and Heal* (4–7). Illus. 1994, HarperCollins LB $17.89 (0-06-020862-7). 64pp. An examination of the properties, appearance, and habitats of many plants that have been important in the past or present in medicine or magic. (Rev: BCCB 4/94; BL 7/94; HB 7–8/94; SLJ 6/94) [581.6]

20234 Garassino, Alessandro. *Plants: Origins and Evolution* (4–8). Illus. Series: Beginnings — Origins and Evolution. 1995, Raintree Steck-Vaughn LB $24.26 (0-8114-3332-3). 48pp. Important concepts of plant evolution are well presented, with coverage of modern botany and its functions. (Rev: BL 4/15/95) [581.3]

20235 Gardner, Robert. *Science Projects About Plants* (5–8). Illus. Series: Science Projects. 1999, Enslow LB $19.95 (0-89490-952-5). 112pp. This experiments book covers seeds, leaves, roots, stems, flowers, and whole plants. (Rev: BL 2/15/99) [580]

20236 Hickman, Pamela. *Starting with Nature Plant Book* (2–4). Illus. by Heather Collins. Series: Starting with Nature. 2000, Kids Can $12.95 (1-55074-483-6); paper $5.95 (1-55074-812-2). 32pp. This introductory account describes groups of plants and plant parts and gives material on state flowers, endangered plants, and outlines of several related activities. (Rev: HBG 10/00; SLJ 7/00) [581]

20237 Himmelman, John. *A Dandelion's Life* (K–2). Illus. Series: Nature Upclose. 1998, Children's LB $24.00 (0-516-21177-3). 32pp. Beginning with a seed floating in the air, this illustrated book traces the life of a dandelion plant. (Rev: BL 12/1/98; HBG 3/99) [583]

20238 Jenkins, Martin. *Fly Traps! Plants That Bite Back* (PS–3). Illus. by David Parkins. Series: Read and Wonder. 1996, Candlewick $15.99 (1-56402-896-8). 32pp. In a picture-book format with simple text, this book entertainingly introduces such flesh-eating flora as the Venus's-flytrap and bladder-worts. (Rev: BCCB 1/97; BL 11/15/96; SLJ 12/96) [583]

20239 Kalman, Bobbie. *How a Plant Grows* (3–5). Illus. by Barbara Bedell. Series: Crabapples. 1996, Crabtree LB $19.96 (0-86505-628-5); paper $5.95 (0-86505-728-1). 32pp. An introduction to plants that covers topics like structure, photosynthesis, pollination, carnivorous plants, and the importance of plants in the food chain. (Rev: SLJ 7/97) [581.5]

20240 Kite, L. Patricia. *Dandelion Adventures* (PS–2). Illus. by Anca Hariton. 1998, Millbrook $20.90 (0-7613-0037-6); paper $6.95 (0-7613-0377-4). 32pp. This appealing picture book describing the life cycle of a dandelion begins with the landing of seed parachutes and ending with new plants producing their own flowers and seeds. (Rev: BL 3/15/98; HBG 3/99; SLJ 7/98) [583]

20241 Kudlinski, Kathleen V. *Dandelions* (2–3). Series: Early Bird Nature Books. 1999, Lerner LB $22.60 (0-8225-3016-3). 48pp. This attractive account, suitable for beginning readers, describes the characteristics of a dandelion and outlines its life cycle. (Rev: BL 10/15/99; HBG 3/00; SLJ 1/00) [583]

20242 Kudlinski, Kathleen V. *Venus Flytraps* (2–5). Illus. Series: Early Bird Nature Books. 1998, Lerner LB $22.60 (0-8225-3015-5). 48pp. This photo-essay uses amazing color photos and a simple text to describe the habitats of the Venus's-flytrap and how and why it kills insects. (Rev: BL 12/1/98; HBG 3/99; SLJ 3/99) [583]

20243 Landau, Elaine. *Endangered Plants* (4–6). Illus. Series: First Books. 1992, Watts paper $6.95 (0-531-15645-1). 64pp. Color photos enhance this look at plants in danger of extinction. (Rev: BL 6/1/92; SLJ 7/92) [581.5]

20244 Lerner, Carol. *Cactus* (4–7). Illus. 1992, Morrow LB $14.93 (0-688-09637-9). 32pp. After explaining the parts of the cactus and how it can exist in near-waterless environments, this account describes different species. (Rev: BCCB 10/92; HB 1–2/93; SLJ 12/92) [635.7]

20245 Lewin, Betsy. *Walk a Green Path* (1–4). Illus. 1995, Lothrop $15.00 (0-688-13425-4). 32pp. Different kinds of plants are introduced in a series of memorable paintings and short poems. (Rev: BL 6/1–15/95; SLJ 4/95) [581]

20246 Llamas, Andreu. *Plants Under the Sea* (4–6). Illus. by Luis Rizo. Series: Incredible World of

Plants. 1996, Chelsea LB $15.95 (0-7910-3468-2). 32pp. Familiar and less common ocean plants are described and pictured, along with their relation to aquatic animal life. Also use *The Vegetation of Rivers, Lakes, and Swamps* (1996). (Rev: SLJ 7/96) [581]

20247 Lucht, Irmgard. *The Red Poppy* (K–3). Trans. by Frank Jacoby-Nelson. Illus. 1995, Hyperion LB $14.49 (0-7868-2043-8). 32pp. A year in the life of a poppy plant is explored in this large-format picture book. (Rev: BCCB 6/95; BL 4/1/95; SLJ 6/95*) [583]

20248 McDonald, Mary Ann. *Sunflowers* (3–5). Illus. Series: Naturebooks: Plants. 1996, Child's World LB $22.79 (1-56766-272-2). 32pp. The growth cycle of sunflowers and their characteristics are covered in this colorful introduction to the popular, useful plant. (Rev: BL 1/1–15/97) [583]

20249 Murray, Peter. *Cactus* (3–5). Illus. Series: Nature Books. 1995, Child's World LB $22.79 (1-56766-191-2). 32pp. Full-page photographs facing large-type pages of text introduce various cacti and their habitats and life. (Rev: BL 12/15/95; SLJ 3/96) [581]

20250 Murray, Peter. *Orchids* (3–5). Illus. Series: Naturebooks: Plants. 1995, Child's World LB $22.79 (1-56766-194-7). 32pp. The structure, habitats, and growth patterns of orchids are introduced with colorful photographs. (Rev: BL 12/1/95) [584]

20251 Nielsen, Nancy J. *Carnivorous Plants* (4–8). Illus. 1992, Watts paper $5.95 (0-531-15644-3). 64pp. A look, with the help of color photos, at flesh-eating plants, such as the Venus's-flytrap. (Rev: BL 6/1/92; SLJ 7/92) [581.5]

20252 Overbeck, Cynthia. *Cactus* (3–6). Illus. by Shabo Hans. 1982, Lerner paper $5.95 (0-8225-9556-7). 48pp. A description of the cactus and how it lives.

20253 Overbeck, Cynthia. *Carnivorous Plants* (4–8). Illus. by Kiyashi Shimizu. 1982, Lerner LB $22.60 (0-8225-1470-2). 48pp. How these plants exist is discussed, plus a mention of several types. ,

20254 Penny, Malcolm. *How Plants Grow* (3–5). Illus. by Stuart Lafford. Series: Nature's Mysteries. 1996, Benchmark LB $22.79 (0-7614-0452-X). 32pp. Topics like flowering, pollination, seed production, and growth are covered in this elementary book about plants. (Rev: SLJ 2/97) [581.5]

20255 *Plants* (K–4). Series: Starting with Science. 1998, Kids Can LB $10.95 (1-55074-193-4). 32pp. Thirteen safe and simple experiments with plants, such as creating "super soil," are presented in this beginning science activity book. (Rev: BL 5/15/98; HBG 10/98; SLJ 5/98) [581]

20256 Pope, Joyce. *Practical Plants* (4–8). Illus. Series: Plant Life. 1991, Facts on File $15.95 (0-8160-2424-3). 62pp. How people use plants for food, medicine, paper and cloth fiber, housing material, and pleasure. (Rev: BL 6/15/91) [581.6]

20257 Posada, Mia. *Dandelions: Stars in the Grass* (PS–2). Illus. by author. 2000, Carolrhoda LB $15.95 (1-57505-383-7). The life cycle of a dandelion is covered in bright acrylic illustrations and a text that includes unusual facts and a recipe for dandelion salad. (Rev: HBG 10/00; SLJ 5/00) [581]

20258 Reading, Susan. *Desert Plants* (4–8). Illus. Series: Plant Life. 1991, Facts on File $15.95 (0-8160-2421-9). 63pp. Varieties of cacti and other desert plants are described with many full-color photos. (Rev: BL 6/15/91) [581]

20259 Reading, Susan. *Plants of the Tropics* (4–8). Illus. Series: Plant Life. 1991, Facts on File $15.95 (0-8160-2423-5). 62pp. Touring the rain forest to see the variety of plants, how they survive, and their relationship with animals. (Rev: BL 6/15/91) [581]

20260 Rockwell, Anne. *One Bean* (PS–2). Illus. by Megan Halsey. 1998, Walker LB $15.85 (0-8027-8649-9). 32pp. This book shows, with step-by-step instructions, how to grow a bean plant and gives details on other bean activities. (Rev: BL 4/15/98; HBG 10/98; SLJ 5/98) [635]

20261 Royston, Angela. *Flowers, Fruits, and Seeds* (K–3). Series: Heinemann First Library. 1999, Heinemann LB $13.95 (1-57572-822-2). 32pp. Through color photos and a brief text, this book introduces the life cycle of various fruits from pollination of flowers through development of the fruit and production of seeds. Also use the companion book by the same author, *How Plants Grow.* (Rev: BL 6/1–15/99; SLJ 1/00) [634]

20262 Royston, Angela. *Life Cycle of a Bean* (2–3). Illus. Series: Life Cycle. 1998, Heinemann $13.95 (1-57572-612-2). 32pp. Using a colorful photograph and a timeline on each page, this book describes the stages in the maturation of a bean plant and its eventual production of a new seed. (Rev: BL 4/15/98; SLJ 7/98) [583]

20263 Royston, Angela. *Plants and Us* (K–3). Series: Heinemann First Library. 1999, Heinemann LB $13.95 (1-57572-825-7). 32pp. Attractive illustrations and a short text are used to explain the relationship between plants and humankind, with material on plants' various uses in everyday life. Also use *Strange Plants* by the same author. (Rev: BL 6/1–15/99) [581]

20264 Silverstein, Alvin, et al. *Plants* (3–6). Illus. Series: Kingdoms of Life. 1996, Twenty-First Century LB $21.40 (0-8050-3519-2). 64pp. Scientific classification of life on earth is explained, focusing on the world of plants and its diversity. (Rev: BL 6/1–15/96; SLJ 7/96) [581]

20265 VanCleave, Janice. *Janice VanCleave's Plants: Mind-Boggling Experiments You Can Turn into Science Fair Projects* (3–7). Illus. 1997, Wiley paper $10.95 (0-471-14687-0). 96pp. Twenty projects and experiments involving plants, their parts, and their growth cycles are presented with clear,

easy-to-follow instructions. (Rev: BL 2/15/97; SLJ 3/97) [581]

20266 Watts, Barrie. *Dandelion* (PS–3). Illus. 1987, Silver Burdett LB $9.95 (0-382-09438-7); paper $3.95 (0-382-24016-2). 24pp. The simple dandelion in close-up photography. (Rev: BL 12/1/87)

20267 Wexler, Jerome. *Queen Anne's Lace* (3–6). Illus. 1994, Albert Whitman LB $14.95 (0-8075-6710-8). 32pp. An examination of this common weed, exploring its structure, roots, seeds, and flowers. (Rev: BCCB 6/94; BL 4/15/94; SLJ 6/94) [583]

Seeds

20268 Burns, Diane L. *Berries, Nuts and Seeds* (4–7). Illus. by John F. McGee. 1996, NorthWord paper $6.95 (1-55971-573-1). 42pp. Each page in this guide is devoted to a description of a single berry, nut, or seed, like the raspberry, pecan, cattail, and thistle blossom. (Rev: BL 2/15/97) [582.13]

20269 Burton, Jane, and Kim Taylor. *The Nature and Science of Seeds* (3–6). Series: Exploring the Science of Nature. 1999, Gareth Stevens LB $14.95 (0-8368-2184-X). 32pp. The composition and functions of seeds are explored in this well-illustrated book that contains a special section of projects and activities involving seeds and plant growth. (Rev: BL 7/99) [582]

20270 Gibbons, Gail. *From Seed to Plant* (PS–3). Illus. 1991, Holiday LB $16.95 (0-8234-0872-8). 32pp. How seeds grow into plants and how flowering plants produce seeds. (Rev: BL 3/1/91; HB 7–8/91; SLJ 7/91) [581.3]

20271 Jordan, Helene J. *How a Seed Grows* (3–6). Illus. by Loretta Krupinski. Series: Let's-Read-and-Find-Out. 1992, HarperCollins LB $15.89 (0-06-020185-1); paper $4.95 (0-06-445107-0). 32pp. A boy and a girl plant seeds and watch them grow. (Rev: BL 8/92; SLJ 7/92) [582]

20272 Kuchalla, Susan. *All About Seeds* (K–3). Illus. by Jane McBee. 1982, Troll paper $3.50 (0-89375-659-8). 32pp. A simple account that explains how and where seeds grow.

20273 Overbeck, Cynthia. *How Seeds Travel* (4–6). Illus. 1982, Lerner LB $22.60 (0-8225-1474-5); paper $5.95 (0-8225-9569-9). 48pp. An explanation of the various ways seeds are dispersed.

20274 Pascoe, Elaine. *Seeds and Seedlings* (4–7). Illus. Series: Nature Close-up. 1996, Blackbirch LB $18.95 (1-56711-178-5). 48pp. The growth cycle of seeds is explained, with many projects on how to plant and raise seedlings. (Rev: BL 12/1/96; SLJ 3/97) [582]

Chemistry

20275 Angliss, Sarah. *Gold* (4–8). Series: The Elements. 1999, Marshall Cavendish LB $15.95 (0-7614-0887-8). 32pp. Easy-to-follow diagrams, fact boxes, and color illustrations accompany an informative text that introduces gold, where it is mined and processed, its properties, value, and uses. (Rev: BL 2/15/00; HBG 10/00) [546]

20276 Beatty, Richard. *Copper* (4–8). Series: The Elements. 2000, Marshall Cavendish LB $15.95 (0-7614-0945-9). 32pp. This book identifies the element copper, defines its properties and describes its uses in everyday life, especially in electrical cables. (Rev: BL 1/1–15/01; SLJ 2/01) [546]

20277 Beatty, Richard. *Phosphorous* (4–8). Series: The Elements. 2000, Marshall Cavendish LB $15.95 (0-7614-0946-7). 32pp. This book describes this nonmetallic element, lists its properties, tells how it behaves, and discusses such uses as matches and fertilizers. (Rev: BL 1/1–15/01; SLJ 2/01) [546]

20278 Beatty, Richard. *Sulfur* (4–8). Series: The Elements. 2000, Marshall Cavendish LB $15.95 (0-7614-0948-3). 32pp. Introduces this nonmetallic element, its characteristics, various compounds, and uses in everyday life, with color photos, easy-to-follow diagrams, fact boxes, and a clear text. (Rev: BL 1/1–15/01; SLJ 2/01) [546]

20279 Burton, Jane, and Kim Taylor. *The Nature and Science of Fire* (3–6). Series: Exploring the Science of Nature. 2001, Gareth Stevens LB $21.27 (0-8368-2198-X). 32pp. An introduction to fire and the chemical processes involved with some safe activities appended. (Rev: BL 3/15/01) [530]

20280 Farndon, John. *Aluminum* (4–8). Series: The Elements. 2000, Marshall Cavendish LB $15.95 (0-7614-0947-5). 32pp. This silvery, metallic element is introduced, with material on its individual characteristics, how it behaves, and its many uses in everyday life. (Rev: BL 1/1–15/01) [546]

20281 Farndon, John. *Calcium* (5–8). 1999, Benchmark LB $15.95 (0-7614-0888-6). 32pp. An attractive, readable book that explains calcium's atomic structure, where and how it occurs in nature, its

reactions, compounds, and uses. (Rev: BL 2/15/00; HBG 10/00; SLJ 6/00) [540]

20282 Farndon, John. *Hydrogen* (5–8). Illus. Series: Elements. 1999, Marshall Cavendish LB $15.95 (0-7614-0886-X). 32pp. As well as explaining hydrogen's place on the periodic table, this account traces the history of its discovery, its properties, reactive combinations, and uses. (Rev: BL 2/15/00; HBG 10/00; SLJ 6/00) [546]

20283 Farndon, John. *Nitrogen* (5–8). Series: The Elements. 1998, Benchmark LB $15.95 (0-7614-0877-0). 32pp. An informative science book that introduces nitrogen's properties, reactions, place in the periodic table, and importance in the human body and the environment. (Rev: HBG 10/99; SLJ 2/99) [540]

20284 Farndon, John. *Oxygen* (5–8). Series: The Elements. 1998, Benchmark LB $15.95 (0-7614-0879-7). 32pp. Oxygen, its properties, uses, and various chemical combinations are covered in this informative text that also discusses the ozone layer. (Rev: HBG 10/99; SLJ 2/99) [540]

20285 Fitzgerald, Karen. *The Story of Nitrogen* (4–6). Illus. Series: First Books. 1997, Watts LB $22.50 (0-531-20248-8). 64pp. Nitrogen is introduced, with material on its atomic structure, properties, uses, and production. (Rev: BL 9/1/97; SLJ 10/97) [546]

20286 Gallant, Roy A. *The Ever-Changing Atom* (5–8). Series: The Story of Science. 1999, Benchmark LB $19.95 (0-7614-0961-0). 80pp. Using a chronological approach, this book traces how and what we have found out about the atom and its structure. (Rev: HBG 3/00; SLJ 2/00) [539]

20287 Madgwick, Wendy. *Super Materials* (K–3). Series: Science Starters. 1999, Raintree Steck-Vaughn LB $15.98 (0-8172-5555-9). 32pp. The properties of various materials are explored in a dozen simple projects using everyday materials: for example, how crystals are formed, why sugar disappears in water, and where metals come from. (Rev: BL 6/1–15/99; HBG 10/99) [540]

20288 Mebane, Robert C., and Thomas R. Rybolt. *Salts and Solids* (4–6). Illus. Series: Everyday Material Science Experiments. 1995, Twenty-First Century LB $18.90 (0-8050-2841-2). 64pp. Each of the experiments that explore the properties of salts and solids is accompanied by an explanation of what should happen and why. (Rev: BL 9/15/95; SLJ 8/95) [530]

20289 Moje, Steven W. *Cool Chemistry: Great Experiments with Simple Stuff* (4–6). Illus. 1999, Sterling LB $14.95 (0-8069-6349-2). 96pp. Simple experiments using easily available materials are presented and grouped under six headings including "Physical Properties," "Liquids," and "Acids and Bases." (Rev: SLJ 12/99) [540]

20290 Richards, Jon. *Chemicals and Reactions* (3–6). Illus. 2000, Millbrook LB $21.90 (0-7613-

1160-2). 32pp. Using common household items, experiments involving chemical reactions are accompanied with sidebars that explain how each works. (Rev: BL 8/00; HBG 3/01) [540]

20291 Uttley, Colin. *Magnesium* (4–8). Series: The Elements. 1999, Marshall Cavendish LB $15.95 (0-7614-0889-4). 32pp. This book explores magnesium, a silvery metallic element important in living organisms, and explains its place in the periodic table, as well as its forms, uses, and properties. (Rev: BL 2/15/00; HBG 10/00) [546]

20292 VanCleave, Janice. *Janice VanCleave's Molecules* (4–6). Illus. 1992, Wiley paper $10.95 (0-471-55054-X). 86pp. The principles of cohesion, adhesion, density, diffusion, and emulsion are explored, with clear line drawings. (Rev: BL 1/15/93; SLJ 2/93) [540]

Geology and Geography

Earth and Geology

20293 Allaby, Michael. *The Environment* (4–7). Series: Inside Look. 2000, Gareth Stevens LB $22.60 (0-8368-2725-2). 48pp. Topics covered in this brief overview of the natural systems of our planet include the ozone layer, greenhouse effect, plant life and food webs, ecosystems and biomes, the water cycle, soil life, and rivers. (Rev: SLJ 3/01) [550]

20294 Ardley, Neil. *The Science Book of Gravity* (3–6). Illus. Series: Science Books. 1992, Harcourt $9.95 (0-15-200621-4). 28pp. Each two-page spread contains information about the properties of gravity and includes projects to demonstrate it. (Rev: BL 10/15/92; SLJ 1/93) [531]

20295 Arnold, Caroline. *Coping with Natural Disasters* (5–7). Illus. 1988, Walker LB $14.85 (0-8027-6717-6). 128pp. How a community returns to life after a natural disaster. (Rev: BCCB 6/88; BL 6/15/88)

20296 Bannan, Jan G. *Letting Off Steam* (3–7). Illus. 1989, Carolrhoda LB $21.27 (0-87614-300-1). 48pp. This book explains and illustrates how underground heat can cause hot springs, geysers, and other phenomena. (Rev: BCCB 12/89; BL 9/15/89; HB 9–10/89; SLJ 9/89) [551.3]

20297 Blobaum, Cindy. *Geology Rocks! 50 Hands-On Activities to Explore the Earth* (4–6). Illus. by Michael Kline. Series: A Kaleidoscope Kids Book. 2000, Williamson paper $10.95 (1-885593-29-5). 96pp. Each chapter introduces a different concept in geology with accompanying projects and plenty of sidebars to furnish interesting information on geologists, land formations, the scientific method, etc. (Rev: SLJ 3/00) [551]

20298 Burton, Virginia Lee. *Life Story* (3–5). Illus. by author. 1989, Houghton $20.00 (0-395-16030-8); paper $9.95 (0-395-52017-7). A work about the changes that have taken place on the earth and in its flora and fauna, from the beginning of time until the present.

20299 Campbell, Ann-Jeanette, and Ronald Rood. *The New York Public Library Incredible Earth: A Book of Answers for Kids* (4–7). Illus. 1996, Wiley paper $12.95 (0-471-14497-5). 192pp. Questions and answers involving science, collected from the reference department of the New York Public Library. (Rev: BL 9/15/96; SLJ 1/97) [550]

20300 Christian, Spencer, and Antonia Felix. *What Makes the Grand Canyon Grand? The World's Most Awe-Inspiring Natural Wonders* (4–6). Series: Spencer Christian's World of Wonders. 1998, Wiley paper $12.95 (0-471-19617-7). 116pp. Chapters on canyons, wild waters, caves, mountains, forests, glaciers, and icebergs are accompanied by many experiments and projects in this book on the world's geographical wonders. (Rev: SLJ 4/98) [550]

20301 Clifford, Nick. *Incredible Earth* (4–7). Illus. Series: Inside Guides. 1996, DK $15.95 (0-7894-1013-3). 44pp. Earth's composition and other geological topics are described in double-page spreads. (Rev: BL 12/1/96; SLJ 2/97) [551]

20302 Cole, Joanna. *The Magic School Bus: Inside the Earth* (2–5). Illus. by Bruce Degen. 1987, Scholastic $15.95 (0-590-40759-7); paper $4.99 (0-590-40760-0). 48pp. In picture-book format, geology is introduced as a school bus journeys to the center of the earth. (Rev: BL 1/1/88)

20303 Dewey, Jennifer O. *Mud Matters* (4–6). 1998, Marshall Cavendish $14.95 (0-7416-5014-9). 65pp. The author, a native of the Southwest, describes all kinds of mud, its characteristics, uses, and the part it played in her childhood, when she became acquainted with flash floods, sinkholes, and other manifestations of mud. (Rev: BL 8/98*) [553.6]

20304 Downs, Sandra. *Shaping the Earth: Erosion* (5–8). Series: Exploring Planet Earth. 2000, Twenty-First Century LB $23.40 (0-7613-1414-8). 64pp. This book explores the force of erosion and how such phenomena as wind, waves, floods, rain, acid rain, freezing, and thawing can change the face of the land. (Rev: HBG 10/00; SLJ 7/00) [551]

20305 Gallant, Roy A. *Dance of the Continents* (5–8). Series: The Story of Science. 1999, Benchmark LB $19.95 (0-7614-0962-9). 80pp. This book covers geological theory from the ancient Greeks to modern plate tectonics with coverage of earthquakes, volcanoes, geysers, and other phenomena. (Rev: HBG 3/00; SLJ 3/00) [551]

20306 Gallant, Roy A. *Geysers: When Earth Roars* (3–6). Illus. 1997, Watts LB $22.50 (0-531-20288-7). 64pp. As well as explaining what geysers are and why they erupt, this account takes the reader on a tour of famous geysers in Russia, Iceland, New Zealand, and the United States. (Rev: BL 12/1/97; HBG 3/98; SLJ 12/97) [551.2]

20307 Gibbons, Gail. *Planet Earth/Inside Out* (2–4). Illus. 1995, Morrow $15.93 (0-688-09681-6). 32pp. Theories about the earth's formation are discussed and information about the earth's interior is given. (Rev: BCCB 9/95; BL 8/95; SLJ 10/95) [550]

20308 Goodman, Billy. *Natural Wonders and Disasters* (4–7). Illus. Series: Planet Earth. 1991, Little, Brown $17.95 (0-316-32016-1). 96pp. Full-color photos help to explain the earth's natural wonders as well as such disasters as floods and typhoons. (Rev: BL 12/1/91; SLJ 1/92) [550]

20309 Goodwin, Peter. *Landslides, Slumps, and Creep* (4–6). Illus. Series: First Books. 1997, Watts LB $22.50 (0-531-20332-8). 64pp. Different types of landslides and avalanches are introduced, with material on their causes and effects and an account of some of the major ones. (Rev: BL 11/1/97; HBG 3/98; SLJ 1/98) [551.3]

20310 Henderson, Doug. *Asteroid Impact* (3–5). Illus. 2000, Dial $16.99 (0-8037-2500-0). 40pp. A fascinating account that traces the history of the world before, during, and after a trillion-ton asteroid struck about 65 million years ago causing the death of many plants and animals including the dinosaurs. (Rev: BL 11/1/00*; HB 11–12/00; HBG 3/01; SLJ 11/00) [567.9]

20311 Hooper, Meredith. *The Pebble in My Pocket: A History of Our Earth* (3–5). Illus. by Chris Coady. 1996, Viking $14.99 (0-670-86259-2). 40pp. From molten rock to the formation of mountains, this is a concise history of the earth. (Rev: BL 7/96; SLJ 4/96) [552]

20312 Lauber, Patricia. *You're Aboard Spaceship Earth* (K–3). Illus. by Holly Keller. Series: Let's-Read-and-Find-Out. 1996, HarperCollins LB $15.89 (0-06-024408-9); paper $4.95 (0-06-445159-3). 32pp. The author describes the earth and its contents as though it were a gigantic spaceship. (Rev: BL 8/96; HB 9–10/96; SLJ 8/96) [550]

20313 McNulty, Faith. *How to Dig a Hole to the Other Side of the World* (2–4). Illus. by Marc Simont. 1979, HarperCollins paper $5.95 (0-06-443218-1). 32pp. A journey to the center of the earth.

20314 O'Neill, Catherine. *Natural Wonders of North America* (4–6). Illus. 1984, National Geographic LB $12.50 (0-87044-519-7). 104pp. Many of the wonders of North America, such as a Mexi-

can volcano and life far north in Alaska, are shown in color photographs.

20315 Parker, Steve. *The Earth* (3–6). Illus. Series: What If. 1995, Millbrook LB $19.90 (1-56294-913-6); paper $5.95 (1-56294-948-9). 32pp. A series of hypothetical questions like "What if the earth were twice as big?" are used to explore the various properties and attributes of the earth. (Rev: SLJ 1/96) [550]

20316 Perham, Molly, and Julian Rowe. *Resources* (4–6). Illus. Series: Mapworlds. 1997, Watts LB $20.00 (0-531-14387-2). 32pp. Using an atlaslike format, this work shows where such natural resources as minerals, oil, and coal are found in the world. (Rev: BL 4/15/97) [333.7]

20317 *Planet Earth: World Geography* (4–8). Illus. 1994, Oxford $40.00 (0-19-910144-2). 160pp. This well-illustrated volume introduces both world geography and earth science. (Rev: SLJ 5/94) [910]

20318 Redfern, Martin. *The Kingfisher Young People's Book of Planet Earth* (4–8). 1999, Kingfisher $19.95 (0-7534-5180-8). 96pp. A useful, enjoyable look at the earth's geology, atmosphere, and weather. (Rev: HBG 10/00; SLJ 2/00) [525]

20319 Rockwell, Anne. *Our Earth* (PS–1). Illus. 1998, Harcourt $13.00 (0-15-201679-1). 24pp. This book introduces very young children to the physical features of the earth, as well as different land formations and landscapes. (Rev: BL 11/1/98; HBG 3/99; SLJ 4/99) [910]

20320 Rothaus, Don P. *Canyons* (2–4). Illus. Series: Biomes of Nature. 1996, Child's World LB $22.79 (1-56766-322-2). 32pp. This book describes what canyons are and how they were formed, along with material on the world's most famous canyons. (Rev: SLJ 3/97) [551.4]

20321 Savan, Beth. *Earthwatch: Earthcycles and Ecosystems* (3–7). Illus. by Pat Cupples. 1992, Addison-Wesley paper $9.95 (0-201-58148-5). 96pp. Earth cycles — such as those of water, earth, and air — are explained; contemporary ecology problems are introduced; and simple activities are outlined. (Rev: SLJ 7/92) [550]

20322 Silverstein, Alvin, et al. *Plate Tectonics* (5–8). Illus. Series: Science Concepts. 1998, Twenty-First Century LB $23.40 (0-7613-3225-1). 64pp. An account that includes an introduction to the earth's crust and mantle, an explanation of plate tectonics theory, and information on the prediction of volcanic eruptions and earthquakes. (Rev: BL 2/1/99; HBG 10/99) [555.1]

20323 Steele, Philip. *Rocking and Rolling* (1–3). Illus. Series: SuperSmarts. 1997, Candlewick $11.99 (0-7636-0303-1). 24pp. A general introduction to the earth that presents basic information on volcanoes, earthquakes, and other geological phenomena. (Rev: HBG 3/98; SLJ 3/98) [551]

20324 VanCleave, Janice. *Janice VanCleave's A+ Projects in Earth Science: Winning Experiments for Science Fairs and Extra Credit* (5–10). Illus. 1999, Wiley $27.95 (0-471-17769-5); paper $12.95 (0-471-17770-9). 240pp. Thirty projects varying in complexity are included in this exploration of topography, minerals, atmospheric composition, the ocean floor, and erosion. (Rev: BL 12/1/98) [550]

20325 VanCleave, Janice. *Janice VanCleave's Gravity* (4–6). Illus. 1992, Wiley paper $10.95 (0-471-55050-7). 86pp. Problems that explain how gravity affects the environment, with clear line drawings. (Rev: BL 1/15/93; SLJ 2/93) [531]

20326 Van Rose, Susanna. *The Earth Atlas* (4–8). Illus. 1994, DK $19.95 (1-56458-626-X). 64pp. An oversize atlas that describes the geography of the earth, supplies cutaways of the interior structure, and introduces various kinds of rocks. (Rev: BL 12/1/94) [912]

20327 Verdet, Jean-Pierre. *Atlas of the Earth* (PS–2). Illus. Series: First Discovery. 1997, Scholastic $12.95 (0-590-96211-6). 24pp. This atlas introduces the different surfaces and regions of the earth, from the ocean floor to the dry stretches of the Sahara desert. (Rev: BL 2/1/98; HBG 3/98) [550]

20328 Watson, Nancy. *Our Violent Earth* (4–8). Illus. 1982, National Geographic LB $12.50 (0-87044-388-7). 104pp. Includes earthquakes, volcanoes, drought, fire and water, and stormy weather.

20329 Zike, Dinah. *The Earth Science Book: Activities for Kids* (3–6). Illus. by Jessie J. Flores. 1993, Wiley paper $12.95 (0-471-57166-0). 119pp. Earth science concepts and environmental issues are presented. (Rev: SLJ 7/93) [551]

20330 Zoehfeld, Kathleen W. *How Mountains Are Made* (K–4). Illus. by James G. Hale. 1995, HarperCollins LB $15.89 (0-06-024510-7). 32pp. In a simple text, such topics as various kinds of mountains, the earth's interior, and plate tectonics are introduced. (Rev: BCCB 9/95; BL 8/95; SLJ 9/95*) [551.8]

Earthquakes and Volcanoes

20331 Archer, Jules. *Earthquake!* (5–7). Illus. Series: Nature's Disasters. 1991, Macmillan LB $16.95 (0-89686-593-2). 48pp. This colorful account discusses the causes and effects of earthquakes and includes a list of famous quakes of the past. (Rev: BCCB 7–8/91; BL 8/91) [551.2]

20332 Asimov, Isaac. *How Did We Find Out About Volcanoes?* (5–7). Illus. by David Wool. 1981, Avon paper $1.95 (0-380-59626-1). 64pp. An overview of volcanoes, from Pompeii to Mount St. Helens.

20333 Berger, Melvin, and Gilda Berger. *Why Do Volcanoes Blow Their Tops?* (3–5). Series: Scholastic Question and Answer. 2000, Scholastic LB $14.95 (0-439-09580-8). 48pp. Answers basic questions about volcanoes and earthquakes with plenty of eye-catching illustrations. (Rev: BL 12/15/00; HBG 3/01; SLJ 2/01) [551.2]

20334 Booth, Basil. *Earthquakes and Volcanoes* (5–8). Illus. Series: Repairing the Damage. 1992, Macmillan LB $13.95 (0-02-711735-9). 46pp. A well-organized photo-essay that explains the interrelationship between earthquakes and volcanoes. (Rev: BL 9/15/92) [551.2]

20335 Branley, Franklyn M. *Volcanoes* (1–3). Illus. by Marc Simont. 1986, HarperCollins paper $4.95 (0-06-445059-7). 32pp. A simple look at the whys and hows of volcanoes. (Rev: BL 6/15/89; HB 5–6/85; SLJ 9/85)

20336 Bunce, Vincent. *Volcanoes* (4–6). Series: Restless Planet. 2000, Raintree Steck-Vaughn LB $25.69 (0-7398-1327-7). 48pp. Different volcanic landforms are illustrated and explained, along with various kinds of eruptions, their effects, and disaster relief efforts. (Rev: HBG 10/00; SLJ 12/00) [551.2]

20337 Drohan, Michele Ingber. *Earthquakes* (2–4). Illus. Series: Natural Disasters. 1999, Rosen $13.50 (0-8239-5285-1). 24pp. Full-page photographs and large type are used in this book that explains the causes and effects of earthquakes. (Rev: BL 9/15/99) [551.22]

20338 Elting, Mary, et al. *Volcanoes and Earthquakes* (4–7). Illus. by Courtney. 1990, Simon & Schuster paper $9.95 (0-671-67217-7). 40pp. Disasters are covered with a you-are-there approach. (Rev: BL 2/1/91) [551.2]

20339 Lauber, Patricia. *Volcano: The Eruption and Healing of Mount St. Helens* (2–5). Illus. 1986, Macmillan $17.99 (0-02-754500-8); paper $8.99 (0-689-71679-6). 64pp. Color photos augment the dramatic story of the eruption, aftermath, and gradual return to life of the volcano. (Rev: BCCB 9/86; BL 8/86; HB 9–10/86)

20340 Levy, Matthys, and Mario Salvadori. *Earthquake Games* (5–8). Illus. 1997, Simon & Schuster $16.00 (0-689-81367-8). 128pp. Games, experiments, and a lucid text answer such questions as what causes earthquakes and volcanoes and what their effects are. (Rev: BL 9/1/97; HBG 3/98; SLJ 12/97) [551.22]

20341 Maslin, Mark. *Earthquakes* (4–6). Series: Restless Planet. 2000, Raintree Steck-Vaughn LB $25.69 (0-7398-1328-5). 48pp. This book explains the causes, measurement, hazards, and effects of both earthquakes and tsunamis. (Rev: HBG 10/00; SLJ 12/00) [551.2]

20342 Meister, Cari. *Earthquakes* (4–6). Illus. Series: Nature's Fury. 1999, ABDO LB $14.95 (1-57765-083-2). 32pp. This account presents a history of earthquakes, how they are predicted, and how to stay safe. Also use *Volcanoes* (1999). (Rev: HBG 3/00; SLJ 12/99) [551.2]

20343 Moores, Eldridge M., ed. *Volcanoes and Earthquakes* (4–6). Illus. Series: Nature Company Discoveries. 1995, Time Life $16.00 (0-7835-4764-1). 64pp. This handsome overview of volcanoes and earthquakes contains many attractive illustrations, including an eight-page foldout. (Rev: BL 1/1–15/96; SLJ 1/96) [551.2]

20344 Murray, Peter. *Volcanoes* (3–5). Illus. Series: Naturebooks: Natural Disasters. 1995, Child's World LB $22.79 (1-56766-197-1). 32pp. The structure and causes of volcanoes are covered, with examples from around the world. (Rev: BL 12/1/95; HB 5–6/95; SLJ 3/96) [551.2]

20345 Rogers, Daniel. *Earthquakes* (3–4). Series: Geography Starts Here. 1999, Raintree Steck-

Vaughn LB $22.83 (0-8172-5546-X). 32pp. Covers many topics including faults, plate movement, shock waves, methods of measurement, and kinds of destruction. (Rev: HBG 10/99; SLJ 7/99) [551.2]

20346 Rogers, Daniel. *Volcanoes* (3–4). Series: Geography Starts Here. 1999, Raintree Steck-Vaughn LB $22.83 (0-8172-5547-8). 32pp. The causes of volcanic eruptions are covered along with how they occur, their effects, and the ecological consequences. (Rev: HBG 10/99; SLJ 7/99) [551.2]

20347 Ruiz, Andres L. *Volcanoes and Earthquakes* (4–7). Series: Sequences of Earth and Space. 1997, Sterling $13.95 (0-8069-9744-3). 32pp. This book covers such topics as tectonic plates, quakes, and tsunamis plus the formation, structure, and eruption of volcanoes. (Rev: BL 12/1/97) [551.21]

20348 Simon, Seymour. *Volcanoes* (1–3). Illus. 1988, Morrow LB $15.88 (0-688-07412-X). 32pp. How volcanoes are formed and erupt, with well-known examples. (Rev: BCCB 10/88; HB 9–10/88; SLJ 12/88)

20349 Sutherland, Lin. *Earthquakes and Volcanoes* (4–8). Illus. Series: Pathfinders. 2000, Reader's Digest $16.99 (1-57584-374-9). 64pp. An oversize volume that uses double-page spreads to introduce earthquakes and volcanoes along with material on major disasters, their causes, and their effects. (Rev: BL 9/15/00; HBG 3/01) [551.2]

20350 Thomas, Margaret. *Volcano!* (5–7). Illus. Series: Nature's Disasters. 1991, Macmillan LB $12.95 (0-89686-595-9). 48pp. This book gives solid information about the causes of volcanic eruptions and their effects and includes famous volcanic disasters of the past. (Rev: BL 8/91) [551.2]

20351 VanCleave, Janice. *Earthquakes: Mind-Boggling Experiments You Can Turn into Science Fair Projects* (4–6). Illus. Series: Spectacular Science Projects. 1993, Wiley paper $10.95 (0-471-57107-5). 88pp. This is a collection of projects involving the movements of the earth, along with good scientific explanations and simple directions. (Rev: BL 5/1/93; SLJ 7/93) [551.2]

20352 VanCleave, Janice. *Janice VanCleave's Volcanoes: Mind-Boggling Experiments You Can Turn into Science Fair Projects* (4–7). Illus. 1994, Wiley paper $10.95 (0-471-30811-0). 89pp. Twenty experiments that explore the properties of erupting volcanoes using simple materials that can often be found around the house. (Rev: BL 7/94; SLJ 8/94) [551.2]

20353 Vogel, Carole G. *Shock Waves Through Los Angeles: The Northridge Earthquake* (3–6). Illus. 1996, Little, Brown $15.95 (0-316-90240-3). 32pp. The 1994 earthquake close to Los Angeles is covered, including causes, rescues, and the incredible destruction. (Rev: BL 10/1/96; SLJ 10/96) [363.3]

20354 Walker, Sally M. *Earthquakes* (3–6). Illus. Series: Earth Watch. 1996, Carolrhoda LB $21.27 (0-87614-888-7). 48pp. A clearly written text and powerful color photos highlight this award-winning book. (Rev: BL 4/15/96; SLJ 6/96) [551.2]

20355 Walker, Sally M. *Volcanoes: Earth's Inner Fire* (3–6). Illus. Series: Earth Watch. 1994, Carolrhoda LB $21.27 (0-87614-812-7). 56pp. Many

color photographs and clear text are used to explain the causes, locations, and effects of volcanoes. (Rev: BL 1/15/95) [551.2]

20356 *Why Do Volcanoes Erupt?* (PS–3). Illus. Series: Why. 1997, DK $9.95 (0-7894-1532-1). 24pp. Using a question-and-answer format, volcanoes are introduced, with material on the causes and effects of volcano eruptions. (Rev: BL 8/97) [550]

Icebergs and Glaciers

20357 Bundey, Nikki. *Ice and the Earth* (3–5). Series: The Science of Weather. 2000, Carolrhoda LB $21.27 (1-57505-472-8). 32pp. Along with some interesting experiments, this book describes how ice affects the earth, how it is created, and what would happen if there was no ice on the earth. Also use a companion work *Ice and People* (2000). (Rev: BL 12/15/00; HBG 3/01) [551.3]

20358 Fowler, Allan. *Icebergs, Ice Caps, and Glaciers* (1–3). Series: Rookie Readers. 1997, Children's LB $19.00 (0-516-20429-7). 32pp. Large type and color illustrations are used to introduce these ice formations, with material on how glaciers move and how pieces of ice caps become icebergs. (Rev: BL 11/15/97; HBG 3/98) [551.31]

20359 Gallant, Roy A. *Glaciers* (3–5). Illus. Series: First Books. 1999, Watts LB $22.00 (0-531-20390-5). 64pp. This book explains the nature of glaciers, how they are formed and move, and how they have changed the face of the earth. (Rev: BL 4/15/99; HBG 10/99) [551.31]

20360 George, Michael. *Glaciers* (3–8). Illus. 1991, Creative Ed. LB $25.30 (0-88682-401-X). 40pp. Formations and types of glaciers, as well as their future effects, are explained. (Rev: BL 12/15/91; SLJ 3/92) [551.3]

20361 Walker, Sally M. *Glaciers: Ice on the Move* (4–7). Illus. 1990, Carolrhoda LB $19.95 (0-87614-373-7). 48pp. This book explains how glaciers are formed, where they are found, and how they move. (Rev: BCCB 9/90; BL 6/15/90; SLJ 8/90) [551.3]

Physical Geography

General and Miscellaneous

20362 Armbruster, Ann. *Wildfires* (4–6). Illus. Series: First Books. 1996, Watts LB $22.50 (0-531-20250-X). 63pp. Introduces types of wildfires, their causes, effects, and possible prevention. (Rev: BL 1/1–15/97) [363.37]

20363 Arnosky, Jim. *Wild and Swampy* (3–5). Illus. 2000, HarperCollins LB $15.89 (0-688-17120-6). 32pp. Paintings and drawings are used effectively to introduce the flora and fauna of a swamp. (Rev: BL 11/1/00; HBG 3/01; SLJ 10/00) [591.768]

20364 Blaustein, Daniel. *The Everglades and the Gulf Coast* (4–7). 1999, Benchmark LB $18.95 (0-7614-0896-7). 64pp. In addition to a tour of the wetlands of the southeastern United States, this book describes how the plants and animals there interact and how this changes human life. (Rev: HBG 10/00; SLJ 4/00) [574.5]

20365 Collard, Sneed B. *Our Natural Homes* (3–6). Illus. by James M. Needham. Series: Our Perfect Planet. 1996, Charlesbridge paper $6.95 (0-88106-928-0). An introduction to the plant and animal life found in such North and South American biomes as tundra, boreal forest, mountains, grasslands, deserts, rain forests, and chaparral. (Rev: SLJ 10/96) [910]

20366 Cone, Patrick. *Wildfire* (3–7). Illus. 1996, Carolrhoda $19.95 (0-87614-936-0); paper $7.95 (1-57505-027-7). 48pp. After a general description of wildfires, discusses their causes, effects, and possible preventive measures that can be taken. (Rev: BL 2/15/97; SLJ 1/97) [574.5]

20367 Dunphy, Madeleine. *Here Is the Wetland* (K–3). Illus. by Wayne McLoughlin. 1996, Hyperion LB $15.49 (0-7868-2136-1). An attractive introduction to wetlands and the animals and plants found there, with colorful full-page paintings. (Rev: SLJ 12/96) [331.91]

20368 Fowler, Allan. *Life in a Wetland* (1–2). Series: Rookie Readers. 1998, Children's LB $18.50 (0-516-20799-7). 32pp. Three or four lines of text facing a full-page photo form the basis of this book that explains what a wetland is and the life found in it. (Rev: BL 9/15/98; HBG 10/99) [574.5]

20369 Fowler, Allan. *The Wonder of a Waterfall* (1–2). Series: Rookie Readers. 1999, Children's LB $18.50 (0-516-20813-6). 32pp. In stunning photographs and large-type text, this book introduces waterfalls, their nature, uses, and beauty. (Rev: BL 7/99; HBG 10/99; SLJ 6/99) [551.48]

20370 Gallant, Roy A. *Limestone Caves* (4–7). Series: First Books. 1998, Watts LB $22.00 (0-531-20293-3). 63pp. Following a general history of caves and their different types, this account focuses on the limestone variety, how it is formed, where it is found, and the creatures that live within it. (Rev: HBG 10/98; SLJ 9/98) [551.4]

20371 George, Jean Craighead. *One Day in the Alpine Tundra* (4–7). Illus. by Walter Gaffney-Kessell. 1984, HarperCollins LB $15.89 (0-690-04326-0). 48pp. An introduction to the geology and ecology of the Alpine Tundra and an exciting story are woven together.

20372 Gibbons, Gail. *Marshes and Swamps* (2–3). Illus. 1998, Holiday LB $16.95 (0-8234-1347-0). 32pp. Fresh and saltwater wetlands are introduced, as well as the amazing variety of animals and plants that are found in them. (Rev: BCCB 4/98; BL 3/15/98; HBG 10/98; SLJ 5/98) [551.41]

20373 Godkin, Celia. *Sea Otter Inlet* (1–3). Illus. by author. 1998, Fitzhenry & Whiteside $15.95 (1-55041-080-6). Ecosystems and the balance of nature are explored in this account of what happens to a kelp bed when the otters are killed or driven off by hunters. (Rev: SLJ 1/99) [574]

20374 Greenaway, Theresa. *Swamp Life* (3–6). Illus. by Jane Burton and Kim Taylor. Series: Look Closer. 1993, DK $9.95 (1-56458-211-6). 32pp. With double-page spreads and many captions, the flora

and fauna of swamps are highlighted. (Rev: BL 8/93; SLJ 8/93) [574]

20375 Guiberson, Brenda Z. *Spoonbill Swamp* (1–3). Illus. by Megan Lloyd. 1995, Holt paper $6.95 (0-8050-3385-8). 32pp. This story depicts a day in the lives of a mother spoonbill and a mother alligator in a southern swamp. (Rev: BL 3/15/92; SLJ 3/92) [591.5]

20376 Hewitt, Sally. *All Kinds of Habitats* (K–3). Series: It's Science! 1999, Children's LB $20.00 (0-516-21181-1). 30pp. Basic information is given in double-page spreads on a variety of habitats including rain forests and grasslands, with material on the plants and animals found in them. (Rev: SLJ 5/99) [574]

20377 Jenkins, Steve. *Hottest, Coldest, Highest, Deepest* (PS–3). Illus. 1998, Houghton $16.00 (0-395-89999-0). 32pp. A geographical picture book describing superlative locations — the deepest lake, highest mountain, and places that are the hottest, coldest, windiest, etc. (Rev: BCCB 1/99; BL 8/98; HBG 3/99; SLJ 8/98) [910]

20378 Kalman, Bobbie, and Jacqueline Langille. *What Is a Biome?* (3–5). Series: Science of Living Things. 1998, Crabtree LB $14.37 (0-86505-875-X); paper $5.36 (0-86505-887-3). 32pp. Different types of ecological communities such as grasslands and deserts are described, with maps, photographs, charts, and short, interesting chapters. (Rev: SLJ 11/98) [591]

20379 Kent, Peter. *Hidden Under the Ground: The World Beneath Your Feet* (3–6). Illus. 1998, Dutton $16.99 (0-525-67552-3). 36pp. This book on our underground world explores such topics as animal life (moles, worms, etc.), medieval dungeons, caves, sewers, subways, and digging tools. (Rev: BL 9/1/98; HBG 3/99; SLJ 11/98) [909]

20380 Kramer, Stephen. *Caves* (3–6). Photos by Kenrick L. Day. Series: Caves. 1995, Carolrhoda LB $19.95 (0-87614-447-4); paper $7.95 (0-87614-896-8). 48pp. Using color photos, diagrams, and maps plus an interesting text, this book supplies a fascinating introduction to caves and their exploration. (Rev: BCCB 7–8/95; BL 4/15/95; SLJ 7/95) [557.4]

20381 Luenn, Nancy. *Squish! A Wetland Walk* (PS–2). Illus. by Ronald Himler. 1994, Atheneum $17.00 (0-689-31842-1). 32pp. A boy's walk in a wetland is used to introduce the plants and animals found there. (Rev: BL 11/1/94; SLJ 11/94) [574.5]

20382 Lye, Keith. *Coasts* (4–7). Illus. 1989, Silver Burdett LB $16.95 (0-382-09790-4). 48pp. The effects and explanation of receding and advancing coastlines. (Rev: BL 5/1/89)

20383 Maynard, Caitlin, and Thane Maynard. *Rain Forests and Reefs: A Kid's-Eye View of the Tropics* (4–8). Illus. 1996, Watts LB $24.00 (0-531-11281-0). 64pp. The flora and fauna of rain forests and coral reefs in Belize are described in text and stunning photos. (Rev: BL 2/15/97; SLJ 3/97*) [574.5]

20384 Perenyi, Constance. *Wild Wild West: Wildlife Habitats of Western North America* (K–3). Illus. 1993, Sasquatch paper $8.95 (0-912365-90-0).

32pp. Ten geographical areas, including the Arctic tundra, Rocky Mountains, Sonoran Desert, and a coral reef, are described and pictured in colorful collages. (Rev: BL 12/15/93; SLJ 12/93) [508.78]

20385 Pipes, Rose. *Islands* (2–4). Series: World Habitats. 1998, Raintree Steck-Vaughn LB $15.98 (0-8172-5009-3). 32pp. The physical characteristics of islands are presented with material on shore life, general geography, and various kinds of wildlife. (Rev: BL 3/15/99; HBG 3/99) [551.4]

20386 Pipes, Rose. *Wetlands* (2–4). Series: World Habitats. 1998, Raintree Steck-Vaughn LB $22.11 (0-8172-5001-8). 32pp. A nicely illustrated and well-laid out book on the ecology of wetlands, their climate, physical features, and plant and animal life. (Rev: BL 5/15/98; HBG 10/98) [574.5]

20387 Podendorf, Illa. *Jungles* (1–4). Illus. 1982, Children's LB $21.00 (0-516-01631-8). The flora and fauna in jungles described simply in this introductory volume.

20388 Regan, Colm. *People of the Islands* (4–6). Series: Wide World. 1998, Raintree Steck-Vaughn LB $25.69 (0-8172-5064-6). 48pp. Island environments are introduced with material on their geography and ecology and how humans live in these environments. (Rev: HBG 3/99; SLJ 2/99) [551.4]

20389 Ricciuti, Edward R. *Chaparral* (5–7). Illus. Series: Biomes of the World. 1996, Benchmark LB $25.64 (0-7614-0137-7). 64pp. The climate, vegetation, and life cycles are described in the chaparral, the biome situated between desert and grassland or forest and grassland, as in western North America from Oregon to Baja California. (Rev: SLJ 7/96) [574.5]

20390 Sauvain, Philip. *Rivers and Valleys* (4–7). Illus. Series: Geography Detectives. 1996, Carolrhoda $19.95 (0-87614-996-4). 32pp. In two-page spreads, rivers and valleys are introduced, with material on geology, flood control, wildlife, and tourism. (Rev: SLJ 3/97) [551.48]

20391 Sayre, April Pulley. *Wetland* (4–7). Illus. Series: Exploring Earth's Biomes. 1996, Twenty-First Century LB $20.40 (0-8050-4086-2). 80pp. The nature of wetlands and the life they support are covered in text and many illustrations. (Rev: BL 6/1–15/96; SLJ 6/96) [574.5]

20392 Siebert, Diane. *Cave* (2–4). Illus. 2000, HarperCollins LB $16.89 (0-688-16448-X). 32pp. In the form of a poem, this account describes caves, their formation, animal life, and such phenomena as stalactites and stalagmites. (Rev: BL 10/1/00; HBG 3/01; SLJ 10/00) [551.44]

20393 Staub, Frank. *America's Wetlands* (4–6). Illus. 1995, Carolrhoda LB $21.27 (0-87614-827-5). 48pp. The ecology of wetlands is described, with emphasis on their importance for the survival of wildlife. (Rev: BL 4/1/95; SLJ 5/95) [574.5]

20394 Steele, Philip. *Islands* (3–5). Illus. Series: Geography Detectives. 1996, Carolrhoda LB $19.95 (0-87614-997-2). 32pp. Double-page spreads introduce islands, their composition, and how they have been changed by humankind. (Rev: BL 9/1/96; SLJ 9/96) [551.4]

20395 Stille, Darlene R. *Wetlands* (2–4). Illus. Series: True Books. 1999, Children's LB $21.50 (0-516-21512-4). 48pp. A simple text and many photographs are used to introduce wetlands, their climate and geography, and the plants and animals that exist there. (Rev: BL 10/15/99) [578.768]

20396 Wood, Jenny. *Waterfalls: Nature's Thundering Splendor* (3–5). Illus. Series: Wonderworks of Nature. 1991, Stevens LB $22.60 (0-8368-0633-6). 32pp. Such waterfalls as Niagara, Sutherland, and Victoria are described with information also on rapids, cascades, and hydroelectric power. (Rev: SLJ 9/92) [551.48]

20397 Young, Allen M. *Lives Intertwined: Relationships Between Plants and Animals* (4–6). Illus. Series: A First Book. 1996, Watts LB $22.50 (0-531-20251-8). 63pp. Using the Central American rain forest as a lab, this account explores the complex relationships and interdependence of its plant and animal life. (Rev: SLJ 4/97) [574.5]

Deserts

20398 Arnold, Caroline. *Watching Desert Wildlife* (3–6). Photos by Arthur Arnold. 1994, Carolrhoda LB $23.93 (0-87614-841-0). 48pp. The desert environment is first explained, and then its wildlife is introduced in text and excellent photographs. (Rev: BL 12/1/94; SLJ 1/95) [574.5]

20399 Arnosky, Jim. *Watching Desert Wildlife* (3–5). Illus. 1998, National Geographic $15.95 (0-7922-7304-4). 32pp. Based on visits to deserts in the Southwest, the author describes and provides paintings of the birds, snakes, lizards, deer, and other animals of the area and their habitats. (Rev: BL 9/15/98; HB 11–12/98; HBG 3/99; SLJ 10/98) [591.754]

20400 Benjamin, Cynthia. *Footprints in the Sand* (PS–1). Illus. by Jacqueline Rogers. Series: Hello Reader! 1999, Scholastic paper $3.99 (0-590-44087-X). In this beginning reader, nine desert animals are introduced as they make their way to their nests or dens. (Rev: SLJ 7/99) [591]

20401 Chambers, Catherine. *Deserts* (3–5). Series: Mapping Earthforms. 2000, Heinemann LB $14.95 (1-57572-522-3). 32pp. Deserts and desert life plus environmental factors that affect deserts are introduced in a large, bold text and numerous illustrations. (Rev: HBG 3/01; SLJ 8/00) [574.5]

20402 Fleisher, Paul. *Saguaro Cactus* (3–5). Series: Webs of Life. 1997, Marshall Cavendish LB $15.95 (0-7614-0433-3). 40pp. An introduction to this gigantic cactus found in the Southwest, with material on how it survives in a hostile environment. (Rev: BL 2/15/98; HBG 3/98) [635.9]

20403 George, Jean Craighead. *One Day in the Desert* (3–6). Illus. by Fred Brenner. 1983, HarperCollins LB $15.89 (0-690-04341-4). 48pp. A day in the desert with both record heat and torrential rain.

20404 Giesecke, Ernestine. *Desert Plants* (K–3). Series: Heinemann First Library. 1999, Heinemann LB $13.95 (1-57572-821-4). 32pp. A colorful beginning book that introduces desert plants and explains a little about their ecosystem and how they have adapted. (Rev: BL 6/1–15/99; SLJ 8/99) [574.4]

20405 Green, Jen. *A Saguaro Cactus* (2–4). Series: Small Worlds. 1999, Crabtree LB $15.96 (0-7787-0134-6); paper $8.06 (0-7787-0148-4). 32pp. The desert ecosystem of the Sonoran Desert is introduced with material on the plants and animals found there. (Rev: SLJ 2/00) [574.5]

20406 Jenkins, Martin. *Deserts* (3–6). Illus. Series: Endangered People and Places. 1996, Lerner LB $22.60 (0-8225-2775-8). 48pp. In this account that combines geography and sociology, deserts and the survival of their inhabitants are described. (Rev: BL 11/15/96; SLJ 11/96) [333.73]

20407 Jernigan, Gisela. *Sonoran Seasons: A Year in the Desert* (3–6). Illus. by E. Wesley Jernigan. 1994, Harbinger paper $10.95 (0-943173-91-4). For every month of the year, a different plant from the Sonoran Desert is introduced, most of them edible. (Rev: SLJ 6/94) [581.5]

20408 Johnson, Rebecca L. *A Walk in the Desert* (2–5). Illus. by Phyllis V. Saroff. Series: Biomes of North America. 2001, Carolrhoda LB $23.93 (1-57505-152-4). 48pp. As well as the climate of the desert, this account covers its flora and fauna and their interactions. (Rev: SLJ 3/01) [574.5]

20409 Lambert, David. *People of the Deserts* (4–6). Series: Wide World. 1998, Raintree Steck-Vaughn LB $25.69 (0-8172-5063-8). 48pp. The physical geography and ecology of desert regions are discussed with material on the human cultures in these areas. (Rev: HBG 3/99; SLJ 2/99) [551.4]

20410 Landau, Elaine. *Desert Mammals* (1–3). Illus. Series: A True Book. 1996, Children's LB $22.00 (0-516-20038-0). 48pp. After brief coverage on what and where deserts are, this account describes some indigenous mammals, like camels, kangaroo rats, antelope jack rabbits, and addaxes. (Rev: SLJ 3/97) [591]

20411 Lesser, Carolyn. *Storm on the Desert* (K–3). Illus. by Ted Rand. 1997, Harcourt $16.00 (0-15-272198-3). 40pp. Pictures and text depict what happens in a desert before, during, and after a violent storm. (Rev: BL 5/1/97; SLJ 5/97) [574.5]

20412 Low, Robert. *Peoples of the Desert* (2–5). Illus. Series: People and Their Environments. 1996, Rosen LB $10.46 (0-8239-2296-0). 24pp. Two nomadic tribes, one from the Sahara and the other from the Kalahari, are featured in this discussion of human life in a desert environment. (Rev: BL 10/15/96; SLJ 1/97) [966]

20413 Lye, Keith. *Deserts* (4–6). Illus. 1987, Silver Burdett LB $12.95 (0-382-09501-4). 48pp. A well-illustrated survey that describes the locations, climate, evolution of, and plant and animal life in the world's deserts. (Rev: BL 2/1/88)

20414 Pipes, Rose. *Hot Deserts* (2–4). Illus. Series: World Habitats. 1998, Raintree Steck-Vaughn LB $22.11 (0-8172-5004-2). 32pp. Color photos and a large, clear text introduce deserts, their climate, vegetation, and the people and animals populating them. (Rev: BL 4/15/98; HBG 10/98) [577.54]

20415 Ricciuti, Edward R. *Desert* (4–6). Illus. Series: Biomes of the World. 1996, Benchmark LB $25.64 (0-7614-0134-2). 64pp. Deserts of the world are identified and described, with coverage on their plant and animal life. (Rev: SLJ 7/96) [574.9]

20416 Ruth, Maria Mudd. *The Deserts of the Southwest* (5–8). Series: Ecosystems of North America. 1998, Benchmark LB $18.95 (0-7614-0899-1). 64pp. The desert ecosystem is presented with material on its plants and animals and how human presence has changed its nature. (Rev: HBG 10/99; SLJ 2/99) [574.5]

20417 Sabin, Louis. *Wonders of the Desert* (1–3). Illus. by Pamela Baldwin Ford. 1982, Troll LB $17.25 (0-89375-574-5); paper $2.50 (0-89375-575-3). 32pp. A fine array of desert flora and fauna is simply introduced.

20418 Savage, Stephen. *Animals of the Desert* (3–6). Illus. Series: Animals by Habitat. 1997, Raintree Steck-Vaughn LB $22.83 (0-8172-4750-5). 32pp. After a discussion of the world's deserts and how they differ, this book introduces five basic animals groups found in deserts, like mammals, birds, and reptiles. (Rev: BL 5/15/97; SLJ 8/97) [591.5]

20419 Sayre, April Pulley. *Desert* (4–7). Illus. Series: Exploring Earth's Biomes. 1994, Twenty-First Century LB $18.90 (0-8050-2825-0). 64pp. After a general introduction to deserts, a specific one is explored in brief chapters with excellent illustrations. (Rev: BL 1/1/95*; SLJ 1/95) [574.5]

20420 Spencer, Guy J. *A Living Desert* (3–5). Illus. 1988, Troll LB $15.35 (0-8167-1169-0); paper $3.95 (0-8167-1170-4). 32pp. An adventure in Arizona's Sonoran Desert. (Rev: BL 8/88)

20421 Steele, Philip. *Deserts* (4–6). Illus. Series: Geography Detectives. 1996, Carolrhoda LB $19.95 (0-87614-998-0). 32pp. This introduction to deserts and the life found in them discusses such topics as the differences between hot and cold deserts, their landscape features, and how they are still being created. (Rev: SLJ 9/96) [574.5]

20422 Stewart, Gail B. *In the Desert* (4–6). Illus. Series: Living Spaces. 1989, Rourke LB $21.27 (0-86592-106-7). 32pp. The hardships faced by people who live in a desert environment. Two other landscapes explored are: *In the Mountains* (1980) and *On the Water* (1989). (Rev: BL 11/1/89) [304.2]

20423 Stille, Darlene R. *Deserts* (2–4). Series: True Books. 1999, Children's LB $21.50 (0-516-21508-6). 48pp. A color photo with six lines of simple text on each page is used to introduced deserts and their characteristics, location, and flora and fauna. (Rev: BL 10/15/99) [574.5]

20424 Storad, Conrad J. *Saguaro Cactus* (3–5). Photos by Paula Jansen. Series: Early Bird Nature Books. 1994, Lerner LB $22.60 (0-8225-3002-3). 48pp. After a general introduction to cacti, this account focuses on the physical appearance and life cycle of the saguaro. (Rev: SLJ 8/94) [583]

20425 Taylor, Barbara. *Desert Life* (3–6). Illus. by Frank Greenaway. Series: Look Closer. 1992, DK $9.95 (1-879431-93-9). 32pp. Clear photos highlight the inhabitants of the desert. (Rev: BL 6/1/92; HB 7–8/92; SLJ 6/92) [574.909]

20426 Twist, Clint. *Deserts* (5–8). Illus. Series: Ecology Watch. 1991, Macmillan LB $17.95 (0-87518-490-1). 45pp. An informative, attractive survey of the specific problems related to the world's deserts, their plants, and animals. (Rev: BL 3/1/92; SLJ 4/92) [574.5]

20427 Wallace, Marianne D. *America's Deserts: Guide to Plants and Animals* (3–5). Illus. 1996, Fulcrum paper $15.95 (1-55591-268-0). 48pp. After a general discussion of the flora and fauna of deserts, this account focuses on specific deserts, like Mojave and Death Valley. (Rev: BL 4/1/96; SLJ 7/96) [574.973]

20428 Wright-Frierson, Virginia. *A Desert Scrapbook: Dawn to Dusk in the Sonoran Desert* (3–5). Illus. 1996, Simon & Schuster $16.00 (0-689-80678-7). 32pp. A day in the life of the Sonoran Desert is described in words and watercolors painted by the author. (Rev: BL 8/96; SLJ 6/96*) [574]

20429 Yolen, Jane. *Welcome to the Sea of Sand* (K–3). Illus. by Laura Regan. 1996, Putnam $16.99 (0-399-22765-2). 32pp. A depiction in text and paintings of the amazing creatures found in a seemingly lifeless desert. (Rev: BL 4/15/96; SLJ 5/96*) [508]

Forests and Rain Forests

20430 Aldis, Rodney. *Rainforests* (5–8). Illus. Series: Ecology Watch. 1991, Macmillan LB $13.95 (0-87518-495-2). 45pp. In an attractive, oversized format, this book discusses how the rain forest evolved, why it is threatened, and the plants and animals specific to it. (Rev: BL 3/1/92; SLJ 4/92) [574.5]

20431 Anderson, Robert. *Forests: Identifying Propaganda Techniques* (5–7). Illus. Series: Opposing Viewpoints Juniors. 1992, Greenhaven LB $16.20 (0-89908-099-5). 36pp. This book examines such issues as acid rain and saving the rain forests from various viewpoints. (Rev: BL 1/15/93) [574.5]

20432 Butterfield, Moira. *Animals in Trees* (K–3). Series: Looking At. 1999, Raintree Steck-Vaughn LB $22.83 (0-7398-0110-4). 32pp. For beginning readers, this book introduces in a simple text and pictures such animals as the squirrel, marmoset, macaw, and ocelot. (Rev: HBG 10/00; SLJ 3/00) [591]

20433 Chinery, Michael. *Poisoners and Pretenders* (5–8). Series: Secrets of the Rainforests. 2000, Crabtree LB $14.97 (0-7787-0219-7); paper $7.16 (0-7787-0229-4). 32pp. After a brief description of a rain forest, this book looks at animals found there and their mimicry, camouflage, venom, natural selection, and adaptation to the environment. Also use *Predators and Prey* (2000). (Rev: SLJ 2/01) [574.5]

20434 Collard, Sneed B. *The Forest in the Clouds* (2–4). Illus. by Michael Rothman. 2000, Charlesbridge $16.95 (0-88106-985-X); paper $6.95 (0-88106-986-8). 32pp. In double-page spreads, the

Monteverde Cloud Forest in Costa Rica is introduced with material on its climate, animals, and plants. (Rev: BL 6/1–15/00; HBG 3/01; SLJ 8/00) [577.34]

20435 Crump, Donald J., ed. *Explore a Tropical Forest* (K–3). Illus. by Barbara Gibson. Series: National Geographic Action Books. 1989, National Geographic $16.00 (0-87044-757-2). Pop-ups and flaps are used to give a three-dimensional look at a tropical rain forest and its flora and fauna. (Rev: SLJ 3/90) [574.5]

20436 Darling, Kathy. *Rain Forest Babies* (K–3). Illus. by Tara Darling. 1996, Walker LB $16.85 (0-8027-8412-7). 32pp. All kinds of baby animals found in the rain forest are introduced in text and full-page color photographs. (Rev: BL 4/15/96; SLJ 4/96) [591]

20437 Dorros, Arthur. *Rain Forest Secrets* (3–5). Illus. 1990, Scholastic $15.95 (0-590-43369-5). 32pp. A picture-book introduction to rain forests. (Rev: BCCB 9/90; BL 9/1/90; SLJ 2/91) [574.5]

20438 Drake, Jane, and Ann Love. *Forestry* (3–4). Illus. by Pat Cupples. Series: America at Work. 1998, Kids Can $12.95 (1-55074-462-3). 31pp. A young boy is taken into a forest where he learns about forestry, the lumbering industry, and associated environmental concerns. (Rev: HBG 3/99; SLJ 12/98) [574.5]

20439 Forsyth, Adrian. *How Monkeys Make Chocolate: Foods and Medicines from the Rainforests* (5–8). Illus. 1995, Firefly $16.95 (1-895688-45-0); paper $9.95 (1-895688-32-9). 48pp. An account of the interdependence of plants, animals, and humans in the world's rain forests. (Rev: BL 12/1/95; SLJ 1/96) [581.6]

20440 Forsyth, Adrian. *Journey Through a Tropical Jungle* (4–8). Illus. 1996, Firefly paper $2.99 (0-920-77526-8). 80pp. A trek through the rain forest in Costa Rica. (Rev: BCCB 4/89; BL 6/1/89; SLJ 5/89)

20441 Fowler, Allan. *Our Living Forests* (1–2). Illus. Series: Rookie Readers. 1999, Children's LB $18.50 (0-516-20811-X). 32pp. With a small format, large type, and color pictures, this book introduces different kinds of forests, and tells how climate affects the kinds of trees and other plant life that grow in them. (Rev: BL 7/99; HBG 10/99) [578.73]

20442 George, Jean Craighead. *One Day in the Tropical Rain Forest* (3–6). Illus. by Gary Allen. 1990, HarperCollins $15.95 (0-690-04767-3). 64pp. The tropical rain forest is introduced in a narrative that proceeds through the course of a day. (Rev: BCCB 3/90; BL 4/15/90; HB 5–6/90; SLJ 8/90) [508]

20443 George, Jean Craighead. *One Day in the Woods* (3–5). Illus. by Gary Allen. 1988, HarperCollins LB $15.89 (0-690-04724-X). 48pp. Following Rebecca's search in the forest for an oven-bird. (Rev: BL 12/15/88; SLJ 2/89)

20444 Gibbons, Gail. *Nature's Green Umbrella: Tropical Rain Forests* (3–5). Illus. 1994, Morrow $15.93 (0-688-12354-6). 32pp. The ecosystem of the rain forest is explained, with material on how these resources should be protected and preserved. (Rev: BL 6/1–15/94; SLJ 7/94) [574.5]

20445 Giesecke, Ernestine. *Forest Plants* (K–3). Series: Heinemann First Library. 1999, Heinemann LB $13.95 (1-57572-823-0). 32pp. Different plants that grow in forests are presented with a full-color photo followed by a few lines of explanatory text. (Rev: BL 6/1–15/99) [574]

20446 Goodman, Susan E. *Bats, Bugs, and Biodiversity: Adventures in the Amazonian Rain Forest* (4–6). Illus. by Michael J. Doolittle. 1995, Simon & Schuster $16.00 (0-689-31943-6). 46pp. Some junior high students learn first-hand about the Amazon rain forest and its endangered ecology. (Rev: BCCB 10/95; BL 8/95; SLJ 7/95*) [508]

20447 Green, Jen. *A Dead Log* (2–4). Series: Small Worlds. 1999, Crabtree LB $15.96 (0-7787-0136-0); paper $8.06 (0-7787-0150-6). 32pp. This book presents the animals and plants that might be associated with a fallen log in a North American deciduous forest. (Rev: SLJ 2/00) [574.5]

20448 Green, Jen. *Rain Forests* (3–6). Illus. Series: Young Scientist Concepts and Projects. 1999, Gareth Stevens LB $16.95 (0-8368-2268-4). 64pp. This work discusses rain forests, where they are found, and the life on a rain forest floor, and outlines several related projects. (Rev: BL 4/15/99) [577.34]

20449 Grupper, Jonathan. *Destination: Rain Forest* (4–6). Illus. 1997, National Geographic $16.00 (0-7922-7018-5). 32pp. Using brilliant photos, this book introduces the rain forest as a habitat, as well as the animals found there. (Rev: BL 11/1/97; HBG 3/98; SLJ 10/97) [578.734]

20450 Hickman, Pamela. *In the Woods* (3–5). Series: See, Make and Do. 1998, Formac paper $9.95 (0-88780-412-8). 64pp. A book about woodland exploration and the animals and plants one might encounter, with several suggestions for craft projects. (Rev: BL 12/1/98) [557.3]

20451 *Inside the Dzanga-Sangha Rain Forest* (4–7). Ed. by Francesca Lyman. Illus. 1998, Workman paper $12.95 (0-7611-0870-X). 128pp. Each page of this book is filled with gorgeous color photos that introduce the rain forest ecosystem, daily life in it, and its rare plants, animals, and insects. (Rev: BL 12/15/98) [508.674]

20452 Johanasen, Heather, and Sindy McKay. *About the Rain Forest* (1–2). Illus. Series: We Both Read. 2000, Treasure Bay $7.99 (1-891327-23-2); paper $3.99 (1-891327-24-0). 44pp. Using side-by-side texts, one for adults and the other for children, this book introduces the rain forest, its climate, ecosystem, and animals. (Rev: BL 7/00) [574.5]

20453 Johnson, Linda Carlson. *Rain Forests: A Pro/Con Issue* (4–8). Series: Hot Issues. 1999, Enslow LB $19.95 (0-7660-1202-6). 64pp. This book describes the rain forests of the world, how political and economic interests are destroying them, efforts to save them, and the pros and cons of conserving them. (Rev: HBG 10/00; SLJ 4/00) [574.5]

20454 Johnson, Rebecca L. *A Walk in the Boreal Forest* (2–4). Illus. by Phyllis V. Saroff. Series: Biomes of North America. 2000, Carolrhoda LB $23.95 (1-57505-156-7). 48pp. This book takes the reader to a forest of tall conifers and tells about its plants and animals and their interdependence. (Rev: BL 10/15/00; HBG 3/01; SLJ 3/01) [574.5]

20455 Johnson, Rebecca L. *A Walk in the Rain Forest* (2–5). Illus. by Phyllis V. Saroff. Series: Biomes of North America. 2001, Carolrhoda LB $23.93 (1-57505-154-0). 48pp. Examines the climate of the rain forest and its flora and fauna. (Rev: SLJ 3/01) [574.5]

20456 Kaplan, Elizabeth. *Taiga* (5–7). Illus. Series: Biomes of the World. 1996, Benchmark LB $25.64 (0-7614-0135-0). 64pp. This account discusses the climate, animal and plant life, soil, and seasonal changes in the taiga, the extensive forest in the Northern Hemisphere. (Rev: SLJ 7/96) [574.5]

20457 Kaplan, Elizabeth. *Temperate Forest* (4–6). Illus. Series: Biomes of the World. 1995, Marshall Cavendish LB $25.64 (0-7614-0082-6). 64pp. Four types of temperate forests are introduced, with material on locations, animals, plants, and possible future problems. (Rev: BL 12/15/95; SLJ 3/96) [574.5]

20458 Klum, Mattias, and Hans Odoo. *Exploring the Rain Forest* (2–5). Illus. 1998, Sterling $14.95 (0-8069-9873-3). 64pp. A chatty, informal guide to the rain forest, with excellent photos and captions. (Rev: BL 3/1/98; SLJ 2/98) [578.734]

20459 Knapp, Brian. *What Do We Know About Rainforests?* (4–6). Illus. Series: Caring for Environments. 1992, Bedrick LB $15.95 (0-87226-358-4). 40pp. A colorful book that surveys the location, terrain, ecology, and importance of rain forests. (Rev: BL 2/15/93; SLJ 1/93) [574]

20460 Lampton, Christopher. *Forest Fire* (4–6). Illus. Series: Disaster! 1974, Millbrook paper $7.95 (1-56294-779-6). 64pp. High interest and low reading level mark this colorful description, especially valuable for scientific insights on causes and results of forests fires. (Rev: BL 1/1/92; SLJ 12/91) [634.9]

20461 Landau, Elaine. *Temperate Forest Mammals* (3–4). Illus. Series: A True Book. 1996, Children's LB $22.00 (0-516-20043-7). 48pp. General information on forests found in temperate climates is followed by material of specific mammals. (Rev: SLJ 4/97) [591]

20462 Lasky, Kathryn. *The Most Beautiful Roof in the World: Exploring the Rainforest Canopy* (3–5). Illus. 1997, Harcourt $18.00 (0-15-100893-4). The canopy of plants and animals found in the rain forest of Belize is explored by the author, a biologist, and her assistant. (Rev: BL 4/1/97*; HB 5–6/97) [574.5]

20463 Lewington, Anna. *Antonio's Rain Forest* (3–5). Illus. by Edward Parker. 1993, Carolrhoda LB $22.60 (0-87614-749-X). 48pp. A first-person narrative by an 8-year-old boy of the rain forest. (Rev: BL 3/1/93; SLJ 3/93) [338]

20464 Lewington, Anna, and Edward Parker. *People of the Rain Forests* (4–7). Series: Wide World.

1998, Raintree Steck-Vaughn LB $25.69 (0-8172-5061-1). 48pp. As well as introducing rain forests, this book describes the people who live there, their tribal customs, their homes — including cities — and their everyday lives. (Rev: HBG 3/99; SLJ 1/99) [574.5]

20465 Low, Robert. *Peoples of the Rain Forest* (2–5). Illus. Series: People and Their Environments. 1996, Rosen LB $15.93 (0-8239-2297-9). 24pp. Human lifestyles in a rain forest environment are introduced, with examples from peoples in Africa, South America, and Borneo. (Rev: BL 10/15/96; SLJ 11/96) [304.2]

20466 Mania, Robert, and Cathy Mania. *A Forest's Life: From Meadow to Mature Woodland* (4–6). Illus. Series: First Books. 1997, Watts LB $22.50 (0-531-20319-0). 64pp. Traces the gradual transformation of a meadow into a forest and of the plants and animals involved. (Rev: BL 12/15/97; SLJ 10/97) [577.3]

20467 Mutel, Cornelia F., and Mary M. Rodgers. *Our Endangered Planet: Tropical Rain Forests* (4–7). Illus. Series: Our Endangered Planet. 1991, Lerner LB $22.60 (0-8225-2503-8); paper $8.95 (0-8225-9629-6). 64pp. Describes tropical rain forests and the environmental dangers they face. (Rev: BL 6/15/91; SLJ 5/91) [333]

20468 Oldfield, Sara. *Rain Forests* (3–6). Illus. Series: Endangered People and Places. 1996, Lerner LB $22.60 (0-8225-2778-2). 48pp. The location, geography, and natural life of rain forests are described, plus material on the threats to these regions and how conservation efforts are proceeding. (Rev: BL 11/15/96; SLJ 1/97) [333.75]

20469 Owens, Caleb. *Deforestation* (2–3). Series: Earth's Conditions. 1999, Child's World LB $15.95 (1-56766-507-1). 32pp. This environmental problem is introduced with material on its causes and its effects on other plants and animals. (Rev: HBG 10/99; SLJ 7/99) [574.5]

20470 Pandell, Karen. *Journey Through the Northern Rainforest* (4–7). Illus. 1999, Dutton $16.99 (0-525-45804-2). 32pp. This book introduces the flora and fauna of the rain forests of the Pacific Northwest with material on how they are currently endangered. (Rev: BL 1/1–15/00; HBG 3/00; SLJ 1/00) [578.734]

20471 Parker, Edward. *Forests for the Future* (4–6). Series: Protecting Our Planet. 1998, Raintree Steck-Vaughn $25.68 (0-8172-4934-6). 48pp. This work comments on the present condition of our forests and the deforestation that threatens the plant and animal world as well as industrial and medical supplies. (Rev: BL 7/98; HBG 10/98) [574.5]

20472 Pascoe, Gwen. *Deep in a Rainforest* (PS–1). Illus. by Veronica Jefferis. 1999, Gareth Stevens LB $14.95 (0-8368-2149-1). 32pp. Picture puzzles and double-page spreads introduce the plants and animals of the rain forest to a young audience. (Rev: BL 5/1/99) [578.734]

20473 Patent, Dorothy Hinshaw. *Fire: Friend or Foe* (4–8). Illus. 1998, Clarion $16.00 (0-395-73081-3). 80pp. This book supplies valuable infor-

mation about forest fires, their causes, effects, benefits, prevention, and the methods used throughout history to combat them. (Rev: BL 11/15/98; HB 1–2/99; HBG 3/99; SLJ 12/98) [577.2]

20474 Pipes, Rose. *Forests and Woodlands* (2–4). Series: World Habitats. 1998, Raintree Steck-Vaughn LB $15.98 (0-8172-5007-7). 32pp. A general description of the physical features of forests is followed by material on climate, wildlife, uses, and protection efforts. (Rev: BL 3/15/99; HBG 3/99) [574.5]

20475 Pipes, Rose. *Rain Forests* (2–4). Illus. Series: World Habitats. 1998, Raintree Steck-Vaughn LB $22.11 (0-8172-5003-4). 32pp. Rain forests are introduced in color photographs and clear text, with material on animal and plant life, climate, and conservation. (Rev: BL 4/15/98; HBG 10/98) [577.4]

20476 Pirotta, Saviour. *People in the Rain Forest* (2–4). Illus. Series: Deep in the Rain Forest. 1998, Raintree Steck-Vaughn LB $15.98 (0-8172-5137-5). 32pp. Rain forests in Peru, Indonesia, and New Guinea are highlighted in this account of the various peoples of the rain forest, their different habitats, how they live, and how their environments are being threatened. (Rev: BL 1/1–15/99; HBG 3/99) [304.2]

20477 Pirotta, Saviour. *Predators in the Rain Forest* (2–5). Series: Deep in the Rain Forest. 1998, Raintree Steck-Vaughn LB $15.98 (0-8172-5132-4). 32pp. This volume filled with large photographs includes material on such predators as the scorpion, anaconda, and crocodile, with related activities such as making a crocodile mask. (Rev: BL 1/1–15/99; HBG 3/99) [574.5]

20478 Pirotta, Saviour. *Rivers in the Rain Forest* (2–4). Illus. Series: Deep in the Rain Forest. 1998, Raintree Steck-Vaughn LB $15.98 (0-8172-5138-3). 32pp. The nature of rivers in the world's rain forests, their uses, and how they are navigated, are discussed with an attached model of a rain forest canoe. (Rev: BL 1/1–15/99; HBG 3/99) [551.48]

20479 Pirotta, Saviour. *Trees and Plants in the Rain Forest* (2–5). Series: Deep in the Rain Forest. 1998, Raintree Steck-Vaughn LB $15.98 (0-8172-5134-0). 32pp. Large photos and hands-on activities introduce the trees and plants of the rain forest, many of which are exported for decoration in our homes. (Rev: BL 1/1–15/99; HBG 3/99; SLJ 1/99) [574.5]

20480 Ricciuti, Edward R. *Rainforest* (4–6). Illus. Series: Biomes of the World. 1995, Marshall Cavendish LB $25.64 (0-7614-0081-8). 64pp. The world's rain forest biome is described, with material on this ecological system, its animals, plants, and current threats of destruction. (Rev: BL 12/15/95) [574.5]

20481 Ross, Suzanne. *What's in the Rainforest?* (3–5). Illus. by author. 1991, Enchanted Rainforest Pr. paper $5.95 (0-9629895-0-9). 48pp. Using an alphabetical approach, this is a well-organized introduction to the plants and animals found in a rain forest. (Rev: SLJ 3/92) [574.5]

20482 Sabin, Francene. *Wonders of the Forest* (1–3). Illus. by Michael Willard. 1982, Troll paper $3.50 (0-89375-573-7). 32pp. An introduction to the trees of the forest in text and pictures. Also use: *Wonders of the Pond* (1982).

20483 Sauvain, Philip. *Rain Forests* (3–5). Illus. Series: Geography Detectives. 1997, Carolrhoda LB $19.93 (1-57505-041-2). 32pp. Identifies and describes the world's rain forests and the lush plants and diverse peoples and animals that live in them, with information on the many industrial threats to rain forests' survival. (Rev: BL 8/97) [574.5]

20484 Savage, Stephen. *Animals of the Rain Forest* (3–6). Illus. Series: Animals by Habitat. 1997, Raintree Steck-Vaughn LB $22.83 (0-8172-4751-3). 32pp. The rain forest habitat is introduced, with focus on the five categories of animal life found there, such as mammals, birds, and amphibians. (Rev: BL 5/15/97) [591.9]

20485 Sayre, April Pulley. *Taiga* (4–7). Illus. Series: Exploring Earth's Biomes. 1994, Twenty-First Century LB $18.90 (0-8050-2830-7). 64pp. This book clearly describes the swampy, carnivorous forest and the wildlife found, for example, in northern Canada, where the tundra ends. (Rev: BL 1/15/95; SLJ 2/95) [574.5]

20486 Sayre, April Pulley. *Temperate Deciduous Forest* (4–7). Illus. Series: Exploring Earth's Biomes. 1994, Twenty-First Century LB $18.90 (0-8050-2828-5). 64pp. Deciduous forests are introduced with material on their composition, uses, and the animal and other plant life found within their community. (Rev: BL 1/1/95*; SLJ 1/95) [574.5]

20487 Sayre, April Pulley. *Tropical Rain Forest* (4–7). Illus. Series: Exploring Earth's Biomes. 1994, Twenty-First Century LB $18.90 (0-8050-2826-9). 64pp. The structure and contents of rain forests are explored with information on the plants, animals, and people that exist in this habitat. (Rev: BL 1/1/95; SLJ 1/95) [574.5]

20488 Silver, Donald M. *Why Save the Rain Forest?* (3–5). Illus. by Patricia J. Wynne. 1993, Messner LB $23.00 (0-671-86609-5); paper $6.95 (0-671-86610-9). 48pp. A handsome volume that shows the amazing diversity of life in a rain forest and the consequences of destroying this environment. (Rev: SLJ 3/94) [574.5]

20489 Staub, Frank. *America's Forests* (3–6). Illus. 1999, Carolrhoda $15.95 (1-57505-265-2). 48pp. Different types of forests that exist in North America are introduced with material on kinds of trees and a basic woodland ecosystem. (Rev: BL 5/1/99; HBG 10/99; SLJ 7/99) [577.3]

20490 Stille, Darlene R. *Tropical Rain Forests* (2–4). Illus. 1999, Children's LB $21.50 (0-516-21511-6). 48pp. The climate and geography of tropical rain forests are discussed with coverage on their plants and animals. (Rev: BL 10/15/99) [578.734]

20491 Taylor, Barbara. *Rain Forest* (3–6). Illus. Series: Look Closer. 1992, DK $9.95 (1-879431-91-2). 32pp. The flora and fauna of rain forests are covered in a series of double-page spreads with informative captions. (Rev: BL 6/1/92; HB 7–8/92; SLJ 6/92) [591.909]

20492 Telford, Carole, and Rod Theodorou. *Up a Rainforest Tree* (3–5). Series: Amazing Journeys.

1997, Heinemann LB $13.95 (1-57572-156-2). 32pp. This trek through the layers of the Amazon rain forest is well organized, but the illustrations are often too small for clarity. (Rev: SLJ 4/98) [574.5]

20493 Thomson, Ruth. *The Rainforest Indians* (K–2). Illus. Series: Footsteps in Time. 1996, Children's LB $17.50 (0-516-08074-1). 24pp. Humorous rhymes accompany paintings that describe eight animals from the rain forest. (Rev: SLJ 11/96) [591]

20494 Woods, Mae. *Insects of the Rain Forest* (2–4). Series: Rain Forest. 1999, ABDO LB $13.95 (1-57765-023-9). 24pp. This book presents the insects found in the rain forest with outstanding photos and an interesting text. Also use *People of the Rain Forest* and *Protecting the Rain Forest* (both 1999). (Rev: HBG 3/00; SLJ 1/00) [574.5]

20495 Wright-Frierson, Virginia. *A North American Rain Forest Scrapbook* (3–5). Illus. 1999, Walker LB $16.89 (0-8027-8680-4). 40pp. Double-page spreads introduce the rain forest on Washington's Olympic Peninsula and discuss its flora and fauna. (Rev: BCCB 6/99; BL 11/1/99; HBG 10/99; SLJ 6/99) [577.34]

Mountains

20496 Chambers, Catherine. *Mountains* (3–5). Series: Mapping Earthforms. 2000, Heinemann LB $14.95 (1-57572-525-8). 32pp. A basic overview of mountains presented in double-page spreads illustrated with photographs, maps, and charts. (Rev: HBG 3/01; SLJ 8/00) [551.4]

20497 Cobb, Vicki. *This Place Is High* (3–5). Illus. by Barbara Lavallee. Series: Imagine Living Here. 1989, Walker LB $13.85 (0-8027-6883-0). Set in the high Andes, this is a book on an unusual climate zone in South America. A companion volume is *This Place Is Wet* (1989), about the rain forest of the Amazon River. (Rev: SLJ 10/89) [551.4]

20498 Collinson, Alan. *Mountains* (5–8). Illus. Series: Ecology Watch. 1992, Macmillan LB $17.95 (0-87518-493-6). 46pp. The flora and fauna of mountainous regions are discussed as well as the need for ecological preservation. (Rev: BL 11/1/92) [574]

20499 Cumming, David. *Mountains* (5–8). Illus. Series: Habitats. 1995, Thomson Learning LB $24.26 (1-56847-388-5). 48pp. Material covered includes the geology of mountains, their formation, and the life they support. (Rev: BL 2/1/96) [551.4]

20500 Green, Jen. *People of the Mountains* (4–6). Series: Wide World. 1998, Raintree Steck-Vaughn LB $25.69 (0-8172-5062-X). 48pp. The geography and ecology of mountain environments are discussed plus material on the human cultures in these areas. (Rev: HBG 3/99; SLJ 2/99) [551.4]

20501 Grupper, Jonathan. *Rocky Mountains* (4–6). Series: Destination. 2001, National Geographic LB $16.95 (0-7922-7722-8). 32pp. This book introduces the Rockies, how they were formed, their composition, and their animals and plants. (Rev: BL 3/1/01) [978]

20502 Landau, Elaine. *Mountain Mammals* (3–4). Illus. Series: A True Book. 1996, Children's LB $22.00 (0-516-20040-2). 48pp. General information on mountain environments is presented, and several typical mammals found in this biome are introduced. (Rev: SLJ 4/97) [591]

20503 Low, Robert. *Peoples of the Mountains* (2–4). Illus. Series: Peoples and Their Environments. 1996, Rosen LB $15.93 (0-8239-2298-7). 24pp. After a definition of a mountain environment, this book tells about people who live in the Himalayas, Andes, and the mountains of China. (Rev: SLJ 1/97) [551.4]

20504 Lye, Keith. *Mountains* (4–6). Illus. 1987, Silver Burdett LB $12.95 (0-382-09498-0). 48pp. Full-color photos, maps, and diagrams highlight this survey of the world's mountains. (Rev: BL 2/1/88)

20505 Pipes, Rose. *Mountains and Volcanoes* (2–4). Series: World Habitats. 1998, Raintree Steck-Vaughn LB $22.11 (0-8172-5006-9). 32pp. This work discusses mountains — their geographic features, evolution, weather, wildlife, and human life — and volcanoes. (Rev: BL 5/15/98; HBG 10/98) [551.4]

20506 Rotter, Charles. *Mountains* (5–8). Illus. Series: Images. 1994, Creative Ed. LB $16.95 (0-88682-596-2). 40pp. How mountains are formed is discussed, with material on how they change and the life they support. (Rev: SLJ 12/94) [551.4]

20507 Steele, Philip. *Mountains* (4–8). Illus. Series: Pocket Facts. 1991, Macmillan LB $15.95 (0-89686-587-8). 32pp. A basic introduction to mountains, aided by color photos and drawings. (Rev: BL 3/15/92) [910]

20508 Stone, Lynn M. *Mountains* (1–4). Illus. 1983, Children's LB $21.00 (0-516-01698-9). 48pp. Mountain ecology is introduced in basic terms with excellent photographs.

20509 Stronach, Neil. *Mountains* (3–6). Illus. Series: Endangered People and Places. 1996, Lerner LB $22.60 (0-8225-2777-4). 48pp. Geological aspects of mountains are covered, as well as the adjustments people make to live in mountainous regions. (Rev: BL 11/15/96; SLJ 11/96) [333.73]

Ponds, Rivers, and Lakes

20510 Amos, William Hopkins. *Life in Ponds and Streams* (PS–3). Illus. 1981, National Geographic LB $16.95 (0-87044-404-2). 32pp. Simple descriptions of pond life, plus outstanding photographs.

20511 Bains, Rae. *Wonders of Rivers* (1–3). Illus. by Yoshi Miyake. 1982, Troll paper $3.50 (0-89375-571-0). 32pp. An explanation of what rivers are and their role in our world.

20512 Cooper, Ann. *Around the Pond* (3–5). Illus. Series: Wild Wonders. 1998, Roberts Rinehart paper $9.95 (1-57098-223-6). 48pp. Using a series of four-page sections, this book describes such pond life as the bullfrog, blackbird, skunk, heron, dragonfly, grebe, turtle, diving beetle, and muskrat. (Rev: BL 12/1/98; SLJ 6/99) [591.763]

20513 Cumming, David. *Rivers and Lakes* (5–8). Illus. Series: Habitats. 1995, Thomson Learning LB $24.26 (1-56847-389-3). 48pp. The plant and animal life that is supported in lakes and rivers is introduced, with information on geology and pollution. (Rev: BL 2/1/96) [551.48]

20514 Ganeri, Anita. *Rivers, Ponds and Lakes* (5–8). Illus. Series: Ecology Watch. 1992, Macmillan LB $17.95 (0-87518-497-9). 46pp. The nature of pollution and the need for environmental protection are stressed in this introduction to water resources. (Rev: BL 11/1/92) [574]

20515 Giesecke, Ernestine. *Pond Plants* (K–3). Series: Heinemann First Library. 1999, Heinemann LB $13.95 (1-57572-826-5). 32pp. Each of the ten pond plants that are introduced are illustrated with a full-color photo plus a few lines of large-print text. (Rev: BL 6/1–15/99) [574]

20516 Giesecke, Ernestine. *River Plants* (K–3). Series: Heinemann First Library. 1999, Heinemann LB $13.95 (1-57572-827-3). 32pp. Color photos and a few lines of simple text are used to introduce about ten plants that are found in rivers. (Rev: BL 6/1–15/99) [574]

20517 Giesecke, Ernestine. *Wetland Plants* (K–3). Series: Heinemann First Library. 1999, Heinemann LB $13.95 (1-57572-830-3). 32pp. About ten common plants found in wetlands are identified and, for each, there is a color photograph and a few lines of explanatory text. (Rev: BL 6/1–15/99; SLJ 8/99) [574]

20518 Heinz, Brian J. *Butternut Hollow Pond* (2–4). Illus. by Bob Marstall. 2000, Millbrook LB $22.90 (0-7613-0268-9). 32pp. This beautiful study of a day and night on a pond introduces many forms of animal life and demonstrates the food chain and the interdependence of creatures. (Rev: BL 1/1–15/01*; HBG 3/01; SLJ 3/01) [591.763]

20519 Hiscock, Bruce. *The Big Rivers: The Missouri, the Mississippi, and the Ohio* (3–5). Illus. 1997, Simon & Schuster $16.00 (0-689-80871-2). 32pp. As well as examining these three rivers, this book gives details on the causes and effects of flooding, with special material on the 1993 floods. (Rev: BL 6/1–15/97; SLJ 7/97) [551.48]

20520 Hoff, Mary, and Mary M. Rodgers. *Our Endangered Planet: Rivers and Lakes* (4–7). Illus. Series: Our Endangered Planet. 1991, Lerner LB $22.60 (0-8225-2501-1). 64pp. The causes and possible cures of water pollution are examined. (Rev: BL 6/15/91; SLJ 5/91) [363.73]

20521 Hunter, Anne. *What's in the Pond?* (PS–2). Illus. by author. 1999, Houghton $4.95 (0-395-91224-5). Attractive color drawings are used to introduce pond life including several insects, a bluegill, a red-winged blackbird, a painted turtle, a frog, a tadpole, and a muskrat. Also use *What's Under the Log?* (1999). (Rev: HBG 3/00; SLJ 11/99) [574]

20522 Kirkpatrick, Rena K. *Look at Pond Life* (K–2). Illus. 1978, Raintree Steck-Vaughn paper $7.00 (0-8114-6901-8). 32pp. An introduction to the subject through brief text and many illustrations.

20523 Pipes, Rose. *Rivers and Lakes* (2–4). Series: World Habitats. 1998, Raintree Steck-Vaughn LB $22.11 (0-8172-5002-6). 32pp. The geographical features of rivers and lakes are introduced with material on plant and animal life found in and around them, and how to protect them in the future. (Rev: BL 5/15/98; HBG 10/98) [574.5]

20524 *The River* (PS–3). Illus. Series: First Discovery. 1993, Scholastic $12.95 (0-590-47128-7). 24pp. Using drawings, overlays, and a concise text, this book for small children describes a river and the life it supports. (Rev: BL 1/1/94) [574.5]

20525 Rowland-Entwistle, Theodore. *Rivers and Lakes* (4–6). Illus. 1987, Silver Burdett LB $20.00 (0-382-09499-9). 48pp. A fact-filled book that emphasizes the need for conservation and care of these important physical features. (Rev: BL 2/1/88)

20526 Sayre, April Pulley. *Lake and Pond* (4–7). Illus. Series: Exploring Earth's Biomes. 1996, Twenty-First Century LB $20.40 (0-8050-4089-7). 80pp. Colorful introduction to lake and pond habitats and the life forms found within them. (Rev: BL 6/1–15/96; SLJ 6/96) [574.05]

20527 Sayre, April Pulley. *River and Stream* (4–7). Illus. Series: Exploring Earth's Biomes. 1996, Twenty-First Century LB $20.40 (0-8050-4088-9). 80pp. In a clearly written, informative style, this book presents material on rivers and streams, their ecology, and the various creatures and plants living in and around them. (Rev: BL 6/1–15/96; SLJ 6/96) [574.5]

20528 Taylor, Barbara. *Pond Life* (3–6). Illus. Series: Look Closer. 1992, DK $9.95 (1-879431-94-7). 32pp. Clear photos and basic information highlight life in the pond. (Rev: BL 6/1/92; HB 7–8/92; SLJ 6/92) [591.92]

20529 Yates, Irene. *From Birth to Death* (1–5). Illus. Series: Life Cycle. 1997, Millbrook LB $20.40 (0-7613-0303-0). 32pp. In double-page spreads, this book gives details on a year of seasonal changes around a pond, with coverage on the interrelationships between plants and animals. (Rev: BL 12/1/97; HBG 3/98; SLJ 1/98) [571.8]

Prairies and Grasslands

20530 Bannatyne-Cugnet, Jo. *A Prairie Year* (3–5). Illus. by Yvette Moore. 1994, Tundra $16.95 (0-88776-334-0). 32pp. A month-by-month account of the experiences and activities involved in prairie life. (Rev: BL 1/15/95; SLJ 2/95) [630]

20531 Butterfield, Moira. *Animals on Plains and Prairies* (K–3). Series: Looking At. 1999, Raintree Steck-Vaughn LB $22.83 (0-7398-0109-0). 32pp. Such grassland animals as the giraffe, termite, vulture, and agama lizard are introduced in this beginning reader. (Rev: HBG 10/00; SLJ 3/00) [574.5]

20532 Collinson, Alan. *Grasslands* (5–8). Illus. Series: Ecology Watch. 1992, Macmillan $17.95 (0-87518-492-8). 46pp. The flora and fauna of a grassland environment are introduced and the ecological balance needed for them to survive. (Rev: BL 11/15/92) [574.5]

20533 Dunphy, Madeleine. *Here Is the African Savanna* (PS–3). Illus. by Tom Leonard. Series: Here Is. 1999, Hyperion LB $15.49 (0-7868-2134-5). 32pp. A cumulative story that introduces the plants and animals of an East African savanna. (Rev: BL 5/15/99; HBG 10/99) [577.4]

20534 Fowler, Allan. *Lands of Grass* (K–2). Illus. Series: Rookie Readers. 2000, Children's LB $19.00 (0-516-21213-3). 32pp. This heavily illustrated, simple book introduces different kinds of grasslands, shows animals found there, and makes a plea for conservation. (Rev: BL 1/1–15/01) [577.4]

20535 Green, Jen. *Under a Stone* (2–4). Series: Small Worlds. 1999, Crabtree LB $15.96 (0-7787-0137-9); paper $8.06 (0-7787-0151-4). 32pp. Highlights the animals and plants found on a North American prairie. (Rev: SLJ 2/00) [574.5]

20536 Hunter, Anne. *What's in the Meadow?* (K–2). Illus. 2000, Houghton $4.95 (0-618-01512-4). 32pp. Ten animals that live in meadows — including the woolly bear caterpillar, spittlebug, firefly, and meadowlark — are introduced with material on this habitat. (Rev: BL 9/15/00; HBG 3/01) [591.74]

20537 Knapp, Brian. *What Do We Know About Grasslands?* (4–6). Illus. 1992, Bedrick LB $15.95 (0-87226-359-2). 40pp. Among the topics covered are the importance of grasslands and their locations, ecology, and outlook. (Rev: BL 2/15/93; SLJ 1/93) [574]

20538 Landau, Elaine. *Grassland Mammals* (1–3). Illus. Series: A True Book. 1996, Children's LB $22.00 (0-516-20039-9). 48pp. After grasslands are defined and located in the world, this book introduces such indigenous mammals as African elephants, prairie dogs, giraffes, and kangaroos. (Rev: SLJ 3/97) [591]

20539 Low, Robert. *Peoples of the Savanna* (2–5). Illus. Series: People and Their Environments. 1996, Rosen LB $15.93 (0-8239-2299-5). 24pp. Describes life in a grassland habitat and how this environment has shaped the lifestyles of the people who live there. (Rev: BL 11/15/96; SLJ 1/97) [304.2]

20540 Ormsby, Alison. *The Prairie* (5–8). Series: Ecosystems of North America. 1998, Benchmark LB $18.95 (0-7614-0897-5). 64pp. This work presents the prairie ecosystem in North America with material on its plants and animals and the impact of human development. (Rev: HBG 10/99; SLJ 2/99) [574.5]

20541 Patent, Dorothy Hinshaw. *Prairies* (3–6). Illus. by William Munoz. 1996, Holiday LB $15.95 (0-8234-1277-6). 40pp. The ecology of prairie environments is covered, with striking photos and clear text. (Rev: BCCB 2/97; BL 11/1/96; SLJ 2/97) [574.5]

20542 Pipes, Rose. *Grasslands* (2–4). Series: World Habitats. 1998, Raintree Steck-Vaughn LB $22.11 (0-8172-5005-0). 32pp. A well-organized account that explains the grassland ecology and gives examples of it around the world using text and pictures. (Rev: BL 5/15/98; HBG 10/98) [574.5]

20543 Ricciuti, Edward R. *Grassland* (4–6). Illus. Series: Biomes of the World. 1996, Benchmark LB

$25.64 (0-7614-0136-9). 64pp. The world's grasslands are identified and described, with material on their vegetation and animal life and the environmental threats they face. (Rev: SLJ 7/96) [574.5]

20544 Rotter, Charles. *The Prairie* (5–8). Illus. Series: Images. 1994, Creative Ed. LB $16.95 (0-88682-598-9). 40pp. The nature of prairie grasslands is introduced, with material on the animals and plants found there. (Rev: SLJ 12/94) [574.5]

20545 Savage, Stephen. *Animals of the Grasslands* (2–6). Illus. Series: Animals by Habitat. 1997, Raintree Steck-Vaughn LB $22.83 (0-8172-4752-1). 32pp. Worldwide locations and characteristics of grasslands are highlighted, with material on such animals as coyotes, zebras, prairie dogs, emus, and termites. (Rev: BL 5/15/97) [591.9]

20546 Sayre, April Pulley. *Grassland* (4–7). Illus. Series: Exploring Earth's Biomes. 1994, Twenty-First Century LB $18.90 (0-8050-2827-7). 64pp. A well-organized, clearly written account that explains what grasslands are and where they exist and the interaction of the creatures who live in this biome. (Rev: BL 1/15/95; SLJ 2/95) [574.5]

20547 Staub, Frank. *America's Prairies* (3–6). Illus. Series: Earth Watch. 1994, Carolrhoda LB $21.27 (0-87614-781-3). 48pp. The three kinds of prairies found in the United States are introduced, with coverage of the animals and plants found in each and the environmental hazards. (Rev: BL 2/1/94) [574.5]

20548 Steele, Philip. *Grasslands* (3–5). Illus. Series: Geography Detectives. 1997, Carolrhoda LB $19.93 (1-57505-042-0). 32pp. Discusses the grassland ecosystem in both temperate and tropical areas, with coverage on how they have been changed by agriculture and urbanization. (Rev: BL 8/97) [574.5]

20549 Stille, Darlene R. *Grasslands* (2–4). Series: True Books. 1999, Children's LB $21.50 (0-516-21509-4). 48pp. Grasslands and prairies are introduced in a book that contains a color picture and six lines of text on each page. (Rev: BL 10/15/99) [574.5]

Rocks, Minerals, and Soil

20550 Bocknek, Jonathan. *The Science of Soil* (2–5). Series: Living Science. 1999, Gareth Stevens LB $14.95 (0-8368-2468-7). 32pp. Various types of soil are introduced with materials on the animals that live in them and the nutrients they contain. (Rev: HBG 10/00; SLJ 1/00) [631.5]

20551 Bourgeois, Paulette. *The Amazing Dirt Book* (3–5). Illus. by Craig Terlson. Series: Children's Activities. 1990, Addison-Wesley paper $8.95 (0-201-55096-2). 80pp. Facts on such appealing matters as dust mites and worms. (Rev: BL 12/1/90; SLJ 3/91) [631.4]

20552 Burton, Jane. *The Nature and Science of Rocks* (3–6). Series: Exploring the Science of Nature. 1998, Gareth Stevens LB $18.60 (0-8368-1945-4). 32pp. An imaginatively illustrated book on how rocks are formed, their different types, their

uses, and how they become soil. (Rev: BL 6/1–15/98; HBG 10/98) [552]

20553 Christian, Spencer, and Antonia Felix. *Is There a Dinosaur in Your Backyard? The World's Most Fascinating Fossils, Rocks, and Minerals* (5–8). Illus. 1998, Wiley paper $12.95 (0-471-19616-9). 128pp. An excellent introduction to earth science, with fascinating information on fossils, rocks, and minerals. (Rev: BL 9/1/98; SLJ 10/98) [552]

20554 Eid, Alain. *1000 Photos of Minerals and Fossils* (5–9). Photos by Michel Viard. 2000, Barron's $24.95 (0-7641-5218-1). 127pp. An oversized, nicely illustrated volume that introduces minerals in their natural and refined states with material on sites, fossils, and jewelry. (Rev: SLJ 10/00) [548]

20555 Flanagan, Alice K. *Rocks* (2–3). Series: Simply Science. 2000, Compass Point LB $14.95 (0-7565-0033-8). 32pp. This book explains how the three types of rocks are formed with examples of each as well as information on erosion and how to be a rock hound. (Rev: SLJ 2/01) [552]

20556 Gallant, Roy A. *Minerals* (3–5). Illus. Series: Kaleidoscope. 2000, Marshall Cavendish $15.95 (0-7614-1039-2). 48pp. An interesting look at minerals and rocks that begins with simple material and moves on to more complex topics such as mineral replacement. (Rev: BL 2/1/01; HBG 3/01) [549]

20557 Gallant, Roy A. *Rocks* (5–8). Series: Earth Sciences. 2000, Marshall Cavendish LB $15.95 (0-7614-1042-2). 48pp. Illustrations and full-spread diagrams introduce rocks and minerals and their properties, forms, and uses. (Rev: BL 3/1/01; HBG 3/01; SLJ 3/01) [552.2]

20558 Gallant, Roy A. *Sand on the Move: The Story of Dunes* (4–6). Illus. Series: First Books. 1997, Watts LB $22.50 (0-531-20334-4). 64pp. Explains where sand comes from, how and why dunes are formed, and what animals and plants live on them. (Rev: BL 12/1/97; HBG 3/98; SLJ 1/98) [551.3]

20559 Gans, Roma. *Let's Go Rock Collecting* (2–4). Illus. by Holly Keller. 1997, HarperCollins LB $15.89 (0-06-027283-X); paper $4.95 (0-06-445170-4). 32pp. An introduction to rocks, how they were formed, their composition, their uses, and how to collect them. (Rev: BL 5/15/97; SLJ 8/97) [552]

20560 Hiscock, Bruce. *The Big Rock* (1–4). Illus. 1988, Macmillan $16.00 (0-689-31402-7). 32pp. Tracing the history of an ancient piece of stone. (Rev: BCCB 10/88; BL 11/1/88)

20561 Kittinger, Jo S. *A Look at Minerals: From Galena to Gold* (4–6). Illus. Series: Earth and Sky Science. 1998, Watts LB $22.00 (0-531-20385-9). 64pp. After discussing the five characteristics of minerals — specific gravity, hardness, cleavage, luster, and streak — this book takes a close look at minerals of all types and describes their formation, appearance, and uses. (Rev: BL 2/1/99; HBG 3/99) [549]

20562 Kittinger, Jo S. *A Look at Rocks: From Coal to Kimberlite* (4–7). Illus. Series: First Books. 1997, Watts LB $22.50 (0-531-20310-7). 64pp. This book describes rocks, rock formations, and famous rocks like Mount Rushmore, with added material on how and why rocks change. (Rev: BL 12/1/97; HBG 3/98; SLJ 1/98) [552]

20563 Klein, James. *Gold Rush! The Young Prospector's Guide to Striking It Rich* (3–6). Illus. 1998, Tricycle Pr. paper $8.95 (1-883672-64-3). 96pp. This book provides a history of gold and gold prospecting and gives tips on good prospecting locations, tools, and what to do if you hit pay dirt. (Rev: BL 4/15/98) [622]

20564 Marzollo, Jean. *I Am a Rock* (1). Illus. by Judith Moffatt. Series: Hello Reader! 1998, Scholastic paper $3.50 (0-590-37222-X). 32pp. In this easy reader, a child named Marble visits the Rock Hall of Fame where one can identify 12 different rocks. (Rev: BL 7/98) [552]

20565 Milne, Jean. *The Story of Diamonds* (5–8). 2000, Linnet LB $21.50 (0-208-02476-X). 113pp. A book that explains where diamonds are found and how they are mined, evaluated, cut, polished, and used as jewels or in industry. (Rev: HBG 10/00; SLJ 6/00) [553.8]

20566 Murphy, Stuart J. *Dave's Down-to-Earth Rock Shop* (1–3). Illus. by Cat B. Smith. 2000, HarperCollins $15.95 (0-06-028018-2); paper $4.95 (0-06-446729-5). 32pp. Dave learns about rock classification in this easy reader about a boy who receives a strange rock from his uncle. (Rev: BL 5/1/00; HBG 10/00; SLJ 4/00) [511.3]

20567 Pellant, Chris. *Collecting Gems and Minerals: Hold the Treasures of the Earth in the Palm of Your Hand* (5–8). Illus. 1998, Sterling $14.95 (0-8069-9760-5). 80pp. After explaining how gems and minerals are formed, this book discusses necessary equipment for the hunter, where to look, how to identify specimens, and how to organize one's collection. (Rev: BL 6/1–15/98; SLJ 8/98) [553.8]

20568 Prager, Ellen J. *Sand* (1–3). Illus. by Nancy Woodman. 2000, National Geographic $15.95 (0-7922-7104-1). 32pp. In this enjoyable, fact-filled book, a seagull disguised as a detective describes how sand is formed, its types, and its composition. (Rev: BL 3/1/00; HBG 10/00; SLJ 4/00) [553.6]

20569 Ricciuti, Edward R., and Margaret W. Carruthers. *National Audubon Society First Field Guide to Rocks and Minerals* (4–6). Series: First Field Guide. 1998, Scholastic $17.95 (0-590-05463-5). More than 450 full-color photographs are included

in this guide to the world's rocks and minerals. (Rev: BL 8/98; SLJ 8/98) [552]

20570 Rutten, Joshua. *Erosion* (2–3). Series: Earth's Conditions. 1999, Child's World LB $15.95 (1-56766-508-X). 32pp. As well as introducing the problem of soil erosion at a beginner's level, this book gives advice on how people can control it. (Rev: HBG 10/99; SLJ 7/99) [631.4]

20571 Spickert, Diane Nelson. *Earthsteps: A Rock's Journey Through Time* (3–6). Illus. 2000, Fulcrum $17.95 (1-55591-986-3). 32pp. The story of a rock and its transformation over 250 million years to a grain of sand. (Rev: BL 1/1–15/01; SLJ 1/01) [551.3]

20572 Staedter, Tracy. *Rocks and Minerals* (4–8). Series: Reader's Digest Pathfinders. 1999, Reader's Digest $16.99 (1-57584-290-4). 64pp. An outstanding introduction to geology is organized in three sections — "Rocks," "Minerals," and "Collecting Rocks and Minerals" — with "discovery paths" featuring personal accounts, hands-on activities, vocabulary, and facts. (Rev: SLJ 11/99) [552]

20573 Stangl, Jean. *Crystals and Crystal Gardens You Can Grow* (4–6). Illus. Series: First Books. 1990, Watts LB $22.50 (0-531-10889-9). 64pp. Introduces the nature and structure of crystals and supplies instruction for experiments on their formation. (Rev: BCCB 5/90; BL 5/15/90; SLJ 8/90) [548.5]

20574 Thorson, Kristine, and Robert Thorson. *Stone Wall Secrets* (3–5). Illus. by Gustav Moore. 1998, Tilbury $16.95 (0-88448-195-6). A history and geology lesson on rocks and their uses, from the shale formed eons ago in prehistoric seas to the construction of a stone fence surrounding a New England farm. (Rev: SLJ 11/98) [552]

20575 VanCleave, Janice. *Rocks and Minerals* (4–6). Illus. Series: Spectacular Science Projects. 1996, Wiley paper $10.95 (0-471-10269-5). 96pp. In easy-to-follow steps, a series of experiments and other activities illustrate the properties and uses of rocks and minerals. (Rev: BL 3/15/96; SLJ 3/96) [552]

20576 Winckler, Suzanne, and Mary M. Rodgers. *Our Endangered Planet: Soil* (4–7). Illus. Series: Our Endangered Planet. 1994, Lerner LB $22.60 (0-8225-2508-9). 72pp. The depletion of our soil resources is the focus of this book, with emphasis on causes and possible solutions. (Rev: BL 5/15/94) [631.4]

Mathematics

General

20577 Aber, Linda Williams. *Who's Got Spots?* (2–3). Illus. by Gioia Fiammenghi. Series: Math Matters. 2000, Kane paper $4.95 (1-57565-099-1). 32pp. In this early math book, there is an outbreak of chicken pox and kids use this opportunity to create charts and graphs to record who has been sick and predict who will stay well. (Rev: SLJ 2/01) [001.4]

20578 Adler, David A. *Fraction Fun* (2–4). Illus. by Nancy Tobin. 1996, Holiday LB $16.95 (0-8234-1259-8). A clear, concise introduction to fractions using plenty of real-life situations as examples and for fun. (Rev: BCCB 12/96; SLJ 11/96) [513.2]

20579 Axelrod, Amy. *Pigs at Odds: Fun with Math and Games* (2–4). Illus. by Sharon McGinley-Nally. 2000, Simon & Schuster $14.00 (0-689-81566-2). In this entertaining concept book starring the Pig family at a carnival, the concept of probability is explored. (Rev: HBG 3/01; SLJ 1/01)

20580 King, Andrew. *Exploring Shapes* (2–5). Illus. Series: Math for Fun. 1998, Millbrook LB $20.90 (0-7613-0851-2). 32pp. Various shapes are introduced in this mathematics book with projects for each shape. (Rev: BL 1/1–15/99; HBG 3/99; SLJ 2/99) [516]

20581 King, Andrew. *Measuring Sizes* (2–5). Series: Math for Fun. 1998, Millbrook LB $20.90 (0-7613-0853-9); paper $5.95 (0-7613-0747-8). 32pp. Interactive projects and games are used to introduce the world of measurement. (Rev: BL 2/15/99; HBG 10/99) [530.8]

20582 Leedy, Loreen. *Measuring Penny* (2–4). Illus. 1998, Holt $16.95 (0-8050-5360-3). 32pp. An attractively illustrated introduction to the world of measurement. (Rev: BL 4/1/98*; HB 7–8/98; HBG 10/98; SLJ 4/98) [530.8]

20583 Leedy, Loreen. *Mission Addition* (PS–3). Illus. 1997, Holiday LB $16.95 (0-8234-1307-1). 32pp. Through many practical applications, the animal creatures of Miss Prime's class explore the mysteries of addition. (Rev: BL 10/15/97; HBG 3/98; SLJ 8/97) [513.2]

20584 Lobosco, Michael L. *Mental Math Workout* (3–7). 1998, Sterling $16.95 (1-895569-27-3). 80pp. There are 34 projects in this book, each of which interestingly explores a different idea or concept in mathematics. (Rev: SLJ 10/98) [510]

20585 Long, Lynette. *Dazzling Division: Games and Activities That Make Math Easy and Fun* (2–5). Illus. 2000, Wiley $12.95 (0-471-36983-7). 122pp. A large-format book that explains division and outlines many activities that explore this concept. (Rev: BL 12/15/00; SLJ 1/01) [513]

20586 Long, Lynette. *Marvelous Multiplication: Games and Activities That Make Math Easy and Fun* (2–5). Illus. 2000, Wiley $12.95 (0-471-36982-9). 122pp. Multiplication is explained in this large-format paperback with cheerful drawings and a number of related activities. (Rev: BL 12/15/00) [513.2]

20587 Losi, Carol A. *The 512 Ants on Sullivan Street* (1–2). Illus. by Patrick Merrell. Series: Hello Math Reader. 1997, Scholastic $1.50 (0-590-30876-9). 32pp. A girl watches ants in a mathematical doubling series (e.g., 1, 2, 4, 8, etc.) as they walk off with picnic food in this easily read math book. (Rev: BL 2/1/98; SLJ 1/98)

20588 Maganzini, Christy. *Cool Math* (4–7). Illus. 1997, Price Stern Sloan paper $6.99 (0-8431-7857-4). 96pp. This book gives a brief history of math, an outline of its basic concepts, and a number of tricks to play on ones' friends. (Rev: BL 11/1/97) [510]

20589 Markle, Sandra. *Discovering Graph Secrets: Experiments, Puzzles, and Games Exploring Graphs* (4–6). Illus. 1997, Simon & Schuster $17.00 (0-689-31942-8). 40pp. An entertaining and informative book that introduces four different graphs and explains their uses. (Rev: BL 2/15/98; HBG 3/98; SLJ 3/98) [001.4]

20590 Murphy, Stuart J. *Betcha!* (1–3). Illus. by S. D. Schindler. Series: MathStart. 1997, Harper-

Collins LB $15.89 (0-06-026769-0). 40pp. The mathematical skill of estimating is introduced in this concept book about guessing the number of jelly beans in a jar. Other skills are explored in *Elevator Magic* and *Just Enough Carrots* (both 1997). (Rev: BL 10/1/97; HBG 3/98; SLJ 1/98) [519.5]

20591 Murphy, Stuart J. *Lemonade for Sale* (1–3). Illus. by Tricia Tusa. Series: MathStart. 1998, HarperCollins LB $14.89 (0-06-027441-7); paper $4.95 (0-06-446715-5). 31pp. Four children operate a lemonade stand and use a bar graph to chart their progress in this simple introduction to graphs. (Rev: HBG 10/98; SLJ 5/98)

20592 Murphy, Stuart J. *Too Many Kangaroo Things to Do!* (1–3). Illus. by Kevin O'Malley. Series: MathStart. 1996, HarperCollins LB $14.89 (0-06-025884-5). 40pp. Addition and multiplication are introduced through the antics of several animals. (Rev: BL 10/15/96; SLJ 12/96) [513.2]

20593 Penner, Lucille R. *Clean-Sweep Campers* (2–3). Illus. by Paige Billin-Frye. Series: Math Matters. 2000, Kane paper $4.95 (1-57565-096-7). 32pp. Using a story about a messy cabin at summer camp, this book effectively introduces fractions. (Rev: SLJ 2/01) [513.2]

20594 *Scholastic Explains Math Homework: Everything Children (and Parents) Need To Survive 2nd and 3rd Grade* (2–3). Series: Scholastic Explains Homework. 1998, Scholastic $14.95 (0-590-39754-0); paper $6.95 (0-590-39757-5). 64pp. Such math topics as patterns, regrouping, telling time, weight and measurement, and problem solving are covered in this overview of primary grades math. (Rev: SLJ 12/98) [510]

20595 Schwartz, David M. *G Is For Googol: A Math Alphabet Book* (3–5). Illus. 1998, Tricycle Pr. $15.95 (1-883672-58-9). 56pp. An alphabet book that uses terms in mathematics, from abacus to zillion, for each letter. (Rev: BL 10/15/98; HBG 3/99) [510]

20596 Stienecker, David L. *Addition* (3–5). Illus. by Richard Maccabe. Series: Discovering Math. 1995, Benchmark LB $22.79 (0-7614-0593-3). 32pp. An introductory math book that explains the principles of addition and gives puzzles and exercises on applying these concepts. Also use *Division, Fractions*, and *Multiplication* (all 1995). (Rev: SLJ 4/96) [510]

20597 VanCleave, Janice. *Janice VanCleave's Math for Every Kid: Easy Activities That Make Learning Math Fun* (3–8). Illus. by Barbara Clark. 1991, Wiley $27.95 (0-471-54693-3); paper $12.95 (0-471-54265-2). 215pp. An entertaining look at math concepts with activities and problems given to illustrate each of them. (Rev: SLJ 12/91) [510]

20598 VanCleave, Janice. *Janice VanCleave's Play and Find Out About Math: Easy Experiments for Young Children* (PS–1). Illus. 1997, Wiley $29.95 (0-471-12937-2); paper $12.95 (0-471-12938-0). 128pp. Simple activities, like measuring one's head and then making a crown, are used to introduce basic math principles. (Rev: BL 12/1/97; SLJ 1/98) [372.7]

20599 Vorderman, Carol. *How Math Works* (5–8). Illus. 1996, Reader's Digest $24.00 (0-89577-850-5). 192pp. Describes mathematics concepts and history, with many related activities. (Rev: BL 11/1/96) [510]

20600 Woods, Mary B., and Michael Woods. *Ancient Computing: From Counting to Calendars* (5–8). Series: Ancient Technologies. 2000, Runestone LB $25.26 (0-8225-2997-1). 88pp. From the invention of the abacus and sundials to the creation of calculators and computers, this is a history of counting with material on the development of the calendar. (Rev: BL 9/15/00; HBG 3/01) [510]

20601 Wyatt, Valerie. *The Math Book for Girls and Other Beings Who Count* (3–6). Illus. 2000, Kids Can $14.95 (1-55074-830-0); paper $9.95 (1-55074-584-0). 64pp. A well-organized, cheerful book that introduces such math concepts as proportion in an entertaining way. (Rev: BCCB 11/00; BL 2/15/01; SLJ 11/00) [510.8]

20602 Ziefert, Harriet. *Rabbit and Hare Divide an Apple* (1–2). Illus. by Emily Bolam. Series: Viking Math Easy-to-Read. 1998, Viking paper $3.99 (0-14-038820-6). 32pp. In this easy reader, the math concept of fractions is taught through a story about Rabbit, Hare, and wily Mr. Raccoon. (Rev: BL 2/1/98; HBG 10/98; SLJ 2/98)

Geometry

20603 Hansen-Smith, Bradford. *The Hands-On Marvelous Ball Book* (4–7). Illus. 1995, W.H. Freeman paper $16.95 (0-7167-6628-0). 48pp. Directions are given for making a variety of geometric forms using such everyday materials as paper plates and bobby pins. (Rev: BL 10/15/95) [516]

20604 King, Andrew. *Plotting Points and Position* (2–5). Illus. Series: Math for Fun. 1998, Millbrook LB $20.90 (0-7613-0852-0). 32pp. An activity book that explores plotting coordinates, measuring angles, and different kinds of symmetry. (Rev: BL 1/1–15/99; HBG 3/99; SLJ 2/99) [516.16]

20605 Riggs, Sandy. *Circles* (2–4). Illus. by Richard Maccabe. Series: Discovering Shapes. 1996, Benchmark LB $22.79 (0-7614-0458-9). 32pp. Circles are introduced through a series of games, puzzles, and crafts. Also use *Triangles* (1996). (Rev: SLJ 2/97) [516]

20606 Stienecker, David L. *Rectangles* (2–4). Series: Discovering Shapes. 1996, Benchmark LB $22.79 (0-7614-0460-0). 32pp. A slim volume in which rectangles are explored through games, art ideas, and problems to solve. Also use *Patterns, Polygons*, and *Three-Dimensional Shapes* (all 1996). (Rev: SLJ 2/97) [516]

20607 VanCleave, Janice. *Geometry for Every Kid: Easy Activities That Make Learning Geometry Fun* (4–6). Illus. Series: Science for Every Kid. 1994, Wiley $29.95 (0-471-31142-1); paper $12.95 (0-471-31141-3). 221pp. Through interesting activities, this book explains geometry from simple shapes and angles to coordinate graphing. (Rev: BL 10/15/94; SLJ 12/94) [516]

Mathematical Puzzles

20608 Adler, David A. *Calculator Riddles* (3–5). Illus. by Cynthia Fisher. 1995, Holiday $14.95 (0-8234-1186-9). 42pp. A series of clever riddles and problems in arithmetic that can be answered using a calculator. (Rev: BL 11/1/95; SLJ 11/95) [513.2]

20609 Adler, David A. *Easy Math Puzzles* (2–5). Illus. by Cynthia Fisher. 1997, Holiday LB $15.95 (0-8234-1283-0). 32pp. A book of challenging, often very tricky math puzzles that sometimes involve the quirks of language and logic. (Rev: BCCB 5/97; BL 3/1/97; SLJ 6/97) [818]

20610 Anno, Mitsumasa. *Anno's Math Games* (PS–2). Illus. by author. 1997, Putnam paper $12.95 (0-698-11671-2). 112pp. Such puzzling mathematical concepts as number squares, classifications of objects, and graphs are imaginatively introduced. (Rev: BCCB 12/87; BL 1/1/88; SLJ 12/87) [793.7]

20611 Blum, Raymond. *Math Tricks, Puzzles and Games* (4–7). Illus. 1994, Sterling $14.95 (0-8069-0582-4). 96pp. Kids who like math will particularly enjoy these tricks, mathematical games and puzzles, and calculator riddles. (Rev: BL 11/1/94) [793.7]

20612 Blum, Raymond. *Mathamusements* (4–6). Illus. by Jeff Sinclair. 1997, Sterling $14.95 (0-8069-9783-4). 95pp. An entertaining collection of math puzzles and activities, many for people with little background in mathematics. (Rev: SLJ 11/97) [513.2]

20613 Burns, Marilyn. *The I Hate Mathematics! Book* (5–8). Illus. by Martha Hairston. 1975, Little, Brown paper $13.95 (0-316-11741-2). 128pp. A lively collection of puzzles and other mind stretchers that illustrate mathematical concepts. Also use: *Math for Smarty Pants: Or Who Says Mathematicians Have Little Pig Eyes* (1982).

20614 Cushman, Jean. *Do You Wanna Bet? Your Chance to Find Out About Probability* (3–6). Illus. by Martha Weston. 1991, Houghton $16.00 (0-395-56516-2). 102pp. A slight plot line aids in the explanation of probability and moves on to guessing games, coin tossing, and breaking codes. (Rev: BCCB 2/92; BL 1/1/92; SLJ 12/91) [519.2]

20615 Ferris, Julie. *Galaxy Getaway: A Math Puzzle Adventure* (2–4). Series: Math for Martians. 2000, Larousse paper $5.95 (0-7534-5276-6). 32pp. Zeno, a young Martian, must solve a number of math problems and decipher codes in order to rescue a pet. Also use: *Planet Omicron: A Math Puzzle Adventure* (2000). (Rev: SLJ 9/00) [793.7]

20616 Gardner, Martin. *Perplexing Puzzles and Tantalizing Teasers* (4–7). Illus. by Laszlo Kubinyi. 1988, Dover paper $5.95 (0-486-25637-5). 256pp. An assortment of math problems, visual teasers, and tricky questions to challenge young, alert minds; perky drawings.

20617 Lobosco, Michael L. *Mental Math Challenges* (5–10). 1999, Sterling LB $16.95 (1-895569-50-8). 80pp. The 37 projects in this fascinating collection involve construction of different mathematical applications, models, games, and drawings

and are grouped under such headings as "Solitaire Games," "Math in Everyday Life Situations," and "Instant Calculations and Mind Reading." (Rev: SLJ 8/99) [510]

20618 Markle, Sandra. *Measuring Up! Experiments, Puzzles, and Games Exploring Measurement* (4–7). Illus. 1995, Atheneum $17.00 (0-689-31904-5). 44pp. This book explains through a series of activities how we measure a number of things like temperature, height of trees and flagpoles, weight, and distance. (Rev: SLJ 1/96*) [512]

20619 Phillips, Louis. *263 Brain Busters: Just How Smart Are You, Anyway?* (4–6). Illus. by James Stevenson. 1985, Puffin paper $4.99 (0-14-031875-5). 87pp. A knowledge of elementary algebra will be helpful in solving some of these brain busters, not all of which are brain twisters. (Rev: BL 2/15/86; SLJ 2/86)

20620 Salvadori, Mario, and Joseph P. Wright. *Math Games for Middle School: Challenges and Skill-Builders for Students at Every Level* (5–8). Illus. 1998, Chicago Review paper $16.95 (1-55652-288-6). 176pp. After explaining the concepts involved in such mathematical topics as geometry, arithmetic, graphing, and linear equations, this work presents a series of puzzles for readers to solve. (Rev: BL 11/1/98) [510]

20621 Sharp, Richard M., and Seymour Metzner. *The Sneaky Square and 113 Other Math Activities for Kids* (4–8). Illus. 1990, TAB $15.95 (0-8306-8474-3); paper $8.95 (0-8306-3474-6). 134pp. Readers are challenged to solve classic as well as new math and logic problems. (Rev: BL 1/1/91) [793.7]

20622 Tang, Greg. *The Grapes of Math: Mind-Stretching Math Riddles* (3–5). Illus. by Harry Briggs. 2001, Scholastic $16.95 (0-439-21033-X). Each riddle and the rhyming clues that accompany it, can be answer by applying simple math skills like adding, subtracting, and multiplying. (Rev: BCCB 3/01; SLJ 3/01) [793.7]

20623 Wells, Alison. *Subtraction* (3–5). Illus. by Richard Maccabe. Series: Discovering Math. 1995, Benchmark LB $22.79 (0-7614-0594-1). 32pp. Principles of subtraction are introduced, with many puzzles and games that apply these concepts in problem-solving situations. (Rev: SLJ 4/96) [510]

20624 Wyler, Rose, and Mary Elting. *Math Fun: Test Your Luck* (4–6). Illus. by Patrick Girouard. Series: Math Fun. 1992, Simon & Schuster LB $10.95 (0-671-74311-2). This book of tricks covers number theory, magic squares, and probabilities. A companion book is: *Math Fun with a Pocket Calculator* (1992). (Rev: SLJ 12/92) [513]

20625 Wyler, Rose, and Mary Elting. *Math Fun with Money Puzzlers* (3–6). Illus. by Patrick Girouard. Series: Math Fun. 1992, Simon & Schuster paper $5.95 (0-671-74314-7). 64pp. Math activities and concepts are presented in a playful way, with cartoonlike artwork. Also use: *Math Fun with Tricky Lines and Shapes* (1992). (Rev: BL 1/15/93) [513]

Numbers and Number Systems

20626 Adler, David A. *Roman Numerals* (2–4). Illus. by Byron Barton. 1977, HarperCollins LB $15.89 (0-690-01302-7). 40pp. The principles involved in Roman numerals and how to write them are detailed.

20627 Anno, Mitsumasa. *Anno's Mysterious Multiplying Jar* (4–6). Illus. by author. 1983, Putnam $19.99 (0-399-20951-4). 48pp. Everyday objects are used to explain factorials.

20628 Burton, Jane, and Kim Taylor. *The Nature and Science of Numbers* (3–6). Series: Exploring the Science of Nature. 2001, Gareth Stevens LB $21.27 (0-8368-2193-9). 32pp. Explores the history of numbers and numbering and counting systems, with well thought-out activities and projects. (Rev: BL 3/15/01) [512]

20629 Fisher, Leonard Everett. *Number Art: Thirteen 123's from Around the World* (5–7). Illus. by author. 1982, Macmillan paper $16.95 (0-02-735240-4). 64pp. The development of numbers in various cultures.

20630 Ganeri, Anita. *The Story of Numbers and Counting* (3–6). Illus. Series: Signs of the Times. 1997, Oxford LB $16.00 (0-19-521258-4). 30pp. A history of the methods of calculating from earliest times to the pocket calculator and computers. (Rev: BL 2/1/97; SLJ 2/97) [513.2]

20631 Geisert, Arthur. *Roman Numerals I to MM: Numberabillia Romana Uno ad Duo Mila* (2–4). Illus. 1996, Houghton $16.00 (0-395-74519-5). 32pp. Using groups of pigs as examples, Roman numerals are introduced, and later other objects test the reader's knowledge. (Rev: BCCB 3/96; BL 5/1/96; HB 9–10/96; SLJ 9/96) [513.5]

20632 Massin. *Fun with Numbers* (2–4). Illus. by Les Chats Pelés. 1995, Harcourt $22.65 (0-15-200962-0). A boy and his dog travel through time from ancient Egypt, Mesopotamia, and Rome, to India and Europe to trace the origins and development of numbers and our counting system. (Rev: SLJ 2/96) [512]

20633 Murphy, Stuart J. *Shark Swimathon* (2–4). Illus. by Lynne W. Cravath. Series: MathStart. 2001, HarperCollins LB $15.89 (0-06-028031-X); paper $4.95 (0-06-446735-X). 40pp. In this number book, a shark swim team practices subtraction of two-digit numbers while trying to reach a goal of 75 laps. (Rev: BL 2/1/01; SLJ 3/01) [513.2]

20634 Schmandt-Besserat, Denise. *The History of Counting* (3–5). Illus. by Michael Hays. 1999, Morrow $17.00 (0-688-14118-8). 48pp. This oversize book traces the history of numbers and counting from primitive people through the Sumerians, Greeks, and Romans to the Arabs who brought Hindu numbers to Europe where this Arabic system was adopted. (Rev: BCCB 11/99; BL 8/99*; HBG 3/00; SLJ 8/99) [513.5]

20635 Schwartz, David M. *How Much Is a Million?* (K–3). Illus. by Steven Kellogg. 1985, Lothrop LB $16.89 (0-688-04050-0); Morrow paper $5.95 (0-

688-09933-5). 40pp. Using images that children can enjoy — such as "one million kids standing on each other's shoulders would be taller than . . ." — the concepts of million, billion, and trillion are explained. (Rev: BCCB 7/85; BL 6/15/85; HB 7–8/85)

20636 Schwartz, David M. *If You Made a Million* (2–5). Illus. by Steven Kellogg. 1989, Lothrop LB $16.93 (0-688-07018-3). 40pp. Exploring mathematical concepts in a delightful way. (Rev: BL 6/15/89)

20637 Schwartz, David M. *On Beyond a Million: An Amazing Math Journey* (2–5). Illus. 1999, Doubleday $15.95 (0-385-32217-8). 32pp. Double-page spreads are used to introduce counting by 10s and give facts about such large numbers as millions, trillions, and ever larger numbers. (Rev: BL 11/1/99; HBG 3/00; SLJ 10/99) [513.5]

20638 Stienecker, David L. *Numbers* (3–5). Illus. by Richard Maccabe. Series: Discovering Math. 1995, Benchmark LB $22.79 (0-7614-0597-6). 32pp. This introductory math book introduces the world of numbers and supplies many problems, with answers at the back of the book. (Rev: SLJ 4/96) [512]

Time, Clocks, and Calendars

20639 Branley, Franklyn M. *Keeping Time: From the Beginning and into the 21st Century* (4–6). Illus. by Jill Weber. 1993, Houghton $13.95 (0-395-47777-8). 106pp. Examines the concept of time and how it has been measured from the sundial to digital watches. (Rev: BL 11/1/93; SLJ 8/93) [529]

20640 Brimner, Larry. *The Official M&M's Brand Book of the Millennium* (1–5). Illus. by Karen E. Pellaton. 1999, Charlesbridge LB $15.95 (0-88106-071-2); paper $6.95 (0-88106-072-0). The M&M kids present a history of the calendar beginning with ancient civilizations including the Babylonians, Romans, and Aztecs, and ending in relatively modern times with England's adoption of the Gregorian calendar in 1752. (Rev: HBG 3/00; SLJ 12/99) [529]

20641 Burns, Marilyn. *This Book Is About Time* (5–7). Illus. 1978, Little, Brown paper $13.95 (0-316-11750-1). This work explores many facets of the concept of time, including a history of the calendar.

20642 Cobb, Annie. *The Long Wait* (1–3). Illus. by Liza Woodruff. Series: Math Matters. 2000, Kane paper $4.95 (1-57565-094-0). 32pp. Introduces the concept of estimating time, using a simple easy-to-read story about two boys waiting in line for a thrill ride. (Rev: SLJ 6/00)

20643 Dolan, Graham. *The Greenwich Guide to Time and the Millennium* (4–7). Illus. by Jeff Edwards. 1999, Heinemann LB $16.95 (1-57572-802-8). 48pp. Covers such subjects as time zones, calendars, centuries, and longitude. (Rev: SLJ 9/99) [529]

20644 Duffy, Trent. *The Clock* (5–9). Illus. by Toby Welles. Series: Turning Points. 2000, Simon & Schuster $17.95 (0-689-82814-4). 80pp. After a general introduction to the concept of time, this visually interesting volume tells how time has been measured with a special focus on clocks and watches and a foldout on how a clock works. (Rev: BCCB 5/00; HBG 10/00; SLJ 5/00) [529]

20645 Ganeri, Anita. *The Story of Time and Clocks* (3–6). Series: Signs of the Times. 1997, Oxford LB $16.00 (0-19-521326-2). 30pp. With the use of double-page spreads and copious illustrations, this account describes how time has been measured in various cultures and tells how clocks and watches developed. (Rev: BL 9/15/97; HBG 3/98; SLJ 11/97) [529]

20646 Maestro, Betsy. *The Story of Clocks and Calendars: Marking a Millennium* (3–5). Illus. by Giulio Maestro. 1999, Lothrop LB $15.93 (0-688-14549-3). 48pp. This book about time explains the various world calendars, past and present, tells how the day got their names, and gives a history of clocks. (Rev: BCCB 5/99; BL 6/1–15/99; HBG 10/99; SLJ 4/99) [909.83]

20647 Matthews, Rupert. *Telling the Time* (3–5). Series: Everyday History. 2000, Watts LB $20.00 (0-531-14588-3). 32pp. This is a fascinating history of the tools used to measure time — from sundials to modern clocks and watches. (Rev: BL 10/15/00) [529]

20648 Murphy, Stuart J. *Get Up and Go!* (1–3). Illus. by Diane Greenseid. Series: MathStart. 1996, HarperCollins LB $15.89 (0-06-025882-9). 40pp. The concept of time as measured by minutes is explored in this imaginative picture book. (Rev: BL 10/15/96; SLJ 12/96) [513.2]

20649 Murphy, Stuart J. *Pepper's Journal: A Kitten's First Year* (1–3). Illus. by Marsha Winborn. Series: MathStart. 2000, HarperCollins LB $15.89 (0-06-027619-3); paper $4.95 (0-06-446723-6). 32pp. The journal of a kitten's first year introduces the months and major holidays of the calendar. (Rev: BL 6/1–15/00; HBG 10/00; SLJ 4/00) [529]

20650 Older, Jules. *Telling Time* (PS–2). Illus. by Megan Halsey. 2000, Charlesbridge $16.95 (0-88106-396-7); paper $6.95 (0-88106-397-5). 32pp. As well as exploring the concept of time, this picture book explains ways in which it is measured and covers topics including how to tell time, calendars, and different kinds of numbers. (Rev: BL 3/1/00; HBG 10/00; SLJ 3/00) [529]

20651 Richards, Kitty. *It's About Time, Max!* (1–3). Illus. by Gioia Fiammenghi. Series: Math Matters. 2000, Kane paper $4.95 (1-57565-088-6). 32pp. After losing his digital watch, a young boy must learn how to tell time using analog timepieces in this easy-to-read concept book. (Rev: SLJ 6/00)

20652 Silverstein, Alvin, et al. *Clocks and Rhythms* (5–8). Illus. 1999, Twenty-First Century LB $23.40 (0-7613-3224-3). 64pp. This book focuses on natu-

ral rhythms of humans, animals, and the environment, including daily or circadian rhythms, monthly cycles, and seasonal patterns. (Rev: BL 9/1/99; HBG 10/99; SLJ 10/99) [571.7]

20653 Skurzynski, Gloria. *On Time: From Seasons to Split Seconds* (2–5). Illus. 2000, National Geographic $17.95 (0-7922-7503-9). 48pp. This heavily illustrated book discusses time and seasons, years, months, and days, with additional coverage on the development of clocks and calendars. (Rev: BL 3/1/00; HBG 10/00; SLJ 7/00) [529]

20654 Sweeney, Joan. *Me Counting Time: From Seconds to Centuries* (K–2). Illus. by Annette Cable. 2000, Crown $12.95 (0-517-80055-1); paper $14.99 (0-517-80056-X). A little girl explains to the reader the various elements of time — seconds, minutes, hours, days, weeks, months, and years. (Rev: HBG 10/00; SLJ 9/00) [529]

20655 Verdet, Andre. *All About Time* (PS–2). Illus. by Celine Bour-Chollet, et al. Series: First Discovery. 1995, Scholastic $12.95 (0-590-42795-4). This book about time includes material on clocks and watches, time zones, seasons, phases of the moon, months of the year, and how a person can budget time. (Rev: SLJ 3/96) [529]

Weights and Measures

20656 Cato, Sheila. *Measuring* (1–4). Illus. by Sami Sweeten. Series: A Question of Math Book. 1999, Carolrhoda LB $18.95 (1-57505-323-3). 32pp. The concept of measurement, what it involves, and several types are covered briefly in a series of double-page spreads each containing a problem. (Rev: HBG 3/00; SLJ 11/99) [530.8]

20657 Ganeri, Anita. *The Story of Weights and Measures* (3–6). Series: Signs of the Times. 1997, Oxford LB $16.00 (0-19-521328-9). 30pp. With the use of double-page spreads, copious illustrations and sidebars describe a history of measurement and weighing systems. (Rev: BL 9/15/97; HBG 3/98; SLJ 11/97) [530.8]

20658 King, Andrew. *Measuring Weight and Time* (2–5). Series: Math for Fun. 1998, Millbrook LB $20.90 (0-7613-0854-7); paper $5.95 (0-7613-0748-6). 32pp. Using interactive games, projects, and colorful artwork, this book explains how we measure weight and time. (Rev: BL 2/15/99; HBG 10/99) [530.8]

20659 Murphy, Stuart J. *Room for Ripley* (2–4). Illus. by Sylvie Wickstrom. Series: MathStart. 1999, HarperCollins LB $15.89 (0-06-446724-4). 33pp. This simple story about a boy filling a fish tank introduces such liquid measurements as a pint and a quart. (Rev: HBG 3/00; SLJ 12/99) [530.8]

Meteorology

General

20660 Kowalski, Kathiann M. *The Everything Kids' Nature Book: Create Clouds, Make Waves, Defy Gravity and Much More!* (4–7). Illus. Series: Everything Kids'. 2000, Adams paper $9.95 (1-58062-321-2). 127pp. Natural phenomena including climate and clouds are explained with a number of hands-on crafts and experiments. (Rev: BL 7/00) [508]

20661 Locker, Thomas. *Cloud Dance* (3–5). Illus. 2000, Harcourt $16.00 (0-15-202231-7). 32pp. This picture book for older readers is a mixture of fiction, science, and art as it describes the beauty of the sky during the different seasons. (Rev: BL 10/1/00; HBG 3/01; SLJ 11/00) [551.5]

20662 Vogel, Carole G. *Nature's Fury: Eyewitness Reports of Natural Disasters* (3–6). Illus. 2000, Scholastic $16.95 (0-590-11502-2). 128pp. Taken from historical archives and newspapers, this book features 13 eyewitness accounts of 13 disasters including flash floods, earthquakes, blizzards, and tornadoes. (Rev: BL 12/15/00; HBG 3/01) [551]

Air

20663 Ardley, Neil. *The Science Book of Air* (3–6). Illus. Series: Science Books. 1991, Harcourt $9.95 (0-15-200578-1). 28pp. Step-by-step illustrations for projects involving air. (Rev: BL 3/1/91; SLJ 5/91) [553.6]

20664 Branley, Franklyn M. *Air Is All Around You* (PS–2). Illus. by Holly Keller. 1986, HarperCollins paper $4.95 (0-06-445048-1). 32pp. Cheery children and an orange cat demonstrate the properties of air. (Rev: BL 4/15/86; SLJ 12/86)

20665 Bundey, Nikki. *Wind and People* (3–5). Series: The Science of Weather. 2000, Carolrhoda LB $21.27 (1-57505-495-7). 32pp. This book, which contains some simple experiments, shows how wind affects our lives — from causing snowdrifts and sandstorms to powering sailboats and creating energy. (Rev: BL 12/15/00; HBG 3/01) [551.5]

20666 Fitzgerald, Karen. *The Story of Oxygen* (4–6). Illus. 1996, Watts LB $22.50 (0-531-20225-9). 63pp. After a discussion of the discovery of oxygen, its roles in nature and chemistry are covered. (Rev: BL 10/15/96; SLJ 9/96) [546]

20667 Fowler, Allan. *Can You See the Wind?* (1–2). Series: Rookie Readers. 1999, Children's LB $18.50 (0-516-20814-4). 32pp. With many color pictures and large type, this book explains what the wind is and how it changes life on earth. (Rev: BL 7/99; HBG 10/99) [551.5]

20668 Gardner, Robert. *Science Project Ideas About Air* (4–7). Series: Science Project Ideas. 1997, Enslow LB $19.95 (0-89490-838-3). 96pp. The properties of air are explored in a series of experiments and projects with easy-to-follow directions. (Rev: BL 12/15/97; HBG 3/98; SLJ 4/98) [678.5]

20669 Gardner, Robert, and David Webster. *Experiments with Balloons* (4–7). Illus. Series: Getting Started in Science. 1995, Enslow LB $20.95 (0-89490-669-0). 104pp. Over a dozen experiments that explore balloons and the properties of air are presented. (Rev: BL 12/1/95; SLJ 3/96) [507.8]

20670 Hoff, Mary, and Mary M. Rodgers. *Atmosphere* (4–7). Illus. Series: Our Endangered Planet. 1995, Lerner LB $22.60 (0-8225-2509-7). 72pp. This account describes the atmosphere and current threats that are endangering it — for example, the ozone layer problem. (Rev: BL 8/95; SLJ 12/95) [363.73]

20671 Madgwick, Wendy. *Up in the Air* (K–3). Illus. Series: Science Starters. 1999, Raintree Steck-Vaughn $15.98 (0-8172-5325-4). 32pp. Concepts and activities related to air are presented in large double-page spreads that deal with topics including air pressure, wind, and how to make a paper airplane. (Rev: BL 6/1–15/99; HBG 10/99) [553]

20672 Mebane, Robert C., and Thomas R. Rybolt. *Air and Other Gases* (4–6). Illus. Series: Everyday Material Science Experiments. 1995, Twenty-First Century LB $18.90 (0-8050-2839-0). 64pp. Basic concepts involving air and other gases are explored in a series of experiments using everyday materials and simple instructions. (Rev: BL 9/15/95; SLJ 8/95) [530.4]

20673 Murphy, Bryan. *Experiment with Air* (2–4). Illus. Series: Science Experiments. 1992, Lerner LB $19.93 (0-8225-2452-X). 32pp. Introduces, in simple terms, concepts involving air pressure, how things fly, and how sound waves travel. (Rev: BL 6/15/92; SLJ 10/92) [533.6]

20674 Murray, Peter. *Professor Solomon Snickerdoodle's Air Science Tricks* (1–3). Illus. by Penny Dann. 1998, Child's World LB $21.36 (1-56766-082-7). 29pp. Professor Snickerdoodle helps a young friend perform several science tricks involving air and follows each with an explanation that shows the property of air. (Rev: SLJ 5/98) [553.6]

20675 Santrey, Laurence. *What Makes the Wind?* (1–3). Illus. by Bert Dodson. 1982, Troll LB $17.25 (0-89375-584-2); paper $3.50 (0-89375-585-0). 32pp. A simple, straightforward account on aspects of weather and the atmosphere.

20676 White, Larry. *Air* (3–6). Illus. by Laurie Hamilton. Series: Simple Experiments for Young Scientists. 1995, Millbrook LB $19.90 (1-56294-471-1). 48pp. Good background information is given, along with a series of simple projects that explore the properties of air. (Rev: SLJ 9/95) [533.6]

20677 Yount, Lisa, and Mary M. Rodgers. *Our Endangered Planet: Air* (4–7). Illus. Series: Our Endangered Planet. 1995, Lerner LB $22.60 (0-8225-2510-0). 72pp. The emphasis in this book is on how air pollution has become a major environmental issue and how everyone can take action to improve air quality. (Rev: BL 10/15/95) [363.73]

Storms

20678 Archer, Jules. *Hurricane!* (5–7). Illus. Series: Nature's Disasters. 1991, Macmillan LB $12.95 (0-89686-597-5). 48pp. In addition to many real-life examples, this book covers the causes of hurricanes and how we can protect ourselves against them. (Rev: BL 8/91) [551.51]

20679 Archer, Jules. *Tornado!* (5–7). Illus. Series: Nature's Disasters. 1991, Macmillan LB $12.95 (0-89686-594-0). 48pp. Full-color photos add to the drama of this weather phenomenon. (Rev: BL 8/91) [551.55]

20680 Armbruster, Ann. *Floods* (4–6). Illus. Series: First Books. 1996, Watts LB $22.50 (0-531-20239-9). 63pp. Describes various kinds of floods and preventive measures against them. (Rev: BL 1/1–15/97) [551.48]

20681 Armbruster, Ann, and Elizabeth Taylor. *Tornadoes* (3–5). Illus. Series: First Books. 1993, Watts paper $6.95 (0-531-15666-4). 64pp. A solid intro-duction to these fearsome storms, including tracking and safety measures. (Rev: BL 12/1/89; SLJ 12/89) [551.55]

20682 Berger, Melvin, and Gilda Berger. *Do Tornadoes Really Twist?* (3–5). Series: Scholastic Question and Answer. 2000, Scholastic LB $14.95 (0-439-09584-0). 48pp. Using a question-and-answer format and lots of excellent illustrations, this book covers children's basic concerns about tornadoes and hurricanes. (Rev: BL 12/15/00; HBG 3/01; SLJ 2/01) [551.5]

20683 Branley, Franklyn M. *Flash, Crash, Rumble, and Roll* (K–3). Illus. by True Kelley. Series: Let's-Read-and-Find-Out. 1999, HarperCollins LB $15.89 (0-06-027859-5); paper $4.95 (0-06-445179-8). 32pp. A new edition of the classic science book that explains the causes and effects of storms to youngsters and contains accompanying activities. Also use: *Rain and Hail* (1983). (Rev: BL 7/99; HBG 10/99; SLJ 6/99) [551.55]

20684 Branley, Franklyn M. *Tornado Alert* (K–4). Illus. by Giulio Maestro. 1988, HarperCollins LB $15.89 (0-690-04688-X); paper $4.95 (0-06-445094-5). 32pp. An explanation of these powerful storms that hold great fear and fascination for children. (Rev: BCCB 9/88; BL 9/1/88; SLJ 11/88)

20685 Bredeson, Carmen. *The Mighty Midwest Flood: Raging Rivers* (4–8). Series: American Disasters. 1999, Enslow LB $18.95 (0-7660-1221-2). 48pp. This account describes the terrible midwestern flood and gives background information on the Mississippi River complex and on the causes of floods. (Rev: BL 10/15/99; HBG 3/00) [363.4]

20686 Burby, Liza N. *Tornadoes* (2–3). Illus. Series: Extreme Weather. 1999, Rosen $12.95 (0-8239-5289-4). 24pp. Using amazing photographs, this book introduces tornadoes with material on their causes, their impact, the possibility of prediction, and where they are commonly found. (Rev: BL 9/15/99) [551.55]

20687 Cole, Joanna. *The Magic School Bus Inside a Hurricane* (2–4). Illus. by Bruce Degen. 1995, Scholastic $15.95 (0-590-44686-X). 48pp. Ms. Frizzle takes her busload of youngsters into the clouds to show where hurricanes come from. (Rev: BCCB 10/95; BL 6/1–15/95; HB 11–12/95; SLJ 9/95) [551.55]

20688 Drohan, Michele Ingber. *Floods* (2–4). Illus. Series: Natural Disasters. 1999, Rosen $13.50 (0-8239-5288-6). 24pp. The causes of floods are explained and their effect on people and places covered in this simple introduction that uses many color photographs. (Rev: BL 9/15/99) [551.48]

20689 Fowler, Allan. *When a Storm Comes Up* (1–2). Illus. Series: Rookie Readers. 1995, Children's LB $19.00 (0-516-06035-X). 32pp. With large type, color photos, and a small format, this effectively introduces storms to young people. (Rev: BL 7/95) [551.55]

20690 Greenberg, Keith E. *Storm Chaser: Into the Eye of a Hurricane* (4–7). Series: Risky Business. 1997, Blackbirch LB $16.95 (1-56711-161-0). 48pp. Tells about the people who track the paths of hurricanes and of the dangers they often face. (Rev: BL 10/15/97; HBG 3/98; SLJ 12/97) [551.55]

20691 Harper, Suzanne. *Lightning: Sheets, Streaks, Beads, and Balls* (4–6). Illus. Series: First Books. 1997, Watts LB $22.50 (0-531-20290-9). 64pp. Describes how thunderclouds form, the causes of lightning, and its various forms. (Rev: BL 5/15/97) [551.5]

20692 Hayden, Kate. *Twisters!* (2–3). Illus. Series: DK Reader. 2000, DK $12.95 (0-7894-5708-3); paper $3.95 (0-7894-5709-1). 32pp. An easy reader that uses a story about Rob, a farmer in Texas, to explain the causes, characteristics, and effects of tornadoes. (Rev: BL 10/1/00; HBG 3/01; SLJ 1/01) [551.55]

20693 Herman, Gail. *Storm Chasers: Tracking Twisters* (2–3). Illus. by Larry Schwinger. Series: All Aboard Reading. 1997, Grosset $13.99 (0-448-41638-7); paper $3.95 (0-448-41624-7). 47pp. Using a fictitious incident as a focus, this account gives good information about tornadoes, their causes and effects, and what to do during a tornado alert. (Rev: HBG 3/98; SLJ 11/97) [551.5]

20694 Hiscock, Bruce. *The Big Storm* (2–5). Illus. 1993, Atheneum $16.00 (0-689-31770-0). 32pp. This picture book traces a violent storm in 1982 from its beginnings on the West Coast, to the deep snows it brought to the Midwest and East Coast. (Rev: BL 11/1/93; SLJ 9/93) [551]

20695 Hopping, Lorraine Jean. *Wild Weather: Blizzards!* (2–3). Illus. by Jody Wheeler. Series: Hello Reader! 1999, Scholastic paper $3.99 (0-590-39730-3). 48pp. After describing several terrible blizzards, there is a discussion of what causes blizzards in this easy reader. (Rev: BCCB 1/99; BL 5/15/99; SLJ 5/99) [551.55]

20696 Hopping, Lorraine Jean. *Wild Weather: Lightning!* (1–4). Illus. by Jody Wheeler. Series: Hello Reader! 1999, Scholastic paper $3.99 (0-590-52285-X). 47pp. The story of lightning from classical mythology to its study using modern computer technology, with tales from survivors of lightning strikes. (Rev: SLJ 8/99) [551.5]

20697 Kahl, Jonathan D. *Storm Warning: Tornadoes and Hurricanes* (3–6). Illus. Series: How's the Weather? 1993, Lerner LB $21.27 (0-8225-2527-5). 64pp. An introduction to tornadoes and hurricanes with information on their causes, characteristics, and effects. (Rev: BL 5/15/93) [551]

20698 Kahl, Jonathan D. *Thunderbolt: Learning About Lightning* (4–6). Illus. Series: How's the Weather? 1994, Lerner LB $21.27 (0-8225-2528-3). 56pp. Causes and effects of lightning and thunder are described, with information on their place in history and in myth. (Rev: BL 6/94; SLJ 5/94) [551.5]

20699 Keller, Ellen. *Floods!* (4–7). Series: Weather Channel. 1999, Simon & Schuster paper $3.99 (0-689-82021-6). 64pp. Beginning with the great flood of 1997, this book uses several personal accounts to describe the various causes and types of floods and their aftermath. (Rev: SLJ 10/99) [363.3]

20700 Kramer, Stephen. *Eye of the Storm* (4–6). Illus. 1997, Putnam $18.99 (0-399-23029-7). 48pp.

A photographer who specializes in severe weather describes some dreadful storms and supplies spectacular full-color illustrations. (Rev: BCCB 4/97; BL 3/15/97; HB 3–4/97; SLJ 3/97*) [778.9]

20701 Kramer, Stephen. *Lightning* (3–6). Illus. by Warren Faidley. Series: Nature in Action. 1992, Carolrhoda LB $19.95 (0-87614-659-0). 48pp. A clear text and many full-color photos explain the hows and whys of lightning. (Rev: BCCB 9/92; BL 6/15/92; SLJ 7/92*) [551.5]

20702 Kramer, Stephen. *Tornado* (3–6). Illus. Series: Nature in Action. 1992, Carolrhoda LB $19.95 (0-87614-660-4). 48pp. This book shows how and where tornadoes usually form and the damage they can cause. (Rev: BL 11/1/92; SLJ 11/92) [551.53]

20703 Lampton, Christopher. *Blizzard* (4–6). Illus. Series: Disaster! 1991, Millbrook paper $5.95 (1-56294-775-3). 64pp. This attractive volume gives a detailed description of the causes of blizzards, some famous examples, and methods of protection during these storms. (Rev: BL 1/1/92; SLJ 1/92) [551.5]

20704 Lampton, Christopher. *Tornado* (4–6). Illus. Series: Disaster! 1991, Millbrook paper $5.95 (1-56294-785-0). 64pp. An appealing layout and sharp color photos add to the detailed, informative text with historical data and examples. (Rev: BL 1/1/92) [551.5]

20705 Lauber, Patricia. *Flood: Wrestling with the Mississippi* (5–8). Illus. 1996, National Geographic $18.95 (0-7922-4141-X). 64pp. An introduction to floods that focuses on the great Mississippi River flood of 1993. (Rev: BL 10/15/96; SLJ 11/96*) [363.3]

20706 Lauber, Patricia. *Hurricanes: Earth's Mightiest Storms* (4–8). Illus. 1996, Scholastic $16.95 (0-590-47406-5). 64pp. Beginning with an actual hurricane that ravaged Long Island in 1938, this account discusses the causes and effects of these mighty storms. (Rev: BCCB 10/96; BL 10/1/96; HB 9–10/96; SLJ 9/96*) [363.3]

20707 Meister, Cari. *Hurricanes* (4–6). Illus. Series: Nature's Fury. 1999, ABDO LB $14.95 (1-57765-080-8). 32pp. A history of hurricanes is included along with material on their causes, effects, and how to stay safe during one. (Rev: HBG 3/00; SLJ 12/99) [551.5]

20708 Murray, Peter. *Floods* (3–5). Illus. Series: Naturebooks: Natural Disasters. 1996, Child's World LB $22.79 (1-56766-214-5). 32pp. Basic information about floods is given, with full-page color photographs facing each page of text. (Rev: BL 1/1–15/97) [363.3]

20709 Murray, Peter. *Hurricanes* (3–5). Illus. Series: Naturebooks: Natural Disasters. 1995, Child's World LB $22.79 (1-56766-196-3). 32pp. Basic information is given about hurricanes in striking photographs and informative large-type text. (Rev: BL 12/15/95; SLJ 3/96) [551.55]

20710 Murray, Peter. *Lightning* (3–5). Illus. Series: Naturebooks: Natural Disasters. 1996, Child's World LB $22.79 (1-56766-215-3). 32pp. The causes and effects of lightning are covered, with many full-page illustrations. (Rev: BL 1/1–15/97) [551.5]

20711 Otfinoski, Steven. *Blizzards* (4–6). Illus. Series: When Disaster Strikes. 1994, Twenty-First Century LB $18.90 (0-8050-3093-X). 64pp. This book explains why blizzards occur, provides safety tips, and tells about famous storms of the past. (Rev: BL 10/15/94; SLJ 9/94) [363.3]

20712 Penner, Lucille R. *Twisters!* (2–3). Illus. by Kazushige Nitta. 1996, Random LB $11.99 (0-679-98271-X); paper $3.99 (0-679-88271-5). An easy-to-read introduction to the causes and effects of tornadoes and hurricanes. (Rev: BL 11/15/96) [551.5]

20713 Rose, Sally. *Tornadoes!* (4–7). Series: Weather Channel. 1999, Simon & Schuster paper $3.99 (0-689-82022-4). 64pp. The causes of tornado formation are covered plus material on types of tornadoes, wind intensity, tracking and forecasting, and safety precautions. (Rev: SLJ 10/99) [551.5]

20714 Rozens, Aleksandrs. *Floods* (4–6). Illus. Series: When Disaster Strikes. 1994, Twenty-First Century LB $22.90 (0-8050-3097-2). 64pp. A history of famous floods is given, plus an account of their causes and effects and survival tips. (Rev: BL 10/15/94; SLJ 9/94) [363.3]

20715 Sherrow, Victoria. *Hurricane Andrew: Nature's Rage* (4–8). Series: American Disasters. 1998, Enslow LB $18.95 (0-7660-1057-0). 48pp. The story of the storm that caused millions of dollars of damage to the Atlantic Coast, told in dramatic text and pictures. (Rev: BL 1/1–15/99; HBG 3/99) [551.5]

20716 Sherrow, Victoria. *Plains Outbreak Tornadoes: Killer Twisters* (4–8). Series: American Disasters. 1998, Enslow LB $18.95 (0-7660-1059-7). 48pp. The causes and effects of the giant tornadoes that occur in the Midwest, with details on some of the most horrendous. (Rev: BL 1/1–15/99; HBG 3/99) [551.55]

20717 Simon, Seymour. *Lightning* (3–6). Illus. 1997, Morrow $15.93 (0-688-14639-2). 32pp. A dramatic, fact-packed description of the causes of lightning, different types, and its effects. (Rev: BL 3/15/97*; SLJ 5/97) [551.319]

20718 Simon, Seymour. *Storms* (3–5). Illus. 1989, Morrow LB $15.93 (0-688-07414-6); paper $5.95 (0-688-11708-2). 32pp. Explaining how storms occur. (Rev: BCCB 3/89; BL 3/1/89; SLJ 4/89)

20719 Simon, Seymour. *Tornadoes* (3–6). Illus. 1999, Morrow LB $15.93 (0-688-14647-3). 32pp. This book explains how and why tornadoes are formed, safety measures that can be taken, and how to predict and track them. (Rev: BCCB 4/99; BL 5/1/99; HBG 10/99; SLJ 6/99) [551.55]

20720 Souza, D. M. *Hurricanes* (3–6). Illus. Series: Nature in Action. 1996, Carolrhoda LB $19.95 (0-87614-861-5); paper $7.95 (0-87614-955-7). 48pp. The causes and effects of hurricanes are covered, as well as forecasting devices. (Rev: BL 8/96; SLJ 11/96) [551.55]

20721 Souza, D. M. *Powerful Waves* (3–6). Illus. 1992, Carolrhoda LB $19.95 (0-87614-661-2).

48pp. Deals with tsunamis — misnamed tidal waves — how they develop, and the disasters they cause. (Rev: BL 11/1/92; SLJ 11/92) [551]

20722 Thompson, Luke. *Tsunamis* (4–10). Series: Natural Disasters. 2000, Children's LB $19.00 (0-516-23368-8); paper $6.95 (0-516-23568-0). 48pp. Using a number of eyewitness accounts, this book tells how tsunamis are created, their movements, and the damage they cause. (Rev: SLJ 3/01) [551.55]

20723 Walters, John. *Flood!* (5–7). Illus. Series: Nature's Disasters. 1991, Macmillan LB $12.95 (0-89686-596-7). 48pp. The dramatic story of floods is enhanced by full-color photos. (Rev: BL 8/91) [551.48]

Water

20724 Ardley, Neil. *The Science Book of Water* (3–6). Illus. Series: Science Books. 1991, Harcourt $9.95 (0-15-200575-7). 28pp. Sinking, floating, and displacement are some of the science projects presented in this full-color book. (Rev: BL 3/1/91; SLJ 5/90) [532]

20725 Asch, Frank. *Water* (PS–1). Illus. 1995, Harcourt $15.00 (0-15-200189-1). 32pp. A simple explanation of the nature of water and its uses, from tears to floodwaters. (Rev: BCCB 4/95; BL 4/15/95; HB 3–4/95; SLJ 5/95) [553.7]

20726 Berger, Melvin, and Gilda Berger. *Water, Water Everywhere: A Book About the Water Cycle* (2–4). Illus. Series: Discovery Readers. 1995, Ideals paper $4.50 (1-57102-042-X). 48pp. In addition to the water cycle, this book discusses a city's water system, sewage, and how to conserve water. (Rev: BL 12/1/95; SLJ 2/96) [551.48]

20727 Brandt, Keith. *What Makes It Rain?* (1–3). Illus. by Yoshi Miyake. 1982, Troll LB $17.25 (0-89375-582-6); paper $3.50 (0-89375-583-4). 32pp. A simple book about the water cycle.

20728 Branley, Franklyn M. *Down Comes the Rain* (5–8). Illus. by James G. Hale. Series: Let's-Read-and-Find-Out. 1997, HarperCollins LB $15.89 (0-06-025338-X). 32pp. An introduction to rain and hail as well as the water cycle. (Rev: BL 9/1/97; HBG 3/98; SLJ 10/97) [551.57]

20729 Bundey, Nikki. *Rain and People* (3–5). Illus. Series: Science of Weather. 2000, Carolrhoda $21.27 (1-57505-494-9). 32pp. This volume describes how fresh water and rain are involved in health, agriculture, construction, and power. A companion volume *Rain and the Earth* (2000), discusses the water cycle, clouds, water pollution, and ecosystems. (Rev: BL 10/15/00; HBG 3/01) [551.57]

20730 Bundey, Nikki. *Snow and the Earth* (3–5). Series: The Science of Weather. 2000, Carolrhoda LB $21.27 (1-57505-471-X). 32pp. This account, with a few experiments, shows how important snow is to the well-being of the earth and its people, animals, and plants. (Rev: BL 12/15/00; HBG 3/01) [551.57]

20731 Cobb, Vicki. *Squirts and Spurts: Science Fun with Water* (3–6). Illus. 2000, Millbrook LB $23.40

(0-7613-1572-1). 48pp. The mechanics behind hydraulics, vacuum pressure, and other forms of moving water are explored in this entertaining activity book that uses a cartoon format. (Rev: BCCB 11/00; BL 10/15/00; HBG 3/01; SLJ 3/01) [507.8]

20732 Farndon, John. *Water* (3–6). Series: Science Experiments. 2000, Marshall Cavendish LB $16.95 (0-7614-1087-2). 32pp. Covers the properties of water, its three states, and the ways it can be manipulated, along with related experiments and projects. (Rev: BL 3/15/01; HBG 3/01) [553.7]

20733 Fiarotta, Noel, and Phyllis Fiarotta. *Great Experiments with H²O* (4–6). Illus. 1997, Sterling paper $9.95 (0-8069-4259-5). 80pp. These simple hands-on experiments demonstrate why water freezes, rises as steam, condenses, and evaporates. (Rev: BL 12/1/97) [553.7]

20734 Fowler, Allan. *It Could Still Be Water* (1–2). Illus. Series: Rookie Readers. 1992, Children's LB $19.00 (0-516-06003-1). 32pp. This is a simple introduction to water and its many uses. It is also available in an oversized "Big Book" edition. (Rev: BL 12/15/92) [553.7]

20735 Gallant, Roy A. *Water* (5–8). Series: Earth Sciences. 2000, Marshall Cavendish LB $15.95 (0-7614-1040-6). 48pp. This work introduces the importance of water on the earth, its three states, and the water cycle. (Rev: BL 3/1/01; HBG 3/01) [551.57]

20736 Hooper, Meredith. *The Drop in My Drink: The Story of Water on Our Planet* (3–6). Illus. by Chris Coady. 1998, Viking $16.99 (0-670-87618-6). 32pp. This richly illustrated account traces the path of a drop of water as it travels in its various states through time and space and describes its role in the evolution of life on earth. (Rev: BL 12/1/98*; HBG 3/99; SLJ 1/99) [551.48]

20737 Locker, Thomas. *Water Dance* (3–5). Illus. 1997, Harcourt $16.00 (0-15-201284-2). 32pp. Using a fictionalized format, this account poetically traces the phases of the water cycle. (Rev: BCCB 5/97; BL 3/1/97; SLJ 4/97) [551]

20738 Madgwick, Wendy. *Water Play* (K–3). Illus. Series: Science Starters. 1999, Raintree Steck-Vaughn $15.98 (0-8172-5326-2). 32pp. The composition, states, and uses of water are explored in large double-page spreads with activities such as constructing a rain measure, observing surface tension, and making a bubble wand. (Rev: BL 6/1–15/99; HBG 10/99) [532]

20739 Marzollo, Jean. *I Am Water* (1–2). Illus. by Judith Moffatt. 1996, Scholastic paper $3.99 (0-590-26587-3). 32pp. In a beginning reader, the various forms of water are introduced. (Rev: BL 9/15/96*) [553.7]

20740 Mebane, Robert C., and Thomas R. Rybolt. *Water and Other Liquids* (4–6). Illus. Series: Everyday Material Science Experiments. 1995, Twenty-First Century LB $18.90 (0-8050-2840-4). 64pp. The properties of water and other liquids are identified and explored in a series of experiments using everyday materials. (Rev: BL 9/15/95; SLJ 8/95) [530.4]

20741 Morgan, Sally, and Adrian Morgan. *Water* (4–7). Illus. Series: Designs in Science. 1994, Facts on File $16.95 (0-8160-2982-2). 48pp. The importance and uses of water are described, with information on water storage, filtering, and conservation, plus activities and experiments. (Rev: BL 7/94) [533.7]

20742 Murphy, Bryan. *Experiment with Water* (2–4). Illus. 1992, Lerner LB $19.93 (0-8225-2453-8). 32pp. Color photos help demonstrate the properties of water through simple activities. (Rev: BL 6/15/92; SLJ 10/92) [532]

20743 O'Neill, Mary. *Water Squeeze* (4–7). Illus. by John Bindon. Series: SOS Planet Earth. 1991, Troll paper $5.95 (0-8167-2081-9). 32pp. Recent problems, such as a massive die-off of seals, are discussed in this look at the threats to our water supply. (Rev: BL 6/15/91) [363.73]

20744 Robinson, Fay. *Where Do Puddles Go?* (1–2). Illus. Series: Rookie Readers. 1995, Children's LB $19.00 (0-516-06036-8). 32pp. In very simple language and many color photographs, the water cycle is introduced to young children. (Rev: BL 7/95) [551.57]

20745 Seuling, Barbara. *Drip! Drop! How Water Gets to Your Tap* (K–2). Illus. by Nancy Tobin. 2000, Holiday $15.95 (0-8234-1459-0). After describing the water cycle, this concise account tells how reservoir water is collected, filtered, and sent through a water-treatment plant before reaching houses and apartments. (Rev: BCCB 1/01; SLJ 2/01) [546]

20746 Walker, Sally M. *Water Up, Water Down: The Hydrologic Cycle* (3–6). Illus. Series: Earth Watch. 1992, Carolrhoda LB $21.27 (0-87614-695-7). 48pp. This includes a description of the water cycle and material on erosion, flooding, caves, and other interesting aspects. (Rev: BL 1/15/93; SLJ 12/92) [551]

20747 White, Larry. *Water* (3–6). Illus. by Laurie Hamilton. Series: Simple Experiments for Young Scientists. 1995, Millbrook LB $20.90 (1-56294-472-X). 48pp. The properties of water and its three states are explored in a series of questions and answers, accompanied by simple projects and experiments. (Rev: HB 3–4/95; SLJ 9/95) [553]

20748 Wick, Walter. *A Drop of Water* (3–6). Illus. 1997, Scholastic $16.95 (0-590-22197-3). 40pp. The properties of water are explored in amazing photographs and activities. (Rev: BCCB 2/97; BL 2/1/97*; HB 3–4/97; SLJ 3/97) [546]

20749 Wyler, Rose. *Raindrops and Rainbows* (K–4). Illus. by Steven J. Petruccio. Series: Outdoor Science. 1989, Simon & Schuster paper $4.95 (0-671-66350-X). 48pp. Many aspects of water and refraction are covered in this simple science book. (Rev: SLJ 9/89) [551.4]

Weather

20750 Allaby, Michael. *Guide to Weather* (3–6). Illus. 2000, DK $19.95 (0-7894-6500-0). 64pp. An oversize book with large illustrations that explores various facets of weather including lightning, tornadoes, and wildfires in a series of attractive double-page spreads. (Rev: BL 12/1/00; HBG 3/01) [551.6]

20751 Arnold, Caroline. *El Niño: Stormy Weather for People and Wildlife* (4–8). Illus. 1998, Clarion $16.00 (0-395-77602-3). 48pp. Discusses the cause and effects of the El Niño current and provides a historic survey, definitions of terms, and many diagrams and photographs. (Rev: BL 10/1/98; HBG 10/99; SLJ 12/98) [551.6]

20752 Berger, Melvin, and Gilda Berger. *Can It Rain Cats and Dogs? Questions and Answers About Weather* (3–5). Series: Question and Answer. 1999, Scholastic $12.95 (0-590-13083-8); paper $5.95 (0-590-08573-X). 148pp. Basic facts about weather are introduced using a question-and-answer format and entertaining illustrations. (Rev: BL 11/15/99; HBG 3/00; SLJ 2/00) [551.5]

20753 Berger, Melvin, and Gilda Berger. *How's the Weather? A Look at Weather and How It Changes* (K–2). Illus. by John E. Cymerman. Series: Discovery Readers. 1993, Ideals paper $4.50 (0-8249-8599-0). 48pp. A basic introduction to weather that touches on such topics as air pressure, water vapor, weather maps, lightning, hurricanes, and tornadoes. (Rev: SLJ 3/94) [551.5]

20754 Branley, Franklyn M. *It's Raining Cats and Dogs: All Kinds of Weather and Why We Have It* (3–6). Illus. 1987, Houghton $16.00 (0-395-33070-X). 128pp. Strange happenings, such as pink and green snowstorms, are mixed in with scientific accounts of the weather. (Rev: BL 7/87; HB 9–10/87)

20755 Branley, Franklyn M. *Snow Is Falling* (1–2). Illus. by Holly Keller. Series: Let's-Read-and-Find-Out. 2000, HarperCollins LB $15.89 (0-06-027991-5); paper $4.95 (0-06-445186-0). 32pp. This simple science book describes snow, its formations, and its effects on people, animals, and the earth. (Rev: BL 2/15/00; HBG 10/00; SLJ 5/00) [551.57]

20756 Breen, Mark, and Kathleen Friestad. *The Kids' Book of Weather Forecasting* (3–5). Illus. Series: Kids Can! 2000, Williamson paper $12.95 (1-885593-39-2). 140pp. This book explains the complex subject of weather forecasting and includes such activities as making a barometer, a rain gauge, and a tornado. (Rev: BL 2/1/01; SLJ 1/01) [551.63]

20757 Burby, Liza N. *Heat Waves and Droughts* (2–3). Illus. Series: Extreme Weather. 1999, Rosen $12.95 (0-8239-5292-4). 24pp. Dramatic photographs illustrate this beginning book on heat waves and droughts and their causes and effects. (Rev: BL 9/15/99) [551.5]

20758 Casey, Denise. *Weather Everywhere* (K–3). Photos by Jackie Gilmore. 1995, Simon & Schuster paper $15.00 (0-02-717777-7). 36pp. A simplified introduction to weather that gives explanations of seasons, wind, precipitation, and clouds. (Rev: SLJ 8/95) [551.5]

20759 Christian, Spencer, and Antonia Felix. *Can It Really Rain Frogs? The World's Strangest Weather Events* (3–7). Series: Spencer Christian's World of Wonders. 1997, Wiley paper $12.95 (0-471-15290-

0). 115pp. Strange facts about the weather are combined with many related activities, experiments, and projects. (Rev: SLJ 4/98) [551.5]

20760 DeWitt, Lynda. *What Will the Weather Be?* (K–3). Illus. by Carolyn Croll. Series: Let's-Read-and-Find-Out. 1993, HarperCollins paper $4.95 (0-06-445113-5). 32pp. An illustrated introduction to weather forecasting. (Rev: BCCB 6/91; BL 5/1/91; SLJ 7/91) [551.6]

20761 Dickinson, Terence. *Exploring the Sky by Day: The Equinox Guide to Weather and Atmosphere* (3–7). Illus. 1989, Firefly $17.95 (0-920656-73-0); paper $9.95 (0-920656-71-4). 72pp. Spectacular photos add to the fascination of this weather explanation. (Rev: BL 3/1/89)

20762 Elsom, Derek. *Weather Explained: A Beginner's Guide to the Elements* (4–8). Illus. Series: Your World Explained. 1997, Holt $18.95 (0-8050-4875-8). 68pp. Basic material on clouds and winds are introduced, followed by a discussion of the world's changing climate, the causes and effects of El Niño, and the problem of global warming. (Rev: BL 3/1/98; HBG 10/98; SLJ 2/98) [551.5]

20763 Facklam, Howard, and Margery Facklam. *Avalanche!* (5–7). Illus. Series: Nature's Disasters. 1991, Macmillan $16.95 (0-89686-598-3). 48pp. Real-life examples and full-color photos add to the drama of this weather phenomenon. (Rev: BL 8/91) [551.3]

20764 Farndon, John. *Weather* (3–6). Illus. Series: Science Experiments. 2000, Marshall Cavendish LB $16.95 (0-7614-1089-9). 32pp. In addition to material on topics including sunlight, winds, clouds, and storms, this book outlines such projects as making a rain gauge and a weather vane. (Rev: BL 3/15/01; HBG 3/01) [551.6]

20765 Fowler, Allan. *What Do You See in a Cloud?* (PS–3). Illus. Series: Rookie Readers. 1996, Children's LB $19.00 (0-516-06056-2). 31pp. Various kinds of clouds and what each signifies are covered in this easy-to-read science book. (Rev: SLJ 8/96) [551.6]

20766 Fowler, Allan. *What's the Weather Today?* (1–3). Illus. Series: Rookie Readers. 1991, Children's LB $18.50 (0-516-04918-6). 32pp. Various kinds of weather are identified in a series of color photographs. (Rev: SLJ 2/92) [551.6]

20767 Gardner, Robert. *Science Project Ideas About Rain* (4–7). Series: Science Project Ideas. 1997, Enslow LB $19.95 (0-89490-843-X). 96pp. Clear explanations and functional drawings and diagrams for a number of activities that study rain, its causes, and its effects. (Rev: BL 12/15/97; HBG 3/98; SLJ 1/98) [551.55]

20768 Gibbons, Gail. *Weather Forecasting* (K–3). Illus. by author. 1987, Macmillan $14.00 (0-02-737250-2); paper $5.99 (0-689-71683-4). 32pp. Touring a weather station during the four seasons. (Rev: BCCB 4/87; BL 4/15/87; SLJ 4/87)

20769 Gibbons, Gail. *Weather Words and What They Mean* (1–3). Illus. by author. 1990, Holiday LB $16.95 (0-8234-0805-1). Various broad terms — such as temperature, air pressure, moisture, and wind — are defined, with breakdowns into more-specific terms. (Rev: BCCB 4/90; SLJ 5/90) [551.6]

20770 Gold, Susan D. *Blame It on El Niño* (5–9). 1999, Raintree Steck-Vaughn LB $25.69 (0-7398-1376-5). 96pp. Covers El Niño, La Niña, how scientists predict and track them, and the effects of each globally. (Rev: HBG 3/00; SLJ 4/00) [551.6]

20771 Harper, Suzanne. *Clouds: From Mare's Tails to Thunderheads* (4–6). Illus. Series: First Books. 1997, Watts LB $22.00 (0-531-20291-7). 64pp. As well as discussing the types of clouds and how they affect climate, this book tells how to predict weather by studying cloud patterns. (Rev: BL 5/15/97) [551.57]

20772 Inkpen, Mick. *Kipper's Book of Weather* (PS–K). Illus. by author. 1995, Harcourt $4.95 (0-15-202295-3); paper $6.00 (0-15-200644-3). Different kinds of weather are introduced through the experiences of Kipper, a lovable dog. (Rev: SLJ 10/99) [551.6]

20773 Kahl, Jonathan D. *Hazy Skies: Weather and the Environment* (4–6). Illus. 1998, Lerner LB $21.27 (0-8225-2530-5). 64pp. After providing a history of air pollution, this book links it to such weather-related topics as the ozone layer and global warming. (Rev: BL 3/15/98; HBG 10/98) [363.73]

20774 Kahl, Jonathan D. *National Audubon Society First Field Guide: Weather* (4–8). Series: Audubon Society First Field Guide. 1998, Scholastic $17.95 (0-590-05469-4). 160pp. Using diagrams, maps, photos, and extensive lists of further sources, this introduction to weather covers a wide range of phenomena from different kinds of clouds and fronts to dust devils and green flash. (Rev: SLJ 4/99) [551.5]

20775 Kahl, Jonathan D. *Weather Watch: Forecasting the Weather* (4–6). Illus. Series: How's the Weather? 1996, Lerner LB $21.27 (0-8225-2529-1). 72pp. Covers the various methods of predicting weather, the history of weather forecasting, and possible future developments. (Rev: BL 6/1–15/96; SLJ 6/96) [551.6]

20776 Kahl, Jonathan D. *Weatherwise: Learning About the Weather* (4–6). Illus. 1992, Lerner LB $21.27 (0-8225-2525-9). 64pp. Topics covered include atmosphere, winds, storms, and forecasting. (Rev: SLJ 8/92) [551.6]

20777 Kahl, Jonathan D. *Wet Weather: Rain Showers and Snowfall* (4–6). Illus. Series: How's the Weather? 1992, Lerner LB $21.27 (0-8225-2526-7). 64pp. A book that concentrates on rain and snow, weather fronts, and such extremes as floods and blizzards. (Rev: BL 1/15/93; SLJ 9/92) [551.577]

20778 Kramer, Stephen. *Avalanche* (3–6). Illus. by Patrick Cone. Series: Nature in Action. 1992, Carolrhoda LB $19.95 (0-87614-422-9). 48pp. Examining different types of snowslides, and how and when they occur. (Rev: BCCB 9/92; BL 6/15/92; SLJ 9/92) [551.57]

20779 Lambert, David. *Weather* (3–5). Illus. 1990, Troll LB $17.25 (0-8167-1979-9); paper $4.95 (0-8167-1980-2). 32pp. An explanation of various kinds of weather and their causes.

20780 Llewellyn, Claire. *Wild, Wet and Windy* (3–5). Series: SuperSmarts. 1997, Candlewick $11.99 (0-7636-0304-X). 24pp. This nicely illustrated book describes various kinds of weather and their causes. (Rev: BL 11/15/97; HBG 3/98) [551.5]

20781 McMillan, Bruce. *The Weather Sky* (4–6). Illus. 1991, Farrar $16.95 (0-374-38261-1). 40pp. A challenging weather book that young children are able to follow. (Rev: BCCB 4/91; BL 4/15/91; HB 7–8/91; SLJ 5/91) [551.6]

20782 Mandell, Muriel. *Simple Weather Experiments with Everyday Materials* (4–7). Illus. by Frances Zweifel. 1991, Sterling paper $5.95 (0-8069-7295-5). 128pp. Includes dozens of carefully described experiments, covering various weather types, instruments, and forecasting. (Rev: BL 7/89; SLJ 4/91) [551.6]

20783 Markle, Sandra. *A Rainy Day* (K–3). Illus. by Cathy Johnson. 1993, Orchard LB $16.99 (0-531-08576-7). 32pp. A simple explanation of how clouds form and why rain falls. (Rev: BCCB 3/93; BL 3/1/93; SLJ 7/93) [551]

20784 Morgan, Sally. *Weather* (4–6). Illus. Series: Nature Company Discoveries. 1996, Time Life $16.00 (0-8094-9370-5). 64pp. Types of weather, their causes, and prediction possibilities are three topics covered, with many colorful illustrations. (Rev: BL 9/15/96) [551.5]

20785 Sayre, April Pulley. *El Nino and La Nina: Weather in the Headlines* (4–8). Illus. 2000, Twenty-First Century LB $24.90 (0-7613-1405-9). 80pp. This book present the real facts about this complex Pacific Ocean phenomenon that produces unusual weather conditions that affect the entire world. (Rev: BL 9/15/00; HBG 3/01) [551.6]

20786 Siebert, Patricia. *Discovering El Nino: How Fable and Fact Together Help Explain the Weather* (3–5). Illus. 1999, Millbrook LB $21.90 (0-7613-1273-0). 32pp. A well-organized science picture book that explains the history, theory, and impact of El Niño and La Niña. (Rev: BL 12/1/99; HBG 3/00; SLJ 1/00) [551.5]

20787 Silverstein, Alvin, et al. *Weather and Climate* (4–7). Illus. Series: Science Concepts. 1998, Twenty-First Century LB $23.40 (0-7613-3223-5). 64pp. This book introduces weather by explaining earth's atmosphere, rotation, and different climates with material on air and water movements, cloud formation, and recent climate changes. (Rev: BL 5/1/99; HBG 10/99) [551.5]

20788 Simon, Seymour. *Weather* (4–6). Illus. 1993, Morrow $14.93 (0-688-10547-5). 40pp. Simple explanations are given for such phenomena as snow and hail, cold and warm fronts, and the atmosphere in this concise introduction to weather. (Rev: BL 9/1/93; SLJ 11/93) [551.5]

20789 Singer, Marilyn. *On the Same Day in March: A Tour of the World's Weather* (1–3). Illus. by Frane Lessac. 2000, HarperCollins LB $15.89 (0-06-028188-X). 40pp. The weather in 17 different places around the world on the same day in March is described in this introduction to climate and seasonal differences. (Rev: BCCB 3/00; BL 2/15/00; HBG 10/00; SLJ 4/00) [551.6]

20790 Souza, D. M. *Northern Lights* (5–7). Illus. 1994, Carolrhoda LB $19.95 (0-87614-799-6); paper $7.95 (0-87614-629-9). 48pp. A description of northern lights and an explanation of what causes them. (Rev: BL 1/15/94) [538]

20791 Stille, Darlene R. *The Greenhouse Effect* (1–3). Illus. Series: New True Books. 1990, Children's LB $21.00 (0-516-01106-5). 48pp. The causes and results of the greenhouse effect are explained. (Rev: BL 1/1/91) [363.73]

20792 Stonehouse, Bernard. *Snow, Ice and Cold* (5–7). 1993, Macmillan LB $21.00 (0-02-788530-5). 45pp. This work tells about how cultures and individuals have adjusted to severe cold climates. (Rev: SLJ 7/93) [551.6]

20793 Suzuki, David, and Barbara Hehner. *Looking at Weather* (3–6). Illus. Series: Looking At. 1991, Stoddart $19.89 (0-471-54753-0); paper $9.95 (0-471-54047-1). 96pp. A brief introduction to various kinds of weather and what causes them, with suggestions for activities and projects. (Rev: SLJ 5/92) [551.6]

20794 VanCleave, Janice. *Janice VanCleave's Weather: Mind-Boggling Experiments You Can Turn into Science Fair Projects* (3–6). Illus. Series: Janice VanCleave's Spectacular Science Projects. 1995, Wiley paper $10.95 (0-471-03231-X). 89pp. Intriguing questions about the weather are answered in 20 easily performed experiments and projects. (Rev: SLJ 8/95) [551.6]

20795 Williams, Terry Tempest, and Ted Major. *The Secret Language of Snow* (4–8). Illus. by Jennifer Dewey. 1984, Pantheon $10.95 (0-394-96574-X). 144pp. Different words for snow in the Eskimo language are used to explore this phenomenon.

20796 *Wind and Weather* (4–6). Illus. Series: Voyages of Discovery. 1995, Scholastic $19.95 (0-590-47646-7). 45pp. Using die-cut pages, transparencies, foldouts, and stickers, this attractively illustrated book explains the atmosphere, weather, storms, climates, and precipitation. (Rev: SLJ 5/96) [551.5]

20797 Wyatt, Valerie. *FAQ Weather* (4–6). Illus. by Brian Share. 2000, Kids Can $12.95 (1-55074-582-4); paper $6.95 (1-55074-815-1). 40pp. Using a question-and-answer format, this book covers many aspects of weather including winds, clouds, precipitation, and global warming. (Rev: HBG 10/00; SLJ 8/00) [551.6]

Physics

General

20798 Bonnet, Bob, and Dan Keen. *Science Fair Projects: Physics* (4–7). Illus. 2000, Sterling $16.95 (0-8069-0707-X). 96pp. This large-format book presents 47 projects demonstrating concepts in physics and using common materials as equipment. (Rev: BL 2/1/00; SLJ 4/00) [530]

20799 Burton, Jane, and Kim Taylor. *The Nature and Science of Bubbles* (3–6). Illus. Series: Exploring the Science of Nature. 1998, Gareth Stevens LB $18.60 (0-8368-1939-X). 32pp. Large type, color photographs, and a lively text are used to explain the nature and composition of various kinds of bubbles. (Rev: BL 6/1–15/98; HBG 10/98) [530.4]

20800 Challoner, Jack. *Big and Small* (K–4). Illus. Series: Start-Up Science. 1996, Raintree Steck-Vaughn LB $24.26 (0-8172-4319-4). 32pp. Information and experiments are combined in this attractive beginner's science book about size. (Rev: SLJ 2/97) [153.7]

20801 Challoner, Jack. *Floating and Sinking* (K–4). Illus. Series: Start-Up Science. 1996, Raintree Steck-Vaughn LB $24.26 (0-8172-4317-8). 32pp. The concepts of floating and sinking are explored in a simple, conversational text with many attractive pictures. (Rev: SLJ 2/97) [530]

20802 Cooper, Christopher. *Matter* (4–8). Illus. Series: Eyewitness Science. 1992, DK $15.95 (1-879431-88-2). 64pp. Lavish illustrations and clear text help to make difficult scientific principles understandable. (Rev: BL 1/15/93; SLJ 12/92) [535]

20803 Davies, Kay, and Wendy Oldfield. *My Boat* (3–6). Illus. Series: First Step Science. 1994, Gareth Stevens LB $21.27 (0-8368-1115-1). 32pp. This simple presentation explains why boats float or sink, stay upright, and can be propelled, with a series of simple activities. (Rev: BL 2/15/95) [623.8]

20804 DiSpezio, Michael A. *Awesome Experiments in Light and Sound* (5–8). Illus. by Catherine Leary. Series: Awesome Experiments. 1999, Sterling

$17.95 (0-8069-9823-7). 160pp. A collection of 73 experiments that deal with such topics as spectra, reflection, and refraction, and vibration, pitch, and resonance. (Rev: SLJ 10/99) [530]

20805 Durant, Penny R. *Bubblemania! Learn the Secrets to Creating Millions of Spectacular Bubbles!* (4–8). 1994, Avon paper $3.99 (0-380-77373-2). 86pp. Through a series of easy experiments, surface tension, bubble formation, and the uses of bubbles are explained. (Rev: SLJ 7/94) [530]

20806 Evans, Neville. *The Science of Gravity* (5–8). Illus. Series: Science World. 2000, Raintree Steck-Vaughn $22.83 (0-7398-1323-4). 32pp. Explores the force of gravity and how it affects our lives, with additional material on air resistance, mass, and invisible forces. (Rev: BL 9/15/00; HBG 10/00) [531]

20807 Friedhoffer, Robert. *Physics Lab in a Hardware Store* (5–8). Illus. Series: Physical Science Labs. 1996, Watts LB $24.00 (0-531-11292-6). 112pp. Using objects like nails, axes, and ladders, a number of principles in physics are introduced. (Rev: BL 12/1/96; SLJ 5/97) [621.9]

20808 Friedhoffer, Robert. *Physics Lab in a Housewares Store* (5–8). Illus. Series: Physical Science Labs. 1996, Watts LB $24.00 (0-531-11293-4). 96pp. Various concepts in physics are demonstrated using such household items as a garlic press and a can opener. (Rev: BL 12/1/96; SLJ 1/97) [621.9]

20809 Gardner, Robert. *Experiments with Bubbles* (4–7). Illus. Series: Getting Started in Science. 1995, Enslow LB $20.95 (0-89490-666-6). 104pp. The properties of bubbles are explored in a series of experiments, each a little more complex than the last. (Rev: BL 12/1/95; SLJ 3/96) [530.4]

20810 Gibson, Gary. *Pushing and Pulling* (3–5). Photos by Roger Vlitos. Illus. by Tony Kenyon. Series: Science for Fun. 1995, Millbrook LB $20.90 (1-56294-630-7). 32pp. In double-page spreads, experiments are described that demonstrate principles of gravity, weight, friction, hydraulic forces, fluid drag, and pulleys. (Rev: SLJ 3/96) [530]

20811 Goodstein, Madeline. *Sports Science Projects: The Physics of Balls in Motion* (5–8). Illus. Series: Science Fair Success. 1999, Enslow LB $19.99 (0-7660-1174-7). 128pp. This book contains 40 projects that use the properties of different sports balls to demonstrate principles of physics. (Rev: BL 2/15/00; HBG 10/00) [530]

20812 Hodge, Deborah, and Adrienne Mason. *Solids, Liquids, and Gases* (K–4). Illus. Series: Starting with Science. 1998, Kids Can $10.95 (1-55074-195-0). 32pp. Uses simple science activities to demonstrate the three states of matter and such phenomena as air pressure and condensation. (Rev: BL 4/15/98; HBG 10/98; SLJ 6/98) [530.4]

20813 Morgan, Sally, and Adrian Morgan. *Materials* (4–7). Illus. Series: Designs in Science. 1994, Facts on File $16.95 (0-8160-2985-7). 48pp. Basic properties of matter and materials are explored in a series of experiments using everyday materials. (Rev: BL 7/94) [620.1]

20814 Nankivell-Aston, Sally, and Dorothy Jackson. *Science Experiments with Forces* (3–6). Series: Science Experiments. 2000, Watts LB $20.00 (0-531-14582-4); paper $6.95 (0-531-15444-0). 32pp. This activity book explains and gives detailed experiments on topics including friction, the forces of gravity and air, and simple phenomena like push and pull. (Rev: SLJ 3/01) [530]

20815 Skurzynski, Gloria. *Zero Gravity* (2–4). Illus. 1994, Bradbury paper $15.00 (0-02-782925-1). 32pp. Weightlessness in space shuttles is explained, with a discussion of orbiting and zero gravity. (Rev: BCCB 10/94; BL 10/15/94; SLJ 10/94) [531]

20816 Zoehfeld, Kathleen W. *What Is the World Made Of? All About Solids, Liquids, and Gases* (1–2). Illus. by Paul Meisel. Series: Let's-Read-and-Find-Out. 1998, HarperCollins LB $15.89 (0-06-027144-2); paper $4.95 (0-06-445163-1). 32pp. This simple science book for beginning readers explains the three states of matter — solid, liquid, and gas. (Rev: BL 11/1/98; HB 9–10/98; HBG 3/99; SLJ 1/99) [530.4]

Energy and Motion

General

20817 Ardley, Neil. *The Science Book of Energy* (3–6). Illus. Series: Science Books. 1992, Harcourt $9.95 (0-15-200611-7). 28pp. This book of experiments introduces the concepts of force and energy through a series of two-page projects. (Rev: BL 3/15/92; HB 9–10/92) [531.6]

20818 Ardley, Neil. *The Science Book of Motion* (3–6). Illus. Series: Science Books. 1992, Harcourt $9.95 (0-15-200622-2). 28pp. This attractive book of experiments discusses the types and characteristics of motion and includes 12 projects to illustrate each. (Rev: BL 10/15/92; SLJ 1/93) [531]

20819 Bonnet, Bob, and Dan Keen. *Science Fair Projects: Energy* (4–6). Illus. 1998, Sterling $16.95 (0-8069-9793-1). 96pp. Such sources of energy as sunlight, batteries, microwave ovens, and lightbulbs

are used in this collection of 55 simple activities about energy and the various forms it takes. (Rev: BL 3/1/98; SLJ 6/98) [531]

20820 Burton, Jane. *The Nature and Science of Energy* (3–6). Series: Exploring the Science of Nature. 1998, Gareth Stevens LB $18.60 (0-8368-1941-1). 32pp. Using large type, color photographs, and clear captioning, this work explores the meaning of energy, its various forms, and its uses. (Rev: BL 6/1–15/98; HBG 10/98) [531]

20821 Challoner, Jack. *Energy* (3–6). Illus. Series: Eyewitness Science. 1993, DK $15.95 (1-56458-232-9). 64pp. A very attractive book that explores the role of energy in our lives and describes its sources and uses. (Rev: SLJ 9/93) [621]

20822 Chandler, Gary, and Kevin Graham. *Alternative Energy Sources* (4–8). Illus. Series: Making a Better World. 1996, Twenty-First Century LB $20.40 (0-8050-4621-6). 64pp. This account explores many varieties of alternative energy and the use of natural resources in environmentally safe ways. (Rev: BL 12/15/96; SLJ 1/97) [333.79]

20823 Cobb, Vicki. *Why Doesn't the Earth Fall Up? And Other Not Such Dumb Questions About Motion* (2–4). Illus. by Ted Enik. 1989, Dutton $14.99 (0-525-67253-2). 40pp. The principles of physics explained for the young. (Rev: BCCB 2/89; BL 11/15/88; SLJ 2/89)

20824 Dann, Sarah. *The Science of Energy* (2–4). 2000, Gareth Stevens LB $19.93 (0-8368-2571-3). 32pp. This book defines energy and describes the energy chain and how energy is transformed into electricity, wind, water, and solar power as well as giving some simple activities. (Rev: HBG 10/00; SLJ 9/00) [531.6]

20825 de Pinna, Simon. *Forces and Motion* (3–5). Series: Science Projects. 1998, Raintree Steck-Vaughn $25.69 (0-8172-4962-1). 48pp. A brief explanation of force and motion is followed by a series of activities, with each double-page spread dealing with a different aspect of the subject. (Rev: BL 3/15/98; HBG 10/98) [531.6]

20826 DiSpezio, Michael A. *Awesome Experiments in Force and Motion* (5–8). Illus. by Catherine Leary. Series: Awesome Experiments. 1999, Sterling LB $17.95 (0-8069-9821-0). 160pp. This cleverly presented book contains more than 70 experiments grouped under five headings: inertia, buoyancy, surface tension, air pressure, and propulsion. (Rev: HBG 10/99; SLJ 7/99) [531.6]

20827 Doherty, Paul, and Don Rathjen. *The Cool Hot Rod and Other Electrifying Experiments on Energy and Matter* (4–8). Illus. Series: Exploratorium Science Snackbook. 1996, Wiley paper $10.95 (0-471-11518-5). 128pp. Based on exhibits at the Exploratorium in San Francisco, this book supplies activities that demonstrate the properties of energy and matter. (Rev: BL 4/15/96; SLJ 7/96) [531]

20828 Doherty, Paul, and Don Rathjen. *The Spinning Blackboard and Other Dynamic Experiments on Force and Motion* (4–8). Illus. Series: Exploratorium Science Snackbook. 1996, Wiley paper $10.95 (0-471-11514-2). 128pp. The many activities in this well-organized, attractive book reveal important characteristics of force and motion. (Rev: BL 4/15/96; SLJ 6/96) [531]

20829 Gardner, Robert. *Experiments with Motion* (4–7). Illus. 1995, Enslow LB $20.95 (0-89490-667-4). 112pp. Projects using simple equipment illustrate the laws of motion and the ways motion differs in various situations. (Rev: BL 2/1/96; SLJ 2/96) [531]

20830 Gutnik, Martin J., and Natalie B. Gutnik. *Projects That Explore Energy* (5–8). Illus. Series: Investigate! 1994, Millbrook LB $21.40 (1-56294-334-0). 72pp. A lucid, well-organized series of projects and experiments that explore power, force, and energy sources and resources. (Rev: BL 8/94; SLJ 6/94) [333.79]

20831 Hawkes, Nigel. *Energy* (4–6). Illus. Series: New Technology. 1994, Twenty-First Century LB $16.90 (0-8050-3419-6). 32pp. Energy sources like water, wind, sunlight, and nuclear fission are described in a series of double-page spreads. (Rev: BL 7/94; SLJ 8/94) [621.044]

20832 Lafferty, Peter. *Force and Motion* (4–8). Illus. Series: Eyewitness Science. 1992, DK $15.95 (1-879431-85-8). 64pp. This account emphasizes the history of scientific discoveries and theories concerning force and motion. (Rev: BL 1/15/93; SLJ 12/92) [531]

20833 Madgwick, Wendy. *On the Move* (K–3). Series: Science Starters. 1999, Raintree Steck-Vaughn LB $15.98 (0-8172-5333-5). 32pp. Energy and motion are explored in this book through a dozen simple activities that use items found in the home to answer questions like why running shoes increase speed, how you keep your balance, and why ice is slippery. (Rev: BL 6/1–15/99; HBG 10/99) [531]

20834 Parker, Steve. *Fuels for the Future* (4–6). Series: Protecting Our Planet. 1998, Raintree Steck-Vaughn $25.68 (0-8172-4937-0). 48pp. After explaining the limits of fossil fuels and commenting on their destructive effects, this account introduces sustainable, planet-friendly alternatives. (Rev: BL 7/98; HBG 10/98) [333.79]

20835 Riley, Peter D. *Energy* (4–5). Series: Cycles in Science. 1998, Heinemann LB $21.36 (1-57572-617-3). 32pp. An overview of the world of energy that touches on topics such as kinds of energy, how potential energy becomes kinetic, nuclear energy, electricity, magnetism, and ecological issues. (Rev: SLJ 7/98) [531.6]

20836 Rybolt, Thomas R., and Robert C. Mebane. *Environmental Experiments About Renewable Energy* (3–5). Illus. Series: Science Experiments for Young People. 1994, Enslow LB $19.95 (0-89490-579-1). 96pp. This book contains 16 easy experiments to answer questions about renewable energy. (Rev: HBG 3/01; SLJ 2/95) [531]

20837 Schultz, Ron. *Looking Inside Sports Aerodynamics* (5–8). Illus. by Peter Aschwanden. Series: X-Ray Vision. 1992, John Muir paper $9.95 (1-56261-065-1). 48pp. Using the effects of gravity, turbulence, drag, and lift, this book explains what

happens when we throw or hit a ball or other object. (Rev: BL 1/15/93) [796]

20838 Silverstein, Alvin, et al. *Energy* (4–7). Illus. Series: Science Concepts. 1998, Twenty-First Century LB $23.40 (0-7613-3222-7). 64pp. Photos, diagrams, and illustrations help introduce six types of energy: electrical, magnetic, light, heat, sound, and nuclear. (Rev: BL 5/1/99; HBG 10/99) [621.042]

20839 Taylor, Kim. *Action* (3–5). Illus. 1992, Wiley $12.95 (0-471-57193-8). 32pp. Explains the principles of movement, including gliding and jumping. (Rev: SLJ 11/92) [530]

20840 White, Larry. *Energy* (3–6). Illus. by Laurie Hamilton. Series: Simple Experiments for Young Scientists. 1995, Millbrook LB $19.90 (1-56294-473-8). 48pp. Simple projects using easily found materials supply answers to a number of questions about energy. (Rev: SLJ 9/95) [531]

20841 Woelfle, Gretchen. *The Wind at Work: An Activity Guide to Windmills* (4–6). Illus. 1997, Chicago Review paper $14.95 (1-55652-308-4). 144pp. The history and uses of windmills are covered, with many fascinating activities. (Rev: BL 9/1/97; SLJ 10/97*) [621.4]

20842 Woodruff, John. *Energy* (3–5). Series: Science Projects. 1998, Raintree Steck-Vaughn $25.69 (0-8172-4961-3). 48pp. The properties, uses, and kinds of energy are covered in a series of double-page spreads that give brief explanations followed by simple activities. (Rev: BL 3/15/98; HBG 10/98) [333]

Coal, Gas, and Oil

20843 Mitgutsch, Ali. *From Swamp to Coal* (2–3). Illus. 1985, Carolrhoda LB $18.60 (0-87614-233-1). 24pp. Much information is simply explained in this account of how coal is formed.

Nuclear Energy

20844 Hawkes, Nigel. *Nuclear Power* (4–6). Illus. 1990, Rourke LB $13.95 (0-685-36380-5). 48pp. Safety and waste disposal, radioisotopes, and an explanation of fission are included in this heavily illustrated book.

20845 Holland, Gini. *Nuclear Energy* (3–6). Illus. Series: Inventors and Inventions. 1996, Marshall Cavendish LB $25.64 (0-7614-0047-8). 63pp. The story of the discoverers of nuclear energy, its uses, and current problems and possibilities are covered, with many color photos. (Rev: BL 7/96; SLJ 9/96) [333.692]

20846 O'Neill, Mary. *Power Failure* (4–7). Illus. by John Bindon. Series: SOS Planet Earth. 1991, Troll paper $4.95 (0-8167-2289-7). 32pp. The Chernobyl nuclear disaster is just one of the problems discussed in this look at an important environmental danger. (Rev: BL 6/15/91) [333.79]

20847 Wilcox, Charlotte. *Powerhouse: Inside a Nuclear Power Plant* (4–8). Illus. 1996, Carolrhoda LB $22.60 (0-87614-945-X); paper $7.95 (0-87614-979-4). 48pp. A history of nuclear energy is followed by a description of how a power plant operates and the dangers that are present. (Rev: BL 10/1/96; SLJ 9/96) [621.48]

Solar Energy

20848 Asimov, Isaac. *How Did We Find Out About Solar Power?* (5–7). Illus. by David Wool. 1981, Walker LB $12.85 (0-8027-6423-1). 64pp. An account that explains what solar power is and how we use it.

20849 Fowler, Allan. *Energy from the Sun* (1–3). Series: Rookie Readers. 1997, Children's LB $19.00 (0-516-20432-7). 32pp. An easy-to-read science book that introduces solar energy and how it is captured and used. (Rev: BL 12/15/97; HBG 3/98) [697.78]

20850 Gardner, Robert. *Science Project Ideas About the Sun* (4–7). Series: Science Project Ideas. 1997, Enslow LB $19.95 (0-89490-845-6). 96pp. The sun and solar energy are the subjects of this book that illustrates important concepts through a number of interesting projects and experiments. (Rev: BL 12/15/97; HBG 3/98; SLJ 1/98) [697.78]

Heat and Fire

20851 Craats, Rennay. *The Science of Fire* (3–5). Series: Living Science. 2000, Gareth Stevens LB $19.93 (0-8368-2680-9). 32pp. This basic book on fire covers chemical basics, fire fighting, conservation issues, and uses of fire in a series of two-page spreads. (Rev: SLJ 3/01) [536]

20852 Darling, David J. *Between Fire and Ice: The Science of Heat* (4–8). Illus. Series: Experiment! 1992, Macmillan LB $17.95 (0-87518-501-0). 60pp. After a discussion of the scientific method, characteristics of heat are described and simple experiments are given to demonstrate these properties. (Rev: BL 10/1/92; SLJ 11/92) [536]

20853 Gardner, Robert, and Eric Kemer. *Science Projects About Temperature and Heat* (4–8). Series: Science Projects. 1994, Enslow LB $20.95 (0-89490-534-1). 128pp. Using household materials, this book clearly outlines procedures and results involving projects that explore heat and temperature. (Rev: SLJ 1/95) [536]

Light and Color

20854 Ardley, Neil. *The Science Book of Color* (3–6). Illus. Series: Science Books. 1991, Harcourt $9.95 (0-15-200576-5). 28pp. Clear color photos enhance the step-by-step directions for science experiments involving color. (Rev: BL 3/1/91; SLJ 5/91) [535.6]

20855 Ardley, Neil. *The Science Book of Light* (3–6). Illus. Series: Science Books. 1991, Harcourt $9.95 (0-15-200577-3). 28pp. Large-type instructions and full-color photographs are included in this

book on science experiments involving light. (Rev: BL 3/1/91; SLJ 5/91) [535]

20856 Asimov, Isaac. *How Did We Find Out About Lasers?* (5–7). Illus. by Erika Kors. 1990, Walker LB $13.85 (0-8027-6936-5). 64pp. A readable introduction to laser science by the veteran writer. (Rev: BL 8/90; SLJ 11/90) [621.36]

20857 Branley, Franklyn M. *Day Light, Night Light: Where Light Comes From* (K–3). Illus. by Stacey Schuett. Series: Let's-Read-and-Find-Out. 1998, HarperCollins LB $15.89 (0-06-027295-3). 32pp. In this book about light, topics like darkness, heat, light sources, reflection, vision, and the speed of light are discussed. (Rev: BL 12/1/97; HBG 10/98; SLJ 2/98) [535]

20858 Burnie, David. *Light* (4–8). Illus. Series: Eyewitness Science. 1992, DK $15.95 (1-879431-79-3). 64pp. Clear explanations and a handsome format make these scientific principles readable. (Rev: BL 1/15/93) [535]

20859 Burton, Jane, and Kim Taylor. *The Nature and Science of Color* (3–6). Illus. Series: Exploring the Science of Nature. 1998, Gareth Stevens LB $18.60 (0-8368-1940-3). 32pp. The nature and composition of color and colors are explained in a lively, large-type text and color photographs. (Rev: BL 6/1–15/98; HBG 10/98) [535]

20860 Burton, Jane, and Kim Taylor. *The Nature and Science of Reflections* (3–6). Series: Exploring the Science of Nature. 2001, Gareth Stevens LB $21.27 (0-8368-2194-7). 32pp. Light, mirrors, and reflection are topics explored in this basic physics book that also contains activities and projects to demonstrate various principles. (Rev: BL 3/15/01) [535]

20861 Darling, David J. *Making Light Work: The Science of Optics* (3–6). Illus. Series: Experiment! 1991, Macmillan LB $17.95 (0-87518-476-6). 64pp. An introduction, with experiments, to the principles of light. (Rev: BL 6/1/92) [535]

20862 Day, Trevor. *Light* (3–5). Illus. Series: Science Projects. 1998, Raintree Steck-Vaughn $25.69 (0-8172-4943-5). 48pp. With explanatory text and simple activities, this account covers such topics as the nature of light, vision, shadows, photography, reflections, refraction, and color. (Rev: BL 3/15/98; HBG 10/98) [538]

20863 Doherty, Paul, et al. *The Magic Wand and Other Bright Experiments on Light and Color* (4–8). Illus. 1995, Wiley paper $10.95 (0-471-11515-0). 128pp. A clearly written, well-organized text with fascinating activities that explore the properties of light and color. (Rev: BL 1/1–15/96; SLJ 1/96) [535]

20864 Farndon, John. *Color* (3–6). Illus. Series: Science Experiments. 2000, Marshall Cavendish LB $16.95 (0-7614-1092-9). 32pp. Topics covered include the spectrum, primary colors, pigment, mixing colors, and color blindness, with many interesting activities such as making a color wheel and creating a spectrum. (Rev: BL 3/15/01; HBG 3/01) [535.6]

20865 Farndon, John. *Lights and Optics* (3–6). Series: Science Experiments. 2000, Marshall Cavendish LB $16.95 (0-7614-1090-2). 32pp. Explores properties of light and optics and outlines projects that apply the principles established. (Rev: BL 3/15/01; HBG 3/01) [535]

20866 Fowler, Allan. *All the Colors of the Rainbow* (1–2). Series: Rookie Readers. 1998, Children's LB $18.50 (0-516-20801-2). 32pp. Using color photographs and three lines of text per page, this book introduces the concept of color to very young readers. (Rev: BL 9/15/98; HBG 10/99) [535]

20867 Fox, Mary V. *Lasers* (3–6). Illus. Series: Inventors and Inventions. 1996, Benchmark LB $25.64 (0-7614-0067-2). 63pp. The history of laser technology, with profiles of several scientists involved in this branch of science and its effects in such areas as medicine. (Rev: BL 3/15/96; SLJ 6/96) [621.36]

20868 Gardner, Robert. *Experiments with Light and Mirrors* (4–7). Illus. 1995, Enslow LB $20.95 (0-89490-668-2). 112pp. Using equipment like mirrors and cardboard, the properties of light are explained and demonstrated. (Rev: BL 2/1/96; SLJ 3/96) [535.2]

20869 Gardner, Robert. *Science Projects About Light* (4–8). Series: Science Projects. 1994, Enslow LB $20.95 (0-89490-529-5). 128pp. This project book contains a wealth of demonstrations that explain the basic principles of light. (Rev: SLJ 1/95) [535]

20870 Gibson, Gary. *Light and Color* (3–5). Illus. Series: Science for Fun. 1995, Millbrook LB $20.90 (1-56294-616-1). 32pp. Underlying scientific principles involving color and light are covered in a series of double-page spreads, each with a different project. (Rev: BL 7/95) [535]

20871 Hecht, Jeff. *Optics: Light for a New Age* (5–8). Illus. 1988, Macmillan $15.95 (0-684-18879-1). 44pp. An overview of optics, including properties of light, optical instruments and laser technology. (Rev: BL 4/1/88)

20872 Krupp, E. C. *The Rainbow and You* (2–3). Illus. by Robin R. Krupp. 2000, HarperCollins LB $15.89 (0-688-15602-9). 32pp. The causes of rainbows are discussed (with directions on how to make your own) plus material on double rainbows, folklore surrounding rainbows, and Isaac Newton's work with them. (Rev: BL 8/00; HBG 10/00; SLJ 5/00) [551.56]

20873 Levine, Shar, and Leslie Johnstone. *The Optics Book: Fun Experiments with Light, Vision and Color* (4–7). Illus. 1999, Sterling $19.95 (0-8069-9947-0). 80pp. This book contains experiments and projects involving such subjects related to light as reflection, refraction, color, polarization, vision, and light rays. (Rev: BL 3/1/99; SLJ 7/99) [535]

20874 Madgwick, Wendy. *Light and Dark* (K–3). Series: Science Starters. 1999, Raintree Steck-Vaughn LB $15.98 (0-8172-5556-7). 32pp. Double-page spreads introduce about a dozen projects that explore the topic of light including demonstrations on how rainbows are formed, why shadows change, and how lenses work. (Rev: BL 6/1–15/99; HBG 10/99) [535.2]

20875 Morgan, Nina. *Lasers* (3–6). Illus. Series: 20th Century Inventions. 1997, Raintree Steck-Vaughn LB $27.12 (0-8172-4812-9). 48pp. This oversize book describes types of lasers and their applications in such fields as CDs and medicine. (Rev: BL 6/1–15/97) [621.36]

20876 Murray, Peter. *Professor Solomon Snickerdoodle's Light Science Tricks* (1–3). Illus. by Penny Dann. 1998, Child's World LB $21.36 (1-56766-148-3). 29pp. This book presents amazing science tricks involving light and explanations that demonstrate its properties. (Rev: SLJ 5/98) [535]

20877 *Why Are Zebras Black and White? Questions Children Ask About Color* (PS–3). Illus. 1996, DK $9.95 (0-7894-1122-9). 32pp. Common questions about colors (e.g., Why is the sea blue?) are answered in simple prose. (Rev: BL 12/1/96; SLJ 1/97) [574.5]

20878 Zubrowski, Bernie. *Mirrors: Finding Out About the Properties of Light* (4–7). Illus. by Roy Doty. 1992, Morrow LB $13.93 (0-688-10592-0). 112pp. In this hands-on approach to science, games and activities entice the reader. (Rev: BL 7/92; SLJ 8/92) [535]

20879 Zubrowski, Bernie. *Shadow Play: Making Pictures with Light and Lenses* (4–6). Illus. by Roy Doty. Series: Boston Children's Museum Activity Books. 1995, Morrow LB $15.93 (0-688-13210-3); paper $7.95 (0-688-13211-1). 112pp. Carefully outlines all sorts of projects involving shadows, from using mirrors to creating a shadow box and a box camera. (Rev: BL 9/1/95; SLJ 10/95) [771]

Magnetism and Electricity

20880 Ardley, Neil. *Electricity* (4–6). Illus. 1992, Macmillan $22.00 (0-02-705665-1). 48pp. This book tells about the types of electricity and how they are produced. (Rev: SLJ 8/92) [537]

20881 Ardley, Neil. *The Science Book of Electricity* (3–6). Illus. Series: Science Books. 1991, Harcourt $9.95 (0-15-200583-8). 29pp. Full-page spreads show step-by-step procedures for projects involving electricity. (Rev: BL 10/15/91) [535]

20882 Ardley, Neil. *The Science Book of Magnets* (3–6). Illus. Series: Science Books. 1991, Harcourt $9.95 (0-15-200581-1). 29pp. Basic properties of magnets and magnetism are explored through a series of projects with clear directions and attractive illustrations. (Rev: BL 10/15/91) [528.4]

20883 Bains, Rae. *Discovering Electricity* (1–3). Illus. by Joel Snyder. 1982, Troll LB $17.25 (0-89375-564-8); paper $3.50 (0-89375-565-6). 32pp. A simple explanation of what makes electricity work.

20884 Berger, Melvin. *Switch On, Switch Off* (K–3). Illus. by Carolyn Croll. 1989, HarperCollins LB $15.89 (0-690-04786-X); paper $4.95 (0-06-

445097-X). 32pp. Explaining the mysteries of electricity. (Rev: BL 4/15/89; HB 5–6/89)

20885 Bocknek, Jonathan. *The Science of Magnets* (2–4). Series: Living Science. 1999, Gareth Stevens LB $19.93 (0-8368-2572-1). 32pp. Different kinds of magnets, magnetic poles and properties, electromagnets, and magnetic animals and medicine are introduced in a series of double-page spreads with some appended activities. (Rev: HBG 10/00; SLJ 9/00) [538.4]

20886 Bonnet, Bob, and Dan Keen. *Science Fair Projects with Electricity and Electronics* (4–8). Illus. 1996, Sterling $17.95 (0-8069-1300-2). 96pp. Details of 46 projects and experiments involving such topics as electric motors and resistance. (Rev: BL 12/1/96; SLJ 12/96) [507.8]

20887 Cole, Joanna. *The Magic School Bus and the Electric Field Trip* (2–4). Illus. by Bruce Degen. Series: Magic School Bus. 1997, Scholastic $15.95 (0-590-44682-7). 56pp. Mrs. Frizzle's class visits a power plant to find out how electricity is made in this entertaining science book filled with facts, jokes, and puns. (Rev: BL 10/15/97; HBG 3/98; SLJ 11/97) [621.3]

20888 Cosner, Sharon. *The Light Bulb* (4–6). Illus. 1984, Walker LB $10.85 (0-8027-6527-0). 64pp. A history of various forms of lighting, the light bulb, and the electrical industry.

20889 de Pinna, Simon. *Electricity* (3–5). Series: Science Projects. 1998, Raintree Steck-Vaughn $24.26 (0-8172-4945-1). 48pp. The properties of electricity are covered in a series of double-page spreads, each of which covers a different aspect of the subject and outlines three or four simple acitivities. (Rev: BL 3/15/98; HBG 10/98) [621.3]

20890 DiSpezio, Michael A. *Awesome Experiments in Electricity and Magnetism* (5–8). Illus. by Catherine Leary. Series: Awesome Experiments. 1999, Sterling LB $17.95 (0-8069-9819-9). 160pp. This book contains more than 70 experiments on such subjects as electrical charges, static electricity, currents, circuits, switches, and magnetism. The presentation is enhanced by entertaining remarks by the author. (Rev: SLJ 7/99) [537]

20891 Evans, Neville. *The Science of a Light Bulb* (5–8). Illus. Series: Science World. 2000, Raintree Steck-Vaughn $22.83 (0-7398-1325-0). 32pp. This work explains how Edison invented the light bulb, describes its parts, and tells how light is produced and how we see it. (Rev: BL 9/15/00; HBG 10/00) [535]

20892 Farndon, John. *Electricity* (3–6). Series: Science Experiments. 2000, Marshall Cavendish LB $16.95 (0-7614-1086-4). 32pp. Each chapter contains information on different aspects and applications of electricity plus experiments that illustrate key principles. (Rev: BL 3/15/01; HBG 3/01) [537]

20893 Fowler, Allan. *What Magnets Can Do* (1–2). Illus. Series: Rookie Readers. 1995, Children's LB $19.00 (0-516-06034-1). 32pp. A basic introduction to magnets and magnetism, with photos, large type, and coverage of interesting topics. (Rev: BL 7/95) [538]

20894 Gardner, Robert. *Science Projects About Electricity and Magnets* (4–8). Series: Science Projects. 1994, Enslow LB $20.95 (0-89490-530-9). 128pp. A wealth of projects that cover the basic principles of electricity and magnetism. (Rev: SLJ 1/95) [537]

20895 Gibson, Gary. *Understanding Electricity* (3–5). Photos by Roger Vlitos. Illus. by Tony Kenyon. Series: Science for Fun. 1995, Millbrook LB $20.90 (1-56294-629-3). 32pp. Using a six-volt battery and a six-volt lightbulb along with other simple household products, electricity is explored in a series of experiments. (Rev: SLJ 3/96) [621.3]

20896 Glover, David. *Batteries, Bulbs, and Wires: Science Facts and Experiments* (3–6). Illus. Series: Young Discoverers. 1993, Kingfisher paper $6.95 (1-85697-933-4). 31pp. Concepts related to magnetism and electricity are revealed in double-page spreads with many activities and connecting text. (Rev: SLJ 12/93) [507]

20897 Good, Keith. *Zap It! Exciting Electricity Activities* (3–7). Series: Design It! 2000, Lerner LB $21.27 (0-8225-3565-3). 30pp. An activity book that explores concepts in electricity and contains projects involving electric circuits, pressure pads, and different kinds of switches. (Rev: HBG 10/00; SLJ 6/00) [537]

20898 Levine, Shar, and Leslie Johnstone. *The Magnet Book* (4–6). Illus. 1997, Sterling $21.95 (0-8069-9943-8). 80pp. Clear drawings, photos, and instructions enhance this book containing more than 30 experiments dealing with magnetism and electricity. (Rev: BL 2/1/98) [538]

20899 Levine, Shar, and Leslie Johnstone. *Shocking Science: Fun and Fascinating Electrical Experiments* (5–8). Illus. 2000, Sterling $19.95 (0-8069-3946-X). 80pp. A large-format book that presents experiments on electricity under these subjects: static-electricity, currents, magnetism, circuits, and electronic boards. (Rev: BL 4/1/00; SLJ 5/00) [537]

20900 Madgwick, Wendy. *Magnets and Sparks* (K–3). Series: Science Starters. 1999, Raintree Steck-Vaughn LB $15.98 (0-8172-5328-9). 32pp. A basic introduction to electricity and magnetism that includes more than a dozen activities using items found in the home to explore topics such as how electricity travels, what magnets attract, and how flashlights work. (Rev: BL 6/1–15/99; HBG 10/99) [537]

20901 Nankivell-Aston, Sally, and Dorothy Jackson. *Science Experiments with Electricity* (3–6). Series: Science Experiments. 2000, Watts LB $20.00 (0-531-14580-8); paper $6.95 (0-531-15443-2). 32pp. This book of simple electricity projects includes building simple switches and circuits with additional material on scientific method and safety. (Rev: SLJ 3/01) [537]

20902 Parker, Steve. *Electricity* (4–8). Illus. Series: Eyewitness Science. 1992, DK $15.95 (1-879431-82-3). 64pp. In double-page spreads with many diagrams and photos, this book covers a history of our knowledge of electricity. (Rev: BL 1/15/93) [537]

20903 Skurzynski, Gloria. *Waves: The Electromagnetic Universe* (4–7). Illus. 1996, National Geographic $16.95 (0-7922-3520-7). 48pp. Wave theory is explained, with many examples from nature and an explanation of the theory's importance. (Rev: BL 12/1/96; SLJ 11/96*) [539.2]

20904 Tomecek, Steve. *Simple Attractions: Phantastic Physical Phenomena* (4–7). Illus. by Arnie Ten. 1995, W.H. Freeman paper $9.95 (0-7167-6632-9). 48pp. A collection of experiments related to magnetic attraction and static cling. (Rev: SLJ 3/96) [538]

20905 VanCleave, Janice. *Janice VanCleave's Electricity: Mind-Boggling Experiments You Can Turn into Science Fair Projects* (5–7). Illus. 1994, Wiley paper $10.95 (0-471-31010-7). 96pp. As well as providing a discussion on the nature of electricity, this book offers 20 informative experiments that move from the very simple to the more complex. (Rev: BL 12/1/94; SLJ 11/94) [537]

20906 VanCleave, Janice. *Magnets: Mind-Boggling Experiments You Can Turn into Science Fair Projects* (4–6). Illus. Series: Spectacular Science Projects. 1993, Wiley paper $10.95 (0-471-57106-7). 88pp. Using magnets and the principles of magnetism, this book offers clear directions in developing many interesting science projects. Also use: *Animals; Gravity;* and *Molecules* (all 1993). (Rev: BL 5/1/93; SLJ 7/93) [538]

20907 Wallace, Joseph. *The Lightbulb* (4–7). Illus. Series: Turning Points. 1999, Simon & Schuster $17.95 (0-689-82816-0). 80pp. After giving a history of the search for a clean, safe light source, this book tells about Thomas Alva Edison and his work to perfect the light bulb. (Rev: BL 10/1/99; HBG 3/00; SLJ 10/99) [621.32]

20908 Whalley, Margaret. *Experiment with Magnets and Electricity* (2–5). Illus. Series: Experiment With. 1994, Lerner LB $19.93 (0-8225-2457-0). 32pp. Principles of magnetism and electricity are covered through a series of simple, fun-to-do experiments using everyday materials. (Rev: BL 3/1/94; SLJ 5/94) [537]

Optical Illusions

20909 Banyai, Istvan. *Re-Zoom* (K–5). Illus. by author. 1995, Viking $15.99 (0-670-86392-0). A remarkable visual journey in which viewers see something that turns out to be part of something larger. (Rev: BCCB 1/96; SLJ 9/95) [152]

20910 Baum, Arline, and Joseph Baum. *Opt: An Illusionary Tale* (1–4). Illus. by authors. 1989, Puffin paper $5.99 (0-14-050573-3). A young prince has a birthday party in the land of Opt, where objects appear and disappear. (Rev: BL 5/15/87; HB 9–10/87; SLJ 6–7/87)

20911 Churchill, E. Richard. *Optical Illusion Tricks and Toys* (4–7). Illus. by James Michaels. 1989, Sterling $12.95 (0-8069-6868-0). 128pp. Sixty-plus opportunities to demonstrate that things look differ-

ent from what they really are. (Rev: BL 7/89) [152.1]

20912 Cobb, Vicki, and Josh Cobb. *Light Action: Amazing Experiments with Optics* (5–8). Illus. 1993, HarperCollins LB $15.89 (0-06-021437-6). 208pp. Activities involving optics such as shadows, focus, reflection, and color. (Rev: BL 1/15/94) [535]

20913 DiSpezio, Michael A. *Optical Illusion Magic: Visual Tricks and Amusements* (3–7). Illus. 2000, Sterling $17.95 (0-8069-6581-9). 80pp. This large-format book presents a series of optical illusions and gives scientific explanations for each. (Rev: BL 3/15/00; SLJ 7/00) [152.14]

20914 Doherty, Paul, et al. *The Cheshire Cat and Other Eye-Popping Experiments on How We See the World* (4–8). Illus. 1995, Wiley paper $10.95 (0-471-11516-9). 128pp. Based on exhibits at the Exploratorium in San Francisco, this attractive volume outlines activities and experiments that explore optics and vision. (Rev: BL 1/1–15/96; SLJ 1/96) [152.14]

20915 Jennings, Terry. *101 Amazing Optical Illusions: Fantastic Visual Tricks* (4–7). Illus. 1997, Sterling $17.95 (0-8069-9462-2). 96pp. In a large-format book, easily followed instructions are given for optical illusions, divided into three groups: sight, perception, and movement. (Rev: BL 9/15/97; SLJ 8/97) [152.14]

20916 Simon, Seymour. *Now You See It, Now You Don't: The Amazing World of Optical Illusions.* Rev. ed. (3–6). Illus. 1998, Morrow $15.00 (0-688-16152-9). 96pp. This interesting discussion of optical illusions uses good illustrations and clear explanations. (Rev: BL 10/15/98; HBG 3/99) [152.14]

20917 Simon, Seymour. *The Optical Illusion Book* (4–6). Illus. by Constance Flera. 1976, Morrow paper $6.95 (0-688-03254-0). 80pp. In addition to illustrations that show several optical illusions, there are explanations for each illusion and a chapter on illusion in art.

20918 Westray, Kathleen. *Picture Puzzler* (3–7). Illus. 1994, Ticknor $13.95 (0-395-70130-9). 32pp. An oversize book that depicts a number of optical illusions and shows how proper focusing can produce different visual patterns. (Rev: BCCB 10/94; BL 7/94; HB 11–12/94; SLJ 8/94*) [152.14]

20919 Wick, Walter. *Walter Wick's Optical Tricks* (3–6). Illus. 1998, Scholastic $13.95 (0-590-22227-9). 45pp. This collection of remarkable photographs demonstrating tricks on the eye and mind also contains explanations of how these optical illusions are accomplished. (Rev: BCCB 10/98; BL 8/98; HB 9–10/98*; HBG 3/99; SLJ 9/98) [151.14]

Simple Machines

20920 Good, Keith. *Gear Up! Marvelous Machine Projects* (3–7). Series: Design It! 2000, Lerner LB $21.27 (0-8225-3566-1). 30pp. Simple machines like pulleys, levers, crankshafts, gear wheels, and conveyor belts are explored in this book of projects that apply the principles behind these machines. (Rev: HBG 10/00; SLJ 6/00) [621.8]

20921 Hodge, Deborah, and Adrienne Mason. *Simple Machines* (K–4). Illus. Series: Starting with Science. 1998, Kids Can $10.95 (1-55074-311-2). 32pp. This activity book uses double-page spreads to present science activities involving pulleys, levers, and other simple machines. (Rev: BL 4/15/98; HBG 10/98; SLJ 6/98) [621.8]

20922 Lampton, Christopher. *Bathtubs, Slides and Roller Coaster Rails: Simple Machines That Are Really Inclined Planes* (3–5). Illus. by Carol Nicklaus. Series: Gateway Simple Machines. 1991, Millbrook paper $4.80 (1-878841-44-0). 32pp. A slim volume that introduces children to the inclined plane. Also use: *Seesaws, Nutcrackers, Brooms: Simple Machines That Are Really Levers* (1991). (Rev: BL 6/15/91) [621]

20923 Stringer, John. *The Science of a Spring* (5–8). Illus. Series: Science World. 2000, Raintree Steck-Vaughn $22.83 (0-7398-1322-6). 32pp. Leaf and coil springs are introduced as well as the balance of forces in physics, the limits of springs, and their uses in such common objects as staplers. (Rev: BL 9/1/00; HBG 10/00; SLJ 8/00) [531]

20924 Welsbacher, Anne. *Inclined Planes* (K–3). Series: Understanding Simple Machines. 2000, Capstone LB $17.26 (0-7368-0610-5). 24pp. As well as showing many examples of inclined planes, this simple physics book outlines activities that apply this knowledge. (Rev: BL 10/15/00; HBG 3/01; SLJ 12/00) [621.8]

20925 Welsbacher, Anne. *Levers* (2–3). Illus. Series: Understanding Simple Machines. 2000, Capstone $17.26 (0-7368-0611-3). 24pp. This work discusses the parts of a lever, the classes of levers, and how these simple machines are used. (Rev: BL 12/1/00; HBG 3/01) [621.8]

20926 Welsbacher, Anne. *Pulleys* (K–3). Series: Understanding Simple Machines. 2000, Capstone LB $17.26 (0-7368-0612-1). 24pp. Gives many examples of pulleys, such as on a flagpole, along with an explanation of their uses and some simple activities. (Rev: BL 10/15/00; HBG 3/01) [621.8]

20927 Welsbacher, Anne. *Screws* (K–3). Series: Understanding Simple Machines. 2000, Capstone LB $17.26 (0-7368-0613-X). 24pp. This simple book on physics explains, with many examples, how screws work and outlines a few hands-on activities. (Rev: BL 10/15/00; HBG 3/01) [621.8]

20928 Welsbacher, Anne. *Wedges* (2–3). Illus. Series: Understanding Simple Machines. 2000, Capstone $17.26 (0-7368-0614-8). 24pp. This book introduces wedges, their parts, and how they are used in axes, knives, scissors, doorstops, and zippers. (Rev: BL 12/1/00; HBG 3/01; SLJ 12/00) [621.8]

20929 Welsbacher, Anne. *Wheels and Axles* (K–3). Series: Understanding Simple Machines. 2000, Capstone LB $17.26 (0-7368-0615-6). 24pp. After showing many examples of wheels (e.g., a steering wheel on a car) and axles (e.g., those found on a wagon), this book explains how they work and their

many applications. (Rev: BL 10/15/00; HBG 3/01) [6621.8]

20930 Whittle, Fran, and Sarah Lawrence. *Simple Machines* (3–5). Illus. Series: Design and Create. 1997, Raintree Steck-Vaughn $25.69 (0-8172-4889-7). 32pp. How to make a cookie crusher and a bubble machine are among the 12 projects nicely presented in double-page spreads to outline each activity and give background information. (Rev: BL 2/1/98; HBG 3/98) [621.8]

Sound

20931 Baker, Wendy, and Andrew Haslam. *Sound* (3–6). Illus. Series: Make It Work! 1993, Macmillan $12.95 (0-689-71665-6). 48pp. The principles of sound are introduced and explained through a series of activities and experiments. (Rev: SLJ 4/93) [530]

20932 Broekel, Ray. *Sound Experiments* (1–4). Illus. 1983, Children's LB $21.00 (0-516-01686-5). 48pp. Simple experiments that introduce the principles of sound to primary school children.

20933 Cobb, Vicki. *Bangs and Twangs: Science Fun with Sound* (3–6). Illus. 2000, Millbrook LB $23.40 (0-7613-1571-3). 48pp. Using a cartoon format, this lively activity book explores different aspects of sound including pitch and the physiology of hearing. (Rev: BCCB 11/00; BL 10/15/00; HBG 3/01; SLJ 3/01) [534.078]

20934 Craats, Rennay. *The Science of Sound* (3–5). Series: Living Science. 2000, Gareth Stevens LB $14.95 (0-8368-2682-5). 32pp. Basic information is given on such sound-related topics as musical instruments, nature's sounds, sounds that people can't hear, echoes, sonar, and sound careers. (Rev: SLJ 3/01) [534]

20935 Darling, David J. *Sounds Interesting: The Science of Acoustics* (3–6). Illus. 1992, Macmillan LB $17.95 (0-87518-477-4). 64pp. A straightforward text provides an in-depth exploration of the science of sound. (Rev: BL 5/1/92) [523]

20936 de Pinna, Simon. *Sound* (3–5). Series: Science Projects. 1998, Raintree Steck-Vaughn $25.69 (0-8172-4944-3). 48pp. The properties of sound are explored in a series of double-page spreads that give simple explanations followed by three or four simple activities. (Rev: BL 3/15/98; HBG 10/98) [534]

20937 Farndon, John. *Sound and Hearing* (3–6). Series: Science Experiments. 2000, Marshall Cavendish LB $16.95 (0-7614-1091-0). 32pp. The properties of sound and the process of hearing are explored with a series of experiments to illustrate different concepts and applications. (Rev: BL 3/15/01; HBG 3/01) [534]

20938 Gibson, Gary. *Hearing Sounds* (3–5). Illus. Series: Science for Fun. 1995, Millbrook LB $20.90 (1-56294-614-5). 32pp. Basic concepts involving sound are introduced through a series of simple activities and projects, with simple instructions and clear, often amusing illustrations. (Rev: BL 7/95) [534]

20939 Kaner, Etta. *Sound Science* (3–5). Illus. by Louise Phillips. 1992, Addison-Wesley paper $11.00 (0-201-56758-X). 96pp. The 40-plus experiments and projects in this book, which can be done with easily obtained materials, explore various aspects of sound. (Rev: SLJ 6/92) [530]

20940 Levine, Shar, and Leslie Johnstone. *The Science of Sound and Music* (4–6). Illus. 2001, Sterling $19.95 (0-8069-7183-5). 80pp. The activities in this book explore sound and its relation to music using materials like drinking glasses, metal coat hangers, rubber bands, and wooden dowels. (Rev: BL 1/1–15/01; SLJ 3/01) [534]

20941 Madgwick, Wendy. *Super Sound* (K–3). Series: Science Starters. 1999, Raintree Steck-Vaughn LB $15.98 (0-8172-5327-0). 32pp. The properties of sound are explored in this book of simple projects that include topics such as how sound travels, whether two ears are better than one, and the possibility of trapping sound. (Rev: BL 6/1–15/99; HBG 10/99) [534]

20942 Morgan, Sally, and Adrian Morgan. *Using Sound* (4–7). Illus. Series: Designs in Science. 1994, Facts on File $16.95 (0-8160-2981-4). 48pp. The properties of sound and their relation to everyday life are covered in the text and a number of experiments using readily available materials. (Rev: BL 7/94) [534]

20943 Pfeffer, Wendy. *Sounds All Around* (PS–2). Illus. by Holly Keller. Series: Let's-Read-and-Find-Out. 1999, HarperCollins LB $15.89 (0-06-027712-2). 32pp. This book about sound covers such topics as decibels, vibration, communication, and radar with examples for the animal kingdom and suggested activities. (Rev: BL 3/1/99; HBG 10/99; SLJ 1/99) [534]

20944 Wright, Lynne. *The Science of Noise* (5–8). Illus. Series: Science World. 2000, Raintree Steck-Vaughn $22.83 (0-7398-1324-2). 32pp. This account describes how sound is produced, how it travels, how we hear it, and how it can be changed. (Rev: BL 9/1/00; HBG 10/00; SLJ 8/00) [534]

Space Exploration

20945 Alston, Edith. *Let's Visit a Space Camp* (2–4). Illus. Series: Let's Visit. 1990, Troll LB $15.35 (0-8167-1743-5); paper $3.50 (0-8167-1744-3). 32pp. Captivating photos of the U.S. Space Camp in Huntsville, Alabama. (Rev: BL 5/1/90; SLJ 7/90) [629.45]

20946 Angliss, Sarah. *Cosmic Journeys: A Beginner's Guide to Space and Time Travel* (5–7). Illus. by Alex Pang, et al. Series: Future Files. 1998, Millbrook LB $22.40 (0-7613-0620-X); paper $8.95 (0-7613-0635-8). 32pp. This book explores such topics as traveling to other solar systems, time travel, black holes, and parallel universes. (Rev: HBG 10/98; SLJ 10/98) [629.4]

20947 Baker, David. *Danger on Apollo 13* (4–7). Illus. 1988, Rourke LB $22.60 (0-86592-871-1). 32pp. The account of the 1970 explosion on a space flight that threatened the lives of three U.S. astronauts. (Rev: BL 12/1/88; SLJ 12/88)

20948 Baker, David. *Factories in Space* (4–8). Illus. 1987, Rourke LB $23.93 (0-86592-409-0). 48pp. The focus is on NASA's plans for a space-orbiting lab. (Rev: BL 2/15/88)

20949 Baker, David. *Peace in Space* (4–8). Illus. 1987, Rourke LB $23.93 (0-86592-408-2). 48pp. A look at the Strategic Defense Initiative, whose purpose is to stop enemy missiles before they reach the earth. (Rev: BL 2/15/88)

20950 Becklake, Sue. *Space, Stars, Planets and Spacecraft* (4–7). Illus. by Brian Delf and Luciano Corbella. Series: See and Explore. 1991, DK $12.95 (1-879-43114-9). 64pp. An explanation of how complex machines work in space and their contribution to life on earth. (Rev: BL 3/1/92; SLJ 5/92) [629.4]

20951 Berliner, Don. *Living in Space* (4–6). Illus. 1993, Lerner LB $22.60 (0-8225-1599-7). 72pp. The living conditions of travelers in space are covered. (Rev: BL 7/93) [629.47]

20952 Blackwood, Gary L. *Alien Astronauts* (4–6). Series: Secrets of the Unexplained. 1998, Benchmark LB $19.95 (0-7614-0469-4). 80pp. As well as

a historical look at UFO sightings, this book covers the types of sightings and the most common varieties. (Rev: HBG 10/99; SLJ 3/99) [001.9]

20953 Bond, Peter. *DK Guide to Space: A Photographic Journey Through the Universe* (4–6). Illus. 1999, DK $19.95 (0-7894-3946-8). 64pp. In double-page spreads this visually exciting work takes the readers on a trip through the solar system and beyond, covering such topics as the Milky Way, space stations, and extraterrestrial life. (Rev: BL 7/99; HBG 3/00; SLJ 9/99) [520]

20954 Branley, Franklyn M. *Floating in Space* (K–3). Illus. by True Kelley. Series: Let's-Read-and-Find-Out. 1998, HarperCollins LB $15.89 (0-06-025433-5). 32pp. Life in space is covered in this book describing weightlessness, space suits, the food astronauts eat, and the activities aboard a space shuttle. (Rev: BCCB 4/98; BL 12/1/97; HBG 10/98; SLJ 2/98) [629.47]

20955 Branley, Franklyn M. *The International Space Station* (K–3). Illus. by True Kelley. Series: Let's-Read-and-Find-Out. 2000, HarperCollins $16.95 (0-06-028702-0); paper $5.95 (0-06-445209-3). 40pp. An easily understood introduction to this massive undertaking. (Rev: BL 9/15/00; HB 1–2/01; HBG 3/01; SLJ 11/00) [629.44]

20956 Branley, Franklyn M. *Is There Life in Outer Space?* (PS–3). Illus. by Edward Miller. Series: Let's-Read-and-Find-Out. 1999, HarperCollins LB $15.89 (0-06-028145-6); paper $4.95 (0-06-445192-5). 31pp. A beginning science book that explores what we know about life on the planets and in outer space. (Rev: HBG 3/00; SLJ 10/99) [523]

20957 Branley, Franklyn M. *Venus: Magellan Explores Our Twin Planet* (4–6). Illus. 1994, HarperCollins LB $15.89 (0-06-020384-6). 64pp. This is an account of the *Magellan* space probe and what it has learned about the structure, motion, and features of the planet Venus. (Rev: BL 8/94; SLJ 6/94) [523.4]

20958 Bredeson, Carmen. *The Challenger Disaster: Tragic Space Flight* (4–8). Series: American Disasters. 1999, Enslow LB $18.95 (0-7660-1222-0). 48pp. An account of the 1986 tragedy. (Rev: BL 10/15/99; HBG 3/00) [629.5]

20959 Bredeson, Carmen. *John Glenn Returns to Orbit: Life on the Space Shuttle* (4–7). Series: Countdown to Space. 2000, Enslow LB $18.95 (0-7660-1304-9). 48pp. This is the story of John Glenn, now a famous politician, his return to space, and the different conditions he encountered. (Rev: BL 8/00; HBG 10/00) [629.4]

20960 Bredeson, Carmen. *NASA Planetary Spacecraft: Galileo, Magellan, Pathfinder, and Voyager* (4–7). Series: Countdown to Space. 2000, Enslow LB $18.95 (0-7660-1303-0). 48pp. This gives a good rundown on the NASA spacecraft used to explore planets, their individual missions, and their findings. (Rev: BL 9/15/00) [629.4]

20961 Bredeson, Carmen. *Our Space Program* (3–5). Series: I Know America. 1999, Millbrook LB $20.90 (0-7613-0952-7). 48pp. This history of the first 50 years of the space program contains material on the space race with the Soviet Union, prominent astronauts, and major successes, failures, and disasters. (Rev: HBG 10/99; SLJ 5/99) [629.45]

20962 Brenner, Barbara. *Planetarium: The Museum That Explores the Many Wonders of Our Solar System* (1–4). Illus. by Ron Miller. Series: Bank Street Museum Book. 1993, Bantam LB $9.50 (0-533-35428-0). 48pp. On a trip to a planetarium, the reader visits outer space and learns about the solar system. (Rev: BL 9/1/93; SLJ 8/93) [520]

20963 Briggs, Carole S. *Women in Space* (4–7). Series: A&E Biography. 1999, Lerner LB $18.95 (0-8225-4937-9). 112pp. Includes profiles of astronauts including Sally Ride, Mae Jemison, Shannon Lucid, Eileen Collins, and two of their Russian counterparts. (Rev: SLJ 5/99) [629.45]

20964 Burns, Khephra, and William Miles. *Black Stars in Orbit: NASA's African American Astronauts* (4–6). Illus. 1994, Harcourt $20.00 (0-15-200432-7); paper $10.00 (0-15-200276-6). 64pp. A history of the contributions of African Americans to NASA and a record of the discrimination they had to overcome. (Rev: BCCB 2/95; BL 2/15/95; SLJ 2/95*) [629.45]

20965 Butterfield, Moira. *Space* (3–8). Illus. Series: Look Inside Cross-Sections. 1994, DK paper $5.95 (1-56458-682-0). 32pp. Double-page spreads introduce such space explorers as *Apollo, Mercury, Viking, Voyager,* and the *Hubble Telescope.* (Rev: BL 2/1/95; SLJ 2/95) [629.47]

20966 Campbell, Ann-Jeanette. *The New York Public Library Amazing Space: A Book of Answers for Kids* (5–8). Illus. by Jessica Wolk-Stanley. 1997, Wiley paper $12.95 (0-471-14498-3). 186pp. This question-and-answer book introduces space exploration, the solar system, individual planets, galaxies, and related phenomena. (Rev: SLJ 7/97) [523]

20967 Campbell, Peter A. *Launch Day* (2–4). Illus. 1995, Millbrook LB $21.40 (1-56294-611-0). 32pp. An account of the shuttle *Atlantis,* including preparations, launching, and the flight and return. (Rev: BL 12/1/95; SLJ 3/96) [629.454]

20968 Casanellas, Antonio. *Great Discoveries and Inventions That Helped Explore Earth and Space* (3–5). Illus. Series: Great Discoveries and Inventions. 2000, Gareth Stevens $21.27 (0-8368-2584-5). In two-page spreads, great inventions such as the Saturn 5 rocket and the seismograph are introduced along with four projects for the young space explorer. (Rev: SLJ 1/01) [629.4]

20969 Charleston, Gordon. *Armstrong Lands on the Moon* (3–6). Illus. Series: Great 20th Century Expeditions. 1994, Dillon LB $20.00 (0-87518-530-4). 32pp. This handy account covers a history of space exploration from the first rockets to the moon landing. (Rev: SLJ 11/94) [523]

20970 Clay, Rebecca. *Space Travel and Exploration* (4–8). Illus. Series: Secrets of Space. 1997, Twenty-First Century LB $20.40 (0-8050-4474-4). 64pp. A history of modern space exploration, covering manned flights, space stations, space probes, and telescopes. (Rev: BL 7/97; SLJ 1/98) [629.5]

20971 Cole, Michael D. *Astronauts: Training for Space* (4–7). Illus. Series: Countdown to Space. 1999, Enslow $18.95 (0-7660-1116-X). 48pp. Focusing mainly on Sally Ride, this account describes the rigorous training of NASA astronauts. (Rev: BL 2/1/99; HBG 10/99) [629.45]

20972 Cole, Michael D. *Challenger: America's Space Tragedy* (4–6). Illus. Series: Countdown to Space. 1995, Enslow LB $18.95 (0-89490-544-9). 48pp. This tragic event is movingly described. Two other titles in this series are *Friendship 7: First American in Orbit* and *Vostok 1: First Human in Space* (both 1995). (Rev: SLJ 2/96) [523]

20973 Cole, Michael D. *Galileo Spacecraft: Mission to Jupiter* (4–7). Series: Countdown to Space. 1999, Enslow LB $18.95 (0-7660-1119-4). 48pp. *Galileo's* journey to Jupiter is described with details of the preparations for the flight and its findings. Photographs, a glossary, and Web sites round out the coverage. (Rev: BL 2/15/99; HBG 10/99; SLJ 5/99) [629.45]

20974 Cole, Michael D. *Moon Base: First Colony on Space* (4–7). Series: Countdown to Space. 1999, Enslow LB $18.95 (0-7660-1118-6). 48pp. A futuristic look at what a space colony on the moon might look like and the problems involved in creating it. (Rev: BL 2/15/99; HBG 10/99; SLJ 5/99) [629.45]

20975 Cole, Michael D. *NASA Space Vehicles: Capsules, Shuttles, and Space Stations* (4–7). Series: Countdown to Space. 2000, Enslow LB $18.95 (0-7660-1308-1). 48pp. Gives a rundown on these specialized vehicles plus a description of space stations and how they operate, with full-color photos and clear, readable text. (Rev: BL 5/15/00; HBG 10/00; SLJ 12/00) [629.4]

20976 Cole, Michael D. *Space Emergency: Astronauts in Danger* (4–8). Illus. Series: Countdown to Space. 2000, Enslow LB $18.95 (0-7660-1307-3). 48pp. An explosion on the command module of *Apollo 13* and a faulty landing bag on *Friendship 7* are two of the emergencies described in this book on crises in space exploration. (Rev: BL 2/1/00; HBG 10/00; SLJ 12/00) [629.45]

20977 Cole, Michael D. *Space Launch Disaster: When Liftoff Goes Wrong* (4–7). Series: Countdown to Space. 2000, Enslow LB $18.95 (0-7660-1309-X). 48pp. This is a rundown of problems that can occur during the liftoff of space vehicles, with examples of actual disasters, many caught on camera. (Rev: BL 3/15/00; HBG 10/00; SLJ 8/00) [629]

20978 Couper, Heather, and Nigel Henbest. *Is Anybody Out There?* (4–7). Illus. 1998, DK $14.95 (0-7894-2798-2). 45pp. Using many illustrations, this work by two British science writers looks at the possibility of intelligent life in space, the forms it might take, and addresses possible communication modes. (Rev: BL 7/98; SLJ 8/98) [576.8]

20979 Davis, Amanda. *Extraterrestrials: Is There Life in Outer Space?* (2–4). Series: Exploring Space. 1997, Rosen LB $15.95 (0-8239-5058-1). 24pp. Colorful illustrations enliven this explanation of the conditions that led to life on earth and to our current quest for proof of life on other planets. (Rev: SLJ 4/98) [001.9]

20980 Dyson, Marianne J. *Space Station Science: Life in Free Fall* (4–7). Illus. 1999, Scholastic $16.95 (0-590-05889-4). 128pp. Written by a former member of a NASA control team, this work explores living and working in space including details on a space station bathroom. (Rev: BL 11/15/99; HBG 10/00; SLJ 12/99) [629.45]

20981 Engelbert, Phillis. *Astronomy and Space: From the Big Bang to the Big Crunch* (4–8). Illus. 1997, Gale $99.00 (0-7876-0942-0). 600pp. Three hundred alphabetically arranged entries about space exploration, including material on the laws and features of the universe, the history of astronomy, important astronauts, famous observatories, and the greenhouse effect. (Rev: SLJ 5/97) [523]

20982 English, June A., and Thomas D. Jones. *Mission: Earth: Voyage to the Home Planet* (4–7). Illus. 1996, Scholastic $16.95 (0-590-48571-7). 48pp. The space program is introduced, with special coverage on the flights of the shuttle *Endeavor* in 1994 and its environmental studies. (Rev: BL 10/15/96; SLJ 10/96) [550]

20983 Fallen, Anne-Catherine. *USA from Space* (4–7). Illus. 1997, Firefly LB $19.95 (1-55209-159-7); paper $7.95 (1-55209-157-0). 48pp. Excellent satellite pictures of parts of the earth are contained in this book, which also explains the value of satellite imagery in tracking pollution, population, and natural disasters. (Rev: BL 3/1/98; SLJ 12/97) [917.3]

20984 Farbman, Melinda, and Frye Gaillard. *Spacechimp: NASA's Ape in Space* (4–7). Series: Countdown to Space. 2000, Enslow LB $18.95 (0-7660-1478-9). 48pp. The story of how animals in general have helped the space program and how one chimp's voyage into space contributed to progress. (Rev: BL 8/00; HBG 10/00) [629.4]

20985 Fox, Mary V. *Rockets* (3–6). Illus. Series: Inventors and Inventions. 1996, Benchmark LB $25.64 (0-7614-0063-X). 63pp. Rocket pioneers are profiled, along with their discoveries and the changes these have caused in the modern world. (Rev: BL 3/15/96; SLJ 3/96) [621.43]

20986 Fox, Mary V. *Satellites* (3–6). Illus. Series: Inventors and Inventions. 1996, Marshall Cavendish LB $25.64 (0-7614-0049-4). 63pp. Details in an informal text and many interesting photos the story of satellites, their uses, and their creators. (Rev: BL 7/96; SLJ 8/96) [629.43]

20987 Gaffney, Timothy R. *Secret Spy Satellites: America's Eyes in Space* (4–7). Series: Countdown to Space. 2000, Enslow LB $18.95 (0-7660-1402-9). 48pp. With sharp illustrations and a strong narrative, this book describes U.S. spy satellites, their purposes, and findings. (Rev: BL 9/15/00) [629.4]

20988 Gallant, Roy A. *Space Stations* (2–4). Illus. Series: Kaleidoscope. 2000, Marshall Cavendish LB $15.95 (0-7614-1035-X). 48pp. This account briefly covers, in text and color pictures, space stations *Salyut, Skylab*, and *Mir* with a little information on the International Space Station. (Rev: BL 1/1–15/01) [629.44]

20989 Graham, Ian. *The Best Book of Spaceships* (1–4). Illus. 1998, Kingfisher $10.95 (0-7534-5133-6). 33pp. This introduction to space exploration pictures various space vehicles, the Hubble telescope, parts of a space suit, and everyday life in space, while also giving simple explanations of gravity and the solar system. (Rev: BL 12/15/98; HBG 3/99; SLJ 3/99) [629.47]

20990 Hawcock, David. *The Amazing Pop-Up, Pull-Out Space Shuttle* (3–5). Illus. 1998, DK $19.95 (0-789-43457-1). More for display than circulation, this interactive book about space shuttles contains a four-foot, fold-out model. (Rev: BL 1/1–15/99) [629.5]

20991 Hehner, Barbara. *First on the Moon: What It Was Like When Man Landed on the Moon* (3–6). Illus. Series: I Was There. 1999, Hyperion $16.99 (0-7868-0489-0). 48pp. Eyewitness accounts are used in this re-creation of the NASA mission that put a man on the moon. (Rev: BCCB 7–8/99; BL 9/15/99; HBG 3/00; SLJ 9/99) [629.45]

20992 Jefferis, David. *Alien Lifesearch: Quest for Extraterrestrial Organisms* (4–6). Illus. Series: Megatech. 1999, Crabtree LB $14.37 (0-7787-0049-6). 32pp. This work explores the possibility of planets supporting life, alien searches, and UFO mysteries. (Rev: BL 8/99) [516.8]

20993 Johnstone, Michael. *The History News in Space* (3–6). Illus. Series: History News. 1999, Candlewick $16.99 (0-7636-0490-9). 32pp. In a newspaper format, this oversize work covers important news about space and space exploration starting with the ancient Greeks and ending with contemporary achievements. (Rev: BL 10/1/99; HBG 10/99; SLJ 6/99) [629.4]

20994 Kennedy, Gregory. *The First Men in Space* (5–7). Illus. Series: World Explorers. 1991, Chelsea LB $19.95 (0-7910-1324-3). 111pp. This book covers the early years and accomplishments of both Soviet and American space programs. (Rev: SLJ 8/91) [629.44]

20995 Kettelkamp, Larry. *ETs and UFOs: Are They Real?* (5–8). Illus. 1996, Morrow $16.00 (0-688-12868-8). 86pp. This account tries to sort out the truth from the massive amount of material on extraterrestrials and unidentified flying objects. (Rev: BL 12/15/96; SLJ 1/97) [001.9]

20996 Kettelkamp, Larry. *Living in Space* (5–7). Illus. 1993, Morrow $14.00 (0-688-10018-X). 128pp. Tells how astronauts live in space and discusses plans for space exploration in the future. (Rev: BL 10/1/93; SLJ 9/93) [629.4]

20997 Landau, Elaine. *Space Disasters* (5–7). Illus. Series: Watts Library. 1999, Watts LB $24.00 (0-531-20345-X); paper $8.95 (0-531-16431-4). 64pp. This work covers four space disasters: *Apollo 1, Soyuz 1, Apollo 13,* and the *Challenger.* (Rev: BL 2/1/00; SLJ 2/00) [363.12]

20998 Lassieur, Allison. *Astronauts* (2–4). Series: True Books. 2000, Children's LB $22.00 (0-516-22000-4). 48pp. Explains how astronauts are chosen and what training they receive, provides material on their duties, and profiles some famous astronauts. (Rev: BL 10/15/00) [629.4]

20999 Lassieur, Allison. *The Space Shuttle* (2–4). Series: True Books. 2000, Children's LB $22.00 (0-516-22003-9). 48pp. This book explains what a space shuttle is, its functions, and how it is operated. (Rev: BL 10/15/00) [629.4]

21000 Markle, Sandra. *Pioneering Space* (5–8). Illus. 1992, Macmillan LB $14.95 (0-689-31748-4). 40pp. Presents basic information on space travel and how people will live in space. (Rev: BL 9/1/92; SLJ 2/93) [629.4]

21001 Marsh, Carole. *Unidentified Flying Objects and Extraterrestrial Life* (4–6). Illus. 1996, Twenty-First Century LB $20.40 (0-8050-4472-8). 64pp. Covers a wide variety of topics associated with UFOs, including the history of famous sightings. (Rev: BL 12/1/96; SLJ 12/96) [001.9]

21002 Maurer, Richard. *Junk in Space* (4–8). Illus. 1989, Simon & Schuster paper $5.95 (0-671-67767-5). 48pp. Discussing the various kinds of space garbage orbiting earth. (Rev: BL 11/15/89) [363]

21003 Miller, Ron. *Rockets* (4–6). Series: Venture Books. 1999, Watts LB $25.00 (0-531-11430-9). 128pp. In spite of mediocre illustrations, this is an exciting history of rockets from ancient Greece through Newton's principles to the mighty Saturn 5. (Rev: SLJ 4/99) [629.54]

21004 Nicolson, Cynthia P. *Exploring Space* (3–5). Illus. Series: Starting with Space. 2000, Kids Can $12.95 (1-55074-711-8). 40pp. A basic book that covers the huge topic of space exploration in a clear, well-organized way. (Rev: BL 12/1/00) [629.4]

21005 Petty, Kate. *You Can Jump Higher on the Moon and Other Amazing Facts About Space Exploration* (2–4). Illus. Series: I Didn't Know That. 1997, Millbrook LB $19.90 (0-7613-0564-5). 32pp. Each double-page spread in this book is used to introduce fascinating facts about space travel and present some related experiments and activities. (Rev: SLJ 10/97) [523]

21006 Ride, Sally, and Susan Okie. *To Space and Back* (3–7). Illus. 1986, Lothrop $19.00 (0-688-06159-1); Morrow paper $12.95 (0-688-09112-1). 96pp. The first American woman in space describes her experiences aboard the shuttle. (Rev: BCCB 10/86; BL 11/1/86; SLJ 11/86)

21007 Scott, Elaine. *Adventure in Space: The Flight to Fix the Hubble* (4–7). Illus. 1995, Hyperion LB $17.49 (0-7868-2031-4). 64pp. A behind-the-scenes look at NASA and the mission to repair the Hubble telescope in 1993. (Rev: BL 7/95*; SLJ 4/95*) [522]

21008 Sipiera, Diane M., and Paul P. Sipiera. *Project Apollo* (2–4). Illus. Series: True Books. 1997, Children's LB $22.00 (0-516-20435-1). 48pp. Using large type and many photos, this book chronicles one of the landmark space projects. (Rev: BL 12/1/97; HBG 3/98) [629.45]

21009 Sipiera, Diane M., and Paul P. Sipiera. *Project Mercury* (2–4). Illus. Series: True Books. 1997, Children's $22.00 (0-516-20443-2). 48pp. An account of this space venture told in large type with many clear photos. (Rev: BL 12/1/97; HBG 3/98; SLJ 1/98) [629.45]

21010 Sipiera, Diane M., and Paul P. Sipiera. *Space Stations* (2–4). Illus. 1997, Children's $22.00 (0-516-20450-5). 48pp. This simple account explains what space stations are, their history, the *Mir* station, and plans for the future. (Rev: BL 2/1/98; HBG 3/98) [629.44]

21011 Souza, D. M. *Space Sailing* (4–6). Illus. 1994, Lerner LB $22.60 (0-8225-2850-9). 64pp. Covers the history and development of these solar-powered spacecraft and discusses future developments. (Rev: BL 1/1/95) [629]

21012 Steele, Philip. *Space Travel* (4–8). Illus. Series: Pocket Facts. 1991, Macmillan LB $3.95 (0-89686-585-1). 32pp. An introduction to space exploration, featuring basic facts and color illustrations. (Rev: BL 3/15/92) [629.4]

21013 Stein, R. Conrad. *Apollo 11* (3–5). Illus. Series: Cornerstones of Freedom. 1992, Children's LB $20.50 (0-516-06651-X). 32pp. In simple text and many pictures, the story of the *Apollo 11* flight to the moon. (Rev: BL 6/1/92) [629.45]

21014 Stewart, Gail B. *In Space* (4–6). Illus. Series: Living Spaces. 1989, Rourke LB $21.27 (0-86592-116-4). 32pp. A richly illustrated account of life in a space colony. (Rev: BL 11/1/89) [919.9]

21015 Stott, Carole. *Space Exploration* (4–8). Series: Eyewitness Books. 1997, Knopf $20.99 (0-679-98563-8). 60pp. An overview of the history of space exploration, with material on the various missions and their findings. (Rev: BL 12/15/97; HBG 3/98; SLJ 1/98) [523]

21016 Sullivan, George. *The Day We Walked on the Moon: A Photo History of Space Exploration* (5–8). Illus. 1990, Scholastic paper $4.95 (0-685-58532-8). 80pp. The history of U.S. space exploration, showing the accomplishments of both the United States and the Soviet Union. (Rev: BL 9/1/90; SLJ 2/91) [629.4]

21017 Uttley, Colin. *Cities in the Sky: A Beginner's Guide to Living in Space* (4–6). Series: Future Files. 1998, Millbrook LB $22.40 (0-7613-0822-9); paper

$8.95 (0-7613-0741-9). 32pp. This account of the future of space exploration covers space stations and possible settlements on the moon and Mars with the problems that must be faced. (Rev: HBG 10/99; SLJ 4/99) [629.47]

21018 Vogt, Gregory L. *Apollo Moonwalks: The Amazing Lunar Missions* (4–7). Series: Countdown to Space. 2000, Enslow LB $18.95 (0-7660-1306-5). 48pp. This account focuses on the moonwalks during the *Apollo 11* expedition and details what was found. (Rev: BL 8/00; HBG 10/00) [629.4]

21019 Vogt, Gregory L. *Spacewalks: The Ultimate Adventures in Orbit* (4–7). Series: Countdown to Space. 2000, Enslow LB $18.95 (0-7660-1305-7). 48pp. This gives a history of spacewalks, tells who were the pioneers, and explains their purpose. (Rev: BL 8/00; HBG 10/00) [629.4]

21020 Wunsch, Susi Trautmann. *The Adventures of Sojourner: The Mission to Mars that Thrilled the World* (5–9). 1998, Mikaya LB $22.95 (0-9650493-5-3); paper $9.95 (0-9650493-6-1). 60pp. This book describes the construction of the *Sojourner* rover and its performance on Mars after landing on July 4, 1997. (Rev: SLJ 2/99*) [629.5]

Technology, Engineering, and Industry

General and Miscellaneous Industries and Inventions

21021 Alphin, Elaine M. *Irons* (3–6). Series: Household History. 1998, Carolrhoda LB $16.95 (1-57505-238-5). 48pp. This book traces the history of this important household appliance and its many uses. (Rev: HBG 10/98; SLJ 7/98) [643]

21022 Alphin, Elaine M. *Toasters* (3–6). Series: Household History. 1998, Carolrhoda LB $16.95 (1-57505-243-1). 48pp. A history of toasters, how they operate, and how they are used. (Rev: HBG 10/98; SLJ 7/98) [643]

21023 Alphin, Elaine M. *Vacuum Cleaners* (3–5). Illus. Series: Household History. 1997, Carolrhoda $22.60 (1-57505-018-8). 48pp. A fascinating history of the vacuum cleaner with an explanation of how it works. (Rev: BL 1/1–15/98; HBG 3/98) [683]

21024 Bryant-Mole, Karen. *Toys* (PS–3). Series: Picture This! 1997, Rigby $18.50 (1-57572-057-4). 24pp. Many toys are shown in this heavily illustrated, interactive book. Also use *Games* (1997). (Rev: BL 10/15/97; SLJ 12/97) [745.592]

21025 Casanellas, Antonio. *Great Discoveries and Inventions That Advanced Industry and Technology* (3–5). Illus. by Ali Garousi. Series: Great Discoveries and Inventions. 2000, Gareth Stevens LB $21.27 (0-8368-2583-7). 32pp. A simple overview of inventions that have changed industrial life plus five backup activities. (Rev: SLJ 1/01) [608]

21026 Corey, Melinda. *Let's Visit a Spaghetti Factory* (2–4). Illus. Series: Let's Visit. 1990, Troll LB $15.35 (0-8167-1741-9). 32pp. This is the story of how durum wheat is used for the pasta dough that is formed into different shapes. (Rev: BL 5/1/90; SLJ 7/90) [670]

21027 Crowther, Robert. *Robert Crowther's Amazing Pop-Up House of Inventions* (2–4). Illus. 2000, Candlewick $14.99 (0-7636-0810-6). Using pop-ups, this book explains the workings of such objects as a stove, computer, washing machine, and a zipper. (Rev: BCCB 12/00; BL 12/1/00; HBG 3/01) [608]

21028 Crump, Donald J., ed. *How Things Work* (5–7). Illus. 1984, National Geographic LB $12.00 (0-87044-430-1). 104pp. A handsome volume that explains how a variety of objects, from toasters to space shuttles, work.

21029 Davis, Gary. *From Rock to Fireworks* (3–6). Series: Changes. 1997, Children's LB $24.00 (0-516-20739-3). 32pp. A photo-essay that shows each of the steps in the process of manufacturing fireworks, with some activities for the reader. (Rev: BL 2/15/98; HBG 10/98) [662.1]

21030 Drake, Jane, and Ann Love. *Mining* (2–4). Illus. by Pat Cupples. Series: America at Work. 1999, Kids Can $12.95 (1-55074-508-5). 31pp. Trish and Jamie learn how the steel blades on their ice skates were made by visiting a mine and then a steel mill and observing the processes in each. (Rev: HBG 3/00; SLJ 11/99) [672]

21031 Erlbach, Arlene. *The Kids' Invention Book* (4–6). Illus. 1997, Lerner LB $22.60 (0-8225-2414-7). 64pp. Beginning with 15-year-old Chester Greenwood, who invented earmuffs in 1873, this book introduces over a dozen young people and their inventions. (Rev: BL 2/1/98; HBG 3/98) [608]

21032 Erlbach, Arlene. *Teddy Bears* (3–5). Illus. 1997, Carolrhoda $22.60 (1-57505-019-6); paper $7.95 (1-57505-222-9). 48pp. Provides the history of the teddy bear, discusses the problem of identifying the first maker, and describes the industry today. (Rev: BL 1/1–15/98; HBG 3/98) [745.594]

21033 Forman, Michael H. *From Wax to Crayon* (2–3). 1997, Children's LB $24.00 (0-516-20708-3). 32pp. Traces the various processes and materials that go into producing the common wax crayon. (Rev: BL 10/15/97) [609]

21034 Gifford, Clive. *How the Future Began: Everyday Life* (4–6). Illus. 2000, Kingfisher $15.95 (0-7534-5268-5). 64pp. This illustrated book speculates on future technological advances in areas including transportation, education, recreation, and biotechnology. (Rev: BL 12/15/00; SLJ 12/00) [600]

21035 Graham, Ian, ed. *How Things Work* (4–6). Illus. Series: Nature Company Discoveries. 1996, Time Life $16.00 (0-8094-9249-0). 64pp. This handsome, well-illustrated volume explains the inner workings of everyday machines and appliances with a special foldout section. (Rev: BL 6/1–15/96) [600]

21036 Hellman, Hal. *Beyond Your Senses: The New World of Sensors* (4–6). Illus. 1997, Lodestar $16.99 (0-525-67533-7). 87pp. Sensors that respond to light, heat, and motion — as in toasters and burglar alarms — are described, with material on robots and their future uses. (Rev: BCCB 7–8/97; HBG 3/98; SLJ 9/97) [609]

21037 Jones, Charlotte F. *Accidents May Happen: Fifty Inventions Discovered by Mistake* (4–6). Illus. 1996, Delacorte $16.95 (0-385-32162-7). 96pp. Fifty products, like dynamite and yo-yos, that came into being by accident. A sequel to *Mistakes That Worked* (1991). (Rev: BCCB 9/96; BL 6/1–15/96; SLJ 6/96) [124]

21038 Jones, Charlotte F. *Mistakes That Worked* (4–6). Illus. by John O'Brien. 1994, Doubleday paper $11.95 (0-385-32043-4). 82pp. An entertaining look at successful mistakes, such as the ice cream vendor who ran out of dishes and invented the cone. (Rev: BCCB 10/91; BL 10/15/91*; SLJ 10/91) [609]

21039 Jones, George. *My First Book of How Things Are Made: Crayons, Jeans, Peanut Butter, Guitars and More* (3–5). Illus. 1995, Scholastic $12.95 (0-590-48004-9). 64pp. The manufacturing process of eight objects common in children's lives — including grape jelly, footballs, orange juice, blue jeans, and books — are enumerated. (Rev: SLJ 2/96) [658.5]

21040 Karnes, Frances A., and Suzanne M. Bean. *Girls and Young Women Inventing: Twenty True Stories About Inventors Plus How You Can Be One Yourself* (4–8). Illus. 1995, Free Spirit paper $12.95 (0-915793-89-X). 168pp. The story of Jennifer Donabar and her electric clock invention plus material on other inventions by young women. (Rev: SLJ 12/95) [658.5]

21041 Kuklin, Susan. *From Head to Toe: How a Doll Is Made* (1–3). Illus. 1994, Hyperion $15.95 (1-56282-666-2). 32pp. The step-by-step creation of a doll is shown using imaginative photos and a text that introduces each worker. (Rev: BCCB 5/94; BL 5/1/94*; HB 5–6/94; SLJ 5/94) [688.7]

21042 Lampton, Christopher. *Chemical Accident* (4–6). Illus. Series: Disaster Book. 1994, Millbrook LB $19.90 (1-56294-316-2). 48pp. Introduces the chemical industry and explains what happens when chemical accidents occur, their effects, and how to prevent them. (Rev: BL 6/1–15/94; SLJ 4/94) [363.17]

21043 Macaulay, David. *The New Way Things Work* (4–10). Illus. by author. 1998, Houghton $35.00 (0-395-93847-3). 400pp. A popular guide that explains the workings of such machines as telephones, parking meters, bicycles, brakes, automobiles, and all the components used in a computer setup. (Rev: HBG 10/99; SLJ 12/98) [621]

21044 *Machines and Inventions* (5–8). Illus. Series: Understanding Science and Nature. 1993, Time Life $17.95 (0-8094-9704-2). 152pp. Double-page spreads are used to explain such inventions as the box camera, printing press, and dynamite. (Rev: BL 1/15/94; SLJ 6/94) [621.8]

21045 Markle, Sandra. *Science Surprises* (4–5). Illus. by June Otani. 1996, Scholastic paper $2.99 (0-590-48401-X). 63pp. Six science surprises — like the invention of photography and the discoveries of penicillin and Velcro/TM — are described, along with 11 fascinating experiments to expand on scientific principles. (Rev: SLJ 7/97) [507]

21046 Mebane, Robert C., and Thomas R. Rybolt. *Plastics and Polymers* (4–6). Illus. Series: Everyday Material Science Experiments. 1995, Twenty-First Century LB $18.90 (0-8050-2843-9). 64pp. The composition, uses, and structure of plastics and polymers are covered in a series of projects with easy procedures and easily procured materials. (Rev: BL 9/15/95; SLJ 10/95) [547.7]

21047 Mitgutsch, Ali. *From Rubber Tree to Tire* (K–2). Illus. by author. 1986, Carolrhoda LB $18.60 (0-87614-297-8). 24pp. The production of rubber explained in easy text. (Rev: BL 12/15/86)

21048 Mitgutsch, Ali. *From Sea to Salt* (2–3). Illus. by author. 1985, Carolrhoda LB $18.60 (0-87614-232-3). 24pp. Beginning with the salt trapped in the earth, simple text and pictures explain the steps that put it on the table. (Rev: BL 7/85; SLJ 9/85)

21049 Mitgutsch, Ali. *From Wood to Paper* (K–2). Illus. by author. 1986, Carolrhoda LB $18.60 (0-87614-296-X). 24pp. Full-color illustrations and easy text explain how paper is made. (Rev: BL 12/15/86)

21050 Parker, Steve. *Fifty-Three and a Half Things That Changed the World and Some That Didn't!* (3–6). Illus. by David West. 1995, Millbrook LB $21.90 (1-56294-603-X). 62pp. A lighthearted look at how various inventions — like clocks, toilets, and the printing press — have changed human history. (Rev: SLJ 8/95) [608]

21051 Paterson, Alan J. *How Glass Is Made* (5–8). Illus. 1985, Facts on File $14.95 (0-8160-0038-7). 32pp. Glossary, diagrams, and color photos highlight this informative look at the business of making glass. (Rev: BL 6/15/85; SLJ 2/86)

21052 Platt, Richard. *Inventions Explained: A Beginner's Guide to Technological Breakthroughs* (4–8). Illus. Series: Your World Explained. 1997, Holt $18.95 (0-8050-4876-6). 69pp. An in-depth look at the changing world of technological innovations, with coverage on systems of transportation, energy, medicine, machinery, and computing. (Rev: BL 3/1/98; HBG 10/98; SLJ 2/98) [609]

21053 Platt, Richard. *The Smithsonian Visual Timeline of Inventions* (3–6). Illus. 1994, DK $16.95 (1-56458-675-8). 64pp. Using a timeline of world events as a framework, a history of inventions is detailed in four main areas of endeavor: communications, health, industry, and travel. (Rev: BL 12/15/94; SLJ 2/95) [609]

21054 Reid, Struan. *Inventions and Trade* (5–8). Illus. Series: Silk and Spice Routes. 1994, Silver Burdett LB $15.95 (0-02-726316-9). 48pp. A history of the trade between China and Europe along the Spice Route and of the technological advances that occurred because of this cultural exchange. (Rev: BL 12/15/94; SLJ 12/94) [382.09]

21055 Rubin, Susan G. *Toilets, Toasters, and Telephones: The How and Why of Everyday Objects* (5–8). Illus. 1998, Harcourt $20.00 (0-15-201421-7). 126pp. In addition to the objects in the title, this book gives details on the invention and design of other familiar household items, such as stoves, vacuum cleaners, bathtubs, and pencils. (Rev: BL 11/1/98; HB 3–4/99; HBG 3/99; SLJ 11/98) [683]

21056 Skurzynski, Gloria. *Almost the Real Things: Simulation in Your High Tech World* (5–8). 1991, Macmillan $15.95 (0-02-778072-4). 64pp. Tells how engineers and scientists simulate events from weightlessness to complex animation. (Rev: BCCB 10/91; BL 10/15/91; HB 11–12/91; SLJ 10/91) [620]

21057 Smith, Elizabeth Simpson. *Paper* (4–8). Illus. 1984, Walker LB $10.85 (0-8027-6569-6). 64pp. The manufacture of paper is described plus its many uses.

21058 Soucie, Gary. *What's the Difference Between . . . Lenses and Prisms and Other Scientific Things?* (3–6). Illus. by Jeff Domm. 1995, Wiley paper $9.95 (0-471-08626-6). 85pp. This book describes the differences in technology between two similar commodities, e.g., soap and detergent; iron and steel. (Rev: SLJ 2/96) [609]

21059 Stone, Tanya. *Snowboards: From Start to Finish* (3–5). Series: Made in the USA. 2000, Blackbirch LB $16.95 (1-56711-480-6). 32pp. A behind-the-scenes look at how snowboards are made and how special problems with their manufacture were solved. (Rev: BL 9/15/00; HBG 3/01; SLJ 12/00) [796.9]

21060 Stone, Tanya. *Teddy Bears: From Start to Finish* (3–5). Series: Made in the USA. 2000, Blackbirch LB $16.95 (1-56711-479-2). 32pp. This book shows how teddy bears are manufactured and how the finished product is put together and marketed. (Rev: BL 9/15/00; HBG 3/01) [688.7]

21061 Thimmesh, Catherine. *Girls Think of Everything* (4–7). Illus. 2000, Houghton $16.00 (0-395-93744-2). 64pp. A fresh, breezy account about women whose inventions include the windshield wiper, chocolate chip cookies, and Glo-paper. (Rev: BCCB 5/00; BL 3/15/00; HB 5–6/00; HBG 10/00; SLJ 4/00) [609.2]

21062 Tucker, Tom. *Brainstorm! The Stories of Twenty American Kid Inventors* (4–7). 1995, Farrar $15.00 (0-374-30944-2). 148pp. A history of young American inventors who produced such innovations as waterskiing, Popsicles, and ear muffs. (Rev: BCCB 10/95; BL 8/95; SLJ 10/95) [609]

21063 Wilcox, Jane. *Why Do We Use That?* (4–6). Illus. Series: Why Do We? 1996, Watts LB $20.00 (0-531-14395-3). 31pp. Explains the origin of such common household items as toothbrushes, pencils, garden tools, games, and toys. (Rev: SLJ 3/97) [608]

21064 Wood, Richard, ed. *Great Inventions* (4–6). Illus. Series: Nature Company Discoveries. 1995, Time Life $16.00 (0-7835-4766-8). 64pp. Some of the world's greatest inventions and inventors are briefly discussed in this well-illustrated book, with a final eight-page foldout section. (Rev: BL 1/1–15/96) [609]

21065 Woods, Samuel. *Recycled Paper* (3–5). Series: Made in the USA. 2000, Blackbirch LB $16.95 (1-56711-395-8). 32pp. The process of recycling paper is covered from the collection of old paper to the production of new paper. (Rev: BL 12/15/00; HBG 3/01; SLJ 12/00) [686.2]

21066 Woods, Samuel G. *Crayons: From Start to Finish* (3–5). Photos by Gale Zucker. Series: Made in the USA. 1999, Blackbirch LB $16.95 (1-56711-390-7). 32pp. A visit to the Crayola crayon factory in Pennsylvania where the reader learns about the production of crayons from basic raw material to the finished boxed product. (Rev: HBG 3/00; SLJ 2/00) [681]

21067 Wulffson, Don L. *The Kid Who Invented the Popsicle and Other Surprising Stories About Inventions* (3–6). 1997, Dutton $13.99 (0-525-65221-3). 128pp. An alphabetically arranged presentation of the stories behind such inventions as animal crackers and zippers. (Rev: BL 2/15/97; SLJ 3/97) [609]

Aeronautics and Airplanes

21068 Baker, Sanna Anderson. *Grandpa Is a Flyer* (2–4). Illus. by Bill Farnsworth. 1995, Albert Whitman LB $15.95 (0-8075-3033-6). 32pp. The life story of a man who was fascinated by flying even as a child in the 1920s. (Rev: BL 4/1/95; SLJ 7/95) [629.1]

21069 Barton, Byron. *Airplanes* (PS). Illus. by author. 1986, HarperCollins LB $15.89 (0-690-04532-8). 32pp. Simple words and brightly colored artwork portray the roles of airplanes. (Rev: BL 8/86; SLJ 9/86)

21070 Bellville, Cheryl Walsh. *The Airplane Book* (2–5). Illus. 1991, Carolrhoda LB $22.60 (0-87614-686-8); paper $5.95 (0-87614-618-3). 48pp. A simple history of flight, from Icarus to the Voyager mission. (Rev: SLJ 2/92) [629.1]

21071 Berliner, Don. *Aviation: Reaching for the Sky* (5–8). Illus. Series: Innovators. 1997, Oliver LB $21.25 (1-881508-33-1). 144pp. A thorough history of aviation, beginning with early hot-air balloons and dirigibles and continuing through the Wright Brothers and Sikorsky's helicopter to supersonic jets. (Rev: SLJ 7/97) [629.133]

21072 Berliner, Don. *Before the Wright Brothers* (4–7). Illus. 1990, Lerner LB $22.60 (0-8225-1588-1). 72pp. The story of the struggle to fly that went on before the Wright brothers. (Rev: BL 6/15/90; SLJ 9/90) [629.133]

21073 Bingham, Caroline. *Big Book of Airplanes* (2–5). Illus. 2001, DK $14.95 (0-7894-6521-3). 32pp. A stunning fact-filled picture book about all kinds of planes, from jumbo jets to the tiny "Gee Bee" and the space plane X-33. (Rev: BL 3/1/01) [629.133]

21074 Cole, Michael D. *TWA Flight 800: Explosion in Midair* (4–8). Series: American Disasters. 1999, Enslow LB $18.95 (0-7660-1217-4). 48pp. A dramatic account of the air tragedy. (Rev: BL 1/1–15/99; HBG 10/99) [629.136]

21075 Curlee, Lynn. *Ships of the Air* (3–6). Illus. 1996, Houghton $14.95 (0-395-69338-1). 32pp. An attractively presented history of dirigibles and hot-air ballooning. (Rev: BCCB 10/96; BL 9/1/96; HB 11–12/96; SLJ 9/96) [629.133]

21076 Darling, David J. *Up and Away: The Science of Flight* (3–6). Illus. 1992, Macmillan LB $17.95 (0-87518-479-0). 64pp. Color photos, clear text, and in-depth experiments explain the science of flight. (Rev: BL 5/1/92; SLJ 3/92) [629.19]

21077 Davis, Meredith. *Up and Away! Taking a Flight* (2–4). Illus. by Ken Dubrowski. 1997, Mondo paper $4.95 (1-57255-214-X). 23pp. An international flight is covered from entering the airport to reaching the final destination. (Rev: SLJ 1/98) [629.133]

21078 Goold, Ian. *The Rutan Voyager* (4–7). Illus. 1988, Rourke LB $22.60 (0-86592-869-X). 32pp. The around-the-world, nonstop flight of Richard Rutan and Jeana Yeager in 1986. (Rev: BL 12/1/88; SLJ 12/88) [910.4]

21079 Haskins, Jim. *Black Eagles: African Americans in Aviation* (5–8). Illus. 1995, Scholastic $14.95 (0-590-45912-0). 176pp. This account traces the contributions made to aviation history by African Americans from before World War I to the astronaut Mae Jemison. (Rev: BL 2/15/95; SLJ 4/95) [629]

21080 Hewish, Mark. *The Young Scientist Book of Jets* (4–7). Illus. 1978, EDC paper $6.95 (0-86020-051-5). An attractive, semicomic book format is used to cover basic material.

21081 Hunter, Ryan Ann. *Take Off!* (PS–1). Illus. by Edward Miller. 2000, Holiday $15.95 (0-8234-1466-3). 32pp. All kinds of airplanes — from the Wright brothers' craft to the 1,000-seat plane of the future — are introduced in this brightly illustrated volume that ends with directions on making a paper airplane. (Rev: BCCB 7–8/00; BL 2/15/00; HBG 10/00; SLJ 9/00) [629.13]

21082 Jefferis, David. *Flight: Fliers and Flying Machines* (3–6). Illus. 1991, Watts $13.95 (0-531-15233-2). 48pp. Beginning with the legend of Icarus, this book chronicles flight to modern times. (Rev: BL 12/15/91; SLJ 3/92) [629.13]

21083 Jennings, Terry. *Planes, Gliders, Helicopters and Other Flying Machines* (3–5). Illus. Series: How Things Work. 1993, Kingfisher LB $13.90 (1-85697-684-X); paper $8.95 (1-85697-869-9). 40pp. In very simple terms with many illustrations, the

principles of flight are introduced with many examples of flying machines pictured and identified. (Rev: BL 6/1–15/93) [629]

21084 Johnstone, Michael. *Planes* (3–6). Illus. Series: Look Inside Cross-Sections. 1994, DK paper $5.95 (1-56458-520-4). 32pp. Cross-sections of such planes as the Fokker triplane, the Concorde, the Boeing 314, and the U.S. B-17 bomber are presented. (Rev: BL 10/15/94; SLJ 9/94) [629.133]

21085 Landau, Elaine. *Air Crashes* (4–7). Series: Watts Library. 1999, Watts LB $24.00 (0-531-20346-8). 63pp. With photographs on almost every page, this book re-creates such air disasters as the Hindenburg, the 1960 Christmas crash, United Airlines Flight 232, and TWA Flight 800. (Rev: SLJ 2/00) [629.136]

21086 Lopez, Donald, ed. *Flight* (4–6). Illus. Series: Nature Company Discoveries. 1995, Time Life $16.00 (0-7835-4761-7). 64pp. A brief, well-illustrated history of human attempts to conquer the skies, with a final eight-page foldout section. (Rev: BL 1/1–15/96) [629.1]

21087 Majoor, Mireille. *Inside the Hindenburg* (4–8). Illus. 2000, Little, Brown $18.95 (0-316-12386-2). 24pp. Fictional stories of two girls aboard the zeppelin are cleverly woven with details about the airship, historic information, and even floor plans of the aircraft. (Rev: BL 2/1/01; SLJ 3/01) [629.133]

21088 Malam, John. *Airport: Behind the Scenes, Check-in to Take-off* (3–5). Illus. Series: Building Works. 2000, Bedrick $16.95 (0-87226-586-2). 32pp. This book supplies an illustrated guided tour of an airport and its facilities plus a history of airports and a glossary of terms. (Rev: BL 7/00; HBG 10/00) [387.7]

21089 Maynard, Chris. *Aircraft* (5–8). Illus. Series: Need for Speed. 1999, Lerner $17.95 (0-8225-2485-6); paper $7.95 (0-8225-9855-8). 32pp. Using double-page spreads, this work introduces high-speed aircraft. (Rev: BL 1/1–15/00; HBG 3/00; SLJ 2/00) [629.133]

21090 Maynard, Christopher. *Airplane* (PS–4). Illus. Series: Mighty Machines. 1995, DK paper $9.95 (0-7894-0211-4). 21pp. Many airplanes are pictured and described, with information on other airport machines and the helicopter. (Rev: BL 12/1/95) [629.136]

21091 Miller, Marilyn. *Behind the Scenes at the Airport* (PS–3). Illus. 1996, Raintree Steck-Vaughn LB $21.40 (0-8172-4086-1). 32pp. Using a question-and-answer approach, the activities that make an airport work are pictured. (Rev: BL 4/15/96; SLJ 12/96) [387.7]

21092 Millspaugh, Ben. *Aviation and Space Science Projects* (5–8). Illus. 1992, TAB paper $10.95 (0-8306-2156-3). 133pp. The principles of flight are explored in 19 projects that vary in difficulty and complexity. (Rev: SLJ 6/92) [629.1]

21093 O'Brien, Patrick. *The Hindenburg* (3–6). Illus. 2000, Holt $17.00 (0-8050-6415-X). 32pp. In this picture book for older readers, the story of the Hindenburg dirigible, its designer, Hugo Eckener, and its ultimate destruction are covered effectively. (Rev: BCCB 9/00; BL 9/1/00; HB 9–10/00; HBG 3/01; SLJ 10/00) [629.133]

21094 Otfinoski, Steven. *Taking Off: Planes Then and Now* (2–4). Illus. Series: Here We Go! 1996, Benchmark LB $22.79 (0-7614-0407-4). 32pp. A history of airplanes that is notable for its informative large-print text and spectacular photos. (Rev: SLJ 2/97) [629.133]

21095 Pallotta, Jerry, and Fred Pallotta. *The Airplane Alphabet Book* (2–4). Illus. by Rob Bolster. 1997, Charlesbridge $16.95 (0-88106-907-8). 32pp. Presents 26 airplanes plus information about the history of flight. (Rev: BL 2/1/97; SLJ 7/97) [629]

21096 Parker, Steve. *High in the Sky* (3–5). Illus. Series: SuperSmarts. 1997, Candlewick $11.99 (0-7636-0128-4). 24pp. This introduction to airplanes and flight uses a magazine-style format, with bright illustrations, many sidebars, quizzes, and double-page spreads. (Rev: BL 8/97; SLJ 1/98) [629.13]

21097 Parker, Steve. *What's Inside Airplanes?* (4–8). Illus. Series: What's Inside? 1995, Bedrick LB $18.95 (0-87226-394-0). 45pp. Elaborate illustrations are used to show various types of airplanes and describe their parts, including pistons, propellers, fuel tanks, and landing gear. (Rev: SLJ 12/95) [629.133]

21098 Provensen, Alice, and Martin Provensen. *The Glorious Flight Across the Channel with Louis Bleriot* (1–5). Illus. by authors. 1983, Puffin paper $4.95 (0-317-63651-0). 40pp. The story of a historic flight by a French aviation pioneer. Caldecott Medal winner, 1984.

21099 Ross, Wilma S. *X-15 Rocket Plane* (3–5). Illus. Series: Those Daring Machines. 1995, Macmillan LB $17.95 (0-89686-831-1). 48pp. A brief history of rocket aircraft is given, with details on the *X-15* and its career. (Rev: BL 2/15/95) [629.133]

21100 Royston, Angela. *Planes* (PS). Illus. by Tim Ridley. Series: Eye Openers. 1992, Macmillan paper $8.99 (0-689-71564-1). 32pp. The concept of airplanes is introduced for preschoolers in this sturdy book with many photographs. (Rev: BL 8/92; SLJ 10/92) [629]

21101 Saunders, Rupert. *Balloon Voyage* (4–7). Illus. 1988, Rourke LB $22.60 (0-86592-870-3). 32pp. The 1987 attempt to cross the Atlantic in a hot-air balloon. (Rev: BL 12/1/88; SLJ 12/88)

21102 Stein, R. Conrad. *The Spirit of St. Louis* (3–5). Illus. Series: Cornerstones of Freedom. 1994, Children's LB $20.50 (0-516-06682-X). 32pp. The record-breaking, trans-Atlantic flight of Lindbergh is re-created with details on the airplane that he flew. (Rev: BL 1/15/95) [629.13]

21103 Stille, Darlene R. *Airplanes* (2–4). Illus. Series: True Books. 1997, Children's LB $22.00 (0-516-20325-8). 48pp. After a short history of flight, this book describes many airplanes and explains how they work. (Rev: BL 9/15/97) [629.133]

21104 Stille, Darlene R. *Blimps* (2–4). Series: True Books. 1997, Children's LB $22.00 (0-516-20327-4). 48pp. A simple introduction to dirigibles and how they work. (Rev: BL 9/15/97) [629]

21105 Stille, Darlene R. *Helicopters* (2–4). Series: True Books. 1997, Children's LB $22.00 (0-516-20335-5). 48pp. A number of types of helicopters are introduced in a simple format with an explanation of how they work. (Rev: BL 9/15/97) [629]

21106 *The Story of Flight* (4–6). Illus. Series: Voyages of Discovery. 1995, Scholastic $19.95 (0-590-47643-2). 45pp. Using die-cut pages, transparencies, foldouts, and stickers, this attractive book traces the history of flight and airplanes from ancient times to the present. (Rev: SLJ 5/96) [629]

21107 Taylor, Richard L. *The First Unrefueled Flight Around the World: The Story of Dick Rutan and Jeana Yeager* (4–6). Illus. 1994, Watts LB $22.00 (0-531-20176-7). 64pp. The story of this remarkable flight around the world during 1986 in a specially designed plane. (Rev: BL 3/15/95; SLJ 3/95) [629.13]

21108 Tessendorf, K. C. *Barnstormers and Daredevils* (5–8). Illus. 1988, Macmillan LB $14.95 (0-689-31346-2). 96pp. True tales for the aviation buff. (Rev: BCCB 4/88; BL 9/15/88; SLJ 10/88)

21109 Tessendorf, K. C. *Wings Around the World: The American World Flight of 1924* (4–8). Illus. 1991, Macmillan LB $14.95 (0-689-31550-3). 104pp. The thrilling story of the four teams that were involved in the first around-the-world flight in 1924. (Rev: SLJ 11/91) [629.132]

21110 Weiss, Harvey. *Strange and Wonderful Aircraft* (4–7). Illus. 1995, Houghton $15.95 (0-395-68716-0). 64pp. Humankind's various attempts to conquer the skies are highlighted, from ancient myths to the success of the Wright brothers. (Rev: BL 2/1/96; SLJ 12/95) [629.13]

21111 Wilkey, Michael. *They Never Gave Up: Adventures in Early Aviation* (5–8). Illus. by author. 1998, Orca paper $9.95 (1-55143-077-0). 115pp. This history of flight in North America emphasizes Canada and its aviation pioneers. (Rev: SLJ 9/98) [629]

21112 Younkin, Paula. *Spirit of St. Louis* (3–5). Illus. Series: Those Daring Machines. 1995, Macmillan LB $17.95 (0-89686-832-X). 48pp. A description of Lindbergh's airplane and the trans-Atlantic flight that made history. (Rev: BL 2/15/95) [629.13]

Building and Construction

General

21113 Adam, Robert. *Buildings: How They Work* (4–6). Illus. 1996, Sterling $14.95 (0-8069-0958-7). 48pp. This well-illustrated volume discusses dwellings, from primitive caves to skyscrapers, and their design, materials, and uses. (Rev: BL 2/15/96) [721]

21114 *Architecture and Construction* (4–6). Illus. Series: Voyages of Discovery. 1995, Scholastic $19.95 (0-590-47644-0). 45pp. An introduction to architecture that spans the subject from simple shelters to such constructions as a Japanese paper house, skyscrapers, castles, and Frank Lloyd Wright's

Fallingwater, with brief text and many illustrations, transparencies, foldouts, stickers, and a spiral binding. (Rev: SLJ 5/96) [720]

21115 Boring, Mel. *Incredible Constructions: And the People Who Built Them* (4–7). Illus. 1985, Walker LB $13.85 (0-8027-6560-2). Hoover Dam, the Statue of Liberty, and other structures are featured in this history of engineering marvels. (Rev: BL 6/1/85; SLJ 8/86)

21116 Cash, Terry. *Bricks* (3–5). Illus. by Ed Barber. Series: Threads. 1990, Garrett LB $15.93 (0-944483-68-2). 26pp. The history of bricks, how they are made, and their many uses are explored. (Rev: BL 2/1/91; SLJ 5/91) [666]

21117 Cooper, Elisha. *Building* (K–2). Illus. 1999, Greenwillow $16.00 (0-688-16494-3). 40pp. A small picture book that portrays the process of changing a vacant city lot into an attractive building. (Rev: BCCB 4/99; BL 6/1–15/99; HB 5–6/99; HBG 10/99; SLJ 5/99) [690]

21118 Corbishley, Mike. *The World of Architectural Wonders* (5–8). Illus. 1997, Bedrick LB $19.95 (0-87226-279-0). 48pp. The story of 14 worldwide architectural wonders, including Stonehenge, the pyramids of Egypt, Chartres Cathedral, the Taj Mahal, and Hoover Dam. (Rev: BL 6/1–15/97; SLJ 7/97) [720]

21119 Darling, David J. *Spiderwebs to Skyscrapers: The Science of Structures* (3–6). Illus. Series: Experiment! 1991, Macmillan LB $13.95 (0-87518-478-2). 57pp. From natural phenomena like birds' nests and spiderwebs to bridges, skyscrapers, and dams, structural engineering is explained with some projects included. (Rev: SLJ 3/92) [690]

21120 Delafosse, Claude. *Construction* (PS–2). Illus. Series: First Discovery. 1997, Scholastic paper $12.95 (0-590-93783-9). 24pp. Various forms of building and their processes are introduced simply with interesting visuals that encourage interaction. (Rev: BL 2/15/97) [338.476]

21121 *Do Buildings Have Bones? First Questions and Answers About Buildings* (PS–3). Illus. Series: Time-Life Library of First Questions and Answers. 1995, Time Life $14.95 (0-7835-0900-6). 48pp. A series of questions and answers supplies basic information about buildings and construction. (Rev: BL 8/95) [720]

21122 Dussling, Jennifer. *Gargoyles: Monsters in Stone* (2–3). Illus. by Peter Church. Series: All Aboard Reading. 1999, Penguin paper $3.99 (0-448-41961-0). 48pp. An easy reader about the origin of gargoyles, their history and purpose, and their use in contemporary architecture. (Rev: BL 10/1/99*; HBG 3/00; SLJ 11/99) [729.5]

21123 Gibbons, Gail. *Up Goes the Skyscraper!* (PS–1). Illus. by author. 1986, Simon & Schuster $14.95 (0-02-736780-0). 32pp. Equipment, construction phases, and workers are depicted in the simple tale of the rise of a skyscraper. (Rev: BL 4/15/86; SLJ 5/86)

21124 Good, Keith. *Build It! Activities for Setting Up Super Structures* (3–7). Series: Design It! 2000, Lerner LB $21.27 (0-8225-3567-X). 30pp. This

book of projects explores ideas for bridges, domes, structures that collapse, and pop-ups in a clear format with good directions. (Rev: HBG 10/00; SLJ 6/00) [624]

21125 Gresko, Marcia S. *The Grand Coulee Dam* (4–6). Illus. Series: Building America. 1999, Blackbirch LB $17.95 (1-56711-174-2). 48pp. The story of the construction of the Grand Coulee Dam, the largest single producer of hydroelectric power in the U.S. since World War II. (Rev: BL 12/1/99; HBG 3/00; SLJ 2/00) [627]

21126 Hill, Lee S. *Bridges Connect* (1–3). Illus. Series: Building Blocks Books. 1997, Carolrhoda $21.27 (1-57505-021-8). 32pp. Using color photos and a simple text, the structure of bridges is introduced. Also use *Canals Are Water Roads* and *Dams Give Us Power* (both 1997). (Rev: BL 9/15/97; SLJ 7/97) [624]

21127 Hill, Lee S. *Monuments Help Us Remember* (1–3). Illus. Series: Building Blocks Books. 2000, Carolrhoda $21.27 (1-57505-475-2). 32pp. This simple book takes the reader on a tour of the world's most famous monuments, including the Statue of Liberty. (Rev: BL 9/15/00; HBG 3/01) [720]

21128 Hill, Lee S. *Roads Take Us Home* (1–3). Illus. Series: Building Blocks Books. 1997, Carolrhoda LB $21.27 (1-57505-022-6). 32pp. Types of roads and their construction are introduced in color photos and a simple text. Also use *Towers Reach High* (1997). (Rev: BL 9/15/97; SLJ 7/97) [388.1]

21129 Hill, Lee S. *Tunnels Go Underground* (1–3). Illus. Series: Building Blocks Books. 2000, Carolrhoda $21.27 (1-57505-429-9). 32pp. Many different kinds of tunnels are covered, from mining tunnels in Pennsylvania to the tunnel that runs under the English Channel. (Rev: BL 9/15/00; HBG 3/01) [725]

21130 Hunter, Ryan Ann. *Cross a Bridge* (PS–2). Illus. by Edward Miller. 1998, Holiday LB $15.95 (0-8234-1340-3). A simple picture book that describes various kinds of bridges. (Rev: BL 4/1/98; HBG 10/98; SLJ 3/98) [625]

21131 Hunter, Ryan Ann. *Dig a Tunnel* (PS–2). Illus. by Edward Miller. 1999, Holiday $15.95 (0-8234-1391-8). 24pp. Beginning with the tunnels dug by animals like moles, this book continues with explanations of how humans have dug tunnels throughout history and the tools they used. (Rev: BCCB 5/99; BL 3/15/99; HBG 10/99; SLJ 4/99) [624.1]

21132 Hunter, Ryan Ann. *Into the Sky* (PS–2). Illus. by Edward Miller. 1998, Holiday $15.95 (0-8234-1372-1). 32pp. This is a heavily illustrated history of the skyscraper (ending with Japan's planned 196-floor Sky City 1000), with details on how they are built and problems encountered during construction. (Rev: BL 9/15/98; HBG 3/99; SLJ 9/98) [720]

21133 Johmann, Carol A., and Elizabeth J. Rieth. *Bridges! Amazing Structures to Design, Build and Test* (4–6). Illus. Series: Kaleidoscope Kids. 1999, Williamson paper $10.95 (1-885593-30-9). 96pp. Bridge construction, design, mechanics, and maintenance are covered in this paperback that also contains several interesting projects. (Rev: BL 1/1–15/00; SLJ 3/00) [624]

21134 Kirkwood, Jon. *The Fantastic Cutaway Book of Giant Buildings* (4–7). Illus. 1997, Millbrook LB $23.90 (0-7613-0615-3); paper $9.95 (0-7613-0629-3). 40pp. Using double-page spreads, outstanding graphics, and many fact boxes, this book features a wide variety of structures including the Statue of Liberty, the pyramids, the Colosseum, churches, operas houses, Grand Central Station, Munich's Olympic stadium, and skyscrapers. (Rev: BL 4/1/98; HBG 10/98) [720]

21135 Lynch, Anne. *Great Buildings* (4–6). Illus. Series: Nature Company Discoveries. 1996, Time Life $16.00 (0-8094-9371-3). 64pp. Some of the world's most impressive structures are introduced, with illustrations and an eight-page foldout. (Rev: BL 9/15/96; SLJ 3/97) [720.9]

21136 Macaulay, David. *Building Big* (5–10). Illus. by author. 2000, Houghton $30.00 (0-395-96331-1). 192pp. This book explains the problems posed by ambitious construction projects such as tunnels, bridges, dams, domes, and skyscrapers. (Rev: HB 1–2/01; HBG 3/01; SLJ 11/00) [720]

21137 Macaulay, David. *Building the Book Cathedral* (4–6). Illus. 1999, Houghton $29.95 (0-395-92147-3). 112pp. In this oversize book, the author describes in words and drawings how he created the book *Cathedral*. (Rev: BCCB 12/99; BL 11/15/99; HB 9–10/99; SLJ 9/99) [726.6]

21138 Macaulay, David. *Unbuilding* (5–8). Illus. by author. 1980, Houghton $18.00 (0-395-29457-6); paper $6.95 (0-395-45360-7). 128pp. A book that explores the concept of tearing down the Empire State Building.

21139 Macaulay, David. *Underground* (5–8). Illus. by author. 1983, Houghton $18.00 (0-395-24739-X); paper $9.95 (0-395-34065-9). An exploration in text and detailed drawings of the intricate network of systems under city streets.

21140 Malam, John. *Hospital: From Accident and Emergency to X-ray* (3–5). Series: Building Works. 2000, Bedrick $16.95 (0-87226-585-4). 32pp. Beginning with a large double gatefold that shows a detailed cutaway illustration of a hospital, this heavily illustrated book proceeds to show every part of the hospital in a series of double-page spreads. (Rev: BL 7/00; HBG 10/00; SLJ 9/00) [725]

21141 Malam, John. *Library: From Ancient Scrolls to the World Wide Web* (3–5). Series: Building Works. 2000, Bedrick $16.95 (0-87226-587-0). 32pp. An outstanding book that first shows the inner workings of a library in a huge double foldout and then proceeds in double-page spreads to describe in detail each part of a library and give a guided tour behind the scenes. (Rev: BL 7/00; HBG 3/01; SLJ 11/00) [027]

21142 Mann, Elizabeth. *The Brooklyn Bridge* (4–7). Illus. Series: Wonders of the World. 1996, Mikaya $19.95 (0-9650493-0-2). 48pp. The story of the building of the Brooklyn Bridge is told through the eyes of a family. (Rev: BL 2/1/97; SLJ 6/97*) [624]

21143 Mellentin, Kath. *Let's Build an Airport* (K–3). Illus. 1998, Zero to Ten LB $14.95 (1-84089-026-6). 32pp. From the decision to build an airport to the opening day celebrations this is a step-by-step account of how an airport is built. (Rev: BL 3/1/99; HBG 3/99) [629.136]

21144 Millard, Anne. *Pyramids* (4–6). Illus. 1996, Kingfisher $16.95 (1-85697-674-2). 64pp. The design, construction, and use of pyramids are explained, primarily those found in Egypt. (Rev: BL 5/1/96; SLJ 6/96) [932]

21145 Neumann, Dietrich. *Joe and the Skyscraper: The Empire State Building in New York City* (2–4). Illus. Series: Where We Live. 2000, Prestel $14.95 (3-7913-2103-X). 32pp. Seen through the eyes of a 16-year-old waterboy, this is the story of the construction of the Empire State Building. (Rev: BL 4/15/00*; SLJ 4/00) [720.483]

21146 Oxlade, Chris. *Skyscrapers* (3–5). Series: Building Amazing Structures. 2000, Heinemann LB $14.95 (1-57572-278-X). 32pp. This colorful book introduces skyscrapers and describes their construction, materials, and functions with many examples of historical and contemporary buildings. Also use *Stadiums* and *Tunnels* (both 2000). (Rev: SLJ 3/01) [720.4]

21147 Platt, Richard. *Stephen Biesty's Incredible Explosions: Exploded Views of Astonishing Things* (4–7). Illus. by Stephen Biesty. 1996, DK $19.95 (0-7894-1024-9). 32pp. Various aspects of buildings, construction, and technology are shown in this book of cutaway illustrations that includes material on such diverse subjects as London's Tower Bridge, the city of Venice, and a futuristic space station. (Rev: SLJ 10/96) [690]

21148 Ricciuti, Edward R. *America's Top 10 Bridges* (3–7). Illus. Series: America's Top 10. 1997, Blackbirch LB $16.95 (1-56711-197-1). 24pp. Using double-page spreads, this book describes such famous American bridges as the Golden Gate. (Rev: BL 1/1–15/98; HBG 3/98; SLJ 2/98) [388]

21149 Richards, Jon. *Diggers and Other Construction Machines* (1–3). Illus. 1999, Millbrook LB $23.90 (0-7613-0905-5). 40pp. An informative book that highlights all kinds of diggers and allied machinery, along with details of tunnel construction. (Rev: BL 8/99; HBG 10/99) [624.1]

21150 Severance, John B. *Skyscrapers: How America Grew Up* (5–9). Illus. 2000, Holiday $18.95 (0-8234-1492-2). 96pp. Beginning with an explanation of the architectural breakthroughs that made the building of skyscrapers possible, this account traces the construction of these buildings from New York's Crystal Palace in 1851 to the present. (Rev: BL 6/1–15/00; HB 9–10/00; HBG 10/00; SLJ 7/00) [720]

21151 Sturges, Philemon. *Bridges Are to Cross* (3–6). Illus. by Giles Laroche. 1998, Putnam $15.99 (0-399-23174-4). 32pp. A series of double-page spreads show the beauty and usefulness of bridges — from the Brooklyn Bridge to Chenonceau, where a bridge is part of the castle. (Rev: BL 12/15/98) [624.2]

21152 Tarsky, Sue. *The Busy Building Book* (PS–2). Illus. by Alex Ayliffe. 1998, Putnam $15.95 (0-399-23137-4). 32pp. An appealing book that uses collages to describe the building of a skyscraper. (Rev: BCCB 3/98; BL 1/1–15/98; HBG 10/98; SLJ 3/98) [690]

21153 Wilkinson, Philip. *Amazing Buildings* (4–7). Illus. by Paolo Donati. 1993, DK $16.95 (1-56458-234-5). 48pp. Twenty famous buildings from around the world are pictured in two-page spreads that include exterior and interior pictures and floor plans. (Rev: BL 9/1/93; SLJ 8/93) [720]

21154 Wilkinson, Philip. *Building* (4–8). Illus. Series: Eyewitness Books. 1995, Knopf $19.00 (0-679-87256-6). 64pp. This introduction to structures discusses engineering, building materials, and types of construction. (Rev: BL 8/95; SLJ 8/95) [690]

21155 Wilkinson, Philip. *Super Structures* (4–6). Illus. Series: Inside Guides. 1996, DK $15.95 (0-7894-1011-7). 44pp. In double-page spreads, the interiors of such structures as oil rigs, skyscrapers, and undersea tunnels are pictured and explained. (Rev: BL 12/15/96; SLJ 2/97) [624.1]

21156 Woods, Mary B., and Michael Woods. *Ancient Construction: From Tents to Towers* (5–8). Illus. Series: Ancient Technologies. 2000, Runestone LB $25.26 (0-8225-2998-X). 88pp. From the Stonehenge and the Colosseum to the Eiffel Tower and the Golden Gate Bridge this is a history of building and construction. (Rev: BL 9/15/00; HBG 3/01) [720]

Houses

21157 DuQuette, Keith. *The House Book* (PS–1). Illus. 1999, Putnam $15.99 (0-399-23183-8). 32pp. This simple picture book looks at the parts of a house — walls, floors, stairs, and so forth — and then puts them together to form a whole. (Rev: BL 7/99; HBG 10/99; SLJ 6/99) [690]

21158 Gallimard Jeunesse and Claude Delafosse. *Houses* (PS–2). Series: First Discovery. 1998, Scholastic $11.95 (0-590-38152-0). 24pp. Sturdy plastic pages and overlays are used to describe the construction of a house and its parts. (Rev: BL 9/15/98; HBG 10/98) [690]

21159 Hill, Lee S. *Homes Keep Us Warm* (1–3). Illus. Series: Building Blocks Books. 2000, Carolrhoda $21.27 (1-57505-430-2). 32pp. This book explores all kinds of homes, from huts made with animal skins to city apartments, farmhouses, and bungalows. (Rev: BL 9/15/00; HBG 3/01) [690]

21160 Knight, Bertram T. *From Mud to House* (3–6). Illus. Series: Changes. 1997, Children's LB $24.00 (0-516-20737-7). 32pp. This book traces the materials and processes used in manufacturing bricks and of their many uses, including the construction of houses. (Rev: BL 2/15/98; HBG 10/98) [666]

21161 Malam, John. *Cleaning the House* (3–5). Series: Everyday History. 2000, Watts LB $20.00 (0-531-14553-0). 32pp. This is a historic overview of how our methods and implements for house cleaning have changed over the years. (Rev: BL 10/15/00; SLJ 1/01) [392]

21162 White, Sylvia. *Welcome Home!* (3–7). Illus. Series: A World of Difference. 1995, Children's LB $21.00 (0-516-08193-4). 32pp. Family dwellings around the world are explored in text and pictures, with material on how they have evolved for different climates and environments. (Rev: BL 7/95; SLJ 12/95) [391.36]

21163 Wood, Tim. *Houses and Homes* (4–8). Series: See Through History. 1997, Viking $17.99 (0-670-86777-2). 48pp. A well-illustrated examination of different kinds of houses and homes, their variations through history, and their structure and parts. (Rev: BL 11/15/97; HBG 10/98; SLJ 4/98) [690]

21164 Yardley, Thompson. *Down the Drain: Explore Your Plumbing* (3–8). Illus. Series: Lighter Look. 1991, Millbrook LB $20.90 (1-878841-28-9). 40pp. This book discusses household plumbing and how it works — and sometimes malfunctions — and gives tips on water conservation. (Rev: SLJ 8/91) [728]

Clothing, Textiles, and Jewelry

21165 Badt, Karin Luisa. *On Your Feet!* (3–7). Illus. Series: A World of Difference. 1994, Children's LB $21.00 (0-516-08189-6). 32pp. Using many drawings, this account describes shoes, their styles, and their purposes in various societies and times. (Rev: BL 1/1/95; SLJ 1/95) [391]

21166 Bryant-Mole, Karen. *Clothes* (K–3). Illus. Series: Picture This! 1997, Rigby $18.50 (1-57572-149-X). 24pp. This book shows what clothes are made of and which should be worn on different occasions. (Rev: BL 10/15/97) [646]

21167 Carlson, Laurie. *Boss of the Plains: The Hat That Won the West* (K–4). Illus. by Holly Meade. 1998, DK $16.95 (0-7894-2479-7). 32pp. The story of John Batterson Stetson and the broad-brimmed hat he produced to protect himself from the sun and the rain in California. (Rev: BCCB 7–8/98; BL 3/1/98; HB 5–6/98*; HBG 10/98; SLJ 4/98) [338.7]

21168 Cole, Trish. *Why Do We Wear That?* (4–6). Illus. Series: Why Do We? 1996, Watts LB $19.00 (0-531-14396-1). 31pp. An overview of fashion in clothes from World War II to the present. (Rev: SLJ 3/97) [646]

21169 *Dazzling! Jewelry of the Ancient World* (5–8). Illus. Series: Buried Worlds. 1995, Lerner LB $23.93 (0-8225-3203-4). 64pp. Using archaeological methods, this account reveals the wonders and beauty of jewelry from various ancient civilizations. (Rev: BL 7/95; SLJ 4/95) [739.27]

21170 Dixon, Annabelle. *Wool* (3–5). Illus. by Ed Barber. Series: Threads. 1990, Garrett LB $15.93 (0-944483-73-9). 26pp. The nature of wool, its origins, and its uses are explored in text and pictures. (Rev: BL 2/1/91) [677.31]

21171 Greenberg, Keith E. *Bill Bowerman and Phil Knight: Building the Nike Empire* (3–4). Illus. by Dick Smolinski. Series: Partners. 1994, Blackbirch LB $9.95 (1-56711-085-1). 47pp. The story of the pair who created the Nike empire and the production of the first "waffle sole" using a waffle iron. (Rev: SLJ 1/95) [391]

21172 Hoobler, Dorothy, and Tom Hoobler. *Vanity Rules: A History of American Fashion and Beauty* (5–8). Illus. 2000, Twenty-First Century LB $25.90 (0-7613-1258-7). 160pp. From the painted bodies of early Native Americans to today's body piercing, this is a history of the quest for personal beauty in America. (Rev: BL 4/1/00; HBG 10/00) [391]

21173 Kalman, Bobbie. *18th Century Clothing* (3–6). Illus. Series: Historic Communities. 1993, Crabtree LB $20.60 (0-86505-492-4); paper $7.95 (0-86505-512-2). 32pp. Many illustrations and simple text show how people of all levels of society dressed in the 18th century. A companion volume is: *19th Century Clothing* (1993). (Rev: BL 8/93; SLJ 9/93) [391]

21174 Keeler, Patricia A., and Francis X. McCall, Jr. *Unraveling Fibers* (3–5). Illus. 1995, Simon & Schuster $16.00 (0-689-31777-8). 36pp. An introduction to plant, animal, and synthetic fibers and how they are used to produce various kinds of cloth. (Rev: BCCB 6/95; BL 8/95; HB 5–6/95; SLJ 6/95) [677]

21175 Knight, Margaret. *Fashion Through the Ages: From Overcoats to Petticoats* (3–8). Illus. by Kim Daziel. 1998, Viking $19.99 (0-670-86521-4). 20pp. Using double-page spreads and flaps, this book explores fashion and dress from the Roman Empire through the 1960s. (Rev: BCCB 2/99; SLJ 4/99) [646]

21176 Lattimore, Deborah N. *I Wonder What's Under There? A Brief History of Underwear* (2–4). Illus. by David A. Carter. 1998, Harcourt $15.95 (0-15-276652-9). Using a number of lift-the-flaps, this work gives a history of Western underwear with a few samples from other cultures. (Rev: BL 1/1–15/99; HBG 3/99) [646]

21177 Lawlor, Laurie. *Where Will This Shoe Take You? A Walk Through the History of Footwear* (5–8). Illus. 1996, Walker LB $18.85 (0-8027-8435-6). 144pp. This is a history of footwear, from sandals worn by the ancients to the sneakers popular today. (Rev: BCCB 1/97; BL 11/15/96; SLJ 5/97) [391]

21178 L'Hommedieu, Arthur J. *From Plant to Blue Jeans* (3–6). Illus. Series: Changes. 1997, Children's LB $24.00 (0-516-20738-5). 32pp. This book begins with the planting of cotton seeds and ends with children wearing blue jeans. (Rev: BL 2/15/98; HBG 10/98) [687]

21179 Maze, Stephanie. *I Want to Be a Fashion Designer* (3–6). Illus. Series: I Want to Be. 2000, Harcourt $18.00 (0-15-201862-8); paper $9.00 (0-15-201938-3). 48pp. This large-format book uses double-page spreads to explore the world of fashion design and covers such topics as trade shows, education, and how a designer works. (Rev: BL 3/1/00; HBG 10/00; SLJ 4/00) [746.9]

21180 Miller, Brandon M. *Dressed for the Occasion* (5–8). Illus. 1999, Lerner $16.95 (0-8225-1738-8). 96pp. A history of men's and women's fashions in the U.S. from the Puritans to the greaser look of

Elvis Presley. (Rev: BCCB 5/99; BL 4/1/99; SLJ 9/99) [391]

21181 Morris, Ann. *Shoes, Shoes, Shoes* (PS–2). Illus. 1995, Lothrop LB $15.00 (0-688-13667-2). 32pp. Thirty-one shoes from a variety of cultures are identified and pictured. (Rev: BCCB 10/95; BL 10/1/95; SLJ 1/96) [391]

21182 Nichelason, Margery G. *Shoes* (3–5). Illus. 1997, Carolrhoda $22.60 (1-57505-047-1). 48pp. From the first shoes worn by the Egyptians to today's latest trends, this is the surprising history of footwear through the years. (Rev: BL 1/1–15/98; HB 5–6/97; HBG 3/98) [391.4]

21183 Power, Vicki. *Vanity* (4–7). Illus. Series: A Very Peculiar History. 1995, Watts LB $22.00 (0-531-14356-2). 48pp. A history of fashion, jewelry, makeup, and other beautifying trends. (Rev: BL 6/1–15/95) [391.6]

21184 Smith, Elizabeth Simpson. *Cloth* (5–8). Illus. 1985, Walker LB $10.85 (0-8027-6577-7). 60pp. The discovery of fiber and how cloth is made. (Rev: BL 8/85; SLJ 11/85)

21185 Straus, Lucy. *The Story of Shoes* (PS). Illus. by Mas Miyamoto. Series: Real Readers. 1989, Raintree Steck-Vaughn LB $19.97 (0-8172-3534-5). 32pp. This easily read account describes how shoes evolved from ancient times. (Rev: BL 2/1/90) [391]

21186 Tythacott, Louise. *Jewelry* (4–8). Illus. Series: Traditions Around the World. 1995, Thomson Learning LB $24.26 (1-56847-229-3). 48pp. A history of jewelry, why it is worn, and the variety of materials and designs used. (Rev: SLJ 7/95) [739.27]

21187 Woods, Samuel G. *Sneakers: From Start to Finish* (3–5). Illus. Series: Made in the USA. 1999, Blackbirch LB $16.95 (1-56711-393-1). 32pp. The manufacture of sneakers is covered in this book that gives a tour of the New Balance Athletic Shoe factory in Lawrence, Massachusetts. (Rev: BL 12/1/99; HBG 3/00; SLJ 3/00) [685]

21188 Young, Robert. *Sneakers: The Shoes We Choose* (3–5). Illus. 1991, Macmillan LB $14.95 (0-87518-460-X). 64pp. A discussion of the history, development, manufacture, and promotion of the shoes that everybody wears. (Rev: BL 6/1/91; SLJ 7/91) [685.31]

21189 Yue, Charlotte, and David Yue. *Shoes: Their History in Words and Pictures* (5–8). Illus. 1997, Houghton $14.95 (0-395-72667-0). 96pp. A history of footwear arranged around topics like protection, status, and fashion. (Rev: BL 4/1/97; HB 5–6/97; SLJ 4/97) [391]

Computers and Automation

21190 Ahmad, Nyla. *CyberSurfer: The OWL Internet Guide for Kids* (4–7). Illus. 1996, Firefly $19.95 (1-895688-50-7). 72pp. Using cartoons, a fast-paced text, and a demonstration disc, the author introduces the Internet, its functions, and important addresses. (Rev: BL 4/1/96; SLJ 9/96) [004.6]

21191 Baker, Christopher W. *Let There Be Life! Animating with the Computer* (4–6). Illus. 1997,

Walker LB $17.85 (0-8027-8473-9). 48pp. An overview of the basics of computer animation, illustrated with stills from feature films, shorts, and commercials. (Rev: BL 1/1–15/98; HBG 3/98) [778.2]

21192 Baker, Christopher W. *Scientific Visualization: The New Eyes of Science* (5–8). Illus. Series: New Century Technology. 2000, Millbrook LB $22.90 (0-7613-1351-6). 48pp. This book explores the ways that computers enable scientists to study the universe beyond the range of the eye and accomplish such miracles as simulating events such as the creation of a black hole. (Rev: BL 4/1/00; HBG 3/01; SLJ 6/00) [507.2]

21193 Baker, Christopher W. *Virtual Reality: Experiencing Illusion* (5–8). Illus. Series: New Century Technology. 2000, Millbrook LB $22.90 (0-7613-1350-8). 48pp. A brief account that explains how computers can synthesize human sensory experiences through digital imaging. (Rev: BL 4/1/00; HBG 3/01; SLJ 6/00) [006]

21194 Brimner, Larry. *E-Mail* (2–5). Illus. Series: True Books. 1997, Children's LB $22.00 (0-516-20332-0). 47pp. A basic introduction to electronic mail that covers topics like what it is, how it works, advantages and disadvantages, symbols, and acronyms. (Rev: SLJ 11/97) [004]

21195 Cook, Peter, and Scott Manning. *Why Doesn't My Floppy Disk Flop? And Other Kids' Computer Questions Answered by the CompuDudes* (3–5). Illus. 1999, Wiley paper $12.95 (0-471-18429-2). 90pp. Using a question-and-answer approach, this book covers hardware, software, the Internet, good computer practices, and the future of computers. (Rev: BL 9/1/99) [004]

21196 Drake, Jim. *Computers All Around Us* (2–4). Illus. Series: Log On to Computers. 1999, Heinemann LB $14.95 (1-57572-784-6). 32pp. An easily read oversize book that explains the many uses of computers in such places as grocery stores, factories, and offices. (Rev: BL 7/99; SLJ 11/99) [004]

21197 Drake, Jim. *Computers and School* (2–4). Series: Log on to Computers. 1999, Heinemann LB $14.95 (1-57572-785-4). 32pp. Large color photographs and a concise text are used to explore the ways computers can be used to gather information to help in school assignments and other related activities. (Rev: BL 7/99; SLJ 12/99) [004]

21198 Drake, Jim. *Play with Computers* (2–4). Series: Log on to Computers. 1999, Heinemann LB $14.95 (1-57572-786-2). 32pp. Double-page spreads featuring large print and bright photographs explore various ways children can use the computer for recreation. (Rev: BL 7/99; SLJ 11/99) [004]

21199 Drake, Jim. *What Is a Computer?* (2–4). Illus. Series: Log on to Computers. 1999, Heinemann LB $14.95 (1-57572-787-0). 32pp. A large-size book that gives a history of computers, explains software and hardware, and relates computers to the everyday life of youngsters. (Rev: BL 7/99; SLJ 12/99) [004]

21200 Fowler, Allan. *It Could Still Be a Robot* (1–3). Illus. Series: Rookie Readers. 1997, Children's LB $19.00 (0-516-20431-9). 32pp. In this easy-to-read book, robots are introduced, along with the tasks they can and cannot do. (Rev: BL 12/1/97; HBG 3/98) [629.8]

21201 Gallimard Jeunesse, et al. *Internet* (PS–2). Series: First Discovery. 2000, Scholastic $12.95 (0-439-14825-1). 24pp. A beginning look at computers and the Internet with large illustrations and clear, simple explanations. (Rev: BL 8/00; SLJ 11/00) [004]

21202 Gascoigne, Marc. *You Can Surf the Net!* (4–7). Illus. 1996, Penguin paper $3.99 (0-14-038265-9). 153pp. After introductory material on how to connect into the Internet, there is an annotated directory of Web sites. (Rev: BL 12/15/96) [004.6]

21203 Graham, Ian. *The World of Computers and Communications* (4–7). Series: Inside Look. 2000, Gareth Stevens LB $22.60 (0-8368-2727-9). 48pp. As well as computers, computer peripherals, and networking, this overview of electronic communications touches on recordings, radar, and calculators. (Rev: SLJ 3/01) [004]

21204 Gralla, Preston. *Online Kids: A Young Surfer's Guide to Cyberspace* (4–7). Illus. 1996, Wiley paper $14.95 (0-471-13545-3). 288pp. An informal guide to online services that includes important addresses. (Rev: BL 7/96; SLJ 9/96) [025.04]

21205 Jefferis, David. *Artificial Intelligence: Robotics and Machine Evolution* (5–7). Series: Megatech. 1999, Crabtree LB $14.37 (0-7787-0046-1); paper $8.06 (0-7787-0056-9). 32pp. This is a survey of the variety of robotic devices in use today, some of the advances that are being made, and a glimpse into the future. (Rev: SLJ 9/99) [004]

21206 Jefferis, David. *Cyber Space: Virtual Reality and the World Wide Web* (4–6). Illus. 1999, Crabtree LB $14.37 (0-7787-0057-7). 32pp. Discusses the world of virtual reality, its uses, applications, and the World Wide Web. (Rev: BL 8/99; SLJ 9/99) [004]

21207 Jortberg, Charles A. *The Internet* (4–6). Illus. Series: Kids and Computers. 1997, ABDO LB $15.95 (1-56239-727-3). 38pp. A history of the Internet, how to use it, and a listing of important sites for kids. (Rev: BL 6/1–15/97; HBG 3/98) [004.6]

21208 Jortberg, Charles A. *Virtual Reality and Beyond* (4–6). Illus. Series: Kids and Computers. 1997, ABDO LB $22.83 (1-56239-728-1). 38pp. An explanation of virtual reality, its uses at present and in the future, and career possibilities. (Rev: BL 6/1–15/97) [006]

21209 Kalbag, Asha. *Build Your Own Web Site* (4–8). Series: Usborne Computer Guides. 1999, EDC paper $8.95 (0-7460-3293-5). 48pp. This title explains how to create a Web site and also discusses the important whys, whens, and wheres. (Rev: SLJ 6/99) [004]

21210 Kazunas, Charnan, and Tom Kazunas. *The Internet for Kids* (2–5). Illus. Series: True Books. 1997, Children's LB $22.00 (0-516-20334-7). 47pp. An easy and attractive introduction that covers such topics as search-and-retrieval tools, networks, addresses, and parts of the Internet, like e-mail and newsgroups. (Rev: SLJ 10/97) [004]

21211 Kazunas, Charnan, and Tom Kazunas. *Personal Computers* (2–4). Illus. Series: True Books. 1997, Children's LB $22.00 (0-516-20338-X). 47pp. Such computer topics as hardware, software, and peripherals are covered, as well as a history of computers from the room-sized ENIAC to modern laptops. (Rev: SLJ 1/98) [004]

21212 Kazunas, Charnan, and Tom Kazunas. *The World Wide Web* (2–4). Illus. Series: True Books. 1997, Children's LB $22.00 (0-516-20345-2). 47pp. Terms like *bookmarks, search engines, hyperlinks,* and *Internet service providers* are explained in this excellent introduction to the World Wide Web. (Rev: SLJ 1/98) [004]

21213 Knittel, John, and Michael Soto. *Everything You Need to Know About the Dangers of Computer Hacking* (5–8). Illus. 2000, Rosen $17.95 (0-8239-3034-3). 64pp. This book points out the differences between a hacker and a cracker and, through this, discusses beneficial and harmful computer actions and how to avoid the latter. (Rev: BL 4/1/00; SLJ 5/00) [364.16]

21214 Lampton, Christopher. *Home Page: An Introduction to Web Page Design* (4–8). Illus. 1997, Watts LB $22.50 (0-531-20255-0). 64pp. The author explains to youngsters clearly and simply how they can design their own Web home pages using offline time. (Rev: BL 7/97; SLJ 2/98) [005.7]

21215 Lampton, Christopher. *The World Wide Web* (4–8). Illus. 1997, Watts LB $22.50 (0-531-20262-3). 64pp. Aspects of the World Wide Web that would be of value and interest to children are covered, with practical suggestions for effective searching. (Rev: BL 7/97; SLJ 2/98) [025.04]

21216 Lauber, Patricia. *Get Ready for Robots!* (K–3). Illus. by True Kelley. 1987, HarperCollins $12.95 (0-690-04576-X). 32pp. An introduction to robots that work in space, under water, and in factories. (Rev: BCCB 3/87; BL 2/15/87; SLJ 6–7/87)

21217 Lawler, Jennifer. *Cyberdanger and Internet Safety: A Hot Issue* (5–10). Series: Hot Issues. 2000, Enslow LB $19.95 (0-7660-1368-5). 64pp. As well as introducing the Internet, this account explains how people abuse it with hidden identities, threatening or obscene material, loss of privacy, hacking, con tricks, pranks, and hoaxes. (Rev: HBG 3/01; SLJ 1/01) [004.6]

21218 Lindsay, Dave, and Bruce Lindsay. *Dave's Quick 'n' Easy Web Pages* (5–9). Illus. 1999, Erin paper $14.95 (0-9690609-7-1). 128pp. Dave, the 14-year-old webmaster of the popular Redwall Abbey Homepage, gives simple, practical, easy-to-follow directions for creating a personal Web page using hypertext markup language (HTML). (Rev: BL 8/99) [005.7]

21219 McCormick, Anita Louise. *The Internet: Surfing the Issues* (5–10). Series: Issues in Focus. 1998, Enslow LB $19.95 (0-89490-956-8). 128pp. A guide to the history, mechanics, and use of the Internet that also covers such topics as surfing, child

pornography, hate groups, and censorship. (Rev: SLJ 12/98) [004]

21220 Pascoe, Elaine, adapt. *Virtual Reality: Beyond the Looking Glass* (4–6). Series: New Explorers. 1997, Blackbirch LB $16.95 (1-56711-228-5). 48pp. An interesting look at virtual reality, its nature, history, uses, and future. (Rev: HBG 3/98; SLJ 6/98) [006]

21221 Perry, Robert L. *Build Your Own Website* (4–7). Illus. Series: Watts Library: Computer Science. 2000, Watts $24.00 (0-531-11756-1); paper $8.95 (0-531-16469-1). 64pp. Clear, jargon-free language is used to explain the basics of Web site construction under various conditions and for various purposes. (Rev: BL 10/15/00) [005.7]

21222 Perry, Robert L. *Personal Computer Communications* (4–7). Illus. Series: Watts Library: Computer Science. 2000, Watts $24.00 (0-531-11758-8); paper $8.95 (0-531-16483-7). 64pp. This work covers such topics as modems, networks, satellite and wireless technology, and the future of communications. (Rev: BL 10/15/00) [004.16]

21223 Sabbeth, Carol. *Kids' Computer Creations: Using Your Computer for Art and Craft Fun* (3–6). Illus. by Loretta Braren. Series: Kids Can! 1995, Williamson paper $12.95 (0-913589-92-6). 158pp. An interesting collection of computer activities grouped by subjects like "Around the House," "Fun and Games," and "Wearable Art." (Rev: SLJ 6/96) [005.1]

21224 Saltveit, Elin Kordahl. *Computer Fun for Everyone: Great Things to Do and Make with Any Computer* (2–5). 1998, Wiley paper $12.95 (0-471-24450-3). 118pp. The 34 projects in this book vary in difficulty and include such activities as making stationery, illustrating stories, producing story chains, and designing rebuses. (Rev: SLJ 7/99) [004]

21225 Skurzynski, Gloria. *Robots: Your High-Tech World* (4–7). Illus. 1990, Macmillan LB $16.95 (0-02-782917-0). 64pp. An overview of robotics and history and an explanation of how robots work. (Rev: BL 11/15/90; HB 1–2/91; SLJ 9/90) [629.8]

21226 Sonenklar, Carol. *Robots Rising* (3–5). Illus. 1999, Holt $15.95 (0-8050-6096-0). 99pp. A fascinating survey of robotics that includes material on current types of robots and their uses. (Rev: BL 1/1–15/00; HB 3–4/00; HBG 3/00; SLJ 1/00) [629.8]

21227 Steinhauser, Peggy L. *Mousetracks: A Kid's Computer Idea Book* (K–5). Illus. 1997, Tricycle Pr. paper $12.95 (1-883672-48-1). 94pp. The 70 projects in this book are designed to help youngsters develop their computer skills. (Rev: SLJ 8/97) [004]

21228 Trumbauer, Lisa. *Computer Fun Math* (3–5). Illus. by Sydney Wright. Series: Click It! 1999, Millbrook LB $20.90 (0-7613-1504-7); paper $5.95 (0-7613-0996-9). 32pp. This book explains how to create simple graphs, charts, and measuring tools, and how to understand math concepts using the computer. Adult help may be required to understand the directions. Also use *Computer Fun Science*. (Rev: HBG 3/00; SLJ 12/99) [004]

21229 Trumbauer, Lisa. *Free Stuff for Kids on the Net* (3–8). Series: Cool Sites. 1999, Millbrook LB $15.90 (0-7613-1508-X); paper $4.95 (0-7613-1025-8). 74pp. A directory of sites that offer free stuff. Also use *Super Sports for Kids on the Net* (1999). (Rev: HBG 3/00; SLJ 11/99) [004]

21230 Trumbauer, Lisa. *Homework Help for Kids on the Net* (4–8). Series: Cool Sites. 2000, Millbrook LB $16.90 (0-7613-1655-8). 75pp. This useful book lists and describes key sites covering general reference, math, language arts, history, geography, and science. (Rev: HBG 10/00; SLJ 7/00) [004]

21231 Wallace, Mark. *101 Things to Do on the Internet* (4–8). Illus. by Isaac Quaye and Ze Wray. Series: Usborne Computer Guides. 1999, EDC paper $9.95 (0-7460-3294-3). 64pp. Each of the double-page spreads in this book focuses on a single subject or theme to be explored on the Internet such as space, music, games, movies, or weather. (Rev: HBG 10/99; SLJ 6/99) [004]

21232 Wilson, Anthony. *Communications* (4–7). Illus. Series: How the Future Began. 1999, Kingfisher $15.95 (0-7534-5179-4). 64pp. The five sections in this book explore the current revolution in communication technology from computers to artificial intelligence. (Rev: BL 11/15/99; HBG 3/00) [621.382]

21233 Wolinsky, Art. *Communicating on the Internet* (4–8). Series: The Internet Library. 1999, Enslow LB $16.95 (0-7660-1260-3). 64pp. This book on how to communicate safely and effectively on the Internet includes material on e-mail problems, computer etiquette, chat rooms, and newsgroups. (Rev: HBG 3/00; SLJ 3/00) [004]

21234 Wolinsky, Art. *Creating and Publishing Web Pages on the Internet* (4–8). Series: The Internet Library. 1999, Enslow LB $16.95 (0-7660-1262-X). 64pp. Using many example Web pages, this book gives practical advice on how to create an interesting, well-organized, safe Web page with links to sites for further information. (Rev: HBG 10/00; SLJ 3/00) [004]

21235 Wolinsky, Art. *The History of the Internet and the World Wide Web* (5–9). Illus. Series: Internet Library. 1999, Enslow $16.95 (0-7660-1261-1). 64pp. This volume explains how the Internet evolved during the Cold War and how it transfers and distributes information. (Rev: BL 12/15/99; HBG 3/00; SLJ 1/00) [004.67]

21236 Wolinsky, Art. *Locating and Evaluating Information on the Internet* (5–9). Illus. 1999, Enslow LB $16.95 (0-7660-1259-X). 64pp. As well as directions on how to complete successful searches on the Internet, this work tells how to determine the usefulness and credibility of Web pages. (Rev: BL 12/15/99; HBG 3/00; SLJ 1/00) [025.04]

21237 Woods, Samuel. *Computer Animation* (3–5). Series: Made in the USA. 2000, Blackbirch LB $16.95 (1-56711-396-6). 32pp. This book explains how computers are used to create animation while tracing the production of a computer-animated com-

mercial from start to completion. (Rev: BL 12/15/00; HBG 3/01; SLJ 12/00) [004]

21238 Wright, David. *Computers* (3–6). Illus. Series: Inventors and Inventions. 1996, Benchmark LB $25.64 (0-7614-0064-8). 63pp. The development of the computer is traced, with brief profiles of important people who brought it into being and an account of the effects of computers on today's world. (Rev: BL 3/15/96; SLJ 6/96) [004]

Electronics

21239 Baker, Wendy, and Andrew Haslam. *Electricity* (3–6). Illus. Series: Make It Work! 1993, Macmillan $12.95 (0-689-71663-X). 48pp. The principles of electricity and how they are applied are explained and activities are provided. (Rev: SLJ 4/93) [537]

21240 Bridgman, Roger. *Electronics* (4–8). Illus. Series: Eyewitness Science. 1993, DK LB $15.95 (1-56458-325-4). 64pp. The field of electronics is introduced through full-color graphics, 3-D models, and detailed captions that explain important experiments, equipment, and concepts. (Rev: BL 11/15/93; SLJ 12/93) [621.38]

21241 Hoare, Stephen. *Digital Revolution* (3–6). Series: 20th Century Inventions. 1998, Raintree Steck-Vaughn LB $24.26 (0-8172-4897-8). 48pp. This work introduces digital technology and such applications as compact discs, television, telephones, DVDs, watches, and cameras. (Rev: HBG 3/99; SLJ 2/99) [621.38]

Machinery

21242 Barton, Byron. *Machines at Work* (PS). Illus. 1987, HarperCollins LB $15.89 (0-690-04573-5). 32pp. All sorts of workers — men and women — with picks and drills and cranes and steamrollers parade across the pages. (Rev: BL 10/1/87)

21243 Berger, Melvin, and Gilda Berger. *Telephones, Televisions and Toilets: How They Work and What Can Go Wrong* (2–3). Illus. by Don Madden. Series: Discovery Readers. 1993, Ideals paper $4.50 (0-8249-8608-3). 48pp. Cartoons and simple text explain the inner workings of these three machines. (Rev: BL 7/93) [632.6]

21244 Biesty, Stephen. *Stephen Biesty's Incredible Pop-Up Cross-Sections* (3–6). Illus. 1995, DK $16.95 (0-7894-0199-1). Pop-ups are used to show cross-sections of a fire engine, helicopter, and space shuttle. (Rev: BL 2/1/96) [690]

21245 Budd, E. S. *Street Cleaners* (PS–K). Illus. Series: Machines at Work. 2000, Child's World LB $21.36 (1-56766-757-0). 24pp. This simple, informative book pictures street cleaning machinery, shows the inside and outside of this equipment, explains how they keep the streets clean, and tells what happens with the dirt they pick up. (Rev: BL 1/1–15/01) [628.4]

21246 Eick, Jean. *Diggers* (PS). Series: Big Machines at Work. 1999, Child's World LB $13.95 (1-56766-529-2). 32pp. Large, clear pictures and a short, simple text explain the parts and uses of diggers. (Rev: BL 4/15/98; HBG 10/99) [629]

21247 Gifford, Clive. *Machines* (5–8). Series: How the Future Began. 2000, Kingfisher $15.95 (0-7534-5188-3). 63pp. This account traces the history of machines in industry, power production, the military, and everyday life and projects future developments. (Rev: HBG 3/01; SLJ 9/00) [623.6]

21248 Hoban, Tana. *Dig, Drill, Dump, Fill* (K–2). Illus. by author. 1975, Greenwillow $15.93 (0-688-84016-7); Morrow paper $3.95 (0-688-11703-1). 32pp. Catching heavy-duty machinery in action.

21249 Jennings, Terry. *Cranes, Dump Trucks, Bulldozers and Other Building Machines* (3–5). Illus. Series: How Things Work. 1993, Kingfisher paper $6.95 (1-85697-865-6). 40pp. All sorts of large equipment used in construction are pictured with simple explanations of their functions and how they operate. (Rev: BL 6/1–15/93; SLJ 6/93) [690]

21250 Kirkwood, Jon. *The Fantastic Cutaway Book of Giant Machines* (4–6). Illus. 1996, Millbrook LB $23.90 (0-7613-0491-6). 40pp. Such giant machines as monster trucks, tunnel borers, and nuclear submarines are introduced in double-page spreads. (Rev: BL 2/15/97) [629.04]

21251 Macaulay, David. *The Way Things Work* (5–8). Illus. by author. 1988, Houghton $29.95 (0-395-42857-2). 400pp. An imaginative look at machine technology. (Rev: BCCB 1/89; BL 1/15/89; HB 3–4/89)

21252 Pluckrose, Henry. *On the Farm* (PS–1). Illus. Series: Machines at Work. 1998, Watts LB $18.00 (0-531-14496-8). 32pp. Large full-page photos and a simple text introduce such farm machines as tractors, plows, milk trucks, seed drills, and harvesters. (Rev: BL 12/1/98; HBG 3/99) [631.3]

21253 Rogers, Hal. *Combines* (PS–K). Illus. Series: Machines at Work. 2000, Child's World LB $21.36 (1-56766-754-6). 24pp. This heavily illustrated book shows the purpose and parts of a combine and how they cut wheat, thresh it, blow away the chaff, and empty their bins. (Rev: BL 1/1–15/01; SLJ 1/01) [633.1]

21254 Rogers, Hal. *Snowplows* (PS–K). Series: Machines at Work. 2000, Child's World LB $21.36 (1-56766-756-2). 24pp. This book introduces snowplows, their uses, and parts, in a series of clear pictures and a short, simple text. (Rev: BL 1/1–15/01) [621]

21255 VanCleave, Janice. *Machines: Mind-Boggling Experiments You Can Turn into Science Fair Projects* (4–6). Illus. Series: Spectacular Science Projects. 1993, Wiley paper $10.95 (0-471-57108-3). 88pp. Simple machines that can be made and operated are featured in this collection of fascinating science projects. (Rev: BL 5/1/93; SLJ 7/93) [521.8]

21256 Wallace, Karen. *Big Machines* (K–2). Series: Eyewitness Reader. 2000, DK LB $12.95 (0-7894-5412-2); paper $3.95 (0-7894-5411-4). 32pp. This

book presents pictures and text on such big machines as a crane, a bulldozer, a front loader, a dump truck, and an excavator. (Rev: HBG 10/00; SLJ 7/00) [621.8]

Metals

21257 Fitzgerald, Karen. *The Story of Iron* (4–6). Illus. Series: First Books. 1997, Watts LB $22.50 (0-531-20270-4). 64pp. Iron's properties, characteristics, uses, and methods of procurement are discussed. (Rev: BL 9/1/97; SLJ 10/97) [669]

21258 Mebane, Robert C., and Thomas R. Rybolt. *Metals* (4–6). Illus. Series: Everyday Material Science Experiments. 1995, Twenty-First Century LB $18.90 (0-8050-2842-0). 64pp. At various levels of difficulty, this is a collection of experiments using common objects that identify and explore the properties of metals. (Rev: BL 9/15/95; SLJ 10/95) [669]

21259 Weitzman, David. *Pouring Iron: A Foundry Ghost Story* (4–6). Illus. 1998, Houghton $15.00 (0-395-84170-4). 40pp. This book describes the workings of the historic, still-functioning Knight Foundry near Sacramento, California — from making molds to pouring the iron — with details of the tools and procedures used. (Rev: BL 12/15/98; HBG 3/99; SLJ 1/99) [669]

Telegraph, Telephone, and Telecommunications

21260 Ganeri, Anita. *The Story of Communications* (3–6). Series: Signs of the Times. 1998, Oxford LB $16.00 (0-19-521411-0). 32pp. A history of communication from prehistoric times to the modern use of telecommunications is given in this well-illustrated account. (Rev: BL 3/15/98; SLJ 5/98) [302]

21261 Gearhart, Sarah. *The Telephone* (4–7). Illus. Series: Turning Points. 1999, Simon & Schuster $17.95 (0-689-82815-2). 80pp. This book describes long-distance communications before the telephone, gives a biography of Alexander Graham Bell, and explains how the telephone was invented. (Rev: BL 10/1/99; HBG 3/00; SLJ 10/99) [384.6]

21262 Oxlade, Chris. *Telecommunications* (3–6). Illus. Series: 20th Century Inventions. 1997, Raintree Steck-Vaughn LB $27.12 (0-8172-4813-7). 48pp. After a brief introduction to telecommunications, this account focuses on such topics as the telephone, telegraph, radio, television, and computers. (Rev: BL 6/1–15/97) [384]

21263 Skurzynski, Gloria. *Get the Message: Telecommunications in Your High-Tech World* (4–6). Illus. 1993, Macmillan LB $17.00 (0-02-778071-6). 64pp. This simple account explains the workings of such machines as the telephone and the fax and the new uses of fiber optics. (Rev: BCCB 5/93; BL 8/93*; HB 7–8/93; SLJ 6/93) [384]

Television, Motion Pictures, Radio, and Recording

21264 Anderson, Carol D., and Robert Sheely. *Techno Lab: How Science Is Changing Entertainment* (4–6). Illus. 1995, Silver Moon $14.95 (1-881889-63-7). 64pp. This fascinating book traces the influence of science and technology on movies, recorded music, television, video games, and virtual reality. (Rev: BL 1/1–15/96; SLJ 12/95) [791.4]

21265 Bentley, Nancy, and Donna Guthrie. *The Young Producer's Video Book: How to Write, Shoot and Direct Your Own Videos* (4–7). Illus. 1995, Millbrook LB $21.90 (1-56294-566-1); paper $7.95 (1-56294-688-9). 64pp. A complete step-by-step manual that begins with choosing equipment and script writing and ends with the finished video. (Rev: BL 2/1/96; SLJ 1/96) [791.45]

21266 Biel, Jackie. *Video* (3–6). Illus. Series: Inventors and Inventions. 1996, Marshall Cavendish LB $25.64 (0-7614-0048-6). 63pp. The story of this important modern invention and the people who brought it into being. (Rev: BL 7/96; SLJ 8/96) [621.388]

21267 Dahl, Lucy. *James and the Giant Peach: The Book and Movie Scrapbook* (3–6). Illus. 1996, Disney $15.95 (0-7868-3106-5); paper $7.95 (0-7868-4085-4). 64pp. Roald Dahl's daughter tells about the making of the movie of her father's book *James and the Giant Peach*. (Rev: BCCB 6/96; BL 4/1/96) [791.43]

21268 Dowd, Ned. *That's a Wrap: How Movies Are Made* (5–7). Illus. 1991, Silver Burdett paper $4.95 (0-382-24376-5). 62pp. Lots of information about moviemaking is contained in this behind-the-scenes movie shoot. (Rev: BCCB 1/92; BL 1/1/92) [791.43]

21269 Francis, Sandy. *At the Movie Theater* (PS–2). Photos by David M. Budd. Series: Field Trips. 1999, Child's World LB $14.95 (1-56766-575-6). 32pp. This photo-essay gives a behind-the-scenes tour of a movie theater including the refreshment stand. (Rev: HBG 3/00; SLJ 2/00) [791.4]

21270 Hahn, Don. *Disney's Animation Magic: A Behind-the-Scenes Look at How an Animated Film Is Made* (4–6). Illus. 1996, Disney $16.89 (0-7868-5041-8). 96pp. Using a team from the Disney studio as case studies, this book traces the various steps and processes involved in creating an animated film. (Rev: BL 9/1/96; SLJ 10/96) [791.43]

21271 Hamilton, Jake. *Special Effects: In Film and Television* (3–8). 1998, DK $17.95 (0-7849-2813-X). 64pp. In double-page spreads, this fascinating book explains how such special effects as shrinking the kids and blowing up the White House are accomplished in movies and on television. (Rev: BL 8/98; SLJ 6/98) [791.43]

21272 Merbreier, W. Carter. *Television: What's Behind What You See* (4–6). Illus. 1996, Farrar $16.00 (0-374-37388-4). 32pp. A grab bag of information about television technology and behind-the-scenes operations of a TV station. (Rev: BCCB 2/96; BL 4/15/96; SLJ 3/96) [384.55]

21273 O'Brien, Lisa. *Lights, Camera, Action! Making Movies and TV from the Inside Out* (4–7). Illus. 1998, Owl $19.95 (1-895688-75-2); paper $12.00 (1-895688-76-0). 64pp. This book explains how a budding actor can break into the television and film business and also describes every facet in a program or movie production schedule. (Rev: BL 6/1–15/98; SLJ 7/98) [791.4]

21274 Oxlade, Chris. *Movies* (3–5). Illus. Series: Science Encounters. 1997, Rigby $22.79 (1-57572-088-4). 32pp. An introduction to movie making that gives a basic history of motion pictures, tells how the film camera works, and covers stunts, different types of film, animation, and computer enhancement. (Rev: SLJ 11/97) [791]

21275 Platt, Richard. *Film* (4–8). Illus. Series: Eyewitness Books. 1992, Knopf $19.00 (0-679-81679-8). 64pp. Through many two-page spreads, the mechanics of motion pictures are explored. (Rev: BL 6/1/92; SLJ 2/93) [791.43]

21276 Riehecky, Janet. *Television* (3–6). Illus. Series: Inventors and Inventions. 1996, Marshall Cavendish LB $25.64 (0-7614-0045-1). 63pp. The history of television and the people behind its development are chronicled, with many photographs and an informal text. (Rev: BL 7/96; SLJ 8/96) [384.55]

21277 Scott, Elaine. *Movie Magic: Behind the Scenes with Special Effects* (4–7). Illus. 1995, Morrow $16.00 (0-688-12477-1). 96pp. The techniques used to produce special effects in movies are explained, with special material on the use of computers. (Rev: BL 2/15/96) [791.43]

21278 Stwertka, Eve, and Albert Stwertka. *Tuning In: The Sounds of the Radio* (3–5). Illus. by Mena Dolobowsky. Series: At Home with Science. 1993, Simon & Schuster paper $5.95 (0-671-69466-9). 40pp. A history of radio technology. (Rev: SLJ 8/93) [621]

Transportation

General

21279 Badt, Karin Luisa. *Let's Go!* (3–7). Illus. Series: A World of Difference. 1995, Children's LB $21.00 (0-516-08195-0). 32pp. A look at various methods of transportation around the world and how they reflect the cultures in which they are found. (Rev: BL 7/95) [629.04]

21280 Burns, Peggy, and Peter Chrisp. *Travel* (3–5). Illus. Series: Stepping Through History. 1995, Thomson Learning LB $5.00 (1-56847-343-5). 32pp. A history of travel and transportation from ancient days to the superjets of today. (Rev: BL 7/95) [629]

21281 Butterfield, Moira. *Look Inside Cross-Sections: Record Breakers* (3–8). Illus. Series: Look Inside Cross-Sections. 1995, DK paper $5.95 (0-7894-0320-X). 32pp. The inner workings of a number of record-breaking speed machines are pictured in a series of cross-sectional diagrams that supply amazing details. (Rev: BL 9/15/95) [629.05]

21282 Davies, Eryl. *Transport: On Land, Road and Rail* (3–6). Illus. Series: Timelines. 1992, Watts $24.00 (0-531-14376-7). 48pp. This survey gives facts, illustrations, and ancedotes about various ways people have traveled on land. (Rev: BL 9/15/92) [629.04]

21283 Graham, Ian. *Cars, Bikes, Trains, and Other Land Machines* (3–5). Illus. Series: How Things Work. 1993, Kingfisher paper $8.95 (1-85697-871-0). 40pp. This book gives a very simple explanation in words, diagrams, and line drawings of how various vehicles operate. (Rev: BL 6/1–15/93; SLJ 5/93) [629.04]

21284 Hamilton, John. *Transportation: A Pictorial History of the Past One Thousand Years* (4–7). Illus. Series: The Millennium. 2000, ABDO $16.95 (1-57765-361-0). 48pp. A history of 1,000 years of transportation that includes animals, ships, trains, bicycles, motorcycles, cars, airplanes, and spacecraft. (Rev: BL 7/00; HBG 10/00; SLJ 10/00) [388.21]

21285 Maynard, Christopher. *Extreme Machines* (3–6). Series: Eyewitness Reader. 2000, DK $12.95 (0-7894-5418-1); paper $3.95 (0-7894-5417-3). 48pp. A visually appealing book that looks at machines from drag cars to helicopters. (Rev: HBG 10/00; SLJ 8/00) [629.04]

21286 Oxlade, Chris. *Fantastic Transport Machines* (3–8). Illus. by David Salariya. Series: X-Ray Picture Books. 1995, Watts LB $25.00 (0-531-14351-1). 48pp. Introduces in double-page spreads such transport machines as motorcycles, cars, trains, ships, submarines, airplanes, and space vehicles. (Rev: SLJ 12/95) [629]

21287 Parker, Steve. *Making Tracks* (3–5). Illus. Series: SuperSmarts. 1997, Candlewick $11.99 (0-7636-0129-2). 24pp. This introduction to various forms of transportation uses bold illustrations, many sidebars, quiz questions, page foldouts, and double-page spreads. (Rev: BL 8/97; SLJ 1/98) [629.04]

21288 Pluckrose, Henry. *On the Move* (PS–1). Illus. 1998, Watts LB $18.00 (0-531-14497-6). 32pp. Machines that help people travel — such as bicycles, cars, buses, ferries, streetcars, airplanes, and wheelchairs — are introduced in full-page color photos and a simple text. (Rev: BL 12/1/98; HBG 3/99) [629.04]

21289 Tong, Willabel L. *Cars, Boats, Trains, and Planes* (PS). Illus. by Jeff Cummins. 1998, Orchard $12.95 (0-531-30058-7). In this interactive book, all kinds of transportation vehicles pop-out at the reader. (Rev: BL 1/1–15/99) [629.04]

21290 Wilson, Anthony. *The Dorling Kindersley Visual Timeline of Transportation* (4–8). Illus. 1995, DK $16.95 (1-56458-880-7). 48pp. A history of transportation from prehistory to possible future developments. (Rev: BL 12/15/95; SLJ 1/96) [629.04]

Automobiles and Trucks

21291 Barton, Byron. *Trucks* (PS). Illus. by author. 1986, HarperCollins LB $15.89 (0-690-04530-1).

32pp. Bright colors and simple text describe the role of trucks. (Rev: BL 8/86; SLJ 9/86)

21292 Bingham, Caroline. *Big Book of Rescue Vehicles* (PS–3). Illus. 2000, DK $14.95 (0-7894-5454-8). 32pp. An oversize picture book that features such vehicles as fire engines, ambulances, rescue helicopters, lifeboats, and airport fire trucks. (Rev: BL 4/15/00; HBG 10/00) [629.04]

21293 Bingham, Caroline. *Big Rig: And Other Massive Machines* (K–3). Illus. Series: Mighty Machines. 1996, DK $9.95 (0-7894-0575-X). 21pp. Eight examples of large machinery and vehicles are used in a series of double-page spreads. (Rev: BL 6/1–15/96; SLJ 7/96) [629.224]

21294 Bingham, Caroline. *Fire Truck* (PS–4). Illus. Series: Mighty Machines. 1995, DK paper $9.95 (0-7894-0212-2). 21pp. A large-size picture book that supplies fascinating facts and pictures about all kinds of fire trucks. (Rev: BL 12/1/95; SLJ 3/96) [628.9]

21295 Bingham, Caroline. *Monster Machines* (PS–1). Illus. 1998, DK $14.95 (0-7894-2796-6). 32pp. Double-page spreads feature such monster machines as tow trucks, tractors, jumbo jets, fire engines, and tractor trailers. (Rev: BL 4/1/98; HBG 10/98) [621.8]

21296 Bingham, Caroline. *Race Car* (PS–3). Illus. Series: Mighty Machines. 1996, DK $9.95 (0-7894-0574-1). 21pp. In a large-size format with lots of visual details, this account introduces special vehicles, how they work, and how powerful they are. (Rev: BL 6/1–15/96) [629.222]

21297 Boucher, Jerry. *Fire Truck Nuts and Bolts* (K–3). Illus. 1993, Carolrhoda LB $22.60 (0-87614-783-X); paper $5.95 (0-87614-619-1). 40pp. An examination of the construction of a fire truck and its many parts. (Rev: BL 11/1/93; SLJ 12/93) [629.255]

21298 Butterfield, Moira. *Bulldozers* (3–8). Illus. Series: Look Inside Cross-Sections. 1995, DK $5.95 (0-7894-0012-X). 32pp. In several richly illustrated double-page spreads, the inner and outer sections of the bulldozer and its parts are introduced along with technical data. (Rev: BL 8/95) [629.225]

21299 Eick, Jean. *Dump Trucks* (PS). Illus. Series: Big Machines at Work. 1999, Child's World LB $13.95 (1-56766-526-8). 32pp. Using many double-page spreads, this work explains the main parts of a dump truck and its functions, particularly in construction. (Rev: BL 4/15/99; HBG 10/99; SLJ 6/99) [732.1]

21300 Eick, Jean. *Forklifts* (PS). Illus. Series: Big Machines at Work. 1999, Child's World LB $13.95 (1-56766-530-6). 32pp. Color photographs and double-page spreads introduce forklifts and the jobs they do. (Rev: BL 4/15/99; HBG 10/99; SLJ 6/99) [621.8]

21301 Eick, Jean. *Garbage Trucks* (PS). Series: Big Machines at Work. 1999, Child's World LB $13.95 (1-56766-528-4). 32pp. This well-illustrated book explores the world of garbage trucks — how they are constructed and how they work. (Rev: BL 4/15/98; HBG 10/99) [629]

21302 Guttmacher, Peter. *Jeep* (4–6). Illus. Series: Those Daring Machines. 1995, Macmillan LB $17.95 (0-89686-830-3). 48pp. A history of this vehicle and its evolution into today's popular sports automobile. (Rev: BL 2/15/95) [629]

21303 Italia, Bob. *Great Auto Makers and Their Cars* (4–6). Illus. 1993, Oliver LB $18.95 (1-881508-08-0). 160pp. The founders of ten automobile companies — like Henry Ford, Horace Dodge, Karl Benz, Soichiro Honda, and Ferruccio Lamborghini — are profiled with details on the obstacles they overcame. (Rev: SLJ 11/93) [629.2]

21304 Johnstone, Michael. *Cars* (3–8). Illus. 1994, DK paper $5.95 (1-56458-681-2). 32pp. Inner and outer details of a wide selection of European and American cars are pictured, ranging from the Model T to the Jeep and Ferrari. (Rev: BL 2/1/95; SLJ 2/95) [629]

21305 McKenna, A. T. *Corvette* (5–7). Series: Ultimate Car. 2000, ABDO LB $15.95 (1-57765-127-8). 32pp. This introduction to this famous sports car includes material on its design, construction, and records it has broken. Similar material appears in companion books *Ferrari*, *Mustang*, and *Porsche* (all 2000). (Rev: BL 3/1/01) [629]

21306 McKenna, A. T. *Jaguar* (5–7). Illus. Series: Ultimate Car. 2000, ABDO LB $15.95 (1-57765-122-7). 32pp. This book traces the history of the Jaguar from 1921 to 2000 with emphasis on current models and how they are made. Also use *Lamborghini* (2000). (Rev: BL 1/1–15/01) [629.222]

21307 Marston, Hope I. *Fire Trucks* (2–5). Illus. 1996, Dutton $15.99 (0-525-65231-0). 48pp. All sorts of fire fighting equipment are introduced in text and color photographs. (Rev: BL 10/15/96; SLJ 9/96) [628.9]

21308 Maurer, Tracy. *License Plates* (3–5). Series: The Rourke Guide to State Symbols. 1999, Rourke LB $19.45 (1-57103-298-3). 48pp. In addition to showing three or four historic and modern license plates for each state, this book includes a few interesting facts and the state motto. (Rev: SLJ 2/00) [629.2]

21309 Mitchell, Joyce Slayton. *Crashed, Smashed, and Mashed* (1–3). Illus. by Steven Borns. 2001, Tricycle Pr. $14.95 (1-58246-034-5). 32pp. Photos and text show an automobile junkyard and describe what happens to old cars when they are recycled. (Rev: BL 3/15/01) [629.2]

21310 Mitchell, Joyce Slayton. *Tractor-Trailer Trucker: A Powerful Truck Book* (2–5). Illus. 2000, Tricycle Pr. $14.95 (1-58246-010-8). 40pp. Written like a manual, this book gives detailed instructions on how to drive and care for a big rig. (Rev: BL 4/1/00; HBG 10/00; SLJ 8/00) [629.2844]

21311 Otfinoski, Steven. *Around the Track: Race Cars Then and Now* (2–4). Series: Here We Go! 1997, Benchmark LB $21.36 (0-7614-0608-5). 32pp. A colorful introduction to race cars, including Grand Prix cars, dragsters, carts, and a few of historical importance. (Rev: HBG 3/98; SLJ 4/98) [629.2]

21312 Otfinoski, Steven. *Behind the Wheel: Cars Then and Now* (2–4). Illus. Series: Here We Go! 1996, Benchmark LB $22.79 (0-7614-0403-1). 32pp. A simple text and spectacular photos are used to give a brief history of cars — past, present, and future. (Rev: SLJ 2/97) [629.27]

21313 Otfinoski, Steven. *To the Rescue: Fire Trucks Then and Now* (1–3). Illus. Series: Here We Go! 1996, Benchmark LB $22.79 (0-7614-0406-6). 32pp. A well-illustrated history of fire trucks, from the horse-drawn ones of yesteryear to the fast, efficient trucks of today. (Rev: SLJ 6/97) [628.9]

21314 Raby, Philip. *Racing Cars* (5–8). Series: Need for Speed. 1999, Lerner LB $17.95 (0-8225-2487-2). 32pp. Using an attention-getting format with plenty of color, action photographs, and sidebars, (called stat and fact files), this book covers such topics as Le Mans, dragsters, the Camel T, dune buggies, and carting. (Rev: BL 1/1–15/00; HBG 3/00; SLJ 2/00) [623.8]

21315 Relf, Patricia. *Tonka Trucks Night and Day* (PS–2). Illus. by Thomas La Padula. 2000, Scholastic $12.95 (0-439-12196-5). 35pp. This book of trucks covers vehicles that are found on a farm, ones that are used for moving, and those that are found at an airport. (Rev: HBG 10/00; SLJ 9/00) [629.24]

21316 Robbins, Ken. *Trucks* (PS–2). Illus. 1999, Simon & Schuster $16.00 (0-689-82664-8). 32pp. This book highlights the massive 18-wheelers known as "big rigs" and describes the work of their drivers. (Rev: BCCB 12/99; BL 9/15/99; HB 9–10/99; HBG 3/00) [629.224]

21317 Savage, Jeff. *Demolition Derby* (3–6). Illus. Series: Action Events. 1996, Crestwood LB $14.95 (0-89686-891-5); paper $4.95 (0-382-39294-9). 48pp. Large action photos are used to convey the thrills of this event, which also highlights car designs and builders and members of the driver's team. Also use *Monster Trucks* and *Trucks and Tractor Pullers* (both 1996). (Rev: SLJ 2/97) [629.23]

21318 Schaefer, Margaret A. *Let's Build a Car* (3–5). Illus. by Patrick T. McRae. 1992, Ideals paper $4.95 (0-8249-8536-2). 32pp. Every page shows a step in car production. (Rev: BL 12/1/90) [629.23]

21319 Simon, Seymour. *Seymour Simon's Book of Trucks* (K–4). 2000, HarperCollins LB $15.89 (0-06-028481-1). A highly appealing book that contains pictures and information on a large number of trucks and the various jobs they do. (Rev: HBG 10/00; SLJ 7/00) [629.28]

21320 Simonds, Christopher. *The Model T Ford* (5–7). Illus. Series: Turning Points. 1991, Silver Burdett LB $17.95 (0-382-24122-3); paper $11.00 (0-382-24117-7). 64pp. The invention and development of the Model T and its impact on America. (Rev: BL 1/15/92) [629.222]

21321 Somerville, Louisa. *Rescue Vehicles* (3–8). Illus. Series: Look Inside Cross-Sections. 1995, DK $5.95 (1-56458-879-3). 32pp. In a series of double-page spreads, different kinds of emergency vehicles are pictured, with detailed diagrams of their interiors and how they work. (Rev: BL 8/95) [629.04]

21322 Steele, Philip. *Cars and Trucks* (3–4). Illus. Series: Pocket Facts. 1991, Macmillan $15.95 (0-89686-521-5). 32pp. An illustrated compendium of basic facts about cars and trucks. (Rev: SLJ 9/91) [629.28]

21323 Stille, Darlene R. *Trucks* (2–4). Series: True Books. 1997, Children's LB $22.00 (0-516-20343-6). 48pp. A simple but informative guide to various kinds of trucks and their uses with a list of places, including Web sites, to get further information. (Rev: BL 9/15/97) [629.24]

21324 Sturges, Philemon. *I Love Trucks!* (PS). Illus. by Shari Halpern. 1999, HarperCollins $12.95 (0-06-027819-6). 32pp. A number of trucks in action are pictured in this simple introduction. (Rev: BCCB 3/99; BL 2/1/99; HBG 10/99; SLJ 3/99) [629.224]

21325 Walker, Sloan, and Andrew Vasey. *The Only Other Crazy Car Book* (3–6). Illus. 1984, Walker LB $11.85 (0-8027-6517-3). 48pp. There is usually one "oddball" auto to a page, including origins and special features, such as the "Roach Coach," which looks like a giant insect.

21326 Whitman, Sylvia. *Get Up and Go! The History of American Road Travel* (5–8). Illus. 1996, Lerner LB $22.60 (0-8225-1735-3). 88pp. From primitive pathways to modern superhighways, this is a history of American roads and the vehicles that traveled them. (Rev: BL 10/15/96; SLJ 10/96) [388.1]

Railroads

21327 Anderson, Peter. *The Transcontinental Railroad* (3–5). Illus. Series: Cornerstones of Freedom. 1996, Children's LB $20.50 (0-516-06635-8). 30pp. The story of building the transcontinental railroad, its many tragedies, and final triumph, with numerous illustrations. (Rev: BL 8/96) [385]

21328 Barton, Byron. *Trains* (PS). Illus. by author. 1986, HarperCollins LB $14.89 (0-690-04534-4). 32pp. Explaining the role of trains for the youngest readers. (Rev: BL 8/86; SLJ 9/86)

21329 *Big Book of Trains: National Railway Museum, York, England* (3–5). Illus. 1998, DK $14.95 (0-7894-3436-9). 32pp. This book begins with the early steam locomotives in England and America and ends with today's bullet trains and monorails. In addition to highlighting in pictures 50 different trains, there is a pullout section on the Channel Tunnel. (Rev: BL 1/1–15/99; HBG 3/99) [625.1]

21330 Collicutt, Paul. *This Train* (PS). Illus. by author. 1999, Farrar $15.00 (0-374-37493-7). Different kinds of trains from different countries are introduced in a very simple text and colorful pictures. (Rev: HBG 3/00; SLJ 10/99) [625.2]

21331 Crews, Donald. *Freight Train* (PS–K). Illus. by author. 1978, Greenwillow $15.93 (0-688-84165-1); Morrow paper $5.95 (0-688-11701-5). 32pp. A description in text and pictures of the vari-

ous cars included in a freight train, from engine to caboose.

21332 Gallimard Jeunesse. *Trains* (PS–2). Illus. Series: First Discovery. 1998, Scholastic $11.95 (0-590-38156-3). 24pp. This colorful book uses a number of overlays to answer basic questions about a variety of trains. (Rev: BL 9/15/98; HBG 10/98) [625.1]

21333 Gibbons, Gail. *Trains* (PS–1). Illus. by author. 1987, Holiday LB $16.95 (0-8234-0640-7); paper $6.95 (0-8234-0699-7). 32pp. Describing the essentials of train transportation. (Rev: BL 5/1/87; SLJ 5/87)

21334 Johnstone, Michael. *Look Inside Cross-Sections: Trains* (3–8). Illus. Series: Look Inside Cross-Sections. 1995, DK paper $6.95 (0-7894-0319-6). 32pp. Cross-sectional drawings with descriptive text are given for ten past and present locomotives. (Rev: BL 9/15/95) [625.1]

21335 Kay, Verla. *Iron Horses* (K–4). Illus. by Michael McCurdy. 1999, Putnam $15.99 (0-399-23119-6). 32pp. In double-page spreads, illustrated with scratchboard drawings, this picture book portrays the labor, hardships, and excitement of constructing the transcontinental railroad. (Rev: BCCB 7–8/99; BL 6/1–15/99; HB 7–8/99; HBG 10/99; SLJ 7/99) [625.4]

21336 Levinson, Nancy S. *She's Been Working on the Railroad* (5–8). Illus. 1997, Dutton $16.99 (0-525-67545-0). 96pp. A history of women's roles as railway workers, including the famous Harvey Girls of the late 1800s. (Rev: BL 9/15/97; HBG 3/98; SLJ 12/97) [331.4]

21337 McNeese, Tim. *America's First Railroads* (4–8). Illus. by Chris Duke. Series: Americans on the Move. 1993, Macmillan $11.95 (0-89686-729-3). 48pp. A history of early railroads and their impact on U.S. history. (Rev: SLJ 8/93) [385]

21338 Murphy, Jim. *Across America on an Emigrant Train* (5–8). Illus. 1993, Clarion $17.00 (0-395-63390-7). 150pp. The cross-country train trip by Robert Louis Stevenson in 1879 is used to present material about the history of railroads. (Rev: BCCB 1/94; BL 12/1/93; SLJ 12/93*) [828]

21339 O'Brien, Patrick. *Steam, Smoke, and Steel: Back in Time with Trains* (K–2). Illus. 2000, Charlesbridge $16.95 (0-88106-969-8); paper $6.95 (0-88106-972-8). 32pp. A boy describes the different trains driven by six generations of his family in this history of railroads and trains. (Rev: BL 7/00; HBG 3/01; SLJ 8/00) [385]

21340 Otfinoski, Steven. *Riding the Rails: Trains Then and Now* (1–3). Illus. Series: Here We Go! 1996, Benchmark LB $22.79 (0-7614-0404-X). 32pp. A copiously illustrated history of trains, with material on how they have evolved through the years. (Rev: SLJ 6/97) [625.4]

21341 Petty, Kate. *Some Trains Run on Water: And Other Amazing Facts About Rail Transportation* (1–3). Illus. by Ross Walton and Jo Moore. Series: I Didn't Know That. 1997, Millbrook LB $19.90 (0-7613-0609-9). 32pp. Strange-but-true facts involving trains, past and present, presented with several projects that don't require adult supervision. (Rev: HBG 10/98; SLJ 3/98) [625.2]

21342 Smith, E. Boyd. *The Railroad Book* (2–4). Illus. by author. 1984, Houghton $18.95 (0-395-34832-3). 56pp. An introduction to railroads via a book originally published in 1913.

21343 Steele, Philip. *Trains* (3–4). Illus. Series: Pocket Facts. 1991, Macmillan LB $15.95 (0-89686-523-1). 32pp. The history of trains plus material on parts, bridges, subways, and the English Channel tunnel. (Rev: SLJ 9/91) [625.2]

21344 Stille, Darlene R. *Trains* (2–4). Illus. Series: True Books. 1997, Children's LB $22.00 (0-516-20342-8). 48pp. A history of railroading is followed by a description of various trains, how they operate, and the men who work on them. (Rev: BL 9/15/97) [625.1]

21345 Weitzman, David. *Locomotive: Building an Eight-Wheeler* (4–6). Illus. by author. 1999, Houghton $16.00 (0-395-69687-9). A handsome picture book that chronicles the two days involved in the production of a wood-burning, eight-wheeled locomotive in 1870. (Rev: HBG 3/00; SLJ 11/99) [625.1]

21346 Yancey, Diane. *Camels for Uncle Sam* (4–7). Illus. 1995, Hendrick-Long $15.95 (0-937460-91-5). 92pp. The story of the experiment to import camels to the Southwest in the 1850s to help in railroad construction. (Rev: BL 9/15/95) [357]

21347 Young, Robert. *The Transcontinental Railroad: America at Its Best?* (4–6). Illus. Series: Both Sides. 1997, Dillon LB $18.95 (0-87518-611-4). 72pp. Various point of view — including those of the workers, business people, and American Indians — are included in this history of the transcontinental railroad. (Rev: BL 9/15/97) [385]

Ships, Boats, and Lighthouses

21348 Adams, Simon. *Titanic* (3–8). Illus. Series: Eyewitness Books. 1999, DK $15.95 (0-7894-4724-X). 60pp. Each double-page spread deals with a different aspect of the *Titanic,* including its construction, accommodations, and the collision. (Rev: BL 11/15/99; HBG 3/00) [910]

21349 Asimov, Isaac, and Elizabeth Kaplan. *How Do Big Ships Float?* (K–3). Illus. Series: Ask Isaac Asimov. 1992, Stevens LB $21.27 (0-8368-0802-9). 24pp. This book explains simply how gravity and buoyancy keep ships afloat. (Rev: BL 6/1–15/93) [623.4]

21350 Ballard, Robert D., and Rick Archbold. *Ghost Liners* (4–7). Illus. 1998, Little, Brown $18.95 (0-316-08020-9). 64pp. This book chronicles the exploration of five 20th-century shipwrecks, including the *Titanic,* the *Empress of Ireland,* the *Lusitania,* the *Britannic,* and the *Andrea Doria.* (Rev: BL 8/98; HBG 3/99; SLJ 9/98) [910.4]

21351 Barton, Byron. *Boats* (PS). Illus. by author. 1986, HarperCollins LB $14.89 (0-690-04536-0). 32pp. Recreational and functional roles of boats are explained in simple text and bright colors. (Rev: BL 8/86; SLJ 9/86)

21352 *Boats* (PS–3). Illus. Series: First Discovery. 1993, Scholastic $12.95 (0-590-47131-7). 24pp. A book for small children that introduces boats from around the world and explains their differences. (Rev: BL 1/1/94) [623.8]

21353 *Boats and Ships* (4–6). Illus. 1996, Scholastic $19.95 (0-590-47647-5). 48pp. Transparencies, flaps, and windows are used to introduce various ships and boats. (Rev: BL 12/15/96) [623]

21354 Bornhoft, Simon. *High Speed Boats* (5–8). Series: Need for Speed. 1999, Lerner LB $17.95 (0-8225-2488-0). 32pp. Using a jazzy, attention-getting format with action photos, side bars for statistics and interesting facts, and different type sizes, this book covers speed boats from the present and future. (Rev: BL 1/1–15/00; HBG 3/00) [629.222]

21355 Butterfield, Moira. *Ships* (3–6). Illus. Series: Look Inside Cross-Sections. 1994, DK paper $5.95 (1-56458-521-2). 32pp. Cross-sections of a variety of ships are shown, including the sunken *Mary Rose* (1545), an old Chinese junk, a fishing trawler, and a World War II aircraft carrier. (Rev: BL 10/15/94; SLJ 9/94) [623.8]

21356 Collicutt, Paul. *This Boat* (PS–3). Illus. 2001, Farrar $15.00 (0-374-37495-3). 32pp. A number of different boats are presented in this picture book, including sailboats, paddle-powered riverboats, a submarine, and an aircraft carrier. (Rev: BL 3/15/01) [623.8]

21357 Delgado, James P. *Wrecks of American Warships* (5–7). Series: Shipwrecks. 2000, Watts LB $24.00 (0-531-20376-X). 64pp. This book describes how underwater archaeologists have discovered and explored such warships as the *Constitution, Philadelphia, Alabama,* and *Arizona.* (Rev: BL 10/15/00) [623.8]

21358 Gibbons, Gail. *Beacons of Light: Lighthouses* (1–3). Illus. 1990, Morrow $15.95 (0-688-07379-4). 32pp. The development of the lighthouse from a hilltop bonfire to the electronic wonders of today. (Rev: BCCB 3/90; BL 2/15/90; HB 3–4/90; SLJ 4/90) [387.1]

21359 Graham, Ian. *Boats, Ships, Submarines and Other Floating Machinery* (4–7). Illus. Series: How Things Work. 1993, Kingfisher paper $6.95 (1-85697-867-2). 40pp. This book explains such scientific principles as wind power and buoyancy and how they apply to a wide range of crafts, including hydrofoils and hovercrafts. (Rev: BL 6/1–15/93; SLJ 5/93) [623.8]

21360 Guiberson, Brenda Z. *Lighthouses: Watchers at Sea* (3–6). Illus. 1995, Holt $15.95 (0-8050-3170-7). 70pp. A history of lighthouses, including their construction, uses, and some exciting stories connected with them. (Rev: BCCB 12/95; BL 11/1/95; SLJ 1/96) [387.1]

21361 Hubble, Richard. *Ships: Sailors and the Sea* (3–6). Illus. Series: Timelines. 1991, Watts $13.95 (0-531-15234-0). 48pp. Includes cutaway views of such ships as the *Titanic* and a modern destroyer. (Rev: BL 12/15/91; SLJ 3/92) [387.2]

21362 Kent, Deborah. *The Titanic* (3–5). Illus. Series: Cornerstones of Freedom. 1993, Children's

LB $20.50 (0-516-06672-2). 32pp. A slim volume with illustrations on each page that describes the building and voyage of the ocean liner. (Rev: BL 2/1/94; SLJ 3/94) [910.9]

21363 Landau, Elaine. *Maritime Disasters* (5–7). Illus. Series: Watts Library. 1999, Watts LB $24.00 (0-531-20344-1); paper $8.95 (0-531-16427-6). 64pp. This book discusses four major maritime disasters: the *Titanic, Lusitania, Morro Castle,* and *Andrea Doria.* (Rev: BL 2/1/00; SLJ 2/00) [910.4]

21364 Lewis, Thomas P. *Clipper Ship* (1–3). Illus. by Joan Sandin. 1992, HarperCollins paper $3.95 (0-06-444160-1). 64pp. An easily read account of our sailing ships.

21365 Lincoln, Margarette. *Amazing Boats* (1–4). Illus. by Mike Dunning. Series: Eyewitness Juniors. 1992, Knopf paper $7.99 (0-679-82770-6). 32pp. What a boat is and what it can do, followed by large photos that show various kinds of boats and ships, plus a text with good general information. (Rev: BL 11/1/92) [623.8]

21366 Maass, Robert. *Tugboats* (1–3). Photos by author. 1997, Holt $15.95 (0-8050-3116-2). This introduction to tugboats explains their types and functions. (Rev: SLJ 5/97) [387.2]

21367 Macaulay, David. *Ship* (4–8). Illus. 1993, Houghton $19.95 (0-395-52439-3). 96pp. Using a fictional 1504 caravel as subject matter, details the parts of the ship and the work undertaken to explore its sunken remains. (Rev: BCCB 11/93; BL 10/15/93; SLJ 11/93) [387.2]

21368 McCurdy, Michael. *The Sailor's Alphabet* (3–6). Illus. 1998, Houghton $16.00 (0-395-84167-4). 32pp. A picture book for older readers in which parts of a 19th-century ship are used to introduce letters of the alphabet. (Rev: BCCB 6/98; BL 4/15/98; HBG 10/98; SLJ 5/98) [387.2]

21369 McNeese, Tim. *Clippers and Whaling Ships* (4–8). Illus. by Chris Duke. Series: Americans on the Move. 1993, Macmillan $16.95 (0-89686-735-8). 48pp. Early American shipping and commerce are discussed. Also use: *West by Steamboat* (1993). (Rev: SLJ 8/93) [623.8]

21370 Maestro, Betsy, and Giulio Maestro. *Ferryboat* (PS–1). Illus. by Giulio Maestro. 1986, HarperCollins LB $15.89 (0-690-04520-4). 32pp. The story of ferryboats, centered around one river crossing. (Rev: BCCB 7–8/86; BL 6/15/86; HB 5–6/86)

21371 Otfinoski, Steven. *Into the Wind: Sailboats Then and Now* (2–4). Illus. Series: Here We Go! 1996, Benchmark LB $22.79 (0-7614-0405-8). 32pp. This simple, well-illustrated account gives a history of sailboats and shows many types and sizes from all over the world, with details on their important features. (Rev: HB 9–10/96; SLJ 2/97) [623.8]

21372 Platt, Richard. *Shipwreck* (4–8). Series: Eyewitness Books. 1997, Knopf LB $20.99 (0-679-98569-X). 60pp. An overview of the causes and consequences of the world's most famous maritime disasters. (Rev: BL 12/15/97) [363]

21373 Platt, Richard. *Stephen Biesty's Cross-Sections Man-of-War* (4–7). Illus. by Stephen Biesty. Series: Incredible Cross-Sections. 1993, DK $16.95

(1-56458-321-X). 32pp. From stem to stern, this is a tour, both inside and outside, of an 18th-century British man-of-war. (Rev: BCCB 1/94; BL 10/1/93; SLJ 1/94*) [359.1]

21374 Purcell, Cindy. *From Glass to Boat* (3–6). Series: Changes. 1997, Children's LB $24.00 (0-516-20736-9). 32pp. This photo-essay shows the process of producing a fiberglass boat with many activities that allow the reader to participate. (Rev: BL 2/15/98; HBG 10/98) [387.2]

21375 Rotner, Shelley. *Boats Afloat* (PS–K). Illus. 1998, Orchard $15.95 (0-531-30112-5). 32pp. Colorful photographs introduce various types of boats to very young children. (Rev: BL 11/1/98; HBG 3/99; SLJ 11/98) [623.8]

21376 *Sailing Ships: A Lift-the-Flap Discovery* (3–6). Illus. by Thomas Bayley. 1998, Orchard $16.95 (0-531-30065-X). This interactive book contains fold-outs of many sailing ships including the *Mayflower* and the *Santa Maria.* (Rev: BL 1/1–15/99; HBG 10/98) [623.8]

21377 Schaefer, Lola M. *Tugboats* (1–3). Series: Transportation Library. 2000, Bridgestone LB $15.93 (0-7368-0505-2). 24pp. A simple description of tugboats, what they do, their parts, and how they operate. (Rev: HBG 10/00; SLJ 8/00) [387.2]

21378 Sloan, Frank. *Titanic.* Rev. ed. (4–6). Illus. Series: First Books. 1998, Raintree Steck-Vaughn $25.69 (0-8172-4091-8). 128pp. This revised edition includes material on passengers' lifestyles, details on the sinking, and efforts to investigate the wreckage some 60 years after the disaster. (Rev: BL 9/1/98; HBG 10/99; SLJ 2/99) [363.12]

21379 Wilkinson, Phillip. *Ships* (4–7). Illus. 2000, Kingfisher $16.95 (0-7534-5280-4). 64pp. Straightforward text and handsome illustrations cover maritime history from the earliest sailing ships and discuss piracy, the slave trade, and superstitions about the sea. (Rev: BL 2/1/01; SLJ 1/01) [623.8]

Weapons, Submarines, and the Armed Forces

21380 Baker, David. *Future Fighters* (4–8). Illus. Series: Military Aircraft. 1989, Rourke LB $18.60 (0-86592-535-6). 48pp. Possible future fighter planes are featured in illustrations and brief text. Also use: *Navy Strike Planes* (1989). (Rev: SLJ 1/90) [358.4]

21381 Day, Malcolm. *The World of Castles and Forts* (4–6). Illus. 1997, Bedrick LB $19.95 (0-87226-278-2). 46pp. This account provides a world history of fortifications, from ancient walled cities to the Maginot Line to nuclear defenses. (Rev: BL 3/1/97; SLJ 2/97) [355.7]

21382 Ferrell, Nancy Warren. *The U.S. Air Force* (4–8). Illus. 1990, Lerner LB $23.93 (0-8225-1433-8). 72pp. This book includes coverage on how to enlist, the ranking system in the Air Force, and today's use of modern technology. (Rev: BL 5/15/91) [358.4]

21383 Ferrell, Nancy Warren. *The U.S. Coast Guard* (4–8). Illus. 1989, Lerner LB $23.93 (0-8225-1431-1). 72pp. History, duties, and opportunities in this story of an arm of the U.S. military. (Rev: BL 5/1/89)

21384 Gartman, Gene. *Life in Army Basic Training* (4–6). Illus. Series: On Duty. 2000, Children's LB $19.00 (0-516-23347-5); paper $6.95 (0-516-23547-8). 48pp. Written by a man who served in the military, this book goes through the routines and demands of basic training with information on weapons and various fitness programs. (Rev: BL 2/1/01) [355.5]

21385 Gilbert, Adrian. *Arms and Armor* (4–8). Illus. by James Field. Series: Then and Now. 1997, Millbrook LB $21.90 (0-7613-0605-6). 32pp. From bows and arrows to missiles and rockets, this is a history of weapons through the ages, presented in double-page spreads with many color drawings and photos. (Rev: HBG 10/98; SLJ 4/98) [355]

21386 Gonen, Rivka. *Charge! Weapons and Warfare in Ancient Times* (5–8). Illus. 1993, Lerner LB $23.93 (0-8225-3201-8). 72pp. Traces the development of weapons from the sticks and stones of cave dwellers to those used in later warfare, like battering rams. (Rev: BCCB 12/93; BL 2/1/94; SLJ 2/94) [355.8]

21387 Hamilton, John. *Weapons of War: A Pictorial History of the Past One Thousand Years* (4–7). Illus. Series: The Millennium. 2000, ABDO $16.95 (1-57765-362-9). 48pp. In a short space, this book traces 1,000 years of weapons including small weaponry, ships, firearms, military airplanes, tanks, missiles, and bombs. (Rev: BL 7/00; HBG 10/00; SLJ 10/00) [623.4]

21388 Holmes, Richard. *Battle* (4–8). Illus. Series: Eyewitness Books. 1995, Knopf LB $20.99 (0-679-97333-8). 64pp. Dramatic illustrations introduce warfare and its consequences. (Rev: BL 12/15/95) [355]

21389 Hughes, Libby. *West Point* (4–6). Illus. Series: Places in American History. 1993, Macmillan LB $18.95 (0-87518-529-0). 72pp. The story of the military academy founded in 1802 and of the life of cadets trained there. (Rev: BL 4/15/93; SLJ 7/93) [355]

21390 Humble, Richard. *A World War Two Submarine* (3–6). Illus. by Mark Bergin. Series: Inside Story. 1991, Bedrick LB $26.50 (0-87226-351-7). 48pp. This account explores the design, construction, and parts of a World War II submarine. (Rev: BL 12/1/91; SLJ 1/92) [359.9]

21391 Keeler, Barbara, and Don Keeler. *Sailing Ship Eagle* (3–5). Illus. Series: Those Daring Machines. 1995, Macmillan paper $5.95 (0-382-24751-5). 48pp. A brief look at the construction and exploits of the U.S. Coast Guard ship. (Rev: BL 2/15/95) [359.9]

21392 Kennedy, Robert C. *Life as a Paratrooper* (4–7). Series: On Duty. 2000, Children's LB $19.00 (0-516-23344-0). 48pp. An easily read account that describes the work, responsibilities, and opportuni-

ties of a paratrooper. Also use: *Life as an Air Force Fighter Pilot* (2000). (Rev: BL 3/1/01) [358.4]

21393 Kennedy, Robert C. *Life as an Army Demolition Expert* (4–6). Illus. Series: On Duty. 2000, Children's LB $19.00 (0-516-23346-7); paper $6.95 (0-516-23546-7). 48pp. This work gives historical background plus an explanation of work today in this specialized area of the U.S. Army. (Rev: BL 2/1/01) [358]

21394 Kennedy, Robert C. *Life in the Army Special Forces* (4–7). Series: On Duty. 2000, Children's LB $19.00 (0-516-23350-5). 48pp. The work, responsibilities, and career possibilities of members of this special army unit are described in this well-illustrated book. (Rev: BL 3/1/01; SLJ 3/01) [335]

21395 Kennedy, Robert C. *Life in the Marines* (4–7). Series: On Duty. 2000, Children's LB $19.00 (0-516-23348-3). 48pp. This branch of the military is examined with material on the special training and responsibilities involved. (Rev: BL 3/1/01) [359.6]

21396 Kennedy, Robert C. *Life with the Navy Seals* (4–7). Series: On Duty. 2000, Children's LB $19.00 (0-516-23351-3). 48pp. This special branch of the U.S. Navy is examined with material on its responsibilities, training, and career opportunities. (Rev: BL 3/1/01) [359]

21397 Meltzer, Milton. *Weapons and Warfare: From the Stone Age to the Space Age* (5–8). Illus. 1996, HarperCollins LB $16.89 (0-06-024876-9). 96pp. Describes the evolution of weapons from clubs to the H-bomb, including how these weapons have been used and misused through the ages. (Rev: BCCB 2/97; BL 12/1/96; SLJ 1/97) [355.02]

21398 Moran, Tom. *The U.S. Army* (4–8). Illus. 1990, Lerner LB $23.93 (0-8225-1434-6). 88pp. A solid overview of the development of the U.S. Army. (Rev: BL 1/1/91) [335]

21399 Payan, Gregory, and Alexander Guelke. *Life on a Submarine* (4–6). Illus. Series: On Duty. 2000, Children's LB $19.00 (0-516-23349-1); paper $6.95 (0-516-23549-4). 48pp. The glamorous and arduous aspects of life aboard a navy submarine are covered, including exercise and sleeping arrangements. (Rev: BL 2/1/01) [359.9]

21400 Pelta, Kathy. *The U.S. Navy* (5–7). Illus. 1990, Lerner LB $23.93 (0-8225-1435-4). 88pp. History and present status and activities of the U.S. Navy. (Rev: BL 12/1/90) [359]

21401 Reef, Catherine. *Black Fighting Men: A Proud History* (4–8). Illus. Series: African American Soldiers. 1994, Twenty-First Century LB $17.90 (0-8050-3106-5). 80pp. A general overview of the contributions that African Americans have made in the armed services. (Rev: BL 9/15/94; SLJ 11/94) [355]

21402 Richie, Jason. *Weapons: Designing the Tools of War* (5–10). Illus. 2000, Oliver LB $19.95 (1-881508-60-9). 144pp. Using separate chapters for different categories of weapons — for example, submarines, battleships, and tanks — this is a history of the development of weaponry from 300 B.C. to today. (Rev: BL 5/1/00; HBG 10/00) [623]

21403 Robertshaw, Andrew. *A Soldier's Life: A Visual History of Soldiers Through the Ages* (4–7). Illus. 1997, Dutton $16.99 (0-525-67550-7). 48pp. Describes a soldier's uniform, equipment, and weapons through the ages, beginning with a Roman soldier in A.D. 50. (Rev: BCCB 6/97; BL 6/1–15/97; SLJ 6/97) [355.02]

21404 Rowan, N. R. *Women in the Marines: The Boot Camp Challenge* (4–8). Illus. Series: Armed Services. 1994, Lerner LB $23.93 (0-8225-1430-3). 72pp. Covers the harrowing basic training that women face in the Marines. (Rev: BCCB 4/94; BL 2/15/94; SLJ 4/94) [359.9]

21405 Schulson, Rachel. *Guns: What You Should Know* (1–3). Illus. by Mary Jones. 1997, Albert Whitman LB $13.95 (0-8075-3093-X). 24pp. An unbiased, appealing book that describes the parts of a gun, introduces different types, explains the destructive power of a bullet, and tells children what to do if they find a gun. (Rev: BL 10/15/97; HBG 3/98; SLJ 12/97) [363.3]

21406 Stein, R. Conrad. *The Manhattan Project* (3–5). Illus. Series: Cornerstones of Freedom. 1993, Children's LB $20.50 (0-516-06670-6). 32pp. The history of the development of the atomic bomb in this country, culminating in its use in World War II. (Rev: BL 11/1/93) [355.8]

21407 Warner, J. F. *The U.S. Marine Corps* (4–8). Illus. Series: Armed Services. 1991, Lerner LB $22.95 (0-8225-1432-X). 88pp. From how to enlist to a discussion of the new technology, this is a well-organized introduction to the U.S. Marine Corps. (Rev: BL 2/1/92; SLJ 2/92) [359.6]

21408 Weiss, Harvey. *Submarines and Other Underwater Craft* (3–7). Illus. 1990, HarperCollins LB $13.89 (0-690-04761-4). 64pp. A good history of submarines that explains many peacetime uses. (Rev: BCCB 6/90; BL 7/90; HB 7–8/90; SLJ 5/90) [359.3]

21409 Woods, Mary B., and Michael Woods. *Ancient Warfare: From Clubs to Catapults* (5–8). Series: Ancient Technologies. 2000, Runestone LB $25.26 (0-8225-2999-8). 96pp. The weaponry of ancient civilizations including Greece and China. (Rev: BCCB 12/00; BL 9/15/00; HBG 3/01) [623]

Recreation

Crafts

General and Miscellaneous

21410 Albregts, Lisa, and Elizabeth Cape. *Best Friends: Tons of Crazy, Cool Things to Do with Your Girlfriends* (4–8). 1998, Chicago Review paper $12.95 (1-55652-326-2). 160pp. Arranged by seasons, this activity book contains crafts, games, dances, snacks, and skits to amuse girls when they get together. (Rev: BL 3/1/99; SLJ 1/99) [796]

21411 Barnes, Emilie, et al. *The Very Best Christmas Ever! A Season of Fun for Girls* (2–5). Illus. by Michal Sparks. 1998, Harvest $14.99 (1-56507-905-1). 32pp. Many useful Christmas craft projects, including activities, recipes, patterns, and ornaments, are the highlight of this book, which also contains a brief story about a group of girls and their Christmas club. (Rev: SLJ 10/98) [745]

21412 Bastyra, Judy. *Fun Food* (1–4). Photos by Michael Michaels and Steve Shott. Illus. by Mei Lim. Series: First Craft Books. 1998, Carolrhoda LB $12.95 (1-57505-204-0). 22pp. This book contains ten projects, each involving three simple steps, that result in such goodies as an ice-cream clown or a shortbread house. (Rev: SLJ 4/98) [745]

21413 Birdseye, Tom. *A Kids' Guide to Building Forts* (5–8). Illus. by Bill Klein. 1993, Harbinger paper $10.95 (0-943173-69-8). 62pp. A guide to the building of 19 kinds of forts, from the very simple to the more complex, some of which can be turned into clubhouses. (Rev: SLJ 9/93) [745.5]

21414 Braman, Arlette N. *Create! The Best Crafts and Activities from Many Lands* (3–6). Illus. by Jo-Ellen Bosson. Series: Kids Around the World. 1999, Wiley paper $12.95 (0-471-29005-X). 116pp. From Amish quilts to Zulu woven baskets this craft book includes both ancient and modern crafts from a variety of cultures, all introduced with clear directions. (Rev: SLJ 12/99) [745]

21415 Bull, Jane. *Change Your Room* (4–8). Photos by Andy Crawford. 1999, DK $14.95 (0-7894-

3956-5). 96pp. A series of inventive projects are outlined for pre- and young teens who want to redecorate their rooms without extensive remodeling. (Rev: HBG 3/00; SLJ 10/99) [745]

21416 Caney, Steven. *Steven Caney's Playbook* (3–5). Illus. 1975, Workman paper $9.95 (0-911104-38-0). 240pp. All sorts of activities involving discarded or inexpensive materials, thoroughly and clearly presented.

21417 Carlson, Laurie. *EcoArt! Earth-Friendly Art and Craft Experiences for 3- to 9-Year-Olds* (K–4). Illus. by Loretta Braren. 1993, Williamson paper $12.95 (0-913589-68-3). 160pp. Over 100 arts and crafts activities using natural, recyclable, or reusable materials. (Rev: BL 2/15/93; SLJ 4/93) [745.5]

21418 Castaldo, Nancy Fusco. *Rainy Day Play! Explore, Create, Discover, Pretend* (PS–1). Illus. by Loretta Braren. Series: A Little Hands Book. 1996, Williamson paper $12.95 (1-885593-00-7). 142pp. A collection of 64 ideas for activities, crafts, and games that are attractively presented and will afford hours of enjoyment. (Rev: SLJ 2/97) [745.5]

21419 Chapman, Gillian, and Pam Robson. *Art from Fabric: With Projects Using Rags, Old Clothing and Remnants* (3–5). Illus. Series: Salvaged! 1995, Thomson Learning LB $21.40 (1-56847-381-8). 32pp. This book contains several creative projects and crafts using old fabrics or fibers, on double-page spreads. (Rev: SLJ 1/96) [745.5]

21420 Cherkerzian, Diane, and Colleen Van Blaricom. *Merry Things to Make* (3–5). Illus. 1999, Boyds Mills paper $7.95 (1-56397-838-5). 64pp. A wide range of craft ideas using simple materials are presented with good step-by-step instructions. (Rev: BL 9/1/99; SLJ 10/99) [745.59]

21421 Civardi, Anne, and Penny King. *Festival Decorations* (2–6). Series: Craft Workshop. 1998, Crabtree LB $22.95 (0-86505-780-X); paper $10.95 (0-86505-790-7). 32pp. These well-organized craft projects include decorations and other items used in a variety of celebrations and ceremonies around the world. (Rev: SLJ 10/98) [745]

21422 Connor, Nikki. *Cardboard Boxes* (1–4). Illus. by Sarah-Jane Neaves. Series: Creative Crafts. 1996, Millbrook LB $19.90 (0-7613-0538-6). A craft book that transforms cardboard boxes into trains, cars, and ships using a few paints, paper, scissors, and a pencil. Also use *Cardboard Tubes, Plastic Bottles,* and *Plastic Cups* (all 1997). (Rev: SLJ 8/97) [745.5]

21423 Corwin, Judith Hoffman. *Christmas Fun* (3–6). Illus. by author. 1982, Silver Burdett paper $5.95 (0-671-49583-6). 64pp. A collection of simple projects that are useful for this holiday, including designs for gifts and decorations.

21424 Corwin, Judith Hoffman. *Easter Crafts* (K–3). Illus. by author. Series: Holiday Crafts. 1994, Watts LB $21.00 (0-531-11145-8). 48pp. A collection of Easter crafts in which bunnies star. (Rev: SLJ 8/94) [745]

21425 Corwin, Judith Hoffman. *Easter Fun* (2–4). Illus. by author. 1984, Silver Burdett paper $5.95 (0-671-53108-5). 64pp. Foods and crafts associated with this holiday are highlighted.

21426 Corwin, Judith Hoffman. *Halloween Crafts: A Holiday Craft Book* (3–5). Illus. Series: Holiday Crafts. 1995, Watts LB $21.00 (0-531-11148-2). 48pp. Following a brief history of Halloween, the author outlines related crafts, including decorations, foods, and costumes. (Rev: BL 9/15/95) [745.594]

21427 Corwin, Judith Hoffman. *Halloween Fun* (3–6). Illus. 1983, Silver Burdett paper $5.95 (0-671-49756-1). 64pp. A wide variety of holiday activities, including party hints and projects.

21428 Corwin, Judith Hoffman. *Valentine Fun* (3–6). Illus. by author. 1983, Silver Burdett paper $5.95 (0-671-49755-3). 64pp. Recipes and craft projects highlight this book of activities.

21429 Craig, Diana. *Making Models: 3-D Creations from Paper and Clay* (4–6). Illus. Series: First Guide. 1993, Millbrook paper $9.95 (1-56294-710-9). 93pp. A craft book that is short on specific directions but filled with interesting projects that will require adult supervision. (Rev: SLJ 10/93) [745]

21430 Deshpande, Chris. *Festival Crafts* (4–7). Illus. Series: World Wide Crafts. 1994, Gareth Stevens LB $22.60 (0-8368-1153-4). 32pp. Thirteen craft projects that relate to such multicultural festivals as Mardi Gras and Mexico's All Souls Day. (Rev: BL 3/1/95; SLJ 1/95) [745.5]

21431 Deshpande, Chris. *Food Crafts* (4–7). Illus. Series: World Wide Crafts. 1994, Gareth Stevens LB $22.60 (0-8368-1154-2). 32pp. Foods become craft materials in this well-illustrated book containing 13 projects. (Rev: BL 3/1/95) [745.5]

21432 Drake, Jane, and Ann Love. *The Kids Summer Handbook* (4–7). Illus. by Heather Collins. 1994, Ticknor $15.95 (0-395-68711-X). 208pp. A handbook of all sorts of outdoor crafts and activities, with several involving whittling, weaving, and knotting. (Rev: BL 4/1/94; SLJ 6/94) [790.1]

21433 Ehlert, Lois. *Snowballs* (PS–3). Illus. 1995, Harcourt $16.00 (0-15-200074-7). 32pp. All kinds of materials are used to create and decorate a snow family in this book of craft ideas. (Rev: BCCB 11/95; BL 12/1/95; SLJ 11/95)

21434 Elffers, Joost, and Saxton Freymann. *Play with Your Pumpkins* (2–6). Photos by John Fortunato. 1998, Stewart, Tabori & Chang $10.95 (1-55670-848-3). 79pp. Photographs of all sorts of pumpkins are used to introduce this craft book on how to carve pumpkins creatively. (Rev: SLJ 1/99) [745]

21435 Engelbreit, Mary. *Hey, Kids! Come Craft with Me* (3–7). Illus. by author. 1999, Meredith $19.95 (0-696-20906-3). 112pp. This book contains dozens of crafts: covering chairs, making twig picture frames, designing patterns for party settings, making greeting cards and stationery, and so forth. (Rev: SLJ 7/99) [745]

21436 Freixenet, Anna. *Creating with Mosaics* (3–6). Series: Crafts for All Seasons. 2000, Blackbirch LB $18.95 (1-56711-440-7). 32pp. This appealing craft book shows how to create attractive mosaics using items like beads, balls of aluminum foil, beans, seeds, and buttons. (Rev: SLJ 2/01) [745]

21437 Gayle, Katie. *Snappy Jazzy Jewelry* (4–7). Illus. 1996, Sterling $14.95 (0-8069-3854-4). 48pp. Making necklaces and earrings are two of the craft projects described, with many helpful photographs. (Rev: BL 5/15/96; SLJ 6/96) [745.594]

21438 Gillis, Jennifer S. *In a Pumpkin Shell: Over 20 Pumpkin Projects for Kids* (3–6). Illus. by Patti Delmonte. 1992, Storey paper $9.95 (0-88266-771-8). 64pp. This book tells how to grow pumpkins and how to have fun with them through a number of craft projects. (Rev: SLJ 10/92) [745.5]

21439 Gould, Roberta. *Kidtopia: 'Round the Country and Back Through Time in 60 Projects* (2–7). 2000, Tricycle Pr. paper $13.95 (1-58246-026-4). 152pp. Divided into sections that cover American history and geography, this book contains many related projects, crafts, party ideas, and games. (Rev: SLJ 12/00) [745]

21440 Gould, Roberta. *Making Cool Crafts and Awesome Art: A Kids' Treasure Trove of Fabulous Fun* (2–5). Photos by author. 1998, Williamson paper $12.95 (1-885593-11-2). 160pp. This welcome addition to craft collections includes simple instructions to make a variety of objects from easy-to-find materials. Many of the projects represent foreign cultures and, in these cases, background material is given. (Rev: SLJ 4/98) [745.5]

21441 Hauser, Jill F. *Gizmos and Gadgets: Creating Science Contraptions That Work (and Knowing Why)* (4–7). Illus. by Michael Kline. Series: A Williamson Kids Can! Book. 1999, Williamson paper $12.95 (1-885593-26-0). 144pp. Outlines the construction of all sorts of gadgets from objects found in kitchen and garage closets and relates each to such scientific topics as motion, energy, balancing, and gravity. (Rev: SLJ 1/00) [745]

21442 Hebert, Holly. *60 Super Simple Crafts* (3–6). Illus. by Leo Abbett. 1996, Lowell House paper $6.95 (1-56565-385-8). 80pp. Simple instructions are given for 60 crafts projects, most of which involve material found in the home or at local craft shops. (Rev: SLJ 2/97) [745.5]

21443 Hendry, Linda. *Making Gift Boxes* (4–8). Illus. by author. Series: Kids Can! 1999, Kids Can paper $5.95 (1-55074-503-4). 40pp. The 14 boxes included in this fine craft book with clear instructions include a photo box, a garden box to grow seeds, a box for storing CDs, and a treasure box with false compartments. (Rev: SLJ 12/99) [745]

21444 Henry, Sandi. *Kids' Art Works! Creating with Color, Design, Texture and More* (K–5). Illus. by Norma Jean Martin-Jourdenais. Series: A Williamson Kids Can! Book. 2000, Williamson paper $12.95 (1-885593-35-X). 138pp. Sixty artistic creations using household materials; for example, a pasta fish, a Swiss cheese candle, and a sandpaper relief print. (Rev: SLJ 3/00) [745]

21445 Hogrogian, Nonny. *Handmade Secret Hiding Places* (3–5). Illus. by author. 1990, Overlook $7.95 (0-87951-033-1). 48pp. The construction of six hiding places from a mud hut to a hideaway made from blankets over chairs is described in words and pictures.

21446 Kerina, Jane. *African Crafts* (5–8). Illus. by Tom Feelings and Marylyn Katzman. 1970, Lion LB $16.50 (0-87460-084-7). Many projects arranged geographically by the region in Africa where they originated.

21447 King, Penny, and Clare Roundhill. *Out of This World: Lots of Space Pictures to Make* (2–6). Illus. Series: Making Pictures. 1997, Rigby $14.95 (1-57572-193-7). 29pp. This craft book introduces 12 space-related activities, like making a rocket from a cardboard tube. Others in the series are *Secrets of the Sea: Lots of Underwater Pictures to Make* and *Spooky Things: Lots of Spooky Pictures to Make* (both 1997). (Rev: SLJ 12/97) [745.5]

21448 Kohl, MaryAnn F., and Jean Potter. *Global Art: Activities, Projects, and Inventions from Around the World* (3–6). Illus. by Rebecca Van Slyke. 1998, Gryphon paper $14.95 (0-87659-190-X). 189pp. A series of crafts that vary in difficulty, are arranged by continent, and explore the world's different cultures and habitats. (Rev: SLJ 10/98) [745]

21449 Lehne, Judith Logan. *The Never-Be-Bored Book: Quick Things to Make When There's Nothing to Do* (4–6). Illus. by Morissa Lipstein. 1993, Sterling $17.95 (0-8069-1254-5). 128pp. Over 40 projects are included in this useful craft book, plus recipes for many ingredients including clay, dough, and natural dyes. (Rev: BL 5/15/93) [745.5]

21450 Lewis, Amanda. *Making Memory Books* (3–6). Illus. by Esperanca Melo. Series: Kids Can! 1999, Kids Can paper $5.95 (1-55074-567-0). 40pp. This craft book shows how to create a book for memorabilia with instructions on creating stencils, decorations, different types of lettering, templates, stamps, etc. (Rev: SLJ 2/00) [745]

21451 Love, Ann, and Jane Drake. *Kids and Grandparents: An Activity Book* (3–6). Illus. by Heather Collins. 2000, Kids Can $17.95 (1-55074-784-3); paper $10.95 (1-55074-492-5). 160pp. A collection

of over 90 games, crafts, recipes, and activities for children and their grandparents together with a "Making Memories" section on creating a memory book, a relative map, and a family tree. (Rev: HBG 10/00; SLJ 5/00) [745]

21452 McGraw, Sheila. *Gifts Kids Can Make* (4–8). Photos by Sheila McGraw and Joy von Tiedemann. 1994, Firefly LB $19.95 (1-895565-36-7); paper $9.95 (1-895565-35-9). 96pp. A craft book that gives directions for making 14 simple gifts, like a cotton sock doll and a hobby horse, by using easily obtainable materials. (Rev: SLJ 12/94) [745]

21453 Merrill, Yvonne Y. *Hands-On Latin America: Art Activities for All Ages* (4–8). Illus. Series: Hands-On. 1998, Kits paper $20.00 (0-9643177-1-0). 84pp. A collection of 30 interesting, affordable arts and crafts projects inspired by the ancient cultures of Latin America. (Rev: BL 9/1/98; SLJ 8/98) [980.07]

21454 Milhous, Katherine. *The Egg Tree* (PS–3). Illus. by author. 1971, Macmillan $16.00 (0-684-12716-4); paper $5.95 (0-689-71568-4). 32pp. This picture book tells how to make a delightful Easter egg tree. Caldecott Medal winner, 1951.

21455 Milord, Susan. *Hands Around the World: 365 Creative Ways to Build Cultural Awareness and Global Respect* (3–6). Illus. 1992, Williamson paper $12.95 (0-913589-65-9). 160pp. One craft, recipe, or project is offered for each day of the year. (Rev: BL 1/1/93; SLJ 1/93) [306]

21456 Moffatt, Judith. *Snow Shapes: A Read-and-Do Book* (1–2). Illus. Series: Hello Reader! 2000, Scholastic $3.99 (0-439-09858-0). 32pp. This beginning reader is also a craft book filled with simple winter projects like making paper snowflakes, snowman ornaments, and a paper chain of squirrels. (Rev: BL 12/1/00) [745.594]

21457 The Muppet Workshop, and Stephanie St. Pierre. *The Muppets Big Book of Crafts: 100 Great Projects to Snip, Sculpt, Stitch, and Stuff* (2–6). Photos by John E. Barrett. Illus. by Stephanie Osser and Matthew Fox. 2000, Workman paper $18.95 (0-7611-0526-3). 322pp. With projects that progress from the easy to the difficult, this amazing book outlines 100 great craft projects arranged by a particular medium (e.g. paper) or technique. (Rev: SLJ 3/00) [745]

21458 National Wildlife Federation. *Wild and Crafty* (1–7). Series: Ranger Rick's NatureScope. 1999, Chelsea LB $19.95 (0-7910-4884-5). 94pp. Step-by-step directions are given for 31 nature crafts (mostly model or puppet making) each with an assigned grade level. (Rev: SLJ 5/99) [745.5]

21459 Needham, Bobbe. *Ecology Crafts for Kids: 50 Great Ways to Make Friends with Planet Earth* (4–7). 1998, Sterling $24.95 (0-8069-0685-5). 144pp. In addition to clear directions for more than 50 projects that use recycled, reused, or natural materials, this book offers pointers on how to be ecologically friendly. A short biography of conservationist John Muir is included. (Rev: SLJ 9/98) [745]

21460 Owen, Cheryl. *My Nature Craft Book* (2–6). Illus. 1993, Little, Brown $15.95 (0-316-67715-9). 96pp. An oversized craft book with such projects as lavender bags and painted stones. (Rev: BL 3/15/93; SLJ 8/93) [745.5]

21461 Pfiffner, George. *Earth-Friendly Holidays: How to Make Fabulous Gifts and Decorations from Reusable Objects* (3–6). Illus. 1995, Wiley paper $12.95 (0-471-12005-7). 128pp. A total of 29 easily executed craft projects for all sorts of holidays, including Valentine's Day, Christmas, and Kwanzaa. (Rev: SLJ 11/95) [745.5]

21462 Pfiffner, George. *Earth-Friendly Outdoor Fun: How to Make Fabulous Games, Gardens, and Other Projects from Reusable Objects* (3–6). Illus. by author. 1996, Wiley paper $12.95 (0-471-14113-5). 128pp. Reusable materials like plastic shopping bags, cardboard, and soda bottles are used to produce a number of items like kites, bowling pins, and a scarecrow. (Rev: SLJ 4/96) [745.5]

21463 Press, Judy. *ArtStarts for Little Hands! Fun and Discoveries for 3- to 7-Year-Olds* (PS–2). Illus. by Karol Kaminski. 2000, Williamson paper $12.95 (1-885593-37-6). 118pp. A fresh and amusing book that presents simple activities using everyday materials under such themes as animals, seasons, transportation, colors, and gardens. (Rev: SLJ 10/00) [745]

21464 Press, Judy. *The Little Hands Big Fun Craft Book: Creative Fun for 2- to 6-Year-Olds* (PS–1). Illus. by Loretta Braren. Series: Little Hands Books. 1996, Williamson paper $12.95 (0-913589-96-9). 142pp. A collection of 75 simple craft projects grouped under such headings as "Animals and Trees," "Friendship," and "Family Fun." (Rev: SLJ 7/96) [745.5]

21465 Press, Judy. *Vroom! Vroom! Making 'Dozers, 'Copters, Trucks, and More* (2–6). Illus. by Michael Kline. Series: Little Hands Books. 1997, Williamson paper $12.95 (1-885593-04-X). 160pp. Both craft and transportation enthusiasts can use this simple guide to making several vehicles with ordinary materials and good step-by-step directions. (Rev: SLJ 8/97) [745.5]

21466 Rhodes, Vicki. *Pumpkin Decorating* (4–8). Illus. 1997, Sterling $11.95 (0-8069-9574-2). 96pp. Clear direction and full-color photos show how to decorate more than 80 pumpkins. (Rev: SLJ 12/97) [745.5]

21467 Rice, Melanie. *The Complete Book of Children's Activities* (PS–K). Illus. by Chris Barker. 1993, Kingfisher paper $9.95 (1-85697-907-5). 120pp. For the very young, this is a collection of learning activities, games, and construction projects. (Rev: BL 5/1/93) [372]

21468 Robins, Deri. *Christmas Fun* (3–6). Illus. by Maggie Downer. 1995, Kingfisher paper $4.95 (1-85697-567-3). 32pp. Crafts, games, and foods are highlighted in this book featuring all sorts of Christmas activities. (Rev: BL 10/1/95) [745]

21469 Robins, Deri, et al. *The Kids Can Do It Book: Fun Things to Make and Do* (PS–3). Illus. by Charlotte Stowell. 1993, Kingfisher paper $9.95 (1-85697-860-5). 80pp. Simple activities like making potato prints, planting a garden, preparing a picnic, and sewing a bath mat are outlined in this delightful book. (Rev: SLJ 1/94) [745]

21470 Roche, Denis. *Art Around the World: Loo-Loo, Boo, and More Art You Can Do* (2–4). Illus. 1998, Houghton $15.00 (0-395-85597-7). 32pp. Eleven art projects, using simple materials (many somewhat difficult for young children to execute), explore the history and geography of areas such as Peru, Java, Bali, and Togo. (Rev: BL 4/1/98; HBG 10/98; SLJ 8/98) [745.5]

21471 Roche, Denis. *Loo-Loo, Boo, and Art You Can Do* (1–4). Illus. 1996, Houghton $14.95 (0-395-75921-8). 32pp. Eleven art projects are introduced by Loo-Loo and her dog, Boo. (Rev: BCCB 9/96; BL 9/15/96; SLJ 8/96) [704]

21472 Ross, Kathy. *Christmas Decorations Kids Can Make* (3–5). Illus. 1999, Millbrook $23.40 (0-7613-1565-9). 64pp. An old-fashioned craft book that uses ordinary materials to create such seasonal gifts and ornaments as figures of the three kings. (Rev: BL 12/15/99; HBG 3/00) [594]

21473 Ross, Kathy. *Christmas Ornaments Kids Can Make* (2–5). Illus. 1998, Millbrook LB $23.40 (0-7613-0366-9). 64pp. Thirty projects for making Christmas ornaments are well-presented in this easy-to-follow craft book. (Rev: BL 10/15/98; HBG 3/99; SLJ 10/98) [745.594]

21474 Ross, Kathy. *Crafts for All Seasons* (3–5). Illus. 2000, Millbrook $19.95 (0-7613-1346-X). 176pp. Drawing widely on the material in the author's four seasonal craft books, this spiral-bound volume contains 80 projects with clear instructions. (Rev: BL 10/15/00) [745.5]

21475 Ross, Kathy. *Crafts for Christian Values* (K–4). Illus. by Sharon L. Holm. 2000, Millbrook LB $24.90 (0-7613-1618-3). 63pp. A book of 28 craft projects, each related to a particular Christian value — such as a bookmark that honors one's parents. (Rev: SLJ 2/01) [745]

21476 Ross, Kathy. *Crafts for Easter* (K–3). Illus. by Sharon L. Holm. 1996, Millbrook LB $21.90 (1-56294-918-7). 48pp. With simple, clear instructions, Easter-related crafts using everyday objects, like making baskets, are described. (Rev: BL 3/1/96) [745.594]

21477 Ross, Kathy. *Crafts for Halloween* (1–3). Illus. by Sharon L. Holm. 1994, Millbrook LB $21.90 (1-56294-411-8). 48pp. Colorful illustrations help explain a number of Halloween craft projects for primary-school youngsters. (Rev: BL 10/15/94; SLJ 1/95) [745]

21478 Ross, Kathy. *Crafts for Kids Who Are Wild About Deserts* (3–5). Illus. Series: Kids Who Are Wild About. 1998, Millbrook LB $22.40 (0-7613-0954-3). 48pp. A book of ingenious craft projects related to deserts, such as an egg-carton rattlesnake and a sand art necklace. (Rev: BL 3/15/99; HBG 10/99; SLJ 4/99) [745.5]

21479 Ross, Kathy. *Crafts for Kids Who Are Wild About Dinosaurs* (3–5). Illus. Series: Crafts for Kids Who Are Wild About. 1997, Millbrook LB $22.40

(0-7613-0053-8); paper $8.95 (0-7613-0177-1). 48pp. Twenty projects involving dinosaurs and using everyday objects are described. (Rev: BL 2/1/97; SLJ 6/97) [745.5]

21480 Ross, Kathy. *Crafts for Kids Who Are Wild About Oceans* (3–5). Illus. Series: Crafts for Kids Who Are Wild About. 1998, Millbrook LB $22.40 (0-7613-0262-X); paper $7.95 (0-7613-0331-6). 48pp. Using excellent illustrations and clear instructions, this book describes a series of ocean-related craft projects such as making a clam puppet and a water-spouting whale. (Rev: BL 4/15/98; HBG 10/98; SLJ 5/98) [745.5]

21481 Ross, Kathy. *Crafts for Kids Who Are Wild About Outer Space* (3–5). Illus. Series: Crafts for Kids Who Are Wild About. 1997, Millbrook LB $22.40 (0-7613-0054-6); paper $7.95 (0-7613-0176-3). 48pp. Various aspects of outer space are presented in 20 craft projects that use commonplace items. (Rev: BL 2/1/97; SLJ 6/97) [745.5]

21482 Ross, Kathy. *Crafts for Kids Who Are Wild About Polar Life* (3–5). Illus. Series: Kids Who Are Wild About. 1998, Millbrook LB $22.40 (0-7613-0955-1). 48pp. A penguin pin, a walrus mask, and an arctic fox cup puppet are three of the clever craft projects related to the Arctic that are found in this volume. (Rev: BL 3/15/99; HBG 10/99; SLJ 4/99) [745.5]

21483 Ross, Kathy. *Crafts for Kids Who Are Wild About Reptiles* (3–5). Illus. Series: Crafts for Kids Who Are Wild About. 1998, Millbrook LB $22.40 (0-7613-0263-8); paper $7.95 (0-7613-0332-4). 48pp. Twenty reptile-related projects such as making a shedding snake and constructing a tiny turtle are included in this clearly written and well-illustrated craft book. (Rev: BL 4/15/98; HBG 10/98; SLJ 5/98) [745.59]

21484 Ross, Kathy. *Crafts for Valentine's Day* (2–5). Illus. by Sharon L. Holm. Series: Holiday Crafts. 1995, Millbrook LB $21.90 (1-56294-489-4). 47pp. Twenty simple holiday projects using readily available materials are described on double-page spreads, with color illustrations and step-by-step instructions. (Rev: SLJ 4/95) [745.5]

21485 Ross, Kathy. *Crafts from Your Favorite Bible Stories* (3–5). Illus. 2000, Millbrook LB $24.90 (0-7613-1619-1). 64pp. Using simple materials such as lunch bags and pipe cleaners, this book offers 27 craft projects from both the Old and New Testaments such as making Noah's ark or Joseph's coat of many colors. (Rev: BL 6/1–15/00; HBG 10/00; SLJ 8/00) [268]

21486 Ross, Kathy. *Crafts from Your Favorite Fairy Tales* (1–5). Illus. by Vicky Enright. 1997, Millbrook LB $22.40 (0-7613-0259-X). 47pp. An unusual craft book that uses such tales as *Cinderella* and *Jack and the Beanstalk* as the inspiration for 20 activities. (Rev: HBG 3/98; SLJ 12/97) [745.5]

21487 Ross, Kathy. *Crafts to Celebrate God's Creation* (3–5). Illus. 2001, Millbrook LB $24.90 (0-7613-1621-3). 64pp. Using the creation story in Genesis as a focus, this craft book gives directions for making such items as a "sunrise puppet," flying

birds, and a beaded pin in the shape of a cross. (Rev: BL 1/1–15/01) [268.432]

21488 Ross, Kathy. *Crafts to Make in the Fall* (3–5). Illus. by Vicky Enright. Series: Crafts for All Seasons. 1998, Millbrook LB $23.40 (0-7613-0318-9); paper $8.95 (0-7613-0335-9). 63pp. Twenty-nine craft projects, with a wide range of difficulty, are included in this book that involves autumn themes and holidays like Columbus Day and Thanksgiving. (Rev: HBG 3/99; SLJ 2/99) [745]

21489 Ross, Kathy. *Crafts to Make in the Spring* (K–4). Illus. by Vicky Enright. 1998, Millbrook LB $23.40 (0-7613-0316-2); paper $8.95 (0-7613-0333-2). 63pp. This book contains 29 simple crafts described in double-page spreads and inspired by spring and such holidays as Passover and Easter. (Rev: HBG 10/98; SLJ 6/98) [745]

21490 Ross, Kathy. *Crafts to Make in the Winter* (K–3). Illus. by Vicky Enright. Series: Crafts for All Seasons. 1999, Millbrook LB $23.40 (0-7613-0319-7). 64pp. The use of accessible materials and good step-by-step instructions make this a fine craft book about making things that are winter-related. (Rev: BL 12/15/99; HBG 3/00; SLJ 1/00) [745.5]

21491 Ross, Kathy. *Every Day Is Earth Day* (2–4). Illus. by Sharon L. Holm. Series: Holiday Crafts. 1995, Millbrook LB $21.90 (1-56294-490-8). 47pp. After a general discussion of Earth Day, presents 20 crafts that reflect an interest in conserving natural resources and recycling materials. (Rev: SLJ 5/95) [745.5]

21492 Ross, Kathy. *Make Yourself a Monster! A Book of Creepy Crafts* (2–5). Illus. by Sharon Hawkins Vargo. 1999, Millbrook LB $22.90 (0-7613-1556-X). 45pp. Twenty 20 monster-themed crafts include making a slimy monster mitt puppet and a Dracula soap dispenser. (Rev: HBG 3/00; SLJ 4/00) [745]

21493 Ross, Kathy. *More Christmas Ornaments Kids Can Make* (2–5). Illus. by Sharon L. Holm. 2000, Millbrook LB $23.90 (0-7613-1755-4). 64pp. Twenty-nine ornaments that can be made easily by primary-school children are described with easy step-by-step instructions. (Rev: BL 9/1/00; HBG 3/01) [745.594]

21494 Sadler, Judy Ann. *The Kids Can Press Jumbo Book of Crafts* (2–6). Illus. by Caroline Price. 1998, Kids Can paper $12.00 (1-55074-375-9). 208pp. This book contains an array of easy and inexpensive craft projects, including making papier-mâché bowls, cord-covered bottles, and collage frames. (Rev: SLJ 12/98) [745]

21495 Sanders, Nancy I. *Old Testament Days: An Activity Guide* (4–6). Illus. 1999, Chicago Review paper $14.95 (1-55652-354-8). 144pp. This craft book contains 80 projects related to incidents in the Old Testament, such as making a sleeping mat similar to that used by Abraham. (Rev: BL 10/15/99; SLJ 12/99) [372.89]

21496 Simons, Robin. *Recyclopedia: Games, Science Equipment and Crafts from Recycled Materials* (5–8). Illus. by author. 1976, Houghton paper $13.95 (0-395-59641-6). Clear directions complemented by good illustrations characterize this book of interesting projects using waste materials.

21497 Sohi, Morteza E. *Look What I Did with a Leaf!* (3–6). Illus. Series: Nature Craft. 1993, Walker LB $15.85 (0-8027-8216-7). Combines nature crafts with field guide material and explains how to make collage animals out of leaves. (Rev: SLJ 12/93) [745]

21498 Sohi, Morteza E. *Look What I Did with a Shell!* (3–6). Illus. 2000, Walker LB $16.85 (0-8027-8723-1). 32pp. Shells are introduced with information on sizes, shapes, color, and contrasts, followed by a series of interesting projects and tips on working with shells. (Rev: BL 7/00; HBG 10/00; SLJ 7/00) [745.55]

21499 Solga, Kim, and Priscilla Hershberger. *Craft Fun!* (2–6). Photos by Pamela Monfort. Series: Art and Activities for Kids. 1997, North Light paper $19.99 (0-89134-834-4). 216pp. This activity book introduces crafts projects on a variety of topics, including card making, costumes, and clothes. (Rev: SLJ 1/98) [745.5]

21500 Supraner, Robyn. *Happy Halloween! Things to Make and Do* (1–3). Illus. by Renzo Barto. 1981, Troll LB $16.65 (0-89375-420-X); paper $3.95 (0-89375-421-8). 48pp. Games, decorations, disguises, and more.

21501 Temko, Florence. *Traditional Crafts from Africa* (2–5). Illus. 1996, Lerner LB $23.93 (0-8225-2936-X). 64pp. Clear instructions and excellent illustrations are used in the presentation of several African craft projects. (Rev: BL 9/1/96; SLJ 10/96) [745]

21502 Temko, Florence. *Traditional Crafts from China* (5–7). Illus. Series: Culture Crafts. 2001, Lerner LB $23.93 (0-8225-2939-4). 64pp. After a few words about crafts in general, this volume carefully outlines a number of projects related to Chinese culture, including instructions for picture scrolls and tanagrams. (Rev: BL 2/15/01) [745]

21503 Temko, Florence. *Traditional Crafts from Mexico and Central America* (3–6). Photos by Robert L. Wolfe and Diane Wolfe. Illus. by Randall Gooch. Series: Culture Crafts. 1996, Lerner LB $23.93 (0-8225-2935-1). 64pp. After a brief introduction to the area, this book describes eight traditional crafts with clear instructions and a number of helpful illustrations. (Rev: BCCB 2/97; SLJ 12/96) [745.5]

21504 Temko, Florence. *Traditional Crafts from the Caribbean* (5–7). Illus. Series: Culture Crafts. 2001, Lerner LB $23.93 (0-8225-2937-8). 64pp. Step-by-step instructions with clear diagrams are given for a number of craft projects related to Caribbean culture including yarn dolls, Puerto Rican masks, and metal cutouts. (Rev: BL 2/15/01) [745]

21505 Thomas, John E., and Danita Pagel. *The Ultimate Book of Kid Concoctions* (PS–4). Illus. by Robb Durr and Zachariah Durr. 1998, Kid Concoctions paper $14.95 (0-9661088-0-9). 80pp. Features about 65 recipes and activities using common kitchen supplies to make items like sidewalk chalk, finger paints, and scratch-and-sniff stickers. (Rev: SLJ 3/98) [745.5]

21506 Treinan, Sarah Jane, ed. *Better Homes and Gardens Incredibly Awesome Crafts for Kids* (4–8). Illus. 1992, Meredith paper $16.95 (0-696-01984-1). 168pp. More than 75 projects — many requiring supervision — for interesting patterns and crafts. (Rev: BL 4/15/92) [745.5]

21507 Trottier, Maxine. *Native Crafts: Inspired by North America's First Peoples* (3–6). Illus. 2000, Kids Can $12.95 (1-55074-854-8); paper $5.95 (1-55074-549-2). 40pp. Sixteen projects (all requiring adult help) from the traditional arts and crafts of Native Americans are presented with step-by-step instructions and pictures of the finished products. (Rev: BL 7/00; HBG 10/00; SLJ 6/00) [745.5]

21508 Umnik, Sharon D., ed. *175 Easy-to-Do Halloween Crafts* (3–5). Illus. 1995, Boyds Mills $6.95 (1-56397-372-3). 63pp. Masks, costumes, and decorations are some of the objects made from common materials in this holiday craft book. (Rev: BL 9/15/95; SLJ 12/95) [745.5]

21509 Wallace, Mary. *I Can Make Toys: So Easy to Make!* (1–3). Photos by author. Series: Greey de Pencier Books. 1994, Firefly $17.95 (1-895688-23-X); paper $9.95 (1-895688-16-7). 31pp. This book contains 11 easy-to-make projects, including a glider, car, bunny, train, and furniture. (Rev: SLJ 11/94) [745]

21510 West, Robin. *My Very Own Birthday: A Book of Cooking and Crafts* (2–4). Photos by Robert L. Wolfe and Diane Wolfe. Illus. by Jackie Urbanovic. Series: My Very Own Holiday. 1996, Carolrhoda LB $21.27 (0-87614-980-8). 64pp. Five birthday parties using different themes are described, along with recipes and craft projects. (Rev: SLJ 5/96) [745.5]

21511 West, Robin. *My Very Own Christmas: A Book of Cooking and Crafts* (PS–1). Illus. by Susan S. Burke. 1993, Carolrhoda LB $21.27 (0-87614-722-8). 64pp. This book contains a variety of Christmas crafts and a number of recipes. (Rev: BL 8/93) [394.2]

21512 Wilkes, Angela. *My First Christmas Activity Book* (4–6). Illus. 1994, DK $12.95 (1-56458-674-X). 48pp. This Christmas craft book concentrates on cards, decorations, and gift-wrapping paper. (Rev: BL 8/94) [745]

21513 Wiseman, Ann S. *Making Things: The Handbook of Creative Discovery*. Rev. ed. (4–8). Illus. by author. 1997, Little, Brown paper $14.70 (0-316-94756-3). 161pp. Children can create an amazing array of objects using this attractive craft book, which also includes many inspirational quotes and sayings. (Rev: SLJ 8/97) [745.5]

21514 *A World of Things to Do* (2–5). Illus. 1987, National Geographic LB $12.50 (0-87044-615-0). 104pp. All sorts of activities for even the most hard to please, from kitchen science experiments to holiday ideas. (Rev: BL 5/15/87)

American Historical Crafts

21515 *Addy's Craft Book: A Look at Crafts from the Past with Projects You Can Make Today* (3–5). Illus. Series: American Girls Pastimes. 1994, Pleasant paper $5.95 (1-56247-124-4). 44pp. A book of handicrafts that re-creates projects popular in 19th-century America during the days of slavery. (Rev: BL 12/15/94) [745.5]

21516 Beard, D. C. *The American Boys' Handy Book: What to Do and How to Do It* (5–7). Illus. 1983, Godine paper $12.95 (0-87923-449-0). 392pp. A facsimile edition of a manual first published in 1882.

21517 Caney, Steven. *Steven Caney's Kids' America* (4–7). Illus. 1978, Workman paper $14.95 (0-911104-80-1). 416pp. Activities that focus on getting children to rediscover parts of America's past.

21518 D'Amato, Janet, and Alex D'Amato. *Indian Crafts* (1–4). Illus. by authors. 1968, Lion LB $16.50 (0-87460-088-X). An excellent introduction to Indian crafts through projects and activities.

21519 *Felicity's Craft Book: A Look at Crafts from the Past with Projects You Can Make Today* (3–5). Illus. Series: American Girls Pastimes. 1994, Pleasant paper $5.95 (1-56247-121-X). 44pp. This craft book outlines projects that were current during the American colonial period. (Rev: BL 12/15/94) [745.5]

21520 Greenwood, Barbara. *Pioneer Crafts* (2–5). 1997, Kids Can paper $4.95 (1-55074-359-7). 40pp. Directions for 17 projects involving such crafts as candle making, soap carving, and basket weaving. (Rev: BL 9/15/97; SLJ 9/97) [745.5]

21521 Kalman, Bobbie. *Pioneer Projects* (3–6). Illus. by Marc Crabtree. Series: Historic Communities. 1997, Crabtree LB $20.60 (0-86505-437-1); paper $7.95 (0-86505-467-3). 32pp. Authentic crafts and activities engaged in by early American settlers are outlined, including step-by-step directions for building a model of a pioneer town. (Rev: BL 7/97; SLJ 8/97) [745.5]

21522 *Kirsten's Craft Book: A Look at Crafts from the Past with Projects You Can Make Today* (3–5). Illus. Series: American Girls Pastimes. 1994, Pleasant paper $5.95 (1-56247-112-0). 45pp. Outlines a number of craft projects that pioneer children enjoyed, like making a calendar stick and a yarn doll. (Rev: BL 12/15/94; SLJ 12/94) [680]

21523 Merrill, Yvonne Y. *Hands-On Rocky Mountains: Art Activities About Anasazi, American Indians, Settlers, Trappers, and Cowboys* (3–6). Illus. 1996, Kits paper $20.00 (0-9643177-2-9). 83pp. People associated with the West are introduced, and, for each, a series of activities and projects are outlined. (Rev: BL 1/1–15/97; SLJ 4/97) [745.5]

21524 *Molly's Craft Book: A Look at Crafts from the Past with Projects You Can Make Today* (3–5). Illus. Series: American Girls Pastimes. 1994, Pleasant paper $5.95 (1-56247-118-X). 44pp. Through a series of craft projects, life between the world wars is re-created. (Rev: BL 12/15/94) [745.5]

21525 *Samantha's Craft Book: A Look at Crafts from the Past with Projects You Can Make Today* (3–5). Illus. Series: American Girls Pastimes. 1994, Pleasant paper $5.95 (1-56247-115-5). 44pp. Twentieth-century American history is reflected in a

series of interesting craft projects. (Rev: BL 12/15/94) [745.5]

21526 Temko, Florence. *Traditional Crafts from Native North America* (2–4). Illus. Series: Culture Crafts. 1997, Lerner LB $23.93 (0-8225-2934-3). 64pp. Introduces the major cultural areas of North American Indians and gives directions for making such objects as baskets, cornhusk dolls, and dream catchers. (Rev: BL 10/1/97; SLJ 7/97) [745.5]

21527 Tull, Mary, et al. *North America* (4–7). Series: Artisans Around the World. 1999, Raintree Steck-Vaughn LB $25.69 (0-7398-0117-1). 48pp. North American folk art is surveyed, from peoples including the Haida of western Canada, New Mexico's Pueblos, the Pennsylvanian German-Americans, and African Americans. (Rev: BL 10/15/99; HBG 3/00) [970]

21528 Yamane, Linda. *Weaving a California Tradition: A Native American Basketmaker* (3–6). Illus. Series: We Are Still Here: Native Americans Today. 1996, Lerner $21.27 (0-8225-2660-3); paper $6.95 (0-8225-9730-6). 48pp. The story of California basket weaving, its present status, and the people who engage in it. (Rev: BL 1/1–15/97; SLJ 2/97) [746.41]

Clay and Other Modeling Crafts

21529 Arima, Elaine. *The Kids 'N' Clay Ceramics Book: HandBuilding and Wheel-Throwing Projects from the Kids 'N' Clay Pottery Studio* (3–8). Illus. 2000, Tricycle Pr. paper $16.95 (1-883672-89-9). 128pp. A ceramic project book for middle and junior high grades that involves creating both handmade and wheel-thrown objects including a breakfast bowl, bookends, and a porcupine. (Rev: BL 3/1/00; SLJ 8/00) [738]

21530 Dixon, Annabelle. *Clay* (3–5). Illus. by Ed Barber. Series: Threads. 1990, Garrett LB $15.93 (0-944483-69-0). 26pp. The nature of clay, where it is found, and its uses in pottery and model crafts are discussed. (Rev: BL 2/1/91; SLJ 4/91) [553.6]

21531 Good, Keith. *Shape It! Magnificent Projects for Molding Materials* (3–7). Series: Design It! 2000, Lerner LB $21.27 (0-8225-3568-8). 30pp. This is a book of craft projects that involve molding materials such as salt dough, plaster, air-drying clay, and edible materials like cookie dough. (Rev: HBG 10/00; SLJ 6/00) [745.5]

21532 MacLeod-Brudenell, Iain. *Animal Crafts* (4–7). Illus. Series: World Wide Crafts. 1994, Gareth Stevens LB $22.60 (0-8368-1151-8). 32pp. The creation of various models of animals related to different cultures is the focus of this craft book containing more than a dozen projects. (Rev: BL 3/1/95; SLJ 1/95) [745.5]

21533 Reid, Barbara. *Fun with Modeling Clay* (1–4). Illus. 1998, Kids Can paper $5.95 (1-55074-510-7). 40pp. After such basics as modeling balls, pancakes, and snakes from clay, this craft book goes on to such projects as fruit baskets, cars and trains, and underwater scenes. (Rev: BL 9/1/98) [731.4]

21534 Rowe, Christine. *The Children's Book of Pottery* (4–7). Illus. 1989, Trafalgar $24.95 (0-7134-5995-6). 64pp. A good British import about pottery making. (Rev: BL 12/1/89) [738.1]

21535 Solga, Kim. *Make Sculptures!* (2–5). Illus. Series: Art and Activities for Kids. 1992, North Light $11.99 (0-89134-420-9). 48pp. This book supplies easy-to-follow instructions on constructing simple sculptures. (Rev: BL 9/1/92; SLJ 11/92) [745.5]

21536 Speechley, Greta. *Clay Modeling* (3–6). Series: Step-by-Step. 2000, Heinemann LB $22.75 (1-57572-326-3). 32pp. This book shows how to create figures including a cat, a tiger, a flowerpot, and a bowl using air-drying clay. (Rev: BL 10/15/00; SLJ 12/00) [745.5]

Costume and Jewelry Making

21537 Casey, Moe. *The Most Excellent Book of Dress Up* (3–5). Illus. Series: Most Excellent Book Of. 1997, Millbrook LB $19.90 (0-7613-0550-5); paper $6.95 (0-7613-0575-0). 32pp. Using many photos and drawings, this colorful book gives easy, step-by-step instructions for making various costumes. (Rev: BL 6/1–15/97; SLJ 8/97) [646.4]

21538 Chernoff, Goldie Taub. *Easy Costumes You Don't Have to Sew* (3–6). Illus. by Margaret A. Hartelius. 1984, Macmillan $13.95 (0-02-718230-4). 48pp. Paper bags, cartons, and old cloth are three of the materials used in making these simple costumes.

21539 Conaway, Judith. *Happy Haunting! Halloween Costumes You Can Make* (2–4). Illus. 1986, Troll LB $16.65 (0-8167-0666-2); paper $3.95 (0-8167-0667-0). 48pp. Simple costumes made with easily obtainable materials. (Rev: BL 12/1/86)

21540 Doney, Meryl. *Jewelry* (5–8). Illus. Series: World Crafts. 1996, Watts LB $21.00 (0-531-14406-2). 32pp. A number of excellent jewelry-making projects from around the world are outlined with easy-to-follow directions and good background cultural information. (Rev: SLJ 1/97) [739.27]

21541 Grisewood, Sara. *Making Jewelry* (3–6). Illus. Series: Step-by-Step. 1995, Kingfisher $13.90 (1-85697-589-4); paper $6.95 (1-85697-588-6). 40pp. A brightly illustrated craft book that tells how to make many kinds of jewelry out of salt dough, modeling clay, felt, and papier-mâché. (Rev: SLJ 1/96) [745.5]

21542 Gryski, Camilla. *Friendship Bracelets* (3–6). Illus. 1993, Morrow paper $6.95 (0-688-12437-2). 48pp. Instructions are given on how to make friendship bracelets from different materials, plus material on creating other forms of jewelry. (Rev: BL 10/1/93; SLJ 9/93) [746]

21543 Gryski, Camilla. *Lanyard: Having Fun with Plastic Lace* (3–6). Illus. by Linda Hendry. 1994, Morrow $15.00 (0-688-13324-X). 32pp. Directions for making a number of bracelets, key chains, and earrings out of lanyards — strips of plastic or other materials. (Rev: BL 3/15/94; SLJ 7/94) [745.57]

21544 Hershberger, Priscilla. *Make Costumes! For Creative Play* (2–5). Illus. and Activities for Kids. 1992, North Light $11.99 (0-89134-450-0). 48pp. This oversized book describes how to make simple costumes with easy to follow directions. (Rev: BL 9/15/92; SLJ 12/92) [616.4]

21545 MacLeod-Brudenell, Iain. *Costume Crafts* (4–7). Illus. Series: World Wide Crafts. 1994, Gareth Stevens LB $22.60 (0-8368-1152-6). 32pp. Multicultural projects involving dress and body decoration are featured in this easily followed craft book. (Rev: BL 3/1/95; SLJ 1/95) [745.5]

21546 Reid, Margarette S. *A String of Beads* (2–4). Illus. by Ashley Wolff. 1997, Dutton $14.99 (0-525-45721-6). 32pp. A unique history of beads and beadwork, combined with a craft book that gives ideas for youngsters creating their own strings of beads. (Rev: BL 8/97*; HBG 3/98; SLJ 11/97*) [745.5]

21547 Sadler, Judy Ann. *Beading: Bracelets, Earrings, Necklaces and More* (4–8). Illus. Series: Kids Can! 1998, Kids Can paper $4.95 (1-55074-338-4). 40pp. Using photographs and simple instructions, directions are given for making a simple beading loom and creating necklaces and bracelets. (Rev: BL 5/15/98) [745.594]

21548 Sadler, Judy Ann. *Beads* (1–4). Illus. Series: Easy Crafts. 1997, Kids Can paper $4.95 (1-55074-182-9). 32pp. Simple to more difficult projects involved with creating beadwork and bead jewelry are presented in this appealing book. (Rev: BL 12/1/97) [746.5]

21549 Sadler, Judy Ann. *Easy Braids, Barrettes and Bows* (3–7). Illus. 1997, Kids Can paper $5.95 (1-55074-325-2). 40pp. Discusses various hairstyles, like cornrows and ponytails, and gives instructions on making pieces of hair jewelry. (Rev: BL 10/15/97; SLJ 11/97) [646.7]

21550 Sensier, Danielle. *Costumes* (5–7). Illus. Series: Traditions Around the World. 1994, Thomson Learning LB $24.26 (1-56847-227-7). 48pp. The rituals and uses involved in costumes are introduced, as well as a general discussion of clothing in various regions and cultures. (Rev: BL 2/1/95; SLJ 3/95) [391]

21551 Solga, Kim. *Make Clothes Fun* (2–5). Illus. Series: Art and Activities for Kids. 1992, North Light $11.95 (0-89134-421-7). 48pp. This oversize book gives easy-to-follow instructions on how to make clothes. Also use: *Make Gifts!* (1991). (Rev: BL 9/1/92; SLJ 11/92) [746.9]

21552 Wallace, Mary. *I Can Make Jewelry* (2–4). Illus. 1997, Firefly $17.95 (1-895688-62-0); paper $6.95 (1-895688-63-9). 32pp. Rings, beads, hair decorations, and necklaces are some of the jewelry for which there are directions to make and wear. (Rev: BL 8/97) [745.5]

21553 Wilkes, Angela. *Dazzling Disguises and Clever Costumes* (4–6). Illus. 1996, DK $14.95 (0-7894-1001-X). 48pp. Step-by-step instructions on how to make a variety of costumes, the materials needed, and information on clever disguises. (Rev: BCCB 11/96; BL 10/1/96; SLJ 12/96) [646.8]

Drawing and Painting

21554 Ames, Lee J. *Draw Fifty Airplanes, Aircraft and Spacecraft* (3–7). Illus. by author. 1987, Doubleday paper $8.95 (0-385-23629-8). 64pp. Simple directions for drawing various airborne articles, from the Wright brothers' plane to the Saturn V rocket. Also use: *Draw Fifty Boats, Ships, Trucks and Trains* (1976); *Draw Fifty Vehicles* (1997); *Draw Fifty Buildings and Other Structures* (1980).

21555 Ames, Lee J. *Draw Fifty Cats* (4–7). Illus. 1986, Doubleday paper $8.95 (0-385-24640-4). 64pp. Step-by-step method of drawing different breeds and poses of cats. Also use: *Draw Fifty Holiday Decorations* (1987). (Rev: BL 11/15/86)

21556 Ames, Lee J. *Draw Fifty Dogs* (4–6). Illus. by author. 1981, Doubleday paper $8.95 (0-385-23431-7). 64pp. Six steps are used to draw several species. Also use: *Draw Fifty Animals* (1985); *Draw Fifty Dinosaurs and Other Prehistoric Animals* (1977); *Draw Fifty Horses* (1984).

21557 Ames, Lee J. *Draw Fifty Famous Cartoons* (4–6). Illus. by author. 1985, Doubleday paper $8.95 (0-385-19521-4). 64pp. How to draw such characters as Dick Tracy and the Flintstones.

21558 Ames, Lee J. *Draw Fifty Monsters, Creeps, Superheroes, Demons, Dragons, Nerds, Dirts, Ghouls, Giants, Vampires, Zombies and Other Curiosa* (4–6). Illus. by author. 1986, Doubleday paper $8.95 (0-385-17639-2). 64pp. How to draw a variety of curiosities.

21559 Ames, Lee J., and Ric Estrada. *Draw 50 Aliens, UFOs, Galaxy Ghouls, Milky Way Marauders, and Other Extraterrestrial Creatures* (3–5). Illus. Series: Draw 50. 1998, Doubleday paper $8.95 (0-385-49145-X). A step-by-step guide to drawing 50 creatures and objects from outer space. (Rev: BL 1/1–15/99; SLJ 6/99) [743]

21560 Arnosky, Jim. *Sketching Outdoors in Summer* (4–7). Illus. 1988, Lothrop $12.95 (0-688-06286-5). 48pp. The artist's appreciation of nature can inspire young enthusiasts. Also use: *Sketching Outdoors in Spring* (1987). (Rev: BL 6/15/88; HB 7–8/88; SLJ 6–7/88)

21561 Baron, Nancy. *Getting Started in Calligraphy* (4–7). Illus. by author. 1979, Sterling $13.95 (0-8069-8840-1). A well-organized text from an experienced teacher of lettering.

21562 Blitz, Bruce. *Blitz: The Fun Book of Cartoon Faces* (5–10). Illus. by author. 1999, Running Pr. paper $12.95 (0-7624-0452-3). 127pp. After a lengthy section on how to create faces, expressions, and character, the second part of this book offers games and tricks based on the skills just learned. (Rev: SLJ 1/00) [741.2]

21563 Butterfield, Moira. *Fun with Paint* (4–8). Illus. Series: Creative Crafts. 1994, Random paper $6.99 (0-679-83942-3). 47pp. This simple introduction to painting covers various media and a number of creative projects, including making your own paints. (Rev: SLJ 3/94) [745]

21564 Carreiro, Carolyn. *Hand-Print Animal Art* (3–5). Illus. by Carolyn Carreiro and A. J. Greenwood. Series: Kids Can! 1997, Williamson paper $14.95 (1-885593-09-0). 144pp. Instructions are given for creating 63 animal shapes by placing paint on one's hands and fingers and stamping them on paper. (Rev: BCCB 3/98; SLJ 4/98) [745.5]

21565 Corbett, Grahame. *You Can Draw Fantastic Animals: A Step-by-Step Guide for Young Artists* (3–6). Illus. Series: You Can Draw. 1997, DK $9.95 (0-7894-1501-1). 21pp. Photos and clever illustrations are used to enliven this book that explains in simple steps how to draw a number of weird animals. (Rev: HBG 3/98; SLJ 2/98) [741.2]

21566 DuBosque, Doug. *Draw Desert Animals* (3–6). Illus. 1996, Peel paper $8.95 (0-939217-26-0). 64pp. Beginning with simple shapes like circles and squares, teaches the reader to draw a variety of desert animals. (Rev: BL 12/15/96; SLJ 3/97) [743]

21567 DuBosque, Doug. *Draw Dinosaurs*. Rev. ed. (3–6). Illus. 1997, Peel paper $8.95 (0-939217-22-8). 64pp. A fine art book that presents easily followed directions for drawing a wide variety of dinosaurs, with interesting facts about each. (Rev: BL 12/15/97) [743.6]

21568 DuBosque, Doug. *Draw! Grassland Animals: A Step-by-Step Guide* (4–7). Illus. by author. 1996, Peel paper $8.95 (0-939217-25-2). 63pp. A step-by-step description of how to draw 31 animals from grasslands around the world. (Rev: SLJ 9/96) [741]

21569 DuBosque, Doug. *Draw Insects* (4–8). Illus. by author. 1998, Peel paper $8.95 (0-939217-28-7). 63pp. In addition to step-by-step instructions for drawing 80 different insects, this book gives information about each species and where it can be found. (Rev: SLJ 6/98) [741]

21570 DuBosque, Doug. *Draw 3-D: A Step-by-Step Guide to Perspective Drawing* (4–9). Illus. by author. 1999, Peel paper $8.95 (0-939217-14-7). 63pp. Using step-by-step directions, this art book explains how to add a third dimension to drawings by using depth, shading, reflections, and multiple vanishing points. (Rev: SLJ 5/99) [741.2]

21571 DuBosque, Doug. *Learn to Draw Now!* (5–8). Illus. by author. Series: Learn to Draw. 1991, Peel paper $8.95 (0-939217-16-3). 64pp. A simple, easily followed manual on how to draw that contains many interesting practice exercises. (Rev: SLJ 8/91) [743]

21572 Emberley, Ed. *Ed Emberley's Big Orange Drawing Book* (2–5). Illus. 1980, Little, Brown paper $9.95 (0-316-23419-2). 96pp. Emberley teaches you to draw many orange things, mostly associated with Halloween.

21573 Emberley, Ed. *Ed Emberley's Drawing Book: Make a World* (2–4). Illus. by author. 1972, Little, Brown paper $6.95 (0-316-23644-6). Illustrations and examples on how to draw objects from flags to faces.

21574 Emberley, Ed. *Ed Emberley's Drawing Book of Faces* (2–5). Illus. 1992, Little, Brown paper $6.95 (0-316-23655-1). 32pp. Step-by-step instructions on how to produce an amusing character from a simple shape.

21575 Ewing, Patrick Aloysius, and Linda L. Louis. *In the Paint* (2–5). Illus. 1999, Abbeville $15.95 (0-7892-0542-4). 64pp. Patrick Ewing talks about his favorite pastime — painting — and how young people can use color, shapes, and texture to create their own works. (Rev: BL 7/99; HBG 10/99; SLJ 11/99) [751]

21576 Goyallon, Jerome. *Drawing Prehistoric Animals* (3–6). Trans. from French by Keith Schiffman. Illus. by author. 1996, Sterling paper $5.95 (0-8069-0979-X). 80pp. Using a system of grids and simple directions, youngsters can draw 30 primitive and prehistoric mammals and Neanderthal man. (Rev: SLJ 5/97) [741.2]

21577 Henson, Paige. *Drawing with Charcoal and Pastels* (3–5). Series: How to Paint and Draw. 1999, Rourke LB $18.45 (1-57103-313-0). 32pp. This book gives background information on charcoal and pastels, shows techniques for using them, suggests ideas and projects, and explains how to clean up when you're finished. Also use *Drawing with Markers* and *Painting with Face Paints* (both 1999). (Rev: SLJ 1/00) [741.2]

21578 Henson, Paige. *Drawing with Pencils* (1–3). Series: How to Paint and Draw. 1999, Rourke LB $18.45 (1-57103-310-6). 32pp. This book contains a little history, information about supplies, and plenty of easy art projects for budding artists. Also use *Painting with Tempera* and *Painting with Watercolors* (both 1999). (Rev: SLJ 2/00) [742]

21579 Kallen, Stuart A. *Eco-Arts and Crafts* (3–4). Illus. Series: Target Earth. 1993, ABDO LB $15.98 (1-56239-208-5). 46pp. In these recycling projects, youngsters are taught how to create their own art supplies, including paper. (Rev: SLJ 3/94) [745]

21580 Lacey, Sue. *Animals* (2–5). Series: Start with Art. 1999, Millbrook LB $21.90 (0-7613-3263-4). 32pp. Various step-by-step projects are introduced using actual artworks to inspire creativity, such as Picasso's model of a goat or a Stubbs painting of a horse. Also use in the same series: *People* (1999). (Rev: HBG 3/00; SLJ 1/00) [741.2]

21581 Levin, Freddie. *1-2-3 Draw: Dinosaurs and Other Prehistoric Animals: A Step by Step Guide* (1–5). Illus. by author. 2000, Peel paper $8.95 (0-939217-41-4). 64pp. Using three basic shapes — circles, ovals, and eggs — the author shows how to draw 24 different prehistoric animals. The same techniques are applied in *1-2-3-Draw: Pets and Farm Animals* (2000). (Rev: SLJ 3/01) [742]

21582 Lewis, Amanda. *Lettering: Make Your Own Cards, Signs, Gifts and More* (3–7). Illus. 1997, Kids Can paper $5.95 (1-55074-232-9). 48pp. Demonstrates lettering techniques, shows how to make letterhead stationery on the computer, and gives material on calligraphy, type, and displays. (Rev: BL 10/15/97; SLJ 1/98) [745.6]

21583 Lightfoot, Marge. *Cartooning for Kids* (3–5). Illus. by author. Series: Greey de Pencier Books. 1993, Firefly $16.95 (1-895688-03-5); paper $8.95 (0-920775-84-5). 64pp. This useful introduction to cartooning shows how to break down figures to basic shapes, how to show movement and gesture,

and how to place people into settings. (Rev: SLJ 2/94) [741.5]

21584 Lincoln, Margaret. *The Most Excellent Book of Face Painting* (3–5). Illus. Series: Most Excellent Book Of. 1997, Millbrook LB $19.90 (0-7613-0551-3); paper $6.95 (0-7613-0576-9). 32pp. Simple step-by-step instructions are given on how to create a wide variety of brilliant faces. (Rev: BL 6/1–15/97; SLJ 8/97) [745.5]

21585 Lynn, Sara, and Diane James. *Play with Paint* (PS–3). Illus. 1993, Carolrhoda LB $19.93 (0-87614-755-4). 24pp. This beginning craft book contains simple projects with brief explanations using everyday materials. A companion volume is: *Play with Paper* (1993). (Rev: BL 5/1/93) [750]

21586 Pellowski, Michael M. *The Art of Making Comic Books* (4–8). Illus. 1995, Lerner LB $21.27 (0-8225-2304-3). 80pp. A history of comic books, with coverage of techniques and details on how to become a comic book artist. (Rev: BCCB 2/96; BL 1/1–15/96; SLJ 1/96) [741.5]

21587 Reinagle, Damon J. *Draw! Medieval Fantasies* (4–8). Illus. 1995, Peel paper $8.95 (0-939217-30-9). 64pp. A how-to drawing book that gives simple instructions on creating such medieval subjects as dragons and castles. (Rev: BL 1/1–15/96; SLJ 3/96) [743]

21588 Reinagle, Damon J. *Draw Alien Fantasies* (3–6). Illus. 1996, Peel paper $8.99 (0-939217-31-7). 64pp. Easy-to-follow directions are given for drawing a number of creatures from outer space. (Rev: BL 12/15/96; SLJ 3/97) [741.2]

21589 Russon, Jacqueline. *Face Painting* (1–4). Photos by Steve Shott. Illus. by Mei Lim. Series: First Craft Books. 1998, Carolrhoda LB $12.95 (1-57505-099-4). 22pp. There are ten simple craft projects in this book that give directions for painting faces to resemble a cat, mermaid, teddy bear, bunny, etc. (Rev: HBG 10/98; SLJ 4/98) [741.2]

21590 Russon, Jacqueline. *Face Painting* (3–7). Illus. Series: First Arts and Crafts. 1994, Thomson Learning LB $21.40 (1-56847-197-1). 32pp. An amazing number of ideas for creative face painting, with clear instructions and many illustrations. (Rev: BL 1/1/95; SLJ 12/94) [745.5]

21591 Sabbeth, Carol. *Crayons and Computers: Computer Art Activities for Kids Ages 4 to 8* (PS–4). 1998, Chicago Review paper $16.95 (1-55652-289-4). 159pp. Using a PC or Mac, any type of printer, and software such as Windows Paintbrush, ClarisWorks, or Kid Pix, this book gives instructions on over 50 craft and project ideas, including using the computer to draw a picture and, after printing it, coloring it. (Rev: SLJ 7/98) [741]

21592 Silver, Patricia. *Face Painting* (1–4). Illus. by Louise Phillips. 2000, Kids Can $12.95 (1-55074-845-9); paper $5.95 (1-55074-689-8). 40pp. A fine introduction to face painting that includes 16 of the most commonly requested faces with rules for safety and cleanup tips. (Rev: BL 9/15/00; SLJ 10/00) [745.5]

21593 Sirett, Dawn. *My First Paint Book* (3–5). Illus. Series: My First. 1994, DK $12.95 (1-56458-

466-6). 48pp. An oversize book that presents many projects, like painting T-shirts and making papier-mâché pins, in double-page spreads. (Rev: BL 5/15/94; SLJ 7/94) [745.5]

21594 Solga, Kim. *Draw!* (2–5). Illus. 1991, North Light $11.99 (0-89134-385-7). 48pp. Ten drawing projects that use color pencils, crayons, charcoal, watercolors, and felt-tip pens. Also use: *Paint!* (1991). (Rev: BL 1/15/92; SLJ 2/92) [741.2]

21595 Solga, Kim, et al. *Art Fun!* (1–6). Photos by Pamela Monfort. Illus. Series: Art and Activities for Kids. 1997, North Light paper $19.99 (0-89134-833-6). 216pp. This activity book introduces projects involving painting, drawing, printmaking, and sculpting. (Rev: SLJ 1/98) [741.2]

21596 Tallarico, Tony. *Drawing and Cartooning All-Star Sports: A Step by Step Guide for the Aspiring Sports Artist* (4–7). Illus. 1998, Putnam paper $9.95 (0-399-52417-7). 94pp. Using simple shapes such as circles and squares, this how-to book gives directions for drawing all sorts of athletes, including football, baseball, and basketball players. (Rev: BL 12/15/98) [743]

21597 Wallace, Mary. *I Can Make Art* (4–8). Photos by author. Series: I Can Make. 1997, Firefly $17.95 (1-895688-64-7); paper $6.95 (1-895688-65-5). 31pp. Art and craft combine in these 12 projects involving such techniques as watercolor, still life, chalk drawing, print-making, and collage. (Rev: SLJ 12/97) [741.2]

21598 Walsh, Patricia. *Aircraft* (3–6). Illus. Series: Draw It! 2000, Heinemann LB $21.36 (1-57572-347-6). 32pp. From the Wright brothers' flying machine to a modern Bell JetRanger helicopter, this chronologically arranged book describes aircraft and gives directions for sketching them. (Rev: BL 2/1/01) [743]

21599 Walsh, Patricia. *Cars* (3–6). Series: Draw It! 2000, Heinemann LB $21.36 (1-57572-348-4). 32pp. Using colored lines to show each step, this book shows how to draw cars in six easy steps. Also use from the same art series: *Dinosaurs, Space Vehicles,* and *Wild Animals* (all 2000). (Rev: BL 3/1/01) [741.2]

21600 Walsh, Patricia. *Woodland Animals* (3–6). Illus. 2000, Heinemann LB $21.36 (1-57572-352-2). 32pp. Introducing a single animal per double-page spread, this book describes such animals as the skunk, woodpecker, and porcupine with clear instructions on how to draw each. (Rev: BL 2/1/01; SLJ 2/01) [743]

Masks and Mask Making

21601 Beaton, Clare. *Masks* (2–4). Illus. Series: Make and Play. 1995, Fitzgerald LB $15.95 (1-887238-02-6). 24pp. Step-by-step directions for making seven different masks. (Rev: BL 1/1/91; SLJ 2/91) [731.785]

21602 Earl, Amanda, and Danielle Sensier. *Masks* (5–7). Illus. Series: Traditions Around the World. 1994, Thomson Learning $24.26 (1-56847-226-9).

48pp. This multicultural introduction to masks discusses their origins and uses in religion, festivals, and the theater. (Rev: BL 2/1/95; SLJ 3/95) [391.43]

21603 Flanagan, Alice K. *Masks!* (3–7). Illus. Series: A World of Difference. 1996, Children's LB $21.00 (0-516-08213-2). 32pp. Describes and illustrates masks from many places and time periods, reflecting different cultures. (Rev: BL 9/15/96; SLJ 11/96) [391]

Paper Crafts

21604 Araki, Chiyo. *Origami in the Classroom* (4–7). Illus. 1965, Tuttle vol. 1 $14.95 (0-8048-0452-4); vol. 2 $14.95 (0-8048-0453-2). In two volumes; each deals with paper crafts for two of the seasons.

21605 Balchin, Judy. *Papier Mâché* (4–7). Illus. Series: Step-by-Step. 2000, Heinemann $15.95 (1-57572-328-X). 32pp. Combines easy-to-follow projects with information on how papier-mâché has been used over the centuries, including applications in construction and furniture. (Rev: BL 10/15/00; SLJ 12/00) [745.54]

21606 Bliss, Helen. *Paper* (3–6). Series: Craft Workshop. 1998, Crabtree LB $22.95 (0-86505-781-8); paper $10.95 (0-86505-791-5). 32pp. This book presents a history of paper as well as various paper-related activities such as making paper, masks, puppets, etc. (Rev: SLJ 9/98) [745]

21607 Borja, Robert, and Corinne Borja. *Making Chinese Papercuts* (4–7). Illus. by authors. 1980, Whitman LB $14.95 (0-8075-4948-7). A clear explanation of an ancient art with many examples and photographs.

21608 Carter, David A., and James Diaz. *The Elements of Pop-Up: A Pop-Up Book for Aspiring Paper Engineers* (3–8). Photos by Keith Sutter. Illus. by authors. 1999, Simon & Schuster $35.00 (0-689-82224-3). Instructions are given for constructing more than 50 pop-ups with working models of each. (Rev: BL 12/15/99; HBG 3/00; SLJ 2/00) [745.5]

21609 Churchill, E. Richard. *Fast and Funny Paper Toys You Can Make* (3–7). Illus. by James Michaels. 1989, Sterling $14.95 (0-8069-5770-0). 128pp. This book takes the reader into a world of toys that move. (Rev: BL 2/1/90; SLJ 4/90) [745.592]

21610 Churchill, E. Richard. *Holiday Paper Projects* (3–6). Illus. by James Michaels. 1993, Sterling $14.95 (0-8069-8512-7). 128pp. Various paper crafts related to holidays are outlined with simple instructions that usually only involve cutting, folding, and pasting. (Rev: SLJ 12/93) [745]

21611 Corwin, Judith Hoffman. *Papercrafts: Origami, Papier-Mâché, and Collage* (1–5). Illus. 1988, Watts LB $20.00 (0-531-10465-6). 72pp. Twenty-four things to do with origami and other paper crafts. (Rev: BL 4/1/87; SLJ 10/88)

21612 Diehn, Gwen. *Making Books That Fly, Fold, Wrap, Hide, Pop Up, Twist, and Turn* (4–8). Illus. 1998, Sterling $19.95 (1-57990-023-2). 112pp. This craft book gives a history of books as well as clear directions on how to produce 18 different folded, wrapped, and pop-up books. (Rev: BL 7/98; SLJ 8/98) [736]

21613 Fiarotta, Phyllis, and Noel Fiarotta. *Papercrafts Around the World* (4–6). Illus. 1996, Sterling $21.95 (0-8069-3990-7). 96pp. Paper crafts and projects from 31 countries are included with easy-to-follow instructions. (Rev: BL 7/96; SLJ 8/96) [745.54]

21614 Fleischman, Paul. *Copier Creations* (3–8). Illus. by David Cain. 1993, HarperCollins $15.00 (0-060-21052-4). 128pp. This craft book shows how to make such items as stationery and decals by using copying machines and common materials. (Rev: BL 7/93) [760]

21615 Garza, Carmen Lomas. *Making Magic Windows: Creating Papel Picado/Cut-Paper Art* (3–7). 1999, Children's Book Pr. paper $9.95 (0-89239-159-6). 61pp. This bilingual book gives directions on making festive papel picado (cut paper) banners associated with the Southwest and Mexican Americans. (Rev: BL 5/1/99) [745.54]

21616 Grummer, Arnold E. *Paper by Kids* (5–7). Illus. 1990, Macmillan $12.95 (0-87518-191-0). 116pp. A clear, well-organized guide to papermaking.

21617 Haas, Rudi, et al. *Egg-Carton Zoo II* (3–7). Illus. 1989, Oxford paper $11.95 (0-19-540718-0). 64pp. How to make animal figures such as a rhino, shark, and pelican with simple tools and egg cartons. (Rev: BL 1/1/90) [745]

21618 Henry, Sandi. *Cut-Paper Play! Dazzling Creations from Construction Paper* (K–5). Illus. by Norma Jean Jourdenais. Series: Kids Can! 1997, Williamson paper $12.95 (1-885593-05-8). 160pp. In this book, which indicates the relative difficulty of each activity, there are projects that include making a desktop robot, a frog, and a mosaic snowman. (Rev: SLJ 9/97) [745.5]

21619 Irvine, Joan. *How to Make Pop-Ups* (3–7). Illus. by Barbara Reid. 1988, Morrow paper $6.95 (0-688-07902-4). 96pp. Instructions on how to create three-dimensional wonders. (Rev: BL 4/15/88; SLJ 3/88)

21620 Irvine, Joan. *How to Make Super Pop-Ups* (4–7). Illus. 1992, Morrow $14.00 (0-688-10690-0); paper $6.95 (0-688-11521-7). 96pp. Lots of ideas and directions for making three-dimensional paper constructions with moving parts. (Rev: BL 1/15/93) [745]

21621 Kelly, Emery J. *Paper Airplanes: Models to Build and Fly* (4–8). Illus. 1997, Lerner LB $23.93 (0-8225-2401-5). 64pp. This is a practical manual on making and flying paper airplanes, with good coverage of the principles of aerodynamics. (Rev: BL 12/1/97; HBG 3/98; SLJ 2/98) [745.592]

21622 *Look What You Can Make with Paper Bags* (3–5). Ed. by Judy Burke. Illus. 1999, Boyds Mills paper $5.95 (1-56397-717-6). 48pp. Paper bags and other easily found materials are used in this series of creative craft projects, some of which require adult help. (Rev: BL 7/99; SLJ 5/99) [745.54]

21623 McGraw, Sheila. *Papier-Mâché for Kids* (3–6). Illus. 1991, Firefly $17.95 (0-920668-92-5); paper $9.95 (0-920668-93-3). 72pp. A well-designed

craft book with instructions for eight projects. (Rev: BL 1/15/92; SLJ 3/92) [745.54]

21624 Powell, Michelle. *Printing* (4–7). Illus. Series: Step-by-Step. 2000, Heinemann $15.95 (1-57572-329-8). 32pp. Various easy-to-follow printing projects are presented along with material on printing methods from ancient Egypt onward. (Rev: BL 10/15/00) [761]

21625 Robins, Deri. *Papier Mâché* (3–6). Illus. by Jim Robins. Series: Step-by-Step. 1993, Kingfisher paper $7.95 (1-85697-926-1). 40pp. This craft book shows how to create such objects as masks, bowls, puppets, and mobiles with papier-mâché. (Rev: SLJ 3/94) [745.54]

21626 Sarasas, Claude. *The ABC's of Origami* (4–6). Illus. 1964, Tuttle $14.95 (0-8048-0000-6). Directions on how to create 26 figures from an albatross to a zebra are given.

21627 Schmidt, Norman. *Paper Birds That Fly* (5–8). Illus. 1997, Sterling $19.95 (1-895569-01-X); paper $12.95 (1-895569-11-7). 96pp. Using the simplest of materials — like paper, patterns, pencils, ruler, scissors, and glue — it is possible to make birds that fly. (Rev: SLJ 7/97) [745.5]

21628 Schwarz, Renée. *Papier-Mâché* (4–6). Illus. by Renee Schwarz. Series: Kids Can! 2000, Kids Can $12.95 (1-55074-833-5); paper $5.95 (1-55074-727-4). 40pp. This work outlines 11 projects in papier-mâché with tips on getting the proper supplies, preparing the paste, and sanding and fixing mistakes. (Rev: HBG 10/00; SLJ 6/00) [745.5]

21629 Seix, Victoria. *Creating with Papier-Mâché* (3–6). Series: Crafts for All Seasons. 2000, Blackbirch LB $18.95 (1-56711-439-3). 32pp. Fifteen projects using either paper strips or paper pulp are outlined in this attractive craft book. (Rev: SLJ 2/01) [745.5]

21630 Siomades, Lorianne, ed. *Look What You Can Make With Boxes: Over 90 Pictured Crafts and Dozens of Other Ideas* (4–6). Photos by Hank Schneider. 1998, Boyds Mills paper $5.95 (1-56397-704-4). 48pp. Different kinds of boxes (cereal, greeting card, etc.) and simple materials, such as glue and paints, are used to create toys, games, decorations, and various useful objects in this easy-to-use craft manual. (Rev: SLJ 6/98) [745.5]

21631 Solga, Kim. *Make Cards!* (2–5). Illus. Series: Art and Activities for Kids. 1992, North Light $11.99 (0-89134-481-0). 48pp. With easy-to-follow instructions, this oversize craft book tells how to make greeting cards for a number of occasions. (Rev: BL 9/15/92; SLJ 12/92) [745.594]

21632 Stowell, Charlotte. *Making Cards* (3–6). Illus. Series: Step-by-Step. 1995, Kingfisher paper $6.95 (1-85697-590-8). 40pp. Directions for making all sorts of greeting cards, including pop-ups, mobiles, and cards for different holidays. (Rev: SLJ 1/96) [745.5]

21633 Temko, Florence. *Paper Gifts and Jewelry* (2–6). Illus. by John Walls. Series: Paper Magic. 1997, Millbrook LB $20.90 (0-7613-0209-3). 45pp. Simple paper projects outlined in this useful craft book include making pleated earrings, unusual gift wraps, and special storage boxes. Also use *Paper Tags and Cards* (1997). (Rev: HBG 3/98; SLJ 9/97) [745.5]

21634 Temko, Florence. *Planes and Other Flying Things* (3–6). Illus. 1996, Millbrook LB $20.90 (0-7613-0041-4); paper $7.95 (0-7613-0082-1). 48pp. This guide to making 19 different paper airplanes begins with the basic glider and moves on to more-complicated spaceships and helicopters. (Rev: BCCB 1/97; BL 1/1–15/97) [745]

21635 Valenta, Barbara. *Pop-o-Mania: How to Create Your Own Pop-Ups* (4–6). Illus. 1997, Dial $16.99 (0-8037-1947-7). 16pp. Pop-ups and instructions are included in this craft book that will require help from an adult. (Rev: BL 12/15/97; HB 5–6/97; SLJ 6/97) [745.5]

21636 Walter, F. Virginia. *Super Toys and Games from Paper* (4–6). Illus. 1993, Sterling $19.95 (1-895569-06-0). 104pp. Directions are given for almost 90 paper toys and games, such as newspaper golf clubs and cardboard-tube hammers. (Rev: BL 1/1/94; SLJ 12/93) [745.592]

21637 Watson, David. *Papermaking* (4–7). Series: Step-by-Step. 2000, Heinemann LB $15.95 (1-57572-327-1). 32pp. This book show how you can use old paper to make new paper and create a number of wonderful art objects following simple step-by-step directions. (Rev: BL 10/15/00) [745.5]

21638 West, Robin. *Dinosaur Discoveries: How to Create Your Own Prehistoric World* (3–6). Illus. 1989, Carolrhoda $19.95 (0-87614-351-6). 72pp. Directions for creating models of dinosaurs using scissors, glue, and construction paper. (Rev: BL 11/15/89; SLJ 12/89) [745.54]

21639 Wilkinson, Beth. *Papermaking for Kids: Simple Steps to Handcrafted Paper* (4–6). Illus. 1997, Gibbs Smith paper $10.95 (0-87905-827-7). 48pp. This craft book gives a brief history of papermaking, then carefully explains in text and detailed color photos how to make paper from a variety of materials. (Rev: BL 4/15/98) [626]

Printmaking

21640 Sadler, Judy Ann. *Prints* (3–7). Illus. 1997, Kids Can paper $4.95 (1-55074-083-0). 32pp. Step-by-step, labeled drawings introduce such printmaking techniques as potato and sponge printing. (Rev: BL 10/15/97; SLJ 1/98) [760]

Sewing and Needle Crafts

21641 Bial, Raymond. *With Needle and Thread: A Book About Quilts* (4–7). Illus. 1996, Houghton $14.95 (0-395-73568-8). 48pp. An attractive introduction to quilts, their history, how they are made, and the people who sew them. (Rev: BCCB 2/96; BL 3/1/96; SLJ 6/96) [746.46]

21642 Falick, Melanie. *Kids Knitting* (4–7). Illus. 1998, Workman $17.95 (1-885183-76-3). 128pp. Exceptionally clear pictures and text are used to present the basics of knitting for girls and boys, with instructions for such projects as backpacks, hats, scarves, and sweaters. (Rev: BL 4/1/98; SLJ 7/98) [746.43]

21643 O'Reilly, Susie. *Knitting and Crochet* (3–5). Illus. Series: Arts and Crafts. 1994, Thomson Learning LB $21.40 (1-56847-221-8). 32pp. A good handicraft book that explains the basic stitches, gives directions for many projects, and encourages young knitters to create their own patterns. (Rev: SLJ 1/95) [745.5]

21644 Sadler, Judy Ann. *Corking* (4–8). Illus. Series: Kids Can! 1998, Kids Can paper $4.95 (1-55074-265-5). 32pp. Provides directions for using the handmade knitting device that creates knit tubes or corks used in making toys and headbands. (Rev: BL 5/15/98) [746.4]

21645 Sadler, Judy Ann. *Making Fleece Crafts* (4–7). Illus. by June Bradford. 2000, Kids Can $12.95 (1-55074-847-5); paper $5.95 (1-55074-739-8). 40pp. Fifteen colorful and inviting projects using fleece including mittens, a scarf, and a jester's hat. (Rev: BL 9/15/00; SLJ 9/00) [745]

21646 Sadler, Judy Ann. *Sewing* (1–4). Illus. Series: Easy Crafts. 1997, Kids Can paper $4.95 (1-55074-101-2). 32pp. Step-by-step illustrations and directions are given for projects like making placemats and decorating clothing. (Rev: BL 12/1/97) [646.2]

21647 Stoppleman, Monica, and Carol Crowe. *Fabric* (3–6). Series: Craft Workshop. 1998, Crabtree LB $22.95 (0-86505-779-6); paper $10.95 (0-86505-789-3). 32pp. A history of fabrics and related craft projects (some of which require adult supervision) make up this brief introduction to an interesting subject. (Rev: SLJ 9/98) [745]

21648 Willing, Karen Bates, and Julie Bates Dock. *Fabric Fun for Kids: Step-by-Step Projects for Children (and Their Grown-ups)* (4–9). 1997, Now & Then LB $17.95 (0-9641820-4-1); paper $12.95 (0-9641820-5-X). 55pp. From simple sewing projects to more complex quilting work, this book gives good step-by-step instructions, provides a rundown on necessary sewing tools and materials, and discusses methods for putting designs on fabrics. (Rev: SLJ 4/98) [746.46]

21649 Wilson, Sule Greg C. *African American Quilting: The Warmth of Tradition* (4–7). Illus. Series: Library of African American Arts and Culture. 1999, Rosen LB $17.95 (0-8239-1854-8). 64pp. This book traces African influences on textile patterns and techniques particularly as they have been applied to quilting by African Americans. (Rev: BL 2/15/00; SLJ 9/99) [746.46]

Toys and Dolls

21650 Churchill, E. Richard. *Paper Science Toys* (4–8). Illus. by James Michaels. 1990, Sterling $14.95 (0-8069-5834-0). 128pp. Forty-eight different toys made from easily obtainable materials. (Rev: BL 2/15/91) [745]

21651 Corbett, Sara. *What a Doll!* (3–7). Illus. Series: A World of Difference. 1996, Children's LB $21.00 (0-516-08211-6). 32pp. Dolls from various world cultures show the similarities and differences in societies. (Rev: BL 9/15/96; SLJ 11/96) [745]

21652 Johnson, Dinah. *Sitting Pretty: A Celebration of Black Dolls* (3–6). Photos by Myles C. Pinkney. 2000, Holt $18.00 (0-8050-6097-9). 45pp. Using photographs and short poems, this account introduces black dolls from Africa, North America, South America, and the Caribbean. (Rev: BL 10/1/00; HBG 3/01; SLJ 10/00) [688.7]

21653 Kay, Helen. *The First Teddy Bear* (K–3). Illus. by Susan Detweiler. 1985, Stemmer $14.95 (0-88045-042-8). 40pp. A simple tale of the history of this well-loved stuffed animal. (Rev: BCCB 2/86; BL 11/15/85; SLJ 1/86)

21654 McGraw, Sheila. *Dolls Kids Can Make* (4–6). Illus. 1995, Firefly LB $19.95 (1-895565-75-8); paper $9.95 (1-895565-74-X). 72pp. Gives directions for making dolls out of washrags, gloves, and old fabrics, with clear instructions on the stitches and techniques involved. (Rev: BL 11/15/95; SLJ 3/96) [745]

21655 Markel, Michelle. *Cornhusk, Silk, and Wishbones: A Book of Dolls from Around the World* (3–6). Illus. 2000, Houghton $15.00 (0-618-05487-1). 48pp. Photographs and double-page spreads present dolls from African, North American, South American, and Asian cultures using an alphabetical approach. (Rev: BL 10/1/00; HBG 3/01; SLJ 11/00) [688.7]

21656 Pfiffner, George. *Earth-Friendly Toys* (3–6). Illus. 1994, Wiley paper $12.95 (0-471-00822-2). 128pp. The author gives clear directions for making a number of dolls using everyday objects like toilet paper tubes and egg cartons. (Rev: BL 7/94) [745]

21657 Sadler, Judy Ann. *Beanbag Buddies and Other Stuffed Toys* (4–7). Illus. by June Bradford. Series: Kids Can! 1999, Kids Can paper $5.95 (1-55074-590-5). 40pp. Using clear directions and many step-by-step illustrations, this book offers many ideas on how to create a variety of stuffed toys. (Rev: SLJ 10/99) [745]

21658 Steele, Philip. *Toys and Games* (2–4). Illus.

2000, Watts $20.00 (0-531-14548-4). A highly visual account that traces the history of toys and games and their uses throughout history from ancient times to today. (Rev: BL 10/15/00; SLJ 6/00) [394]

21659 *The Ultimate LEGO Book* (K–3). Illus. 1999, DK $19.95 (0-7894-4691-X). 128pp. In addition to stunning photos of LEGO constructions, this account gives a history of the company, tells about model makers, and provides details on competitions open to youngsters. (Rev: BL 2/1/00) [688.1]

Woodworking

21660 Ainsworth, Ken. *Building a Shelf and a Bike Rack* (3–5). Illus. Series: Building Together. 1998, Annick LB $16.95 (1-55037-555-5); paper $5.95 (1-55037-513-X). 24pp. Stressing the need for parental participation, this book introduces woodworking techniques and shows how to build storage units including a shelf and a bike rack. (Rev: BL 2/15/99) [684]

21661 Ainsworth, Ken. *Building a Solitaire Game and a Peg Board* (3–5). Illus. 1998, Annick LB $16.95 (1-55037-554-7); paper $5.95 (1-55037-512-1). 24pp. Plans are given for building game boards, along with information on tools, techniques, safety tips, and the need for adult participation. (Rev: BL 2/15/99) [684]

21662 Gibbons, Gail. *Tool Book* (K–3). Illus. by author. 1982, Holiday LB $16.95 (0-8234-0444-7); paper $6.95 (0-8234-0694-6). 32pp. An introduction to various simple tools and their uses.

21663 Hendry, Linda, and Lisa Rebnord. *Making Picture Frames* (4–6). Photos by Frank Baldassarra. Illus. by Linda Hendry. Series: Kids Can! 1999, Kids Can paper $5.95 (1-55074-505-0). 40pp. This clearly illustrated book presents basic picture-frame construction plus variations for more appealing products. (Rev: SLJ 5/99) [684]

21664 Walker, Lester. *Housebuilding for Children* (4–7). Illus. 1977, Overlook paper $13.95 (0-87951-332-2). 176pp. The construction of six different kinds of houses, including a tree house, is clearly described in text and pictures.

Hobbies

General and Miscellaneous

21665 Adkins, Jan. *The Art and Industry of Sandcastles* (4–6). Illus. 1982, Walker paper $9.95 (0-8027-7205-6). This is an illustrated guide to basic construction of sandcastles plus amazing background information.

21666 Adkins, Jan. *String: Tying It Up, Tying It Down* (5–8). Illus. 1992, Macmillan LB $13.95 (0-684-18875-9). 48pp. With a text that reads like a novel, this book instructs and entertains readers in the art of knot tying. (Rev: BL 4/15/92; SLJ 6/92) [677]

21667 Demi. *Kites: Magic Wishes That Fly Up to the Sky* (PS–2). Illus. 1999, Crown LB $18.99 (0-517-80050-0). 40pp. After a short story about painting kites, this book describes several different kites and the holidays associated with them. (Rev: BCCB 6/99; BL 3/1/99; HBG 10/99; SLJ 6/99) [394.26]

21668 Goodman, Michael. *Model Railroading* (5–8). Illus. Series: Hobby Guides. 1993, Crestwood LB $17.95 (0-89686-620-3). 48pp. As well as describing the basics of model railroading as a hobby, this account discusses clubs, displays, and organizations. (Rev: SLJ 2/94) [625.1]

21669 Goodman, Michael. *Radio Control Models* (5–8). Illus. Series: Hobby Guides. 1993, Crestwood LB $17.95 (0-89686-622-X). 48pp. Gives practical advice on getting started in this fascinating hobby, with good background information on radio control models plus coverage on equipment, competitions, and organizations. (Rev: SLJ 2/94) [621]

21670 Kiralfy, Bob. *The Most Excellent Book of How to Be a Cheerleader* (3–5). Series: Most Excellent Book Of. 1997, Millbrook LB $19.90 (0-7613-0617-X); paper $6.95 (0-7613-0631-5). 32pp. A step-by-step guide to cheerleading, with examples of moves and chants and tips on how to look the part. (Rev: BL 11/15/97; HBG 10/98; SLJ 3/98) [761.6]

21671 Mitchelson, Mitch. *The Most Excellent Book of How to Be a Juggler* (3–5). Series: Most Excellent Book Of. 1997, Millbrook LB $19.90 (0-7613-0618-8); paper $6.95 (0-7613-0632-3). 32pp. A step-by-step guide to juggling, with examples of techniques, routines, and tips for giving an effective performance. (Rev: BL 11/15/97; HBG 10/98) [790]

21672 Perkins, Catherine. *The Most Excellent Book of How to Be a Clown* (3–5). Illus. 1996, Millbrook LB $19.90 (0-7613-0486-X); paper $6.95 (0-7613-0499-1). 32pp. Hints on makeup and presentations plus suggestions for routines are given for aspiring clowns. (Rev: BL 6/1–15/96; SLJ 6/96) [791.3]

21673 Walker, Lester. *Block Building for Children: Making Buildings of the World with the Ultimate Construction Toy* (2–6). Illus. 1995, Overlook $22.95 (0-87951-609-7). 167pp. The 18 block-building projects in this book include a city of the future and the Emerald City of Oz. (Rev: SLJ 1/96) [621]

21674 Young, Robert. *Miniature Vehicles* (4–6). Illus. Series: Collectibles. 1993, Dillon LB $18.95 (0-87518-518-5). 71pp. A guide for young collectors of miniature vehicles that tells about current sources, how models are manufactured, and where famous collections can be found. (Rev: BL 10/1/93) [629.22]

Cooking

21675 *Addy's Cook Book: A Peek at Dining in the Past with Meals You Can Cook Today* (3–5). Illus. Series: American Girls Pastimes. 1994, Pleasant paper $5.95 (1-56247-123-6). 44pp. This cookbook deals with foods prepared and served during the days of slavery in 19th-century America. (Rev: BCCB 2/95; BL 12/15/94; SLJ 4/95) [641.5]

21676 Bisignano, Alphonse. *Cooking the Italian Way* (5–8). Illus. 1982, Lerner LB $19.93 (0-8225-0906-7). 48pp. Fifteen recipes plus a description of the country, markets, and dinner tables.

21677 Björk, Christina. *Elliot's Extraordinary Cookbook* (3–5). Trans. by Joan Sandin. Illus. by Lena Anderson. 1991, R&S $11.95 (91-29-59658-0). 64pp. A friendly book that takes the reader step by step through food preparation. (Rev: BCCB 5/91; SLJ 5/91) [641]

21678 Blain, Diane. *The Boxcar Children Cookbook* (3–5). Illus. by L. Kate Deal and Eileen M. Neill. 1991, Whitman paper $9.95 (0-8075-0856-X). 96pp. Each of the simple recipes in this book is related to the Boxcar Children series. (Rev: BL 1/15/92; SLJ 11/91) [641]

21679 Brown, Karen. *Kids Are Cookin': All-Time-Favorite Recipes That Kids Love to Cook* (3–6). Illus. 1997, Meadowbrook Pr. LB $8.00 (0-671-57552-X). 200pp. This attractive book of kids' favorite recipes includes franks and beans, grilled cheese, and milkshakes plus a number of breakfast dishes, snacks, and desserts. (Rev: BL 6/1–15/97; SLJ 7/97) [641.5]

21680 Buck-Murray, Marian. *The Mash and Smash Cookbook: Fun and Yummy Recipes Every Kid Can Make!* (3–6). Illus. 1997, Wiley paper $12.95 (0-471-17969-8). 128pp. A collection of recipes that are named to appeal to kids, with interesting sidebars containing background information about the ingredients. (Rev: BL 1/1–15/98; SLJ 2/98) [641.5]

21681 Bugni, Alice. *Moose Racks, Bear Tracks, and Other Alaska Kidsnacks: Cooking with Kids Has Never Been So Easy!* (K–5). Illus. by Shannon Cartwright. 1999, Sasquatch paper $8.95 (1-57061-214-5). This clever, fanciful book contains recipes and step-by-step instructions for the preparation of 25 easy-to-make snacks with enticing names. (Rev: SLJ 12/99) [641]

21682 Chung, Okwha, and Judy Monroe. *Cooking the Korean Way* (5–7). Illus. 1988, Lerner LB $19.93 (0-8225-0921-0). 48pp. Tempting recipes and a brief look at where they come from. (Rev: BL 8/88; SLJ 9/88)

21683 Colen, Kimberly. *Peas and Honey: Recipes for Kids (with a Pinch of Poetry)* (3–6). Illus. 1995, Boyds Mills $15.95 (1-56397-062-7). 64pp. A collection of recipes for each daily meal plus appropriate poetry and food facts. (Rev: BL 1/1/95; SLJ 3/95) [641.5]

21684 Cook, Deanna F. *The Kids' Multicultural Cookbook: Food and Fun Around the World* (3–6). Illus. 1995, Williamson paper $12.95 (0-913589-91-8). 160pp. This collection of activities, recipes, and games includes material on various regions of the world. (Rev: BL 3/15/96; SLJ 2/96) [641.59]

21685 Coronado, Rosa. *Cooking the Mexican Way* (5–8). Illus. 1982, Lerner LB $19.93 (0-8225-0907-5); paper $5.95 (0-8225-9614-8). 48pp. Easy-to-follow instructions are given for typical Mexican foods.

21686 Corwin, Judith Hoffman. *Cookie Fun* (4–6). Illus. by author. 1988, Simon & Schuster paper $5.95 (0-671-55019-5). 64pp. Simple recipes for delicious cookies in this reissued cookbook.

21687 Cotler, Amy. *The Secret Garden Cookbook: Recipes Inspired by Frances Hodgson Burnett's The Secret Garden* (4–8). Illus. by Prudence See. 1999, HarperCollins $15.95 (0-06-027740-8). 128pp. A collection of 42 recipes inspired by *The Secret Garden* arranged under such headings as "Yorkshire Breakfasts" and "Dickon's Cottage Food." (Rev: HBG 10/99; SLJ 7/99) [641.5]

21688 Coyle, Rena. *My First Baking Book* (4–6). Illus. by Tedd Arnold. 1988, Workman paper $9.95 (0-89480-579-7). 144pp. Bialosky Bear offers several fun treats to make, with the emphasis on cooking safety. (Rev: BL 1/1/89; SLJ 1/89)

21689 Coyle, Rena. *My First Cookbook* (4–7). Illus. 1985, Workman paper $10.95 (0-89480-846-X). 128pp. Fifty recipes, including pancakes, salads, and tacos, and an emphasis on safety. (Rev: BL 4/15/86; SLJ 4/86)

21690 D'Amico, Joan, and Karen Eich Drummond. *The Healthy Body Cookbook: Fun Activities and Delicious Recipes for Kids* (4–6). Illus. by Tina Cash-Walsh. 1999, Wiley paper $12.95 (0-471-18888-3). 192pp. The 56 recipes in this book are arranged according to the part of the body they benefit, e.g., heart, muscles, teeth, hair, nerves. (Rev: SLJ 2/99) [641]

21691 D'Amico, Joan, and Karen Eich Drummond. *The Science Chef Travels Around the World* (4–7). Illus. 1996, Wiley paper $12.95 (0-471-11779-X). 192pp. Recipes from around the world also include the scientific principles of various cooking and baking processes. (Rev: BL 2/1/96; SLJ 3/96) [641.5]

21692 D'Amico, Joan, and Karen Eich Drummond. *The United States Cookbook: Fabulous Foods and Fascinating Facts from All 50 States* (4–6). Illus. by Jeff Cline and Tina Cash-Walsh. 2000, Wiley paper $12.95 (0-471-35839-8). 186pp. This cookbook, which is divided into seven regions and then individual states, gives basic information about each state followed by tempting recipes and food and cooking tips. (Rev: BL 5/15/00; SLJ 5/00) [641]

21693 Davis, Robin. *The Star Wars Cookbook: Wookiee Cookies and Other Galactic Recipes* (3–5). Photos by Frankie Frankeny. 1998, Chronicle $14.95 (0-8118-2184-6). 60pp. Standard recipes, many using prepared foods, are recycled using *Star Wars* lingo in a spiral-bound cookbook. (Rev: SLJ 1/99) [641]

21694 *Desserts Around the World* (4–6). Illus. by Robert L. Wolfe and Diane Wolfe. Series: Easy Menu Ethnic Cookbooks. 1992, Lerner LB $19.93 (0-8225-0926-1). 56pp. This book gives recipes and background material on simple desserts as prepared in different countries and cultures. (Rev: BL 6/15/92) [641.8]

21695 Dooley, Norah. *Everybody Cooks Rice* (K–3). Illus. 1991, Carolrhoda LB $15.95 (0-87614-412-1); paper $6.95 (0-87614-591-8). 32pp. A story that shows the different ways Americans cook and eat rice. (Rev: BCCB 5/91; BL 4/15/91; SLJ 6/91) [641.6]

21696 *Felicity's Cook Book: A Peek at Dining in the Past with Meals You Can Cook Today* (3–5). Illus. Series: American Girls Pastimes. 1994, Pleasant paper $5.95 (1-56247-120-1). 44pp. This book, a mixture of history and recipes, re-creates meals that were current during the colonial period in American history. (Rev: BL 12/15/94) [641.5]

21697 Fison, Josie, and Felicity Dahl. *Roald Dahl's Revolting Recipes* (4–6). Illus. by Quentin Blake. 1994, Viking $15.99 (0-670-85836-6). 32pp. Recipes are given for all the dishes mentioned in Roald Dahl's books. (Rev: BCCB 3/95; BL 1/15/95; SLJ 3/95) [641.5]

21698 Frankeny, Frankie, and Wesley Martin. *The Star Wars Cookbook II: Darth Malt and More Galactic Recipes* (3–5). Photos by Frankie Frankeny. 2000, Chronicle $15.95 (0-8118-2803-4). 62pp. A delightful cookbook with 29 recipes in five categories: breakfasts, snacks, main courses, desserts, and drinks. (Rev: SLJ 11/00) [641]

21699 Gardella, Tricia, comp. *Writers in the Kitchen: Children's Book Authors Share Memories of Their Favorite Recipes* (4–6). 1998, Boyds Mills paper $14.95 (1-56397-713-3). 247pp. One hundred and fifty authors and illustrators of children's books, including Paula Danziger and Jerry Spinelli, talk about food and share a favorite recipe. (Rev: SLJ 12/98) [641]

21700 Germaine, Elizabeth, and Ann L. Burckhardt. *Cooking the Australian Way* (3–7). Illus. by Robert L. Wolfe and Diane Wolfe. Series: Easy Menu Ethnic Cookbooks. 1990, Lerner LB $19.93 (0-8225-0923-7). 48pp. Recipes from Australia and an introduction to their food and eating habits. (Rev: SLJ 2/91) [641]

21701 Gillies, Judi, and Jennifer Glossop. *The Kids Can Press Jumbo Cookbook* (5–8). Illus. 2000, Kids Can paper $14.95 (1-55074-621-9). 256pp. After a few cooking tips, this book provides recipes that range from the simple (scrambled eggs) to the difficult (crepes and carrot cake). (Rev: BL 5/1/00; SLJ 6/00) [641.8]

21702 Goodwin, Bob, and Candi Perez. *A Taste of Spain* (4–6). Illus. Series: Food Around the World. 1995, Thomson Learning LB $22.83 (1-56847-188-2). 48pp. Basic information is given about the history and culture of Spain, followed by material on Spanish food and a group of representative recipes. (Rev: SLJ 3/95) [641]

21703 Goss, Gary. *Blue Moon Soup: A Family Cookbook* (4–6). Illus. 1999, Little, Brown $16.95 (0-316-32991-6). 64pp. As well as eight to ten soup recipes for each of the seasons, this book gives related recipes for breads, salads, and snacks. (Rev: BL 11/1/99; HBG 3/00; SLJ 9/99) [641.8]

21704 Hargittai, Magdolna. *Cooking the Hungarian Way* (5–7). Illus. 1986, Lerner LB $19.93 (0-8225-0916-4). 48pp. An Easy Menu Ethnic Cookbook, with information about Hungarian history and food. (Rev: BL 10/15/86)

21705 Harrison, Supenn, and Judy Monroe. *Cooking the Thai Way* (5–7). Illus. 1986, Lerner LB $19.93 (0-8225-0917-2). 48pp. Such recipes as Thai salads are included in this Easy Menu Ethnic Cookbook, along with history and information about Thai food. (Rev: BL 10/15/86)

21706 Hill, Barbara W. *Cooking the English Way* (5–8). Illus. 1982, Lerner LB $19.93 (0-8225-0903-

2). 48pp. Menus from breakfast through dinner are outlined plus national customs.

21707 *Holiday Cooking Around the World* (4–6). Illus. 1988, Lerner LB $19.93 (0-8225-0922-9); paper $5.95 (0-8225-9573-7). 52pp. Recipes for holiday treats from around the world. (Rev: BL 1/15/89; SLJ 1/89)

21708 Hughes, Helga. *Cooking the Swiss Way* (5–8). Photos by Robert L. Wolfe and Diane Wolfe. Illus. Series: Easy Menu Ethnic Cookbooks. 1995, Lerner LB $19.93 (0-8225-0930-X). 47pp. After a general introduction to Switzerland, this book colorfully discusses its food and produce and gives a number of tempting recipes. (Rev: SLJ 7/95) [641]

21709 Katzen, Mollie. *Honest Pretzels: And 64 Other Amazing Recipes for Cooks Ages 8 and Up* (4–6). Illus. 1999, Tricycle Pr. $19.95 (1-883672-88-0). 192pp. Here is a collection of 64 vegetarian recipes designed for older children. (Rev: BL 11/1/99; HBG 3/00; SLJ 9/99) [641.5]

21710 Katzen, Mollie, and Ann Henderson. *Pretend Soup and Other Real Recipes: A Cookbook for Preschoolers and Up* (PS–3). Illus. by Mollie Katzen. 1994, Tricycle Pr. $16.95 (1-883672-06-6). 95pp. Using pictures as well as text, 17 simple recipes are presented that are easy enough for youngsters to prepare with little supervision. (Rev: HB 7–8/94; SLJ 6/94*) [641]

21711 Kaufman, Cheryl Davidson. *Cooking the Caribbean Way* (5–7). Illus. 1988, Lerner LB $19.93 (0-8225-0920-2). 48pp. A variety of dishes featuring the spices and fresh fruits that come from these islands. (Rev: BL 8/88; SLJ 9/88)

21712 *Kids' First Cookbook: Delicious-Nutritious Treats to Make Yourself!* (K–3). 1999, American Cancer Society $13.95 (0-944235-19-0). 88pp. A cookbook with 53 nutritionally sound recipes plus information on how to read a food label, kitchen safety, and a guide to the food pyramid. (Rev: SLJ 3/00) [641]

21713 *Kirsten's Cook Book: A Peek at Dining in the Past with Meals You Can Cook Today* (3–5). Illus. Series: American Girls Pastimes. 1994, Pleasant paper $5.95 (1-56247-111-2). 44pp. Describes the food that pioneer Swedish families ate in the United States and gives 17 simple recipes. (Rev: BCCB 2/95; BL 12/15/94; SLJ 10/94) [641.5]

21714 Krizmanic, Judy. *The Teen's Vegetarian Cookbook* (5–10). Illus. by Matthew Wawiorka. 1999, Viking $15.99 (0-670-87426-4). 186pp. An attractive cookbook that focuses on healthy eating through vegetarianism and features clearly written recipes using commonly found ingredients. (Rev: SLJ 6/99) [641.5]

21715 MacDonald, Kate. *The Anne of Green Gables Cookbook* (4–7). Illus. by Barbara Dilella. 1987, Oxford $14.95 (0-19-540496-3). 48pp. The granddaughter of the Anne series, MacDonald combines heritage and expertise in 25 enticing recipes. (Rev: BL 1/1/87)

21716 McKenley, Yvonne. *A Taste of the Caribbean* (4–6). Illus. Series: Food Around the World. 1995, Thomson Learning LB $22.83 (1-56847-187-4).

48pp. Describes the food of the Caribbean islands, gives several recipes, and supplies basic background information on Caribbean history and culture. (Rev: SLJ 3/95) [641]

21717 MacLeod, Elizabeth. *Bake It and Build It* (2–6). Illus. 1998, Kids Can paper $5.95 (1-55074-427-5). 40pp. This combination cooking and craft book shows how to make objects such as a cookie castle, an edible flower wreath, and cookie flowers out of various kinds of cookies, oatmeal, and different doughs. (Rev: BL 12/1/98; SLJ 1/99) [745.5]

21718 Madavan, Vijay. *Cooking the Indian Way* (5–8). Illus. 1985, Lerner LB $19.93 (0-8225-0911-3). 52pp. Cultural information is detailed plus both vegetarian and nonvegetarian recipes. (Rev: SLJ 9/85)

21719 Mayer, Marianna. *The Mother Goose Cookbook: Rhymes and Recipes for the Very Young* (1–3). Illus. by Carol Schwartz. 1998, Morrow $11.95 (0-688-15242-2). 40pp. Rather complex recipes for such dishes as pease porridge and plum pudding are accompanied by the traditional rhymes that inspired them. (Rev: BL 4/1/98; HBG 10/98; SLJ 4/98) [641.5]

21720 Medearis, Angela Shelf, and Michael R. Medearis. *Cooking* (5–8). Illus. 1997, Twenty-First Century $18.90 (0-8050-4484-1). 80pp. This account traces the contributions of African Americans to cooking and food. (Rev: BL 2/15/98; SLJ 11/97) [641.59]

21721 *Molly's Cook Book: A Peek at Dining in the Past with Meals You Can Cook Today* (3–5). Illus. Series: American Girls Pastimes. 1994, Pleasant paper $5.95 (1-56247-117-1). 44pp. A look at life between the world wars is given in this cookbook with recipes that reflect those times. (Rev: BL 12/15/94) [641.5]

21722 Monroe, Lucy. *Creepy Cuisine: Revolting Recipes that Look Disgusting But Taste Divine* (4–7). Illus. by Dianne O. Burke. 1993, Random $5.99 (0-679-84402-3). 79pp. Recipes that bear such revolting names as Pus Pockets and Worms au Gratin actually contain directions for preparing delicious food, plus all sorts of cooking techniques and tips. (Rev: BCCB 10/93; SLJ 12/93) [641]

21723 Nabwire, Constance. *Cooking the African Way* (5–8). Illus. 1988, Lerner LB $19.93 (0-8225-0919-9); paper $5.95 (0-8225-9564-8). 48pp. Clear instructions highlight these African recipes. (Rev: BCCB 5/89; BL 3/15/89)

21724 Nathan, Joan. *The Children's Jewish Holiday Kitchen: 70 Ways to Have Fun with Your Kids and Make Your Family's Celebrations Special* (4–6). Illus. 1995, Schocken $24.00 (0-8052-4130-2). 176pp. Seventy recipes arranged by holiday and by the degree of difficulty and need for supervision. (Rev: BL 10/15/95) [641.5]

21725 Nguyen, Chi, and Judy Monroe. *Cooking the Vietnamese Way* (5–8). Illus. 1985, Lerner LB $19.93 (0-8225-0914-8). 48pp. Information about the country is given plus recipes for native dishes and even how to eat with chopsticks. (Rev: SLJ 9/85)

21726 Numeroff, Laura. *Mouse Cookies: 10 Easy-to-Make Cookie Recipes* (2–4). Illus. by Felicia

Bond. Series: Laura Geringer Books. 1995, Harper-Festival $13.95 (0-694-00633-5). 25pp. A spiral-bound book that contains amusing illustrations and ten recipes that are spinoffs from the author's *If You Give a Mouse a Cookie* (1985). (Rev: SLJ 11/95) [641]

21727 Osseo-Asare, Fran. *A Good Soup Attracts Chairs: A First African Cookbook for American Kids* (4–8). Illus. 1993, Pelican $18.95 (0-88289-816-7). 160pp. The more than 35 recipes from Ghana found in this book include peanut butter stew and palm nut soup. (Rev: BL 10/15/93; SLJ 8/93) [641.5]

21728 Parnell, Helga. *Cooking the German Way* (5–7). Illus. 1988, Lerner LB $19.93 (0-8225-0918-0). 48pp. Includes such treats as Black Forest Torte and Apple Cake. (Rev: BL 8/88)

21729 Parnell, Helga. *Cooking the South American Way* (4–6). Illus. by Robert L. Wolfe and Diane Wolfe. 1992, Lerner LB $19.93 (0-8225-0925-3). 48pp. Great recipes and basic data about where the foods come from. (Rev: BL 6/15/92) [641]

21730 *The Please Touch Cookbook* (K–3). Illus. 1990, Silver Burdett LB $7.95 (0-671-70558-X). 64pp. A good beginning cookbook with some 70 recipes. (Rev: SLJ 10/90) [641.5]

21731 Plotkin, Gregory, and Rita Plotkin. *Cooking the Russian Way* (5–7). Illus. 1986, Lerner LB $19.93 (0-8225-0915-6). 48pp. Included along with history and information are such recipes as Russian honey spice cake, in this Easy Menu Ethnic Cookbook. (Rev: BL 10/15/86)

21732 Pratt, Dianne. *Hey Kids! You're Cookin' Now! A Global Awareness Cooking Adventure* (4–6). Illus. 1998, Harvest Hill $19.95 (1-886862-07-9). 160pp. Seventeen cooking projects, along with the necessary recipes and directions, are including in this handy volume dealing with such edibles as pizza and chocolate pudding and some non-edibles such as glue and play clay. (Rev: BL 12/15/98; SLJ 3/99) [641.5]

21733 Pulleyn, Micah, and Sarah Bracken. *Kids in the Kitchen: 100 Delicious, Fun and Healthy Recipes to Cook and Bake* (3–5). Illus. 1994, Sterling $24.95 (0-8069-0447-X). 112pp. Gives background information on food preparation for boys and girls plus lots of recipes, many of which require no cooking. (Rev: BL 7/94; SLJ 8/94) [641.5]

21734 Ralph, Judy, and Ray Gompf. *The Peanut Butter Cookbook for Kids* (5–7). Illus. 1995, Hyperion LB $15.49 (0-7868-2110-8); paper $10.95 (0-7868-1028-9). 96pp. An amazing collection of recipes involving peanut butter, including soups, snacks, and main dishes. (Rev: BL 10/1/95; SLJ 9/95) [641.6]

21735 Rotner, Shelley, and Julia P. Hellums. *Hold the Anchovies!* (K–2). Illus. 1996, Orchard LB $16.99 (0-531-08857-X). 32pp. The pizza, its ingredients, and methods of preparation are presented with a recipe for basic pizza dough. (Rev: BL 9/15/96; SLJ 10/96) [641.8]

21736 *Samantha's Cook Book: A Peek at Dining in the Past with Meals You Can Cook Today* (3–5).

Illus. Series: American Girls Pastimes. 1994, Pleasant paper $5.95 (1-56247-114-7). 44pp. Twentieth-century American history is reflected in a series of recipes for easily prepared meals. (Rev: BL 12/15/94; SLJ 10/94) [641]

21737 Scherie, Strom. *Stuffin' Muffin: Muffin Pan Cooking for Kids* (4–6). Illus. by Dave Ferry. 1982, Young People's Pr. paper $18.95 (0-9606964-9-0). 100pp. A variety of foods without sugar or salt that can be made in muffin tins.

21738 Skrepcinski, Denice, et al. *Cody Coyote Cooks! A Southwest Cookbook for Kids* (4–6). Illus. 1996, Tricycle Pr. paper $14.95 (1-883672-37-6). 96pp. Recipes along with legends, history, and geographical facts highlight this book about cooking and eating in Texas, Arizona, and New Mexico. (Rev: BL 10/15/96; SLJ 10/96) [641]

21739 Supraner, Robyn. *Quick and Easy Cookbook* (1–3). Illus. by Renzo Barto. 1981, Troll LB $16.65 (0-89375-438-2). 48pp. A good introductory cookbook with 22 recipes.

21740 Van der Linde, Polly, and Tasha Van der Linde. *Around the World in Eighty Dishes* (3–7). Illus. by Horst Lemke. 1971, Scroll $12.95 (0-87592-007-1). 88pp. The compilers and testers of these recipes from many continents are two little girls, eight and ten years old.

21741 *Vegetarian Cooking Around the World* (5–7). Illus. Series: Easy Menu Ethnic Cookbooks. 1992, Lerner LB $19.95 (0-8225-0927-X). 48pp. Vegetarian meal recipes from the Americas, Africa, Asia, Europe, and Australia. (Rev: BL 2/15/93) [641.5]

21742 Villios, Lynne W. *Cooking the Greek Way* (5–8). Illus. 1984, Lerner LB $19.93 (0-8225-0910-5). 52pp. The young cook is introduced to the cuisine of Greece, with a chapter covering utensils and ingredient needs and a glossary of basic cooking terms. Recipes are varied and easy to prepare.

21743 Waldee, Lynne Marie. *Cooking the French Way* (5–8). Illus. 1982, Lerner LB $19.93 (0-8225-0904-0). 48pp. A nicely illustrated introduction to French recipes including breads and sauces.

21744 Walker, Barbara M. *The Little House Cookbook* (5–7). Illus. by Garth Williams. 1979, HarperCollins paper $9.95 (0-06-446090-8). 256pp. Frontier food, such as green pumpkin pie from the Little House books, served up in tasty, easily used recipes.

21745 Warner, Margaret Brink, and Ruth Ann Hayward. *What's Cooking? Favorite Recipes from Around the World* (5–8). Illus. 1981, Little, Brown $16.95 (0-316-35252-7). Eighty-nine recipes from teenagers around the world are given in simple terms.

21746 Warshaw, Hallie. *The Sleepover Cookbook* (4–8). Photos by Julie Brown. 2000, Sterling $19.95 (0-8069-4497-8). 126pp. Easy-to-prepare goodies for all kinds of sleepovers are outlined with color photographs on each spread. (Rev: HBG 10/00; SLJ 7/00) [641]

21747 Webb, Lois S. *Holidays of the World Cookbook for Students* (5–8). 1995, Oryx paper $35.00 (0-89774-884-0). 264pp. This excellent cookbook contains 388 recipes that represent holidays in 136 countries, including many from various regions of the United States. (Rev: SLJ 1/96) [641]

21748 Weston, Reiko. *Cooking the Japanese Way* (5–8). Illus. 1983, Lerner LB $19.93 (0-8225-0905-9). 48pp. Directions for preparing traditional foods are given along with lists of terms, ingredients, and utensils.

21749 White, Linda. *Cooking on a Stick: Campfire Recipes for Kids* (3–6). Illus. 1996, Gibbs Smith paper $8.95 (0-87905-727-0). 48pp. In addition to covering campfire cooking, this book discusses equipment and fire making. (Rev: BL 4/1/96) [641.5]

21750 Wilkes, Angela. *The Children's Quick and Easy Cookbook* (4–6). Illus. 1997, DK $16.95 (0-7894-2026-0). 96pp. Not nearly as "quick and easy" as the title would suggest, this book nevertheless contains some good recipes in an attractive format. (Rev: BL 12/15/97; HBG 3/98; SLJ 1/98) [641.5]

21751 Williamson, Sarah A., and Zachary Williamson. *Kids Cook! Fabulous Food for the Whole Family* (4–6). Illus. by Loretta Trezzo-Baren. 1992, Williamson paper $12.95 (0-913589-61-6). 157pp. Using recipes at three levels of difficulty, this book contains 153 recipes of foods that are fun to prepare. (Rev: SLJ 7/92) [641.5]

21752 Winston, Mary, ed. *American Heart Association Kids' Cookbook* (3–7). Illus. by Joan Holub. 1993, Times Bks. $16.00 (0-8129-1930-0). 128pp. An exceptional cookbook with outstanding healthful recipes and many nutritional tips. (Rev: BL 10/1/93*) [641.5]

21753 Wishik, Cindy S. *Kids Dish It Up . . . Sugar-Free: A Versatile Teaching Tool for Beginning Cooks* (3–5). Illus. 1982, Peninsula paper $11.95 (0-918146-22-4). 160pp. From soup to nuts with sugar-free recipes.

21754 Yu, Ling. *Cooking the Chinese Way* (5–8). Illus. 1982, Lerner LB $19.93 (0-8225-0902-4). 48pp. From appetizers to desserts, with attractive illustrations.

21755 Zalben, Jane Breskin. *Beni's Family Cookbook: For the Jewish Holidays* (4–8). Illus. 1996, Holt $19.95 (0-8050-3735-7). 91pp. This entertaining collection of recipes is arranged around the Jewish calendar. (Rev: BL 9/15/96; SLJ 2/97) [641.5]

21756 Zalben, Jane Breskin. *To Every Season: A Family Holiday Cookbook* (4–8). Illus. 1999, Simon & Schuster $19.95 (0-689-81797-5). 112pp. Arranged by the name of the holiday (from New Year's Day to Kwanzaa), this book explains the importance of each holiday and supplies a total of 69 recipes for the 16 American holidays highlighted. (Rev: BL 12/1/99; HBG 3/00; SLJ 2/00) [641.5]

21757 Zamojska-Hutchins, Danuta. *Cooking the Polish Way* (5–8). Illus. 1984, Lerner LB $19.93 (0-8225-0909-1). 52pp. Simple Polish recipes include traditional dishes such as pierogi. Glossary of terms, plus listing of utensils and ingredients used.

21758 Zanzarella, Marianne. *The Good Housekeeping Illustrated Children's Cookbook* (5–8). Illus. 1997, Morrow $17.95 (0-688-13375-4). 176pp. A visually appealing cookbook containing a number of recipes that require adult supervision. (Rev: BL 12/15/97; HBG 3/98; SLJ 1/98) [641.5]

Gardening

21759 Björk, Christina. *Linnea's Windowsill Garden* (1–5). Trans. by Joan Sandin. Illus. by Lena Anderson. 1988, Farrar $13.00 (91-29-59064-7). 60pp. Linnea takes readers on a tour of her indoor garden. (Rev: BCCB 12/88; BL 1/15/89; SLJ 11/88) [635]

21760 Burns, Kate, and Dawn Apperley. *How Does Your Garden Grow?* (K–2). Illus. 1998, Levinson $10.95 (1-899607-51-X). In this interactive garden book, flowers and vegetables pop-up from seeds. (Rev: BL 1/1–15/99; SLJ 1/99) [635]

21761 Dietl, Ulla. *The Plant-and-Grow Project Book* (PS–3). Illus. 1994, Sterling $14.95 (0-8069-0456-9). 48pp. Contains a series of projects involving indoor gardening and growing such plants as cotton, corn, eggplant, and wheat. (Rev: BL 1/15/94) [635.9]

21762 Eclare, Melanie. *A Handful of Sunshine* (2–4). Illus. 2000, Ragged Bears $16.95 (1-929927-14-2). 32pp. In this beginner's gardening book, little Tilda plants a sunflower seed and tends it until she harvests the seeds for next year. (Rev: BCCB 12/00; BL 11/1/00; SLJ 12/00) [635.9]

21763 Kite, L. Patricia. *Gardening Wizardry for Kids* (3–6). 1995, Barron's paper $14.95 (0-8120-1317-4). 220pp. A guide to windowsill and kitchen gardens, with informative explanations, projects and experiments. (Rev: BL 8/95) [635]

21764 Lerner, Carol. *My Backyard Garden* (4–6). Illus. 1998, Morrow $16.00 (0-688-14755-0). 48pp. Advice and inspiration are supplied in this book about planting and caring for a backyard vegetable garden. (Rev: BL 3/15/98; HBG 10/98; SLJ 4/98) [635]

21765 Lerner, Carol. *My Indoor Garden* (3–7). Illus. 1999, Morrow LB $15.93 (0-688-14754-2). 48pp. Pen-and-watercolor drawings are used to illustrate this guide to indoor gardening, the necessary tools, conditions, and the types of suitable plants. (Rev: BL 6/1–15/99; HB 7–8/99; HBG 10/99; SLJ 4/99) [635.9]

21766 Lovejoy, Sharon. *Roots, Shoots, Buckets and Boots: Gardening Together with Children* (1–4). Illus. by author. 1999, Workman $24.95 (0-7611-1765-2); paper $13.95 (0-7611-1056-9). 159pp. A fine how-to book on gardening with lore, tips, techniques, and ideas for adults and children to share including a list of the top 20 plans for kids. (Rev: SLJ 2/00) [635]

21767 Maass, Robert. *Garden* (1–3). Illus. 1998, Holt $15.95 (0-8050-5477-4). 32pp. Photographs of children gardening are used with a simple text to explain plants and their cultivation, including annuals, perennials, bulbs, planting, and composting. (Rev: BL 6/1–15/98; HBG 10/98; SLJ 4/98) [635]

21768 MacLeod, Elizabeth. *Grow It Again* (3–5). Illus. Series: Kids Can! 1999, Kids Can paper $5.95 (1-55074-558-1). 40pp. Using discarded parts of plants — carrot tops, avocado pits, and potato buds

— this guide shows how to grow new vegetables and fruits and supplies a few tasty recipes and interesting projects. (Rev: BL 6/1–15/99; SLJ 6/99) [635]

21769 Maurer, Tracy Nelson. *Growing Flowers* (1–4). Series: Green Thumb Guides. 2000, Rourke LB $21.27 (1-55916-251-1). 24pp. A very simple gardening guide that includes material on what, where, and when to plant plus information on weeding, watering, and other gardening tips. Also use *Growing House Plants* and *Growing Vegetables* (both 2000). (Rev: SLJ 1/01) [635]

21770 Morris, Karyn. *The Kids Can Press Jumbo Book of Gardening* (3–6). Illus. 2000, Kids Can $14.95 (1-55074-690-1). 240pp. Some of the topics covered in this information-packed volume include fruit, vegetable, and flower gardens; native plants; gardens that attract wildlife; and group projects. (Rev: BL 7/00) [635]

21771 Rhoades, Diane. *Garden Crafts for Kids: 50 Great Reasons to Get Your Hands Dirty* (3–6). Illus. 1995, Sterling $21.95 (0-8069-0998-6). 144pp. A complete guide for the beginning gardener, from choosing the right spot, to selecting seeds and plants, preparing the soil, and growing healthy plants. (Rev: SLJ 8/95*) [635]

21772 Rosen, Michael J., ed. *Down to Earth* (5–8). Illus. 1998, Harcourt $18.00 (0-15-201341-5). 64pp. The work of 41 children's authors and illustrators has been collected for this volume of stories, projects, recipes, and other material on the joys of gardening and its allied activities. (Rev: BCCB 7–8/98; BL 4/1/98; HBG 10/98; SLJ 4/98) [635]

21773 Smith, Maggie. *This Is Your Garden* (PS–1). Illus. 1998, Crown $14.00 (0-517-70992-9). 32pp. In this gardening manual for the very young, topics such as planting a garden, using proper tools, and caring for the garden are covered in a simple text and watercolor-charcoal drawings. (Rev: BL 5/1/98; HBG 10/98; SLJ 6/98) [635]

21774 Van Hage, Mary An. *Little Green Thumbs* (3–6). Photos by Lucy Tizard. Illus. by Bettina Paterson. 1996, Millbrook LB $21.40 (1-56294-270-0). 32pp. An activity book that offers 12 indoor and outdoor projects for each of the seasons, like building a dinosaur-theme terrarium or planting an orange tree. (Rev: SLJ 7/96) [635]

21775 Walker, Lois. *Get Growing! Exciting Indoor Plant Projects for Kids* (2–6). Illus. 1991, Wiley paper $10.95 (0-471-54488-4). 101pp. This project book shows how to grow 11 common food plants, such as beans and pineapples, indoors. (Rev: SLJ 11/91) [635]

Magic

21776 Baker, James W. *Illusions Illustrated: A Professional Magic Show for Young Performers* (5–8). Illus. by Jeanette Swofford. 1994, Lerner paper $6.95 (0-8225-9512-5). 120pp. Directions on how to put on a magic show with ten different tricks.

21777 Broekel, Ray, and Laurence B. White. *Abra-Ca-Dazzle: Easy Magic Tricks* (3–5). Illus. by Mary

Thelen. 1982, Whitman LB $13.95 (0-8075-0121-2). 48pp. Twenty-five simple but impressive tricks for the beginner.

21778 Broekel, Ray, and Laurence B. White. *Hocus Pocus: Magic You Can Do* (4–6). Illus. by Mary Thelen. 1984, Whitman LB $13.95 (0-8075-3350-5). 48pp. Twenty simple tricks for beginners.

21779 Charles, Kirk. *Amazing Coin Tricks* (3–5). Illus. 1995, Child's World LB $21.36 (1-56766-084-3). 24pp. Ten simple coin tricks, including how to pull one from the air, are presented in this beginner's magic book. Also use *Amazing String Tricks* (1995). (Rev: BL 11/15/95) [793.8]

21780 Cobb, Vicki. *Magic . . . Naturally! Science Entertainments and Amusements* (4–6). Illus. 1993, HarperCollins LB $16.89 (0-06-022475-4). 150pp. A group of experiments that demonstrate the magic found in many scientific phenomena. (Rev: BL 10/15/93; SLJ 10/93) [793.8]

21781 Day, Jon. *Let's Make Magic: Over 40 Tricks You Can Do* (4–7). Illus. by Chris Fisher. 1992, Kingfisher paper $12.95 (1-85697-806-0). 96pp. Using items generally found at home, the author shows readers how they can make magic. (Rev: BL 10/15/92; SLJ 11/92 & 7/93) [793.2]

21782 Eldin, Peter. *The Most Excellent Book of How to Be a Magician* (3–5). Illus. 1996, Millbrook LB $19.90 (0-7613-0458-4); paper $6.95 (0-7613-0473-8). 32pp. Practical advice for would-be magicians, with simple tricks explained and tips on presentation. (Rev: BL 6/1–15/96; SLJ 6/96) [793.8]

21783 Friedhoffer, Robert. *Magic and Perception: The Art and Science of Fooling the Senses* (5–7). Illus. 1996, Watts LB $25.00 (0-531-11254-3). 109pp. Simple directions for magic tricks that involve altering perceptions. (Rev: BL 7/96; SLJ 9/96) [793.8]

21784 Gordon, Henry. *It's Magic* (4–6). Illus. 1989, Prometheus paper $13.00 (0-87975-545-8). 92pp. A treasury of simple magic tricks. (Rev: BL 12/1/89) [793.8]

21785 Leyton, Lawrence. *My First Magic Book: A Life-Size Guide to Making and Performing Magic Tricks* (3–5). Illus. 1993, DK $12.95 (1-56458-319-8). 48pp. A large-format book that explains how to perform some puzzling tricks and make the props to accompany them. (Rev: BL 12/15/93; SLJ 4/94) [793.8]

21786 McMaster, Shawn. *Magic Tricks: Absolutely Everything You Need to Know About Magic!* (3–6). Illus. by Mike Moran. 2000, Lowell House paper $9.95 (0-7373-0231-3). 119pp. As well as a number of tricks, this book gives a history of sleight-of-hand performances and spells out the skills required to become a magician. (Rev: SLJ 8/00) [793.8]

21787 McMaster, Shawn. *60 Super Simple Magic Tricks* (3–6). Illus. by Leo Abbett. 1996, Lowell House paper $6.95 (1-56565-384-X). 80pp. Simple instructions are used to describe clearly 60 magic tricks, with additional information on effective presentations and examples of magician's patter. (Rev: SLJ 2/97) [783.9]

21788 Presto, Fay. *Magic for Kids* (3–6). Illus. 1999, Kingfisher paper $10.95 (0-7534-5210-3). 72pp. Step-by-step instructions are given for 20 tricks sure to please the young amateur magician. (Rev: BL 11/15/99) [793.8]

21789 Rigney, Francis. *A Beginner's Book of Magic* (4–6). Illus. 1963, Devin $8.25 (0-8159-5103-5). This is a do-it-yourself book of tricks, magic, and stunts.

21790 Russell, Tom. *Magic Step-by-Step* (3–6). Illus. 1997, Sterling $17.95 (0-8069-9533-5). 80pp. Step-by-step instructions for such areas of magic as disappearing acts and tricks involving cards and coins. (Rev: SLJ 8/97) [793.8]

21791 White, Laurence B., and Ray Broekel. *Razzle Dazzle! Magic Tricks for You* (3–5). Illus. 1987, Whitman LB $13.95 (0-8075-6857-0). 48pp. A clever collection of mystifying tricks explained clearly in text, diagrams, and witty cartoonlike illustrations. (Rev: BL 1/1/88)

21792 Wyler, Rose, and Gerald Ames. *Spooky Tricks* (1–3). Illus. 1994, HarperCollins paper $3.95 (0-06-444172-5). 64pp. Magic tricks with spooky trappings are explained clearly, with helpful illustrations. (Rev: BL 9/15/94; SLJ 7/95) [793.8]

Model Making

21793 Bliss, Helen, and Ruth Thomson. *Models* (2–6). Series: Craft Workshop. 1998, Crabtree LB $22.95 (0-86505-778-8); paper $10.95 (0-86505-788-5). 32pp. A well-organized craft book that offers instruction on how to make miniature objects from various countries and cultures. (Rev: SLJ 10/98) [745]

21794 Harris, Jack C. *Plastic Model Kits* (5–8). Illus. Series: Hobby Guides. 1993, Crestwood LB $21.00 (0-89686-623-8). 48pp. The hobby of making plastic models from kits is introduced, with good background information for both the novice and the expert. (Rev: SLJ 2/94) [745]

21795 Schmidt, Norman. *Fabulous Paper Gliders* (5–10). 1998, Sterling $19.95 (1-895569-21-4). 96pp. This book can serve two purposes: as a guide to building 16 model gliders and as a history of how these motorless planes developed. (Rev: SLJ 6/98) [745]

21796 Simon, Seymour. *The Paper Airplane Book* (3–6). Illus. by Byron Barton. 1971, Puffin paper $5.99 (0-14-030925-X). Using how-to-make paper airplanes as the takeoff point, the author explains why planes fly and how changes in their construction can cause variations in flight.

Photography and Filmmaking

21797 Evans, Art. *First Photos: How Kids Can Take Great Pictures* (4–6). Illus. 1993, Photo Data Research paper $9.95 (0-9626508-7-0). 64pp. Focuses on disposable cameras and gives good tips on topics like composition, light, point of view, and camera handling. (Rev: BL 12/15/92; SLJ 9/93) [770]

21798 Gibbons, Gail. *Click! A Book About Cameras and Taking Pictures* (K–3). Illus. 1997, Little, Brown $14.95 (0-316-30976-1). 32pp. As well as describing the workings of a camera, this simple guide tells how to take good pictures indoors and out. (Rev: BL 4/1/97; SLJ 5/97) [771]

21799 Hilton, Jonathan, and Barrie Watts. *Photography* (4–6). Illus. Series: First Guide. 1994, Millbrook LB $23.90 (1-56294-398-7). 96pp. Basic photographic equipment is introduced, with techniques and tips on taking a variety of photos, from still lifes to portraits. (Rev: BL 12/15/94) [770]

21800 King, Dave. *My First Photography Book* (4–7). Illus. Series: My First. 1994, DK $12.95 (1-56458-673-1). 48pp. A manual on how to use your camera creatively, with many interesting projects outlined. (Rev: BL 1/15/95; SLJ 12/94) [771]

21801 Lasky, Kathryn. *Think Like an Eagle: At Work with a Wildlife Photographer* (3–7). Illus. by Christopher G. Knight and Jack Swedberg. 1992, Little, Brown $15.95 (0-316-51519-1). 48pp. Following a wildlife photographer through the seasons and across the country. (Rev: BCCB 3/92; BL 6/1/92; SLJ 4/92) [778.9]

21802 Morgan, Terri, and Shmuel Thaler. *Photography: Take Your Best Shot* (5–8). Illus. 1991, Lerner LB $21.27 (0-8225-2302-7). 72pp. A comprehensive and well-put-together guide to photography. (Rev: BL 10/1/91) [771]

21803 Price, Susanna, and Tim Stephens. *Click! Fun with Photography* (4–8). Illus. 1997, Sterling $14.95 (0-8069-9541-6). 48pp. A fine introduction to photography that covers both beginning and advanced topics including the operation of various cameras, exposure, lighting, different types of photography, and filters. (Rev: SLJ 8/97) [770]

21804 Varriale, Jim. *Take a Look Around: Photography Activities for Young People* (5–8). Illus. 1999, Millbrook LB $23.90 (0-7613-1265-X). 32pp. Photographs taken by children in a summer camp photography class illustrate the importance of such elements as light and camera angles, framing, creating mood, and photographing action. (Rev: BL 3/15/00; HBG 3/00; SLJ 12/99) [770]

21805 Wallace, Joseph. *The Camera* (4–7). Series: Turning Points. 2000, Simon & Schuster $17.95 (0-

689-82813-6). 80pp. This is a basic history of photography — with a focus on the development of the camera and its impact on our lives. (Rev: BL 8/00; HBG 3/01) [778.59]

Stamp, Coin, and Other Types of Collecting

21806 Dobkin, Bonnie. *Collecting* (1–2). Illus. by Rick Hackney. Series: Rookie Readers. 1993, Children's LB $18.00 (0-516-02015-3). 32pp. For beginning readers, this rhyming story tells about the joys and problems of being a collector. (Rev: BL 3/1/94) [737]

21807 Dyson, Cindy. *Rare and Interesting Stamps* (5–8). Illus. Series: Costume, Tradition, and Culture: Reflecting on the Past. 1998, Chelsea LB $16.95 (0-7910-5171-4). 64pp. This work tells the story behind 25 unusual stamps including Britain's first one-penny stamp with a portrait of Queen Victoria. (Rev: BL 3/15/99; HBG 10/99) [769.56]

21808 Owens, Thomas S. *Collecting Baseball Cards* (4–6). Illus. 1993, Millbrook LB $22.40 (1-56294-254-9). 80pp. A basic introduction to this hobby, with a history of baseball cards and how they can be priced. (Rev: BL 8/93; SLJ 6/93) [796]

21809 Owens, Thomas S. *Collecting Baseball Memorabilia* (4–6). Illus. 1996, Millbrook LB $23.40 (1-56294-579-3). 96pp. Ticket stubs, team schedules, autographs, and other related items are described, with hints for collectors on how to get them and how to organize and preserve a collection. (Rev: SLJ 6/96) [796.357]

21810 Owens, Thomas S. *Collecting Basketball Cards* (4–6). Illus. 1998, Millbrook LB $23.90 (0-7613-0418-5). 80pp. A thorough discussion of the hobby of collecting basketball cards with particularly good advice for the beginner. (Rev: BL 1/1–15/99; HBG 3/99; SLJ 3/99) [796.323]

21811 Owens, Thomas S. *Collecting Comic Books: A Young Person's Guide* (5–8). Illus. 1995, Millbrook LB $25.90 (1-56294-580-7). 80pp. A beginner's guide to comic book collecting, with sections on kinds of collections, sources, and organizations. (Rev: BL 2/1/96; SLJ 1/96) [741.5]

Jokes, Puzzles, Riddles, Word Games

Jokes and Riddles

21812 Adler, David A. *The Dinosaur Princess and Other Prehistoric Riddles* (2–6). Illus. 1988, Holiday LB $14.95 (0-8234-0686-5). 64pp. An assortment of jokes and riddles and laughs with dinosaurs as the focus. (Rev: BL 5/1/88; SLJ 9/88)

21813 Beisner, Monika. *Monika Beisner's Book of Riddles* (2–4). Illus. by author. 1987, Farrar paper $3.95 (0-374-45317-9). 32pp. The answers to these 101 riddles are found in the illustrations.

21814 Bierhorst, John. *Lightning Inside You and Other Native American Riddles* (2–6). Illus. by Louise Brierley. 1992, Morrow $14.00 (0-688-09582-8). 104pp. Many subjects and difficulty levels are presented in this collection of 140 riddles from North, South, and Central America. (Rev: BCCB 7–8/92; BL 6/15/92; HB 9–10/92; SLJ 7/92) [398.6]

21815 Brown, Marc. *Spooky Riddles* (1–4). Illus. by author. 1983, Random $7.99 (0-394-86093-4). 48pp. Simply read riddles involving ghosts, vampires, and so on.

21816 Burns, Diane L., and Andy Burns. *Home on the Range: Ranch-Style Riddles* (2–5). Illus. by Susan S. Burke. Series: You Must Be Joking! 1994, Lerner LB $14.60 (0-8225-2341-8). A collection of zany riddles about life on the range. (Rev: SLJ 8/94) [818]

21817 Charlip, Remy. *Arm in Arm: A Collection of Connections, Endless Tales, Reiterations, and Other Echolalia* (K–3). Illus. 1997, Tricycle Pr. $15.95 (1-883672-50-3). 48pp. Verbal and visual plays on words are revealed through a series of riddles, jokes, and puzzles. (Rev: BL 9/1/97; HBG 3/98) [808]

21818 Christopher, Matt. *Baseball Jokes and Riddles* (2–4). Illus. 1996, Little, Brown paper $4.50 (0-316-14081-3). 48pp. Trivia and lots of jokes and riddles about baseball highlight this amusing collection. (Rev: BL 4/1/96; SLJ 6/96) [796.357]

21819 Cole, Joanna, and Stephanie Calmenson, eds. *Ready . . . Set . . . Read — and Laugh! A Funny Treasury for Beginning Readers* (1–3). Illus. 1995, Doubleday $17.95 (0-385-32119-8). 144pp. This easy-to-read book contains a small collection of stories, jokes, and riddles. (Rev: BL 10/1/95; SLJ 10/95)

21820 Cole, Joanna, and Stephanie Calmenson. *Why Did the Chicken Cross the Road? And Other Riddles Old and New* (2–4). Illus. by Alan Tiegreen. 1994, Morrow LB $14.93 (0-688-12203-5). 64pp. A lively collection of clever riddles arranged by broad subject or type. (Rev: BL 10/15/94; SLJ 9/94)

21821 Corwin, Judith Hoffman. *My First Riddles* (PS). Illus. 1998, HarperFestival $9.95 (0-694-01109-6). 24pp. A beginning riddle book that features nine simple riddles and many cheery illustrations. (Rev: BCCB 9/98; BL 6/1–15/98; HBG 10/98; SLJ 7/98)

21822 Eckstein, Joan, and Joyce Gleit. *The Best Joke Book for Kids Number 4* (3–6). Illus. by Joe Kohl. 1991, Avon paper $3.50 (0-380-76263-3). 64pp. There are riddles, knock-knocks, jokes, and tongue twisters in this book arranged by subjects. (Rev: BL 9/15/91) [793.73]

21823 Hall, Katy, and Lisa Eisenberg. *Creepy Riddles* (1–3). Illus. by S. D. Schindler. Series: Easy-to-Read. 1998, Dial LB $13.89 (0-8037-1685-0). 48pp. A very funny group of riddles involving horror creatures and creepy situations that will be ideal for Halloween. (Rev: BCCB 10/98; BL 9/15/98; HBG 3/99; SLJ 10/98) [818]

21824 Hall, Katy, and Lisa Eisenberg. *Kitty Riddles* (1–2). Illus. by R. W. Alley. Series: Dial Easy-to-Read. 2000, Dial $13.99 (0-8037-2116-1). 40pp. This book for beginning readers contains 34 jokes involving puns about cats and their antics. (Rev: BL 2/15/00; HBG 10/00; SLJ 4/00) [818]

21825 Hills, Tad. *Knock, Knock! Who's There? My First Book of Knock-Knock Jokes* (PS–1). Illus. by author. 2000, Simon & Schuster $6.99 (0-689-83413-6). Using flaps to conceal answers, this is an amusing collection of old and new knock-knock jokes. (Rev: SLJ 8/00) [818]

21826 Jansen, John. *Class Act: Riddles for School* (3–5). Illus. by Susan S. Burke. Series: You Must Be Joking! 1995, Lerner paper $3.95 (0-8225-9673-3). Riddles that take schools, students, and teachers as their subjects. Also use *Playing Possum: Riddles About Kangaroos, Koalas, and Other Marsupials* (1995). (Rev: SLJ 9/95)

21827 Joyce, Susan, comp. and ed. *ABC School Riddles* (2–5). Illus. by Freddie Levin. 2001, Peel $13.95 (0-939217-54-6). This simple book presents one riddle for each letter of the alphabet. (Rev: SLJ 1/01)

21828 Keller, Charles. *Astronuts: Space Jokes and Riddles* (1–4). Illus. 1991, Simon & Schuster paper $2.95 (0-671-73984-0). Mostly original, clever jokes on a popular subject. (Rev: BCCB 6/85; BL 6/15/85; SLJ 9/85)

21829 Keller, Charles. *Ballpoint Bananas and Other Jokes for Kids* (3–6). Illus. by David Barrios. 1976, Simon & Schuster paper $5.95 (0-671-66965-6). Zany American riddles, rhymes, and contemporary jokes.

21830 Keller, Charles. *Driving Me Crazy: Fun on Wheels Jokes* (2–6). Illus. by Lee Lorenz. 1989, Pippin $13.95 (0-945912-05-6). A collection of jokes and riddles that deal with driving and vehicles. (Rev: BL 7/89) [398]

21831 Keller, Charles. *It's Raining Cats and Dogs: Cat and Dog Jokes* (2–6). Illus. by Robert Quackenbush. 1988, Pippin $13.95 (0-945912-01-3). 40pp. Pleasing nonsense for young readers. Also use: *Colossal Fossils: Dinosaur Riddles* (1991, Simon & Schuster paper). (Rev: BCCB 11/88; BL 2/15/89; SLJ 2/89)

21832 Keller, Charles. *King Henry the Ape: Animal Jokes* (2–6). Illus. by Edward Frascino. 1990, Pippin LB $13.95 (0-945912-08-0). 40pp. Animal guffaws sure to delight young readers. (Rev: BL 3/15/90; SLJ 4/90) [818]

21833 Keller, Charles. *The Planet of the Grapes: Show Biz Jokes and Riddles* (2–5). Illus. by Mischa Richter. 1992, Pippin $13.95 (0-945912-17-X). All the performing arts are included in this collection of zany jokes. (Rev: SLJ 12/92) [808.7]

21834 Keller, Charles, ed. *Take Me to Your Liter: Science and Math Jokes* (3–6). Illus. by Gregory Filling. 1991, Pippin LB $13.95 (0-945912-13-7). 40pp. Jokes and silly riddles about a serious subject. (Rev: BL 5/15/91; SLJ 7/91) [398.2]

21835 Leslie, Amanda. *Flappy Waggy Wiggly* (PS–K). Illus. 1999, Dutton $12.99 (0-525-46182-5). 40pp. An interactive book in which answers to a series of animal riddles are found in pictures under the flaps. (Rev: BCCB 7–8/99; BL 8/99; HBG 10/99; SLJ 6/99)

21836 Lewis, J. Patrick. *Riddle-Lightful: Oodles of Little Riddle-Poems* (PS–3). Illus. by Debbie Tilley. 1998, Knopf LB $18.99 (0-679-98760-6). Picture clues abound in this charming book of rhyming riddles based on childhood experiences. (Rev: BL 12/1/98; HBG 3/99) [818]

21837 Maestro, Giulio. *Riddle Roundup* (3–5). Illus. 1989, Houghton paper $6.95 (0-89919-537-7). 64pp. Puns, homonyms, and homographs for word-play lovers. (Rev: BL 12/15/89; SLJ 2/90) [818]

21838 Maestro, Marco. *Geese Find the Missing Piece: School Time Riddle Rhymes* (1–2). Illus. by Giulio Maestro. Series: I Can Read. 1999, HarperCollins LB $14.89 (0-06-026221-4). 48pp. An easy reader that contains 21 humorous riddles for new readers. (Rev: BL 10/1/99; HBG 3/00; SLJ 12/99)

21839 Maestro, Marco, and Giulio Maestro. *What Do You Hear When Cows Sing? And Other Silly Riddles* (1–3). Illus. 1996, HarperCollins LB $14.89 (0-06-024949-8). 48pp. Silly riddles and even sillier answers.are found in this delightful joke book. (Rev: BL 1/1–15/96; SLJ 3/96) [398.8]

21840 Marzollo, Jean. *I Spy: Gold Challenger!* (2–5). Illus. by Walter Wick. Series: I Spy. 1998, Scholastic $12.95 (0-590-04296-3). 40pp. Objects are hidden in each photo in this puzzle book with appropriate riddles under each picture. (Rev: BL 1/1–15/99; HBG 3/99) [793.735]

21841 Marzollo, Jean. *I Spy Spooky Night* (2–5). Illus. by Walter Wick. 1996, Scholastic $13.95 (0-590-48137-1). 40pp. Riddles give clues to objects hidden in accompanying pictures. (Rev: BL 9/15/96; SLJ 9/96*) [793.73]

21842 Most, Bernard. *Pets in Trumpets and Other Word-Play Riddles* (1–3). Illus. 1991, Harcourt $12.95 (0-15-261210-6). 32pp. Finding words within other words is the basis of this wordplay book. (Rev: BL 10/15/91; SLJ 3/92) [818]

21843 Most, Bernard. *Zoodles* (PS–2). Illus. 1992, Harcourt $13.95 (0-15-299969-8). 32pp. An iguana who hogs all the food is a "piguana" in this riddle book that combines animal names. (Rev: BL 10/15/92; SLJ 1/93) [818]

21844 Peterson, Scott. *Plugged In: Electric Riddles* (3–5). Illus. by Susan S. Burke. Series: You Must Be Joking! 1995, Lerner paper $1.98 (0-8225-9700-4). Very funny jokes and riddles that involve appliances found around the house. (Rev: SLJ 9/95)

21845 Rosen, Michael, sel. *Walking the Bridge of Your Nose* (1–5). Illus. by Chloe Cheese. 1995, Kingfisher $14.95 (1-85697-596-7). 61pp. A collection of riddles, puns, tongue twisters, sayings, and chants that have fun with the English language. (Rev: SLJ 1/96) [818]

21846 Rosenbloom, Joseph. *Biggest Riddle Book in the World* (3–6). Illus. by Joyce Behr. 1979, Sterling paper $7.95 (0-8069-8884-3). About 2,000 old and new riddles arranged under various subjects and amusingly illustrated.

21847 Rosenbloom, Joseph. *Spooky Riddles and Jokes* (2–4). Illus. by Sanford Hoffman. 1987, Sterling paper $4.95 (0-8069-6736-6). 128pp. Riddles based on ghosts, werewolves, and other creatures. Also use: *Giggles, Gags and Groaners* (1987). (Rev: BL 11/1/87)

21848 Rosenbloom, Joseph. *Sports Riddles* (2–5). Illus. by Sam Q. Weissman. 1982, Harcourt $8.95 (0-15-277994-9). 64pp. A collection of riddles divided by various sports.

21849 Rosenbloom, Joseph. *The World's Best Sports Riddles and Jokes* (2–6). Illus. by Sanford Hoffman. 1988, Sterling paper $3.95 (0-8069-6846-6). 128pp. Young sports fans will enjoy these gaffaws. (Rev: BL 5/1/88)

21850 Rosenbloom, Joseph. *The Zaniest Riddle Book in the World* (3–6). Illus. by Sanford Hoffman. 1984, Sterling paper $4.95 (0-8069-6252-6). 128pp. A riddle book arranged by topics.

21851 Schwartz, Alvin. *Witcracks: Jokes and Jests from American Folklore* (3–6). Illus. by Glen Rounds. 1973, HarperCollins LB $14.89 (0-397-31475-2). 128pp. All sorts of humor associated with America's past, from old riddles to knock-knock jokes.

21852 Sloat, Teri, and Robert Sloat. *Rib-Ticklers: A Book of Punny Animals* (2–4). Illus. 1995, Lothrop $15.00 (0-688-12519-0). 32pp. Using different animals as focal points, this book contains a choice collection of jokes, puns, and riddles. (Rev: BL 6/1–15/95; SLJ 7/95) [818]

21853 Spires, Elizabeth. *Riddle Road: Puzzles in Poems and Pictures* (1–4). Illus. by Erik Blegvad. 1999, Simon & Schuster $15.00 (0-689-81783-5). 32pp. Using rhymes and picture clues, 26 riddles involving common or household objects are presented. (Rev: BCCB 5/99; BL 7/99; HB 5–6/99; HBG 10/99; SLJ 5/99) [811]

21854 Spires, Elizabeth. *With One White Wing* (1–4). Illus. by Erik Blegvad. 1995, Simon & Schuster paper $14.00 (0-689-50622-8). 32pp. A collection of literate riddles culled from sources such as Mother Goose and Tolkien. (Rev: BCCB 2/96; BL 10/1/95; SLJ 9/95*) [811]

21855 Steig, William. *C D B!* (3–6). Illus. by author. 1987, Simon & Schuster paper $3.95 (0-671-66689-4). 48pp. When each set of letters and/or numbers is repeated aloud and riddle buffs apply a bit of imagination, the amusing caption accompanying each cartoon becomes apparent. Also use: *C D C!* (1986, Farrar).

21856 Swanson, June. *Out to Dry: Riddles About Deserts* (2–5). Illus. by Susan S. Burke. Series: You Must Be Joking! 1994, Lerner LB $14.60 (0-8225-2343-4). A cornucopia of groaners dealing with deserts. More riddles can be found in *Summit Up: Riddles About Mountains* (1994). (Rev: SLJ 8/94) [818.5]

21857 Terban, Marvin. *Funny You Should Ask: How to Make Up Jokes and Riddles with Wordplay* (4–6). Illus. by John O'Brien. 1992, Houghton paper $7.95 (0-395-58113-3). 64pp. How word manipulation works and how kids can become schoolyard hams. (Rev: BCCB 2/93; BL 10/1/92; SLJ 12/92) [808.7]

21858 Thaler, Mike. *Frankenstein's Pantyhose* (2–4). Illus. 1990, Avon paper $2.50 (0-380-75613-7). 92pp. This collection of jokes and riddles contains a special section of cigar jokes. (Rev: BL 3/15/90)

21859 Young, Frederica. *Super-Duper Jokes* (3–6). Illus. by Chris Murphy. 1993, Farrar paper $4.95 (0-374-47353-6). 97pp. An enjoyable collection of var-ious kinds of jokes, including silly definitions. (Rev: BL 7/93; SLJ 7/93) [818]

21860 Ziefert, Harriet. *Math Riddles* (1–3). Illus. by Andrea Baruffi. 1997, Penguin paper $3.50 (0-14-038541-X). 32pp. Comic riddles using numbers are amusingly presented in this easy reader. (Rev: BL 8/97; SLJ 12/97)

Puzzles

21861 Adshead, Paul. *Puzzle Island* (2–5). Illus. 1991, Child's Play $13.99 (0-85953-402-2); paper $7.99 (0-85953-403-0). 24pp. This puzzle book contains visual clues to decode a secret message and learn the identity of an extinct species. (Rev: BL 6/1/91) [793.73]

21862 Baxter, Nicola. *Parallel Universe* (4–6). Illus. by Mike Taylor. 1997, Watts LB $24.00 (0-531-14465-8). 41pp. Picture puzzles in which the reader must find 20 anachronisms in each of 13 scenes from different historical periods. (Rev: HBG 3/98; SLJ 2/98)

21863 Burnie, Richard. *Monumental Mazes* (2–5). Illus. by author. 1999, Knopf $14.95 (0-375-80155-3). Features facts on famous structures, such as the Eiffel Tower, and a cunning collection of mazes to solve. (Rev: HBG 3/00; SLJ 2/00) [793.7]

21864 Burns, Marilyn. *The Book of Think (or How to Solve a Problem Twice Your Size)* (5–7). Illus. by Martha Weston. 1976, Little, Brown paper $13.95 (0-316-11743-9). A stimulating collection of puzzles to make children think; informally and entertainingly presented.

21865 Chalk, Gary. *Hide and Seek in History* (K–3). Illus. by author. 1997, DK $14.95 (0-7894-1500-3). Using double-page spreads, this picture book introduces eight periods in history from ancient Egypt and Rome to the French Revolution and the U.S. Wild West. (Rev: SLJ 12/97) [793.73]

21866 Gardner, Martin. *Classic Brainteasers* (4–6). Illus. 1995, Sterling $14.95 (0-8069-1260-X). 96pp. An entertaining book of classic puzzles that involve math, science, and logic. (Rev: BL 5/1/95) [793.73]

21867 Handford, Martin. *Where's Waldo? In Hollywood* (3–6). Illus. 1993, Candlewick $14.95 (1-56402-044-4). 32pp. Waldo can be found in a series of movie sets from silent movies and lavish musicals to the present-day blockbuster. (Rev: BL 12/15/93; SLJ 2/94)

21868 McMillan, Bruce. *Sense Suspense: A Guessing Game for the Five Senses* (PS–1). Illus. 1994, Scholastic $15.95 (0-590-47904-0). 32pp. A puzzle book that introduces the five senses and challenges youngsters to determine objects from close-up details. (Rev: BCCB 12/94; BL 12/1/94; SLJ 12/94*) [793.73]

21869 Madgwick, Wendy. *Citymaze!* (3–5). Illus. 1995, Millbrook LB $17.90 (1-56294-561-0). 40pp. Each of the maze puzzles in this book introduces a famous city, e.g., Moscow, Delhi, Paris, and London. (Rev: BCCB 4/95; BL 3/1/95; SLJ 6/95) [793.73]

21870 Marzollo, Jean. *I Spy: A Book of Picture Riddles* (K–4). Illus. 1992, Scholastic $13.95 (0-590-45087-5). 48pp. Readers are asked to search out certain items from collages or montages. (Rev: BCCB 2/92; BL 5/15/92; SLJ 4/92) [793.73]

21871 Marzollo, Jean. *I Spy: Extreme Challenger: A Book of Picture Riddles* (K–3). Photos by alter Wick. 2000, Scholastic $13.95 (0-439-19900-X). 40pp. This book contains 12 double-page picture puzzles with accompanying riddles. (Rev: BL 10/1/00; HBG 3/01; SLJ 12/00) [793.73]

21872 Marzollo, Jean. *I Spy Fantasy: A Book of Picture Riddles* (1–3). Illus. by Walter Wick. 1994, Scholastic $12.95 (0-590-46295-4). 40pp. In a series of photographic collages, children are challenged to find hidden objects. (Rev: BL 12/1/94; SLJ 10/94) [793.3]

21873 Marzollo, Jean. *I Spy Super Challenger! A Book of Picture Riddles* (PS–2). Illus. by Walter Wick. Series: I Spy. 1997, Scholastic $12.95 (0-590-34128-6). 32pp. This detailed picture puzzle book defies the reader to find a needle in the haystack, as well as other eye-dazzling problems. (Rev: BL 10/1/97; HBG 3/98; SLJ 9/97) [793.735]

21874 Marzollo, Jean. *I Spy Treasure Hunt: A Book of Picture Riddles* (K–3). Illus. by Walter Wick. Series: I Spy. 1999, Scholastic $12.95 (0-439-04244-5). 40pp. A series of picture puzzles in which children are asked to find hidden objects in the illustrations as well as solving the mystery of the pirate's hidden treasure. (Rev: BL 11/15/99; HBG 10/00; SLJ 1/00) [793.73]

21875 Rogers, Paul. *What Can You See?* (PS–2). Illus. by Kazuko. 1998, Doubleday $15.95 (0-385-32603-3). Cut-paper collages are used to create a minute world in which readers are asked to identify various objects. (Rev: HBG 3/99; SLJ 1/99)

21876 Swinburne, Stephen R. *Guess Whose Shadow?* (PS–K). Illus. 1999, Boyds Mills $15.95 (1-56397-724-9). Shadows are introduced in a series of photographs and then readers are asked to identify objects by their shadows. (Rev: BCCB 4/99; BL 3/1/99; HBG 10/99; SLJ 4/99) [770]

Word Games

21877 Agee, Jon. *Go Hang a Salami! I'm a Lasagna Hog! And Other Palindromes* (3–6). Illus. 1992, Farrar $14.41 (0-374-33473-0). 74pp. A humorous look at groups of letters or numbers that read the same backward and forward. (Rev: BCCB 10/92*;

BL 2/1/93) [793]

21878 Agee, Jon. *Sit on a Potato Pan, Otis!* (3–6). Illus. 1999, Farrar $14.41 (0-374-31808-5). 80pp. A collection of palindromes with matching humorous illustrations. (Rev: BCCB 2/99; BL 3/1/99; HB 3–4/99; HBG 10/99; SLJ 3/99) [793.734]

21879 Cole, Joanna, and Stephanie Calmenson, eds. *Six Sick Sheep: 101 Tongue Twisters* (3–6). Illus. by Alan Tiegreen. 1993, Morrow $14.93 (0-688-11140-8). 64pp. Some well-known tongue twisters as well as games, contests, and stories. (Rev: BL 3/15/93; SLJ 4/93) [818]

21880 Davis, Lee. *P. B. Bear's Treasure Hunt* (K–2). Photos by Dave King. 1995, DK $12.95 (0-7894-0214-9). Toys and other objects are used to represent 88 words in this intriguing rebus book. (Rev: SLJ 4/96)

21881 de Vicq de Cumptich, Roberto. *Bembo's Zoo* (4–8). Illus. 2000, Holt $17.95 (0-8050-6382-X). 32pp. A mature alphabet book that that jumbles letters to create a picture of each animal from A to Z. (Rev: BCCB 5/00; BL 6/1–15/00; HB 5–6/00; HBG 10/00; SLJ 5/00) [793.73]

21882 McMillan, Bruce, and Brett McMillan. *Puniddles* (2–4). Illus. 1982, Houghton paper $6.95 (0-395-32076-3). Objects in photographs are used to illustrate word combinations.

21883 Most, Bernard. *Hippopotamus Hunt* (1–3). Illus. 1994, Harcourt $14.95 (0-15-234520-5). 32pp. Explores the pastime of finding words within words and, using *hippopotamus* as an example, comes up with 53 new words. (Rev: BL 9/1/94; SLJ 11/94)

21884 Rosenbloom, Joseph. *World's Toughest Tongue Twisters* (3–5). Illus. 1987, Sterling paper $4.95 (0-8069-6596-7). 128pp. More than 500 tongue twisters, alphabetically from A to Z.

21885 Schnur, Steven. *Autumn: An Alphabet Acrostic* (K–3). Illus. by Leslie Evans. 1997, Clarion $15.00 (0-395-77043-2). 32pp. An alphabet book that uses autumn and acrostic poems as a framework. (Rev: BL 9/1/97; HBG 3/98; SLJ 9/97) [793.73]

21886 Tucker, Sian. *What Do You See? Come Look with Me: My First Lift-the-Flap Word Search Book* (PS). Illus. 1998, Simon $12.95 (0-689-81847-5). Readers search for the items pictured at the bottom of the page by lifting a series of flaps in this interactive book. (Rev: BL 1/1–15/99)

21887 Van Dyke, Janice. *Captivating Cryptograms* (5–8). 1996, Sterling paper $5.95 (0-8069-4890-6). 128pp. A collection of 400 cryptograms based on famous quotes, with the names of the authors also included. (Rev: SLJ 8/96) [793.73]

Mysteries, Monsters, Curiosities, and Trivia

21888 Allen, Eugenie. *The Best Ever Kids' Book of Lists* (4–8). Illus. 1991, Avon paper $2.95 (0-380-76357-5). 128pp. Trivia buffs will enjoy these data bits under such headings as Nature's Most Lethal Weapons and Revolting Eating Habits. (Rev: BL 12/15/91) [031.02]

21889 Ash, Russell. *Factastic Book of 1001 Lists* (5–10). 1999, DK $19.95 (0-7894-3769-4); paper $14.95 (0-7894-3412-1). 208pp. A collection of fantastic facts arranged under such subjects as space, the earth, science, countries, the arts, and world sports. (Rev: SLJ 7/99) [500]

21890 Asimov, Isaac, and Greg Walz-Chojnacki. *UFOs: True Mysteries or Hoaxes?* (3–4). Illus. Series: Isaac Asimov's New Library of the Universe. 1995, Gareth Stevens LB $21.27 (0-8368-1198-4). 32pp. This brief account examines the supposed sightings of alien craft from a skeptical viewpoint. (Rev: SLJ 4/95) [001.9]

21891 Ballinger, Erich. *Monster Manual: A Complete Guide to Your Favorite Creatures* (5–8). Illus. 1994, Lerner LB $19.95 (0-8225-0722-6). 144pp. This A-to-Z introduction to monsters includes Dracula, King Kong, and Rambo plus activities and material on people behind some of these creations, like Boris Karloff. (Rev: BL 12/1/94; SLJ 3/95) [001.9]

21892 Blackwood, Gary L. *Extraordinary Events and Oddball Occurrences* (4–7). Illus. Series: Secrets of the Unexplained. 1999, Marshall Cavendish LB $19.95 (0-7614-0748-0). 80pp. A book that covers such unusual occurrences as strange things falling from the sky, teleportation, and unexplained appearances and disappearances. (Rev: BL 3/1/00; HBG 10/00) [001.9]

21893 Blackwood, Gary L. *Fateful Forebodings* (4–6). Series: Secrets of the Unexplained. 1998, Benchmark LB $19.95 (0-7614-0467-8). 80pp. This book covers the origins and practices of such forms of fortune telling as astrology, tarot-card reading, tea-leaf reading, and the I Ching. (Rev: HBG 10/99; SLJ 3/99) [133.3]

21894 Blackwood, Gary L. *Long-Ago Lives* (4–7). Illus. Series: Secrets of the Unexplained. 1999, Marshall Cavendish LB $19.95 (0-7614-0747-2). 80pp. This book explores the subject of reincarnation. (Rev: BL 3/1/00; HBG 10/00) [133.9]

21895 Blackwood, Gary L. *Paranormal Powers* (4–6). Series: Secrets of the Unexplained. 1998, Benchmark LB $19.95 (0-7614-0468-6). 80pp. This book explores psychic abilities such as telepathy, clairvoyance, precognition, body magnetism, pain control, and spoon bending. (Rev: HBG 10/99; SLJ 3/99) [001.9]

21896 Campbell, Peter A. *Alien Encounters* (5–7). Illus. 2000, Millbrook LB $23.90 (0-7613-1402-4). 48pp. An overview of eight supposed encounters between humans and aliens. (Rev: BL 7/00; HBG 10/00; SLJ 4/00) [001.9]

21897 Choron, Sandy, and Harry Choron. *The Book of Lists for Kids* (4–6). Illus. 1995, Houghton paper $11.00 (0-395-70815-X). 396pp. Amazing trivia on such subjects as toys, books, education, online services, and family and friends is included in this volume that is fun for browsing. (Rev: BL 2/15/96) [031.02]

21898 Cohen, Daniel. *Ghosts of the Deep* (5–7). 1993, Putnam $14.95 (0-399-22435-1). 103pp. A collection of ghost stories involving sailors and pirates who met untimely ends. (Rev: BL 11/15/93; SLJ 3/94) [133.1]

21899 Cohen, Daniel. *The Ghosts of War* (4–6). 1990, Putnam $13.95 (0-399-22200-6). 82pp. Tales about spirits who died in war. (Rev: BCCB 9/90; BL 6/1/90) [133.1]

21900 Cohen, Daniel. *Phone Call from a Ghost: Strange Tales from Modern America* (4–6). Illus. 1990, Pocket paper $3.50 (0-671-68242-3). 112pp. Stories about weird happenings to famous and average people. (Rev: BCCB 11/88; BL 6/1/88; SLJ 8/88)

21901 Cohen, Daniel. *The World's Most Famous Ghosts* (6–8). 1989, Pocket paper $2.99 (0-671-

69145-7). 112pp. A report in ten short chapters of better-known incidents accredited to ghosts.

21902 Corbett, Sara. *Hold Everything!* (3–7). Illus. Series: A World of Difference. 1996, Children's LB $21.00 (0-516-08212-4). 32pp. Containers like pots and pourers from various cultures of the world are used to illustrate human diversity. (Rev: BL 9/15/96) [688.8]

21903 Crisp, Tony. *Super Minds: People with Amazing Mind Power* (4–7). Illus. by Mary Kuper. 1999, Element Books paper $4.95 (1-901881-03-2). 128pp. Near-death experiences, feral children's case histories, and the strange mental powers of such people as Eileen Garrett of telepathy fame and Henry Keller are included in this book about unusual mental capacities and happenings. (Rev: SLJ 5/99) [001.9]

21904 Deem, James M. *How to Find a Ghost* (5–8). Illus. 1990, Avon paper $3.25 (0-380-70829-9). 144pp. Explaining what one can do to have a supernatural experience. (Rev: BCCB 11/88; BL 11/1/88; SLJ 11/88)

21905 Deem, James M. *How to Hunt Buried Treasure* (4–7). Illus. by True Kelley. 1992, Houghton $16.95 (0-395-58799-9). 192pp. Tales of lost mines and pirate ships are part of the lure of this attractive guidebook. (Rev: BL 9/15/92; SLJ 10/92) [622.19]

21906 Deem, James M. *How to Read Your Mother's Mind* (5–7). Illus. by True Kelley. 1994, Houghton $17.00 (0-395-62426-6). 192pp. Various aspects of ESP are introduced, including the pros and cons about its existence and a test to determine one's own ESP powers. (Rev: BCCB 3/94; BL 3/1/94; SLJ 7/94) [133.8]

21907 Donkin, Andrew. *Atlantis: The Lost City?* (2–4). Illus. Series: DK Reader. 2000, DK $12.95 (0-7894-6681-3). 48pp. The first part of this book discusses the legend of Atlantis; the second half tells of the search for this lost city at sites around the world. (Rev: BL 12/15/00) [001.94]

21908 Donkin, Andrew. *Bermuda Triangle* (2–4). Series: Eyewitness Reader. 2000, DK $12.95 (0-7894-5416-5); paper $3.95 (0-7894-5415-7). 48pp. An easily read study of the Bermuda Triangle that favors explanations leaning toward the supernatural — blaming UFOs or the lost continent of Atlantis. (Rev: HBG 10/00; SLJ 8/00) [001.9]

21909 Farndon, John. *Eyewitness Question and Answer Book* (2–4). Illus. Series: Eyewitness Juniors. 1993, DK $16.95 (1-56458-347-3). 64pp. A browsing book that answers all sorts of questions in three categories: nature, history, and inventions. (Rev: BL 1/1/94) [031]

21910 French, Jackie. *The Little Book of Big Questions* (3–6). Illus. by Martha Newbigging. 2000, Annick $19.95 (1-55037-655-1); paper $9.95 (1-55037-654-3). 127pp. Fifteen subject-oriented chapters cover such areas as the universe, animal intelligence, extraterrestrials, and mortality. (Rev: HBG 3/01; SLJ 11/00) [001.9]

21911 Heller, Ruth. *A Sea Within a Sea: Secrets of the Sargasso* (3–5). Illus. by author. 2000, Grosset LB $16.99 (0-448-42417-7). Fact and fiction are combined in this poetic introduction to the Sargasso Sea and the Bermuda Triangle. (Rev: SLJ 3/01) [972.9]

21912 Hepplewhite, Peter, and Neil Tonge. *Alien Encounters* (5–8). Series: The Unexplained. 1998, Sterling $14.95 (0-8069-3869-2). 47pp. This book is filled with reports of strange and unexplained events, such as encounters with aliens and UFOs. Also use *Hauntings: The World of Spirits and Ghosts, Mysterious Places,* and *The Uncanny* (all 1998). (Rev: HBG 3/99; SLJ 10/98) [001.9]

21913 Herbst, Judith. *The Mystery of UFOs* (3–5). Illus. by Greg Clarke. 1997, Simon & Schuster $16.00 (0-689-31652-6). 40pp. An open-minded history of reported encounters with UFOs and aliens from space. (Rev: BL 12/1/97; HB 11–12/97; HBG 3/98; SLJ 11/97) [001.9]

21914 Huang, Chungliang Al. *The Chinese Book of Animal Powers* (5–7). Illus. 1999, HarperCollins LB $16.89 (0-06-027729-7). 40pp. The 12 animals of the Chinese zodiac are introduced in double-page spreads, and the characteristics and powers of each are outlined. (Rev: BCCB 12/99; BL 1/1–15/00; HBG 3/00) [133.5]

21915 Hubbard-Brown, Janet. *The Curse of the Hope Diamond* (4–7). Illus. 1991, Avon paper $2.99 (0-380-76222-6). 96pp. A mystery style introduces historical information. (Rev: BL 12/15/91) [736.23]

21916 Innes, Brian. *The Bermuda Triangle* (4–7). Illus. Series: Unsolved Mysteries. 1999, Raintree Steck-Vaughn LB $24.26 (0-8172-5485-4). 48pp. The author explores many theories that have been proposed to explain the disappearances that have occurred in this area off the southeast coast of the U.S. (Rev: BL 5/15/99; HBG 10/99) [001.94]

21917 Innes, Brian. *The Cosmic Joker* (4–7). Illus. Series: Unsolved Mysteries. 1999, Raintree Steck-Vaughn LB $24.26 (0-8172-5487-0). 48pp. This book introduces Charles Fort, the Cosmic Joker, and the many strange facts and coincidences he has uncovered. (Rev: BL 5/15/99; HBG 10/99; SLJ 9/99) [001.94]

21918 Innes, Brian. *Giant Humanlike Beasts* (4–7). Series: Unsolved Mysteries. 1999, Raintree Steck-Vaughn LB $16.98 (0-8172-5484-6). 48pp. This account explores stories about the abominable snowman, or yeti, and other sightings of primitive creatures while questioning the possibility of living links with Neanderthals. (Rev: BL 5/15/99; HBG 10/99; SLJ 9/99) [001.9]

21919 Innes, Brian. *Millennium Prophecies* (4–7). Illus. Series: Unsolved Mysteries. 1999, Raintree Steck-Vaughn LB $24.26 (0-8172-5486-2). 48pp. The predictions concerning the millennium of Nostradamus, Edgar Cayce, and other soothsayers are reported here. (Rev: BL 5/15/99; HBG 10/99; SLJ 9/99) [133.3]

21920 Jackson, Ellen. *The Book of Slime* (2–4). Illus. by Jan Davey Ellis. 1997, Millbrook LB $21.40 (0-7613-0042-2). 32pp. Describes various forms of slime in nature, including human mucus and saliva, along with their uses, slime jokes, and some recipes. (Rev: BL 3/15/97; SLJ 6/97) [001.9]

21921 Jenkins, Steve. *Duck's Breath and Mouse Pie: A Collection of Animal Superstitions* (2–4). Illus. 1994, Ticknor $14.95 (0-395-69688-7). 48pp. With breathtaking collages, 17 superstitions about animals and their origins are explored. (Rev: BL 10/1/94; SLJ 9/94) [398.24]

21922 Kemp, Gillian. *Tea Leaves, Herbs, and Flowers: Fortune-Telling the Gypsy Way* (5–9). Illus. by Mary Kuper. Series: Elements of the Extraordinary. 1998, Element Books paper $5.95 (1-901881-92-X). 128pp. This book tells how to prepare tea and read the leaves for significant signs as well as how to determine the secret messages that can be conveyed through flowers. (Rev: SLJ 1/99) [133.3]

21923 Knight, David C. *Best True Ghost Stories of the 20th Century* (5–8). Illus. 1984, Simon & Schuster paper $5.95 (0-671-66557-X). 64pp. Twenty tales of apparitions and poltergeists.

21924 Krull, Kathleen. *They Saw the Future: Oracles, Psychics, Scientists, Great Thinkers, and Pretty Good Guessers* (5–9). Illus. 1999, Simon & Schuster $19.99 (0-689-81295-7). 112pp. This chronological survey of people who professed to see into the future includes the Oracle at Delphi, Nostradamus, Jules Verne, Leonardo da Vinci, and Jeane Dixon. (Rev: BCCB 6/99; BL 6/1–15/99*; HB 5–6/99; HBG 10/99; SLJ 7/99) [133.3]

21925 Landau, Elaine. *ESP* (4–6). Illus. Series: Mysteries of Science. 1996, Millbrook LB $20.90 (0-7613-0012-0). 48pp. The amazing phenomenon known as extrasensory perception is explored in an account that separates fact from fiction. (Rev: BL 10/15/96; SLJ 11/96) [133.8]

21926 Landau, Elaine. *Fortune Telling* (4–6). Illus. Series: Mysteries of Science. 1996, Millbrook LB $20.90 (0-7613-0013-9). 48pp. Various methods of future telling are covered, with material that debunks the claims of supposed clairvoyants. (Rev: BL 10/15/96; SLJ 11/96) [133.3]

21927 Landau, Elaine. *Ghosts* (4–6). Illus. Series: Mysteries of Science. 1995, Millbrook LB $20.90 (1-56294-544-0). 48pp. A slim volume that presents information pro and con on the controversy concerning the existence of ghosts. (Rev: BL 12/15/95; SLJ 4/96) [133.1]

21928 Landau, Elaine. *The Loch Ness Monster* (4–6). Illus. Series: Mysteries of Science. 1993, Millbrook LB $20.90 (1-56294-347-2). 48pp. Evidence for and against the existence of the Loch Ness monster is presented in a compact format with drawings and color photos. (Rev: BL 1/1/94; SLJ 2/94) [001.9]

21929 Landau, Elaine. *Near-Death Experiences* (4–6). Illus. Series: Mysteries of Science. 1995, Millbrook LB $20.90 (1-56294-543-2). 48pp. An objective account that surveys the evidence concerning the possible truth behind reported near-death experiences. (Rev: BL 12/15/95; SLJ 4/96) [133.9]

21930 Landau, Elaine. *Sasquatch: Wild Man of North America* (4–6). Illus. Series: Mysteries of Science. 1993, Millbrook LB $20.90 (1-56294-348-0). 48pp. Sightings and arguments concerning the supposed existence of this monster from the American Northwest are presented in a concise text and attractive format. (Rev: BL 1/1/94) [001.9]

21931 Landau, Elaine. *UFOs* (4–6). Illus. Series: Mysteries of Science. 1995, Millbrook LB $20.90 (1-56294-542-4). 48pp. The controversy concerning UFO sightings is reported in an objective way, with many intriguing photographs. (Rev: BL 12/15/95; SLJ 4/96) [001.9]

21932 Larkspur, Penelope. *The Secret Life of Fairies* (3–5). Illus. 1999, Kids Can $14.95 (1-55074-547-6). 32pp. This account presents an inside look at fairy life including homes, dress, and food. (Rev: BL 11/1/99; HBG 3/00) [813.48]

21933 Levine, Michael. *The Kid's Address Book: Over 2,000 Addresses of Celebrities, Athletes, Entertainers, and More . . . Just for Kids* (3–8). Illus. 1994, Putnam paper $9.95 (0-399-51875-4). 219pp. This directory lists the names and addresses of over 2,000 celebrities, sports figures, and politicians. (Rev: BL 1/1/95) [920]

21934 Lorenz, Albert, and Joy Schlen. *Buried Blueprints: Maps and Sketches of Lost Worlds and Mysterious Places* (3–8). Illus. by authors. 1999, Abrams $19.95 (0-8109-4110-4). Fact and fiction are mixed in this exploration of locales including the Seven Cities of Gold, Egyptian cities, Atlantis, and the Lost World created by Sir Arthur Conan Doyle. (Rev: HBG 3/00; SLJ 2/00) [001.9]

21935 Maynard, Christopher. *Informania: Ghosts* (4–8). Illus. Series: Informania. 1999, Candlewick $16.99 (0-7636-0758-4). 92pp. This book about ghosts includes coverage of sightings around the world, items needed to be a ghost hunter, and a chart of typical haunting sights. (Rev: HBG 3/00; SLJ 12/99) [133.1]

21936 Mitton, Jacqueline. *Informania: Aliens* (3–5). Series: Informania. 1999, Candlewick $15.99 (0-7636-0492-5). 92pp. A spiral-bound book that covers sighting of UFOs, research on extraterrestrial communication, and a rundown on aliens in the movies. (Rev: HBG 10/99; SLJ 7/99) [001.9]

21937 Morgan, Rowland. *In the Next Three Seconds* (3–6). Illus. by Rod Josey and Kira Josey. 1997, Lodestar $14.99 (0-525-67551-5). 32pp. This book of curiosities outlines events that could occur in three seconds, minutes, hours, days, weeks, and so on, to three million years. (Rev: SLJ 9/97) [001.9]

21938 Myers, Janet Nuzum. *Strange Stuff: True Stories of Odd Places and Things* (5–8). Illus. by Maj-Britt Hagsted. 1999, Linnet LB $19.50 (0-208-02405-0). 104pp. A browser's delight that covers topics such as voodoo, zombies, poisonous snakes, quicksand, Bigfoot, the Bermuda Triangle, and mermaids. (Rev: HBG 3/00; SLJ 7/99) [001.9]

21939 Nickell, Joe. *The Magic Detectives: Join Them in Solving Strange Mysteries* (3–7). Illus. 1989, Prometheus paper $12.00 (0-87975-547-4). 115pp. Each of the 30 brief chapters explores a mysterious phenomenon, such as Bigfoot. (Rev: BCCB 12/89; BL 12/1/89) [133]

21940 *1001 Questions and Answers* (3–7). Illus. 1995, DK $16.95 (1-7894-0205-X). 64pp. More than 1,000 fascinating questions and amazing answers covering science and invention, history, the natural world, and recreation are detailed, with matching photographs. (Rev: BL 1/1–15/96) [031.02]

21941 O'Neill, Catherine. *Amazing Mysteries of the World* (3–8). Illus. 1983, National Geographic LB $12.50 (0-87044-502-2). 104pp. Stonehenge, Easter Island, and Bigfoot are three of the many mysteries explored.

21942 Oxlade, Chris. *The Mystery of Crop Circles* (4–6). Series: Can Science Solve? 1999, Heinemann LB $15.95 (1-57572-804-4). 32pp. This book examines the strange phenomenon known as crop circles, unusual circular patterns that appear in crop fields, and covers the various theories about them. (Rev: SLJ 8/99) [001.9]

21943 Oxlade, Chris. *The Mystery of the Bermuda Triangle* (4–6). Series: Can Science Solve? 1999, Heinemann LB $15.95 (1-57572-811-7). 32pp. A variety of natural explanations are examined in this dramatic presentation of material on the Bermuda Triangle. (Rev: SLJ 1/00) [001.9]

21944 Parker, Steve. *Frankenstein* (4–6). Illus. Series: In the Footsteps Of. 1995, Millbrook LB $21.90 (1-56294-647-1). 40pp. This introduction to the Mary Shelley novel supplies background information, the basic story, and a description of the screen adaptations. (Rev: SLJ 1/96) [398.24]

21945 Pipe, Jim. *Dracula* (4–6). Illus. Series: In the Footsteps Of. 1995, Millbrook LB $21.90 (1-56294-646-3). 40pp. The origins and content of Bram Stoker's novel are examined, with information on other vampire stories and a rundown on bloodsucking insects and animals. (Rev: SLJ 1/96) [001.9]

21946 Powell, Jillian. *Body Decoration* (4–8). Illus. Series: Traditions Around the World. 1995, Thomson Learning LB $24.26 (1-56847-276-5). 48pp. An interesting book that explains the uses of body decoration in history and discusses tattooing, face painting, and body piercing. (Rev: SLJ 7/95) [617]

21947 Powell, Jillian. *The Supernatural* (4–6). Illus. Series: Mysteries Of. 1996, Millbrook LB $22.90 (0-7613-0455-X). 40pp. Topics like ghosts, UFOs, alien abductions, witchcraft, and out-of-body experiences are discussed. (Rev: SLJ 6/96) [001.9]

21948 Reid, Lori. *Hand Reading: Discover Your Future* (5–9). Illus. by Paul Dowling. Series: Elements of the Extraordinary. 1998, Element Books paper $5.95 (1-901881-82-2). 125pp. Simple illustrations are used to describe the characteristics of the human palm and how these can be used in palmistry. (Rev: SLJ 1/99) [133.3]

21949 Ross, Stewart. *Secret Societies* (5–7). Illus. Series: Fact or Fiction. 1996, Millbrook paper $6.95 (0-7613-0510-6). 48pp. This colorful work explores cults, gangs, and secret clans throughout history, from ancient Japan to today. (Rev: BL 10/15/96; SLJ 4/97) [366]

21950 Scalora, Suza. *The Fairies: Photographic Evidence of the Existence of Another World* (3–5). Illus. 1999, HarperCollins $19.95 (0-06-028234-7). 48pp. The author spent a year investigating the phe-

nomenon of fairies and the results, including names, sightings, location, history, and photographs, are found in this intriguing book. (Rev: BL 11/1/99; HBG 3/00; SLJ 1/00) [001.9]

21951 Schwartz, Alvin. *Gold and Silver, Silver and Gold: Tales of Hidden Treasure* (4–8). Illus. 1993, Farrar paper $8.95 (0-374-42583-3). All sorts of treasure tales, from Captain Kidd to buried coins in a vacant lot. (Rev: BCCB 1/89; HB 3–4/89; SLJ 2/89)

21952 Simon, Seymour. *Strange Mysteries from Around the World*. Rev. ed. (4–6). Illus. 1997, Morrow $16.00 (0-688-14636-8). 64pp. An updating of the 1980 title that describes nine unusual events, such as strange lights that periodically appear in the sky. (Rev: BL 2/15/97; SLJ 4/97) [001.9]

21953 Tambini, Michael. *Future* (4–9). Series: Eyewitness Books. 1998, Knopf LB $20.00 (0-679-99317-7). The world of the future is explored in this oversize, richly illustrated book. (Rev: BL 8/98; HBG 3/99) [133.3]

21954 Tesar, Jenny. *America's Top 10 Curiosities* (3–7). Illus. Series: America's Top 10. 1997, Blackbirch LB $16.95 (1-56711-199-8). 24pp. Using double-page spreads, this book describes such phenomena as the Marfa Mystery Lights in Texas, the Flaming Fountain in South Dakota, and the Seattle Space Needle. (Rev: BL 1/1–15/98; HBG 3/98) [508.73]

21955 Tesar, Jenny. *Kidbits* (4–7). Illus. by Robert Italiano. 1998, Blackbirch $29.95 (1-56711-169-6). 320pp. A compendium of odd facts and statistics, including a list of Ben and Jerry's top ten flavors. (Rev: SLJ 11/98) [031]

21956 Walker, Paul R. *Bigfoot and Other Legendary Creatures* (4–6). Illus. by William Noonan. 1992, Harcourt $18.00 (0-15-207147-4). 56pp. Facts, legends, and seven original stories are included in this collection of material about several legendary creatures. (Rev: BL 2/15/92; SLJ 3/92) [001.9]

21957 Wallace, Holly. *The Mystery of Atlantis* (4–6). Series: Can Science Solve? 1999, Heinemann LB $15.95 (1-57572-803-6). 32pp. This account examines the efforts to prove the existence of the lost continent of Atlantis and looks at theories concerning its location and destruction. (Rev: SLJ 8/99) [001.9]

21958 Wallace, Holly. *The Mystery of the Abominable Snowman* (4–6). Series: Can Science Solve? 1999, Heinemann LB $15.95 (1-57572-810-9). 32pp. The possible existence of the abominable snowman is explored in this dramatic account with eye-catching illustrations. (Rev: SLJ 1/00) [001.9]

21959 Watts, Claire, and Robert Nicholson. *Super Heroes* (3–6). Illus. Series: Info Adventure. 1995, Thomson Learning paper $6.00 (1-56847-316-8). 31pp. An introduction to many mythical and legendary heroes plus coverage on such modern marvels as Batman, James Bond, Tarzan, the Terminator, and Indiana Jones. (Rev: SLJ 12/95) [001.9]

21960 Wilkinson, Philip. *A Celebration of Customs and Rituals of the World* (5–8). Illus. 1996, Facts on File $40.00 (0-8160-3479-6). 224pp. Discusses customs and rituals connected with birth, death, marriage, and coming-of-age. (Rev: BL 4/1/96) [394.2]

21961 Wilson, Colin. *Mysteries of the Universe* (5–8). Illus. Series: Unexplained. 1997, DK $14.95 (0-7894-2165-8). 37pp. Such world mysteries as the Shroud of Turin, showers of fish, and life on Mars are explored in this book of curiosities. Also use *UFOs and Aliens* (1997). (Rev: BL 2/1/98; HBG 3/98; SLJ 2/98) [001.9]

21962 Wood, Ted. *Ghosts of the Southwest: The Phantom Gunslinger and Other Real-Life Hauntings* (4–6). Illus. 1997, Walker LB $17.85 (0-8027-8483-6). 48pp. A trip through Arizona, New Mexico, Texas, and Oklahoma, with stops in locales where ghosts reside. (Rev: BL 3/1/97; SLJ 4/97) [133.1]

21963 Wood, Ted. *Ghosts of the West Coast: The Lost Souls of the Queen Mary and Other Real-Life Hauntings* (3–6). Illus. 1999, Walker LB $17.85 (0-8027-8669-3). 48pp. A chronicle of reported sightings of ghosts in California, Oregon, and Washington with information on who saw the phantoms, and when and where. (Rev: BCCB 7–8/99; BL 4/15/99; HBG 10/99; SLJ 6/99) [133.1]

21964 Yolen, Jane, and Heidi E. Y. Stemple. *Meet the Monsters* (K–2). Illus. by Patricia Ludlow. 1996, Walker LB $16.85 (0-8027-8442-9). A number of strange creatures — like zombies, vampires, mummies, and Medusa — are introduced in double-page spreads. (Rev: SLJ 11/96) [001.9]

Sports and Games

General and Miscellaneous

21965 Aaseng, Nathan. *True Champions: Great Athletes and Their Off-the-Field Heroics* (5–8). Illus. 1993, Walker LB $15.85 (0-8027-8247-7). 130pp. These stories illustrate brave true-life sports incidents. (Rev: SLJ 6/93) [793]

21966 Ajmera, Maya K., and Michael Regan. *Let the Games Begin!* (3–5). Illus. 2000, Charlesbridge LB $16.95 (0-88106-067-4); paper $6.95 (0-88106-068-2). 32pp. This book examines the philosophy of sports and sportsmanship with double-page spreads on topics such as practice, teamwork, competition, and rules. (Rev: BL 4/1/00; HBG 10/00; SLJ 5/00) [796]

21967 Alexander, Kyle. *Pro Wrestling's Most Punishing Finishing Moves* (4–7). Series: Pro Wrestling Legends. 2000, Chelsea LB $17.95 (0-7910-5833-6). 64pp. This book describes the most effective finishing moves in the sport of wrestling and fighters who use them. (Rev: BL 3/1/01; HBG 3/01) [796.8]

21968 Alexander, Kyle. *The Women of Pro Wrestling* (4–7). Illus. Series: Pro Wrestling Legends. 2000, Chelsea LB $17.95 (0-7910-5839-5); paper $8.95 (0-7910-5840-9). 64pp. After introducing several famous women pro wrestlers, this account describes women's roles in this sport in and out of the ring. (Rev: BL 10/15/00; HBG 3/01) [796.812]

21969 Allison, Linda. *The Sierra Club Summer Book* (3–6). Illus. by author. 1989, Little, Brown paper $7.95 (0-316-03433-9). 160pp. All sorts of activities on how to spend a summer day in this updated activity book.

21970 Alter, Judith. *Rodeos: The Greatest Show on Dirt* (4–7). Illus. Series: First Books. 1996, Watts LB $22.50 (0-531-20245-3). 64pp. Includes a history of rodeos, standard events, rules, legendary performers, and women in rodeos. (Rev: SLJ 3/97) [791.8]

21971 Anderson, Dave. *The Story of Golf* (4–8). Illus. 1998, Morrow $16.00 (0-688-15796-3).

192pp. A history of golf, highlighting the careers of some of its great stars, plus material on the lure of the game, golf architecture, and caddies. (Rev: BL 5/15/98; HB 9–10/98; HBG 10/98) [796.35]

21972 *The Baby's Game Book* (PS). Ed. by Isabel Wilner. Illus. by Sam Williams. 2000, Greenwillow $23.95 (0-688-15916-8). 48pp. Games like pat-a-cake and rub-a-dub-dub are included in this collection of games for babies and toddlers. (Rev: BL 5/15/00; HB 7–8/00; HBG 10/00; SLJ 5/00) [649]

21973 Barrett, Norman. *Hang Gliding* (3–5). Illus. 1988, Watts LB $20.00 (0-531-10350-1). 32pp. Basic techniques of this thrill-seeking sport. (Rev: BL 5/15/88; SLJ 11/88)

21974 Bellville, Cheryl Walsh. *Flying in a Hot Air Balloon* (3–5). Illus. 1993, Carolrhoda LB $22.60 (0-87614-750-3). 48pp. An introduction to hot-air ballooning past and present that uses a rally in Minnesota as a framework. (Rev: BCCB 3/94; BL 1/1/94; SLJ 2/94) [797.5]

21975 Bellville, Cheryl Walsh. *Rodeo* (1–3). Illus. by author. 1985, Lerner paper $5.95 (0-87614-492-X). 32pp. A brief introduction to rodeos, highlighted with color photos. (Rev: BL 4/1/85; HB 7–8/85; SLJ 4/85)

21976 Bizley, Kirk. *Inline Skating* (4–7). Series: Radical Sports. 1999, Heinemann LB $15.95 (1-57572-942-3). 32pp. As well as a history of inline skating, this book tells how to get started and gives information on equipment, techniques, terms, and safety. (Rev: SLJ 4/00) [796]

21977 Boardman, Bob. *Red Hot Peppers: The Skookum Book of Jump Rope Games, Rhymes, and Fancy Footwork* (3–6). Illus. by Diane Boardman. 1993, Sasquatch paper $8.95 (0-912365-74-9). 64pp. A collection of directions for jump-rope and other games, from simple to highly complex. (Rev: BL 7/93) [796.2]

21978 Brimner, Larry. *Bobsledding and the Luge* (2–4). Series: True Books. 1997, Children's LB $22.00 (0-516-20436-X). 48pp. An introduction to the history, rules techniques, and people involved in these two hazardous winter sports. (Rev: BL 1/1–15/98; HBG 3/98; SLJ 2/98) [796]

21979 Brimner, Larry. *Rock Climbing* (4–6). Illus. 1997, Watts LB $22.50 (0-531-20269-0). 64pp. Equipment, techniques, and safety tips are covered in this basic introduction to rock climbing. (Rev: BL 6/1–15/97) [796.5]

21980 Brooks, Philip. *United States* (4–6). Illus. Series: Games People Play! 1996, Children's LB $23.50 (0-516-04442-7). 64pp. Amateur and professional sports in the United States are covered, along with games we play and other forms of recreation. (Rev: SLJ 11/96) [796]

21981 Bryant-Mole, Karen. *Games* (PS–3). Series: Picture This! 1997, Rigby $18.50 (1-57572-151-1). 24pp. Various games are introduced, with material on where they are played and the importance of healthy recreation. (Rev: BL 10/15/97) [790]

21982 Chalmers, Aldie. *In-Line Skating* (3–6). Illus. Series: Fantastic Book Of. 1997, Millbrook LB $22.40 (0-7613-0623-4). 40pp. This introduction to inline skating covers equipment, safety gear, stretching exercises, drills, techniques, and tips for beginners. (Rev: HBG 3/98; SLJ 3/98) [796.9]

21983 Cole, Joanna. *Anna Banana: 101 Jump-Rope Rhymes* (2–4). Illus. by Alan Tiegreen. 1989, Morrow $16.00 (0-688-07788-9); paper $7.95 (0-688-08809-0). 64pp. Rhymes grouped according to jumping style. (Rev: BL 5/1/89)

21984 Cole, Joanna, and Stephanie Calmenson. *The Eentsy, Weentsy Spider* (PS–1). Illus. by Alan Tiegreen. 1991, Morrow paper $6.95 (0-688-10805-9). 64pp. Thirty-eight rhymes that demonstrate the fun children have performing the actions. (Rev: BL 10/15/91; SLJ 10/91) [793.4]

21985 Cole, Joanna, and Stephanie Calmenson. *Fun on the Run: Travel Games and Songs* (3–6). Illus. by Alan Tiegreen. 1999, Morrow $17.00 (0-688-14660-0). 126pp. Good descriptions with detailed playing steps are given in this inventive book of games useful when traveling, particularly by car. (Rev: HBG 3/00; SLJ 10/99) [790]

21986 Cole, Joanna, and Stephanie Calmenson. *Marbles: 101 Ways to Play* (4–6). Illus. 1998, Morrow $16.00 (0-688-12205-1). 128pp. After a short history of marbles, this book explains their types, describes various playing surfaces, and gives directions for playing 12 different games. (Rev: BL 5/15/98; HBG 10/98; SLJ 5/98) [796]

21987 Cole, Joanna, and Stephanie Calmenson. *Pin the Tail on the Donkey and Other Party Games* (K–3). Illus. by Alan Tiegreen. 1993, Morrow LB $14.93 (0-688-11892-5). 48pp. A picture book with 20 simple party games. (Rev: BL 8/93) [793]

21988 Coleman, Lori. *Beginning Strength Training* (4–7). Photos by Jimmy Clarke. Series: Beginning Sports. 1998, Lerner LB $22.60 (0-8225-3511-4). 64pp. This abridged version of *Jeff Savage's Fundamental Strength Training* is a beginner's book on body development. (Rev: HBG 10/99; SLJ 2/99) [796]

21989 Cook, Nick. *Downhill In-Line Skating* (5–8). Series: Extreme Sports. 2000, Capstone LB $21.26

(0-7368-0482-X). 48pp. Downhill inline skating is introduced with material on its history, equipment, skills, and competitions. (Rev: HBG 10/00; SLJ 8/00) [796]

21990 Crisfield, Deborah. *Winning Volleyball for Girls* (5–7). Illus. 1995, Facts on File $24.95 (0-8160-3033-2). 160pp. An excellent introduction to volleyball that gives girls information on rules, strategies, and techniques. (Rev: BCCB 3/96; BL 9/1/95) [796.32]

21991 Crisman, Ruth. *Racing the Iditarod Trail* (4–6). Illus. 1993, Macmillan LB $14.95 (0-87518-523-1). 72pp. The origins and history of the great Alaskan dog sledding race, the Iditarod. (Rev: SLJ 6/93) [979.8]

21992 Crossingham, John, and Sarah Dann. *Volleyball in Action* (4–6). Series: Sports in Action. 1999, Crabtree LB $14.97 (0-7787-0164-6); paper $5.36 (0-7787-0176-X). 32pp. This well-organized account introduces volleyball and supplies information on techniques, equipment, rules, and safety considerations. (Rev: SLJ 6/00) [796.32]

21993 Crum, Robert. *Let's Rodeo! Young Buckaroos and the World's Wildest Sport* (3–5). Illus. 1996, Simon & Schuster paper $17.00 (0-689-80075-4). 48pp. Various events in a typical rodeo are covered in this interesting photo-essay. (Rev: BCCB 12/96; BL 11/1/96; SLJ 9/96) [791.8]

21994 Curtis, Bruce, and Jay Morelli. *Beginning Golf* (5–8). Illus. 2000, Sterling $19.95 (0-8069-4970-8). 96pp. Beginning with an overview of golf, equipment, swing, full-play, and short game, and moving on to more complex topics, this fully illustrated volume is a fine introduction to golf. (Rev: BL 9/1/00; SLJ 1/01) [796.352]

21995 Davidson, Bob. *Hillary and Tenzing Climb Everest* (4–6). Illus. Series: Great 20th Century Expeditions. 1993, Dillon LB $13.95 (0-87518-534-7). 32pp. A description in text and photographs of many early attempts to conquer Everest, with emphasis on the successful 1953 expedition. (Rev: BL 9/15/93; SLJ 9/93) [796.5]

21996 Ditchfield, Christin. *Wrestling* (2–4). Illus. Series: True Books. 2000, Children's LB $21.50 (0-516-21611-2); paper $6.95 (0-516-27033-8). 48pp. This simple introduction to wrestling contains material on its history and how it is played and judged. (Rev: BL 9/15/00) [796.8]

21997 Dolan, Ellen M. *Susan Butcher and the Iditarod Trail* (5–7). Illus. 1993, Walker LB $15.85 (0-8027-8212-4). 112pp. This book tells about the history of the Iditarod sled dog race and of Susan Butcher who entered the race in 1978. (Rev: BL 4/1/93; SLJ 4/93) [798.8]

21998 Drake, Jane, and Ann Love. *The Kids Summer Games Book* (3–6). Illus. 1998, Kids Can paper $10.95 (1-55074-465-8). 176pp. This book includes a section on teams as well as ideas and rules for summer games, in and out of the water. (Rev: BL 5/15/98; SLJ 5/98) [796]

21999 Edwards, Chris. *The Young Inline Skater* (4–6). Illus. 1996, DK $15.95 (0-7894-1124-5). 35pp. From skate maintenance to important techniques, this book describes inline skating, with an emphasis on safety. (Rev: BL 11/15/96; SLJ 11/96) [792.2]

22000 Erlbach, Arlene. *Sidewalk Games Around the World* (3–5). Illus. 1997, Millbrook LB $23.90 (0-7613-0008-2). 64pp. Informal sidewalk games from 26 countries are introduced, with material on the country and the games and their rules. (Rev: BL 5/1/97; SLJ 5/97) [796.1]

22001 Fine, John C. *Free Spirits in the Sky* (3–5). Illus. 1994, Atheneum $14.95 (0-689-31705-0). 32pp. With color photos on each page, this book gives a history of ballooning, tells how balloons fly, and explains the different types. (Rev: BL 1/15/94; SLJ 3/94) [797.5]

22002 Flowers, Sarah. *Sports in America* (5–8). Illus. 1996, Lucent LB $18.96 (1-56006-178-2). 112pp. Problems in the modern sports world like commercialism, racism, and drugs are discussed in a straightforward way. (Rev: BL 9/1/96) [306.4]

22003 Gay, Kathlyn. *They Don't Wash Their Socks! Sports Superstitions* (3–5). Illus. by John Kerschbaum. 1990, Walker LB $14.85 (0-8027-6917-9). 114pp. Superstitions from many sports are highlighted. (Rev: SLJ 6/90) [796]

22004 Grayson, Marion F. *Let's Do Fingerplays* (PS–2). Illus. by Nancy Weyl. 1962, Luce $14.95 (0-88331-003-1). Comprehensive collection of finger plays under such headings as "Things That Go," "Animal Antics," and "Holidays."

22005 Greenberg, Keith E. *Rodeo Clown: Laughs and Danger in the Ring* (2–5). Illus. Series: Risky Business. 1995, Blackbirch LB $16.95 (1-56711-152-1). 32pp. This career book goes behind the scenes at a rodeo and shows that there is a great deal of danger involved in being a rodeo clown. (Rev: BCCB 9/95; SLJ 8/95) [791.8]

22006 Gryski, Camilla. *Cat's Cradle, Owl's Eyes: A Book of String Games* (4–7). Illus. by Tom Sankey. 1984, Morrow LB $15.93 (0-688-03940-5); paper $6.95 (0-688-03941-3). 80pp. Explanations of 21 string figures, plus variations.

22007 Gryski, Camilla. *Let's Play: Traditional Games of Childhood* (K–3). Illus. by Dusan Petricic. 1998, Kids Can $14.95 (1-55074-497-6). 47pp. A few of the games and activities that are described in this helpful manual are jacks, marbles, hopscotch, clapping games, and jump-rope rhymes. (Rev: HBG 10/98; SLJ 5/98) [790]

22008 Gryski, Camilla. *Many Stars and More String Games* (4–8). Illus. by Tom Sankey. 1985, Morrow paper $7.95 (0-688-05792-6). 80pp. Figures taken from a range of cultures to be mastered by agile fingers. (Rev: BL 12/15/85; SLJ 1/86)

22009 Gryski, Camilla. *Super String Games* (4–6). Illus. by Tom Sankey. 1988, Morrow paper $6.95 (0-688-07684-X). 80pp. Advanced string games with harder-to-learn patterns. (Rev: BL 3/1/88; SLJ 8/88)

22010 Hall, Godfrey. *Games* (5–7). Illus. Series: Traditions Around the World. 1995, Thomson Learning LB $24.26 (1-56847-345-1). 48pp. An oversize book that covers, in text and large color

pictures, various games played in geographical regions around the world. (Rev: BL 6/1–15/95; SLJ 9/95) [790.1]

22011 Hammond, Tim. *Sports* (4–8). Illus. 1988, Knopf LB $20.99 (0-394-99616-X). 64pp. Two dozen varieties of sports, including equipment, history, and rules. (Rev: BCCB 11/88; BL 12/1/88; SLJ 12/88)

22012 Harris, Jack C. *Adventure Gaming* (5–8). Illus. Series: Hobby Guides. 1993, Crestwood $17.95 (0-89686-621-1). 48pp. Clear, easy-to-read information is given, with coverage of all kinds of adventure games, including war and role-playing games and those that deal with magic and sorcery. (Rev: SLJ 2/94) [793.92]

22013 Hayhurst, Chris. *Wakeboarding! Throw a Tantrum* (4–8). Series: Extreme Sports. 2000, Rosen LB $17.95 (0-8239-3008-4). 64pp. This new water sport is described with material on the equipment needed and the necessary safety precautions. (Rev: BL 6/1–15/00; SLJ 8/00) [797.1]

22014 Hort, Lenny. *Treasure Hunts! Treasure Hunts! Treasure and Scavenger Hunts to Play with Friends and Family* (3–6). 2000, HarperCollins $15.95 (0-688-17245-8); paper $4.95 (0-688-17177-X). 80pp. This book supplies information for all sorts of treasure-hunting games with material on number of players, and where, when, and how to play. (Rev: BL 6/1–15/00; HBG 10/00; SLJ 11/00) [796.1]

22015 Hoyt-Goldsmith, Diane. *Lacrosse: The National Game of the Iroquois* (3–6). Illus. 1998, Holiday $16.95 (0-8234-1360-8). 32pp. After an introduction to the Iroquois Confederacy, this book traces the history of lacrosse and its past and present roles in the life of the Iroquois. (Rev: BL 6/1–15/98; HBG 10/98; SLJ 6/98) [796.3]

22016 Hu, Evaleen. *A Big Ticket: Sports and Commercialism* (4–7). Illus. 1998, Lerner LB $16.95 (0-8225-3305-7). 96pp. This well-organized book explains the connections between sports and the media, including broadcast rights, endorsement contracts, pop culture, and the impact of television. (Rev: BL 7/98; HBG 10/98) [338.4]

22017 Hughes, Sarah. *Let's Jump Rope* (1–3). 2000, Children's LB $13.50 (0-516-23114-6); paper $4.95 (0-516-23039-5). 24pp. Colorful action photographs and a simple text are used to show the basics of rope jumping as described by young Christina. (Rev: SLJ 2/01) [796]

22018 Hughes, Sarah. *Let's Play Hopscotch* (1–3). 2000, Children's LB $13.50 (0-516-23112-X); paper $4.95 (0-516-23037-9). 24pp. Action photos and a simple text explain how to play hopscotch. (Rev: SLJ 2/01) [796.1]

22019 Hughes, Sarah. *Let's Play Jacks* (1–3). 2000, Children's LB $13.50 (0-516-23113-8); paper $4.95 (0-516-23038-7). 24pp. A little girl explains the rules of the game of jacks and how to play it. (Rev: SLJ 2/01) [790.1]

22020 Hull, Mary. *The Composite Guide to Golf* (5–7). Series: Composite Guide. 1998, Chelsea LB $15.95 (0-7910-4726-1). 64pp. An introduction to the game of golf and its history, along with high-lights of the game's pioneers and some current stars such as Tiger Woods. (Rev: HBG 10/98; SLJ 9/98) [796.352]

22021 Hunter, Matt. *Pro Wrestling's Greatest Tag Teams* (4–7). Series: Pro Wrestling Legends. 2000, Chelsea LB $17.95 (0-7910-5835-2). 64pp. This title covers such tag teams as the Road Warriors, the Midnight Express, the Nasty Boys, Public Enemy, and Harlem Heat. (Rev: BL 10/15/00; HBG 3/01) [796.8]

22022 Hunter, Matt. *Ric Flair: The Story of the Wrestler They Call "The Natural Boy"* (4–7). Series: Pro Wrestling Legends. 2000, Chelsea LB $17.95 (0-7910-5825-5). 64pp. The story of the wrestler who has been at the top of his sport for most of the last three decades. (Rev: BL 10/15/00; HBG 3/01) [796.8]

22023 Irwin, Dawn. *Inline Skating* (3–6). Series: Superguides. 2000, DK $9.95 (0-7894-6542-6). 48pp. The basics of inline skating are covered with many color photographs that illustrate moves and tactics. (Rev: BL 8/00) [796]

22024 Janicot, Didier, and Gilbert Pouillart. *Judo Techniques andTactics* (4–7). Trans. from French by Yana Melnikova. 2000, Sterling $19.95 (0-8069-1970-1). 104pp. An informative manual that gives material on self-defense techniques and training tips for each level of judo from yellow up to black belt. (Rev: SLJ 3/01) [796.8]

22025 Jenkins, Steve. *The Top of the World: Climbing Mount Everest* (2–6). Illus. by author. 1999, Houghton $16.00 (0-395-94218-7). After a history of climbing on Mount Everest, the author discusses necessary equipment, climbing routes, dangers, and the physical effects on climbers. (Rev: BCCB 4/99; HBG 10/99; SLJ 5/99) [796.5]

22026 Kaminker, Laura. *In-Line Skating! Get Aggressive* (5–8). Series: Extreme Sports. 1999, Rosen Central LB $17.95 (0-8239-3012-2). 64pp. This book provides information for both beginning and advanced inline skaters and covers topics including equipment, history, techniques, and safety tips. (Rev: SLJ 4/00) [796]

22027 Kauchak, Therese. *Good Sports: Winning, Losing, and Everything in Between* (3–6). Illus. 1999, Pleasant paper $8.95 (1-56247-747-1). 95pp. Upbeat advice for girls on how to participate effectively in sports, with material on preparation, team efforts, practice, cooperation, and good and bad behavior. (Rev: BCCB 12/99; BL 3/1/00; SLJ 11/99) [796]

22028 Klingel, Cynthia, and Robert B. Noyed. *In-Line Skating* (K–2). Series: Wonder Books. 2000, Child's World LB $21.36 (1-56766-816-X). 24pp. A page of large-print text faces a full-color photograph in this easy-to-read introduction to inline skating, the equipment involved, and safety measures necessary. (Rev: SLJ 3/01) [792.2]

22029 Knotts, Bob. *Weightlifting* (2–4). Illus. Series: True Books. 2000, Children's LB $21.50 (0-516-21067-X); paper $6.95 (0-516-27032-X). 48pp. The sport of weightlifting is introduced in large-

type text and many color photographs. (Rev: BL 9/15/00) [796.4]

22030 Kramer, S. A. *To the Top! Climbing the World's Highest Mountain* (2–4). Illus. by Thomas La Padula. 1993, Random paper $3.99 (0-679-83885-6). 47pp. An account of how Edmund Hillary and Tenzing Norgay conquered Mount Everest in 1953. (Rev: BCCB 6/93; SLJ 8/93) [796.5]

22031 Krause, Peter. *Fundamental Golf* (5–8). Photos by Andy King. Series: Fundamental Sports. 1995, Lerner LB $22.60 (0-8225-3454-1). 64pp. A clear introduction to golf that covers history, equipment, swings, rules, and courses. (Rev: SLJ 9/95) [796.352]

22032 Lankford, Mary D. *Hopscotch Around the World* (2–4). Illus. by Karen Milone. 1992, Morrow LB $15.93 (0-688-08420-6). 48pp. A description of 19 hopscotch variations played in 16 countries around the world. (Rev: BCCB 6/92; BL 3/15/92; SLJ 4/92) [796.2]

22033 Levine, Shar, and Robert Bowden. *Awesome Yo-Yo Tricks* (4–6). Illus. 2000, Sterling paper $10.95 (0-8069-4468-4). 96pp. A wealth of information about yo-yos is included in this volume: their history and physics, types, the National Yo-Yo Museum, and, most important, step-by-step directions for mastering a number of tricks and techniques. (Rev: BL 6/1–15/00; SLJ 8/00) [796.2]

22034 Levine, Shar, and Vicki Scudamore. *Marbles: A Player's Guide* (3–5). Illus. 1999, Sterling $16.95 (0-8069-4262-2). 96pp. A careful description of 30 games involving marbles with a visual dictionary that classifies marbles. (Rev: BL 3/15/99; SLJ 4/99) [796.2]

22035 Marchon-Arnaud, Catherine. *A Gallery of Games* (5–7). Illus. by Marc Schwartz. Series: Young Artisan. 1994, Ticknor $12.95 (0-395-68379-3). 60pp. Historical information, clear directions, and rules of each game are supplied, but young novices might find some of these projects difficult. (Rev: BL 4/1/94; SLJ 3/94) [745]

22036 Mayo, Terry. *The Illustrated Rules of In-line Hockey* (3–5). Illus. by Ned Butterfield. Series: Illustrated Sports. 1996, Ideals paper $6.95 (1-57102-064-0). 32pp. An introduction to inline hockey, with a history of the sport, an explanation of the rules, a look at different positions and signals, and discussion of sportsmanship. (Rev: SLJ 8/96) [796.2]

22037 Miller, Thomas. *Taking Time Out: Recreation and Play* (5–8). Illus. Series: Our Human Family. 1995, Blackbirch LB $22.45 (1-56711-128-9). 80pp. Divided into five broad geographic areas, this account describes how people enjoy themselves at play in various cultures. (Rev: SLJ 1/96) [794]

22038 Moss, Marissa. *Dr. Amelia's Boredom Survival Guide: First Aid for Rainy Days, Boring Errands, Waiting Rooms, Whatever!* (3–5). Illus. by author. Series: Amelia. 1999, Pleasant paper $5.95 (1-56247-794-3). A humorous collection of 51 activities to allay boredom: listing good and gross food, eye tricks, and making up jump-rope songs are just three examples. (Rev: SLJ 7/99) [796]

22039 Nash, Bruce, and Allan Zullo. *The Greatest Sports Stories Never Told* (4–6). Illus. by John Gampert. 1993, Simon & Schuster paper $8.95 (0-671-75938-8). 96pp. From a variety of sports, this is a collection of 27 unusual but true stories. (Rev: BL 5/15/93; SLJ 6/93) [796]

22040 Nicholson, Lois. *The Composite Guide to Lacrosse* (4–8). Series: The Composite Guide. 1998, Chelsea LB $15.95 (0-7910-4719-9). 64pp. A fine guide to lacrosse, giving its history, how it is played today, and portraits of the game's greatest players. (Rev: HBG 3/99; SLJ 12/98) [796.34]

22041 Orozco, Jose-Luis. *Diez Deditos and Other Play Rhymes and Action Songs from Latin America* (PS–1). Illus. by Elisa Kleven. 1997, Dutton $18.99 (0-525-45736-4). 48pp. Thirty-four finger rhymes and songs in English and the original Spanish are included in this attractive collection. (Rev: BCCB 3/98; BL 1/1–15/98; HB 3–4/98; HBG 3/98) [782.42]

22042 Paros, Lawrence, and Ben Joshua Paros. *Smash Caps: The Official Milkcap Fun Book* (3–6). Illus. by Kuo W. Yang. 1995, Avon paper $7.99 (0-380-78459-9). 55pp. An introduction to POGS, a game originally from Hawaii, which is played with caps from different bottles. (Rev: SLJ 1/96) [796]

22043 Patent, Dorothy Hinshaw. *A Family Goes Hunting* (4–8). Illus. by William Munoz. 1991, Houghton $14.95 (0-395-52004-5). 64pp. One family is followed through hunting season in this photo-essay. (Rev: BCCB 11/91; BL 12/15/91; SLJ 11/91) [799]

22044 Payan, Gregory. *Essential Snowmobiling for Teens* (5–9). Series: Outdoor Life. 2000, Children's LB $19.00 (0-516-23358-0); paper $6.95 (0-516-23558-3). 48pp. The invention of the snowmobile is covered plus material on license requirements, trail permits, equipment, clothing, safety, driving techniques, and maintenance. (Rev: SLJ 2/01) [796.94]

22045 Perry, Phyllis J. *Ballooning* (4–6). Illus. 1996, Watts LB $22.00 (0-531-20234-8). 63pp. Following a history of ballooning, this account describes the parts of balloons and provides race statistics. (Rev: BL 2/1/97; SLJ 2/97) [629.133]

22046 Perry, Phyllis J. *Soaring* (4–7). Illus. Series: First Books. 1997, Watts LB $22.50 (0-531-20258-5). 64pp. Covers the history of gliders, scientific principles — like lift, thrust, and drag — and the sport of soaring and the equipment needed for it. (Rev: BL 7/97) [797.5]

22047 Platt, Richard. *Everest: Reaching the World's Highest Peak* (4–8). Illus. by Russell Barnet and John James. 2000, DK $14.95 (0-7894-6167-6). 48pp. Traces the history of mountain climbing with a focus on the many expeditions to Mount Everest and ending with the discovery of the body of George Mallory in 1999. (Rev: SLJ 10/00) [796.5]

22048 *Play Like a Girl: A Celebration of Women in Sports* (5–9). Ed. by Sue Macy and Jane Gottesman. Illus. 1999, Holt $15.95 (0-8050-6071-5). 32pp. This is a tribute to women in sports using material culled from books, photo archives, newspapers, and magazines. (Rev: BCCB 10/99; BL 7/99; HBG 10/00; SLJ 9/99) [796]

22049 *Racing on the Tour de France: And Other Stories of Sports* (4–6). Illus. 1989, Zaner-Bloser $10.95 (0-88309-546-7). 63pp. A collection of sports articles reprinted from the past 20 years of the magazine Highlights for Children. (Rev: SLJ 3/90) [796]

22050 Roberts, Jeremy. *Rock and Ice Climbing! Top the Tower* (4–8). Illus. Series: Extreme Sports. 2000, Rosen $17.95 (0-8239-3009-2). 64pp. This book on climbing covers the dangers of climbing, climbing styles, equipment, techniques, and venues, and profiles some young climbers. (Rev: BL 3/15/00; SLJ 8/00) [796.52]

22051 Roberts, Robin. *Sports for Life: How Athletes Have More Fun* (5–8). Illus. Series: Get in the Game. 2000, Millbrook LB $21.90 (0-7613-1407-5). 48pp. This account, mainly for girls, explains how to enjoy sports through applying discipline, patience, cooperation, health, and the fun of competition. (Rev: BL 1/1–15/01; HBG 3/01) [796]

22052 Ross, Dan. *Pro Wrestling's Greatest Wars* (4–7). Illus. 2000, Chelsea LB $17.95 (0-7910-5837-9); paper $8.95 (0-7910-5838-7). 64pp. Some of the great feuds in wrestling history, such as Harlem Heat vs. the Nasty Boys, are described in this fast read. (Rev: BL 10/15/00; HBG 3/01) [796.812]

22053 Ross, Dan. *The Story of the Wrestler They Call "The Rock"* (4–7). Series: Pro Wrestling Legends. 2000, Chelsea LB $17.95 (0-7910-5831-X). 64pp. This is the story of the third-generation wrestler known as "The Rock." (Rev: BL 10/15/00; HBG 3/01) [796.8]

22054 Rowe, Julian. *Recreation* (4–7). Illus. Series: Science Encounters. 1997, Rigby $22.79 (1-57572-092-2). 32pp. Shows how science is used in theme park rides, backpacking and camping equipment, computer games, television, scuba diving, and hang gliding. (Rev: SLJ 10/97) [796]

22055 Rowe, Julian. *Sports* (4–7). Illus. Series: Science Encounters. 1997, Rigby $22.79 (1-57572-089-2). 32pp. Shows how science is used in such sports-related topics as the design of equipment, protective clothing, and sports medicine. (Rev: SLJ 10/97) [796]

22056 Ryan, Pat. *Rock Climbing* (4–7). Illus. Series: World of Sports. 2000, Smart Apple Media $15.95 (1-887068-57-0). 32pp. In addition to covering the origins and evolution of rock climbing, this book discusses the basics of the sport, equipment, and star athletes. (Rev: BL 9/15/00) [796.52]

22057 Savage, Jeff. *Top 10 Sports Bloopers and Who Made Them* (4–7). Illus. Series: Sports Top 10. 2000, Enslow LB $18.95 (0-7660-1271-9). 48pp. This collection of ten famous sports mistakes also gives good background information on the perpetrators and the causes of the errors. (Rev: BL 9/15/00; HBG 10/00; SLJ 10/00) [796]

22058 Shahan, Sherry. *Dashing Through the Snow: The Story of the Jr. Iditarod* (4–7). Illus. 1997, Millbrook LB $22.40 (0-7613-0208-5); paper $9.95 (0-7613-0143-7). 48pp. All aspects of the 150-mile Junior Iditarod are touched upon in this account, including how these young mushers communicate with their dogs. (Rev: BL 3/1/97; SLJ 4/97) [798]

22059 Sheely, Robert, and Louis Bourgeois. *Sports Lab: How Science Has Changed Sports* (4–7). Illus. Series: Science Lab. 1994, Silver Moon $14.95 (1-881889-49-1). 60pp. Traces the effect on sports of applying findings from such branches of science as aerodynamics, psychology, and medicine. (Rev: SLJ 9/94) [617.1]

22060 Sherman, Josepha. *Barrel Racing* (4–6). Series: Rodeo. 2000, Heinemann LB $21.36 (1-57572-503-7). 32pp. Barrel racing training, skills, equipment, and schedules are covered here. Three other titles on rodeo events are *Bronc Riding, Bull Riding* and *Steer Wrestling* (all 2000). (Rev: BL 10/15/00; HBG 3/01; SLJ 8/00) [791.8]

22061 Sherman, Josepha. *Ropers and Riders* (4–6). Series: Rodeo. 2000, Heinemann LB $21.36 (1-57572-506-1). 32pp. A colorful book that features these stars of the rodeo, their skills, training, and lifestyles. (Rev: BL 10/15/00; HBG 3/01; SLJ 9/00) [791.8]

22062 Sherman, Josepha. *Welcome to the Rodeo!* (4–6). Illus. Series: Rodeo. 2000, Heinemann $14.95 (1-57572-508-8). 32pp. An introduction to rodeos with material on the various riding and roping competitions and on famous rodeo stars. (Rev: BL 10/15/00; HBG 3/01; SLJ 9/00) [791.8]

22063 Simmons, Richard. *The Young Golfer: A Young Enthusiast's Guide to Golf* (4–10). 1999, DK $15.95 (0-7894-4712-6). 48pp. A brief history of golf is followed by explanations of the course, equipment, scoring, rules, grip, swing, shots, and playing tips. (Rev: HBG 10/00; SLJ 1/00) [796.352]

22064 Sobol, Donald J. *Encyclopedia Brown's Book of Wacky Sports* (3–6). Illus. by Ted Enik. 1984, Morrow $16.00 (0-688-03884-0). 112pp. A spin-off from the popular series, this is actually a book about wacky "happenings" in sports, covering a wide range of high school, college, and pro sports.

22065 Steiner, Andy. *Girl Power on the Playing Field: A Book About Girls, Their Goals, and Their Struggles* (5–10). Series: Girl Power. 2000, Lerner LB $25.26 (0-8225-2690-5). 96pp. This book explains women's roles in sports with good personal guidance for young girls on participation and goals. (Rev: HBG 10/00; SLJ 6/00) [796]

22066 Steiner, Andy. *A Sporting Chance: Sports and Gender* (5–7). Illus. 1995, Lerner LB $22.60 (0-8225-3300-6). 96pp. The lack of equality between men and women in sports is covered in this account, ranging from Little League to professional levels. (Rev: BL 1/1–15/96; SLJ 1/96) [796]

22067 Stott, Dorothy. *The Big Book of Games* (K–2). Illus. by author. 1998, Dutton $17.99 (0-525-45454-3). 64pp. Grouped into three sections (party games, outdoor games, and singing games), this book contains more than 40 favorite childhood games complete with excellent instructions on how to play each. (Rev: HBG 3/99; SLJ 3/99) [790.1]

22068 Sullivan, George. *Any Number Can Play: The Numbers Athletes Wear* (4–8). Illus. 2000, Millbrook LB $22.90 (0-7613-1557-8). 80pp. A fasci-

nating glimpse at players' devotion to their assigned numbers, along with information on retired and banned numbers and who uses the number 13. (Rev: BL 12/15/00; HBG 3/01; SLJ 2/01) [796]

22069 Sullivan, George. *Don't Step on the Foul Line: Sports Superstitions* (4–8). Illus. 2000, Millbrook LB $22.90 (0-7613-1558-6). 80pp. This is an intriguing look at superstitions, customs, and traditions associated with many different sports. (Rev: BL 12/15/00; HBG 3/01; SLJ 2/01) [796.357]

22070 Todd, Susan. *Boredom Blasters: Hours and Miles of Games and Activities to Make Time Fly* (1–6). Illus. by David Vordtriede. 2000, EFG paper $9.99 (0-9630222-9-6). 88pp. Seventy-seven ideas for games and pastimes that can be played in small spaces and are suitable for single or multiple players. (Rev: SLJ 11/00) [793]

22071 Willard, Keith. *Ballooning* (4–7). Illus. Series: World of Sports. 2000, Smart Apple Media $15.95 (1-887068-51-1). 32pp. This brief introduction to ballooning mentions star balloonists, different kinds of ballooning, the origins of this sport, and how one becomes proficient at it. (Rev: BL 9/15/00) [797.5]

22072 Williamson, Susan. *Summer Fun! 60 Activities for a Kid-Perfect Summer* (2–6). Illus. by Michael Kline. Series: A Williamson Kids Can! Book. 1999, Williamson paper $12.95 (1-885593-33-3). 138pp. Sixty quiet activities — including making up riddles, learning sign language, and bug hunts — are presented with black-and-white cartoons. (Rev: SLJ 8/99) [796]

22073 Willker, Joshua D. G. *Everything You Need to Know About the Dangers of Sports Gambling* (5–10). Illus. Series: Need to Know Library. 2000, Rosen LB $17.95 (0-8239-3229-X). 64pp. This brief, well-written book surveys the world of gambling on sports, its legal and illegal aspects, and how it has ruined the careers of many fine athletes. (Rev: BL 1/1–15/01) [796]

22074 Witt, Alexa. *It's Great to Skate! An Easy Guide to In-line Skating* (K–2). Illus. by Nate Evans. 2000, Simon & Schuster paper $3.99 (0-689-82590-0). 30pp. A beginner's book on the basics of inline skating with material on safety measures and equipment. (Rev: SLJ 4/00) [796]

22075 Wood, Ted. *Iditarod Dream: Dusty and His Sled Dogs Compete in Alaska's Jr. Iditarod* (2–5). Illus. 1996, Walker $17.85 (0-8027-8407-0). 48pp. Dusty, a 15-year-old Alaskan boy, prepares for and later enters the 158-mile Junior Iditarod. (Rev: BCCB 4/96; BL 3/15/96; SLJ 5/96) [798]

22076 Wulffson, Don L. *Toys! Amazing Stories Behind Some Great Inventions* (4–6). Illus. 2000, Holt $15.95 (0-8050-6196-7). 136pp. The story behind such toys as Mr. Potato Head, Slinky, Silly Putty, kites, checkers, and Parcheesi is told in 25 illustrated chapters each dealing with a different game or toy. (Rev: BCCB 6/00; BL 6/1–15/00; HBG 3/01; SLJ 9/00) [688.7]

22077 Young, Robert. *Sports Cards* (3–6). Illus. Series: Collectibles. 1993, Macmillan LB $13.95 (0-87518-519-3). 71pp. This book presents a history of trading cards and gives material both on their production and on how to collect them. (Rev: SLJ 8/93) [796]

Automobile Racing

22078 Andretti, Michael, et al. *Michael Andretti at Indianapolis* (3–7). Illus. by Douglas Carver. 1993, Simon & Schuster paper $5.95 (0-671-79674-7). 64pp. Readers experience the Indianapolis 500 from the driver's viewpoint. (Rev: BL 7/92; SLJ 6/92) [796.7]

22079 Benson, Michael. *Crashes and Collisions* (5–8). Illus. Series: Race Car Legends. 1997, Chelsea $16.95 (0-7910-4435-1). 64pp. This exciting book chronicles several multicar pileups and gives short profiles of some who have survived them. (Rev: HBG 3/98; SLJ 2/98) [629.228]

22080 *Formula 1 Motor Racing Book* (5–8). Illus. 1996, DK $16.95 (0-7894-0440-0). 64pp. A fascinating introduction to the world of Grand Prix racing with material on car care and maintenance. (Rev: BL 12/15/96) [796.72]

22081 Kirkwood, Jon. *The Fantastic Book of Car Racing* (4–6). Illus. Series: Fantastic Book Of. 1997, Millbrook LB $22.40 (0-7613-0565-3). 39pp. A heavily illustrated book with foldout sections on the subject of car racing, its excitement, and its allure. (Rev: SLJ 8/97) [796.7]

22082 Savage, Jeff. *Drag Racing* (4–8). Illus. Series: Action Events. 1996, Crestwood LB $14.95 (0-89686-890-7); paper $4.95 (0-382-39293-0). 48pp. The thrill of drag racing is conveyed through action photos and a simple text. Also use *Mud Racing* and *Super Cross Motorcycle Racing* (both 1996). (Rev: SLJ 2/97) [796.7]

22083 Sullivan, George. *Burnin' Rubber: Behind the Scenes in Stock Car Racing* (4–6). 1998, Millbrook LB $21.90 (0-7613-1256-0). 48pp. A look at NASCAR racing, with interesting behind-the-scenes information on this uniquely American sport. (Rev: HBG 3/99; SLJ 1/99) [796.7]

Baseball

22084 Anderson, Joan. *Batboy: An Inside Look at Spring Training* (3–6). Illus. 1996, Dutton $16.99 (0-525-67511-6). 48pp. A photo-essay that highlights the work and pleasures of being a bat boy. (Rev: BCCB 3/96; BL 4/1/96; HB 5–6/96; SLJ 3/96) [796.357]

22085 Aylesworth, Thomas G. *The Kids' World Almanac of Baseball* (4–8). Illus. 1996, World Almanac $8.95 (0-88687-787-3). 288pp. An entertaining compendium of baseball facts. (Rev: BL 6/1/90) [796.357]

22086 Brundage, Buz. *Be a Better Hitter: Baseball Basics* (5–9). Illus. 2000, Sterling $17.95 (0-8069-2461-6). 96pp. Covers baseball hitting techniques including grip stance, bunting, swing, contact, and

follow-through. (Rev: BL 6/1–15/00; SLJ 9/00) [796.357]

22087 Christopher, Matt. *Great Moments in Baseball History* (3–5). 1996, Little, Brown paper $4.95 (0-316-14130-5). 104pp. Describes nine important baseball events, involving such luminaries as Babe Ruth and Reggie Jackson. (Rev: SLJ 5/96) [796.357]

22088 Dunnahoo, Terry, et al. *Baseball Hall of Fame* (4–6). Illus. Series: Halls of Fame. 1994, Macmillan LB $17.95 (0-89686-849-4). 48pp. In addition to providing a description of the Cooperstown, N.Y., museum, this book discusses the origins of the game, rules, and great players. (Rev: BL 9/1/94) [796.357]

22089 Egan, Terry, et al. *The Good Guys of Baseball: Sixteen True Sports Stories* (3–6). Illus. 1997, Simon & Schuster paper $18.00 (0-689-80212-9). 111pp. Sixteen true stories, many featuring well-known players, that celebrate the hard work and dedication that baseball demands of a serious player. (Rev: SLJ 5/97) [796.357]

22090 Egan, Terry, et al. *The Macmillan Book of Baseball Stories* (4–6). Illus. 1992, Macmillan LB $16.00 (0-02-733280-2). 112pp. These sentimental, true baseball stories demonstrate strong values, tradition, and the fun of the game. (Rev: BL 1/15/93) [796]

22091 Gardner, Robert, and Dennis Shortelle. *The Forgotten Players: The Story of Black Baseball in America* (5–8). Illus. 1993, Walker LB $13.85 (0-8027-8249-3). 120pp. The trials of black baseball in America are revealed along with little-known aspects of U.S. baseball. (Rev: BL 2/15/93; SLJ 4/93) [769.357]

22092 Gay, Douglas, and Kathlyn Gay. *The Not-So-Minor Leagues* (5–8). Illus. 1996, Millbrook LB $22.40 (1-56294-921-7). 96pp. The history, importance, and present status of the minor leagues in baseball. (Rev: BL 5/15/96; SLJ 6/96) [796.357]

22093 Gibbons, Gail. *My Baseball Book* (PS–3). Illus. 2000, HarperCollins $5.95 (0-688-17137-0). An attractive introduction to baseball that describes the playing field, positions, equipment, and game plays. (Rev: BCCB 4/00; BL 5/1/00; HBG 10/00; SLJ 6/00) [796.357]

22094 Hanmer, Trudy J. *The All-American Girls Professional Baseball League* (5–8). Illus. Series: American Events. 1994, New Discovery LB $18.95 (0-02-742595-9). 96pp. As well as discussing the AAGPBL, this account describes women in baseball prior to the league and recent attempts to play at all levels from Little League to the majors. (Rev: SLJ 3/95) [796.357]

22095 Healy, Dennis. *The Illustrated Rules of Baseball* (3–5). Illus. Series: Illustrated Sports. 1995, Ideals paper $6.95 (1-57102-017-9). 32pp. The baseball diamond, playing positions, equipment, and rules are covered in this introduction to baseball. (Rev: BL 7/95; SLJ 5/95) [798.357]

22096 Horenstein, Henry. *Baseball in the Barrios* (2–4). Illus. 1997, Harcourt $16.00 (0-15-200499-8). 36pp. A fifth-grader introduces baseball as it is played in the barrios of Caracas, Venezuela. (Rev: BL 4/15/97; HB 7–8/97; SLJ 6/97) [796.357]

22097 Isadora, Rachael. *Nick Plays Baseball* (2–4). Illus. 2001, Putnam $15.99 (0-399-23231-1). 32pp. Using a fictional story about Nick and his team as a framework, this oversize picture book gives information on batting, pitching, equipment, playing positions, and the rules of the game. (Rev: BCCB 2/01; BL 2/15/01) [796.357]

22098 Jensen, Julie. *Beginning Baseball* (3–5). Photos by Andy King. Series: Beginning Sports. 1995, Lerner LB $22.60 (0-8225-3505-X). 80pp. The fundamentals of baseball — like throwing, hitting, fielding, and baserunning — are presented, along with a history of the game. (Rev: SLJ 2/96) [796.357]

22099 Kasoff, Jerry. *Baseball Just for Kids: Skills, Strategies and Stories to Make You a Better Ballplayer* (3–7). Illus. 1996, Grand Slam paper $12.95 (0-9645826-7-8). 159pp. Baseball rules, techniques, tips, jokes, and trivia are included in this book that shows that the author loves the game. (Rev: SLJ 4/97) [796.357]

22100 Kelley, James. *Baseball* (2–6). Illus. Series: Eyewitness Books. 2000, DK $15.95 (0-7894-5241-3). 60pp. Using double-page spreads, amazing photos, and an interesting text, this book covers topics including baseball legends, playing techniques, history, and jargon. (Rev: BL 6/1–15/00; HBG 10/00) [796.357]

22101 Kellogg, David. *True Stories of Baseball's Hall of Famers* (4–8). Illus. 2000, Bluewood $8.95 (0-912517-41-7). 144pp. Using a chronological approach, this book profiles 60 Hall of Famers and tells why each is there. (Rev: BL 10/15/00) [796.357]

22102 Kisseloff, Jeff. *Who Is Baseball's Greatest Hitter?* (5–8). Illus. 2000, Holt $15.95 (0-8050-6013-8). 122pp. The author introduces a number of strong candidates for the title of baseball's greatest hitter. (Rev: BL 5/1/00; HBG 10/00; SLJ 7/00) [796.357]

22103 Kreutzer, Peter, and Ted Kerley. *Little League's Official How-to-Play Baseball Handbook* (4–8). Illus. 1990, Doubleday paper $11.95 (0-385-24700-1). 210pp. This guidebook covers all the basics of baseball and supplies strategies for playing various positions. (Rev: BL 5/15/90) [796.357]

22104 Layden, Joe. *The Great American Baseball Strike* (5–8). Illus. Series: Headliners. 1995, Millbrook LB $23.40 (1-56294-930-6). 64pp. A story of the baseball strike that did great damage to the sport and alienated the fans. (Rev: BL 11/15/95; SLJ 1/96) [331.89]

22105 Mackin, Bob. *Record-Breaking Baseball Trivia* (5–8). 2000, Douglas & McIntyre paper $6.95 (1-55054-757-7). 128pp. Questions, answers, and quizzes cover topics including baseball history, team play, World Series facts, and trivia from the plate and mound. (Rev: BL 9/15/00) [796.357]

22106 Macy, Sue. *A Whole New Ball Game: The Story of the All-American Girls Professional Baseball League* (5–8). Illus. 1993, Holt $14.95 (0-8050-1942-1). 140pp. A fascinating look at the All-American Girls Professional Baseball League that

functioned from 1945 to 1954. (Rev: SLJ 5/93*) [796.357]

22107 Nash, Bruce, and Allan Zullo. *The Baseball Hall of Shame: Young Fans' Edition* (5–8). Illus. 1990, Pocket paper $2.99 (0-671-69354-9). 133pp. Baseball blunders by players, managers, umpires, and even groundskeepers are reported on. (Rev: SLJ 7/90) [796.357]

22108 Newman, Gerald. *Happy Birthday, Little League* (3–6). Illus. 1989, Watts LB $22.00 (0-531-10687-X). 64pp. A half-century tribute to Little League baseball, filled with impressive statistics. (Rev: BCCB 4/89; BL 4/1/89; SLJ 5/89)

22109 Nitz, Kristin Wolden. *Softball* (5–9). Series: Play-by-Play. 2000, Lerner paper $7.95 (0-8225-9875-2). 80pp. Good basic information about softball is given including history, rules, equipment, and positions. (Rev: SLJ 9/00) [796.357]

22110 Owens, Thomas S. *The Atlanta Braves Baseball Team* (4–6). Series: Great Sports Teams. 1998, Enslow LB $17.95 (0-7660-1021-X). 48pp. Provides a history of the Atlanta Braves and highlights their most famous players and exciting seasons. (Rev: BL 5/15/98; HBG 10/98) [796.357]

22111 Patrick, Jean L. S. *The Girl Who Struck Out Babe Ruth* (2–3). Illus. by Jeni Reeves. 2000, Lerner $21.27 (1-57505-397-7); paper $5.95 (1-57505-455-8). 48pp. In 1931, 17-year-old Jackie Mitchell, a pitcher in the minor leagues, played in an exhibition game in which she struck out Babe Ruth and Lou Gehrig. (Rev: BCCB 6/00; BL 4/15/00; HBG 10/00; SLJ 8/00) [796.357]

22112 Pietrusza, David. *The Baltimore Orioles Baseball Team* (4–6). Series: Great Sports Teams. 2000, Enslow LB $18.95 (0-7660-1283-2). 48pp. Covers the history of the Baltimore Orioles, the team's best players, and its performance today and tomorrow. (Rev: BL 5/15/00; HBG 10/00) [796.357]

22113 Pietrusza, David. *The New York Yankees Baseball Team* (4–6). Illus. 1998, Enslow LB $17.95 (0-7660-1018-X). 48pp. A brief, well-illustrated account of the history of the Yankees, with emphasis on star players and important coaches. (Rev: BL 4/1/98; HBG 10/98) [796.357]

22114 Pietrusza, David. *The San Francisco Giants Baseball Team* (4–6). Series: Great Sports Teams. 2000, Enslow LB $18.95 (0-7660-1284-0). 48pp. Plenty of sports action is included in this introduction to the past, present, and future of the San Francisco Giants. (Rev: BL 5/15/00; HBG 10/00) [795.357]

22115 Preller, James. *McGwire and Sosa: A Season to Remember* (4–7). Illus. 1998, Simon & Schuster paper $5.99 (0-689-82871-3). 32pp. An oversize paperback that traces the baseball season that brought Sosa and McGwire to the nation's attention and made them sports heroes. (Rev: BL 1/1–15/99) [796.357]

22116 Ritter, Lawrence S. *The Story of Baseball*. Rev. ed. (4–8). 1999, Morrow $16.95 (0-688-16264-9). 224pp. First published in 1983, this is the third edition of this standard work that gives material on the history of the game, how it is played, famous teams and players, plus lots of statistics. (Rev: HBG 10/99; SLJ 4/99) [796.357]

22117 Smyth, Ian. *The Young Baseball Player* (4–7). Illus. 1998, DK $15.95 (0-7894-2825-3). 37pp. A good beginner's guide to baseball that explains, through illustrations and text, the fundamentals of baseball, the roles of each position, basic skills, and a little of the sport's history. (Rev: BL 6/1–15/98; HBG 10/98; SLJ 6/98) [796.357]

22118 Stewart, Wayne. *Baseball Bafflers* (4–7). Illus. 2000, Sterling paper $5.95 (0-8069-6561-4). 96pp. Using anecdotes, quotes, and statistics, this book describes some of baseball's most unusual plays and strategies. (Rev: BL 2/1/00) [796.357]

22119 Sublett, Anne. *The Illustrated Rules of Softball* (3–5). Illus. by Patrick Kelley. Series: Illustrated Sports. 1996, Ideals paper $6.95 (1-57102-063-2). 32pp. After a brief history of baseball, this account presents an explanation of rules and a look at various positions and signals, plus a glossary and discussion of sportsmanship. (Rev: SLJ 8/96) [796.357]

22120 Sullivan, George. *All About Baseball* (4–6). Illus. 1989, Putnam paper $9.95 (0-399-21734-7). 128pp. The basics of the game in an appealing format. (Rev: BL 5/1/89)

22121 Sullivan, George. *Glovemen: Twenty-Seven of Baseball's Greatest* (4–7). Illus. 1996, Simon & Schuster $18.00 (0-689-31991-6). 72pp. A history of the role of defensemen in baseball and profiles of 27 of the greatest. (Rev: BL 5/15/96; SLJ 8/96) [796.357]

22122 Thomson, Peggy. *Take Me Out to the Bat and Ball Factory* (2–5). Illus. 1998, Albert Whitman $14.95 (0-8075-7737-5). 32pp. This tour of a bat and ball factory not only explains how wood and aluminum bats are made and the composition and manufacture of balls but also supplies trivia and interesting lore about the game. (Rev: BL 6/1–15/98; HBG 10/98; SLJ 6/98) [688.357]

22123 Tuttle, Dennis R. *Life in the Minor Leagues* (4–6). Illus. Series: Baseball Legends. 1999, Chelsea LB $16.95 (0-7910-5160-9). 64pp. An introduction to the minor leagues, how they developed, their organization, famous players, and daily life within the teams. (Rev: BL 8/99; HBG 10/99) [796.357]

22124 Young, Robert. *Game Day: Behind the Scenes at a Ballpark* (3–5). 1998, Carolrhoda LB $22.60 (1-57505-084-6). 48pp. This photo-essay depicts all the activities that occur at a major league ballpark (Camden Yards in Baltimore, Maryland) on the day of a game — from early food deliveries to the work of cleanup crews afterward. (Rev: BCCB 12/98; BL 11/15/98; HBG 3/99; SLJ 1/99) [796.357]

22125 Young, Robert. *A Personal Tour of Camden Yards* (4–7). Series: How It Was. 1999, Lerner LB $23.93 (0-8225-3578-5). 64pp. Designed to remind fans of famous old ballparks, this book visits Camden Yards, home of the Baltimore Orioles. The reader inspects the field, visits the old warehouse

and views the game from a sky box. (Rev: BL 6/1–15/99; HBG 10/99) [796.357]

Basketball

22126 Anderson, Dave. *The Story of Basketball* (4–8). Illus. 1997, Morrow $16.00 (0-688-14316-4). 208pp. An updated introduction to the history, rules, players, and teams involved in basketball. (Rev: BL 1/1–15/98; HBG 3/98; SLJ 10/97) [796.32]

22127 Aretha, David. *The Seattle SuperSonics Basketball Team* (4–6). Illus. Series: Great Sports Teams. 1999, Enslow LB $18.95 (0-7660-1102-X). 48pp. A history of the Seattle SuperSonics is given, with information on famous players past and present and descriptions of important games. (Rev: BL 3/15/99; HBG 10/99) [796.323]

22128 Bennett, Frank. *The Illustrated Rules of Basketball* (3–5). Illus. 1994, Ideals paper $6.95 (1-57102-021-7). 32pp. Following the history of basketball, provides a detailed discussion of each rule. (Rev: BL 9/15/94; SLJ 11/94) [796.323]

22129 Dixon, Tamecka, and Judith Cohen. *You Can Be a Woman Basketball Player* (3–6). Illus. 1999, Cascade Pass $13.95 (1-880599-40-6); paper $7.00 (1-880599-38-4). 40pp. As well as the story of Tamecka Dixon, a player on the Los Angeles Sparks, this book explains the fundamentals of basketball, its positions, and the duties of each team member. (Rev: BL 8/99; SLJ 9/99) [796.323]

22130 Dunnahoo, Terry, et al. *Basketball Hall of Fame* (4–6). Illus. Series: Halls of Fame. 1994, Macmillan LB $13.95 (0-89686-850-8). 48pp. As well as describing the functions of the Basketball Hall of Fame, this book explains how the sport evolved and tells about some of the great players. (Rev: BL 9/1/94; SLJ 8/94) [796.323]

22131 Gibbons, Gail. *My Basketball Book* (K–2). Illus. 2000, HarperCollins $5.95 (0-688-17140-0). 24pp. This small-format paperback book contains the basics of basketball with coverage of equipment, positions, and rules. (Rev: BL 9/15/00; HBG 3/01; SLJ 11/00) [796.323]

22132 Glenn, Mike. *Lessons in Success from the NBA's Top Players* (5–7). Illus. 1998, Visions 3000 paper $14.95 (0-9649795-5-1). 126pp. This noted sportsman tells about his career in the NBA while introducing each of the NBA teams and its strengths. (Rev: BL 7/98) [796.323]

22133 Kramer, S. A. *Hoop Stars* (2–3). Illus. by Mitchell Heinze. 1995, Putnam paper $3.99 (0-448-40943-7). 48pp. Hakeem Olajuwon, Charles Barkley, Shaquille O'Neal, and David Robinson are the NBA stars briefly profiled in this beginning reader. (Rev: BL 1/1–15/96; SLJ 3/96) [796.323]

22134 Lace, William W. *The Houston Rockets Basketball Team* (5–8). Series: Great Sports Teams. 1997, Enslow LB $18.95 (0-89490-792-1). 48pp. A profile of the Houston Rockets, with sketches of their key players. (Rev: BL 10/15/97; HBG 3/98) [796.323]

22135 Lace, William W. *The Los Angeles Lakers Basketball Team* (4–6). Illus. Series: Great Sports Teams. 1998, Enslow LB $17.95 (0-7660-1020-1). 48pp. After a short introduction on Magic Johnson, this account focuses on the history of the team on which he played, with emphasis on their finest moments, their star players, and famous coaches. (Rev: BL 4/1/98; HBG 10/98) [796.323]

22136 Lannin, Joanne. *A History of Basketball for Girls and Women: From Bloomers to the Big Leagues* (5–9). Illus. Series: Sports Legacy. 2000, Lerner LB $26.60 (0-8225-3331-6); paper $9.95 (0-8225-9863-9). 144pp. From the creation of basketball in 1891 to today, this account describes women's roles in its inception and development. (Rev: BL 1/1–15/01; HBG 3/01) [796.323]

22137 Morris, Greggory. *Basketball Basics* (4–6). Illus. by Tim Engelland. 1979, Prentice Hall $6.95 (0-13-072256-1). A player and coach explain four specific skills to young players.

22138 Mullin, Chris. *Basketball* (3–6). Illus. Series: Superguides. 2000, DK $9.95 (0-7894-5426-2). 44pp. This attractive guide to basketball has an introduction by Chris Mullin and covers topics including the history of the sport, the court, rules, and basic movements. (Rev: BL 6/1–15/00; HBG 10/00) [796.323]

22139 Mullin, Chris, and Brian Coleman. *The Young Basketball Player* (4–7). Illus. 1995, DK $15.95 (0-7894-0220-3). 45pp. Such basketball techniques as dribbling, passing, and scoring are described, along with brief material on the history of the sport and on equipment. (Rev: BL 11/1/95; SLJ 1/96) [796.323]

22140 Owens, Thomas S. *The Chicago Bulls Basketball Team* (5–8). Illus. Series: Great Sports Teams. 1997, Enslow LB $18.95 (0-89490-793-X). 48pp. A history of the Chicago Bulls, with emphasis on the various stars who have made the team famous. (Rev: BL 10/15/97; HBG 3/98) [796.323]

22141 Parselle, Matt. *Basketball: Learn How to Be a Star Player* (3–5). Illus. by Mel Pickering. Series: Sports Club. 2000, Two-Can $9.95 (1-58728-000-0). 32pp. This basic book on basketball explains different kinds of passes and the rules of the game, as well as giving some history and profiles of a few important players. (Rev: SLJ 3/01) [796.323]

22142 Pietrusza, David. *The Phoenix Suns Basketball Team* (5–8). Series: Great Sports Teams. 1997, Enslow LB $18.95 (0-89490-795-6). 48pp. Introduces the history of the Phoenix Suns and their key players. (Rev: BL 10/15/97; HBG 3/98) [796.323]

22143 Ponti, James. *WNBA: Stars of Women's Basketball* (5–8). 1999, Pocket paper $4.99 (0-671-03275-5). 121pp. This book on women's professional basketball not only profiles the teams but also gives interesting sketches, three or four pages long, of the key players. (Rev: SLJ 8/99) [796.323]

22144 Preller, James. *NBA Game Day: An Inside Look at the NBA* (3–8). Illus. 1997, Scholastic paper $10.95 (0-590-76742-9). 48pp. A photo-essay on a day in the life of the NBA, from the morning workout to the custodian sweeping the court after the evening game. (Rev: BL 1/1–15/98; HBG 3/98) [796.323]

22145 Roberts, Robin. *Basketball Year: What It's Like to Be a Woman Pro* (4–6). Illus. Series: Get in the Game. 2000, Millbrook $21.90 (0-7613-1406-7). 48pp. This account follows women of the WNBA as they train, travel, play games, and try to lead normal lives. (Rev: BL 9/1/00; HBG 10/00; SLJ 8/00) [796.323]

22146 Rogers, Glenn. *The San Antonio Spurs Basketball Team* (5–8). Series: Great Sports Teams. 1997, Enslow LB $18.95 (0-89490-797-2). 48pp. Profiles of important players and stories behind important games are included in this profile of the San Antonio Spurs. (Rev: BL 10/15/97; HBG 3/98) [796.323]

22147 Rutledge, Rachel. *The Best of the Best in Basketball* (4–7). Illus. Series: Women in Sports. 1998, Millbrook LB $22.90 (0-7613-1301-X); paper $6.95 (0-7613-0443-6). 64pp. After a history of basketball, this account highlights women's role and covers today's most important female players. (Rev: BL 2/15/99; HBG 10/99; SLJ 3/99) [796.323]

22148 Schulz, Randy. *The New York Knicks Basketball Team* (4–6). Series: Great Sports Teams. 2000, Enslow LB $18.95 (0-7660-1281-6). 48pp. The New York Nicks are profiled with material on the team's history, greatest players, and most exciting games. (Rev: BL 9/15/00) [796.323]

22149 Sullivan, George. *All About Basketball* (5–8). Illus. 1991, Putnam paper $9.99 (0-399-21793-2). 160pp. An ideal explanation for those who know little or nothing about the game. (Rev: BL 1/1/92) [296.323]

22150 Vancil, Mark. *NBA Basketball Offense Basics* (4–8). Illus. 1996, Sterling $17.95 (0-8069-4892-2). 96pp. Action photos and lively text demonstrate such techniques as dribbling, passing, and shooting. (Rev: BL 9/1/96) [796.332]

22151 Weatherspoon, Teresa, et al. *Teresa Weatherspoon's Basketball for Girls* (5–10). 1999, Wiley paper $14.95 (0-471-31784-5). 120pp. This introduction to the game and guide to playing basketball effectively stresses teamwork and the fun of playing. (Rev: SLJ 8/99) [796.32]

Bicycles

22152 Bach, Julie. *Bicycling* (4–7). Illus. Series: World of Sports. 2000, Smart Apple Media $15.95 (1-887068-53-8). 32pp. A brief introduction to bicycling that gives material on the origins and evolution of the sport, equipment, and techniques, plus coverage of the sport's star athletes. (Rev: BL 9/15/00) [796.6]

22153 Bizley, Kirk. *Mountain Biking* (4–7). Series: Radical Sports. 1999, Heinemann LB $15.95 (1-57572-944-X). 32pp. Color photographs and a simple text introduce mountain biking, its history, equipment, skills, and safety concerns. (Rev: SLJ 5/00) [796.6]

22154 Brimner, Larry. *Mountain Biking* (5–7). Illus. 1997, Watts LB $22.50 (0-531-20243-7). 64pp. An attractive book that includes information on the history of mountain bikes, their construction, and how to choose, use, and maintain one. (Rev: BL 9/1/97; SLJ 8/97) [796.6]

22155 Ditchfield, Christin. *Cycling* (2–4). Illus. Series: True Books. 2000, Children's LB $21.50 (0-516-21061-0); paper $6.95 (0-516-27024-9). 48pp. A simply written introduction to the sport of cycling with material on competitions, equipment, and the history of the sport. (Rev: BL 9/15/00) [796.6]

22156 Erlbach, Arlene. *Bicycles* (3–5). Illus. Series: How It's Made. 1994, Lerner LB $19.93 (0-8225-2388-4); paper $6.95 (0-8225-9740-3). 48pp. The story of the bicycle is told, from its early design to the sleek machines of today. (Rev: BL 3/15/95) [629]

22157 Gibbons, Gail. *Bicycle Book* (K–4). Illus. 1995, Holiday LB $16.95 (0-8234-1199-0). 32pp. A short book that covers such topics as the history of the bicycle, its types, care tips, and safety rules. (Rev: BL 12/1/95; SLJ 1/96) [629.227]

22158 Hayhurst, Chris. *Bicycle Stunt Riding!* (4–8). Series: Extreme Sports. 2000, Rosen LB $17.95 (0-8239-3011-4). 64pp. In this book, readers will learn about stunts like the vert and mega spin as well as finding out about the bikes and the safety equipment needed to start this sport. (Rev: BL 6/1–15/00) [629]

22159 Hayhurst, Chris. *Mountain Biking: Get on the Trail* (4–8). Illus. Series: Extreme Sports. 2000, Rosen $17.95 (0-8239-3013-0). 64pp. Stressing safety throughout, this book covers topics including the history of mountain biking, why mountain bikes are different than others, and riding techniques. (Rev: BL 3/15/00; SLJ 8/00) [796.6]

22160 Jensen, Julie. *Beginning Mountain Biking* (4–6). Photos by Andy King. Series: Beginning Sports. 1996, Lerner LB $21.27 (0-8225-3509-2). 63pp. A very simple, short account that introduces mountain biking to a young audience. (Rev: SLJ 2/97) [796.6]

22161 Loewen, Nancy. *Bicycle Safety* (K–2). Illus. by Penny Dann. 1996, Child's World LB $18.50 (1-56766-260-9). 24pp. Safety rules for bicycle riding are outlined and then illustrated by cartoons that show right and wrong behavior. Also use *Traffic Safety* (1996). (Rev: SLJ 1/97) [629.227]

22162 Lord, Trevor. *Amazing Bikes* (1–4). Illus. by Peter Downs. Series: Eyewitness Juniors. 1992, Knopf paper $9.99 (0-679-82772-2). 32pp. An explanation of bicycles plus many illustrations showing various types. (Rev: BL 11/1/92) [629.227]

22163 Maestro, Betsy, and Giulio Maestro. *Bike Trip* (2–4). Illus. 1992, HarperCollins $16.00 (0-06-022731-1). 32pp. Young Joshua tells a simple story of a bike trip he takes with his family from their rural home into town. (Rev: BL 1/1/92; SLJ 3/92) [796.6]

22164 Molzahn, Arlene Bourgeois. *Extreme Mountain Biking* (5–8). Series: Extreme Sports. 2000, Capstone LB $21.26 (0-7368-0483-8). 48pp. This introduction to mountain biking includes material

on its history, equipment, safety concerns, skills, and competitions. (Rev: HBG 10/00; SLJ 8/00) [796.6]

22165 Otfinoski, Steven. *Pedaling Along: Bikes Then and Now* (1–3). Illus. Series: Here We Go! 1996, Benchmark LB $22.79 (0-7614-0402-3). 32pp. A copiously illustrated history of bicycles, from their invention to modern bikes. (Rev: SLJ 6/97) [629]

Camping and Backpacking

22166 Ching, Jacqueline. *Camping: Have Fun, Be Smart* (3–6). Series: Explore the Outdoors. 2000, Rosen LB $19.95 (0-8239-3173-0). 64pp. A basic introduction to camping that includes material on setting up a camp, gear and clothing, and different types of tents. (Rev: SLJ 1/01) [796.54]

22167 Drake, Jane, and Ann Love. *The Kids Campfire Book* (4–6). Illus. 1998, Kids Can paper $9.95 (1-55074-539-5). 128pp. A thorough guide to good camping that includes such topics as how to choose wood for the fire, recipes for cooking over the fire, games and songs, tips on wildlife exploration, and stories to tell around the campfire. (Rev: BL 3/15/98; HBG 10/98; SLJ 4/98) [796.54]

22168 Hooks, Kristine. *Essential Hiking for Teens* (5–9). Series: Outdoor Life. 2000, Children's LB $19.00 (0-516-23357-2); paper $6.95 (0-516-23557-5). 48pp. This book on hiking covers such topics as clothing, equipment, safety, first aid, trails, planning hikes, and calculating hiking time. (Rev: SLJ 2/01) [796.54]

22169 McManus, Patrick F. *Kid Camping from Aaaaiii! to Zip* (5–7). Illus. by Roy Doty. 1979, Avon paper $3.99 (0-380-71311-X). 128pp. A practical camping guide presented in an amusing way.

Chess

22170 Berg, Barry. *Opening Moves: The Making of a Very Young Chess Champion* (2–5). Illus. 2000, Little, Brown $15.95 (0-316-91339-1). 48pp. Michael Thaler began playing chess at age 4. Now 8 years old, he discusses his life, important chess lessons, and plays from several of his important games. (Rev: BCCB 3/00; BL 3/1/00; HBG 10/00; SLJ 7/00) [793.1]

22171 Kidder, Harvey. *The Kids' Book of Chess* (4–8). Illus. by Kimberly Bulcken. 1990, Workman paper $15.95 (0-89480-767-6). 96pp. Using their origins in the Middle Ages as a focus, this book explains each chess piece and the basics of the game. (Rev: SLJ 2/91) [794.1]

22172 Nottingham, Ted, et al. *Chess for Children* (4–6). Illus. 1994, Sterling $16.95 (0-8069-0452-6). 128pp. Three experts explain chess, the meaning and use of each piece, strategies, famous games, and the accomplishments of famous players. (Rev: BL 5/1/94) [794.1]

22173 Nottingham, Ted, and Bob Wade. *Winning Chess: Piece by Piece* (4–8). Illus. 1999, Sterling $16.95 (0-8069-9955-1). 128pp. This book is for chess players who already know the basics and are ready to improve their techniques. (Rev: BL 11/15/99) [794.1]

Fishing

22174 Bailey, John. *The Young Fishing Enthusiast: A Practical Guide for Kids* (5–10). 1999, DK $15.95 (0-7894-3965-4). 48pp. Using many photos including underwater ones, this book covers all aspects of fishing — gear and tackle, casting, lures and bait, fly-fishing, fish anatomy, landing your catch, and bobber fishing. (Rev: HBG 10/99; SLJ 7/99) [799.1]

22175 Fitzgerald, Ron. *Essential Fishing for Teens* (4–10). 2000, Children's LB $19.00 (0-516-23355-6); paper $6.95 (0-516-23555-9). 48pp. A thorough introduction to fishing that covers such topics as bait, boat, fly, and big-game fishing with material on equipment and the perfect fishing spot. (Rev: SLJ 3/01) [799.1]

22176 Morey, Shaun. *Incredible Fishing Stories for Kids* (3–6). Illus. 1993, Incredible Fishing Stories paper $11.95 (0-9633691-1-3). 96pp. These true stories tell how young anglers have made record catches. (Rev: BL 9/1/93)

22177 Schmidt, Gerald D. *Let's Go Fishing: A Book for Beginners* (4–7). Illus. by Brian W. Payne. 1990, Roberts Rinehart paper $11.95 (0-911797-84-X). 96pp. This practical guide to freshwater fishing includes material on tackle and kinds of fish. (Rev: BL 3/1/91; SLJ 5/91) [799.1]

22178 Solomon, Dane. *Fishing: Have Fun, Be Smart* (3–6). Illus. Series: Explore the Outdoors. 2000, Rosen $19.95 (0-8239-3168-4). This introduction to fishing includes material on fresh and salt water varieties and the equipment needed. (Rev: SLJ 1/01) [799.1]

Football

22179 Buckley, James, Jr. *America's Greatest Game: The Real Story of Football and the NFL* (4–7). Illus. 1998, Hyperion $16.95 (0-7868-0433-5). 64pp. A lavishly illustrated introduction to football and its history, with special material on the NFL and key players of yesterday and today. (Rev: BL 11/15/98; SLJ 2/99) [796.332]

22180 DiLorenzo, J. J. *The Miami Dolphins Football Team* (5–8). Series: Great Sports Teams. 1997, Enslow LB $18.95 (0-89490-796-4). 48pp. A history of the Miami Dolphins that focuses on their brightest stars and best moments on the field. (Rev: BL 10/15/97; HBG 3/98) [796.332]

22181 Dunnahoo, Terry, et al. *Pro Football Hall of Fame* (4–6). Illus. Series: Halls of Fame. 1994, Macmillan LB $13.95 (0-89686-851-6). 48pp. The story of the Football Hall of Fame, its contents and history, plus many asides about the origins of American football and its star players. (Rev: BL 7/94; SLJ 8/94) [796.332]

22182 Gibbons, Gail. *My Football Book* (K–2). Illus. 2000, HarperCollins $5.95 (0-688-17139-7). 24pp. Equipment, the playing field, positions, and basic rules are covered in this small-format paperback introduction to football. (Rev: BL 9/15/00; HBG 3/01; SLJ 11/00) [796.332]

22183 Kessler, Leonard. *Kick, Pass, and Run* (1–2). Illus. 1996, HarperCollins LB $15.89 (0-06-027105-1); paper $3.95 (0-06-444210-1). 64pp. An easily read reissue of a book that introduces football and its rules. (Rev: BL 11/15/96) [796.332]

22184 Lace, William W. *The Dallas Cowboys Football Team* (5–8). Illus. Series: Great Sports Teams. 1997, Enslow LB $18.95 (0-89490-791-3). 48pp. After discussing the Dallas championship in 1973, this book traces the history of the team and supplies plenty of sports action. (Rev: BL 10/15/97; HBG 3/98) [796.332]

22185 Lace, William W. *The Pittsburgh Steelers Football Team* (4–6). Series: Great Sports Teams. 1999, Enslow LB $18.95 (0-7660-1099-6). 48pp. Using action photos and numerous quotes, this is a history of the Steelers and an account of their most famous moments. (Rev: BL 4/15/98; HBG 10/99) [796.332]

22186 Molzahn, Arlene Bourgeois. *The San Francisco 49ers Football Team* (4–6). Series: Great Sports Teams. 2000, Enslow LB $18.95 (0-7660-1280-8). 48pp. As well as giving a history of this great team, this short book describes the team's best players. (Rev: BL 9/15/00) [796.48]

22187 Owens, Thomas S., and Diana Star Helmer. *Football* (4–7). Series: Game Plan. 1998, Twenty-First Century LB $23.40 (0-7613-3233-2). 64pp. An insider's book about professional football that covers such topics as game preparation, strategy, player selection, and business aspects, with many references to actual situations and players. (Rev: HBG 10/99; SLJ 6/99) [796.48]

22188 Patey, R. L. *The Illustrated Rules of Football* (3–5). Illus. by Eleanor Hoyt. Series: Illustrated Sports. 1995, Ideals paper $6.95 (1-57102-049-7). 32pp. Introduces football's basic plays and techniques, equipment, and the rules. (Rev: BL 10/15/95; SLJ 1/96) [796.332]

22189 Stewart, Mark. *Football: A History of the Gridiron Game* (4–6). Illus. 1998, Watts LB $32.00 (0-531-11493-7). 144pp. A history of football from rugbylike competitions in England to the big-business sport it is today. (Rev: BL 4/1/99; HBG 10/99) [796.332]

22190 Sullivan, George. *All About Football* (3–5). Illus. 1990, Putnam paper $9.99 (0-399-21907-2). 128pp. Numerous photos aid in the telling of the game's development, history, complexities, and notable personalities through the years. (Rev: BCCB 12/87; BL 2/1/88)

Gymnastics

22191 Bragg, Linda Wallenberg. *Fundamental Gymnastics* (3–6). Photos by Andy King. Illus. Series: Fundamental Sports. 1995, Lerner LB $22.60 (0-8225-3453-3). 80pp. A brief history of gymnastics is given, including six events for boys and four for girls and basic moves and workouts. (Rev: SLJ 3/96) [796.44]

22192 Ditchfield, Christin. *Gymnastics* (2–4). Illus. Series: True Books. 2000, Children's LB $21.50 (0-516-21063-7); paper $6.95 (0-516-27026-5). 48pp. A simple introduction to gymnastics that describes some of the events, their history, and the equipment. (Rev: BL 9/15/00) [796.44]

22193 Gutman, Dan. *Gymnastics* (5–8). Illus. 1996, Viking $15.99 (0-670-86949-X). 212pp. In addition to a history of gymnastics from the ancient Greeks to the 1996 Olympics, this account explains the different competitive events and how they are judged. (Rev: BL 5/1/96; SLJ 8/96) [796.44]

22194 Jackman, Joan. *Gymnastics* (3–6). Illus. Series: Superguides. 2000, DK $9.95 (0-7894-5430-0). 44pp. Excellent photos, fact boxes, and a good format are used to introduce gymnastics, with material on history, rules, and basic movements. (Rev: BL 6/1–15/00; HBG 10/00; SLJ 8/00) [796.44]

22195 Jackman, Joan. *The Young Gymnast* (4–7). Illus. 1995, DK $15.95 (1-56458-677-4). 45pp. After a history of the sport, the required equipment and clothing are outlined, followed by extensive material on each of the specific skills involved. (Rev: BL 9/1/95; SLJ 7/95) [796.44]

22196 Kuklin, Susan. *Going to My Gymnastics Class* (4–6). Illus. 1991, Macmillan LB $13.95 (0-02-751236-3). 40pp. The experiences of preschoolers at gymnastics class. (Rev: BCCB 10/91; BL 8/91; SLJ 12/91) [796.44]

22197 Readhead, Lloyd. *Gymnastics* (3–6). Illus. Series: Fantastic Book Of. 1997, Millbrook LB $22.40 (0-7613-0622-6). 32pp. Covers gymnastics techniques, training, warm-up exercises, and equipment, with an eight-page foldout section on competitions. (Rev: BL 3/15/98; HBG 3/98) [796.44]

Horsemanship

22198 Binder, Sibylle Luise, and Gefion Wolf. *Riding for Beginners* (5–10). Trans. from German by Elisabeth E. Reinersmann. 1999, Sterling LB $19.95 (0-8069-6205-4). 144pp. A straightforward text, beautiful color photos and illustrations, and an attractive layout are used to explain the English and Western styles of riding and give tips for the novice. (Rev: SLJ 8/99) [798.4]

22199 Damrell, Liz. *With the Wind* (PS–1). Illus. by Stephen Marchesi. 1991, Smithmark $4.98 (0-831-76779-0). 32pp. The feelings of a boy as he goes horseback riding through the country. (Rev: BL 3/1/91; SLJ 6/91) [799.1]

22200 Davis, Caroline. *The Young Equestrian* (5–8). Illus. 2000, Firefly $29.95 (1-55209-495-2); paper $19.95 (1-55209-484-7). 128pp. With a generous use of color photos, this account devotes chapters to riding aids and techniques, choosing schools and proper equipment, buying and caring for a horse, and competitions. (Rev: BL 2/15/01; SLJ 2/01) [798.2]

22201 Feldman, Jane. *I Am a Rider* (3–6). Illus. Series: Young Dreamers. 2000, Random $14.99 (0-679-88664-8). 48pp. Thirteen-year-old Eve Shinerock describes her riding experience and competitions on her horse Lightning as well as sharing many good tips that Eve learned from her mother, a riding instructor. (Rev: BL 9/1/00; HBG 10/00; SLJ 7/00) [798.2]

22202 Green, Lucinda. *Riding* (3–6). Series: Superguides. 2000, DK $9.95 (0-7894-5428-9). 64pp. The basics of horseback riding are described with step-by-instructions plus details on horses and their care in this heavily illustrated account. (Rev: BL 8/00; SLJ 1/01) [798.2]

22203 Green, Lucinda. *The Young Rider* (4–6). Illus. 1993, DK $15.95 (1-56458-320-1). 64pp. A wide range of topics are covered in this introduction to riding and horse care. (Rev: BL 10/15/93; SLJ 12/93) [798.2]

22204 Haas, Jessie. *Safe Horse, Safe Rider: A Young Rider's Guide to Responsible Horsekeeping* (4–7). Illus. 1994, Storey paper $16.95 (0-88266-700-9). 160pp. This guide to horsemanship stresses safety and covers such topics as understanding horse behavior. (Rev: BL 1/1/95) [636.1]

22205 Henderson, Carolyn. *Improve Your Riding Skills* (3–6). Illus. Series: DK Riding Club. 1999, DK LB $12.95 (0-7894-4264-7). 48pp. Coverage on trotting, galloping, and jumping is included, plus a discussion of mounting and special types of riding. (Rev: BL 8/99; HBG 10/99) [798.2]

22206 Kirksmith, Tommie. *Ride Western Style: A Guide for Young Riders* (4–8). Illus. 1991, Howell Book House $16.95 (0-87605-895-0). 212pp. A guide on Western-style riding for use in conjunction with a supervised riding program. (Rev: BL 4/1/92) [798.2]

22207 Knotts, Bob. *Equestrian Events* (2–4). Illus. Series: True Books. 2000, Children's LB $21.50 (0-516-21062-9); paper $6.95 (0-516-27025-7). 48pp. Various horseback riding events are introduced with material on their history and how they are judged. (Rev: BL 9/15/00) [798.2]

22208 Winter, Ginny L. *The Riding Book* (K–3). Illus. by author. 1963, Astor-Honor $8.95 (0-8392-3031-1). An introductory account for the very young rider.

Ice Hockey

22209 Adelson, Bruce. *Hat Trick Trivia: Secrets, Statistics, and Little-Known Facts About Hockey* (4–7). Illus. 1998, Lerner LB $23.93 (0-8225-3315-5). 64pp. History, statistics, and trivia are combined in this lively discussion of hockey and its players. (Rev: BL 1/1–15/99) [796.962]

22210 Aretha, David. *The Montreal Canadiens Hockey Team* (4–6). Series: Great Sports Teams. 1998, Enslow LB $17.95 (0-7660-1022-8). 48pp. This book contains a history of the team and a run-down of their most valuable players and most exciting seasons. (Rev: BL 5/15/98; HBG 10/98) [796.48]

22211 Ayers, Tom. *The Illustrated Rules of Ice Hockey* (3–5). Illus. by Eleanor Hoyt. Series: Illustrated Sports. 1995, Ideals paper $6.95 (1-57102-048-9). 32pp. This book introduces the dimensions and parts of a hockey rink, the player's equipment, and basic rules of ice hockey. (Rev: BL 10/15/95; SLJ 1/96) [796.962]

22212 Foley, Mike. *Fundamental Hockey* (4–8). Photos by Andy King. Series: Fundamental Sports. 1996, Lerner LB $22.60 (0-8225-3456-8). 80pp. The basics of ice hockey are introduced, plus a brief history of the sport and an explanation of what the various players do. (Rev: SLJ 3/96) [796.962]

22213 Jensen, Julie, adapt. *Beginning Hockey* (4–8). Photos by Andy King. Series: Beginning Sports. 1996, Lerner LB $22.60 (0-8225-3506-8). 80pp. An introduction to hockey, its history, and the techniques and skills used by the players. (Rev: SLJ 3/96) [796.964]

22214 O'Shei, Tim. *The Detroit Red Wings Hockey Team* (4–6). Series: Great Sports Teams. 2000, Enslow LB $18.95 (0-7660-1282-4). 48pp. Profiles the Detroit Red Wings, their history, great moments from the past, and famous players. (Rev: BL 9/15/00) [796.962]

22215 Sullivan, George. *All About Hockey* (4–6). Illus. 1998, Putnam $15.99 (0-399-23172-2); paper $9.99 (0-399-23173-0). 160pp. Topics covered in this introduction to ice hockey include rules, skills, types of plays, history, and profiles of famous players. (Rev: BL 3/1/99; HBG 3/99; SLJ 3/99) [796.962]

22216 Wilson, Stacy. *The Hockey Book for Girls* (4–7). Illus. 2000, Kids Can $12.95 (1-55074-860-2); paper $6.95 (1-55074-719-3). 40pp. This book, by the former captain of Canada's women's Olympic hockey team, introduces ice hockey's rules, positions, strategies, and training and includes interviews with star players. (Rev: BL 3/1/01; HBG 3/01; SLJ 12/00) [796.962]

Ice Skating

22217 Blackstone, Margaret. *This Is Figure Skating* (K–3). Illus. by John O'Brien. 1998, Holt $15.95 (0-8050-3706-3). 32pp. Two young girls on an outdoor rink share their knowledge of skates and ice skating and introduce the sport to others in this simple picture book. (Rev: BL 11/15/98; HBG 3/99; SLJ 10/98) [796.91]

22218 Boo, Michael. *The Story of Figure Skating* (5–8). Illus. 1998, Morrow $16.00 (0-688-15820-X). 210pp. Beginning with skates made of bone and walrus teeth, this account traces the history of ice skating with decade-by-decade coverage from 1950

to the 1998 Olympics. (Rev: BL 11/1/98; HBG 3/99; SLJ 12/98) [796.91]

22219 Brimner, Larry. *Speed Skating* (2–4). Illus. Series: True Books. 1997, Children's $22.00 (0-516-20451-3). 48pp. The story of speed skating: its history, equipment, techniques, and place in the Olympic Games. (Rev: BL 1/1–15/98; HBG 3/98; SLJ 2/98) [796.91]

22220 Cranston, Patty. *The Best on Ice: The World's Top Figure Skaters* (2–5). Illus. 1999, Kids Can paper $4.95 (1-55074-581-6). 32pp. This book on figure skating focuses on the careers of three young stars: Michelle Kwan, Todd Eldredge, and Tara Lipinski. (Rev: BL 10/15/99) [796.91]

22221 Cranston, Patty. *Magic on Ice* (3–6). Illus. 1998, Kids Can paper $5.95 (1-55074-455-0). 48pp. Using a large format and double-page spreads, this book covers the terminology and the training involved in ice skating plus profiles of the important people involved. (Rev: BL 11/1/98; SLJ 10/98) [796.91]

22222 Gutman, Dan. *Ice Skating: From Axels to Zambonis* (5–8). Illus. 1995, Viking $14.99 (0-670-86013-1). 196pp. A complete guide to ice skating that includes a history, information on techniques, biographies, a chronology, and a list of champions. (Rev: BL 10/1/95; SLJ 12/95) [796.91]

22223 Helmer, Diana Star, and Thomas S. Owens. *The History of Figure Skating* (2–4). Series: Sports Throughout History. 2000, Rosen LB $17.26 (0-8239-5472-2). 24pp. This book gives a history of figure skating and information on equipment, along with biographical details on famous skaters. (Rev: SLJ 12/00) [796.91]

22224 Macnow, Glen. *The Philadelphia Flyers Hockey Team* (4–6). Series: Great Sports Teams. 2000, Enslow LB $18.95 (0-7660-1279-4). 48pp. With a generous number of color and black-and-white photos, this slim book traces the history of the Philadelphia Flyers, their star players, and their greatest successes. (Rev: BL 3/15/00; HBG 10/00) [796.964]

22225 Morrissey, Peter. *Ice Skating* (3–8). 2000, DK $9.95 (0-7894-5427-0). 45pp. This is an excellent introduction to ice skating with basic well-illustrated material on skates, techniques, skills, and safety. Also published as *The Young Ice Skater* (1998). (Rev: BL 6/1–15/00; HBG 10/00; SLJ 5/00) [796.91]

22226 Morrissey, Peter. *The Young Ice Skater: A Young Enthusiast's Guide to Ice Skating* (3–8). Photos by Andy Crawford. 1998, DK $15.95 (0-7894-3422-9). 37pp. This manual covers skating topics such as the equipment needed, warm-up exercises, easy and difficult steps, and career opportunities. (Rev: HBG 3/99; SLJ 10/98) [796.91]

22227 Wilkes, Debbi. *The Figure Skating Book: A Young Person's Guide to Figure Skating* (4–8). Illus. 2000, Firefly LB $19.95 (1-55209-444-8); paper $12.95 (1-55209-445-6). 128pp. The author, an Olympic silver medalist, gives practical advice on figure skating from buying skates to simple and complicated skating techniques. (Rev: BL 7/00; SLJ 4/00) [796.9]

22228 Winter, Ginny L. *The Skating Book* (K–3). Illus. by author. 1963, Astor-Honor $8.95 (0-8392-3035-4). A beginning account for the young skater.

Indoor Games

22229 Cole, Joanna, and Stephanie Calmenson. *Crazy Eights and Other Card Games* (2–5). Illus. by Alan Tiegreen. 1994, Morrow $16.00 (0-688-12199-3). 80pp. Twenty tried-and-true card games, like spit and go fish, are explained with easy instructions. (Rev: BL 4/15/94; SLJ 6/94) [795.4]

22230 Collis, Len. *Card Games for Children* (K–6). Illus. by Terry Carter and Bob George. 1989, Barron's paper $6.95 (0-8120-4290-5). 95pp. A collection of 41 card games with easily followed directions involving different numbers of players. (Rev: SLJ 3/90) [795.4]

22231 Eldin, Peter. *The Most Excellent Book of How to Do Card Tricks* (3–5). Illus. Series: Most Excellent Book Of. 1996, Millbrook LB $19.90 (0-7613-0525-4); paper $6.95 (0-7613-0504-1). 32pp. This how-to book also contains "easy step-by-step instructions for a brilliant performance." (Rev: BL 10/15/96; SLJ 2/97) [795.4]

22232 Erlbach, Arlene. *Video Games* (4–6). Illus. 1995, Lerner LB $19.93 (0-8225-2389-2). 48pp. An explanation of how video games came to be, how they are constructed, and how they work. (Rev: BL 8/95; SLJ 6/95) [794.8]

22233 Hetzer, Linda. *Rainy Days and Saturdays* (3–6). Illus. 1996, Workman paper $10.95 (1-56305-513-9). 227pp. About 150 activities are outlined on topics like sports, science, and cooking for youngsters confined indoors. (Rev: BL 6/1–15/96; SLJ 7/96) [793]

22234 Jones, Michelle. *The American Girls Party Book* (3–5). Illus. 1998, Pleasant paper $7.95 (1-56247-677-7). 78pp. For each of the six American Girls, three thematic parties are outlined complete with games, crafts, and food recipes. (Rev: BL 1/1–15/99) [793.2]

22235 Lankford, Mary D. *Dominoes Around the World* (3–5). Illus. 1998, Morrow $16.00 (0-688-14051-3). 40pp. After providing the history of dominoes, the author presents eight versions of the game as played in such places as Malta, Vietnam, and the United States. (Rev: BL 3/15/98; HBG 10/98; SLJ 4/98) [795.3]

22236 McCoy, Elin. *Cards for Kids: Games, Tricks and Amazing Facts* (3–6). Illus. by Tom Huffman. 1991, Macmillan $13.95 (0-02-765461-3). 150pp. Tells the history of playing cards and introduces 42 games suitable for youngsters. (Rev: SLJ 3/92) [795.4]

22237 Sheinwold, Alfred. *101 Best Family Card Games* (4–8). Illus. by Myron Miller. 1993, Sterling paper $4.95 (0-8069-8635-2). 128pp. A book filled with games enjoyed by many age groups. (Rev: BL 2/15/93) [795.4]

22238 Silbaugh, Elizabeth. *Let's Play Cards! A First Book of Card Games* (2–3). Illus. by Jef

Kaminsky. 1996, Simon & Schuster $14.00 (0-689-80802-X); paper $3.99 (0-689-80801-1). 47pp. Five card games, including one type of solitaire, are introduced, along with a history of playing cards and a description of the deck. (Rev: BCCB 9/96; SLJ 10/96) [795.4]

22239 Skurzynski, Gloria. *Know the Score: Video Games in Your High-Tech World* (4–6). Illus. 1994, Bradbury $16.95 (0-02-782922-7). 64pp. The history and design of video games are discussed, with material on necessary hardware and current technology in the field. (Rev: BCCB 7–8/94; BL 3/1/94; SLJ 4/94) [794.8]

Motor Bikes and Motorcycles

22240 Hendrickson, Steve. *Enduro Racing* (3–6). Series: Motorcycles. 2000, Capstone LB $21.26 (0-7368-0477-3). 48pp. A straightforward, heavily illustrated introduction to Enduro motorcycle racing with material on history, equipment, skills, and safety. (Rev: HBG 10/00; SLJ 10/00) [796.7]

22241 Raby, Philip, and Simon Nix. *Motorbikes* (5–8). Illus. Series: Need for Speed. 1999, Lerner $17.95 (0-8225-2486-4); paper $7.95 (0-8225-9854-X). 32pp. A variety of motorbikes are introduced including dirt, motorcross, and land speed bikes. (Rev: BL 1/1–15/00; HBG 3/00; SLJ 2/00) [629.227]

22242 Youngblood, Ed. *Dirt Track Racing* (3–6). Series: Motorcycles. 2000, Capstone LB $21.26 (0-7368-0474-9). 48pp. Dirt track motorcycle racing is introduced, with material on its history, courses, skills required, and safety considerations. Also use *Hillclimbing* (2000). (Rev: HBG 10/00; SLJ 10/00) [796.7]

Olympic Games

22243 Anderson, Dave. *The Story of the Olympics*. Rev. ed. (4–9). 2000, HarperCollins $15.95 (0-688-16734-9). 168pp. This book on the Olympics is divided into two parts: the first gives historical highlights, the second profiles famous personalities and their trials and tribulations. (Rev: HBG 10/00; SLJ 6/00) [796.48]

22244 Brimner, Larry. *The Winter Olympics* (2–4). Illus. Series: True Books. 1997, Children's $22.00 (0-516-20456-4). 48pp. Describes the various sports in the Winter Olympics and gives a general history of the games and their goals and symbols. (Rev: BL 1/1–15/98; HBG 3/98; SLJ 2/98) [796.98]

22245 Crowther, Robert. *Robert Crowther's Pop-Up Olympics* (3–5). Illus. 1996, Candlewick $19.99 (1-56402-801-1). 12pp. A history of the Olympics is given, and many of the events are illustrated with pop-ups. (Rev: BL 2/1/96) [796.4]

22246 Currie, Stephen. *The Olympic Games* (5–8). Series: Overview. 1999, Lucent LB $17.96 (1-56006-395-5). 111pp. This book covers both the ancient and modern games in concise text and fine illustrations. (Rev: BL 9/15/99) [796.49]

22247 Glubok, Shirley, and Alfred Tamarin. *Olympic Games in Ancient Greece* (5–8). Illus. 1976, Harper-Collins LB $16.89 (0-06-022048-1). 128pp. Using a fictitious Olympiad set in the 5th century B.C., the authors offer a great deal of background information in an imaginative, satisfying way.

22248 Haycock, Kate. *Skiing* (4–8). Illus. Series: Olympic Sports. 1992, Macmillan LB $13.00 (0-89686-669-6). 32pp. The Winter Olympic events in skiing are discussed. (Rev: SLJ 4/92) [796.93]

22249 Knotts, Bob. *The Summer Olympics* (2–4). Illus. Series: True Books. 2000, Children's LB $21.50 (0-516-21064-5); paper $6.95 (0-516-27029-X). 48pp. This simple account gives a short history of the Olympic games, a rundown on the events, and an introduction to a few Olympic stars. (Rev: BL 8/00) [796.4809]

22250 Kristy, Davida. *Coubertin's Olympics: How the Games Began* (5–8). Illus. 1995, Lerner LB $26.60 (0-8225-3327-8); paper $10.95 (0-8225-9713-6). 128pp. The story of Baron Pierre de Coubertin, who established the modern Olympic Games. (Rev: BL 8/95; SLJ 11/95) [338.4]

22251 Middleton, Haydn. *Ancient Olympic Games* (3–7). Series: Olympics. 1999, Heinemann LB $22.79 (1-57572-450-2). 32pp. This account describes the first Olympic Games, the nature of the events, and when and where they were held. (Rev: BL 4/15/00; SLJ 1/00) [796.49]

22252 Middleton, Haydn. *Crises at the Olympics* (3–7). Illus. Series: Olympics. 1999, Heinemann LB $22.79 (1-57572-452-9). 32pp. This account describes some of the scandals, controversies, and tragedies that have occurred at the Olympic Games including the 1972 terrorism attack in Munich and the current drug testing of athletes. (Rev: BL 12/15/99; SLJ 1/00) [796.48]

22253 Middleton, Haydn. *Great Olympic Moments* (3–7). Series: Olympics. 1999, Heinemann LB $22.79 (1-57572-451-0). 32pp. Some of the great Olympic moments in modern times are retold in this exciting book. (Rev: BL 4/15/00) [796.49]

22254 Middleton, Haydn. *Modern Olympic Games* (3–7). Illus. 1999, Heinemann LB $22.79 (1-57572-453-7). 32pp. This account gives a history of the games from 1896 to the present with material on how new events are chosen and how the winter games came into being. (Rev: BL 12/15/99) [796.48]

22255 Oxlade, Chris, and David Ballheimer. *Olympics* (4–8). Illus. Series: Eyewitness Books. 1999, Knopf LB $20.99 (0-375-90222-8). 60pp. Double-page spreads cover the ancient games, the rebirth of the modern Olympics, and the events of the winter and summer games plus material on equipment and past stars. (Rev: SLJ 12/99) [796.48]

22256 Ross, Stewart. *The Original Olympics* (4–7). Illus. Series: Ancient Greece. 2000, Bedrick LB $18.95 (0-87226-596-X). 48pp. Using a fictional narrative involving a day at the Olympic Games, this attractive book gives details on the types of events, the history of the games, and the roles of

athletes in Greek life. (Rev: BL 1/1–15/01; HBG 10/00; SLJ 8/00) [796.48]

22257 Sandelson, Robert. *Ice Sports* (4–8). Illus. Series: Olympic Sports. 1992, Macmillan LB $21.00 (0-89686-667-X). 32pp. Discusses Winter Olympic events, such as bobsledding and ice hockey. (Rev: SLJ 4/92) [796.91]

22258 Woff, Richard. *The Ancient Greek Olympics* (4–6). Illus. 2000, Oxford $16.95 (0-19-521581-8). 32pp. A thoughtful, interesting account that supplies details on the origins, events, and athletes of the Olympics in ancient Greece. (Rev: BL 1/1–15/00; HBG 10/00; SLJ 5/00) [796.48]

Running and Jogging

22259 Savage, Jeff. *Running* (4–6). Illus. Series: Working Out. 1995, Silver Burdett LB $17.95 (0-89686-855-9); paper $7.95 (0-382-24948-8). 48pp. An introduction to running and its benefits, with information on how to begin, safety considerations, and a training schedule. (Rev: SLJ 10/95) [796.4]

Sailing and Boating

22260 Ditchfield, Christin. *Kayaking, Canoeing, Rowing, and Yachting* (2–4). Illus. Series: True Books. 2000, Children's LB $21.50 (0-516-21610-4); paper $6.95 (0-516-27027-3). 48pp. Introduces a range of water sports in a simple text with many color photos. (Rev: BL 9/15/00) [797.1]

22261 Hackler, Lew. *Boating with Cap'n Bob and Matey: An Encyclopedia for Kids of All Ages* (K–3). Illus. by Bobby Basnight. 1989, Seascape $12.95 (0-931595-03-7). 32pp. A guide for the very young on boating, which includes basic terms and useful tips. (Rev: SLJ 10/89) [796.125]

22262 Kalman, Bobbie. *A Canoe Trip* (2–4). Illus. 1995, Crabtree LB $19.96 (0-86505-619-6); paper $5.95 (0-86505-719-2). 32pp. Covers the parts of a canoe, safety considerations, and basic strokes. Also use *Summer Camp* (1994). (Rev: SLJ 7/95) [797.1]

22263 Revell, Phil. *Kayaking* (4–7). Series: Radical Sports. 1999, Heinemann LB $15.95 (1-57572-943-1). 32pp. A history of kayaks and kayaking is given followed by material on basic skills, equipment, safety concerns, and competitions. (Rev: SLJ 5/00) [797.1]

22264 Thompson, Luke. *Essential Boating for Teens* (4–10). Series: Outdoor Life. 2000, Children's LB $19.00 (0-516-23352-1); paper $6.95 (0-516-23552-4). 48pp. Topics covered in this introduction to boats and boating include canoes and rowboats, powerboats, sailboats, maneuvering techniques, and safety tips. (Rev: SLJ 3/01) [797]

22265 Wilson, Rich. *Racing a Ghost Ship: The Incredible Journey of Great American II* (3–6). Illus. 1996, Walker LB $17.85 (0-8027-8417-8). 48pp. Photos, maps, and diagrams enliven this account of a voyage from San Francisco around the

Cape Horn to Boston in 1993. (Rev: BL 10/1/96; SLJ 11/96) [910.4]

Self-Defense

22266 Casey, Kevin K. *Judo* (4–6). Illus. by Jean Dixon. Series: Illustrated History of Martial Arts. 1994, Rourke LB $14.95 (0-86593-369-3). 32pp. How-to information on judo is given, plus a fascinating history of this martial art. Also use, from the same series, *Kung Fu* and *Tae Kwon Do* (both 1997). (Rev: SLJ 1/95) [796.8]

22267 Knotts, Bob. *Martial Arts* (2–4). Illus. Series: True Books. 2000, Children's LB $21.50 (0-516-21609-0); paper $6.95 (0-516-27028-1). 48pp. This simple sports book with large type and many color photos introduces karate and other martial arts with material on their history and how they are judged. (Rev: BL 9/15/00) [796.8]

22268 Leder, Jane M. *Karate* (3–5). Illus. 1992, Bancroft-Sage LB $14.95 (0-944280-34-X); paper $5.95 (0-944280-39-0). 47pp. Some topics covered are the history of karate, basic stances, kicks and punches, and different kinds of competitions. (Rev: SLJ 10/92) [796.8]

22269 Mitchell, David. *Martial Arts* (3–8). Series: Superguides. 2000, DK $9.95 (0-7894-5431-9). 64pp. After introducing the various kinds of martial arts, this heavily illustrated book gives step-by-step instructions on how to master basic moves and techniques and how to achieve success in these sports. (Rev: BL 6/1–15/00; HBG 10/00; SLJ 5/00) [796.8]

22270 Mitchell, David. *The Young Martial Arts Enthusiast* (5–8). Photos by Andy Crawford. 1997, DK $15.95 (0-7894-1508-9). 64pp. Double-page spreads and plenty of full-color photos are used in this history of the martial arts, which explains how to perform various stances and self-defense techniques. (Rev: SLJ 7/97) [796.8]

22271 Morris, Ann. *Karate Boy* (K–3). Illus. 1996, Dutton $15.99 (0-525-45337-7). 32pp. A visit to David's karate class is used as an opportunity to explain the basics of this sport. (Rev: BCCB 9/96; BL 8/96; SLJ 8/96) [796.815]

22272 Queen, J. Allen. *Learn Karate* (4–8). 1999, Sterling $17.95 (0-8069-8136-9). 80pp. This instruction manual gives little background information but is excellent for coverage of the basics, kicks, blocks, punches, and stances. (Rev: SLJ 5/99) [796.8]

22273 Rafkin, Louise. *The Tiger's Eye, the Bird's Fist: A Beginner's Guide to the Martial Arts* (4–7). Illus. 1997, Little, Brown paper $12.95 (0-316-73464-0). 144pp. Short articles cover such topics as the history of the martial arts, lore and legends associated with them, techniques, and several biographical profiles of important people in the field. (Rev: BL 6/1–15/97; SLJ 7/97) [796.8]

22274 Yates, Keith D., and Bryan Robbins. *Tae Kwon Do for Kids* (4–8). 1999, Sterling paper $5.95 (0-8069-1761-X). 96pp. An introduction to the Korean form of self-defense known as Tae Kwon

Do with coverage of different kicks, stances, blocks, and warm-up exercises. (Rev: SLJ 6/99) [796.8]

Skateboarding

22275 Burke, L. M. *Skateboarding! Surf the Pavement* (5–8). Series: Extreme Sports. 1999, Rosen Central LB $17.95 (0-8239-3014-9). 64pp. This book supplies information for beginning and advanced skateboarders with coverage of history, techniques, equipment, and safety considerations. (Rev: SLJ 4/00) [796]

22276 Werner, Doug. *Skateboarder's Start-Up: A Beginner's Guide to Skateboarding* (4–8). 2000, Tracks paper $11.95 (1-884654-13-4). 144pp. Using a question-and-answer format, this introduction to skateboarding covers such subjects as equipment, history, and basic skating and technical tricks. (Rev: SLJ 12/00) [795.2]

Snowboarding

22277 Brimner, Larry. *Snowboarding* (4–6). Illus. Series: First Books. 1997, Watts LB $22.50 (0-531-20313-1). 64pp. Introduces the sport of snowboarding, its equipment, clothing, rules, techniques, and competitions. (Rev: BL 11/1/97; HBG 3/98; SLJ 2/98) [796.9]

22278 Davis, Steve. *Snowboarding* (3–6). Series: Superguides. 2000, DK $9.95 (0-7894-6541-8). 48pp. The basics of snowboarding are presented with step-by-step instructions and information on equipment in this heavily illustrated book. (Rev: BL 8/00) [796.9]

22279 Fraser, Andy. *Snowboarding* (4–7). Series: Radical Sports. 1999, Heinemann LB $15.95 (1-57572-946-6). 32pp. This book covers the history of snowboarding, the equipment and clothing needed, techniques, terms, and how to get started. (Rev: SLJ 4/00) [796.9]

22280 Hayhurst, Chris. *Snowboarding! Shred the Powder* (5–8). Series: Extreme Sports. 1999, Rosen Central LB $17.95 (0-8239-3010-6). 64pp. The book supplies both beginning and advanced information on this sport including material on history, equipment, techniques, and safety considerations. (Rev: SLJ 4/00) [796.9]

22281 Iguchi, Bryan. *The Young Snowboarder* (5–8). Illus. 1997, DK $15.95 (0-7894-2062-7). 37pp. Using middle-schoolers as models in the photos, this account describes basic skills, equipment, and techniques plus material on freestyle riding and slalom racing. (Rev: BL 11/15/97; HBG 3/98; SLJ 2/98) [796.1]

22282 Jensen, Julie, adapt. *Beginning Snowboarding* (4–8). Photos by Jimmy Clarke. Illus. Series: Beginning Sports. 1996, Lerner LB $22.60 (0-8225-3507-6). 64pp. Snowboarding is introduced, with material on equipment, basic maneuvers, types of competitions, and advanced stunts. (Rev: SLJ 3/96) [796.9]

22283 Lurie, Jon. *Fundamental Snowboarding* (4–8). Photos by Jimmy Clarke. Illus. Series: Fundamental Sports. 1996, Lerner LB $22.60 (0-8225-3457-6). 64pp. With eye-catching photos, the equipment and principles of snowboarding are covered, with material on basic and advanced maneuvers, skills, and stunts. (Rev: SLJ 3/96) [796.9]

22284 Sullivan, George. *Snowboarding: A Complete Guide for Beginners* (4–6). Illus. 1997, Penguin paper $6.99 (0-14-056181-1). 48pp. A complete manual to snowboarding, a new sport that gained Olympic status in 1998. (Rev: BL 1/1–15/97; SLJ 3/97) [796.9]

Soccer

22285 Baddiel, Ivor. *Soccer* (5–9). Illus. 1998, DK $16.95 (0-7894-2795-8); paper $12.95 (0-7894-3071-1). 92pp. A well-illustrated account dealing with such subjects as a history of the sport, techniques, tactics, positions, great teams and players, and the rules of the game. (Rev: BL 9/1/98; HBG 10/98; SLJ 8/98) [796.344]

22286 Bizley, Kirk. *Soccer* (K–2). Series: You Can Do It! 1999, Heinemann LB $13.95 (1-57572-962-8). 24pp. Colorful photos and cartoons are used to cover basic topics about soccer: warm-up exercises, moves, playing areas, rules, and safety. (Rev: SLJ 1/00) [796.334]

22287 Blackall, Bernie. *Soccer* (4–8). Illus. by Vasja Koman. Series: Top Sport. 1999, Heinemann LB $14.95 (1-57572-840-0). 32pp. This introduction to soccer covers history, equipment, rules, skills, and a few male and female stars. (Rev: SLJ 12/99) [796.334]

22288 Blackstone, Margaret. *This Is Soccer* (PS–1). Illus. by John O'Brien. 1999, Holt $15.95 (0-8050-2801-3). 32pp. Using numerous illustrations, this book explains the game of soccer including equipment and moves. (Rev: BCCB 4/99; BL 4/15/99; HBG 10/99; SLJ 5/99) [796.334]

22289 Coleman, Lori. *Soccer* (5–9). Series: Play-by-Play. 2000, Lerner paper $7.95 (0-8225-9876-0). 64pp. A fine introduction to the rules, equipment, and tactics of soccer with historical coverage through 1999. (Rev: SLJ 9/00) [796.334]

22290 Fischer, George. *The Illustrated Laws of Soccer* (3–5). Illus. 1994, Ideals paper $6.95 (1-57102-020-9). 32pp. The history, equipment, field, and rules of soccer are given. (Rev: BL 9/15/94; SLJ 11/94) [796.334]

22291 Gibbons, Gail. *My Soccer Book* (PS–3). Illus. 2000, HarperCollins $5.95 (0-688-17138-9). This accessible guide describes the playing field, equipment, rules, and the method of scoring. (Rev: BCCB 4/00; BL 5/1/00; HBG 10/00; SLJ 6/00) [796.334]

22292 Helmer, Diana Star, and Thomas S. Owens. *The History of Soccer* (2–4). Series: Sports Throughout History. 2000, Rosen LB $17.26 (0-8239-5467-6). 24pp. In addition to a history of soccer, this book

profiles some championship players. (Rev: SLJ 12/00) [796.334]

22293 Hornby, Hugh. *Soccer* (3–7). Photos by Andy Crawford. Series: Eyewitness Books. 2000, DK $15.95 (0-7894-5245-6). 61pp. A heavily illustrated introduction to soccer with material on history, rules, playing fields, and a few key players. (Rev: HBG 3/01; SLJ 9/00) [796.334]

22294 Howard, Dale E. *Soccer Stars* (3–6). Illus. 1994, Children's LB $22.00 (0-516-08047-4). 48pp. As well as introducing key U.S. players, this account includes a glossary of soccer terms. (Rev: BL 9/1/94) [796.334]

22295 Klingel, Cynthia, and Robert B. Noyed. *Soccer* (K–2). Series: Wonder Books. 2000, Child's World LB $21.36 (1-56766-805-4). 24pp. A beginning reader that gives basic information about soccer, the main activities, equipment, and uniforms. (Rev: SLJ 3/01) [796.334]

22296 Lineker, Gary. *Soccer* (3–8). Series: Superguides. 2000, DK $9.95 (0-7894-5425-4). 44pp. Bright clear photographs and a straightforward text explain the fundamentals of soccer and give sound advice on improving one's game. (Rev: BL 6/1–15/00; HBG 10/00; SLJ 8/00) [796.334]

22297 Lineker, Gary. *The Young Soccer Player* (2–5). Illus. 1994, DK $9.95 (1-56458-592-1). 32pp. A seasoned soccer player gives a good introduction to the sport, many useful tips for beginners, and techniques for improving one's game. (Rev: BL 7/94; SLJ 7/94) [796.334]

22298 Miller, Marla. *All-American Girls: The U.S. Women's National Soccer Team* (4–8). 1999, Pocket paper $4.99 (0-671-03599-1). 221pp. The story of the members of the U.S. Women's National Soccer Team, their accomplishments, and their advice to young female soccer players. (Rev: SLJ 8/99) [796.334]

22299 Owens, Thomas S., and Diana Star Helmer. *Soccer* (5–8). Series: Game Plan. 2000, Twenty-First Century LB $23.40 (0-7613-1400-8). 64pp. This introduction to soccer covers the different positions, game strategy, and memorable games and players of the past. (Rev: HBG 10/00; SLJ 7/00) [796.334]

22300 Page, Jason. *Soccer: Learn How to Be a Star Player* (3–5). Illus. by Mel Pickering. Series: Sports Club. 2000, Two-Can $9.95 (1-58728-001-9). 32pp. Soccer rules are explained along with some important plays and techniques, a little history, and profiles of important players. (Rev: SLJ 3/01) [796.334]

22301 Scott, Nina Savin. *The Thinking Kid's Guide to Successful Soccer* (3–6). Illus. 1999, Millbrook LB $18.90 (0-7613-0324-3). 96pp. Using true anecdotes and concrete examples, this is a practical guide to playing better soccer and having fun. (Rev: BL 5/15/99; HBG 10/99; SLJ 4/99) [796.344]

22302 Venturini, Tisha Lea, and Judith Cohen. *You Can Be a Woman Soccer Player* (2–5). Illus. 2000, Cascade Pass $13.95 (1-880599-49-X); paper $7.00 (1-880599-48-1). 40pp. This is basically a biography of Venturini, a World Cup soccer player, plus tips on how to play the game and a brief history of the sport. (Rev: BL 10/1/00) [796.334]

Surfing

22303 Barker, Amanda. *Windsurfing* (4–7). Series: Radical Sports. 1999, Heinemann LB $15.95 (1-57572-948-2). 32pp. After a history of windsurfing, this book describes equipment, safety tips, and basic skills. (Rev: SLJ 5/00) [797.2]

22304 Voeller, Edward. *Extreme Surfing* (5–8). Series: Surfing. 2000, Capstone LB $21.26 (0-7368-0485-4). 48pp. An introduction to surfing that contains material on equipment, history, skills, safety considerations, and competitions. (Rev: HBG 10/00; SLJ 8/00) [797]

Swimming and Diving

22305 Bizley, Kirk. *Swimming* (K–2). Series: You Can Do It! 1999, Heinemann LB $13.95 (1-57572-963-6). 24pp. A beginners guide to swimming with material on topics including water wings, basic strokes, and safety rules. (Rev: SLJ 1/00) [797.2]

22306 Cross, Rick. *Swimming* (3–8). Series: Superguides. 2000, DK $9.95 (0-7894-5432-7). 44pp. Using bright photos of children and pros, this is a basic guide to swimming with step-by-step instructions on strokes and techniques. (Rev: BL 6/1–15/00; HBG 10/00; SLJ 5/00) [797.2]

22307 Ditchfield, Christin. *Swimming and Diving* (2–4). Illus. Series: True Books. 2000, Children's LB $21.50 (0-516-21065-3); paper $6.95 (0-516-27030-3). 48pp. Large print and an informative text cover the sport of swimming, with material on the history of the sport, different strokes and dives, competitions, and famous swimmers. (Rev: BL 8/00) [797.2]

22308 Peterson, Sue H. *Swim with Me: A New Fun Approach to Learning to Swim* (PS–2). Illus. by Rama Von Baringer. 1999, Tricycle Pr. $12.95 (1-883672-94-5). 20pp. This book is intended for parents who are trying to prepare their children for swimming by showing how to teach floating, jumping in, gliding, proper breathing, and how to feel at home in the water. (Rev: SLJ 9/99) [797.2]

22309 Rouse, Jeff. *The Young Swimmer* (3–6). Illus. 1997, DK $15.95 (0-7894-1533-X). 37pp. An illustrated introduction to swimming that provides history, techniques, and a rundown on various strokes. (Rev: BL 8/97; SLJ 2/98) [797.2]

22310 Vander Hook, Sue. *Scuba Diving* (4–7). Illus. Series: World of Sports. 2000, Smart Apple Media $15.95 (1-887068-59-7). 32pp. After a section on star scuba divers, this account describes the origins and evolution of the sport, its equipment, hazards, and techniques. (Rev: BL 9/15/00) [797.2]

Tennis

22311 Blackall, Bernie. *Tennis* (4–8). Illus. by Vasja Koman. Series: Top Sport. 1999, Heinemann LB $14.95 (1-57572-842-7). 32pp. Double-page spreads present topics including the history of tennis, its equipment and rules, and important skills, plus a rundown on famous stars of the sport. (Rev: SLJ 12/99) [796.342]

22312 Gilbert, Nancy. *Wimbledon* (4–6). Illus. Series: Great Moments in Sports. 1991, Creative Ed. LB $21.30 (0-88682-319-6). 32pp. This brief history of the famous tennis tournament in England highlights some of the major players. (Rev: BL 1/1/92) [796.342]

22313 Muskat, Carrie. *The Composite Guide to Tennis* (5–7). Series: Composite Guide. 1998, Chelsea LB $15.95 (0-7910-4728-8). 64pp. Past and present tennis stars are mentioned along with a general introduction to the game. (Rev: HBG 10/98; SLJ 9/98) [796.342]

22314 Rutledge, Rachel. *The Best of the Best in Tennis* (4–7). Illus. 1998, Millbrook LB $22.90 (0-7613-1303-6); paper $6.95 (0-7613-0445-2). 64pp. Using a lively text and many color photos, this work gives a history of women in tennis and a rundown of today's most important female players. (Rev: BL 2/15/99; HBG 10/99; SLJ 3/99) [796.342]

22315 Tym, Wanda. *The Illustrated Rules of Tennis* (3–5). Illus. Series: Illustrated Sports. 1995, Ideals paper $6.95 (1-57102-016-0). 32pp. Such topics as equipment, the tennis court, scoring, and the rules are covered in this introduction to tennis. (Rev: BL 7/95; SLJ 6/95) [796.342]

22316 Vicario, Arantxa S. *The Young Tennis Player* (4–6). Illus. 1996, DK $15.95 (0-7894-0473-7). 45pp. Different types of play, tennis techniques, and warm-up exercises are covered in text and striking illustrations. (Rev: BL 5/1/96; SLJ 6/96) [796.342]

Track and Field

22317 Hughes, Morgan. *Track and Field: The Jumps: Instructional Guide to Track and Field* (4–8). Series: Compete Like a Champion. 2001, Rourke LB $26.60 (1-57103-290-8). 48pp. This book includes material on the long jump, the triple jump, the high jump, and the pole vault, along with training tips. Also use in the same series: *Track and Field: Middle and Long Distance Runs* and *Track and Field: The Sprints* (both 2001). (Rev: SLJ 3/01) [796.42]

22318 Jackson, Colin. *The Young Track and Field Athlete* (4–7). Illus. 1996, DK $15.95 (0-7894-0855-4); paper $9.95 (0-7894-0474-5). 32pp. Each track and field event is explained thoroughly in text and pictures, with tips on techniques and conditioning exercises. (Rev: BL 4/15/96; SLJ 8/96) [796.42]

22319 Knotts, Bob. *Track and Field* (2–4). Illus. Series: True Books. 2000, Children's LB $21.50 (0-516-21066-1); paper $6.95 (0-516-27031-1). 48pp. Various track and field events are introduced in a simple text with material on their history and how they are judged. (Rev: BL 9/15/00) [796.42]

Author/Illustrator Index

Authors and illustrators are arranged alphabetically by last name, followed by book titles—which are also arranged alphabetically—and the text entry number. Book titles may refer to those that appear as a main entry or as an internal entry mentioned in the annotation. Fiction titles are indicated by (F) following the entry number.

Aamodt, Alice (jt. author). *Wolf Pack*, 19126
Aardema, Verna. *Anansi Does the Impossible!* 10637
Bimwili and the Zimwi, 10638
A Bookworm Who Hatched, 12487
Koi and the Kola Nuts, 10640
The Lonely Lioness and the Ostrich Chicks, 10641
Rabbit Makes a Monkey of Lion, 10642
Sebgugugu the Glutton, 10643
Aardema, Verna, ed. *Why Mosquitoes Buzz in People's Ears*, 10644
Aardema, Verna, reteller. *Bringing the Rain to Kapiti Plain*, 10639
Aaron, Jane. *No More Secrets for Me*, 17735
When I'm Afraid, 17601
When I'm Angry, 17602
Aaseng, Nathan. *Barry Sanders*, 13625
Business Builders in Computers, 13201
Business Builders in Oil, 12633
Carl Lewis, 13663
Construction, 13202
Dwight Gooden, 13457
Florence Griffith Joyner, 13660
Invertebrates, 19599
Jose Canseco, 13441
Meat-Eating Plants, 20222
The Peace Seekers, 13723
Poisonous Creatures, 18601
Sports Great David Robinson, 13567
Sports Great John Stockton, 13576
Sports Great Michael Jordan, 13535
Top 10 Basketball Scoring Small Forwards, 13360
True Champions, 21965
Wildshots, 17769

Yearbooks in Science: 1940–1949, 18272
Yearbooks in Science: 1930–1939, 18271
You Are the Explorer, 14326
Aaseng, Rolfe E. *Augsburg Story Bible*, 17237
Abbett, Leo. *60 Super Simple Crafts*, 21442
60 Super Simple Magic Tricks, 21787
Abbink, Emily. *Colors of the Navajo*, 15917
Missions of the Monterey Bay Area, 16758
Abbott, Deborah. *One TV Blasting and a Pig Outdoors*, 8874(F)
Abbott, Kate. *Mystery at Echo Cliffs*, 6727(F)
Abbott, Tony. *Danger Guys*, 6728(F)
Abeel, Samantha. *What Once Was White*, 17899
Abells, Chana Byers. *The Children We Remember*, 14809
Aber, Linda Williams. *Who's Got Spots?* 20577
Abercrombie, Barbara. *Charlie Anderson*, 5111(F)
Michael and the Cats, 5112(F)
Abolafia, Yossi. *Harry in Trouble*, 6582(F)
Harry's Pony, 6583(F)
It's Valentine's Day, 11851
Moving Day, 2271(F)
Abraham-Podietz, Eva (jt. author). *Ten Thousand Children*, 14851
Accardo, Anthony. *Where Did You Get Those Eyes?* 17648
Ace, Katherine. *The Creek*, 15965
The Pawnee, 15966
The Shawnee, 15955
Ackerman, Diane. *Bats*, 19018
Ackerman, Karen. *Araminta's Paint Box*, 4567(F)
Bingleman's Midway, 2903(F)

By the Dawn's Early Light, 3500(F)
The Leaves in October, 8395(F)
Song and Dance Man, 3501(F)
This Old House, 2987(F)
The Tin Heart, 4568(F)
Ackerman, Ned. *Spirit Horse*, 9143(F)
Acosta, Cristina. *When Woman Became the Sea*, 11416
Ada, Alma F. *The Christmas Tree/El Arbol de Navidad*, 5741(F)
Dear Peter Rabbit, 941(F)
Friend Frog, 1722(F)
The Gold Coin, 4896(F)
Jordi's Star, 942(F)
The Lizard and the Sun, 11392
The Malachite Palace, 10375(F)
My Name Is Maria Isabel, 7331(F)
The Three Golden Oranges, 11133
Under the Royal Palms, 15692
Yours Truly, Goldilocks, 943(F)
Adam, Robert. *Buildings*, 21113
Adams, Adrienne. *The Christmas Party*, 5742(F)
The Easter Bunny That Overslept, 5966(F)
The Easter Egg Artists, 5962(F)
The Great Valentine's Day Balloon Race, 6160(F)
The Shoemaker and the Elves, 10906
A Woggle of Witches, 5980(F)
Adams, Barbara J. *The Go-Around Dollar*, 2988
New York City, 16645
Adams, Cynthia. *The Mysterious Case of Sir Arthur Conan Doyle*, 12532
Adams, Eric J. *On the Day His Daddy Left*, 4897(F)
Adams, Faith. *El Salvador*, 15656
Nicaragua, 15657

Adams, Jean Ekman. *Clarence Goes Out West and Meets a Purple Horse*, 1723(F)

Adams, Jeanie. *Going for Oysters*, 4569(F)

Adams, Jonathan. *Zoom City*, 13871

Adams, Kathleen (jt. author). *On the Day His Daddy Left*, 4897(F)

Adams, Lisa K. *Dealing with Teasing*, 17693

Adams, Lynn. *How Many Feet? How Many Tails?* 392(F)
Where's That Bone? 235(F)

Adams, McCrea. *Tipi*, 15918

Adams, Mary A. *Whoopi Goldberg*, 12389

Adams, Richard. *Watership Down*, 7544(F)

Adams, Sarah. *Asana and the Animals*, 11804

Adams, Simon. *Junior Chronicle of the 20th Century*, 14543
Titanic, 21348
Visual Timeline of the 20th Century, 14577
World War II, 14810

Addy, Sharon Hart. *Right Here on This Spot*, 4570(F)
A Visit with Great-Grandma, 3502(F)

Adedjouma, Davida, ed. *The Palm of My Heart*, 11747

Adeeb, Bonnetta (jt. author). *Nigeria*, 15008

Adeeb, Hassan. *Nigeria*, 15008

Adeleke, Tunde. *Songhay*, 15009

Adelson, Bruce. *Hat Trick Trivia*, 22209

Adinolfi, JoAnn. *The Birthday Letters*, 5719(F)
The Egyptian Polar Bear, 944(F)
Liar, Liar, Pants on Fire, 8732(F)
Mrs. Cole on an Onion Roll and Other School Poems, 11549
My Teacher's Secret Life, 5512(F)
Outrageous, Bodacious Boliver Boggs! 4176(F)
Tina's Diner, 4071(F)

Adkins, Jan. *The Art and Industry of Sandcastles*, 21665
String, 21666

Adler, C. S. *Always and Forever Friends*, 8246(F)
Daddy's Climbing Tree, 8550(F)
Ghost Brother, 7545(F)
Good-bye Pink Pig, 7546(F)
Help, Pink Pig! 7547(F)
Her Blue Straw Hat, 7381(F)
The Lump in the Middle, 8551(F)
The Magic of the Glits, 8247(F)
More Than a Horse, 7146(F)
Not Just a Summer Crush, 8248(F)
One Sister Too Many, 7382(F)
One Unhappy Horse, 7147(F)
The Silver Coach, 8396(F)
What's to Be Scared Of, Suki? 8552(F)

Willie, the Frog Prince, 8553(F)
Winning, 10267(F)

Adler, David A. *America's Champion Swimmer*, 13684
Andy and Tamika, 7383(F)
The Babe and I, 4571(F)
Calculator Riddles, 20608
Cam Jansen and the Barking Treasure Mystery, 6729(F)
Cam Jansen and the Birthday Mystery, 6730(F)
Cam Jansen and the Catnapping Mystery, 6731(F)
Cam Jansen and the Ghostly Mystery, 6732(F)
Cam Jansen and the Mystery at the Haunted House, 6733(F)
Cam Jansen and the Mystery of Flight 54, 6734(F)
Cam Jansen and the Mystery of the Chocolate Fudge Sale, 6735(F)
Cam Jansen and the Scary Snake Mystery, 6736(F)
Cam Jansen and the Triceratops Pops Mystery, 6737(F)
Chanukah in Chelm, 6067(F)
Child of the Warsaw Ghetto, 14811
Christopher Columbus, 12095
The Dinosaur Princess and Other Prehistoric Riddles, 21812
Easy Math Puzzles, 20609
Fraction Fun, 20578
Hiding from the Nazis, 14812
Hilde and Eli, 14813
How Tall How Short How Far Away, 366
Jackie Robinson, 13486
The Kids' Catalog of Jewish Holidays, 17450
Lou Gehrig, 13453
The Many Troubles of Andy Russell, 8554(F)
My Writing Day, 12488
Parachuting Hamsters and Andy Russell, 6738(F)
A Picture Book of Abraham Lincoln, 13063
A Picture Book of Amelia Earhart, 12107
A Picture Book of Anne Frank, 13796
A Picture Book of Benjamin Franklin, 12878
A Picture Book of Christopher Columbus, 12096
A Picture Book of Davy Crockett, 12102
A Picture Book of Eleanor Roosevelt, 13178
A Picture Book of Florence Nightingale, 13840
A Picture Book of Frederick Douglass, 12708
A Picture Book of George Washington, 13113

A Picture Book of George Washington Carver, 13251
A Picture Book of Harriet Tubman, 12795
A Picture Book of Helen Keller, 13164
A Picture Book of Jackie Robinson, 13487
A Picture Book of Jesse Owens, 13664
A Picture Book of John F. Kennedy, 13058
A Picture Book of Louis Braille, 13757
A Picture Book of Martin Luther King, Jr., 12739
A Picture Book of Patrick Henry, 12898
A Picture Book of Paul Revere, 12958
A Picture Book of Robert E. Lee, 12925
A Picture Book of Rosa Parks, 12773
A Picture Book of Sacagawea, 12988
A Picture Book of Simon Bolivar, 13754
A Picture Book of Sojourner Truth, 12789
A Picture Book of Thomas Jefferson, 13046
A Picture Book of Thurgood Marshall, 12763
Roman Numerals, 20626
School Trouble for Andy Russell, 10024(F)
Shape Up! 319(F)
We Remember the Holocaust, 14814
Young Cam Jansen and the Baseball Mystery, 6179(F)
Young Cam Jansen and the Dinosaur Game, 6180(F)
Young Cam Jansen and the Ice Skate Mystery, 6181(F)
Young Cam Jansen and the Missing Cookie, 6182(F)
Young Cam Jansen and the Pizza Shop Mystery, 6183(F)

Adler, Naomi. *Play Me a Story*, 10528

Adler, Susan S. *Meet Samantha*, 9511(F)

Adlerman, Daniel. *Africa Calling*, 5113(F)

Adlerman, Kimberly. *Africa Calling*, 5113(F)

Adoff, Arnold. *All the Colors of the Race*, 11522
The Basket Counts, 11994
Black Is Brown Is Tan, 3503(F)
In for Winter, Out for Spring, 11934
Love Letters, 11523
Malcolm X, 12759

The Return of Rex and Ethel, 7148(F)

Street Music, 11524

Touch the Poem, 11525

Adorjan, Carol. *I Can!* 2989(F)

WKID, 12009(F)

Adshead, Paul. *Puzzle Island*, 21861

Ae-ro, Yoo. *The Two Love Stars*, 10731

Aesop. *The Aesop for Children*, 11048

Aesop's Fables, 11049, 11050

Fables of Aesop, 11051

The Tortoise and the Hare, 11052

The Town Mouse and the Country Mouse, 11053

Afanasyev, Alexander, ed. *Russian Fairy Tales*, 11080

Agassi, Martine. *Hands Are Not for Hitting*, 2990(F)

Agee, Jon. *Elvis Lives! and Other Anagrams*, 14020

Go Hang a Salami! I'm a Lasagna Hog! 21877

The Halloween House, 6050(F)

The Incredible Painting of Felix Clousseau, 945(F)

Mean Margaret, 8079(F)

The Return of Freddy Legrand, 4072(F)

Sit on a Potato Pan, Otis! 21878

So Many Dynamos! 14021

Who Ordered the Jumbo Shrimp? 14022

Agell, Charlotte. *To the Island*, 1724(F)

Up the Mountain, 1725(F)

Ageorges, Veronique. *The Arabs in the Golden Age*, 15556

Aggs, Patrice. *Bye-Bye, Babies!* 3317(F)

Florizella and the Wolves, 10426(F)

Mr. Pam Pam and the Hullabazoo, 1074(F)

The Visitor, 1726(F)

Why the Sea Is Salty, 11123

Ahiagble, Gilbert Bobbo. *Master Weaver from Ghana*, 15010

Ahlberg, Allan. *The Bravest Ever Bear*, 1727(F)

The Ghost Train, 6184(F)

It Was a Dark and Stormy Night, 2904(F)

Mockingbird, 616

Monkey Do! 1728(F)

The Mysteries of Zigomar, 11854

The Snail House, 946(F)

Ahlberg, Janet. *It Was a Dark and Stormy Night*, 2904(F)

Ahmad, Nyla. *CyberSurfer*, 21190

Ahrens, Robin Isabel. *Dee and Bee*, 4073(F)

Aiello, Laurel. *Janice VanCleave's Food and Nutrition for Every Kid*, 18212

Janice VanCleave's Solar System, 18533

Science Around the World, 18326

Aiken, Joan. *Dangerous Games*, 6739(F)

The Wolves of Willoughby Chase, 6740(F)

Ainsworth, Ken. *Building a Shelf and a Bike Rack*, 21660

Building a Solitaire Game and a Peg Board, 21661

Aja, Christopher. *The Sea Monster's Secret*, 11231

Ajhar, Brian. *A Burst of Firsts*, 11628

The Giggler Treatment, 7709(F)

Pinocchio, 1410(F)

Ajmera, Maya K. *Children from Australia to Zimbabwe*, 14328

Let the Games Begin! 21966

To Be a Kid, 14327

Akintola, Ademola. *The River That Went to the Sky*, 10698

Alan, H. M. *Child's Guide to the Mass*, 17221

Alarcon, Francisco X. *Angels Ride Bikes and Other Fall Poems*, 11935

From the Bellybutton of the Moon and Other Summer Poems, 11526

Laughing Tomatoes and Other Spring Poems/Jitomates Risueños y Otros Poemas de Primavera, 11527

Alarcon, Karen Beaumont. *Louella Mae, She's Run Away!* 4074(F)

Albee, Sarah. *The Dragon's Scales*, 6185(F)

I Can Do It! 6186(F)

Albert, Burton. *Journey of the Nightly Jaguar*, 11770

Windsongs and Rainbows, 4369(F)

Albert, Shirley. *Doll Party*, 6187(F)

Alborough, Jez. *Duck in the Truck*, 1729(F)

Hug, 1730(F)

My Friend Bear, 947(F)

Watch Out! Big Bro's Coming! 948(F)

Where's My Teddy? 1731(F)

Albregts, Lisa. *Best Friends*, 21410

Alcantara, Ricardo. *Dog and Cat*, 1732(F)

Alcock, Vivien. *The Haunting of Cassie Palmer*, 7548(F)

The Red-Eared Ghosts, 7549(F)

Singer to the Sea God, 9023(F)

The Stonewalkers, 7550(F)

Stranger at the Window, 6741(F)

The Trial of Anna Cotman, 6742(F)

Alcorn, Stephen. *I, Too, Sing America*, 11753

My America, 11603

Alcott, Louisa May. *Little Women*, 7384(F)

An Old Fashioned Thanksgiving, 9703(F)

The Quiet Little Woman, 9704(F)

Alcraft, Rob. *Valley of the Kings*, 14602

Zoom City, 13871

Alda, Arlene. *Arlene Alda's ABC*, 1(F)

Arlene Alda's 1 2 3, 367(F)

Hurry Granny Annie, 4075(F)

Aldana, Patricia, ed. *Jade and Iron*, 11434

Aldape, Virginia Totorica. *David, Donny, and Darren*, 17641

Nicole's Story, 17936

Alderson, Brian. *The Arabian Nights; or, Tales Told by Sheherezade During a Thousand Nights and One Night*, 11180

Alderson, Brian, reteller. *The Tale of the Turnip*, 10943

Alderson, Sue Ann. *Pond Seasons*, 11936

Aldis, Rodney. *Polar Lands*, 15792

Rainforests, 20430

Aldrich, Kent A. *Fine Print*, 13304

Aldridge, Eve. *Hurry Granny Annie*, 4075(F)

Sarah's Story, 1220(F)

Aldridge, Josephine Haskell. *A Possible Tree*, 4370(F)

Alegre, Hermes. *The Mats*, 4578(F)

Alessandrello, Anna. *The Earth*, 18426

Alexander, Anita. *Gingersnaps*, 17538

Alexander, Bryan. *An Eskimo Family*, 15793

What Do We Know About the Inuit? 15794

Alexander, Cherry (jt. author). *An Eskimo Family*, 15793

What Do We Know About the Inuit? 15794

Alexander, Ellen. *Fireflies in the Night*, 19452

Alexander, Kyle. *Pro Wrestling's Most Punishing Finishing Moves*, 21967

The Women of Pro Wrestling, 21968

Alexander, Lloyd. *The Book of Three*, 7551(F)

The Cat Who Wished to Be a Man, 7552(F)

The Drackenberg Adventure, 6743(F)

The First Two Lives of Lukas-Kasha, 7553(F)

Gypsy Rizka, 6744(F)

How the Cat Swallowed Thunder, 1733(F)

The Jedera Adventure, 6745(F)

Time Cat, 7554(F)

The Wizard in the Tree, 7555(F)

Alexander, Martha. *A You're Adorable*, 71(F)

And My Mean Old Mother Will Be Sorry, Blackboard Bear, 949(F)

How My Library Grew, by Dinah, 2991(F)

Understood Betsy, 7401(F)

Where Does the Sky End, Grandpa? 3504(F)

You're a Genius, Blackboard Bear, 617(F)

Alexander, Nina. *Alison Rides the Rapids*, 6746(F)

Alexander, Sally H. *Do You Remember the Color Blue? And Other Questions Kids Ask About Blindness*, 17900

Alexander, Sue. *Behold the Trees*, 4572(F)

One More Time, Mama, 3505(F)

Small Plays for Special Days, 12010

There's More . . . Much More, 1734(F)

World Famous Muriel and the Magic Mystery, 6188(F)

Alexeieff, Alexander. *Russian Fairy Tales*, 11080

Alford, Jan. *I Can't Believe I Have to Do This*, 9770(F)

Ali, Sharifah Enayat. *Afghanistan*, 15145

Aliki. *All By Myself!* 2992(F)

At Mary Bloom's, 5114(F)

Best Friends Together Again, 3977(F)

Christmas Tree Memories, 5743(F)

Corn Is Maize, 20169

Digging Up Dinosaurs, 14373

Dinosaur Bones, 14374

Feelings, 152

Fossils Tell of Long Ago, 14375

Hello! Good-bye! 2993(F)

How a Book Is Made, 13990

The Listening Walk, 3893(F)

Manners, 2994

Marianthe's Story, 4573(F)

A Medieval Feast, 14752

Mummies Made in Egypt, 14603

My Feet, 18045

My Five Senses, 18129

My Hands, 18046

My Visit to the Aquarium, 20020

My Visit to the Dinosaurs, 14376

My Visit to the Zoo, 20021

Nice New Neighbors, 1851(F)

The Story of Johnny Appleseed, 12842

The Two of Them, 7385(F)

We Are Best Friends, 3978(F)

Welcome, Little Baby, 3506(F)

William Shakespeare and the Globe, 12590

Aliotta, Jerome J. *The Puerto Ricans*, 17539

Allaby, Michael. *The Environment*, 20293

Guide to Weather, 20750

Allan, Jonathan. *Don't Wake the Baby!* 9771(F)

Allan, Nicholas. *The Bird*, 4076(F)

Jesus' Christmas Party, 9705(F)

Allard, Denise. *Greece*, 15370

Allard, Harry. *The Cactus Flower Bakery*, 1735(F)

Miss Nelson Has a Field Day, 5466(F)

Miss Nelson Is Missing! 5467(F)

The Stupids Have a Ball, 4077(F)

The Stupids Take Off, 4078(F)

Allen, Debbie. *Brothers of the Knight*, 10376

Dancing in the Wings, 4898(F)

Allen, Eugenie. *The Best Ever Kids' Book of Lists*, 21888

Allen, Gary. *One Day in the Tropical Rain Forest*, 20442

One Day in the Woods, 20443(F)

Allen, Graham. *The Prairie Dog*, 19194

Allen, Jonathan. *Burton and Stanley*, 8003(F)

Joe Lion's Big Boots, 6515(F)

Mucky Moose, 1736(F)

Simply Delicious! 1388(F)

Allen, Joy. *A Dollar for Penny*, 446(F)

Allen, Judy. *Are You a Butterfly?* 19539

Are You a Ladybug? 19528

Are You a Snail? 19600

Are You a Spider? 19571

Seal, 5115(F)

Whale, 950(F)

Allen, Judy, ed. *Anthology for the Earth*, 16952

Allen, Laura. *Where Does the Night Hide?* 644(F)

Allen, Laura J. *Rollo and Tweedy and the Ghost at Dougal Castle*, 6189(F)

Allen, Marjorie. *Changes*, 4371(F)

Allen, Paula Gunn. *As Long As the Rivers Flow*, 12634

Allen, Thomas B. *The Chalk Box Kid*, 4914(F)

The Days Before Now, 12508

Good-bye, Charles Lindbergh, 4599(F)

Littlejim, 9556(F)

Littlejim's Dreams, 9557(F)

Littlejim's Gift, 9734(F)

Mountain Valor, 9481(F)

Once in the Country, 11613

Over Back, 4496(F)

A Place Called Freedom, 4822(F)

Summer Wheels, 8262(F)

Where Does the Night Hide? 644(F)

Aller, Susan Bivin. *Emma and the Night Dogs*, 2905(F)

Alley, R. *Hey, Little Baby!* 3055(F)

Alley, R. W. *Animals on Board*, 523(F)

The Bull and the Fire Truck, 6424(F)

Detective Dinosaur Lost and Found, 6666(F)

The Emperor's Birthday Suit, 6716(F)

Family Reunion, 11702

Follow That Puppy! 4228(F)

Kitty Riddles, 21824

A Know-Nothing Birthday, 5725(F)

Mrs. Toggle's Beautiful Blue Shoe, 4278(F)

Mrs. Toggle's Zipper, 4279(F)

Old Winter, 1506(F)

Paddington Bear, 1833(F)

Paddington Bear All Day, 1834(F)

Paddington Bear and the Busy Bee Carnival, 12(F)

Paddington Bear and the Christmas Surprise, 5756(F)

Paddington Bear Goes to Market, 1835(F)

School Isn't Fair, 5471(F)

Serena Katz, 4270(F)

The Teeny Tiny Woman, 6551(F)

Thanksgiving Day at Our House, 6138

Who Said Boo? 11827

Young Arthur Ashe, 13643

Allibone, Judith. *Jody's Beans*, 4420(F)

Allison, Diane. *The Case of the Elevator Duck*, 7158(F)

Allison, Linda. *Blood and Guts*, 18047

The Sierra Club Summer Book, 21969

Allman, Barbara. *Her Piano Sang*, 12337

Allon, Jeffrey. *Ten Holiday Jewish Children's Stories*, 17468(F)

Almond, David. *Heaven Eyes*, 7556(F)

Skellig, 7557(F)

Aloof, Andrew. *Baby Animals*, 5392

Alper, Ann Fitzpatrick. *Harry McNairy, Tooth Fairy*, 951(F)

Alphin, Elaine M. *Irons*, 21021

Toasters, 21022

Tournament of Time, 7558(F)

Vacuum Cleaners, 21023

Alrawi, Karim. *The Girl Who Lost Her Smile*, 4574(F)

Alston, Edith. *Let's Visit a Space Camp*, 20945

Alter, Judith. *Amusement Parks, Roller Coasters, Ferris Wheels, and Cotton Candy*, 14263

Beauty Pageants, 14264

Callie Shaw, Stable Boy, 10268(F)

Christopher Reeve, 12450

Cissie Palmer, 13174

Luke and the Van Zandt County War, 9512(F)

Maggie and a Horse Named Devildust, 7149(F)

Maggie and the Search for Devil-dust, 7150(F)
Meet Me at the Fair, 14265
Rodeos, 21970
The Santa Fe Trail, 16284
Wild West Shows, 14266
Altman, Joyce. *Dear Bronx Zoo*, 20022
Lunch at the Zoo, 20023
Altman, Linda Jacobs. *Amelia's Road*, 4899(F)
Arkansas, 16828
Big Dogs, 19936
California, 16759
The California Gold Rush in American History, 16285
The Legend of Freedom Hill, 9339(F)
Parrots, 19882
The Pullman Strike of 1894, 16444
Small Dogs, 19937
Altman, Susan. *Extraordinary Black Americans*, 12635
Altschuler, Franz. *One Hundred Favorite Folktales*, 10621
Alvarez, Julia. *How Tia Lola Came to ~~Visit~~ Stay*, 7386(F)
The Secret Footprints, 11417
Alvord, Douglas. *Sarah's Boat*, 10269(F)
Amado, Elisa. *Barrilete*, 15658
Amato, Mary. *The Word Eater*, 7559(F)
Ambrus, Victor G. *Favorite Stories of the Ballet*, 14297
The Iliad, 11486
Moby Dick, 9304(F)
Pinocchio, 7661(F)
Amdur, Melissa. *Anthony Quinn*, 12449
Linda Ronstadt, 12460
Amery, Heather, comp. *The Usborne Children's Songbook*, 14234
Ames, Gerald (jt. author). *Spooky Tricks*, 21792
Ames, Lee J. *Draw Fifty Airplanes, Aircraft and Spacecraft*, 21554
Draw Fifty Aliens, UFOs, Galaxy Ghouls, Milky Way Marauders, and Other Extraterrestrial Creatures, 21559
Draw Fifty Cats, 21555
Draw Fifty Dogs, 21556
Draw Fifty Famous Cartoons, 21557
Draw Fifty Monsters, Creeps, Superheroes, Demons, Dragons, Nerds, Dirts, Ghouls, Giants, Vampires, Zombies and Other Curiosa, 21558
Ames, Mildred. *Grandpa Jake and the Grand Christmas*, 9706(F)
Amiri, Fahimeh. *The Monkey Bridge*, 10802
Ammon, Richard. *An Amish Christmas*, 5744(F)
An Amish Wedding, 17161

An Amish Year, 17162
Conestoga Wagons, 16286
Amoore, Susannah. *Motley the Cat*, 1737(F)
Amos, William Hopkins. *Life in Ponds and Streams*, 20510
Amoss, Berthe. *Lost Magic*, 7560(F)
Amper, Thomas. *Booker T. Washington*, 12812
Amstel, Marsha. *Sybil Ludington's Midnight Ride*, 16189
Amstey, David. *The Wizard in the Woods*, 8164(F)
Amstutz, Andre. *The Ghost Train*, 6184(F)
Monkey Do! 1728(F)
Anastasio, Dina. *The Case of the Glacier Park Swallow*, 6747(F)
The Case of the Grand Canyon Eagle, 6748(F)
Anaya, Rudolfo A. *Elegy on the Death of Cesar Chavez*, 11528
Farolitos for Abuelo, 5745(F)
The Farolitos of Christmas, 5746(F)
Maya's Children, 11393
My Land Sings, 11323
Roadrunner's Dance, 1738(F)
Ancona, George. *The American Family Farm*, 20046
Barrio, 16760
Carnaval, 17333
Charro, 15599
Cowboys, 16900
Cuban Kids, 15693
Fiesta Fireworks, 4575(F)
Fiesta U.S.A., 17334
The Golden Lion Tamarin Comes Home, 18921
Handtalk, 14012
Handtalk Birthday, 5673(F)
Handtalk School, 14017(F)
Handtalk Zoo, 5116(F)
Let's Dance! 14271
Man and Mustang, 19983
Pablo Remembers, 15600
The Pinata Maker/El Piñatero, 15601
Powwow, 15919
Ancona, George (jt. author). *Handtalk School*, 14017(F)
Ancona, Mary Beth (jt. author). *Handtalk*, 14012
Handtalk Zoo, 5116(F)
Anda, Michael O. *Yoruba*, 15011
Andersen, Bethanne. *But God Remembered*, 17320
Kindle Me a Riddle, 4704(F)
A Prayer for the Earth, 5649(F)
Seven Brave Women, 3682(F)
Ten Queens, 13738
Andersen, Hans Christian. *The Emperor and the Nightingale*, 10377(F)
The Emperor's New Clothes, 10378(F), 10379(F), 10380(F), 10381(F)

The Fir Tree, 10382(F)
Hans Christian Andersen Fairy Tales, 10383(F)
The Little Match Girl, 10384(F)
The Little Mermaid, 10385(F)
The Little Mermaid and Other Fairy Tales, 10386(F)
The Snow Queen, 10387(F)
The Steadfast Tin Soldier, 10388(F)
Stories from Hans Christian Andersen, 10389
The Swan's Stories, 10390(F)
Thumbelina, 10391(F)
Thumbeline, 10392(F)
The Tinderbox, 10393(F), 10394(F)
The Top and the Ball, 10395(F)
The Ugly Duckling, 10396(F)
Anderson, Bob. *Obo*, 952(F)
Anderson, Carol D. *Techno Lab*, 21264
Anderson, Catherine C. *Jackie Kennedy Onassis*, 13172
Anderson, Dave. *The Story of Basketball*, 22126
The Story of Golf, 21971
The Story of the Olympics, 22243
Anderson, David A. *The Origin of Life on Earth*, 10645
The Rebellion of Humans, 4372(F)
Anderson, Janet S. *Sunflower Sal*, 2995(F)
Anderson, Jeff. *Greek Myths*, 11462
Anderson, Joan. *The American Family Farm*, 20046
Batboy, 22084
Cowboys, 16900
Pioneer Children of Appalachia, 9340(F)
Rookie, 13580
Spanish Pioneers of the Southwest, 16287
Anderson, Joel. *Jonah's Trash . . . God's Treasure*, 17238
Anderson, Kathy P. *Illinois*, 16527
Anderson, Kevin J. *Stars Wars*, 10141(F)
Anderson, Laurie Halse. *Fight for Life*, 7151(F)
No Time for Mother's Day, 5609(F)
Saudi Arabia, 15534
Turkey Pox, 6132(F)
Anderson, Lena. *Elliot's Extraordinary Cookbook*, 21677
Linnea in Monet's Garden, 13876(F)
Linnea's Almanac, 18578
Linnea's Windowsill Garden, 21759
Stina, 3507(F)
Tea for Ten, 368(F)
Anderson, Linda. *On Top of Old Smoky*, 11360
Anderson, Lydia M. *Champion for Children's Health*, 13134
Stateswoman to the World, 13185
Anderson, Margaret J. *Bizarre Insects*, 19423

Carl Linnaeus, 13316
Charles Darwin, 13264
Children of Summer, 9024(F)
Isaac Newton, 13333
Anderson, Mary. *Suzy's Secret Snoop Society*, 6749(F)
Anderson, Peggy Perry. *Out to Lunch*, 1739(F)
To the Tub, 6190(F)
Anderson, Peter. *A Grand Canyon Journey*, 16595
The Pony Express, 16288
The Transcontinental Railroad, 21327
Anderson, Robert. *Forests*, 20431
Anderson, Scoular. *A Puzzling Day in the Land of the Pharaohs*, 14604
Anderson, William. *Laura's Album*, 12626
Pioneer Girl, 12627
Ando, Noriyuki. *Shin's Tricycle*, 14860
Andreae, Giles. *Cock-a-doodle-doo! Barnyard Hullabaloo*, 1740(F)
Love Is a Handful of Honey, 1741(F)
Rumble in the Jungle, 11771
Andreasen, Dan. *The Bite of the Gold Bug*, 9535(F)
By the Dawn's Early Light, 14161
Changes for Felicity, 9214(F)
Felicity Learns a Lesson, 9215(F)
Felicity's Surprise, 9216(F)
Halley Came to Jackson, 3568(F)
Little Clearing in the Woods, 9457(F)
Little House in Brookfield, 9458(F)
Pioneer Girl, 12627
Rose Red and the Bear Prince, 10882
Streets of Gold, 16283
We Played Marbles, 2971(F)
Andretti, Michael. *Michael Andretti at Indianapolis*, 22078
Andrew, Ian. *Back to the Blue*, 5329(F)
The Midnight Man, 660(F)
Premlata and the Festival of Lights, 8996(F)
Andrew, Robert. *Castles*, 14785
Andrews, Benny. *The Hickory Chair*, 4960
Sky Sash So Blue, 4677(F)
Andrews, Ian. *Pompeii*, 14710
Andrews, Jan. *Pa's Harvest*, 16445
Very Last First Time, 4576(F)
Andrews, Jean F. *The Secret in the Dorm Attic*, 6750(F)
Andriani, Renee W. *Annabel the Actress Starring in Gorilla My Dreams*, 9806(F)
Andronik, Catherine M. *Hatshepsut, His Majesty, Herself*, 13807
Andryszewski, Tricia. *Bill Bradley*, 12858
Kosovo, 15259

The Seminoles, 15920
Step by Step Along the Appalachian Trail, 15859
Step by Step Along the Pacific Crest Trail, 16761
Anema, Durlynn. *Louise Arner Boyd*, 12075
Anflick, Charles. *Resistance*, 14815
Angeletti, Roberta. *The Cave Painter of Lascaux*, 13937
The Minotaur of Knossos, 7561(F)
Nefertari, Princess of Egypt, 14605
Vulca the Etruscan, 14711
Angell, Judie. *The Buffalo Nickel Blues Band*, 8249(F)
Angelo, Valenti. *Roller Skates*, 9622(F)
Angelou, Maya. *My Painted House, My Friendly Chicken, and Me*, 13872
Angliss, Sarah. *Cosmic Journeys*, 20946
Future World, 18273
Gold, 20275
Anglund, Joan Walsh. *In a Pumpkin Shell*, 2(F)
Nibble Nibble Mousekin, 10901
Anholt, Catherine. *Bear and Baby*, 953(F)
Billy and the Big New School, 5468(F)
The Candlewick Book of First Rhymes, 822
Catherine and Laurence Anholt's Big Book of Families, 3508(F)
Come Back, Jack! 954(F)
Harry's Home, 2996(F)
Here Come the Babies, 3509
Sophie and the New Baby, 3510(F)
The Twins, Two by Two, 619(F)
What I Like, 2997(F)
Anholt, Laurence. *Billy and the Big New School*, 5468(F)
Camille and the Sunflowers, 4577(F)
Leonardo and the Flying Boy, 9025(F)
Sophie and the New Baby, 3510(F)
Stone Girl, Bone Girl, 13227
Summerhouse, 955(F)
Anholt, Laurence (jt. author). *Bear and Baby*, 953(F)
Catherine and Laurence Anholt's Big Book of Families, 3508(F)
Come Back, Jack! 954(F)
Harry's Home, 2996(F)
Here Come the Babies, 3509
The Twins, Two by Two, 619(F)
What I Like, 2997(F)
Anno, Mitsumasa. *Anno's Alphabet*, 3(F)
Anno's Counting Book, 369(F)
Anno's Magic Seeds, 370(F)
Anno's Math Games, 20610
Anno's Mysterious Multiplying Jar, 20627
The Magic Pocket, 11649

Annunziata, Jane (jt. author). *Help Is on the Way*, 17927
Ansary, Mir T. *Afghanistan*, 15146
Columbus Day, 17335
Labor Day, 17336
Martin Luther King Jr. Day, 17337
Memorial Day, 17338
Veterans Day, 17339
Anstey, Caroline. *The Glass Bird*, 8043(F)
Moles Can Dance, 2059(F)
Anstey, David. *Wizard in Wonderland*, 8165(F)
Antle, Nancy. *Sam's Wild West Christmas*, 5747(F)
Antoine, Héloïse. *Curious Kids Go to Preschool*, 2998(F)
Antram, David. *Across America*, 16088
Exploring the Polar Regions, 15804
Anzaldua, Gloria. *Prietita and the Ghost Woman*, 7562(F)
Apfel, Necia H. *Orion, the Hunter*, 18537
Appel, Marty. *Joe DiMaggio*, 13448
Appelbaum, Diana. *Cocoa Ice*, 8250(F)
Giants in the Land, 16096
Appelt, Kathi. *Bat Jamboree*, 371(F)
Bats Around the Clock, 1743(F)
Bats on Parade, 372(F)
Bayou Lullaby, 620(F)
Cowboy Dreams, 621(F)
Elephants Aloft, 956(F)
I See the Moon, 622(F)
Kissing Tennessee, 8555(F)
Oh, My Baby, Little One, 1744(F)
Toddler Two-Step, 373(F)
Watermelon Day, 2999(F)
Apperley, Dawn. *Animal Moves*, 18794
Hello Little Chicks, 1745(F)
Hide and Seek, 4400(F)
Nighty-Night, 623(F)
Apperley, Dawn (jt. author). *How Does Your Garden Grow?* 21760
Appiah, Peggy. *Tales of an Ashanti Father*, 10646
Apple, Margot. *Angel's Mother's Baby*, 7421(F)
Angel's Mother's Boyfriend, 7422(F)
Big Mama, 3095(F)
The Boy Who Ate Dog Biscuits, 7298(F)
Brave Martha, 624(F)
Bunny's Night Out, 776(F)
Casey's New Hat, 3154(F)
The Great Rescue Operation, 8173(F)
Have I Got Dogs! 5170(F)
Just Like My Dad, 3155(F)
Sheep in a Jeep, 6654(F)
Sheep in a Shop, 5723(F)
Sheep Out to Eat, 6655(F)

Sheep Take a Hike, 2685(F)
Sheep Trick or Treat, 6048(F)
Applegate, Stan. *The Devil's High-way*, 9341(F)
Aragon, Jane C. *Salt Hands*, 5118(F)
Arai, Tomie. *China's Bravest Girl*, 10745
Sachiko Means Happiness, 5066(F)
Araki, Chiyo. *Origami in the Class-room*, 21604
Araten, Harry. *The Jewish Child's First Book of Why*, 17477
Seven Animal Stories for Children, 17249
Araujo, Frank P. *Nekane, the Lamina and the Bear*, 11134
The Perfect Orange, 10647
Arbuckle, Scott. *Chico and Dan*, 7234(F)
Zeb, the Cow's on the Roof Again! 9256(F)
Arcellana, Francisco. *The Mats*, 4578(F)
Archambault, John. *The Birth of a Whale*, 5119
Archambault, John (jt. author). *Barn Dance!* 2481(F)
Chicka Chicka Boom Boom, 89(F)
The Ghost-Eye Tree, 2957(F)
Here Are My Hands, 3310(F)
Knots on a Counting Rope, 7353(F)
Listen to the Rain, 3311(F)
The Magic Pumpkin, 6032(F)
Up and Down on the Merry-Go-Round, 3312(F)
White Dynamite and Curly Kidd, 2958(F)
Archambault, Matthew. *Seasons of the Trail*, 9368(F)
Archbold, Rick (jt. author). *Ghost Liners*, 21350
Safari, 18607
Archer, Chris. *Alien Blood*, 10142(F)
Archer, Jules. *Earthquake!* 20331
Hurricane! 20678
To Save the Earth, 13203
Tornado! 20679
Archibald, Erika F. *A Sudanese Fam-ily*, 17540
Archipowa, Anastassija. *The Emper-or's New Clothes*, 10492(F)
The Little Match Girl, 10493
Ardalan, Hayde. *Milton*, 1746(F)
Ardley, Neil. *Electricity*, 20880
The Science Book of Air, 20663
The Science Book of Color, 20854
The Science Book of Electricity, 20881
The Science Book of Energy, 20817
The Science Book of Gravity, 20294
The Science Book of Light, 20855
The Science Book of Magnets, 20882
The Science Book of Motion, 20818
The Science Book of the Senses, 18130

The Science Book of Things That Grow, 20223
The Science Book of Water, 20724
A Young Person's Guide to Music, 14119
Arenson, Roberta. *A Caribbean Counting Book*, 402(F)
Manu and the Talking Fish, 10786
One, Two, Skip a Few! First Num-ber Rhymes, 545
Aretha, David. *The Montreal Canadi-ens Hockey Team*, 22210
The Seattle SuperSonics Basketball Team, 22127
Argent, Kerry. *Derek the Knitting Dinosaur*, 1816(F)
Gotcha! 2266(F)
One Woolly Wombat, 599(F)
Sleepy Bears, 677(F)
Thank You, Santa, 5954(F)
Wombat Divine, 5817(F)
Argent, Kerry (jt. author). *One Wool-ly Wombat*, 599(F)
Argueta, Manlio. *Magic Dogs of the Volcanoes*, 957(F)
Arima, Elaine. *The Kids 'N' Clay Ceramics Book*, 21529
Arkhurst, Joyce Cooper. *The Adven-tures of Spider*, 10648
Arkin, Alan. *Cassie Loves Beethoven*, 7563(F)
The Lemming Condition, 7564(F)
Armbruster, Ann. *The American Flag*, 13968
Floods, 20680
Lake Huron, 16528
Lake Ontario, 16529
Tornadoes, 20681
Wildfires, 20362
Armistead, John. *The $66 Summer*, 8251(F)
Armitage, David. *My Brother Sammy*, 4948(F)
Armour, Peter. *Stop That Pickle!* 958(F)
Armstrong, Carole. *Lives and Leg-ends of the Saints*, 17163
Armstrong, Jennifer. *Patrick Doyle Is Full of Blarney*, 10270(F)
Pierre's Dream, 4079(F)
Pockets, 3000(F)
The Snowball, 959(F)
Spirit of Endurance, 15795
Steal Away, 9257(F)
Sunshine, Moonshine, 6191(F)
Theodore Roosevelt, 9513(F)
Armstrong, Kristin. *Lance Armstrong*, 13676
Armstrong, Nancy M. *Navajo Long Walk*, 9144(F)
Armstrong, Nichola. *Ant*, 19508
Armstrong, Pam. *Young Explorer's Guide to Undersea Life*, 19622
Armstrong, Robb. *Drew and the Bub Daddy Showdown*, 8556(F)
Runnin' with the Big Dawgs, 10271(F)

Armstrong, William H. *Sounder*, 7387(F)
Arnaktauyok, Germaine. *A Sled Dog for Moshi*, 5151(F)
Arndt, Ursula. *Fireworks, Picnics, and Flags*, 17363
Lilies, Rabbits and Painted Eggs, 17433
Shamrocks, Harps and Shillelaghs, 17341
Arno, Iris Hiskey. *I Like a Snack on an Iceberg*, 5120(F)
Arnold, Ann. *Fanny at Chez Panisse*, 16951
Arnold, Arthur P. *Stone Age Farmers Beside the Sea*, 15334
Arnold, Caroline. *The Ancient Cliff Dwellers of Mesa Verde*, 15921
Australian Animals, 18602
Baby Whale Rescue, 19775
Bat, 19019
Bobcats, 19073
Cats, 19915
Children of the Settlement Houses, 16446
Coping with Natural Disasters, 20295
Dinosaur Mountain, 14377
Dinosaurs All Around, 14378
Easter Island, 15222
El Niño, 20751
Giant Shark, 14379
A Guide Dog Puppy Grows Up, 19938
House Sparrows Everywhere, 19213
Killer Whale, 19774
Lion, 19074
Mealtime for Zoo Animals, 18795
Mother and Baby Zoo Animals, 18866
Noisytime for Zoo Animals, 18796
Ostriches and Other Flightless Birds, 19214
Pele, 13707
Playtime for Zoo Animals, 18797
Saving the Peregrine Falcon, 19319
Shockers of the Sea and Other Electrical Animals, 19694
Sleepytime for Zoo Animals, 18798
South American Animals, 18603
Splashtime for Zoo Animals, 18799
Stone Age Farmers Beside the Sea, 15334
Stories in Stone, 13941
Tule Elk, 19147
A Walk on the Great Barrier Reef, 15223
Watching Desert Wildlife, 20398
Zebra, 18922
Arnold, Helen. *Egypt*, 15495
France, 15296
Kenya, 14914
Mexico, 15602
Russia, 15404

Arnold, Jeanne. *Carlos and the Carnival*, 5726(F)
Carlos and the Cornfield/Carlos y la Milpa de Maiz, 4839(F)
Carlos and the Skunk, 4328(F)
Arnold, Katya. *The Adventures of Snowwoman*, 5748(F)
Duck, Duck, Goose? 1747(F)
It Happened Like This, 9896(F)
Me Too! 1748(F)
Meow! 1749(F)
Onions and Garlic, 11156
That Apple Is Mine! 11081
Arnold, Katya, reteller. *Me Too!* 1748(F)
That Apple Is Mine! 11081
Arnold, Lynda. *My Mommy Has AIDS*, 17937
Arnold, Marsha Diane. *The Bravest of Us All*, 2906(F)
The Chicken Salad Club, 3511(F)
The Pumpkin Runner, 4579(F)
Arnold, Syrah. *Stories from the Caribbean*, 11418
Arnold, Tedd. *Axle Annie*, 4277(F)
Five Ugly Monsters, 625(F)
Huggly Takes a Bath, 626(F)
Inside a Barn in the Country, 5157(F)
Inside a House That Is Haunted, 5986(F)
Inside a Zoo in the City, 6259(F)
My First Baking Book, 21688
My Working Mom, 1195(F)
No Jumping on the Bed! 960(F)
The Roly-Poly Spider, 2653(F)
Arnold, Tim. *Natural History from A to Z*, 18604
The Three Billy Goats Gruff, 11117
The Winter Mittens, 961(F)
Arnosky, Jim. *All About Owls*, 19357
All About Rattlesnakes, 18753
All About Turkeys, 19215
All About Turtles, 18777
Arnosky's Ark, 19390
Beaver Pond, Moose Pond, 4373(F)
Big Jim and the White-Legged Moose, 5121(F)
Crinkleroot's Book of Animal Tracking, 18800
Crinkleroot's Guide to Knowing Animal Habitats, 18905
Crinkleroot's Guide to Knowing the Birds, 4374
Crinkleroot's Guide to Knowing the Trees, 20193
Crinkleroot's Guide to Walking in Wild Places, 4375
Crinkleroot's Nature Almanac, 18576
Crinkleroot's 25 Birds Every Child Should Know, 19216
Crinkleroot's 25 Fish Every Child Should Know, 19695
Crinkleroot's Visit to Crinkle Cove, 4376(F)

Empty Lot, 4427(F)
Little Lions, 5122(F)
Long Spikes, 7152(F)
A Manatee Morning, 5123(F)
Otters Under Water, 5124
Rabbits and Raindrops, 1750(F)
Raccoons and Ripe Corn, 18923
Rattlesnake Dance, 1751(F)
Sketching Outdoors in Summer, 21560
Watching Desert Wildlife, 20399
Watching Water Birds, 19346
Wild and Swampy, 20363
Arnsteen, Katy K. *Grandpa Doesn't Know It's Me*, 3668(F)
Let's Celebrate Valentine's Day, 6177
Aroner, Miriam. *The Kingdom of Singing Birds*, 11140
Aronson, Billy. *Meteors*, 18503
Aronson, Virginia. *Venus Williams*, 13654
Arora Lal, Sunandini. *India*, 15094
Arredia, Joni. *Sex, Boys and You*, 17603
Arredondo, Francisco. *Metamorphosis*, 18663
Arrhenius, Peter. *The Penguin Quartet*, 1752(F)
Arrigoni, Patricia. *Harpo*, 5125(F)
Arrington, Frances. *Bluestem*, 9342(F)
Arrowood, Clinton. *Frogs and Ballet*, 14280
Arroyo, Andrea. *The Legend of the Lady Slipper*, 9167
Arthur, Alex. *Shell*, 18924
Arthur, Joe (jt. author). *It Came From Ohio! My Life as a Writer*, 12602
Artley, Bob. *Once Upon a Farm*, 20047
Artone, Lara. *Why Are You Calling Me a Barbarian?* 14738
Artzybasheff, Boris. *Gay-Neck*, 7273(F)
Aruego, Jose. *Alligator Arrived with Apples*, 33(F)
Alligators and Others All Year Long, 2038(F)
Antarctic Antics, 11812
Birthday Rhymes, Special Times, 5688
The Chick and the Duckling, 2125(F)
Five Little Ducks, 563(F)
Gregory, the Terrible Eater, 2684(F)
Herman the Helper, 2319(F)
How Chipmunk Got His Stripes, 11221
Leo the Late Bloomer, 2320(F)
Little Louie the Baby Bloomer, 3753(F)
Lizard's Home, 2680(F)
Look What I Can Do! 906(F)
Mouse in Love, 2322(F)

Mushroom in the Rain, 2742(F)
One Duck, Another Duck, 560(F)
Rockabye Crocodile, 1753(F)
Safe, Warm, and Snug, 18862
They Thought They Saw Him, 5425(F)
We Hide, You Seek, 297(F)
Where Does the Sun Go at Night? 1193(F)
Whose Mouse Are You? 2323(F)
Asbjornsen, Peter C. *The Man Who Kept House*, 11119
Norwegian Folk Tales, 11120
The Three Billy Goats Gruff, 11118
Asbury, Kelly. *Bonnie's Blue House*, 3001(F)
Asch, Devin. *Baby Duck's New Friend*, 1754(F)
Asch, Frank. *Baby Bird's First Nest*, 1755(F)
Barnyard Lullaby, 627(F)
Bear Shadow, 1756(F)
Bear's Bargain, 1757(F)
Cactus Poems, 11937
Dear Brother, 1764(F)
The Earth and I, 4377(F)
Good Night, Baby Bear, 628(F)
Hands Around Lincoln School, 10025(F)
Happy Birthday, Moon, 1758(F)
Insects from Outer Space, 1765(F)
Just Like Daddy, 1759(F)
The Last Puppy, 5126(F)
Moonbear's Dream, 1760(F)
Moonbear's Pet, 1761(F)
Moondance, 1762(F)
One Man Show, 12500
Sand Cake, 1763(F)
Song of the North, 11938
The Sun Is My Favorite Star, 4378(F)
Water, 20725
Ziggy Piggy and the Three Little Pigs, 10944
Asch, Frank (jt. author). *Baby Duck's New Friend*, 1754(F)
Aschenbrenner, Gerald. *Jack, the Seal and the Sea*, 4379(F)
Aschwanden, Peter. *Looking Inside Sports Aerodynamics*, 20837
Looking Inside Sunken Treasure, 14539
Looking Inside Telescopes and the Night Sky, 18413
Aseltine, Lorraine. *First Grade Can Wait*, 5469(F)
I'm Deaf and It's Okay, 17901(F)
Ash, Rhiannon. *Roman Colosseum*, 14712
Ash, Russell. *Factastic Book of 1001 Lists*, 21889
Great Wonders of the World, 14578
Incredible Comparisons, 18274
Ash, Russell, ed. *Aesop's Fables*, 11054
Ashabranner, Brent. *Badge of Valor*, 16646

A Date with Destiny, 16647
The Lion's Whiskers and Other Ethiopian Tales, 10649
The New African Americans, 17541
No Better Hope, 16648
Their Names to Live, 16649
Ashbe, Jeanne. *What's Inside*, 298(F)
Ashby, Ruth. *Elizabethan England*, 15335
The Orangutan, 18989
Asher, Sandy. *Stella's Dancing Days*, 5127(F)
Where Do You Get Your Ideas? 14064
Asher, Sandy, ed. *With All My Heart, With All My Mind*, 7332(F)
Ashforth, Camilla. *Calamity*, 1766(F)
Monkey Tricks, 1767(F)
Who Do You Love? 800(F)
Ashley, Bernard. *Cleversticks*, 5470(F)
Ashman, Linda. *Castles, Caves, and Honeycombs*, 5128(F)
Asian Cultural Center for Unesco, ed. *Folk Tales from Asia for Children Everywhere*, 10719
Asikinack, Bill. *Exploration into North America*, 16075
Asimov, Isaac. *Astronomy in Ancient Times*, 18377
Cosmic Debris, 18375
Death from Space, 14380
How Did We Find Out About Comets? 18504
How Did We Find Out About Lasers? 20856
How Did We Find Out About Solar Power? 20848
How Did We Find Out About Volcanoes? 20332
How Do Big Ships Float? 21349
The Moon, 18440
Mysteries of Deep Space, 18376
The Red Planet, 18455
UFOs, 21890
Asimov, Isaac (jt. author). *Norby and the Court Jester*, 10145(F)
Norby and the Invaders, 10146(F)
Norby and the Oldest Dragon, 10147(F)
Norby Finds a Villain, 10148(F)
Norby, the Mixed-up Robot, 10149(F)
Asimov, Janet. *Norby and the Court Jester*, 10145(F)
Norby and the Invaders, 10146(F)
Norby and the Oldest Dragon, 10147(F)
Norby and the Terrified Taxi, 10143(F)
Norby Finds a Villain, 10148(F)
Norby, the Mixed-up Robot, 10149(F)
The Package in Hyperspace, 10144(F)
Askar, Saoussan (jt. author). *From Far Away*, 5040(F)

Aspenwall, Margaret (jt. author). *Alexander Calder and His Magical Mobiles*, 12196
Asquith, Ros. *My Do It!* 3512(F)
Astrella, Mark. *The Butterfly Alphabet Book*, 19543
Hello Ocean, 4526(F)
Ata, Te. *Baby Rattlesnake*, 11210
Atkins, Jeannine. *Aani and the Tree Huggers*, 8982(F)
Get Set! Swim! 3002(F)
Mary Anning and the Sea Dragon, 13228
A Name on the Quilt, 4900(F)
Robin's Home, 1768(F)
Atkinson, Mary (jt. author). *The Snake Book*, 18763
Atwater, Florence (jt. author). *Mr. Popper's Penguins*, 9772(F)
Atwater, Richard. *Mr. Popper's Penguins*, 9772(F)
Atwell, Debby. *Barn*, 4580(F)
River, 4380(F)
Atwood, Margaret. *Princess Prunella and the Purple Peanut*, 7565(F)
Auch, Herm. *I Was a Third Grade Science Project*, 9773(F)
Auch, Mary Jane. *Angel and Me and the Bayside Bombers*, 10272(F)
Bantam of the Opera, 1769(F)
Bird Dogs Can't Fly, 1770(F)
The Easter Egg Farm, 962(F)
Eggs Mark the Spot, 1771(F)
Frozen Summer, 9258(F)
Hen Lake, 1772(F)
I Was a Third Grade Science Project, 9773(F)
Journey to Nowhere, 9259(F)
Monster Brother, 963(F)
The Nutquacker, 5749(F)
Peeping Beauty, 1773(F)
The Road to Home, 9260(F)
Seven Long Years Until College, 8557(F)
Troll Teacher, 1646(F)
Audry, Andrew C. *How Babies Are Made*, 18236
Audryszewski, Tricia. *The Reform Party*, 17093
Auerbacher, Inge. *I Am a Star*, 14816
August, Louise. *In the Month of Kislev*, 6081(F)
Milk and Honey, 17490
The Way Meat Loves Salt, 11151
Why on This Night? A Passover Haggadah for Family Celebration, 17479
Augustin, Byron. *Qatar*, 15535
Augustin, Rebecca A. (jt. author). *Qatar*, 15535
Auld, Mary. *Daniel in the Lions' Den*, 17239
David and Goliath, 17240
Moses in the Bulrushes, 17242
The Story of Jonah, 17243
Auld, Mary, reteller. *Exodus from Egypt*, 17241

Austin, Margot. *A Friend for Growl Bear*, 1774(F)
Austin, Michael. *The Horned Toad Prince*, 10434(F)
Austin, Virginia. *Kate's Giants*, 2936(F)
Avakian, Monique. *A Historical Album of Massachusetts*, 16650
A Historical Album of New York, 16651
Reformers, 13724
Averill, Esther. *King Philip*, 12980
Avi. *Abigail Takes the Wheel*, 9514(F)
The Barn, 9343(F)
Captain Grey, 6752(F)
The Christmas Rat, 6753(F)
Ereth's Birthday, 7566(F)
The Fighting Ground, 9220(F)
Finding Providence, 4581(F)
Man from the Sky, 6754(F)
Midnight Magic, 9026(F)
Perloo the Bold, 7567(F)
Poppy, 7568(F)
Poppy and Rye, 7569(F)
Ragweed, 7570(F)
S.O.R. Losers, 10273(F)
Something Upstairs, 6755(F)
Tom, Babette, and Simon, 7571(F)
What Do Fish Have to Do with Anything? 8558(F)
Who Stole the Wizard of Oz? 6756(F)
Who Was That Masked Man, Anyway? 9643(F)
Windcatcher, 6757(F)
Avi-Yonah, Michael. *Dig This!* 14519
Piece by Piece! 13938
Avikian, Monique. *The Mejii Restoration and the Rise of Modern Japan*, 14579
Axelrod, Alan, ed. *Songs of the Wild West*, 14139
Axelrod, Amy. *Pigs at Odds*, 20579(F)
Pigs Go to Market, 9707(F)
Pigs in the Pantry, 1775(F)
Pigs on a Blanket, 1776(F)
Pigs Will Be Pigs, 1777(F)
Axelrod, Toby. *In the Camps*, 14817
Rescuers Defying the Nazis, 14818
Axelrod-Contrada, Joan. *The Lizzie Borden "Axe Murder" Trial*, 16447
Axeman, Lois. *Just Like Me*, 6541(F)
Axtell, David. *We're Going on a Lion Hunt*, 2907(F)
Axworthy, Anni. *Along Came Toto*, 1778(F)
Anni's India Diary, 8983(F)
Guess What I Am, 299(F)
Guess What I'll Be, 300(F)
Ayazi-Hashjin, Sherry. *Rap and Hip Hop*, 14120
Aye, Nila. *When I'm Big*, 1139(F)
Ayer, Eleanor. *Adolf Hitler*, 13810

Charles Dickens, 12527
Colorado, 16596
Germany, 15321
In the Ghettos, 14819
Our Flag, 13969
Our National Monuments, 15849
Ruth Bader Ginsburg, 12886
Ayers, Tom. *The Illustrated Rules of Ice Hockey*, 22211
Aylesworth, Jim. *Aunt Pitty Patty's Piggy*, 1779(F)
The Completed Hickory Dickory Dock, 823
The Folks in the Valley, 4(F)
The Full Belly Bowl, 964(F)
The Gingerbread Man, 10945
The Good-Night Kiss, 629(F)
My Sister's Rusty Bike, 965(F)
Old Black Fly, 5(F)
One Crow, 374(F)
The Tale of Tricky Fox, 966(F)
Teddy Bear Tears, 630(F)
Through the Night, 3513(F)
Wake Up, Little Children, 4381(F)
Aylesworth, Thomas G. *Eastern Great Lakes*, 16530
The Kids' World Almanac of Baseball, 22085
The Pacific, 16762
The Southeast, 16829
The Southwest, 16901
Upper Atlantic, 16652
Aylesworth, Virginia L. (jt. author). *Eastern Great Lakes*, 16530
The Pacific, 16762
The Southeast, 16829
The Southwest, 16901
Upper Atlantic, 16652
Ayliffe, Alex. *The Busy Building Book*, 21152
Island in the Sun, 15695
Oh No, Anna! 3151(F)
Pirates Ahoy! 4027(F)
Something Special, 5519(F)
Where's Bear? 2434(F)
Ayliffe, Alex (jt. author). *Let's Go, Anna!* 4152(F)
Not Again, Anna! 3634(F)
Ayo, Yvonne. *Africa*, 14899
Ayodo, Awuor. *Luo*, 14915
Ayres, Becky. *Salt Lake City*, 16597
Ayres, Katherine. *Silver Dollar Girl*, 9344(F)
Under Copp's Hill, 9515(F)
Voices at Whisper Bend, 9644(F)
Ayres, Pam. *Guess What?* 301(F)
Ayto, Russell. *Baby Bird*, 2041(F)
Ella and the Naughty Lion, 1078(F)
You'll Grow Soon, Alex, 5076(F)
Azarian, Mary. *Barn Cat*, 574(F)
Faraway Summer, 9560(F)
A Gardener's Alphabet, 6(F)
Snowflake Bentley, 12191
A Symphony for the Sheep, 4768(F)
Azevedo, Fernando. *Baby High, Baby Low*, 161(F)
Azuonye, Chukwuma. *Edo*, 15012

Babbitt, Natalie. *Bub; or, The Very Best Thing*, 967(F)
The Devil's Other Storybook, 7572(F)
The Devil's Storybook, 7573(F)
The Eyes of the Amaryllis, 7388(F)
Goody Hall, 6758(F)
Kneeknock Rise, 6759(F)
Ouch! 10883
Phoebe's Revolt, 4582(F)
The Search for Delicious, 7574(F)
Tuck Everlasting, 7575(F)
Baca, Maria. *Maya's Children*, 11393
Bacchin, Giorgio. *A Day with a Cheyenne*, 16003
A Day with a Chumash, 15986
A Day with a Miller, 9066(F)
A Day with a Mimbres, 15935
A Day with a Pueblo, 16013
Bach, Julie. *Bicycling*, 22152
Hillary Rodham Clinton, 13144
Bachem, Paul. *The Bushwhacker*, 9477(F)
Shadows in the Glasshouse, 16154(F)
The Wreck of the Ethie, 6906(F)
Back, Christine. *Bean and Plant*, 20076(F)
Chicken and Egg, 19302
Spider's Web, 19572
Tadpole and Frog, 18713
Backer, Marni. *Emma and the Night Dogs*, 2905(F)
The Lady in the Box, 5870(F)
A Little Bit of Rob, 3924(F)
Backstein, Karen. *The Blind Men and the Elephant*, 6192
Bacon, Katharine Jay. *Finn*, 6760(F)
Bacon, Paul. *Susanna of the Alamo*, 9294(F)
Teammates, 13371
Baddiel, Ivor. *Soccer*, 22285
Bader, Bonnie. *East Side Story*, 9516(F)
Bader, Philip. *France*, 15297
Iran, 15536
Badt, Karin Luisa. *Hair There and Everywhere*, 18177
Let's Go! 21279
The Mississippi Flood of 1993, 16531
On Your Feet! 21165
Pass the Bread! 20077
Baehr, Patricia. *Mouse in the House*, 4080(F)
School Isn't Fair, 5471(F)
Baer, Edith. *This Is the Way We Eat Our Lunch*, 3003(F)
This Is the Way We Go to School, 5546
Baer, Gene. *Thump, Thump, Rat-a-Tat-Tat*, 3004(F)
Bagert, Brod. *Chicken Socks*, 11529
Bagnold, Enid. *National Velvet*, 7153(F)

Bahr, Mary. *If Nathan Were Here*, 4901(F)
Bahti, Tom. *When Clay Sings*, 13942
Baicker-McKee, Carol. *Mapped Out!* 14361
Baier, Joan Foley. *Luvella's Promise*, 9517(F)
Bailer, Darice. *The Last Rail*, 9345(F)
Bailey, Carolyn Sherwin. *Miss Hickory*, 7576(F)
Bailey, Debbie. *Happy Birthday*, 5661(F)
Let's Pretend, 969(F)
Bailey, Gerald. *Talking to Animals*, 18891
Bailey, Jill. *Birds*, 19217
How Fish Swim, 19696
How Spiders Make Their Webs, 19573
Mosquito, 19424
Bailey, John. *The Young Fishing Enthusiast*, 22174
Bailey, LaWanda. *Miss Myrtle Frag, the Grammar Nag*, 14023
Bailey, Linda. *Adventures in Ancient Egypt*, 14606
Adventures in the Middle Ages, 7577(F)
How Can I Be a Detective If I Have to Baby-Sit? 6761(F)
How Come the Best Clues Are Always in the Garbage? 6762(F)
What's a Daring Detective Like Me Doing in the Doghouse? 6763(F)
When Addie Was Scared, 2908(F)
Bailey, Wendy. *When Addie Was Scared*, 2908(F)
Baillie, Marilyn. *Little Wonders*, 18868
Side by Side, 18606
Bailly, Sharon. *Pass It On!* 14066
Baines, John. *Japan*, 15116
Keeping the Air Clean, 16989
The United States, 15860
Bains, Rae. *Discovering Electricity*, 20883
Wonders of Rivers, 20511
Bair, Diane. *Bat Watching*, 19020
Butterfly Watching, 19540
Deer Watching, 19148
Eagle Watching, 19320
Sea Turtle Watching, 18778
Tide Pool Life Watching, 19853
Whale Watching, 19776
Baird, Audrey B. *Storm Coming!* 11939
Baiul, Oksana. *Oksana*, 13587
Baker, Alan. *Black and White Rabbit's ABC*, 7(F)
Brown Rabbit's Day, 154(F)
Brown Rabbit's Shape Book, 320(F)
Gray Rabbit's Odd One Out, 155(F)

Little Rabbits' First Time Book, 156(F)

Little Rabbits' First Word Book, 6193

White Rabbit's Color Book, 260(F)

Baker, Barbara. *Digby and Kate and the Beautiful Day*, 6194(F)

N-O Spells No! 6195(F)

Oh, Emma, 7389(F)

One Saturday Afternoon, 6196(F)

Third Grade Is Terrible, 5472(F)

Baker, Beth. *Sylvia Earle*, 13267

Baker, Chris. *Prosper's Mountain*, 10402(F)

Baker, Christopher W. *Let There Be Life! Animating with the Computer*, 21191

Scientific Visualization, 21192

Virtual Reality, 21193

Baker, David. *Danger on Apollo 13*, 20947

Factories in Space, 20948

Future Fighters, 21380

Peace in Space, 20949

Baker, Garin. *Can I Pray with My Eyes Open?* 17516

Baker, James W. *Illusions Illustrated*, 21776

Baker, Jeannie. *The Hidden Forest*, 7578(F)

The Story of Rosy Dock, 4583

Where the Forest Meets the Sea, 7579(F)

Window, 3005(F)

Baker, Joe. *I Am Wings*, 11564

Baker, Karen Lee. *Seneca*, 5129(F)

Baker, Keith. *Big Fat Hen*, 375(F)

Cat Tricks, 1780(F)

The Dove's Letter, 970(F)

Elephants Aloft, 956(F)

Hide and Snake, 4081(F)

The Magic Fan, 971(F)

Quack and Count, 376(F)

Sometimes, 6197(F)

Who Is the Beast? 1781(F)

Baker, Leslie. *Looking for Angels*, 3184(F)

Our Old House, 3464(F)

Paris Cat, 4584(F)

Rabbit and the Moon, 11319

A Song for Lena, 4681(F)

Baker, Sanna Anderson. *Grandpa Is a Flyer*, 21068

Mississippi Going North, 4382(F)

Baker, Valerie (jt. author). *Traveling in Grandma's Day*, 16493

Baker, Wendy. *Earth*, 18427

Electricity, 21239

Plants, 20225

Sound, 20931

Balan, Bruce. *Buoy*, 7580(F)

Balcavage, Dynise. *Ludwig van Beethoven*, 12320

Balcells, Jacqueline. *The Enchanted Raisin*, 10397(F)

Balcer, Bernadette. *Philadelphia*, 16653

Balchin, Judy. *Papier Mâché*, 21605

Baldwin, Guy. *Oklahoma*, 16532

Baldwin, Robert F. *Daily Life in Ancient and Modern Beijing*, 15053

New England Whaler, 16225

Baldwin-Ford, Pamela. *Tatterhood and Other Tales*, 10603

Bale, Andrew. *Bears*, 19047

Bale, Karen A. (jt. author). *Cave-In*, 9273(F)

Death Valley, 9359(F)

Fire, 9543(F)

Flood, 6825(F)

Hurricane, 9274(F)

Shipwreck, 9544(F)

Train Wreck, 6826(F)

Balestrino, Philip. *The Skeleton Inside You*, 18165

Balgassi, Haemi. *Peacebound Trains*, 8984(F)

Tae's Sonata, 7333(F)

Balian, Lorna. *Amelia's Nine Lives*, 5130(F)

Humbug Potion, 8(F)

Humbug Witch, 972(F)

Leprechauns Never Lie, 973(F)

A Sweetheart for Valentine, 6161(F)

Wilbur's Space Machine, 974(F)

Balit, Christina. *Atlantis*, 11459

Zoo in the Sky, 18549

Balkwill, Fran. *Cells Are Us*, 18048

Balkwill, Richard. *Clothes and Crafts in Ancient Egypt*, 14607

Ball, Jacqueline A. *The Leopard Son*, 19075

Ballard, Carol. *The Heart and Circulatory System*, 18086

How Do Our Ears Hear? 18131

How Do Our Eyes See? 18132

How Do We Feel and Touch? 18133

How Do We Move? 18166

How Do We Taste and Smell? 18134

How Do We Think? 18109

The Skeleton and Muscular System, 18167

The Stomach and Digestive System, 18095

Ballard, Robert D. *Exploring the Bismarck*, 14820

Exploring the Titanic, 19873

Ghost Liners, 21350

Ballard, Robin. *Good-bye, House*, 3006(F)

My Day, Your Day, 3007(F)

Tonight and Tomorrow, 631(F)

When I Am a Sister, 3514(F)

When We Get Home, 632(F)

Ballheimer, David (jt. author). *Olympics*, 22255

Ballinger, Erich. *Detective Dictionary*, 17062

Monster Manual, 21891

Balouch, Kristen. *The King and the Three Thieves*, 11181

Bancroft, Bronwyn. *Big Rain Coming*, 4657(F)

Bancroft, Catherine. *Felix's Hat*, 1782(F)

Bancroft, Henrietta. *Animals in Winter*, 18801

Bandon, Alexandra. *Asian Indian Americans*, 17542

Dominican Americans, 17543

West Indian Americans, 17544

Banfill, A. Scott. *Forest Child*, 1370(F)

Nicholi, 5808(F)

Bang, Molly. *Common Ground*, 4383(F)

David's Landing, 8793(F)

Delphine, 975(F)

Goose, 1783(F)

The Grey Lady and the Strawberry Snatcher, 907(F)

The Paper Crane, 976(F)

Ten, Nine, Eight, 377(F)

When Sophie Gets Angry — Really, Really Angry, 4902(F)

Wiley and the Hairy Man, 11324

Yellow Ball, 3008(F)

Bangura, Abdul Karim. *Kipsigis*, 14916

Banim, Lisa. *American Dreams*, 4585(F)

Drums at Saratoga, 9221(F)

The Hessian's Secret Diary, 9222(F)

A Spy in the King's Colony, 9223(F)

Banks, Jacqueline T. *Egg-Drop Blues*, 8875(F)

Banks, Kate. *Alphabet Soup*, 977(F)

And If the Moon Could Talk, 633(F)

Baboon, 5131(F)

The Bird, the Monkey, and the Snake in the Jungle, 1784(F)

Howie Bowles and Uncle Sam, 9774(F)

Howie Bowles, Secret Agent, 6764(F)

The Night Worker, 634(F)

Banks, Lynne Reid. *Alice-by-Accident*, 8397(F)

Angela and Diabola, 7581(F)

The Fairy Rebel, 10398(F)

Harry the Poisonous Centipede, 7582(F)

The Indian in the Cupboard, 7583(F)

The Key to the Indian, 7584(F)

The Mystery of the Cupboard, 7585(F)

The Return of the Indian, 7586(F)

The Secret of the Indian, 7587(F)

Banks, Merry. *Animals of the Night*, 5132

Banks, Sara H. *Abraham's Battle*, 9463(F)

A Net to Catch Time, 4586(F)
Under the Shadow of Wings, 9645(F)
Banks, Timothy. *No Pets Allowed*, 1471(F)
Bankston, John. *Alyssa Milano*, 12423
Bannan, Jan G. *Letting Off Steam*, 20296
Bannatyne-Cugnet, Jo. *A Prairie Year*, 20530
Bannerman, Helen. *The Story of Little Babaji*, 978(F)
Bany-Winters, Lisa. *On Stage*, 14320
Show Time! 14321
Banyai, Istvan. *Poems for Children Nowhere Near Old Enough to Vote*, 11915
Re-Zoom, 20909
Zoom, 908(F)
Baquedano, Elizabeth. *Aztec, Inca and Maya*, 15603
Baralt, Luis A. *Turkey*, 15260
Baranski, Joan Sullivan. *Round Is a Pancake*, 321(F)
Barasch, Lynne. *Old Friends*, 979(F)
Radio Rescue, 9518(F)
Rodney's Inside Story, 1785(F)
Barber, Antonia. *Catkin*, 10399
The Ghosts, 7588(F)
The Mousehole Cat, 1786(F)
Shoes of Satin, Ribbons of Silk, 14272
Barber, Antonia, reteller. *Apollo and Daphne*, 11460
Barber, Barbara E. *Allie's Basketball Dream*, 3009(F)
Saturday at The New You, 3010(F)
Barber, Ed. *Bricks*, 21116
Clay, 21530
Wood, 20205
Wool, 21170
Barber, James. *Presidents*, 12636
Barber, Nicola. *The Search for Gold*, 14544
The Search for Lost Cities, 14520
The Search for Sunken Treasure, 14521
Barber, Phyllis. *Legs*, 7154(F)
Barber, Tina. *Stories from the Caribbean*, 11418
Barbosa, Rogerio Andrade. *African Animal Tales*, 10650
Barbot, Daniel. *A Bicycle for Rosaura*, 1787(F)
Barbour, Karen. *I Have an Olive Tree*, 4609(F)
Little Nino's Pizzeria, 3515(F)
Marvelous Math, 11602
Street Music, 11524
Barden, Renardo. *Gangs*, 17063
Bare, Colleen S. *Never Kiss an Alligator!* 18698
Sammy, Dog Detective, 19939
Barfuss, Matto H. *My Cheetah Family*, 19076

Barger, Jan (jt. author). *Bible Stories for the Young*, 17281
Barghusen, Joan. *Daily Life in Ancient and Modern Rome*, 15371
Baringer, Rama Von. *Swim with Me*, 22308
Barish, Wendy (jt. author). *The French Resistance*, 14863
Barker, Amanda. *Windsurfing*, 22303
Barker, Chris. *The Complete Book of Children's Activities*, 21467
Barker, Henry. *Egyptian Gods and Goddesses*, 14608
Barker, Margot. *What Is Martin Luther King, Jr. Day?* 5610
Barker, Marjorie. *Magical Hands*, 5662(F)
Barkin, Carol. *The New Complete Babysitter's Handbook*, 16938
Barkin, Carol (jt. author). *How to Be School Smart*, 17614
How to Write Super School Reports, 14091
How to Write Terrific Book Reports, 14092
How to Write Your Best Book Report, 14093
Social Smarts, 17636
Barkley, James. *Sounder*, 7387(F)
Barlas, Bob. *Canada*, 15564
Jamaica, 15694
Welcome to Canada, 15565
Barlowe, Wayne D. *An Alphabet of Dinosaurs*, 14408
Barmeier, Jim. *The Brain*, 18110
Barnard, Bryn. *Gorillas*, 19010
Barner, Bob. *Bugs! Bugs! Bugs!* 19425
Dem Bones, 18168
Fish Wish, 5133(F)
To Everything, 17244
Which Way to the Revolution? 157(F)
Barnes, Emilie. *The Very Best Christmas Ever!* 21411
Barnes, Joyce Annette. *Promise Me the Moon*, 8559(F)
Barnes, Laura T. *Teeny Tiny Ernest*, 1788(F)
Barnes, Suzanne. *Cradles in the Trees*, 19222
Barnes, Trevor. *The Kingfisher Book of Religions*, 17164
Barnes-Murphy, Frances. *The Fables of Aesop*, 11055
Barnes-Murphy, Rowan. *One Hungry Cat*, 568(F)
Barnet, Nancy. *Where's the Fly?* 323(F)
Barnet, Russell. *Everest*, 22047
Barnett, Moneta. *Sister*, 7438(F)
Barnwell, Ysaye M. *No Mirrors in My Nana's House*, 3516(F)
Baroin, Catherine. *Tubu*, 14917
Baron, Alan. *The Magic Globe*, 14348

Red Fox and the Baby Bunnies, 1789(F)
The Red Fox Monster, 1790(F)
Baron, Nancy. *Getting Started in Calligraphy*, 21561
Barracca, Debra. *Maxi, the Hero*, 1791(F)
Barracca, Sal (jt. author). *Maxi, the Hero*, 1791(F)
Barraclough, John. *Mohandas Gandhi*, 13801
Mother Teresa, 13852
Barre, Michel. *Animal Senses*, 18802
How Animals Protect Themselves, 18895
Barrett, Angela. *Beware Beware*, 1239(F)
The Emperor's New Clothes, 10379(F)
Joan of Arc, 13813
Barrett, Anna Pearl. *Juneteenth*, 17340(F)
Barrett, Jalma. *Bobcat*, 19077
Cougar, 19078
Feral Cat, 19079
Lynx, 19080
Barrett, Jennifer. *The Seven Treasure Hunts*, 9795(F)
Barrett, John M. *Daniel Discovers Daniel*, 3517(F)
Barrett, Judith. *Animals Should Definitely Not Wear Clothing*, 4082(F)
Benjamin's 365 Birthdays, 5663(F)
Cloudy with a Chance of Meatballs, 980(F)
I Knew Two Who Said Moo, 378(F)
Pickles to Pittsburgh, 981(F)
Things That Are Most in the World, 982(F)
Barrett, Marvin. *Meet Thomas Jefferson*, 13047
Barrett, Mary Brigid. *Day Care Days*, 3518(F)
Leaf Baby, 3011(F)
The Man of the House at Huffington Row, 5750(F)
Snow Baby, 3012(F)
Barrett, Norman. *Hang Gliding*, 21973
Barrett, Peter. *Dinosaur Babies*, 5361
Moses the Kitten, 5258(F)
Only One Woof, 7220(F)
S-S-Snakes! 18774
Barrett, Robert. *Dust for Dinner*, 6700(F)
Barrett, Ron. *Animals Should Definitely Not Wear Clothing*, 4082(F)
Benjamin's 365 Birthdays, 5663(F)
Cloudy with a Chance of Meatballs, 980(F)
Pickles to Pittsburgh, 981(F)
Barrett, Tracy. *Anna of Byzantium*, 9027(F)
Growing Up in Colonial America, 16097

Kentucky, 16830

Virginia, 16831

Barrie, J. M. *Peter Pan*, 7589(F), 7590(F)

Barringer, Sarah. *Picnic Farm*, 3335(F)

Barrios, David. *Ballpoint Bananas and Other Jokes for Kids*, 21829

Barron, Rex. *The Big Bug Ball*, 2374(F)

Eggbert, 1527(F)

Fed Up! A Feast of Frazzled Foods, 9(F)

Barron, T. A. *Where Is Grandpa?* 4903(F)

Barrow, Ann. *The Final Cut*, 10278(F)

Full Court Fever, 10279(F)

Ghost Horse, 6681(F)

On the Line, 10280(F)

Barrow, Lloyd H. *Science Fair Projects Investigating Earthworms*, 19601

Barrows, Allison. *The Artist's Friends*, 3013(F)

Barry, Robert. *Mr. Willowby's Christmas Tree*, 5751(F)

Barsotti, Monica. *Why Are You Calling Me a Barbarian?* 14738

Barth, Edna. *Lilies, Rabbits and Painted Eggs*, 17433

Shamrocks, Harps and Shillelaghs, 17341

Bartholomew, Lois Thompson. *The White Dove*, 6765(F)

Bartlett, Alison. *Charlie's Checklist*, 2356(F)

A Cow, a Bee, a Cookie, and Me, 3221(F)

Growing Frogs, 5212(F)

Oliver's Fruit Salad, 3631(F)

Oliver's Vegetables, 4151(F)

Over in the Grasslands, 610(F)

Paddiwak and Cozy, 5186(F)

Ten Bright Eyes, 196(F)

Bartlett, Paula. *Chessie, the Travelin' Man*, 5269(F)

Bartlett, Susan. *Seal Island School*, 10026(F)

Barto, Renzo. *Happy Halloween! Things to Make and Do*, 21500

Plenty of Puppets to Make, 14307

Quick and Easy Cookbook, 21739

Science Secrets, 18351

Bartoletti, Susan Campbell. *A Coal Miner's Bride*, 9519(F)

Dancing with Dziadziu, 9520(F)

Growing Up in Coal Country, 16448

Kids on Strike! 16449

No Man's Land, 9464(F)

Barton, Byron. *Airplanes*, 21069

Airport, 5547(F)

Boats, 21351

Bones, Bones, Dinosaur Bones, 5134(F)

Building a House, 3014(F)

Dinosaurs, Dinosaurs, 14381

Gila Monsters Meet You at the Airport, 4314(F)

A Girl Called Al, 8292(F)

Good Morning, Chick, 11089

I Want to Be an Astronaut, 6766(F)

The Little Red Hen, 10946

Machines at Work, 21242

The Paper Airplane Book, 21796

Roman Numerals, 20626

The Snopp on the Sidewalk and Other Poems, 11809

The Three Bears, 10947

Trains, 21328

Truck Song, 5600(F)

Trucks, 21291

Wee Little Woman, 4083(F)

Where's the Bear? 5369(F)

Barton, Harriett. *Books and Libraries*, 13999

Geography from A to Z, 14344

Barton, Jill. *Baby Duck and the Bad Eyeglasses*, 2199(F)

The Caterpillow Fight, 2407(F)

The Happy Hedgehog Band, 2796(F)

In the Rain with Baby Duck, 2200(F)

Little Mo, 2799(F)

Off to School, Baby Duck! 2201(F)

What Baby Wants, 3861(F)

You're the Boss, Baby Duck! 2202(F)

Barton, Marylys. *Adventures of Monkey King*, 10752(F)

Bartone, Elisa. *American Too*, 3015(F)

Peppe the Lamplighter, 4587(F)

Baruffi, Andrea. *Math Riddles*, 21860(F)

Barwin, Gary. *The Magic Mustache*, 983(F)

Barwin, Steven. *Slam Dunk*, 10274(F)

Base, Graeme. *The Discovery of Dragons*, 9775(F)

The Eleventh Hour, 6767(F)

Jabberwocky, 11860

Lewis Carroll's Jabberwocky, 11855

The Sign of the Seahorse, 984(F)

The Worst Band in the Universe, 10150(F)

Bash, Barbara. *Desert Giant*, 20226

Phantom of the Prairie, 5315(F)

Urban Roosts, 19303

Baskin, Leonard. *Alberic the Wise*, 9049(F)

Animals That Ought to Be, 11901

Did You Say Ghosts? 1412(F)

Ten Times Better, 514(F)

Baskin-Salzberg, Anita. *Turtles*, 18779

Baskwill, Jane. *Somewhere*, 4384(F)

Basnight, Bobby. *Boating with Cap'n Bob and Matey*, 22261

Bass, Jules. *Herb, the Vegetarian Dragon*, 1792(F)

Bassede, Francine. *A Day with the Bellyflops*, 1793(F)

George Paints His House, 1794(F)

George's Store at the Shore, 379(F)

Bassett, Jeni. *The Biggest Pumpkin Ever*, 6022(F)

It's Groundhog Day! 5631(F)

Bassis, Volodymyr. *Ukraine*, 15405, 15406

Basso, Bill. *Bat Bones and Spider Stew*, 6041(F)

Ghost Dog, 7906(F)

Bastian, Lois Brunner. *Chipmunk Family*, 19192

Bastyra, Judy. *Fun Food*, 21412

Bat-Ami, Miriam. *Sea, Salt, and Air*, 4904(F)

Batchelor, Mary, ed. *Children's Prayers*, 17511

Bate, Lucy. *Little Rabbit's Loose Tooth*, 1795(F)

Bateman, Noel. *Egyptian Stories*, 10674

Bateman, Robert. *Safari*, 18607

Bateman, Teresa. *Leprechaun Gold*, 985(F)

The Ring of Truth, 9776(F)

Bates, Ivan. *All By Myself*, 1796(F)

Big Truck and Little Truck, 1041(F)

The Dark at the Top of the Stairs, 2408(F)

Just One! 2409(F)

Just You and Me, 2410(F)

Bates, Katherine L. *America the Beautiful*, 14232

Bates, Matthew. *What Is Martin Luther King, Jr. Day?* 5610

Bateson-Hill, Margaret. *Lao Lao of Dragon Mountain*, 986(F)

Shota and the Star Quilt, 3016(F)

Batman, Teresa. *Harp O' Gold*, 987(F)

Batt, Tanya. *The Fabrics of Fairytale*, 10529

Batten, John D. *Celtic Fairy Tales*, 11003

English Fairy Tales, 11004

Indian Fairy Tales, 10794

Batten, Mary. *Hungry Plants*, 20227

The Winking, Blinking Sea, 19623

Battle-Lavert, Gwendolyn. *The Music in Derrick's Heart*, 3519(F)

Off to School, 4905(F)

The Shaking Bag, 988(F)

Bauch, Patricia L. *Dance, Tanya*, 3017(F)

Bauer, Caroline Feller, ed. *Halloween*, 9708(F)

Rainy Day, 11530

Bauer, Louisa. *The Glass Mountain*, 10938

Bauer, Marion Dane. *Alison's Puppy*, 7155(F)

Bear's Hiccups, 6198(F)

Christmas in the Forest, 5752(F)

A Dream of Queens and Castles, 8252(F)

An Early Winter, 8876(F)

Ghost Eye, 7591(F)

Grandmother's Song, 3520(F)

If You Were Born a Kitten, 18869

Jason's Bears, 3018(F)

On My Honor, 6768(F)

Sleep, Little One, Sleep, 635(F)

A Taste of Smoke, 7592(F)

Touch the Moon, 7593(F)

Turtle Dreams, 6199(F)

When I Go Camping with Grandma, 4385(F)

A Writer's Story from Life to Fiction, 12506

Bauer, Steven. *A Cat of a Different Color*, 7594(F)

The Strange and Wonderful Tale of Robert McDoodle, 4084(F)

Bauld, Jane Scoggins. *We Need Librarians*, 17738

We Need Principals, 17739

Baum, Arline. *Opt*, 20910

Baum, Joseph. *Opt*, 20910

Baum, L. Frank. *The Marvelous Land of Oz*, 7595(F)

The Wizard of Oz, 989(F), 7596(F), 7597(F), 7598(F)

The Wonderful Wizard of Oz, 7599(F), 7600(F), 7601(F)

Baum, Roger S. *Dorothy of Oz*, 7602(F)

Baumbusch, Brigitte. *Animals Observed*, 13873

Figuring Figures, 13874

Baumgart, Klaus. *Don't Be Afraid, Tommy*, 4906(F)

Laura's Christmas Star, 5753(F)

Where Are You, Little Green Dragon? 1797(F)

Bausum, Ann. *Dragon Bones and Dinosaur Eggs*, 13226

Baviera, Rocco. *A Boy Called Slow*, 9146(F)

Dream Weaver, 4487(F)

First Painter, 1338(F)

Bawden, Nina. *Granny the Pag*, 7390(F)

Humbug, 7391(F)

Off the Road, 10151(F)

The Real Plato Jones, 8398(F)

Baxter, Nicola. *Parallel Universe*, 21862(F)

Baxter, Robert. *The Adventures of Eros and Psyche*, 11503

Jason and the Golden Fleece, 11496

Baxter, Sylvia. *Zulu Fireside Tales*, 10712

Bay, Ann Phillips. *The Kid's Guide to the Smithsonian*, 17104

Bayley, Nicola. *All for the Newborn Baby*, 5912(F)

Fun with Mrs. Thumb, 1394(F)

The Mousehole Cat, 1786(F)

Bayley, Thomas. *Sailing Ships*, 21376

Baylor, Byrd. *The Best Town in the World*, 3019(F)

The Desert Is Theirs, 15922

Desert Voices, 11772

Guess Who My Favorite Person Is, 3521(F)

Hawk, I'm Your Brother, 7156(F)

If You Are a Hunter of Fossils, 4386(F)

I'm in Charge of Celebrations, 10251(F)

Moon Song, 11211

One Small Blue Bead, 4588(F)

The Other Way to Listen, 302(F)

The Way to Start a Day, 11531

When Clay Sings, 13942

Baynes, Pauline. *The Lion, the Witch and the Wardrobe*, 7911(F)

Thanks Be to God, 17512

Baynton, Martin. *Why Do You Love Me?* 3522(F)

Bazilian, Barbara. *The Red Shoes*, 10400(F)

Beach, Milo Cleveland. *The Adventures of Rama*, 10787

Bealer, Alex W. *Only the Names Remain*, 15923

Beales, Valerie. *Emma and Freckles*, 7157(F)

Bean, Suzanne M. (jt. author). *Girls and Young Women Inventing*, 21040

Girls and Young Women Leading the Way, 17147

Beard, D. C. *The American Boys' Handy Book*, 21516

Beard, Darleen Bailey. *The Flimflam Man*, 9777(F)

The Pumpkin Man from Piney Creek, 5981(F)

Twister, 2909(F)

Bearden, Romare. *A Visit to the Country*, 5278(F)

Beardshaw, Rosalind. *Fran's Flower*, 3054(F)

Beaton, Clare. *How Big Is a Pig?* 158(F)

Masks, 21601

Mother Goose Remembers, 824(F)

One Moose, Twenty Mice, 380(F)

Zoe and Her Zebra, 10(F)

Beaton, Clare, comp. *Mother Goose Remembers*, 824(F)

Beaton, Margaret. *Senegal*, 15013

Beattie, Owen. *Buried in Ice*, 15566

Beatty, Patricia. *Who Comes with Cannons?* 9465(F)

Beatty, Richard. *Copper*, 20276

Phosphorous, 20277

Sulfur, 20278

Beaty, Dave. *Moths and Butterflies*, 19541

Waterfowl, 19308

Beaty, Sandy. *Champion of Arbor Day*, 13326

Beaude, Pierre-Marie. *The Book of Creation*, 17245

Beaudry, Jo. *Carla Goes to Court*, 17011

Bechard, Margaret. *My Mom Married the Principal*, 7392(F)

My Sister, My Science Report, 10027(F)

Bechtold, Lisze. *Buster, the Very Shy Dog*, 6200(F)

Beck, Andrea. *Elliot Bakes a Cake*, 5664(F)

Elliot's Bath, 990(F)

Elliot's Emergency, 991(F)

Beck, Ian. *Emily and the Golden Acorn*, 992(F)

Home Before Dark, 636(F)

Owl and the Pussycat, 11888

Read Me a Fairy Tale, 10435(F)

Beck, Scott. *Pepito the Brave*, 1798(F)

Becker, Bonny. *The Christmas Crocodile*, 5754(F)

Tickly Prickly, 303(F)

Beckett, Harry. *Lake Erie*, 15861

Lake Superior, 15862

Waterways to the Great Lakes, 15863

Beckett, Wendy. *A Child's Book of Prayer in Art*, 17513

The Duke and the Peasant, 13946

Becklake, Sue. *All About Space*, 18378

Space, Stars, Planets and Spacecraft, 20950

Becnel, Barbara Cottman (jt. author). *Gangs and Drugs*, 17090

Bedard, Michael. *The Clay Ladies*, 3020(F)

The Divide, 12515

Emily, 8253(F)

Glass Town, 14067

Sitting Ducks, 1799(F)

Beddows, Eric. *Joyful Noise*, 11781

Who Shrank My Grandmother's House? 11558

Bedell, Barbara. *How a Plant Grows*, 20239

A Koala Is Not a Bear! 19181

The Victorian Home, 13897

What Is a Primate? 19000

Bee, Peta. *Living with Asthma*, 17938

Beecroft, Simon. *Super Humans*, 17898

Beeke, Jemma. *The Brand New Creature*, 993(F)

The Rickety Barn Show, 1800(F)

Beeke, Tiphanie (jt. author). *The Brand New Creature*, 993(F)

Beeler, Selby B. *Throw Your Tooth on the Roof*, 10531

Been, Dwight. *Waking Upside Down*, 1230(F)

Begay, Shonto. *The Mud Pony*, 11223

The Native American Book of Knowledge, 16067

The Native American Book of Life, 16068

Begin, Maryjane. *Before I Go to Sleep*, 705(F)
The Porcupine Mouse, 2605(F)

Beh-Eger, Dorita (jt. author). *I Heal*, 17984

Beha, Philippe. *Biscuits in the Cupboard*, 11803

Behan, Brendan. *The King of Ireland's Son*, 10948

Behler, John L. *National Audubon Society First Field Guide*, 18678

Behr, Joyce. *Biggest Riddle Book in the World*, 21846

Behrens, June. *Fiesta!* 3523(F)
Gung Hay Fat Choy, 17342
Missions of the Central Coast, 16763

Behrman, Carol H. *The Ding Dong Clock*, 381(F)

Beier, Ellen. *The 18 Penny Goose*, 9254(F)
Mrs. Peachtree's Bicycle, 4316(F)
The Paint Brush Kid, 8574(F)
The Promise Quilt, 4804(F)
Remember the Ladies, 13124
Sybil Ludington's Midnight Ride, 16189

Beil, Karen M. *A Cake All for Me!* 825(F)
Fire in Their Eyes, 17806
Grandma According to Me, 3524(F)

Beirne, Barbara. *Children of the Ecuadorean Highlands*, 15723

Beisner, Monika. *Monika Beisner's Book of Riddles*, 21813

Belafonte, Harry. *Island in the Sun*, 15695

Bell, Anthea. *Jack in Luck*, 10884
Swan Lake, 14273

Bell, David C. *Scholastic Kid's Almanac for the 21st Century*, 14353

Bell, Elisabeth. *The Little Red Hen and the Ear of Wheat*, 10975

Bell, Hilari. *Songs of Power*, 10152(F)

Bell, Lili. *The Sea Maidens of Japan*, 4589(F)

Bell, Mike. *Roman Colosseum*, 14712

Bell, Neill. *The Book of Where*, 14330

Bell, Rachael. *Cows*, 20048
Ireland, 15336

Bell, Robert A. (jt. author). *My First Book About Space*, 18514

Bellairs, John. *The Curse of the Blue Figurine*, 7603(F)
The Ghost in the Mirror, 7604(F)
The Mansion in the Mist, 7605(F)

Beller, Susan P. *Billy Yank and Johnny Reb*, 16387
The Confederate Ladies of Richmond, 16388

Bellingham, Brenda. *Lilly's Good Deed*, 8254(F)

Belloc, Hilaire. *Jim, Who Ran Away from His Nurse, and Was Eaten by a Lion*, 9778(F)

Bellows, Cathy. *The Grizzly Sisters*, 1801(F)

Bellville, Cheryl Walsh. *The Airplane Book*, 21070
American Bison, 18925
Cranberries, 20079
Flying in a Hot Air Balloon, 21974
Rodeo, 21975

Below, Halina. *Chestnut Dreams*, 4387(F)

Belpré, Pura. *Firefly Summer*, 9130(F)

Belsky, Vera. *King Philip*, 12980

Belton, Sandra. *Ernestine and Amanda*, 8255(F), 8256(F)
McKendree, 8560(F)
May'naise Sandwiches and Sunshine Tea, 3979(F)
Members of the C.L.U.B, 8257(F)
Mysteries on Monroe Street, 8258(F)

Bemelmans, Ludwig. *Madeline*, 4590(F)
Madeline in America and Other Holiday Tales, 4591(F)

Ben-Ezer, Ehud. *Hosni the Dreamer*, 11182

Benagh, Jim. *Sports Great Herschel Walker*, 13636

Benchley, Nathaniel. *George the Drummer Boy*, 4592(F)
A Ghost Named Fred, 6201(F)
Oscar Otter, 6202(F)
Red Fox and His Canoe, 6203(F)
Sam the Minuteman, 4593(F)

Bendall-Brunello, John. *My Goose Betsy*, 5140(F)
When I Grow Bigger, 3080(F)
Yum, Yum, Yummy, 2804(F)

Bender, Michael. *All the World's a Stage*, 12591

Bender, Robert. *The A to Z Beastly Jamboree*, 382(F)
Barnyard Song, 2147(F)
The Chizzywink and the Alamagoozlum, 2260(F)
Lima Beans Would Be Illegal, 7606(F)
Swine Divine, 1938(F)

Bender, Robert, comp. *Lima Beans Would Be Illegal*, 7606(F)

Bendick, Jeanne. *Comets and Meteors*, 18505
Exploring an Ocean Tide Pool, 19854
Markets, 16932
Moons and Rings, 18506
The Planets, 18456
The Stars, 18538
The Sun, 18558
The Universe, 18379

Bendick, Robert (jt. author). *Markets*, 16932

Benedict, Kitty. *The Fall of the Bastille*, 15298
The Literary Crowd, 12157

Benedict, William. *The Big Red Bus*, 5573(F)
Winnie All Day Long, 5404(F)

Beneduce, Ann Keay. *Jack and the Beanstalk*, 10949
A Weekend with Winslow Homer, 12239

Bengamin, Alan. *Curious Critters*, 1802(F)

Benge, Geoff (jt. author). *George Washington Carver, What Do You See?* 13252

Benge, Janet. *George Washington Carver, What Do You See?* 13252

Benjamin, A. H. *It Could Have Been Worse*, 1803(F)

Benjamin, Anne. *Young Rosa Parks*, 12774

Benjamin, Carol Lea. *The Wicked Stepdog*, 8561(F)

Benjamin, Cynthia. *Footprints in the Sand*, 20400

Benjamin, Floella. *Skip Across the Ocean*, 826(F)

Benjamin, Saragail Katzman. *My Dog Ate It*, 10028(F)

Benner, Cheryl. *Dan's Pants*, 3176(F)

Bennett, Barbara J. *Stonewall Jackson*, 12906

Bennett, Cathereen L. *Will Rogers*, 12457

Bennett, Cherie. *Zink*, 8877(F)

Bennett, David. *One Cow Moo Moo!* 383(F)

Bennett, David, ed. *A Treasury of Witches and Wizards*, 7607(F)

Bennett, Evelyn. *Frederick Douglass and the War Against Slavery*, 12709

Bennett, Frank. *The Illustrated Rules of Basketball*, 22128

Bennett, Gary. *Rainy's Powwow*, 9173(F)

Bennett, Gay. *A Family in Sri Lanka*, 15147

Bennett, Jill. *Round the Christmas Tree*, 5790(F)

Bennett, Jill, comp. *Seaside Poems*, 11533

Bennett, Jill, ed. *A Cup of Starshine*, 11532
Spooky Poems, 11534

Bennett, Linda. *The Night Sky Book*, 18396

Bennett, Nneka. *Cherish Me!* 3452(F)
Gettin' Through Thursday, 3588(F)
Juma and the Honey Guide, 5135(F)
A Pony for Jeremiah, 9413(F)

Solo Girl, 6577(F)
You Are My Perfect Baby, 3453(F)
Bennett, Olivia. *A Family in Egypt*, 15496
Bennett, Paul. *Escaping from Enemies*, 18896
Bennett, William J., ed. *The Book of Virtues for Young People*, 10252
The Children's Book of Virtues, 3022
Benson, Kathleen (jt. author). *African Beginnings*, 14907
Bound for America, 16251
Carter G. Woodson, 12822
Count Your Way Through Brazil, 15740
Count Your Way Through France, 15309
Count Your Way Through Greece, 15385
Count Your Way Through Ireland, 15350
Space Challenger, 12079
Benson, Laura Lee. *Washington, D.C.*, 16654
Benson, Michael. *Crashes and Collisions*, 22079
Gloria Estefan, 12380
Benson, Patrick. *The Book of Hob Stories*, 7956(F)
Let the Lynx Come In, 1357(F)
The Little Boat, 3202(F)
The Minpins, 1095(F)
Owl Babies, 2802(F)
The Sea-Thing Child, 1241(F)
The Wind in the Willows, 7754(F)
Bentley, Judith. *"Dear Friend,"* 16226
Bentley, Nancy. *Putting On a Play*, 12011
Writing Mysteries, Movies, Monster Stories, and More, 14068
The Young Producer's Video Book, 21265
Bentley, Nancy (jt. author). *The Young Journalist's Book*, 14086
Benton, Michael. *Dinosaur and Other Prehistoric Animal Factfinder*, 14382
Dinosaurs, 14383
Bercaw, Edna Coe. *Halmoni's Day*, 5473(F)
Berelson, Howard. *Viva Mexico!* 13818
Berendes, Mary. *Australia*, 15224
Beluga Whales, 19777
Deer, 19149
Mexico, 15604
Piranhas, 19697
Spain, 15471
Berends, Polly. *The Case of the Elevator Duck*, 7158(F)
Berenstain, Jan. *Bears in the Night*, 6204(F)
The Berenstain Bears in the Dark, 1804(F)

Inside, Outside, Upside Down, 159(F)
Berenstain, Jan (jt. author). *Bears in the Night*, 6204(F)
The Berenstain Bears in the Dark, 1804(F)
Inside, Outside, Upside Down, 159(F)
Berenstain, Stan. *Bears in the Night*, 6204(F)
The Berenstain Bears in the Dark, 1804(F)
Inside, Outside, Upside Down, 159(F)
Berenzy, Alix. *A Frog Prince*, 10401(F)
Home at Last, 18848
Into the Sea, 18783
Touch the Moon, 7593(F)
Beres, Cynthia Breslin. *Longhouse*, 15924
Beres, Samantha. *101 Things Every Kid Should Know About Science*, 18275
Berg, Barry. *Opening Moves*, 22170
Berg, Cami. *D Is for Dolphin*, 11(F)
Berg, Elizabeth. *Ethiopia*, 14918
Nigeria, 15014
USA, 15864, 15865
Berg, Elizabeth (jt. author). *Welcome to the USA*, 15878
Berg, Lois Anne. *An Eritrean Family*, 17545
Berger, Barbara Helen. *Angels on a Pin*, 995(F)
The Donkey's Dream, 5755(F)
Gwinna, 7608(F)
The Jewel Heart, 996(F)
A Lot of Otters, 997(F)
Berger, Gilda. *Celebrate! Stories of the Jewish Holidays*, 17451
Berger, Gilda (jt. author). *Can It Rain Cats and Dogs? Questions and Answers About Weather*, 20752
Did Dinosaurs Live in Your Backyard? Questions And Answers About Dinosaurs, 14385
Do Stars Have Points? 18380
Do Tornadoes Really Twist? 20682
Do Whales Have Belly Buttons? Questions and Answers About Whales and Dolphins, 19625
How Do Flies Walk Upside Down? Questions and Answers About Insects, 19429
How's the Weather? 20753
Mummies of the Pharaohs, 14609
Round and Round the Money Goes, 16918
Screech! 19021
Telephones, Televisions and Toilets, 21243
Water, Water Everywhere, 20726
What Do Animals Do in Winter? 18902
Where Are the Stars During the Day? 18539

Where Did Your Family Come From? 17546
Where Does the Mail Go? 17105
The Whole World in Your Hands, 14362
Why Do Volcanoes Blow Their Tops? 20333
Why Don't Haircuts Hurt? 18050
Berger, Melvin. *Buzz! A Book About Insects*, 19426
Can It Rain Cats and Dogs? Questions and Answers About Weather, 20752
Chirping Crickets, 19427
Chomp! 19751
Did Dinosaurs Live in Your Backyard? Questions And Answers About Dinosaurs, 14385
Discovering Jupiter, 18457
Dive! A Book of Deep-Sea Creatures, 19624
Do Stars Have Points? 18380
Do Tornadoes Really Twist? 20682
Do Whales Have Belly Buttons? Questions and Answers About Whales and Dolphins, 19625
Germs Make Me Sick! 17939
Growl! 19038
How Do Flies Walk Upside Down? Questions and Answers About Insects, 19429
How's the Weather? 20753
Killer Bugs, 19428
Look Out for Turtles! 18780
Mighty Dinosaurs, 14384
Mummies of the Pharaohs, 14609
Oil Spill! 16990
Round and Round the Money Goes, 16918
Screech! 19021
The Story of Folk Music, 14140
Switch On, Switch Off, 20884
Telephones, Televisions and Toilets, 21243
Water, Water Everywhere, 20726
What Do Animals Do in Winter? 18902
Where Are the Stars During the Day? 18539
Where Did Your Family Come From? 17546
Where Does the Mail Go? 17105
The Whole World in Your Hands, 14362
Why Do Volcanoes Blow Their Tops? 20333
Why Don't Haircuts Hurt? 18050
Why I Sneeze, Shiver, Hiccup, and Yawn, 18049
The World of Dance, 14274
Berger, Phil. *Michael Jordan*, 13536
Berger, Terry. *I Have Feelings*, 17604
Bergherr, Mary. *Earth Day*, 5636
Bergin, Mark. *An Egyptian Pyramid*, 14649
Inca Town, 15759

Magellan, 12141

Marco Polo, 12148

A Medieval Castle, 14777

A World War Two Submarine, 21390

Bergin, Mark (jt. author). *A 16th Century Galleon*, 15477

Bergren, Kris (jt. author). *Ishi*, 15939

Bergsma, Jody. *The Right Touch*, 18264

Bergum, Constance R. *Grandma Buffalo, May and Me*, 3908(F)

The Sunsets of Miss Olivia Wiggins, 3763(F)

Berkeley, Jon. *Scarlette Beane*, 1663(F)

Berkeley, Laura. *The Seeds of Peace*, 998(F)

The Spirit of the Maasai Man, 999(F)

Berkes, Marianne. *Marsh Music*, 1805(F)

Berleth, Richard. *Mary Patten's Voyage*, 9261(F)

Samuel's Choice, 9224(F)

Berliner, Don. *Aviation*, 21071

Before the Wright Brothers, 21072

Living in Space, 20951

Berliner, Franz. *Wildebeest*, 1806(F)

Berlow, Leonard (jt. author). *You're Too Sweet*, 17951

Berman, Claire. *"What Am I Doing in a Step-Family?"* 17642

Berman, Ruth. *American Bison*, 18925

Ants, 19506

Buzzing Rattlesnakes, 18754

Climbing Tree Frogs, 18714

Fishing Bears, 19039

Peacocks, 19218

Spinning Spiders, 19574

Squeaking Bats, 19022

Watchful Wolves, 19117

Bernard, Robin. *Juma and the Honey Guide*, 5135(F)

Bernard, Virginia. *Eliza Down Under*, 8925(F)

Bernardin, James. *Big Men, Big Country*, 11389

Casey Jones's Fireman, 11336

Little Folk, 10624

Bernards, Neal. *Elections*, 17094

The Palestinian Conflict, 15537

Population, 17009

Bernards, Neal (jt. author). *Prisons*, 17086

Bernhard, Durga. *Eagles*, 19321

Earth, Sky, Wet, Dry, 160(F)

Happy New Year! 17343

Prairie Dogs, 19193

A Ride on Mother's Back, 3525

Trouble, 10682

The Way of the Willow Branch, 3023(F)

Bernhard, Emery. *Eagles*, 19321

Happy New Year! 17343

Prairie Dogs, 19193

A Ride on Mother's Back, 3525

The Way of the Willow Branch, 3023(F)

Bernier-Grand, Carmen T. *In the Shade of the Nispero Tree*, 7334(F)

Poet and Politician of Puerto Rico, 12935

Bernos de Gasztold, Carmen. *Prayers from the Ark*, 17514

Bernstein, Daryl. *Better Than a Lemonade Stand!* 16939

Bernstein, Margery. *My Brother, the Pest*, 6205(F)

Bernstein, Ross. *Gary Payton*, 13562

Bernstein, Sharon C. *A Family That Fights*, 4907(F)

Bernstein, Zena. *Mrs. Frisby and the Rats of NIMH*, 7999(F)

Berry, Carrie. *A Confederate Girl*, 9466

Berry, Holly. *Arctic Fives Arrive*, 555(F)

Market Day, 4610(F)

Old MacDonald Had a Farm, 14172

Roughing It on the Oregon Trail, 8123(F)

Berry, James. *Don't Leave an Elephant to Go and Chase a Bird*, 10651

First Palm Trees, 10652

Isn't My Name Magical? Sister and Brother Poems, 11748

Rough Sketch Beginning, 11940

Berry, James, ed. *Classic Poems to Read Aloud*, 11535

Bertrand, Diane Gonzales. *Alicia's Treasure*, 7393(F)

Family, Familia, 3526(F)

Sip, Slurp, Soup, Soup/Caldo, Caldo, Caldo, 3527(F)

Bertrand, Philippe. *First Times*, 3036(F)

Beshore, George. *Science in Ancient China*, 15054

Science in Early Islamic Culture, 15486

Beskow, Elsa. *Pelle's New Suit*, 4594(F)

Bess, Clayton. *The Truth About the Moon*, 4388(F)

Best, Alyse. *Miss Best's Etiquette for Young People*, 17634

Best, Cari. *Getting Used to Harry*, 4908(F)

Last Licks, 3024(F)

Montezuma's Revenge, 1807(F)

Red Light, Green Light, Mama and Me, 3025(F)

Three Cheers for Catherine the Great! 5665(F)

Betancourt, Jeanne. *My Name Is Brain/Brian*, 8878(F)

Puppy Love, 8399(F)

Betz, Adrienne, comp. *Scholastic Treasury of Quotations for Children*, 14069

Bevan, Finn. *Beneath the Earth*, 10532

Cities of Splendor, 10533

Bial, Raymond. *Amish Home*, 17165

The Apache, 15925

Cajun Home, 16832

The Cheyenne, 15926

The Comanche, 15927

Corn Belt Harvest, 20170

The Fresh Grave, 7609(F)

Frontier Home, 16289

The Ghost of Honeymoon Creek, 7610(F)

Ghost Towns of the American West, 16290

The Haida, 15928

A Handful of Dirt, 18608

The Huron, 15929

Mist over the Mountains, 16833

The Ojibwe, 15930

One-Room School, 15866

Portrait of a Farm Family, 20049

The Pueblo, 15931

The Seminole, 15932

Shaker Home, 17166

The Strength of These Arms, 16227

The Underground Railroad, 16228

Where Lincoln Walked, 13064

With Needle and Thread, 21641

Bianchi, John. *Is the Spaghetti Ready?* 6322(F)

The Lab Rats of Doctor Eclair, 1808(F)

New at the Zoo, 6323(F)

Troubles with Bubbles, 6324(F)

Welcome Back to Pokeweed Public School, 5474(F)

Biard, Philippe. *Pyramids*, 14621

Bible. *And It Was Good*, 17246

The Ark, 17247

Give Us This Day, 17515

The Lord Is My Shepherd, 17248

The Nativity, 17409

Bickel, Cindy (jt. author). *Tiger Math*, 20027

Biedrzycki, David. *Dory Story*, 4504(F)

The Freshwater Alphabet Book, 19642

Underwater Counting, 549(F)

Biel, Jackie. *Video*, 21266

Biel, Timothy. *Charlemagne*, 13767

Bierhorst, John. *Doctor Coyote*, 11394

Lightning Inside You and Other Native American Riddles, 21814

The Woman Who Fell from the Sky, 11214

Bierhorst, John, ed. *The Dancing Fox*, 11204

The Deetkatoo, 11212

The Monkey's Haircut, 11395

Bierhorst, John, sel. *On the Road of Stars*, 11213

Bierman, Carol. *Journey to Ellis Island*, 17547

Biesele, Megan. *San*, 14965

Biesiot, Elizabeth. *Natural Treasures Field Guide for Kids*, 18577

Biesty, Stephen. *Castles*, 14789

Stephen Biesty's Cross-Sections Man-of-War, 21373

Stephen Biesty's Incredible Explosions, 21147

Stephen Biesty's Incredible Pop-Up Cross-Sections, 21244

Biet, Pascal. *Mice Make Trouble*, 1003(F)

Wolf! 1818(F)

Bigham, Julia. *The 60s*, 13875

Bileck, Marvin. *Rain Makes Applesauce*, 4302(F)

Billin-Frye, Paige. *A Box Can Be Many Things*, 6589(F)

Clean-Sweep Campers, 20593

Flower Girl, 6380(F)

Lulu's Lemonade, 419(F)

This Is the Pumpkin, 6027(F)

This Is the Turkey, 6148(F)

Billings, Henry. *Antarctica*, 15796

Billings, John. *My Pet Crocodile and Other Slightly Outrageous Verse*, 11856

Billingsley, Franny. *The Folk Keeper*, 7611(F)

Well Wished, 7612(F)

Binch, Caroline. *Boundless Grace*, 4683(F)

Down by the River, 846

Newborn, 3687(F)

Starring Grace, 8302(F)

Binder, Sibylle Luise. *Riding for Beginners*, 22198

Bindon, John. *Air Scare*, 17001

Nature in Danger, 19407

Power Failure, 20846

Water Squeeze, 20743

Bines, Gary. *The Usborne Complete Book of Astronomy and Space*, 18400

The Usborne Complete Book of the Microscope, 19809

Bing, Christopher. *Ernest L. Thayer's Casey at the Bat*, 12007

Bingham, Caroline. *Big Book of Airplanes*, 21073

Big Book of Rescue Vehicles, 21292

Big Rig, 21293

Fire Truck, 21294

Monster Machines, 21295

Race Car, 21296

Bingham, Mindy. *Minou*, 1809(F)

Bini, Renata, reteller. *A World Treasury of Myths, Legends, and Folktales*, 10534

Biondi, Janet. *D Is for Dolphin*, 11(F)

Birch, Beverley. *Marie Curie*, 13260

Shakespeare's Stories, 12044, 12045, 12046

Birch, David. *The King's Chessboard*, 10788

Birch, Linda. *When the People Are Away*, 2270(F)

Birchall, Mark. *Be Quiet, Parrot!* 6719(F)

Rabbit's Wooly Sweater, 1810(F)

The Wrong Overcoat, 2554(F)

Bircher, William. *A Civil War Drummer Boy*, 9467

Birchmore, Daniel A. *The White Curtain*, 1000(F)

Bird, Bettina (jt. author). *Whales*, 19799

Bird, E. J. *The Rainmakers*, 9145(F)

Birdseye, Debbie H. *Under Our Skin*, 17548

What I Believe, 17167

Birdseye, Debbie H. (jt. author). *She'll Be Comin' Round the Mountain*, 4085(F)

Birdseye, Tom. *Airmail to the Moon*, 3026(F)

The Eye of the Stone, 7613(F)

I'm Going to Be Famous, 9779(F)

Just Call Me Stupid, 8400(F)

A Kids' Guide to Building Forts, 21413

A Regular Flood of Mishap, 3528(F)

She'll Be Comin' Round the Mountain, 4085(F)

Soap! Soap! Don't Forget the Soap! 11325

Tarantula Shoes, 8562(F)

Tucker, 8401(F)

Waiting for Baby, 3529(F)

Birdseye, Tom (jt. author). *Under Our Skin*, 17548

What I Believe, 17167

Birkbeck, Paul. *The Emperor and the Nightingale*, 10517(F)

Birmingham, Christian. *A Baby for Grace*, 3941(F)

The Sea of Tranquillity, 4673(F)

The Silver Swan, 5351(F)

The Windhover, 5143(F)

Wombat Goes Walkabout, 2510(F)

Birney, Betty G. *Pie's in the Oven*, 4086(F)

Tyrannosaurus Tex, 1811(F)

Bischoff, Ilse. *Gigi*, 7731(F)

Bishop, Adela. *The Easter Wolf*, 5963(F)

Bishop, Claire Huchet. *Five Chinese Brothers*, 4087(F)

Twenty and Ten, 9646(F)

Bishop, Gavin. *Little Rabbit and the Sea*, 1812(F)

Stay Awake, Bear! 1813(F)

The Video Shop Sparrow, 2922(F)

Bishop, Nic. *Digging for Bird-Dinosaurs*, 14386

Red-Eyed Tree Frog, 18717

The Secrets of Animal Flight, 19220

Bishop, Roma. *My First Pop-up Book of Prehistoric Animals*, 14387

Bishop, Rudine Sims, comp. *Wonders*, 11941

Bisignano, Alphonse. *Cooking the Italian Way*, 21676

Bisson, Terry (jt. author). *Be First in the Universe*, 10241(F)

Bittinger, Ned. *The Blue and the Gray*, 9469(F)

The Matzah That Papa Brought Home, 6094(F)

Rocking Horse Christmas, 3350(F)

Bittner, Wolfgang. *Wake Up, Grizzly!* 3530(F)

Bizley, Kirk. *Inline Skating*, 21976

Mountain Biking, 22153

Soccer, 22286

Swimming, 22305

Bjarkman, Peter C. *Duke Snider*, 13503

Roberto Clemente, 13442

Sports Great Dominique Wilkins, 13581

Sports Great Scottie Pippen, 13563

Top 10 Baseball Base Stealers, 13361

Top 10 Basketball Slam Dunkers, 13362

Björk, Christina. *Elliot's Extraordinary Cookbook*, 21677

Linnea in Monet's Garden, 13876(F)

Linnea's Almanac, 18578

Linnea's Windowsill Garden, 21759

Vendela in Venice, 9028(F)

Bjorkland, Ruth. *Kansas*, 16533

Bjorkman, Steve. *Aliens for Lunch*, 6330(F)

Germs! Germs! Germs! 17971

Heart to Heart, 2679(F)

Invisible Stanley, 1015(F)

Lots of Lice, 17972

Seeds, 4043(F)

Thanksgiving Is . . ., 6133(F)

This Is the Way We Eat Our Lunch, 3003(F)

This Is the Way We Go to School, 5546

Black, Sheila. *Sitting Bull and the Battle of the Little Bighorn*, 12995

Black, Sonia. *Hanging Out with Mom*, 6206(F)

Black, Wallace B. *America Prepares for War*, 14821

Bataan and Corregidor, 14822

Battle of Britain, 14823

Battle of the Atlantic, 14824

Battle of the Bulge, 14825

Blockade Runners and Ironclads, 16389

Bombing Fortress Europe, 14826

D-Day, 14827
Desert Warfare, 14828
Flattops at War, 14829
Guadalcanal, 14830
Hiroshima and the Atomic Bomb, 14831
Invasion of Italy, 14832
Island Hopping in the Pacific, 14833
Iwo Jima and Okinawa, 14834
Jungle Warfare, 14835
Pearl Harbor! 14836
Russia at War, 14837
Slaves to Soldiers, 16390
Victory in Europe, 14838
War Behind the Lines, 14839
Blackall, Bernie. *Soccer*, 22287
Tennis, 22311
Blacklock, Dyan. *Pankration*, 9029(F)
Blackman, Cally. *The 20s and 30s*, 16450
Blackstone, Margaret. *Girl Stuff*, 18249
This Is Figure Skating, 22217
This Is Soccer, 22288
Blackstone, Stella. *Baby High, Baby Low*, 161(F)
Baby Rock, Baby Roll, 3027(F)
Bear About Town, 1814(F)
Bear in a Square, 322(F)
Bear on a Bike, 6207(F)
Bear's Busy Family, 1815(F)
Can You See the Red Balloon? 162(F)
Grandma Went to Market, 384(F)
Making Minestrone, 3028(F)
You and Me, 163(F)
Blackwood, Gary L. *Alien Astronauts*, 20952
Extraordinary Events and Oddball Occurrences, 21892
Fateful Forebodings, 21893
Life on the Oregon Trail, 16291
Long-Ago Lives, 21894
Moonshine, 9521(F)
Paranormal Powers, 21895
The Shakespeare Stealer, 9079(F)
Shakespeare's Scribe, 9080(F)
Blackwood, Mary. *Derek the Knitting Dinosaur*, 1816(F)
Blades, Ann. *Back to the Cabin*, 2910(F)
A Boy of Tache, 6769(F)
A Dog Came, Too, 4760
Mary of Mile 18, 8563(F)
Pettranella, 4869(F)
Pond Seasons, 11936
A Salmon for Simon, 2824(F)
Too Small, 11141
Bladholm, Cheri. *Small Gifts in God's Hands*, 17300
Blain, Diane. *The Boxcar Children Cookbook*, 21678
Blair, Bonnie. *A Winning Edge*, 13679

Blair, Margaret Whitman. *Brothers at War*, 7614(F)
Blake, Arthur. *The Scopes Trial*, 16451
Blake, Claire. *The Paper Chain*, 17940
Blake, Quentin. *All Join In*, 11536
The Best of Michael Rosen, 11682
A Christmas Carol, 9720(F)
Clown, 909(F)
Dick King-Smith's Alphabeasts, 73(F)
The Enormous Crocodile, 1995(F)
George's Marvelous Medicine, 7695(F)
Matilda, 10045(F)
Mrs. Armitage and the Big Wave, 4088(F)
Of Quarks, Quasars and Other Quirks, 11857
Roald Dahl's Revolting Recipes, 21697
The Seven Voyages of Sinbad the Sailor, 11202
The Witches, 7698(F)
Wizzil, 1594(F)
Blake, Robert J. *Akiak*, 5136(F)
The Angel of Mill Street, 5949(F)
Dog, 5137(F)
Fledgling, 5138(F)
Mississippi Mud, 11726
The Perfect Spot, 3531(F)
Riptide, 5448(F)
Spray, 1001(F)
Yudonsi, 3029(F)
Blakeman, Sarah. *Elephant*, 19160
Blakemore, Sally. *Extremely Weird Endangered Species*, 19402
Blakemore, Sally (jt. author). *I Really Want a Dog*, 5142(F)
Blakeslee, Ann R. *A Different Kind of Hero*, 9346(F)
Summer Battles, 9522(F)
Blanc, Esther S. *Berchick*, 5139(F)
Bland, Celia. *Harriet Beecher Stowe*, 12603
Blaney, Martine. *Jungle Animals*, 5393
Blankley, Kathy. *The King and the Tortoise*, 10701
Blanquet, Claire-Helene. *Miró*, 13877
Blashfield, Jean F. *Arizona*, 16598
The California Gold Rush, 16292
Colorado, 16599
Delaware, 16655
England, 15337
Horse Soldiers, 16391
Italy, 15372
Mines and Minie Balls, 16392
Norway, 15438
The Oregon Trail, 16293
Virginia, 16834
Wisconsin, 16534
Women at the Front, 16393
Blashfield, Jean F. (jt. author). *America Prepares for War*, 14821

Bataan and Corregidor, 14822
Battle of Britain, 14823
Battle of the Atlantic, 14824
Battle of the Bulge, 14825
Bombing Fortress Europe, 14826
D-Day, 14827
Desert Warfare, 14828
Flattops at War, 14829
Guadalcanal, 14830
Hiroshima and the Atomic Bomb, 14831
Invasion of Italy, 14832
Island Hopping in the Pacific, 14833
Iwo Jima and Okinawa, 14834
Jungle Warfare, 14835
Pearl Harbor! 14836
Russia at War, 14837
Victory in Europe, 14838
War Behind the Lines, 14839
Blassingame, Wyatt. *The Look-It-Up Book of Presidents*, 12637
Blatchford, Claire H. *Going with the Flow*, 8879(F)
Nick's Mission, 6770(F)
Nick's Secret, 6771(F)
Blauer, Ettagale. *Ghana*, 15015
Madagascar, 14966
Morocco, 14956
South Africa, 14967
Swaziland, 14968
Uganda, 14919
Blaustein, Daniel. *The Everglades and the Gulf Coast*, 20364
Bledsoe, Lucy Jane. *The Big Bike Race*, 10275(F)
Tracks in the Snow, 6772(F)
Bledsoe, Sara. *Colorado*, 16600
Blegel, Michael D. *Jesse Owens*, 13665
Langston Hughes, 12552
Paul Robeson, 12453
Satchel Paige, 13476
Sojourner Truth, 12792
Blegvad, Erik. *Anna Banana and Me*, 3980(F)
Around My Room, 11916
First Friends, 6208(F)
The Gammage Cup, 7858(F)
Hurry, Hurry, Mary Dear, 3535(F)
I Like to Be Little, 3499(F)
Little Little Sister, 10412(F)
Riddle Road, 21853
The Tenth Good Thing About Barney, 5100(F)
With One White Wing, 21854
Blegvad, Lenore. *Anna Banana and Me*, 3980(F)
First Friends, 6208(F)
Once Upon a Time and Grandma, 3532(F)
A Sound of Leaves, 4909(F)
Bleifeld, Maurice. *Experimenting with a Microscope*, 18300
Bliss, Corinne D. *Electra and the Charlotte Russe*, 9780(F)
The Littlest Matryoshka, 1002(F)

Matthew's Meadow, 7615(F)
Snow Day, 6209(F)
Bliss, Helen. *Models*, 21793
Paper, 21606
Blitz, Bruce. *Blitz*, 21562
Blizzard, Gladys S. *Come Look with Me*, 13878, 13879, 13880
Blobaum, Cindy. *Geology Rocks!* 20297
Blocksma, Mary. *Yoo Hoo, Moon!* 6210(F)
Blondon, Herve. *Waiting to Sing*, 3743(F)
The Well of the Wind, 7738(F)
Blood, Charles L. *The Goat in the Rug*, 1817(F)
Bloom, Becky. *Mice Make Trouble*, 1003(F)
Wolf! 1818(F)
Bloom, Lloyd. *Arthur, for the Very First Time*, 9933(F)
Ghost Catcher, 7785(F)
The Green Book, 10244(F)
Like Jake and Me, 3742(F)
Poems for Jewish Holidays, 11837
Thanksgiving with Me, 6159(F)
When Uncle Took the Fiddle, 3181(F)
Bloom, Suzanne. *The Bus for Us*, 4089(F)
Blos, Joan W. *Bedtime!* 637(F)
Brooklyn Doesn't Rhyme, 9523(F)
The Days Before Now, 12508
A Gathering of Days, 9262(F)
The Grandpa Days, 3533(F)
Hello, Shoes! 164(F)
The Heroine of the Titanic, 4595(F)
Bloyd, Sunni. *Animal Rights*, 18609
Blue, Rose. *Chris Rock*, 12455
Colin Powell, 12949
Good Yontif, 910(F)
Madeleine Albright, 12838
Me and Einstein, 8880(F)
People of Peace, 13725
The White House Kids, 12638
Blue, Rose (jt. author). *Belle Starr and the Wild West*, 12965
Christa McAuliffe, 12137
John Muir, 13329
Blum, Raymond. *Math Tricks, Puzzles and Games*, 20611
Mathamusements, 20612
Blumberg, Rhoda. *Bloomers!* 4596
Commodore Perry in the Land of the Shogun, 15117
Jumbo, 19161
Shipwrecked! The True Adventures of a Japanese Boy, 13833
What's the Deal? Jefferson, Napoleon, and the Louisiana Purchase, 16229
Blume, Judy. *Are You There God? It's Me, Margaret*, 8564(F)
Blubber, 8565(F)
Deenie, 8881(F)
Freckle Juice, 9781(F)
Fudge-a-Mania, 9782(F)

Iggie's House, 7335(F)
It's Not the End of the World, 8402(F)
Otherwise Known as Sheila the Great, 8566(F)
The Pain and the Great One, 3534(F)
Starring Sally J. Freedman as Herself, 9783(F)
Tales of a Fourth Grade Nothing, 9784(F)
Then Again, Maybe I Won't, 8567(F)
Tiger Eyes, 8568(F)
Blumenthal, Deborah. *The Chocolate-Covered-Cookie Tantrum*, 4910(F)
Blundell, Kim. *First Book of the Keyboard*, 14226
Bluthenthal, Diana C. *Hot Fudge Hero*, 6228(F)
The La-di-da Hare, 11895
Nana Hannah's Piano, 3541(F)
The Youngest Fairy Godmother Ever, 1321(F)
Bluthenthal, Diana Cain. *Matilda the Moocher*, 3981(F)
Bly, Nellie (jt. author). *Nellie Bly's Book*, 13139
Blythe, Gary. *This Is the Star*, 5806(F)
The Whales' Song, 1568(F)
Bo, Ben. *The Edge*, 10277(F)
Board, Perry. *Thomas's Sheep and the Great Geography Test*, 76(F)
Boardman, Bob. *Red Hot Peppers*, 21977
Boardman, Diane. *Red Hot Peppers*, 21977
Boast, Clare. *France*, 15299
Russia, 15408
Boateng, Faustine Ama. *Asante*, 15016
Boatwright, Phil. *Nothing Here But Trees*, 4860(F)
Bobak, Cathy. *As the Roadrunner Runs*, 1227(F)
The Big Monkey Mix-up, 2943(F)
Burton and the Giggle Machine, 9870(F)
Bochak, Grayce. *The Long Silk Strand*, 1687(F)
Bock, Hal. *David Robinson*, 13568
Bock, William Sauts. *Indians of the Northeast Woodlands*, 16041
Only the Names Remain, 15923
Bocknek, Jonathan. *The Science of Magnets*, 20885
The Science of Plants, 20228
The Science of Soil, 20550
Boddy, Joe. *K'tonton's Sukkot Adventure*, 1672(F)
K'tonton's Yom Kippur Kitten, 6122(F)
Bode, Janet. *Food Fight*, 17941
For Better, For Worse, 17643

Bodecker, N. M. *Hurry, Hurry, Mary Dear*, 3535(F)
Bodett, Tom. *Williwaw*, 6773(F)
Bodkin, Odds. *The Banshee Train*, 2911(F)
The Crane Wife, 10811
Ghost of the Southern Belle, 7616(F)
Bodmer, Karl. *An Indian Winter*, 15954
Bodnar, Judit Z. *Tale of a Tail*, 1819(F)
A Wagonload of Fish, 10853
Boehm, Arlene. *Jack in Search of Art*, 1820(F)
Boelts, Darwin (jt. author). *Kids to the Rescue!* 18215
Boelts, Maribeth. *Big Daddy, Frog Wrestler*, 1821(F)
Dry Days, Wet Nights, 1822(F)
Grace and Joe, 3982(F)
A Kid's Guide to Staying Safe Around Water, 18214
Kids to the Rescue! 18215
Little Bunny's Cool Tool Set, 1823(F)
Little Bunny's Pacifier Plan, 1824(F)
Little Bunny's Preschool Countdown, 5475(F)
Summer's End, 5476(F)
Boerst, William J. *Edgar Rice Burroughs*, 12513
Isaac Asimov, 12501
Time Machine, 12618
Boesky, Amy. *Planet Was*, 1004(F)
Bofill, Francesc. *Jack and the Beanstalk/Juan y los frijoles magicos*, 10950
Bogacki, Tomek. *The Bird, the Monkey, and the Snake in the Jungle*, 1784(F)
Cat and Mouse, 1825(F)
Cat and Mouse in the Night, 1826(F)
Cat and Mouse in the Snow, 1827(F)
Five Creatures, 3720(F)
My First Garden, 4389(F)
The Story of a Blue Bird, 1828(F)
Bogan, Paulette. *Spike in the City*, 1829(F)
Bogart, Jo Ellen. *Gifts*, 3536(F)
Jeremiah Learns to Read, 3030(F)
Boggs, Cary. *W. D. the Wonder Dog*, 1830(F)
Bogot, Howard I., reteller. *Seven Animal Stories for Children*, 17249
Bogot, Mary K. (jt. author). *Seven Animal Stories for Children*, 17249
Bograd, Larry. *Colorado Summer*, 7159(F)
Bohlmeijer, Arno. *Something Very Sorry*, 8403(F)
Boies, Alex. *Imani in the Belly*, 10657

Boiko, Claire. *Children's Plays for Creative Actors*, 12012

Boiry, Veronique. *Chagall*, 13905

Boitano, Brian. *Boitano's Edge*, 13588

Bolaane, Maitseo. *Batswana*, 14969

Bolam, Emily. *Bearobics*, 550(F)
Clara Ann Cookie, 3968(F)
Clara Ann Cookie, Go to Bed! 819(F)
I Swapped My Dog, 4365(F)
Little Red Riding Hood, 10942
Louie's Goose, 4951(F)
Mother Goose Math, 905(F)
One Smiling Sister, 409(F)
A Polar Bear Can Swim, 18865
The Princess and the Pea, 10527(F)
Rabbit and Hare Divide an Apple, 20602(F)
Talk, Baby! 3970(F)
The Twelve Days of Christmas, 14216
Waiting for Baby, 3971(F)

Bolick, Nancy O. *Mail Call!* 17106
Shaker Inventions, 17168
Shaker Villages, 17169

Bollen, Roger. *Alistair in Outer Space*, 1536(F)
Alistair Underwater, 1537(F)
Alistair's Time Machine, 4293(F)
Bobo Crazy, 10230(F)
The Parakeet Girl, 6621(F)

Bolognese, Don. *Abigail Takes the Wheel*, 9514(F)
Buddy, 19957
Buffalo Bill and the Pony Express, 6273(F)
First Flight, 6657(F)
George the Drummer Boy, 4592(F)
Pocahontas, 12987
Wagon Wheels, 6222(F)

Bolognese, Don (jt. author). *Daniel Boone*, 12084
Pocahontas, 12987

Bolster, Rob. *The Airplane Alphabet Book*, 21095
The Cheerios Counting Book, 506(F)
Going Lobstering, 3355(F)

Bolton, Linda. *Cubism*, 13881
Impressionism, 13882
Pop Art, 13950

Boltz, Dan (jt. author). *Dan's Pants*, 3176(F)

Bomans, Godfried. *Eric in the Land of the Insects*, 7617(F)

Bomzer, Barry. *Dirt Bike Racer*, 10299(F)

Bonafoux, Pascal. *A Weekend with Rembrandt*, 12288

Bonar, Samantha. *Asteroids*, 18507
Comets, 18508

Bond, Adrienne. *Sugarcane House and Other Stories About Mr. Fat*, 7618(F)

Bond, Denny. *Sleepy Little Owl*, 2132(F)

Bond, Felicia. *The Big Green Pocketbook*, 3372(F)
Big Red Barn, 5144(F)
If You Give a Moose a Muffin, 2537(F)
If You Give a Mouse a Cookie, 2538(F)
If You Give a Pig a Pancake, 2539(F)
If You Take a Mouse to the Movies, 2540(F)
Mouse Cookies, 21726
Poinsettia and Her Family, 1831(F)
The Sky Is Full of Stars, 18541
Tumble Bumble, 1832(F)

Bond, Higgins. *Susie King Taylor*, 12785
When I Was Little, 3715(F)

Bond, Michael. *A Bear Called Paddington*, 9785(F)
Paddington at Large, 9786(F)
Paddington Bear, 1833(F)
Paddington Bear All Day, 1834(F)
Paddington Bear and the Busy Bee Carnival, 12(F)
Paddington Bear and the Christmas Surprise, 5756(F)
Paddington Bear Goes to Market, 1835(F)
Paddington's 1, 2, 3, 385(F)
Paddington's Opposites, 165(F)
Paddington's Storybook, 9787(F)

Bond, Nancy. *Career Ideas for Kids Who Like Art*, 17779
Career Ideas for Kids Who Like Computers, 17796
Career Ideas for Kids Who Like Math, 17761
Career Ideas for Kids Who Like Science, 17835
Career Ideas for Kids Who Like Sports, 17762
Career Ideas for Kids Who Like Talking, 17780
Career Ideas for Kids Who Like Writing, 17781

Bond, Peter. *DK Guide to Space*, 20953

Bond, Rebecca. *Bravo, Maurice!* 3537(F)
Just Like a Baby, 3538(F)

Bond, Ruskin. *Binya's Blue Umbrella*, 8985(F)

Bonforte, Lisa. *Otter on His Own*, 19729

Bonner, Rog. *Moo Moo, Brown Cow*, 613(F)

Bonners, Susan. *Edwina Victorious*, 8569(F)
A Penguin Year, 19368
The Silver Balloon, 8259(F)
Why Does the Cat Do That? 19916

Bonnet, Bob. *Science Fair Projects*, 18301, 20819, 18381, 20798
Science Fair Projects with Electricity and Electronics, 20886

Bonnett-Rampersaud, Louise. *Polly Hopper's Pouch*, 1836(F)

Bonning, Tony. *Another Fine Mess*, 1837(F)

Bonsall, Crosby. *The Case of the Scaredy Cats*, 6211(F)
Mine's Best, 6212(F)
Piggle, 6213(F)
Tell Me Some More, 6214(F)
Who's a Pest? 6215(F)
Who's Afraid of the Dark? 6216(F)

Bonson, Richard. *Great Wonders of the World*, 14578

Bontemps, Arna. *The Pasteboard Bandit*, 1005(F)

Boo, Michael. *The Story of Figure Skating*, 22218

Boon, Debbie. *My Gran*, 3539(F)

Booth, Basil. *Earthquakes and Volcanoes*, 20334

Booth, David. *The Dust Bowl*, 4597(F)

Booth, George. *The Ballymara Flood*, 4334(F)
Possum Come a-Knockin', 2775(F)
Wacky Wednesday, 492(F)

Booth, Martin. *Panther*, 6774(F)

Bootman, Colin. *In My Momma's Kitchen*, 3824(F)
The Music in Derrick's Heart, 3519(F)
Oh, No, Toto! 4849(F)
Young Frederick Douglass, 12710

Borchard, Therese. *Taste and See*, 17170

Borden, Louise. *A. Lincoln and Me*, 4598(F)
Albie the Lifeguard, 3031(F)
Caps, Hats, Socks, and Mittens, 4390(F)
The Day Eddie Met the Author, 10029(F)
Fly High! The Story of Bessie Coleman, 12090
Good-bye, Charles Lindbergh, 4599(F)
Good Luck, Mrs. K.! 5477(F)
Just in Time for Christmas, 5757(F)
The Little Ships, 9081(F)
The Neighborhood Trucker, 5549(F)
Sleds on Boston Common, 9185(F)
Thanksgiving Is . . ., 6133(F)

Borden, Louise (jt. author). *Paperboy*, 4716(F)

Borders, Christine. *Gram Makes a House Call*, 7394(F)

Boring, Mel. *Incredible Constructions*, 21115

Borja, Corinne. *Making Chinese Papercuts*, 21607

Borja, Robert. *Making Chinese Papercuts*, 21607

Borlenghi, Patricia. *Chaucer the Cat and the Animal Pilgrims*, 10535

Bornhoft, Simon. *High Speed Boats*, 21354

Bornoff, Nick. *Japan*, 15118

Borns, Steven. *Crashed, Smashed, and Mashed*, 21309

Bornstein, Harry. *Nursery Rhymes from Mother Goose Told in Signed English*, 827

Bornstein, Ruth. *The Dancing Man*, 1006(F)
Little Gorilla, 1838(F)
Mama One, Mama Two, 3789(F)
Rabbit's Good News, 1839(F)

Bornstein, Sandy. *What Makes You What You Are*, 18034

Boroson, Martin. *Becoming Me*, 17250

Borton, Lady. *Junk Pile!* 4090(F)

Bortz, Fred. *Martian Fossils on Earth? The Story of Meteorite ALH 84001*, 18382

Bos, Burny. *Alexander the Great*, 1840(F)
Fun with the Molesons, 7620(F)
Leave It to the Molesons! 1841(F)

Bosak, Susan V. *Something to Remember Me By*, 3540(F)

Boss, Sarah Jane. *Mary's Story*, 17251

Bosschaert, Greet. *Teenie Bird and How She Learned to Fly*, 1842(F)

Bosson, Jo-Ellen. *Create! The Best Crafts and Activities from Many Lands*, 21414

Bosson, Victor. *The Fox's Kettle*, 1334(F)

Bostock, Mike. *Gentle Giant Octopus*, 19727
Imagine You Are a Crocodile, 5445(F)
Pond Year, 4481(F)

Boston, David. *The Dancing Turtle*, 11436

Bottner, Barbara. *Bootsie Barker Ballerina*, 6217(F)
Bootsie Barker Bites, 4911(F)
Marsha Is Only a Flower, 6218(F)
Nana Hannah's Piano, 3541(F)
Two Messy Friends, 6219(F)

Bouchard, David. *The Dragon New Year*, 5611(F)
The Great Race, 10738
If Sarah Will Take Me, 11537

Boucher, Jerry. *Fire Truck Nuts and Bolts*, 21297

Boucher, Joelle. *The Seventh Walnut*, 4510

Bouis, Antonina W. (jt. author). *A Letter for Daria*, 13589

Boulais, Sue. *Andres Galarraga*, 13452
Gloria Estefan, 12381
Katie Holmes, 12401
Liv Tyler, 12479
Tommy Nunez, 13553
Vanessa Williams, 12483

Boulais, Sue (jt. author). *Trent Dimas*, 13683

Boulton, Jane. *Only Opal*, 4600

Bouma, Paddy. *Valentine*, 3569(F)

Bour, Daniele. *Little Brown Bear Does Not Want to Eat*, 2349(F)

Bour-Chollet, Celine. *All About Time*, 20655

Bourgeois, Louis (jt. author). *Sports Lab*, 22059

Bourgeois, Paulette. *The Amazing Dirt Book*, 20551
Big Sarah's Little Boots, 3032(F)
Changes in You and Me, 18250
Fire Fighters, 3033
Franklin and the Thunderstorm, 1843(F)
Franklin Goes to the Hospital, 1844(F)
Franklin's Bad Day, 1845(F)
Franklin's Class Trip, 1849(F)
Franklin's Classic Treasury, 1846(F)
Franklin's Classic Treasury, Volume II, 1847(F)
Franklin's Friendship Treasury, 1848(F)
Garbage Collectors, 3034
The Moon, 18441
Police Officers, 17807
Postal Workers, 17740
The Sun, 18559
Too Many Chickens! 4091(F)

Bourre, Martine. *Max, the Stubborn Little Wolf*, 2269(F)

Bowden, Joan. *Why the Tides Ebb and Flow*, 1007(F)

Bowden, Robert (jt. author). *Awesome Yo-Yo Tricks*, 22033

Bowdish, Lynea. *Brooklyn, Bugsy, and Me*, 8570(F)
Living with My Stepfather Is like Living with a Moose, 8404(F)

Bowen, Andy Russell. *The Back of Beyond*, 16076
Flying Against the Wind, 12143
A Head Full of Notions, 13286
A World of Knowing, 12885

Bowen, Betsy. *Gathering*, 386(F)
Shingebiss, 11315
Tracks in the Wild, 18610

Bowen, Fred. *The Final Cut*, 10278(F)
Full Court Fever, 10279(F)
On the Line, 10280(F)
Playoff Dreams, 10281(F)
T.J.'s Secret Pitch, 10282(F)

Bower, Tamara. *The Shipwrecked Sailor*, 11183

Bowermaster, Jon (jt. author). *Over the Top of the World*, 15836

Bowers, Tim. *Little Whistle*, 1533(F)

Bowers, Vivien. *Crime Science*, 17064
Wow Canada! Exploring This Land from Coast to Coast to Coast, 15567

Bowes, Deborah. *The Ballet Book*, 14275

Bowie, C. W. *Busy Toes*, 4092(F)

Bowler, Ray. *The Beast in the Bathtub*, 2726(F)

Bowman, Crystal. *Ivan and the Dynamos*, 10283(F)

Bowman, Leslie. *The Canada Geese Quilt*, 8723(F)
The Copper Lady, 6599(F)
The Cuckoo Child, 7236(F)
The Fiddler of the Northern Lights, 1305(F)
Hannah, 8922(F)
Orcas Around Me, 3354

Bowman-Kruhm, Mary. *Everything You Need to Know About Down Syndrome*, 17942

Bown, Deni. *Color Fun*, 261
Happy Times, 166(F)
Let's Count, 387

Bowring, Joanne. *Let Me Explain*, 18246

Boyajian, Ann. *Hello, Shoes!* 164(F)

Boyd, Aaron. *Tiger Woods*, 13711

Boyd, Candy Dawson. *Charlie Pippin*, 8405(F)

Boyd, Lizi. *Willy and the Cardboard Boxes*, 1008(F)

Boyle, Alison. *Twinkle, Twinkle, Little Star*, 828(F)

Boyle, Doe. *Otter on His Own*, 19729

Boynton, Sandra. *A Is for Angry*, 13(F)
Bob, 5758(F)
Hey! Wake Up! 3035(F)

Brace, Eric. *The Day My Dogs Became Guys*, 1396(F)
It's Disgusting — and We Ate It! True Food Facts from Around the World — and Throughout History! 20045
The Krazees, 1607(F)
My Brother Is from Outer Space, 3829(F)
Punctuation Power, 14112

Brace, Steve. *Bangladesh*, 15148
From Beans to Batteries, 4601(F)
Ghana, 15017

Bracken, Sarah (jt. author). *Kids in the Kitchen*, 21733

Bradby, Marie. *The Longest Wait*, 3542(F)
Momma, Where Are You From? 4602(F)
More Than Anything Else, 4603(F)

Bradford, June. *Beanbag Buddies and Other Stuffed Toys*, 21657
Making Fleece Crafts, 21645

Bradley, Catherine. *Freedom of Movement*, 17016

Bradley, David, ed. *The Encyclopedia of Civil Rights in America*, 17026

Bradley, Kimberly Brubaker. *One-of-a-Kind Mallie*, 9524(F)

Ruthie's Gift, 9525(F)
Weaver's Daughter, 9263(F)
Bradman, Tony. *A Goodnight Kind of Feeling*, 1850(F)
Michael, 4093(F)
Bradshaw, Gillian. *The Land of Gold*, 7621(F)
Brady, April A. *Kwanzaa Karamu*, 17344
Brady, Irene. *Peeping in the Shell*, 19256
Brady, Kimberley Smith. *Keeper for the Sea*, 4391(F)
Bragg, Linda Wallenberg. *Fundamental Gymnastics*, 22191
Bragg, Ruth G. *Alphabet Out Loud*, 14(F)
Braginetz, Donna. *Seismosaurus*, 14438
Braine, Susan. *Drumbeat . . . Heartbeat*, 15934
Braman, Arlette N. *Create! The Best Crafts and Activities from Many Lands*, 21414
Brami, Elisabeth. *First Times*, 3036(F)
Brammer, Erin M. *The Sea Maidens of Japan*, 4589(F)
Bramwell, Martyn. *Central and South America*, 14331
Europe, 15257
How Maps Are Made, 14363
Mapping Our World, 14364
Mapping the Seas and Airways, 14365
Maps in Everyday Life, 14366
North America and the Caribbean, 15562
Branch, Muriel M. *Juneteenth*, 17345
Pennies to Dollars, 12811
Branch, Muriel M. (jt. author). *Dear Ellen Bee*, 9487(F)
Brandenberg, Alexa. *Chop, Simmer, Season*, 3037(F)
I Am Me! 3038(F)
Brandenberg, Franz. *Nice New Neighbors*, 1851(F)
Brandenburg, Jim. *An American Safari*, 16535
Sand and Fog, 14970
Scruffy, 7160(F)
To the Top of the World, 19118
Brandi, Lillian. *Encyclopedia Brown, Boy Detective*, 7075(F)
Brandt, Amy. *Benjamin Comes Back/Benjamin regresa*, 4912(F)
When Katie Was Our Teacher/Cuando Katie era nuestra maestra, 5478(F)
Brandt, Keith. *Daniel Boone*, 12081
Discovering Trees, 20194
John Paul Jones, 12913
Marie Curie, 13261
What Makes It Rain? 20727
Wonders of the Seasons, 4392(F)
Brandt, Sue R. *State Flags*, 13970
State Trees, 15850

Branford, Henrietta. *Fire, Bed, and Bone*, 9082(F)
Prosper's Mountain, 10402(F)
White Wolf, 7161(F)
Branley, Franklyn M. *Air Is All Around You*, 20664
The Big Dipper, 18540
Day Light, Night Light, 20857
Down Comes the Rain, 20728
Flash, Crash, Rumble, and Roll, 20683
Floating in Space, 20954
The International Space Station, 20955
Is There Life in Outer Space? 20956
It's Raining Cats and Dogs, 20754
Keeping Time, 20639
The Planets in Our Solar System, 18458
The Sky Is Full of Stars, 18541
Snow Is Falling, 20755
Star Guide, 18542
The Sun, 18560
The Sun and the Solar System, 18509
Sunshine Makes the Seasons, 18561
Tornado Alert, 20684
Venus, 20957
Volcanoes, 20335
What Happened to the Dinosaurs? 14388
What Makes Day and Night? 18428
What the Moon Is Like, 18442
Brannon, Tom. *Baker, Baker, Cookie Maker*, 6374(F)
Braren, Loretta. *EcoArt!* 21417
Kids' Computer Creations, 21223
The Kids' Science Book, 18322
The Kids' Wildlife Book, 18667
The Little Hands Big Fun Craft Book, 21464
Rainy Day Play! 21418
Shapes, Sizes and More Surprises! 253(F)
Brashares, Ann. *Steve Jobs*, 12911
Bratman, Fred. *War in the Persian Gulf*, 15487
Bratun, Katy. *A Head Is For Hats*, 6639(F)
Bratvold, Gretchen. *Oregon*, 16764
Wisconsin, 16536
Braun, Barbara. *A Weekend with Diego Rivera*, 12293
Braun, Trudi. *My Goose Betsy*, 5140(F)
Bray, Rosemary L. *Martin Luther King*, 12740
Braybrooks, Ann. *Plenty of Pockets*, 4094(F)
Brazell, Derek. *Cleversticks*, 5470(F)
Brazelton, T. Berry. *Going to the Doctor*, 3039
Breathed, Berkeley. *Edwurd Fudwupper Fibbed Big*, 1009(F)
The Last Basselope, 7622(F)

Breckler, Rosemary K. *Sweet Dried Apples*, 8986(F)
Bredeson, Carmen. *American Writers of the 20th Century*, 12158
The Battle of the Alamo, 16230
The Challenger Disaster, 20958
Fire in Oakland, California, 16765
Gus Grissom, 12119
John Glenn Returns to Orbit, 20959
The Mighty Midwest Flood, 20685
The Moon, 18443
NASA Planetary Spacecraft, 20960
Neil Armstrong, 12072
Our Space Program, 20961
Shannon Lucid, 12135
The Spindletop Gusher, 16902
Texas, 16903
Tide Pools, 19855
Breen, Mark. *The Kids' Book of Weather Forecasting*, 20756
Breese, Gillian. *The Amazing Adventures of Teddy Tum Tum*, 1852(F)
Breeze, Lynn. *Pickle and the Ball*, 3040(F)
Breinburg, Petronella. *Stories from the Caribbean*, 11418
Breitenbucher, Cathy. *Bonnie Blair*, 13680
Brenda, Aminah. *The Shaking Bag*, 988(F)
Brennan, Herbie. *The Mystery Machine*, 10153(F)
Brennan, Linda Crotta. *Flannel Kisses*, 3041(F)
Marshmallow Kisses, 3042(F)
Brennan, Neil. *River Friendly, River Wild*, 11619
Brenner, Barbara. *Beavers Beware!* 6220(F)
The Boy Who Loved to Draw, 12310
Chibi, 5141
The Color Wizard, 6221(F)
Group Soup, 1853(F)
If You Were There in 1492, 16077
If You Were There in 1776, 16190
Planetarium, 20962
Thinking About Ants, 19507
Wagon Wheels, 6222(F)
Where's That Insect? 19430
Where's That Reptile? 18679
Brenner, Barbara, ed. *The Earth Is Painted Green*, 11942
Brenner, Barbara, sel. *Voices*, 11538
Brenner, Fred. *The Drinking Gourd*, 9308(F)
One Day in the Desert, 20403
Brenner, Martha. *Abe Lincoln's Hat*, 13065
Brent, Isabelle. *The Fairy Tales of Oscar Wilde*, 10478(F)
Breslow, Susan. *I Really Want a Dog*, 5142(F)
Bresnick-Perry, Roslyn. *Leaving for America*, 4604

Brett, Jan. *Armadillo Rodeo*, 1854(F)
Berlioz Bear, 1855(F)
Christmas Trolls, 5759(F)
Comet's Nine Lives, 1856(F)
Fritz and the Beautiful Horses, 1857(F)
Gingerbread Baby, 10951(F)
The Hat, 1858(F)
Hedgie's Surprise, 1859(F)
The Mitten, 10854
The Mother's Day Mice, 5613(F)
The Night Before Christmas, 11843
Noelle of the Nutcracker, 7834(F)
The Owl and the Pussycat, 11887
St. Patrick's Day in the Morning, 5615(F)
Scary, Scary Halloween, 5985(F)
Town Mouse, Country Mouse, 1860(F)
Trouble with Trolls, 1010(F)
The Valentine Bears, 6163(F)
The Wild Christmas Reindeer, 5760(F)
Brett, Jan, reteller. *Beauty and the Beast*, 10866
Brett, Jessica. *Animals on the Go*, 18926
Brett-Surman, Michael. *James Gurney*, 14389
Brewer, Dan (jt. author). *Silver Seeds*, 11978
Brewer, Janet Neff. *In God's Image*, 18251
Brewster, Hugh. *Anastasia's Album*, 15409
Brewster, Patience. *Bear and Roly-Poly*, 2865(F)
Bear's Christmas Surprise, 5956(F)
A Hive for the Honeybee, 7885(F)
Queen of the May, 10440(F)
Rabbit Inn, 1861(F)
There's More . . . Much More, 1734(F)
Yoo Hoo, Moon! 6210(F)
Brewton, Sara, ed. *Of Quarks, Quasars and Other Quirks*, 11857
Brickman, Robin. *A Log's Life*, 20215
Starfish, 19721
Swallows in the Birdhouse, 5426
Bridges, Margaret Park. *Am I Big or Little?* 3543(F)
If I Were Your Father, 3544(F)
If I Were Your Mother, 3545(F)
Will You Take Care of Me? 1862(F)
Bridges, Ruby. *Through My Eyes*, 16497
Bridgman, Roger. *Electronics*, 21240
Bridwell, Norman. *Clifford Makes a Friend*, 6223(F)
Clifford's Good Deeds, 1863(F)
Clifford's Halloween, 5982(F)
Brier, Peggy. *Southern Fried Rat and Other Gruesome Tales*, 11330

Brierley, Louise. *Lightning Inside You and Other Native American Riddles*, 21814
When the World Was Young, 10588
Briggs, Carole S. *Women in Space*, 20963
Briggs, Harry. *The Grapes of Math*, 20622
Briggs, Raymond. *The Bear*, 1011(F)
Father Christmas, 5761(F)
Jim and the Beanstalk, 1012(F)
The Snowman, 911(F)
Briggs-Bunting, Jane. *Laddie of the Light*, 7162(F)
Brighton, Catherine. *The Fossil Girl*, 13229
Brill, Marlene T. *Allen Jay and the Underground Railroad*, 6224(F)
Building the Capital City, 16656
Diary of a Drummer Boy, 9468(F)
Guatemala, 15659
Guyana, 15725
Illinois, 16537
Indiana, 16538
James Buchanan, 13009
John Adams, 13002
Let Women Vote! 17027
Mongolia, 15149
Tooth Tales from Around the World, 10536
Brillhart, Julie. *When Daddy Came to School*, 3546(F)
When Daddy Took Us Camping, 2912(F)
Brimner, Larry. *Bees*, 19515
Bobsledding and the Luge, 21978
Butterflies and Moths, 19542
Cat on Wheels, 1864(F)
Cats! 6225(F)
Cockroaches, 19431
Cowboy Up! 6226(F)
Dinosaurs Dance, 6227(F)
E-Mail, 21194
Earth, 18429
Flies, 19432
If Dogs Had Wings, 1865(F)
Jupiter, 18459
Mars, 18460
Mercury, 18461
Merry Christmas, Old Armadillo, 5762(F)
A Migrant Family, 17132
Mountain Biking, 22154
The Names Project, 17943
Neptune, 18462
The Official M&M's Brand Book of the Millennium, 20640
Pluto, 18463
Polar Mammals, 18927
Praying Mantises, 19433
Rock Climbing, 21979
Saturn, 18464
Snowboarding, 22277
Speed Skating, 22219
Unusual Friendships, 18579
Uranus, 18465
Venus, 18466

The Winter Olympics, 22244
Brinckloe, Julie. *Fireflies!* 4393(F)
The Hunky-Dory Dairy, 7913(F)
Brink, Benjamin. *David's Story*, 18037
Brinn, Ruth Esrig. *Jewish Holiday Crafts for Little Hands*, 17452
Brisley, Joyce Lankester. *More Milly-Molly-Mandy*, 3043(F)
Brisson, Pat. *Bertie's Picture Day*, 9788(F)
Hot Fudge Hero, 6228(F)
Kate Heads West, 3044(F)
Little Sister, Big Sister, 6229(F)
Sky Memories, 8571(F)
The Summer My Father Was Ten, 3045(F)
Wanda's Roses, 3046(F)
Britt, Gary. *Birds*, 19243
Britt, Grant. *Charlie Sifford*, 13709
Brittain, Bill. *All the Money in the World*, 7623(F)
Devil's Donkey, 7624(F)
Dr. Dredd's Wagon of Wonders, 6775(F)
The Ghost from Beneath the Sea, 7625(F)
The Mystery of the Several Sevens, 7626(F)
Who Knew There'd Be Ghosts? 6776(F)
Wings, 7627(F)
Brittingham, Geoffrey. *Where Does the Mail Go?* 17105
Britton, Tamara L. *Greece*, 15373
Brock, Alice M. *Mooses Come Walking*, 5240(F)
Brock, Betty. *No Flying in the House*, 1866(F)
Brockmann, Carolee. *Going for Great*, 8260(F)
Broda, Ron. *Butterflies*, 19563
Have You Seen Bugs? 19472
Brodie, James Michael (jt. author). *Sweet Words So Brave*, 14076
Brodmann, Aliana. *The Gift*, 6068(F)
Brodmann, Aliana, reteller. *Such a Noise!* 11142
Brody, J. J. *A Day with a Mimbres*, 15935
Brody, Janis. *Your Body*, 17694
Brodzinsky, Anne Braff. *The Mulberry Bird*, 1867(F)
Broekel, Ray. *Abra-Ca-Dazzle*, 21777
Dangerous Fish, 19698
Hocus Pocus, 21778
Snakes, 18755
Sound Experiments, 20932
Broekel, Ray (jt. author). *Razzle Dazzle!* 21791
Brogger, Lilian. *Wildebeest*, 1806(F)
Broida, Marian. *Ancient Egyptians and Their Neighbors*, 14610
Brokaw, Nancy Steele. *Leaving Emma*, 8572(F)

Bronikowski, Ken. *Sarah Winnemucca*, 13001

Bronson, Linda. *Crookjaw*, 1064(F)
Round and Square, 357(F)
Teatime with Emma Buttersnap, 20128

Brontë, Charlotte. *Jane Eyre*, 6777(F)

Brook, Donna. *The Journey of English*, 13978

Brook, Larry. *Daily Life in Ancient and Modern Timbuktu*, 15018

Brooke, Lauren. *Heartland*, 7163(F)

Brooke, William J. *A Is for AAR-RGH!* 9789(F)

Brooker, Kyrsten. *Isabella Abnormella and the Very, Very Finicky Queen of Trouble*, 1352(F)
Nothing Ever Happens on 90th Street, 3412(F)

Brooks, Alan. *Frogs Jump*, 388(F)

Brooks, Bruce. *Billy*, 10284(F)
Boot, 10285(F)
Cody, 10286(F)
Dooby, 10287(F)
Everywhere, 8261(F)
NBA by the Numbers, 389(F)
Prince, 10288(F)
Reed, 10289(F)
Shark, 10290(F)
Throwing Smoke, 7628(F)
Vanishing, 8882(F)
Woodsie, 10291(F)

Brooks, Erik. *The Practically Perfect Pajamas*, 1868(F)

Brooks, Gwendolyn. *Bronzeville Boys and Girls*, 11749

Brooks, Jim. *Mik-Shrok*, 7020(F)

Brooks, Karen Stormer. *I Bought a Baby Chicken*, 454(F)

Brooks, Nan. *Making Minestrone*, 3028(F)

Brooks, Nigel. *Country Mouse Cottage*, 1013(F)
Town Mouse House, 4605(F)

Brooks, Philip. *Extraordinary Jewish Americans*, 12639
Georgia O'Keeffe, 12275
Mary Cassatt, 12199
Oprah Winfrey, 12484
United States, 21980
The United States Holocaust Memorial Museum, 16657

Brooks, Ron. *Motor Bill and the Lovely Caroline*, 2805(F)
Rosie and Tortoise, 2856(F)

Brooks, Victor. *African Americans in the Civil War*, 16394
Civil War Forts, 16395
Secret Weapons in the Civil War, 16396

Brophy, Ann. *John Ericsson*, 13278

Broutin, Christian. *The Jungle Book*, 7243(F)

Brower, Pauline. *Missions of the Inland Valleys*, 16766

Brown, Alan. *Nikki and the Rocking Horse*, 3547(F)
What I Believe, 17171
The Windhover, 5143(F)

Brown, Angela McHaney. *Carpenter*, 17785

Brown, Bradford. *Addy Saves the Day*, 9608(F)

Brown, Calef. *Dutch Sneakers and Flea Keepers*, 11858
Polkabats and Octopus Slacks, 7629(F)

Brown, Craig. *What Good Is a Cactus?* 9169(F)

Brown, Dan. *Impatient Pamela Asks*, 5000(F)
Impatient Pamela Calls 9-1-1, 3266(F)
A Picture Book of George Washington Carver, 13251
A Picture Book of Sacagawea, 12988

Brown, Dennis L. *A Sweet, Sweet Basket*, 3072(F)

Brown, Don. *Alice Ramsey's Grand Adventure*, 2913
One Giant Leap, 12073
Rare Treasure, 13230
Ruth Law Thrills a Nation, 12129
Uncommon Traveler, 12128

Brown, Dottie. *Delaware*, 16658
Kentucky, 16835
New Hampshire, 16659
Ohio, 16539

Brown, F. K. *Last Hurdle*, 7164(F)

Brown, Fern G. *Daisy and the Girl Scouts*, 13168
Franklin Pierce, 13089
Special Olympics, 17902

Brown, Gene. *Discovery and Settlement*, 16098
The 1992 Election, 17095
The Struggle to Grow, 16452

Brown, Greg (jt. author). *Kirby Puckett*, 13478
Reach Higher, 13565
A Winning Edge, 13679

Brown, Isabel Bodor. *The Magic Hill*, 10464(F)

Brown, Jane. *Defenders of the Universe*, 6919(F)
Marvin's Best Christmas Present Ever, 5896(F)
The Smallest Cow in the World, 5046(F)

Brown, Jeff. *Flat Stanley*, 1014(F)
Invisible Stanley, 1015(F)

Brown, Judith G. *The Best Christmas Pageant Ever*, 9757(F)
Maudie in the Middle, 7489(F)
The Miracle of Saint Nicholas, 1675(F)

Brown, Karen. *Kids Are Cookin'*, 21679

Brown, Kathryn. *A Bear for All Seasons*, 2108(F)
Climb into My Lap, 11545

From Lullaby to Lullaby, 1182(F)
The Littlest Matryoshka, 1002(F)
Old Thunder and Miss Raney, 1100(F)
The Old Woman Who Named Things, 5399(F)
Stella's Dancing Days, 5127(F)
Tough Boris, 2930(F)

Brown, Ken. *Dilly-Dally and the Nine Secrets*, 2421(F)
King of the Woods, 2006(F)
Mucky Pup, 1869(F)
Mucky Pup's Christmas, 5763(F)
Nellie's Knot, 1870(F)
The Scarecrow's Hat, 1871(F)
The Wolf Is Coming! 2422(F)

Brown, Laurie Krasny. *Dinosaurs Alive and Well!* 3047
Dinosaurs Divorce, 17644
How to Be a Friend, 3983(F)
Rex and Lilly Family Time, 6230(F)
Rex and Lilly Schooltime, 6231(F)
Visiting the Art Museum, 3048(F)
What's the Big Secret? Talking About Sex with Girls and Boys, 18252
When Dinosaurs Die, 17695

Brown, Laurie Krasny (jt. author).
The Bionic Bunny Show, 1892(F)

Brown, Marc. *Arthur Accused*, 6232(F)
Arthur and the Crunch Cereal Contest, 4095(F)
Arthur and the Scare-Your-Pants-Off Club, 6233(F)
Arthur Lost and Found, 1872(F)
Arthur Makes the Team, 6234(F)
Arthur Meets the President, 1873(F)
Arthur Writes a Story, 1874(F)
Arthur's April Fool, 5612(F)
Arthur's Birthday, 5666(F)
Arthur's Chicken Pox, 1875(F)
Arthur's Christmas, 5764(F)
Arthur's Computer Disaster, 1876(F)
Arthur's Eyes, 1877(F)
Arthur's Family Treasury, 1878(F)
Arthur's Family Vacation, 1879(F)
Arthur's First Sleepover, 1880(F)
Arthur's Halloween, 5983(F)
Arthur's Mystery Envelope, 1881(F)
Arthur's New Puppy, 1882(F)
Arthur's Really Helpful Bedtime Book, 10403(F)
Arthur's Really Helpful Word Book, 14024
Arthur's Teacher Moves In, 1883(F)
Arthur's Teacher Trouble, 1884(F)
Arthur's Thanksgiving, 6134(F)
Arthur's TV Trouble, 1885(F)
Arthur's Underwear, 1886(F)
Arthur's Valentine, 6162(F)
The Bionic Bunny Show, 1892(F)

Buster's Dino Dilemma, 6435(F)
D.W. Flips, 1887(F)
D.W., Go to Your Room! 3548(F)
D.W. Rides Again! 1888(F)
D.W.'s Lost Blankie, 1889(F)
D.W. the Picky Eater, 1890(F)
D.W. Thinks Big, 1891(F)
Dinosaurs, Beware! A Safety Guide, 3049(F)
Dinosaurs Divorce, 17644
The Family Read-Aloud Christmas Treasury, 5866
How to Be a Friend, 3983(F)
Little Witch's Big Night, 6004(F)
Party Rhymes, 11539
Perfect Pigs, 1893(F)
Play Rhymes, 829
Rex and Lilly Family Time, 6230(F)
Rex and Lilly Schooltime, 6231(F)
Scared Silly! 7630(F)
Spooky Riddles, 21815
There's No Place Like Home, 6235(F)
The True Francine, 3984(F)
What's the Big Secret? Talking About Sex with Girls and Boys, 18252
When Dinosaurs Die, 17695
Why the Tides Ebb and Flow, 1007(F)
Witches Four, 1016(F)
Brown, Marc, ed. *Party Rhymes*, 11539
Brown, Marc (jt. author). *Dinosaurs Alive and Well!* 3047
Dinosaurs Divorce, 17644
Visiting the Art Museum, 3048(F)
Brown, Marcia. *Backbone of the King*, 11326
Dick Whittington and His Cat, 10952
Shadow, 171(F)
Sing a Song of Popcorn, 11551
Stone Soup, 10867
Brown, Margaret Wise. *Another Important Book*, 3050(F)
Big Red Barn, 5144(F)
Bumble Bee, 5145(F)
Bunny's Noisy Book, 1894(F)
The Diggers, 5550
Goodnight Moon, 638(F)
I Like Stars, 6236(F)
The Little Scarecrow Boy, 1017(F)
Love Songs of the Little Bear, 11540
Red Light, Green Light, 3051(F)
The Runaway Bunny, 1895(F)
The Sleepy Men, 639(F)
Under the Sun and the Moon and Other Poems, 11943
Wait Till the Moon Is Full, 4394(F)
Wheel on the Chimney, 5146(F)
Brown, Marion M. *Singapore*, 15150
Brown, Marty. *Webmaster*, 17786
Brown, Mary B. *Tiger with Wings*, 19360
Brown, Paula. *Moon Jump*, 390(F)

Brown, Richard. *Baby Buggy, Buggy Baby*, 14063(F)
Gone Fishing, 3777(F)
Brown, Rick. *Kate Heads West*, 3044(F)
Let's Be Animals, 5439(F)
The Princess and the Potty, 3281(F)
Put a Fan in Your Hat! 18303
Rockabye Farm, 693(F)
Uncle Chuck's Truck, 5552(F)
Brown, Ruth. *Ben's Christmas Carol*, 5816(F)
The Big Sneeze, 4096(F)
Blossom Comes Home, 5257(F)
Cry Baby, 3549(F)
Holly, 5765(F)
Ladybug, Ladybug, 830
Mad Summer Night's Dream, 1018(F)
The Shy Little Angel, 3052(F)
Smudge, the Little Lost Lamb, 5259(F)
Toad, 18715
Brown, Sterling. *First Lady of the Air*, 12153
Tailypo, 11368
Brown, Susan M. *You're Dead, David Borelli*, 8406(F)
Brown, Susan Taylor. *Can I Pray with My Eyes Open?* 17516
Brown, Tricia. *Children of the Midnight Sun*, 16767
Chinese New Year, 17346
The City by the Bay, 16768
Hello, Amigos! 5667(F)
Someone Special, Just Like You, 4913(F)
Browne, Anthony. *My Dad*, 1019(F)
Piggybook, 1896(F)
Voices in the Park, 3053(F)
Willy the Dreamer, 1897(F)
Willy's Pictures, 9790(F)
Browne, Eileen. *No Problem*, 1898(F)
Tick-Tock, 1899(F)
Browne, Jane. *Little Stowaway*, 2979(F)
My Wicked Stepmother, 5010(F)
Browne, Philippa-Alys. *A Gaggle of Geese*, 18928
Kangaroos Have Joeys, 5147
Browne, Rollo. *An Aboriginal Family*, 15225
Browne, Vee. *Owl*, 19358
Brownell, Barbara. *Spin's Really Wild U.S.A. Tour*, 15867
Brownell, Shawn Costello. *Mommy Far, Mommy Near*, 5047(F)
Browning, Tom. *Santa's Time Off*, 3316(F)
Brownlie, Alison. *Nigeria*, 15019
South Africa, 14971
West Africa, 15020
Brownlow, Mike. *Way Out West with a Baby*, 4606(F)

Brownrigg, Sheri. *Hearts and Crafts*, 17504
Broyles, Anne. *Shy Mama's Halloween*, 5984(F)
Bruce, Lisa. *Fran's Flower*, 3054(F)
Oliver's Alphabets, 15(F)
Bruchac, James (jt. author). *How Chipmunk Got His Stripes*, 11221
When the Chenoo Howls, 11222
Bruchac, Joseph. *The Arrow over the Door*, 9225(F)
Between Earth and Sky, 11215
A Boy Called Slow, 9146(F)
Crazy Horse's Vision, 9147(F)
Dog People, 11216
Flying with the Eagle, Racing the Great Bear, 11217
Gluskabe and the Four Wishes, 11218
The Heart of a Chief, 9148(F)
How Chipmunk Got His Stripes, 11221
Native American Animal Stories, 11219
Native Plant Stories, 11220
Pushing Up the Sky, 12013
Seeing the Circle, 12509
Squanto's Journey, 17491
Tell Me a Tale, 14070
Thirteen Moons on Turtle's Back, 11929
The Trail of Tears, 15936
When the Chenoo Howls, 11222
Bruchac, Joseph (jt. author). *Makiawisug*, 7722(F)
Bruemmer, Fred. *Seals*, 19734
Brumbeau, Jeff. *The Quiltmaker's Gift*, 1020(F)
Brundage, Buz. *Be a Better Hitter*, 22086
Brunelli, Roberto. *A Family Treasury of Bible Stories*, 17252
Brunkus, Denise. *Chocolatina*, 1319(F)
The Creepy Computer Mystery, 6455(F)
I Shop with My Daddy, 6477(F)
Junie B. Jones and a Little Monkey Business, 9951(F)
Junie B. Jones and her Big Fat Mouth, 10118(F)
Junie B. Jones and the Stupid Smelly Bus, 9953(F)
Junie B. Jones and the Yucky Blucky Fruitcake, 10119(F)
Junie B. Jones Has a Monster Under Her Bed, 6568(F)
Junie B. Jones Loves Handsome Warren, 6569(F)
The Karate Class Mystery, 6456(F)
The Luckiest Leprechaun, 1318(F)
Marsha Is Only a Flower, 6218(F)
Parents' Night Fright, 6458(F)
Samantha the Snob, 4939(F)
Brunning, Bob. *Heavy Metal*, 14121
1960s Pop, 14122

Rock 'n' Roll, 14123

Bruns, Roger A. *Billy the Kid*, 12851
Jesse James, 12908
John Wesley Powell, 12151

Brusca, Maria C. *Three Friends*, 391(F)

Brust, Beth Wagner. *The Amazing Paper Cuttings of Hans Christian Andersen*, 12491

Bruun, Bertel (jt. author). *The Human Body*, 18051

Bruun, Ruth Dowling. *The Human Body*, 18051

Bryan, Ashley. *All Night, All Day*, 14141
Aneesa Lee and the Weaver's Gift, 11581
Ashley Bryan's ABC of African American Poetry, 11750
Beat the Story-Drum, Pum-Pum, 10653
Carol of the Brown King, 5849
Christmas Gif', 17430
Climbing Jacob's Ladder, 17295
The House with No Door, 11722
Lion and the Ostrich Chicks and Other African Folk Tales, 10654
The Night Has Ears, 10655
Sing to the Sun, 11541
The Story of Lightning and Thunder, 10656
The Sun Is So Quiet, 11756
Turtle Knows Your Name, 11419
What a Morning! 14205
What a Wonderful World, 14259(F)
Why Leopard Has Spots, 10710

Bryan, Ashley, ed. *All Night, All Day*, 14141

Bryan, Diana. *The Fisherman and His Wife*, 10897

Bryan, Jenny. *Breathing*, 18123
Digestion, 18096
Living with Diabetes, 17944
Movement, 18169
The Pulse of Life, 18087
Smell, Taste and Touch, 18135
What's Wrong with Me? 17945

Bryan, Mike (jt. author). *Cal Ripken Jr.*, 13481
Cal Ripken, Jr., 13482

Bryant, Bonnie. *Horse Crazy*, 7165(F)

Bryant, Jennifer. *Jane Sayler*, 17842
Louis Braille, 13758

Bryant, Louella. *The Black Bonnet*, 9264(F)

Bryant, Michael. *Bein' with You This Way*, 11766
Booker T. Washington, 12813
Come Sunday, 3186(F)
Family Celebrations, 5644
Lost in the Tunnel of Time, 6823(F)
Madam C. J. Walker, 12810
Treemonisha, 9596(F)
A World of Holidays! 17347
Zora Neale Hurston, 12554

Bryant, Michael (jt. author). *The Story of Nat Love*, 12757

Bryant-Mole, Karen. *Blue*, 262(F)
Clothes, 21166
Drugs, 17861
Food, 20078
Games, 21981
Toys, 21024

Bryer, Diana. *The Girl Who Loved Coyotes*, 11321

Brynie, Faith Hickman. *Six-Minute Nature Experiments*, 18302

Bubley, Esther. *How Kittens Grow*, 19933

Buchanan, Debby (jt. author). *It Rained on the Desert Today*, 11944

Buchanan, Jane. *Gratefully Yours*, 9347(F)

Buchanan, Ken. *It Rained on the Desert Today*, 11944
This House Is Made of Mud, 4395(F)

Buchanan, Yvonne. *Fly, Bessie, Fly*, 12093
Follow the Drinking Gourd, 9268(F)
God Inside of Me, 1502(F)
Juneteenth Jamboree, 9767(F)

Buchholz, Quint. *The Collector of Moments*, 3985(F)
Sleep Well, Little Bear, 640(F)

Buchs, Thomas. *One Giant Leap*, 7017(F)

Buchwald, Ann (jt. author). *What to Do When and Why*, 17640

Buchwald, Emilie. *Gildaen*, 7631(F)

Buck, Nola. *Hey, Little Baby!* 3055(F)
How a Baby Grows, 3550(F)
Oh, Cats! 5148(F)
Santa's Short Suit Shrunk, 5766(F)
Sid and Sam, 6237(F)

Buck, Pearl. *The Big Wave*, 8573(F)

Buck-Murray, Marian. *The Mash and Smash Cookbook*, 21680

Buckley, Helen E. *Grandfather and I*, 3551(F)
Where Did Josie Go? 4097(F)

Buckley, James, Jr. *America's Greatest Game*, 22179

Buckvar, Felice. *Dangerous Dream*, 9647(F)

Budd, E. S. *Street Cleaners*, 21245

Budd, Jackie. *The Best Book of Ponies*, 19984
Horse and Pony Breeds, 19985
Horse and Pony Care, 19986
Horses, 19987
Learning to Ride Horses and Ponies, 19988

Budiansky, Stephen. *The World According to Horses*, 19989

Buehner, Caralyn. *Fanny's Dream*, 3552(F)
I Did It, I'm Sorry, 167(F)

Buehner, Mark. *Fanny's Dream*, 3552(F)
Harvey Potter's Balloon Farm, 1435(F)
I Am the Cat, 11811
I Did It, I'm Sorry, 167(F)
Maxi, the Hero, 1791(F)
My Life with the Wave, 1081(F)
My Monster Mama Loves Me So, 1351(F)

Buell, Janet. *Bog Bodies*, 14489
Greenland Mummies, 14490
Ice Maiden of the Andes, 14491

Buetter, Barbara M. *Simple Puppets from Everyday Materials*, 14303

Buetter, Barbara MacDonald. *Simple Puppets from Everyday Materials*, 14303

Buetter, George. *Simple Puppets from Everyday Materials*, 14303

Buffett, Jimmy. *The Jolly Mon*, 1021(F)
Trouble Dolls, 1022(F)

Buffett, Savannah (jt. author). *The Jolly Mon*, 1021(F)
Trouble Dolls, 1022(F)

Buffie, Margaret. *The Watcher*, 7632(F)

Bugni, Alice. *Moose Racks, Bear Tracks, and Other Alaska Kidsnacks*, 21681

Buholzer, Theres. *Life of the Snail*, 19602

Bulcken, Kimberly. *The Kids' Book of Chess*, 22171

Bull, Angela. *Flying Ace*, 12108

Bull, Jane. *Change Your Room*, 21415
The Halloween Book, 17442

Bull, Peter. *The Usborne Complete Book of Astronomy and Space*, 18400

Bulla, Clyde Robert. *The Chalk Box Kid*, 4914(F)
Daniel's Duck, 6238(F)
A Lion to Guard Us, 9186(F)
The Paint Brush Kid, 8574(F)
Shoeshine Girl, 8575(F)
Singing Sam, 6239(F)
Squanto, Friend of the Pilgrims, 12997
The Story of Valentine's Day, 17505
The Sword in the Tree, 9083(F)

Bullard, Lisa. *Not Enough Beds!* 16(F)

Buller, Jon. *Captain Zap and the Evil Baron von Fishhead*, 6240(F)
Felix and the 400 Frogs, 6241(F)

Buller, Jon (jt. author). *Toad on the Road*, 6629(F)
Toad Takes Off, 6630(F)

Bullock, Kathleen. *It Chanced to Rain*, 1900(F)
She'll Be Comin' Round the Mountain, 14142

Bulmer-Thomas, Barbara. *Journey Through Mexico*, 15605
Bunce, Vincent. *Volcanoes*, 20336
Bundey, Nikki. *Ice and the Earth*, 20357
Rain and People, 20729
Snow and the Earth, 20730
Wind and People, 20665
Bunnett, Rochelle. *Friends in the Park*, 4915
Bunson, Margaret. *St. Joan of Arc*, 13811
Bunson, Matthew (jt. author). *St. Joan of Arc*, 13811
Bunting, Eve. *Blackwater*, 8576(F)
The Blue and the Gray, 9469(F)
Butterfly House, 4396(F)
Can You Do This, Old Badger? 1901(F)
Cheyenne Again, 9149(F)
Coffin on a Case, 6778(F)
Dandelions, 9526(F)
The Day Before Christmas, 5767(F)
The Day the Whale Came, 3056(F)
A Day's Work, 3553(F)
December, 5768(F)
Doll Baby, 8577(F)
Dreaming of America, 4607(F)
Ducky, 1023(F)
Flower Garden, 3554(F)
Fly Away Home, 4916(F)
Ghost's Hour, Spook's Hour, 4917(F)
Going Home, 4608(F)
The Hideout, 6779(F)
How Many Days to America? A Thanksgiving Story, 6135(F)
I Am the Mummy Heb-Nefert, 8960(F)
I Don't Want to Go to Camp, 3057(F)
I Have an Olive Tree, 4609(F)
Is Anybody There? 8407(F)
Jin Woo, 3555(F)
The Man Who Could Call Down Owls, 1024(F)
Market Day, 4610(F)
The Memory String, 3556(F)
The Mother's Day Mice, 5613(F)
My Backpack, 4098(F)
Nasty, Stinky Sneakers, 9791(F)
Night of the Gargoyles, 1025(F)
Night Tree, 5769(F)
No Nap, 641(F)
On Call Back Mountain, 4918(F)
Once Upon a Time, 12511
Our Teacher's Having a Baby, 5479(F)
A Perfect Father's Day, 5614(F)
A Picnic in October, 3557(F)
The Pumpkin Fair, 3058(F)
Red Fox Running, 5149(F)
Riding the Tiger, 1026(F)
St. Patrick's Day in the Morning, 5615(F)
Scary, Scary Halloween, 5985(F)
Secret Place, 4397(F)

Sharing Susan, 8408(F)
Smoky Night, 3059(F)
So Far from the Sea, 4611(F)
Some Frog! 7166(F)
Someday a Tree, 4398(F)
Someone Is Hiding on Alcatraz Island, 6780(F)
Summer Wheels, 8262(F)
Sunflower House, 4399(F)
Sunshine Home, 3558(F)
Swan in Love, 1902(F)
Train to Somewhere, 9348(F)
Trouble on the T-Ball Team, 2914(F)
A Turkey for Thanksgiving, 6136(F)
Twinnies, 4919(F)
The Valentine Bears, 6163(F)
The Wall, 3559(F)
The Wednesday Surprise, 3560(F)
Who Was Born This Special Day? 5770(F)
Your Move, 8578(F)
Bunting, Jane. *My First ABC*, 17(F)
Burandt, Harriet. *Tales from the Homeplace*, 9527(F)
Burbank, Jon. *Nepal*, 15151
Burby, Liza N. *Heat Waves and Droughts*, 20757
Mae Jemison, 12126
Tornadoes, 20686
Burch, Joann J. *Chico Mendes*, 13323
A Fairy-Tale Life, 12492
Fine Print, 13304
Jefferson Davis, 12872
Marian Wright Edelman, 13150
Burch, Robert. *Christmas with Ida Early*, 9709(F)
Ida Early Comes over the Mountain, 7395(F)
Queenie Peavy, 8579(F)
Burchard, Peter. *Squanto, Friend of the Pilgrims*, 12997
Burckhardt, Ann L. (jt. author). *Cooking the Australian Way*, 21700
Burden-Patmon, Denise. *Imani's Gift at Kwanzaa*, 9710(F)
Burdett, Lois. *Hamlet for Kids*, 12047
Burdick, Jeri. *Sailor Cats*, 2850(F)
Burford, Betty. *Chocolate by Hershey*, 12899
Burford, Kay. *Kimako's Story*, 3255(F)
Burgan, Michael. *Belgium*, 15397
England, 15338
Maryland, 16836
Burger, Carl. *Old Yeller*, 7199(F)
Burger, Leslie. *Red Cross/Red Crescent*, 17017
Sister Cities in a World of Difference, 14332
United Nations High Commission for Refugees, 17018
Burgess, Jan. *Food and Digestion*, 18097

Burgess, Lord (jt. author). *Island in the Sun*, 15695
Burgess, Mark. *Dogs' Night*, 2218(F)
Harriet and the Crocodiles, 2797(F)
Burgess, Melvin. *The Copper Treasure*, 9084(F)
The Cry of the Wolf, 7167(F)
The Earth Giant, 7633(F)
Kite, 7168(F)
Burgess, Thornton W. *Old Mother West Wind*, 1903(F)
Burgin, Norma. *Mouse, Look Out!* 2810(F)
Burke, Dianne O. *Creepy Cuisine*, 21722
Burke, Jennifer S. *Cloudy Days*, 6242(F)
Burke, L. M. *Skateboarding!* 22275
Burke, Patrick. *Eastern Europe*, 15261
Burke, Susan S. *Class Act*, 21826(F)
Home on the Range, 21816
My Very Own Christmas, 21511
Out to Dry, 21856
Plugged In, 21844(F)
Burke, Timothy R. *Tugboats in Action*, 4612(F)
Burke-Weiner, Kimberly. *The Maybe Garden*, 3060(F)
Burkholder, Kelly. *Pen Pals*, 14071
Plays, 12014
Poetry, 11542
Stories, 14072
Burks, Brian. *Walks Alone*, 15937(F)
Wrango, 9349(F)
Burleigh, Robert. *Black Whiteness*, 12087
Flight, 12134
Hercules, 11461
Home Run, 13497
Hoops, 11995
It's Funny Where Ben's Train Takes Him, 1027(F)
Lookin' for Bird in the Big City, 4613(F)
A Man Named Thoreau, 12605
Messenger, Messenger, 3061(F)
Who Said That? 12640
Burnard, Damon. *The Amazing Adventures of Soupy Boy!* 7634(F)
Burger! 7635(F)
Pork and Beef's Great Adventure, 7636(F)
Burnett, Frances Hodgson. *A Little Princess*, 4920(F), 7396(F)
The Secret Garden, 8263(F)
Burnham, Philip. *Gbaya*, 14920
Burnie, David. *How Nature Works*, 18580
Light, 20858
Mammals, 18611
Tree, 20195
Burnie, David (jt. author). *Birds*, 19217

Burnie, Richard. *Monumental Mazes*, 21863

Burningham, John. *Chitty Chitty Bang Bang*, 7728(F)
Hey! 5150(F)
Mr. Gumpy's Motor Car, 2915(F)
Whaddayamean, 1028(F)

Burns, Andy (jt. author). *Home on the Range*, 21816

Burns, Bree. *Harriet Tubman*, 12796

Burns, Diane L. *Berries, Nuts and Seeds*, 20268
Cranberries, 20079
Frogs, Toads and Turtles, 18680
Home on the Range, 21816
Sugaring Season, 20080

Burns, Howard M. *The Boy Who Saved the Town*, 4829(F)

Burns, Kate. *Hide and Seek*, 4400(F)
How Does Your Garden Grow? 21760
Jump Like a Frog! 304(F)

Burns, Khephra. *Black Stars in Orbit*, 20964

Burns, Marilyn. *The Book of Think (or How to Solve a Problem Twice Your Size)*, 21864
The Greedy Triangle, 1029(F)
The Hanukkah Book, 17453
How Many Feet? How Many Tails? 392(F)
I Am Not a Short Adult, 17028
The I Hate Mathematics! Book, 20613
This Book Is About Time, 20641

Burns, Peggy. *The Mail*, 16919
Money, 16920
News, 14073
Stores and Markets, 16933
Travel, 21280
Writing, 13979

Burr, Claudia. *Broken Shields*, 15606
Cinco de Mayo, 15607
When the Viceroy Came, 15608

Burr, Dan. *Keisha Discovers Harlem*, 9583(F)

Burrell, Roy. *Oxford First Ancient History*, 14580
The Romans, 14713

Burrowes, Adjoa J. *Grandma's Purple Flowers*, 3561(F)
My Steps, 3102(F)

Bursik, Rose. *Amelia's Fantastic Flight*, 1030(F)

Burstein, Chaya M. *The Jewish Kids Catalog*, 17454

Burt, Denise. *Kangaroos*, 19176
Koalas, 19177

Burton, Jane. *Egg*, 18917
Fox, 19131
The Nature and Science of Autumn, 18562
The Nature and Science of Bubbles, 20799
The Nature and Science of Color, 20859

The Nature and Science of Energy, 20820
The Nature and Science of Fire, 20279
The Nature and Science of Fossils, 14390
The Nature and Science of Numbers, 20628
The Nature and Science of Reflections, 20860
The Nature and Science of Rocks, 20552
The Nature and Science of Seeds, 20269
The Nature and Science of Shells, 19771
The Nature and Science of Survival, 18581
The Nature and Science of Waste, 16974
Swamp Life, 20374

Burton, Katherine. *One Gray Mouse*, 393

Burton, Robert. *Egg*, 18917

Burton, Tim. *The Nightmare Before Christmas*, 9711(F)

Burton, Virginia Lee. *Life Story*, 20298
The Little House, 3062(F)
Mike Mulligan and His Steam Shovel, 5551(F)

Busby, Cylin. *The Chicken-Fried Rat*, 8580(F)

Buscaglia, Leo. *A Memory for Tino*, 8264(F)

Busch, Phyllis S. *Backyard Safaris*, 18582

Buscher, Sarah. *Mairead Corrigan and Betty Williams*, 15339

Bush, John. *The Fish Who Could Wish*, 1904(F)

Bush, Lawrence. *Emma Ansky-Levine and Her Mitzvah Machine*, 7637(F)

Bush, Timothy. *Bach's Big Adventure*, 4711(F)
Ferocious Girls, Steamroller Boys, and Other Poems in Between, 11859

Bushe, Claire. *Angels, Prophets, Rabbis and Kings*, 11157

Bushey, Jeanne. *A Sled Dog for Moshi*, 5151(F)

Bushnell, Jack. *Circus of the Wolves*, 5152(F)
Sky Dancer, 5153(F)

Buss, Fran L. *Journey of the Sparrows*, 7336(F)

Bussell, Darcey. *Ballet*, 14276
The Young Dancer, 14277

Busser, Marianne. *King Bobble*, 4099(F)

Butcher, Jim. *Jackie Robinson and the Story of All-Black Baseball*, 13494

Butcher, Kristin. *The Runaways*, 8581(F)

Butler, Chris. *The Moon and Riddles Diner and the Sunnyside Cafe*, 11927

Butler, Daphne. *France*, 15300
Italy, 15374
U.S.A., 15868

Butler, Dori Hillestad. *M Is for Minnesota*, 16540

Butler, Dorothy. *Another Happy Tale*, 4100(F)
My Brown Bear Barney at the Party, 5668(F)

Butler, Jerry. *A Drawing in the Sand*, 13951
Sweet Words So Brave, 14076

Butler, John. *Baby Animals*, 5245(F)
Bashi, Elephant Baby, 5374(F)
Little Elephant Thunderfoot, 5236(F)
Little Sibu, 5237(F)
Maya, Tiger Cub, 5375(F)
Pi-Shu, the Little Panda, 5154(F)
Polar Star, 5238(F)
While You Were Sleeping, 394(F)

Butler, Jon. *Religion in Colonial America*, 16099

Butler, Kristi T. *Rip's Secret Spot*, 6243(F)

Butler, Philippa. *Pawprints in Time*, 4614(F)

Butler, Susan. *The Hermit Thrush Sings*, 10154(F)

Butterfield, Moira. *Animals in Trees*, 20432
Animals on Plains and Prairies, 20531
Bulldozers, 21298
Fast, Strong, and Striped, 18929
Fun with Paint, 21563
Hansel and Gretel, 12015
Little Red Riding Hood, 12016
Look Inside Cross-Sections, 21281
Richard Orr's Nature Cross-Sections, 16953
Ships, 21355
Space, 20965

Butterfield, Ned. *The Ghost of Gracie Mansion*, 9302(F)
The Illustrated Rules of In-line Hockey, 22036

Butterworth, Nick. *Jasper's Beanstalk*, 1905(F)
Jingle Bells, 5771(F)
My Dad Is Awesome, 3562(F)
The Rescue Party, 1031(F)

Butterworth, Oliver. *The Enormous Egg*, 9792(F)

Buttfield, Helen. *The Secret Life of Fishes*, 19654

Buttner, Thom. *Smoking Stinks!!* 8668(F)

Butts, Ellen R. *Carl Sagan*, 13345
Eugenie Clark, 13258

Butts, Nancy. *Cheshire Moon*, 8883(F)
The Door in the Lake, 10155(F)

Byard, Carole. *Africa Dream,*
4671(F)
The Black Snowman, 5881(F)
Grandmama's Joy, 3661(F)
Have a Happy . . ., 9766(F)
Working Cotton, 3476(F)
Byars, Betsy. *The Animal, the Veg-
etable and John D. Jones,*
8265(F)
Ant Plays Bear, 6244(F)
Beans on the Roof, 7397(F)
*The Blossoms and the Green Phan-
tom,* 7398(F)
*The Burning Questions of Bingo
Brown,* 10030(F)
The Cartoonist, 8582(F)
The Computer Nut, 10156(F)
Cracker Jackson, 8409(F)
The Cybil War, 9793(F)
The Dark Stairs, 6781(F)
Dead Letter, 6782(F)
Death's Door, 6783(F)
The 18th Emergency, 10031(F)
The Glory Girl, 7399(F)
The Golly Sisters Go West, 4101(F)
The Golly Sisters Ride Again,
6245(F)
Hooray for the Golly Sisters!
6246(F)
The House of Wings, 8583(F)
McMummy, 7638(F)
Me Tarzan, 9794(F)
The Midnight Fox, 7169(F)
The Moon and I, 12514
My Brother, Ant, 6247(F)
My Dog, My Hero, 7171(F)
The Night Swimmers, 8584(F)
The Pinballs, 8266(F)
The Seven Treasure Hunts, 9795(F)
The Summer of the Swans, 8884(F)
Tarot Says Beware, 6784(F)
Tornado, 7170(F)
Trouble River, 9350(F)
*The Two-Thousand-Pound
Goldfish,* 8410(F)
The Winged Colt of Casa Mia,
7639(F)
Byers, Helen. *Colors of Japan,* 15130
*Count Your Way Through
Germany,* 15325
Byers, Patricia. *The Kids' Money
Book,* 16940
Byles, Monica. *Experiment with
Plants,* 20229
Experiment with Senses, 18136
Byman, Jeremy. *Carl Sagan,* 13346
Madam Secretary, 12839
Tim Duncan, 13520
Bynum, Jane K. *Bubbe and Gram,*
3677(F)
Bynum, Janie. *Altoona Baboona,*
1906(F)
Otis, 1907(F)
Byrd, Robert. *Finn MacCoul and His
Fearless Wife,* 10953
*Saint Francis and the Christmas
Donkey,* 5772(F)

Byrd, Samuel. *Dancing with the Indians,* 3318(F)
Keep on Singing, 12345
*A Picture Book of Frederick Dou-
glass,* 12708
A Picture Book of Harriet Tubman,
12795
Byrne, Connell P. *Millions of Miles
to Mars,* 18475

Cabban, Vanessa. *Bertie and Small
and the Brave Sea Journey,*
1032(F)
Down in the Woods at Sleepytime,
774(F)
Love Is a Handful of Honey,
1741(F)
Cable, Annette. *I Fly,* 2965(F)
Me and My Amazing Body, 18081
Me and My Family Tree, 3910
Me and My Place in Space, 18420
Me Counting Time, 20654
Me on the Map, 14372
Cabrera, Jane. *Dog's Day,* 1908(F)
Eggday, 2043(F)
Over in the Meadow, 395
Panda Big and Panda Small,
1909(F)
Rory and the Lion, 4102(F)
Cadnum, Michael. *Heat,* 10292(F)
Caduto, Michael J. *Earth Tales from
Around the World,* 10537
Cadwallader, Sharon. *Cookie
McCorkle and the Case of the
Emerald Earrings,* 6785(F)
Caes, Charles J. *The Young Zillion-
aire's Guide to the Stock
Market,* 16921
Caffey, Donna. *Yikes — Lice!* 17946
Cahoon, Heather. *Word Play ABC,*
18(F)
Cain, David. *Copier Creations,*
21614
*The New York Public Library Kid's
Guide to Research,* 14089
Cain, Sheridan. *Look Out for the Big
Bad Fish!* 1910(F)
Why So Sad, Brown Rabbit?
1911(F)
Caines, Jeannette. *Abby,* 3563(F)
I Need a Lunch Box, 3063(F)
Just Us Women, 2916(F)
Cairns, Julia. *Off to the Sweet Shores
of Africa,* 897
The Spider Weaver, 10707
Calabro, Marian. *The Perilous Jour-
ney of the Donner Party,* 16294
Calcagnino, Steve (jt. author). *The
Body Book,* 4522
Calder, Kate (jt. author). *The Life of a
Miner,* 16329
Women of the West, 16330
Caldwell, V. M. *The Ocean Within,*
8585(F)
Calhoun, Mary. *Blue-Ribbon Henry,*
1912(F)
Cross-Country Cat, 1913(F)

Flood, 8586(F)
Hot-Air Henry, 1914(F)
Katie John, 8411(F)
Callahan, Dorothy. *Julie Krone,*
13694
Callan, Lyndall (jt. author). *Dirt on
Their Skirts,* 4805(F)
Callen, Larry. *Who Kidnapped the
Sheriff?* 9796(F)
Calmenson, Stephanie. *Gator Hal-
loween,* 9797(F)
Get Well, Gators! 9798(F)
*Marigold and Grandma on the
Town,* 6248(F)
My Dog's the Best! 6249(F)
Roller Skates! 6250(F)
Rosie, 19940
Shaggy, Waggy Dogs (and Others),
19941
The Teeny Tiny Teacher, 10954
Calmenson, Stephanie (jt. author).
*Crazy Eights and Other Card
Games,* 22229
The Eentsy, Weentsy Spider, 21984
Fun on the Run, 21985
Give a Dog a Bone, 7176(F)
Marbles, 21986
*Pin the Tail on the Donkey and
Other Party Games,* 21987
Ready . . . Set . . . Read! 6280(F)
*Ready . . . Set . . . Read — and
Laugh!* 21819(F)
Six Sick Sheep, 21879
*Why Did the Chicken Cross the
Road?* 21820(F)
Calvert, Patricia. *Bigger,* 9351(F)
Glennis, Before and After, 8412(F)
Great Lives, 12641
Michael, Wait for Me, 8587(F)
Sooner, 9352(F)
Writing to Richie, 8588(F)
Calvert, Roz. *Zora Neale Hurston,*
12553
Camburn, Carol A. *Teeny Tiny
Ernest,* 1788(F)
Cameron, Alice. *The Cat Sat on the
Mat,* 5155(F)
Cameron, Ann. *Gloria's Way,*
8589(F)
Julian, Dream Doctor, 5669(F)
Julian's Glorious Summer, 6251(F)
The Kidnapped Prince, 13791
More Stories Huey Tells, 9799(F)
*The Secret Life of Amanda K.
Woods,* 8590(F)
The Stories Julian Tells, 7400(F)
Cameron, Eleanor. *The Court of the
Stone Children,* 7640(F)
Mr. Bass's Planetoid, 10157(F)
*The Wonderful Flight to the Mush-
room Planet,* 10158(F)
Cameron, Marie. *Clever Katya,*
11090
Cameron, Rod. *Breaking the Chains
of the Ancient Warrior,*
10372(F)

Cameron, Scott. *Beethoven Lives Upstairs*, 9065(F)
David and Goliath, 17263
Maple Moon, 11225(F)
The Token Gift, 9002(F)
Camm, Martin. *Frog*, 18716
Journey Through Canada, 15596
Journey Through China, 15084
Journey Through Japan, 15140
Journey Through Mexico, 15605
Camp, Carole Ann. *American Astronomers*, 13204
Camp, Lindsay. *The Biggest Bed in the World*, 3564(F)
Why? 1033(F)
Campbell, Ann. *Once upon a Princess and a Pea*, 10404(F)
Campbell, Ann-Jeanette. *Dora's Box*, 1034(F)
The New York Public Library Amazing Space, 20966
The New York Public Library Incredible Earth, 20299
Campbell, Jim. *Baseball's Greatest Pitchers*, 13384
Joe Louis, 13586
Wonder Women of Sports, 13385
Campbell, Kumari. *Prince Edward Island*, 15568
Campbell, Louisa. *Phoebe's Fabulous Father*, 3565(F)
A World of Holidays! 17347
Campbell, Peter A. *Alien Encounters*, 21896
Launch Day, 20967
Campbell, Rod. *Dear Zoo*, 5156(F)
Campitelli, Sara. *Mammolina*, 13835
Canadeo, Anne. *Ralph Lauren*, 12924
Caney, Steven. *Steven Caney's Kids' America*, 21517
Steven Caney's Playbook, 21416
Canfield, Dorothy. *Understood Betsy*, 7401(F)
Canfield, Jack. *Chicken Soup for Little Souls*, 4921(F)
Cann, Helen. *Mary's Story*, 17251
Cann, Kate. *Living in the World*, 17133
Cannon, Ann Edwards. *I Know What You Do When I Go to School*, 4103(F)
Cannon, Annie. *The Bat in the Boot*, 4401(F)
Ma Jiang and the Orange Ants, 4799(F)
Tale of a Tadpole, 5370(F)
Cannon, Janell. *Crickwing*, 1917(F)
Stellaluna, 1918(F)
Trupp, 1919(F)
Verdi, 1920(F)
Cannon, Karen. *A Special Place for Charlee*, 7266(F)
Canyon, Christopher. *The Ever-Living Tree*, 20219
Grand Canyon, 16643

The Tree in the Ancient Forest, 16966
Cape, Elizabeth (jt. author). *Best Friends*, 21410
Capek, Michael. *Artistic Trickery*, 13883
Jamaica, 15696, 15697
Murals, 13884
Caple, Kathy. *The Friendship Tree*, 6252(F)
Hillary to the Rescue, 2917(F)
The Purse, 3064(F)
Well Done, Worm! 6253(F)
The Wimp, 1921(F)
Caple, Laurie A. *Bird Watching with Margaret Morse Nice*, 13336
Clyde Tombaugh and the Search for Planet X, 13350
Wildlife Watching with Charles Eastman, 13268
Capote, Truman. *A Christmas Memory*, 9712(F)
The Thanksgiving Visitor, 8592(F)
Cappetta, Cynthia. *Chairs, Chairs, Chairs!* 6254(F)
Capucilli, Alyssa Satin. *Bathtime for Biscuit*, 6255(F)
Biscuit, 6256(F)
Biscuit Finds a Friend, 6257(F)
Biscuit's New Trick, 6258(F)
Biscuit's Valentine's Day, 6164(F)
Happy Birthday, Biscuit! 5670(F)
Happy Thanksgiving, Biscuit! 6137(F)
Inside a Barn in the Country, 5157(F)
Inside a House That Is Haunted, 5986(F)
Inside a Zoo in the City, 6259(F)
The Potty Book for Boys, 3065(F)
Carbone, Elisa. *Sarah and the Naked Truth*, 10032(F)
Starting School with an Enemy, 10033(F)
Storm Warriors, 9528(F)
Cardo, Horacio. *The Story of Chess*, 7641(F)
Carey, Charles W. *The Emancipation Proclamation*, 16397
George Washington Carver, 13253
Carey, Janet. *Molly's Fire*, 9648(F)
Carey, Peter. *The Big Bazoohley*, 6786(F)
Carey, Vicky. *Mark T-W-A-I-N!* 12607
Carle, Eric. *Brown Bear, Brown Bear, What Do You See?* 283(F)
Do You Want to Be My Friend? 912(F)
Does a Kangaroo Have a Mother, Too? 5158
Draw Me a Star, 1035(F)
Dream Snow, 5773(F)
Eric Carle's Animals Animals, 11816

Eric Carle's Dragons Dragons and Other Creatures That Never Were, 11735
Eric Carle's Treasury of Classic Stories for Children by Aesop, Hans Christian Andersen, and the Brothers Grimm, 10538
Flora and Tiger, 12198
From Head to Toe, 168
The Grouchy Ladybug, 1922(F)
Have You Seen My Cat? 5159(F)
Hello, Red Fox, 263(F)
The Hole in the Dike, 4670(F)
The Honeybee and the Robber, 1923(F)
Little Cloud, 1036(F)
The Mixed-Up Chameleon, 1924(F)
My Apron, 3566(F)
My Very First Book of Words, 6260
1, 2, 3 to the Zoo, 396(F)
Papa, Please Get the Moon for Me, 1037(F)
Polar Bear, Polar Bear, What Do You Hear? 5340(F)
Roosters Off to See the World, 397(F)
The Secret Birthday Message, 5671(F)
The Tiny Seed, 4402(F)
Today Is Monday, 14235
The Very Busy Spider, 1925(F)
The Very Clumsy Click Beetle, 1926(F)
The Very Hungry Caterpillar, 5160(F)
The Very Lonely Firefly, 1927(F)
The Very Quiet Cricket, 1928(F)
Carlesimo, Cheryl (jt. author). *The Saturday Kid*, 4835(F)
Carling, Amelia Lau. *Mama and Papa Have a Store*, 4615(F)
Carlson, Jeffrey D. *A Historical Album of Minnesota*, 16541
Carlson, Kit. *Bringing Up Baby*, 18870
Carlson, Kit (jt. author). *The Leopard Son*, 19075
Carlson, Laurie. *Boss of the Plains*, 21167
Classical Kids, 14581
Colonial Kids, 16100
EcoArt! 21417
Westward Ho! 16295
Carlson, Lori M. *Hurray for Three Kings' Day!* 5774(F)
Sol a Sol, 11543
Carlson, Lori M., ed. *You're On! Seven Plays in English and Spanish*, 12017
Carlson, Margaret. *The Canning Season*, 7402(F)
Carlson, Nancy. *ABC I Like Me!* 19(F)
Arnie and the New Kid, 4922(F)
Harriet and the Garden, 1929(F)
Harriet's Halloween Candy, 5987(F)

Hooray for Grandparents' Day! 5480(F)

I Like Me! 1930(F)

It's Going to Be Perfect! 3567(F)

Look Out Kindergarten, Here I Come! 5481(F)

Loudmouth George and the Cornet, 1931(F)

Carlson, Natalie Savage. *The Family Under the Bridge,* 8267(F)

Carlson, Nolan. *Summer and Shiner,* 7172(F)

Carlsson, Bo Kage. *Sweden,* 15439

Carlstrom, Nancy White. *Better Not Get Wet, Jesse Bear,* 1932(F)

Blow Me a Kiss, Miss Lilly, 3986(F)

Does God Know How to Tie Shoes? 17172(F)

Guess Who's Coming, Jesse Bear, 1933(F)

Happy Birthday, Jesse Bear! 5672(F)

How Do You Say It Today, Jesse Bear? 1934(F)

I'm Not Moving, Mama! 1935(F)

Let's Count It Out, Jesse Bear, 398(F)

Midnight Dance of the Snowshoe Hare, 11945

Raven and River, 1936(F)

The Snow Speaks, 3066(F)

Swim the Silver Sea, Joshie Otter, 643(F)

Thanksgiving Day at Our House, 6138

The Way to Wyatt's House, 1038(F)

What a Scare, Jesse Bear, 5988(F)

Where Does the Night Hide? 644(F)

Where Is Christmas, Jesse Bear? 5775(F)

Who Said Boo? 11827

Wild Wild Sunflower Child Anna, 4403(F)

Carlyle, Carolyn. *Mercy Hospital,* 6787(F)

Carmack, Lisa Jobe. *Philippe in Monet's Garden,* 1039(F)

Carmi, Daniella. *Samir and Yonatan,* 8926(F)

Carmi, Giora. *The Chanukkah Guest,* 6083(F)

The Greatest of All, 10818

A Journey to Paradise, 11152

The Old Woman and Her Pig, 11009

The Rooster Prince, 8193(F)

Carmichael, Clay. *Bear at the Beach,* 1937(F)

Used-Up Bear, 1040(F)

Carnabuci, Anthony. *The Gift,* 6068(F)

Carnell, Suzanne, ed. *A Treasury of Pet Stories,* 7173(F)

Carney, Margaret. *At Grandpa's Sugar Bush,* 3067(F)

Carolin, Roger, ed. *Incredible Plants,* 20230

Caron, Mona. *The Boy Without a Name,* 11196

Caron, Romi. *Little Wonders,* 18868

Side by Side, 18606

Carow, Leslie. *Marjory Stoneman Douglas,* 13266

Carpenter, Angelica S. *Frances Hodgson Burnett,* 12512

Robert Louis Stevenson, 12599

Carpenter, Eric. *Young Thurgood Marshall,* 12764

Carpenter, F. R. *Tales of a Chinese Grandmother,* 10739

Carpenter, Mark L. *Brazil,* 15726

Carpenter, Mary Chapin. *Halley Came to Jackson,* 3568(F)

Carpenter, Nancy. *Bus Riders,* 3993(F)

Can You Dance, Dalila? 5003(F)

Lester's Dog, 2939(F)

Loud Emily, 4256(F)

Masai and I, 8967(F)

Mysteries on Monroe Street, 8258(F)

Only a Star, 5811(F)

A Picnic in October, 3557(F)

A Sister's Wish, 3717(F)

Sitti's Secrets, 4781(F)

Twinnies, 4919(F)

Twister, 2909(F)

Washing the Willow Tree Loon, 5341(F)

Carpenter, Stephen. *A Bad Case of the Giggles,* 11881

Miles of Smiles, 11882

The Three Billy Goats Gruff, 10955

Carr, Jan. *Big Truck and Little Truck,* 1041(F)

Dark Day, Light Night, 4923(F)

Frozen Noses, 3987(F)

Swine Divine, 1938(F)

Carran, Betty B. *Romania,* 15262

Carreiro, Carolyn. *Hand-Print Animal Art,* 21564

Carrick, Carol. *The Accident,* 4924(F)

Big Old Bones, 4104(F)

Left Behind, 2918(F)

Lost in the Storm, 5161(F)

Melanie, 1042(F)

Mothers Are Like That, 5162(F)

Patrick's Dinosaurs, 4925(F)

Patrick's Dinosaurs on the Internet, 1043(F)

Sleep Out, 2919(F)

Stay Away from Simon! 9265(F)

The Upside-Down Cake, 8593(F)

Valentine, 3569(F)

Whaling Days, 19778

What Happened to Patrick's Dinosaurs? 1939(F)

Carrick, Donald. *The Accident,* 4924(F)

Big Old Bones, 4104(F)

Doctor Change, 7658(F)

Ghost's Hour, Spook's Hour, 4917(F)

Going the Moose Way Home, 2346(F)

Journey to Topaz, 7379(F)

Left Behind, 2918(F)

Lost in the Storm, 5161(F)

Patrick's Dinosaurs, 4925(F)

Sleep Out, 2919(F)

Stay Away from Simon! 9265(F)

The Wednesday Surprise, 3560(F)

What Happened to Patrick's Dinosaurs? 1939(F)

Yellow Blue Jay, 8705(F)

Carrick, Paul. *Mothers Are Like That,* 5162(F)

Carrier, Lark. *A Christmas Promise,* 5776(F)

Do Not Touch, 169(F)

There Was a Hill . . ., 305(F)

Carrier, Roch. *The Boxing Champion,* 4926(F)

A Happy New Year's Day, 5616(F)

Carrillo, Louis. *Edward James Olmos,* 12438

Oscar de la Renta, 12829

Carrington, Cheryl. *Kwanzaa,* 5655

Carrington, Marsha Gray. *Jake Johnson,* 4311(F)

Sometimes I Feel Like a Storm Cloud, 3124(F)

Carrion, Esther. *The Empire of the Czars,* 15410

Carris, Joan. *Just a Little Ham,* 7174(F)

Carroll, Bob. *Napoleon Bonaparte,* 13839

Pancho Villa, 13864

Carroll, Lewis. *Alice in Wonderland,* 7642(F)

Alice's Adventures in Wonderland, 7643(F), 7644(F), 7645(F)

Alice's Adventures in Wonderland and Through the Looking Glass, 7646(F)

Jabberwocky, 11860

Through the Looking Glass, and What Alice Found There, 7647(F)

Carroll, Michael. *Are We Moving to Mars?* 18486

Carroll, Pamela. *Life in a Tidal Pool,* 19867

Carroll, Thomas. *The Colony,* 7648(F)

Carroll, Walter. *Life in a Tidal Pool,* 19867

Carrow, Robert. *Put a Fan in Your Hat!* 18303

Carrozza, John. *Tundra Discoveries,* 15843

Carruthers, Margaret W. (jt. author). *National Audubon Society First Field Guide to Rocks and Minerals,* 20569

Carryl, Charles E. *The Walloping Window-Blind,* 11861

Carson, Mary Kay. *Epilepsy*, 17947

Cart, Chris. *The Formerly Great Alexander Family*, 8522(F)

Carter, Abby. *Baseball Ballerina*, 6293(F)
Baseball Ballerina Strikes Out! 6294(F)
Busy O'Brien and the Great Bubble Gum Blowout, 9969(F)
Never Ride Your Elephant to School, 4193(F)
No Copycats Allowed! 6354(F)

Carter, Alden R. *Big Brother Dustin*, 3570(F)
Crescent Moon, 9529(F)
Dustin's Big School Day, 5482(F)
I'm Tougher Than Asthma! 17949
Seeing Things My Way, 4927
Stretching Ourselves, 17948

Carter, Andy. *George Washington Carver*, 13254

Carter, Anne. *Tall in the Saddle*, 1044(F)

Carter, Carol. *Big Brother Dustin*, 3570(F)

Carter, Carol S. *Dustin's Big School Day*, 5482(F)

Carter, David. *The Nutcracker*, 10885

Carter, David A. *Cars! Cars! Cars!* 5584(F)
Curious Critters, 1802(F)
The Elements of Pop-Up, 21608
How to Be an Ocean Scientist in Your Own Home, 18348
I Wonder What's Under There? A Brief History of Underwear, 21176
In a Dark, Dark Wood, 2920(F)
More Bugs in Boxes, 170(F)

Carter, Don. *See You Soon Moon*, 3079(F)
Wake Up House! Rooms Full of Poems, 11631

Carter, Donna Renee. *Music in the Family*, 3571(F)

Carter, Dorothy. *Bye, Mis' Lela*, 4928(F)
Wilhe'mina Miles After the Stork Night, 3572(F)

Carter, Gail G. *May'naise Sandwiches and Sunshine Tea*, 3979(F)

Carter, Noelle (jt. author). *The Nutcracker*, 10885

Carter, Siri M. (jt. author). *I'm Tougher Than Asthma!* 17949

Carter, Terry. *Card Games for Children*, 22230

Cartwright, Reg. *The Band over the Hill*, 2243(F)
The Boat of Many Rooms, 4213(F)
James and the Rain, 487(F)
The Lot at the End of My Block, 5581(F)
The Three Golden Oranges, 11133
What Does the Rabbit Say? 5246(F)

Cartwright, Shannon. *Alaska's Three Bears*, 5227(F)
Moose Racks, Bear Tracks, and Other Alaska Kidsnacks, 21681
Turnagain Ptarmigan! Where Did You Go? 1212(F)

Cartwright, Stephen. *Ted in a Red Bed*, 6288(F)
The Usborne Children's Songbook, 14234

Carus, Marianne, ed. *That's Ghosts for You*, 7649(F)

Caruso, Sandra. *The Young Actor's Book of Improvisation*, 14322

Carusone, Al. *Don't Open the Door After the Sun Goes Down*, 7650(F)

Carusone, Albert R. *The Boy with Dinosaur Hands*, 7651(F)

Carver, Douglas. *Michael Andretti at Indianapolis*, 22078

Carwardine, Mark. *Killer Whale*, 19779

Cary, Alice. *Jean Craighead George*, 12541
Katherine Paterson, 12575

Casad, Mary Brooke. *Bluebonnet at the Marshall Train Depot*, 1940(F)

Casale, Paul. *Return of the Home Run Kid*, 10310(F)

Casanellas, Antonio. *Great Discoveries and Inventions That Advanced Industry and Technology*, 21025
Great Discoveries and Inventions That Helped Explore Earth and Space, 20968
Great Discoveries and Inventions That Improved Human Health, 18019

Casanova, Mary. *Curse of a Winter Moon*, 9030(F)
The Hunter, 10740
Moose Tracks, 6788(F)
Riot, 8594(F)
Stealing Thunder, 7175(F)
Wolf Shadows, 6789(F)

Casden, Ron (jt. author). *A Noteworthy Tale*, 1427(F)

Caseley, Judith. *Chloe in the Know*, 8595(F)
Dorothy's Darkest Days, 8596(F)
Field Day Friday, 5483(F)
Harry and Arney, 7403(F)
Jorah's Journal, 8597(F)
Mama Coming and Going, 3573(F)
Mickey's Class Play, 5484(F)
Mr. Green Peas, 5163(F)
Praying to A. L, 8598(F)
Priscilla Twice, 4929(F)
Starring Dorothy Kane, 7404(F)
Witch Mama, 5989(F)

Caselli, Giovanni. *Greek Myths*, 11494
An Ice Age Hunter, 8950(F)

In Search of Knossos, 14522
In Search of Troy, 14523
In Search of Tutankhamun, 14611

Casey, Denise. *Weather Everywhere*, 20758

Casey, Jane C. *Millard Fillmore*, 13033
William Howard Taft, 13105

Casey, Kevin K. *Judo*, 22266

Casey, Moe. *The Most Excellent Book of Dress Up*, 21537

Casey, Patricia. *The Best Thing About a Puppy*, 5261(F)
I Like Monkeys Because . . ., 18997

Cash, Rosanne. *Penelope Jane*, 10405(F)

Cash, Terry. *Bricks*, 21116

Cash-Walsh, Tina. *The Healthy Body Cookbook*, 21690
The United States Cookbook, 21692

Casilla, Robert. *Con Mi Hermano/With My Brother*, 3859(F)
Jackie Robinson, 13486
Jalapeno Bagels, 3952(F)
The Legend of Mexicatl, 11402
The Little Painter of Sabana Granda, 4762(F)
A Picture Book of Eleanor Roosevelt, 13178
A Picture Book of Jackie Robinson, 13487
A Picture Book of Jesse Owens, 13664
A Picture Book of John F. Kennedy, 13058
A Picture Book of Martin Luther King, Jr., 12739
A Picture Book of Rosa Parks, 12773
A Picture Book of Simon Bolivar, 13754
A Picture Book of Thurgood Marshall, 12763
The Pool Party, 8821(F)
Rodeo Day, 5434(F)
The Train to Lulu's, 3223(F)

Casparian, Marguerite. *Ada's Pal*, 5321(F)

Cassatt, Mary. *A Child's Book of Lullabies*, 737(F)

Cassedy, Sylvia. *Behind the Attic Wall*, 7652(F)

Cassels, Jean. *Earthmates*, 11792
Fantastic Frogs, 18736

Cassidy, Sean. *The Chicken Cat*, 2443(F)

Cassie, Brian. *The Butterfly Alphabet Book*, 19543
National Audubon Society First Field Guide, 18681, 20196
Say It Again, 18612
Shells, 19772

Castaldo, Nancy Fusco. *Rainy Day Play!* 21418

Castaneda, Omar S. *Abuela's Weave*, 4616(F)

Castle, Caroline. *For Every Child*, 17019
Gorgeous! 1941(F)
Castle, Kate. *Ballet*, 14278
My Ballet Book, 14279
Castor, Harriet, ed. *Ballet Stories*, 10253(F)
Castro, Antonio. *Barry*, 6364
Jane Goodall, 13299
Castro, Nick (jt. author). *What's Going on Down There?* 18258
Catalano, Dominic. *Bernard's Bath*, 2136(F)
Bernard's Nap, 688(F)
Frog Went A-Courting, 14143
Merry Christmas, Old Armadillo, 5762(F)
Santa and the Three Bears, 5777(F)
Sleeping Beauty, 10494
Catalano, Julie. *The Mexican Americans*, 17549
Catalanotto, Peter. *Book*, 11646
Circle of Thanks, 1163(F)
Dad and Me, 3574(F)
Dreamplace, 4749(F)
Dylan's Day Out, 1942(F)
Getting Used to the Dark, 11723
Letter to the Lake, 3449(F)
The Longest Wait, 3542(F)
My House Has Stars, 736(F)
The Painter, 3575(F)
The Rolling Store, 4693(F)
Who Came Down That Road? 3291(F)
Catlett, Elizabeth. *Lift Every Voice and Sing*, 14157
Cato, Sheila. *Addition*, 399(F)
Division, 400(F)
Measuring, 20656
Catrow, David. *Cinderella Skeleton*, 10496(F)
The Emperor's Old Clothes, 1337(F)
The Fungus that Ate My School, 1131(F)
The Long, Long Letter, 4321(F)
The Million-Dollar Bear, 2950(F)
Over the River and Through the Wood, 6140(F)
Rotten Teeth, 4317(F)
That's Good! That's Bad! 4122(F)
There Was an Old Witch, 6042(F)
Westward Ho, Carlotta! 4147(F)
Who Said That? 12640
Why Lapin's Ears Are Long and Other Tales from the Louisiana Bayou, 11335
Caudill, Rebecca. *A Certain Small Shepherd*, 9713(F)
Did You Carry the Flag Today, Charley? 10034(F)
A Pocketful of Cricket, 5485(F)
Cauley, Lorinda Bryan. *The Beginning of the Armadilloes*, 7242(F)
The Goodnight Circle, 722(F)
The Trouble with Tyrannosaurus Rex, 1943(F)

Caumartin, Francois. *Now You See Them, Now You Don't*, 1944(F)
Cavan, Seamus. *The Irish-American Experience*, 17550
W. E. B. Du Bois and Racial Relations, 12717
Cavanagh, Helen. *The Last Piper*, 6790(F)
Panther Glade, 8599(F)
Cave, Katherine. *Henry's Song*, 1945(F)
Cazet, Denys. *Annie, Bea, and Chi Chi Dolores*, 92(F)
Dancing, 3576(F)
A Fish in His Pocket, 1946(F)
Minnie and Moo and the Musk of Zorro, 6261(F)
Minnie and Moo and the Thanksgiving Tree, 6139(F)
Minnie and Moo Go Dancing, 6262(F)
Minnie and Moo Go to Paris, 6263(F)
Minnie and Moo Go to the Moon, 6264(F)
Never Poke a Squid, 5990(F)
Night Lights, 645(F)
Nothing at All, 1947(F)
Cecala, Frank. *What Makes You What You Are*, 18034
Cech, John. *Django*, 11327
First Snow, Magic Snow, 11082
My Grandmother's Journey, 4617(F)
Cecil, Ivon. *Kirby Kelvin and the Not-Laughing Lessons*, 4105(F)
Cecil, Laura. *The Frog Princess*, 11083
Noah and the Space Ark, 1045(F)
Cecil, Laura, ed. *A Thousand Yards of Sea*, 1046(F)
Cecil, Mirabel. *Ruby the Christmas Donkey*, 5778(F)
Cecil, Randy. *Little Red Cowboy Hat*, 4219(F)
The Runaway Tortilla, 11362
The Singing Chick, 2723(F)
Cefrey, Holly. *Coping with Cancer*, 17950
Celdart, William. *The Return of the Indian*, 7586(F)
Celenza, Anna Harwell. *The Farewell Symphony*, 9031(F)
Celsi, Teresa. *Jesse Jackson and Political Power*, 12727
Rosa Parks and the Montgomery Bus Boycott, 12775
Cendrars, Blaise. *Shadow*, 171(F)
Cepeda, Joe. *Big Bushy Mustache*, 3902(F)
Captain Bob Sets Sail, 3410(F)
Gracias, the Thanksgiving Turkey, 6141(F)
Juan Bobo Goes to Work, 4774(F)
Koi and the Kola Nuts, 10640
Nappy Hair, 3207(F)

The Old Man and His Door, 4836(F)
Pumpkin Fiesta, 4893(F)
Rip's Secret Spot, 6243(F)
Vroomaloom, 1085(F)
We Were Tired of Living in a House, 3432(F)
What a Truly Cool World, 10686
Cerasini, Marc. *Diana*, 13781
Cerullo, Mary. *Coral Reef*, 19655
Dolphins, 19681
Lobsters, 19672
The Octopus, 19722
Sea Soup, 19626
The Truth About Great White Sharks, 19752
Cha, Chue. *Dia's Story Cloth*, 15153
Cha, Dia. *Dia's Story Cloth*, 15153
Cha, Nhia Thao. *Dia's Story Cloth*, 15153
Chaconas, Dori. *On a Wintry Morning*, 3577(F)
Chadwick, Roxane. *Amelia Earhart*, 12109
Chadwick, Tim. *Cabbage Moon*, 1948(F)
Chaiet, Donna. *The Safe Zone*, 18216
Chaikin, Miriam. *Clouds of Glory*, 17253
Joshua in the Promised Land, 17255
Menorahs, Mezuzas, and Other Jewish Symbols, 17455
A Nightmare in History, 14840
Chaikin, Miriam, adapt. *Exodus*, 17254
Chalfonte, Jessica. *I Am Muslim*, 17173
Chalk, Gary. *Hide and Seek in History*, 21865
Mariel of Redwall, 7823(F)
Martin the Warrior, 7825(F)
Mossflower, 7827(F)
Salamandastron, 7830(F)
Chall, Marsha Wilson. *Bonaparte*, 1949(F)
Happy Birthday, America! 5617(F)
Rupa Raises the Sun, 1047(F)
Sugarbush Spring, 3578(F)
Challoner, Jack. *Big and Small*, 20800
Energy, 20821
Floating and Sinking, 20801
Wet and Dry, 18803
Chalmers, Aldie. *In-Line Skating*, 21982
Chalmers, Mary. *Marigold and Grandma on the Town*, 6248(F)
Chamberlain, Margaret. *A Busy Day for a Good Grandmother*, 3795(F)
Dog Donovan, 5256(F)
Chamberlain, Sarah. *The Button Box*, 3854(F)
Chambers, Catherine. *Africa*, 14900
All Saints, All Souls, and Halloween, 17443

Carnival, 17348
Chinese New Year, 17349
Christmas, 17410
Deserts, 20401
Easter, 17434
The Elephants' Ears, 1048(F)
Mountains, 20496
Oceans and Seas, 19814
West African States, 15021
Chambers, Veronica. *Amistad Rising*, 16231
Marisol and Magdalena, 8413(F)
Chambliss, Maxie. *Fat Fanny, Beanpole Bertha and the Boys*, 7495(F)
I'm a Big Brother, 3583(F)
My Big Boy Potty Book, 3076(F)
One Up, One Down, 3901(F)
Tomorrow Is Daddy's Birthday, 5732(F)
Champion, Joyce. *Emily and Alice Again*, 3988(F)
Champion, Neil. *Portugal*, 15472
Chan, Harvey. *The Charlotte Stories*, 4190(F)
The Child's Story, 1123(F)
Ghost Train, 8231(F)
Music for the Tsar of the Sea, 11100
Three Monks, No Water, 10775
ttuM, 6908(F)
Chan, Wilson. *Why Does That Man Have Such a Big Nose?* 3371(F)
Chancellor, Deborah. *Tiger Tales*, 19081
Chandler, Clare. *Harvest Celebrations*, 17350
Chandler, Gary. *Alternative Energy Sources*, 20822
Guardians of Wildlife, 19391
Kids Who Make a Difference, 16954
Natural Foods and Products, 20081
Protecting Our Air, Land, and Water, 16991
Recycling, 16975
Chandler, Karen. *Keeper of the Swamp*, 3642(F)
Chandra, Deborah. *A Is for Amos*, 20(F)
Miss Mabel's Table, 401(F)
Chang, Margaret. *The Beggar's Magic*, 10741
The Cricket Warrior, 10742
Da Wei's Treasure, 10743
In the Eye of War, 9649(F)
Chang, Perry. *Florida*, 16837
Chang, Raymond (jt. author). *The Beggar's Magic*, 10741
The Cricket Warrior, 10742
Da Wei's Treasure, 10743
In the Eye of War, 9649(F)
Chang, Warren. *Encyclopedia Brown and the Case of the Sleeping Dog*, 7073(F)

Chanin, Michael. *The Chief's Blanket*, 4618(F)
Grandfather Four Winds and Rising Moon, 9150(F)
Chantland, Loren. *Chocolate by Hershey*, 12899
Chapin, Patrick. *Cookie McCorkle and the Case of the Emerald Earrings*, 6785(F)
My Friend, O'Connell, 9980(F)
Chaplin, Susan Gibbons. *I Can Sign My ABCs*, 21(F)
Chapman, Gillian. *Art from Fabric*, 21419
The Aztecs, 15609
The Egyptians, 14612
Exploring Time, 18304
The Greeks, 14674
Making Shaped Books, 13991
The Romans, 14714
Chapman, Jane. *Dora's Eggs*, 2744(F)
The Emperor's Egg, 19372
Happy and Honey, 6351(F)
Honey Helps, 6352(F)
One Duck Stuck, 569(F)
Run with the Wind, 2591(F)
Smudge, 2747(F)
The Story of Christmas, 17417
The Very Noisy Night, 699(F)
Chapman, Lee. *Doggie Dreams*, 1950(F)
Eight Animals on the Town, 2071(F)
Chapman, Lynne. *The Rickety Barn Show*, 1800(F)
Chapman, Nancy Kapp. *Doggie Dreams*, 1950(F)
Chapman, Robert. *A Gift for Abuelita*, 4746(F)
Chappell, Warren. *The Ghost in the Noonday Sun*, 9847(F)
Light in the Forest, 9174(F)
Charbonnet, Gabrielle. *Competition Fever*, 10293(F)
Chardiet, Bernice. *The Best Teacher in the World*, 5486(F)
Chardiet, Bernice (jt. author). *Where's That Insect?* 19430
Where's That Reptile? 18679
Charles, Faustin. *A Caribbean Counting Book*, 402(F)
The Selfish Crocodile, 1951(F)
Charles, Kirk. *Amazing Coin Tricks*, 21779
Charles, N. N. *What Am I?* 172(F)
Charles, Oz. *How Does Soda Get into the Bottle?* 20082
Charles, Veronika M. *The Crane Girl*, 10406(F)
Stretch, Swallow and Stare, 1049(F)
Charleston, Gordon. *Armstrong Lands on the Moon*, 20969
Peary Reaches the North Pole, 12146
Charlip, Remy. *Arm in Arm*, 21817

Handtalk, 14012
Handtalk Birthday, 5673(F)
Hooray for Me! 3068(F)
Mother Mother I Feel Sick Send for the Doctor Quick Quick Quick, 1050(F)
Peanut Butter Party, 20083
Sleepytime Rhyme, 646(F)
Why I Will Never Ever Ever Ever Have Enough Time to Read This Book, 4106(F)
Charlish, Anne. *Divorce*, 17645
Charlton, Nancy Lee. *Derek's Dog Days*, 1051(F)
Chartier, Normand. *All Stuck Up*, 11347
Do You See Mouse? 1990(F)
Chase, Richard. *Grandfather Tales*, 11328
Chasemore, Richard. *Star Wars Episode I*, 14318
Chast, Roz. *Meet My Staff*, 4231(F)
Chastain, Madye Lee. *The Cow-Tail Switch*, 10659
Chau, Tungwai. *The Runaway Rice Cake*, 5620(F)
Chaucer, Geoffrey. *Canterbury Tales*, 9085(F)
Chavarria-Chairez, Becky. *Magda's Tortillas/Las tortillas de Magda*, 5674(F)
Chayka, Doug. *Beekeepers*, 3213(F)
Yanni Rubbish, 4787(F)
Cheaney, J. B. *The Playmaker*, 9086(F)
Chee, Cheng-Khee. *Old Turtle*, 2872(F)
Cheese, Chloe. *The Babies Are Coming!* 3209(F)
Walking the Bridge of Your Nose, 21845
Chekhov, Anton. *Kashtanka*, 5164(F)
Chen, Jian Jiang. *Lord of the Cranes*, 10744
Chen, Ju-Hong. *The Tale of Aladdin and the Wonderful Lamp*, 11189
Chen, Kerstin. *Lord of the Cranes*, 10744
Chen, Yong. *Miz Fannie Mae's Fine New Easter Hat*, 1413(F)
Cheng, Andrea. *Grandfather Counts*, 403(F)
Cheon, Winnie. *Toddler Two*, 597(F)
Cherkerzian, Diane. *Merry Things to Make*, 21420
Chermayeff, Ivan. *Feathery Facts*, 19221
Furry Facts, 18613
The Hole Story, 3320(F)
Scaly Facts, 18682
The Three Languages, 10911
Chernoff, Goldie Taub. *Easy Costumes You Don't Have to Sew*, 21538
Cherry, Lynne. *Archie, Follow Me*, 1952(F)

The Armadillo from Amarillo, 1953(F)

The Dragon and the Unicorn, 1052(F)

The Great Kapok Tree, 4404(F)

If I Were in Charge of the World and Other Worries, 11730

Making a Difference in the World, 12518

A River Ran Wild, 16992

The Shaman's Apprentice, 4619(F)

The Snail's Spell, 1530(F)

Where Butterflies Grow, 4817

Who's Sick Today? 1954(F)

Chesak-Liberace, Lina. *Polly Hopper's Pouch,* 1836(F)

Chesanow, Neil. *Where Do I Live?* 173

Chesaux, Lisa Canney. *Philippe in Monet's Garden,* 1039(F)

Chesi, Matteo. *The Atlas of the Bible Lands,* 15518

Chess, Victoria. *The Beautiful Butterfly,* 11139

Ghosts! 6637(F)

Good Night Dinosaurs, 2689(F)

A Hippopotamusn't and Other Animal Verses, 11797

Jim, Who Ran Away from His Nurse, and Was Eaten by a Lion, 9778(F)

King Long Shanks, 10526(F)

The Little Buggers, 11798

The Sheriff of Rottenshot, 11912

Slither McCreep and His Brother, 2262(F)

Spider Kane and the Mystery Under the May-Apple, 7000(F)

Tommy at the Grocery Store, 2157(F)

Chessa, Francesca. *Farm Friends Clean Up,* 2116(F)

Chessare, Michele. *The Ghost from Beneath the Sea,* 7625(F)

A Lion to Guard Us, 9186(F)

Rainy Day, 11530

Who Knew There'd Be Ghosts? 6776(F)

Chester, Jonathan. *Busy Penguins,* 5401(F)

Splash! A Penguin Counting Book, 512(F)

Chesworth, Michael. *Aunt CeeCee, Aunt Belle, and Mama's Surprise,* 5720(F)

Grand-Gran's Best Trick, 8695(F)

Pippi Longstocking's After-Christmas Party, 5865(F)

Pippi to the Rescue, 6949(F)

Pippi's Extraordinary Ordinary Day, 9918(F)

Swish! 2959(F)

Touchdown Mars! An ABC Adventure, 146(F)

Chiago, Michael. *Sing Down the Rain,* 14253

Chiappe, Luis (jt. author). *The Tiniest Giants,* 14399

Chiarelli, Brunetto. *The Atlas of World Cultures,* 14333

Chicoine, Stephen D. *A Liberian Family,* 15022

Spain, 15473

Child, John. *The Crusades,* 14754

Child, Lauren. *Beware of the Storybook Wolves,* 1053(F)

Clarice Bean, Guess Who's Babysitting? 4107(F)

Clarice Bean, That's Me, 4930(F)

I Want a Pet, 4108(F)

I Will Never Not Ever Eat a Tomato, 4109(F)

Child, Lydia M. *Over the River and Through the Wood,* 6140(F)

Childers, Norman. *Tears for Ashan,* 8972(F)

Childress, Diana. *Prehistoric People of North America,* 14492

Childs, Sam. *Gorgeous!* 1941(F)

Chin, Charlie. *China's Bravest Girl,* 10745

Chin, Steven A. *Dragon Parade,* 5618

When Justice Failed, 12922

Chin, Yin-lien C., ed. *Traditional Chinese Folktales,* 10746

Chin-Lee, Cynthia. *A Is for Asia,* 22(F)

A Is for the Americas, 23

Chinery, Michael. *Ant,* 19508

Butterfly, 19544

Frog, 18716

How Bees Make Honey, 19516

Poisoners and Pretenders, 20433

Snake, 18756

Spider, 19575

Ching, Jacqueline. *Camping,* 22166

Chinn, Karen. *Sam and the Lucky Money,* 3069(F)

Chisholm, Jane. *The Usborne Book of World History Dates,* 14546

Chislett, Gail. *Whump,* 647(F)

Chmielarz, Sharon. *Down at Angel's,* 5779(F)

Cho, Shinta. *The Gas We Pass,* 18098

Chocolate, Deborah M. *Imani in the Belly,* 10657

Kente Colors, 15023

My First Kwanzaa Book, 5619

NEATE to the Rescue! 6791(F)

On the Day I Was Born, 3579(F)

The Piano Man, 3580(F)

Chodos-Irvine, Margaret. *Buzz,* 3486(F)

Chodzin, Sherab. *The Wisdom of the Crows and Other Buddhist Tales,* 10720

Choi, Sook N. *Echoes of the White Giraffe,* 8987(F)

Halmoni and the Picnic, 3581(F)

Yunmi and Halmoni's Trip, 4620(F)

Choi, Yangsook. *Basket Weaver and Catches Many Mice,* 1188(F)

New Cat, 1955(F)

Nim and the War Effort, 9669(F)

Rice Is Life, 20093

This Next New Year, 5658(F)

Choldenko, Gennifer. *Moonstruck,* 4110(F)

Chollat, Emilie. *Ackamarackus,* 2366(F)

Chorao, Kay. *The Baby's Bedtime Book,* 648(F)

The Cats Kids, 1956(F)

The Christmas Story, 5780(F)

The Good-bye Book, 5099(F)

Here Comes Kate, 6265(F)

I'm Terrific, 2682(F)

Knock at the Door and Other Baby Action Rhymes, 832

The Little Country Town, 778(F)

Little Farm by the Sea, 3070(F)

My Mama Says There Aren't Any Zombies, Ghosts, Vampires, Creatures, Demons, Monsters, Fiends, Goblins, or Things, 4341(F)

Number One Number Fun, 404(F)

Pig and Crow, 1957(F)

Choron, Harry (jt. author). *The Book of Lists for Kids,* 21897

Choron, Sandy. *The Book of Lists for Kids,* 21897

Choyce, Lesley. *Carrie's Crowd,* 8268(F)

Chrisman, Arthur B. *Shen of the Sea,* 8988(F)

Chrisp, Peter. *Alexander the Great,* 13747

The Aztecs, 15610

The Colosseum, 14715

The Parthenon, 14675

The Whalers, 19780

Chrisp, Peter (jt. author). *Travel,* 21280

Christelow, Eileen. *The Completed Hickory Dickory Dock,* 823

The Five-Dog Night, 4111(F)

Five Little Monkeys Jumping on the Bed, 405(F)

Five Little Monkeys Sitting in a Tree, 406(F)

Five Little Monkeys Wash the Car, 1958(F)

Five Little Monkeys with Nothing to Do, 1959(F)

The Great Pig Escape, 1960(F)

Jerome Camps Out, 1961(F)

The Mysterious Cases of Mr. Pin, 6976(F)

Not Until Christmas, Walter! 5781(F)

The Pumpkin Fair, 3058(F)

The Robbery at the Diamond Dog Diner, 1962(F)

Secondhand Star, 10106(F)

What Do Authors Do? 14074

What Do Illustrators Do? 17770

Will It Ever Be My Birthday? 5676(F)

Christelow, Eileen, reteller. *Five Little Monkeys Jumping on the Bed,* 405(F)

Christensen, Bonnie. *Breaking into Print,* 14000

Christian, Frank (jt. author). *Dancin' in the Kitchen,* 3644(F)

Christian, Mary Blount. *Sebastian (Super Sleuth) and the Bone to Pick Mystery,* 6792(F)

Sebastian (Super Sleuth) and the Copycat Crime, 6793(F)

The Toady and Dr. Miracle, 6266(F)

Christian, Peggy. *The Bookstore Mouse,* 7653(F)

Chocolate, a Glacier Grizzly, 5165(F)

If You Find a Rock, 4405(F)

Christian, Spencer. *Can It Really Rain Frogs?* 20759

Is There a Dinosaur in Your Backyard? The World's Most Fascinating Fossils, Rocks, and Minerals, 20553

What Makes the Grand Canyon Grand? 20300

Christiana, David. *Drawer in a Drawer,* 649(F)

The First Snow, 1054(F)

I Am the Mummy Heb-Nefert, 8960(F)

The Mouse Bride, 1982(F)

Poppy's Puppet, 1178(F)

Silver Morning, 4505(F)

The Tale I Told Sasha, 1685(F)

A Tooth Fairy's Tale, 1055(F)

Christiansen, C. B. *I See the Moon,* 7405(F)

A Snowman on Sycamore Street, 8269(F)

Sycamore Street, 3989(F)

Christiansen, Candace. *The Mitten Tree,* 3071(F)

Christiansen, Lee. *Eagle Boy,* 1651(F)

Turtle, Turtle, Watch Out! 18789

Christie, Gregory. *The Palm of My Heart,* 11747

Richard Wright and the Library Card, 4771(F)

Christopher, Andre. *Top 10 Men's Tennis Players,* 13363

Christopher, John. *When the Tripods Came,* 10159(F)

The White Mountains, 10160(F)

Christopher, Matt. *Baseball Jokes and Riddles,* 21818

Baseball Turnaround, 10294(F)

The Captain Contest, 10295(F)

The Catcher's Mask, 10296(F)

Center Court Sting, 10297(F)

The Comeback Challenge, 10298(F)

Dirt Bike Racer, 10299(F)

The Dog That Called the Pitch, 10300(F)

The Dog That Pitched a No-Hitter, 10301(F)

Great Moments in Baseball History, 22087

Hat Trick, 10302(F)

The Hit-Away Kid, 10303(F)

The Hockey Machine, 10304(F)

In the Huddle with John Elway, 13607

In the Huddle with . . . Steve Young, 13637

Mountain Bike Mania, 10305(F)

On the Course with . . . Tiger Woods, 13712

On the Court with . . . Grant Hill, 13527

On the Court with . . . Michael Jordan, 13537

On the Ice with . . . Wayne Gretzky, 13686

On the Mound with . . . Greg Maddux, 13469

Operation Baby-Sitter, 10306(F)

Penalty Shot, 10307(F)

Prime-Time Pitcher, 10308(F)

Red-Hot Hightops, 10309(F)

Return of the Home Run Kid, 10310(F)

Roller Hockey Radicals, 10311(F)

Shortstop from Tokyo, 10312(F)

Snowboard Maverick, 10313(F)

Soccer Halfback, 10314(F)

Soccer Scoop, 10315(F)

Spike It! 10316(F)

Stranger in Right Field, 10317(F)

Tennis Ace, 10318(F)

Christopher, Peter. *Westward with Columbus,* 16079

Chrustowski, Rick. *Bright Beetle,* 19529

Chrystie, Frances N. *Pets,* 19883

Chui, Terry. *Projects for a Healthy Planet,* 16960

Chung, Okwha. *Cooking the Korean Way,* 21682

Church, Caroline Jayne. *Hugo and the Bully Frogs,* 2699(F)

Nine Naughty Kittens, 478(F)

Church, Peter. *Gargoyles,* 21122

Churchill, E. Richard. *Fast and Funny Paper Toys You Can Make,* 21609

Holiday Paper Projects, 21610

Optical Illusion Tricks and Toys, 20911

Paper Science Toys, 21650

Chwast, Eve. *Leaf Baby,* 3011(F)

Snow Baby, 3012(F)

Chwast, Jacqueline. *The Hungry Black Bag,* 2761(F)

Starlight and Candles, 6095(F)

Chwast, Seymour. *The Alphabet Parade,* 24(F)

Moonride, 820(F)

Traffic Jam, 1056(F)

Ciardi, John. *Doodle Soup,* 11862

The Hopeful Trout and Other Limericks, 11863

You Read to Me, I'll Read to You, 11864

Ciavonne, Jean. *Carlos, Light the Farolito,* 5783(F)

Cibula, Matt. *The Contrary Kid,* 4112(F)

How to Be the Greatest Writer in the World, 14075

What's Up With You, Taquandra Fu? 1057(F)

Ciencin, Scott. *Dinoverse,* 10161(F)

Cieslawski, Steve. *At the Crack of the Bat,* 12001

Cimarusti, Marie Torres. *Peek-a-Moo!* 5166(F)

Civardi, Anne. *Festival Decorations,* 21421

Clair, Donna. *Carlos, Light the Farolito,* 5783(F)

Clancy, Frances. *An American Face,* 4941(F)

Clapp, John. *King of Shadows,* 7669(F)

Clare, John D. *Fourteenth-Century Towns,* 14755

Clare, John D., ed. *Ancient Greece,* 14676

Classical Rome, 14716

First World War, 14806

Knights in Armor, 14756

Pyramids of Ancient Egypt, 14613

The Vikings, 15440

The Voyages of Christopher Columbus, 12097

Clark, Alan M. *The Twilight Gate,* 8062(F)

Clark, Anne. *Hanukkah,* 17456

Clark, Barbara. *Janice VanCleave's Math for Every Kid,* 20597

Clark, Brenda. *Big Sarah's Little Boots,* 3032(F)

Franklin and the Thunderstorm, 1843(F)

Franklin Goes to the Hospital, 1844(F)

Franklin's Bad Day, 1845(F)

Franklin's Class Trip, 1849(F)

Franklin's Classic Treasury, 1846(F)

Franklin's Classic Treasury, Volume II, 1847(F)

Franklin's Friendship Treasury, 1848(F)

Franklin's Neighborhood, 2250(F)

Clark, Clara Gillow. *Willie and the Rattlesnake King,* 6794(F)

Clark, Colin. *Journey Through Italy,* 15375

Clark, David. *Don't Do That!* 4269(F)

Insect Soup, 11806

The Trouble with Ben, 2593(F)

Clark, Emma C. *Across the Blue Mountains,* 4113(F)

Beware of the Aunts! 5938(F)
Catch That Hat! 1058(F)
Don't Worry, Alfie, 2602(F)
Elf Hill, 10450(F)
The Frog Princess, 11083
Greek Myths, 11488
I Have a Song to Sing, O! 14257
I Love You, Blue Kangaroo!
   1059(F)
Noah and the Space Ark, 1045(F)
Patch Finds a Friend, 2603(F)
A Thousand Yards of Sea, 1046(F)
Too Tired, 2768(F)
Where Are You, Blue Kangaroo?
   1060(F)
Clark, Lorna. *All We Needed to Say,*
   11701
Clark, Margaret, comp. *A Treasury of*
   Dragon Stories, 7654(F)
Clark, Sue. *Hanukkah! A Three-*
   Dimensional Celebration, 17465
Clarke, Gillian, comp. *The Whisper-*
   ing Room, 11544
Clarke, Ginjer L. *Baby Alligator,*
   18699
Clarke, Greg. *The Mystery of UFOs,*
   21913
Clarke, Gus. *E I E I O,* 14144
Nothing But Trouble, 4114(F)
Clarke, Sue. *The Tombs of the*
   Pharaohs, 14614
Claro, Nicole. *The Cherokee Indians,*
   15938
Clary, Margie Willis. *A Sweet, Sweet*
   Basket, 3072(F)
Classen, Martin. *A Safe Home for*
   Manatees, 19737
Claverie, Jean. *Little Lou,* 4621(F)
The Perfume of Memory, 10469(F)
Clay, Julie. *The Stars That Shine,*
   10255(F)
Clay, Rebecca. *Space Travel and*
   Exploration, 20970
Stars and Galaxies, 18543
Clay, Wil. *Two Hundred Thirteen*
   Valentines, 10039(F)
Claybourne, Anna. *The Usborne*
   Book of Treasure Hunting,
   14334
Claybourne, Anna, reteller. *Greek*
   Myths, 11462
Clayton, Elaine. *Five Alien Elves,*
   9747(F)
The Ghost of Lizard Light, 8217(F)
The Yeoman's Daring Daughter
   and the Princes in the Tower,
   9087(F)
Clayton, Gordon. *Foal,* 20002
Clayton, Lawrence. *Alcohol Drug*
   Dangers, 17862
Diet Pill Drug Dangers, 17863
Claytor, Constance (jt. author).
   African Americans Who Were
   First, 12691
Cleary, Beverly. *Dear Mr. Henshaw,*
   8600(F)
Ellen Tebbits, 9800(F)

Emily's Runaway Imagination,
   9801(F)
Henry Huggins, 9802(F)
The Hullabaloo ABC, 25(F)
Mitch and Amy, 10035(F)
Muggie Maggie, 6267(F)
Otis Spofford, 9803(F)
Petey's Bedtime Story, 650(F)
Ramona the Pest, 7406(F)
Ramona's World, 7407(F)
The Real Hole, 2921(F)
Runaway Ralph, 9804(F)
Sister of the Bride, 7408(F)
Socks, 7409(F)
Strider, 8601(F)
Cleary, Brian P. *Hairy, Scary, Ordi-*
   nary, 14025
A Mink, a Fink, a Skating Rink,
   14026
Cleaver, Bill (jt. author). *Grover,*
   8602(F)
Cleaver, Elizabeth. *The Loon's Neck-*
   lace, 11313
Cleaver, Vera. *Grover,* 8602(F)
Clemenston, John. *How the Animals*
   Got Their Colors, 10608
Clement, Gary. *Don't Dig So Deep,*
   Nicholas! 1224(F)
The Great Poochini, 1963(F)
Just Stay Put, 11143
Clement, Rod. *Edwina the Emu,*
   2304(F)
Frank's Great Museum Adventure,
   4115(F)
Grandpa's Teeth, 4116(F)
Just Another Ordinary Day,
   1061(F)
Clement-Davies, David. *Trojan*
   Horse, 11463
Clements, Andrew. *Bright Christmas,*
   5784(F)
Circus Family Dog, 1964(F)
Double Trouble in Walla Walla,
   4117(F)
Frindle, 10036(F)
The Janitor's Boy, 10037(F)
The Landry News, 10038(F)
Noah and the Ark and the Animals,
   17256
Temple Cat, 4622(F)
Workshop, 3073
Clements, Gillian. *The Picture Histo-*
   ry of Great Inventors, 13205
The Truth About Castles, 14757
Clementson, John. *Big Brother, Little*
   Sister, 11500(F)
Clemesha, David (jt. author). *My Dog*
   Toby, 5465(F)
Cleveland, David. *The April Rabbits,*
   407(F)
Clifford, Daniel. *The Wind Wagon,*
   9303(F)
Clifford, Eth. *Family for Sale,*
   8414(F)
Flatfoot Fox and the Case of the
   Bashful Beaver, 7655(F)

Flatfoot Fox and the Case of the
   Missing Schoolhouse, 6268(F)
Flatfoot Fox and the Case of the
   Missing Whoooo, 1965(F)
Flatfoot Fox and the Case of the
   Nosy Otter, 6269(F)
Harvey's Horrible Snake Disaster,
   9805(F)
Harvey's Mystifying Raccoon Mix-
   Up, 6795(F)
Help! I'm a Prisoner in the
   Library, 6796(F)
The Remembering Box, 8415(F)
Scared Silly, 6797(F)
Clifford, Judy. *Midnight Magic,*
   1202(F)
Clifford, Mary Louise. *The Land and*
   People of Afghanistan, 15154
Clifford, Nick. *Incredible Earth,*
   20301
Clifton, Lucille. *Everett Anderson's*
   Christmas Coming, 5785(F)
Everett Anderson's Goodbye,
   11751
The Lucky Stone, 7410(F)
Some of the Days of Everett Ander-
   son, 11752
The Times They Used to Be,
   9530(F)
Climo, Lindee. *Chester's Barn,*
   5167(F)
Climo, Shirley. *Atalanta's Race,*
   11464
City! Washington, D.C., 16660
The Cobweb Christmas, 5786(F)
The Egyptian Cinderella, 10658
King of the Birds, 10539
The Korean Cinderella, 10721
Magic and Mischief, 10956
The Persian Cinderella, 10407
Stolen Thunder, 11518
A Treasury of Mermaids, 10540
Climo, Shirley, comp. and reteller. *A*
   Pride of Princesses, 10408(F)
Climo, Shirley, reteller. *The Little*
   Red Ant and the Great Big
   Crumb, 11396
Cline, Jeff. *The United States Cook-*
   book, 21692
Cline-Ransome, Lesa. *Satchel Paige,*
   13475
Clinton, Catherine. *The Black*
   Soldier, 15869
I, Too, Sing America, 11753
Scholastic Encyclopedia of the
   Civil War, 16398
Clinton, Susan. *Benjamin Harrison,*
   13040
Herbert Hoover, 13043
James Madison, 13081
Clough, B. W. *An Impossumble Sum-*
   mer, 7411(F)
Clouse, Nancy L. *Pink Paper Swans,*
   4021(F)
Sebgugugu the Glutton, 10643
Clutton-Brock, Juliet. *Dog,* 19942

Clymer, Eleanor. *My Mother Is the Smartest Woman in the World,* 7412(F)

Clyne, Densey. *Spotlight on Spiders,* 19576

Coady, Chris. *The Drop in My Drink,* 20736
The Pebble in My Pocket, 20311

Coalson, Glo. *Blackberry Booties,* 3153(F)
Brave as a Mountain Lion, 3414(F)
The Chosen Baby, 17690
Emily Just in Time, 5080(F)
Hi, 3415(F)
On Mother's Lap, 4828(F)

Coats, Laura J. *Ten Little Animals,* 408(F)

Coats, Lucy. *One Smiling Sister,* 409(F)

Coatsworth, Elizabeth. *The Cat Who Went to Heaven,* 10409(F)
Song of the Camels, 11828

Cobb, Allan B. *Super Science Projects About Animals and Their Habitats,* 18614
Super Science Projects About Oceans, 19815

Cobb, Annie. *The Long Wait,* 20642(F)
Wheels! 6270(F)

Cobb, Josh (jt. author). *Light Action,* 20912

Cobb, Mary. *The Quilt-Block History of Pioneer Days,* 16296
A Sampler View of Colonial Life, 16101

Cobb, Vicki. *Bangs and Twangs,* 20933
Bet You Can't! Science Impossibilities to Fool You, 18306
Don't Try This at Home! Science Fun for Kids on the Go, 18307
Follow Your Nose, 18137
Light Action, 20912
Magic . . . Naturally! 21780
Science Experiments You Can Eat, 18305
Squirts and Spurts, 20731
This Place Is Crowded, 15119
This Place Is High, 20497
This Place Is Wild, 14921
Wanna Bet? 18308
Why Doesn't the Earth Fall Up? 20823
You Gotta Try This! 18309
Your Tongue Can Tell, 18138

Coburn, Broughton. *Triumph on Everest,* 12123

Coburn, Jewell Reinhart. *Domitila,* 11397

Coburn, Jewell Reinhart, adapt. *Jouanah,* 10837

Cocca-Leffler, Maryann. *Bus Route to Boston,* 3074(F)
Clams All Year, 4118(F)
I Don't Want to Go to Camp, 3057(F)

Ice-Cold Birthday, 6271(F)
Jumping Day, 3122(F)
Jungle Halloween, 5991(F)
Missing, 4931(F)
Mr. Tanen's Ties, 5487(F)
Tea Party for Two, 6581(F)
Thanksgiving at the Tappletons', 6155(F)
Wanda's Roses, 3046(F)

Cockcroft, Jason. *A Flag for Grandma,* 3666(F)

Cocke, William. *A Historical Album of Virginia,* 16838

Coconis, Ted. *The Summer of the Swans,* 8884(F)

Cody, Tod. *The Cowboy's Handbook,* 17741

Coerr, Eleanor. *The Big Balloon Race,* 6272(F)
Buffalo Bill and the Pony Express, 6273(F)
Chang's Paper Pony, 6274(F)
The Josefina Story Quilt, 6275(F)
Mieko and the Fifth Treasure, 8989(F)
Sadako, 14841
Sadako and the Thousand Paper Cranes, 13847

Coffelt, Nancy. *Dogs in Space,* 1062(F)
Good Night, Sigmund, 5168(F)
Tom's Fish, 1063(F)

Coffey, Maria. *A Cat in a Kayak,* 1966(F)
Jungle Islands, 15226

Coffey, Tim. *Red Berry Wool,* 2080(F)

Coffey, Wayne. *Katarina Witt,* 13596

Coffin, Tom. *Coyote in Love with a Star,* 11227

Cogancherry, Helen. *Don't Hurt Me, Mama,* 5087(F)
The Floating House, 4820(F)
Here Comes the Mystery Man, 4821(F)
I Am Not a Crybaby, 5077(F)
I'm Deaf and It's Okay, 17901(F)
The Real Tooth Fairy, 3746(F)
Sarah, Also Known as Hannah, 7500(F)
Who Is a Stranger and What Should I Do? 17704
Words in Our Hands, 5015(F)

Cohat, Elisabeth. *The Seashore,* 19856

Cohen, Barbara. *The Carp in the Bathtub,* 7413(F)
David, 13780
Here Come the Purim Players! 6069(F)
Molly's Pilgrim, 3582(F)
Thank You, Jackie Robinson, 10319(F)
Two Hundred Thirteen Valentines, 10039(F)

Cohen, Carol Lee. *Digger Pig and the Turnip,* 10958

Cohen, Caron L. *Crookjaw,* 1064(F)
How Many Fish? 6276(F)
The Mud Pony, 11223
Where's the Fly? 323(F)

Cohen, Daniel. *The Alaska Purchase,* 16769
Dangerous Ghosts, 7656(F)
George W. Bush, 13013
Ghostly Tales of Love and Revenge, 7657(F)
Ghosts of the Deep, 21898
The Ghosts of War, 21899
Great Ghosts, 6798(F)
The Modern Ark, 19392
Phantom Animals, 18615
Phone Call from a Ghost, 21900
Prohibition, 16453
Pteranodon, 14391
Railway Ghosts and Highway Horrors, 11329
Southern Fried Rat and Other Gruesome Tales, 11330
The World's Most Famous Ghosts, 21901

Cohen, Izhar. *A B C Discovery! An Alphabet Book of Picture Puzzles,* 26

Cohen, Joel H. *Norman Rockwell,* 12294
R. L. Stine, 12601

Cohen, Judith (jt. author). *You Can Be a Woman Astronomer,* 17825
You Can Be a Woman Basketball Player, 22129
You Can Be a Woman Soccer Player, 22302
You Can Be a Woman Softball Player, 13450

Cohen, Miriam. *Best Friends,* 5488(F)
Down in the Subway, 1065(F)
Mimmy and Sophie, 4623(F)
Will I Have a Friend? 5489(F)

Cohen, Sheldon. *The Boxing Champion,* 4926(F)

Cohen-Posey, Kate. *How to Handle Bullies, Teasers and Other Meanies,* 17698

Cohn, Amy L., ed. *From Sea to Shining Sea,* 14145

Cohn, Janice. *The Christmas Menorahs,* 17457
Molly's Rosebush, 4932(F)

Coil, Suzanne M. *Poisonous Plants,* 20231

Colbeck, Martyn. *Little Big Ears,* 19167

Colbert, Jan, ed. *Dear Dr. King,* 17029

Colbert, Margaret. *Discovering Dinosaur Babies,* 14469

Colbert, Nancy A. *Lou Hoover,* 13159

Coldrey, Jennifer. *Strawberry,* 20139

Cole, Babette. *Bad Habits! (or The Taming of Lucretzia Crum),* 4119(F)

Hair in Funny Places, 18253
Hurrah for Ethelyn, 1967(F)
Mommy Laid an Egg! 18237
The Trouble with Mom, 1066(F)
The Un-Wedding, 4933(F)
Cole, Brock. *Alpha and the Dirty Baby*, 1067(F)
Buttons, 4120(F)
Gaffer Samson's Luck, 8381(F)
The Giant's Toe, 10410(F)
The Indian in the Cupboard, 7583(F)
The Winter Wren, 1068(F)
Cole, Henry. *Barefoot*, 4639(F)
Dinorella, 2051(F)
Ed and Fred Flea, 2050(F)
Four Famished Foxes and Fosdyke, 2052(F)
Honk! 2054(F)
I Took a Walk, 4406(F)
Jack's Garden, 3075(F)
Little Dogs Say "Rough!" 4346(F)
Livingstone Mouse, 2055(F)
Moosetache, 2558(F)
Moosletoe, 5894(F)
Roar! A Noisy Counting Book, 427(F)
Some Smug Slug, 2056(F)
The Wacky Wedding, 35(F)
Who Bop? 2399(F)
The Worrywarts, 2057(F)
Zipping, Zapping, Zooming Bats, 19023
Cole, Joanna. *Anna Banana*, 21983
Asking About Sex and Growing Up, 18254
Bony-Legs, 11084
Bully Trouble, 6277(F)
Crazy Eights and Other Card Games, 22229
Doctor Change, 7658(F)
Don't Tell the Whole World! 3990(F)
The Eentsy, Weentsy Spider, 21984
A Fish Hatches, 19699
Fun on the Run, 21985
Golly Gump Swallowed a Fly, 1069(F)
How You Were Born, 18238
Hungry, Hungry Sharks, 19753
I'm a Big Brother, 3583(F)
The Magic School Bus, 16993, 20302, 18052
The Magic School Bus and the Electric Field Trip, 20887
The Magic School Bus Explores the Senses, 18139
The Magic School Bus in the Time of the Dinosaurs, 14392
The Magic School Bus Inside a Beehive, 19517
The Magic School Bus Inside a Hurricane, 20687
The Magic School Bus Lost in the Solar System, 18510(F)
The Magic School Bus on the Ocean Floor, 19816

Marbles, 21986
The Missing Tooth, 6278(F)
My Big Boy Potty Book, 3076(F)
My New Kitten, 5169
The New Baby at Your House, 17646
Norma Jean, Jumping Bean, 6279(F)
On the Bus with Joanna Cole, 12519
Pin the Tail on the Donkey and Other Party Games, 21987
Riding Silver Star, 19990
Why Did the Chicken Cross the Road? 21820(F)
You Can't Smell a Flower with Your Ear! 18140
Your Insides, 18053
Cole, Joanna, ed. *Give a Dog a Bone*, 7176(F)
Ready . . . Set . . . Read! 6280(F)
Ready . . . Set . . . Read — and Laugh! 21819(F)
Six Sick Sheep, 21879
Cole, Joanna (jt. author). *Gator Halloween*, 9797(F)
Get Well, Gators! 9798(F)
Cole, Julia. *My Parents' Divorce*, 17647
Cole, Melanie. *Celine Dion*, 12375
Chuck Norris, 12427
Famous People of Hispanic Heritage, 17551
Jimmy Smits, 12469
Mariah Carey, 12365
Mary Joe Fernandez, 13647
Cole, Michael D. *Astronauts*, 20971
Challenger, 20972
Galileo Spacecraft, 20973
Hubble Space Telescope, 18383
John F. Kennedy, 13059
John Glenn, 12887
The L.A. Riots, 16498
Living on Mars, 18467
Moon Base, 20974
NASA Space Vehicles, 20975
The Siege at Waco, 16839
Space Emergency, 20976
Space Launch Disaster, 20977
TWA Flight 800, 21074
Walt Disney, 12224
Cole, Trish. *Why Do We Wear That?* 21168
Cole, William. *Have I Got Dogs!* 5170(F)
Cole, William, ed. *An Arkful of Animals*, 11773
Poem Stew, 11865
A Zooful of Animals, 11774
Coleman, Brian (jt. author). *The Young Basketball Player*, 22139
Coleman, Evelyn. *The Foot Warmer and the Crow*, 9266(F)
The Riches of Oseola McCarty, 12758
To Be a Drum, 3077(F)
White Socks Only, 4624(F)

Coleman, Janet W. *Fast Eddie*, 7659(F)
Coleman, Lori. *Beginning Strength Training*, 21988 ·
My Pet Fish, 19980
Soccer, 22289
Coleman, Mary Ann. *The Dreams of Hummingbirds*, 11946
Coleman, Michael. *Escape Key*, 6799(F)
One, Two, Three, Oops! 410(F)
Weirdo's War, 6800(F)
Colen, Kimberly. *Peas and Honey*, 21683
Coles, Robert. *The Story of Ruby Bridges*, 16499(F)
Collard, Sneed B. *Animal Dads*, 18871
Birds of Prey, 19322
The Forest in the Clouds, 20434
Lizard Island, 19656
Making Animal Babies, 18918
1,000 Years Ago on Planet Earth, 14335
Our Natural Homes, 20365
A Whale Biologist at Work, 19781
Colle, Gisela. *The Star Tree*, 5787(F)
Collicott, Sharleen. *The Chicken Sisters*, 2534(F)
Collicutt, Paul. *This Boat*, 21356
This Train, 21330
Collier, Bryan. *These Hands*, 763(F)
Uptown, 3078(F)
Collier, Christopher. *The American Revolution, 1763–1783*, 16191
Andrew Jackson's America, 1824–1850, 16232
Building a New Nation, 1789–1801, 16233
A Century of Immigration, 1820–1924, 15870
The Civil War, 1860–1865, 16399
Clash of Cultures, Prehistory–1638, 16102
Creating the Constitution, 1787, 16192
The French and Indian War, 16103
Hispanic America, Texas and the Mexican War, 1835–1850, 16234
Indians, Cowboys, and Farmers, 16297
The Jeffersonian Republicans, 1800–1823, 16235
The Paradox of Jamestown, 16104
Pilgrims and Puritans, 16105
Progressivism, the Great Depression, and the New Deal, 16454
Reconstruction and the Rise of Jim Crow, 1864–1896, 16455
The Rise of Industry, 1860–1900, 16456
The Rise of the Cities, 15871
Slavery and the Coming of the Civil War, 1831–1861, 16236
The United States Enters the World Stage, 16457

Collier, Christopher (jt. author). *The Clock*, 9267(F)
My Brother Sam Is Dead, 9226(F)
Collier, James Lincoln. *The Clock*, 9267(F)
The Corn Raid, 9187(F)
My Brother Sam Is Dead, 9226(F)
Collier, James Lincoln (jt. author). *The American Revolution, 1763–1783*, 16191
Andrew Jackson's America, 1824–1850, 16232
Building a New Nation, 1789–1801, 16233
A Century of Immigration, 1820–1924, 15870
The Civil War, 1860–1865, 16399
Clash of Cultures, Prehistory–1638, 16102
Creating the Constitution, 1787, 16192
The French and Indian War, 16103
Hispanic America, Texas and the Mexican War, 1835–1850, 16234
Indians, Cowboys, and Farmers, 16297
The Jeffersonian Republicans, 1800–1823, 16235
The Paradox of Jamestown, 16104
Pilgrims and Puritans, 16105
Progressivism, the Great Depression, and the New Deal, 16454
Reconstruction and the Rise of Jim Crow, 1864–1896, 16455
The Rise of Industry, 1860–1900, 16456
The Rise of the Cities, 15871
Slavery and the Coming of the Civil War, 1831–1861, 16236
The United States Enters the World Stage, 16457
Collier, Mary Jo. *The King's Giraffe*, 4625(F)
Collier, Peter (jt. author). *The King's Giraffe*, 4625(F)
Collier-Morales, Roberta. *With Love, to Earth's Endangered Peoples*, 17571
Collington, Peter. *Clever Cat*, 1968(F)
A Small Miracle, 9714(F)
Collins, David R. *Casimir Pulaski*, 13844
The Country Artist, 12579
Farmworker's Friend, 12825
Ishi, 15939
Lee Iacocca, 12905
Mark T-W-A-I-N! 12607
Tales for Hard Times, 12528
Tiger Woods, 13713
Tiger Woods, Golfing Champion, 13714
To the Point, 12622
Washington Irving, 12555
Woodrow Wilson, 13121
Write a Book for Me, 12547

Zachary Taylor, 13106
Collins, Heather. *Kids and Grandparents*, 21451
The Kids' Summer Handbook, 21432
The Last Safe House, 9281(F)
A New Duck, 19310
A New Frog, 18726
A Pioneer Thanksgiving, 17499
Starting with Nature Bird Book, 19234
Starting with Nature Plant Book, 20236
Writing, 14098
Collins, James L. *John Brown and the Fight Against Slavery*, 12861
The Mountain Men, 12056
Collins, Judy. *My Father*, 14146
Collins, Mary. *The Industrial Revolution*, 15872
Mount Vernon, 16840
The Smithsonian Institution, 16661
The Spanish-American War, 16458
Collins, Pat L. *Waiting for Baby Joe*, 3584(F)
Collins, Ross. *The No-Nothings and Their Baby*, 4234(F)
What If? 1619(F)
Collins, Sheila Hebert. *Jolie Blonde and the Three Heberts*, 10959
Collins, Sheila Hebert, reteller. *Les Trois Cochons*, 10960
Collinson, Alan. *Grasslands*, 20532
Mountains, 20498
Pollution, 16994
Collis, Len. *Card Games for Children*, 22230
Collodi, Carlo. *The Adventures of Pinocchio*, 7660(F)
Pinocchio, 7661(F), 7662(F)
Colman, Hila. *Diary of a Frantic Kid Sister*, 8603(F)
Colman, Penny. *Fannie Lou Hamer and the Fight for the Vote*, 12725
Girls, 15873
Madam C. J. Walker, 12807
Strike! 15874
Toilets, Bathtubs, Sinks, and Sewers, 18191
Colon, Ernie. *Bruce Coville's UFOs*, 10167(F)
Colon, Raul. *A Band of Angels*, 7346(F)
Buoy, 7580(F)
Celebration! 5652(F)
Hercules, 11461
My Mama Had a Dancing Heart, 3659(F)
Secrets from the Dollhouse, 1628(F)
The Snowman's Path, 1482(F)
Tomas and the Library Lady, 3331(F)
A Weave of Words, 10863
Colum, Padraic. *The Children's Homer*, 11465

The Golden Fleece and the Heroes Who Lived Before Achilles, 11466
Columbus, Christopher. *The Log of Christopher Columbus' First Voyage to America in the Year 1492 as Copied Out in Brief by Bartholomew Las Casas*, 12098
Coman, Carolyn. *What Jamie Saw*, 8416(F)
Comissiong, Lynette. *Mind Me Good Now!* 11420
Compestine, Ying Chang. *The Runaway Rice Cake*, 5620(F)
Comport, Sally Wern. *Brave Margaret*, 11031
Compton, Joanne (jt. author). *Granny Greenteeth and the Noise in the Night*, 1070(F)
Compton, Kenn. *Granny Greenteeth and the Noise in the Night*, 1070(F)
Conaway, Judith. *Happy Haunting!* 21539
Happy Thanksgiving! 17492
Conboy, Fiona (jt. author). *Welcome to Mexico*, 15623
Condon, Ken. *Sky Scrape/City Scape*, 11744
Condra, Estelle. *See the Ocean*, 4407(F)
Condy, Roy. *Christopher Changes His Name*, 4294(F)
Cone, Molly. *Mishmash*, 7177(F)
The Story of Shabbat, 17458
Cone, Patrick. *Avalanche*, 20778
Wildfire, 20366
Conford, Ellen. *And This Is Laura*, 7414(F)
Annabel the Actress Starring in Gorilla My Dreams, 9806(F)
Annabel the Actress Starring in Just a Little Extra, 9807(F)
A Case for Jenny Archer, 6801(F)
Dear Lovey Hart, I Am Desperate, 10040(F)
Diary of a Monster's Son, 10162(F)
The Frog Princess of Pelham, 9808(F)
Hail, Hail Camp Timberwood, 8604(F)
Jenny Archer to the Rescue, 9809(F)
A Job for Jenny Archer, 9810(F)
My Sister the Witch, 9811(F)
Nibble, Nibble, Jenny Archer, 9812(F)
What's Cooking, Jenny Archer? 9813(F)
Conlin, Susan. *All My Feelings at Preschool*, 5490(F)
Conlon, Laura. *People of Mexico*, 15611
Conlon-McKenna, Marita. *Fields of Home*, 9088(F)
Under the Hawthorn Tree, 9089(F)
Conly, Jane L. *Crazy Lady!* 8605(F)

R-T, Margaret, and the Rats of NIMH, 7663(F)

Racso and the Rats of NIMH, 7664(F)

What Happened on Planet Kid, 8606(F)

While No One Was Watching, 8607(F)

Connelly, Bernardine. *Follow the Drinking Gourd*, 9268(F)

Connelly, Gwen. *Let's Celebrate Thanksgiving*, 6152

Connelly, John P. *You're Too Sweet*, 17951

Conner, Eulala. *Amazing World of Ants*, 19513

Connolly, James E. *Why the Possum's Tail Is Bare*, 11224

Connolly, Jay. *Dwight D. Eisenhower*, 13029

Connolly, Peter. *The Romans*, 14713

Connolly, Sean. *Claude Monet*, 12264

Henry Moore, 12268

Leonardo da Vinci, 12212

Nelson Mandela, 13827

Paul Cézanne, 12204

Paul Klee, 12247

Vincent Van Gogh, 12305

Connor, Nikki. *Cardboard Boxes*, 21422

Conord, Bruce W. *Bill Cosby*, 12369

Cesar Chavez, 12826

Conover, Chris. *The Lion's Share*, 1071(F)

Conrad, Donna. *See You Soon Moon*, 3079(F)

Conrad, Pam. *Animal Lullabies*, 651(F)

Blue Willow, 8990(F)

Don't Go Near That Rabbit, Frank! 7178(F)

Our House, 7415(F)

Pedro's Journal, 8927(F)

Prairie Songs, 8608(F)

Prairie Visions, 12865

Staying Nine, 8609(F)

Stonewords, 7665(F)

This Mess, 1969(F)

The Tub Grandfather, 1072(F)

The Tub People, 1073(F)

The Tub People's Christmas, 5788(F)

Zoe Rising, 7666(F)

Conteh-Morgan, Jane. *Cow Moo Me*, 5319(F)

Little Fish, Lost, 2774(F)

Cony, Frances. *Hansel and Gretel*, 12015

Little Red Riding Hood, 12016

Old MacDonald Had a Farm, 14147

Cook, Deanna F. *FamilyFun's Parties*, 17351

The Kids' Multicultural Cookbook, 21684

Kids' Pumpkin Projects, 20171

Cook, Donald. *Abe Lincoln's Hat*, 13065

The Bravest Dog Ever, 6680

Cook, Jean Thor. *Room for a Stepdaddy*, 3585(F)

Cook, Joel. *The Rats' Daughter*, 10541

Whistling the Morning In, 11976

Cook, Nick. *Downhill In-Line Skating*, 21989

Roller Coasters; or, I Had So Much Fun, I Almost Puked, 14267

Cook, Peter. *Why Doesn't My Floppy Disk Flop?* 21195

Cook, Scott. *Ling Cho and His Three Friends*, 4791(F)

A Net to Catch Time, 4586(F)

Cooke, Andy. *Little Tiger Goes Shopping*, 2103(F)

One Cow Moo Moo! 383(F)

Ups and Downs, 17715

When Your Parents Split Up . . ., 17688

Cooke, Trish. *The Grandad Tree*, 3586(F)

Mr. Pam Pam and the Hullabazoo, 1074(F)

So Much, 5675(F)

When I Grow Bigger, 3080(F)

Cooley, Brian. *Make-a-Saurus*, 14393

Coolidge, Olivia. *Greek Myths*, 11467

Coolidge, Susan. *What Katy Did*, 8610(F)

Cooling, Wendy. *Farmyard Tales from Far and Wide*, 10542

Cools, Els. *Albery and Lila*, 2660(F)

Coombs, Karen Mueller. *Children of the Dust Days*, 16459

Flush! Treating Wastewater, 16976

Jackie Robinson, 13488

Coombs, Patricia. *Dorrie and the Haunted Schoolhouse*, 1075(F)

Cooney, Barbara. *Basket Moon*, 4806(F)

The Best Christmas, 9739(F)

Chanticleer and the Fox, 11546

Eleanor, 13179

Emily, 8253(F)

Hattie and the Wild Waves, 4626(F)

Island Boy, 3587(F)

Only Opal, 4600

Ox-Cart Man, 4674(F)

Peter and the Wolf, 10481(F)

Roxaboxen, 3301(F)

Cooney, Barbara, reteller. *Chanticleer and the Fox*, 11546

Cooney, Helen. *Underwater Animals*, 19627

Cooper, Ann. *Along the Seashore*, 19857

Around the Pond, 20512

In the Forest, 18930

Cooper, Christopher. *Matter*, 20802

Cooper, Elisha. *Ballpark*, 3081(F)

Building, 21117

Country Fair, 3082(F)

Cooper, Emilie (jt. author). *Journey Through Australia*, 15227

Cooper, Floyd. *African Beginnings*, 14907

Be Good to Eddie Lee, 4957(F)

Bound for America, 16251

Chita's Christmas Tree, 5846(F)

Coming Home, 12551

Cumbayah, 14148

Faraway Drums, 1323(F)

Freedom School, Yes! 4740(F)

The Girl Who Loved Caterpillars, 10825

Granddaddy's Street Songs, 3604(F)

Grandpa's Face, 3662(F)

How Sweet the Sound, 14247

I Have Heard of a Land, 9443(F)

Imani's Gift at Kwanzaa, 9710(F)

Jaguarundi, 7782(F)

Laura Charlotte, 3639(F)

Ma Dear's Aprons, 4757(F)

Mandela, 13828

Meet Danitra Brown, 11759

Miz Berlin Walks, 4066(F)

On Mardi Gras Day, 5650(F)

Papa Tells Chita a Story, 4686(F)

Pass It On, 11761

Pulling the Lion's Tail, 10681

Shake Rag, 5016(F)

Sweet, Sweet Memory, 5108

Tree of Hope, 4742(F)

When Africa Was Home, 4880(F)

Cooper, Helen. *Christmas Stories for the Very Young*, 5782(F)

Pumpkin Soup, 1970(F)

Cooper, Ilene. *Absolutely Lucy*, 8611(F)

Choosing Sides, 10320(F)

The Dead Sea Scrolls, 17257

Lucy on the Loose, 6802(F)

Queen of the Sixth Grade, 8270(F)

Cooper, James Fenimore. *Last of the Mohicans*, 9151(F)

Cooper, Jason. *Beef*, 20084

Dairy Products, 20085

Poultry, 20086

Cooper, Kay. *Where Did You Get Those Eyes?* 17648

Who Put the Cannon in the Courthouse Square? 14547

Why Do You Speak as You Do? 13980

Cooper, Martha. *Anthony Reynoso*, 17552

Cooper, Melrose. *Gettin' Through Thursday*, 3588(F)

Pets! 1971(F)

Cooper, Michael. *Klondike Fever*, 15571

Cooper, Michael L. *Indian School*, 15940

Cooper, Patrick. *Never Trust a Squirrel!* 1972(F)

Cooper, Rod. *Journey Through Australia*, 15227

Cooper, Roscoe. *The Great Pyramid*, 14615

Cooper, Susan. *The Boggart*, 7667(F)
The Boggart and the Monster, 7668(F)
Danny and the Kings, 5789(F)
Dawn of Fear, 8271(F)
King of Shadows, 7669(F)
Matthew's Dragon, 652(F)
Seaward, 7670(F)
Silver on the Tree, 7671(F)
Tam Lin, 10963

Cooper, Susan, reteller. *The Selkie Girl*, 10961
The Silver Cow, 10962

Corbella, Luciano. *The Space Atlas*, 18385
Space, Stars, Planets and Spacecraft, 20950

Corbett, Grahame. *You Can Draw Fantastic Animals*, 21565

Corbett, Sara. *Hold Everything!* 21902
Shake, Rattle, and Strum, 14218
What a Doll! 21651

Corbett, Scott. *The Lemonade Trick*, 9814(F)

Corbin, William. *Me and the End of the World*, 8612(F)

Corbishley, Mike. *Growing Up in Ancient Rome*, 14717
How Do We Know Where People Came From? 14524
The Medieval World, 14758
What Do We Know About Prehistoric People? 14493
The World of Architectural Wonders, 21118

Corcoran, Barbara. *Family Secrets*, 7416(F)
The Potato Kid, 8613(F)

Cordes, Helen. *Girl Power in the Classroom*, 17699
Girl Power in the Mirror, 17700

Cordoba, Yasmine A. *Igloo*, 15797

Cordova, Amy. *Abuelita's Heart*, 4408(F)

Corentin, Philippe. *Papa!* 653(F)

Corey, Dorothy. *Will It Ever Be My Birthday?* 5676(F)
Will There Be a Lap for Me? 3589(F)
You Go Away, 3083(F)

Corey, Jim. *Dolphin Babies*, 19692

Corey, Melinda. *Let's Visit a Spaghetti Factory*, 21026

Corey, Shana. *You Forgot Your Skirt, Amelia Bloomer!* 4627(F)

Coristine, Philip. *Serena and the Wild Doll*, 1076(F)

Cornelissen, Cornelia. *Soft Rain*, 9152(F)

Cornell, Laura. *Before You Were Born*, 18228
Earl's Too Cool for Me, 4020(F)

Tell Me Again About the Night I Was Born, 3596(F)
Today I Feel Silly, 4940(F)
Where Do Balloons Go? 1091(F)

Cornette. *Purple Coyote*, 1077(F)

Cornfield, Robin Bell. *Dreamtime*, 664

Cornish, Mary Hofstrand. *On the Stairs*, 2340(F)

Corona, Laurel. *Brazil*, 15728
Ethiopia, 14922
Kenya, 14923
Norway, 15441
Poland, 15263
Scotland, 15340
South Africa, 14972

Coronado, Rosa. *Cooking the Mexican Way*, 21685

Corpi, Lucha. *Where Fireflies Dance*, 4628(F)

Corral, Hannah (jt. author). *A Child's Glacier Bay*, 16770

Corral, Kimberly. *A Child's Glacier Bay*, 16770

Corrin, Sara, ed. *Round the Christmas Tree*, 5790(F)

Corrin, Stephen (jt. author). *Round the Christmas Tree*, 5790(F)

Corvino, Lucy. *Clever Quicksolve Whodunit Puzzles*, 7091(F)

Corwin, Judith Hoffman. *Christmas Fun*, 21423
Colonial American Crafts, 16106
Cookie Fun, 21686
Easter Crafts, 21424
Easter Fun, 21425
Halloween Crafts, 21426
Halloween Fun, 21427
Harvest Festivals Around the World, 17493
Jewish Holiday Fun, 17459
My First Riddles, 21821(F)
Papercrafts, 21611
Thanksgiving Fun, 17494
Valentine Fun, 21428

Cory, Steve. *Daily Life in Ancient and Modern Mexico City*, 15612

Cory, Steven. *Pueblo Indian*, 15941

Corzine, Phyllis. *The Black Death*, 14759

Cosby, Bill. *The Best Way to Play*, 8272(F)
The Day I Was Rich, 4934(F)
My Big Lie, 8614(F)
One Dark and Scary Night, 6281(F)
Shipwreck Saturday, 6282(F)
Super-Fine Valentine, 6283(F)

Cosgrove, John O'Hara. *Carry On, Mr. Bowditch*, 12086
The Log of Christopher Columbus' First Voyage to America in the Year 1492 as Copied Out in Brief by Bartholomew Las Casas, 12098

Cosner, Sharon. *The Light Bulb*, 20888

Cossi, Olga. *Harp Seals*, 19730

Costabel, Eva D. *The Early People of Florida*, 15942

Costantino, Valeria. *Ask Me Anything About the Presidents*, 12689

Costello, Emily. *Realm of the Panther*, 19082

Cote, Nancy. *The Borrowed Hanukkah Latkes*, 6072(F)
The Can-Do Thanksgiving, 6150(F)
Fireflies, Peach Pies and Lullabies, 5004(F)
Flip-Flops, 3084(F)
Gretchen Groundhog, It's Your Day! 5633(F)
I Like Your Buttons! 3272(F)
Palm Trees, 3991(F)
When I Feel Angry, 2710(F)

Cotler, Amy. *The Secret Garden Cookbook*, 21687

Cottam, Clarence (jt. author). *Insects*, 19504

Cottle, Joan. *Emily's Shoes*, 6284(F)

Cottone-Kolthoff, Carol. *Chocolate, a Glacier Grizzly*, 5165(F)

Cottonwood, Joe. *Danny Ain't*, 8615(F)

Cottringer, Anne. *Ella and the Naughty Lion*, 1078(F)
Movie Magic, 6285(F)

Cotts, Claire B. *The Christmas Gift*, 5853(F)
Manuela's Gift, 5684(F)

Couch, Greg. *The Cello of Mr. O*, 4631(F)
First Palm Trees, 10652
Moon Ball, 1710(F)
Wild Child, 762(F)
The Windigo's Return, 11320
Winter Waits, 1483(F)

Coucher, Helen. *Rain Forest*, 4409(F)

Couloumbis, Audrey. *Getting Near to Baby*, 8417(F)

Coulson, Jane. *Sam's New Baby*, 3652(F)

Coulter, George. *Science in Art*, 18310

Coulter, Hope N. *Uncle Chuck's Truck*, 5552(F)

Coulter, Shirley (jt. author). *Science in Art*, 18310

Councell, Ruth T. *Once upon a Bedtime Story*, 10631

Coupe, Sheena. *Sharks*, 19754

Couper, Heather. *Big Bang*, 18384
Is Anybody Out There? 20978
The Space Atlas, 18385

Couri, Kathy. *Sweets and Treats*, 11575

Couric, Katie. *The Brand New Kid*, 5491(F)

Courlander, Harold. *The Cow-Tail Switch*, 10659

Coursen, Valerie. *Mordant's Wish*, 1973(F)

Courtney. *Volcanoes and Earth-quakes*, 20338
Courtney, Richard. *Dinosaurs Everywhere!* 14426
Courtney-Clarke, Margaret. *My Painted House, My Friendly Chicken, and Me*, 13872
Cousineau, Normand. *Hairs on Bears*, 4292(F)
Cousins, Lucy. *Happy Birthday, Maisy*, 5677(F)
Humpty Dumpty and Other Nursery Rhymes, 833(F)
Jack and Jill and Other Nursery Rhymes, 834(F)
Katy Cat and Beaky Boo, 1079(F)
The Lucy Cousins Book of Nursery Rhymes, 835
Maisy at the Farm, 1974(F)
Maisy Dresses Up, 1975(F)
Maisy Drives the Bus, 1976(F)
Maisy Goes Swimming, 1977(F)
Maisy Goes to School, 1978(F)
Maisy Makes Gingerbread, 1979(F)
Maisy's Pool, 6286(F)
Maisy's Pop-Up Playhouse, 3085(F)
Noah's Ark, 17258
Where Are Maisy's Friends? 1980(F)
Za-Za's Baby Brother, 1981(F)
Cousins, Margaret. *Ben Franklin of Old Philadelphia*, 12879
Cousins, Steven. *Frankenbug*, 10163(F)
Cousteau Society. *Penguins*, 19369
Seals, 19731
Couvillon, Alice (jt. author). *Mimi and Jean-Paul's Cajun Mardi Gras*, 5639(F)
Covey, Rosemary Feit. *Hearsay*, 10768(F)
Covey, Traci O. *Mapped Out!* 14361
Coville, Bruce. *Aliens Ate My Homework*, 10041(F)
Aliens Stole My Body, 10164(F)
The Attack of the Two-Inch Teacher, 10165(F)
The Dragonslayers, 7672(F)
Fortune's Journey, 9353(F)
The Ghost in the Big Brass Bed, 7673(F)
The Ghost Wore Grey, 6803(F)
Goblins in the Castle, 7674(F)
I Left My Sneakers in Dimension X, 10168(F)
I Was a Sixth Grade Alien, 10169(F)
Into the Land of the Unicorns, 7675(F)
Jennifer Murdley's Toad, 7676(F)
Jeremy Thatcher, Dragon Hatcher, 7677(F)
The Lapsnatcher, 3590(F)
The Monster's Ring, 7678(F)
My Grandfather's House, 4935(F)

My Teacher Fried My Brains, 10170(F)
Odder Than Ever, 7679(F)
The Skull of Truth, 7680(F)
Song of the Wanderer, 7681(F)
Space Brat 4, 10171(F)
William Shakespeare's Macbeth, 12048
William Shakespeare's Romeo and Juliet, 12049
The World's Worst Fairy Godmother, 7682(F)
Coville, Bruce, comp. and ed. *Bruce Coville's UFOs*, 10167(F)
Coville, Bruce, ed. *Bruce Coville's Alien Visitors*, 10166(F)
Coville, Katherine. *Aliens Ate My Homework*, 10041(F)
I Left My Sneakers in Dimension X, 10168(F)
The Monster's Ring, 7678(F)
The Summer I Shrank My Grandmother, 8219(F)
Covington, Karen. *Creators*, 12159
Covington, Karen (jt. author). *The Literary Crowd*, 12157
Cowan, Catherine. *My Friend the Piano*, 1080(F)
Cowan, Catherine, trans. and adapt. *My Life with the Wave*, 1081(F)
Cowcher, Helen. *Jaguar*, 5171(F)
Tigress, 5172(F)
Whistling Thorn, 4629
Cowdrey, Richard. *Animal Lullabies*, 651(F)
Animals on the Go, 18926
Cowell, Cressida. *Don't Do That, Kitty Kilroy!* 3591(F)
What Shall We Do with the Boo-Hoo Baby? 654(F)
Cowen-Fletcher, Jane. *Baby Angels*, 1082(F)
It Takes a Village, 4630(F)
Mama Zooms, 3592(F)
Cowles, Rose. *Dog Tales*, 10484(F)
Cowley, Joy. *Agapanthus Hum and Major Bark*, 6287(F)
Agapanthus Hum and the Eyeglasses, 9815(F)
Big Moon Tortilla, 4936(F)
Gracias, the Thanksgiving Turkey, 6141(F)
The Mouse Bride, 1982(F)
Red-Eyed Tree Frog, 18717
The Rusty, Trusty Tractor, 5553(F)
Singing Down the Rain, 1083(F)
Starbright and the Dream Eater, 10172(F)
The Video Shop Sparrow, 2922(F)
Cowley, Marjorie. *Anooka's Answer*, 8951(F)
Dar and the Spear-Thrower, 8952(F)
Cox, Christine. *The Girl Who Swam with the Fish*, 11292
Cox, Clinton. *African American Healers*, 13206

African American Teachers, 12642
Come All You Brave Soldiers, 16193
Cox, Judy. *Mean, Mean Maureen Green*, 8616(F)
Now We Can Have a Wedding! 3086(F)
Rabbit Pirates, 1983(F)
Third Grade Pet, 9816(F)
Weird Stories from the Lonesome Cafe, 9817(F)
The West Texas Chili Monster, 1084(F)
Cox, Phil Roxbee. *Ted in a Red Bed*, 6288(F)
Cox, Ted. *Whitney Houston*, 12404
Coxe, Molly. *Big Egg*, 6289(F)
Hot Dog, 6290(F)
R Is for Radish! 6291(F)
6 Sticks, 412(F)
Coxon, Michele. *The Cat Who Lost His Purr*, 1984(F)
Coy, John. *Night Driving*, 3593(F)
Strong to the Hoop, 10321(F)
Vroomaloom, 1085(F)
Coy, Ron Hilbert. *The Deetkatoo*, 11212
Coyle, Rena. *My First Baking Book*, 21688
My First Cookbook, 21689
Craats, Rennay. *The Science of Fire*, 20851
The Science of Sound, 20934
Crabtree, Marc. *Pioneer Projects*, 21521
Craddock, Sonia. *Sleeping Boy*, 7683(F)
Cradock-Watson, Jane. *Cars*, 5598
Dinosaurs, 14467
Craft, Charlotte. *King Midas and the Golden Touch*, 11468
Craft, K. Y. *Cinderella*, 10411(F)
Craft, Kinuko. *Baba Yaga and Vasilisa the Brave*, 11105
Bailey's Window, 7912(F)
King Midas and the Golden Touch, 11468
Pegasus, 11492
Craig, Claire. *Animal Babies*, 18872
Explorers and Traders, 16078
Incredible Creatures, 18931
Craig, Diana. *Making Models*, 21429
Craig, Helen. *The Bowl of Fruit*, 2042(F)
The Bunny Who Found Easter, 5979(F)
Crumbling Castle, 7787(F)
Foggy Friday, 2635(F)
One Windy Wednesday, 1520(F)
The Random House Book of Nursery Stories, 10543
This Is the Bear, 848
This Is the Bear and the Bad Little Girl, 2178(F)
This Is the Bear and the Scary Night, 2179(F)

The Town Mouse and the Country Mouse, 11056
Turnover Tuesday, 4286(F)
Craig, Ruth. *Malu's Wolf*, 8953(F)
Craighead, Charles. *The Eagle and the River*, 19323
Cramer, Mark. *Cuba*, 15698
Crane, Walter. *Household Stories of the Brothers Grimm*, 10899
Cranston, Patty. *The Best on Ice*, 22220
Magic on Ice, 22221
Crary, Elizabeth. *I'm Frustrated*, 4937(F)
Cravath, Lynne W. *My First Action Rhymes*, 874
A My Name Is . . ., 84(F)
One Little, Two Little, Three Little Pilgrims, 6143(F)
The Penny Pot, 531
Shark Swimathon, 20633
Spunky Monkeys on Parade, 532(F)
Tiny and Bigman, 2933(F)
Tomboy Trouble, 6724(F)
The Two Sillies, 1246(F)
Cray, Jordan. *Dead Man's Hand*, 6804(F)
Shiver, 6805(F)
Creagh, Carson. *Mammals*, 18932
Things with Wings, 18616
Creagh, Carson, ed. *Reptiles*, 18683
Crebbin, June. *Cows in the Kitchen*, 9818(F)
Danny's Duck, 5492(F)
Fly by Night, 1985(F)
The Train Ride, 3087(F)
Creech, Sharon. *Absolutely Normal Chaos*, 8617(F)
Bloomability, 10042(F)
Chasing Redbird, 8618(F)
Fishing in the Air, 1086(F)
Pleasing the Ghost, 7684(F)
The Wanderer, 6806(F)
Creel, Ann Howard. *Nowhere, Now Here*, 8619(F)
Water at the Blue Earth, 9354(F)
Crelinstein, Jeffrey. *To the Limit*, 18054
Crenson, Victoria. *Bay Shore Park*, 16955
Crenson, Victoria (jt. author). *Thinking*, 18121
Cresp, Gael. *The Tale of Gilbert Alexander Pig*, 1986(F)
Crespo, George. *Lizard Sees the World*, 2758(F)
Cresswell, Helen. *Posy Bates, Again!* 9819(F)
The Secret World of Polly Flint, 7685(F)
Time Out, 7686(F)
The Watchers, 7687(F)
Cressy, Mik. *Purple Is Best*, 6590(F)
Creswick, Paul. *Robin Hood*, 10964
Cretzmeyer, Stacy. *Your Name Is Renée*, 14842
Crew, Gary. *Bright Star*, 4938(F)

Crewe, Sabrina. *The Bear*, 19040
The Bee, 19518
The Prairie Dog, 19194
The Salmon, 19700
Crews, Donald. *Bicycle Race*, 5554(F)
Bigmama's, 3594
Blue Sea, 342(F)
Carousel, 3088(F)
Cloudy Day Sunny Day, 6292(F)
Each Orange Had Eight Slices, 443
Flying, 5555(F)
Freight Train, 21331
Harbor, 5556(F)
How Many Snails? 444(F)
Inside Freight Train, 5557(F)
More Than One, 575
Night at the Fair, 3089(F)
Parade, 3090(F)
Rain, 4470(F)
Sail Away, 2923(F)
School Bus, 5558(F)
Shortcut, 3091(F)
Ten Black Dots, 413(F)
This Is the Sunflower, 4535(F)
Truck, 913(F)
Crews, Nina. *A High, Low, Near, Far, Loud, Quiet Story*, 174(F)
I'll Catch the Moon, 1087(F)
One Hot Summer Day, 3092(F)
Snowball, 3093(F)
We, the People, 11615
When Will Sarah Come? 3708(F)
You Are Here, 1088(F)
Crilley, Mark. *Akiko in the Sprubly Islands*, 10173(F)
Akiko on the Planet Smoo, 10174(F)
Crimi, Carolyn. *Don't Need Friends*, 1987(F)
Outside, Inside, 3094(F)
Crisfield, Deborah. *Louisville Slugger Book of Great Hitters*, 13364
Winning Volleyball for Girls, 21990
Crisman, Ruth. *Racing the Iditarod Trail*, 21991
Crisp, Marty. *Black and White*, 1988(F)
My Dog, Cat, 7179(F)
Ratzo, 7180(F)
Crisp, Tony. *Super Minds*, 21903
Crist-Evans, Craig. *Moon over Tennessee*, 9470(F)
Cristaldi, Kathryn. *Baseball Ballerina*, 6293(F)
Baseball Ballerina Strikes Out! 6294(F)
Princess Lulu Goes to Camp, 6295(F)
Samantha the Snob, 4939(F)
Cristini, Ermanno. *In My Garden*, 914(F)
Crockcroft, Jason. *The Dandelion Wish*, 1250(F)
Crocker, Debbie. *Learn the Value of Trust*, 184

Crockett-Blassingame, Linda. *See the Ocean*, 4407(F)
Crofford, Emily. *Born in the Year of Courage*, 8991(F)
Frontier Surgeons, 13318
Healing Warrior, 13311
A Place to Belong, 9531(F)
Croll, Carolyn. *The Big Balloon Race*, 6272(F)
Clara and the Bookwagon, 6454(F)
The Great Pyramid, 14615
Switch On, Switch Off, 20884
Too Many Babas, 6296(F)
What Will the Weather Be? 20760
Cromie, Alice. *Taiwan*, 15155
Crompton, Jack. *Mountains to Climb*, 8842(F)
Cronin, Doreen. *Click, Clack, Moo*, 1989(F)
Crook, Connie Brummel. *Maple Moon*, 11225(F)
Crosbie, Michael J. *Arches to Zigzags*, 27
Crosby, Jeff. *Egyptian Gods and Goddesses*, 14608
Crosher, Judith. *Ancient Egypt*, 14616
Technology in the Time of Ancient Egypt, 14617
Cross, Gillian. *The Great American Elephant Chase*, 9532(F)
Pictures in the Dark, 7688(F)
Cross, Rick. *Swimming*, 22306
Cross, Robin. *Children and War*, 14843
Crosse, Joanna. *A Child's Book of Angels*, 7689(F)
Crossingham, John. *Volleyball in Action*, 21992
Crossley-Holland, Kevin. *The World of King Arthur and His Court*, 10965
Crossley-Holland, Kevin (jt. author). *Tales from the Mabinogion*, 11040
Crossman, David A. *The Secret of the Missing Grave*, 6807(F)
Croswell, Ken. *See the Stars*, 18386
Crouch, Marcus. *Ivan*, 11085
Crowe, Carol (jt. author). *Fabric*, 21647
Crowe, Elizabeth. *Jirohattan*, 9677(F)
Crowther, Robert. *Dump Trucks and Diggers*, 5559(F)
My Pop-Up Surprise ABC, 28(F)
My Pop-Up Surprise 123, 414(F)
Robert Crowther's Amazing Pop-Up House of Inventions, 21027
Robert Crowther's Pop-Up Olympics, 22245
Crozon, Alain. *I Can Fly!* 175(F)
Cruise, Robin. *Fiona's Private Pages*, 8273(F)
The Top-Secret Journal of Fiona Claire Jardin, 8620(F)

Crum, Anna-Maria L. *Slugs, Bugs, and Salamanders*, 18644
Crum, Robert. *Eagle Drum*, 15943
Let's Rodeo! 21993
Crume, Marion. *Do You See Mouse?* 1990(F)
Crummel, Susan Stevens. *Tumbleweed Stew*, 6297(F)
Crummel, Susan Stevens (jt. author). *Cook-a-Doodle-Doo!* 2724(F)
My Big Dog, 2725(F)
Shoe Town, 6684(F)
Crump, Donald J., ed. *Amazing Animals of Australia*, 18933
Animal Architects, 18906
Explore a Tropical Forest, 20435
How Animals Behave, 18804
How Things Work, 21028
Secrets of Animal Survival, 18805
Crunk, Tony. *Big Mama*, 3095(F)
Cruz, Barbara C. *Rubén Blades*, 12357
Cruz, Ray. *Alexander and the Terrible, Horrible, No Good, Very Bad Day*, 3927(F)
Alexander, Who Used to Be Rich Last Sunday, 6706(F)
Baseball Fever, 10339(F)
Cruz Martinez, Alejandro. *The Woman Who Outshone the Sun*, 11135
Cryan-Hicks, Kathryn. *W. E. B. Du Bois*, 12718
Cryan-Hicks, Kathryn, ed. *Pride and Promise*, 16460
Cuetara, Mittie. *The Crazy Crawler Crane and Other Very Short Truck Stories*, 5560(F)
Cuffari, Richard. *The Cartoonist*, 8582(F)
The Odyssey of Ben O'Neal, 7096(F)
Thank You, Jackie Robinson, 10319(F)
The Winged Colt of Casa Mia, 7639(F)
Cuffie, Terrasita A. *Maya Angelou*, 12494
Cullen, Lynn. *The Mightiest Heart*, 10966
Stink Bomb, 10043(F)
The Three Lives of Harris Harper, 8418(F)
Cullinan, Bernice E., ed. *A Jar of Tiny Stars*, 11547
Cumming, David. *The Ganges Delta and Its People*, 15095
India, 15096, 15097
Mountains, 20499
Rivers and Lakes, 20513
Russia, 15411
Cummings, Pat. *Angel Baby*, 3595(F)
Carousel, 1089(F)
Clean Your Room, Harvey Moon! 4121(F)
Go Fish, 7522(F)
I Need a Lunch Box, 3063(F)

Just Us Women, 2916(F)
Lulu's Birthday, 5695(F)
My Aunt Came Back, 836(F)
Pickin' Peas, 2423(F)
Purrrrr, 5173(F)
Storm in the Night, 5090(F)
Talking with Artists, 13953
Cummings, Pat, ed., 13952
Cummings, Priscilla. *A Face First*, 8621(F)
Cummings, Rhoda (jt. author). *The Survival Guide for Kids with LD (Learning Differences)*, 17907
Cummins, Jeff. *Cars, Boats, Trains, and Planes*, 21289
Cummins, Julie. *The Inside-Outside Book of Libraries*, 13992
Cuneo, Diane. *Mary Louise Loses Her Manners*, 1090(F)
Cuneo, Mary L. *Mail for Husher Town*, 655(F)
Cunningham, Chet. *Chief Crazy Horse*, 12971
Cunningham, Julia. *Burnish Me Bright*, 8885(F)
Cupples, Pat. *Earthwatch*, 20321
Farming, 20052
Fishing, 19848
Forestry, 20438
Hands On, Thumbs Up, 14014
Lu and Clancy's Crime Science, 17065
Lu and Clancy's Secret Codes, 13967
Mining, 21030
The Science Book for Girls and Other Intelligent Beings, 18371
Sportsworks, 18068
Curlee, Lynn. *Into the Ice*, 15798
Liberty, 16662
Rushmore, 16542
Ships of the Air, 21075
Curless, Allan. *Dogs' Night*, 2218(F)
Outcast of Redwall, 7828(F)
Curran, Emily (jt. author). *Science Sensations*, 18370
Curran, Wanda L. *Your Guinea Pig*, 19884
Currey, Anna. *Tickling Tigers*, 1992(F)
Truffle's Christmas, 5791(F)
Currie, Philip J. *The Newest and Coolest Dinosaurs*, 14394
Currie, Stephen. *Adoption*, 17649
The Olympic Games, 22246
Curry, Barbara K. *Sweet Words So Brave*, 14076
Curry, Jane L. *Back in the Beforetime*, 9153(F)
The Big Smith Snatch, 6808(F)
The Christmas Knight, 10967
The Great Smith House Hustle, 6809(F)
Little Little Sister, 10412(F)
Moon Window, 7690(F)

Robin Hood and His Merry Men, 10968
Robin Hood in the Greenwood, 10969
A Stolen Life, 9188(F)
Turtle Island, 11226
What the Dickens! 9269(F)
Curry, Tom. *The Bootmaker and the Elves*, 1361(F)
Comes a Wind, 4352(F)
Curtis, Bruce. *Beginning Golf*, 21994
Curtis, Chara M. *No One Walks on My Father's Moon*, 8929(F)
Curtis, Christopher Paul. *Bud, Not Buddy*, 8622(F)
The Watsons Go to Birmingham — 1963, 7337(F)
Curtis, Gavin. *The Bat Boy and His Violin*, 10322(F)
Curtis, Jamie Lee. *Tell Me Again About the Night I Was Born*, 3596(F)
Today I Feel Silly, 4940(F)
Where Do Balloons Go? 1091(F)
Curtis, Sandra R. *Gabriel's Ark*, 8623(F)
Curtiss, A. B. *In the Company of Bears*, 1993(F)
Cushman, Doug. *Aunt Eater Loves a Mystery*, 6298(F)
Aunt Eater's Mystery Halloween, 5992(F)
Aunt Eater's Mystery Vacation, 6299(F)
Halloween Mice! 6044(F)
Inspector Hopper, 6300(F)
The Mystery of King Karfu, 6810(F)
The Mystery of the Monkey's Maze, 6811(F)
Porcupine's Pajama Party, 6367(F)
Valentine Mice! 6175(F)
What Dads Can't Do, 2873(F)
What Moms Can't Do, 2874(F)
Cushman, Jean. *Do You Wanna Bet?* 20614
Cushman, Karen. *The Ballad of Lucy Whipple*, 9355(F)
Matilda Bone, 9090(F)
Cuthbert, Susan, comp. *The Classic Treasury of Children's Prayers*, 17519
Cutler, Jane. *The Cello of Mr. O*, 4631(F)
Darcy and Gran Don't Like Babies, 3597(F)
'Gator Aid, 9820(F)
Mr. Carey's Garden, 5174(F)
My Wartime Summers, 9650(F)
No Dogs Allowed, 9821(F)
Rats! 9822(F)
The Song of the Molimo, 9533(F)
Spaceman, 8886(F)
Cutts, David. *More About Dinosaurs*, 14395

Cuyler, Margery. *The Battlefield Ghost*, 7691(F)
The Biggest, Best Snowman, 1092(F)
Fat Santa, 5792(F)
From Here to There, 3096(F)
100th Day Worries, 415(F)
Roadsigns, 11469
That's Good! That's Bad! 4122(F)
Weird Wolf, 7692(F)
Cvijanovic, Adam. *The Ledgerbook of Thomas Blue Eagle*, 9160(F)
Cwiklik, Robert. *A. Philip Randolph and the Labor Movement*, 12781
Bill Clinton, 13022
King Philip and the War with the Colonists, 12981
Malcolm X and Black Pride, 12760
Sequoyah and the Cherokee Alphabet, 12993
Stokely Carmichael and Black Power, 12706
Cymerman, John E. *How's the Weather?* 20753
It's Just a Game, 3128(F)
Cyrus, Kurt. *The Mousery*, 2594(F)
Oddhopper Opera, 11947
Slow Train to Oxmox, 1093(F)
Tangle Town, 4123(F)
There's Nothing to D-o-o-o! 2485(F)
Cytron, Barry. *Fire! The Library Is Burning*, 16663
Czarnota, Lorna MacDonald. *Medieval Tales That Kids Can Read and Tell*, 10544
Czech, Jan M. *An American Face*, 4941(F)
Czernecki, Stefan. *The Cricket's Cage*, 10747
The Girl Who Lost Her Smile, 4574(F)
Mama God, Papa God, 11428
Mr. Belinsky's Bagels, 4042(F)
Pancho's Pinata, 5793
The Sleeping Bread, 11398
Zorah's Magic Carpet, 1094(F)

Da Rif, Andrea. *Where Did You Put Your Sleep?* 752(F)
Dabcovich, Lydia. *Annushka's Voyage*, 4848(F)
Feathers, 11148
The Keys to My Kingdom, 837
The Polar Bear Son, 11205
Dacey, Bob. *Miriam's Cup*, 17478
Dadey, Debbie. *Cherokee Sister*, 9154(F)
King of the Kooties, 10044(F)
Leprechauns Don't Play Basketball, 7693(F)
Shooting Star, 12429
Will Rogers, 12458(F)
Dahan, Andre. *Squiggle's Tale*, 1994(F)
Dahl, Felicity (jt. author). *Roald Dahl's Revolting Recipes*, 21697

Dahl, Lucy. *James and the Giant Peach*, 21267
Dahl, Michael. *The Horizontal Man*, 6812(F)
Dahl, Roald. *Boy*, 12520(F)
Charlie and the Chocolate Factory, 7694(F)
The Enormous Crocodile, 1995(F)
George's Marvelous Medicine, 7695(F)
James and the Giant Peach, 7696(F), 12018(F)
Magic Finger, 7697(F)
Matilda, 10045(F)
The Minpins, 1095(F)
The Roald Dahl Treasury, 10256
The Witches, 7698(F)
The Wonderful Story of Henry Sugar and Six More, 7699(F)
Dahlberg, Maurine F. *Play to the Angel*, 9651(F)
Daily, Don. *Callie Ann and Mistah Bear*, 11375
Daily, Robert. *The Code Talkers*, 14844
Daitch, Richard W. *Northwest Territories*, 15572
Dakos, Kalli. *The Bug in Teacher's Coffee*, 11866
Don't Read This Book, Whatever You Do! 11867
Mrs. Cole on an Onion Roll and Other School Poems, 11549
Dal Sasso, Cristiano. *Animals*, 14396
Dale, Elizabeth. *How Long?* 176(F)
Dale, Penny. *All About Alice*, 4124(F)
Big Brother, Little Brother, 3598(F)
The Mushroom Hunt, 20187
My Shadow, 11718
Night Night, Cuddly Bear, 799(F)
Once There Were Giants, 3468(F)
Rosie's Babies, 3931(F)
Ten Play Hide-and-Seek, 656(F)
Wake Up, Mr. B.! 1096(F)
When the Teddy Bears Came, 3932(F)
Dale, Shelley (jt. author). *Tales from the Homeplace*, 9527(F)
Daley, William. *The Chinese Americans*, 17553
Dalgliesh, Alice. *The Bears on Hemlock Mountain*, 5175(F)
Courage of Sarah Noble, 9189(F)
The Thanksgiving Story, 6142(F)
D'Allance, Mireille. *Bear's Christmas Star*, 5794(F)
Dallinger, Jane. *Grasshoppers*, 19434
Spiders, 19577
Dallinger, Rebecca. *Allison's Story*, 10105
Dalokay, Vedat. *Sister Shako and Kolo the Goat*, 13779
Daly, Carla. *Damien the Dragon*, 8047(F)
Daly, Catherine. *Whiskers*, 18806

Daly, Jim. *Sugarbush Spring*, 3578(F)
Daly, Jude. *Fair, Brown and Trembling*, 10413(F)
Gift of the Sun, 4333(F)
The Stone, 11187
Daly, Judy. *The Star-Bearer*, 11186
Daly, Niki. *The Boy on the Beach*, 3097(F)
Bravo, Zan Angelo! 4632(F)
The Dinosaurs Are Back and It's All Your Fault Edward! 4177(F)
Fly, Eagle, Fly! 10670
Jamela's Dress, 4633(F)
Mama, Papa, and Baby Joe, 1097(F)
My Dad, 4942(F)
Not So Fast, Songololo, 4634(F)
One Round Moon and a Star for Me, 3804(F)
Papa Lucky's Shadow, 3599(F)
Red Light, Green Light, Mama and Me, 3025(F)
Daly, Niki (jt. author). *The Dinosaurs Are Back and It's All Your Fault Edward!* 4177(F)
D'Amato, Alex. *Indian Crafts*, 21518
D'Amato, Janet. *Indian Crafts*, 21518
Damerow, Gail. *Your Chickens*, 20050
Your Goats, 20051
D'Amico, Joan. *The Healthy Body Cookbook*, 21690
The Science Chef, 20087
The Science Chef Travels Around the World, 21691
The United States Cookbook, 21692
Damon, Duane. *When This Cruel War Is Over*, 16400
Damrell, Liz. *With the Wind*, 22199
Dana, Barbara. *Zucchini Out West*, 7181(F)
Dang, Xuan-Quang. *To Swim in Our Own Pond*, 14113
Daniel, Alan. *Bunnicula*, 9885(F)
Bunnicula Escapes! 6902(F)
The Dream Collector, 695(F)
Get Out of Bed! 4241(F)
The Orchestra, 14228
Return to Howliday Inn, 9889(F)
Sody Salleratus, 11331
Daniel, Claire. *The Chick That Wouldn't Hatch*, 6301(F)
Daniel, Lea. *Bunnicula Escapes!* 6902(F)
The Dream Collector, 695(F)
Get Out of Bed! 4241(F)
Sody Salleratus, 11331
Daniels, Teri. *The Feet in the Gym*, 5493(F)
G-Rex, 1098(F)
Just Enough, 3098(F)
Danis, Naomi. *Walk with Me*, 3099(F)
Dann, Colin. *Nobody's Dog*, 7182(F)

Dann, Penny. *Bicycle Safety,* 22161
Emergencies, 18220
Professor Solomon Snickerdoodle's Air Science Tricks, 20674
Professor Solomon Snickerdoodle's Light Science Tricks, 20876
What Are Friends For? 2154(F)
What Will I Do Without You? 2155(F)
Dann, Sarah. *The Science of Energy,* 20824
Dann, Sarah (jt. author). *Volleyball in Action,* 21992
Danneberg, Julie. *First Day Jitters,* 3100(F)
D'Antonio, Nancy. *Our Baby from China,* 3600(F)
Danza, Jennifer. *The Friendship of Milly and Tug,* 7497(F)
Danziger, Paula. *Amber Brown Goes Fourth,* 9823(F)
Amber Brown Is Feeling Blue, 9824(F)
Amber Brown Is Not a Crayon, 9825(F)
Amber Brown Sees Red, 9826(F)
Amber Brown Wants Extra Credit, 8419(F)
Forever Amber Brown, 8420(F)
I, Amber Brown, 9827(F)
It's Justin Time, Amber Brown, 6302(F)
P.S. Longer Letter Later, 8274(F)
Snail Mail No More, 8275(F)
You Can't Eat Your Chicken Pox, Amber Brown, 9828(F)
Darby, Jean. *Douglas MacArthur,* 12930
Dwight D. Eisenhower, 13028
Martin Luther King, Jr., 12741
Darian-Smith, Kate. *The Australian Outback and Its People,* 15229
Exploration into Australia, 15228
Darley, Felix O. *Rip Van Winkle and the Legend of Sleepy Hollow,* 7816(F)
Darling, Benjamin. *Valerie and the Silver Pear,* 3601(F)
Darling, Christina. *Mirror,* 1099(F)
Darling, David J. *Between Fire and Ice,* 20852
Making Light Work, 20861
Sounds Interesting, 20935
Spiderwebs to Skyscrapers, 21119
Up and Away, 21076
Darling, Kathy. *ABC Cats,* 29(F)
ABC Dogs, 19944
Amazon ABC, 30(F)
Arctic Babies, 15799
Chameleons, 18743
Desert Babies, 18873
Komodo Dragon, 18744
Lemurs on Location, 18990
Lions, 19083
Rain Forest Babies, 20436
Seashore Babies, 19628
There's a Zoo on You! 18055

Walrus, 19732
Darling, Kathy (jt. author). *Bet You Can't! Science Impossibilities to Fool You,* 18306
Don't Try This at Home! Science Fun for Kids on the Go, 18307
How to Babysit an Orangutan, 18991
Wanna Bet? 18308
You Gotta Try This! 18309
Darling, Louis. *Ellen Tebbits,* 9800(F)
The Enormous Egg, 9792(F)
Henry Huggins, 9802(F)
Mr. Bass's Planetoid, 10157(F)
Otis Spofford, 9803(F)
Ramona the Pest, 7406(F)
Runaway Ralph, 9804(F)
Darling, Tara. *ABC Cats,* 29(F)
ABC Dogs, 19944
Amazon ABC, 30(F)
Arctic Babies, 15799
Chameleons, 18743
Desert Babies, 18873
How to Babysit an Orangutan, 18991
Komodo Dragon, 18744
Rain Forest Babies, 20436
Seashore Babies, 19628
Walrus, 19732
Darrow, Sharon. *Old Thunder and Miss Raney,* 1100(F)
Darwin, Beatrice. *Socks,* 7409(F)
Das, Prodeepta. *I Is for India,* 15098
Rice, 20130
Dash, Joan. *The World at Her Fingertips,* 13165
Dash, Paul. *Traditions from the Caribbean,* 15699
Datlow, Ellen, ed. *A Wolf at the Door,* 10414(F)
Datnow, Claire. *American Science Fiction and Fantasy Writers,* 12160
Edwin Hubble, 13309
Daugherty, James. *Abe Lincoln Grows Up,* 13075
Andy and the Lion, 1996(F)
Joe Magarac and His U.S.A. Citizen Papers, 11383
The Landing of the Pilgrims, 16107
D'Aujourd'Hui, Nicolas. *The Strongest Mouse in the World,* 2829(F)
D'Aulaire, Edgar. *D'Aulaire's Book of Greek Myths,* 11470
D'Aulaire, Ingri. *D'Aulaire's Book of Greek Myths,* 11470
Davalos, Felipe. *All the Way to Morning,* 696(F)
Gone Forever! An Alphabet of Extinct Animals, 19405
The Lizard and the Sun, 11392
Our Lady of Guadalupe, 17216
The Secret Stars, 5920(F)
Davenier, Christine. *Leon and Albertine,* 1997(F)

The Low-Down Laundry Line Blues, 3806(F)
Mabel Dancing, 700(F)
The Other Dog, 2355(F)
Very Best (Almost) Friends, 11729
Davenport, Meg. *Circus! A Pop-Up Adventure,* 14268
Davenport, Zoe. *Animals,* 5176
David, Lawrence. *Beetle Boy,* 1101(F)
David, Rosalie. *Growing Up in Ancient Egypt,* 14618
David, Thomas (jt. author). *Marc Chagall,* 12208
Davidson, Bob. *Hillary and Tenzing Climb Everest,* 21995
Davidson, Margaret. *The Story of Jackie Robinson,* 13489
Davidson, Sue. *Getting the Real Story,* 12643
Davie, Helen K. *Animals in Winter,* 18801
Ladder to the Sky, 11234
The Night Rainbow, 15802
The Star Maiden, 11235
What Lives in a Shell? 18916
Davies, Eryl. *Transport,* 21282
Davies, Kath. *Amelia Earhart Flies Around the World,* 12110
Davies, Kay. *My Apple,* 20140
My Boat, 20803
Davies, Nicola. *Big Blue Whale,* 19782
Davies, Sally J. K. *When William Went Away,* 3992(F)
Why Did We Have to Move Here? 4943(F)
Davies, Valentine. *Miracle on 34th Street,* 9715(F)
Davis, Amanda. *Extraterrestrials,* 20979
Davis, Aubrey. *Bone Button Borscht,* 11144
The Enormous Potato, 11086
Sody Salleratus, 11331
Davis, Burke. *Black Heroes of the American Revolution,* 12644
Davis, Caroline. *The Young Equestrian,* 22200
Davis, Donald. *Jack and the Animals,* 11332(F)
Davis, Gary. *From Rock to Fireworks,* 21029
Submarine Wahoo, 14845
Davis, Gibbs. *The Other Emily,* 5494(F)
Davis, Jack E. *Bedhead,* 4258(F)
Dr. Jekyll, Orthodontist, 7757(F)
A Ghost Named Wanda, 7758(F)
Mary Louise Loses Her Manners, 1090(F)
Music over Manhattan, 4994(F)
My Son, the Time Traveler, 10189(F)
Davis, Jennifer. *Before You Were Born,* 18228

Davis, Karen. *Star Light, Star Bright*, 657(F)

Davis, Kate. *I Hate to Go to Bed!* 658(F)

Davis, Kathleen. *Killer Bees*, 19519

Davis, Katie. *Who Hoots?* 5177(F)
Who Hops? 1998(F)

Davis, Lambert. *Baby Whales Drink Milk*, 19786
The Bells of Christmas, 9729(F)
The Jolly Mon, 1021(F)
Rikki-Tikki-Tavi, 1309(F)
Trouble Dolls, 1022(F)

Davis, Lee. *The Lifesize Animal Opposites Book*, 18617
P. B. Bear's Treasure Hunt, 21880(F)

Davis, Lucile. *Alabama*, 16841
The Mayo Brothers, 13319
Puerto Rico, 15700

Davis, Meredith. *Up and Away!* 21077

Davis, Nelle. *The Best Worst Day*, 10067(F)

Davis, Patricia A. *Brian's Bird*, 5178(F)

Davis, Rich. *Tiny Goes to the Library*, 6517(F)
Tiny's Bath, 6518(F)
When Tiny Was Tiny, 6519(F)

Davis, Robin. *The Star Wars Cookbook*, 21693

Davis, Russell (jt. author). *The Lion's Whiskers and Other Ethiopian Tales*, 10649

Davis, Steve. *Snowboarding*, 22278

Davis, Tim. *Mice of the Westing Wind*, 6303(F)

Davis, Wendy. *From Metal to Music*, 14219
Working at a Marine Institute, 17843

Davis, Yvonne. *The Girl Who Wore Too Much*, 10840
Slop! A Welsh Folktale, 11013
Tuck-Me-In Tales, 735

Davison, Katherine. *Moon Magic*, 10722

Davol, Marguerite W. *Batwings and the Curtain of Night*, 1999(F)
Black, White, Just Right! 3602(F)
The Heart of the Wood, 4410(F)
How Snake Got His Hiss, 1102(F)
The Loudest, Fastest, Best Drummer in Kansas, 1103(F)
Papa Alonzo Leatherby, 9829(F)
The Paper Dragon, 1104(F)

Dawson, Imogen. *Clothes and Crafts in Ancient Aztec Times*, 15613
Clothes and Crafts in the Middle Ages, 14760
Food and Feasts in the Middle Ages, 14761

Dawson, Zoe. *China*, 15056
Japan, 15120
South Africa, 14973

Day, Alexandra. *Boswell Wide Awake*, 659(F)
Carl Goes to Daycare, 2000(F)
Carl Makes a Scrapbook, 1105(F)
Carl's Afternoon in the Park, 2001(F)
Carl's Birthday, 5678(F)
Carl's Christmas, 2002(F)
Carl's Masquerade, 915(F)
The Christmas We Moved to the Barn, 5795(F)
Darby, the Special-Order Pup, 1106(F)
Follow Carl! 2003(F)
Frank and Ernest on the Road, 2004(F)
Frank and Ernest Play Ball, 2005(F)
Mirror, 1099(F)

Day, David. *King of the Woods*, 2006(F)

Day, Jon. *Let's Make Magic*, 21781

Day, Larry. *William's House*, 9200(F)

Day, Malcolm. *The World of Castles and Forts*, 21381

Day, Marie. *Quennu and the Cave Bear*, 4635(F)

Day, Nancy. *The Horseshoe Crab*, 19673
Your Travel Guide to Ancient Egypt, 14619
Your Travel Guide to Ancient Greece, 14677
Your Travel Guide to Ancient Mayan Civilization, 15661
Your Travel Guide to Civil War America, 16401
Your Travel Guide to Colonial America, 16108
Your Travel Guide to Renaissance Europe, 14797

Day, Nancy Raines. *A Kitten's Year*, 5179(F)
The Lion's Whiskers, 10660

Day, Noreha Yussof. *Kancil and the Crocodiles*, 10838

Day, Rob. *Walt Whitman*, 12623

Day, Trevor. *Light*, 20862
The Random House Book of 1001 Questions and Answers About the Human Body, 18056
Youch! 18618

Daziel, Kim. *Fashion Through the Ages*, 21175

Deady, Kathleen W. *Egypt*, 15497
Kansas Facts and Symbols, 16543
Kentucky Facts and Symbols, 16842

Deal, Jim. *Way Down Deep*, 19630

Deal, L. Kate. *The Boxcar Children Cookbook*, 21678

Dean, Julia. *A Year on Monhegan Island*, 16664

Dean, Ruth. *Life in the American Colonies*, 16109

de Anda, Diane. *The Ice Dove and Other Stories*, 7417(F)

Deane, Bill. *Top 10 Baseball Home Run Hitters*, 13365
Top 10 Men's Baseball Hitters, 13366

Deane, Peter M. G. (jt. author). *Coping with Allergies*, 17996

De Angeli, Marguerite. *Copper-Toed Boots*, 9534(F)
The Door in the Wall, 9091(F)

De Angelis, Gina. *The Black Cowboys*, 16298
Gregory Hines, 12400
Jackie Robinson, 13490
Science and Medicine, 13207
The Wild West, 16299

De Angelis, Therese. *Wonders of the Ancient World*, 14582

Dearborn, Sabrina, ed. *A Child's Book of Blessings*, 17520

Dearth, Greg. *Secrets on 26th Street*, 9565(F)
Voices at Whisper Bend, 9644(F)
Watcher in the Piney Woods, 9483(F)

de Beer, Hans. *Alexander the Great*, 1840(F)
Bernard Bear's Amazing Adventure, 2007(F)
King Bobble, 4099(F)
Leave It to the Molesons! 1841(F)
Little Polar Bear and the Husky Pup, 2008(F)
Little Polar Bear Finds a Friend, 2009(F)
Little Polar Bear, Take Me Home! 2010(F)

DeBiasi, Antoinette. *A Child's Day*, 16476
Colonial Crafts, 16142

Debon, Nicolas. *The Warlord's Puzzle*, 4795(F)

De Bourgoing, Pascale. *Vegetables in the Garden*, 20172

De Brunhoff, Jean. *The Story of Babar, the Little Elephant*, 2011(F)

De Brunhoff, Laurent. *Babar and the Succotash Bird*, 2012(F)

De Capua, Sarah. *J.C. Watts, Jr. Character Counts*, 12968

Decesare, Angelo. *Flip's Fantastic Journal*, 2013(F)

DeClements, Barthe. *The Bite of the Gold Bug*, 9535(F)
Liar, Liar, 10046(F)
Nothing's Fair in Fifth Grade, 10047(F)
Sixth Grade Can Really Kill You, 10048(F)
Wake Me at Midnight, 6813(F)

Dee, Catherine. *The Girls' Guide to Life*, 17134

Dee, Catherine, ed. *The Girls' Book of Wisdom*, 17701

Dee, Ruby. *Two Ways to Count to Ten*, 10661

Deeble, Mark. *The Crocodile Family Book*, 18700

Deedy, Carmen A. *Agatha's Feather Bed*, 3603(F)
The Library Dragon, 1107(F)
The Secret of Old Zeb, 6814(F)
The Yellow Star, 9652(F)

Deegan, Paul J. *Sandra Day O'Connor*, 12938
Supreme Court Book, 17012

Deem, James M. *Bodies from the Bog*, 14494
How to Find a Ghost, 21904
How to Hunt Buried Treasure, 21905
How to Make a Mummy Talk, 14620
How to Read Your Mother's Mind, 21906
The Very Real Ghost Book of Christina Rose, 7700(F)

Deer, Victoria. *Kenya*, 14924

Deeter, Catherine. *The Return of Rex and Ethel*, 7148(F)
Seymour Bleu, 264(F)

Deetlefs, Rene. *The Song of Six Birds*, 4636(F)

DeFelice, Cynthia. *The Apprenticeship of Lucas Whitaker*, 9270(F)
Clever Crow, 5180(F)
Cold Feet, 7701(F)
The Dancing Skeleton, 11333
Death at Devil's Bridge, 6815(F)
Devil's Bridge, 6816(F)
The Ghost of Fossil Glen, 7702(F)
The Light on Hogback Hill, 8276(F)
Lostman's River, 6817(F)
Nowhere to Call Home, 9536(F)
The Strange Night Writing of Jessamine Colter, 10175(F)
Three Perfect Peaches, 10868
Weasel, 9356(F)
Willy's Silly Grandma, 4125(F)

Degen, Bruce. *Better Not Get Wet, Jesse Bear*, 1932(F)
Daddy Is a Doodlebug, 2014(F)
Guess Who's Coming, Jesse Bear, 1933(F)
Happy Birthday, Jesse Bear! 5672(F)
How Do You Say It Today, Jesse Bear? 1934(F)
If You Were a Writer, 14101
Jamberry, 2015(F)
The Josefina Story Quilt, 6275(F)
Let's Count It Out, Jesse Bear, 398(F)
The Magic School Bus, 16993, 20302, 18052
The Magic School Bus and the Electric Field Trip, 20887
The Magic School Bus Explores the Senses, 18139

The Magic School Bus in the Time of the Dinosaurs, 14392
The Magic School Bus Inside a Beehive, 19517
The Magic School Bus Inside a Hurricane, 20687
The Magic School Bus Lost in the Solar System, 18510(F)
The Magic School Bus on the Ocean Floor, 19816
Sailaway Home, 2016(F)
What a Scare, Jesse Bear, 5988(F)
Where Is Christmas, Jesse Bear? 5775(F)

De Groat, Diane. *Annie Pitts, Burger Kid*, 9830(F)
Armadillos Sleep in Dugouts, 18912
Attaboy, Sam! 9923(F)
DeDe Takes Charge! 8461(F)
Dr. Ruth Talks to Kids, 18270
The Great Summer Camp Catastrophe, 8174(F)
Happy Birthday to You, You Belong in a Zoo, 5679(F)
It Goes Eeeeeeeeeeeee! 10065(F)
Jingle Bells, Homework Smells, 5796(F)
Little Rabbit's Loose Tooth, 1795(F)
Our Teacher's Having a Baby, 5479(F)
A Pinky Is a Baby Mouse, 18880
Pots and Pans, 4184(F)
Roses Are Pink, Your Feet Really Stink, 6165(F)
See You Around, Sam! 9925(F)
Some Days, Other Days, 3837(F)
Sunshine Home, 3558(F)
Tough-Luck Karen, 10086(F)
Trick or Treat, Smell My Feet, 5993(F)
A Turkey for Thanksgiving, 6136(F)
Where Is Everybody? 97(F)

DeGross, Monalisa. *Donavan's Word Jar*, 7418(F)
Granddaddy's Street Songs, 3604(F)

de Hugo, Pierre. *The Seashore*, 19856

Deines, Brian. *Bear on the Train*, 5298(F)
Charlotte, 16203
SkySisters, 11316

Deitch, Kenneth. *Dwight D. Eisenhower*, 13029

DeJong, Meindert. *Along Came a Dog*, 7183(F)
The House of Sixty Fathers, 9653(F)
Hurry Home, Candy, 7184(F)
Wheel on the School, 9032(F)

de Kiefte, Kees. *The Girl Who Could Fly*, 10197(F)
Yang the Third and Her Impossible Family, 8497(F)

Del Negro, Janice. *Lucy Dove*, 7703(F)

Del Prado, Dana. *Terror Below!* 19755

Delacre, Lulu. *Arroz con Leche*, 14236
The Bossy Gallito, 11422
Golden Tales, 11435
Las Navidades, 14197
Salsa Stories, 7419(F)
Señor Cat's Romance and Other Favorite Stories from Latin America, 11439

Delacre, Lulu, ed. *Arroz con Leche*, 14236

Delafosse, Claude. *Animals*, 13885
Bees, 19520
Butterflies, 19545
Construction, 21120
Frogs, 18718
Hidden World, 18387
Landscapes, 13886
Paintings, 13887
Portraits, 13888
Pyramids, 14621
Tools, 5561(F)
Under the Ground, 18934
Under the Sea, 19629
Whales, 19783

Delafosse, Claude (jt. author). *Houses*, 21158

Delamare, David. *Midnight Farm*, 1579(F)

de la Mare, Walter. *The Turnip*, 10886

Delaney, Janet. *Frog Face*, 3880(F)

Delaney, Mark. *The Vanishing Chip*, 6818(F)

Delaney, Michael. *Deep Doo-Doo and the Mysterious E-mail*, 6819(F)

Delaney, Molly. *Andrew Wants a Dog*, 5293(F)

Delaney, Ned. *The Cactus Flower Bakery*, 1735(F)

DeLange, Alex P. *Sip, Slurp, Soup, Soup/Caldo, Caldo, Caldo*, 3527(F)

Delano, Marfe Ferguson. *Kangaroos*, 2017(F)
Sea Otters, 19733
Tigers, 19084

de la Pena, Terri (jt. author). *A Is for the Americas*, 23

de Larrea, Victoria. *Pinatas and Paper Flowers*, 17394

deLeiris, Lucia. *Antarctic Journal*, 15806

Delf, Brian. *Space, Stars, Planets and Spacecraft*, 20950

Delgado, James P. *Native American Shipwrecks*, 15944
Shipwrecks from the Westward Movement, 16300
Wrecks of American Warships, 21357

Delgado, María Isabel. *Chave's Memories/Los Recuerdos de Chave,* 4637(F)

Delisle, Jim. *Kidstories,* 12645

Della Piana, Leandro. *Black Heroes of the Wild West,* 12687

Dell'Oro, Suzanne Paul. *Hiding Toads,* 18719

Tunneling Earthworms, 19603

Delmonte, Patti. *In a Pumpkin Shell,* 21438

DeLong, Faith. *Mystery at Echo Cliffs,* 6727(F)

Delton, Judy. *Angel Bites the Bullet,* 7420(F)

Angel Spreads Her Wings, 9033(F)

Angel's Mother's Baby, 7421(F)

Angel's Mother's Boyfriend, 7422(F)

Back Yard Angel, 7423(F)

Blue Skies, French Fries, 4126(F)

Cookies and Crutches, 6304(F)

Halloween Helpers, 9716(F)

Kitty from the Start, 10049(F)

My Mom Made Me Go to Camp, 3101(F)

The Perfect Christmas Gift, 5797(F)

Tricks and Treats, 9717(F)

DelVecchio, Ellen (jt. author). *Big City Port,* 5587(F)

De Magalhaes, Roberto Carvalho. *Prehistory,* 14397

de Marcken, Gail. *The Quiltmaker's Gift,* 1020(F)

Demarco, Neil. *The Children's Atlas of World History,* 14336

Demarest, Chris L. *The Animals' Song,* 1222(F)

April Fool! 6725(F)

Beep Beep, Vroom Vroom! 223(F)

The Butterfly Jar, 11661

The Cowboy ABC, 31

The Cows Are Going to Paris, 2293(F)

Derek's Dog Days, 1051(F)

A Dozen Dozens, 259(F)

Firefighters A to Z, 32(F)

Honk! 2018(F)

If Dogs Had Wings, 1865(F)

Smart Dog, 2354(F)

Someday We'll Have Very Good Manners, 4366(F)

Train, 5562(F)

What Would Mama Do? 2073(F)

When Cows Come Home, 2173(F)

Zookeeper Sue, 2019(F)

DeMarsh, Mary (jt. author). *Three Perfect Peaches,* 10868

Demas, Corinne. *The Disappearing Island,* 4411(F)

Hurricane! 2924(F)

If Ever I Return Again, 9271(F)

Nina's Waltz, 3605(F)

Dematons, Charlotte. *Looking for Cinderella,* 1108(F)

de Mejo, Oscar. *Does God Have a Big Toe?* 17272

Demers, Barbara. *Willa's New World,* 6820(F)

Demi. *Buddha,* 17175

Buddha Stories, 17176

The Dalai Lama, 13777

The Donkey and the Rock, 10723

The Dragon's Tale and Other Animal Fables of the Chinese Zodiac, 10748

The Emperor's New Clothes, 10415(F)

The Empty Pot, 10749

Eucalyptus Wings, 1268(F)

Grass Sandals, 9015

The Greatest Treasure, 10750

Happy New Year! Kung-Hsi Fa-Ts' Ai! 5621(F)

In the Eyes of the Cat, 11821

Kites, 21667

Liang and the Magic Paintbrush, 1109(F)

One Grain of Rice, 10789

De Montano, Marty Kreipe. *Coyote in Love with a Star,* 11227

Demunn, Michael. *The Earth Is Good,* 4412(F)

Demuth, Patricia. *Achoo! All About Colds,* 17952

Cradles in the Trees, 19222

Johnny Appleseed, 12843

Snakes, 18757

Those Amazing Ants, 19509

Way Down Deep, 19630

Denenberg, Barry. *The Journal of Ben Uchida,* 9654(F)

The Journal of William Thomas Emerson, 9227(F)

One Eye Laughing, The Other Weeping, 9655(F)

So Far from Home, 9537(F)

Stealing Home, 13491

Dengler, Marianna. *Fiddlin' Sam,* 4944(F)

The Worry Stone, 11228

Denim, Sue. *The Dumb Bunnies,* 2020(F)

The Dumb Bunnies' Easter, 5964(F)

The Dumb Bunnies Go to the Zoo, 2021(F)

Make Way for Dumb Bunnies, 2022(F)

Denise. *Baby Rock, Baby Roll,* 3027(F)

Denise, Christopher. *Digger Pig and the Turnip,* 10958

The Great Redwall Feast, 7819(F)

Rabbit and Turtle Go to School, 6334(F)

Dennen, Sue. *Alphabet Art,* 117(F)

Dennis, Peter. *Tiger Tales,* 19081

Dennis, Wesley. *Album of Horses,* 19996

King of the Wind, 7216(F)

Misty of Chincoteague, 7217(F)

Denny, Sidney. *The Ancient Splendor of Prehistoric Cahokia,* 14495

Denslow, Sharon P. *Big Wolf and Little Wolf,* 2023(F)

Bus Riders, 3993(F)

Hazel's Circle, 5181(F)

On the Trail with Miss Pace, 4413(F)

Denslow, W. W. *The Wonderful Wizard of Oz,* 7599(F), 7600(F)

Denti, Susanna. *The Book of You,* 17608

Denton, Kady M. *I Wished for a Unicorn,* 1231(F)

If I Were Your Father, 3544(F)

If I Were Your Mother, 3545(F)

Toes Are to Tickle, 3386(F)

Would They Love a Lion? 1110(F)

Denton, Terry. *Night Noises,* 5685(F)

Denzel, Justin. *Boy of the Painted Cave,* 8954(F)

dePaola, Tomie. *Alice Nizzy Nazzy,* 1276(F)

The Art Lesson, 5495(F)

The Baby Sister, 3606(F)

The Badger and the Magic Fan, 10816

Big Anthony, 1111(F)

Bill and Pete, 1112(F)

Bill and Pete Go Down the Nile, 2024(F)

Bill and Pete to the Rescue, 2025(F)

Bonjour, Mr. Satie, 2026(F)

Charlie Needs a Cloak, 4414(F)

Christopher, 13768

The Cloud Book, 4415(F)

The Clown of God, 5798(F)

The Comic Adventures of Old Mother Hubbard and Her Dog, 838

Country Angel Christmas, 5799(F)

Days of the Blackbird, 11057(F)

The Eagle and the Rainbow, 11409

An Early American Christmas, 5800(F)

Erandi's Braids, 4759(F)

Fin M'Coul, 10970

Four Stories for Four Seasons, 2027(F)

Francis, 13793

Ghost Poems, 11731

Helga's Dowry, 4127(F)

Here We All Are, 12524

The Hunter and the Animals, 916(F)

I Love You, Mouse, 5233(F)

Jamie O'Rourke and the Big Potato, 10971

Jamie O'Rourke and the Pooka, 1113(F)

Kit and Kat, 6305(F)

The Knight and the Dragon, 2028(F)

The Lady of Guadalupe, 5622(F)

The Legend of Old Befana, 5801(F)

The Legend of the Bluebonnet, 11229

The Legend of the Persian Carpet, 11184

The Legend of the Poinsettia, 11399

Little Grunt and the Big Egg, 2029(F)

Maggie and the Monster, 812(F)

Mary, 17259

Merry Christmas, Strega Nona, 5802(F)

Mice Squeak, We Speak, 5410(F)

Miracle on 34th Street, 9715(F)

The Miracles of Jesus, 17260

The Mysterious Giant of Barletta, 11058

The Night Before Christmas, 11839

The Night of Las Posadas, 5803(F)

Now One Foot, Now the Other, 4945(F)

Oliver Button Is a Sissy, 4946(F)

On My Way, 12525(F)

Pages of Music, 5854(F)

Pancakes for Breakfast, 4128(F)

The Parables of Jesus, 17261

Patrick, 13842

Petook, 5969(F)

The Popcorn Book, 20088

The Quicksand Book, 4416(F)

The Quilt Story, 3252(F)

Shh! We're Writing the Constitution, 17056

Sing, Pierrot, Sing, 1114(F)

Strega Nona, 11059, 11060

Strega Nona Meets Her Match, 1115(F)

Strega Nona Takes a Vacation, 1116(F)

The Surprise Party, 6585(F)

The Tale of Rabbit and Coyote, 11403

Tom, 3607(F)

Tomie dePaola's Book of Bible Stories, 17262

Tomie dePaola's Favorite Nursery Tales, 10545

Tomie dePaola's Mother Goose, 873

Tony's Bread, 11061

26 Fairmount Avenue, 12526

The Unicorn and the Moon, 1117(F)

The Vanishing Pumpkin, 6018(F)

Watch Out for the Chicken Feet in Your Soup, 3608(F)

dePaola, Tomie, ed. *The Clown of God*, 5798(F)

Tomie dePaola's Favorite Nursery Tales, 10545

dePaola, Tomie, reteller. *Fin M'Coul*, 10970

The Legend of Old Befana, 5801(F)

The Legend of the Bluebonnet, 11229

DePauw, Sandra A. *The Don't-Give-Up-Kid and Learning Differences*, 4964(F)

de Pinna, Simon. *Electricity*, 20889

Forces and Motion, 20825

Sound, 20936

Derby, Sally. *Jacob and the Stranger*, 7704(F)

King Kenrick's Splinter, 4129(F)

The Mouse Who Owned the Sun, 2030(F)

My Steps, 3102(F)

De Regniers, Beatrice S. *David and Goliath*, 17263

Little Sister and the Month Brothers, 11087

May I Bring a Friend? 4130(F)

So Many Cats! 416(F)

De Regniers, Beatrice S., ed. *Sing a Song of Popcorn*, 11551

deRosa, Dee. *My Favorite Ghost*, 7036(F)

Soccer Circus, 6861(F)

Soccer Mania! 10366(F)

DeRoy, Craig. *We Can Work it Out*, 17724

deRubertis, Barbara. *A Collection for Kate*, 417(F)

Count on Pablo, 418(F)

Deena's Lucky Penny, 6306(F)

Lulu's Lemonade, 419(F)

de Ruiz, Dana C. *La Causa*, 17135

Dervaux, Isabelle. *The Sky Is Always in the Sky*, 11621

DeSantis, Laura. *Come Home with Me*, 3245(F)

de Sauza, James. *Brother Anansi and the Cattle Ranch/El Hermano Anansi y el Rancho de Ganada*, 11400

Descamps-Lequime, Sophie. *The Ancient Greeks*, 14678

de Seve, Peter. *Finn McCoul*, 10985

Deshpande, Chris. *Festival Crafts*, 21430

Food Crafts, 21431

Desimini, Lisa. *All Year Round*, 4417(F)

Anansi Does the Impossible! 10637

Doodle Dandies, 11629

Good Mousekeeping, 11894

The Great Peace March, 14254

How the Stars Fell into the Sky, 11285

Love Letters, 11523

The Magic Weaver of Rugs, 11286

Moon Soup, 1118(F)

Northwoods Cradle Song, 814(F)

Sun and Moon, 1119(F)

Touch the Poem, 11525

Tulip Sees America, 2967(F)

Desmoinaux, Christel. *Mrs. Hen's Big Surprise*, 2031(F)

De Souza, Philip (jt. author). *The Roman News*, 14726

DeSpain, Pleasant. *The Dancing Turtle*, 11436

Sweet Land of Story, 11334

DeSpain, Pleasant, reteller. *Thirty-Three Multicultural Tales to Tell*, 10546

Desputeaux, Helene. *Baby Science*, 18230

Munschworks 2, 4243(F)

de Trevino, Elizabeth. *I, Juan de Pareja*, 9034(F)

Detweiler, Susan. *The First Teddy Bear*, 21653

Detz, Joan. *You Mean I Have to Stand Up and Say Something?* 14077

Devaney, John. *America Goes to War*, 14846

Bo Jackson, 13614

Winners of the Heisman Trophy, 13367

De Varona, Frank. *Benito Juarez*, 13817

Simon Bolivar, 13755

DeVelasco, Joe. *The Twenty-Four Days Before Christmas*, 9743(F)

Deverell, Catherine. *Stradivari's Singing Violin*, 9035(F)

de Vicq de Cumptich, Roberto. *Bembo's Zoo*, 21881

Devito, Anna. *If You Sailed on the Mayflower*, 16156

DeVito, Pam. *We'll Paint the Octopus Red*, 3447(F)

Devlin, Harry. *Cranberry Easter*, 5965(F)

Old Black Witch! 1120(F)

Devlin, Harry (jt. author). *Cranberry Easter*, 5965(F)

Cranberry Valentine, 6166(F)

Old Black Witch! 1120(F)

Devlin, Wende. *Cranberry Easter*, 5965(F)

Cranberry Valentine, 6166(F)

Old Black Witch! 1120(F)

Devon, Paddie. *The Grumpy Shepherd*, 17264(F)

De Vos, Philip. *Carnival of the Animals*, 11776

De Vries, Anke. *My Elephant Can Do Almost Anything*, 2032(F)

Piggy's Birthday Dream, 2033(F)

Dewan, Ted. *Crispin*, 1121(F)

The Sorcerer's Apprentice, 1122(F)

Dewar, Bob. *Ivan*, 11085

Dewdney, Anna. *What You Do Is Easy, What I Do Is Hard*, 2867(F)

Dewey, Ariane. *Alligator Arrived with Apples*, 33(F)

Alligators and Others All Year Long, 2038(F)

Antarctic Antics, 11812

Birthday Rhymes, Special Times, 5688

The Chick and the Duckling, 2125(F)

Five Little Ducks, 563(F)

Gregory, the Terrible Eater, 2684(F)

Herman the Helper, 2319(F)

How Chipmunk Got His Stripes, 11221

Lizard's Home, 2680(F)

Mouse in Love, 2322(F)

Mushroom in the Rain, 2742(F)

One Duck, Another Duck, 560(F)

Rockabye Crocodile, 1753(F)

Safe, Warm, and Snug, 18862

They Thought They Saw Him, 5425(F)

We Hide, You Seek, 297(F)

Where Does the Sun Go at Night? 1193(F)

Dewey, Ariane (jt. author). *Rockabye Crocodile*, 1753(F)

We Hide, You Seek, 297(F)

Dewey, Jennifer. *New Questions and Answers About Dinosaurs*, 14471

The Secret Language of Snow, 20795

The Song of the Sea Otter, 19736

Dewey, Jennifer O. *Antarctic Journal*, 15800

Bedbugs in Our House, 19435

Faces Only a Mother Could Love, 18874

Family Ties, 18875

Mud Matters, 20303

Navajo Summer, 8421(F)

Poison Dart Frogs, 18720

Rattlesnake Dance, 18758

Dewey, Jennifer Owings. *Strange Nests*, 19307

DeWitt, Lynda. *What Will the Weather Be?* 20760

de Wolf, Alex. *Mop to the Rescue*, 1545(F)

Mop's Backyard Concert, 1546(F)

Dexter, Alison. *The Blessing Seed*, 17305

The Seeds of Peace, 998(F)

Dexter, Catherine. *A Is for Apple, W Is for Witch*, 7705(F)

Alien Game, 10176(F)

I Dream of Murder, 6821(F)

Safe Return, 9036(F)

Dexter, Robin. *Young Arthur Ashe*, 13643

De Young, C. Coco. *A Letter to Mrs. Roosevelt*, 9538(F)

De Zutter, Hank. *Who Says a Dog Goes Bow-Wow?* 5182

Dhanjal, Beryl. *Amritsar*, 15099

What Do We Know About Sikhism? 17177

Dhilawala, Sakina. *Armenia*, 15412

Diakite, Baba Wague. *The Hatseller and the Monkeys*, 10662

The Hunterman and the Crocodile, 10663

Diakite, Baba Wague, reteller. *The Hatseller and the Monkeys*, 10662

Diamond, Donna. *Beat the Turtle Drum*, 8670(F)

Bridge to Terabithia, 8355(F)

Dianov, Alisher. *Forty Fortunes*, 11201

Melanie, 1042(F)

Diaz, David. *Be Not Far from Me*, 17294

December, 5768(F)

The Disappearing Alphabet, 11926

Going Home, 4608(F)

Jump Rope Magic, 1553(F)

The Little Scarecrow Boy, 1017(F)

Neighborhood Odes, 11708

Shadow Story, 1683(F)

Smoky Night, 3059(F)

The Wanderer, 6806(F)

Wilma Unlimited, 13670

Diaz, James. *The Elements of Pop-Up*, 21608

DiCamillo, Kate. *Because of Winn-Dixie*, 8624(F)

The Tiger Rising, 8625(F)

Dick, Judy. *Sefer Ha-Aggadah*, 11163

Dickens, Charles. *The Child's Story*, 1123(F)

A Christmas Carol, 9718(F), 9719(F), 9720(F), 9721(F)

The Magic Fish-bone, 7706(F)

Dickey, Glenn. *Jerry Rice*, 13623

Dickinson, Emily. *A Brighter Garden*, 11552

Dickinson, Joan D. *Bill Gates*, 13294

Dickinson, Peter. *Chuck and Danielle*, 7707(F)

Noli's Story, 8955(F)

Suth's Story, 8956(F)

Dickinson, Rebecca. *Monster Cake*, 5680(F)

Dickinson, Terence. *Exploring the Sky by Day*, 20761

Other Worlds, 18511

Dicks, Jan T. *The House That Crack Built*, 17894

Dickson, Louise. *Lu and Clancy's Crime Science*, 17065

Dickson, Mora. *Tales of an Ashanti Father*, 10646

Diehn, Gwen. *Making Books That Fly, Fold, Wrap, Hide, Pop Up, Twist, and Turn*, 21612

Dieterichs, Shelley. *Uh Oh! Gotta Go!* 3298

Dietl, Ulla. *The Plant-and-Grow Project Book*, 21761

DiFiori, Larry. *I Can Do It!* 6186(F)

We Just Moved! 6440(F)

Di Franco, J. Philip. *The Italian Americans*, 17554

di Gaudesi, Andrea Ricciardi. *The Incredible Journey to the Beginning of Time*, 14555

Dilella, Barbara. *The Anne of Green Gables Cookbook*, 21715

Diller, Harriet. *Big Band Sound*, 3103(F)

The Faraway Drawer, 3104(F)

Dilley, Becki. *Sixty Fingers, Sixty Toes*, 18229

Dilley, Keith (jt. author). *Sixty Fingers, Sixty Toes*, 18229

Dillon, Diane. *Aida*, 14136

Brother to the Wind, 1664(F)

The Color Wizard, 6221(F)

The Girl Who Dreamed Only Geese and Other Stories of the Far North, 11209

The Girl Who Spun Gold, 10914

Her Stories, 11340

Honey, I Love, and Other Love Poems, 11757

The Hundred Penny Box, 7483(F)

The People Could Fly, 11341

Pish, Posh, Said Hieronymus Bosch, 1682

The Sorcerer's Apprentice, 1684(F)

The Tale of the Mandarin Ducks, 10826

What Am I? 172(F)

Why Mosquitoes Buzz in People's Ears, 10644

Dillon, Diane (jt. author). *To Every Thing There Is a Season*, 17178

Dillon, Jana. *Jeb Scarecrow's Pumpkin Patch*, 1124(F)

Lucky O'Leprechaun, 5623(F)

Lucky O'Leprechaun Comes to America, 1125(F)

Dillon, Leo. *Aida*, 14136

Brother to the Wind, 1664(F)

The Color Wizard, 6221(F)

The Girl Who Dreamed Only Geese and Other Stories of the Far North, 11209

The Girl Who Spun Gold, 10914

Her Stories, 11340

Honey, I Love, and Other Love Poems, 11757

The Hundred Penny Box, 7483(F)

The People Could Fly, 11341

Pish, Posh, Said Hieronymus Bosch, 1682

The Sorcerer's Apprentice, 1684(F)

The Tale of the Mandarin Ducks, 10826

To Every Thing There Is a Season, 17178

What Am I? 172(F)

Why Mosquitoes Buzz in People's Ears, 10644

Dillons, The. *Wind Child*, 10467(F)

DiLorenzo, J. J. *The Miami Dolphins Football Team*, 22180

Dils, Tracey E. *Samuel L. Jackson*, 12409

Dineen, Jacqueline. *Frederic Chopin*, 12325

The Skeleton and Movement, 18170

Dineen, Jacqueline (jt. author). *The Mediterranean*, 14597

People Who Changed the World, 13745

Dingle, Derek T. *First in the Field*, 13492

Dingus, Lowell. *Searching for Velociraptor*, 14400
The Tiniest Giants, 14399
What Color Is That Dinosaur? 14398

Dingus, Lowell (jt. author). *A Nest of Dinosaurs*, 14455

Dionetti, Michelle. *Painting the Wind*, 12306

Dionysia. *Ling Ling*, 2687(F)

Diouf, Sylviane. *Kings and Queens of Central Africa*, 14925
Kings and Queens of East Africa, 14926
Kings and Queens of Southern Africa, 14974
Kings and Queens of West Africa, 15025

Diouf, Sylviane (jt. author). *Growing Up in Crawfish Country*, 16861

DiPiazza, Domenica. *Arkansas*, 16843

DiSalvo-Ryan, DyAnne. *The American Wei*, 3367(F)
The Bravest Cat! 6315(F)
The Christmas Knight, 10967
A Dog Like Jack, 5183(F)
George Washington's Mother, 13200
Grandpa's Corner Store, 3105(F)
If I Were President, 17126
Is It Hanukkah Yet? 6092(F)
Kate Skates, 6547(F)
The Mommy Exchange, 3694(F)
Nina, Nina Ballerina, 6549(F)
Nina, Nina, Star Ballerina, 6550(F)
Now We Can Have a Wedding! 3086(F)
Our Eight Nights of Hanukkah, 6107(F)
The Real Hole, 2921(F)
True Blue, 6328(F)

Disher, Garry. *The Bamboo Flute*, 8930(F)
Switch Cat, 5184(F)

DiSpezio, Michael A. *Awesome Experiments in Electricity and Magnetism*, 20890
Awesome Experiments in Force and Motion, 20826
Awesome Experiments in Light and Sound, 20804
Optical Illusion Magic, 20913

Ditchfield, Christin. *Cycling*, 22155
Gymnastics, 22192
Kayaking, Canoeing, Rowing, and Yachting, 22260
Sports Great Michael Chang, 13646
Swimming and Diving, 22307
Top 10 American Women's Olympic Gold Medalists, 13368
Wrestling, 21996

Diterlizzi, Tony. *Jimmy Zangwow's Out-of-This-World Moon Pie Adventure*, 1126(F)

Diviny, Sean. *Halloween Motel*, 5994(F)

DiVito, Anna. *I Want Answers and a Parachute*, 8508(F)
Striking It Rich, 16338

Dixon, Ann. *Blueberry Shoe*, 5185(F)

Dixon, Annabelle. *Clay*, 21530
Wool, 21170

Dixon, Dougal. *Be a Dinosaur Detective*, 14403
Dougal Dixon's Amazing Dinosaurs, 14404
Dougal Dixon's Dinosaurs, 14405
Questions and Answers About Dinosaurs, 14406
The Search for Dinosaurs, 14407

Dixon, Jean. *Judo*, 22266

Dixon, Tamecka. *You Can Be a Woman Basketball Player*, 22129

Dixon, Tennessee. *Berchick*, 5139(F)
The Heroine of the Titanic, 4595(F)
Jessica and the Wolf, 5017(F)
The Princess and the Peacocks, 9111(F)

Dobkin, Bonnie. *Collecting*, 21806
Everybody Says, 6307(F)
Go-With Words, 14027

Dobson, Clive. *Tex*, 5377(F)

Dobson, David. *Can We Save Them? Endangered Species of North America*, 19393

Dobson, Mary. *Greek Grime*, 14679
Mouldy Mummies, 14622
Vile Vikings, 15443

Dock, Julie Bates (jt. author). *Fabric Fun for Kids*, 21648

Dockray, Tracy. *Am I Big or Little?* 3543(F)

Dodd, Anne W. *Footprints and Shadows*, 3107(F)
The Story of the Sea Glass, 3609(F)

Dodd, Emma. *Dog's Colorful Day*, 177(F)

Dodd, Lynley. *Hairy Maclary and Zachary Quack*, 6308(F)
Sniff-Snuff-Snap! 420(F)

Dodds, Dayle Ann. *The Color Box*, 265(F)
Ghost and Pete, 5995(F)
The Great Divide, 421(F)
Sing, Sophie! 4131(F)

Dodds, Siobhan. *Grumble-Rumble!* 2034(F)
Ting-a-ling! 3108(F)
Words and Pictures, 6309(F)

Dodge, Bill. *Megan in Ancient Greece*, 9054(F)

Dodge, Katharine. *Sweet Dreams of the Wild*, 661

Dodson, Bert. *Buffalo Thunder*, 4889(F)
Chicken Soup for Little Souls, 4921(F)

Grandpa Was a Cowboy, 2977(F)
Hannah's Fancy Notions, 9617(F)
Thomas, 9246(F)
What Makes the Wind? 20675
Wonders of the Sea, 19836
Young Frederick Douglass, 12715

Dodson, Liz B. *Count Your Way Through Brazil*, 15740
Count Your Way Through India, 15103
Korean Holidays and Festivals, 15177

Dodson, Peter. *An Alphabet of Dinosaurs*, 14408

Doherty, Berlie. *Fairy Tales*, 10416(F)
The Midnight Man, 660(F)
Paddiwak and Cozy, 5186(F)
Street Child, 9092(F)

Doherty, Craig A. *The Empire State Building*, 16665
The Erie Canal, 16237
The Gateway Arch, 16544
The Golden Gate Bridge, 16771
Hoover Dam, 16601
Mount Rushmore, 16545
The Sears Tower, 16546
The Statue of Liberty, 16666
The Washington Monument, 16667

Doherty, Katherine M. (jt. author). *The Empire State Building*, 16665
The Erie Canal, 16237
The Gateway Arch, 16544
The Golden Gate Bridge, 16771
Hoover Dam, 16601
Mount Rushmore, 16545
The Sears Tower, 16546
The Statue of Liberty, 16666
The Washington Monument, 16667

Doherty, Kieran. *Explorers, Missionaries, and Trappers*, 12646
Puritans, Pilgrims, and Merchants, 16110
Soldiers, Cavaliers, and Planters, 16111
William Bradford, 12856

Doherty, Paul. *The Cheshire Cat and Other Eye-Popping Experiments on How We See the World*, 20914
The Cool Hot Rod and Other Electrifying Experiments on Energy and Matter, 20827
The Magic Wand and Other Bright Experiments on Light and Color, 20863
The Spinning Blackboard and Other Dynamic Experiments on Force and Motion, 20828

Dolan, Edward F. *America in World War I*, 14807
America in World War II, 14847
The American Civil War, 16402
The American Revolution, 16194
Beyond the Frontier, 16301

Dolan, Ellen M. *Susan Butcher and the Iditarod Trail*, 21997
Thomas Alva Edison, 13270
Dolan, Graham. *The Greenwich Guide to Time and the Millennium*, 20643
Dolan, Sean. *Charles Barkley*, 13512
Juan Ponce de Leon, 12149
Dolan, Terrance. *Julio Cesar Chavez*, 13583
Dolin, Nick. *Basketball Stars*, 13369
Dollinger, Renate. *The Rabbi Who Flew*, 1127(F)
Dolobowsky, Mena. *Tuning In*, 21278
Domanska, Janina. *If All the Seas Were One Sea*, 851
The Trumpeter of Krakow, 9051(F)
Domi. *The Night the Moon Fell*, 11412
Señora Reganona, 773(F)
Domínguez, Domitila. *The Story of Colors/La Historia de los Colores*, 11410
Dominic, Gloria, adapt. *Brave Bear and the Ghosts*, 11230
Domm, Jeff. *What's the Difference Between . . . Lenses and Prisms and Other Scientific Things?* 21058
Donahue, John. *An Island Far from Home*, 9471(F)
Donaldson, Joan. *A Pebble and a Pen*, 16238(F)
Donaldson, Julia. *The Gruffalo*, 2035(F)
Donati, Paolo. *Amazing Buildings*, 21153
Doner, Kim. *Buffalo Dreams*, 5187(F)
Green Snake Ceremony, 4870(F)
Doney, Meryl. *Jewelry*, 21540
Puppets, 14304
Doney, Todd. *Empire Dreams*, 9635(F)
Doney, Todd L. W. *January Rides the Wind*, 4503(F)
Sleeping Beauty, 14289
Doniger, Nancy. *Gingersnaps*, 17538
Morning, Noon, and Night, 11725
Donkin, Andrew. *Atlantis*, 21907
Bermuda Triangle, 21908
Going for Gold! 13370
Donnelly, Judy. *The Titanic*, 6310
True-Life Treasure Hunts, 14525
Tut's Mummy, 6311
Who Shot the President? 13060
Donnelly, Karen. *Everything You Need to Know About Lyme Disease*, 17953
Donnelly, Liza. *Dinosaur Beach*, 1128(F)
Dinosaur Garden, 1129(F)
Dinosaurs' Christmas, 5804(F)
Donohue, Dorothy. *Believing Sophie*, 4985(F)
Big and Little on the Farm, 5188(F)

Dear Daddy, 3879(F)
Frozen Noses, 3987(F)
No Time for Mother's Day, 5609(F)
Turkey Pox, 6132(F)
Veggie Soup, 2036(F)
Donohue, Shiobhan. *Kristi Yamaguchi*, 13598
Donoughue, Carol. *The Mystery of the Hieroglyphs*, 14623
Donze, Lisa. *Squanto and the First Thanksgiving*, 12998
Dooley, Norah. *Everybody Bakes Bread*, 3109(F)
Everybody Cooks Rice, 21695
Everybody Serves Soup, 5805(F)
Dooley, Virginia. *Tubes In My Ears*, 18038
Dooling, Michael. *A Long Way to Go*, 9602(F)
Mary Anning and the Sea Dragon, 13228
Mary McLean and the St. Patrick's Day Parade, 5632(F)
The Memory Coat, 4891(F)
Robin Hook, Pirate Hunter! 1302(F)
Straw Sense, 8978(F)
Thomas Jefferson, 13049
Doolittle, Bev. *The Forest Has Eyes*, 310
Doolittle, Michael. *Chopsticks for My Noodle Soup*, 15161
Doolittle, Michael J. *Bats, Bugs, and Biodiversity*, 20446
Dore, Gustave. *Perrault's Fairy Tales*, 10877
Doren, Marion. *Nell of Blue Harbor*, 8422(F)
Dorflinger, Carolyn. *Tomorrow Is Mom's Birthday*, 5681(F)
Dorfman, Elena. *When Learning Is Tough*, 17930
Doris, Ellen. *Entomology*, 19436
Meet the Arthropods, 19604
Ornithology, 19223
Woods, Ponds, and Fields, 18583
Dorman, N. B. *Petey and Miss Magic*, 8626(F)
Dorrie, Doris. *Lottie's Princess Dress*, 4132(F)
Dorris, Michael. *Sees Behind Trees*, 9155(F)
Dorros, Arthur. *Abuela*, 1130(F)
Ant Cities, 19510
Elephant Families, 19162
Feel the Wind, 4418(F)
The Fungus that Ate My School, 1131(F)
Rain Forest Secrets, 20437
Ten Go Tango, 422(F)
A Tree Is Growing, 20197
What Makes Day and Night? 18428
Dorsey, Bob. *The Pet-Sitters*, 7302(F)
Dorson, Mercedes. *Tales from the Rain Forest*, 11437

Dosier, Susan. *Civil War Cooking*, 16403
Colonial Cooking, 16112
Dossenbach, Hans D. *Beware! We Are Poisonous*, 18935
Dossenbach, Hans D. (jt. author). *EyeOpeners!* 18807
Dossenbach, Monika. *EyeOpeners!* 18807
Dotlich, Rebecca. *Away We Go!* 6312(F)
Lemonade Sun and Other Summer Poems, 11553
Sweet Dreams of the Wild, 661
What Is a Triangle? 324
What Is Round? 325(F)
What Is Square? 326(F)
D'Ottavi, Francesca. *The Myths and Civilization of the Ancient Egyptians*, 14661
The Myths and Civilization of the Ancient Greeks, 14696
Doty, Eldon C. *Zoo Clues*, 20024
Doty, Roy. *How to Write Your Best Book Report*, 14093
Kid Camping from Aaaaiii! to Zip, 22169
Mirrors, 20878
Shadow Play, 20879
Tales of a Fourth Grade Nothing, 9784(F)
Doucet, Bob. *The Field Mouse and the Dinosaur Named Sue*, 2808(F)
Doucet, Sharon Arms. *Fiddle Fever*, 8423(F)
Why Lapin's Ears Are Long and Other Tales from the Louisiana Bayou, 11335
Dougherty, Terri. *Mark McGwire*, 13467
Sammy Sosa, 13504
Douglas, Ann. *Baby Science*, 18230
Before You Were Born, 18239
The Family Tree Detective, 17650
Douglas, Eric. *Get That Pest!* 6313(F)
Douglas, Kirk. *The Broken Mirror*, 9656(F)
Kirk Douglas's Young Heroes of the Bible, 17265
Douglas-Hamilton, Oria. *The Elephant Family Book*, 19163
Douty, Sheila Cornell. *You Can Be a Woman Softball Player*, 13450
Douzou, Olivier. *The Wolf's Lunch*, 2037(F)
Dow, Lesley. *Alligators and Crocodiles*, 18701
Whales, 19784
Dowd, Ned. *That's a Wrap*, 21268
Dowden, Anne O. *The Clover and the Bee*, 20232
Poisons in Our Path, 20233
Dowell, Frances O'Roark. *Dovey Coe*, 7424(F)
Dowling, Paul. *Hand Reading*, 21948

Down, Mike. *Bear*, 19041

Downer, Maggie. *Christmas Fun*, 21468

Downey, Lynn. *Sing, Henrietta! Sing!* 4133(F)

This Is the Earth That God Made, 17266

Downing, Julie. *Cabbage Rose*, 10430(F)

The Chicken Salad Club, 3511(F)

Daniel's Gift, 5835(F)

A First Bible Story Book, 17285

Lullaby and Good Night, 662(F)

The Magpies' Nest, 10977

Mozart Tonight, 12333

Mr. Griggs' Work, 3407(F)

A Ride on the Red Mare's Back, 1345(F)

Sonia Begonia, 7034(F)

Water Voices, 10265(F)

White Snow, Blue Feather, 4419(F)

Downing, Julie, comp. *Lullaby and Good Night*, 662(F)

Downs, Peter. *Amazing Bikes*, 22162

Downs, Sandra. *Shaping the Earth*, 20304

Doyle, Brian. *Spud Sweetgrass*, 6822(F)

Doyle, Charlotte. *You Can't Catch Me*, 1132(F)

Doyle, Debra. *Groogleman*, 10177(F)

Knight's Wyrd, 7708(F)

Doyle, Malachy. *Jody's Beans*, 4420(F)

Tales from Old Ireland, 10972

Well, a Crocodile Can! 5189(F)

Doyle, Richard. *King of the Golden River or the Black Brother*, 8054(F)

Doyle, Roddy. *The Giggler Treatment*, 7709(F)

Dragonwagon, Crescent. *Alligator Arrived with Apples*, 33(F)

Alligators and Others All Year Long, 2038(F)

Annie Flies the Birthday Bike, 6314(F)

The Bat in the Dining Room, 4134(F)

Brass Button, 1133(F)

Half a Moon and One Whole Star, 663(F)

Home Place, 3110(F)

The Itch Book, 3111(F)

This Is the Bread I Baked for Ned, 3112(F)

Winter Holding Spring, 8627(F)

Drake, Jane. *Farming*, 20052

Forestry, 20438

The Kids Camp-fire Book, 22167

The Kids Summer Games Book, 21998

The Kids' Summer Handbook, 21432

Mining, 21030

Drake, Jane (jt. author). *Fishing*, 19848

Kids and Grandparents, 21451

The Kids Book of the Far North, 15816

The Kids Guide to the Millennium, 14346

Drake, Jim. *Computers All Around Us*, 21196

Computers and School, 21197

Play with Computers, 21198

What Is a Computer? 21199

Dramer, Kim. *China*, 15057

People's Republic of China, 15058

Draper, Charla L. *Cooking on Nine-teenth Century Whaling Ships*, 15875

Draper, Rochelle. *The World at His Fingertips*, 13761

Draper, Sharon M. *Lost in the Tunnel of Time*, 6823(F)

Shadows of Caesar's Creek, 6824(F)

Drawson, Blair. *Arachne Speaks*, 11480

Flying Dimitri, 1134(F)

Mary Margaret's Tree, 1135(F)

Dreier, Ted (jt. author). *Moozie's Kind Adventure*, 2511(F)

Dreifuss, Donald. *Pumpkin Pie*, 2898(F)

Drescher, Henrik. *The Boy Who Ate Around*, 1136(F)

Klutz, 4135(F)

Runaway Opposites, 11736

Simon's Book, 1137(F)

Drescher, Joan. *Your Family, My Family*, 17651

Drew, Bonnie. *Fast Cash for Kids*, 16941

Drew, Helen. *My First Music Book*, 14220

Drew, Noel (jt. author). *Fast Cash for Kids*, 16941

Drexler, Sam. *Lost in Spillville*, 7710(F)

Dreyer, Ellen. *Speechless in New York*, 8628(F)

Driemen, J. E. *Winston Churchill*, 13769

Drimmer, Frederick. *Incredible People*, 12647

Driscoll, Laura. *The Bravest Cat!* 6315(F)

Drogues, Valerie. *Battleship Missouri*, 14848

Drohan, Michele Ingber. *Earthquakes*, 20337

Floods, 20688

Dronzek, Laura. *The Adventure of Louey and Frank*, 2848(F)

Oh! 1234(F)

Drucker, Malka. *The Family Treasury of Jewish Holidays*, 17460

The Sea Monster's Secret, 11231

Drucker, Mort. *Tomatoes from Mars*, 1714(F)

Whitefish Will Rides Again! 4363(F)

Drucker, Olga L. *Kindertransport*, 14849

Drummond, Allan. *Casey Jones*, 4638(F)

Stories Told by Mother Teresa, 17222

The Willow Pattern Story, 1138(F)

Drummond, Karen Eich (jt. author). *The Healthy Body Cookbook*, 21690

The Science Chef, 20087

The Science Chef Travels Around the World, 21691

The United States Cookbook, 21692

Drumtra, Stacy. *Face-Off*, 10323(F)

Drury, Tim. *When I'm Big*, 1139(F)

Duane, Diane. *Deep Wizardry*, 7711(F)

So You Want to Be a Wizard, 7712(F)

Dubanevich, Arlene. *Pig William*, 2039(F)

Dubois, Claude K. *Hello, Sweetie Pie*, 2528(F)

I Love You So Much, 2529(F)

Dubois, Jill. *Colombia*, 15729

Greece, 15376

Israel, 15517

Dubois, Muriel. *Alaska*, 16772

Maryland, 16844

Wyoming, 16602

Dubois, Muriel L. *I Like Music*, 17771

I Like Sports, 17742

New Hampshire, 16668

du Bois, William Pene. *A Certain Small Shepherd*, 9713(F)

Magic Finger, 7697(F)

Twenty and Ten, 9646(F)

Twenty-One Balloons, 9831(F)

William's Doll, 3976(F)

DuBosque, Doug. *ABC Animal Riddles*, 67

ABC Nature Riddles, 68(F)

Alphabet Riddles, 69(F)

Draw Desert Animals, 21566

Draw Dinosaurs, 21567

Draw! Grassland Animals, 21568

Draw Insects, 21569

Draw 3-D, 21570

Learn to Draw Now! 21571

Dubowski, Cathy E. *Pirate School*, 6316(F)

Robert E. Lee, 12926

Shark Attack! 19756

Snug Bug, 6317(F)

Dubowski, Mark. *Pirate School*, 6316(F)

Dubowski, Mark (jt. author). *Snug Bug*, 6317(F)

Dubrovin, Vivian. *Storytelling Adventures*, 14078

Storytelling for the Fun of It, 14079

Dubrowski, Ken. *Up and Away!* 21077

Dudash, C. Michael. *The Quiet Little Woman*, 9704(F)

Duden, Jane. *1950s*, 16500
1940s, 16461
Dudley, Ebet. *The World of Insects*, 19499
Dudley, Karen. *Giant Pandas*, 19185
Great African Americans in Government, 12648
Dudley, William. *The Environment*, 16995
The U.S. Constitution, 17054
Dudzinski, Kathleen. *Meeting Dolphins*, 19682
Dué, Andrea. *The Atlas of the Bible Lands*, 15518
Duey, Kathleen. *Agnes May Gleason*, 9539(F)
Amelina Carrett, 9472(F)
Anisett Lundberg, 9357(F)
Cave-In, 9273(F)
Celou Sudden Shout, Idaho, 1826, 9156(F)
Death Valley, 9359(F)
Ellen Elizabeth Hawkins, 9540(F)
Evie Peach, 9272(F)
Fire, 9543(F)
Flood, 6825(F)
Hurricane, 9274(F)
Josie Poe, 9657(F)
Nell Dunne, 9541(F)
Rosa Moreno, 9542(F)
Sarah Anne Hartford, 9190(F)
Shipwreck, 9544(F)
Train Wreck, 6826(F)
Willow Chase, 9358(F)
Duffey, Betsy. *Alien for Rent*, 9832(F)
A Boy in the Doghouse, 5190(F)
Coaster, 8424(F)
Cody Unplugged, 9833(F)
Cody's Secret Admirer, 9834(F)
The Gadget War, 9835(F)
Hey, New Kid! 9836(F)
How to Be Cool in the Third Grade, 6318(F)
Puppy Love, 7185(F)
Spotlight on Cody, 8629(F)
Utterly Yours, Booker Jones, 8630(F)
Virtual Cody, 9837(F)
The Wild Things, 5191(F)
Duffy, Daniel. *Molly's Pilgrim*, 3582(F)
Theodoric's Rainbow, 9055(F)
Duffy, James. *Radical Red*, 9545(F)
Uncle Shamus, 8277(F)
Duffy, Trent. *The Clock*, 20644
Dugan, Barbara. *Good-bye, Hello*, 10050(F)
Dugan, Karen M. *Bicycle Riding*, 11630
Halmoni and the Picnic, 3581(F)
School Spirit, 10084(F)
Tea Party Today, 11709
Yunmi and Halmoni's Trip, 4620(F)
Duggan, Paul. *Two Skeletons on the Telephone*, 11868

Duggleby, John. *Artist in Overalls*, 12312
Story Painter, 12252
Dugin, Andrej (jt. author). *The Brave Little Tailor*, 10887
Dugina, Olga. *The Brave Little Tailor*, 10887
Duke, Chris. *America's First Railroads*, 21337
Clippers and Whaling Ships, 21369
Duke, Kate. *Archaeologists Dig for Clues*, 14526
Aunt Isabel Tells a Good One, 2040(F)
Don't Tell the Whole World! 3990(F)
Mr. Big Brother, 6412(F)
One Guinea Pig Is Not Enough, 423(F)
One Saturday Afternoon, 6196(F)
The Show-and-Tell Frog, 6553(F)
Twenty Is Too Many, 424(F)
Dumas, Philippe. *A Farm*, 15341
Dunbar, Fiona. *Every Buddy Counts*, 525(F)
Dunbar, James. *When I Was Young*, 3610(F)
Dunbar, Joyce. *Baby Bird*, 2041(F)
The Bowl of Fruit, 2042(F)
Eggday, 2043(F)
Four Fierce Kittens, 5192(F)
The Pig Who Wished, 2044(F)
The Sand Children, 1140(F)
Tell Me Something Happy Before I Go to Sleep, 665(F)
Ten Little Mice, 425(F)
This Is the Star, 5806(F)
The Very Small, 666(F)
Dunbar, Paul Laurence. *Jump Back, Honey*, 11754
Duncan, Alice Faye. *Miss Viola and Uncle Ed Lee*, 4136(F)
Willie Jerome, 3611(F)
Duncan, Beverly. *Red-Spotted Newt*, 18685
Unseen Rainbows, Silent Songs, 18818
A Water Snake's Year, 18759
Duncan, Debbie. *When Molly Was in the Hospital*, 3113(F)
Duncan, Jane. *Brave Janet Reachfar*, 7425(F)
Duncan, Lois. *A Gift of Magic*, 8425(F)
I Walk at Night, 2045(F)
The Longest Hair in the World, 1141(F)
Wonder Kid Meets the Evil Lunch Snatcher, 10051(F)
Dunfield, Robb T. *If Sarah Will Take Me*, 11537
Dunford, Mick. *France*, 15301
Dunlap, Julie. *Birds in the Bushes*, 13335
Eye on the Wild, 12187
Parks for the People, 12941

Dunlop, Eileen. *Finn's Island*, 7426(F)
Finn's Search, 8278(F)
The Ghost by the Sea, 7713(F)
Websters' Leap, 7714(F)
Dunmore, Helen. *Brother Brother, Sister Sister*, 8631(F)
Dunn, Carolyn. *A Pie Went By*, 1142(F)
Dunn, Joan W. *Waiting for Baby Joe*, 3584(F)
Dunn, John. *Advertising*, 16934
Dunn, John M. *Life During the Black Death*, 14762
Dunn, Judy. *The Little Puppy*, 5193(F)
The Little Rabbit, 4421(F)
Dunn, Opal. *Hippety-Hop Hippety-Hay*, 11554
Dunn, Phoebe. *Farm Animals*, 4422(F)
The Little Puppy, 5193(F)
The Little Rabbit, 4421(F)
Dunn-Ramsey, Marcy. *Cats Add Up! Math Activities by Marilyn Burns*, 540(F)
Dunnahoo, Terry. *Baseball Hall of Fame*, 22088
Basketball Hall of Fame, 22130
Boston's Freedom Trail, 16113
Pro Football Hall of Fame, 22181
Dunning, Mike. *Amazing Birds of Prey*, 19335
Amazing Boats, 21365
Dunning, Stephen, ed. *Reflections on a Gift of Watermelon Pickle and Other Modern Verse*, 11555
Dunnington, Tom. *Go-With Words*, 14027
I Love Cats, 6514(F)
Dunphy, Madeleine. *Here Is the African Savanna*, 20533
Here Is the Arctic Winter, 15801
Here Is the Coral Reef, 19657
Here Is the Wetland, 20367
Dunrea, Olivier. *Appearing Tonight! Mary Heather Elizabeth Livingstone*, 4947(F)
Bear Noel, 5807(F)
The Boy Who Loved to Draw, 12310
Eppie M. Says . . ., 4137(F)
The Painter Who Loved Chickens, 4138(F)
The Rusty, Trusty Tractor, 5553(F)
The Trow-Wife's Treasure, 1143(F)
Duntze, Dorothee. *The Emperor's New Clothes*, 10378(F)
The Six Swans, 10908
Dupasquier, Philippe. *A Sunday with Grandpa*, 3612(F)
duPont, Lindsay Harper. *I'm Not Going to Chase the Cat Today!* 2170(F)
Dupont, Philippe. *The Cheetah*, 19085

Duquennoy, Jacques. *The Ghosts' Trip to Loch Ness*, 1144(F)
Operation Ghost, 7715(F)
DuQuette, Keith. *The House Book*, 21157
Duran, Silvia. *Big Cats*, 19101
Duranceau, Suzanne. *Hickory, Dickory, Dock*, 2518(F)
Piece of Jungle, 4874(F)
Durand, Delphine. *Beetle Boy*, 1101(F)
Durant, Alan. *Big Bad Bunny*, 2046(F)
Durant, Alan, sel. *Sports Stories*, 10324(F)
Durant, Penny R. *Bubblemania!* 20805
When Heroes Die, 8632(F)
Durbin, William. *The Broken Blade*, 8928(F)
The Journal of Sean Sullivan, 9360(F)
Wintering, 8931(F)
Durham, Sarah. *Rose and Sebastian*, 4067(F)
What Do You See When You Shut Your Eyes? 3495(F)
Durr, Robb. *The Ultimate Book of Kid Concoctions*, 21505
Durr, Zachariah. *The Ultimate Book of Kid Concoctions*, 21505
Durrant, Lynda. *The Beaded Moccasins*, 9157(F)
Betsy Zane, the Rose of Fort Henry, 9228(F)
Echohawk, 9191(F)
Turtle Clan Journey, 9192(F)
Durrell, Julie. *Halloween Hide-and-Seek*, 6016(F)
Starring Rosie, 8660(F)
Durrett, Deanne. *Dominique Moceanu*, 13702
Dusikova, Maja. *Good-Bye, Vivi!* 5071(F)
Rapunzel, 10903
Silent Night, Holy Night, 14209
Dussling, Jennifer. *Bugs! Bugs! Bugs!* 19437
Gargoyles, 21122
Planets, 18512
Stars, 18544
DuTemple, Lesley A. *Jacques Cousteau*, 12101
North American Cranes, 19224
North American Moose, 19150
Polar Bears, 19042
Sweden, 15444
Tigers, 19086
Whales, 19785
Dutton, Roderic. *An Arab Family*, 15538
Duvall, Jill D. *The Cayuga*, 15945
Chef Ki Is Serving Dinner! 17743
Meet Rory Hohenstein, a Professional Dancer, 17772
The Mohawk, 15946

Who Keeps the Water Clean? Ms. Schindler! 17824
Duvoisin, Roger. *Hide and Seek Fog*, 4553(F)
Petunia, 2047(F)
White Snow Bright Snow, 3458(F)
Dvorson, Alexa. *The Hitler Youth*, 14850
Dwight, Laura. *We Can Do It!* 17903
Dwyer, Kathleen M. *What Do You Mean I Have a Learning Disability?* 17904
What Do You Mean I Have Attention Deficit Disorder? 17905
Dwyer, Mindy. *Aurora*, 1145(F)
Coyote in Love, 11232
Quilt of Dreams, 3613(F)
Dwyer, Mindy, reteller. *Coyote in Love*, 11232
Dyer, Alan. *Space*, 18388
Dyer, Jane. *Animal Crackers*, 667(F)
Child of Faerie, Child of Earth, 6065(F)
I Love You Like Crazy Cakes, 4735(F)
If Anything Ever Goes Wrong at the Zoo, 1233(F)
My Father, 14146
Oh, My Baby, Little One, 1744(F)
The Patchwork Lady, 5737(F)
Picnic with Piggins, 2891(F)
The Sick Day, 3790(F)
The Snow Speaks, 3066(F)
Talking Like the Rain, 11616
The Three Bears Holiday Rhyme Book, 5659
Time for Bed, 678(F)
When Mama Comes Home Tonight, 3903(F)
Dygard, Thomas J. *River Danger*, 6827(F)
Second Stringer, 10325(F)
Dylan, Bob. *Man Gave Names to All the Animals*, 14237
Dypold, Pat. *One Cow Coughs*, 498(F)
Twist with a Burger, Jitter with a Bug, 3287(F)
Dyson, Cindy. *Janet Jackson*, 12407
Rare and Interesting Stamps, 21807
Dyson, John. *Westward with Columbus*, 16079
Dyson, Marianne J. *Space Station Science*, 20980
Dzapla, Carole. *The Easter Wolf*, 5963(F)

Eachus, Jennifer. *The Big Big Sea*, 4559(F)
Daddy, Will You Miss Me? 3783(F)
I'm Sorry, 4026(F)
Eagle, Ellen. *The Jenny Summer*, 8291(F)
Star Guide, 18542
Eagle, Mike. *A Flag for Our Country*, 13976
The Trojan Horse, 14688

Eagle Walking Turtle. *Full Moon Stories*, 11233
Earl, Amanda. *Masks*, 21602
Earle, Ann. *Zipping, Zapping, Zooming Bats*, 19023
Earle, Sylvia A. *Dive! My Adventures in the Deep Frontier*, 19631
Hello, Fish! 19658
Sea Critters, 19632
Early, Margaret. *Ali Baba and the Forty Thieves*, 11193
Robin Hood, 10973
Romeo and Juliet, 9037(F)
Sleeping Beauty, 10869
William Tell, 10855
Early, Theresa S. *New Mexico*, 16904
Easley, Maryann. *I Am the Ice Worm*, 6828(F)
East, Jacqueline. *The Big Bad Rumor*, 2497(F)
East, Stella. *Dreamstones*, 1625(F)
Eastman, David. *Story of Dinosaurs*, 14409
What Is a Fish? 19701
Eastman, P. D. *Are You My Mother?* 6319(F)
Eastman, Patricia. *Sometimes Things Change*, 6320(F)
Easton, Patricia H. *A Week at the Fair*, 6829(F)
Easwaran, Eknath. *The Monkey and the Mango*, 4423(F)
Eaton, Deborah. *No One Told the Aardvark*, 1146(F)
The Rainy Day Grump, 6321(F)
Eberhart, Donald G. *Great Grizzly Wilderness*, 19046
Eboch, Chris. *The Well of Sacrifice*, 9131(F)
Eccleshare, Julia, ed. *First Poems*, 11556
Echewa, T. Obinkaram. *The Magic Tree*, 10664
Eckert, Allan W. *Incident at Hawk's Hill*, 7186(F)
Return to Hawk's Hill, 9158(F)
Eckhouse, Morris. *Bob Feller*, 13451
Eckstein, Joan. *The Best Joke Book for Kids Number 4*, 21822
Eclare, Melanie. *A Handful of Sunshine*, 21762
Edelman, Marian Wright. *Stand for Children*, 17030
Edelson, Paula. *Nancy Kerrigan*, 13592
Edelson, Wendy. *The Baker's Dozen*, 5919
Edens, Cooper. *An ABC of Fashionable Animals*, 34(F)
The Animal Mall, 2048(F)
How Many Bears? 426(F)
Nicholi, 5808(F)
Santa Cows, 5809(F)
Edens, Cooper, sel. *The Glorious Mother Goose*, 839(F)

Edens, Cooper (jt. author). *The Christmas We Moved to the Barn*, 5795(F)
Darby, the Special-Order Pup, 1106(F)
Edens, John. *Glorious Days, Dreadful Days*, 16202
The Time Machine, 10246(F)
Edgett, Ken (jt. author). *Touchdown Mars! An ABC Adventure*, 146(F)
Edmiston, Jim. *The Emperor Who Forgot His Birthday*, 5682(F)
Edmonds, I. G. *Ooka the Wise*, 10812
Edmonds, Walter. *The Matchlock Gun*, 9193(F)
Eduar, Gilles. *Dream Journey*, 668(F)
Jooka Saves the Day, 2049(F)
Edward, Pamela Duncan. *Ed and Fred Flea*, 2050(F)
Edwards, Becky. *My Brother Sammy*, 4948(F)
Edwards, Chris. *The Young Inline Skater*, 21999
Edwards, Frank B. *Is the Spaghetti Ready?* 6322(F)
New at the Zoo, 6323(F)
Troubles with Bubbles, 6324(F)
Edwards, Jeff. *The Greenwich Guide to Time and the Millennium*, 20643
Edwards, Julie Andrews. *Little Bo*, 7187(F)
Edwards, Linda Strauss. *Thirteen Ways to Sink a Sub*, 10066(F)
Edwards, Mark. *The Sand Children*, 1140(F)
Edwards, Michelle. *A Baker's Portrait*, 4949(F)
Pa Lia's First Day, 10052(F)
Edwards, Pamela Duncan. *Barefoot*, 4639(F)
Dinorella, 2051(F)
Four Famished Foxes and Fosdyke, 2052(F)
The Grumpy Morning, 2053(F)
Honk! 2054(F)
Livingstone Mouse, 2055(F)
Roar! A Noisy Counting Book, 427(F)
Some Smug Slug, 2056(F)
The Wacky Wedding, 35(F)
The Worrywarts, 2057(F)
Edwards, Richard. *Amazing Animal Alphabet*, 36(F)
Copy Me, Copycub, 2058(F)
Fly with the Birds, 3114(F)
Moles Can Dance, 2059(F)
Moon Frog, 11777
Edwards, Roberta. *Five Silly Fishermen*, 6325(F)
Edwards, Roland. *Tigers*, 2060(F)
Egan, Robert. *From Wheat to Pasta*, 20089
Egan, Terry. *The Good Guys of Baseball*, 22089

The Macmillan Book of Baseball Stories, 22090
Egan, Tim. *Burnt Toast on Davenport Street*, 2061(F)
Chestnut Cove, 4139(F)
Distant Feathers, 1147(F)
Friday Night at Hodges' Cafe, 2062(F)
Metropolitan Cow, 2063(F)
Egger-Bovet, Howard. *Book of the American Civil War*, 16404
US Kids History, 16114
Egger-Bovet, Howard (jt. author). *Brown Paper School USKids History*, 16278
Egielski, Richard. *Amy's Eyes*, 7859(F)
Buz, 1148(F)
"Fire! Fire!" Said Mrs. McGuire, 863
The Gingerbread Boy, 10974
Jazper, 2064(F)
Louis the Fish, 1713(F)
Oh, Brother, 4362(F)
Three Magic Balls, 1149(F)
The Tub Grandfather, 1072(F)
The Tub People, 1073(F)
The Tub People's Christmas, 5788(F)
Ehlert, Lois. *Angel Hide and Seek*, 315(F)
Chicka Chicka Boom Boom, 89(F)
Circus, 3115
Color Farm, 266(F)
Color Zoo, 267(F)
Crocodile Smile, 14188
Cuckoo/Cucu, 11401
Eating the Alphabet, 37(F)
Feathers for Lunch, 4424(F)
Fish Eyes, 428(F)
Growing Vegetable Soup, 3116(F)
Hands, 3117(F)
Market Day, 3118(F)
Mole's Hill, 2065(F)
Moon Rope, 11438
Nuts to You! 2066(F)
A Pair of Socks, 1426(F)
Red Leaf, Yellow Leaf, 4425(F)
Snowballs, 21433(F)
Thump, Thump, Rat-a-Tat-Tat, 3004(F)
Top Cat, 2067(F)
Under My Nose, 12533
Waiting for Wings, 19546
Ehrenhaft, Daniel. *Marc Andreessen*, 13225
Ehrlich, Amy. *Leo, Zack, and Emmie*, 6326(F)
Lucy's Winter Tale, 4950(F)
Ehrlich, Amy, ed. *When I Was Your Age*, 12161
Ehrlich, Fred. *A Class Play with Ms. Vanilla*, 6327(F)
Ehrlich, H. M. *Louie's Goose*, 4951(F)

Ehrlich, Robert. *What If? Mind-Boggling Science Questions for Kids*, 18276
Eichenberg, Fritz. *Ape in a Cape*, 38(F)
Eick, Jean. *Bulldozers*, 5563
Concrete Mixers, 5564
Diggers, 21246
Dump Trucks, 21299
Forklifts, 21300
Garbage Trucks, 21301
Eid, Alain. *1000 Photos of Minerals and Fossils*, 20554
Eige, Lillian. *Dangling*, 8633(F)
Eilenberg, Max. *Cowboy Kid*, 669(F)
Einhorn, Edward. *Paradox in Oz*, 7716(F)
Einzig, Susan. *Tom's Midnight Garden*, 8009(F)
Eisenberg, Lisa (jt. author). *Creepy Riddles*, 21823
Kitty Riddles, 21824
The Paxton Cheerleaders, 10072(F)
Eisenberg, Phyllis R. *You're My Nikki*, 3614(F)
Eisner, Will. *The Last Knight*, 9038(F)
The Princess and the Frog, 10417
Eitan, Ora. *Astro Bunnies*, 1358(F)
Cowboy Bunnies, 2400(F)
Dance, Sing, Remember, 17476
Hanna's Sabbath Dress, 6116(F)
Inch by Inch, 14169
No Milk! 5194(F)
Sun Is Falling, Night Is Calling, 723(F)
Eitzen, Allan. *Alphabestiary*, 11818
Distant Thunder, 9242(F)
Totem Poles, 15952
Willie's Birthday, 6687(F)
Ekoomiak, Normee. *Arctic Memories*, 15573
Eldin, Peter. *The Most Excellent Book of How to Be a Magician*, 21782
The Most Excellent Book of How to Do Card Tricks, 22231
Elffers, Joost. *Play with Your Pumpkins*, 21434
Elffers, Joost (jt. author). *How Are You Peeling? Foods with Moods*, 4961
One Lonely Sea Horse, 437(F)
Elgar, Rebecca. *Jack*, 2068(F)
Tiger and the New Baby, 3632(F)
Tiger and the Temper Tantrum, 3633(F)
Elgar, Susan. *The Brothers Gruesome*, 1150(F)
Eliot, T. S. *Growltiger's Last Stand*, 11778
Elish, Dan. *Harriet Tubman and the Underground Railroad*, 12797
James Meredith and School Desegregation, 12772
Vermont, 16669

Washington, D.C., 16670

Elivia. *The Uninvited Guest and Other Jewish Holiday Tales*, 17475

Ellerbee, Linda. *Girl Reporter Blows Lid Off Town!* 10053(F)

Elliott, David. *The Cool Crazy Crickets*, 8279(F)

Elliott, Donald. *Frogs and Ballet*, 14280

Elliott, Leslee. *Mind-Blowing Mammals*, 18620

Ellis, Deborah. *The Breadwinner*, 8992(F)

Ellis, Jan Davey. *The Autumn Equinox*, 17370
The Book of Slime, 21920
Toad Overload, 16968
Turn of the Century, 14557

Ellis, Rafaela. *Dwight D. Eisenhower*, 13030
Martin Van Buren, 13111

Ellis, Royston. *Madagascar*, 14975
Trinidad, 15701

Ellis, Sarah. *Next Stop!* 3119(F)
Out of the Blue, 8426(F)

Ellis, Tim. *Chicken Socks*, 11529

Ellis, Veronica F. *Afro-Bets First Book About Africa*, 8961(F)
Wynton Marsalis, 12420

Ellison, Suzanne Pierson. *Best of Enemies*, 9473(F)

Ellsworth, Mary Ellen. *Gertrude Chandler Warner and the Boxcar Children*, 12616

Ellwand, David. *Alfred's Camera*, 306(F)
Alfred's Party, 5683(F)
Midas Mouse, 2069(F)

Ellwand, Ruth (jt. author). *Midas Mouse*, 2069(F)

Elmer, Howard. *Blues*, 14126

Elmer, Robert. *Chasing the Wind*, 9039(F)
Far from the Storm, 6830(F)
Follow the Star, 6831(F)
Into the Flames, 9658(F)

Elsdale, Bob. *Mac Side Up*, 2070(F)

Else, George, ed. *Insects and Spiders*, 19438

Elsom, Derek. *Weather Explained*, 20762

Elste, Joan. *True Blue*, 6328(F)

Elting, Mary. *Volcanoes and Earthquakes*, 20338

Elting, Mary (jt. author). *Math Fun*, 20624
Math Fun with Money Puzzlers, 20625

Elwell, Peter. *Three Brave Women*, 3800(F)
Time Out, 7686(F)

Ely, Paul. *Eerie Feary Feeling*, 6014(F)

Elya, Susan Middleton. *Eight Animals on the Town*, 2071(F)
Say Hola to Spanish, 13981

Say Hola to Spanish at the Circus, 2925(F)

Emberley, Barbara. *Drummer Hoff*, 14238

Emberley, Ed. *The Big Dipper*, 18540
Drummer Hoff, 14238
Ed Emberley's Big Orange Drawing Book, 21572
Ed Emberley's Drawing Book, 21573
Ed Emberley's Drawing Book of Faces, 21574
Go Away, Big Green Monster! 670(F)
Three, 13954

Emberley, Michael. *Happy Birth Day!* 3670(F)
Hi New Baby! 3671(F)
It's Perfectly Normal, 18260
It's So Amazing, 18261

Emberley, Rebecca. *My Colors/Mis Colores*, 268(F)
My Mother's Secret Life, 1151(F)
My Numbers/Mis Numeros, 429(F)
My Opposites/Mis Opuestos, 178(F)
My Shapes/Mis Formas, 327(F)
Taking a Walk/Caminando, 4640(F)
Three Cool Kids, 11122

Emerling, Dorothy. *In the Forest*, 18930

Emerson, Anthony Chee. *Songs of Shiprock Fair*, 9181(F)

Emerson, Kathy L. *Making Headlines*, 13136
The Mystery of the Missing Bagpipes, 6832(F)

Emerson, Sally, comp. *Nursery Rhyme Songbook with Easy Music to Play for Piano and Guitar*, 840(F)

Emerson, Sally, ed. *The Nursery Treasury*, 841

Emmert, Michelle. *I'm the Big Sister Now*, 17906

Emory, Jerry. *Nightprowlers*, 18621

Emsden, Katharine. *Voices from the West*, 16302

Emsden, Katharine, ed. *Coming to America*, 17555

Enderle, Judith R. *Nell Nugget and the Cow Caper*, 2926(F)
Six Creepy Sheep, 5996(F)
Six Sandy Sheep, 2072(F)
Something's Happening on Calabash Street, 3120(F)
Upstairs, 1152(F)
What Would Mama Do? 2073(F)
What's the Matter, Kelly Beans? 8634(F)
Where Are You, Little Zack? 430(F)

Endicott, James. *Listen to the Rain*, 3311(F)

Engel, Dean. *Ezra Jack Keats*, 12246

Engel, Diana. *Circle Song*, 671(F)

Fishing, 3615(F)
Holding On, 7427(F)

Engelbert, Phillis. *Astronomy and Space*, 20981

Engelbreit, Mary. *Hey, Kids! Come Craft with Me*, 21435

Engelhart, Margaret S. (jt. author). *They Sought a New World*, 16152

Engelland, Tim. *Basketball Basics*, 22137

Engfer, LeeAnne. *Maine*, 16671
My Pet Cats, 19917
My Pet Hamster and Gerbils, 19885
My Pet Lizards, 19886

Engh, M. J. *The House in the Snow*, 6833(F)

England, Linda. *The Old Cotton Blues*, 4952(F)
3 Kids Dreamin', 8280(F)

Englander, Roger. *Opera! What's All the Screaming About?* 14127

English, June A. *Mission: Earth*, 20982

English, Karen. *Big Wind Coming!* 2927(F)
Francie, 7338(F)
Just Right Stew, 4140(F)
Nadia's Hands, 5625(F)
Neeny Coming, Neeny Going, 3994(F)
Speak English for Us, Marisol! 3616(F)

Engvick, William. *Lullabies and Night Songs*, 14149

Enik, Ted. *Encyclopedia Brown's Book of Wacky Sports*, 22064
Why Doesn't the Earth Fall Up? 20823

Enos, Randall. *Inchworm and a Half*, 556(F)

Enright, Elizabeth. *Gone-Away Lake*, 6834(F)
Tatsinda, 1153(F)
Thimble Summer, 7428(F)

Enright, Vicky. *Crafts from Your Favorite Fairy Tales*, 21486
Crafts to Make in the Fall, 21488
Crafts to Make in the Spring, 21489
Crafts to Make in the Winter, 21490

Epanya, Christian. *Konte Chameleon Fine, Fine, Fine! A West African Folktale*, 2289(F)

Ephraim, Shelly Schonebaum. *Shalom Shabbat*, 6121(F)

Ephron, Amy, reteller. *Swan Lake*, 14281

Ephron, Delia. *The Girl Who Changed the World*, 7717(F)

Epple, Wolfgang. *Barn Owls*, 19359

Epps, Melanie. *Into the Jungle*, 2940(F)

Epstein, Rachel. *Anne Frank*, 13797
Estee Lauder, 12923
W. K. Kellogg, 12917

Ercelawn, Ayesha. *New Zealand*, 15230

Erdogan, Buket. *Mouse at Night*, 2165(F)

Mouse's First Christmas, 5937(F)

Mouse's First Halloween, 6055(F)

Erdosh, George. *The African American Kitchen*, 20090

Erdrich, Louise. *The Birchbark House*, 9159(F)

Erickson, Darren. *Caterpillarology*, 19568

Ladybugology, 19538

Erickson, John R. *The Case of the Vanishing Fishhook*, 7188(F)

Hank the Cowdog, 6329(F)

Moonlight Madness, 7718(F)

Erickson, Paul. *Daily Life on a Southern Plantation 1853*, 16239

Erickson, Richard. *New England Whaler*, 16225

Pueblo Indian, 15941

Sodbuster, 16382

Ericsson, Jennifer A. *The Most Beautiful Kid in the World*, 3617(F)

No Milk! 5194(F)

Eriksson, Eva. *If You Didn't Have Me*, 8776(F)

Is It Magic? 5006(F)

Rosa, 5309(F)

Rosa Goes to Daycare, 2377(F)

Sam's Ball, 5014(F)

Sam's Potty, 3282(F)

Erkel, Michael. *The Amish*, 17179

Erlbach, Arlene. *Bicycles*, 22156

Happy Birthday, Everywhere! 17352

Happy New Year, Everywhere! 17353

Kent State, 16501

The Kids' Invention Book, 21031

Sidewalk Games Around the World, 22000

Soda Pop, 20091

Teddy Bears, 21032

Video Games, 22232

Worth the Risk, 17605

Erlbruch, Wolf. *Mrs. Meyer the Bird*, 5195(F)

Ermitage, Kathleen. *Recreation Director*, 17744

Veterinarian, 17844

Ernst, Judith. *The Golden Goose King*, 10790

Ernst, Kathleen. *Retreat from Gettysburg*, 9474(F)

Trouble at Fort La Pointe, 9361(F)

Ernst, Lisa Campbell. *Bear's Day*, 3121(F)

Bubba and Trixie, 2074(F)

Cat's Play, 5196(F)

The Chick That Wouldn't Hatch, 6301(F)

Duke the Dairy Delight Dog, 2075(F)

Ginger Jumps, 2076(F)

Goldilocks Returns, 10418(F)

Gumshoe Goose, Private Eye, 6443(F)

The Letters Are Lost! 39(F)

Little Red Riding Hood, 2077(F)

The Luckiest Kid on the Planet, 4141(F)

Miss Penny and Mr. Grubbs, 4142(F)

Potato, 4737(F)

Sam Johnson and the Blue Ribbon Quilt, 4641(F)

Stella Louella's Runaway Book, 4143(F)

Up to Ten and Down Again, 431(F)

Walter's Tail, 2078(F)

When Bluebell Sang, 2079(F)

Esbensen, Barbara J. *Baby Whales Drink Milk*, 19786

Jumping Day, 3122(F)

Ladder to the Sky, 11234

The Night Rainbow, 15802

Sponges Are Skeletons, 19719

The Star Maiden, 11235

Tiger with Wings, 19360

Who Shrank My Grandmother's House? 11558

Esiason, Boomer. *A Boy Named Boomer*, 13608

Essley, Roger. *Angels in the Dust*, 9612(F)

Esterl, Arnica. *Okino and the Whales*, 1154(F)

Esterman, M. M. *A Fish That's a Box*, 13955

Estes, Eleanor. *The Hundred Dresses*, 10054(F)

Estes, Kristyn Rehling. *Manuela's Gift*, 5684(F)

Estrada, Pau. *The April Fool's Day Mystery*, 6962(F)

Button Soup, 1446(F)

Little Red Riding Hood/Caperucita roja, 10900

Estrada, Ric (jt. author). *Draw 50 Aliens, UFOs, Galaxy Ghouls, Milky Way Marauders, and Other Extraterrestrial Creatures*, 21559

Etchemendy, Nancy. *The Power of Un*, 7719(F)

Etra, Jonathan. *Aliens for Breakfast*, 10178(F)

Aliens for Lunch, 6330(F)

Etre, Lisa. *One White Sail*, 441(F)

Ets, Marie Hall. *Just Me*, 5197(F)

Nine Days to Christmas, 5810(F)

Play with Me, 5198(F)

Ettlinger, Doris. *Janice VanCleave's Insects and Spiders*, 19496

Eugene, Toni. *Hide and Seek*, 18882

Evans, Art. *First Photos*, 21797

Evans, Dilys, comp. *Fairies, Trolls and Goblins Galore*, 11559

Evans, Dilys, ed. *Monster Soup and Other Spooky Poems*, 1155

Weird Pet Poems, 11779

Evans, Douglas. *Apple Island; or, the Truth About Teachers*, 9838(F)

The Classroom at the End of the Hall, 10179(F)

The Elevator Family, 9839(F)

Math Rashes and Other Classroom Tales, 9840(F)

So What Do You Do? 8635(F)

Evans, Katie. *Hunky Dory Ate It*, 5199(F)

Evans, Leslie. *Autumn*, 21885

Spring, 127

Evans, Lezlie. *Can You Count Ten Toes? Count to 10 in 10 Different Languages*, 432

If I Were the Wind, 3618(F)

Rain Song, 4426(F)

Snow Dance, 3123(F)

Sometimes I Feel Like a Storm Cloud, 3124(F)

Evans, Mari. *Dear Corinne, Tell Somebody! A Book About Secrets*, 8636(F)

Evans, Mark. *Fish*, 19981

Guinea Pigs, 19887

Hamster, 19888

Kitten, 19918

Puppy, 19945

Rabbit, 19889

Evans, Nate. *It's Great to Skate!* 22074

The Mixed-Up Zoo of Professor Yahoo, 4144

Tiffany Dino Works Out, 2683(F)

Evans, Neville. *The Science of a Light Bulb*, 20891

The Science of Gravity, 20806

Evans, Shane W. *Down the Winding Road*, 3724(F)

Shaq and the Beanstalk, 10472(F)

Everett, Percival. *The One That Got Away*, 4145(F)

Everitt, Betsy. *The Happy Hippopotami*, 2480(F)

Mean Soup, 4146(F)

Popcorn, 6537(F)

Up the Ladder, Down the Slide, 3125(F)

Evernden, Margery (jt. author). *Of Swords and Sorcerers*, 11000

Eversole, Robyn. *The Gift Stone*, 4642(F)

Red Berry Wool, 2080(F)

Everts, Tammy. *Really Weird Animals*, 18936

Everts, Tammy (jt. author). *A Child's Day*, 16476

Customs and Traditions, 16331

Evetts-Secker, Josephine. *The Barefoot Book of Father and Son Tales*, 10547

The Barefoot Book of Mother and Son Tales, 10548

Ewart, Claire. *The Dwarf, the Giant, and the Unicorn*, 1187(F)

The Legend of the Persian Carpet, 11184

Sister Yessa's Story, 17280(F)
Ewing, Carolyn. *The Cold and Hot Winter*, 8307(F)
Moose and Friends, 2347(F)
The Nutcracker Ballet, 6371(F)
Phoebe's Parade, 5638(F)
Wake Up, City! 3457(F)
Ewing, Patrick Aloysius. *In the Paint*, 21575
Exquemelin, A. O. *Exquemelin and the Pirates of the Caribbean*, 12117
Eyles, Heather. *Well, I Never!* 1156(F)
Ezra, Mark. *The Frightened Little Owl*, 2081(F)
The Hungry Otter, 2082(F)

Faber, Doris. *The Amish*, 17179
Eleanor Roosevelt, 13180
Nature and the Environment, 13208
Faber, Harold (jt. author). *Nature and the Environment*, 13208
Facchini, Fiorenzo. *Humans*, 14496
Facklam, Howard. *Avalanche!* 20763
Bacteria, 19805
Insects, 19439
Parasites, 18622
Viruses, 17954
Facklam, Margery. *The Big Bug Book*, 19440
Bugs for Lunch, 18808
Do Not Disturb, 18903
Only a Star, 5811(F)
Spiders and Their Web Sites, 19578
Tracking Dinosaurs in the Gobi, 14410
Facklam, Margery (jt. author). *Avalanche!* 20763
Bacteria, 19805
Insects, 19439
Parasites, 18622
Viruses, 17954
Facklam, Paul. *The Big Bug Book*, 19440
Fadden, David K. *Cave of Falling Water*, 9208(F)
Native American Animal Stories, 11219
Skywoman, 11299
Fadden, John K. *Native American Animal Stories*, 11219
Fadden, John Kahionhes. *Skywoman*, 11299
Fagan, Cary. *Gogol's Coat*, 4643(F)
The Market Wedding, 8637(F)
Faidley, Warren. *Lightning*, 20701
Fain, Kathleen. *Once upon a Lily Pad*, 2743(F)
Fain, Moira. *The Christmas Dolls*, 5908(F)
Snow Day, 5496(F)
Fair, David. *The Fabulous Four Skunks*, 2083(F)
Fair, Jeff. *Black Bears*, 19043
Fair, Sylvia. *The Bedspread*, 3126(F)

Fakih, Kimberly O. *High on the Hog*, 7429(F)
Falconer, Ian. *Olivia*, 2084(F)
Falconer, Kieran. *Peru*, 15731
Falda, Dominique. *The Treasure Chest*, 2085(F)
Falick, Melanie. *Kids Knitting*, 21642
Falk, Barbara B. *The Same Wind*, 4473(F)
Falk, John H. *Bubble Monster*, 18311
Falkof, Lucille. *George Washington*, 13114
Helen Gurley Brown, 12507
Lyndon B. Johnson, 13056
Falla, Dominique (jt. author). *Woodlore*, 20211
Fallen, Anne-Catherine. *USA from Space*, 20983
Falwell, Cathryn. *Christmas for 10*, 5812(F)
Dragon Tooth, 4953(F)
Feast for 10, 433(F)
Hands! 18064
It's About Time! 194
The Letter Jesters, 13993
New Moon, 4540(F)
P. J. and Puppy, 3127(F)
Shape Space, 328(F)
We Have a Baby, 3619(F)
Word Wizard, 179(F)
Fancher, Lou. *Bambi*, 7299(F)
Coppelia, 14283(F)
Horsefly, 1248(F)
I Walk at Night, 2045(F)
The Lost Boy and the Monster, 1602(F)
My Many Colored Days, 289(F)
Peach and Blue, 1300(F)
Silver Seeds, 11978
Fang, Linda. *The Ch'i-lin Purse*, 10751
Fannon, Cecilia. *Leaders*, 17745
Faranda, Brigid. *Pizza!* 20115
Farber, Erica. *Ooey Gooey*, 6331(F)
Farber, Norma. *Without Wings, Mother, How Can I Fly?* 3620(F)
Farbman, Melinda. *Spacechimp*, 20984
Faría, Rosana. *Niña Bonita*, 1373(F)
Farjeon, Eleanor. *Elsie Piddock Skips in Her Sleep*, 1157(F)
Morning Has Broken, 14239
Farley, Carol. *The Case of the Haunted Health Club*, 6835(F)
The Case of the Vanishing Villain, 6836(F)
Mr. Pak Buys a Story, 10724
Farley, Rick. *Capturing Nature*, 12190
Farley, Steven. *The Black Stallion's Shadow*, 7189(F)
Farley, Walter. *Black Stallion*, 7190(F)
Man O' War, 19991
Farmer, Andrew. *Brain*, 18113
Ears, 18148

Eyes, 18145
Heart and Lungs, 18078
Farmer, Jacqueline. *Bananas!* 20141
Farmer, Nancy. *Casey Jones's Fireman*, 11336
Do You Know Me? 8962(F)
Farmer, Patti. *What's He Doing Now?* 3621(F)
Farndon, John. *Aluminum*, 20280
Calcium, 20281
Color, 20864
Electricity, 20892
Eyewitness Question and Answer Book, 21909
Hydrogen, 20282
Lights and Optics, 20865
Nitrogen, 20283
Oxygen, 20284
Sound and Hearing, 20937
Water, 20732
Weather, 20764
Farnes, Catherine. *Snow*, 8887(F)
Farnsworth, Bill. *The Buffalo Jump*, 9177(F)
Grandpa Is a Flyer, 21068
The Last Rail, 9345(F)
Mississippi Going North, 4382(F)
Shannon, 9574(F), 9575(F)
The Stars in My Geddoh's Sky, 3802(F)
When Abraham Talked to the Trees, 13079
Farrell, John. *It's Just a Game*, 3128(F)
Farrell, Mame. *Bradley and the Billboard*, 10326(F)
Marrying Malcolm Murgatroyd, 8281(F)
Farris, Pamela J. *Young Mouse and Elephant*, 10665
Fassler, David. *What's a Virus, Anyway?* 17955
Fassler, Joan. *Howie Helps Himself*, 8888(F)
Fatras, Andre. *The Penguin*, 19370
Faulkner, Keith. *The Big Yawn*, 5201(F)
David Dreaming of Dinosaurs, 5202(F)
The Long-Nosed Pig, 2086(F)
My Colors, 269(F)
The Scared Little Bear, 672(F)
The Wide-Mouthed Frog, 2087(F)
Faulkner, Matt. *Black Belt*, 7720(F)
Favole, Robert J. *Through the Wormhole*, 7721(F)
Fawcett, Melissa Jayne. *Makiawisug*, 7722(F)
Fazio, Brenda Lena. *Grandfather's Story*, 3622(F)
Fazio, Wende. *Times Square*, 16672
West Virginia, 16845
Fazzi, Maura. *The Circus of Mystery*, 6837(F)
Fearnley, Jan. *Little Robin's Christmas*, 5813(F)
A Special Something, 3623(F)

Fearrington, Ann. *Christmas Lights*, 5814(F)

Fedden, Mary. *Motley the Cat*, 1737(F)

Feder, Jane. *Table, Chair, Bear*, 13982

Feder, Paula K. *The Feather-Bed Journey*, 4644(F)

Where Does the Teacher Live? 6332(F)

Feelings, Tom. *African Crafts*, 21446

To Be a Slave, 17574

Tommy Traveler in the World of Black History, 17556

Feeney, Kathy. *Puerto Rico Facts and Symbols*, 15702

Rhode Island Facts and Symbols, 16673

South Dakota Facts and Symbols, 16547

Tennessee, 16846

Utah, 16603

Vermont Facts and Symbols, 16674

Washington, D.C. Facts and Symbols, 16675

West Virginia, 16847

Feeney, Stephanie. *A Is for Aloha*, 4645(F)

Hawaii Is a Rainbow, 16773

Sand to Sea, 19633

Feiffer, Jules. *Bark, George*, 2088(F)

I Lost My Bear, 2928(F)

The Man in the Ceiling, 9841(F)

The Phantom Tollbooth, 7849(F)

Some Things Are Scary, 3201(F)

Feinberg, Barbara S. *Abraham Lincoln's Gettysburg Address*, 16405

Black Tuesday, 16462

The Cabinet, 17107

The Changing White House, 16676

Constitutional Amendments, 17055

Edith Kermit Carow Roosevelt, 13177

Electing the President, 17108

John McCain, 12933

The National Government, 17109

Patricia Ryan Nixon, 13171

State Governments, 17129

Term Limits for Congress? 17110

Feinstein, Stephen. *The 1960s*, 16504

The 1970s, 16503

The 1980s, 16502

Feinstein, Steve. *Egypt in Pictures*, 15498

Israel in Pictures, 15519

Turkey in Pictures, 15266

Feldman, Eve B. *That Cat!* 7191(F)

Feldman, Heather. *The Story of the Golden Retriever*, 19946

Feldman, Jane. *I Am a Dancer*, 14282

I Am a Rider, 22201

Feldman, Lynne. *Good Yontif*, 910(F)

Felix, Antonia (jt. author). *Can It Really Rain Frogs?* 20759

Is There a Dinosaur in Your Backyard? The World's Most Fascinating Fossils, Rocks, and Minerals, 20553

What Makes the Grand Canyon Grand? 20300

Felix, Monique. *Hundreds of Fish*, 5460(F)

Feller, Marsha (jt. author). *Fanciful Faces and Handbound Books*, 14080

Feller, Ron. *Fanciful Faces and Handbound Books*, 14080

Fellows, Rebecca Nevers. *A Lei for Tutu*, 3624(F)

Fellows, Stan. *The Copper Tin Cup*, 3876(F)

The Dog Who Walked with God, 11295

Felstead, Cathie. *Adam, Adam, What Do You See?* 17304

Big Wolf and Little Wolf, 2023(F)

The Circle of Days, 17203

Who Made Me? 1627(F)

Felts, Shirley. *The Secret World of Polly Flint*, 7685(F)

Feltwell, John. *Butterflies and Moths*, 19547

Fenner, Carol. *The King of Dragons*, 8638(F)

Randall's Wall, 8639(F)

Yolonda's Genius, 7430(F)

Ferguson, Alane. *The Practical Joke War*, 9842(F)

Stardust, 8640(F)

Ferguson, Alane (jt. author). *Cliff-Hanger*, 7058(F)

Deadly Waters, 7059(F)

Ghost Horses, 7060(F)

The Hunted, 7061(F)

Rage of Fire, 7062(F)

Wolf Stalker, 7063(F)

Ferguson, Amos. *Under the Sunday Tree*, 11580

Ferguson, Dwayne. *Kid Caramel, Private Investigator*, 6838(F)

Ferguson, Dwayne J. *Case of the Missing Ankh*, 6839(F)

Fernandes, Eugenie. *Aaron's Awful Allergies*, 4973(F)

Baby Dreams, 673(F)

Before You Were Born, 18239

A Cat in a Kayak, 1966(F)

A Difficult Day, 4954(F)

Lavender Moon, 2937(F)

The Memory Horse, 3192(F)

Ribbon Rescue, 3337(F)

Rise and Shine, 14255

Sleepy Little Mouse, 1158(F)

Fernandes, Kim. *One Gray Mouse*, 393

Sleepy Little Mouse, 1158(F)

Fernandez, Jose B. *Jose de San Martin*, 13846

Fernandez, Laura. *Glass Town*, 14067

Jeremiah Learns to Read, 3030(F)

Little Dog Moon, 4854(F)

The Magnificent Piano Recital, 5055(F)

Prairie Willow, 4855(F)

Tchaikovsky Discovers America, 9566(F)

Fernando. *Baby Rock, Baby Roll*, 3027(F)

Ferrari, Maria. *What Is a Triangle?* 324

What Is Round? 325(F)

Ferrell, Nancy Warren. *The U.S. Air Force*, 21382

The U.S. Coast Guard, 21383

Ferri, Giuliano. *And God Created Squash*, 17284(F)

A Baby Born in Bethlehem, 17420

Ferrie, Richard. *The World Turned Upside Down*, 16195

Ferris, Helen, ed. *Favorite Poems Old and New*, 11560

Ferris, Jeri. *Arctic Explorer*, 12120

Go Free or Die, 12798

Native American Doctor, 12982

Walking the Road to Freedom, 12790

What Are You Figuring Now? 13233

What I Had Was Singing, 12344

Ferris, Jeri Chase. *Remember the Ladies*, 13124

Thomas Jefferson, 13048

With Open Hands, 12769

Ferris, Julie. *Galaxy Getaway*, 20615

Shakespeare's London, 15342

Ferro, Jennifer. *Brazilian Foods and Culture*, 15732

Italian Foods and Culture, 15377

Jewish Foods and Culture, 17461

Ferroa, Peggy. *China*, 15059

Ferrón, Miguel. *Birds Conquer the Sky*, 19247

Ferrón, Miriam. *Birds Conquer the Sky*, 19247

Ferry, Dave. *Stuffin' Muffin*, 21737

Fertl, Dagmar. *Bears*, 19044

Fertl, Dagmar (jt. author). *Wolves and Their Relatives*, 19141

Fetz, Ingrid. *Maurice's Room*, 7434(F)

Once I Was a Plum Tree, 8703(F)

Feuer, Elizabeth. *Lost Summer*, 8282(F)

Few, Roger. *Macmillan Children's Guide to Endangered Animals*, 19394

Fiammenghi, Gioia. *Chocolate Fever*, 9993(F)

A Collection for Kate, 417(F)

Eagle-Eye Ernie Comes to Town, 6571(F)

The Green Magician Puzzle, 6572(F)

I Love to Sneeze, 6631(F)

It's About Time, Max! 20651(F)

An Occasional Cow, 9882(F)

Who's Got Spots? 20577

Why Do Dogs Do That? 19978

Fiarotta, Noel. *Great Experiments with H²O*, 20733

Fiarotta, Noel (jt. author). *Papercrafts Around the World*, 21613

Fiarotta, Phyllis. *Papercrafts Around the World*, 21613

Fiarotta, Phyllis (jt. author). *Great Experiments with H²O*, 20733

Fiedler, Joseph Daniel. *The Crystal Heart*, 10842

Hatshepsut, His Majesty, Herself, 13807

Field, Catherine. *China*, 15060

Field, Edward. *Magic Words*, 11930

Field, Eugene. *Wynken, Blynken, and Nod*, 674

Field, James. *The Age of Discovery*, 14575

Arms and Armor, 21385

The Modern World, 14574

Field, Rachel. *Calico Bush*, 9194(F)

General Store, 3129(F)

Hitty, 7723(F)

Prayer for a Child, 17522

Fielding, Ann (jt. author). *Sand to Sea*, 19633

Fielding, David. *Acacia Terrace*, 15256

Fields, Julia. *The Green Lion of Zion Street*, 8283(F)

Fields, T. S. *Danger in the Desert*, 6840(F)

Missing in the Mountains, 6841(F)

Fife, Dale H. *Empty Lot*, 4427(F)

Figley, Marty R. *Noah's Wife*, 17267

Figueredo, D. H. *When This World Was New*, 4955(F)

Filbin, Dan. *Arizona*, 16604

Filling, Gregory. *Take Me to Your Liter*, 21834

Fillon, Mike. *Young Superstars of Tennis*, 13655

Finch, Linda. *A Lei for Tutu*, 3624(F)

The Seven Gods of Luck, 10820

Finch, Margo. *The Lunch Bunch*, 6333(F)

Finch, Mary. *The Little Red Hen and the Ear of Wheat*, 10975

Finch, Sheila. *Tiger in the Sky*, 10180(F)

Finchler, Judy. *Miss Malarkey Doesn't Live in Room 10*, 5497(F)

Miss Malarkey Won't Be In Today, 5498(F)

Testing Miss Malarkey, 5499(F)

Findon, Joanne. *When Night Eats the Moon*, 7724(F)

Fine, Anne. *Bad Dreams*, 7725(F)

Step by Wicked Step, 7431(F)

The Tulip Touch, 8889(F)

Fine, Doreen. *What Do We Know About Judaism?* 17180

Fine, Edith Hope. *Gary Paulsen*, 12576

Under the Lemon Moon, 4956(F)

Fine, Howard. *Ding Dong Ding Dong*, 2557(F)

A Piggie Christmas, 14199

Piggie Pie! 1450(F)

The Upstairs Cat, 1327(F)

Zak's Lunch, 1451(F)

Zoom Broom, 1452(F)

Fine, John C. *Free Spirits in the Sky*, 22001

Fink, Deborah F. *It's a Family Thanksgiving! A Celebration of an American Tradition for Children and Their Families*, 17495

Finkelstein, Norman H. *The Emperor General*, 12931

The Way Things Never Were, 16505

Finlayson, Reggie. *Colin Powell*, 12950

Nelson Mandela, 13829

Finley, Carol. *Aboriginal Art of Australia*, 13889

The Art of African Masks, 13935

Art of the Far North, 13943

Finley, Mary Peace. *White Grizzly*, 9362(F)

Finney, Kathryn Kunz. *For Heaven's Sake*, 3873(F)

I Don't Want to Talk About It, 5053(F)

Finney, Pat. *The Courage Seed*, 4811(F)

Fiodorov, Mikhail. *A Family Treasury of Bible Stories*, 17252

A World Treasury of Myths, Legends, and Folktales, 10534

Fiore, Peter M. *The Boston Tea Party*, 16151

Dear Willie Rudd, 3658(F)

Keeper for the Sea, 4391(F)

One Christmas Dawn, 5909(F)

Firth, Barbara. *At the Edge of the Forest*, 5312(F)

Bears in the Forest, 19072

Can't You Sleep, Little Bear? 798(F)

Good Job, Little Bear, 2795(F)

The Grumpalump, 2177(F)

Let's Go Home, Little Bear, 2798(F)

A Song for Little Toad, 679(F)

Tom Rabbit, 1658(F)

You and Me, Little Bear, 2803(F)

Fischer, George. *The Illustrated Laws of Soccer*, 22290

Fischer, Hans. *The Bremem Town Musicians*, 10892

Fischer, Marsha. *Miami*, 16848

Fischer, Maureen M. *Nineteenth Century Lumber Camp Cooking*, 15876

Fischer-Nagel, Andreas (jt. author). *Fir Trees*, 20198

The Housefly, 19441

Life of the Butterfly, 19548

Life of the Honeybee, 19521

Life of the Ladybug, 19530

Fischer-Nagel, Heiderose. *Fir Trees*, 20198

The Housefly, 19441

Life of the Butterfly, 19548

Life of the Honeybee, 19521

Life of the Ladybug, 19530

Fisher, Aileen. *Sing of the Earth and Sky*, 11561

Year-Round Programs for Young Players, 12019

Fisher, Chris. *Let's Make Magic*, 21781

Under the Moon, 7733(F)

Fisher, Cynthia. *Calculator Riddles*, 20608

Can You Guess Where We're Going? 3489(F)

Deena's Lucky Penny, 6306(F)

Easy Math Puzzles, 20609

The Sky Is Falling! 6521(F)

The Worst Kid Who Ever Lived on Eighth Avenue, 6446(F)

Fisher, Enid. *Emotional Ups and Downs*, 17702

The Great Dinosaur Record Book, 14411

They Lived with the Dinosaurs, 14412

Fisher, Frederick. *Costa Rica*, 15662

Indonesia, 15156

Israel, 15520

Fisher, Gary L. *The Survival Guide for Kids with LD (Learning Differences)*, 17907

Fisher, Iris L. *Katie-Bo*, 3625(F)

Fisher, James T. *Catholics in America*, 17181

Fisher, Jeff. *A Picture Book of Amelia Earhart*, 12107

Fisher, Leonard Everett. *The ABC Exhibit*, 40(F)

Alexander Graham Bell, 13236

Alphabet Art, 13890

Anasazi, 15947

Celebrations, 11835

A Circle of Seasons, 11969

Cyclops, 11471

David and Goliath, 17268

Festivals, 17383

Galileo, 13289

Gandhi, 13802

The Gods and Goddesses of Ancient Egypt, 14624

Gods and Goddesses of the Ancient Maya, 11446

Gutenberg, 13305

The Hatters, 16115

If You Ever Meet a Whale, 11801

Kinderdike, 10856

Marie Curie, 13262

Monticello, 16849

Moses, 17269

Number Art, 20629

The Oregon Trail, 16303

The Papermakers, 16116

Sailboat Lost, 1159(F)

Sky, Sea, the Jetty, and Me, 4428(F)
The Spotted Pony, 9738(F)
Theseus and the Minotaur, 11472
The Three Princes, 11190
To Bigotry No Sanction, 17182
The Tower of London, 15343
Up in the Air, 11970
William Tell, 10857
Fisher, Lillian M. *Brave Bessie,* 12091
Fisher, Teresa. *France,* 15302, 15303, 15304
Fishkin, Shelley Fisher (jt. author). *The Encyclopedia of Civil Rights in America,* 17026
Fishman, Cathy G. *On Hanukkah,* 17462
On Passover, 6070
On Purim, 17463
On Rosh Hashanah and Yom Kippur, 17464
Fison, Josie. *Roald Dahl's Revolting Recipes,* 21697
Fitch, Florence Mary. *A Book About God,* 17183
Fitch, Sheree. *If You Could Wear My Sneakers!* 11869
Fitchett, Gordon. *Cinderella,* 10500(F)
The Twelve Princesses, 10888
Fittipaldi, Cica. *African Animal Tales,* 10650
Fitz-Gerald, Christine A. *Julia Dent Grant,* 13157
Fitz-Gerald, Christine Maloney. *William Henry Harrison,* 13041
Fitzgerald, Gerald. *Casey at the Bat,* 12006
In My Pocket, 9689(F)
Fitzgerald, Joanne. *Ten Small Tales,* 10572
Fitzgerald, John D. *The Great Brain,* 9843(F)
Fitzgerald, Karen. *The Story of Iron,* 21257
The Story of Nitrogen, 20285
The Story of Oxygen, 20666
Fitzgerald, Patrick J. *Bear Attacks,* 19045
Croc and Gator Attacks, 18702
Fitzgerald, Ron. *Essential Fishing for Teens,* 22175
Fitzhugh, Louise. *Harriet the Spy,* 10055(F)
Nobody's Family Is Going to Change, 7432(F)
Fitzpatrick, Marie-Louise. *Lizzy and Skunk,* 3130(F)
The Long March, 15948
Flack, Marjorie. *Angus and the Ducks,* 5203(F)
Ask Mr. Bear, 2089(F)
The Country Bunny and the Little Gold Shoes, 5968(F)
Flake, Sharon. *The Skin I'm In,* 10056(F)

Flammang, James M. *Robert Fulton,* 13287
Flanagan, Alice K. *Ask Nurse Pfaff, She'll Help You!* 17798
A Busy Day at Mr. Kang's Grocery Store, 3131
Buying a Pet from Ms. Chavez, 3132(F)
Call Mr. Vasquez, He'll Fix It! 3133
Choosing Eyeglasses with Mrs. Koutris, 3134
Coach John and His Soccer Team, 3135(F)
A Day in Court with Mrs. Trinh, 17746
Desert Birds, 19225
Dolley Payne Todd Madison, 13169
Dr. Friedman Helps Animals, 17845
Dr. Kanner, Dentist with a Smile, 17799
Exploring Parks with Ranger Dockett, 17747
Flying an Agricultural Plane with Mr. Miller, 17836
Here Comes Mr. Eventoff with the Mail! 3136(F)
Learning About Bees from Mr. Krebs, 19522
Learning Is Fun with Mrs. Perez, 3137
Masks! 21603
Mr. Paul and Mr. Luecke Build Communities, 17787
Mr. Santizo's Tasty Treats! 3138
Mr. Yee Fixes Cars, 3139
Mrs. Scott's Beautiful Art, 17773
Ms. Davison, Our Librarian, 3140
Ms. Murphy Fights Fires, 17808
Night Birds, 19226
Raising Cows on the Koebel's Farm, 17748
Riding the Ferry with Captain Cruz, 3141
Riding the School Bus with Mrs. Kramer, 3142(F)
Rocks, 20555
Seabirds, 19347
Songbirds, 19227
A Visit to the Gravesens' Farm, 3143(F)
The Wilsons, a House-Painting Team, 3144
The Zieglers and Their Apple Orchard, 17749
Flather, Lisa. *Bugs, Beetles, and Butterflies,* 19503
Just Dog, 2551(F)
My Bear and Me, 3307(F)
Ten Silly Dogs, 434(F)
Whale Journey, 5213(F)
Flavin, Teresa. *City Kids,* 11608
Escape North! The Story of Harriet Tubman, 12799

Fly High! The Story of Bessie Coleman, 12090
The Old Cotton Blues, 4952(F)
Silver Rain Brown, 3684(F)
Fleck, Earl. *Chasing Bears,* 6842(F)
Flegg, Aubrey. *Katie's War,* 9093(F)
Flegg, Jim. *Animal Builders,* 18907
Animal Communication, 18892
Animal Families, 18876
Animal Hunters, 18810
Animal Movement, 18809
Fleischer, Jane. *Tecumseh,* 12999
Fleischman, Paul. *Big Talk,* 11562
The Borning Room, 9363(F)
Bull Run, 16406
Copier Creations, 21614
The Half-a-Moon Inn, 6843(F)
I Am Phoenix, 11780
Joyful Noise, 11781
Lost! A Story in String, 3626(F)
Seedfolks, 7339(F)
Weslandia, 1160(F)
Fleischman, Paul, ed. *Cannibal in the Mirror,* 17606
Fleischman, Sid. *Bandit's Moon,* 9364(F)
By the Great Horn Spoon, 9844(F)
A Carnival of Animals, 9845(F)
Chancy and the Grand Rascal, 9846(F)
The Ghost in the Noonday Sun, 9847(F)
The Ghost on Saturday Night, 9848(F)
Humbug Mountain, 9849(F)
Jim Ugly, 9365(F)
McBroom Tells the Truth, 9850(F)
The Midnight Horse, 7726(F)
Mr. Mysterious and Company, 9851(F)
The Scarebird, 3145(F)
The 13th Floor, 7727(F)
The Whipping Boy, 6844(F)
Fleischner, Jennifer. *The Dred Scott Case,* 16240
I Was Born a Slave, 12730
Fleisher, Paul. *Coral Reef,* 19659
Gorillas, 18992
Life Cycles of a Dozen Diverse Creatures, 18623
Oak Tree, 20199
Saguaro Cactus, 20402
Tide Pool, 19858
Fleishman, Seymour. *Gus Loves His Happy Home,* 1617(F)
Sometimes Things Change, 6320(F)
Fleming, Alice. *P. T. Barnum,* 12353
Fleming, Bill (jt. author). *Puppy Care and Critters, Too!* 19962
Fleming, Candace. *A Big Cheese for the White House,* 4646(F)
Gabriella's Song, 4647(F)
The Hatmaker's Sign, 9229(F)
Westward Ho, Carlotta! 4147(F)
When Agnes Caws, 2929(F)
Fleming, Denise. *Barnyard Banter,* 5204(F)

Count! 435(F)
The Everything Book, 180(F)
In the Small, Small Pond, 4429(F)
In the Tall, Tall Grass, 5205(F)
Lunch, 2090(F)
Mama Cat Has Three Kittens, 2091(F)
Time to Sleep, 2092(F)
Where Once There Was a Wood, 3146(F)
Fleming, Ian. *Chitty Chitty Bang Bang*, 7728(F)
Fleming, Robert. *Rescuing a Neighborhood*, 17136
Fleming, Virginia. *Be Good to Eddie Lee*, 4957(F)
Flera, Constance. *The Optical Illusion Book*, 20917
Flesher, Vivienne. *Lullaby Raft*, 754(F)
An Mei's Strange and Wondrous Journey, 3812(F)
Fletcher, Corina (jt. author). *Ghoul School*, 1512(F)
Fletcher, Ralph. *Buried Alive*, 11563
Fig Pudding, 7433(F)
Flying Solo, 10057(F)
Grandpa Never Lies, 3627(F)
How Writers Work, 14081
I Am Wings, 11564
Ordinary Things, 11948
Relatively Speaking, 11565
Spider Boy, 8641(F)
Tommy Trouble and the Magic Marble, 8642(F)
Twilight Comes Twice, 4430(F)
Fletcher, Susan. *Flight of the Dragon Kyn*, 7729(F)
Shadow Spinner, 8993(F)
Sign of the Dove, 7730(F)
The Stuttgart Nanny Mafia, 8427(F)
Flint, David. *The Baltic States*, 15413
China, 15061
Egypt, 15499
Great Britain, 15344
Mexico, 15614
The Russian Federation, 15414
South Africa, 14976
The United Kingdom, 15345
Floca, Brian. *Dinosaurs at the Ends of the Earth*, 14413
Five Trucks, 5565(F)
The Frightful Story of Harry Walfish, 10058(F)
From Boys to Men, 17706
Let's Fly a Kite, 348(F)
Luck with Potatoes, 1299(F)
Solomon Sneezes, 6663(F)
Sports! Sports! Sports! A Poetry Collection, 12005
Where Are You, Little Zack? 430(F)
Flood, Nancy Bo. *I'll Go to School If . . .*, 5500(F)
Flora, James. *The Fabulous Firework Family*, 4648(F)
Grandpa's Ghost Stories, 6845(F)

Florczak, Robert. *Birdsong*, 4563(F)
The Magic Fish-bone, 7706(F)
The Persian Cinderella, 10407
The Rainbow Bridge, 11318
Rough Sketch Beginning, 11940
Flores, Jessie J. *The Earth Science Book*, 20329
Florian, Douglas. *Beast Feast*, 11782
Bing Bang Boing, 11870
In the Swim, 11783
Insectlopedia, 11784
Laugh-Eteria, 11871
Lizards, Frogs, and Polliwogs, 11785
Mammalabilia, 11786
Monster Motel, 1161(F)
On the Wing, 11787
A Pig Is Big, 329(F)
A Summer Day, 4431(F)
Turtle Day, 5206(F)
Very Scary, 6019(F)
Winter Eyes, 11949
Flory, Verdon. *You Can Call Me Willy*, 5094(F)
Flower, Renee. *School Supplies*, 11604
Flowers, Sarah. *Sports in America*, 22002
Floyd, Lucy. *Rabbit and Turtle Go to School*, 6334(F)
Flynn, Amy. *Doll Party*, 6187(F)
Flynn, Barbara. *Gildaen*, 7631(F)
Flynn, Gabriel. *Venus and Serena Williams*, 13656
Flynn, Jean. *Annie Oakley*, 12430
Foa, Maryclare. *Odin's Family*, 11520
Songs Are Thoughts, 11669
Fogarty, Pat. *Meet Thomas Jefferson*, 13047
Fogelin, Adrian. *Crossing Jordan*, 8284(F)
Foggo, Cheryl. *One Thing That's True*, 8428(F)
Foley, Erin. *Ecuador*, 15733
Foley, June. *Susanna Siegelbaum Gives Up Guys*, 9852(F)
Foley, Mike. *Fundamental Hockey*, 22212
Foley, Sheila, ed. *Faith Unfurled*, 16117
Follett, Ken. *The Power Twins*, 10181(F)
Fong, Ryan T. *Global Warning*, 6975(F)
Fontaine, Joel. *Long Ago in Oregon*, 11626
Fontanel, Beatrice. *Monsters*, 18937
The Penguin, 19370
Fonteyn, Margot. *Coppelia*, 14283(F)
Foon, Stanley Wong Hoo. *The Dancing Dragon*, 5654(F)
Forberg, Ati. *The Magic of the Glits*, 8247(F)
Samurai of Gold Hill, 9634(F)
Forbes, Anna. *Kids with AIDS*, 17956

When Someone You Know Has AIDS, 17957
Forbes, Bart. *How Many Miles to Jacksonville?* 4698(F)
Forbes, Esther. *Johnny Tremain*, 9230(F)
Ford, Barbara. *Saint Louis*, 16548
Walt Disney, 12225
Ford, Bernette G. (jt. author). *Bright Eyes, Brown Skin*, 3226(F)
Ford, Carin T. *Legends of American Dance and Choreography*, 12162
Ford, Christine. *Snow!* 3147(F)
Ford, George. *Afro-Bets First Book About Africa*, 8961(F)
Bright Eyes, Brown Skin, 3226(F)
Hanging Out with Mom, 6206(F)
Jamal's Busy Day, 6419(F)
The Story of Ruby Bridges, 16499(F)
Wild, Wild Hair, 6358(F)
Ford, Harry. *The Young Astronomer*, 18389
Ford, Juwanda G. *K Is for Kwanzaa*, 5626
Ford, M. Thomas. *Paula Abdul*, 12341
Ford, Miela. *Bear Play*, 5207(F)
Little Elephant, 5208(F)
Mom and Me, 5209(F)
My Day in the Garden, 3148(F)
On My Own, 2093(F)
Sunflower, 4432(F)
Watch Us Play, 6335(F)
What Color Was the Sky Today? 181(F)
Ford, Pamela Baldwin. *Amazing World of Dinosaurs*, 14421
Wonders of the Desert, 20417
Ford, Roxanne (jt. author). *David Robinson*, 13569
Ford, Wayne. *Fast, Strong, and Striped*, 18929
Foreman, Michael. *After the War Was Over*, 12232
The Arabian Nights; or, Tales Told by Sheherezade During a Thousand Nights and One Night, 11180
Arthur, 11019(F)
Jack's Fantastic Voyage, 1162(F)
The Little Reindeer, 5815(F)
The Little Ships, 9081(F)
Michael Foreman's Christmas Treasury, 17416
Michael Foreman's Mother Goose, 843
Rock-A-Doodle-Do! 10889(F)
Seal Surfer, 4958(F)
Seasons of Splendor, 10795
Forest, Crista. *Moon in Bear's Eyes*, 19070
Shockers of the Sea and Other Electrical Animals, 19694
Forest, Heather. *The Baker's Dozen*, 11337

Stone Soup, 10870
Wisdom Tales from Around the World, 10549
The Woman Who Flummoxed the Fairies, 10976
Wonder Tales from Around the World, 10550
Forman, James D. *Becca's Story*, 9475(F)
Forman, Michael H. *Arctic Tundra*, 15803
From Wax to Crayon, 21033
Fornari, Giuliano. *The Body Atlas*, 18069
Inside the Body, 18059
Forrest, Sandra. *We All Scream for Ice Cream*, 20133
Forrester, Sandra. *Dust from Old Bones*, 9275(F)
Wheel of the Moon, 9195(F)
Forsey, Chris. *Flying Ace*, 12108
Fossil Detective, 14463
The Stars, 18538
Forsyth, Adrian. *The Architecture of Animals*, 18908
How Monkeys Make Chocolate, 20439
Journey Through a Tropical Jungle, 20440
Forsyth, Elizabeth (jt. author). *The Disease Book*, 17967
Know About AIDS, 17968
Know About Mental Illness, 17969
Living with Asthma, 17970
Forten, Charlotte. *A Free Black Girl Before the Civil War*, 16241
Fortney, Mary T. *Fire Station Number 4*, 17809
Fortnum, Peggy. *A Bear Called Paddington*, 9785(F)
Paddington's Storybook, 9787(F)
Fortunato, Frank. *Sports Great Alonzo Mourning*, 13550
Wayne Gretzky, 13687
Forward, Toby. *Ben's Christmas Carol*, 5816(F)
Fosberg, John. *Cookie Shapes*, 330(F)
Foster, Alan Dean. *The Hand of Dinotopia*, 10182(F)
Foster, Elizabeth. *Gigi*, 7731(F)
Foster, Evelyn. *The Mermaid of Cafur*, 7732(F)
Foster, Genevieve. *George Washington's World*, 15877
Foster, Joanna. *The Magpies' Nest*, 10977
Foster, Joanna (jt. author). *George Washington's World*, 15877
Foster, John, comp. *First Verses*, 11566
Let's Celebrate, 11829
Foster, Leila M. *Afghanistan*, 15157
Benjamin Franklin, 12880
Italy, 15378
Jordan, 15539
Kuwait, 15540

Oman, 15541
Saudi Arabia, 15542
The Story of the Persian Gulf War, 15488
Foster, Lynne. *Exploring the Grand Canyon*, 16605
Foster, Merrell L. *Iraq*, 15543
Foster, Travis. *The Feet in the Gym*, 5493(F)
Fowler, Allan. *All the Colors of the Rainbow*, 20866
Animals on the Move, 18811
Animals Under the Ground, 18624
Arms and Legs and Other Limbs, 18058
The Best Way to See a Shark, 19757
The Biggest Animal Ever, 19787
The Biggest Animal on Land, 18938
Can You See the Wind? 20667
The Chicken or the Egg? 19228
Corn — On and Off the Cob, 20173
The Dewey Decimal System, 13994
Energy from the Sun, 20849
Friendly Dolphins, 19683
Frogs and Toads and Tadpoles Too! 18721
Giant Pandas, 19186
Hard-to-See Animals, 18883
Horses, Horses, Horses, 19992
How Animals See Things, 18812
How Do You Know It's Fall? 18563
How Do You Know It's Summer? 18564
Icebergs, Ice Caps, and Glaciers, 20358
If It Weren't for Farmers, 20053
It Could Still Be a Cat, 19919
It Could Still Be a Dinosaur, 14414
It Could Still Be a Mammal, 18939
It Could Still Be a Robot, 21200
It Could Still Be a Tree, 20200
It Could Still Be Endangered, 19395
It Could Still Be Water, 20734
It's a Good Thing There Are Insects, 19442
Knowing About Noses, 18141
Lands of Grass, 20534
The Library of Congress, 13995
Life in a Wetland, 20368
North, South, East, and West, 182
Of Mice and Rats, 19195
Our Living Forests, 20441
Raccoons, 18940
Shellfish Aren't Fish, 19674
A Snail's Pace, 19605
So That's How the Moon Changes Shape! 18444
Spiders Are Not Insects, 19579
Star of the Sea, 19720
The Sun Is Always Shining Somewhere, 18565
The Sun's Family of Planets, 18468
Taking Root, 20174

Thanks to Cows, 20054
These Birds Can't Fly, 19229
Turtles Take Their Time, 18781
What Do You See in a Cloud? 20765
What Magnets Can Do, 20893
What's the Weather Today? 20766
When a Storm Comes Up, 20689
The Wonder of a Waterfall, 20369
Woolly Sheep and Hungry Goats, 20055
Fowler, Christine. *Shota and the Star Quilt*, 3016(F)
Fowler, Jim. *Beautiful*, 3628(F)
Dolphin Adventure, 19684
Fowler, Susi G. *Albertina, the Animals, and Me*, 9853(F)
Albertina the Practically Perfect, 8285(F)
Beautiful, 3628(F)
Circle of Thanks, 1163(F)
Fowler, Verna. *The Menominee*, 15949
Fowlkes, Nancy D. *The Old Woman Who Lived in a Vinegar Bottle*, 10458
Fox, Anne L. *Ten Thousand Children*, 14851
Fox, Christyan. *Goodnight Piggy-Wiggy*, 2094(F)
Fox, Dan, ed. *Go in and out the Window*, 14150
Fox, Diane. *Goodnight PiggyWiggy*, 2094(F)
Fox, Mary V. *Bahrain*, 15544
Cyprus, 15267
Douglas MacArthur, 12932
Iran, 15545
Lasers, 20867
New Zealand, 15231
Rockets, 20985
Satellites, 20986
Somalia, 14928
Tunisia, 14957
Fox, Matthew. *The Muppets Big Book of Crafts*, 21457
Fox, Mem. *A Bedtime Story*, 676(F)
Feathers and Fools, 1164(F)
Guess What? 4148(F)
Harriet, You'll Drive Me Wild! 4959(F)
Hattie and the Fox, 2095(F)
Koala Lou, 2096(F)
Night Noises, 5685(F)
Possum Magic, 2097(F)
Shoes from Grandpa, 4149(F)
Sleepy Bears, 677(F)
Sophie, 3629(F)
The Straight Line Wonder, 1165(F)
Time for Bed, 678(F)
Tough Boris, 2930(F)
Whoever You Are, 3630(F)
Wilfrid Gordon McDonald Partridge, 3995(F)
Wombat Divine, 5817(F)
Zoo-Looking, 5210(F)

Fox, Paula. *Amzat and His Brothers*, 11062

How Many Miles to Babylon? 6846(F)

Maurice's Room, 7434(F)

Monkey Island, 8643(F)

One-Eyed Cat, 8429(F)

Radiance Descending, 8644(F)

The Slave Dancer, 9276(F)

The Stone-Faced Boy, 8645(F)

The Village by the Sea, 8646(F)

Western Wind, 8647(F)

Fox-Davies, Sarah. *Little Beaver and the Echo*, 2419(F)

Little Caribou, 5211(F)

Moon Frog, 11777

Walk with a Wolf, 19125

Foxx, Jeffrey J. *Angela Weaves a Dream*, 15685

Fradin, Dennis B. *Alabama*, 16850

Alaska, 16774

Arizona, 16606

Arkansas, 16856

Astronomy, 18390

Bound for the North Star, 16242

California, 16775

The Cheyenne, 15950

Colorado, 16607

Columbus Day, 17354

The Connecticut Colony, 16118

Explorers, 12057

Georgia, 16851

The Georgia Colony, 16119

Hawaii, 16776

Hiawatha, 12974

Ida B. Wells, 12816

Illinois, 16549

Iowa, 16550

Is There Life on Mars? 18469

Kentucky, 16852

Louis Braille, 13759

Maine, 16677

Maria de Sautuola, 13848

The Maryland Colony, 16120

Massachusetts, 16678

Michigan, 16551

Missouri, 16552

Montana, 16608

New Hampshire, 16679

The New Hampshire Colony, 16121

New Jersey, 16680

The New Jersey Colony, 16122

New York, 16681

The New York Colony, 16123

North Carolina, 16853

Ohio, 16553

Oregon, 16777

Pennsylvania, 16682

The Pennsylvania Colony, 16124

Pioneers, 16304

The Planet Hunters, 18470

The Republic of Ireland, 15346

The Rhode Island Colony, 16125

Samuel Adams, 12836

Searching for Alien Life, 18391

The Shoshoni, 15951

The South Carolina Colony, 16126

Tennessee, 16854

Texas, 16905

Utah, 16609

Valentine's Day, 17506

Vermont, 16683

Virginia, 16855

The Virginia Colony, 16127

Washington, D.C., 16684

"We Have Conquered Pain," 13209

Wyoming, 16610

Fradin, Dennis B. (jt. author). *New Mexico*, 16906

Fradin, Judith B. *New Mexico*, 16906

Fradin, Judith B. (jt. author).

Arkansas, 16856

Ida B. Wells, 12816

Oregon, 16777

Wyoming, 16610

Fraggalosch, Audrey. *Great Grizzly Wilderness*, 19046

Fraifield, Denise. *Baby High, Baby Low*, 161(F)

Frame, Paul. *Katie John*, 8411(F)

Frampton, David. *Clouds of Glory*, 17253

Jerusalem, Shining Still, 15524

Joshua in the Promised Land, 17255

Just So Stories, 7245(F)

Of Swords and Sorcerers, 11000

Riding the Tiger, 1026(F)

Whaling Days, 19778

Francis, John. *Animal Hide and Seek*, 18913

Francis, Sandy. *At the Movie Theater*, 21269

Francisco, Melissa. *Shaker Inventions*, 17168

Franco, Betsy. *Why the Frog Has Big Eyes*, 6336(F)

Franco-Feeney, Betsy. *James Bear and the Goose Gathering*, 1340(F)

Frank, Anne. *Anne Frank*, 13798

Frank, John. *The Tomb of the Boy King*, 14625

Frank, Josette, ed. *Poems to Read to the Very Young*, 11567

Frank, Nicole. *Argentina*, 15734

Welcome to Egypt, 15500

Welcome to Greece, 15380

Welcome to Italy, 15379

Welcome to the USA, 15878

Frank, Steven. *Dennis Rodman*, 13573

Frankel, Alona. *Joshua's Book of Clothes*, 3149(F)

Frankeny, Frankie. *The Star Wars Cookbook II*, 21698

Franklin, Kristine L. *Dove Song*, 8430(F)

The Gift, 4433(F)

Iguana Beach, 3150(F)

Lone Wolf, 8431(F)

Nerd No More, 9854(F)

The Shepherd Boy, 2931(F)

When the Monkeys Came Back, 4434(F)

Franklin, Kristine L., ed. *Out of the Dump*, 15663

Franklin, Paula A. (jt. author). *Proudly Red and Black*, 12664

Franklin, Sharon. *Mexico and Central America*, 15615

Scandinavia, 15446

Southwest Pacific, 15232

Franson, Leanne. *The Girl Who Hated Books*, 1463(F)

I Miss Franklin P. Shuckles, 4045(F)

Jessica Takes Charge, 3764(F)

Frantz, Jennifer. *Totem Poles*, 15952

Frascino, Edward. *King Henry the Ape*, 21832

Nanny Noony and the Dust Queen, 2098(F)

Nanny Noony and the Magic Spell, 1166(F)

The Trumpet of the Swan, 8201(F)

Frasconi, Antonio. *Elijah the Slave*, 11171

If the Owl Calls Again, 11800

Platero y Yo/Platero and I, 7229

Fraser, Andy. *Snowboarding*, 22279

Fraser, Betty. *A House Is a House for Me*, 200(F)

The Llama Who Had No Pajama, 11596

Pets in a Jar, 19908

Fraser, Douglas. *David and Goliath*, 17309

Fraser, Mary Ann. *Armadillos and Other Unusual Animals*, 18962

In Search of the Grand Canyon, 16611

A Mission for the People, 16778

Piranhas and Other Wonders of the Jungle, 18653

The Stargazer's Guide to the Galaxy, 18408

Vicksburg, 16407

Where Are the Night Animals? 18813

Why Frogs Are Wet, 18725

Frasier, Debra. *Miss Alaineus*, 8648(F)

On the Day You Were Born, 4435(F)

Out of the Ocean, 4436(F)

Fraustino, Lisa Rowe. *The Hickory Chair*, 4960

Frazee, Marla. *Everywhere Babies*, 3322(F)

Harriet, You'll Drive Me Wild! 4959(F)

Hush, Little Baby, 14155

On the Morn of Mayfest, 1578(F)

The Seven Silly Eaters, 4182(F)

That Kookoory! 2107(F)

World Famous Muriel and the Magic Mystery, 6188(F)

Frazer, Simon. *The Mushroom Hunt*, 20187

Frazier, Nancy. *Frida Kahlo*, 12243
Fredeen, Charles. *Kansas*, 16554
Nellie Bly, 13137
New Jersey, 16685
South Carolina, 16857
Fredericks, Anthony D. *Animal Sharpshooters*, 18897
Cannibal Animals, 18814
Slugs, 19606
Tadpole Tales and Other Totally Terrific Treats for Readers Theatre, 12020
Zebras, 18941
Freedland, Sara. *Hanukkah! A Three-Dimensional Celebration*, 17465
Freedman, Florence B. *It Happened in Chelm*, 11145
Two Tickets to Freedom, 9476(F)
Freedman, Florence B. (jt. author). *Ezra Jack Keats*, 12246
Freedman, Russell. *Babe Didrikson Zaharias*, 13720
Buffalo Hunt, 15953
Children of the Wild West, 16305
Cowboys of the Wild West, 16306
Franklin Delano Roosevelt, 13096
Give Me Liberty! The Story of the Declaration of Independence, 16196
Immigrant Kids, 16463
An Indian Winter, 15954
Kids at Work, 12901
Lincoln, 13066
Martha Graham, 12390
Out of Darkness, 13760
Freedman, Suzanne. *Ida B. Wells-Barnett and the Anti-Lynching Crusade*, 12817
Madeleine Albright, 12840
Freeman, Charles, ed. *The Ancient Greeks*, 14680
Freeman, Don. *Bearymore*, 2099(F)
Corduroy, 2100(F)
Dandelion, 2101(F)
Gregory's Shadow, 2102(F)
Mop Top, 4150(F)
A Rainbow of My Own, 1167(F)
Freeman, Dorothy R. *Kwanzaa*, 17356
St. Patrick's Day, 17355
Freeman, Grace R. (jt. author). *Inside the Synagogue*, 17224
Freeman, Julie. *The Magic Horse*, 11199
Freeman, Martha. *Fourth Grade Weirdo*, 10059(F)
The Polyester Grandpa, 9855(F)
The Trouble with Cats, 8649(F)
Freeman, Mylo. *Shanti*, 2556(F)
Freeman, Suzanne. *The Cuckoo's Child*, 8650(F)
Freixenet, Anna. *Creating with Mosaics*, 21436
Fremon, David K. *The Alaska Purchase in American History*, 16779

The Jim Crow Laws and Racism in American History, 16464
French, Fiona. *Jamil's Clever Cat*, 10791
Lord of the Animals, 11236
Pepi and the Secret Names, 8187(F)
French, Fiona, reteller. *Jamil's Clever Cat*, 10791
French, Jackie. *The Little Book of Big Questions*, 21910
French, Michael (jt. author). *Basher Five-Two*, 12144
French, Simon. *Change the Locks*, 8432(F)
French, Vanessa. *Africa Brothers and Sisters*, 4717(F)
French, Vivian. *Caterpillar Caterpillar*, 19549
A Christmas Star Called Hannah, 5818(F)
Growing Frogs, 5212(F)
The Kingfisher Book of Fairy Tales, 10420(F)
Let's Go, Anna! 4152(F)
Little Tiger Goes Shopping, 2103(F)
Not Again, Anna! 3634(F)
Oh No, Anna! 3151(F)
Oliver's Fruit Salad, 3631(F)
Oliver's Vegetables, 4151(F)
Once upon a Time, 1168(F)
One Ballerina Two, 436(F)
Red Hen and Sly Fox, 2104(F)
A Song for Little Toad, 679(F)
The Story of Christmas, 17417
The Thistle Princess, 10421(F)
Tiger and the New Baby, 3632(F)
Tiger and the Temper Tantrum, 3633(F)
Under the Moon, 7733(F)
Whale Journey, 5213(F)
Why the Sea Is Salty, 11123
Frenck, Hal. *Tecumseh*, 12999
Freschet, Gina. *Naty's Parade*, 4649(F)
Freymann, Saxton. *How Are You Peeling? Foods with Moods*, 4961
One Lonely Sea Horse, 437(F)
Freymann, Saxton (jt. author). *Play with Your Pumpkins*, 21434
Fridell, Ron. *Amphibians in Danger*, 18684
Frieden, Sarajo. *The Care and Feeding of Fish*, 1169(F)
Friedhoffer, Robert. *Magic and Perception*, 21783
Physics Lab in a Hardware Store, 20807
Physics Lab in a Housewares Store, 20808
Science Lab in a Supermarket, 18312
Friedman, Aileen. *A Cloak for the Dreamer*, 8651(F)
The King's Commissioners, 438(F)

Friedman, Ina R. *How My Parents Learned to Eat*, 3635(F)
Friedman, Jim. *The Mysterious Misadventures of Foy Rin Jin*, 2105(F)
Friedman, Judi. *Operation Siberian Crane*, 19230
Friedman, Judith. *Adoption Is for Always*, 3650(F)
After Charlotte's Mom Died, 5083(F)
At Daddy's on Saturdays, 8662(F)
Baby's Bris, 6123(F)
I Speak English for My Mom, 7376(F)
Losing Uncle Tim, 8466(F)
A Safe Place, 5092(F)
Stacy Had a Little Sister, 5045(F)
Tell Me a Mitzvah, 17155
Friedman, Lise. *First Lessons in Ballet*, 14284
Friedman, Mel (jt. author). *Color Me Criminal*, 7125(F)
Friedman, Robin. *How I Survived My Summer Vacation*, 9856(F)
Friedman, Susan L. (jt. author). *All My Feelings at Preschool*, 5490(F)
Friedrich, Elizabeth. *Leah's Pony*, 4650(F)
Friedrich, Otto (jt. author). *The Easter Bunny That Overslept*, 5966(F)
Friedrich, Priscilla. *The Easter Bunny That Overslept*, 5966(F)
Friend, Catherine. *My Head Is Full of Colors*, 1170(F)
Silly Ruby, 6337(F)
Friend, David. *Baseball, Football, Daddy and Me*, 3636(F)
Frienz, D. J. *Where Will Nana Go Next?* 4153(F)
Fries, Claudia. *A Pig Is Moving In!* 2106(F)
Friesen, Gayle. *Men of Stone*, 8652(F)
Friestad, Kathleen (jt. author). *The Kids' Book of Weather Forecasting*, 20756
Frisch, Carlienne. *Wyoming*, 16612
Frissen. *Yann and the Whale*, 1171(F)
Fritz, Jean. *Around the World in a Hundred Years*, 12058
Brady, 9277(F)
Bully for You, Teddy Roosevelt! 13101
The Cabin Faced West, 9231(F)
The Double Life of Pocahontas, 12984
George Washington's Breakfast, 9232(F)
George Washington's Mother, 13200
The Great Little Madison, 13082
Harriet Beecher Stowe and the Beecher Preachers, 12604

Homesick, 12536
Just a Few Words, Mr. Lincoln, 16408
Make Way for Sam Houston, 12903
Shh! We're Writing the Constitution, 17056
Surprising Myself, 12537
Where Do You Think You're Going, Christopher Columbus? 12099
Why Don't You Get a Horse, Sam Adams? 12837
Why Not, Lafayette? 13825
Will You Sign Here, John Hancock? 12896
You Want Women to Vote, Lizzie Stanton? 13192
Fritz, Ron. *My Dog Talks*, 6381(F)
Froehlich, Margaret W. *That Kookoory!* 2107(F)
Froese, Deborah. *The Wise Washerman*, 10725
Froman, Nan. *What's That Bug?* 19443
Fromental, Jean-Luc. *Broadway Chicken*, 7734(F)
Fromer, Julie. *Jane Goodall*, 13299
Fromm, Pete. *Monkey Tag*, 8653(F)
Frost, Helen. *Drinking Water*, 18192
Eating Right, 18193
Feeling Angry, 17607
The Fruit Group, 20142
The Grain Group, 20092
Frost, Jonathan. *Gowanus Dogs*, 5214(F)
Frost, Kristi. *Kitoto the Mighty*, 10702
Frost, Robert. *Birches*, 11950
The Runaway, 11788
Stopping by Woods on a Snowy Evening, 11568
A Swinger of Birches, 11569
You Come Too, 11570
Froud, Brian. *Are All the Giants Dead?* 7996(F)
Froud, Wendy. *A Midsummer Night's Faery Tale*, 7735(F)
Fruisen, Catherine Myler. *My Mother's Pearls*, 3637(F)
Fuchs, Bernie. *Raising Yoder's Barn*, 3494(F)
The Wolves, 19122
Fuchs, Diane M. *A Bear for All Seasons*, 2108(F)
Fuchshuber, Annegert. *Augsburg Story Bible*, 17237
Two Peas in a Pod, 439(F)
Fuenmayor, Morella. *A Bicycle for Rosaura*, 1787(F)
The Spirit of Tio Fernando, 5634(F)
Fuge, Charles (jt. author). *Whale Is Stuck*, 2180(F)
Fuhr, Ute (jt. author). *Whales*, 19783
Fulk, Ken (jt. author). *Shake, Rattle and Roll*, 236(F)
This and That, 237(F)

Fulkerston, Chuck. *The Shawnee*, 15955
Fuller, Barbara. *Britain*, 15347
Germany, 15322
Fuller, Elizabeth. *My Brown Bear Barney at the Party*, 5668(F)
Fullick, Ann. *Charles Darwin*, 13265
Louis Pasteur, 13338
Funai, Mamoru. *Dolphin*, 19687
Funston, Sylvia. *Animal Feelings*, 18815
Animal Smarts, 18816
The Book of You, 17608
Mummies, 14548
Furlong, Arlene. *Argentina*, 15735
Furlong, Kate A. *Mexico*, 15616
Futran, Eric. *A Baby's Coming to Your House!* 18234
Somewhere Today, 251(F)

Gaarder, Jostein. *Hello? Is Anybody There?* 7736(F)
Gaber, Susan. *The Baker's Dozen*, 11337
Bit by Bit, 4301(F)
The Brave Little Parrot, 10800
Jordi's Star, 942(F)
The Language of Birds, 11104
Pierre's Dream, 4079(F)
Raisel's Riddle, 11170
Small Talk, 11959
The Stable Where Jesus Was Born, 5827
Stone Soup, 10870
When Winter Comes, 5441(F)
The Woman Who Flummoxed the Fairies, 10976
Gabhart, Ann. *Two of a Kind*, 8286(F)
Gabor, A. *Polish Americans*, 17557
Gabrielpillai, Matilda. *Bosnia and Herzegovina*, 15268
Gabrielson, Ira N. (jt. author). *Birds*, 19301
Gac-Artigas, Alejandro. *Yo, Alejandro*, 12830
Gackenbach, Dick. *A Bag Full of Pups*, 5215(F)
Barker's Crime, 1172(F)
Claude the Dog, 5819(F)
Harry and the Terrible Whatzit, 1173(F)
Mighty Tree, 4437
The Monster in the Third Dresser Drawer and Other Stories About Adam Joshua, 7516(F)
With Love from Gran, 3638(F)
Gadbois, Nick. *Looking Inside Sunken Treasure*, 14539
Looking Inside Telescopes and the Night Sky, 18413
Gaeddert, Louann. *Breaking Free*, 9278(F)
Hope, 9366(F)
Gaff, Jackie. *1900–20*, 13891
Gaffney, Timothy R. *Secret Spy Satellites*, 20987

Gaffney-Kessell, Walter. *Daddy Will Be There*, 3657(F)
One Day in the Alpine Tundra, 20371
Gag, Wanda. *Millions of Cats*, 5216(F)
Gage, Wilson. *My Stars, It's Mrs. Gaddy*, 4154(F)
Gaillard, Frye (jt. author). *Spacechimp*, 20984
Gaines, Ann Graham. *Britney Spears*, 12470
Jim Bowie, 12855
Matthew Henson and the North Pole Expedition, 12121
Melissa Joan Hart, 12396
The Panama Canal in American History, 15664
Steve Jobs, 12912
Gal, Laszlo. *Islands*, 3900(F)
The Parrot, 11063
Tiktala, 1567(F)
Gal, Raffaella (jt. author). *The Parrot*, 11063
Galan, Mark. *There's Still Time*, 19396
Galante, Louis R. *The World of the Pharaoh*, 14646
Galbraith, Kathryn O. *Holding onto Sunday*, 7435(F)
Laura Charlotte, 3639(F)
Look! Snow! 3152(F)
Roommates, 6338(F)
Roommates Again, 8287(F)
Something Suspicious, 6847(F)
Galchutt, David. *There Was Magic Inside*, 1174(F)
Galdone, Joanna. *The Tailypo*, 11338
Galdone, Paul. *Basil of Baker Street*, 8148(F)
The Complete Story of the Three Blind Mice, 852(F)
The Dog Who Wouldn't Be, 7272(F)
The Elves and the Shoemaker, 10895
George Washington's Breakfast, 9232(F)
The Gingerbread Boy, 10978
Henny Penny, 10979
The Lemonade Trick, 9814(F)
The Little Red Hen, 10980
The Magic Porridge Pot, 1175(F)
The Monkey and the Crocodile, 10792
Over in the Meadow, 440(F)
Puss in Boots, 10878
Rumpelstiltskin, 10904
The Sword in the Tree, 9083(F)
The Tailypo, 11338
The Three Bears, 10981
The Three Billy Goats Gruff, 11124
Three Ducks Went Wandering, 5391(F)
Three Little Kittens, 844
The Three Little Pigs, 10982
The Turtle and the Monkey, 10847

Galeron, Henri. *Dinosaurs*, 14401

Galicich, Anne. *The German Americans*, 17558

Galindo, Mary Sue. *Icy Watermelon / Sandia fria*, 3640(F)

Gallagher, Catharine. *The Boy Who Sat by the Window*, 8477(F)

Gallagher, Jim. *Ferdinand Magellan and the First Voyage Around the World*, 12140

Shania Twain, 12478

Gallagher, Kristin Ellersbusch. *Cottontail Rabbits*, 19196

Gallagher, S. Saelig. *Blue Willow*, 8990(F)

Gallant, Jonathan R. *The Tales Fossils Tell*, 14415

Gallant, Roy A. *Comets, Asteroids, and Meteorites*, 18393

Dance of the Continents, 20305

Early Humans, 14497

Earth's Place in Space, 18430

The Ever-Changing Atom, 20286

Fossils, 14416

Geysers, 20306

Glaciers, 20359

The Life Stories of Stars, 18394

Limestone Caves, 20370

Minerals, 20556

Planets, 18471

Rocks, 20557

Sand on the Move, 20558

Space Stations, 20988

Stars, 18545

Water, 20735

Gallardo, Evelyn. *Among the Orangutans*, 13288

Gallimard Jeunesse. *Atlas of Islands*, 14338

Dogs, 19947

Fish, 19702

Houses, 21158

Internet, 21201

Lions, 19087

Monkeys and Apes, 18993

Native Americans, 15956

Trains, 21332

Gallimard Jeunesse (jt. author). *Vegetables in the Garden*, 20172

Galloway, Priscilla. *Aleta and the Queen*, 11473(F)

Daedalus and the Minotaur, 11474

Galouchko, Annouchka Gravel. *The Walking Stick*, 4856(F)

Galvez, Daniel. *It Doesn't Have to Be This Way*, 7367(F)

Galvin, Irene F. *Japan*, 15121

Galvin, Laura Gates. *Bumblebee at Apple Tree Lane*, 5217(F)

Gamble, Kim. *Dear Fred*, 5059(F)

Gamgee, John. *Journey Through France*, 15305

Gamlin, Linda. *Evolution*, 14498

Gammell, Stephen. *Airmail to the Moon*, 3026(F)

Come a Tide, 3290(F)

Dancing Teepees, 11931

Is That You, Winter? 1176(F)

Monster Mama, 1525(F)

More Scary Stories to Tell in the Dark, 11380

Old Black Fly, 5(F)

Once Upon MacDonald's Farm, 14151

Once Upon MacDonald's Farm . . ., 5218(F)

A Regular Rolling Noah, 4220(F)

The Relatives Came, 3869(F)

Scary Stories 3, 7046(F)

Scary Stories to Tell in the Dark, 11381

Song and Dance Man, 3501(F)

Twigboy, 1177(F)

Wake Up, Bear . . . It's Christmas! 5820(F)

Who Kidnapped the Sheriff? 9796(F)

Will's Mammoth, 929(F)

The Wing Shop, 1706(F)

Gampert, John. *The Greatest Sports Stories Never Told*, 22039

Gan, Delice. *Sweden*, 15447

Gandolfi, Peter. *Jerusalem 3000*, 15526

Ganeri, Anita. *The Ancient Romans*, 14718

Exploration into India, 15100

Growing Up, 17184

How Would You Survive as an Ancient Roman? 14719

The Hunt for Food, 18625

I Remember Bosnia, 15269

I Wonder Why the Sea Is Salty, 19817

Inside the Body, 18059

Journey's End, 17357

The Kingfisher First Science Encyclopedia, 18277

New Beginnings, 17358

Out of the Ark, 17185

Rivers, Ponds and Lakes, 20514

The Search for Tombs, 14527

The Story of Communications, 21260

The Story of Maps and Navigation, 14367

The Story of Numbers and Counting, 20630

The Story of Time and Clocks, 20645

The Story of Weights and Measures, 20657

The Story of Writing and Printing, 13996

Wedding Days, 17359

What Do We Know About Buddhism? 17186

What Do We Know About Hinduism? 17187

The Young Person's Guide to Shakespeare, 12050

The Young Person's Guide to the Ballet, 14285

The Young Person's Guide to the Orchestra, 14221

Ganeri, Anita (jt. author). *The Search for Sunken Treasure*, 14521

Gannett, Ruth. *Miss Hickory*, 7576(F)

My Father's Dragon, 9857(F)

My Mother Is the Most Beautiful Woman in the World, 11109

Gans, Roma. *How Do Birds Find Their Way?* 19231

Let's Go Rock Collecting, 20559

Gantos, Jack. *Back to School for Rotten Ralph*, 2109(F)

Happy Birthday, Rotten Ralph, 5686(F)

Heads or Tails, 6848(F)

Jack on the Tracks, 6849(F)

Jack's New Power, 9132(F)

Joey Pigza Loses Control, 8654(F)

Joey Pigza Swallowed the Key, 8890(F)

Not So Rotten Ralph, 2110(F)

Rotten Ralph, 2111(F)

Rotten Ralph's Rotten Christmas, 5821(F)

Rotten Ralph's Rotten Romance, 6167(F)

Rotten Ralph's Show and Tell, 2112(F)

Rotten Ralph's Trick or Treat, 5998(F)

Wedding Bells for Rotten Ralph, 2113(F)

Gantschev, Ivan. *Where Is Mr. Mole?* 2114(F)

Where the Moon Lives, 2115(F)

Gao, R. L. *Adventures of Monkey King*, 10752(F)

Garassino, Alessandro. *Life*, 14499

Plants, 20234

Garaway, Margaret K. *Ashkii and His Grandfather*, 4651(F)

Garay, Luis. *A Handful of Seeds*, 4689(F)

The Long Road, 4652(F)

Pedrito's Day, 4653(F)

Popol Vuh, 11411

Garber, Sean. *Where Will Nana Go Next?* 4153(F)

Garcia, Carolyn. *Moonboy*, 6339(F)

Garcia, Cheo (jt. author). *Pick a Pet*, 5387(F)

Garcia, Geronimo. *A Gift from PapaDiego*, 3870(F)

Grandma Fina and Her Wonderful Umbrellas/La Abuelita Fina y Sus Sombrillas Maravillosas, 4295(F)

Garcia, Guy. *Spirit of the Maya*, 15665

Garcia, Jerry. *There Ain't No Bugs on Me*, 14241

Garcia, Stephanie. *Snapshots from the Wedding*, 3436(F)

Garcia, T. R. *The Town Mouse and the Country Mouse*, 11053

Gardella, Tricia. *Blackberry Booties*, 3153(F)
Casey's New Hat, 3154(F)
Just Like My Dad, 3155(F)
Gardella, Tricia, comp. *Writers in the Kitchen*, 21699
Garden, Nancy. *Holly's Secret*, 8655(F)
Gardiner, John Reynolds. *General Butterfingers*, 6850(F)
Stone Fox, 7340(F)
Top Secret, 9858(F)
Gardiner, Lindsey. *Here Come Poppy and Max*, 3156(F)
Gardner, Jane M. *Henry Moore*, 12269
Gardner, Martin. *Classic Brainteasers*, 21866
Perplexing Puzzles and Tantalizing Teasers, 20616
Gardner, Richard A. *Boys and Girls Book About Divorce*, 17652
The Girls and Boys Book About Good and Bad Behavior, 17609
Gardner, Robert. *Celebrating Earth Day*, 17360
Experiments with Balloons, 20669
Experiments with Bubbles, 20809
Experiments with Light and Mirrors, 20868
Experiments with Motion, 20829
The Forgotten Players, 22091
Kitchen Chemistry, 18313
Projects in Space Science, 18314
Science Around the House, 18315
Science Project Ideas About Air, 20668
Science Project Ideas About Animal Behavior, 18817
Science Project Ideas About Rain, 20767
Science Project Ideas About the Moon, 18445
Science Project Ideas About the Sun, 20850
Science Project Ideas About Trees, 20201
Science Projects About Electricity and Magnets, 20894
Science Projects About Light, 20869
Science Projects About Plants, 20235
Science Projects About Temperature and Heat, 20853
Science Projects About the Human Body, 18060
Garelick, May. *Look at the Moon*, 680(F)
What Makes a Bird a Bird? 19232
Garelli, Cristina. *Farm Friends Clean Up*, 2116(F)
Garfield, James B. *Follow My Leader*, 8891(F)
Garland, Michael. *Electra and the Charlotte Russe*, 9780(F)

An Elf for Christmas, 5822(F)
Icarus Swinebuckle, 2117(F)
Leah's Pony, 4650(F)
Garland, Sherry. *Cabin 102*, 7737(F)
A Line in the Sand, 9279(F)
The Lotus Seed, 7341(F)
My Father's Boat, 3641(F)
The Silent Storm, 6851(F)
The Summer Sands, 3157(F)
Vietnam, 15158
Voices of the Alamo, 16243
Garne, S. T. *By a Blazing Blue Sea*, 4654(F)
One White Sail, 441(F)
Garner, Alan. *Once upon a Time*, 10551
The Well of the Wind, 7738(F)
Garner, Alan, reteller. *The Little Red Hen*, 10983
Garnett, Ron. *Great Black Heroes*, 13213(F)
Garns, Allen. *The Gift Stone*, 4642(F)
Gonna Sing My Head Off! 14162
When I Go Camping with Grandma, 4385(F)
Garousi, Ali. *Great Discoveries and Inventions That Advanced Industry and Technology*, 21025
Garrett, Ann. *Keeper of the Swamp*, 3642(F)
What's for Lunch? 5219(F)
Garrigue, Sheila. *The Eternal Spring of Mr. Ito*, 9659(F)
Garrison, Barbara. *Look at the Moon*, 680(F)
One Room School, 14877
Only One, 460(F)
Garrison, Christian. *The Dream Eater*, 10813
Garrison, Susan. *How Emily Blair Got Her Fabulous Hair*, 4155(F)
Garrity, Jennifer Johnson. *The Bushwhacker*, 9477(F)
Gartman, Gene. *Life in Army Basic Training*, 21384
Garwood, Val. *The World of the Pirate*, 14549
Garza, Carmen Lomas. *Magic Windows*, 16907
Making Magic Windows, 21615
Garza, Hedda. *Frida Kahlo*, 12244
Gascoigne, Christina. *Ruby the Christmas Donkey*, 5778(F)
Gascoigne, Marc. *You Can Surf the Net!* 21202
Gasque, Dale Blackwell. *Pony Trouble*, 7192(F)
Gates, Donald. *The Summer of Stanley*, 2949(F)
Gates, Doris. *Blue Willow*, 7436(F)
A Fair Wind for Troy, 11475
Lord of the Sky, 11476
Gates, Phil. *The History News*, 18020
Nature Got There First, 18278
Gates, Richard. *Conservation*, 16956
Gatti, Anne, reteller. *The Magic Flute*, 14128

Gauch, Patricia L. *Bravo, Tanya*, 4962(F)
Christina Katerina and Fats and the Great Neighborhood War, 3996(F)
Christina Katerina and the Great Bear Train, 3643(F)
Noah, 17270
Poppy's Puppet, 1178(F)
Presenting Tanya, the Ugly Duckling, 4963(F)
Tanya and Emily in a Dance for Two, 3997(F)
Tanya and the Magic Wardrobe, 3158(F)
This Time, Tempe Wick? 9233(F)
Gauthier, Gail. *Club Earth*, 10183(F)
The Hero of Ticonderoga, 10060(F)
My Life Among the Aliens, 10184(F)
A Year with Butch and Spike, 10061(F)
Gay, Douglas. *The Not-So-Minor Leagues*, 22092
Gay, Kathlyn. *Civil War*, 16409
Korean War, 16506
Persian Gulf War, 15489
Revolutionary War, 16197
Science in Ancient Greece, 14681
Spanish-American War, 16465
They Don't Wash Their Socks! 22003
Vietnam War, 16507
War of 1812, 16244
World War I, 14808
World War II, 14852
Gay, Kathlyn (jt. author). *The Not-So-Minor Leagues*, 22092
Gay, Marie-Louise. *The Christmas Orange*, 5824(F)
The Fabulous Song, 4162(F)
Fat Charlie's Circus, 4156(F)
How to Take Your Grandmother to the Museum, 3960(F)
On My Island, 1179(F)
Rumpelstiltskin, 10890
Stella, 3159(F)
Stella, Queen of the Snow, 3160(F)
Yuck, a Love Story, 1191(F)
Gay, Marie-Louise, adapt. *Rumpelstiltskin*, 10890
Gay, Marie-Louise (jt. author). *Dreams Are More Real than Bathtubs*, 5522(F)
Gay, Martin (jt. author). *Civil War*, 16409
Korean War, 16506
Persian Gulf War, 15489
Revolutionary War, 16197
Spanish-American War, 16465
Vietnam War, 16507
War of 1812, 16244
World War I, 14808
World War II, 14852
Gayle, Katie. *Snappy Jazzy Jewelry*, 21437

Gearhart, Sarah. *The Telephone*, 21261

Gedatus, Gus. *Violence in Public Places*, 17137

Geehan, Wayne. *Twenty Thousand Leagues Under the Sea*, 7112(F)

Geer, Charles. *Plain Girl*, 8820(F)

Geeslin, Campbell. *How Nanita Learned to Make Flan*, 1180(F)
On Ramon's Farm, 5220(F)

Gehm, Charles C. *Soup*, 8358(F)

Gehret, Jeanne. *The Don't-Give-Up-Kid and Learning Differences*, 4964(F)

Geiger, John (jt. author). *Buried in Ice*, 15566

Geis, Jacqueline. *Where the Buffalo Roam*, 11951

Geisert, Arthur. *After the Flood*, 17271
The Ark, 17247
Desert Town, 3161(F)
The Etcher's Studio, 1181(F)
Mountain Town, 3162(F)
Oink, 2118(F)
Oink Oink, 917(F)
Pigs from A to Z, 41(F)
Pigs from 1 to 10, 442(F)
River Town, 3163
Roman Numerals I to MM, 20631

Geisert, Arthur (jt. author). *Haystack*, 20056
Prairie Town, 3164(F)

Geisert, Bonnie. *Desert Town*, 3161(F)
Haystack, 20056
Mountain Town, 3162(F)
Prairie Town, 3164(F)
River Town, 3163

Gelber, Carol. *Love and Marriage Around the World*, 17361
Masks Tell Stories, 14550

Geldart, William. *The Fairy Rebel*, 10398(F)

Gellman, Marc. *"Always Wear Clean Underwear!" and Other Ways Parents Say "I Love You."* 17653
Does God Have a Big Toe? 17272
God's Mailbox, 17273
How Do You Spell God? 17188
Lost and Found, 17703

Gelman, Amy. *My Pet Ferrets*, 19890

Gelman, Rita G. *Monkeys and Apes of the World*, 18994
Pizza Pat, 6340(F)
Queen Esther Saves Her People, 6071
Rice Is Life, 20093

Gelsanliter, Wendy. *Dancin' in the Kitchen*, 3644(F)

Gennings, Sara. *The Atocha Treasure*, 19874

Gentieu, Penny. *Baby! Talk!* 3645(F)
Grow! Babies! 18231
Wow! Babies! 3646(F)

Geoghegan, Adrienne. *Dogs Don't Wear Glasses*, 4157(F)

George, Bob. *Card Games for Children*, 22230

George, Charles. *Idaho*, 16613
Montana, 16614

George, Charles (jt. author). *Civil Rights Marches*, 17559
Jimmy Carter, 13015
Luis Munoz Marin, 12936

George, Jean Craighead. *Arctic Son*, 4655(F)
The Cry of the Crow, 7193(F)
Dear Katie, the Volcano Is a Girl, 4438(F)
Elephant Walk, 5221(F)
Everglades, 16858
The First Thanksgiving, 17496
Frightful's Mountain, 7194(F)
Giraffe Trouble, 5222(F)
How to Talk to Your Cat, 19920
How to Talk to Your Dog, 19948
Julie, 6852(F)
Julie of the Wolves, 6853(F)
Julie's Wolf Pack, 6854(F)
Look to the North, 5223(F)
Morning, Noon, and Night, 18626
Nutik, the Wolf Pup, 4656(F)
One Day in the Alpine Tundra, 20371
One Day in the Desert, 20403
One Day in the Tropical Rain Forest, 20442
One Day in the Woods, 20443(F)
Rhino Romp, 5224(F)
Snow Bear, 5225(F)
The Summer of the Falcon, 8656(F)
The Talking Earth, 6855(F)
There's an Owl in the Shower, 7195(F)

George, Kristine O'Connell. *The Great Frog Race and Other Poems*, 11952
Little Dog Poems, 11789
Old Elm Speaks, 11953
Toasting Marshmallows, 11954

George, Linda. *Alcatraz*, 16780
Civil Rights Marches, 17559
Jimmy Carter, 13015
Luis Munoz Marin, 12936

George, Linda (jt. author). *Idaho*, 16613
Montana, 16614

George, Lindsay B. *Box Turtle at Long Pond*, 4441(F)

George, Lindsay Barrett. *Around the Pond*, 4439(F)
Around the World, 5226(F)
In the Snow, 4440(F)
My Bunny and Me, 681(F)

George, Michael. *Glaciers*, 20360
The Sun, 18566
Wolves, 19119

George, Twig C. *A Dolphin Named Bob*, 7196(F)
Jellies, 19660
Swimming with Sharks, 6856(F)

George, William T. *Box Turtle at Long Pond*, 4441(F)

George-Kanentiio, Douglas M. (jt. author). *Skywoman*, 11299

George-Warren, Holly. *Shake, Rattle and Roll*, 14129

Gerard, Elena. *Even a Little Is Something*, 8995(F)

Geras, Adele. *The Fabulous Fantoras*, 9859(F)
The Fabulous Fantoras, Book Two, 7739(F)
From Lullaby to Lullaby, 1182(F)
The Random House Book of Opera Stories, 14130

Gerber, Carole. *Firefly Night*, 682(F)
Hush! 683(F)

Gerber, Mary Jane. *A Gift for Ampato*, 9141(F)

Gerber, Pesach. *Nine Spoons*, 6119(F)

Gergely, Tibor. *Wheel on the Chimney*, 5146(F)

Gerig, Sibyl G. *Fiddlin' Sam*, 4944(F)
The Worry Stone, 11228

Geringer, Laura. *The Pomegranate Seeds*, 11477
A Three Hat Day, 4158(F)

Gerke, Pamela. *Multicultural Plays for Children Grades K–3*, 12021

Germaine, Elizabeth. *Cooking the Australian Way*, 21700

Germein, Katrina. *Big Rain Coming*, 4657(F)

Gernand, Renee. *The Cuban Americans*, 17560

Gerrard, Roy. *Croco'Nile*, 4658(F)
The Favershams, 12534
The Roman Twins, 4659(F)
Sir Cedric, 4660(F)
Wagons West! 2932(F)

Gershator, David. *Bread Is for Eating*, 3165(F)
Palampam Day, 1183(F)

Gershator, David (jt. author). *Greetings, Sun*, 4661(F)

Gershator, Phillis. *Greetings, Sun*, 4661(F)
Only One Cowry, 10666
Tiny and Bigman, 2933(F)
Tukama Tootles the Flute, 11421
When It Starts to Snow, 2119(F)
Zzzng! Zzzng! Zzzng! A Yoruba Tale, 10667

Gershator, Phillis (jt. author). *Bread Is for Eating*, 3165(F)
Palampam Day, 1183(F)

Gershom, Griffith. *Journey to Freedom*, 9338(F)

Gershwin, George. *Summertime*, 14242

Gerson, Corrine. *My Grandfather the Spy*, 6857(F)

Gerstein, Mordicai. *The Absolutely Awful Alphabet*, 42
Albert and the Angels, 9752(F)

Bedtime, Everybody! 684(F)
Behind the Couch, 1184(F)
Daisy's Garden, 2120(F)
Frankenstein Moved In on the Fourth Floor, 6944(F)
The Giant, 7740(F)
The Jar of Fools, 11155(F)
Jonah and the Two Great Fish, 17274
The Mountains of Tibet, 4662(F)
Noah and the Great Flood, 17275
Queen Esther, the Morning Star, 17466
The Shadow of a Flying Bird, 11146
Something Queer at the Library, 6946(F)
Something Queer in the Wild West, 6947(F)
Stop Those Pants! 1185(F)
The Wild Boy, 4663
Gerstenfeld, Sheldon L. *Zoo Clues,* 20024
Geter, Tyrone. *Dawn and the Round To-It,* 3898(F)
Sunday Week, 3729(F)
White Socks Only, 4624(F)
Willie Jerome, 3611(F)
Getz, David. *Almost Famous,* 9860(F)
Floating Home, 1186(F)
Frozen Girl, 15736
Frozen Man, 14500
Life on Mars, 18472
Purple Death, 17958
Gewing, Lisa. *Mama, Daddy, Baby and Me,* 3647(F)
Ghazi, Suhaib Hamid. *Ramadan,* 5627
Ghent, Natale. *Piper,* 7197(F)
Gherman, Beverly. *The Mysterious Rays of Dr. Roentgen,* 13343
Norman Rockwell, 12295
Robert Louis Stevenson, 12600
Ghez, Andrea Mia. *You Can Be a Woman Astronomer,* 17825
Ghigna, Charles. *Christmas Is Coming,* 11830
Mice Are Nice, 6341(F)
Ghigna, Debra (jt. author). *Christmas Is Coming,* 11830
Giacobello, John. *Everything You Need to Know About Anxiety and Panic Attacks,* 17908
Gianfriddo, Fran. *Tooth Fairy Travels,* 7790(F)
Giannini, Enzo. *Zorina Ballerina,* 2121(F)
Gibala-Broxholm, Janice. *Let Me Do It!* 4159(F)
Gibbie, Mike. *Small Brown Dog's Bad Remembering Day,* 2122(F)
Gibbons, Faye. *Hook Moon Night,* 7741(F)
Mama and Me and the Model T, 4160(F)
Mountain Wedding, 4161(F)

Gibbons, Gail. *Apples,* 20143
The Art Box, 13892
Bats, 19024
Beacons of Light, 21358
Behold . . . the Dragons! 10552
Bicycle Book, 22157
Boat Book, 5566(F)
Cats, 19921
Check It Out, 13997
Click! A Book About Cameras and Taking Pictures, 21798
Deadline! 14082
Dinosaurs, 14417
Dogs, 19949
Easter, 5967
Emergency! 5567
Exploring the Deep, Dark Sea, 19818
Farming, 20057
Fire! Fire! 3166(F)
Frogs, 18722
From Path to Highway, 16686
From Seed to Plant, 20270
The Great St. Lawrence Seaway, 15574
Gulls . . . Gulls . . . Gulls, 19348
Halloween, 17444
The Honey Makers, 19523
How a House Is Built, 3167
Knights in Shining Armor, 14763
Marshes and Swamps, 20372
The Milk Makers, 20094
Monarch Butterfly, 19550
The Moon Book, 18446
My Baseball Book, 22093
My Basketball Book, 22131
My Football Book, 22182
My Soccer Book, 22291
Nature's Green Umbrella, 20444
New Road! 5568(F)
Paper, Paper Everywhere, 3168(F)
Penguins! 19371
Pigs, 18942
Pirates, 14551
Planet Earth/Inside Out, 20307
The Planets, 18473
Playgrounds, 183(F)
The Post Office Book, 17111
Prehistoric Animals, 14418
The Pumpkin Book, 20175
Rabbits, Rabbits and More Rabbits! 19891
The Reasons for Seasons, 4442
St. Patrick's Day, 17362
Santa Who? 5823(F)
Sea Turtles, 18782
The Seasons of Arnold's Apple Tree, 4443(F)
Sharks, 19758
Soaring with the Wind, 19324
Spiders, 19580
Stargazers, 18546
Sun Up, Sun Down, 18567
Sunken Treasure, 19875
Thanksgiving Day, 17497
Tool Book, 21662
Trains, 21333(F)

Up Goes the Skyscraper! 21123
Valentine's Day, 17507
Weather Forecasting, 20768
Weather Words and What They Mean, 20769
Whales, 19788
Wolves, 19120
Yippee-Yay! 16307
Giblin, James Cross. *The Amazing Life of Benjamin Franklin,* 12881
The Dwarf, the Giant, and the Unicorn, 1187(F)
Fireworks, Picnics, and Flags, 17363
The Mystery of the Mammoth Bones, 14419
The Riddle of the Rosetta Stone, 14626
Thomas Jefferson, 13049
Gibson, Barbara. *Explore a Tropical Forest,* 20435
Star Wars, 10247(F)
Gibson, Gary. *Hearing Sounds,* 20938
Light and Color, 20870
Making Shapes, 18316
Making Things Change, 18317
Pushing and Pulling, 20810
Understanding Electricity, 20895
Gibson, Karen Bush. *Child Care Workers,* 17750
Emergency Medical Technicians, 17800
Mississippi Facts and Symbols, 16859
Nevada Facts and Symbols, 16615
North Dakota Facts and Symbols, 16555
Oklahoma Facts and Symbols, 16556
Giddens, Sandra. *Escape,* 14853
Gieck, Charlene. *Bald Eagles,* 19325
Giesecke, Ernestine. *Desert Plants,* 20404
Forest Plants, 20445
Frederic Remington, 12290
Governments Around the World, 17020
Local Government, 17131
Mary Cassatt, 12200
National Government, 17112
Pond Plants, 20515
River Plants, 20516
Seashore Plants, 19859
State Government, 17130
Wetland Plants, 20517
Gietzen, Jean. *If You're Missing Baby Jesus,* 9722(F)
Gifaldi, David. *Ben, King of the River,* 4965(F)
Toby Scudder, Ultimate Warrior, 8657(F)
Giff, Patricia Reilly. *The Beast in Ms. Rooney's Room,* 6342(F)
Fourth Grade Celebrity, 10062(F)

Garbage Juice for Breakfast, 6343(F)

The Gift of the Pirate Queen, 8658(F)

A Glass Slipper for Rosie, 7437(F)

Good Luck, Ronald Morgan! 6344(F)

Happy Birthday, Ronald Morgan! 5687(F)

Have You Seen Hyacinth Macaw? 6858(F)

In the Dinosaur's Paw, 6345(F)

Kidnap at the Catfish Cafe, 6859(F)

Laura Ingalls Wilder, 12628

Left-Handed Shortstop, 10327(F)

Lily's Crossing, 9660(F)

Look Out, Washington, D.C.! 10063(F)

Love, from the Fifth-Grade Celebrity, 8288(F)

Mary Moon Is Missing, 6860(F)

Mother Teresa, 13853

Next Stop, New York City! 6346(F)

Nory Ryan's Song, 9094(F)

Not-So-Perfect Rosie, 9861(F)

Pet Parade, 5501(F)

Poopsie Pomerantz, Pick Up Your Feet, 8659(F)

The Powder Puff Puzzle, 6347(F)

Purple Climbing Days, 6348(F)

Rat Teeth, 8433(F)

Ronald Morgan Goes to Bat, 4966(F)

Starring Rosie, 8660(F)

Sunny-Side Up, 6349(F)

Today Was a Terrible Day, 5502(F)

Turkey Trouble, 9723(F)

Giffard, Hannah. *Is There Room on the Bus?* 554(F)

Gifford, Clive. *How the Future Began,* 21034

Machines, 21247

Giganti, Paul. *Each Orange Had Eight Slices,* 443

How Many Snails? 444(F)

Gilbert, Adrian. *Arms and Armor,* 21385

The French Revolution, 15306

Gilbert, Alma, ed. *Maxfield Parrish,* 13956

Gilbert, Anne Y. *A Christmas Star Called Hannah,* 5818(F)

Gilbert, Lyn. *The Song of Six Birds,* 4636(F)

Gilbert, Nancy. *Wimbledon,* 22312

Gilbert, Suzie. *Hawk Hill,* 7198(F)

Gilbert, Tom. *Roberto Clemente,* 13443

Gilbert, Yvonne. *Night of the White Stag,* 10431(F)

Per and the Dala Horse, 1237(F)

Gilchrist, Cherry. *A Calendar of Festivals,* 10553

Stories from the Silk Road, 10554

Sun-Day, Moon-Day, 10555

Gilchrist, Jan S. *Angels,* 11579

Big Friend, Little Friend, 3182(F)

Easter Parade, 7342(F)

Everett Anderson's Christmas Coming, 5785(F)

First Pink Light, 3660(F)

For the Love of the Game, 11996

Honey, I Love, 3999(F)

I Can Draw a Weeposaur and Other Dinosaurs, 11873

Lemonade Sun and Other Summer Poems, 11553

Lift Ev'ry Voice and Sing, 14158

Nathaniel Talking, 11758

Singing Down the Rain, 1083(F)

Waiting for Christmas, 5828(F)

Water, Water, 3183(F)

William and the Good Old Days, 3664(F)

Gilchrist, Jan Spivey. *Indigo and Moonlight Gold,* 3648(F)

Gilden, Mel. *Outer Space and All That Junk,* 10185(F)

The Pumpkins of Time, 10186(F)

Giles, Gail. *Breath of the Dragon,* 8994(F)

Gilfoy, Bruce. *Whisper Whisper Jesse, Whisper Whisper Josh,* 5051(F)

Gilks, Helen. *Bears,* 19047

Gill, Janet. *Basket Weaver and Catches Many Mice,* 1188(F)

Gill, Madeline. *The Spring Hat,* 2123(F)

Gill, Margery. *Dawn of Fear,* 8271(F)

Gill, Shelly. *Alaska's Three Bears,* 5227(F)

Gillard, Denise. *Music from the Sky,* 3649(F)

Gilleece, David. *In the Land of the Big Red Apple,* 9403(F)

Little House on Rocky Edge, 9405(F)

Gillerlain, Gayle, reteller. *The Reverend Thomas's False Teeth,* 1189(F)

Gillespie, Jessie. *The Birds' Christmas Carol,* 9768(F)

Gillespie, Sarah. *A Pioneer Farm Girl,* 16308

Gillette, J. Lynett. *Dinosaur Ghosts,* 14420

Gillies, Judi. *The Kids Can Press Jumbo Cookbook,* 21701

Gilliland, Hap. *Flint's Rock,* 8434(F)

Gilliland, Judith Heide. *Not in the House, Newton!* 1190(F)

Steamboat! The Story of Captain Blanche Leathers, 12130

Gilliland, Judith Heide (jt. author). *The Day of Ahmed's Secret,* 4678(F)

House of Wisdom, 8957(F)

Sami and the Time of the Troubles, 4679(F)

Gillis, Jennifer S. *In a Pumpkin Shell,* 21438

Gillman, Alec. *Fast Eddie,* 7659(F)

Green Truck Garden Giveaway, 3313(F)

Toad or Frog, Swamp or Bog? 18584

Gillmor, Don. *The Christmas Orange,* 5824(F)

The Fabulous Song, 4162(F)

Yuck, a Love Story, 1191(F)

Gillooly, Eileen, ed. *Rudyard Kipling,* 11571

Gilman, Phoebe. *The Gypsy Princess,* 1192(F)

Something from Nothing, 11147

Gilmore, Rachna. *Mina's Spring of Colors,* 8435(F)

Gilson, Jamie. *Bug in a Rug,* 10064(F)

Hello, My Name Is Scrambled Eggs, 8289(F)

It Goes Eeeeeeeeeeeee! 10065(F)

Soccer Circus, 6861(F)

Thirteen Ways to Sink a Sub, 10066(F)

Gilvan-Cartwright, Christopher. *Becoming Me,* 17250

Ginsburg, Mirra. *Across the Stream,* 2124(F)

The Chinese Mirror, 10726

Clay Boy, 11088

Good Morning, Chick, 11089

Where Does the Sun Go at Night? 1193(F)

Ginsburg, Mirra, adapt. *The Sun's Asleep Behind the Hill,* 685(F)

Ginsburg, Mirra, trans. *The Chick and the Duckling,* 2125(F)

Giovanni, Nikki. *Knoxville, Tennessee,* 11755

The Sun Is So Quiet, 11756

Giovanopoulos, Paul. *How Many Miles to Babylon?* 6846(F)

Learning to Say Good-bye, 17717

Gipson, Fred. *Old Yeller,* 7199(F)

Girard, Linda Walvoord. *Adoption Is for Always,* 3650(F)

Alex, the Kid with AIDS, 8661(F)

At Daddy's on Saturdays, 8662(F)

My Body Is Private, 18255

We Adopted You, Benjamin Koo, 17654(F)

Who Is a Stranger and What Should I Do? 17704

You Were Born on Your Very First Birthday, 18240

Young Frederick Douglass, 12710

Girl Scouts of the U.S.A. *Sing Together,* 14243

Girnis, Meg. *A B C for You and Me,* 43(F)

Girouard, Patrick. *I Have a Weird Brother Who Digested a Fly,* 18100

Math Fun, 20624

Math Fun with Money Puzzlers, 20625

More or Less a Mess, 6429(F)

Yikes-Lice! 17946

Gish, Steven. *Ethiopia,* 14929

Gittins, Anne. *Tales from the South Pacific Islands,* 10848

Giudici, Vittorio. *The Sistine Chapel,* 14798

Giuliano, Katie. *All the Way to God,* 686(F)

Giuliano, Michael (jt. author). *All the Way to God,* 686(F)

Giuliano Children. *All the Way to God,* 686(F)

Givens, Steven J. *Levi Dust,* 9280(F)

Givens, Terryl. *Dragon Scales and Willow Leaves,* 1194(F)

Glanzman, Louis. *The Bears' House,* 10127(F)
  The Noonday Friends, 8376(F)
  Pippi Longstocking, 9917(F)

Glaser, Byron. *Round the Garden,* 4444(F)

Glaser, Isabel Joshlin, ed. *Dreams of Glory,* 11572

Glaser, Linda. *Beautiful Bats,* 19025
  The Borrowed Hanukkah Latkes, 6072(F)
  Compost! 3169
  Fabulous Frogs, 18723
  Magnificent Monarchs, 19551
  Our Big Home, 3170(F)
  Spectacular Spiders, 19581
  Tanya's Big Green Dream, 8663(F)
  Wonderful Worms, 19607

Glaser, Omri. *Round the Garden,* 4444(F)

Glass, Andrew. *Ananse's Feast,* 10699
  Bad Guys, 12649
  Bewildered for Three Days, 4664(F)
  Cajun, 4851(F)
  Crabby Cratchitt, 2956(F)
  Devil's Donkey, 7624(F)
  Dr. Dredd's Wagon of Wonders, 6775(F)
  Easy Work! An Old Tale, 11128
  Grizz! 1301(F)
  Monster Manners, 1511(F)
  A Right Fine Life, 9367(F)
  She'll Be Comin' Round the Mountain, 4085(F)
  Soap! Soap! Don't Forget the Soap! 11325
  The Tale of Willie Monroe, 10828

Glass, Julie. *Counting Sheep,* 445(F)
  A Dollar for Penny, 446(F)

Glass, Tom. *Even a Little Is Something,* 8995(F)

Glasser, Robin P. *Alexander, Who's Not (Do You Hear Me? I Mean It!) Going to Move,* 3928(F)
  Super-Completely and Totally the Messiest, 4342(F)
  You Can't Take a Balloon into the Metropolitan Museum, 938(F)
  You Can't Take a Balloon into the National Gallery, 4875(F)

Glassman, Bruce. *Wilma Mankiller,* 12976

Glassman, Miriam. *Box Top Dreams,* 8664(F)

Glassman, Peter. *My Working Mom,* 1195(F)

Glaze, Lynn. *Seasons of the Trail,* 9368(F)

Gleasner, Diana C. *The Movies (Inventions That Changed Our Lives),* 14309

Gleeson, Brian. *Finn McCoul,* 10985
  The Savior Is Born, 5825

Gleit, Joyce (jt. author). *The Best Joke Book for Kids Number 4,* 21822

Gleitzman, Morris. *Puppy Fat,* 8436(F)
  Sticky Beak, 8892(F)

Gleman, Amy. *Connecticut,* 16687

Glenn, Mike. *Lessons in Success from the NBA's Top Players,* 22132

Glibbery, Caroline. *Join the Total Fitness Gang,* 18194

Glick, Beth. *God Must Like Cookies, Too,* 6118(F)
  The Great Monarch Butterfly Chase, 1493(F)

Gliori, Debi. *Mr. Bear Says, Are You There, Baby Bear?* 2126(F)
  Mr. Bear Says Peek-a-Boo, 2127(F)
  Mr. Bear to the Rescue, 2128(F)
  Mr. Bear's New Baby, 2129(F)
  Mr. Bear's Vacation, 2130(F)
  New Big House, 3651(F)
  No Matter What, 2131(F)
  Oliver's Alphabets, 15(F)
  The Snow Lambs, 5228(F)
  Tell Me Something Happy Before I Go to Sleep, 665(F)
  The Very Small, 666(F)
  What Can I Give Him? 5826(F)

Gloeckner, Phoebe. *The Chicken-Fried Rat,* 8580(F)

Glossop, Jennifer (jt. author). *The Kids Can Press Jumbo Cookbook,* 21701

Glover, David. *Batteries, Bulbs, and Wires,* 20896

Glover, Savion. *Savion!* 12465

Glubok, Shirley. *Great Lives,* 12163
  Olympic Games in Ancient Greece, 22247

Goble, Paul. *Adopted by the Eagles,* 11237
  Buffalo Woman, 11238
  Crow Chief, 11239
  Death of the Iron Horse, 4665(F)
  Dream Wolf, 1196(F)
  The Gift of the Sacred Dog, 11240
  The Girl Who Loved Wild Horses, 5229(F)
  The Great Race, 11241
  Hau Kola Hello Friend, 12542
  Her Seven Brothers, 11242

I Sing for the Animals, 4445
Iktomi and the Berries, 11243
Iktomi and the Boulder, 11244
Iktomi and the Buffalo Skull, 11245
Iktomi and the Coyote, 11246
Iktomi Loses His Eyes, 11247
The Legend of the White Buffalo Woman, 11248
The Lost Children, 11249
Love Flute, 11250
Remaking the Earth, 11251
The Return of the Buffaloes, 11252

Goble, Paul, reteller. *Star Boy,* 11253

Godard, Alex. *Idora,* 4666(F)
  Mama, Across the Sea, 3171(F)

Godden, Rumer. *Listen to the Nightingale,* 8665(F)
  Premlata and the Festival of Lights, 8996(F)
  The Rocking Horse Secret, 6862(F)

Godfrey, Jan. *Sam's New Baby,* 3652(F)

Godfrey, Neale S. *Neale S. Godfrey's Ultimate Kids' Money Book,* 16942

Godkin, Celia. *Kit,* 7328(F)
  Sea Otter Inlet, 20373

Godon, Ingrid. *Curious Kids Go to Preschool,* 2998(F)
  What Shall We Do with the Boo-Hoo Baby? 654(F)

Godwin, Laura. *Barnyard Prayers,* 687
  The Flower Girl, 3172(F)
  Forest, 6350(F)
  Happy and Honey, 6351(F)
  Honey Helps, 6352(F)
  Little White Dog, 270(F)

Godwin, Laura (jt. author). *The Doll People,* 7951(F)

Goembel, Ponder. *Good Day, Good Night,* 5417(F)
  "Hi, Pizza Man!" 4345(F)
  The Night Iguana Left Home, 2426(F)

Goennel, Heidi. *I Pretend,* 1197(F)

Gofen, Ethel C. *Cultures of the World,* 15737
  France, 15307

Goffe, Toni. *The Emperor's New Clothes,* 10380(F)
  The Legend of Lightning Larry, 1569(F)
  The Legend of Slappy Hooper, 11384

Gogol, Nikolai. *The Nose,* 7743(F)
  Sorotchintzy Fair, 1198(F)

Gogol, Sara. *Katy Steding,* 13575
  A Mien Family, 15159

Goh, Sui Noi. *China,* 15062
  Welcome to China, 15063

Gold, Alison L. *Memories of Anne Frank,* 13799
  A Special Fate, 13851

Gold, Bernice. *My Four Lions,* 1199(F)

Gold, Caroline. *The Crooked Apple Tree*, 3222(F)

Gold, Carolyn J. *Dragonfly Secret*, 8437(F)

Gold, John C. *Environments of the Western Hemisphere*, 14339

Gold, Julie. *From a Distance*, 11573

Gold, Rebecca. *Steve Wozniak*, 13353

Gold, Susan D. *Alzheimer's Disease*, 17959

Attention Deficit Disorder, 17909

Blame It on El Niño, 20770

Governments of the Western Hemisphere, 14552

Indian Treaties, 15957

Land Pacts, 15879

Religions of the Western Hemisphere, 17189

Gold-Vukson, Marji. *The Colors of My Jewish Year*, 6073(F)

Goldberg, Jake. *Hawaii*, 16781

Miguel de Cervantes, 12517

Goldberg, Sue. *Dear Bronx Zoo*, 20022

Goldenstern, Joyce. *Lost Cities*, 14528

Goldentyer, Debra. *Child Abuse*, 17655

Divorce, 17656

Street Violence, 17138

Goldin, Augusta. *Ducks Don't Get Wet*, 19309

Goldin, Barbara D. *Coyote and the Fire Stick*, 11254

The Girl Who Lived with the Bears, 11255

Journeys with Elijah, 17276

A Mountain of Blintzes, 6074(F)

The Passover Journey, 17467

Ten Holiday Jewish Children's Stories, 17468(F)

While the Candles Burn, 9724(F)

The World's Birthday, 6075(F)

Goldin, David. *Go-Go-Go!* 1200(F)

Lost Cat, 5247(F)

Golding, Kim. *Alphababies*, 44(F)

Counting Kids, 447(F)

Golding, Theresa Martin. *Kat's Surrender*, 8666(F)

Golding, Vivien. *Traditions from Africa*, 14901

Goldish, Meish. *Immigration*, 17561

Our Supreme Court, 17013

Goldman, Molly Rose (jt. author). *How to Take Your Grandmother to the Museum*, 3960(F)

Goldsen, Louise. *Colors*, 271

Fruit, 20144

The Ladybug and Other Insects, 19444

Weather, 4446

Goldsmith, Howard. *Sleepy Little Owl*, 2132(F)

The Twiddle Twins' Haunted House, 7744(F)

Goldstein, Bobbye S., comp. *Sweets and Treats*, 11575

Goldstein, Bobbye S., ed. *Inner Chimes*, 11574

Goldstein, Bobbye S., sel. *Birthday Rhymes, Special Times*, 5688

Goldstein, Ernest. *The Statue Abraham Lincoln*, 13957(F)

Goldstein, Margaret J. *Brett Hull*, 13693

Jackie Joyner-Kersee, 13661

Goldstein, Peggy. *Long Is a Dragon*, 14083

Goldstone, Bruce. *The Beastly Feast*, 2133(F)

Golembe, Carla. *Annabelle's Big Move*, 5230(F)

Dog Magic, 4163(F)

Golenbock, Peter. *Hank Aaron*, 13430

Teammates, 13371

Goley, Elaine P. *Learn the Value of Trust*, 184

Gollub, Matthew. *Cool Melons Turn to Frogs! The Life and Poems of Issa*, 12556

The Jazz Fly, 2134(F)

Ten Oni Drummers, 1201(F)

The Twenty-Five Mixtec Cats, 7745(F)

Gomez, Elizabeth. *The Upside Down Boy/El niño de cabeza*, 10074(F)

Gomi, Taro. *Everyone Poops*, 3173

I Lost My Dad, 4967(F)

My Friends, 3174(F)

Spring Is Here, 4447(F)

Who Ate It? 3175(F)

Gompf, Ray (jt. author). *The Peanut Butter Cookbook for Kids*, 21734

Gondosch, Linda. *The Monsters of Marble Avenue*, 9862(F)

Gonen, Rivka. *Charge!* 21386

Fired Up! 13939

Gonzales, Edward. *Farolitos for Abuelo*, 5745(F)

The Farolitos of Christmas, 5746(F)

Gonzalez, Christina. *Prietita and the Ghost Woman*, 7562(F)

Gonzalez, Joaquin L. *The Philippines*, 15233

Gonzalez, Lucia M. *The Bossy Gallito*, 11422

Señor Cat's Romance and Other Favorite Stories from Latin America, 11439

Gonzalez, Maya Christina. *Angels Ride Bikes and Other Fall Poems*, 11935

From the Bellybutton of the Moon and Other Summer Poems, 11526

Laughing Tomatoes and Other Spring Poems/Jitomates Risueños y Otros Poemas de Primavera, 11527

My Very Own Room/ Mi propio cuartito, 3360(F)

Gonzalez, Ralfka. *My First Book of Proverbs/Mi Primer Libro de Dichos*, 14028

Gooch, Randall. *Traditional Crafts from Mexico and Central America*, 21503

Good, Keith. *Build It!* 21124

Gear Up! 20920

Shape It! 21531

Zap It! 20897

Good, Merle. *Dan's Pants*, 3176(F)

Reuben and the Blizzard, 3653(F)

Reuben and the Quilt, 3654(F)

Goodale, Rebecca. *Island Dog*, 918(F)

Goodall, Jane. *The Chimpanzee Family Book*, 18995

Dr. White, 2135(F)

The Eagle and the Wren, 11339

My Life with the Chimpanzees, 13300

With Love, 18996

Goodall, John S. *Creepy Castle*, 919(F)

Paddy Under Water, 920(F)

The Story of a Farm, 4667(F)

The Story of a Main Street, 921(F)

Goode, Diane. *A Child's Garden of Verses*, 11717

Cinderella, 10422(F)

The Dinosaur's New Clothes, 10423(F)

The Dream Eater, 10813

Goode, Molly. *Mama Loves*, 6353(F)

Goodell, Jon. *Mice Are Nice*, 6341(F)

Goodhart, Pippa. *Noah Makes a Boat*, 17277

Goodman, Alan. *Nickelodeon's The Big Help Book*, 17139

Goodman, Billy. *Natural Wonders and Disasters*, 20308

Goodman, Jim. *Thailand*, 15160

Goodman, Joan E. *Bernard's Bath*, 2136(F)

Bernard's Nap, 688(F)

Beyond the Sea of Ice, 12125

Hope's Crossing, 9234(F)

Songs from Home, 8438(F)

The Winter Hare, 9095(F)

Goodman, Michael. *Model Railroading*, 21668

Radio Control Models, 21669

Goodman, Susan. *Chopsticks for My Noodle Soup*, 15161

Goodman, Susan E. *Animal Rescue*, 18627

Bats, Bugs, and Biodiversity, 20446

Stones, Bones, and Petroglyphs, 15958

Ultimate Field Trip 4, 16245

Ultimate Field Trip 3, 19860

Unseen Rainbows, Silent Songs, 18818

Goodman, Vivienne. *Guess What?* 4148(F)

Goodnough, David. *Cult Awareness,* 17190
Eating Disorders, 17960
Goodrich, Carter. *A Christmas Carol,* 9721(F)
Goodsmith, Lauren. *The Children of Mauritania,* 15027
Goodstein, Madeline. *Sports Science Projects,* 20811
Goodwin, Bob. *A Taste of Spain,* 21702
Goodwin, Peter. *Landslides, Slumps, and Creep,* 20309
Goodwin, William. *India,* 15101
Goold, Ian. *The Rutan Voyager,* 21078
Goolsby, Abe. *Jonah's Trash . . . God's Treasure,* 17238
Goom, Bridget. *A Family in Singapore,* 15162
Goor, Nancy. *Shadows,* 185(F)
Williamsburg, 16128
Goor, Ron. *Shadows,* 185(F)
Williamsburg, 16128
Goor, Ron (jt. author). *Backyard Insects,* 19488
Gorbachev, Valeri. *Fool of the World and the Flying Ship,* 10858
Little Bunny's Sleepless Night, 768(F)
Nicky and the Big, Bad Wolves, 2137(F)
Nicky and the Fantastic Birthday Gift, 2138(F)
Peter's Picture, 2139(F)
So Much in Common, 2245(F)
What If? 11793
Where Is the Apple Pie? 2140(F)
Young Mouse and Elephant, 10665
Gorbaty, Norman. *Earthdance,* 4528
Gordeeva, Ekaterina. *A Letter for Daria,* 13589
Gordon, Amy. *Midnight Magic,* 1202(F)
When JFK Was My Father, 8667(F)
Gordon, Ginger (jt. author). *Anthony Reynoso,* 17552
Gordon, Henry. *It's Magic,* 21784
Gordon, Judith (jt. author). *A Better Safe Than Sorry Book,* 18256
Did the Sun Shine Before You Were Born? 18257
Gordon, Lynn. *The Witch's Revenge,* 5999(F)
Gordon, Melanie Apel. *Let's Talk About Dyslexia,* 17910
Let's Talk About Head Lice, 17961
Gordon, Mike. *Taste,* 18163
Gordon, Ruth. *Feathers,* 11148
Gordon, Sol. *A Better Safe Than Sorry Book,* 18256
Did the Sun Shine Before You Were Born? 18257
Gordon, Stephanie Jacob (jt. author). *Something's Happening on Calabash Street,* 3120(F)

Gore, Leonid. *Behold the Trees,* 4572(F)
Clockwork, 8029(F)
King Kenrick's Splinter, 4129(F)
Lucy Dove, 7703(F)
The Malachite Palace, 10375(F)
The Pomegranate Seeds, 11477
The Story of Hanukkah, 6117
Who Was Born This Special Day? 5770(F)
Gorey, Edward. *The Shrinking of Treehorn,* 9874(F)
You Read to Me, I'll Read to You, 11864
Gorman, Carol. *Dork in Disguise,* 9863(F)
Jennifer-the-Jerk Is Missing, 6863(F)
Lizard Flanagan, Supermodel?? 9864(F)
Gormley, Beatrice. *Best Friend Insurance,* 7746(F)
Fifth Grade Magic, 7747(F)
First Ladies, 12650
The Magic Mean Machine, 9865(F)
Mail-Order Wings, 7748(F)
Miriam, 8963(F)
More Fifth Grade Magic, 7749(F)
Paul's Volcano, 10187(F)
Wanted, 10188(F)
Gorog, Judith. *In a Messy, Messy Room,* 7750(F)
Gorrell, Gena K. *Catching Fire,* 17810
Heart and Soul, 13841
Gorski, Jason. *The Science Explorer Out and About,* 18336
Gorsline, Douglas. *Cowboys,* 16309
North American Indians, 15959
Gorsline, Douglas (jt. author). *Cowboys,* 16309
North American Indians, 15959
Gorsline, Marie. *Cowboys,* 16309
North American Indians, 15959
Gorton, Julia. *My Two Hands, My Two Feet,* 804(F)
Super Sand Castle Saturday, 230(F)
Ten Rosy Roses, 513(F)
The Terrible Twos, 3177(F)
Gosnell, Kelvin. *Belarus, Ukraine, and Moldova,* 15416
Gosney, Joy. *Naughty Parents,* 4164(F)
Goss, Gary. *Blue Moon Soup,* 21703
Goss, Linda. *The Frog Who Wanted to Be a Singer,* 2141(F)
Gosselin, Kim. *Smoking Stinks!!* 8668(F)
Got, Yves. *Sweet Dreams, Sam,* 186(F)
Goto, Scott. *Heat Wave,* 1298(F)
Shoeshine Whittaker, 4202(F)
Shooting Star, 12429
Will Rogers, 12458(F)
Gott, Barry. *Patches Lost and Found,* 5295(F)

Gottfried, Ted. *Eleanor Roosevelt,* 13181
Steven Spielberg, 12473
Gottlieb, Dale. *Watermelon Day,* 2999(F)
Where Jamaica Go? 4165(F)
Gould, Deborah. *Aaron's Shirt,* 3178(F)
Camping in the Temple of the Sun, 2934(F)
Gould, Marilyn. *Golden Daffodils,* 8893(F)
Gould, Roberta. *Kidtopia,* 21439
Making Cool Crafts and Awesome Art, 21440
Goulding, June. *Dracula Steps Out,* 8037(F)
Monster Train, 1499(F)
Gourbault, Martine. *Grace and Joe,* 3982(F)
I Went to the Bay, 5348
Mr. McGratt and the Ornery Cat, 5255(F)
Room for a Stepdaddy, 3585(F)
Gourbault, Martine (jt. author). *No Dragons for Tea,* 1468(F)
Gourley, Catherine. *Good Girl Work,* 16466
Media Wizards, 14084
Sharks! 19759
Welcome to Felicity's World, 1774, 16129
Welcome to Molly's World, 1944, 14854
Welcome to Samantha's World, 1904, 16467
Wheels of Time, 13280
Gourse, Leslie. *Gloria Estefan,* 12382
Wynton Marsalis, 12421
Gove, Doris. *My Mother Talks to Trees,* 3655(F)
One Rainy Night, 5231(F)
Red-Spotted Newt, 18685
A Water Snake's Year, 18759
Gowell, Elizabeth T. *Fountains of Life,* 19819
Life in the Deep Sea, 19820
Whales and Dolphins, 19634
Gowing, Toby. *Addie's Dakota Winter,* 9395(F)
Addie's Long Summer, 9396(F)
Goyallon, Jerome. *Drawing Prehistoric Animals,* 21576
Grabowski, John. *Jackie Robinson,* 13493
The Northwest, 16782
Sports Great Emmitt Smith, 13632
Willie Mays, 13473
Grabowski, John F. *Canada,* 15575
The Death Penalty, 17066
Spain, 15474
Grabowski, Patricia (jt. author). *The Northwest,* 16782
Grace, Catherine O. (jt. author). *I Want to Be a Veterinarian,* 17854

I Want to Be an Astronaut, 17758
Grace, Eric S. *Seals*, 19734
  Sharks, 19760
Grace, Robert. *Changes for Samantha*, 9630(F)
Gradisher, Martha. *A Class Play with Ms. Vanilla*, 6327(F)
Graeber, Charlotte. *Fudge*, 7200(F)
  Nobody's Dog, 7201(F)
Graef, Renee. *Going to Town*, 4877(F)
  The Nutcracker, 10932(F)
Graff, Nancy P. *In the Hush of the Evening*, 689(F)
  The Strength of the Hills, 20058
Graff, Polly (jt. author). *Helen Keller*, 13166
Graff, Stewart. *Helen Keller*, 13166
Grafton, Allison (jt. author). *Projects for a Healthy Planet*, 16960
Graham, Bob. *Benny*, 2142(F)
  Max, 1203(F)
  Poems for the Very Young, 11684
  Queenie, One of the Family, 5232(F)
  The Red Woolen Blanket, 3179(F)
  Rose Meets Mr. Wintergarten, 3180(F)
  Spirit of Hope, 3656(F)
  This Is Our House, 5063(F)
Graham, Christine. *When Pioneer Wagons Rumbled West*, 4668(F)
Graham, Georgia. *The Strongest Man This Side of Cremona*, 2935(F)
  Tyler's New Boots, 2960(F)
Graham, Harriet. *A Boy and His Bear*, 9096(F)
Graham, Ian. *The Best Book of Spaceships*, 20989
  The Best Book of the Moon, 18447
  Boats, Ships, Submarines and Other Floating Machinery, 21359
  Cars, Bikes, Trains, and Other Land Machines, 21283
  Crime-Fighting, 17067
  Fakes and Forgeries, 17068
  The World of Computers and Communications, 21203
Graham, Ian, ed. *How Things Work*, 21035
Graham, Joan B. *Flicker Flash*, 11577
  Splish Splash, 11578
Graham, John. *I Love You, Mouse*, 5233(F)
Graham, Kevin (jt. author). *Alternative Energy Sources*, 20822
  Guardians of Wildlife, 19391
  Kids Who Make a Difference, 16954
  Natural Foods and Products, 20081
  Protecting Our Air, Land, and Water, 16991
  Recycling, 16975

Graham, Lorenz. *How God Fix Jonah*, 17278
Graham, Margaret B. *Be Nice to Spiders*, 2143(F)
Graham, Mark. *Baby Talk*, 3696(F)
  Charlie Anderson, 5111(F)
  Come Meet Muffin! 2545(F)
  The Dream Jar, 3846(F)
  If I Were Queen of the World, 1236(F)
  Michael and the Cats, 5112(F)
  Miss Opal's Auction, 4053(F)
  Murphy and Kate, 7223(F)
  My Father's Hands, 3868(F)
  Roommates, 6338(F)
  Sarah's Sleepover, 5061(F)
  Shadows Are About, 3358(F)
Graham, Paula W. *Speaking of Journals*, 14085
Graham, Ruth B. *One Wintry Night*, 17418(F)
Graham, Steve. *Dear Old Donegal*, 4669(F)
Graham, Thomas. *Day Breaks*, 4557(F)
Graham-Barber, Lynda. *Doodle Dandy!* 17364
  Gobble! 17498
  Ho Ho Ho! 17419
  Mushy! 17508
  Toad or Frog, Swamp or Bog? 18584
Grahame, Kenneth. *The Adventures of Mr. Toad*, 7751(F)
  Duck Song, 2144(F)
  The Reluctant Dragon, 10424(F)
  The River Bank, 7752(F)
  The Wind in the Willows, 7753(F), 7754(F), 7755(F)
  A Wind in the Willows Christmas, 9725(F)
Gralla, Preston. *Online Kids*, 21204
Gralley, Jean. *Hogula*, 6000(F)
Gramatky, Hardie. *Little Toot*, 5569(F)
Grambling, Lois G. *Can I Have a Stegosaurus, Mom? Can I? Please!?* 4166(F)
  Daddy Will Be There, 3657(F)
  Happy Valentine's Day, Miss Hildy! 6168(F)
Grambling, Louis. *Miss Hildy's Missing Cape Caper*, 6001(F)
Grambo, Rebecca L. *Eagles*, 19326
Granados, Christine. *Christina Aguilera*, 12343
  Enrique Iglesias, 12406
  Rosie O'Donnell, 12433
GrandPré, Mary. *Batwings and the Curtain of Night*, 1999(F)
  Harry Potter and the Prisoner of Azkaban, 8050(F)
  Pockets, 3000(F)
Granfield, Linda. *Amazing Grace*, 14152
  Circus, 14269
  Cowboy, 16310

High Flight, 12570
  The Legend of the Panda, 10753
  Silent Night, 14202(F)
Granger, Judith. *Amazing World of Dinosaurs*, 14421
Granström, Brita. *Art School*, 13909
  Eyes, Nose, Fingers, and Toes, 18062
  Honk! Honk! 1392(F)
  My Body, Your Body, 18832
  Science School, 18328
Granström, Brita (jt. author). *Art School*, 13909
  My Body, Your Body, 18832
  Science School, 18328
  Supermom, 3796(F)
Grant, Donald. *Atlas of Countries*, 14329
Grant, Donald (jt. author). *Atlas of Islands*, 14338
Grant, Leigh. *Kid Power*, 7493(F)
  Shoeshine Girl, 8575(F)
Grant, Neil. *Eric the Red*, 13792
  The Vikings, 15448
Grant, Neil, ed. *The Egyptians*, 14627
Grant, R. G. *Genocide*, 17021
  The Seventies, 16508
Grant, Richard. *Cretaceous Dinosaur World*, 14422
  Dinosaur Babies, 14423
  The Great Dinosaur Record Book, 14411
  Jurassic Dinosaur World, 14424
  They Lived with the Dinosaurs, 14412
Grassby, Donna. *A Seaside Alphabet*, 45(F)
Grassy, John. *National Audubon Society First Field Guide*, 18943
Graston, Arlene. *Thumbelina*, 10391(F)
Grau, Andrea. *Dance*, 14286
Gravelle, Jennifer (jt. author). *The Period Book*, 18259
Gravelle, Karen. *Growing Up in a Holler in the Mountains*, 16860
  Growing Up in Crawfish Country, 16861
  Growing Up Where the Partridge Drums Its Wings, 15960
  The Period Book, 18259
  What's Going on Down There? 18258
Graves, Bonnie. *The Best Worst Day*, 10067(F)
  No Copycats Allowed! 6354(F)
Graves, Elizabeth. *An Ancient Castle*, 9097(F)
Graves, Keith. *Armadillo Tattletale*, 2290(F)
  Frank Was a Monster Who Wanted to Dance, 1204(F)
  Pet Boy, 1205(F)
Graves, Robert. *An Ancient Castle*, 9097(F)

Gravett, Christopher. *The World of the Medieval Knight*, 14764

Gray, Cissy. *To Find the Way*, 8940(F)

Gray, Dianne E. *Holding Up the Earth*, 8669(F)

Gray, Elizabeth Janet. *Adam of the Road*, 9040(F)

Gray, Kes. *Eat Your Peas*, 4167(F)

The Get Well Soon Book, 2145(F)

Gray, Libba M. *Dear Willie Rudd*, 3658(F)

Is There Room on the Feather Bed? 1206(F)

The Little Black Truck, 5570(F)

Miss Tizzy, 3998(F)

My Mama Had a Dancing Heart, 3659(F)

Small Green Snake, 2146(F)

When Uncle Took the Fiddle, 3181(F)

Gray, Luli. *Falcon's Egg*, 7756(F)

Gray, Valerie A. *Jason Kidd*, 13542

Grayson, Marion F. *Let's Do Finger-plays*, 22004

Greaves, Margaret. *Sarah's Lion*, 10425(F)

Stories from the Ballet, 14287

Greaves, Nick. *When Hippo Was Hairy*, 10668

Grebu, Devis. *The King's Chess-board*, 10788

Green, Anne Canevari. *Adopting Pets*, 19892

Becoming Best Friends with Your Iguana, Snake, or Turtle, 19894

Fats, 20168

Pattern Fish, 192(F)

Walk on the Wild Side! 18661

Green, Carl R. *Allan Pinkerton*, 12947

Billy the Kid, 12852

Butch Cassidy, 12867

Confederate Generals of the Civil War, 12652

The Dalton Gang, 16311

David Robinson, 13569

Doc Holliday, 12902

Jackie Joyner-Kersee, 13662

Jesse James, 12909

Judge Roy Bean, 12849

Union Generals of the Civil War, 12653

Wild Bill Hickok, 12900

Wyatt Earp, 12874

The Younger Brothers, 12651

Green, Carl R. (jt. author). *Babe Ruth*, 13500

Bill Pickett, 12443

Billie Jean King, 13650

Brigham Young, 12969

Buffalo Bill Cody, 12869

Calamity Jane, 12864

Daniel Boone, 12085

Davy Crockett, 12103

Dorothy Hamill, 13591

Joe DiMaggio, 13449

John C. Fremont, 12118

Kareem Abdul-Jabbar, 13511

Kit Carson, 12088

Richard King, 12921

Sacagawea, 12991

Zebulon Pike, 12147

Green, Connie J. *Emmy*, 8439(F)

Green, Donnie Lee. *Why Alligator Hates Dog*, 11372

Green, Jen. *Alcohol*, 17864

A Dead Log, 20447

Dealing with Racism, 17140

Exploring the Polar Regions, 15804

A Family from South Africa, 14977

Insects, 19445

Our New Baby, 17657

People of the Mountains, 20500

Racism, 17141

Rain Forests, 20448

A Saguaro Cactus, 20405

Under a Stone, 20535

Green, Jonathan. *Crosby*, 4000(F)

Noah, 17270

Green, Ken. *Florence Kelley*, 12916

Green, Lucinda. *Riding*, 22202

The Young Rider, 22203

Green, Meg. *The Young Zillionaire's Guide to Investments and Savings*, 16922

Green, Norma B. *The Hole in the Dike*, 4670(F)

Green, Norman. *Christopher Columbus*, 16083

Knights of the Round Table, 10991

Green, Rebecca L. *Merina*, 14978

Green, Robert. *Alexander the Great*, 13748

Cleopatra, 13773

Hannibal, 13806

Herod the Great, 13809

Julius Caesar, 13763

King George III, 13805

King Henry VIII, 13808

Queen Elizabeth I, 13787

Queen Elizabeth II, 13790

Queen Victoria, 13863

Tutankhamun, 13861

"Vive La France," 14855

William the Conqueror, 13868

Green, Robina. *Brain*, 18113

Ears, 18148

Eyes, 18145

Heart and Lungs, 18078

Muscles and Bones, 18172

Green, Roger L. *Adventures of Robin Hood*, 10988

Green, Ruby. *My First Oxford Book of Stories*, 10453(F)

Green, Septima. *Top 10 Women Gymnasts*, 13372

Green, Shirley Leamon. *A B C for You and Me*, 43(F)

Green, Tamara. *Cretaceous Dinosaur World*, 14422

Dinosaur Babies, 14423

Exercise Is Fun! 18195

Jurassic Dinosaur World, 14424

Greenaway, Frank. *Amazing Bats*, 19026

Cave Life, 18629

Desert Life, 20425

Shoreline, 19869

Greenaway, Theresa. *Paws and Claws*, 18819

The Plant Kingdom, 20032

Swamp Life, 20374

Greenberg, Blu. *King Solomon and the Queen of Sheba*, 17279(F)

Greenberg, Dan. *Frogs*, 18724

Whales, 19789

Greenberg, David T. *Bugs!* 11790

Whatever Happened to Humpty Dumpty? 11872

Greenberg, Doreen. *A Drive to Win*, 13545

Sword of a Champion, 13704

Greenberg, Jan. *Chuck Close, Up Close*, 12211

Frank O. Gehry, 12233

Greenberg, Judith E. *A Girl's Guide to Growing Up*, 17610

Young People's Letters to the President, 17113

Greenberg, Keith E. *Adolescent Rights*, 17031

Bill and Hillary, 13023

Bill Bowerman and Phil Knight, 21171

Bomb Squad Officer, 17811

Bosnia, 15270

Disease Detective, 17962

Family Abuse, 17705

A Haitian Family, 15703

Jesse Ventura, 13710

Magic Johnson, 13532

Marine Biologist, 17826

Out of the Gang, 17069

Photojournalist, 17774

Rodeo Clown, 22005

Rwanda, 14930

Smokejumper, 17812

Storm Chaser, 20690

Stunt Woman, 12106

Test Pilot, 12076

Window Washer, 17751

Zack's Story, 17658

Greenberg, Mark (jt. author). *Amazon Diary*, 7093(F)

Greenberg, Martin H., ed. *A Newbery Christmas*, 9726(F)

A Newbery Halloween, 6864(F)

A Newbery Zoo, 7202(F)

Greenberg, Melanie H. *Blessings*, 6076

Greenberg, Melanie Hope. *Boats for Bedtime*, 5582(F)

Down in the Subway, 1065(F)

On My Street, 6520(F)

Greenberg, Michael (jt. author). *A Drive to Win*, 13545

Sword of a Champion, 13704

Greenblatt, Miriam. *Alexander the Great and Ancient Greece*, 13749
Franklin D. Roosevelt, 13097
Peter the Great and Tsarist Russia, 13843
Greenburg, Dan. *Dr. Jekyll, Orthodontist*, 7757(F)
A Ghost Named Wanda, 7758(F)
Great-Grandpa's in the Litter Box, 7759(F)
My Son, the Time Traveler, 10189(F)
Greene, Bette. *Philip Hall Likes Me, I Reckon Maybe*, 8290(F)
Greene, Carol. *Benjamin Franklin*, 12882
Firefighters Fight Fires, 17813
The Golden Locket, 4168(F)
Hi, Clouds, 6355(F)
The Jenny Summer, 8291(F)
Police Officers Protect People, 17814
The 13 Days of Halloween, 6002(F)
Veterinarians Help Animals, 17846
Where Is That Cat? 5234(F)
Greene, Constance C. *Beat the Turtle Drum*, 8670(F)
A Girl Called Al, 8292(F)
Greene, Ellin. *Billy Beg and His Bull*, 10989
The Little Golden Lamb, 10990
Greene, Jacqueline D. *Marie*, 9041(F)
The Maya, 15666
One Foot Ashore, 9042(F)
Powwow, 15961
Slavery in Ancient Egypt and Mesopotamia, 14583
Slavery in Ancient Greece and Rome, 14584
Greene, Jeffrey. *Just My Dad and Me*, 3752(F)
The Rain, 4480(F)
Greene, Joshua M. (jt. author). *Hanuman*, 10796
Greene, Meg. *Lauryn Hill*, 12399
Matt Damon, 12373
Slave Young, Slave Long, 16246
Greene, Rhonda Gowler. *Barnyard Song*, 2147(F)
The Stable Where Jesus Was Born, 5827
When a Line Bends . . . A Shape Begins, 331(F)
Greene, Sheppard M. (jt. author). *We All Sing with the Same Voice*, 14252
Greene, Stephanie. *Not Just Another Moose*, 2148(F)
Owen Foote, Frontiersman, 6865(F)
Owen Foote, Money Man, 9866(F)
Owen Foote, Second Grade Strongman, 10068(F)
Owen Foote, Soccer Star, 10328(F)
Show and Tell, 10069(F)

Greenfield, Eloise. *Africa Dream*, 4671(F)
Angels, 11579
Big Friend, Little Friend, 3182(F)
Childtimes, 17562
Easter Parade, 7342(F)
First Pink Light, 3660(F)
For the Love of the Game, 11996
Grandmama's Joy, 3661(F)
Grandpa's Face, 3662(F)
Honey, I Love, 3999(F)
Honey, I Love, and Other Love Poems, 11757
I Can Draw a Weeposaur and Other Dinosaurs, 11873
Koya DeLaney and the Good Girl Blues, 7343(F)
Mary McLeod Bethune, 12701
Nathaniel Talking, 11758
Rosa Parks, 12776
She Come Bringing Me That Little Baby Girl, 3663(F)
Sister, 7438(F)
Under the Sunday Tree, 11580
Water, Water, 3183(F)
William and the Good Old Days, 3664(F)
Greenfield, Giles. *Chaucer the Cat and the Animal Pilgrims*, 10535
Greenfield, Karen R. *Sister Yessa's Story*, 17280(F)
Greenfield, Monica. *Waiting for Christmas*, 5828(F)
Greenseid, Diane. *Chicken for a Day*, 6535(F)
Follow Me! 2630(F)
Get Up and Go! 20648
Mrs. Piccolo's Easy Chair, 1265(F)
We Had a Picnic This Sunday Past, 3958(F)
When Aunt Lena Did the Rhumba, 3759(F)
Wilson Sat Alone, 4005(F)
Greenspun, Adele Aron. *Bunny and Me*, 1207(F)
Greenstein, Elaine. *Dreaming*, 690(F)
Matzo Ball Moon, 6103(F)
The Mitten Tree, 3071(F)
Mrs. Rose's Garden, 1208(F)
Greenwald, Sheila. *Mariah Delany's Author-of-the-Month Club*, 9867(F)
My Fabulous New Life, 8671(F)
Stucksville, 10070(F)
Greenwood, A. J. *Hand-Print Animal Art*, 21564
Greenwood, Barbara. *The Last Safe House*, 9281(F)
Pioneer Crafts, 21520
A Pioneer Sampler, 15576
A Pioneer Thanksgiving, 17499
Greer, Gery. *Billy the Ghost and Me*, 6356(F)
Max and Me and the Time Machine, 7760(F)
Max and Me and the Wild West, 10190(F)

This Island Isn't Big Enough for the Four of Us! 9868(F)
Greger, C. Shana. *Cry of the Benu Bird*, 10669
Gregorowski, Christopher. *Fly, Eagle, Fly!* 10670
Gregory, Deborah. *Wishing on a Star*, 8293(F)
Gregory, Kristiana. *Across the Wide and Lonesome Prairie*, 9369(F)
Cleopatra VII, 8964(F)
Five Smooth Stones, 9235(F)
The Great Railroad Race, 9370(F)
Orphan Runaways, 9546(F)
The Stowaway, 9282(F)
The Winter of Red Snow, 9236(F)
Gregory, Philippa. *Florizella and the Wolves*, 10426(F)
Gregory, Tony. *The Dark Ages*, 14585
Gregory, Valiska. *Kate's Giants*, 2936(F)
Looking for Angels, 3184(F)
A Valentine for Norman Noggs, 6169(F)
When Stories Fell Like Shooting Stars, 7761(F)
Gregson, Susan R. *Stress Management*, 17911
Greisman, Joan (jt. author). *A First Thesaurus*, 14061
Grejniec, Michael. *From Anne to Zach*, 90(F)
Good Morning, Good Night, 187
What Do You Like? 3185(F)
Gresko, Marcia S. *Brazil*, 15738
The Grand Coulee Dam, 21125
India, 15102
Israel, 15546
Letters Home from Canada, 15577
Letters Home from China, 15064
Letters Home from Egypt, 15501
Letters Home from Greece, 15382
Letters Home from Israel, 15521
Letters Home from Japan, 15122
Letters Home from Russia, 15417
Letters Home from Scotland, 15348
Gretz, Susanna. *Duck Takes Off*, 2149(F)
Frog, Duck, and Rabbit, 2150(F)
Rabbit Food, 2151(F)
Grieg, Sibyl G. *The Underbed*, 704(F)
Grier, Ella. *Seven Days of Kwanzaa*, 17365
Griese, Arnold. *Anna's Athabaskan Summer*, 4448(F)
Grifalconi, Ann. *Don't Leave an Elephant to Go and Chase a Bird*, 10651
Everett Anderson's Goodbye, 11751
In the Rainfield, 10708
The Lion's Whiskers, 10660
The Midnight Fox, 7169(F)
The Secret Soldier, 13191
Tiny's Hat, 4968(F)

Tio Armando, 3683(F)
The Village of Round and Square Houses, 10671
Griffey, Harriet. *Secrets of the Mummies*, 14553
Griffin, Adele. *Dive*, 8440(F)
The Other Shepards, 8441(F)
Sons of Liberty, 8442(F)
Split Just Right, 8443(F)
Griffin, Lana T. *The Navajo*, 15962
Griffin, Peni R. *The Brick House Burglars*, 6866(F)
A Dig in Time, 7762(F)
Margo's House, 7763(F)
Switching Well, 10191(F)
The Treasure Bird, 6867(F)
Griffin, Sandra U. *Earth Circles*, 691(F)
Griffith, Gershom. *Jumping the Broom*, 4892(F)
Off to School, 4905(F)
A Picture Book of Sojourner Truth, 12789
Griffith, Helen V. *Alex and the Cat*, 6357(F)
Cougar, 7764(F)
Dinosaur Habitat, 7765(F)
Foxy, 7203(F)
Georgia Music, 3665(F)
Grandaddy and Janetta Together, 7439(F)
How Many Candles? 5689(F)
"Mine Will," Said John, 5235(F)
Griffith, Jonathan. *New Zealand*, 15234
Scotland, 15349
Griffiths, Dean. *Ballerinas Don't Wear Glasses*, 3797(F)
Griffiths, Diana. *Australia*, 15235
Grigg, Carol. *The Great Change*, 8850(F)
The Singing Snowbear, 2152(F)
Grimes, Nikki. *Aneesa Lee and the Weaver's Gift*, 11581
At Break of Day, 17191(F)
Come Sunday, 3186(F)
A Dime a Dozen, 11582
Hopscotch Love, 11583
Is It Far to Zanzibar? Poems About Tanzania, 11874
Meet Danitra Brown, 11759
My Man Blue, 11760
A Pocketful of Poems, 11584
Shoe Magic, 11585
Wild, Wild Hair, 6358(F)
Grimm, Edward. *The Doorman*, 4969(F)
Grimm, Phyllis W. *Crayfish*, 19675
Grimm Brothers. *The Brave Little Tailor*, 10891
The Bremem Town Musicians, 10892
The Complete Grimm's Fairy Tales, 10893
Dear Mili, 10894
The Elves and the Shoemaker, 10895, 10896

The Fisherman and His Wife, 10897
The Frog Prince, 10427(F), 10898
Household Stories of the Brothers Grimm, 10899
Little Red Riding Hood/Caperucita roja, 10900
Nibble Nibble Mousekin, 10901
Rapunzel, 10902, 10903
Rumpelstiltskin, 10904, 10905
The Shoemaker and the Elves, 10906, 10907
The Six Swans, 10908
Snow White and the Seven Dwarves, 10909
The Three Feathers, 10910
The Three Languages, 10911
The Water of Life, 10912
The Wolf and the Seven Little Kids, 10913
Grinaway, Ray. *The Best Book of Sharks*, 19763
Grindley, Sally. *Bible Stories for the Young*, 17281
Breaking the Spell, 7766(F)
A Flag for Grandma, 3666(F)
The Giant Postman, 6359(F)
Little Elephant Thunderfoot, 5236(F)
Little Sibu, 5237(F)
A New Room for William, 4970(F)
Polar Star, 5238(F)
Silly Goose and Dizzy Duck Play Hide-and-Seek, 2153(F)
What Are Friends For? 2154(F)
What Will I Do Without You? 2155(F)
Why Is the Sky Blue? 2156(F)
Grinsted, Katherine. *Spain*, 15475
Grisewood, Sara. *Making Jewelry*, 21541
Grisman, David (jt. author). *There Ain't No Bugs on Me*, 14241
Grobler, Piet. *Carnival of the Animals*, 11776
Grody, Carl W. *Sports Great Mitch Richmond*, 13566
Groner, Judye. *All About Hanukkah*, 6077
All About Passover, 17469
All About Sukkot, 17470
Thank You, God! 17523
Grooms, Molly. *We Are Bears*, 5239(F)
Gross, Gwen, ed. *Knights of the Round Table*, 10991
Gross, Ruth Belov. *True Stories About Abraham Lincoln*, 13067
You Don't Need Words! 14013
Grosshandler-Smith, Janet. *Working Together Against Drinking and Driving*, 17865
Grossman, Bill. *Donna O'Neeshuck Was Chased by Some Cows*, 4169(F)
My Little Sister Ate One Hare, 448(F)

Timothy Tunny Swallowed a Bunny, 4170(F)
Tommy at the Grocery Store, 2157(F)
Grossman, Mendel. *My Secret Camera*, 14856
Grossman, Nancy. *Did You Carry the Flag Today, Charley?* 10034(F)
Grossman, Robert. *The 18th Emergency*, 10031(F)
What Could a Hippopotamus Be? 2759(F)
Grossman, Susan. *Piranhas*, 19703
Grossman, Virginia. *Ten Little Rabbits*, 449(F)
Grosz, Peter. *The Special Gifts*, 5829(F)
Grot, Rich. *Alison Rides the Rapids*, 6746(F)
Keisha Discovers Harlem, 9583(F)
Groth, B. L., ed. *Home Is Where We Live*, 8672(F)
Grove, Vicki. *The Crystal Garden*, 8294(F)
Destiny, 8673(F)
Reaching Dustin, 8295(F)
Grover, Max. *Amazing and Incredible Counting Stories*, 450(F)
Miss Mabel's Table, 401(F)
The Night Before Christmas, 11847
Where Go the Boats? 11720
Grover, Wayne. *Dolphin Adventure*, 19684
Dolphin Freedom, 6868(F)
Dolphin Treasure, 6869(F)
Gruber, Wilhelm. *The Upside-Down Reader*, 6360(F)
Gruelle, Johnny. *How Raggedy Ann Got Her Candy Heart*, 1209(F)
Raggedy Ann and Andy and the Camel with the Wrinkled Knees, 1210(F)
Raggedy Ann Stories, 1211(F)
Gruenberg, Hannah C. *Felix's Hat*, 1782(F)
Grummer, Arnold E. *Paper by Kids*, 21616
Grunwald, Lisa. *Now Soon Later*, 188(F)
Grupper, Jonathan. *Destination*, 15236, 19635, 15805, 20449
Rocky Mountains, 20501
Grutman, Jewel H. *The Ledgerbook of Thomas Blue Eagle*, 9160(F)
Gryski, Camilla. *Cat's Cradle, Owl's Eyes*, 22006
Friendship Bracelets, 21542
Hands On, Thumbs Up, 14014
Lanyard, 21543
Let's Play, 22007
Many Stars and More String Games, 22008
Super String Games, 22009
Guarino, Deborah. *Is Your Mama a Llama?* 2158(F)
Guarnaccia, Steven. *Busy, Busy City Street*, 4235(F)

Goldilocks and the Three Bears, 10987

Guarnieri, Paolo. *A Boy Named Giotto*, 4672(F)

Guarnotta, Lucia. *We Are Bears*, 5239(F)

Guccione, Leslie D. *Come Morning*, 16247(F)

Guelke, Alexander (jt. author). *Life on a Submarine*, 21399

Guenther, James. *Turnagain Ptarmigan! Where Did You Go?* 1212(F)

Guernsey, JoAnn B. *Hillary Rodham Clinton*, 13145
Tipper Gore, 13155

Guest, C. Z. *Tiny Green Thumbs*, 2159(F)

Guest, Elissa Haden. *Iris and Walter*, 8674(F)

Guest, Elissa Haden (jt. author). *Girl Stuff*, 18249

Guettier, Benedicte. *The Father Who Had 10 Children*, 3667(F)

Guevara, Susan. *Chato and the Party Animals*, 5724(F)
Chato's Kitchen, 2708(F)
The King's Commissioners, 438(F)

Guiberson, Brenda Z. *Cactus Hotel*, 4449
Exotic Species, 18628
Into the Sea, 18783
Lighthouses, 21360
Mummy Mysteries, 14501
Spoonbill Swamp, 20375
Tales of the Haunted Deep, 7767(F)
Teddy Roosevelt's Elk, 19151

Guilfoile, Elizabeth. *Nobody Listens to Andrew*, 6361(F)

Guittard, Charles. *The Romans*, 14720

Gukova, Julia. *All Mixed-Up!* 4171(F)
Serena and the Wild Doll, 1076(F)
Who Stole the Gold? 2830(F)

Gulatta, Charles. *Extraordinary Women in Politics*, 13726

Gundersheimer, Karen. *Find Cat, Wear Hat*, 3187(F)
The Very Little Boy, 3267(F)

Gunderson, Mary. *American Indian Cooking Before 1500*, 15963
Cooking on the Lewis and Clark Expedition, 16080
Oregon Trail Cooking, 16312
Southern Plantation Cooking, 16248

Gunning, Monica. *Under the Breadfruit Tree*, 11586

Gunzl, Christiane. *Cave Life*, 18629

Guravich, Dan. *Harp Seal Pups*, 19741

Gurian, Michael. *From Boys to Men*, 17706

Gurne, James. *The Hand of Dinotopia*, 10182(F)

Gurney, James. *James Gurney*, 14389

Gurney, John S. *The Bald Bandit*, 6047(F)
The Deadly Dungeon, 7037(F)
The Goose's Gold, 7038(F)
Leprechauns Don't Play Basketball, 7693(F)
Upchuck and the Rotten Willy, 8183(F)

Gustafson, John. *Planets, Moons and Meteors*, 18513
Stars, Clusters and Galaxies, 18547

Gustafson, Scott. *Scott Gustafson's Animal Orchestra*, 451(F)

Gustavson, Adam. *Good Luck, Mrs. K.!* 5477(F)

Gusti. *Danny, the Angry Lion*, 5005(F)
Dog and Cat, 1732(F)

Gutelle, Andrew. *Baseball's Best*, 6362

Gutfreund, Geraldine M. *Vanishing Animal Neighbors*, 19397
Yearbooks in Science: 1970–1979, 18279

Guthrie, Arlo. *Mooses Come Walking*, 5240(F)

Guthrie, Donna. *Frankie Murphy's Kiss List*, 10071(F)
Grandpa Doesn't Know It's Me, 3668(F)
The Witch Who Lives Down the Hall, 1213(F)
The Young Author's Do-It-Yourself Book, 14087
The Young Journalist's Book, 14086

Guthrie, Donna (jt. author). *How to Write, Recite, and Delight in All Kinds of Poetry*, 14090
Putting On a Play, 12011
Writing Mysteries, Movies, Monster Stories, and More, 14068
The Young Producer's Video Book, 21265

Guthrie, Woody. *Howdi Do*, 14153
This Land Is Your Land, 14154

Gutierrez, Rudy. *All for the Better*, 12824
La Causa, 17135

Gutman, Anne. *Gaspard on Vacation*, 2160(F)
Lisa's Airplane Trip, 2161(F)

Gutman, Bill. *Adopting Pets*, 19892
Alonzo Mourning, 13551
Anfernee Hardaway, 13525
Barry Sanders, 13626
Be Aware of Danger, 18217
Becoming Best Friends with Your Hamster, Guinea Pig, or Rabbit, 19893
Becoming Best Friends with Your Iguana, Snake, or Turtle, 19894

Becoming Your Bird's Best Friend, 19895
Becoming Your Cat's Best Friend, 19922
Becoming Your Dog's Best Friend, 19950
Bo Jackson, 13615
Brett Favre, 13609, 13610
Cal Ripken, Jr. Baseball's Iron Man, 13479
David Robinson, 13570
Frank Thomas, 13507
Gail Devers, 13658
Grant Hill, 13528
Greg Maddux, 13470
Hakeem Olajuwon, 13554
Harmful to Your Health, 17963
Hazards at Home, 18218
Juan Gonzalez, 13456
Julie Krone, 13695
Ken Griffey, Jr. Baseball's Best, 13459
Ken Griffey, Sr., and Ken Griffey, Jr., 13458
Magic Johnson, 13533
Michael Jordan, 13538, 13539
Recreation Can Be Risky, 18219
Steve Young, 13638
Tara Lipinski, 13594
Tiger Woods, 13715
Troy Aikman, 13600

Gutman, Dan. *Babe and Me*, 7768(F)
Gymnastics, 22193
Honus and Me, 7769(F)
Ice Skating, 22222
Jackie and Me, 7770(F)
The Kid Who Ran for President, 9869(F)
Virtually Perfect, 10192(F)

Gutnik, Martin J. *Experiments That Explore Acid Rain*, 16996
Projects That Explore Energy, 20830

Gutnik, Natalie B. (jt. author). *Projects That Explore Energy*, 20830

Guttmacher, Peter. *Jeep*, 21302

Guy, Ginger F. *Black Crow, Black Crow*, 1214(F)
¡Fiesta! 452(F)

Guzner, Vlad. *The Keeper of Ugly Sounds*, 1411(F)

Guzzetti, Paula. *The Last Hawaiian Queen*, 12928
The White House, 16688

Guzzi, George. *Blue Feather's Vision*, 16149

Gwynne, Fred. *Pondlarker*, 2162(F)

Haas, Dorothy. *Burton and the Giggle Machine*, 9870(F)

Haas, Irene. *The Maggie B*, 1215(F)
A Summertime Song, 1216(F)

Haas, Jessie. *Be Well, Beware*, 7204(F)
Beware and Stogie, 7205(F)
A Blue for Beware, 7206(F)

Chipmunk! 5241(F)
Clean House, 9871(F)
Fire! My Parents' Story, 16689
A Horse Like Barney, 7207(F)
Hurry! 3188(F)
Mowing, 5242(F)
No Foal Yet, 5243(F)
Safe Horse, Safe Rider, 22204
Sugaring, 4450(F)
Unbroken, 8675(F)
Will You, Won't You? 8676(F)
Haas, Rudi. *Egg-Carton Zoo II,* 21617
Haas, Shelly O. *Grandma's Soup,* 4993(F)
The Kingdom of Singing Birds, 11140
Listening to Crickets, 13248
The Magic of Kol Nidre, 17487
Sara's Secret, 8919(F)
Thank You, God! 17523
Haban, Rita D. *How Proudly They Wave,* 13971
Hacker, Carlotta. *Explorers,* 12059
Great African Americans in History, 12654
Great African Americans in Jazz, 12164
Great African Americans in the Arts, 12165
Humanitarians, 13727
Nobel Prize Winners, 13728
Rebels, 13729
Scientists, 13210
Hackler, Lew. *Boating with Cap'n Bob and Matey,* 22261
Hackney, Rick. *Collecting,* 21806
Haddix, Margaret P. *Among the Hidden,* 10193(F)
Running Out of Time, 7771(F)
Haddock, Patricia. *San Francisco,* 16783
Haddon, Mark. *The Sea of Tranquility,* 4673(F)
Hader, Berta. *The Big Snow,* 4451(F)
Hader, Elmer. *The Big Snow,* 4451(F)
Haderer, Kurt. *Journey to Native Americans,* 15964
Hadithi, Mwenye. *Hot Hippo,* 2163(F)
Haduch, Bill. *Food Rules! The Stuff You Munch, Its Crunch, Its Punch, and Why You Sometimes Lose Your Lunch,* 18099
Haefele, Steve. *Oh Say Can You Say Di-no-saur?* 14482
Haffner, Marianne. *Bats! Amazing and Mysterious Creatures of the Night,* 19027
Hafner, Marylin. *And Then What?* 1696(F)
Bully Trouble, 6277(F)
The Candy Witch, 1322(F)
Germs Make Me Sick! 17939
Happy Father's Day, 5630(F)
It's Thanksgiving, 11850
Lucille's Snowsuit, 2342(F)

Lunch Bunnies, 2343(F)
The Missing Tooth, 6278(F)
Molly and Emmett's Camping Adventure, 1217(F)
Mommies Don't Get Sick, 4172(F)
My Stars, It's Mrs. Gaddy, 4154(F)
Purim Play, 6114(F)
Science Fair Bunnies, 2344(F)
Show and Tell Bunnies, 5513(F)
A Year with Molly and Emmett, 4173(F)
Hagen, Jeff. *Hiawatha Passing,* 692(F)
Hagerman, Jennifer. *Adventurous Spirit,* 13342
Hagsted, Maj-Britt. *Strange Stuff,* 21938
Hague, Kathleen. *Alphabears,* 46(F)
Calendarbears, 4452(F)
Ten Little Bears, 453(F)
Hague, Michael. *Alphabears,* 46(F)
The Book of Dragons, 7772(F)
Calendarbears, 4452(F)
The Children's Book of Faith, 17174
The Children's Book of Virtues, 3022
A Child's Book of Prayers, 17518
Michael Hague's Family Christmas Treasury, 9727
Michael Hague's Magical World of Unicorns, 7773(F)
Mother Goose, 869
Old Mother West Wind, 1903(F)
The Perfect Present, 5830(F)
Peter Pan, 7589(F)
Rootabaga Stories, 9984(F), 9985(F)
South Pacific, 9676(F)
The Teddy Bears' Picnic, 14249
Ten Little Bears, 453(F)
The 23rd Psalm, 17326
The Velveteen Rabbit, 8209(F)
The Wizard of Oz, 7596(F), 7598(F)
Hague, Michael, ed. *The Book of Dragons,* 7772(F)
Hahn, Don. *Disney's Animation Magic,* 21270
Hahn, Elizabeth. *The Creek,* 15965
The Pawnee, 15966
Hahn, Mary D. *Anna All Year Round,* 9547(F)
Anna on the Farm, 8677(F)
As Ever, Gordy, 8678(F)
Daphne's Book, 8296(F)
The Doll in the Garden, 7774(F)
Following My Own Footsteps, 8444(F)
Following the Mystery Man, 6870(F)
The Gentleman Outlaw and Me-Eli, 9371(F)
The Jellyfish Season, 8445(F)
Promises to the Dead, 9478(F)
The Spanish Kidnapping Disaster, 6871(F)

Stepping on the Cracks, 9661(F)
Tallahassee Higgins, 8446(F)
Time for Andrew, 7775(F)
Wait Till Helen Comes, 7776(F)
Hairs, Joya. *Barrilete,* 15658
Hairston, Martha. *The I Hate Mathematics! Book,* 20613
Hakim, Joy. *An Age of Extremes,* 16468
All the People, 16509
The First Americans, 15967
From Colonies to Country, 16130
Liberty for All? 16410
Liberty for All? 2nd ed, 16249
Making Thirteen Colonies, 16131
The New Nation, 16313
Reconstruction and Reform, 16469
Sourcebook, 15880
War, Peace, and All That Jazz, 16470
War, Terrible War, 16411
Hakim, Rita. *Martin Luther King, Jr. and the March Toward Freedom,* 12742
Haldane, Suzanne (jt. author). *Lakota Hoop Dancer,* 12414
Hale, Anna W. *The Mayflower People,* 16132
Hale, Bruce. *The Chameleon Wore Chartreuse,* 7777(F)
Farewell, My Lunchbag, 7778(F)
The Mystery of Mr. Nice, 7779(F)
Hale, Christine. *Billy and Emma,* 2487(F)
Hale, Christy. *The Complete Poems to Solve,* 11724
Elizabeti's Doll, 4844(F)
Mama Elizabeti, 4845(F)
Those Calculating Crows! 1661(F)
Hale, Irina. *The Naughty Crow,* 5244(F)
Hale, James G. *Down Comes the Rain,* 20728
How Mountains Are Made, 20330
Through Moon and Stars and Night Skies, 3923(F)
Who's Going to Take Care of Me? 5025(F)
Hale, Sarah Josepha. *Mary Had a Little Lamb,* 845
Haley, Amanda. *Dee and Bee,* 4073(F)
It's a Baby's World, 3189(F)
Haley, Gail E. *Altogether, One at a Time,* 8730(F)
A Story, a Story, 10672
Halfmann, Janet. *Life in a Garden,* 18630
Life in the Sea, 19636
Hall, Amanda. *The Storytelling Star,* 10607
Sun-Day, Moon-Day, 10555
Hall, David E. *Living with Learning Disabilities,* 17912
Hall, Derek. *Baby Animals,* 5245(F)
Hall, Diane (jt. author). *Celebrate!* 17404, 17405

Celebrate! In Central America, 17406

Hall, Donald. *Lucy's Christmas,* 5831(F)

The Man Who Lived Alone, 11587

The Milkman's Boy, 9548(F)

Old Home Day, 7440(F)

Ox-Cart Man, 4674(F)

When Willard Met Babe Ruth, 10329(F)

Hall, Donald, ed. *The Oxford Book of Children's Verse in America,* 11588

Hall, Eleanor J. *Garbage,* 16978

Hall, Elizabeth. *Child of the Wolves,* 7208(F)

Venus Among the Fishes, 7780(F)

Hall, Godfrey. *Games,* 22010

Hall, Jacque. *What Does the Rabbit Say?* 5246(F)

Hall, Katy. *Creepy Riddles,* 21823

Kitty Riddles, 21824

The Paxton Cheerleaders, 10072(F)

Hall, Kirsten. *At the Carnival,* 6363(F)

Hall, Lynn. *Barry,* 6364

Here Comes Zelda Claus and Other Holiday Disasters, 9728(F)

The Secret Life of Dagmar Schultz, 9872(F)

Windsong, 7209(F)

Hall, Margaret. *Credit Cards and Checks,* 16923

Money, 16924

Your Allowance, 16943

Hall, Martin. *Charlie and Tess,* 2164(F)

Hall, Melanie. *In Our Image,* 5651

July Is a Mad Mosquito, 11968

On Hanukkah, 17462

On Passover, 6070

On Purim, 17463

On Rosh Hashanah and Yom Kippur, 17464

Hall, Nancy Christen. *Mouse at Night,* 2165(F)

Hall, Wendell E. *Race with Buffalo,* 11322

Hall, Zoe. *The Apple Pie Tree,* 4453(F)

Fall Leaves Fall! 4454(F)

It's Pumpkin Time! 6003(F)

The Surprise Garden, 4455(F)

Hallensleben, Georg. *And If the Moon Could Talk,* 633(F)

Baboon, 5131(F)

Isabelle and the Angel, 1386(F)

The Night Worker, 634(F)

Pauline, 2166(F)

Hallensleben, Georg (jt. author). *Gaspard on Vacation,* 2160(F)

Lisa's Airplane Trip, 2161(F)

Halley, Ned. *Disasters,* 14340

Farm, 20059

Halliburton, Warren J. *African Industries,* 14902

African Landscapes, 14903

African Wildlife, 18631

Africa's Struggle for Independence, 14904

Africa's Struggle to Survive, 14905

Celebrations of African Heritage, 14906

Halliwell, Sarah, ed. *The Renaissance,* 14799

Halls, Kelly M. *Dino-Trekking,* 14425

I Bought a Baby Chicken, 454(F)

Hallworth, Grace, ed. *Down by the River,* 846

Hally, Greg. *Once There Was a Bull . . . (frog),* 2822(F)

Halperin, Wendy A. *Bonaparte,* 1949(F)

The Full Belly Bowl, 964(F)

Homeplace, 3423(F)

Hunting the White Cow, 5409(F)

The Lampfish of Twill, 7921(F)

Love Is . . . , 17707

Once upon a Company, 16944

Sophie and Rose, 3275(F)

The Trolls, 9883(F)

When Chickens Grow Teeth, 4174(F)

Halpern, Joan. *The Carp in the Bathtub,* 7413(F)

Halpern, Shari. *The Apple Pie Tree,* 4453(F)

Fall Leaves Fall! 4454(F)

Hush, Little Baby, 708(F)

I Love Trucks! 21324

It's Pumpkin Time! 6003(F)

Little Robin Redbreast, 855(F)

No, No, Titus! 5343(F)

The Surprise Garden, 4455(F)

Tickly Prickly, 303(F)

Halsey, Megan. *Circus 1-2-3,* 455(F)

One Bean, 20260

Pumpkin Day, Pumpkin Night, 3857(F)

Telling Time, 20650

3 Pandas Planting, 456(F)

Who Wakes Rooster? 5345(F)

Halstead, Virginia. *Spectacular Science,* 11960

Ten-Second Rainshowers, 11645

Halter, Susan (jt. author). *No One Told the Aardvark,* 1146(F)

Haluska, Vicki. *The Arapaho Indians,* 15968

Halverson, Lydia. *Jack and the Beanstalk,* 11015

A Visit with Great-Grandma, 3502(F)

Halvorsen, Lisa. *Letters Home from Grand Canyon,* 16616

Letters Home from Yosemite, 16784

Letters Home from Zimbabwe, 14979

Letters Home from Zion, 16617

Hamanaka, Sheila. *All the Colors of the Earth,* 3190(F)

Class Clown, 10081(F)

Class President, 10082(F)

The Heart of the Wood, 4410(F)

The Hokey Pokey, 4208(F)

I Look Like a Girl, 1218(F)

In Search of the Spirit, 15123

The Journey, 17563

Molly the Brave and Me, 6548(F)

School's Out, 7459(F)

A Visit to Amy-Claire, 4029(F)

Hamilton, DeWitt. *Sad Days, Glad Days,* 4971(F)

Hamilton, Jake. *Special Effects,* 21271

Hamilton, Janice. *Canada,* 15578, 15579

Quebec, 15580

Hamilton, John. *The Attorney General Through Janet Reno,* 12957

Transportation, 21284

Weapons of War, 21387

Hamilton, Kersten. *The Butterfly Book,* 19552

Hamilton, Laurie. *Air,* 20676

Energy, 20840

Water, 20747

Hamilton, Martha. *How and Why Stories,* 10556

Noodlehead Stories, 10557

Stories in My Pocket, 14088

Hamilton, Morse. *Belching Hill,* 10814

The Garden of Eden Motel, 7441(F)

Hamilton, Virginia. *The All Jahdu Storybook,* 7781(F)

The Bells of Christmas, 9729(F)

Bluish, 7442(F)

Cousins, 8679(F)

Drylongso, 8680(F)

The Girl Who Spun Gold, 10914

Her Stories, 11340

The House of Dies Drear, 6872(F)

Jaguarundi, 7782(F)

Justice and Her Brothers, 7443(F)

M. C. Higgins, the Great, 7444(F)

The Mystery of Drear House, 6873(F)

The People Could Fly, 11341

Plain City, 8447(F)

A Ring of Tricksters, 10558

Second Cousins, 8681(F)

When Birds Could Talk and Bats Could Sing, 11342

Zeely, 8682(F)

Hamlin, Janet. *Escape to the Forest,* 9684(F)

Hamm, Diane J. *Daughter of Suqua,* 9161(F)

How Many Feet in the Bed? 457(F)

Laney's Lost Momma, 3191(F)

Rockabye Farm, 693(F)

Hammer, Loretta J. *The Tree That Owns Itself,* 8932(F)

Hammerslough, Jane. *Everything You Need to Know About Skin Care,* 18196

Hammond, Tim. *Sports,* 22011

Hampton, Wilborn. *Kennedy Assassinated! The World Mourns*, 13061

Han, Carolyn. *Why Snails Have Shells*, 10754

Han, Oki S. *Basho and the Fox*, 4775(F)

Han, Suzanne C. *The Rabbit's Tail*, 10727

Han, Yu-Mei. *Round Is a Pancake*, 321(F)

Hanan, Jessica. *When Someone You Love Is Addicted*, 17866

Hancock, Lyn. *Nunavut*, 15581

Handelman, Dorothy. *Get the Ball, Slim*, 6449(F)
I Like Mess, 6450(F)
I'll Do It Later, 6695(F)
Let Me Help! 6696(F)
Molly in the Middle, 6538(F)
Mud! 6661(F)
My Brother, the Pest, 6205(F)
The New Kid, 6410(F)
No New Pants! 6452(F)
The Rainy Day Grump, 6321(F)

Handford, Martin. *Where's Waldo?* 21867(F)

Handson, Rick. *Count Your Way Through Israel*, 15522

Handville, Robert. *Lord of the Sky*, 11476

Hanel, Wolfram. *Abby*, 7210(F)
Little Elephant's Song, 2167(F)
Mary and the Mystery Dog, 7211(F)
Mia the Beach Cat, 6365(F)
Old Mahony and the Bear Family, 6366(F)
Rescue at Sea! 6874(F)

Hanke, Karen. *The Jazz Fly*, 2134(F)

Hanley, Sally. *A. Philip Randolph*, 12782

Hanly, Sheila. *The Big Book of Animals*, 18632

Hanmer, Trudy J. *The All-American Girls Professional Baseball League*, 22094

Hanna, Cheryl. *The Story of Stagecoach Mary Fields*, 12722

Hanna, Jack. *Jungle Jack Hanna's Safari Adventure*, 18633
Jungle Jack Hanna's What Zookeepers Do, 20025

Hanrahan, Brendan. *My Sisters Love My Clothes*, 3669(F)

Hans, Shabo. *Cactus*, 20252

Hansard, Peter. *I Like Monkeys Because . . .*, 18997

Hansen, Biruta A. *Parading with Piglets*, 47(F)

Hansen, Brooks. *Caesar's Antlers*, 7783(F)

Hansen, Elvig. *Guinea Pig*, 19896

Hansen, Joyce. *Breaking Ground, Breaking Silence*, 16690
The Captive, 9283(F)
The Gift-Giver, 8297(F)

I Thought My Soul Would Rise and Fly, 9549(F)
Women of Hope, 12655
Yellow Bird and Me, 8298(F)

Hansen, Mark V. (jt. author). *Chicken Soup for Little Souls*, 4921(F)

Hansen, Ole Steen. *Denmark*, 15449
Vietnam, 15163

Hansen, Ron. *The Shadowmaker*, 7784(F)

Hansen, Rosanna. *My First Book About Space*, 18514

Hansen-Smith, Bradford. *The Hands-On Marvelous Ball Book*, 20603

Hanson, Mary Elizabeth. *Snug*, 2168(F)

Hanson, Peter E. *Buttons for General Washington*, 4812(F)
Keep the Lights Burning, Abbie, 6597

Hanson, Regina. *The Face at the Window*, 4675(F)
The Tangerine Tree, 4972(F)

Hanson, Rick. *Columbus Day*, 17382
I Pledge Allegiance, 6688

Hanze. *Yann and the Whale*, 1171(F)

Harber, Frances. *The Brothers' Promise*, 11149

Harbison, Elizabeth M. *Loaves of Fun*, 20095

Harbour, Elizabeth. *The Thistle Princess*, 10421(F)

Hard, Charlotte. *Polly Molly Woof Woof*, 2388(F)

Harder, Dan. *A Child's California*, 16785
Colliding with Chris, 1219(F)

Harding, Donal. *The Leaving Summer*, 6875(F)

Hardy, Sian. *A Treasury of Christmas Stories*, 9730(F)

Hardy, Tad. *Lost Cat*, 5247(F)

Hare, Tony. *Animal Fact-File*, 18944

Hargittai, Magdolna. *Cooking the Hungarian Way*, 21704

Hargrove, Jim. *Abraham Lincoln*, 13068
Dwight D. Eisenhower, 13031
Germany, 15324
Harry S. Truman, 13108
Lyndon B. Johnson, 13057
Martin Van Buren, 13112
Thomas Jefferson, 13050

Haring, Keith. *Big*, 189(F)
Ten, 458(F)

Hariton, Anca. *Butterfly Story*, 19553
Compost! 3169
Dandelion Adventures, 20240

Harjo, Joy. *The Good Luck Cat*, 5248(F)

Harker, Lesley. *My Family's Changing*, 17689

Harkonen, Reijo. *The Children of China*, 15065
The Children of Egypt, 15502

Harlan, Judith. *Mamphela Ramphele*, 13845

Sounding the Alarm, 13244

Harley, Avis. *Fly with Poetry*, 11589

Harley, Bill. *Nothing Happened*, 694(F)
Sarah's Story, 1220(F)
Sitting Down to Eat, 2169(F)

Harlow, Joan Hiat. *Star in the Storm*, 6876(F)

Harman, Amanda. *Elephants*, 19164
Leopards, 19088
Manatees and Dugongs, 19735
Rhinoceroses, 18945
Sharks, 19761
South American Monkeys, 18998
Tigers, 19089
Whales, 19790

Harmon, Dan. *Juan Ponce de León and the Search for the Fountain of Youth*, 12150

Harmon, Rod. *American Civil Rights Leaders*, 12656

Harms, Ann M. (jt. author). *Dear Dr. King*, 17029

Harness, Cheryl. *Aaron's Shirt*, 3178(F)
Abe Lincoln Goes to Washington, 1837–1865, 13069
The Amazing Impossible Erie Canal, 16250
Fudge, 7200(F)
George Washington, 13115
Ghosts of the Twentieth Century, 14554
Ghosts of the White House, 15881
Mark Twain and the Queens of the Mississippi, 12608
Midnight in the Cemetery, 48(F)
The Night Before Christmas, 11840
Papa's Christmas Gift, 11831
Remember the Ladies, 12657
They're Off! 16314
Three Young Pilgrims, 9196(F)
Young Abe Lincoln, 13070
Young John Quincy, 13004
Young Teddy Roosevelt, 13102

Harp, David. *Swanfall*, 19311

Harper, Dan. *Telling Time with Big Mama Cat*, 190(F)

Harper, Isabelle. *My Cats Nick and Nora*, 5249(F)
Our New Puppy, 5250(F)

Harper, Jessica. *I Forgot My Shoes*, 4175(F)
I'm Not Going to Chase the Cat Today! 2170(F)

Harper, Jo. *The Legend of Mexicatl*, 11402
Outrageous, Bodacious Boliver Boggs! 4176(F)
Prairie Dog Pioneers, 4676(F)

Harper, Josephine (jt. author). *Prairie Dog Pioneers*, 4676(F)

Harper, Judith E. *African Americans and the Revolutionary War*, 16198
Maya Angelou, 12495

Harper, Piers. *Cabbage Moon*, 1948(F)
If You Love a Bear, 1221(F)
Harper, Suzanne. *Clouds*, 20771
Lightning, 20691
Harper, Suzanne (jt. author). *Boitano's Edge*, 13588
Harrah, Madge. *My Brother, My Enemy*, 9237(F)
The Nobody Club, 8683(F)
Harrell, Beatrice O. *Longwalker's Journey*, 9162(F)
Harrington, Denis J. *Sports Great Jim Kelly*, 13617
Top 10 Women Tennis Players, 13373
Harris, Alan. *The Great Voyager Adventure*, 18515
Harris, Annie (jt. author). *Painting*, 13930
Harris, Aurand (jt. author). *Plays Children Love, Volume II*, 12022
Harris, Cottrell J. *Music in the Family*, 3571(F)
Harris, Emily. *Lighthouse Dog to the Rescue*, 5362(F)
Harris, Geraldine. *Gods and Pharaohs from Egyptian Mythology*, 11447
Harris, Jack C. *Adventure Gaming*, 22012
Plastic Model Kits, 21794
Harris, Jacqueline L. *Communicable Diseases*, 17964
Drugs and Disease, 17867
Hereditary Diseases, 17965
Harris, Jim. *Jack and the Giant*, 11343
Slim and Miss Prim, 9898(F)
The Three Little Dinosaurs, 10992
The Three Little Javelinas, 2403(F)
The Tortoise and the Jackrabbit, 11066(F)
Harris, Jim, reteller. *The Three Little Dinosaurs*, 10992
Harris, Joel Chandler. *Brer Rabbit and Boss Lion*, 11344
Jump! The Adventures of Brer Rabbit, 11345
Harris, Laurie L., ed. *Biography for Beginners*, 12658
Biography Today, 13211
Harris, Lee. *Never Let Your Cat Make Lunch for You*, 2171(F)
Harris, Nathaniel. *Mummies*, 14628
Harris, Nicholas. *The Incredible Journey to the Beginning of Time*, 14555
The Incredible Journey to the Depths of the Ocean, 19876
The Incredible Journey to the Planets, 18474
Harris, Pamela. *Hot, Cold, Shy, Bold*, 191
Harris, Pamela K. *Clarinets*, 14222
Harris, Robie H. *Happy Birth Day!* 3670(F)

Hi New Baby! 3671(F)
It's Perfectly Normal, 18260
It's So Amazing, 18261
Harris, Susan Y. (jt. author). *Daisy's Garden*, 2120(F)
Harris, Trudy. *100 Days of School*, 459(F)
Pattern Fish, 192(F)
Harris, Zoe. *Pinatas and Smiling Skeletons*, 17366
Harrison, Barbara. *A Ripple of Hope*, 12919
Theo, 9662(F)
Harrison, Carol. *Dinosaurs Everywhere!* 14426
Harrison, Cora. *The Famine Secret*, 9098(F)
The Secret of Drumshee Castle, 9099(F)
The Secret of the Seven Crosses, 9100(F)
Harrison, David L. *The Animals' Song*, 1222(F)
The Boy Who Counted Stars, 11590
A Farmer's Garden, 2172(F)
The Purchase of Small Secrets, 11591
A Thousand Cousins, 11592
When Cows Come Home, 2173(F)
Wild Country, 11955
Harrison, George H. *Backyard Bird Watching for Kids*, 19233
Harrison, Joanna. *Dear Bear*, 2174(F)
When Mom Turned into a Monster, 1223(F)
Where's That Cat? 5031(F)
Harrison, Maggie. *Angels on Roller Skates*, 7445(F)
Lizzie's List, 7446(F)
Harrison, Michael, comp. *The Oxford Treasury of Time Poems*, 11594
Harrison, Michael, ed. *The Oxford Book of Story Poems*, 11593
Harrison, Stuart. *Fit for Life*, 18202
Harrison, Supenn. *Cooking the Thai Way*, 21705
Harrison, Ted. *Children of the Yukon*, 6877(F)
The Cremation of Sam McGee, 11694
A Northern Alphabet, 49(F)
O Canada, 15582
Harrison, Troon. *Aaron's Awful Allergies*, 4973(F)
Don't Dig So Deep, Nicholas! 1224(F)
The Dream Collector, 695(F)
The Floating Orchard, 1225(F)
Lavender Moon, 2937(F)
The Memory Horse, 3192(F)
Harshman, Marc. *All the Way to Morning*, 696(F)
Only One, 460(F)
The Storm, 4974(F)
Harshman, Terry Webb. *Porcupine's Pajama Party*, 6367(F)

Harston, Jerry. *Bill and Hillary*, 13023
Dick Rutan and Jena Yeager, 12066
Hart, Alison. *Hostage*, 6878(F)
Shadow Horse, 7212(F)
Hart, Avery. *Ancient Greece!* 14682
Knights and Castles, 14765
Pyramids! 50 Hands-on Activities to Experience Ancient Egypt, 14629
Hart, Celia. *What Do We Know About Hinduism?* 17187
What Do We Know About Judaism? 17180
Hart, George, ed. *Ancient Egypt*, 14630
Hart, Jane, ed. *Singing Bee! A Collection of Favorite Children's Songs*, 14244
Hart, Philip S. *Up in the Air*, 12092
Hart, Tony. *Leonardo da Vinci*, 12213
Michelangelo, 12259
Picasso, 12280
Toulouse-Lautrec, 12303
Hartas, Leo. *Haunted Castle*, 6879(F)
Mimi and the Dream House, 2800(F)
Mimi and the Picnic, 2801(F)
Mimi's Christmas, 3467(F)
Hartelius, Margaret A. *Easy Costumes You Don't Have to Sew*, 21538
Monster Math Picnic, 500(F)
Monster Math School Time, 209(F)
Monster Money, 501(F)
Harter, Debbie. *The Animal Boogie*, 2175(F)
Bear About Town, 1814(F)
Bear in a Square, 322(F)
Bear on a Bike, 6207(F)
Bear's Busy Family, 1815(F)
Can You See the Red Balloon? 162(F)
Herb, the Vegetarian Dragon, 1792(F)
Walking Through the Jungle, 1226(F)
Hartley, Donald. *Trojan Horse*, 14698
Hartley, Karen. *Caterpillar*, 19554
Centipede, 19446
Cockroach, 19447
Fly, 19448
Grasshopper, 19449
Head Louse, 19450
Hearing in Living Things, 18820
Ladybug, 19531
Snail, 19608
Spider, 19582
Termite, 19451
Hartling, Peter. *Ben Loves Anna*, 8684(F)
Hartman, Gail. *As the Crow Flies*, 193(F)
As the Roadrunner Runs, 1227(F)

Hartman, Laura. *If It Weren't for Benjamin (I'd Always Get to Lick the Icing Spoon)*, 3681(F)

Hartman, Thomas (jt. author). *How Do You Spell God?* 17188

Lost and Found, 17703

Hartmann, Wendy. *The Dinosaurs Are Back and It's All Your Fault Edward!* 4177(F)

Hartry, Nancy. *Jocelyn and the Ballerina*, 4178(F)

Hartung, Susan Kathleen. *Dear Juno*, 3831(F)

Hartzog, John Daniel. *Everyday Science Experiments in the Kitchen*, 18318

Everyday Science Experiments with Food, 20096

Harvey, Amanda. *My Friend John*, 4070(F)

Up the Chimney, 10999

Harvey, Bonnie Carman. *Jane Addams*, 13127

Harvey, Brett. *My Prairie Christmas*, 5832(F)

Harvey, Miles. *The Fall of the Soviet Union*, 15418

Look What Came from China, 15066

Look What Came from Egypt, 15503

Look What Came from France, 15308

Look What Came from Italy, 15383

Look What Came from Japan, 15124

Look What Came from Mexico, 15617

Look What Came from Russia, 15419

Women's Voting Rights, 17032

Harvey, Paul. *How to Make a Chemical Volcano and Other Mysterious Experiments*, 18324

Harvey, Roland. *My Place in Space*, 18395

Harvill, Kitty. *Jack and the Animals*, 11332(F)

Sitting Down to Eat, 2169(F)

Harwood, Chuck. *Hot-Tempered Farmers*, 10194(F)

Hasday, Judy. *Keri Russell*, 12461

Hasegawa, Tomoko. *Contemplating Your Bellybutton*, 18232

Haseley, Dennis. *Crosby*, 4000(F)

Ghost Catcher, 7785(F)

Haskamp, Steve. *Roadsigns*, 11469

Haskins, Francine. *I Remember "121,"* 3672

Haskins, Jim. *African Beginnings*, 14907

Amazing Grace, 12937

Bayard Rustin, 12783

Bill Cosby, 12370

Black, Blue, and Gray, 16412

Black Eagles, 21079

Bound for America, 16251

Carter G. Woodson, 12822

Count Your Way Through Brazil, 15740

Count Your Way Through China, 15067

Count Your Way Through France, 15309

Count Your Way Through Germany, 15325

Count Your Way Through Greece, 15385

Count Your Way Through India, 15103

Count Your Way Through Ireland, 15350

Count Your Way Through Israel, 15522

Count Your Way Through Italy, 15384

Count Your Way Through Japan, 15125

Count Your Way Through Russia, 15420

Count Your Way Through the Arab World, 15547

The Day Fort Sumter Was Fired On, 16413

The Day Martin Luther King, Jr., Was Shot, 16510

Freedom Rides, 17033

I Have a Dream, 12743

The Life and Death of Martin Luther King, Jr., 12744

One More River to Cross, 12659

Space Challenger, 12079

Sports Great Magic Johnson, 13534

Haskins, Jim (jt. author). *I Am Rosa Parks*, 12778

Haskins, Lori. *Ducks in Muck*, 6368(F)

Haslam, Andrew (jt. author). *Earth*, 18427

Electricity, 21239

Plants, 20225

Sound, 20931

Hasler, Eveline. *The Giantess*, 4975(F)

Hasselriis, Else. *Shen of the Sea*, 8988(F)

Hasselriis, Malthe. *Tales of a Chinese Grandmother*, 10739

Hassett, Ann. *We Got My Brother at the Zoo*, 3673(F)

Hassett, Ann (jt. author). *Cat Up a Tree*, 4179(F)

Charles of the Wild, 2176(F)

We Got My Brother at the Zoo, 3673(F)

Hassett, John. *Cat Up a Tree*, 4179(F)

Charles of the Wild, 2176(F)

We Got My Brother at the Zoo, 3673(F)

Hassig, Susan M. *Iraq*, 15548

Panama, 15668

Hastings, Kathryn K. *Fanciful Faces and Handbound Books*, 14080

Hastings, Selina. *The Children's Illustrated Bible*, 17282

Hastings, Selina, reteller. *Sir Gawain and the Loathly Lady*, 10993

Hathaway, Jim. *Cameroon in Pictures*, 15028

Hatherly, Janelle. *Dolphins and Porpoises*, 19685

Hathorn, Elizabeth. *The Tram to Bondi Beach*, 6369(F)

Hathorn, Libby. *Freya's Fantastic Surprise*, 5503(F)

Sky Sash So Blue, 4677(F)

Hatrick, Gloria. *Masks*, 7786(F)

Hatt, Christine. *The American West*, 16315

Slavery, 15882

Haugaard, Erik C. *A Boy's Will*, 9101(F)

Under the Black Flag, 6880(F)

Haugaard, Kay. *No Place*, 7344(F)

Haughton, Emma. *Alcohol*, 17868

Living with Deafness, 17913

Rainy Day, 3674(F)

A Right to Smoke? 17869

Hauman, Doris. *The Little Engine That Could*, 5592(F)

Hauman, George. *The Little Engine That Could*, 5592(F)

Hausam, Josephine Sander (jt. author). *Welcome to Italy*, 15379

Hausam, Josephine Sanders. *Italy*, 15386

Hauser, Jill F. *Gizmos and Gadgets*, 21441

Science Play! 18319

Hauser, Pierre. *Illegal Aliens*, 17142

Hausherr, Rosmarie. *Celebrating Families*, 3675(F)

What Food Is This? 20097

Hausman, Gerald. *Cats of Myth*, 10559

Doctor Bird, 11423

Dogs of Myth, 10560

The Story of Blue Elk, 11256

Tom Cringle, 9284(F)

Hausman, Loretta (jt. author). *Cats of Myth*, 10559

Dogs of Myth, 10560

Hautzig, David. *At the Supermarket*, 3193

On the Air, 14310

Hautzig, Deborah. *Beauty and the Beast*, 10428

Little Witch Goes to School, 6370(F)

Little Witch's Big Night, 6004(F)

The Nutcracker Ballet, 6371(F)

Hautzig, Esther. *On the Air*, 14310

Havard, Christian. *The Fox*, 19121

Havelin, Kate. *Child Abuse*, 17708

Family Violence, 17659

Haverstock, Nathan A. *Brazil in Pictures*, 15741

Cuba in Pictures, 15705

Nicaragua in Pictures, 15669
Paraguay in Pictures, 15742
Havill, Juanita. *Jamaica and Brianna*, 4001(F)
Jamaica and the Substitute Teacher, 5504(F)
Jamaica's Blue Marker, 4002(F)
Jamaica's Find, 3194(F)
Sato and the Elephants, 8965(F)
Treasure Map, 3676(F)
Hawcock, David. *The Amazing Pop-Up Pull-Out Body in a Book*, 18061
The Amazing Pop-Up, Pull-Out Space Shuttle, 20990
Hawes, Judy. *Fireflies in the Night*, 19452
Why Frogs Are Wet, 18725
Hawkes, Kevin. *And to Think That We Thought That We'd Never Be Friends*, 1243(F)
Boogie Bones, 1359(F)
Dreamland, 3411(F)
Imagine That! Poems of Never-Was, 11876
Jason's Bears, 3018(F)
Marven of the Great North Woods, 2951(F)
My Friend the Piano, 1080(F)
My Little Sister Ate One Hare, 448(F)
Painting the Wind, 12306
Timothy Tunny Swallowed a Bunny, 4170(F)
The Turnip, 10886
Weslandia, 1160(F)
Hawkes, Nigel. *Energy*, 20831
Nuclear Power, 20844
Hawkins, Colin. *Come for a Ride on the Ghost Train*, 1228(F)
Hey Diddle Diddle, 847
Hawkins, Jacqui. *Come for a Ride on the Ghost Train*, 1228(F)
Hey Diddle Diddle, 847
Hawkins, Jacqui (jt. author). *Come for a Ride on the Ghost Train*, 1228(F)
Hey Diddle Diddle, 847
Hawks, Robert. *The Richest Kid in the World*, 6881(F)
Hawthorne, Nathaniel. *Wonder Book and Tanglewood Tales*, 11478
Hawxhurst, Joan C. *Bubbe and Gram*, 3677(F)
Hayashi, Nancy. *Bunny Bungalow*, 2645(F)
My Two Grandmothers, 3827(F)
Haycock, Kate. *Skiing*, 22248
Hayden, Kate. *Twisters!* 20692
Hayden, Melissa, ed. *The Nutcracker Ballet*, 14288
Hayes, Ann. *Meet the Marching Smithereens*, 14223
Meet the Orchestra, 14224
Hayes, Daniel. *Eye of the Beholder*, 9873(F)
Hayes, Donna. *Brandy*, 12358

Hayes, Geoffrey. *The Secret of Foghorn Island*, 6372(F)
Thump and Plunk, 6701(F)
Treasure of the Lost Lagoon, 6373(F)
Hayes, Joe. *Little Gold Star/Estrellita de oro*, 11346
A Spoon for Every Bite, 3195(F)
Hayes, Sarah. *The Candlewick Book of Fairy Tales*, 10429
Crumbling Castle, 7787(F)
Eat Up, Gemma, 3196(F)
The Grumpalump, 2177(F)
Happy Christmas, Gemma, 5833(F)
Lucy Anna and the Finders, 1229(F)
This Is the Bear, 848
This Is the Bear and the Bad Little Girl, 2178(F)
This Is the Bear and the Scary Night, 2179(F)
Hayhurst, Chris. *Bicycle Stunt Riding!* 22158
Mountain Biking, 22159
Snowboarding! 22280
Wakeboarding! Throw a Tantrum, 22013
Hayles, Karen. *Whale Is Stuck*, 2180(F)
Hayles, Marsha. *Beach Play*, 3197(F)
Pet of a Pet, 2181(F)
Haynes, Max. *Dinosaur Island*, 2938(F)
Grandma's Gone to Live in the Stars, 3678(F)
Ticklemonster and Me, 3679(F)
Hays, Michael. *Abiyoyo*, 10713
Because You're Lucky, 5081(F)
The History of Counting, 20634
Kevin and His Dad, 3899(F)
The Tin Heart, 4568(F)
Hayward, Linda. *All Stuck Up*, 11347
Baby Moses, 17283
Baker, Baker, Cookie Maker, 6374(F)
The First Thanksgiving, 17500
Hello, House! 11348
Hayward, Ruth Ann (jt. author). *What's Cooking?* 21745
Haywood, Carolyn. *"B" Is for Betsy*, 10073(F)
Haywood, John, ed. *The Romans*, 14721
Hazelaar, Cor. *Zoo Dreams*, 697(F)
Hazell, Rebecca. *The Barefoot Book of Heroic Children*, 13730
Heroes, 13731
Hazeltine, Alice I., ed. *The Year Around*, 11956
Hazen, Barbara S. *Digby*, 6375(F)
Even If I Did Something Awful? 3680(F)
If It Weren't for Benjamin (I'd Always Get to Lick the Icing Spoon), 3681(F)
Mommy's Office, 3198(F)
Stay, Fang, 5251(F)

That Toad Is Mine! 4003(F)
Tight Times, 5252(F)
Where Do Bears Sleep? 698(F)
Hazen-Hammond, Susan. *Thunder Bear and Ko*, 15969
Head, Judith. *Culebra Cut*, 9133(F)
Heal, Gillian. *Grandpa Bear's Fantastic Scarf*, 2182(F)
Heale, Jay. *Portugal*, 15476
South Africa, 14980
Heale, Jonathan. *Lady Muck*, 2486(F)
The Ugly Duckling, 10466(F)
Healy, Dennis. *The Illustrated Rules of Baseball*, 22095
Heaney, Marie, reteller. *The Names Upon the Harp*, 10994
Heap, Sue. *Cowboy Baby*, 3199(F)
Cowboy Kid, 669(F)
Harry the Explorer, 10235(F)
Hearn, Diane D. *Bad Luck Boswell*, 2183(F)
Bear's Hiccups, 6198(F)
Down Dairy Farm Road, 5026(F)
Turtle Dreams, 6199(F)
Hearne, Betsy. *Eli's Ghost*, 6882(F)
Eliza's Dog, 7213(F)
Listening for Leroy, 8685(F)
Seven Brave Women, 3682(F)
Who's in the Hall? A Mystery in Four Chapters, 6883(F)
Wishes, Kisses, and Pigs, 7788(F)
Heath, Amy. *Sofie's Role*, 5834(F)
Heatwole, Marsha. *Jambo, Watoto!* 2483(F)
Hebert, Holly. *60 Super Simple Crafts*, 21442
Hecht, Jeff. *Optics*, 20871
Heckman, Philip. *Waking Upside Down*, 1230(F)
Hedderwick, Mairi. *Brave Janet Reachfar*, 7425(F)
Venus Peter Saves the Whale, 2644(F)
Hedlund, Carey. *Night Fell at Harry's Farm*, 3200(F)
Hedlund, Irene. *Mighty Mountain and the Three Strong Women*, 10815
Heegaard, Mary E. *Coping with Death and Grief*, 17709
Heelan, Jamee Riggio. *The Making of My Special Hand*, 17914
Rolling Along, 17915
Heerboth, Sharon (jt. author). *Movies*, 14312
Heerden, Marjorie van. *Baby Dance*, 3912(F)
Hegel, Annette. *Saturday Is Pattyday*, 5043(F)
Hehenberger, Shelly. *Isn't My Name Magical? Sister and Brother Poems*, 11748
Hehner, Barbara. *First on the Moon*, 20991
Hehner, Barbara (jt. author). *Journey to Ellis Island*, 17547
Looking at Senses, 18164

Looking at the Body, 18080
Looking at Weather, 20793
Hehrlich, Gretel. *A Blizzard Year*, 7447(F)
Heidbreder, Robert. *I Wished for a Unicorn*, 1231(F)
Heide, Florence Parry. *The Day of Ahmed's Secret*, 4678(F)
House of Wisdom, 8957(F)
It's About Time! 194
Oh, Grow Up! 4976(F)
Sami and the Time of the Troubles, 4679(F)
The Shrinking of Treehorn, 9874(F)
Some Things Are Scary, 3201(F)
Tio Armando, 3683(F)
Heidelbach, Nikolaus. *Where the Girls Are*, 50(F)
Heilbroner, Joan. *Tom the TV Cat*, 6376(F)
Heiligman, Deborah. *From Caterpillar to Butterfly*, 19555
The Mysterious Ocean Highway, 19849
The New York Public Library Kid's Guide to Research, 14089
Heilman, Joan R. *Tons of Trash*, 16979
Heine, Helme. *The Boxer and the Princess*, 2184(F)
Friends, 2185(F)
Friends Go Adventuring, 2186(F)
The Pearl, 2187(F)
The Pigs' Wedding, 2188(F)
Seven Wild Pigs, 2189(F)
Heinlen, Marieka. *Hands Are Not for Hitting*, 2990(F)
Heinrichs, Ann. *Arizona*, 16618
Arkansas, 16862
Brazil, 15743
California, 16786
China, 15068
Egypt, 15504
Florida, 16863
Indiana, 16557
Japan, 15126, 15127
Louisa Catherine Johnson Adams, 13126
Mexico, 15618
Montana, 16619
Nepal, 15164
Ohio, 16558
Pennsylvania, 16691
Rhode Island, 16692
South Africa, 14981
Texas, 16908
Tibet, 15165
Venezuela, 15744
Heinrichs, Susan. *The Atlantic Ocean*, 19821
Heinst, Marie. *My First Number Book*, 461
Heintze, Ty. *Valley of the Eels*, 10195(F)
Heinz, Brian J. *Butternut Hollow Pond*, 20518
The Monsters' Test, 6005(F)

Nanuk, 5253(F)
The Wolves, 19122
Heinze, Mitchell. *Hoop Stars*, 22133
Heisel, Sharon E. *Precious Gold, Precious Jade*, 9372(F)
Wrapped in a Riddle, 6884(F)
Heitler, Susan M. *David Decides About Thumbsucking*, 4977(F)
Hellard, Susan. *Baby Lemur*, 2190(F)
Leonardo da Vinci, 12213
Michelangelo, 12259
Picasso, 12280
Toulouse-Lautrec, 12303
Helldorfer, M. C. *Cabbage Rose*, 10430(F)
Daniel's Gift, 5835(F)
Hog Music, 9373(F)
Night of the White Stag, 10431(F)
Phoebe and the River Flute, 10432(F)
Silver Rain Brown, 3684(F)
Spook House, 6885(F)
Heller, Debbe. *Building a Dream*, 12702
Heller, Julek. *The Minstrel in the Tower*, 9071(F)
Heller, Nicholas. *Elwood and the Witch*, 2191(F)
Ogres! Ogres! Ogres! A Feasting Frenzy from A to Z, 51(F)
Peas, 1232(F)
Heller, Ruth. *Behind the Mask*, 14029
Chickens Aren't the Only Ones, 4456(F)
The Egyptian Cinderella, 10658
Fantastic! Wow! and Unreal! A Book About Interjections and Conjunctions, 14030
Fine Lines, 12546
"Galápagos" Means "Tortoises." 18634
King of the Birds, 10539
Kites Sail High, 14031
The Korean Cinderella, 10721
Many Luscious Lollipops, 14032
Merry-Go-Round, 14033
Mine, All Mine, 14034
A Sea Within a Sea, 21911
Up, Up and Away, 14035
Hellman, Hal. *Beyond Your Senses*, 21036
Hellums, Julia P. (jt. author). *Hold the Anchovies!* 21735
Helman, Andrea. *Northwest Animal Babies*, 18877
O Is for Orca, 52(F)
1, 2, 3 Moose, 462
Helmer, Diana Star. *The History of Figure Skating*, 22223
The History of Soccer, 22292
Let's Talk About When Someone You Know Is in a Nursing Home, 17857
Helmer, Diana Star (jt. author). *Football*, 22187
Soccer, 22299

Helmer, Jean. *Amazing World of Butterflies and Moths*, 19569
Helmer, Marilyn. *Fog Cat*, 5254(F)
Mr. McGratt and the Ornery Cat, 5255(F)
Henba, Bobbie. *Pianna*, 3374(F)
Henbest, Nigel (jt. author). *Big Bang*, 18384
Is Anybody Out There? 20978
The Space Atlas, 18385
Hench, Larry L. *Boing-Boing the Bionic Cat*, 7789(F)
Henderickson, Karen. *Baby and I Can Play and Fun with Toddlers*, 3685
Henderson, Aileen K. *The Monkey Thief*, 6886(F)
The Summer of the Bonepile Monster, 6887(F)
Treasure of Panther Peak, 8686(F)
Henderson, Ann (jt. author). *Pretend Soup and Other Real Recipes*, 21710
Henderson, Carolyn. *Horse and Pony Breeds*, 19993
Horse and Pony Care, 19994
Horse and Pony Shows and Events, 19995
Improve Your Riding Skills, 22205
Henderson, Doug. *Asteroid Impact*, 20310
Henderson, Douglas. *Dinosaur Ghosts*, 14420
Dinosaur Tree, 20202
Living with Dinosaurs, 14435
Henderson, Harry. *Stephen Hawking*, 13308
Henderson, Kathy. *The Baby Dances*, 3686(F)
The Little Boat, 3202(F)
Newborn, 3687(F)
The Storm, 4457(F)
A Year in the City, 4458(F)
Henderson, Meryl. *The Purchase of Small Secrets*, 11591
Hendra, Sue. *Henry's Song*, 1945(F)
Numbers, 463
Oliver's Wood, 2192(F)
Opposites, 231(F)
Hendrick, Mary J. *If Anything Ever Goes Wrong at the Zoo*, 1233(F)
Hendrickson, Ann-Marie. *Nat Turner*, 12805
Hendrickson, Steve. *Enduro Racing*, 22240
Hendry, Diana. *Dog Donovan*, 5256(F)
The Very Noisy Night, 699(F)
Hendry, Linda. *Jocelyn and the Ballerina*, 4178(F)
The Kids Can Press French and English Phrase Book, 14096
Lanyard, 21543
Making Gift Boxes, 21443
Making Picture Frames, 21663
Heneghan, James. *Wish Me Luck*, 9663(F)

Henkes, Kevin. *The Biggest Boy*, 332(F)
The Birthday Room, 8448(F)
Chester's Way, 4004(F)
Chrysanthemum, 2193(F)
Circle Dogs, 333(F)
Clean Enough, 3203(F)
Good-bye, Curtis, 3204(F)
Julius, the Baby of the World, 2194(F)
Lilly's Purple Plastic Purse, 5505(F)
Oh! 1234(F)
Owen, 2195(F)
Protecting Marie, 7214(F)
Sheila Rae, the Brave, 2196(F)
Shhhh, 3688(F)
Sun and Spoon, 8687(F)
Two Under Par, 8449(F)
A Weekend with Wendell, 2197(F)
Wemberly Worried, 2198(F)
The Zebra Wall, 7448(F)
Henneberger, Robert. *The Wonderful Flight to the Mushroom Planet*, 10158(F)
Hennessy, B. G. *Busy Dinah Dinosaur*, 6377(F)
Corduroy's Halloween, 6006(F)
Meet Dinah Dinosaur, 6378(F)
One Little, Two Little, Three Little Pilgrims, 6143(F)
Road Builders, 5571
Henricksson, John. *Rachel Carson*, 13245
Henry, Barb. *Baby Moses*, 17283
Henry, Christopher. *The Electoral College*, 17114
Presidential Conventions, 17096
Henry, Greg. *Chickens! Chickens!* 4271(F)
Henry, Joanne L. *A Clearing in the Forest*, 9374(F)
Henry, Marguerite. *Album of Horses*, 19996
Brown Sunshine, 7215(F)
King of the Wind, 7216(F)
Misty of Chincoteague, 7217(F)
Mustang, Wild Spirit of the West, 7218(F)
San Domingo, 7219(F)
Henry, Marie H. *Christmas Is Coming!* 5877(F)
Henry, O. *The Gift of the Magi*, 9731(F)
Henry, Sandi. *Cut-Paper Play!* 21618
Kids' Art Works! 21444
Henry, Sondra (jt. author). *Israel*, 15531
Henry, Wolcott. *Sea Critters*, 19632
Henson, Paige. *Drawing with Charcoal and Pastels*, 21577
Drawing with Pencils, 21578
Henstra, Friso. *The Mouse Who Owned the Sun*, 2030(F)
Why Not? 3219(F)
Henterly, Jamichael. *Good Night, Garden Gnome*, 1235(F)

Young Arthur, 11032
Heo, Yumi. *A Is for Asia*, 22(F)
Father's Rubber Shoes, 3689(F)
The Green Frogs, 10728
The Lonely Lioness and the Ostrich Chicks, 10641
One Afternoon, 3205(F)
One Sunday Morning, 3690(F)
Pets! 1971(F)
So Say the Little Monkeys, 11444
Yoshi's Feast, 10817
Hepplewhite, Peter. *Alien Encounters*, 21912
Hepworth, Cathi. *ANTics!* 53(F)
Bug Off! A Swarm of Insect Words, 14036
While You Are Asleep, 3237(F)
Herbert, Don. *Mr. Wizard's Experiments for Young Scientists*, 18320
Mr. Wizard's Supermarket Science, 18321
Herbert, Janis. *The Civil War for Kids*, 16414
Leonardo da Vinci for Kids, 12214
Herbst, Judith. *The Mystery of UFOs*, 21913
Herda, D. J. *Environmental America*, 16693, 16787, 16864, 16909
Ethnic America, 16694, 16910
Herman, Charlotte. *How Yussel Caught the Gefilte Fish*, 6078(F)
Max Malone Makes a Million, 8299(F)
Herman, Gail. *Double-Header*, 6379(F)
Flower Girl, 6380(F)
Just Like Mike, 8688(F)
My Dog Talks, 6381(F)
Storm Chasers, 20693
Tooth Fairy Travels, 7790(F)
Herman, Gail, reteller. *The Lion and the Mouse*, 11064
Herman, R. A. *Pal the Pony*, 6382(F)
Hermann, Spring. *Geronimo*, 12972
R. C. Gorman, 12235
Seeing Lessons, 9285(F)
Hermes, Jules. *The Children of Bolivia*, 15745
Children of Guatemala, 15670
The Children of India, 15104
The Children of Micronesia, 15237
The Children of Morocco, 14958
Hermes, Patricia. *Calling Me Home*, 9375(F)
Cheat the Moon, 8450(F)
The Cousins Club, 8689(F)
Heads, I Win, 8451(F)
I Hate Being Gifted, 8300(F)
Kevin Corbett Eats Flies, 9875(F)
Nothing but Trouble, 9876(F)
Our Strange New Land, 9197(F)
Westward to Home, 9376(F)
You Shouldn't Have to Say Goodbye, 8452(F)
Herndon, Ernest. *The Secret of Lizard Island*, 6888(F)

Herold, Maggie R. *A Very Important Day*, 3206(F)
Herrera, Juan Felipe. *Calling the Doves/El Canto de las Palomas*, 12548
The Upside Down Boy/El niño de cabeza, 10074(F)
Herriot, James. *Blossom Comes Home*, 5257(F)
Moses the Kitten, 5258(F)
Only One Woof, 7220(F)
Smudge, the Little Lost Lamb, 5259(F)
Herron, Carolivia. *Nappy Hair*, 3207(F)
Herschler, Mildred Barger. *The Darkest Corner*, 8453(F)
Hershberger, Priscilla. *Make Costumes!* 21544
Hershberger, Priscilla (jt. author). *Craft Fun!* 21499
Hershenhorn, Esther. *There Goes Lowell's Party!* 5690(F)
Herzig, Alison C. *Bronco Busters*, 5260(F)
Mystery on October Road, 6889(F)
Herzog, George (jt. author). *The Cow-Tail Switch*, 10659
Hess, Debra. *Wilson Sat Alone*, 4005(F)
Hess, Mark. *Drummer Boy*, 9505(F)
Hercules, 11484
Hess, Paul. *Once There Was a Hoodie*, 1365(F)
Phoebe and the River Flute, 10432(F)
The Pig in a Wig, 2418(F)
Polar Animals, 18964
Hesse, Karen. *Come On, Rain!* 3208(F)
Just Juice, 8690(F)
Lester's Dog, 2939(F)
Letters from Rifka, 9550(F)
A Light in the Storm, 9479(F)
Poppy's Chair, 3691(F)
Sable, 7221(F)
Stowaway, 8933(F)
A Time of Angels, 9551(F)
Hest, Amy. *The Babies Are Coming!* 3209(F)
Baby Duck and the Bad Eyeglasses, 2199(F)
The Crack-of-Dawn Walkers, 3692(F)
Gabby Growing Up, 5691(F)
The Great Green Notebook of Katie Roberts, 8691(F)
How to Get Famous in Brooklyn, 3210(F)
In the Rain with Baby Duck, 2200(F)
Jamaica Louise James, 3693(F)
Mabel Dancing, 700(F)
The Mommy Exchange, 3694(F)
Nana's Birthday Party, 5692(F)
Off to School, Baby Duck! 2201(F)

The Private Notebook of Katie Roberts, Age 11, 8692(F)
The Purple Coat, 3211(F)
Rosie's Fishing Trip, 3695(F)
When Jessie Came Across the Sea, 9043(F)
You're the Boss, Baby Duck! 2202(F)
Hester, Sallie. *A Covered Wagon Girl*, 16316
Hestler, Anna. *Yemen*, 15549
Hetfield, Jamie. *The Yoruba of West Africa*, 15029
Hetzer, Linda. *Rainy Days and Saturdays*, 22233
Hewett, Richard. *The Ancient Cliff Dwellers of Mesa Verde*, 15921
Bat, 19019
Killer Whale, 19774
Mealtime for Zoo Animals, 18795
Noisytime for Zoo Animals, 18796
Ostriches and Other Flightless Birds, 19214
Tule Elk, 19147
Hewett, Richard (jt. author). *Baby Whale Rescue*, 19775
Hewish, Mark. *The Young Scientist Book of Jets*, 21080
Hewitt, Kathryn. *Animals from Mother Goose*, 850
Flower Garden, 3554(F)
Lives of the Artists, 12171
Lives of the Athletes, 13386
Lives of the Presidents, 12670
Lives of the Writers, 12173
Songs of Praise, 17200
Sunflower House, 4399(F)
The Three Sillies, 10995
The Worry Week, 6948(F)
Hewitt, Kathryn, adapt. *The Three Sillies*, 10995
Hewitt, Richard. *Stories in Stone*, 13941
Hewitt, Sally. *All Kinds of Habitats*, 20376
The Five Senses, 18142
Heyer, Carol. *A Christmas Carol*, 5857(F)
Dinosaurs! 14465
The Gift of the Magi, 9731(F)
Here Come the Brides, 17371
Robin Hood, 10996
Heyer, Marilee. *The Weaving of a Dream*, 10755
Heyman, Ken. *Hats, Hats, Hats*, 3333(F)
Loving, 3818
Heymsfeld, Carla. *Coaching Ms. Parker*, 10330(F)
Heyward, DuBose. *The Country Bunny and the Little Gold Shoes*, 5968(F)
Hiatt, Fred. *Baby Talk*, 3696(F)
If I Were Queen of the World, 1236(F)
Hickcox, Ruth. *Great-grandmother's Treasure*, 7449(F)

Hickman, Janet. *Jericho*, 7450(F)
Susannah, 9377(F)
Hickman, Martha W. *And God Created Squash*, 17284(F)
A Baby Born in Bethlehem, 17420
Robert Lives with His Grandparents, 3697(F)
When Andy's Father Went to Prison, 4978(F)
Hickman, Pamela. *Animal Senses*, 18821
Animals Eating, 18822
Animals in Motion, 18823
Bug Book, 19453
In the Woods, 20450
A New Duck, 19310
A New Frog, 18726
The Night Book, 18280
Starting with Nature Bird Book, 19234
Starting with Nature Plant Book, 20236
Tree Book, 20203
Hickman, Pamela M. *Birdwise*, 19235
Hickox, Rebecca. *The Golden Sandal*, 11185
Per and the Dala Horse, 1237(F)
Hicks, Peter. *Ancient Greece*, 14683
Hicks, Ray. *The Jack Tales*, 11349
Hidaka, Masako. *Girl from the Snow Country*, 4680(F)
Higashi, Sandra. *Round the Garden*, 4444(F)
Higgins, Maria Mihalik. *Cats*, 19090
Higginson, Mel. *Scientists Who Study Ancient Temples and Tombs*, 17827
Scientists Who Study Fossils, 17828
Scientists Who Study Ocean Life, 17829
Scientists Who Study the Earth, 17830
Scientists Who Study Wild Animals, 17831
Wildlife of Mexico, 15619
High, Linda O. *Barn Savers*, 3212(F)
Beekeepers, 3213(F)
A Christmas Star, 5836(F)
Hound Heaven, 7222(F)
Maizie, 8454(F)
A Stone's Throw from Paradise, 8455(F)
The Summer of the Great Divide, 8693(F)
Under New York, 16695
Highet, Alistair. *The Yellow Train*, 1238(F)
Highlights for Children, ed. *Ashanti Festival*, 10258(F)
Hightower, Paul. *Galileo*, 13290
Highwater, Jamake. *Anpao*, 11257
Songs for the Seasons, 11957
Higney, Gene-Michael (jt. author). *What's for Lunch?* 5219(F)
Higton, Bernard A. (jt. author). *Aesop's Fables*, 11054

Hildebrandt, Ziporah. *This Is Our Seder*, 17472
Hildick, E. W. *The Case of the Absent Author*, 6890(F)
The Case of the Wiggling Wig, 6891(F)
Hester Bidgood, 9198(F)
The Purloined Corn Popper, 6892(F)
Hilgartner, Beth. *A Murder for Her Majesty*, 6893(F)
Hill, Anne E. *Jennifer Lopez*, 12415
Sandra Bullock, 12363
Hill, Anthony. *The Burnt Stick*, 8934(F)
Hill, Barbara W. *Cooking the English Way*, 21706
Hill, Christine M. *Robert Ballard*, 12077
Ten Terrific Authors for Teens, 12166
Hill, Donna. *Shipwreck Season*, 9286(F)
Hill, Earl. *Haiti Through Its Holidays*, 15720
Hill, Elizabeth S. *Bird Boy*, 8997(F)
Hill, Eric. *Spot at Home*, 2203(F)
Spot Counts from 1 to 10, 464(F)
Spot Goes to a Party, 2204(F)
Spot Goes to School, 6383(F)
Spot Goes to the Circus, 6384(F)
Spot Goes to the Park, 2205(F)
Spot Looks at Colors, 272(F)
Spot Sleeps Over, 2206(F)
Spot's Baby Sister, 2207(F)
Spot's Big Book of Colors, Shapes and Numbers, 195(F)
Spot's Big Book of Words, 14037(F)
Hill, Kirkpatrick. *Toughboy and Sister*, 6894(F)
Winter Camp, 6895(F)
The Year of Miss Agnes, 10075(F)
Hill, Lee S. *Bridges Connect*, 21126
Farms Feed the World, 20060
Get Around in the City, 5572
Homes Keep Us Warm, 21159
Monuments Help Us Remember, 21127
Parks Are to Share, 16957
Roads Take Us Home, 21128
Tunnels Go Underground, 21129
Hill, Margaret Bateson. *Masha and the Firebird*, 7791(F)
Hill, Susan. *Beware Beware*, 1239(F)
The Christmas Collection, 9732(F)
The Glass Angels, 9733(F)
King of Kings, 5837(F)
Hill, Trish. *Somewhere*, 4384(F)
Hill, William. *The Magic Bicycle*, 10196(F)
Hill-Jackson, Troy. *Aliens in Woodford*, 7883(F)
The Ghost of Captain Briggs, 6929(F)
Hillenbrand, Will. *Asher and the Capmakers*, 6082(F)

Awfully Short for the Fourth Grade, 8216(F)
The Biggest, Best Snowman, 1092(F)
Counting Crocodiles, 2688(F)
Coyote and the Fire Stick, 11254
Down by the Station, 2208(F)
The Golden Sandal, 11185
The House That Drac Built, 6049(F)
Kiss the Cow! 1519(F)
The Last Snake in Ireland, 1372(F)
The Tale of Ali Baba and the Forty Thieves, 1303(F)
The Treasure Chest, 10772
Wicked Jack, 11391
Hillerman, Tony, ed. *The Boy Who Made Dragonfly*, 11258
Hillert, Margaret. *The Sky Is Not So Far Away*, 701
Hills, Tad. *Knock, Knock! Who's There?* 21825
A Name on the Quilt, 4900(F)
Tom Cringle, 9284(F)
Hilton, Jonathan. *Photography*, 21799
Hilton, Nette. *Andrew Jessup*, 4006(F)
Hilts, Len. *Timmy O'Dowd and the Big Ditch*, 9287(F)
Himler, Ronald. *Animals of the Night*, 5132
The Apaches, 16045
Bess's Log Cabin Quilt, 9401(F)
The Best Town in the World, 3019(F)
A Brand Is Forever, 7304(F)
The Cherokees, 16046
A Christmas Star, 5836(F)
Dakota Dugout, 4857(F)
A Day's Work, 3553(F)
Eli's Ghost, 6882(F)
Fly Away Home, 4916(F)
The Hopis, 16048
I'm Going to Pet a Worm Today and Other Poems, 11796
The Iroquois, 16049
Katie's Trunk, 4858(F)
The Log Cabin Christmas, 5847(F)
The Log Cabin Quilt, 4687(F)
Mark Twain and Huckleberry Finn, 12612
Moon Song, 11211
The Navajos, 16050
The Nez Perce, 16051
One Small Blue Bead, 4588(F)
Pearl Harbor Is Burning! 9668(F)
Redcoats and Petticoats, 9239(F)
The Roses in My Carpets, 4712(F)
Sadako and the Thousand Paper Cranes, 13847
Sand in My Shoes, 3259(F)
The Seminoles, 16052
The Sioux, 16053
Someday a Tree, 4398(F)
Squish! 20381
Train to Somewhere, 9348(F)

Trouble for Lucy, 9441(F)
The Wall, 3559(F)
Winter Holding Spring, 8627(F)
Himmelman, John. *The Animal Rescue Club*, 6385(F)
Charlotte Shakespeare and Annie the Great, 10076(F)
The Clover County Carrot Contest, 6386(F)
A Dandelion's Life, 20237
An Earthworm's Life, 19609
Honest Tulio, 4007(F)
A House Spider's Life, 19583
A Hummingbird's Life, 19236
J.J. Versus the Baby-sitter, 4180(F)
A Ladybug's Life, 19532
Lights Out! 4181(F)
A Luna Moth's Life, 19556
A Monarch Butterfly's Life, 19557
Mort the Sport, 2321(F)
A Pill Bug's Life, 18635
A Slug's Life, 19610
Sound the Shofar! A Story for Rosh Hashanah and Yom Kippur, 6088(F)
The Ups and Downs of Simpson Snail, 6387(F)
Wanted, 3698(F)
A Wood Frog's Life, 18727
Hincks, Gary. *The Incredible Journey to the Planets*, 18474
Hincks, Joseph. *Dinosaur Dictionary*, 14427
Hindley, Judy. *The Best Thing About a Puppy*, 5261(F)
The Big Red Bus, 5573(F)
Eyes, Nose, Fingers, and Toes, 18062
Into the Jungle, 2940(F)
Ten Bright Eyes, 196(F)
Hinds, Kathryn. *The Castle*, 14766
Cats, 19923
The Church, 14767
The City, 14768
The Countryside, 14769
Hamsters and Gerbils, 19897
Rabbits, 19898
Hines, Anna Grossnickle. *Bean Soup*, 2209(F)
Bean's Games, 5262(F)
Bouncing on the Bed, 3264(F)
Daddy Makes the Best Spaghetti, 3699(F)
Even If I Spill My Milk? 3700(F)
Grandma Gets Grumpy, 3701(F)
My Own Big Bed, 702(F)
Pieces, 11958
What Can You Do in the Rain? 3214(F)
What Can You Do in the Snow? 3215(F)
What Can You Do in the Sun? 3216(F)
When the Goblins Came Knocking, 6007(F)
When We Married Gary, 3702(F)

Hines, Bob. *Lost Wild America*, 19403
Hines, Gary. *A Christmas Tree in the White House*, 5838(F)
Hines-Stephens, Sarah. *Bean Soup*, 2209(F)
Bean's Games, 5262(F)
Hinke, George. *Joseph's Story*, 17429
Hinton, Tim. *Robert Lives with His Grandparents*, 3697(F)
Hintz, Martin. *Chile*, 15746
Hawaii, 16788
Iowa, 16559
Israel, 15523
Louisiana, 16865
Michigan, 16560
Minnesota, 16561
Missouri, 16562
The Netherlands, 15398
North Carolina, 16866
North Dakota, 16563
Norway, 15450
Switzerland, 15271
Hintz, Stephen (jt. author). *Israel*, 15523
North Carolina, 16866
Hippely, Hilary H. *Adventure on Klickitat Island*, 1240(F)
A Song for Lena, 4681(F)
Hirsch, Karen. *Ellen Anders on Her Own*, 8301(F)
Hirschfeld, Robert. *The Kids' Science Book*, 18322
Hirschfelder, Arlene. *Kick Butts! A Kid's Action Guide to a Tobacco-Free America*, 17870
Hirschfelder, Arlene, ed. *Rising Voices*, 9163(F)
Hirschfelder, Arlene B. *Photo Odyssey*, 16081
Hirschi, Ron. *Octopuses*, 19723
Salmon, 19704
Spring, 4459
What Is a Bird? 19237
What Is a Cat? 5263
What Is a Horse? 5264
When Morning Comes, 18824
When Night Comes, 18825
Where Do Cats Live? 5265
Hirsh, Marilyn. *Potato Pancakes All Around*, 6079(F)
Hirst, Mike. *A Flavor of India*, 15105
Freedom of Belief, 17034
The History of Emigration from Scotland, 15351
Hirst, Robin. *My Place in Space*, 18395
Hirst, Sally (jt. author). *My Place in Space*, 18395
Hirt-Manheimer, Judith (jt. author). *A Candle for Grandpa*, 17488
Hiscock, Bruce. *The Big Rivers*, 20519
The Big Rock, 20560
The Big Storm, 20694
When Will It Snow? 4460(F)

Hiser, Constance. *Night of the Were-poodle*, 7792(F)

Hiskey, Iris. *Hannah the Hippo's No Mud Day*, 2210(F)

Hissey, Jane. *Little Bear Lost*, 2211(F)

Hitchcock, Sharon. *The Day Sun Was Stolen*, 11284

Hite, Sid. *Stick and Whittle*, 9378(F)

Hitzeroth, Deborah. *Movies*, 14312

Thurgood Marshall, 12765

Hjelmeland, Andy. *Prisons*, 17070

Ho, Minfong. *Hush!* 703(F)

Ho, Siow Yen. *South Korea*, 15166

Hoade, Lonnie F. (jt. author). *When a Parent Goes to Jail*, 17092

Hoare, Stephen. *Digital Revolution*, 21241

Hoban, Julia. *Amy Loves the Rain*, 3217(F)

Amy Loves the Snow, 3218(F)

Quick Chick, 6388(F)

Hoban, Lillian. *Amy Loves the Rain*, 3217(F)

Amy Loves the Snow, 3218(F)

Arthur's Back to School Day, 6389(F)

Arthur's Birthday Party, 6390(F)

Arthur's Camp-Out, 6391(F)

Arthur's Christmas Cookies, 5839(F)

Arthur's Great Big Valentine, 6170(F)

Arthur's Halloween Costume, 6008(F)

Arthur's Honey Bear, 6392(F)

Arthur's Loose Tooth, 6393(F)

Best Friends, 5488(F)

Best Friends for Frances, 6396(F)

Caps, Hats, Socks, and Mittens, 4390(F)

"E" Is for Elisa, 7458(F)

Elisa in the Middle, 9892(F)

Ever-Clever Elisa, 10083(F)

I Never Did That Before, 11656

Quick Chick, 6388(F)

Ready . . . Set . . . Robot! 6394(F)

Silly Tilly's Thanksgiving Dinner, 6144(F)

Silly Tilly's Valentine, 6171(F)

Where Does the Teacher Live? 6332(F)

Will I Have a Friend? 5489(F)

Hoban, Phoebe (jt. author). *Ready . . . Set . . . Robot!* 6394(F)

Hoban, Russell. *Bedtime for Frances*, 6395(F)

Best Friends for Frances, 6396(F)

The Sea-Thing Child, 1241(F)

Trouble on Thunder Mountain, 7793(F)

Hoban, Sarah. *Daily Life in Ancient and Modern Paris*, 15310

Hoban, Tana. *Black on White*, 197(F)

A Children's Zoo, 18946

Circles, Triangles, and Squares, 334(F)

Colors Everywhere, 273(F)

Construction Zone, 5574

Count and See, 465(F)

Cubes, Cones, Cylinders, and Spheres, 335

Dig, Drill, Dump, Fill, 21248

Exactly the Opposite, 198(F)

I Read Signs, 307(F)

Is It Larger? Is It Smaller? 336(F)

Is It Red? Is It Yellow? Is It Blue? 274(F)

Is It Rough? Is It Smooth? Is It Shiny? 308(F)

Let's Count, 466

Little Elephant, 5208(F)

Look Again! 309(F)

More, Fewer, Less, 467

Of Colors and Things, 275(F)

1, 2, 3, 468(F)

Over, Under and Through and Other Spacial Concepts, 337(F)

Red, Blue, Yellow Shoe, 276(F)

Shapes, Shapes, Shapes, 338(F)

So Many Circles, So Many Squares, 339

26 Letters and 99 Cents, 54(F)

What Is That? 199(F)

Hobbie, Holly. *Toot and Puddle*, 55(F), 2212(F), 2213(F), 5693(F)

Hobbs, Valerie. *Carolina Crow Girl*, 8694(F)

Charlie's Run, 8456(F)

Hobbs, Will. *Beardream*, 1242(F)

Howling Hill, 2214(F)

Jason's Gold, 6896(F)

Hoberman, Mary Ann. *And to Think That We Thought That We'd Never Be Friends*, 1243(F)

The Eensy-Weensy Spider, 14245

A Fine Fat Pig, 11791

A House Is a House for Me, 200(F)

It's Simple, Said Simon, 1244(F)

The Llama Who Had No Pajama, 11596

Miss Mary Mack, 1245(F), 11350

One of Each, 2215(F)

The Seven Silly Eaters, 4182(F)

The Two Sillies, 1246(F)

Hoberman, Mary Ann, ed. *My Song Is Beautiful*, 11597

Hobkirk, Lori. *Madam C. J. Walker*, 12808

Hobson, Sally. *Another Fine Mess*, 1837(F)

Chicken Little, 2216(F)

Parcel for Stanley, 2852(F)

Red Hen and Sly Fox, 2104(F)

Three Bags Full, 2657(F)

Hocker, Kirsten. *Mary and the Mystery Dog*, 7211(F)

Mia the Beach Cat, 6365(F)

Hoctor, Sarah K. *Changes*, 4980(F)

Hodge, Deborah. *Bears*, 19048

Beavers, 19197

Deer, Moose, Elk and Caribou, 19152

Eagles, 19327

Simple Machines, 20921

Solids, Liquids, and Gases, 20812

Whales, 19791

Wild Cats, 19091

Wild Dogs, 19123

Hodge, Susie. *Ancient Egyptian Art*, 14631

Ancient Greek Art, 14684

Ancient Roman Art, 14722

Prehistoric Art, 14502

Hodges, C. Walter. *The Silver Sword*, 9687(F)

Hodges, Margaret. *Brother Francis and the Friendly Beasts*, 4682

Gulliver in Lilliput, 7795(F)

The Hero of Bremen, 10915

Joan of Arc, 13812

Molly Limbo, 1247(F)

St. George and the Dragon, 10998

Silent Night, 5840(F)

The True Tale of Johnny Appleseed, 12844

Up the Chimney, 10999

Hodges, Margaret, ed. *Comus*, 7794(F)

Don Quixote and Sancho Panza, 9044(F)

Hauntings, 10561

Hodges, Margaret, reteller. *The Kitchen Knight*, 10997

Of Swords and Sorcerers, 11000

Hodgkins, Fran. *Animals Among Us*, 18636

Hodgman, Ann. *My Babysitter Is a Vampire*, 9877(F)

Hoellwarth, Cathryn C. *The Under-bed*, 704(F)

Hoestlandt, Jo. *Star of Fear, Star of Hope*, 9664(F)

Hofer, Angelika. *The Lion Family Book*, 19092

Hofer, Ernst. *Hans Christian Andersen's The Snow Queen*, 10501(F)

Silent Night, 14202(F)

Hofer, Nelly. *Hans Christian Andersen's The Snow Queen*, 10501(F)

Silent Night, 14202(F)

Hoff, Carol. *Johnny Texas*, 9379(F)

Hoff, Mary. *Atmosphere*, 20670

Gloria Steinem, 13195

Life on Land, 19398

Our Endangered Planet, 16997, 19822, 20520

Hoff, Syd. *Albert the Albatross*, 6397(F)

Arturo's Baton, 4183(F)

Barkley, 6398(F)

Barney's Horse, 6399(F)

Danny and the Dinosaur, 6400(F)

Danny and the Dinosaur Go to Camp, 6401(F)

Don't Be My Valentine, 6173(F)

Duncan the Dancing Duck, 2217(F)
Grizzwold, 6402(F)
Happy Birthday, Danny and the Dinosaur! 6403(F)
I Saw You in the Bathtub and Other Folk Rhymes, 6638(F)
The Lighthouse Children, 6404(F)
Mrs. Brice's Mice, 6405(F)
Sammy the Seal, 6406(F)
Stanley, 6407(F)
Where's Prancer? 5841(F)
Hoffman, Alice. *Aquamarine*, 7796(F)
Horsefly, 1248(F)
Hoffman, E. T. A. *The Nutcracker*, 10916
The Strange Child, 10917
Hoffman, Mary. *An Angel Just Like Me*, 5842(F)
The Barefoot Book of Brother and Sister Tales, 10433(F)
Boundless Grace, 4683(F)
Clever Katya, 11090
Parables, 17286
Starring Grace, 8302(F)
Sun, Moon, and Stars, 10563
Three Wise Women, 5843(F)
A Twist in the Tail, 10564
Hoffman, Mary, reteller. *A First Bible Story Book*, 17285
A First Book of Myths, 10562
Hoffman, Nancy. *South Carolina*, 16867
Hoffman, Rosekrans. *Jane Yolen's Mother Goose Songbook*, 904
Jane Yolen's Old MacDonald Songbook, 14195
Pignic, 101(F)
The Truth About the Moon, 4388(F)
Where Do Little Girls Grow? 3774(F)
Hoffman, Sanford. *Spooky Riddles and Jokes*, 21847
The World's Best Sports Riddles and Jokes, 21849
The Zaniest Riddle Book in the World, 21850
Hofmeyr, Dianne. *The Star-Bearer*, 11186
The Stone, 11187
Hofsepian, Sylvia A. *Why Not?* 3219(F)
Hogrogian, Nonny. *Always Room for One More*, 14165
The Contest, 11091
The Golden Bracelet, 11188
Handmade Secret Hiding Places, 21445
I Am Eyes Ni Macho, 4867(F)
One Fine Day, 10859
Hol, Coby. *The Birth of the Moon*, 1249(F)
Holch, Gregory. *The Things with Wings*, 7797(F)
Holcomb, Jerry Kimble. *The Chinquapin Tree*, 6897(F)

Holcomb, Nan. *Andy Finds a Turtle*, 4979(F)
Holden, Dwight. *Grand-Gran's Best Trick*, 8695(F)
Holden, Robert. *The Pied Piper of Hamelin*, 10918
Holder, Jimmy. *Why the Banana Split*, 4347(F)
Holeman, Linda. *Promise Song*, 8935(F)
Holford, David M. *Herbert Hoover*, 13044
Holl, Kristi D. *First Things First*, 8696(F)
Hidden in the Fog, 8457(F)
Just Like a Real Family, 7451(F)
No Strings Attached, 7452(F)
Holland, Cheri. *Maccabee Jamboree*, 469(F)
Holland, Gay. *Magnificent Monarchs*, 19551
Spectacular Spiders, 19581
Holland, Gini. *The Empire State Building*, 16696
Nelson Mandela, 13830
Nuclear Energy, 20845
Rosa Parks, 12777
Holland, Heather. *How the Reindeer Got Their Antlers*, 5867(F)
Holland, Isabelle. *The Journey Home*, 9380(F)
Paperboy, 9552(F)
The Promised Land, 9288(F)
Holler, Anne. *Pocahontas*, 12985
Holley, Vanessa. *Kai*, 8979(F)
Holliday, Keaf. *Haircuts at Sleepy Sam's*, 3446(F)
Holling, Holling C. *Minn of the Mississippi*, 18784
Paddle-to-the-Sea, 15883
Pagoo, 19676
Seabird, 19349
Tree in the Trail, 9381(F)
Hollyer, Beatrice. *Wake Up, World! A Day in the Life of Children Around the World*, 14341
Holm, Anne. *North to Freedom*, 9665(F)
Holm, Jenni. *Our Only May Amelia*, 7453(F)
Holm, John. *Ice Cream*, 20104
Holm, Sharon L. *Beautiful Bats*, 19025
The Best Birthday Parties Ever! 17396
Crafts for Christian Values, 21475
Crafts for Easter, 21476
Crafts for Halloween, 21477
Crafts for Kwanzaa, 5647
Crafts for Valentine's Day, 21484
Every Day Is Earth Day, 21491
Experiments That Explore Acid Rain, 16996
Happy New Year, Everywhere! 17353
More Christmas Ornaments Kids Can Make, 21493

Holman, Felice. *Slake's Limbo*, 6898(F)
Holman, Karlyn. *Little Brother Moose*, 5284(F)
Holman, Sandy Lynne. *Grandpa, Is Everything Black Bad?* 3703(F)
Holmes, Anita. *Can You Find Us?* 18884
Flowers and Friends, 20035
I Can Save the Earth, 16958
Insect Detector, 19454
Holmes, Barbara W. *Charlotte Shakespeare and Annie the Great*, 10076(F)
Holmes, Bonnie. *Quaking Aspen*, 20204
Holmes, Dawn. *Thomas's Sitter*, 3856(F)
Holmes, Gerald L. *The Case of the Vanishing Fishhook*, 7188(F)
Hank the Cowdog, 6329(F)
Holmes, Richard. *Battle*, 21388
Holmes, Sally. *The Complete Fairy Tales of Charles Perrault*, 10876
Holohan, Maureen. *Catch Shorty by Rosie*, 10331(F)
Everybody's Favorite, 10332(F)
Left Out, 10333(F)
Holsonback, Anita. *Monkey See, Monkey Do*, 5266(F)
Holt, Daniel D., sel. *Tigers, Frogs, and Rice Cakes*, 10729
Holt, David, ed. *More Ready-to-Tell Tales from Around the World*, 10565
Holt, Denver W. (jt. author). *Owls*, 19361
Holt, Kimberly Willis. *Dancing in Cadillac Light*, 7454(F)
Mister and Me, 8458(F)
When Zachary Beaver Came to Town, 8303(F)
Holtz, Thomas R., Jr. (jt. author). *James Gurney*, 14389
Holtzman, Jon. *Samburu*, 14931
Holub, Joan. *American Heart Association Kids' Cookbook*, 21752
Boo Who? 6009(F)
Deena's Lucky Penny, 6306(F)
Hector's Hiccups, 6708(F)
How to Find Lost Treasure in All 50 States and Canada, Too! 14529
I Have a Weird Brother Who Digested a Fly, 18100
Why Do Cats Meow? 19924
Why Do Dogs Bark? 19951
Holyoke, Nancy. *Help! A Girl's Guide to Divorce and Stepfamilies*, 17660
Oops! 17635
Hom, Nancy. *Judge Rabbit and the Tree Spirit*, 10844
Nine-in-One, Grr! Grr! 10846
Homer. *The Odyssey*, 11479
Honan, Linda. *Spend the Day in Ancient Egypt*, 14632

Honey, Elizabeth. *Don't Pat the Wombat*, 9878(F)
Stella Street, and Everything That Happened, 9879(F)
Honeycutt, Natalie. *The All New Jonah Twist*, 10077(F)
Granville Jones, 9880(F)
Invisible Lissa, 10078(F)
Josie's Beau, 8304(F)
Twilight in Grace Falls, 8459(F)
Honeywood, Varnette P. *The Day I Was Rich*, 4934(F)
One Dark and Scary Night, 6281(F)
Shake It to the One That You Love the Best, 14170
Hong, Lily T. *The Empress and the Silkworm*, 4684(F)
How the Ox Star Fell from Heaven, 10756
Two of Everything, 10757
Honig, Debbie (jt. author). *Growing Money*, 16925
Hoobler, Dorothy. *The First Decade*, 9553(F)
Florence Robinson, 9554(F)
The Italian American Family Album, 17565
Lost Civilizations, 14530
Priscilla Foster, 9199(F)
Real American Girls Tell Their Own Stories, 15884
The Second Decade, 9555(F)
Vanity Rules, 21172
Hoobler, Dorothy (jt. author). *Sally Bradford*, 9480(F)
Hoobler, Thomas. *Lost Civilizations*, 14530
Sally Bradford, 9480(F)
Hoobler, Thomas (jt. author). *The First Decade*, 9553(F)
Florence Robinson, 9554(F)
The Italian American Family Album, 17565
Priscilla Foster, 9199(F)
Real American Girls Tell Their Own Stories, 15884
Hoobler, Tom (jt. author). *The Second Decade*, 9555(F)
Vanity Rules, 21172
Hood, Susan. *I Am Mad!* 6408(F)
Look! I Can Read! 6409(F)
National Audubon Society First Field Guide to Wildflowers, 20036
The New Kid, 6410(F)
Hood, Thomas. *Before I Go to Sleep*, 705(F)
Hook, Frances. *We Laughed a Lot, My First Day of School*, 5542(F)
Hook, Richard. *Growing Up in Aztec Times*, 15654
Little Bighorn, 16057
Stories from Native North America, 11291
Hooks, Bell. *Happy to Be Nappy*, 3220(F)

Hooks, Kristine. *Essential Hiking for Teens*, 22168
Hooks, William H. *Circle of Fire*, 7345(F)
Freedom's Fruit, 9289(F)
The Girl Who Could Fly, 10197(F)
The Legend of the Christmas Rose, 5844(F)
The Mighty Santa Fe, 3704(F)
Mr. Baseball, 6411(F)
Mr. Big Brother, 6412(F)
Pioneer Cat, 9382(F)
Snowbear Whittington, 11351
The Three Little Pigs and the Fox, 11352
Hooper, Maureen B. *The Christmas Drum*, 5845(F)
Hooper, Meredith. *Antarctic Journal*, 15806
A Cow, a Bee, a Cookie, and Me, 3221(F)
Dogs' Night, 2218(F)
The Drop in My Drink, 20736
The Pebble in My Pocket, 20311
River Story, 4461(F)
Tom's Rabbit, 5267(F)
Hoopes, Lyn Littlefield. *My Own Home*, 2219(F)
Hopcraft, Carol C. (jt. author). *How It Was with Dooms*, 19093
Hopcraft, Xan. *How It Was with Dooms*, 19093
Hopkins, Beverly H. *Changes*, 4980(F)
Hopkins, Dave. *Cars*, 5598
Dinosaurs, 14467
Jungle Animals, 5393
Hopkins, Ellen. *Orcas*, 19792
Hopkins, Jackie Mims. *The Horned Toad Prince*, 10434(F)
Hopkins, Lee Bennett. *Animals from Mother Goose*, 850
Been to Yesterdays, 11599
Marvelous Math, 11602
Spectacular Science, 11960
The Writing Bug, 12549
Hopkins, Lee Bennett, ed. *April Bubbles Chocolate*, 11598
Blast Off! 11607
Extra Innings, 11997
Good Books, Good Times, 11600
Hand in Hand, 11601
Happy Birthday, 5694
Hey-How for Halloween! 11832
Opening Days, 11998
School Supplies, 11604
Small Talk, 11959
Song and Dance, 11605
Surprises, 11606
Hopkins, Lee Bennett, sel. *All God's Children*, 17524
My America, 11603
Hopkinson, Deborah. *A Band of Angels*, 7346(F)
Birdie's Lighthouse, 2941(F)
Maria's Comet, 4685(F)
Pearl Harbor, 14857

Sweet Clara and the Freedom Quilt, 9290(F)
Hopler, Brigitta. *Marc Chagall*, 12207
Hopper, Nancy J. *Ape Ears and Beaky*, 6899(F)
Cassandra — Live at Carnegie Hall! 9666(F)
Hopping, Lorraine Jean. *Wild Weather*, 20695, 20696
Horenstein, Henry. *A Is for . . .?* 56
Baseball in the Barrios, 22096
My Mom's a Vet, 17847
Horn, Peter. *When I Grow Up . . .*, 2220(F)
Horn, Sandra Ann. *The Dandelion Wish*, 1250(F)
Hornby, Hugh. *Soccer*, 22293
Horner, Abigail (jt. author). *Country Mouse Cottage*, 1013(F)
Town Mouse House, 4605(F)
Hornsby, Christopher. *Take a Look, It's in a Book*, 14313
Horosko, Marian. *Sleeping Beauty*, 14289
Horowitz, Anthony. *The Devil and His Boy*, 9102(F)
Horowitz, Ruth. *Crab Moon*, 5268(F)
Horrell, Sarah. *The History of Emigration from Eastern Europe*, 14556
Horse, Harry. *A Friend for Little Bear*, 2221(F)
Hort, Lenny. *How Many Stars in the Sky?* 706(F)
The Seals on the Bus, 14246
Tie Your Socks and Clap Your Feet, 11875
Treasure Hunts! Treasure Hunts! Treasure and Scavenger Hunts to Play with Friends and Family, 22014
Horton, Casey. *Apes*, 18999
Bears, 19049
Dolphins, 19686
Eagles, 19328
The Jews, 17566
Parrots, 19238
Wolves, 19124
Horton, Joan. *Halloween Hoots and Howls*, 11833
Horton, Madelyn. *The Importance of Mother Jones*, 13161
Horton, Tom. *Swanfall*, 19311
Horvath, Betty. *Sir Galahad, Mr. Longfellow, and Me*, 7455(F)
Horvath, Penny. *Everything on a Waffle*, 8697(F)
Horvath, Polly. *The Happy Yellow Car*, 9881(F)
An Occasional Cow, 9882(F)
The Trolls, 9883(F)
When the Circus Came to Town, 9884(F)
Hosking, David. *Animal Communication*, 18892
Animal Families, 18876

Animal Movement, 18809

Hossack, Sylvie. *Green Mango Magic*, 8305(F)

Hossack, Sylvie A. *The Flying Chickens of Paradise Lane*, 8306(F)

Hosten, James. *The Original Freddie Ackerman*, 6907(F)

Hotvedt, Kris. *The Little Ghost Who Wouldn't Go Away/El pequeño fantasma que no queria irse*, 8052(F)

Houbre, Gilbert. *Vegetables in the Garden*, 20172

Houghton, Diane R. *Helpin' Bugs*, 4024(F)

Houghton, Eric. *The Crooked Apple Tree*, 3222(F)

Houk, Randy. *Chessie, the Travelin' Man*, 5269(F)

Houle, Tim. *Kirby Puckett*, 13478

Houselander, Caryll. *Petook*, 5969(F)

Houston, Gloria. *Bright Freedom's Song*, 9291(F)

Littlejim, 9556(F)

Littlejim's Dreams, 9557(F)

Littlejim's Gift, 9734(F)

Mountain Valor, 9481(F)

My Great-Aunt Arizona, 3705

Houston, James. *Fire into Ice*, 12240

Frozen Fire, 6900(F)

Tikta'liktak, 11206

Hovanec, Erin M. *Get Involved!* 17611

Hovey, Kate. *Arachne Speaks*, 11480

Howard, Arthur. *Cosmo Zooms*, 2222(F)

Mr. Putter and Tabby Bake the Cake, 5913(F)

Mr. Putter and Tabby Fly the Plane, 6609(F)

Mr. Putter and Tabby Paint the Porch, 9981(F)

Mr. Putter and Tabby Pick the Pears, 6610(F)

Mr. Putter and Tabby Pour the Tea, 6611(F)

Mr. Putter and Tabby Take the Train, 6612(F)

Mr. Putter and Tabby Toot the Horn, 6613(F)

100th Day Worries, 415(F)

When I Was Five, 4008(F)

Howard, Dale E. *India*, 15106

Soccer Stars, 22294

Howard, Elizabeth F. *Aunt Flossie's Hats (and Crab Cakes Later)*, 3706(F)

Chita's Christmas Tree, 5846(F)

Lulu's Birthday, 5695(F)

Papa Tells Chita a Story, 4686(F)

The Train to Lulu's, 3223(F)

Virgie Goes to School with Us Boys, 4981(F)

What's in Aunt Mary's Room? 3707(F)

When Will Sarah Come? 3708(F)

Howard, Ellen. *The Chickenhouse House*, 9383(F)

Edith, Herself, 8894(F)

The Gate in the Wall, 9103(F)

The Log Cabin Christmas, 5847(F)

The Log Cabin Quilt, 4687(F)

Murphy and Kate, 7223(F)

Howard, Ginger. *William's House*, 9200(F)

Howard, Kim. *The Chief's Blanket*, 4618(F)

A Cloak for the Dreamer, 8651(F)

Percy to the Rescue, 2698(F)

Howard, Milly. *The Case of the Dog-napped Cat*, 6901(F)

Howard, Nancy S. *Jacob Lawrence*, 13958

William Sidney Mount, 12271

Howard, Paul. *The Bravest Ever Bear*, 1727(F)

Classic Poetry, 11683

Mockingbird, 616

Rosie's Fishing Trip, 3695(F)

A Year in the City, 4458(F)

Howard, Pauline Rodriguez. *Family, Familia*, 3526(F)

Icy Watermelon / Sandia fria, 3640(F)

Howard, Richard. *The Strength of the Hills*, 20058

Howarth, Sarah. *Colonial People*, 16133

Colonial Places, 16134

The Middle Ages, 14770

What Do We Know About the Middle Ages? 14771

Howe, Deborah. *Bunnicula*, 9885(F)

Teddy Bear's Scrapbook, 2223(F)

Howe, James. *Bunnicula Escapes!* 6902(F)

Bunnicula Strikes Again! 9886(F)

Creepy-Crawly Birthday, 5696(F)

Dew Drop Dead, 6903(F)

Horace and Morris But Mostly Dolores, 2224(F)

The Hospital Book, 18039

I Wish I Were a Butterfly, 2225(F)

Morgan's Zoo, 7798(F)

The New Nick Kramer; or, My Life as a Baby-sitter, 9887(F)

A Night Without Stars, 8698(F)

Nighty-Nightmare, 9888(F)

Pinky and Rex and the Bully, 8699(F)

Pinky and Rex and the Double-Dad Weekend, 7456(F)

Pinky and Rex and the Just-Right Pet, 7224(F)

Pinky and Rex and the Mean Old Witch, 6413(F)

Pinky and Rex and the New Baby, 6414(F)

Pinky and Rex and the New Neighbors, 6415(F)

Pinky and Rex and the Perfect Pumpkin, 8700(F)

Pinky and Rex and the School Play, 6416(F)

Pinky and Rex Get Married, 6417(F)

Pinky and Rex Go to Camp, 6418(F)

Playing with Words, 12550

Return to Howliday Inn, 9889(F)

Scared Silly, 6010(F)

There's a Dragon in My Sleeping Bag, 1251(F)

There's a Monster Under My Bed, 707(F)

When You Go to Kindergarten, 5506

Howe, James (jt. author). *Bunnicula*, 9885(F)

Teddy Bear's Scrapbook, 2223(F)

Howe, John. *Jack and the Beanstalk*, 11001

Knights, 14772

Howell, Kathleen C. *The Singing Green*, 11971

Howell, Troy. *A Boy's Will*, 9101(F)

Favorite Greek Myths, 11499

Favorite Norse Myths, 11519

Fox in a Trap, 7100(F)

Lucy's Winter Tale, 4950(F)

The Maiden on the Moor, 11035

Mermaid Tales from Around the World, 10597

The Night Swimmers, 8584(F)

Under Copp's Hill, 9515(F)

Howell, Will C. *I Call It Sky*, 4463(F)

Howey, Paul. *Garth Brooks*, 12360

Howker, Janni. *Walk with a Wolf*, 19125

Howland, Naomi. *ABCDrive!* 57(F)

Latkes, Latkes, Good to Eat, 6080(F)

Howlett, Bud. *I'm New Here*, 5507(F)

Hoyt, Eleanor. *The Illustrated Rules of Football*, 22188

The Illustrated Rules of Ice Hockey, 22211

Hoyt-Goldsmith, Diane. *Apache Rodeo*, 15970

Arctic Hunter, 15807

Buffalo Days, 15971

Celebrating Chinese New Year, 17367

Celebrating Hanukkah, 17473

Celebrating Kwanzaa, 17368

Celebrating Passover, 17474

Day of the Dead, 7347(F)

Hoang Anh, 17567

Lacrosse, 22015

Las Posadas, 17421

Mardi Gras, 17369

Migrant Worker, 17143

Potlatch, 15972

Pueblo Storyteller, 15973

Hru, Dakari. *Joshua's Masai Mask*, 4982(F)

Hsu-Flanders, Lillian. *Dumpling Soup*, 5645(F)

Hu, Evaleen. *A Big Ticket*, 22016
Hu, Ying-Hwa. *An Angel Just Like Me*, 5842(F)
The Case of the Shrunken Allowance, 567(F)
Coming Home, 13455
Jingle Dancer, 3434(F)
The Legend of Freedom Hill, 9339(F)
Make a Joyful Sound, 11767
Mei-Mei Loves the Morning, 5438(F)
Sam and the Lucky Money, 3069(F)
Zora Hurston and the Chinaberry Tree, 3810
Huang, Benrei. *Big Daddy, Frog Wrestler*, 1821(F)
Let's Go Riding in Our Strollers, 3309(F)
Moon Sandwich Mom, 2246(F)
Mr. Pak Buys a Story, 10724
Mrs. Sato's Hens, 516(F)
One Hundred Is a Family, 572(F)
This Is the Earth That God Made, 17266
Huang, Chungliang Al. *The Chinese Book of Animal Powers*, 21914
Huang, Zhong-Yang. *The Dragon New Year*, 5611(F)
The Great Race, 10738
Hubbard, Coleen (jt. author). *Colorado Summer*, 7159(F)
Hubbard, Eleanor. *The Fisherman and His Wife*, 10520
Hubbard, Jim. *Lives Turned Upside Down*, 17144
Hubbard, Louise Garff. *Grandfather's Gold Watch*, 4688(F)
Hubbard, Patricia. *My Crayons Talk*, 1252(F)
Trick or Treat Countdown, 6011(F)
Hubbard, Woodleigh. *Imaginary Menagerie*, 5318(F)
Once I Was . . ., 205(F)
The Precious Gift, 11259
Hubbard, Woodleigh Marx. *All That You Are*, 17612
Hubbard-Brown, Janet. *The Curse of the Hope Diamond*, 21915
The Secret of Roanoke Island, 16135
Hubbell, Patricia. *Boo! Halloween Poems and Limericks*, 6012
Bouncing Time, 5270(F)
City Kids, 11608
Earthmates, 11792
Pots and Pans, 4184(F)
Sidewalk Trip, 3224(F)
Wrapping Paper Romp, 3225(F)
Hubbell, Will. *Pumpkin Jack*, 6013(F)
Hubble, Richard. *Ships*, 21361
Huber, Carey. *Nature Explorer*, 18585
Huck, Charlotte. *A Creepy Countdown*, 470(F)
Toads and Diamonds, 10871

Huckins, David. *W. E. B. Du Bois*, 12718
Hucko, Bruce. *A Rainbow at Night*, 15974
Hudson, Cheryl W. *Bright Eyes, Brown Skin*, 3226(F)
Hold Christmas in Your Heart, 5848(F)
Hudson, Cheryl W. (jt. author). *How Sweet the Sound*, 14247
In Praise of Our Fathers and Our Mothers, 12167
Hudson, Jan. *Sweetgrass*, 9164(F)
Hudson, Karen E. *The Will and the Way*, 12311
Hudson, Wade. *Afro-Bets Book of Black Heroes from A to Z*, 12660
Anthony's Big Surprise, 10079(F)
How Sweet the Sound, 14247
Jamal's Busy Day, 6419(F)
Hudson, Wade, comp. *In Praise of Our Fathers and Our Mothers*, 12167
Hudson, Wade, ed. *Pass It On*, 11761
Huegel, Kelly. *Young People and Chronic Illness*, 17966
Huert, Catherine. *Megan in Ancient Greece*, 9054(F)
Huffman, Bunny P. *Nihancan's Feast of Beaver*, 11263
Huffman, Tom. *Cards for Kids*, 22236
The Dove Dove, 14047
Punching the Clock, 14051
Small Plays for Special Days, 12010
Hughes, Arthur. *Sing Song*, 11686
Hughes, Carol. *Jack Black and the Ship of Thieves*, 7799(F)
Toots and the Upside-Down House, 7800(F)
Hughes, Dean. *Brad and Butter Play Ball*, 10334(F)
End of the Race, 10335(F)
Family Pose, 8701(F)
Home Run Hero, 10336(F)
Now We're Talking, 10337(F)
Nutty and the Case of the Ski-Slope Spy, 6904(F)
Nutty, the Movie Star, 9890(F)
Nutty's Ghost, 7801(F)
Play Ball, 10338(F)
Re-Elect Nutty! 10080(F)
Hughes, E. Thomas (jt. author). *Buried Treasure*, 20178
Hughes, George. *Help! I'm a Prisoner in the Library*, 6796(F)
Scared Silly, 6797(F)
Hughes, Helga. *Cooking the Swiss Way*, 21708
Hughes, Langston. *Carol of the Brown King*, 5849
The Sweet and Sour Animal Book, 58(F)
Hughes, Langston (jt. author). *The Pasteboard Bandit*, 1005(F)

Hughes, Libby. *Madam Prime Minister*, 13860
Valley Forge, 16199
West Point, 21389
Hughes, Meredith S. *Buried Treasure*, 20178
Cool as a Cucumber, Hot as a Pepper, 20098
Flavor Foods, 20099
Glorious Grasses, 20100
Spill the Beans and Pass the Peanuts, 20176
Stinky and Stringy, 20177
Tall and Tasty, 20145
Yes, We Have Bananas, 20146
Hughes, Monica. *The Golden Aquarians*, 10198(F)
A Handful of Seeds, 4689(F)
Hughes, Monica, sel. *What If?* 7802(F)
Hughes, Morgan. *Track and Field*, 22317
Hughes, Morgan E. *Mario Lemieux*, 13697
Hughes, Neal. *Marvin Redpost*, 6620(F)
Hughes, Sarah. *Let's Jump Rope*, 22017
Let's Play Hopscotch, 22018
Let's Play Jacks, 22019
Hughes, Shirley. *Abel's Moon*, 3709(F)
Alfie and the Birthday Surprise, 4983(F)
Alfie's ABC, 59(F)
Alfie's 1-2-3, 471(F)
Being Together, 3227(F)
The Big Alfie and Annie Rose Storybook, 3710(F)
The Big Alfie Out of Doors Storybook, 3711(F)
Bouncing, 3228(F)
Chatting, 3229(F)
Colors, 277(F)
Dogger, 4984(F)
Enchantment in the Garden, 7803(F)
The Lion and the Unicorn, 9667(F)
Out and About, 4464(F)
Rhymes for Annie Rose, 11609
Stories by Firelight, 1253(F)
Tales of Trotter Street, 3230(F)
Two Shoes, New Shoes, 3231(F)
Hughes, Ted. *How the Whale Became and Other Stories*, 1254(F)
The Mermaid's Purse, 11961
Hugo, Victor. *The Hunchback of Notre Dame*, 9045(F)
Huling, Phil. *Moses in Egypt*, 17293
Huliska-Beith, Laura. *The Book of Bad Ideas*, 4185(F)
Hull, Mary. *The Composite Guide to Golf*, 22020
Ethnic Violence, 17145
Hull, Mary E. *Mary Todd Lincoln*, 13167

Shays' Rebellion and the Constitution in American History, 16252

Hull, Richard. *The Alphabet from Z to A*, 141(F)

My Sister's Rusty Bike, 965(F)

Hull, Robert. *The Aztecs*, 15620

Greece, 14685

Hull, Robert, reteller. *Egyptian Stories*, 10674

Hulme, Joy N. *Eerie Feary Feeling*, 6014(F)

How to Write, Recite, and Delight in All Kinds of Poetry, 14090

Sea Squares, 472

Through the Open Door, 9558(F)

What If? 11793

Humble, Richard. *A 16th Century Galleon*, 15477

A World War Two Submarine, 21390

Hume, Lotta Carswell. *Favorite Children's Stories from China and Tibet*, 10758

Humphrey, Kathryn L. *Pompeii*, 14723

Humphreys, Rob. *Czech Republic*, 15272

Humphries, Tudor. *Are You a Butterfly?* 19539

Are You a Ladybug? 19528

Are You a Snail? 19600

Are You a Spider? 19571

Hiding, 3232(F)

Seal, 5115(F)

Whale, 950(F)

Hundal, Nancy. *Prairie Summer*, 11962

Huneck, Stephen. *Sally Goes to the Beach*, 5271(F)

Hunt, Angela E. *The Tale of Three Trees*, 11353

Hunt, Irene. *Across Five Aprils*, 9482(F)

No Promises in the Wind, 8702(F)

Hunt, Jonathan. *Bestiary*, 60

Jumbo, 19161

Leif's Saga, 9046(F)

Hunt, Joyce (jt. author). *A First Look at Dogs*, 19970

A First Look at Ducks, Geese, and Swans, 19316

Hunt, Robert. *Halmoni's Day*, 5473(F)

Hunter, Anne. *Nocturne*, 4565(F)

On Grandpa's Farm, 3409(F)

Possum and the Peeper, 2226(F)

Possum's Harvest Moon, 2227(F)

What's in the Meadow? 20536

What's in the Pond? 20521

What's in the Tide Pool? 19861

Hunter, Edith Fisher. *Child of the Silent Night*, 13140

Hunter, Evan. *Me and Mr. Stenner*, 8460(F)

Hunter, Matt. *Pro Wrestling's Greatest Tag Teams*, 22021

Ric Flair, 22022

Hunter, Mollie. *Gilly Martin the Fox*, 11002

The Mermaid Summer, 7804(F)

Hunter, Ryan Ann. *Cross a Bridge*, 21130

Dig a Tunnel, 21131

Into the Sky, 21132

Take Off! 21081

Hunter, Sally M. *Four Seasons of Corn*, 15975

Hunter, Sara H. *The Unbreakable Code*, 9165(F)

Hunter, Shaun. *Great African Americans in the Olympics*, 13374

Leaders in Medicine, 13212

Visual and Performing Artists, 12168

Hurd, Clement. *Goodnight Moon*, 638(F)

The Runaway Bunny, 1895(F)

Hurd, Edith Thacher. *I Dance in My Red Pajamas*, 3712(F)

The Song of the Sea Otter, 19736

Starfish, 19721

Hurd, Thacher. *Art Dog*, 2228(F)

Little Mouse's Big Valentine, 6172(F)

Mama Don't Allow, 2229(F)

Mystery on the Docks, 2230(F)

Santa Mouse and the Ratdeer, 5850(F)

Zoom City, 3233(F)

Hurford, John. *Another Happy Tale*, 4100(F)

Hurmence, Belinda. *A Girl Called Boy*, 7805(F)

Hurst, Brian Seth (jt. author). *A Pig Tale*, 2527(F)

Hurst, Carol Otis. *Through the Lock*, 9559(F)

Hurwitz, Eugene. *Working Together Against Homelessness*, 17146

Hurwitz, Jane. *Choosing a Career in Animal Care*, 17848

Hurwitz, Johanna. *The Adventures of Ali Baba Bernstein*, 6420(F)

Aldo Applesauce, 9891(F)

Anne Frank, 13800

Baseball Fever, 10339(F)

Class Clown, 10081(F)

Class President, 10082(F)

The Cold and Hot Winter, 8307(F)

DeDe Takes Charge! 8461(F)

The Down and Up Fall, 7457(F)

"E" Is for Elisa, 7458(F)

Elisa in the Middle, 9892(F)

Ever-Clever Elisa, 10083(F)

Faraway Summer, 9560(F)

The Hot and Cold Summer, 8308(F)

The Just Desserts Club, 8309(F)

Leonard Bernstein, 12323

A Llama in the Family, 7225(F)

Llama in the Library, 7226(F)

New Shoes for Silvia, 3234(F)

Once I Was a Plum Tree, 8703(F)

One Small Dog, 7227(F)

Ozzie on His Own, 8310(F)

PeeWee's Tale, 7806(F)

School Spirit, 10084(F)

School's Out, 7459(F)

Spring Break, 8311(F)

Starting School, 10085(F)

Summer with Elisa, 8704(F)

Tough-Luck Karen, 10086(F)

The Up and Down Spring, 8312(F)

Yellow Blue Jay, 8705(F)

Hurwitz, Johanna, ed. *Birthday Surprises*, 10259(F)

Hurwitz, Sue (jt. author). *Working Together Against Homelessness*, 17146

Husain, Shahrukh. *The Barefoot Book of Stories from the Opera*, 14131

What Do We Know About Islam? 17192

Husberg, Rob. *Better Than a Lemonade Stand!* 16939

Huser, Glen. *Touch of the Clown*, 8706(F)

Husted, Marty. *Firefly Night*, 682(F)

Hush! 683(F)

Hutchins, Hazel. *Believing Sophie*, 4985(F)

It's Raining, Yancy and Bear, 1255(F)

One Duck, 5272(F)

The Prince of Tarn, 7807(F)

Tess, 8462(F)

Two So Small, 1256(F)

Hutchins, Pat. *Changes, Changes*, 922(F)

Don't Forget the Bacon! 4186(F)

The Doorbell Rang, 3235(F)

Good-Night, Owl! 2231(F)

Happy Birthday, Sam, 5697(F)

It's My Birthday, 5698(F)

Little Pink Pig, 2232(F)

One Hunter, 473(F)

Rosie's Walk, 2233(F)

Shrinking Mouse, 340(F)

Silly Billy! 1257(F)

The Surprise Party, 2234(F)

Ten Red Apples, 474(F)

Titch, 3713(F)

The Very Worst Monster, 1258(F)

What Game Shall We Play? 2235(F)

Which Witch Is Which? 6015(F)

Hutchins, Roger. *Trojan Horse*, 14698

Hutchinson, Duane. *The Gunny Wolf and Other Fairy Tales*, 10566

Hutchinson, Sascha. *Snap!* 2778(F)

Hutchison, Paula. *The Year Around*, 11956

Huth, Holly. *Twilight*, 1259(F)

Huth, Holly Young. *Darkfright*, 1260(F)

The Son of the Sun and the Daughter of the Moon, 11125

Hutton, Warwick. *The Cricket Warrior*, 10742
Moses in the Bulrushes, 17287
Odysseus and the Cyclops, 11481
Perseus, 11482
The Selkie Girl, 10961
The Silver Cow, 10962
Tam Lin, 10963
Theseus and the Minotaur, 11483
The Tinderbox, 10393(F)
The Trojan Horse, 14686
Hutton, Warwick, adapt. *Moses in the Bulrushes*, 17287
Huxley, Dee. *Mr. Nick's Knitting*, 4060(F)
Remember Me, 3945(F)
Huynh, Quang Nhuong. *The Land I Lost*, 8998(F)
Water Buffalo Days, 15167
Hyatt, Patricia Rusch. *Coast to Coast with Alice*, 9561(F)
Hyde, Dayton O. *Mr. Beans*, 6905(F)
Hyde, Lawrence E. (jt. author). *Meeting Death*, 17858
Hyde, Margaret O. *Alcohol 101*, 17873
The Disease Book, 17967
Know About Abuse, 17710
Know About AIDS, 17968
Know About Drugs, 17871
Know About Mental Illness, 17969
Know About Smoking, 17872
Living with Asthma, 17970
Meeting Death, 17858
Hyland, Hilary. *The Wreck of the Ethie*, 6906(F)
Hyland, Rebecca. *No One Walks on My Father's Moon*, 8929(F)
Hyman, Miles. *Broadway Chicken*, 7734(F)
Hyman, Trina S. *The Adventures of Hershel of Ostropol*, 11153
Bearskin, 1494(F)
Canterbury Tales, 9085(F)
Cat Poems, 11799
A Child's Calendar, 11987
A Child's Christmas in Wales, 11853
A Christmas Carol, 9718(F)
Christmas Poems, 11836
Comus, 7794(F)
A Connecticut Yankee in King Arthur's Court, 8161(F)
Ghost Eye, 7591(F)
The Golem, 11162
Haunts, 7960(F)
Hershel and the Hanukkah Goblins, 6084(F)
Iron John, 10923
The Kitchen Knight, 10997
Magic in the Mist, 1304(F)
The Night Journey, 9057(F)
Rapunzel, 10902
St. George and the Dragon, 10998
Star Mother's Youngest Child, 5884(F)
Tight Times, 5252(F)

The Water of Life, 10912
Why Don't You Get a Horse, Sam Adams? 12837
Will You Sign Here, John Hancock? 12896
Winter Poems, 11981
Witch Poems, 11732
Hynes, Robert. *Crawdad Creek*, 4533(F)
Meeting Trees, 4534(F)
Hyppolite, Joanne. *Ola Shakes It Up*, 8707(F)

Iannone, Catherine. *Pocahontas*, 12986
Ibazebo, Isimeme. *Exploration into Africa*, 14908
Ibbotson, Eva. *Island of the Aunts*, 7808(F)
The Secret of Platform 13, 7809(F)
Which Witch? 7810(F)
Icanberry, Mark. *Picnic on a Cloud*, 7811(F)
Ichikawa, Satomi. *Bravo, Tanya*, 4962(F)
Dance, Tanya, 3017(F)
The First Bear in Africa! 1261(F)
Grandpa's Soup, 1284(F)
Presenting Tanya, the Ugly Duckling, 4963(F)
Tanya and Emily in a Dance for Two, 3997(F)
Tanya and the Magic Wardrobe, 3158(F)
Ichord, Loretta Frances. *Hasty Pudding, Johnnycakes, and Other Good Stuff*, 16136
Toothworms and Spider Juice, 18021
Iguchi, Bryan. *The Young Snowboarder*, 22281
Igus, Toyomi. *Going Back Home*, 12313
I See the Rhythm, 14132
Two Mrs. Gibsons, 3714(F)
When I Was Little, 3715(F)
Igus, Toyomi, ed. *Great Women in the Struggle*, 12661
Ilgenfritz, Elizabeth. *Anne Hutchinson*, 13160
Illsley, Linda. *The Caribbean*, 15706
Mexico, 15621
Imai, Miko. *Wuzzy Takes Off*, 2367(F)
Imershein, Betsy. *Trucks*, 5575(F)
Immell, Myra H. *Tecumseh*, 13000
Immell, William H. (jt. author). *Tecumseh*, 13000
Impey, Rose. *Read Me a Fairy Tale*, 10435(F)
Ingemanson, Donna. *Something's Happening on Calabash Street*, 3120(F)
Ingham, Richard. *France*, 15311
Ingle, Lester (jt. author). *Seashores*, 19872
Inglis, Jane. *Fiber*, 20159

Proteins, 20160
Ingman, Bruce. *Lost Property*, 5273(F)
A Night on the Tiles, 709(F)
When Martha's Away, 2236(F)
Ingpen, Robert. *Generals Who Changed the World*, 13746
The Magical East, 15052
The Mediterranean, 14597
People Who Changed the World, 13745
The Poppykettle Papers, 7893(F)
Scientists Who Changed the World, 13224
Who Is the World For? 1487(F)
Ingraham, Erick. *Blue-Ribbon Henry*, 1912(F)
Cross-Country Cat, 1913(F)
Flood, 8586(F)
Hot-Air Henry, 1914(F)
Ingram, W. Scott. *Oregon*, 16789
Inkpen, Mick. *Billy's Beetle*, 4187(F)
The Great Pet Sale, 2237(F)
Kipper, 2238(F)
Kipper's Book of Colors, 278(F)
Kipper's Book of Numbers, 475(F)
Kipper's Book of Opposites, 201(F)
Kipper's Book of Weather, 20772
Kipper's Christmas Eve, 5851(F)
Kipper's Snowy Day, 2239(F)
Nothing, 1262(F)
Picnic, 2240(F)
Wibbly Pig Can Make a Tent, 2241(F)
Inkpen, Mick (jt. author). *Jasper's Beanstalk*, 1905(F)
Innes, Brian. *The Bermuda Triangle*, 21916
The Cosmic Joker, 21917
Giant Humanlike Beasts, 21918
Millennium Prophecies, 21919
Mysterious Healing, 18022
Powers of the Mind, 18111
Inserra, Rose. *The Kalahari*, 14982
Intrater, Roberta G. *The Christmas Puppy*, 7228(F)
Smile! 3236(F)
Inwald, Robin. *Cap It Off with a Smile*, 17613
Iofin, Michael. *A Coat for the Moon and Other Jewish Tales*, 11167
Iosa, Ann. *Where Do I Live?* 173
Irbinskas, Heather. *How Jackrabbit Got His Very Long Ears*, 2242(F)
Irvine, Georgeanne. *Protecting Endangered Species at the San Diego Zoo*, 19399
Irvine, Joan. *How to Make Pop-Ups*, 21619
How to Make Super Pop-Ups, 21620
Irving, James G. *Fishes*, 19718
Irving, Washington. *The Legend of Sleepy Hollow*, 7812(F), 7813(F)
Rip Van Winkle, 7814(F), 7815(F)

Rip Van Winkle and the Legend of Sleepy Hollow, 7816(F)
Irwin, Dawn. *Inline Skating*, 22023
Irwin, Hadley. *Jim-Dandy*, 9384(F)
The Lilith Summer, 8708(F)
The Original Freddie Ackerman, 6907(F)
Isaacs, Anne. *Cat Up a Tree*, 11794
Swamp Angel, 4188(F)
Treehouse Tales, 9562(F)
Isaacs, Gwynne L. *While You Are Asleep*, 3237(F)
Isaacs, Sally Senzell. *America in the Time of Franklin Delano Roosevelt*, 16471
America in the Time of Martin Luther King Jr., 16511
America in the Time of Susan B. Anthony, 16472
Life in a Colonial Town, 16137
Life in a Hopi Village, 15976
Life on a Pioneer Homestead, 16317
Life on a Southern Plantation, 16253
Isadora, Rachael. *ABC Pop!* 61(F)
Ben's Trumpet, 4986(F)
Caribbean Dream, 4690(F)
City Seen from A to Z, 62(F)
I See, 18143
I Touch, 18144
Lili at Ballet, 3238(F)
Lili Backstage, 3716(F)
Lili on Stage, 3239(F)
Listen to the City, 3240(F)
Max, 4189(F)
Nick Plays Baseball, 22097
1 2 3 Pop! 476
Sophie Skates, 3241(F)
A South African Night, 5274(F)
Isadora, Rachael, reteller. *The Steadfast Tin Soldier*, 10436
Isadora, Rachel. *Ben's Trumpet*, 4986(F)
City Seen from A to Z, 62(F)
I See, 18143
I Touch, 18144
The Little Mermaid, 10385(F)
Max, 4189(F)
The Steadfast Tin Soldier, 10436
Isenbart, Hans-Heinrich. *Birth of a Foal*, 19997
Isherwood, Shirley. *The Band over the Hill*, 2243(F)
Flora the Frog, 4987(F)
Ishinabe, Fusako. *Spring Snowman*, 1263(F)
Ishizuka, Kathy. *Asian American Authors*, 12169
Iskowitz, Joel. *A Candle for Grandpa*, 17488
Emma Ansky-Levine and Her Mitzvah Machine, 7637(F)
Ghosts Don't Get Goose Bumps, 7129(F)
Isler, Claudia. *Caught in the Middle*, 17661

Isles, Joanna. *A Child's Garden of Verses*, 11716
Isom, Joan Shaddox. *The First Starry Night*, 4691(F)
Israel, Fred L. *The Amish*, 17568
Italia, Bob. *Al Gore*, 12891
Amy Grant, 12393
Anita Hill, 12726
Clara Hale, 13158
Great Auto Makers and Their Cars, 21303
Ross Perot, 12946
Italiano, Bob. *Scholastic Kid's Almanac for the 21st Century*, 14353
Italiano, Robert. *Kidbits*, 21955
Ito, Tom. *Abraham Lincoln*, 13071
The Importance of John Muir, 13328
Ivanko, John D. (jt. author). *To Be a Kid*, 14327
Iverson, Carlyn. *How Insects Build Their Amazing Homes*, 19482
How Mammals Build Their Amazing Homes, 18911
Ivimey, John W. *The Complete Story of the Three Blind Mice*, 852(F)
Iwai, Melissa. *Gramps and the Fire Dragon*, 766(F)
Night Shift Daddy, 782(F)
Iwasaki, Chihiro. *Snow White and the Seven Dwarves*, 10909
Swan Lake, 14273
Izcoa, Carmen Rivera, adapt. *Mediopollito/Half-a-Chick*, 11424

Jabar, Cynthia. *Bored Blue?* 3242(F)
The Frog Who Wanted to Be a Singer, 2141(F)
Game Time! 225(F)
The Greatest Gymnast of All, 227
How Many How Many How Many, 603(F)
A Koala for Katie, 3776(F)
Rain Song, 4426(F)
Snow Dance, 3123(F)
Jackman, Joan. *Gymnastics*, 22194
The Young Gymnast, 22195
Jackson, Alison. *I Know an Old Lady Who Swallowed a Pie*, 6145(F)
Jackson, Bobby L., reteller. *Little Red Ronnika*, 10919
Jackson, Colin. *The Young Track and Field Athlete*, 22318
Jackson, Dave. *Abandoned on the Wild Frontier*, 9385(F)
The Betrayer's Fortune, 9047(F)
Quest for the Lost Prince, 13837
The Runaway's Revenge, 9292(F)
The Thieves of Tyburn Square, 9293(F)
Jackson, Donna M. *The Bone Detectives*, 17071
The Wildlife Detectives, 18637

Jackson, Dorothy (jt. author). *Science Experiments with Electricity*, 20901
Science Experiments with Forces, 20814
Jackson, Ellen. *The Autumn Equinox*, 17370
The Book of Slime, 21920
Brown Cow, Green Grass, Yellow Mellow Sun, 4465(F)
Cinder Edna, 10437(F)
Here Come the Brides, 17371
The Impossible Riddle, 11092
The Precious Gift, 11259
Turn of the Century, 14557
The Winter Solstice, 18568
Jackson, Jean. *Big Lips and Hairy Arms*, 1264(F)
Mrs. Piccolo's Easy Chair, 1265(F)
Thorndike and Nelson, 2244(F)
Jackson, Jeff. *The Silly Chicken*, 2677(F)
Jackson, Julian. *Quest for the Lost Prince*, 13837
Jackson, Lawrence. *Newfoundland and Labrador*, 15583
Jackson, Nancy. *Photographers*, 12170
Jackson, Neta (jt. author). *Abandoned on the Wild Frontier*, 9385(F)
The Betrayer's Fortune, 9047(F)
Quest for the Lost Prince, 13837
The Runaway's Revenge, 9292(F)
The Thieves of Tyburn Square, 9293(F)
Jackson, Shelley. *Do You Know Me?* 8962(F)
Escape South, 9320(F)
The Old Woman and the Wave, 1266(F)
Willy's Silly Grandma, 4125(F)
Jackson, Shirley. *The Witchcraft of Salem Village*, 16138
Jacob, Murv. *Dog People*, 11216
Jacobi, Kathryn. *The Half-a-Moon Inn*, 6843(F)
Tomorrow's Wizard, 7942(F)
Jacobs, Francine. *Follow That Trash!* 16980
Jacobs, Jimmy. *Moonlight Through the Pines*, 11354
Jacobs, Joseph. *Celtic Fairy Tales*, 11003
English Fairy Tales, 11004
Indian Fairy Tales, 10794
Jacobs, Judy. *Indonesia*, 15168
Jacobs, Kate. *A Sister's Wish*, 3717(F)
Jacobs, Laurie A. *So Much in Common*, 2245(F)
Jacobs, Lee. *The Orthopedist*, 18023
Jacobs, Paul S. *James Printer*, 9238(F)
Jacobs, Shannon K. *Healers of the Wild*, 17849
Jacobs, William J. *Ellis Island*, 16697
Great Lives, 17035

Mother Teresa, 13854

War with Mexico, 16254

Jacobsen, Karen. *Farm Animals*, 20061

Jacobson, Jennifer Richard. *Moon Sandwich Mom*, 2246(F)

A Net of Stars, 1267(F)

Jacobson, Rick. *Glass Town*, 14067

Little Dog Moon, 4854(F)

The Magnificent Piano Recital, 5055(F)

Prairie Willow, 4855(F)

Tchaikovsky Discovers America, 9566(F)

Jacobus, Tim. *My Sister the Witch*, 9811(F)

Jacques, Brian. *The Bellmaker*, 7817(F)

Castaways of the Flying Dutchman, 7818(F)

The Great Redwall Feast, 7819(F)

The Legend of Luke, 7820(F)

The Long Patrol, 7821(F)

Lord Brocktree, 7822(F)

Mariel of Redwall, 7823(F)

Marlfox, 7824(F)

Martin the Warrior, 7825(F)

Mattimeo, 7826(F)

Mossflower, 7827(F)

Outcast of Redwall, 7828(F)

The Pearls of Lutra, 7829(F)

Salamandastron, 7830(F)

Seven Strange and Ghostly Tales, 7831(F)

Jacques, Laura. *At Home in the Rain Forest*, 4882

Going to a Horse Farm, 5276

Sweet Magnolia, 4718(F)

Jaeger, Winifred (jt. author). *The Round Book*, 14251

Jaffe, Nina. *The Cow of No Color*, 10567

The Golden Flower, 11425

In the Month of Kislev, 6081(F)

The Mysterious Visitor, 17193

Tales for the Seventh Day, 11150

The Uninvited Guest and Other Jewish Holiday Tales, 17475

The Way Meat Loves Salt, 11151

Jaffrey, Madhur. *Seasons of Splendor*, 10795

Jahn-Clough, Lisa. *ABC Yummy*, 63(F)

Missing Molly, 4009(F)

My Friend and I, 4010(F)

1 2 3 Yippie, 477(F)

Jakes, John. *Susanna of the Alamo*, 9294(F)

Jakob, Donna. *Tiny Toes*, 3243(F)

Jakobsen, Kathy. *My New York*, 16698

This Land Is Your Land, 14154

Jakoubek, Robert E. *James Farmer and the Freedom Rides*, 12721

Walter White and the Power of Organized Protest, 12821

Jam, Teddy. *The Charlotte Stories*, 4190(F)

The Fishing Summer, 2942(F)

The Stoneboat, 4011(F)

ttuM, 6908(F)

The Year of Fire, 3718(F)

Jambor, Louis. *Little Women*, 7384(F)

James, Ann. *Midnight Babies*, 1680(F)

James, Barbara. *Animal Rights*, 18638

James, Betsy. *The Dream Stair*, 710(F)

Flashlight, 3244(F)

Tadpoles, 3719(F)

James, Derek. *Who Stole the Wizard of Oz?* 6756(F)

James, Diane (jt. author). *Play with Paint*, 21585

James, Elizabeth. *How to Be School Smart*, 17614

How to Write Super School Reports, 14091

How to Write Terrific Book Reports, 14092

How to Write Your Best Book Report, 14093

Social Smarts, 17636

James, Elizabeth (jt. author). *The New Complete Babysitter's Handbook*, 16938

James, Ellen Foley. *Little Bull*, 5275(F)

James, J. Alison. *The Drums of Noto Hanto*, 4692(F)

Eucalyptus Wings, 1268(F)

James, John. *An Egyptian Pyramid*, 14649

Everest, 22047

Medieval Cathedral, 14778

A Roman Villa, 14733

James, Kennon. *George Washington Carver, What Do You See?* 13252

James, Laura. *Michelle Kwan*, 13593

James, Louise. *How We Know About the Egyptians*, 14633

How We Know About the Greeks, 14687

The Romans, 14724

The Vikings, 15452

James, Mary. *Frankenlouse*, 8463(F)

Shoebag, 7832(F)

The Shuteyes, 7833(F)

James, Rhian N. *Scramcat*, 2249(F)

James, Robert (jt. author). *Lies (People Believe) About Animals*, 18856

James, Shirley K. *Going to a Horse Farm*, 5276

James, Simon. *Dear Mr. Blueberry*, 2247(F)

Leon and Bob, 4012(F)

Sally and the Limpet, 1269(F)

The Wild Woods, 5277(F)

Jameson, W. C. *Buried Treasures of the Atlantic Coast*, 14531

Buried Treasures of the Great Plains, 16564

Jane, Pamela. *The Big Monkey Mix-up*, 2943(F)

Halloween Hide-and-Seek, 6016(F)

Noelle of the Nutcracker, 7834(F)

Janeczko, Paul B. *How to Write Poetry*, 14094

The Place My Words Are Looking For, 11610

Poetry from A to Z, 14095

That Sweet Diamond, 11999

Janeway, Elizabeth. *The Vikings*, 15453

Jango-Cohen, Judith. *Clinging Sea Horses*, 19705

Crocodiles, 18703

Janicot, Didier. *Judo Techniques andTactics*, 22024

Janin, Hunt. *Saudi Arabia*, 15551

Janisch, Heinz. *Noah's Ark*, 17288(F)

Janover, Caroline. *How Many Days Until Tomorrow?* 8709(F)

Zipper, 8895(F)

Janovitz, Marilyn. *Hey Diddle Diddle*, 849

Little Fox, 2248(F)

What Could Be Keeping Santa? 5852(F)

Jansen, John. *Class Act*, 21826(F)

January, Brendan. *The Assassination of Abraham Lincoln*, 13072

The Emancipation Proclamation, 16415

Fort Sumter, 16416

Ireland, 15353

The Jamestown Colony, 16139

John Brown's Raid on Harpers Ferry, 16255

The Lincoln-Douglas Debates, 16256

The National Mall, 16699

The New York Public Library Amazing Mythology, 11448

Reconstruction, 16473

Science in Colonial America, 16140

Science in the Renaissance, 14800

Janulewicz, Mike. *Yikes! Your Body, Up Close*, 18063

Jaques, Faith. *The Orchard Book of Nursery Rhymes*, 893

Jaramillo, Raquel. *Ride, Baby, Ride!* 1270(F)

Jarecka, Danuta. *Joseph and His Coat of Many Colors*, 17292

Jarrell, Randall. *The Bat-Poet*, 7835(F)

Jarrett, Clare. *Catherine and the Lion*, 1271(F)

Jarrow, Gail. *Beyond the Magic Sphere*, 8710(F)

If Phyllis Were Here, 7460(F)

Naked Mole-Rats, 19198

Jarvis, Kila. *Owls*, 19361

Jarvis, Robin. *The Dark Portal*, 7836(F)

Jarzyna, Dave. *Slump*, 8711(F)

Jaskol, Julie. *City of Angels*, 16790

Jasper, Alvin C. *The American Flag*, 13974

Jaspersohn, William. *Cookies*, 16949
Ice Cream, 20101
The Two Brothers, 9563(F)
A Week in the Life of an Airline Pilot, 17837

Jauck, Andrea. *Assateague*, 19998

Javna, John. *50 Simple Things Kids Can Do to Save the Earth*, 16959

Jay, Alison. *The Classic Treasury of Children's Prayers*, 17519
Picture This . . ., 202(F)
The Shore Beyond, 1281(F)
William and the Night Train, 1295(F)

Jay, Betsy. *Jane vs. the Tooth Fairy*, 4191(F)
Swimming Lessons, 4988(F)

Jedrosa, Aleksander. *Eyes*, 18145

Jefferis, David. *Alien Lifesearch*, 20992
Artificial Intelligence, 21205
Cloning, 18035
Cyber Space, 21206
Flight, 21082

Jefferis, Veronica. *Deep in a Rainforest*, 20472

Jeffers, H. Paul. *Legends of Santa Claus*, 17422

Jeffers, Susan. *Black Beauty*, 5408(F)
Hiawatha, 11641
Lassie Come-Home, 7321(F)
Love Songs of the Little Bear, 11540
McDuff and the Baby, 5449(F)
McDuff Comes Home, 5450(F)
McDuff Moves In, 5451(F)
McDuff's New Friend, 5950(F)
Rachel Field's Hitty, 8196(F)
Stopping by Woods on a Snowy Evening, 11568

Jeffrey, Laura S. *Al Gore*, 12892
Christa McAuliffe, 12136
Great American Businesswomen, 12662
Guion Bluford, 12080

Jemison, Mary. *The Diary of Mary Jemison*, 15977

Jendresen, Erik. *The First Story Ever Told*, 11440

Jendresen, Erik, reteller. *Hanuman*, 10796

Jenkins, Debra R. *I See the Moon*, 622(F)
I Wanted to Know All About God, 17199
My Freedom Trip, 15193

Jenkins, Emily. *Five Creatures*, 3720(F)

Jenkins, Leonard. *If I Only Had a Horn*, 12349

Mayfield Crossing, 7363(F)

Jenkins, Martin. *Chameleons Are Cool*, 18745
Deserts, 20406
The Emperor's Egg, 19372
Fly Traps! 20238
Wings, Stings and Wriggly Things, 18639

Jenkins, Priscilla B. *Falcons Nest on Skyscrapers*, 19329
A Nest Full of Eggs, 19239
A Safe Home for Manatees, 19737

Jenkins, Sandra. *Flip-Flap*, 203

Jenkins, Steve. *Animal Dads*, 18871
Big and Little, 341(F)
Biggest, Strongest, Fastest, 18640
Duck's Breath and Mouse Pie, 21921
Elephants Swim, 18845
Hottest, Coldest, Highest, Deepest, 20377
Into the A, B, Sea, 119
Looking Down, 923(F)
Making Animal Babies, 18918
This Big Sky, 11975
The Top of the World, 22025
What Do You Do When Something Wants to Eat You? 18898

Jenness, Aylette. *Come Home with Me*, 3245(F)

Jennings, Coleman A., ed. *Plays Children Love, Volume II*, 12022

Jennings, Dana A. *Me, Dad, and Number 6*, 5576(F)

Jennings, Linda. *Nine Naughty Kittens*, 478(F)
Scramcat, 2249(F)

Jennings, Patrick. *Faith and the Electric Dogs*, 7837(F)
Faith and the Rocket Cat, 7838(F)
Putnam and Pennyroyal, 8464(F)

Jennings, Paul. *Unreal!* 10260(F)

Jennings, Richard W. *Orwell's Luck*, 7839(F)

Jennings, Sharon. *The Bye-Bye Pie*, 3721(F)
Franklin's Neighborhood, 2250(F)
Into My Mother's Arms, 3246(F)

Jennings, Sharon (jt. author).
Franklin's Class Trip, 1849(F)

Jennings, Terry. *Cranes, Dump Trucks, Bulldozers and Other Building Machines*, 21249
101 Amazing Optical Illusions, 20915
Planes, Gliders, Helicopters and Other Flying Machines, 21083
Wood, 20205

Jennis, Paul. *The Phantom of the Opera*, 6939(F)

Jenny, Christine. *The Toady and Dr. Miracle*, 6266(F)

Jensen, Dorothea. *The Riddle of Penncroft Farm*, 7840(F)

Jensen, Julie. *Beginning Baseball*, 22098
Beginning Mountain Biking, 22160

Jensen, Julie, adapt. *Beginning Hockey*, 22213
Beginning Snowboarding, 22282

Jenssen, Hans. *Star Wars Episode I*, 14318

Jeppson, Ann-Sofie. *Here Comes Pontus!* 7841(F)

Jepson, Beth. *I Don't Want to Go to Justin's House Anymore*, 4998(F)

Jerabek, Ilka. *The Monkey and the Mango*, 4423(F)

Jeram, Anita. *All Pigs Are Beautiful*, 5291
All Together Now, 2251(F)
Bill's Belly Button, 2252(F)
Birthday Happy, Contrary Mary, 5699(F)
Daisy Dare, 2253(F)
Dick King-Smith's Animal Friends, 19899
Guess How Much I Love You, 732(F)
I Love Guinea Pigs, 19900
My Hen Is Dancing, 20073
Puppy Love, 19955

Jermyn, Leslie. *Brazil*, 15747
Colombia, 15748
Mexico, 15622
Paraguay, 15749
Peru, 15750
Welcome to Mexico, 15623

Jernegan, Laura. *A Whaling Captain's Daughter*, 16474

Jernigan, E. Wesley. *Agave Blooms Just Once*, 64(F)
Sonoran Seasons, 20407

Jernigan, Gisela. *Agave Blooms Just Once*, 64(F)
Sonoran Seasons, 20407

Jerome, Karen A. *If Nathan Were Here*, 4901(F)

Jeschke, Susan. *Perfect the Pig*, 2254(F)

Jessel, Camilla. *Ballet School*, 14290
The Kitten Book, 19925
The Puppy Book, 19952

Jessop, Joanne. *The X-Ray Picture Book of Big Buildings of the Ancient World*, 14586

Jessup, Harley. *Grandma Summer*, 4466(F)
Just Enough, 3098(F)

Jestadt, Peter. *City at Night*, 16971

Jewell, Nancy. *Five Little Kittens*, 711(F)
Sailor Song, 712(F)
Two Silly Trolls, 6421(F)

Jezek, Alisandra. *Miloli's Orchids*, 2944(F)

Jia, Bo. *The Trip Back Home*, 4890(F)

Jiguang, Xin. *The Giant Panda*, 19187

Jimenez, Francisco. *The Christmas Gift*, 5853(F)
La Mariposa, 4989(F)

Jimenez, Juan Ramon. *Platero y Yo/Platero and I*, 7229

Joachim, Claude. *The Rebellion of Humans*, 4372(F)

Jobb, Jamie. *The Night Sky Book*, 18396

Jocelyn, Marthe. *Earthly Astonishments*, 9564(F)
Hannah and the Seven Dresses, 5700(F)
Hannah's Collections, 5508(F)
Invisible Day, 7842(F)
The Invisible Harry, 7843(F)

Jockel, Nils. *Bruegel's Tower of Babel*, 13895

Johanasen, Heather. *About the Rain Forest*, 20452

Johansen, Hanna. *Dinosaur with an Attitude*, 7844(F)

Johansen, K. V. *Pippin and the Bones*, 6422(F)
Pippin Takes a Bath, 2255(F)

Johmann, Carol A. *Bridges! Amazing Structures to Design, Build and Test*, 21133
Going West! 16318

John, Helen. *All-of-a-Kind Family*, 7527(F)

John Paul II, Pope. *For the Children*, 17194

Johns, Elizabeth. *Sunflower Sal*, 2995(F)

Johnson, Adrian. *What! Cried Granny*, 731(F)

Johnson, Amy. *To the Point*, 12622

Johnson, Angela. *The Aunt in Our House*, 3722(F)
Do Like Kyla, 3723(F)
Down the Winding Road, 3724(F)
The Leaving Morning, 3247(F)
Maniac Monkeys on Magnolia Street, 8313(F)
One of Three, 3725(F)
The Other Side, 11763
Rain Feet, 3248(F)
The Rolling Store, 4693(F)
Shoes Like Miss Alice's, 3249(F)
Songs of Faith, 8465(F)
Tell Me a Story, Mama, 3726(F)
Those Building Men, 5577(F)
The Wedding, 3727(F)
When I Am Old with You, 3728(F)
When Mules Flew on Magnolia Street, 8314(F)

Johnson, Annabel. *The Grizzly*, 6909(F)
I Am Leaper, 7845(F)

Johnson, Anne E. *Jazz Tap*, 14291

Johnson, Arden. *The Lost Tooth Club*, 4192(F)

Johnson, Beth Griffis. *100 Days of School*, 459(F)

Johnson, Bruce (jt. author). *Apples, Alligators and Also Alphabets*, 66(F)

Johnson, Cathy. *A Rainy Day*, 20783

Johnson, Charles. *Pieces of Eight*, 7846(F)

Johnson, Crockett. *The Carrot Seed*, 1320(F)
Harold and the Purple Crayon, 6423(F)

Johnson, D. B. *Henry Hikes to Fitchburg*, 2256(F)

Johnson, Dave, ed. *Movin'*, 11611

Johnson, David. *The Beggar's Magic*, 10741

Johnson, David A. *Old Mother Hubbard*, 853

Johnson, Dinah. *All Around Town*, 4694
Quinnie Blue, 4695(F)
Sitting Pretty, 21652
Sunday Week, 3729(F)

Johnson, Dolores. *Big Meeting*, 3959(F)
The Children's Book of Kwanzaa, 17372
Grandma's Hands, 3730(F)
My Mom Is My Show-and-Tell, 5509(F)
Now Let Me Fly, 4696(F)
Seminole Diary, 4697
What Kind of Baby-Sitter Is This? 3250(F)
What Will Mommy Do When I'm at School? 3731(F)
Your Dad Was Just Like You, 3732(F)

Johnson, Doug. *Never Ride Your Elephant to School*, 4193(F)

Johnson, Edgar (jt. author). *The Grizzly*, 6909(F)

Johnson, Emily Rhoads. *Write Me If You Dare!* 8712(F)

Johnson, Eric W. *People, Love, Sex, and Families*, 18262

Johnson, Gillian. *My Sister Gracie*, 2257(F)

Johnson, Herschel. *A Visit to the Country*, 5278(F)

Johnson, James W. *The Creation*, 17290
Lift Every Voice and Sing, 14157, 14156
Lift Ev'ry Voice and Sing, 14158

Johnson, Jane. *My Dear Noel*, 12580
Now Soon Later, 188(F)

Johnson, Jean. *Firefighters A to Z*, 65(F)

Johnson, Jinny. *Children's Guide to Insects and Spiders*, 19455
Simon & Schuster Children's Guide to Birds, 19240
Simon and Schuster Children's Guide to Sea Creatures, 19637

Johnson, Julie. *Being Angry*, 17615
Bullies and Gangs, 17711
My Stepfamily, 17662

Johnson, Karen. *I Can't Wait Until I'm Old Enough to Hunt with Dad*, 2946(F)

Johnson, Kipchak. *Worm's Eye View*, 18323

Johnson, Larry. *Knoxville, Tennessee*, 11755
Soccer Halfback, 10314(F)
Train, 3451(F)
Wilma Rudolph, 13672

Johnson, Laurie K. *Clouds of Terror*, 9452(F)

Johnson, Layne. *Abuelito Eats with His Fingers*, 3771(F)
Ben, King of the River, 4965(F)
Brad and Butter Play Ball, 10334(F)
Brian's Bird, 5178(F)
On the Day His Daddy Left, 4897(F)

Johnson, Linda C. *Mother Teresa*, 13855
Our Constitution, 17057
Our National Symbols, 15851

Johnson, Linda Carlson. *Rain Forests*, 20453

Johnson, Lindsay L. *Hurricane Henrietta*, 1272(F)

Johnson, Lois W. *Escape into the Night*, 9295(F)
Midnight Rescue, 9296(F)

Johnson, Lonni S. *The Story of Z*, 102(F)

Johnson, Meredith. *The Bathwater Gang*, 9998(F)
Ben and Becky in the Haunted House, 6491(F)
Wanna Bet? 18308

Johnson, Neil. *All in a Day's Work*, 17753
Fire and Silk, 2945

Johnson, Odette. *Apples, Alligators and Also Alphabets*, 66(F)

Johnson, Pamela. *Do Not Disturb*, 18903
Monster Bugs, 19478
A Mouse's Tale, 2258(F)

Johnson, Paul. *An Appalachian Mother Goose*, 892
Insects Are My Life, 5323(F)
Lost, 5279(F)
Mr. Persnickety and Cat Lady, 4194(F)
Too Quiet for These Old Bones, 4312(F)
A Traveling Cat, 5322(F)

Johnson, Paul B. *Bearhide and Crow*, 1273(F)
The Cow Who Wouldn't Come Down, 1274(F)
Farmers' Market, 3251(F)
Lost, 5279(F)
Mr. Persnickety and Cat Lady, 4194(F)
Old Dry Frye, 11355
A Perfect Pork Stew, 1275(F)
The Pig Who Ran a Red Light, 2259(F)

Johnson, Rebecca L. *Braving the Frozen Frontier*, 15808

The Great Barrier Reef, 19661
Investigating the Ozone Hole, 16998
A Walk in the Boreal Forest, 20454
A Walk in the Desert, 20408
A Walk in the Rain Forest, 20455
A Walk in the Tundra, 15809
Johnson, Rick L. *Jim Abbott*, 13432
Johnson, Robert (jt. author). *Shona*, 15006
Johnson, Scott. *I Can't Wait Until I'm Old Enough to Hunt with Dad*, 2946(F)
Safe at Second, 10340(F)
Johnson, Stephen. *On a Wintry Morning*, 3577(F)
A Roman Fort, 14725
Johnson, Stephen T. *Alphabet City*, 13983
City by Numbers, 479
The Girl Who Wanted a Song, 1540(F)
Hoops, 11995
Love as Strong as Ginger, 3779(F)
The Nutcracker Ballet, 14288
Johnson, Steve. *Bambi*, 7299(F)
Coppelia, 14283(F)
The Frog Prince Continued, 10499(F)
Horsefly, 1248(F)
I Walk at Night, 2045(F)
The Lost Boy and the Monster, 1602(F)
My Many Colored Days, 289(F)
Peach and Blue, 1300(F)
The Salamander Room, 5344(F)
Silver Seeds, 11978
Johnson, Sylvia A. *Albatrosses of Midway Island*, 19241
Apple Trees, 20147
Bats, 19028
Beetles, 19533
Crabs, 19677
Elephant Seals, 19738
Ferrets, 18947
Fireflies, 19456
How Leaves Change, 20206
Inside an Egg, 19304
Ladybugs, 19534
Mapping the World, 14368
Morning Glories, 20037
Penguins, 19373
Roses Red, Violets Blue, 20038
Silkworms, 19611
Snails, 19612
Snakes, 18760
Songbirds, 19305
Tree Frogs, 18728
Wasps, 19524
Water Insects, 19457
Wheat, 20102
Wolf Pack, 19126
Johnson-Petrov, Arden. *Bow-Wow Birthday*, 5735(F)
A Farmer's Garden, 2172(F)
Johnston, Joyce. *Alaska*, 16791
Maryland, 16868

Washington, D.C., 16700
Johnston, Marianne. *Dealing with Anger*, 17616
Dealing with Bullying, 17712
From the Dinosaurs of the Past to the Birds of the Present, 14428
Let's Talk About Being Shy, 17713
Let's Talk About Going to a Funeral, 17859
Let's Talk About Going to the Hospital, 18040
Sharks Past and Present, 19762
Johnston, Norma. *Over Jordan*, 9297(F)
Remember the Ladies, 17036
Johnston, Tony. *Alice Nizzy Nazzy*, 1276(F)
The Badger and the Magic Fan, 10816
The Barn Owls, 5280(F)
Bigfoot Cinderrrrrella, 10438
The Bull and the Fire Truck, 6424(F)
The Chizzywink and the Alamagoozlum, 2260(F)
The Cowboy and the Black-Eyed Pea, 10439(F)
Day of the Dead, 5628(F)
Desert Song, 4467(F)
Fishing Sunday, 3733(F)
How Many Miles to Jacksonville? 4698(F)
The Iguana Brothers, 2261(F)
It's About Dogs, 11795
The Magic Maguey, 4699(F)
My Mexico/México Mío, 11612
An Old Shell, 11964
Once in the Country, 11613
Pages of Music, 5854(F)
The Quilt Story, 3252(F)
Slither McCreep and His Brother, 2262(F)
The Soup Bone, 6017(F)
Sparky and Eddie, 6425(F), 6426(F)
The Tale of Rabbit and Coyote, 11403
Uncle Rain Cloud, 3734(F)
The Vanishing Pumpkin, 6018(F)
Very Scary, 6019(F)
The Wagon, 4700(F)
Johnstone, Leslie (jt. author). *Everyday Science*, 18325
Fun with Your Microscope, 19806
The Magnet Book, 20898
The Microscope Book, 19807
The Optics Book, 20873
Science Around the World, 18326
The Science of Sound and Music, 20940
Shocking Science, 20899
Silly Science, 18327
Johnstone, Michael. *Cars*, 21304
The History News, 16082
The History News in Space, 20993
Look Inside Cross-Sections, 21334
Planes, 21084

Jolin, Dominique. *It's Not Fair!* 3735(F)
Jonas, Ann. *Aardvarks, Disembark!* 17291
Bird Talk, 5281(F)
Color Dance, 279(F)
Reflections, 3253(F)
Round Trip, 4195(F)
Splash! 480(F)
The Trek, 1277(F)
Two Bear Cubs, 5282(F)
Watch William Walk, 4196(F)
When You Were a Baby, 3254(F)
Jonell, Lynne. *I Need a Snake*, 4197(F)
It's My Birthday, Too! 5701(F)
Let's Play Rough! 3736(F)
Mom Pie, 3737(F)
Mommy Go Away! 1278(F)
Jones, Amy Robin. *Kwanzaa*, 17373
Jones, Betty. *A Child's Seasonal Treasury*, 4468(F)
Jones, Bill T. *Dance*, 14292
Jones, Bob. *Jelly Belly*, 8815(F)
Jones, Carol. *The Cat Sat on the Mat*, 5155(F)
The Hare and the Tortoise, 11065
Old MacDonald Had a Farm, 14171
This Old Man, 14184
Town Mouse Country Mouse, 2263(F)
What's the Time, Mr. Wolf? 2264(F)
Jones, Charlotte F. *Accidents May Happen*, 21037
Eat Your Words, 20103
Fingerprints and Talking Bones, 17072
Mistakes That Worked, 21038
Yukon Gold, 16792
Jones, Diana Wynne. *Charmed Life*, 7847(F)
Jones, Elizabeth McDavid. *Secrets on 26th Street*, 9565(F)
Watcher in the Piney Woods, 9483(F)
Jones, Elizabeth Orton. *Prayer for a Child*, 17522
Jones, George. *My First Book of How Things Are Made*, 21039
Jones, Helen. *40s and 50s*, 13896
Jones, Helga. *Venezuela*, 15751
Jones, Jennifer B. *Dear Mrs. Ryan, You're Ruining My Life*, 9893(F)
Heetunka's Harvest, 11260
Jones, Jenny. *Happy Birthday, Amelia*, 5712(F)
Jones, John R. *Dinosaur Hunters*, 14444
Jones, John R. (jt. author). *Madagascar*, 14975
Jones, Joy. *Tambourine Moon*, 1279(F)
Jones, Lois Mailou. *Wonders*, 11941
Jones, Lynda. *Great Black Heroes*, 13213(F)

Kids Around the World Celebrate! 17374

Jones, Marcia T. (jt. author). *Leprechauns Don't Play Basketball*, 7693(F)

Jones, Margaret. *Tales from the Mabinogion*, 11040

Jones, Mary. *Guns*, 21405

Jones, Michelle. *The American Girls Party Book*, 22234

Jones, Miranda. *The Floating Orchard*, 1225(F)

Jones, Rebecca C. *Matthew and Tilly*, 4013(F)

The President Has Been Shot! 15885

Jones, Richard C. *Princess September and the Nightingale*, 10462(F)

Jones, Robert F. *Jake*, 19953

Jones, Schuyler. *Pygmies of Central Africa*, 14932

Jones, Terry. *The Lady and the Squire*, 9048(F)

Jones, Thomas D. (jt. author). *Mission: Earth*, 20982

Jones, Veda Boyd. *Ewan McGregor*, 12419

Jonke, Tim. *The Tale of Three Trees*, 11353

Joos, Frederic. *Kiss It Better*, 2552(F)

Joos, Louis. *Oregon's Journey*, 1496(F)

Joosse, Barbara M. *Alien Brain Fryout*, 6910(F)

Anna and the Cat Lady, 8713(F)

Ghost Trap, 6911(F)

I Love You the Purplest, 3738(F)

Lewis and Papa, 4701(F)

The Losers Fight Back, 10341(F)

Mama, Do You Love Me? 3739(F)

The Morning Chair, 3740(F)

Nugget and Darling, 5283(F)

Pieces of the Picture, 8714(F)

Snow Day! 4469(F)

Jordan, Billy. *Lion*, 19094

Jordan, Deloris. *Salt in His Shoes*, 4990(F)

Jordan, Denise. *Susie King Taylor*, 12785

Jordan, Helene J. *How a Seed Grows*, 20271

Jordan, June. *Kimako's Story*, 3255(F)

Jordan, Mary K. *Losing Uncle Tim*, 8466(F)

Jordan, Roslyn M. (jt. author). *Salt in His Shoes*, 4990(F)

Jordan, Sandra. *Down on Casey's Farm*, 713(F)

Jordan, Sandra (jt. author). *Chuck Close, Up Close*, 12211

Frank O. Gehry, 12233

Jordan, Taylor. *Hiccup*, 6427(F)

Jordan, William Chester, ed. *The Middle Ages*, 14773

Jorg, Sabine. *Mina and the Bear*, 1280(F)

Jorgensen, David. *Wind Says Good Night*, 769(F)

Jorgensen, Gail. *Crocodile Beat*, 2265(F)

Gotcha! 2266(F)

Jorgensen, Lisa. *Grand Trees of America*, 20207

Jorisch, Stephane. *The Magic Mustache*, 983(F)

Jortberg, Charles A. *The Internet*, 21207

Virtual Reality and Beyond, 21208

Joseph, Lynn. *Coconut Kind of Day*, 11614

The Color of My Words, 8715(F)

Fly, Bessie, Fly, 12093

An Island Christmas, 9735(F)

Jump Up Time, 4702(F)

The Mermaid's Twin Sister, 11426

A Wave in Her Pocket, 11427

Joseph, Paul. *Calvin Coolidge*, 13026

Harry S. Truman, 13109

Richard Nixon, 13087

Warren G. Harding, 13038

Josephson, Judith P. *Allan Pinkerton*, 12948

Josey, Kira. *In the Next Three Seconds*, 21937

Josey, Rod. *In the Next Three Seconds*, 21937

Joslin, Mary. *The Goodbye Boat*, 3741(F)

The Shore Beyond, 1281(F)

The Tale of the Heaven Tree, 1282(F)

Joslin, Sesyle. *What Do You Say, Dear?* 4991(F)

Jourdenais, Norma Jean. *Cut-Paper Play!* 21618

Joyce, Susan. *ABC Animal Riddles*, 67

ABC Nature Riddles, 68(F)

Alphabet Riddles, 69(F)

Joyce, Susan, comp. and ed. *ABC School Riddles*, 21827(F)

Joyce, William. *Bently and Egg*, 2267(F)

Buddy, 7230(F)

George Shrinks, 7848(F)

Humphrey's Bear, 801(F)

The Leaf Men and the Brave Good Bugs, 2268(F)

Rolie Polie Olie, 1283(F)

Shoes, 3482(F)

Snowie Rolie, 5855(F)

The World of William Joyce Scrapbook, 13959

Joysmith, Brenda. *Hush Songs*, 793

Jubb, Kendahl J. *Bold and Bright*, 18888

Flashy Fantastic Rain Forest Frogs, 18734

Slinky Scaly Slithery Snakes, 18772

Judd, Naomi. *Naomi Judd's Guardian Angels*, 14248

Judes, Marie-Odile. *Max, the Stubborn Little Wolf*, 2269(F)

Judkis, Jim. *Let's Talk About It*, 17677, 17931, 17678

Judson, Karen. *Abraham Lincoln*, 13073

Isaac Asimov, 12502

Jukes, Mavis. *Getting Even*, 8315(F)

Growing Up, 18263

Like Jake and Me, 3742(F)

Junakovic, Svjetlan. *Colors*, 1570(F)

Jung, Sung-Hoon. *South Korea*, 15169

Jungman, Ann. *When the People Are Away*, 2270(F)

Jurmain, Suzanne. *Freedom's Sons*, 16257

Juster, Norton. *Alberic the Wise*, 9049(F)

As, 14038

The Phantom Tollbooth, 7849(F)

Kabatova-Taborska, Zdenka. *Salt Is Sweeter Than Gold*, 10862

Kachur, Wanda G. *The Nautilus*, 8896(F)

Kaczman, James. *When a Line Bends . . . A Shape Begins*, 331(F)

Kadmon, Cristina. *Little Elephant's Song*, 2167(F)

Luke the Lionhearted, 5402(F)

When I Grow Up . . ., 2220(F)

Kadodwala, Dilip. *Divali*, 17375

Holi, 17376

Kadono, Eiko. *Grandpa's Soup*, 1284(F)

Kaergel, Julia. *Lottie's Princess Dress*, 4132(F)

Kagda, Falaq. *Algeria*, 14959

Hong Kong, 15170

Kagda, Sakina. *Lithuania*, 15274

Norway, 15454

Kahl, Jonathan D. *Hazy Skies*, 20773

National Audubon Society First Field Guide, 20774

Storm Warning, 20697

Thunderbolt, 20698

Weather Watch, 20775

Weatherwise, 20776

Wet Weather, 20777

Kahle, Peter V. T. *Shakespeare's The Tempest*, 12051

Kahn, Katherine J. *Jewish Holiday Crafts for Little Hands*, 17452

Matzah Ball, 6105(F)

Sammy Spider's First Passover, 6111(F)

Sammy Spider's First Rosh Hashanah, 6112(F)

Sammy Spider's First Shabbat, 6113(F)

Kahn, Sharon. *Kacy and the Space Shuttle Secret*, 10199(F)

Kairi, Wambui. *Kenya*, 14933

Kajikawa, Kimiko. *Sweet Dreams*, 18826

Yoshi's Feast, 10817

Kajpust, Melissa. *A Dozen Silk Diapers*, 10920
The Peacock's Pride, 10797
Kakkak, Dale. *Ininatig's Gift of Sugar*, 16069
The Sacred Harvest, 16027
Kalan, Robert. *Blue Sea*, 342(F)
Moving Day, 2271(F)
Rain, 4470(F)
Kalas, Sybille. *The Goose Family Book*, 19312
The Wild Horse Family Book, 19999
Kalb, Jonah. *What Every Kid Should Know*, 17617
Kalbacken, Joan. *Badgers*, 18948
The Food Pyramid, 20161
Food Safety, 20162
Recycling, 16981
Vitamins and Minerals, 20163
White-Tailed Deer, 19153
Kalbacken, Joan (jt. author). *Foxes*, 19129
Kalbag, Asha. *Build Your Own Web Site*, 21209
Kallen, Stuart A. *Eco-Arts and Crafts*, 21579
Egypt, 15505
Exploring the Origins of the Universe, 18397
Life Among the Pirates, 14558
Life on the American Frontier, 16319
Life on the Underground Railroad, 16258
The 1950s, 16512
Rosie O'Donnell, 12434
The Salem Witch Trials, 16141
Thurgood Marshall, 12766
Kalman, Bobbie. *AB Sea*, 19638
Bandannas, Chaps, and Ten-Gallon Hats, 16320
Canada, 15584, 15585, 15586
Canada Celebrates Multiculturalism, 15587
A Canoe Trip, 22262
Celebrating the Powwow, 15978
A Child's Day, 16476
Christmas Long Ago from A to Z, 70(F)
Colonial Crafts, 16142
Colonial Life, 16143
Customs and Traditions, 16331
18th Century Clothing, 21173
Fort Life, 16332
The General Store, 16259
The Gristmill, 16321
Home Crafts, 16322
Hooray for Sheep Farming! 20062
How a Plant Grows, 20239
How Animals Communicate, 18893
How Do Animals Adapt? 18827
In the Barn, 16323
The Kitchen, 16324
Life in the Coral Reef, 19662
The Life of a Miner, 16329
Life on a Plantation, 16260

Mexico, 15624, 15625, 15626
19th Century Girls and Women, 16475
A One-Room School, 16325
Penguins, 19374
Pioneer Projects, 21521
Settler Sayings, 16326
Spanish Missions, 15886
The Victorian Home, 13897
Vietnam, 15171, 15172, 15173
Visiting a Village, 16327
Web Weavers and Other Spiders, 19584
What Are Food Chains and Webs? 18586
What Is a Biome? 20378
What Is a Life Cycle? 18587
What Is a Marsupial? 19178
What Is a Primate? 19000
What Is a Rodent? 19199
What Is a Whale? 19639
What Is an Amphibian? 18686
Who Settled the West? 16328
Women of the West, 16330
Kalman, Bobbie (jt. author). *How Do Animals Move?* 18863
A Koala Is Not a Bear! 19181
Really Weird Animals, 18936
Kalman, Esther. *Tchaikovsky Discovers America*, 9566(F)
Kalman, Maira. *Hey Willy, See the Pyramids*, 714(F)
Next Stop Grand Central, 3256(F)
Ooh-La-La (Max in Love), 2272(F)
Sayonara, Mrs. Kackleman, 4703(F)
Swami on Rye, 7850(F)
Kaloustian, Rosanne. *Cemetery Quilt*, 5065(F)
Kamal, Aleph. *The Bird Who Was an Elephant*, 8999(F)
Kamen, Gloria. *Hidden Music*, 12332
Kipling, 12559
Lisa and Her Soundless World, 8900(F)
Siggy's Spaghetti Works, 20129
Kamerman, Sylvia E., ed. *Christmas Play Favorites for Young People*, 12023
Great American Events on Stage, 12024
Thirty Plays from Favorite Stories, 12025
Kaminker, Laura. *In-Line Skating!* 22026
Kaminski, Karol. *ArtStarts for Little Hands!* 21463
Kaminsky, Jef. *"I Can't Take You Anywhere!"* 4248(F)
Let's Play Cards! 22238
Poppy and Ella, 2273(F)
Kaminsky, Marty. *Uncommon Champions*, 13375
Kamish, Daniel. *The Night the Scary Beasties Popped Out of My Head*, 1285(F)

Kamish, David. *The Night the Scary Beasties Popped Out of My Head*, 1285(F)
Kandel, Bethany. *Trevor's Story*, 17663
Kandoian, Ellen. *Summer's End*, 5476(F)
Kane, Henry B. *All Day Long*, 11647
One at a Time, 11648
Kanefield, Teri. *Rivka's Way*, 9050(F)
Kaner, Etta. *Animal Defenses*, 18899
Sound Science, 20939
Kang, Johanna. *Star of Fear, Star of Hope*, 9664(F)
Kanitkar, V. P. *Hinduism*, 17195
Kantor, MacKinlay. *Gettysburg*, 16417
Kantor, Susan, ed. *One-Hundred-and-One African-American Read-Aloud Stories*, 10261(F)
Kaplan, Elizabeth. *Taiga*, 20456
Temperate Forest, 20457
Tundra, 15810
Kaplan, Elizabeth (jt. author). *How Do Big Ships Float?* 21349
Kaplan, Gisela (jt. author). *Iran*, 15558
Kaplan, Howard. *Waiting to Sing*, 3743(F)
Kaplan, John. *Mom and Me*, 3744
Kaplan, William. *One More Border*, 14858
Kappeler, Markus (jt. author). *The Giant Panda*, 19187
Karas, G. Brian. *Bebe's Bad Dream*, 4198(F)
The Best Teacher in the World, 5486(F)
The Bone Keeper, 7936(F)
Bootsie Barker Ballerina, 6217(F)
Car Wash, 3439(F)
The Case of the Climbing Cat, 6600(F)
Cinder-Elly, 10465
Don't Read This Book, Whatever You Do! 11867
Follow the Leader, 3429(F)
Give Me Half! 226(F)
Good Knight, 772(F)
The High-Rise Private Eyes, 8059(F)
Home on the Bayou, 4992(F)
I Know an Old Lady, 14159
In the Hush of the Evening, 689(F)
Missing Mittens, 529
Mr. Carey's Garden, 5174(F)
My Crayons Talk, 1252(F)
On the Trail with Miss Pace, 4413(F)
Penelope Jane, 10405(F)
Raising Sweetness, 4323(F)
Saving Sweetness, 4324(F)
The Seals on the Bus, 14246
Sleepless Beauty, 4237(F)
The Spider Who Created the World, 2420(F)

Throw Your Tooth on the Roof, 10531

Truman's Aunt Farm, 4281(F)

The Windy Day, 3257(F)

Karas, Phyllis. *For Lucky's Sake,* 6912(F)

Karim, Roberta. *Kindle Me a Riddle,* 4704(F)

This Is a Hospital, Not a Zoo! 1286(F)

Karkonen, Reijo. *The Children of Nepal,* 15174

Karkowsku, Nancy. *Grandma's Soup,* 4993(F)

Karlin, Nurit. *The April Rabbits,* 407(F)

The Fat Cat Sat on the Mat, 6428(F)

The Tooth Witch, 1287(F)

Karlins, Mark. *Music over Manhattan,* 4994(F)

Salmon Moon, 1288(F)

Karlitz, Gail. *Growing Money,* 16925

Karnes, Frances A. *Girls and Young Women Inventing,* 21040

Girls and Young Women Leading the Way, 17147

Karon, Jan. *Jeremy,* 7851(F)

Karpinski, John E. *Somebody Somewhere Knows My Name,* 8749(F)

Karr, Kathleen. *Gold-Rush Phoebe,* 9386(F)

The Great Turkey Walk, 9298(F)

The Lighthouse Mermaid, 9567(F)

Man of the Family, 9568(F)

Oregon, Sweet Oregon, 9387(F)

Skullduggery, 9299(F)

Spy in the Sky, 9484(F)

Karwoski, Gail L. *Seaman,* 7231(F)

Karwoski, Gail L. (jt. author). *The Tree That Owns Itself,* 8932(F)

Kasamatsu, Shiro. *The Inch-High Samurai,* 10822

Kaschula, Russel. *Xhosa,* 14983

Kasoff, Jerry. *Baseball Just for Kids,* 22099

Kasperson, James. *Little Brother Moose,* 5284(F)

Kassem, Lou. *A Summer for Secrets,* 7852(F)

Kassinger, Ruth. *U.S. Census,* 17115

Kassirer, Sue. *Joseph and His Coat of Many Colors,* 17292

Kastner, Jill. *Aurora Means Dawn,* 4819(F)

Barnyard Big Top, 4199(F)

Beardream, 1242(F)

Down at Angel's, 5779(F)

Howling Hill, 2214(F)

In November, 4530(F)

The Lizard Man of Crabtree County, 4252(F)

The Shepherd Boy, 2931(F)

Songs for the Ancient Forest, 1362(F)

The Stone Dancers, 4764(F)

True Stories About Abraham Lincoln, 13067

The Waterfall, 2953(F)

You're My Nikki, 3614(F)

Kastner, Joseph. *John James Audubon,* 12189

Kasza, Keiko. *Don't Laugh, Joe!* 2274(F)

Dorothy and Mikey, 2275(F)

A Mother for Choco, 2276(F)

The Rat and the Tiger, 2277(F)

When the Elephant Walks, 5285(F)

Katan, Norma Jean. *Hieroglyphics,* 14634

Katchen, Carole. *That Sweet Diamond,* 11999

Katcher, Ruth (jt. author). *My Heroes, My People,* 16344

Katella-Cofrancesco, Kathy. *Children's Causes,* 17148

Economic Causes, 17149

Katin, Miriam. *Tubes In My Ears,* 18038

Katz, Avi. *God Said Amen,* 1543(F)

King Solomon and the Queen of Sheba, 17279(F)

Katz, Avner. *Tortoise Solves a Problem,* 2278(F)

Katz, Bobbi. *Germs! Germs! Germs!* 17971

Lots of Lice, 17972

Truck Talk, 5578

We, the People, 11615

Katz, David. *You Can Be a Woman Astronomer,* 17825

Katz, Karen. *The Colors of Us,* 3258(F)

Counting Kisses, 715(F)

Over the Moon, 3745(F)

Katz, Susan. *Snowdrops for Cousin Ruth,* 8467(F)

Katz, Welwyn W. *Beowulf,* 11126

Out of the Dark, 8716(F)

Time Ghost, 10200(F)

Katz, William L. *Black People Who Made the Old West,* 12663

Proudly Red and Black, 12664

Katzen, Mollie. *Honest Pretzels,* 21709

Pretend Soup and Other Real Recipes, 21710

Katzman, Marylyn. *African Crafts,* 21446

Kauchak, Therese. *Good Sports,* 22027

Kaufman, Cheryl Davidson. *Cooking the Caribbean Way,* 21711

Kaulbach, Kathy. *Lilly's Good Deed,* 8254(F)

Kaur-Singh, Kanwaljit. *Sikh Gurdwara,* 17196

Kavanagh, Jack. *Dizzy Dean,* 13447

Grover Cleveland Alexander, 13434

Rogers Hornsby, 13462

Sports Great Joe Montana, 13620

Sports Great Larry Bird, 13514

Sports Great Patrick Ewing, 13523

Walter Johnson, 13466

Kavasch, E. Barrie. *The Seminoles,* 15979

Kawasaki, Shauna Mooney. *Too Many Cooks,* 6131(F)

Kay, Helen. *The First Teddy Bear,* 21653

Kay, Verla. *Covered Wagons, Bumpy Trails,* 4705(F)

Gold Fever, 4706(F)

Iron Horses, 21335

Kaye, Buddy. *A You're Adorable,* 71(F)

Kaye, Judith. *The Life of Daniel Hale Williams,* 13352

Kaye, Marilyn. *Amy, Number Seven,* 10201(F)

Cabin Six Plays Cupid, 8316(F)

A Friend Like Phoebe, 8317(F)

Happily Ever After, 8468(F)

Real Heroes, 8717(F)

The Real Tooth Fairy, 3746(F)

Kaye, Rosalind Charney. *Sweet Strawberries,* 3821(F)

Kazuko. *What Can You See?* 21875(F)

Kazunas, Charnan. *The Internet for Kids,* 21210

Personal Computers, 21211

The World Wide Web, 21212

Kazunas, Tom (jt. author). *The Internet for Kids,* 21210

Personal Computers, 21211

The World Wide Web, 21212

Keams, Geri. *Snail Girl Brings Water,* 13944

Kearney, David. *Sports Stories,* 10324(F)

Keats, Ezra Jack. *Apt. 3,* 4014(F)

Goggles! 4015(F)

Jennie's Hat, 4200(F)

John Henry, 11356

Louie, 4995(F)

Maggie and the Pirate, 2947(F)

One Red Sun, 481(F)

Regards to the Man in the Moon, 1289(F)

The Snowy Day, 4471(F)

The Trip, 6020(F)

Two Tickets to Freedom, 9476(F)

Whistle for Willie, 4016(F)

Keats, Ezra Jack, illus. *The Little Drummer Boy,* 14203

Keefauver, John. *The Three-Day Traffic Jam,* 7853(F)

Keefer, Janice Kulyk. *Anna's Goat,* 4707(F)

Keegan, Marcia. *Pueblo Girls,* 15980

Keegan, Shannon. *Heetunka's Harvest,* 11260

Keehn, Sally M. *The First Horse I See,* 7232(F)

I Am Regina, 9166(F)

Keeler, Barbara. *Sailing Ship Eagle,* 21391

Keeler, Don (jt. author). *Sailing Ship Eagle*, 21391

Keeler, Patricia A. *Unraveling Fibers*, 21174

Keen, Dan (jt. author). *Science Fair Projects*, 18301, 20819, 18381, 20798

Science Fair Projects with Electricity and Electronics, 20886

Keenan, Sheila. *More or Less a Mess*, 6429(F)

Keene, Ann T. *Earthkeepers*, 13214

Keene, Carolyn. *Love Times Three*, 8718(F)

Keene, Chuck (jt. author). *National Audubon Society First Field Guide*, 18943

Keens-Douglas, Richardo. *Mama God, Papa God*, 11428

The Miss Meow Pageant, 1290(F)

Keep, Linda Lowery. *Hannah and the Angels*, 6913(F)

Keeping, Charles. *Beowulf*, 11037

Keeter, Susan. *The Piano*, 4770(F)

Kehoe, Michael. *A Book Takes Root*, 13998

Kehret, Peg. *The Blizzard Disaster*, 7854(F)

Danger at the Fair, 6914(F)

Don't Tell Anyone, 6915(F)

Earthquake Terror, 6916(F)

Frightmares, 7233(F), 6917(F)

I'm Not Who You Think I Am, 8719(F)

My Brother Made Me Do It, 8720(F)

Searching for Candlestick Park, 6918(F)

The Secret Journey, 8966(F)

Shelter Dogs, 19954

Sisters Long Ago, 7461(F)

Small Steps, 17973

The Volcano Disaster, 7855(F)

Keiko, Narahashi. *Who Said Red?* 288(F)

Keillor, Garrison. *The Sandy Bottom Orchestra*, 8318(F)

Keith, Eros. *The House of Dies Drear*, 6872(F)

The Slave Dancer, 9276(F)

Keith, Harold. *Chico and Dan*, 7234(F)

Rifles for Watie, 9485(F)

Kelch, Joseph W. *Millions of Miles to Mars*, 18475

Kelleher, D. V. *Defenders of the Universe*, 6919(F)

Keller, Beverly. *Desdemona*, 9894(F)

Keller, Charles. *Astronuts*, 21828

Ballpoint Bananas and Other Jokes for Kids, 21829

Driving Me Crazy, 21830

It's Raining Cats and Dogs, 21831

King Henry the Ape, 21832

The Planet of the Grapes, 21833

Keller, Charles, ed. *Take Me to Your Liter*, 21834

Keller, Ellen. *Floods!* 20699

Keller, Holly. *Air Is All Around You*, 20664

Angela's Top-Secret Computer Club, 6920(F)

Be a Friend to Trees, 20209

A Bed Full of Cats, 6430(F)

The Best Bug Parade, 346(F)

Brave Horace, 2279(F)

From Tadpole to Frog, 18735

Geraldine and Mrs. Duffy, 2280(F)

Geraldine's Big Snow, 2281(F)

Geraldine's Blanket, 2282(F)

Growing Like Me, 18596

Harry and Tuck, 3747(F)

Hear Your Heart, 18091

Jacob's Tree, 4996(F)

Let's Go Rock Collecting, 20559

Merry Christmas, Geraldine, 5856(F)

Snakes Are Hunters, 18761

Snow Is Falling, 20755

Sounds All Around, 20943

Sponges Are Skeletons, 19719

That's Mine, Horace, 2283(F)

What I See, 6431(F)

What's It Like to Be a Fish? 19982

Who Eats What? 18590

You're Aboard Spaceship Earth, 20312

Keller, Katie. *Seven Loaves of Bread*, 1697(F)

Turnip Soup, 4247(F)

Keller, Laurie. *Open Wide*, 18184

The Scrambled States of America, 1291(F)

Keller, Stella. *Ice Cream*, 20104

Kellerhals-Stewart, Heather. *Brave Highland Heart*, 4708(F)

Kelley, Brent. *Keith Van Horn*, 13578

Lisa Leslie, 13544

Kelley, Ellen A. *The Lucky Lizard*, 7856(F)

Kelley, Emily. *Christmas Around the World*, 17423

Kelley, Gary. *William Shakespeare's Macbeth*, 12048

Kelley, James. *Baseball*, 22100

Kelley, Marty. *Fall Is Not Easy*, 1292(F)

The Rules, 4201(F)

Kelley, Patrick. *The Illustrated Rules of Softball*, 22119

Kelley, True. *Basketball Buddies*, 6512(F)

Day by Day a Week Goes Round, 244(F)

Flash, Crash, Rumble, and Roll, 20683

Floating in Space, 20954

Football Friends, 6511(F)

Get Ready for Robots! 21216

How Many Teeth? 18189

How to Hunt Buried Treasure, 21905

How to Read Your Mother's Mind, 21906

I Really Want a Dog, 5142(F)

The International Space Station, 20955

Look at Your Eyes, 18162

Month by Month a Year Goes Round, 245(F)

My Dog Toby, 5465(F)

Roller Skates! 6250(F)

The Skeleton Inside You, 18165

Three Stories You Can Read to Your Cat, 6524(F)

Three Stories You Can Read to Your Dog, 6525(F)

What the Moon Is Like, 18442

Kellogg, David. *True Stories of Baseball's Hall of Famers*, 22101

Kellogg, Steven. *A-hunting We Will Go!* 716

Abby, 3563(F)

Aster Aardvark's Alphabet Adventures, 72(F)

The Baby Beebee Bird, 742(F)

A Beasty Story, 2478(F)

Can I Keep Him? 3748(F)

Chicken Little, 2284(F)

Come Here, Cat, 6543(F)

Frogs Jump, 388(F)

Give the Dog a Bone, 482(F)

The Great Christmas Kidnapping Caper, 9765(F)

The Great Quillow, 8146(F)

How Much Is a Million? 20635

If You Made a Million, 20636

Is Your Mama a Llama? 2158(F)

Jack and the Beanstalk, 11005

Johnny Appleseed, 12845

Leo, Zack, and Emmie, 6326(F)

The Missing Mitten Mystery, 1293(F)

Paul Bunyan, 11357

Pecos Bill, 11358

Ralph's Secret Weapon, 1294(F)

Sally Ann Thunder Ann Whirlwind Crockett, 11359

The Three Little Pigs, 11006

The Three Sillies, 11007

Yankee Doodle, 14193

Kellogg, Steven, reteller. *Chicken Little*, 2284(F)

Pecos Bill, 11358

Kelly, Emery J. *Paper Airplanes*, 21621

Kelly, Eric P. *The Trumpeter of Krakow*, 9051(F)

Kelly, Evelyn B. *Katarina Witt*, 13597

Kelly, Geoff. *Power and Glory*, 4283(F)

Kelly, Irene. *Stories of the Songs of Christmas*, 14207

Kelly, J. *Superstars of Women's Basketball*, 13376

Kelly, Jo. *Why So Sad, Brown Rabbit?* 1911(F)

Kelly, Jo'Anne. *The Peacock's Pride*, 10797
Som See and the Magic Elephant, 1441(F)
Kelly, Kate (jt. author). *Everything You Need to Know About American History Homework*, 14118
Kelly, Laura. *A Carol for Christmas*, 5939(F)
The Pumpkin Man from Piney Creek, 5981(F)
Tabitha, 5433(F)
Kelly, Maddox. *The Clock*, 9267(F)
Kelly, Martin. *The Ants Came Marching*, 1742(F)
Kelly, Mij. *William and the Night Train*, 1295(F)
Kelly, Sheila (jt. author). *The A.D.D. Book for Kids*, 17933
Feeling Thankful, 3398
Kelly, Sheila M. (jt. author). *About Twins*, 17680
Lots of Dads, 17681
Kelsey, Elin. *Finding Out About Dinosaurs*, 14429
Finding Out About Whales, 19793
Kelso, Richard. *Building a Dream*, 12702
Walking for Freedom, 17037
Kemer, Eric (jt. author). *Science Projects About Temperature and Heat*, 20853
Kemp, Gillian. *Tea Leaves, Herbs, and Flowers*, 21922
Kemp, Moira. *Grandma Chickenlegs*, 11102
Helpful Betty Solves a Mystery, 2509(F)
Kempton, Kate. *The World Beyond the Waves*, 7857(F)
Kendall, Carol. *The Gammage Cup*, 7858(F)
Sweet and Sour, 10759
Kendall, Jane. *Miranda Goes to Hollywood*, 9569(F)
Kendall, Martha E. *Nellie Bly*, 13138
Kendall, Robert. *Mike's Kite*, 503(F)
Kendall, Russ. *Eskimo Boy*, 15811
Sara Morton's Day, 16184
Tapenum's Day, 16185
Kendall, Sarita. *The Incas*, 15752
Ransom for a River Dolphin, 7235(F)
Kendrick, Dennis. *The Fox with Cold Feet*, 6662(F)
Kenna, Kathleen. *A People Apart*, 17197
Kennaway, Adrienne. *Hot Hippo*, 2163(F)
Kennedy, Dorothy M., ed. *Make Things Fly*, 11965
Kennedy, Dorothy M. (jt. author). *Talking Like the Rain*, 11616
Kennedy, Doug. *Six Foolish Fishermen*, 11378
Kennedy, Gregory. *The First Men in Space*, 20994

Kennedy, Jimmy. *The Teddy Bears' Picnic*, 14249
Kennedy, Mike (jt. author). *Home Run Heroes*, 13413
Kennedy, Nick. *Dan Marino*, 13619
Kennedy, Pamela. *A Christmas Carol*, 5857(F)
A Christmas Celebration, 17424
An Easter Celebration, 17436
Kennedy, Richard. *Amy's Eyes*, 7859(F)
Kennedy, Robert C. *Life as a Paratrooper*, 21392
Life as an Army Demolition Expert, 21393
Life in the Army Special Forces, 21394
Life in the Marines, 21395
Life with the Navy Seals, 21396
Kennedy, Trish. *Baseball Card Crazy*, 7462(F)
Kennedy, X. J. *Brats*, 11877
The Eagle as Wide as the World, 7860(F)
Elympics, 2285(F)
Fresh Brats, 11878
Uncle Switch, 11879
Kennedy, X. J., ed. *Talking Like the Rain*, 11616
Kenny, Chantal Lacourciere. *The Kids Can Press French and English Phrase Book*, 14096
Kent, Deborah. *African-Americans in the Thirteen Colonies*, 16144
The American Revolution, 16200
Amsterdam, 15399
Beijing, 15069
Boston, 16701
Dallas, 16911
Delaware, 16702
The Disability Rights Movement, 17038
Dublin, 15354
In Colonial New England, 16145
Iowa, 16565
The Lincoln Memorial, 16703
Maine, 16704
Mexico, 15627
Moscow, 15422
New Mexico, 16912
New York City, 16705
Puerto Rico, 15708
Rio de Janeiro, 15753
St. Petersburg, 15423
Salem, Massachusetts, 16146
San Francisco, 16793
Thurgood Marshall and the Supreme Court, 12767
The Titanic, 21362
Tokyo, 15129
Utah, 16620
The Vietnam War, 16513
Wyoming, 16621
Kent, Jack. *The Caterpillar and the Polliwog*, 2286(F)
Joey, 2287(F)

Kent, Jacqueline C. *Women in Medicine*, 13215
Kent, Peter. *Fabulous Feasts*, 14559
Go to Jail! 14342
Hidden Under the Ground, 20379
Quest for the West, 9388(F)
A Slice Through a City, 14532
Kent, Peter (jt. author). *Career Ideas for Kids Who Like Computers*, 17796
Career Ideas for Kids Who Like Sports, 17762
Kent, Susan. *Let's Talk About Needing Extra Help at School*, 17714
Let's Talk About Stuttering, 17916
Kent, Zachary. *Andrew Johnson*, 13054
Calvin Coolidge, 13027
The Civil War, 16418
George Armstrong Custer, 12871
George Bush, 13010
George Washington, 13116
Grover Cleveland, 13021
John F. Kennedy, 13062
John Quincy Adams, 13005
The Persian Gulf War, 16514
Ronald Reagan, 13093
Rutherford B. Hayes, 13042
Theodore Roosevelt, 13103
Ulysses S. Grant, 13036
William McKinley, 13080
William Seward, 12961
Williamsburg, 16147
Zachary Taylor, 13107
Kenyon, Tony. *I Wonder Why the Sea Is Salty*, 19817
Making Shapes, 18316
Pushing and Pulling, 20810
Understanding Electricity, 20895
Kerby, Mona. *Robert E. Lee*, 12927
Kerina, Jane. *African Crafts*, 21446
Kerins, Tony. *The Baby Dances*, 3686(F)
The Brave Ones, 1296(F)
The Christmas Tree Tangle, 5873(F)
Little Clancy's New Drum, 4472(F)
Kerley, Barbara. *Songs of Papa's Island*, 4709(F)
Kerley, Ted (jt. author). *Little League's Official How-to-Play Baseball Handbook*, 22103
Kern, Noris. *I Love You with All My Heart*, 2288(F)
Kerr, Daisy. *Keeping Clean*, 18197
Kerr, Janet. *The Quiet Little Farm*, 5286(F)
Kerr, M. E. *Dinky Hocker Shoots Smack!* 9895(F)
Kerr, Rita. *Texas Footprints*, 9389(F)
Kerrod, Robin. *Asteroids, Comets, and Meteors*, 18516
Jupiter, 18476
The Moon, 18448
Pets and Farm Animals, 18828
Planet Earth, 18431
Saturn, 18477

The Solar System, 18517

The Sun, 18569

Uranus, Neptune, and Pluto, 18478

Kerschbaum, John. *They Don't Wash Their Socks!* 22003

Kertes, Joseph. *The Gift*, 9737(F)

Kerven, Rosalind. *Id-ul-Fitr*, 17377

Keselman, Gabriela. *The Gift*, 5702(F)

Kessel, Joyce K. *Squanto and the First Thanksgiving*, 12998

Valentine's Day, 17509

Kesselman, Wendy. *Sand in My Shoes*, 3259(F)

Kessler, Brad. *Moses in Egypt*, 17293

Kessler, Cristina. *All the King's Animals*, 19400

Jubela, 5287(F)

Konte Chameleon Fine, Fine, Fine! A West African Folktale, 2289(F)

My Great-Grandmother's Gourd, 4710(F)

Kessler, Ethel. *Stan the Hot Dog Man*, 6432(F)

Kessler, Leonard. *Here Comes the Strikeout*, 6433(F)

Kick, Pass, and Run, 22183

Last One In Is a Rotten Egg, 6434(F)

Kessler, Leonard (jt. author). *Stan the Hot Dog Man*, 6432(F)

Kest, Kristin. *Bumblebee at Apple Tree Lane*, 5217(F)

Ketcham, Sallie. *Bach's Big Adventure*, 4711(F)

Ketchum, Liza. *The Gold Rush*, 16333

Into a New Country, 12665

Orphan Journey Home, 9300(F)

Ketchum, Lynne (jt. author). *Carla Goes to Court*, 17011

Kettelkamp, Larry. *ETs and UFOs*, 20995

Living in Space, 20996

Ketteman, Helen. *Armadillo Tattletale*, 2290(F)

Bubba, The Cowboy Prince, 1297(F)

Grandma's Cat, 5288(F)

Heat Wave, 1298(F)

I Remember Papa, 3260(F)

Luck with Potatoes, 1299(F)

Mama's Way, 3749(F)

Shoeshine Whittaker, 4202(F)

Kettner, Christine. *An Ordinary Cat*, 2291(F)

Key, Alexander. *The Forgotten Door*, 10202(F)

Keyworth, Valerie. *New Zealand*, 15238

Khan, Rukhsana. *The Roses in My Carpets*, 4712(F)

Khanduri, Kamini (jt. author). *Greek Myths*, 11462

Kharms, Daniil. *First, Second*, 483(F)

It Happened Like This, 9896(F)

Kherdian, David. *The Golden Bracelet*, 11188

Kherdian, Jeron. *The Road from Home*, 13821

Khng, Pauline. *Myanmar*, 15175

Kibbey, Marsha. *My Grammy*, 4997(F)

Kidd, Diana. *Onion Tears*, 7348(F)

Kidd, Richard. *Almost Famous Daisy!* 4713(F)

Kidd, Ronald. *Sammy Carducci's Guide to Women*, 9897(F)

Kidd, Ronald, ed. *On Top of Old Smoky*, 11360

Kiddell-Monroe, Joan. *West Indian Folk Tales*, 11432

Kidder, Harvey. *The Kids' Book of Chess*, 22171

Shortstop from Tokyo, 10312(F)

Kieffer, Christa. *You Were Born on Your Very First Birthday*, 18240

Kiefte, Kees de. *Chuck and Danielle*, 7707(F)

Kiesler, Kate. *Across America, I Love You*, 3780(F)

A Blizzard Year, 7447(F)

Bright Christmas, 5784(F)

Crab Moon, 5268(F)

Grandfather's Christmas Camp, 5868(F)

The Great Frog Race and Other Poems, 11952

Old Elm Speaks, 11953

Temple Cat, 4622(F)

Twilight Comes Twice, 4430(F)

Kiki. *My Head Is Full of Colors*, 1170(F)

Kilborne, Sarah S. *Leaving Vietnam*, 15176

Peach and Blue, 1300(F)

Kilby, Don. *The Prairie Fire*, 4810(F)

Killcoyne, Hope Lourie. *The Lost Village of Central Park*, 9301(F)

Killeen, Richard. *The Easter Rising*, 15355

Killien, Christi. *Artie's Brief*, 8721(F)

Killilea, Maria. *Newf*, 5289(F)

Killion, Bette. *The Same Wind*, 4473(F)

Kim, Jody. *Nightfeathers*, 11659

Kim, Joung Un. *Duck Song*, 2144(F)

Why the Frog Has Big Eyes, 6336(F)

A Year for Kiko, 3485(F)

Kimber, Kevin. *A First Book of Myths*, 10562

Kimmel, Elizabeth C. *Balto and the Great Race*, 16794

Ice Story, 15812

In the Stone Circle, 7861(F)

Kimmel, Eric A. *The Adventures of Hershel of Ostropol*, 11153

Anansi and the Moss-Covered Rock, 10675

Anansi and the Talking Melon, 10676

Anansi Goes Fishing, 10677

Asher and the Capmakers, 6082(F)

Baba Yaga, 11093

Be Not Far from Me, 17294

Bearhead, 11094

Bernal and Florinda, 11136

Billy Lazroe and the King of the Sea, 11361

The Birds' Gift, 11095

Boots and His Brothers, 11127

The Chanukkah Guest, 6083(F)

Count Silvernose, 9052(F)

Easy Work! An Old Tale, 11128

Four Dollars and Fifty Cents, 2948(F)

The Four Gallant Sisters, 10921

Gershon's Monster, 11154

The Gingerbread Man, 11008

The Goose Girl, 10922

The Greatest of All, 10818

Grizz! 1301(F)

Hershel and the Hanukkah Goblins, 6084(F)

I Know Not What, I Know Not Where, 11096

I Took My Frog to the Library, 4203(F)

Iron John, 10923

The Jar of Fools, 11155(F)

The Magic Dreidels, 6085(F)

Montezuma and the Fall of the Aztecs, 11404

The Old Woman and Her Pig, 11009

One Eye, Two Eyes, Three Eyes, 11097

Onions and Garlic, 11156

Rimonah of the Flashing Sword, 10678

Robin Hook, Pirate Hunter! 1302(F)

The Rooster's Antlers, 10760

The Runaway Tortilla, 11362

Seven at One Blow, 10924

Sirko and the Wolf, 10860

The Spotted Pony, 9738(F)

Squash It! A True and Ridiculous Tale, 11137

Sword of the Samurai, 10819

The Tale of Aladdin and the Wonderful Lamp, 11189

The Tale of Ali Baba and the Forty Thieves, 1303(F)

Ten Suns, 10761

The Three Princes, 11190

Three Sacks of Truth, 10872

The Two Mountains, 11405

Website of the Warped Wizard, 7862(F)

When Mindy Saved Hanukkah, 6086(F)

Kimmel, Margaret Mary. *Magic in the Mist*, 1304(F)

Kimmelman, Leslie. *Dance, Sing, Remember*, 17476

The Runaway Latkes, 6087(F)

Sound the Shofar! A Story for Rosh Hashanah and Yom Kippur, 6088(F)

Kincade, Nancy. *Even If I Did Something Awful?* 3680(F)

My Mother Is the Smartest Woman in the World, 7412(F)

Kinch, Michael P. *Warts*, 18178

Kincher, Jonni. *Psychology for Kids II*, 17618

Kindersley, Anabel (jt. author). *Celebrations!* 17378

Children Just Like Me, 14343

Kindersley, Barnabas. *Celebrations!* 17378

Children Just Like Me, 14343

Kinerk, Robert. *Slim and Miss Prim*, 9898(F)

King, Andrew. *Exploring Shapes*, 20580

Measuring Sizes, 20581

Measuring Weight and Time, 20658

Plotting Points and Position, 20604

King, Bob. *Sitting on the Farm*, 2292(F)

King, Colin. *My "a" Sound Box*, 103(F)

King, Dave. *Birds*, 19279

Counting Book, 411(F)

My First Photography Book, 21800

Night-time Animals, 18846

Seashore, 19863

King, David. *Lexington and Concord*, 16201

King, David C. *Al Capone and the Roaring Twenties*, 12866

Benedict Arnold and the American Revolution, 12847

Colonial Days, 16148

Egypt, 15506

First Facts About American Heroes, 12666

First Facts About U.S. History, 15887

Freedom of Assembly, 17039

Pioneer Days, 16334

Victorian Days, 16477

World War II Days, 14859

King, Deborah. *The Flight of the Snow Geese*, 5290(F)

King, Elizabeth. *Quinceanera*, 17379, 17380

King, Hazel. *Milk and Yogurt*, 20105

King, John. *Bedouin*, 15490

A Family from Iraq, 15553

King, Martin Luther, Jr. *I Have a Dream*, 17040

King, Penny. *Animals*, 13898

Myths and Legends, 13899

Out of This World, 21447

Sports and Games, 13900

King, Penny (jt. author). *Festival Decorations*, 21421

King, Sandra. *Shannon*, 15981

King, Sarah E. *Maya Angelou Greeting the Morning*, 12496

King, Stephen M. *Henry and Amy (right-way-round and upside down)*, 4017(F)

The Pocket Dogs, 1681(F)

King, Tara Calahan. *Enemy Pie*, 4030(F)

Odd Velvet, 4059(F)

King, Wilma. *Children of the Emancipation*, 16419

King-Smith, Dick. *All Pigs Are Beautiful*, 5291

Animal Stories, 7863(F)

Charlie Muffin's Miracle Mouse, 7864(F)

The Cuckoo Child, 7236(F)

Dick King-Smith's Alphabeasts, 73(F)

Dick King-Smith's Animal Friends, 19899

Harriet's Hare, 10203(F)

Harry's Mad, 6921(F)

Hogsel and Gruntel and Other Animal Stories, 7865(F)

I Love Guinea Pigs, 19900

The Invisible Dog, 7237(F)

Jenius, 7238(F)

A Mouse Called Wolf, 7866(F)

Mr. Ape, 9899(F)

Mysterious Miss Slade, 8319(F)

Pigs Might Fly, 7867(F)

Puppy Love, 19955

The Roundhill, 7868(F)

The School Mouse, 7869(F)

Smasher, 7239(F)

Sophie Hits Six, 7240(F)

Sophie Is Seven, 8722(F)

Sophie's Lucky, 7241(F)

Spider Sparrow, 8897(F)

The Stray, 7463(F)

The Water Horse, 7870(F)

Kingman, Lee. *The Best Christmas*, 9739(F)

The Luck of the Miss L, 6922(F)

Kinkade, Sheila. *Children of the Philippines*, 15239

Kinsey, Helen (jt. author). *The Bear That Heard Crying*, 1307(F)

Kinsey-Warnock, Natalie. *As Long As There Are Mountains*, 7871(F)

The Bear That Heard Crying, 1307(F)

The Canada Geese Quilt, 8723(F)

The Fiddler of the Northern Lights, 1305(F)

If Wishes Were Horses, 9570(F)

In the Language of Loons, 8724(F)

On a Starry Night, 1306(F)

The Summer of Stanley, 2949(F)

When Spring Comes, 4474(F)

Kinter, Judith. *King of Magic, Man of Glass*, 10925

Kipling, Rudyard. *The Beginning of the Armadilloes*, 7242(F)

Gunga Din, 11617

How the Camel Got His Hump, 1308(F)

The Jungle Book, 7243(F), 7244(F)

Just So Stories, 7245(F), 7246(F)

Rikki-Tikki-Tavi, 1309(F), 7872(F)

Kiralfy, Bob. *The Most Excellent Book of How to Be a Cheerleader*, 21670

Kirby, David. *The Cows Are Going to Paris*, 2293(F)

Kirby, Philippa. *Glorious Days, Dreadful Days*, 16202

Kirk, Daniel. *Bigger*, 3261(F)

Breakfast at the Liberty Diner, 4714(F)

Chugga-Chugga Choo Choo, 5580(F)

The Diggers, 5550

How the Wind Plays, 1355(F)

Humpty Dumpty, 854(F)

Hush, Little Alien, 717(F)

Lucky's 24-Hour Garage, 3262(F)

Moondogs, 1310(F)

Snow Family, 3750(F)

Trash Trucks! 1311(F)

Kirk, David. *Little Miss Spider*, 2294(F)

Little Miss Spider at Sunny Patch School, 2295(F)

Miss Spider's ABC, 74(F)

Miss Spider's New Car, 2296(F)

Miss Spider's Tea Party, 2297(F)

Miss Spider's Wedding, 2298(F)

Nova's Ark, 2299(F)

Kirkpatrick, Karey. *Disney's James and the Giant Peach*, 1312(F)

Kirkpatrick, Katherine. *Redcoats and Petticoats*, 9239(F)

Trouble's Daughter, 9201(F)

Kirkpatrick, Rena K. *Look at Pond Life*, 20522

Kirksmith, Tommie. *Ride Western Style*, 22206

Kirkwood, Jon. *The Fantastic Book of Car Racing*, 22081

The Fantastic Cutaway Book of Giant Buildings, 21134

The Fantastic Cutaway Book of Giant Machines, 21250

Kirsten, Lincoln, adapt. *Puss in Boots*, 10873

Kirtland, Mark. *Why Do We Do That?* 17637

Kirwan, Anna. *Juliet*, 9104(F)

Kiser, Kevin. *Buzzy Widget*, 4204(F)

Kisor, Henry (jt. author). *One TV Blasting and a Pig Outdoors*, 8874(F)

Kisseloff, Jeff. *Who Is Baseball's Greatest Hitter?* 22102

Kitamura, Satoshi. *Cat Is Sleepy*, 2300(F)

Fly with the Birds, 3114(F)

From Acorn to Zoo and Everything in Between in Alphabetical Order, 75(F)

In the Attic, 1444(F)

Me and My Cat? 1313(F)

Sheep in Wolves' Clothing, 2301(F)

When Sheep Cannot Sleep, 484(F)

Kitano, Harry. *The Japanese Americans*, 17569

Kitchel, JoAnn E. *The Farewell Symphony*, 9031(F)
Tales of the Shimmering Sky, 10591

Kitchen, Bert. *And So They Build*, 18909
The Barn Owl, 19367
The Frog, 18740
The Lion and the Mouse and Other Aesop's Fables, 11072
The Otter, 18965
The Rabbit, 19211
Tom's Rabbit, 5267(F)
When Hunger Calls, 18641

Kite, L. Patricia. *Blood-Feeding Bugs and Beasts*, 18642
Dandelion Adventures, 20240
Gardening Wizardry for Kids, 21763
Maya Angelou, 12497

Kite, Patricia. *Down in the Sea*, 19678, 19663, 19724, 19640

Kittelsen, Theodor. *Norwegian Folk Tales*, 11120

Kittinger, Jo S. *Dead Log Alive!* 20208
A Look at Minerals, 20561
A Look at Rocks, 20562
Stories in Stone, 14430

Kiuchi, Tatsuro. *The Eagle's Gift*, 11207
The Fox Maiden, 7950(F)
Mysterious Tales of Japan, 10581
The Seasons and Someone, 4477(F)
Tsubu the Little Snail, 10836

Kjelgaard, James A. *Big Red*, 7247(F)

Klare, Roger. *Gregor Mendel*, 13322

Klass, Sheila S. *Kool Ada*, 8725(F)
Little Women Next Door, 8726(F)
A Shooting Star, 9571(F)
The Uncivil War, 8727(F)

Klassen, Heather. *I Don't Want to Go to Justin's House Anymore*, 4998(F)

Klausmeier, Robert. *Cowboy*, 16335

Klausner, Janet. *Sequoyah's Gift*, 12994

Klayman, Michael (jt. author). *Sharing Blessings*, 17480

Klebanoff, Susan. *Ups and Downs*, 17715

Klein, Bill. *A Kids' Guide to Building Forts*, 21413

Klein, James. *Gold Rush! The Young Prospector's Guide to Striking It Rich*, 20563

Klein, Michael. *Do People Grow on Family Trees?* 17692

Klein, Norma. *Mom, the Wolfman and Me*, 7464(F)

Klein, Robin. *The Sky in Silver Lace*, 7465(F)

Klein, Suzanna. *Womenfolk and Fairy Tales*, 10592

Klein, Tom. *Loon Magic for Kids*, 19242

Kleven, Elisa. *Abuela*, 1130(F)
B Is for Bethlehem, 149(F)
The City by the Bay, 16768
Diez Deditos and Other Play Rhymes and Action Songs from Latin America, 22041
Hooray, A Piñata! 5703(F)
The Magic Maguey, 4699(F)
A Monster in the House, 1314(F)
Our Big Home, 3170(F)
The Paper Princess, 1315(F)
The Puddle Pail, 2302(F)

Kleven, Sandy. *The Right Touch*, 18264

Kline, Michael. *The Beast in You!* 14505
Geology Rocks! 20297
Gizmos and Gadgets, 21441
Going West! 16318
Science Play! 18319
Summer Fun! 22072
Vroom! Vroom! 21465

Kline, Suzy. *Herbie Jones*, 10087(F)
Herbie Jones and the Dark Attic, 8320(F)
Horrible Harry and the Ant Invasion, 4018(F)
Horrible Harry and the Christmas Surprise, 5858(F)
Horrible Harry and the Purple People, 7873(F)
Horrible Harry at Halloween, 10088(F)
Horrible Harry Goes to the Moon, 5510(F)
Horrible Harry Moves Up to Third Grade, 10089(F)
Marvin and the Mean Words, 8728(F)
Marvin and the Meanest Girl, 10090(F)
Mary Marony and the Chocolate Surprise, 8729(F)
Molly's in a Mess, 9900(F)
Orp, 9901(F)
Orp and the Chop Suey Burgers, 9902(F)
Orp and the FBI, 6923(F)
Orp Goes to the Hoop, 9903(F)
Song Lee and the "I Hate You" Notes, 10091(F)
Song Lee in Room 2B, 5511(F)
Who's Orp's Girlfriend? 9904(F)

Klingel, Cynthia. *Coretta Scott King*, 12735
In-Line Skating, 22028
Soccer, 22295

Klinting, Lars. *Bruno the Baker*, 5704(F)
Bruno the Tailor, 2303(F)

Kliros, Thea. *God Is Like . . . Three Parables for Children*, 17227
Sand Castle, 4064(F)
What Can You Do in the Rain? 3214(F)

What Can You Do in the Snow? 3215(F)

What Can You Do in the Sun? 3216(F)

Klise, Kate. *Letters from Camp*, 9905(F)
Regarding the Fountain, 9906(F)

Klots, Steve. *Richard Allen*, 12700

Klove, Lars. *I See a Sign*, 14015

Kluchi, Tatsuro. *The Lotus Seed*, 7341(F)

Klum, Mattias. *Exploring the Rain Forest*, 20458

Klyce, Katherine P. *Kenya, Jambo!* 14935

Knapp, Brian. *What Do We Know About Grasslands?* 20537
What Do We Know About Rainforests? 20459

Knapp, Ron. *American Generals of World War II*, 12667
Andre Agassi, 13641
Barry Sanders, 13627
Bloodsuckers, 18643
Bobby Bonilla, 13439
Charles Barkley, 13513
Chris Webber, 13579
Mummies, 14533
Sports Great Barry Sanders, 13628
Sports Great Bo Jackson, 13616
Sports Great Isiah Thomas, 13577
Sports Great Orel Hershiser, 13461
Steve Young, 13639
Top 10 American Men Sprinters, 13377
Top 10 American Men's Olympic Gold Medalists, 13378
Top 10 Basketball Centers, 13379
Top 10 Basketball Scorers, 13380
Top 10 Hockey Scorers, 13381
Top 10 NFL Super Bowl Most Valuable Players, 13382

Knapp, Ruthie. *American Art*, 13960
Egyptian Art, 13940
Impressionist Art, 13901

Kneen, Maggie. *The Lonely Scarecrow*, 1492(F)
Milly's Wedding, 2741(F)
Thimbleberry Stories, 2648(F)
"Too Many Cooks . . ." and Other Proverbs, 10568
When You're Not Looking, 485(F)

Kneidel, Sally. *Pet Bugs*, 19458
Slugs, Bugs, and Salamanders, 18644

Kniffke, Sophie. *Weather*, 4446

Knight, Amelia S. *The Way West*, 16336

Knight, Bertram T. *From Cow to Ice Cream*, 20106
From Mud to House, 21160
Working at a Zoo, 17850

Knight, Christopher G. *A Baby for Max*, 3765(F)
Days of the Dead, 15628
Monarchs, 19558
Think Like an Eagle, 21801

Knight, David C. *Best True Ghost Stories of the 20th Century*, 21923

Knight, Dawn. *Mischief, Mad Mary, and Me*, 7248(F)

Knight, Hilary. *Eloise at Christmas-time*, 5936(F)
Happy Birthday, 5694
Hello, Mrs. Piggle-Wiggle, 7934(F)
Hilary Knight's the Twelve Days of Christmas, 14204

Knight, James E. *Blue Feather's Vision*, 16149

Knight, Joan MacPhail. *Charlotte in Giverny*, 9053(F)

Knight, Margaret. *Fashion Through the Ages*, 21175

Knight, Margy B. *Africa Is Not a Country*, 14909
Talking Walls, 14534, 14560
Who Belongs Here? 17570

Knight, Maxwell B. (jt. author). *A Baby for Max*, 3765(F)

Knittel, John. *Everything You Need to Know About the Dangers of Computer Hacking*, 21213

Knotts, Bob. *Equestrian Events*, 22207
Martial Arts, 22267
The Summer Olympics, 22249
Track and Field, 22319
Weightlifting, 22029

Knowles, Sheena. *Edwina the Emu*, 2304(F)

Knowlton, Jack. *Books and Libraries*, 13999
Geography from A to Z, 14344
Maps and Globes, 14369

Knowlton, Laurie L. *God Be in My Heart*, 17527
The Nativity, 5859(F)

Knudson, R. R. *Rinehart Lifts*, 10342(F)

Knutson, Barbara. *How the Guinea Fowl Got Her Spots*, 10679

Knutson, Kimberley. *Beach Babble*, 3263(F)
Bed Bouncers, 718(F)
Jungle Jamboree, 1316(F)

Kobre, Faige. *A Sense of Shabbat*, 6089

Koch, Michelle. *World Water Watch*, 4475

Koci, Marta. *Sarah's Bear*, 2305(F)

Kodama, Tatsuharu. *Shin's Tricycle*, 14860

Koehler, Phoebe. *The Day We Met You*, 3751(F)
Making Room, 2306(F)

Koehler-Pentacoff, Elizabeth. *Louise the One and Only*, 10092(F)

Koenig, Viviane. *A Family Treasury of Myths from Around the World*, 11449

Koeppen, Peter. *Pedro's Journal*, 8927(F)
A Swinger of Birches, 11569

Koertge, Ron. *The Heart of the City*, 8321(F)

Koh, Frances M. *Adopted from Asia*, 17664
Korean Holidays and Festivals, 15177

Kohen, Elizabeth. *Spain*, 15478

Kohl, Joe. *The Best Joke Book for Kids Number 4*, 21822

Kohl, MaryAnn F. *Global Art*, 21448
Making Make-Believe, 12026

Kohl, Susan. *The Ghost of Gracie Mansion*, 9302(F)

Kohler, Keith. *The Titanic*, 6310

Kohn, Alexandra (jt. author). *The Wisdom of the Crows and Other Buddhist Tales*, 10720

Koide, Tan. *May We Sleep Here Tonight?* 2307(F)

Koide, Yasuko. *May We Sleep Here Tonight?* 2307(F)

Koike, Hiro. *Apple Trees*, 20147

Koja, Stephan. *Claude Monet*, 12265

Kolar, Bob. *Do You Want to Play? A Book About Being Friends*, 4019(F)

Kolatch, Alfred J. *The Jewish Child's First Book of Why*, 17477

Kolbisen, Irene M. *Wiggle-Butts and Up-Faces*, 4999(F)

Koller, Jackie F. *Bouncing on the Bed*, 3264(F)
Dragon Quest, 7874(F)
The Dragonling, 7875(F)
If I Had One Wish . . ., 7876(F)
Impy for Always, 8322(F)
Mole and Shrew, 5629(F)
Nickommoh! A Thanksgiving Celebration, 6146
No Such Thing, 719(F)
Nothing to Fear, 9572(F)
One Monkey Too Many, 486(F)
The Promise, 9740(F)

Komaiko, Leah. *Annie Bananie and the Pain Sisters*, 9907(F)
Earl's Too Cool for Me, 4020(F)
Just My Dad and Me, 3752(F)
My Perfect Neighborhood, 1317(F)

Koman, Vasja. *Soccer*, 22287
Tennis, 22311

Kometiani, Lela. *Grandpa, Is Everything Black Bad?* 3703(F)

Komoda, Beverly. *The Too Hot Day*, 2308(F)
The Winter Day, 2309(F)

Konigsburg, E. L. *About the B'nai Bagels*, 9908(F)
Altogether, One at a Time, 8730(F)
Amy Elizabeth Explores Bloomingdale's, 3265(F)
Father's Arcane Daughter, 6924(F)
From the Mixed-Up Files of Mrs. Basil E. Frankweiler, 6925(F)
Jennifer, Hecate, Macbeth, William McKinley, and Me, Elizabeth, 8323(F)

Samuel Todd's Book of Great Inventions, 9909
Silent to the Bone, 6926(F)
T-Backs, T-Shirts, Coat, and Suit, 8731(F)
The View from Saturday, 8324(F)

Koon-Chiu, Lo. *Favorite Children's Stories from China and Tibet*, 10758

Koontz, Robin M. *Chicago and the Cat*, 2310(F)

Koopmans, Loek. *Cinderella*, 10475(F)

Kopka, Deborah. *Norway*, 15455

Kopper, Lisa. *Daisy Knows Best*, 2311(F)
Daisy's Babies, 2312(F)
Jafta, 4733(F)
Stories from the Ballet, 14287

Kops, Deborah (jt. author). *Scholastic Kid's Almanac for the 21st Century*, 14353

Koralek, Jenny. *Cat and Kit*, 5292(F)
Night Ride to Nanna's, 720(F)

Korman, Bernice (jt. author). *The D-Poems of Jeremy Bloom*, 11880
The Last-Place Sports Poems of Jeremy Bloom, 12000

Korman, Gordon. *The Chicken Doesn't Skate*, 9910(F)
The D-Poems of Jeremy Bloom, 11880
The Last-Place Sports Poems of Jeremy Bloom, 12000
Liar, Liar, Pants on Fire, 8732(F)
Nose Pickers from Outer Space! 10204(F)
The 6th Grade Nickname Game, 10093(F)
Something Fishy at Macdonald Hall, 10094(F)
The Twinkle Squad, 10095(F)
The Zucchini Warriors, 10096(F)

Korman, Justine. *The Luckiest Leprechaun*, 1318(F)

Korman, Susan. *Megan in Ancient Greece*, 9054(F)

Kornblatt, Marc. *Understanding Buddy*, 8325(F)

Kors, Erika. *How Did We Find Out About Lasers?* 20856

Kortum, Jeanie. *Ghost Vision*, 7877(F)

Koscielniak, Bruce. *The Fabulous Four Skunks*, 2083(F)
Geoffrey Groundhog Predicts the Weather, 2313(F)
Hear, Hear, Mr. Shakespeare, 4715(F)
The Story of the Incredible Orchestra, 14225

Koshkin, Alexander. *The Angel and the Donkey*, 17315
Atalanta's Race, 11464
Images of God, 17314
The Little Humpbacked Horse, 11116

Stolen Thunder, 11518

Koski, Mary. *Impatient Pamela Asks*, 5000(F)

Impatient Pamela Calls 9-1-1, 3266(F)

Koslow, Philip. *Dahomey*, 15030

El Cid, 13772

John Hancock, 12897

Kosmer, Ellen. *Spend the Day in Ancient Egypt*, 14632

Kosoff, Susan (jt. author). *The Young Actor's Book of Improvisation*, 14322

Koss, Amy Goldman. *The Ashwater Experiment*, 8469(F)

The Girls, 8733(F)

How I Saved Hanukkah, 9741(F)

Smoke Screen, 8734(F)

Stranger in Dadland, 8470(F)

The Trouble with Zinny Weston, 8326(F)

Kossman, Nina. *Behind the Border*, 13824

Kostyal, K. M. *Trial by Ice*, 12155

Kotzwinkle, William. *The Million-Dollar Bear*, 2950(F)

Trouble in Bugland, 6927(F)

Kovacs, Deborah. *Beneath Blue Waters*, 19641

Dive to the Deep Ocean, 19877

Off to Sea, 19878

Kovalski, Maryann. *The Big Storm*, 5437(F)

Brenda and Edward, 2314(F)

The Cake That Mack Ate, 4282(F)

Omar on Ice, 2315(F)

Princess Prunella and the Purple Peanut, 7565(F)

Queen Nadine, 2316(F)

The Seven Chairs, 4724(F)

Take Me Out to the Ballgame, 14160

The Wheels on the Bus, 14250

Kowalski, Kathiann M. *The Everything Kids' Nature Book*, 20660

Kozar, Richard. *Daniel Boone and the Exploration of the Frontier*, 12082

Kozielski, Dolores (jt. author). *Halloween Fun for Everyone*, 17449

Kraan, Hanna. *Flowers for the Wicked Witch*, 7878(F)

Tales of the Wicked Witch, 7879(F)

The Wicked Witch Is at It Again, 7880(F)

Kraft, Betsy Harvey. *Mother Jones*, 13162

Kraft, Erik. *Chocolatina*, 1319(F)

Krahenbuhl, Eddy. *The Cathedral Builders*, 13949

Krahn, Fernando. *Laughing Time*, 11917

Kramer, Alan. *How to Make a Chemical Volcano and Other Mysterious Experiments*, 18324

Kramer, Barbara. *Alice Walker*, 12615

John Glenn, 12888

Neil Armstrong, 12074

Ron Howard, 12405

Sally Ride, 12154

Tipper Gore, 13156

Trailblazing American Women, 12668

Kramer, Jackie. *You Can Learn Sign Language!* 14016

Kramer, Robin. *1, 2, 3 Thanksgiving!* 539(F)

Will You Come Back for Me? 3920(F)

Kramer, S. A. *Baseball's Greatest Hitters*, 13383

Baseball's Greatest Pitchers, 13384

Hoop Stars, 22133

Tiger Woods, 13716

To the Top! 22030

Wonder Women of Sports, 13385

Kramer, Stephen. *Avalanche*, 20778

Caves, 20380

Eye of the Storm, 20700

How to Think Like a Scientist, 18282

Lightning, 20701

Theodoric's Rainbow, 9055(F)

Tornado, 20702

Kramer, Sydelle. *Wagon Train*, 9390(F)

Kranendonk, Anke. *Just a Minute*, 2317(F)

Kranz, Leslie Shuman. *Grey Neck*, 2643(F)

Krasilovsky, Phyllis. *The Very Little Boy*, 3267(F)

Kraske, Robert. *Asteroids*, 18518

The Voyager's Stone, 19823

Krasno, Rena. *Floating Lanterns and Golden Shrines*, 17381

Kneeling Carabao and Dancing Giants, 15240

Kratoville, Betty Lou. *Vasco da Gama*, 12105

Kraus, Robert. *Big Squeak, Little Squeak*, 2318(F)

Herman the Helper, 2319(F)

How Spider Saved Halloween, 6021(F)

Leo the Late Bloomer, 2320(F)

Little Louie the Baby Bloomer, 3753(F)

Mort the Sport, 2321(F)

Mouse in Love, 2322(F)

Whose Mouse Are You? 2323(F)

Krause, Peter. *Fundamental Golf*, 22031

Krause, Robert. *Sun and Moon*, 10736

Krauss, Ronnie. *Take a Look, It's in a Book*, 14313

Krauss, Ruth. *The Carrot Seed*, 1320(F)

The Growing Story, 4476(F)

A Hole Is to Dig, 204(F)

A Very Special House, 5001(F)

You're Just What I Need, 3754(F)

Kredel, Fritz. *The Adventures of Pinocchio*, 7660(F)

Krehbiel, Randy. *Little Bighorn*, 16337

Kreiner, Anna. *Let's Talk About Drug Abuse*, 17874

Kreisler, Ken (jt. author). *Citybook*, 3399(F)

Faces, 3400

Nature Spy, 4523

Ocean Day, 4524(F)

Kreiswirth, Kinny. *All About Hanukkah*, 6077

All About Passover, 17469

All About Sukkot, 17470

It's a Family Thanksgiving! A Celebration of an American Tradition for Children and Their Families, 17495

Krementz, Jill. *How It Feels to Be Adopted*, 17665

How It Feels When a Parent Dies, 17716

How It Feels When Parents Divorce, 17666

A Storyteller's Story, 12573

A Visit to Washington, D.C., 16706

Krenina, Katya. *At the Wish of the Fish*, 11099

The Birds' Gift, 11095

The House of Boo, 6028(F)

How Yussel Caught the Gefilte Fish, 6078(F)

The Magic Dreidels, 6085(F)

Tooth Tales from Around the World, 10536

Krensky, Stephen. *Arthur and the Big Blow-Up*, 7881(F)

Breaking into Print, 14000

Buster's Dino Dilemma, 6435(F)

Christopher Columbus, 16083

Dinosaurs, Beware! A Safety Guide, 3049(F)

Four Against the Odds, 13216

How Santa Got His Job, 9742(F)

Lionel at School, 6436(F)

Lionel in the Spring, 6437(F)

Lionel in the Summer, 6438(F)

Louise Goes Wild, 9911(F)

Louise, Soccer Star? 10343(F)

Louise Takes Charge, 10097(F)

My Loose Tooth, 6439(F)

My Teacher's Secret Life, 5512(F)

Perfect Pigs, 1893(F)

Striking It Rich, 16338

Taking Flight, 13354

We Just Moved! 6440(F)

Who Really Discovered America? 16084

Witch Hunt, 16150

The Youngest Fairy Godmother Ever, 1321(F)

Krensky, Stephen (jt. author). *Dinosaurs, Beware! A Safety Guide*, 3049(F)

Perfect Pigs, 1893(F)

Kress, Camille. *Purim!* 6090(F)
Tot Shabbat, 6091(F)
Kress, Nancy. *Yanked!* 10205(F)
Kress, Stephen W. *Project Puffin*, 19350
Kretzer-Malvehy, Terry. *Passage to Little Bighorn*, 7882(F)
Kreutzer, Peter. *Little League's Official How-to-Play Baseball Handbook*, 22103
Krevitsky, Nik. *It Happened in Chelm*, 11145
Krischanitz, Raoul. *Nobody Likes Me!* 2324(F)
Krisher, Trudy. *Kathy's Hats*, 5002(F)
Krishnaswami, Uma. *The Broken Tusk*, 17198
Stories of the Flood, 10569
Krishnaswami, Uma, reteller. *Shower of Gold*, 10798
Krishnaswamy, Uma. *And Land Was Born*, 10804
Kristy, Davida. *Coubertin's Olympics*, 22250
George Balanchine, 12350
Krizmanic, Judy. *The Teen's Vegetarian Cookbook*, 21714
Kroeber, Theodora. *A Green Christmas*, 5860(F)
Ishi, Last of the Tribe, 12975
Kroeger, Mary Kay. *Paperboy*, 4716(F)
Kroeger, Mary Kay (jt. author). *Fly High! The Story of Bessie Coleman*, 12090
Krohn, Katherine. *Everything You Need to Know About Birth Order*, 17667
Rosie O'Donnell, 12435
Women of the Wild West, 12669
Krohn, Katherine E. *Elvis Presley*, 12444
Lucille Ball, 12351
Kroll, Steven. *Andrew Wants a Dog*, 5293(F)
The Biggest Pumpkin Ever, 6022(F)
The Boston Tea Party, 16151
By the Dawn's Early Light, 14161
The Candy Witch, 1322(F)
Ellis Island, 15888
Happy Father's Day, 5630(F)
It's Groundhog Day! 5631(F)
Lewis and Clark, 12131
Mary McLean and the St. Patrick's Day Parade, 5632(F)
New Kid in Town, 10344(F)
Oh, Tucker! 5294(F)
Oh, What a Thanksgiving! 6147(F)
Patches Lost and Found, 5295(F)
Patrick's Tree House, 8327(F)
Queen of the May, 10440(F)
When I Dream of Heaven, 9573(F)
William Penn, 12945
Kroll, Virginia. *Africa Brothers and Sisters*, 4717(F)
Beginnings, 3755(F)

Butterfly Boy, 3756(F)
Can You Dance, Dalila? 5003(F)
Faraway Drums, 1323(F)
Fireflies, Peach Pies and Lullabies, 5004(F)
Hands! 18064
I Wanted to Know All About God, 17199
Masai and I, 8967(F)
Motherlove, 5296
Pink Paper Swans, 4021(F)
The Seasons and Someone, 4477(F)
She Is Born, 3757(F)
Sweet Magnolia, 4718(F)
With Love, to Earth's Endangered Peoples, 17571
Krommes, Beth. *Grandmother Winter*, 1518(F)
Kroninger, Stephen. *If I Crossed the Road*, 1324(F)
Psssst! It's Me . . . the Bogeyman, 1456(F)
Tie Your Socks and Clap Your Feet, 11875
Kroupa, Melanie. *A Little Touch of Monster*, 5007(F)
Krudop, Walter L. *Black Whiteness*, 12087
Crossing the Delaware, 16209
The Good-Night Kiss, 629(F)
My Great-Grandmother's Gourd, 4710(F)
One Rainy Night, 5231(F)
One Small Lost Sheep, 5883(F)
Our Neighbor Is a Strange, Strange Man, 13331
Wake Up, Little Children, 4381(F)
Krudop, Walter Lyon. *The Man Who Caught Fish*, 1325(F)
Something Is Growing, 1326(F)
Krueger, Richard. *The Dinosaurs*, 14431
Krulik, Nancy. *Is It Hanukkah Yet?* 6092(F)
Krull, Kathleen. *A Kids' Guide to America's Bill of Rights*, 17058
Lives of Extraordinary Women, 13732
Lives of the Artists, 12171
Lives of the Athletes, 13386
Lives of the Musicians, 12172
Lives of the Presidents, 12670
Lives of the Writers, 12173
Maria Molina and the Days of the Dead, 4719(F)
One Nation, Many Tribes, 15982
They Saw the Future, 21924
Wilma Unlimited, 13670
Wish You Were Here, 15889
Krull, Kathleen, ed. *Gonna Sing My Head Off!* 14162
Songs of Praise, 17200
Krumgold, Joseph. *Onion John*, 8735(F)
Krupinski, Loretta. *Best Friends*, 4720(F)
Celia's Island Journal, 4850

Fabulous Frogs, 18723
How a Seed Grows, 20271
Into the Woods, 18645
Lost in the Fog, 6928(F)
Tiny Green Thumbs, 2159(F)
A Visit from Saint Nicholas and Santa Mouse, Too! 5885(F)
Where Is That Cat? 5234(F)
Why Do Leaves Change Color? 20210
Wonderful Worms, 19607
Krupp, E. C. *The Moon and You*, 18449
The Rainbow and You, 20872
Krupp, Robin R. *The Moon and You*, 18449
The Rainbow and You, 20872
Kruse, Brandon. *Why Do You Speak as You Do?* 13980
Krush, Beth. *The Borrowers*, 7997(F)
Emily's Runaway Imagination, 9801(F)
Gone-Away Lake, 6834(F)
Poor Stainless, 7998(F)
Sister of the Bride, 7408(F)
Krush, Joe. *The Borrowers*, 7997(F)
Emily's Runaway Imagination, 9801(F)
Gone-Away Lake, 6834(F)
Poor Stainless, 7998(F)
Sister of the Bride, 7408(F)
Kruusval, Catarina. *Here Comes Pontus!* 7841(F)
No Clothes Today! 3268(F)
Krykorka, Vladyana. *Arctic Stories*, 4722(F)
Munschworks 3, 4245
My Arctic 1, 2, 3, 488(F)
Whump, 647(F)
Kubiak, Kasi. *The Nativity*, 5859(F)
Kubinyi, Laszlo. *The Boy Who Made Dragonfly*, 11258
Perplexing Puzzles and Tantalizing Teasers, 20616
Shadows in the Glasshouse, 16154(F)
Under Copp's Hill, 9515(F)
The Wizard in the Tree, 7555(F)
Kubler, Annie. *From Beans to Batteries*, 4601(F)
Kuchalla, Susan. *All About Seeds*, 20272
Birds, 19243
Kuchera, Kathleen. *Your Skin and Mine*, 18180
Kudler, David. *The Seven Gods of Luck*, 10820
Kudlinski, Kathleen V. *Dandelions*, 20241
Pearl Harbor Is Burning! 9668(F)
Popcorn Plants, 20179
Rachel Carson, 13246
Shannon, 9574(F), 9575(F)
Shannon, Lost and Found, 9576(F)
Venus Flytraps, 20242
Kudrna, C. Imbior. *To Bathe a Boa*, 2325(F)

Kueffner, Sue. *Our New Baby*, 6441(F)

Kuhn, Betsy. *Angels of Mercy*, 14861
Not Exactly Nashville, 8328(F)
Top 10 Jockeys, 13387

Kuhn, Bob. *Big Red*, 7247(F)

Kuhn, Dwight. *Lucky Mouse*, 19206

Kuhne, Heinz. *Leonardo da Vinci*, 12215

Kuhner, Peter (jt. author). *The Circus of Mystery*, 6837(F)

Kui, Wang. *The Wise Washerman*, 10725

Kuklin, Susan. *Fighting Fires*, 5579
From Head to Toe, 21041
Going to My Gymnastics Class, 22196
How My Family Lives in America, 3758

Kuklin, Susan (jt. author). *Dance*, 14292

Kule, Elaine. *Arkansas Facts and Symbols*, 16869
Delaware Facts and Symbols, 16707
Idaho Facts and Symbols, 16622
Iowa Facts and Symbols, 16566

Kulling, Monica. *Bears*, 19050
Edgar Badger's Balloon Day, 5705(F)
Eleanor Everywhere, 13182
Escape North! The Story of Harriet Tubman, 12799

Kulman, Andrew. *Moo in the Morning*, 3306(F)
Red Light Stop, Green Light Go, 4205(F)

Kummer, Patricia K. *Cote d'Ivoire*, 15031

Kunhardt, Edith. *I'm Going to Be a Police Officer*, 3269(F)

Kunstler, James Howard. *Annie Oakley*, 12431

Kuper, Mary. *Super Minds*, 21903
Tea Leaves, Herbs, and Flowers, 21922

Kupfer, Andrew (jt. author). *Night City*, 3936(F)

Kurelek, William. *A Northern Nativity*, 17425
A Prairie Boy's Summer, 12250
They Sought a New World, 16152

Kurnizki, Kimberly L. Dawson.
Igloo, 15797
Longhouse, 15924
Pueblo, 16026
Tipi, 15918

Kuroi, Ken. *Midnight Dance of the Snowshoe Hare*, 11945
Swim the Silver Sea, Joshie Otter, 643(F)

Kuropas, Myron B. *Ukrainians in America*, 17572

Kurosaki, Yoshio. *Japanese Children's Favorite Stories*, 10827

Kurth, Linda Moore. *Keiko's Story*, 19794

Kurtis-Kleinman, Eileen. *When Aunt Lena Did the Rhumba*, 3759(F)

Kurts, Charles. *These Are the Voyages*, 10206(F)

Kurtz, Christopher (jt. author). *Only a Pigeon*, 4721(F)

Kurtz, Jane. *Ethiopia*, 14936
Faraway Home, 3760(F)
Fire on the Mountain, 10680
I'm Sorry, Almira Ann, 9391(F)
Only a Pigeon, 4721(F)
Pulling the Lion's Tail, 10681
River Friendly, River Wild, 11619
The Storyteller's Beads, 8968(F)
Trouble, 10682

Kushner, Karen (jt. author). *Because Nothing Looks Like God*, 17201

Kushner, Lawrence. *Because Nothing Looks Like God*, 17201

Kushner, Nina. *The Democratic Republic of the Congo*, 15032

Kuskin, Karla. *Dogs and Dragons, Trees and Dreams*, 11620
I Am Me, 3761(F)
James and the Rain, 487(F)
Jerusalem, Shining Still, 15524
The Philharmonic Gets Dressed, 3270(F)
The Sky Is Always in the Sky, 11621
Soap Soup and Other Verses, 6442
Thoughts, Pictures, and Words, 12560
The Upstairs Cat, 1327(F)

Kustanowitz, Esther. *The Hidden Children of the Holocaust*, 14862

Kusugak, Michael (jt. author). *Munschworks 3*, 4245

Kusugak, Michael A. *Arctic Stories*, 4722(F)
My Arctic 1, 2, 3, 488(F)

Kutner, Merrily. *Z Is for Zombie*, 6023(F)

Kutschbach, Doris. *The Blue Rider*, 13902

Kvasnosky, Laura McGee. *Mr. Chips!* 5297(F)
See You Later, Alligator, 2326(F)
Zelda and Ivy, 2327(F)
Zelda and Ivy and the Boy Next Door, 2328(F)
Zelda and Ivy One Christmas, 5861(F)

Kwas, Susan Estelle. *The Story of Valentine's Day*, 17505

Kwitz, Mary D. *Gumshoe Goose, Private Eye*, 6443(F)

Kyrias, Rhonda. *A Window of Time*, 3769(F)

Labastida, Aurora (jt. author). *Nine Days to Christmas*, 5810(F)

Labatt, Mary. *Aliens in Woodford*, 7883(F)
The Ghost of Captain Briggs, 6929(F)
Strange Neighbors, 7884(F)

LaBonte, Gail. *The Llama*, 18949
The Miniature Horse, 20000

Labrosse, Darcia. *The Grumpy Morning*, 2053(F)
If You Could Wear My Sneakers! 11869

Lacapa, Michael. *The Magic Hummingbird*, 11268

Lace, William W. *The Dallas Cowboys Football Team*, 22184
The Houston Rockets Basketball Team, 22134
Leaders and Generals, 13733
The Los Angeles Lakers Basketball Team, 22135
The Pittsburgh Steelers Football Team, 22185
Sports Great Nolan Ryan, 13501
Top 10 Football Quarterbacks, 13388
Top 10 Football Rushers, 13389

Lacey, Mike. *Divorce and Separation*, 17682
Drinking Alcohol, 17888
Feeling Violent, 17630

Lacey, Sue. *Animals*, 21580

Lachner, Dorothea. *Andrew's Angry Words*, 1328(F)
Danny, the Angry Lion, 5005(F)
Meredith, 1329(F)
Meredith's Mixed-up Magic, 1330(F)

Lachtman, Ofelia Dumas. *Call Me Consuelo*, 6930(F)

Lacome, Julie. *A Was Once an Apple Pie*, 11883
Guess What? 301(F)
I'm a Jolly Farmer, 1331(F)

Lacy, Mike. *Anorexia and Bulimia*, 17994
Dyslexia, 17995

Lade, Roger. *The Most Excellent Book of How to Be a Puppeteer*, 14305

Laden, Nina. *Bad Dog*, 2329(F)
The Blues of Flats Brown, 2525(F)
Peek-a-Who? 4206(F)
Ready, Set, Go! 3271(F)
Roberto, 2330(F)
When Pigasso Met Mootisse, 2331(F)

LaDoux, Rita C. *Georgia*, 16870
Iowa, 16567
Louisiana, 16871
Missouri, 16568
Montana, 16623
Oklahoma, 16569

Ladwig, Tim. *The Lord's Prayer*, 17528
Morning Has Broken, 14239
Probity Jones and the Fear Not Angel, 1659(F)
Psalm Twenty-Three, 17316
Silent Night, 5840(F)

LaFave, Kim. *Fire Fighters*, 3033
Garbage Collectors, 3034
Police Officers, 17807

Postal Workers, 17740

Lafaye, A. *Nissa's Place*, 8736(F)
Strawberry Hill, 8329(F)
The Year of the Sawdust Man, 8471(F)

Lafferty, Peter. *Force and Motion*, 20832

Lafford, Stuart. *The Bee*, 19518
How Plants Grow, 20254

Lafrance, Marie. *Mind Me Good Now!* 11420
The Miss Meow Pageant, 1290(F)

Lagarrigue, Jerome. *Freedom Summer*, 4061(F)
My Man Blue, 11760

Lagercrantz, Rose. *Is It Magic?* 5006(F)

Lagercrantz, Samuel (jt. author). *Is It Magic?* 5006(F)

Laird, Elizabeth. *Secret Friends*, 8898(F)
When the World Began, 10683

Lake, Mary D., reteller. *The Royal Drum*, 10684

Lakin, Patricia. *Dad and Me in the Morning*, 3762(F)
Hurricane! 4478(F)

Lalicki, Tom. *Spellbinder*, 12402

Lally, Soinbhe. *A Hive for the Honeybee*, 7885(F)

LaMarche, Jim. *Albert*, 1428(F)
The Carousel, 1524(F)
Little Oh, 4767(F)
The Raft, 4479(F)
The Rainbabies, 10463(F)
The Walloping Window-Blind, 11861

Lamb, Christine. *A Tale of Two Rice Birds*, 10841

Lamb, Nancy. *The Great Mosquito, Bull, and Coffin Caper*, 8330(F)

Lamb, Susan C. *My Great-Aunt Arizona*, 3705

Lambase, Barbara. *Donnatalee*, 1611(F)
The Garden of Happiness, 4551(F)

Lambert, David. *DK Guide to Dinosaurs*, 14432
The Kingfisher Young People's Book of Oceans, 19824
The Mediterranean Sea, 19825
The Pacific Ocean, 19826
People of the Deserts, 20409
Polar Regions, 15813
Seas and Oceans, 19827
Weather, 20779

Lambert, Jonathan. *The Big Yawn*, 5201(F)
David Dreaming of Dinosaurs, 5202(F)
The Long-Nosed Pig, 2086(F)
My Colors, 269(F)
The Scared Little Bear, 672(F)
The Wide-Mouthed Frog, 2087(F)

Lambert, Kathy K. *Martin Luther King, Jr.*, 12745

Lambert, Mark. *The Brain and Nervous System*, 18112
The Lungs and Breathing, 18124

Lambert, Martha L. (jt. author). *Why Do You Love Me?* 3881(F)

Lambert, Paulette L. *Charlie Young Bear*, 4863(F)
Quest for Courage, 9176(F)

Lambert, Sally Anne. *Hippety-Hop Hippety-Hay*, 11554
Slender Ella and Her Fairy Hogfather, 6624(F)
Too Close Friends, 2634(F)

Lambert, Stephen. *Bedtime!* 637(F)
Fly by Night, 1985(F)
Nobody Rides the Unicorn, 1417(F)
Secret in the Mist, 3338(F)
The Train Ride, 3087(F)

Lambourne, Mike. *Down the Hatch*, 18101

Lambroza, Shlomo. *Boris Yeltsin*, 13869

Laminack, Lester L. *The Sunsets of Miss Olivia Wiggins*, 3763(F)

Lamm, C. Drew. *The Prog Frince*, 10441(F)

Lamont, Priscilla. *Our House*, 3860(F)
Playtime Rhymes, 858

Lamorisse, Albert. *The Red Balloon*, 4723(F)

Lampert, Emily. *A Little Touch of Monster*, 5007(F)

Lamprell, Klay. *Scaly Things*, 18687

Lampton, Christopher. *Bathtubs, Slides and Roller Coaster Rails*, 20922
Blizzard, 20703
Chemical Accident, 21042
Epidemic, 17974
Famine, 20043
Forest Fire, 20460
Home Page, 21214
Tidal Wave, 19850
Tornado, 20704
The World Wide Web, 21215

Lampton, Christopher (jt. author). *Endangered Species*, 19422

Lamson, Sharon (jt. author). *The Barn at Gun Lake*, 7102(F)

Lamstein, Sarah M. *Annie's Shabbat*, 6093
I Like Your Buttons! 3272(F)

Lamut, Sonja. *And the Cow Said Moo!* 5363(F)
How Many Candles? 5689(F)

Lancome, Julie. *Ruthie's Big Old Coat*, 2332(F)

Landa, Norbert. *Little Bear's Christmas*, 5862(F)

Landa, Peter. *The Sign of the Chrysanthemum*, 9008(F)

Landalf, Helen. *The Secret Night World of Cats*, 1332(F)

Landau, Elaine. *Air Crashes*, 21085
Allergies, 17975
Angelfish, 19706
Apples, 20148
The Assyrians, 14635
The Babylonians, 14636
Bananas, 20149
Bill Clinton and His Presidency, 13024
Blindness, 17917
Cancer, 17976
Corn, 20180
The Curse of Tutankhamen, 14637
Deafness, 17918
Desert Mammals, 20410
Diabetes, 17977
Electric Fish, 19707
Endangered Plants, 20243
Epilepsy, 17978
ESP, 21925
Fortune Telling, 21926
Ghosts, 21927
Grassland Mammals, 20538
Hooked, 17875
Jellyfish, 19664
John F. Kennedy Jr., 12918
Joined at Birth, 18065
Jupiter, 18479
Living with Albinism, 17919
The Loch Ness Monster, 21928
Maritime Disasters, 21363
Mars, 18480
Mountain Mammals, 20502
Multiple Births, 18241
Near-Death Experiences, 21929
Neptune, 18481
The Ottawa, 15983
Parkinson's Disease, 17979
Piranhas, 19708
Sasquatch, 21930
Saturn, 18482
Sea Horses, 19709
Short Stature, 18066
Siamese Fighting Fish, 19710
Sibling Rivalry, 17668
Space Disasters, 20997
Standing Tall, 18067
State Birds, 15852
State Flowers, 15853
The Sumerians, 14638
Temperate Forest Mammals, 20461
UFOs, 21931
Wheat, 20107
Wild Children, 17619

Landmann, Bimba. *A Boy Named Giotto*, 4672(F)

Landon, Lucinda. *Meg Mackintosh and the Mystery at the Medieval Castle*, 6931(F)
Meg Mackintosh and the Mystery at the Soccer Match, 6932(F)
Meg Mackintosh and the Mystery in the Locked Library, 6933(F)

Landsman, Susan. *What Happened to Amelia Earhart?* 12111

Landstrom, Lena. *Will Gets a Haircut*, 4207(F)

Landstrom, Lena (jt. author). *Boo and Baa at Sea*, 2333(F)

Boo and Baa in a Party Mood, 2334(F)
Boo and Baa in the Woods, 2335(F)
Will Gets a Haircut, 4207(F)
Will Goes to the Beach, 3273(F)
Will Goes to the Post Office, 3274(F)
Landstrom, Olof. *Benny's Had Enough!* 2376(F)
Boo and Baa at Sea, 2333(F)
Boo and Baa in a Party Mood, 2334(F)
Boo and Baa in the Woods, 2335(F)
Santa's Winter Vacation, 5931(F)
Will Gets a Haircut, 4207(F)
Will Goes to the Beach, 3273(F)
Will Goes to the Post Office, 3274(F)
Lane, Brian. *Investigation of Murder*, 17073
Lane, Daniel. *Santa Cows*, 5809(F)
Valerie and the Silver Pear, 3601(F)
Lane, Daniel (jt. author). *The Animal Mall*, 2048(F)
Lane, Kim. *The Usborne Complete Book of the Microscope*, 19809
Lanfredi, Judy. *Halloween Fun for Everyone*, 17449
The Year You Were Born, 1986, 17390
Lang, Andrew, ed. *The Arabian Nights Entertainments*, 11191
Blue Fairy Book, 10442(F)
Lang, Aubrey. *Eagles*, 19330
Lang, Cecily. *Annie's Shabbat*, 6093
A Birthday Basket for Tia, 5713(F)
Pablo's Tree, 3815(F)
Lang, Glenna. *The Children's Hour*, 11639
The Runaway, 11788
Lang, Susan. *Nature in Your Backyard*, 18588
Lang, Susan S. *More Nature in Your Backyard*, 18589
Langford, Alton. *Whales*, 6531(F)
Langham, Tony (jt. author). *The Amazing Adventures of Teddy Tum Tum*, 1852(F)
Langille, Jacqueline (jt. author). *What Are Food Chains and Webs?* 18586
What Is a Biome? 20378
What Is a Life Cycle? 18587
What Is a Rodent? 19199
What Is an Amphibian? 18686
Langley, Andrew. *Alexander the Great*, 13750
Amelia Earhart, 12112
Castle at War, 14774
Hans Christian Andersen, 12493
Medieval Life, 14775
Renaissance, 14801
The Roman News, 14726
Shakespeare's Theatre, 13903
Langley, Andrew (jt. author). *What I Believe*, 17171

Langley, Jonathan. *The Biggest Bed in the World*, 3564(F)
Missing! 1333(F)
My First Dictionary, 14043
Langley, Myrtle. *Religion*, 17202
Langreuter, Jutta. *Little Bear and the Big Fight*, 2336(F)
Little Bear Brushes His Teeth, 2337(F)
Little Bear Is a Big Brother, 2338(F)
Langstaff, John. *Frog Went A-Courtin'*, 14163
Langstaff, John, ed. *Climbing Jacob's Ladder*, 17295
What a Morning! 14205
Langstaff, John (jt. author). *Sally Go Round the Moon*, 14164
Langstaff, Nancy. *Sally Go Round the Moon*, 14164
Langston, Laura. *The Fox's Kettle*, 1334(F)
Langton, Jane. *The Fledgling*, 7886(F)
The Queen's Necklace, 10443(F)
Salt, 11098
The Time Bike, 7887(F)
Langton, Roger. *A First Book of Myths*, 10562
Lanino, Deborah. *Maria's Comet*, 4685(F)
Nina's Waltz, 3605(F)
Lankford, Mary D. *Christmas Around the World*, 17426
Dominoes Around the World, 22235
Hopscotch Around the World, 22032
Quinceañera, 17620
Lannin, Joanne. *A History of Basketball for Girls and Women*, 22136
Lansky, Bruce. *Happy Birthday to Me!* 11834
Sweet Dreams, 721(F)
Lansky, Bruce, ed. *A Bad Case of the Giggles*, 11881
Girls to the Rescue Book 2, 10571
Miles of Smiles, 11882
Newfangled Fairy Tales, Book 1, 7888(F)
No More Homework! No More Tests! Kids' Favorite Funny School Poems, 11622
Lansky, Bruce, sel. *Girls to the Rescue*, 10570
Lansky, Vicki. *It's Not Your Fault, KoKo Bear*, 2339(F)
Lanteigne, Helen. *The Seven Chairs*, 4724(F)
Lanting, Frans. *Albatrosses of Midway Island*, 19241
Lantz, Francess. *Mom, There's a Pig in My Bed!* 7249(F)
A Royal Kiss, 8331(F)
Stepsister from the Planet Weird, 8472(F)
Lantz, Paul. *Blue Willow*, 7436(F)

The Matchlock Gun, 9193(F)
La Padula, Thomas. *To the Top!* 22030
Tonka Big Book of Trucks, 5593
Tonka Trucks Night and Day, 21315
True-Life Treasure Hunts, 14525
La Pierre, Yvette. *Native American Rock Art*, 15984
Welcome to Josefina's World, 1824, 16339
La Prise, Larry. *The Hokey Pokey*, 4208(F)
Larimer, Donna. *Mama, Daddy, Baby and Me*, 3647(F)
Larios, Julie Hofstrand. *On the Stairs*, 2340(F)
Larios, Richard (jt. author). *La Causa*, 17135
Larkspur, Penelope. *The Secret Life of Fairies*, 21932
Laroche, Giles. *Bridges Are to Cross*, 21151
The Color Box, 265(F)
Laronde, Gary. *Juneteenth*, 17340(F)
Larose, Linda. *Jessica Takes Charge*, 3764(F)
Larrabee, Lisa. *Grandmother Five Baskets*, 11261(F)
Larrañaga, Ana Martín. *The Big Wide-Mouthed Frog*, 2341(F)
Busy Dinah Dinosaur, 6377(F)
Meet Dinah Dinosaur, 6378(F)
Woo! The Not-So-Scary Ghost, 1335(F)
Larrecq, John. *Broderick*, 2555(F)
A Green Christmas, 5860(F)
A Single Speckled Egg, 4212(F)
Larsen, Anita. *Psychic Sleuths*, 17074
Larson, Bonni (jt. author). *Watakame's Journey*, 11407
Larson, Jean Russell. *The Fish Bride and Other Gypsy Tales*, 10861
Larson, Jennifer (jt. author). *Jackie Joyner-Kersee*, 13661
Larson, Kirby. *Cody and Quinn, Sitting in a Tree*, 6444(F)
The Magic Kerchief, 1336(F)
Lascaro, Rita. *Down on the Farm*, 5706(F)
Laser, Michael. *The Rain*, 4480(F)
6–321, 8737(F)
Lasker, Joe. *All Kinds of Families*, 17685
The Cobweb Christmas, 5786(F)
He's My Brother, 8899(F)
How Do I Feel? 7514(F)
Howie Helps Himself, 8888(F)
Nick Joins In, 5008(F)
The Way Mothers Are, 2663(F)
Lasky, Kathryn. *Alice Rose and Sam*, 9392(F)
A Baby for Max, 3765(F)
A Brilliant Streak, 12609
Cloud Eyes, 11262
Days of the Dead, 15628

Double Trouble Squared, 7889(F)
Dreams in the Golden Country, 9577(F)
Elizabeth I, 9105(F)
The Emperor's Old Clothes, 1337(F)
First Painter, 1338(F)
The Gates of the Wind, 1339(F)
Hercules, 11484
Interrupted Journey, 18785
The Journal of Augustus Pelletier, 16085
A Journey to the New World, 9202(F)
Lucille's Snowsuit, 2342(F)
Lunch Bunnies, 2343(F)
Marie Antoinette, 9056(F)
Marven of the Great North Woods, 2951(F)
Monarchs, 19558
The Most Beautiful Roof in the World, 20462
The Night Journey, 9057(F)
Pond Year, 4481(F)
Science Fair Bunnies, 2344(F)
Shadows in the Dawn, 19001
Shadows in the Water, 7890(F)
Show and Tell Bunnies, 5513(F)
Sophie and Rose, 3275(F)
Sugaring Time, 20108
The Tantrum, 5009(F)
Think Like an Eagle, 21801
Vision of Beauty, 12809
Lass, Bonnie. *Who Took the Cookies from the Cookie Jar?* 2345(F)
Lassieur, Allison. *Astronauts,* 20998
Head Lice, 17980
The Inuit, 15814
The Moon, 18450
Scorpions, 19585
The Space Shuttle, 20999
The Sun, 18570
Lassig, Jurgen. *Spiny,* 7891(F)
Latham, Jean Lee. *Carry On, Mr. Bowditch,* 12086
Lathrop, Dorothy P. *Hitty,* 7723(F)
Latimer, Clay. *Muhammad Ali,* 13582
Latimer, Jim. *Going the Moose Way Home,* 2346(F)
The Irish Piper, 10926
James Bear and the Goose Gathering, 1340(F)
Moose and Friends, 2347(F)
Latimer, Jonathan P. *Backyard Birds,* 19244
Birds of Prey, 19331
Bizarre Birds, 19245
Shorebirds, 19246
Lattimore, Deborah N. *Arabian Nights,* 11192
Cinderhazel, 6024(F)
The Dragon's Robe, 10444(F)
The Flame of Peace, 9134(F)
Fool and the Phoenix, 9000(F)
Frida María, 7250(F)
Gittel's Hands, 1577(F)

I Wonder What's Under There? A Brief History of Underwear, 21176
The Lady with the Ship on Her Head, 4209(F)
The Winged Cat, 8969(F)
Lattimore, Eleanor F. *Little Pear,* 4725(F)
Lauber, Patricia. *Be a Friend to Trees,* 20209
Dinosaurs Walked Here, 14433
Flood, 20705
Fur, Feathers, and Flippers, 18646
Get Ready for Robots! 21216
How Dinosaurs Came to Be, 14434
How We Learned the Earth Is Round, 18432
Hurricanes, 20706
Living with Dinosaurs, 14435
Lost Star, 12113
Painters of the Caves, 14503
Purrfectly Purrfect, 7892(F)
Seeing Earth from Space, 18433
Snakes Are Hunters, 18761
Summer of Fire, 16624
Tales Mummies Tell, 14535
The Tiger Has a Toothache, 17851
The True-or-False Book of Cats, 19926
The True-or-False Book of Horses, 20001
Volcano, 20339
What You Never Knew About Fingers, Forks, and Chopsticks, 17638
Who Eats What? 18590
You're Aboard Spaceship Earth, 20312
Laufer, Peter. *Made in Mexico,* 15629
Laughlin, Rosemary. *John D. Rockefeller,* 12960
Laurabeatriz. *Tales of the Amazon,* 11441
Lauré, Jason. *Angola,* 14984
Bangladesh, 15179
Botswana, 14985
Namibia, 14986
Zambia, 14987
Zimbabwe, 14988
Lauré, Jason (jt. author). *Ghana,* 15015
Madagascar, 14966
Morocco, 14956
South Africa, 14967
Swaziland, 14968
Uganda, 14919
Lauren, Jill. *Succeeding with LD,* 17920
Laurgaard, Rachel K. *Patty Reed's Doll,* 9393(F)
Lauter, Richard. *The War with Grandpa,* 7517(F)
Lauture, Denizé. *Running the Road to ABC,* 10098(F)
Lavallee, Barbara. *The Gift,* 4433(F)
Mama, Do You Love Me? 3739(F)

This Place Is Crowded, 15119
This Place Is High, 20497
Uno, Dos, Tres, 520(F)
Lavender, David. *Mother Earth, Father Sky,* 15985
Lavies, Bianca. *Backyard Hunter,* 19459
Compost Critters, 19460
A Gathering of Garter Snakes, 18762
Monarch Butterflies, 19559
Lavis, Steve. *Little Mouse Has a Busy Day,* 6445(F)
Lavitt, Edward. *Nihancan's Feast of Beaver,* 11263
Lawler, Jennifer. *Cyberdanger and Internet Safety,* 21217
Drug Testing in Schools, 17876
Lawlor, Laurie. *Addie Across the Prairie,* 9394(F)
Addie's Dakota Winter, 9395(F)
Addie's Forever Friend, 9578(F)
Addie's Long Summer, 9396(F)
Adventure on the Wilderness Road, 9397(F)
Come Away with Me, 9579(F)
Gold in the Hills, 9398(F)
How to Survive Third Grade, 5514(F)
The Real Johnny Appleseed, 12846
West Along the Wagon Road, 1852, 9399(F)
Where Will This Shoe Take You? 21177
Window on the West, 12242
The Worst Kid Who Ever Lived on Eighth Avenue, 6446(F)
Lawlor, Veronica. *I Was Dreaming to Come to America,* 16708
Lawn, John. *Daniel Boone,* 12081
Lawrence, Iain. *The Smugglers,* 9106(F)
The Wreckers, 9107(F)
Lawrence, Jacob. *Harriet and the Promised Land,* 12800
Toussaint L'Ouverture, 13826
Lawrence, John. *The Christmas Collection,* 9732(F)
King of Kings, 5837(F)
Lawrence, Michael. *Baby Loves Hugs and Kisses,* 3766(F)
The Poppykettle Papers, 7893(F)
Lawrence, Sarah (jt. author). *Simple Machines,* 20930
Lawrie, Robin. *Dreams,* 12750
The Lion, the Witch and the Wardrobe, 7910(F)
Lawson, Barbara Spilman (jt. author). *Jambo, Watoto!* 2483(F)
Lawson, Don. *The French Resistance,* 14863
Lawson, Julie. *Bear on the Train,* 5298(F)
Cougar Cove, 7251(F)
The Dragon's Pearl, 10762
Emma and the Silk Train, 4726(F)
Goldstone, 6934(F)

Midnight in the Mountains, 4482(F)

Turns on a Dime, 8473(F)

Lawson, Robert. *Adam of the Road*, 9040(F)

Ben and Me, 9912(F)

Captain Kidd's Cat, 9913(F)

The Fabulous Flight, 7894(F)

Mr. Popper's Penguins, 9772(F)

Mr. Revere and I, 9914(F)

Rabbit Hill, 7895(F)

The Story of Ferdinand, 2348(F)

Lawston, Lisa. *A Pair of Red Sneakers*, 4210(F)

Lawton, Clive. *The Story of the Holocaust*, 14864

Layden, Joe. *The Great American Baseball Strike*, 22104

Layefsky, Virginia. *Impossible Things*, 7896(F)

Layne, Steven L. *Thomas's Sheep and the Great Geography Test*, 76(F)

Layton, George. *The Swap*, 8738(F)

Layton, Lesley. *Singapore*, 15180

Layton, Neal. *Nothing Scares Us*, 3483(F)

Rover, 4287(F)

Smile If You're Human, 1341(F)

Lazare, Jerry. *Queenie Peavy*, 8579(F)

Lazo, Caroline. *Arthur Ashe*, 13644

Eleanor Roosevelt, 13183

Elie Wiesel, 12624

Gloria Steinem, 13196

Jimmy Carter, 13016

Lech Walesa, 13866

The Terra Cotta Army of Emperor Qin, 15070

Wilma Mankiller, 12977

Leach, Norman. *My Wicked Stepmother*, 5010(F)

Leaf, Munro. *The Story of Ferdinand*, 2348(F)

Leahy, Philippa. *Spain*, 15479

Lear, Edward. *A Was Once an Apple Pie*, 11883

Complete Nonsense Book of Edward Lear, 11884

Daffy Down Dillies, 11885

An Edward Lear Alphabet, 77

Nonsense Songs, 11886

The Owl and the Pussycat, 11887

Owl and the Pussycat, 11888

The Owl and the Pussycat, 11889, 11890

The Quangle Wangle's Hat, 11891

Lear, Ruth Denise. *Boing-Boing the Bionic Cat*, 7789(F)

Lears, Laurie. *Ben Has Something to Say*, 8739(F)

Ian's Walk, 5011(F)

Waiting for Mr. Goose, 5012(F)

Leary, Catherine. *Awesome Experiments in Electricity and Magnetism*, 20890

Awesome Experiments in Force and Motion, 20826

Awesome Experiments in Light and Sound, 20804

Leavy, Una. *Irish Fairy Tales and Legends*, 11010

Lebenson, Richard. *Merlin's Mistake*, 7988(F)

Le Blanc, Andre. *Snow Treasure*, 9673(F)

Lebrun, Claude. *Little Brown Bear Does Not Want to Eat*, 2349(F)

LeCain, Errol. *Growltiger's Last Stand*, 11778

Lechon, Daniel. *The Desert Is My Mother/El Desierto Es Mi Madre*, 11974

Leder, Dora. *I Was So Mad!* 5078(F)

I'm Busy, Too, 5540(F)

Julian's Glorious Summer, 6251(F)

Just a Little Ham, 7174(F)

Oh, That Cat! 5415(F)

The Plum Tree War, 8362(F)

Leder, Jane M. *Karate*, 22268

A Russian Jewish Family, 17573

Lee, Alan. *Black Ships Before Troy*, 11510

The Wanderings of Odysseus, 11511

Lee, Barbara. *Working in Health Care and Wellness*, 17801

Working in Music, 17775

Working in Sports and Recreation, 17754

Working with Animals, 17852

Lee, Dennis. *The Ice Cream Store*, 11892

Lee, Dom. *Baseball Saved Us*, 5037(F)

Heroes, 7358(F)

Passage to Freedom, 14873

Lee, Fran. *Classical Kids*, 14581

Sense-Abilities, 18150

Show Time! 14321

Lee, Georgia. *A Day with a Chumash*, 15986

Lee, Hector Viveros. *Can You Top That?* 4250(F)

Get Set! Swim! 3002(F)

Lee, Huy Voun. *At the Beach*, 13984

Cardinal and Sunflower, 5372(F)

In the Park, 13985(F)

In the Snow, 13986(F)

1, 2, 3, Go! 489

Lee, Ileana C. *Kneeling Carabao and Dancing Giants*, 15240

Lee, Jared. *Snake Camp*, 6682(F)

Lee, Jeanne. *Jam! The Story of Jazz Music*, 14133

Lee, Jeanne M. *The Ch'i-lin Purse*, 10751

I Once Was a Monkey, 10799

The Song of Mu Lan, 10763

Toad Is the Uncle of Heaven, 10839

Lee, Jody. *Anne of Green Gables*, 8764(F)

Lee, Jordan. *Coping with Braces and Other Orthodontic Work*, 18185

Lee, Lauren. *Stella*, 7349(F)

Lee, Marie G. *Night of the Chupacabras*, 6935(F)

Lee, Martin. *The Seminoles*, 15987

Lee, Milly. *Nim and the War Effort*, 9669(F)

Lee, Paul. *Amistad Rising*, 16231

The Good Luck Cat, 5248(F)

Hank Aaron, 13430

Lee, Robert J. *The Magic Pumpkin*, 6032(F)

The Summer Sands, 3157(F)

Lee, Sally. *San Antonio*, 16913

Lee, Sandra. *Anteaters*, 18950

Giant Pandas, 19188

Skunks, 18951

Lee, Tan Chung. *Finland*, 15456, 15457

Lee, Tanith. *Islands in the Sky*, 7897(F)

Wolf Tower, 7898(F)

Lee, Tzexa Cherta (jt. author). *Jouanah*, 10837

Lee, Victor. *Rainbow Wings*, 1529(F)

Where Did All the Dragons Go? 1514(F)

Leedahl, Shelley A. *The Bone Talker*, 1342(F)

Leedy, Loreen. *Blast Off to Earth!* 4483

Celebrate the 50 States! 15890

The Dragon Halloween Party, 6025(F)

The Edible Pyramid, 20164

Fraction Action, 490

The Furry News, 2350(F)

The Great Trash Bash, 2351(F)

How Humans Make Friends, 1343(F)

Mapping Penny's World, 5299(F)

Measuring Penny, 20582

Messages in the Mailbox, 14097

Mission Addition, 20583

The Monster Money Book, 2352(F)

Pingo the Plaid Panda, 2353(F)

Postcards from Pluto, 18519

The Potato Party and Other Troll Tales, 1344(F)

Subtraction Action, 491(F)

2 x 2=Boo! 6026(F)

Waiting for Baby, 3529(F)

Who's Who in My Family? 3767(F)

Leeming, David A., ed. *The Children's Dictionary of Mythology*, 11450

Leemis, Ralph. *Smart Dog*, 2354(F)

Leeper, David R. *The Diary of David R. Leeper*, 16340

Leer, Rebecca. *A Spoon for Every Bite*, 3195(F)

Leeson, Pat (jt. author). *Black Bear*, 19051

Panda, 19189

Leeson, Tom. *Black Bear*, 19051

Panda, 19189

Left Hand Bull, Jacqueline. *Lakota Hoop Dancer*, 12414

Legge, David. *Bamboozled*, 3768(F)
Tom Goes to Kindergarten, 2857(F)
Leghorn, Lindsay. *Proud of Our Feelings*, 3276(F)
Le Guin, Ursula K. *Catwings*, 7899(F)
Jane on Her Own, 7900(F)
A Ride on the Red Mare's Back, 1345(F)
Wonderful Alexander and the Catwings, 7901(F)
Lehmberg, Janice (jt. author). *American Art*, 13960
Egyptian Art, 13940
Impressionist Art, 13901
Lehn, Barbara. *What Is a Scientist?* 17832
What Is a Teacher? 5515(F)
Lehne, Judith Logan. *The Never-Be-Bored Book*, 21449
Lehr, Norma. *Dance of the Crystal Skull*, 7902(F)
Haunting at Black Water Cove, 7903(F)
The Secret of the Floating Phantom, 6936(F)
The Shimmering Ghost of Riversend, 6937(F)
Lehrman, Robert. *The Store That Mama Built*, 9580(F)
Lehtinen, Ritva. *The Grandchildren of the Incas*, 15754
Leibowitz, Julie. *Finding Your Place*, 17669
Leigh, Nila K. *Learning to Swim in Swaziland*, 14989
Leigh, Tom. *Bone Poems*, 11660
Leigh, Vanora. *Mental Illness*, 17981
Leighton, Audrey O. *A Window of Time*, 3769(F)
Leighton, Robert. *What's Going on Down There?* 18258
Leiner, Alan. *Poems That Sing to You*, 11721
Leland, Dorothy K. *Sallie Fox*, 9400(F)
Lelooska, Chief. *Echoes of the Elders*, 11264
Lember, Barbara Hirsch. *A Book of Fruit*, 20150
If You Find a Rock, 4405(F)
The Shell Book, 19773
Lemelman, Martin. *The Wise Shoemaker of Studena*, 4736(F)
Lemieux, Margo. *The Fiddle Ribbon*, 3770(F)
Lemieux, Michele. *Amahl and the Night Visitors*, 5882(F)
Stormy Night, 8740(F)
Lemke, Elisabeth. *Marc Chagall*, 12208
Lemke, Horst. *Around the World in Eighty Dishes*, 21740
Lemke, Nancy. *Missions of the Southern Coast*, 16795

Lemoine, Georges. *The Book of Creation*, 17245
L'Engle, Madeleine. *Meet the Austins*, 7466(F)
The Other Dog, 2355(F)
The Twenty-Four Days Before Christmas, 9743(F)
A Wrinkle in Time, 10207(F)
Lennon, Joan. *There's a Kangaroo in My Soup!* 7904(F)
Lennox, Elsie. *Little Obie and the Kidnap*, 9450(F)
Lenski, Lois. *Betsy-Tacy*, 10103(F)
Strawberry Girl, 9581(F)
Lent, Blair. *The Beastly Feast*, 2133(F)
The Little Match Girl, 10384(F)
Tikki Tikki Tembo, 10766
Leo, Jana. *Cat Nap*, 19105
Count Us In, 562(F)
Shake, Rattle and Roll, 236(F)
This and That, 237(F)
Leodhas, Sorche Nic. *Always Room for One More*, 14165
Leon, Sharon (jt. author). *Thurgood Marshall*, 12765
Leon, Vicki. *Outrageous Women of Ancient Times*, 13734
Outrageous Women of the Middle Ages, 13735
Leonard, Marcia. *Best Friends*, 6447(F)
Dan and Dan, 6448(F)
Get the Ball, Slim, 6449(F)
I Like Mess, 6450(F)
My Pal Al, 6451(F)
No New Pants! 6452(F)
Leonard, Richard. *The Story of Sacajawea*, 12989
Leonard, Tom. *Discovering Jupiter*, 18457
Here Is the African Savanna, 20533
Here Is the Coral Reef, 19657
Under the Sun and the Moon and Other Poems, 11943
Whiskers, 18806
Leopold, Niki Clark. *Once I Was . . .*, 205(F)
Leplar, Anna C. *Flora the Frog*, 4987(F)
Lepthien, Emilie U. *The Cherokee*, 15988
The Choctaw, 15989
Coyotes, 19127
Foxes, 19129
Giraffes, 19175
Grizzlies, 19052
Iceland, 15458
Llamas, 18952
Manatees, 19739
Monarch Butterflies, 19560
Penguins, 19375
Peru, 15755
The Philippines, 15241
Polar Bears, 19053
Sea Turtles, 18786
Skunks, 18953

South Dakota, 16570
Walruses, 19740
Wolves, 19128
Lepthien, Emilie U. (jt. author). *Recycling*, 16981
Lerman, Rory S. *Charlie's Checklist*, 2356(F)
Lerner, Carol. *Cactus*, 20244
My Backyard Garden, 21764
My Indoor Garden, 21765
Leroe, E. W. *Monster Vision*, 7905(F)
Leroe, Ellen. *Ghost Dog*, 7906(F)
H.O.W.L. High, 7907(F)
Racetrack Robbery, 6938(F)
Leroux, Gaston. *The Phantom of the Opera*, 6939(F)
Les Chats Pelés. *Fun with Numbers*, 20632
LeShan, Eda. *Learning to Say Goodbye*, 17717
When Grownups Drive You Crazy, 17670
Le Sieg, Theo. *Ten Apples Up on Top*, 6453(F)
Wacky Wednesday, 492(F)
Lesinski, Jeanne. *Bill Gates*, 13295
Lesinski, Jeanne M. *Exotic Invaders*, 18647
Leslie, Amanda. *Are Chickens Stripy?* 2357(F)
Flappy Waggy Wiggly, 21835(F)
Leslie, Clare W. *Nature All Year Long*, 18591
Lessac, Frane. *The Bird Who Was an Elephant*, 8999(F)
The Chalk Doll, 3843(F)
The Distant Talking Drum, 11977
O Christmas Tree, 5907(F)
On the Same Day in March, 20789
Queen Esther Saves Her People, 6071
Lessem, Don. *Dinosaur Worlds*, 14436
Ornithomimids, 14437
Seismosaurus, 14438
Supergiants! 14439
Troodon, 14440
Lesser, Carolyn. *Dig Hole, Soft Mole*, 5300(F)
The Goodnight Circle, 722(F)
Great Crystal Bear, 5301(F)
Spots, 493
Storm on the Desert, 20411
Lessum, Don. *Dinosaurs to Dodos*, 19401
Lester, Alison. *Alice and Aldo*, 78(F)
Celeste Sails to Spain, 3277(F)
Isabella's Bed, 1346(F)
My Farm, 4727
The Quicksand Pony, 6940(F)
Tessa Snaps Snakes, 4022(F)
When Frank Was Four, 3278(F)
Lester, Helen. *Author*, 12561
Hooway for Wodney Wat, 2358(F)
It Wasn't My Fault, 4211(F)
Listen, Buddy, 2359(F)

Me First, 2360(F)
Pookins Gets Her Way, 1347(F)
A Porcupine Named Fluffy, 2361(F)
Princess Penelope's Parrot, 1348(F)
Tacky and the Emperor, 2362(F)
Tacky in Trouble, 2363(F)
Tacky the Penguin, 2364(F)
Three Cheers for Tacky, 2365(F)
The Wizard, the Fairy and the Magic Chicken, 1349(F)
Lester, Helen (jt. author). *Wuzzy Takes Off*, 2367(F)
Lester, Julius. *Ackamarackus*, 2366(F)
Albidaro and the Mischievous Dream, 1350(F)
Black Cowboy, Wild Horses, 4728(F)
How Many Spots Does a Leopard Have? 10685
Long Journey Home, 7350(F)
To Be a Slave, 17574
What a Truly Cool World, 10686
When the Beginning Began, 17296
Lester, Mike. *A Is for Salad*, 79(F)
Lester, Robin. *Wuzzy Takes Off*, 2367(F)
Lesynski, Loris. *Dirty Dog Boogie*, 11623
Le Tord, Bijou. *A Bird or Two*, 4729(F)
A Blue Butterfly, 13904
God's Little Seeds, 17297
Noah's Tree, 17298(F)
Le Tord, Bijou, ed. *Sing a New Song*, 17299
Letzig, Michael. *Trick or Treat Countdown*, 6011(F)
Leuck, Laura. *My Baby Brother Has Ten Tiny Toes*, 494(F)
My Monster Mama Loves Me So, 1351(F)
Sun Is Falling, Night Is Calling, 723(F)
Teeny, Tiny Mouse, 280(F)
Levenson, George. *Pumpkin Circle*, 20181
Leverich, Kathleen. *Best Enemies Forever*, 8332(F)
Daisy, 8741(F)
The New You, 8742(F)
Levering, Robert. *If You Lived with the Sioux Indians*, 15996
Levert, Mireille. *Goldilocks and the Three Bears*, 10986
Tiny Toes, 3243(F)
LeVert, Suzanne. *Hillary Rodham Clinton*, 13146
Louisiana, 16872
Massachusetts, 16709
Levete, Sarah. *Being Jealous*, 17718
Levey, Judith, ed. *The Macmillan Picture Wordbook*, 14039
Levigne, Heather (jt. author). *What Is a Marsupial?* 19178

What Is a Primate? 19000
What Is a Whale? 19639
Levin, Betty. *Away to Me, Moss*, 7252(F)
The Banished, 7908(F)
Creature Crossing, 7253(F)
Fire in the Wind, 6941(F)
Gift Horse, 7254(F)
Island Bound, 6942(F)
Look Back, Moss, 7255(F)
Shadow-Catcher, 6943(F)
Starshine and Sunglow, 8333(F)
Levin, Freddie. *ABC School Riddles*, 21827(F)
1-2-3 Draw, 21581
Levin, Pam. *Tyra Banks*, 12352
Levin, Pamela. *Susan B. Anthony*, 13130
Levin, Ted. *Cactus Poems*, 11937
Song of the North, 11938
Levine, Abby. *Gretchen Groundhog, It's Your Day!* 5633(F)
This Is the Pumpkin, 6027(F)
This Is the Turkey, 6148(F)
Levine, Anna. *Running on Eggs*, 8936(F)
Levine, David. *Fables of Aesop*, 11051
Levine, Edna S. *Lisa and Her Soundless World*, 8900(F)
Levine, Ellen. *Anna Pavlova*, 12441
Darkness Over Denmark, 14865
If Your Name Was Changed at Ellis Island, 17575
The Tree That Would Not Die, 4730
Levine, Evan. *Not the Piano, Mrs. Medley!* 4484(F)
Levine, Gail C. *Cinderellis and the Glass Hill*, 10445(F)
Dave at Night, 9582(F)
Ella Enchanted, 10446(F)
The Fairy's Mistake, 10447(F)
Princess Sonora and the Long Sleep, 10448(F)
The Princess Test, 10449(F)
The Wish, 7909(F)
Levine, Melinda. *Eight Days of Hanukkah*, 6130(F)
The School Mural, 5544(F)
Water for One, Water for Everyone, 589(F)
Levine, Michael. *The Kid's Address Book*, 21933
Levine, Shar. *Awesome Yo-Yo Tricks*, 22033
Everyday Science, 18325
Fun with Your Microscope, 19806
The Magnet Book, 20898
Marbles, 22034
The Microscope Book, 19807
The Optics Book, 20873
Projects for a Healthy Planet, 16960
Science Around the World, 18326
The Science of Sound and Music, 20940
Shocking Science, 20899

Silly Science, 18327
Levinson, Marilyn. *No Boys Allowed*, 8474(F)
Levinson, Nancy S. *Clara and the Bookwagon*, 6454(F)
She's Been Working on the Railroad, 21336
Levitin, Sonia. *Annie's Promise*, 7467(F)
Boom Town, 4731(F)
Dream Freedom, 8970(F)
Journey to America, 9670(F)
A Single Speckled Egg, 4212(F)
Taking Charge, 4732(F)
Levitt, Sidney. *You Don't Get a Carrot Unless You're a Bunny*, 6030(F)
Levoy, Myron. *The Magic Hat of Mortimer Wintergreen*, 9915(F)
The Witch of Fourth Street and Other Stories, 7468(F)
Levy, Constance. *A Crack in the Clouds and Other Poems*, 11624
I'm Going to Pet a Worm Today and Other Poems, 11796
A Tree Place and Other Poems, 11966
When Whales Exhale and Other Poems, 11625
Levy, David H., ed. *Stars and Planets*, 18548
Levy, Elizabeth. *The Creepy Computer Mystery*, 6455(F)
Frankenstein Moved In on the Fourth Floor, 6944(F)
If You Were There When They Signed the Constitution, 17059
The Karate Class Mystery, 6456(F)
Keep Ms. Sugarman in the Fourth Grade, 10099(F)
A Mammoth Mix-Up, 6945(F)
My Life as a Fifth-Grade Comedian, 8743(F)
The Mystery of the Missing Dog, 6457(F)
Parents' Night Fright, 6458(F)
Seventh Grade Tango, 10100(F)
Something Queer at the Library, 6946(F)
Something Queer in the Wild West, 6947(F)
Third Grade Bullies, 8334(F)
Wolfman Sam, 7469(F)
Levy, Janice. *Abuelito Eats with His Fingers*, 3771(F)
The Spirit of Tio Fernando, 5634(F)
Totally Uncool, 5013(F)
Levy, Matthys. *Earthquake Games*, 20340
Levy, Pamela R. *Otto's Rainy Day*, 3493(F)
Levy, Pat (jt. author). *Rome*, 14744
Levy, Patricia. *Ireland*, 15356
Nigeria, 15033
Switzerland, 15275
Tibet, 15181

Levy, Robert. *Escape from Exile*, 10208(F)
Lewin, Betsy. *Araminta's Paint Box*, 4567(F)
Aunt Minnie McGranahan, 3845(F)
Booby Hatch, 5302(F)
The Boy Who Counted Stars, 11590
Chubbo's Pool, 2368(F)
Click, Clack, Moo, 1989(F)
Doodle Dandy! 17364
Dumpy La Rue, 2866(F)
Elephant Quest, 19165
Gobble! 17498
Ho Ho Ho! 17419
Is It Far to Zanzibar? Poems About Tanzania, 11874
The Lunch Box Surprise, 6478(F)
Mushy! 17508
My Tooth Is About to Fall Out, 6479(F)
No Such Thing, 719(F)
Promises, 3955(F)
Purrfectly Purrfect, 7892(F)
Recess Mess, 6480(F)
Sharing Time Troubles, 6481(F)
Snake Alley Band, 2542(F)
A Thousand Cousins, 11592
Walk a Green Path, 20245
Weird! 17445
What If the Shark Wears Tennis Shoes? 748(F)
What's the Matter, Habibi? 2369(F)
Wiley Learns to Spell, 6459(F)
Lewin, Betsy (jt. author). *Elephant Quest*, 19165
Gorilla Walk, 19002
Lewin, Hugh. *Jafta*, 4733(F)
Lewin, Ted. *A. Lincoln and Me*, 4598(F)
Ali, Child of the Desert, 4743(F)
The Always Prayer Shawl, 4782(F)
American Too, 3015(F)
Barn Savers, 3212(F)
Brother Francis and the Friendly Beasts, 4682
Cowboy Country, 2969(F)
The Day of Ahmed's Secret, 4678(F)
The Disappearing Island, 4411(F)
The Doorman, 4969(F)
Elephant Quest, 19165
Gorilla Walk, 19002
Just in Time for Christmas, 5757(F)
Lost Moose, 5419(F)
Matthew's Meadow, 7615(F)
National Velvet, 7153(F)
Nilo and the Tortoise, 5303(F)
The Originals, 11819
Paperboy, 4716(F)
Peppe the Lamplighter, 4587(F)
The Potato Man, 3296(F)
The Reindeer People, 15815
Sacred River, 15108
Sami and the Time of the Troubles, 4679(F)
Sea Watch, 11820

The Search for Grissi, 8811(F)
The Secret of the Indian, 7587(F)
The Storytellers, 4734(F)
Touch and Go, 12254
Lewington, Anna. *Antonio's Rain Forest*, 20463
People of the Rain Forests, 20464
What Do We Know About the Amazonian Indians? 15756
Lewis, Amanda. *Lettering*, 21582
Making Memory Books, 21450
Writing, 14098
Lewis, Barbara A. *The Kid's Guide to Service Projects*, 17150
The Kid's Guide to Social Action, 17621
Lewis, Barbara S. *Being Your Best*, 17622
Lewis, Beverly. *Catch a Falling Star*, 8744(F)
The Chicken Pox Panic, 7470(F)
The Crazy Christmas Angel Mystery, 9744(F)
Frog Power, 10101(F)
Holly's First Love, 8335(F)
Night of the Fireflies, 8745(F)
Whispers down the Lane, 8475(F)
Lewis, Brian (jt. author). *City of Angels*, 16790
Lewis, C. S. *The Lion, the Witch and the Wardrobe*, 7910(F), 7911(F)
Lewis, Celeste (jt. author). *Lost*, 5279(F)
Lewis, Claudia. *Long Ago in Oregon*, 11626
Lewis, Cynthia C. *Dilly's Big Sister Diary*, 3772(F)
Dilly's Summer Camp Diary, 9916(F)
Hello, Alexander Graham Bell Speaking, 13237
Lewis, Cynthia Copeland. *Dilly's Big Sister Diary*, 3772(F)
Dilly's Summer Camp Diary, 9916(F)
Lewis, E. B. *The Bat Boy and His Violin*, 10322(F)
Big Boy, 4772(F)
Creativity, 4047(F)
Dirt on Their Skirts, 4805(F)
Down the Road, 3878(F)
Faraway Home, 3760(F)
Fire on the Mountain, 10680
I Love My Hair! 3450(F)
The Jazz of Our Street, 3420(F)
Little Cliff and the Porch People, 3911(F)
The Magic Tree, 10664
My Rows and Piles of Coins, 4773(F)
Only a Pigeon, 4721(F)
The Other Side, 4063(F)
Virgie Goes to School with Us Boys, 4981(F)
Lewis, Elizabeth Foreman. *Young Fu of the Upper Yangtze*, 9001(F)

Lewis, H. *Can I Have a Stegosaurus, Mom? Can I? Please!?* 4166(F)
Lewis, J. Patrick. *At the Wish of the Fish*, 11099
Black Swan/White Crow, 11822
The Boat of Many Rooms, 4213(F)
The Bookworm's Feast, 11627
Boshblobberbosh, 11893
A Burst of Firsts, 11628
Doodle Dandies, 11629
Earth Verses and Water Rhymes, 11967
Freedom Like Sunlight, 11764
Good Mousekeeping, 11894
A Hippopotamusn't and Other Animal Verses, 11797
The House of Boo, 6028(F)
Isabella Abnormella and the Very, Very Finicky Queen of Trouble, 1352(F)
July Is a Mad Mosquito, 11968
The La-di-da Hare, 11895
The Little Buggers, 11798
Night of the Goat Children, 1353(F)
One Dog Day, 7256(F)
Riddle-Lightful, 21836
Lewis, Kevin. *Chugga-Chugga Choo Choo*, 5580(F)
The Lot at the End of My Block, 5581(F)
Lewis, Kim. *Emma's Lamb*, 5304(F)
First Snow, 2952(F)
Floss, 5305(F)
Friends, 4023(F)
Just Like Floss, 5306(F)
Little Calf, 5307(F)
My Friend Harry, 3279(F)
The Shepherd Boy, 3280(F)
Lewis, Maggie. *Morgy Makes His Move*, 8746(F)
Lewis, Naomi, reteller. *Elf Hill*, 10450(F)
Lewis, Richard. *All of You Was Singing*, 11406
Lewis, Rob. *Grandpa at the Beach*, 6460(F)
Hide-and-Seek with Grandpa, 3773(F)
Too Much Trouble for Grandpa, 6461(F)
Lewis, Rose. *I Love You Like Crazy Cakes*, 4735(F)
Lewis, Stephen. *Growing Money*, 16925
Lewis, Thomas P. *Clipper Ship*, 21364
Hill of Fire, 15630
Lewis, Zoe. *Keisha Discovers Harlem*, 9583(F)
Lewison, Wendy C. *The Princess and the Potty*, 3281(F)
Shy Vi, 2370(F)
Lexau, Joan M. *Don't Be My Valentine*, 6173(F)
Striped Ice Cream, 7471(F)

Leyton, Lawrence. *My First Magic Book*, 21785
L'Hommedieu, Arthur J. *From Plant to Blue Jeans*, 21178
Working at a Museum, 17755
Li, Xiao Jun. *Nekane, the Lamina and the Bear*, 11134
The Perfect Orange, 10647
Liatsos, Sandra O. *Bicycle Riding*, 11630
Libura, Krystyna. *What the Aztecs Told Me*, 15631
Licata, Renora. *Princess Diana*, 13782
Lichtenberg, Andre. *Brazil*, 15757
Lichtenheld, Tom. *Everything I Know About Pirates*, 14561
Liddell, Janice. *Imani and the Flying Africans*, 11363
Lidz, Jane. *Zak*, 2371(F)
Lieber, Susan F. *Parks for the People*, 12941
Lieberman, Syd. *The Wise Shoemaker of Studena*, 4736(F)
Lieblich, Irene. *The Power of Light*, 9761(F)
Liebman, Dan. *I Want to Be a Doctor*, 17802
I Want to Be a Police Officer, 17815
I Want to Be a Vet, 17853
Lied, Kate. *Potato*, 4737(F)
Liedahl, Brian. *I Speak for the Women*, 13197
Liersch, Anne. *A House Is Not a Home*, 2372(F)
Lies, Brian. *Flatfoot Fox and the Case of the Bashful Beaver*, 7655(F)
Flatfoot Fox and the Case of the Missing Schoolhouse, 6268(F)
Flatfoot Fox and the Case of the Missing Whoooo, 1965(F)
Flatfoot Fox and the Case of the Nosy Otter, 6269(F)
Hamlet and the Enormous Chinese Dragon Kite, 2373(F)
Liestman, Vicki. *Columbus Day*, 17382
Life, Kay. *Finding a Job for Daddy*, 3801(F)
Muggie Maggie, 6267(F)
Poppy's Chair, 3691(F)
Veronica's First Year, 5056(F)
When Mommy Is Sick, 3889(F)
Ligasan, Darryl. *Allie's Basketball Dream*, 3009(F)
Caravan, 4756(F)
Lightburn, Ron. *Waiting for the Whales*, 3788(F)
Lightfoot, Marge. *Cartooning for Kids*, 21583
Lill, Debra. *Music and Drum*, 11681
Lillegard, Dee. *The Big Bug Ball*, 2374(F)
James A. Garfield, 13035
James K. Polk, 13091

John Tyler, 13110
Nevada, 16625
Richard Nixon, 13088
Wake Up House! Rooms Full of Poems, 11631
Lilly, Charles. *Philip Hall Likes Me, I Reckon Maybe*, 8290(F)
Runaway to Freedom, 9322(F)
Lilly, Melinda. *Kwian and the Lazy Sun*, 10687
Lilly, Melinda, reteller. *Spider and His Son Find Wisdom*, 10688
Wanyana and Matchmaker Frog, 10689
Zimani's Drum, 10690
Lim, Mei. *Face Painting*, 21589
Fun Food, 21412
Limberland, Dennis. *The Cheyenne*, 15990
Limburg, Peter R. *Weird!* 17445
Limmer, Milly J. *Where Do Little Girls Grow?* 3774(F)
Lin, Grace. *Round Is a Mooncake*, 362(F)
The Ugly Vegetables, 3775(F)
Linch, Tanya. *Look Out for the Big Bad Fish!* 1910(F)
My Duck, 1354(F)
This and That, 2748(F)
Lincoln, Abraham. *The Gettysburg Address*, 16420
Lincoln, Margaret. *The Most Excellent Book of Face Painting*, 21584
Lincoln, Margarette. *Amazing Boats*, 21365
Lindberg, Becky T. *Chelsea Martin Turns Green*, 8336(F)
Thomas Tuttle, Just in Time, 10102(F)
Lindberg, Dean. *Can You Catch a Falling Star?* 18525
Can You Hitch a Ride on a Comet? 18526
Where's the Big Dipper? 18553
Lindbergh, Anne. *Bailey's Window*, 7912(F)
The Hunky-Dory Dairy, 7913(F)
Nobody's Orphan, 8476(F)
The People in Pineapple Place, 7914(F)
The Prisoner of Pineapple Place, 7915(F)
Three Lives to Live, 7916(F)
The Worry Week, 6948(F)
Lindbergh, Reeve. *The Awful Aardvarks Go to School*, 80(F)
The Awful Aardvarks Shop for School, 2375(F)
The Circle of Days, 17203
Nobody Owns the Sky, 12094
North Country Spring, 4485(F)
Lindblad, Lisa. *The Serengeti Migration*, 14937
Lindenbaum, Pija. *Boodil, My Dog*, 5308(F)

Lindgren, Astrid. *Christmas in the Stable*, 5863(F)
I Don't Want to Go to Bed, 724(F)
I Want to Go to School, Too! 5516(F)
Lotta's Christmas Surprise, 5864(F)
Lotta's Easter Surprise, 5970(F)
Pippi Longstocking, 9917(F)
Pippi Longstocking's After-Christmas Party, 5865(F)
Pippi to the Rescue, 6949(F)
Pippi's Extraordinary Ordinary Day, 9918(F)
Ronia, the Robber's Daughter, 7917(F)
The Tomten, 4738(F)
Lindgren, Barbro. *Benny's Had Enough!* 2376(F)
Rosa, 5309(F)
Rosa Goes to Daycare, 2377(F)
Sam's Ball, 5014(F)
Sam's Potty, 3282(F)
Lindley, Thomas. *Look-Alikes Jr.*, 359
Lindop, Edmund. *Dwight D. Eisenhower, John F. Kennedy, Lyndon B. Johnson*, 12671
George Washington, Thomas Jefferson, Andrew Jackson, 12672
James K. Polk, Abraham Lincoln, Theodore Roosevelt, 12673
Panama and the United States, 15672
Political Parties, 17097
Richard M. Nixon, Jimmy Carter, Ronald Reagan, 12674
Woodrow Wilson, Franklin D. Roosevelt, Harry S. Truman, 12675
Lindquist, Jennie D. *The Little Silver House*, 7472(F)
Lindquist, Susan H. *Summer Soldiers*, 9584(F)
Wander, 7257(F)
Lindsay, Bruce (jt. author). *Dave's Quick 'n' Easy Web Pages*, 21218
Lindsay, Dave. *Dave's Quick 'n' Easy Web Pages*, 21218
Lindsay, Janice. *The Milly Stories*, 7918(F)
Lindsay, Jeanne W. *Do I Have a Daddy? A Story About a Single-Parent Child*, 17671
Lindsay, William. *DK Great Dinosaur Atlas*, 14441
Prehistoric Life, 14504
Lindstrom, Jack. *Happy Birthday to Me!* 11834
Lineker, Gary. *Soccer*, 22296
The Young Soccer Player, 22297
Ling, Bettina. *Maya Lin*, 12255
Ling, Bettina (jt. author). *Mairead Corrigan and Betty Williams*, 15339

Ling, Lim Bee (jt. author). *Welcome to China*, 15063

Ling, Mary. *Amazing Wolves, Dogs, and Foxes*, 19130

Butterfly, 19561

Foal, 20002

Fox, 19131

Owl, 19362

Penguin, 19376

The Snake Book, 18763

Lings, Stephen. *Down a River*, 15908

Duck, 19315

Inside a Coral Reef, 19669

Link, Martin (jt. author). *The Goat in the Rug*, 1817(F)

Linn, David. *Great Ghosts*, 6798(F)

Linn, Warren. *Happy Birthday, Frankie*, 1670(F)

Linnea, Sharon. *Princess Ka'iulani*, 13819

Raoul Wallenberg, 13867

Linton, Patricia (jt. author). *The Young Dancer*, 14277

Linzer, Lila. *Once Upon an Island*, 11429

Lionel. *Peekaboo Babies*, 495(F)

Lionni, Leo. *Alexander and the Wind-Up Mouse*, 2378(F)

The Biggest House in the World, 2379(F)

An Extraordinary Egg, 2380(F)

Fish Is Fish, 2381(F)

Frederick, 2382(F)

Inch by Inch, 2383(F)

Little Blue and Little Yellow, 281(F)

Matthew's Dream, 2384(F)

Mr. McMouse, 2385(F)

Swimmy, 2386(F)

Tillie and the Wall, 2387(F)

Lipkind, William. *Finders Keepers*, 5310(F)

Lipman, Jean. *Alexander Calder and His Magical Mobiles*, 12196

Lippert, Margaret H. (jt. author). *Why Leopard Has Spots*, 10710

Lippincott, Gary. *The Bookstore Mouse*, 7653(F)

Jennifer Murdley's Toad, 7676(F)

Jeremy Thatcher, Dragon Hatcher, 7677(F)

Lippman, Peter. *Science Experiments You Can Eat*, 18305

Lipson, Michael. *How the Wind Plays*, 1355(F)

Lipstein, Morissa. *The Never-Be-Bored Book*, 21449

Liptak, Karen. *North American Indian Survival Skills*, 15991

Lisandrelli, Elaine S. *Bob Dole, Legendary Senator*, 12873

Jack London, 12563

Lishak, Anthony. *Row Your Boat*, 14166

Lisi, Victoria. *If I Were the Wind*, 3618(F)

Snowbear Whittington, 11351

Lisker, Emily. *Just Rewards, or Who Is That Man in the Moon and What's He Doing Up There Anyway?* 10769

Sol a Sol, 11543

Lisker, Sonia O. *Freckle Juice*, 9781(F)

Leonard Bernstein, 12323

Lisle, Janet T. *Afternoon of the Elves*, 7919(F)

Angela's Aliens, 10209(F)

The Art of Keeping Cool, 9671(F)

The Gold Dust Letters, 7920(F)

The Lampfish of Twill, 7921(F)

Looking for Juliette, 7922(F)

The Lost Flower Children, 7923(F)

A Message from the Match Girl, 6950(F)

Lister, Maree. *England*, 15357

Welcome to England, 15358

Litchfield, Ada B. *A Button in Her Ear*, 18146

A Cane in Her Hand, 8901(F)

Words in Our Hands, 5015(F)

Litchfield, Jo. *The Usborne Book of Everyday Words*, 14055

Litchman, Kristin Embry. *All Is Well*, 9585(F)

Lithgow, John. *The Remarkable Farkle McBride*, 4214(F)

Litowinsky, Olga. *Boats for Bedtime*, 5582(F)

Littell, Mary Ann. *Heroin Drug Dangers*, 17877

Little, Claire St Louis. *The Goodbye Boat*, 3741(F)

Little, Emily. *The Trojan Horse*, 14688

Little, Jean. *The Belonging Place*, 8747(F)

Different Dragons, 7258(F)

Emma's Magic Winter, 6462(F)

Emma's Yucky Brother, 6463(F)

From Anna, 8902(F)

Little, Kimberly Griffiths. *Enchanted Runner*, 6951(F)

Little, Lessie Jones (jt. author). *Childtimes*, 17562

Little, Mimi O. *Yoshiko and the Foreigner*, 4739(F)

Littlechild, George. *A Man Called Raven*, 1645(F)

What's the Most Beautiful Thing You Know About Horses? 5440(F)

Littlefield, Holly. *Colors of Japan*, 15130

Fire at the Triangle Factory, 9586(F)

Littlesugar, Amy. *Freedom School, Yes!* 4740(F)

Jonkonnu, 4741(F)

Marie in Fourth Position, 9058(F)

A Portrait of Spotted Deer's Grandfather, 7351(F)

Shake Rag, 5016(F)

The Spinner's Daughter, 9203(F)

Tree of Hope, 4742(F)

Littlewood, Valerie. *The Glass Angels*, 9733(F)

Litty, Julie. *Dr. White*, 2135(F)

Litzinger, Rosanne. *Leprechaun Gold*, 985(F)

The Little Golden Lamb, 10990

Louella Mae, She's Run Away! 4074(F)

The Magic Kerchief, 1336(F)

Rupa Raises the Sun, 1047(F)

Sing, Sophie! 4131(F)

The Someday House, 3424(F)

Song Bird, 10704

You Can't Catch Me, 1132(F)

Liu, Lesley. *Cat and Cat-face*, 1605(F)

Livingston, Francis. *The Fiddle Ribbon*, 3770(F)

Livingston, Myra Cohn. *B Is for Baby*, 81(F)

A Circle of Seasons, 11969

Cricket Never Does, 11823

Festivals, 17383

Flights of Fancy and Other Poems, 11633

I Never Told and Other Poems, 11636

Keep on Singing, 12345

Remembering and Other Poems, 11637

Up in the Air, 11970

Livingston, Myra Cohn, ed. *Cat Poems*, 11799

Celebrations, 11835

Christmas Poems, 11836

I Am Writing a Poem About . . . a Game of Poetry, 11634

I Like You, If You Like Me, 11635

If the Owl Calls Again, 11800

If You Ever Meet a Whale, 11801

Lots of Limericks, 11896

Poems for Jewish Holidays, 11837

Roll Along, 11638

Valentine Poems, 11838

Llamas, Andreu. *Birds Conquer the Sky*, 19247

The Era of the Dinosaurs, 14442

Plants Under the Sea, 20246

Llewellyn, Claire. *The Best Book of Bugs*, 19461

The Best Book of Sharks, 19763

The Big Book of Bones, 18829

Chocolate, 20109

Disguises and Surprises, 18885

Milk, 20110

My First Book of Time, 206

Our Planet Earth, 14345

Peanuts, 20111

Potatoes, 20182

Some Bugs Glow in the Dark, 19462

Some Snakes Spit Poison and Other Amazing Facts About Snakes, 18764

Spiders Have Fangs, 19586

What's for Lunch? Bread, 20112

What's for Lunch? Eggs, 20113
What's for Lunch? Oranges, 20151
What's for Lunch? Peas, 20183
Wild, Wet and Windy, 20780
Lloyd, David. *Polly Molly Woof Woof*, 2388(F)
Lloyd, Emily. *Catch of the Day*, 6952(F)
Forest Slump, 6953(F)
Lloyd, Mary Anne. *Sandbox Scientist*, 18346
Lloyd, Megan. *Baba Yaga*, 11093
Cactus Hotel, 4449
Chirping Crickets, 19427
Falcons Nest on Skyscrapers, 19329
The Gingerbread Doll, 5934(F)
The Gingerbread Man, 11008
How We Learned the Earth Is Round, 18432
The Little Old Lady Who Was Not Afraid of Anything, 1688(F)
Look Out for Turtles! 18780
A Regular Flood of Mishap, 3528(F)
Seven at One Blow, 10924
Spoonbill Swamp, 20375
Surprises, 11606
Too Many Pumpkins, 4351(F)
What Color Is Camouflage? 18887
Lloyd-Jones, Karen. *Butterflies Fly*, 19570
Spiders Spin Webs, 19598
Lobb, Janice. *Dig and Sow! How Do Plants Grow?* 18592
Splish! Splosh! Why Do We Wash? 4486
Lobban, John. *Paddington's 1, 2, 3*, 385(F)
Paddington's Opposites, 165(F)
Lobby, Ted. *Jessica and the Wolf*, 5017(F)
Lobe, Mira. *Christoph Wants a Party*, 5707(F)
Lobel, Anita. *Away from Home*, 82(F)
The Dwarf Giant, 10451(F)
My Day in the Garden, 3148(F)
A New Coat for Anna, 3969(F)
On Market Street, 83(F)
One Lighthouse, One Moon, 207(F)
The Rose in My Garden, 5311(F)
Singing Bee! A Collection of Favorite Children's Songs, 14244
This Quiet Lady, 3975(F)
Toads and Diamonds, 10871
Lobel, Arnold. *Dinosaur Time*, 14459
Fables, 2389(F)
Frog and Toad Are Friends, 6464(F)
Grasshopper on the Road, 6465(F)
Gregory Griggs and Other Nursery Rhyme People, 866
Greg's Microscope, 19810
I'll Fix Anthony, 3929(F)

Ming Lo Moves the Mountain, 4215(F)
Mouse Soup, 6466(F)
Mouse Tales, 6467(F)
Nightmares, 11677
On Market Street, 83(F)
Oscar Otter, 6202(F)
Owl at Home, 6468(F)
The Quarreling Book, 3973(F)
The Random House Book of Poetry for Children, 11679
Red Fox and His Canoe, 6203(F)
The Rose in My Garden, 5311(F)
Sam the Minuteman, 4593(F)
Small Pig, 6469(F)
A Three Hat Day, 4158(F)
Tyrannosaurus Was a Beast, 11810
Uncle Elephant, 6470(F)
Whiskers and Rhymes, 856
Lobosco, Michael L. *Mental Math Challenges*, 20617
Mental Math Workout, 20584
Locker, Thomas. *Between Earth and Sky*, 11215
Cloud Dance, 20661
The First Thanksgiving, 17496
Grandfather's Christmas Tree, 5929(F)
Home, 15854
In Blue Mountains, 16710
The Man Who Paints, 12562
Thirteen Moons on Turtle's Back, 11929
Water Dance, 20737
Lodge, Bernard. *Cloud Cuckoo Land*, 1356(F)
Grandma Went to Market, 384(F)
Mouldylocks, 5708(F)
Noah Makes a Boat, 17277
Tanglebird, 2390(F)
There Was an Old Woman Who Lived in a Glove, 857
Lodge, Bernard (jt. author). *The Grand Old Duke of York*, 886
Lodge, Jo. *Busy Farm*, 496(F)
Lodge, Katherine. *The Clever Cowboy*, 1364(F)
Loehr, Mallory. *Water Wishes*, 7924(F)
Loehr, Mallory, adapt. *Babe*, 6471(F)
Loeper, John J. *Going to School in 1776*, 16153
Meet the Drakes on the Kentucky Frontier, 16341
Meet the Wards on the Oregon Trail, 16342
Loewen, Nancy. *Atlanta*, 16873
Bicycle Safety, 22161
Emergencies, 18220
Philadelphia, 16711
Seattle, 16796
Washington, D.C., 16712
Loewen, Nancy, ed. *Walt Whitman*, 12623
Loewer, Peter. *Pond Water Zoo*, 19808

Lofting, Hugh. *The Story of Doctor Dolittle*, 7925(F)
Loftis, Chris. *The Boy Who Sat by the Window*, 8477(F)
Lofts, Pamela. *Koala Lou*, 2096(F)
Loftus, Barbara. *Egyptian Stories*, 10674
Loggia, Wendy. *A Puppy of My Own*, 7259(F)
Loh, Morag. *Tucking Mommy In*, 725(F)
Lohstoeter, Lori. *Beatrice's Goat*, 4750(F)
By a Blazing Blue Sea, 4654(F)
Friend Frog, 1722(F)
Iguana Beach, 3150(F)
Lomas, Clare. *The 80s and 90s*, 16515
Lomas Garza, Carmen. *Family Pictures/Cuadros de Familia*, 17576
In My Family/En Mi Familia, 3283(F)
Lonborg, Rosemary. *Helpin' Bugs*, 4024(F)
London, Jack. *White Fang*, 7260(F)
London, Jonathan. *Ali, Child of the Desert*, 4743(F)
At the Edge of the Forest, 5312(F)
Baby Whale's Journey, 5313(F)
The Candystore Man, 3284(F)
Dream Weaver, 4487(F)
The Eyes of Gray Wolf, 7261(F)
Froggy Gets Dressed, 2391(F)
Froggy Goes to Bed, 726(F)
Froggy Goes to School, 2392(F)
Froggy Learns to Swim, 2393(F)
Froggy Plays Soccer, 2394(F)
Froggy's First Kiss, 2395(F)
Froggy's Halloween, 6029(F)
Gone Again Ptarmigan, 19248
Hurricane! 4744(F)
Ice Bear and Little Fox, 5314(F)
A Koala for Katie, 3776(F)
Let the Lynx Come In, 1357(F)
Let's Go, Froggy! 2396(F)
The Lion Who Has Asthma, 5018(F)
Liplap's Wish, 2397(F)
Moshi Moshi, 4745(F)
Panther, 19095
Phantom of the Prairie, 5315(F)
Red Wolf Country, 5316(F)
Shawn and Keeper and the Birthday Party, 6472(F)
Shawn and Keeper Show-and-Tell, 6473(F)
Snuggle Wuggle, 727(F)
The Waterfall, 2953(F)
What Do You Love? 728(F)
What Newt Could Do for Turtle, 2398(F)
Who Bop? 2399(F)
Wiggle Waggle, 5317(F)
London, Jonathan (jt. author). *Thirteen Moons on Turtle's Back*, 11929

London, Sara. *Firehorse Max*, 4216(F)

Long, Barbara. *Jim Thorpe*, 13674

Long, Cathryn J. *The Middle East in Search of Peace*, 15491

Long, Earlene. *Gone Fishing*, 3777(F)

Long, Laurel. *The Magic Nesting Doll*, 10471(F)

The Mightiest Heart, 10966

Long, Laurie S. *Amy's (Not So) Great Camp-Out*, 2962(F)

Sarah's Incredible Idea, 3347(F)

Long, Lynette. *Dazzling Division*, 20585

Dealing with Addition, 497(F)

Marvelous Multiplication, 20586

Long, Melinda. *Hiccup Snickup*, 4217(F)

When Papa Snores, 3778(F)

Long, Sylvia. *Bugs for Lunch*, 18808

Deck the Hall, 14206

Hawk Hill, 7198(F)

Hush Little Baby, 729(F)

Liplap's Wish, 2397(F)

Sylvia Long's Mother Goose, 894

Ten Little Rabbits, 449(F)

Longfellow, Henry Wadsworth. *The Children's Hour*, 11639

The Children's Own Longfellow, 11640

Hiawatha, 11641

The Midnight Ride of Paul Revere, 11642

Paul Revere's Ride, 11643, 11644

Longfellow, Layne. *Imaginary Menagerie*, 5318(F)

Look, Lenore. *Love as Strong as Ginger*, 3779(F)

Loomis, Christine. *Across America, I Love You*, 3780(F)

Astro Bunnies, 1358(F)

Cowboy Bunnies, 2400(F)

In the Diner, 3285(F)

One Cow Coughs, 498(F)

Rush Hour, 3286(F)

Loomis, Jennifer A. *A Duck in a Tree*, 19313

Loos, Pamela. *Elizabeth Cady Stanton*, 13193

Lopez, Donald, ed. *Flight*, 21086

Lopez, Loretta. *The Birthday Swap*, 5709(F)

Say Hola to Spanish, 13981

Say Hola to Spanish at the Circus, 2925(F)

Lopshire, Robert. *Big Max*, 6579(F)

Put Me in the Zoo, 6474(F)

Lorbiecki, Marybeth. *Children of Vietnam*, 15182

Of Things Natural, Wild, and Free, 13315

Sister Anne's Hands, 5517(F)

Lorbiecki, Marybeth (jt. author). *Earthwise at Home*, 16961

Lord, Bette Bao. *In the Year of the Boar and Jackie Robinson*, 7352(F)

Lord, John Vernon. *The Giant Jam Sandwich*, 4218(F)

Lord, Richard. *Germany*, 15326, 15327

Lord, Trevor. *Amazing Bikes*, 22162

Loredo, Betsy. *Faraway Families*, 7473(F)

Loredo, Elizabeth. *Boogie Bones*, 1359(F)

Lorenz, Albert. *Buried Blueprints*, 21934

Lorenz, Lee. *Driving Me Crazy*, 21830

A Weekend in the City, 2401(F)

Lorraine, Walter. *McBroom Tells the Truth*, 9850(F)

Los, Marek. *Lookin' for Bird in the Big City*, 4613(F)

Losi, Carol A. *The 512 Ants on Sullivan Street*, 20587(F)

Losordo, Stephen. *Cow Moo Me*, 5319(F)

Lott, Sheena. *Midnight in the Mountains*, 4482(F)

Lottridge, Celia B. *Music for the Tsar of the Sea*, 11100

Something Might Be Hiding, 5019(F)

Ten Small Tales, 10572

Ticket to Canada, 8937(F)

The Wind Wagon, 9303(F)

Lottridge, Celia B., reteller. *The Name of the Tree*, 10691

LoTurco, Laura. *Huskings, Quiltings, and Barn Raisings*, 16171

Shaker Villages, 17169

Lougheed, Robert. *Mustang, Wild Spirit of the West*, 7218(F)

San Domingo, 7219(F)

Louie, Ai-Ling, reteller. *Yeh-Shen*, 10764

Louis, Allen. *Calico Bush*, 9194(F)

Louis, Linda L. (jt. author). *In the Paint*, 21575

Louise, Karen. *The Deep*, 5106(F)

Loulan, JoAnn. *Period*, 18265

Loumaye, Jacqueline. *Chagall*, 13905

Degas, 13906

Van Gogh, 13907

Lound, Karen. *Girl Power in the Family*, 17719

Lourie, Peter. *Erie Canal*, 16713

The Lost Treasure of Captain Kidd, 6954(F)

Lost Treasure of the Inca, 15758

Mississippi River, 15891

Rio Grande, 15892

Yukon River, 15588

Love, Ann. *Fishing*, 19848

Kids and Grandparents, 21451

The Kids Book of the Far North, 15816

The Kids Guide to the Millennium, 14346

Love, Ann (jt. author). *Farming*, 20052

Forestry, 20438

The Kids Camp-fire Book, 22167

The Kids Summer Games Book, 21998

The Kids Summer Handbook, 21432

Mining, 21030

Love, D. Anne. *Bess's Log Cabin Quilt*, 9401(F)

I Remember the Alamo, 9587(F)

My Lone Star Summer, 8748(F)

Three Against the Tide, 9486(F)

A Year Without Rain, 9588(F)

Love, Hallie N., reteller. *Watakame's Journey*, 11407

Love, Judy. *First Day Jitters*, 3100(F)

Kirby Kelvin and the Not-Laughing Lessons, 4105(F)

Loveday, John. *Goodbye, Buffalo Sky*, 9402(F)

Lovejoy, Sharon. *Roots, Shoots, Buckets and Boots*, 21766

Lovelace, Maud H. *Betsy-Tacy*, 10103(F)

The Trees Kneel at Christmas, 9745(F)

Loverance, Rowena. *Ancient Greece*, 14689

Loveridge, Emma. *Egypt*, 15507

Lovett, Sarah. *Extremely Weird Endangered Species*, 19402

Low, Alice. *The Macmillan Book of Greek Gods and Heroes*, 11485

Stories to Tell a Five-Year-Old, 1360(F)

The Witch Who Was Afraid of Witches, 9746(F)

Low, Alice, ed. *The Family Read-Aloud Christmas Treasury*, 5866

Stories to Tell a Six-Year-Old, 10104(F)

Low, Joseph. *Mice Twice*, 2402(F)

Low, Robert. *Peoples of the Desert*, 20412

Peoples of the Mountains, 20503

Peoples of the Rain Forest, 20465

Peoples of the Savanna, 20539

Low, William. *Chinatown*, 5635(F)

Lowe, David. *Australia*, 15242

Lowe, David (jt. author). *The Australian Outback and Its People*, 15229

Lowell, Susan. *The Bootmaker and the Elves*, 1361(F)

Cindy Ellen, 10452(F)

I Am Lavina Cumming, 9589(F)

Little Red Cowboy Hat, 4219(F)

The Three Little Javelinas, 2403(F)

The Tortoise and the Jackrabbit, 11066(F)

Lowenheim, Al. *The Girls and Boys Book About Good and Bad Behavior*, 17609
Lowenstein, Sallie. *Evan's Voice*, 10210(F)
Lowery, Linda. *Aunt Clara Brown*, 12705
Earth Day, 5636
Earthwise at Home, 16961
Georgia O'Keeffe, 12276
Laurie Tells, 8478(F)
Martin Luther King Day, 12746
Pablo Picasso, 12281
Somebody Somewhere Knows My Name, 8749(F)
Twist with a Burger, Jitter with a Bug, 3287(F)
Wilma Mankiller, 12978
Lowry, Judith. *Home to Medicine Mountain*, 9178(F)
Lowry, Lois. *Anastasia, Absolutely*, 9919(F)
Anastasia at This Address, 9920(F)
Anastasia on Her Own, 9921(F)
Anastasia's Chosen Career, 9922(F)
Attaboy, Sam! 9923(F)
Gathering Blue, 7926(F)
Looking Back, 12565
Number the Stars, 9672(F)
The One Hundredth Thing About Caroline, 9924(F)
See You Around, Sam! 9925(F)
Stay! Keeper's Story, 7927(F)
Switcharound, 9926(F)
Us and Uncle Fraud, 7474(F)
Zooman Sam! 9927(F)
Lowry, Patrick. *The Amazing Adventures of Teddy Tum Tum*, 1852(F)
Lubach, Vanessa. *Hurricane!* 4478(F)
Lubar, David. *Hidden Talents*, 7928(F)
Lubin, Leonard. *R-T, Margaret, and the Rats of NIMH*, 7663(F)
Racso and the Rats of NIMH, 7664(F)
Luborsky, Ellen (jt. author). *Ups and Downs*, 17715
Luby, Thia. *Children's Book of Yoga*, 18198
Lucado, Max. *Small Gifts in God's Hands*, 17300
Lucas, Cedric. *Big Wind Coming!* 2927(F)
The Crab Man, 4862(F)
Frederick Douglass, 12713
The Leaving, 4843(F)
Night Golf, 5034(F)
What's in Aunt Mary's Room? 3707(F)
Lucas, Daryl J. *The Baker Bible Dictionary for Kids*, 17204
Lucas, Eileen. *The Cherokees*, 15992
Civil Rights, 17041
Cracking the Wall, 17042

Elizabeth Dole, 13149
Vincent van Gogh, 12307
Lucas, Gail. *The White Curtain*, 1000(F)
Lucht, Irmgard. *The Red Poppy*, 20247
Luciani, Brigitte. *How Will We Get to the Beach?* 2954(F)
Ludlow, Patricia. *Meet the Monsters*, 21964
Ludwig, Warren. *The Cowboy and the Black-Eyed Pea*, 10439(F)
Ludy, Mark. *The Grump*, 3288(F)
Luenn, Nancy. *Celebrations of Light*, 17384
A Gift for Abuelita, 4746(F)
The Miser on the Mountain, 11265
Mother Earth, 4488(F)
Nessa's Fish, 4747(F)
Nessa's Story, 4748(F)
Otter Play, 5320(F)
Songs for the Ancient Forest, 1362(F)
Squish! 20381
Luger, Harriett. *Bye, Bye, Bali Kai*, 8479(F)
Lukes, Bonnie L. *How to Be a Reasonably Thin Teenage Girl*, 18199
Luks, Peggy. *Me and Einstein*, 8880(F)
Lum, Bernice. *Pippin and the Bones*, 6422(F)
Pippin Takes a Bath, 2255(F)
Lum, Kate. *What! Cried Granny*, 731(F)
Lumpkin, Susan. *Small Cats*, 19096
Lumpkin, Susan (jt. author). *Dangerous Animals*, 18971
Lund, Gary. *Coyote Stories for Children*, 11304
Lund, Jillian. *Two Cool Coyotes*, 2404(F)
Lund, John. *Malinda Martha Meets Mariposa*, 12039
Lund, Kristin. *Star Wars, Episode I*, 14314
Lunelli, Giuliano. *Puss in Boots*, 10880
The Special Gifts, 5829(F)
Teddy's Easter Secret, 5977(F)
Lunge-Larsen, Lise. *The Legend of the Lady Slipper*, 9167
The Troll with No Heart in His Body, 11129
Lunn, Carolyn. *A Whisper Is Quiet*, 6475(F)
Lunn, Janet. *Charlotte*, 16203
Come to the Fair, 3289(F)
The Hollow Tree, 9240(F)
Lupton, Hugh, reteller. *Tales of Wisdom and Wonder*, 10573
Lurie, Alison. *The Black Geese*, 11101
Lurie, Jon. *Allison's Story*, 10105
Fundamental Snowboarding, 22283

Lush, Debbie (jt. author). *Moon Tales*, 10619
Luthardt, Kevin. *Mine!* 5020(F)
Luthringer, Chelsea. *So What Is Citizenship Anyway?* 17043
Lutz, Norma Jean. *Britney Spears*, 12471
Business and Industry, 12676
Celine Dion, 12376
The History of Third Parties, 17098
J. C. Watts, 12815
John Paul Jones, 12914
Lychack, William. *Russia*, 15424
Lydecker, Laura. *Mouse in the House*, 4080(F)
Lye, Keith. *Coasts*, 20382
Deserts, 20413
Mountains, 20504
The World Today, 14587
Lynch, Amy. *Nashville*, 16874
Lynch, Anne. *Great Buildings*, 21135
Lynch, Chris. *Gold Dust*, 10345(F)
The Wolf Gang, 9928(F)
Lynch, P. J. *The Candlewick Book of Fairy Tales*, 10429
Catkin, 10399
The Christmas Miracle of Jonathan Toomey, 5957(F)
East o' the Sun and West o' the Moon, 11121
Grandad's Prayers of the Earth, 3957(F)
The King of Ireland's Son, 10948
Melisande, 10468(F)
The Names Upon the Harp, 10994
When Jessie Came Across the Sea, 9043(F)
Lynch, Tom. *Fables from Aesop*, 11067
Lynch, Wayne. *Arctic Alphabet*, 15817
Eagles, 19330
Penguins! 19377
Lynch, Wendy. *Bach*, 12317
Dr. Seuss, 12538
Mozart, 12334
Lyne, Alice. *A My Name Is . . .*, 84(F)
Lyne, Sandford, comp. *Ten-Second Rainshowers*, 11645
Lynn, Sara. *Clothes*, 208(F)
Play with Paint, 21585
Lynne, Cherry. *Flute's Journey*, 19249
Lyon, David. *The Biggest Truck*, 5583(F)
The Runaway Duck, 2405(F)
Lyon, George E. *Ada's Pal*, 5321(F)
Book, 11646
Come a Tide, 3290(F)
Counting on the Woods, 499
Dreamplace, 4749(F)
Five Live Bongos, 3781(F)
One Lucky Girl, 2955(F)
The Outside Inn, 1363(F)
A Regular Rolling Noah, 4220(F)
A Sign, 17776
Together, 4025

A Traveling Cat, 5322(F)
Who Came Down That Road?
    3291(F)
A Wordful Child, 12567
Lyon, Tammie. *An Alligator Ate My
    Brother*, 1442(F)
Grumpy Bunnies, 806(F)
Lyons, Mary E. *Catching the Fire*,
    12302
Dear Ellen Bee, 9487(F)
Master of Mahogany, 12220
Painting Dreams, 12231
Starting Home, 12286
Stitching Stars, 12287
Lyons, Mary E., ed. *Raw Head,
    Bloody Bones*, 11364
Talking with Tebe, 12241
Lytle, John. *Robin Hood and His
    Merry Men*, 10968
Lytle, Robert A. *Three Rivers Cross-
    ing*, 7929(F)

Ma, Wenhai. *The Swan's Gift*,
    1554(F)
Maass, Robert. *Fire Fighters*, 17816
Garbage, 16982
Garden, 21767
*Mommy's in the Hospital Having a
    Baby*, 18043
Tugboats, 21366
UN Ambassador, 12841
When Autumn Comes, 4489
When Summer Comes, 4490
McAfee, Toby. *Say No and Know
    Why*, 17896
McAllister, Angela. *The Clever Cow-
    boy*, 1364(F)
McAllister, Margaret. *Hold My Hand
    and Run*, 9108(F)
McAllister-Stammen, Jo Ellen. *Bears
    Out There*, 1528(F)
Teddy Bear Tears, 630(F)
Macaulay, David. *BAAA*, 7930(F)
Black and White, 10262(F)
Building Big, 21136
Building the Book Cathedral,
    21137
Castle, 14776
Cathedral, 13947
City, 14727
Mill, 16261
The New Way Things Work, 21043
Pyramid, 14639
Rome Antics, 9059(F)
Ship, 21367
Shortcut, 3292(F)
Unbuilding, 21138
Underground, 21139
The Way Things Work, 21251
Why the Chicken Crossed the Road,
    2406(F)
Macaulay, Kitty. *The Butterflies'
    Promise*, 3830(F)
McBee, Jane. *All About Seeds*, 20272
McBratney, Sam. *The Caterpillow
    Fight*, 2407(F)

The Dark at the Top of the Stairs,
    2408(F)
Guess How Much I Love You,
    732(F)
I'm Sorry, 4026(F)
Just One! 2409(F)
Just You and Me, 2410(F)
Once There Was a Hoodie, 1365(F)
McBratney, Sam, reteller. *Celtic
    Myths*, 11011
McBride, Angus. *Growing Up in
    Ancient Egypt*, 14618
Growing Up in Viking Times,
    15468
MacBride, Roger L. *In the Land of
    the Big Red Apple*, 9403(F)
Little Farm in the Ozarks, 9404(F)
Little House on Rocky Edge,
    9405(F)
New Dawn on Rocky Ridge,
    9406(F)
McBrier, Page. *Beatrice's Goat*,
    4750(F)
Maccabe, Richard. *Addition*, 20596
Circles, 20605
Numbers, 20638
Subtraction, 20623
McCaffery, Janet. *Hey-How for Hal-
    loween!* 11832
McCain, Becky Ray. *Grandmother's
    Dreamcatcher*, 733(F)
McCall, Francis X., Jr. (jt. author).
    Unraveling Fibers, 21174
McCall, Rebecca Haley.
    Shelterwood, 4541(F)
McCann, Jerry. *Girls Who Rocked
    the World 2*, 13742
Maccarone, Grace. *Cars! Cars! Cars!*
    5584(F)
A Child Was Born, 17427
The Gym Day Winner, 6476(F)
I Shop with My Daddy, 6477(F)
The Lunch Box Surprise, 6478(F)
Monster Math Picnic, 500(F)
Monster Math School Time, 209(F)
Monster Money, 501(F)
My Tooth Is About to Fall Out,
    6479(F)
Recess Mess, 6480(F)
Sharing Time Troubles, 6481(F)
Maccarone, Grace (jt. author). *The
    Best Teacher in the World*,
    5486(F)
McCarthy, Betty. *Utah*, 16626
McCarthy, Bobette. *The Tantrum*,
    5009(F)
McCarthy, Cathy. *The Ojibwa*, 15993
McCarthy, Pat. *Daniel Boone*, 12083
Thomas Paine, 12943
MacCarthy, Patricia. *Boom, Baby,
    Boom, Boom!* 1387(F)
Cat and Kit, 5292(F)
Down the Dragon's Tongue,
    3304(F)
McCarthy, Ralph F. *The Inch-High
    Samurai*, 10822
The Moon Princess, 10823

McCarthy-Tucker, Sherri. *Coping
    with Special-Needs Classmates*,
    17921
McCarty, Nick, reteller. *The Iliad*,
    11486
McCarty, Peter. *Baby Steps*, 3293(F)
Little Bunny on the Move, 2411(F)
Night Driving, 3593(F)
McCaughrean, Geraldine. *The
    Bronze Cauldron*, 10574
The Crystal Pool, 10575
God's Kingdom, 17301
God's People, 17302
The Golden Hoard, 11451
Grandma Chickenlegs, 11102
Greek Gods and Goddesses, 11487
Greek Myths, 11488
*How the Reindeer Got Their
    Antlers*, 5867(F)
My First Oxford Book of Stories,
    10453(F)
The Nutcracker, 14293
A Pack of Lies, 7931(F)
*The Random House Book of Stories
    from the Ballet*, 14294
The Silver Treasure, 10576
Starry Tales, 10577
The Stones Are Hatching, 7932(F)
Unicorns! Unicorns! 2412(F)
McCaughrean, Geraldine, adapt.
    Moby Dick, 9304(F)
McCaul, Laura. *I Can Sign My ABCs*,
    21(F)
McCave, Marta E. *Counting Heads,
    and More*, 17116
McClain, Margaret S. *Bellboy*,
    6955(F)
McClintock, Barbara. *Animal Fables
    from Aesop*, 11068
Aunt Pitty Patty's Piggy, 1779(F)
*The Fantastic Drawings of
    Danielle*, 4751(F)
The Gingerbread Man, 10945
A Little Princess, 4920(F)
The Tale of Tricky Fox, 966(F)
When Mindy Saved Hanukkah,
    6086(F)
McClintock, Mike. *Stop That Ball!*
    6482(F)
McCloskey, Kevin. *Mrs. Fitz's
    Flamingos*, 1366(F)
McCloskey, Robert. *Burt Dow,
    Deep-Water Man*, 4221(F)
Henry Reed, Inc., 9973(F)
Homer Price, 9929(F)
Lentil, 4222(F)
One Morning in Maine, 3782(F)
Time of Wonder, 4491(F)
McClung, Robert M. *Lost Wild
    America*, 19403
McClure, Gillian. *Selkie*, 11012
McClure, Judy. *Healers and
    Researchers*, 13217
McCollum, Sean. *Australia*, 15243,
    15244
Kenya, 14938, 14939
Poland, 15276, 15277

McConnell, Mary. *A Quilt for Elizabeth*, 3919(F)
McCord, David. *All Day Long*, 11647
One at a Time, 11648
McCord, Kathleen G. *Adam Mouse's Book of Poems*, 11972
Don't Be Afraid, Amanda, 7966(F)
McCormick, Anita Louise. *The Internet*, 21219
McCormick, Dell J. *Paul Bunyan Swings His Axe*, 11365
McCormick, Wendy. *Daddy, Will You Miss Me?* 3783(F)
The Night You Were Born, 3784(F)
McCourt, Lisa. *Chicken Soup for Little Souls*, 5021(F)
I Love You, Stinky Face, 734(F)
I Miss You, Stinky Face, 3785(F)
It's Time for School, Stinky Face, 5518(F)
The Rain Forest Counts! 502(F)
McCourt, Lisa, adapt. *Della Splatnuk, Birthday Girl*, 5710(F)
McCourt, Lisa (jt. author). *The Long and Short of It*, 350(F)
McCoy, Elin. *Cards for Kids*, 22236
McCrady, Lady. *Science Sensations*, 18370
McCreary, Jane. *Round and Round the Money Goes*, 16918
McCue, Lisa. *Bunny's Noisy Book*, 1894(F)
Corduroy's Halloween, 6006(F)
The Lion and the Mouse, 11064
Mama Loves, 6353(F)
My Mom Made Me Go to Camp, 3101(F)
The Perfect Christmas Gift, 5797(F)
Polar Babies, 19064
The Puppy Who Wanted a Boy, 5935(F)
Sebastian (Super Sleuth) and the Bone to Pick Mystery, 6792(F)
Snot Stew, 8181(F)
McCullough, L. E. *"Now I Get It!" Vol. I*, 12027
Plays from Fairy Tales, 12028
Plays from Mythology, 12029
Plays of America from American Folklore for Children Grades K–6, 12030
Plays of the Wild West, 12031
Stories of the Songs of Christmas, 14207
McCully, Emily Arnold. *Amzat and His Brothers*, 11062
Annie Flies the Birthday Bike, 6314(F)
Beautiful Warrior, 4752(F)
Beavers Beware! 6220(F)
Best Friend Insurance, 7746(F)
Black Is Brown Is Tan, 3503(F)
The Boston Coffee Party, 16212
The Divide, 12515
The Field of the Dogs, 8006(F)
Fifth Grade Magic, 7747(F)

First Snow, 2413(F)
Four Hungry Kittens, 924(F)
Gertrude's Pocket, 8758(F)
The Grandma Mix-Up, 6483(F)
Grandmas at Bat, 6484(F)
Grandma's at the Lake, 6485(F)
The Grandpa Days, 3533(F)
The Halloween Candy Mystery, 6963(F)
How to Eat Fried Worms, 9976(F)
Hurry! 3294(F)
I Dance in My Red Pajamas, 3712(F)
Leo the Magnificat, 5339(F)
The Magic Mean Machine, 9865(F)
Mail-Order Wings, 7748(F)
Mirette and Bellini Cross Niagara Falls, 4753(F)
Mirette on the High Wire, 4754(F)
Monk Camps Out, 2414(F)
More Fifth Grade Magic, 7749(F)
Mouse Practice, 5022(F)
My Real Family, 2415(F)
Old Home Day, 7440(F)
An Outlaw Thanksgiving, 9407(F)
Picnic, 925(F)
The Pirate Queen, 12145
Popcorn at the Palace, 4223(F)
Rabbit Pirates, 1983(F)
School, 926(F)
Speak Up, Blanche! 2416(F)
Starring Mirette and Bellini, 1367(F)
Ten Go Tango, 422(F)
Wanted, 10188(F)
McCurdy, Michael. *An Algonquian Year*, 15994
American Tall Tales, 11370
The Bone Man, 11300
The Gettysburg Address, 16420
Giants in the Land, 16096
Hannah's Farm, 4492(F)
Iron Horses, 21335
Lucy's Christmas, 5831(F)
The Sailor's Alphabet, 21368
The Seasons Sewn, 16350
Trapped by the Ice, 15818
War and the Pity of War, 11670
The Way West, 16336
McCusker, Paul. *Arin's Judgment*, 7933(F)
McCutcheon, John. *Happy Adoption Day!* 3786
McCutcheon, Marc. *The Beast in You!* 14505
Grandfather's Christmas Camp, 5868(F)
McDaniel, Lurlene. *To Live Again*, 8903(F)
McDaniel, Melissa. *Arizona*, 16627
The Sac and Fox Indians, 15995
Spike Lee, 12412
W. E. B. DuBois, 12719
McDermott, Dennis. *Gilly Martin the Fox*, 11002
The Golden Goose, 10927

McDermott, Gerald. *Anansi, the Spider*, 10692
Coyote, 11266
The Fox and the Stork, 11069
Musicians of the Sun, 11408
Raven, 11267
The Stonecutter, 10824
Zomo the Rabbit, 10693
MacDonald, Alan. *Beware of the Bears!* 2417(F)
The Pig in a Wig, 2418(F)
MacDonald, Amy. *Cousin Ruth's Tooth*, 4224(F)
Let's Go, 3295(F)
Little Beaver and the Echo, 2419(F)
No More Nice, 9930(F)
Rachel Fister's Blister, 4225(F)
The Spider Who Created the World, 2420(F)
MacDonald, Betty. *Hello, Mrs. Piggle-Wiggle*, 7934(F)
McDonald, Brigitte. *Fun with Numbers*, 551
Fun with Patterns, 232
McDonald, Brix. *Riding on the Wind*, 9408(F)
MacDonald, Elizabeth. *Dilly-Dally and the Nine Secrets*, 2421(F)
John's Picture, 1368(F)
Mike's Kite, 503(F)
The Wolf Is Coming! 2422(F)
MacDonald, Fiona. *Albert Einstein*, 13275
Ancient African Town, 15035
A Child's Eye View of History, 14347
Exploring the World, 12060
A Greek Temple, 14690
How Would You Survive as an Aztec? 15632
I Wonder Why Greeks Built Temples and Other Questions About Ancient Greece, 14691
I Wonder Why Romans Wore Togas and Other Questions About Ancient Rome, 14728
Inca Town, 15759
Magellan, 12141
Marco Polo, 12148
A Medieval Castle, 14777
Medieval Cathedral, 14778
The Middle Ages, 14779
The Roman Colosseum, 14729
A Samurai Castle, 15131
A 16th Century Mosque, 15492
The Stone Age News, 14506
Women in a Changing World, 14588
Women in Ancient Egypt, 14640
Women in Ancient Greece, 14692
Women in Ancient Rome, 14730
Women in Medieval Times, 14780
Women in 19th-Century America, 15855
Women in 19th-Century Europe, 14589

MacDonald, George. *At the Back of the North Wind*, 7935(F)
The Golden Key, 10454(F)
The Light Princess, 10455(F), 10456(F)
The Princess and the Goblin, 10457(F)
Sir Gibbie, 9109(F)
MacDonald, James D. (jt. author). *Groogleman*, 10177(F)
Knight's Wyrd, 7708(F)
MacDonald, Kate. *The Anne of Green Gables Cookbook*, 21715
MacDonald, Margaret Read. *The Old Woman Who Lived in a Vinegar Bottle*, 10458
Peace Tales, 10579
Pickin' Peas, 2423(F)
The Round Book, 14251
The Skit Book, 12032
Slop! A Welsh Folktale, 11013
Tuck-Me-In Tales, 735
MacDonald, Margaret Read, comp. *Earth Care*, 10578
MacDonald, Margaret Read, reteller. *The Girl Who Wore Too Much*, 10840
McDonald, Mary Ann. *Anacondas*, 18765
Boas, 18766
Chimpanzees, 19003
Cobras, 18767
Doves, 19250
Garter Snakes, 18768
Grasshoppers, 19463
Grizzlies, 19054
Jays, 19251
Lemurs, 19004
Leopards, 19097
Reindeer, 19154
Sunflowers, 20248
Toucans, 19252
Woodpeckers, 19253
MacDonald, Maryann. *Hedgehog Bakes a Cake*, 6486(F)
Rosie and the Poor Rabbits, 2424(F)
Rosie's Baby Tooth, 2425(F)
Secondhand Star, 10106(F)
McDonald, Megan. *Beezy and Funnybone*, 6487(F)
Beezy at Bat, 6488(F)
Beezy Magic, 6489(F)
The Bone Keeper, 7936(F)
Insects Are My Life, 5323(F)
Judy Moody, 10107(F)
Lucky Star, 6490(F)
My House Has Stars, 736(F)
The Night Iguana Left Home, 2426(F)
The Potato Man, 3296(F)
Shadows in the Glasshouse, 16154(F)
Tundra Mouse, 5869(F)
Whoo-oo Is It? 5324(F)
McDonald, Mercedes. *How Snake Got His Hiss*, 1102(F)

Macdonald, Robert. *Islands of the Pacific Rim and Their People*, 15245
MacDonald, Suse. *Alphabatics*, 85(F)
Elephants on Board, 2427(F)
I Love You, 11651
Look Whooo's Counting, 504(F)
Nanta's Lion, 4755(F)
Peck Slither and Slide, 18830
Sea Shapes, 343(F)
Who Says a Dog Goes Bow-Wow? 5182
McDonnell, Christine. *It's a Deal, Dogboy*, 8750(F)
McDonnell, Flora. *Flora McDonnell's ABC*, 86(F)
I Love Animals, 2428(F)
I Love Boats, 5585(F)
The Mermaid's Purse, 11961
Splash! 2429(F)
McDonnell, Janet. *Animal Camouflage*, 18886
Animal Communication, 18894
McDonough, Yona Z. *The Dollhouse Magic*, 9590(F)
Sisters in Strength, 12677
McDowell, Robert E. (jt. author). *Nihancan's Feast of Beaver*, 11263
MacEachern, Stephen. *The Family Tree Detective*, 17650
McElfresh, Lynn E. *Can You Feel the Thunder?* 8751(F)
McElligott, Matt. *The Spooky Book*, 4261(F)
McElligott, Matthew. *The Truth About Cousin Ernie's Head*, 3787(F)
Uncle Frank's Pit, 4226(F)
McElmurry, Jill. *Mad About Plaid*, 1369(F)
McElrath-Eslick, Lori. *Da Wei's Treasure*, 10743
Does God Know How to Tie Shoes? 17172(F)
Mommy Poems, 11655
McElroy, Lisa Tucker. *Meet My Grandmother*, 17833, 12939, 12877
McEvoy, Greg. *The Ice Cream King*, 4227(F)
McEwen, Katharine. *Cows in the Kitchen*, 9818(F)
Here Comes Tabby Cat, 6598(F)
I Know How My Cells Make Me Grow, 18076
I Know How We Fight Germs, 17993
I Know Where My Food Goes, 18102
I Know Why I Brush My Teeth, 18188
McFarland, Lyn Rossiter. *The Pirate's Parrot*, 7937(F)
McFarlane, Marilyn. *Sacred Myths*, 17205

McFarlane, Sheryl. *Waiting for the Whales*, 3788(F)
McGaffey, Leta. *Honduras*, 15673
McGaw, Laurie. *Journey to Ellis Island*, 17547
Polar the Titanic Bear, 16486
Something to Remember Me By, 3540(F)
McGee, John F. *Berries, Nuts and Seeds*, 20268
McGee, Marni. *Forest Child*, 1370(F)
McGeorge, Constance W. *Boomer Goes to School*, 5325(F)
Boomer's Big Day, 5326(F)
Boomer's Big Surprise, 2430(F)
Snow Riders, 1371(F)
Waltz of the Scarecrows, 3297(F)
McGibbon, Robin. *New Kids on the Block*, 12425
McGill, Alice. *In the Hollow of Your Hand*, 14167
Molly Bannaky, 12848
McGill, Allyson. *The Swedish Americans*, 17577
MacGill-Callahan, Sheila. *The Last Snake in Ireland*, 1372(F)
McGinley, Sharon. *The Friendly Beasts*, 14208
McGinley-Nally, Sharon. *Django*, 11327
First Snow, Magic Snow, 11082
Hazel's Circle, 5181(F)
My Grandmother's Journey, 4617(F)
Pigs at Odds, 20579(F)
Pigs Go to Market, 9707(F)
Pigs in the Pantry, 1775(F)
Pigs on a Blanket, 1776(F)
Pigs Will Be Pigs, 1777(F)
McGinty, Alice B. *Software Designer*, 17788
Staying Healthy, 18186
McGirr, Nancy (jt. author). *Out of the Dump*, 15663
McGough, Roger. *Until I Met Dudley*, 5586(F)
McGovern, Ann. *If You Lived in Colonial Times*, 16155
If You Lived with the Sioux Indians, 15996
If You Sailed on the Mayflower, 16156
The Lady in the Box, 5870(F)
The Secret Soldier, 13191
Too Much Noise, 11014
McGovern, Ann, adapt. *Stone Soup*, 10874
McGowan, Gary (jt. author). *Breaking Ground, Breaking Silence*, 16690
McGowen, Tom. *Adventures in Archaeology*, 14536
The Battle for Iwo Jima, 14866
The Beginnings of Science, 18283
Germany's Lightning War, 14867

Giant Stones and Earth Mounds, 14507
"Go for Broke," 14868
Sink the Bismarck, 14869
Yearbooks in Science: 1900–1919, 18284
Yearbooks in Science: 1960–1969, 18285
McGrath, Barbara Barbieri. *The Baseball Counting Book*, 505
The Cheerios Counting Book, 506(F)
McGrath, Bob. *Uh Oh! Gotta Go!* 3298
McGrath, Patrick. *The Lewis and Clark Expedition*, 16086
McGrath, Susan. *The Amazing Things Animals Do*, 18831
McGraw, Eloise. *The Moorchild*, 7938(F)
Tangled Webb, 6956(F)
McGraw, Sheila. *Dolls Kids Can Make*, 21654
Gifts Kids Can Make, 21452
Papier-Mâché for Kids, 21623
Pussycats Everywhere! 5327(F)
McGregor, Barbara. *Purple Delicious Blackberry Jam*, 4263(F)
MacGregor, Cynthia. *Ten Steps to Staying Safe*, 18221
What to Do If You Get Lost, 18222
McGregor, Merideth. *Cowgirl*, 3299
McGrory, Anik. *A Mountain of Blintzes*, 6074(F)
Mouton's Impossible Dream, 2431(F)
MacGrory, Yvonne. *The Secret of the Ruby Ring*, 10211(F)
McGuigan, Mary Ann. *Where You Belong*, 8337(F)
McGuinness, Diane. *My First Phonics Book*, 14099
McGuire, Leslie. *Brush Your Teeth, Please*, 2432(F)
Victims, 17151
McGuire, Paula. *AIDS*, 17982
Alcohol, 17878
McGuirk, Leslie. *Tucker Flips!* 5328(F)
Tucker Off His Rocker, 2433(F)
Machado, Ana María. *Niña Bonita*, 1373(F)
Machlin, Mikki. *My Name Is Not Gussie*, 9591(F)
Macht, Merle. *Doodle Soup*, 11862
Macht, Norman L. *Babe Ruth*, 13498
Christy Mathewson, 13472
Cy Young, 13510
Frank Robinson, 13485
Lou Gehrig, 13454
Roberto Alomar, 13435
Sandra Day O'Connor, 12940
Sojourner Truth, 12791
Ty Cobb, 13446
McInerney, Claire. *Find It!* 14001
McIntosh, Jon. *The Longest Hair in the World*, 1141(F)

Witch Way to the Beach, 1393(F)
Mack, Tracy. *Drawing Lessons*, 8480(F)
Mack-Williams, Kibibi V. *Mossi*, 15036
Mackain, Bonnie. *One Hundred Hungry Ants*, 557(F)
A Remainder of One, 558(F)
Mackay, Claire, sel. *Laughs*, 9931(F)
MacKay, Donald. *The Stone-Faced Boy*, 8645(F)
McKay, Hilary. *The Amber Cat*, 7939(F)
Dog Friday, 7262(F)
Dolphin Luck, 7475(F)
The Exiles, 7476(F)
The Exiles at Home, 7477(F)
The Exiles in Love, 7478(F)
Pirates Ahoy! 4027(F)
Where's Bear? 2434(F)
McKay, Lawrence, Jr. *Caravan*, 4756(F)
McKay, Patricia. *Ireland*, 15359
McKay, Robert A. *Grandfather's Day*, 7528(F)
McKay, Sharon E. *Charlie Wilcox*, 9060(F)
McKay, Sindy. *Ben and Becky in the Haunted House*, 6491(F)
McKay, Sindy, adapt. *Jack and the Beanstalk*, 11015
McKay, Sindy (jt. author). *About the Rain Forest*, 20452
McKay, Susan. *France*, 15312
Spain, 15480
Switzerland, 15278
McKay, Susan (jt. author). *Welcome to Australia*, 15251
McKean, Thomas. *The Secret of the Seven Willows*, 7940(F)
McKeating, Eileen. *Laura Ingalls Wilder*, 12628
Ozzie on His Own, 8310(F)
McKee, David. *Elmer Again*, 2435(F)
Elmer and the Kangaroo, 2436(F)
Elmer and the Lost Teddy Bear, 2437(F)
Elmer and Wilbur, 2438(F)
Elmer in the Snow, 2439(F)
Elmer Takes Off, 2440(F)
I Can Too! 2441(F)
Zebra's Hiccups, 2442(F)
McKee, Tim. *No More Strangers Now*, 14990
Mackel, Kathy. *Can of Worms*, 10212(F)
Eggs in One Basket, 10213(F)
A Season of Comebacks, 10346(F)
McKellar, Shona, comp. *Playtime Rhymes*, 858
McKellar, Shona, ed. *A Child's Book of Lullabies*, 737(F)
McKelvey, Douglas Kaine. *The Angel Knew Papa and the Dog*, 7941(F)

Macken, Walter. *Island of the Great Yellow Ox*, 6957(F)
McKenley, Yvonne. *A Taste of the Caribbean*, 21716
McKenna, A. T. *Corvette*, 21305
Jaguar, 21306
McKenna, Colleen O'Shaughnessy. *Camp Murphy*, 8338(F)
Fifth Grade, 8752(F)
Live from the Fifth Grade, 10108(F)
Mother Murphy, 9932(F)
McKenna, Virginia. *Back to the Blue*, 5329(F)
McKerns, Dorothy. *The Kid's Guide to Good Grammar*, 14040
Mackey, Stephen. *Cat Up a Tree*, 11794
McKibbon, Hugh William. *The Token Gift*, 9002(F)
McKie, Roy. *Mr. Wizard's Supermarket Science*, 18321
McKie, Todd. *First He Made the Sun*, 17332
Mackin, Bob. *Record-Breaking Baseball Trivia*, 22105
McKinley, Robin. *The Door in the Hedge*, 10459(F)
MacKinnon, Christy. *Silent Observer*, 17922
MacKinnon, Debbie. *Eye Spy Colors*, 282(F)
Eye Spy Shapes, 344(F)
My Day, 3300(F)
McKissack, Fredrick (jt. author). *Booker T. Washington*, 12813
Carter G. Woodson, 12823
Christmas in the Big House, Christmas in the Quarters, 16262
Frederick Douglass, 12711
George Washington Carver, 13255
Ida B. Wells-Barnett, 12818
Jesse Owens, 13665
Langston Hughes, 12552
Let My People Go, 9306(F)
Louis Armstrong, 12347
Madam C. J. Walker, 12810
Marian Anderson, 12346
Martin Luther King, Jr., 12747
Mary Church Terrell, 12786
Mary McLeod Bethune, 12703
Messy Bessey's Family Reunion, 6493(F)
Messy Bessey's Holidays, 6494(F)
Paul Robeson, 12453
Rebels Against Slavery, 16263
Satchel Paige, 13476
Sojourner Truth, 12792
Zora Neale Hurston, 12554
McKissack, Patricia. *Booker T. Washington*, 12813
Can You Imagine? 12568
Carter G. Woodson, 12823
Christmas in the Big House, Christmas in the Quarters, 16262
Color Me Dark, 9592(F)
The Dark-Thirty, 11366

Frederick Douglass, 12711
George Washington Carver, 13255
The Honest-to-Goodness Truth, 5023(F)
Ida B. Wells-Barnett, 12818
Jesse Owens, 13665
Langston Hughes, 12552
Let My People Go, 9306(F)
Louis Armstrong, 12347
Ma Dear's Aprons, 4757(F)
Madam C. J. Walker, 12810
Marian Anderson, 12346
Martin Luther King, Jr., 12747
Mary Church Terrell, 12786
Mary McLeod Bethune, 12703
The Maya, 15674
Messy Bessey's Family Reunion, 6493(F)
Messy Bessey's Holidays, 6494(F)
Monkey-Monkey's Trick, 6492(F)
Nzingha, 8971(F)
Paul Robeson, 12453
A Picture of Freedom, 9305(F)
Rebels Against Slavery, 16263
Run Away Home, 9409(F)
Satchel Paige, 13476
Sojourner Truth, 12792
Zora Neale Hurston, 12554
MacLachlan, Patricia. *All the Places to Love*, 7479(F)
Arthur, for the Very First Time, 9933(F)
Cassie Binegar, 7480(F)
The Facts and Fictions of Minna Pratt, 8753(F)
Journey, 8481(F)
Mama One, Mama Two, 3789(F)
Sarah, Plain and Tall, 9410(F)
Seven Kisses in a Row, 7481(F)
The Sick Day, 3790(F)
Skylark, 9411(F)
Three Names, 4758(F)
Through Grandpa's Eyes, 3791(F)
Tomorrow's Wizard, 7942(F)
Unclaimed Treasures, 8754(F)
McLain, Gary. *The Indian Way*, 9168(F)
McLaren, Chesley. *You Forgot Your Skirt, Amelia Bloomer!* 4627(F)
McLaren, Clemence. *Dance for the Land*, 8904(F)
McLarey, Kristina Thermaenius. *When You Take a Pig to a Party*, 5711(F)
McLarey, Myra (jt. author). *When You Take a Pig to a Party*, 5711(F)
McLaughlin, Molly. *Dragonflies*, 19464
Earthworms, Dirt, and Rotten Leaves, 19613
Maclay, Elise. *The Forest Has Eyes*, 310
McLean, Andrew. *Switch Cat*, 5184(F)
Maclean, Colin. *Nursery Rhyme Songbook with Easy Music to*

Play for Piano and Guitar, 840(F)
The Nursery Treasury, 841
McLean, Dirk. *Play Mas! A Carnival ABC*, 87(F)
Maclean, Moira. *Nursery Rhyme Songbook with Easy Music to Play for Piano and Guitar*, 840(F)
The Nursery Treasury, 841
McLean, Mollie. *Adventures of Greek Heroes*, 11489
McLean, Virginia O. (jt. author). *Kenya, Jambo!* 14935
McLellan, Stephanie Simpson. *The Chicken Cat*, 2443(F)
McLenighan, Valjean. *China*, 15071
MacLeod, Elizabeth. *Alexander Graham Bell*, 13238
Bake It and Build It, 21717
Dinosaurs, 14443
Grow It Again, 21768
I Heard a Little Baa, 5330(F)
McLeod, Emilie W. *The Bear's Bicycle*, 2444(F)
MacLeod-Brudenell, Iain. *Animal Crafts*, 21532
Costume Crafts, 21545
McLerran, Alice. *The Ghost Dance*, 15997
Roxaboxen, 3301(F)
McLester, L. Gordon. *The Oneida*, 15998
McLoone, Margo. *Women Explorers of the Air*, 12061
Women Explorers of the Mountains, 12062
Women Explorers of the World, 12063
McLoone, Margo (jt. author). *The Blackbirch Kid's Almanac of Geography*, 14357
McLoughland, Beverly. *A Hippo's a Heap and Other Animal Poems*, 11802
McLoughlin, Wayne. *Here Is the Wetland*, 20367
McLuskey, Krista. *Entrepreneurs*, 13736
McMahon, Patricia. *Dancing Wheels*, 17923
Listen for the Bus, 5024
One Belfast Boy, 15360
Six Words, Many Turtles, and Three Days in Hong Kong, 15072
Summer Tunes, 8905(F)
McMane, Fred. *Hakeem Olajuwon*, 13555
Scottie Pippen, 13564
McManus, Patrick F. *Kid Camping from Aaaaiii! to Zip*, 22169
McMaster, Shawn. *Magic Tricks*, 21786
60 Super Simple Magic Tricks, 21787

McMillan, Brett (jt. author). *Puniddles*, 21882
McMillan, Bruce. *Apples, How They Grow*, 20152
The Baby Zoo, 20026
A Beach for the Birds, 19254
Eating Fractions, 507
Ghost Doll, 1374(F)
Gletta the Foal, 5331(F)
Going on a Whale Watch, 19795
Grandfather's Trolley, 3792(F)
Jelly Beans for Sale, 508
Mouse View, 311(F)
My Horse of the North, 20003
Nights of the Pufflings, 19351
One, Two, One Pair! 509
Penguins at Home, 19378
Puffins Climb, Penguins Rhyme, 19379
Puniddles, 21882
The Remarkable Riderless Runaway Tricycle, 1375(F)
Salmon Summer, 16797
Sense Suspense, 21868
Step by Step, 3793(F)
Summer Ice, 15819
The Weather Sky, 20781
Wild Flamingos, 19255
McMillan, Bruce (jt. author). *The Picture That Mom Drew*, 13908
MacMillan, Dianne. *Destination Los Angeles*, 16798
Missions of the Los Angeles Area, 16799
MacMillan, Dianne M. *Cheetahs*, 19098
Diwali, 17385
Elephants, 19166
Japanese Children's Day and the Obon Festival, 15132
Mardi Gras, 17386
Martin Luther King, Jr. Day, 17387
Mexican Independence Day and Cinco de Mayo, 15633
Presidents Day, 17388
Thanksgiving Day, 17501
MacMillan, Dianne M. (jt. author). *Kwanzaa*, 17356
McMullan, Jim. *The Earth Is Good*, 4412(F)
Hey, Pipsqueak! 1376(F)
No No, Jo! 2445(F)
Papa's Song, 739(F)
McMullan, Kate. *Dinosaur Hunters*, 14444
Hey, Pipsqueak! 1376(F)
If You Were My Bunny, 738(F)
The New Kid at School, 7943(F)
No No, Jo! 2445(F)
Papa's Song, 739(F)
McNair, Joseph. *Barbara Jordan*, 12732
Leontyne Price, 12446
McNair, Sylvia. *Chile*, 15760
Connecticut, 16714
India, 15109
Indonesia, 15183

Korea, 15184

Massachusetts, 16715

New Hampshire, 16716

Rhode Island, 16717

Vermont, 16718

McNamee, Graham. *Nothing Wrong with a Three-Legged Dog*, 8755(F)

McNaught, Harry. *Astronomy Today*, 18403

McNaughton, Colin. *Boo!* 2446(F)

Captain Abdul's Pirate School, 1377(F)

Making Friends with Frankenstein, 11897

Oomph! A Preston Pig Story, 2447(F)

Oops! 2448(F)

Preston's Goal! 2449(F)

Shh! (Don't Tell Mr. Wolf!), 2450(F)

Suddenly! 2451(F)

Who's Been Sleeping in My Porridge? 11898

Who's That Banging on the Ceiling? 1378(F)

Wish You Were Here (And I Wasn't), 11899

Yum! 2452(F)

McNeal, Laura (jt. author). *The Dog Who Lost His Bob*, 5332(F)

McNeal, Tom. *The Dog Who Lost His Bob*, 5332(F)

McNeese, Tim. *America's Early Canals*, 16264

America's First Railroads, 21337

Clippers and Whaling Ships, 21369

The Panama Canal, 15675

McNeil, Florence. *Sail Away*, 1379(F)

McNeil, Keith. *Colonial and Revolution Songbook*, 14168

McNeil, Rusty (jt. author). *Colonial and Revolution Songbook*, 14168

McNeill, Sarah. *The Middle Ages*, 14781

McNey, Martha. *Leslie's Story*, 17924

Macnow, Glen. *David Robinson*, 13571

Ken Griffey, Jr, 13460

The Philadelphia Flyers Hockey Team, 22224

Shaquille O'Neal, 13557

Sports Great Cal Ripken, Jr., 13480

Sports Great Troy Aikman, 13601

McNulty, Faith. *The Elephant Who Couldn't Forget*, 2453(F)

How to Dig a Hole to the Other Side of the World, 20313

How Whales Walked into the Sea, 19796

The Lady and the Spider, 5333(F)

Orphan, 4493

Peeping in the Shell, 19256

A Snake in the House, 5334(F)

When I Lived with Bats, 19029

McPhail, David. *Angel Pig and the Hidden Christmas*, 5945(F)

The Bear's Bicycle, 2444(F)

The Bear's Toothache, 2454(F)

Big Brown Bear, 6495(F)

A Bug, a Bear, and a Boy, 6496(F)

The Day the Sheep Showed Up, 6497(F)

Drawing Lessons from a Bear, 2455(F)

Edward and the Pirates, 1380(F)

Farm Morning, 3302(F)

First Flight, 2456(F)

A Friend for Growl Bear, 1774(F)

A Girl, a Goat, and a Goose, 6498(F)

The Glerp, 2457(F)

The Great Race, 6499(F)

The Ice Cream Store, 11892

If You Were My Bunny, 738(F)

In Flight with David McPhail, 12569

John Pig's Halloween, 6059(F)

Lost! 2458(F)

Mole Music, 2459(F)

On a Starry Night, 1306(F)

The Party, 1381(F)

Pig Pig Gets a Job, 2460(F)

Pigs Ahoy! 2461(F)

Pigs Aplenty, Pigs Galore! 2462(F)

The Puddle, 1382(F)

Sail Away, 1379(F)

Santa's Book of Names, 5871(F)

Sisters, 3794(F)

Snow Lion, 6500(F)

Tall in the Saddle, 1044(F)

Ten Cats Have Hats, 510(F)

Those Can-Do Pigs, 2463(F)

Tinker and Tom and the Star Baby, 1383(F)

Twilight, 1259(F)

Uncle Terrible, 8208(F)

Why a Disguise? 4254(F)

McPhail, David (jt. author). *Sail Away*, 1379(F)

McPherson, Stephanie S. *I Speak for the Women*, 13197

Martha Washington, 13198

Ordinary Genius, 13276

Peace and Bread, 13128

Rooftop Astronomer, 13324

Sisters Against Slavery, 12894

TV's Forgotten Hero, 13279

The Workers' Detective, 13306

McQuade, Jacqueline. *At Preschool with Teddy Bear*, 2464(F)

At the Petting Zoo with Teddy Bear, 2465(F)

Christmas with Teddy Bear, 5872(F)

Teddy Bears Trim the Tree, 5955(F)

McQuarrie, Ralph (jt. author). *Stars Wars*, 10141(F)

McQueen, Kelly (jt. author). *What's a Virus, Anyway?* 17955

McQuillan, Mary. *The Get Well Soon Book*, 2145(F)

MacQuitty, Miranda. *Ocean*, 19828

McRae, Patrick T. *Let's Build a Car*, 21318

Macro, Chris (jt. author). *Hearing in Living Things*, 18820

Ladybug, 19531

Snail, 19608

McSwigan, Marie. *Snow Treasure*, 9673(F)

McTaggart, David. *John's Picture*, 1368(F)

McVilly, Walter, reteller. *Ali Baba and the Forty Thieves*, 11193

Macy, Sue. *A Whole New Ball Game*, 22106

Madama, John. *Clambake*, 16022

Desktop Publishing, 14002

Madavan, Vijay. *Cooking the Indian Way*, 21718

Madden, Don. *The Sun*, 18560

Telephones, Televisions and Toilets, 21243

The Wartville Wizard, 1384(F)

Maddox, Tony. *Ducks Disappearing*, 536(F)

Madgwick, Wendy. *Citymaze!* 21869

Light and Dark, 20874

Magnets and Sparks, 20900

On the Move, 20833

Super Materials, 20287

Super Sound, 20941

Up in the Air, 20671

Water Play, 20738

Madin, Kate (jt. author). *Beneath Blue Waters*, 19641

Madinaveitia, Horacio. *Sir Robert's Little Outing*, 1385(F)

Mado, Michio. *The Magic Pocket*, 11649

Madrigal, Antonio H. *Blanca's Feather*, 5335(F)

The Eagle and the Rainbow, 11409

Erandi's Braids, 4759(F)

Maeno, Itoko. *Minou*, 1809(F)

Shadow and the Ready Time, 5411(F)

Thank You, Meiling, 2753(F)

Maestro, Betsy. *Bats*, 19030

Big City Port, 5587(F)

Bike Trip, 22163

Coming to America, 17578

Ferryboat, 21370

How Do Apples Grow? 20153

A More Perfect Union, 17060

The New Americans, 16157

A Sea Full of Sharks, 19764

Snow Day, 4494

The Story of Clocks and Calendars, 20646

The Story of Money, 16926

The Story of Religion, 17206

Struggle for a Continent, 16158

Taxi, 3303(F)

The Voice of the People, 17117

Why Do Leaves Change Color? 20210

Maestro, Giulio. *Bats*, 19030
Big City Port, 5587(F)
The Dinosaur Is the Biggest Animal That Ever Lived, 18292
Eight Ate, 14048
Ferryboat, 21370
Geese Find the Missing Piece, 21838(F)
Guppies in Tuxedos, 14049
How Do Apples Grow? 20153
In a Pickle and Other Funny Idioms, 14050
It Figures! 14111
The New Americans, 16157
Riddle Roundup, 21837
A Sea Full of Sharks, 19764
Snow Day, 4494
The Story of Clocks and Calendars, 20646
The Story of Money, 16926
The Story of Religion, 17206
Sunshine Makes the Seasons, 18561
Taxi, 3303(F)
Too Hot to Hoot, 14052
Tornado Alert, 20684
The Voice of the People, 17117
Your Foot's on My Feet! 14053

Maestro, Giulio (jt. author). *Bike Trip*, 22163
Ferryboat, 21370
A More Perfect Union, 17060
What Do You Hear When Cows Sing? 21839

Maestro, Marco. *Geese Find the Missing Piece*, 21838(F)
What Do You Hear When Cows Sing? 21839

Maganzini, Christy. *Cool Math*, 20588

Magdanz, James. *Go Home, River*, 4495(F)

Maggio, Viqui. *Absolutely Angels*, 11521

Magine, John. *We Are Monsters*, 1449(F)

Magnier, Thierry. *Isabelle and the Angel*, 1386(F)

Magnuson, Diana. *Buffalo*, 18955
Owl, 19358
The Trail of Tears, 15936

Magocsi, Paul R. *The Russian Americans*, 17579

Magorian, Michelle. *Who's Going to Take Care of Me?* 5025(F)

Maguire, Gregory. *Crabby Cratchitt*, 2956(F)
Five Alien Elves, 9747(F)
Four Stupid Cupids, 7944(F)
The Good Liar, 9674(F)
Seven Spiders Spinning, 7945(F)
Six Haunted Hairdos, 8339(F)

Maguire, Kerry. *Oh, the Places He Went*, 12539

Magurn, Susan. *Singing Sam*, 6239(F)

Mahler, Joseph. *The Itch Book*, 3111(F)

Mahr, Juli. *The Mailbox Mice Mystery*, 6501(F)

Mahy, Margaret. *The Blood-and-Thunder Adventure on Hurricane Peak*, 7946(F)
Boom, Baby, Boom, Boom! 1387(F)
Bubble Trouble and Other Poems and Stories, 11900
A Busy Day for a Good Grandmother, 3795(F)
The Chewing-Gum Rescue, 10460(F)
The Christmas Tree Tangle, 5873(F)
Clancy's Cabin, 6958(F)
Down the Dragon's Tongue, 3304(F)
The Five Sisters, 7947(F)
The Horribly Haunted School, 7948(F)
Making Friends, 5336(F)
My Mysterious World, 12571
The Pirate Uncle, 6959(F)
Raging Robots and Unruly Uncles, 10214(F)
The Seven Chinese Brothers, 10765
Simply Delicious! 1388(F)
A Summery Saturday Morning, 3305(F)
A Tall Story and Other Tales, 7949(F)
Tangled Fortunes, 6960(F)
Tick Tock Tales, 1389(F)

Mai, Vo-Dinh. *The Brocaded Slipper and Other Vietnamese Tales*, 10845

Maifair, Linda Lee. *Batter Up, Bailey Benson!* 10347(F)
The Case of the Bashed-Up Bicycle, 6961(F)
Go Figure, Gabriella Grant! 10348(F)

Mainland, Pauline. *A Yoga Parade of Animals*, 18200

Maione, Heather H. *Princess Lulu Goes to Camp*, 6295(F)
Stories to Tell a Five-Year-Old, 1360(F)

Mair, Jacqueline. *The Bottle Imp*, 8130(F)

Maisner, Heather. *The Magic Globe*, 14348

Maitland, Barbara. *The Bear Who Didn't Like Honey*, 2466(F)
The Bookstore Ghost, 6502(F)
Moo in the Morning, 3306(F)
My Bear and Me, 3307(F)

Maizlish, Lisa. *The Ring*, 1390(F)

Majewska, Maria. *Ten Little Mice*, 425(F)

Majewski, Dawn. *Because Nothing Looks Like God*, 17201

Majewski, Stephen. *Sports Great Jerome Bettis*, 13603
Terrell Davis, 13605

Majno, Mary Lee. *The Lost Village of Central Park*, 9301(F)

Majoor, Mireille. *Inside the Hindenburg*, 21087

Major, Beverly. *Over Back*, 4496(F)

Major, Ted (jt. author). *The Secret Language of Snow*, 20795

Majure, Janet. *Elections*, 17099

Mak, Kam. *The Dragon Prince*, 10776
The Year of the Panda, 7303(F)

Makris, Kathryn. *The Five Cat Club*, 8340(F)

Malam, John. *Airport*, 21088
Ancient Egypt, 14641
Beatrix Potter, 12581
Claude Monet, 12266
Cleaning the House, 21161
Exploring Ancient Greece, 14693
Gods and Goddesses, 14694
Greek Town, 14695
Hospital, 21140
Leonardo da Vinci, 12216
Library, 21141
Mesopotamia and the Fertile Crescent, 14642
Myths and Civilization of the Ancient Romans, 11490
Pieter Bruegel, 12194
Song and Dance, 14134
Theater, 14323
Thor Heyerdahl, 12122
Vincent van Gogh, 12308
Wolfgang Amadeus Mozart, 12335

Maland, Nick. *Big Blue Whale*, 19782

Malaspina, Ann. *Children's Rights*, 17044

Malcolm, Peter. *Libya*, 14961

Male, Alan. *Ladybug*, 19531
Mosquito, 19424
Snail, 19608
Spider, 19575
Spiders and Their Web Sites, 19578

Mali, Jane L. (jt. author). *Mystery on October Road*, 6889(F)

Mallat, Kathy. *Brave Bear*, 2467(F)
The Picture That Mom Drew, 13908
Seven Stars More! 740(F)

Mallett, David. *Inch by Inch*, 14169

Mallory, Kenneth. *A Home by the Sea*, 19404

Mallory, Marilynn H. *My Mother Talks to Trees*, 3655(F)

Malnig, Anita. *Where the Waves Break*, 19862

Malone, Mary. *James Madison*, 13083
Maya Lin, 12256
Will Rogers, 12459

Malone, Michael. *A Guatemalan Family*, 15676

Malone, Nola L. *Earrings!* 4340(F)
King of the Playground, 5041(F)
N-O Spells No! 6195(F)

Malone, Peter. *The Adventures of Odysseus*, 11501
Brother Sun, Sister Moon, 13794
The Magic Flute, 14128
Star Shapes, 4497(F)
A World of Words, 138
Maloney, Peter. *The Magic Hockey Stick*, 1391(F)
Redbird at Rockefeller Center, 5874(F)
Malotki, Ekkehart, comp. *The Magic Hummingbird*, 11268
Malterre, Elona. *The Last Wolf of Ireland*, 7263(F)
Mama, Raouf. *The Barefoot Book of Tropical Tales*, 10580
Why Goats Smell Bad and Other Stories from Benin, 10694
Mamdani, Shelby. *Traditions from China*, 15073
Traditions from India, 15110
Mammano, Julie. *Rhinos Who Skateboard*, 2468(F)
Rhinos Who Snowboard, 2469(F)
Rhinos Who Surf, 2470(F)
Manchess, Gregory. *Nanuk*, 5253(F)
Mandel, Peter. *Say Hey! A Song of Willie Mays*, 13474
Mandell, Muriel. *Simple Kitchen Experiments*, 20114
Simple Weather Experiments with Everyday Materials, 20782
Manders, John. *Dirt Boy*, 1582(F)
The Dragon's Scales, 6185(F)
King Snake, 2703(F)
What You Never Knew About Fingers, Forks, and Chopsticks, 17638
Z Is for Zombie, 6023(F)
Manes, Stephen. *An Almost Perfect Game*, 10349(F)
Chocolate-Covered Ants, 9934(F)
Make Four Million Dollars by Next Thursday! 9935(F)
Mangan, Anne. *The Smallest Bear*, 2471(F)
Mangas, Brian. *Follow That Puppy!* 4228(F)
You Don't Get a Carrot Unless You're a Bunny, 6030(F)
Mangelsen, Thomas D. *Spring*, 4459
When Night Comes, 18825
Mania, Cathy. *Woodpecker in the Backyard*, 19257
Mania, Cathy (jt. author). *A Forest's Life*, 20466
Mania, Robert. *A Forest's Life*, 20466
Mania, Robert (jt. author). *Woodpecker in the Backyard*, 19257
Manitonquat. *The Children of the Morning Light*, 11269
Mann, Elizabeth. *The Brooklyn Bridge*, 21142
The Great Pyramid, 14643
The Great Wall, 15074
Machu Picchu, 15761

The Panama Canal, 15677
The Roman Colosseum, 14731
Mann, Kenny. *Egypt, Kush, Aksum*, 14962
Ghana, Mali, Songhay, 15037
Manna, Anthony L. *Mr. Semolina-Semolinus*, 11070
Manna, Giovanni. *You and Me*, 163(F)
Mannetti, William. *Dinosaurs in Your Backyard*, 14445
Manning, Jane. *Cindy Ellen*, 10452(F)
Drip, Drop, 6709(F)
Lost Little Angel, 1495(F)
That Toad Is Mine! 4003(F)
Manning, Karen. *AIDS*, 17983
Manning, Linda. *Dinosaur Days*, 210(F)
Manning, Mick. *Art School*, 13909
Honk! Honk! 1392(F)
My Body, Your Body, 18832
Science School, 18328
Supermom, 3796(F)
Manning, Scott (jt. author). *Why Doesn't My Floppy Disk Flop?* 21195
Mansell, Dom. *My Old Teddy*, 3308(F)
Manson, Ainslie. *Ballerinas Don't Wear Glasses*, 3797(F)
A Dog Came, Too, 4760
Just Like New, 4761(F)
Manson, Christopher. *Black Swan/White Crow*, 11822
Till Year's Good End, 14784
The Tree in the Wood, 859
Mantegazza, Giovanna. *The Hippopotamus*, 5337
Mantell, Paul (jt. author). *Ancient Greece!* 14682
Knights and Castles, 14765
Pyramids! 50 Hands-on Activities to Experience Ancient Egypt, 14629
Manuel, Lynn. *The Night the Moon Blew Kisses*, 4498(F)
Manushkin, Fran. *Let's Go Riding in Our Strollers*, 3309(F)
The Matzah That Papa Brought Home, 6094(F)
Miriam's Cup, 17478
The Perfect Christmas Picture, 5875(F)
Starlight and Candles, 6095(F)
Mara, William P. *The Fragile Frog*, 18729
Marcellino, Fred. *I, Crocodile*, 2472(F)
Ouch! 10883
Puss in Boots, 10879
The Steadfast Tin Soldier, 10388(F)
The Story of Little Babaji, 978(F)
The Wainscott Weasel, 8080(F)
Marchand, Peter. *What Good Is a Cactus?* 9169(F)
Marchant, Kerena. *Id-Ul-Fitr*, 17389

Marchesi, Stephen. *Don Quixote and Sancho Panza*, 9044(F)
Martin Luther King, Jr., and the March on Washington, 16518
The Mysterious Rays of Dr. Roentgen, 13343
Railway Ghosts and Highway Horrors, 11329
Silver, 7322(F)
Terror Below! 19755
With the Wind, 22199
Marchi, Paola. *The Hippopotamus*, 5337
Marchon-Arnaud, Catherine. *A Gallery of Games*, 22035
Marciano, John Bemelmans (jt. author). *Madeline in America and Other Holiday Tales*, 4591(F)
Marcos, Subcomandante. *The Story of Colors/La Historia de los Colores*, 11410
Marcus, Leonard S. *A Caldecott Celebration*, 12174
Marden, Priscilla. *Oliver*, 2853(F)
Margolin, Malcolm, ed. *Native Ways*, 15999
Mariconda, Barbara. *Witch Way to the Beach*, 1393(F)
Marie, D. *Tears for Ashan*, 8972(F)
Marino, Jan. *Eighty-Eight Steps to September*, 8906(F)
For the Love of Pete, 8482(F)
Mario, Heidi Stetson. *I'd Rather Have an Iguana*, 3798(F)
Mariotti, Mario. *Hands Off!* 927(F)
Hanimations, 928(F)
Mark, Jan. *Fun with Mrs. Thumb*, 1394(F)
The Midas Touch, 11491
The Tale of Tobias, 17303(F)
Markel, Michelle. *Cornhusk, Silk, and Wishbones*, 21655
Gracias, Rosa, 3799(F)
Markel, Rita J. *Jimi Hendrix*, 12397(F)
Markes, Julie. *Good Thing You're Not an Octopus!* 1395(F)
Market, Jenny. *Moose*, 19155
Penguins, 19380
Markham, Lois. *Avi*, 12503
Colombia, 15762
Harvest, 17502
Lois Lowry, 12566
Markham, Marion M. *The April Fool's Day Mystery*, 6962(F)
The Halloween Candy Mystery, 6963(F)
The St. Patrick's Day Shamrock Mystery, 6964(F)
The Thanksgiving Day Parade Mystery, 6965(F)
Markle, Sandra. *After the Spill*, 16800
Creepy, Crawly Baby Bugs, 19465
Creepy, Spooky Science, 18329
Discovering Graph Secrets, 20589

Down, Down, Down in the Ocean, 19829
Exploring Autumn, 18330
Exploring Winter, 18571
Gone Forever! An Alphabet of Extinct Animals, 19405
Growing Up Wild, 19055
Icky, Squishy Science, 18331
Measuring Up! 20618
Outside and Inside Alligators, 18704
Outside and Inside Bats, 19031
Outside and Inside Birds, 19258
Outside and Inside Dinosaurs, 14446
Outside and Inside Kangaroos, 19179
Outside and Inside Sharks, 19765
Outside and Inside Snakes, 18769
Outside and Inside Spiders, 19587
Pioneering Frozen Worlds, 15820
Pioneering Space, 21000
A Rainy Day, 20783
Science Surprises, 21045
Science to the Rescue, 18332
Super Cool Science, 15821
Super Science Secrets, 18333
Markle, William (jt. author). *Gone Forever! An Alphabet of Extinct Animals*, 19405
Markoe, Merrill. *The Day My Dogs Became Guys*, 1396(F)
Marks, Alan. *Abby*, 7210(F)
How Long? 176(F)
The Little Green Goose, 2651(F)
The Midsummer Bride, 1473(F)
Ragged Bear, 3474(F)
Ring-a-Ring O'Roses and Ding, Dong Bell, 861
With Love, 18996
Marks, Alan, ed. *Over the Hills and Far Away*, 860
Markun, Patricia M. *It's Panama's Canal!* 15678
The Little Painter of Sabana Granda, 4762(F)
Marlow, Eric. *Rosa Parks*, 12776
Marlowe, Sam. *Learning About Dedication from the Life of Frederick Douglass*, 12712
Marquez, Heron. *Destination San Juan*, 15709
Destination Veracruz, 15634
Latin Sensations, 12175
Marr, John S. *Breath of Air and a Breath of Smoke*, 17879
Marrella, Maria Pia. *Seven Kisses in a Row*, 7481(F)
Marrin, Albert. *Struggle for a Continent*, 16159
The War for Independence, 16204
Marriott, Pat. *The Wolves of Willoughby Chase*, 6740(F)
Mars, W. T. *Adventures of Greek Heroes*, 11489
Marschall, Ken. *Exploring the Titanic*, 19873

On Board the Titanic, 7094(F)
Marsh, Carole. *AIDS to Zits*, 18266
Asteroids, Comets, and Meteors, 18520
Unidentified Flying Objects and Extraterrestrial Life, 21001
Marsh, Dilleen. *Some Answers Are Loud, Some Answers Are Soft*, 3368(F)
Marsh, T. J. *Way Out in the Desert*, 5338(F)
Marsh, T. J. (jt. author). *Somewhere in the Ocean*, 898(F)
Marshak, Samuel. *The Absentminded Fellow*, 4229(F)
Marshak, Samuel, reteller. *The Month-Brothers*, 11103
Marshall, Edward. *Three by the Sea*, 6503(F)
Marshall, Felicia. *Down Home at Miss Dessa's*, 4049(F)
Keepers, 5102(F)
Molasses Man, 3803(F)
Marshall, James. *All the Way Home*, 4306(F)
Fox Outfoxed, 6504(F)
George and Martha, 2473(F)
George and Martha Round and Round, 2474(F)
How Beastly! 11928
James Marshall's Mother Goose, 862
Miss Nelson Has a Field Day, 5466(F)
Miss Nelson Is Missing! 5467(F)
Old Mother Hubbard and Her Wonderful Dog, 877
The Owl and the Pussycat, 11890
The Piggy in the Puddle, 2595(F)
The Stupids Have a Ball, 4077(F)
The Stupids Take Off, 4078(F)
Swine Lake, 2475(F)
Three by the Sea, 6503(F)
What's the Matter with Carruthers? A Bedtime Story, 741(F)
Yummers! 2476(F)
Yummers Too, 2477(F)
Marshall, James, reteller. *Hansel and Gretel*, 10928
Marshall, Janet. *Banana Moon*, 312(F)
A Honey of a Day, 4499(F)
Look Once, Look Twice, 88(F)
Marshall, Lynne. *Juliet*, 9104(F)
Marstall, Bob. *Butternut Hollow Pond*, 20518
Down, Down, Down in the Ocean, 19829
An Extraordinary Life, 19565
Fire in the Forest, 16965
The Lady and the Spider, 5333(F)
Mitch and Amy, 10035(F)
Marston, Elsa. *The Ancient Egyptians*, 14644
The Fox Maiden, 7950(F)
Lebanon, 15555

Marston, Hope I. *Fire Trucks*, 21307
Martchenko, Michael. *Alligator Baby*, 4239(F)
Andrew's Loose Tooth, 4240(F)
From Far Away, 5040(F)
Munschworks, 4242(F)
Munschworks 3, 4245
Munschworks 2, 4243(F)
Stephanie's Ponytail, 4244(F)
We Share Everything! 5521(F)
Martell, Hazel M. *The Ancient Chinese*, 15075
The Celts, 15361
Civilizations of Peru, Before 1535, 15763
Exploring Africa, 14910
The Great Pyramid, 14645
The Kingfisher Book of the Ancient World, 14590
The Myths and Civilization of the Ancient Greeks, 14696
Myths and Civilization of the Celts, 11452
Native Americans and Mesa Verde, 16000
Over 6,000 Years Ago, 14508
Roman Town, 14732
The Vikings and Jorvik, 15459
Martin, Alexander C. (jt. author). *Flowers*, 20042
Trees, 20221
Martin, Ann M. *The Doll People*, 7951(F)
Leo the Magnificat, 5339(F)
Ten Kids, No Pets, 7482(F)
Martin, Ann M. (jt. author). *P.S. Longer Letter Later*, 8274(F)
Snail Mail No More, 8275(F)
Martin, Annie-Claude. *The Ancient Greeks*, 14678
The Romans, 14720
Martin, Bill, Jr. *Adam, Adam, What Do You See?* 17304
Barn Dance! 2481(F)
A Beasty Story, 2478(F)
Brown Bear, Brown Bear, What Do You See? 283(F)
Chicka Chicka Boom Boom, 89(F)
Chicken Chuck, 2479(F)
"Fire! Fire!" Said Mrs. McGuire, 863
The Ghost-Eye Tree, 2957(F)
The Happy Hippopotami, 2480(F)
Here Are My Hands, 3310(F)
Knots on a Counting Rope, 7353(F)
Listen to the Rain, 3311(F)
The Maestro Plays, 4230(F)
The Magic Pumpkin, 6032(F)
Old Devil Wind, 6031(F)
Polar Bear, Polar Bear, What Do You Hear? 5340(F)
Swish! 2959(F)
Up and Down on the Merry-Go-Round, 3312(F)
White Dynamite and Curly Kidd, 2958(F)

Martin, C. L. G. *The Blueberry Train*, 4763(F)
Down Dairy Farm Road, 5026(F)
Three Brave Women, 3800(F)
Martin, Christopher. *Mohandas Gandhi*, 13803
Martin, Clovis. *A Whisper Is Quiet*, 6475(F)
Martin, David. *Five Little Piggies*, 864(F)
Monkey Business, 6505(F)
Martin, Francesca. *Clever Tortoise*, 10695
The Honey Hunters, 10673
Martin, Jacqueline B. *Grandmother Bryant's Pocket*, 9204(F)
Green Truck Garden Giveaway, 3313(F)
Higgins Bend Song and Dance, 1397(F)
The Lamp, the Ice, and the Boat Called Fish, 15822
Snowflake Bentley, 12191
Washing the Willow Tree Loon, 5341(F)
Martin, John F. *A Message for General Washington*, 9249(F)
Martin, Joseph Plumb. *A Revolutionary War Soldier*, 16205
Martin, Josephine. *The Snow Tree*, 5910(F)
Martin, Les. *Humbug*, 6966(F)
Martin, Linda. *Watch Them Grow*, 18593
When Dinosaurs Go to School, 2482(F)
Martin, Linda R. *Brave Wolf and the Thunderbird*, 11279
Martin, Mary Jane. *From Anne to Zach*, 90(F)
Martin, Nora. *The Stone Dancers*, 4764(F)
Martin, Patricia A. *Chimpanzees*, 19005
Gorillas, 19006
Lemurs, Lorises, and Other Lower Primates, 19007
Memory Jug, 8483(F)
Monkeys of Asia and Africa, 19008
Orangutans, 19009
Travels with Rainie Marie, 8484(F)
Martin, Paul D. *Messengers to the Brain*, 18147
Science, 18286
Martin, Rafe. *The Boy Who Lived with the Seals*, 11270
The Brave Little Parrot, 10800
The Eagle's Gift, 11207
Foolish Rabbit's Big Mistake, 10801
The Language of Birds, 11104
The Monkey Bridge, 10802
Mysterious Tales of Japan, 10581
The Rough-Face Girl, 11271
A Storyteller's Story, 12573
Will's Mammoth, 929(F)

Martin, Terri. *A Family Trait*, 6967(F)
Martin, Wesley (jt. author). *The Star Wars Cookbook II*, 21698
Martin-James, Kathleen. *Building Beavers*, 19200
Sturdy Turtles, 18787
Martin-Jourdenais, Norma Jean. *Kids' Art Works!* 21444
Martinet, Jeanne, comp. *The Year You Were Born, 1986*, 17390
Martinez, Ed. *Hurray for Three Kings' Day!* 5774(F)
Too Many Tamales, 5921(F)
Martinez, Elizabeth Coonrod. *Edward James Olmos*, 12439
Henry Cisneros, 12828
The Mexican-American Experience, 17580
Sor Juana, 12557
Martinez, Leovigildo. *The Twenty-Five Mixtec Cats*, 7745(F)
Martino, Teresa. *Pizza!* 20115
Martino, Val. *The Witch's Revenge*, 5999(F)
Marton, Jirina. *Lady Kaguya's Secret*, 10821
You Can Go Home Again, 4765(F)
Maruki, Toshi. *Hiroshima No Pika*, 14870
Marupin, Melissa. *Benjamin Banneker*, 13234
Maruska, Edward J. *Salamanders*, 18688
Marvin, Fred. *Grover*, 8602(F)
Marvin, Isabel R. *A Bride for Anna's Papa*, 9593(F)
Marvis, Barbara. *Famous People of Asian Ancestry*, 12678
Famous People of Hispanic Heritage, 12679
Rafael Palmeiro, 13477
Robert Rodriguez, 12456
Selena, 12466
Marvis, Barbara (jt. author). *Tommy Nunez*, 13553
Marx, David F. *Canada*, 15589
Marx, Patricia. *Meet My Staff*, 4231(F)
Marx, Trish. *Echoes of World War II*, 14871
I Heal, 17984
One Boy from Kosovo, 15279
Marzollo, Dan (jt. author). *Basketball Buddies*, 6512(F)
Marzollo, Jean. *Basketball Buddies*, 6512(F)
Football Friends, 6511(F)
Happy Birthday, Martin Luther King, 12748
I Am a Rock, 20564
I Am an Apple, 6506(F)
I Am Water, 20739
I Love You, 11651
I Spy, 21870, 21871, 21840
I Spy Christmas, 5876
I Spy Fantasy, 21872

I Spy Funhouse, 4232
I Spy School Days, 211(F)
I Spy Spooky Night, 21841
I Spy Super Challenger! A Book of Picture Riddles, 21873
I Spy Treasure Hunt, 21874
I'm a Caterpillar, 6507(F)
Mama Mama, 5342(F)
My First Book of Biographies, 13737
Once upon a Springtime, 6508(F)
Slam Dunk Saturday, 10350(F)
Snow Angel, 1398(F)
Soccer Cousins, 6509(F)
Soccer Sam, 6510(F)
Ten Cats Have Hats, 510(F)
Masheris, Robert. *The Dreams of Hummingbirds*, 11946
Masiello, Ralph. *The Flag We Love*, 13975
The Frog Alphabet Book . . . and Other Awesome Amphibians, 109(F)
Masini, Beatrice. *A Brave Little Princess*, 1399(F)
Maslac, Evelyn Hughes. *Finding a Job for Daddy*, 3801(F)
Maslin, Mark. *Earthquakes*, 20341
Masoff, Joy. *American Revolution*, 16206
Colonial Times, 1600–1700, 16160
Emergency, 18041
Fire! 17817
Mason, Adrienne. *Living Things*, 18334
Lu and Clancy's Secret Codes, 13967
Mealworms, 19535
Mason, Adrienne (jt. author). *Simple Machines*, 20921
Solids, Liquids, and Gases, 20812
Mason, Antony. *Aztec Times*, 15635
Leonardo da Vinci, 12217
Viking Times, 15460
Mason, Cherie. *Wild Fox*, 19132
Mason, Jane B. *Hellow, Two-Wheeler!* 6513(F)
Massari, Francesca. *Everything You Need to Know About Cancer*, 17985
Massart, Nadine. *Degas*, 13906
Massey, Cal. *My First Kwanzaa Book*, 5619
Massie, Diane Redfield. *The Baby Beebee Bird*, 742(F)
Massie, Elizabeth. *Jambo, Watoto!* 2483(F)
Patsy's Discovery, 9241(F)
Massin. *Fun with Numbers*, 20632
Masson, Jeffrey Moussaieff. *Dogs Have the Strangest Friends*, 18833
Masson, Sophie. *Serafin*, 7952(F)
Masterman-Smith, Virginia. *First Mate Tate*, 8756(F)
Masters, Anthony. *Heroic Stories*, 12064

Masters, Nancy Robinson. *Kansas*, 16571

Mastin, Colleayn O. (jt. author). *The Newest and Coolest Dinosaurs*, 14394

Masuda, Modoki. *Water Insects*, 19457

Masurel, Claire. *Christmas Is Coming!* 5877(F)
No, No, Titus! 5343(F)
Ten Dogs in the Window, 511(F)
Too Big! 3314(F)

Mata, Marta. *Goldilocks and the Three Bears/Ricitos de Oro y los tres osos*, 11016

Matas, Carol. *A Meeting of the Minds*, 10215(F)
Of Two Minds, 7953(F)
Out of Their Minds, 7954(F)

Mataya, David. *Earthwise at Home*, 16961
Tales for Hard Times, 12528

Matero, Robert. *Animals Asleep*, 18834
The Birth of a Humpback Whale, 19797

Mather, Karen Trella. *Silas*, 7955(F)

Mathers, Douglas. *Brain*, 18113
Ears, 18148

Mathers, Petra. *A Cake for Herbie*, 91(F)
Grandmother Bryant's Pocket, 9204(F)
How Nanita Learned to Make Flan, 1180(F)
I Need a Snake, 4197(F)
It's My Birthday, Too! 5701(F)
Lottie's New Beach Towel, 3315(F)
Lottie's New Friend, 2484(F)
Mom Pie, 3737(F)
Mommy Go Away! 1278(F)
On Ramon's Farm, 5220(F)
Tell Me a Season, 4544(F)

Mathews, Judith. *Nathaniel Willy, Scared Silly*, 11367
There's Nothing to D-o-o-o! 2485(F)

Mathews, Sally S. *The Sad Night*, 15636

Mathieu, Joe. *Chimps Don't Wear Glasses*, 2535(F)
Dogs Don't Wear Sneakers, 2536(F)

Mathis, Melissa. *Earthsong*, 14176
Grandad Bill's Song, 5109(F)

Mathis, Melissa Bay. *Animal House*, 1400(F)

Mathis, Sharon Bell. *The Hundred Penny Box*, 7483(F)
Running Girl, 10351(F)

Matje, Martin. *Celeste*, 1401(F)
Harry and Lulu, 1712(F)
Wallace Hoskins, 1717(F)
When It Starts to Snow, 2119(F)

Matson, Nancy. *The Boy Trap*, 10109(F)

Mattern, Joanne. *Coming to America*, 9594(F)
Safety at School, 18223
Safety on the Go, 18224

Matthaei, Gay (jt. author). *The Ledgerbook of Thomas Blue Eagle*, 9160(F)

Matthews, Andrew. *Marduk the Mighty and Other Stories of Creation*, 10582

Matthews, Bethan. *Lizzie's List*, 7446(F)

Matthews, Bonnie. *Annie Ate Apples*, 123(F)
A Dog's Best Friend, 19966

Matthews, Caitlin. *The Barefoot Book of Princesses*, 10461
The Blessing Seed, 17305
While the Bear Sleeps, 9748(F)

Matthews, Caitlin (jt. author). *The Wizard King and Other Spellbinding Tales*, 10584

Matthews, Derek. *Living in the World*, 17133

Matthews, Downs. *Harp Seal Pups*, 19741

Matthews, John. *Giants, Ghosts and Goblins*, 10583
The Wizard King and Other Spellbinding Tales, 10584

Matthews, Mary. *Magid Fasts for Ramadan*, 7354(F)

Matthews, Rupert. *Cooking a Meal*, 14349
Telling the Time, 20647

Matthews, Tom L. *Always Inventing*, 13239
Light Shining Through the Mist, 13284

Matthias, Catherine. *I Love Cats*, 6514(F)
Over-Under, 212(F)

Mattingley, Christobel. *The Magic Saddle*, 5878(F)

Mattox, Cheryl W., ed. *Shake It to the One That You Love the Best*, 14170

Mattson, Mark. *Scholastic Environmental Atlas of the United States*, 16962

Matze, Claire Sidhom. *The Stars in My Geddoh's Sky*, 3802(F)

Mau, Christine. *Twelve Lizards Leaping*, 14213

Maugham, W. Somerset. *Princess September and the Nightingale*, 10462(F)

Maurer, Donna. *Annie, Bea, and Chi Chi Dolores*, 92(F)

Maurer, Richard. *Junk in Space*, 21002
The Wild Colorado, 16087

Maurer, Tracy. *License Plates*, 21308

Maurer, Tracy Nelson. *Growing Flowers*, 21769

Mauser, Pat Rhoads. *Patti's Pet Gorilla*, 5027(F)

Mavor, Salley. *The Hollyhock Wall*, 1657(F)
Mary Had a Little Lamb, 845

Mavor, Salley, ed. *You and Me*, 11652

Max, Jill, ed. *Spider Spins a Story*, 11272

May, Darcy. *The Dragons of North Chittendon*, 8068(F)

May, Kara. *Joe Lion's Big Boots*, 6515(F)

May, Kathy L. *Molasses Man*, 3803(F)

May, Robin. *Plains Indians of North America*, 16001

Maybarduk, Linda. *The Dancer Who Flew*, 12428

Mayberry, Jodine. *Business Leaders Who Built Financial Empires*, 12680

Mayer, Bill. *Brer Rabbit and Boss Lion*, 11344

Mayer, Marianna. *Baba Yaga and Vasilisa the Brave*, 11105
Beauty and the Beast, 10875
Iron John, 10585
The Mother Goose Cookbook, 21719
Pegasus, 11492
The Prince and the Pauper, 9110(F)
The Twelve Apostles, 17306
Women Warriors, 10586
Young Jesus of Nazareth, 17307
Young Mary of Nazareth, 17308

Mayer, Mercer. *East of the Sun and West of the Moon*, 11130
Everyone Knows What a Dragon Looks Like, 4353(F)
The Great Brain, 9843(F)
Ooey Gooey, 6331(F)
Shibumi and the Kitemaker, 1402(F)
You're the Scaredy-Cat, 5028(F)

Mayers, Florence Cassen. *ABC*, 93(F), 94(F)
Baseball ABC, 95(F)
A Russian ABC, 96(F)

Mayerson, Evelyn Wilde. *The Cat Who Escaped from Steerage*, 9595(F)

Mayes, Dave (jt. author). *Killer Bees*, 19519

Mayfield, Thomas Jefferson. *Adopted by Indians*, 16002

Mayhew, James. *Katie and the Mona Lisa*, 1403(F)
Katie Meets the Impressionists, 1404(F)

Maynard, Bill. *Incredible Ned*, 1405(F)
Pondfire, 6968(F)
Quiet, Wyatt! 5029(F)
Rock River, 6969(F)
Santa's Time Off, 3316(F)

Maynard, Caitlin. *Rain Forests and Reefs*, 20383

Maynard, Chris. *Aircraft*, 21089
Maynard, Christopher. *Airplane*, 21090
Amazing Animal Babies, 18878
The Best Book of Dinosaurs, 14447
Extreme Machines, 21285
The History News, 14563
Informania, 21935, 19766
Jobs People Do, 17756
Micromonsters, 18648
Pirates! Raiders of the High Seas, 12065
The Young Scientist Book of Stars and Planets, 18398
Maynard, Jacqui. *I Know Where My Food Goes*, 18102
Maynard, Meredy. *Dreamcatcher*, 7264(F)
Maynard, Thane. *Ostriches*, 19259
Maynard, Thane (jt. author). *Rain Forests and Reefs*, 20383
Mayne, William. *The Book of Hob Stories*, 7956(F)
Hob and the Goblins, 7957(F)
Hob and the Peddler, 7958(F)
Lady Muck, 2486(F)
Mayo, Diana. *Exodus from Egypt*, 17241
The Story of Jonah, 17243
Mayo, Gretchen Will. *Anna and the Cat Lady*, 8713(F)
Big Trouble for Tricky Rabbit! 11273
Earthmaker's Tales, 11274
Here Comes Tricky Rabbit! 11275
Meet Tricky Coyote! 11276
Star Tales, 11277
That Tricky Coyote! 11278
Whale Brother, 4838(F)
Mayo, Gretchen Will, reteller. *Big Trouble for Tricky Rabbit!* 11273
Meet Tricky Coyote! 11276
Mayo, Margaret. *Brother Sun, Sister Moon*, 13794
When the World Was Young, 10588
Mayo, Margaret, reteller. *Magical Tales from Many Lands*, 10587
Mayo, Terry. *The Illustrated Rules of In-line Hockey*, 22036
Mayper, Monica. *Come and See*, 5879(F)
Maze, Stephanie. *I Want to Be a Dancer*, 17777
I Want to Be a Fashion Designer, 21179
I Want to Be a Firefighter, 17818
I Want to Be a Veterinarian, 17854
I Want to Be an Astronaut, 17758
I Want to Be an Engineer, 17789
I Want to Be an Environmentalist, 17757
Mazer, Abby. *The Amazing Days of Abby Hayes*, 10352(F)
Mazer, Anne. *The Fixits*, 4233(F)
The No-Nothings and Their Baby, 4234(F)

The Salamander Room, 5344(F)
A Sliver of Glass and Other Uncommon Tales, 7959(F)
Mazer, Anne, ed. *America Street*, 7355(F)
Mazer, Harry. *Snow Bound*, 6970(F)
The Wild Kid, 6971(F)
Mazer, Norma Fox. *Good Night, Maman*, 9675(F)
Mrs. Fish, Ape and Me, the Dump Queen, 8341(F)
Mazille, Capucine. *A Is for Apple, W Is for Witch*, 7705(F)
Mazor, Barry. *Multimedia and New Media Developer*, 17790
Mazzola, Frank. *The Cheerios Counting Book*, 506(F)
Mazzola, Frank, Jr. *Counting Is for the Birds*, 19260
Mazzucco, Jennifer. *I Know What You Do When I Go to School*, 4103(F)
Little Johnny Buttermilk, 11041
Meacham, Margaret. *Oyster Moon*, 6972(F)
Meachum, Virginia. *Rosie O'Donnell*, 12436
Steven Spielberg, 12474
Mead, Alice. *Billy and Emma*, 2487(F)
Crossing the Starlight Bridge, 9170(F)
Girl of Kosovo, 9061(F)
Junebug, 8485(F)
Junebug and the Reverend, 8486(F)
Soldier Mom, 8487(F)
Walking the Edge, 8488(F)
Meade, Holly. *Boss of the Plains*, 21167
Cocoa Ice, 8250(F)
Hush! 703(F)
John Willy and Freddy McGee, 2488(F)
Pie's in the Oven, 4086(F)
Small Green Snake, 2146(F)
Steamboat! The Story of Captain Blanche Leathers, 12130
When Papa Snores, 3778(F)
Meadows, Graham. *Cats*, 19927
Dogs, 19956
Horses, 20004
Meadows, James. *Jesse Jackson*, 12728
Meadows, Matthew. *Pablo Picasso*, 12282
Mebane, Robert C. *Air and Other Gases*, 20672
Metals, 21258
Plastics and Polymers, 21046
Salts and Solids, 20288
Water and Other Liquids, 20740
Mebane, Robert C. (jt. author). *Environmental Experiments About Renewable Energy*, 20836
Mechler, Gary. *National Audubon Society First Field Guide*, 18399
Meddaugh, Susan. *Beast*, 1406(F)

The Best Halloween of All, 6064(F)
The Best Place, 2489(F)
Bimwili and the Zimwi, 10638
Cinderella's Rat, 1407(F)
Five Little Piggies, 864(F)
Good Zap, Little Grog, 2863(F)
Hog-Eye, 2490(F)
The Hopeful Trout and Other Limericks, 11863
Martha and Skits, 2491(F)
Martha Blah Blah, 1408(F)
Martha Calling, 2492(F)
Martha Speaks, 2493(F)
Martha Walks the Dog, 2494(F)
The Most Beautiful Kid in the World, 3617(F)
No Nap, 641(F)
A Perfect Father's Day, 5614(F)
Tree of Birds, 2495(F)
Two Ways to Count to Ten, 10661
The Witches' Supermarket, 6033(F)
Medearis, Angela Shelf. *The Adventures of Sugar and Junior*, 8342(F)
Annie's Gifts, 5030(F)
Bye-Bye, Babies! 3317(F)
Cooking, 21720
Dance, 14295
Dancing with the Indians, 3318(F)
Dare to Dream, 12736
The Ghost of Sifty Sifty Sam, 1409(F)
Haunts, 7960(F)
Here Comes the Snow, 6516(F)
Music, 14135
Poppa's Itchy Christmas, 5880(F)
Poppa's New Pants, 3319(F)
Princess of the Press, 12819
Rum-a-Tum-Tum, 4766(F)
Seven Spools of Thread, 5637(F)
The Singing Man, 10696
The Spray-Paint Mystery, 6973(F)
Tailypo, 11368
Too Much Talk, 10697
Medearis, Angela Shelf, reteller. *Treemonisha*, 9596(F)
Medearis, Angela Shelf (jt. author). *Daisy and the Doll*, 7356(F)
Medearis, Michael. *Daisy and the Doll*, 7356(F)
Medearis, Michael R. (jt. author). *Cooking*, 21720
Dance, 14295
Music, 14135
Medicine Crow, Joe. *Brave Wolf and the Thunderbird*, 11279
Medina, Jane. *My Name Is Jorge*, 11653
Medlicott, Mary, ed. and sel. *The River That Went to the Sky*, 10698
Medlock, Scott. *Extra Innings*, 11997
Opening Days, 11998
Mee, Sue. *1900–20*, 16478
Meeker, Clare Hodgson. *Lootas, Little Wave Eater*, 19742
A Tale of Two Rice Birds, 10841

Who Wakes Rooster? 5345(F)

Meeks, Arone R. *Enora and the Black Crane*, 7961(F)

Meeuwissen, Tony. *Remarkable Animals*, 2496(F)

Megale, Marina. *Baby and I Can Play and Fun with Toddlers*, 3685
Kids to the Rescue! 18215

Meggs, Libby Phillips. *Go Home! The True Story of James the Cat*, 5346(F)

Meichun, Zhong. *Finland*, 15461

Meidell, Sherry. *When Pioneer Wagons Rumbled West*, 4668(F)

Meier, Gisela. *Minorities*, 17581

Meier, Max. *Amazing Spiders*, 19594
Chameleons, 18747
Lizards, 18748

Meisel, Jacqueline D. *Australia*, 15246

Meisel, Paul. *Busy Buzzing Bumblebees and Other Tongue Twisters*, 6636
A Cake All for Me! 825(F)
The Fixits, 4233(F)
Go Away, Dog, 6544(F)
How to Talk to Your Cat, 19920
Howard and the Sitter Surprise, 1462(F)
I Wish My Brother Was a Dog, 1571(F)
Lunch Money and Other Poems About School, 11695
Monkey-Monkey's Trick, 6492(F)
Mr. Baseball, 6411(F)
The Three Little Pigs, 11018
The Tortoise and the Hare, 11071
We All Sing with the Same Voice, 14252
What Is the World Made Of? All About Solids, Liquids, and Gases, 20816
Why Do You Love Me? 3881(F)
Why I Sneeze, Shiver, Hiccup, and Yawn, 18049
Wizard and Wart in Trouble, 6670(F)
Your Insides, 18053

Meisner, James. *American Revolutionaries and Founders of the Nation*, 12681

Meister, Cari. *Busy, Busy City Street*, 4235(F)
Earthquakes, 20342
Grand Canyon, 16628
Hurricanes, 20707
Tiny Goes to the Library, 6517(F)
Tiny's Bath, 6518(F)
When Tiny Was Tiny, 6519(F)
Yellowstone National Park, 16629

Mekibel, Shoshana. *Here Come the Purim Players!* 6069(F)
A Thread of Kindness, 11169

Melanson, Luc. *Little Kim's Doll*, 4894(F)

Meli, Franco. *A Day with a Cheyenne*, 16003

Mellage, Nanette. *Coming Home*, 13455

Mellentin, Kath. *Let's Build an Airport*, 21143

Mellett, Peter. *Pyramids*, 14350

Melling, David. *Over the Moon! Best Loved Nursery Rhymes*, 865(F)
Where Are You? 2700(F)

Melmed, Laura K. *I Love You As Much . . .* , 743(F)
Jumbo's Lullaby, 744(F)
Little Oh, 4767(F)
Moishe's Miracle, 6096(F)
The Rainbabies, 10463(F)

Melnicove, Mark (jt. author). *Africa Is Not a Country*, 14909

Melnyczuk, Peter. *Red Fox*, 19144

Melo, Esperanca. *Making Memory Books*, 21450

Meltzer, Milton. *Carl Sandburg*, 12587
Driven from the Land, 16479
Food, 20116
Hold Your Horses! 20005
Mary McLeod Bethune, 12704
Ten Queens, 13738
There Comes a Time, 15893
Weapons and Warfare, 21397
Witches and Witch-Hunts, 14564

Melville, Kirsty. *Splash! A Penguin Counting Book*, 512(F)

Menard, Valerie. *Cristina Saralegui*, 12464
Jennifer Lopez, 12416
Oscar De La Hoya, 13584
Ricky Martin, 12422
Trent Dimas, 13683
Winona Ryder, 12462

Menchin, Scott. *The Day the Whale Came*, 3056(F)
Man Gave Names to All the Animals, 14237
Plenty of Pockets, 4094(F)

Mendez, Adriana. *Cubans in America*, 17582

Mendez, Phil. *The Black Snowman*, 5881(F)

Mendoza, Lunita. *Philippines*, 15247

Menick, Stephen. *The Muffin Child*, 9062(F)

Mennen, Ingrid. *One Round Moon and a Star for Me*, 3804(F)

Mennie, Steve. *The Fish Princess*, 1667(F)

Menotti, Gian Carlo. *Amahl and the Night Visitors*, 5882(F)

Merbreier, W. Carter. *Television*, 21272

Mercati, Cynthia. *Wagons Ho! A Diary of the Oregon Trail*, 9412(F)

Mercredi, Morningstar. *Fort Chipewyan Homecoming*, 16004

Meres, Jonathan. *The Big Bad Rumor*, 2497(F)

Meret, Sasha. *Make Things Fly*, 11965

Merlo, Claudio. *The History of Art*, 13910

Merrell, Patrick. *The 512 Ants on Sullivan Street*, 20587(F)

Merriam, Eve. *The Hole Story*, 3320(F)
Low Song, 3321(F)
On My Street, 6520(F)
The Singing Green, 11971
Ten Rosy Roses, 513(F)
Where Is Everybody? 97(F)
Where's That Cat? 5031(F)

Merrick, Patrick. *Bears*, 19056
Cardinals, 19261
Caterpillars, 19562
Eagles, 19332
Earthworms, 19614
Easter Bunnies, 17437
Fourth of July Fireworks, 17391
Loons, 19262
Raccoons, 18954
Ticks, 19466
Toads, 18730

Merrill, Jean. *The Girl Who Loved Caterpillars*, 10825
The Pushcart War, 9936(F)
The Toothpaste Millionaire, 9937(F)

Merrill, Linda. *The Princess and the Peacocks*, 9111(F)

Merrill, Yvonne Y. *Hands-On Latin America*, 21453
Hands-On Rocky Mountains, 21523

Merriman, Rachel. *Silly Ruby*, 6337(F)
The Tale of Tobias, 17303(F)

Messenger, Norman. *Hob and the Goblins*, 7957(F)
Jack and the Beanstalk, 11043
The Little Red Hen, 10983
Once upon a Time, 10551

Metaxas, Eric. *The Birthday ABC*, 98(F)
Stormalong, 11369

Metaxas, Eric, adapt. *Pinocchio*, 1410(F)

Metaxas, Eric, reteller. *David and Goliath*, 17309

Metcalf, Florence E. *A Peek at Japan*, 15133

Mets, Marilyn. *The Baseball Birthday Party*, 6584(F)
Scaredy Dog, 5430(F)

Mettler, Rene. *Birds*, 19219

Metzger, Lois. *Barry's Sister*, 8489(F)
Missing Girls, 8490(F)

Metzner, Seymour (jt. author). *The Sneaky Square and 113 Other Math Activities for Kids*, 20621

Meyer, Carolyn. *Anastasia*, 9063(F)
Beware, Princess Elizabeth, 9112(F)
Gideon's People, 8491(F)
Jubilee Journey, 7484(F)

Rio Grande Stories, 7357(F)

Meyer, Donald, ed. *Views from Our Shoes*, 17925

Meyer, Eleanor Walsh. *The Keeper of Ugly Sounds*, 1411(F)

Meyer, Louise (jt. author). *Master Weaver from Ghana*, 15010

Meyer, Susan E. *Mary Cassatt*, 12201

Meyerowitz, Rick. *Rip Van Winkle*, 7815(F)

Meyers, Bob. *Johnny Texas*, 9379(F)

Meyers, Madeleine, ed. *Cherokee Nation*, 16005
Forward into Light, 17045

Meyers, Susan. *Everywhere Babies*, 3322(F)

Mgadla, Part T. (jt. author). *Batswana*, 14969

Mi-ae, Lee. *The Two Love Stars*, 10731

Michaels, Elizabeth. *Patty Reed's Doll*, 9393(F)

Michaels, James. *Fast and Funny Paper Toys You Can Make*, 21609
Holiday Paper Projects, 21610
Optical Illusion Tricks and Toys, 20911
Paper Science Toys, 21650

Michaels, Steve. *Healing Warrior*, 13311

Michaels, William. *Clare and Her Shadow*, 3805(F)

Michels, Tilde. *What a Beautiful Day!* 4500(F)

Michelson, Richard. *Animals That Ought to Be*, 11901
Did You Say Ghosts? 1412(F)
Grandpa's Gamble, 6097(F)
Ten Times Better, 514(F)

Michener, James A. *South Pacific*, 9676(F)

Micich, Paul. *The Littlest Angel*, 1614(F)
Someone Was Watching, 7003(F)

Micklethwait, Lucy. *A Child's Book of Art*, 13911, 13912
A Child's Book of Play in Art, 13913
Spot a Cat, 13914

Micklethwait, Lucy, ed. *I Spy*, 99(F)

Micklos, John. *Leonard Nimoy*, 12426

Micucci, Charles. *The Life and Times of the Honeybee*, 19525
The Life and Times of the Peanut, 20117

Middleton, Don. *Dealing with Competitiveness*, 17720
Jaguars, 19099
Tigers, 19100

Middleton, Haydn. *Ancient Olympic Games*, 22251
Cleopatra, 13774
Crises at the Olympics, 22252
Great Olympic Moments, 22253

Henry Ford, 13281
Modern Olympic Games, 22254
Thomas Edison, 13271
William Shakespeare, 12592

Midge, Tiffany. *Buffalo*, 18955

Migdale, Lawrence. *Buffalo Days*, 15971
Celebrating Hanukkah, 17473
Celebrating Kwanzaa, 17368
Hoang Anh, 17567
Pueblo Storyteller, 15973

Migdale, Lawrence (jt. author). *A Child's California*, 16785

Miglio, Paige. *Crocky Dilly*, 1604(F)
One More Bunny, 604(F)
So Many Bunnies, 143(F)

Miklowitz, Gloria D. *Masada*, 8938(F)

Mikolaycak, Charles. *Bearhead*, 11094
Exodus, 17254
He Is Risen, 17441
The Hero of Bremen, 10915
The Man Who Could Call Down Owls, 1024(F)

Miksovsky, Katja (jt. author). *Claude Monet*, 12265

Miles, Betty. *Goldilocks and the Three Bears*, 11017
Just the Beginning, 7485(F)
The Sky Is Falling! 6521(F)
The Three Little Pigs, 11018
The Tortoise and the Hare, 11071

Miles, Elizabeth. *Dorothy of Oz*, 7602(F)
Louie and Dan Are Friends, 2604(F)
Molly Limbo, 1247(F)

Miles, J. C. *First Book of the Keyboard*, 14226

Miles, Lisa. *The Usborne Complete Book of Astronomy and Space*, 18400

Miles, Miska. *Annie and the Old One*, 8757(F)
Gertrude's Pocket, 8758(F)

Miles, William (jt. author). *Black Stars in Orbit*, 20964

Milgrim, David. *Cows Can't Fly*, 2498(F)
Patrick's Dinosaurs on the Internet, 1043(F)
Why Benny Barks, 6522(F)

Milhous, Katherine. *The Egg Tree*, 21454

Milich, Melissa. *Miz Fannie Mae's Fine New Easter Hat*, 1413(F)

Milivojevic, JoAnn. *Puerto Rico*, 15710, 15711
Serbia, 15280

Mill, Eleanor. *A Button in Her Ear*, 18146
A Cane in Her Hand, 8901(F)

Millais, Raoul. *Elijah and Pin-Pin*, 2499(F)

Millar, Heather. *Spain in the Age of Exploration*, 15481

Millard, Anne. *Pyramids*, 21144
A Street Through Time, 14351
The World of the Pharaoh, 14646

Millard, Kerry. *Nim's Island*, 6999(F)

Millen, C. M. *The Low-Down Laundry Line Blues*, 3806(F)
A Symphony for the Sheep, 4768(F)

Miller, Arthur. *Spain*, 15482

Miller, Brandon M. *Buffalo Gals*, 16343
Dressed for the Occasion, 21180
Just What the Doctor Ordered, 18024

Miller, Cameron. *Woodlore*, 20211

Miller, Dawn M. *David Robinson*, 13572

Miller, Debbie S. *A Caribou Journey*, 19156
Disappearing Lake, 16801
A Polar Bear Journey, 19057
River of Life, 16802

Miller, Dorothy R. *The Clearing*, 6974(F)
Home Wars, 8492(F)

Miller, Edna. *Mousekin's Family*, 2500(F)
Patches Finds a New Home, 5347(F)

Miller, Edward. *The Animal Mall*, 2048(F)
Circus Shapes, 347(F)
Cross a Bridge, 21130
Dig a Tunnel, 21131
Into the Sky, 21132
Is There Life in Outer Space? 20956
Take Off! 21081

Miller, Elizabeth I. *Just Like Home*, 5032(F)

Miller, Gus. *Hats Off for the Fourth of July!* 5660(F)

Miller, H. R. *Five Children and It*, 7987(F)

Miller, Helen L. *Everyday Plays for Boys and Girls*, 12033
First Plays for Children, 12034

Miller, J. Philip. *We All Sing with the Same Voice*, 14252

Miller, Jane. *Farm Alphabet Book*, 100(F)
Farm Counting Book, 515(F)

Miller, Jay. *American Indian Families*, 16006
American Indian Festivals, 16007
American Indian Foods, 16008
American Indian Games, 16009
Native Americans, 16010

Miller, Judi. *My Crazy Cousin Courtney*, 8343(F)
Purple Is My Game, Morgan Is My Name, 8493(F)

Miller, Kathryn Ann. *Did My First Mother Love Me?* 5033(F)

Miller, Lyle. *Boomer's Kids*, 9629(F)
Christopher Columbus, 12095
Uncle Carmello, 7543(F)

Miller, Margaret. *Baby Faces*, 3807(F)
Baby Food, 3323(F)
Big and Little, 4028
Can You Guess? 213(F)
Family Time, 3324(F)
Friends! 17731
Guess Who? 4236(F)
How You Were Born, 18238
I Love Colors, 284(F)
Me and My Bear, 3325(F)
My New Kitten, 5169
The New Baby at Your House, 17646
Riding Silver Star, 19990
Twins! 17684
What's on My Head? 3808(F)
Who Uses This? 3326
Miller, Marilyn. *Behind the Scenes at the Airport*, 21091
Behind the Scenes at the Hospital, 18042
Behind the Scenes at the Shopping Mall, 16935
Behind the Scenes at the TV News Studio, 14315
Thanksgiving, 17503
The Transcontinental Railroad, 16265
Words That Built a Nation, 15894
Miller, Marla. *All-American Girls*, 22298
Miller, Mary Beth. *Handtalk School*, 14017(F)
Miller, Michaela. *Guinea Pigs*, 19901
Miller, Millie. *The United States of America*, 15895
Miller, Myron. *101 Best Family Card Games*, 22237
Miller, Natalie. *The Statue of Liberty*, 16719
Miller, Phyllis (jt. author). *House of Shadows*, 7995(F)
Miller, Robert. *The Story of Nat Love*, 12757
Miller, Robert H. *A Pony for Jeremiah*, 9413(F)
The Story of Stagecoach Mary Fields, 12722
Miller, Ron. *Planetarium*, 20962
Rockets, 21003
Miller, Ruth. *I Went to the Bay*, 5348
Miller, Sara S. *Chickens*, 20063
Cows, 20064
Flies, 19467
Frogs and Toads, 18731
Goats, 20065
Horses and Rhinos, 18956
Owls, 19363
Perching Birds of North America, 19263
Pigs, 20066
Rodents, 19201
Salamanders, 18689
Sheep, 20067
Shorebirds, 19352

Snakes and Lizards, 18690
Three More Stories You Can Read to Your Dog, 6523(F)
Three Stories You Can Read to Your Cat, 6524(F)
Three Stories You Can Read to Your Dog, 6525(F)
True Bugs, 19468
Waterfowl, 19314
Miller, Shannon. *Winning Every Day*, 13701
Miller, Susan. *Cowboy Up!* 6226(F)
Miller, Susan Martins. *Betsy Ross*, 13188
Miller, Thomas. *Taking Time Out*, 22037
Miller, Tom. *Can a Coal Scuttle Fly?* 12263
Miller, Virginia. *Be Gentle!* 2501(F)
Eat Your Dinner! 2502(F)
Go to Bed! 745(F)
I Love You Just the Way You Are, 746(F)
On Your Potty! 3327(F)
Miller, William. *The Bus Ride*, 4769(F)
Frederick Douglass, 12713
A House by the River, 3809(F)
Night Golf, 5034(F)
The Piano, 4770(F)
Richard Wright and the Library Card, 4771(F)
Tituba, 12788
Zora Hurston and the Chinaberry Tree, 3810
Milligan, Bryce. *With the Wind, Kevin Dolan*, 9414(F)
Millman, Isaac. *Moses Goes to a Concert*, 5035(F)
Moses Goes to School, 5036(F)
Mills, Claudia. *Cally's Enterprise*, 8759(F)
Dinah for President, 10110(F)
Dinah Forever, 8760(F)
Dinah in Love, 9938(F)
Gus and Grandpa, 6526(F)
Gus and Grandpa and Show-and-Tell, 6527(F)
Gus and Grandpa and the Christmas Cookies, 6528(F)
Gus and Grandpa and the Two-Wheeled Bike, 8761(F)
Gus and Grandpa at the Hospital, 6529(F)
Gus and Grandpa Ride the Train, 6530(F)
Lizzie at Last, 10111(F)
Losers, Inc, 10112(F)
One Small Lost Sheep, 5883(F)
Phoebe's Parade, 5638(F)
Standing Up to Mr. O, 10113(F)
A Visit to Amy-Claire, 4029(F)
You're a Brave Man, Julius Zimmerman, 9939(F)
Mills, Judith C. *The Boy Who Stuck Out His Tongue*, 11177
The Stonehook Schooner, 9597(F)

Mills, Lauren. *Fairy Wings*, 1414(F)
The Goblin Baby, 1415(F)
The Rag Coat, 8762(F)
Mills, Yaroslava. *The Mitten*, 10864
Millspaugh, Ben. *Aviation and Space Science Projects*, 21092
Millyard, Karen (jt. author). *City at Night*, 16971
Milman, Barbara. *Light in the Shadows*, 14872
Milne, A. A. *The Magic Hill*, 10464(F)
Pooh's Bedtime Book, 7962(F)
The World of Christopher Robin, 11654
The World of Pooh, 7963(F)
Milne, Jean. *The Story of Diamonds*, 20565
Milne, Terry. *The Polka Dot Horse*, 1618(F)
Milner, Angela, ed. *Dinosaurs*, 14448
Milner, Angela (jt. author). *Dinosaur*, 14456
Milo, Francesco. *The Story of Architecture*, 13915
Milone, Karen. *Amelia Earhart*, 12115
Hopscotch Around the World, 22032
Marie Curie, 13261
Milord, Susan. *Bird Tales from Near and Far*, 10589
Hands Around the World, 21455
Mexico! 15638
Tales Alive! 10590
Milord, Susan, reteller. *Tales of the Shimmering Sky*, 10591
Milton, Joyce. *Bats*, 19032
Bears Are Curious, 19058
Big Cats, 19101
Gorillas, 19010
Marching to Freedom, 12749
Mummies, 14647
Whales, 6531(F)
Wild, Wild Wolves, 6532
Min, Laura. *Mrs. Sato's Hens*, 516(F)
Min, Willemien. *Peter's Patchwork Dream*, 1416(F)
Minahan, John A. *Abigail's Drum*, 9307(F)
Minard, Rosemary, ed. *Womenfolk and Fairy Tales*, 10592
Minarik, Else Holmelund. *Little Bear*, 6533(F)
No Fighting, No Biting! 6534(F)
Miner, Chalise. *Rain Forest Girl*, 17672
Miner, Julia. *The Unbreakable Code*, 9165(F)
Ming, Li. *Hanuman*, 10796
Pegasus, the Flying Horse, 11517
Minor, Wendell. *Abe Lincoln Remembers*, 13078
Arctic Son, 4655(F)
Everglades, 16858
Grand Canyon, 16630

Grassroots, 11689
Heartland, 11696
A Lucky Thing, 11692
Mojave, 11983
Morning, Noon, and Night, 18626
Pumpkin Heads! 6034(F)
Red Fox Running, 5149(F)
Snow Bear, 5225(F)
Minter, Daniel. *The Foot Warmer and the Crow*, 9266(F)
Seven Spools of Thread, 5637(F)
Minters, Frances. *Chicken for a Day*, 6535(F)
Cinder-Elly, 10465
Sleepless Beauty, 4237(F)
Mintz, Barbara (jt. author). *Hieroglyphics*, 14634
Miotto, Enrico. *The Universe*, 18401
Mirable, Lisa. *The Berlin Wall*, 15328
Miralles, Jose. *Little Sure Shot*, 12432
Miranda, Anne. *Baby-Sit!* 3328(F)
Beep! Beep! 5588(F)
Does a Mouse Have a House? 18910
Monster Math, 517(F)
Night Songs, 747(F)
Pignic, 101(F)
To Market, To Market, 3329(F)
Vroom, Chugga, Vroom-Vroom, 518(F)
Mirocha, Paul. *How Do Birds Find Their Way?* 19231
Hungry Plants, 20227
I Am Lavina Cumming, 9589(F)
Oil Spill! 16990
Mirpuri, Gouri. *Indonesia*, 15186
Mistry, Nilesh. *The Illustrated Book of Myths*, 11455
Turtle Bay, 5365(F)
Mitakidou, Christodoula (jt. author). *Mr. Semolina-Semolinus*, 11070
Mitchell, Adrian. *Nobody Rides the Unicorn*, 1417(F)
Twice My Size, 5349(F)
The Ugly Duckling, 10466(F)
Mitchell, Anastasia. *Silly Science Tricks (with Professor Solomon Snickerdoodle)*, 18337
Mitchell, Barbara. *America, I Hear You*, 12326
Between Two Worlds, 12510
"Good Morning Mr. President," 12588
A Pocketful of Goobers, 13256
Raggin', 12330
Shoes for Everyone, 12770
We'll Race You, Henry, 13282
The Wizard of Sound, 13272
Mitchell, David. *Martial Arts*, 22269
The Young Martial Arts Enthusiast, 22270
Mitchell, Hayley R. *The Wolf*, 19133
Mitchell, Hetty. *Martin Luther King Day*, 12746
The Wizard of Sound, 13272

Mitchell, Joyce Slayton. *Crashed, Smashed, and Mashed*, 21309
Tractor-Trailer Trucker, 21310
Mitchell, Judith. *The Dragonling*, 7875(F)
Mitchell, Kathy. *Beauty and the Beast*, 10428
Jane Eyre, 6777(F)
Mitchell, Lori. *Different Just Like Me*, 3330(F)
Mitchell, Margaree King. *Uncle Jed's Barber Shop*, 9598(F)
Mitchell, Mark. *Kacy and the Space Shuttle Secret*, 10199(F)
Mitchell, Nancy. *Global Warning*, 6975(F)
Mitchell, Pratima. *Gandhi*, 13804
Mitchell, Rhonda. *Little Red Ronnika*, 10919
Rain Feet, 3248(F)
The Talking Cloth, 3811(F)
Mitchell, Tracy. *The Great Divide*, 421(F)
Mitchelson, Mitch. *The Most Excellent Book of How to Be a Juggler*, 21671
Mitgutsch, Ali. *From Rubber Tree to Tire*, 21047
From Sea to Salt, 21048
From Swamp to Coal, 20843
From Wood to Paper, 21049
Mitra, Annie. *The Blind Men and the Elephant*, 6192
Mitton, Jacqueline. *Galileo*, 13291
Informania, 21936
Zoo in the Sky, 18549
Mitton, Jacqueline (jt. author). *The Young Oxford Book of Astronomy*, 18402
Mitton, Simon. *The Young Oxford Book of Astronomy*, 18402
Miya, Ann. *Nothing Happened*, 694(F)
Miyake, Yoshi. *Miloli's Orchids*, 2944(F)
Moshi Moshi, 4745(F)
What Makes It Rain? 20727
Wonders of Rivers, 20511
Miyamoto, Mas. *The Story of Shoes*, 21185
Miyazaki, Hibiki. *Making the World*, 258(F)
Miyazaki, Yoshi. *Making the World*, 258(F)
Moche, Dinah L. *Astronomy Today*, 18403
Mochizuki, Ken. *Baseball Saved Us*, 5037(F)
Heroes, 7358(F)
Passage to Freedom, 14873
Mockford, Caroline. *Cleo the Cat*, 5350(F)
The Elephants' Ears, 1048(F)
What's This? 4501
Modarressi, Mitra. *Monster Stew*, 1418(F)
Yard Sale! 1419(F)

Modell, Frank. *One Zillion Valentines*, 6174(F)
Modesitt, Jeanne. *It's Hanukkah!* 6098(F)
Little Bunny's Easter Surprise, 5971(F)
Mama, If You Had a Wish, 2503(F)
Sometimes I Feel Like a Mouse, 214(F)
The Story of Z, 102(F)
Moe, Jorgen (jt. author). *The Man Who Kept House*, 11119
Norwegian Folk Tales, 11120
Moehn, Heather. *Everything You Need to Know When Someone You Know Has Leukemia*, 17986
World Holidays, 17207
Moeri, Louise. *The Devil in Ol' Rosie*, 9599(F)
Save Queen of Sheba, 9415(F)
Star Mother's Youngest Child, 5884(F)
Moers, Hermann. *Katie and the Big, Brave Bear*, 1420(F)
Moeschl, Richard. *Exploring the Sky*, 18404
Moeyaert, Bart. *Bare Hands*, 7265(F)
Moffatt, Judith. *Bats*, 19032
I Am a Rock, 20564
I Am an Apple, 6506(F)
I Am Water, 20739
I'm a Caterpillar, 6507(F)
Pumpkin Faces, 239(F)
Snakes, 18757
Snow Shapes, 21456
Two Crows Counting, 546(F)
Who Stole the Cookies? 6536(F)
Moffett, Jami. *Did My First Mother Love Me?* 5033(F)
Do I Have a Daddy? A Story About a Single-Parent Child, 17671
Mohan, Claire J. *Saint Maximilian Kolbe*, 13822
The Young Life of Mother Teresa of Calcutta, 13856
The Young Life of Pope John Paul II, 13816
Mohr, Joseph. *Silent Night, Holy Night*, 14209
Mohr, Mark. *The Storm*, 4974(F)
Mohr, Nicholasa. *All for the Better*, 12824
The Magic Shell, 8763(F)
Moignot, Daniel. *Fire Fighting*, 5589(F)
Tools, 5561(F)
Moiz, Azra. *Taiwan*, 15187
Moje, Steven W. *Cool Chemistry*, 20289
Moktefi, Mokhtar. *The Arabs in the Golden Age*, 15556
Molan, Christine. *Growing Up in Ancient Rome*, 14717
Molk, Laurel. *Good Job, Oliver!* 2504(F)
Off We Go! 2890(F)

Mollel, Tololwa M. *Ananse's Feast*, 10699
Big Boy, 4772(F)
The Flying Tortoise, 10700
The King and the Tortoise, 10701
Kitoto the Mighty, 10702
My Rows and Piles of Coins, 4773(F)
The Orphan Boy, 10703
Shadow Dance, 8973
Song Bird, 10704
Subira Subira, 10705
To Dinner, for Dinner, 10706
Moller, Anne. *A Letter to Santa Claus*, 5952(F)
Molnar-Fenton, Stephan. *An Mei's Strange and Wondrous Journey*, 3812(F)
Molzahn, Arlene Bourgeois. *Extreme Mountain Biking*, 22164
The San Francisco 49ers Football Team, 22186
Top 10 American Women Sprinters, 13390
Mombourquette, Paul. *Emma and the Silk Train*, 4726(F)
Fog Cat, 5254(F)
Monaco, Octavia. *A Brave Little Princess*, 1399(F)
Monceaux, Morgan. *My Heroes, My People*, 16344
Monchaux, Marie-Claude. *The Trees Kneel at Christmas*, 9745(F)
Moncure, Jane Belk. *My "a" Sound Box*, 103(F)
Monjo, F. N. *The Drinking Gourd*, 9308(F)
Monk, Isabell. *Family*, 3813(F)
Hope, 3814(F)
Monke, Ingrid. *Boston*, 16720
Monks, Lydia. *The Cat Barked?* 2505(F)
City Pig, 2811(F)
Mad Dog McGraw, 1633(F)
Monroe, Chris. *Totally Uncool*, 5013(F)
Monroe, Jean Guard. *They Dance in the Sky*, 11280
Monroe, Judy. *Inhalant Drug Dangers*, 17880
Steroid Drug Dangers, 17881
Monroe, Judy (jt. author). *Cooking the Korean Way*, 21682
Cooking the Thai Way, 21705
Cooking the Vietnamese Way, 21725
Monroe, Lucy. *Creepy Cuisine*, 21722
Monsell, Mary Elise. *The Mysterious Cases of Mr. Pin*, 6976(F)
Toohy and Wood, 7964(F)
Underwear! 2506(F)
Monson-Burton, Marianne, comp. *Girls Know Best 2*, 17721
Montáñez, Nívea O. *Mediopollito/Half-a-Chick*, 11424

Montavon, Jay. *The Curse of King Tut's Tomb*, 14648
Monte, Richard. *The Flood Tales*, 17310
Monteith, David. *Hellow, Two-Wheeler!* 6513(F)
Montejo, Victor, reteller. *Popol Vuh*, 11411
Montes, Marisa. *Juan Bobo Goes to Work*, 4774(F)
Something Wicked's in Those Woods, 7965(F)
Montez, Michele. *50 Simple Things Kids Can Do to Save the Earth*, 16959
Montezinos, Nina S. *Joe Joe*, 3417(F)
Look! Snow! 3152(F)
Montgomery, L. M. *Anne of Green Gables*, 8764(F)
Christmas with Anne and Other Holiday Stories, 9749(F)
Montgomery, Lucy. *Onion Tears*, 7348(F)
Montgomery, Michael. *Johnny Appleseed*, 12843
Montgomery, Michael G. *Night Rabbits*, 5371(F)
Montgomery, Sy. *The Man-Eating Tigers of Sundarbans*, 19102
The Snake Scientist, 18770
Montijo, Yolanda (jt. author). *Native Ways*, 15999
Montresor, Beni. *May I Bring a Friend?* 4130(F)
Montserrat, Pep. *The Gift*, 5702(F)
Moody, Barbara S. *When a Parent Goes to Jail*, 17092
Moody, Richard. *Over 65 Million Years Ago*, 14449
Moon, Lily. *The Bearer of Gifts*, 5925(F)
Moon, Nicola. *Happy Birthday, Amelia*, 5712(F)
Something Special, 5519(F)
Moon, Pat. *The Spying Game*, 8765(F)
Mooney, Bill (jt. author). *More Ready-to-Tell Tales from Around the World*, 10565
Mooney, David. *Say It Again*, 18612
Mooney, Martin. *Brett Favre*, 13611
The Comanche Indians, 16011
Moorcroft, Christine. *The Taj Mahal*, 15111
Moore, Barbara (jt. author). *The Nine-Ton Cat*, 13964
Moore, Bobbie. *Pioneer Days*, 16334
Moore, Clement Clarke. *The Night Before Christmas*, 11839, 11840, 11841, 11842, 11843, 11844, 11845, 11846, 11847, 11848
The Teddy Bears' Night Before Christmas, 11849
A Visit from Saint Nicholas and Santa Mouse, Too! 5885(F)

Moore, Cyd. *I Love You, Bunny Rabbit*, 3349(F)
I Love You, Stinky Face, 734(F)
I Miss You, Stinky Face, 3785(F)
It's Time for School, Stinky Face, 5518(F)
Jane Yolen's Songs of Summer, 14194
What Is the Full Moon Full Of? 4257(F)
Where Is the Night Train Going? 11710
Moore, Elaine. *Roly-Poly Puppies*, 519(F)
Moore, Elizabeth. *Mimi and Jean-Paul's Cajun Mardi Gras*, 5639(F)
Moore, Emily. *Whose Side Are You On?* 8766(F)
Moore, Eva. *Buddy*, 19957
Moore, Gustav. *Earth Cycles*, 18438
Stone Wall Secrets, 20574
Moore, Inga. *The River Bank*, 7752(F)
Six-Dinner Sid, 2507(F)
Moore, Jo. *Some Trains Run on Water*, 21341
Spiders Have Fangs, 19586
Moore, Lillian. *Adam Mouse's Book of Poems*, 11972
Don't Be Afraid, Amanda, 7966(F)
I Never Did That Before, 11656
Poems Have Roots, 11973
Moore, Lillian (jt. author). *Hooray for Me!* 3068(F)
Moore, Martha. *Under the Mermaid Angel*, 8344(F)
Moore, Miriam. *Koi's Python*, 8974(F)
The Kwanzaa Contest, 9750(F)
Moore, Patrick. *Comets and Shooting Stars*, 18521
The Planets, 18483
The Stars, 18550
The Sun and Moon, 18522
Moore, Robin. *Hercules*, 11493
Moore, Ruth Nulton. *Distant Thunder*, 9242(F)
Moore, Yvette. *A Prairie Year*, 20530
Moores, Eldridge M., ed. *Volcanoes and Earthquakes*, 20343
Moores, Ian. *The Science Factory*, 18343
Moorman, Margaret. *Light the Lights!* 5640
Mora, Francisco. *Delicious Hullabaloo*, 2508(F)
Listen to the Desert/Oye al Desierto, 4502
The Little Red Ant and the Great Big Crumb, 11396
Mora, Pat. *A Birthday Basket for Tia*, 5713(F)
Confetti, 11657
Delicious Hullabaloo, 2508(F)

The Desert Is My Mother/El Desierto Es Mi Madre, 11974
Listen to the Desert/Oye al Desierto, 4502
The Night the Moon Fell, 11412
Pablo's Tree, 3815(F)
The Rainbow Tulip, 5038(F)
This Big Sky, 11975
Tomas and the Library Lady, 3331(F)
Uno, Dos, Tres, 520(F)
Moraes, Odilon. *The Bear Who Didn't Like Honey*, 2466(F)
Moragne, Wendy. *Allergies*, 17987
Dyslexia, 17926
Moran, Alex. *Popcorn*, 6537(F)
Moran, Mike. *Magic Tricks*, 21786
Moran, Rosslyn. *Farmyard Tales from Far and Wide*, 10542
Moran, Tom. *The U.S. Army*, 21398
Morck, Irene. *Tyler's New Boots*, 2960(F)
Mordan, C. B. *Lost! A Story in String*, 3626(F)
Mordvinoff, Nicolas. *Finders Keepers*, 5310(F)
Morehead, Debby. *A Special Place for Charlee*, 7266(F)
Moreillon, Judi. *Sing Down the Rain*, 14253
Morell, Abelardo. *Alice's Adventures in Wonderland*, 7643(F)
Morelli, Jay (jt. author). *Beginning Golf*, 21994
Moreno, René King. *¡Fiesta!* 452(F)
Under the Lemon Moon, 4956(F)
Moreton, Daniel. *I Knew Two Who Said Moo*, 378(F)
La Cucaracha Martina, 11430
Lost! 6698(F)
What Day Is It? 6699(F)
Morey, Eileen. *Eleanor Roosevelt*, 13184
Morey, Shaun. *Incredible Fishing Stories for Kids*, 22176(F)
Morey, Walt. *Gentle Ben*, 7267(F)
Scrub Dog of Alaska, 7268(F)
Year of the Black Pony, 7269(F)
Morgan, Adrian (jt. author). *Materials*, 20813
Using Sound, 20942
Water, 20741
Morgan, Cheryl Koenig. *The Everglades*, 16875
Morgan, Gwyneth. *Life in a Medieval Village*, 14782
Morgan, Jill. *Blood Brothers*, 7967(F)
Morgan, Kate. *The Story of Things*, 14565
Morgan, Mary. *Asleep in a Heap*, 811(F)
Bloomers! 4596
Buba Leah and Her Paper Children, 3863(F)
Daddies, 3852(F)
Gentle Rosie, 3332(F)

Hannah and Jack, 5354(F)
I'm the Boss! 3954(F)
Our Puppies Are Growing, 19960
The Tiger Has a Toothache, 17851
The Way to Wyatt's House, 1038(F)
Morgan, Michaela. *Helpful Betty Solves a Mystery*, 2509(F)
Morgan, Nina. *The Caribbean and the Gulf of Mexico*, 19830
Lasers, 20875
Mother Teresa, 13857
The North Sea and the Baltic Sea, 19831
Morgan, Pierre. *The Miser on the Mountain*, 11265
Snow Pumpkin, 4038(F)
Sometimes Moon, 3877(F)
The Squiggle, 1547(F)
Morgan, Rowland. *In the Next Three Seconds*, 21937
Morgan, Sally. *Acid Rain*, 16999
Animals and Their World, 18835
Flowers, Trees, and Fruits, 20044
Materials, 20813
The Ozone Hole, 17000
Using Sound, 20942
Water, 20741
Weather, 20784
Morgan, Sally (jt. author). *Ultimate Atlas of Almost Everything*, 14352
Morgan, Terri. *Chris Mullin*, 13552
Gabrielle Reece, 13708
Junior Seau, 13630
Photography, 21802
Steve Young, 13640
Morgan, Tessa. *Do Sharks Ever . . . ?* 19769
Morgane, Wendy. *New Jersey*, 16721
Morgenstern, Susie. *Secret Letters from 0 to 10*, 9940(F)
Mori, Hana. *Jirohattan*, 9677(F)
Mori, Midori. *Neem the Half-Boy*, 11200
Morimoto, Junko. *The Two Bullies*, 1421(F)
Morin, Isobel V. *Politics, American Style*, 17100
Women Chosen for Public Office, 12682
Morin, Leane. *Shy Mama's Halloween*, 5984(F)
Morin, Paul. *Animal Dreaming*, 10849
At Break of Day, 17191(F)
The Dragon's Pearl, 10762
Flags, 4853(F)
The Ghost Dance, 15997
The Orphan Boy, 10703
Panther, 19095
Morley, Jacqueline. *Across America*, 16088
Egyptian Myths, 11453
An Egyptian Pyramid, 14649
How Would You Survive as a Viking? 15462

How Would You Survive as an Ancient Egyptian? 14650
How Would You Survive in the American West? 16345
The Living Tomb, 14651
A Renaissance Town, 14802
A Roman Villa, 14733
Shakespeare's Theater, 14324
Viking Town, 15463
Morley, Jacqueline, reteller. *Greek Myths*, 11494
Morninghouse, Sundaira. *Nightfeathers*, 11659
Moroney, Christopher. *Babe*, 6471(F)
Moroney, Lynn. *Moontellers*, 7968(F)
Morozumi, Atsuko. *My Friend Gorilla*, 1422(F)
One Gorilla, 521(F)
The Reindeer Christmas, 5905(F)
Morpurgo, Michael. *Arthur*, 11019(F)
The Butterfly Lion, 7270(F)
Escape from Shangri-La, 7486(F)
The Ghost of Grania O'Malley, 8907(F)
The Silver Swan, 5351(F)
Wombat Goes Walkabout, 2510(F)
Morrell, Darby. *Orphan*, 4493
Morrill, Leslie. *Back Yard Angel*, 7423(F)
A Boy in the Doghouse, 5190(F)
Creepy-Crawly Birthday, 5696(F)
Fourth Grade Celebrity, 10062(F)
Left-Handed Shortstop, 10327(F)
Love, from the Fifth-Grade Celebrity, 8288(F)
Morgan's Zoo, 7798(F)
Nighty-Nightmare, 9888(F)
Poopsie Pomerantz, Pick Up Your Feet, 8659(F)
Rat Teeth, 8433(F)
Scared Silly, 6010(F)
Stay, Fang, 5251(F)
Totally Disgusting, 8182(F)
Morris, Ann. *The Baby Book*, 3816
The Daddy Book, 3817
Families, 17673
Hats, Hats, Hats, 3333(F)
Houses and Homes, 3334(F)
Karate Boy, 22271
Loving, 3818
The Mommy Book, 3819
Play, 215
Shoes, Shoes, Shoes, 21181
Teamwork, 216
Weddings, 5641
Work, 217
Morris, Bob. *Crispin the Terrible*, 1423(F)
Morris, Gerald. *The Savage Damsel and the Dwarf*, 7969(F)
The Squire, His Knight, and His Lady, 9113(F)
The Squire's Tale, 9114(F)
Morris, Gilbert. *The Dangerous Voyage*, 10216(F)

Journey to Freedom, 7970(F)
Vanishing Clues, 7971(F)
Morris, Greggory. *Basketball Basics*, 22137
Morris, Jackie. *The Fourth Wise Man*, 5930(F)
How the Whale Became and Other Stories, 1254(F)
Mariana and the Merchild, 11442
Out of the Ark, 17185
Parables, 17286
The Time of the Lion, 5366(F)
Morris, Jeffrey. *The FDR Way*, 13098
The Jefferson Way, 13051
The Washington Way, 13117
Morris, Juddi. *At Home with the Presidents*, 12683
Tending the Fire, 12257
Morris, Judy K. *The Kid Who Ran for Principal*, 10114(F)
Nightwalkers, 7271(F)
Morris, Karyn. *The Kids Can Press Jumbo Book of Gardening*, 21770
Morris, Kim. *Molly in the Middle*, 6538(F)
Morris, Neil. *Ancient Egypt*, 14652
The Atlas of Ancient Egypt, 14653
Morris, Robert A. *Dolphin*, 19687
Morris, Winifred. *What If the Shark Wears Tennis Shoes?* 748(F)
Morrison, Gordon. *Bald Eagle*, 19333
Oak Tree, 20212
Morrison, Lillian. *I Scream, You Scream*, 11902
Whistling the Morning In, 11976
Morrison, Lillian, ed. *At the Crack of the Bat*, 12001
Slam Dunk, 12002
Morrison, Marion. *Belize*, 15679
Brazil, 15764
Colombia, 15765
Cuba, 15712, 15713
Ecuador, 15766
Indians of the Andes, 15767
Paraguay, 15768
Peru, 15769
Uruguay, 15770
Venezuela, 15771
Morrison, Slade (jt. author). *The Big Box*, 7972(F)
Morrison, Taylor. *Antonio's Apprenticeship*, 13948
Cheetah, 19103
Civil War Artist, 16421
The Neptune Fountain, 9064(F)
Morrison, Toni. *The Big Box*, 7972(F)
Morrissey, Dean. *The Christmas Ship*, 5886(F)
Ship of Dreams, 749(F)
Morrissey, Peter. *Ice Skating*, 22225
The Young Ice Skater, 22226
Morrow, Mary Frances. *Sarah Winnemucca*, 13001

Mortimer, Anne. *A Kitten's Year*, 5179(F)
Morton, Christine. *Picnic Farm*, 3335(F)
Morton, Jane. *Moozie's Kind Adventure*, 2511(F)
Morton, Robert. *The Bear*, 19040
Mosatche, Harriet S. *Too Old for This, Too Young for That! Your Survival Guide for the Middle-School Years*, 18267
Moscovitch, Arlene. *Egypt, the Culture*, 14654
Egypt, the Land, 15508
Mosel, Arlene. *Tikki Tikki Tembo*, 10766
Moseng, Elisabeth. *Just One More Story*, 10507(F)
Moser, Barry. *The All Jahdu Storybook*, 7781(F)
Appalachia, 3403
Around the World in Eighty Days, 7111(F)
Bingleman's Midway, 2903(F)
The Bird House, 8056(F)
A Brilliant Streak, 12609
Cloud Eyes, 11262
Dippers, 7989(F)
East of the Sun and West of the Moon, 12041
Ever Heard of an Aardwolf? 18649
Ghost Horse of the Mounties, 11805
Good and Perfect Gifts, 9751(F)
Grandpa's Gamble, 6097(F)
Journey, 8481(F)
Jump! The Adventures of Brer Rabbit, 11345
Just So Stories, 7246(F)
My Cats Nick and Nora, 5249(F)
On Call Back Mountain, 4918(F)
Our New Puppy, 5250(F)
Pilgrim's Progress, 8070(F)
Prayers from the Ark, 17514
A Ring of Tricksters, 10558
Telling Time with Big Mama Cat, 190(F)
Those Building Men, 5577(F)
When Birds Could Talk and Bats Could Sing, 11342
When Willard Met Babe Ruth, 10329(F)
Moser, Cara. *Telling Time with Big Mama Cat*, 190(F)
Moser, Diane (jt. author). *Exploring the Reaches of the Solar System*, 18531
Moser, Madeline. *Ever Heard of an Aardwolf?* 18649
Moses, Amy. *Doctors Help People*, 17803
Moses, Brian. *Winking, Blinking, Wiggling, and Waggling*, 18836
Moses, Will. *The Legend of Sleepy Hollow*, 7973(F)
Rip Van Winkle, 7974(F)
Silent Night, 5887(F)

Mosher, Kiki. *Learning About Bravery from the Life of Harriet Tubman*, 12801
Learning About Fairness from the Life of Susan B. Anthony, 13131
Learning About Honesty from the Life of Abraham Lincoln, 13074
Learning About Leadership from the Life of George Washington, 13118
Mosher, Richard. *The Taxi Navigator*, 8345(F)
Moss, Carol. *Science in Ancient Mesopotamia*, 14655
Moss, Cynthia. *Little Big Ears*, 19167
Moss, Deborah M. *Lee, the Rabbit with Epilepsy*, 5039(F)
Moss, Jeff. *Bone Poems*, 11660
The Butterfly Jar, 11661
Moss, Joanne. *The Fox and the Rooster and Other Tales*, 10599
The Smallest Bear, 2471(F)
Moss, Lloyd. *Zin! Zin! Zin! A Violin*, 14227(F)
Moss, Marissa. *The All-New Amelia*, 8346(F)
Amelia Takes Command, 8767(F)
Amelia Works It Out, 8768(F)
Amelia's Family Ties, 8494(F)
Dr. Amelia's Boredom Survival Guide, 22038
Emma's Journal, 9243(F)
Hannah's Journal, 9600(F)
The Lapsnatcher, 3590(F)
Luv, Amelia Luv, Nadia, 8347(F)
Mel's Diner, 3336(F)
Rachel's Journal, 9416(F)
Regina's Big Mistake, 5520(F)
True Heart, 9417(F)
Moss, Miriam. *Jigsaw*, 1424(F)
Moss, P. Buckley. *Reuben and the Blizzard*, 3653(F)
Reuben and the Quilt, 3654(F)
Most, Bernard. *A B C T-Rex*, 104(F)
Catbirds and Dogfish, 18650
Catch Me If You Can! 6539(F)
Cock-A-Doodle-Moo! 2512(F)
The Cow That Went Oink, 2513(F)
Dinosaur Cousins? 14450
A Dinosaur Named After Me, 5352
Dinosaur Questions, 14451
Happy Holidaysaurus! 17392
Hippopotamus Hunt, 21883(F)
How Big Were the Dinosaurs? 14452
If the Dinosaurs Came Back, 2514(F)
A Pair of Protoceratops, 218(F)
Pets in Trumpets and Other Word-Play Riddles, 21842
A Trio of Triceratops, 219(F)
The Very Boastful Kangaroo, 6540(F)

Whatever Happened to the Dinosaurs? 4238(F)

Where to Look for a Dinosaur, 14453

Z-Z-Zoink! 2515(F)

Zoodles, 21843

Mostue, Trude. *Wild About Animals*, 18957

Mostyn, David. *Dad, You're Not Funny and Other Poems*, 11922

Motchkavitz, Leslie (jt. author). *The Kid's Guide to Good Grammar*, 14040

Mother Goose. *Gregory Griggs and Other Nursery Rhyme People*, 866

Mother Goose, 867, 868(F), 869, 870(F)

Real Mother Goose, 871

The Real Mother Goose Clock Book, 872

Tomie dePaola's Mother Goose, 873

Mott, Evelyn Clarke. *Balloon Ride*, 2961

Steam Train Ride, 5590

Mould, Chris. *Frankenstein*, 10217(F)

Mound, Laurence. *Amazing Insects*, 19469

Mount, Arthur. *Picnic on a Cloud*, 7811(F)

Mowat, Farley. *The Dog Who Wouldn't Be*, 7272(F)

Moxley, Sheila. *The Arabian Nights*, 11195

Joy to the World, 9756

Marduk the Mighty and Other Stories of Creation, 10582

Skip Across the Ocean, 826(F)

Stone Girl, Bone Girl, 13227

Moyer, Marshall M. *Rollo Bones, Canine Hypnotist*, 2516(F)

Mozelle, Shirley. *The Pig Is in the Pantry, the Cat Is on the Shelf*, 2517(F)

Mudge, Jacqueline. *Kevin Nash*, 13705

Mueller, Virginia. *Monster's Birthday Hiccups*, 5714(F)

Muggamin, Howard. *The Jewish Americans*, 17583

Muirden, James. *Seeing Stars*, 18405

Mukerji, Dhan Gopal. *Gay-Neck*, 7273(F)

Mulcahy, Robert. *Medical Technology*, 13218

Muldoon, Kathleen M. *Princess Pooh*, 3820(F)

Mulford, Philippa Greene. *The Holly Sisters on Their Own*, 7487(F)

Mullarkey, Lisa Geurdes. *The Witch's Portraits*, 7975(F)

Muller, Eric. *While You're Waiting for the Food to Come*, 18335

Muller, Robin. *Hickory, Dickory, Dock*, 2518(F)

Muller, Thomas. *What a Beautiful Day!* 4500(F)

Mullin, Caryl Cude. *A Riddle of Roses*, 7976(F)

Mullin, Chris. *Basketball*, 22138

The Young Basketball Player, 22139

Mullin, Rita Thievon. *Who's for Dinner?* 18837

Mullins, Patricia. *Crocodile Beat*, 2265(F)

Hattie and the Fox, 2095(F)

The Magic Saddle, 5878(F)

One Horse Waiting for Me, 522(F)

Shoes from Grandpa, 4149(F)

Mulvany, Martha. *The Story of the Boxer*, 19958

Mulvihill, Margaret. *The Treasury of Saints and Martyrs*, 17208

Munan, Heidi. *Malaysia*, 15188

Munduruku, Daniel. *Tales of the Amazon*, 11441

Munoz, Claudio. *Shadow*, 5356(F)

Muñoz, William. *Baby Horses*, 5359

Dogs, 19961

A Family Goes Hunting, 22043

Gray Wolf, Red Wolf, 19136

Horses, 20007

Ospreys, 19354

Prairie Dogs, 19203

Prairies, 20541

Waiting Alligators, 18705

Watchful Wolves, 19117

West by Covered Wagon, 16349

Where the Bald Eagles Gather, 19338

Where the Wild Horses Roam, 20008

Munro, Margaret. *The Story of Life on Earth*, 14454

Munro, Roxie. *Crocodiles, Camels and Dugout Canoes*, 12071

The Inside-Outside Book of Libraries, 13992

Munsch, Robert. *Alligator Baby*, 4239(F)

Andrew's Loose Tooth, 4240(F)

From Far Away, 5040(F)

Get Out of Bed! 4241(F)

Mud Puddle, 1425(F)

Munschworks, 4242(F)

Munschworks 3, 4245

Munschworks 2, 4243(F)

Ribbon Rescue, 3337(F)

Stephanie's Ponytail, 4244(F)

We Share Everything! 5521(F)

Munsinger, Lynn. *An Arkful of Animals*, 11773

Bugs! 11790

Dinosaurs Forever, 11817

Don't Need Friends, 1987(F)

Group Soup, 1853(F)

Hedgehog Bakes a Cake, 6486(F)

Hello, House! 11348

Hooway for Wodney Wat, 2358(F)

It Wasn't My Fault, 4211(F)

Just a Little Bit, 2762(F)

Listen, Buddy, 2359(F)

Me First, 2360(F)

Monster's Birthday Hiccups, 5714(F)

My New Boy, 6575(F)

Nothing Sticks Like a Shadow, 2763(F)

One Hungry Monster, 542(F)

One Monkey Too Many, 486(F)

Pookins Gets Her Way, 1347(F)

A Porcupine Named Fluffy, 2361(F)

Princess Penelope's Parrot, 1348(F)

Rooter Remembers, 2549(F)

Tacky and the Emperor, 2362(F)

Tacky in Trouble, 2363(F)

Tacky the Penguin, 2364(F)

The Teeny Tiny Ghost, 6062(F)

Three Cheers for Tacky, 2365(F)

Turtle Time, 787(F)

Underwear! 2506(F)

What Grandmas Do Best/What Grandpas Do Best, 3825(F)

What Mommies Do Best/What Daddies Do Best, 2541(F)

Whooo's Haunting the Teeny Tiny Ghost? 6063(F)

The Wizard, the Fairy and the Magic Chicken, 1349(F)

A Zooful of Animals, 11774

Munson, Derek. *Enemy Pie*, 4030(F)

Munson, Sammye. *Today's Tejano Heroes*, 12684

The Muppet Workshop. *The Muppets Big Book of Crafts*, 21457

Murawski, Darlyne A. *Bug Faces*, 19470

Murdico, Suzanne J. *Coyote Attacks*, 19134

Drug Abuse, 17882

Murdocca, Sal. *Big Numbers*, 548(F)

The Clue of the Left-Handed Envelope, 7080(F)

Dinosaurs, 14458

Dinosaurs Before Dark, 6554(F)

Double Trouble in Walla Walla, 4117(F)

The Monsters' Test, 6005(F)

A Pig Tale, 2527(F)

Tom the TV Cat, 6376(F)

Two for Stew, 4255(F)

Murphy, Bryan. *Experiment with Air*, 20673

Experiment with Water, 20742

Murphy, Camay C. (jt. author). *Can a Coal Scuttle Fly?* 12263

Murphy, Charles R. *What Once Was White*, 17899

Murphy, Chris. *Super-Duper Jokes*, 21859

Murphy, Chuck. *Bow Wow*, 345(F)

Chuck Murphy's Black Cat White Cat, 220(F)

Color Surprises, 285(F)

Murphy, Church. *Jack and the Beanstalk*, 11020

Murphy, Claire R. *Caribou Girl*, 11208

Murphy, David. *Beep! Beep!* 5588(F)
Vroom, Chugga, Vroom-Vroom, 518(F)

Murphy, Elspeth C. *The Mystery of the Dancing Angels*, 6977(F)
The Mystery of the Eagle Feather, 6978(F)
The Mystery of the Haunted Light-house, 6979(F)
The Mystery of the Hobo's Message, 6980(F)

Murphy, Jill. *Jeffrey Strangeways*, 9941(F)
The Last Noo-Noo, 4246(F)
The Worst Witch, 7977(F)

Murphy, Jim. *Across America on an Emigrant Train*, 21338
Blizzard! The Storm that Changed America, 16480
The Great Fire, 16572
The Journal of James Edmond Pease, 9488(F)
Pick and Shovel Poet, 12523
West to a Land of Plenty, 9418(F)
A Young Patriot, 16207

Murphy, Mary. *Caterpillar's Wish*, 2519(F)
Here Comes Spring, 5353(F)
Here Comes the Rain, 2520(F)
I Am an Artist, 2521(F)
I Feel Happy and Sad and Angry and Glad, 2522(F)
I Like It When . . ., 2523(F)
If . . ., 221(F)
Roxie and Bo Together, 2524(F)
Some Things Change, 222(F)
You Smell, 18149

Murphy, Nora. *A Hmong Family*, 17584

Murphy, Pat. *The Science Explorer Out and About*, 18336

Murphy, Patti Beling. *Day Care Days*, 3518(F)

Murphy, Rita. *Black Angels*, 7359(F)
Night Flying, 7978(F)

Murphy, Shirley Rousseau. *Wind Child*, 10467(F)

Murphy, Stuart J. *Animals on Board*, 523(F)
Beep Beep, Vroom Vroom! 223(F)
The Best Bug Parade, 346(F)
The Best Vacation Ever, 224(F)
Betcha! 20590
Circus Shapes, 347(F)
Dave's Down-to-Earth Rock Shop, 20566
Divide and Ride, 524
Every Buddy Counts, 525(F)
A Fair Bear Share, 526(F)
Game Time! 225(F)
Get Up and Go! 20648
Give Me Half! 226(F)
The Greatest Gymnast of All, 227
Henry the Fourth, 527
Jump, Kangaroo, Jump! 528

Lemonade for Sale, 20591(F)
Let's Fly a Kite, 348(F)
Missing Mittens, 529
Monster Musical Chairs, 530(F)
A Pair of Socks, 1426(F)
The Penny Pot, 531
Pepper's Journal, 20649
Probably Pistachio, 228
Rabbit's Pajama Party, 229
Room for Ripley, 20659
Shark Swimathon, 20633
Spunky Monkeys on Parade, 532(F)
Super Sand Castle Saturday, 230(F)
Too Many Kangaroo Things to Do! 20592

Murray, Dennis. *The Stars Are Wait-ing*, 750(F)

Murray, Peter. *Beetles*, 19536
Cactus, 20249
Dreams, 12750
Floods, 20708
Hurricanes, 20709
Lightning, 20710
Mushrooms, 20188
Orchids, 20250
Parrots, 19264
Porcupines, 19202
Professor Solomon Snickerdoodle's Air Science Tricks, 20674
Professor Solomon Snickerdoodle's Light Science Tricks, 20876
Redwoods, 20213
Roses, 20039
Scorpions, 19588
Silly Science Tricks (with Professor Solomon Snickerdoodle), 18337
Snails, 19615
Tarantulas, 19589
Volcanoes, 20344

Murrell, Kathleen Berton. *Russia*, 15426

Murrow, Liza Ketchum. *The Ghost of Lost Island*, 6981(F)

Musgrave, Susan. *Dreams Are More Real than Bathtubs*, 5522(F)

Musgrove, Margaret. *The Spider Weaver*, 10707

Muskat, Carrie. *The Composite Guide to Tennis*, 22313
Sammy Sosa, 13505

Musleah, Rahel. *Sharing Blessings*, 17480
Why on This Night? A Passover Haggadah for Family Celebra-tion, 17479

Mussari, Mark. *Suzanne De Passe*, 13148

Mutchnick, Brenda. *A Noteworthy Tale*, 1427(F)

Mutel, Cornelia F. *Our Endangered Planet*, 20467

Muten, Burleigh. *Grandmothers' Sto-ries*, 10593

Muth, Jon J. *Come On, Rain!* 3208(F)

Gershon's Monster, 11154
Why I Will Never Ever Ever Ever Have Enough Time to Read This Book, 4106(F)

Myers, Anna. *Captain's Command*, 9678(F)
Graveyard Girl, 9601(F)
The Keeping Room, 9244(F)
Red-Dirt Jessie, 7274(F)
Rosie's Tiger, 8495(F)
Spotting the Leopard, 7275(F)
When the Bough Breaks, 8769(F)

Myers, Arthur. *The Cheyenne*, 16012

Myers, Christopher. *Black Cat*, 7276(F)
Wings, 11495(F)

Myers, Christopher (jt. author). *Turnip Soup*, 4247(F)

Myers, Christopher A. (jt. author). *Galapagos*, 15772

Myers, Edward. *Hostage*, 6982(F)

Myers, Jack. *On the Trail of the Komodo Dragon*, 18287
What Happened to the Mammoths? And Other Explorations of Sci-ence in Action, 18838

Myers, Janet Nuzum. *Strange Stuff*, 21938

Myers, Laurie. *Earthquake in the Third Grade*, 10115(F)
Guinea Pigs Don't Talk, 10116(F)
Surviving Brick Johnson, 8348(F)

Myers, Lynne B. *Galapagos*, 15772
Turnip Soup, 4247(F)

Myers, Paul (jt. author). *Dear Okla-homa City, Get Well Soon*, 16578

Myers, Steve (jt. author). *Anorexia and Bulimia*, 17994
Divorce and Separation, 17682
Drinking Alcohol, 17888
Dyslexia, 17995
Feeling Violent, 17630

Myers, Tim. *Basho and the Fox*, 4775(F)

Myers, Walter Dean. *Amistad*, 16266
Angel to Angel, 11765
At Her Majesty's Request, 13756
The Blues of Flats Brown, 2525(F)
The Journal of Biddy Owens, 10353(F)
The Journal of Joshua Loper, 9419(F)
The Journal of Scott Pendleton Collins, 9679(F)
Malcolm X, 12761, 12762
Me, Mop, and the Moondance Kid, 10354(F)
145th Street, 7360(F)
Toussaint L'Ouverture, 13826

Myler, Terry. *The Secret of the Ruby Ring*, 10211(F)

Myller, Rolf. *How Big Is a Foot?* 349(F)

Naava. *Three Pandas*, 2809(F)

Nabwire, Constance. *Cooking the African Way*, 21723

Nadel, Laurie. *The Kremlin Coup*, 15427

Naden, Corinne J. *Belle Starr and the Wild West*, 12965
Christa McAuliffe, 12137
Jason and the Golden Fleece, 11496
John Muir, 13329
Ronald McNair, 12139

Naden, Corinne J. (jt. author). *Chris Rock*, 12455
Colin Powell, 12949
Madeleine Albright, 12838
People of Peace, 13725
The White House Kids, 12638

Nagda, Ann Whitehead. *Dear Whiskers*, 8349(F)
Tiger Math, 20027

Nagel, Karen. *The Lunch Line*, 535(F)

Naidoo, Beverley. *Journey to Jo'burg*, 7361(F)
No Turning Back, 8975(F)

Nail, Jim. *Whose Tracks Are These?* 18839

Nakata, Hiroe. *Lucky Pennies and Hot Chocolate*, 3890(F)

Nam, Yeoh Hong (jt. author). *Welcome to Greece*, 15380

Namioka, Lensey. *The Laziest Boy in the World*, 4776(F)
The Loyal Cat, 4777(F)
Yang the Eldest and His Odd Jobs, 7488(F)
Yang the Second and Her Secret Admirers, 8496(F)
Yang the Third and Her Impossible Family, 8497(F)

Nanao, Jun. *Contemplating Your Bellybutton*, 18232

Nankivell-Aston, Sally. *Science Experiments with Electricity*, 20901
Science Experiments with Forces, 20814

Napoli, Donna Jo. *Albert*, 1428(F)
Changing Tunes, 8498(F)
Jimmy, the Pickpocket of the Palace, 7979(F)
The Prince of the Pond, 7980(F)
Shelley Shock, 10117(F)
Stones in Water, 9680(F)
Trouble on the Tracks, 8939(F)

Narahashi, Keiko. *A Is for Amos*, 20(F)
A Fawn in the Grass, 4529(F)
Is That Josie? 751(F)
The Magic Purse, 10833
Rain Talk, 4538(F)
Two Girls Can! 4031(F)
What's What? 243(F)
Who Wants One? 580(F)
Without Wings, Mother, How Can I Fly? 3620(F)

Naranjo, Tito E. *A Day with a Pueblo*, 16013

Nardo, Don. *The Age of Augustus*, 14734
France, 15313
Greece, 15387
Greek and Roman Mythology, 11497
Greek and Roman Science, 14591
Greek and Roman Sport, 14592
Julius Caesar, 13764
Teen Sexuality, 18268
Walt Disney, 12226
The War Against Iraq, 15493

Nascimbene, Yan. *The Beautiful Christmas Tree*, 3498(F)

Nascimbeni, Barbara. *The Real Winner*, 2526(F)
Santa's Gift, 5891(F)
Small Brown Dog's Bad Remembering Day, 2122(F)
What If? 1573(F)

Nash, Bruce. *The Baseball Hall of Shame*, 22107
The Greatest Sports Stories Never Told, 22039

Nash, Margaret. *Secret in the Mist*, 3338(F)

Nash, Scott. *Henry the Fourth*, 527
Martian Rock, 1572(F)
Monster Musical Chairs, 530(F)
Oh, Tucker! 5294(F)
Over the Moon, 2771(F)
Pet of a Pet, 2181(F)
Saturday Night at the Dinosaur Stomp, 2686(F)
Six Hogs on a Scooter, 2711(F)

Nason, Thomas W. *You Come Too*, 11570

Natchev, Alexi. *Nathaniel Willy, Scared Silly*, 11367
Night of the Goat Children, 1353(F)
Peter and the Blue Witch Baby, 11111
A Wagonload of Fish, 10853
Wet World, 3430(F)

Nathan, Amy. *The Kids' Allowance Book*, 16945
Surviving Homework, 17623
The Young Musician's Survival Guide, 17778

Nathan, Cheryl. *The Long and Short of It*, 350(F)
The Rain Forest Counts! 502(F)

Nathan, Emma. *What Do You Call a Group of Butterflies? And Other Insect Groups*, 19471

Nathan, Joan. *The Children's Jewish Holiday Kitchen*, 21724

National Wildlife Federation. *Wild and Crafty*, 21458

Natti, Susanna. *Cam Jansen and the Mystery at the Haunted House*, 6733(F)
Cam Jansen and the Mystery of Flight 54, 6734(F)

Cam Jansen and the Mystery of the Chocolate Fudge Sale, 6735(F)
Good Luck, Ronald Morgan! 6344(F)
Happy Birthday, Ronald Morgan! 5687(F)
Lionel at School, 6436(F)
Lionel in the Spring, 6437(F)
Lionel in the Summer, 6438(F)
Puppy Love, 7185(F)
Ronald Morgan Goes to Bat, 4966(F)
Today Was a Terrible Day, 5502(F)
The Wild Things, 5191(F)
Young Cam Jansen and the Baseball Mystery, 6179(F)
Young Cam Jansen and the Ice Skate Mystery, 6181(F)
Young Cam Jansen and the Pizza Shop Mystery, 6183(F)

Naylor, Phyllis Reynolds. *The Agony of Alice*, 8770(F)
Alice in April, 8771(F)
Alice In-Between, 9942(F)
Alice in Rapture, Sort Of, 9943(F)
Alice the Brave, 8772(F)
All But Alice, 8773(F)
Beetles, Lightly Toasted, 9944(F)
Being Danny's Dog, 8499(F)
Bernie and the Bessledorf Ghost, 7981(F)
The Bodies in the Bessledorf Hotel, 6983(F)
The Bomb in the Bessledorf Bus Depot, 6984(F)
Boys Against Girls, 9945(F)
Carlotta's Kittens and the Club of Mysteries, 6985(F)
Danny's Desert Rats, 9946(F)
Ducks Disappearing, 536(F)
Eddie, Incorporated, 8774(F)
The Face in the Bessledorf Funeral Parlor, 6986(F)
The Fear Place, 6987(F)
The Girls' Revenge, 9947(F)
The Grand Escape, 7982(F)
The Healing of Texas Jake, 7983(F)
"I Can't Take You Anywhere!" 4248(F)
Jade Green, 7984(F)
Josie's Troubles, 8350(F)
Keeping a Christmas Secret, 5889(F)
King of the Playground, 5041(F)
Maudie in the Middle, 7489(F)
Night Cry, 8775(F)
Old Sadie and the Christmas Bear, 5890(F)
One of the Third-Grade Thonkers, 6988(F)
Outrageously Alice, 9948(F)
Peril in the Bessledorf Parachute Factory, 6989(F)
Reluctantly Alice, 8500(F)
Saving Shiloh, 7277(F)
Shiloh, 7278(F)

Shiloh Season, 7279(F)
A Spy Among the Girls, 9949(F)
Sweet Strawberries, 3821(F)
A Traitor Among the Boys, 9950(F)
The Treasure of Bessledorf Hill, 6990(F)
Near, Holly. *The Great Peace March*, 14254
Neasi, Barbara J. *Just Like Me*, 6541(F)
Neaves, Sarah-Jane. *Cardboard Boxes*, 21422
Needham, Bobbe. *Ecology Crafts for Kids*, 21459
Needham, James M. *Can We Save Them? Endangered Species of North America*, 19393
One Tiger Growls, 601
Our Natural Homes, 20365
Needham, Kate (jt. author). *The Usborne Book of Everyday Words*, 14055
Neely, Keith. *Everybody Says*, 6307(F)
Negri, Rocco. *Journey Outside*, 8125(F)
Trouble River, 9350(F)
Negrin, Fabian. *Dora's Box*, 1034(F)
Oscar Wilde's The Selfish Giant, 10518(F)
The Secret Footprints, 11417
Neibart, Wally. *Hurricane Henrietta*, 1272(F)
Neidigh, Sherry. *Black and White*, 1988(F)
Neilan, Eujin Kim. *In the Moonlight Mist*, 10735
Neill, Eileen M. *The Boxcar Children Cookbook*, 21678
Neill, John R. *The Marvelous Land of Oz*, 7595(F)
Neimark, Anne E. *Myth Maker*, 12606
Neitzel, Shirley. *The Bag I'm Taking to Grandma's*, 3339(F)
The Dress I'll Wear to the Party, 6542(F)
I'm Taking a Trip on My Train, 5591(F)
Nelson, Annika. *Dancing with Dziadziu*, 9520(F)
Nelson, Cyndi (jt. author). *The United States of America*, 15895
Nelson, Donna. *Blue Ribbon Blues*, 7078(F)
Nelson, Jennie Anne. *Pieces of Eight*, 7846(F)
Nelson, Kadir. *Big Jabe*, 1434(F)
Brothers of the Knight, 10376
Dancing in the Wings, 4898(F)
Salt in His Shoes, 4990(F)
Nelson, Kristin L. *Clever Raccoons*, 18958
Nelson, S. D. *Crazy Horse's Vision*, 9147(F)
Gift Horse, 11281

Nelson, Sharlene. *Bull Whackers to Whistle Punks*, 16346
William Boeing, 12853
Nelson, Ted (jt. author). *Bull Whackers to Whistle Punks*, 16346
William Boeing, 12853
Nelson, Theresa. *The Empress of Elsewhere*, 8351(F)
Nelson, Vaunda M. *Beyond Mayfield*, 7362(F)
Mayfield Crossing, 7363(F)
Nemiroff, Marc A. *Help Is on the Way*, 17927
Nerlove, Miriam. *Easter*, 5972(F)
Flowers on the Wall, 4778(F)
Halloween, 6035(F)
Hanukkah, 6099(F)
I Can! 2989(F)
Passover, 6100(F)
Purim, 6101(F)
Shabbat, 6102
The Ten Commandments, 17311
Thanksgiving, 6149(F)
Nesbit, Edith. *The Best of Shakespeare*, 12052
The Deliverers of Their Country, 7985(F)
The Enchanted Castle, 7986(F)
Five Children and It, 7987(F)
Melisande, 10468(F)
Nesbitt, Jan. *A Tall Story and Other Tales*, 7949(F)
Nesbitt, Kris. *My Amazon River Day*, 15773
Neshama, Rivvy. *Nat Turner and the Virginia Slave Revolt*, 12806
Ness, Caroline. *The Ocean of Story*, 10803
Ness, Evaline. *A Pocketful of Cricket*, 5485(F)
Sam, Bangs and Moonshine, 5042(F)
Some of the Days of Everett Anderson, 11752
Netherton, John. *Red-Eyed Tree Frogs*, 18732
Nethery, Mary. *Hannah and Jack*, 5354(F)
Mary Veronica's Egg, 5355(F)
Netzley, Patricia D. *Japan*, 15134
Neuberger, Anne E. *The Girl-Son*, 9003(F)
Neugebauer, Charise. *The Real Winner*, 2526(F)
Santa's Gift, 5891(F)
Neuhaus, David. *I Can Save the Earth*, 16958
Neumann, Dietrich. *Joe and the Skyscraper*, 21145
Neuschwander, Cindy. *Amanda Bean's Amazing Dream*, 537(F)
Newbigging, Martha. *The Little Book of Big Questions*, 21910
Newbold, Greg. *Winter Lullaby*, 18904
Newby, Dick. *Jamil's Clever Cat*, 10791

Newcome, Zita. *Toddlerobics*, 3340(F), 3341(F)
Newfield, Marcia. *Where Did You Put Your Sleep?* 752(F)
Newman, Barbara. *The Illustrated Book of Ballet Stories*, 14296
Newman, Colin. *How Fish Swim*, 19696
The Salmon, 19700
Newman, Gerald. *Happy Birthday, Little League*, 22108
Newman, Leslea. *Cats, Cats, Cats!* 1429(F)
Matzo Ball Moon, 6103(F)
Remember That, 3822(F)
Saturday Is Pattyday, 5043(F)
Too Far Away to Touch, 5044(F)
Newman, Michael. *Brandy*, 12359
Newman, Robert. *The Case of the Baker Street Irregular*, 6991(F)
Merlin's Mistake, 7988(F)
Newman, Shirlee P. *The African Slave Trade*, 16267
Child Slavery in Modern Times, 17022
The Creek, 16014
The Inuits, 15823
Isabella, 9135(F)
Slavery in the United States, 15896
Newsom, Carol. *Impy for Always*, 8322(F)
A Memory for Tino, 8264(F)
Newsom, Tom. *The Mystery of the Cupboard*, 7585(F)
Newsome, Jill. *Shadow*, 5356(F)
Newton, David E. *Black Holes and Supernovae*, 18406
Yearbooks in Science: 1920–1929, 18288
Newton, Jill. *All About Color*, 295(F)
All About Pattern, 318(F)
Newton, Michael. *Walking for Freedom*, 17037
Newton, Patricia Montgomery. *Old Sadie and the Christmas Bear*, 5890(F)
Newton-John, Olivia. *A Pig Tale*, 2527(F)
Neye, Emily. *Butterflies*, 19563
NgCheong-Lum, Roseline. *France*, 15314
Haiti, 15714
Tahiti, 15248
Nguyen, Chi. *Cooking the Vietnamese Way*, 21725
Ngwane, Zolani. *Zulu*, 14992
Ng'weno, Fleur. *Kenya*, 14941
Nichelason, Margery G. *Homeless or Hopeless?* 17152
Shoes, 21182
Nichol, Barbara. *Beethoven Lives Upstairs*, 9065(F)
Biscuits in the Cupboard, 11803
Dippers, 7989(F)
Nicholls, Delia (jt. author). *Dolphins and Porpoises*, 19685

Nichols, Grace. *Asana and the Animals*, 11804

Nichols, Joan Kane. *New Orleans*, 16876

Nicholson, Darrel. *Wild Boars*, 18959

Nicholson, Dorinda M. *Pearl Harbor Child*, 14874

Nicholson, Lois. *Babe Ruth*, 13499
The Composite Guide to Lacrosse, 22040
Michael Jackson, 12408

Nicholson, Peggy. *The Case of the Furtive Firebug*, 8352(F)

Nicholson, Robert (jt. author). *Super Heroes*, 21959

Nicholson, William. *The Wind Singer*, 7990(F)

Nickell, Joe. *The Magic Detectives*, 21939

Nickens, Linda. *Imani and the Flying Africans*, 11363

Nickerson, Barbara. *Shakespeare's The Tempest*, 12051

Nicklaus, Carol. *Bathtubs, Slides and Roller Coaster Rails*, 20922

Nickle, John. *The Ant Bully*, 1430(F)
Things That Are Most in the World, 982(F)
TV Rex, 1431(F)

Nickles, Greg (jt. author). *Spanish Missions*, 15886

Nicolle, David. *Medieval Knights*, 14783

Nicolson, Cynthia P. *The Earth*, 18434
Exploring Space, 21004
The Planets, 18484
The Stars, 18551

Nidenoff, Michelle. *Kids Around the World Celebrate!* 17374

Nielsen, Laura F. *Jeremy's Muffler*, 4249(F)

Nielsen, Nancy J. *Carnivorous Plants*, 20251

Nielsen, Virginia. *Batty Hattie*, 7281(F)

Nightingale, Sandy. *Cider Apples*, 1432(F)
A Giraffe on the Moon, 1433(F)

Nigiortis, Theodore (jt. author). *No More Dodos*, 19406

Nigoghossian, Christine Willis. *Discovering Trees*, 20194

Nikcolai, Margaret. *Kitaq Goes Ice Fishing*, 9171(F)

Nikly, Michelle. *The Perfume of Memory*, 10469(F)

Nikola-Lisa, W. *America*, 3342(F)
Bein' with You This Way, 11766
Can You Top That? 4250(F)
Hallelujah! A Christmas Celebration, 5892(F)
One Hole in the Road, 538(F)
1, 2, 3 Thanksgiving! 539(F)
Shake Dem Halloween Bones, 6036(F)

Till Year's Good End, 14784
The Year with Grandma Moses, 13961

Nile, Richard. *Australian Aborigines*, 15249

Niles, Nancy. *Changes for Samantha*, 9630(F)

Nilsen, Anna. *Art Fraud Detective*, 13916

Nilsson, Jenny L. (jt. author). *The Sandy Bottom Orchestra*, 8318(F)

Nilsson, Ulf. *If You Didn't Have Me*, 8776(F)

Nimmo, Jenny. *Orchard of the Crescent Moon*, 7991(F)

Nirgiotis, Nicholas. *No More Dodos*, 19406
West by Waterway, 16347

Nitta, Kazushige. *Twisters!* 20712

Nitz, Kristin Wolden. *Softball*, 22109

Nivola, Claire A. *Elisabeth*, 4779(F)

Nix, Simon (jt. author). *Motorbikes*, 22241

Nixon, Joan Lowery. *Aggie's Home*, 9420(F)
Ann's Story, 9205(F)
Caesar's Story, 9206(F)
Circle of Love, 9421(F)
David's Search, 9422(F)
Ghost Town, 6992(F)
Gus and Gertie and the Missing Pearl, 7992(F)
If You Were a Writer, 14101
Maggie Forevermore, 8501(F)
Nancy's Story, 9207(F)
Search for the Shadowman, 6993(F)
Who Are You? 6994(F)
Will's Choice, 9423(F)

Njoku, Onwuka N. *Mbundu*, 14942

Nnoromele, Salome. *Life Among the Ibo Women of Nigeria*, 15039
Somalia, 14943

Nobisso, Josephine. *John Blair and the Great Hinckley Fire*, 16481

Noble, Sheilagh. *More!* 3343(F)

Noble, Trinka Hakes. *Meanwhile, Back at the Ranch*, 4251(F)

Noblet, Yves. *Kalifax*, 8145(F)

Nodar, Carmen Santiago. *Abuelita's Paradise*, 3823(F)

Nodelman, Perry. *A Completely Different Place*, 7993(F)

Nodelman, Perry (jt. author). *A Meeting of the Minds*, 10215(F)
Of Two Minds, 7953(F)
Out of Their Minds, 7954(F)

Nodset, Joan L. *Come Here, Cat*, 6543(F)
Go Away, Dog, 6544(F)
Who Took the Farmer's Hat? 6545(F)

Nofi, Albert A. *Spies in the Civil War*, 16422
The Underground Railroad and the Civil War, 16268

Nofziger, Harold H. *And It Was Good*, 17246

Nolan, Dennis. *Androcles and the Lion*, 11498
Fairy Wings, 1414(F)
Red Flower Goes West, 4859(F)
Sherwood, 9129(F)
Wolf Child, 8958(F)

Nolan, Lucy. *The Lizard Man of Crabtree County*, 4252(F)

Nolan, Paul T. *Folk Tale Plays Round the World*, 12035

Nolan, Peggy. *The Spy Who Came in from the Sea*, 6995(F)

Nolen, Jerdine. *Big Jabe*, 1434(F)
Harvey Potter's Balloon Farm, 1435(F)
In My Momma's Kitchen, 3824(F)
Raising Dragons, 1436(F)

Noll, Cheryl K. *Victorian Days*, 16477
World War II Days, 14859

Noll, Sally. *Sunflower*, 4432(F)
What Color Was the Sky Today? 181(F)

Nollen, Tim. *Czech Republic*, 15281

Nolte, Larry. *Tiger Woods*, 13713
Tiger Woods, Golfing Champion, 13714

Nolting, Karen Stray (jt. author). *Backyard Birds*, 19244
Birds of Prey, 19331
Bizarre Birds, 19245
Shorebirds, 19246

Nomura, Noriko S. *I Am Shinto*, 17209

Nomura, Takaaki. *Grandpa's Town*, 4780(F)

Nones, Eric Jon. *Angela's Wings*, 1437(F)
The Canary Prince, 10470(F)

Noon, Steve. *A Street Through Time*, 14351

Noonan, Don. *Mr. Wizard's Experiments for Young Scientists*, 18320

Noonan, Julia. *Bath Day*, 3344(F)
Hare and Rabbit, 6546(F)
You're Just What I Need, 3754(F)

Noonan, R. A. *Enter at Your Own Risk*, 7994(F)

Noonan, William. *Bigfoot and Other Legendary Creatures*, 21956
Great Crystal Bear, 5301(F)

Norac, Carl. *Hello, Sweetie Pie*, 2528(F)
I Love You So Much, 2529(F)

Nordstrom, Joe. *The Mystery of the Eagle Feather*, 6978(F)
The Mystery of the Haunted Lighthouse, 6979(F)

Nordstrom, Judy. *Concord and Lexington*, 16208

Noreika, Robert. *Marsh Music*, 1805(F)
A Moon for Seasons, 11986

Norell, Mark A. *A Nest of Dinosaurs*, 14455

Norell, Mark A. (jt. author). *Searching for Velociraptor*, 14400

Norman, David. *Dinosaur*, 14456

Norman, Howard. *The Girl Who Dreamed Only Geese and Other Stories of the Far North*, 11209

Trickster and the Fainting Birds, 11282

Normandin, Christine, ed. *Spirit of the Cedar People*, 11283

Norris, Leslie. *Albert and the Angels*, 9752(F)

North, Peter. *Australia*, 15250

Welcome to Australia, 15251

North, Sterling. *Rascal*, 7282(F)

Norton, Andre. *House of Shadows*, 7995(F)

Norton, Lindy. *Myths and Legends*, 13899

Sports and Games, 13900

Norton, Mary. *Are All the Giants Dead?* 7996(F)

The Borrowers, 7997(F)

Poor Stainless, 7998(F)

Nottingham, Ted. *Chess for Children*, 22172

Winning Chess, 22173

Nottridge, Rhoda. *Additives*, 20165

Fats, 20166

Sugars, 20118

Vitamins, 20167

Novak, Matt. *Ghost and Pete*, 5995(F)

Jazzbo and Googy, 2530(F)

Jazzbo Goes to School, 2531(F)

Mouse TV, 2532(F)

Newt, 2533(F)

The Pillow War, 4253(F)

The Robobots, 1438(F)

Noyed, Robert B. (jt. author). *In-Line Skating*, 22028

Soccer, 22295

Numeroff, Laura. *The Chicken Sisters*, 2534(F)

Chimps Don't Wear Glasses, 2535(F)

Dogs Don't Wear Sneakers, 2536(F)

If You Give a Moose a Muffin, 2537(F)

If You Give a Mouse a Cookie, 2538(F)

If You Give a Pig a Pancake, 2539(F)

If You Take a Mouse to the Movies, 2540(F)

Mouse Cookies, 21726

Two for Stew, 4255(F)

What Grandmas Do Best/What Grandpas Do Best, 3825(F)

What Mommies Do Best/What Daddies Do Best, 2541(F)

Why a Disguise? 4254(F)

Nunes, Susan. *The Last Dragon*, 3345(F)

To Find the Way, 8940(F)

Nurmi, Karl E. (jt. author). *The Grandchildren of the Incas*, 15754

Nutt, Ken. *I Am Phoenix*, 11780

Nuwer, Hank. *The Legend of Jesse Owens*, 13666

Nwaezeigwe, Nwankwo T. *Ngoni*, 14993

Nwanunobi, C. O. *Malinke*, 15040

Soninke, 15041

Nyberg, John. *Bruce Coville's UFOs*, 10167(F)

Nye, Bill. *Bill Nye the Science Guy's Big Blast of Science*, 18338

Bill Nye the Science Guy's Big Blue Ocean, 19832

Nye, Naomi S. *Benito's Dream Bottle*, 753(F)

Come with Me, 11663

Lullaby Raft, 754(F)

Sitti's Secrets, 4781(F)

Nygaard, Elizabeth. *Snake Alley Band*, 2542(F)

Nyman, Elisabeth. *The Top and the Ball*, 10395(F)

O Flatharta, Antoine. *The Prairie Train*, 1439(F)

Oakley, Graham. *The Church Mice and the Ring*, 2543(F)

Hetty and Harriet, 2544(F)

Oates, Joyce Carol. *Come Meet Muffin!* 2545(F)

Ober, Carol. *How Music Came to the World*, 11413

Ober, Hal. *How Music Came to the World*, 11413

Oberle, Joseph. *Anchorage*, 16803

Oberman, Sheldon. *The Always Prayer Shawl*, 4782(F)

By the Hanukkah Light, 6104(F)

The Shaman's Nephew, 15824

The Wisdom Bird, 17312(F)

O'Book, Irene. *Maybe My Baby*, 3346(F)

O'Brien, Anne S. *Africa Is Not a Country*, 14909

Jamaica and Brianna, 4001(F)

Jamaica and the Substitute Teacher, 5504(F)

Jamaica's Blue Marker, 4002(F)

Jamaica's Find, 3194(F)

Jouanah, 10837

The Princess and the Beggar, 10732

Talking Walls, 14534, 14560

Who Belongs Here? 17570

O'Brien, John. *The Bookworm's Feast*, 11627

Buzzy Widget, 4204(F)

Daffy Down Dillies, 11885

Dear Old Donegal, 4669(F)

The Farmer in the Dell, 876

Funny You Should Ask, 21857

The Irish Piper, 10926

Mistakes That Worked, 21038

Mother Hubbard's Christmas, 5893(F)

Myrna Never Sleeps, 1472(F)

Poof! 1440(F)

Six Creepy Sheep, 5996(F)

Six Sandy Sheep, 2072(F)

This Is Figure Skating, 22217

This Is Soccer, 22288

The Twelve Days of Christmas, 14214

Tyrannosaurus Tex, 1811(F)

Uncle Switch, 11879

The West Texas Chili Monster, 1084(F)

O'Brien, Lisa. *Lights, Camera, Action! Making Movies and TV from the Inside Out*, 21273

O'Brien, Patrick. *Bottoms Up!* 18853

Gigantic! How Big Were the Dinosaurs? 14457

The Hindenburg, 21093

The Making of a Knight, 9115(F)

Steam, Smoke, and Steel, 21339

Storm Coming! 11939

Teddy Roosevelt's Elk, 19151

A Wasp Is Not a Bee, 18672

O'Brien, Robert C. *Mrs. Frisby and the Rats of NIMH*, 7999(F)

O'Brien, Steven. *Pancho Villa*, 13865

O'Brien-Palmer, Michelle. *Sense-Abilities*, 18150

O'Byrne-Pelham, Fran (jt. author). *Philadelphia*, 16653

O'Callahan, Jay. *Herman and Marguerite*, 2546(F)

Orange Cheeks, 3826(F)

O'Callahan, Laura. *Herman and Marguerite*, 2546(F)

Ochiltree, Dianne. *Cats Add Up! Math Activities by Marilyn Burns*, 540(F)

Ochoa, George. *The Assassination of Julius Caesar*, 14735

The Fall of Quebec and the French and Indian War, 16161

The New York Public Library Amazing Hispanic American History, 17585

Ochs, Carol P. *When I'm Alone*, 541(F)

O'Connor, Barbara. *Barefoot Dancer*, 12377

Beethoven in Paradise, 8502(F)

Katherine Dunham, 12378

Mammolina, 13835

Me and Rupert Goody, 8353(F)

The Soldiers' Voice, 12584

The World at His Fingertips, 13761

O'Connor, David. *Gods and Pharaohs from Egyptian Mythology*, 11447

O'Connor, Jane. *Amy's (Not So) Great Camp-Out*, 2962(F)

Coaching Ms. Parker, 10330(F)

Kate Skates, 6547(F)

Molly the Brave and Me, 6548(F)

Nina, Nina Ballerina, 6549(F)
Nina, Nina, Star Ballerina, 6550(F)
Sarah's Incredible Idea, 3347(F)
The Teeny Tiny Woman, 6551(F)
O'Connor, Jim. *Jackie Robinson and the Story of All-Black Baseball*, 13494
O'Connor, Karen. *Dan Thuy's New Life in America*, 17586
The Herring Gull, 19353
A Kurdish Family, 17587
San Diego, 16804
Vietnam, 15189, 15190
O'Connor, Maureen. *Equal Rights*, 17023
Oda, Kancho. *The Moon Princess*, 10823
O'Dell, Scott. *Black Star, Bright Dawn*, 6996(F)
Island of the Blue Dolphins, 6997(F)
My Name Is Not Angelica, 9136(F)
Sarah Bishop, 9245(F)
Sing Down the Moon, 9489(F)
Streams to the River, River to the Sea, 9424(F)
O'Dell, Scott (jt. author). *Venus Among the Fishes*, 7780(F)
Odijk, Pamela. *The Aztecs*, 15639
The Chinese, 15076
The Egyptians, 14656
The Greeks, 14697
The Incas, 15774
The Israelites, 15525
The Japanese, 15135
The Mayas, 15680
The Phoenicians, 14593
The Romans, 14736
The Sumerians, 14657
The Vikings, 15464
Odinoski, Steve. *Georgia*, 16877
O'Donnell, Annie. *Computer Animator*, 17791
O'Donnell, Elizabeth Lee. *Patrick's Day*, 5642(F)
Odoo, Hans (jt. author). *Exploring the Rain Forest*, 20458
Oechsli, Kelly. *Mice at Bat*, 6552(F)
Scruffy, 6567(F)
Space Dog and the Pet Show, 10242(F)
Oeltjenbruns, Joni. *Not Enough Beds!* 16(F)
Ogami, Nancy. *1 to 10 and Back Again*, 544(F)
Ogbaa, Kalu. *Igbo*, 15042
Ogburn, Jacqueline K. *The Jukebox Man*, 3348(F)
The Magic Nesting Doll, 10471(F)
Ogden, Sam. *Going to the Doctor*, 3039
Ogle, Nancy Gray. *Wild Cats*, 19091
O'Grady, Scott. *Basher Five-Two*, 12144
Ohi, Ruth. *Adam's Daycare*, 3351(F)
The Bye-Bye Pie, 3721(F)
Into My Mother's Arms, 3246(F)

It's Raining, Yancy and Bear, 1255(F)
Next Stop! 3119(F)
One Duck, 5272(F)
Tess, 8462(F)
Two So Small, 1256(F)
Ohlsson, Ib. *Celebration*, 17393
It Happened in America, 15897
A Moon in Your Lunch Box, 784
Ohmi, Ayano (jt. author). *In Search of the Spirit*, 15123
O'Huigin, Sean. *Ghost Horse of the Mounties*, 11805
O'Keefe, Mary. *Christmas Is Coming*, 11830
O'Keefe, Susan Heyboer. *Angel Prayers*, 17529
Good Night, God Bless, 755(F)
One Hungry Monster, 542(F)
Okeke, Chika. *Kongo*, 14944
Okie, Susan (jt. author). *To Space and Back*, 21006
Okimoto, Jean D. *Blumpoe the Grumpoe Meets Arnold the Cat*, 5357(F)
Olaleye, Isaac. *Bitter Bananas*, 4783(F)
The Distant Talking Drum, 11977
In the Rainfield, 10708
Lake of the Big Snake, 4784(F)
Olawsky, Lynn A. *Colors of Mexico*, 15640
Olbinski, Tomek. *The Peaceable Kingdom*, 8245(F)
Old, Wendie C. *George Washington*, 13119
James Monroe, 13085
Louis Armstrong: King of Jazz, 12348
Marian Wright Edelman, 13151
Stacy Had a Little Sister, 5045(F)
Thomas Jefferson, 13052
The Wright Brothers, 13355
Older, Effin. *My Two Grandmothers*, 3827(F)
Older, Jules. *Telling Time*, 20650
Oldfield, Sara. *Rain Forests*, 20468
Oldfield, Wendy (jt. author). *My Apple*, 20140
My Boat, 20803
Oleksa, Nancy. *The Chickenhouse House*, 9383(F)
Oleksy, Walter. *The Philippines*, 15252
Princess Diana, 13783
Video Game Designer, 17792
Web Page Designer, 17793
Olesen, Jens (jt. author). *Chicken and Egg*, 19302
Oliver, Marilyn Tower. *Alcatraz Prison in American History*, 16805
Gangs, 17075
Olivera, Fernando. *The Woman Who Outshone the Sun*, 11135
Oliviero, Jamie. *The Day Sun Was Stolen*, 11284

Som See and the Magic Elephant, 1441(F)
Olivo, Richard (jt. author). *Close, Closer, Closest*, 355
Oller, Erika. *Cats, Cats, Cats!* 1429(F)
Ollikainen, Nina. *When Molly Was in the Hospital*, 3113(F)
Olney, Ross R. *The Farm Combine*, 20068
Lyn St. James, 13429
Olsen, Glenda P. *Birds of Prey*, 19334
Olson, Ann W. *Counting on the Woods*, 499
Olson, Mary W. *An Alligator Ate My Brother*, 1442(F)
Nice Try, Tooth Fairy, 1443(F)
Oluikpe, Benson O. *Swazi*, 14994
Oluonye, Mary N. *Madagascar*, 14995
South Africa, 14996, 14997
Olyff, Clotilde. *1 2 3 . . .*, 543(F)
O'Malia, Carol. *Edgar Badger's Balloon Day*, 5705(F)
The Royal Drum, 10684
O'Malley, Kevin. *Big Squeak, Little Squeak*, 2318(F)
Bud, 2547(F)
The Candystore Man, 3284(F)
Chanukah in Chelm, 6067(F)
Cinder Edna, 10437(F)
Colliding with Chris, 1219(F)
Halloween Pie, 6056(F)
Jump, Kangaroo, Jump! 528
Leo Cockroach . . . Toy Tester, 2548(F)
Miss Malarkey Doesn't Live in Room 10, 5497(F)
Miss Malarkey Won't Be In Today, 5498(F)
Pet Detectives, 2881(F)
The Planets in Our Solar System, 18458
Rosie's Fiddle, 1521(F)
Testing Miss Malarkey, 5499(F)
Too Many Kangaroo Things to Do! 20592
Velcome, 6037(F)
Who Killed Cock Robin? 6998(F)
O'Neal, Shaquille. *Shaq and the Beanstalk*, 10472(F)
Oneal, Zibby. *Grandma Moses*, 12270
A Long Way to Go, 9602(F)
O'Neill, Alexis. *Loud Emily*, 4256(F)
O'Neill, Amanda. *Dogs*, 19959
O'Neill, Catharine. *J. B. Wigglebottom and the Parade of Pets*, 10128(F)
O'Neill, Catherine. *Amazing Mysteries of the World*, 21941
Natural Wonders of North America, 20314
O'Neill, Chris. *Being Angry*, 17615
Being Jealous, 17718
Bullies and Gangs, 17711

Dealing with Racism, 17140
My Parents' Divorce, 17647
Our New Baby, 17657
O'Neill, Cynthia, ed. *Goddesses, Heroes and Shamans*, 11454
O'Neill, Laurie A. *The Boston Tea Party*, 16162
Little Rock, 17046
Wounded Knee, 16015
O'Neill, Mary. *Air Scare*, 17001
Hailstones and Halibut Bones, 11665
Nature in Danger, 19407
Power Failure, 20846
Water Squeeze, 20743
O'Neill, Terry. *The Homeless*, 17153
Ongman, Gudrun. *The Sleep Ponies*, 756(F)
Ontal, Carlo. *Best Wishes*, 12586
Ontario Science Centre Staff. *Scienceworks*, 18339
Sportsworks, 18068
Ontiveros, Martin. *Ricky Ricotta's Giant Robot*, 1475(F)
Ricky Ricotta's Giant Robot vs. the Mutant Mosquitoes from Mercury, 1476(F)
Onyefulu, Ifeoma. *A Is for Africa*, 106(F)
Chidi Only Likes Blue, 4785(F)
Grandfather's Work, 4786(F)
Ogbo, 15043
A Triangle for Adaora, 351(F)
Opgenoorth, Winfried. *Christoph Wants a Party*, 5707(F)
Opie, Iona. *Humpty Dumpty and Other Rhymes*, 879(F)
Opie, Iona, ed. *The Classic Fairy Tales*, 10473(F)
Here Comes Mother Goose, 878
I Saw Esau, 11903
My Very First Mother Goose, 880(F)
Opie, Peter (jt. author). *The Classic Fairy Tales*, 10473(F)
I Saw Esau, 11903
Oppel, Kenneth. *Peg and the Whale*, 8000(F)
Silverwing, 8001(F)
Sunwing, 8002(F)
Oppenheim, Joanne. *Have You Seen Bugs?* 19472
Rooter Remembers, 2549(F)
The Show-and-Tell Frog, 6553(F)
Oppenheim, Shulamith Levey. *I Love You, Bunny Rabbit*, 3349(F)
Iblis, 11194
What Is the Full Moon Full Of? 4257(F)
Yanni Rubbish, 4787(F)
Oram, Hiawyn. *Badger's Bad Mood*, 2550(F)
Badger's Bring Something Party, 5715(F)
In the Attic, 1444(F)
Just Dog, 2551(F)
Kiss It Better, 2552(F)

Not-So-Grizzly Bear Stories, 10595
Princess Chamomile Gets Her Way, 1445(F)
Princess Chamomile's Garden, 2553(F)
The Wrong Overcoat, 2554(F)
Oram, Hiawyn, reteller. *Counting Leopard's Spots*, 10709
O'Reilly, Susie. *Knitting and Crochet*, 21643
Orgel, Doris. *Button Soup*, 1446(F)
Don't Call Me Slob-o, 8777(F)
The Lion and the Mouse and Other Aesop's Fables, 11072
Two Crows Counting, 546(F)
Orgill, Roxane. *If I Only Had a Horn*, 12349
Shout, Sister, Shout! Ten Girl Singers Who Shaped a Century, 12176
Orlev, Uri. *The Island on Bird Street*, 9681(F)
Ormai, Stella. *I Am Leaper*, 7845(F)
Ormerod, Jan. *The Chewing-Gum Rescue*, 10460(F)
Eat Up, Gemma, 3196(F)
Grandfather and I, 3551(F)
Happy Christmas, Gemma, 5833(F)
Jan Ormerod's To Baby with Love, 881(F)
Joe Can Count, 547(F)
Midnight Pillow Fight, 757(F)
Miss Mouse's Day, 1447(F)
Ms. MacDonald Has a Class, 5523(F)
One Ballerina Two, 436(F)
Sky Dancer, 5153(F)
A Twist in the Tail, 10564
Where Did Josie Go? 4097(F)
Who's Whose? 3828(F)
Ormondroyd, Edward. *Broderick*, 2555(F)
Ormsby, Alison. *The Prairie*, 20540
Ormsby, Lawrence. *Mountain Animals in Danger*, 19420
Ocean Animals in Danger, 19421
O'Rourke, Frank. *Burton and Stanley*, 8003(F)
O'Rourke, Page Eastburn. *Bananas!* 20141
Orozco, Jose-Luis. *Diez Deditos and Other Play Rhymes and Action Songs from Latin America*, 22041
Orr, Katherine. *My Grandpa and the Sea*, 4788(F)
Story of a Dolphin, 5358(F)
Orr, Richard. *Richard Orr's Nature Cross-Sections*, 16953
Orr, Wendy. *Ark in the Park*, 7283(F)
A Light in Space, 10218(F)
Nim's Island, 6999(F)
Ortakales, Denise. *Planets*, 18512
Ortega, Jose. *Fiesta!* 3966(F)
Ortiz, Fran. *Hello, Amigos!* 5667(F)
Osband, Gillian. *Castles*, 14785

Osborn, Kathy. *I Forgot My Shoes*, 4175(F)
Osborne, Mary Pope. *Adaline Falling Star*, 9425(F)
American Tall Tales, 11370
Dinosaurs Before Dark, 6554(F)
Favorite Greek Myths, 11499
Favorite Medieval Tales, 10596
Favorite Norse Myths, 11519
Kate and the Beanstalk, 9116
The Life of Jesus in Masterpieces of Art, 17313
Mummies in the Morning, 1448(F)
My Brother's Keeper, 9490(F)
My Secret War, 9682(F)
One World, Many Religions, 17210
Rocking Horse Christmas, 3350(F)
Spider Kane and the Mystery Under the May-Apple, 7000(F)
Standing in the Light, 9172(F)
Osborne, Mary Pope, ed. *Mermaid Tales from Around the World*, 10597
Osborne, Mary Pope (jt. author). *Dinosaurs*, 14458
Osborne, Will. *Dinosaurs*, 14458
Oseki, Iku. *The Firefly Star*, 11138
O'Shaughnessy, Tam (jt. author). *The Mystery of Mars*, 18485
O'Shea, Maria. *Saudi Arabia*, 15557
Turkey, 15282
O'Shea, Pat. *The Hounds of the Morrigan*, 8004(F)
O'Shei, Tim. *The Detroit Red Wings Hockey Team*, 22214
Osiecki, Lori. *Jane vs. the Tooth Fairy*, 4191(F)
Swimming Lessons, 4988(F)
Osinski, Alice. *Andrew Jackson*, 13045
The Chippewa, 16016
The Eskimo, 15825
Franklin D. Roosevelt, 13099
The Navajo, 16017
The Nez Perce, 16018
The Sioux, 16019
Woodrow Wilson, 13122
Osinski, Christine. *A Busy Day at Mr. Kang's Grocery Store*, 3131
Call Mr. Vasquez, He'll Fix It! 3133
Ms. Davison, Our Librarian, 3140
Riding the Ferry with Captain Cruz, 3141
The Wilsons, a House-Painting Team, 3144
Osofsky, Audrey. *Dreamcatcher*, 758(F)
My Buddy, 8908(F)
Osseo-Asare, Fran. *A Good Soup Attracts Chairs*, 21727
Osser, Stephanie. *The Muppets Big Book of Crafts*, 21457
Ostendorf, Ned. *Carter G. Woodson*, 12823
George Washington Carver, 13255
Mary Church Terrell, 12786

Ostrow, Vivian. *My Brother Is from Outer Space*, 3829(F)

Otani, June. *Chibi*, 5141
Little Dog Poems, 11789
Science Surprises, 21045

Otero, Ben. *Mary Patten's Voyage*, 9261(F)

Otfinoski, Steven. *Around the Track*, 21311
Behind the Wheel, 21312
Blizzards, 20711
Bugsy Siegel and the Postwar Boom, 12964
Into the Wind, 21371
John Wilkes Booth and the Civil War, 12854
Oprah Winfrey, 12485
Pedaling Along, 22165
Riding the Rails, 21340
Speaking Up, Speaking Out, 14102
Taking Off, 21094
To the Rescue, 21313

Otis, James. *Toby Tyler*, 7001(F)

Ott, Margaret V. (jt. author). *I've Got an Idea!* 13310

Otten, Charlotte F. *January Rides the Wind*, 4503(F)

Otto, Carolyn. *Our Puppies Are Growing*, 19960
Pioneer Church, 4789(F)
What Color Is Camouflage? 18887

Oughton, Jerrie. *How the Stars Fell into the Sky*, 11285
The Magic Weaver of Rugs, 11286

Ouwendijk, George. *Santas of the World*, 17428

Ovadia, Tali (jt. author). *You Can Learn Sign Language!* 14016

Ovecka, Janice. *Cave of Falling Water*, 9208(F)

Ovenden, Denys. *Snake*, 18756

Ovenell-Carter, Julie. *Adam's Daycare*, 3351(F)
The Butterflies' Promise, 3830(F)

Overbeck, Cynthia. *Ants*, 19511
Cactus, 20252
Carnivorous Plants, 20253
Cats, 19928
Elephants, 19168
How Seeds Travel, 20273

Overend, Jenni. *Welcome with Love*, 18242

Owen, Cheryl. *My Nature Craft Book*, 21460

Owens, Caleb. *Deforestation*, 20469

Owens, Gail. *The Cybil War*, 9793(F)
Encyclopedia Brown and the Case of the Disgusting Sneakers, 7071(F)
Hail, Hail Camp Timberwood, 8604(F)
The Hot and Cold Summer, 8308(F)
I'm the Big Sister Now, 17906
Molly's Rosebush, 4932(F)
Poison Ivy and Eyebrow Wigs, 10122(F)

Sad Days, Glad Days, 4971(F)
Tac's Island, 8363(F)
The Up and Down Spring, 8312(F)
Vinegar Pancakes and Vanishing Cream, 9970(F)

Owens, Gay. *All Alone After School*, 5086(F)

Owens, L. L. *The Code of the Drum*, 9491(F)

Owens, Mary Beth. *Be Blest*, 17530
A Caribou Alphabet, 107(F)
The Story of the Sea Glass, 3609(F)

Owens, Thomas S. *The Atlanta Braves Baseball Team*, 22110
The Chicago Bulls Basketball Team, 22140
Collecting Baseball Cards, 21808
Collecting Baseball Memorabilia, 21809
Collecting Basketball Cards, 21810
Collecting Comic Books, 21811
Football, 22187
Soccer, 22299

Owens, Thomas S. (jt. author). *The History of Figure Skating*, 22223
The History of Soccer, 22292

Oxenbury, Helen. *Alice's Adventures in Wonderland*, 7644(F)
Dressing, 930(F)
Farmer Duck, 2794(F)
Helen Oxenbury's ABC of Things, 108(F)
It's My Birthday, 5716(F)
So Much, 5675(F)
The Three Little Wolves and the Big Bad Pig, 2764(F)
Tom and Pippo Go Shopping, 3352(F)
Tom and Pippo Read a Story, 3353(F)
We're Going on a Bear Hunt, 2966(F)

Oxlade, Chris. *Crime Detection*, 17076
Fantastic Transport Machines, 21286
Movies, 21274
The Mystery of Black Holes, 18407
The Mystery of Crop Circles, 21942
The Mystery of the Bermuda Triangle, 21943
Olympics, 22255
Skyscrapers, 21146
Telecommunications, 21262

Oxlade, Chris (jt. author). *The Kingfisher First Science Encyclopedia*, 18277

Oyibo, Papa. *Big Brother, Little Sister*, 11500(F)

Pace, Lorenzo. *Jalani and the Lock*, 4790(F)

Pacilio, V. J. *Ling Cho and His Three Friends*, 4791(F)

Packard, Edward. *Big Numbers*, 548(F)

Packard, Mary. *We Are Monsters*, 1449(F)
When I Am Big, 6555(F)

Pacoe, Elaine. *The Right to Vote*, 17047

Padt, Maartje. *Shanti*, 2556(F)

Page, Debra. *Orcas Around Me*, 3354

Page, Jason. *Soccer*, 22300

Page, Katherine H. *Christie and Company in the Year of the Dragon*, 7002(F)

Page, Ken. *Shoes Like Miss Alice's*, 3249(F)

Pagel, Danita (jt. author). *The Ultimate Book of Kid Concoctions*, 21505

Paige, David. *A Day in the Life of a Marine Biologist*, 17834

Pak, Soyung. *Dear Juno*, 3831(F)

Pak, Yu Cha. *Benito's Dream Bottle*, 753(F)
From Here to There, 3096(F)

Palacios, Argentina. *Viva Mexico!* 13818

Paladino, Catherine. *One Good Apple*, 19408

Palatini, Margie. *Bedhead*, 4258(F)
Ding Dong Ding Dong, 2557(F)
Good as Goldie, 4259(F)
Moosetache, 2558(F)
Moosletoe, 5894(F)
Piggie Pie! 1450(F)
The Wonder Worm Wars, 8778(F)
Zak's Lunch, 1451(F)
Zoom Broom, 1452(F)

Palazzo, Tony. *The Biggest and the Littlest Animals*, 18651
Magic Crayon, 1453(F)

Paley, Joan. *I Like Stars*, 6236(F)
Little White Duck, 2847(F)
Unbeatable Beaks, 19289

Palin, Nicki. *The Nutcracker*, 14293

Pallotta, Fred (jt. author). *The Airplane Alphabet Book*, 21095

Pallotta, Jerry. *The Airplane Alphabet Book*, 21095
Dory Story, 4504(F)
The Freshwater Alphabet Book, 19642
The Frog Alphabet Book . . . and Other Awesome Amphibians, 109(F)
Going Lobstering, 3355(F)
Underwater Counting, 549(F)

Pallotta, Jerry (jt. author). *The Butterfly Alphabet Book*, 19543

Palmer, Jan. *Ballet Magic*, 3391(F)
How Raggedy Ann Got Her Candy Heart, 1209(F)
The Moon's Choice, 1598(F)
Raggedy Ann and Andy and the Camel with the Wrinkled Knees, 1210(F)
The Toothpaste Millionaire, 9937(F)

Palmer, Kate S. *How Many Feet in the Bed?* 457(F)

Upstairs, 1152(F)

Palmisciano, Diane. *A Case for Jenny Archer*, 6801(F)
Getting Used to Harry, 4908(F)
Hannah and the Whistling Teakettle, 2972(F)
Jenny Archer to the Rescue, 9809(F)
A Job for Jenny Archer, 9810(F)
Last Licks, 3024(F)
Montezuma's Revenge, 1807(F)
Nibble, Nibble, Jenny Archer, 9812(F)
Patti's Pet Gorilla, 5027(F)
What's Cooking, Jenny Archer? 9813(F)

Pami, Louise T. (jt. author). *Oh, No, Toto!* 4849(F)

Pandell, Karen. *Journey Through the Northern Rainforest*, 20470

Panek, Dennis. *Splash, Splash*, 5412(F)

Pang, Alex. *Cosmic Journeys*, 20946
101 Science Tricks, 18345

Pang, Guek-Cheng. *Mongolia*, 15192

Pank, Rachel. *Sonia and Barnie and the Noise in the Night*, 759(F)

Paolilli, Paul. *Silver Seeds*, 11978

Papademetriou, Lisa. *My Pen Pal, Pat*, 6556(F)
You're in Big Trouble, Brad! 6557(F)

Paparone, Pamela. *Fire Fighters*, 5414(F)
Five Little Ducks, 842(F)
How a Baby Grows, 3550(F)
Low Song, 3321(F)
Mail for Husher Town, 655(F)
Nobody Owns the Sky, 12094
Ten Dirty Pigs, Ten Clean Pigs, 570(F)
Ten Dogs in the Window, 511(F)
Who Built the Ark? 14260

Papineau, Lucie. *Gontrand and the Crescent Moon*, 1454(F)

Paradis, Susan. *My Daddy*, 3832(F)

Paradise, Susan. *Brass Button*, 1133(F)

Paraskevas, Betty. *Gracie Graves and the Kids from Room 402*, 11904
Hoppy and Joe, 2559(F)
Junior Kroll, 11667
Junior Kroll and Company, 11905
Nibbles O'Hare, 5973(F)
On the Day the Tall Ships Sailed, 5643(F)
The Tangerine Bear, 1455(F)

Paraskevas, Michael. *Gracie Graves and the Kids from Room 402*, 11904
Hoppy and Joe, 2559(F)
Junior Kroll, 11667
Junior Kroll and Company, 11905
Nibbles O'Hare, 5973(F)
On the Day the Tall Ships Sailed, 5643(F)

The Tangerine Bear, 1455(F)

Parillo, Tony. *Michelangelo's Surprise*, 4792(F)

Paris, Alan. *Jerusalem 3000*, 15526

Pariser, Michael. *Elie Wiesel*, 12625

Parish, Herman. *Amelia Bedelia 4 Mayor*, 6558(F)
Bravo, Amelia Bedelia! 6559(F)
Good Driving, Amelia Bedelia, 6560(F)

Parish, Peggy. *Amelia Bedelia*, 6561(F)
Amelia Bedelia Goes Camping, 6562(F)
The Cats' Burglar, 6563(F)
Dinosaur Time, 14459
Good Hunting, Blue Sky, 6564(F)
Haunted House, 8005(F)
Merry Christmas, Amelia Bedelia, 5895(F)
No More Monsters for Me! 6565(F)
Play Ball, Amelia Bedelia, 6566(F)
Scruffy, 6567(F)

Park, Barbara. *Buddies*, 8354(F)
Don't Make Me Smile, 8503(F)
The Graduation of Jake Moon, 8504(F)
Junie B. Jones and a Little Monkey Business, 9951(F)
Junie B. Jones and her Big Fat Mouth, 10118(F)
Junie B. Jones and Some Sneaky Peeky Spying, 9952(F)
Junie B. Jones and the Stupid Smelly Bus, 9953(F)
Junie B. Jones and the Yucky Blucky Fruitcake, 10119(F)
Junie B. Jones Has a Monster Under Her Bed, 6568(F)
Junie B. Jones Is a Beauty Shop Guy, 9954(F)
Junie B. Jones Loves Handsome Warren, 6569(F)
Junie B. Jones Smells Something Fishy, 9955(F)
The Kid in the Red Jacket, 9956(F)
Operation, 9957(F)
Psssst! It's Me . . . the Bogeyman, 1456(F)

Park, Frances. *My Freedom Trip*, 15193
The Royal Bee, 4793(F)

Park, Ginger (jt. author). *My Freedom Trip*, 15193
The Royal Bee, 4793(F)

Park, Linda Sue. *The Kite Fighters*, 9004(F)
Seesaw Girl, 9005(F)

Parker, Barbara Keevil. *North American Wolves*, 19135
Susan B. Anthony, 13132

Parker, Cam. *A Horse in New York*, 7284(F)

Parker, Edward. *Antonio's Rain Forest*, 20463
Forests for the Future, 20471

Parker, Edward (jt. author). *People of the Rain Forests*, 20464

Parker, Jane. *The Fantastic Book of Horses*, 20006

Parker, Jane (jt. author). *Collecting Fossils*, 14460

Parker, Janice. *Cockroaches, Cocoons, and Honeycombs*, 19473
Great African Americans in Film, 12685
Political Leaders, 13740
The Science of Insects, 19474

Parker, Nancy W. *Bugs*, 19475
Locks, Crocs, and Skeeters, 15682
Money, Money, Money, 16927

Parker, Nancy Winslow. *The Bag I'm Taking to Grandma's*, 3339(F)
Black Crow, Black Crow, 1214(F)
Bugs, 19475
The Dress I'll Wear to the Party, 6542(F)
General Store, 3129(F)
The Goat in the Rug, 1817(F)
I'm Taking a Trip on My Train, 5591(F)
Paul Revere's Ride, 11643

Parker, Philip. *Global Cities*, 16972

Parker, Robert Andrew. *Aunt Skilly and the Stranger*, 4329(F)
An Autumn Tale, 6057(F)
Circus of the Wolves, 5152(F)
Cold Feet, 7701(F)
The Dancing Skeleton, 11333
Grandfather Tang's Story, 1624(F)
Guess Who My Favorite Person Is, 3521(F)
Gunga Din, 11617
The Hatmaker's Sign, 9229(F)
The Monkey's Haircut, 11395
The People with Five Fingers, 11287
The Sounds of Summer, 7316(F)
A Spring Story, 7104(F)
The Woman Who Fell from the Sky, 11214

Parker, Steve. *Blood*, 18088
The Body Atlas, 18069
Brain and Nerves, 18114
The Brain and Nervous System, 18115
Brain Surgery for Beginners, 18116
Collecting Fossils, 14460
Digestion, 18103
The Earth, 20315
Electricity, 20902
Fifty-Three and a Half Things That Changed the World and Some That Didn't! 21050
Frankenstein, 21944
Fuels for the Future, 20834
High in the Sky, 21096
The Human Body, 18070
Lungs, 18125
The Lungs and Respiratory System, 18126
Making Tracks, 21287

Medicine, 18025

Professor Protein's Fitness, Health, Hygiene and Relaxation Tonic, 18201

The Reproductive System, 18243

Seashore, 19863

Senses, 18151

Sharks, 19767

Shocking, Slimy, Stinky, Shiny Science Experiments, 18340

Skeleton, 18171

Ultimate Atlas of Almost Everything, 14352

Waste, Recycling and Re-Use, 16983

What's Inside Airplanes? 21097

Parker, Vic. *Bearobics,* 550(F)

Parker-Rees, Guy. *Big Bad Bunny,* 2046(F)

Parkins, David. *Aunt Nancy and Cousin Lazybones,* 4285(F)

Aunt Nancy and Old Man Trouble, 1517(F)

Fly Traps! 20238

No Problem, 1898(F)

Sophie Hits Six, 7240(F)

Tick-Tock, 1899(F)

Parkinson, Kathy. *Dry Days, Wet Nights,* 1822(F)

Little Bunny's Cool Tool Set, 1823(F)

Little Bunny's Pacifier Plan, 1824(F)

Little Bunny's Preschool Countdown, 5475(F)

Mama and Daddy Bear's Divorce, 5084(F)

The Paper Chain, 17940

Parks, Rosa. *Dear Mrs. Parks,* 17048

I Am Rosa Parks, 12778

Parmenter, Wayne. *If Your Name Was Changed at Ellis Island,* 17575

Parnall, Peter. *Annie and the Old One,* 8757(F)

Become a Bird and Fly! 1526(F)

The Desert Is Theirs, 15922

Desert Voices, 11772

Hawk, I'm Your Brother, 7156(F)

If You Are a Hunter of Fossils, 4386(F)

The Other Way to Listen, 302(F)

Spaces, 1457(F)

The Way to Start a Day, 11531

Parnell, Helga. *Cooking the German Way,* 21728

Cooking the South American Way, 21729

Paros, Ben Joshua (jt. author). *Smash Caps,* 22042

Paros, Lawrence. *Smash Caps,* 22042

Parr, Jan. *Amelia Earhart,* 12114

Parr, Todd. *The Best Friends Book,* 2560(F)

Do's and Don'ts, 3356(F)

The Feelings Book, 4260(F)

Parramon, J. M. *Hearing,* 18152

Sight, 18153

Smell, 18154

Taste, 18155

Touch, 18156

Parramon, Merce. *How Our Blood Circulates,* 18089

Parrilli, Mary Em (jt. author). *The Cheyenne,* 15990

Parris, Ronald. *Hausa,* 15044

Rendille, 14945

Parry-Jones, Jemima. *Amazing Birds of Prey,* 19335

Parselle, Matt. *Basketball,* 22141

Parsons, Alexandra. *Amazing Birds,* 19265

Amazing Mammals, 18960

Amazing Snakes, 18771

Amazing Spiders, 19590

Fit for Life, 18202

Parsons, Tom. *Pierre Auguste Renoir,* 12291

Partis, Joanne. *Stripe,* 2561(F)

Partridge, Elizabeth. *Oranges on Golden Mountain,* 4794(F)

Paschkis, Julie. *Happy Adoption Day!* 3786

Play All Day, 1458(F)

Pascoe, Elaine. *Ants,* 19512

Beetle, 19537

The Brooklyn Bridge, 16723

Butterflies and Moths, 19564

Crickets and Grasshoppers, 19476

Earthworms, 19616

First Facts About the Presidents, 12686

Flies, 19477

Scholastic Kid's Almanac for the 21st Century, 14353

Seeds and Seedlings, 20274

Slime, Molds, and Fungus, 20189

Snails and Slugs, 19617

Tadpoles, 18733

Pascoe, Elaine, adapt. *Mysteries of the Rain Forest,* 13341

New Dinosaurs, 14461

Virtual Reality, 21220

Pascoe, Gwen. *Deep in a Rainforest,* 20472

Pasqua, Sandra M. *The Navajo Nation,* 16020

Passaro, John. *Colin Powell,* 12951

Frederick Douglass, 12714

Passen, Lisa. *Attack of the 50-Foot Teacher,* 6038(F)

Passicot, Monique. *The Day the Rabbi Disappeared,* 11166

Pasternak, Ceel. *Cool Careers for Girls in Computers,* 17794

Cool Careers for Girls in Engineering, 17795

Cool Careers for Girls in Food, 17759

Cool Careers for Girls in Health, 17804

Cool Careers for Girls in Sports, 17760

Cool Careers for Girls with Animals, 17855

Pastore, Clare. *Fiona McGilray's Story,* 9603(F)

Pastuchiv, Olga. *Minas and the Fish,* 1459(F)

Pate, Rodney. *My Body Is Private,* 18255

Pateman, Robert. *Belgium,* 15400

Bolivia, 15775

Egypt, 15509

Kenya, 14946

Patent, Dorothy Hinshaw. *The American Alligator,* 18706

Apple Trees, 20214

Baby Horses, 5359

Back to the Wild, 20028

The Bald Eagle Returns, 19336

Bold and Bright, 18888

Deer and Elk, 19157

Dogs, 19961

Eagles of America, 19337

A Family Goes Hunting, 22043

Fire, 20473

Flashy Fantastic Rain Forest Frogs, 18734

Gray Wolf, Red Wolf, 19136

Great Ice Bear, 19059

Homesteading, 16348

Horses, 20007

In Search of Maiasaurs, 14462

The Incredible Story of China's Buried Warriors, 15077

Looking at Bears, 19060

Looking at Penguins, 19381

Lost City of Pompeii, 14737

Mystery of the Lascaux Cave, 14509

Ospreys, 19354

Pigeons, 19266

Polar Bears, 19061

Prairie Dogs, 19203

Prairies, 20541

Return of the Wolf, 7285(F)

Secrets of the Ice Man, 14510

Shaping the Earth, 18436

Slinky Scaly Slithery Snakes, 18772

Treasures of the Spanish Main, 14537

West by Covered Wagon, 16349

Where the Bald Eagles Gather, 19338

Where the Wild Horses Roam, 20008

Wild Turkeys, 19267

Paterson, Alan J. *How Glass Is Made,* 21051

Paterson, Bettina. *Little Green Thumbs,* 21774

Paterson, Diane. *Abuelita's Paradise,* 3823(F)

All Kinds of Children, 4831

Camping in the Temple of the Sun, 2934(F)

The Christmas Drum, 5845(F)

Gracias, Rosa, 3799(F)

Let Me Do It! 4159(F)

You Go Away, 3083(F)

Paterson, John. *Images of God*, 17314

Paterson, Katherine. *The Angel and the Donkey*, 17315

Angels and Other Strangers, 9753(F)

Bridge to Terabithia, 8355(F)

Celia and the Sweet, Sweet Water, 1460(F)

Come Sing, Jimmy Jo, 7490(F)

The Field of the Dogs, 8006(F)

The Great Gilly Hopkins, 8779(F)

Jacob Have I Loved, 7491(F)

Jip, His Story, 9309(F)

The King's Equal, 1461(F)

Marvin's Best Christmas Present Ever, 5896(F)

The Master Puppeteer, 9006(F)

Of Nightingales That Weep, 9007(F)

Park's Quest, 8505(F)

Parzival, 11021

Preacher's Boy, 8780(F)

The Sign of the Chrysanthemum, 9008(F)

The Smallest Cow in the World, 5046(F)

The Tale of the Mandarin Ducks, 10826

Who Am I? 17211

The Wide-Awake Princess, 10474(F)

Paterson, Katherine (jt. author). *Images of God*, 17314

Patey, R. L. *The Illustrated Rules of Football*, 22188

Patilla, Peter. *Fun with Numbers*, 551

Fun with Patterns, 232

Fun with Shapes, 352(F)

Fun with Sizes, 353(F)

Measuring, 354

Patterns, 233

Patneaude, David. *Dark Starry Morning*, 8007(F)

Haunting at Home Plate, 10355(F)

The Last Man's Reward, 8356(F)

Someone Was Watching, 7003(F)

Paton, Priscilla. *Howard and the Sitter Surprise*, 1462(F)

Patrick, Denise Lewis. *The Adventures of Midnight Son*, 9310(F)

The Car Washing Street, 3357(F)

The Longest Ride, 9492(F)

Red Dancing Shoes, 3833(F)

Patrick, Diane. *The Executive Branch*, 17118

Family Celebrations, 5644

Martin Luther King, Jr., 12751

Patrick, Jean L. S. *The Girl Who Struck Out Babe Ruth*, 22111

Patrick, Pamela. *An Amish Christmas*, 5744(F)

An Amish Wedding, 17161

Through the Night, 3513(F)

Patrick-Wexler, Diane. *Barbara Jordan*, 12733

Colin Powell, 12952

Toni Morrison, 12574

Patschke, Steve. *The Spooky Book*, 4261(F)

Patterson, Francine. *Koko-Love! Conversations with a Signing Gorilla*, 19011

Patterson, Jose. *Angels, Prophets, Rabbis and Kings*, 11157

Israel, 15527

Pattison, Darcy. *The Wayfinder*, 8008(F)

Patton, Don. *Armadillos*, 18961

Pythons, 18773

Sea Turtles, 18788

Patz, Nancy. *Moses Supposes His Toeses Are Roses*, 882

Sarah Bear and Sweet Sidney, 2562(F)

Patz, Nancy, reteller. *Moses Supposes His Toeses Are Roses*, 882

Paul, Ann W. *All by Herself*, 11668

Eight Hands Round, 110(F)

Hello Toes! Hello Feet! 234(F)

The Seasons Sewn, 16350

Shadows Are About, 3358(F)

Silly Sadie, Silly Samuel, 6570(F)

Paul, Anne Whitford. *Everything to Spend the Night*, 111(F)

Paul, Korky. *The Fish Who Could Wish*, 1904(F)

Professor Puffendorf's Secret Potions, 1631(F)

Winnie Flies Again, 4337(F)

Paul, Tessa. *By the Seashore*, 19864

In Fields and Meadows, 18652

Paulsen, Gary. *Alida's Song*, 8781(F)

Brian's Return, 8782(F)

Call Me Francis Tucket, 9426(F)

Canoe Days, 5360(F)

The Cookcamp, 8783(F)

Escape from Fire Mountain, 7004(F)

Guts, 12577

Harris and Me, 9958(F)

The Legend of Red Horse Cavern, 7005(F)

The Rock Jockeys, 7006(F)

The Schernoff Discoveries, 8357(F)

Soldier's Heart, 9493(F)

The Tortilla Factory, 20119

The Transall Saga, 10219(F)

Tucket's Gold, 9427(F)

Tucket's Home, 9428(F)

Tucket's Ride, 9429(F)

Worksong, 3359(F)

Paulsen, Ruth W. *Canoe Days*, 5360(F)

The Tortilla Factory, 20119

Worksong, 3359(F)

Pawagi, Manjusha. *The Girl Who Hated Books*, 1463(F)

Paxton, Tom. *The Jungle Baseball Game*, 2563(F)

The Marvelous Toy, 3834(F)

Payan, Gregory. *Essential Snowmobiling for Teens*, 22044

Life on a Submarine, 21399

Paye, Won-Ldy. *Why Leopard Has Spots*, 10710

Payne, Brian W. *Let's Go Fishing*, 22177

Payne, C. F. *Meet Molly*, 9691(F)

The Remarkable Farkle McBride, 4214(F)

Payne, Elizabeth. *The Pharaohs of Ancient Egypt*, 14658

Payne, Emmy. *Katy No-Pocket*, 2564(F)

Payne, Lauren M. *We Can Get Along*, 17624

Payne, Susan (jt. author). *Gingersnaps*, 17538

Payne, Tom. *Cats!* 6225(F)

Lemonade Stand, 6705(F)

Payson, Dale. *The Lucky Stone*, 7410(F)

Peacock, Carol Antoinette. *Mommy Far, Mommy Near*, 5047(F)

Sugar Was My Best Food, 17988

Peacock, Judith. *Anger Management*, 17625

Bipolar Disorder, 17989

Depression, 17723

Peacock, Louise. *Crossing the Delaware*, 16209

Pearce, Philippa. *Tom's Midnight Garden*, 8009(F)

Who's Afraid? And Other Strange Stories, 7007(F)

Pearce, Q. L. *Armadillos and Other Unusual Animals*, 18962

Great Predators of the Land, 18840

Piranhas and Other Wonders of the Jungle, 18653

The Stargazer's Guide to the Galaxy, 18408

Pearl, Sydelle. *Elijah's Tears*, 9754(F)

Pearson, Debora (jt. author). *52 Days by Camel*, 14963

Jungle Islands, 15226

Pearson, Gayle. *The Secret Box*, 8784(F)

Pearson, Kit. *A Handful of Time*, 8506(F)

Pearson, Maggie. *The Fox and the Rooster and Other Tales*, 10599

The Headless Horseman and Other Ghoulish Tales, 10600

Pearson, Susan. *Eagle-Eye Ernie Comes to Town*, 6571(F)

The Green Magician Puzzle, 6572(F)

Silver Morning, 4505(F)

Well, I Never! 1464(F)

Pearson, Tracey Campbell. *The Awful Aardvarks Go to School*, 80(F)

The Awful Aardvarks Shop for School, 2375(F)

G-Rex, 1098(F)

No Dogs Allowed, 9821(F)

The Purple Hat, 4262(F)

Where Does Joe Go? 5897(F)

Peck, Beth. *A Christmas Memory*, 9712(F)
The Day Before Christmas, 5767(F)
The House on Maple Street, 4800(F)
How Many Days to America? A Thanksgiving Story, 6135(F)
Matthew and Tilly, 4013(F)
The Thanksgiving Visitor, 8592(F)
Peck, Ira. *Elizabeth Blackwell*, 13242
Nellie Bly's Book, 13139
Peck, Marshall H. *Amazing Rescues*, 6656
Peck, Richard. *The Ghost Belonged to Me*, 8010(F)
The Great Interactive Dream Machine, 10220(F)
A Long Way from Chicago, 9604(F)
Strays Like Us, 8507(F)
A Year Down Yonder, 7492(F)
Peck, Robert Newton. *Arly*, 10120(F)
The Cowboy Ghost, 7008(F)
A Day No Pigs Would Die, 9605(F)
Higbee's Halloween, 9959(F)
Nine Man Tree, 7009(F)
Soup, 8358(F)
Peddle, Daniel. *Snow Day*, 931(F)
Pedersen, Janet. *Bravo, Mildred and Ed!* 2806(F)
A Friend Like Ed, 2807(F)
Jake and the Copycats, 6593(F)
A Weed Is a Seed, 3484(F)
Pedersen, Judy. *On the Road of Stars*, 11213
Seedfolks, 7339(F)
When Night Time Comes Near, 760(F)
Peduzzi, Kelli. *Shaping a President*, 16724
Peek, Merle. *Roll Over! A Counting Song*, 552(F)
Peers, Judi. *Shark Attack*, 10356(F)
Peet, Bill. *Big Bad Bruce*, 1465(F)
Bill Peet, 12279
The Caboose Who Got Loose, 1466(F)
Cock-a-Doodle Dudley, 2565(F)
Cowardly Clyde, 2566(F)
Eli, 2567(F)
Encore for Eleanor, 2568(F)
The Gnats of Knotty Pine, 2569(F)
Jennifer and Josephine, 1467(F)
Whingdingdilly, 2570(F)
The Wump World, 4506(F)
Zella, Zack, and Zodiac, 2571(F)
Peffer-Engels, John. *The Benin Kingdom of West Africa*, 15045
Pegram, Laura. *Daughter's Day Blues*, 3835(F)
Peguero, Adrian. *Lionel and Amelia*, 2572(F)
Peguero, Gerard. *Lionel and Amelia*, 2572(F)
Peguero, Leone. *Lionel and Amelia*, 2572(F)
Peifer, Charles. *Houston*, 16914

Soldier of Destiny, 12944
Pekarik, Andrew. *Painting*, 13917
Pelham, David. *A Is for Animals*, 112(F)
Pelizzoli, Francesca. *Lao Lao of Dragon Mountain*, 986(F)
Pellant, Chris. *Collecting Gems and Minerals*, 20567
Pellaton, Karen E. *The Official M&M's Brand Book of the Millennium*, 20640
Pellegrini, Nina. *Families Are Different*, 3836(F)
Pelletier, David. *The Graphic Alphabet*, 113(F)
Pelletier, Gilles. *Come to the Fair*, 3289(F)
A Happy New Year's Day, 5616(F)
Pellowski, Anne. *The Storytelling Handbook*, 14103
Pellowski, Michael M. *The Art of Making Comic Books*, 21586
Pels, Winslow. *Iron John*, 10585
Stone Soup, 10874
Pelta, Kathy. *California*, 16806
Cattle Trails, 16351
Discovering Christopher Columbus, 12100
Eastern Trails, 16269
The Royal Roads, 16352
The U.S. Navy, 21400
Pelz, Ruth. *Black Heroes of the Wild West*, 12687
Women of the Wild West, 12688
Pembleton, Seliesa. *The Armadillo*, 18963
The Pileated Woodpecker, 19268
Pendleton, Lorann (jt. author). *Native Americans*, 16063
Pendleton, Scott. *The Ultimate Guide to Student Contests, Grades K–6*, 17626
Pendziwol, Jean. *No Dragons for Tea*, 1468(F)
Penisten, John. *Honolulu*, 16807
Penn, Malka. *The Hanukkah Ghosts*, 9755(F)
Penner, Lucille R. *Celebration*, 17393
Clean-Sweep Campers, 20593
Dinosaur Babies, 5361
Eating the Plates, 16163
The Liberty Tree, 16210
Lights Out! 553(F)
Monster Bugs, 19478
S-S-Snakes! 18774
Twisters! 20712
Where's That Bone? 235(F)
Penney, Ian. *Ian Penney's Book of Nursery Rhymes*, 883(F)
A Noteworthy Tale, 1427(F)
Pennington, Daniel. *Itse Selu*, 16021
Penny, Malcolm. *Giant Panda*, 19190
How Bats "See" in the Dark, 19033
How Plants Grow, 20254

The Indian Ocean, 19833
Our Environment, 16963
Polar Bear, 19062
The Polar Seas, 15826
Peppe, Rodney. *The Magic Toy Box*, 1469(F)
Percy, Graham. *The Cock, the Mouse, and the Little Red Hen*, 10957
A Cup of Starshine, 11532
Elympics, 2285(F)
The Mailbox Mice Mystery, 6501(F)
Perdrizet, Marie-Pierre. *The Cathedral Builders*, 13949
Perenyi, Constance. *Wild Wild West*, 20384
Perez, Amada Irma. *My Very Own Room/ Mi propio cuartito*, 3360(F)
Perez, Candi (jt. author). *A Taste of Spain*, 21702
Perez, Frank. *Dolores Huerta*, 12832
Raul Julia, 12833
Perez, Gloria Osuna. *Little Gold Star/Estrellita de oro*, 11346
Perez, L. King. *Ghoststalking*, 8011(F)
Perez, Lucia Angela. *Little Gold Star/Estrellita de oro*, 11346
Perez, N. A. *Breaker*, 9606(F)
Perham, Molly. *People*, 14511
Resources, 20316
Wildlife, 18654
Perkins, Catherine. *The Most Excellent Book of How to Be a Clown*, 21672
Perkins, Lynne Rae. *All Alone in the Universe*, 8359(F)
Home Lovely, 4507(F)
Perl, Lila. *The Great Ancestor Hunt*, 17674
It Happened in America, 15897
Mummies, Tombs, and Treasure, 14659
Pinatas and Paper Flowers, 17394
Pernoud, Regine. *A Day with a Miller*, 9066(F)
A Day with a Noble-woman, 14786
A Day with a Stonecutter, 14787
Perols, Sylvaine. *Atlas of Plants*, 20224
Colors, 271
The Human Body, 18071
The Ladybug and Other Insects, 19444
Perrault, Charles. *Cinderella*, 10475(F)
The Complete Fairy Tales of Charles Perrault, 10876
Perrault's Fairy Tales, 10877
Puss in Boots, 10878, 10879, 10880
Perrault, Charles, reteller. *Cinderella, Puss in Boots, and Other Favorite Tales*, 10476(F)

Perrin, Gerry. *Hau Kola Hello Friend*, 12542
Perrin, Randy. *Time Like a River*, 8012(F)
Perrone, Donna. *Shadow Dance*, 8973
Perrow, Angeli. *Lighthouse Dog to the Rescue*, 5362(F)
Perry, Chris. *A Yoga Parade of Animals*, 18200
Perry, Phyllis J. *Armor to Venom*, 18900
  Ballooning, 22045
  Bats, 19034
  Crafty Canines, 19137
  The Crocodilians, 18707
  Freshwater Giants, 19643
  Hide and Seek, 18889
  Sea Stars and Dragons, 19711
  The Snow Cats, 19104
  Soaring, 22046
Perry, Rebecca. *Lots of Limericks*, 11896
Perry, Robert L. *Build Your Own Website*, 21221
  Personal Computer Communications, 21222
Perry, Sarah. *If . . .*, 1470(F)
Persun, Morgan Reed. *No Pets Allowed*, 1471(F)
Pertzoff, Alexander. *Three Names*, 4758(F)
Peters, Andrew. *Salt Is Sweeter Than Gold*, 10862
Peters, Andrew F. *Strange and Spooky Stories*, 10601
Peters, Celeste A. *Peppers, Popcorn, and Pizza*, 20120
Peters, David. *Supergiants!* 14439
Peters, Julie A. *How Do You Spell G-E-E-K?* 8360(F)
  Revenge of the Snob Squad, 8785(F)
  Romance of the Snob Squad, 9960(F)
Peters, Lisa Westberg. *Cold Little Duck, Duck, Duck*, 2573(F)
  October Smiled Back, 4508(F)
  Purple Delicious Blackberry Jam, 4263(F)
  The Sun, the Wind, and the Rain, 4509(F)
Peters, Patricia. *Nursery Rhymes from Mother Goose Told in Signed English*, 827
Peters, Russell. *Clambake*, 16022
Peters, Sonja. *A Family from Germany*, 15329
Peters, Stephanie True. *Gary Paulsen*, 12578
Peters, Stephen. *Pennsylvania*, 16725
Peterseil, Tehila. *The Safe Place*, 8786(F)
Petersen, David. *Bryce Canyon National Park*, 16631
  Dinosaur National Monument, 16632

Grand Canyon National Park, 16633
  Great Smoky Mountains National Park, 16878
  North America, 14354
  Rocky Mountain National Park, 16634
  South America, 15777
  Yellowstone National Park, 16635
Petersen, P. J. *Can You Keep a Secret?* 10121(F)
  I Hate Weddings, 9961(F)
  I Want Answers and a Parachute, 8508(F)
  Liars, 7010(F)
  My Worst Friend, 8361(F)
  Some Days, Other Days, 3837(F)
  White Water, 7011(F)
Petersen-Fleming, Judy. *Puppy Care and Critters, Too!* 19962
Petersham, Maud. *The Rooster Crows*, 884
Petersham, Miska. *The Rooster Crows*, 884
Peterson, Beth. *Myrna Never Sleeps*, 1472(F)
  No Turning Back, 8013(F)
Peterson, Cris. *Century Farm*, 20069
  Extra Cheese, Please! 20070
  Harvest Year, 20121
  Horsepower, 20009
Peterson, Dawn. *Ellie Bear and the Fly-Away Fly*, 2642(F)
Peterson, Donna. *Gran's Bees*, 3917(F)
Peterson, Ingela. *The Penguin Quartet*, 1752(F)
Peterson, Jeanne Whitehouse. *I Have a Sister, My Sister Is Deaf*, 5048(F)
Peterson, Mary. *Cat on Wheels*, 1864(F)
Peterson, Melissa. *Hasta La Vista, Blarney!* 7012(F)
Peterson, Scott. *Plugged In*, 21844(F)
Peterson, Stephanie. *Peek-a-Moo!* 5166(F)
Peterson, Sue H. *Swim with Me*, 22308
Petit, Genevieve. *The Seventh Walnut*, 4510
Petrén, Birgitta. *Why Are You Calling Me a Barbarian?* 14738
Petricic, Dusan. *Bone Button Borscht*, 11144
  The Enormous Potato, 11086
  Let's Play, 22007
Petrie, Catherine. *Joshua James Likes Trucks*, 6574(F)
Petrone, Valeria. *Ducks in Muck*, 6368(F)
Petruccio, Steven J. *Great White Shark*, 19770
  Raindrops and Rainbows, 20749
  The Starry Sky, 18425
Petry, Ann. *Tituba of Salem Village*, 9209(F)

Pettit, Jayne. *Jane Goodall*, 13301
  Michelangelo, 12260
  A Time to Fight Back, 14875
Petty, Kate. *Horse Heroes*, 20010
  Rabbits, 19902
  Some Trains Run on Water, 21341
  The Sun Is a Star, 18409
  You Can Jump Higher on the Moon and Other Amazing Facts About Space Exploration, 21005
Pevsner, Stella. *Is Everyone Moon-burned But Me?* 8787(F)
  Sing for Your Father, Su Phan, 9009(F)
  Would My Fortune Cookie Lie? 8509(F)
Pfeffer, Susan Beth. *Devil's Den*, 8510(F)
  Kid Power, 7493(F)
  Who Were They Really? The True Stories Behind Famous Characters, 14004
Pfeffer, Wendy. *From Tadpole to Frog*, 18735
  A Log's Life, 20215
  Mute Swans, 19269
  Polar Bears, 19063
  Popcorn Park Zoo, 20029
  Sounds All Around, 20943
  What's It Like to Be a Fish? 19982
Pfeifer, Kathryn B. *Henry O. Flipper*, 12723
  The 761st Tank Battalion, 14876
Pfeiffer, Christine. *Chicago*, 16573
  Poland, 15283
Pfiffner, George. *Earth-Friendly Holidays*, 21461
  Earth-Friendly Outdoor Fun, 21462
  Earth-Friendly Toys, 21656
Pfister, Marcus. *Dazzle the Dinosaur*, 2574(F)
  Hopper's Treetop Adventure, 2575(F)
  Make a Wish, Honey Bear! 5717(F)
  Milo and the Magical Stones, 2576(F)
  Milo and the Mysterious Island, 2577(F)
  Penguin Pete, Ahoy! 2578(F)
  The Rainbow Fish, 2579(F)
  Rainbow Fish and the Big Blue Whale, 2580(F)
  The Rainbow Fish Board Book, 2581(F)
  Rainbow Fish to the Rescue! 2582(F)
Pfitsch, Patricia C. *Keeper of the Light*, 9607(F)
Pflaum, Rosalynd. *Marie Curie and Her Daughter Irene*, 13219
Pfleger, Andrea F. *Surprising Myself*, 12537
Pfleger, Susanne. *A Day with Picasso*, 12283
  Henri Rousseau, 12298

Pflueger, Lynda. *Dolley Madison*, 13170
Jeb Stuart, 12967
Mark Twain, 12610
Stonewall Jackson, 12907
Thomas Nast, 12272
Pham, LeUyen. *Can You Do This, Old Badger?* 1901(F)
Phelps, Ethel Johnston. *The Maid of the North*, 10602
Tatterhood and Other Tales, 10603
Phifer, Kate Gilbert. *Tall and Small*, 18072
Philbrick, Rodman. *The Fire Pony*, 8511(F)
REM World, 10221(F)
Philip, Neil. *The Arabian Nights*, 11195
Celtic Fairy Tales, 11022
The Illustrated Book of Myths, 11455
Mythology, 11456
Philip, Neil, ed. *Christmas Fairy Tales*, 10477(F)
The Fairy Tales of Oscar Wilde, 10478(F)
In a Sacred Manner I Live, 16023
Songs Are Thoughts, 11669
War and the Pity of War, 11670
Philip, Neil, reteller. *The Adventures of Odysseus*, 11501
Odin's Family, 11520
Phillips, Anne. *The Franklin Delano Roosevelt Memorial*, 16726
Phillips, Francis. *The Sun Is a Star*, 18409
Phillips, Joan. *My New Boy*, 6575(F)
Phillips, Louis. *Ask Me Anything About the Presidents*, 12689
263 Brain Busters, 20619
Phillips, Louise. *Face Painting*, 21592
I Heard a Little Baa, 5330(F)
Sound Science, 20939
Phillips, Mildred. *And the Cow Said Moo!* 5363(F)
Phillips-Duke, Barbara J. *Digby*, 6375(F)
Picard, Barbara Leonie. *The Midsummer Bride*, 1473(F)
Picart, Gabriel. *Alison Rides the Rapids*, 6746(F)
Pichon, Liz. *Twilight Verses, Moonlight Rhymes*, 795
Pickels, Dwayne E. *Roman Myths, Heroes, and Legends*, 14739
Pickering, Jane. *Down a River*, 15908
Inside a Coral Reef, 19669
Pickering, Marianne. *Lessons for Life*, 17627
Pickering, Mel. *Basketball*, 22141
Soccer, 22300
Pickering, Robert. *The People*, 14512
Pidgeon, Jean. *Brush Your Teeth, Please*, 2432(F)
The Snowball, 959(F)
Pienkowski, Jan. *Colors*, 286(F)

Sally Go Round the Moon, 14164
Pierard, John. *My Babysitter Is a Vampire*, 9877(F)
My Teacher Fried My Brains, 10170(F)
Pierce, Roxanne H. (jt. author). *Oh, Grow Up!* 4976(F)
Tio Armando, 3683(F)
Pierce, Tamora. *Briar's Book*, 8014(F)
The Circle Opens, 8015(F)
Daja's Book, 8016(F)
First Test, 8017(F)
Page, 9117(F)
Tris's Book, 8018(F)
Pierre, Stephanie St. (jt. author). *The Muppets Big Book of Crafts*, 21457
Piers, Helen. *Is There Room on the Bus?* 554(F)
Who's in My Bed? 2583(F)
Pietrusza, David. *The Baltimore Orioles Baseball Team*, 22112
The New York Yankees Baseball Team, 22113
The Phoenix Suns Basketball Team, 22142
The San Francisco Giants Baseball Team, 22114
Smoking, 17883
Top 10 Baseball Managers, 13391
Pignataro, Anna. *Unknown*, 5431(F)
Pilbeam, Mavis. *Japan Under the Shoguns, 1185–1868*, 15136
Pilegard, Virginia Walton. *The Warlord's Puzzle*, 4795(F)
Pilkey, Dav. *The Adventures of Captain Underpants*, 9962(F)
Big Dog and Little Dog Making a Mistake, 6576(F)
Captain Underpants and the Attack of the Talking Toilets, 9963(F)
Captain Underpants and the Invasion of the Incredibly Naughty Cafeteria Ladies from Outer Space (and the Subsequent Assault of the Equally Evil Lunchroom Zombie Nerds), 9964(F)
Captain Underpants and the Perilous Plot of Professor Poopypants, 9965(F)
Dog Breath, 2584(F)
Dogzilla, 5364(F)
Dragon's Merry Christmas, 5898(F)
The Dumb Bunnies, 2020(F)
The Dumb Bunnies' Easter, 5964(F)
The Dumb Bunnies Go to the Zoo, 2021(F)
God Bless the Gargoyles, 1474(F)
The Hallo-Wiener, 6039(F)
Make Way for Dumb Bunnies, 2022(F)
The Moonglow Roll-o-Rama, 2585(F)

The Paperboy, 3361(F)
Ricky Ricotta's Giant Robot, 1475(F)
Ricky Ricotta's Giant Robot vs. the Mutant Mosquitoes from Mercury, 1476(F)
The Silly Gooses, 2586(F)
When Cats Dream, 1477(F)
Pilling, Ann. *Creation*, 10604
A Kingfisher Treasury of Bible Stories, Poems, and Prayers for Bedtime, 17212
The Year of the Worm, 7013(F)
Pimm, Paul. *Living with Cerebral Palsy*, 17990
Pincus, Dion. *Everything You Need to Know About Cerebral Palsy*, 17991
Pincus, Harriet. *Tell Me a Mitzi*, 3883(F)
The Wedding Procession of the Rag Doll and the Broom Handle and Who Was in It, 1539(F)
Pinczes, Elinor J. *Arctic Fives Arrive*, 555(F)
Inchworm and a Half, 556(F)
One Hundred Hungry Ants, 557(F)
A Remainder of One, 558(F)
Pingry, Patricia A. *Joseph's Story*, 17429
Pinkney, Andrea D. *Bill Pickett*, 12442
Dear Benjamin Banneker, 13235
Duke Ellington, 12379
Hold Fast to Dreams, 7364(F)
Let It Shine, 12690
Raven in a Dove House, 8788(F)
Silent Thunder, 9494(F)
Solo Girl, 6577(F)
Pinkney, Brian. *The Adventures of Sparrowboy*, 1478(F)
Bill Pickett, 12442
The Boy and the Ghost, 1541(F)
Cendrillon, 10495
Cosmo and the Robot, 1479(F)
Cut from the Same Cloth, 11376
The Dark-Thirty, 11366
Dear Benjamin Banneker, 13235
Duke Ellington, 12379
The Faithful Friend, 11431
Happy Birthday, Martin Luther King, 12748
In the Time of the Drums, 9321(F)
Jojo's Flying Side Kick, 5049(F)
Max Found Two Sticks, 3362(F)
Sukey and the Mermaid, 11379
A Wave in Her Pocket, 11427
Pinkney, Jerry. *The Adventures of Spider*, 10648
Aesop's Fables, 11073
Albidaro and the Mischievous Dream, 1350(F)
Black Cowboy, Wild Horses, 4728(F)
Childtimes, 17562
Drylongso, 8680(F)

The Green Lion of Zion Street,
8283(F)
Half a Moon and One Whole Star,
663(F)
Home Place, 3110(F)
In for Winter, Out for Spring,
11934
Journeys with Elijah, 17276
The Jungle Book, 7244(F)
The Little Match Girl, 10479(F)
Mary McLeod Bethune, 12701
New Shoes for Silvia, 3234(F)
Rabbit Makes a Monkey of Lion,
10642
Rikki-Tikki-Tavi, 7872(F)
Roll of Thunder, Hear My Cry,
7526(F)
Turtle in July, 11813
The Ugly Duckling, 10480(F)
Wild Wild Sunflower Child Anna,
4403(F)
Pinkney, Myles C. *Shades of Black,*
3363(F)
Pinkney, Sandra L. *Shades of Black,*
3363(F)
Pinkwater, Daniel. *Author's Day,*
4264(F)
The Big Orange Splot, 4265(F)
Bongo Larry, 2587(F)
Borgel, 10222(F)
Doodle Flute, 4032(F)
Fat Men from Space, 9966(F)
The Hoboken Chicken Emergency,
9967(F)
Ice Cream Larry, 2588(F)
The Magic Pretzel, 8019(F)
Mush, a Dog from Space, 10223(F)
Ned Feldman, Space Pirate,
10224(F)
The Phantom of the Lunch Wagon,
1480(F)
Rainy Morning, 4266(F)
Second-Grade Ape, 6578(F)
Wallpaper from Space, 10225(F)
Wempires, 1481(F)
The Werewolf Club, 9968(F)
Wolf Christmas, 5899(F)
Young Larry, 2589(F)
Pinkwater, Daniel (jt. author). *Super-*
puppy, 19963
Pinkwater, Jill. *Bongo Larry,* 2587(F)
Ice Cream Larry, 2588(F)
Rainy Morning, 4266(F)
Second-Grade Ape, 6578(F)
Superpuppy, 19963
Wallpaper from Space, 10225(F)
Wolf Christmas, 5899(F)
Young Larry, 2589(F)
Pinto, Venantius J. *Aani and the Tree*
Huggers, 8982(F)
Pipe, Jim. *Dracula,* 21945
The Giant Book of Bugs and
Creepy Crawlies, 19479
The Giant Book of Creatures of the
Night, 18841
The Giant Book of Snakes and
Slithery Creatures, 18691

Medieval Castle, 14788
Trojan Horse, 14698
The Werewolf, 8020(F)
Piper, Watty. *The Little Engine That*
Could, 5592(F)
Pipes, Rose. *Coasts and Shores,*
19865
Forests and Woodlands, 20474
Grasslands, 20542
Hot Deserts, 20414
Islands, 20385
Mountains and Volcanoes, 20505
Rain Forests, 20475
Rivers and Lakes, 20523
Tundra and Cold Deserts, 15827
Wetlands, 20386
Pippen, Scottie. *Reach Higher,* 13565
Pirner, Connie W. *Even Little Kids*
Get Diabetes, 17992
Pirotta, Saviour. *Jerusalem,* 15528
People in the Rain Forest, 20476
Pirates and Treasure, 14566
Predators in the Rain Forest,
20477
Rivers in the Rain Forest, 20478
Rome, 15388
Trees and Plants in the Rain
Forest, 20479
Turtle Bay, 5365(F)
Pirotta, Saviour, reteller. *Joy to the*
World, 9756
Pitcher, Caroline. *Are You Spring?*
2590(F)
Mariana and the Merchild, 11442
Run with the Wind, 2591(F)
The Time of the Lion, 5366(F)
Pitkanen, Matti. *The Children of*
China, 15065
The Children of Egypt, 15502
The Children of Nepal, 15174
The Grandchildren of the Incas,
15754
Pitkanen, Matti A. *The Grandchil-*
dren of the Vikings, 15465
Pittman, Helena Clare. *The Angel*
Tree, 5900(F)
The Snowman's Path, 1482(F)
Still-Life Stew, 3364(F)
Sunrise, 559(F)
Uncle Phil's Diner, 3838(F)
Pitts, Paul. *Racing the Sun,* 7365(F)
Place, François. *The Last Giants,*
8021(F)
Place, Robin. *Bodies from the Past,*
14513
Plain, Nancy. *The Man Who Painted*
Indians, 12203
Platt, Chris. *Race the Wind!* 7286(F)
Willow King, 7287(F)
Platt, Kin. *Big Max,* 6579(F)
Platt, Richard. *Castle Diary,* 9118(F)
Castles, 14789
Everest, 22047
Film, 21275
In the Beginning, 14567
Inventions Explained, 21052
Pirate, 14568

Shipwreck, 21372
The Smithsonian Visual Timeline of
Inventions, 21053
Spy, 17077
Stephen Biesty's Cross-Sections
Man-of-War, 21373
Stephen Biesty's Incredible Body,
18073
Stephen Biesty's Incredible Cross-
Sections, 13918
Stephen Biesty's Incredible Explo-
sions, 21147
Playe, Stephen. *Celtic Myths,* 11011
Plazy, Gilles. *A Weekend with*
Rousseau, 12299
Plecas, Jennifer. *Agapanthus Hum*
and Major Bark, 6287(F)
Agapanthus Hum and the Eyeglass-
es, 9815(F)
Emma's Magic Winter, 6462(F)
Emma's Yucky Brother, 6463(F)
Good Night, Good Knight, 6692(F)
The Outside Dog, 6580(F)
The Pig Is in the Pantry, the Cat Is
on the Shelf, 2517(F)
Snow Day! 4469(F)
Wrapping Paper Romp, 3225(F)
Plenkowski, Jan. *Good Night,* 761(F)
Plewes, Andrew. *The Girl Who Lived*
with the Bears, 11255
Plotkin, Gregory. *Cooking the Russ-*
ian Way, 21731
Plotkin, Mark J. (jt. author). *The*
Shaman's Apprentice, 4619(F)
Plotkin, Rita (jt. author). *Cooking the*
Russian Way, 21731
Plourde, Lynn. *Pigs in the Mud in the*
Middle of the Rud, 4267(F)
Wild Child, 762(F)
Winter Waits, 1483(F)
Pluckrose, Henry. *Egypt,* 15510
France, 15315
On the Farm, 21252
On the Move, 21288
Plume, Ilse. *The Queen's Necklace,*
10443(F)
Salt, 11098
The Shoemaker and the Elves,
10907
Sleepy Book, 821(F)
Pocock, Rita. *Annabelle and the Big*
Slide, 3365(F)
Podendorf, Illa. *Animals of Sea and*
Shore, 19644
Jungles, 20387
Spiders, 19591
Podwal, Mark. *The Angel's Mistake,*
11159
The Demons' Mistake, 11160
Golem, 11158
The Menorah Story, 17481
You Never Know, 11161
Pogany, Willy. *The Children's*
Homer, 11465
The Golden Fleece and the Heroes
Who Lived Before Achilles,
11466

Pohrt, Tom. *Coyote Goes Walking*, 11289
The Tomb of the Boy King, 14625
Trickster and the Fainting Birds, 11282

Polacco, Patricia. *Appelemando's Dreams*, 1484(F)
Aunt Chip and the Great Triple Creek Dam Affair, 3366(F)
Babushka Baba Yaga, 4796(F)
Babushka's Doll, 1485(F)
Babushka's Mother Goose, 10605
The Bee Tree, 4033(F)
The Butterfly, 4797(F)
Chicken Sunday, 5974(F)
I Can Hear the Sun, 8022(F)
In Enzo's Splendid Gardens, 4268(F)
The Keeping Quilt, 3839(F)
Luba and the Wren, 11106
Mrs. Katz and Tush, 4034(F)
Mrs. Mack, 5367(F)
My Ol' Man, 3840(F)
My Rotten Redheaded Older Brother, 3841(F)
Picnic at Mudsock Meadow, 6040(F)
Pink and Say, 9495(F)
Rechenka's Eggs, 1486(F)
Some Birthday! 5718(F)
Thank You, Mr. Falker, 5050(F)
Thunder Cake, 3842(F)
The Trees of the Dancing Goats, 5901(F)
Uncle Vova's Tree, 5902(F)
Welcome Comfort, 5903(F)

Policoff, Stephen Phillip. *Cesar's Amazing Journey*, 2592(F)

Polikoff, Barbara G. *Life's a Funny Proposition, Horatio*, 8512(F)

Polisar, Barry L. *Don't Do That!* 4269(F)
Insect Soup, 11806
The Trouble with Ben, 2593(F)

Politi, Leo. *Song of the Swallows*, 5368(F)

Polking, Kirk. *Oceanographers and Explorers of the Sea*, 13220

Pollack, Eileen. *Whisper Whisper Jesse, Whisper Whisper Josh*, 5051(F)

Pollack, Jill S. *Shirley Chisholm*, 12707

Pollack, Lou M. *The Girls' Book of Wisdom*, 17701

Pollack, Pam (jt. author). *Where's That Cat?* 5031(F)

Polland, Barbara K. *We Can Work it Out*, 17724

Pollard, Michael. *Alexander Graham Bell*, 13240
The Amazon, 15778
The Ganges, 15112
Margaret Mead, 13320
The Mississippi, 16574
The Nile, 14911
People Who Care, 13741

The Rhine, 15330
The Yangtze, 15078

Pollard, Michael (jt. author). *Generals Who Changed the World*, 13746
The Magical East, 15052
Scientists Who Changed the World, 13224

Pollock, Penny. *The Turkey Girl*, 11290

Pomeranc, Marion Hess. *The American Wei*, 3367(F)
The Can-Do Thanksgiving, 6150(F)
The Hand-Me-Down Horse, 4798(F)

Pomerantz, Charlotte. *The Birthday Letters*, 5719(F)
The Chalk Doll, 3843(F)
Halfway to Your House, 11672
If I Had a Paka, 11673
The Mousery, 2594(F)
One Duck, Another Duck, 560(F)
The Outside Dog, 6580(F)
The Piggy in the Puddle, 2595(F)
Serena Katz, 4270(F)
Where's the Bear? 5369(F)
You're Not My Best Friend Anymore, 4035(F)

Pomeroy, Diana. *One Potato*, 561
Wildflower ABC, 114(F)

Poncet, Sally. *Antarctic Encounter*, 15828

Pond, Mildred. *Mother Teresa*, 13858

Pons, Bernadette. *Tickle Tum!* 2776(F)

Ponti, James. *WNBA*, 22143

Poole, Amy Lowry. *The Ant and the Grasshopper*, 11074
How the Rooster Got His Crown, 10767

Poole, Josephine. *Joan of Arc*, 13813

Pooley, Sarah. *It's Raining, It's Pouring*, 11674

Pope, Joyce. *Fossil Detective*, 14463
Living Fossils, 18655
Practical Plants, 20256

Poploff, Michelle. *Bat Bones and Spider Stew*, 6041(F)
Busy O'Brien and the Great Bubble Gum Blowout, 9969(F)
Tea Party for Two, 6581(F)

Popp, K. Wendy. *Sister Anne's Hands*, 5517(F)

Poppel, Hans. *Salmon Moon*, 1288(F)
Such a Noise! 11142

Porfirio, Guy. *Happy Birthday, America!* 5617(F)

Porte, Barbara A. *If You Ever Get Lost*, 7494(F)

Porte, Barbara Ann. *Black Elephant with a Brown Ear (in Alabama)*, 13962
Chickens! Chickens! 4271(F)
Fat Fanny, Beanpole Bertha and the Boys, 7495(F)
Harry in Trouble, 6582(F)

Harry's Pony, 6583(F)
Hearsay, 10768(F)
Ma Jiang and the Orange Ants, 4799(F)
Tale of a Tadpole, 5370(F)

Porter, A. P. *Greg LeMond*, 13698
Kwanzaa, 17395
Minnesota, 16575
Nebraska, 16576
Zina Garrison, 13648

Porter, Barbara J. *Some Answers Are Loud, Some Answers Are Soft*, 3368(F)

Porter, Connie. *Addy Learns a Lesson*, 9496(F)
Addy Saves the Day, 9608(F)

Porter, Janice L. *Allen Jay and the Underground Railroad*, 6224(F)
Aunt Clara Brown, 12705
Colors of Mexico, 15640
Colors of the Navajo, 15917
Count Your Way Through Greece, 15385
Family, 3813(F)
Hope, 3814(F)
Kwanzaa, 17395
M Is for Minnesota, 16540
Pablo Picasso, 12281

Porter, Pat G. *Della Splatnuk, Birthday Girl*, 5710(F)

Porter, Sue. *Little Wolf and the Giant*, 2596(F)

Porter, Tracey. *Treasures in the Dust*, 8789(F)

Porter, Walter. *The Same Sun Was in the Sky*, 4873(F)

Porter-Gaylord, Laurel. *I Love My Daddy Because . . .*, 3844(F)

Portnoy, Mindy A. *Matzah Ball*, 6105(F)

Portwood, Andrew. *Dragon Scales and Willow Leaves*, 1194(F)

Posada, Mia. *Dandelions*, 20257

Posell, Elsa. *Horses*, 20011
Whales and Other Sea Mammals, 19798

Posey, Lee. *Night Rabbits*, 5371(F)

Posner, Mitch. *Kai, a Big Decision*, 8976(F)

Potter, Beatrix. *The Complete Adventures of Peter Rabbit*, 2597(F)
The Tales of Peter Rabbit and Benjamin Bunny, 2598(F)

Potter, Giselle. *The Big Box*, 7972(F)
Gabriella's Song, 4647(F)
The Honest-to-Goodness Truth, 5023(F)
Kate and the Beanstalk, 9116
Mr. Semolina-Semolinus, 11070
Three Cheers for Catherine the Great! 5665(F)
When Agnes Caws, 2929(F)

Potter, Jean. *Science in Seconds with Toys*, 18341

Potter, Jean (jt. author). *Global Art*, 21448

Potter, Joan. *African Americans Who Were First*, 12691

Potter, Katherine. *Naming the Cat*, 5373(F)

Potter, Keith R. *Cat Nap*, 19105
Count Us In, 562(F)
Shake, Rattle and Roll, 236(F)
This and That, 237(F)

Pouillart, Gilbert (jt. author). *Judo Techniques andTactics*, 22024

Poulin, Stephane. *The King's Giraffe*, 4625(F)

Pow, Tom. *Who Is the World For?* 1487(F)

Powe-Temperley, Kitty. *The 60s*, 16516

Powell, Consie. *Old Dog Cora and the Christmas Tree*, 5904(F)

Powell, David. *Cougar Cove*, 7251(F)

Powell, E. Sandy. *Washington*, 16808

Powell, Jillian. *Adoption*, 17675
Animal Rights, 18656
Body Decoration, 21946
Drug Trafficking, 17078
Eggs, 19270
Exercise and Your Health, 18203
Family Breakup, 17676
Food and Your Health, 18204
Fruit, 20154
A History of France Through Art, 15316
Milk, 20122
Pasta, 20123
The Supernatural, 21947
Talking About Bullying, 17725
Talking About Disability, 17928

Powell, John Wesley. *Conquering the Grand Canyon*, 16636

Powell, Michelle. *Printing*, 21624

Powell, Phelan. *Alicia Silverstone*, 12468
Garth Brooks, 12361(F)
Hanson, 12395
Jeff Gordon, 13428
Sarah Michelle Gellar, 12388

Powell, Polly. *Just Dessert*, 4272(F)
Monster Math, 517(F)

Powell, Sandy. *Rats*, 19204

Powell, Susan (jt. author). *The Kalahari*, 14982

Powell, Suzanne. *The Pueblos*, 16024

Power, Vicki. *Vanity*, 21183

Powers, Daniel. *Dear Katie, the Volcano Is a Girl*, 4438(F)
Jiro's Pearl, 1488(F)

Powers, Mary Ellen. *Our Teacher's in a Wheelchair*, 17929

Powers, Tom. *Steven Spielberg*, 12475

Powledge, Fred. *Pharmacy in the Forest*, 18026

Powling, Chris. *Roald Dahl*, 12521

Powzyk, Joyce. *In Search of Lemurs*, 19012

Poydar, Nancy. *The Adventures of Sugar and Junior*, 8342(F)

Beezy and Funnybone, 6487(F)
Beezy at Bat, 6488(F)
Beezy Magic, 6489(F)
Busy Bea, 4273(F)
Chelsea Martin Turns Green, 8336(F)
Cool Ali, 1489(F)
First Day, Hooray! 5524(F)
In the Diner, 3285(F)
Mailbox Magic, 4274(F)
Scrabble Creek, 3956(F)
Snip, Snip . . . Snow! 5525(F)
Snow Day, 6209(F)
Will There Be a Lap for Me? 3589(F)

Poynter, Margaret. *Killer Asteroids*, 18523
The Leakeys, 13313
Marie Curie, 13263
Top 10 American Women's Figure Skaters, 13392

Prager, Annabelle. *The Baseball Birthday Party*, 6584(F)
The Surprise Party, 6585(F)

Prager, Ellen J. *Sand*, 20568

Pragoff, Fiona. *My Apple*, 20140
Where Is Alice's Bear? 6586(F)

Prater, John. *Again!* 2599(F)
The Greatest Show on Earth, 2963(F)
On Top of the World, 2600(F)
Once upon a Picnic, 1490(F)
Once upon a Time, 1168(F)

Pratt, Dianne. *Hey Kids! You're Cookin' Now! A Global Awareness Cooking Adventure*, 21732

Pratt, Helen Jay. *The Hawaiians*, 16809

Pratt, Kristin J. *A Swim Through the Sea*, 115(F)
A Walk in the Rainforest, 116(F)

Pratt, Paula B. *Jane Goodall*, 13302
Martha Graham, 12391

Pratt, Pierre. *Sassy Gracie*, 4296(F)

Prebeg, Rick A. *Jungle Jack Hanna's What Zookeepers Do*, 20025

Prebeg, Rick A. (jt. author). *Jungle Jack Hanna's Safari Adventure*, 18633

Preiss, Byron, ed. *The Best Children's Books in the World*, 1491(F)

Preller, James. *Cardinal and Sunflower*, 5372(F)
McGwire and Sosa, 22115
NBA Game Day, 22144

Prelutsky, Jack. *The Baby Uggs Are Hatching*, 2601(F)
Beneath a Blue Umbrella, 885
Dog Days, 11979
The Dragons Are Singing Tonight, 11808
The Gargoyle on the Roof, 11675
It's Raining Pigs and Noodles, 11909
It's Snowing! It's Snowing! 4511(F)

It's Thanksgiving, 11850
It's Valentine's Day, 11851
Monday's Troll, 11676
The New Kid on the Block, 11910
Nightmares, 11677
A Pizza the Size of the Sun, 11678
Ride a Purple Pelican, 11911
The Sheriff of Rottenshot, 11912
The Snopp on the Sidewalk and Other Poems, 11809
Something Big Has Been Here, 11913
Tyrannosaurus Was a Beast, 11810

Prelutsky, Jack, ed. *The Beauty of the Beast*, 11807
For Laughing Out Loud, 11908
The Random House Book of Poetry for Children, 11679

Prelutsky, Jack (jt. author). *Hooray for Diffendoofer Day!* 4309(F)

Prentzas, G. S. *Thurgood Marshall*, 12768

Presilla, Maricel E. *Life Around the Lake*, 15641
Mola, 13945

Presnall, Judith J. *Animals That Glow*, 18657
Circuses, 14270
Rachel Carson, 13247

Press, H. J. *Giant Book of Science Experiments*, 18342

Press, Judy. *Alphabet Art*, 117(F)
ArtStarts for Little Hands! 21463
The Kids' Natural History Book, 14464
The Little Hands Big Fun Craft Book, 21464
Vroom! Vroom! 21465

Press, Petra. *Indians of the Northwest*, 16025
Puerto Ricans, 17588

Press, Skip. *Candice and Edgar Bergen*, 12177
Mark Twain, 12611
Natalie and Nat King Cole, 12178

Presto, Fay. *Magic for Kids*, 21788

Preston, Julia (jt. author). *The Kids' Money Book*, 16940

Preston, Tim. *The Lonely Scarecrow*, 1492(F)

Preus, Margi (jt. author). *The Legend of the Lady Slipper*, 9167

Preussler, Otfried. *The Satanic Mill*, 8023(F)

Price, Caroline. *The Kids Can Press Jumbo Book of Crafts*, 21494

Price, David. *Rosa Parks*, 12777

Price, Hope Lynne. *These Hands*, 763(F)

Price, Leontyne, reteller. *Aida*, 14136

Price, Mathew. *Don't Worry, Alfie*, 2602(F)
Patch Finds a Friend, 2603(F)

Price, Moe. *The Reindeer Christmas*, 5905(F)

Price, Reynolds. *A Perfect Friend*, 8024(F)

Price, Steven D. *The Kids' Book of the American Quarter Horse*, 20012
Price, Susanna. *Click!* 21803
Priceman, Marjorie. *The Brand New Kid*, 5491(F)
Cousin Ruth's Tooth, 4224(F)
Dancin' in the Kitchen, 3644(F)
Emeline at the Circus, 3369(F)
For Laughing Out Loud, 11908
Froggie Went A-Courting, 14173
How Emily Blair Got Her Fabulous Hair, 4155(F)
My Nine Lives, 8025(F)
One of Each, 2215(F)
Rachel Fister's Blister, 4225(F)
Serefina under the Circumstances, 5729(F)
What Zeesie Saw on Delancey Street, 4802(F)
When Zaydeh Danced on Eldridge Street, 6106(F)
Zin! Zin! Zin! A Violin, 14227(F)
Priddy, Roger. *Baby's Book of Animals*, 18879
Baby's Book of Nature, 238
Baby's Book of the Body, 3370(F)
My Big Book of Everything, 4512
Priebe, Jennifer. *The Peregrine Falcon*, 19339
Priebe, Mac. *The Peregrine Falcon*, 19339
Priest, Robert. *The Old Pirate of Central Park*, 4275(F)
The Town That Got Out of Town, 8026(F)
Prigger, Mary Skillings. *Aunt Minnie McGranahan*, 3845(F)
Primavera, Elise. *Auntie Claus*, 5906(F)
Christina Katerina and the Great Bear Train, 3643(F)
Make Way for Sam Houston, 12903
Raising Dragons, 1436(F)
Prince, Jane. *It's Not Your Fault, KoKo Bear*, 2339(F)
Pringle, Laurence. *Animal Monsters*, 18658
Bats! Strange and Wonderful, 19035
Coral Reefs, 19665
Dinosaurs! 14465
Elephant Woman, 13327
The Environmental Movement, 16964
Everybody Has a Bellybutton, 18074
An Extraordinary Life, 19565
Fire in the Forest, 16965
Hearing, 18157
Naming the Cat, 5373(F)
Nature! Wild and Wonderful, 12583
Oil Spills, 17002
One Room School, 14877
Scorpion Man, 19592
Smell, 18158

Smoking, 17884
Taste, 18159
Touch, 18160
Vanishing Ozone, 17003
Printup, Erwin. *Giving Thanks*, 11305
Prior, Katherine. *The History of Emigration from China and Southeast Asia*, 15079
Indian Subcontinent, 15113
Ireland, 15363
Prior, R. W. N. *The Great Monarch Butterfly Chase*, 1493(F)
Pritchard, Louise. *My Pony Book*, 20013
Probosz, Kathilyn S. *Martha Graham*, 12392
Proimos, James. *The Loudness of Sam*, 4276(F)
Prokofiev, Sergei. *Peter and the Wolf*, 10481(F), 11107
Propp, Vera W. *When the Soldiers Were Gone*, 9683(F)
Prose, Francine. *The Angel's Mistake*, 11159
The Demons' Mistake, 11160
You Never Know, 11161
Prosmitsky, Jenya. *Hairy, Scary, Ordinary*, 14025
A Mink, a Fink, a Skating Rink, 14026
Provensen, Alice. *The Glorious Flight Across the Channel with Louis Bleriot*, 21098
My Fellow Americans, 12692
A Visit to William Blake's Inn, 11737
The Voyage of the Ludgate Hill, 11738
Provensen, Martin. *The Glorious Flight Across the Channel with Louis Bleriot*, 21098
A Visit to William Blake's Inn, 11737
The Voyage of the Ludgate Hill, 11738
Provensen, Martin (jt. author). *The Glorious Flight Across the Channel with Louis Bleriot*, 21098
Proysen, Alf. *Little Old Mrs. Pepperpot and Other Stories*, 8027(F)
Prum, Deborah Mazzotta. *Rats, Bulls, and Flying Machines*, 14803
Prunier, James. *Dinosaurs*, 14401
Pryor, Bonnie. *The Dream Jar*, 3846(F)
The House on Maple Street, 4800(F)
Joseph, 9497(F)
Joseph's Choice — 1861, 9498(F)
Louie and Dan Are Friends, 2604(F)
Luke, 9430(F)
Luke on the High Seas, 9311(F)
Marvelous Marvin and the Pioneer Ghost, 8028(F)

Marvelous Marvin and the Wolfman Mystery, 7014(F)
The Plum Tree War, 8362(F)
Poison Ivy and Eyebrow Wigs, 10122(F)
The Porcupine Mouse, 2605(F)
Thomas, 9246(F)
Thomas in Danger, 9210(F)
Toenails, Tonsils, and Tornadoes, 7496(F)
Vinegar Pancakes and Vanishing Cream, 9970(F)
Ptacek, Greg. *Champion for Children's Health*, 13134
Puckett, Kirby. *Kirby Puckett*, 13478
Puddephatt, Neal. *Classic Horse and Pony Stories*, 7288(F)
Pudles, Daniel (jt. author). *Twice My Size*, 5349(F)
Puig, J. J. (jt. author). *Hearing*, 18152
Sight, 18153
Smell, 18154
Taste, 18155
Touch, 18156
Pullein-Thompson, Diana, ed. *Classic Horse and Pony Stories*, 7288(F)
Pulleyn, Micah. *Kids in the Kitchen*, 21733
Pullman, Philip. *Clockwork*, 8029(F)
Count Karlstein, 8030(F)
The Firework-Maker's Daughter, 8031(F)
I Was a Rat! 8032(F)
Pulver, Harry. *Find It!* 14001
Pulver, Robin. *Axle Annie*, 4277(F)
Mrs. Toggle's Beautiful Blue Shoe, 4278(F)
Mrs. Toggle's Zipper, 4279(F)
Way to Go, Alex! 5052(F)
Purcell, Cindy. *From Glass to Boat*, 21374
Puricelli, Luigi. *In My Garden*, 914(F)
Putini, Elisabetta (jt. author). *Why Are You Calling Me a Barbarian?* 14738
Putnam, James. *Pyramid*, 14660
Pyle, Howard. *Bearskin*, 1494(F)
The Garden Behind the Moon, 8033(F)
Men of Iron, 9119(F)
The Merry Adventures of Robin Hood, 11023
Otto of the Silver Hand, 9067(F)
The Story of King Arthur and His Knights, 11024
The Story of the Grail and the Passing of Arthur, 11025
The Swan Maiden, 10482(F)
The Wonder Clock, 10483(F)

Quackenbush, Robert. *Batbaby*, 2606(F)
Benjamin Franklin and His Friends, 12883

Henry's Awful Mistake, 2607(F)
It's Raining Cats and Dogs, 21831
James Madison and Dolley Madison and Their Times, 13084
Lost in the Amazon, 2608(F)
Where Did Your Family Come From? 17546
The Whole World in Your Hands, 14362
Quasha, Jennifer. *The Manx*, 19929
Shorthaired Cats in America, 19930
Quattlebaum, Mary. *Aunt CeeCee, Aunt Belle, and Mama's Surprise*, 5720(F)
Quay, M. J. *Bellybuttons Are Navels*, 4537
Quaye, Isaac. *101 Things to Do on the Internet*, 21231
Queen, J. Allen. *Learn Karate*, 22272
Quie, Sarah. *The Myths and Civilization of the Ancient Egyptians*, 14661
Quigley, Sebastian. *The Incredible Journey to the Planets*, 18474
Quindlen, Anna. *Happily Ever After*, 8034(F)
Quiner, Krista. *Dominique Moceanu*, 13703
Quinlan, Patricia. *My Dad Takes Care of Me*, 3847(F)
Quinlan, Susan. *The Case of the Mummified Pigs and Other Mysteries in Nature*, 18595
Quinlan, Susan E. *Puffins*, 19271
Quinn, Stephen C. *What Color Is That Dinosaur?* 14398
Quinsey, Mary Beth. *Why Does That Man Have Such a Big Nose?* 3371(F)
Quiri, Patricia R. *The American Flag*, 13972
The Bill of Rights, 17049
The Declaration of Independence, 16211
Ellis Island, 16727
The Lewis and Clark Expedition, 16089
The White House, 16728

Ra, Carol (jt. author). *The Sun Is Up*, 11985
Raatma, Lucia. *Libraries*, 14005
Maya Angelou, 12498
Rabatti, Alessandro. *The Incredible Journey to the Beginning of Time*, 14555
Rabe, Berniece. *Hiding Mr. McMulty*, 9609(F)
Where's Chimpy? 3848(F)
Rabe, Monica. *Sweden*, 15466
Rabe, Tish. *On Beyond Bugs!* 19480
There's No Place Like Space, 18410
Raber, Thomas R. *Joe Montana*, 13621

Rabin, Staton. *Casey Over There*, 4801(F)
Rabinovich, Abraham. *Teddy Kollek*, 13823
Rabinowitz, Sandy. *Colorado Summer*, 7159(F)
Raby, Philip. *Motorbikes*, 22241
Racing Cars, 21314
Raczek, Linda. *Stories from Native North America*, 11291
Raczek, Linda Theresa. *Rainy's Powwow*, 9173(F)
Radcliffe, Theresa. *Bashi, Elephant Baby*, 5374(F)
Maya, Tiger Cub, 5375(F)
Rader, Laura. *At the Carnival*, 6363(F)
A Book of Friends, 17729
A Book of Hugs, 3395(F)
A Book of Kisses, 3396(F)
A Hippo's a Heap and Other Animal Poems, 11802
Presents for Santa, 5961(F)
Sleepy-O! 14196
When I Am Big, 6555(F)
Radford, Derek. *Harry at the Garage*, 2609(F)
Radin, Ruth Yaffe. *All Joseph Wanted*, 8790(F)
Escape to the Forest, 9684(F)
Tac's Island, 8363(F)
Radlauer, Ruth. *Honor the Flag*, 13973
Radley, Gail. *Odd Man Out*, 8364(F)
Radunsky, Eugenia (jt. author). *Yucka Drucka Droni*, 4280(F)
Radunsky, Vladimir. *An Edward Lear Alphabet*, 77
Howdi Do, 14153
The Maestro Plays, 4230(F)
Yucka Drucka Droni, 4280(F)
Rae, Jennifer. *Dog Tales*, 10484(F)
Rael, Elsa O. *What Zeesie Saw on Delancey Street*, 4802(F)
When Zaydeh Danced on Eldridge Street, 6106(F)
Raffi. *Five Little Ducks*, 563(F)
Rise and Shine, 14255
Rafkin, Louise. *The Tiger's Eye, the Bird's Fist*, 22273
Ragins, Charles. *Anna's Athabaskan Summer*, 4448(F)
Raglin, Tim. *The Birthday ABC*, 98(F)
Five Creepy Creatures, 6676(F)
Five Goofy Ghosts, 6677(F)
How the Camel Got His Hump, 1308(F)
The 13 Days of Halloween, 6002(F)
Ragz, M. M. *French Fries up Your Nose*, 10123(F)
Lost Little Angel, 1495(F)
Rahaman, Vashanti. *O Christmas Tree*, 5907(F)
Read for Me, Mama, 3849(F)
Rahm, Debra L. (jt. author). *Red Cross/Red Crescent*, 17017

Sister Cities in a World of Difference, 14332
United Nations High Commission for Refugees, 17018
Raible, Alton. *The Egypt Game*, 8371(F)
The Witches of Worm, 8916(F)
Raimondo, Lois. *The Little Lama of Tibet*, 17213
Raine, Patricia. *Orange Cheeks*, 3826(F)
Rainis, Kenneth G. *Crime-Solving Science Projects*, 17079
Raja, Monisha. *Faraway Families*, 7473(F)
Rajendra, Sundran (jt. author). *Australia*, 15253
Rajendra, Vijeya. *Australia*, 15253
Iran, 15558
Ralph, Judy. *The Peanut Butter Cookbook for Kids*, 21734
Rambeck, Richard. *Bonnie Blair*, 13681
Martina Hingis, 13649
Mia Hamm, 13689
Michael Jordan, 13540
Monica Seles, 13653
Pete Sampras, 13651
Rebecca Lobo, 13546
Tara Lipinski, 13595
Tiger Woods, 13717
Ramirez, Michael Rose. *The Little Ant/La Hormiga Chiquita*, 2610(F)
Ramsey, Marcy. *My Dog's the Best!* 6249(F)
One Dog Day, 7256(F)
Oyster Moon, 6972(F)
Ramstad, Ralph L. *Birds in the Bushes*, 13335
John Brown, 12862
Science Fiction Pioneer, 12613
With Open Hands, 12769
Ramulshah, Mano. *Pakistan*, 15194
Rand, Gloria. *Baby in a Basket*, 4803(F)
The Cabin Key, 3850(F)
Fighting for the Forest, 4513(F)
A Home for Spooky, 5376(F)
Willie Takes a Hike, 2611(F)
Rand, Ted. *Baby in a Basket*, 4803(F)
Barn Dance! 2481(F)
The Bear That Heard Crying, 1307(F)
The Cabin Key, 3850(F)
Can I Be Good? 5429(F)
Fighting for the Forest, 4513(F)
The Football That Won . . ., 2968(F)
The Ghost-Eye Tree, 2957(F)
Grandma According to Me, 3524(F)
Here Are My Hands, 3310(F)
A Home for Spooky, 5376(F)
How Whales Walked into the Sea, 19796
The Hullabaloo ABC, 25(F)

In the Palace of the Ocean King, 10503(F)
Jezebel's Spooky Spot, 3394(F)
Keepers, 11691
Knots on a Counting Rope, 7353(F)
Let's Play Rough! 3736(F)
Mailing May, 3922(F)
Mama and Me and the Model T, 4160(F)
The Memory String, 3556(F)
Mountain Wedding, 4161(F)
My Buddy, 8908(F)
My Father's Boat, 3641(F)
The Night Before Christmas, 11841
Night Tree, 5769(F)
Nutik, the Wolf Pup, 4656(F)
Paul Revere's Ride, 11644
Salt Hands, 5118(F)
Secret Place, 4397(F)
A Snake in the House, 5334(F)
Storm on the Desert, 20411
The Sun, the Wind, and the Rain, 4509(F)
The Tree That Would Not Die, 4730
Up and Down on the Merry-Go-Round, 3312(F)
White Dynamite and Curly Kidd, 2958(F)
Willie Takes a Hike, 2611(F)
With a Dog Like That, a Kid Like Me . . ., 1523(F)
Randolph, Sallie G. (jt. author). *Shaker Inventions*, 17168
Shaker Villages, 17169
Rane, Walter. *Meet Kit*, 9632(F)
Rankin, Joan. *Scaredy Cat*, 2612(F)
Wow! It's Great Being a Duck, 2613(F)
You're Somebody Special, Walliwigs! 2614(F)
Rankin, Laura. *The Handmade Alphabet*, 14018
The Handmade Counting Book, 564(F)
Ransford, Sandy. *The Otter*, 18965
Ransom, Candice. *The Big Green Pocketbook*, 3372(F)
Children of the Civil War, 16423
The Christmas Dolls, 5908(F)
Danger at Sand Cave, 6588(F)
Fire in the Sky, 9610(F)
Jimmy Crack Corn, 9611(F)
Listening to Crickets, 13248
One Christmas Dawn, 5909(F)
The Promise Quilt, 4804(F)
We're Growing Together, 3851(F)
Ransom, Jeanie Franz. *I Don't Want to Talk About It*, 5053(F)
Ransome, Arthur. *The Fool of the World and the Flying Ship*, 11108
Swallows and Amazons, 7015(F)
Winter Holiday, 7016(F)
Ransome, James E. *Aunt Flossie's Hats (and Crab Cakes Later)*, 3706(F)
Bimmi Finds a Cat, 7308(F)

Bonesy and Isabel, 5385(F)
The Creation, 17290
Dark Day, Light Night, 4923(F)
Do Like Kyla, 3723(F)
Freedom's Fruit, 9289(F)
How Many Stars in the Sky? 706(F)
The Jukebox Man, 3348(F)
Let My People Go, 9306(F)
The Old Dog, 5110(F)
Quinnie Blue, 4695(F)
Red Dancing Shoes, 3833(F)
Rum-a-Tum-Tum, 4766(F)
Satchel Paige, 13475
The Secret of the Stones, 11377
Sweet Clara and the Freedom Quilt, 9290(F)
Uncle Jed's Barber Shop, 9598(F)
The Wagon, 4700(F)
Your Move, 8578(F)
Ranville, Myrelene. *Tex*, 5377(F)
Rao, Sandhya, reteller. *And Land Was Born*, 10804
Raphael, Elaine. *Daniel Boone*, 12084
Pocahontas, 12987
Rappaport, Doreen. *The Boston Coffee Party*, 16212
Dirt on Their Skirts, 4805(F)
Freedom River, 9312(F)
Rappoport, Ken. *Bobby Bonilla*, 13440
Guts and Glory, 13393
Nolan Ryan, 13502
Sports Great Eric Lindros, 13699
Sports Great Wayne Gretzky, 13688
Tim Duncan, 13521
Top 10 Basketball Legends, 13394
Rascal. *Oregon's Journey*, 1496(F)
Raschka, Chris. *Another Important Book*, 3050(F)
Arlene Sardine, 2615(F)
The Blushful Hippopotamus, 2616(F)
Can't Sleep, 764(F)
Elizabeth Imagined an Iceberg, 8035(F)
Fishing in the Air, 1086(F)
The Four Corners of the Sky, 10635
Happy to Be Nappy, 3220(F)
Like Likes Like, 1497(F)
Movin', 11611
Mysterious Thelonious, 12424
A Poke in the I, 11907
Ring! Yo? 3373(F)
Simple Gifts, 14174
Yo! Yes? 4036(F)
Rash, Andy. *The Robots Are Coming*, 11914
Raskin, Ellen. *Figgs and Phantoms*, 8036(F)
The Mysterious Disappearance of Leon (I Mean Noel), 9971(F)
Raskin, Lawrie. *52 Days by Camel*, 14963
Rasmussen, R. Kent. *Pueblo*, 16026

Rasmussen, Wendy. *There's a Kangaroo in My Soup!* 7904(F)
Rasovsky, Yuri (jt. author). *WKID*, 12009(F)
Rassmus, Jens. *Farmer Enno and His Cow*, 1498(F)
Ratcliffe, Annelle W. *Window of Time*, 8194(F)
Rathjen, Don (jt. author). *The Cool Hot Rod and Other Electrifying Experiments on Energy and Matter*, 20827
The Spinning Blackboard and Other Dynamic Experiments on Force and Motion, 20828
Rathmann, Peggy. *Bootsie Barker Bites*, 4911(F)
Good Night, Gorilla, 2617(F)
Officer Buckle and Gloria, 5378(F)
Ruby the Copycat, 5054(F)
10 Minutes till Bedtime, 565(F)
Ratnett, Michael. *Dracula Steps Out*, 8037(F)
Monster Train, 1499(F)
Rattigan, Jama Kim. *Dumpling Soup*, 5645(F)
Truman's Aunt Farm, 4281(F)
Rau, Christopher (jt. author). *George Lucas*, 12417
Rau, Dana Meachen. *A Box Can Be Many Things*, 6589(F)
George Lucas, 12417
One Giant Leap, 7017(F)
Purple Is Best, 6590(F)
The Solar System, 18524
Rauth, Leslie. *Maryland*, 16879
Rauzon, Mark. *Golden Eagles of Devil Mountain*, 19340
Hummingbirds, 19272
Parrots, 19273
Seabirds, 19274
Vultures, 19275
Ravaglia, Paola. *The Atlas of the Bible Lands*, 15518
The Atlas of World Cultures, 14333
Raven, Margot T. *Angels in the Dust*, 9612(F)
Rawlings, Marjorie Kinnan. *The Yearling*, 7289(F)
Rawlins, Carol B. *The Colorado River*, 15898
The Orinoco River, 15779
Rawlins, Donna. *Tucking Mommy In*, 725(F)
Rawlinson, Jonathan. *Discovering the Titanic*, 19879
Rawls, Wilson. *Summer of the Monkeys*, 7290(F)
Ray, Deborah Kogan. *All Joseph Wanted*, 8790(F)
The Barn Owls, 5280(F)
I Have a Sister, My Sister Is Deaf, 5048(F)
My Prairie Christmas, 5832(F)
Sky Words, 11984
Sweet Dried Apples, 8986(F)
Through Grandpa's Eyes, 3791(F)

Wagon Train, 9390(F)

Ray, Jane. *From a Distance*, 11573
Hansel and Gretel, 10929
Magical Tales from Many Lands, 10587
Sun, Moon, and Stars, 10563

Ray, Jane, reteller. *Hansel and Gretel*, 10929

Ray, Karen. *The T.F. Letters*, 8791(F)

Ray, Mary L. *Basket Moon*, 4806(F)
Mud, 4514(F)
Pianna, 3374(F)
Pumpkins, 1500(F)
Red Rubber Boot Day, 3375(F)
Shaker Boy, 4807(F)

Raya-Norman, Faye. *Wolf Songs*, 765(F)

Rayevsky, Robert. *Bernal and Florinda*, 11136
Joan of Arc, 13812
The Sleepy Men, 639(F)
Squash It! A True and Ridiculous Tale, 11137
Three Sacks of Truth, 10872
Under New York, 16695

Raymond, Larry. *When Andy's Father Went to Prison*, 4978(F)

Raymond, Victoria. *Brown Cow, Green Grass, Yellow Mellow Sun*, 4465(F)
Bumble Bee, 5145(F)
Still-Life Stew, 3364(F)

Rayner, Mary. *Pigs Might Fly*, 7867(F)

Rayyan, Omar. *Count Silvernose*, 9052(F)
King Midas, 11508
Ramadan, 5627
Rimonah of the Flashing Sword, 10678
The Ring of Truth, 9776(F)

Read, Andrew. *Porpoises*, 19688

Readhead, Lloyd. *Gymnastics*, 22197

Reading, Susan. *Desert Plants*, 20258
Plants of the Tropics, 20259

Ready, Anna. *Mississippi*, 16880

Reasoner, Charles. *Brave Bear and the Ghosts*, 11230
Spider and His Son Find Wisdom, 10688
Wanyana and Matchmaker Frog, 10689
Who Drives This? 1501(F)
Zimani's Drum, 10690

Rebman, Renee C. *Life on Ellis Island*, 16729

Rebnord, Lisa (jt. author). *Making Picture Frames*, 21663

Recknagel, Friedrich. *Meg's Wish*, 4037(F)

Recorvits, Helen. *Goodbye, Walter Malinski*, 9613(F)

Reczuch, Karen. *The Dust Bowl*, 4597(F)
Just Like New, 4761(F)

Morning on the Lake, 4558(F)

Reddix, Valerie. *Dragon Kite of the Autumn Moon*, 4808(F)

Reddy, Francis (jt. author). *Astronomy in Ancient Times*, 18377

Reddy, Michelle (jt. author). *Dolphin Babies*, 19692

Redenbaugh, Vicki Jo. *Green Beans*, 3914(F)
Pug, Slug, and Doug the Thug, 2649(F)
When I'm Alone, 541(F)

Redfern, Martin. *The Kingfisher Young People's Book of Planet Earth*, 20318
The Kingfisher Young People's Book of Space, 18411

Rediger, Pat. *Great African Americans in Business*, 12693
Great African Americans in Civil Rights, 12694
Great African Americans in Entertainment, 12179
Great African Americans in Literature, 12180
Great African Americans in Music, 12181
Great African Americans in Sports, 13395

Redmond, Ian. *Gorilla*, 19013

Redmond, Shirley-Raye. *Grampa and the Ghost*, 8038(F)

Reed, Gregory J. (jt. author). *Dear Mrs. Parks*, 17048

Reed, Lynn Rowe. *The Halloween Showdown*, 6046(F)

Reed, Mike. *The Bug in Teacher's Coffee*, 11866
Catching the Wild Waiyuuzee, 3950(F)
Shake Dem Halloween Bones, 6036(F)

Reed, Neil. *The Storm Seal*, 5444(F)

Reed-Jones, Carol. *The Tree in the Ancient Forest*, 16966

Reeder, Carolyn. *Across the Lines*, 9499(F)
Captain Kate, 9500(F)
Shades of Gray, 9501(F)

Reedy, Jerry. *Oklahoma*, 16577

Reef, Catherine. *Albert Einstein*, 13277
Arlington National Cemetery, 16881
Black Fighting Men, 21401
Buffalo Soldiers, 16353
Civil War Soldiers, 16424
George Gershwin, 12327
Gettysburg, 16425
The Lincoln Memorial, 16730
Monticello, 16882
Mount Vernon, 16883
Ralph David Abernathy, 12699
The Supreme Court, 17014
Washington, D.C., 16731

Reef, Kristensen. *Colin Powell*, 12953

Rees, Celia. *The Truth Out There*, 7019(F)

Rees, Mary. *Spooky Poems*, 11534

Rees, Rosemary. *The Ancient Egyptians*, 14662
The Ancient Greeks, 14699
The Ancient Romans, 14740
The Aztecs, 15642
The Incas, 15780

Reese, Della. *God Inside of Me*, 1502(F)

Reeve, Kirk. *Lolo and Red-Legs*, 7291(F)

Reeves, Diane Lindsey. *Career Ideas for Kids Who Like Art*, 17779
Career Ideas for Kids Who Like Computers, 17796
Career Ideas for Kids Who Like Math, 17761
Career Ideas for Kids Who Like Science, 17835
Career Ideas for Kids Who Like Sports, 17762
Career Ideas for Kids Who Like Talking, 17780
Career Ideas for Kids Who Like Writing, 17781

Reeves, Howard W. *There Was an Old Witch*, 6042(F)

Reeves, Jeni. *The Girl Who Struck Out Babe Ruth*, 22111

Reeves, Mona R. *The Spooky Eerie Night Noise*, 5379(F)

Regan, Colm. *People of the Islands*, 20388

Regan, Dana. *Messy Bessey's Family Reunion*, 6493(F)
Messy Bessey's Holidays, 6494(F)

Regan, Dian C. *Daddies*, 3852(F)
The Friendship of Milly and Tug, 7497(F)
Monsters and My One True Love, 8039(F)
Monsters in Cyberspace, 10226(F)
Monsters in the Attic, 8040(F)
Princess Nevermore, 10227(F)

Regan, Laura. *Dig Hole, Soft Mole*, 5300(F)
Mama Mama, 5342(F)
Spots, 493
Tiger Trail, 5456(F)
Welcome to the Green House, 4566
Welcome to the Ice House, 15847
Welcome to the Sea of Sand, 20429
Wolf Watch, 5457(F)

Regan, Michael (jt. author). *Let the Games Begin!* 21966

Regguinti, Gordon. *The Sacred Harvest*, 16027

Reich, Janet. *Gus and the Green Thing*, 2618(F)

Reich, Susanna. *Clara Schumann*, 12338

Reichstein, Alexander. *The Eagle and the Wren*, 11339
Mina and the Bear, 1280(F)
Special Delivery, 3937(F)

Reid, Barbara. *Fun with Modeling Clay*, 21533

Gifts, 3536(F)

How to Make Pop-Ups, 21619

The Party, 3853(F)

Reid, Lori. *Hand Reading*, 21948

Reid, Margarette S. *The Button Box*, 3854(F)

A String of Beads, 21546

Reid, Struan. *Alexander Graham Bell*, 13241

The Children's Atlas of Lost Treasures, 14538

Cultures and Civilizations, 14355

Inventions and Trade, 21054

John Logie Baird, 13232

Reilly, Mary J. *Mexico*, 15643

Reimers, David M. *A Land of Immigrants*, 17589

Reinagle, Damon J. *Draw!* 21587

Draw Alien Fantasies, 21588

Reiner, Annie. *A Visit to the Art Galaxy*, 1503(F)

Reingold-Reiss, Debra. *Puppy Care and Critters, Too!* 19962

Reinhard, Johan. *Discovering the Inca Ice Maiden*, 15781

Reisberg, Mira. *Just Like Home*, 5032(F)

Leaving for America, 4604

Uncle Nacho's Hat, 9138(F)

Where Fireflies Dance, 4628(F)

Reisberg, Veg. *Baby Rattlesnake*, 11210

Reiser, Lynn. *Cherry Pies and Lullabies*, 3855(F)

Earthdance, 5526(F)

Little Clam, 2619(F)

My Cat Tuna, 5380(F)

The Surprise Family, 5381(F)

Tomorrow on Rocky Pond, 3376(F)

Tortillas and Lullabies, 4809(F)

Two Mice in Three Fables, 2620(F)

Reiss, Johanna. *The Upstairs Room*, 9685(F)

Reiss, Kathryn. *Paperquake*, 8792(F)

Reit, Seymour. *Behind Rebel Lines*, 13152

Rekela, George R. *Brett Favre*, 13612

Karl Malone, 13548

Sports Great Anfernee Hardaway, 13526

Relf, Patricia. *A Dinosaur Named Sue*, 14466

Tonka Big Book of Trucks, 5593

Tonka Trucks Night and Day, 21315

Remington, Gwen. *The Sioux*, 16028

Remkiewicz, Frank. *Froggy Gets Dressed*, 2391(F)

Froggy Goes to Bed, 726(F)

Froggy Goes to School, 2392(F)

Froggy Learns to Swim, 2393(F)

Froggy Plays Soccer, 2394(F)

Froggy's First Kiss, 2395(F)

Froggy's Halloween, 6029(F)

The Great Mosquito, Bull, and Coffin Caper, 8330(F)

Hiccup, 6427(F)

Horrible Harry and the Ant Invasion, 4018(F)

Horrible Harry and the Christmas Surprise, 5858(F)

Horrible Harry and the Purple People, 7873(F)

Horrible Harry Goes to the Moon, 5510(F)

Incredible Ned, 1405(F)

Let's Go, Froggy! 2396(F)

Quiet, Wyatt! 5029(F)

Rabbit's Pajama Party, 229

Remphry, Martin. *When I Was Young*, 3610(F)

Rendon, Marcie R. *Powwow Summer*, 16029

Rendon, Maria. *Touching the Distance*, 11932

Reneaux, J. J. *Haunted Bayou*, 11371

How Animals Saved the People, 10606

Why Alligator Hates Dog, 11372

Renfro, Nancy. *Puppet Show Made Easy!* 14306

Renne. *Animal Males and Females*, 18659

Animals Trails and Tracks, 18842

Renner, Michelle. *The Girl Who Swam with the Fish*, 11292

Rennert, Richard S. *Jesse Owens*, 13667

Rennert, Richard S., ed. *Book of Firsts*, 13396

Reno, Alain. *Gontrand and the Crescent Moon*, 1454(F)

Repchuk, Caroline. *The Snow Tree*, 5910(F)

Repp, Gloria. *Mik-Shrok*, 7020(F)

Resnick, Abraham. *The Commonwealth of Independent States*, 15428

Resnick, Sandi W. *Apple Valley Year*, 4555(F)

Retan, Walter, ed. *Piggies, Piggies, Piggies*, 2621(F)

Revell, Phil. *Kayaking*, 22263

Revels, Robert. *Neem the Half-Boy*, 11200

Rex, Michael. *Brooms Are for Flying!* 6043(F)

Floating Home, 1186(F)

My Fire Engine, 2964(F)

My Race Car, 5594

The Painting Gorilla, 2622(F)

Snuggle Wuggle, 727(F)

Sunrise, 559(F)

Who Builds? 5595(F)

Who Digs? 5596(F)

Wiggle Waggle, 5317(F)

Rey, H. A. *Cecily G. and the Nine Monkeys*, 2623(F)

Curious George, 2624(F)

Curious George Flies a Kite, 2626(F)

Curious George Learns the Alphabet, 118(F)

Find the Constellations, 18552

Katy No-Pocket, 2564(F)

Whiteblack the Penguin Sees the World, 2625(F)

Rey, H. A. (jt. author). *Curious George and the Dump Truck*, 2627(F)

Rey, Margaret. *Curious George and the Dump Truck*, 2627(F)

Curious George Flies a Kite, 2626(F)

Rey, Margaret (jt. author). *Whiteblack the Penguin Sees the World*, 2625(F)

Reyher, Becky. *My Mother Is the Most Beautiful Woman in the World*, 11109

Reynolds, Adrian. *Baby Loves Hugs and Kisses*, 3766(F)

Harry and the Snow King, 1676(F)

Pete and Polo's Big School Adventure, 1504(F)

Sammy and the Dinosaurs, 1677(F)

Silly Goose and Dizzy Duck Play Hide-and-Seek, 2153(F)

Toby's Doll's House, 5722(F)

Reynolds, David West. *Star Wars*, 14316, 14317

Star Wars Episode I, 14318, 14319

Reynolds, Helen. *The 40s and 50s*, 16517

Reynolds, Jan. *Amazon Basin*, 15782

Frozen Land, 15829

Himalaya, 15195

Mongolia, 15196

Reynolds, Lura Schield (jt. author). *Maudie in the Middle*, 7489(F)

Reynolds, Marilyn. *The Magnificent Piano Recital*, 5055(F)

The Prairie Fire, 4810(F)

Reynolds, Pat. *All the Better to See You With!* 3942(F)

Reynolds, Peter H. *Serendipity*, 3455(F)

Reynolds, Quentin. *The Wright Brothers*, 13356

Rhee, Nami. *Magic Spring*, 10733

Rheingrover, Jean S. *Veronica's First Year*, 5056(F)

Rhoades, Diane. *Garden Crafts for Kids*, 21771

Rhodes, Lisa R. *Barbara Jordan*, 12734

Coretta Scott King, 12737

Rhodes, Timothy (jt. author). *Pancho's Pinata*, 5793

The Sleeping Bread, 11398

Rhodes, Vicki. *Pumpkin Decorating*, 21466

Ricchiardi, Sherry. *Bosnia*, 15284

Ricci, Regolo. *Gogol's Coat*, 4643(F)

The Market Wedding, 8637(F)

Ricciuti, Edward R. *America's Top 10 Bridges*, 21148

Birds, 19276

Chaparral, 20389
Crustaceans, 19679
Desert, 20415
Grassland, 20543
National Audubon Society First Field Guide to Rocks and Minerals, 20569
Ocean, 19834
Rainforest, 20480
What on Earth Is a Capybara? 19205
What on Earth Is a Pout? 19712
Wildlife Special Agent, 17119
Rice, Chris. *My First Body Book*, 18075
Rice, David L. *Because Brian Hugged His Mother*, 3377(F)
Lifetimes, 18289
Rice, Dorothy M. (jt. author). *Pennies to Dollars*, 12811
Rice, Eve. *Sam Who Never Forgets*, 5382(F)
Rice, Melanie. *The Complete Book of Children's Activities*, 21467
Rice, Melanie (jt. author). *My First Body Book*, 18075
Rice, Oliver D. *Lone Woman of Ghalas-Hat*, 16810
Rice, Terence M. G. *Russia*, 15429
Rich, Anna. *Annie's Gifts*, 5030(F)
Dare to Dream, 12736
From My Window, 3487(F)
Joshua's Masai Mask, 4982(F)
Just Right Stew, 4140(F)
Saturday at The New You, 3010(F)
Rich, Susan. *Africa South of the Sahara*, 14912
Richard, Christopher. *Brazil*, 15783
Richards, Caroline Cowles. *A 19th Century Schoolgirl*, 16270
Richards, Jean. *The First Olympic Games*, 11502
Richards, Jon. *Chemicals and Reactions*, 20290
Diggers and Other Construction Machines, 21149
The Science Factory, 18343
Richards, Kitty. *It's About Time, Max!* 20651(F)
Richards, Norman. *Monticello*, 16884
Richards, Roy. *101 Science Surprises*, 18344
101 Science Tricks, 18345
Richardson, Bill. *After Hamelin*, 8042(F)
Richardson, Gillian. *Saskatchewan*, 15590
Richardson, I. M. *The Adventures of Eros and Psyche*, 11503
Richardson, Jean. *The Bear Who Went to the Ballet*, 1505(F)
The Courage Seed, 4811(F)
Thomas's Sitter, 3856(F)
Richardson, John. *Budgie at Bendick's Point*, 1715(F)
Richardson, Joy. *Inside the Museum*, 13919

Looking at Faces in Art, 13920
Looking at Pictures, 13921
Richardson, Judith B. *David's Landing*, 8793(F)
Old Winter, 1506(F)
Richardson, Mark. *Eric in the Land of the Insects*, 7617(F)
Richardson, Nancy Ann (jt. author). *Winning Every Day*, 13701
Richardson, Ruth. *My Own Home*, 2219(F)
Richardson, Sandy. *The Girl Who Ate Chicken Feet*, 8794(F)
Richemont, Enid. *The Glass Bird*, 8043(F)
The Time Tree, 8044(F)
Riches, Judith. *Tigers*, 2060(F)
Richie, Jason. *Weapons*, 21402
Richler, Mordecai. *Jacob Two-Two's First Spy Case*, 9972(F)
Richman, Daniel A. *James E. Carter*, 13017
Richmond, Robin. *Children in Art*, 13922
Richter, Conrad. *Light in the Forest*, 9174(F)
Richter, Mischa. *The Planet of the Grapes*, 21833
Rickarby, Laura A. *Ulysses S. Grant and the Strategy of Victory*, 13037
Rickey, Ann Heiskell. *Bugs and Critters I Have Known*, 11980
Ridd, Stephen, ed. *Julius Caesar in Gaul and Britain*, 14741
Riddell, Chris. *The Birthday Presents*, 5727(F)   ·
A Little Bit of Winter, 2731(F)
The Swan's Stories, 10390(F)
Until I Met Dudley, 5586(F)
Riddell, Edwina. *100 First Words to Say with Your Baby*, 3378(F)
Riddle, Sue. *Gotta Go! Gotta Go!* 4549(F)
Riddle, Tohby. *The Great Escape from City Zoo*, 2628(F)
The Singing Hat, 1507(F)
Ride, Sally. *The Mystery of Mars*, 18485
To Space and Back, 21006
Ridgewell, Jenny. *Fruit and Vegetables*, 20124
Ridley, Sarah (jt. author). *The Princess and the Peacocks*, 9111(F)
Ridley, Tim. *Planes*, 21100
Ridlon, Marci. *Sun Through the Window*, 11680
Riecken, Nancy. *Today Is the Day*, 5057(F)
Riehecky, Janet. *Greece*, 15389
The Mystery of the Missing Money, 7021(F)
The Mystery of the UFO, 7022(F)
Television, 21276
Rieper-Bastian, Marlies. *The Upside-Down Reader*, 6360(F)

Rieth, Elizabeth J. (jt. author).
Bridges! Amazing Structures to Design, Build and Test, 21133
Going West! 16318
Riggio, Anita. *Beware the Brindlebeast*, 10485
A Moon in My Teacup, 5911(F)
Noah's Wife, 17267
Riggs, Sandy. *Circles*, 20605
Rigney, Francis. *A Beginner's Book of Magic*, 21789
Riha, Susanne. *Animal Journeys*, 18843
Animals and the Seasons, 4515(F)
Animals at Rest, 18844
Riley, Gail B. *Top 10 NASCAR Drivers*, 13397
Wah Ming Chang, 12210
Riley, Jeni. *First Word Book*, 14041
Riley, John. *Benjamin Franklin*, 12884
George Washington Carver, 13257
John Paul Jones, 12915
Riley, Linda C. *Elephants Swim*, 18845
Riley, Linnea. *Mouse Mess*, 2629(F)
The 12 Days of Christmas, 14211
Riley, Linnea A. *Outside, Inside*, 3094(F)
Riley, Peter D. *Earth*, 18437
Energy, 20835
Rimland, Mark. *The Secret Night World of Cats*, 1332(F)
Rinaldi, Angelo. *Rainy Day*, 3674(F)
Rinaldi, Ann. *Amelia's War*, 9502(F)
The Blue Door, 9313(F)
Cast Two Shadows, 9247(F)
The Journal of Jasper Jonathan Pierce, 9211(F)
Keep Smiling Through, 9686(F)
My Heart Is on the Ground, 9175(F)
The Second Bend in the River, 9431(F)
The Staircase, 9432(F)
Rinard, Judith E. *Amazing Animals of the Sea*, 19743
Zoos Without Cages, 20030
Ring, Elizabeth. *Lucky Mouse*, 19206
Night Flier, 19566
Rachel Carson, 13249
What Rot! 16984
Ring, Susan. *Polar Babies*, 19064
Ringgold, Faith. *Bonjour, Lonnie*, 1508(F)
Dinner at Aunt Connie's House, 12695
If a Bus Could Talk, 12779
The Invisible Princess, 10486(F) ·
My Dream of Martin Luther King, 12752
Tar Beach, 1509(F)
Rinn, Miriam. *The Saturday Secret*, 8513(F)
Riordan, James. *The Coming of Night*, 10711

Favorite Stories of the Ballet, 14297

King Arthur, 11026

The Songs My Paddle Sings, 11293

The Storytelling Star, 10607

The Twelve Labors of Hercules, 11504

Riordan, James, reteller. *Korean Folk-Tales*, 10734

Ripken, Cal, Jr. *Cal Ripken Jr.*, 13481

Cal Ripken, Jr., 13482

Ripley, Catherine. *Why Do Stars Twinkle?* 4516

Why Does Popcorn Pop? and Other Kitchen Questions, 20125

Why Is Soap So Slippery? 3379

Riskind, Mary. *Apple Is My Sign*, 8909(F)

Riswold, Gilbert. *The Grizzly*, 6909(F)

Ritchie, David. *Frontier Life*, 16354

Ritchie, Scot. *Why Do Stars Twinkle?* 4516

Why Does Popcorn Pop? and Other Kitchen Questions, 20125

Why Is Soap So Slippery? 3379

Ritter, John H. *Choosing Up Sides*, 10357(F)

Ritter, Lawrence S. *The Story of Baseball*, 22116

Ritz, Karen. *Ben Has Something to Say*, 8739(F)

Between Two Worlds, 12510

Child of the Warsaw Ghetto, 14811

The Country Artist, 12579

Earthquake in the Third Grade, 10115(F)

Ellis Island, 15888

A Family That Fights, 4907(F)

Frontier Surgeons, 13318

The Ghost of Popcorn Hill, 8225(F)

Hiding from the Nazis, 14812

Hilde and Eli, 14813

Ian's Walk, 5011(F)

Kate Shelley and the Midnight Express, 6715(F)

My Grammy, 4997(F)

A Picture Book of Anne Frank, 13796

Remember That, 3822(F)

Seneca Chief, Army General, 12979

Sisters Against Slavery, 12894

Valentine's Day, 17509

Waiting for Mr. Goose, 5012(F)

Rius, Maria. *Hearing*, 18152

Sight, 18153

Smell, 18154

Taste, 18155

Touch, 18156

Rivers, Karen. *Waiting to Dive*, 10358(F)

Rix, Jamie. *The Last Chocolate Cookie*, 1510(F)

Rizo, Luis. *The Era of the Dinosaurs*, 14442

Plants Under the Sea, 20246

Roach, Marilynne K. *Encounters with the Invisible World*, 7023(F)

In the Days of the Salem Witchcraft Trials, 16164

Roalf, Peggy. *Cats*, 13923

Dogs, 13924

Robart, Rose. *The Cake That Mack Ate*, 4282(F)

Robb, Don. *Hail to the Chief*, 17101

Robb, Laura, ed. *Music and Drum*, 11681

Robbins, Bryan (jt. author). *Tae Kwon Do for Kids*, 22274

Robbins, Jane. *The Young Life of Mother Teresa of Calcutta*, 13856

Robbins, Ken. *Autumn Leaves*, 20216

Make Me a Peanut Butter Sandwich (and a Glass of Milk), 3380

Thunder on the Plains, 18966

Trucks, 21316

Robbins, Neal. *Ronald W. Reagan*, 13094

Robbins, Paul R. *Crack and Cocaine Drug Dangers*, 17885

Robbins, Ruth. *Baboushka and the Three Kings*, 11110

Ishi, Last of the Tribe, 12975

Robbins, Sandra. *The Firefly Star*, 11138

Roberts, Bethany. *Follow Me!* 2630(F)

Gramps and the Fire Dragon, 766(F)

Halloween Mice! 6044(F)

Monster Manners, 1511(F)

Valentine Mice! 6175(F)

Roberts, David. *Ghoul School*, 1512(F)

Roberts, David T. *Spinning Spiders*, 19574

Roberts, Elizabeth. *Georgia, Armenia, and Azerbaijan*, 15430

Roberts, Jack L. *Nelson Mandela*, 13831

Oskar Schindler, 13849

Roberts, Jeremy. *Rock and Ice Climbing! Top the Tower*, 22050

Saint Joan of Arc, 13814

Roberts, Michael. *Mumbo Jumbo*, 14042

Roberts, Paul C., ed. *Ancient Rome*, 14742

Roberts, Robin. *Basketball Year*, 22145

Careers for Women Who Love Sports, 17763

Sports for Life, 22051

Roberts, Russell. *Lincoln and the Abolition of Slavery*, 16426

Roberts, Willo Davis. *The Absolutely True Story*, 7024(F)

Baby-Sitting Is a Dangerous Job, 7025(F)

Caught! 7026(F)

Don't Hurt Laurie! 8795(F)

Hostage, 7027(F)

Jo and the Bandit, 9433(F)

The Kidnappers, 7028(F)

Megan's Island, 7029(F)

Pawns, 8514(F)

The Pet-Sitting Peril, 7030(F)

Scared Stiff, 7031(F)

Secrets at Hidden Valley, 8796(F)

Sugar Isn't Everything, 8910(F)

What Are We Going to Do About David? 8515(F)

What Could Go Wrong? 7032(F)

Robertshaw, Andrew. *A Soldier's Life*, 21403

Robertson, Bruce. *Marguerite Makes a Book*, 9068(F)

Robertson, Graham. *Looking at Penguins*, 19381

Robertson, James. *My Backyard History Book*, 14573

Robertson, Keith. *Henry Reed, Inc.*, 9973(F)

Robertson, M. P. *The Egg*, 1513(F)

Robertson, Mark. *A Treasury of Dragon Stories*, 7654(F)

Robertson, Matthew. *Insects and Spiders*, 19481

Robertson, Stuart. *The Odyssey*, 11479

Robertus, Polly M. *The Dog Who Had Kittens*, 5383(F)

Robinet, Harriette G. *Children of the Fire*, 9614(F)

Forty Acres and Maybe a Mule, 9615(F)

If You Please, President Lincoln, 9137(F)

The Twins, the Pirates, and the Battle of New Orleans, 9314(F)

Walking to the Bus-Rider Blues, 7366(F)

Washington City Is Burning, 9315(F)

Robins, Arthur. *The Last Chocolate Cookie*, 1510(F)

Mission Ziffoid, 1522(F)

The Teeny Tiny Woman, 11027

Robins, Deri. *Christmas Fun*, 21468

The Kids Can Do It Book, 21469

Papier Mâché, 21625

The Stone in the Sword, 9120(F)

Robins, Jim. *Papier Mâché*, 21625

Robins, Jim (jt. author). *The Stone in the Sword*, 9120(F)

Robins, Joan. *Addie Meets Max*, 6591(F)

Robinson, Alan J. *Here Is the Arctic Winter*, 15801

Robinson, Aminah. *Elijah's Angel*, 5646(F)

Sophie, 3629(F)

To Be a Drum, 3077(F)

Robinson, Barbara. *The Best Christmas Pageant Ever*, 9757(F)
The Best School Year Ever, 9974(F)
My Brother Louis Measures Worms and Other Louis Stories, 9975(F)
Robinson, Charles. *All the Money in the World*, 7623(F)
A Clearing in the Forest, 9374(F)
Journey Home, 7378(F)
Journey to America, 9670(F)
Just a Few Words, Mr. Lincoln, 16408
Pioneer Cat, 9382(F)
A Taste of Blackberries, 8814(F)
There's No Such Thing as a Chanukah Bush, Sandy Goldstein, 9762(F)
Robinson, Claire. *Bears*, 19065
Chimpanzees, 19014
Crocodiles, 18708
Elephants, 19169
Lions, 19106
Penguin, 19383
Penguins, 19384
Robinson, Ed. *Sand to Sea*, 19633
Robinson, Fay. *Fantastic Frogs*, 18736
Great Snakes! 18775
Pilots Fly Planes, 17838
Singing Robins, 19277
Vegetables, Vegetables! 20184
We Love Fruit! 20155
Where Did All the Dragons Go? 1514(F)
Where Do Puddles Go? 20744
Robinson, Fay (jt. author). *Nathaniel Willy, Scared Silly*, 11367
Robinson, Lynn. *The Shaking Bag*, 988(F)
Robinson, Mary. *The Amazing Valvano and the Mystery of the Hooded Rat*, 7033(F)
Robinson, Nancy K. *Angela and the Broken Heart*, 7498(F)
Countess Veronica, 8797(F)
Robinson, Tim. *Tobias, the Quig and the Rumplenut Tree*, 1515(F)
Robinson, W. Wright. *How Insects Build Their Amazing Homes*, 19482
How Mammals Build Their Amazing Homes, 18911
Incredible Facts About the Ocean, 19835
Robson, Pam. *Banana*, 20156
Body Language, 17628
Corn, 20185
Honey, 20126
Rice, 20127
Robson, Pam (jt. author). *Art from Fabric*, 21419
Exploring Time, 18304
Making Shaped Books, 13991
Roby, Cynthia. *When Learning Is Tough*, 17930

Roca, Francois. *The Yellow Train*, 1238(F)
Rocca, Frank. *Tales from the South Pacific Islands*, 10848
Rocco, Joe. *Halloween Motel*, 5994(F)
Roche, Denis. *Art Around the World*, 21470
Brave Georgie Goat, 2631(F)
Can You Count Ten Toes? Count to 10 in 10 Different Languages, 432
Loo-Loo, Boo, and Art You Can Do, 21471
Ollie All Over, 3381(F)
Only One Ollie, 566(F)
The Teeny Tiny Teacher, 10954
Roche, Orla. *The Famine Secret*, 9098(F)
The Secret of Drumshee Castle, 9099(F)
Rocheleau, Paul (jt. author). *The Shaker's Dozen*, 594
Rochette. *Purple Coyote*, 1077(F)
Rochford, Dierdre. *Rights for Animals?* 18660
Rock, Lois. *I Wish Tonight*, 767(F)
Rock, Maxine. *Totally Fun Things to Do with Your Dog*, 19965
Rocklin, Joanne. *The Case of the Backyard Treasure*, 6592(F)
The Case of the Shrunken Allowance, 567(F)
For Your Eyes Only, 10124(F)
Jake and the Copycats, 6593(F)
One Hungry Cat, 568(F)
Sonia Begonia, 7034(F)
Strudel Stories, 7499(F)
The Very Best Hanukkah Gift, 9758(F)
Rockwell, Anne. *The Boy Who Wouldn't Obey*, 11414
Bumblebee, Bumblebee, Do You Know Me? A Garden Guessing Game, 4517(F)
Career Day, 5527(F)
Ducklings and Pollywogs, 4518(F)
Ferryboat Ride! 3382(F)
The First Snowfall, 4520(F)
Growing Like Me, 18596
Halloween Day, 6045(F)
Hugo at the Park, 2632(F)
I Fly, 2965(F)
Long Ago Yesterday, 3383(F)
Mr. Panda's Painting, 287(F)
No! No! No! 5058(F)
One Bean, 20260
Only Passing Through, 12793
Our Earth, 20319
Our Stars, 18412
Our Yard Is Full of Birds, 5384
Pots and Pans, 3384(F)
Pumpkin Day, Pumpkin Night, 3857(F)
The Robber Baby, 11505
Romulus and Remus, 11506
Show and Tell Day, 5528(F)

The Storm, 4519(F)
The Story Snail, 6594(F)
Sweet Potato Pie, 6595(F)
Thanksgiving Day, 6151(F)
Valentine's Day, 6176(F)
What Happens to a Hamburger, 18105
What We Like, 3385
Rockwell, Anne, reteller. *Romulus and Remus*, 11506
Rockwell, Harlow. *The First Snowfall*, 4520(F)
My Dentist, 18187
Rockwell, Harlow (jt. author). *The First Snowfall*, 4520(F)
Rockwell, Lizzy. *Career Day*, 5527(F)
Ducklings and Pollywogs, 4518(F)
Good Enough to Eat, 18205
Halloween Day, 6045(F)
Hello Baby! 3858(F)
A Nest Full of Eggs, 19239
Our Yard Is Full of Birds, 5384
Pots and Pans, 3384(F)
Show and Tell Day, 5528(F)
Thanksgiving Day, 6151(F)
Valentine's Day, 6176(F)
Rockwell, Norman. *Willie Was Different*, 2633(F)
Rockwell, Thomas. *How to Eat Fried Worms*, 9976(F)
Rodanas, Kristina. *The Story of Blue Elk*, 11256
Rodanas, Kristina, adapt. *The Dragonfly's Tale*, 11294
Rodda, Emily. *Finders Keepers*, 10228(F)
The Pigs Are Flying, 8045(F)
Power and Glory, 4283(F)
Yay! 4284(F)
Roddie, Shen. *Toes Are to Tickle*, 3386(F)
Too Close Friends, 2634(F)
Rodell, Susanna. *Dear Fred*, 5059(F)
Roden, Katie. *The Mummy*, 8046(F)
Solving International Crime, 17080
Terrorism, 17081
Rodgers, Frank. *Who's Afraid of the Ghost Train?* 5060(F)
Rodgers, Mary. *Freaky Friday*, 9977(F)
Rodgers, Mary M. (jt. author). *Atmosphere*, 20670
Life on Land, 19398
Our Endangered Planet, 20677, 16997, 19822, 17010, 20520, 20576, 20467
Rodolph, Stormy. *Quest for Courage*, 9176(F)
Rodowsky, Colby. *Hannah in Between*, 8516(F)
Not My Dog, 7292(F)
Spindrift, 8517(F)
The Turnabout Shop, 8798(F)
Rodriguez, Bobbie. *Sarah's Sleepover*, 5061(F)

Rodriguez, Ingrid. *The Lion Who Saw Himself in the Water*, 11198
Rodriguez, Janel. *Gloria Estefan*, 12383
Nely Galan, 12831
Rodriguez, Luis J. *America Is Her Name*, 5062(F)
It Doesn't Have to Be This Way, 7367(F)
Roe, Eileen. *Con Mi Hermano/With My Brother*, 3859(F)
Roeckelein, Katrina. *Making Up Megaboy*, 8847(F)
Roehm, Michelle. *Girls Who Rocked the World 2*, 13742
Roehm, Michelle, comp. *Girls Know Best*, 17726
Roessel, Monty. *Kinaalda*, 16030
Songs from the Loom, 16031
Roffe, Mike. *Comets and Meteors*, 18505
Moons and Rings, 18506
The Planets, 18456
The Sun, 18558
The Universe, 18379
Roffey, Maureen. *The Grand Old Duke of York*, 886
Let's Go, 3295(F)
Rogasky, Barbara. *The Golem*, 11162
Winter Poems, 11981
Rogers, Barbara Radcliffe. *Canada*, 15591
The Dominican Republic, 15716
Toronto, 15592
Rogers, Daniel. *Earthquakes*, 20345
Volcanoes, 20346
Rogers, Emma. *Our House*, 3860(F)
Rogers, Forest. *Belching Hill*, 10814
Rogers, Fred. *Let's Talk About It*, 17677, 17931, 17678
Rogers, Glenn. *The San Antonio Spurs Basketball Team*, 22146
Rogers, Hal. *Combines*, 21253
Milking Machines, 20071
Snowplows, 21254
Rogers, Jacqueline. *Ballerina Dreams*, 12481
A Big, Spooky House, 11390
A Boy Named Boomer, 13608
Don't Call Me Toad! 7055(F)
Emma and Freckles, 7157(F)
Even More Short and Shivery, 10611
Fairies, Trolls and Goblins Galore, 11559
Five Live Bongos, 3781(F)
Footprints in the Sand, 20400
The Ghost of Sifty Sifty Sam, 1409(F)
Monster Soup and Other Spooky Poems, 1155
Once upon a Springtime, 6508(F)
Patrick's Day, 5642(F)
Roly-Poly Puppies, 519(F)
The Saddest Time, 17732
Snow Angel, 1398(F)
The Stars Are Waiting, 750(F)

Story Time for Little Porcupine, 2702(F)
There Goes Lowell's Party! 5690(F)
Tiptoe into Kindergarten, 5529(F)
Walk with Me, 3099(F)
Weird Pet Poems, 11779
Rogers, Kirsteen. *The Usborne Complete Book of the Microscope*, 19809
Rogers, Lure (jt. author). *The Dominican Republic*, 15716
Rogers, Paul. *What Can You See?* 21875(F)
Rogers, Paul (jt. author). *Our House*, 3860(F)
Rogers, Sally. *Earthsong*, 14176
Rogers, Stillman D. *Montreal*, 15593
Rogers, Stillman D. (jt. author). *Canada*, 15591
Toronto, 15592
Rogl, Manfred. *Barn Owls*, 19359
Rogo, Thomas Paul. *A Surfrider's Odyssey*, 7035(F)
Rohling, Claudia. *We Can Get Along*, 17624
Rohmann, Eric. *The Cinder-Eyed Cats*, 1516(F)
The Prairie Train, 1439(F)
Rohmer, Harriet. *Uncle Nacho's Hat*, 9138(F)
Rohmer, Harriet, ed. *Just Like Me*, 13925
Rohmer, Harriet (jt. author). *Magic Windows*, 16907
Rojankovsky, Feodor. *The Cabin Faced West*, 9231(F)
Frog Went A-Courtin', 14163
Roland, Timothy. *Come Down Now, Flying Cow!* 6596(F)
Rolfe, John (jt. author). *Michael Jordan*, 13536
Rollings, Susan. *New Shoes, Red Shoes*, 3387(F)
Rollins, Charlemae H., ed. *Christmas Gif'*, 17430
Rollo, Vera F. *The American Flag*, 13974
Rolph, Mic. *Cells Are Us*, 18048
Romain, Trevor. *Bullies Are a Pain in the Brain*, 17727
Cliques, Phonies, and Other Baloney, 17728
How to Do Homework Without Throwing Up, 17629
Roman, Irena. *The Voice from the Mendelsohns' Maple*, 8802(F)
Romero, Maritza. *Selena Perez*, 12467
Rood, Ronald (jt. author). *The New York Public Library Incredible Earth*, 20299
Roop, Connie. *Walk on the Wild Side!* 18661
Roop, Connie, ed. *Pilgrim Voices*, 16165

Roop, Connie (jt. author). *Buttons for General Washington*, 4812(F)
Capturing Nature, 12190
China, 15080
A City Album, 3388
Egypt, 15511
An Eye for an Eye, 9248(F)
A Farm Album, 15899
Girl of the Shining Mountains, 9434(F)
Good-Bye for Today, 9316(F)
Grace's Letter to Lincoln, 9503(F)
A Home Album, 15900
Keep the Lights Burning, Abbie, 6597
Let's Celebrate Christmas, 17431
Let's Celebrate Halloween, 17446
Let's Celebrate Thanksgiving, 6152
Let's Celebrate Valentine's Day, 6177
Martin Luther King, Jr., 12753
Off the Map, 16090
A School Album, 3389
Seasons of the Crane, 19278
Susan B. Anthony, 13133
Vietnam, 15197
Westward, Ho, Ho, Ho! 16355
Roop, Peter. *The Buffalo Jump*, 9177(F)
Buttons for General Washington, 4812(F)
China, 15080
A City Album, 3388
Egypt, 15511
An Eye for an Eye, 9248(F)
A Farm Album, 15899
Girl of the Shining Mountains, 9434(F)
Good-Bye for Today, 9316(F)
Grace's Letter to Lincoln, 9503(F)
A Home Album, 15900
Keep the Lights Burning, Abbie, 6597
Let's Celebrate Christmas, 17431
Let's Celebrate Halloween, 17446
Let's Celebrate Thanksgiving, 6152
Let's Celebrate Valentine's Day, 6177
Martin Luther King, Jr., 12753
A School Album, 3389
Seasons of the Crane, 19278
Susan B. Anthony, 13133
Vietnam, 15197
Westward, Ho, Ho, Ho! 16355
Roop, Peter, ed. *Capturing Nature*, 12190
Off the Map, 16090
Roop, Peter (jt. author). *Pilgrim Voices*, 16165
Walk on the Wild Side! 18661
Roos, Stephen. *The Gypsies Never Came*, 8911(F)
My Favorite Ghost, 7036(F)
Twelve-Year-Old Vows Revenge After Being Dumped by Extraterrestrial on First Date, 9978(F)

Root, Barry. *April Bubbles Chocolate*, 11598
Brave Potatoes, 1591(F)
Cowboy Dreams, 621(F)
Fishing Sunday, 3733(F)
Messenger, Messenger, 3061(F)
Old Devil Wind, 6031(F)
Pumpkins, 1500(F)
Saturday Night Jamboree, 3935(F)
Two Cool Cows, 2709(F)
Root, Betty. *My First Dictionary*, 14043
Root, Kimberly B. *Billy Beg and His Bull*, 10989
Birdie's Lighthouse, 2941(F)
Boots and His Brothers, 11127
Bronco Busters, 5260(F)
Gulliver in Lilliput, 7795(F)
In a Messy, Messy Room, 7750(F)
Junk Pile! 4090(F)
The Peddler's Gift, 6115(F)
The Toll-Bridge Troll, 1698(F)
The True Tale of Johnny Appleseed, 12844
Root, Phyllis. *All for the Newborn Baby*, 5912(F)
Aunt Nancy and Cousin Lazybones, 4285(F)
Aunt Nancy and Old Man Trouble, 1517(F)
Foggy Friday, 2635(F)
Grandmother Winter, 1518(F)
Here Comes Tabby Cat, 6598(F)
Kiss the Cow! 1519(F)
One Duck Stuck, 569(F)
One Windy Wednesday, 1520(F)
Rosie's Fiddle, 1521(F)
Turnover Tuesday, 4286(F)
What Baby Wants, 3861(F)
Rootes, David. *The Arctic*, 15830
Roraback, Robin. *This Is Our Seder*, 17472
Roraff, Susan. *Chile*, 15784
Rosa-Casanova, Sylvia. *Mama Provi and the Pot of Rice*, 3390(F)
Rosales, Melodye. *Addy Learns a Lesson*, 9496(F)
Irene Jennie and the Christmas Masquerade, 4833(F)
On the Day I Was Born, 3579(F)
A Strawbeater's Thanksgiving, 4834(F)
Rosales, Melodye Benson. *Leola and the Honeybears*, 11028
Rose, David. *Passover*, 17482
Rose, David S. *Teddy Bear's Scrapbook*, 2223(F)
There's a Dragon in My Sleeping Bag, 1251(F)
There's a Monster Under My Bed, 707(F)
Rose, Deborah L. *Into the A, B, Sea*, 119
The Rose Horse, 9616(F)
Rose, Emma. *Ballet Magic*, 3391(F)
Pumpkin Faces, 239(F)

Rose, Gill (jt. author). *Passover*, 17482
Rose, LaVera. *Grandchildren of the Lakota*, 16032
Rose, Mary Catherine. *Clara Barton*, 13135
Rose, Sally. *Tornadoes!* 20713
Rose, Ted. *The Banshee Train*, 2911(F)
John Blair and the Great Hinckley Fire, 16481
Roseman, Kenneth. *The Other Side of the Hudson*, 7368(F)
Rosemarin, Ike. *South Africa*, 14998
Rosemffet, Gustavo. *Wake Up, Grizzly!* 3530(F)
Rosemont School of the Holy Child Students. *My Mommy Has AIDS*, 17937
Rosen, Dorothy S. *A Fire in Her Bones*, 12929
Rosen, Dorothy S. (jt. author). *The Magician's Apprentice*, 9121(F)
Rosen, Michael. *The Best of Michael Rosen*, 11682
Michael Rosen's ABC, 120(F)
Mission Ziffoid, 1522(F)
Rover, 4287(F)
This Is Our House, 5063(F)
Rosen, Michael, ed. *Poems for the Very Young*, 11684
Rosen, Michael, sel. *Classic Poetry*, 11683
Walking the Bridge of Your Nose, 21845
Rosen, Michael J. *The Blessing of the Animals*, 8799(F)
Bonesy and Isabel, 5385(F)
The Dog Who Walked with God, 11295
Elijah's Angel, 5646(F)
Food Fight, 11685
How the Animals Got Their Colors, 10608
Our Eight Nights of Hanukkah, 6107(F)
A School for Pompey Walker, 9317(F)
A Thanksgiving Wish, 6153(F)
We're Going on a Bear Hunt, 2966(F)
With a Dog Like That, a Kid Like Me . . ., 1523(F)
Rosen, Michael J., ed. *Down to Earth*, 21772
Food Fight, 11685
Purr . . . Children's Book Illustrators Brag About Their Cats, 19931
South and North, East and West, 10609
Rosen, Sidney. *Can You Catch a Falling Star?* 18525
Can You Hitch a Ride on a Comet? 18526
The Magician's Apprentice, 9121(F)

Where Does the Moon Go? 18452
Where's the Big Dipper? 18553
Rosen, Sybil. *Speed of Light*, 7369(F)
Rosenberg, Liz. *A Big and a Little Alphabet*, 121(F)
The Carousel, 1524(F)
Monster Mama, 1525(F)
The Silence in the Mountains, 3862(F)
Rosenberg, Marsha Sarah. *Everything You Need to Know When a Brother or Sister Is Autistic*, 17932
Rosenberg, Maxine B. *Living with a Single Parent*, 17679
Mommy's in the Hospital Having a Baby, 18043
Rosenberry, Vera. *Anne Frank*, 13800
A Big and a Little Alphabet, 121(F)
Big Lips and Hairy Arms, 1264(F)
Binya's Blue Umbrella, 8985(F)
The Outside Inn, 1363(F)
Run, Jump, Whiz, Splash, 3392(F)
Savitri, 10806
Thorndike and Nelson, 2244(F)
Together, 4025
Vera Runs Away, 5064(F)
Vera's First Day of School, 5530(F)
When Vera Was Sick, 3393(F)
Who Is in the Garden? 4521
Rosenblatt, Lynn. *Monarch Magic!* 19567
Rosenbloom, Joseph. *Biggest Riddle Book in the World*, 21846
Spooky Riddles and Jokes, 21847
Sports Riddles, 21848
The World's Best Sports Riddles and Jokes, 21849
World's Toughest Tongue Twisters, 21884
The Zaniest Riddle Book in the World, 21850
Rosenblum, Richard. *Brooklyn Dodger Days*, 4813
Rosenburg, John. *William Parker*, 9318(F)
Young George Washington, 13120
Rosenfield, Lynn (jt. author). *When Your Parents Split Up . . .*, 17688
Rosenthal, Kit. *Arches to Zigzags*, 27
Rosenthal, Lisa. *A Dog's Best Friend*, 19966
Rosenthal, Marc. *The Absentminded Fellow*, 4229(F)
First, Second, 483(F)
The Straight Line Wonder, 1165(F)
Yo, Aesop! Get a Load of These Fables, 9979(F)
Rosenthal, Paul. *Yo, Aesop! Get a Load of These Fables*, 9979(F)
Rosenthal, Steve. *Arches to Zigzags*, 27
Rosner, Ruth. *I Hate My Best Friend*, 8365(F)

Ross, Adrienne. *In the Quiet*, 8518(F)
Ross, Alice. *The Copper Lady*, 6599(F)
Jezebel's Spooky Spot, 3394(F)
Ross, Alice (jt. author). *Cemetery Quilt*, 5065(F)
Ross, Christine. *A Pillow for My Mom*, 5073(F)
Ross, Dan. *Pro Wrestling's Greatest Wars*, 22052
The Story of the Wrestler They Call "The Rock," 22053
Ross, Dave. *A Book of Friends*, 17729
A Book of Hugs, 3395(F)
A Book of Kisses, 3396(F)
Ross, Edward S. *Yellowjackets*, 19526
Ross, Eileen. *The Halloween Showdown*, 6046(F)
Ross, Gaby. *Damien the Dragon*, 8047(F)
Ross, Jim, ed. *Dear Oklahoma City, Get Well Soon*, 16578
Ross, Kathy. *The Best Birthday Parties Ever!* 17396
Christmas Decorations Kids Can Make, 21472
Christmas Ornaments Kids Can Make, 21473
Crafts for All Seasons, 21474
Crafts for Christian Values, 21475
Crafts for Easter, 21476
Crafts for Halloween, 21477
Crafts for Hanukkah, 17483
Crafts for Kids Who Are Wild About Deserts, 21478
Crafts for Kids Who Are Wild About Dinosaurs, 21479
Crafts for Kids Who Are Wild About Oceans, 21480
Crafts for Kids Who Are Wild About Outer Space, 21481
Crafts for Kids Who Are Wild About Polar Life, 21482
Crafts for Kids Who Are Wild About Reptiles, 21483
Crafts for Kwanzaa, 5647
Crafts for Valentine's Day, 21484
Crafts from Your Favorite Bible Stories, 21485
Crafts from Your Favorite Fairy Tales, 21486
Crafts to Celebrate God's Creation, 21487
Crafts to Make in the Fall, 21488
Crafts to Make in the Spring, 21489
Crafts to Make in the Winter, 21490
Every Day Is Earth Day, 21491
The Jewish Holiday Craft Book, 6108
Make Yourself a Monster! 21492
More Christmas Ornaments Kids Can Make, 21493
Ross, Kent. *Cemetery Quilt*, 5065(F)

Ross, Kent (jt. author). *The Copper Lady*, 6599(F)
Jezebel's Spooky Spot, 3394(F)
Ross, Lillian. *Buba Leah and Her Paper Children*, 3863(F)
Ross, Lillian H. *Daughters of Eve*, 17317
Sarah, Also Known as Hannah, 7500(F)
Ross, Michael. *Fish Watching with Eugenie Clark*, 13259
Ross, Michael E. *Become a Bird and Fly!* 1526(F)
Bird Watching with Margaret Morse Nice, 13336
Bug Watching with Charles Henry Turner, 13351
Caterpillarology, 19568
Cricketology, 19483
Earth Cycles, 18438
Exploring the Earth with John Wesley Powell, 12152
Flower Watching with Alice Eastwood, 13269
Ladybugology, 19538
Millipedeology, 19618
Nature Art with Chiura Obata, 12274
Pond Watching with Ann Morgan, 13325
Rolypolyology, 18662
Sandbox Scientist, 18346
Snailology, 19619
Spiderology, 19593
Wildlife Watching with Charles Eastman, 13268
Wormology, 19620
Ross, Pat. *Hannah's Fancy Notions*, 9617(F)
Ross, Ramon R. *The Dancing Tree*, 8519(F)
Ross, Stewart. *Bandits and Outlaws*, 17082
Conquerors and Explorers, 14569
Cowboys, 16356
Daily Life, 14700
Greek Theatre, 14701
Knights, 14790
Mark Twain and Huckleberry Finn, 12612
The Original Olympics, 22256
Oxford Children's Book of the 20th Century, 14570
Secret Societies, 21949
Spies and Traitors, 17083
Ross, Suzanne. *What's in the Rainforest?* 20481
Ross, Terry. *Well, I Never!* 1156(F)
Ross, Tom. *Eggbert*, 1527(F)
Ross, Tony. *Amber Brown Is Not a Crayon*, 9825(F)
Animals, 13885
The Boy Who Lost His Belly Button, 1689(F)
I, Amber Brown, 9827(F)
I Want My Dinner, 4288(F)
I Want to Be, 4289(F)

It's Justin Time, Amber Brown, 6302(F)
Little Wolf's Book of Badness, 2851(F)
Little Wolf's Diary of Daring Deeds, 8203(F)
Little Wolf's Haunted Hall for Small Horrors, 8204(F)
Meanwhile, Back at the Ranch, 4251(F)
Michael, 4093(F)
Portraits, 13888
Silly Silly, 2636(F)
Sloth's Shoes, 5738(F)
Wash Your Hands! 3397(F)
What Did I Look Like When I Was a Baby? 2862(F)
Why? 1033(F)
You Can't Eat Your Chicken Pox, Amber Brown, 9828(F)
Ross, Tony, reteller. *Goldilocks and the Three Bears*, 11029
Hansel and Gretel, 10930
Ross, Wilma S. *X-15 Rocket Plane*, 21099
Rossel, Seymour. *Sefer Ha-Aggadah*, 11163
Rossetti, Christina. *Sing Song*, 11686
Rossi, Pamela. *Grandmother's Song*, 3520(F)
Rossiter, Nan P. *Rugby and Rosie*, 19967
The Way Home, 5386(F)
Rossiter, Phyllis. *Moxie*, 9618(F)
Rotblatt, Steven. *The Kid's Guide to the Smithsonian*, 17104
Rotenberg, Lisa. *Rodeo Pup*, 2637(F)
Roth, Carol. *Little Bunny's Sleepless Night*, 768(F)
Ten Dirty Pigs, Ten Clean Pigs, 570(F)
Roth, Robert. *Journey of the Nightly Jaguar*, 11770
Mama Provi and the Pot of Rice, 3390(F)
Tiger Woman, 10779
When the Monkeys Came Back, 4434(F)
Roth, Roger. *Billy the Ghost and Me*, 6356(F)
Fishing for Methuselah, 4290(F)
The Invisible Dog, 7237(F)
Roth, Susan L. *The Biggest Frog in Australia*, 10850
Cinnamon's Day Out, 2638(F)
Happy Birthday Mr. Kang, 5721(F)
Leon's Story, 17052
Made in Mexico, 15629
Night-Time Numbers, 571(F)
Rothaus, Don P. *Canyons*, 20320
Moray Eels, 19645
Warthogs, 18967
Rothenberg, Joan. *Inside-Out Grandma*, 6109(F)
Matzah Ball Soup, 6110(F)
Yettele's Feathers, 11164

Rothero, Chris. *Over 6,000 Years Ago*, 14508

Rothman, Michael. *The Forest in the Clouds*, 20434
Jaguar in the Rain Forest, 5396(F)
Tyrannosaurus Time, 14468

Rotner, Shelley. *The A.D.D. Book for Kids*, 17933
About Twins, 17680
Action Alphabet, 122(F)
Boats Afloat, 21375
The Body Book, 4522
Changes, 4371(F)
Citybook, 3399(F)
Close, Closer, Closest, 355
Faces, 3400
Feeling Thankful, 3398
Hold the Anchovies! 21735
Lots of Dads, 17681
Nature Spy, 4523
Ocean Day, 4524(F)
Pick a Pet, 5387(F)
Wheels Around, 5597

Rotter, Charles. *Mountains*, 20506
The Prairie, 20544

Rottman, S. L. *Hero*, 8800(F)

Roucha, Claudine. *Van Gogh*, 13907

Rougelot, Marilyn C. *Mimi and Jean-Paul's Cajun Mardi Gras*, 5639(F)

Roundhill, Clare (jt. author). *Animals*, 13898
Myths and Legends, 13899
Out of This World, 21447
Sports and Games, 13900

Rounds, Glen. *Beaver*, 19207
The Blind Colt, 7293(F)
Cowboys, 3401(F)
Four Dollars and Fifty Cents, 2948(F)
I Know an Old Lady Who Swallowed a Fly, 14177
Ol' Paul, the Mighty Logger, 11373
Once We Had a Horse, 5388(F)
Sod Houses on the Great Plains, 9435
Wild Horses, 5389
Witcracks, 21851

Rounds, Glen, ed. *I Know an Old Lady Who Swallowed a Fly*, 14177

Rouse, Jeff. *The Young Swimmer*, 22309

Rouss, Sylvia A. *Sammy Spider's First Passover*, 6111(F)
Sammy Spider's First Rosh Hashanah, 6112(F)
Sammy Spider's First Shabbat, 6113(F)

Row, Richard. *Murder on the Canadian*, 7127(F)

Rowan, Kate. *I Know How My Cells Make Me Grow*, 18076
I Know How We Fight Germs, 17993
I Know Why I Brush My Teeth, 18188

Rowan, N. R. *Women in the Marines*, 21404

Rowan, Pete. *Big Head*, 18077

Rowand, Phyllis. *The Growing Story*, 4476(F)

Rowe, Christine. *The Children's Book of Pottery*, 21534

Rowe, Gavin. *The Frightened Little Owl*, 2081(F)
The Hungry Otter, 2082(F)

Rowe, Jeannette. *Whose Feet?* 5390(F)

Rowe, John. *Monkey Trouble*, 2639(F)
Rabbit Moon, 2640(F)
She Is Born, 3757(F)
Smudge, 2641(F)

Rowe, John A. *The Elf's Hat*, 2838(F)
Monkey Trouble, 2639(F)

Rowe, Julian. *Music*, 14137
Recreation, 22054
Sports, 22055

Rowe, Julian (jt. author). *People*, 14511
Resources, 20316
Wildlife, 18654

Rowell, Jonathan. *Malaysia*, 15198

Rowinski, Kate. *Ellie Bear and the Fly-Away Fly*, 2642(F)

Rowland, Della. *The Story of Sacajawea*, 12989

Rowland, Jada. *Miss Tizzy*, 3998(F)

Rowland-Entwistle, Theodore. *Rivers and Lakes*, 20525

Rowley, John. *Harriet Tubman*, 12802

Rowling, J. K. *Harry Potter and the Chamber of Secrets*, 8048(F)
Harry Potter and the Goblet of Fire, 8049(F)
Harry Potter and the Prisoner of Azkaban, 8050(F)
Harry Potter and the Sorcerer's Stone, 8051(F)

Roy, Indrapramit. *The Very Hungry Lion*, 10809

Roy, Ron. *The Bald Bandit*, 6047(F)
The Deadly Dungeon, 7037(F)
The Goose's Gold, 7038(F)
Three Ducks Went Wandering, 5391(F)

Royal, Kxao (jt. author). *San*, 14965

Royen, Mary Morgan Van. *Where Do Bears Sleep?* 698(F)

Royse, Jane. *Moozie's Kind Adventure*, 2511(F)

Royston, Angela. *Baby Animals*, 5392
Birds, 19279
Cars, 5598
Dinosaurs, 14467
Eat Well, 18206
Fire Fighters, 17819
Flowers, Fruits, and Seeds, 20261
Insects and Crawly Creatures, 19484

Jungle Animals, 5393
Life Cycle of a Bean, 20262
Life Cycle of a Dog, 19968
Life Cycle of a Frog, 18737
Life Cycle of a Guinea Pig, 19903
Life Cycle of a Kangaroo, 19180
Life Cycle of a Mushroom, 20190
Life Cycle of a Salmon, 19713
Life Cycle of an Oak Tree, 20217
Night-time Animals, 18846
Planes, 21100
Plants and Us, 20263
Sea Animals, 5394
Truck Trouble, 17839
Where Do Babies Come From? 18244

Rozakis, Laurie. *Dick Rutan and Jena Yeager*, 12066
Homelessness, 17154
Teen Pregnancy, 18269

Rozens, Aleksandrs. *Floods*, 20714

Rubalcaba, Jill. *A Place in the Sun*, 8977(F)
The Wadjet Eye, 8941(F)

Rubel, David. *Scholastic Atlas of the United States*, 15901
Scholastic Encyclopedia of the Presidents and Their Times, 12696

Rubel, Nicole. *Back to School for Rotten Ralph*, 2109(F)
A Cowboy Named Ernestine, 4291(F)
Happy Birthday, Rotten Ralph, 5686(F)
Not So Rotten Ralph, 2110(F)
The One and Only Me, 3896(F)
Rotten Ralph, 2111(F)
Rotten Ralph's Rotten Christmas, 5821(F)
Rotten Ralph's Rotten Romance, 6167(F)
Rotten Ralph's Show and Tell, 2112(F)
Rotten Ralph's Trick or Treat, 5998(F)
Wedding Bells for Rotten Ralph, 2113(F)

Rubenstein, Len. *Entomology*, 19436

Rubin, David. *Kitaq Goes Ice Fishing*, 9171(F)

Rubin, Mark. *The Orchestra*, 14228

Rubin, Susan G. *Fireflies in the Dark*, 14878
Toilets, Toasters, and Telephones, 21055

Rubinger, Diane. *The Writing Bug*, 12549

Rubinstein, Gillian. *Under the Cat's Eye*, 10229(F)

Rucki, Ani. *When the Earth Wakes*, 4525(F)

Ruckman, Ivy. *In Care of Cassie Tucker*, 9619(F)
Night of the Twisters, 7039(F)
Spell It M-U-R-D-E-R, 7040(F)

Ruddick, Bob (jt. author). *Billy the Ghost and Me*, 6356(F)
Max and Me and the Time Machine, 7760(F)
Max and Me and the Wild West, 10190(F)
This Island Isn't Big Enough for the Four of Us! 9868(F)
Rudolph, Marguerita. *Grey Neck*, 2643(F)
Ruelle, Karen G. *Snow Valentines*, 6178(F)
The Thanksgiving Beast Feast, 6154(F)
Ruepp, Krista. *Horses in the Fog*, 7294(F)
Midnight Rider, 7295(F)
Ruff, Donna. *Acorn Magic*, 5422(F)
Eleanor Roosevelt, 13180
Grandma Moses, 12270
The Missing Sunflowers, 5423(F)
Ruff, Sue. *Bats*, 19036
Ruffin, Frances E. *Martin Luther King, Jr., and the March on Washington*, 16518
Ruffins, Reynold. *The Gift of the Crocodile*, 10502(F)
Running the Road to ABC, 10098(F)
There Was an Old Lady Who Swallowed a Trout! 14182
Ruhl, Greg. *In the Time of Knights*, 14795
Lost Temple of the Aztecs, 15652
Ruiz, Ana. *My First Book of Proverbs/Mi Primer Libro de Dichos*, 14028
Ruiz, Andres L. *Evolution*, 14514
Metamorphosis, 18663
Volcanoes and Earthquakes, 20347
Ruiz, Aristides. *There's No Place Like Space*, 18410
Wish for a Fish, 19653
Ruiz, Joseph J. *The Little Ghost Who Wouldn't Go Away/El pequeño fantasma que no queria irse*, 8052(F)
Rumford, James. *The Cloudmakers*, 4814(F)
The Island-Below-the-Star, 11374
Seeker of Knowledge, 13766
Rummel, Jack. *Mexico*, 15644
Runningwolf, Michael. *On the Trail of Elder Brother*, 11296
Rupert, Rona. *Straw Sense*, 8978(F)
Rupp, Rebecca. *The Dragon of Lonely Island*, 8053(F)
Rusch, Amy. *Moose Tales*, 6702(F)
Ruschak, Lynette. *Annie Ate Apples*, 123(F)
Rush, Barbara. *The Kids' Catalog of Passover*, 17484
Rush, Barbara (jt. author). *A Coat for the Moon and Other Jewish Tales*, 11167
Rush, Christopher. *Venus Peter Saves the Whale*, 2644(F)

Rush, Ken. *The Seltzer Man*, 4815(F)
What About Emma? 5395(F)
Rushton, Lucy. *Birth Customs*, 17214
Ruskin, John. *King of the Golden River or the Black Brother*, 8054(F)
Russell, Barbara T. *Blue Lightning*, 8055(F)
Last Left Standing, 8801(F)
Russell, Ching Yeung. *Child Bride*, 9010(F)
First Apple, 9011(F)
Lichee Tree, 9012(F)
Moon Festival, 9759(F)
Water Ghost, 9013(F)
Russell, Francine (jt. author). *The Safe Zone*, 18216
Russell, Linda. *Caribou Girl*, 11208
Russell, Lynne. *Summerhouse*, 955(F)
Three Wise Women, 5843(F)
Russell, Marion. *Along the Santa Fe Trail*, 16357
Russell, P. Craig. *Fairy Tales of Oscar Wilde*, 10419
The Fairy Tales of Oscar Wilde, v. 3, 10487
Russell, Tom. *Magic Step-by-Step*, 21790
Russmann, Edna R. *Nubian Kingdoms*, 14663
Russo, Marisabina. *The Big Brown Box*, 3864(F)
Good-bye, Curtis, 3204(F)
Grandpa Abe, 3865(F)
Hannah's Baby Sister, 3866(F)
I Don't Want to Go Back to School, 5531(F)
Mama Talks Too Much, 3402(F)
A Visit to Oma, 3867(F)
Russo, Monica. *Watching Nature*, 18597
Russon, Jacqueline. *Face Painting*, 21589, 21590
Ruth, Amy. *Louisa May Alcott*, 12489
Queen Latifah, 12410
Wilma Rudolph, 13671
Ruth, Amy (jt. author). *American Revolutionaries and Founders of the Nation*, 12681
Ruth, Maria Mudd. *The Deserts of the Southwest*, 20416
Firefighting, 17820
Rutherford, Jenny. *The Gift of the Pirate Queen*, 8658(F)
Rutherford, Meg. *Big Panda, Little Panda*, 2733(F)
Rutledge, Rachel. *The Best of the Best in Basketball*, 22147
The Best of the Best in Figure Skating, 13398
The Best of the Best in Gymnastics, 13399
The Best of the Best in Soccer, 13400

The Best of the Best in Tennis, 22314
The Best of the Best in Track and Field, 13401
Marion Jones, 13659
Mia Hamm, 13690
Rutten, Joshua. *Erosion*, 20570
Ryan, Mary C. *My Friend, O'Connell*, 9980(F)
The Voice from the Mendelsohns' Maple, 8802(F)
Ryan, Mary E. *Me, My Sister, and I*, 8803(F)
Ryan, Pam M. *Amelia and Eleanor Go for a Ride*, 4816(F)
Armadillos Sleep in Dugouts, 18912
Esperanza Rising, 9620(F)
The Flag We Love, 13975
Hello Ocean, 4526(F)
One Hundred Is a Family, 572(F)
A Pinky Is a Baby Mouse, 18880
Riding Freedom, 9436(F)
Ryan, Pat. *Rock Climbing*, 22056
Ryan, Patrick. *Poland*, 15286
South Africa, 14999
South Korea, 15199
Ryan, Susannah. *Coming to America*, 17578
Darcy and Gran Don't Like Babies, 3597(F)
Sparky and Eddie, 6425(F), 6426(F)
You Don't Need Words! 14013
Ryan-Lush, Geraldine. *Hairs on Bears*, 4292(F)
Rybolt, Thomas R. *Environmental Experiments About Renewable Energy*, 20836
Rybolt, Thomas R. (jt. author). *Air and Other Gases*, 20672
Metals, 21258
Plastics and Polymers, 21046
Salts and Solids, 20288
Water and Other Liquids, 20740
Rydell, Katy. *Wind Says Good Night*, 769(F)
Ryden, Hope. *ABC of Crawlers and Flyers*, 124(F)
Wild Horse Summer, 8804(F)
Wild Horses I Have Known, 20014
Wildflowers Around the Year, 20040
Ryder, Joanne. *Bears Out There*, 1528(F)
Each Living Thing, 4527(F)
Earthdance, 4528
A Fawn in the Grass, 4529(F)
Jaguar in the Rain Forest, 5396(F)
My Father's Hands, 3868(F)
Rainbow Wings, 1529(F)
The Snail's Spell, 1530(F)
Tyrannosaurus Time, 14468
Where Butterflies Grow, 4817
Ryder, Nora L. *In the Wild*, 18968
Rylant, Cynthia. *Appalachia*, 3403
Bear Day, 770(F)

Best Wishes, 12586
The Bird House, 8056(F)
Bless Us All, 17531
A Blue-Eyed Daisy, 8805(F)
The Blue Hill Meadows, 7501(F)
The Bookshop Dog, 5397(F)
Bunny Bungalow, 2645(F)
The Case of the Climbing Cat,
    6600(F)
Cat Heaven, 1531(F)
Children of Christmas, 9760(F)
The Cookie-Store Cat, 2646(F)
Dog Heaven, 5398(F)
Every Living Thing, 7296(F)
An Everyday Book, 3404(F)
Everyday Children, 3405(F)
Everyday House, 3406(F)
Give Me Grace, 17532
Gooseberry Park, 8057(F)
The Great Gracie Chase, 1532(F)
The Heavenly Village, 8058(F)
*Henry and Mudge and Annie's
    Good Move*, 6601(F)
*Henry and Mudge and Annie's Per-
    fect Pet*, 6602(F)
*Henry and Mudge and the Careful
    Cousin*, 6603(F)
*Henry and Mudge and the Sneaky
    Crackers*, 6604(F)
*Henry and Mudge and the Starry
    Night*, 6605(F)
*Henry and Mudge and the Wild
    Wind*, 6606(F)
*Henry and Mudge and Their Snow-
    man Plan*, 6607(F)
*Henry and Mudge in the Family
    Trees*, 6608(F)
The High-Rise Private Eyes,
    8059(F)
In Aunt Lucy's Kitchen, 7502(F)
In November, 4530(F)
The Islander, 8060(F)
A Little Shopping, 7503(F)
Little Whistle, 1533(F)
Missing May, 8806(F)
Mr. Griggs' Work, 3407(F)
*Mr. Putter and Tabby Bake the
    Cake*, 5913(F)
*Mr. Putter and Tabby Fly the
    Plane*, 6609(F)
*Mr. Putter and Tabby Paint the
    Porch*, 9981(F)
*Mr. Putter and Tabby Pick the
    Pears*, 6610(F)
*Mr. Putter and Tabby Pour the
    Tea*, 6611(F)
*Mr. Putter and Tabby Take the
    Train*, 6612(F)
*Mr. Putter and Tabby Toot the
    Horn*, 6613(F)
Night in the Country, 771(F)
*The Old Woman Who Named
    Things*, 5399(F)
Poppleton, 6614(F)
Poppleton and Friends, 6615(F)
Poppleton Everyday, 6616(F)
Poppleton Forever, 6617(F)

Poppleton Has Fun, 2647(F)
Poppleton in Fall, 6618(F)
Poppleton in Spring, 6619(F)
The Relatives Came, 3869(F)
Scarecrow, 1534(F)
Silver Packages, 5914(F)
Some Good News, 7504(F)
Special Gifts, 7505(F)
Thimbleberry Stories, 2648(F)
This Year's Garden, 4531(F)
Tulip Sees America, 2967(F)
The Van Gogh Cafe, 8061(F)
The Whales, 4532(F)
Rymill, Linda R. *Good Knight*,
    772(F)

Saaf, David. *Elemenopeo*, 2897(F)
Saaf, Donald. *Animal Music*, 2896(F)
    Pushkin Meets the Bundle, 2899(F)
    Pushkin Minds the Bundle, 2900(F)
    Train Song, 5608(F)
    Wee G, 2901(F)
Sabbeth, Alex. *Rubber-Band Banjos
    and a Java Jive Bass*, 14229
Sabbeth, Carol. *Crayons and Com-
    puters*, 21591
    Kids' Computer Creations, 21223
Sabin, Francene. *Amazing World of
    Ants*, 19513
    Amelia Earhart, 12115
    Louis Pasteur, 13339
    Wonders of the Forest, 20482
Sabin, Louis. *Amazing World of But-
    terflies and Moths*, 19569
    Thomas Alva Edison, 13273
    Wonders of the Desert, 20417
    Wonders of the Sea, 19836
Sabir, C. Ogbu. *Scott Joplin*, 12331
Sabuda, Robert. *Arthur and the
    Sword*, 11030(F)
    A B C Disney, 125(F)
    The Blizzard's Robe, 1535(F)
    Cookie Count, 3408(F)
    Earth Verses and Water Rhymes,
    11967
    Movable Mother Goose, 887(F)
    The Paper Dragon, 1104(F)
    Saint Valentine, 17510
    Tutankhamen's Gift, 13862
    The Twelve Days of Christmas,
    14212
    The Wonderful Wizard of Oz,
    7601(F)
Sachar, Louis. *Holes*, 7041(F)
    Marvin Redpost, 7297(F),
    10125(F), 9982(F), 6620(F),
    8807(F)
    *Sideways Arithmetic from Wayside
    School*, 9983(F)
    Sixth Grade Secrets, 8366(F)
    Wayside School Is Falling Down,
    10126(F)
Sachi, Karla. *Turtle Songs*, 10852
Sachs, Betsy. *The Boy Who Ate Dog
    Biscuits*, 7298(F)
Sachs, Marilyn. *The Bears' House*,
    10127(F)

Fran Ellen's House, 8520(F)
JoJo and Winnie, 7506(F)
JoJo and Winnie Again, 7507(F)
Surprise Party, 7508(F)
Sadler, Judy Ann. *Beading*, 21547
    Beads, 21548
    *Beanbag Buddies and Other Stuffed
    Toys*, 21657
    Corking, 21644
    Easy Braids, Barrettes and Bows,
    21549
    *The Kids Can Press Jumbo Book of
    Crafts*, 21494
    Making Fleece Crafts, 21645
    Prints, 21640
    Sewing, 21646
Sadler, Marilyn. *Alistair in Outer
    Space*, 1536(F)
    Alistair Underwater, 1537(F)
    Alistair's Time Machine, 4293(F)
    Bobo Crazy, 10230(F)
    The Parakeet Girl, 6621(F)
Sadu, Itah. *Christopher Changes His
    Name*, 4294(F)
Saenz, Benjamin Alire. *A Gift from
    PapaDiego*, 3870(F)
    *Grandma Fina and Her Wonderful
    Umbrellas/La Abuelita Fina y
    Sus Sombrillas Maravillosas*,
    4295(F)
Sage, James. *Coyote Makes Man*,
    11297
    Sassy Gracie, 4296(F)
Sahlhoff, Carl. *Friends in the Park*,
    4915
Saign, Geoffrey. *The African Cats*,
    19107
    The Great Apes, 19015
Saiko, Tatyana (jt. author). *Russia*,
    15431
St. George, Judith. *Betsy Ross*, 13189
    *Dear Dr. Bell . . . Your Friend,
    Helen Keller*, 12697
    Sacagawea, 12990
    So You Want to Be President?
    17120
Saint James, Synthia. *The Gifts of
    Kwanzaa*, 5648
    Girls Together, 5103(F)
    Greetings, Sun, 4661(F)
    *Hallelujah! A Christmas Celebra-
    tion*, 5892(F)
    Neeny Coming, Neeny Going,
    3994(F)
    No Mirrors in My Nana's House,
    3516(F)
    Sunday, 3871(F)
    To Dinner, for Dinner, 10706
    Tukama Tootles the Flute, 11421
St. John, Jetty. *A Family in Chile*,
    15785
St. Pierre, Stephanie. *Our National
    Anthem*, 14233
Sakade, Florence, ed. *Japanese Chil-
    dren's Favorite Stories*, 10827
Sakai, Kimiko. *Sachiko Means Hap-
    piness*, 5066(F)

Sakurai, Gail. *Asian-Americans in the Old West*, 16358
The Jamestown Colony, 16166
The Liberty Bell, 16732
The Library of Congress, 16733
The Louisiana Purchase, 16271
Paul Revere, 12959
The Thirteen Colonies, 16167
Salak, John. *Drugs in Society*, 17886
Violent Crime, 17084
Salariya, David. *Fantastic Transport Machines*, 21286
Salerno, Steven. *Chicken Chuck*, 2479(F)
Salisbury, Cynthia. *Phillis Wheatley*, 12619
Salisbury, Graham. *Jungle Dogs*, 8808(F)
Salk, Larry. *Mending Peter's Heart*, 7326(F)
Salkeld, Audrey. *Mystery on Everest*, 12142
Sallah, Tijan M. *Wolof*, 15046
Saller, Carol. *Florence Kelley*, 12916
Pug, Slug, and Doug the Thug, 2649(F)
Working Children, 15856
Saller, Carol (jt. author). *George Washington Carver*, 13254
Sallnow, John. *Russia*, 15431
Salmansohn, Pete (jt. author). *Project Puffin*, 19350
Salsi, Lynn (jt. author). *The Jack Tales*, 11349
Salsitz, Rhoni V. *The Twilight Gate*, 8062(F)
Salten, Felix. *Bambi*, 7299(F), 7300(F)
Saltveit, Elin Kordahl. *Computer Fun for Everyone*, 21224
Saltzberg, Barney. *The Flying Garbanzos*, 4297(F)
Mrs. Morgan's Lawn, 5067(F)
Phoebe and the Spelling Bee, 5532(F)
Show-and-Tell, 5533(F)
The Soccer Mom from Outer Space, 4298(F)
There's a Zoo in Room 22, 133(F)
This Is a Great Place for a Hot Dog Stand, 1538(F)
Where, Oh, Where Is My Underwear? 4299(F)
Saltzberg, Barney (jt. author). *Two for Stew*, 4255(F)
Saltzman, David. *The Jester Has Lost His Jingle*, 4818(F)
Salvadori, Mario. *Math Games for Middle School*, 20620
Salvadori, Mario (jt. author). *Earthquake Games*, 20340
Salzberg, Allen (jt. author). *Turtles*, 18779
Salzmann, Mary Elizabeth. *Circles*, 356(F)
Sammis, Fran. *Cities and Towns*, 16973

Measurements, 14356
Samoyault, Tiphaine. *Alphabetical Order*, 13987
Sampson, Mary Beth (jt. author). *Star of the Circus*, 2650(F)
Sampson, Michael. *The Football That Won . . .*, 2968(F)
Star of the Circus, 2650(F)
Sampson, Michael (jt. author). *Adam, Adam, What Do You See?* 17304
Swish! 2959(F)
Sams, B. B. *A Pair of Red Sneakers*, 4210(F)
Samton, Sheila W. *Jamaica Louise James*, 3693(F)
Moon to Sun, 573(F)
A Tree for Me, 600(F)
Samuels, Amy. *Follow That Fin! Studying Dolphin Behavior*, 19689
Samuels, Barbara. *Aloha, Dolores*, 4300(F)
Duncan and Dolores, 5400(F)
Samuelson, Mary Lou. *The Coyote*, 19138
Samuelson, Mary Lou (jt. author). *The African Rhinos*, 18970
Sanchez, Enrique O. *A Is for the Americas*, 23
Abuela's Weave, 4616(F)
Amelia's Road, 4899(F)
Confetti, 11657
The Golden Flower, 11425
Lupe and Me, 8825(F)
Palampam Day, 1183(F)
Speak English for Us, Marisol! 3616(F)
When This World Was New, 4955(F)
Sanchez, Enrique O. (jt. author). *Maria Molina and the Days of the Dead*, 4719(F)
Sand, George. *The Castle of Pictures and Other Stories*, 10488(F)
Sandak, Cass R. *Congressional Committees*, 17121
Lobbying, 17122
The National Debt, 17123
The United States, 15902
Sandburg, Carl. *Abe Lincoln Grows Up*, 13075
Grassroots, 11689
The Huckabuck Family and How They Raised Popcorn in Nebraska and Quit and Came Back, 3872(F)
Poems for Children Nowhere Near Old Enough to Vote, 11915
Rootabaga Stories, 9984(F), 9985(F)
The Sandburg Treasury, 11690(F)
The Wedding Procession of the Rag Doll and the Broom Handle and Who Was in It, 1539(F)
Sandelson, Robert. *Ice Sports*, 22257
Sandeman, Anna. *Babies*, 18245
Blood, 18090

Brain, 18117
Eating, 18104
Senses, 18161
Skin, Teeth, and Hair, 18179
Sanders, Mark. *The White House*, 16734
Sanders, Nancy I. *A Kid's Guide to African American History*, 15903
Old Testament Days, 21495
Sanders, Pete. *Anorexia and Bulimia*, 17994
Bullying, 17730
Divorce and Separation, 17682
Drinking Alcohol, 17888
Dyslexia, 17995
Feeling Violent, 17630
Smoking, 17887
Sanders, Scott R. *Aurora Means Dawn*, 4819(F)
Crawdad Creek, 4533(F)
The Floating House, 4820(F)
Here Comes the Mystery Man, 4821(F)
Meeting Trees, 4534(F)
A Place Called Freedom, 4822(F)
Sanderson, Ruth. *The Animal, the Vegetable and John D. Jones*, 8265(F)
The Crystal Mountain, 10610
Don't Hurt Laurie! 8795(F)
The Night Before Christmas, 11842
Papa Gatto, 10489
Rose Red and Snow White, 10490(F)
Tapestries, 17318
Where Have the Unicorns Gone? 1711(F)
Sandford, John. *The Dog Who Lost His Bob*, 5332(F)
I Like a Snack on an Iceberg, 5120(F)
The Leprechaun in the Basement, 5653(F)
Tale of a Tail, 1819(F)
Sandin, Joan. *As the Crow Flies*, 5105(F)
Clipper Ship, 21364
Daniel's Duck, 6238(F)
From Anna, 8902(F)
Hill of Fire, 15630
The Lemming Condition, 7564(F)
The Long Way to a New Land, 4823(F)
The Long Way Westward, 9621(F)
Pioneer Bear, 6622(F)
Sandler, Martin W. *Vaqueros*, 16359
Sandoval, Dolores. *Be Patient, Abdul*, 4824(F)
Sandoz, Eduard. *Greek Myths*, 11467
Sandved, Kjell B. *The Butterfly Alphabet*, 126(F)
Sanfield, Steve. *Bit by Bit*, 4301(F)
The Girl Who Wanted a Song, 1540(F)
Just Rewards, or Who Is That Man in the Moon and What's He

Doing Up There Anyway?
10769

Sanfilippo, Margaret. *The Code of the Drum*, 9491(F)
Coming to America, 9594(F)
Exploring the Grand Canyon, 16605

Sanford, William R. *Babe Ruth*, 13500
Bill Pickett, 12443
Billie Jean King, 13650
Brigham Young, 12969
Buffalo Bill Cody, 12869
Calamity Jane, 12864
The Chisholm Trail in American History, 16360
Daniel Boone, 12085
Davy Crockett, 12103
Dorothy Hamill, 13591
Joe DiMaggio, 13449
John C. Fremont, 12118
Kareem Abdul-Jabbar, 13511
Kit Carson, 12088
Richard King, 12921
Sacagawea, 12991
Zebulon Pike, 12147

Sanford, William R. (jt. author).
Allan Pinkerton, 12947
Billy the Kid, 12852
Butch Cassidy, 12867
Confederate Generals of the Civil War, 12652
The Dalton Gang, 16311
Doc Holliday, 12902
Jesse James, 12909
Judge Roy Bean, 12849
Union Generals of the Civil War, 12653
Wild Bill Hickok, 12900
Wyatt Earp, 12874

San Jose, Christine. *The Little Match Girl*, 10493
Sleeping Beauty, 10494

San Jose, Christine, reteller. *Cinderella*, 10491(F)
The Emperor's New Clothes, 10492(F)

Sankey, Tom. *Cat's Cradle, Owl's Eyes*, 22006
Many Stars and More String Games, 22008
Super String Games, 22009

Sanroman, Susana. *Señora Reganona*, 773(F)

Sansevere, J. R. (jt. author). *Ooey Gooey*, 6331(F)

Sansevero, Tony. *The Attack of the Two-Inch Teacher*, 10165(F)
Sing, Henrietta! Sing! 4133(F)

Sansone, Adele. *The Little Green Goose*, 2651(F)

San Souci, Daniel. *Cowpokes*, 2976(F)
The Gifts of Wali Dad, 10805
Ice Bear and Little Fox, 5314(F)
In the Moonlight Mist, 10735
Island Magic, 3907(F)

The Legend of Sleepy Hollow, 7812(F)
Montezuma and the Fall of the Aztecs, 11404
A Possible Tree, 4370(F)
Red Wolf Country, 5316(F)
Two Bear Cubs, 11298
Vassilisa the Wise, 11113

San Souci, Robert D. *The Boy and the Ghost*, 1541(F)
Brave Margaret, 11031
Callie Ann and Mistah Bear, 11375
Cendrillon, 10495
Cinderella Skeleton, 10496(F)
Cut from the Same Cloth, 11376
Even More Short and Shivery, 10611
The Faithful Friend, 11431
Little Gold Star, 10497(F)
N. C. Wyeth's Pilgrims, 16168
Peter and the Blue Witch Baby, 11111
The Secret of the Stones, 11377
Six Foolish Fishermen, 11378
Two Bear Cubs, 11298
Young Arthur, 11032

San Souci, Robert D., reteller. *Sukey and the Mermaid*, 11379
A Terrifying Taste of Short and Shivery, 8063(F)
A Weave of Words, 10863
The White Cat, 10498(F)

Santangelo, Colony Elliot. *Brother Wolf of Gubbio*, 11075

Santella, Andrew. *The Assassination of Robert F. Kennedy*, 12920
The Battle of the Alamo, 16272
The Chisholm Trail, 16361
Illinois, 16579
Impeachment, 17124
Jackie Robinson Breaks the Color Line, 13495
Mount Rushmore, 16580
Thomas Jefferson, 13053

Santiago, Chiori. *Home to Medicine Mountain*, 9178(F)

Santiago, Rose Mary. *The Clever Boy and the Terrible, Dangerous Animal*, 11197

Santini, Debrah. *Cinderella*, 10491(F)
When Young Melissa Sweeps, 3460(F)

Santore, Charles. *A Stowaway on Noah's Ark*, 17319(F)
William the Curious, 2652(F)
The Wizard of Oz, 7597(F)

Santoro, Christopher. *Bears Are Curious*, 19058
A Pie Went By, 1142(F)

Santoro, Scott. *Isaac the Ice Cream Truck*, 1542(F)

Santow, Dan. *Elizabeth Bloomer Ford*, 13154
Jacqueline Bouvier Kennedy Onassis, 13173

Santrey, Laurence. *Davy Crockett*, 12104
Discovering the Stars, 18554
Jim Thorpe, 13675
What Makes the Wind? 20675
Young Frederick Douglass, 12715

Sanvoisin, Eric. *The Ink Drinker*, 8064(F)
A Straw for Two, 8065(F)

Saport, Linda. *All the Pretty Little Horses*, 618
The Face at the Window, 4675(F)
Subira Subira, 10705

Saport, Lynn. *Jump Up Time*, 4702(F)

Saraceni, Claudia. *Goya*, 12236

Sarasas, Claude. *The ABC's of Origami*, 21626

Sardegna, Jill. *The Roly-Poly Spider*, 2653(F)

Sargent, Sarah. *Weird Henry Berg*, 8066(F)

Saroff, Phyllis V. *Taste and See*, 17170
A Walk in the Boreal Forest, 20454
A Walk in the Desert, 20408
A Walk in the Rain Forest, 20455

Sarrazin, Marisol. *Hamsters Don't Glow in the Dark*, 7323(F)

Sasaki, Ellen. *The Riddle*, 4046(F)

Sasaki, Goro. *Me, Dad, and Number 6*, 5576(F)

Sasso, Sandy Eisenberg. *But God Remembered*, 17320
For Heaven's Sake, 3873(F)
God in Between, 17215
God Said Amen, 1543(F)
A Prayer for the Earth, 5649(F)

Sateren, Shelley Swanson. *The Humane Societies*, 18664

Sathre, Vivian. *J. B. Wigglebottom and the Parade of Pets*, 10128(F)
Leroy Potts Meets the McCrooks, 6623(F)
On Grandpa's Farm, 3409(F)
Slender Ella and Her Fairy Hogfather, 6624(F)

Sato, Yuko. *Ladybugs*, 19534
Roses Red, Violets Blue, 20038

Sattler, Helen R. *The Book of North American Owls*, 19364
The Earliest Americans, 16033

Sauber, Robert. *Florence Robinson*, 9554(F)
The Goose Girl, 10922
I Know Not What, I Know Not Where, 11096
Operation, 9957(F)
Sirko and the Wolf, 10860
The Storm, 4519(F)
The Swan Maiden, 10482(F)

Saul, Carol P. *Barn Cat*, 574(F)

Saul, Wendy (jt. author). *On the Bus with Joanna Cole*, 12519

Saulnier, Karen L. (jt. author). *Nursery Rhymes from Mother Goose Told in Signed English*, 827

Saunders, Dave. *Brave Jack*, 2654(F)
Dibble and Dabble, 2655(F)
Snowtime, 2656(F)
Who's in My Bed? 2583(F)

Saunders, Julie (jt. author). *Brave Jack*, 2654(F)
Dibble and Dabble, 2655(F)
Snowtime, 2656(F)

Saunders, Rupert. *Balloon Voyage*, 21101

Saunders, Susan. *The Curse of the Cat Mummy*, 7042(F)
The Ghost Who Ate Chocolate, 7043(F)
Lucky Lady, 7301(F)

Saunderson, Jane. *Heart and Lungs*, 18078
Muscles and Bones, 18172

Sauvain, Philip. *Oceans*, 19837
Rain Forests, 20483
Rivers and Valleys, 20390

Sauve, Gordon. *Dinosaurs*, 14443

Savadier, Elivia. *A Bedtime Story*, 676(F)
Treasure Map, 3676(F)

Savage, Ann. *Dig and Sow! How Do Plants Grow?* 18592
Paws and Claws, 18819

Savage, Douglas J. *Ironclads and Blockades in the Civil War*, 16427
Prison Camps in the Civil War, 16428
Women in the Civil War, 16429

Savage, Jeff. *Aerobics*, 18207
Andre Agassi, 13642
Barry Bonds, 13438
Cal Ripken, Jr., 13483
Cowboys and Cow Towns of the Wild West, 16362
Deion Sanders, 13629
Demolition Derby, 21317
Drag Racing, 22082
Emmitt Smith, 13633
Fundamental Strength Training, 18208
Grant Hill, 13529
Gunfighters of the Wild West, 16363
Home Run Kings, 13402
Julie Krone, Unstoppable Jockey, 13696
Junior Seau, 13631
Kobe Bryant, 13515
Kristi Yamaguchi, 13599
Pioneering Women of the Wild West, 16364
Running, 22259
Sports Great Brett Favre, 13613
Sports Great Juwan Howard, 13531
Thurman Thomas, 13635
Tiger Woods, 13718

Top 10 Basketball Point Guards, 13403
Top 10 Football Sackers, 13404
Top 10 Heisman Trophy Winners, 13405
Top 10 Physically Challenged Athletes, 13406
Top 10 Professional Football Coaches, 13407
Top 10 Sports Bloopers and Who Made Them, 22057

Savage, Stephen. *Amphibians*, 18692
Animals of the Desert, 20418
Animals of the Grasslands, 20545
Animals of the Oceans, 19646
Animals of the Rain Forest, 20484
Birds, 19280
Duck, 19315
Fish, 19714
Insects, 19485
Mammals, 18969
Reptiles, 18693
Skin, 18847

Savan, Beth. *Earthwatch*, 20321

Savin, Deborah. *Whales*, 19799

Savory, Phyllis. *Zulu Fireside Tales*, 10712

Sawaya, Linda D. *How to Get Famous in Brooklyn*, 3210(F)
The Little Ant/La Hormiga Chiquita, 2610(F)

Sawyer, Kem Knapp. *Marjory Stoneman Douglas*, 13266

Sawyer, Liz. *Anorexia and Bulimia*, 17994
Dyslexia, 17995

Sawyer, Lori. *Grandmother Five Baskets*, 11261(F)

Sawyer, Ruth. *Roller Skates*, 9622(F)

Sawyers, June S. *Famous Firsts of Scottish-Americans*, 17590

Say, Allen. *Allison*, 5068(F)
The Bicycle Man, 4825(F)
The Boy of the Three-Year Nap, 10830
El Chino, 13685
Emma's Rug, 5069(F)
Grandfather's Journey, 3874(F)
How My Parents Learned to Eat, 3635(F)
The Lost Lake, 3875(F)
River Dream, 1544(F)
The Sign Painter, 8809(F)
Stranger in the Mirror, 8067(F)
Tea with Milk, 15137
Tree of Cranes, 5915(F)

Sayer, Chloe. *The Incas*, 15786

Sayles, Elizabeth. *Albie the Lifeguard*, 3031(F)
Five Little Kittens, 711(F)
The Little Black Truck, 5570(F)
The Marvelous Toy, 3834(F)
Millions of Snowflakes, 3427(F)
Not in the House, Newton! 1190(F)
The Rainbow Tulip, 5038(F)
This Mess, 1969(F)

Saylor-Marchant, Linda. *Hammer*, 12394

Sayre, April Pulley. *Antarctica*, 15831
Asia, 15051
Coral Reef, 19666
Desert, 20419
El Nino and La Nina, 20785
Endangered Birds of North America, 19409
Grassland, 20546
Home at Last, 18848
If You Should Hear a Honey Guide, 14947
Lake and Pond, 20526
Ocean, 19838
Put On Some Antlers and Walk Like a Moose, 18665
River and Stream, 20527
Seashore, 19866
Splish! Splash! Animal Baths, 18849
Taiga, 20485
Temperate Deciduous Forest, 20486
Tropical Rain Forest, 20487
Tundra, 15832
Turtle, Turtle, Watch Out! 18789
Wetland, 20391

Scalora, Suza. *The Fairies*, 21950

Scamell, Ragnhild. *Three Bags Full*, 2657(F)
Toby's Doll's House, 5722(F)

Scarborough, Kate (jt. author). *Exploration into North America*, 16075

Scarry, Huck. *Looking into the Middle Ages*, 14791

Scarry, Richard. *Lowly Worm Joins the Circus*, 6625(F)
Mr. Fixit's Magnet Machine, 6626(F)
Pie Rats Ahoy! 2658(F)
Richard Scarry's Best Word Book Ever, 14044
Richard Scarry's Lowly Worm Word Book, 240(F)

Schaap, Martine. *Mop to the Rescue*, 1545(F)
Mop's Backyard Concert, 1546(F)

Schachner, Judith Byron. *The Grannyman*, 2659(F)
How the Cat Swallowed Thunder, 1733(F)
I Know an Old Lady Who Swallowed a Pie, 6145(F)
Mr. Emerson's Cook, 9623(F)
The Prince of the Pond, 7980(F)
Willy and May, 5916(F)

Schade, Susan. *Space Rock*, 6628(F)
Toad on the Road, 6629(F)
Toad Takes Off, 6630(F)

Schade, Susan (jt. author). *Captain Zap and the Evil Baron von Fishhead*, 6240(F)
Felix and the 400 Frogs, 6241(F)

Schaefer, Carole L. *The Copper Tin Cup*, 3876(F)
Down in the Woods at Sleepytime, 774(F)
Snow Pumpkin, 4038(F)
Sometimes Moon, 3877(F)
The Squiggle, 1547(F)
Schaefer, Lola M. *Chinese New Year*, 17397
Cinco de Mayo, 17398
Henry Ford, 13283
This Is the Sunflower, 4535(F)
Tugboats, 21377
The Wright Brothers, 13357
Schaefer, Margaret A. *Let's Build a Car*, 21318
Schaeffer, Edith. *Mei Fuh*, 9014(F)
Schaeffer, Susan F. *The Dragons of North Chittendon*, 8068(F)
Schaer, Miriam. *Katie-Bo*, 3625(F)
Schafer, John. *ABC Career Book for Girls/El Libro de Carreras para Niñas*, 17767(F)
Schafer, Susan. *The Galapagos Tortoise*, 18790
The Komodo Dragon, 18746
Lizards, 19904
Turtles, 18791
Schaffer, Amanda. *All God's Children*, 17524
Schaffer, Donna. *Pillbugs*, 19486
Silkworms, 19487
Schami, Rafik. *Albery and Lila*, 2660(F)
Schanzer, Rosalyn. *Escaping to America*, 17591
Gold Fever! Tales from the California Gold Rush, 16365
How We Crossed the West, 16091
Maccabee Jamboree, 469(F)
Ten Good Rules, 17325
The True-or-False Book of Horses, 20001
Scharff-Kniemeyer, Marlis. *Little Bear's Christmas*, 5862(F)
Scharfstein, Sol. *Understanding Israel*, 15529
Understanding Jewish Holidays and Customs, 17485
Scharl, Josef. *The Complete Grimm's Fairy Tales*, 10893
Scheader, Catherine. *Lorraine Hansberry*, 12544
Schecter, Ellen. *The Big Idea*, 7370(F)
The Family Haggadah, 17486
I Love to Sneeze, 6631(F)
The Pet-Sitters, 7302(F)
Scheer, Julian. *Rain Makes Applesauce*, 4302(F)
Scheffler, Axel. *The Gruffalo*, 2035(F)
Scheffler, Ursel. *Be Brave, Little Lion!* 6632(F)
Grandpa's Amazing Computer, 7509(F)

The Man with the Black Glove, 7044(F)
The Spy in the Attic, 7045(F)
Taking Care of Sister Bear, 2661(F)
Who Has Time for Little Bear? 2662(F)
Scheidl, Gerda M. *Andy's Wild Animal Adventure*, 1548(F)
Schemenauer, Elma. *Iran*, 15559
Japan, 15138
Schenker, Dona. *The Secret Circle*, 10129(F)
Schepp, Steven (jt. author). *How Babies Are Made*, 18236
Scherer, Jeffrey. *One Snowy Day*, 6633(F)
Scherie, Strom. *Stuffin' Muffin*, 21737
Schertle, Alice. *Down the Road*, 3878(F)
I Am the Cat, 11811
Keepers, 11691
A Lucky Thing, 11692
Schiaffino, Mariarosa. *Goya*, 12236
Schick, Eleanor. *Mama*, 5070(F)
My Navajo Sister, 4039(F)
Navajo ABC, 136(F)
Navajo Wedding Day, 4826(F)
Schick, Eleanor (jt. author). *Navajo ABC*, 136(F)
Schick, Joel. *My Robot Buddy*, 10239(F)
Wayside School Is Falling Down, 10126(F)
Schields, Gretchen. *The Chinese Siamese Cat*, 5428(F)
The Moon Lady, 9017(F)
Schille, Marjett. *How Many Bears?* 426(F)
Schimpky, David (jt. author). *Fort Life*, 16332
Schindel, John. *Busy Penguins*, 5401(F)
Dear Daddy, 3879(F)
Frog Face, 3880(F)
Schindelman, Joseph. *Charlie and the Chocolate Factory*, 7694(F)
Schindler, S. D. *Are We There Yet, Daddy?* 255(F)
The Bat in the Dining Room, 4134(F)
Betcha! 20590
A Big Cheese for the White House, 4646(F)
Big Pumpkin, 1576(F)
Catwings, 7899(F)
Children of Christmas, 9760(F)
Clever Crow, 5180(F)
Covered Wagons, Bumpy Trails, 4705(F)
Creepy Riddles, 21823
Don't Fidget a Feather! 2690(F)
The Earth Is Painted Green, 11942
Every Living Thing, 7296(F)
First Night, 3496(F)
Gold Fever, 4706(F)

Hog Music, 9373(F)
How Many Fish? 6276(F)
How Santa Got His Job, 9742(F)
I Love My Buzzard, 4310(F)
If You Should Hear a Honey Guide, 14947
Not the Piano, Mrs. Medley! 4484(F)
Oh, What a Thanksgiving! 6147(F)
The Smash-up Crash-up Derby, 3419(F)
Those Amazing Ants, 19509
The Three Little Pigs and the Fox, 11352
A Tree Is Growing, 20197
Tundra Mouse, 5869(F)
Whatever Happened to Humpty Dumpty? 11872
Whoo-oo Is It? 5324(F)
Whuppity Stoorie, 11044
Schindler, Steven. *Night Creatures*, 18988
Schlaepfer, Gloria G. *The African Rhinos*, 18970
Schlaepfer, Gloria G. (jt. author). *The Coyote*, 19138
Schleichert, Elizabeth. *Sitting Bull*, 12996
Schleifer, Jay. *Methamphetamine*, 17889
Our Declaration of Independence, 16213
Schlein, Miriam. *Discovering Dinosaur Babies*, 14469
More Than One, 575
Round and Square, 357(F)
Sleep Safe, Little Whale, 775(F)
The Way Mothers Are, 2663(F)
What the Dinosaurs Saw, 576
What's a Penguin Doing in a Place Like This? 19385
The Year of the Panda, 7303(F)
Schlen, Joy. *Buried Blueprints*, 21934
Schlessinger, Laura C. *Why Do You Love Me?* 3881(F)
Schlieper, Anne. *The Best Fight*, 10130(F)
Schlissel, Lillian. *Black Frontiers*, 16366
Schmandt-Besserat, Denise. *The History of Counting*, 20634
Schmid, Eleonore. *The Living Earth*, 18598
The Three Feathers, 10910
Schmidt, Annie M. G. *Minnie*, 8069(F)
Schmidt, Diane. *Where's Chimpy?* 3848(F)
Schmidt, Gary. *William Bradford*, 12857
Schmidt, Gary D. *Anson's Way*, 9122(F)
The Blessing of the Lord, 17321
Pilgrim's Progress, 8070(F)
Saint Ciaran, 13771

Schmidt, Gary D., ed. *Robert Frost*, 11693

Schmidt, Gerald D. *Let's Go Fishing*, 22177

Schmidt, Jeremy. *In the Village of the Elephants*, 19170
Two Lands, One Heart, 15200

Schmidt, Karen L. *Hannah the Hippo's No Mud Day*, 2210(F)
The Jungle Baseball Game, 2563(F)
What Do You Love? 728(F)

Schmidt, Michael J. (jt. author). *In the Forest with the Elephants*, 15205

Schmidt, Norman. *Fabulous Paper Gliders*, 21795
Paper Birds That Fly, 21627

Schmitt, Lois. *Smart Spending*, 16936

Schnakenberg, Robert E. *Cynthia Cooper*, 13519
Kobe Bryant, 13516
Teammates, 13408

Schneider, Antonie. *The Birthday Bear*, 6634(F)
Good-Bye, Vivi! 5071(F)
Luke the Lionhearted, 5402(F)

Schneider, Christine M. *Jeremy's Muffler*, 4249(F)
Picky Mrs. Pickle, 4303(F)

Schneider, Elizabeth Ann. *Ndebele*, 15000

Schneider, Howie. *Blumpoe the Grumpoe Meets Arnold the Cat*, 5357(F)
Chewy Louie, 1549(F)

Schneider, Jost. *Lynx*, 19108

Schneider, Meg. *Help! My Teacher Hates Me*, 17631

Schneider, Mical. *Between the Dragon and the Eagle*, 8942(F)

Schneider, R. M. *Add It, Dip It, Fix It*, 14045

Schnieper, Claudia. *Amazing Spiders*, 19594
Chameleons, 18747
Lizards, 18748
Snakes, 18776

Schnitter, Jane T. *Let Me Explain*, 18246

Schnur, Steven. *Autumn*, 21885
The Koufax Dilemma, 10359(F)
Night Lights, 577(F)
The Shadow Children, 8071(F)
Spring, 127
Spring Thaw, 4536(F)
Summer, 128(F)

Schnurnberger, Lynn. *Kids Love New York!* 16735

Schoberle, Cecile. *Creepy, Spooky Science*, 18329
Icky, Squishy Science, 18331

Schodorf, Timothy. *Baseball Card Crazy*, 7462(F)

Schoell, William. *Magic Man*, 12476

Schoen, Mark. *Bellybuttons Are Navels*, 4537

Schoenherr, Ian. *Jonkonnu*, 4741(F)
Marie in Fourth Position, 9058(F)
Newf, 5289(F)

Schoenherr, John. *Bear*, 2664(F)
Gentle Ben, 7267(F)
Incident at Hawk's Hill, 7186(F)
Julie of the Wolves, 6853(F)
Owl Moon, 5463(F)
Pigs in the Mud in the Middle of the Rud, 4267(F)
Rascal, 7282(F)
Rebel, 5403(F)

Schofield, Den. *Danger at Sand Cave*, 6588(F)

Scholder, Fritz. *Anpao*, 11257

Scholte van Mast, Ruth. *Grandpa's Amazing Computer*, 7509(F)

Scholz, Jackson. *The Football Rebels*, 10360(F)

Schomp, Virginia. *The Bottlenose Dolphin*, 19690
He Fought for Freedom, 12716
If You Were a Ballet Dancer, 17782
If You Were a Construction Worker, 17797
If You Were a Doctor, 17805
If You Were a Farmer, 17764
If You Were a Firefighter, 17821
If You Were a Musician, 17783
If You Were a Pilot, 17840
If You Were a Police Officer, 17822
If You Were a Teacher, 17765
If You Were a Truck Driver, 17841
If You Were a Veterinarian, 17856
If You Were an Astronaut, 17766
New York, 16736
Russia, 15432

Schories, Pat. *Bathtime for Biscuit*, 6255(F)
Biscuit Finds a Friend, 6257(F)
Biscuit's New Trick, 6258(F)
Biscuit's Valentine's Day, 6164(F)
Happy Birthday, Biscuit! 5670(F)
Happy Thanksgiving, Biscuit! 6137(F)
Teeny, Tiny Mouse, 280(F)

Schott, Jane A. *Dian Fossey and the Mountain Gorillas*, 13285

Schotter, Roni. *Bunny's Night Out*, 776(F)
Captain Bob Sets Sail, 3410(F)
Captain Snap and the Children of Vinegar Lane, 4040(F)
Dreamland, 3411(F)
Nothing Ever Happens on 90th Street, 3412(F)
Purim Play, 6114(F)

Schouweiler, Thomas. *Germans in America*, 17592

Schraff, Anne. *American Heroes of Exploration and Flight*, 12067
Are We Moving to Mars? 18486
Woodrow Wilson, 13123

Schram, Peninnah. *Ten Classic Jewish Children's Stories*, 11165

Schrepfer, Margaret. *Switzerland*, 15287

Schrier, Jeffrey. *On the Wings of Eagles*, 4827(F)

Schroder, Ron (jt. author). *King Bobble*, 4099(F)

Schroeder, Alan. *The Tale of Willie Monroe*, 10828

Schroeder, Binette. *The Frog Prince*, 10898

Schroeder, Lisa Golden. *California Gold Rush Cooking*, 16367

Schroeder, Russell, ed. *Walt Disney*, 12227

Schubert, Dieter (jt. author). *Abracadabra*, 1550(F)
Amazing Animals, 18666
Bear's Egg, 2665(F)
There's a Hole in My Bucket, 2666(F)
Wild Will, 4041(F)

Schubert, Ingrid. *Abracadabra*, 1550(F)
Amazing Animals, 18666
Bear's Egg, 2665(F)
There's a Hole in My Bucket, 2666(F)
Wild Will, 4041(F)

Schubert, Leda. *Winnie All Day Long*, 5404(F)

Schubert, Ulli. *Harry's Got a Girlfriend!* 6635(F)

Schuch, Steve. *A Symphony of Whales*, 5405(F)

Schuett, Stacey. *Beginnings*, 3755(F)
Christina Katerina and Fats and the Great Neighborhood War, 3996(F)
Come and See, 5879(F)
Day Light, Night Light, 20857
The Feather-Bed Journey, 4644(F)
Flashlight, 3244(F)
Forest, 6350(F)
Grace's Letter to Lincoln, 9503(F)
Grandmother's Dreamcatcher, 733(F)
Night Lights, 577(F)
Purple Mountain Majesties, 12505
Rhino Romp, 5224(F)
Spring Thaw, 4536(F)
When Spring Comes, 4474(F)

Schulson, Rachel. *Guns*, 21405

Schultz, Ron. *Looking Inside Sports Aerodynamics*, 20837
Looking Inside Sunken Treasure, 14539
Looking Inside Telescopes and the Night Sky, 18413

Schultz, Suzy. *Crossing Jordan*, 8284(F)

Schulz, Andrea. *North Carolina*, 16885

Schulz, Janet. *The Workers' Detective*, 13306

Schulz, Randy. *The New York Knicks Basketball Team*, 22148

Schumaker, Ward. *In My Garden*, 578(F)

Toddler Two-Step, 373(F)

Schuman, Michael. *Delaware*, 16737

Schuman, Michael A. *Bill Cosby*, 12371

Franklin D. Roosevelt, 13100

Martin Luther King, Jr., 12754

Theodore Roosevelt, 13104

Schur, Maxine R. *The Peddler's Gift*, 6115(F)

Schurfranz, Vivian. *A Message for General Washington*, 9249(F)

Schusky, Ernest L. (jt. author). *The Ancient Splendor of Prehistoric Cahokia*, 14495

Schutzer, Dena. *The Reverend Thomas's False Teeth*, 1189(F)

3 Kids Dreamin', 8280(F)

Schuurmans, Hilde. *Sidney Won't Swim*, 2667(F)

Schwabach, Karen. *Thailand*, 15201

Schwabacher, Martin. *Elephants*, 19171

The Huron Indians, 16034

Minnesota, 16581

Superstars of Women's Tennis, 13409

Schwarts, Joyce R. (jt. author). *Carl Sagan*, 13345

Schwartz, Alvin. *Busy Buzzing Bumblebees and Other Tongue Twisters*, 6636

Ghosts! 6637(F)

Gold and Silver, Silver and Gold, 21951(F)

I Saw You in the Bathtub and Other Folk Rhymes, 6638(F)

More Scary Stories to Tell in the Dark, 11380

Scary Stories 3, 7046(F)

Witcracks, 21851

Schwartz, Alvin, ed. *Scary Stories to Tell in the Dark*, 11381

Whoppers, 11382

Schwartz, Amy. *Annabelle Swift, Kindergartner*, 5534(F)

Blow Me a Kiss, Miss Lilly, 3986(F)

The Crack-of-Dawn Walkers, 3692(F)

Gabby Growing Up, 5691(F)

How I Captured a Dinosaur, 2668(F)

How to Catch an Elephant, 4304(F)

Nana's Birthday Party, 5692(F)

Old MacDonald, 14178

The Purple Coat, 3211(F)

Some Babies, 3413(F)

A Teeny Tiny Baby, 3882(F)

Wish You Were Here, 15889

The Witch Who Lives Down the Hall, 1213(F)

Schwartz, Carol. *Lee, the Rabbit with Epilepsy*, 5039(F)

The Maiden of Northland, 11131

The Mother Goose Cookbook, 21719

Sea Squares, 472

Thinking About Ants, 19507

What the Dinosaurs Saw, 576

Where's That Insect? 19430

Schwartz, Cherie Karo (jt. author). *The Kids' Catalog of Passover*, 17484

Schwartz, Daniel. *The House of Wings*, 8583(F)

Schwartz, David M. *G Is For Googol*, 20595

How Much Is a Million? 20635

If You Hopped Like a Frog, 241

If You Made a Million, 20636

On Beyond a Million, 20637

Schwartz, Ellen. *Jesse's Star*, 9069(F)

Mr. Belinsky's Bagels, 4042(F)

Schwartz, Henry. *How I Captured a Dinosaur*, 2668(F)

Schwartz, Howard. *The Day the Rabbi Disappeared*, 11166

Schwartz, Howard, sel. and reteller. *A Coat for the Moon and Other Jewish Tales*, 11167

Schwartz, Joyce R. (jt. author). *Eugenie Clark*, 13258

Schwartz, Marc. *A Gallery of Games*, 22035

Schwartz, Michael. *La Donna Harris*, 12973

Luis Rodriguez, 12835

Schwartz, Perry. *Carolyn's Story*, 17683

Schwartz, Robert H. *Coping with Allergies*, 17996

Schwartz, Roslyn. *The Mole Sisters and the Busy Bees*, 2669(F)

The Mole Sisters and the Piece of Moss, 1551(F)

Schwartz, Virginia Frances. *Send One Angel Down*, 9319(F)

Schwarz, Renée. *Papier-Mâché*, 21628

Schweiger-Dmi'el, Itzhak. *Hanna's Sabbath Dress*, 6116(F)

Schweninger, Ann. *Amanda Pig and Her Best Friend Lollipop*, 6703(F)

Oliver and Albert, Friends Forever, 6704(F)

Schwinger, Larry. *Storm Chasers*, 20693

Wild, Wild Wolves, 6532

Scieszka, Jon. *The Frog Prince Continued*, 10499(F)

The Good, the Bad and the Goofy, 1552(F)

It's All Greek to Me, 8072(F)

Knights of the Kitchen Table, 7047(F)

Math Curse, 5535(F)

See You Later, Gladiator, 10231(F)

Squids Will Be Squids, 9986(F)

The Stinky Cheese Man, 4305(F)

Summer Reading Is Killing Me, 8073(F)

The True Story of the Three Little Pigs, 11033

Tut, Tut, 8074(F)

Scioscia, Mary. *Bicycle Rider*, 12784

Scollon, E. W. (jt. author). *Goners*, 10236(F), 10237(F)

Scoones, Simon. *A Family from Vietnam*, 15202

Scott, Ann H. *A Brand Is Forever*, 7304(F)

Brave as a Mountain Lion, 3414(F)

Cowboy Country, 2969(F)

Hi, 3415(F)

On Mother's Lap, 4828(F)

Scott, C. Anne. *Lizard Meets Ivana the Terrible*, 8367(F)

Old Jake's Skirts, 3416(F)

Scott, Carey. *Kittens*, 19932

Scott, Deborah. *The Kid Who Got Zapped Through Time*, 8075(F)

Scott, Elaine. *Adventure in Space*, 21007

Close Encounters, 18414

Friends! 17731

Funny Papers, 13926

Movie Magic, 21277

Twins! 17684

Scott, Geoffrey. *Labor Day*, 17399

Scott, Margaret. *Help Is on the Way*, 17927

Scott, Michael. *Ecology*, 16967

Scott, Nina Savin. *The Thinking Kid's Guide to Successful Soccer*, 22301

Scott, Steve. *Splish Splash*, 11578

Teddy Bear, Teddy Bear, 888(F)

Scott-Mitchell, Clare. *Cinderella*, 10500(F)

Scrace, Carolyn. *Dinosaurs and Other Prehistoric Creatures*, 14470

Scrimger, Richard. *A Nose for Adventure*, 10232(F)

The Nose from Jupiter, 9987(F)

The Way to Schenectady, 9988(F)

Scrofani, Joseph M. *Lost in the Devil's Desert*, 7057(F)

Scruggs, Afi-Odelia. *Jump Rope Magic*, 1553(F)

Scruton, Clive. *A Goodnight Kind of Feeling*, 1850(F)

Scudamore, Vicki (jt. author). *Marbles*, 22034

Scuderi, Lucia. *To Fly*, 5406(F)

Scull, Marie-Louise. *The Skit Book*, 12032

Seabrooke, Brenda. *The Boy Who Saved the Town*, 4829(F)

The Care and Feeding of Dragons, 8076(F)

The Haunting at Stratton Falls, 7048(F)

The Swan's Gift, 1554(F)

The Vampire in My Bathtub, 8077(F)

Sean, J. A. *Jane Goodall*, 13303

Sebastian, John. *J.B.'s Harmonica*, 2670(F)

Sebestyen, Ouida. *Words by Heart*, 9624(F)

Seddon, Tony. *Animal Parenting*, 18920

Sedgwick, Marcus. *Floodland*, 8078(F)

See, Prudence. *The Secret Garden Cookbook*, 21687

Seeber, Dorothea P. *A Pup Just for Me/A Boy Just for Me*, 5407(F)

Seeger, Pete, adapt. *Abiyoyo*, 10713

Seeley, Laura L. *Agatha's Feather Bed*, 3603(F)
The Book of Shadowboxes, 129(F)
Cats Vanish Slowly, 11815

Seelig, Renate. *The Giantess*, 4975(F)

Segal, John. *The Musicians of Bremen*, 10939

Segal, Lore. *All the Way Home*, 4306(F)
Tell Me a Mitzi, 3883(F)

Sehnert, Chris W. *Top 10 Sluggers*, 13410

Seibert, Patricia. *Mush!* 2970
Toad Overload, 16968

Seibold, J. Otto. *Free Lunch*, 2671(F)
Going to the Getty, 16811
Mr. Lunch Takes a Plane Ride, 2672(F)
Penguin Dreams, 1555(F)

Seibold, J. Otto (jt. author). *Olive, the Other Reindeer*, 5947(F)

Seidensticker, John, ed. *Dangerous Animals*, 18971

Seidler, Tor. *Mean Margaret*, 8079(F)
The Silent Spillbills, 7305(F)
The Wainscott Weasel, 8080(F)

Seidman, David. *The Young Zillionaire's Guide to Supply and Demand*, 16928

Seix, Victoria. *Creating with Papier-Mâché*, 21629

Selby, Anna. *Spain*, 15484

Selby, Jennifer. *Bear Day*, 770(F)
The Seed Bunny, 2673(F)

Selden, Bernice. *The Story of Walt Disney, Maker of Magical Worlds*, 12228

Selden, George. *Chester Cricket's Pigeon Ride*, 2674(F)
The Cricket in Times Square, 8081(F)
The Genie of Sutton Place, 8082(F)
Harry Kitten and Tucker Mouse, 8083(F)

Seldman, David. *Adam Sandler*, 12463

Selfridge, John W. *Pablo Picasso*, 12284

Selgin, Peter. *S.S. Gigantic Across the Atlantic*, 4307(F)

Sellier, Marie. *Cézanne from A to Z*, 12205
Matisse from A to Z, 13927

Selsam, Millicent E. *Backyard Insects*, 19488
Egg to Chick, 19306
A First Look at Dogs, 19970
A First Look at Ducks, Geese, and Swans, 19316
Greg's Microscope, 19810
How Kittens Grow, 19933
How Puppies Grow, 19969

Seltzer, Isadore. *The House I Live In*, 13963
The Man Who Tricked a Ghost, 10778
This Is the Bread I Baked for Ned, 3112(F)
Tree of Dreams, 10629

Seltzer, Meyer. *Here Comes the Recycling Truck!* 16985

Selven, Maniam. *Shower of Gold*, 10798

Selway, Martina. *Don't Forget to Write*, 3884(F)

Selznick, Brian. *Amelia and Eleanor Go for a Ride*, 4816(F)
Barnyard Prayers, 687
The Boy of a Thousand Faces, 7049(F)
Our House, 7415(F)

Sendak, Maurice. *Along Came a Dog*, 7183(F)
The Bat-Poet, 7835(F)
Chicken Soup with Rice, 4308(F)
Dear Mili, 10894
The Golden Key, 10454(F)
Hector Protector, and As I Went over the Water, 889
Higglety Pigglety Pop! or There Must Be More to Life, 8084(F)
A Hole Is to Dig, 204(F)
The House of Sixty Fathers, 9653(F)
Hurry Home, Candy, 7184(F)
I Saw Esau, 11903
In Grandpa's House, 7510(F)
Kenny's Window, 1556(F)
Let's Be Enemies, 4051(F)
The Light Princess, 10455(F)
Little Bear, 6533(F)
Lullabies and Night Songs, 14149
Maurice Sendak's Really Rosie, 1557(F)
The Moon Jumpers, 1632(F)
Mr. Rabbit and the Lovely Present, 2902(F)
No Fighting, No Biting! 6534(F)
The Nutcracker, 10916
The Nutshell Library, 242(F)
Outside Over There, 1558(F)
Pierre, 5072(F)
Seven Little Monsters, 579(F)
Swine Lake, 2475(F)
Very Far Away, 1559(F)
A Very Special House, 5001(F)
What Do You Say, Dear? 4991(F)

Wheel on the School, 9032(F)
Where the Wild Things Are, 1560(F)
Zlateh the Goat and Other Stories, 11175

Sendak, Philip. *In Grandpa's House*, 7510(F)

Senior, Helen. *Butterfly*, 19544

Senior, Kathryn. *Dinosaurs and Other Prehistoric Creatures*, 14470

Senisi, Ellen B. *For My Family, Love, Allie*, 3885(F)
Hurray for Pre-K! 5536(F)
Just Kids, 8912(F)
Kindergarten Kids, 5537
Reading Grows, 14007

Senna, Carl. *Colin Powell*, 12954

Sensier, Danielle. *Costumes*, 21550

Sensier, Danielle (jt. author). *Masks*, 21602

Senungetuk, Vivian. *Wise Words of Paul Tiulana*, 16812

Serafin, Kim. *Everything You Need to Know About Being a Vegetarian*, 18209

Seredy, Kate. *The Good Master*, 9070(F)

Serfozo, Mary. *Benjamin Bigfoot*, 5538(F)
A Head Is For Hats, 6639(F)
Joe Joe, 3417(F)
Rain Talk, 4538(F)
What's What? 243(F)
Who Said Red? 288(F)
Who Wants One? 580(F)

Seros, Kathleen, adapt. *Sun and Moon*, 10736

Serraillier, Ian. *The Silver Sword*, 9687(F)

Serrano, Francisco. *Our Lady of Guadalupe*, 17216

Servello, Joe. *Daniel Discovers Daniel*, 3517(F)
Trouble in Bugland, 6927(F)

Service, Pamela F. *Phantom Victory*, 7050(F)
Stinker from Space, 10233(F)
Stinker's Return, 10234(F)
Storm at the Edge of Time, 8085(F)
Vision Quest, 8086(F)

Service, Robert W. *The Cremation of Sam McGee*, 11694

Setaro, John F. (jt. author). *Alcohol 101*, 17873

Settel, Joanne. *Exploding Ants*, 18850

Setterington, Ken. *Hans Christian Andersen's The Snow Queen*, 10501(F)

Seuling, Barbara. *Drip! Drop!* 20745
Oh No, It's Robert, 9989(F)
To Be a Writer, 14107
Winter Lullaby, 18904

Seuss, Dr. *And to Think That I Saw It on Mulberry Street*, 1561(F)

Bartholomew and the Oobleck, 1562(F)

The Butter Battle Book, 1563(F)

The Cat in the Hat, 6640(F)

Dr. Seuss' ABC, 130(F)

The 500 Hats of Bartholomew Cubbins, 1564(F)

Green Eggs and Ham, 6641(F)

Hooray for Diffendoofer Day! 4309(F)

Hop on Pop, 6642(F)

Horton Hears a Who! 2675(F)

How the Grinch Stole Christmas, 5917(F)

Hunches in Bunches, 2676(F)

I Am Not Going to Get Up Today! 6643(F)

I Can Lick Thirty Tigers Today and Other Stories, 6644(F)

I Can Read with My Eyes Shut! 6645(F)

The Lorax, 4539(F)

My Many Colored Days, 289(F)

Oh Say Can You Say? 6646(F)

Oh, the Places You'll Go! 3418(F)

On Beyond Zebra! 1565(F)

Sevastiades, Philemon D. *I Am Eastern Orthodox,* 17217

I Am Protestant, 17218

I Am Roman Catholic, 17219

Severance, John B. *Skyscrapers,* 21150

Winston Churchill, 13770

Severs, Vesta-Nadine. *Jennifer Love Hewitt,* 12398

Sevier, Marti (jt. author). *England,* 15357

Welcome to England, 15358

Sewall, Marcia. *Animal Song,* 890

Captain Snap and the Children of Vinegar Lane, 4040(F)

The Golden Locket, 4168(F)

The Green Mist, 11034

The Marzipan Moon, 8206(F)

The Morning Chair, 3740(F)

Nickommoh! A Thanksgiving Celebration, 6146

People of the Breaking Day, 16035

The Pilgrims of Plimoth, 16169

Sable, 7221(F)

Sarah, Plain and Tall, 9410(F)

Saying Good-bye to Grandma, 3915(F)

Stone Fox, 7340(F)

Thunder from the Clear Sky, 16170

Sewell, Anna. *Black Beauty,* 5408(F)

Sewell, Helen. *The Bears on Hemlock Mountain,* 5175(F)

The Thanksgiving Story, 6142(F)

Seymour, Tres. *Hunting the White Cow,* 5409(F)

I Love My Buzzard, 4310(F)

Jake Johnson, 4311(F)

Our Neighbor Is a Strange, Strange Man, 13331

The Smash-up Crash-up Derby, 3419(F)

Too Quiet for These Old Bones, 4312(F)

We Played Marbles, 2971(F)

Sgouros, Charissa. *A Pillow for My Mom,* 5073(F)

Shachat, Andrew. *Stop That Pickle!* 958(F)

Shackell, John. *Fit for Life,* 18202

Shader, Laurel (jt. author). *Environmental Diseases,* 18018

Shaffer, Terea D. *The Singing Man,* 10696

Shah, Idries. *The Boy Without a Name,* 11196

The Clever Boy and the Terrible, Dangerous Animal, 11197

The Lion Who Saw Himself in the Water, 11198

The Magic Horse, 11199

Neem the Half-Boy, 11200

The Silly Chicken, 2677(F)

Shahan, Sherry. *Dashing Through the Snow,* 22058

Frozen Stiff, 7051(F)

Shaik, Fatima. *The Jazz of Our Street,* 3420(F)

On Mardi Gras Day, 5650(F)

Shakespeare, William. *The Tempest,* 8087(F)

William Shakespeare, 12053

Shalant, Phyllis. *Bartleby of the Mighty Mississippi,* 8088(F)

Look What We've Brought You from Vietnam, 17593

Shange, Ntozake. *White Wash,* 5074(F)

Shank, Ned. *The Sanyasin's First Day,* 4830(F)

Shannon, David. *The Acrobat and the Angel,* 10881

The Amazing Christmas Extravaganza, 5918(F)

A Bad Case of Stripes, 5075(F)

The Boy Who Lived with the Seals, 11270

The Bunyans, 1699(F)

David Goes to School, 5539(F)

Encounter, 9142(F)

How Georgie Radbourn Saved Baseball, 10361(F)

How Many Spots Does a Leopard Have? 10685

No, David! 3886(F)

The Rain Came Down, 4313(F)

The Rough-Face Girl, 11271

Sacred Places, 11743

Shannon, George. *Frog Legs,* 2678(F)

Heart to Heart, 2679(F)

Lizard's Home, 2680(F)

Seeds, 4043(F)

Spring, 11824

Still More Stories to Solve, 10612

Stories to Solve, 10613

This Is the Bird, 3887(F)

True Lies, 10614

Shannon, Margaret. *Elvira,* 1566(F)

Gullible's Troubles, 2681(F)

Shannon, Mark. *The Acrobat and the Angel,* 10881

Shannon, Mike. *Johnny Bench,* 13437

Shapiro, Arnold L. *Mice Squeak, We Speak,* 5410(F)

Shapiro, Irwin. *Joe Magarac and His U.S.A. Citizen Papers,* 11383

Shapiro, Marc. *J. K. Rowling,* 12585

Share, Brian. *FAQ Weather,* 20797

Sharkey, Niamh. *The Gigantic Turnip,* 11114

Tales of Wisdom and Wonder, 10573

Sharmat, Craig (jt. author). *Nate the Great and the Tardy Tortoise,* 6652(F)

Sharmat, Marjorie W. *Getting Something on Maggie Marmelstein,* 10131(F)

Gila Monsters Meet You at the Airport, 4314(F)

I'm Terrific, 2682(F)

Nate the Great, 6647(F), 6653(F)

Nate the Great and Me, 6648(F)

Nate the Great and the Fishy Prize, 6649(F)

Nate the Great and the Monster Mess, 6650(F)

Nate the Great and the Tardy Tortoise, 6652(F)

Nate the Great Saves the King of Sweden, 6651(F)

Tiffany Dino Works Out, 2683(F)

Sharmat, Mitchell. *Gregory, the Terrible Eater,* 2684(F)

Sharmat, Mitchell (jt. author). *Nate the Great,* 6653(F)

Sharp, Gene. *Hi, Clouds,* 6355(F)

Over-Under, 212(F)

Sharp, Richard M. *The Sneaky Square and 113 Other Math Activities for Kids,* 20621

Sharpe, Jim. *Rudyard Kipling,* 11571

Sharpe, Susan. *Spirit Quest,* 7052(F)

Waterman's Boy, 7053(F)

Sharrar, Jack (jt. author). *Great Scenes and Monologues for Children,* 14325

Sharratt, Nick. *Do Knights Take Naps?* 1626(F)

Eat Your Peas, 4167(F)

The Green Queen, 290(F)

Mrs. Pirate, 4315(F)

Seaside Poems, 11533

Snazzy Aunties, 3888(F)

Spider Storch's Carpool Catastrophe, 8540(F)

Spider Storch's Fumbled Field Trip, 10019(F)

Spider Storch's Music Mess, 10139(F)

The Time It Took Tom, 3421(F)

Sharth, Sharon. *Finches,* 19281

Rabbits, 19208

Shavick, Andrea. *Roald Dahl,* 12522

You'll Grow Soon, Alex, 5076(F)
Shaw, Brian. *The Baseball Counting Book*, 505
Shaw, Charles. *It Looked Like Spilt Milk*, 313(F)
Shaw, Eve. *Grandmother's Alphabet*, 131(F)
Shaw, Janet. *Happy Birthday Kirsten!* 9437(F)
Kirsten Learns a Lesson, 9438(F)
Shaw, Nancy. *Sheep in a Jeep*, 6654(F)
Sheep in a Shop, 5723(F)
Sheep Out to Eat, 6655(F)
Sheep Take a Hike, 2685(F)
Sheep Trick or Treat, 6048(F)
Shaw-MacKinnon, Margaret. *Tiktala*, 1567(F)
Shaw-Smith, Emma. *Bread Is for Eating*, 3165(F)
A Pocketful of Stars, 777
Shawver, Margaret. *What's Wrong with Grandma? A Family's Experience with Alzheimer's*, 8521(F)
Shea, George. *Amazing Rescues*, 6656
First Flight, 6657(F)
Shea, Pegi Deitz. *Ekatarina Gordeeva*, 13590
I See Me! 3422(F)
The Impeachment Process, 17125
New Moon, 4540(F)
Shearer, Alex. *Professor Sniff and the Lost Spring Breezes*, 8089(F)
The Summer Sisters and the Dance Disaster, 8090(F)
Sheather, Allan. *Neptune's Nursery*, 19647
Sheather, Allan (jt. author). *One Less Fish*, 598
Shecter, Ben. *Getting Something on Maggie Marmelstein*, 10131(F)
A Ghost Named Fred, 6201(F)
Shed, Greg. *Butterfly House*, 4396(F)
Casey Over There, 4801(F)
Dandelions, 9526(F)
I Remember Papa, 3260(F)
The Language of Doves, 4876(F)
Moontellers, 7968(F)
A Net of Stars, 1267(F)
Squanto's Journey, 17491
Shedd, Warner. *The Kids' Wildlife Book*, 18667
Sheehan, Patricia. *Côte d'Ivoire*, 15048
Luxembourg, 15401
Moldova, 15433
Sheehan, Patty. *Shadow and the Ready Time*, 5411(F)
Sheehan, Sean. *Ancient Rome*, 14743
Austria, 15288
Cambodia, 15203
Great African Kingdoms, 14913
Jamaica, 15717
Malta, 15258
Pakistan, 15204

Rome, 14744
Turkey, 15289
Sheely, Robert. *Sports Lab*, 22059
Sheely, Robert (jt. author). *Techno Lab*, 21264
Shefelman, Janice. *Comanche Song*, 9439(F)
Shefelman, Tom. *Comanche Song*, 9439(F)
Shein, Lori. *AIDS*, 17997
Sheindlin, Judy. *Win or Lose by How You Choose!* 17632
Sheinwold, Alfred. *101 Best Family Card Games*, 22237
Shelby, Anne. *Homeplace*, 3423(F)
The Someday House, 3424(F)
Shelby, Fay (jt. author). *Lost in Spillville*, 7710(F)
Sheldon, Dyan. *Harry the Explorer*, 10235(F)
My Brother Is a Superhero, 7511(F)
The Whales' Song, 1568(F)
Shellard, Dominic. *William Shakespeare*, 12593
Shelly, Jeff. *Website of the Warped Wizard*, 7862(F)
Shelowitz, Holly Anne. *Oh, Baby!* 18233
Shemie, Bonnie. *Houses of Adobe*, 16036
Houses of Bark, 16037
Houses of China, 15081
Houses of Snow, Skin and Bones, 15833
Mounds of Earth and Shell, 16038
Shemin, Margaretha. *The Little Riders*, 9688(F)
Shems, Ed. *Everyday Science*, 18325
Silly Science, 18327
Shenandoah-Tekalihwa: Khwa, Joanne. *Skywoman*, 11299
Shepard, Aaron. *The Baker's Dozen*, 5919
The Crystal Heart, 10842
Forty Fortunes, 11201
The Gifts of Wali Dad, 10805
The Legend of Lightning Larry, 1569(F)
The Legend of Slappy Hooper, 11384
The Maiden of Northland, 11131
Master Man, 10714
The Sea King's Daughter, 11112
Shepard, Aaron, reteller. *Savitri*, 10806
Shepard, Claudia. *Lake of the Big Snake*, 4784(F)
Shepard, E. H. *Pooh's Bedtime Book*, 7962(F)
The Reluctant Dragon, 10424(F)
The Wind in the Willows, 7753(F)
The World of Christopher Robin, 11654
The World of Pooh, 7963(F)
Shepard, Ernest H. *Winnie-the-Pooh's ABC*, 132(F)

Shephard, Marie T. *Maria Montessori*, 13836
Shepherd, Donna Walsh. *Auroras*, 18415
The Aztecs, 15645
The Klondike Gold Rush, 15594
Tundra, 15834
Uranus, 18487
Shepherd, Jennifer. *Canada*, 15595
Shepherd, Roni. *Third Grade Is Terrible*, 5472(F)
Sheppard, Jeff. *Splash, Splash*, 5412(F)
Sherkin-Langer, Ferne. *When Mommy Is Sick*, 3889(F)
Sherlock, Patti. *Four of a Kind*, 7054(F)
Sherlock, Philip M., ed. *West Indian Folk Tales*, 11432
Sherman, Eileen B. *Independence Avenue*, 9625(F)
Sherman, Josepha. *Barrel Racing*, 22060
Bill Gates, 13296
Jeff Bezos, 12850
Merlin's Kin, 10615
Rachel the Clever and Other Jewish Folktales, 11168
Ropers and Riders, 22061
Told Tales, 10616
Vassilisa the Wise, 11113
Welcome to the Rodeo! 22062
Sherman, Paul (jt. author). *Naked Mole-Rats*, 19198
Sherrow, Victoria. *Bill Clinton*, 13025
Endangered Mammals of North America, 19410
The Exxon Valdez, 16813
Freedom of Worship, 17050
The Gecko, 18749
Hillary Rodham Clinton, 13147
Hurricane Andrew, 20715
Huskings, Quiltings, and Barn Raisings, 16171
The Iroquois Indians, 16039
Joseph McCarthy and the Cold War, 12934
Life During the Gold Rush, 16368
The Maya Indians, 15683
The Oklahoma City Bombing, 16582
Phillis Wheatley, 12620
Plains Outbreak Tornadoes, 20716
The Porcupine, 18972
San Francisco Earthquake, 1989, 16814
Sports Great Pete Sampras, 13652
The Triangle Factory Fire, 16482
Wilma Rudolph, 13672, 13673
The World Trade Center Bombing, 16738
Shetterly, Robert. *The Dwarf-Wizard of Uxmal*, 11415
Shetterly, Susan Hand. *The Dwarf-Wizard of Uxmal*, 11415
Shelterwood, 4541(F)

Shields, Carol D. *Colors*, 1570(F)
Day by Day a Week Goes Round, 244(F)
I Wish My Brother Was a Dog, 1571(F)
Lucky Pennies and Hot Chocolate, 3890(F)
Lunch Money and Other Poems About School, 11695
Martian Rock, 1572(F)
Month by Month a Year Goes Round, 245(F)
Saturday Night at the Dinosaur Stomp, 2686(F)
Shields, Sue. *Chameleons Are Cool*, 18745
Shiffman, Lena. *Keeping a Christmas Secret*, 5889(F)
My First Book of Words, 14046(F)
When I Lived with Bats, 19029
Shih, Bernadette L. *Ling Ling*, 2687(F)
Shimin, Symeon. *Onion John*, 8735(F)
Zeely, 8682(F)
Shimizu, Kiyashi. *Carnivorous Plants*, 20253
Shimmen, Andrea (jt. author). *Australia*, 15242
Shine, Andrea. *Big Band Sound*, 3103(F)
Count Your Way Through France, 15309
Danger at the Breaker, 6712(F)
The Faraway Drawer, 3104(F)
Stradivari's Singing Violin, 9035(F)
The Summer My Father Was Ten, 3045(F)
Shine, Deborah S., ed. *Make a Joyful Sound*, 11767
Shipman, Ronnie W. *I'll Go to School If . . .*, 5500(F)
Shipton, Jonathan. *What If?* 1573(F)
Shipton, Paul. *The Mighty Skink*, 8091(F)
Shirley, David. *Alabama*, 16886
Gloria Estefan, 12384
Thomas Nast, 12273
Shirley, Jean (jt. author). *Frances Hodgson Burnett*, 12512
Robert Louis Stevenson, 12599
Shlichta, Joe. *Thirty-Three Multicultural Tales to Tell*, 10546
Shoemaker, Hurst H. (jt. author). *Fishes*, 19718
Shollar, Leah. *A Thread of Kindness*, 11169
Shone, Rob. *Professor Protein's Fitness, Health, Hygiene and Relaxation Tonic*, 18201
Shore, Judie. *Birdwise*, 19235
Shore, Nancy. *Spice Girls*, 12472
Short, Joan. *Platypus*, 18973
Whales, 19799
Shortall, Leonard. *The Bully of Barkham Street*, 8375(F)

Encyclopedia Brown, Boy Detective, 7075(F)
Mishmash, 7177(F)
Shortelle, Dennis (jt. author). *The Forgotten Players*, 22091
Shorto, Russell. *David Farragut and the Great Naval Blockade*, 12876
Jane Fonda, 12387
Shott, Stephen. *Sea Animals*, 5394
Shough, Carol Gandee. *All the Mamas*, 3891(F)
All the Papas, 3892(F)
Showers, Paul. *Hear Your Heart*, 18091
How Many Teeth? 18189
The Listening Walk, 3893(F)
Look at Your Eyes, 18162
Sleep Is for Everyone, 18118
What Happens to a Hamburger, 18105
Your Skin and Mine, 18180
Shrader, Christine N. *Gluskabe and the Four Wishes*, 11218
Shreve, Susan. *The Formerly Great Alexander Family*, 8522(F)
Ghost Cats, 8092(F)
Goodbye, Amanda the Good, 7512(F)
Jonah, the Whale, 8810(F)
Joshua T. Bates in Trouble Again, 10132(F)
Shropshire, Sandy. *The Buffalo Train Ride*, 18987
Shuck, Vicki. *If You're Missing Baby Jesus*, 9722(F)
Shue, Kenneth. *Hiawatha Passing*, 692(F)
Shui, Amy. *China*, 15082
Shulevitz, Uri. *Dawn*, 4542(F)
The Fool of the World and the Flying Ship, 11108
The Fools of Chelm and Their History, 11172
The Golden Goose, 10931
Hosni the Dreamer, 11182
Rain Rain Rivers, 4543(F)
The Secret Room, 10617
Snow, 3425(F)
The Strange and Exciting Adventures of Jeremiah Hash, 8093(F)
Toddlecreek Post Office, 3426(F)
The Treasure, 3894(F)
What Is a Wise Bird Like You Doing in a Silly Tale Like This? 1574(F)
Shulman, Janet. *The Nutcracker*, 10932(F)
Shupe, Bobbi. *Storytelling Adventures*, 14078
Storytelling for the Fun of It, 14079
Shura, Mary Francis. *Don't Call Me Toad!* 7055(F)
The Josie Gambit, 8368(F)
The Search for Grissi, 8811(F)
The Sunday Doll, 8812(F)

Shute, Linda. *How I Named the Baby*, 3895(F)
The Other Emily, 5494(F)
Princess Pooh, 3820(F)
We Adopted You, Benjamin Koo, 17654(F)
Shuter, Jane. *The Acropolis*, 14702
Ancient Egypt, 14664
The Ancient Egyptians, 14665
Builders, Traders and Craftsmen, 14703
Carisbrooke Castle, 15364
Cities and Citizens, 14704
Discoveries, Inventions and Ideas, 14705
Egypt, 14666
Farmers and Fighters, 14706
Mesa Verde, 16040
The Middle Ages, 14792
The Renaissance, 14804
Shuter, Jane, ed. *Charles Ball and American Slavery*, 16273
Christabel Bielenberg and Nazi Germany, 15331
Francis Parkman and the Plains Indians, 16369
Helen Williams and the French Revolution, 15317
Sarah Royce and the American West, 16370
Shyer, Marlene Fanta. *Welcome Home, Jellybean*, 8913(F)
Sibbald, Jean H. *The Manatee*, 19744
Strange Eating Habits of Sea Creatures, 19648
Sibbick, John. *Gods and Pharaohs from Egyptian Mythology*, 11447
Heroes, Gods and Emperors from Roman Mythology, 11512
Sibley, Norman. *Sun and Moon*, 10736
Siddals, Mary M. *I'll Play With You*, 1575(F)
Millions of Snowflakes, 3427(F)
Tell Me a Season, 4544(F)
Sidjakov, Nicholas. *Baboushka and the Three Kings*, 11110
Sidman, Joyce. *Just Us Two*, 11982
Sidney, Margaret. *The Five Little Peppers and How They Grew*, 7513(F)
Siebel, Fritz. *Amelia Bedelia*, 6561(F)
Stop That Ball! 6482(F)
Tell Me Some More, 6214(F)
Who Took the Farmer's Hat? 6545(F)
Siebert, Diane. *Cave*, 20392
Heartland, 11696
Mississippi, 15904
Mojave, 11983
Train Song, 5599(F)
Truck Song, 5600(F)
Siebert, Patricia. *Discovering El Nino*, 20786
Siebold, Jan. *Rope Burn*, 8523(F)

Siegel, Alice. *The Blackbirch Kid's Almanac of Geography*, 14357

Siegel, Beatrice. *Indians of the Northeast Woodlands*, 16041

Siegel, Bruce H. *Coming of Age*, 9990(F)

The Magic of Kol Nidre, 17487

Siegel, Danny. *Tell Me a Mitzvah*, 17155

Siegel, Dorothy S. *Ann Richards*, 13176

Siegelson, Kim L. *Escape South*, 9320(F)

In the Time of the Drums, 9321(F)

Siegen-Smith, Nikki, comp. *A Pocketful of Stars*, 777

Siegrist, Wes. *Realm of the Panther*, 19082

Sierra, F. John. *My Mexico/México Mío*, 11612

Sierra, Judy. *Antarctic Antics*, 11812

The Beautiful Butterfly, 11139

Counting Crocodiles, 2688(F)

The Dancing Pig, 10851

The Gift of the Crocodile, 10502(F)

Good Night Dinosaurs, 2689(F)

The House That Drac Built, 6049(F)

Tasty Baby Belly Buttons, 10829

There's a Zoo in Room 22, 133(F)

Sierra, Judy, ed. *Nursery Tales Around the World*, 10618

Sieveking, Anthea. *Eye Spy Colors*, 282(F)

My Day, 3300(F)

Silbaugh, Elizabeth. *Let's Play Cards!* 22238

Sill, Cathryn. *About Birds*, 19282

About Insects, 19489

About Mammals, 18974

About Reptiles, 18694

Sill, John. *About Birds*, 19282

About Insects, 19489

About Mammals, 18974

About Reptiles, 18694

Sills, Leslie. *Inspirations*, 12182

Visions, 12183

Silox-Jarrett, Diane. *Heroines of the American Revolution*, 16214

Silsbe, Brenda. *Just One More Color*, 4545(F)

Silva, Simon. *La Mariposa*, 4989(F)

Silver, Donald M. *Extinction Is Forever*, 18668

Why Save the Rain Forest? 20488

Silver, Patricia. *Face Painting*, 21592

Silver, Stan. *Cal Ripken, Jr.*, 13482

Silveria, Gordon. *The Greedy Triangle*, 1029(F)

Silverman, Erica. *Big Pumpkin*, 1576(F)

Don't Fidget a Feather! 2690(F)

Fixing the Crack of Dawn, 3428(F)

Follow the Leader, 3429(F)

Gittel's Hands, 1577(F)

The Halloween House, 6050(F)

Mrs. Peachtree's Bicycle, 4316(F)

On the Morn of Mayfest, 1578(F)

Raisel's Riddle, 11170

Silverman, Jerry. *Children's Songs*, 14179

Singing Our Way West, 14180

Silverman, Maida. *Israel*, 15530

Silverman, Robin L. *A Bosnian Family*, 17594

Silverstein, Alvin. *Allergies*, 17998

The Black-Footed Ferret, 18975

The California Condor, 19341

The Circulatory System, 18092

Clocks and Rhythms, 20652

Common Colds, 17999

Cuts, Scrapes, Scabs, Scars, 18181

Different Dogs, 19971

The Digestive System, 18106

Dogs, 19972

Eat Your Vegetables! Drink Your Milk! 18210

Energy, 20838

The Excretory System, 18107

Fats, 20168

The Florida Panther, 19109

Fungi, 20191

The Grizzly Bear, 19066

Invertebrates, 19621

Is That a Rash? 18182

Life in a Tidal Pool, 19867

Lyme Disease, 18000

The Manatee, 19745

Monerans and Protists, 19811

The Muscular System, 18173

The Mustang, 20015

The Nervous System, 18119

The Peregrine Falcon, 19342

A Pet or Not? 19905

Photosynthesis, 20033

Plants, 20264

Plate Tectonics, 20322

Pocket Pets, 19907

The Red Wolf, 19139

The Reproductive System, 18247

The Respiratory System, 18127

The Sea Otter, 19746

Sickle Cell Anemia, 18001

The Skeletal System, 18174

Sleep, 18227

Snakes and Such, 19906

Sore Throats and Tonsillitis, 18002

The Spotted Owl, 19365

Staying Safe, 18226

Symbiosis, 18599

Tooth Decay and Cavities, 18190

Vertebrates, 18669

Weather and Climate, 20787

Silverstein, Herma. *The Alamo*, 16274

Yearbooks in Science: 1990 and Beyond, 18291

Silverstein, Shel. *Falling Up*, 11697

Lafcadio, the Lion Who Shot Back, 7306(F)

Where the Sidewalk Ends, 11698

Who Wants a Cheap Rhinoceros? 2691(F)

Silverstein, Virginia (jt. author). *Different Dogs*, 19971

Dogs, 19972

Life in a Tidal Pool, 19867

Photosynthesis, 20033

Pocket Pets, 19907

Symbiosis, 18599

Silverstone, Michael. *Rigoberta Menchu*, 15684

Sim, Dorrith M. *In My Pocket*, 9689(F)

Simison, D. J. *Book of the American Civil War*, 16404

Simmonds, Nicola. *The Making of My Special Hand*, 17914

Rolling Along, 17915

Simmons, Alex. *Denzel Washington*, 12480

John Lucas, 13547

Simmons, Elly. *Calling the Doves/El Canto de las Palomas*, 12548

Magic Dogs of the Volcanoes, 957(F)

Simmons, Jane. *Come Along, Daisy!* 2692(F)

Daisy and the Beastie, 2693(F)

Daisy and the Egg, 2694(F)

Daisy Says Coo! 2695(F)

Daisy's Favorite Things, 2696(F)

Ebb and Flo and the Greedy Gulls, 5413(F)

Ebb and Flo and the New Friend, 2697(F)

Simmons, Richard. *The Young Golfer*, 22063

Simmons, Steven J. *Percy to the Rescue*, 2698(F)

Simms, Laura. *The Bone Man*, 11300

Rotten Teeth, 4317(F)

Simon, Carly. *Midnight Farm*, 1579(F)

Simon, Charnan. *Brigham Young*, 12970

Chester A. Arthur, 13007

Come! Sit! Speak! 6659(F)

Franklin Pierce, 13090

Hollywood at War, 14879

I Like to Win! 6660(F)

Martha Dandridge Curtis Washington, 13199

Molly Brown, 12863

Mud! 6661(F)

One Happy Classroom, 581(F)

Walt Disney, 12229

Simon, Francesca. *Calling All Toddlers*, 246(F)

Hugo and the Bully Frogs, 2699(F)

Toddler Time, 11699

Where Are You? 2700(F)

Simon, Norma. *All Kinds of Children*, 4831

All Kinds of Families, 17685

Fire Fighters, 5414(F)

How Do I Feel? 7514(F)

I Am Not a Crybaby, 5077(F)

I Was So Mad! 5078(F)

I Wish I Had My Father, 5079(F)

I'm Busy, Too, 5540(F)

Oh, That Cat! 5415(F)

The Saddest Time, 17732

The Story of Hanukkah, 6117

Wet World, 3430(F)

Simon, Seymour. *Animals Nobody Loves,* 18670

Big Cats, 19110

Bones, 18175

The Brain, 18120

Comets, Meteors, and Asteroids, 18527

Crocodiles and Alligators, 18709

Destination, 18488, 18489

The Dinosaur Is the Biggest Animal That Ever Lived, 18292

From Paper Airplanes to Outer Space, 12596

Galaxies, 18555

Gorillas, 19016

The Heart, 18093

How to Be an Ocean Scientist in Your Own Home, 18348

Jupiter, 18490

Lightning, 20717

Mars, 18491

The Moon, 18453

Muscles, 18176

Neptune, 18492

New Questions and Answers About Dinosaurs, 14471

Now You See It, Now You Don't, 20916

The On-Line Spaceman and Other Cases, 7056(F)

The Optical Illusion Book, 20917

Our Solar System, 18528

Out of Sight, 18293

The Paper Airplane Book, 21796

Pets in a Jar, 19908

Ride the Wind, 18671

Saturn, 18493

Seymour Simon's Book of Trucks, 21319

Sharks, 19768

Spring Across America, 18572

The Stars, 18556

Storms, 20718

Strange Mysteries from Around the World, 21952

The Sun, 18573

They Swim the Seas, 18851

They Walk the Earth, 18852

Tornadoes, 20719

The Universe, 18416

Uranus, 18494

Volcanoes, 20348

Weather, 20788

Simon, Seymour, ed. *Star Walk,* 11700

Simonds, Christopher. *The Model T Ford,* 21320

Samuel Slater's Mill and the Industrial Revolution, 16275

Simonds, Patricia. *The Founding of the AFL and the Rise of Organized Labor,* 16483

Simons, Jamie. *Goners,* 10236(F), 10237(F)

Simons, Robin. *Recyclopedia,* 21496

Simont, Marc. *Ant Plays Bear,* 6244(F)

The Elephant Who Couldn't Forget, 2453(F)

The Goose That Almost Got Cooked, 2701(F)

How to Dig a Hole to the Other Side of the World, 20313

In the Year of the Boar and Jackie Robinson, 7352(F)

Many Moons, 10511(F)

My Brother, Ant, 6247(F)

Nate the Great, 6647(F)

Nate the Great and Me, 6648(F)

Nate the Great and the Fishy Prize, 6649(F)

Nate the Great and the Tardy Tortoise, 6652(F)

Nate the Great Saves the King of Sweden, 6651(F)

No More Monsters for Me! 6565(F)

The Philharmonic Gets Dressed, 3270(F)

The Stray Dog, 5416(F)

Top Secret, 9858(F)

A Tree Is Nice, 4556(F)

Volcanoes, 20335

What Happened to the Dinosaurs? 14388

Simpson, Carolyn. *Coping with Asthma,* 18003

Everything You Need to Know About Asthma, 18004

Simpson, Judith. *Mighty Dinosaurs,* 14472

Simpson, Judith, ed. *Ancient China,* 15083

Sims, Blanche. *The Beast in Ms. Rooney's Room,* 6342(F)

Drugs and Our World, 17893

Eddie, Incorporated, 8774(F)

Garbage Juice for Breakfast, 6343(F)

I Took My Frog to the Library, 4203(F)

In the Dinosaur's Paw, 6345(F)

Next Stop, New York City! 6346(F)

The Powder Puff Puzzle, 6347(F)

Purple Climbing Days, 6348(F)

Soccer Sam, 6510(F)

Sunny-Side Up, 6349(F)

Where Are the Stars During the Day? 18539

Sims, J. Michael. *Young Claus,* 8094(F)

Sincic, Alan. *Edward Is Only a Fish,* 8095(F)

Sinclair, Jeff. *Mathamusements,* 20612

Sing, Rachel. *Chinese New Year's Dragon,* 7371(F)

Singer, Beverly R. (jt. author). *Rising Voices,* 9163(F)

Singer, Bill. *The Fox with Cold Feet,* 6662(F)

Singer, Isaac Bashevis. *A Day of Pleasure,* 12597

Elijah the Slave, 11171

The Fools of Chelm and Their History, 11172

The Power of Light, 9761(F)

Stories for Children, 11173

When Shlemiel Went to Warsaw and Other Stories, 11174

Zlateh the Goat and Other Stories, 11175

Singer, Marilyn. *All We Needed to Say,* 11701

Bottoms Up! 18853

The Circus Lunicus, 8096(F)

A Dog's Gotta Do What a Dog's Gotta Do, 19973

Family Reunion, 11702

Good Day, Good Night, 5417(F)

In the Palace of the Ocean King, 10503(F)

Josie to the Rescue, 9991(F)

The Maiden on the Moor, 11035

On the Same Day in March, 20789

The One and Only Me, 3896(F)

Prairie Dogs Kiss and Lobsters Wave, 18854

Sky Words, 11984

Solomon Sneezes, 6663(F)

Turtle in July, 11813

A Wasp Is Not a Bee, 18672

Singer, Paula. *David Decides About Thumbsucking,* 4977(F)

Singh, Rina. *The Foolish Men of Agra,* 10807

Moon Tales, 10619

Sinnott, Susan. *Charley Waters Goes to Gettysburg,* 16430

Doing Our Part, 14880

Our Burden of Shame, 14881

Sarah Childress Polk, 1803–1891, 13175

Welcome to Addy's World, 1864, 16431

Welcome to Kirsten's World, 1854, 16371

Sinykin, Sheri C. *A Matter of Time,* 8097(F)

Siomades, Lorianne. *The Itsy Bitsy Spider,* 14181(F)

Kangaroo and Cricket, 247(F)

My Box of Color, 291(F)

A Place to Bloom, 3431(F)

Three Little Kittens, 891(F)

Siomades, Lorianne, ed. *Look What You Can Make With Boxes,* 21630

Sioras, Efstathia. *Greece,* 15390

Sipiera, Diane M. *Constellations,* 18557

The Hubble Space Telescope, 18417

Project Apollo, 21008

Project Mercury, 21009

Space Stations, 21010

Sipiera, Paul P. *Comets and Meteor Showers*, 18529
Gerald Ford, 13034
The Solar System, 18530
Sipiera, Paul P. (jt. author). *Constellations*, 18557
The Hubble Space Telescope, 18417
Project Apollo, 21008
Project Mercury, 21009
Space Stations, 21010
Siracusa, Catherine. *No Mail for Mitchell*, 6664(F)
Sirett, Dawn. *My First Paint Book*, 21593
Sirimarco, Elizabeth. *At the Bank*, 16950
Sirvaitis, Karen. *Florida*, 16887
Michigan, 16583
Tennessee, 16888
Utah, 16637
Virginia, 16889
Sis, Peter. *Alphabet Soup*, 977(F)
Dinosaur! 932(F)
The Dragons Are Singing Tonight, 11808
Fire Truck, 1580(F)
The Gargoyle on the Roof, 11675
Halloween, 9708(F)
Komodo! 5418(F)
Madlenka, 1581(F)
The Midnight Horse, 7726(F)
Monday's Troll, 11676
The Scarebird, 3145(F)
Ship Ahoy! 933(F)
Sleep Safe, Little Whale, 775(F)
Starry Messenger, 13292
Stories to Solve, 10613
Trucks Trucks Trucks, 5601(F)
Waving, 582(F)
Sisulu, Elinor B. *The Day Gogo Went to Vote*, 4832(F)
Sita, Lisa. *Coming of Age*, 17400
Indians of the Great Plains, 16042
Indians of the Southwest, 16043
Worlds of Belief, 17220
Sivertson, Liz. *North Country Spring*, 4485(F)
Siy, Alexandra. *The Eeyou*, 16044
Footprints on the Moon, 18454
The Great Astrolabe Reef, 19667
The Waorani, 15787
Skarmeta, Antonio. *The Composition*, 9139(F)
Skerry, Brian. *A Whale on Her Own*, 19800
Skiles, Janet. *The Birth of a Whale*, 5119
Skira-Venturi, Rosabianca. *A Weekend with Degas*, 12221
Skofield, James. *Detective Dinosaur*, 6665(F)
Detective Dinosaur Lost and Found, 6666(F)
Skolsky, Mindy W. *Hannah and the Whistling Teakettle*, 2972(F)

Love from Your Friend, Hannah, 9626(F)
Skorpen, Liesel Moak. *We Were Tired of Living in a House*, 3432(F)
Skrepcinski, Denice. *Cody Coyote Cooks!* 21738
Skudder, Hyla. *Whose Tracks Are These?* 18839
Skurzynski, Gloria. *Almost the Real Things*, 21056
Cliff-Hanger, 7058(F)
Deadly Waters, 7059(F)
Discover Mars, 18495
Get the Message, 21263
Ghost Horses, 7060(F)
Good-bye, Billy Radish, 8369(F)
The Hunted, 7061(F)
Know the Score, 22239
Lost in the Devil's Desert, 7057(F)
The Minstrel in the Tower, 9071(F)
On Time, 20653
Rage of Fire, 7062(F)
Robots, 21225
Waves, 20903
Wolf Stalker, 7063(F)
Zero Gravity, 20815
Slade, Arthur G. *The Haunting of Drang Island*, 8098(F)
Slaight, Craig, ed. *Great Scenes and Monologues for Children*, 14325
Slangerup, Erik Jon. *Dirt Boy*, 1582(F)
Slate, Joseph. *Crossing the Trestle*, 8524(F)
Miss Bindergarten Celebrates the 100th Day of Kindergarten, 248(F)
Miss Bindergarten Stays Home from Kindergarten, 5541(F)
The Secret Stars, 5920(F)
Story Time for Little Porcupine, 2702(F)
Slater, Teddy. *Stay in Line*, 583(F)
Slattery, Zara. *Dark as a Midnight Dream*, 11733
Slaughter, Hope. *Buckley and Wilberta*, 6667(F)
A Cozy Place, 4044(F)
Slavin, Bill. *Adventures in the Middle Ages*, 7577(F)
The Bone Talker, 1342(F)
How the Second Grade Got $8,205.50 to Visit the Statue of Liberty, 4368(F)
The Hunchback of Notre Dame, 9045(F)
The Moon, 18441
Sitting on the Farm, 2292(F)
Too Many Chickens! 4091(F)
Slavin, Ed. *Jimmy Carter*, 13018
Slawski, Wolfgang. *Harry's Got a Girlfriend!* 6635(F)
Sleator, William. *The Beasties*, 8099(F)
Boltzmon! 10238(F)
The Boxes, 8100(F)

Rewind, 8101(F)
Slepian, Jan. *Back to Before*, 8102(F)
The Broccoli Tapes, 7515(F)
Emily Just in Time, 5080(F)
Lost Moose, 5419(F)
The Mind Reader, 8813(F)
Slier, Deborah. *Farm Animals*, 5420(F)
Hello Baby, 3897(F)
Sloan, Christopher. *Feathered Dinosaurs*, 14473
Sloan, Frank. *Titanic*, 21378
Sloat, Robert (jt. author). *Rib-Ticklers*, 21852
Sloat, Teri. *Dance on a Sealskin*, 4885(F)
Farmer Brown Goes Round and Round, 1583(F)
Farmer Brown Shears His Sheep, 1584(F)
Patty's Pumpkin Patch, 134(F)
Rib-Ticklers, 21852
There Was an Old Lady Who Swallowed a Trout! 14182
The Thing That Bothered Farmer Brown, 4318(F)
Slobodkin, Louis. *The Hundred Dresses*, 10054(F)
Slobodkina, Esphyr. *Caps for Sale*, 4319(F)
Slonim, David. *The Flying Flea, Callie, and Me*, 8185(F)
Moishe's Miracle, 6096(F)
Old Jake's Skirts, 3416(F)
Slotboom, Wendy. *King Snake*, 2703(F)
Slote, Alfred. *Finding Buck McHenry*, 10362(F)
Hang Tough, Paul Mather, 8914(F)
My Robot Buddy, 10239(F)
Slovenz-Low, Madeline (jt. author). *Lion Dancer*, 5656
Small, David. *As*, 14038
The Christmas Crocodile, 5754(F)
Fenwick's Suit, 8103(F)
The Gardener, 4841(F)
George Washington's Cows, 8104(F)
The Huckabuck Family and How They Raised Popcorn in Nebraska and Quit and Came Back, 3872(F)
Imogene's Antlers, 1585(F)
The Journey, 7521(F)
The Library, 3443(F)
The Money Tree, 1596(F)
Paper John, 1586(F)
Petey's Bedtime Story, 650(F)
So You Want to Be President? 17120
Smalls, Irene. *Because You're Lucky*, 5081(F)
Dawn and the Round To-It, 3898(F)
Irene Jennie and the Christmas Masquerade, 4833(F)

Jenny Reen and the Jack Muh Lantern, 6051(F)
Kevin and His Dad, 3899(F)
A Strawbeater's Thanksgiving, 4834(F)
Smart, Paul. *Everything You Need to Know About Mononucleosis*, 18005
Smath, Jerry. *Double-Header*, 6379(F)
Lights Out! 553(F)
Pretzel and Pop's Closetful of Stories, 6668(F)
Smee, Nicola. *The Tusk Fairy*, 1587(F)
Smith, A. G. *Where Am I? The Story of Maps and Navigation*, 14370
Smith, Adam. *A Historical Album of Kentucky*, 16890
Smith, Alastair (jt. author). *The Usborne Complete Book of Astronomy and Space*, 18400
Smith, Alvin. *Shadow of a Bull*, 8864(F)
Smith, Ardeane Heiskell. *Bugs and Critters I Have Known*, 11980
Smith, Barry. *Grandma Rabbitty's Visit*, 2704(F)
Smith, Betsy. *Jimmy Carter, President*, 13019
Smith, Carter. *The Jamestown Colony*, 16174
The Korean War, 16519
Smith, Carter, ed. *The Arts and Sciences*, 16172
Behind the Lines, 16432
Daily Life, 16173
1863, 16433
The First Battles, 16434
The Founding Presidents, 16276
Presidents in a Time of Change, 16520
Presidents of a Growing Country, 16484
Presidents of a World Power, 16485
Presidents of a Young Republic, 16277
Smith, Carter, III (jt. author). *A Historical Album of New York*, 16651
Smith, Cat B. *Angel and Me and the Bayside Bombers*, 10272(F)
Bedtime! 790
Boom Town, 4731(F)
Dave's Down-to-Earth Rock Shop, 20566
Feliciana Feydra LeRoux, 2978(F)
Feliciana Meets d'Loup Garou, 1621(F)
General Butterfingers, 6850(F)
The Loudest, Fastest, Best Drummer in Kansas, 1103(F)
The Monsters of Marble Avenue, 9862(F)
Peter's Trucks, 5607(F)
Taking Charge, 4732(F)

Smith, Charles R. *Rimshots*, 12003
Short Takes, 12004
Tall Tales, 10363(F)
Smith, Charles R., Jr. *Brown Sugar Babies*, 3433(F)
Smith, Craig. *Yay!* 4284(F)
Smith, Cynthia Leitich. *Jingle Dancer*, 3434(F)
Smith, Dede. *A Bookworm Who Hatched*, 12487
Smith, Dodie. *The Hundred and One Dalmatians*, 8105(F)
Smith, Doris Buchanan. *A Taste of Blackberries*, 8814(F)
Smith, E. Boyd. *The Farm Book*, 20072
The Railroad Book, 21342
Smith, E. S. *Bear Bryant*, 13604
Smith, Elizabeth Simpson. *Cloth*, 21184
Coming Out Right, 12089
Paper, 21057
Smith, Elva (jt. author). *The Year Around*, 11956
Smith, George. *Pawprints in Time*, 4614(F)
Smith, J. Gerard. *Popcorn Park Zoo*, 20029
Smith, Jane D. *Charlie Is a Chicken*, 8370(F)
Smith, Janice Lee. *The Monster in the Third Dresser Drawer and Other Stories About Adam Joshua*, 7516(F)
Wizard and Wart at Sea, 6669(F)
Wizard and Wart in Trouble, 6670(F)
Smith, Jessie Willcox. *At the Back of the North Wind*, 7935(F)
The Princess and the Goblin, 10457(F)
Smith, John. *You Can Learn Sign Language!* 14016
Smith, Joseph A. *Be Well, Beware*, 7204(F)
Benjamin Bigfoot, 5538(F)
Chipmunk! 5241(F)
Clay Boy, 11088
A Creepy Countdown, 470(F)
Danny and the Kings, 5789(F)
Elwood and the Witch, 2191(F)
How Do You Spell God? 17188
Hurry! 3188(F)
Jim Ugly, 9365(F)
Matthew's Dragon, 652(F)
"Mine Will," Said John, 5235(F)
Mowing, 5242(F)
No Foal Yet, 5243(F)
Ogres! Ogres! Ogres! A Feasting Frenzy from A to Z, 51(F)
Starshine and Sunglow, 8333(F)
Sugaring, 4450(F)
Smith, Juliet Stanwell. *The Rocking Horse Secret*, 6862(F)
Smith, K. C. *Ancient Shipwrecks*, 14594
Exploring for Shipwrecks, 14540

Shipwrecks of the Explorers, 14541
Smith, Katherine S. (jt. author). *A Historical Album of Kentucky*, 16890
Smith, Kathie Billingslea. *Thinking*, 18121
Smith, Kathryn M. *All My Feelings at Preschool*, 5490(F)
Smith, L. J. *Heart of Valor*, 8106(F)
Smith, Lane. *Disney's James and the Giant Peach*, 1312(F)
Glasses, 9992(F)
The Good, the Bad and the Goofy, 1552(F)
The Happy Hocky Family, 1588(F)
Hooray for Diffendoofer Day! 4309(F)
James and the Giant Peach, 7696(F)
Knights of the Kitchen Table, 7047(F)
Math Curse, 5535(F)
Squids Will Be Squids, 9986(F)
The Stinky Cheese Man, 4305(F)
Summer Reading Is Killing Me, 8073(F)
Tut, Tut, 8074(F)
Smith, Lawrence Beall. *Rebecca of Sunnybrook Farm*, 7536(F)
Smith, Linda W. *Louis Pasteur*, 13340
Smith, Maggie. *Achoo! All About Colds*, 17952
Counting Our Way to Maine, 584(F)
Dear Daisy, Get Well Soon, 2705(F)
Desser the Best Ever Cat, 5421(F)
Everything to Spend the Night, 111(F)
Ferryboat Ride! 3382(F)
Good Thing You're Not an Octopus! 1395(F)
This Is Your Garden, 21773
Smith, Marisa, ed. *The Seattle Children's Theatre*, 12036
Smith, Mark. *Pay Attention, Slosh!* 8915(F)
Smith, Mavis. *Follow That Trash!* 16980
Mind Your Manners, Ben Bunny, 17639
Stars, 18544
You Can't Smell a Flower with Your Ear! 18140
Smith, Miranda. *Living Earth*, 18600
Smith, Nigel. *The Houses of Parliament*, 15365
Smith, Patricia C. (jt. author). *As Long As the Rivers Flow*, 12634
Smith, Patrick Clark (jt. author). *On the Trail of Elder Brother*, 11296
Smith, Pohla. *Superstars of Women's Figure Skating*, 13411
Smith, Robert K. *Chocolate Fever*, 9993(F)

Jelly Belly, 8815(F)

The War with Grandpa, 7517(F)

Smith, Roland. *African Elephants*, 19172

The Captain's Dog, 9440(F)

Cats in the Zoo, 19111

In the Forest with the Elephants, 15205

Jaguar, 7064(F)

Journey of the Red Wolf, 19140

The Last Lobo, 7065(F)

Sasquatch, 7066(F)

Vultures, 19283

Smith, Rosie (jt. author). *Captain Pajamas*, 4350(F)

Whatley's Quest, 7126

Smith, Sally J. *Dragon Soup*, 1686(F)

Grandfather Four Winds and Rising Moon, 9150(F)

Smith, Sherwood. *Court Duel*, 8107(F)

Crown Duel, 8108(F)

Wren's War, 8109(F)

Smith, Stephen J. *Shy Vi*, 2370(F)

Smith, Susan M. *The Booford Summer*, 7307(F)

Smith, Theresa. *The Story Snail*, 6594(F)

Zzzng! Zzzng! Zzzng! A Yoruba Tale, 10667

Smith, Tony. *Jigsaw*, 1424(F)

Smith, Wendy. *The Blood-and-Thunder Adventure on Hurricane Peak*, 7946(F)

The Giant Postman, 6359(F)

Making Friends, 5336(F)

Tick Tock Tales, 1389(F)

Smith, William J. *Around My Room*, 11916

Here Is My Heart, 11704

Laughing Time, 11917

Smith, William J., comp. *The Sun Is Up*, 11985

Smith-Baranzini, Marlene. *Brown Paper School USKids History*, 16278

Smith-Baranzini, Marlene (jt. author). *Book of the American Civil War*, 16404

US Kids History, 16114

Smith-Moore, J. J. *Honor the Flag*, 13973

Smolinski, Dick. *Bill Bowerman and Phil Knight*, 21171

Smothers, Ethel Footman. *Moriah's Pond*, 7372(F)

Smucker, Barbara. *Runaway to Freedom*, 9322(F)

Smyth, Iain (jt. author). *Old MacDonald Had a Farm*, 14147

Smyth, Ian. *The Young Baseball Player*, 22117

Smyth, Karen C. *Crystal*, 19801

Smythe, Anne. *Islands*, 3900(F)

Snape, Charles. *Frog Odyssey*, 2706(F)

Snape, Juliet. *Frog Odyssey*, 2706(F)

Snedden, Robert. *Medical Ethics*, 18027

Technology in the Time of Ancient Rome, 14745

Yuck! 19812

Sneed, Brad. *The Bravest of Us All*, 2906(F)

Higgins Bend Song and Dance, 1397(F)

The Pumpkin Runner, 4579(F)

The Strange and Wonderful Tale of Robert McDoodle, 4084(F)

Watch Out for Bears! The Adventures of Henry and Bruno, 6722(F)

Snelson, Karin. *Seattle*, 16815

Sneve, Virginia Driving Hawk. *The Apaches*, 16045

The Cherokees, 16046

The Cheyennes, 16047

The Hopis, 16048

The Iroquois, 16049

The Navajos, 16050

The Nez Perce, 16051

The Seminoles, 16052

The Sioux, 16053

The Trickster and the Troll, 8110(F)

Sneve, Virginia Driving Hawk, ed. *Dancing Teepees*, 11931

Snicket, Lemony. *The Austere Academy*, 9123(F)

The Bad Beginning, 7067(F)

The Miserable Mill, 7068(F)

The Wide Window, 7069(F)

Snider, Jackie. *Secret Pal Surprises*, 4062(F)

Snihura, Ulana. *I Miss Franklin P. Shuckles*, 4045(F)

Snodgrass, Mary Ellen. *Acid Rain*, 17004

Air Pollution, 17005

Solid Waste, 16986

Snow, Alan. *Stories from Hans Christian Andersen*, 10389

The Truth About Cats, 2707(F)

Snow, Pegeen. *Atlanta*, 16891

Snyder, Carol. *God Must Like Cookies, Too*, 6118(F)

One Up, One Down, 3901(F)

Snyder, Dianne. *The Boy of the Three-Year Nap*, 10830

Snyder, Joel. *Discovering Electricity*, 20883

Story of Dinosaurs, 14409

Snyder, Zilpha Keatley. *Cat Running*, 8525(F)

The Diamond War, 8816(F)

The Egypt Game, 8371(F)

Gib and the Gray Ghost, 9627(F)

Gib Rides Home, 9628(F)

The Gypsy Game, 8372(F)

The Headless Cupid, 7070(F)

The Runaways, 8817(F)

The Trespassers, 8111(F)

The Witches of Worm, 8916(F)

So, Meilo. *The Beauty of the Beast*, 11807

The Emperor and the Nightingale, 10377(F)

It's Simple, Said Simon, 1244(F)

The Tale of the Heaven Tree, 1282(F)

Tasty Baby Belly Buttons, 10829

Wishbones, 10773

Sobat, Vera. *Little Bear and the Big Fight*, 2336(F)

Little Bear Brushes His Teeth, 2337(F)

Little Bear Is a Big Brother, 2338(F)

Sobel, Ileene Smith. *Moses and the Angels*, 17322

Sobey, Ed. *Car Smarts*, 18349

Wrapper Rockets and Trombone Straws, 18350

Sobol, Donald J. *Encyclopedia Brown and the Case of the Disgusting Sneakers*, 7071(F)

Encyclopedia Brown and the Case of the Mysterious Handprints, 7072(F)

Encyclopedia Brown and the Case of the Sleeping Dog, 7073(F)

Encyclopedia Brown and the Case of the Slippery Salamander, 7074(F)

Encyclopedia Brown, Boy Detective, 7075(F)

Encyclopedia Brown's Book of Wacky Sports, 22064

My Name Is Amelia, 10240(F)

Socias, Marcel. *How Our Blood Circulates*, 18089

Soentpiet, Chris K. *Around Town*, 3435

Coolies, 4895(F)

Jin Woo, 3555(F)

The Last Dragon, 3345(F)

Molly Bannaky, 12848

Momma, Where Are You From? 4602(F)

More Than Anything Else, 4603(F)

Peacebound Trains, 8984(F)

A Sign, 17776

The Silence in the Mountains, 3862(F)

Silver Packages, 5914(F)

So Far from the Sea, 4611(F)

Something Beautiful, 3490(F)

Where Is Grandpa? 4903(F)

Sogabe, Aki. *Aesop's Fox*, 11076

The Loyal Cat, 4777(F)

Oranges on Golden Mountain, 4794(F)

Sogabe, Aki, reteller. *Aesop's Fox*, 11076

Sohi, Morteza E. *Look What I Did with a Leaf!* 21497

Look What I Did with a Shell! 21498

Soinale, Laura. *Sojourner Truth*, 12794

Sokol, Bill. *Time Cat*, 7554(F)
Sola, Michele. *Angela Weaves a Dream*, 15685
Solbert, Ronni. *Bronzeville Boys and Girls*, 11749
  The Pushcart War, 9936(F)
Solga, Kim. *Art Fun!* 21595
  Craft Fun! 21499
  Draw! 21594
  Make Cards! 21631
  Make Clothes Fun, 21551
  Make Sculptures! 21535
Solheim, James. *It's Disgusting — and We Ate It! True Food Facts from Around the World — and Throughout History!* 20045
Solomon, Dane. *Fishing*, 22178
Solomon, Debra. *How Come Planet Earth?* 18297
Soman, David. *The Aunt in Our House*, 3722(F)
  Great-grandmother's Treasure, 7449(F)
  The Leaving Morning, 3247(F)
  Mommy's Office, 3198(F)
  One More Time, Mama, 3505(F)
  One of Three, 3725(F)
  Only One Cowry, 10666
  Tell Me a Story, Mama, 3726(F)
  This Is the Bird, 3887(F)
  The Wedding, 3727(F)
  When I Am Old with You, 3728(F)
  You're Not My Best Friend Anymore, 4035(F)
Somary, Wolfgang. *Night and the Candlemaker*, 8112(F)
Somdahl, Gary L. *Marijuana Drug Dangers*, 17890
Somerlott, Robert. *The Lincoln Assassination in American History*, 16435
Somerville, Charles C. *Bubble Monster*, 18311
Somerville, Louisa. *Rescue Vehicles*, 21321
Sommerdorf, Norma. *An Elm Tree and Three Sisters*, 4546(F)
Sonenklar, Carol. *Bug Boy*, 8113(F)
  Bug Girl, 8114(F)
  Mighty Boy, 8818(F)
  My Own Worst Enemy, 8819(F)
  Robots Rising, 21226
Sonneborn, Liz. *The Cheyenne Indians*, 16054
  The New York Public Library Amazing Native American History, 16055
Soper, Patrick. *Jolie Blonde and the Three Heberts*, 10959
  Les Trois Cochons, 10960
Sorel, Edward. *Johnny on the Spot*, 1589(F)
  The Saturday Kid, 4835(F)
Sorensen, Henri. *A Book About God*, 17183
  Daddy Played Music for the Cows, 3471(F)

Footprints and Shadows, 3107(F)
  Hurricane! 4744(F)
  I Love You As Much . . ., 743(F)
  Jumbo's Lullaby, 744(F)
  My Grandfather's House, 4935(F)
  Robert Frost, 11693
Sorensen, Virginia. *Miracles on Maple Hill*, 7518(F)
  Plain Girl, 8820(F)
Sorra, Kristin. *Venola in Love*, 10014(F)
Soto, Gary. *Big Bushy Mustache*, 3902(F)
  Canto Familiar, 11707
  The Cat's Meow, 8115(F)
  Chato and the Party Animals, 5724(F)
  Chato's Kitchen, 2708(F)
  Crazy Weekend, 7076(F)
  Local News, 7373(F)
  Neighborhood Odes, 11708
  Novio Boy, 12037
  The Old Man and His Door, 4836(F)
  Petty Crimes, 7374(F)
  The Pool Party, 8821(F)
  Snapshots from the Wedding, 3436(F)
  Summer on Wheels, 9994(F)
  Taking Sides, 7375(F)
  Too Many Tamales, 5921(F)
Soto, Gloria (jt. author). *Life Around the Lake*, 15641
Soto, Michael (jt. author). *Everything You Need to Know About the Dangers of Computer Hacking*, 21213
Sotzek, Hannelore. *A Koala Is Not a Bear!* 19181
Soucie, Gary. *What's the Difference Between . . . Lenses and Prisms and Other Scientific Things?* 21058
Souhami, Jessica. *The Black Geese*, 11101
  No Dinner! The Story of the Old Woman and the Pumpkin, 10843
  Old MacDonald, 14183
  Rama and the Demon King, 10808
Southern, Randy. *Ruled Out*, 8943(F)
Southwell, Jandelyn. *The Little Country Town*, 778(F)
Souza, D. M. *Catch Me If You Can*, 18750
  Eight Legs, 19595
  Frogs, Frogs Everywhere, 18738
  Hurricanes, 20720
  Insects Around the House, 19490
  Northern Lights, 20790
  Powerful Waves, 20721
  Roaring Reptiles, 18710
  Sea Creatures with Many Arms, 19725
  Sea Snakes, 19649
  Shy Salamanders, 18695
  Space Sailing, 21011

What Bit Me? 19491
  What's a Lemming? 19209
  What's Under That Shell? 18792
Sovak, Jan. *The Newest and Coolest Dinosaurs*, 14394
Sovka, David. *The Microscope Book*, 19807
Sowler, Sandie. *Amazing Armored Animals*, 18901
Spackman, Jeff. *Boo! Halloween Poems and Limericks*, 6012
Spagnoli, Cathy. *Judge Rabbit and the Tree Spirit*, 10844
Spain, Valerie. *Meet Maya Angelou*, 12499
Spalding, Andrea. *The Keeper and the Crows*, 8116(F)
  Me and Mr. Mah, 5082(F)
  Sarah May and the New Red Dress, 1590(F)
Spangenburg, Ray. *Exploring the Reaches of the Solar System*, 18531
Sparks, Michal. *The Very Best Christmas Ever!* 21411
Spaulding, Dean T. *Feeding Our Feathered Friends*, 19284
  Housing Our Feathered Friends, 19285
  Watching Our Feathered Friends, 19286
Speare, Elizabeth G. *The Bronze Bow*, 8944(F)
  The Sign of the Beaver, 9212(F)
  The Witch of Blackbird Pond, 9213(F)
Spearing, Craig. *Prairie Dog Pioneers*, 4676(F)
Spears, Rick. *Dino-Trekking*, 14425
Spedden, Daisy C. S. *Polar the Titanic Bear*, 16486
Speechley, Greta. *Clay Modeling*, 21536
Speed, Toby. *Brave Potatoes*, 1591(F)
  Two Cool Cows, 2709(F)
  Water Voices, 10265(F)
Speidel, Sandra. *Coconut Kind of Day*, 11614
  Fixing the Crack of Dawn, 3428(F)
  The Neighborhood Trucker, 5549(F)
  Songs for the Seasons, 11957
Speirs, John. *The Case of the Backyard Treasure*, 6592(F)
  A Fair Bear Share, 526(F)
  The Key to the Playhouse, 8394(F)
Spellman, Susan. *A Small Treasury of Christmas*, 17432
  A Small Treasury of Easter, 11852
Spelman, Cornelia Maude. *After Charlotte's Mom Died*, 5083(F)
  Mama and Daddy Bear's Divorce, 5084(F)
  When I Feel Angry, 2710(F)
  Your Body Belongs to You, 17733

Spence, Amy (jt. author). *Clickety Clack*, 4320(F)
Spence, Annora. *W. D. the Wonder Dog*, 1830(F)
Spence, Jim. *No One Told the Aardvark*, 1146(F)
Spence, Rob. *Clickety Clack*, 4320(F)
Spencer, Eve. *A Flag for Our Country*, 13976
Spencer, Guy J. *A Living Desert*, 20420
Spencer, Laurie. *The Kwanzaa Contest*, 9750(F)
Spencer, Shannon. *Ireland*, 15366
Spengler, Kenneth J. *A Campfire for Cowboy Billy*, 1634(F)
 How Jackrabbit Got His Very Long Ears, 2242(F)
 Somewhere in the Ocean, 898(F)
 Way Out in the Desert, 5338(F)
Spengler, Margaret. *Clickety Clack*, 4320(F)
Speregen, Devra. *Phone Call from a Flamingo*, 8822(F)
Sperry, Armstrong. *Call It Courage*, 7077(F)
Spetter, Jung-Hee. *Just a Minute*, 2317(F)
 Lily and Trooper's Fall, 3437(F)
 Lily and Trooper's Spring, 779(F)
 Lily and Trooper's Summer, 780(F)
 Piggy's Birthday Dream, 2033(F)
Spickert, Diane Nelson. *Earthsteps*, 20571
Spiegelman, Art. *Little Lit*, 10504(F)
Spier, Peter. *Last Hurdle*, 7164(F)
 The Little Riders, 9688(F)
 Noah's Ark, 17323
 People, 3438(F)
Spier, Peter, reteller. *Noah's Ark*, 17323
Spies, Karen B. *Barbara Bush*, 13141
 Buffalo Bill Cody, 12870
 Denver, 16638
 George Bush, 13011
 Isolation vs. Intervention, 17024
 Our Presidency, 17102
Spilka, Arnold. *Bumples, Fumdidlers, and Jellybeans*, 11918
Spillman, Fredrika. *The Maybe Garden*, 3060(F)
 Year of the Black Pony, 7269(F)
Spinelli, Eileen. *Coming Through the Blizzard*, 5922(F)
 Lizzie Logan Gets Married, 9995(F)
 Lizzie Logan, Second Banana, 9996(F)
 Lizzie Logan Wears Purple Sunglasses, 9997(F)
 Naptime, Laptime, 781(F)
 Night Shift Daddy, 782(F)
 Six Hogs on a Scooter, 2711(F)
 Somebody Loves You, Mr. Hatch, 5085(F)
 Song for the Whooping Crane, 11814

Tea Party Today, 11709
Thanksgiving at the Tappletons', 6155(F)
When Mama Comes Home Tonight, 3903(F)
Where Is the Night Train Going? 11710
Spinelli, Jerry. *The Bathwater Gang*, 9998(F)
 Blue Ribbon Blues, 7078(F)
 Crash, 7519(F)
 Knots in My Yo-Yo String, 12598
 The Library Card, 9999(F)
 Maniac Magee, 8823(F)
 There's a Girl in My Hammerlock, 10364(F)
 Tooter Pepperday, 10000(F)
 Wringer, 8824(F)
Spinner, Stephanie. *Be First in the Universe*, 10241(F)
 Born to Be Wild, 8117(F)
 Little Sure Shot, 12432
 Snake Hair, 11507
Spinner, Stephanie (jt. author). *Aliens for Breakfast*, 10178(F)
 Aliens for Lunch, 6330(F)
Spires, Elizabeth. *The Mouse of Amherst*, 8118(F)
 Riddle Road, 21853
 With One White Wing, 21854
Spirin, Gennady. *The Christmas Story*, 5923
 The Crane Wife, 10811
 The Easter Story, 17435
 Jack and the Beanstalk, 10949
 Joy to the World, 9736(F)
 Kashtanka, 5164(F)
 The Nose, 7743(F)
 Philipok, 5543(F)
 The Sea King's Daughter, 11112
 Sorotchintzy Fair, 1198(F)
 The Tempest, 8087(F)
 The White Cat, 10498(F)
Spirn, Michele. *Birth*, 17401
 The Bridges in London, 7079(F)
 A Know-Nothing Birthday, 5725(F)
 A Know-Nothing Halloween, 6052(F)
 The Know-Nothings Talk Turkey, 6156(F)
 New Year, 17402
Spiros, Dean. *Frank Thomas*, 13508
 Top 10 Hockey Goalies, 13412
 Troy Aikman, 13602
Spivak, Dawnine. *Grass Sandals*, 9015
Splear, Elise Lee. *Growing Seasons*, 16487
Spohn, Cliff. *Baseball's Best*, 6362
Spohn, Kate. *Chick's Daddy*, 2712(F)
 Dog and Cat Make a Splash, 2713(F)
 Dog and Cat Shake a Leg, 6671(F)
 The Mermaids' Lullaby, 783(F)
 Turtle and Snake at Work, 6672(F)
 Turtle and Snake Go Camping, 6673(F)

Spooner, Michael. *A Moon in Your Lunch Box*, 784
Sporn, Michael. *White Wash*, 5074(F)
Spowart, Robin. *Inside, Outside Christmas*, 5924(F)
 It's Hanukkah! 6098(F)
 Little Bunny's Easter Surprise, 5971(F)
 Mama, If You Had a Wish, 2503(F)
 The Night the Moon Blew Kisses, 4498(F)
 Sometimes I Feel Like a Mouse, 214(F)
 To Rabbittown, 1668(F)
Springer, Harriett. *A First Look at Dogs*, 19970
 A First Look at Ducks, Geese, and Swans, 19316
Springer, Nancy. *I Am Mordred*, 8119(F)
 Red Wizard, 8120(F)
 Sky Rider, 8121(F)
Springer, Sally. *A Costume for Noah*, 6120(F)
Springett, Martin. *The Follower*, 1622(F)
 The Wise Old Woman, 10834
Sproule, Anna. *Great Britain*, 15367
 Thomas Edison, 13274
 The Wright Brothers, 13358
Sprung, Barbara. *Death*, 17860
 Stress, 17734
Spudvilas, Anne. *Big Cat Dreaming*, 3943(F)
 Bright Star, 4938(F)
Spurll, Barbara. *The Flying Tortoise*, 10700
Spurr, Elizabeth. *The Long, Long Letter*, 4321(F)
 Lupe and Me, 8825(F)
 Mama's Birthday Surprise, 7520(F)
Squire, Ann. *101 Questions and Answers About Backyard Wildlife*, 18673
 101 Questions and Answers About Pets and People, 19909
 Understanding Man's Best Friend, 19974
Squire, Ann O. *Anteaters, Sloths, and Armadillos*, 18976
 Spiders of North America, 19596
Sreenivasan, Jyotsna. *Aruna's Journeys*, 9016(F)
 Ela Bhatt, 13753
Srinivasan, Rodbika. *India*, 15114
Staake, Bob. *My Little ABC Book*, 135(F)
 My Little 123 Book, 585(F)
Stadler, John. *The Adventures of Snail at School*, 6674(F)
 Animal Cafe, 2714(F)
 The Cats of Mrs. Calamari, 4322(F)
 Hooray for Snail! 2715(F)
 Ready, Set, Go! 6675(F)

Staedter, Tracy. *Rocks and Minerals*, 20572

Staermose, Robert. *The Horribly Haunted School*, 7948(F)

Stahl, Ben F. *Dreaming of America*, 4607(F)

Stalcup, Ann. *On the Home Front*, 14882
Ukrainian Egg Decoration, 17439

Stalio, Ivan. *The Myths and Civilization of the Ancient Egyptians*, 14661
The Myths and Civilization of the Ancient Greeks, 14696

Stamaty, Mark Alan. *Too Many Time Machines*, 8122(F)

Stammen, JoEllen M. *The Angel Tree*, 5900(F)
If You Were Born a Kitten, 18869
Jubela, 5287(F)
Sleep, Little One, Sleep, 635(F)
Swan in Love, 1902(F)
Wild Fox, 19132

Stamper, Judith B. *Five Creepy Creatures*, 6676(F)
Five Goofy Ghosts, 6677(F)
Space Race, 6678(F)
Tic-Tac-Toe, 6679(F)

Stanbridge, Joanne. *My Four Lions*, 1199(F)

Stanchak, John. *Civil War*, 16436

Standiford, Natalie. *The Bravest Dog Ever*, 6680
Space Dog and the Pet Show, 10242(F)

Stanek, Muriel. *All Alone After School*, 5086(F)
Don't Hurt Me, Mama, 5087(F)
I Speak English for My Mom, 7376(F)
We Came from Vietnam, 17595

Stangl, Jean. *Crystals and Crystal Gardens You Can Grow*, 20573
What Makes You Cough, 18079

Stanley, Diane. *Bard of Avon*, 12594
Charles Dickens, 12529
Cleopatra, 13775
Elena, 9140(F)
Good Queen Bess, 13788
Joan of Arc, 13815
The Last Princess, 13820
Leonardo da Vinci, 12218
Michelangelo, 12261
The Month-Brothers, 11103
The Mulberry Bird, 1867(F)
Raising Sweetness, 4323(F)
Roughing It on the Oregon Trail, 8123(F)
Rumpelstiltskin's Daughter, 10505(F)
Saving Sweetness, 4324(F)
Shaka, 13850

Stanley, Fay. *The Last Princess*, 13820

Stanley, George E. *The Clue of the Left-Handed Envelope*, 7080(F)

The Day the Ants Got Really Mad, 8124(F)
Ghost Horse, 6681(F)
Hershell Cobwell and the Miraculous Tattoo, 10001(F)
Snake Camp, 6682(F)

Stanley, Jerry. *Children of the Dust Bowl*, 16488
Frontier Merchants, 16372

Stanley, Mandy. *First Word Book*, 14041

Stanley, Phyllis M. *American Environmental Heroes*, 13221

Stanley, Sanna. *Monkey Sunday*, 4837(F)

Stanton, Sue. *Child's Guide to the Mass*, 17221

Stark, Al. *Zimbabwe*, 15002

Starkman, Neal. *The Riddle*, 4046(F)

Starosta, Paul. *The Frog*, 18739

Staub, Frank. *Alligators*, 18711
America's Forests, 20489
America's Prairies, 20547
America's Wetlands, 20393
Children of Belize, 15686
Children of Cuba, 15718
Children of Dominica, 15719
Children of Hawaii, 16816
The Children of the Sierra Madre, 15646
Children of the Tlingit, 16817
Children of Yucatan, 15647
Herons, 19355
Manatees, 19747
Mountain Goats, 18977
Prairie Dogs, 19210
Sea Lions, 19748
Yellowstone's Cycle of Fire, 16639

Staub, Leslie. *Bless This House*, 17534
Whoever You Are, 3630(F)

Stauffer, Stacey. *Leonardo DiCaprio*, 12374

Staunton, Ted. *Two False Moves*, 8373(F)

Stawicki, Andrew. *A People Apart*, 17197

Steadman, Barbara. *Clancy's Cabin*, 6958(F)

Stearman, Kaye. *Homelessness*, 17025

Steedman, Scott. *The Egyptian News*, 14667
Egyptian Town, 14668
A Frontier Fort on the Oregon Trail, 16373
How Would You Survive as an American Indian? 16056

Steele, Mary. *Featherbys*, 8374(F)

Steele, Mary Q. *Journey Outside*, 8125(F)

Steele, Philip. *Astronomy*, 18418
The Aztec News, 15648
The Best Book of Mummies, 14669
Cars and Trucks, 21322
Castles, 14793

Clothes and Crafts in Ancient Greece, 14707
Clothes and Crafts in Roman Times, 14746
Clothes and Crafts in Victorian Times, 14358
Deserts, 20421
The Egyptians and the Valley of the Kings, 14670
Food and Feasts in Ancient Rome, 14747
Germany, 15332
Going to School, 14008
Grasslands, 20548
The Incas and Machu Picchu, 15788
Islands, 20394
Journey Through China, 15084
Knights, 14794
Little Bighorn, 16057
Mountains, 20507
Pirates, 14571
Rocking and Rolling, 20323
Space Travel, 21012
Toys and Games, 21658
Trains, 21343
Tundra, 15835
Vampire Bats and Other Creatures of the Night, 18674

Steele, Robert G. *Dad and Me in the Morning*, 3762(F)

Steen, Bill. *Children of Clay*, 16061

Steen, Sandra. *Car Wash*, 3439(F)
Colonial Williamsburg, 16175
Independence Hall, 16739

Steen, Susan (jt. author). *Car Wash*, 3439(F)
Colonial Williamsburg, 16175
Independence Hall, 16739

Steenkamer, Paul. *Dale Earnhardt*, 13427

Steer, Dugald. *Just One More Story*, 10507(F)

Steffens, Bradley. *Addiction*, 17891
Emily Dickinson, 12530
Jesse Jackson, 12729

Steffler, Shawn. *Just One More Color*, 4545(F)

Stefoff, Rebecca. *Abraham Lincoln*, 13076
Al Gore, 12893
Ant, 19514
Chameleon, 18751
Children of the Westward Trail, 16374
The Colonies, 16176
Crab, 19680
Exploring the New World, 16092
First Frontier, 16375
George H. W. Bush, 13012
Gloria Estefan, 12385
Horses, 20016
Idaho, 16640
Lewis and Clark, 16093
Octopus, 19726
Oregon, 16818
Owl, 19366

Penguin, 19386
Revolutionary War, 16215
Sea Horse, 19715
Utah, 16641
The War of 1812, 16279
Steger, Will. *Over the Top of the World*, 15836
Steig, Jeanne. *Consider the Lemming*, 11919
A Handful of Beans, 10508(F)
Steig, William. *Abel's Island*, 8126(F)
The Amazing Bone, 4325(F)
Brave Irene, 2973(F)
C D B! 4326, 21855
Caleb and Kate, 1592(F)
Consider the Lemming, 11919
Doctor De Soto, 2716(F)
Doctor De Soto Goes to Africa, 2717(F)
Dominic, 8127(F)
Farmer Palmer's Wagon Ride, 2718(F)
The Flying Latke, 6124(F)
Gorky Rises, 2719(F)
A Handful of Beans, 10508(F)
Pete's a Pizza, 4327(F)
The Real Thief, 8128(F)
Solomon the Rusty Nail, 2720(F)
Spinky Sulks, 5088(F)
Sylvester and the Magic Pebble, 2721(F)
Tiffky Doofky, 2722(F)
The Toy Brother, 1593(F)
Wizzil, 1594(F)
Stein, R. Conrad. *Apollo 11*, 21013
The Assassination of Martin Luther King, Jr., 12755
Athens, 15391
Austria, 15291
The Aztec Empire, 15649
The Battle of the Little Bighorn, 16058
Berlin, 15333
The Bill of Rights, 17061
The Boston Tea Party, 16177
Cairo, 15512
The California Gold Rush, 16376
Cape Town, 15003
Chicago, 16584
Chuck Yeager Breaks the Sound Barrier, 12156
Ellis Island, 16740
The Great Depression, 16489
Greece, 15392
In the Spanish West, 16377
The Iran Hostage Crisis, 15560
The Korean War, 16521
Lewis and Clark, 12132
The Manhattan Project, 21406
Mexico, 15650
Mexico City, 15651
Minnesota, 16585
Nevada, 16642
New Hampshire, 16741
New Jersey, 16742

On the Old Western Frontier, 16378
Oregon, 16819
Paris, 15318
Powers of the Supreme Court, 17015
The Roaring Twenties, 16490
Rome, 15393
Seattle, 16820
South Carolina, 16892
The Spirit of St. Louis, 21102
The Trail of Tears, 16059
Valley Forge, 16216
Washington, 16821
Washington, D.C., 16743
West Virginia, 16893
World War II in Europe, 14883
World War II in the Pacific, 14884
Stein, Sara Bonnett. *About Dying*, 5089(F)
About Handicaps, 17934
A Hospital Story, 18044
Oh, Baby! 18233
On Divorce, 17686
The Science Book, 18294
That New Baby, 17687
Steiner, Andy. *Girl Power on the Playing Field*, 22065
A Sporting Chance, 22066
Steiner, Barbara. *Foghorn Flattery and the Dancing Horses*, 7081(F)
Oliver Dibbs to the Rescue! 10002(F)
Whale Brother, 4838(F)
Steiner, Joan. *Look-Alikes*, 314
Look-Alikes Jr., 359
Steinhauser, Peggy L. *Mousetracks*, 21227
Steins, Richard. *Alcohol Abuse*, 17892
The Allies Against the Axis, 14885
Censorship, 17156
Colonial America, 16178
Exploration and Settlement, 16094
Hungary, 15292
Leontyne Price, 12447
The Nation Divides, 16437
A Nation Is Born, 16217
Our Elections, 17103
Our National Capital, 16744
The Postwar Years, 14595
Shiloh, 16438
Steirnagle, Michael. *Billy Lazroe and the King of the Sea*, 11361
Steltzer, Ulli. *Building an Igloo*, 15837
Stelzig, Christine. *Can You Spot the Leopard?* 13936
Stem, Jacqueline. *The Cellar in the Woods*, 7082(F)
Stemple, Adam (jt. author). *Jane Yolen's Mother Goose Songbook*, 904
Jane Yolen's Old MacDonald Songbook, 14195

Stemple, Heidi E. Y. (jt. author).
Dear Mother, Dear Daughter, 11745
Meet the Monsters, 21964
An Unsolved Mystery from History, 7141(F)
Stemple, Jason. *A Letter from Phoenix Farm*, 12632
Once upon Ice, 11991
Snow, Snow, 11992
Stenmark, Victoria. *The Singing Chick*, 2723(F)
Stepanchuk, Carol. *Red Eggs and Dragon Boats*, 15085
Stephens, Pat. *Animal Defenses*, 18899
Animal Feelings, 18815
Bears, 19048
Stephens, Tim (jt. author). *Click!* 21803
Steptoe, Javaka. *Do You Know What I'll Do?* 3972(F)
In Daddy's Arms I Am Tall, 11762
A Pocketful of Poems, 11584
Steptoe, John. *All the Colors of the Race*, 11522
Baby Says, 3904(F)
Creativity, 4047(F)
Mufaro's Beautiful Daughters, 10715
She Come Bringing Me That Little Baby Girl, 3663(F)
Stevie, 3905(F)
Steptoe, John, reteller. *The Story of Jumping Mouse*, 11301
Sterman, Betsy. *Saratoga Secret*, 9323(F)
Stermer, Dugald. *Ghost Vision*, 7877(F)
Stern, Maggie. *Acorn Magic*, 5422(F)
George and Diggety, 6683(F)
The Missing Sunflowers, 5423(F)
Steven, Kenneth. *The Bearer of Gifts*, 5925(F)
Stevens, Ann Shepard. *Strange Nests*, 19307
Stevens, Bernardine S. *Colonial American Craftspeople*, 16179
Stevens, Bryna. *Frank Thompson*, 13153
Stevens, Carla. *A Book of Your Own*, 14108
Trouble for Lucy, 9441(F)
Stevens, Chambers. *Magnificent Monologues for Kids*, 12038
Stevens, Jan R. *Carlos and the Carnival*, 5726(F)
Carlos and the Cornfield/Carlos y la Milpa de Maiz, 4839(F)
Carlos and the Skunk, 4328(F)
Twelve Lizards Leaping, 14213
Stevens, Janet. *Anansi and the Moss-Covered Rock*, 10675
Anansi and the Talking Melon, 10676
Anansi Goes Fishing, 10677
Cook-a-Doodle-Doo! 2724(F)

Coyote Steals the Blanket, 11302
The Dog Who Had Kittens, 5383(F)
From Pictures to Words, 14109
The Gates of the Wind, 1339(F)
My Big Dog, 2725(F)
Old Bag of Bones, 11303
The Quangle Wangle's Hat, 11891
Shoe Town, 6684(F)
To Market, To Market, 3329(F)
Tops and Bottoms, 11385
The Tortoise and the Hare, 11052
Tumbleweed Stew, 6297(F)
Stevens, Kathleen. *Aunt Skilly and the Stranger*, 4329(F)
The Beast in the Bathtub, 2726(F)
Stevens, Kathryn. *Halloween Jack-o'-Lanterns*, 17447
Stevens, Mary. *Nobody Listens to Andrew*, 6361(F)
Stevens, Rick. *God's Quiet Things*, 4548(F)
Stevens, Rita. *Andrew Johnson*, 13055
Chester A. Arthur, 13008
Stevenson, Harvey. *As the Crow Flies*, 193(F)
Big, Scary Wolf, 785(F)
Bye, Mis' Lela, 4928(F)
The Chocolate-Covered-Cookie Tantrum, 4910(F)
Good Books, Good Times, 11600
Grandpa Never Lies, 3627(F)
Grandpa's House, 3906(F)
Sam the Zamboni Man, 2975(F)
The Tangerine Tree, 4972(F)
Wilhe'mina Miles After the Stork Night, 3572(F)
Stevenson, James. *The Baby Uggs Are Hatching*, 2601(F)
The Bones in the Cliff, 7083(F)
Candy Corn, 11711
Christmas at Mud Flat, 5926(F)
Cornflakes, 11712
"Could Be Worse!" 2974(F)
Don't Make Me Laugh, 4330(F)
Don't You Know There's a War On? 4840
Fun/No Fun, 3440
Georgia Music, 3665(F)
Happily Ever After, 8034(F)
Heat Wave at Mud Flat, 2727(F)
I Am Not Going to Get Up Today! 6643(F)
I Know a Lady, 4069(F)
It's Raining Pigs and Noodles, 11909
July, 3441
Just Around the Corner, 11713
The Most Amazing Dinosaur, 2728(F)
Mud Flat April Fool, 6685(F)
The Mud Flat Mystery, 8129(F)
Mud Flat Spring, 2729(F)
The New Kid on the Block, 11910
A Pizza the Size of the Sun, 11678
Popcorn, 3442(F)
Rolling Rose, 1595(F)

Sam the Zamboni Man, 2975(F)
Something Big Has Been Here, 11913
263 Brain Busters, 20619
The Unprotected Witness, 7084(F)
What's Under My Bed? 786(F)
Worse Than the Worst, 4331(F)
The Worst Goes South, 2730(F)
Yard Sale, 4332(F)
Stevenson, Laura C. *Happily After All*, 8526(F)
Stevenson, Monica. *The Teddy Bears' Night Before Christmas*, 11849
Stevenson, Peter. *Raging Robots and Unruly Uncles*, 10214(F)
Stevenson, Robert Louis. *The Bottle Imp*, 8130(F)
A Child's Garden of Verses, 11714, 11715, 11716, 11717
My Shadow, 11718
Poetry for Young People, 11719
The Strange Case of Dr. Jekyll and Mr. Hyde, 10243(F)
Where Go the Boats? 11720
Stevenson, Sucie. *Emily and Alice Again*, 3988(F)
Henry and Mudge and Annie's Good Move, 6601(F)
Henry and Mudge and Annie's Perfect Pet, 6602(F)
Henry and Mudge and the Careful Cousin, 6603(F)
Henry and Mudge and the Sneaky Crackers, 6604(F)
Henry and Mudge and the Starry Night, 6605(F)
Henry and Mudge and the Wild Wind, 6606(F)
Henry and Mudge and Their Snowman Plan, 6607(F)
Henry and Mudge in the Family Trees, 6608(F)
Stewart, Alex. *Keeping Clean*, 18211
Sending a Letter, 13965
Stewart, Arvis. *A Gift of Magic*, 8425(F)
The Macmillan Book of Greek Gods and Heroes, 11485
Stewart, Dianne. *Gift of the Sun*, 4333(F)
Stewart, Don. *Itse Selu*, 16021
Stewart, Elisabeth J. *Bimmi Finds a Cat*, 7308(F)
On the Long Trail Home, 9179(F)
Stewart, Gail B. *Alexander the Great*, 13751
Chicago, 16586
Diabetes, 18006
F. Scott Fitzgerald, 12535
Gangs, 17085
Houston, 16915
In Space, 21014
In the Desert, 20422
In the Polar Regions, 15838
Los Angeles, 16822
New York, 16745

1900s, 16491
Stewart, Jennifer J. *If That Breathes Fire, We're Toast!* 8131(F)
Stewart, Judy. *A Family in Morocco*, 14964
A Family in Sudan, 14948
Stewart, Marjabelle Young. *What to Do When and Why*, 17640
Stewart, Mark. *Alex Rodriguez*, 13496
Derek Jeter, 13464
Football, 22189
Home Run Heroes, 13413
Kobe Bryant, 13517
Peyton Manning, 13618
Randy Moss, 13622
Se Ri Pak, 13706
Sweet Victory, 13677
Terrell Davis, 13606
Tim Duncan, 13522
Venus and Serena Williams, 13657
Stewart, Melissa. *Birds*, 19287
Fishes, 19716
Insects, 19492
Life Without Light, 18675
Mammals, 18978
Science in Ancient India, 15115
Stewart, Paul. *The Birthday Presents*, 5727(F)
A Little Bit of Winter, 2731(F)
Stewart, Roger. *The Best Book of Sharks*, 19763
Movie Magic, 6285(F)
Stewart, Sarah. *The Gardener*, 4841(F)
The Journey, 7521(F)
The Library, 3443(F)
The Money Tree, 1596(F)
Stewart, Wayne. *Baseball Bafflers*, 22118
Stewart, Whitney. *The 14th Dalai Lama*, 13778
Sir Edmund Hillary, 12124
Stewig, John W. *Clever Gretchen*, 1597(F)
King Midas, 11508
The Moon's Choice, 1598(F)
Stickland, Henrietta. *The Christmas Bear*, 5927(F)
Stickland, Henrietta (jt. author). *Dinosaur Roar!* 2732(F)
Stickland, Paul. *The Christmas Bear*, 5927(F)
Dinosaur Roar! 2732(F)
Truck Jam, 5602(F)
Stickler, Soma Han. *Tigers, Frogs, and Rice Cakes*, 10729
Stienecker, David L. *Addition*, 20596
Countries, 14572
Maps, 14371
Numbers, 20638
Rectangles, 20606
States, 15905
The World, 14359
Stier, Catherine. *If I Were President*, 17126

Stiles, Martha Bennett. *Island Magic*, 3907(F)

Sarah the Dragon Lady, 8826(F)

Still, James. *An Appalachian Mother Goose*, 892

Stille, Darlene R. *Airplanes*, 21103

Blimps, 21104

The Circulatory System, 18094

Deserts, 20423

The Digestive System, 18108

Grasslands, 20549

The Greenhouse Effect, 20791

Helicopters, 21105

The Nervous System, 18122

Oceans, 19839

The Ozone Hole, 17006

The Respiratory System, 18128

Trains, 21344

Tropical Rain Forests, 20490

Trucks, 21323

Water Pollution, 17007

Wetlands, 20395

Stillerman, Marci. *Nine Spoons*, 6119(F)

Stillman, Susan. *Windsongs and Rainbows*, 4369(F)

Stilwell, Stella. *Living Fossils*, 18655

Stilz, Carol C. *Grandma Buffalo, May and Me*, 3908(F)

Stimson, Joan. *Big Panda, Little Panda*, 2733(F)

Stine, R. L. *It Came From Ohio! My Life as a Writer*, 12602

Nightmare Hour, 8132(F)

Stirnweis, Shannon. *Last of the Mohicans*, 9151(F)

Stock, Catherine. *Birthday Present*, 5728(F)

By the Dawn's Early Light, 3500(F)

Doll Baby, 8577(F)

Easter Surprise, 5975(F)

Gugu's House, 4842(F)

Gus and Grandpa, 6526(F)

Gus and Grandpa and Show-and-Tell, 6527(F)

Gus and Grandpa and the Christmas Cookies, 6528(F)

Gus and Grandpa at the Hospital, 6529(F)

Gus and Grandpa Ride the Train, 6530(F)

Halloween Monster, 6053(F)

An Island Christmas, 9735(F)

Island Summer, 3444(F)

Justin and the Best Biscuits in the World, 8846(F)

Miss Viola and Uncle Ed Lee, 4136(F)

Oh, Emma, 7389(F)

Painted Dreams, 4878(F)

The Sanyasin's First Day, 4830(F)

Street Talk, 11727

Tap-Tap, 4879(F)

Thanksgiving Treat, 6157(F)

Today Is the Day, 5057(F)

Too Far Away to Touch, 5044(F)

A Very Important Day, 3206(F)

The Willow Umbrella, 4560(F)

Stockdale, Linda. *ABC Career Book for Girls/El Libro de Carreras para Niñas*, 17767(F)

Stockdale, Susan. *Nature's Paintbrush*, 18855

Some Sleep Standing Up, 5424

Stoddard, Sandol. *Turtle Time*, 787(F)

Stoeke, Janet M. *Hide and Seek*, 3445(F)

Hunky Dory Ate It, 5199(F)

Stoeke, Janet Morgan. *Five Little Kitty Cats*, 586(F)

A Friend for Minerva Louise, 2734(F)

Hide and Seek, 3445(F)

Minerva Louise at School, 2735(F)

Minerva Louise at the Fair, 2736(F)

One Little Puppy Dog, 587(F)

Stojic, Manya. *Rain*, 2737(F)

Stoker, Wayne (jt. author). *Nevada*, 16625

Stolz, Mary. *A Ballad of the Civil War*, 9504(F)

The Bully of Barkham Street, 8375(F)

Casebook of a Private (Cat's) Eye, 7085(F)

Emmett's Pig, 6686(F)

Go Fish, 7522(F)

Night of Ghosts and Hermits, 19868

The Noonday Friends, 8376(F)

Storm in the Night, 5090(F)

Stone, B. J. *Ola's Wake*, 7523(F)

Stone, Barbara. *In the Company of Bears*, 1993(F)

Stone, Debbie L. (jt. author). *Alligators and Crocodiles*, 18712

Stone, Jason. *Grizzly Bear*, 19067

Polar Bear, 19068

Stone, Jody (jt. author). *Grizzly Bear*, 19067

Stone, Judy (jt. author). *Polar Bear*, 19068

Stone, Kazuko. *Cool Melons Turn to Frogs! The Life and Poems of Issa*, 12556

Dorobo the Dangerous, 1650(F)

Ten Oni Drummers, 1201(F)

Stone, Kazuko G. *Aligay Saves the Stars*, 2738(F)

Stone, Lynn M. *Baboons*, 19017

Back from the Edge, 18979

Cougars, 19112, 19113

Eagles, 19343

Endangered Animals, 19411

Grizzlies, 19069

Mountains, 20508

Penguins, 19387, 19388

Sandhill Cranes, 19288

Swans, 19317

Vultures, 19344

Stone, Phoebe. *All the Blue Moons at the Wallace Hotel*, 8527(F)

Go Away, Shelley Boo! 4048(F)

What Night Do the Angels Wander? 5928(F)

When the Wind Bears Go Dancing, 1599(F)

Stone, Ras. *Play Mas! A Carnival ABC*, 87(F)

Stone, Tanya. *Snowboards*, 21059

Teddy Bears, 21060

Stone, Tanya L. *America's Top 10 National Monuments*, 15857

Diana, 13784

Rosie O'Donnell, 12437

Stone, Victoria (jt. author). *The Crocodile Family Book*, 18700

Stonehouse, Bernard. *Snow, Ice and Cold*, 20792

Whales, 19802

Stoops, Erik D. *Alligators and Crocodiles*, 18712

Dolphins, 19691

Whales, 19803

Wolves and Their Relatives, 19141

Stoppleman, Monica. *Fabric*, 21647

Storad, Conrad J. *Saguaro Cactus*, 20424

Tarantulas, 19597

Storer, Pat. *Your Puppy, Your Dog*, 19975

Stork, Lise. *My Sisters Love My Clothes*, 3669(F)

Storm, Theodor. *Little Hobbin*, 788(F)

Storring, Rod. *A Doctor's Life*, 18028

Stott, Carole. *Out of This World*, 18419

Space Exploration, 21015

Stott, Dorothy. *Baby-Sit*, 3328(F)

The Big Book of Games, 22067

Our New Baby, 6441(F)

Stow, Jenny. *The Coming of Night*, 10711

Darkfright, 1260(F)

Growing Pains, 2739(F)

Stowe, Cynthia. *Not-So-Normal Norman*, 7309(F)

Stowe, Cynthia M. *The Second Escape of Arthur Cooper*, 9324(F)

Stowell, Charlotte. *The Kids Can Do It Book*, 21469

Making Cards, 21632

Step-by-Step Making Books, 14009

Strachan, Ian. *The Flawed Glass*, 8917(F)

The Iliad, 11509

Strand, Claudia. *Hello, Fruit Face! The Paintings of Giuseppe Arcimboldo*, 12188

Strand, Keith. *Grandfather's Christmas Tree*, 5929(F)

Strassburg, Brian. *The Contrary Kid*, 4112(F)

How to Be the Greatest Writer in the World, 14075

Miss Myrtle Frag, the Grammar Nag, 14023

What's Up With You, Taquandra Fu? 1057(F)

Strasser, Todd. *The Diving Bell*, 9180(F)

Gator Prey, 7086(F)

Help! I'm Trapped in Obedience School, 8133(F)

Here Comes Heavenly, 10003(F)

Hey Dad, Get a Life! 8134(F)

Kidnap Kids, 10004(F)

Pastabilities, 8135(F)

Shark Bite, 7087(F)

Straub, Deborah G., ed. *African American Voices*, 15906

Straus, Lucy. *The Story of Shoes*, 21185

Strauss, Linda Leopold. *A Fairy Called Hilary*, 8136(F)

Strauss, Peggy Guthart. *Relieve the Squeeze*, 18007

Strauss, Susan. *Coyote Stories for Children*, 11304

When Woman Became the Sea, 11416

Stray, P. J. *Secrets of the Mayan Ruins*, 7088(F)

Strazzabosco, Jeanne M. *Learning About Determination from the Life of Gloria Estefan*, 12386

Learning About Dignity from the Life of Martin Luther King, Jr., 12756

Learning About Forgiveness from the Life of Nelson Mandela, 13832

Learning About Responsibility from the Life of Colin Powell, 12955

Streich, Oliver. *Albery and Lila*, 2660(F)

Streissguth, Thomas. *Egypt*, 15513, 15514

Jesse Owens, 13668

John Brown, 12862

John Glenn, 12889

Lewis and Clark, 12133

Mary Cassatt, 12202

Queen Cleopatra, 13776

Rocket Man, 13298

Say It with Music, 12322

Science Fiction Pioneer, 12613

Writer of the Plains, 12516

Streissguth, Tom. *Jack London*, 12564

Stren, Patti. *The Mysterious Misadventures of Foy Rin Jin*, 2105(F)

Strete, Craig Kee. *The Lost Boy and the Monster*, 1602(F)

They Thought They Saw Him, 5425(F)

The World in Grandfather's Hands, 8528(F)

Strickland, Brad. *The Beast Under the Wizard's Bridge*, 7089(F)

The Specter from the Magician's Museum, 7090(F)

When Mack Came Back, 7310(F)

The Wrath of the Grinning Ghost, 8137(F)

Strickland, Dorothy S., ed. *Families*, 11768

Strickland, Michael R. *Haircuts at Sleepy Sam's*, 3446(F)

Poems That Sing to You, 11721

Strickland, Michael R. (jt. author). *Families*, 11768

Strickland, Paul. *Dinosaur Stomp*, 2740(F)

Stringer, John. *The Science of a Spring*, 20923

Stringer, Lauren. *Castles, Caves, and Honeycombs*, 5128(F)

Mud, 4514(F)

Red Rubber Boot Day, 3375(F)

Scarecrow, 1534(F)

Strohmeier, Lenice U. *Hurricane!* 2924(F)

Strom, Maria Diaz. *Rainbow Joe and Me*, 1603(F)

Strom, Yale. *Quilted Landscape*, 17596

Stromoski, Rick. *Chairs, Chairs, Chairs!* 6254(F)

Stronach, Neil. *Mountains*, 20509

Strongbow, Dyanne. *Big Moon Tortilla*, 4936(F)

Stroud, Bettye. *Down Home at Miss Dessa's*, 4049(F)

The Leaving, 4843(F)

Stroud, Jonathan. *Ancient Rome*, 14748

Strudwick, Leslie. *Athletes*, 13414

Strugnell, Ann. *Julian, Dream Doctor*, 5669(F)

The Stories Julian Tells, 7400(F)

Stuart, Chad. *The Ballymara Flood*, 4334(F)

Stuart, Dee. *The Astonishing Armadillo*, 18980

Bats, 19037

Stuart, Gene S. *Wildlife Alert*, 19412

Stuart, Sara Brown. *Bellboy*, 6955(F)

Stuart-Clark, Christopher (jt. author). *The Oxford Book of Story Poems*, 11593

The Oxford Treasury of Time Poems, 11594

Sturges, Jo. *France*, 15319

Sturges, Philemon. *Bridges Are to Cross*, 21151

Crocky Dilly, 1604(F)

I Love Trucks! 21324

The Little Red Hen (Makes a Pizza), 11036

Sacred Places, 17223

Ten Flashing Fireflies, 588(F)

Sturges, Philemon (jt. author). *Who Took the Cookies from the Cookie Jar?* 2345(F)

Sturman, Susan. *Kansas City*, 16587

Sturtevant, Katherine. *At the Sign of the Star*, 9124(F)

Stutson, Caroline. *Cowpokes*, 2976(F)

Stutz, Hans-Peter B. (jt. author). *Bats! Amazing and Mysterious Creatures of the Night*, 19027

Stuve-Bodeen, Stephanie. *Elizabeti's Doll*, 4844(F)

Mama Elizabeti, 4845(F)

We'll Paint the Octopus Red, 3447(F)

Stux, Erica. *Writing for Freedom*, 13143

Stwertka, Albert (jt. author). *Microscope*, 19813

Tuning In, 21278

Stwertka, Eve. *Microscope*, 19813

Tuning In, 21278

Stynes, Barbara W. *Walking with Mama*, 4547(F)

Sublett, Anne. *The Illustrated Rules of Softball*, 22119

Suen, Anastasia. *Delivery*, 3448(F)

Willie's Birthday, 6687(F)

Window Music, 3909(F)

Sugarman, Joan G. *Inside the Synagogue*, 17224

Sugita, Toru. *Floating Lanterns and Golden Shrines*, 17381

Suhr, Mandy. *Taste*, 18163

Sukach, Jim. *Clever Quicksolve Whodunit Puzzles*, 7091(F)

Sullivan, Ann. *Molly Maguire*, 10365(F)

Sullivan, Arthur. *I Have a Song to Sing, O!* 14257

Sullivan, Barbara. *Marvin Redpost*, 9982(F), 8807(F)

Sullivan, Charles. *Imaginary Gardens*, 11963

Sullivan, Charles, ed. *Children of Promise*, 15907

Sullivan, George. *All About Baseball*, 22120

All About Basketball, 22149

All About Football, 22190

All About Hockey, 22215

Any Number Can Play, 22068

Burnin' Rubber, 22083

The Civil War at Sea, 16439

The Day the Women Got the Vote, 17051

The Day We Walked on the Moon, 21016

Don't Step on the Foul Line, 22069

Glovemen, 22121

Great Lives, 13415

How the White House Really Works, 16746

In the Line of Fire, 13743

Picturing Lincoln, 13077

Portraits of War, 16440

Presidents at Play, 17127

Quarterbacks! 13416

Ronald Reagan, 13095

Sluggers! 13417

Snowboarding, 22284
To the Bottom of the Sea, 19880
Sullivan, Margaret. *The Philippines*, 15254
Sullivan, Michael J. *Mark Messier*, 13700
Sports Great Shaquille O'Neal, 13558
Top 10 Baseball Pitchers, 13418
Sullivan, Michael J. (jt. author). *Darryl Strawberry*, 13506
Sullivan, Otha Richard. *African American Inventors*, 13222
Sullivan, Silky. *Grandpa Was a Cowboy*, 2977(F)
Summer, L. S. *The March on Washington*, 16522
Rosa Parks, 12780
Summers, Kate. *Milly's Wedding*, 2741(F)
Summers, Susan. *The Fourth Wise Man*, 5930(F)
Sun, Chyng Feng. *Cat and Cat-face*, 1605(F)
Sundling, Charles W. *Cowboys of the Frontier*, 16379
Explorers of the Frontier, 16380
Native Americans of the Frontier, 16060
Pioneers of the Frontier, 16381
Sundstrom, Mary. *Extremely Weird Endangered Species*, 19402
Sundvall, Viveca L. *Santa's Winter Vacation*, 5931(F)
Suomalainen, Sami. *Mud Puddle*, 1425(F)
Super, Gretchen. *Drugs and Our World*, 17893
Super, Neil. *Daniel "Chappie" James*, 12731
Super, Terri. *The Three Little Pigs*, 895
Supraner, Lauren (jt. author). *Plenty of Puppets to Make*, 14307
Supraner, Robyn. *Happy Halloween! Things to Make and Do*, 21500
Plenty of Puppets to Make, 14307
Quick and Easy Cookbook, 21739
Science Secrets, 18351
Supree, Burton (jt. author). *Mother Mother I Feel Sick Send for the Doctor Quick Quick Quick*, 1050(F)
Susman, Edward. *Multiple Sclerosis*, 18008
Sussman, Susan. *Lies (People Believe) About Animals*, 18856
There's No Such Thing as a Chanukah Bush, Sandy Goldstein, 9762(F)
Susuki, Masaharu. *Wheat*, 20102
Sutcliff, Rosemary. *Black Ships Before Troy*, 11510
The Wanderings of Odysseus, 11511
Sutcliff, Rosemary, reteller. *Beowulf*, 11037

Sutcliffe, Jane. *Babe Didrikson Zaharias*, 13721
Jesse Owens, 13669
Sutcliffe, Justin. *Rosie*, 19940
Shaggy, Waggy Dogs (and Others), 19941
Sutcliffe, Mandy. *Night Ride to Nanna's*, 720(F)
Suteyev, V. *Mushroom in the Rain*, 2742(F)
Sutherland, Dorothy B. *Wales*, 15368
Sutherland, Kelly Stribling. *Tales for the Seventh Day*, 11150
Sutherland, Lin. *Earthquakes and Volcanoes*, 20349
Sutherland, Marc. *The Waiting Place*, 789(F)
Sutherland, Zena, ed. *The Orchard Book of Nursery Rhymes*, 893
Suzan, Gerardo. *Blanca's Feather*, 5335(F)
Butterfly Boy, 3756(F)
Suzan, Sophia. *Angel Prayers*, 17529
Suzuki, David. *Looking at Senses*, 18164
Looking at the Body, 18080
Looking at Weather, 20793
Svend Otto S. *The Man Who Kept House*, 11119
Swain, Gwenyth. *Bookworks*, 14010
Civil Rights Pioneer, 12787
Pennsylvania, 16747
The Road to Seneca Falls, 13194
Smiling, 17633
Swain, Ruth Freeman. *Bedtime!* 790
Swamp, Chief Jake. *Giving Thanks*, 11305
Swan, Erin Pembrey. *Camels and Pigs*, 19158
Kangaroos and Koalas, 19182
Land Predators of North America, 18981
Swan, Susan. *John Paul Jones*, 12913
Jungle Drum, 5461(F)
Just Us Two, 11982
Louis Pasteur, 13339
Mummies, 14647
Plays Children Love, Volume II, 12022
Snake Hair, 11507
Swan-Jackson, Alys. *When Your Parents Split Up . . .*, 17688
Swann, Brian. *The House with No Door*, 11722
Touching the Distance, 11932
Swanson, Diane. *Animals Eat the Weirdest Things*, 18857
Feet That Suck and Feed, 18858
Noses That Plow and Poke, 18859
Otters, 19749
Tails That Talk and Fly, 18860
Teeth That Stab and Grind, 18861
Swanson, Gloria M. *I've Got an Idea!* 13310
Swanson, June. *I Pledge Allegiance*, 6688

Out to Dry, 21856
Swanson, Susan M. *Getting Used to the Dark*, 11723
Letter to the Lake, 3449(F)
Swartz, Nancy Sohn. *In Our Image*, 5651
Sweat, Lynn. *Amelia Bedelia Goes Camping*, 6562(F)
Bravo, Amelia Bedelia! 6559(F)
The Cats' Burglar, 6563(F)
Good Driving, Amelia Bedelia, 6560(F)
Merry Christmas, Amelia Bedelia, 5895(F)
What Is a Fish? 19701
Swedberg, Jack. *Think Like an Eagle*, 21801
Sweeney, Diane. *Dolphin Babies*, 19692
Sweeney, Jacqueline. *Critter Day*, 6689(F)
Sweeney, Joan. *Bijou, Bonbon and Beau*, 4846(F)
Me and My Amazing Body, 18081
Me and My Family Tree, 3910
Me and My Place in Space, 18420
Me Counting Time, 20654
Me on the Map, 14372
Once upon a Lily Pad, 2743(F)
Suzette and the Puppy, 4847(F)
Sweet, Melissa. *Bat Jamboree*, 371(F)
Bats Around the Clock, 1743(F)
Bats on Parade, 372(F)
Blast Off! 11607
Bouncing Time, 5270(F)
Leaving Vietnam, 15176
Love and Kisses, 1690(F)
Marvelous Marvin and the Wolfman Mystery, 7014(F)
Naptime, Laptime, 781(F)
On Christmas Day in the Morning, 14210
Pinky and Rex and the Double-Dad Weekend, 7456(F)
Pinky and Rex and the Mean Old Witch, 6413(F)
Pinky and Rex and the New Baby, 6414(F)
Pinky and Rex and the New Neighbors, 6415(F)
Pinky and Rex and the School Play, 6416(F)
Pinky and Rex Get Married, 6417(F)
Pinky and Rex Go to Camp, 6418(F)
Rosie and the Poor Rabbits, 2424(F)
Rosie's Baby Tooth, 2425(F)
Sycamore Street, 3989(F)
Will You Take Care of Me? 1862(F)
Sweet, Stephen. *Super Humans*, 17898
Sweeten, Sami. *Addition*, 399(F)
Division, 400(F)

Measuring, 20656
Wolf, 1606(F)
Sweetland, Nancy. *God's Quiet Things*, 4548(F)
Sweetland, Sally. *God in Between*, 17215
Sweetwater, Jesse. *Bouki Dances the Kokioko*, 11433
The Dancing Pig, 10851
Sweetzer, Anna Leah. *Treason Stops at Oyster Bay*, 9250(F)
Swenson, May. *The Complete Poems to Solve*, 11724
Swentzell, Rina. *Children of Clay*, 16061
Swift, Hildegarde. *Little Red Lighthouse and the Great Gray Bridge*, 5603(F)
Swinburne, Stephen R. *Coyote*, 19142
Guess Whose Shadow? 21876
In Good Hands, 19345
Lots and Lots of Zebra Stripes, 360
Moon in Bear's Eyes, 19070
Once a Wolf, 19143
Safe, Warm, and Snug, 18862
Swallows in the Birdhouse, 5426
Unbeatable Beaks, 19289
Water for One, Water for Everyone, 589(F)
What's a Pair? What's a Dozen? 590
What's Opposite? 249(F)
Swinimer, Ciarunji C. *Pokot*, 14950
Swofford, Jeanette. *Illusions Illustrated*, 21776
Swope, Sam. *Gotta Go! Gotta Go!* 4549(F)
The Krazees, 1607(F)
Sykes, Julie. *Dora's Eggs*, 2744(F)
Hurry, Santa! 5932(F)
I Don't Want to Take a Bath, 2745(F)
Little Tiger's Big Surprise! 2746(F)
Smudge, 2747(F)
This and That, 2748(F)
Sylvada, Peter. *A Symphony of Whales*, 5405(F)
Sylvestre, Daniel. *Two Skeletons on the Telephone*, 11868
Symank, Yvonne. *Chave's Memories/Los Recuerdos de Chave*, 4637(F)
Szabo, Corinne. *Sky Pioneer*, 12116
Szekeres, Cyndy. *The Deep Blue Sky Twinkles with Stars*, 791(F)
I Can Count 100 Bunnies, 591(F)
I Love My Busy Book, 250(F)
Learn to Count, Funny Bunnies, 592(F)
Szilagyi, Mary. *Night in the Country*, 771(F)
This Year's Garden, 4531(F)
Szumski, Bonnie. *Prisons*, 17086

Taback, Simms. *Joseph Had a Little Overcoat*, 11176

Road Builders, 5571
Too Much Noise, 11014
Two Little Witches, 6066(F)
When I First Came to This Land, 4367(F)
Taber, Anthony. *The Boy Who Stopped Time*, 1608(F)
Taberski, Sharon, ed. *Morning, Noon, and Night*, 11725
Tabor, Nancy María Grande. *Bottles Break*, 8827(F)
Tackach, James. *Hank Aaron*, 13431
James Baldwin, 12504
Tafuri, Nancy. *Across the Stream*, 2124(F)
The Barn Party, 5427(F)
The Biggest Boy, 332(F)
Counting to Christmas, 5933(F)
Early Morning in the Barn, 934(F)
Have You Seen My Duckling? 2749(F)
I Love You, Little One, 792(F)
If I Had a Paka, 11673
Junglewalk, 935(F)
Silly Little Goose! 2750(F)
Snowy Flowy Blowy, 4550(F)
Spots, Feathers, and Curly Tails, 6690(F)
This Is the Farmer, 4335(F)
What the Sun Sees/What the Moon Sees, 1609(F)
Who's Counting? 593(F)
Will You Be My Friend? 6691(F)
Tagholm, Sally. *Ancient Egypt*, 14671
The Barn Owl, 19367
The Frog, 18740
The Rabbit, 19211
Tagliaferro, Linda. *Bruce Lee*, 12411
Destination New York, 16748
Tait, Les. *The Clay Ladies*, 3020(F)
Taitz, Emily. *Israel*, 15531
Takabayashi, Mari. *Flannel Kisses*, 3041(F)
Marshmallow Kisses, 3042(F)
Rush Hour, 3286(F)
Sidewalk Trip, 3224(F)
Takahashi, Hideko. *Beach Play*, 3197(F)
The Ding Dong Clock, 381(F)
Good Night, God Bless, 755(F)
My Loose Tooth, 6439(F)
Takamado, Princess. *Katie and the Dream-Eater*, 10831
Takao, Yuko. *A Winter Concert*, 2751(F)
Takaya, Julia (jt. author). *Chibi*, 5141
Talbert, Marc. *Small Change*, 7092(F)
Star of Luis, 8828(F)
A Sunburned Prayer, 7524(F)
The Trap, 7311(F)
Talbot, Frank H., ed. *Under the Sea*, 19840
Talbott, Hudson. *Amazon Diary*, 7093(F)
Forging Freedom, 14886

King Arthur and the Round Table, 11038
Lancelot, 11039
O'Sullivan Stew, 1610(F)
Talbott, Hudson, reteller. *King Arthur and the Round Table*, 11038
Tallarico, Tony. *Drawing and Cartooning All-Star Sports*, 21596
Find Freddie, 2752(F)
Tallchief, Maria. *Tallchief*, 12477
Talley, Linda. *Thank You, Meiling*, 2753(F)
Tallman, Edward. *Garth Brooks*, 12362
Shaquille O'Neal, 13559
Tamar, Erika. *Donnatalee*, 1611(F)
The Garden of Happiness, 4551(F)
The Midnight Train Home, 9442(F)
Soccer Mania! 10366(F)
Tamarin, Alfred (jt. author). *Olympic Games in Ancient Greece*, 22247
Tambini, Michael. *Future*, 21953
Tames, Richard. *Auguste Rodin*, 12297
Exploration into Japan, 15139
Journey Through Canada, 15596
Journey Through Japan, 15140
Michelangelo Buonarroti, 12262
Tamura, David. *When Justice Failed*, 12922
Tan, Amy. *The Chinese Siamese Cat*, 5428(F)
The Moon Lady, 9017(F)
Tan, Sheri. *Seiji Ozawa*, 12440
Tanaka, Shelley. *The Buried City of Pompeii*, 14749(F)
Discovering the Iceman, 14515
Graveyards of the Dinosaurs, 14474
In the Time of Knights, 14795
Lost Temple of the Aztecs, 15652
On Board the Titanic, 7094(F)
Tanaka, Shelley (jt. author). *One More Border*, 14858
Tang, Charles. *The Mystery of the Hidden Painting*, 7123(F)
Tang, Fay (jt. author). *Sing for Your Father, Su Phan*, 9009(F)
Tang, Greg. *The Grapes of Math*, 20622
Tanner, Tim. *Off the Map*, 16090
Tao, Wang. *Exploration into China*, 15086
Tapahonso, Luci. *Navajo ABC*, 136(F)
Songs of Shiprock Fair, 9181(F)
Tarbescu, Edith. *Annushka's Voyage*, 4848(F)
The Boy Who Stuck Out His Tongue, 11177
Targ, Harry R. (jt. author). *Guatemala*, 15659
Tarpley, Natasha A. *I Love My Hair!* 3450(F)

Tarry, Linda (jt. author). *King Solomon and the Queen of Sheba*, 17279(F)

Tarsky, Sue. *The Busy Building Book*, 21152

Tashjian, Janet. *Multiple Choice*, 8829(F)

Tru Confessions, 7525(F)

Tate, Don. *Say Hey! A Song of Willie Mays*, 13474

Tate, Eleanora E. *African American Musicians*, 12184

Tate, Lindsey. *Teatime with Emma Buttersnap*, 20128

Taulbert, Clifton L. *Little Cliff and the Porch People*, 3911(F)

Tauss, Herbert. *The Shadow Children*, 8071(F)

Tavares, Matt. *Zachary's Ball*, 1612(F)

Taylor, Alastair. *Swollobog*, 1613(F)

Taylor, Ann. *Baby Dance*, 3912(F)

Taylor, Barbara. *Animal Hide and Seek*, 18913

Animal Homes, 18914

Arctic and Antarctic, 15839

Coral Reef, 19668

Desert Life, 20425

Oxford First Book of Animals, 18982

Pond Life, 20528

Rain Forest, 20491

The Really Deadly and Dangerous Dinosaur, 14475

The Really Sinister Savage Shark, 19650

Shoreline, 19869

Taylor, Bonnie Highsmith. *Ezra*, 19114

Taylor, Bridget S. *Happy Valentine's Day, Miss Hildy!* 6168(F)

Harry McNairy, Tooth Fairy, 951(F)

Miss Hildy's Missing Cape Caper, 6001(F)

Phoebe's Fabulous Father, 3565(F)

Taylor, C. J. *Firedancers*, 3930(F)

The Ghost and Lone Warrior, 11306

How We Saw the World, 11307

The Secret of the White Buffalo, 11308

Taylor, Cheryl M. *Snug*, 2168(F)

Song and Dance, 11605

Taylor, Clark. *The House That Crack Built*, 17894

Taylor, Cora. *Vanishing Act*, 7095(F)

Taylor, Dahl. *Voices at Whisper Bend*, 9644(F)

Taylor, Dave. *Endangered Forest Animals*, 19413

Endangered Grassland Animals, 19414

Endangered Wetland Animals, 19415

Taylor, Elizabeth (jt. author). *Tornadoes*, 20681

Taylor, Harriet P. *Brother Wolf*, 11309

Coyote and the Laughing Butterflies, 11310

Coyote Places the Stars, 11311

Secrets of the Stone, 2754(F)

Ulaq and the Northern Lights, 2755(F)

When Bear Stole the Chinook, 11312

Taylor, John W. *Talking to Animals*, 18891

Taylor, Kenny. *Puffins*, 19356

Taylor, Kim. *Action*, 20839

Butterfly, 19561

Egg, 18917

Owl, 19362

Swamp Life, 20374

Taylor, Kim (jt. author). *The Nature and Science of Autumn*, 18562

The Nature and Science of Bubbles, 20799

The Nature and Science of Color, 20859

The Nature and Science of Fire, 20279

The Nature and Science of Fossils, 14390

The Nature and Science of Numbers, 20628

The Nature and Science of Reflections, 20860

The Nature and Science of Seeds, 20269

The Nature and Science of Shells, 19771

The Nature and Science of Survival, 18581

The Nature and Science of Waste, 16974

Taylor, Lawrie. *The Elephant Truck*, 5436(F)

Taylor, Leighton. *The Atlantic Ocean*, 19841

Creeps from the Deep, 19651

The Mediterranean Sea, 19842

Taylor, Livingston. *Can I Be Good?* 5429(F)

Taylor, M. W. *Harriet Tubman*, 12803

Taylor, Marilyn. *Faraway Home*, 9690(F)

Taylor, Maureen. *Through the Eyes of Your Ancestors*, 16441

Taylor, Michael. *The Indian Way*, 9168(F)

Taylor, Mike. *Parallel Universe*, 21862(F)

Some Bugs Glow in the Dark, 19462

Spiders Have Fangs, 19586

Taylor, Mildred D. *Roll of Thunder, Hear My Cry*, 7526(F)

Taylor, Nicole. *Baby*, 18248

Taylor, Penny (jt. author). *Koi's Python*, 8974(F)

The Kwanzaa Contest, 9750(F)

Taylor, Richard L. *The First Flight*, 13359

The First Human-Powered Flight, 12138

The First Unrefueled Flight Around the World, 21107

Taylor, Scott. *Fiesta!* 3523(F)

Taylor, Stephen. *Music from the Sky*, 3649(F)

One More Border, 14858

Taylor, Sydney. *All-of-a-Kind Family*, 7527(F)

Taylor, Theodore. *Air Raid — Pearl Harbor*, 14887

The Cay, 8377(F)

The Hostage, 7312(F)

The Odyssey of Ben O'Neal, 7096(F)

Timothy of the Cay, 7097(F)

The Trouble with Tuck, 7313(F)

Tuck Triumphant, 7314(F)

Taylor, William. *Agnes the Sheep*, 7315(F)

Numbskulls, 7098(F)

Tazewell, Charles. *The Littlest Angel*, 1614(F)

Tchana, Katrin. *Oh, No, Toto!* 4849(F)

The Serpent Slayer and Other Stories of Strong Women, 10717

Teague, Allison L. *Prince of the Fairway*, 13719

Teague, Ken. *Growing Up in Ancient China*, 15087

Teague, Mark. *Baby Tamer*, 4336(F)

The Great Gracie Chase, 1532(F)

How Do Dinosaurs Say Goodnight? 816(F)

The Iguana Brothers, 2261(F)

The Lost and Found, 1615(F)

One Halloween Night, 6054(F)

Pigsty, 2756(F)

Poppleton, 6614(F)

Poppleton and Friends, 6615(F)

Poppleton Everyday, 6616(F)

Poppleton Forever, 6617(F)

Poppleton Has Fun, 2647(F)

Poppleton in Fall, 6618(F)

Poppleton in Spring, 6619(F)

The Secret Shortcut, 1616(F)

Sweet Dream Pie, 1702(F)

Teague, Mark (jt. author). *The Flying Dragon Room*, 1704(F)

Teare, Brad. *Dance, Pioneer, Dance!* 4866(F)

Techner, David. *A Candle for Grandpa*, 17488

Teckentrup, Britta. *Coyote Makes Man*, 11297

Kancil and the Crocodiles, 10838

Well, a Crocodile Can! 5189(F)

Teeters, Peggy. *Jules Verne*, 12614

Telander, Todd. *Exploring an Ocean Tide Pool*, 19854

Telemaque, Eleanor Wong. *Haiti Through Its Holidays*, 15720
Telford, Carole. *Down a River*, 15908
Inside a Coral Reef, 19669
Through a Termite City, 19493
Up a Rainforest Tree, 20492
Temko, Florence. *Paper Gifts and Jewelry*, 21633
Planes and Other Flying Things, 21634
Traditional Crafts from Africa, 21501
Traditional Crafts from China, 21502
Traditional Crafts from Mexico and Central America, 21503
Traditional Crafts from Native North America, 21526
Traditional Crafts from the Caribbean, 21504
Temple, Bob. *Chihuahuas*, 19976
Jack Russell Terriers, 19977
Temple, Charles. *Train*, 3451(F)
Templeton, Ty. *Batman Gotham Adventures*, 8138(F)
Ten, Arnie. *Simple Attractions*, 20904
Tenniel, John. *Alice's Adventures in Wonderland and Through the Looking Glass*, 7646(F)
Through the Looking Glass, and What Alice Found There, 7647(F)
Tenquist, Alasdair. *Egypt*, 15515
Nigeria, 15049
Terban, Marvin. *Checking Your Grammar*, 14110
The Dove Dove, 14047
Eight Ate, 14048
Funny You Should Ask, 21857
Guppies in Tuxedos, 14049
In a Pickle and Other Funny Idioms, 14050
It Figures! 14111
Punching the Clock, 14051
Punctuation Power, 14112
Too Hot to Hoot, 14052
Your Foot's on My Feet! 14053
Terkel, Susan N. *Colonial American Medicine*, 16180
Terlson, Craig. *The Amazing Dirt Book*, 20551
Terreson, Jeffrey. *Animal Homes*, 18915
Terris, Daniel (jt. author). *A Ripple of Hope*, 12919
Terry, Michael (jt. author). *The Selfish Crocodile*, 1951(F)
Terry, Michael Bad Hand. *Daily Life in a Plains Indian Village*, 16062
Terry, Will. *Pizza Pat*, 6340(F)
Terzian, Alexandra M. *The Kids' Multicultural Art Book*, 13928
Tesar, Jenny. *America's Top 10 Curiosities*, 21954

America's Top 10 National Parks, 15909
Fungi, 20192
Kidbits, 21955
Shrinking Forests, 20218
Threatened Oceans, 19843
The Waste Crisis, 16987
What on Earth Is a Bustard? 19290
What on Earth Is a Quokka? 19183
Teskey, Donald. *Fields of Home*, 9088(F)
Tessendorf, K. C. *Barnstormers and Daredevils*, 21108
Over the Edge, 15840
Wings Around the World, 21109
Tessitore, John. *Kofi Annan*, 13752
Tessler, Stephanie G. (jt. author). *Nell Nugget and the Cow Caper*, 2926(F)
Six Creepy Sheep, 5996(F)
Six Sandy Sheep, 2072(F)
Upstairs, 1152(F)
What Would Mama Do? 2073(F)
What's the Matter, Kelly Beans? 8634(F)
Where Are You, Little Zack? 430(F)
Testa, Fulvio. *Aesop's Fables*, 11049
Time to Get Out, 2757(F)
Testa, Maria. *Nine Candles*, 8830(F)
Someplace to Go, 8831(F)
Thumbs Up, Rico! 8918(F)
Tester, Sylvia Root. *We Laughed a Lot, My First Day of School*, 5542(F)
Tews, Susan. *The Gingerbread Doll*, 5934(F)
Lizard Sees the World, 2758(F)
Thaler, Mike. *Frankenstein's Pantyhose*, 21858
What Could a Hippopotamus Be? 2759(F)
Thaler, Shmuel (jt. author). *Chris Mullin*, 13552
Photography, 21802
Steve Young, 13640
Thapar, Valmik. *Tiger*, 19115
Tharlet, Eve. *The Brave Little Tailor*, 10891
The Emperor's New Clothes, 10381(F)
Happy Birthday, Davy! 5736(F)
How Will We Get to the Beach? 2954(F)
Jack in Luck, 10884
Little Pig, Bigger Trouble, 2760(F)
Merry Christmas, Davy! 5953(F)
What Have You Done, Davy? 2839(F)
What's the Matter, Davy? 2840(F)
Where Have You Gone, Davy? 2841(F)
Why Are You Fighting, Davy? 2842(F)
Will You Mind the Baby, Davy? 2843(F)
Thaxter, Celia. *Celia's Island Journal*, 4850

Thayer, Ernest Lawrence. *Casey at the Bat*, 12006
Ernest L. Thayer's Casey at the Bat, 12007
Thayer, Jane. *Gus Loves His Happy Home*, 1617(F)
The Puppy Who Wanted a Boy, 5935(F)
Thelen, Mary. *Abra-Ca-Dazzle*, 21777
Hocus Pocus, 21778
Theodorou, Rod. *Across the Solar System*, 18532
Along the Seashore, 19870
Amphibians, 18696
From the Arctic to Antarctica, 15841
Insects, 19494
Theodorou, Rod (jt. author). *Down a River*, 15908
Inside a Coral Reef, 19669
Through a Termite City, 19493
Up a Rainforest Tree, 20492
Theroux, Phyllis. *Serefina under the Circumstances*, 5729(F)
Thesman, Jean. *Calling the Swan*, 8832(F)
When the Road Ends, 8529(F)
Thiel, Elizabeth. *The Polka Dot Horse*, 1618(F)
Thiele, Bob (jt. author). *What a Wonderful World*, 14259(F)
Thiesing, Lisa. *Me and You*, 3913(F)
Two Silly Trolls, 6421(F)
Thimmesh, Catherine. *Girls Think of Everything*, 21061
Thomas, Angela T. *The Blueberry Train*, 4763(F)
The Mighty Santa Fe, 3704(F)
Thomas, David Hurst, ed. *Native Americans*, 16063
Thomas, Dawn C. *Kai*, 8979(F)
Thomas, Dylan. *A Child's Christmas in Wales*, 11853
Thomas, Elizabeth. *Green Beans*, 3914(F)
Thomas, Frances. *What If?* 1619(F)
Thomas, Gwyn. *Tales from the Mabinogion*, 11040
Thomas, Jane Resh. *Behind the Mask*, 13789
Celebration! 5652(F)
Courage at Indian Deep, 7099(F)
Fox in a Trap, 7100(F)
The Princess in the Pigpen, 8139(F)
Saying Good-bye to Grandma, 3915(F)
Scaredy Dog, 5430(F)
Thomas, John E. *The Ultimate Book of Kid Concoctions*, 21505
Thomas, Joyce C. *The Bowlegged Rooster and Other Tales That Signify*, 8140(F)
Cherish Me! 3452(F)
Hush Songs, 793
I Have Heard of a Land, 9443(F)

You Are My Perfect Baby, 3453(F)
Thomas, Margaret. *Volcano!* 20350
Thomas, Naturi. *Uh-oh! It's Mama's Birthday!* 3916(F)
Thomas, Pamela. *Brooklyn Pops Up*, 16749
Thomas, Pat. *My Family's Changing*, 17689
Thomas, Paul. *The Central Asian States*, 15435
Thomas, Peggy. *Big Cat Conservation*, 19416
Bird Alert, 19417
Marine Mammal Preservation, 19418
Reptile Rescue, 19419
Thomas, Shelley M. *A Baby's Coming to Your House!* 18234
Good Night, Good Knight, 6692(F)
Somewhere Today, 251(F)
Thomas, Valerie. *Winnie Flies Again*, 4337(F)
Thomas, Velma M. *Lest We Forget*, 9325
Thomassie, Tynia. *Cajun*, 4851(F)
Feliciana Feydra LeRoux, 2978(F)
Feliciana Meets d'Loup Garou, 1621(F)
Thompson, Alexa. *Nova Scotia*, 15597
Thompson, Carol. *Baby Days*, 3454(F)
First Verses, 11566
A New Room for William, 4970(F)
Oonga Boonga, 4355(F)
Piggy Goes to Bed, 6693(F)
Thompson, Colin. *The Last Alchemist*, 8141(F)
Looking for Atlantis, 8142(F)
Unknown, 5431(F)
Thompson, Ellen. *The Fighting Ground*, 9220(F)
Thompson, Ian. *Brain and Nerves*, 18114
The Science Factory, 18343
The Sun Is a Star, 18409
Super Humans, 17898
What Do We Know About the Amazonian Indians? 15756
Thompson, Jan. *Christian Festivals*, 17403
Thompson, Jeffrey. *The Midnight Ride of Paul Revere*, 11642
Thompson, John. *Christmas in the Big House, Christmas in the Quarters*, 16262
The Dead Sea Scrolls, 17257
O Jerusalem, 11742
A Thanksgiving Wish, 6153(F)
Thompson, K. Dyble. *Because Brian Hugged His Mother*, 3377(F)
My Name Is Maria Isabel, 7331(F)
Thompson, Karmen. *Meet the Marching Smithereens*, 14223
Meet the Orchestra, 14224
Thompson, Kate. *Switchers*, 8143(F)
Wild Blood, 8144(F)

Thompson, Kathleen. *New York*, 16750
Pennsylvania, 16751
Thompson, Kay. *Eloise at Christmastime*, 5936(F)
Thompson, Lauren. *Love One Another*, 17440
Mouse's First Christmas, 5937(F)
Mouse's First Halloween, 6055(F)
One Riddle, One Answer, 10510(F)
Thompson, Luke. *Essential Boating for Teens*, 22264
Tsunamis, 20722
Thompson, Margot. *Make a Change Opposites*, 252(F)
Make a Change Shapes, 361(F)
Thompson, Mary. *Andy and His Yellow Frisbee*, 5091(F)
Gran's Bees, 3917(F)
My Brother Matthew, 3918(F)
Thompson, Richard. *The Follower*, 1622(F)
Thompson, Sharon. *Freya's Fantastic Surprise*, 5503(F)
Thompson, Sharon E. *Built for Speed*, 19116
Death Trap, 14476
Thompson, Stith, ed. *One Hundred Favorite Folktales*, 10621
Thompson, Stuart (jt. author). *China*, 15082
Thomson, Melissa (jt. author). *Life in the American Colonies*, 16109
Thomson, Neil (jt. author). *A Family in Thailand*, 15208
Thomson, Pat. *Beware of the Aunts!* 5938(F)
Thomson, Peggy. *The Nine-Ton Cat*, 13964
Siggy's Spaghetti Works, 20129
Take Me Out to the Bat and Ball Factory, 22122
Thomson, Ruth. *A Family in Thailand*, 15208
The Rainforest Indians, 20493
Rice, 20130
Thomson, Ruth (jt. author). *Models*, 21793
Thomson, Tracy. *Ahmek*, 8188(F)
Thong, Roseanne. *Round Is a Mooncake*, 362(F)
Thornburg, Linda (jt. author). *Cool Careers for Girls in Computers*, 17794
Cool Careers for Girls in Engineering, 17795
Cool Careers for Girls in Food, 17759
Cool Careers for Girls in Health, 17804
Cool Careers for Girls in Sports, 17760
Thornburgh, Rebecca. *Count on Pablo*, 418(F)
Thornburgh, Rebecca M. *My First Day at Camp*, 6711(F)
One Happy Classroom, 581(F)

Thorne-Thomsen, Kathleen. *Frank Lloyd Wright for Kids*, 12314
The Shaker's Dozen, 594
Thornhill, Jan. *Before and After*, 18983
Thornley, Stew. *Emmitt Smith*, 13634
Frank Thomas, 13509
Grant Hill, 13530
Jerry Rice, 13624
Mark McGwire, 13468
Roberto Alomar, 13436
Shawn Kemp, 13541
Sports Great Dennis Rodman, 13574
Sports Great Greg Maddux, 13471
Sports Great Reggie Miller, 13549
Top 10 Football Receivers, 13419
Thornton, Duncan. *Kalifax*, 8145(F)
Thornton, Peter J. *Everybody Bakes Bread*, 3109(F)
Everybody Serves Soup, 5805(F)
Thorpe, Jim. *T.J.'s Secret Pitch*, 10282(F)
Thorson, Kristine. *Stone Wall Secrets*, 20574
Thorson, Robert (jt. author). *Stone Wall Secrets*, 20574
Thrasher, Thomas. *Gunfighters*, 12698
The Importance of William Shakespeare, 12595
Thurber, James. *The Great Quillow*, 8146(F)
Many Moons, 10511(F)
The White Deer, 10512(F)
Thurman, Mark. *Carrie's Crowd*, 8268(F)
Thury, Fredrick H. *The Last Straw*, 9763(F)
Thyacott, Louise. *Musical Instruments*, 14230
Tibbitts, Alison Davis. *James K. Polk*, 13092
Tibbles, Jean-Paul. *Watcher in the Piney Woods*, 9483(F)
Tibo, Gilles. *The Cowboy Kid*, 8147(F)
Simon and the Snowflakes, 1623(F)
Tick, Gabriel David (jt. author). *Slam Dunk*, 10274(F)
Tidd, Louise Vitellaro. *The Best Pet Yet*, 6694(F)
I'll Do It Later, 6695(F)
Let Me Help! 6696(F)
Lost and Found, 6697(F)
Tiegreen, Alan. *Anna Banana*, 21983
Asking About Sex and Growing Up, 18254
Blue Skies, French Fries, 4126(F)
Cookies and Crutches, 6304(F)
Crazy Eights and Other Card Games, 22229
The Eentsy, Weentsy Spider, 21984
Fun on the Run, 21985
Halloween Helpers, 9716(F)
Pin the Tail on the Donkey and Other Party Games, 21987

Six Sick Sheep, 21879
Why Did the Chicken Cross the Road? 21820(F)
Tiffault, Benette W. *A Quilt for Elizabeth*, 3919(F)
Tildes, Phyllis L. *Animals*, 5432(F)
Animals in Camouflage, 18890
Calico's Cousins, 19934
Counting on Calico, 595(F)
Tillage, Leon W. *Leon's Story*, 17052
Tiller, Ruth. *Cats Vanish Slowly*, 11815
Tillery, Angelo. *A Pride of Princesses*, 10408(F)
Tilley, Debbie. *God's Mailbox*, 17273
Never Let Your Cat Make Lunch for You, 2171(F)
Oops! 17635
Riddle-Lightful, 21836
Tillotson, Katherine. *Nice Try, Tooth Fairy*, 1443(F)
Songs of Papa's Island, 4709(F)
Tilton, Rafael. *Mother Teresa*, 13859
Timmel, Carol Ann. *Tabitha*, 5433(F)
Timmers, Leo. *Monkey See, Monkey Do*, 5266(F)
Tipp, Stacey L. *Causes of Crime*, 17087
Child Abuse, 17157
Tippins, Sherill. *Donna Karan*, 13163
Michael Eisner, 12875
Titherington, Jeanne. *It's Snowing! It's Snowing!* 4511(F)
Pumpkin Pumpkin, 4552(F)
Tito, E. Tina. *Liberation*, 14888
Titus, Eve. *Basil of Baker Street*, 8148(F)
Tjong-Khing, The. *Andrew's Angry Words*, 1328(F)
Tobias, Tobi. *Serendipity*, 3455(F)
Tobias, Tobi, ed. *A World of Words*, 138
Tobin, Nancy. *Drip! Drop!* 20745
Fraction Fun, 20578
How Tall How Short How Far Away, 366
Shape Up! 319(F)
Tocci, Salvatore. *Science Fair Success in the Hardware Store*, 18352
Science Fair Success Using Supermarket Products, 18353
Toda, Kyoko. *Animal Faces*, 18984
Todd, Janette. *My Pet Crocodile and Other Slightly Outrageous Verse*, 11856
Todd, Justin. *The Whispering Room*, 11544
Todd, Pamela. *Pig and the Shrink*, 10005(F)
Todd, Susan. *Boredom Blasters*, 22070
Toddy, Irving. *Cheyenne Again*, 9149(F)

Toft, Kim Michelle. *Neptune's Nursery*, 19647
One Less Fish, 598
Toht, David W. *Sodbuster*, 16382
Tolan, Stephanie S. *The Face in the Mirror*, 8149(F)
Ordinary Miracles, 8833(F)
Save Halloween! 8530(F)
Who's There? 8150(F)
Tolkien, J. R. R. *The Hobbit*, 8151(F)
Roverandom, 8152(F)
Tolliver, Ruby C. *Boomer's Kids*, 9629(F)
I Love You, Daisy Phew, 8834(F)
Sarita, Be Brave, 7377(F)
Tolstoy, Aleksei. *The Gigantic Turnip*, 11114
Tolstoy, Leo. *Philipok*, 5543(F)
Tom, Linda C. *Nursery Rhymes from Mother Goose Told in Signed English*, 827
Tomcheck, Ann Heinrichs. *The Hopi*, 16064
Tomczyk, Mary. *Shapes, Sizes and More Surprises!* 253(F)
Tomecek, Steve. *Simple Attractions*, 20904
Tomei, Lorna. *Rosie and Michael*, 4052(F)
Tomes, Margot. *Homesick*, 12536
The Lap-Time Song and Play Book, 903
Little Sister and the Month Brothers, 11087
The Shadowmaker, 7784(F)
The Soup Bone, 6017(F)
Ty's One-Man Band, 3470(F)
Where Do You Think You're Going, Christopher Columbus? 12099
Tomey, Ingrid. *Grandfather's Day*, 7528(F)
Tomlinson, Theresa. *Child of the May*, 9125(F)
Little Stowaway, 2979(F)
Tomoko. *A Peek at Japan*, 15133
Tomova, Veselina. *A Dozen Silk Diapers*, 10920
Tompert, Ann. *A Carol for Christmas*, 5939(F)
Grandfather Tang's Story, 1624(F)
The Hungry Black Bag, 2761(F)
Just a Little Bit, 2762(F)
Nothing Sticks Like a Shadow, 2763(F)
Saint Nicholas, 17225
Will You Come Back for Me? 3920(F)
Tompsett, Norman (jt. author). *Canada*, 15564
Welcome to Canada, 15565
Tong, Willabel L. *Cars, Boats, Trains, and Planes*, 21289
Tonge, Neil (jt. author). *Alien Encounters*, 21912
Tooke, Susan. *A Seaside Alphabet*, 45(F)
Tope, Lily R. *Philippines*, 15255

Topek, Susan Remick. *A Costume for Noah*, 6120(F)
Shalom Shabbat, 6121(F)
Ten Good Rules, 17325
Topper, Frank. *A Historical Album of New Jersey*, 16752
Tore, Bob. *Win or Lose by How You Choose!* 17632
Toriseva, JoNelle. *Rodeo Day*, 5434(F)
Torrence, Susan. *A Cozy Place*, 4044(F)
Torres, John. *Derek Jeter*, 13465
Kobe Bryant, 13518
Mia Hamm, 13691
Torres, John A. *Darryl Strawberry*, 13506
Hakeem Olajuwon, 13556
Sports Great Jason Kidd, 13543
Sports Great Oscar De La Hoya, 13585
Top 10 Basketball Three-Point Shooters, 13420
Top 10 NBA Finals Most Valuable Players, 13421
Torres, Leyla. *Liliana's Grandmothers*, 3921(F)
Saturday Sancocho, 4852(F)
Subway Sparrow, 3456(F)
Towers, Elisabeth (jt. author). *The Oneida*, 15998
Towne, Mary. *Steve the Sure*, 8835(F)
Townley, Roderick. *The Great Good Thing*, 10513(F)
Townsend, Brad. *Shaquille O'Neal*, 13560
Townsend, Tom. *The Trouble with an Elf*, 8153(F)
Toye, William. *The Loon's Necklace*, 11313
Toynton, Evelyn. *Growing Up in America*, 16280
Tracqui, Valerie. *The Brown Bear*, 19071
Tracqui, Valerie (jt. author). *The Cheetah*, 19085
Tracy, Libba. *It Rained on the Desert Today*, 11944
This House Is Made of Mud, 4395(F)
Trahey, Jane. *The Clovis Caper*, 10006(F)
Trapani, Iza. *How Much Is That Doggie in the Window?* 14258
The Itsy Bitsy Spider, 14185
Mary Had a Little Lamb, 896(F)
Row Row Row Your Boat, 14186
Shoo Fly! 794(F)
Tomorrow Is Mom's Birthday, 5681(F)
What Am I? 5435
Trapani, Iza, reteller. *How Much Is That Doggie in the Window?* 14258
Mary Had a Little Lamb, 896(F)

Trapani, Margi. *Working Together Against Gang Violence*, 17088

Travers, Will. *Elephant*, 19173

The Elephant Truck, 5436(F)

Travis, George. *State Facts*, 15910

Travis, Lucille. *Redheaded Orphan*, 9444(F)

Traylor, Betty. *Buckaroo*, 8531(F)

Traylor, Bill. *Black Elephant with a Brown Ear (in Alabama)*, 13962

Treat, Rose. *The Seaweed Book*, 19652

Treays, Rebecca, ed. *The Usborne Book of Everyday Words*, 14055

Tregebov, Rhea. *The Big Storm*, 5437(F)

Treherne, Katie T. *The Light Princess*, 10456(F)

The Little Mermaid, 10514(F)

Tatsinda, 1153(F)

Treherne, Katie T., reteller. *The Little Mermaid*, 10514(F)

Treinan, Sarah Jane, ed. *Better Homes and Gardens Incredibly Awesome Crafts for Kids*, 21506

Trembath, Don. *Frog Face and the Three Boys*, 10367(F)

Tresselt, Alvin. *Hide and Seek Fog*, 4553(F)

Rain Drop Splash, 4554(F)

Wake Up, City! 3457(F)

White Snow Bright Snow, 3458(F)

Tresselt, Alvin, ed. *The Mitten*, 10864

Trezzo-Baren, Loretta. *Kids Cook! Fabulous Food for the Whole Family*, 21751

Trimble, Marcia. *Malinda Martha Meets Mariposa*, 12039

Trimble, Patti. *Lost!* 6698(F)

What Day Is It? 6699(F)

Trinca, Rod. *One Woolly Wombat*, 599(F)

Tripp, Janet. *Lorraine Hansberry*, 12545

Tripp, Valerie. *Changes for Felicity*, 9214(F)

Changes for Samantha, 9630(F)

Felicity Learns a Lesson, 9215(F)

Felicity's Surprise, 9216(F)

Happy Birthday, Josefina! A Springtime Story, 9445(F)

Josefina Saves the Day, 9446(F)

Kit Learns a Lesson, 9631(F)

Meet Josefina, 9447(F)

Meet Kit, 9632(F)

Meet Molly, 9691(F)

Tripp, Wallace. *A Great Big Ugly Man Came Up and Tied His Horse to Me*, 11920

No Flying in the House, 1866(F)

Play Ball, Amelia Bedelia, 6566(F)

Rose's Are Red, Violet's Are Blue and Other Silly Poems, 11921

Tripp, Wallace, ed. *A Great Big Ugly Man Came Up and Tied His Horse to Me*, 11920

Trist, Glenda, comp. *A Child's Book of Prayers*, 17535

Trivas, Irene. *Black, White, Just Right!* 3602(F)

Emma's Christmas, 5940(F)

My First Book of Biographies, 13737

One-Eyed Cat, 8429(F)

One Lucky Girl, 2955(F)

The Pain and the Great One, 3534(F)

Soccer Cousins, 6509(F)

Three Perfect Peaches, 10868

Trouble on the T-Ball Team, 2914(F)

Trivizas, Eugene. *The Three Little Wolves and the Big Bad Pig*, 2764(F)

Trojer, Thomas. *Goya*, 12236

Trottier, Maxine. *A Circle of Silver*, 8945(F)

Dreamstones, 1625(F)

Flags, 4853(F)

Little Dog Moon, 4854(F)

Native Crafts, 21507

Prairie Willow, 4855(F)

A Safe Place, 5092(F)

The Tiny Kite of Eddie Wing, 5093(F)

The Walking Stick, 4856(F)

Troupe, Quincy. *Take It to the Hoop, Magic Johnson*, 12008

Troy, Don. *Booker T. Washington*, 12814

Harriet Ross Tubman, 12804

W. E. B. Du Bois, 12720

Trueman, Terry. *Stuck in Neutral*, 8836(F)

Truesdell, Sue. *Addie Meets Max*, 6591(F)

Circus Family Dog, 1964(F)

Donna O'Neeshuck Was Chased by Some Cows, 4169(F)

The Golly Sisters Go West, 4101(F)

The Golly Sisters Ride Again, 6245(F)

Hooray for the Golly Sisters! 6246(F)

How to Talk to Your Dog, 19948

Nugget and Darling, 5283(F)

Santa's Short Suit Shrunk, 5766(F)

This Is a Hospital, Not a Zoo! 1286(F)

Trumbauer, Lisa. *Computer Fun Halloween*, 17448

Computer Fun Math, 21228

Free Stuff for Kids on the Net, 21229

Homework Help for Kids on the Net, 21230

Trumble, Kelly. *Cat Mummies*, 14672

Trynan, Amit. *Frog Legs*, 2678(F)

Tryon, Leslie. *Albert's Alphabet*, 139(F)

Albert's Ballgame, 3459(F)

Albert's Birthday, 5730(F)

Albert's Christmas, 5941(F)

Albert's Field Trip, 2765(F)

Albert's Halloween, 2766(F)

Albert's Play, 2767(F)

Albert's Thanksgiving, 6158(F)

Dear Peter Rabbit, 941(F)

Yours Truly, Goldilocks, 943(F)

Tseng, Grace. *White Tiger, Blue Serpent*, 10770

Tseng, Jean. *The City of Dragons*, 1709(F)

Dragon Kite of the Autumn Moon, 4808(F)

The Ghost Fox, 10525(F)

The Khan's Daughter, 10737

Maples in the Mist, 11650

Sato and the Elephants, 8965(F)

The Seven Chinese Brothers, 10765

A Treasury of Mermaids, 10540

White Tiger, Blue Serpent, 10770

Tseng, Mou-Sien. *The City of Dragons*, 1709(F)

Dragon Parade, 5618

The Ghost Fox, 10525(F)

The Khan's Daughter, 10737

Maples in the Mist, 11650

Sato and the Elephants, 8965(F)

A Treasury of Mermaids, 10540

White Tiger, Blue Serpent, 10770

Tsubakiyama, Margaret. *Lice Are Lousy! All About Headlice*, 18009

Mei-Mei Loves the Morning, 5438(F)

Tsukushi. *The Drums of Noto Hanto*, 4692(F)

Tucker, Kathy. *Do Cowboys Ride Bikes?* 4338(F)

Do Knights Take Naps? 1626(F)

Do Pirates Take Baths? 2980(F)

The Leprechaun in the Basement, 5653(F)

Tucker, Patricia (jt. author). *There's a Wolf in the Classroom!* 19145

Tucker, Sian. *What Do You See? Come Look with Me*, 21886(F)

Tucker, Stephen (jt. author). *The Time It Took Tom*, 3421(F)

Tucker, Terry Ward. *Moonlight and Mill Whistles*, 9633(F)

Tucker, Tom. *Brainstorm!* 21062

Tudor, Tasha. *A Brighter Garden*, 11552

A Child's Garden of Verses, 11714

Give Us This Day, 17515

The Great Corgiville Kidnapping, 8154(F)

A Little Princess, 7396(F)

The Lord Is My Shepherd, 17248

The Night Before Christmas, 11845

The Secret Garden, 8263(F)

Tuitel, Johnnie. *The Barn at Gun Lake*, 7102(F)

Tull, Mary. *North America*, 21527

Northern Asia, 15209

Tulloch, Shirley. *Who Made Me?* 1627(F)

Tung, Jeffrey Dao-Sheng (jt. author). *The Chinese-American Experience*, 17600

Tunis, John R. *The Kid from Tomkinsville*, 10368(F)

Tunnell, Michael O. *Halloween Pie*, 6056(F)

Mailing May, 3922(F)

School Spirits, 8155(F)

Turbak, Gary. *Mountain Animals in Danger*, 19420

Ocean Animals in Danger, 19421

Turck, Mary C. *The Civil Rights Movement for Kids*, 16523

Turk, Ruth. *Charlie Chaplin*, 12367

Ray Charles, 12368

Rosalynn Carter, 13142

Turley, Peggy. *The Pasteboard Bandit*, 1005(F)

Turnbull, Andy. *By Truck to the North*, 15842

Turnbull, Ann. *Maroo of the Winter Caves*, 8959(F)

Too Tired, 2768(F)

Turner, Ann. *Abe Lincoln Remembers*, 13078

Angel Hide and Seek, 315(F)

Apple Valley Year, 4555(F)

Dakota Dugout, 4857(F)

Drummer Boy, 9505(F)

Dust for Dinner, 6700(F)

Elfsong, 8156(F)

Finding Walter, 8157(F)

The Girl Who Chased Away Sorrow, 9182(F)

Grasshopper Summer, 9448(F)

Katie's Trunk, 4858(F)

Let's Be Animals, 5439(F)

Mississippi Mud, 11726

A Moon for Seasons, 11986

Red Flower Goes West, 4859(F)

Secrets from the Dollhouse, 1628(F)

Street Talk, 11727

Through Moon and Stars and Night Skies, 3923(F)

Turner, Barbara J. *A Little Bit of Rob*, 3924(F)

Turner, Glennette Tilley. *Running for Our Lives*, 9326(F)

The Underground Railroad in Illinois, 16281

Turner, Megan W. *Instead of Three Wishes*, 8158(F)

The Queen of Attolia, 8159(F)

The Thief, 8160(F)

Turner, Nancy Byrd. *When Young Melissa Sweeps*, 3460(F)

Turner, Priscilla. *The War Between the Vowels and the Consonants*, 140(F)

Turner, Steve. *Dad, You're Not Funny and Other Poems*, 11922

Turner, Whitney. *The War Between the Vowels and the Consonants*, 140(F)

Tusa, Tricia. *Bunnies in My Head*, 3461(F)

Lemonade for Sale, 20591(F)

Maebelle's Suitcase, 1629(F)

Stay Away from the Junkyard, 4050(F)

Tuttle, Dennis R. *Life in the Minor Leagues*, 22123

Twain, Mark. *Adventures of Huckleberry Finn*, 10007(F)

A Connecticut Yankee in King Arthur's Court, 8161(F)

The Stolen White Elephant, 7103(F)

Tweddle, Dominic. *Growing Up in Viking Times*, 15468

Tweit, Susan J. *Meet the Wild Southwest*, 16916

Twinem, Neecy. *Baby Alligator*, 18699

Changing Colors, 18752

High in the Trees, 19184

Twist, Clint. *Deserts*, 20426

Magellan and da Gama, 12069

Seas and Oceans, 19844

Tyers, Jenny. *When It Is Night, When It Is Day*, 796(F)

Tylden-Wright, Jenny. *Coming Through the Blizzard*, 5922(F)

Tyler, Deborah. *The Greeks and Troy*, 14708

Japan, 15141

Tyler, Gillian. *The Snail House*, 946(F)

Tym, Wanda. *The Illustrated Rules of Tennis*, 22315

Tyrrell, Frances. *Woodland Christmas*, 14217

Tythacott, Louise. *Dance*, 14299

Jewelry, 21186

Tzannes, Robin. *Professor Puffendorf's Secret Potions*, 1631(F)

Uchida, Yoshiko. *The Bracelet*, 9692(F)

The Happiest Ending, 7529(F)

A Jar of Dreams, 7530(F)

Journey Home, 7378(F)

Journey to Topaz, 7379(F)

Magic Listening Cap, 10832

The Magic Purse, 10833

Samurai of Gold Hill, 9634(F)

The Wise Old Woman, 10834

Udechukwu, Ada. *Herero*, 15004

Udry, Janice May. *Let's Be Enemies*, 4051(F)

The Moon Jumpers, 1632(F)

Thump and Plunk, 6701(F)

A Tree Is Nice, 4556(F)

Uff, Caroline. *Happy Birthday, Lulu!* 5731(F)

Hello, Lulu, 3925(F)

Lulu's Busy Day, 3462(F)

Uhlberg, Myron. *Flying over Brooklyn*, 8162(F)

Mad Dog McGraw, 1633(F)

Ulmer, Wendy K. *A Campfire for Cowboy Billy*, 1634(F)

Ulrich, George. *Divide and Ride*, 524

The Frog Prince, 10427(F)

Make Four Million Dollars by Next Thursday! 9935(F)

Thomas Alva Edison, 13273

Umnik, Sharon D., ed. *175 Easy-to-Do Halloween Crafts*, 21508

Un Kim, Joung. *The Gift of Driscoll Lipscomb*, 294(F)

UNESCO. *700 Science Experiments for Everyone*, 18354

Unger, Karen (jt. author). *Too Old for This, Too Young for That! Your Survival Guide for the Middle-School Years*, 18267

Ungerer, Tomi. *Crictor*, 2769(F)

Flat Stanley, 1014(F)

Flix, 2770(F)

Tortoni Tremolo, 1635(F)

Ungs, Tim. *Shaquille O'Neal*, 13561

Superstars of Men's Soccer, 13422

Unobagha, Uzo. *Off to the Sweet Shores of Africa*, 897

Unwin, David. *The New Book of Dinosaurs*, 14477

Prehistoric Life, 14516

Unwin, Nora S. *Amos Fortune, Free Man*, 12724

Unzner, Christa. *A House Is Not a Home*, 2372(F)

Meredith, 1329(F)

Meredith's Mixed-up Magic, 1330(F)

Updike, David. *An Autumn Tale*, 6057(F)

The Sounds of Summer, 7316(F)

A Spring Story, 7104(F)

Updike, John. *A Child's Calendar*, 11987

Upitis, Alvis. *Extra Cheese, Please!* 20070

Harvest Year, 20121

Upton, Barbara. *Adventure on Klickitat Island*, 1240(F)

Urbanovic, Jackie. *My Very Own Birthday*, 21510

Ure, Jean. *The Children Next Door*, 8163(F)

Muddy Four Paws, 7317(F)

Skinny Melon and Me, 8837(F)

The Wizard in the Woods, 8164(F)

Wizard in Wonderland, 8165(F)

U'Ren, Andrea. *Pugdog*, 1636(F)

Uschan, Michael V. *The 1940s*, 16492

Usher, Kerry. *Heroes, Gods and Emperors from Roman Mythology*, 11512

Uttley, Colin. *Cities in the Sky*, 21017

Magnesium, 20291

Utton, Peter. *Dig and Sow! How Do Plants Grow?* 18592

Nikki and the Rocking Horse, 3547(F)

Splish! Splosh! Why Do We Wash?
4486

Uyehara, Elizabeth. *Love One Another*, 17440

Vachula, Monica. *Tea with an Old Dragon*, 9642(F)

Vaes, Alain. *Puss in Boots*, 10873

Vagin, Vladimir. *Celia and the Sweet, Sweet Water*, 1460(F)
The Enormous Carrot, 11387
Insects from Outer Space, 1765(F)
The King's Equal, 1461(F)
The Nutcracker Ballet, 14300(F)
Peter and the Wolf, 11115
The Twelve Days of Christmas, 14215

Vagin, Vladimir (jt. author). *Dear Brother*, 1764(F)
Insects from Outer Space, 1765(F)

Vail, Rachel. *Daring to Be Abigail*, 8838(F)
Ever After, 8839(F)
If You Only Knew, 8378(F)
Not That I Care, 10133(F)
Over the Moon, 2771(F)
Please, Please, Please, 8379(F)

Vainio, Pirkko. *The Best of Friends*, 2772(F)
The Christmas Angel, 5942(F)
The Dream House, 1637(F)

Valenta, Barbara. *Pop-o-Mania*, 21635

Valet, P. M. *Colors*, 271
Fruit, 20144

Valgardson, W. D. *Garbage Creek and Other Stories*, 10266(F)
Sarah and the People of Sand River, 8946
Winter Rescue, 7105(F)

Valientes, Corazones. *Tortillas and Lullabies*, 4809(F)

Van Allsburg, Chris. *Bad Day at Riverbend*, 1638(F)
Ben's Dream, 1639(F)
The Garden of Abdul Gasazi, 2981(F)
Jumanji, 1640(F)
Just a Dream, 1641(F)
The Mysteries of Harris Burdick, 936(F)
The Polar Express, 5943(F)
The Stranger, 1642(F)
The Sweetest Fig, 8167(F)
Two Bad Ants, 2773(F)
The Widow's Broom, 1643(F)
The Wreck of the Zephyr, 8168(F)
The Wretched Stone, 1644(F)
The Z Was Zapped, 14056

Vanasse, Deb. *Out of the Wilderness*, 7106(F)

Van Blaricom, Colleen (jt. author). *Merry Things to Make*, 21420

Van Camp, Richard. *A Man Called Raven*, 1645(F)

What's the Most Beautiful Thing You Know About Horses?
5440(F)

Vancil, Mark. *NBA Basketball Offense Basics*, 22150

VanCleave, Janice. *Bugs C*, 19495
Dinosaurs for Every Kid, 14478
Earthquakes, 20351
Geometry for Every Kid, 20607
The Human Body for Every Kid, 18082
Janice VanCleave's A+ Projects in Earth Science, 20324
Janice VanCleave's Animals, 18355
Janice VanCleave's Biology for Every Kid, 18356
Janice VanCleave's Earth Science for Every Kid, 18357
Janice VanCleave's Ecology for Every Kid, 16969
Janice VanCleave's Electricity, 20905
Janice VanCleave's Food and Nutrition for Every Kid, 18212
Janice VanCleave's Gravity, 20325
Janice VanCleave's Guide to More of the Best Science Fair Projects, 18358
Janice VanCleave's Guide to the Best Science Fair Projects, 18359
Janice VanCleave's Insects and Spiders, 19496
Janice VanCleave's Math for Every Kid, 20597
Janice VanCleave's Molecules, 20292
Janice VanCleave's Oceans for Every Kid, 19845
Janice VanCleave's Plants, 20265
Janice VanCleave's Play and Find Out About Math, 20598
Janice VanCleave's Play and Find Out About Nature, 18360
Janice VanCleave's Play and Find Out About Science, 18361
Janice VanCleave's Play and Find Out About the Human Body, 18083
Janice VanCleave's Solar System, 18533
Janice VanCleave's 203 Icy, Freezing, Frosty, Cool and Wild Experiments, 18362
Janice VanCleave's 202 Oozing, Bubbling, Dripping and Bouncing Experiments, 18363
Janice VanCleave's Volcanoes, 20352
Janice VanCleave's Weather, 20794
Machines, 21255
Magnets, 20906
Rocks and Minerals, 20575

Vande Griek, Susan. *A Gift for Ampato*, 9141(F)

Vande Velde, Vivian. *A Coming Evil*, 8169(F)
Ghost of a Hanged Man, 8170(F)
The Rumpelstiltskin Problem, 10515(F)
Smart Dog, 8171(F)
Tales from the Brothers Grimm and the Sisters Weird, 10933
There's a Dead Person Following My Sister Around, 8172(F)
Troll Teacher, 1646(F)

Vandenbroeck, Fabricio. *My Name Is Jorge*, 11653
Once When the World Was Green, 1660(F)
Torch Fishing with the Sun, 4881(F)
Uncle Rain Cloud, 3734(F)

Vanderbeek, Don. *Stormalong*, 11369

van der Linde, Laurel. *From Mustangs to Movie Stars*, 20017

Van der Linde, Polly. *Around the World in Eighty Dishes*, 21740

Van der Linde, Tasha (jt. author). *Around the World in Eighty Dishes*, 21740

Van Draanen, Wendelin. *Sammy Keyes and the Hollywood Mummy*, 7107(F)
Sammy Keyes and the Hotel Thief, 7108(F)
Sammy Keyes and the Runaway Elf, 9764(F)
Sammy Keyes and the Sisters of Mercy, 7109(F)
Sammy Keyes and the Skeleton Man, 7110(F)

Van Dusen, Chris. *Down to the Sea with Mr. Magee*, 1647(F)
Silas, 7955(F)

Van Dyck, Sara. *Insect Wars*, 19497

Van Dyke, Janice. *Captivating Cryptograms*, 21887

Vander Els, Betty. *The Bombers' Moon*, 9693(F)

Vander Hook, Sue. *Scuba Diving*, 22310

Van Fenema, Joyce. *Netherlands*, 15402

Van Fleet, Matthew. *One Yellow Lion*, 254(F)

van Garderen, Ilse. *Meg's Wish*, 4037(F)

Van Gelder, Richard G. (jt. author). *Animals in Winter*, 18801

van Haeringen, Annemarie. *Tales of the Wicked Witch*, 7879(F)

Van Hage, Mary An. *Little Green Thumbs*, 21774

Van Kampen, Vlasta. *Dinosaur Days*, 210(F)
My Dad Takes Care of Me, 3847(F)

Van Laan, Nancy. *In a Circle Long Ago*, 11314
Little Fish, Lost, 2774(F)
The Magic Bean Tree, 11443

Moose Tales, 6702(F)
Possum Come a-Knockin', 2775(F)
Round and Round Again, 4339(F)
Shingebiss, 11315
So Say the Little Monkeys, 11444
Tickle Tum! 2776(F)
A Tree for Me, 600(F)
When Winter Comes, 5441(F)
With a Whoop and a Holler, 11388
Van Leeuwen, Jean. *Amanda Pig and Her Best Friend Lollipop*, 6703(F)
Dear Mom, You're Ruining My Life, 8532(F)
The Great Christmas Kidnapping Caper, 9765(F)
The Great Rescue Operation, 8173(F)
The Great Summer Camp Catastrophe, 8174(F)
Hannah of Fairfield, 9251(F)
Hannah's Helping Hands, 9252(F)
Hannah's Winter of Hope, 9253(F)
Nothing Here But Trees, 4860(F)
Oliver and Albert, Friends Forever, 6704(F)
The Strange Adventures of Blue Dog, 1648(F)
The Tickle Stories, 3926(F)
Van Mil, Al. *The Tiny Kite of Eddie Wing*, 5093(F)
Van Nutt, Julia. *A Cobtown Christmas*, 9327(F)
The Monster in the Shadows, 10008(F)
The Mystery of Mineral Gorge, 9328(F)
Pignapped! 10009(F)
Pumpkins from the Sky? 4861(F)
Van Nutt, Robert. *A Cobtown Christmas*, 9327(F)
The Junior Thunder Lord, 10777
Pumpkins from the Sky? 4861(F)
The Savior Is Born, 5825
Van Oosting, James. *The Last Payback*, 8840(F)
Van Rose, Susanna. *The Earth Atlas*, 20326
Van Rynbach, Iris. *Five Little Pumpkins*, 6058(F)
Washington, D.C., 16654
Vansickle, Lisa. *The Secret Little City*, 8175(F)
Van Slyke, Rebecca. *Global Art*, 21448
Van Steenwyk, Elizabeth. *The California Gold Rush*, 16383
The California Missions, 16823
Dwight David Eisenhower, President, 13032
Frontier Fever, 18029
Mathew Brady, 12859
Seneca Chief, Army General, 12979
Three Dog Winter, 7531(F)
When Abraham Talked to the Trees, 13079

Van Wert, Faye. *Empty Pockets*, 3463(F)
Van West, Patricia E. *The Crab Man*, 4862(F)
Van Wright, Cornelius. *An Angel Just Like Me*, 5842(F)
The Case of the Shrunken Allowance, 567(F)
Coming Home, 13455
Daughter's Day Blues, 3835(F)
Ginger Brown, 6723(F)
A House by the River, 3809(F)
Jingle Dancer, 3434(F)
The Legend of Freedom Hill, 9339(F)
Make a Joyful Sound, 11767
Mei-Mei Loves the Morning, 5438(F)
Sam and the Lucky Money, 3069(F)
Zora Hurston and the Chinaberry Tree, 3810
Van Wyk, Gary N. *Basotho*, 15005
Shona, 15006
Van Zandt, Eleanor. *A History of the United States Through Art*, 15912
Van Zyle, Jon. *Baby Whale's Journey*, 5313(F)
A Caribou Journey, 19156
Disappearing Lake, 16801
The Eyes of Gray Wolf, 7261(F)
Gone Again Ptarmigan, 19248
Lewis and Papa, 4701(F)
A Polar Bear Journey, 19057
Raven and River, 1936(F)
River of Life, 16802
Vare, Ethlie A. *Adventurous Spirit*, 13342
Vargo, Sharon Hawkins. *Make Yourself a Monster!* 21492
Vargo, Vanessa. *Zebra Talk*, 5442(F)
Varley, Susan. *Badger's Bad Mood*, 2550(F)
Badger's Bring Something Party, 5715(F)
Badger's Parting Gifts, 2777(F)
Princess Chamomile Gets Her Way, 1445(F)
Princess Chamomile's Garden, 2553(F)
Why Is the Sky Blue? 2156(F)
Varriale, Jim. *Kids Dance*, 14301
Take a Look Around, 21804
Varvasovszky, Laszlo. *Henry in Shadowland*, 1649(F)
Vasconcellos, Daniel. *The Dog That Pitched a No-Hitter*, 10301(F)
Hat Trick, 10302(F)
Operation Baby-Sitter, 10306(F)
Vasey, Andrew (jt. author). *The Only Other Crazy Car Book*, 21325
Vaugelade, Anais. *The War*, 8176(F)
Vaughan, Marcia. *The Dancing Dragon*, 5654(F)
Dorobo the Dangerous, 1650(F)
Lemonade Stand, 6705(F)
Snap! 2778(F)

Vaughan, Marcia K. *Abbie Against the Storm*, 9329(F)
Vaughan, Richard Lee. *Eagle Boy*, 1651(F)
Vazquez, Ana Maria B. *Panama*, 15687
Vazquez, Carlos. *America Is Her Name*, 5062(F)
Vazquez, Sarah. *The School Mural*, 5544(F)
Vecchione, Glen. *100 First Prize Make It Yourself Science Fair Projects*, 18364
Vega, Anne. *Magda's Tortillas/Las tortillas de Magda*, 5674(F)
Veggeberg, Scott. *Lyme Disease*, 18010
Velasquez, Eric. *Journey to Jo'burg*, 7361(F)
The Piano Man, 3580(F)
Velikan, Phil. *A Drive to Win*, 13545
Sword of a Champion, 13704
Velthuijs, Max. *Crocodile's Masterpiece*, 2779(F)
Venezia, Mike. *Alexander Calder*, 12197
Andy Warhol, 12309
The Beatles, 12355
Da Vinci, 12219
Dorothea Lange, 12251
Edgar Degas, 12222
El Greco, 12230
Francisco Goya, 12237
Frida Kahlo, 12245
George Gershwin, 12328
Giotto, 12234
Henri Matisse, 12258
Igor Stravinsky, 12339
Jacob Lawrence, 12253
Johann Sebastian Bach, 12318
Leonard Bernstein, 12324
Ludwig Van Beethoven, 12321
Marc Chagall, 12209
Monet, 12267
Norman Rockwell, 12296
Paul Cézanne, 12206
Paul Klee, 12248
Peter Tchaikovsky, 12340
Picasso, 12285
Pierre Auguste Renoir, 12292
Rembrandt, 12289
Vennema, Peter (jt. author). *Bard of Avon*, 12594
Charles Dickens, 12529
Cleopatra, 13775
Good Queen Bess, 13788
Shaka, 13850
Venokur, Ross. *The Amazing Frecktacle*, 8177(F)
The Cookie Company, 8178(F)
Ventura, Marco. *The Strange Adventures of Blue Dog*, 1648(F)
Ventura, Piero. *Food*, 20131
Great Composers, 12185
Venturini, Tisha Lea. *You Can Be a Woman Soccer Player*, 22302
Verba, Joan M. *North Dakota*, 16588

Verboven, Agnes. *Ducks Like to Swim*, 2780(F)

Verdet, Andre. *All About Time*, 20655

Verdet, Jean-Pierre. *Atlas of the Earth*, 20327

The Universe, 18421

verDorn, Bethea. *Day Breaks*, 4557(F)

Vergoth, Karin. *Endangered Species*, 19422

Verheyden-Hilliard, Mary Ellen. *Mathematician and Computer Scientist, Caryn Navy*, 13332

Scientist and Activist, Phyllis Stearner, 13347

Scientist and Physician, Judith Pachciarz, 13337

Scientist and Strategist, June Rooks, 13344

Scientist and Teacher, Anne Barrett Swanson, 13349

Verne, Jules. *Around the World in Eighty Days*, 7111(F)

Twenty Thousand Leagues Under the Sea, 7112(F)

Vernerey, Denise (jt. author). *The Ancient Greeks*, 14678

Verniero, Joan C. *You Can Call Me Willy*, 5094(F)

Vernon, Roland. *Introducing Gershwin*, 12329

Introducing Mozart, 12336

Verougstraete, Randy. *Neale S. Godfrey's Ultimate Kids' Money Book*, 16942

Versola, Anna R. (jt. author). *Children from Australia to Zimbabwe*, 14328

Vesey, Amanda. *The Princess and the Frog*, 1652(F)

Vicario, Arantxa S. *The Young Tennis Player*, 22316

Vick, Helen H. *Shadow*, 9183(F)

Vidal, Beatriz. *Bringing the Rain to Kapiti Plain*, 10639

The Magic Bean Tree, 11443

Vieira, Linda. *The Ever-Living Tree*, 20219

Grand Canyon, 16643

Viesti, Joe. *Celebrate!* 17404, 17405

Celebrate! In Central America, 17406

Vigil, Angel. *¡Teatro!* 12040

Viglucci, Patricia C. *Sun Dance at Turtle Rock*, 8533(F)

Vigna, Judith. *Boot Weather*, 1653(F)

I Wish Daddy Didn't Drink So Much, 5095(F)

My Two Uncles, 5096(F)

Saying Goodbye to Daddy, 5097(F)

Uncle Alfredo's Zoo, 1654(F)

When Eric's Mom Fought Cancer, 5098(F)

Vigor, John. *Danger, Dolphins, and Ginger Beer*, 7113(F)

Villios, Lynne W. *Cooking the Greek Way*, 21742

Villoldo, Alberto (jt. author). *The First Story Ever Told*, 11440

Vincent, Benjamin. *Bluebonnet at the Marshall Train Depot*, 1940(F)

Vincent, Gabrielle. *A Day, a Dog*, 7318(F)

Ernest and Celestine at the Circus, 2781(F)

Halfway to Your House, 11672

Vinge, Joan D. *The Random House Book of Greek Myths*, 11513

Vinton, Ken. *Alphabet Antics*, 14114

Viola, Herman J. *It Is a Good Day to Die*, 16065

Viorst, Judith. *Alexander and the Terrible, Horrible, No Good, Very Bad Day*, 3927(F)

Alexander, Who Used to Be Rich Last Sunday, 6706(F)

Alexander, Who's Not (Do You Hear Me? I Mean It!) Going to Move, 3928(F)

The Alphabet from Z to A, 141(F)

Earrings! 4340(F)

The Good-bye Book, 5099(F)

If I Were in Charge of the World and Other Worries, 11730

I'll Fix Anthony, 3929(F)

My Mama Says There Aren't Any Zombies, Ghosts, Vampires, Creatures, Demons, Monsters, Fiends, Goblins, or Things, 4341(F)

Rosie and Michael, 4052(F)

Sad Underwear and Other Complications, 11923

Super-Completely and Totally the Messiest, 4342(F)

The Tenth Good Thing About Barney, 5100(F)

Visconti, Guido. *The Genius of Leonardo*, 9072(F)

Viscott, David (jt. author). *What Every Kid Should Know*, 17617

Vishaka. *Our Most Dear Friend*, 17226

Vishniac, Roman. *A Day of Pleasure*, 12597

Vitale, Stefano. *The Folks in the Valley*, 4(F)

Magic Words, 11930

Nursery Tales Around the World, 10618

Sailor Song, 712(F)

Too Much Talk, 10697

When Stories Fell Like Shooting Stars, 7761(F)

Vitkus-Weeks, Jessica. *Television*, 17784

Vivas, Julie. *I Went Walking*, 3477(F)

Let the Celebrations Begin! 9076(F)

Let's Eat! 3965(F)

Let's Go Visiting, 609(F)

The Nativity, 17409

Our Granny, 3944(F)

Possum Magic, 2097(F)

The Tram to Bondi Beach, 6369(F)

Welcome with Love, 18242

Wilfrid Gordon McDonald Partridge, 3995(F)

Vivelo, Jackie. *Chills in the Night*, 8179(F)

Vivian, Bart. *Imagine*, 1655(F)

Vizurraga, Susan. *Miss Opal's Auction*, 4053(F)

Our Old House, 3464(F)

Vo-Dinh, Mai. *The Land I Lost*, 8998(F)

Voake, Charlotte. *Alphabet Adventure*, 142(F)

Caterpillar Caterpillar, 19549

Elsie Piddock Skips in Her Sleep, 1157(F)

Ginger, 5443(F)

Here Comes the Train, 3465(F)

Voce, Louise. *The Owl and the Pussycat*, 11889

What Newt Could Do for Turtle, 2398(F)

Voeller, Edward. *Extreme Surfing*, 22304

The Red-Crowned Crane, 19291

Voetberg, Julie. *I Am a Home Schooler*, 3466

Vogel, Carole G. *Legends of Landforms*, 10622

Nature's Fury, 20662

Shock Waves Through Los Angeles, 20353

Vogiel, Eva. *Invisible Chains*, 10134(F)

Vogt, Gregory L. *Apollo Moonwalks*, 21018

Asteroids, Comets, and Meteors, 18534

Deep Space Astronomy, 18423

Earth, 18439

John Glenn's Return to Space, 12890

Jupiter, 18496

Mars, 18497

Mercury, 18498

Neptune, 18499

Pluto, 18500

Saturn, 18501

The Solar System, 18535

Spacewalks, 21019

The Sun, 18574

Uranus, 18502

Voigt, Cynthia. *Bad, Badder, Baddest*, 10010(F)

Bad Girls, 10011(F)

The Callender Papers, 7114(F)

Dicey's Song, 7532(F)

It's Not Easy Being Bad, 10135(F)

Vojtech, Anna. *Elephant Walk*, 5221(F)

Giraffe Trouble, 5222(F)

Otter Play, 5320(F)

The Son of the Sun and the Daughter of the Moon, 11125

Song of the Camels, 11828
Ten Flashing Fireflies, 588(F)
Volkmann, Roy. *Curious Kittens*, 2782(F)
Von Ahnen, Katherine. *Charlie Young Bear*, 4863(F)
Heart of Naosaqua, 9184(F)
Von Konigslow, Andrea Wayne. *Bing and Chutney*, 4054(F)
Von Mason, Stephen. *Brother Anansi and the Cattle Ranch/El Hermano Anansi y el Rancho de Ganada*, 11400
Von Schmidt, Eric. *By the Great Horn Spoon*, 9844(F)
Chancy and the Grand Rascal, 9846(F)
The Ghost on Saturday Night, 9848(F)
Humbug Mountain, 9849(F)
Mr. Mysterious and Company, 9851(F)
Vorderman, Carol. *How Math Works*, 20599
Vordtriede, David. *Boredom Blasters*, 22070
Vos, Ida. *Anna Is Still Here*, 9694(F)
Dancing on the Bridge at Avignon, 9073(F)
Hide and Seek, 9695(F)
The Key Is Lost, 9696(F)
Voss, Gisela. *Museum Colors*, 13929
Voth, Danna. *Kidsource*, 18365
Vulliamy, Clara. *Danny's Duck*, 5492(F)
Ellen and Penguin, 4055(F)
Good Night, Baby, 797(F)
My Baby Brother Has Ten Tiny Toes, 494(F)
Vuong, Lynette Dyer. *The Brocaded Slipper and Other Vietnamese Tales*, 10845

Waas, Uli. *The Birthday Bear*, 6634(F)
Waber, Bernard. *An Anteater Named Arthur*, 2783(F)
Bearsie Bear and the Surprise Sleepover Party, 2784(F)
Bernard, 2785(F)
Do You See a Mouse? 4343(F)
Funny, Funny Lyle, 2786(F)
Gina, 4056(F)
The House on East 88th Street, 2787(F)
Ira Says Goodbye, 2788(F)
Ira Sleeps Over, 5101(F)
A Lion Named Shirley Williamson, 2789(F)
Lyle at Christmas, 5944(F)
Lyle at the Office, 2790(F)
The Mouse That Snored, 2791(F)
The Snake, 2792(F)
You Look Ridiculous, Said the Rhinoceros to the Hippopotamus, 2793(F)

You're a Little Kid with a Big Heart, 1656(F)
Waboose, Jan B. *Firedancers*, 3930(F)
Morning on the Lake, 4558(F)
SkySisters, 11316
Wachter, Oralee. *No More Secrets for Me*, 17735
Wacker, Grant. *Religion in Nineteenth Century America*, 15913
Waddell, Martin. *The Big Big Sea*, 4559(F)
Can't You Sleep, Little Bear? 798(F)
Farmer Duck, 2794(F)
Good Job, Little Bear, 2795(F)
The Happy Hedgehog Band, 2796(F)
Harriet and the Crocodiles, 2797(F)
The Hollyhock Wall, 1657(F)
Let's Go Home, Little Bear, 2798(F)
Little Mo, 2799(F)
Little Obie and the Flood, 9449(F)
Little Obie and the Kidnap, 9450(F)
Mimi and the Dream House, 2800(F)
Mimi and the Picnic, 2801(F)
Mimi's Christmas, 3467(F)
Night Night, Cuddly Bear, 799(F)
Once There Were Giants, 3468(F)
Owl Babies, 2802(F)
Rosie's Babies, 3931(F)
Tom Rabbit, 1658(F)
When the Teddy Bears Came, 3932(F)
Who Do You Love? 800(F)
You and Me, Little Bear, 2803(F)
Yum, Yum, Yummy, 2804(F)
Wade, Bob (jt. author). *Winning Chess*, 22173
Wade, Linda R. *Badlands*, 16589
Hannibal, 16590
James Carter, 13020
Montgomery, 16524
St. Augustine, 16894
Warren G. Harding, 13039
Wade, Mary D. *Ada Byron Lovelace*, 13317
Guadalupe Quintanilla, 12834
I Am Houston, 12904
Wadsworth, Ginger. *Giant Sequoia Trees*, 20220
John Burroughs, 13243
John Muir, 13330
Laura Ingalls Wilder, 12629
One Tiger Growls, 601
Rachel Carson, 13250
Susan Butcher, 13682
Tomorrow Is Daddy's Birthday, 5732(F)
Tundra Discoveries, 15843
Wagener, Gerda. *The Ghost in the Classroom*, 8180(F)

Wagerin, Walter. *Probity Jones and the Fear Not Angel*, 1659(F)
Waggoner, Karen. *Partners*, 8380(F)
Wagner, David. *Makiawisug*, 7722(F)
Wagner, Jane. *J.T.*, 8841(F)
Wagner, Jenny. *Motor Bill and the Lovely Caroline*, 2805(F)
Wagner, Karen. *Bravo, Mildred and Ed!* 2806(F)
A Friend Like Ed, 2807(F)
Wahl, Jan. *The Field Mouse and the Dinosaur Named Sue*, 2808(F)
Humphrey's Bear, 801(F)
Little Johnny Buttermilk, 11041
Mabel Ran Away with the Toys, 3933(F)
Once When the World Was Green, 1660(F)
Three Pandas, 2809(F)
Wainwright, Richard M. *Mountains to Climb*, 8842(F)
Waite, Judy. *Mouse, Look Out!* 2810(F)
The Storm Seal, 5444(F)
Wakefield, Ali. *Those Calculating Crows!* 1661(F)
Wakeman, Nancy. *Babe Didrikson Zaharias*, 13722
Wakiyama, Hanako. *Too Big!* 3314(F)
Waldee, Lynne Marie. *Cooking the French Way*, 21743
Waldherr, Kris. *The Book of Goddesses*, 11457
Waldman, Jackie. *Teens with the Courage to Give*, 17736
Waldman, Neil. *America the Beautiful*, 14232
Bayou Lullaby, 620(F)
By the Hanukkah Light, 6104(F)
The Gold Coin, 4896(F)
The Golden City, 15532
Masada, 14596
Mother Earth, 4488(F)
Nessa's Fish, 4747(F)
Nessa's Story, 4748(F)
The Passover Journey, 17467
The Starry Night, 1662(F)
The Wisdom Bird, 17312(F)
Wounded Knee, 16066
Waldron, Ann. *Francisco Goya*, 12238
Waldron, Jan L. *Angel Pig and the Hidden Christmas*, 5945(F)
John Pig's Halloween, 6059(F)
Walker, Alice. *To Hell with Dying*, 8843(F)
Walker, Barbara K., ed. *A Treasury of Turkish Folktales for Children*, 10865
Walker, Barbara M. *The Little House Cookbook*, 21744
Walker, Jane C. *John Quincy Adams*, 13006
Walker, Lester. *Block Building for Children*, 21673

Housebuilding for Children, 21664
Walker, Lois. *Get Growing!* 21775
Walker, Niki. *How Do Animals Move?* 18863
Walker, Pamela. *Pray Hard*, 8844(F)
Walker, Paul R. *Big Men, Big Country*, 11389
Bigfoot and Other Legendary Creatures, 21956
Giants! 10623
Little Folk, 10624
Pride of Puerto Rico, 13444
Walker, Richard. *The Barefoot Book of Pirates*, 10625
The Barefoot Book of Trickster Tales, 10626
The Kingfisher First Human Body Encyclopedia, 18084
A Right to Die? 17158
Walker, Sally M. *Dolphins*, 19693
Earthquakes, 20354
The 18 Penny Goose, 9254(F)
Glaciers, 20361
Hippos, 18985
Manatees, 19750
Mary Anning, 13231
Rhinos, 18986
Sea Horses, 19717
Volcanoes, 20355
Water Up, Water Down, 20746
Walker, Sloan. *The Only Other Crazy Car Book*, 21325
Wall, Bill. *The Cove of Cork*, 9330(F)
Wallace, Andrea. *Lucky Star*, 6490(F)
Not Just Another Moose, 2148(F)
Wallace, Barbara Brooks. *Cousins in the Castle*, 7115(F)
Ghosts in the Gallery, 7116(F)
Peppermints in the Parlor, 7117(F)
Sparrows in the Scullery, 9126(F)
The Twin in the Tavern, 7118(F)
Wallace, Bill. *Beauty*, 7533(F)
Blackwater Swamp, 7119(F)
Coyote Autumn, 7319(F)
Danger in Quicksand Swamp, 7120(F)
A Dog Called Kitty, 7320(F)
Eye of the Great Bear, 7121(F)
Ferret in the Bedroom, Lizards in the Fridge, 10012(F)
Never Say Quit, 10369(F)
Red Dog, 9451(F)
Snot Stew, 8181(F)
Totally Disgusting, 8182(F)
Trapped in Death Cave, 7122(F)
True Friends, 8534(F)
Upchuck and the Rotten Willy, 8183(F)
Watchdog and the Coyotes, 8184(F)
Wallace, Bill (jt. author). *The Flying Flea, Callie, and Me*, 8185(F)
That Furball Puppy and Me, 8186(F)

Wallace, Carol. *The Flying Flea, Callie, and Me*, 8185(F)
That Furball Puppy and Me, 8186(F)
Wallace, Daisy, ed. *Ghost Poems*, 11731
Witch Poems, 11732
Wallace, Holly. *The Mystery of Atlantis*, 21957
The Mystery of the Abominable Snowman, 21958
Wallace, Ian. *Boy of the Deeps*, 4864(F)
Duncan's Way, 3934(F)
Hansel and Gretel, 10934
The Name of the Tree, 10691
Sarah and the People of Sand River, 8946
Very Last First Time, 4576(F)
A Winter's Tale, 2982(F)
The Year of Fire, 3718(F)
Wallace, John. *The Flower Girl*, 3172(F)
Grump, 813(F)
Tiny Rabbit Goes to a Birthday Party, 5733(F)
Wallace, Joseph. *The Camera*, 21805
The Lightbulb, 20907
Wallace, Karen. *Bears in the Forest*, 19072
A Bed for the Winter, 6707(F)
Big Machines, 21256
City Pig, 2811(F)
Duckling Days, 19318
Gentle Giant Octopus, 19727
Imagine You Are a Crocodile, 5445(F)
My Hen Is Dancing, 20073
Red Fox, 19144
Scarlette Beane, 1663(F)
Tale of a Tadpole, 18741
Wild Baby Animals, 18881
Wallace, Marianne D. *America's Deserts*, 20427
Wallace, Mark. *101 Things to Do on the Internet*, 21231
Wallace, Mary. *I Can Make Art*, 21597
I Can Make Jewelry, 21552
I Can Make Puppets, 14308
I Can Make Toys, 21509
The Inuksuk Book, 15844
Wallace, Nancy E. *Apples, Apples, Apples*, 2812(F)
Paperwhite, 4057(F)
Rabbit's Bedtime, 802(F)
A Taste of Honey, 2813(F)
Tell-A-Bunny, 5734(F)
Wallis, Diz. *Battle of the Beasts*, 10935
Something Nasty in the Cabbages, 10516(F)
Wallner, Alexandra. *Abigail Adams*, 13125
An Alcott Family Christmas, 5946(F)
Beatrix Potter, 12582

Betsy Ross, 13190
A Christmas Tree in the White House, 5838(F)
The Farmer in the Dell, 14187
The First Air Voyage in the United States, 12078
Laura Ingalls Wilder, 12630
A Picture Book of Abraham Lincoln, 13063
A Picture Book of Benjamin Franklin, 12878
A Picture Book of George Washington, 13113
A Picture Book of Helen Keller, 13164
A Picture Book of Louis Braille, 13757
A Picture Book of Patrick Henry, 12898
A Picture Book of Robert E. Lee, 12925
A Picture Book of Thomas Jefferson, 13046
Sergio and the Hurricane, 4865(F)
Wallner, John. *Aldo Applesauce*, 9891(F)
Hello, My Name Is Scrambled Eggs, 8289(F)
A Picture Book of Abraham Lincoln, 13063
A Picture Book of Benjamin Franklin, 12878
A Picture Book of Christopher Columbus, 12096
A Picture Book of Davy Crockett, 12102
A Picture Book of Florence Nightingale, 13840
A Picture Book of George Washington, 13113
A Picture Book of Helen Keller, 13164
A Picture Book of Louis Braille, 13757
A Picture Book of Patrick Henry, 12898
A Picture Book of Robert E. Lee, 12925
A Picture Book of Thomas Jefferson, 13046
Walls, John. *Paper Gifts and Jewelry*, 21633
Walpole, Brenda. *175 Science Experiments to Amuse and Amaze Your Friends*, 18366
Walpole, Peter. *The Healer of Harrow Point*, 8845(F)
Walraven, Ilja. *My Elephant Can Do Almost Anything*, 2032(F)
Walrod, Amy. *Horace and Morris But Mostly Dolores*, 2224(F)
Walsh, Ellen S. *For Pete's Sake*, 2814(F)
Hop Jump, 2815(F)
Mouse Count, 602(F)
Mouse Paint, 2816(F)
Pip's Magic, 2817(F)

Samantha, 2818(F)
You Silly Goose, 2819(F)
Walsh, Jill Paton. Fireweed, 9697(F)
Gaffer Samson's Luck, 8381(F)
The Green Book, 10244(F)
Pepi and the Secret Names, 8187(F)
Walsh, Melanie. Do Donkeys Dance? 5446(F)
Do Monkeys Tweet? 5447
Do Pigs Have Stripes? 4344(F)
Hide and Sleep, 803(F)
Ned's Rainbow, 3469(F)
Walsh, Patricia. Aircraft, 21598
Cars, 21599
Woodland Animals, 21600
Walsh, V. L. (jt. author). Penguin Dreams, 1555(F)
Walsh, Vivian. Olive, the Other Reindeer, 5947(F)
Walsh, Vivian (jt. author). Free Lunch, 2671(F)
Going to the Getty, 16811
Mr. Lunch Takes a Plane Ride, 2672(F)
Walter, F. Virginia. Super Toys and Games from Paper, 21636
Walter, Mildred P. Brother to the Wind, 1664(F)
Have a Happy . . . , 9766(F)
Justin and the Best Biscuits in the World, 8846(F)
Kwanzaa, 5655
Mariah Keeps Cool, 8535(F)
Ty's One-Man Band, 3470(F)
Walter, Mildren P. Suitcase, 10370(F)
Walter, Virginia. "Hi, Pizza Man!" 4345(F)
Making Up Megaboy, 8847(F)
Walters, Catherine. Are You There, Baby Bear? 2820(F)
Charlie and Tess, 2164(F)
Never Trust a Squirrel! 1972(F)
Walters, Eric. Three on Three, 10371(F)
War of the Eagles, 8947(F)
Walters, John. Flood! 20723
Walters, Julie. God Is Like . . . Three Parables for Children, 17227
Walters, Virginia. Are We There Yet, Daddy? 255(F)
Walters, William (jt. author). Flint's Rock, 8434(F)
Walton, Darwin McBeth. Dance, Kayla! 8536(F)
Walton, Rick. The Bear Came Over to My House, 2821(F)
Dance, Pioneer, Dance! 4866(F)
How Many How Many How Many, 603(F)
Little Dogs Say "Rough!" 4346(F)
My Two Hands, My Two Feet, 804(F)
Noah's Square Dance, 1665(F)
Once There Was a Bull . . . (frog), 2822(F)

One More Bunny, 604(F)
So Many Bunnies, 143(F)
Why the Banana Split, 4347(F)
Walton, Ross. Some Trains Run on Water, 21341
Walty, Margaret. The Elves and the Shoemaker, 10896
Rock-a-Bye Baby, 14175
Walz-Chojnacki, Greg (jt. author). UFOs, 21890
Wanasundera, Nanda P. Sri Lanka, 15211
Wanbli Numpa Afraid of Hawk (jt. author). A Boy Becomes a Man at Wounded Knee, 16072
Wang, Lu. Traditional Chinese Folktales, 10746
Wang, Rosalind C. The Magical Starfruit Tree, 10771
The Treasure Chest, 10772
Wangari, Esther. Ameru, 14952
Wangberg, James K. Do Bees Sneeze? And Other Questions Kids Ask About Insects, 19498
Wanous, Suzanne. Sara's Secret, 8919(F)
Warburton, Lois. The Beginning of Writing, 14011
Ward, Amy. The Little Red Hen (Makes a Pizza), 11036
Ward, Brian. Epidemic, 18011
Ward, Helen. The Hare and the Tortoise, 11077
The King of the Birds, 10627
Living Fossils, 18655
Ward, Jennifer. Somewhere in the Ocean, 898(F)
Ward, Jennifer (jt. author). Way Out in the Desert, 5338(F)
Ward, John. The Bus Ride, 4769(F)
The Car Washing Street, 3357(F)
Families, 11768
I Call It Sky, 4463(F)
Kente Colors, 15023
Poppa's Itchy Christmas, 5880(F)
Poppa's New Pants, 3319(F)
Seven Days of Kwanzaa, 17365
Ward, Keith. Black Stallion, 7190(F)
Ward, Leila. I Am Eyes Ni Macho, 4867(F)
Ward, Lynd. The Biggest Bear, 2983(F)
Brady, 9277(F)
The Cat Who Went to Heaven, 10409(F)
Johnny Tremain, 9230(F)
Little Red Lighthouse and the Great Gray Bridge, 5603(F)
The Silver Pony, 937(F)
Swiss Family Robinson, 7136(F)
Ward, Lynd (jt. author). Little Red Lighthouse and the Great Gray Bridge, 5603(F)
Ward, Nathalie. Do Sharks Ever . . .? 19769
Ward, Nick. Farmer George and the Fieldmice, 2823(F)

Ward, Sally G. The Anesthesiologist, 18030
Laney's Lost Momma, 3191(F)
Wardlaw, Lee. Bow-Wow Birthday, 5735(F)
Bubblemania, 20132
Hector's Hiccups, 6708(F)
101 Ways to Bug Your Parents, 10013(F)
Saturday Night Jamboree, 3935(F)
We All Scream for Ice Cream, 20133
Ware, Cheryl. Catty-Cornered, 8537(F)
Venola in Love, 10014(F)
Ware, Jim. Crazy Jacob, 8948(F)
Warhola, James. The Bear Came Over to My House, 2821(F)
Bigfoot Cinderrrrella, 10438
Bubba, The Cowboy Prince, 1297(F)
If You Hopped Like a Frog, 241
The Mystery of the Several Sevens, 7626(F)
The Tinderbox, 10394(F)
Well, I Never! 1464(F)
Warner, Gertrude C. The Mystery of the Hidden Painting, 7123(F)
Warner, J. F. Rhode Island, 16753
The U.S. Marine Corps, 21407
Warner, John F. Colonial American Home Life, 16181
Warner, John F. (jt. author). The Case of the Furtive Firebug, 8352(F)
Warner, Margaret Brink. What's Cooking? 21745
Warner, Sally. Accidental Lily, 8848(F)
Finding Hattie, 10136(F)
How to Be a Real Person (in Just One Day), 8538(F)
Leftover Lily, 8382(F)
Private Lily, 10015(F)
Sort of Forever, 8383(F)
Sweet and Sour Lily, 10137(F)
Totally Confidential, 8849(F)
Warner, Sunny. Madison Finds a Line, 1666(F)
The Magic Sewing Machine, 4868(F)
Warnes, Tim. Counting Leopard's Spots, 10709
Have You Got My Purr? 2845(F)
Hurry, Santa! 5932(F)
I Don't Want to Take a Bath, 2745(F)
It Could Have Been Worse, 1803(F)
Little Tiger's Big Surprise! 2746(F)
Warnick, Elsa. Bedtime, 805(F)
Ride the Wind, 18671
Song for the Whooping Crane, 11814
Warren, Andrea. Orphan Train Rider, 15914
Pioneer Girl, 16384

Surviving Hitler, 14889

Warren, Harry. *Ashkii and His Grandfather*, 4651(F)

Warrick, Karen Clemens. *Louisa May Alcott*, 12490

Warshaw, Hallie. *The Sleepover Cookbook*, 21746

Warshaw, Jerry. *Joshua James Likes Trucks*, 6574(F)

Warshaw, Mal. *The Hospital Book*, 18039

Warter, Fred. *Annie Oakley*, 12431

Wartski, Maureen C. *A Boat to Nowhere*, 9018(F)

Washburn, Lucia. *Dinosaur Babies*, 14486

I See Me! 3422(F)

Look to the North, 5223(F)

Motherlove, 5296

Sunshine, Moonshine, 6191(F)

Terrible Tyrannosaurs, 14487

Washburne, Carolyn K. *Drug Abuse*, 17895

Washington, Donna. *A Big, Spooky House*, 11390

Washington, George. *George-isms*, 16182

Wasson, Valentina P. *The Chosen Baby*, 17690

Waterlow, Julia. *The Atlantic Ocean*, 19846

China, 15088, 15089

A Family from Bosnia, 15294

A Family from China, 15090

A Family from Guatemala, 15688

The Red Sea and the Arabian Gulf, 19847

Waters, Alice. *Fanny at Chez Panisse*, 16951

Waters, Elizabeth. *Painting*, 13930

Waters, Fiona. *The Emperor and the Nightingale*, 10517(F)

Oscar Wilde's The Selfish Giant, 10518(F)

Waters, Fiona, comp. *Dark as a Midnight Dream*, 11733

Waters, John F. *Night Raiders Along the Cape*, 9255(F)

Waters, Kate. *Lion Dancer*, 5656

Mary Geddy's Day, 9217(F)

On the Mayflower, 16183

Sara Morton's Day, 16184

Tapenum's Day, 16185

Waters, Tony. *Flick*, 7329(F)

Waterton, Betty. *Pettranella*, 4869(F)

A Salmon for Simon, 2824(F)

Watkins, Richard. *Gladiator*, 14750

Watkins, Sherrin. *Green Snake Ceremony*, 4870(F)

Watling, James. *Along the Santa Fe Trail*, 16357

The Devil's Highway, 9341(F)

Discovering the Stars, 18554

Finding Providence, 4581(F)

The First Thanksgiving, 17500

Samuel's Choice, 9224(F)

The Tree That Owns Itself, 8932(F)

Tut's Mummy, 6311

Witch Hunt, 16150

Wonders of the Seasons, 4392(F)

Watson, Amy. *The Folk Art Counting Book*, 605

Watson, Clyde. *Applebet*, 144(F)

Love's a Sweet, 11734

Watson, David. *Papermaking*, 21637

Watson, Lyall. *Warriors, Warthogs, and Wisdom*, 12617

Watson, Mary. *The Butterfly Seeds*, 4871(F)

The Market Lady and the Mango Tree, 4872(F)

My Own Big Bed, 702(F)

Watson, Nancy. *Our Violent Earth*, 20328

Watson, Patrick. *Ahmek*, 8188(F)

Watson, Pete. *The Market Lady and the Mango Tree*, 4872(F)

Watson, Richard J. *The Dream Stair*, 710(F)

The High Rise Glorious Skittle Skat Roarious Sky Pie Angel Food Cake, 8205(F)

One Wintry Night, 17418(F)

Watson, Wendy. *Applebet*, 144(F)

Boo! It's Halloween, 6060(F)

Doctor Coyote, 11394

Happy Easter Day! 5976

Hurray for the Fourth of July, 5657(F)

Love's a Sweet, 11734

Sleep Is for Everyone, 18118

Tales for a Winter's Eve, 2825(F)

Wattenberg, Jane. *Henny-Penny*, 11042

Watts, Barrie. *Apple Tree*, 20157

Dandelion, 20266

Hamster, 19910

Honeybee, 19527

Potato, 20186

Tomato, 20134

Watts, Barrie (jt. author). *Photography*, 21799

Watts, Bernadette. *The Fir Tree*, 10382(F)

Happy Birthday, Harvey Hare! 2826(F)

Harvey Hare, 2827(F)

Harvey Hare's Christmas, 5948(F)

The Lion and the Mouse, 11078

The Snow Queen, 10387(F)

The Town Mouse and the Country Mouse, 11079

The Ugly Duckling, 10396(F)

The Wolf and the Seven Little Kids, 10913

Watts, Bernadette, reteller. *The Lion and the Mouse*, 11078

Watts, Claire. *Super Heroes*, 21959

Watts, Irene N. *The Fish Princess*, 1667(F)

Good-Bye Marianne, 9074(F)

Remember Me, 9698(F)

Watts, J. F. *The Irish Americans*, 17597

Watts, James. *Back in the Beforetime*, 9153(F)

Brats, 11877

Fresh Brats, 11878

Good Hunting, Blue Sky, 6564(F)

Watts, Jeri Hanel. *Keepers*, 5102(F)

Waugh, Charles G. (jt. author). *A Newbery Christmas*, 9726(F)

A Newbery Halloween, 6864(F)

A Newbery Zoo, 7202(F)

Waugh, Sylvia. *The Mennyms*, 8189(F)

Mennyms Alive, 8190(F)

Mennyms Alone, 8191(F)

Mennyms in the Wilderness, 8192(F)

Space Race, 10245(F)

Wawiorka, Matthew. *The Teen's Vegetarian Cookbook*, 21714

Wax, Wendy. *Empire Dreams*, 9635(F)

Say No and Know Why, 17896

Waxman, Sydell, reteller. *The Rooster Prince*, 8193(F)

Wayland, April Halprin. *To Rabbittown*, 1668(F)

Waysman, Dvora. *Back of Beyond*, 7124(F)

Weatherby, Mark A. *My Dinosaur*, 1669(F)

Weatherford, Carole Boston. *Juneteenth Jamboree*, 9767(F)

Sink or Swim, 16895

The Sound that Jazz Makes, 14138

Weatherly, Myra. *William Marshal*, 13834

Women Pirates, 12070

Weatherspoon, Teresa. *Teresa Weatherspoon's Basketball for Girls*, 22151

Weaver, Robyn M. *John Grisham*, 12543

Webb, Denise. *The Same Sun Was in the Sky*, 4873(F)

Webb, Lois S. *Holidays of the World Cookbook for Students*, 21747

Webb, Marcus. *The United States*, 15915

Webb, Ray. *Daily Life in Ancient and Modern Beijing*, 15053

Daily Life in Ancient and Modern Mexico City, 15612

Daily Life in Ancient and Modern Rome, 15371

Webb, Sophie. *My Season with Penguins*, 19389

Webber, Desiree Morrison. *The Buffalo Train Ride*, 18987

Weber, Bruce (jt. author). *Savion!* 12465

Weber, Jill. *Harp O' Gold*, 987(F)

Keeping Time, 20639

Weber, Michael. *The American Revolution*, 16218

Our Congress, 17128

Our National Parks, 15916

Yorktown, 16219

The Young Republic, 16282

Weber, Valerie. *Traveling in Grand-ma's Day*, 16493

Webster, David (jt. author). *Experiments with Balloons*, 20669
Science Project Ideas About Animal Behavior, 18817

Webster, Vera. *Plant Experiments*, 18367

Webster-Doyle, Terrence. *Breaking the Chains of the Ancient Warrior*, 10372(F)

Wechsler, Doug. *Bizarre Birds*, 19292

Weeks, Sarah. *Crocodile Smile*, 14188
Drip, Drop, 6709(F)
Guy Time, 10016(F)
Happy Birthday, Frankie, 1670(F)
Mrs. McNosh and the Great Big Squash, 1671(F)
Mrs. McNosh Hangs Up Her Wash, 4348(F)
Piece of Jungle, 4874(F)
Regular Guy, 10017(F)
Splish, Splash! 6710(F)

Wegman, William. *Cinderella*, 10519(F)
Little Red Riding Hood, 10936
My Town, 2828(F)
Triangle, Square, Circle, 363(F)

Wegner, Fritz. *The Tale of the Turnip*, 10943

Wehrman, Richard. *The Rabbit's Tail*, 10727

Wehrman, Vicki. *Sweet Dreams*, 721(F)

Wei Liu, Shao. *Chinese New Year's Dragon*, 7371(F)
The Magical Starfruit Tree, 10771

Weide, Bruce. *There's a Wolf in the Classroom!* 19145

Weidensaul, Scott. *National Audubon Society First Field Guide to Birds*, 19293

Weidner, Teri. *Your Body Belongs to You*, 17733

Weidt, Maryann N. *Daddy Played Music for the Cows*, 3471(F)
Mr. Blue Jeans, 12966
Oh, the Places He Went, 12539
Revolutionary Poet, 12621
Stateswoman to the World, 13185

Weigelt, Udo. *The Strongest Mouse in the World*, 2829(F)
Who Stole the Gold? 2830(F)

Weihs, Erika. *An Elm Tree and Three Sisters*, 4546(F)
Menorahs, Mezuzas, and Other Jewish Symbols, 17455

Weil, Ann. *Michael Dorris*, 12531

Weilerstein, Sadie R. *K'tonton's Sukkot Adventure*, 1672(F)
K'tonton's Yom Kippur Kitten, 6122(F)

Weinberg, Karen. *Window of Time*, 8194(F)

Weiner, Jonathan. *Nadia's Hands*, 5625(F)

Weinhaus, Karen Ann. *The Perfect Christmas Picture*, 5875(F)
Poem Stew, 11865

Weinman, Brad. *Myth Maker*, 12606
Tales from the Brothers Grimm and the Sisters Weird, 10933

Weinstein, Ellen. *Ben Loves Anna*, 8684(F)

Weintraub, Aileen. *Everything You Need to Know About Being a Baby-sitter*, 16947

Weir, Joan. *The Witcher*, 8949(F)

Weisgard, Leonard. *Courage of Sarah Noble*, 9189(F)
Favorite Poems Old and New, 11560
Hailstones and Halibut Bones, 11665
Rain Drop Splash, 4554(F)
Red Light, Green Light, 3051(F)

Weisman, Joanne B. (jt. author). *Dwight D. Eisenhower*, 13029

Weiss, Bernard P. *I Am Jewish*, 17228

Weiss, Ellen. *Color Me Criminal*, 7125(F)
My First Day at Camp, 6711(F)
My Teacher Sleeps in School, 2831(F)
Odd Jobs, 17768
So Many Cats! 416(F)
A Very Noisy Girl, 1694(F)

Weiss, Ellen (jt. author). *Born to Be Wild*, 8117(F)

Weiss, George D. *What a Wonderful World*, 14259(F)

Weiss, Harvey. *Strange and Wonderful Aircraft*, 21110
Submarines and Other Underwater Craft, 21408

Weiss, Jacqueline Shachter. *Young Brer Rabbit*, 11445

Weiss, Jonathan H. *Breathe Easy*, 18012

Weiss, Leatie. *My Teacher Sleeps in School*, 2831(F)

Weiss, Mitch (jt. author). *How and Why Stories*, 10556
Noodlehead Stories, 10557
Stories in My Pocket, 14088

Weiss, Nicki. *If You're Happy and You Know It*, 14189
The World Turns Round and Round, 3472(F)

Weiss, Stefanie Iris. *Everything You Need to Know About Being a Vegan*, 18213

Weissman, Bari. *Come! Sit! Speak!* 6659(F)
From Caterpillar to Butterfly, 19555
Goldilocks and the Three Bears, 11017
Golly Gump Swallowed a Fly, 1069(F)

Weissman, Paul (jt. author). *The Great Voyager Adventure*, 18515

Weissman, Sam Q. *Sports Riddles*, 21848

Weissmann, Joe. *Mummies*, 14548

Weitzman, David. *Great Lives*, 13223
Locomotive, 21345
My Backyard History Book, 14573
Old Ironsides, 9331(F)
Pouring Iron, 21259

Weitzman, Elizabeth. *I Am Jewish American*, 17599
Let's Talk About Foster Homes, 17691
Let's Talk About Smoking, 17897
Let's Talk About When Someone You Love Has Alzheimer's Disease, 18013

Weitzman, Jacqueline Preiss. *You Can't Take a Balloon into The Metropolitan Museum*, 938(F)
You Can't Take a Balloon into the National Gallery, 4875(F)

Welch, Catherine A. *Children of the Relocation Camps*, 14891
Clouds of Terror, 9452(F)
Danger at the Breaker, 6712(F)
Ida B. Wells-Barnett, 12820
Margaret Bourke-White, 12192, 12193

Welch, Leona N. *Kai*, 8980(F)

Welch, R. C. *Scary Stories for Stormy Nights*, 8195(F)

Welch, Sheila K. *Don't Call Me Marda*, 8920(F)
The Shadowed Unicorn, 7534(F)

Welch, Willy. *Grumpy Bunnies*, 806(F)

Welden, Amelie. *Girls Who Rocked the World*, 13744

Well, Ann (jt. author). *Raul Julia*, 12833

Weller, Frances W. *The Angel of Mill Street*, 5949(F)
Riptide, 5448(F)

Welles, Toby. *The Clock*, 20644

Wellington, Monica. *Bunny's First Snowflake*, 807(F)
Bunny's Rainbow Day, 2832(F)
Night City, 3936(F)
Night House, Bright House, 1673(F)
Squeaking of Art, 13931

Wells, Alison. *Subtraction*, 20623

Wells, Daryl. *Two Mrs. Gibsons*, 3714(F)

Wells, Donna. *Biotechnology*, 18036

Wells, H. G. *The Time Machine*, 10246(F)

Wells, Haru. *The Master Puppeteer*, 9006(F)
Of Nightingales That Weep, 9007(F)

Wells, Robert. *Can You Count to a Googol?* 606(F)

Wells, Robert E. *Is a Blue Whale the Biggest Thing There Is?* 364(F)
What's Faster Than a Speeding Cheetah? 18864
What's Smaller Than a Pygmy Shrew? 365(F)
Wells, Rosemary. *The Bear Went Over the Mountain*, 899(F)
Benjamin's Treasure, 2861(F)
Bingo, 3473(F)
Bunny Money, 2833(F)
Emily's First 100 Days of School, 607(F)
The Fisherman and His Wife, 10520
Goodnight Max, 808(F)
Here Comes Mother Goose, 878
Humpty Dumpty and Other Rhymes, 879(F)
The Itsy-Bitsy Spider, 900(F)
The Language of Doves, 4876(F)
Lassie Come-Home, 7321(F)
McDuff and the Baby, 5449(F)
McDuff Comes Home, 5450(F)
McDuff Moves In, 5451(F)
McDuff's New Friend, 5950(F)
Mary on Horseback, 12860
Max Cleans Up, 2834(F)
Max's Bath, 2835(F)
Max's Bedtime, 809(F)
Morris's Disappearing Bag, 5951(F)
My Very First Mother Goose, 880(F)
Old MacDonald, 14190
Rachel Field's Hitty, 8196(F)
Read to Your Bunny, 2836(F)
Streets of Gold, 16283
Timothy Goes to School, 2837(F)
Yoko, 4058(F)
Wells, Rosemary, reteller. *Jack and the Beanstalk*, 11043
Wells, Rosemary (jt. author). *Tallchief*, 12477
Wells, Ruth. *A to Zen*, 145(F)
The Farmer and the Poor God, 10835
Welply, Michael. *Viking Times*, 15460
Welsbacher, Anne. *Flying Brown Pelicans*, 19294
Inclined Planes, 20924
James Monroe, 13086
John Adams, 13003
Levers, 20925
New York, 16754
Pulleys, 20926
Screws, 20927
Wading Birds, 19295
Wedges, 20928
Wheels and Axles, 20929
Weninger, Brigitte. *The Elf's Hat*, 2838(F)
Happy Birthday, Davy! 5736(F)
A Letter to Santa Claus, 5952(F)
Merry Christmas, Davy! 5953(F)
Ragged Bear, 3474(F)

Special Delivery, 3937(F)
What Have You Done, Davy? 2839(F)
What's the Matter, Davy? 2840(F)
Where Have You Gone, Davy? 2841(F)
Why Are You Fighting, Davy? 2842(F)
Will You Mind the Baby, Davy? 2843(F)
Wenngren, Anders. *Bringing Up Baby*, 18870
Cats, 19090
Who's for Dinner? 18837
Wensell, Ulises. *Taking Care of Sister Bear*, 2661(F)
Who Has Time for Little Bear? 2662(F)
Wenzel, Angela. *Gustav Klimt*, 12249
Rene Magritte, 13932
Wenzel, David. *Fairy Tales of the Brothers Grimm*, 10521
Hauntings, 10561
The Liberty Tree, 16210
Wenzel, Greg. *More About Dinosaurs*, 14395
Werenko, Lisa V. (jt. author). *Circus! A Pop-Up Adventure*, 14268
Werenskiold, Erik. *Norwegian Folk Tales*, 11120
Werlin, Nancy. *Are You Alone on Purpose?* 8921(F)
Werner, Doug. *Skateboarder's Start-Up*, 22276
Werner, Thomas. *The Sky Is Not So Far Away*, 701
Wesley, Mary. *Haphazard House*, 8197(F)
Wesley, Valerie W. *Freedom's Gifts*, 7535(F)
West, Alan. *José Martí*, 12572
Roberto Clemente, 13445
West, Colin. *"Buzz, Buzz, Buzz,"* Went the Bumblebee, 2844(F)
One Day in the Jungle, 316(F)
West, David. *Fifty-Three and a Half Things That Changed the World and Some That Didn't!* 21050
West, Delno C. *Braving the North Atlantic*, 16095
Uncle Sam and Old Glory, 15858
West, Jean M. (jt. author). *Braving the North Atlantic*, 16095
Uncle Sam and Old Glory, 15858
West, Judy. *Have You Got My Purr?* 2845(F)
West, Kipling. *A Rattle of Bones*, 6061(F)
West, Robin. *Dinosaur Discoveries*, 21638
My Very Own Birthday, 21510
My Very Own Christmas, 21511
West, Tracey. *Costa Rica*, 15689, 15690
Fire in the Valley, 9636(F)
Mr. Peale's Bones, 9332(F)

Voyage of the Half Moon, 8198(F)
Westall, Robert. *Ghost Abbey*, 8199(F)
Westcott, Nadine Bernard. *The Best Vacation Ever*, 224(F)
The Bookstore Ghost, 6502(F)
Do Cowboys Ride Bikes? 4338(F)
Do Pirates Take Baths? 2980(F)
The Eensy-Weensy Spider, 14245
Even Little Kids Get Diabetes, 17992
Farmer Brown Goes Round and Round, 1583(F)
Farmer Brown Shears His Sheep, 1584(F)
The Giant Vegetable Garden, 1674(F)
Hello Toes! Hello Feet! 234(F)
I Know an Old Lady Who Swallowed a Fly, 14191
Is There Room on the Feather Bed? 1206(F)
I've Been Working on the Railroad, 14192
Kathy's Hats, 5002(F)
The Lady with the Alligator Purse, 11924(F)
The Lion Who Has Asthma, 5018(F)
Miss Mary Mack, 1245(F), 11350
Mrs. McNosh and the Great Big Squash, 1671(F)
Mrs. McNosh Hangs Up Her Wash, 4348(F)
Oh, Cats! 5148(F)
Oh, Grow Up! 4976(F)
Peanut Butter and Jelly, 4349(F)
Planet Was, 1004(F)
Round and Round Again, 4339(F)
The Thing That Bothered Farmer Brown, 4318(F)
Westcott, Nadine Bernard, ed. *Never Take a Pig to Lunch and Other Poems About the Fun of Eating*, 11925
Westcott, Patsy. *Living with Blindness*, 17935
Living with Epilepsy, 18014
Living with Leukemia, 18015
Westerduin, Anne. *Ducks Like to Swim*, 2780(F)
Westerfeld, Scott. *Watergate*, 16525
Westerman, Johanna. *Wynken, Blynken, and Nod*, 674
Westervelt, Virginia Veeder. *Here Comes Eleanor*, 13186
Westheimer, Ruth. *Dr. Ruth Talks to Kids*, 18270
Westman, Barbara. *My Perfect Neighborhood*, 1317(F)
Weston, Carol. *The Diary of Melanie Martin; or, How I Survived Matt the Brat, Michelangelo, and the Leaning Tower of Pizza*, 9075(F)
Private and Personal, 17737
Weston, Martha. *Apple Juice Tea*, 3938(F)

Bad Baby Brother, 3939(F)

Bet You Can't! Science Impossibilities to Fool You, 18306

The Book of Think (or How to Solve a Problem Twice Your Size), 21864

Cats Are Like That, 6713(F)

Do You Wanna Bet? 20614

The Hanukkah Book, 17453

How Will the Easter Bunny Know? 5978(F)

I Am Not a Short Adult, 17028

Nate the Great, 6653(F)

Nate the Great and the Monster Mess, 6650(F)

Owen Foote, Money Man, 9866(F)

Space Guys, 6714(F)

Tuck in the Pool, 2846(F)

Weston, Reiko. *Cooking the Japanese Way*, 21748

Westray, Kathleen. *A Color Sampler*, 292

Picture Puzzler, 20918

Westridge Young Writers Workshop. *Kids Explore America's Jewish Heritage*, 17229

Westrup, Hugh. *The Mammals*, 14479

Maurice Strong, 13348

Wethered, Peggy. *Touchdown Mars! An ABC Adventure*, 146(F)

Wetterer, Charles M. (jt. author). *The Snow Walker*, 16494

Wetterer, Margaret K. *Clyde Tombaugh and the Search for Planet X*, 13350

Kate Shelley and the Midnight Express, 6715(F)

The Snow Walker, 16494

Wexler, Jerome. *Pet Gerbils*, 19911

Pet Hamsters, 19912

Queen Anne's Lace, 20267

Weyl, Nancy. *Let's Do Fingerplays*, 22004

Whalen, Sharla S. *Friends on Ice*, 9453(F)

Meet the Friends, 9637(F)

Whalley, Margaret. *Experiment with Magnets and Electricity*, 20908

Wharton, Jennifer Heyd. *Suzette and the Puppy*, 4847(F)

Whatley, Bruce. *Captain Pajamas*, 4350(F)

Elvis Presley's the First Noel, 14198

My First Nursery Rhymes, 875

The Night Before Christmas, 11846

There Ain't No Bugs on Me, 14241

Whatley's Quest, 7126

Whayne, Susanne S. *Night Creatures*, 18988

The World of Insects, 19499

Wheeler, Cindy. *Bookstore Cat*, 5452(F)

The Emperor's Birthday Suit, 6716(F)

More Simple Signs, 14019

Wheeler, Doug (jt. author). *Fairy Tales of the Brothers Grimm*, 10521

Wheeler, Jill C. *Coretta Scott King*, 12738

Princess Caroline of Monaco, 13765

Wheeler, Jody. *An Old Fashioned Thanksgiving*, 9703(F)

Wild Weather, 20695, 20696

Wheeler, Leslie. *Jane Addams*, 13129

Wheeler, Sara. *Greetings from Antarctica*, 15845

Wheeler, Susan. *Holly Pond Hill*, 17536

Whelan, Gloria. *Farewell to the Island*, 9333(F)

Hannah, 8922(F)

Homeless Bird, 9019(F)

The Miracle of Saint Nicholas, 1675(F)

Miranda's Last Stand, 9454(F)

Next Spring an Oriole, 9455(F)

Once on This Island, 9334(F)

Return to the Island, 9456(F)

Silver, 7322(F)

Welcome to Starvation Lake, 10138(F)

Whelan, Olwyn. *A Child's Book of Angels*, 7689(F)

Whelan, Olwyn (jt. author). *The Mermaid of Cafur*, 7732(F)

Whipple, Catherine. *Shannon*, 15981

Whipple, Laura. *Eric Carle's Dragons Dragons and Other Creatures That Never Were*, 11735

Whipple, Laura, ed. *Eric Carle's Animals Animals*, 11816

Whippo, Walt. *Little White Duck*, 2847(F)

Whitaker, Malle N. *Toxic Threat*, 17008

Whitcomb, Mary E. *Odd Velvet*, 4059(F)

Whitcraft, Melissa. *The Hudson River*, 16755

The Tigris and Euphrates Rivers, 15494

White, Alana J. *Sacagawea*, 12992

White, Carolyn. *The Adventure of Louey and Frank*, 2848(F)

Whuppity Stoorie, 11044

White, Dana. *George Lucas*, 12418

White, Diana. *Ballerina Dreams*, 12481

White, E. B. *Charlotte's Web*, 8200(F)

The Trumpet of the Swan, 8201(F)

White, Ellen E. *Jim Abbott*, 13433

Voyage on the Great Titanic, 9638(F)

White, Kathryn. *When They Fight*, 2849(F)

White, Keinyo. *Jenny Reen and the Jack Muh Lantern*, 6051(F)

Uh-oh! It's Mama's Birthday! 3916(F)

White, Larry. *Air*, 20676

Energy, 20840

Water, 20747

White, Laurence B. *Razzle Dazzle!* 21791

White, Laurence B. (jt. author). *Abra-Ca-Dazzle*, 21777

Hocus Pocus, 21778

White, Linda. *Cooking on a Stick*, 21749

Too Many Pumpkins, 4351(F)

White, Linda Arms. *Comes a Wind*, 4352(F)

White, Michael. *Aztec Times*, 15635

Galileo Galilei, 13293

Isaac Newton, 13334

White, Michael P. *The Library Dragon*, 1107(F)

The Secret of Old Zeb, 6814(F)

White, Mike. *Nelson Mandela*, 13830

White, Nancy. *Why Do Dogs Do That?* 19978

White, Nancy (jt. author). *The Kids' Science Book*, 18322

White, Rosalyn. *Heart of Gold*, 10793

White, Sylvia. *Welcome Home!* 21162

White, Tekla N. *Missions of the San Francisco Bay Area*, 16824

White, William. *All About the Frog*, 18742

White Deer of Autumn. *The Great Change*, 8850(F)

The Native American Book of Knowledge, 16067

The Native American Book of Life, 16068

Whitelaw, Nancy. *Lady Diana Spencer*, 13785

More Perfect Union, 12895

William Tecumseh Sherman, 12963

Whitesel, Cheryl Aylward. *Rebel*, 9020(F)

Whitfield, Philip. *Macmillan Children's Guide to Dinosaurs and Other Prehistoric Animals*, 14480

Whitman, Candace. *The Night Is Like an Animal*, 810(F)

Now It Is Morning, 3940(F)

Robin's Home, 1768(F)

Snow! 3147(F)

Zoo-Looking, 5210(F)

Whitman, John. *Star Wars*, 10247(F)

Whitman, Sylvia. *Children of the World War II Home Front*, 14892

Get Up and Go! 21326

Immigrant Children, 16495

This Land Is Your Land, 16970

Uncle Sam Wants You! 14893

V Is for Victory, 14894

Whitmore, Arvella. *The Bread Winner*, 9639(F)

Trapped between the Lash and the Gun, 8202(F)

Whitney, Jean. *I'm Frustrated*, 4937(F)

Whittingham, Kim. *Six-Minute Nature Experiments*, 18302

Whittington, Mary K. *The Patchwork Lady*, 5737(F)

Whittle, Emily. *Sailor Cats*, 2850(F)

Whittle, Fran. *Simple Machines*, 20930

Whittock, Martyn. *The Roman Empire*, 14751

Whybrow, Ian. *A Baby for Grace*, 3941(F)
Harry and the Snow King, 1676(F)
Little Wolf's Book of Badness, 2851(F)
Little Wolf's Diary of Daring Deeds, 8203(F)
Little Wolf's Haunted Hall for Small Horrors, 8204(F)
Parcel for Stanley, 2852(F)
Sammy and the Dinosaurs, 1677(F)

Whyman, Kate. *The Animal Kingdom*, 18676

Whyte, Harlinah. *Japan*, 15142
Thailand, 15212

Whyte, Mariam. *Bangladesh*, 15213

Whyte, Mary. *Boomer Goes to School*, 5325(F)
Boomer's Big Day, 5326(F)
Boomer's Big Surprise, 2430(F)
I Love You the Purplest, 3738(F)
Mama's Way, 3749(F)
Snow Riders, 1371(F)
The Tickle Stories, 3926(F)
Waltz of the Scarecrows, 3297(F)

Wiberg, Harald. *Christmas in the Stable*, 5863(F)
The Tomten, 4738(F)

Wichlinski, Andrew. *Platypus*, 18973

Wick, Walter. *A Drop of Water*, 20748
I Spy, 21840
I Spy Christmas, 5876
I Spy Fantasy, 21872
I Spy School Days, 211(F)
I Spy Spooky Night, 21841
I Spy Super Challenger! A Book of Picture Riddles, 21873
I Spy Treasure Hunt, 21874
Walter Wick's Optical Tricks, 20919

Wickham, Martha. *Superstars of Women's Track and Field*, 13423

Wickstrom, Lois. *Oliver*, 2853(F)

Wickstrom, Sylvie. *Five Silly Fishermen*, 6325(F)
Little Witch Goes to School, 6370(F)
Room for Ripley, 20659
Silly Sadie, Silly Samuel, 6570(F)
This Old House, 2987(F)

Wickstrom, Thor. *The Brothers' Promise*, 11149

Hiccup Snickup, 4217(F)
I'm Not Moving, Mama! 1935(F)
Noah's Square Dance, 1665(F)

Widener, Terry. *America's Champion Swimmer*, 13684
The Babe and I, 4571(F)
Lou Gehrig, 13453
Peg and the Whale, 8000(F)
Shoe Magic, 11585
Tambourine Moon, 1279(F)

Widman, Christine. *The Willow Umbrella*, 4560(F)

Widom, Dianne. *Go Home, River*, 4495(F)

Wiebe, Darren. *Global Warning*, 6975(F)

Wiebe, Trina. *Hamsters Don't Glow in the Dark*, 7323(F)

Wieler, Diana. *To the Mountains by Morning*, 5453(F)

Wiencirz, Gerlinde. *Teddy's Easter Secret*, 5977(F)

Wiener, Lori S. *Be a Friend*, 18016

Wiener, Paul. *Patrick Ewing*, 13524

Wiese, Jim. *Cosmic Science*, 18424
Detective Science, 17089
Head to Toe Science, 18085
Magic Science, 18368
Rocket Science, 18369

Wiese, Kurt. *Five Chinese Brothers*, 4087(F)

Wiesel, Elie. *King Solomon and His Magic Ring*, 17327

Wiesmuller, Dieter. *The Adventures of Marco and Polo*, 2854(F)

Wiesner, David. *Free Fall*, 939(F)
Hurricane, 2984(F)
June 29, 1999, 1678(F)
Man from the Sky, 6754(F)
Night of the Gargoyles, 1025(F)
Sector 7, 1679(F)
Tuesday, 2855(F)

Wiggin, Kate Douglas. *The Birds' Christmas Carol*, 9768(F)
Rebecca of Sunnybrook Farm, 7536(F)

Wijngaard, Juan. *The Midas Touch*, 11491
Sir Gawain and the Loathly Lady, 10993

Wik, Lars. *Baby's First Words*, 153

Wikland, Ilon. *I Don't Want to Go to Bed*, 724(F)
I Want to Go to School, Too! 5516(F)
Lotta's Christmas Surprise, 5864(F)
Lotta's Easter Surprise, 5970(F)

Wikler, Madeline. *The Colors of My Jewish Year*, 6073(F)

Wikler, Madeline (jt. author). *All About Hanukkah*, 6077
All About Passover, 17469
All About Sukkot, 17470
Thank You, God! 17523

Wilbur, C. Keith. *Revolutionary Medicine 1700–1800*, 16220

The Revolutionary Soldier 1775–1783, 16221

Wilbur, Frances. *The Dog with Golden Eyes*, 7324(F)

Wilbur, Richard. *The Disappearing Alphabet*, 11926
Opposites, 14057
The Pig in the Spigot, 14058
Runaway Opposites, 11736

Wilburn, Kathy. *The Gingerbread Boy*, 10984

Wilcox, Cathy. *Andrew Jessup*, 4006(F)

Wilcox, Charlotte. *Mummies and Their Mysteries*, 17230
Mummies, Bones, and Body Parts, 14517
Powerhouse, 20847
Trash! 16988

Wilcox, Jane. *Why Do We Celebrate That?* 17407
Why Do We Use That? 21063

Wilcox, Jonathan. *Iceland*, 15469

Wild, Margaret. *All the Better to See You With!* 3942(F)
Big Cat Dreaming, 3943(F)
Let the Celebrations Begin! 9076(F)
Midnight Babies, 1680(F)
Mr. Nick's Knitting, 4060(F)
Our Granny, 3944(F)
The Pocket Dogs, 1681(F)
Remember Me, 3945(F)
Rosie and Tortoise, 2856(F)
Thank You, Santa, 5954(F)
Tom Goes to Kindergarten, 2857(F)

Wilde, Oscar. *Happy Prince*, 10522(F)

Wilder, Laura Ingalls. *Going to Town*, 4877(F)
Little House in the Big Woods, 7537(F)
West from Home, 7538(F)

Wildsmith, Brian. *Birds by Brian Wildsmith*, 19296
The Bremen Town Band, 10937
Brian Wildsmith's Amazing World of Words, 14059
Exodus, 17328
Jesus, 17329
Joseph, 17330
Katie and the Dream-Eater, 10831
Mother Goose, 867
Saint Francis, 13795
Seasons, 4561(F)
Wake Up, Wake Up! 5454(F)
What the Moon Saw, 256(F)

Wildsmith, Rebecca (jt. author). *Wake Up, Wake Up!* 5454(F)

Wiles, Deborah. *Freedom Summer*, 4061(F)

Wiley, Melissa. *On Tide Mill Lane*, 9335(F)

Wilgus, David. *Here There Be Dragons*, 8236(F)
Here There Be Ghosts, 8237(F)

Wilhelm, Hans. *I Lost My Tooth!* 6717(F)

I'll Always Love You, 5455(F)

It's Too Windy! 6718(F)

More Bunny Trouble, 2858(F)

The Royal Raven, 2859(F)

Tyrone the Horrible, 2860(F)

Wilkerson, J. L. *A Doctor to Her People,* 12983

From Slave to World-Class Horseman, 13678

Scribe of the Great Plains, 12589

Wilkerson, J. L. (jt. author). *Champion of Arbor Day,* 13326

Wilkes, Angela. *The Best Book of Ballet,* 14302

The Big Book of Dinosaurs, 14481

The Children's Quick and Easy Cookbook, 21750

Dazzling Disguises and Clever Costumes, 21553

My First Christmas Activity Book, 21512

My First Word Board Book, 3475(F)

See How I Grow, 18235

Your World, 18295

Wilkes, Debbi. *The Figure Skating Book,* 22227

Wilkes, Maria D. *Little Clearing in the Woods,* 9457(F)

Little House in Brookfield, 9458(F)

Little Town at the Crossroads, 9459(F)

Wilkes, Sybella. *One Day We Had to Run!* 14953

Wilkey, Michael. *They Never Gave Up,* 21111

Wilkin, Eloise. *Poems to Read to the Very Young,* 11567

Wilkinson, Beth. *Papermaking for Kids,* 21639

Wilkinson, Brenda. *African American Women Writers,* 12186

Wilkinson, Philip. *Amazing Buildings,* 21153

The Art Gallery, 13933

Building, 21154

A Celebration of Customs and Rituals of the World, 21960

Generals Who Changed the World, 13746

The Magical East, 15052

The Mediterranean, 14597

People Who Changed the World, 13745

Scientists Who Changed the World, 13224

Super Structures, 21155

Wilkinson, Phillip. *Ships,* 21379

Wilkon, Jozef. *Katie and the Big, Brave Bear,* 1420(F)

Wilkowski, Susan. *Baby's Bris,* 6123(F)

Willard, Keith. *Ballooning,* 22071

Willard, Michael. *Wonders of the Forest,* 20482

Willard, Nancy. *An Alphabet of Angels,* 147(F)

Cracked Corn and Snow Ice Cream, 20074

East of the Sun and West of the Moon, 12041

The Good-Night Blessing Book, 17537

The High Rise Glorious Skittle Skat Roarious Sky Pie Angel Food Cake, 8205(F)

The Marzipan Moon, 8206(F)

The Moon and Riddles Diner and the Sunnyside Cafe, 11927

Pish, Posh, Said Hieronymus Bosch, 1682

Shadow Story, 1683(F)

The Sorcerer's Apprentice, 1684(F)

The Tale I Told Sasha, 1685(F)

The Tortilla Cat, 8207(F)

Uncle Terrible, 8208(F)

A Visit to William Blake's Inn, 11737

The Voyage of the Ludgate Hill, 11738

Willey, Bee. *The Golden Hoard,* 11451

Michael Rosen's ABC, 120(F)

Nonsense Songs, 11886

River Story, 4461(F)

The Silver Treasure, 10576

Willey, Lynne. *The Universe,* 18379

Willey, Margaret. *Thanksgiving with Me,* 6159(F)

Willhoite, Michael. *Daddy's Roommate,* 3946(F)

Daddy's Wedding, 3947(F)

Williams, Arlene. *Dragon Soup,* 1686(F)

Williams, Berkeley. *Grandfather Tales,* 11328

Williams, Brenda (jt. author). *The Age of Discovery,* 14575

Williams, Brian. *The Age of Discovery,* 14575

The Modern World, 14574

Williams, Carol Ann. *Tsubu the Little Snail,* 10836

Williams, Carol L. *Carolina Autumn,* 8851(F)

Christmas in Heaven, 8852(F)

If I Forget, You Remember, 8853(F)

My Angelica, 8384(F)

Williams, Earl P. *What You Should Know About the American Flag,* 13977

Williams, Garth. *Bedtime for Frances,* 6395(F)

Beneath a Blue Umbrella, 885

Benjamin's Treasure, 2861(F)

Charlotte's Web, 8200(F)

Chester Cricket's Pigeon Ride, 2674(F)

The Cricket in Times Square, 8081(F)

Emmett's Pig, 6686(F)

The Family Under the Bridge, 8267(F)

Harry Kitten and Tucker Mouse, 8083(F)

J.B.'s Harmonica, 2670(F)

The Little House Cookbook, 21744

Little House in the Big Woods, 7537(F)

The Little Silver House, 7472(F)

Ride a Purple Pelican, 11911

Wait Till the Moon Is Full, 4394(F)

Williams, Jared T. *Return of the Wolf,* 7285(F)

Williams, Jay. *Everyone Knows What a Dragon Looks Like,* 4353(F)

Williams, Jennifer (jt. author). *Stringbean's Trip to the Shining Sea,* 3479(F)

Williams, Karen L. *One Thing I'm Good At,* 8854(F)

Painted Dreams, 4878(F)

A Real Christmas This Year, 9769(F)

Tap-Tap, 4879(F)

When Africa Was Home, 4880(F)

Williams, Laura. *The Executioner's Daughter,* 9127(F)

Williams, Laura E. *Behind the Bedroom Wall,* 9077(F)

The Ghost Stallion, 7325(F)

The Long Silk Strand, 1687(F)

The Spider's Web, 9078(F)

Torch Fishing with the Sun, 4881(F)

Up a Creek, 8539(F)

Williams, Laura Ellen. *A B C Kids,* 148(F)

Williams, Linda. *The Little Old Lady Who Was Not Afraid of Anything,* 1688(F)

Williams, Marcia. *The Adventures of Robin Hood,* 11045

Bravo, Mr. William Shakespeare! 12054

Fabulous Monsters, 11458

Greek Myths for Young Children, 11514

The Iliad and the Odyssey, 11515

Tales from Shakespeare, 12055

Williams, Marcia, reteller. *The Iliad and the Odyssey,* 11515

Williams, Margery. *The Velveteen Rabbit,* 8209(F)

Williams, Neva. *Patrick DesJarlait,* 12223

Williams, Nick. *How Birds Fly,* 19297

Williams, Richard. *Herbie Jones and the Dark Attic,* 8320(F)

Lewis and Clark, 12131

Williams, Richard A. *The Legend of the Christmas Rose,* 5844(F)

Williams, Rose. *The Book of Fairies,* 10628

Williams, Rozanne Lanczak. *The Coin Counting Book,* 608(F)

Williams, Sam. *The Baby's Game Book*, 21972

The Baby's Word Book, 14060

A Child Was Born, 17427

Cold Little Duck, Duck, Duck, 2573(F)

My Do It! 3512(F)

Teddy Bears Trim the Tree, 5955(F)

Williams, Sherley A. *Girls Together*, 5103(F)

Working Cotton, 3476(F)

Williams, Sophy. *The Night You Were Born*, 3784(F)

Williams, Stanley. *Gangs and Drugs*, 17090

Williams, Sue. *Carnival of the Animals*, 14124

I Went Walking, 3477(F)

Let's Go Visiting, 609(F)

Williams, Suzanne. *Made in China*, 15091

Secret Pal Surprises, 4062(F)

Williams, Suzanne (jt. author). *Pinatas and Smiling Skeletons*, 17366

Williams, Terry Tempest. *The Secret Language of Snow*, 20795

Williams, Vera B. *A Chair for My Mother*, 3948(F)

Cherries and Cherry Pits, 3478(F)

Hooray for Me! 3068(F)

Lucky Song, 3949(F)

"More More More," Said the Baby, 4354(F)

Scooter, 8385(F)

Stringbean's Trip to the Shining Sea, 3479(F)

Three Days on a River in a Red Canoe, 2985(F)

Williams-Andriani, Renee. *Shawn and Keeper and the Birthday Party*, 6472(F)

Shawn and Keeper Show-and-Tell, 6473(F)

Williams-Garcia, Rita. *Catching the Wild Waiyuuzee*, 3950(F)

Williamson, Gwyneth. *Beware of the Bears!* 2417(F)

One, Two, Three, Oops! 410(F)

Williamson, Ray A. (jt. author). *They Dance in the Sky*, 11280

Williamson, Sarah A. *Kids Cook! Fabulous Food for the Whole Family*, 21751

Williamson, Susan. *Summer Fun!* 22072

Williamson, Zachary (jt. author). *Kids Cook! Fabulous Food for the Whole Family*, 21751

Willing, Karen Bates. *Fabric Fun for Kids*, 21648

Willingham, Fred. *Busy Toes*, 4092(F)

Willis, Jeanne. *Be Quiet, Parrot!* 6719(F)

The Boy Who Lost His Belly Button, 1689(F)

Sloth's Shoes, 5738(F)

Susan Laughs, 5104(F)

What Did I Look Like When I Was a Baby? 2862(F)

Willis, Karen. *Vietnam*, 15214

Willis, Nancy C. *The Robins in Your Backyard*, 19298

Willis, Patricia. *The Barn Burner*, 7539(F)

Out of the Storm, 8855(F)

Willker, Joshua D. G. *Everything You Need to Know About the Dangers of Sports Gambling*, 22073

Willner-Pardo, Gina. *Daphne Eloise Slater, Who's Tall for Her Age*, 8856(F)

Figuring Out Frances, 8386(F)

Jumping into Nothing, 8857(F)

Spider Storch's Carpool Catastrophe, 8540(F)

Spider Storch's Desperate Deal, 10018(F)

Spider Storch's Fumbled Field Trip, 10019(F)

Spider Storch's Music Mess, 10139(F)

Spider Storch's Teacher Torture, 10140(F)

When Jane-Marie Told My Secret, 8387(F)

Willow, Diane. *At Home in the Rain Forest*, 4882

Science Sensations, 18370

Wills, Charles A. *Alabama*, 16896

A Historical Album of California, 16825

A Historical Album of Colorado, 16644

A Historical Album of Florida, 16897

A Historical Album of Georgia, 16898

A Historical Album of Illinois, 16591

A Historical Album of Michigan, 16592

A Historical Album of Ohio, 16593

A Historical Album of Oregon, 16826

A Historical Album of Pennsylvania, 16756

A Historical Album of Texas, 16917

Pearl Harbor, 14895

Wills, Charles A. (jt. author). *A Historical Album of New Jersey*, 16752

Wills, Patricia. *Danger Along the Ohio*, 9460(F)

Wilmore, Kathy. *A Day in the Life of a Colonial Innkeeper*, 16186

A Day in the Life of a Colonial Wigmaker, 16187

Wilmot, Jeanne (jt. author). *Tales from the Rain Forest*, 11437

Wilner, Isabel. *B Is for Bethlehem*, 149(F)

Wilner, Yvonne. *Butterflies Fly*, 19570

Wilsdon, Christina. *National Audubon Society First Field Guide to Insects*, 19500

The Solar System, 18536

Wilson, Anna. *Over in the Grasslands*, 610(F)

Wilson, Anne. *I Wish Tonight*, 767(F)

Masha and the Firebird, 7791(F)

Wilson, Anthony. *Communications*, 21232

The Dorling Kindersley Visual Timeline of Transportation, 21290

Wilson, Antoine. *The Young Zillionaire's Guide to Distributing Goods and Services*, 16930

Wilson, April. *Magpie Magic*, 940(F)

Wilson, Barbara K. *Acacia Terrace*, 15256

Wilson, Barbara K., reteller. *Wishbones*, 10773

Wilson, Colin. *Mysteries of the Universe*, 21961

Wilson, Dick. *"What Am I Doing in a Step-Family?"* 17642

Wilson, Don E. (jt. author). *Bats*, 19036

Wilson, Eric. *Murder on the Canadian*, 7127(F)

Wilson, Jacqueline. *Bad Girls*, 8858(F)

Double Act, 7540(F)

Elsa, Star of the Shelter, 8541(F)

The Lottie Project, 8859(F)

Wilson, Janet. *Amazing Grace*, 14152

Anna's Goat, 4707(F)

At Grandpa's Sugar Bush, 3067(F)

Buried in Ice, 15566

The Gadget War, 9835(F)

How to Be Cool in the Third Grade, 6318(F)

Imagine That! 14576

The Ingenious Mr. Peale, 12278

Sarah May and the New Red Dress, 1590(F)

What's He Doing Now? 3621(F)

Wilson, Janet (jt. author). *Me and Mr. Mah*, 5082(F)

Wilson, John. *Striped Ice Cream*, 7471(F)

Wilson, Johnniece M. *Poor Girl*, 8860(F)

Robin on His Own, 8861(F)

Wilson, Kathleen A. *The Origin of Life on Earth*, 10645

Wilson, Laura. *How I Survived the Oregon Trail*, 9461(F)

Wilson, Mary Ann (jt. author). *Make-a-Saurus*, 14393

Wilson, Nancy H. *Becoming Felix*, 8542(F)

Bringing Nettie Back, 8923(F)
Flapjack Waltzes, 8862(F)
Old People, Frogs, and Albert, 8388(F)
The Reason for Janey, 8543(F)
Wilson, Reginald. *Think About Our Rights*, 17053
Wilson, Rich. *Racing a Ghost Ship*, 22265
Wilson, Richard. *The Book of Where*, 14330
Wilson, Roberta. *Patrick's Tree House*, 8327(F)
Wilson, Sarah. *Good Zap, Little Grog*, 2863(F)
Love and Kisses, 1690(F)
Wilson, Sharon. *The Day Gogo Went to Vote*, 4832(F)
Freedom's Gifts, 7535(F)
The Grandad Tree, 3586(F)
Wilson, Stacy. *The Hockey Book for Girls*, 22216
Wilson, Sule Greg C. *African American Quilting*, 21649
Kwanzaa! 17408
Wilson, Susan. *Egypt*, 15516
Wilson, Susan L. (jt. author). *Welcome to Egypt*, 15500
Wilson, Suzan. *Stephen King*, 12558
Wilson, Tona (jt. author). *Three Friends*, 391(F)
Wilson, Valerie Wesley (jt. author). *Afro-Bets Book of Black Heroes from A to Z*, 12660
Wilson, Wayne. *Freddie Prinze, Jr.*, 12448
Julia Roberts, 12452
Wilson-Max, Ken. *Dexter Gets Dressed!* 3480(F)
Flush the Potty, 3481(F)
Furaha Means Happy, 14116
Halala Means Welcome, 13988
K Is for Kwanzaa, 5626
Little Green Tow Truck, 5605
Little Red Plane, 5606(F)
Max, 2864(F)
Max Loves Sunflowers, 4562(F)
Max's Starry Night, 1691(F)
Tic-Tac-Toe, 6679(F)
Wake Up, Sleep Tight, 257(F)
Wilton, Nicholas. *Feathers and Fools*, 1164(F)
Wimmer, Mike. *All the Places to Love*, 7479(F)
Bully for You, Teddy Roosevelt! 13101
Flight, 12134
Home Run, 13497
Staying Nine, 8609(F)
Summertime, 14242
Train Song, 5599(F)
Winborn, Marsha. *Digby and Kate and the Beautiful Day*, 6194(F)
Fat Santa, 5792(F)
Grandma's Cat, 5288(F)
Pepper's Journal, 20649
Probably Pistachio, 228

A Valentine for Norman Noggs, 6169(F)
Winch, John. *Keeping Up with Grandma*, 3951(F)
The Old Man Who Loved to Sing, 1692(F)
The Old Woman Who Loved to Read, 1693(F)
Winckler, Suzanne. *Our Endangered Planet*, 15846, 17010, 20576
Windham, Sophie. *The Mermaid and Other Sea Poems*, 11988
Unicorns! Unicorns! 2412(F)
Windling, Terri (jt. author). *A Midsummer Night's Faery Tale*, 7735(F)
A Wolf at the Door, 10414(F)
Winer, Yvonne. *Spiders Spin Webs*, 19598
Winfield, Alison. *The Impossible Riddle*, 11092
Wing, Natasha L. *Jalapeno Bagels*, 3952(F)
Wingerter, Linda S. *One Riddle, One Answer*, 10510(F)
Winget, Mary. *Eleanor Roosevelt*, 13187
Winkelman, Barbara Gaines. *The Panama Canal*, 15691
Winkleman, John S. *Firehouse*, 17823
Police Patrol, 17091
Winkleman, Katherine K. *Firehouse*, 17823
Police Patrol, 17091
Winkler, Allan M. *Cassie's War*, 9699(F)
Winkler, David. *Scotty and the Gypsy Bandit*, 8389(F)
Winkler, Kathy. *Radiology*, 18031
Winner, Cherie. *Coyotes*, 19146
Salamanders, 18697
The Sunflower Family, 20041
Woodpeckers, 19299
Winnick, Karen B. *Mr. Lincoln's Whiskers*, 4883(F)
Sybil's Night Ride, 4884(F)
Winograd, Deborah. *My Color Is Panda*, 293(F)
Winslow, Barbara. *Dance on a Sealskin*, 4885(F)
Winslow, Mimi. *Loggers and Railroad Workers*, 16385
Winston, Mary, ed. *American Heart Association Kids' Cookbook*, 21752
Winter, Ginny L. *The Riding Book*, 22208
The Skating Book, 22228
Winter, Jane K. *Chile*, 15790
Italy, 15394
Venezuela, 15791
Winter, Jeanette. *Cowboy Charlie*, 12300
Day of the Dead, 5628(F)
Eight Hands Round, 110(F)

Follow the Drinking Gourd, 4886(F)
Josefina, 611(F)
My Baby, 4887(F)
My Name Is Georgia, 12277
Sebastian, 12319
Shaker Boy, 4807(F)
The Tortilla Cat, 8207(F)
The World's Birthday, 6075(F)
Winter, Jonah. *Fair Ball! 14 Great Stars from Baseball's Negro Leagues*, 13424
Winter, Laurel. *Growing Wings*, 8210(F)
Winter, Milo. *The Aesop for Children*, 11048
Winter, Susan. *The Bear Who Went to the Ballet*, 1505(F)
Calling All Toddlers, 246(F)
Copy Me, Copycub, 2058(F)
I Can, 3953(F)
Toddler Time, 11699
Winters, Jeanette. *The House That Jack Built*, 901
Winters, Kay. *How Will the Easter Bunny Know?* 5978(F)
The Teeny Tiny Ghost, 6062(F)
Tiger Trail, 5456(F)
Whooo's Haunting the Teeny Tiny Ghost? 6063(F)
Wolf Watch, 5457(F)
Winther, Barbara. *Plays from African Tales*, 12042
Plays from Hispanic Tales, 12043
Winthrop, Elizabeth. *As the Crow Flies*, 5105(F)
Asleep in a Heap, 811(F)
The Battle for the Castle, 8211(F)
Bear and Roly-Poly, 2865(F)
Bear's Christmas Surprise, 5956(F)
The Castle in the Attic, 8212(F)
Dumpy La Rue, 2866(F)
I'm the Boss! 3954(F)
The Little Humpbacked Horse, 11116
Maggie and the Monster, 812(F)
Promises, 3955(F)
Shoes, 3482(F)
A Very Noisy Girl, 1694(F)
Winthrop, Elizabeth, adapt. *He Is Risen*, 17441
Winton, Tim. *The Deep*, 5106(F)
Lockie Leonard, Scumbuster, 10020(F)
Wise, William. *Dinosaurs Forever*, 11817
Nell of Branford Hall, 9128(F)
Wiseman, Ann S. *Making Things*, 21513
Wiseman, Ann S. (jt. author). *Adventures of Greek Heroes*, 11489
Wiseman, Bernard. *Barber Bear*, 6720(F)
Morris and Boris at the Circus, 6721(F)
Wiseman, David. *Jeremy Visick*, 8213(F)

Wishik, Cindy S. *Kids Dish It Up . . . Sugar-Free*, 21753
Wishinsky, Frieda. *Each One Special*, 5107(F)
The Man Who Made Parks, 12942
Nothing Scares Us, 3483(F)
Oonga Boonga, 4355(F)
Wisler, G. Clifton. *All for Texas*, 9462(F)
Caleb's Choice, 9336(F)
The Drummer Boy of Vicksburg, 9506(F)
Mr. Lincoln's Drummer, 9507(F)
Mustang Flats, 9508(F)
Run the Blockade, 9509(F)
This New Land, 9218(F)
Wismer, Donald. *Starluck*, 10248(F)
Wisniewski, David. *Ducky*, 1023(F)
Elfwyn's Saga, 11132
Golem, 11178
I'll Play With You, 1575(F)
Master Man, 10714
Rain Player, 4888(F)
The Secret Knowledge of Grown-ups, 10021(F)
Sundiata, 10718
Tough Cookie, 1695(F)
The Warrior and the Wise Man, 10523(F)
The Wave of the Sea-Wolf, 11317
Workshop, 3073
Wister, Sally. *A Colonial Quaker Girl*, 16222
Withington, William A. *Southeast Asia*, 15215
Withrow, Sarah. *Bat Summer*, 8390(F)
Witschonke, Alan. *Hail to the Chief*, 17101
Witt, Alexa. *It's Great to Skate!* 22074
Wittbold, Maureen. *Mending Peter's Heart*, 7326(F)
Wittels, Harriet. *A First Thesaurus*, 14061
Wittlinger, Ellen. *Gracie's Girl*, 8391(F)
Wittmann, Patricia. *Buffalo Thunder*, 4889(F)
Clever Gretchen, 1597(F)
Scrabble Creek, 3956(F)
Wittstock, Laura W. *Ininatig's Gift of Sugar*, 16069
Woelfle, Gretchen. *The Wind at Work*, 20841
Woff, Richard. *The Ancient Greek Olympics*, 22258
Bright-Eyed Athena, 11516
Wohl, Lauren L. *Christopher Davis's Best Year Yet*, 8863(F)
Wohnoutka, Mike. *Counting Sheep*, 445(F)
Wojciechowska, Maia. *Shadow of a Bull*, 8864(F)
Wojciechowski, Susan. *Beany and the Dreaded Wedding*, 8865(F)

Beany (Not Beanhead) and the Magic Crystal, 8214(F)
The Best Halloween of All, 6064(F)
The Christmas Miracle of Jonathan Toomey, 5957(F)
Don't Call Me Beanhead! 10022(F)
Wojtowycz, David. *Animal ABC*, 150(F)
Animal Antics from 1 to 10, 612(F)
Rumble in the Jungle, 11771
Wolcott, Dyanna. *Dog Days*, 11979
I Am Me, 3761(F)
Wolf, Bernard. *Beneath the Stone*, 15653
Cuba, 15721
Homeless, 17159
If I Forget Thee, O Jerusalem, 15533
Wolf, Elizabeth. *Way to Go, Alex!* 5052(F)
Wolf, Gefion (jt. author). *Riding for Beginners*, 22198
Wolf, Gita. *The Very Hungry Lion*, 10809
Wolf, Jake. *And Then What?* 1696(F)
What You Do Is Easy, What I Do Is Hard, 2867(F)
Wolf, Sallie. *Peter's Trucks*, 5607(F)
Wolfe, Art. *Northwest Animal Babies*, 18877
1, 2, 3 Moose, 462
Wolfe, Diane. *Cooking the Australian Way*, 21700
Cooking the South American Way, 21729
Desserts Around the World, 21694
Wolfe, Gillian. *Oxford First Book of Art*, 13934
Wolfe, Robert L. *Cooking the Australian Way*, 21700
Cooking the South American Way, 21729
Desserts Around the World, 21694
Wolfert, Adrienne. *Making Tracks*, 9640(F)
Wolff, Ashley. *Doctor Bird*, 11423
Each Living Thing, 4527(F)
I Love My Daddy Because . . ., 3844(F)
Miss Bindergarten Celebrates the 100th Day of Kindergarten, 248(F)
Miss Bindergarten Stays Home from Kindergarten, 5541(F)
Some Things Go Together, 3974(F)
Splish, Splash! 6710(F)
Stella and Roy Go Camping, 2986(F)
A String of Beads, 21546
Who Took the Cookies from the Cookie Jar? 2345(F)
Wolff, Barbara. *Egg to Chick*, 19306
Wolff, Ferida. *Halloween Fun for Everyone*, 17449
Seven Loaves of Bread, 1697(F)

Watch Out for Bears! The Adventures of Henry and Bruno, 6722(F)
A Weed Is a Seed, 3484(F)
A Year for Kiko, 3485(F)
Wolff, Jason. *That Furball Puppy and Me*, 8186(F)
Wolff, Patricia R. *The Toll-Bridge Troll*, 1698(F)
Wolff, Rick. *Brooks Robinson*, 13484
Wolff, Virginia E. *Bat 6*, 10373(F)
Wolfish, Martin (jt. author). *Changes in You and Me*, 18250
Wolfman, Ira. *Do People Grow on Family Trees?* 17692
Wolfman, Judy. *Life on a Pig Farm*, 20075
Wolfson, Evelyn. *From the Earth to Beyond the Sky*, 18032
Growing Up Indian, 16070
Wolfson, Margaret O. *Turtle Songs*, 10852
Wolinsky, Art. *Communicating on the Internet*, 21233
Creating and Publishing Web Pages on the Internet, 21234
The History of the Internet and the World Wide Web, 21235
Locating and Evaluating Information on the Internet, 21236
Wolitzer, Hilma. *Wish You Were Here*, 8544(F)
Wolk-Stanley, Jessica. *The New York Public Library Amazing Space*, 20966
Wolkstein, Diane. *Bouki Dances the Kokioko*, 11433
Wolkstein, Diane, reteller. *The Glass Mountain*, 10938
Wollard, Kathy. *How Come?* 18296
How Come Planet Earth? 18297
Wolpert, Tom. *Whale Magic for Kids*, 19804
Whitetail Magic for Kids, 19159
Womack, Alfred. *Going to the Doctor*, 3039
Wong, Janet S. *Buzz*, 3486(F)
Grump, 813(F)
Night Garden, 11739
The Rainbow Hand, 11740
A Suitcase of Seaweed and Other Poems, 11741
This Next New Year, 5658(F)
The Trip Back Home, 4890(F)
Wong, Jeanyee. *The Alphabet Atlas*, 151(F)
Wong, Olive. *From My Window*, 3487(F)
Wong, Ovid K. *Giant Pandas*, 19191
Woo, Yolanda Garfias. *Pinatas and Smiling Skeletons*, 17366
Wood, A. J. *Amazing Animals*, 5458
Beautiful Birds, 5459
Hidden Pictures, 317
Wood, Angela. *Buddhist Temple*, 17231
Christian Church, 17232

Hindu Mandir, 17233
Jewish Festivals, 17489
Jewish Synagogue, 17234
Judaism, 17235
Muslim Mosque, 17236
Wood, Audrey. *Birdsong*, 4563(F)
The Bunyans, 1699(F)
The Christmas Adventure of Space Elf Sam, 5958(F)
Elbert's Bad Word, 1700(F)
The Flying Dragon Room, 1704(F)
Heckedy Peg, 10524(F)
Jubal's Wish, 2868(F)
King Bidgood's in the Bathtub, 4356(F)
Little Penguin's Tale, 2869(F)
The Napping House, 4357(F)
The Napping House Wakes Up, 3488(F)
Oh My Baby Bear! 2870(F)
Piggies, 1705(F)
The Rainbow Bridge, 11318
Red Racer, 4358(F)
The Rude Giants, 1701(F)
Silly Sally, 2871(F)
Sweet Dream Pie, 1702(F)
Tickleoctopus, 1703(F)
Wood, Beverley. *Dogstar*, 8215(F)
Wood, Bruce Robert. *The Christmas Adventure of Space Elf Sam*, 5958(F)
Wood, Chris (jt. author). *Dogstar*, 8215(F)
Wood, Clare. *Everybody Has a Bellybutton*, 18074
Wood, Dan (jt. author). *Jesse Jackson*, 12729
Wood, Don. *Heckedy Peg*, 10524(F)
Jubal's Wish, 2868(F)
King Bidgood's in the Bathtub, 4356(F)
The Napping House, 4357(F)
The Napping House Wakes Up, 3488(F)
Piggies, 1705(F)
Tickleoctopus, 1703(F)
Wood, Don (jt. author). *Piggies*, 1705(F)
Wood, Douglas. *Grandad's Prayers of the Earth*, 3957(F)
Making the World, 258(F)
Northwoods Cradle Song, 814(F)
Old Turtle, 2872(F)
Rabbit and the Moon, 11319
What Dads Can't Do, 2873(F)
What Moms Can't Do, 2874(F)
The Windigo's Return, 11320
Wood, Ellen. *Hundreds of Fish*, 5460(F)
Wood, Gerald. *Ancient African Town*, 15035
Exploring Africa, 14910
Exploring the World, 12060
Wood, Jakki. *Across the Big Blue Sea*, 4359(F)
Fiddle-i-fee, 902(F)
Four Fierce Kittens, 5192(F)

Moo Moo, Brown Cow, 613(F)
Wood, Jenny. *Coral Reefs*, 19670
Waterfalls, 20396
Wood, John D. *Easy Geography Activities*, 14360
Wood, June R. *About Face*, 8392(F)
The Man Who Loved Clowns, 8866(F)
Turtle on a Fence Post, 8867(F)
When Pigs Fly, 8868(F)
Wood, Leigh. *The Crow Indians*, 16071
Wood, Marion. *Growing Up in Aztec Times*, 15654
The World of Native Americans, 14518
Wood, Michele. *Christmas Soul*, 17414
Going Back Home, 12313
I See the Rhythm, 14132
Wood, Nancy. *The Girl Who Loved Coyotes*, 11321
Wood, Richard. *Diana*, 13786
Wood, Richard, ed. *Great Inventions*, 21064
Wood, Robert W. *Easy Geography Activities*, 14360
Wood, Ted. *A Boy Becomes a Man at Wounded Knee*, 16072
Ghosts of the Southwest, 21962
Ghosts of the West Coast, 21963
Iditarod Dream, 22075
In the Village of the Elephants, 19170
Wood, Ted (jt. author). *Two Lands, One Heart*, 15200
Wood, Tim. *The Aztecs*, 15655
Houses and Homes, 21163
The Renaissance, 14805
Wood, Tim (jt. author). *Ancient Greece*, 14689
Woodbury, Mary. *Brad's Universe*, 8545(F)
Wooden, Lenny. *A Terrifying Taste of Short and Shivery*, 8063(F)
Woodford, Susan. *The Parthenon*, 14709
Woodhouse, Jane. *Joseph Turner*, 12304
Pieter Bruegel, 12195
Woodhouse, Jayne. *Louis Braille*, 13762
Woodman, Allen (jt. author). *The Cows Are Going to Paris*, 2293(F)
Woodman, Nancy. *Sand*, 20568
Sea-Fari Deep, 7128(F)
Woodruff, Elvira. *Awfully Short for the Fourth Grade*, 8216(F)
Can You Guess Where We're Going? 3489(F)
Dear Austin, 9337(F)
"Dear Napoleon, I Know You're Dead, But . . ." 7541(F)
The Ghost of Lizard Light, 8217(F)
Ghosts Don't Get Goose Bumps, 7129(F)

The Memory Coat, 4891(F)
Orphan of Ellis Island, 8218(F)
The Secret Funeral of Slim Jim the Snake, 8869(F)
The Summer I Shrank My Grandmother, 8219(F)
The Wing Shop, 1706(F)
Woodruff, John. *Energy*, 20842
Woodruff, Liza. *Amanda Bean's Amazing Dream*, 537(F)
The Long Wait, 20642(F)
Mabel Ran Away with the Toys, 3933(F)
Woods, Andrew. *Young Reggie Jackson*, 13463
Woods, Geraldine. *Animal Experimentation and Testing*, 18677
The Oprah Winfrey Story, 12486
Science in Ancient Egypt, 14673
Science of the Early Americas, 15563
Woods, Geraldine (jt. author). *Bill Cosby*, 12372
Woods, Harold. *Bill Cosby*, 12372
Woods, Mae. *Charles Schulz*, 12301
Dr. Seuss, 12540
Insects of the Rain Forest, 20494
Laura Ingalls Wilder, 12631
Woods, Mary (jt. author). *Ancient Agriculture*, 14598
Ancient Machines from Wedges to Waterwheels, 14599
Woods, Mary B. *Ancient Communication*, 13966
Ancient Computing, 20600
Ancient Construction, 21156
Ancient Warfare, 21409
Woods, Mary B. (jt. author). *Ancient Medicine*, 14600
Ancient Transportation, 14601
Woods, Michael. *Ancient Agriculture*, 14598
Ancient Machines from Wedges to Waterwheels, 14599
Ancient Medicine, 14600
Ancient Transportation, 14601
Woods, Michael (jt. author). *Ancient Communication*, 13966
Ancient Computing, 20600
Ancient Construction, 21156
Ancient Warfare, 21409
Woods, Samuel. *Computer Animation*, 21237
The Pediatrician, 18033
Recycled Paper, 21065
Woods, Samuel G. *Chocolate*, 20136
Crayons, 21066
Guitars, 14231
Sneakers, 21187
Woods, Shirley. *Black Nell*, 7327(F)
Kit, 7328(F)
Woodson, Jacqueline. *The Other Side*, 4063(F)
Sweet, Sweet Memory, 5108
We Had a Picnic This Sunday Past, 3958(F)

Woodtor, Dee Parmer. *Big Meeting*, 3959(F)

Woog, Adam. *The Beatles*, 12356
Elvis Presley, 12445
Harry Houdini, 12403

Wool, David. *How Did We Find Out About Solar Power?* 20848
How Did We Find Out About Volcanoes? 20332

Wooldridge, Connie N. *Wicked Jack*, 11391

Worcester, Don. *Cowboy with a Camera, Erwin E. Smith*, 16386

Wormell, Christopher. *Blue Rabbit and Friends*, 2875(F)
Blue Rabbit and the Runaway Wheel, 2876(F)
Puff-Puff, Chugga-Chugga, 2877(F)

Wormell, Mary. *Hilda Hen's Happy Birthday*, 5739(F)
Hilda Hen's Scary Night, 2878(F)
Hilda Hen's Search, 2879(F)
Why Not? 2880(F)

Worth, Bonnie. *Oh Say Can You Say Di-no-saur?* 14482
Wish for a Fish, 19653

Worth, Richard. *Poverty*, 17160
Robert Mugabe of Zimbabwe, 13838

Worthen, Bonnie (jt. author). *Period*, 18265

Wotjowycz, David. *Cock-a-doodle-doo! Barnyard Hullabaloo*, 1740(F)

Wray, Thomas (jt. author). *Home Is Where We Live*, 8672(F)

Wray, Ze. *101 Things to Do on the Internet*, 21231

Wrede, Patricia C. *Book of Enchantments*, 8220(F)

Wright, Beth. *Count Your Way Through Ireland*, 15350
Count Your Way Through Italy, 15384

Wright, Betty R. *Christina's Ghost*, 8221(F)
The Dollhouse Murders, 7130(F)
The Ghost Comes Calling, 8222(F)
The Ghost in Room 11, 8223(F)
A Ghost in the Family, 7131(F)
A Ghost in the House, 8224(F)
The Ghost of Popcorn Hill, 8225(F)
Haunted Summer, 8226(F)
The Moonlight Man, 8227(F)
Out of the Dark, 8228(F)
Pet Detectives, 2881(F)
Rosie and the Dance of the Dinosaurs, 8924(F)
The Summer of Mrs. MacGregor, 8393(F)
Too Many Secrets, 7132(F)
The Wish Master, 8870(F)

Wright, Blanche Fisher. *Real Mother Goose*, 871
The Real Mother Goose Clock Book, 872

Wright, Cliff. *Are You Spring?* 2590(F)
Santa's Ark, 5959(F)
When They Fight, 2849(F)

Wright, Courtni C. *Journey to Freedom*, 9338(F)
Jumping the Broom, 4892(F)

Wright, David. *Computers*, 21238

Wright, David K. *Arthur Ashe*, 13645
Brunei, 15216
Burma, 15217
John Lennon, 12413
Paul Robeson, 12454
Vietnam, 15218

Wright, Jane C. *The Sun Is Up*, 11985

Wright, Joan Richards (jt. author). *Bugs*, 19475

Wright, Joseph P. (jt. author). *Math Games for Middle School*, 20620

Wright, Lynn F. *Flick*, 7329(F)

Wright, Lynne. *The Science of Noise*, 20944

Wright, Pamela (jt. author). *Bat Watching*, 19020
Butterfly Watching, 19540
Deer Watching, 19148
Eagle Watching, 19320
Sea Turtle Watching, 18778
Tide Pool Life Watching, 19853
Whale Watching, 19776

Wright, Rachel. *Paris 1789*, 15320
The Viking News, 15470

Wright, Susan K. *Dead Letters*, 7133(F)
The Secret of the Old Graveyard, 7134(F)

Wright, Sydney. *Computer Fun Halloween*, 17448
Computer Fun Math, 21228

Wright-Frierson, Virginia. *A Desert Scrapbook*, 20428
First Grade Can Wait, 5469(F)
An Island Scrapbook, 19871
A North American Rain Forest Scrapbook, 20495
We're Growing Together, 3851(F)

Wroble, Lisa A. *Kids During the Great Depression*, 16496
Kids in Colonial Times, 16188

Wu, Dana Ying-Hul. *The Chinese-American Experience*, 17600

Wu, Leslie. *Bijou, Bonbon and Beau*, 4846(F)

Wu, Norbert. *A City Under the Sea*, 19671

Wu, Priscilla. *The Abacus Contest*, 9021(F)

Wukovits, John F. *Bill Gates*, 13297
Butch Cassidy, 12868
Colin Powell, 12956
George W. Bush, 13014
Jesse James, 12910
Jim Carrey, 12366
Life as a POW, 14896
Life of an American Soldier in Europe, 14897

Wulffson, Don L. *The Kid Who Invented the Popsicle and Other Surprising Stories About Inventions*, 21067
Toys! Amazing Stories Behind Some Great Inventions, 22076

Wummer, Amy. *Look! I Can Read!* 6409(F)

Wundrow, Deanna. *Jungle Drum*, 5461(F)

Wunsch, Marjory. *When You Take a Pig to a Party*, 5711(F)

Wunsch, Susi Trautmann. *The Adventures of Sojourner*, 21020

Wyatt, Valerie. *FAQ Weather*, 20797
The Math Book for Girls and Other Beings Who Count, 20601
The Science Book for Girls and Other Intelligent Beings, 18371

Wyeth, N. C. *N. C. Wyeth's Pilgrims*, 16168
Rip Van Winkle, 7814(F)
Robin Hood, 10964
The Yearling, 7289(F)

Wyeth, Sharon D. *The Dinosaur Tooth*, 7135(F)
Ginger Brown, 6723(F)
Once on This River, 9219(F)
A Piece of Heaven, 8871(F)
Something Beautiful, 3490(F)
Tomboy Trouble, 6724(F)

Wyler, Rose. *Math Fun*, 20624
Math Fun with Money Puzzlers, 20625
Raindrops and Rainbows, 20749
Science Fun with Peanuts and Popcorn, 18372
Science Fun with Toy Boats and Planes, 18373
Spooky Tricks, 21792
The Starry Sky, 18425

Wyman, Cherie R. *Labor Day*, 17399

Wynne, Patricia J. *Extinction Is Forever*, 18668
The Human Body, 18051
Hungry, Hungry Sharks, 19753
Why Save the Rain Forest? 20488

Wynne Jones, Diana. *Fantasy Stories*, 8229(F)

Wynne-Jones, Tim. *Lord of the Fries*, 8872(F)
Some of the Kinder Planets, 8230(F)

Wyse, Lois. *How to Take Your Grandmother to the Museum*, 3960(F)

Wyss, Johann D. *Swiss Family Robinson*, 7136(F)

Xiong, Blia. *Nine-in-One, Grr! Grr!* 10846

Xuan, Yong-Sheng. *The Dragon Lover and Other Chinese Proverbs*, 10774

Xuan, Yongsheng. *The Laziest Boy in the World*, 4776(F)

The Rooster's Antlers, 10760
Ten Suns, 10761
That's Ghosts for You, 7649(F)

Yaccarino, Dan. *Away We Go!*
6312(F)
Circle Dogs, 333(F)
Come with Me, 11663
Deep in the Jungle, 2882(F)
Five Little Pumpkins, 5997(F)
Good Night, Mr. Night, 815(F)
Little White Dog, 270(F)
An Octopus Followed Me Home,
4360(F)
One Hole in the Road, 538(F)
*Sammy Keyes and the Hollywood
Mummy*, 7107(F)
So Big! 5462(F)
Trashy Town, 3497(F)
*Zoom! Zoom! Zoom! I'm Off to the
Moon*, 1707(F)
Yacowitz, Caryn. *Pumpkin Fiesta*,
4893(F)
Yaffe, Rebecca M. *When a Parent
Goes to Jail*, 17092
Yagyu, Genichiro. *All About Scabs*,
18183
Yakovetic, Ed. *Great Predators of
the Land*, 18840
Yalowitz, Paul. *Catty-Cornered*,
8537(F)
Mary Veronica's Egg, 5355(F)
Moonstruck, 4110(F)
Nell Nugget and the Cow Caper,
2926(F)
The Runaway Latkes, 6087(F)
Somebody Loves You, Mr. Hatch,
5085(F)
The Spooky Eerie Night Noise,
5379(F)
Yamaka, Sara. *The Gift of Driscoll
Lipscomb*, 294(F)
Yamane, Linda. *Weaving a Califor-
nia Tradition*, 21528
Yamazaki, Sanae. *Ooka the Wise*,
10812
Yancey, Diane. *Camels for Uncle
Sam*, 21346
Leaders of the North and South,
16442
Strategic Battles, 16443
Zoos, 20031
Yang, Belle. *Chili-Chili-Chin-Chin*,
2883(F)
Yang, Dori Jones. *The Secret Voice
of Gina Zhang*, 8873(F)
Yang, Kuo W. *Smash Caps*, 22042
Yannuzzi, Della A. *Mae Jemison*,
12127
Yao-wen, Li (jt. author). *Sweet and
Sour*, 10759
Yardley, Joanna. *The Bracelet*,
9692(F)
The Hand-Me-Down Horse,
4798(F)
*It's Funny Where Ben's Train
Takes Him*, 1027(F)

Yardley, Thompson. *Buy Now, Pay
Later*, 16937
Down the Drain, 21164
Down the Hatch, 18101
Yaroshevskaya, Kim. *Little Kim's
Doll*, 4894(F)
Yashima, Taro. *Crow Boy*, 5545(F)
Umbrella, 3491(F)
Yates, Elizabeth. *Amos Fortune, Free
Man*, 12724
Yates, Irene. *All About Color*, 295(F)
All About Pattern, 318(F)
From Birth to Death, 20529
Yates, Keith D. *Tae Kwon Do for
Kids*, 22274
Yates, Sarah. *Alberta*, 15598
Ybanez, Terry. *The Christmas
Tree/El Arbol de Navidad*,
5741(F)
Ye, Ting-xing. *Three Monks, No
Water*, 10775
Yee, Brenda Shannon. *Sand Castle*,
4064(F)
Yee, Josie. *Thomas Goes to the Cir-
cus*, 1620(F)
Yee, Patrick. *Rosie Rabbit's Colors*,
296(F)
Winter Rabbit, 2884(F)
Yee, Paul. *Ghost Train*, 8231(F)
Yee, Wong H. *Big Black Bear*,
2885(F)
Eek! There's a Mouse in the House,
4361(F)
Fireman Small, 3492(F)
Get That Pest! 6313(F)
Hamburger Heaven, 2886(F)
Here Come Trainmice! 2887(F)
Mrs. Brown Went to Town, 2888(F)
The Officer's Ball, 2889(F)
Yektai, Niki. *Bears at the Beach*,
614(F)
Triplets, 3961(F)
Yen, Clara. *Why Rat Comes First*,
1708(F)
Yeoh, Hong Nam. *Greece*, 15395
Yeoman, John. *The Seven Voyages of
Sinbad the Sailor*, 11202
Yep, Laurence. *The Amah*, 8546(F)
The Case of the Firecrackers,
7137(F)
The Case of the Goblin Pearls,
7138(F)
The Case of the Lion Dance,
7139(F)
The City of Dragons, 1709(F)
Cockroach Cooties, 7140(F)
The Cook's Family, 10023(F)
Dragon of the Lost Sea, 8232(F)
The Dragon Prince, 10776
Dream Soul, 8547(F)
The Ghost Fox, 10525(F)
Hiroshima, 9700(F)
The Imp That Ate My Homework,
8233(F)
The Journal of Wong Ming-Chung,
9641(F)
The Junior Thunder Lord, 10777

The Khan's Daughter, 10737
Later, Gator, 7330(F)
The Magic Paintbrush, 8234(F)
The Man Who Tricked a Ghost,
10778
Ribbons, 8548(F)
Thief of Hearts, 7380(F)
Tiger Woman, 10779
Tree of Dreams, 10629
Yerxa, Leo. *Last Leaf First
Snowflake to Fall*, 4564(F)
Yezerski, Thomas F. *Mimmy and
Sophie*, 4623(F)
Queen of the World, 5740(F)
Spy in the Sky, 9484(F)
Together in Pinecone Patch,
4065(F)
Yim, Natasha. *Otto's Rainy Day*,
3493(F)
Yin. *Coolies*, 4895(F)
Ying-Hwa. *Daughter's Day Blues*,
3835(F)
Yoder, Dot. *Andy Finds a Turtle*,
4979(F)
Yolen, Jane. *Boots and the Seven
Leaguers*, 8235(F)
Child of Faerie, Child of Earth,
6065(F)
Color Me a Rhyme, 11989
*Commander Toad and the Voyage
Home*, 10249(F)
Dear Mother, Dear Daughter,
11745
The Devil's Arithmetic, 9701(F)
The Emperor and the Kite, 10780
Encounter, 9142(F)
Fairies' Ring, 10630
Grandad Bill's Song, 5109(F)
Here There Be Dragons, 8236(F)
Here There Be Ghosts, 8237(F)
House, House, 16757
How Beastly! 11928
*How Do Dinosaurs Say Good-
night?* 816(F)
*Jane Yolen's Mother Goose Song-
book*, 904
*Jane Yolen's Old MacDonald
Songbook*, 14195
King Long Shanks, 10526(F)
A Letter from Phoenix Farm, 12632
Meet the Monsters, 21964
Merlin, 8238(F)
Milk and Honey, 17490
Miz Berlin Walks, 4066(F)
Moon Ball, 1710(F)
The Musicians of Bremen, 10939
Nocturne, 4565(F)
O Jerusalem, 11742
Off We Go! 2890(F)
Once upon a Bedtime Story, 10631
The Originals, 11819
Owl Moon, 5463(F)
Passager, 8239(F)
Pegasus, the Flying Horse, 11517
Picnic with Piggins, 2891(F)
The Pictish Child, 8240(F)
Raising Yoder's Barn, 3494(F)

Sacred Places, 11743
The Sea Man, 8241(F)
Sea Watch, 11820
Snow, Snow, 11992
Tea with an Old Dragon, 9642(F)
The Three Bears Holiday Rhyme Book, 5659
An Unsolved Mystery from History, 7141(F)
Water Music, 11993
Welcome to the Green House, 4566
Welcome to the Ice House, 15847
Welcome to the Sea of Sand, 20429
Where Have the Unicorns Gone? 1711(F)
Wizard's Hall, 8242(F)
The Wizard's Map, 8243(F)
Yolen, Jane, ed. Alphabestiary, 11818
Camelot, 11046
Jane Yolen's Songs of Summer, 14194
The Lap-Time Song and Play Book, 903
Mother Earth, Father Sky, 11990
Once upon Ice, 11991
Sherwood, 9129(F)
Sky Scrape/City Scape, 11744
Sleep Rhymes Around the World, 817
Yorinks, Adrienne. The Alphabet Atlas, 151(F)
Stand for Children, 17030
Yorinks, Arthur. The Alphabet Atlas, 151(F)
The Flying Latke, 6124(F)
Harry and Lulu, 1712(F)
Hey, Al, 2892(F)
Louis the Fish, 1713(F)
Oh, Brother, 4362(F)
Tomatoes from Mars, 1714(F)
Whitefish Will Rides Again! 4363(F)
York, Carol B. The Key to the Playhouse, 8394(F)
York, Sarah Mountbatten-Windsor, Duchess of. Budgie at Bendick's Point, 1715(F)
Yoshi. A to Zen, 145(F)
The Butterfly Hunt, 8244(F)
The Farmer and the Poor God, 10835
The First Story Ever Told, 11440
Magical Hands, 5662(F)
Yoshida, Hideo C. Why Rat Comes First, 1708(F)
Yoshino, Shin. Cats, 19928
Young, Allen M. Lives Intertwined, 20397
Young, Caroline (jt. author). The Usborne Book of Treasure Hunting, 14334
Young, Dan. Big Brother Dustin, 3570(F)
Dustin's Big School Day, 5482(F)
Young, Ed. All of You Was Singing, 11406

Bicycle Rider, 12784
Bitter Bananas, 4783(F)
Cat and Rat, 2893
Desert Song, 4467(F)
Donkey Trouble, 10632
Dreamcatcher, 758(F)
The Emperor and the Kite, 10780
Foolish Rabbit's Big Mistake, 10801
Happy Prince, 10522(F)
The Hunter, 10740
I Wish I Were a Butterfly, 2225(F)
Iblis, 11194
Lon Po Po, 10781
The Lost Horse, 10782
Monkey King, 1716(F)
Mouse Match, 10783
Night Visitors, 10784
October Smiled Back, 4508(F)
Pinocchio, 7662(F)
A Pup Just for Me/A Boy Just for Me, 5407(F)
Sadako, 14841
Seven Blind Mice, 10810
The Turkey Girl, 11290
Voices of the Heart, 13989
Yeh-Shen, 10764
Young Fu of the Upper Yangtze, 9001(F)
Young, Frederica. Super-Duper Jokes, 21859
Young, Jay. The Art of Science, 18374
Young, Jeff C. Top 10 Basketball Shot-Blockers, 13425
Young, Jerry. Amazing Bats, 19026
Amazing Birds, 19265
Amazing Mammals, 18960
Amazing Wolves, Dogs, and Foxes, 19130
Insects and Crawly Creatures, 19484
Young, Judy D. (jt. author). Race with Buffalo, 11322
Stories from the Days of Christopher Columbus, 10633
Young, Karen Romano. Arctic Investigations, 19881
Young, Kathy O. Once upon a Princess and a Pea, 10404(F)
Young, Ken. Cy Young Award Winners, 13426
Young, Mary O. Chicken Soup for Little Souls, 5021(F)
Sea, Salt, and Air, 4904(F)
Young, Noela. Finders Keepers, 10228(F)
The Pigs Are Flying, 8045(F)
Young, Richard, ed. Race with Buffalo, 11322
Stories from the Days of Christopher Columbus, 10633
Young, Robert. The Chewing Gum Book, 20137
Game Day, 22124
Miniature Vehicles, 21674
Money, 16931

A Personal Tour of Camden Yards, 22125
A Personal Tour of La Purisima, 16827
A Personal Tour of Mesa Verde, 16073
A Personal Tour of Monticello, 16899
The Real Patriots of the American Revolution, 16223
Sneakers, 21188
Sports Cards, 22077
The Transcontinental Railroad, 21347
Young, Ronder T. Learning by Heart, 7542(F)
Moving Mama to Town, 8549(F)
Young, Ruth. One Crow, 374(F)
Young, Selina. First Poems, 11556
My Favorite Word Book, 14062
The Pig Who Wished, 2044(F)
A Summery Saturday Morning, 3305(F)
Young, Sue. Writing with Style, 14117
Youngblood, Ed. Dirt Track Racing, 22242
Younger, Barbara. Purple Mountain Majesties, 12505
Younker, Linda Q. What Is a Cat? 5263
What Is a Horse? 5264
Where Do Cats Live? 5265
Younkin, Paula. Spirit of St. Louis, 21112
V-2 Rockets, 14898
Yount, Lisa. Antoine Lavoisier, 13312
Antoni van Leeuwenhoek, 13314
Cancer, 18017
Our Endangered Planet, 20677
William Harvey, 13307
Yu, Ling. Cooking the Chinese Way, 21754
Taiwan in Pictures, 15219
Yuditskaya, Tatyana. The Four Gallant Sisters, 10921
A Spy in the King's Colony, 9223(F)
Yue, Charlotte. Armor, 14796
The Igloo, 15848
Shoes, 21189
The Wigwam and the Longhouse, 16074
Yue, David. The Wigwam and the Longhouse, 16074
Yue, David (jt. author). Armor, 14796
The Igloo, 15848
Shoes, 21189
The Wigwam and the Longhouse, 16074
Yumoto, Kazumi. The Friends, 9022(F)
Yusufali, Jabeen. Pakistan, 15220

Zabar, Abbie. 55 Friends, 615(F)

Zadrzynska, Ewa. *The Peaceable Kingdom*, 8245(F)

Zafuto, Charles. *Lone Woman of Ghalas-Hat*, 16810

Zagwyn, Deborah Turney. *Apple Batter*, 3962(F)
Turtle Spring, 5464(F)
The Winter Gift, 5960(F)

Zahares, Wade. *Delivery*, 3448(F)
Window Music, 3909(F)

Zak, Drahos. *The Brothers Gruesome*, 1150(F)
The Pied Piper of Hamelin, 10918

Zakarin, Debra M. *The Ultimate Baby-Sitter's Handbook*, 16948

Zakowski, Connie. *The Insect Book*, 19502

Zalben, Jane Breskin. *Beni's Family Cookbook*, 21755
Beni's First Chanukah, 6125(F)
Beni's First Wedding, 3963(F)
Happy New Year, Beni, 6126(F)
Inner Chimes, 11574
Leo and Blossom's Sukkah, 6127(F)
Miss Violet's Shining Day, 2894(F)
Papa's Latkes, 6128(F)
Pearl Plants a Tree, 2895(F)
Pearl's Eight Days of Chanukah, 6129
Pearl's Marigolds for Grandpa, 3964(F)
To Every Season, 21756

Zallinger, Jean Day. *The Earliest Americans*, 16033
Great Snakes! 18775

Zallinger, Peter. *Dinosaurs and Other Archosaurs*, 14483
Prehistoric Animals, 14484

Zambreno, Mary F. *Journeyman Wizard*, 7143(F)

Zamojska-Hutchins, Danuta. *Cooking the Polish Way*, 21757

Zamorano, Ana. *Let's Eat!* 3965(F)

Zanes, Julia. *The Snow Child*, 6726(F)

Zannos, Susan. *Cesar Chavez*, 12827
Drew Barrymore, 12354
Hollywood Hulk Hogan, 13692
Paula Abdul, 12342
Robin Williams, 12482
Sandra Bullock, 12364

Zanzarella, Marianne. *The Good Housekeeping Illustrated Children's Cookbook*, 21758

Zapater, Beatriz M. *Fiesta!* 3966(F)

Zarin, Cynthia. *Rose and Sebastian*, 4067(F)
Wallace Hoskins, 1717(F)
What Do You See When You Shut Your Eyes? 3495(F)

Zarins, Joyce A. *The Go-Around Dollar*, 2988
How to Survive Third Grade, 5514(F)
The Story of Things, 14565

Zaunders, Bo. *Crocodiles, Camels and Dugout Canoes*, 12071

Zawadzki, Marek. *Okino and the Whales*, 1154(F)

Zeaman, John. *Birds*, 19300
Climbing onto the Horse's Back, 20019
Exotic Pets, 19913
From Pests to Pets, 19914
How the Wolf Became the Dog, 19979
Why the Cat Chose Us, 19935

Zeinert, Karen. *Those Courageous Women of the Civil War*, 9510
Those Remarkable Women of the American Revolution, 16224
To Touch the Stars, 9702(F)
The Valiant Women of the Vietnam War, 16526

Zeinert, Karen, ed. *The Memoirs of Andrew Sherburne*, 12962

Zeitlin, Steve. *The Four Corners of the Sky*, 10635

Zeitlin, Steve (jt. author). *The Cow of No Color*, 10567

Zekauskas, Felicia (jt. author). *The Magic Hockey Stick*, 1391(F)
Redbird at Rockefeller Center, 5874(F)

Zeldich, Arieh. *I Wish I Had My Father*, 5079(F)

Zeldis, Malcah. *A Fine Fat Pig*, 11791
Martin Luther King, 12740
Spring, 11824

Zeleza, Tiyambe. *Maasai*, 14954
Mijikenda, 14955

Zelinsky, Paul O. *Dear Mr. Henshaw*, 8600(F)
The Enchanted Castle, 7986(F)
Rapunzel, 10940
Rumpelstiltskin, 10905
Strider, 8601(F)
The Sun's Asleep Behind the Hill, 685(F)
Swamp Angel, 4188(F)
The Wheels on the Bus, 14262

Zelinsky, Paul O., adapt., 14261

Zemach, Harve. *Duffy and the Devil*, 11047
Mommy, Buy Me a China Doll, 3967(F)
A Penny a Look, 4364(F)
The Princess and Froggie, 1718(F)

Zemach, Kaethe. *The Character in the Book*, 1719(F)

Zemach, Kaethe (jt. author). *The Princess and Froggie*, 1718(F)

Zemach, Margot. *The Chinese Mirror*, 10726
Duffy and the Devil, 11047
It Could Always Be Worse, 11179
Jake and Honeybunch Go to Heaven, 1720(F)
Mommy, Buy Me a China Doll, 3967(F)
A Penny a Look, 4364(F)

The Princess and Froggie, 1718(F)
The Three Wishes, 10941
When Shlemiel Went to Warsaw and Other Stories, 11174

Zeman, Anne. *Everything You Need to Know About American History Homework*, 14118

Zeman, Ludmila. *The First Red Maple Leaf*, 1721(F)
Sindbad, 11203

Zemser, Amy Bronwen. *Beyond the Mango Tree*, 8981(F)

Zerbetz, Evon. *Blueberry Shoe*, 5185(F)

Zerner, Amy. *The Dream Quilt*, 818(F)
Scheherazade's Cat, 10636

Zerner, Jessie S. *Scheherazade's Cat*, 10636

Zerner, Jessie S. (jt. author). *The Dream Quilt*, 818(F)
Scheherazade's Cat, 10636

Zhang, Ange. *The Fishing Summer*, 2942(F)
Grandfather Counts, 403(F)
The Stoneboat, 4011(F)
To the Mountains by Morning, 5453(F)
Winter Rescue, 7105(F)

Zhang, Christopher Zhong-Yuan. *The Royal Bee*, 4793(F)

Zhang, Song Nan. *The Children of China*, 15092
Cowboy on the Steppes, 15093
The Legend of the Panda, 10753
A Little Tiger in the Chinese Night, 12316
The Man Who Made Parks, 12942
A Time of Golden Dragons, 10785

Zhensun, Zheng. *A Young Painter*, 12315

Zhong-Yuan, Christopher. *Moon Festival*, 9759(F)

Ziborova, Dasha. *Crispin the Terrible*, 1423(F)

Ziefert, Harriet. *Animal Music*, 2896(F)
April Fool! 6725(F)
Baby Buggy, Buggy Baby, 14063(F)
Bugs, Beetles, and Butterflies, 19503
Clara Ann Cookie, 3968(F)
Clara Ann Cookie, Go to Bed! 819(F)
A Dozen Dozens, 259(F)
Eight Days of Hanukkah, 6130(F)
Elemenopeo, 2897(F)
First He Made the Sun, 17332
First Night, 3496(F)
Hats Off for the Fourth of July! 5660(F)
I Swapped My Dog, 4365(F)
Little Red Riding Hood, 10942
Math Riddles, 21860(F)
Moonride, 820(F)
A New Coat for Anna, 3969(F)

A Polar Bear Can Swim, 18865
Presents for Santa, 5961(F)
Pumpkin Pie, 2898(F)
Pushkin Meets the Bundle, 2899(F)
Pushkin Minds the Bundle, 2900(F)
Rabbit and Hare Divide an Apple, 20602(F)
Sleepy-O! 14196
The Snow Child, 6726(F)
Someday We'll Have Very Good Manners, 4366(F)
Talk, Baby! 3970(F)
Train Song, 5608(F)
Two Little Witches, 6066(F)
Waiting for Baby, 3971(F)
Wee G, 2901(F)
When I First Came to This Land, 4367(F)
Ziefert, Harriet, ed. *Mother Goose Math*, 905(F)
Ziefert, Harriet, reteller. *The Princess and the Pea*, 10527(F)
Ziegler, Jack. *Mr. Knocky*, 4068(F)
Ziehler-Martin, Richard. *Snail Girl Brings Water*, 13944
Wolf Songs, 765(F)
Ziesk, Edra. *Margaret Mead*, 13321
Zike, Dinah. *The Earth Science Book*, 20329
Zim, Herbert S. *Birds*, 19301
Fishes, 19718
Flowers, 20042
Insects, 19504
Seashores, 19872
Trees, 20221
Zimelman, Nathan. *How the Second Grade Got $8,205.50 to Visit the Statue of Liberty*, 4368(F)
Zimmer, Dirk. *Bony-Legs*, 11084
King of Magic, Man of Glass, 10925
One Eye, Two Eyes, Three Eyes, 11097
The One That Got Away, 4145(F)
Seven Spiders Spinning, 7945(F)
Weird Wolf, 7692(F)
Zimmerman, Andrea. *My Dog Toby*, 5465(F)
Trashy Town, 3497(F)

Zimmerman, Chanda K. *Detroit*, 16594
Zimmerman, Howard. *Dinosaurs! The Biggest Baddest Strangest Fastest*, 14485
Zimmerman, Jerry. *The Lunch Line*, 535(F)
Space Race, 6678(F)
Zimmerman, Werner. *Brave Highland Heart*, 4708(F)
Zimmermann, H. Werner. *Each One Special*, 5107(F)
Zimmermann, Robert. *The Gambia*, 15050
Sri Lanka, 15221
Zindel, Paul. *Raptor*, 7144(F)
Zinovieff, Sofka. *Greece*, 15396
Zipko, Stephen J. *Toxic Threat*, 17008
Zirpoli, Jane. *Roots in the Outfield*, 10374(F)
Ziter, Cary B. *When Turtles Come to Town*, 18793
Zmolek, Sandy D. *Wiggle-Butts and Up-Faces*, 4999(F)
Zoehfeld, Kathleen W. *Dinosaur Babies*, 14486
Fossil Fever, 7145(F)
Great White Shark, 19770
How Mountains Are Made, 20330
Terrible Tyrannosaurs, 14487
What Is the World Made Of? All About Solids, Liquids, and Gases, 20816
What Lives in a Shell? 18916
Zolkower, Edie Stoltz. *Too Many Cooks*, 6131(F)
Zolotow, Charlotte. *The Beautiful Christmas Tree*, 3498(F)
The Bunny Who Found Easter, 5979(F)
Do You Know What I'll Do? 3972(F)
I Know a Lady, 4069(F)
I Like to Be Little, 3499(F)
Mr. Rabbit and the Lovely Present, 2902(F)
My Friend John, 4070(F)
The Old Dog, 5110(F)

The Quarreling Book, 3973(F)
Sleepy Book, 821(F)
Some Things Go Together, 3974(F)
This Quiet Lady, 3975(F)
William's Doll, 3976(F)
Zonderman, Jon. *Environmental Diseases*, 18018
Zubrowski, Bernie. *Making Waves*, 19852
Mirrors, 20878
Shadow Play, 20879
Soda Science, 20138
Zuchora-Walske, Christine. *Giant Octopuses*, 19728
Leaping Grasshoppers, 19505
Peeking Prairie Dogs, 19212
Zucker, David. *Uncle Carmello*, 7543(F)
Zudeck, Darryl S. *Prairie Songs*, 8608(F)
Prairie Visions, 12865
Zullo, Allan (jt. author). *The Baseball Hall of Shame*, 22107
The Greatest Sports Stories Never Told, 22039
Zurlo, Tony. *Japan*, 15143
Zweifel, Frances. *Science Fair Projects*, 18301, 18381
Simple Weather Experiments with Everyday Materials, 20782
Zwerger, Lisbeth. *Aesop's Fables*, 11050
Alice in Wonderland, 7642(F)
A Christmas Carol, 9719(F)
The Deliverers of Their Country, 7985(F)
Hans Christian Andersen Fairy Tales, 10383(F)
Little Hobbin, 788(F)
Noah's Ark, 17288(F)
The Strange Child, 10917
Thumbeline, 10392(F)
The Wizard of Oz, 989(F)
Zwierzynska-Coldicott, Aldona Maria. *Poland*, 15295
Zwolak, Paul. *Something Might Be Hiding*, 5019(F)
Zymet, Cathy Alter. *LeAnn Rimes*, 12451

Title Index

This index contains both main entry and internal titles cited in the entries. References are to entry numbers, not page numbers. All fiction titles are indicated by (F), following the entry number.

A B C Discovery! An Alphabet Book of Picture Puzzles, 26
A B C Disney, 125(F)
A B C for You and Me, 43(F)
A B C Kids, 148(F)
A B C T-Rex, 104(F)
The A.D.D. Book for Kids, 17933
A-hunting We Will Go! 716
A Is for . . .? 56
A Is for AARRGH! 9789(F)
A Is for Africa, 106(F)
A Is for Aloha, 4645(F)
A Is for Amos, 20(F)
A Is for Angry, 13(F)
A Is for Animals, 112(F)
A Is for Apple, W Is for Witch, 7705(F)
A Is for Artist, 13870
A Is for Asia, 22(F)
A Is for Salad, 79(F)
A Is for the Americas, 23
A. Lincoln and Me, 4598(F)
A. Philip Randolph, 12782
A. Philip Randolph and the Labor Movement, 12781
The A to Z Beastly Jamboree, 382(F)
A to Zen, 145(F)
A Was Once an Apple Pie, 11883
A You're Adorable, 71(F)
Aani and the Tree Huggers, 8982(F)
Aardvarks, Disembark! 17291
Aaron's Awful Allergies, 4973(F)
Aaron's Shirt, 3178(F)
AB Sea, 19638
The Abacus Contest, 9021(F)
Abandoned on the Wild Frontier, 9385(F)
Abbie Against the Storm, 9329(F)
Abby (Illus. by Steven Kellogg), 3563(F)
  (Illus. by Alan Marks), 7210(F)
ABC, 93(F)
ABC, 94(F)
ABC Animal Riddles, 67
ABC Career Book for Girls/El Libro de Carreras para Niñas, 17767(F)
ABC Cats, 29(F)

ABC Dogs, 19944
The ABC Exhibit, 40(F)
ABC I Like Me! 19(F)
ABC Nature Riddles, 68(F)
ABC of Crawlers and Flyers, 124(F)
An ABC of Fashionable Animals, 34(F)
ABC Pop! 61(F)
ABC School Riddles, 21827(F)
ABC Yummy, 63(F)
ABCDrive! 57(F)
The ABC's of Origami, 21626
Abe Lincoln Goes to Washington, 1837–1865, 13069
Abe Lincoln Grows Up, 13075
Abe Lincoln Remembers, 13078
Abe Lincoln's Hat, 13065
Abel's Island, 8126(F)
Abel's Moon, 3709(F)
Abigail Adams, 13125
Abigail Takes the Wheel, 9514(F)
Abigail's Drum, 9307(F)
Abiyoyo, 10713
Aboriginal Art of Australia, 13889
An Aboriginal Family, 15225
About Birds, 19282
About Dying, 5089(F)
About Face, 8392(F)
About Handicaps, 17934
About Insects, 19489
About Mammals, 18974
About Phobias, 5089(F)
About Reptiles, 18694
About the B'nai Bagels, 9908(F)
About the Rain Forest, 20452
About Twins, 17680
Abra-Ca-Dazzle, 21777
Abracadabra, 1550(F)
Abraham Lincoln, 13068, 13071, 13073, 13076
Abraham Lincoln's Gettysburg Address, 16405
Abraham's Battle, 9463(F)
The Absentminded Fellow, 4229(F)
Absolutely Angels, 11521
The Absolutely Awful Alphabet, 42
Absolutely Lucy, 8611(F)

Absolutely Normal Chaos, 8617(F)
The Absolutely True Story, 7024(F)
Abuela, 1130(F)
Abuela's Weave, 4616(F)
Abuelita's Heart, 4408(F)
Abuelita's Paradise, 3823(F)
Abuelito Eats with His Fingers, 3771(F)
Acacia Terrace, 15256
The Accident, 4924(F)
Accidental Lily, 8848(F)
Accidents May Happen, 21037
Achoo! All About Colds, 17952
Acid Rain, 16999, 17004
Ackamarackus, 2366(F)
Acorn Magic, 5422(F)
The Acrobat and the Angel, 10881
The Acropolis, 14702
Across America, 16088
Across America, I Love You, 3780(F)
Across America on an Emigrant Train, 21338
Across Five Aprils, 9482(F)
Across the Big Blue Sea, 4359(F)
Across the Blue Mountains, 4113(F)
Across the Lines, 9499(F)
Across the Solar System, 18532
Across the Stream, 2124(F)
Across the Wide and Lonesome Prairie, 9369(F)
Action, 20839
Action Alphabet, 122(F)
Ada Byron Lovelace, 13317
Adaline Falling Star, 9425(F)
Adam, Adam, What Do You See? 17304
Adam Mouse's Book of Poems, 11972
Adam of the Road, 9040(F)
Adam Sandler, 12463
Adam's Daycare, 3351(F)
Ada's Pal, 5321(F)
Add It, Dip It, Fix It, 14045
Addiction, 17891
Addie Across the Prairie, 9394(F)
Addie Meets Max, 6591(F)

Addie Runs Away, 6591(F)
Addie's Dakota Winter, 9395(F)
Addie's Forever Friend, 9578(F)
Addie's Long Summer, 9396(F)
Addition (Illus. by Richard Mac-
    cabe), 20596
    (Illus. by Sami Sweeten), 399(F)
Additives, 20165
Addy Learns a Lesson, 9496(F)
Addy Saves the Day, 9608(F)
Addy's Cook Book, 21675
Addy's Craft Book, 21515
Adolescent Rights, 17031
Adolf Hitler, 13810
Adopted by Indians, 16002
Adopted by the Eagles, 11237
Adopted from Asia, 17664
The Adopted One, 5089(F)
Adopting Pets, 19892
Adoption, 17649, 17675
Adoption Is for Always, 3650(F)
Adventure Gaming, 22012
Adventure in Space, 21007
The Adventure of Louey and Frank,
    2848(F)
Adventure on Klickitat Island,
    1240(F)
Adventure on the Wilderness Road,
    9397(F)
Adventures in Ancient Egypt, 14606
Adventures in Archaeology, 14536
Adventures in the Middle Ages,
    7577(F)
The Adventures of Ali Baba Bern-
    stein, 6420(F)
The Adventures of Captain Under-
    pants, 9962(F)
The Adventures of Eros and Psyche,
    11503
Adventures of Greek Heroes, 11489
The Adventures of Hercules, 11503
The Adventures of Hershel of
    Ostropol, 11153
Adventures of Huckleberry Finn,
    10007(F)
The Adventures of Marco and Polo,
    2854(F)
The Adventures of Midnight Son,
    9310(F), 9492(F)
Adventures of Monkey King,
    10752(F)
The Adventures of Mr. Toad,
    7751(F)
The Adventures of Odysseus, 11501
The Adventures of Pinocchio,
    7660(F)
The Adventures of Rama, 10787
Adventures of Robin Hood, 10988
The Adventures of Robin Hood,
    11045
The Adventures of Snail at School,
    6674(F)
The Adventures of Snowwoman,
    5748(F)
The Adventures of Sojourner, 21020
The Adventures of Sparrowboy,
    1478(F)
The Adventures of Spider, 10648
The Adventures of Sugar and Junior,
    8342(F)
The Adventures of Treehorn, 9874(F)

Adventurous Spirit, 13342
Advertising, 16934
Aerobics, 18207
The Aesop for Children, 11048
Aesop's Fables, 11054, 11073
    (Illus. by Fulvio Testa), 11049
    (Illus. by Lisbeth Zwerger), 11050
Aesop's Fox, 11076
Afghanistan, 15145, 15146, 15157
Afghanistan in Pictures, 15144
Africa, 14899, 14900
Africa Brothers and Sisters, 4717(F)
Africa Calling, 5113(F)
Africa Dream, 4671(F)
Africa Is Not a Country, 14909
Africa South of the Sahara, 14912
African American Healers, 13206
African American Inventors, 13222
The African American Kitchen,
    20090
African American Musicians, 12184
African American Quilting, 21649
African American Teachers, 12642
African American Voices, 15906
African American Women Writers,
    12186
African Americans and the Revolu-
    tionary War, 16198
African Americans in the Civil War,
    16394
African-Americans in the Thirteen
    Colonies, 16144
African Americans Who Were First,
    12691
African Animal Tales, 10650
African Beginnings, 14907
The African Cats, 19107
African Crafts, 21446
African Elephants, 19172
African Industries, 14902
African Landscapes, 14903
The African Rhinos, 18970
The African Slave Trade, 16267
African Wildlife, 18631
Africa's Struggle for Independence,
    14904
Africa's Struggle to Survive, 14905
Afro-Bets Book of Black Heroes
    from A to Z, 12660
Afro-Bets First Book About Africa,
    8961(F)
After Charlotte's Mom Died, 5083(F)
After Hamelin, 8042(F)
After the Flood, 17271
After the Spill, 16800
After the War Was Over, 12232
Afternoon of the Elves, 7919(F),
    12036
Again! 2599(F)
Agapanthus Hum and Major Bark,
    6287(F)
Agapanthus Hum and the Eyeglasses,
    9815(F)
Agatha's Feather Bed, 3603(F)
Agave Blooms Just Once, 64(F)
The Age of Augustus, 14734
The Age of Discovery, 14575
An Age of Extremes, 16468
Aggie's Home, 9420(F)
Agnes May Gleason, 9539(F)
Agnes the Sheep, 7315(F)

The Agony of Alice, 8770(F)
Ahmek, 8188(F)
Aida, 14136
AIDS, 17982, 17983, 17997
AIDS to Zits, 18266
Air, 20676
Air and Other Gases, 20672
Air Crashes, 21085
Air Is All Around You, 20664
Air Pollution, 17005
Air Raid — Pearl Harbor, 14887
Air Scare, 17001
Aircraft, 21089, 21598
Airmail to the Moon, 3026(F)
Airplane, 21090
The Airplane Alphabet Book, 21095
The Airplane Book, 21070
Airplanes, 21103
    (Illus. by Byron Barton), 21069
Airport, 5547(F), 21088
Akiak, 5136(F)
Akiko in the Sprubly Islands,
    10173(F)
Akiko on the Planet Smoo, 10174(F)
Al Capone and the Roaring Twenties,
    12866
Al Gore, 12891, 12892, 12893
Alabama, 16841, 16850, 16886,
    16896
The Alamo, 16274
Alaska, 16772, 16774, 16791
The Alaska Purchase, 16769
The Alaska Purchase in American
    History, 16779
Alaska's Three Bears, 5227(F)
Albatrosses of Midway Island, 19241
Alberic the Wise, 9049(F)
Albert, 1428(F)
Albert and the Angels, 9752(F)
Albert Einstein, 13275, 13277
Albert the Albatross, 6397(F)
Alberta, 15598
Albertina, the Animals, and Me,
    9853(F)
Albertina the Practically Perfect,
    8285(F)
Albert's Alphabet, 139(F)
Albert's Ballgame, 3459(F)
Albert's Birthday, 5730(F)
Albert's Christmas, 5941(F)
Albert's Field Trip, 2765(F)
Albert's Halloween, 2766(F)
Albert's Play, 2767(F)
Albert's Thanksgiving, 6158(F)
Albery and Lila, 2660(F)
Albidaro and the Mischievous
    Dream, 1350(F)
Albie the Lifeguard, 3031(F)
Album of Horses, 19996
Alcatraz, 16780
Alcatraz Prison in American History,
    16805
Alcohol, 17864, 17868, 17878
Alcohol Abuse, 17892
Alcohol Drug Dangers, 17862
Alcohol 101, 17873
An Alcott Family Christmas, 5946(F)
Aldo Applesauce, 9891(F)
Aldo Ice Cream, 9891(F)
Aleta and the Queen, 11473(F)
Alex and the Cat, 6357(F)

Alex Rodriguez, 13496

Alex, the Kid with AIDS, 8661(F)

Alexander and the Terrible, Horrible, No Good, Very Bad Day, 3927(F)

Alexander and the Wind-Up Mouse, 2378(F)

Alexander Calder, 12197

Alexander Calder and His Magical Mobiles, 12196

Alexander Graham Bell, 13236, 13238, 13240, 13241

Alexander the Great, 1840(F), 13747, 13748, 13750, 13751 (Illus. by Hans de Beer),

Alexander the Great and Ancient Greece, 13749

Alexander, Who Used to Be Rich Last Sunday, 6706(F)

Alexander, Who's Not (Do You Hear Me? I Mean It!) Going to Move, 3928(F)

Alfie and the Birthday Surprise, 4983(F)

Alfie's ABC, 59(F)

Alfie's 1-2-3, 471(F)

Alfred's Camera, 306(F)

Alfred's Party, 5683(F)

Algeria, 14959

An Algonquian Year, 15994

Ali Baba and the Forty Thieves, 11193

Ali, Child of the Desert, 4743(F)

Alice and Aldo, 78(F)

Alice-by-Accident, 8397(F)

Alice in April, 8771(F)

Alice In-Between, 9942(F)

Alice in Rapture, Sort Of, 9943(F)

Alice in Wonderland, 7642(F)

Alice Nizzy Nazzy, 1276(F)

Alice Ramsey's Grand Adventure, 2913

Alice Rose and Sam, 9392(F)

Alice the Brave, 8772(F)

Alice Walker, 12615

Alice's Adventures in Wonderland, 7645(F) (Illus. by Abelardo Morell), 7643(F) (Illus. by Helen Oxenbury), 7644(F)

Alice's Adventures in Wonderland and Through the Looking Glass, 7646(F)

Alicia Silverstone, 12468

Alicia's Treasure, 7393(F)

Alida's Song, 8781(F)

Alien Astronauts, 20952

Alien Blood, 10142(F)

Alien Brain Fryout, 6910(F)

Alien Encounters, 21896, 21912

Alien for Rent, 9832(F)

Alien Game, 10176(F)

Alien Lifesearch, 20992

Alien Terror, 10142(F)

Aliens Ate My Homework, 10041(F)

Aliens for Breakfast, 10178(F)

Aliens for Lunch, 6330(F)

Aliens in Woodford, 7883(F)

Aliens Stole My Body, 10164(F)

Aligay Saves the Stars, 2738(F)

Alison Rides the Rapids, 6746(F)

Alison's Puppy, 7155(F)

Alistair in Outer Space, 1536(F)

Alistair Underwater, 1537(F)

Alistair's Time Machine, 4293(F)

All About Alice, 4124(F)

All About Baseball, 22120

All About Basketball, 22149

All About Color, 295(F)

All About Football, 22190

All About Hanukkah, 6077

All About Hockey, 22215

All About Owls, 19357

All About Passover, 17469

All About Pattern, 318(F)

All About Rattlesnakes, 18753

All About Sam, 9922(F)

All About Scabs, 18183

All About Seeds, 20272

All About Space, 18378

All About Stacy, 6345(F)

All About Sukkot, 17470

All About the Frog, 18742

All About Time, 20655

All About Turkeys, 19215

All About Turtles, 18777

All Alone After School, 5086(F)

All Alone in the Universe, 8359(F)

All-American Girls, 22298

The All-American Girls Professional Baseball League, 22094

All Around Town, 4694

All But Alice, 8773(F)

All By Herself, 11668

All By Myself, 1796(F)

All By Myself! 2992(F)

All Day Long, 11647

All for Texas, 9462(F)

All for the Better, 12824

All for the Newborn Baby, 5912(F)

All God's Children, 17524

All in a Day's Work, 17753

All in the Blue Unclouded Weather, 7465(F)

All Is Well, 9585(F)

The All Jahdu Storybook, 7781(F)

All Join In, 11536

All Joseph Wanted, 8790(F)

All Kinds of Children, 4831

All Kinds of Families, 17685

All Kinds of Habitats, 20376

All Mixed-Up! 4171(F)

All My Feelings at Preschool, 5490(F)

The All-New Amelia, 8346(F)

The All New Jonah Twist, 10077(F)

All Night, All Day, 14141

All-of-a-Kind Family, 7527(F)

All of Our Noses Are Here and Other Noodle Tales, 6638(F)

All of You Was Singing, 11406

All Pigs Are Beautiful, 5291

All Saints, All Souls, and Halloween, 17443

All Stuck Up, 11347

All That You Are, 17612

All the Better to See You With! 3942(F)

All the Blue Moons at the Wallace Hotel, 8527(F)

All the Colors of the Earth, 3190(F)

All the Colors of the Race, 11522

All the Colors of the Rainbow, 20866

All the King's Animals, 19400

All the Mamas, 3891(F)

All the Money in the World, 7623(F)

All the Papas, 3892(F)

All the People, 16509

All the Places to Love, 7479(F)

All the Pretty Little Horses, 618

All the Way Home, 4306(F)

All the Way to God, 686(F)

All the Way to Morning, 696(F)

All the World's a Stage, 12591

All Together Now, 2251(F)

All We Needed to Say, 11701

All Year Round, 4417(F)

Allan Pinkerton, 12947, 12948

Allen Jay and the Underground Railroad, 6224(F)

Allergies, 17975, 17987, 17998

The Allies Against the Axis, 14885

Allie's Basketball Dream, 3009(F)

Alligator Arrived with Apples, 33(F)

An Alligator Ate My Brother, 1442(F)

Alligator Baby, 4239(F)

Alligators, 18711

Alligators All Around, 242(F)

Alligators and Crocodiles, 18701, 18712

Alligators and Others All Year Long, 2038(F)

Allison, 5068(F)

Allison's Story, 10105

Almost Famous, 9860(F)

Almost Famous Daisy! 4713(F)

An Almost Perfect Game, 10349(F)

Almost the Real Things, 21056

Aloha, Dolores, 4300(F)

Along Came a Dog, 7183(F)

Along Came Toto, 1778(F)

Along the Santa Fe Trail, 16357

Along the Seashore, 19857, 19870

Alonzo Mourning, 13551

Alpha and the Dirty Baby, 1067(F)

Alphababies, 44(F)

Alphabatics, 85(F)

Alphabears, 46(F)

Alphabestiary, 11818

Alphabet Adventure, 142(F)

Alphabet Antics, 14114

Alphabet Art, 117(F), 13890

The Alphabet Atlas, 151(F)

Alphabet City, 13983

The Alphabet from Z to A, 141(F)

An Alphabet of Angels, 147(F)

An Alphabet of Dinosaurs, 14408

Alphabet Out Loud, 14(F)

The Alphabet Parade, 24(F)

Alphabet Riddles, 69(F)

Alphabet Soup, 977(F)

Alphabetical Order, 13987

Alternative Energy Sources, 20822

Altogether, One at a Time, 8730(F)

Altoona Baboona, 1906(F)

Aluminum, 20280

Always and Forever Friends, 8246(F)

Always Inventing, 13239

The Always Prayer Shawl, 4782(F)

Always Room for One More, 14165

"Always Wear Clean Underwear!" and Other Ways Parents Say "I Love You." 17653
Alyssa Milano, 12423
Alzheimer's Disease, 17959
Am I Big or Little? 3543(F)
The Amah, 8546(F)
Amahl and the Night Visitors, 5882(F)
Amanda Bean's Amazing Dream, 537(F)
Amanda Pig and Her Best Friend Lollipop, 6703(F)
The Amazing Adventures of Soupy Boy! 7634(F)
The Amazing Adventures of Teddy Tum Tum, 1852(F)
Amazing and Incredible Counting Stories, 450(F)
Amazing Animal Alphabet, 36(F)
Amazing Animal Babies, 18878
Amazing Animals, 5458, 18666
Amazing Animals of Australia, 18933
Amazing Animals of the Sea, 19743
Amazing Armored Animals, 18901
Amazing Bats, 19026
Amazing Bikes, 22162
Amazing Birds, 19265
Amazing Birds of Prey, 19335
Amazing Boats, 21365
The Amazing Bone, 4325(F)
Amazing Buildings, 21153
The Amazing Christmas Extravaganza, 5918(F)
Amazing Coin Tricks, 21779
The Amazing Days of Abby Hayes, 10352(F)
The Amazing Dirt Book, 20551
The Amazing Frecktacle, 8177(F)
Amazing Grace, 12937, 14152
The Amazing Impossible Erie Canal, 16250
Amazing Insects, 19469
The Amazing Life of Benjamin Franklin, 12881
Amazing Mammals, 18960
Amazing Mysteries of the World, 21941
The Amazing Paper Cuttings of Hans Christian Andersen, 12491
The Amazing Pop-Up Pull-Out Body in a Book, 18061
The Amazing Pop-Up, Pull-Out Space Shuttle, 20990
Amazing Rescues, 6656
Amazing Snakes, 18771
Amazing Spiders, 19590
(Illus. by Max Meier), 19594
Amazing String Tricks, 21779
The Amazing Things Animals Do, 18831
The Amazing Valvano and the Mystery of the Hooded Rat, 7033(F)
Amazing Wolves, Dogs, and Foxes, 19130
Amazing World of Ants, 19513
Amazing World of Butterflies and Moths, 19569
Amazing World of Dinosaurs, 14421
The Amazon, 15778

Amazon ABC, 30(F)
Amazon Basin, 15782
Amazon Diary, 7093(F)
Amber Brown Goes Fourth, 9823(F)
Amber Brown Is Feeling Blue, 9824(F)
Amber Brown Is Not a Crayon, 9825(F)
Amber Brown Sees Red, 9826(F)
Amber Brown Wants Extra Credit, 8419(F)
The Amber Cat, 7939(F)
Amelia and Eleanor Go for a Ride, 4816(F)
Amelia Bedelia, 6561(F)
Amelia Bedelia and the Baby, 6566(F)
Amelia Bedelia and the Surprise Shower, 6561(F)
Amelia Bedelia 4 Mayor, 6558(F)
Amelia Bedelia Goes Camping, 6562(F)
Amelia Bedelia Helps Out, 6566(F)
Amelia Bedelia's Family Album, 6562(F)
Amelia Earhart, 12109, 12112, 12114, 12115
Amelia Earhart Flies Around the World, 12110
Amelia Takes Command, 8767(F)
Amelia Works It Out, 8768(F)
Amelia's Family Ties, 8494(F)
Amelia's Fantastic Flight, 1030(F)
Amelia's Nine Lives, 5130(F)
Amelia's Road, 4899(F)
Amelia's War, 9502(F)
Amelina Carrett, 9472(F)
America, 3342(F)
America Goes to War, 14846
America, I Hear You, 12326
America in the Time of Franklin Delano Roosevelt, 16471
America in the Time of Martin Luther King Jr., 16511
America in the Time of Susan B. Anthony, 16472
America in World War I, 14807
America in World War II, 14847
America Prepares for War, 14821
America Is Her Name, 5062(F)
America Street, 7355(F)
America the Beautiful, 14232
The American Alligator, 18706
American Art, 13960
American Astronomers, 13204
American Bison, 18925
The American Boys' Handy Book, 21516
American Civil Rights Leaders, 12656
The American Civil War, 16402
American Dreams, 4585(F)
American Environmental Heroes, 13221
An American Face, 4941(F)
The American Family Farm, 20046
The American Flag, 13968, 13972
(Illus. by Alvin C. Jasper), 13974
American Generals of World War II, 12667

The American Girls Party Book, 22234
American Heart Association Kids' Cookbook, 21752
American Heroes of Exploration and Flight, 12067
American Indian Cooking Before 1500, 15963
American Indian Families, 16006
American Indian Festivals, 16007
American Indian Foods, 16008
American Indian Games, 16009
The American Revolution, 16194, 16218, 16200
American Revolution, 16206
The American Revolution, 1763–1783, 16191
American Revolutionaries and Founders of the Nation, 12681
An American Safari, 16535
American Science Fiction and Fantasy Writers, 12160
American Tall Tales, 11370
American Too, 3015(F)
The American Wei, 3367(F)
The American West, 16315
American Writers of the 20th Century, 12158
America's Champion Swimmer, 13684
America's Deserts, 20427
America's Early Canals, 16264
America's First Railroads, 21337
America's Forests, 20489
America's Greatest Game, 22179
America's Prairies, 20547
America's Top 10 Bridges, 21148
America's Top 10 Curiosities, 21954
America's Top 10 National Monuments, 15857
America's Top 10 National Parks, 15909
America's Top 10 Rivers, 15909
America's Wetlands, 20393
Ameru, 14952
The Amish, 17568
(Illus. by Michael Erkel), 17179
An Amish Christmas, 5744(F)
Amish Home, 17165
An Amish Wedding, 17161
An Amish Year, 17162
Amistad, 16266
Amistad Rising, 16231
Among the Hidden, 10193(F)
Among the Orangutans, 13288
Amos Fortune, Free Man, 12724
Amphibians, 18692, 18696
Amphibians in Danger, 18684
Amritsar, 15099
Amsterdam, 15399
Amusement Parks, Roller Coasters, Ferris Wheels, and Cotton Candy, 14263
Amy Elizabeth Explores Bloomingdale's, 3265(F)
Amy Grant, 12393
Amy Loves the Rain, 3217(F)
Amy Loves the Snow, 3218(F)
Amy Loves the Sun, 3217(F)
Amy, Number Seven, 10201(F)
Amy's Eyes, 7859(F)

Amy's (Not So) Great Camp-Out, 2962(F)
Amzat and His Brothers, 11062
Anacondas, 18765
Ananse's Feast, 10699
Anansi and the Moss-Covered Rock, 10675
Anansi and the Talking Melon, 10676
Anansi Does the Impossible! 10637
Anansi Goes Fishing, 10677
Anansi, the Spider, 10692
Anasazi, 15947
Anastasia, 9063(F)
Anastasia, Absolutely, 9919(F)
Anastasia at This Address, 9920(F)
Anastasia Has the Answers, 9921(F)
Anastasia on Her Own, 9921(F)
Anastasia's Album, 15409
Anastasia's Chosen Career, 9922(F)
Anchorage, 16803
Ancient African Town, 15035
Ancient Agriculture, 14598
An Ancient Castle, 9097(F)
Ancient China, 15083
The Ancient Chinese, 15075
The Ancient Cliff Dwellers of Mesa Verde, 15921
Ancient Communication, 13966
Ancient Computing, 20600
Ancient Construction, 21156
Ancient Egypt, 14616, 14630, 14641, 14652, 14664, 14671
Ancient Egyptian Art, 14631
The Ancient Egyptians, 14644, 14662, 14665
Ancient Egyptians and Their Neighbors, 14610
Ancient Greece, 14676, 14683, 14689
Ancient Greece! 14682
Ancient Greek Art, 14684
The Ancient Greek Olympics, 22258
The Ancient Greeks, 14678, 14680, 14699
Ancient Machines from Wedges to Waterwheels, 14599
Ancient Medicine, 14600
Ancient Olympic Games, 22251
Ancient Roman Art, 14722
The Ancient Romans, 14718, 14740
Ancient Rome, 14742, 14743, 14748
Ancient Shipwrecks, 14594
The Ancient Splendor of Prehistoric Cahokia, 14495
Ancient Transportation, 14601
Ancient Warfare, 21409
And God Created Squash, 17284(F)
And If the Moon Could Talk, 633(F)
And It Was Good, 17246
And Land Was Born, 10804
And Maggie Makes Three, 8501(F)
And My Mean Old Mother Will Be Sorry, Blackboard Bear, 949(F)
. . . And Now Miguel, 8735(F)
And So They Build, 18909
And the Cow Said Moo! 5363(F)
And Then What? 1696(F)
And This Is Laura, 7414(F)
And to Think That I Saw It on Mulberry Street, 1561(F)

And to Think That We Thought That We'd Never Be Friends, 1243(F)
Andre Agassi, 13641, 13642
Andres Galarraga, 13452
Andrew Jackson, 13045
Andrew Jackson's America, 1824–1850, 16232
Andrew Jessup, 4006(F)
Andrew Johnson, 13054, 13055
Andrew Wants a Dog, 5293(F)
Andrew's Angry Words, 1328(F)
Andrew's Loose Tooth, 4240(F)
Androcles and the Lion, 11498
Andy and His Yellow Frisbee, 5091(F)
Andy and Tamika, 7383(F)
Andy and the Lion, 1996(F)
Andy Finds a Turtle, 4979(F)
Andy Warhol, 12309
Andy's Wild Animal Adventure, 1548(F)
Aneesa Lee and the Weaver's Gift, 11581
The Anesthesiologist, 18030
Anfernee Hardaway, 13525
Angel and Me and the Bayside Bombers, 10272(F)
The Angel and the Donkey, 17315
Angel Baby, 3595(F)
Angel Bites the Bullet, 7420(F)
Angel Hide and Seek, 315(F)
Angel in Charge, 7422(F)
An Angel Just Like Me, 5842(F)
The Angel Knew Papa and the Dog, 7941(F)
The Angel of Mill Street, 5949(F)
Angel Pig and the Hidden Christmas, 5945(F)
Angel Prayers, 17529
Angel Spreads Her Wings, 9033(F)
Angel to Angel, 11765
The Angel Tree, 5900(F)
Angela and Diabola, 7581(F)
Angela and the Broken Heart, 7498(F)
Angela Weaves a Dream, 15685
Angela's Airplane, 4245
Angela's Aliens, 10209(F)
Angela's Top-Secret Computer Club, 6920(F)
Angela's Wings, 1437(F)
Angelfish, 19706
Angels, 11579
Angels and Other Strangers, 9753(F)
Angels in the Dust, 9612(F)
The Angel's Mistake, 11159
Angel's Mother's Baby, 7421(F)
Angel's Mother's Boyfriend, 7422(F)
Angel's Mother's Wedding, 7422(F)
Angels of Mercy, 14861
Angels on a Pin, 995(F)
Angels on Roller Skates, 7445(F)
Angels, Prophets, Rabbis and Kings, 11157
Angels Ride Bikes and Other Fall Poems, 11935
Anger Management, 17625
Angola, 14984
Angus and the Cat, 5203(F)
Angus and the Ducks, 5203(F)
Angus Lost, 5203(F)

Animal ABC, 150(F)
Animal Antics from 1 to 10, 612(F)
Animal Architects, 18906
Animal Babies, 18872
The Animal Boogie, 2175(F)
Animal Builders, 18907
Animal Cafe, 2714(F)
Animal Camouflage, 18886
Animal Communication, 18894
(Illus. by David Hosking), 18892
Animal Crackers, 667(F)
Animal Crafts, 21532
Animal Dads, 18871
Animal Defenses, 18899
Animal Dreaming, 10849
Animal Experimentation and Testing, 18677
Animal Fables from Aesop, 11068
Animal Fact-File, 18944
Animal Faces, 18984
Animal Families, 18876
Animal Feelings, 18815
Animal Hide and Seek, 18913
Animal Homes, 5117, 18914, 18915
Animal House, 1400(F)
Animal Hunters, 18810
Animal Journeys, 18843
The Animal Kingdom, 18676
Animal Lullabies, 651(F)
Animal Males and Females, 18659
The Animal Mall, 2048(F)
Animal Monsters, 18658
Animal Movement, 18809
Animal Moves, 18794
Animal Music, 2896(F)
Animal Noises, 18794
Animal Parenting, 18920
Animal Rescue, 18627
The Animal Rescue Club, 6385(F)
Animal Rights, 18609, 18638, 18656
Animal Senses, 18802, 18821
Animal Sharpshooters, 18897
Animal Smarts, 18816
Animal Song, 890
Animal Stories, 7863(F)
The Animal, the Vegetable and John D. Jones, 8265(F)
Animals, 5176, 5432(F), 13898, 20906, 21580
(Illus. by Tony Ross), 13885, 14396
Animals Among Us, 18636
Animals and the Seasons, 4515(F)
Animals and Their World, 18835
Animals Asleep, 18834
Animals at Rest, 18844
Animals Eat the Weirdest Things, 18857
Animals Eating, 18822
Animals from Mother Goose, 850
Animals in Camouflage, 18890
Animals in Motion, 18823
Animals in Trees, 20432
Animals in Winter, 18801
Animals Nobody Loves, 18670
Animals Observed, 13873
Animals of Sea and Shore, 19644
Animals of the Desert, 20418
Animals of the Grasslands, 20545
Animals of the Night, 5132
Animals of the Oceans, 19646

Animals of the Rain Forest, 20484
Animals on Board, 523(F)
Animals on Plains and Prairies, 20531
Animals on the Go, 18926
Animals on the Move, 18811
Animals Should Definitely Not Act Like People, 4082(F)
Animals Should Definitely Not Wear Clothing, 4082(F)
The Animals' Song, 1222(F)
Animals That Glow, 18657
Animals That Ought to Be, 11901
Animals Trails and Tracks, 18842
Animals Under the Ground, 18624
Anisett Lundberg, 9357(F)
Anita Hill, 12726
Ann Richards, 13176
Anna All Year Round, 9547(F)
Anna and the Cat Lady, 8713(F)
Anna Banana, 21983
Anna Banana and Me, 3980(F)
Anna Is Still Here, 9694(F)
Anna of Byzantium, 9027(F)
Anna on the Farm, 8677(F)
Anna Pavlova, 12441
Annabel the Actress Starring in Gorilla My Dreams, 9806(F)
Annabel the Actress Starring in Just a Little Extra, 9807(F)
Annabelle and the Big Slide, 3365(F)
Annabelle Swift, Kindergartner, 5534(F)
Annabelle's Big Move, 5230(F)
Anna's Athabaskan Summer, 4448(F)
Anna's Goat, 4707(F)
Anne Frank, 13797, 13798, 13800
Anne Hutchinson, 13160
Anne of Green Gables, 12036
    (Illus. by Jody Lee), 8764(F)
The Anne of Green Gables Cookbook, 21715
Annie and the Old One, 8757(F)
Annie Ate Apples, 123(F)
Annie Bananie and the Pain Sisters, 9907(F)
Annie, Bea, and Chi Chi Dolores, 92(F)
Annie Flies the Birthday Bike, 6314(F)
Annie Oakley, 12430, 12431
Annie Pitts, Burger Kid, 9830(F)
Annie's Gifts, 5030(F)
Annie's Pet, 6221(F)
Annie's Promise, 7467(F)
Annie's Shabbat, 6093
Anni's India Diary, 8983(F)
Anno's Alphabet, 3(F)
Anno's Counting Book, 369(F)
Anno's Magic Seeds, 370(F)
Anno's Math Games, 20610
Anno's Mysterious Multiplying Jar, 20627
Ann's Story, 9205(F)
Annushka's Voyage, 4848(F)
Anooka's Answer, 8951(F)
Anorexia and Bulimia, 17994
Another Fine Mess, 1837(F)
Another Happy Tale, 4100(F)
Another Important Book, 3050(F)

Another Mouse to Feed, 2319(F)
Anpao, 11257
Anson's Way, 9122(F)
Ant, 19514
    (Illus. by Nichola Armstrong), 19508
Ant and the Elephant, 2566(F)
The Ant and the Grasshopper, 11074
The Ant Bully, 1430(F)
Ant Cities, 19510
Ant Plays Bear, 6244(F)
Antarctic Antics, 11812
Antarctic Encounter, 15828
Antarctic Journal, 15800, 15806
Antarctica, 15796, 15831
An Anteater Named Arthur, 2783(F)
Anteaters, 18950
Anteaters, Sloths, and Armadillos, 18976
Anthology for the Earth, 16952
Anthony Quinn, 12449
Anthony Reynoso, 17552
Anthony's Big Surprise, 10079(F)
ANTics! 53(F)
Antoine Lavoisier, 13312
Antoni van Leeuwenhoek, 13314
Antonio's Apprenticeship, 13948
Antonio's Rain Forest, 20463
Ants, 19506, 19511, 19512
The Ants Came Marching, 1742(F)
Any Number Can Play, 22068
The Apache, 15925
Apache Rodeo, 15970
The Apaches, 16045
Ape Ears and Beaky, 6899(F)
Ape in a Cape, 38(F)
Apes, 18999
Apollo and Daphne, 11460
Apollo 11, 21013
Apollo Moonwalks, 21018
Appalachia, 3403
An Appalachian Mother Goose, 892
Appearing Tonight! Mary Heather Elizabeth Livingstone, 4947(F)
Appelemando's Dreams, 1484(F)
Apple Batter, 3962(F)
Apple Is My Sign, 8909(F)
Apple Island; or, the Truth About Teachers, 9838(F)
Apple Juice Tea, 3938(F)
The Apple Pie Tree, 4453(F)
Apple Tree, 20157
Apple Trees, 20214
    (Illus. by Hiro Koike), 20147
Apple Valley Year, 4555(F)
Applebet, 144(F)
Apples, 20143, 20148
Apples, Alligators and Also Alphabets, 66(F)
Apples, Apples, Apples, 2812(F)
Apples, How They Grow, 20152
The Apprenticeship of Lucas Whitaker, 9270(F)
April Bubbles Chocolate, 11598
April Fool! 6725(F)
The April Fool's Day Mystery, 6962(F)
The April Rabbits, 407(F)
Apt. 3, 4014(F)
Aquamarine, 7796(F)
An Arab Family, 15538

Arabian Nights, 11192, 11202
The Arabian Nights, 11195
The Arabian Nights Entertainments, 11191
The Arabian Nights; or, Tales Told by Sheherezade During a Thousand Nights and One Night, 11180
The Arabs in the Golden Age, 15556
Arachne Speaks, 11480
Araminta's Paint Box, 4567(F)
The Arapaho Indians, 15968
Archaeologists Dig for Clues, 14526
Arches to Zigzags, 27
Archie, Follow Me, 1952(F)
Architecture and Construction, 21114
The Architecture of Animals, 18908
The Arctic, 15830
Arctic Alphabet, 15817
Arctic and Antarctic, 15839
Arctic Babies, 15799
Arctic Explorer, 12120
Arctic Fives Arrive, 555(F)
Arctic Hunter, 15807
Arctic Investigations, 19881
Arctic Memories, 15573
Arctic Son, 4655(F)
Arctic Stories, 4722(F)
Arctic Tundra, 15803
Are All the Giants Dead? 7996(F)
Are Chickens Stripy? 2357(F)
Are We Moving to Mars? 18486
Are We There Yet, Daddy? 255(F)
Are You a Butterfly? 19539
Are You a Ladybug? 19528
Are You a Snail? 19600
Are You a Spider? 19571
Are You Alone on Purpose? 8921(F)
Are You My Mother? 6319(F)
Are You Spring? 2590(F)
Are You There, Baby Bear? 2820(F)
Are You There God? It's Me, Margaret, 8564(F)
Argentina, 15734, 15735
Argentina in Pictures, 15722
Arin's Judgment, 7933(F)
Arizona, 16598, 16604, 16606, 16618, 16627
The Ark, 17247
Ark in the Park, 7283(F)
Arkansas, 16828, 16843, 16856, 16862
Arkansas Facts and Symbols, 16869
An Arkful of Animals, 11773
Arlene Alda's ABC, 1(F)
Arlene Alda's 1 2 3, 367(F)
Arlene Sardine, 2615(F)
Arlington National Cemetery, 16881
Arly, 10120(F)
Arm in Arm, 21817
The Armadillo, 18963
The Armadillo from Amarillo, 1953(F)
Armadillo Rodeo, 1854(F)
Armadillo Tattletale, 2290(F)
Armadillos, 18961
Armadillos and Other Unusual Animals, 18962
Armadillos Sleep in Dugouts, 18912
Armenia, 15403, 15412
Armor, 14796
Armor to Venom, 18900

Arms and Armor, 21385
Arms and Legs and Other Limbs, 18058
Armstrong Lands on the Moon, 20969
Arnie and the New Kid, 4922(F)
Arnosky's Ark, 19390
Around My Room, 11916
Around the Pond, 4439(F), 20512
Around the Track, 21311
Around the World, 5226(F)
Around the World in a Hundred Years, 12058
Around the World in Eighty Days, 7111(F)
Around the World in Eighty Dishes, 21740
Around Town, 3435
The Arrow over the Door, 9225(F)
Arroz con Leche, 14236
The Art and Industry of Sandcastles, 21665
Art Around the World, 21470
The Art Box, 13892
Art Dog, 2228(F)
Art Fraud Detective, 13916
Art from Fabric, 21419
Art Fun! 21595
The Art Gallery, 13933
The Art Lesson, 5495(F)
The Art of African Masks, 13935
The Art of Keeping Cool, 9671(F)
The Art of Making Comic Books, 21586
The Art of Science, 18374
Art of the Far North, 13943
Art School, 13909
Arthur, 11019(F)
Arthur Accused, 6232(F)
Arthur and the Big Blow-Up, 7881(F)
Arthur and the Crunch Cereal Contest, 4095(F)
Arthur and the Scare-Your-Pants-Off Club, 6233(F)
Arthur and the Sword, 11030(F)
Arthur Ashe, 13644, 13645
Arthur Babysits, 1873(F)
Arthur, for the Very First Time, 9933(F)
Arthur Goes to Camp, 1877(F)
Arthur Lost and Found, 1872(F)
Arthur Makes the Team, 6234(F)
Arthur Meets the President, 1873(F)
Arthur Writes a Story, 1874(F)
Arthur's April Fool, 5612(F)
Arthur's Baby, 1878(F)
  (Illus. by Marc Brown), 1884(F)
Arthur's Back to School Day, 6389(F)
Arthur's Birthday, 1878(F), 5666(F)
Arthur's Birthday Party, 6390(F)
Arthur's Camp-Out, 6391(F)
Arthur's Chicken Pox, 1875(F)
Arthur's Christmas, 5764(F)
Arthur's Christmas Cookies, 5839(F)
Arthur's Computer Disaster, 1876(F)
Arthur's Eyes, 1877(F)
Arthur's Family Treasury, 1878(F)
Arthur's Family Vacation, 1878(F), 1879(F)

Arthur's First Sleepover, 1880(F)
Arthur's Funny Money, 6392(F)
Arthur's Great Big Valentine, 6170(F)
Arthur's Halloween, 5983(F)
Arthur's Halloween Costume, 6008(F)
Arthur's Honey Bear, 6392(F)
Arthur's Loose Tooth, 6393(F)
Arthur's Mystery Envelope, 1881(F)
Arthur's New Puppy, 1882(F)
Arthur's Nose, 1877(F)
Arthur's Pen Pal, 6392(F)
Arthur's Pet Business, 1873(F)
Arthur's Prize Reader, 6392(F)
Arthur's Really Helpful Bedtime Book, 10403(F)
Arthur's Really Helpful Word Book, 14024
Arthur's Teacher Moves In, 1883(F)
Arthur's Teacher Trouble, 1884(F)
Arthur's Thanksgiving, 6134(F)
Arthur's Tooth, 1884(F)
Arthur's TV Trouble, 1885(F)
Arthur's Underwear, 1886(F)
Arthur's Valentine, 6162(F)
Artie's Brief, 8721(F)
Artificial Intelligence, 21205
Artist in Overalls, 12312
Artistic Trickery, 13883
The Artist's Friends, 3013(F)
The Arts and Sciences, 16172
ArtStarts for Little Hands! 21463
Arturo's Baton, 4183(F)
Aruna's Journeys, 9016(F)
As, 14038
As Ever, Gordy, 8678(F)
As Long As the Rivers Flow, 12634
As Long As There Are Mountains, 7871(F)
As the Crow Flies, 193(F), 5105(F)
As the Roadrunner Runs, 1227(F)
Asana and the Animals, 11804
Asante, 15016
Ashanti Festival, 10258(F)
Asher and the Capmakers, 6082(F)
Ashkii and His Grandfather, 4651(F)
Ashley Bryan's ABC of African American Poetry, 11750
The Ashwater Experiment, 8469(F)
Asia, 15051
Asian American Authors, 12169
Asian-Americans in the Old West, 16358
Asian Indian Americans, 17542
Ask Me Anything About the Presidents, 12689
Ask Mr. Bear, 2089(F)
Ask Nurse Pfaff, She'll Help You! 17798
Ask the Bones, 6751(F)
Asking About Sex and Growing Up, 18254
Asleep in a Heap, 811(F)
The Assassination of Abraham Lincoln, 13072
The Assassination of Julius Caesar, 14735
The Assassination of Martin Luther King, Jr., 12755

The Assassination of Robert F. Kennedy, 12920
Assateague, 19998
The Assyrians, 14635
Aster Aardvark's Alphabet Adventures, 72(F)
Asteroid Impact, 20310
Asteroids, 18507, 18518
Asteroids, Comets, and Meteors, 18516, 18520, 18534
The Astonishing Armadillo, 18980
Astro Bunnies, 1358(F)
Astronauts, 20971, 20998
Astronomy, 18390, 18418
Astronomy and Space, 20981
Astronomy in Ancient Times, 18377
Astronomy Today, 18403
Astronuts, 21828
At Break of Day, 17191(F)
At Daddy's on Saturdays, 8662(F)
At Grandpa's Sugar Bush, 3067(F)
At Her Majesty's Request, 13756
At Home in the Rain Forest, 4882
At Home with the Presidents, 12683
At Mary Bloom's, 5114(F)
At Preschool with Teddy Bear, 2464(F)
At the Back of the North Wind, 7935(F)
At the Bank, 16950
At the Beach, 13984
At the Carnival, 6363(F)
At the Crack of the Bat, 12001
At the Edge of the Forest, 5312(F)
At the Hotel, Larry, 2589(F)
At the Movie Theater, 21269
At the Petting Zoo with Teddy Bear, 2465(F)
At the Shore, 3324(F)
At the Sign of the Star, 9124(F)
At the Supermarket, 3193
At the Wish of the Fish, 11099
Atalanta's Race, 11464
Athens, 15391
Athletes, 13414
Atlanta, 16873, 16891
The Atlanta Braves Baseball Team, 22110
The Atlantic Ocean, 19821, 19841, 19846
Atlantis, 11459, 21907
The Atlas of Ancient Egypt, 14653
Atlas of Animals, 18605
Atlas of Countries, 14329
Atlas of Islands, 14338
Atlas of People, 14488
Atlas of Plants, 20224
The Atlas of the Bible Lands, 15518
Atlas of the Earth, 20327
The Atlas of World Cultures, 14333
Atmosphere, 20670
The Atocha Treasure, 19874
Attaboy, Sam! 9923(F)
Attack of the 50-Foot Teacher, 6038(F)
The Attack of the Two-Inch Teacher, 10165(F)
Attention Deficit Disorder, 17909
The Attorney General Through Janet Reno, 12957
Augsburg Story Bible, 17237

Auguste Rodin, 12297
Aunt CeeCee, Aunt Belle, and Mama's Surprise, 5720(F)
Aunt Chip and the Great Triple Creek Dam Affair, 3366(F)
Aunt Clara Brown, 12705
Aunt Eater Loves a Mystery, 6298(F)
Aunt Eater's Mystery Halloween, 5992(F)
Aunt Eater's Mystery Vacation, 6299(F)
Aunt Flossie's Hats (and Crab Cakes Later) (Illus. by Cedric Lucas), 3707(F)
(Illus. by James E. Ransome), 3706(F)
The Aunt in Our House, 3722(F)
Aunt Isabel Tells a Good One, 2040(F)
Aunt Minnie McGranahan, 3845(F)
Aunt Nancy and Cousin Lazybones, 4285(F)
Aunt Nancy and Old Man Trouble, 1517(F)
Aunt Pitty Patty's Piggy, 1779(F)
Aunt Skilly and the Stranger, 4329(F)
Auntie Claus, 5906(F)
Aurora, 1145(F)
Aurora Means Dawn, 4819(F)
Auroras, 18415
The Austere Academy, 9123(F)
Australia, 15224, 15235, 15242, 15243, 15244, 15246, 15250, 15253
Australian Aborigines, 15249
Australian Animals, 18602
The Australian Outback and Its People, 15229
Austria, 15288, 15291
Author, 12561
Author Talk, 14065
Author's Day, 4264(F)
Autumn, 21885
Autumn Across America, 18572
The Autumn Equinox, 17370
Autumn Leaves, 20216
An Autumn Tale, 6057(F)
Avalanche, 20778
Avalanche! 20763
Avi, 12503
Aviation, 21071
Aviation and Space Science Projects, 21092
Away from Home, 82(F)
Away to Me, Moss, 7252(F)
Away We Go! 6312(F)
Awesome Experiments in Electricity and Magnetism, 20890
Awesome Experiments in Force and Motion, 20826
Awesome Experiments in Light and Sound, 20804
Awesome Yo-Yo Tricks, 22033
The Awful Aardvarks Go to School, 80(F)
The Awful Aardvarks Shop for School, 2375(F)
Awfully Short for the Fourth Grade, 8216(F)
Axle Annie, 4277(F)
The Aztec Empire, 15649

Aztec, Inca and Maya, 15603
The Aztec News, 15648
Aztec Times, 15635
The Aztecs, 15609, 15610, 15620, 15639, 15642, 15645, 15655

B Is for Baby, 81(F)
B Is for Bethlehem, 149(F)
"B" Is for Betsy, 10073(F)
BAAA, 7930(F)
Baba Yaga, 11093
Baba Yaga and Vasilisa the Brave, 11105
Babar and the Succotash Bird, 2012(F)
Babe, 6471(F), 7863(F)
The Babe and I, 4571(F)
Babe and Me, 7768(F)
Babe Didrikson Zaharias, 13720, 13721, 13722
Babe Ruth, 13498, 13499, 13500
Babies, 18245
The Babies Are Coming! 3209(F)
Baboon, 5131(F)
Baboons, 19017
Baboushka and the Three Kings, 11110
Babushka Baba Yaga, 4796(F)
Babushka's Doll, 1485(F)
Babushka's Mother Goose, 10605
Baby, 18248, 18867
Baby Alligator, 18699
Baby and I Can Play and Fun with Toddlers, 3685
Baby Angels, 1082(F)
Baby Animals, 5245(F), 5392
Baby Bear's Treasury, 968(F)
The Baby Beebee Bird, 742(F)
Baby Bird, 2041(F)
Baby Bird's First Nest, 1755(F)
The Baby Book, 3816
A Baby Born in Bethlehem, 17420
Baby Buggy, Buggy Baby, 14063(F)
Baby Dance, 3912(F)
The Baby Dances, 3686(F)
Baby Days, 3454(F)
Baby Dreams, 673(F)
Baby Duck and the Bad Eyeglasses, 2199(F)
Baby Duck's New Friend, 1754(F)
Baby Faces, 3807(F)
Baby Food, 3323(F)
A Baby for Grace, 3941(F)
A Baby for Max, 3765(F)
Baby High, Baby Low, 161(F)
Baby Horses, 5359
Baby in a Basket, 4803(F)
Baby Lemur, 2190(F)
Baby Loves Hugs and Kisses, 3766(F)
Baby Moses, 17283
Baby Rattlesnake, 11210
Baby Rock, Baby Roll, 3027(F)
Baby Says, 3904(F)
Baby Science, 18230
The Baby Sister, 3606(F)
A Baby Sister for Frances, 6396(F)
Baby-Sit, 3328(F)
Baby-Sitting Is a Dangerous Job, 7025(F)
Baby Steps, 3293(F)

Baby Talk, 3696(F)
Baby! Talk! 3645(F)
Baby Tamer, 4336(F)
The Baby Uggs Are Hatching, 2601(F)
Baby Whale Rescue, 19775
Baby Whales Drink Milk, 19786
Baby Whale's Journey, 5313(F)
The Baby Zoo, 20026
The Babylonians, 14636
The Baby's Bedtime Book, 648(F)
Baby's Book of Animals, 18879
Baby's Book of Nature, 238
Baby's Book of the Body, 3370(F)
Baby's Bris, 6123(F)
A Baby's Coming to Your House! 18234
Baby's First Words, 153
The Baby's Game Book, 21972
The Baby's Word Book, 14060
Baby's Words, 3897(F)
Bach, 12317
Bach's Big Adventure, 4711(F)
Back from the Edge, 18979
Back in the Beforetime, 9153(F)
Back of Beyond, 7124(F)
The Back of Beyond, 16076
Back to Before, 8102(F)
Back to School for Rotten Ralph, 2109(F)
Back to School with Betsy, 10073(F)
Back to the Blue, 5329(F)
Back to the Cabin, 2910(F)
Back to the Wild, 20028
Back Yard Angel, 7423(F)
Backbone of the King, 11326
Backyard Bird Watching for Kids, 19233
Backyard Birds, 19244
Backyard Hunter, 19459
Backyard Insects, 19488
Backyard Safaris, 18582
Bacteria, 19805
Bad Baby Brother, 3939(F)
Bad, Badder, Baddest, 10010(F)
The Bad Beginning, 7067(F)
A Bad Case of Stripes, 5075(F)
A Bad Case of the Giggles, 11881
Bad Day at Riverbend, 1638(F)
Bad Dog, 2329(F)
Bad Dreams, 7725(F)
Bad Girls, 8858(F), 10011(F)
Bad Guys, 12649
Bad Habits! (or The Taming of Lucretzia Crum), 4119(F)
Bad Luck Boswell, 2183(F)
Badge of Valor, 16646
The Badger and the Magic Fan, 10816
Badgers, 18948
Badger's Bad Mood, 2550(F)
Badger's Bring Something Party, 5715(F)
Badger's Parting Gifts, 2777(F)
Badlands, 16589
A Bag Full of Pups, 5215(F)
The Bag I'm Taking to Grandma's, 3339(F)
Bahrain, 15544
Bailey's Window, 7912(F)
Bake It and Build It, 21717

Baker, Baker, Cookie Maker, 6374(F)
The Baker Bible Dictionary for Kids, 17204
The Baker's Dozen, 5919, 11337
A Baker's Portrait, 4949(F)
The Bald Bandit, 6047(F)
Bald Eagle, 19333
The Bald Eagle Returns, 19336
Bald Eagles, 19325
The Ballad of Lucy Whipple, 9355(F)
A Ballad of the Civil War, 9504(F)
Ballerina Dreams, 12481
Ballerinas Don't Wear Glasses, 3797(F)
Ballet, 14276, 14278
The Ballet Book, 14275
Ballet Magic, 3391(F)
Ballet School, 14290
Ballet Stories, 10253(F)
Balloon Ride, 2961
Balloon Voyage, 21101
Ballooning, 22045, 22071
Ballpark, 3081(F)
Ballpoint Bananas and Other Jokes for Kids, 21829
The Ballymara Flood, 4334(F)
The Baltic States, 15413
The Baltimore Orioles Baseball Team, 22112
Balto and the Great Race, 16794
Bambi, 7299(F), 7300(F)
The Bamboo Flute, 8930(F)
Bamboozled, 3768(F)
Banana, 20156
Banana Moon, 312(F)
Bananas, 20149
Bananas! 20141
A Band of Angels, 7346(F)
The Band over the Hill, 2243(F)
Bandannas, Chaps, and Ten-Gallon Hats, 16320
Bandits and Outlaws, 17082
Bandit's Moon, 9364(F)
Bangladesh, 15148, 15179, 15213
Bangs and Twangs, 20933
The Banished, 7908(F)
The Banshee Train, 2911(F)
Bantam of the Opera, 1769(F)
Barbara Bush, 13141
Barbara Jordan, 12732, 12733, 12734
Barber Bear, 6720(F)
Bard of Avon, 12594
Bare Hands, 7265(F)
Barefoot, 4639(F)
The Barefoot Book of Brother and Sister Tales, 10433(F)
The Barefoot Book of Father and Son Tales, 10547
The Barefoot Book of Heroic Children, 13730
The Barefoot Book of Mother and Son Tales, 10548
The Barefoot Book of Pirates, 10625
The Barefoot Book of Princesses, 10461
The Barefoot Book of Stories from the Opera, 14131
The Barefoot Book of Trickster Tales, 10626

The Barefoot Book of Tropical Tales, 10580
Barefoot Dancer, 12377
A Bargain for Frances, 6395(F)
Bark, George, 2088(F)
Barker's Crime, 1172(F)
Barkley, 6398(F)
Barn, 4580(F)
The Barn, 9343(F)
The Barn at Gun Lake, 7102(F)
The Barn Burner, 7539(F)
Barn Cat, 574(F)
Barn Dance! 2481(F)
The Barn Owl, 19367
Barn Owls, 19359
The Barn Owls, 5280(F)
The Barn Party, 5427(F)
Barn Savers, 3212(F)
Barney's Horse, 6399(F)
Barnstormers and Daredevils, 21108
Barnyard Banter, 5204(F)
Barnyard Big Top, 4199(F)
Barnyard Lullaby, 627(F)
Barnyard Prayers, 687
Barnyard Song, 2147(F)
Barrel Racing, 22060
Barrilete, 15658
Barrio, 16760
Barry, 6364
Barry Bonds, 13438
Barry Sanders, 13625, 13626, 13627
Barry's Sister, 8489(F)
Bartholomew and the Oobleck, 1562(F)
Bartleby of the Mighty Mississippi, 8088(F)
Baseball, 22100
Baseball ABC, 95(F)
Baseball Bafflers, 22118
Baseball Ballerina, 6293(F)
Baseball Ballerina Strikes Out! 6294(F)
The Baseball Birthday Party, 6584(F)
Baseball Card Crazy, 7462(F)
The Baseball Counting Book, 505
Baseball Fever, 10339(F)
Baseball, Football, Daddy and Me, 3636(F)
Baseball Hall of Fame, 22088
The Baseball Hall of Shame, 22107
Baseball in the Barrios, 22096
Baseball Jokes and Riddles, 21818
Baseball Just for Kids, 22099
Baseball Saved Us, 5037(F)
Baseball Turnaround, 10294(F)
Baseball's Best, 6362
Baseball's Greatest Hitters, 13383
Baseball's Greatest Pitchers, 13384
Basher Five-Two, 12144
Bashi, Elephant Baby, 5374(F)
Basho and the Fox, 4775(F)
Basil in the Wild West, 8148(F)
Basil of Baker Street, 8148(F)
The Basket Counts, 11994
Basket Moon, 4806(F)
Basket Weaver and Catches Many Mice, 1188(F)
Basketball, 22138, 22141
Basketball Basics, 22137
Basketball Buddies, 6512(F)
Basketball Hall of Fame, 22130

Basketball Stars, 13369
Basketball Year, 22145
Basotho, 15005
Bat, 19019
Bat Bones and Spider Stew, 6041(F)
The Bat Boy and His Violin, 10322(F)
The Bat in the Boot, 4401(F)
The Bat in the Dining Room, 4134(F)
Bat Jamboree, 371(F)
The Bat-Poet, 7835(F)
Bat 6, 10373(F)
Bat Summer, 8390(F)
Bat Watching, 19020
Bataan and Corregidor, 14822
Batbaby, 2606(F)
Batboy, 22084
Bath Day, 3344(F)
Bathtime for Biscuit, 6255(F)
Bathtubs, Slides and Roller Coaster Rails, 20922
The Bathwater Gang, 9998(F)
Batman Gotham Adventures, 8138(F)
Bats, 19018, 19024, 19028, 19030, 19032, 19034, 19036, 19037
Bats! Amazing and Mysterious Creatures of the Night, 19027
Bats Around the Clock, 1743(F)
Bats, Bugs, and Biodiversity, 20446
Bats on Parade, 372(F)
Bats! Strange and Wonderful, 19035
Batswana, 14969
Batter Up, Bailey Benson! 10347(F)
Batteries, Bulbs, and Wires, 20896
Battle, 21388
The Battle for Iwo Jima, 14866
The Battle for the Castle, 8211(F)
Battle of Britain, 14823
The Battle of the Alamo, 16230, 16272
Battle of the Atlantic, 14824
Battle of the Beasts, 10935
Battle of the Bulge, 14825
The Battle of the Little Bighorn, 16058
The Battlefield Ghost, 7691(F)
Battleship Missouri, 14848
Batty Hattie, 7281(F)
Batwings and the Curtain of Night, 1999(F)
Bay Shore Park, 16955
Bayard Rustin, 12783
Bayou Lullaby, 620(F)
Be a Better Hitter, 22086
Be a Dinosaur Detective, 14403
Be a Friend, 18016
Be a Friend to Trees, 20209
Be Aware of Danger, 18217
Be Blest, 17530
Be Brave, Little Lion! 6632(F)
Be First in the Universe, 10241(F)
Be Gentle! 2501(F)
Be Good to Eddie Lee, 4957(F)
Be Nice to Spiders, 2143(F)
Be Not Far from Me, 17294
Be Patient, Abdul, 4824(F)
Be Quiet, Parrot! 6719(F)
Be Well, Beware, 7204(F)
Beach Babble, 3263(F)
A Beach for the Birds, 19254
Beach Play, 3197(F)

Beacons of Light, 21358
The Beaded Moccasins, 9157(F)
Beading, 21547
Beads, 21548
Bean and Plant, 20076(F)
Bean Soup, 2209(F)
Beanbag Buddies and Other Stuffed
  Toys, 21657
Bean's Games, 5262(F)
Beans on the Roof, 7397(F)
Beany and the Dreaded Wedding,
  8865(F)
Beany (Not Beanhead) and the Magic
  Crystal, 8214(F)
Bear, 2664(F), 19041
The Bear, 1011(F)
  (Illus. by Robert Morton), 19040
Bear About Town, 1814(F)
Bear and Baby, 953(F)
Bear and Roly-Poly, 2865(F)
Bear at the Beach, 1937(F)
Bear Attacks, 19045
Bear Bryant, 13604
A Bear Called Paddington, 9785(F)
The Bear Came Over to My House,
  2821(F)
Bear Day, 770(F)
A Bear for All Seasons, 2108(F)
Bear in a Square, 322(F)
Bear Noel, 5807(F)
Bear on a Bike, 6207(F)
Bear on the Train, 5298(F)
Bear Play, 5207(F)
Bear Shadow, 1756(F)
Bear Tales, 10530
The Bear That Heard Crying,
  1307(F)
The Bear Went Over the Mountain,
  899(F)
The Bear Who Didn't Like Honey,
  2466(F)
The Bear Who Went to the Ballet,
  1505(F)
Beardream, 1242(F)
The Bearer of Gifts, 5925(F)
Bearhead, 11094
Bearhide and Crow, 1273(F)
Bearobics, 550(F)
Bears, 19044, 19049, 19056, 19065
  (Illus. by Andrew Bale), 19047,
  19048, 19050
Bears Are Curious, 19058
Bears at the Beach, 614(F)
Bear's Bargain, 1757(F)
The Bear's Bicycle, 2444(F)
Bear's Busy Family, 1815(F)
Bear's Christmas Star, 5794(F)
Bear's Christmas Surprise, 5956(F)
Bear's Day, 3121(F)
Bear's Egg, 2665(F)
Bear's Hiccups, 6198(F)
The Bears' House, 10127(F)
Bears in the Forest, 19072
Bears in the Night, 6204(F)
The Bears on Hemlock Mountain,
  5175(F)
Bears on Wheels, 6204(F)
Bears Out There, 1528(F)
The Bear's Toothache, 2454(F)
Bearsie Bear and the Surprise Sleep-
  over Party, 2784(F)

Bearskin, 1494(F)
Bearymore, 2099(F)
Beast, 1406(F)
Beast Feast, 11782
The Beast in Ms. Rooney's Room,
  6342(F)
The Beast in the Bathtub, 2726(F)
The Beast in You! 14505
The Beast Under the Wizard's
  Bridge, 7089(F)
The Beasties, 8099(F)
The Beastly Feast, 2133(F)
A Beasty Story, 2478(F)
Beat the Story-Drum, Pum-Pum,
  10653
Beat the Turtle Drum, 8670(F)
The Beatles, 12355, 12356
Beatrice's Goat, 4750(F)
Beatrix Potter, 12581, 12582
Beautiful, 3628(F)
Beautiful Bats, 19025
Beautiful Birds, 5459
The Beautiful Butterfly, 11139
The Beautiful Christmas Tree,
  3498(F)
Beautiful Warrior, 4752(F)
Beauty, 7533(F)
Beauty and the Beast, 10866
  (Illus. by Marianna Mayer), 10875
  (Illus. by Marianna Mayer), 10875
  (Illus. by Kathy Mitchell), 10428
The Beauty of the Beast, 11807
Beauty Pageants, 14264
Beaver, 19207
Beaver Pond, Moose Pond, 4373(F)
Beavers, 19197
Beavers Beware! 6220(F)
Bebe's Bad Dream, 4198(F)
Because Brian Hugged His Mother,
  3377(F)
Because Nothing Looks Like God,
  17201
Because of Winn-Dixie, 8624(F)
Because You're Lucky, 5081(F)
Becca's Story, 9475(F)
Become a Bird and Fly! 1526(F)
Becoming Best Friends with Your
  Hamster, Guinea Pig, or Rabbit,
  19893
Becoming Best Friends with Your
  Iguana, Snake, or Turtle, 19894
Becoming Felix, 8542(F)
Becoming Me, 17250
Becoming Your Bird's Best Friend,
  19895
Becoming Your Cat's Best Friend,
  19922
Becoming Your Dog's Best Friend,
  19950
Bed Bouncers, 718(F)
A Bed for the Winter, 6707(F)
A Bed Full of Cats, 6430(F)
Bedbugs in Our House, 19435
Bedhead, 4258(F)
Bedouin, 15490
The Bedspread, 3126(F)
Bedtime, 805(F), 3021(F)
Bedtime! (Illus. by Stephen Lam-
  bert), 637(F)
  (Illus. by Cat B. Smith), 790
Bedtime, Everybody! 684(F)

Bedtime for Frances, 6395(F)
A Bedtime Story, 676(F)
The Bee, 19518
The Bee Tree, 4033(F)
Beef, 20084
Beekeepers, 3213(F)
Been to Yesterdays, 11599
Beep! Beep! 5588(F)
Beep Beep, Vroom Vroom! 223(F)
Bees, 19515, 19520
Beethoven in Paradise, 8502(F)
Beethoven Lives Upstairs, 9065(F)
Beetle, 19537
Beetle Boy, 1101(F)
Beetles, 19533, 19536
Beetles, Lightly Toasted, 9944(F)
Beezus and Ramona, 7406(F)
Beezy and Funnybone, 6487(F)
Beezy at Bat, 6488(F)
Beezy Magic, 6489(F)
Before and After, 18983
Before I Go to Sleep, 705(F)
Before the Wright Brothers, 21072
Before You Were Born, 18228,
  18239
The Beggar's Magic, 10741
A Beginner's Book of Magic, 21789
Beginning Baseball, 22098
Beginning Golf, 21994
Beginning Hockey, 22213
Beginning Mountain Biking, 22160
The Beginning of the Armadilloes,
  7242(F)
The Beginning of Writing, 14011
Beginning Snowboarding, 22282
Beginning Strength Training, 21988
Beginnings, 3755(F)
The Beginnings of Science, 18283
Behind Rebel Lines, 13152
Behind the Attic Wall, 7652(F)
Behind the Bedroom Wall, 9077(F)
Behind the Border, 13824
Behind the Couch, 1184(F)
Behind the Lines, 16432
Behind the Mask, 13789, 14029
Behind the Scenes at the Airport,
  21091
Behind the Scenes at the Hospital,
  18042
Behind the Scenes at the Shopping
  Mall, 16935
Behind the Scenes at the TV News
  Studio, 14315
Behind the Wheel, 21312
Behold . . . the Dragons! 10552
Behold the Trees, 4572(F)
Beijing, 15069
Bein' with You This Way, 11766
Being Angry, 17615
Being Danny's Dog, 8499(F),
  9946(F)
Being Jealous, 17718
Being Together, 3227(F)
Being Your Best, 17622
Belarus, 15407
Belarus, Ukraine, and Moldova,
  15416
Belching Hill, 10814
Belgium, 15397, 15400
Believing Sophie, 4985(F)
Belize, 15679

Bellboy, 6955(F)
Belle Starr and the Wild West, 12965
The Bellmaker, 7817(F)
The Bells of Christmas, 9729(F)
Bellybuttons Are Navels, 4537
The Belonging Place, 8747(F)
Beluga Whales, 19777
Bembo's Zoo, 21881
Ben and Becky in the Haunted House, 6491(F)
Ben and Me, 9912(F)
Ben and the Porcupine, 2919(F)
The Ben Franklin Book of Easy and Incredible Experiments, 18298
Ben Franklin of Old Philadelphia, 12879
Ben Has Something to Say, 8739(F)
Ben, King of the River, 4965(F)
Ben Loves Anna, 8684(F)
Beneath a Blue Umbrella, 885
Beneath Blue Waters, 19641
Beneath the Earth, 10532
Beneath the Stone, 15653
Benedict Arnold and the American Revolution, 12847
The Benin Kingdom of West Africa, 15045
Beni's Family Cookbook, 21755
Beni's First Chanukah, 6125(F)
Beni's First Wedding, 3963(F)
Benito Juarez, 13817
Benito's Dream Bottle, 753(F)
Benjamin Banneker, 13234
Benjamin Bigfoot, 5538(F)
Benjamin Comes Back/Benjamin regresa, 4912(F)
Benjamin Franklin, 12880, 12882, 12884
Benjamin Franklin and His Friends, 12883
Benjamin Harrison, 13040
Benjamin's First Book, 994(F)
Benjamin's 365 Birthdays, 5663(F)
Benjamin's Toys, 994(F)
Benjamin's Treasure, 2861(F)
Benny, 2142(F)
Benny's Had Enough! 2376(F)
Ben's Christmas Carol, 5816(F)
Ben's Dream, 1639(F)
Ben's Trumpet, 4986(F)
Bently and Egg, 2267(F)
Beowulf, 11126
  (Illus. by Charles Keeping), 11037
Berchick, 5139(F)
The Berenstain Bears in the Dark, 1804(F)
Berlin, 15333
The Berlin Wall, 15328
Berlioz Bear, 1855(F)
Bermuda Triangle, 21908
The Bermuda Triangle, 21916
Bernal and Florinda, 11136
Bernard, 2785(F)
Bernard Bear's Amazing Adventure, 2007(F)
Bernard's Bath, 2136(F)
Bernard's Nap, 688(F)
Bernie and the Bessledorf Ghost, 7981(F)
Berries, Nuts and Seeds, 20268

Bertie and Small and the Brave Sea Journey, 1032(F)
Bertie and Small and the Fast Bike Ride, 1032(F)
Bertie's Picture Day, 9788(F)
Bess's Log Cabin Quilt, 9401(F)
The Best Bad Thing, 7530(F)
The Best Birthday Parties Ever! 17396
The Best Book of Ballet, 14302
The Best Book of Bugs, 19461
The Best Book of Dinosaurs, 14447
The Best Book of Mummies, 14669
The Best Book of Ponies, 19984
The Best Book of Sharks, 19763
The Best Book of Spaceships, 20989
The Best Book of the Moon, 18447
The Best Bug Parade, 346(F)
The Best Children's Books in the World, 1491(F)
The Best Christmas, 9739(F)
The Best Christmas Pageant Ever, 9757(F)
Best Enemies Forever, 8332(F)
The Best Ever Kids' Book of Lists, 21888
The Best Fight, 10130(F)
Best Friend Insurance, 7746(F)
Best Friends, 4720(F), 6447(F)
  (Illus. by Lillian Hoban), 5488(F), 21410
The Best Friends Book, 2560(F)
Best Friends for Frances, 6396(F)
Best Friends Together Again, 3977(F)
The Best Halloween of All, 6064(F)
The Best Joke Book for Kids Number 4, 21822
The Best-Laid Plans of Jonah Twist, 10077(F)
Best of Enemies, 9473(F)
The Best of Friends, 2772(F)
The Best of Michael Rosen, 11682
The Best of Shakespeare, 12052
The Best of the Best in Basketball, 22147
The Best of the Best in Figure Skating, 13398
The Best of the Best in Gymnastics, 13399
The Best of the Best in Soccer, 13400
The Best of the Best in Tennis, 22314
The Best of the Best in Track and Field, 13401
The Best on Ice, 22220
The Best Pet Yet, 6694(F)
The Best Place, 2489(F)
The Best School Year Ever, 9974(F)
The Best Teacher in the World, 5486(F)
The Best Thing About a Puppy, 5261(F)
The Best Town in the World, 3019(F)
Best True Ghost Stories of the 20th Century, 21923
The Best Vacation Ever, 224(F)
The Best Way to Play, 8272(F)
The Best Way to See a Shark, 19757
Best Wishes, 12586
The Best Worst Day, 10067(F)

Bestiary, 60
Bet You Can! Science Possibilities to Fool You, 18306
Bet You Can't! Science Impossibilities to Fool You, 18306
Betcha! 20590
The Betrayer's Fortune, 9047(F)
Betsy and Billy, 10073(F)
Betsy and Tacy Go Downtown, 10103(F)
Betsy and Tacy Go over the Big Hill, 10103(F)
Betsy and the Boys, 10073(F)
Betsy in Spite of Herself, 10103(F)
Betsy Ross, 13188, 13189, 13190
Betsy-Tacy, 10103(F)
Betsy-Tacy and Tib, 10103(F)
Betsy Zane, the Rose of Fort Henry, 9228(F)
Better Homes and Gardens Incredibly Awesome Crafts for Kids, 21506
Better Not Get Wet, Jesse Bear, 1932(F)
A Better Safe Than Sorry Book, 18256
Better Than a Lemonade Stand! 16939
Between Earth and Sky, 11215
Between Fire and Ice, 20852
Between the Dragon and the Eagle, 8942(F)
Between Two Worlds, 12510
Beware and Stogie, 7205(F)
Beware Beware, 1239(F)
Beware of the Aunts! 5938(F)
Beware of the Bears! 2417(F)
Beware of the Storybook Wolves, 1053(F)
Beware, Princess Elizabeth, 9112(F)
Beware the Brindlebeast, 10485
Beware! We Are Poisonous, 18935
Bewildered for Three Days, 4664(F)
Beyond Mayfield, 7362(F)
Beyond the Frontier, 16301
Beyond the Magic Sphere, 8710(F)
Beyond the Mango Tree, 8981(F)
Beyond the Sea of Ice, 12125
Beyond Your Senses, 21036
Bible Stories for the Young, 17281
Bicycle Book, 22157
A Bicycle for Rosaura, 1787(F)
The Bicycle Man, 4825(F)
Bicycle Race, 5554(F)
Bicycle Rider, 12784
Bicycle Riding, 11630
Bicycle Safety, 22161
Bicycle Stunt Riding! 22158
Bicycles, 22156
Bicycling, 22152
Big, 189(F)
The Big Alfie and Annie Rose Storybook, 3710(F)
The Big Alfie Out of Doors Storybook, 3711(F)
A Big and a Little Alphabet, 121(F)
Big and Little, 341(F), 4028
Big and Little on the Farm, 5188(F)
Big and Small, 20800
Big Anthony, 1111(F)
Big Anthony and the Magic Ring, 11059

Big Bad Bruce, 1465(F)
Big Bad Bunny, 2046(F)
The Big Bad Rumor, 2497(F)
The Big Balloon Race, 6272(F)
Big Band Sound, 3103(F)
Big Bang, 18384
The Big Bazoohley, 6786(F)
The Big Big Sea, 4559(F)
The Big Bike Race, 10275(F)
Big Black Bear, 2885(F)
Big Blue Whale, 19782
Big Book of Airplanes, 21073
The Big Book of Animals, 18632
The Big Book of Bones, 18829
The Big Book of Dinosaurs, 14481
The Big Book of Games, 22067
The Big Book of Nature Projects, 18299
Big Book of Rescue Vehicles, 21292
Big Book of Trains, 21329
The Big Box, 7972(F)
Big Boy, 4772(F)
Big Brother Dustin, 3570(F)
Big Brother, Little Brother, 3598(F)
Big Brother, Little Sister, 11500(F)
Big Brown Bear, 6495(F)
The Big Brown Box, 3864(F)
The Big Bug Ball, 2374(F)
The Big Bug Book, 19440
Big Bushy Mustache, 3902(F)
Big Cat Conservation, 19416
Big Cat Dreaming, 3943(F)
Big Cats, 19110
  (Illus. by Silvia Duran), 19101
A Big Cheese for the White House, 4646(F)
Big City Port, 5587(F)
Big Daddy, Frog Wrestler, 1821(F)
The Big Dipper, 18540
Big Dog and Little Dog Making a Mistake, 6576(F)
Big Dogs, 19936
Big Egg, 6289(F)
Big Fat Hen, 375(F)
Big Friend, Little Friend, 3182(F)
The Big Green Pocketbook, 3372(F)
Big Head, 18077
The Big Idea, 7370(F)
Big Jabe, 1434(F)
Big Jim and the White-Legged Moose, 5121(F)
Big Lips and Hairy Arms, 1264(F)
Big Machines, 21256
Big Mama, 3095(F)
Big Max, 6579(F)
Big Meeting, 3959(F)
Big Men, Big Country, 11389
The Big Monkey Mix-up, 2943(F)
Big Moon Tortilla, 4936(F)
Big Numbers, 548(F)
Big Old Bones, 4104(F)
The Big Orange Splot, 4265(F)
Big Panda, Little Panda, 2733(F)
Big Pumpkin, 1576(F)
Big Rain Coming, 4657(F)
Big Red, 7247(F)
Big Red Barn, 5144(F)
The Big Red Bus, 5573(F)
Big Red Fire Truck, 5605
Big Rig, 21293
The Big Rivers, 20519

The Big Rock, 20560
Big Sarah's Little Boots, 3032(F)
Big, Scary Wolf, 785(F)
The Big Smith Snatch, 6808(F)
The Big Sneeze, 4096(F)
The Big Snow, 4451(F)
A Big, Spooky House, 11390
Big Squeak, Little Squeak, 2318(F)
The Big Storm, 20694
  (Illus. by Maryann Kovalski), 5437(F)
Big Talk, 11562
A Big Ticket, 22016
Big Trouble for Tricky Rabbit! 11273
Big Truck and Little Truck, 1041(F)
The Big Wave, 8573(F)
The Big Wide-Mouthed Frog, 2341(F)
Big Wind Coming! 2927(F)
Big Wolf and Little Wolf, 2023(F)
The Big Yawn, 5201(F)
Bigfoot and Other Legendary Creatures, 21956
Bigfoot Cinderrrrrella, 10438
Bigger, 3261(F), 9351(F), 9352(F)
The Biggest and the Littlest Animals, 18651
The Biggest Animal Ever, 19787
The Biggest Animal on Land, 18938
The Biggest Bear, 2983(F)
The Biggest Bed in the World, 3564(F)
The Biggest, Best Snowman, 1092(F)
The Biggest Boy, 332(F)
The Biggest Frog in Australia, 10850
The Biggest House in the World, 2379(F)
The Biggest Pumpkin Ever, 6022(F)
Biggest Riddle Book in the World, 21846
Biggest, Strongest, Fastest, 18640
The Biggest Truck, 5583(F)
Bigmama's, 3594
Bijou, Bonbon and Beau, 4846(F)
Bike Trip, 22163
Bikes, Cars, Trucks and Trains, 5548
Bill and Hillary, 13023
Bill and Pete, 1112(F)
Bill and Pete Go Down the Nile, 2024(F)
Bill and Pete to the Rescue, 2025(F)
Bill Bowerman and Phil Knight, 21171
Bill Bradley, 12858
Bill Clinton, 13022, 13025
Bill Clinton and His Presidency, 13024
Bill Cosby, 12369, 12370, 12371, 12372
Bill Gates, 13294, 13295, 13296, 13297
Bill Nye the Science Guy's Big Blast of Science, 18338
Bill Nye the Science Guy's Big Blue Ocean, 19832
The Bill of Rights, 17049, 17061
Bill Peet, 12279
Bill Pickett, 12442, 12443
Billie Jean King, 13650
A Billion for Boris, 9977(F)

Bill's Belly Button, 2252(F)
Billy, 10284(F)
Billy and Emma, 2487(F)
Billy and the Big New School, 5468(F)
Billy Beg and His Bull, 10989
Billy Lazroe and the King of the Sea, 11361
Billy the Ghost and Me, 6356(F)
Billy the Kid, 12851, 12852
Billy Yank and Johnny Reb, 16387
Billy's Beetle, 4187(F)
Bimmi Finds a Cat, 7308(F)
Bimwili and the Zimwi, 10638
Bing and Chutney, 4054(F)
Bing Bang Boing, 11870
Bingleman's Midway, 2903(F)
Bingo, 3473(F)
Binya's Blue Umbrella, 8985(F)
Biography for Beginners, 12658
Biography Today, 13211
The Bionic Bunny Show, 1892(F)
Biotechnology, 18036
Bipolar Disorder, 17989
Bipolar Disorder and Depression, 17909
The Birchbark House, 9159(F)
Birches, 11950
The Bird, 4076(F)
Bird Alert, 19417
Bird Boy, 8997(F)
Bird Dogs Can't Fly, 1770(F)
The Bird House, 8056(F)
A Bird or Two, 4729(F)
Bird Tales from Near and Far, 10589
Bird Talk, 5281(F)
The Bird, the Monkey, and the Snake in the Jungle, 1784(F)
Bird Watching with Margaret Morse Nice, 13336
The Bird Who Was an Elephant, 8999(F)
Birdie's Lighthouse, 2941(F)
Birds, 19217, 19276, 19280, 19287, 19301
  (Illus. by Gary Britt), 19243
  (Illus. by Dave King), 19279
  (Illus. by Rene Mettler), 19219, 19300
Birds by Brian Wildsmith, 19296
The Birds' Christmas Carol, 9768(F)
Birds Conquer the Sky, 19247
The Birds' Gift, 11095
Birds in the Bushes, 13335
Birds of Prey, 19322, 19331, 19334
Birdsong, 4563(F)
Birdwise, 19235
Birth, 17401
Birth Customs, 17214
Birth of a Foal, 19997
The Birth of a Humpback Whale, 19797
The Birth of a Whale, 5119
The Birth of the Moon, 1249(F)
The Birthday ABC, 98(F)
A Birthday Basket for Tia, 5713(F)
The Birthday Bear, 6634(F)
Birthday Happy, Contrary Mary, 5699(F)
The Birthday Letters, 5719(F)
The Birthday Party Mystery, 6965(F)

Birthday Present, 5728(F)
The Birthday Presents, 5727(F)
Birthday Rhymes, Special Times, 5688
The Birthday Room, 8448(F)
Birthday Surprises, 10259(F)
The Birthday Swap, 5709(F)
Biscuit, 6256(F)
Biscuit Finds a Friend, 6257(F)
Biscuits in the Cupboard, 11803
Biscuit's New Trick, 6258(F)
Biscuit's Valentine's Day, 6164(F)
Bit by Bit, 4301(F)
The Bite of the Gold Bug, 9535(F)
Bitter Bananas, 4783(F)
Bizarre Birds, 19245, 19292
Bizarre Insects, 19423
Black and White, 10262(F)
  (Illus. by Sherry Neidigh), 1988(F)
Black and White Rabbit's ABC, 7(F)
Black Angels, 7359(F)
Black Bear, 19051
Black Bears, 19043
Black Beauty, 5408(F)
Black Belt, 7720(F)
Black, Blue, and Gray, 16412
The Black Bonnet, 9264(F)
Black Cat, 7276(F)
The Black Cauldron, 7551(F)
Black Cowboy, Wild Horses, 4728(F)
The Black Cowboys, 16298
Black Crow, Black Crow, 1214(F)
The Black Death, 14759
Black Eagles, 21079
Black Elephant with a Brown Ear (in Alabama), 13962
Black Fighting Men, 21401
The Black-Footed Ferret, 18975
Black Frontiers, 16366
The Black Geese, 11101
Black Gold, 7216(F)
Black Hearts in Battersea, 6740(F)
Black Heroes of the American Revolution, 12644
Black Heroes of the Wild West, 12687
Black Holes, 18557
Black Holes and Supernovae, 18406
Black Is Brown Is Tan, 3503(F)
Black Nell, 7327(F)
Black on White, 197(F)
Black People Who Made the Old West, 12663
Black Ships Before Troy, 11510
The Black Snowman, 5881(F)
The Black Soldier, 15869
Black Stallion, 7190(F)
The Black Stallion Returns, 7190(F)
The Black Stallion's Shadow, 7189(F)
Black Star, Bright Dawn, 6996(F)
Black Stars in Orbit, 20964
Black Swan/White Crow, 11822
Black Tuesday, 16462
Black, White, Just Right! 3602(F)
Black Whiteness, 12087
Blackberry Booties, 3153(F)
The Blackbirch Kid's Almanac of Geography, 14357
Blackwater, 8576(F)

Blackwater Swamp, 7119(F)
Blame It on El Niño, 20770
Blanca's Feather, 5335(F)
Blast Off! 11607
Blast Off to Earth! 4483
Bless This House, 17534
Bless Us All, 17531
The Blessing of the Animals, 8799(F)
The Blessing of the Lord, 17321
The Blessing Seed, 17305
Blessings, 6076
Blimps, 21104
The Blind Colt, 7293(F)
The Blind Men and the Elephant, 6192
Blindness, 17917
Blitz, 21562
Blitzkrieg, 14823
Blizzard, 20703
The Blizzard Disaster, 7854(F)
Blizzard! The Storm that Changed America, 16480
A Blizzard Year, 7447(F)
Blizzards, 20711
The Blizzard's Robe, 1535(F)
Block Building for Children, 21673
Blockade Runners and Ironclads, 16389
Blood, 18088, 18090
Blood and Guts, 18047
The Blood-and-Thunder Adventure on Hurricane Peak, 7946(F)
Blood Brothers, 7967(F)
Blood-Feeding Bugs and Beasts, 18642
Bloodsuckers, 18643
Bloomability, 10042(F)
Bloomers! 4596
Blossom Comes Home, 5257(F)
A Blossom Promise, 7398(F)
The Blossoms and the Green Phantom, 7398(F)
The Blossoms Meet the Vulture Lady, 7398(F)
Blow Me a Kiss, Miss Lilly, 3986(F)
Blubber, 8565(F)
Blue, 262(F)
The Blue and the Gray, 9469(F)
A Blue Butterfly, 13904
The Blue Darter and Other Sports Stories, 10276(F)
The Blue Door, 9313(F)
A Blue-Eyed Daisy, 8805(F)
Blue Fairy Book, 10442(F)
Blue Feather's Vision, 16149
A Blue for Beware, 7206(F)
The Blue Hill Meadows, 7501(F)
Blue Lightning, 8055(F)
Blue Moon Soup, 21703
Blue Rabbit and Friends, 2875(F)
Blue Rabbit and the Runaway Wheel, 2876(F)
Blue Ribbon Blues, 7078(F)
Blue-Ribbon Henry, 1912(F)
The Blue Rider, 13902
Blue Sea, 342(F)
Blue Skies, French Fries, 4126(F)
Blue Willow (Illus. by S. Saelig Gallagher), 8990(F)
  (Illus. by Paul Lantz), 7436(F)
Blueberries for Sal, 3782(F)

Blueberry Shoe, 5185(F)
The Blueberry Train, 4763(F)
Bluebonnet at the Marshall Train Depot, 1940(F)
Blues, 14126
The Blues of Flats Brown, 2525(F)
Bluestem, 9342(F)
Bluish, 7442(F)
Blumpoe the Grumpoe Meets Arnold the Cat, 5357(F)
The Blushful Hippopotamus, 2616(F)
Bo Jackson, 13614, 13615
Boas, 18766
Boat Book, 5566(F)
The Boat of Many Rooms, 4213(F)
A Boat to Nowhere, 9018(F)
Boating with Cap'n Bob and Matey, 22261
Boats, 21352
  (Illus. by Byron Barton), 21351
Boats Afloat, 21375
Boats and Ships, 21353
Boats for Bedtime, 5582(F)
Boats, Ships, Submarines and Other Floating Machinery, 21359
Bob, 5758(F)
Bob Dole, Legendary Senator, 12873
Bob Feller, 13451
Bobby Bonilla, 13439, 13440
Bobcat, 19077
Bobcats, 19073
Bobo Crazy, 10230(F)
Bobsledding and the Luge, 21978
Bodies from the Bog, 14494
Bodies from the Past, 14513
The Bodies in the Bessledorf Hotel, 6983(F)
The Body Atlas, 18069
The Body Book, 4522
Body Decoration, 21946
Body Language, 17628
Bog Bodies, 14489
The Boggart, 7667(F)
The Boggart and the Monster, 7668(F)
Boing-Boing the Bionic Cat, 7789(F)
Boitano's Edge, 13588
Bold and Bright, 18888
Bolivia, 15775
Bolivia in Pictures, 15724
Boltzmon! 10238(F)
The Bomb in the Bessledorf Bus Depot, 6984(F)
Bomb Squad Officer, 17811
The Bombers' Moon, 9693(F)
Bombing Fortress Europe, 14826
Bonaparte, 1949(F)
Bone Button Borscht, 11144
The Bone Detectives, 17071
The Bone Keeper, 7936(F)
The Bone Man, 11300
Bone Poems, 11660
The Bone Talker, 1342(F)
Bones, 18175
Bones, Bones, Dinosaur Bones, 5134(F)
The Bones in the Cliff, 7083(F)
Bonesy and Isabel, 5385(F)
Bongo Larry, 2587(F)
Bonjour, Lonnie, 1508(F)
Bonjour, Mr. Satie, 2026(F)

Bonnie Blair, 13680, 13681
Bonnie's Blue House, 3001(F)
Bony-Legs, 11084
Boo! 2446(F)
Boo and Baa at Sea, 2333(F)
Boo and Baa Get Wet, 2335(F)
Boo and Baa in a Party Mood, 2334(F)
Boo and Baa in the Woods, 2335(F)
Boo and Baa in Windy Weather, 2334(F)
Boo and Baa on a Cleaning Spree, 2333(F)
Boo! Halloween Poems and Limericks, 6012
Boo! It's Halloween, 6060(F)
Boo Who? 6009(F)
Booby Hatch, 5302(F)
Boodil, My Dog, 5308(F)
The Booford Summer, 7307(F)
Boogie Bones, 1359(F)
Book, 11646
A Book About God, 17183
The Book of Bad Ideas, 4185(F)
The Book of Creation, 17245
The Book of Dragons, 7772(F)
Book of Enchantments, 8220(F)
The Book of Fairies, 7619, 10628
Book of Firsts, 13396
A Book of Friends, 17729
A Book of Fruit, 20150
The Book of Goddesses, 11457
The Book of Hob Stories, 7956(F)
A Book of Hugs, 3395(F)
A Book of Kisses, 3396(F)
The Book of Lists for Kids, 21897
The Book of North American Owls, 19364
The Book of Shadowboxes, 129(F)
The Book of Slime, 21920
Book of the American Civil War, 16404
The Book of Think (or How to Solve a Problem Twice Your Size), 21864
The Book of Three, 7551(F)
The Book of Virtues for Young People, 10252
The Book of Where, 14330
The Book of You, 17608
A Book of Your Own, 14108
A Book Takes Root, 13998
Booker T. Washington, 12812, 12813, 12814
Books and Libraries, 13999
The Bookshop Dog, 5397(F)
Bookstore Cat, 5452(F)
The Bookstore Ghost, 6502(F)
The Bookstore Mouse, 7653(F)
Bookworks, 14010
A Bookworm Who Hatched, 12487
The Bookworm's Feast, 11627
Boom, Baby, Boom, Boom! 1387(F)
Boom Town, 4731(F)
Boomer Goes to School, 5325(F)
Boomer's Big Day, 5326(F)
Boomer's Big Surprise, 2430(F)
Boomer's Kids, 9629(F)
Boomtowns of the West, 16328
Boot, 10285(F)
Boot Weather, 1653(F)

The Bootmaker and the Elves, 1361(F)
Boots and His Brothers, 11127
Boots and the Seven Leaguers, 8235(F)
Bootsie Barker Ballerina, 6217(F)
Bootsie Barker Bites, 4911(F)
Bored Blue? 3242(F)
Boredom Blasters, 22070
Borgel, 10222(F)
Boris Yeltsin, 13869
Born in the Year of Courage, 8991(F)
Born to Be Wild, 8117(F)
Born to Trot, 7216(F)
The Borning Room, 9363(F)
The Borrowed Hanukkah Latkes, 6072(F)
The Borrowers, 7997(F)
The Borrowers Afield, 7997(F)
The Borrowers Afloat, 7997(F)
The Borrowers Aloft, 7997(F)
The Borrowers Avenged, 7997(F)
Boshblobberbosh, 11893
Bosnia, 15270, 15284
Bosnia and Herzegovina, 15268
A Bosnian Family, 17594
Boss of the Plains, 21167
The Bossy Gallito, 11422
Boston, 16701, 16720
The Boston Coffee Party, 16212
The Boston Tea Party, 16162, 16177
   (Illus. by Peter M. Fiore), 16151
Boston Tea Party, 16149
Boston's Freedom Trail, 16113
Boswell Wide Awake, 659(F)
Botswana, 14985
The Bottle Imp, 8130(F)
The Bottlenose Dolphin, 19690
Bottles Break, 8827(F)
Bottoms Up! 18853
Bouki Dances the Kokioko, 11433
Bouncing, 3228(F)
Bouncing on the Bed, 3264(F)
Bouncing Time, 5270(F)
Bound for America, 16251
Bound for the North Star, 16242
Boundless Grace, 4683(F)
Bow Wow, 345(F)
Bow-Wow Birthday, 5735(F)
The Bowl of Fruit, 2042(F)
The Bowlegged Rooster and Other Tales That Signify, 8140(F)
A Box Can Be Many Things, 6589(F)
Box Top Dreams, 8664(F)
Box Turtle at Long Pond, 4441(F)
The Boxcar Children Cookbook, 21678
The Boxer and the Princess, 2184(F)
The Boxes, 8100(F)
The Boxing Champion, 4926(F)
Boy, 12520(F)
A Boy and His Bear, 9096(F)
The Boy and the Ghost, 1541(F)
A Boy Becomes a Man at Wounded Knee, 16072
A Boy Called Slow, 9146(F)
A Boy in the Doghouse, 5190(F)
A Boy Named Boomer, 13608
A Boy Named Giotto, 4672(F)

The Boy of a Thousand Faces, 7049(F)
A Boy of Tache, 6769(F)
Boy of the Deeps, 4864(F)
Boy of the Painted Cave, 8954(F)
The Boy of the Three-Year Nap, 10830
The Boy on the Beach, 3097(F)
The Boy Trap, 10109(F)
The Boy Who Ate Around, 1136(F)
The Boy Who Ate Dog Biscuits, 7298(F)
The Boy Who Counted Stars, 11590
The Boy Who Lived with the Seals, 11270
The Boy Who Lost His Belly Button, 1689(F)
The Boy Who Loved to Draw, 12310
The Boy Who Made Dragonfly, 11258
The Boy Who Sat by the Window, 8477(F)
The Boy Who Saved the Town, 4829(F)
The Boy Who Stopped Time, 1608(F)
The Boy Who Stuck Out His Tongue, 11177
The Boy Who Wouldn't Obey, 11414
The Boy with Dinosaur Hands, 7651(F)
The Boy Without a Name, 11196
Boys Against Girls, 9945(F)
Boys and Girls Book About Divorce, 17652
A Boy's Will, 9101(F)
The Bracelet, 9692(F)
Brad and Butter Play Ball, 10334(F)
Bradley and the Billboard, 10326(F)
Brad's Universe, 8545(F)
Brady, 9277(F)
A Braid of Lives, 15933
Brain, 18117
   (Illus. by Andrew Farmer), 18113
The Brain, 18110, 18120
Brain and Nerves, 18114
The Brain and Nervous System, 18112, 18115
Brain Surgery for Beginners, 18116
Brainstorm! 21062
A Brand Is Forever, 7304(F)
The Brand New Creature, 993(F)
The Brand New Kid, 5491(F)
Brandy, 12358, 12359
Brass Button, 1133(F)
Brats, 11877
Brave as a Mountain Lion, 3414(F)
Brave Bear, 2467(F)
Brave Bear and the Ghosts, 11230
Brave Bessie, 12091
Brave Georgie Goat, 2631(F)
Brave Highland Heart, 4708(F)
Brave Horace, 2279(F)
Brave Irene, 2973(F)
Brave Jack, 2654(F)
Brave Janet Reachfar, 7425(F)
The Brave Little Parrot, 10800
A Brave Little Princess, 1399(F)
The Brave Little Tailor, 10887
   (Illus. by Eve Tharlet), 10891
Brave Margaret, 11031

Brave Martha, 624(F)
The Brave Ones, 1296(F)
Brave Potatoes, 1591(F)
Brave Wolf and the Thunderbird, 11279
The Bravest Cat! 6315(F)
The Bravest Dog Ever, 6680
The Bravest Ever Bear, 1727(F)
The Bravest of Us All, 2906(F)
Braving the Frozen Frontier, 15808
Braving the North Atlantic, 16095
Bravo, Amelia Bedelia! 6559(F)
Bravo, Maurice! 3537(F)
Bravo, Mildred and Ed! 2806(F)
Bravo, Mr. William Shakespeare! 12054
Bravo, Tanya, 4962(F)
Bravo, Zan Angelo! 4632(F)
Brazil, 15726, 15728, 15738, 15743, 15747, 15757, 15764, 15783
Brazil in Pictures, 15741
Brazilian Foods and Culture, 15732
Bread and Jam for Frances, 6395(F)
Bread, Bread, Bread, 3333(F)
Bread Is for Eating, 3165(F)
The Bread Winner, 9639(F)
The Breadwinner, 8992(F)
Breaker, 9606(F)
Breakfast at the Liberty Diner, 4714(F)
Breakfast Time, 3344(F)
Breaking Free, 9278(F)
Breaking Ground, Breaking Silence, 16690
Breaking into Print, 14000
Breaking the Chains of the Ancient Warrior, 10372(F)
Breaking the Spell, 7766(F)
Breath of Air and a Breath of Smoke, 17879
Breath of the Dragon, 8994(F)
Breathe Easy, 18012
Breathing, 18123
The Bremem Town Musicians, 10892
The Bremen Town Band, 10937
Brenda and Edward, 2314(F)
Brer Rabbit and Boss Lion, 11344
Brett Favre, 13609, 13610, 13611, 13612
Brett Hull, 13693
Brian Wildsmith's Amazing World of Words, 14059
Brian's Bird, 5178(F)
Brian's Return, 8782(F)
Brian's Winter, 8782(F)
Briar's Book, 8014(F)
The Brick House Burglars, 6866(F)
Bricks, 21116
A Bride for Anna's Papa, 9593(F)
Bridge to Terabithia, 8355(F)
Bridges! Amazing Structures to Design, Build and Test, 21133
Bridges Are to Cross, 21151
Bridges Connect, 21126
The Bridges in London, 7079(F)
Brigham Young, 12969, 12970
Bright Beetle, 19529
Bright Christmas, 5784(F)
Bright-Eyed Athena, 11516
Bright Eyes, Brown Skin, 3226(F)

Bright Freedom's Song, 9291(F)
Bright Star, 4938(F)
Bright Star Shining, 11826
A Brighter Garden, 11552
Brighty of the Grand Canyon, 7219(F)
A Brilliant Streak, 12609
Bringing Nettie Back, 8923(F)
Bringing the Rain to Kapiti Plain, 10639
Bringing Up Baby, 18870
Britain, 15347
Britney Spears, 12470, 12471
Broadway Chicken, 7734(F)
The Brocaded Slipper and Other Vietnamese Tales, 10845
The Broccoli Tapes, 7515(F)
Broderick, 2555(F)
The Broken Blade, 8928(F), 8931(F)
Broken Days, 9313(F)
The Broken Mirror, 9656(F)
Broken Shields, 15606
The Broken Tusk, 17198
Bronc Riding, 22060
Bronco Busters, 5260(F)
The Bronze Bow, 8944(F)
The Bronze Cauldron, 10574
Bronzeville Boys and Girls, 11749
The Brooklyn Bridge, 16723, 21142
Brooklyn, Bugsy, and Me, 8570(F)
Brooklyn Dodger Days, 4813
Brooklyn Doesn't Rhyme, 9523(F)
Brooklyn Pops Up, 16749
Brooks Robinson, 13484
Brooms Are for Flying! 6043(F)
Brother Anansi and the Cattle Ranch/El Hermano Anansi y el Rancho de Ganada, 11400
Brother Brother, Sister Sister, 8631(F)
Brother Francis and the Friendly Beasts, 4682
Brother Sun, Sister Moon, 13794
Brother to the Wind, 1664(F)
Brother Wolf, 11309
Brother Wolf of Gubbio, 11075
Brothers at War, 7614(F)
The Brothers Gruesome, 1150(F)
Brothers of the Knight, 10376
The Brothers' Promise, 11149
The Brown Bear, 19071
Brown Bear, Brown Bear, What Do You See? 283(F)
Brown Cow, Green Grass, Yellow Mellow Sun, 4465(F)
Brown, Fierce, and Furry, 18929
Brown Paper School USKids History, 16278
Brown Rabbit's Day, 154(F)
Brown Rabbit's Shape Book, 320(F)
Brown Sugar Babies, 3433(F)
Brown Sunshine, 7215(F)
Bruce Coville's Alien Visitors, 10166(F)
Bruce Coville's UFOs, 10167(F)
Bruce Lee, 12411
Bruegel's Tower of Babel, 13895
Brunei, 15216
Bruno the Baker, 5704(F)
Bruno the Tailor, 2303(F)
Brush Your Teeth, Please, 2432(F)

Bryce Canyon National Park, 16631
Bub; or, The Very Best Thing, 967(F)
Buba Leah and Her Paper Children, 3863(F)
Bubba and Trixie, 2074(F)
Bubba, The Cowboy Prince, 1297(F)
Bubbe and Gram, 3677(F)
Bubble Monster, 18311
Bubble Trouble and Other Poems and Stories, 11900
Bubblemania, 20132
Bubblemania! 20805
Buckaroo, 8531(F)
Buckley and Wilberta, 6667(F)
Bud, 2547(F)
Bud, Not Buddy, 8622(F)
Buddha, 17175
Buddha Stories, 17176
Buddhist Temple, 17231
Buddies, 8354(F)
Buddy, 7230(F), 19957
Budgie at Bendick's Point, 1715(F)
Budgie the Little Helicopter, 1715(F)
Buffalo, 18955
Buffalo Bill and the Pony Express, 6273(F)
Buffalo Bill Cody, 12869, 12870
Buffalo Days, 15971
Buffalo Dreams, 5187(F)
Buffalo Gals, 16343
Buffalo Hunt, 15953
The Buffalo Jump, 9177(F)
The Buffalo Nickel Blues Band, 8249(F)
Buffalo Soldiers, 16353
Buffalo Thunder, 4889(F)
The Buffalo Train Ride, 18987
Buffalo Woman, 11238
A Bug, a Bear, and a Boy, 6496(F)
Bug Book, 19453
Bug Boy, 8113(F)
Bug Faces, 19470
Bug Girl, 8114(F)
Bug in a Rug, 10064(F)
The Bug in Teacher's Coffee, 11866
Bug Off! A Swarm of Insect Words, 14036
Bug Watching with Charles Henry Turner, 13351
Bugs, 19475
Bugs! 11790
Bugs and Critters I Have Known, 11980
Bugs, Beetles, and Butterflies, 19503
Bugs! Bugs! Bugs! 19425, 19437
Bugs C, 19495
Bugs for Lunch, 18808
Bugsy Siegel and the Postwar Boom, 12964
Build It! 21124
Build Your Own Web Site, 21209
Build Your Own Website, 21221
Builders, Traders and Craftsmen, 14703
Building, 21117, 21154
Building a Dream, 12702
Building a House, 3014(F)
Building a New Nation, 1789–1801, 16233

Building a Shelf and a Bike Rack, 21660
Building a Solitaire Game and a Peg Board, 21661
Building an Igloo, 15837
Building Beavers, 19200
Building Big, 21136
Building the Book Cathedral, 21137
Building the Capital City, 16656
Buildings, 21113
Built for Speed, 19116
The Bull and the Fire Truck, 6424(F)
Bull Riding, 22060
Bull Run, 16406
Bull Whackers to Whistle Punks, 16346
Bulldozers, 5563, 21298
Bullies and Gangs, 17711
Bullies Are a Pain in the Brain, 17727
Bully for You, Teddy Roosevelt! 13101
The Bully of Barkham Street, 8375(F)
Bully Trouble, 6277(F)
Bullying, 17730
Bumble Bee, 5145(F)
Bumblebee at Apple Tree Lane, 5217(F)
Bumblebee, Bumblebee, Do You Know Me? A Garden Guessing Game, 4517(F)
Bumples, Fumdidlers, and Jellybeans, 11918
Bunnicula, 9885(F), 9886(F)
Bunnicula Escapes! 6902(F)
Bunnicula Strikes Again! 9886(F)
Bunnies in My Head, 3461(F)
Bunny and Me, 1207(F)
Bunny Bungalow, 2645(F)
Bunny Money, 2833(F)
The Bunny Who Found Easter (Illus. by Helen Craig), 5979(F)
(Illus. by Helen Craig), 5979(F)
Bunny's First Snowflake, 807(F)
Bunny's Night Out, 776(F)
Bunny's Noisy Book, 1894(F)
Bunny's Rainbow Day, 2832(F)
The Bunyans, 1699(F)
Buoy, 7580(F)
Burger! 7635(F)
Buried Alive, 11563
Buried Blueprints, 21934
The Buried City of Pompeii, 14749(F)
Buried in Ice, 15566
Buried Treasure, 20178
Buried Treasures of New England, 14531
Buried Treasures of the Atlantic Coast, 14531
Buried Treasures of the Great Plains, 16564
Burma, 15217
Burnin' Rubber, 22083
The Burning Questions of Bingo Brown, 10030(F)
Burnish Me Bright, 8885(F)
The Burnt Stick, 8934(F)
Burnt Toast on Davenport Street, 2061(F)

A Burst of Firsts, 11628
Burt Dow, Deep-Water Man, 4221(F)
Burton and Stanley, 8003(F)
Burton and the Giggle Machine, 9870(F)
The Bus for Us, 4089(F)
The Bus Ride, 4769(F)
Bus Riders, 3993(F)
Bus Route to Boston, 3074(F)
The Bushwhacker, 9477(F)
Business and Industry, 12676
Business Builders in Computers, 13201
Business Builders in Oil, 12633
Business Leaders Who Built Financial Empires, 12680
Buster, the Very Shy Dog, 6200(F)
Buster's Dino Dilemma, 6435(F)
Busy Baby, 3897(F)
Busy Bea, 4273(F)
The Busy Building Book, 21152
Busy, Busy City Street, 4235(F)
Busy Buzzing Bumblebees and Other Tongue Twisters, 6636
A Busy Day at Mr. Kang's Grocery Store, 3131
A Busy Day for a Good Grandmother, 3795(F)
Busy Dinah Dinosaur, 6377(F)
Busy Farm, 496(F)
Busy O'Brien and the Great Bubble Gum Blowout, 9969(F)
Busy Penguins, 5401(F)
Busy Toes, 4092(F)
But God Remembered, 17320
Butch Cassidy, 12867, 12868
The Butter Battle Book, 1563(F)
Butterflies, 19545
(Illus. by Ron Broda), 19563
Butterflies and Moths, 19542, 19547, 19564
Butterflies Fly, 19570
The Butterflies' Promise, 3830(F)
Butterfly (Illus. by Helen Senior), 19544
(Illus. by Kim Taylor), 19561
The Butterfly, 4797(F)
The Butterfly Alphabet, 126(F)
The Butterfly Alphabet Book, 19543
The Butterfly Book, 19552
Butterfly Boy, 3756(F)
Butterfly House, 4396(F)
The Butterfly Hunt, 8244(F)
The Butterfly Jar, 11661
The Butterfly Lion, 7270(F)
The Butterfly Seeds, 4871(F)
Butterfly Story, 19553
Butterfly Watching, 19540
Butternut Hollow Pond, 20518
The Button Box, 3854(F)
A Button in Her Ear, 18146
Button Soup, 1446(F)
Buttons, 4120(F)
Buttons for General Washington, 4812(F)
Buy Now, Pay Later, 16937
Buying a Pet from Ms. Chavez, 3132(F)
Buz, 1148(F)
Buzz, 3486(F)
Buzz! A Book About Insects, 19426

"Buzz, Buzz, Buzz," Went the Bumblebee, 2844(F)
Buzzing Rattlesnakes, 18754
Buzzy Widget, 4204(F)
By a Blazing Blue Sea, 4654(F)
By the Dawn's Early Light, 3500(F), 14161
By the Great Horn Spoon, 9844(F)
By the Hanukkah Light, 6104(F)
By the Seashore, 19864
By the Shores of Silver Lake, 7537(F)
By Truck to the North, 15842
Bye-Bye, Babies! 3317(F)
Bye, Bye, Bali Kai, 8479(F)
The Bye-Bye Pie, 3721(F)
Bye, Mis' Lela, 4928(F)

C D B! 4326, 21855
C D C! 21855
Cabbage Moon, 1948(F)
Cabbage Rose, 10430(F)
The Cabin Faced West, 9231(F)
The Cabin Key, 3850(F)
Cabin 102, 7737(F)
Cabin Six Plays Cupid, 8316(F)
The Cabinet, 17107
The Caboose Who Got Loose, 1466(F)
A Cache of Jewels and Other Collective Nouns, 14035
Cactus, 20244, 20249
(Illus. by Shabo Hans), 20252
The Cactus Flower Bakery, 1735(F)
Cactus Hotel, 4449
Cactus Poems, 11937
Caesar's Antlers, 7783(F)
Caesar's Story, 9206(F)
Cairo, 15512
Cajun, 4851(F)
Cajun Home, 16832
A Cake All for Me! 825(F)
A Cake for Herbie, 91(F)
The Cake That Mack Ate, 4282(F)
Cal Ripken Jr., 13481
Cal Ripken, Jr., 13482, 13483
Cal Ripken, Jr. Baseball's Iron Man, 13479
Calamity, 1766(F)
Calamity Jane, 12864
Calcium, 20281
Calculator Riddles, 20608
A Caldecott Celebration, 12174
Caleb and Kate, 1592(F)
Caleb's Choice, 9336(F)
A Calendar of Festivals, 10553
Calendarbears, 4452(F)
Calico Bush, 9194(F)
Calico Captive, 9213(F)
Calico's Cousins, 19934
California, 16759, 16775, 16786, 16806
The California Condor, 19341
The California Gold Rush, 16292, 16376, 16383
California Gold Rush Cooking, 16367
The California Gold Rush in American History, 16285
The California Missions, 16823
Call It Courage, 7077(F)

Call Me Consuelo, 6930(F)
Call Me Francis Tucket, 9426(F)
Call Mr. Vasquez, He'll Fix It! 3133
The Callender Papers, 7114(F)
Callie Ann and Mistah Bear, 11375
Callie Shaw, Stable Boy, 10268(F)
Calling All Toddlers, 246(F)
Calling Me Home, 9375(F)
Calling the Doves/El Canto de las Palomas, 12548
Calling the Swan, 8832(F)
Cally's Enterprise, 8759(F)
Calvin Coolidge, 13026, 13027
Cam Jansen and the Barking Treasure Mystery, 6729(F)
Cam Jansen and the Birthday Mystery, 6730(F)
Cam Jansen and the Catnapping Mystery, 6731(F)
Cam Jansen and the Ghostly Mystery, 6732(F)
Cam Jansen and the Mystery at the Haunted House, 6733(F)
Cam Jansen and the Mystery of Flight 54, 6734(F)
Cam Jansen and the Mystery of the Chocolate Fudge Sale, 6735(F)
Cam Jansen and the Scary Snake Mystery, 6736(F)
Cam Jansen and the Triceratops Pops Mystery, 6737(F)
Cambodia, 15203
Cambodia in Pictures, 15152
Camelot, 11046
Camels and Pigs, 19158
Camels for Uncle Sam, 21346
The Camera, 21805
Cameroon in Pictures, 15028
Camille and the Sunflowers, 4577(F)
Camp Ghost-Away, 4126(F)
Camp Murphy, 8338(F)
A Campfire for Cowboy Billy, 1634(F)
Camping, 22166
Camping in the Temple of the Sun, 2934(F)
Camy Baker's Body Electric, 17696
Camy Baker's How to be Popular in the Sixth Grade, 8591(F)
Camy Baker's It Must be Love, 17696
Camy Baker's Love You Like a Sister, 17697
Can a Coal Scuttle Fly? 12263
Can Do, Jenny Archer, 9809(F)
The Can-Do Thanksgiving, 6150(F)
Can I Be Good? 5429(F)
Can I Have a Stegosaurus, Mom? Can I? Please!? 4166(F)
Can I Keep Him? 3748(F)
Can I Pray with My Eyes Open? 17516
Can It Rain Cats and Dogs? Questions and Answers About Weather, 20752
Can It Really Rain Frogs? 20759
Can of Worms, 10212(F)
Can We Save Them? Endangered Species of North America, 19393
Can You Catch a Falling Star? 18525

Can You Count Ten Toes? Count to 10 in 10 Different Languages, 432
Can You Count to a Googol? 606(F)
Can You Dance, Dalila? 5003(F)
Can You Do This, Old Badger? 1901(F)
Can You Feel the Thunder? 8751(F)
Can You Find Us? 18884
Can You Guess? 213(F)
Can You Guess Where We're Going? 3489(F)
Can You Hitch a Ride on a Comet? 18526
Can You Imagine? 12568
Can You Keep a Secret? 10121(F)
Can You See the Red Balloon? 162(F)
Can You See the Wind? 20667
Can You Spot the Leopard? 13936
Can You Top That? 4250(F)
Canada, 15564, 15575, 15578, 15579, 15584, 15585, 15586, 15589, 15591, 15595
Canada Celebrates Multiculturalism, 15587
The Canada Geese Quilt, 8723(F)
Canada in Pictures, 15569
Canals Are Water Roads, 21126
The Canary Prince, 10470(F)
Cancer, 17976, 18017
Candice and Edgar Bergen, 12177
A Candle for Grandpa, 17488
The Candlewick Book of Animal Tales, 1915(F)
The Candlewick Book of Bear Stories, 1916(F)
The Candlewick Book of Bedtime Stories, 642(F)
The Candlewick Book of Fairy Tales, 10429
The Candlewick Book of First Rhymes, 822
Candy Corn, 11711
The Candy Corn Contest, 6345(F)
The Candy Witch, 1322(F)
The Candystore Man, 3284(F)
A Cane in Her Hand, 8901(F)
Cannibal Animals, 18814
Cannibal in the Mirror, 17606
The Canning Season, 7402(F)
Canoe Days, 5360(F)
A Canoe Trip, 22262
Can't Sleep, 764(F)
Can't You Sleep, Little Bear? 798(F)
Canterbury Tales, 9085(F)
Canto Familiar, 11707
Canyons, 20320
Cap It Off with a Smile, 17613
Cape Town, 15003
Caps for Sale, 4319(F)
Caps, Hats, Socks, and Mittens, 4390(F)
Captain Abdul's Pirate School, 1377(F)
Captain Bob Sets Sail, 3410(F)
The Captain Contest, 10295(F)
Captain Grey, 6752(F)
Captain Kate, 9500(F)
Captain Kidd's Cat, 9913(F)
Captain Pajamas, 4350(F)

Captain Snap and the Children of Vinegar Lane, 4040(F)
Captain Underpants and the Attack of the Talking Toilets, 9963(F)
Captain Underpants and the Invasion of the Incredibly Naughty Cafeteria Ladies from Outer Space (and the Subsequent Assault of the Equally Evil Lunchroom Zombie Nerds), 9964(F)
Captain Underpants and the Perilous Plot of Professor Poopypants, 9965(F)
Captain Zap and the Evil Baron von Fishhead, 6240(F)
Captain's Command, 9678(F)
The Captain's Dog, 9440(F)
Captivating Cryptograms, 21887
The Captive, 9283(F)
Capturing Nature, 12190
Car Smarts, 18349
Car Wash, 3439(F)
The Car Washing Street, 3357(F)
Caravan, 4756(F)
Card Games for Children, 22230
Cardboard Boxes, 21422
Cardboard Tubes, 21422
Cardinal and Sunflower, 5372(F)
Cardinals, 19261
Cards for Kids, 22236
The Care and Feeding of Dragons, 8076(F)
The Care and Feeding of Fish, 1169(F)
Career Day, 5527(F)
Career Ideas for Kids Who Like Art, 17779
Career Ideas for Kids Who Like Computers, 17796
Career Ideas for Kids Who Like Math, 17761
Career Ideas for Kids Who Like Science, 17835
Career Ideas for Kids Who Like Sports, 17762
Career Ideas for Kids Who Like Talking, 17780
Career Ideas for Kids Who Like Writing, 17781
Careers for Women Who Love Sports, 17763
The Caribbean, 15706
The Caribbean and the Gulf of Mexico, 19830
A Caribbean Counting Book, 402(F)
Caribbean Dream, 4690(F)
A Caribou Alphabet, 107(F)
Caribou Girl, 11208
A Caribou Journey, 19156
Carisbrooke Castle, 15364
Carl Goes to Daycare, 2000(F)
Carl Lewis, 13663
Carl Linnaeus, 13316
Carl Makes a Scrapbook, 1105(F)
Carl Sagan, 13345, 13346
Carl Sandburg, 12587
Carla Goes to Court, 17011
Carlos and the Carnival, 5726(F)
Carlos and the Cornfield/Carlos y la Milpa de Maiz, 4839(F)
Carlos and the Skunk, 4328(F)

Carlos, Light the Farolito, 5783(F)
Carlotta's Kittens and the Club of Mysteries, 6985(F)
Carl's Afternoon in the Park, 2001(F)
Carl's Birthday, 5678(F)
Carl's Christmas, 2002(F)
Carl's Masquerade, 915(F)
Carnaval, 17333
Carnival, 17348
A Carnival of Animals, 9845(F)
Carnival of the Animals, 11776, 14124
Carnivorous Plants, 20251
  (Illus. by Kiyashi Shimizu), 20253
A Carol for Christmas, 5939(F)
Carol of the Brown King, 5849
Carolina Autumn, 8851(F)
Carolina Crow Girl, 8694(F)
Carolyn's Story, 17683
Carousel, 1089(F)
  (Illus. by Donald Crews), 3088(F)
The Carousel, 1524(F)
The Carp in the Bathtub, 7413(F)
Carpenter, 17785
Carrie's Crowd, 8268(F)
The Carrot Seed, 1320(F)
Carry On, Mr. Bowditch, 12086
Cars, 21304, 21599
  (Illus. by Jane Cradock-Watson), 5598
Cars and Trucks, 21322
Cars, Bikes, Trains, and Other Land Machines, 21283
Cars, Boats, Trains, and Planes, 21289
Cars! Cars! Cars! 5584(F)
Carter G. Woodson, 12822, 12823
Cartooning for Kids, 21583
The Cartoonist, 8582(F)
A Case for Jenny Archer, 6801(F)
The Case of the Absent Author, 6890(F)
The Case of the Backyard Treasure, 6592(F)
The Case of the Baker Street Irregular, 6991(F)
The Case of the Bashed-Up Bicycle, 6961(F)
The Case of the Cat's Meow, 6211(F)
The Case of the Climbing Cat, 6600(F)
The Case of the Dognapped Cat, 6901(F)
The Case of the Double Cross, 6211(F)
The Case of the Dumb Bells, 6211(F)
The Case of the Elevator Duck, 7158(F)
The Case of the Firecrackers, 7137(F)
The Case of the Furtive Firebug, 8352(F)
The Case of the Glacier Park Swallow, 6747(F)
The Case of the Goblin Pearls, 7138(F)
The Case of the Grand Canyon Eagle, 6748(F)
The Case of the Haunted Health Club, 6835(F)

The Case of the Hungry Stranger, 6211(F)
The Case of the Lion Dance, 7139(F)
The Case of the Lost Lookalike, 6836(F)
Case of the Missing Ankh, 6839(F)
The Case of the Missing Monkey, 6600(F)
The Case of the Mummified Pigs and Other Mysteries in Nature, 18595
The Case of the Scaredy Cats, 6211(F)
The Case of the Shrunken Allowance, 567(F)
The Case of the Vanishing Fishhook, 7188(F)
The Case of the Vanishing Villain, 6836(F)
The Case of the Wiggling Wig, 6891(F)
Casebook of a Private (Cat's) Eye, 7085(F)
Casey at the Bat, 12006
Casey Jones, 4638(F)
Casey Jones's Fireman, 11336
Casey Over There, 4801(F)
Casey's New Hat, 3154(F)
Casimir Pulaski, 13844
Cassandra — Live at Carnegie Hall! 9666(F)
Cassie Binegar, 7480(F)
Cassie Loves Beethoven, 7563(F)
Cassie's War, 9699(F)
Cast Two Shadows, 9247(F)
Castaways of the Flying Dutchman, 7818(F)
Castle, 14776
The Castle, 14766
Castle at War, 14774
Castle Diary, 9118(F)
The Castle in the Attic, 8212(F)
The Castle of Llyr, 7551(F)
The Castle of Pictures and Other Stories, 10488(F)
Castles, 14753, 14793
  (Illus. by Robert Andrew), 14785
  (Illus. by Stephen Biesty), 14789
Castles, Caves, and Honeycombs, 5128(F)
Cat and Cat-face, 1605(F)
Cat and Kit, 5292(F)
Cat and Mouse, 1825(F)
Cat and Mouse in the Night, 1826(F)
Cat and Mouse in the Snow, 1827(F)
Cat and Rat, 2893
The Cat Barked? 2505(F)
Cat Heaven, 1531(F)
A Cat in a Kayak, 1966(F)
The Cat in the Hat, 6640(F)
The Cat in the Hat Comes Back! 6640(F)
Cat Is Sleepy, 2300(F)
Cat Mummies, 14672
Cat Nap, 19105
A Cat of a Different Color, 7594(F)
Cat on Wheels, 1864(F)
Cat Poems, 11799
Cat Running, 8525(F)
The Cat Sat on the Mat, 5155(F)
Cat Tricks, 1780(F)

Cat Up a Tree, 4179(F)
  (Illus. by Stephen Mackey), 11794
The Cat Who Escaped from Steerage, 9595(F)
The Cat Who Lost His Purr, 1984(F)
The Cat Who Went to Heaven, 10409(F)
The Cat Who Wished to Be a Man, 7552(F)
Catbirds and Dogfish, 18650
Catch a Falling Star, 8744(F)
Catch Me If You Can, 18750
Catch Me If You Can! 6539(F)
Catch of the Day, 6952(F)
Catch Shorty by Rosie, 10331(F)
Catch That Hat! 1058(F)
The Catcher's Mask, 10296(F)
Catching Fire, 17810
Catching the Fire, 12302
Catching the Wild Waiyuuzee, 3950(F)
Caterpillar, 19554
The Caterpillar and the Polliwog, 2286(F)
Caterpillar Caterpillar, 19549
Caterpillarology, 19568
Caterpillars, 19562
Caterpillar's Wish, 2519(F)
The Caterpillow Fight, 2407(F)
Cathedral, 13947
The Cathedral Builders, 13949
Catherine and Laurence Anholt's Big Book of Families, 3508(F)
Catherine and the Lion, 1271(F)
Catholics in America, 17181
Catkin, 10399
Cats, 13923, 19090, 19915, 19923, 19927
  (Illus. by Gail Gibbons), 19921
  (Illus. by Shin Yoshino), 19928
Cats! 6225(F)
Cats Add Up! Math Activities by Marilyn Burns, 540(F)
Cats Are Like That, 6713(F)
The Cats' Burglar, 6563(F)
Cats, Cats, Cats! 1429(F)
Cat's Cradle, Owl's Eyes, 22006
Cats in the Zoo, 19111
The Cats Kids, 1956(F)
The Cat's Meow, 8115(F)
The Cats of Mrs. Calamari, 4322(F)
Cats of Myth, 10559
Cat's Play, 5196(F)
  (Illus. by Lisa Campbell Ernst), 3121(F)
Cats Vanish Slowly, 11815
Cattle Trails, 16351
Catty-Cornered, 8537(F)
Catwings, 7899(F)
Catwings Return, 7899(F)
Caught! 7026(F)
Caught in the Middle, 17661
Causes of Crime, 17087
Cave, 20392
Cave-In, 9273(F)
Cave Life, 18629
Cave of Falling Water, 9208(F)
The Cave Painter of Lascaux, 13937
Caves, 20380
The Cay, 8377(F)
The Cayuga, 15945

Cecily G. and the Nine Monkeys, 2623(F)
Celebrate! 17404, 17405
Celebrate! In Central America, 17406
Celebrate! Stories of the Jewish Holidays, 17451
Celebrate the 50 States! 15890
Celebrating Chinese New Year, 17367
Celebrating Earth Day, 17360
Celebrating Families, 3675(F)
Celebrating Hanukkah, 17473
Celebrating Kwanzaa, 17368
Celebrating Passover, 17474
Celebrating the Powwow, 15978
Celebration, 17393
Celebration! 5652(F)
A Celebration of Customs and Rituals of the World, 21960
Celebrations, 11835
Celebrations! 17378
Celebrations of African Heritage, 14906
Celebrations of Light, 17384
The Celery Stalks at Midnight, 9885(F)
Celeste, 1401(F)
Celeste Sails to Spain, 3277(F)
Celia and the Sweet, Sweet Water, 1460(F)
Celia's Island Journal, 4850
Celine Dion, 12375, 12376
Cell Wars, 18048
The Cellar in the Woods, 7082(F)
The Cello of Mr. O, 4631(F)
Cells Are Us, 18048
Celou Sudden Shout, Idaho, 1826, 9156(F)
Celtic Fairy Tales, 11022
  (Illus. by John D. Batten), 11003
Celtic Myths, 11011
The Celts, 15361
Cemetery Quilt, 5065(F)
Cendrillon, 10495
Censorship, 17156
Center Court Sting, 10297(F)
Centerburg Tales, 9929(F)
Centipede, 19446
Central and South America, 14331
The Central Asian States, 15435
Century Farm, 20069
A Century of Immigration, 1820–1924, 15870
A Certain Small Shepherd, 9713(F)
Cesar Chavez, 12826, 12827
Cesar's Amazing Journey, 2592(F)
Cézanne from A to Z, 12205
Chagall, 13905
A Chair for My Mother, 3948(F)
Chairs, Chairs, Chairs! 6254(F)
The Chalk Box Kid, 4914(F)
The Chalk Doll, 3843(F)
Challenger, 20972
The Challenger Disaster, 20958
Chameleon, 18751
The Chameleon Wore Chartreuse, 7777(F)
Chameleons, 18743, 18747
Chameleons Are Cool, 18745
Champion for Children's Health, 13134

Champion of Arbor Day, 13326
Chancy and the Grand Rascal, 9846(F)
Change the Locks, 8432(F)
Change Your Room, 21415
Changes, 4371(F), 4980(F)
Changes, Changes, 922(F)
Changes for Felicity, 9214(F)
Changes . . . for Girls, 18250
Changes for Kirsten, 9437(F)
Changes for Molly, 9691(F)
Changes for Samantha, 9630(F)
Changes in You and Me, 18250
Changing Colors, 18752
Changing Tunes, 8498(F)
The Changing White House, 16676
Chang's Paper Pony, 6274(F)
Chanticleer and the Fox, 11546
Chanukah in Chelm, 6067(F)
The Chanukkah Guest, 6083(F)
Chaparral, 20389
The Character in the Book, 1719(F)
Charge! 21386
Charlemagne, 13767
Charles Ball and American Slavery, 16273
Charles Barkley, 13512, 13513
Charles Darwin, 13264, 13265
Charles Dickens, 12527, 12529
Charles of the Wild, 2176(F)
Charles Schulz, 12301
Charley Waters Goes to Gettysburg, 16430
Charlie and Tess, 2164(F)
Charlie and the Chocolate Factory, 7694(F)
Charlie and the Great Glass Elevator, 7694(F)
Charlie Anderson, 5111(F)
Charlie Chaplin, 12367
Charlie Is a Chicken, 8370(F)
Charlie Muffin's Miracle Mouse, 7864(F)
Charlie Needs a Cloak, 4414(F)
Charlie Pippin, 8405(F)
Charlie Sifford, 13709
Charlie Wilcox, 9060(F)
Charlie Young Bear, 4863(F)
Charlie's Checklist, 2356(F)
Charlie's Run, 8456(F)
Charlotte, 16203
Charlotte in Giverny, 9053(F)
Charlotte Shakespeare and Annie the Great, 10076(F)
The Charlotte Stories, 4190(F)
Charlotte's Web, 8200(F)
Charmed Life, 7847(F)
Charro, 15599
Chasing Bears, 6842(F)
Chasing Redbird, 8618(F)
Chasing the Wind, 9039(F)
Chato and the Party Animals, 5724(F)
Chato's Kitchen, 2708(F)
Chatter with the Angels, 14125
Chatting, 3229(F)
Chaucer the Cat and the Animal Pilgrims, 10535
Chave's Memories/Los Recuerdos de Chave, 4637(F)
Cheat the Moon, 8450(F)

Check It Out, 13997
Checking Your Grammar, 14110
The Cheerios Counting Book, 506(F)
Cheetah, 19103
The Cheetah, 19085
Cheetahs, 19098
Chef Ki Is Serving Dinner! 17743
Chelsea Martin Turns Green, 8336(F)
Chemical Accident, 21042
Chemicals and Reactions, 20290
Cherish Me! 3452(F)
The Cherokee, 15988
The Cherokee Indians, 15938
Cherokee Nation, 16005
Cherokee Sister, 9154(F)
The Cherokees, 15992, 16046
Cherries and Cherry Pits, 3478(F)
Cherry Pies and Lullabies, 3855(F)
The Cheshire Cat and Other Eye-Popping Experiments on How We See the World, 20914
Cheshire Moon, 8883(F)
Chess for Children, 22172
Chessie, the Travelin' Man, 5269(F)
Chester A. Arthur, 13007, 13008
Chester Cricket's New Home, 2674(F)
Chester Cricket's Pigeon Ride, 2674(F)
Chester the Worldly Pig, 2567(F)
Chester's Barn, 5167(F)
Chester's Way, 4004(F)
Chestnut Cove, 4139(F)
Chestnut Dreams, 4387(F)
The Chewing Gum Book, 20137
The Chewing-Gum Rescue, 10460(F)
Chewy Louie, 1549(F)
The Cheyenne, 15926, 15950, 15990, 16012
Cheyenne Again, 9149(F)
The Cheyenne Indians, 16054
The Cheyennes, 16047
The Ch'i-lin Purse, 10751
Chibi, 5141
Chicago, 16573, 16584, 16586
Chicago and the Cat, 2310(F)
The Chicago Bulls Basketball Team, 22140
The Chick and the Duckling, 2125(F)
The Chick That Wouldn't Hatch, 6301(F)
Chicka Chicka Boom Boom, 89(F)
Chicken and Egg, 19302
The Chicken Cat, 2443(F)
Chicken Chuck, 2479(F)
The Chicken Doesn't Skate, 9910(F)
Chicken for a Day, 6535(F)
The Chicken-Fried Rat, 8580(F)
Chicken Little, 2216(F)
  (Illus. by Steven Kellogg), 2284(F)
The Chicken or the Egg? 19228
The Chicken Pox Panic, 7470(F)
The Chicken Salad Club, 3511(F)
The Chicken Sisters, 2534(F)
Chicken Socks, 11529
Chicken Soup for Little Souls, 4921(F), 5021(F)
Chicken Soup for the Kid's Soul, 10254
Chicken Soup with Rice, 4308(F)
Chicken Sunday, 5974(F)

The Chickenhouse House, 9383(F)
Chickens, 20063
Chickens Aren't the Only Ones, 4456(F)
Chickens! Chickens! 4271(F)
Chick's Daddy, 2712(F)
Chico and Dan, 7234(F)
Chico Mendes, 13323
Chidi Only Likes Blue, 4785(F)
Chief Crazy Horse, 12971
The Chief's Blanket, 4618(F)
Chihuahuas, 19976
Child Abuse, 17157, 17655, 17708
Child Bride, 9010(F)
Child Care Workers, 17750
Child of Faerie, Child of Earth, 6065(F)
Child of the May, 9125(F)
Child of the Silent Night, 13140
Child of the Warsaw Ghetto, 14811
Child of the Wolves, 7208(F)
Child Slavery in Modern Times, 17022
A Child Was Born, 17427
Children and War, 14843
Children from Australia to Zimbabwe, 14328
Children in Art, 13922
Children Just Like Me, 14343
The Children Next Door, 8163(F)
Children of Belize, 15686
The Children of Bolivia, 15745
The Children of China, 15092
  (Illus. by Matti Pitkanen), 15065
Children of Christmas, 9760(F)
Children of Clay, 16061
Children of Cuba, 15718
Children of Dominica, 15719
The Children of Egypt, 15502
Children of Guatemala, 15670
Children of Hawaii, 16816
The Children of India, 15104
The Children of Mauritania, 15027
The Children of Micronesia, 15237
The Children of Morocco, 14958
The Children of Nepal, 15174
Children of Promise, 15907
Children of Summer, 9024(F)
Children of the Civil War, 16423
Children of the Dust Bowl, 16488
Children of the Dust Days, 16459
Children of the Ecuadorean Highlands, 15723
Children of the Emancipation, 16419
Children of the Fire, 9614(F)
Children of the Midnight Sun, 16767
The Children of the Morning Light, 11269
Children of the Philippines, 15239
Children of the Relocation Camps, 14891
Children of the Settlement Houses, 16446
The Children of the Sierra Madre, 15646
Children of the Tlingit, 16817
Children of the Westward Trail, 16374
Children of the Wild West, 16305
Children of the World War II Home Front, 14892

Children of the Yukon, 6877(F)
Children of Vietnam, 15182
Children of Yucatan, 15647
The Children We Remember, 14809
The Children's Atlas of Lost Treasures, 14538
The Children's Atlas of World History, 14336
The Children's Book of Faith, 17174
The Children's Book of Kwanzaa, 17372
The Children's Book of Poems, Prayers and Meditations, 17517
The Children's Book of Pottery, 21534
The Children's Book of Virtues, 3022
Children's Book of Yoga, 18198
Children's Causes, 17148
The Children's Dictionary of Mythology, 11450
Children's Guide to Insects and Spiders, 19455
Children's History of the 20th Century, 14545
The Children's Homer, 11465
The Children's Hour, 11639
The Children's Illustrated Bible, 17282
The Children's Jewish Holiday Kitchen, 21724
The Children's Own Longfellow, 11640
Children's Plays for Creative Actors, 12012
Children's Prayers, 17511
The Children's Quick and Easy Cookbook, 21750
Children's Rights, 17044
Children's Songs, 14179
A Children's Zoo, 18946
A Child's Book of Angels, 7689(F)
A Child's Book of Art, 13911, 13912
A Child's Book of Blessings, 17520
A Child's Book of Lullabies, 737(F)
A Child's Book of Play in Art, 13913
A Child's Book of Prayer in Art, 17513
A Child's Book of Prayers, 17518, 17535
A Child's Calendar, 11987
A Child's California, 16785
A Child's Christmas in Wales (Illus. by Trina S. Hyman), 11853
  (Illus. by Trina S. Hyman), 11853
A Child's Day, 16476
A Child's Eye View of History, 14347
A Child's Garden of Verses, 11715
  (Illus. by Diane Goode), 11717
  (Illus. by Joanna Isles), 11716
  (Illus. by Tasha Tudor), 11714
A Child's Glacier Bay, 16770
Child's Guide to the Mass, 17221
A Child's Seasonal Treasury, 4468(F)
The Child's Story, 1123(F)
A Child's Treasury of Nursery Rhymes, 831(F)
Childtimes, 17562
Chile, 15746, 15760, 15784, 15790

Chile in Pictures, 15741
Chili-Chili-Chin-Chin, 2883(F)
Chills in the Night, 8179(F)
The Chimpanzee Family Book, 18995
Chimpanzees, 19003, 19005, 19014, 19017
Chimps Don't Wear Glasses, 2535(F)
China, 15056, 15057, 15059, 15060, 15061, 15062, 15068, 15071, 15080, 15082, 15088, 15089
China in Pictures, 15055
China's Bravest Girl, 10745
Chinatown, 5635(F)
The Chinese, 15076
The Chinese-American Experience, 17600
The Chinese Americans, 17553
The Chinese Book of Animal Powers, 21914
The Chinese Mirror, 10726
Chinese New Year, 17346, 17349, 17397
Chinese New Year's Dragon, 7371(F)
The Chinese Siamese Cat, 5428(F)
The Chinquapin Tree, 6897(F)
Chipmunk! 5241(F)
Chipmunk Family, 19192
The Chippewa, 16016
Chirping Crickets, 19427
The Chisholm Trail, 16361
The Chisholm Trail in American History, 16360
Chita's Christmas Tree, 5846(F)
Chitty Chitty Bang Bang, 7728(F)
The Chizzywink and the Alamagoozlum, 2260(F)
Chloe in the Know, 8595(F)
Chocolate, 20109, 20136
Chocolate, a Glacier Grizzly, 5165(F)
Chocolate by Hershey, 12899
Chocolate-Covered Ants, 9934(F)
The Chocolate-Covered-Cookie Tantrum, 4910(F)
Chocolate Fever, 9993(F)
Chocolatina, 1319(F)
The Choctaw, 15989
Chomp! 19751
Choosing a Career in Animal Care, 17848
Choosing Eyeglasses with Mrs. Koutris, 3134
Choosing Sides, 10320(F)
Choosing Up Sides, 10357(F)
Chop, Simmer, Season, 3037(F)
Chopsticks for My Noodle Soup, 15161
The Chosen Baby, 17690
Chris Mullin, 13552
Chris Rock, 12455
Chris Webber, 13579
Christa McAuliffe, 12136, 12137
Christabel Bielenberg and Nazi Germany, 15331
Christian Church, 17232
Christian Festivals, 17403
Christie and Company in the Year of the Dragon, 7002(F)
Christina Aguilera, 12343

Christina Katerina and Fats and the Great Neighborhood War, 3996(F)
Christina Katerina and the Great Bear Train, 3643(F)
Christina's Ghost, 8221(F)
Christmas, 17410
The Christmas Adventure of Space Elf Sam, 5958(F)
The Christmas Angel, 5942(F)
Christmas Around the World, 17423, 17426
Christmas at Mud Flat, 5926(F)
The Christmas Bear, 5927(F)
A Christmas Carol (Illus. by Quentin Blake), 9720(F)
  (Illus. by Carter Goodrich), 9721(F)
  (Illus. by Carol Heyer), 5857(F)
  (Illus. by Trina S. Hyman), 9718(F)
  (Illus. by Lisbeth Zwerger), 9719(F)
A Christmas Celebration, 17424
The Christmas Collection, 9732(F)
The Christmas Crocodile, 5754(F)
Christmas Decorations Kids Can Make, 21472
The Christmas Dolls, 5908(F)
The Christmas Drum, 5845(F)
Christmas Fairy Tales, 10477(F)
Christmas for 10, 5812(F)
Christmas Fun (Illus. by Judith Hoffman Corwin), 21423
  (Illus. by Maggie Downer), 21468
Christmas Gif', 17430
The Christmas Gift, 5853(F)
Christmas in Canada, 15570
Christmas in Colonial and Early America, 17411
Christmas in Greece, 17412
Christmas in Heaven, 8852(F)
Christmas in Switzerland, 17413
Christmas in the Big House, Christmas in the Quarters, 16262
Christmas in the Forest, 5752(F)
Christmas in the Stable, 5863(F)
Christmas Is Coming, 11830
Christmas Is Coming! 5877(F)
The Christmas Knight, 10967
Christmas Lights, 5814(F)
Christmas Long Ago from A to Z, 70(F)
A Christmas Memory, 9712(F)
The Christmas Menorahs, 17457
The Christmas Miracle of Jonathan Toomey, 5957(F)
The Christmas Orange, 5824(F)
Christmas Ornaments Kids Can Make, 21473
The Christmas Party, 5742(F)
Christmas Play Favorites for Young People, 12023
Christmas Poems, 11836
The Christmas Present Mystery, 6963(F)
A Christmas Promise, 5776(F)
The Christmas Puppy, 7228(F)
The Christmas Rat, 6753(F)
The Christmas Ship, 5886(F)
Christmas Soul, 17414
A Christmas Star, 5836(F)

A Christmas Star Called Hannah, 5818(F)
Christmas Stories for the Very Young, 5782(F)
The Christmas Story, 5780(F), 5923
The Christmas Tree/El Arbol de Navidad, 5741(F)
A Christmas Tree in the White House, 5838(F)
Christmas Tree Memories, 5743(F)
The Christmas Tree Tangle, 5873(F)
Christmas Trolls, 5759(F)
The Christmas We Moved to the Barn, 5795(F)
Christmas with Anne and Other Holiday Stories, 9749(F)
Christmas with Ida Early, 9709(F)
Christmas with Teddy Bear, 5872(F)
Christoph Wants a Party, 5707(F)
Christopher, 13768
Christopher Changes His Name, 4294(F)
Christopher Columbus, 12095, 16083
Christopher Davis's Best Year Yet, 8863(F)
Christopher Reeve, 12450
Christy Mathewson, 13472
Chrysanthemum, 2193(F)
Chubbo's Pool, 2368(F)
Chuck and Danielle, 7707(F)
Chuck Close, Up Close, 12211
Chuck Murphy's Black Cat White Cat, 220(F)
Chuck Norris, 12427
Chuck Yeager Breaks the Sound Barrier, 12156
Chugga-Chugga Choo Choo, 5580(F)
The Church, 14767
The Church Mice and the Ring, 2543(F)
Cider Apples, 1432(F)
Cinco de Mayo, 15607, 17398
Cinder Edna, 10437(F)
Cinder-Elly, 10465
The Cinder-Eyed Cats, 1516(F)
Cinderella, 10411(F), 10519(F)
  (Illus. by Gordon Fitchett), 10500(F)
  (Illus. by Loek Koopmans), 10475(F)
  (Illus. by P. J. Lynch), 10429
  (Illus. by Debrah Santini), 10491(F),
  15607
Cinderella, Puss in Boots, and Other Favorite Tales, 10476(F)
Cinderella Skeleton, 10496(F)
Cinderella's Rat, 1407(F)
Cinderellis and the Glass Hill, 10445(F)
Cinderhazel, 6024(F)
Cindy Ellen, 10452(F)
Cinnamon's Day Out, 2638(F)
Circle Dogs, 333(F)
The Circle of Days, 17203
Circle of Fire, 7345(F)
Circle of Love, 9421(F)
A Circle of Seasons, 11969
A Circle of Silver, 8945(F)
Circle of Thanks, 1163(F)
The Circle Opens, 8015(F)

Circle Song, 671(F)
Circles, 356(F)
  (Illus. by Richard Maccabe), 20605
Circles, Triangles, and Squares, 334(F)
The Circulatory System, 18092, 18094
Circus, 3115, 14269
Circus! A Pop-Up Adventure, 14268
Circus Family Dog, 1964(F)
The Circus Lunicus, 8096(F)
The Circus of Mystery, 6837(F)
Circus of the Wolves, 5152(F)
Circus 1-2-3, 455(F)
Circus Shapes, 347(F)
Circuses, 14270
Cissie Palmer, 13174
Cities and Citizens, 14704
Cities and Towns, 16973
Cities in the Sky, 21017
Cities of Splendor, 10533
The City, 14768
City, 14727
A City Album, 3388
City at Night, 16971
City by Numbers, 479
The City by the Bay, 16768
City Kids, 11608
City of Angels, 16790
The City of Dragons, 1709(F)
City of Gold and Lead, 10160(F)
City Pig, 2811(F)
City Seen from A to Z, 62(F)
A City Under the Sea, 19671
City! Washington, D.C., 16660
Citybook, 3399(F)
Citymaze! 21869
Civil Rights, 17041
Civil Rights Marches, 17559
The Civil Rights Movement for Kids, 16523
Civil Rights Pioneer, 12787
Civil War, 16409, 16436
The Civil War, 16418
Civil War Artist, 16421
The Civil War at Sea, 16439
Civil War Cooking, 16403
A Civil War Drummer Boy, 9467
The Civil War, 1860–1865, 16399
The Civil War for Kids, 16414
Civil War Forts, 16395
Civil War Soldiers, 16424
Civilizations of Peru, Before 1535, 15763
Clambake, 16022
Clams All Year, 4118(F)
Clancy's Cabin, 6958(F)
Clara and the Bookwagon, 6454(F)
Clara Ann Cookie, 3968(F)
Clara Ann Cookie, Go to Bed! 819(F)
Clara Barton, 13135
Clara Hale, 13158
Clara Schumann, 12338
Clare and Her Shadow, 3805(F)
Clarence Goes Out West and Meets a Purple Horse, 1723(F)
Clarice Bean, Guess Who's Babysitting? 4107(F)
Clarice Bean, That's Me, 4930(F)
Clarinets, 14222

Clash of Cultures, Prehistory–1638, 16102
Class Act, 21826(F)
Class Clown, 10081(F)
A Class Play with Ms. Vanilla, 6327(F)
Class President, 10082(F)
Classic Brainteasers, 21866
The Classic Fairy Tales, 10473(F)
Classic Horse and Pony Stories, 7288(F)
Classic Poems to Read Aloud, 11535
Classic Poetry, 11683
The Classic Treasury of Children's Prayers, 17519
Classical Kids, 14581
Classical Rome, 14716
The Classroom at the End of the Hall, 10179(F)
Claude Monet, 12264, 12265, 12266
Claude the Dog, 5819(F)
Clay, 21530
Clay Boy, 11088
The Clay Ladies, 3020(F)
Clay Modeling, 21536
Clean Enough, 3203(F)
Clean House, 9871(F)
Clean-Sweep Campers, 20593
The Clean-up Crew, 8340(F)
Clean Your Room, Harvey Moon! 4121(F)
Cleaning the House, 21161
The Clearing, 6974(F)
A Clearing in the Forest, 9374(F)
Cleo the Cat, 5350(F)
Cleopatra, 13773, 13774
    (Illus. by Diane Stanley), 13775
Cleopatra VII, 8964(F)
The Clever Boy and the Terrible, Dangerous Animal, 11197
Clever Cat, 1968(F)
The Clever Cowboy, 1364(F)
Clever Crow, 5180(F)
Clever Gretchen, 1597(F)
Clever Katya, 11090
Clever Quicksolve Whodunit Puzzles, 7091(F)
Clever Raccoons, 18958
Clever Tortoise, 10695
Cleversticks, 5470(F)
Click! 21803
Click! A Book About Cameras and Taking Pictures, 21798
Click, Clack, Moo, 1989(F)
Clickety Clack, 4320(F)
Cliff-Hanger, 7058(F)
Clifford at the Circus, 1863(F)
Clifford Goes to Hollywood, 1863(F)
Clifford Makes a Friend, 6223(F)
Clifford Takes a Trip, 1863(F)
Clifford the Big Red Dog, 1863(F)
Clifford the Small Red Puppy, 1863(F)
Clifford's Good Deeds, 1863(F)
Clifford's Halloween, 5982(F)
Clifford's Tricks, 1863(F)
Climb into My Lap, 11545
Climbing Jacob's Ladder, 17295
Climbing onto the Horse's Back, 20019
Climbing Tree Frogs, 18714

Clinging Sea Horses, 19705
Clipper Ship, 21364
Clippers and Whaling Ships, 21369
Cliques, Phonies, and Other Baloney, 17728
A Cloak for the Dreamer, 8651(F)
The Clock (Illus. by Maddox Kelly), 9267(F)
    (Illus. by Toby Welles), 20644
Clocks and Rhythms, 20652
Clockwork, 8029(F)
Cloning, 18035
Close, Closer, Closest, 355
Close Encounters, 18414
Cloth, 21184
Clothes, 21166
    (Illus. by Sara Lynn), 208(F)
Clothes and Crafts in Ancient Aztec Times, 15613
Clothes and Crafts in Ancient Egypt, 14607
Clothes and Crafts in Ancient Greece, 14707
Clothes and Crafts in Roman Times, 14746
Clothes and Crafts in the Middle Ages, 14760
Clothes and Crafts in Victorian Times, 14358
The Cloud Book, 4415(F)
Cloud Cuckoo Land, 1356(F)
Cloud Dance, 20661
Cloud Eyes, 11262
The Cloudmakers, 4814(F)
Clouds, 20771
Clouds of Glory, 17253
Clouds of Terror, 9452(F)
Cloudy Day Sunny Day, 6292(F)
Cloudy Days, 6242(F)
Cloudy with a Chance of Meatballs, 980(F)
The Clover and the Bee, 20232
The Clover County Carrot Contest, 6386(F)
The Clovis Caper, 10006(F)
Clown, 909(F)
The Clown of God, 5798(F)
Club Earth, 10183(F)
The Clue of the Left-Handed Envelope, 7080(F)
Clyde Tombaugh and the Search for Planet X, 13350
Coach John and His Soccer Team, 3135(F)
A Coal Miner's Bride, 9519(F)
Coast to Coast with Alice, 9561(F)
Coaster, 8424(F)
Coasts, 20382
Coasts and Shores, 19865
A Coat for the Moon and Other Jewish Tales, 11167
Cobras, 18767
A Cobtown Christmas, 9327(F)
The Cobweb Christmas, 5786(F)
Cock-a-doodle-doo! Barnyard Hullabaloo, 1740(F)
Cock-a-Doodle Dudley, 2565(F)
Cock-A-Doodle-Moo! 2512(F)
The Cock, the Mouse, and the Little Red Hen, 10957

Cockroach, 19447
Cockroach Cooties, 7140(F)
Cockroaches, 19431
Cockroaches, Cocoons, and Honeycombs, 19473
Cocoa Ice, 8250(F)
Coconut Kind of Day, 11614
The Code of the Drum, 9491(F)
The Code Talkers, 14844
Cody, 10286(F)
Cody and Quinn, Sitting in a Tree, 6444(F)
Cody Coyote Cooks! 21738
Cody Unplugged, 9833(F)
Cody's Secret Admirer, 9834(F)
Coffin on a Case, 6778(F)
The Coin Counting Book, 608(F)
The Cold and Hot Winter, 8307(F)
Cold Feet, 7701(F)
Cold Little Duck, Duck, Duck, 2573(F)
Colin Powell, 12951, 12952, 12953, 12956
Colin Powell, 12949, 12950, 12954
Collecting, 21806
Collecting Baseball Cards, 21808
Collecting Baseball Memorabilia, 21809
Collecting Basketball Cards, 21810
Collecting Comic Books, 21811
Collecting Fossils, 14460
Collecting Gems and Minerals, 20567
A Collection for Kate, 417(F)
The Collector of Moments, 3985(F)
Colliding with Chris, 1219(F)
Colombia, 15729, 15748, 15762, 15765
Colombia in Pictures, 15727
Colonial America, 16178
Colonial American Crafts, 16106
Colonial American Craftspeople, 16179
Colonial American Home Life, 16181
Colonial American Medicine, 16180
Colonial and Revolution Songbook, 14168
Colonial Cooking, 16112
Colonial Crafts, 16142
Colonial Days, 16148
Colonial Kids, 16100
Colonial Life, 16143
Colonial People, 16133
Colonial Places, 16134
A Colonial Quaker Girl, 16222
Colonial Times, 1600–1700, 16160
A Colonial Town, 16142
Colonial Williamsburg, 16175
The Colonies, 16176
The Colony, 7648(F)
Color, 20864
The Color Box, 265(F)
Color Dance, 279(F)
Color Farm, 266(F)
Color Fun, 261
Color Me a Rhyme, 11989
Color Me Criminal, 7125(F)
Color Me Dark, 9592(F)
The Color of My Words, 8715(F)
A Color Sampler, 292

Color Surprises, 285(F)
The Color Wizard, 6221(F)
Color Zoo, 267(F)
Colorado, 16596, 16599, 16600,
  16607
The Colorado River, 15898
Colorado Summer, 7159(F)
Colors (Illus. by Shirley Hughes),
  277(F)
  (Illus. by Svjetlan Junakovic),
  1570(F)
  (Illus. by Jan Pienkowski), 286(F)
  (Illus. by P. M. Valet), 271
Colors Everywhere, 273(F)
Colors of Japan, 15130
Colors of Mexico, 15640
The Colors of My Jewish Year,
  6073(F)
Colors of the Navajo, 15917
The Colors of Us, 3258(F)
Colossal Fossils, 21831
The Colosseum, 14715
Columbus Day, 17335, 17354
  (Illus. by Rick Hanson), 17382
The Comanche, 15927
The Comanche Indians, 16011
Comanche Song, 9439(F)
Combines, 20071, 21253
Come a Tide, 3290(F)
Come All You Brave Soldiers, 16193
Come Along, Daisy! 2692(F)
Come and See, 5879(F)
Come Away with Me, 9579(F)
Come Back, Amelia Bedelia, 6566(F)
Come Back, Jack! 954(F)
Come Down Now, Flying Cow!
  6596(F)
Come for a Ride on the Ghost Train,
  1228(F)
Come Here, Cat, 6543(F)
Come Home with Me, 3245(F)
Come Look with Me, 13878, 13879,
  13880
Come Meet Muffin! 2545(F)
Come Morning, 16247(F)
Come On, Rain! 3208(F)
Come Sing, Jimmy Jo, 7490(F)
Come! Sit! Speak! 6659(F)
Come Sunday, 3186(F)
Come to the Fair, 3289(F)
Come with Me, 11663
The Comeback Challenge, 10298(F)
Comes a Wind, 4352(F)
Comets, 18508
Comets and Meteor Showers, 18529
Comets and Meteors, 18505
Comets and Shooting Stars, 18521
Comets, Asteroids, and Meteorites,
  18393
Comets, Meteors, and Asteroids,
  18527
Comet's Nine Lives, 1856(F)
The Comic Adventures of Old Moth-
  er Hubbard and Her Dog, 838
A Coming Evil, 8169(F)
Coming Home, 12551, 13455
Coming of Age, 9990(F), 17400
The Coming of Night, 10711
Coming Out Right, 12089
Coming Through the Blizzard,
  5922(F)

Coming to America, (Illus. by Mar-
  garet Sanfilippo), 9594(F),
  17555,
  (Illus. by Susannah Ryan), 17578
Commander Toad and the Voyage
  Home, 10249(F)
Commodore Perry in the Land of the
  Shogun, 15117
Common Colds, 17999
Common Ground, 4383(F)
The Commonwealth of Independent
  States, 15428
Communicable Diseases, 17964
Communicating on the Internet,
  21233
Communications, 21232
Competition Fever, 10293(F)
The Complete Adventures of Peter
  Rabbit, 2597(F)
The Complete Book of Children's
  Activities, 21467
The Complete Dog Book for Kids,
  19943
The Complete Fairy Tales of Charles
  Perrault, 10876
The Complete Grimm's Fairy Tales,
  10893
Complete Nonsense Book of Edward
  Lear, 11884
The Complete Poems to Solve, 11724
The Complete Story of the Three
  Blind Mice, 852(F)
The Completed Hickory Dickory
  Dock, 823
A Completely Different Place,
  7993(F)
The Composite Guide to Golf, 22020
The Composite Guide to Lacrosse,
  22040
The Composite Guide to Tennis,
  22313
The Composition, 9139(F)
Compost! 3169
Compost Critters, 19460
Computer Animation, 21237
Computer Animator, 17791
Computer Fun for Everyone, 21224
Computer Fun Halloween, 17448
Computer Fun Math, 21228
Computer Fun Science, 21228
The Computer Nut, 10156(F)
Computers, 21238
Computers All Around Us, 21196
Computers and School, 21197
Comus, 7794(F)
Con Mi Hermano/With My Brother,
  3859(F)
Concord and Lexington, 16208
Concrete Mixers, 5564
Conestoga Wagons, 16286
Confederate Generals of the Civil
  War, 12652
A Confederate Girl, 9466
The Confederate Ladies of Rich-
  mond, 16388
Confetti, 11657
Congressional Committees, 17121
Connecticut, 16687, 16714
The Connecticut Colony, 16118
A Connecticut Yankee in King
  Arthur's Court, 8161(F)

Conquering the Grand Canyon,
  16636
Conquerors and Explorers, 14569
Conservation, 16956
Consider the Lemming, 11919
Constellations, 18557
Constitutional Amendments, 17055
Construction, 13202, 21120
Construction Zone, 5574
Contemplating Your Bellybutton,
  18232
The Contest, 11091
The Contrary Kid, 4112(F)
Contrary Mary, 2253(F)
Cook-a-Doodle-Doo! 2724(F)
The Cookcamp, 8781(F), 8783(F)
The Cookie Company, 8178(F)
Cookie Count, 3408(F)
Cookie Fun, 21686
Cookie McCorkle and the Case of the
  Emerald Earrings, 6785(F)
Cookie McCorkle and the Case of the
  Polka-Dot Safecracker, 6785(F)
Cookie Shapes, 330(F)
The Cookie-Store Cat, 2646(F)
Cookies, 16949
Cookies and Crutches, 6304(F)
Cooking, 21720
Cooking a Meal, 14349
Cooking on a Stick, 21749
Cooking on Nineteenth Century
  Whaling Ships, 15875
Cooking on the Lewis and Clark
  Expedition, 16080
Cooking the African Way, 21723
Cooking the Australian Way, 21700
Cooking the Caribbean Way, 21711
Cooking the Chinese Way, 21754
Cooking the English Way, 21706
Cooking the French Way, 21743
Cooking the German Way, 21728
Cooking the Greek Way, 21742
Cooking the Hungarian Way, 21704
Cooking the Indian Way, 21718
Cooking the Italian Way, 21676
Cooking the Japanese Way, 21748
Cooking the Korean Way, 21682
Cooking the Mexican Way, 21685
Cooking the Polish Way, 21757
Cooking the Russian Way, 21731
Cooking the South American Way,
  21729
Cooking the Swiss Way, 21708
Cooking the Thai Way, 21705
Cooking the Vietnamese Way, 21725
The Cook's Family, 10023(F)
Cool Ali, 1489(F)
Cool as a Cucumber, Hot as a Pep-
  per, 20098
Cool Careers for Girls in Computers,
  17794
Cool Careers for Girls in Engineer-
  ing, 17795
Cool Careers for Girls in Food,
  17759
Cool Careers for Girls in Health,
  17804
Cool Careers for Girls in Sports,
  17760
Cool Careers for Girls with Animals,
  17855

Cool Chemistry, 20289
The Cool Crazy Crickets, 8279(F)
The Cool Hot Rod and Other Electrifying Experiments on Energy and Matter, 20827
Cool Math, 20588
Cool Melons Turn to Frogs! The Life and Poems of Issa, 12556
Coolies, 4895(F)
Coot Club, 7016(F)
Copier Creations, 21614
Coping with Allergies, 17996
Coping with Asthma, 18003
Coping with Braces and Other Orthodontic Work, 18185
Coping with Cancer, 17950
Coping with Death and Grief, 17709
Coping with Natural Disasters, 20295
Coping with Special-Needs Classmates, 17921
Coppelia, 14283(F)
Copper, 20276
The Copper Lady, 6599(F)
The Copper Tin Cup, 3876(F)
Copper-Toed Boots, 9534(F)
The Copper Treasure, 9084(F)
Copy Me, Copycub, 2058(F)
Coral Reef, 19655, 19659, 19666, 19668
Coral Reefs, 19665, 19670
Corduroy, 2100(F)
Corduroy's Halloween, 6006(F)
Coretta Scott King, 12735, 12737, 12738
Corking, 21644
Corn, 20180, 20185
Corn Belt Harvest, 20170
Corn Is Maize, 20169
Corn — On and Off the Cob, 20173
The Corn Raid, 9187(F)
Cornflakes, 11712
Cornhusk, Silk, and Wishbones, 21655
Corrie's Secret Pal, 2962(F)
Corvette, 21305
Cosmic Debris, 18375
The Cosmic Joker, 21917
Cosmic Journeys, 20946
Cosmic Science, 18424
Cosmo and the Robot, 1479(F)
Cosmo Zooms, 2222(F)
Costa Rica, 15662, 15689, 15690
Costa Rica in Pictures, 15660
Costume Crafts, 21545
A Costume for Noah, 6120(F)
Costumes, 21550
Cote d'Ivoire, 15031
Côte d'Ivoire, 15048
Cote d'Ivoire (Ivory Coast) in Pictures, 15024
Cottontail Rabbits, 19196
Coubertin's Olympics, 22250
Cougar, 7764(F), 19078
Cougar Cove, 7251(F)
Cougars, 19112, 19113
"Could Be Worse!" 2974(F)
Count! 435(F)
Count and See, 465(F)
Count Karlstein, 8030(F)
Count on Pablo, 418(F)
Count Silvernose, 9052(F)

Count Us In, 562(F)
Count Your Way Through Brazil, 15740
Count Your Way Through China, 15067
Count Your Way Through France, 15309
Count Your Way Through Germany, 15325
Count Your Way Through Greece, 15385
Count Your Way Through India, 15103
Count Your Way Through Ireland, 15350
Count Your Way Through Israel, 15522
Count Your Way Through Italy, 15384
Count Your Way Through Japan, 15125
Count Your Way Through Russia, 15420
Count Your Way Through the Arab World, 15547
Countess Veronica, 8797(F)
Counting and Numbers, 399(F)
Counting Book, 411(F)
Counting Crocodiles, 2688(F)
Counting Heads, and More, 17116
Counting Is for the Birds, 19260
Counting Kids, 447(F)
Counting Kisses, 715(F)
Counting Leopard's Spots, 10709
Counting on Calico, 595(F)
Counting on the Woods, 499
Counting Our Way to Maine, 584(F)
Counting Sheep, 445(F)
Counting to Christmas, 5933(F)
Countries, 14572
Country Angel Christmas, 5799(F)
The Country Artist, 12579
The Country Bunny and the Little Gold Shoes, 5968(F)
Country Fair, 3082(F)
Country Mouse Cottage, 1013(F)
The Countryside, 14769
Courage at Indian Deep, 7099(F)
Courage of Sarah Noble, 9189(F)
The Courage Seed, 4811(F)
Court Duel, 8107(F)
The Court of the Stone Children, 7640(F)
Cousin Ruth's Tooth, 4224(F)
Cousins, 8679(F), 8681(F)
The Cousins Club, 8689(F)
Cousins in the Castle, 7115(F)
The Cove of Cork, 9330(F)
A Covered Wagon Girl, 16316
Covered Wagons, Bumpy Trails, 4705(F)
A Cow, a Bee, a Cookie, and Me, 3221(F)
Cow Moo Me, 5319(F)
The Cow of No Color, 10567
The Cow-Tail Switch, 10659
The Cow That Went Oink, 2513(F)
The Cow Who Wouldn't Come Down, 1274(F)
Cowardly Clyde, 2566(F)
Cowboy, 16310, 16335

The Cowboy ABC, 31
The Cowboy and the Black-Eyed Pea, 10439(F)
Cowboy Baby, 3199(F)
Cowboy Bunnies, 2400(F)
Cowboy Charlie, 12300
Cowboy Cooking, 16312
Cowboy Country, 2969(F)
Cowboy Dreams, 621(F)
The Cowboy Ghost, 7008(F)
Cowboy Kid, 669(F)
The Cowboy Kid, 8147(F)
A Cowboy Named Ernestine, 4291(F)
Cowboy on the Steppes, 15093
Cowboy Up! 6226(F)
Cowboy with a Camera, Erwin E. Smith, 16386
Cowboys, 3401(F), 16356
    (Illus. by George Ancona), 16900
    (Illus. by Douglas Gorsline), 16309
Cowboys and Cow Towns of the Wild West, 16362
The Cowboy's Handbook, 17741
Cowboys of the Frontier, 16379
Cowboys of the Wild West, 16306
Cowgirl, 3299
Cowpokes, 2976(F)
Cows, 20048, 20064
The Cows Are Going to Paris, 2293(F)
Cows Can't Fly, 2498(F)
Cows in the Kitchen, 9818(F)
The Coyote, 19138
Coyote, 11266, 19142
Coyote and the Fire Stick, 11254
Coyote and the Grasshoppers, 11230
Coyote and the Laughing Butterflies, 11310
Coyote Attacks, 19134
Coyote Autumn, 7319(F)
Coyote Goes Walking, 11289
Coyote in Love, 11232
Coyote in Love with a Star, 11227
Coyote Makes Man, 11297
Coyote Places the Stars, 11311
Coyote Steals the Blanket, 11302
Coyote Stories for Children, 11304
Coyotes, 19127, 19146
A Cozy Place, 4044(F)
Crab, 19680
The Crab Man, 4862(F)
Crab Moon, 5268(F)
Crabby Cratchitt, 2956(F)
Crabs, 19677
Crack and Cocaine Drug Dangers, 17885
A Crack in the Clouds and Other Poems, 11624
The Crack-of-Dawn Walkers, 3692(F)
Cracked Corn and Snow Ice Cream, 20074
Cracker Jackson, 8409(F)
Cracking the Wall, 17042
Cradles in the Trees, 19222
Craft Fun! 21499
Crafts for All Seasons, 21474
Crafts for Christian Values, 21475
Crafts for Easter, 21476
Crafts for Halloween, 21477

Crafts for Hanukkah, 17483
Crafts for Kids Who Are Wild About Deserts, 21478
Crafts for Kids Who Are Wild About Dinosaurs, 21479
Crafts for Kids Who Are Wild About Oceans, 21480
Crafts for Kids Who Are Wild About Outer Space, 21481
Crafts for Kids Who Are Wild About Polar Life, 21482
Crafts for Kids Who Are Wild About Reptiles, 21483
Crafts for Kwanzaa, 5647
Crafts for Valentine's Day, 21484
Crafts from Your Favorite Bible Stories, 21485
Crafts from Your Favorite Fairy Tales, 21486
Crafts to Celebrate God's Creation, 21487
Crafts to Make in the Fall, 21488
Crafts to Make in the Spring, 21489
Crafts to Make in the Winter, 21490
Crafty Canines, 19137
Cranberries, 20079
Cranberry Easter, 5965(F)
Cranberry Valentine, 6166(F)
The Crane Girl, 10406(F)
The Crane Wife, 10811
Cranes, Dump Trucks, Bulldozers and Other Building Machines, 21249
Crash, 7519(F)
Crashed, Smashed, and Mashed, 21309
Crashes and Collisions, 22079
Crawdad Creek, 4533(F)
Crayfish, 19675
Crayons, 21066
Crayons and Computers, 21591
The Crazy Christmas Angel Mystery, 9744(F)
The Crazy Crawler Crane and Other Very Short Truck Stories, 5560(F)
Crazy Eights and Other Card Games, 22229
Crazy Horse's Vision, 9147(F)
Crazy Jacob, 8948(F)
Crazy Lady! 8605(F)
Crazy Weekend, 7076(F)
Create! The Best Crafts and Activities from Many Lands, 21414
Creating and Publishing Web Pages on the Internet, 21234
Creating the Constitution, 1787, 16192
Creating with Mosaics, 21436
Creating with Papier-Mâché, 21629
The Creation, 17290
Creation, 10604
Creativity, 4047(F)
Creators, 12159
Creature Crossing, 7253(F)
Credit Cards and Checks, 16923
The Creek, 16014
    (Illus. by Katherine Ace), 15965
Creeps from the Deep, 19651
Creepy Castle, 919(F)
The Creepy Computer Mystery, 6455(F)

A Creepy Countdown, 470(F)
Creepy, Crawly Baby Bugs, 19465
Creepy-Crawly Birthday, 5696(F)
Creepy Cuisine, 21722
Creepy Riddles, 21823
Creepy, Spooky Science, 18329
The Cremation of Sam McGee, 11694
Crescent Moon, 9529(F)
Cretaceous Dinosaur World, 14422
The Cricket in Times Square, 8081(F)
Cricket Never Does, 11823
The Cricket Warrior, 10742
Cricketology, 19483
Crickets and Grasshoppers, 19476
The Cricket's Cage, 10747
Crickwing, 1917(F)
Crictor, 2769(F)
Crime Detection, 17076
Crime-Fighting, 17067
Crime Science, 17064
Crime-Solving Science Projects, 17079
Crinkleroot's Book of Animal Tracking, 18800
Crinkleroot's Guide to Knowing Animal Habitats, 18905
Crinkleroot's Guide to Knowing the Birds, 4374
Crinkleroot's Guide to Knowing the Trees, 20193
Crinkleroot's Guide to Walking in Wild Places, 4375
Crinkleroot's Nature Almanac, 18576
Crinkleroot's 25 Birds Every Child Should Know, 19216
Crinkleroot's 25 Fish Every Child Should Know, 19695
Crinkleroot's Visit to Crinkle Cove, 4376(F)
Crises at the Olympics, 22252
Crispin, 1121(F)
Crispin the Terrible, 1423(F)
Cristina Saralegui, 12464
Critter Day, 6689(F)
Croc and Gator Attacks, 18702
Crocky Dilly, 1604(F)
Crocodile Beat, 2265(F)
The Crocodile Family Book, 18700
Crocodile Smile, 14188
Crocodiles, 18703, 18708
Crocodiles and Alligators, 18709
Crocodiles, Camels and Dugout Canoes, 12071
Crocodile's Masterpiece, 2779(F)
The Crocodilians, 18707
Croco'Nile, 4658(F)
The Crooked Apple Tree, 3222(F)
Crookjaw, 1064(F)
Crosby, 4000(F)
Cross a Bridge, 21130
Cross-Country Cat, 1913(F)
Crossing Jordan, 8284(F)
Crossing the Delaware, 16209
Crossing the Starlight Bridge, 9170(F)
Crossing the Trestle, 8524(F)
Crow Boy, 5545(F)
Crow Chief, 11239
The Crow Indians, 16071

Crown Duel, 8108(F)
Crumbling Castle, 7787(F)
The Crusades, 14754
Crustaceans, 19679
Cry Baby, 3549(F)
Cry of the Benu Bird, 10669
The Cry of the Crow, 7193(F)
The Cry of the Wolf, 7167(F)
Crystal, 19801
The Crystal Garden, 8294(F)
The Crystal Heart, 10842
The Crystal Mountain, 10610
The Crystal Pool, 10575
Crystals and Crystal Gardens You Can Grow, 20573
Cuba, 15698, 15712, 15713, 15721
Cuba in Pictures, 15705
The Cuban Americans, 17560
Cuban Kids, 15693
Cubans in America, 17582
Cubes, Cones, Cylinders, and Spheres, 335
Cubism, 13881
The Cuckoo Child, 7236(F)
Cuckoo/Cucu, 11401
The Cuckoo's Child, 8650(F)
Culebra Cut, 9133(F)
Cult Awareness, 17190
Cultures and Civilizations, 14355
Cultures of the World, 15737
Cumbayah, 14148
A Cup of Starshine, 11532
Curious Cats, 11775
Curious Critters, 1802(F)
Curious George, 2624(F)
Curious George and the Dump Truck, 2627(F)
Curious George and the Puppies, 1991(F)
Curious George at the Parade, 2627(F)
Curious George Flies a Kite, 2626(F)
Curious George Gets a Medal, 2624(F)
Curious George Goes Camping, 2627(F)
Curious George Goes to a Movie, 1991(F)
Curious George Goes to the Hospital, 2626(F)
Curious George Learns the Alphabet, 118(F)
Curious George Makes Pancakes, 1991(F)
Curious George Rides a Bike, 2624(F)
Curious George Takes a Job, 2624(F)
Curious George's Dream, 1991(F)
Curious Kids Go to Preschool, 2998(F)
Curious Kittens, 2782(F)
Curse of a Winter Moon, 9030(F)
The Curse of King Tut's Tomb, 14648
The Curse of the Blue Figurine, 7603(F)
The Curse of the Cat Mummy, 7042(F)
The Curse of the Hope Diamond, 21915
The Curse of Tutankhamen, 14637

Customs and Traditions, 16331
Cut from the Same Cloth, 11376
Cut-Paper Play! 21618
Cuts, Scrapes, Scabs, Scars, 18181
Cy Young, 13510
Cy Young Award Winners, 13426
Cyber Space, 21206
Cyberdanger and Internet Safety, 21217
CyberSurfer, 21190
The Cybil War, 9793(F)
Cycling, 22155
Cyclops, 11471
Cynthia Cooper, 13519
Cyprus, 15267
Cyprus in Pictures, 15264
Cyrus the Unsinkable Sea Serpent, 2567(F)
Czech Republic, 15272, 15281
Czech Republic in Pictures, 15265

D-Day, 14827
D Is for Dolphin, 11(F)
The D-Poems of Jeremy Bloom, 11880
D.W. All Wet, 1887(F)
D.W. Flips, 1887(F)
D.W., Go to Your Room! 3548(F)
D.W. Rides Again! 1888(F)
D.W.'s Lost Blankie, 1889(F)
D.W. the Picky Eater, 1890(F)
D.W. Thinks Big, 1891(F)
Da Vinci, 12219
Da Wei's Treasure, 10743
Dad and Me, 3574(F)
Dad and Me in the Morning, 3762(F)
Dad, You're Not Funny and Other Poems, 11922
Daddies, 3852(F)
Daddy and I, 3182(F)
The Daddy Book, 3817
Daddy Is a Doodlebug, 2014(F)
Daddy Makes the Best Spaghetti, 3699(F)
Daddy Played Music for the Cows, 3471(F)
Daddy Poems, 11548
Daddy Will Be There, 3657(F)
Daddy, Will You Miss Me? 3783(F)
Daddy's Climbing Tree, 8550(F)
Daddy's Roommate, 3946(F)
Daddy's Wedding, 3947(F)
Daedalus and the Minotaur, 11474
Daffy Down Dillies, 11885
Dahomey, 15030
Daily Life, 14700, 16173
Daily Life in a Plains Indian Village, 16062
Daily Life in Ancient and Modern Beijing, 15053
Daily Life in Ancient and Modern Mexico City, 15612
Daily Life in Ancient and Modern Paris, 15310
Daily Life in Ancient and Modern Rome, 15371
Daily Life in Ancient and Modern Timbuktu, 15018
Daily Life on a Southern Plantation 1853, 16239
Dairy Products, 20085

Daisy, 8741(F)
Daisy and the Beastie, 2693(F)
Daisy and the Doll, 7356(F)
Daisy and the Egg, 2694(F)
Daisy and the Girl Scouts, 13168
Daisy Dare, 2253(F)
Daisy Knows Best, 2311(F)
Daisy Says Coo! 2695(F)
Daisy's Babies, 2312(F)
Daisy's Day Out, 2695(F)
Daisy's Favorite Things, 2696(F)
Daisy's Garden, 2120(F)
Daja's Book, 8016(F)
Dakota Dugout, 4857(F)
The Dalai Lama, 13777
Dale Earnhardt, 13427
Dallas, 16911
The Dallas Cowboys Football Team, 22184
The Dalton Gang, 16311
Damien the Dragon, 8047(F)
Dams Give Us Power, 21126
Dan and Dan, 6448(F)
Dan Marino, 13619
Dan Thuy's New Life in America, 17586
Dance, 14286, 14292, 14295, 14299
Dance for the Land, 8904(F)
Dance, Kayla! 8536(F)
Dance of the Continents, 20305
Dance of the Crystal Skull, 7902(F)
Dance on a Sealskin, 4885(F)
Dance, Pioneer, Dance! 4866(F)
Dance, Sing, Remember, 17476
Dance, Tanya, 3017(F)
The Dancer Who Flew, 12428
Dancers, 13923
Dancin' in the Kitchen, 3644(F)
Dancing, 3576(F)
The Dancing Dragon, 5654(F)
The Dancing Fox, 11204
Dancing in Cadillac Light, 7454(F)
Dancing in the Wings, 4898(F)
The Dancing Man, 1006(F)
Dancing on the Bridge at Avignon, 9073(F)
The Dancing Pig, 10851
The Dancing Skeleton, 11333
Dancing Teepees, 11931
The Dancing Tree, 8519(F)
The Dancing Turtle, 11436
Dancing Wheels, 17923
Dancing with Dziadziu, 9520(F)
Dancing with the Indians, 3318(F)
Dandelion, 20266
  (Illus. by Don Freeman), 2101(F)
Dandelion Adventures, 20240
The Dandelion Wish, 1250(F)
Dandelions,
  (Illus. by Greg Shed), 9526(F), 20241, 20257
A Dandelion's Life, 20237
Danger Along the Ohio, 9460(F)
Danger at Sand Cave, 6588(F)
Danger at the Breaker, 6712(F)
Danger at the Fair, 6914(F)
Danger, Dolphins, and Ginger Beer, 7113(F)
Danger Guys, 6728(F)
Danger Guys Blast Off! 6728(F)

Danger in Quicksand Swamp, 7120(F)
Danger in the Desert, 6840(F)
Danger on Apollo 13, 20947
Dangerous Animals, 18971
Dangerous Dream, 9647(F)
Dangerous Fish, 19698
Dangerous Games, 6739(F)
Dangerous Ghosts, 7656(F)
The Dangerous Voyage, 10216(F)
Dangling, 8633(F)
Daniel Boone, 12081, 12083, 12084, 12085
Daniel Boone and the Exploration of the Frontier, 12082
Daniel "Chappie" James, 12731
Daniel Discovers Daniel, 3517(F)
Daniel in the Lions' Den, 17239
Daniel's Duck, 6238(F)
Daniel's Gift, 5835(F)
Danny Ain't, 8615(F)
Danny and the Dinosaur, 6400(F)
Danny and the Dinosaur Go to Camp, 6401(F)
Danny and the Kings, 5789(F)
Danny and the Merry-Go-Round, 4979(F)
Danny, the Angry Lion, 5005(F)
Danny's Desert Rats, 9946(F)
Danny's Duck, 5492(F)
Dan's Pants, 3176(F)
Daphne Eloise Slater, Who's Tall for Her Age, 8856(F)
Daphne's Book, 8296(F)
Dar and the Spear Thrower, 8951(F)
Dar and the Spear-Thrower, 8952(F)
Darby, the Special-Order Pup, 1106(F)
Darcy and Gran Don't Like Babies, 3597(F)
Dare to Dream, 12736
Daring to Be Abigail, 8838(F)
The Dark Ages, 14585
Dark as a Midnight Dream, 11733
The Dark at the Top of the Stairs, 2408(F)
Dark Day, Light Night, 4923(F)
The Dark Is Rising, 7671(F)
The Dark Portal, 7836(F)
The Dark Stairs, 6781(F)
Dark Starry Morning, 8007(F)
The Dark-Thirty, 11366
The Darkest Corner, 8453(F)
Darkfright, 1260(F)
Darkness Over Denmark, 14865
Darryl Strawberry, 13506
Dashing Through the Snow, 22058
The Dastardly Murder of Dirty Pete, 6796(F)
A Date with Destiny, 16647
Daughter of Suqua, 9161(F)
Daughter's Day Blues, 3835(F)
Daughters of Eve, 17317
D'Aulaire's Book of Greek Myths, 11470
Dave at Night, 9582(F)
Dave's Down-to-Earth Rock Shop, 20566
Dave's Quick 'n' Easy Web Pages, 21218
David, 13780

David and Goliath, 17240, 17268
  (Illus. by Scott Cameron), 17263
  (Illus. by Douglas Fraser), 17309
David Decides About Thumbsucking,
  4977(F)
David, Donny, and Darren, 17641
David Dreaming of Dinosaurs,
  5202(F)
David Farragut and the Great Naval
  Blockade, 12876
David Goes to School, 5539(F)
David Robinson, 13568, 13569,
  13570, 13571, 13572
David's Father, 4242(F)
David's Landing, 8793(F)
David's Search, 9422(F)
David's Story, 18037
Davy Crockett, 12103, 12104
Dawn, 4542(F)
Dawn and the Round To-It, 3898(F)
Dawn of Fear, 8271(F)
A Day, a Dog, 7318(F)
The Day Before Christmas, 5767(F)
Day Breaks, 4557(F)
Day by Day a Week Goes Round,
  244(F)
Day Care Days, 3518(F)
The Day Eddie Met the Author,
  10029(F)
The Day Fort Sumter Was Fired On,
  16413
The Day Gogo Went to Vote,
  4832(F)
The Day I Was Rich, 4934(F)
A Day in Court with Mrs. Trinh,
  17746
A Day in the Life of a Colonial
  Innkeeper, 16186
A Day in the Life of a Colonial Wig-
  maker, 16187
A Day in the Life of a Marine Biolo-
  gist, 17834
Day Light, Night Light, 20857
The Day Martin Luther King, Jr.,
  Was Shot, 16510
The Day My Dogs Became Guys,
  1396(F)
A Day No Pigs Would Die, 9605(F)
The Day of Ahmed's Secret, 4678(F)
A Day of Pleasure, 12597
Day of the Dead, 5628(F), 7347(F)
The Day Sun Was Stolen, 11284
The Day the Ants Got Really Mad,
  8124(F)
The Day the Rabbi Disappeared,
  11166
The Day the Sheep Showed Up,
  6497(F)
The Day the Whale Came, 3056(F)
The Day the Women Got the Vote,
  17051
The Day We Met You, 3751(F)
The Day We Walked on the Moon,
  21016
A Day with a Cheyenne, 16003
A Day with a Chumash, 15986
A Day with a Miller, 9066(F)
A Day with a Mimbres, 15935
A Day with a Noble-woman, 14786
A Day with a Pueblo, 16013
A Day with a Stonecutter, 14787

A Day with Picasso, 12283
A Day with the Bellyflops, 1793(F)
The Days Before Now, 12508
Days Like This, 11550
Days of the Blackbird, 11057(F)
Days of the Dead, 15628
Days with Frog and Toad, 6464(F)
A Day's Work, 3553(F)
Dazzle the Dinosaur, 2574(F)
Dazzling! 21169
Dazzling Disguises and Clever Cos-
  tumes, 21553
Dazzling Division, 20585
Dead Letter, 6782(F)
Dead Letters, 7133(F)
A Dead Log, 20447
Dead Log Alive! 20208
Dead Man's Hand, 6804(F)
The Dead Sea Scrolls, 17257
Deadline! 14082
The Deadly Dungeon, 7037(F)
Deadly Waters, 7059(F)
Deafness, 17918
Dealing with Addition, 497(F)
Dealing with Anger, 17616
Dealing with Bullying, 17712
Dealing with Competitiveness, 17720
Dealing with Racism, 17140
Dealing with Secrets, 17720
Dealing with Teasing, 17693
Dear Austin, 9337(F)
Dear Bear, 2174(F)
Dear Benjamin Banneker, 13235
Dear Bronx Zoo, 20022
Dear Brother, 1764(F)
Dear Corinne, Tell Somebody! A
  Book About Secrets, 8636(F)
Dear Daddy, 3879(F)
Dear Daisy, Get Well Soon, 2705(F)
Dear Dr. Bell . . . Your Friend, Helen
  Keller, 12697
Dear Dr. King, 17029
Dear Ellen Bee, 9487(F)
Dear Fred, 5059(F)
"Dear Friend," 16226
Dear Juno, 3831(F)
Dear Katie, the Volcano Is a Girl,
  4438(F)
Dear Lovey Hart, I Am Desperate,
  10040(F)
Dear Mili, 10894
Dear Mom, You're Ruining My Life,
  8532(F)
Dear Mother, Dear Daughter, 11745
Dear Mr. Blueberry, 2247(F)
Dear Mr. Henshaw, 8600(F)
Dear Mrs. Parks, 17048
Dear Mrs. Ryan, You're Ruining My
  Life, 9893(F)
"Dear Napoleon, I Know You're
  Dead, But . . ." 7541(F)
Dear Oklahoma City, Get Well Soon,
  16578
Dear Old Donegal, 4669(F)
Dear Peter Rabbit (Illus. by Leslie
  Tryon), 941(F)
  (Illus. by Leslie Tryon), 943(F)
Dear Whiskers, 8349(F)
Dear Willie Rudd, 3658(F)
Dear Zoo, 5156(F)
Death, 17860

Death at Devil's Bridge, 6815(F)
Death Customs, 17214
Death from Space, 14380
Death of the Iron Horse, 4665(F)
The Death Penalty, 17066
Death Trap, 14476
Death Valley, 9359(F)
Death Valley National Park, 16631
Death's Door, 6783(F)
December, 5768(F)
December Secrets, 6345(F)
Deck the Hall, 14206
The Declaration of Independence,
  16211
DeDe Takes Charge! 8461(F)
Dee and Bee, 4073(F)
Deena's Lucky Penny, 6306(F)
Deenie, 8881(F)
The Deep, 5106(F)
The Deep Blue Sky Twinkles with
  Stars, 791(F)
Deep Doo-Doo and the Mysterious
  E-mail, 6819(F)
Deep in a Rainforest, 20472
Deep in the Jungle, 2882(F)
Deep Space Astronomy, 18423
Deep Wizardry, 7711(F)
Deer, 19149
Deer and Elk, 19157
Deer, Moose, Elk and Caribou,
  19152
Deer Watching, 19148
The Deetkatoo, 11212
Defenders of the Universe, 6919(F)
Deforestation, 20469
Degas, 13906
Deion Sanders, 13629
Delaware, 16655, 16658, 16702,
  16737
Delaware Facts and Symbols, 16707
Delicious Hullabaloo, 2508(F)
The Deliverers of Their Country,
  7985(F)
Delivery, 3448(F)
Della Splatnuk, Birthday Girl,
  5710(F)
Delphine, 975(F)
Dem Bones, 18168
Demeter and Persephone, 11503
The Democratic Republic of the
  Congo, 15032
Demolition Derby, 21317
The Demons' Mistake, 11160
Denmark, 15449
Denmark in Pictures, 15442
Dennis Rodman, 13573
Denver, 16638
Denzel Washington, 12480
Depend on Katie John, 8411(F)
Depression, 17723
Derek Jeter, 13464, 13465
Derek the Knitting Dinosaur, 1816(F)
Derek's Dog Days, 1051(F)
Desdemona, 9894(F)
Desert, 20415, 20419
Desert Babies, 18873
Desert Birds, 19225
Desert Giant, 20226
The Desert Is My Mother/El Desierto
  Es Mi Madre, 11974
The Desert Is Theirs, 15922

Desert Life, 20425
Desert Mammals, 20410
Desert Plants, 20258, 20404
A Desert Scrapbook, 20428
Desert Song, 4467(F)
Desert Town, 3161(F)
Desert Voices, 11772
Desert Warfare, 14828
Deserts, 20401, 20406, 20413, 20421, 20423, 20426
The Deserts of the Southwest, 20416
Desktop Publishing, 14002
Desser the Best Ever Cat, 5421(F)
Desserts Around the World, 21694
Destination, 15236, 15805, 18488, 18489, 19635, 20449
Destination Los Angeles, 16798
Destination New York, 16748
Destination San Juan, 15709
Destination Veracruz, 15634
Destiny, 8673(F)
Detective Dictionary, 17062
Detective Dinosaur, 6665(F)
Detective Dinosaur Lost and Found, 6666(F)
Detective Science, 17089
Detroit, 16594
The Detroit Red Wings Hockey Team, 22214
The Devil and His Boy, 9102(F)
The Devil in Ol' Rosie, 9599(F)
The Devil's Arithmetic, 9701(F)
Devil's Bridge, 6816(F)
Devil's Den, 8510(F)
Devil's Donkey, 7624(F)
The Devil's Highway, 9341(F)
The Devil's Other Storybook, 7572(F)
The Devil's Storybook, 7573(F)
Dew Drop Dead, 6903(F)
The Dewey Decimal System, 13994
Dexter Gets Dressed! 3480(F)
Diabetes, 17977, 18006
The Diamond in the Window, 7886(F)
The Diamond War, 8816(F)
Dian Fossey and the Mountain Gorillas, 13285
Diana, 13781, 13784, 13786
Diary of a Drummer Boy, 9468(F)
Diary of a Frantic Kid Sister, 8603(F)
Diary of a Monster's Son, 10162(F)
The Diary of David R. Leeper, 16340
The Diary of Mary Jemison, 15977
The Diary of Melanie Martin; or, How I Survived Matt the Brat, Michelangelo, and the Leaning Tower of Pizza, 9075(F)
Dia's Story Cloth, 15153
Dibble and Dabble, 2655(F)
Dicey's Song, 7532(F)
Dick King-Smith's Alphabeasts, 73(F)
Dick King-Smith's Animal Friends, 19899
Dick Rutan and Jena Yeager, 12066
Dick Whittington and His Cat, 10952
Did Dinosaurs Live in Your Backyard? Questions And Answers About Dinosaurs, 14385

Did My First Mother Love Me? 5033(F)
Did the Sun Shine Before You Were Born? 18257
Did You Carry the Flag Today, Charley? 10034(F)
Did You Say Ghosts? 1412(F)
Diet Pill Drug Dangers, 17863
Diez Deditos and Other Play Rhymes and Action Songs from Latin America, 22041
Different Dogs, 19971
Different Dragons, 7258(F)
Different Just Like Me, 3330(F)
A Different Kind of Hero, 9346(F)
A Difficult Day, 4954(F)
Dig a Tunnel, 21131
Dig and Sow! How Do Plants Grow? 18592
Dig, Drill, Dump, Fill, 21248
Dig Hole, Soft Mole, 5300(F)
A Dig in Time, 7762(F)
Dig This! 14519
Digby, 6375(F)
Digby and Kate and the Beautiful Day, 6194(F)
Digestion, 18096, 18103
The Digestive System, 18106, 18108
Digger Pig and the Turnip, 10958
Diggers, 21246
The Diggers, 5550
Diggers and Dump Trucks, 5598
Diggers and Other Construction Machines, 21149
Digging for Bird-Dinosaurs, 14386
Digging Up Dinosaurs, 14373
Digital Revolution, 21241
Dilly-Dally and the Nine Secrets, 2421(F)
Dilly's Big Sister Diary, 3772(F)
Dilly's Summer Camp Diary, 9916(F)
A Dime a Dozen, 11582
Dinah for President, 10110(F)
Dinah Forever, 8760(F)
Dinah in Love, 9938(F)
The Ding Dong Clock, 381(F)
Ding Dong Ding Dong, 2557(F)
Dinky Hocker Shoots Smack! 9895(F)
Dinner at Aunt Connie's House, 12695
Dino-Trekking, 14425
Dinorella, 2051(F)
Dinosaur, 14456
Dinosaur! 932(F)
Dinosaur and Other Prehistoric Animal Factfinder, 14382
Dinosaur Babies (Illus. by Peter Barrett), 5361
  (Illus. by Richard Grant), 14423
  (Illus. by Lucia Washburn), 14486
Dinosaur Beach, 1128(F)
Dinosaur Bones, 14374
Dinosaur Cousins? 14450
Dinosaur Days, 210(F)
Dinosaur Dictionary, 14427
Dinosaur Discoveries, 21638
Dinosaur Garden, 1129(F)
Dinosaur Ghosts, 14420
Dinosaur Habitat, 7765(F)

Dinosaur Hunters, 14444
The Dinosaur Is the Biggest Animal That Ever Lived, 18292
Dinosaur Island, 2938(F)
Dinosaur Mountain, 14377
A Dinosaur Named After Me, 5352
A Dinosaur Named Sue, 14466
Dinosaur National Monument, 16632
The Dinosaur Princess and Other Prehistoric Riddles, 21812
Dinosaur Questions, 14451
Dinosaur Roar! 2732(F)
Dinosaur Stomp, 2740(F)
Dinosaur Time, 14459
The Dinosaur Tooth, 7135(F)
Dinosaur Tree, 20202
Dinosaur with an Attitude, 7844(F)
Dinosaur Worlds, 14436
Dinosaurs, 14383, 14402, 14417, 14443, 14448, 14458, 21599
  (Illus. by Jane Cradock-Watson), 14467
  (Illus. by James Prunier), 14401
The Dinosaurs, 14431
Dinosaurs! 14465
Dinosaurs Alive and Well! 3047
Dinosaurs All Around, 14378
Dinosaurs and Other Archosaurs, 14483
Dinosaurs and Other Prehistoric Creatures, 14470
The Dinosaurs Are Back and It's All Your Fault Edward! 4177(F)
Dinosaurs Are Different, 14376
Dinosaurs at the Ends of the Earth, 14413
Dinosaurs Before Dark, 6554(F)
Dinosaurs, Beware! A Safety Guide, 3049(F)
Dinosaurs' Christmas, 5804(F)
Dinosaurs Dance, 6227(F)
Dinosaurs, Dinosaurs, 14381
Dinosaurs Divorce, 17644
Dinosaurs Everywhere! 14426
Dinosaurs for Every Kid, 14478
Dinosaurs Forever, 11817
Dinosaurs in Your Backyard, 14445
The Dinosaur's New Clothes, 10423(F)
Dinosaurs! The Biggest Baddest Strangest Fastest, 14485
Dinosaurs to Dodos, 19401
Dinosaurs Travel, 3047
Dinosaurs Walked Here, 14433
Dinotopia Lost, 10182(F)
Dinoverse, 10161(F)
Dippers, 7989(F)
Dirt Bike Racer, 10299(F)
Dirt Bike Runaway, 10299(F)
Dirt Boy, 1582(F)
Dirt on Their Skirts, 4805(F)
Dirt Track Racing, 22242
Dirty Dog Boogie, 11623
The Disability Rights Movement, 17038
The Disappearing Alphabet, 11926
The Disappearing Island, 4411(F)
Disappearing Lake, 16801
Disasters, 14340
Discover Mars, 18495

Discoveries, Inventions and Ideas, 14705
Discovering Christopher Columbus, 12100
Discovering Dinosaur Babies, 14469
Discovering El Nino, 20786
Discovering Electricity, 20883
Discovering Graph Secrets, 20589
Discovering Jupiter, 18457
Discovering the Iceman, 14515
Discovering the Inca Ice Maiden, 15781
Discovering the Stars, 18554
Discovering the Titanic, 19879
Discovering Trees, 20194
Discovery and Settlement, 16098
The Discovery of Dragons, 9775(F)
The Disease Book, 17967
Disease Detective, 17962
Disguises and Surprises, 18885
Disney's Animation Magic, 21270
Disney's James and the Giant Peach, 1312(F)
Distant Feathers, 1147(F)
The Distant Talking Drum, 11977
Distant Thunder, 9242(F)
Divali, 17375
Dive, 8440(F)
Dive! A Book of Deep-Sea Creatures, 19624
Dive! My Adventures in the Deep Frontier, 19631
Dive to the Deep Ocean, 19877
The Divide, 12515
Divide and Ride, 524
The Diving Bell, 9180(F)
Division (Illus. by Richard Maccabe), 20596
  (Illus. by Sami Sweeten), 400(F)
Divorce, 17645, 17656
Divorce and Separation, 17682
Diwali, 17385
Dizzy Dean, 13447
Django, 11327
DK Great Dinosaur Atlas, 14441
DK Guide to Dinosaurs, 14432
DK Guide to Space, 20953
DNA Is Here to Stay, 18048
Do Bears Give Bear Hugs? 18619
Do Bees Sneeze? And Other Questions Kids Ask About Insects, 19498
Do Buildings Have Bones? 21121
Do Cowboys Ride Bikes? 4338(F)
Do Crocodiles Moo? 2357(F)
Do Donkeys Dance? 5446(F)
Do I Have a Daddy? A Story About a Single-Parent Child, 17671
Do Knights Take Naps? 1626(F)
Do Like Kyla, 3723(F)
Do Monkeys Tweet? 5447
Do Not Disturb, 18903
Do Not Touch, 169(F)
Do People Grow on Family Trees? 17692
Do Pigs Have Stripes? 4344(F)
Do Pirates Take Baths? 2980(F)
Do Sharks Ever . . .? 19769
Do Skyscrapers Touch the Sky? 3106
Do Stars Have Points? 18380
Do Tornadoes Really Twist? 20682

Do Whales Have Belly Buttons? Questions and Answers About Whales and Dolphins, 19625
Do You Know Me? 8962(F)
Do You Know What I'll Do? 3972(F)
Do You Remember the Color Blue? And Other Questions Kids Ask About Blindness, 17900
Do You See a Mouse? 4343(F)
Do You See Mouse? 1990(F)
Do You Wanna Bet? 20614
Do You Want to Be My Friend? 912(F)
Do You Want to Play? A Book About Being Friends, 4019(F)
Doc Holliday, 12902
Doctor Bird, 11423
Doctor Change, 7658(F)
Doctor Coyote, 11394
Doctor De Soto, 2716(F)
Doctor De Soto Goes to Africa, 2717(F)
A Doctor to Her People, 12983
Doctors Help People, 17803
A Doctor's Life, 18028
Does a Kangaroo Have a Mother, Too? 5158
Does a Mouse Have a House? 18910
Does God Have a Big Toe? 17272
Does God Know How to Tie Shoes? 17172(F)
Dog, 5137(F), 19942
Dog and Cat, 1732(F)
Dog and Cat Make a Splash, 2713(F)
Dog and Cat Shake a Leg, 6671(F)
Dog Breath, 2584(F)
A Dog Called Kitty, 7320(F)
A Dog Came, Too, 4760
Dog Days, 11979
Dog Donovan, 5256(F)
Dog Friday, 7262(F)
Dog Heaven, 5398(F)
Dog Is Thirsty, 2300(F)
A Dog Like Jack, 5183(F)
Dog Magic, 4163(F)
A Dog on Barkham Street, 8375(F)
Dog People, 11216
Dog Tales, 10484(F)
The Dog That Called the Pitch, 10300(F)
The Dog That Pitched a No-Hitter, 10301(F)
The Dog Who Had Kittens, 5383(F)
The Dog Who Lost His Bob, 5332(F)
The Dog Who Walked with God, 11295
The Dog Who Wouldn't Be, 7272(F)
The Dog with Golden Eyes, 7324(F)
Dog Years, 10137(F)
Dogger, 4984(F)
Doggie Dreams, 1950(F)
Dogs, 13924, 19947, 19956, 19959
  (Illus. by Gail Gibbons), 19949, 19961, 19972
Dogs and Dragons, Trees and Dreams, 11620
A Dog's Best Friend, 19966
Dog's Colorful Day, 177(F)
Dog's Day, 1908(F)
Dogs Don't Wear Glasses, 4157(F)
Dogs Don't Wear Sneakers, 2536(F)

A Dog's Gotta Do What a Dog's Gotta Do, 19973
Dogs Have the Strangest Friends, 18833
Dogs in Space, 1062(F)
Dogs' Night, 2218(F)
Dogs of Myth, 10560
Dogstar, 8215(F)
Dogzilla, 5364(F)
Doing Our Part, 14880
Doll Baby, 8577(F)
The Doll in the Garden, 7774(F)
Doll Party, 6187(F)
The Doll People, 7951(F)
A Dollar for Penny, 446(F)
Dolley Madison, 13170
Dolley Payne Todd Madison, 13169
The Dollhouse Magic, 9590(F)
The Dollhouse Murders, 7130(F)
Dolls Kids Can Make, 21654
Dolores Huerta, 12832
Dolphin, 19687
Dolphin Adventure, 19684
Dolphin Babies, 19692
Dolphin Freedom, 6868(F)
Dolphin Luck, 7475(F)
A Dolphin Named Bob, 7196(F)
Dolphin Treasure, 6869(F)
Dolphins, 19681, 19686, 19691, 19693
Dolphins and Porpoises, 19685
Dominic, 8127(F)
Dominican Americans, 17543
The Dominican Republic, 15716
Dominican Republic in Pictures, 15705
Dominique Moceanu, 13702, 13703
Dominoes Around the World, 22235
Domitila, 11397
Don Quixote and Sancho Panza, 9044(F)
Donavan's Word Jar, 7418(F)
The Donkey and the Rock, 10723
Donkey Trouble, 10632
The Donkey's Dream, 5755(F)
Donna Karan, 13163
Donna O'Neeshuck Was Chased by Some Cows, 4169(F)
Donnatalee, 1611(F)
Don't Be Afraid, Amanda, 7966(F)
Don't Be Afraid, Tommy, 4906(F)
Don't Be My Valentine, 6173(F)
Don't Call Me Beanhead! 10022(F)
Don't Call Me Marda, 8920(F)
Don't Call Me Slob-o, 8777(F)
Don't Call Me Toad! 7055(F)
Don't Dig So Deep, Nicholas! 1224(F)
Don't Do That! 4269(F)
Don't Do That, Kitty Kilroy! 3591(F)
Don't Fidget a Feather! 2690(F)
Don't Forget the Bacon! 4186(F)
Don't Forget to Write, 3884(F)
The Don't-Give-Up-Kid and Learning Differences, 4964(F)
Don't Go into the Graveyard! 7994(F)
Don't Go Near That Rabbit, Frank! 7178(F)
Don't Hurt Laurie! 8795(F)
Don't Hurt Me, Mama, 5087(F)

Don't Laugh, Joe! 2274(F)
Don't Leave an Elephant to Go and Chase a Bird, 10651
Don't Make Me Laugh, 4330(F)
Don't Make Me Smile, 8503(F)
Don't Need Friends, 1987(F)
Don't Open the Door After the Sun Goes Down, 7650(F)
Don't Pat the Wombat, 9878(F)
Don't Read This Book, Whatever You Do! 11867
Don't Step on the Foul Line, 22069
Don't Tell Anyone, 6915(F)
Don't Tell the Whole World! 3990(F)
Don't Try This at Home! Science Fun for Kids on the Go, 18307
Don't Wake the Baby! 9771(F)
Don't Wake Up Mama! 406(F)
Don't Worry, Alfie, 2602(F)
Don't You Know There's a War On? 4840
Dooby, 10287(F)
Doodle Dandies, 11629
Doodle Dandy! 17364
Doodle Flute, 4032(F)
Doodle Soup, 11862
The Door in the Hedge, 10459(F)
The Door in the Lake, 10155(F)
The Door in the Wall, 9091(F)
The Doorbell Rang, 3235(F)
The Doorman, 4969(F)
Dora's Box, 1034(F)
Dora's Eggs, 2744(F)
Dork in Disguise, 9863(F)
Dorling Kindersley Children's Atlas, 14337
The Dorling Kindersley Visual Timeline of Transportation, 21290
Dorobo the Dangerous, 1650(F)
Dorothea Lange, 12251
Dorothy and Mikey, 2275(F)
Dorothy Hamill, 13591
Dorothy of Oz, 7602(F)
Dorothy's Darkest Days, 8596(F)
Dorrie and the Haunted Schoolhouse, 1075(F)
Dory Story, 4504(F)
Do's and Don'ts, 3356(F)
Double Act, 7540(F)
The Double Dabble Surprise, 7470(F)
Double-Header, 6379(F)
The Double Life of Pocahontas, 12984
Double Trouble in Walla Walla, 4117(F)
Double Trouble Squared, 7889(F)
Dougal Dixon's Amazing Dinosaurs, 14404
Dougal Dixon's Dinosaurs, 14405
Douglas MacArthur, 12930, 12932
The Dove Dove, 14047
Dove Song, 8430(F)
Doves, 19250
The Dove's Letter, 970(F)
Dovey Coe, 7424(F)
Down a River, 15908
The Down and Up Fall, 7457(F)
Down at Angel's, 5779(F)
Down by the River, 846

Down by the Station, 2208(F)
Down Comes the Rain, 20728
Down Dairy Farm Road, 5026(F)
Down, Down, Down in the Ocean, 19829
Down Home at Miss Dessa's, 4049(F)
Down in the Sea, 19640, 19663, 19678, 19724
Down in the Subway, 1065(F)
Down in the Woods at Sleepytime, 774(F)
Down on Casey's Farm, 713(F)
Down on the Farm, 5706(F)
Down the Dragon's Tongue, 3304(F)
Down the Drain, 21164
Down the Hatch, 18101
Down the Road, 3878(F)
Down the Winding Road, 3724(F)
Down to Earth, 21772
Down to the Sea with Mr. Magee, 1647(F)
Downhill In-Line Skating, 21989
A Dozen Dozens, 259(F)
A Dozen Silk Diapers, 10920
Dr. Amelia's Boredom Survival Guide, 22038
Dr. Dredd's Wagon of Wonders, 6775(F)
Dr. Friedman Helps Animals, 17845
Dr. Jekyll, Orthodontist, 7757(F)
Dr. Kanner, Dentist with a Smile, 17799
Dr. Ruth Talks to Kids, 18270
Dr. Seuss, 12538, 12540
Dr. Seuss' ABC, 130(F)
Dr. White, 2135(F)
The Drackenberg Adventure, 6743(F)
Dracula, 21945
Dracula Is a Pain in the Neck, 6944(F)
Dracula Steps Out, 8037(F)
Drag Racing, 22082
The Dragon and the Unicorn, 1052(F)
Dragon Bones and Dinosaur Eggs, 13226
The Dragon Halloween Party, 6025(F)
A Dragon in the Family, 7874(F)
Dragon Kite of the Autumn Moon, 4808(F)
The Dragon Lover and Other Chinese Proverbs, 10774
The Dragon New Year, 5611(F)
The Dragon of Lonely Island, 8053(F)
Dragon of the Lost Sea, 8232(F)
Dragon Parade, 5618
The Dragon Prince, 10776
Dragon Quest, 7874(F)
Dragon Scales and Willow Leaves, 1194(F)
Dragon Soup, 1686(F)
Dragon Tooth, 4953(F)
Dragonflies, 19464
Dragonfly Secret, 8437(F)
The Dragonfly's Tale, 11294
The Dragonling, 7875(F)
The Dragons Are Singing Tonight, 11808

Dragon's Merry Christmas, 5898(F)
Dragon's Milk, 7730(F)
The Dragons of Blueland, 9857(F)
The Dragons of North Chittendon, 8068(F)
The Dragon's Pearl, 10762
The Dragon's Robe, 10444(F)
The Dragon's Scales, 6185(F)
The Dragon's Tale and Other Animal Fables of the Chinese Zodiac, 10748
The Dragonslayers, 7672(F)
Draugr, 8098(F)
Draw! 21587, 21594
Draw Alien Fantasies, 21588
Draw Desert Animals, 21566
Draw Dinosaurs, 21567
Draw Fifty Airplanes, Aircraft and Spacecraft, 21554
Draw Fifty Aliens, UFOs, Galaxy Ghouls, Milky Way Marauders, and Other Extraterrestrial Creatures, 21559
Draw Fifty Animals, 21556
Draw Fifty Boats, Ships, Trucks and Trains, 21554
Draw Fifty Buildings and Other Structures, 21554
Draw Fifty Cats, 21555
Draw Fifty Dinosaurs and Other Prehistoric Animals, 21556
Draw Fifty Dogs, 21556
Draw Fifty Famous Cartoons, 21557
Draw Fifty Holiday Decorations, 21555
Draw Fifty Horses, 21556
Draw Fifty Monsters, Creeps, Superheroes, Demons, Dragons, Nerds, Dirts, Ghouls, Giants, Vampires, Zombies and Other Curiosa, 21558
Draw Fifty Vehicles, 21554
Draw! Grassland Animals, 21568
Draw Insects, 21569
Draw Me a Star, 1035(F)
Draw 3-D, 21570
Drawer in a Drawer, 649(F)
Drawing and Cartooning All-Star Sports, 21596
A Drawing in the Sand, 13951
Drawing Lessons, 8480(F)
Drawing Lessons from a Bear, 2455(F)
Drawing Prehistoric Animals, 21576
Drawing with Charcoal and Pastels, 21577
Drawing with Markers, 21577
Drawing with Pencils, 21578
The Dreadful Future of Blossom Culp, 8010(F)
The Dream Collector, 695(F)
The Dream Eater, 10813
Dream Freedom, 8970(F)
The Dream House, 1637(F)
The Dream Jar, 3846(F)
Dream Journey, 668(F)
A Dream of Queens and Castles, 8252(F)
The Dream Quilt, 818(F)
Dream Snow, 5773(F)
Dream Soul, 8547(F)
The Dream Stair, 710(F)

Dream Weaver, 4487(F)
Dream Wolf, 1196(F)
Dreamcatcher, 7264(F)
  (Illus. by Ed Young), 758(F)
Dreaming, 690(F)
Dreaming of America, 4607(F)
Dreamland, 3411(F)
Dreamplace, 4749(F)
Dreams, 12750
Dreams Are More Real than Bath-
  tubs, 5522(F)
Dreams in the Golden Country,
  9577(F)
Dreams of Glory, 11572
The Dreams of Hummingbirds,
  11946
Dreamstones, 1625(F)
Dreamtime, 664
The Dred Scott Case, 16240
The Dress I'll Wear to the Party,
  6542(F)
Dressed for the Occasion, 21180
Dressing, 930(F)
Drew and the Bub Daddy Show-
  down, 8556(F)
Drew Barrymore, 12354
Drinking Alcohol, 17888
The Drinking Gourd, 9308(F)
Drinking Water, 18192
Drip, Drop, 6709(F)
Drip! Drop! 20745
A Drive to Win, 13545
Driven from the Land, 16479
Driving Me Crazy, 21830
The Drop in My Drink, 20736
A Drop of Water, 20748
Drug Abuse, 17882, 17895
Drug Testing in Schools, 17876
Drug Trafficking, 17078
Drugs, 17861
Drugs and Disease, 17867
Drugs and Our World, 17893
Drugs and Sports, 18268
Drugs in Society, 17886
Drumbeat . . . Heartbeat, 15934
Drummer Boy, 9505(F)
The Drummer Boy of Vicksburg,
  9506(F)
Drummer Hoff, 14238
Drums, 14222
Drums at Saratoga, 9221(F)
The Drums of Noto Hanto, 4692(F)
Dry Days, Wet Nights, 1822(F)
Drylongso, 8680(F)
Dublin, 15354
Duck, 19315
Duck, Duck, Goose? 1747(F)
A Duck in a Tree, 19313
Duck in the Truck, 1729(F)
Duck Is Dirty, 2300(F)
Duck Song, 2144(F)
Duck Takes Off, 2149(F)
Duckling Days, 19318
Ducklings and Pollywogs, 4518(F)
Duck's Breath and Mouse Pie, 21921
Ducks Disappearing, 536(F)
Ducks Don't Get Wet, 19309
Ducks in Muck, 6368(F)
Ducks Like to Swim, 2780(F)
Ducky, 1023(F)
Duffy and the Devil, 11047

The Duke and the Peasant, 13946
Duke Ellington, 12379
Duke Snider, 13503
Duke the Dairy Delight Dog, 2075(F)
The Dumb Bunnies, 2020(F)
The Dumb Bunnies' Easter, 5964(F)
The Dumb Bunnies Go to the Zoo,
  2021(F)
Dump Trucks, 21299
Dump Trucks and Diggers, 5559(F)
Dumpling Soup, 5645(F)
Dumpy La Rue, 2866(F)
Duncan and Dolores, 5400(F)
Duncan the Dancing Duck, 2217(F)
Duncan's Way, 3934(F)
The Dust Bowl, 4597(F)
Dust for Dinner, 6700(F)
Dust from Old Bones, 9275(F)
Dustin's Big School Day, 5482(F)
Dustland, 7443(F)
Dutch Sneakers and Flea Keepers,
  11858
The Dwarf Giant, 10451(F)
The Dwarf, the Giant, and the Uni-
  corn, 1187(F)
The Dwarf-Wizard of Uxmal, 11415
Dwight D. Eisenhower, 13028,
  13029, 13030, 13031
Dwight D. Eisenhower, John F.
  Kennedy, Lyndon B. Johnson,
  12671
Dwight David Eisenhower, President,
  13032
Dwight Gooden, 13457
Dylan's Day Out, 1942(F)
Dyslexia, 17926
  (Illus. by Mike Lacy), 17995

E I E I O, 14144
"E" Is for Elisa, 7458(F)
E-Mail, 21194
Each Living Thing, 4527(F)
Each One Special, 5107(F)
Each Orange Had Eight Slices, 443
The Eagle and the Rainbow, 11409
The Eagle and the River, 19323
The Eagle and the Wren, 11339
The Eagle as Wide as the World,
  7860(F)
Eagle Boy, 1651(F)
Eagle Drum, 15943
Eagle-Eye Ernie Comes to Town,
  6571(F)
Eagle Watching, 19320
Eagles, 19321, 19326, 19327, 19328,
  19332, 19343
  (Illus. by Wayne Lynch), 19330
The Eagle's Gift, 11207
Eagles of America, 19337
The Earliest Americans, 16033
Earl's Too Cool for Me, 4020(F)
An Early American Christmas,
  5800(F)
Early Humans, 14497
Early Morning in the Barn, 934(F)
The Early People of Florida, 15942
An Early Winter, 8876(F)
Earrings! 4340(F)
Ears, 18148
Earth, 18427, 18429, 18437, 18439
The Earth, 18426, 18434, 20315

The Earth and I, 4377(F)
The Earth Atlas, 20326
Earth Care, 10578
Earth Circles, 691(F)
Earth Cycles, 18438
Earth Day, 5636
Earth-Friendly Holidays, 21461
Earth-Friendly Outdoor Fun, 21462
Earth-Friendly Toys, 21656
The Earth Giant, 7633(F)
The Earth Is Good, 4412(F)
The Earth Is Painted Green, 11942
The Earth Science Book, 20329
Earth, Sky, Wet, Dry, 160(F)
Earth Tales from Around the World,
  10537
Earth Verses and Water Rhymes,
  11967
Earthdance, 5526(F)
  (Illus. by Norman Gorbaty), 4528
Earthkeepers, 13214
Earthly Astonishments, 9564(F)
Earthmaker's Tales, 11274
Earthmates, 11792
Earthquake! 20331
Earthquake Games, 20340
Earthquake in the Third Grade,
  10115(F)
Earthquake Terror, 6916(F)
Earthquakes, 20337, 20341, 20342,
  20345, 20351, 20354
Earthquakes and Volcanoes, 20334,
  20349
Earth's Place in Space, 18430
Earthsong, 14176
Earthsteps, 20571
Earthwatch, 20321
Earthwise at Home, 16961
Earthwise at Play, 16961
Earthwise at School, 16961
Earthworms, 19614, 19616
Earthworms, Dirt, and Rotten
  Leaves, 19613
An Earthworm's Life, 19609
East o' the Sun and West o' the
  Moon, 11121
East of the Sun and West of the
  Moon, 11130, 12041
East Side Story, 9516(F)
Easter, 5972(F), 17434
  (Illus. by Gail Gibbons), 5967
Easter Bunnies, 17437
The Easter Bunny That Overslept,
  5966(F)
An Easter Celebration, 17436
Easter Crafts, 21424
The Easter Egg Artists, 5962(F)
The Easter Egg Farm, 962(F)
Easter Fun, 21425
Easter Island, 15222
Easter Parade, 7342(F)
The Easter Rising, 15355
The Easter Story, 17435
Easter Surprise, 5975(F)
The Easter Wolf, 5963(F)
Eastern Europe, 15261
Eastern Great Lakes, 16530
Eastern Trails, 16269
Easy Braids, Barrettes and Bows,
  21549

Easy Costumes You Don't Have to Sew, 21538
Easy Geography Activities, 14360
Easy Math Puzzles, 20609
Easy Work! An Old Tale, 11128
Eat, Babies, Eat! 3317(F)
Eat Up, Gemma, 3196(F)
Eat Well, 18206
Eat Your Dinner! 2502(F)
Eat Your Peas, 4167(F)
Eat Your Vegetables! Drink Your Milk! 18210
Eat Your Words, 20103
Eating, 18104
Eating Disorders, 17960
Eating Fractions, 507
Eating Right, 18193
Eating the Alphabet, 37(F)
Eating the Plates, 16163
Ebb and Flo and the Greedy Gulls, 5413(F)
Ebb and Flo and the New Friend, 2697(F)
Echoes of the Elders, 11264
Echoes of the White Giraffe, 8987(F)
Echoes of World War II, 14871
Echohawk, 9191(F), 9192(F)
Eco-Arts and Crafts, 21579
EcoArt! 21417
Ecology, 16967
Ecology Crafts for Kids, 21459
Economic Causes, 17149
Ecuador, 15733, 15766
Ecuador in Pictures, 15730
Ed and Fred Flea, 2050(F)
Ed Emberley's Big Orange Drawing Book, 21572
Ed Emberley's Drawing Book, 21573
Ed Emberley's Drawing Book of Faces, 21574
Eddie, Incorporated, 8774(F)
Edgar Badger's Balloon Day, 5705(F)
Edgar Degas, 12222
Edgar Rice Burroughs, 12513
The Edge, 10277(F)
The Edible Pyramid, 20164
Edith, Herself, 8894(F)
Edith Kermit Carow Roosevelt, 13177
Edna St. Vincent Millay, 11557
Edo, 15012
Edward and the Pirates, 1380(F)
Edward Is Only a Fish, 8095(F)
Edward James Olmos, 12438, 12439
An Edward Lear Alphabet, 77
Edwin Hubble, 13309
Edwina the Emu, 2304(F)
Edwina Victorious, 8569(F)
Edwurd Fudwupper Fibbed Big, 1009(F)
Eek! There's a Mouse in the House, 4361(F)
The Eensy-Weensy Spider, 14245
The Eentsy, Weentsy Spider, 21984
Eerie Feary Feeling, 6014(F)
The Eeyou, 16044
Egg, 18917
The Egg, 1513(F)
Egg-Carton Zoo II, 21617
Egg-Drop Blues, 8875(F)

Egg to Chick, 19306
The Egg Tree, 21454
Eggbert, 1527(F)
Eggday, 2043(F)
Eggs, 19270
Eggs in One Basket, 10213(F)
Eggs Mark the Spot, 1771(F)
Egypt, 14666, 15495, 15497, 15499, 15504, 15505, 15506, 15507, 15509, 15510, 15511, 15513, 15514, 15515, 15516
The Egypt Game, 8371(F)
Egypt in Pictures, 15498
Egypt, Kush, Aksum, 14962
Egypt, the Culture, 14654
Egypt, the Land, 15508
Egypt, the People, 15508
Egyptian Art, 13940
The Egyptian Cinderella, 10658
Egyptian Gods and Goddesses, 14608
Egyptian Myths, 11453
The Egyptian News, 14667
The Egyptian Polar Bear, 944(F)
An Egyptian Pyramid, 14649
Egyptian Stories, 10674
Egyptian Town, 14668
The Egyptians, 14612, 14627, 14656
The Egyptians and the Valley of the Kings, 14670
Eight Animals on the Town, 2071(F)
Eight Ate, 14048
Eight Days of Hanukkah, 6130(F)
Eight Hands Round, 110(F)
Eight Legs, 19595
The 18 Penny Goose, 9254(F)
1863, 16433
18th Century Clothing, 21173
The 18th Emergency, 10031(F)
The 80s and 90s, 16515
Eighty-Eight Steps to September, 8906(F)
Ekatarina Gordeeva, 13590
El Chino, 13685
El Cid, 13772
The El Dorado Adventure, 6743(F)
El Greco, 12230
El Niño, 20751
El Nino and La Nina, 20785
El Salvador, 15656
Ela Bhatt, 13753
Elbert's Bad Word, 1700(F)
Eleanor, 13179
Eleanor Everywhere, 13182
Eleanor Roosevelt, 13180, 13181, 13183, 13184, 13187
Electing the President, 17108
Elections, 17094, 17099
The Electoral College, 17114
Electra and the Charlotte Russe, 9780(F)
Electric Fish, 19707
Electricity, 20880, 20889, 20892, 20902, 21239
Electronics, 21240
Elegy on the Death of Cesar Chavez, 11528
Elemenopeo, 2897(F)
The Elements of Pop-Up, 21608
Elena, 9140(F)
Elephant, 19160, 19173

Elephant Families, 19162
The Elephant Family Book, 19163
Elephant Quest, 19165
Elephant Seals, 19738
The Elephant Truck, 5436(F)
Elephant Walk, 5221(F)
The Elephant Who Couldn't Forget, 2453(F)
Elephant Woman, 13327
Elephants, 19164, 19166, 19168, 19169, 19171
Elephants Aloft, 956(F)
The Elephants' Ears, 1048(F)
Elephants on Board, 2427(F)
Elephants Swim, 18845
The Elevator Family, 9839(F)
Elevator Magic, 20590
The 11th Commandment, 5624
The Eleventh Hour, 6767(F)
An Elf for Christmas, 5822(F)
Elf Hill, 10450(F)
The Elf's Hat, 2838(F)
Elfsong, 8156(F)
Elfwyn's Saga, 11132
Eli, 2567(F)
Elie Wiesel, 12624, 12625
Elijah and Pin-Pin, 2499(F)
Elijah the Slave, 11171
Elijah's Angel, 5646(F)
Elijah's Tears, 9754(F)
Eli's Ghost, 6882(F)
Elisa in the Middle, 9892(F)
Elisabeth, 4779(F)
Eliza Down Under, 8925(F)
Elizabeth Blackwell, 13242
Elizabeth Bloomer Ford, 13154
Elizabeth Cady Stanton, 13193
Elizabeth Dole, 13149
Elizabeth I, 9105(F)
Elizabeth Imagined an Iceberg, 8035(F)
Elizabethan England, 15335
Elizabeti's Doll, 4844(F)
Eliza's Dog, 7213(F)
Ella, 2567(F)
Ella and the Naughty Lion, 1078(F)
Ella Enchanted, 10446(F)
Ella of All-of-a-Kind Family, 7527(F)
Ellen and Penguin, 4055(F)
Ellen Anders on Her Own, 8301(F)
Ellen Elizabeth Hawkins, 9540(F)
Ellen Tebbits, 9800(F)
Ellie Bear and the Fly-Away Fly, 2642(F)
Elliot Bakes a Cake, 5664(F)
Elliot's Bath, 990(F)
Elliot's Emergency, 991(F)
Elliot's Extraordinary Cookbook, 21677
Ellis Island, 15888, 16697, 16727, 16740
An Elm Tree and Three Sisters, 4546(F)
Elmer Again, 2435(F)
Elmer and the Dragon, 9857(F)
Elmer and the Kangaroo, 2436(F)
Elmer and the Lost Teddy Bear, 2437(F)
Elmer and Wilbur, 2438(F)
Elmer in the Snow, 2439(F)

Elmer Takes Off, 2440(F)
Eloise at Christmastime, 5936(F)
Elsa, Star of the Shelter, 8541(F)
Elsie Piddock Skips in Her Sleep, 1157(F)
The Elves and the Shoemaker (Illus. by Paul Galdone), 10895
   (Illus. by Margaret Walty), 10896
Elvira, 1566(F)
Elvis Lives! and Other Anagrams, 14020
Elvis Presley, 12445, 12444
Elvis Presley's the First Noel, 14198
Elwood and the Witch, 2191(F)
Elympics, 2285(F)
The Emancipation Proclamation, 16397, 16415
Emeline at the Circus, 3369(F)
Emergencies, 18220
Emergency, 18041
Emergency! 5567
Emergency Medical Technicians, 17800
Emily, 8253(F)
Emily and Alice Again, 3988(F)
Emily and the Golden Acorn, 992(F)
Emily Dickinson, 12530
Emily Just in Time, 5080(F)
Emily's First 100 Days of School, 607(F)
Emily's Runaway Imagination, 9801(F)
Emily's Shoes, 6284(F)
Emma and Freckles, 7157(F)
Emma and the Night Dogs, 2905(F)
Emma and the Silk Train, 4726(F)
Emma Ansky-Levine and Her Mitzvah Machine, 7637(F)
Emma's Christmas, 5940(F)
Emma's Journal, 9243(F)
Emma's Lamb, 5304(F)
Emma's Magic Winter, 6462(F)
Emma's Rug, 5069(F)
Emma's Yucky Brother, 6463(F)
Emmett's Pig, 6686(F)
Emmitt Smith, 13633, 13634
Emmy, 8439(F)
Emotional Ups and Downs, 17702
The Emperor and the Kite, 10780
The Emperor and the Nightingale
   (Illus. by Paul Birkbeck), 10517(F)
   (Illus. by Meilo So), 10377(F)
The Emperor General, 12931
The Emperor Who Forgot His Birthday, 5682(F)
The Emperor's Birthday Suit, 6716(F)
The Emperor's Egg, 19372
The Emperor's New Clothes, 10415(F)
   (Illus. by Anastassija Archipowa), 10492(F)
   (Illus. by Angela Barrett), 10379(F)
   (Illus. by Dorothee Duntze), 10378(F)
   (Illus. by Toni Goffe), 10380(F)
   (Illus. by Eve Tharlet), 10381(F)
The Emperor's Old Clothes, 1337(F)
Empire Dreams, 9635(F)
The Empire of the Czars, 15410

The Empire State Building, 16665, 16696
The Empress and the Silkworm, 4684(F)
The Empress of Elsewhere, 8351(F)
Empty Lot, 4427(F)
Empty Pockets, 3463(F)
The Empty Pot, 10749
The Enchanted Castle, 7986(F)
The Enchanted Raisin, 10397(F)
Enchanted Runner, 6951(F)
Enchantment in the Garden, 7803(F)
Encore for Eleanor, 2568(F)
Encounter, 9142(F)
Encounters with the Invisible World, 7023(F)
Encyclopedia Brown and the Case of the Dead Eagles, 7075(F)
Encyclopedia Brown and the Case of the Disgusting Sneakers, 7071(F)
Encyclopedia Brown and the Case of the Mysterious Handprints, 7072(F)
Encyclopedia Brown and the Case of the Secret Pitch, 7072(F)
Encyclopedia Brown and the Case of the Sleeping Dog, 7073(F)
Encyclopedia Brown and the Case of the Slippery Salamander, 7074(F)
Encyclopedia Brown and the Case of the Treasure Hunt, 7072(F)
Encyclopedia Brown, Boy Detective, 7075(F)
Encyclopedia Brown Finds the Clues, 7075(F)
Encyclopedia Brown Gets His Man, 7075(F)
Encyclopedia Brown Keeps the Peace, 7075(F)
Encyclopedia Brown Lends a Hand, 7072(F)
Encyclopedia Brown Sets the Pace, 7075(F)
Encyclopedia Brown's Book of Wacky Sports, 22064
The Encyclopedia of Civil Rights in America, 17026
End of the Race, 10335(F)
Endangered Animals, 19411
Endangered Birds of North America, 19409
Endangered Forest Animals, 19413
Endangered Grassland Animals, 19414
Endangered Mammals of North America, 19410
Endangered Mountain Animals, 19415
Endangered Plants, 20243
Endangered Species, 19422
Endangered Wetland Animals, 19415
Enduro Racing, 22240
Enemy Pie, 4030(F)
Energy, 20821, 20831, 20835, 20838, 20842
   (Illus. by Laurie Hamilton), 20840
Energy from the Sun, 20849
England, 15337, 15338, 15357
English Fairy Tales, 11004
Enora and the Black Crane, 7961(F)
The Enormous Carrot, 11387
The Enormous Crocodile, 1995(F)

The Enormous Egg, 9792(F)
The Enormous Potato, 11086
Enrique Iglesias, 12406
Enter at Your Own Risk, 7994(F)
Entomology, 19436
Entrepreneurs, 13736
The Environment, 16995, 20293
Environmental America, 16693, 16787, 16864, 16909
Environmental Diseases, 18018
Environmental Experiments About Renewable Energy, 20836
The Environmental Movement, 16964
Environments of the Western Hemisphere, 14339
Epidemic, 17974, 18011
Epilepsy, 17947, 17978
Eppie M. Says . . ., 4137(F)
Equal Rights, 17023
Equestrian Events, 22207
The Era of the Dinosaurs, 14442
Erandi's Braids, 4759(F)
Ereth's Birthday, 7566(F)
Eric Carle's Animals Animals, 11816
Eric Carle's Dragons Dragons and Other Creatures That Never Were, 11735
Eric Carle's Treasury of Classic Stories for Children by Aesop, Hans Christian Andersen, and the Brothers Grimm, 10538
Eric in the Land of the Insects, 7617(F)
Eric the Red, 13792
The Erie Canal, 16237
Erie Canal, 16713
An Eritrean Family, 17545
Ernest and Celestine at the Circus, 2781(F)
Ernest L. Thayer's Casey at the Bat, 12007
Ernestine and Amanda, 8255(F), 8256(F)
Erosion, 20570
Escape, 14853
Escape from Exile, 10208(F)
Escape from Fire Mountain, 7004(F)
Escape from Shangri-La, 7486(F)
Escape into the Night, 9295(F)
Escape Key, 6799(F)
Escape North! The Story of Harriet Tubman, 12799
Escape South, 9320(F)
Escape to the Forest, 9684(F)
Escaping from Enemies, 18896
Escaping to America, 17591
The Eskimo, 15825
Eskimo Boy, 15811
An Eskimo Family, 15793
ESP, 21925
Esperanza Rising, 9620(F)
Essential Boating for Teens, 22264
Essential Fishing for Teens, 22175
Essential Hiking for Teens, 22168
Essential Snowmobiling for Teens, 22044
Estee Lauder, 12923
The Etcher's Studio, 1181(F)
The Eternal Spring of Mr. Ito, 9659(F)

Ethiopia, 14918, 14922, 14929, 14936
Ethiopia in Pictures, 14927
Ethnic America, 16694, 16910
Ethnic Violence, 17145
ETs and UFOs, 20995
Eucalyptus Wings, 1268(F)
Eugenie Clark, 13258
Europe, 15257
Evan's Voice, 10210(F)
Even a Little Is Something, 8995(F)
Even If I Did Something Awful? 3680(F)
Even If I Spill My Milk? 3700(F)
Even Little Kids Get Diabetes, 17992
Even More Short and Shivery, 10611
Ever After, 8839(F)
The Ever-Changing Atom, 20286
Ever-Clever Elisa, 10083(F)
Ever Heard of an Aardwolf? 18649
The Ever-Living Tree, 20219
Everest, 22047
Everett Anderson's Christmas Coming, 5785(F)
Everett Anderson's Goodbye, 11751
Everett Anderson's Nine Month Long, 11752
Everglades, 16858
The Everglades, 16875
The Everglades and the Gulf Coast, 20364
Every Buddy Counts, 525(F)
Every Day Is Earth Day, 21491
Every Living Thing, 7296(F)
Everybody Bakes Bread, 3109(F)
Everybody Cooks Rice, 21695
Everybody Has a Bellybutton, 18074
Everybody Says, 6307(F)
Everybody Serves Soup, 5805(F)
Everybody's Favorite, 10332(F)
An Everyday Book, 3404(F)
Everyday Children, 3405(F)
Everyday Garden, 3405(F)
Everyday House, 3406(F)
Everyday Pets, 3406(F)
Everyday Plays for Boys and Girls, 12033
Everyday Science, 18325
Everyday Science Experiments in the Kitchen, 18318
Everyday Science Experiments with Food, 20096
Everyday Town, 3406(F)
Everyone Knows What a Dragon Looks Like, 4353(F)
Everyone Poops, 3173
The Everything Book, 180(F)
Everything I Know About Pirates, 14561
The Everything Kids' Nature Book, 20660
Everything on a Waffle, 8697(F)
Everything to Spend the Night, 111(F)
Everything You Need to Know About American History Homework, 14118
Everything You Need to Know About Anxiety and Panic Attacks, 17908

Everything You Need to Know About Asthma, 18004
Everything You Need to Know About Being a Baby-sitter, 16947
Everything You Need to Know About Being a Vegan, 18213
Everything You Need to Know About Being a Vegetarian, 18209
Everything You Need to Know About Birth Order, 17667
Everything You Need to Know About Cancer, 17985
Everything You Need to Know About Cerebral Palsy, 17991
Everything You Need to Know About Down Syndrome, 17942
Everything You Need to Know About Lyme Disease, 17953
Everything You Need to Know About Math Homework, 14118
Everything You Need to Know About Mononucleosis, 18005
Everything You Need to Know About Science Homework, 14118
Everything You Need to Know About Skin Care, 18196
Everything You Need to Know About the Dangers of Computer Hacking, 21213
Everything You Need to Know About the Dangers of Sports Gambling, 22073
Everything You Need to Know When a Brother or Sister Is Autistic, 17932
Everything You Need to Know When Someone You Know Has Leukemia, 17986
Everywhere, 8261(F)
Everywhere Babies, 3322(F)
Evie Peach, 9272(F)
Evolution, 14498, 14514
Ewan McGregor, 12419
Exactly the Opposite, 198(F)
The Excretory System, 18107
The Executioner's Daughter, 9127(F)
The Executive Branch, 17118
Exercise and Your Health, 18203
Exercise Is Fun! 18195
The Exiles, 7476(F)
The Exiles at Home, 7477(F)
The Exiles in Love, 7478(F)
Exodus, 17328
   (Illus. by Charles Mikolaycak), 17254
Exodus from Egypt, 17241
Exotic Invaders, 18647
Exotic Pets, 19913
Exotic Species, 18628
Experiment with Air, 20673
Experiment with Magnets and Electricity, 20908
Experiment with Plants, 20229
Experiment with Senses, 18136
Experiment with Water, 20742
Experimenting with a Microscope, 18300
Experiments That Explore Acid Rain, 16996
Experiments with Balloons, 20669
Experiments with Bubbles, 20809

Experiments with Light and Mirrors, 20868
Experiments with Motion, 20829
Exploding Ants, 18850
Exploration and Settlement, 16094
Exploration into Africa, 14908
Exploration into Australia, 15228
Exploration into China, 15086
Exploration into India, 15100
Exploration into Japan, 15139
Exploration into North America, 16075
Explore a Tropical Forest, 20435
Explorers, 12057, 12059
Explorers and Traders, 16078
Explorers, Missionaries, and Trappers, 12646
Explorers of the Frontier, 16380
Exploring Africa, 14910
Exploring an Ocean Tide Pool, 19854
Exploring Ancient Greece, 14693
Exploring Autumn, 18330
Exploring for Shipwrecks, 14540
Exploring Parks with Ranger Dockett, 17747
Exploring Shapes, 20580
Exploring Space, 21004
Exploring the Bismarck, 14820
Exploring the Deep, Dark Sea, 19818
Exploring the Earth with John Wesley Powell, 12152
Exploring the Grand Canyon, 16605
Exploring the New World, 16092
Exploring the Origins of the Universe, 18397
Exploring the Polar Regions, 15804
Exploring the Rain Forest, 20458
Exploring the Reaches of the Solar System, 18531
Exploring the Sky, 18404
Exploring the Sky by Day, 20761
Exploring the Titanic, 19873
Exploring the World, 12060
Exploring Time, 18304
Exploring Winter, 18571
Exquemelin and the Pirates of the Caribbean, 12117
Extinction Is Forever, 18668
Extra Cheese, Please! 20070
Extra Innings, 11997
Extraordinary Black Americans, 12635
An Extraordinary Egg, 2380(F)
Extraordinary Events and Oddball Occurrences, 21892
Extraordinary Jewish Americans, 12639
An Extraordinary Life, 19565
Extraordinary Women in Politics, 13726
Extraterrestrials, 20979
Extreme Machines, 21285
Extreme Mountain Biking, 22164
Extreme Surfing, 22304
Extremely Weird Endangered Species, 19402
The Exxon Valdez, 16813
Eye Book, 6453(F)
An Eye for an Eye, 9248(F)
Eye of the Beholder, 9873(F)
Eye of the Great Bear, 7121(F)

The Eye of the Stone, 7613(F)
Eye of the Storm, 20700
Eye on the Wild, 12187
Eye Spy Colors, 282(F)
Eye Spy Shapes, 344(F)
EyeOpeners! 18807
Eyes, 18145
Eyes, Nose, Fingers, and Toes, 18062
The Eyes of Gray Wolf, 7261(F)
The Eyes of the Amaryllis, 7388(F)
Eyewitness Question and Answer
 Book, 21909
Ezra, 19114
Ezra Jack Keats, 12246

F. Scott Fitzgerald, 12535
Fables, 2389(F)
Fables from Aesop, 11067
Fables of Aesop, 11051
The Fables of Aesop, 11055
Fabric, 21647
Fabric Fun for Kids, 21648
The Fabrics of Fairytale, 10529
The Fabulous Fantoras, 9859(F)
The Fabulous Fantoras, Book Two,
 7739(F)
Fabulous Feasts, 14559
The Fabulous Firework Family,
 4648(F)
The Fabulous Flight, 7894(F)
The Fabulous Four Skunks, 2083(F)
Fabulous Frogs, 18723
Fabulous Monsters, 11458
Fabulous Paper Gliders, 21795
The Fabulous Song, 4162(F)
The Face at the Window, 4675(F)
A Face First, 8621(F)
The Face in the Bessledorf Funeral
 Parlor, 6986(F)
The Face in the Mirror, 8149(F)
Face-Off, 10323(F)
Face Painting, 21590
 (Illus. by Mei Lim), 21589
 (Illus. by Louise Phillips), 21592
Faces, 3400
Faces Only a Mother Could Love,
 18874
Factastic Book of 1001 Lists, 21889
Factories in Space, 20948
The Facts and Fictions of Minna
 Pratt, 8753(F)
Fair Ball! 14 Great Stars from Base-
 ball's Negro Leagues, 13424
A Fair Bear Share, 526(F)
Fair, Brown and Trembling,
 10413(F)
A Fair Wind for Troy, 11475
The Fairies, 21950
Fairies' Ring, 10630
Fairies, Trolls and Goblins Galore,
 11559
A Fairy Called Hilary, 8136(F)
The Fairy Rebel, 10398(F)
A Fairy-Tale Life, 12492
Fairy Tales, 10416(F)
Fairy Tales of Oscar Wilde, 10419
The Fairy Tales of Oscar Wilde,
 10478(F)
The Fairy Tales of Oscar Wilde, v. 3,
 10487

Fairy Tales of the Brothers Grimm,
 10521
Fairy Wings, 1414(F)
The Fairy's Mistake, 10447(F)
Faith and the Electric Dogs, 7837(F)
Faith and the Rocket Cat, 7838(F)
Faith Unfurled, 16117
The Faithful Friend, 11431
Fakes and Forgeries, 17068
Falcon's Egg, 7756(F)
Falcons Nest on Skyscrapers, 19329
Fall Is Not Easy, 1292(F)
Fall Leaves Fall! 4454(F)
The Fall of Quebec and the French
 and Indian War, 16161
The Fall of the Bastille, 15298
The Fall of the Soviet Union, 15418
Falling Up, 11697
Families, 11768, 13923, 17673
Families Are Different, 3836(F)
Family, 3813(F)
Family Abuse, 17705
Family Breakup, 17676
Family Celebrations, 5644
Family, Familia, 3526(F)
Family for Sale, 8414(F)
A Family from Bosnia, 15294
A Family from China, 15090
A Family from Germany, 15329
A Family from Guatemala, 15688
A Family from Iraq, 15553
A Family from South Africa, 14977
A Family from Vietnam, 15202
A Family Goes Hunting, 22043
The Family Haggadah, 17486
A Family in Chile, 15785
A Family in Egypt, 15496
A Family in Morocco, 14964
A Family in Singapore, 15162
A Family in Sri Lanka, 15147
A Family in Sudan, 14948
A Family in Thailand, 15208
Family Pictures/Cuadros de Familia,
 17576
Family Pose, 8701(F)
The Family Read-Aloud Christmas
 Treasury, 5866
Family Reunion, 11702
Family Secrets, 7416(F)
A Family That Fights, 4907(F)
Family Ties, 18875
Family Time, 3324(F)
A Family Trait, 6967(F)
A Family Treasury of Bible Stories,
 17252
The Family Treasury of Jewish Holi-
 days, 17460
A Family Treasury of Myths from
 Around the World, 11449
A Family Treasury of Prayers, 17521
The Family Tree Detective, 17650
The Family Under the Bridge,
 8267(F)
Family Violence, 17659
FamilyFun's Parties, 17351
Famine, 20043
The Famine Secret, 9098(F)
Famous Firsts of Scottish-Americans,
 17590
Famous People of Asian Ancestry,
 12678

Famous People of Hispanic Heritage,
 12679, 17551
Famous People of Hispanic Heritage,
 vol. 3, 12679
Famous People of Hispanic Heritage,
 vol. 2, 12679
The Famous Stanley Kidnapping
 Case, 7070(F)
Fanciful Faces and Handbound
 Books, 14080
Fannie Lou Hamer and the Fight for
 the Vote, 12725
Fanny at Chez Panisse, 16951
Fanny's Dream, 3552(F)
The Fantastic Book of Car Racing,
 22081
The Fantastic Book of Horses, 20006
The Fantastic Cutaway Book of
 Giant Buildings, 21134
The Fantastic Cutaway Book of
 Giant Machines, 21250
The Fantastic Drawings of Danielle,
 4751(F)
Fantastic Frogs, 18736
Fantastic Transport Machines, 21286
Fantastic! Wow! and Unreal! A Book
 About Interjections and Conjunc-
 tions, 14030
Fantasy Stories, 8229(F)
FAQ Weather, 20797
Far from the Storm, 6830(F)
The Faraway Drawer, 3104(F)
Faraway Drums, 1323(F)
Faraway Families, 7473(F)
Faraway Home, 9690(F)
 (Illus. by E. B. Lewis), 3760(F)
Faraway Summer, 9560(F)
Farewell, My Lunchbag, 7778(F)
The Farewell Symphony, 9031(F)
Farewell to Shady Glade, 2566(F)
Farewell to the Island, 9333(F)
A Farm, 15341
Farm, 20059
The Farm, 16149
A Farm Album, 15899
Farm Alphabet Book, 100(F)
Farm Animals, 5200, 5420(F)
 (Illus. by Phoebe Dunn), 4422(F)
 (Illus. by Karen Jacobsen), 20061
The Farm Book, 20072
The Farm Combine, 20068
Farm Counting Book, 515(F)
Farm Friends Clean Up, 2116(F)
Farm Morning, 3302(F)
The Farmer and the Poor God, 10835
Farmer Boy, 7537(F)
Farmer Brown Goes Round and
 Round, 1583(F)
Farmer Brown Shears His Sheep,
 1584(F)
Farmer Duck, 2794(F)
Farmer Enno and His Cow, 1498(F)
Farmer George and the Fieldmice,
 2823(F)
Farmer George and the Lost Chick,
 2823(F)
The Farmer in the Dell, 876, 14187
Farmer Palmer's Wagon Ride,
 2718(F)
Farmers and Fighters, 14706
A Farmer's Garden, 2172(F)

Farmers' Market, 3251(F)
Farming (Illus. by Pat Cupples), 20052
(Illus. by Gail Gibbons), 20057
Farms Feed the World, 20060
Farmworker's Friend, 12825
Farmyard Tales from Far and Wide, 10542
Farolitos for Abuelo, 5745(F)
The Farolitos of Christmas, 5746(F)
Fashion Through the Ages, 21175
Fast and Funny Paper Toys You Can Make, 21609
Fast Cash for Kids, 16941
Fast Eddie, 7659(F)
Fast, Strong, and Striped, 18929
The Fat Cat Sat on the Mat, 6428(F)
Fat Charlie's Circus, 4156(F)
Fat Fanny, Beanpole Bertha and the Boys, 7495(F)
Fat Men from Space, 9966(F)
Fat Santa, 5792(F)
Fateful Forebodings, 21893
Father Christmas, 5761(F)
The Father Who Had 10 Children, 3667(F)
Father's Arcane Daughter, 6924(F)
Father's Rubber Shoes, 3689(F)
Fats, 20166
(Illus. by Anne Canevari Green), 20168
The Favershams, 12534
Favorite Children's Stories from China and Tibet, 10758
Favorite Greek Myths, 11499
Favorite Medieval Tales, 10596
Favorite Norse Myths, 11519
Favorite Poems Old and New, 11560
Favorite Stories of the Ballet, 14297
A Fawn in the Grass, 4529(F)
The FDR Way, 13098
The Fear Place, 6987(F)
Feast for 10, 433(F)
The Feather-Bed Journey, 4644(F)
Featherbys, 8374(F)
Feathered Dinosaurs, 14473
Feathers, 11148
Feathers and Fools, 1164(F)
Feathers for Lunch, 4424(F)
Feathery Facts, 19221
Fed Up! A Feast of Frazzled Foods, 9(F)
Feeding Our Feathered Friends, 19284
Feel the Wind, 4418(F)
Feeling Angry, 17607
Feeling Happy, 17607
Feeling Scared, 17607
Feeling Thankful, 3398
Feeling Violent, 17630
Feelings, 152
The Feelings Book, 4260(F)
The Feet in the Gym, 5493(F)
Feet That Suck and Feed, 18858
Feliciana Feydra LeRoux, 2978(F)
Feliciana Meets d'Loup Garou, 1621(F)
Felicity Learns a Lesson, 9215(F)
Felicity Saves the Day, 9214(F)
Felicity's Cook Book, 21696
Felicity's Craft Book, 21519

Felicity's Surprise, 9216(F)
Felix and the 400 Frogs, 6241(F)
Felix's Hat, 1782(F)
Fenwick's Suit, 8103(F)
Feral Cat, 19079
Ferdinand Magellan and the First Voyage Around the World, 12140
Ferocious Girls, Steamroller Boys, and Other Poems in Between, 11859
Ferrari, 21305
Ferret in the Bedroom, Lizards in the Fridge, 10012(F)
Ferrets, 18947
Ferryboat, 21370
Ferryboat Ride! 3382(F)
Festival Crafts, 21430
Festival Decorations, 21421
Festivals, 17383
Fiber, 20159
Fiddle Fever, 8423(F)
Fiddle-i-fee, 902(F)
The Fiddle Ribbon, 3770(F)
The Fiddler of the Northern Lights, 1305(F)
Fiddlin' Sam, 4944(F)
Field Day Friday, 5483(F)
The Field Mouse and the Dinosaur Named Sue, 2808(F)
The Field of the Dogs, 8006(F)
Fields of Home, 9088(F)
¡Fiesta! 452(F)
Fiesta! (Illus. by Jose Ortega), 3966(F)
(Illus. by Scott Taylor), 3523(F)
Fiesta Fireworks, 4575(F)
Fiesta U.S.A., 17334
Fifth Grade, 8752(F)
Fifth Grade Magic, 7747(F)
55 Friends, 615(F)
50 Simple Things Kids Can Do to Recycle, 16977
50 Simple Things Kids Can Do to Save the Earth, 16959
Fifty-Three and a Half Things That Changed the World and Some That Didn't! 21050
52 Days by Camel, 14963
Fig Pudding, 7433(F)
Figgs and Phantoms, 8036(F)
Fight for Life, 7151(F)
Fighting Fires, 5579
Fighting for the Forest, 4513(F)
The Fighting Ground, 9220(F)
The Figure Skating Book, 22227
Figuring Figures, 13874
Figuring Out Frances, 8386(F)
Film, 21275
Fin M'Coul, 10970
The Final Cut, 10278(F)
Finches, 19281
Find Cat, Wear Hat, 3187(F)
Find Freddie, 2752(F)
Find It! 14001
Find the Constellations, 18552
Finders Keepers (Illus. by Nicolas Mordvinoff), 5310(F)
(Illus. by Noela Young), 10228(F)
Finding a Job for Daddy, 3801(F)
Finding Buck McHenry, 10362(F)
Finding Hattie, 10136(F)

Finding Out About Dinosaurs, 14429
Finding Out About Whales, 19793
Finding Providence, 4581(F)
Finding Walter, 8157(F)
Finding Your Place, 17669
A Fine Fat Pig, 11791
Fine Lines, 12546
Fine Print, 13304
Fingerprints and Talking Bones, 17072
Finland, 15456, 15457, 15461
Finland in Pictures, 15445
Finn, 6760(F)
Finn McCoul, 10985
Finn MacCoul and His Fearless Wife, 10953
Finn's Island, 7426(F)
Finn's Search, 8278(F)
Fiona McGilray's Story, 9603(F)
Fiona's Private Pages, 8273(F)
The Fir Tree, 10382(F)
Fir Trees, 20198
Fire, 9543(F), 20473
Fire! 17817
Fire and Silk, 2945
Fire at the Triangle Factory, 9586(F)
Fire, Bed, and Bone, 9082(F)
Fire Fighters, 17816, 17819
(Illus. by Kim LaFave), 3033
(Illus. by Pamela Paparone), 5414(F)
Fire Fighting, 5589(F)
Fire! Fire! 3166(F)
"Fire! Fire!" Said Mrs. McGuire, 863
A Fire in Her Bones, 12929
Fire in Oakland, California, 16765
Fire in the Forest, 16965
Fire in the Sky, 9610(F)
Fire in the Valley, 9636(F)
Fire in the Wind, 6941(F)
Fire in Their Eyes, 17806
Fire into Ice, 12240
Fire! My Parents' Story, 16689
Fire on the Mountain, 10680
The Fire Pony, 8511(F)
Fire Station Number 4, 17809
Fire! The Library Is Burning, 16663
Fire Truck, 1580(F), 21294
Fire Truck Nuts and Bolts, 21297
Fire Trucks, 21307
Fired Up! 13939
Firedancers, 3930(F)
Firefighters A to Z, 32(F), 65(F)
Firefighters Fight Fires, 17813
Firefighting, 17820
Fireflies, 19456
Fireflies! 4393(F)
Fireflies in the Dark, 14878
Fireflies in the Night, 19452
Fireflies, Peach Pies and Lullabies, 5004(F)
Firefly Night, 682(F)
The Firefly Star, 11138
Firefly Summer, 9130(F)
Firehorse Max, 4216(F)
Firehouse, 17823
Fireman Small, 3492(F)
Fireweed, 9697(F)
The Firework-Maker's Daughter, 8031(F)
Fireworks, Picnics, and Flags, 17363

The First Air Voyage in the United States, 12078
The First Americans, 15967
The First Amphibians, 14442
First Apple, 9011(F)
The First Battles, 16434
The First Bear in Africa! 1261(F)
A First Bible Story Book, 17285
A First Book of Myths, 10562
First Book of the Keyboard, 14226
The First Christmas, 17415
First Day, Hooray! 5524(F)
First Day Jitters, 3100(F)
The First Decade, 9553(F)
First Facts About American Heroes, 12666
First Facts About the Presidents, 12686
First Facts About U.S. History, 15887
First Flight, 2456(F), 6657(F)
The First Flight, 13359
The First Four Years, 7537(F)
First Friends, 6208(F)
First Frontier, 16375
First Grade Can Wait, 5469(F)
First Grade Takes a Test, 5488(F)
First He Made the Sun, 17332
The First Horse I See, 7232(F)
The First Human-Powered Flight, 12138
First in the Field, 13492
First Ladies, 12650
First Lady of the Air, 12153
First Lessons in Ballet, 14284
A First Look at Bats, 19316
A First Look at Dogs, 19970
A First Look at Ducks, Geese, and Swans, 19316
First Mate Tate, 8756(F)
The First Men in Space, 20994
First Night, 3496(F)
The First Noel, 14200
The First Olympic Games, 11502
First on the Moon, 20991
First Painter, 1338(F)
First Palm Trees, 10652
First Photos, 21797
First Pink Light, 3660(F)
First Plays for Children, 12034
First Poems, 11556
First Questions and Answers About the Human Body, 18057
The First Red Maple Leaf, 1721(F)
First, Second, 483(F)
First Snow, 2952(F)
  (Illus. by Emily Arnold McCully), 2413(F)
The First Snow, 1054(F)
First Snow, Magic Snow, 11082
The First Snowfall, 4520(F)
The First Starry Night, 4691(F)
The First Story Ever Told, 11440
The First Teddy Bear, 21653
First Test, 8017(F)
The First Thanksgiving (Illus. by Thomas Locker), 17496
  (Illus. by James Watling), 17500
A First Thesaurus, 14061
First Things First, 8696(F)
First Times, 3036(F)

The First Two Lives of Lukas-Kasha, 7553(F)
The First Unrefueled Flight Around the World, 21107
First Verses, 11566
First Word Book, 14041
First World War, 14806
Fish, 19702, 19714, 19981
The Fish Bride and Other Gypsy Tales, 10861
Fish Eyes, 428(F)
Fish Face, 6342(F)
A Fish Hatches, 19699
A Fish in His Pocket, 1946(F)
Fish Is Fish, 2381(F)
The Fish Princess, 1667(F)
A Fish That's a Box, 13955
Fish Watching with Eugenie Clark, 13259
The Fish Who Could Wish, 1904(F)
Fish Wish, 5133(F)
The Fisherman and His Wife (Illus. by Diana Bryan), 10897
  (Illus. by Eleanor Hubbard), 10520
Fishes, 19716
  (Illus. by James G. Irving), 19718
Fishing, 3615(F)
  (Illus. by Pat Cupples), 19848, 22178
Fishing Bears, 19039
Fishing for a Dream, 675
Fishing for Methuselah, 4290(F)
Fishing in the Air, 1086(F)
The Fishing Summer, 2942(F)
Fishing Sunday, 3733(F)
Fishy Facts, 18613
Fit for Life, 18202
Five Alien Elves, 9747(F)
The Five Cat Club, 8340(F)
Five Children and It, 7987(F)
Five Chinese Brothers, 4087(F)
Five Creatures, 3720(F)
Five Creepy Creatures, 6676(F)
The Five-Dog Night, 4111(F)
Five Goofy Ghosts, 6677(F)
Five Green and Speckled Frogs, 1742(F)
The 500 Hats of Bartholomew Cubbins, 1564(F)
The 512 Ants on Sullivan Street, 20587(F)
Five Little Ducks, 563(F), 842(F)
Five Little Kittens, 711(F)
Five Little Kitty Cats, 586(F)
Five Little Monkeys Jumping on the Bed, 405(F)
Five Little Monkeys Sitting in a Tree, 406(F)
Five Little Monkeys Wash the Car, 1958(F)
Five Little Monkeys with Nothing to Do, 1959(F)
The Five Little Peppers and How They Grew, 7513(F)
Five Little Piggies, 864(F)
Five Little Pumpkins, 6058(F)
  (Illus. by Dan Yaccarino), 5997(F)
Five Live Bongos, 3781(F)
The Five Senses, 18142
Five Silly Fishermen, 6325(F)
The Five Sisters, 7947(F)

Five Smooth Stones, 9235(F)
Five Trucks, 5565(F)
Five Ugly Monsters, 625(F)
Fixing the Crack of Dawn, 3428(F)
The Fixits, 4233(F)
A Flag for Grandma, 3666(F)
A Flag for Our Country, 13976
The Flag We Love, 13975
Flags, 4853(F)
The Flame of Peace, 9134(F)
Flannel Kisses, 3041(F)
Flapjack Waltzes, 8862(F)
Flappy Waggy Wiggly, 21835(F)
Flash, Crash, Rumble, and Roll, 20683
Flashlight, 3244(F)
Flashy Fantastic Rain Forest Frogs, 18734
Flat Stanley, 1014(F)
Flatfoot Fox and the Case of the Bashful Beaver, 7655(F)
Flatfoot Fox and the Case of the Missing Eye, 6269(F)
Flatfoot Fox and the Case of the Missing Schoolhouse, 6268(F)
Flatfoot Fox and the Case of the Missing Whoooo, 1965(F)
Flatfoot Fox and the Case of the Nosy Otter, 6269(F)
Flattops at War, 14829
Flavor Foods, 20099
A Flavor of India, 15105
The Flawed Glass, 8917(F)
Fledgling, 5138(F)
The Fledgling, 7886(F)
Flick, 7329(F)
Flicker Flash, 11577
Flies, 19432, 19467, 19477
Flight, 12134, 21082, 21086
Flight of the Dragon Kyn, 7729(F)
The Flight of the Snow Geese, 5290(F)
Flights of Fancy and Other Poems, 11633
The Flimflam Man, 9777(F)
Flint's Rock, 8434(F)
Flip-Flap, 203
Flip-Flops, 3084(F)
Flip's Fantastic Journal, 2013(F)
Flix, 2770(F)
Floating and Sinking, 20801
Floating Home, 1186(F)
The Floating House, 4820(F)
Floating in Space, 20954
Floating Lanterns and Golden Shrines, 17381
The Floating Orchard, 1225(F)
Flood, 6825(F), 8586(F), 20705
Flood! 20723
The Flood Tales, 17310
Floodland, 8078(F)
Floods, 20680, 20688, 20708, 20714
Floods! 20699
Flora and Tiger, 12198
Flora McDonnell's ABC, 86(F)
Flora the Frog, 4987(F)
Florence Griffith Joyner, 13660
Florence Kelley, 12916
Florence Robinson, 9554(F)
Florida, 16837, 16863, 16887
The Florida Panther, 19109

Florizella and the Wolves, 10426(F)
Floss, 5305(F)
Flower Garden, 3554(F)
Flower Girl, 6380(F)
The Flower Girl, 3172(F)
Flower Watching with Alice East-
wood, 13269
Flowers, 20034, 20042
Flowers and Friends, 20035
Flowers for the Wicked Witch,
7878(F)
Flowers, Fruits, and Seeds, 20261
Flowers on the Wall, 4778(F)
Flowers, Trees, and Fruits, 20044
Flush the Potty, 3481(F)
Flush! Treating Wastewater, 16976
Flute's Journey, 19249
Fly, 19448
Fly Away Home, 4916(F)
Fly, Bessie, Fly, 12093
Fly by Night, 1985(F)
Fly, Eagle, Fly! 10670
Fly High! The Story of Bessie Cole-
man, 12090
Fly, Homer, Fly, 2570(F)
Fly Traps! 20238
Fly with Poetry, 11589
Fly with the Birds, 3114(F)
Flying, 5555(F)
Flying Ace, 12108
Flying Against the Wind, 12143
Flying an Agricultural Plane with Mr.
Miller, 17836
Flying Brown Pelicans, 19294
The Flying Chickens of Paradise
Lane, 8306(F)
Flying Dimitri, 1134(F)
The Flying Dragon Room, 1704(F)
The Flying Flea, Callie, and Me,
8185(F)
The Flying Garbanzos, 4297(F)
Flying in a Hot Air Balloon, 21974
The Flying Latke, 6124(F)
Flying over Brooklyn, 8162(F)
Flying Solo, 10057(F)
The Flying Tortoise, 10700
Flying with the Eagle, Racing the
Great Bear, 11217
Foal, 20002
Fog Cat, 5254(F)
Foggy Friday, 2635(F)
Foghorn Flattery and the Dancing
Horses, 7081(F)
The Folk Art Counting Book, 605
The Folk Keeper, 7611(F)
Folk Tale Plays Round the World,
12035
Folk Tales from Asia for Children
Everywhere, 10719
The Folks in the Valley, 4(F)
Follow Carl! 2003(F)
Follow Me! 2630(F)
Follow My Leader, 8891(F)
Follow That Fin! Studying Dolphin
Behavior, 19689
Follow That Puppy! 4228(F)
Follow That Trash! 16980
Follow the Drinking Gourd, 4886(F),
9268(F)
Follow the Leader, 3429(F)
Follow the Star, 6831(F)

Follow Your Nose, 18137
The Follower, 1622(F)
Following My Own Footsteps,
8444(F)
Following the Mystery Man, 6870(F)
Food, 20078, 20116, 20131
Food and Digestion, 18097
Food and Feasts in Ancient Rome,
14747
Food and Feasts in the Middle Ages,
14761
Food and Your Health, 18204
Food Crafts, 21431
Food Fight, 11685, 17941
Food in Grandma's Day, 16493
The Food Pyramid, 20161
Food Rules! The Stuff You Munch,
Its Crunch, Its Punch, and Why
You Sometimes Lose Your Lunch,
18099
Food Safety, 20162
Fool and the Phoenix, 9000(F)
Fool of the World and the Flying
Ship, 10858
The Fool of the World and the Flying
Ship, 11108
The Foolish Men of Agra, 10807
Foolish Rabbit's Big Mistake, 10801
The Fools of Chelm and Their Histo-
ry, 11172
Foot Book, 6640(F)
The Foot Warmer and the Crow,
9266(F)
Football, 22187, 22189
Football Friends, 6511(F)
The Football Rebels, 10360(F)
The Football That Won . . ., 2968(F)
Footprints and Shadows, 3107(F)
Footprints in the Sand, 20400
Footprints on the Moon, 18454
For Better, For Worse, 17643
For Every Child, 17019
For Heaven's Sake, 3873(F)
For Laughing Out Loud, 11908
For Lucky's Sake, 6912(F)
For My Family, Love, Allie, 3885(F)
For Our Children, 14240
For Pete's Sake, 2814(F)
For the Children, 17194
For the Love of Pete, 8482(F)
For the Love of the Game, 11996
For Your Eyes Only, 10124(F)
Force and Motion, 20832
Forces and Motion, 20825
Forest, 6350(F)
Forest Child, 1370(F)
Forest Fire, 20460
The Forest Has Eyes, 310
The Forest in the Clouds, 20434
Forest Plants, 20445
Forest Slump, 6953(F)
Forestry, 20438
Forests, 20431
Forests and Woodlands, 20474
Forests for the Future, 20471
A Forest's Life, 20466
Forever Amber Brown, 8420(F)
Forging Freedom, 14886
The Forgotten Door, 10202(F)
The Forgotten Players, 22091
Forklifts, 21300

The Formerly Great Alexander Fami-
ly, 8522(F)
Formula 1 Motor Racing Book,
22080
Fort Chipewyan Homecoming, 16004
Fort Life, 16332
Fort Sumter, 16416
The 40s and 50s, 16517
40s and 50s, 13896
Fortune Telling, 21926
Fortune's Journey, 9353(F)
Forty Acres and Maybe a Mule,
9615(F)
Forty Fortunes, 11201
Forward into Light, 17045
Fossil Detective, 14463
Fossil Fever, 7145(F)
The Fossil Girl, 13229
Fossils, 14416
Fossils Tell of Long Ago, 14375
The Founding of the AFL and the
Rise of Organized Labor, 16483
The Founding Presidents, 16276
Fountains of Life, 19819
Four Against the Odds, 13216
4B Goes Wild, 10066(F)
The Four Corners of the Sky, 10635
Four Dollars and Fifty Cents,
2948(F)
Four Famished Foxes and Fosdyke,
2052(F)
Four Fierce Kittens, 5192(F)
The Four Gallant Sisters, 10921
Four Hungry Kittens, 924(F)
Four of a Kind, 7054(F)
Four Seasons of Corn, 15975
Four Stories for Four Seasons,
2027(F)
Four Stupid Cupids, 7944(F)
Fourteenth-Century Towns, 14755
The 14th Dalai Lama, 13778
Fourth Grade Celebrity, 10062(F)
Fourth Grade Weirdo, 10059(F)
Fourth of July Fireworks, 17391
The Fourth Wise Man, 5930(F)
Fowl Play, Desdemona, 9894(F)
Fox, 19131
The Fox, 19121
The Fox and the Rooster and Other
Tales, 10599
The Fox and the Stork, 11069
Fox in a Trap, 7100(F)
Fox in Socks, 6642(F)
The Fox Maiden, 7950(F)
Fox Outfoxed, 6504(F)
The Fox Steals Home, 10312(F)
The Fox with Cold Feet, 6662(F)
Foxes, 19129
The Fox's Kettle, 1334(F)
Foxy, 7203(F)
Fraction Action, 490
Fraction Fun, 20578
Fractions, 20596
The Fragile Flag, 7886(F)
The Fragile Frog, 18729
Fran Ellen's House, 8520(F)
France, 15296, 15297, 15299, 15300,
15301, 15302, 15303, 15304,
15307, 15311, 15312, 15313,
15314, 15315, 15319
Frances Hodgson Burnett, 12512

Francie, 7338(F)
Francis, 13793
Francis Parkman and the Plains Indians, 16369
Francisco Goya, 12237, 12238
Frank and Ernest on the Road, 2004(F)
Frank and Ernest Play Ball, 2005(F)
Frank Lloyd Wright for Kids, 12314
Frank O. Gehry, 12233
Frank Robinson, 13485
Frank Thomas, 13153, 13507, 13508, 13509
Frank Was a Monster Who Wanted to Dance, 1204(F)
Frankenbug, 10163(F)
Frankenlouse, 8463(F)
Frankenstein, 10217(F), 21944
Frankenstein Moved In on the Fourth Floor, 6944(F)
Frankenstein's Pantyhose, 21858
Frankie Murphy's Kiss List, 10071(F)
Franklin and the Thunderstorm, 1843(F)
Franklin D. Roosevelt, 13097, 13099, 13100
Franklin Delano Roosevelt, 13096
The Franklin Delano Roosevelt Memorial, 16726
Franklin Goes to the Hospital, 1844(F)
Franklin Has a Sleepover, 1848(F)
Franklin Pierce, 13089, 13090
Franklin's Bad Day (Illus. by Brenda Clark), 1845(F)
(Illus. by Brenda Clark), 1848(F)
Franklin's Class Trip, 1849(F)
Franklin's Classic Treasury, 1846(F)
Franklin's Classic Treasury, Volume II, 1847(F)
Franklin's Friendship Treasury, 1848(F)
Franklin's Neighborhood, 2250(F)
Franklin's Secret Club, 1848(F)
Frank's Great Museum Adventure, 4115(F)
Fran's Flower, 3054(F)
Freaky Friday, 9977(F)
Freckle Juice, 9781(F)
Freddie Prinze, Jr., 12448
Frederic Chopin, 12325
Frederic Remington, 12290
Frederick, 2382(F)
Frederick Douglass, 12711, 12713, 12714
Frederick Douglass and the War Against Slavery, 12709
A Free Black Girl Before the Civil War, 16241
Free Fall, 939(F)
Free Lunch, 2671(F)
Free Spirits in the Sky, 22001
Free Stuff for Kids on the Net, 21229
Freedom Like Sunlight, 11764
Freedom of Assembly, 17039
Freedom of Belief, 17034
Freedom of Movement, 17016
Freedom of Worship, 17050
Freedom Rides, 17033
Freedom River, 9312(F)

Freedom School, Yes! 4740(F)
Freedom Summer, 4061(F)
Freedom's Fruit, 9289(F)
Freedom's Gifts, 7535(F)
Freedom's Sons, 16257
Freight Train, 21331
The French and Indian War, 16103
French Fries up Your Nose, 10123(F)
The French Resistance, 14863
The French Revolution, 15306
Fresh Brats, 11878
The Fresh Grave, 7609(F)
The Freshwater Alphabet Book, 19642
Freshwater Giants, 19643
Freya's Fantastic Surprise, 5503(F)
Frida Kahlo, 12243, 12244, 12245
Frida María, 7250(F)
Friday Night at Hodges' Cafe, 2062(F)
A Friend for Growl Bear, 1774(F)
A Friend for Little Bear, 2221(F)
A Friend for Minerva Louise, 2734(F)
Friend Frog, 1722(F)
A Friend Like Ed, 2807(F)
A Friend Like Phoebe, 8317(F)
The Friendly Beasts, 14208
Friendly Dolphins, 19683
Friends, 2186(F), 4023(F)
    (Illus. by Helme Heine), 2185(F)
The Friends, 9022(F)
Friends! 17731
Friends Go Adventuring, 2186(F)
Friends in the Park, 4915
Friends on Ice, 9453(F)
Friendship Bracelets, 21542
The Friendship of Milly and Tug, 7497(F)
Friendship 7, 20972
The Friendship Tree, 6252(F)
The Frightened Little Owl, 2081(F)
The Frightful Story of Harry Walfish, 10058(F)
Frightful's Mountain, 7194(F)
Frightmares, 6917(F), 7233(F)
Frindle, 10036(F)
Fritz and the Beautiful Horses, 1857(F)
Frog, 18716
The Frog, 18739, 18740
The Frog Alphabet Book . . . and Other Awesome Amphibians, 109(F)
Frog and Toad All Year, 6464(F)
Frog and Toad Are Friends, 6464(F)
Frog and Toad Together, 6464(F)
Frog, Duck, and Rabbit, 2150(F)
Frog Face, 3880(F)
Frog Face and the Three Boys, 10367(F)
Frog in the Middle, 2149(F)
Frog Legs, 2678(F)
Frog Odyssey, 2706(F)
Frog Power, 10101(F)
A Frog Prince, 10401(F)
The Frog Prince, 10427(F), 10898
The Frog Prince Continued, 10499(F)
The Frog Princess, 11083
The Frog Princess of Pelham, 9808(F)

Frog Went A-Courtin', 14163
Frog Went A-Courting, 14143
The Frog Who Wanted to Be a Singer, 2141(F)
Froggie Went A-Courting, 14173
Froggy Gets Dressed, 2391(F)
Froggy Goes to Bed, 726(F)
Froggy Goes to School, 2392(F)
Froggy Learns to Swim, 2393(F)
Froggy Plays Soccer, 2394(F)
Froggy's First Kiss, 2395(F)
Froggy's Halloween, 6029(F)
Frogs, 18718, 18722, 18724
Frogs and Ballet, 14280
Frogs and Toads, 18731
Frogs and Toads and Tadpoles Too! 18721
Frogs, Frogs Everywhere, 18738
Frogs Jump, 388(F)
Frogs, Toads and Turtles, 18680
From a Distance, 11573
From Acorn to Zoo and Everything in Between in Alphabetical Order, 75(F)
From Anna, 8902(F)
From Anne to Zach, 90(F)
From Beans to Batteries, 4601(F)
From Birth to Death, 20529
From Boys to Men, 17706
From Caterpillar to Butterfly, 19555
From Colonies to Country, 16130
From Cow to Ice Cream, 20106
From Far Away, 5040(F)
From Glass to Boat, 21374
From Head to Toe, 168, 21041
From Here to There, 3096(F)
From Lullaby to Lullaby, 1182(F)
From Metal to Music, 14219
From Mud to House, 21160
From Mustangs to Movie Stars, 20017
From My Window, 3487(F)
From Paper Airplanes to Outer Space, 12596
From Path to Highway, 16686
From Pests to Pets, 19914
From Pictures to Words, 14109
From Plant to Blue Jeans, 21178
From Rock to Fireworks, 21029
From Rubber Tree to Tire, 21047
From Sea to Salt, 21048
From Sea to Shining Sea, 14145
From Seed to Plant, 20270
From Slave to World-Class Horseman, 13678
From Swamp to Coal, 20843
From Tadpole to Frog, 18735
From the Arctic to Antarctica, 15841
From the Bellybutton of the Moon and Other Summer Poems, 11526
From the Dinosaurs of the Past to the Birds of the Present, 14428
From the Earth to Beyond the Sky, 18032
From the Mixed-Up Files of Mrs. Basil E. Frankweiler, 6925(F)
From Wax to Crayon, 21033
From Wheat to Pasta, 20089
From Wood to Paper, 21049
Frontier Fever, 18029

A Frontier Fort on the Oregon Trail, 16373
Frontier Home, 16289
Frontier Life, 16354
Frontier Merchants, 16372
Frontier Surgeons, 13318
Frozen Fire, 6900(F)
Frozen Girl, 15736
Frozen Land, 15829
Frozen Man, 14500
Frozen Noses, 3987(F)
Frozen Stiff, 7051(F)
Frozen Summer, 9258(F), 9260(F)
Fruit, 20154
   (Illus. by P. M. Valet), 20144
Fruit and Vegetables, 20124
The Fruit Group, 20142
Fudge, 7200(F)
Fudge-a-Mania, 9782(F)
Fuels for the Future, 20834
The Full Belly Bowl, 964(F)
Full Court Fever, 10279(F)
Full Moon Stories, 11233
Fun Food, 21412
Fun/No Fun, 3440
Fun on the Run, 21985
Fun with Modeling Clay, 21533
Fun with Mrs. Thumb, 1394(F)
Fun with Numbers (Illus. by Les Chats Pelés), 20632
   (Illus. by Brigitte McDonald), 551
Fun with Paint, 21563
Fun with Patterns, 232
Fun with Shapes, 352(F)
Fun with Sizes, 353(F)
Fun with the Molesons, 7620(F)
Fun with Your Microscope, 19806
Fundamental Golf, 22031
Fundamental Gymnastics, 22191
Fundamental Hockey, 22212
Fundamental Snowboarding, 22283
Fundamental Strength Training, 18208
Fungi, 20191, 20192
The Fungus that Ate My School, 1131(F)
Funny, Funny Lyle, 2786(F)
Funny Papers, 13926
Funny You Should Ask, 21857
Fur, Feathers, and Flippers, 18646
Furaha Means Happy, 14116
Furry Facts, 18613
The Furry News, 2350(F)
Future, 21953
Future Fighters, 21380
Future World, 18273

G Is For Googol, 20595
G-Rex, 1098(F)
Gabby Growing Up, 5691(F)
Gabriella's Song, 4647(F)
Gabrielle Reece, 13708
Gabriel's Ark, 8623(F)
The Gadget War, 9835(F)
Gaffer Samson's Luck, 8381(F)
A Gaggle of Geese, 18928
Gail Devers, 13658
Galapagos, 15772
"Galápagos" Means "Tortoises." 18634
The Galapagos Tortoise, 18790

Galaxies, 18392, 18555, 18557
Galaxy Getaway, 20615
Galileo, 13289, 13290, 13291
Galileo Galilei, 13293
Galileo Spacecraft, 20973
A Gallery of Games, 22035
The Gambia, 15050
Game Day, 22124
Game Time! 225(F)
Games, 21981, 22010
The Gammage Cup, 7858(F)
Gander's Pond, 2042(F)
Gandhi, 13802, 13804
The Ganges, 15112
The Ganges Delta and Its People, 15095
Gangs, 17063, 17075, 17085
Gangs and Drugs, 17090
Garbage, 16978, 16982
Garbage Collectors, 3034
Garbage Creek and Other Stories, 10266(F)
Garbage Juice for Breakfast, 6343(F)
Garbage Trucks, 21301
Garden, 21767
The Garden Behind the Moon, 8033(F)
Garden Crafts for Kids, 21771
The Garden of Abdul Gasazi, 2981(F)
The Garden of Eden Motel, 7441(F)
The Garden of Happiness, 4551(F)
The Gardener, 4841(F)
A Gardener's Alphabet, 6(F)
Gardening Wizardry for Kids, 21763
The Gargoyle on the Roof, 11675
Gargoyles, 21122
Garter Snakes, 18768
Garth Brooks, 12360, 12361(F), 12362
Gary Paulsen, 12576, 12578
Gary Payton, 13562
The Gas We Pass, 18098
Gaspard on Vacation, 2160(F)
The Gate in the Wall, 9103(F)
The Gates of the Wind, 1339(F)
The Gateway Arch, 16544
The Gathering, 7443(F)
Gathering, 386(F)
Gathering Blue, 7926(F)
A Gathering of Days, 9262(F)
A Gathering of Garter Snakes, 18762
'Gator Aid, 9820(F)
Gator Halloween, 9797(F)
Gator Prey, 7086(F)
Gay-Neck, 7273(F)
Gbaya, 14920
Gear Up! 20920
The Gecko, 18749
Geese Find the Missing Piece, 21838(F)
General Butterfingers, 6850(F)
General Store (Illus. by Nancy Winslow Parker), 3129(F)
   (Illus. by Nancy Winslow Parker), 3129(F)
The General Store, 16259
Generals Who Changed the World, 13746
The Genie of Sutton Place, 8082(F)
The Genius of Leonardo, 9072(F)

Genocide, 17021
Gentle Ben, 7267(F)
Gentle Giant Octopus, 19727
Gentle Rosie, 3332(F)
The Gentleman Outlaw and Me-Eli, 9371(F)
Geoffrey Groundhog Predicts the Weather, 2313(F)
Geography from A to Z, 14344
Geology Rocks! 20297
Geometry for Every Kid, 20607
George and Diggety, 6683(F)
George and Martha, 2473(F)
George and Martha Back in Town, 2473(F)
George and Martha Encore, 2473(F)
George and Martha One Fine Day, 2473(F)
George and Martha Rise and Shine, 2473(F)
George and Martha Round and Round, 2474(F)
George and Martha Tons of Fun, 2473(F)
George Armstrong Custer, 12871
George Balanchine, 12350
George Bush, 13010, 13011
George Gershwin, 12327, 12328
George H. W. Bush, 13012
George-isms, 16182
George Lucas, 12417, 12418
George Paints His House, 1794(F)
George Shrinks, 7848(F)
George the Drummer Boy, 4592(F)
George W. Bush, 13013, 13014
George Washington, 13114, 13115, 13116, 13119
George Washington Carver, 13253, 13254, 13255, 13257
George Washington Carver, What Do You See? 13252
George Washington, Thomas Jefferson, Andrew Jackson, 12672
George Washington's Breakfast, 9232(F)
George Washington's Cows, 8104(F)
George Washington's Mother, 13200
George Washington's World, 15877
George's Marvelous Medicine, 7695(F)
George's Store at the Shore, 379(F)
Georgia, 15415, 16851, 16870, 16877
Georgia, Armenia, and Azerbaijan, 15430
The Georgia Colony, 16119
Georgia Music, 3665(F)
Georgia O'Keeffe, 12275, 12276
Gerald Ford, 13034
Geraldine and Mrs. Duffy, 2280(F)
Geraldine's Big Snow, 2281(F)
Geraldine's Blanket, 2282(F)
The German Americans, 17558
Germans in America, 17592
Germany, 15321, 15322, 15324, 15326, 15327, 15332
Germany in Pictures, 15323
Germany's Lightning War, 14867
Germs! Germs! Germs! 17971
Germs Make Me Sick! 17939
Geronimo, 12972

Gershon's Monster, 11154
Gertrude Chandler Warner and the Boxcar Children, 12616
Gertrude's Pocket, 8758(F)
Get Around in the City, 5572
Get Around in the Country, 5572
Get Growing! 21775
Get Involved! 17611
Get Out of Bed! 4241(F)
Get Ready, Baby, 3323(F)
Get Ready for Robots! 21216
Get Set! Swim! 3002(F)
Get That Pest! 6313(F)
Get the Ball, Slim, 6449(F)
Get the Message, 21263
Get Up and Go! 20648, 21326
Get Well, Gators! 9798(F)
The Get Well Soon Book, 2145(F)
Gettin' Through Thursday, 3588(F)
Getting Even, 8315(F)
Getting Near to Baby, 8417(F)
Getting Something on Maggie Marmelstein, 10131(F)
Getting Started in Calligraphy, 21561
Getting the Real Story, 12643
Getting Used to Harry, 4908(F)
Getting Used to the Dark, 11723
Gettysburg, 16417, 16425
The Gettysburg Address, 16420
Geysers, 20306
Ghana, 15015, 15017
Ghana in Pictures, 15026
Ghana, Mali, Songhay, 15037
Ghost Abbey, 8199(F)
The Ghost and Lone Warrior, 11306
Ghost and Pete, 5995(F)
The Ghost Belonged to Me, 8010(F)
Ghost Brother, 7545(F)
The Ghost by the Sea, 7713(F)
Ghost Catcher, 7785(F)
Ghost Cats, 8092(F)
The Ghost Comes Calling, 8222(F)
The Ghost Dance, 15997
Ghost Dog, 7906(F)
Ghost Doll, 1374(F)
Ghost Eye, 7591(F)
The Ghost-Eye Tree, 2957(F)
The Ghost Fox, 10525(F)
The Ghost from Beneath the Sea, 7625(F)
Ghost Horse, 6681(F)
Ghost Horse of the Mounties, 11805
Ghost Horses, 7060(F)
The Ghost in Room 11, 8223(F)
The Ghost in the Big Brass Bed, 7673(F)
The Ghost in the Classroom, 8180(F)
A Ghost in the Family, 7131(F)
A Ghost in the House, 8224(F)
The Ghost in the Mirror, 7604(F)
The Ghost in the Noonday Sun, 9847(F)
The Ghost in the Third Row, 6803(F)
Ghost Liners, 21350
A Ghost Named Fred, 6201(F)
A Ghost Named Wanda, 7758(F)
Ghost of a Hanged Man, 8170(F)
The Ghost of Captain Briggs, 6929(F)
The Ghost of Fossil Glen, 7702(F)

The Ghost of Gracie Mansion, 9302(F)
The Ghost of Grania O'Malley, 8907(F)
The Ghost of Honeymoon Creek, 7610(F)
The Ghost of Lizard Light, 8217(F)
The Ghost of Lost Island, 6981(F)
The Ghost of Popcorn Hill, 8225(F)
The Ghost of Sifty Sifty Sam, 1409(F)
Ghost of the Southern Belle, 7616(F)
The Ghost on Saturday Night, 9848(F)
Ghost Poems, 11731
The Ghost Stallion, 7325(F)
Ghost Town, 6992(F)
Ghost Towns of the American West, 16290
Ghost Train, 8231(F)
The Ghost Train, 6184(F)
Ghost Trap, 6911(F)
Ghost Vision, 7877(F)
The Ghost Who Ate Chocolate, 7043(F)
The Ghost Wore Grey, 6803(F)
Ghostly Tales of Love and Revenge, 7657(F)
Ghosts, 21927
The Ghosts, 7588(F)
Ghosts! 6637(F)
Ghosts Don't Get Goose Bumps, 7129(F)
Ghost's Hour, Spook's Hour, 4917(F)
Ghosts I Have Been, 8010(F)
Ghosts in the Gallery, 7116(F)
Ghosts of the Deep, 21898
Ghosts of the Southwest, 21962
Ghosts of the Twentieth Century, 14554
Ghosts of the West Coast, 21963
Ghosts of the White House, 15881
The Ghosts of War, 21899
The Ghosts' Trip to Loch Ness, 1144(F)
Ghoststalking, 8011(F)
Ghoul School, 1512(F)
The Giant, 7740(F)
The Giant Book of Bugs and Creepy Crawlies, 19479
The Giant Book of Creatures of the Night, 18841
Giant Book of Science Experiments, 18342
The Giant Book of Snakes and Slithery Creatures, 18691
Giant Humanlike Beasts, 21918
The Giant Jam Sandwich, 4218(F)
Giant Octopuses, 19728
Giant Panda, 19190
The Giant Panda, 19187
Giant Pandas, 19185, 19186, 19188, 19191
The Giant Postman, 6359(F)
Giant Sequoia Trees, 20220
Giant Shark, 14379
Giant Stones and Earth Mounds, 14507
Giant Turtle, 19726

The Giant Vegetable Garden, 1674(F)
The Giantess, 4975(F)
Giants! 10623
Giants, Ghosts and Goblins, 10583
Giants in the Land, 16096
The Giant's Toe, 10410(F)
Gib and the Gray Ghost, 9627(F)
Gib Rides Home, 9627(F), 9628(F)
Gideon's People, 8491(F)
The Gift, 9737(F)
  (Illus. by Anthony Carnabuci), 6068(F)
  (Illus. by Barbara Lavallee), 4433(F)
  (Illus. by Pep Montserrat), 5702(F)
A Gift for Abuelita, 4746(F)
A Gift for Ampato, 9141(F)
A Gift from PapaDiego, 3870(F)
The Gift-Giver, 8297(F)
Gift Horse, 7254(F), 11281
The Gift of Driscoll Lipscomb, 294(F)
A Gift of Magic, 8425(F)
The Gift of the Crocodile, 10502(F)
The Gift of the Magi (Illus. by Carol Heyer), 9731(F)
  (Illus. by Carol Heyer), 9731(F)
The Gift of the Pirate Queen, 8658(F)
The Gift of the Sacred Dog, 11240
Gift of the Sun, 4333(F)
The Gift Stone, 4642(F)
Gifts, 3536(F)
Gifts Kids Can Make, 21452
The Gifts of Kwanzaa, 5648
The Gifts of Wali Dad, 10805
Gigantic! How Big Were the Dinosaurs? 14457
The Gigantic Turnip, 11114
The Giggler Treatment, 7709(F)
Giggles, Gags and Groaners, 21847
Gigi, 7731(F)
Gigi in America, 7731(F)
Gila Monsters Meet You at the Airport, 4314(F)
Gildaen, 7631(F)
Gilly Martin the Fox, 11002
Gina, 4056(F)
Ginger, 5443(F)
Ginger Brown, 6723(F)
Ginger Jumps, 2076(F)
Gingerbread Baby, 10951(F)
The Gingerbread Boy, 10974
  (Illus. by Paul Galdone), 10978
  (Illus. by Kathy Wilburn), 10984
The Gingerbread Doll, 5934(F)
The Gingerbread Man (Illus. by Megan Lloyd), 11008
  (Illus. by Barbara McClintock), 10945
Gingersnaps, 17538
Giotto, 12234
Giraffe, 19174
A Giraffe on the Moon, 1433(F)
Giraffe Trouble, 5222(F)
Giraffes, 19175
A Girl, a Goat, and a Goose, 6498(F)
A Girl Called Al, 8292(F)
A Girl Called Boy, 7805(F)
Girl from the Snow Country, 4680(F)
Girl of Kosovo, 9061(F)

Girl of the Shining Mountains, 9434(F)
Girl Power in the Classroom, 17699
Girl Power in the Family, 17719
Girl Power in the Mirror, 17700
Girl Power on the Playing Field, 22065
Girl Reporter Blows Lid Off Town! 10053(F)
Girl Reporter Sinks School! 10053(F)
The Girl-Son, 9003(F)
Girl Stuff, 18249
The Girl Who Ate Chicken Feet, 8794(F)
The Girl Who Changed the World, 7717(F)
The Girl Who Chased Away Sorrow, 9182(F)
The Girl Who Could Fly, 10197(F)
The Girl Who Dreamed Only Geese and Other Stories of the Far North, 11209
The Girl Who Hated Books, 1463(F)
The Girl Who Lived with the Bears, 11255
The Girl Who Lost Her Smile, 4574(F)
The Girl Who Loved Caterpillars, 10825
The Girl Who Loved Coyotes, 11321
The Girl Who Loved Wild Horses, 5229(F)
The Girl Who Spun Gold, 10914
The Girl Who Struck Out Babe Ruth, 22111
The Girl Who Swam with the Fish, 11292
The Girl Who Wanted a Song, 1540(F)
The Girl Who Wore Too Much, 10840
The Girls, 8733(F)
Girls, 15873
The Girls and Boys Book About Good and Bad Behavior, 17609
Girls and Young Women Inventing, 21040
Girls and Young Women Leading the Way, 17147
The Girls' Book of Wisdom, 17701
A Girl's Guide to Growing Up, 17610
The Girls' Guide to Life, 17134
Girls Know Best, 17726
Girls Know Best 2, 17721
The Girls' Revenge, 9947(F)
Girls Think of Everything, 21061
Girls to the Rescue, 10570
Girls to the Rescue Book 2, 10571
Girls Together, 5103(F)
Girls Who Rocked the World, 13744
Girls Who Rocked the World 2, 13742
Gittel's Hands, 1577(F)
Give a Dog a Bone, 7176(F)
Give Me Grace, 17532
Give Me Half! 226(F)
Give Me Liberty! The Story of the Declaration of Independence, 16196
Give the Dog a Bone, 482(F)

Give Us This Day, 17515
Giving, 3228(F)
Giving Thanks, 11305
Gizmos and Gadgets, 21441
Glaciers, 20359, 20360, 20361
Gladiator, 14750
The Glass Angels, 9733(F)
The Glass Bird, 8043(F)
The Glass Mountain, 10938
A Glass Slipper for Rosie, 7437(F)
Glass Town, 14067
Glasses, 9992(F)
Glennis, Before and After, 8412(F)
The Glerp, 2457(F)
Gletta the Foal, 5331(F)
Global Art, 21448
Global Cities, 16972
Global Warning, 6975(F)
Gloria Estefan, 12380, 12381, 12382, 12383, 12384, 12385
Gloria Steinem, 13195, 13196
Gloria's Way, 8589(F)
The Glorious Christmas Songbook, 14201
Glorious Days, Dreadful Days, 16202
The Glorious Flight Across the Channel with Louis Bleriot, 21098
Glorious Grasses, 20100
The Glorious Mother Goose, 839(F)
The Glory Girl, 7399(F)
A Glory of Unicorns, 7742(F)
Glovemen, 22121
Gluskabe and the Four Wishes, 11218
The Gnats of Knotty Pine, 2569(F)
The Go-Around Dollar, 2988
Go Away, Big Green Monster! 670(F)
Go Away, Dog, 6544(F)
Go Away, Shelley Boo! 4048(F)
Go Figure, Gabriella Grant! 10348(F)
Go Fish, 7522(F)
"Go for Broke" 14868
Go Free or Die, 12798
Go-Go-Go! 1200(F)
Go Hang a Salami! I'm a Lasagna Hog! 21877
Go Home, River, 4495(F)
Go Home! The True Story of James the Cat, 5346(F)
Go in and out the Window, 14150
Go to Bed! 745(F)
Go to Jail! 14342
Go to Sleep, Daisy, 2696(F)
Go-With Words, 14027
The Goat in the Rug, 1817(F)
Goats, 20065
Gobble! 17498
The Goblin Baby, 1415(F)
Goblins in the Castle, 7674(F)
God Be in My Heart, 17527
God Bless the Gargoyles, 1474(F)
God in Between, 17215
God Inside of Me, 1502(F)
God Is Like . . . Three Parables for Children, 17227
God Must Like Cookies, Too, 6118(F)
God Said Amen, 1543(F)
Goddesses, Heroes and Shamans, 11454

Gods and Goddesses, 14694
The Gods and Goddesses of Ancient Egypt, 14624
Gods and Goddesses of the Ancient Maya, 11446
Gods and Pharaohs from Egyptian Mythology, 11447
God's Kingdom, 17301
God's Little Seeds, 17297
God's Mailbox, 17273
God's People, 17302
God's Quiet Things, 4548(F)
Goggles! 4015(F)
Gogol's Coat, 4643(F)
Going Back Home, 12313
Going for Gold! 13370
Going for Great, 8260(F)
Going for Oysters, 4569(F)
Going Home, 4608(F)
Going Lobstering, 3355(F)
Going on a Whale Watch, 19795
Going the Moose Way Home, 2346(F)
Going to a Horse Farm, 5276
Going to My Gymnastics Class, 22196
Going to School, 14008
Going to School in 1776, 16153
Going to the Doctor, 3039
Going to the Getty, 16811
Going to Town, 4877(F)
Going West! 16318
Going with the Flow, 8879(F)
Gold, 20275
Gold and Silver, Silver and Gold, 21951(F)
The Gold Coin, 4896(F)
Gold Dust, 10345(F)
The Gold Dust Letters, 7920(F)
Gold Fever, 4706(F)
Gold Fever! Tales from the California Gold Rush, 16365
Gold in the Hills, 9398(F)
The Gold Rush, 16333
Gold-Rush Phoebe, 9386(F)
Gold Rush! The Young Prospector's Guide to Striking It Rich, 20563
The Golden Aquarians, 10198(F)
The Golden Bracelet, 11188
The Golden City, 15532
Golden Daffodils, 8893(F)
Golden Eagles of Devil Mountain, 19340
The Golden Fleece and the Heroes Who Lived Before Achilles, 11466
The Golden Flower, 11425
The Golden Gate Bridge, 16771
The Golden Goose, 10927, 10931
The Golden Goose King, 10790
The Golden Hoard, 11451
The Golden Key, 10454(F)
The Golden Lion Tamarin Comes Home, 18921
The Golden Locket, 4168(F)
The Golden Sandal, 11185
Golden Tales, 11435
Goldilocks and the Three Bears, 11029
   (Illus. by Mireille Levert), 10986 10987
   (Illus. by Bari Weissman), 11017

Goldilocks and the Three Bears/Rici-
tos de Oro y los tres osos, 11016
Goldilocks Returns, 10418(F)
Goldstone, 6934(F)
Golem, 11158, 11178
The Golem, 11162
Golly Gump Swallowed a Fly,
1069(F)
The Golly Sisters Go West, 4101(F)
The Golly Sisters Ride Again,
6245(F)
Gone Again Ptarmigan, 19248
Gone-Away Lake, 6834(F)
Gone Fishing, 3777(F)
Gone Forever! An Alphabet of
Extinct Animals, 19405
Goners, 10236(F), 10237(F)
Gonna Sing My Head Off! 14162
Gontrand and the Crescent Moon,
1454(F)
Good and Perfect Gifts, 9751(F)
Good as Goldie, 4259(F)
Good Books, Good Times, 11600
Good-bye, Billy Radish, 8369(F)
The Good-bye Book, 5099(F)
Good-bye, Charles Lindbergh,
4599(F)
Good-bye, Curtis, 3204(F)
Good-Bye for Today, 9316(F)
Good-bye, Hello, 10050(F)
Good-bye, House, 3006(F)
Good-Bye Marianne, 9074(F)
Good-bye Pink Pig, 7546(F)
Good-Bye, Vivi! 5071(F)
Good Day, Good Night, 5417(F)
Good Driving, Amelia Bedelia,
6560(F)
Good Enough to Eat, 18205
Good Girl Work, 16466
The Good Guys of Baseball, 22089
The Good Housekeeping Illustrated
Children's Cookbook, 21758
Good Hunting, Blue Sky, 6564(F)
Good Job, Little Bear, 2795(F)
Good Job, Oliver! 2504(F)
Good Knight, 772(F)
The Good Liar, 9674(F)
The Good Luck Cat, 5248(F)
Good Luck, Mrs. K.! 5477(F)
Good Luck, Ronald Morgan! 6344(F)
The Good Master, 9070(F)
Good Morning, Chick, 11089
Good Morning, Good Night, 187
"Good Morning Mr. President"
12588
Good Mousekeeping, 11894
Good Night, 761(F)
Good Night, Baby, 797(F)
Good Night, Baby Bear, 628(F)
The Good-Night Blessing Book,
17537
Good Night Dinosaurs, 2689(F)
Good Night, Garden Gnome, 1235(F)
Good Night, God Bless, 755(F)
Good Night, Good Knight, 6692(F)
Good Night, Gorilla, 2617(F)
The Good-Night Kiss, 629(F)
Good Night, Maman, 9675(F)
Good Night, Mr. Night, 815(F)
Good-Night, Owl! 2231(F)
Good Night, Sigmund, 5168(F)

Good Night, Sleep Tight, 11576
Good Queen Bess, 13788
A Good Soup Attracts Chairs, 21727
Good Sports, 22027
The Good, the Bad and the Goofy,
1552(F)
Good Thing You're Not an Octopus!
1395(F)
Good Yontif, 910(F)
Good Zap, Little Grog, 2863(F)
Goodbye, Amanda the Good,
7512(F)
The Goodbye Boat, 3741(F)
Goodbye, Buffalo Sky, 9402(F)
Goodbye House, 1756(F)
Goodbye, Walter Malinski, 9613(F)
The Goodnight Circle, 722(F)
A Goodnight Kind of Feeling,
1850(F)
Goodnight Max, 808(F)
Goodnight Moon, 638(F)
The Goodnight Moon Room, 638(F)
Goodnight PiggyWiggy, 2094(F)
Goody Hall, 6758(F)
Goose, 1783(F)
The Goose Family Book, 19312
The Goose Girl, 10922
The Goose That Almost Got Cooked,
2701(F)
Gooseberry Park, 8057(F)
The Goose's Gold, 7038(F)
Gorgeous! 1941(F)
Gorilla, 19013
Gorilla Walk, 19002
Gorillas, 18992, 19006, 19010,
19016, 19017
Gorky Rises, 2719(F)
Gotcha! 2266(F)
Gotta Go! Gotta Go! 4549(F)
Governments Around the World,
17020
Governments of the Western Hemi-
sphere, 14552
Gowanus Dogs, 5214(F)
Goya, 12236
Grace and Joe, 3982(F)
Grace's Letter to Lincoln, 9503(F)
Gracias, Rosa, 3799(F)
Gracias, the Thanksgiving Turkey,
6141(F)
Gracie Graves and the Kids from
Room 402, 11904
Gracie's Girl, 8391(F)
The Graduation of Jake Moon,
8504(F)
The Grain Group, 20092
Gram Makes a House Call, 7394(F)
Grampa and the Ghost, 8038(F)
Gramps and the Fire Dragon, 766(F)
Grand Canyon, 16628, 16630, 16643
A Grand Canyon Journey, 16595
Grand Canyon National Park, 16633
The Grand Coulee Dam, 21125
The Grand Escape, 7982(F)
Grand-Gran's Best Trick, 8695(F)
The Grand Old Duke of York, 886
Grand Trees of America, 20207
Grandad Bill's Song, 5109(F)
The Grandad Tree, 3586(F)
Grandaddy and Janetta, 7439(F)

Grandaddy and Janetta Together,
7439(F)
Grandaddy's Place, 7439(F)
(Illus. by James Stevenson),
3665(F)
Grandaddy's Stars, 7439(F)
Grandad's Prayers of the Earth,
3957(F)
The Grandchildren of the Incas,
15754
Grandchildren of the Lakota, 16032
The Grandchildren of the Vikings,
15465
Granddaddy's Street Songs, 3604(F)
Grandfather and I, 3551(F)
Grandfather Counts, 403(F)
Grandfather Four Winds and Rising
Moon, 9150(F)
Grandfather Tales, 11328
Grandfather Tang's Story, 1624(F)
Grandfather's Christmas Camp,
5868(F)
Grandfather's Christmas Tree,
5929(F)
Grandfather's Day, 7528(F)
Grandfather's Gold Watch, 4688(F)
Grandfather's Journey, 3874(F)
Grandfather's Story, 3622(F)
Grandfather's Trolley, 3792(F)
Grandfather's Work, 4786(F)
Grandma According to Me, 3524(F)
Grandma Buffalo, May and Me,
3908(F)
Grandma Chickenlegs, 11102
Grandma Fina and Her Wonderful
Umbrellas/La Abuelita Fina y Sus
Sombrillas Maravillosas, 4295(F)
Grandma Gets Grumpy, 3701(F)
The Grandma Mix-Up, 6483(F)
Grandma Moses, 12270
Grandma Rabbitty's Visit, 2704(F)
Grandma Summer, 4466(F)
Grandma Went to Market, 384(F)
Grandmama's Joy, 3661(F)
Grandmas at Bat, 6484(F)
Grandma's at the Lake, 6485(F)
Grandma's Cat, 5288(F)
Grandma's Gone to Live in the Stars,
3678(F)
Grandma's Hands, 3730(F)
Grandma's Purple Flowers, 3561(F)
Grandma's Soup, 4993(F)
Grandmother and I, 3551(F)
Grandmother Bryant's Pocket,
9204(F)
Grandmother Five Baskets, 11261(F)
Grandmother Winter, 1518(F)
Grandmother's Alphabet, 131(F)
Grandmother's Dreamcatcher, 733(F)
Grandmother's Song, 3520(F)
Grandmothers' Stories, 10593
Grandpa Abe, 3865(F)
Grandpa at the Beach, 6460(F)
Grandpa Bear's Fantastic Scarf,
2182(F)
Grandpa Comes to Stay, 3773(F)
The Grandpa Days, 3533(F)
Grandpa Doesn't Know It's Me,
3668(F)
Grandpa Is a Flyer, 21068

Grandpa, Is Everything Black Bad? 3703(F)
Grandpa Jake and the Grand Christmas, 9706(F)
Grandpa Never Lies, 3627(F)
Grandpa Was a Cowboy, 2977(F)
Grandpa's Amazing Computer, 7509(F)
Grandpa's Corner Store, 3105(F)
Grandpa's Face, 3662(F)
Grandpa's Gamble, 6097(F)
Grandpa's Ghost Stories, 6845(F)
Grandpa's House, 3906(F)
Grandpa's Soup, 1284(F)
Grandpa's Teeth, 4116(F)
Grandpa's Town, 4780(F)
Granny Greenteeth and the Noise in the Night, 1070(F)
Granny the Pag, 7390(F)
The Grannyman, 2659(F)
Gran's Bees, 3917(F)
Grant Hill, 13528, 13529, 13530
Granville Jones, 9880(F)
The Grapes of Math, 20622
The Graphic Alphabet, 113(F)
Grass Sandals, 9015
Grasshopper, 19449
Grasshopper on the Road, 6465(F)
Grasshopper Summer, 9448(F)
Grasshoppers, 19434, 19463
Grassland, 20543, 20546
Grassland Mammals, 20538
Grasslands, 20532, 20542, 20548, 20549
Grassroots, 11689
Gratefully Yours, 9347(F)
Graveyard Girl, 9601(F)
Graveyards of the Dinosaurs, 14474
Gravity, 20906
Gray Rabbit's Odd One Out, 155(F)
Gray Wolf, Red Wolf, 19136
Great African Americans in Business, 12693
Great African Americans in Civil Rights, 12694
Great African Americans in Entertainment, 12179
Great African Americans in Film, 12685
Great African Americans in Government, 12648
Great African Americans in History, 12654
Great African Americans in Jazz, 12164
Great African Americans in Literature, 12180
Great African Americans in Music, 12181
Great African Americans in Sports, 13395
Great African Americans in the Arts, 12165
Great African Americans in the Olympics, 13374
Great African Kingdoms, 14913
The Great American Baseball Strike, 22104
Great American Businesswomen, 12662

The Great American Elephant Chase, 9532(F)
Great American Events on Stage, 12024
The Great Ancestor Hunt, 17674
The Great Apes, 19015
The Great Astrolabe Reef, 19667
Great Auto Makers and Their Cars, 21303
The Great Barrier Reef, 19661
A Great Big Ugly Man Came Up and Tied His Horse to Me, 11920
Great Black Heroes, 13213(F)
The Great Brain, 9843(F)
The Great Brain at the Academy, 9843(F)
The Great Brain Does It Again, 9843(F)
The Great Brain Reforms, 9843(F)
Great Britain, 15344, 15367
Great Buildings, 21135
The Great Change, 8850(F)
The Great Christmas Kidnapping Caper, 9765(F)
Great Composers, 12185
The Great Corgiville Kidnapping, 8154(F)
Great Crystal Bear, 5301(F)
The Great Depression, 16489
Great Dinosaur Hunters, 14423
The Great Dinosaur Record Book, 14411
Great Discoveries and Inventions That Advanced Industry and Technology, 21025
Great Discoveries and Inventions That Helped Explore Earth and Space, 20968
Great Discoveries and Inventions That Improved Human Health, 18019
The Great Divide, 421(F)
The Great Escape from City Zoo, 2628(F)
Great Experiments with H$_2$O, 20733
The Great Fire, 16572
The Great Frog Race and Other Poems, 11952
Great Ghosts, 6798(F)
The Great Gilly Hopkins, 8779(F)
Great Girl Stories, 10257(F)
The Great Good Thing, 10513(F)
The Great Gracie Chase, 1532(F)
Great-grandmother's Treasure, 7449(F)
Great-Grandpa's in the Litter Box, 7759(F)
The Great Green Notebook of Katie Roberts, 8691(F)
Great Grizzly Wilderness, 19046
Great Ice Bear, 19059
The Great Interactive Dream Machine, 10220(F)
Great Inventions, 21064
The Great Kapok Tree, 4404(F)
The Great Little Madison, 13082
Great Lives, 12163, 12641, 13223, 13415, 17035
Great Moments in Baseball History, 22087

The Great Monarch Butterfly Chase, 1493(F)
The Great Mosquito, Bull, and Coffin Caper, 8330(F)
Great Olympic Moments, 22253
The Great Peace March, 14254
The Great Pet Sale, 2237(F)
The Great Pig Escape, 1960(F)
The Great Poochini, 1963(F)
Great Predators of the Land, 18840
Great Predators of the Sea, 18840
The Great Pyramid, 14615, 14643, 14645
The Great Quillow, 8146(F)
The Great Race, 6499(F)
(Illus. by Zhong-Yang Huang), 10738
11241
The Great Railroad Race, 9370(F)
The Great Redwall Feast, 7819(F)
The Great Rescue Operation, 8173(F)
The Great St. Lawrence Seaway, 15574
Great Scenes and Monologues for Children, 14325
The Great Smith House Hustle, 6809(F)
Great Smoky Mountains National Park, 16878
Great Snakes! 18775
The Great Summer Camp Catastrophe, 8174(F)
The Great Trash Bash, 2351(F)
The Great Turkey Walk, 9298(F)
The Great Valentine's Day Balloon Race, 6160(F)
The Great Voyager Adventure, 18515
The Great Wall, 15074
Great White Shark, 19770
Great Women in the Struggle, 12661
Great Wonders of the World, 14578
The Greatest Gymnast of All, 227
The Greatest of All, 10818
The Greatest Show on Earth, 2963(F)
The Greatest Sports Stories Never Told, 22039
The Greatest Treasure, 10750
Greece, 14685, 15370, 15373, 15376, 15387, 15389, 15390, 15392, 15395, 15396
Greece in Pictures, 15381
The Greedy Triangle, 1029(F)
Greek and Roman Mythology, 11497
Greek and Roman Science, 14591
Greek and Roman Sport, 14592
Greek Gods and Goddesses, 11487
Greek Grime, 14679
Greek Myths, 11462
(Illus. by Giovanni Caselli), 11494
(Illus. by Emma C. Clark), 11488
(Illus. by Eduard Sandoz), 11467
Greek Myths for Young Children, 11514
A Greek Temple, 14690
Greek Theatre, 14701
Greek Town, 14695
The Greeks, 14674, 14697
The Greeks and Troy, 14708
Green Beans, 3914(F)
The Green Book, 10244(F)

A Green Christmas, 5860(F)
Green Eggs and Ham, 6641(F)
Green Fairy Book, 10442(F)
The Green Frogs, 10728
The Green Lion of Zion Street,
    8283(F)
The Green Magician Puzzle, 6572(F)
Green Mango Magic, 8305(F)
The Green Mist, 11034
The Green Queen, 290(F)
Green Snake Ceremony, 4870(F)
The Green Team, 8340(F)
Green Truck Garden Giveaway,
    3313(F)
The Greenhouse Effect, 20791
Greenland Mummies, 14490
The Greenwich Guide to Time and
    the Millennium, 20643
Greenwitch, 7671(F)
Greetings from Antarctica, 15845
Greetings, Sun, 4661(F)
Greg LeMond, 13698
Greg Maddux, 13470
Gregor Mendel, 13322
Gregory Griggs and Other Nursery
    Rhyme People, 866
Gregory Hines, 12400
Gregory, the Terrible Eater, 2684(F)
Gregory's Shadow, 2102(F)
Greg's Microscope, 19810
Gretchen Groundhog, It's Your Day!
    5633(F)
Grey Fairy Book, 10442(F)
The Grey King, 7671(F)
The Grey Lady and the Strawberry
    Snatcher, 907(F)
Grey Neck, 2643(F)
The Gristmill, 16321
Grizz! 1301(F)
Grizzlies, 19052, 19054, 19069
The Grizzly, 6909(F)
Grizzly Bear, 19067
The Grizzly Bear, 19066
The Grizzly Sisters, 1801(F)
Grizzwold, 6402(F)
Groogleman, 10177(F)
Groom Your Room, 13893
The Grouchy Ladybug, 1922(F)
Group Soup, 1853(F)
Grover, 8602(F)
Grover Cleveland, 13021
Grover Cleveland Alexander, 13434
Grow! Babies! 18231
Grow It Again, 21768
Growing Flowers, 21769
Growing Frogs, 5212(F)
Growing House Plants, 21769
Growing Like Me, 18596
Growing Money, 16925
Growing Pains, 2739(F)
Growing Seasons, 16487
The Growing Story, 4476(F)
Growing Up, 17184, 18263
Growing Up in a Holler in the Moun-
    tains, 16860
Growing Up in America, 16280
Growing Up in Ancient China, 15087
Growing Up in Ancient Egypt, 14618
Growing Up in Ancient Rome, 14717
Growing Up in Aztec Times, 15654
Growing Up in Coal Country, 16448

Growing Up in Colonial America,
    16097
Growing Up in Crawfish Country,
    16861
Growing Up in Viking Times, 15468
Growing Up Indian, 16070
Growing Up Where the Partridge
    Drums Its Wings, 15960
Growing Up Wild, 19055
Growing Vegetable Soup, 3116(F)
Growing Vegetables, 21769
Growing Wings, 8210(F)
Growl! 19038
Growltiger's Last Stand, 11778
The Gruffalo, 2035(F)
Grumble-Rumble! 2034(F)
Grump, 813(F)
The Grump, 3288(F)
The Grumpalump, 2177(F)
Grumpy Bunnies, 806(F)
The Grumpy Morning, 2053(F)
The Grumpy Shepherd, 17264(F)
Guadalcanal, 14830
Guadalupe Quintanilla, 12834
Guardians of Wildlife, 19391
Guatemala, 15659
Guatemala in Pictures, 15667
A Guatemalan Family, 15676
Guess How Much I Love You,
    732(F)
Guess What? (Illus. by Vivienne
    Goodman), 4148(F)
    (Illus. by Julie Lacome), 301(F)
Guess What I Am, 299(F)
Guess What I'll Be, 300(F)
Guess Who? 4236(F)
Guess Who My Favorite Person Is,
    3521(F)
Guess Who's Coming, Jesse Bear,
    1933(F)
Guess Whose Shadow? 21876
Gugu's House, 4842(F)
A Guide Dog Puppy Grows Up,
    19938
Guide to Weather, 20750
Guinea Pig, 19896
Guinea Pigs, 19887, 19901
Guinea Pigs Don't Talk, 10116(F)
Guion Bluford, 12080
Guitars, 14231
Gullible's Troubles, 2681(F)
Gulliver in Lilliput, 7795(F)
Gulls . . . Gulls . . . Gulls, 19348
Gumshoe Goose, Private Eye,
    6443(F)
Gunfighters, 12698
Gunfighters of the Wild West, 16363
Gung Hay Fat Choy, 17342
Gunga Din, 11617
The Gunny Wolf and Other Fairy
    Tales, 10566
Guns, 21405
Guppies in Tuxedos, 14049
Gus and Gertie and the Missing
    Pearl, 7992(F)
Gus and Grandpa, 6526(F)
Gus and Grandpa and Show-and-
    Tell, 6527(F)
Gus and Grandpa and the Christmas
    Cookies, 6528(F)

Gus and Grandpa and the Two-
    Wheeled Bike, 8761(F)
Gus and Grandpa at the Hospital,
    6529(F)
Gus and Grandpa Ride the Train,
    6530(F)
Gus and the Green Thing, 2618(F)
Gus Grissom, 12119
Gus Loves His Happy Home,
    1617(F)
Gustav Klimt, 12249
Gutenberg, 13305
Guts, 12577
Guts and Glory, 13393
Guy Time, 10016(F)
Guyana, 15725
Guyana in Pictures, 15739
Gwinna, 7608(F)
The Gym Day Winner, 6476(F)
Gymnastics, 22192, 22193, 22194,
    22197
The Gypsies Never Came, 8911(F)
The Gypsy Game, 8372(F)
The Gypsy Princess, 1192(F)
Gypsy Rizka, 6744(F)

H.O.W.L. High, 7907(F)
The Haida, 15928
Hail, Hail Camp Timberwood,
    8604(F)
Hail to the Chief, 17101
Hailstones and Halibut Bones, 11665
Hair in Funny Places, 18253
Hair There and Everywhere, 18177
Haircuts at Sleepy Sam's, 3446(F)
Hairs on Bears, 4292(F)
Hairy Horror, 7905(F)
Hairy Maclary and Zachary Quack,
    6308(F)
Hairy, Scary, Ordinary, 14025
Haiti, 15714
Haiti in Pictures, 15704
Haiti Through Its Holidays, 15720
A Haitian Family, 15703
Hakeem Olajuwon, 13554, 13555,
    13556
Halala Means Welcome, 13988
Half a Moon and One Whole Star,
    663(F)
The Half-a-Moon Inn, 6843(F)
Halfway to Your House, 11672
Hallelujah! A Christmas Celebration,
    5892(F)
Halley Came to Jackson, 3568(F)
The Hallo-Wiener, 6039(F)
Halloween, 6035(F), 9708(F)
    (Illus. by Gail Gibbons), 17444
The Halloween Book, 17442
The Halloween Candy Mystery,
    6963(F)
Halloween Crafts, 21426
Halloween Day, 6045(F)
Halloween Fun, 21427
Halloween Fun for Everyone, 17449
Halloween Helpers, 9716(F)
Halloween Hide-and-Seek, 6016(F)
Halloween Hoots and Howls, 11833
The Halloween House, 6050(F)
Halloween Jack-o'-Lanterns, 17447
Halloween Mice! 6044(F)
Halloween Monster, 6053(F)

Halloween Motel, 5994(F)
Halloween Pie, 6056(F)
The Halloween Showdown, 6046(F)
Halmoni and the Picnic, 3581(F)
Halmoni's Day, 5473(F)
Hamburger Heaven, 2886(F)
Hamlet and the Enormous Chinese Dragon Kite, 2373(F)
Hamlet for Kids, 12047
Hammer, 12394
Hamster, 19888, 19910
Hamsters and Gerbils, 19897
Hamsters Don't Glow in the Dark, 7323(F)
Hand in Hand, 11601
The Hand-Me-Down Horse, 4798(F)
The Hand of Dinotopia, 10182(F)
Hand-Print Animal Art, 21564
Hand Reading, 21948
Hand Rhymes, 829
A Handful of Beans, 10508(F)
A Handful of Dirt, 18608
A Handful of Seeds, 4689(F)
A Handful of Sunshine, 21762
A Handful of Time, 8506(F)
The Handmade Alphabet, 14018
The Handmade Counting Book, 564(F)
Handmade Secret Hiding Places, 21445
Hands, 3117(F)
Hands! 18064
Hands Are Not for Hitting, 2990(F)
Hands Around Lincoln School, 10025(F)
Hands Around the World, 21455
Hands Off! 927(F)
Hands-On Latin America, 21453
The Hands-On Marvelous Ball Book, 20603
Hands-On Rocky Mountains, 21523
Hands On, Thumbs Up, 14014
Handtalk, 14012
Handtalk Birthday, 5673(F)
Handtalk School, 14017(F)
Handtalk Zoo, 5116(F)
Hang Gliding, 21973
Hang Tough, Paul Mather, 8914(F)
Hanging Out with Mom, 6206(F)
Hanimations, 928(F)
Hank Aaron, 13430, 13431
Hank the Cowdog, 6329(F)
Hannah, 8922(F)
Hannah and Jack, 5354(F)
Hannah and the Angels, 6913(F)
Hannah and the Seven Dresses, 5700(F)
Hannah and the Whistling Teakettle, 2972(F)
Hannah in Between, 8516(F)
Hannah of Fairfield, 9251(F)
Hannah the Hippo's No Mud Day, 2210(F)
Hannah's Baby Sister, 3866(F)
Hannah's Collections, 5508(F)
Hannah's Fancy Notions, 9617(F)
Hannah's Farm, 4492(F)
Hannah's Helping Hands, 9252(F)
Hannah's Journal, 9600(F)
Hannah's Winter of Hope, 9253(F)
Hanna's Sabbath Dress, 6116(F)

Hannibal, 13806, 16590
Hans Christian Andersen, 12493
Hans Christian Andersen Fairy Tales, 10383(F)
Hans Christian Andersen's The Snow Queen, 10501(F)
Hansel and Gretel, 10928, 10930, 10934
(Illus. by Frances Cony), 12015
(Illus. by Jane Ray), 10929
Hanson, 12395
Hanukkah, 6099(F), 17456
Hanukkah! A Three-Dimensional Celebration, 17465
The Hanukkah Book, 17453
The Hanukkah Ghosts, 9755(F)
A Hanukkah Treasury, 17471
Hanuman, 10796
Haphazard House, 8197(F)
The Happiest Ending, 7529(F)
Happily After All, 8526(F)
Happily Ever After, 8468(F)
(Illus. by James Stevenson), 8034(F)
Happy Adoption Day! 3786
Happy and Honey, 6351(F)
Happy Birth Day! 3670(F)
Happy Birthday, 5661(F)
(Illus. by Hilary Knight), 5694
Happy Birthday, Amelia, 5712(F)
Happy Birthday, America! 5617(F)
Happy Birthday, Biscuit! 5670(F)
Happy Birthday, Danny and the Dinosaur! 6403(F)
Happy Birthday, Davy! 5736(F)
Happy Birthday, Everywhere! 17352
Happy Birthday, Felicity, 9214(F)
Happy Birthday, Frankie, 1670(F)
Happy Birthday, Harvey Hare! 2826(F)
Happy Birthday, Jesse Bear! 5672(F)
Happy Birthday, Josefina! A Spring-time Story, 9445(F)
Happy Birthday, Kirsten! 9437(F)
Happy Birthday, Little League, 22108
Happy Birthday, Lulu! 5731(F)
Happy Birthday, Maisy, 5677(F)
Happy Birthday, Martin Luther King, 12748
Happy Birthday, Molly! 9691(F)
Happy Birthday, Moon, 1758(F)
Happy Birthday Mr. Kang, 5721(F)
Happy Birthday, Ronald Morgan! 5687(F)
Happy Birthday, Rotten Ralph, 5686(F)
Happy Birthday, Sam, 5697(F)
Happy Birthday Samantha, 9630(F)
Happy Birthday to Me! 11834
Happy Birthday to You, You Belong in a Zoo, 5679(F)
Happy Christmas, Gemma, 5833(F)
Happy Days, 3324(F)
Happy Easter Day! 5976
Happy Father's Day, 5630(F)
Happy Halloween! Things to Make and Do, 21500
Happy Haunting! 21539
The Happy Hedgehog Band, 2796(F)
The Happy Hippopotami, 2480(F)

The Happy Hocky Family, 1588(F)
Happy Holidaysaurus! 17392
Happy New Year! 17343
Happy New Year, Beni, 6126(F)
Happy New Year, Everywhere! 17353
Happy New Year! Kung-Hsi Fa-Ts' Ai! 5621(F)
A Happy New Year's Day, 5616(F)
Happy Prince, 10522(F)
Happy Thanksgiving! 17492
Happy Thanksgiving, Biscuit! 6137(F)
Happy Times, 166(F)
Happy to Be Nappy, 3220(F)
Happy Valentine's Day, Miss Hildy! 6168(F)
The Happy Yellow Car, 9881(F)
Harbor, 5556(F)
Hard-to-See Animals, 18883
Hare and Rabbit, 6546(F)
The Hare and the Tortoise, 11065, 11077
Harmful to Your Health, 17963
Harold and the Purple Crayon, 6423(F)
Harold's Circus, 6423(F)
Harold's Trip to the Sky, 6423(F)
Harp O' Gold, 987(F)
Harp Seal Pups, 19741
Harp Seals, 19730
Harpo, 5125(F)
Harriet and the Crocodiles, 2797(F)
Harriet and the Garden, 1929(F)
Harriet and the Promised Land, 12800
Harriet and the Roller Coaster, 1929(F)
Harriet and Walt, 1929(F)
Harriet Beecher Stowe, 12603
Harriet Beecher Stowe and the Beecher Preachers, 12604
Harriet Ross Tubman, 12804
Harriet the Spy, 10055(F)
Harriet Tubman, 12796, 12802, 12803
Harriet Tubman and the Underground Railroad, 12797
Harriet, You'll Drive Me Wild! 4959(F)
Harriet's Halloween Candy, 5987(F)
Harriet's Hare, 10203(F)
Harriet's Recital, 1929(F)
Harris and Me, 9958(F)
Harry and Arney, 7403(F)
Harry and Lulu, 1712(F)
Harry and the Snow King, 1676(F)
Harry and the Terrible Whatzit, 1173(F)
Harry and Tuck, 3747(F)
Harry at the Garage, 2609(F)
Harry Cat's Pet Puppy, 8081(F)
Harry Houdini, 12403
Harry in Trouble, 6582(F)
Harry Kitten and Tucker Mouse, 8083(F)
Harry McNairy, Tooth Fairy, 951(F)
Harry Potter and the Chamber of Secrets, 8048(F)
Harry Potter and the Goblet of Fire, 8049(F)

Harry Potter and the Prisoner of Azk-aban, 8050(F)
Harry Potter and the Sorcerer's Stone, 8051(F)
Harry S. Truman, 13108, 13109
Harry the Explorer, 10235(F)
Harry the Poisonous Centipede, 7582(F)
Harry's Got a Girlfriend! 6635(F)
Harry's Home, 2996(F)
Harry's Mad, 6921(F)
Harry's Pony, 6583(F)
Harvest, 17502
Harvest Celebrations, 17350
Harvest Festivals Around the World, 17493
Harvest Year, 20121
Harvey Hare, 2827(F)
Harvey Hare's Christmas, 5948(F)
Harvey Potter's Balloon Farm, 1435(F)
Harvey's Horrible Snake Disaster, 9805(F)
Harvey's Mystifying Raccoon Mix-Up, 6795(F)
Hasta La Vista, Blarney! 7012(F)
Hasty Pudding, Johnnycakes, and Other Good Stuff, 16136
The Hat, 1858(F)
Hat Trick, 10302(F)
Hat Trick Trivia, 22209
The Hating Book, 3973(F)
The Hatmaker's Sign, 9229(F)
Hats, Hats, Hats, 3333(F)
Hats Off for the Fourth of July! 5660(F)
The Hatseller and the Monkeys, 10662
Hatshepsut, His Majesty, Herself, 13807
The Hatters, 16115
Hattie and the Fox, 2095(F)
Hattie and the Wild Waves, 4626(F)
Hau Kola Hello Friend, 12542
Haunted Bayou, 11371
Haunted Castle, 6879(F)
Haunted House, 8005(F)
The Haunted Skateboard, 7043(F)
Haunted Summer, 8226(F)
Haunting at Black Water Cove, 7903(F)
Haunting at Home Plate, 10355(F)
The Haunting at Stratton Falls, 7048(F)
The Haunting of Cassie Palmer, 7548(F)
The Haunting of Drang Island, 8098(F)
Hauntings, 10561, 21912
Haunts, 7960(F)
Hausa, 15044
Have a Happy . . ., 9766(F)
Have I Got Dogs! 5170(F)
Have You Got My Purr? 2845(F)
Have You Seen Bugs? 19472
Have You Seen Hyacinth Macaw? 6858(F)
Have You Seen My Cat? 5159(F)
Have You Seen My Duckling? 2749(F)
Hawaii, 16776, 16781, 16788

Hawaii Is a Rainbow, 16773
The Hawaiians, 16809
Hawk Hill, 7198(F)
Hawk, I'm Your Brother, 7156(F)
Haystack, 20056
Hazards at Home, 18218
Hazel's Circle, 5181(F)
Hazy Skies, 20773
He Fought for Freedom, 12716
He Is Risen, 17441
A Head Full of Notions, 13286
A Head Is For Hats, 6639(F)
Head Lice, 17980
Head Louse, 19450
Head to Toe Science, 18085
The Headless Cupid, 7070(F)
The Headless Horseman and Other Ghoulish Tales, 10600
The Headless Horseman Rides Tonight, 11677
Heads, I Win, 8451(F)
Heads or Tails, 6848(F)
Heads or Tales, 9132(F)
The Healer of Harrow Point, 8845(F)
Healers and Researchers, 13217
Healers of the Wild, 17849
The Healing of Texas Jake, 7983(F)
Healing Warrior, 13311
A Healthy Body, 18206
The Healthy Body Cookbook, 21690
Hear, Hear, Mr. Shakespeare, 4715(F)
Hear Your Heart, 18091
Hearing, 18157
    (Illus. by Maria Rius), 18152
Hearing in Living Things, 18820
Hearing Sounds, 20938
Hearsay, 10768(F)
The Heart, 18093
The Heart and Circulatory System, 18086
Heart and Lungs, 18078
Heart and Soul, 13841
The Heart of a Chief, 9148(F)
Heart of Gold, 10793
Heart of Naosaqua, 9184(F)
The Heart of the City, 8321(F)
The Heart of the Wood, 4410(F)
Heart of Valor, 8106(F)
Heart to Heart, 2679(F), 11595
Heartland, 7163(F), 11696
Hearts and Crafts, 17504
Heat, 10292(F)
Heat Wave, 1298(F)
Heat Wave at Mud Flat, 2727(F)
Heat Waves and Droughts, 20757
Heather, 8741(F)
Heaven Eyes, 7556(F)
Heaven to Betsy, 10103(F)
The Heavenly Village, 8058(F)
Heavy Metal, 14121
Heckedy Peg, 10524(F)
Hector Protector, and As I Went over the Water, 889
Hector's Hiccups, 6708(F)
Hedgehog Bakes a Cake, 6486(F)
Hedgie's Surprise, 1859(F)
Heetunka's Harvest, 11260
Helen Gurley Brown, 12507
Helen Keller, 13166

Helen Oxenbury's ABC of Things, 108(F)
Helen Williams and the French Revolution, 15317
Helga's Dowry, 4127(F)
Helicopters, 21105
Hello, Alexander Graham Bell Speaking, 13237
Hello, Amigos! 5667(F)
Hello Baby, 3897(F)
Hello Baby! 3858(F)
Hello, Fish! 19658
Hello, Fruit Face! The Paintings of Giuseppe Arcimboldo, 12188
Hello! Good-bye! 2993(F)
Hello, House! 11348
Hello? Is Anybody There? 7736(F)
Hello Little Chicks, 1745(F)
Hello Little Ducks, 1745(F)
Hello Little Lamb, 1745(F)
Hello Little Piglet, 1745(F)
Hello, Lulu, 3925(F)
Hello, Mrs. Piggle-Wiggle, 7934(F)
Hello, My Name Is Scrambled Eggs, 8289(F)
Hello Ocean, 4526(F)
Hello, Red Fox, 263(F)
Hello, Shoes! 164(F)
Hello, Sweetie Pie, 2528(F)
Hello Toes! Hello Feet! 234(F)
Hellow, Two-Wheeler! 6513(F)
Help! A Girl's Guide to Divorce and Stepfamilies, 17660
Help! I'm a Prisoner in the Library, 6796(F)
Help! I'm Trapped in Obedience School, 8133(F)
Help Is on the Way, 17927
Help! My Teacher Hates Me, 17631
Help, Pink Pig! 7547(F)
Helpful Betty Solves a Mystery, 2509(F)
Helpful Betty to the Rescue, 2509(F)
Helpin' Bugs, 4024(F)
Hen Lake, 1772(F)
Henny Penny, 10979
Henny-Penny, 11042
Henri Matisse, 12258
Henri Rousseau, 12298
Henry and Amy (right-way-round and upside down), 4017(F)
Henry and Beezus, 9802(F)
Henry and Mudge and Annie's Good Move, 6601(F)
Henry and Mudge and Annie's Perfect Pet, 6602(F)
Henry and Mudge and the Careful Cousin, 6603(F)
Henry and Mudge and the Sneaky Crackers, 6604(F)
Henry and Mudge and the Starry Night, 6605(F)
Henry and Mudge and the Wild Wind, 6606(F)
Henry and Mudge and Their Snowman Plan, 6607(F)
Henry and Mudge in the Family Trees, 6608(F)
Henry and Ribsy, 9802(F)
Henry and the Clubhouse, 9802(F)
Henry and the Paper Route, 9802(F)

Henry Cisneros, 12828
Henry Ford, 13281, 13283
Henry Hikes to Fitchburg, 2256(F)
Henry Huggins, 9802(F)
Henry in Shadowland, 1649(F)
Henry Moore, 12268, 12269
Henry O. Flipper, 12723
Henry Reed, Inc., 9973(F)
Henry Reed's Baby-Sitting Service, 9973(F)
Henry Reed's Big Show, 9973(F)
Henry Reed's Journey, 9973(F)
Henry the Fourth, 527
Henry's Awful Mistake, 2607(F)
Henry's Important Date, 2607(F)
Henry's Song, 1945(F)
Her Blue Straw Hat, 7381(F)
Her Piano Sang, 12337
Her Seven Brothers, 11242
Her Stories, 11340
Herb, the Vegetarian Dragon, 1792(F)
Herbert Hoover, 13043, 13044
Herbie Jones, 10087(F)
Herbie Jones and the Class Gift, 10087(F)
Herbie Jones and the Dark Attic, 8320(F)
Herbie Jones and the Monster Ball, 10087(F)
Hercules, 11484, 11493
  (Illus. by Raul Colon), 11461
Here Are My Hands, 3310(F)
Here Come Poppy and Max, 3156(F)
Here Come the Babies, 3509
Here Come the Brides, 17371
Here Come the Purim Players! 6069(F)
Here Come Trainmice! 2887(F)
Here Comes Eleanor, 13186
Here Comes Heavenly, 10003(F)
Here Comes Kate, 6265(F)
Here Comes Mother Goose, 878
Here Comes Mr. Eventoff with the Mail! 3136(F)
Here Comes Pontus! 7841(F)
Here Comes Spring, 5353(F)
Here Comes Tabby Cat, 6598(F)
Here Comes the Mystery Man, 4821(F)
Here Comes the Rain, 2520(F)
Here Comes the Recycling Truck! 16985
Here Comes the Snow, 6516(F)
Here Comes the Strikeout, 6433(F)
Here Comes the Train, 3465(F)
Here Comes Tricky Rabbit! 11275
Here Comes Zelda Claus and Other Holiday Disasters, 9728(F)
Here Is My Heart, 11704
Here Is the African Savanna, 20533
Here Is the Arctic Winter, 15801
Here Is the Coral Reef, 19657
Here Is the Wetland, 20367
Here There Be Dragons, 8236(F)
Here There Be Ghosts, 8237(F)
Here We All Are, 12524
Hereditary Diseases, 17965
Herero, 15004
Herman and Marguerite, 2546(F)
Herman the Helper, 2319(F)

The Hermit Thrush Sings, 10154(F)
Hero, 8800(F)
The Hero of Bremen, 10915
The Hero of Ticonderoga, 10060(F)
Herod the Great, 13809
Heroes, 7358(F), 13731
Heroes, Gods and Emperors from Roman Mythology, 11512
Heroic Stories, 12064
Heroin Drug Dangers, 17877
The Heroine of the Titanic, 4595(F)
Heroines of the American Revolution, 16214
Herons, 19355
The Herring Gull, 19353
Hershel and the Hanukkah Goblins, 6084(F)
Hershell Cobwell and the Miraculous Tattoo, 10001(F)
He's My Brother, 8899(F)
The Hessian's Secret Diary, 9222(F)
Hester Bidgood, 9198(F)
Hetty and Harriet, 2544(F)
Hey! 5150(F)
Hey, Al, 2892(F)
Hey Dad, Get a Life! 8134(F)
Hey Diddle Diddle (Illus. by Colin Hawkins), 847
  (Illus. by Marilyn Janovitz), 849
Hey-How for Halloween! 11832
Hey, Kids! Come Craft with Me, 21435
Hey Kids! You're Cookin' Now! A Global Awareness Cooking Adventure, 21732
Hey, Little Baby! 3055(F)
Hey, New Kid! 9836(F)
Hey, Pipsqueak! 1376(F)
Hey, Tabby Cat! 6598(F)
Hey! Wake Up! 3035(F)
Hey Willy, See the Pyramids, 714(F)
Hi, 3415(F)
Hi, Clouds, 6355(F)
Hi New Baby! 3671(F)
"Hi, Pizza Man!" 4345(F)
Hiawatha, 11641, 12974
Hiawatha Passing, 692(F)
Hiccup, 6427(F)
Hiccup Snickup, 4217(F)
The Hickory Chair, 4960
Hickory, Dickory, Dock, 2518(F)
The Hidden Children of the Holocaust, 14862
The Hidden Forest, 7578(F)
Hidden in the Fog, 8457(F)
Hidden Music, 12332
Hidden Pictures, 317
Hidden Talents, 7928(F)
Hidden Under the Ground, 20379
Hidden World, 18387
Hide and Seek, 4400(F), 9695(F), 18882, 18889
  (Illus. by Janet M. Stoeke), 3445(F)
Hide and Seek Fog, 4553(F)
Hide and Seek in History, 21865
Hide-and-Seek with Grandpa, 3773(F)
Hide and Sleep, 803(F)
Hide and Snake, 4081(F)
The Hideout, 6779(F)
Hiding, 3229(F), 3232(F)

Hiding from the Nazis, 14812
Hiding Mr. McMulty, 9609(F)
Hiding Toads, 18719
Hieroglyphics, 14634
Higbee's Halloween, 9959(F)
Higgins Bend Song and Dance, 1397(F)
Higglety Pigglety Pop! or There Must Be More to Life, 8084(F)
High Flight, 12570
High in the Sky, 21096
High in the Trees, 19184
The High King, 7551(F)
A High, Low, Near, Far, Loud, Quiet Story, 174(F)
High on the Hog, 7429(F)
The High Rise Glorious Skittle Skat Roarious Sky Pie Angel Food Cake, 8205(F)
The High-Rise Private Eyes, 8059(F)
High Speed Boats, 21354
Hilary Knight's the Twelve Days of Christmas, 14204
Hilda Hen's Happy Birthday, 5739(F)
Hilda Hen's Scary Night, 2878(F)
Hilda Hen's Search, 2879(F)
Hilde and Eli, 14813
Hill of Fire, 15630
Hillary and Tenzing Climb Everest, 21995
Hillary Rodham Clinton, 13144, 13145, 13146, 13147
Hillary to the Rescue, 2917(F)
Hillclimbing, 22242
Himalaya, 15195
The Hindenburg, 21093
Hindu Mandir, 17233
Hinduism, 17195
Hippety-Hop Hippety-Hay, 11554
The Hippopotamus, 5337
Hippopotamus Hunt, 21883(F)
A Hippopotamusn't and Other Animal Verses, 11797
Hippos, 18985
A Hippo's a Heap and Other Animal Poems, 11802
Hiroshima, 9700(F)
Hiroshima and the Atomic Bomb, 14831
Hiroshima No Pika, 14870
Hispanic America, Texas and the Mexican War, 1835–1850, 16234
A Historical Album of California, 16825
A Historical Album of Colorado, 16644
A Historical Album of Florida, 16897
A Historical Album of Georgia, 16898
A Historical Album of Illinois, 16591
A Historical Album of Kentucky, 16890
A Historical Album of Massachusetts, 16650
A Historical Album of Michigan, 16592
A Historical Album of Minnesota, 16541
A Historical Album of New Jersey, 16752

A Historical Album of New York, 16651
A Historical Album of Ohio, 16593
A Historical Album of Oregon, 16826
A Historical Album of Pennsylvania, 16756
A Historical Album of Texas, 16917
A Historical Album of Virginia, 16838
The History News, 14563, 16082, 18020
The History News in Space, 20993
The History of Art, 13910
A History of Basketball for Girls and Women, 22136
The History of Counting, 20634
The History of Emigration from China and Southeast Asia, 15079
The History of Emigration from Eastern Europe, 14556
The History of Emigration from Scotland, 15351
The History of Figure Skating, 22223
A History of France Through Art, 15316
The History of Moviemaking, 14311
The History of Printmaking, 13894
The History of Soccer, 22292
The History of the Internet and the World Wide Web, 21235
A History of the United States Through Art, 15912
The History of Third Parties, 17098
The Hit-Away Kid, 10303(F)
The Hitler Youth, 14850
Hitty, 7723(F)
A Hive for the Honeybee, 7885(F)
A Hmong Family, 17584
Ho Ho Ho! 17419
Hoang Anh, 17567
Hob and the Goblins, 7957(F)
Hob and the Peddler, 7958(F)
The Hobbit (Illus. by J. R. R. Tolkien), 8151(F)
(Illus. by J. R. R. Tolkien), 8151(F)
The Hoboken Chicken Emergency, 9967(F)
The Hockey Book for Girls, 22216
The Hockey Machine, 10304(F)
Hocus Pocus, 21778
Hog-Eye, 2490(F)
Hog Music, 9373(F)
Hogsel and Gruntel and Other Animal Stories, 7865(F)
Hogula, 6000(F)
The Hokey Pokey, 4208(F)
Hold Christmas in Your Heart, 5848(F)
Hold Everything! 21902
Hold Fast to Dreams, 7364(F)
Hold My Hand and Run, 9108(F)
Hold the Anchovies! 21735
Hold Your Horses! 20005
Holding On, 7427(F)
Holding onto Sunday, 7435(F)
Holding Up the Earth, 8669(F)
The Hole in the Dike, 4670(F)
A Hole Is to Dig, 204(F)
The Hole Story, 3320(F)
Holes, 7041(F)

Holi, 17376
Holiday Cooking Around the World, 21707
Holiday Paper Projects, 21610
Holidays of the World Cookbook for Students, 21747
The Hollow Tree, 9240(F)
Holly, 5765(F)
Holly Pond Hill, 17536
The Holly Sisters on Their Own, 7487(F)
The Hollyhock Wall, 1657(F)
Holly's First Love, 8335(F)
Holly's Secret, 8655(F)
Hollywood at War, 14879
Hollywood Hulk Hogan, 13692
Home, 15854
A Home Album, 15900
Home at Last, 18848
Home Before Dark, 636(F)
A Home by the Sea, 19404
Home Crafts, 16322
A Home for Spooky, 5376(F)
Home Is Where We Live, 8672(F)
Home Lovely, 4507(F)
Home on the Bayou, 4992(F)
Home on the Range, 21816
Home Page, 21214
Home Place, 3110(F)
Home Run, 13497
Home Run Hero, 10336(F)
Home Run Heroes, 13413
Home Run Kings, 13402
Home to Medicine Mountain, 9178(F)
Home Wars, 8492(F)
Homecoming, 7532(F)
Homeless, 17159
The Homeless, 17153
Homeless Bird, 9019(F)
Homeless Children, 18268
Homeless or Hopeless? 17152
Homelessness, 17025, 17154
Homeplace, 3423(F)
Homer Price, 9929(F)
Homes Keep Us Warm, 21159
Homesick, 6689(F), 12536
Homesteading, 16348
Homework Help for Kids on the Net, 21230
Honduras, 15673
Honduras in Pictures, 15671
Honest Pretzels, 21709
The Honest-to-Goodness Truth, 5023(F)
Honest Tulio, 4007(F)
Honey, 20126
Honey Helps, 6352(F)
The Honey Hunters, 10673
Honey, I Love, 3999(F)
Honey, I Love, and Other Love Poems, 11757
The Honey Makers, 19523
A Honey of a Day, 4499(F)
Honeybee, 19527
The Honeybee and the Robber, 1923(F)
Hong Kong, 15170
Honk! (Illus. by Henry Cole), 2054(F)

(Illus. by Chris L. Demarest), 2018(F)
Honk! Honk! 1392(F)
Honolulu, 16807
Honor the Flag, 13973
Honoring Our Ancestors, 17564
Honus and Me, 7769(F)
Hook Moon Night, 7741(F)
Hooked, 17875
Hoop Stars, 22133
Hoops, 11995
Hooray, A Piñata! 5703(F)
Hooray for Diffendoofer Day! 4309(F)
Hooray for Grandparents' Day! 5480(F)
Hooray for Me! 3068(F)
Hooray for Sheep Farming! 20062
Hooray for Snail! 2715(F)
Hooray for the Golly Sisters! 6246(F)
Hooray for Truckmice! 2887(F)
Hoover Dam, 16601
Hooway for Wodney Wat, 2358(F)
Hop Jump, 2815(F)
Hop on Pop, 6642(F)
Hope, 9366(F)
(Illus. by Janice L. Porter), 3814(F)
The Hopeful Trout and Other Limericks, 11863
Hope's Crossing, 9234(F)
The Hopi, 16064
The Hopis, 16048
Hopper's Treetop Adventure, 2575(F)
Hoppy and Joe, 2559(F)
Hopscotch Around the World, 22032
Hopscotch Love, 11583
Horace and Morris But Mostly Dolores, 2224(F)
The Horizontal Man, 6812(F)
The Horned Toad Prince, 10434(F)
Horrible Harry and the Ant Invasion, 4018(F)
Horrible Harry and the Christmas Surprise, 5858(F)
Horrible Harry and the Purple People, 7873(F)
Horrible Harry at Halloween, 10088(F)
Horrible Harry Goes to the Moon, 5510(F)
Horrible Harry Moves Up to Third Grade, 10089(F)
The Horribly Haunted School, 7948(F)
The Horse and His Boy, 7911(F)
Horse and Pony Breeds, 19985, 19993
Horse and Pony Care, 19986, 19994
Horse and Pony Shows and Events, 19995
Horse Crazy, 7165(F)
Horse Heroes, 20010
A Horse in New York, 7284(F)
A Horse Like Barney, 7207(F)
Horse Shy, 7165(F)
Horse Soldiers, 16391
Horsefly, 1248(F)
Horsepower, 20009
Horses, 19987, 20004, 20011, 20016
(Illus. by William Munoz), 20007

Horses and Rhinos, 18956
Horses, Horses, Horses, 19992
Horses in the Fog, 7294(F)
The Horseshoe Crab, 19673
Horton Hatches the Egg, 2675(F)
Horton Hears a Who! 2675(F)
Hosni the Dreamer, 11182
Hospital, 21140
The Hospital Book, 18039
A Hospital Story, 18044
Hostage, 6878(F), 6982(F), 7027(F)
The Hostage, 7312(F)
Hot-Air Henry, 1914(F)
The Hot and Cold Summer, 8308(F)
Hot, Cold, Shy, Bold, 191
Hot Deserts, 20414
Hot Dog, 6290(F)
Hot Fudge Hero, 6228(F)
Hot Hippo, 2163(F)
Hot-Tempered Farmers, 10194(F)
Hottest, Coldest, Highest, Deepest,
  20377
Hound Heaven, 7222(F)
The Hounds of the Morrigan,
  8004(F)
The House Book, 21157
A House by the River, 3809(F)
A House for Hermit Crab, 1925(F)
House, House, 16757
The House I Live In, 13963
The House in the Snow, 6833(F)
A House Is a House for Me, 200(F)
A House Is Not a Home, 2372(F)
The House of Boo, 6028(F)
The House of Dies Drear, 6872(F)
House of Shadows, 7995(F)
The House of Sixty Fathers, 9653(F)
The House of Wings, 8583(F)
House of Wisdom, 8957(F)
The House on East 88th Street,
  2787(F)
The House on Maple Street, 4800(F)
House Sparrows Everywhere, 19213
A House Spider's Life, 19583
The House That Crack Built, 17894
The House That Drac Built, 6049(F)
The House That Jack Built, 901
The House with No Door, 11722
Housebuilding for Children, 21664
The Housefly, 19441
Household Stories of the Brothers
  Grimm, 10899
Houses, 21158
Houses and Homes, 3334(F), 21163
Houses of Adobe, 16036
Houses of Bark, 16037
Houses of China, 15081
The Houses of Parliament, 15365
Houses of Snow, Skin and Bones,
  15833
Housing Our Feathered Friends,
  19285
Houston, 16914, 16915
The Houston Rockets Basketball
  Team, 22134
How a Baby Grows, 3550(F)
How a Book Is Made, 13990
How a House Is Built, 3167
How a Plant Grows, 20239
How a Seed Grows, 20271
How About a Hug, 4979(F)

How and Why Stories, 10556
How Animals Behave, 18804
How Animals Communicate, 18893
How Animals Protect Themselves,
  18895
How Animals Saved the People,
  10606
How Animals See Things, 18812
How Are You Peeling? Foods with
  Moods, 4961
How Babies Are Made, 18236
How Bats "See" in the Dark, 19033
How Beastly! 11928
How Bees Make Honey, 19516
How Big Is a Foot? 349(F)
How Big Is a Pig? 158(F)
How Big Is the Ocean? 4462
How Big Were the Dinosaurs? 14452
How Birds Fly, 19297
How Can I Be a Detective If I Have
  to Baby-Sit? 6761(F)
How Chipmunk Got His Stripes,
  11221
How Come? 18296
How Come Planet Earth? 18297
How Come the Best Clues Are
  Always in the Garbage? 6762(F)
How Did We Find Out About
  Comets? 18504
How Did We Find Out About
  Lasers? 20856
How Did We Find Out About Solar
  Power? 20848
How Did We Find Out About Volca-
  noes? 20332
How Dinosaurs Came to Be, 14434
How Do Animals Adapt? 18827
How Do Animals Move? 18863
How Do Apples Grow? 20153
How Do Big Ships Float? 21349
How Do Birds Find Their Way?
  19231
How Do Dinosaurs Say Goodnight?
  816(F)
How Do Flies Walk Upside Down?
  Questions and Answers About
  Insects, 19429
How Do I Feel? 7514(F)
How Do Our Ears Hear? 18131
How Do Our Eyes See? 18132
How Do We Feel and Touch? 18133
How Do We Know Where People
  Came From? 14524
How Do We Move? 18166
How Do We Taste and Smell? 18134
How Do We Think? 18109
How Do You Know It's Fall? 18563
How Do You Know It's Summer?
  18564
How Do You Say It Today, Jesse
  Bear? 1934(F)
How Do You Spell G-E-E-K?
  8360(F)
How Do You Spell God? 17188
How Does Soda Get into the Bottle?
  20082
How Does Your Garden Grow?
  21760
How Dogs Really Work! 2707(F)
How Droofus the Dragon Lost His
  Head, 2570(F)

How Emily Blair Got Her Fabulous
  Hair, 4155(F)
How Fish Swim, 19696
How Georgie Radbourn Saved Base-
  ball, 10361(F)
How Glass Is Made, 21051
How God Fix Jonah, 17278
How Humans Make Friends, 1343(F)
How I Captured a Dinosaur, 2668(F)
How I Named the Baby, 3895(F)
How I Saved Hanukkah, 9741(F)
How I Survived My Summer Vaca-
  tion, 6803(F), 9856(F)
How I Survived the Oregon Trail,
  9461(F)
How Insects Build Their Amazing
  Homes, 19482
How It Feels to Be Adopted, 17665
How It Feels When a Parent Dies,
  17716
How It Feels When Parents Divorce,
  17666
How It Was with Dooms, 19093
How Jackrabbit Got His Very Long
  Ears, 2242(F)
How Kittens Grow, 19933
How Leaves Change, 20206
How Long? 176(F)
How Mammals Build Their Amazing
  Homes, 18911
How Many Bears? 426(F)
How Many Candles? 5689(F)
How Many Days to America? A
  Thanksgiving Story, 6135(F)
How Many Days Until Tomorrow?
  8709(F)
How Many Feet? How Many Tails?
  392(F)
How Many Feet in the Bed? 457(F)
How Many Fish? 6276(F)
How Many How Many How Many,
  603(F)
How Many Miles to Babylon?
  6846(F)
How Many Miles to Jacksonville?
  4698(F)
How Many Snails? 444(F)
How Many Spots Does a Leopard
  Have? 10685
How Many Stars in the Sky? 706(F)
How Many Teeth? 18189
How Maps Are Made, 14363
How Math Works, 20599
How Monkeys Make Chocolate,
  20439
How Mountains Are Made, 20330
How Much Is a Million? 20635
How Much Is That Doggie in the
  Window? 14258
How Music Came to the World,
  11413
How My Family Lives in America,
  3758
How My Library Grew, by Dinah,
  2991(F)
How My Parents Learned to Eat,
  3635(F)
How Nanita Learned to Make Flan,
  1180(F)
How Nature Works, 18580
How Our Blood Circulates, 18089

How Plants Grow, 20261
  (Illus. by Stuart Lafford), 20254
How Proudly They Wave, 13971
How Puppies Grow, 19969
How Raggedy Ann Got Her Candy
  Heart, 1209(F)
How Santa Got His Job, 9742(F)
How Seeds Travel, 20273
How Snake Got His Hiss, 1102(F)
How Spider Saved Halloween,
  6021(F)
How Spiders Make Their Webs,
  19573
How Sweet the Sound, 14247
How Tall How Short How Far Away,
  366
How the Animals Got Their Colors,
  10608
How the Camel Got His Hump,
  1308(F)
How the Cat Swallowed Thunder,
  1733(F)
How the Future Began, 21034
How the Grinch Stole Christmas,
  5917(F)
How the Guinea Fowl Got Her Spots,
  10679
How the Ox Star Fell from Heaven,
  10756
How the Reindeer Got Their Antlers,
  5867(F)
How the Rooster Got His Crown,
  10767
How the Second Grade Got
  $8,205.50 to Visit the Statue of
  Liberty, 4368(F)
How the Stars Fell into the Sky,
  11285
How the Whale Became and Other
  Stories, 1254(F)
How the White House Really Works,
  16746
How the Wind Plays, 1355(F)
How the Wolf Became the Dog,
  19979
How Things Work, 21028, 21035
How Tia Lola Came to Visit Stay,
  7386(F)
How to Babysit an Orangutan, 18991
How to Be a Friend, 3983(F)
How to Be a Real Person (in Just One
  Day), 8538(F)
How to Be a Reasonably Thin
  Teenage Girl, 18199
How to Be an Ocean Scientist in
  Your Own Home, 18348
How to Be Cool in the Third Grade,
  6318(F)
How to Be School Smart, 17614
How to Be the Greatest Writer in the
  World, 14075
How to Catch an Elephant, 4304(F)
How to Dig a Hole to the Other Side
  of the World, 20313
How to Do Homework Without
  Throwing Up, 17629
How to Eat Fried Worms, 9976(F)
How to Find a Ghost, 21904
How to Find Lost Treasure in All 50
  States and Canada, Too! 14529

How to Get Famous in Brooklyn,
  3210(F)
How to Handle Bullies, Teasers and
  Other Meanies, 17698
How to Hunt Buried Treasure, 21905
How to Make a Chemical Volcano
  and Other Mysterious Experiments,
  18324
How to Make a Mummy Talk, 14620
How to Make Pop-Ups, 21619
How to Make Super Pop-Ups, 21620
How to Read Your Mother's Mind,
  21906
How to Survive Third Grade,
  5514(F)
How to Take Your Grandmother to
  the Museum, 3960(F)
How to Talk to Your Cat, 19920
How to Talk to Your Dog, 19948
How to Think Like a Scientist, 18282
How to Write Poetry, 14094
How to Write, Recite, and Delight in
  All Kinds of Poetry, 14090
How to Write Super School Reports,
  14091
How to Write Terrific Book Reports,
  14092
How to Write Your Best Book
  Report, 14093
How We Crossed the West, 16091
How We Know About the Egyptians,
  14633
How We Know About the Greeks,
  14687
How We Learned the Earth Is Round,
  18432
How We Saw the World, 11307
How Whales Walked into the Sea,
  19796
How Will the Easter Bunny Know?
  5978(F)
How Will We Get to the Beach?
  2954(F)
How Would You Survive as a
  Viking? 15462
How Would You Survive as an
  American Indian? 16056
How Would You Survive as an
  Ancient Egyptian? 14650
How Would You Survive as an
  Ancient Roman? 14719
How Would You Survive as an
  Aztec? 15632
How Would You Survive in the
  American West? 16345
How Writers Work, 14081
How You Were Born, 18238
How Yussel Caught the Gefilte Fish,
  6078(F)
Howard and the Sitter Surprise,
  1462(F)
Howdi Do, 14153
Howie Bowles and Uncle Sam,
  9774(F)
Howie Bowles, Secret Agent,
  6764(F)
Howie Helps Himself, 8888(F)
Howliday Inn, 9885(F)
Howling Hill, 2214(F)
How's the Weather? 20753
The Hubble Space Telescope, 18417

Hubble Space Telescope, 18383
Hubert's Hair-Raising Adventure,
  2567(F)
The Huckabuck Family and How
  They Raised Popcorn in Nebraska
  and Quit and Came Back, 3872(F)
The Hudson River, 16755
Hug, 1730(F)
Huge Harold, 2570(F)
Huggly Takes a Bath, 626(F)
Hugo and the Bully Frogs, 2699(F)
Hugo at the Park, 2632(F)
The Hullabaloo ABC, 25(F)
The Human Body, 18070
  (Illus. by Sylvaine Perols), 18071
  (Illus. by Patricia J. Wynne), 18051
The Human Body for Every Kid,
  18082
The Humane Societies, 18664
Humanitarians, 13727
Humans, 14496
Humbug, 6966(F), 7391(F)
Humbug Mountain, 9849(F)
Humbug Potion, 8(F)
Humbug Witch, 972(F)
Hummingbirds, 19272
A Hummingbird's Life, 19236
Humphrey's Bear, 801(F)
Humpty Dumpty, 854(F)
  (Illus. by Colin Hawkins), 847
Humpty Dumpty and Other Nursery
  Rhymes, 833(F)
Humpty Dumpty and Other Rhymes,
  879(F)
The Hunchback of Notre Dame,
  9045(F)
Hunches in Bunches, 2676(F)
The Hundred and One Dalmatians,
  8105(F)
The Hundred Dresses, 10054(F)
The Hundred Penny Box, 7483(F)
Hundreds of Fish, 5460(F)
Hungary, 15292
Hungary in Pictures, 15273
The Hungry Black Bag, 2761(F)
Hungry, Hungry Sharks, 19753
The Hungry Otter, 2082(F)
Hungry Plants, 20227
Hunky Dory Ate It, 5199(F)
The Hunky-Dory Dairy, 7913(F)
The Hunt for Food, 18625
Hunt for Hector, 2752(F)
The Hunted, 7061(F)
The Hunter, 10740
The Hunter and the Animals, 916(F)
The Hunterman and the Crocodile,
  10663
Hunting the White Cow, 5409(F)
The Huron, 15929
The Huron Indians, 16034
Hurrah for Ethelyn, 1967(F)
Hurray for Ali Baba Bernstein,
  6420(F)
Hurray for Pre-K! 5536(F)
Hurray for the Fourth of July,
  5657(F)
Hurray for Three Kings' Day!
  5774(F)
Hurricane, 2984(F), 9274(F)
Hurricane! 20678
  (Illus. by Vanessa Lubach),

4478(F)
(Illus. by Henri Sorensen), 4744(F)
(Illus. by Lenice U. Strohmeier),
2924(F)
Hurricane Andrew, 20715
Hurricane Harry, 8595(F)
Hurricane Henrietta, 1272(F)
Hurricanes, 20706, 20707, 20709,
20720
Hurry! 3294(F)
(Illus. by Joseph A. Smith),
3188(F)
Hurry Granny Annie, 4075(F)
Hurry Home, Candy, 7184(F)
Hurry, Hurry, Mary Dear, 3535(F)
Hurry, Santa! 5932(F)
Hush! 683(F), 703(F)
Hush, Little Alien, 717(F)
Hush, Little Baby, 708(F), 729(F),
14155
Hush Songs, 793
Huskings, Quiltings, and Barn Rais-
ings, 16171
Hydrogen, 20282

I Am a Dancer, 14282
I Am a Home Schooler, 3466
I Am a Rider, 22201
I Am a Rock, 20564
I Am a Star, 14816
I Am an Apple, 6506(F)
I Am an Artist, 2521(F)
I Am Angela, 6920(F)
I Am Eastern Orthodox, 17217
I Am Eyes Ni Macho, 4867(F)
I Am Houston, 12904
I Am Jewish, 17228
I Am Jewish American, 17599
I Am Lavina Cumming, 9589(F)
I Am Leaper, 7845(F)
I Am Mad! 6408(F)
I Am Me, 3761(F)
I Am Me! 3038(F)
I Am Mordred, 8119(F)
I Am Muslim, 17173
I Am Not a Crybaby, 5077(F)
I Am Not a Short Adult, 17028
I Am Not Going to Get Up Today!
6643(F)
I Am Phoenix, 11780
I Am Protestant, 17218
I Am Regina, 9166(F)
I Am Roman Catholic, 17219
I Am Rosa Parks, 12778
I Am Shinto, 17209
I Am the Cat, 11811
I Am the Ice Worm, 6828(F)
I Am the Mummy Heb-Nefert,
8960(F)
I Am Water, 20739
I Am Wings, 11564
I Am Writing a Poem About . . . a
Game of Poetry, 11634
I, Amber Brown, 9827(F)
I Bought a Baby Chicken, 454(F)
I Call It Sky, 4463(F)
I Can, 3953(F)
I Can! 2989(F)
I Can Count 100 Bunnies, 591(F)
I Can Do It! 6186(F)

I Can Draw a Weeposaur and Other
Dinosaurs, 11873
I Can Fly! 175(F)
I Can Hear the Sun, 8022(F)
I Can Lick Thirty Tigers Today and
Other Stories, 6644(F)
I Can Make Art, 21597
I Can Make Jewelry, 21552
I Can Make Puppets, 14308
I Can Make Toys, 21509
I Can Read with My Eyes Shut!
6645(F)
I Can Roll, 175(F)
I Can Save the Earth, 16958
I Can Sign My ABCs, 21(F)
I Can Too! 2441(F)
I Can't Believe I Have to Do This,
9770(F)
"I Can't Take You Anywhere!"
4248(F)
I Can't Wait Until I'm Old Enough to
Hunt with Dad, 2946(F)
I, Crocodile, 2472(F)
I Dance in My Red Pajamas, 3712(F)
I Did It, I'm Sorry, 167(F)
I Don't Want to Go Back to School,
5531(F)
I Don't Want to Go to Bed, 724(F)
I Don't Want to Go to Camp,
3057(F)
I Don't Want to Go to Justin's House
Anymore, 4998(F)
I Don't Want to Take a Bath, 2745(F)
I Don't Want to Talk About It,
5053(F)
I Dream of Murder, 6821(F)
I Feel Happy and Sad and Angry and
Glad, 2522(F)
I Fly, 2965(F)
I Forgot My Shoes, 4175(F)
I Had Trouble in Getting to Solla
Sollew, 2676(F)
I Hate Being Gifted, 8300(F)
The I Hate Mathematics! Book,
20613
I Hate My Best Friend, 8365(F)
I Hate to Go to Bed! 658(F)
I Hate Weddings, 9961(F)
I Have a Dream, 12743, 17040
I Have a Sister, My Sister Is Deaf,
5048(F)
I Have a Song to Sing, O! 14257
I Have a Weird Brother Who Digest-
ed a Fly, 18100
I Have an Olive Tree, 4609(F)
I Have Feelings, 17604
I Have Heard of a Land, 9443(F)
I Heal, 17984
I Heard a Little Baa, 5330(F)
I Imagine Angels, 17525
I Is for India, 15098
I, Juan de Pareja, 9034(F)
I Knew Two Who Said Moo, 378(F)
I Know a Lady, 4069(F)
I Know an Old Lady, 14159
I Know an Old Lady Who Swallowed
a Fly (Illus. by Glen Rounds),
14177
(Illus. by Nadine Bernard West-
cott), 14191

I Know an Old Lady Who Swallowed
a Pie, 6145(F)
I Know How My Cells Make Me
Grow, 18076
I Know How We Fight Germs, 17993
I Know Not What, I Know Not
Where, 11096
I Know What You Do When I Go to
School, 4103(F)
I Know Where My Food Goes,
18102
I Know Why I Brush My Teeth,
18188
I Left My Sneakers in Dimension X,
10168(F)
I Like a Snack on an Iceberg,
5120(F)
I Like It When . . ., 2523(F)
I Like Me! 1930(F)
I Like Mess, 6450(F)
I Like Monkeys Because . . ., 18997
I Like Music, 17771
I Like Sports, 17742
I Like Stars, 6236(F)
I Like to Be Little, 3499(F)
I Like to Win! 6660(F)
I Like You, If You Like Me, 11635
I Like Your Buttons! 3272(F)
I Look Like a Girl, 1218(F)
I Lost My Bear, 2928(F)
I Lost My Dad, 4967(F)
I Lost My Tooth! 6717(F)
I Love Animals, 2428(F)
I Love Boats, 5585(F)
I Love Cats, 6514(F)
I Love Colors, 284(F)
I Love Guinea Pigs, 19900
I Love My Busy Book, 250(F)
I Love My Buzzard, 4310(F)
I Love My Daddy Because . . .,
3844(F)
I Love My Hair! 3450(F)
I Love My Mommy Because . . .,
3844(F)
I Love to Sneeze, 6631(F)
I Love Trucks! 21324
I Love You, 11651
I Love You As Much . . ., 743(F)
I Love You, Blue Kangaroo! 1059(F)
I Love You, Bunny Rabbit, 3349(F)
I Love You, Daisy Phew, 8834(F)
I Love You Just the Way You Are,
746(F)
I Love You Like Crazy Cakes,
4735(F)
I Love You, Little One, 792(F)
I Love You, Mouse, 5233(F)
I Love You So Much, 2529(F)
I Love You, Stinky Face, 734(F)
I Love You the Purplest, 3738(F)
I Love You with All My Heart,
2288(F)
I Make a Cake, 2521(F)
I Make Music, 3182(F)
I Miss Franklin P. Shuckles, 4045(F)
I Miss You, Stinky Face, 3785(F)
I Need a Lunch Box, 3063(F)
I Need a Snake, 4197(F)
I Never Did That Before, 11656
I Never Told and Other Poems,
11636

I Once Was a Monkey, 10799
I Pledge Allegiance, 6688
I Pretend, 1197(F)
I Read Signs, 307(F)
I Read Symbols, 307(F)
I Really Want a Dog, 5142(F)
I Remember Bosnia, 15269
I Remember "121" 3672
I Remember Papa, 3260(F)
I Remember the Alamo, 9587(F)
I Saw Esau, 11903
I Saw You in the Bathtub and Other
  Folk Rhymes, 6638(F)
I Scream, You Scream, 11902
I See, 18143
I See a Sign, 14015
I See Me! 3422(F)
I See the Moon, 7405(F)
  (Illus. by Debra R. Jenkins), 622(F)
I See the Rhythm, 14132
I Shop with My Daddy, 6477(F)
I Sing for the Animals, 4445
I Speak English for My Mom,
  7376(F)
I Speak for the Women, 13197
I Spy, 99(F), 21840, 21870, 21871
I Spy Christmas, 5876
I Spy Fantasy, 21872
I Spy Funhouse, 4232
I Spy School Days, 211(F)
I Spy Spooky Night, 21841
I Spy Super Challenger! A Book of
  Picture Riddles, 21873
I Spy Treasure Hunt, 21874
I Swapped My Dog, 4365(F)
I Thought My Soul Would Rise and
  Fly, 9549(F)
I, Too, Sing America, 11753
I Took a Walk, 4406(F)
I Took My Frog to the Library,
  4203(F)
I Touch, 18144
I Walk at Night, 2045(F)
I Want a Pet, 4108(F)
I Want Answers and a Parachute,
  8508(F)
I Want My Dinner, 4288(F)
I Want to Be, 4289(F)
I Want to Be a Chef, 17752
I Want to Be a Dancer, 17777
I Want to Be a Doctor, 17802
I Want to Be a Fashion Designer,
  21179
I Want to Be a Firefighter, 17818
I Want to Be a Police Officer, 17815
I Want to Be a Vet, 17853
I Want to Be a Veterinarian, 17854
I Want to Be an Astronaut, 17758
  (Illus. by Byron Barton), 6766(F)
I Want to Be an Engineer, 17789
I Want to Be an Environmentalist,
  17757
I Want to Go to School, Too!
  5516(F)
I Wanted to Know All About God,
  17199
I Was a Rat! 8032(F)
I Was a Sixth Grade Alien, 10169(F)
I Was a Third Grade Science Project,
  9773(F)
I Was Born a Slave, 12730

I Was Dreaming to Come to Ameri-
  ca, 16708
I Was So Mad! 5078(F)
I Went to the Bay, 5348
I Went Walking, 3477(F)
I Will Never Not Ever Eat a Tomato,
  4109(F)
I Wish Daddy Didn't Drink So
  Much, 5095(F)
I Wish I Had My Father, 5079(F)
I Wish I Were a Butterfly, 2225(F)
I Wish My Brother Was a Dog,
  1571(F)
I Wish That I Had Duck Feet,
  6453(F)
I Wish Tonight, 767(F)
I Wished for a Unicorn, 1231(F)
I Wonder What's Under There? A
  Brief History of Underwear, 21176
I Wonder Why Greeks Built Temples
  and Other Questions About Ancient
  Greece, 14691
I Wonder Why Romans Wore Togas
  and Other Questions About Ancient
  Rome, 14728
I Wonder Why the Sea Is Salty,
  19817
Ian Penney's Book of Nursery
  Rhymes, 883(F)
Ian's Walk, 5011(F)
Iblis, 11194
Icarus Swinebuckle, 2117(F)
An Ice Age Hunter, 8950(F)
Ice and People, 20357
Ice and the Earth, 20357
The Ice Bear, 7908(F)
Ice Bear and Little Fox, 5314(F)
Ice-Cold Birthday, 6271(F)
Ice Cream, 20101
  (Illus. by John Holm), 20104
Ice Cream Colors, 330(F)
The Ice Cream King, 4227(F)
Ice Cream Larry, 2588(F)
The Ice Cream Store, 11892
The Ice Dove and Other Stories,
  7417(F)
Ice Is . . . Whee! 6355(F)
Ice Maiden of the Andes, 14491
Ice Skating, 22222, 22225
Ice Sports, 22257
Ice Story, 15812
Icebergs, Ice Caps, and Glaciers,
  20358
Iceland, 15458, 15469
Iceland in Pictures, 15451
Icky, Squishy Science, 18331
Icy Watermelon / Sandia fria,
  3640(F)
I'd Rather Have an Iguana, 3798(F)
Id-ul-Fitr, 17377, 17389
Ida B. Wells, 12816
Ida B. Wells-Barnett, 12818, 12820
Ida B. Wells-Barnett and the Anti-
  Lynching Crusade, 12817
Ida Early Comes over the Mountain,
  7395(F)
Idaho, 16613, 16640
Idaho Facts and Symbols, 16622
Iditarod Dream, 22075
Idora, 4666(F)
If . . ., 221(F)

If a Bus Could Talk, 12779
If All the Seas Were One Sea, 851
If Anything Ever Goes Wrong at the
  Zoo, 1233(F)
If Dogs Had Wings, 1865(F)
If Ever I Return Again, 9271(F)
If I Crossed the Road, 1324(F)
If I Forget Thee, O Jerusalem, 15533
If I Forget, You Remember, 8853(F)
If I Had a Paka, 11673
If I Had One Wish . . ., 7876(F)
If I Only Had a Horn, 12349
If I Ran the Circus, 2675(F)
If I Ran the Zoo, 2675(F)
If I Were in Charge of the World and
  Other Worries, 11730
If I Were President, 17126
If I Were Queen of the World,
  1236(F)
If I Were the Wind, 3618(F)
If I Were Your Father, 3544(F)
If I Were Your Mother, 3545(F)
If It Weren't for Benjamin (I'd
  Always Get to Lick the Icing
  Spoon), 3681(F)
If It Weren't for Farmers, 20053
If Nathan Were Here, 4901(F)
If Phyllis Were Here, 7460(F)
If . . ., 1470(F)
If Sarah Will Take Me, 11537
If That Breathes Fire, We're Toast!
  8131(F)
If the Dinosaurs Came Back, 2514(F)
If the Owl Calls Again, 11800
If Wishes Were Horses, 9570(F)
If You Are a Hunter of Fossils,
  4386(F)
If You Could Wear My Sneakers!
  11869
If You Didn't Have Me, 8776(F)
If You Ever Get Lost, 7494(F)
If You Ever Meet a Whale, 11801
If You Find a Rock, 4405(F)
If You Give a Moose a Muffin,
  2537(F)
If You Give a Mouse a Cookie,
  2538(F)
If You Give a Pig a Pancake, 2539(F)
If You Hopped Like a Frog, 241
If You Lived in Colonial Times,
  16155
If You Lived with the Sioux Indians,
  15996
If You Love a Bear, 1221(F)
If You Made a Million, 20636
If You Only Knew, 8378(F)
If You Please, President Lincoln,
  9137(F)
If You Sailed on the Mayflower,
  16156
If You Should Hear a Honey Guide,
  14947
If You Take a Mouse to the Movies,
  2540(F)
If You Were a Ballet Dancer, 17782
If You Were a Construction Worker,
  17797
If You Were a Doctor, 17805
If You Were a Farmer, 17764
If You Were a Firefighter, 17821
If You Were a Musician, 17783

If You Were a Pilot, 17840
If You Were a Police Officer, 17822
If You Were a Teacher, 17765
If You Were a Truck Driver, 17841
If You Were a Veterinarian, 17856
If You Were a Writer, 14101
If You Were an Astronaut, 17766
If You Were Born a Kitten, 18869
If You Were My Bunny, 738(F)
If You Were There in 1492, 16077
If You Were There in 1776, 16190
If You Were There When They Signed the Constitution, 17059
If Your Name Was Changed at Ellis Island, 17575
If You're Happy and You Know It, 14189
If You're Missing Baby Jesus, 9722(F)
Igbo, 15042
Iggie's House, 7335(F)
Igloo, 15797
The Igloo, 15848
Igor Stravinsky, 12339
Iguana Beach, 3150(F)
The Iguana Brothers, 2261(F)
Iktomi and the Berries, 11243
Iktomi and the Boulder, 11244
Iktomi and the Buffalo Skull, 11245
Iktomi and the Coyote, 11246
Iktomi Loses His Eyes, 11247
Iliad, 11510
The Iliad, 11509
(Illus. by Victor G. Ambrus), 11486
The Iliad and the Odyssey, 11515
I'll Always Love You, 5455(F)
I'll Catch the Moon, 1087(F)
I'll Do It Later, 6695(F)
I'll Fix Anthony, 3929(F)
I'll Go to School If . . ., 5500(F)
I'll Play With You, 1575(F)
Illegal Aliens, 17142
Illinois, 16527, 16537, 16549, 16579
Illusions Illustrated, 21776
The Illustrated Book of Ballet Stories, 14296
The Illustrated Book of Myths, 11455
The Illustrated Laws of Soccer, 22290
The Illustrated Rules of Baseball, 22095
The Illustrated Rules of Basketball, 22128
The Illustrated Rules of Football, 22188
The Illustrated Rules of Ice Hockey, 22211
The Illustrated Rules of In-line Hockey, 22036
The Illustrated Rules of Softball, 22119
The Illustrated Rules of Tennis, 22315
The Illyrian Adventure, 6743(F)
I'm a Big Brother, 3583(F)
I'm a Big Sister, 3583(F)
I'm a Caterpillar, 6507(F)
I'm a Jolly Farmer, 1331(F)
I'm Busy, Too, 5540(F)
I'm Deaf and It's Okay, 17901(F)

I'm Frustrated, 4937(F)
I'm Going to Be a Police Officer, 3269(F)
I'm Going to Be Famous, 9779(F)
I'm Going to Pet a Worm Today and Other Poems, 11796
I'm in Charge of Celebrations, 10251(F)
I'm Mad, 4937(F)
I'm New Here, 5507(F)
I'm Not Going to Chase the Cat Today! 2170(F)
I'm Not Moving, Mama! 1935(F)
I'm Not Who You Think I Am, 8719(F)
I'm Out of My Body . . . Please Leave a Message, 7757(F)
I'm Proud, 4937(F)
I'm Sorry, 4026(F)
I'm Sorry, Almira Ann, 9391(F)
I'm Taking a Trip on My Train, 5591(F)
I'm Terrific, 2682(F)
I'm the Big Sister Now, 17906
I'm the Boss! 3954(F)
I'm Tougher Than Asthma! 17949
Images of God, 17314
Imaginary Gardens, 11963
Imaginary Menagerie, 5318(F)
Imagine, 1655(F)
Imagine That! 14576
Imagine That! Poems of Never-Was, 11876
Imagine You Are a Crocodile, 5445(F)
Imani and the Flying Africans, 11363
Imani in the Belly, 10657
Imani's Gift at Kwanzaa, 9710(F)
Immigrant Children, 16495
Immigrant Kids, 16463
Immigration, 17561
Imogene's Antlers, 1585(F)
The Imp That Ate My Homework, 8233(F)
Impatient Pamela Asks, 5000(F)
Impatient Pamela Calls 9-1-1, 3266(F)
Impeachment, 17124
The Impeachment Process, 17125
The Importance of John Muir, 13328
The Importance of Mother Jones, 13161
The Importance of William Shakespeare, 12595
The Impossible Riddle, 11092
Impossible Things, 7896(F)
An Impossumble Summer, 7411(F)
Impressionism, 13882
Impressionist Art, 13901
Improve Your Riding Skills, 22205
Impy for Always, 8322(F)
In a Circle Long Ago, 11314
In a Dark, Dark Wood, 2920(F)
In a Messy, Messy Room, 7750(F)
In a Pickle and Other Funny Idioms, 14050
In a Pumpkin Shell, 2(F), 21438
In a Sacred Manner I Live, 16023
In Aunt Lucy's Kitchen, 7502(F)
In Blue Mountains, 16710
In Care of Cassie Tucker, 9619(F)

In Colonial New England, 16145
In Daddy's Arms I Am Tall, 11762
In Enzo's Splendid Gardens, 4268(F)
In Every Tiny Grain of Sand, 17526
In Fields and Meadows, 18652
In Flight with David McPhail, 12569
In for Winter, Out for Spring, 11934
In God's Image, 18251
In Good Hands, 19345
In Grandpa's House, 7510(F)
In-Line Skating, 21982, 22028
In-Line Skating! 22026
In My Family/En Mi Familia, 3283(F)
In My Garden, 578(F)
(Illus. by Ermanno Cristini), 914(F)
In My Momma's Kitchen, 3824(F)
In My Pocket, 9689(F)
In November, 4530(F)
In Our Image, 5651
In Praise of Our Fathers and Our Mothers, 12167
In Search of Knossos, 14522
In Search of Lemurs, 19012
In Search of Maiasaurs, 14462
In Search of the Grand Canyon, 16611
In Search of the Spirit, 15123
In Search of Troy, 14523
In Search of Tutankhamun, 14611
In Space, 21014
In the Attic, 1444(F)
In the Barn, 16323
In the Beginning, 14567
In the Camps, 14817
In the Company of Bears, 1993(F)
In the Days of the Salem Witchcraft Trials, 16164
In the Desert, 20422
In the Diner, 3285(F)
In the Dinosaur's Paw, 6345(F)
In the Eye of War, 9649(F)
In the Eyes of the Cat, 11821
In the Forest, 18930
In the Forest with the Elephants, 15205
In the Ghettos, 14819
In the Hollow of Your Hand, 14167
In the Huddle with John Elway, 13607
In the Huddle with . . . Steve Young, 13637
In the Hush of the Evening, 689(F)
In the Land of the Big Red Apple, 9403(F)
In the Language of Loons, 8724(F)
In the Line of Fire, 13743
In the Middle Colonies, 16145
In the Month of Kislev, 6081(F)
In the Moonlight Mist, 10735
In the Mountains, 20422
In the Next Three Seconds, 21937
In the Paint, 21575
In the Palace of the Ocean King, 10503(F)
In the Park, 13985(F)
In the Piney Woods, 7372(F)
In the Polar Regions, 15838
In the Quiet, 8518(F)
In the Rain with Baby Duck, 2200(F)
In the Rainfield, 10708

In the Shade of the Nispero Tree, 7334(F)
In the Small, Small Pond, 4429(F)
In the Snow, 4440(F), 13986(F)
In the Southern Colonies, 16145
In the Spanish West, 16377
In the Stone Circle, 7861(F)
In the Swim, 11783
In the Tall, Tall Grass, 5205(F)
In the Time of Knights, 14795
In the Time of the Drums, 9321(F)
In the Village of the Elephants, 19170
In the Wild, 18968
In the Woods, 20450
In the Year of the Boar and Jackie Robinson, 7352(F)
Inca Town, 15759
The Incas, 15752, 15774, 15780, 15786
The Incas and Machu Picchu, 15788
Inch by Inch, 2383(F), 14169
The Inch-High Samurai, 10822
Inchworm and a Half, 556(F)
Incident at Hawk's Hill, 9158(F) (Illus. by John Schoenherr), 7186(F)
Inclined Planes, 20924
Incredible Comparisons, 18274
Incredible Constructions, 21115
Incredible Creatures, 18931
Incredible Earth, 20301
Incredible Facts About the Ocean, 19835
Incredible Fishing Stories for Kids, 22176(F)
The Incredible Journey to the Beginning of Time, 14555
The Incredible Journey to the Depths of the Ocean, 19876
The Incredible Journey to the Planets, 18474
Incredible Ned, 1405(F)
The Incredible Painting of Felix Clousseau, 945(F)
Incredible People, 12647
Incredible Plants, 20230
The Incredible Story of China's Buried Warriors, 15077
Independence Avenue, 9625(F)
Independence Hall, 16739
India, 15094, 15096, 15097, 15101, 15102, 15106, 15109, 15114
India in Pictures, 15107
Indian Crafts, 21518
Indian Fairy Tales, 10794
The Indian in the Cupboard, 7583(F)
The Indian Ocean, 19833
Indian School, 15940
Indian Subcontinent, 15113
Indian Treaties, 15957
The Indian Way, 9168(F)
An Indian Winter, 15954
Indiana, 16538, 16557
Indians, Cowboys, and Farmers, 16297
Indians of the Andes, 15767
Indians of the Great Plains, 16042
Indians of the Northeast Woodlands, 16041
Indians of the Northwest, 16025

Indians of the Southwest, 16043
Indigo and Moonlight Gold, 3648(F)
Indonesia, 15156, 15168, 15183, 15186
The Industrial Revolution, 15872
Informania, 19766, 21935, 21936
The Ingenious Mr. Peale, 12278
Inhalant Drug Dangers, 17880
Ininatig's Gift of Sugar, 16069
The Ink Drinker, 8064(F)
Inline Skating, 21976, 22023
Inner Chimes, 11574
The Insect Book, 19502
Insect Detector, 19454
Insect Soup, 11806
Insect Wars, 19497
Insectlopedia, 11784
Insects, 19439, 19445, 19485, 19492, 19494, 19504
Insects and Crawly Creatures, 19484
Insects and Spiders, 19438, 19481
Insects Are My Life, 5323(F)
Insects Around the House, 19490
Insects from Outer Space, 1765(F)
Insects in the Garden, 19490
Insects of the Rain Forest, 20494
Inside a Barn in the Country, 5157(F)
Inside a Coral Reef, 19669
Inside a House That Is Haunted, 5986(F)
Inside a Zoo in the City, 6259(F)
Inside an Egg, 19304
Inside Freight Train, 5557(F)
Inside Out, 18281
Inside-Out Grandma, 6109(F)
The Inside-Outside Book of Libraries, 13992
Inside, Outside Christmas, 5924(F)
Inside, Outside, Upside Down, 159(F)
Inside the Body, 18059
Inside the Dzanga-Sangha Rain Forest, 20451
Inside the Hindenburg, 21087
Inside the Museum, 13919
Inside the Synagogue, 17224
Inspector Hopper, 6300(F)
Inspirations, 12182
Instead of Three Wishes, 8158(F)
The International Space Station, 20955
Internet, 21201
The Internet, 21207, 21219
The Internet for Kids, 21210
Interrupted Journey, 18785
Into a New Country, 12665
Into My Mother's Arms, 3246(F)
Into the A, B, Sea, 119
Into the Flames, 9658(F)
Into the Ice, 15798
Into the Jungle, 2940(F)
Into the Land of the Unicorn, 7681(F)
Into the Land of the Unicorns, 7675(F)
Into the Sea, 18783
Into the Sky, 21132
Into the Wind, 21371
Into the Woods, 18645
Introducing Gershwin, 12329
Introducing Mozart, 12336

The Inuit, 15814
The Inuits, 15823
The Inuksuk Book, 15844
Invasion of Italy, 14832
Inventions and Trade, 21054
Inventions Explained, 21052
Invertebrates, 19599, 19621
Investigating the Ozone Hole, 16998
Investigation of Murder, 17073
Invisible Chains, 10134(F)
Invisible Day, 7842(F)
The Invisible Dog, 7237(F)
The Invisible Harry, 7843(F)
Invisible Lissa, 10078(F)
The Invisible Princess, 10486(F)
Invisible Stanley, 1015(F)
Iowa, 16550, 16559, 16565, 16567
Iowa Facts and Symbols, 16566
Ira Says Goodbye, 2788(F)
Ira Sleeps Over, 5101(F)
Iran, 15536, 15545, 15558, 15559
The Iran Hostage Crisis, 15560
Iran in Pictures, 15550
Iraq, 15543, 15548
Ireland, 15336, 15353, 15356, 15359, 15363, 15366
Ireland in Pictures, 15352
Irene Jennie and the Christmas Masquerade, 4833(F)
Iris and Walter, 8674(F)
The Irish-American Experience, 17550
The Irish Americans, 17597
Irish Fairy Tales and Legends, 11010
The Irish Piper, 10926
Irish Red, 7247(F)
Iron Horses, 21335
Iron John (Illus. by Trina S. Hyman), 10923
(Illus. by Winslow Pels), 10585
Ironclads and Blockades in the Civil War, 16427
Irons, 21021
The Iroquois, 16049
The Iroquois Indians, 16039
Is a Blue Whale the Biggest Thing There Is? 364(F)
Is Anybody Out There? 20978
Is Anybody There? 8407(F)
Is Everyone Moonburned But Me? 8787(F)
Is It Far to Zanzibar? Poems About Tanzania, 11874
Is It Hanukkah Yet? 6092(F)
Is It Larger? Is It Smaller? 336(F)
Is It Magic? 5006(F)
Is It Red? Is It Yellow? Is It Blue? 274(F)
Is It Rough? Is It Smooth? Is It Shiny? 308(F)
Is That a Rash? 18182
Is That Josie? 751(F)
Is That You, Winter? 1176(F)
Is the Spaghetti Ready? 6322(F)
Is There a Dinosaur in Your Backyard? The World's Most Fascinating Fossils, Rocks, and Minerals, 20553
Is There Life in Outer Space? 20956
Is There Life on Mars? 18469
Is There Room on the Bus? 554(F)

Is There Room on the Feather Bed? 1206(F)
Is Your Mama a Llama? 2158(F)
Isaac Asimov, 12501, 12502
Isaac Newton, 13333, 13334
Isaac the Ice Cream Truck, 1542(F)
Isabella, 9135(F)
Isabella Abnormella and the Very, Very Finicky Queen of Trouble, 1352(F)
Isabella's Bed, 1346(F)
Isabelle and the Angel, 1386(F)
Ishi, 15939
Ishi, Last of the Tribe, 12975
The Island-Below-the-Star, 11374
Island Bound, 6942(F)
Island Boy, 3587(F)
An Island Christmas, 9735(F)
Island Dog, 918(F)
An Island Far from Home, 9471(F)
Island Hopping in the Pacific, 14833
Island in the Sun, 15695
Island Magic, 3907(F)
Island of the Aunts, 7808(F)
Island of the Blue Dolphins, 6997(F)
Island of the Great Yellow Ox, 6957(F)
The Island on Bird Street, 9681(F)
An Island Scrapbook, 19871
Island Summer, 3444(F)
The Islander, 8060(F)
Islands, 20385, 20394
    (Illus. by Laszlo Gal), 3900(F)
Islands in the Sky, 7897(F)
Islands of the Pacific Rim and Their People, 15245
Isn't My Name Magical? Sister and Brother Poems, 11748
Isolation vs. Intervention, 17024
Israel, 15517, 15520, 15523, 15527, 15530, 15531, 15546
Israel in Pictures, 15519
The Israelites, 15525
It Came From Ohio! My Life as a Writer, 12602
It Chanced to Rain, 1900(F)
It Could Always Be Worse, 11179
It Could Have Been Worse, 1803(F)
It Could Still Be a Cat, 19919
It Could Still Be a Dinosaur, 14414
It Could Still Be a Mammal, 18939
It Could Still Be a Robot, 21200
It Could Still Be a Tree, 20200
It Could Still Be Endangered, 19395
It Could Still Be Water, 20734
It Doesn't Have to Be This Way, 7367(F)
It Figures! 14111
It Goes Eeeeeeeeeeeee! 10065(F)
It Happened in America, 15897
It Happened in Chelm, 11145
It Happened Like This, 9896(F)
It Is a Good Day to Die, 16065
It Looked Like Spilt Milk, 313(F)
It Rained on the Desert Today, 11944
It Takes a Village, 4630(F)
It Was a Dark and Stormy Night, 2904(F)
It Wasn't My Fault, 4211(F)
The Italian American Family Album, 17565

The Italian Americans, 17554
Italian Foods and Culture, 15377
Italy, 15372, 15374, 15378, 15386, 15394
The Itch Book, 3111(F)
It's a Baby's World, 3189(F)
It's a Deal, Dogboy, 8750(F)
It's a Family Thanksgiving! A Celebration of an American Tradition for Children and Their Families, 17495
It's a Good Thing There Are Insects, 19442
It's About Dogs, 11795
It's About Time! 194
It's About Time, Max! 20651(F)
It's All Greek to Me, 8072(F)
It's Disgusting — and We Ate It! True Food Facts from Around the World — and Throughout History! 20045
It's Funny Where Ben's Train Takes Him, 1027(F)
It's Going to Be Perfect! 3567(F)
It's Great to Skate! 22074
It's Groundhog Day! 5631(F)
It's Hanukkah! 6098(F)
It's Just a Game, 3128(F)
It's Justin Time, Amber Brown, 6302(F)
It's Magic, 21784
It's My Birthday, 5698(F), 5716(F)
It's My Birthday, Too! 5701(F)
It's Not Easy Being Bad, 10135(F)
It's Not Fair! 3735(F)
It's Not the End of the World, 8402(F)
It's Not Your Fault, KoKo Bear, 2339(F)
It's Panama's Canal! 15678
It's Perfectly Normal, 18260
It's Pumpkin Time! 6003(F)
It's Raining Cats and Dogs, 20754, 21831
It's Raining, It's Pouring, 11674
It's Raining Pigs and Noodles, 11909
It's Raining, Yancy and Bear, 1255(F)
It's Simple, Said Simon, 1244(F)
It's Snowing! It's Snowing! 4511(F)
It's So Amazing, 18261
It's Thanksgiving, 11850
It's Time for School, Stinky Face, 5518(F)
It's Too Windy! 6718(F)
It's Valentine's Day, 11851
Itse Selu, 16021
The Itsy Bitsy Spider, 14181(F), 14185
The Itsy-Bitsy Spider, 900(F)
Ivan, 11085
Ivan and the Dynamos, 10283(F)
I've Been Working on the Railroad, 14192
I've Got an Idea! 13310
Iwo Jima and Okinawa, 14834

J.B.'s Harmonica, 2670(F)
J. B. Wigglebottom and the Parade of Pets, 10128(F)
J. C. Watts, 12815

J.C. Watts, Jr. Character Counts, 12968
J.J. Versus the Baby-sitter, 4180(F)
J. K. Rowling, 12585
J.T., 8841(F)
Jabberwocky, 11855
    (Illus. by Graeme Base), 11860
Jack, 2068(F)
Jack and Jill and Other Nursery Rhymes, 834(F)
Jack and the Animals, 11332(F)
Jack and the Beanstalk, 11001, 11005, 11020
    (Illus. by Lydia Halverson), 11015
    (Illus. by Norman Messenger), 11043
    (Illus. by Gennady Spirin), 10949
Jack and the Beanstalk/Juan y los frijoles magicos, 10950
Jack and the Giant, 11343
Jack Black and the Ship of Thieves, 7799(F)
Jack in Luck, 10884
Jack in Search of Art, 1820(F)
Jack London, 12563, 12564
Jack on the Tracks, 6849(F)
Jack Russell Terriers, 19977
The Jack Tales, 11349
    (Illus. by Berkeley Williams), 11328
Jack, the Seal and the Sea, 4379(F)
Jackie and Me, 7770(F)
Jackie Joyner-Kersee, 13661, 13662
Jackie Kennedy Onassis, 13172
Jackie Robinson, 13486, 13488, 13490, 13493
Jackie Robinson and the Story of All-Black Baseball, 13494
Jackie Robinson Breaks the Color Line, 13495
Jack's Fantastic Voyage, 1162(F)
Jack's Garden, 3075(F)
Jack's New Power, 9132(F)
Jacob and Esau, 17240
    (Illus. by Diana Mayo), 17241
Jacob and the Stranger, 7704(F)
Jacob Have I Loved, 7491(F)
Jacob Lawrence, 12253, 13958
Jacob Two-Two's First Spy Case, 9972(F)
Jacob's Tree, 4996(F)
Jacqueline Bouvier Kennedy Onassis, 13173
Jacques Cousteau, 12101
Jade and Iron, 11434
Jade Green, 7984(F)
Jafta, 4733(F)
Jafta and the Wedding, 4733(F)
Jafta's Father, 4733(F)
Jafta's Mother, 4733(F)
Jaguar, 5171(F), 7064(F), 21306
Jaguar in the Rain Forest, 5396(F)
Jaguars, 19099
Jaguarundi, 7782(F)
Jake, 19953
Jake and Honeybunch Go to Heaven, 1720(F)
Jake and the Copycats, 6593(F)
Jake Johnson, 4311(F)
Jalani and the Lock, 4790(F)
Jalapeno Bagels, 3952(F)

Jam! The Story of Jazz Music, 14133
Jamaica, 15694, 15696, 15697, 15717
Jamaica and Brianna, 4001(F)
Jamaica and the Substitute Teacher, 5504(F)
Jamaica in Pictures, 15707
Jamaica Louise James, 3693(F)
Jamaica Tag-Along, 3194(F)
Jamaica's Blue Marker, 4002(F)
Jamaica's Find, 3194(F)
Jamal's Busy Day, 6419(F)
Jamberry, 2015(F)
Jambo, Watoto! 2483(F)
Jamela's Dress, 4633(F)
James A. Garfield, 13035
James and the Giant Peach, 7696(F), 12018(F), 21267
James and the Rain, 487(F)
James Baldwin, 12504
James Bear and the Goose Gathering, 1340(F)
James Bear's Pie, 1340(F)
James Buchanan, 13009
James Carter, 13020
James E. Carter, 13017
James Farmer and the Freedom Rides, 12721
James Gurney, 14389
James K. Polk, 13091, 13092
James K. Polk, Abraham Lincoln, Theodore Roosevelt, 12673
James Madison, 13081, 13083
James Madison and Dolley Madison and Their Times, 13084
James Marshall's Mother Goose, 862
James Meredith and School Desegregation, 12772
James Monroe, 13085, 13086
James Printer, 9238(F)
Jamestown, 16149
The Jamestown Colony, 16139, 16166, 16174
Jamie O'Rourke and the Big Potato, 10971
Jamie O'Rourke and the Pooka, 1113(F)
Jamil's Clever Cat, 10791
Jan Ormerod's To Baby with Love, 881(F)
Jane Addams, 13127, 13129
Jane Eyre, 6777(F)
Jane Fonda, 12387
Jane Goodall, 13299, 13301, 13302, 13303
Jane on Her Own, 7900(F)
Jane Sayler, 17842
Jane vs. the Tooth Fairy, 4191(F)
Jane Yolen's Mother Goose Songbook, 904
Jane Yolen's Old MacDonald Songbook, 14195
Jane Yolen's Songs of Summer, 14194
Janet Jackson, 12407
Janice VanCleave's A+ Projects in Earth Science, 20324
Janice VanCleave's Animals, 18355
Janice VanCleave's Biology for Every Kid, 18356

Janice VanCleave's Earth Science for Every Kid, 18357
Janice VanCleave's Ecology for Every Kid, 16969
Janice VanCleave's Electricity, 20905
Janice VanCleave's Food and Nutrition for Every Kid, 18212
Janice VanCleave's Gravity, 20325
Janice VanCleave's Guide to More of the Best Science Fair Projects, 18358
Janice VanCleave's Guide to the Best Science Fair Projects, 18359
Janice VanCleave's Insects and Spiders, 19496
Janice VanCleave's Math for Every Kid, 20597
Janice VanCleave's Molecules, 20292
Janice VanCleave's Oceans for Every Kid, 19845
Janice VanCleave's Plants, 20265
Janice VanCleave's Play and Find Out About Math, 20598
Janice VanCleave's Play and Find Out About Nature, 18360
Janice VanCleave's Play and Find Out About Science, 18361
Janice VanCleave's Play and Find Out About the Human Body, 18083
Janice VanCleave's Solar System, 18533
Janice VanCleave's 203 Icy, Freezing, Frosty, Cool and Wild Experiments, 18362
Janice VanCleave's 202 Oozing, Bubbling, Dripping and Bouncing Experiments, 18363
Janice VanCleave's Volcanoes, 20352
Janice VanCleave's Weather, 20794
The Janitor's Boy, 10037(F)
January Rides the Wind, 4503(F)
Japan, 15116, 15118, 15120, 15121, 15126, 15127, 15134, 15138, 15141, 15142, 15143
Japan in Pictures, 15128
Japan Under the Shoguns, 1185–1868, 15136
The Japanese, 15135
The Japanese Americans, 17569
Japanese Children's Day and the Obon Festival, 15132
Japanese Children's Favorite Stories, 10827
A Jar of Dreams, 7530(F)
The Jar of Fools, 11155(F)
A Jar of Tiny Stars, 11547
Jason and the Golden Fleece, 11496
Jason Kidd, 13542
Jason's Bears, 3018(F)
Jason's Gold, 6896(F)
Jasper's Beanstalk, 1905(F)
Jays, 19251
Jazper, 2064(F)
The Jazz Fly, 2134(F)
The Jazz of Our Street, 3420(F)
Jazz Tap, 14291
Jazzbo and Googy, 2530(F)
Jazzbo Goes to School, 2531(F)

Jean Craighead George, 12541
Jeb Scarecrow's Pumpkin Patch, 1124(F)
Jeb Stuart, 12967
The Jedera Adventure, 6745(F)
Jeep, 21302
Jeff Bezos, 12850
Jeff Gordon, 13428
Jefferson Davis, 12872
The Jefferson Way, 13051
The Jeffersonian Republicans, 1800–1823, 16235
Jeffrey Strangeways, 9941(F)
Jellies, 19660
Jelly Beans for Sale, 508
Jelly Belly, 8815(F)
Jellyfish, 19664
The Jellyfish Season, 8445(F)
Jenius, 7238(F)
Jennie's Hat, 4200(F)
Jennifer and Josephine, 1467(F)
Jennifer, Hecate, Macbeth, William McKinley, and Me, Elizabeth, 8323(F)
Jennifer Lopez, 12415, 12416
Jennifer Love Hewitt, 12398
Jennifer Murdley's Toad, 7676(F)
Jennifer-the-Jerk Is Missing, 6863(F)
Jenny Archer to the Rescue, 9809(F)
Jenny Reen and the Jack Muh Lantern, 6051(F)
The Jenny Summer, 8291(F)
Jeremiah Learns to Read, 3030(F)
Jeremy, 7851(F)
Jeremy Thatcher, Dragon Hatcher, 7677(F)
Jeremy Visick, 8213(F)
Jeremy's Muffler, 4249(F)
Jericho, 7450(F)
Jerome Camps Out, 1961(F)
Jerry Rice, 13623, 13624
Jerusalem, 15528
Jerusalem, Shining Still, 15524
Jerusalem 3000, 15526
Jesse Bear, What Will You Wear? 1932(F)
Jesse Jackson, 12728, 12729
Jesse Jackson and Political Power, 12727
Jesse James, 12908, 12909, 12910
Jesse Owens, 13665, 13667, 13668, 13669
Jesse Ventura, 13710
Jesse's Star, 9069(F)
Jessica and the Wolf, 5017(F)
Jessica Takes Charge, 3764(F)
The Jester Has Lost His Jingle, 4818(F)
Jesus, 17329
Jesus' Christmas Party, 9705(F)
Jesus of Nazareth, 17289
The Jewel Heart, 996(F)
Jewelry, 21186, 21540
The Jewish Americans, 17583
The Jewish Child's First Book of Why, 17477
Jewish Festivals, 17489
Jewish Foods and Culture, 17461
The Jewish Holiday Craft Book, 6108

Jewish Holiday Crafts for Little Hands, 17452
Jewish Holiday Fun, 17459
The Jewish Kids Catalog, 17454
Jewish Synagogue, 17234
The Jews, 17566
Jezebel's Spooky Spot, 3394(F)
Jigsaw, 1424(F)
Jim Abbott, 13432, 13433
Jim and the Beanstalk, 1012(F)
Jim Bowie, 12855
Jim Carrey, 12366
The Jim Crow Laws and Racism in American History, 16464
Jim-Dandy, 9384(F)
Jim Meets the Thing, 5489(F)
Jim Thorpe, 13674, 13675
Jim Ugly, 9365(F)
Jim, Who Ran Away from His Nurse, and Was Eaten by a Lion, 9778(F)
Jimi Hendrix, 12397(F)
Jimmy Carter, 13015, 13016, 13018
Jimmy Carter, President, 13019
Jimmy Crack Corn, 9611(F)
Jimmy Smits, 12469
Jimmy, the Pickpocket of the Palace, 7979(F)
Jimmy Zangwow's Out-of-This-World Moon Pie Adventure, 1126(F)
Jim's Dog Muffins, 5489(F)
Jin Woo, 3555(F)
Jingle Bells, 5771(F)
Jingle Bells, Homework Smells, 5796(F)
Jingle Dancer, 3434(F)
Jip, His Story, 9309(F)
Jirohattan, 9677(F)
Jiro's Pearl, 1488(F)
Jo and the Bandit, 9433(F)
Joan of Arc, 13812, 13815
  (Illus. by Angela Barrett), 13813
A Job for Jenny Archer, 9810(F)
Jobs People Do, 17756
Jocelyn and the Ballerina, 4178(F)
Jody's Beans, 4420(F)
Joe and the Skyscraper, 21145
Joe Can Count, 547(F)
Joe DiMaggio, 13448, 13449
Joe Joe, 3417(F)
Joe Lion's Big Boots, 6515(F)
Joe Louis, 13586
Joe Magarac and His U.S.A. Citizen Papers, 11383
Joe Montana, 13621
Joey, 2287(F)
Joey Pigza Loses Control, 8654(F)
Joey Pigza Swallowed the Key, 8890(F)
Johann Sebastian Bach, 12318
John Adams, 13002, 13003
John Blair and the Great Hinckley Fire, 16481
John Brown, 12862
John Brown and the Fight Against Slavery, 12861
John Brown's Raid on Harpers Ferry, 16255
John Burroughs, 13243
John C. Fremont, 12118
John D. Rockefeller, 12960

John Ericsson, 13278
John F. Kennedy, 13059, 13062
John F. Kennedy Jr., 12918
John Glenn, 12887, 12888, 12889
John Glenn Returns to Orbit, 20959
John Glenn's Return to Space, 12890
John Grisham, 12543
John Hancock, 12897
John Henry, 11356
John James Audubon, 12189
John Lennon, 12413
John Logie Baird, 13232
John Lucas, 13547
John McCain, 12933
John Muir, 13329, 13330
John Paul Jones, 12913, 12914, 12915
John Pig's Halloween, 6059(F)
John Quincy Adams, 13005, 13006
John Tyler, 13110
John Wesley Powell, 12151
John Wilkes Booth and the Civil War, 12854
John Willy and Freddy McGee, 2488(F)
Johnny Appleseed (Illus. by Steven Kellogg), 12845
  (Illus. by Michael Montgomery), 12843
Johnny Bench, 13437
Johnny on the Spot, 1589(F)
Johnny Texas, 9379(F)
Johnny Tremain, 9230(F)
John's Picture, 1368(F)
Join the Total Fitness Gang, 18194
Joined at Birth, 18065
JoJo and Winnie, 7506(F)
JoJo and Winnie Again, 7507(F)
Jojo's Flying Side Kick, 5049(F)
Jolie Blonde and the Three Heberts, 10959
The Jolly Mon, 1021(F)
Jonah and the Two Great Fish, 17274
Jonah, the Whale, 8810(F)
Jonah's Trash . . . God's Treasure, 17238
Jonkonnu, 4741(F)
Jooka Saves the Day, 2049(F)
Jorah's Journal, 8597(F)
Jordan, 15539
Jordan in Pictures, 15552
Jordi's Star, 942(F)
Jo's Boys, 7384(F)
Jose Canseco, 13441
Jose de San Martin, 13846
José Martí, 12572
Josefina, 611(F)
Josefina Learns a Lesson, 9447(F)
Josefina Saves the Day, 9446(F)
The Josefina Story Quilt, 6275(F)
Joseph, 9497(F), 17330
Joseph and His Coat of Many Colors, 17292
Joseph Had a Little Overcoat, 11176
Joseph McCarthy and the Cold War, 12934
Joseph Turner, 12304
Joseph's Choice — 1861, 9498(F)
Joseph's Story, 17429
Joshua in the Promised Land, 17255
Joshua James Likes Trucks, 6574(F)

Joshua T. Bates in Trouble Again, 10132(F)
Joshua's Book of Clothes, 3149(F)
Joshua's Masai Mask, 4982(F)
The Josie Gambit, 8368(F)
Josie Poe, 9657(F)
Josie to the Rescue, 9991(F)
Josie's Beau, 8304(F)
Josie's Troubles, 8350(F)
Jouanah, 10837
The Journal of Augustus Pelletier, 16085
The Journal of Ben Uchida, 9654(F)
The Journal of Biddy Owens, 10353(F)
The Journal of James Edmond Pease, 9488(F)
The Journal of Jasper Jonathan Pierce, 9211(F)
The Journal of Joshua Loper, 9419(F)
The Journal of Scott Pendleton Collins, 9679(F)
The Journal of Sean Sullivan, 9360(F)
The Journal of William Thomas Emerson, 9227(F)
The Journal of Wong Ming-Chung, 9641(F)
Journey, 8481(F)
The Journey, 7521(F), 17563
The Journey Back, 9685(F)
Journey Home, 7378(F)
The Journey Home, 9380(F)
The Journey of English, 13978
Journey of the Nightly Jaguar, 11770
Journey of the Red Wolf, 19140
Journey of the Sparrows, 7336(F)
Journey Outside, 8125(F)
Journey Through a Tropical Jungle, 20440
Journey Through Australia, 15227
Journey Through Canada, 15596
Journey Through China, 15084
Journey Through France, 15305
Journey Through Italy, 15375
Journey Through Japan, 15140
Journey Through Mexico, 15605
Journey Through the Northern Rain-forest, 20470
Journey to America, 9670(F)
Journey to Ellis Island, 17547
Journey to Freedom, 7970(F), 9338(F)
Journey to Jo'burg, 7361(F)
Journey to Monticello, 16149
Journey to Native Americans, 15964
Journey to Nowhere, 9258(F), 9259(F), 9260(F)
A Journey to Paradise, 11152
A Journey to the New World, 9202(F)
Journey to Topaz, 7379(F)
Journeyman Wizard, 7143(F)
Journey's End, 17357
Journeys with Elijah, 17276
Joy to the World, 9736(F), 9756
Joyful Noise, 11781
Juan Bobo Goes to Work, 4774(F)
Juan Gonzalez, 13456
Juan Ponce de Leon, 12149

Juan Ponce de León and the Search for the Fountain of Youth, 12150
Jubal's Wish, 2868(F)
Jubela, 5287(F)
Jubilee Journey, 7484(F)
Judaism, 17235
Judge Rabbit and the Tree Spirit, 10844
Judge Roy Bean, 12849
Judo, 22266
Judo Techniques andTactics, 22024
Judy Moody, 10107(F)
The Jukebox Man, 3348(F)
Jules Verne, 12614
Julia Dent Grant, 13157
Julia Roberts, 12452
Julian, Dream Doctor, 5669(F)
Julian, Secret Agent, 6251(F)
Julian's Glorious Summer, 6251(F)
Julie, 6852(F)
Julie Krone, 13694, 13695
Julie Krone, Unstoppable Jockey, 13696
Julie of the Wolves, 6853(F)
Julie's Wolf Pack, 6854(F)
Juliet, 9104(F)
Julio Cesar Chavez, 13583
Julius Caesar, 13763, 13764
Julius Caesar in Gaul and Britain, 14741
Julius, the Baby of the World, 2194(F)
July, 3441
July Is a Mad Mosquito, 11968
Juma and the Honey Guide, 5135(F)
Jumanji, 1640(F)
Jumbo, 19161
Jumbo's Lullaby, 744(F)
Jump Back, Honey, 11754
Jump, Kangaroo, Jump! 528
Jump Like a Frog! 304(F)
Jump Rope Magic, 1553(F)
Jump! The Adventures of Brer Rabbit, 11345
Jump Up Time, 4702(F)
Jumping Day, 3122(F)
Jumping into Nothing, 8857(F)
Jumping the Broom, 4892(F)
June 29, 1999, 1678(F)
Junebug, 8485(F)
Junebug and the Reverend, 8486(F)
Juneteenth, 17340(F), 17345
Juneteenth Jamboree, 9767(F)
Jungle Animals, 5393
The Jungle Baseball Game, 2563(F)
The Jungle Book, 7243(F), 7244(F)
Jungle Dogs, 8808(F)
Jungle Drum, 5461(F)
Jungle Halloween, 5991(F)
Jungle Islands, 15226
Jungle Jack Hanna's Safari Adventure, 18633
Jungle Jack Hanna's What Zookeepers Do, 20025
Jungle Jamboree, 1316(F)
Jungle Warfare, 14835
Jungles, 20387
Junglewalk, 935(F)
Junie B. Jones and a Little Monkey Business, 9951(F)

Junie B. Jones and her Big Fat Mouth, 10118(F)
Junie B. Jones and Some Sneaky Peeky Spying, 9952(F)
Junie B. Jones and the Stupid Smelly Bus, 9953(F)
Junie B. Jones and the Yucky Blucky Fruitcake, 10119(F)
Junie B. Jones Has a Monster Under Her Bed, 6568(F)
Junie B. Jones Is a Beauty Shop Guy, 9954(F)
Junie B. Jones Is Not a Crook, 6568(F)
Junie B. Jones Loves Handsome Warren, 6569(F)
Junie B. Jones Smells Something Fishy, 9955(F)
Junior Chronicle of the 20th Century, 14543
Junior Kroll, 11667
Junior Kroll and Company, 11905
Junior Seau, 13630, 13631
The Junior Thunder Lord, 10777
Junk in Space, 21002
Junk Pile! 4090(F)
Jupiter, 18459, 18476, 18479, 18490, 18496
Jurassic Dinosaur World, 14424
Just a Dream, 1641(F)
Just a Few Words, Mr. Lincoln, 16408
Just a Little Bit, 2762(F)
Just a Little Ham, 7174(F)
Just a Minute, 2317(F)
Just Another Ordinary Day, 1061(F)
Just Around the Corner, 11713
Just Call Me Stupid, 8400(F)
Just Dessert, 4272(F)
The Just Desserts Club, 8309(F)
Just Dog, 2551(F)
Just Enough, 3098(F)
Just Enough Carrots, 20590
Just in Time for Christmas, 5757(F)
Just Juice, 8690(F)
Just Kids, 8912(F)
Just Like a Baby, 3538(F)
Just Like a Real Family, 7451(F)
Just Like Daddy, 1759(F)
Just Like Floss, 5306(F)
Just Like Home, 5032(F)
Just Like Me, 6541(F), 13925
Just Like Mike, 8688(F)
Just Like My Dad, 3155(F)
Just Like New, 4761(F)
Just Me, 5197(F)
Just My Dad and Me, 3752(F)
Just One! 2409(F)
Just One More Color, 4545(F)
Just One More Story, 10507(F)
Just Rewards, or Who Is That Man in the Moon and What's He Doing Up There Anyway? 10769
Just Right Stew, 4140(F)
Just So Stories (Illus. by David Frampton), 7245(F)
  (Illus. by Barry Moser), 7246(F)
Just Stay Put, 11143
Just Tell Me When We're Dead! 6796(F)
Just the Beginning, 7485(F)

Just Us Two, 11982
Just Us Women, 2916(F)
Just What the Doctor Ordered, 18024
Just You and Me, 2410(F)
Justice and Her Brothers, 7443(F)
Justin and the Best Biscuits in the World, 8846(F)
Justin Morgan Had a Horse, 7219(F)

K Is for Kwanzaa, 5626
Kacy and the Space Shuttle Secret, 10199(F)
Kai, 8979(F), 8980(F)
Kai, a Big Decision, 8976(F)
The Kalahari, 14982
Kalifax, 8145(F)
Kancil and the Crocodiles, 10838
Kangaroo and Cricket, 247(F)
Kangaroos, 2017(F), 19176
Kangaroos and Koalas, 19182
Kangaroos Have Joeys, 5147
Kansas, 16533, 16554, 16571
Kansas City, 16587
Kansas Facts and Symbols, 16543
Karate, 22268
Karate Boy, 22271
The Karate Class Mystery, 6456(F)
Kareem Abdul-Jabbar, 13511
Karl Malone, 13548
Kashtanka, 5164(F)
Kat Kong, 5364(F)
Katarina Witt, 13596, 13597
Kate and the Beanstalk, 9116
Kate Heads West, 3044(F)
Kate on the Coast, 3044(F)
Kate Shelley and the Midnight Express, 6715(F)
Kate Skates, 6547(F)
Kate's Giants, 2936(F)
Katherine Dunham, 12378
Katherine Paterson, 12575
Kathy's Hats, 5002(F)
Katie and the Big, Brave Bear, 1420(F)
Katie and the Dream-Eater, 10831
Katie and the Mona Lisa, 1403(F)
Katie-Bo, 3625(F)
Katie Holmes, 12401
Katie John, 8411(F)
Katie John and Heathcliff, 8411(F)
Katie Meets the Impressionists, 1404(F)
Katie's Trunk, 4858(F)
Katie's War, 9093(F)
Kat's Surrender, 8666(F)
Katy and the Big Snow, 5551(F)
Katy Cat and Beaky Boo, 1079(F)
Katy No-Pocket, 2564(F)
Katy Steding, 13575
Kavik the Wolf Dog, 7268(F)
Kayaking, 22263
Kayaking, Canoeing, Rowing, and Yachting, 22260
Kazakhstan, 15421
Keep Ms. Sugarman in the Fourth Grade, 10099(F)
Keep on Singing, 12345
Keep Smiling Through, 9686(F)
Keep the Lights Burning, Abbie, 6597
The Keeper and the Crows, 8116(F)

Keeper for the Sea, 4391(F)
Keeper of the Light, 9607(F)
Keeper of the Swamp, 3642(F)
The Keeper of Ugly Sounds, 1411(F)
Keepers (Illus. by Felicia Marshall),
    5102(F)
    (Illus. by Ted Rand), 11691
Keeping a Christmas Secret, 5889(F)
Keeping Clean, 18197, 18211
The Keeping Quilt, 3839(F)
The Keeping Room, 9244(F)
Keeping the Air Clean, 16989
Keeping Time, 20639
Keeping Up with Grandma, 3951(F)
Keiko's Story, 19794
Keisha Discovers Harlem, 9583(F)
Keith Van Horn, 13578
Ken Griffey, Jr, 13460
Ken Griffey, Jr. Baseball's Best,
    13459
Ken Griffey, Sr., and Ken Griffey,
    Jr., 13458
Kennedy Assassinated! The World
    Mourns, 13061
Kenny's Window, 1556(F)
Kent State, 16501
Kente Colors, 15023
Kentucky, 16830, 16835, 16852
Kentucky Facts and Symbols, 16842
Kenya, 14914, 14923, 14924, 14933,
    14938, 14939, 14941, 14946
Kenya in Pictures, 14934
Kenya, Jambo! 14935
Keri Russell, 12461
Kermit the Hermit, 2567(F)
Kevin and His Dad, 3899(F)
Kevin Corbett Eats Flies, 9875(F)
Kevin Nash, 13705
The Key Is Lost, 9696(F)
The Key to the Indian, 7584(F)
The Key to the Playhouse, 8394(F)
The Keys to My Kingdom, 837
Keystone Kids, 10368(F)
The Khan's Daughter, 10737
Kick Butts! A Kid's Action Guide to
    a Tobacco-Free America, 17870
Kick, Pass, and Run, 22183
Kick, Pass and Run, 6433(F)
Kid Camping from Aaaaiii! to Zip,
    22169
Kid Caramel, Private Investigator,
    6838(F)
The Kid from Tomkinsville,
    10368(F)
The Kid in the Red Jacket, 9956(F)
The Kid Next Door and Other
    Headaches, 7516(F)
Kid Power, 7493(F)
The Kid Who Got Zapped Through
    Time, 8075(F)
The Kid Who Invented the Popsicle
    and Other Surprising Stories About
    Inventions, 21067
The Kid Who Only Hit Homers,
    10312(F)
The Kid Who Ran for President,
    9869(F)
The Kid Who Ran for Principal,
    10114(F)
Kidbits, 21955
Kidnap at the Catfish Cafe, 6859(F)

Kidnap Kids, 10004(F)
The Kidnapped Prince, 13791
The Kidnappers, 7028(F)
The Kid's Address Book, 21933
The Kids' Allowance Book, 16945
Kids and Grandparents, 21451
Kids Are Cookin', 21679
Kids Around the World Celebrate!
    17374
Kids' Art Works! 21444
Kids at Work, 12901
The Kids' Book of Chess, 22171
The Kids' Book of the American
    Quarter Horse, 20012
The Kids Book of the Far North,
    15816
The Kids' Book of Weather Forecast-
    ing, 20756
The Kids Camp-fire Book, 22167
The Kids Can Do It Book, 21469
The Kids Can Press French and Eng-
    lish Phrase Book, 14096
The Kids Can Press Jumbo Book of
    Crafts, 21494
The Kids Can Press Jumbo Book of
    Gardening, 21770
The Kids Can Press Jumbo Cook-
    book, 21701
The Kids Can Press Spanish and
    English Phrase Book, 14096
The Kids' Catalog of Jewish Holi-
    days, 17450
The Kids' Catalog of Passover,
    17484
Kids' Computer Creations, 21223
Kids Cook! Fabulous Food for the
    Whole Family, 21751
Kids Dance, 14301
Kids Dish It Up . . . Sugar-Free,
    21753
Kids During the Great Depression,
    16496
Kids Explore America's Jewish Her-
    itage, 17229
Kids' First Cookbook, 21712
A Kid's Guide to African American
    History, 15903
A Kids' Guide to America's Bill of
    Rights, 17058
A Kids' Guide to Building Forts,
    21413
The Kid's Guide to Good Grammar,
    14040
The Kid's Guide to Service Projects,
    17150
The Kid's Guide to Social Action,
    17621
A Kid's Guide to Staying Safe
    Around Water, 18214
The Kids Guide to the Millennium,
    14346
The Kid's Guide to the Smithsonian,
    17104
Kids in Colonial Times, 16188
Kids in the Kitchen, 21733
The Kids' Invention Book, 21031
Kids Knitting, 21642
Kids Love New York! 16735
The Kids' Money Book, 16940
The Kids' Multicultural Art Book,
    13928

The Kids' Multicultural Cookbook,
    21684
The Kids 'N' Clay Ceramics Book,
    21529
The Kids' Natural History Book,
    14464
Kids on Strike! 16449
Kids' Pumpkin Projects, 20171
The Kids' Science Book, 18322
The Kids Summer Games Book,
    21998
The Kids Summer Handbook, 21432
Kids to the Rescue! 18215
Kids Who Make a Difference, 16954
The Kids' Wildlife Book, 18667
Kids with AIDS, 17956
The Kids' World Almanac of Base-
    ball, 22085
Kidsource, 18365
Kidstories, 12645
Kidtopia, 21439
Killer Asteroids, 18523
Killer Bees, 19519
Killer Bugs, 19428
Killer Whale, 19779
    (Illus. by Richard Hewett), 19774
Kimako's Story, 3255(F)
Kinaalda, 16030
Kinderdike, 10856
Kindergarten Kids, 5537
Kindertransport, 14849
Kindle Me a Riddle, 4704(F)
Kindness, 10730
The King and the Three Thieves,
    11181
The King and the Tortoise, 10701
King Arthur, 11026
King Arthur and the Round Table,
    11038
King Bidgood's in the Bathtub,
    4356(F)
King Bobble, 4099(F)
King George III, 13805
King Henry the Ape, 21832
King Henry VIII, 13808
King Kenrick's Splinter, 4129(F)
King Long Shanks, 10526(F)
King Midas, 11508
King Midas and the Golden Touch,
    11468
The King of Dragons, 8638(F)
The King of Ireland's Son, 10948
King of Kings, 5837(F)
King of Magic, Man of Glass, 10925
King of Shadows, 7669(F)
King of the Birds, 10539
The King of the Birds, 10627
King of the Golden River or the
    Black Brother, 8054(F)
King of the Kooties, 10044(F)
King of the Playground, 5041(F)
King of the Wind, 7216(F)
King of the Woods, 2006(F)
King Philip, 12980
King Philip and the War with the
    Colonists, 12981
King Snake, 2703(F)
King Solomon and His Magic Ring,
    17327
King Solomon and the Queen of
    Sheba, 17279(F)

The Kingdom of Singing Birds, 11140
The Kingfisher Book of Fairy Tales, 10420(F)
The Kingfisher Book of Religions, 17164
The Kingfisher Book of the Ancient World, 14590
The Kingfisher First Human Body Encyclopedia, 18084
The Kingfisher First Science Encyclopedia, 18277
A Kingfisher Treasury of Bible Stories, Poems, and Prayers for Bedtime, 17212
The Kingfisher Young People's Book of Oceans, 19824
The Kingfisher Young People's Book of Planet Earth, 20318
The Kingfisher Young People's Book of Space, 18411
Kings and Queens of Central Africa, 14925
Kings and Queens of East Africa, 14926
Kings and Queens of Southern Africa, 14974
Kings and Queens of West Africa, 15025
The King's Chessboard, 10788
The King's Commissioners, 438(F)
The King's Equal, 1461(F)
The King's Giraffe, 4625(F)
Kipling, 12559
Kipper, 2238(F)
Kipper's Book of Colors, 278(F)
Kipper's Book of Numbers, 475(F)
Kipper's Book of Opposites, 201(F)
Kipper's Book of Weather, 20772
Kipper's Christmas Eve, 5851(F)
Kipper's Snowy Day, 2239(F)
Kipsigis, 14916
Kirby Kelvin and the Not-Laughing Lessons, 4105(F)
Kirby Puckett, 13478
Kirk Douglas's Young Heroes of the Bible, 17265
Kirsten Learns a Lesson, 9438(F)
Kirsten Saves the Day, 9437(F)
Kirsten's Cook Book, 21713
Kirsten's Craft Book, 21522
Kirsten's Surprise, 9438(F)
A Kiss for Little Bear, 6533(F)
Kiss It Better, 2552(F)
Kiss the Cow! 1519(F)
Kissing Tennessee, 8555(F)
Kit, 7328(F)
Kit and Kat, 6305(F)
Kit Carson, 12088
Kit Learns a Lesson, 9631(F)
Kitaq Goes Ice Fishing, 9171(F)
The Kitchen, 16324
Kitchen Chemistry, 18313
The Kitchen Knight, 10997
Kite, 7168(F)
The Kite Fighters, 9004(F)
Kites, 21667
Kites Sail High, 14031
Kitoto the Mighty, 10702
Kitten, 19918
The Kitten Book, 19925

Kittens, 19932
Kitten's Nap, 2712(F)
A Kitten's Year, 5179(F)
Kitty from the Start, 10049(F)
Kitty Riddles, 21824
Klondike Fever, 15571
The Klondike Gold Rush, 15594
Klutz, 4135(F)
Kneeknock Rise, 6759(F)
Kneeling Carabao and Dancing Giants, 15240
The Knight and the Dragon, 2028(F)
Knights, 14772, 14790, 14794
Knights and Castles, 14765
Knights in Armor, 14756
Knights in Shining Armor, 14763
Knights of the Kitchen Table, 7047(F)
Knights of the Round Table, 10991
Knight's Wyrd, 7708(F)
Knitting and Crochet, 21643
Knitwits, 7098(F)
Knock at a Star, 11618
Knock at the Door and Other Baby Action Rhymes, 832
Knock, Knock! Who's There? 21825
Knots in My Yo-Yo String, 12598
Knots on a Counting Rope, 7353(F)
Know About Abuse, 17710
Know About AIDS, 17968
Know About Drugs, 17871
Know About Mental Illness, 17969
Know About Smoking, 17872
A Know-Nothing Birthday, 5725(F)
A Know-Nothing Halloween, 6052(F)
The Know-Nothings Talk Turkey, 6156(F)
Know the Score, 22239
Knowing About Noses, 18141
Knoxville, Tennessee, 11755
A Koala for Katie, 3776(F)
A Koala Is Not a Bear! 19181
Koala Lou, 2096(F)
Koalas, 19177
Kobe Bryant, 13515, 13516, 13517, 13518
Kofi Annan, 13752
Koi and the Kola Nuts, 10640
Koi's Python, 8974(F)
Koko-Love! Conversations with a Signing Gorilla, 19011
Komodo! 5418(F)
The Komodo Dragon, 18746
Komodo Dragon, 18744
Kongo, 14944
Konte Chameleon Fine, Fine, Fine! A West African Folktale, 2289(F)
Kool Ada, 8725(F)
Korea, 15184
The Korean Cinderella, 10721
Korean Folk-Tales, 10734
Korean Holidays and Festivals, 15177
Korean War, 16506
The Korean War, 16519, 16521
Kosovo, 15259
The Koufax Dilemma, 10359(F)
Koya DeLaney and the Good Girl Blues, 7343(F)
The Krazees, 1607(F)

The Kremlin Coup, 15427
Kristi Yamaguchi, 13598, 13599
K'tonton's Sukkot Adventure, 1672(F)
K'tonton's Yom Kippur Kitten, 6122(F)
Kung Fu, 22266
A Kurdish Family, 17587
Kuwait, 15540
Kwanzaa, 5655, 17356, 17373
    (Illus. by Janice L. Porter), 17395
Kwanzaa! 17408
The Kwanzaa Contest, 9750(F)
Kwanzaa Karamu, 17344
Kwian and the Lazy Sun, 10687

The L.A. Riots, 16498
La Causa, 17135
La Cucaracha Martina, 11430
The La-di-da Hare, 11895
La Donna Harris, 12973
La Mariposa, 4989(F)
The Lab Rats of Doctor Eclair, 1808(F)
Labor Day, 17336
    (Illus. by Cherie R. Wyman), 17399
Lacrosse, 22015
Ladder to the Sky, 11234
Laddie of the Light, 7162(F)
The Lady and the Spider, 5333(F)
The Lady and the Squire, 9048(F)
Lady Diana Spencer, 13785
The Lady in the Box, 5870(F)
Lady Kaguya's Secret, 10821
Lady Muck, 2486(F)
The Lady of Guadalupe, 5622(F)
The Lady with the Alligator Purse, 11924(F)
The Lady with the Ship on Her Head, 4209(F)
Ladybug, 19531
The Ladybug and Other Insects, 19444
Ladybug, Ladybug, 830
Ladybugology, 19538
Ladybugs, 19534
A Ladybug's Life, 19532
Lafcadio, the Lion Who Shot Back, 7306(F)
Lake and Pond, 20526
Lake Erie, 15861
Lake Huron, 16528
Lake Michigan, 16528
Lake of the Big Snake, 4784(F)
Lake Ontario, 16529
Lake Superior, 15862, 16528
Lakota Hoop Dancer, 12414
Lamborghini, 21306
The Lamp, the Ice, and the Boat Called Fish, 15822
The Lampfish of Twill, 7921(F)
Lance Armstrong, 13676
Lancelot, 11039
The Land and People of Afghanistan, 15154
The Land I Lost, 8998(F)
The Land of Gold, 7621(F)
A Land of Immigrants, 17589
Land Pacts, 15879
Land Pollution, 17005

Land Predators of North America, 18981
The Landing of the Pilgrims, 16107
The Landry News, 10038(F)
Lands of Grass, 20534
Landscapes, 13886, 13898
Landslides, Slumps, and Creep, 20309
Laney's Lost Momma, 3191(F)
Langston Hughes, 12552
The Language of Birds, 11104
The Language of Doves, 4876(F)
Lanyard, 21543
Lao Lao of Dragon Mountain, 986(F)
Laos in Pictures, 15178
The Lap-Time Song and Play Book, 903
The Lapsnatcher, 3590(F)
Las Navidades, 14197
Las Posadas, 17421
Lasers, 20867, 20875
Lassie Come-Home, 7321(F)
The Last Alchemist, 8141(F)
The Last Basselope, 7622(F)
The Last Battle, 7911(F)
The Last Chocolate Cookie, 1510(F)
The Last Dragon, 3345(F)
The Last Giants, 8021(F)
The Last Hawaiian Queen, 12928
Last Hurdle, 7164(F)
The Last Knight, 9038(F)
Last Leaf First Snowflake to Fall, 4564(F)
Last Left Standing, 8801(F)
Last Licks, 3024(F)
The Last Lobo, 7065(F)
The Last Man's Reward, 8356(F)
The Last Noo-Noo, 4246(F)
Last of the Mohicans, 9151(F)
Last One In Is a Rotten Egg, 6434(F)
  (Illus. by Leonard Kessler), 6433(F)
The Last Payback, 8840(F)
The Last Piper, 6790(F)
The Last-Place Sports Poems of Jeremy Bloom, 12000
The Last Princess, 13820
The Last Puppy, 5126(F)
The Last Rail, 9345(F)
The Last Safe House, 9281(F)
The Last Snake in Ireland, 1372(F)
The Last Straw, 9763(F)
The Last Wolf of Ireland, 7263(F)
Later, Gator, 7330(F)
Latin Sensations, 12175
Latkes, Latkes, Good to Eat, 6080(F)
Laugh-Eteria, 11871
Laughing Time, 11917
Laughing Tomatoes and Other Spring Poems/Jitomates Risueños y Otros Poemas de Primavera, 11527
Laughs, 9931(F)
Launch Day, 20967
Laura Charlotte, 3639(F)
Laura Ingalls Wilder, 12628, 12629, 12630, 12631
Laura's Album, 12626
Laura's Christmas Star, 5753(F)
Laurie Tells, 8478(F)
Lauryn Hill, 12399
Lavender Moon, 2937(F)

The Laziest Boy in the World, 4776(F)
Lazy Lions, Lucky Lambs, 6348(F)
Leaders, 17745
Leaders and Generals, 13733
Leaders in Medicine, 13212
Leaders of the North and South, 16442
Leaf Baby, 3011(F)
The Leaf Men and the Brave Good Bugs, 2268(F)
Leah's Pony, 4650(F)
The Leakeys, 13313
LeAnn Rimes, 12451
Leaping Grasshoppers, 19505
Learn Karate, 22272
Learn the Value of Patience, 184
Learn the Value of Trust, 184
Learn the Value of Understanding Others, 184
Learn to Count, Funny Bunnies, 592(F)
Learn to Draw Now! 21571
Learning About Bees from Mr. Krebs, 19522
Learning About Bravery from the Life of Harriet Tubman, 12801
Learning About Dedication from the Life of Frederick Douglass, 12712
Learning About Determination from the Life of Gloria Estefan, 12386
Learning About Dignity from the Life of Martin Luther King, Jr., 12756
Learning About Fairness from the Life of Susan B. Anthony, 13131
Learning About Forgiveness from the Life of Nelson Mandela, 13832
Learning About Honesty from the Life of Abraham Lincoln, 13074
Learning About Leadership from the Life of George Washington, 13118
Learning About Responsibility from the Life of Colin Powell, 12955
Learning by Heart, 7542(F)
Learning Is Fun with Mrs. Perez, 3137
Learning to Ride Horses and Ponies, 19988
Learning to Say Good-bye, 17717
Learning to Swim in Swaziland, 14989
Leave It to the Molesons! 1841(F)
The Leaves in October, 8395(F)
The Leaving, 4843(F)
Leaving Emma, 8572(F)
Leaving for America, 4604
The Leaving Morning, 3247(F)
Leaving Point, 9693(F)
The Leaving Summer, 6875(F)
Leaving Vietnam, 15176
Lebanon, 15555
Lebanon in Pictures, 15554
Lech Walesa, 13866
The Ledgerbook of Thomas Blue Eagle, 9160(F)
Lee Iacocca, 12905
Lee, the Rabbit with Epilepsy, 5039(F)
Left Behind, 2918(F)
Left-Handed Shortstop, 10327(F)

Left Out, 10333(F)
Leftover Lily, 8382(F)
The Legend of Freedom Hill, 9339(F)
The Legend of Jesse Owens, 13666
The Legend of Lightning Larry, 1569(F)
The Legend of Luke, 7820(F)
The Legend of Mexicatl, 11402
The Legend of Old Befana, 5801(F)
The Legend of Red Horse Cavern, 7005(F)
The Legend of Slappy Hooper, 11384
The Legend of Sleepy Hollow, 7813(F), 7973(F)
  (Illus. by Daniel San Souci), 7812(F)
The Legend of the Bluebonnet, 11229
The Legend of the Christmas Rose, 5844(F)
The Legend of the Lady Slipper, 9167
The Legend of the Panda, 10753
The Legend of the Persian Carpet, 11184
The Legend of the Poinsettia, 11399
The Legend of the White Buffalo Woman, 11248
Legends of American Dance and Choreography, 12162
Legends of Landforms, 10622
Legends of Santa Claus, 17422
Legs, 7154(F)
A Lei for Tutu, 3624(F)
Leif's Saga, 9046(F)
The Lemming Condition, 7564(F)
Lemonade for Sale, 20591(F)
Lemonade Stand, 6705(F)
Lemonade Sun and Other Summer Poems, 11553
The Lemonade Trick, 9814(F)
Lemurs, 19004
Lemurs, Lorises, and Other Lower Primates, 19007
Lemurs on Location, 18990
Lentil, 4222(F)
Leo and Blossom's Sukkah, 6127(F)
Leo Cockroach . . . Toy Tester, 2548(F)
Leo the Late Bloomer, 2320(F)
Leo the Magnificat, 5339(F)
Leo, Zack, and Emmie, 6326(F)
Leola and the Honeybears, 11028
Leon and Albertine, 1997(F)
Leon and Bob, 4012(F)
Leonard Bernstein, 12323, 12324
Leonard Nimoy, 12426
Leonardo and the Flying Boy, 9025(F)
Leonardo da Vinci, 12212, 12215, 12216, 12217, 12218
  (Illus. by Susan Hellard), 12213
Leonardo da Vinci for Kids, 12214
Leonardo DiCaprio, 12374
Leon's Story, 17052
Leontyne Price, 12446, 12447
The Leopard Son, 19075
Leopards, 19088, 19097
Leprechaun Gold, 985(F)
The Leprechaun in the Basement, 5653(F)

Leprechauns Don't Play Basketball, 7693(F)
Leprechauns Never Lie, 973(F)
Leroy Potts Meets the McCrooks, 6623(F)
Les Trois Cochons, 10960
Leslie's Story, 17924
Lessons for Life, 17627
Lessons in Success from the NBA's Top Players, 22132
Lest We Forget, 9325
Lester's Dog, 2939(F)
Let It Shine, 12690
Let Me Do It! 4159(F)
Let Me Explain, 18246
Let Me Help! 6696(F)
Let My People Go, 9306(F)
Let the Celebrations Begin! 9076(F)
Let the Circle Be Unbroken, 7526(F)
Let the Games Begin! 21966
Let the Lynx Come In, 1357(F)
Let There Be Life! Animating with the Computer, 21191
Let Women Vote! 17027
Let's Be Animals, 5439(F)
Let's Be Enemies, 4051(F)
Let's Build a Car, 21318
Let's Build an Airport, 21143
Let's Celebrate, 11829
Let's Celebrate Christmas, 17431
Let's Celebrate Halloween, 17446
Let's Celebrate Thanksgiving, 6152
Let's Celebrate Valentine's Day, 6177
Let's Count, 387, 466
Let's Count It Out, Jesse Bear, 398(F)
Let's Dance! 14271
Let's Do Fingerplays, 22004
Let's Eat! 3965(F)
Let's Fly a Kite, 348(F)
Let's Go, 3295(F)
Let's Go! 21279
Let's Go, Anna! 4152(F)
Let's Go Fishing, 22177
Let's Go, Froggy! 2396(F)
Let's Go Home, Little Bear, 2798(F)
Let's Go Riding in Our Strollers, 3309(F)
Let's Go Rock Collecting, 20559
Let's Go Visiting, 609(F)
Let's Jump Rope, 22017
Let's Make Magic, 21781
Let's Play, 22007
Let's Play Cards! 22238
Let's Play Hopscotch, 22018
Let's Play Jacks, 22019
Let's Play Rough! 3736(F)
Let's Pretend, 969(F)
    (Illus. by Maureen Roffey), 3295(F)
Let's Rodeo! 21993
Let's Talk About Being Afraid, 17713
Let's Talk About Being Shy, 17713
Let's Talk About Drug Abuse, 17874
Let's Talk About Dyslexia, 17910
Let's Talk About Foster Homes, 17691
Let's Talk About Going to a Funeral, 17859

Let's Talk About Going to the Hospital, 18040
Let's Talk About Head Lice, 17961
Let's Talk About It, 17677, 17678, 17931
Let's Talk About Needing Extra Help at School, 17714
Let's Talk About Smoking, 17897
Let's Talk About Staying in a Shelter, 17691
Let's Talk About Stuttering, 17916
Let's Talk About When a Parent Dies, 17691
Let's Talk About When Someone You Know Is in a Nursing Home, 17857
Let's Talk About When Someone You Love Has Alzheimer's Disease, 18013
Let's Talk About Your Parents' Divorce, 17691
Let's Visit a Space Camp, 20945
Let's Visit a Spaghetti Factory, 21026
A Letter for Daria, 13589
A Letter from Phoenix Farm, 12632
The Letter Jesters, 13993
A Letter to Mrs. Roosevelt, 9538(F)
A Letter to Santa Claus, 5952(F)
Letter to the Lake, 3449(F)
Lettering, 21582
The Letters Are Lost! 39(F)
Letters from Camp, 9905(F)
Letters from Rifka, 9550(F)
Letters Home from Canada, 15577
Letters Home from China, 15064
Letters Home from Egypt, 15501
Letters Home from Grand Canyon, 16616
Letters Home from Greece, 15382
Letters Home from Israel, 15521
Letters Home from Japan, 15122
Letters Home from Russia, 15417
Letters Home from Scotland, 15348
Letters Home from Yosemite, 16616, 16784
Letters Home from Zimbabwe, 14979
Letters Home from Zion, 16617
Letting Off Steam, 20296
Levers, 20925
Levi Dust, 9280(F)
Lewis and Clark, 12131, 12132, 12133, 16093
The Lewis and Clark Expedition, 16086, 16089
Lewis and Papa, 4701(F)
Lewis Carroll's Jabberwocky, 11855
Lexington and Concord, 16201
Liang and the Magic Paintbrush, 1109(F)
Liar, Liar, 10046(F)
Liar, Liar, Pants on Fire, 8732(F)
Liars, 7010(F)
Liberation, 14888
Liberia in Pictures, 15034
A Liberian Family, 15022
Liberty, 16662
The Liberty Bell, 16732
Liberty for All? 16410
Liberty for All? 2nd ed, 16249

The Liberty Tree, 16210
Librarians A to Z, 65(F)
Libraries, 14005
The Library, 3443(F)
Library, 21141
The Library Card, 9999(F)
The Library Dragon, 1107(F)
The Library of Congress, 13995, 16733
Libya, 14961
Libya in Pictures, 14960
Lice Are Lousy! All About Headlice, 18009
License Plates, 21308
Lichee Tree, 9012(F)
Lies (People Believe) About Animals, 18856
Life, 14499, 14562
Life Among the Ibo Women of Nigeria, 15039
Life Among the Pirates, 14558
The Life and Death of Martin Luther King, Jr., 12744
The Life and Times of the Honeybee, 19525
The Life and Times of the Peanut, 20117
Life Around the Lake, 15641
Life as a Paratrooper, 21392
Life as a POW, 14896
Life as an Air Force Fighter Pilot, 21392
Life as an Army Demolition Expert, 21393
Life Cycle of a Bean, 20262
Life Cycle of a Dog, 19968
Life Cycle of a Frog, 18737
Life Cycle of a Guinea Pig, 19903
Life Cycle of a Kangaroo, 19180
Life Cycle of a Mushroom, 20190
Life Cycle of a Salmon, 19713
Life Cycle of an Oak Tree, 20217
Life Cycles of a Dozen Diverse Creatures, 18623
Life During the Black Death, 14762
Life During the Gold Rush, 16368
Life in a Colonial Town, 16137
Life in a Garden, 18630
Life in a Hopi Village, 15976
Life in a Medieval Village, 14782
Life in a Tidal Pool, 19867
Life in a Wetland, 20368
Life in America's First Cities, 16137
Life in Army Basic Training, 21384
Life in Ponds and Streams, 20510
Life in the American Colonies, 16109
Life in the Army Special Forces, 21394
Life in the Coral Reef, 19662
Life in the Deep Sea, 19820
Life in the Marines, 21395
Life in the Minor Leagues, 22123
Life in the Sea, 19636
The Life of a Miner, 16329
Life of an American Soldier in Europe, 14897
The Life of Daniel Hale Williams, 13352
The Life of Jesus in Masterpieces of Art, 17313
Life of the Butterfly, 19548

Life of the Honeybee, 19521
Life of the Ladybug, 19530
Life of the Snail, 19602
Life on a Pig Farm, 20075
Life on a Pioneer Homestead, 16317
Life on a Plantation, 16260
Life on a Southern Plantation, 16253
Life on a Submarine, 21399
Life on Ellis Island, 16729
Life on Land, 19398
Life on Mars, 18472
Life on the American Frontier, 16319
Life on the Oregon Trail, 16291, 16317
Life on the Underground Railroad, 16258
The Life Stories of Stars, 18394
Life Story, 20298
Life with the Navy Seals, 21396
Life Without Light, 18675
Life's a Funny Proposition, Horatio, 8512(F)
The Lifesize Animal Opposites Book, 18617
Lifetimes, 18289
Lift Every Voice and Sing, 14156, 14157
Lift Ev'ry Voice and Sing, 14158
Light, 20858, 20862
Light Action, 20912
Light and Color, 20870
Light and Dark, 20874
The Light Bulb, 20888
A Light in Space, 10218(F)
A Light in the Attic, 11698
Light in the Forest, 9174(F)
Light in the Shadows, 14872
A Light in the Storm, 9479(F)
The Light on Hogback Hill, 8276(F)
The Light Princess (Illus. by Maurice Sendak), 10455(F)
   (Illus. by Katie T. Treherne), 10456(F)
Light Shining Through the Mist, 13284
Light the Lights! 5640
The Lightbulb, 20907
The Lighthouse Children, 6404(F)
Lighthouse Dog to the Rescue, 5362(F)
The Lighthouse Mermaid, 9567(F)
Lighthouses, 21360
Lightning, 20691, 20710, 20717
   (Illus. by Warren Faidley), 20701
Lightning Inside You and Other Native American Riddles, 21814
Lights and Optics, 20865
Lights, Camera, Action! Making Movies and TV from the Inside Out, 21273
Lights Out! 4181(F)
   (Illus. by Jerry Smath), 553(F)
Like Jake and Me, 3742(F)
Like Likes Like, 1497(F)
A Likely Place, 8646(F)
Lili at Ballet, 3238(F)
Lili Backstage, 3716(F)
Lili on Stage, 3239(F)
Liliana's Grandmothers, 3921(F)
Lilies, Rabbits and Painted Eggs, 17433

The Lilith Summer, 8708(F)
Lilly's Good Deed, 8254(F)
Lilly's Purple Plastic Purse, 5505(F)
Lily and Trooper's Fall, 3437(F)
Lily and Trooper's Spring, 779(F)
Lily and Trooper's Summer, 780(F)
Lily and Trooper's Winter, 3437(F)
Lily's Crossing, 9660(F)
Lima Beans Would Be Illegal, 7606(F)
Limestone Caves, 20370
Lincoln, 13066
Lincoln and the Abolition of Slavery, 16426
The Lincoln Assassination in American History, 16435
The Lincoln-Douglas Debates, 16256
The Lincoln Memorial, 16703, 16730
Linda Ronstadt, 12460
A Line in the Sand, 9279(F)
Ling Cho and His Three Friends, 4791(F)
Ling Ling, 2687(F)
Linnea in Monet's Garden, 13876(F)
Linnea's Almanac, 18578
Linnea's Windowsill Garden, 21759
Lion, 19074, 19094
The Lion and the Mouse, 11064, 11078
The Lion and the Mouse and Other Aesop's Fables, 11072
Lion and the Ostrich Chicks and Other African Folk Tales, 10654
The Lion and the Unicorn, 9667(F)
Lion Dancer, 5656
The Lion Family Book, 19092
A Lion Named Shirley Williamson, 2789(F)
The Lion, the Witch and the Wardrobe, 7910(F), 7911(F)
A Lion to Guard Us, 9186(F)
The Lion Who Has Asthma, 5018(F)
The Lion Who Saw Himself in the Water, 11198
Lionel and Amelia, 2572(F)
Lionel at School, 6436(F)
Lionel in the Spring, 6437(F)
Lionel in the Summer, 6438(F)
Lions, 19083, 19087, 19106
The Lion's Share, 1071(F)
The Lion's Whiskers, 10660
The Lion's Whiskers and Other Ethiopian Tales, 10649
Liplap's Wish, 2397(F)
Lisa and Her Soundless World, 8900(F)
Lisa Leslie, 13544
Lisa's Airplane Trip, 2161(F)
Listen, Buddy, 2359(F)
Listen for the Bus, 5024
Listen to the City, 3240(F)
Listen to the Desert/Oye al Desierto, 4502
Listen to the Nightingale, 8665(F)
Listen to the Rain, 3311(F)
Listening for Leroy, 8685(F)
Listening to Crickets, 13248
The Listening Walk, 3893(F)
The Literary Crowd, 12157
Lithuania, 15274

The Little Ant/La Hormiga Chiquita, 2610(F)
Little Bear, 6533(F)
Little Bear and the Big Fight, 2336(F)
Little Bear Brushes His Teeth, 2337(F)
Little Bear Goes to Kindergarten, 2337(F)
Little Bear Is a Big Brother, 2338(F)
Little Bear Lost, 2211(F)
Little Bear's Christmas, 5862(F)
Little Bear's Friend, 6533(F)
Little Bear's Visit, 6533(F)
Little Beaver and the Echo, 2419(F)
Little Big Ears, 19167
Little Bighorn, 16337
   (Illus. by Richard Hook), 16057
A Little Bit of Rob, 3924(F)
A Little Bit of Winter, 2731(F)
Little Black Sambo, 978(F)
The Little Black Truck, 5570(F)
Little Blue and Little Yellow, 281(F)
Little Bo, 7187(F)
The Little Boat, 3202(F)
The Little Book of Big Questions, 21910
Little Boy Blue and Other Rhymes, 879(F)
Little Brother Moose, 5284(F)
Little Brown Bear Does Not Want to Eat, 2349(F)
Little Brown Bear Is Growing Up, 2349(F)
Little Brown Bear Wants to Be Read To, 2349(F)
The Little Buggers, 11798
Little Bull, 5275(F)
Little Bunny on the Move, 2411(F)
Little Bunny's Cool Tool Set, 1823(F)
Little Bunny's Easter Surprise, 5971(F)
Little Bunny's Pacifier Plan, 1824(F)
Little Bunny's Preschool Countdown, 5475(F)
Little Bunny's Sleepless Night, 768(F)
Little Calf, 5307(F)
Little Caribou, 5211(F)
Little Clam, 2619(F)
Little Clancy's New Drum, 4472(F)
Little Clearing in the Woods, 9457(F)
Little Cliff and the Porch People, 3911(F)
Little Cloud, 1036(F)
The Little Country Town, 778(F)
Little Dog Moon, 4854(F)
Little Dog Poems, 11789
Little Dogs Say "Rough!" 4346(F)
The Little Drummer Boy, 14203
Little Elephant, 5208(F)
Little Elephant Thunderfoot, 5236(F)
Little Elephant's Song, 2167(F)
The Little Engine That Could, 5592(F)
Little Farm by the Sea, 3070(F)
Little Farm in the Ozarks, 9404(F)
Little Fish, Lost, 2774(F)
Little Folk, 10624
Little Fox, 2248(F)

The Little Ghost Who Wouldn't Go Away/El pequeño fantasma que no quería irse, 8052(F)
Little Gold Star, 10497(F)
Little Gold Star/Estrellita de oro, 11346
The Little Golden Lamb, 10990
Little Gorilla, 1838(F)
The Little Green Goose, 2651(F)
Little Green Thumbs, 21774
Little Green Tow Truck, 5605
Little Grunt and the Big Egg, 2029(F)
The Little Hands Big Fun Craft Book, 21464
Little Hobbin, 788(F)
The Little House, 3062(F)
The Little House Cookbook, 21744
Little House in Brookfield, 9458(F)
Little House in the Big Woods (Illus. by Renee Graef), 4877(F)
(Illus. by Garth Williams), 7537(F)
Little House on Rocky Edge, 9405(F)
Little House on the Prairie, 7537(F)
The Little Humpbacked Horse, 11116
Little Johnny Buttermilk, 11041
Little Kim's Doll, 4894(F)
The Little Lama of Tibet, 17213
Little Lamb, 5307(F)
Little League's Official How-to-Play Baseball Handbook, 22103
Little Lions, 5122(F)
Little Lit, 10504(F)
Little Little Sister, 10412(F)
Little Lou, 4621(F)
Little Louie the Baby Bloomer, 3753(F)
The Little Match Girl, 10479(F)
(Illus. by Anastassija Archipowa), 10493
(Illus. by Blair Lent), 10384(F)
Little Men, 7384(F)
The Little Mermaid (Illus. by Rachel Isadora), 10385(F)
(Illus. by Alan Snow), 10389
(Illus. by Katie T. Treherne), 10514(F)
The Little Mermaid and Other Fairy Tales, 10386(F)
Little Miss Spider, 2294(F)
Little Miss Spider at Sunny Patch School, 2295(F)
Little Mo, 2799(F)
Little Mouse Has a Busy Day, 6445(F)
Little Mouse Has an Adventure, 6445(F)
Little Mouse's Big Valentine, 6172(F)
Little Nino's Pizzeria, 3515(F)
Little Obie and the Flood, 9449(F)
Little Obie and the Kidnap, 9450(F)
Little Oh, 4767(F)
The Little Old Lady Who Was Not Afraid of Anything, 1688(F)
Little Old Mrs. Pepperpot and Other Stories, 8027(F)
The Little Painter of Sabana Granda, 4762(F)
Little Pear, 4725(F)

Little Penguin's Tale, 2869(F)
Little Pig, Bigger Trouble, 2760(F)
Little Pink Pig, 2232(F)
Little Polar Bear and the Husky Pup, 2008(F)
Little Polar Bear Finds a Friend, 2009(F)
Little Polar Bear, Take Me Home! 2010(F)
A Little Princess (Illus. by Barbara McClintock), 4920(F)
(Illus. by Tasha Tudor), 7396(F)
Little Puppy, 5307(F)
The Little Puppy, 5193(F)
The Little Rabbit, 4421(F)
Little Rabbit and the Sea, 1812(F)
Little Rabbits' First Time Book, 156(F)
Little Rabbits' First Word Book, 6193
Little Rabbit's Loose Tooth, 1795(F)
The Little Red Ant and the Great Big Crumb, 11396
Little Red Cowboy Hat, 4219(F)
The Little Red Hen, 10946, 10980
(Illus. by Paul Galdone), 10980
(Illus. by Norman Messenger), 10983
The Little Red Hen and the Ear of Wheat, 10975
The Little Red Hen (Makes a Pizza), 11036
Little Red Lighthouse and the Great Gray Bridge, 5603(F)
Little Red Plane, 5606(F)
Little Red Riding Hood, 2077(F), 10936
(Illus. by Emily Bolam), 10942
(Illus. by Frances Cony), 12016
Little Red Riding Hood/Caperucita roja, 10900
Little Red Ronnika, 10919
The Little Reindeer, 5815(F)
The Little Riders, 9688(F)
Little Robin Redbreast, 855(F)
Little Robin's Christmas, 5813(F)
Little Rock, 17046
The Little Scarecrow Boy, 1017(F)
The Little Ships, 9081(F)
A Little Shopping, 7503(F)
Little Sibu, 5237(F)
The Little Silver House, 7472(F)
Little Sister and the Month Brothers, 11087
Little Sister, Big Sister, 6229(F)
Little Stowaway, 2979(F)
Little Sure Shot, 12432
Little Tiger Goes Shopping, 2103(F)
A Little Tiger in the Chinese Night, 12316
Little Tiger's Big Surprise! 2746(F)
Little Toot, 5569(F)
A Little Touch of Monster, 5007(F)
Little Town at the Crossroads, 9459(F)
Little Whistle, 1533(F)
Little White Dog, 270(F)
Little White Duck, 2847(F)
Little Witch Goes to School, 6370(F)
Little Witch's Big Night, 6004(F)
Little Wolf and the Giant, 2596(F)

Little Wolf's Book of Badness, 2851(F)
Little Wolf's Diary of Daring Deeds, 8203(F)
Little Wolf's Haunted Hall for Small Horrors, 8204(F)
Little Women, 7384(F)
Little Women Next Door, 8726(F)
Little Wonders, 18868
Littlejim, 9556(F)
Littlejim's Dreams, 9557(F)
Littlejim's Gift, 9734(F)
The Littlest Angel, 1614(F)
The Littlest Matryoshka, 1002(F)
Liv Tyler, 12479
Live from the Fifth Grade, 10108(F)
Lives, 11632
Lives and Legends of the Saints, 17163
Lives Intertwined, 20397
Lives of Extraordinary Women, 13732
Lives of the Artists, 12171
Lives of the Athletes, 13386
Lives of the Musicians, 12172
Lives of the Presidents, 12670
Lives of the Writers, 12173
Lives Turned Upside Down, 17144
A Living Desert, 20420
Living Earth, 18600
The Living Earth, 18598
Living Fossils, 18655
Living in Space, 20951, 20996
Living in the World, 17133
Living on Mars, 18467
Living Things, 18334
The Living Tomb, 14651
Living with a Single Parent, 17679
Living with Albinism, 17919
Living with Asthma, 17938, 17970
Living with Blindness, 17935
Living with Cerebral Palsy, 17990
Living with Deafness, 17913
Living with Diabetes, 17944
Living with Dinosaurs, 14435
Living with Epilepsy, 18014
Living with Learning Disabilities, 17912
Living with Leukemia, 18015
Living with My Stepfather Is like Living with a Moose, 8404(F)
Livingstone Mouse, 2055(F)
The Lizard and the Sun, 11392
Lizard Flanagan, Supermodel?? 9864(F)
Lizard Island, 19656
The Lizard Man of Crabtree County, 4252(F)
Lizard Meets Ivana the Terrible, 8367(F)
Lizard Sees the World, 2758(F)
Lizards, 19904
(Illus. by Max Meier), 18748
Lizards, Frogs, and Polliwogs, 11785
Lizard's Home, 2680(F)
Lizzie at Last, 10111(F)
The Lizzie Borden "Axe Murder" Trial, 16447
Lizzie Logan Gets Married, 9995(F)
Lizzie Logan, Second Banana, 9996(F)

Lizzie Logan Wears Purple Sunglass-
  es, 9997(F)
Lizzie's List, 7446(F)
Lizzy and Skunk, 3130(F)
The Llama, 18949
A Llama in the Family, 7225(F)
Llama in the Library, 7226(F)
The Llama Who Had No Pajama,
  11596
Llamas, 18952
Loaves of Fun, 20095
Lobbying, 17122
Lobsters, 19672
Local Government, 17131
Local News, 7373(F)
Locating and Evaluating Information
  on the Internet, 21236
The Loch Ness Monster, 21928
Locked in the Library! 6435(F)
Lockie Leonard, Scumbuster,
  10020(F)
Locks, Crocs, and Skeeters, 15682
Locomotive, 21345
The Log Cabin Christmas, 5847(F)
The Log Cabin Quilt, 4687(F)
The Log of Christopher Columbus'
  First Voyage to America in the
  Year 1492 as Copied Out in Brief
  by Bartholomew Las Casas, 12098
Loggers and Railroad Workers,
  16385
A Log's Life, 20215
Lois Lowry, 12566
Lolo and Red-Legs, 7291(F)
Lon Po Po, 10781
Lone Wolf, 8431(F)
Lone Woman of Ghalas-Hat, 16810
The Lonely Lioness and the Ostrich
  Chicks, 10641
The Lonely Scarecrow, 1492(F)
Long Ago in Oregon, 11626
Long-Ago Lives, 21894
Long Ago Yesterday, 3383(F)
The Long and Short of It, 350(F)
Long Is a Dragon, 14083
Long Journey Home, 7350(F)
The Long, Long Letter, 4321(F)
The Long March, 15948
The Long-Nosed Pig, 2086(F)
The Long Patrol, 7821(F)
The Long Road, 4652(F)
The Long Secret, 10055(F)
The Long Silk Strand, 1687(F)
Long Spikes, 7152(F)
The Long Wait, 20642(F)
A Long Way from Chicago, 7492(F),
  9604(F)
The Long Way to a New Land,
  4823(F)
A Long Way to Go, 9602(F)
The Long Way Westward, 9621(F)
Long Winter, 7537(F)
The Longest Hair in the World,
  1141(F)
The Longest Ride, 9492(F)
The Longest Wait, 3542(F)
Longhouse, 15924
Longwalker's Journey, 9162(F)
Loo-Loo, Boo, and Art You Can Do,
  21471
Look Again! 309(F)

Look-Alikes, 314
Look-Alikes Jr., 359
A Look at Minerals, 20561
Look at Pond Life, 20522
A Look at Rocks, 20562
Look at the Moon, 680(F)
Look at Your Eyes, 18162
Look Back, Moss, 7255(F)
Look for Lisa, 2752(F)
Look! I Can Read! 6409(F)
Look Inside Cross-Sections, 21281,
  21334
The Look-It-Up Book of Presidents,
  12637
Look Once, Look Twice, 88(F)
Look Out for the Big Bad Fish!
  1910(F)
Look Out for Turtles! 18780
Look Out Kindergarten, Here I
  Come! 5481(F)
Look Out, Washington, D.C.!
  10063(F)
Look! Snow! 3152(F)
Look to the North, 5223(F)
Look What Came from China, 15066
Look What Came from Egypt, 15503
Look What Came from France,
  15308
Look What Came from Italy, 15383
Look What Came from Japan, 15124
Look What Came from Mexico,
  15617
Look What Came from Russia,
  15419
Look What I Can Do! 906(F)
Look What I Did with a Leaf! 21497
Look What I Did with a Shell! 21498
Look What We've Brought You from
  Vietnam, 17593
Look What You Can Make With
  Boxes, 21630
Look What You Can Make with
  Paper Bags, 21622
Look Whooo's Counting, 504(F)
Look Who's Hatching! 18919
Lookin' for Bird in the Big City,
  4613(F)
Looking at Bears, 19060
Looking at Faces in Art, 13920
Looking at Nature, 13873
Looking at Penguins, 19381
Looking at Pictures, 13921
Looking at Senses, 18164
Looking at the Body, 18080
Looking at Weather, 20793
Looking Back, 12565
Looking Down, 923(F)
Looking for Angels, 3184(F)
Looking for Atlantis, 8142(F)
Looking for Cinderella, 1108(F)
Looking for Juliette, 7922(F)
Looking Inside Sports Aerodynam-
  ics, 20837
Looking Inside Sunken Treasure,
  14539
Looking Inside Telescopes and the
  Night Sky, 18413
Looking into the Middle Ages, 14791
Loon Magic for Kids, 19242
Loons, 19262
The Loon's Necklace, 11313

Lootas, Little Wave Eater, 19742
The Lorax, 4539(F)
Lord Brocktree, 7822(F)
The Lord Is My Shepherd, 17248
Lord of the Animals, 11236
Lord of the Cranes, 10744
Lord of the Fries, 8872(F)
Lord of the Sky, 11476
The Lord's Prayer, 17528
Loretta P. Sweeney, Where Are You?
  6858(F)
Lorraine Hansberry, 12544, 12545
Los Angeles, 16822
The Los Angeles Lakers Basketball
  Team, 22135
The Losers Fight Back, 10341(F)
Losers, Inc., 9939(F)
Losers, Inc, 10112(F)
Losing Uncle Tim, 8466(F)
Lost, 5279(F)
Lost! 2458(F)
  (Illus. by Daniel Moreton), 6698(F)
Lost! A Story in String, 3626(F)
Lost and Found, 6697(F), 17703
The Lost and Found, 1615(F)
The Lost Boy and the Monster,
  1602(F)
Lost Cat, 5247(F)
The Lost Children, 11249
Lost Cities, 14528
Lost City of Pompeii, 14737
Lost Civilizations, 14530
The Lost Flower Children, 7923(F)
The Lost Horse, 10782
Lost in Spillville, 7710(F)
Lost in the Amazon, 2608(F)
Lost in the Devil's Desert, 7057(F)
Lost in the Fog, 6928(F)
Lost in the Storm, 5161(F)
Lost in the Tunnel of Time, 6823(F)
The Lost Lake, 3875(F)
Lost Little Angel, 1495(F)
Lost Magic, 7560(F)
Lost Moose, 5419(F)
Lost Property, 5273(F)
Lost Star, 12113
Lost Summer, 8282(F)
Lost Temple of the Aztecs, 15652
The Lost Tooth Club, 4192(F)
The Lost Treasure of Captain Kidd,
  6954(F)
Lost Treasure of the Inca, 15758
The Lost Village of Central Park,
  9301(F)
Lost Wild America, 19403
Lostman's River, 6817(F)
The Lot at the End of My Block,
  5581(F)
A Lot of Otters, 997(F)
Lots and Lots of Zebra Stripes, 360
Lots of Dads, 17681
Lots of Lice, 17972
Lots of Limericks, 11896
Lotta's Christmas Surprise, 5864(F)
Lotta's Easter Surprise, 5970(F)
The Lottie Project, 8859(F)
Lottie's New Beach Towel, 3315(F)
Lottie's New Friend, 2484(F)
Lottie's Princess Dress, 4132(F)
The Lotus Seed, 7341(F)
Lou Gehrig, 13453, 13454

Lou Hoover, 13159
Loud Emily, 4256(F)
The Loudest, Fastest, Best Drummer in Kansas, 1103(F)
Loudmouth George and the Big Race, 1931(F)
Loudmouth George and the Cornet, 1931(F)
Loudmouth George and the Fishing Trip, 1931(F)
Loudmouth George and the New Neighbors, 1931(F)
Loudmouth George and the Sixth-Grade Bully, 1931(F)
The Loudness of Sam, 4276(F)
Louella Mae, She's Run Away! 4074(F)
Louie, 4995(F)
Louie and Dan Are Friends, 2604(F)
Louie's Goose, 4951(F)
Louis Armstrong, 12347, 12348
Louis Braille, 13758, 13759, 13762
Louis Pasteur, 13338, 13339, 13340
Louis the Fish, 1713(F)
Louisa Catherine Johnson Adams, 13126
Louisa May Alcott, 12489, 12490
Louise Arner Boyd, 12075
Louise Goes Wild, 9911(F)
Louise, Soccer Star? 10343(F)
Louise Takes Charge, 10097(F)
Louise the One and Only, 10092(F)
Louisiana, 16865, 16871, 16872
The Louisiana Purchase, 16271
Louisville Slugger Book of Great Hitters, 13364
Lovable Lyle, 2787(F)
Love and Kisses, 1690(F)
Love and Marriage Around the World, 17361
Love as Strong as Ginger, 3779(F)
Love Flute, 11250
Love, from the Fifth-Grade Celebrity, 8288(F)
Love from Your Friend, Hannah, 9626(F)
Love Is . . ., 17707
Love Is a Handful of Honey, 1741(F)
Love Letters, 11523
Love One Another, 17440
Love Songs of the Little Bear, 11540
Love Times Three, 8718(F)
Love's a Sweet, 11734
Loving, 3818
The Low-Down Laundry Line Blues, 3806(F)
Low Song, 3321(F)
Lowly Worm Joins the Circus, 6625(F)
The Loyal Cat, 4777(F)
Lu and Clancy's Crime Science, 17065
Lu and Clancy's Secret Codes, 13967
Luba, 14992
Luba and the Wren, 11106
Lucille Ball, 12351
Lucille's Snowsuit, 2342(F)
The Luck of the Miss L, 6922(F)
Luck with Potatoes, 1299(F)
The Luckiest Kid on the Planet, 4141(F)

The Luckiest Leprechaun, 1318(F)
The Luckiest One of All, 2566(F)
Lucky Bear, 6575(F)
Lucky Dog Days, 4126(F)
Lucky Lady, 7301(F)
The Lucky Lizard, 7856(F)
Lucky Mouse, 19206
Lucky O'Leprechaun, 5623(F)
Lucky O'Leprechaun Comes to America, 1125(F)
Lucky Pennies and Hot Chocolate, 3890(F)
Lucky Song, 3949(F)
Lucky Star, 6490(F)
The Lucky Stone, 7410(F)
A Lucky Thing, 11692
Lucky's 24-Hour Garage, 3262(F)
Lucy Anna and the Finders, 1229(F)
The Lucy Cousins Book of Nursery Rhymes, 835
Lucy Dove, 7703(F)
Lucy on the Loose, 6802(F)
Lucy's Christmas, 5831(F)
Lucy's Winter Tale, 4950(F)
Ludwig van Beethoven, 12320, 12321
Luis Munoz Marin, 12936
Luis Rodriguez, 12835
Luke, 9430(F)
Luke and the Van Zandt County War, 9512(F)
Luke on the High Seas, 9311(F)
Luke the Lionhearted, 5402(F)
Lullabies, 730
Lullabies and Night Songs, 14149
Lullaby and Good Night, 662(F)
Lullaby Raft, 754(F)
Lulu's Birthday, 5695(F)
Lulu's Busy Day, 3462(F)
Lulu's Lemonade, 419(F)
The Lump in the Middle, 8551(F)
A Luna Moth's Life, 19556
Lunch, 2090(F)
Lunch at the Zoo, 20023
The Lunch Box Surprise, 6478(F)
The Lunch Bunch, 6333(F)
Lunch Bunnies, 2343(F)
The Lunch Line, 535(F)
Lunch Money and Other Poems About School, 11695
Lungs, 18125
The Lungs and Breathing, 18124
The Lungs and Respiratory System, 18126
Luo, 14915
Lupe and Me, 8825(F)
Luv, Amelia Luv, Nadia, 8347(F)
Luvella's Promise, 9517(F)
Luxembourg, 15401
Lyle and the Birthday Party, 2787(F)
Lyle at Christmas, 5944(F)
Lyle at the Office, 2790(F)
Lyle Finds His Mother, 2787(F)
Lyle, Lyle, Crocodile, 2787(F)
Lyme Disease, 18000, 18010
Lyn St. James, 13429
Lyndon B. Johnson, 13056, 13057
Lynx, 19080, 19108

M. C. Higgins, the Great, 7444(F)
M Is for Minnesota, 16540

Ma Dear's Aprons, 4757(F)
Ma Jiang and the Orange Ants, 4799(F)
Maasai, 14954
Mabel Dancing, 700(F)
Mabel Ran Away with the Toys, 3933(F)
Mac Side Up, 2070(F)
McBroom and the Great Race, 9850(F)
McBroom Tells the Truth, 9850(F)
Maccabee Jamboree, 469(F)
McDuff and the Baby, 5449(F)
McDuff Comes Home, 5450(F)
McDuff Moves In, 5451(F)
McDuff's New Friend, 5950(F)
McElligot's Pool, 1562(F)
McGwire and Sosa, 22115
Machines, 21247, 21255
Machines and Inventions, 21044
Machines at Work, 21242
Machu Picchu, 15761
McKendree, 8560(F)
The Macmillan Book of Baseball Stories, 22090
The Macmillan Book of Greek Gods and Heroes, 11485
Macmillan Children's Guide to Dinosaurs and Other Prehistoric Animals, 14480
Macmillan Children's Guide to Endangered Animals, 19394
The Macmillan Picture Wordbook, 14039
McMummy, 7638(F)
Mad About Plaid, 1369(F)
Mad As a Wet Hen! and Other Funny Idioms, 14047
Mad Dog McGraw, 1633(F)
Mad Summer Night's Dream, 1018(F)
Madagascar, 14966, 14975, 14995
Madagascar in Pictures, 14991
Madam C. J. Walker, 12807, 12808, 12810
Madam Prime Minister, 13860
Madam Secretary, 12839
Made in China, 15091
Made in Mexico, 15629
Madeleine Albright, 12838, 12840
Madeline, 4590(F)
Madeline in America and Other Holiday Tales, 4591(F)
Madison Finds a Line, 1666(F)
Madlenka, 1581(F)
Mae Jemison, 12126, 12127
Maebelle's Suitcase, 1629(F)
The Maestro Plays, 4230(F)
Magda's Tortillas/Las tortillas de Magda, 5674(F)
Magellan, 12141
Magellan and da Gama, 12069
Maggie and a Horse Named Devildust, 7149(F)
Maggie and the Monster, 812(F)
Maggie and the Pirate, 2947(F)
Maggie and the Search for Devildust, 7150(F)
The Maggie B, 1215(F)
Maggie Forevermore, 8501(F)

Maggie Marmelstein for President, 10131(F)
Maggie, Too, 8501(F)
Magic and Mischief, 10956
Magic and Perception, 21783
The Magic Bean Tree, 11443
The Magic Bicycle, 10196(F)
Magic Crayon, 1453(F)
The Magic Detectives, 21939
Magic Dogs of the Volcanoes, 957(F)
The Magic Dreidels, 6085(F)
The Magic Fan, 971(F)
Magic Finger, 7697(F)
The Magic Fish-bone, 7706(F)
The Magic Flute, 14128
Magic for Kids, 21788
The Magic Globe, 14348
The Magic Hat of Mortimer Winter-green, 9915(F)
The Magic Hill, 10464(F)
The Magic Hockey Stick, 1391(F)
The Magic Horse, 11199
The Magic Hourglass, 14348
The Magic Hummingbird, 11268
Magic in the Mist, 1304(F)
Magic Johnson, 13532, 13533
The Magic Kerchief, 1336(F)
Magic Listening Cap, 10832
The Magic Maguey, 4699(F)
Magic Man, 12476
The Magic Mean Machine, 9865(F)
The Magic Mustache, 983(F)
Magic . . . Naturally! 21780
The Magic Nesting Doll, 10471(F)
The Magic of Kol Nidre, 17487
The Magic of the Glits, 8247(F)
Magic on Ice, 22221
The Magic Paintbrush, 8234(F)
The Magic Pocket, 11649
The Magic Porridge Pot, 1175(F)
The Magic Pretzel, 8019(F)
The Magic Pumpkin, 6032(F)
The Magic Purse, 10833
The Magic Saddle, 5878(F)
The Magic School Bus, 16993, 18052, 20302
The Magic School Bus and the Electric Field Trip, 20887
The Magic School Bus Explores the Senses, 18139
The Magic School Bus in the Time of the Dinosaurs, 14392
The Magic School Bus Inside a Beehive, 19517
The Magic School Bus Inside a Hurricane, 20687
The Magic School Bus Lost in the Solar System, 18510(F)
The Magic School Bus on the Ocean Floor, 19816
Magic Science, 18368
The Magic Sewing Machine, 4868(F)
The Magic Shell, 8763(F)
Magic Spring, 10733
Magic Step-by-Step, 21790
The Magic Toy Box, 1469(F)
The Magic Tree, 10664
Magic Tricks, 21786
The Magic Wand and Other Bright Experiments on Light and Color, 20863

The Magic Weaver of Rugs, 11286
Magic Windows, 16907
Magic Words, 11930
The Magical East, 15052
Magical Hands, 5662(F)
The Magical Starfruit Tree, 10771
Magical Tales from Many Lands
    (Illus. by Gretchen Will Mayo), 11276
    (Illus. by Jane Ray), 10587
The Magician's Apprentice, 9121(F)
The Magician's Nephew, 7911(F)
Magid Fasts for Ramadan, 7354(F)
Magnesium, 20291
The Magnet Book, 20898
Magnets, 20906
Magnets and Sparks, 20900
Magnificent Monarchs, 19551
Magnificent Monologues for Kids, 12038
The Magnificent Piano Recital, 5055(F)
Magpie Magic, 940(F)
The Magpies' Nest, 10977
The Maid of the North, 10602
The Maiden of Northland, 11131
The Maiden on the Moor, 11035
The Mail, 16919
Mail Call! 17106
Mail for Husher Town, 655(F)
Mail-Order Wings, 7748(F)
Mailbox Magic, 4274(F)
The Mailbox Mice Mystery, 6501(F)
Mailing May, 3922(F)
Maine, 16671, 16677, 16704
Mairead Corrigan and Betty Williams, 15339
Maisy at the Farm, 1974(F)
Maisy Dresses Up, 1975(F)
Maisy Drives the Bus, 1976(F)
Maisy Goes Swimming, 1977(F)
Maisy Goes to Bed, 1977(F)
Maisy Goes to School, 1978(F)
Maisy Goes to the Playground, 1978(F)
Maisy Makes Gingerbread, 1979(F)
Maisy Takes a Bath, 1976(F)
Maisy's Bedtime, 1975(F)
    (Illus. by Lucy Cousins), 6286(F)
Maisy's Pool, 1979(F)
    (Illus. by Lucy Cousins), 6286(F)
Maisy's Pop-Up Playhouse, 3085(F)
Maizie, 8454(F)
Make a Change Opposites, 252(F)
Make a Change Shapes, 361(F)
Make a Joyful Sound, 11767
Make-a-Saurus, 14393
Make a Wish, Honey Bear! 5717(F)
Make Cards! 21631
Make Clothes Fun, 21551
Make Costumes! 21544
Make Four Million Dollars by Next Thursday! 9935(F)
Make Gifts! 21551
Make Me a Peanut Butter Sandwich (and a Glass of Milk), 3380
Make Sculptures! 21535
Make Things Fly, 11965
Make Up Your Mind, Marshal, 3347(F)

Make Way for Dumb Bunnies, 2022(F)
Make Way for Sam Houston, 12903
Make Yourself a Monster! 21492
Makiawisug, 7722(F)
Making a Difference in the World, 12518
Making Animal Babies, 18918
Making Babies, 5089(F)
Making Books That Fly, Fold, Wrap, Hide, Pop Up, Twist, and Turn, 21612
Making Cards, 21632
Making Chinese Papercuts, 21607
Making Cool Crafts and Awesome Art, 21440
Making Fleece Crafts, 21645
Making Friends, 5336(F)
Making Friends with Frankenstein, 11897
Making Gift Boxes, 21443
Making Headlines, 13136
Making Jewelry, 21541
Making Light Work, 20861
Making Magic Windows, 16907, 21615
Making Make-Believe, 12026
Making Memory Books, 21450
Making Minestrone, 3028(F)
Making Models, 21429
The Making of a Knight, 9115(F)
The Making of My Special Hand, 17914
Making Picture Frames, 21663
Making Room, 2306(F)
Making Shaped Books, 13991
Making Shapes, 18316
Making the World, 258(F)
Making Things, 21513
Making Things Change, 18317
Making Thirteen Colonies, 16131
Making Tracks, 9640(F), 21287
Making Up Megaboy, 8847(F)
Making Waves, 19852
The Malachite Palace, 10375(F)
Malawi in Pictures, 14940
Malaysia, 15188, 15198
Malaysia in Pictures, 15185
Malcolm X and Black Pride, 12760
Malcolm X, 12759, 12761, 12762
Malinda Martha Meets Mariposa, 12039
Malinke, 15040
Malta, 15258
Malu's Wolf, 8953(F)
Mama, 5070(F)
Mama, Across the Sea, 3171(F)
Mama and Daddy Bear's Divorce, 5084(F)
Mama and Me and the Model T, 4160(F)
Mama and Papa Have a Store, 4615(F)
Mama Birds, Baby Birds, 3248(F)
Mama Cat Has Three Kittens, 2091(F)
Mama Coming and Going, 3573(F)
Mama, Daddy, Baby and Me, 3647(F)
Mama, Do You Love Me? 3739(F)
Mama Don't Allow, 2229(F)

Mama Elizabeti, 4845(F)
Mama God, Papa God, 11428
Mama, If You Had a Wish, 2503(F)
Mama Loves, 6353(F)
Mama Mama, 5342(F)
Mama One, Mama Two, 3789(F)
Mama, Papa, and Baby Joe, 1097(F)
Mama Provi and the Pot of Rice, 3390(F)
Mama Talks Too Much, 3402(F)
Mama Zooms, 3592(F)
Mama's Birthday Surprise, 7520(F)
Mama's Way, 3749(F)
Mammalabilia, 11786
Mammals, 18611, 18932, 18969, 18978
The Mammals, 14479
Mammolina, 13835
A Mammoth Mix-Up, 6945(F)
Mamphela Ramphele, 13845
Man and Mustang, 19983
A Man Called Raven, 1645(F)
The Man-Eating Tigers of Sundarbans, 19102
Man from the Sky, 6754(F)
Man Gave Names to All the Animals, 14237
The Man in the Ceiling, 9841(F)
A Man Named Thoreau, 12605
Man O' War, 19991
Man of the Family, 9568(F)
The Man of the House at Huffington Row, 5750(F)
The Man Who Caught Fish, 1325(F)
The Man Who Could Call Down Owls, 1024(F)
The Man Who Kept House, 11119
The Man Who Lived Alone, 11587
The Man Who Loved Clowns, 8866(F)
The Man Who Made Parks, 12942
The Man Who Painted Indians, 12203
The Man Who Paints, 12562
The Man Who Tricked a Ghost, 10778
The Man with the Black Glove, 7044(F)
The Manatee, 19744, 19745
A Manatee Morning, 5123(F)
Manatees, 19739, 19747, 19750
Manatees and Dugongs, 19735
Mandela, 13828
The Manhattan Project, 21406
Maniac Magee, 8823(F)
Maniac Monkeys on Magnolia Street, 8313(F)
Manners, 2994
The Mansion in the Mist, 7605(F)
Manu and the Talking Fish, 10786
Manuela's Gift, 5684(F)
The Manx, 19929
The Many Faces of the Face, 13874
Many Luscious Lollipops, 14032
Many Moons (Illus. by Marc Simont), 10511(F)
(Illus. by Marc Simont), 10511(F)
Many Stars and More String Games, 22008
The Many Troubles of Andy Russell, 8554(F)

Maple Moon, 11225(F)
Maples in the Mist, 11650
Mapped Out! 14361
Mapping Our World, 14364
Mapping Penny's World, 5299(F)
Mapping the Seas and Airways, 14365
Mapping the World, 14368
Maps, 14371
Maps and Globes, 14369
Maps in Everyday Life, 14366
Marbles, 21986, 22034
Marc Andreessen, 13225
Marc Chagall, 12207, 12208, 12209
The March on Washington, 16522
Marching to Freedom, 12749
Marco Polo, 12148
Mardi Gras, 17369, 17386
Marduk the Mighty and Other Stories of Creation, 10582
Margaret Bourke-White, 12192, 12193
Margaret Mead, 13320, 13321
Margo's House, 7763(F)
Marguerite Makes a Book, 9068(F)
Maria de Sautuola, 13848
Maria Molina and the Days of the Dead, 4719(F)
Maria Montessori, 13836
Mariah Carey, 12365
Mariah Delany's Author-of-the-Month Club, 9867(F)
Mariah Keeps Cool, 8535(F)
Marian Anderson, 12346
Marian Wright Edelman, 13150, 13151
Mariana and the Merchild, 11442
Marianthe's Story, 4573(F)
Maria's Comet, 4685(F)
Marie, 9041(F)
Marie Antoinette, 9056(F)
Marie Curie, 13260, 13261, 13262, 13263
Marie Curie and Her Daughter Irene, 13219
Marie in Fourth Position, 9058(F)
Mariel of Redwall, 7823(F)
Marigold and Grandma on the Town, 6248(F)
Marijuana Drug Dangers, 17890
Marine Biologist, 17826
Marine Mammal Preservation, 19418
Mario Lemieux, 13697
Marion Jones, 13659
Marisol and Magdalena, 8413(F)
Maritime Disasters, 21363
Marjory Stoneman Douglas, 13266
Mark McGwire, 13467, 13468
Mark Messier, 13700
Mark T-W-A-I-N! 12607
Mark Twain, 12610, 12611
Mark Twain and Huckleberry Finn, 12612
Mark Twain and the Queens of the Mississippi, 12608
Market Day, 3118(F), 4610(F)
The Market Lady and the Mango Tree, 4872(F)
The Market Wedding, 8637(F)
Markets, 16932
Marlfox, 7824(F)

Maroo of the Winter Caves, 8959(F)
Marrying Malcolm Murgatroyd, 8281(F)
Mars, 18460, 18476, 18480, 18491, 18497
Marsh Music, 1805(F)
Marsha Is Only a Flower, 6218(F)
Marshes and Swamps, 20372
Marshmallow Kisses, 3042(F)
Martha and Skits, 2491(F)
Martha Blah Blah, 1408(F)
Martha Calling, 2492(F)
Martha Dandridge Curtis Washington, 13199
Martha Graham, 12390, 12391, 12392
Martha Speaks, 2493(F)
Martha Walks the Dog, 2494(F)
Martha Washington, 13198
Martial Arts, 22267, 22269
Martian Fossils on Earth? The Story of Meteorite ALH 84001, 18382
Martian Rock, 1572(F)
Martin Luther King, 12740
Martin Luther King Day, 12746
Martin Luther King, Jr., 12741, 12745, 12747, 12751, 12753, 12754
Martin Luther King, Jr., and the March on Washington, 16518
Martin Luther King, Jr. and the March Toward Freedom, 12742
Martin Luther King Jr. Day, 17337
Martin Luther King, Jr. Day, 17387
Martin the Warrior, 7825(F)
Martin Van Buren, 13111, 13112
Martina Hingis, 13649
The Marvelous Land of Oz, 7595(F)
Marvelous Marvin and the Pioneer Ghost, 8028(F)
Marvelous Marvin and the Wolfman Mystery, 7014(F)
Marvelous Math, 11602
Marvelous Multiplication, 20586
The Marvelous Toy, 3834(F)
Marven of the Great North Woods, 2951(F)
Marvin and the Mean Words, 8728(F)
Marvin and the Meanest Girl, 10090(F)
Marvin Redpost, 6620(F), 7297(F), 8807(F), 9982(F), 10125(F)
Marvin's Best Christmas Present Ever, 5896(F)
Mary, 17259
Mary and the Mystery Dog, 7211(F)
Mary Anning, 13231
Mary Anning and the Sea Dragon, 13228
Mary Cassatt, 12199, 12200, 12201, 12202
Mary Church Terrell, 12786
Mary Geddy's Day, 9217(F)
Mary Had a Little Lamb (Illus. by Salley Mavor), 845
(Illus. by Iza Trapani), 896(F)
Mary Joe Fernandez, 13647
Mary Louise Loses Her Manners, 1090(F)

Mary McLean and the St. Patrick's Day Parade, 5632(F)
Mary McLeod Bethune, 12701, 12703, 12704
Mary Margaret's Tree, 1135(F)
Mary Marony and the Chocolate Surprise, 8729(F)
Mary Moon Is Missing, 6860(F)
Mary of Mile 18, 8563(F)
Mary on Horseback, 12860
Mary Patten's Voyage, 9261(F)
Mary Todd Lincoln, 13167
Mary Veronica's Egg, 5355(F)
Maryland, 16836, 16844, 16868, 16879
The Maryland Colony, 16120
Mary's Story, 17251
The Marzipan Moon, 8206(F)
Masada, 8938(F), 14596
Masai and I, 8967(F)
The Mash and Smash Cookbook, 21680
Masha and the Firebird, 7791(F)
Masks, 7786(F), 21601, 21602
Masks! 21603
Masks Tell Stories, 14550
Massachusetts, 16678, 16709, 16715
Master Man, 10714
Master of Mahogany, 12220
The Master Puppeteer, 9006(F)
Master Weaver from Ghana, 15010
The Matchlock Gun, 9193(F)
Materials, 20813
The Math Book for Girls and Other Beings Who Count, 20601
Math Curse, 5535(F)
Math for Smarty Pants, 20613
Math Fun, 20624
Math Fun with a Pocket Calculator, 20624
Math Fun with Money Puzzlers, 20625
Math Fun with Tricky Lines and Shapes, 20625
Math Games for Middle School, 20620
Math Rashes and Other Classroom Tales, 9840(F)
Math Riddles, 21860(F)
Math Tricks, Puzzles and Games, 20611
Mathamusements, 20612
Mathematician and Computer Scientist, Caryn Navy, 13332
Mathew Brady, 12859
Matilda, 10045(F)
Matilda Bone, 9090(F)
Matilda the Moocher, 3981(F)
Matisse from A to Z, 13927
The Mats, 4578(F)
Matt Damon, 12373
Matter, 20802
A Matter of Time, 8097(F)
Matthew and Tilly, 4013(F)
Matthew Henson and the North Pole Expedition, 12121
Matthew's Dragon, 652(F)
Matthew's Dream, 2384(F)
Matthew's Meadow, 7615(F)
Mattimeo, 7826(F)
Matzah Ball, 6105(F)

Matzah Ball Soup, 6110(F)
The Matzah That Papa Brought Home, 6094(F)
Matzo Ball Moon, 6103(F)
Maudie in the Middle, 7489(F)
Maurice Sendak's Really Rosie, 1557(F)
Maurice Strong, 13348
Maurice's Room, 7434(F)
Max, 1203(F)
  (Illus. by Rachel Isadora), 4189(F)
  (Illus. by Ken Wilson-Max), 2864(F)
Max and Me and the Time Machine, 7760(F)
Max and Me and the Wild West, 10190(F)
Max Cleans Up, 2834(F)
Max Found Two Sticks, 3362(F)
Max Loves Sunflowers, 4562(F)
Max Malone and the Great Cereal Rip-Off, 8299(F)
Max Malone Makes a Million, 8299(F)
Max, the Stubborn Little Wolf, 2269(F)
Maxfield Parrish, 13956
Maxi, the Hero, 1791(F)
Max's Bath, 2835(F)
Max's Bedtime, 809(F)
Max's Ride, 2835(F)
Max's Starry Night, 1691(F)
Max's Toys, 2835(F)
May I Bring a Friend? 4130(F)
May We Sleep Here Tonight? 2307(F)
The Maya, 15666, 15674
Maya Angelou, 12494, 12495, 12497, 12498
Maya Angelou Greeting the Morning, 12496
The Maya Indians, 15683
Maya Lin, 12255, 12256
Maya, Tiger Cub, 5375(F)
The Mayas, 15680
Maya's Children, 11393
The Maybe Garden, 3060(F)
Maybe My Baby, 3346(F)
Mayfield Crossing, 7362(F)
  (Illus. by Leonard Jenkins), 7363(F)
The Mayflower People, 16132
May'naise Sandwiches and Sunshine Tea, 3979(F)
The Mayo Brothers, 13319
Mbundu, 14942
Me and Einstein, 8880(F)
Me and Mr. Mah, 5082(F)
Me and Mr. Stenner, 8460(F)
Me and My Amazing Body, 18081
Me and My Bear, 3325(F)
Me and My Cat? 1313(F)
Me and My Family Tree, 3910
Me and My Little Brain, 9843(F)
Me and My Place in Space, 18420
Me and Rupert Goody, 8353(F)
Me and the End of the World, 8612(F)
Me and You, 3913(F)
Me Counting Time, 20654
Me, Dad, and Number 6, 5576(F)

Me First, 2360(F)
Me, Mop, and the Moondance Kid, 10354(F)
Me, My Sister, and I, 8803(F)
Me on the Map, 14372
Me Tarzan, 9794(F)
Me, Too, 3953(F)
Me Too! 1748(F)
Mealtime for Zoo Animals, 18795
Mealworms, 19535
Mean Margaret, 8079(F)
Mean, Mean Maureen Green, 8616(F)
Mean Soup, 4146(F)
The Meanest Thing to Say, 8272(F)
Meanwhile, Back at the Ranch, 4251(F)
Measurements, 14356
Measuring, 354
  (Illus. by Sami Sweeten), 20656
Measuring Penny, 20582
Measuring Sizes, 20581
Measuring Up! 20618
Measuring Weight and Time, 20658
Meat-Eating Plants, 20222
Media Wizards, 14084
Medical Ethics, 18027
Medical Technology, 13218
Medicine, 18025
A Medieval Castle, 14777
Medieval Castle, 14788
Medieval Cathedral, 14778
A Medieval Feast, 14752
Medieval Knights, 14783
Medieval Life, 14775
Medieval Tales That Kids Can Read and Tell, 10544
The Medieval World, 14758
Mediopollito/Half-a-Chick, 11424
The Mediterranean, 14597
The Mediterranean Sea, 19825, 19842
Meet Danitra Brown, 11759
Meet Dinah Dinosaur, 6378(F)
Meet Josefina, 9447(F)
Meet Kirsten, 9438(F)
Meet Kit, 9632(F)
Meet Maya Angelou, 12499
Meet Me at the Fair, 14265
Meet Molly, 9691(F)
Meet My Grandmother, 12877, 12939, 17833
Meet My Staff, 4231(F)
Meet Rory Hohenstein, a Professional Dancer, 17772
Meet Samantha, 9511(F)
Meet the Arthropods, 19604
Meet the Austins, 7466(F)
Meet the Drakes on the Kentucky Frontier, 16341
Meet the Friends, 9637(F)
Meet the Marching Smithereens, 14223
Meet the Molesons, 1841(F)
Meet the Monsters, 21964
Meet the Orchestra, 14224
Meet the Wards on the Oregon Trail, 16342
Meet the Wild Southwest, 16916
Meet Thomas Jefferson, 13047
Meet Tricky Coyote! 11276

Meeting Death, 17858
Meeting Dolphins, 19682
A Meeting of the Minds, 10215(F)
Meeting Trees, 4534(F)
Meg Mackintosh and the Case of the Curious Whale Watch, 6931(F)
Meg Mackintosh and the Mystery at the Medieval Castle, 6931(F)
Meg Mackintosh and the Mystery at the Soccer Match, 6932(F)
Meg Mackintosh and the Mystery in the Locked Library, 6933(F)
Megan in Ancient Greece, 9054(F)
Megan's Island, 7029(F)
Meg's Wish, 4037(F)
Mei Fuh, 9014(F)
Mei-Mei Loves the Morning, 5438(F)
An Mei's Strange and Wondrous Journey, 3812(F)
The Mejii Restoration and the Rise of Modern Japan, 14579
Melanie, 1042(F)
Melisande, 10468(F)
Melissa Joan Hart, 12396
Mel's Diner, 3336(F)
Members of the C.L.U.B, 8257(F)
The Memoirs of Andrew Sherburne, 12962
Memorial Day, 17338
Memories of Anne Frank, 13799
The Memory Coat, 4891(F)
A Memory for Tino, 8264(F)
The Memory Horse, 3192(F)
Memory Jug, 8483(F)
The Memory String, 3556(F)
Men of Iron, 9119(F)
Men of Stone, 8652(F)
Mending Peter's Heart, 7326(F)
The Mennyms, 8189(F)
Mennyms Alive, 8190(F)
Mennyms Alone, 8191(F)
Mennyms in the Wilderness, 8192(F)
The Menominee, 15949
The Menorah Story, 17481
Menorahs, Mezuzas, and Other Jewish Symbols, 17455
Mental Illness, 17981
Mental Math Challenges, 20617
Mental Math Workout, 20584
Meow! 1749(F)
Meow Monday, 2635(F)
Mercury, 18461, 18498
Mercury and Venus, 18476
Mercy Hospital, 6787(F)
Meredith, 1329(F)
Meredith's Mixed-up Magic, 1330(F)
Merina, 14978
Merle the High Flying Squirrel, 2570(F)
Merlin, 8238(F)
Merlin's Kin, 10615
Merlin's Mistake, 7988(F)
The Mermaid and Other Sea Poems, 11988
The Mermaid of Cafur, 7732(F)
The Mermaid Summer, 7804(F)
Mermaid Tales from Around the World, 10597
The Mermaids' Lullaby, 783(F)
The Mermaid's Purse, 11961

The Mermaid's Twin Sister, 11426
The Merry Adventures of Robin Hood, 11023
Merry Christmas, Amelia Bedelia, 5895(F)
Merry Christmas, Davy! 5953(F)
Merry Christmas, Geraldine, 5856(F)
Merry Christmas, Old Armadillo, 5762(F)
Merry Christmas, Strega Nona, 5802(F)
Merry-Go-Round, 14033
Merry Things to Make, 21420
Mesa Verde, 16040
Mesopotamia and the Fertile Crescent, 14642
A Message for General Washington, 9249(F)
A Message from the Match Girl, 6950(F)
Messages in the Mailbox, 14097
Messenger, Messenger, 3061(F)
Messengers to the Brain, 18147
Messy Bessey's Family Reunion, 6493(F)
Messy Bessey's Holidays, 6494(F)
Metals, 21258
Metamorphosis, 18663
Meteors, 18503
Methamphetamine, 17889
Metropolitan Cow, 2063(F)
The Mexican-American Experience, 17580
The Mexican Americans, 17549
Mexican Independence Day and Cinco de Mayo, 15633
Mexico, 15198, 15602, 15604, 15614, 15616, 15618, 15621, 15622, 15624, 15625, 15626, 15627, 15643, 15644, 15650
Mexico! 15638
Mexico and Central America, 15615
Mexico City, 15651
Mexico in Pictures, 15637
Mia Hamm, 13689, 13690, 13691
Mia the Beach Cat, 6365(F)
Miami, 16848
The Miami Dolphins Football Team, 22180
Mice Are Nice, 6341(F)
Mice at Bat, 6552(F)
Mice Make Trouble, 1003(F)
Mice of the Westing Wind, 6303(F)
Mice Squeak, We Speak, 5410(F)
Mice Twice, 2402(F)
Michael, 4093(F)
Michael and the Cats, 5112(F)
Michael Andretti at Indianapolis, 22078
Michael Bird Boy, 2027(F)
Michael Dorris, 12531
Michael Eisner, 12875
Michael Foreman's Christmas Treasury, 17416
Michael Foreman's Mother Goose, 843
Michael Hague's Family Christmas Treasury, 9727
Michael Hague's Family Easter Treasury, 17438

Michael Hague's Magical World of Unicorns, 7773(F)
Michael Jackson, 12408
Michael Jordan, 13536, 13538, 13539, 13540
Michael Rosen's ABC, 120(F)
Michael, Wait for Me, 8587(F)
Michelangelo, 12260, 12261
   (Illus. by Susan Hellard), 12259
Michelangelo Buonarroti, 12262
Michelangelo's Surprise, 4792(F)
Michelle Kwan, 13593
Michigan, 16551, 16560, 16583
Mickey's Class Play, 5484(F)
Micromonsters, 18648
Microscope, 19813
The Microscope Book, 19807
Midas Mouse, 2069(F)
The Midas Touch, 11491
The Middle Ages, 14770, 14773, 14779, 14781, 14792
The Middle East in Search of Peace, 15491
Midnight Babies, 1680(F)
Midnight Dance of the Snowshoe Hare, 11945
Midnight Farm, 1579(F)
The Midnight Fox, 7169(F)
The Midnight Horse, 7726(F)
Midnight in the Cemetery, 48(F)
Midnight in the Mountains, 4482(F)
Midnight Magic, 9026(F)
   (Illus. by Judy Clifford), 1202(F)
The Midnight Man, 660(F)
Midnight Pillow Fight, 757(F)
Midnight Rescue, 9296(F)
The Midnight Ride of Paul Revere, 11642
Midnight Rider, 7295(F)
The Midnight Train Home, 9442(F)
The Midsummer Bride, 1473(F)
A Midsummer Night's Faery Tale, 7735(F)
Mieko and the Fifth Treasure, 8989(F)
A Mien Family, 15159
The Mightiest Heart, 10966
Mighty Boy, 8818(F)
Mighty Dinosaurs, 14384, 14472
The Mighty Midwest Flood, 20685
Mighty Mountain and the Three Strong Women, 10815
The Mighty Santa Fe, 3704(F)
The Mighty Skink, 8091(F)
Mighty Tree, 4437
A Migrant Family, 17132
Migrant Worker, 17143
Miguel de Cervantes, 12517
Mijikenda, 14955
Mik-Shrok, 7020(F)
Mike Mulligan and His Steam Shovel, 5551(F)
Mike's Kite, 503(F)
Miles of Smiles, 11882
Milk, 20110, 20122
Milk and Cookies, 1759(F)
Milk and Honey, 17490
Milk and Yogurt, 20105
The Milk Makers, 20094
Milking Machines, 20071
The Milkman's Boy, 9548(F)

Mill, 16261
Millard Fillmore, 13033
Millennium Falcon, 10247(F)
Millennium Prophecies, 21919
The Million-Dollar Bear, 2950(F)
Millions of Cats, 5216(F)
Millions of Miles to Mars, 18475
Millions of Snowflakes, 3427(F)
Millipedeology, 19618
The Milly Stories, 7918(F)
Milly's Wedding, 2741(F)
Milo and the Magical Stones, 2576(F)
Milo and the Mysterious Island, 2577(F)
Miloli's Orchids, 2944(F)
Milton, 1746(F)
Milton the Early Riser, 2319(F)
Mimi and Jean-Paul's Cajun Mardi Gras, 5639(F)
Mimi and the Dream House, 2800(F)
Mimi and the Picnic, 2801(F)
Mimi's Christmas, 3467(F)
Mimmy and Sophie, 4623(F)
Mina and the Bear, 1280(F)
Minas and the Fish, 1459(F)
Mina's Spring of Colors, 8435(F)
Mind-Blowing Mammals, 18620
Mind Me Good Now! 11420
The Mind Reader, 8813(F)
Mind Your Manners, Ben Bunny, 17639
Mine! 5020(F)
Mine, All Mine, 14034
"Mine Will," Said John, 5235(F)
Minerals, 20556
Minerva Louise at School, 2735(F)
Minerva Louise at the Fair, 2736(F)
Mines and Minie Balls, 16392
Mine's the Best, 6212(F)
Ming Lo Moves the Mountain, 4215(F)
The Miniature Horse, 20000
Miniature Vehicles, 21674
Mining, 21030
A Mink, a Fink, a Skating Rink, 14026
Minn of the Mississippi, 18784
Minnesota, 16561, 16575, 16581, 16585
Minnie, 8069(F)
Minnie and Moo and the Musk of Zorro, 6261(F)
Minnie and Moo and the Thanksgiving Tree, 6139(F)
Minnie and Moo Go Dancing, 6262(F)
Minnie and Moo Go to Paris, 6263(F)
Minnie and Moo Go to the Moon, 6264(F)
Minnie and Moo Save the Earth, 6263(F)
Minorities, 17581
The Minotaur of Knossos, 7561(F)
Minou, 1809(F)
The Minpins, 1095(F)
The Minstrel in the Tower, 9071(F)
The Miracle of Saint Nicholas, 1675(F)
Miracle on 34th Street, 9715(F)

The Miracles of Jesus, 17260
Miracles on Maple Hill, 7518(F)
Miranda Goes to Hollywood, 9569(F)
Miranda's Last Stand, 9454(F)
Mirette and Bellini Cross Niagara Falls, 4753(F)
Mirette on the High Wire, 4754(F)
Miriam, 8963(F)
Miriam's Cup, 17478
Miró, 13877
Mirror, 1099(F)
Mirrors, 20878
Mischief, Mad Mary, and Me, 7248(F)
The Miser on the Mountain, 11265
The Miserable Mill, 7068(F)
Mishmash, 7177(F)
Mishmash and the Robot, 7177(F)
Mishmash and the Sauerkraut Mystery, 7177(F)
Miss Alaineus, 8648(F)
Miss Best's Etiquette for Young People, 17634
Miss Bindergarten Celebrates the 100th Day of Kindergarten, 248(F)
Miss Bindergarten Stays Home from Kindergarten, 5541(F)
Miss Hickory, 7576(F)
Miss Hildy's Missing Cape Caper, 6001(F)
Miss Mabel's Table, 401(F)
Miss Malarkey Doesn't Live in Room 10, 5497(F)
Miss Malarkey Won't Be In Today, 5498(F)
Miss Mary Mack, 1245(F), 11350
The Miss Meow Pageant, 1290(F)
Miss Mouse's Day, 1447(F)
Miss Myrtle Frag, the Grammar Nag, 14023
Miss Nelson Has a Field Day, 5466(F)
Miss Nelson Is Back, 5467(F)
Miss Nelson Is Missing! 5467(F)
Miss Opal's Auction, 4053(F)
Miss Penny and Mr. Grubbs, 4142(F)
Miss Spider's ABC, 74(F)
Miss Spider's New Car, 2296(F)
Miss Spider's Tea Party, 2297(F)
Miss Spider's Wedding, 2298(F)
Miss Tizzy, 3998(F)
Miss Viola and Uncle Ed Lee, 4136(F)
Miss Violet's Shining Day, 2894(F)
Missing, 4931(F)
Missing! 1333(F)
Missing Girls, 8490(F)
Missing in the Mountains, 6841(F)
Missing May, 8806(F)
The Missing Mitten Mystery, 1293(F)
Missing Mittens, 529
Missing Molly, 4009(F)
The Missing Sunflowers, 5423(F)
The Missing Tooth, 6278(F)
Mission, 20982
Mission Addition, 20583
A Mission for the People, 16778
Mission Ziffoid, 1522(F)
Missions of the Central Coast, 16763

Missions of the Inland Valleys, 16766
Missions of the Los Angeles Area, 16799
Missions of the Monterey Bay Area, 16758
Missions of the San Francisco Bay Area, 16824
Missions of the Southern Coast, 16795
Mississippi, 15904, 16880
The Mississippi, 16574
Mississippi Facts and Symbols, 16859
The Mississippi Flood of 1993, 16531
Mississippi Going North, 4382(F)
Mississippi Mud, 11726
Mississippi River, 15891
Missouri, 16552, 16562, 16568
Mist over the Mountains, 16833
Mistakes That Worked, 21038
Mister and Me, 8458(F)
Misty of Chincoteague, 7217(F)
Mitch and Amy, 10035(F)
The Mitten, 10854
  (Illus. by Yaroslava Mills), 10864
The Mitten Tree, 3071(F)
The Mixed-Up Chameleon, 1924(F)
The Mixed-Up Zoo of Professor Yahoo, 4144
Miz Berlin Walks, 4066(F)
Miz Fannie Mae's Fine New Easter Hat, 1413(F)
Moby Dick, 9304(F)
Mockingbird, 616
Model Railroading, 21668
The Model T Ford, 21320
Models, 21793
The Modern Ark, 19392
Modern Olympic Games, 22254
The Modern World, 14574
Mohandas Gandhi, 13801, 13803
The Mohawk, 15946
Moishe's Miracle, 6096(F)
Mojave, 11983
Mola, 13945
Molasses Man, 3803(F)
Moldova, 15425, 15433
Mole and Shrew, 5629(F)
Mole Music, 2459(F)
The Mole Sisters and the Busy Bees, 2669(F)
The Mole Sisters and the Piece of Moss, 1551(F)
The Mole Sisters and the Rainy Day, 1551(F)
The Mole Sisters and the Wavy Wheat, 2669(F)
Molecules, 20906
Moles Can Dance, 2059(F)
Mole's Hill, 2065(F)
Molly and Emmett's Camping Adventure, 1217(F)
Molly Bannaky, 12848
Molly Brown, 12863
Molly in the Middle, 6538(F)
Molly Learns a Lesson, 9691(F)
Molly Limbo, 1247(F)
Molly Maguire, 10365(F)
Molly Saves the Day, 9691(F)

Molly the Brave and Me, 6548(F)
Molly's Cook Book, 21721
Molly's Craft Book, 21524
Molly's Fire, 9648(F)
Molly's in a Mess, 9900(F)
Molly's Pilgrim, 3582(F)
Molly's Rosebush, 4932(F)
Molly's Store, 6689(F)
Molly's Surprise, 9691(F)
Mom and Me, 3744, 5209(F)
Mom Pie, 3737(F)
Mom, the Wolfman and Me, 7464(F)
Mom, There's a Pig in My Bed!
7249(F)
Momma, Where Are You From?
4602(F)
Mommies Don't Get Sick, 4172(F)
The Mommy Book, 3819
Mommy, Buy Me a China Doll,
3967(F)
The Mommy Exchange, 3694(F)
Mommy Far, Mommy Near, 5047(F)
Mommy Go Away! 1278(F)
Mommy Laid an Egg! 18237
Mommy Poems, 11655
Mommy's in the Hospital Having a
Baby, 18043
Mommy's Office, 3198(F)
Monarch Butterflies, 19559, 19560
Monarch Butterfly, 19550
A Monarch Butterfly's Life, 19557
Monarch Magic! 19567
Monarchs, 19558
Monday's Troll, 11676
Monerans and Protists, 19811
Monet, 12267
Money, 16920, 16924, 16931
Money, Money, Money, 16927
The Money Tree, 1596(F)
Mongolia, 15149, 15192, 15196
Monica Seles, 13653
Monika Beisner's Book of Riddles,
21813
Monk Camps Out, 2414(F)
The Monkey and the Crocodile,
10792
The Monkey and the Mango, 4423(F)
The Monkey Bridge, 10802
Monkey Business, 6505(F)
Monkey Do! 1728(F)
Monkey Island, 8643(F)
Monkey King, 1716(F)
Monkey-Monkey's Trick, 6492(F)
Monkey See, Monkey Do, 5266(F)
Monkey Sunday, 4837(F)
Monkey Tag, 8653(F)
The Monkey Thief, 6886(F)
Monkey Tricks, 1767(F)
Monkey Trouble, 6505(F)
(Illus. by John A. Rowe), 2639(F)
Monkeys and Apes, 18993
Monkeys and Apes of the World,
18994
The Monkey's Haircut, 11395
Monkeys of Asia and Africa, 19008
Monkeys of Central and South Amer-
ica, 19008
Monster Brother, 963(F)
Monster Bugs, 19478
Monster Cake, 5680(F)
A Monster in the House, 1314(F)

The Monster in the Shadows,
10008(F)
The Monster in the Third Dresser
Drawer and Other Stories About
Adam Joshua, 7516(F)
Monster Machines, 21295
Monster Mama, 1525(F)
Monster Manners, 1511(F)
Monster Manual, 21891
Monster Math, 517(F)
Monster Math Picnic, 500(F)
Monster Math School Time, 209(F)
Monster Money, 501(F)
The Monster Money Book, 2352(F)
Monster Motel, 1161(F)
Monster Musical Chairs, 530(F)
Monster Soup and Other Spooky
Poems, 1155
Monster Stew, 1418(F)
Monster Train, 1499(F)
Monster Trucks, 21317
Monster Vision, 7905(F)
Monsters, 18937
Monsters and My One True Love,
8039(F)
Monster's Birthday Hiccups, 5714(F)
Monsters in Cyberspace, 10226(F)
Monsters in the Attic, 8040(F)
The Monsters of Marble Avenue,
9862(F)
The Monster's Ring, 7678(F)
The Monsters' Test, 6005(F)
Montana, 16608, 16614, 16619,
16623
Montezuma and the Fall of the
Aztecs, 11404
Montezuma's Revenge, 1807(F)
Montgomery, 16524
The Month-Brothers, 11103
Month by Month a Year Goes
Round, 245(F)
Monticello, 16882, 16884
(Illus. by Leonard Everett Fisher),
16849
Montreal, 15593
The Montreal Canadiens Hockey
Team, 22210
Monumental Mazes, 21863
Monuments Help Us Remember,
21127
Moo in the Morning, 3306(F)
Moo Moo, Brown Cow, 613(F)
The Moon, 18440, 18443, 18448,
18450, 18453
(Illus. by Bill Slavin), 18441
The Moon and I, 12514
The Moon and Riddles Diner and the
Sunnyside Cafe, 11927
The Moon and You, 18449
Moon Ball, 1710(F)
Moon Base, 20974
The Moon Book, 18446
Moon Festival, 9759(F)
A Moon for Seasons, 11986
Moon Frog, 11777
Moon in Bear's Eyes, 19070
A Moon in My Teacup, 5911(F)
A Moon in Your Lunch Box, 784
Moon Jump, 390(F)
The Moon Jumpers, 1632(F)
The Moon Lady, 9017(F)

Moon Magic, 10722
Moon over Tennessee, 9470(F)
The Moon Princess, 10823
Moon Rope, 11438
Moon Sandwich Mom, 2246(F)
Moon Song, 11211
Moon Soup, 1118(F)
Moon Tales, 10619
Moon to Sun, 573(F)
Moon Window, 7690(F)
Moonbear's Dream, 1760(F)
Moonbear's Pet, 1761(F)
Moonboy, 6339(F)
Mooncake, 1758(F)
Moondance, 1762(F)
Moondogs, 1310(F)
Moongame, 1758(F)
The Moonglow Roll-o-Rama,
2585(F)
Moonlight and Mill Whistles,
9633(F)
Moonlight Madness, 7718(F)
The Moonlight Man, 8227(F)
Moonlight Through the Pines, 11354
Moonride, 820(F)
Moons and Rings, 18506
The Moon's Choice, 1598(F)
Moonshine, 9521(F)
Moonstruck, 4110(F)
Moontellers, 7968(F)
The Moorchild, 7938(F)
Moose, 19155
Moose and Friends, 2347(F)
Moose Racks, Bear Tracks, and
Other Alaska Kidsnacks, 21681
Moose Tales, 6702(F)
Moose Tracks, 6788(F)
Mooses Come Walking, 5240(F)
Moosetache, 2558(F)
Moosletoe, 5894(F)
Moozie's Kind Adventure, 2511(F)
Mop to the Rescue, 1545(F)
Mop Top, 4150(F)
Mop's Backyard Concert, 1546(F)
Mop's Treasure Hunt, 1546(F)
Moray Eels, 19645
Mordant's Wish, 1973(F)
More! 3343(F)
More About Dinosaurs, 14395
More About Paddington, 9785(F)
More Adventures of the Great Brain,
9843(F)
More Bugs in Boxes, 170(F)
More Bunny Trouble, 2858(F)
More Celtic Fairy Tales, 11003
More Christmas Ornaments Kids Can
Make, 21493
More, Fewer, Less, 467
More Fifth Grade Magic, 7749(F)
More Milly-Molly-Mandy, 3043(F)
More Minds, 7954(F)
"More More More," Said the Baby,
4354(F)
More Nature in Your Backyard,
18589
More or Less a Mess, 6429(F)
More Perfect Union, 12895
A More Perfect Union, 17060
More Ready-to-Tell Tales from
Around the World, 10565

More Scary Stories to Tell in the Dark, 11380
More Science Experiments You Can Eat, 18305
More Simple Signs, 14019
More Spice than Sugar, 11658
More Stories Huey Tells, 9799(F)
More Stories Julian Tells, 6251(F)
More Than a Horse, 7146(F)
More Than Anything Else, 4603(F)
More Than One, 575
Morgan's Zoo, 7798(F)
Morgy Makes His Move, 8746(F)
Moriah's Pond, 7372(F)
The Morning Chair, 3740(F)
Morning Glories, 20037
Morning Has Broken, 14239
Morning, Noon, and Night, 11725, 18626
Morning on the Lake, 4558(F)
Morocco, 14956
Morris and Boris at the Circus, 6721(F)
Morris Goes to School, 6721(F)
Morris's Disappearing Bag, 5951(F)
Mort the Sport, 2321(F)
Moscow, 15422
Moses, 17269
Moses and the Angels, 17322
Moses Goes to a Concert, 5035(F)
Moses Goes to School, 5036(F)
Moses in Egypt, 17293
Moses in the Bulrushes, 17242
    (Illus. by Warwick Hutton), 17287
    (Illus. by Diana Mayo), 17243
Moses Supposes His Toeses Are Roses, 882
Moses the Kitten, 5258(F)
Moshi Moshi, 4745(F)
Mosquito, 19424
Mossflower, 7827(F)
Mossi, 15036
The Most Amazing Dinosaur, 2728(F)
The Most Beautiful Kid in the World, 3617(F)
The Most Beautiful Roof in the World, 20462
The Most Excellent Book of Dress Up, 21537
The Most Excellent Book of Face Painting, 21584
The Most Excellent Book of How to Be a Cheerleader, 21670
The Most Excellent Book of How to Be a Clown, 21672
The Most Excellent Book of How to Be a Juggler, 21671
The Most Excellent Book of How to Be a Magician, 21782
The Most Excellent Book of How to Be a Puppeteer, 14305
The Most Excellent Book of How to Do Card Tricks, 22231
Mother and Baby Zoo Animals, 18866
Mother Earth, 4488(F)
Mother Earth, Father Sky, 11990, 15985
A Mother for Choco, 2276(F)
Mother Goose, 867, 868(F), 869

Mother Goose, 870(F)
The Mother Goose Cookbook, 21719
Mother Goose Math, 905(F)
Mother Goose Remembers, 824(F)
Mother Hubbard's Christmas, 5893(F)
Mother Jones, 13162
Mother Mother I Feel Sick Send for the Doctor Quick Quick Quick, 1050(F)
Mother Murphy, 9932(F)
Mother Teresa, 13852, 13853, 13854, 13855, 13857, 13858, 13859
Motherlove, 5296
Mothers Are Like That, 5162(F)
The Mother's Day Mice, 5613(F)
Moths and Butterflies, 19541
Motley the Cat, 1737(F)
Motor Bill and the Lovely Caroline, 2805(F)
Motorbikes, 22241
Mouldy Mummies, 14622
Mouldylocks, 5708(F)
Mounds of Earth and Shell, 16038
Mount Rushmore, 16545, 16580
Mount Vernon, 16840, 16883
Mountain Animals in Danger, 19420
Mountain Bike Mania, 10305(F)
Mountain Biking, 22153, 22154, 22159
Mountain Goats, 18977
Mountain Mammals, 20502
The Mountain Men, 12056
Mountain Men of the Frontier, 16380
A Mountain of Blintzes, 6074(F)
Mountain Town, 3162(F)
Mountain Valor, 9481(F)
Mountain Wedding (Illus. by Ted Rand), 4160(F)
    (Illus. by Ted Rand), 4161(F)
Mountains, 20496, 20498, 20499, 20504, 20506, 20507, 20508, 20509
Mountains and Volcanoes, 20505
The Mountains of Tibet, 4662(F)
Mountains to Climb, 8842(F)
The Mouse and the Motorcycle, 9804(F)
Mouse at Night, 2165(F)
The Mouse Bride, 1982(F)
A Mouse Called Wolf, 7866(F)
Mouse Cookies, 21726
Mouse Count, 602(F)
Mouse in Love, 2322(F)
Mouse in the House, 4080(F)
Mouse, Look Out! 2810(F)
Mouse Match, 10783
Mouse Mess, 2629(F)
The Mouse of Amherst, 8118(F)
The Mouse of the Westing Wind, 6303(F)
Mouse Paint, 2816(F)
Mouse Practice, 5022(F)
Mouse Soup, 6466(F)
Mouse Tales, 6467(F)
The Mouse That Snored, 2791(F)
Mouse TV, 2532(F)
Mouse View, 311(F)
The Mouse Who Owned the Sun, 2030(F)
The Mousehole Cat, 1786(F)

Mousekin's Close Call, 2500(F)
Mousekin's Fables, 2500(F)
Mousekin's Family, 2500(F)
The Mousery, 2594(F)
Mouse's First Christmas, 5937(F)
Mouse's First Halloween, 6055(F)
A Mouse's Tale, 2258(F)
Mousetracks, 21227
Mouton's Impossible Dream, 2431(F)
Movable Mother Goose, 887(F)
Movement, 18169
Movie Magic, 6285(F), 21277
Movies, 14312, 21274
The Movies (Inventions That Changed Our Lives), 14309
Movin', 11611
Moving Day, 2271(F)
Moving Mama to Town, 8549(F)
Mowing, 5242(F)
Moxie, 9618(F)
Mozart, 12334
Mozart Tonight, 12333
Mr. Ape, 9899(F)
Mr. Baseball, 6411(F)
Mr. Bass's Planetoid, 10157(F)
Mr. Beans, 6905(F)
Mr. Bear Says, Are You There, Baby Bear? 2126(F)
Mr. Bear Says Good Night, 2127(F)
Mr. Bear Says I Love You, 2127(F)
Mr. Bear Says Peek-a-Boo, 2127(F)
Mr. Bear to the Rescue, 2128(F)
Mr. Bear's New Baby, 2129(F)
Mr. Bear's Vacation, 2130(F)
Mr. Belinsky's Bagels, 4042(F)
Mr. Big Brother, 6412(F)
Mr. Blue Jeans, 12966
Mr. Carey's Garden, 5174(F)
Mr. Chips! 5297(F)
Mr. Duvall Reports the News, 17743
Mr. Emerson's Cook, 9623(F)
Mr. Fixit's Magnet Machine, 6626(F)
Mr. Green Peas, 5163(F)
Mr. Griggs' Work, 3407(F)
Mr. Gumpy's Motor Car, 2915(F)
Mr. Gumpy's Outing, 2915(F)
Mr. Knocky, 4068(F)
Mr. Lincoln's Drummer, 9507(F)
Mr. Lincoln's Whiskers, 4883(F)
Mr. Lunch Takes a Plane Ride, 2672(F)
Mr. McGratt and the Ornery Cat, 5255(F)
Mr. McMouse, 2385(F)
Mr. Mysterious and Company, 9851(F)
Mr. Nick's Knitting, 4060(F)
Mr. Pak Buys a Story, 10724
Mr. Pam Pam and the Hullabazoo, 1074(F)
Mr. Panda's Painting, 287(F)
Mr. Paul and Mr. Luecke Build Communities, 17787
Mr. Peale's Bones, 9332(F)
Mr. Persnickety and Cat Lady, 4194(F)
Mr. Popper's Penguins, 9772(F)
Mr. Putter and Tabby Bake the Cake, 5913(F)

Mr. Putter and Tabby Fly the Plane, 6609(F)
Mr. Putter and Tabby Paint the Porch, 9981(F)
Mr. Putter and Tabby Pick the Pears, 6610(F)
Mr. Putter and Tabby Pour the Tea, 6611(F)
Mr. Putter and Tabby Row the Boat, 6609(F)
Mr. Putter and Tabby Take the Train, 6612(F)
Mr. Putter and Tabby Toot the Horn, 6613(F)
Mr. Putter and Tabby Walk the Dog, 6611(F)
Mr. Rabbit and the Lovely Present, 2902(F)
Mr. Revere and I, 9914(F)
Mr. Santizo's Tasty Treats! 3138
Mr. Semolina-Semolinus, 11070
Mr. Sugar Came to Town/La Visita del Señor Azucar, 11400
Mr. Tanen's Ties, 5487(F)
Mr. Willowby's Christmas Tree, 5751(F)
Mr. Wizard's Experiments for Young Scientists, 18320
Mr. Wizard's Supermarket Science, 18321
Mr. Yee Fixes Cars, 3139
Mrs. Armitage and the Big Wave, 4088(F)
Mrs. Brice's Mice, 6405(F)
Mrs. Brown Went to Town, 2888(F)
Mrs. Cole on an Onion Roll and Other School Poems, 11549
Mrs. Fish, Ape and Me, the Dump Queen, 8341(F)
Mrs. Fitz's Flamingos, 1366(F)
Mrs. Frisby and the Rats of NIMH, 7999(F)
Mrs. Hen's Big Surprise, 2031(F)
Mrs. Katz and Tush, 4034(F)
Mrs. Mack, 5367(F)
Mrs. McNosh and the Great Big Squash, 1671(F)
Mrs. McNosh Hangs Up Her Wash, 4348(F)
Mrs. Meyer the Bird, 5195(F)
Mrs. Morgan's Lawn, 5067(F)
Mrs. Peachtree's Bicycle, 4316(F)
Mrs. Piccolo's Easy Chair, 1265(F)
Mrs. Piggle-Wiggle, 7934(F)
Mrs. Piggle-Wiggle's Farm, 7934(F)
Mrs. Piggle-Wiggle's Magic, 7934(F)
Mrs. Pirate, 4315(F)
Mrs. Rose's Garden, 1208(F)
Mrs. Sato's Hens, 516(F)
Mrs. Scott's Beautiful Art, 17773
Mrs. Toggle's Beautiful Blue Shoe, 4278(F)
Mrs. Toggle's Zipper, 4279(F)
Ms. Davison, Our Librarian, 3140
Ms. MacDonald Has a Class, 5523(F)
Ms. Moja Makes Beautiful Clothes, 17743
Ms. Murphy Fights Fires, 17808
Much Ado About Aldo, 9891(F)
Mucky Moose, 1736(F)

Mucky Pup, 1869(F)
Mucky Pup's Christmas, 5763(F)
Mud, 4514(F)
Mud! 6661(F)
Mud Flat April Fool, 6685(F)
The Mud Flat Mystery, 8129(F)
Mud Flat Spring, 2729(F)
Mud Matters, 20303
The Mud Pony, 11223
Mud Puddle, 1425(F)
Mud Racing, 22082
Muddy Four Paws, 7317(F)
Mufaro's Beautiful Daughters, 10715
The Muffin Child, 9062(F)
Muggie Maggie, 6267(F)
Muhammad Ali, 13582
The Mulberry Bird, 1867(F)
Multicultural Plays for Children Grades 4–6, 12021
Multicultural Plays for Children Grades K–3, 12021
Multimedia and New Media Developer, 17790
Multiple Births, 18241
Multiple Choice, 8829(F)
Multiple Sclerosis, 18008
Multiplication (Illus. by Richard Maccabe), 20596
  (Illus. by Sami Sweeten), 400(F)
Mumbo Jumbo, 14042
Mummies, 14533, 14628
  (Illus. by Susan Swan), 14647
  (Illus. by Joe Weissmann), 14548
Mummies and Their Mysteries, 17230
Mummies, Bones, and Body Parts, 14517
Mummies in the Morning, 1448(F)
Mummies Made in Egypt, 14603
Mummies of the Pharaohs, 14609
Mummies, Tombs, and Treasure, 14659
The Mummy, 8046(F)
Mummy Mysteries, 14501
The Mummy, the Will, and the Crypt, 7603(F)
Munschworks, 4242(F)
Munschworks 2, 4243(F)
Munschworks 3, 4245
The Muppets Big Book of Crafts, 21457
Murals, 13884
A Murder for Her Majesty, 6893(F)
Murder on the Canadian, 7127(F)
Murphy and Kate, 7223(F)
Muscles, 18176
Muscles and Bones, 18172
The Muscular System, 18173
Museum Colors, 13929
Museum Numbers, 13929
Museum Shapes, 13929
Mush! 2970
Mush, a Dog from Space, 10223(F)
The Mushroom Hunt, 20187
Mushroom in the Rain, 2742(F)
Mushrooms, 20188
Mushy! 17508
Music, 14135, 14137
  (Illus. by Svjetlan Junakovic), 1570(F)
Music and Drum, 11681

Music for the Tsar of the Sea, 11100
Music from the Sky, 3649(F)
The Music in Derrick's Heart, 3519(F)
Music in the Family, 3571(F)
Music, Music for Everyone, 3948(F)
Music over Manhattan, 4994(F)
Musical Instruments, 14230
The Musicians of Bremen, 10939
Musicians of the Sun, 11408
Muslim Mosque, 17236
Mustang, 21305
The Mustang, 20015
Mustang Flats, 9508(F)
Mustang, Wild Spirit of the West, 7218(F)
Mute Swans, 19269
My "a" Sound Box, 103(F)
My Amazon River Day, 15773
My America, 11603
My Angelica, 8384(F)
My Apple, 20140
My Apron, 3566(F)
My Arctic 1, 2, 3, 488(F)
My Aunt Came Back, 836(F)
My Baby, 4887(F)
My Baby Brother Has Ten Tiny Toes, 494(F)
My Babysitter Is a Vampire, 9877(F)
My Backpack, 4098(F)
My Backyard Garden, 21764
My Backyard History Book, 14573
My Ballet Book, 14279
My Baseball Book, 22093
My Basketball Book, 22131
My Bear and Me, 3307(F)
My Best Friends, 3324(F)
My Big Alphabet Book, 105(F)
My Big Book of Everything, 4512
My Big Boy Potty Book, 3076(F)
My Big Counting Book, 533(F)
My Big Dog, 2725(F)
My Big Girl Potty Book, 3076(F)
My Big Lie, 8614(F)
My Boat, 20803
My Body Is Private, 18255
My Body, Your Body, 18832
My Box of Color, 291(F)
My Brother, Ant, 6247(F)
My Brother Is a Superhero, 7511(F)
My Brother Is from Outer Space, 3829(F)
My Brother Louis Measures Worms and Other Louis Stories, 9975(F)
My Brother Made Me Do It, 8720(F)
My Brother Matthew, 3918(F)
My Brother, My Enemy, 9237(F)
My Brother Sam Is Dead, 9226(F)
My Brother Sammy, 4948(F)
My Brother, the Pest, 6205(F)
My Brother's Keeper, 9490(F)
My Brown Bear Barney at the Party, 5668(F)
My Buddy, 8908(F)
My Bunny and Me, 681(F)
My "c" Sound Box, 103(F)
My Cat Tuna, 5380(F)
My Cats Nick and Nora, 5249(F)
My Cheetah Family, 19076
My Color Is Panda, 293(F)
My Colors, 269(F)

My Colors/Mis Colores, 268(F)
My Crayons Talk, 1252(F)
My Crazy Cousin Courtney, 8343(F)
My "d" Sound Box, 103(F)
My Dad, 1019(F), 4942(F)
My Dad Is Awesome, 3562(F)
My Dad Takes Care of Me, 3847(F)
My Daddy, 3832(F)
My Day, 3300(F)
My Day in the Garden, 3148(F)
My Day, Your Day, 3007(F)
My Dear Noel, 12580
My Dentist, 18187
My Dinosaur, 1669(F)
My Do It! 3512(F)
My Dog Ate It, 10028(F)
My Dog, Cat, 7179(F)
My Dog, My Hero, 7171(F)
My Dog Talks, 6381(F)
My Dog Toby, 5465(F)
My Dog Truffle, 5380(F)
My Dog's the Best! 6249(F)
My Doll, Keshia, 3182(F)
My Dream of Martin Luther King, 12752
My Drum, 20140
My Duck, 1354(F)
My Elephant Can Do Almost Any-thing, 2032(F)
My Fabulous New Life, 8671(F)
My Family's Changing, 17689
My Farm, 4727
My Father, 14146
My Father's Boat, 3641(F)
My Father's Dragon, 9857(F)
My Father's Hands, 3868(F)
My Favorite Ghost, 7036(F)
My Favorite Word Book, 14062
My Feet, 18045
My Fellow Americans, 12692
My Fire Engine, 2964(F)
My First ABC, 17(F)
My First Action Rhymes, 874
My First Baking Book, 21688
My First Body Book, 18075
My First Book About Space, 18514
My First Book of Biographies, 13737
My First Book of How Things Are Made, 21039
My First Book of Proverbs/Mi Primer Libro de Dichos, 14028
My First Book of Time, 206
My First Book of Words, 14046(F)
My First Christmas Activity Book, 21512
My First Christmas Board Book, 5888(F)
My First Cookbook, 21689
My First Day at Camp, 6711(F)
My First Dictionary, 14043
My First Garden, 4389(F)
My First Kwanzaa Book, 5619
My First Look at Numbers, 534
My First Magic Book, 21785
My First Music Book, 14220
My First Number Book, 461
My First Nursery Rhymes, 875
My First Oxford Book of Poems, 11662
My First Oxford Book of Stories, 10453(F)

My First Paint Book, 21593
My First Phonics Book, 14099
My First Photography Book, 21800
My First Pop-up Book of Prehistoric Animals, 14387
My First Riddles, 21821(F)
My First Word Board Book, 3475(F)
My Five Senses, 18129
My Football Book, 22182
My Four Lions, 1199(F)
My Freedom Trip, 15193
My Friend and I, 4010(F)
My Friend Bear, 947(F)
My Friend Gorilla, 1422(F)
My Friend Harry, 3279(F)
My Friend John, 4070(F)
My Friend, O'Connell, 9980(F)
My Friend the Piano, 1080(F)
My Friends, 3174(F)
My Goose Betsy, 5140(F)
My Grammy, 4997(F)
My Gran, 3539(F)
My Grandfather the Spy, 6857(F)
My Grandfather's House, 4935(F)
My Grandmother's Journey, 4617(F)
My Grandpa and the Sea, 4788(F)
My Great-Aunt Arizona, 3705
My Great-Grandmother's Gourd, 4710(F)
My Hands, 18046
My Head Is Full of Colors, 1170(F)
My Heart Is on the Ground, 9175(F)
My Hen Is Dancing, 20073
My Heroes, My People, 16344
My Horse of the North, 20003
My House Has Stars, 736(F)
My House/Mi Casa, 4640(F)
My Indoor Garden, 21765
My Land Sings, 11323
My Life Among the Aliens, 10184(F)
My Life as a Fifth-Grade Comedian, 8743(F)
My Life with the Chimpanzees, 13300
My Life with the Wave, 1081(F)
My Little ABC Book, 135(F)
My Little 123 Book, 585(F)
My Little Sister Ate One Hare, 448(F)
My Lone Star Summer, 8748(F)
My Loose Tooth, 6439(F)
My Mama Had a Dancing Heart, 3659(F)
My Mama Says There Aren't Any Zombies, Ghosts, Vampires, Crea-tures, Demons, Monsters, Fiends, Goblins, or Things, 4341(F)
My Man Blue, 11760
My Many Colored Days, 289(F)
My Mexico/México Mío, 11612
My Mom Is My Show-and-Tell, 5509(F)
My Mom Made Me Go to Camp, 3101(F)
My Mom Married the Principal, 7392(F)
My Mommy Has AIDS, 17937
My Mom's a Vet, 17847
My Monster Mama Loves Me So, 1351(F)

My Mother Is the Most Beautiful Woman in the World, 11109
My Mother Is the Smartest Woman in the World, 7412(F)
My Mother Talks to Trees, 3655(F)
My Mother's Pearls, 3637(F)
My Mother's Secret Life, 1151(F)
My Mysterious World, 12571
My Name Is Amelia, 10240(F)
My Name Is Brain/Brian, 8878(F)
My Name Is Georgia, 12277
My Name Is Jorge, 11653
My Name Is Maria Isabel, 7331(F)
My Name Is Not Angelica, 9136(F)
My Name Is Not Gussie, 9591(F)
A My Name Is . . ., 84(F)
My Nature Craft Book, 21460
My Navajo Sister, 4039(F)
My New Boy, 6575(F)
My New Kitten, 5169
My New York, 16698
My Nine Lives, 8025(F)
My Numbers/Mis Numeros, 429(F)
My Ol' Man, 3840(F)
My Old Teddy, 3308(F)
My Opposites/Mis Opuestos, 178(F)
My Own Big Bed, 702(F)
My Own Home, 2219(F)
My Own Worst Enemy, 8819(F)
My Painted House, My Friendly Chicken, and Me, 13872
My Pal Al, 6451(F)
My Parents' Divorce, 17647
My Pen Pal, Pat, 6556(F)
My Perfect Neighborhood, 1317(F)
My Pet Cats, 19917
My Pet Crocodile and Other Slightly Outrageous Verse, 11856
My Pet Ferrets, 19890
My Pet Fish, 19980
My Pet Hamster and Gerbils, 19885
My Pet Lizards, 19886
My Place in Space, 18395
My Pony Book, 20013
My Pop-Up Surprise ABC, 28(F)
My Pop-Up Surprise 123, 414(F)
My Prairie Christmas, 5832(F)
My Race Car, 5594
My Real Family, 2415(F)
My Robot Buddy, 10239(F)
My Rotten Redheaded Older Brother, 3841(F)
My Rows and Piles of Coins, 4773(F)
My Season with Penguins, 19389
My Secret Camera, 14856
My Secret War, 9682(F)
My Shadow, 11718
My Shapes/Mis Formas, 327(F)
My Side of the Mountain, 7194(F)
My Sister Gracie, 2257(F)
My Sister, My Science Report, 10027(F)
My Sister the Witch, 9811(F)
My Sisters Love My Clothes, 3669(F)
My Sister's Rusty Bike, 965(F)
My Soccer Book, 22291
My Son, the Time Traveler, 10189(F)
My Song Is Beautiful, 11597
My Stars, It's Mrs. Gaddy, 4154(F)

My Stepfamily, 17662
My Steps, 3102(F)
My Teacher Fried My Brains, 10170(F)
My Teacher Sleeps in School, 2831(F)
My Teacher's Secret Life, 5512(F)
My Tooth Is About to Fall Out, 6479(F)
My Town, 2828(F)
My Trip to Alpha I, 10239(F)
My Two Grandmothers, 3827(F)
My Two Hands, My Two Feet, 804(F)
My Two Uncles, 5096(F)
My Very First Book of Words, 6260
My Very First Mother Goose, 880(F)
My Very Own Birthday, 21510
My Very Own Christmas, 21511
My Very Own Room/ Mi propio cuartito, 3360(F)
My Visit to the Aquarium, 20020
My Visit to the Dinosaurs, 14376
My Visit to the Zoo, 20021
My Wartime Summers, 9650(F)
My Wicked Stepmother, 5010(F)
My Wish for Tomorrow, 10263(F)
My Working Mom, 1195(F)
My Worst Friend, 8361(F)
My Writing Day, 12488
Myanmar, 15175
Myrna Never Sleeps, 1472(F)
Mysteries of Deep Space, 18376
The Mysteries of Harris Burdick, 936(F)
Mysteries of the Rain Forest, 13341
Mysteries of the Universe, 21961
The Mysteries of Zigomar, 11854
Mysteries on Monroe Street, 8258(F)
The Mysterious Case of Sir Arthur Conan Doyle, 12532
The Mysterious Cases of Mr. Pin, 6976(F)
The Mysterious Disappearance of Leon (I Mean Noel), 9971(F)
The Mysterious Giant of Barletta, 11058
Mysterious Healing, 18022
The Mysterious Misadventures of Foy Rin Jin, 2105(F)
Mysterious Miss Slade, 8319(F)
The Mysterious Ocean Highway, 19849
Mysterious Places, 21912
The Mysterious Rays of Dr. Roentgen, 13343
Mysterious Tales of Japan, 10581
Mysterious Thelonious, 12424
The Mysterious Visitor, 17193
Mysteriously Yours, Maggie Marmelstein, 10131(F)
Mystery at Echo Cliffs, 6727(F)
Mystery Explosion! 7102(F)
The Mystery Machine, 10153(F)
The Mystery of Atlantis, 21957
The Mystery of Black Holes, 18407
The Mystery of Crop Circles, 21942
The Mystery of Drear House, 6873(F)
The Mystery of King Karfu, 6810(F)
The Mystery of Mars, 18485

The Mystery of Mineral Gorge, 9328(F)
The Mystery of Mr. Nice, 7779(F)
The Mystery of the Abominable Snowman, 21958
The Mystery of the Bermuda Triangle, 21943
The Mystery of the Cupboard, 7585(F)
The Mystery of the Dancing Angels, 6977(F)
The Mystery of the Eagle Feather, 6978(F)
The Mystery of the Haunted Lighthouse, 6979(F)
The Mystery of the Hidden Painting, 7123(F)
The Mystery of the Hieroglyphs, 14623
The Mystery of the Hobo's Message, 6980(F)
Mystery of the Lascaux Cave, 14509
The Mystery of the Mammoth Bones, 14419
Mystery of the Melted Diamonds, 6836(F)
The Mystery of the Missing Bagpipes, 6832(F)
The Mystery of the Missing Dog, 6457(F)
The Mystery of the Missing Money, 7021(F)
The Mystery of the Monkey's Maze, 6811(F)
The Mystery of the Several Sevens, 7626(F)
The Mystery of the UFO, 7022(F)
The Mystery of UFOs, 21913
Mystery on Everest, 12142
Mystery on October Road, 6889(F)
Mystery on the Docks, 2230(F)
Myth Maker, 12606
Mythology, 11456
The Myths and Civilization of the Ancient Egyptians, 14661
The Myths and Civilization of the Ancient Greeks, 14696
Myths and Civilization of the Ancient Romans, 11490
Myths and Civilization of the Celts, 11452
Myths and Legends, 13899

N. C. Wyeth's Pilgrims, 16168
N-O Spells No! 6195(F)
Nadia's Hands, 5625(F)
Naked Mole-Rats, 19198
The Name of the Tree, 10691
A Name on the Quilt, 4900(F)
The Names Project, 17943
The Names Upon the Harp, 10994
Namibia, 14986
Naming the Cat, 5373(F)
Nana Hannah's Piano, 3541(F)
Nana's Birthday Party, 5692(F)
Nancy Kerrigan, 13592
Nancy's Story, 9207(F)
Nanny Noony and the Dust Queen, 2098(F)
Nanny Noony and the Magic Spell, 1166(F)

Nanta's Lion, 4755(F)
Nanuk, 5253(F)
Naomi Judd's Guardian Angels, 14248
Napoleon Bonaparte, 13839
The Napping House, 4357(F)
The Napping House Wakes Up, 3488(F)
Nappy Hair, 3207(F)
Naptime, Laptime, 781(F)
NASA Planetary Spacecraft, 20960
NASA Space Vehicles, 20975
Nashville, 16874
Nasty, Stinky Sneakers, 9791(F)
Nasty the Snowman, 7905(F)
Nat Turner, 12805
Nat Turner and the Virginia Slave Revolt, 12806
Natalie and Nat King Cole, 12178
Nate the Great, 6647(F), 6653(F)
Nate the Great and Me, 6648(F)
Nate the Great and the Fishy Prize, 6649(F)
Nate the Great and the Lost List, 6647(F)
Nate the Great and the Missing Key, 6647(F)
Nate the Great and the Monster Mess, 6650(F)
Nate the Great and the Phony Clue, 6647(F)
Nate the Great and the Snowy Trail, 6647(F)
Nate the Great and the Sticky Case, 6647(F)
Nate the Great and the Tardy Tortoise, 6652(F)
Nate the Great Goes Down in the Dumps, 6649(F)
Nate the Great Goes Undercover, 6647(F)
Nate the Great Saves the King of Sweden, 6651(F)
Nate the Great Stalks Stupidweed, 6649(F)
Nathaniel Talking, 11758
Nathaniel Willy, Scared Silly, 11367
The Nation Divides, 16437
A Nation Is Born, 16217
National Audubon Society First Field Guide, 18399, 18678, 18681, 18943, 20196, 20774
National Audubon Society First Field Guide to Birds, 19293
National Audubon Society First Field Guide to Insects, 19500
National Audubon Society First Field Guide to Rocks and Minerals, 20569
National Audubon Society First Field Guide to Wildflowers, 20036
The National Debt, 17123
National Government, 17112
The National Government, 17109
The National Mall, 16699
National Velvet, 7153(F)
Native American Animal Stories, 11219
The Native American Book of Knowledge, 16067

The Native American Book of Life, 16068
Native American Doctor, 12982
Native American Rock Art, 15984
Native American Shipwrecks, 15944
Native Americans, 15956, 16010, 16063
Native Americans and Mesa Verde, 16000
Native Americans of the Frontier, 16060
Native Crafts, 21507
Native Plant Stories, 11220
Native Ways, 15999
The Nativity, 5859(F), 17409
Natural Foods and Products, 20081
Natural History from A to Z, 18604
Natural Treasures Field Guide for Kids, 18577
Natural Wonders and Disasters, 20308
Natural Wonders of North America, 20314
Nature All Year Long, 18591
The Nature and Science of Autumn, 18562
The Nature and Science of Bubbles, 20799
The Nature and Science of Color, 20859
The Nature and Science of Energy, 20820
The Nature and Science of Fire, 20279
The Nature and Science of Fossils, 14390
The Nature and Science of Numbers, 20628
The Nature and Science of Reflections, 20860
The Nature and Science of Rocks, 20552
The Nature and Science of Seeds, 20269
The Nature and Science of Shells, 19771
The Nature and Science of Spring, 18562
The Nature and Science of Summer, 18562
The Nature and Science of Survival, 18581
The Nature and Science of Waste, 16974
The Nature and Science of Winter, 18562
Nature and the Environment, 13208
Nature Art with Chiura Obata, 12274
Nature Explorer, 18585
Nature Got There First, 18278
Nature in Danger, 19407
Nature in Your Backyard, 18588
Nature Spy, 4523
Nature! Wild and Wonderful, 12583
Nature's Fury, 20662
Nature's Green Umbrella, 20444
Nature's Paintbrush, 18855
Naty's Parade, 4649(F)
Nauala and Her Secret Wolf, 9100(F)
The Naughty Crow, 5244(F)
Naughty Parents, 4164(F)

The Nautilus, 8896(F)
The Navajo, 15962, 16017
Navajo ABC, 136(F)
Navajo Long Walk, 9144(F)
The Navajo Nation, 16020
Navajo Summer, 8421(F)
Navajo Wedding Day, 4826(F)
The Navajos, 16050
Navy Strike Planes, 21380
NBA Basketball Offense Basics, 22150
NBA by the Numbers, 389(F)
NBA Game Day, 22144
Ndebele, 15000
Neale S. Godfrey's Ultimate Kids' Money Book, 16942
Near-Death Experiences, 21929
The Nearsighted Neighbor, 6961(F)
NEATE to the Rescue! 6791(F)
Nebraska, 16576
The Necessary Cat, 7280(F)
Ned Feldman, Space Pirate, 10224(F)
Ned's Rainbow, 3469(F)
Neem the Half-Boy, 11200
Neeny Coming, Neeny Going, 3994(F)
Nefertari, Princess of Egypt, 14605
Neighborhood Odes, 11708
The Neighborhood Trucker, 5549(F)
Neil Armstrong, 12072, 12074
Nekane, the Lamina and the Bear, 11134
Nell Dunne, 9541(F)
Nell Nugget and the Cow Caper, 2926(F)
Nell of Blue Harbor, 8422(F)
Nell of Branford Hall, 9128(F)
Nellie Bly, 13137, 13138
Nellie Bly's Book, 13139
Nellie's Knot, 1870(F)
Nelson Mandela, 13827, 13829, 13831
    (Illus. by Mike White), 13830
Nely Galan, 12831
Nepal, 15151, 15164
Neptune, 18462, 18481, 18492, 18496, 18499
The Neptune Fountain, 9064(F)
Neptune's Nursery, 19647
Nerd No More, 9854(F)
The Nervous System, 18119, 18122
Nessa's Fish, 4747(F)
Nessa's Story, 4748(F)
A Nest Full of Eggs, 19239
A Nest of Dinosaurs, 14455
Net Bandits, 6799(F)
A Net of Stars, 1267(F)
A Net to Catch Time, 4586(F)
Netherlands, 15402
The Netherlands, 15398
Nevada, 16625, 16642
Nevada Facts and Symbols, 16615
The Never-Be-Bored Book, 21449
Never Kiss an Alligator! 18698
Never Let Your Cat Make Lunch for You, 2171(F)
Never Poke a Squid, 5990(F)
Never Ride Your Elephant to School, 4193(F)
Never Say Quit, 10369(F)

Never Take a Pig to Lunch and Other Poems About the Fun of Eating, 11925
Never Trust a Squirrel! 1972(F)
The New African Americans, 17541
The New Americans, 16157
New at the Zoo, 6323(F)
The New Baby at Your House, 17646
New Beginnings, 17358
New Big House, 3651(F)
The New Book of Dinosaurs, 14477
New Cat, 1955(F)
A New Coat for Anna, 3969(F)
The New Complete Babysitter's Handbook, 16938
New Dawn on Rocky Ridge, 9406(F)
New Dinosaurs, 14461
A New Duck, 19310
New England Whaler, 16225
A New Frog, 18726
New Hampshire, 16659, 16668, 16679, 16716, 16741
The New Hampshire Colony, 16121
New Jersey, 16680, 16685, 16721, 16742
The New Jersey Colony, 16122
The New Kid, 6410(F)
The New Kid at School, 7943(F)
New Kid in Town, 10344(F)
The New Kid on the Block, 11910
New Kids on the Block, 12425
New Mexico, 16904, 16906, 16912
New Moon, 4540(F), 14100, 16946
New Moon on Friendship, 17722
The New Nation, 16313
The New Nick Kramer; or, My Life as a Baby-sitter, 9887(F)
The New One, 8875(F)
New Orleans, 16876
New Questions and Answers About Dinosaurs, 14471
New Road! 5568(F)
A New Room for William, 4970(F)
New Shoes for Silvia, 3234(F)
New Shoes, Red Shoes, 3387(F)
The New Way Things Work, 21043
New Year, 17402
New York, 16681, 16736, 16745, 16750, 16754
New York City, 16645, 16705
The New York Colony, 16123
The New York Knicks Basketball Team, 22148
The New York Public Library Amazing Hispanic American History, 17585
The New York Public Library Amazing Mythology, 11448
The New York Public Library Amazing Native American History, 16055
The New York Public Library Amazing Space, 20966
The New York Public Library Incredible Earth, 20299
The New York Public Library Kid's Guide to Research, 14089
The New York Yankees Baseball Team, 22113
The New You, 8742(F)

New Zealand, 15230, 15231, 15234, 15238
A Newbery Christmas, 9726(F)
Newbery Girls, 10264(F)
A Newbery Halloween, 6864(F)
A Newbery Zoo, 7202(F)
Newborn, 3687(F)
The Newest and Coolest Dinosaurs, 14394
Newf, 5289(F)
Newfangled Fairy Tales, Book 1, 7888(F)
Newfoundland and Labrador, 15583
News, 14073
Newt, 2533(F)
Next Spring an Oriole, 9455(F)
Next Stop! 3119(F)
Next Stop Grand Central, 3256(F)
Next Stop, New York City! 6346(F)
The Nez Perce, 16018
    (Illus. by Ronald Himler), 16051
Ngoni, 14993
Nibble, Nibble, Jenny Archer, 9812(F)
Nibble Nibble Mousekin, 10901
Nibbles O'Hare, 5973(F)
Nicaragua, 15657
Nicaragua in Pictures, 15669
Nice New Neighbors, 1851(F)
Nice Try, Tooth Fairy, 1443(F)
Nicholi, 5808(F)
Nick Joins In, 5008(F)
Nick Plays Baseball, 22097
Nickelodeon's The Big Help Book, 17139
Nickommoh! A Thanksgiving Celebration, 6146
Nick's Mission, 6770(F)
Nick's Secret, 6771(F)
Nicky and the Big, Bad Wolves, 2137(F)
Nicky and the Fantastic Birthday Gift, 2138(F)
Nicole's Story, 17936
Nigeria, 15008, 15014, 15019, 15033, 15049
Nigeria in Pictures, 15038
Night and the Candlemaker, 8112(F)
Night at the Fair, 3089(F)
The Night Before Christmas, 11844, 11847, 11848
    (Illus. by Jan Brett), 11843
    (Illus. by Tomie dePaola), 11839
    (Illus. by Cheryl Harness), 11840
    (Illus. by Ted Rand), 11841
    (Illus. by Ruth Sanderson), 11842
    (Illus. by Tasha Tudor), 11845
    (Illus. by Bruce Whatley), 11846
Night Birds, 19226
The Night Book, 18280
Night City, 3936(F)
Night Creatures, 18988
Night Cry, 8775(F)
Night Driving, 3593(F)
Night Fell at Harry's Farm, 3200(F)
Night Flier, 19566
Night Flying, 7978(F)
Night Garden, 11739
Night Golf, 5034(F)
The Night Has Ears, 10655
Night House, Bright House, 1673(F)

The Night Iguana Left Home, 2426(F)
Night in the Country, 771(F)
The Night Is Like an Animal, 810(F)
The Night Journey, 9057(F)
Night, Knight, 14063(F)
Night Lights, 577(F), 645(F)
Night Night, Cuddly Bear, 799(F)
Night Noises, 5685(F)
Night of Ghosts and Hermits, 19868
The Night of Las Posadas, 5803(F)
Night of the Chupacabras, 6935(F)
Night of the Fireflies, 8745(F)
Night of the Gargoyles, 1025(F)
Night of the Goat Children, 1353(F)
Night of the Twisters, 7039(F)
Night of the Werepoodle, 7792(F)
Night of the White Stag, 10431(F)
A Night on the Tiles, 709(F)
Night Rabbits, 5371(F)
Night Raiders Along the Cape, 9255(F)
The Night Rainbow, 15802
Night Ride to Nanna's, 720(F)
Night Shift Daddy, 782(F)
The Night Sky Book, 18396
Night Songs, 747(F)
The Night Swimmers, 8584(F)
The Night the Moon Blew Kisses, 4498(F)
The Night the Moon Fell, 11412
The Night the Scary Beasties Popped Out of My Head, 1285(F)
Night-time Animals, 18846
Night-Time Numbers, 571(F)
Night Tree, 5769(F)
Night Visitors, 10784
A Night Without Stars, 8698(F)
The Night Worker, 634(F)
The Night You Were Born, 3784(F)
Nightbirds on Nantucket, 6740(F)
Nightfeathers, 11659
The Nightmare Before Christmas, 9711(F)
Nightmare Hour, 8132(F)
A Nightmare in History, 14840
Nightmares, 11677
Nightprowlers, 18621
Nights of the Pufflings, 19351
Nightwalkers, 7271(F)
Nighty-Night, 623(F)
Nighty-Nightmare, 9888(F)
Nihancan's Feast of Beaver, 11263
Nikki and the Rocking Horse, 3547(F)
The Nile, 14911
Nilo and the Tortoise, 5303(F)
Nim and the War Effort, 9669(F)
Nim's Island, 6999(F)
Niña Bonita, 1373(F)
Nina, Nina Ballerina, 6549(F)
Nina, Nina, Star Ballerina, 6550(F)
Nina's Waltz, 3605(F)
Nine Candles, 8830(F)
Nine Days to Christmas, 5810(F)
Nine-in-One, Grr! Grr! 10846
Nine Man Tree, 7009(F)
Nine Naughty Kittens, 478(F)
Nine Spoons, 6119(F)
The Nine-Ton Cat, 13964
1900–20, 13891, 16478

1900s, 16491
1910s, 16491
1920s, 16491
1930s, 16491
1940s, 16461
The 1940s, 16492
1950s, 16500
The 1950s, 16512
1960s, 16500
The 1960s, 16504
1960s Pop, 14122
1970s, 16500
The 1970s, 16503
1970s Pop, 14122
The 1980s, 16502
The 1992 Election, 17095
Nineteenth Century Lumber Camp Cooking, 15876
19th Century Clothing, 21173
19th Century Girls and Women, 16475
A 19th Century Schoolgirl, 16270
Nissa's Place, 8736(F)
Nitrogen, 20283
No Arm in Left Field, 10312(F)
No Better Hope, 16648
No Boys Allowed, 8316(F), 8474(F)
No Clothes Today! 3268(F)
No Copycats Allowed! 6354(F)
No, David! 3886(F)
No Dinner! The Story of the Old Woman and the Pumpkin, 10843
No Dogs Allowed, 9821(F)
No Dragons for Tea, 1468(F)
No Fighting, No Biting! 6534(F)
No Flying in the House, 1866(F)
No Foal Yet, 5243(F)
No Good in Art, 5489(F)
No Jumping on the Bed! 960(F)
No Mail for Mitchell, 6664(F)
No Man's Land, 9464(F)
No Matter What, 2131(F)
No Milk! 5194(F)
No Mirrors in My Nana's House, 3516(F)
No More Dodos, 19406
No More Homework! No More Tests! Kids' Favorite Funny School Poems, 11622
No More Monsters for Me! 6565(F)
No More Nice, 9930(F)
No More Secrets for Me, 17735
No More Strangers Now, 14990
No Nap, 641(F)
No New Pants! 6452(F)
No No, Jo! 2445(F)
No! No! No! 5058(F)
No, No, Titus! 5343(F)
The No-Nothings and Their Baby, 4234(F)
No One Told the Aardvark, 1146(F)
No One Walks on My Father's Moon, 8929(F)
No Pets Allowed, 1471(F)
No Place, 7344(F)
No Problem, 1898(F)
No Promises in the Wind, 8702(F)
No Strings Attached, 7452(F)
No Such Thing, 719(F)
No Such Things, 2566(F)
No Time for Mother's Day, 5609(F)

No Turning Back, 8013(F), 8975(F)
Noah, 17270
Noah and the Ark and the Animals, 17256
Noah and the Great Flood, 17275
Noah and the Space Ark, 1045(F)
Noah Makes a Boat, 17277
Noah's Ark, 17240, 17258
    (Illus. by Peter Spier), 17323
    (Illus. by Lisbeth Zwerger), 17288(F)
Noah's Square Dance, 1665(F)
Noah's Tree, 17298(F)
Noah's Wife, 17267
Nobel Prize Winners, 13728
The Nobody Club, 8683(F)
Nobody Likes Me! 2324(F)
Nobody Listens to Andrew, 6361(F)
Nobody Owns the Sky, 12094
Nobody Rides the Unicorn, 1417(F)
Nobody's Dog, 7182(F), 7201(F)
Nobody's Family Is Going to Change, 7432(F)
Nobody's Orphan, 8476(F)
Nocturne, 4565(F)
Noelle of the Nutcracker, 7834(F)
Noisytime for Zoo Animals, 18796
Nolan Ryan, 13502
Noli's Story, 8955(F)
Nonsense Songs, 11886
Noodlehead Stories, 10557
The Noonday Friends, 8376(F)
Norby and the Court Jester, 10145(F)
Norby and the Invaders, 10146(F)
Norby and the Oldest Dragon, 10147(F)
Norby and the Queen's Necklace, 10148(F)
Norby and the Terrified Taxi, 10143(F)
Norby Finds a Villain, 10148(F)
Norby, the Mixed-up Robot, 10149(F)
Norby's Other Secret, 10149(F)
Norma Jean, Jumping Bean, 6279(F)
Norman Rockwell, 12294, 12295, 12296
North America, 14354, 21527
North America and the Caribbean, 15562
North American Cranes, 19224
North American Indian Survival Skills, 15991
North American Indians, 15959
North American Moose, 19150
A North American Rain Forest Scrapbook, 20495
North American Wolves, 19135
The North Atlantic Coast, 16722
North Carolina, 16853, 16866, 16885
North Country Spring, 4485(F)
North Dakota, 16563, 16588
North Dakota Facts and Symbols, 16555
The North Sea and the Baltic Sea, 19831
North, South, East, and West, 182
North to Freedom, 9665(F)
A Northern Alphabet, 49(F)
Northern Asia, 15209
Northern Ireland in Pictures, 15362

Northern Lights, 20790
A Northern Nativity, 17425
The Northwest, 16782
Northwest Animal Babies, 18877
Northwest Territories, 15572
Northwoods Cradle Song, 814(F)
Norway, 15438, 15441, 15450, 15454, 15455
Norwegian Folk Tales, 11120
Nory Ryan's Song, 9094(F)
The Nose, 7743(F)
A Nose for Adventure, 10232(F)
The Nose from Jupiter, 9987(F)
Nose Pickers from Outer Space! 10204(F)
Noses That Plow and Poke, 18859
Not Again, Anna! 3634(F)
Not Enough Beds! 16(F)
Not Exactly Nashville, 8328(F)
Not Just a Summer Crush, 8248(F)
Not Just Another Moose, 2148(F)
The Not-Just-Anybody Family, 7398(F)
Not My Dog, 7292(F)
Not One Damsel in Distress, 10594
Not So Fast, Songololo, 4634(F)
Not-So-Grizzly Bear Stories, 10595
The Not-So-Jolly Roger, 7047(F)
The Not-So-Minor Leagues, 22092
Not-So-Normal Norman, 7309(F)
Not-So-Perfect Rosie, 9861(F)
Not So Rotten Ralph, 2110(F)
Not That I Care, 10133(F)
Not the Piano, Mrs. Medley! 4484(F)
Not Until Christmas, Walter! 5781(F)
A Noteworthy Tale, 1427(F)
Nothing, 1262(F)
Nothing at All, 1947(F)
Nothing but Trouble, 9876(F)
    (Illus. by Gus Clarke), 4114(F)
Nothing Ever Happens on 90th Street, 3412(F)
Nothing Happened, 694(F)
Nothing Here But Trees, 4860(F)
Nothing Scares Us, 3483(F)
Nothing Sticks Like a Shadow, 2763(F)
Nothing to Fear, 9572(F)
Nothing Wrong with a Three-Legged Dog, 8755(F)
Nothing's Fair in Fifth Grade, 10047(F)
Nova Scotia, 15597
Nova's Ark, 2299(F)
Novio Boy, 12037
"Now Get It Right" Volume II, 12027
"Now I Get It!" Vol. I, 12027
Now I Know Better, 18225
Now It Is Morning, 3940(F)
Now Let Me Fly, 4696(F)
Now One Foot, Now the Other, 4945(F)
Now Soon Later, 188(F)
Now We Can Have a Wedding! 3086(F)
Now We're Talking, 10337(F)
Now You See It, Now You Don't, 20916

Now You See Them, Now You Don't, 1944(F)
Nowhere, Now Here, 8619(F)
Nowhere to Call Home, 9536(F)
Nubian Kingdoms, 14663
Nuclear Energy, 20845
Nuclear Power, 20844
Nugget and Darling, 5283(F)
Number Art, 20629
Number One Number Fun, 404(F)
Number the Stars, 9672(F)
Numbers, 463
    (Illus. by Richard Maccabe), 20638
Numbskulls, 7098(F)
Nunavut, 15581
Nursery Rhyme Songbook with Easy Music to Play for Piano and Guitar, 840(F)
Nursery Rhymes from Mother Goose Told in Signed English, 827
Nursery Tales Around the World, 10618
The Nursery Treasury, 841
The Nutcracker, 10885
    (Illus. by Renee Graef), 10932(F)
    (Illus. by Nicki Palin), 14293
    (Illus. by Maurice Sendak), 10916
The Nutcracker Ballet, 14300(F)
    (Illus. by Carolyn Ewing), 6371(F)
    (Illus. by Stephen T. Johnson), 14288
Nutik, the Wolf Pup, 4656(F)
The Nutquacker, 5749(F)
Nutritional Diseases, 18018
Nuts to You! 2066(F)
The Nutshell Library, 242(F)
Nutty and the Case of the Ski-Slope Spy, 6904(F)
Nutty, the Movie Star, 9890(F)
Nutty's Ghost, 7801(F)
Nzingha, 8971(F)

O Canada, 15582
O Christmas Tree, 5907(F)
O Is for Orca, 52(F)
O Jerusalem, 11742
Oak Tree, 20199, 20212
Obo, 952(F)
An Occasional Cow, 9882(F)
Ocean, 19828, 19834, 19838
Ocean Animals in Danger, 19421
Ocean Day, 4524(F)
The Ocean of Story, 10803
The Ocean Within, 8585(F)
Oceanographers and Explorers of the Sea, 13220
Oceans, 19837, 19839
Oceans and Seas, 19814
October Smiled Back, 4508(F)
Octopus, 19726
The Octopus, 19722
An Octopus Followed Me Home, 4360(F)
Octopuses, 19723
Odd Jobs, 17768
Odd Man Out, 8364(F)
Odd Velvet, 4059(F)
Odder Than Ever, 7679(F)
Oddhopper Opera, 11947
Odin's Family, 11520
Odysseus and the Cyclops, 11481

Odyssey, 11511
The Odyssey, 11479
The Odyssey of Ben O'Neal, 7096(F)
Of Colors and Things, 275(F)
Of Mice and Rats, 19195
Of Nightingales That Weep, 9007(F)
Of Quarks, Quasars and Other
  Quirks, 11857
Of Swords and Sorcerers, 11000
Of Things Natural, Wild, and Free,
  13315
Of Two Minds, 7953(F), 7954(F)
Off the Map, 16090
Off the Road, 10151(F)
Off to School, 4905(F)
Off to School, Baby Duck! 2201(F)
Off to Sea, 19878
Off to the Sweet Shores of Africa,
  897
Off We Go! 2890(F)
Officer Buckle and Gloria, 5378(F)
The Officer's Ball, 2889(F)
The Official M&M's Brand Book of
  the Millennium, 20640
Ogbo, 15043
Ogres! Ogres! Ogres! A Feasting
  Frenzy from A to Z, 51(F)
Oh! 1234(F)
Oh, Baby! 18233
Oh, Brother, 4362(F)
Oh, Cats! 5148(F)
Oh, Emma, 7389(F)
Oh, Grow Up! 4976(F)
Oh My Baby Bear! 2870(F)
Oh, My Baby, Little One, 1744(F)
Oh No, Anna! 3151(F)
Oh No, It's Robert, 9989(F)
Oh, No, Toto! 4849(F)
Oh Say Can You Say? 6646(F)
Oh Say Can You Say Di-no-saur?
  14482
Oh, That Cat! 5415(F)
Oh, the Places He Went, 12539
Oh, the Places You'll Go! 3418(F)
Oh, Tucker! 5294(F)
Oh, What a Thanksgiving! 6147(F)
Ohio, 16539, 16553, 16558
Oil Spill! 16990
Oil Spills, 17002
Oink, 2118(F)
Oink Oink, 917(F)
The Ojibwa, 15993
The Ojibwe, 15930
The Okay Book, 3356(F)
Okino and the Whales, 1154(F)
Oklahoma, 16532, 16569, 16577
The Oklahoma City Bombing, 16582
Oklahoma Facts and Symbols, 16556
Oksana, 13587
Ol' Paul, the Mighty Logger, 11373
Ola Shakes It Up, 8707(F)
Ola's Wake, 7523(F)
Old Bag of Bones, 11303
Old Black Fly, 5(F)
Old Black Witch! 1120(F)
The Old Cotton Blues, 4952(F)
Old Devil Wind, 6031(F)
The Old Dog, 5110(F)
Old Dog Cora and the Christmas
  Tree, 5904(F)
Old Dry Frye, 11355

Old Elm Speaks, 11953
An Old Fashioned Thanksgiving,
  9703(F)
Old Friends, 979(F)
Old Home Day, 7440(F)
Old Ironsides, 9331(F)
Old Jake's Skirts, 3416(F)
Old MacDonald, 14178, 14183
  (Illus. by Rosemary Wells), 14190
Old MacDonald Had a Farm, 14147
  (Illus. by Holly Berry), 14172
  (Illus. by Carol Jones), 14171
Old Mahony and the Bear Family,
  6366(F)
The Old Man and His Door, 4836(F)
The Old Man Who Loved to Sing,
  1692(F)
Old Mother Hubbard, 853
Old Mother Hubbard and Her Won-
  derful Dog, 877
Old Mother West Wind, 1903(F)
Old People, Frogs, and Albert,
  8388(F)
The Old Pirate of Central Park,
  4275(F)
Old Sadie and the Christmas Bear,
  5890(F)
An Old Shell, 11964
Old Testament Days, 21495
Old Thunder and Miss Raney,
  1100(F)
Old Turtle, 2872(F)
Old Winter, 1506(F)
The Old Woman and Her Pig, 11009
The Old Woman and the Wave,
  1266(F)
The Old Woman Who Lived in a
  Vinegar Bottle, 10458
The Old Woman Who Loved to
  Read, 1693(F)
The Old Woman Who Named
  Things, 5399(F)
Old Yeller, 7199(F)
Olive, the Other Reindeer, 5947(F)
Oliver, 2853(F)
Oliver and Albert, Friends Forever,
  6704(F)
Oliver Button Is a Sissy, 4946(F)
Oliver Dibbs and the Dinosaur
  Cause, 10002(F)
Oliver Dibbs to the Rescue! 10002(F)
Oliver's Alphabets, 15(F)
Oliver's Fruit Salad, 3631(F)
Oliver's Vegetables, 4151(F)
Oliver's Wood, 2192(F)
Olivia, 2084(F)
Ollie All Over, 3381(F)
Ollie Forgot, 960(F)
The Olympic Games, 22246
Olympic Games in Ancient Greece,
  22247
Olympics, 22255
Oman, 15541
Omar on Ice, 2315(F)
Omega Station, 10239(F)
On a Starry Night, 1306(F)
On a Wintry Morning, 3577(F)
On Beyond a Million, 20637
On Beyond Bugs! 19480
On Beyond Zebra! 1565(F)
On Board the Titanic, 7094(F)

On Call Back Mountain, 4918(F)
On Christmas Day in the Morning,
  14210
On Divorce, 17686
On Grandpa's Farm, 3409(F)
On Hanukkah, 17462
The On-Line Spaceman and Other
  Cases, 7056(F)
On Mardi Gras Day, 5650(F)
On Market Street, 83(F)
On Mother's Lap, 4828(F)
On My Honor, 6768(F)
On My Horse, 3999(F)
On My Island, 1179(F)
On My Own, 2093(F)
On My Street, 6520(F)
On My Way, 12525(F)
On Passover, 6070
On Purim, 17463
On Ramon's Farm, 5220(F)
On Rosh Hashanah and Yom Kippur,
  17464
On Stage, 14320
On the Air, 14310
On the Banks of Plum Creek,
  7537(F)
On the Bus with Joanna Cole, 12519
On the Course with . . . Tiger Woods,
  13712
On the Court with . . . Grant Hill,
  13527
On the Court with . . . Michael Jor-
  dan, 13537
On the Day His Daddy Left, 4897(F)
On the Day I Was Born, 3579(F)
On the Day the Tall Ships Sailed,
  5643(F)
On the Day You Were Born, 4435(F)
On the Farm, 21252
On the Go, 3818
On the Home Front, 14882
On the Ice with . . . Wayne Gretzky,
  13686
On the Line, 10280(F)
On the Long Trail Home, 9179(F)
On the Mayflower, 16183
On the Morn of Mayfest, 1578(F)
On the Mound with . . . Greg Mad-
  dux, 13469
On the Move, 20833, 21288
On the Old Western Frontier, 16378
On the River, 573(F)
On the Road of Stars, 11213
On the Same Day in March, 20789
On the Stairs, 2340(F)
On the Trail of Elder Brother, 11296
On the Trail of the Komodo Dragon,
  18287
On the Trail with Miss Pace, 4413(F)
On the Water, 20422
On the Wing, 11787
On the Wings of Eagles, 4827(F)
On Tide Mill Lane, 9335(F)
On Time, 20653
On Top of Old Smoky, 11360
On Top of the World, 2600(F)
On Your Feet! 21165
On Your Potty! 3327(F)
Once a Wolf, 19143
Once I Was . . ., 205(F)
Once I Was a Plum Tree, 8703(F)

Once in the Country, 11613
Once on This Island, 9333(F), 9334(F)
Once on This River, 9219(F)
Once There Was a Bull . . . (frog), 2822(F)
Once There Was a Hoodie, 1365(F)
Once There Were Giants, 3468(F)
Once upon a Bedtime Story, 10631
Once upon a Company, 16944
Once Upon a Farm, 20047
Once upon a Lily Pad, 2743(F)
Once upon a Picnic, 1490(F)
Once upon a Princess and a Pea, 10404(F)
Once upon a Springtime, 6508(F)
Once Upon a Time, 12511
  (Illus. by John Prater), 1168(F)
Once upon a Time, 10551
Once Upon a Time and Grandma, 3532(F)
Once Upon an Island, 11429
Once upon Ice, 11991
Once Upon MacDonald's Farm, 14151
Once Upon MacDonald's Farm . . ., 5218(F)
Once We Had a Horse, 5388(F)
Once When the World Was Green, 1660(F)
One Afternoon, 3205(F)
The One and Only Me, 3896(F)
One at a Time, 11648
One Ballerina Two, 436(F)
One Bean, 20260
One Belfast Boy, 15360
One Boy from Kosovo, 15279
One Christmas Dawn, 5909(F)
One Cow Coughs, 498(F)
One Cow Moo Moo! 383(F)
One Crow, 374(F)
One Dark and Scary Night, 6281(F)
One Day in the Alpine Tundra, 20371
One Day in the Desert, 20403
One Day in the Jungle, 316(F)
One Day in the Tropical Rain Forest, 20442
One Day in the Woods, 20443(F)
One Day We Had to Run! 14953
One Dog Day, 7256(F)
One Duck, 5272(F)
One Duck, Another Duck, 560(F)
One Duck Stuck, 569(F)
One Eye Laughing, The Other Weeping, 9655(F)
One Eye, Two Eyes, Three Eyes, 11097
One-Eyed Cat, 8429(F)
One Fine Day, 10859
One Fish, Two Fish, Red Fish, Blue Fish, 6642(F)
One Foot Ashore, 9042(F)
One Giant Leap, 7017(F), 12073
One Good Apple, 19408
One Gorilla, 521(F)
One Grain of Rice, 10789
One Gray Mouse, 393
One Guinea Pig Is Not Enough, 423(F)
One Halloween Night, 6054(F)

One Happy Classroom, 581(F)
One Hole in the Road, 538(F)
One Horse Waiting for Me, 522(F)
One Hot Summer Day, 3092(F)
145th Street, 7360(F)
One-Hundred-and-One African-American Read-Aloud Stories, 10261(F)
100 Days of School, 459(F)
One Hundred Favorite Folktales, 10621
100 First Prize Make It Yourself Science Fair Projects, 18364
100 First Words to Say with Your Baby, 3378(F)
One Hundred Hungry Ants, 557(F)
One Hundred Is a Family, 572(F)
101 Amazing Optical Illusions, 20915
101 Best Family Card Games, 22237
101 Questions and Answers About Backyard Wildlife, 18673
101 Questions and Answers About Pets and People, 19909
101 Science Surprises, 18344
101 Science Tricks, 18345
101 Things Every Kid Should Know About Science, 18275
101 Things to Do on the Internet, 21231
101 Ways to Bug Your Parents, 10013(F)
175 Easy-to-Do Halloween Crafts, 21508
175 Science Experiments to Amuse and Amaze Your Friends, 18366
One Hundred Years of Poetry for Children, 11664
100th Day Worries, 415(F)
The One Hundredth Thing About Caroline, 9924(F)
One Hungry Cat, 568(F)
One Hungry Monster, 542(F)
One Hunter, 473(F)
One Less Fish, 598
One Lighthouse, One Moon, 207(F)
One Little Puppy Dog, 587(F)
One Little, Two Little, Three Little Pilgrims, 6143(F)
One Lonely Sea Horse, 437(F)
One Lucky Girl, 2955(F)
One Man Show, 12500
One Monkey Too Many, 486(F)
One Moose, Twenty Mice, 380(F)
One More Border, 14858
One More Bunny, 604(F)
One More River to Cross, 12659
One More Time, Mama, 3505(F)
One Morning in Maine, 3782(F)
One Nation, Many Tribes, 15982
One-of-a-Kind Mallie, 9524(F)
One of Each, 2215(F)
One of the Third-Grade Thonkers, 6988(F)
One of Three, 3725(F)
One Potato, 561
One Rainy Night, 5231(F)
One Red Sun, 481(F)
One Riddle, One Answer, 10510(F)
A One-Room School, 16325
One Room School, 14877

One-Room School, 15866
One Round Moon and a Star for Me, 3804(F)
One Saturday Afternoon, 6196(F)
One Sister Too Many, 7382(F)
One Small Blue Bead, 4588(F)
One Small Dog, 7227(F)
One Small Lost Sheep, 5883(F)
One Smiling Sister, 409(F)
One Snowy Day, 6633(F)
One Sunday Morning, 3690(F)
The One That Got Away, 4145(F)
One Thing I'm Good At, 8854(F)
One Thing That's True, 8428(F)
1000 Makers of the Millennium, 13739
1001 Questions and Answers, 21940
1000 Photos of Minerals and Fossils, 20554
1,000 Years Ago on Planet Earth, 14335
One Tiger Growls, 601
1 to 10 and Back Again, 544(F)
One TV Blasting and a Pig Outdoors, 8874(F)
One, Two, One Pair! 509
One, Two, Skip a Few! First Number Rhymes, 545
1, 2, 3, 468(F)
1-2-3 Draw, 21581
1, 2, 3, Go! 489
1, 2, 3 Moose, 462
One, Two, Three, Oops! 410(F)
1 2 3 Pop! 476
1 2 3 . . ., 543(F)
1, 2, 3 Thanksgiving! 539(F)
1, 2, 3 to the Zoo, 396(F)
1 2 3 Yippie, 477(F)
One Unhappy Horse, 7147(F)
One Up, One Down, 3901(F)
One Was Johnny, 242(F)
One White Sail, 441(F)
One Windy Wednesday, 1520(F)
One Wintry Night, 17418(F)
One Woolly Wombat, 599(F)
One World, Many Religions, 17210
One Yellow Lion, 254(F)
One Zillion Valentines, 6174(F)
The Oneida, 15998
Onion John, 8735(F)
Onion Tears, 7348(F)
Onions and Garlic, 11156
Online Kids, 21204
Only a Pigeon, 4721(F)
Only a Star, 5811(F)
Only One, 460(F)
Only One Cowry, 10666
Only One Ollie, 566(F)
Only One Woof, 7220(F)
Only Opal, 4600
The Only Other Crazy Car Book, 21325
Only Passing Through, 12793
Only the Names Remain, 15923
Ooey Gooey, 6331(F)
Ooh-La-La (Max in Love), 2272(F)
Ooka the Wise, 10812
Oomph! A Preston Pig Story, 2447(F)
Oonga Boonga, 4355(F)
Oops! 2448(F), 17635

Open Wide, 18184
Opening Days, 11998
Opening Moves, 22170
Opera! What's All the Screaming About? 14127
Operation, 9957(F)
Operation Baby-Sitter, 10306(F)
Operation Ghost, 7715(F)
Operation Siberian Crane, 19230
Opposites (Illus. by Sue Hendra), 231(F)
　(Illus. by Richard Wilbur), 14057
Oprah Winfrey, 12484, 12485
The Oprah Winfrey Story, 12486
Opt, 20910
The Optical Illusion Book, 20917
Optical Illusion Magic, 20913
Optical Illusion Tricks and Toys, 20911
Optics, 20871
The Optics Book, 20873
Orange Cheeks, 3826(F)
Orange Fairy Book, 10442(F)
Oranges on Golden Mountain, 4794(F)
The Orangutan, 18989
Orangutans, 19009
Orcas, 19792
Orcas Around Me, 3354
The Orchard Book of Nursery Rhymes, 893
Orchard of the Crescent Moon, 7991(F)
The Orchestra, 14228
Orchids, 20250
An Ordinary Cat, 2291(F)
Ordinary Genius, 13276
Ordinary Miracles, 8833(F)
Ordinary Things, 11948
Oregon, 16764, 16777, 16789, 16818, 16819
Oregon, Sweet Oregon, 9387(F)
The Oregon Trail, 16293, 16303
Oregon Trail Cooking, 16312
Oregon's Journey, 1496(F)
Origami in the Classroom, 21604
The Origin of Life on Earth, 10645
The Original Freddie Ackerman, 6907(F)
The Original Olympics, 22256
The Originals, 11819
The Orinoco River, 15779
Orion, the Hunter, 18537
Ornithology, 19223
Ornithomimids, 14437
Orp, 9901(F)
Orp and the Chop Suey Burgers, 9902(F)
Orp and the FBI, 6923(F)
Orp Goes to the Hoop, 9903(F)
Orphan, 4493
The Orphan Boy, 10703
Orphan Journey Home, 9300(F)
Orphan of Ellis Island, 8218(F)
Orphan Runaways, 9546(F)
Orphan Train Rider, 15914
The Orthopedist, 18023
Orwell's Luck, 7839(F)
Oscar De La Hoya, 13584
Oscar de la Renta, 12829
Oscar Otter, 6202(F)

Oscar Wilde's The Selfish Giant, 10518(F)
Osceola, 12771
Oskar Schindler, 13849
Ospreys, 19354
Ostriches, 19259
Ostriches and Other Flightless Birds, 19214
O'Sullivan Stew, 1610(F)
The Other Dog, 2355(F)
The Other Emily, 5494(F)
The Other Shepards, 8441(F)
The Other Side, 4063(F), 11763
The Other Side of the Hudson, 7368(F)
The Other Way to Listen, 302(F)
Other Worlds, 18511
Otherwise Known as Sheila the Great, 8566(F)
Otis, 1907(F)
Otis Spofford, 9803(F)
The Ottawa, 15983
The Otter, 18965
Otter on His Own, 19729
Otter Play, 5320(F)
Otters, 19749
Otters Under Water, 5124
Otto of the Silver Hand, 9067(F)
Otto's Rainy Day, 3493(F)
Ouch! 10883
Our Baby from China, 3600(F)
Our Big Home, 3170(F)
Our Burden of Shame, 14881
Our Congress, 17128
Our Constitution, 17057
Our Declaration of Independence, 16213
Our Earth, 20319
Our Eight Nights of Hanukkah, 6107(F)
Our Elections, 17103
Our Endangered Planet, 15846, 16997, 17010, 19822, 20467, 20520, 20576, 20677
Our Environment, 16963, 18594
Our Flag, 13969
Our Granny, 3944(F)
Our House, 3860(F), 7415(F)
Our Lady of Guadalupe, 17216
Our Living Forests, 20441
Our Most Dear Friend, 17226
Our National Anthem, 14233
Our National Capital, 16744
Our National Monuments, 15849
Our National Parks, 15916
Our National Symbols, 15851
Our Natural Homes, 20365
Our Neighbor Is a Strange, Strange Man, 13331
Our New Baby (Illus. by Chris O'Neill), 17657
　(Illus. by Dorothy Stott), 6441(F)
Our New Puppy, 5250(F)
Our Old House, 3464(F)
Our Only May Amelia, 7453(F)
Our Planet Earth, 14345
Our Planet, 18435
Our Presidency, 17102
Our Puppies Are Growing, 19960
Our Satellite, 18451
Our Solar System, 18528

Our Space Program, 20961
Our Stars, 18412
Our Strange New Land, 9197(F)
Our Supreme Court, 17013
Our Teacher's Having a Baby, 5479(F)
Our Teacher's in a Wheelchair, 17929
Our Violent Earth, 20328
Our Yard Is Full of Birds, 5384
Out and About, 4464(F)
Out of Darkness, 13760
Out of Sight, 18293
Out of the Ark, 17185
Out of the Blue, 8426(F)
Out of the Dark, 8228(F), 8716(F)
Out of the Dump, 15663
Out of the Gang, 17069
Out of the Ocean, 4436(F)
Out of the Storm, 8855(F)
Out of the Wilderness, 7106(F)
Out of Their Minds, 7954(F)
Out of This World, 18419, 21447
Out to Dry, 21856
Out to Lunch, 1739(F)
Outcast of Redwall, 7828(F)
Outer Space and All That Junk, 10185(F)
Outlaw Red, 7247(F)
An Outlaw Thanksgiving, 9407(F)
Outrageous, Bodacious Boliver Boggs! 4176(F)
Outrageous Women of Ancient Times, 13734
Outrageous Women of the Middle Ages, 13735
Outrageously Alice, 9948(F)
Outside and Inside Alligators, 18704
Outside and Inside Bats, 19031
Outside and Inside Birds, 19258
Outside and Inside Dinosaurs, 14446
Outside and Inside Kangaroos, 19179
Outside and Inside Sharks, 19765
Outside and Inside Snakes, 18769
Outside and Inside Spiders, 19587
The Outside Dog, 6580(F)
The Outside Inn, 1363(F)
Outside, Inside, 3094(F)
Outside Over There, 1558(F)
Over Back, 4496(F)
Over in the Grasslands, 610(F)
Over in the Meadow, 395, 440(F)
Over Jordan, 9297(F)
Over Sea, Under Stone, 7671(F)
Over 6,000 Years Ago, 14508
Over 65 Million Years Ago, 14449
Over the Edge, 15840
Over the Hills and Far Away, 860
Over the Moon, 2771(F), 3745(F)
Over the Moon! Best Loved Nursery Rhymes, 865(F)
Over the River and Through the Wood, 6140(F)
Over the Top of the World, 15836
Over-Under, 212(F)
Over, Under and Through and Other Spacial Concepts, 337(F)
Owen, 2195(F)
Owen Foote, Frontiersman, 6865(F)
Owen Foote, Money Man, 9866(F)

Owen Foote, Second Grade Strongman, 10068(F)
Owen Foote, Soccer Star, 10328(F)
Owl, 19366
   (Illus. by Diana Magnuson), 19358
   (Illus. by Kim Taylor), 19362
Owl and the Pussycat, 11888
The Owl and the Pussycat (Illus. by Jan Brett), 11887
   (Illus. by James Marshall), 11890
   (Illus. by Louise Voce), 11889
Owl at Home, 6468(F)
Owl Babies, 2802(F)
Owl Moon, 5463(F)
Owls, 19361, 19363
Ox-Cart Man, 4674(F)
The Oxford Book of Children's Verse in America, 11588
The Oxford Book of Story Poems, 11593
Oxford Children's Book of the 20th Century, 14570
Oxford First Ancient History, 14580
Oxford First Book of Animals, 18982
Oxford First Book of Art, 13934
The Oxford Illustrated Book of American Children's Poems, 11666
The Oxford Treasury of Time Poems, 11594
The Oxford Treasury of World Stories, 10598
Oxygen, 20284
Oyster Moon, 6972(F)
Oz, 14003
The Ozone Hole, 17000, 17006
Ozzie on His Own, 8310(F)

P. B. Bear's Treasure Hunt, 21880(F)
P. J. and Puppy, 3127(F)
P.S. Longer Letter Later, 8274(F)
P. T. Barnum, 12353
Pa Lia's First Day, 10052(F)
Pablo Picasso, 12282, 12284
   (Illus. by Janice L. Porter), 12281
Pablo Remembers, 15600
Pablo's Tree, 3815(F)
The Pacific, 16762
The Pacific Ocean, 19826
A Pack of Lies, 7931(F)
The Package in Hyperspace, 10144(F)
Paddington Abroad, 9785(F)
Paddington at Large, 9786(F)
Paddington at Work, 9785(F)
Paddington Bear, 1833(F)
Paddington Bear All Day, 1834(F)
Paddington Bear and the Busy Bee Carnival, 12(F)
Paddington Bear and the Christmas Surprise, 5756(F)
Paddington Bear Goes to Market, 1835(F)
Paddington Goes to Town, 9785(F)
Paddington Helps Out, 9785(F)
Paddington's 1, 2, 3, 385(F)
Paddington's Opposites, 165(F)
Paddington's Storybook, 9787(F)
Paddiwak and Cozy, 5186(F)
Paddle-to-the-Sea, 15883
Paddy Under Water, 920(F)
Page, 9117(F)

Pages of Music, 5854(F)
Pagoo, 19676
The Pain and the Great One, 3534(F)
Paint! 21594
The Paint Brush Kid, 8574(F)
Painted Dreams, 4878(F)
The Painter, 3575(F)
The Painter Who Loved Chickens, 4138(F)
Painters of the Caves, 14503
Painting, 13917, 13930
Painting Dreams, 12231
The Painting Gorilla, 2622(F)
Painting the Wind, 12306
Painting with Face Paints, 21577
Painting with Tempera, 21578
Painting with Watercolors, 21578
Paintings, 13887
A Pair of Protoceratops, 218(F)
A Pair of Red Sneakers, 4210(F)
A Pair of Socks, 1426(F)
Pajama Time! 3035(F)
Pakistan, 15194, 15204, 15220
Pakistan in Pictures, 15191
Pal the Pony, 6382(F)
Palampam Day, 1183(F)
The Palestinian Conflict, 15537
The Palm of My Heart, 11747
Palm Trees, 3991(F)
Pamela Camel, 2566(F)
Panama, 15668, 15687
Panama and the United States, 15672
The Panama Canal, 15675, 15677, 15691
The Panama Canal in American History, 15664
Panama in Pictures, 15681
Pancakes for Breakfast, 4128(F)
Pancho Villa, 13864, 13865
Pancho's Pinata, 5793
Panda, 19189
Panda Big and Panda Small, 1909(F)
Panda's New Toy, 2042(F)
Pankration, 9029(F)
Panther, 6774(F), 19095
Panther Glade, 8599(F)
Papa! 653(F)
Papa Alonzo Leatherby, 9829(F)
Papa Gatto, 10489
Papa Lucky's Shadow, 3599(F)
Papa, Please Get the Moon for Me, 1037(F)
Papa Tells Chita a Story, 4686(F)
Papa's Christmas Gift, 11831
Papa's Latkes, 6128(F)
Papa's Song, 739(F)
Paper, 21057, 21606
The Paper Airplane Book, 21796
Paper Airplanes, 21621
The Paper Bag Princess, 4242(F)
Paper Birds That Fly, 21627
Paper by Kids, 21616
The Paper Chain, 17940
The Paper Crane, 976(F)
The Paper Dragon, 1104(F)
Paper Gifts and Jewelry, 21633
Paper John, 1586(F)
Paper, Paper Everywhere, 3168(F)
The Paper Princess, 1315(F)
Paper Science Toys, 21650
Paper Tags and Cards, 21633

Paperboy, 9552(F)
   (Illus. by Ted Lewin), 4716(F)
The Paperboy, 3361(F)
Papercrafts, 21611
Papercrafts Around the World, 21613
The Papermakers, 16116
Papermaking, 21637
Papermaking for Kids, 21639
Paperquake, 8792(F)
Paperwhite, 4057(F)
Papier Mâché, 21605
   (Illus. by Jim Robins), 21625
Papier-Mâché, 21628
Papier-Mâché for Kids, 21623
Parables, 17286
The Parables of Jesus, 17261
Parachuting Hamsters and Andy Russell, 6738(F)
Parade, 3090(F)
Parading with Piglets, 47(F)
Paradox in Oz, 7716(F)
The Paradox of Jamestown, 16104
Paraguay, 15749, 15768
Paraguay in Pictures, 15742
The Parakeet Girl, 6621(F)
Parallel Universe, 21862(F)
Paranormal Powers, 21895
Parasites, 18622
Parcel for Stanley, 2852(F)
Parents' Night Fright, 6458(F)
Paris, 15318
Paris Cat, 4584(F)
Paris 1789, 15320
Parkinson's Disease, 17979
Parks Are to Share, 16957
Parks for the People, 12941
Park's Quest, 8505(F)
The Parrot, 11063
Parrots, 19238, 19264, 19273, 19882
The Parthenon, 14675, 14709
Partners, 8380(F)
The Party, 1381(F), 3853(F)
Party Rhymes, 11539
Parzival, 11021
Pa's Harvest, 16445
Pass It On, 11761
Pass It On! 14066
Pass the Bread! 20077
Passage to Freedom, 14873
Passage to Little Bighorn, 7882(F)
Passager, 8239(F)
Passover, 6100(F), 17482
The Passover Journey, 17467
Pasta, 20123
Pastabilities, 8135(F)
The Pasteboard Bandit, 1005(F)
Patch and the Rabbits, 2603(F)
Patch Finds a Friend, 2603(F)
Patches Finds a New Home, 5347(F)
Patches Lost and Found, 5295(F)
The Patchwork Lady, 5737(F)
Patricia Ryan Nixon, 13171
Patrick, 13842
Patrick DesJarlait, 12223
Patrick Doyle Is Full of Blarney, 10270(F)
Patrick Ewing, 13524
Patrick's Day, 5642(F)
Patrick's Dinosaurs, 4925(F)
Patrick's Dinosaurs on the Internet, 1043(F)

Patrick's Tree House, 8327(F)
Patsy's Discovery, 9241(F)
Pattern Fish, 192(F)
Patterns, 233, 20606
Patti's Pet Gorilla, 5027(F)
Patty Reed's Doll, 9393(F)
Patty's Pumpkin Patch, 134(F)
Paul Bunyan, 11357
Paul Bunyan Swings His Axe, 11365
Paul Cézanne, 12204, 12206
Paul Klee, 12247, 12248
Paul Revere, 12959
Paul Revere's Ride (Illus. by Nancy Winslow Parker), 11643
    (Illus. by Ted Rand), 11644
Paul Robeson, 12453, 12454
Paula Abdul, 12341, 12342
Pauline, 2166(F)
Paul's Volcano, 10187(F)
The Pawnee, 15966
Pawns, 8514(F)
Pawprints in Time, 4614(F)
Paws and Claws, 18819
The Paxton Cheerleaders, 10072(F)
Pay Attention, Slosh! 8915(F)
Peace and Bread, 13128
Peace in Space, 20949
The Peace Seekers, 13723
Peace Tales, 10579
The Peaceable Kingdom, 8245(F)
Peacebound Trains, 8984(F)
Peach and Blue, 1300(F)
Peacocks, 19218
The Peacock's Pride, 10797
Peanut Butter, 20091
Peanut Butter and Jelly, 4349(F)
The Peanut Butter Cookbook for Kids, 21734
Peanut Butter Party, 20083
Peanut Butter Pilgrims, 4126(F)
Peanuts, 20111
The Pearl, 2187(F)
Pearl Harbor, 14857, 14895
Pearl Harbor! 14836
Pearl Harbor Child, 14874
Pearl Harbor Is Burning! 9668(F)
Pearl Plants a Tree, 2895(F)
Pearl's Eight Days of Chanukah, 6129
Pearl's Marigolds for Grandpa, 3964(F)
The Pearls of Lutra, 7829(F)
Peary Reaches the North Pole, 12146
Peas, 1232(F)
Peas and Honey, 21683
A Pebble and a Pen, 16238(F)
The Pebble in My Pocket, 20311
Peck Slither and Slide, 18830
Pecos Bill, 11358
Pedaling Along, 22165
The Peddler's Gift, 6115(F)
The Pediatrician, 18033
Pedrito's Day, 4653(F)
Pedro's Journal, 8927(F)
Peek-a-Boo! 3236(F)
Peek-a-Moo! 5166(F)
Peek-a-Who? 4206(F)
A Peek at Japan, 15133
Peekaboo Babies, 495(F)
Peeking Prairie Dogs, 19212
Peeping Beauty, 1773(F)

Peeping in the Shell, 19256
PeeWee's Tale, 7806(F)
Peg and the Whale, 8000(F)
Pegasus, 11492
Pegasus, the Flying Horse, 11517
Pegasus, the Winged Horse, 11496
Pele, 13707
Pelicans, 19343
Pelle's New Suit, 4594(F)
Pen Pals, 14071
Penalty Shot, 10307(F)
Penelope Jane, 10405(F)
Penguin, 19376, 19383, 19386
The Penguin, 19370
Penguin Dreams, 1555(F)
Penguin Pete, Ahoy! 2578(F)
The Penguin Quartet, 1752(F)
A Penguin Year, 19368
Penguins, 19369, 19373, 19374, 19375, 19380, 19382, 19384, 19387, 19388
Penguins! 19371, 19377
Penguins at Home, 19378
Pennies to Dollars, 12811
Pennsylvania, 16682, 16691, 16725, 16747, 16751
The Pennsylvania Colony, 16124
A Penny a Look, 4364(F)
The Penny Pot, 531
People, 14511, 21580
    (Illus. by Peter Spier), 3438(F)
The People, 14512
A People Apart, 17197
The People Could Fly, 11341
People from Mother Goose, 850
The People in Pineapple Place, 7914(F)
People in the Rain Forest, 20476
People, Love, Sex, and Families, 18262
People of Mexico, 15611
People of Peace, 13725
People of the Breaking Day, 16035
People of the Deserts, 20409
People of the Islands, 20388
People of the Mountains, 20500
People of the Rain Forest, 20494
People of the Rain Forests, 20464
People Who Care, 13741
People Who Changed the World, 13745
The People with Five Fingers, 11287
Peoples of the Desert, 20412
Peoples of the Mountains, 20503
Peoples of the Rain Forest, 20465
Peoples of the Savanna, 20539
People's Republic of China, 15058
Pepi and the Secret Names, 8187(F)
Pepito the Brave, 1798(F)
Peppe the Lamplighter, 4587(F)
Peppermints in the Parlor, 7117(F)
Pepper's Journal, 20649
Peppers, Popcorn, and Pizza, 20120
Per and the Dala Horse, 1237(F)
Perching Birds of North America, 19263
Percy to the Rescue, 2698(F)
The Peregrine Falcon, 19342
    (Illus. by Jennifer Priebe), 19339
The Perfect Christmas Gift, 5797(F)

The Perfect Christmas Picture, 5875(F)
A Perfect Father's Day, 5614(F)
A Perfect Friend, 8024(F)
The Perfect Orange, 10647
Perfect Pigs, 1893(F)
A Perfect Pork Stew, 1275(F)
The Perfect Present, 5830(F)
The Perfect Spot, 3531(F)
Perfect the Pig, 2254(F)
The Perfume of Memory, 10469(F)
Peril in the Bessledorf Parachute Factory, 6989(F)
The Perilous Journey of the Donner Party, 16294
Period, 18265
The Period Book, 18259
Perloo the Bold, 7567(F)
Perplexing Puzzles and Tantalizing Teasers, 20616
Perrault's Fairy Tales, 10877
Perseus, 11482
Perseus and Medusa, 11496
The Persian Cinderella, 10407
Persian Gulf War, 15489
The Persian Gulf War, 16514
Personal Computer Communications, 21222
Personal Computers, 21211
A Personal Tour of Camden Yards, 22125
A Personal Tour of La Purisima, 16827
A Personal Tour of Mesa Verde, 16073
A Personal Tour of Monticello, 16899
Peru, 15198, 15731, 15750, 15755, 15769
Peru in Pictures, 15776
Pet Boy, 1205(F)
Pet Bugs, 19458
Pet Detectives, 2881(F)
Pet Gerbils, 19911
Pet Hamsters, 19912
Pet of a Pet, 2181(F)
A Pet or Not? 19905
Pet Parade, 5501(F)
The Pet-Sitters, 7302(F)
The Pet-Sitting Peril, 7030(F)
Pet Stories, 6573(F)
Pete and Polo's Big School Adventure, 1504(F)
Pete Sampras, 13651
Peter and the Blue Witch Baby, 11111
Peter and the Wolf, 11115
    (Illus. by Barbara Cooney), 10481(F)
    (Illus. by Sergei Prokofiev), 11107
Peter Duck, 7015(F)
Peter Pan, 7590(F)
    (Illus. by Michael Hague), 7589(F)
Peter Tchaikovsky, 12340
Peter the Great and Tsarist Russia, 13843
Peter's Patchwork Dream, 1416(F)
Peter's Picture, 2139(F)
Peter's Trucks, 5607(F)
Pete's a Pizza, 4327(F)
Petey and Miss Magic, 8626(F)

Petey's Bedtime Story, 650(F)
Petook, 5969(F)
Pets, 19883
Pets! 1971(F)
Pets and Farm Animals, 18828
Pets in a Jar, 19908
Pets in Trumpets and Other Word-Play Riddles, 21842
Pettranella, 4869(F)
Petty Crimes, 7374(F)
Petunia, 2047(F)
Peyton Manning, 13618
Phantom Animals, 18615
The Phantom of the Lunch Wagon, 1480(F)
The Phantom of the Opera, 6939(F)
Phantom of the Prairie, 5315(F)
The Phantom Tollbooth, 7849(F)
Phantom Victory, 7050(F)
The Pharaohs of Ancient Egypt, 14658
Pharmacy in the Forest, 18026
Philadelphia, 16653, 16711
The Philadelphia Flyers Hockey Team, 22224
The Philharmonic Gets Dressed, 3270(F)
Philip Hall Likes Me, I Reckon Maybe, 8290(F)
Philipok, 5543(F)
Philippe in Monet's Garden, 1039(F)
Philippines, 15247, 15255
The Philippines, 15233, 15241, 15252, 15254
Phillis Wheatley, 12619, 12620
Phoebe and the River Flute, 10432(F)
Phoebe and the Spelling Bee, 5532(F)
Phoebe's Fabulous Father, 3565(F)
Phoebe's Parade, 5638(F)
Phoebe's Revolt, 4582(F)
The Phoenicians, 14593
The Phoenix and the Carpet, 7987(F)
The Phoenix Suns Basketball Team, 22142
Phone Call from a Flamingo, 8822(F)
Phone Call from a Ghost, 21900
Phosphorous, 20277
Photo Odyssey, 16081
Photographers, 12170
Photography, 21799, 21802
Photojournalist, 17774
Photosynthesis, 20033
Physics Lab in a Hardware Store, 20807
Physics Lab in a Housewares Store, 20808
Pi-Shu, the Little Panda, 5154(F)
Pia Toya, 11288
Pianna, 3374(F)
The Piano, 4770(F)
The Piano Man, 3580(F)
Picasso, 12285
 (Illus. by Susan Hellard), 12280
Pick a Pet, 5387(F)
Pick and Shovel Poet, 12523
Pickin' Peas, 2423(F)
Pickle and the Ball, 3040(F)
PIckle and the Blanket, 3040(F)
Pickle and the Blocks, 3040(F)
Pickle and the Box, 3040(F)

Pickles to Pittsburgh, 981(F)
Picky Mrs. Pickle, 4303(F)
Picnic (Illus. by Mick Inkpen), 2240(F)
 (Illus. by Emily Arnold McCully), 925(F)
Picnic at Mudsock Meadow, 6040(F)
Picnic Farm, 3335(F)
A Picnic in October, 3557(F)
Picnic on a Cloud, 7811(F)
Picnic with Piggins, 2891(F)
The Pictish Child, 8240(F)
A Picture Book of Abraham Lincoln, 13063
A Picture Book of Amelia Earhart, 12107
A Picture Book of Anne Frank, 13796
A Picture Book of Benjamin Franklin, 12878
A Picture Book of Christopher Columbus, 12096
A Picture Book of Davy Crockett, 12102
A Picture Book of Eleanor Roosevelt, 13178
A Picture Book of Florence Nightin-gale, 13840
A Picture Book of Frederick Dou-glass, 12708
A Picture Book of George Washing-ton, 13113
A Picture Book of George Washing-ton Carver, 13251
A Picture Book of Harriet Tubman, 12795
A Picture Book of Helen Keller, 13164
A Picture Book of Jackie Robinson, 13487
A Picture Book of Jesse Owens, 13664
A Picture Book of John F. Kennedy, 13058
A Picture Book of Louis Braille, 13757
A Picture Book of Martin Luther King, Jr., 12739
A Picture Book of Patrick Henry, 12898
A Picture Book of Paul Revere, 12958
A Picture Book of Robert E. Lee, 12925
A Picture Book of Rosa Parks, 12773
A Picture Book of Sacagawea, 12988
A Picture Book of Simon Bolivar, 13754
A Picture Book of Sojourner Truth, 12789
A Picture Book of Thomas Jefferson, 13046
A Picture Book of Thurgood Mar-shall, 12763
A Picture for Harold's Room, 6423(F)
The Picture History of Great Inven-tors, 13205
A Picture of Freedom, 9305(F)
Picture Puzzler, 20918
The Picture That Mom Drew, 13908

Picture This . . ., 202(F)
Pictures in the Dark, 7688(F)
Picturing Lincoln, 13077
Pie Rats Ahoy! 2658(F)
A Pie Went By, 1142(F)
Piece by Piece! 13938
A Piece of Heaven, 8871(F)
Piece of Jungle, 4874(F)
Pieces, 11958
Pieces of Eight, 7846(F)
Pieces of the Picture, 8714(F)
The Pied Piper of Hamelin, 10918
Pierre, 5072(F)
Pierre Auguste Renoir, 12291, 12292
Pierre's Dream, 4079(F)
Pie's in the Oven, 4086(F)
Pieter Bruegel, 12194, 12195
Pig and Crow, 1957(F)
Pig and the Shrink, 10005(F)
The Pig in a Wig, 2418(F)
The Pig in the Spigot, 14058
A Pig Is Big, 329(F)
The Pig Is in the Pantry, the Cat Is on the Shelf, 2517(F)
A Pig Is Moving In! 2106(F)
Pig Pig Gets a Job, 2460(F)
A Pig Tale, 2527(F)
The Pig Who Ran a Red Light, 2259(F)
The Pig Who Wished, 2044(F)
Pig William, 2039(F)
Pigeons, 19266
A Piggie Christmas, 14199
Piggie Pie! 1450(F)
Piggies, 1705(F)
Piggies, Piggies, Piggies, 2621(F)
Piggins, 2891(F)
Piggins and the Royal Wedding, 2891(F)
Piggle, 6213(F)
Piggy Goes to Bed, 6693(F)
The Piggy in the Puddle, 2595(F)
Piggybook, 1896(F)
Piggy's Birthday Dream, 2033(F)
Piglet's Bath, 2712(F)
Pignapped! 10009(F)
Pignic, 101(F)
Pigs, 18942, 20048, 20066
 (Illus. by Michael Martchenko), 4243(F)
Pigs Ahoy! 2461(F)
Pigs Aplenty, Pigs Galore! 2462(F)
The Pigs Are Flying, 8045(F)
Pigs at Odds, 20579(F)
Pigs from A to Z, 41(F)
Pigs from 1 to 10, 442(F)
Pigs Go to Market, 9707(F)
Pigs in the Mud in the Middle of the Rud, 4267(F)
Pigs in the Pantry, 1775(F)
Pigs Might Fly, 7867(F)
Pigs on a Blanket, 1776(F)
The Pigs' Wedding, 2188(F)
Pigs Will Be Pigs, 1777(F)
Pigsty, 2756(F)
The Pileated Woodpecker, 19268
Pilgrim Voices, 16165
Pilgrims and Puritans, 16105
The Pilgrims of Plimoth, 16169
Pilgrim's Progress, 8070(F)
A Pill Bug's Life, 18635

Pillbugs, 19486
A Pillow for My Mom, 5073(F)
The Pillow War, 4253(F)
Pilots Fly Planes, 17838
Pin the Tail on the Donkey and Other
  Party Games, 21987
The Pinata Maker/El Piñatero, 15601
Pinatas and Paper Flowers, 17394
Pinatas and Smiling Skeletons, 17366
The Pinballs, 8266(F)
Pingo the Plaid Panda, 2353(F)
Pink and Say, 9495(F)
Pink Paper Swans, 4021(F)
The Pinkish, Purplish, Bluish Egg,
  2570(F)
Pinky and Rex, 6417(F)
Pinky and Rex and the Bully,
  8699(F)
Pinky and Rex and the Double-Dad
  Weekend, 7456(F)
Pinky and Rex and the Just-Right
  Pet, 7224(F)
Pinky and Rex and the Mean Old
  Witch, 6413(F)
Pinky and Rex and the New Baby,
  6414(F)
Pinky and Rex and the New Neigh-
  bors, 6415(F)
Pinky and Rex and the Perfect Pump-
  kin, 8700(F)
Pinky and Rex and the School Play,
  6416(F)
Pinky and Rex and the Spelling Bee,
  6413(F)
Pinky and Rex Get Married, 6417(F)
Pinky and Rex Go to Camp, 6418(F)
A Pinky Is a Baby Mouse, 18880
Pinocchio, 1410(F)
  (Illus. by Victor G. Ambrus),
  7661(F)
  (Illus. by Ed Young), 7662(F)
Pioneer Bear, 6622(F)
Pioneer Cat, 9382(F)
Pioneer Children of Appalachia,
  9340(F)
Pioneer Church, 4789(F)
Pioneer Crafts, 21520
Pioneer Days, 16334
A Pioneer Farm Girl, 16308
Pioneer Girl, 12627, 16384
Pioneer Projects, 21521
A Pioneer Sampler, 15576
A Pioneer Thanksgiving, 17499
Pioneering Frozen Worlds, 15820
Pioneering Space, 21000
Pioneering Women of the Wild West,
  16364
Pioneers, 16304
Pioneers of the Frontier, 16381
Piper, 7197(F)
Pippi Goes on Board, 9917(F)
Pippi in the South Seas, 9917(F)
Pippi Longstocking (Illus. by
  Michael Chesworth), 9918(F)
  (Illus. by Louis Glanzman),
  9917(F)
Pippi Longstocking's After-Christ-
  mas Party, 5865(F)
Pippi to the Rescue, 6949(F)
Pippin and the Bones, 6422(F)
Pippin Takes a Bath, 2255(F)

Pippi's Extraordinary Ordinary Day,
  9918(F)
Pip's Magic, 2817(F)
Piranhas, 19697, 19703, 19708
Piranhas and Other Wonders of the
  Jungle, 18653
Pirate, 14568
The Pirate Queen, 12145
Pirate School, 6316(F)
The Pirate Uncle, 6959(F)
Pirates, 14551, 14571
Pirates Ahoy! 4027(F)
Pirates and Treasure, 14566
The Pirate's Parrot, 7937(F)
Pirates! Raiders of the High Seas,
  12065
Pish, Posh, Said Hieronymus Bosch,
  1682
The Pittsburgh Steelers Football
  Team, 22185
Pizza! 20115
Pizza Pat, 6340(F)
A Pizza the Size of the Sun, 11678
Pizza Zombies, 7905(F)
A Place Called Freedom, 4822(F)
A Place in the Sun, 8977(F)
The Place My Words Are Looking
  For, 11610
A Place to Belong, 9531(F)
A Place to Bloom, 3431(F)
Plain City, 8447(F)
Plain Girl, 8820(F)
Plains Indians of North America,
  16001
Plains Outbreak Tornadoes, 20716
Planes, 21084
  (Illus. by Tim Ridley), 21100
Planes and Other Flying Things,
  21634
Planes, Gliders, Helicopters and
  Other Flying Machines, 21083
Planet Earth, 18431, 20317
Planet Earth/Inside Out, 20307
The Planet Hunters, 18470
The Planet of the Grapes, 21833
Planet Omicron, 20615
Planet Was, 1004(F)
Planetarium, 20962
Planets, 18471
  (Illus. by Denise Ortakales), 18512
The Planets, 18456, 18473, 18483,
  18484
The Planets in Our Solar System,
  18458
Planets, Moons and Meteors, 18513
The Plant-and-Grow Project Book,
  21761
Plant Experiments, 18367
The Plant Kingdom, 20032
Planting a Rainbow, 3116(F)
Plants, 20225, 20234, 20255, 20264
Plants and Us, 20263
Plants of the Tropics, 20259
Plants Under the Sea, 20246
Plastic Bottles, 21422
Plastic Cups, 21422
Plastic Model Kits, 21794
Plastics and Polymers, 21046
Plate Tectonics, 20322
Platero y Yo/Platero and I, 7229
Platypus, 18973

Play, 215
Play All Day, 1458(F)
Play Ball, 10338(F)
Play Ball, Amelia Bedelia, 6566(F)
Play Like a Girl, 22048
Play Mas! A Carnival ABC, 87(F)
Play Me a Story, 10528
Play Rhymes, 829
Play to the Angel, 9651(F)
Play with Computers, 21198
Play with Me, 5198(F)
Play with Paint, 21585
Play with Paper, 21585
Play with Your Pumpkins, 21434
Playgrounds, 183(F)
Playing, 3227(F)
Playing Possum, 21826(F)
Playing with Words, 12550
The Playmaker, 9086(F)
Playoff Dreams, 10281(F)
Plays, 12014
Plays Children Love, Volume II,
  12022
Plays from African Tales, 12042
Plays from Fairy Tales, 12028
Plays from Hispanic Tales, 12043
Plays from Mythology, 12029
Plays of America from American
  Folklore for Children Grades K–6,
  12030
Plays of the Wild West, 12031
Playtime, 3021(F)
Playtime for Zoo Animals, 18797
Playtime Rhymes, 858
Please, Please, Please, 8379(F)
The Please Touch Cookbook, 21730
Pleasing the Ghost, 7684(F)
Plenty of Pockets, 4094(F)
Plenty of Puppets to Make, 14307
Plotting Points and Position, 20604
Plows, 20071
Plugged In, 21844(F)
The Plum Tree War, 8362(F)
Pluto, 18463, 18496, 18500
Pocahontas, 12985, 12986, 12987
The Pocket Dogs, 1681(F)
A Pocket for Corduroy, 2100(F)
Pocket Pets, 19907
A Pocketful of Cricket, 5485(F)
A Pocketful of Goobers, 13256
A Pocketful of Poems, 11584
A Pocketful of Stars, 777
Pockets, 3000(F)
Poem Stew, 11865
Poems for Children Nowhere Near
  Old Enough to Vote, 11915
Poems for Jewish Holidays, 11837
Poems for the Very Young, 11684
Poems Have Roots, 11973
Poems That Sing to You, 11721
Poems to Read to the Very Young,
  11567
Poet and Politician of Puerto Rico,
  12935
Poetry, 11542
Poetry for Young People, 11671,
  11719, 11906
Poetry from A to Z, 14095
Poinsettia and Her Family, 1831(F)
Poinsettia and the Firefighters,
  1831(F)

Poison Dart Frogs, 18720
Poison Ivy and Eyebrow Wigs, 10122(F)
Poisoners and Pretenders, 20433
Poisonous Creatures, 18601
Poisonous Plants, 20231
Poisons in Our Path, 20233
A Poke in the I, 11907
Pokot, 14950
Poland, 15263, 15276, 15277, 15283, 15286, 15295
Polar Animals, 18964
Polar Babies, 19064
Polar Bear, 19062, 19068
A Polar Bear Can Swim, 18865
A Polar Bear Journey, 19057
Polar Bear, Polar Bear, What Do You Hear? 5340(F)
The Polar Bear Son, 11205
Polar Bears, 19042, 19053, 19061, 19063
The Polar Express, 5943(F)
Polar Lands, 15792
Polar Mammals, 18927
Polar Regions, 15813
The Polar Seas, 15826
Polar Star, 5238(F)
Polar the Titanic Bear, 16486
Police Officers, 17807
Police Officers A to Z, 65(F)
Police Officers Protect People, 17814
Police Patrol, 17091
Polish Americans, 17557
Political Leaders, 13740
Political Parties, 17097
Politics, American Style, 17100
The Polka Dot Horse, 1618(F)
Polkabats and Octopus Slacks, 7629(F)
Pollution, 16994
Polly Hopper's Pouch, 1836(F)
Polly Molly Woof Woof, 2388(F)
The Polyester Grandpa, 9855(F)
Polygons, 20606
The Pomegranate Seeds, 11477
Pompeii, 14710, 14723
Pond Life, 20528
Pond Plants, 20515
Pond Seasons, 11936
Pond Watching with Ann Morgan, 13325
Pond Water Zoo, 19808
Pond Year, 4481(F)
Pondfire, 6968(F)
Pondlarker, 2162(F)
The Pony Express, 16288
A Pony for Jeremiah, 9413(F)
Pony Trouble, 7192(F)
Poof! 1440(F)
Pooh's Bedtime Book, 7962(F)
Pookins Gets Her Way, 1347(F)
Pool of Fire, 10160(F)
The Pool Party, 8821(F)
Poopsie Pomerantz, Pick Up Your Feet, 8659(F)
Poor Girl, 8860(F)
Poor Stainless, 7998(F)
Pop, 14121
Pop Art, 13950
Pop-o-Mania, 21635

Popcorn, 3442(F)
   (Illus. by Betsy Everitt), 6537(F)
Popcorn at the Palace, 4223(F)
The Popcorn Book, 20088
Popcorn Park Zoo, 20029
Popcorn Plants, 20179
Popol Vuh, 11411
Poppa's Itchy Christmas, 5880(F)
Poppa's New Pants, 3319(F)
Poppleton, 6614(F)
Poppleton and Friends, 6615(F)
Poppleton Everyday, 6616(F)
Poppleton Forever, 6617(F)
Poppleton Has Fun, 2647(F)
Poppleton in Fall, 6618(F)
Poppleton in Spring, 6619(F)
Poppy, 7568(F)
Poppy and Ella, 2273(F)
Poppy and Rye, 7569(F)
The Poppykettle Papers, 7893(F)
Poppy's Chair, 3691(F)
Poppy's Puppet, 1178(F)
Population, 17009
The Porcupine, 18972
The Porcupine Mouse, 2605(F)
A Porcupine Named Fluffy, 2361(F)
Porcupines, 19202
Porcupine's Pajama Party, 6367(F)
Pork and Beef's Great Adventure, 7636(F)
Porpoises, 19688
Porsche, 21305
Portrait of a Farm Family, 20049
A Portrait of Spotted Deer's Grandfather, 7351(F)
Portraits, 13898
   (Illus. by Tony Ross), 13888
Portraits of War, 16440
Portugal, 15472, 15476
Portugal in Pictures, 15483
A Possible Tree, 4370(F)
Possum and the Peeper, 2226(F)
Possum Come a-Knockin', 2775(F)
Possum Magic, 2097(F)
Possum's Harvest Moon, 2227(F)
The Post Office Book, 17111
Postal Workers, 17740
Postal Workers A to Z, 65(F)
Postcards from Pluto, 18519
The Postwar Years, 14595
Posy Bates, Again! 9819(F)
Potato, 4737(F), 20186
The Potato Kid, 8613(F)
The Potato Man, 3296(F)
Potato Pancakes All Around, 6079(F)
The Potato Party and Other Troll Tales, 1344(F)
Potatoes, 20182
Potlatch, 15972
Pots and Pans (Illus. by Diane De Groat), 4184(F)
   (Illus. by Lizzy Rockwell), 3384(F)
The Potters, 16115
The Potty Book for Boys, 3065(F)
The Potty Book for Girls, 3065(F)
Poultry, 20086
Pouring Iron, 21259
Poverty, 17160
The Powder Puff Puzzle, 6347(F)
Power and Glory, 4283(F)
Power Failure, 20846

The Power of Light, 9761(F)
The Power of Un, 7719(F)
The Power Twins, 10181(F)
Powerful Waves, 20721
Powerhouse, 20847
Powers of the Mind, 18111
Powers of the Supreme Court, 17015
Powwow, 15919, 15961
Powwow Summer, 16029
The Practical Joke War, 9842(F)
Practical Plants, 20256
The Practically Perfect Pajamas, 1868(F)
The Prairie, 20540, 20544
A Prairie Boy's Summer, 12250
A Prairie Boy's Winter, 12250
The Prairie Dog, 19194
Prairie Dog Pioneers, 4676(F)
Prairie Dogs, 19210
   (Illus. by Durga Bernhard), 19193
   (Illus. by William Munoz), 19203
Prairie Dogs Kiss and Lobsters Wave, 18854
The Prairie Fire, 4810(F)
Prairie Songs, 8608(F)
Prairie Summer, 11962
Prairie Town, 3164(F)
The Prairie Train, 1439(F)
Prairie Visions, 12865
Prairie Willow, 4855(F)
A Prairie Year, 20530
Prairies, 20541
Pray Hard, 8844(F)
Prayer for a Child, 17522
A Prayer for the Earth, 5649(F)
Prayers from the Ark, 17514
Praying Mantis, 19726
Praying Mantises, 19433
Praying to A. L., 8598(F)
Preacher's Boy, 8780(F)
The Precious Gift, 11259
Precious Gold, Precious Jade, 9372(F)
Predators and Prey, 20433
Predators in the Rain Forest, 20477
Prehistoric Animals, 14418
   (Illus. by Peter Zallinger), 14484
Prehistoric Art, 14502
Prehistoric Life, 14504, 14516
Prehistoric People of North America, 14492
Prehistory, 14397
Premlata and the Festival of Lights, 8996(F)
Presenting Tanya, the Ugly Duckling, 4963(F)
Presents for Santa, 5961(F)
The President Has Been Shot! 15885
Presidential Conventions, 17096
Presidents, 12636
Presidents at Play, 17127
Presidents Day, 17388
Presidents in a Time of Change, 16520
Presidents of a Growing Country, 16484
Presidents of a World Power, 16485
Presidents of a Young Republic, 16277
Preston's Goal! 2449(F)

Pretend Soup and Other Real Recipes, 21710
Pretzel and Pop's Closetful of Stories, 6668(F)
Pride and Promise, 16460
A Pride of Princesses, 10408(F)
Pride of Puerto Rico, 13444
Prietita and the Ghost Woman, 7562(F)
Prime-Time Pitcher, 10308(F)
Prince, 10288(F)
The Prince and the Pauper, 9110(F)
Prince Caspian, 7911(F)
Prince Edward Island, 15568
The Prince of Tarn, 7807(F)
Prince of the Fairway, 13719
The Prince of the Pond, 7980(F)
The Princess and Froggie, 1718(F)
The Princess and the Beggar, 10732
The Princess and the Frog, 1652(F), 10417
The Princess and the Goblin, 10457(F)
The Princess and the Pea, 10527(F)
The Princess and the Peacocks, 9111(F)
The Princess and the Potty, 3281(F)
Princess Caroline of Monaco, 13765
Princess Chamomile Gets Her Way, 1445(F)
Princess Chamomile's Garden, 2553(F)
Princess Diana, 13782, 13783
The Princess in the Pigpen, 8139(F)
Princess Ka'iulani, 13819
Princess Lulu Goes to Camp, 6295(F)
Princess Nevermore, 10227(F)
Princess of the Press, 12819
Princess Penelope's Parrot, 1348(F)
Princess Pooh, 3820(F)
Princess Prunella and the Purple Peanut, 7565(F)
Princess September and the Nightingale, 10462(F)
Princess Sonora and the Long Sleep, 10448(F)
The Princess Test, 10449(F)
Printing, 21624
Prints, 21640
Priscilla Foster, 9199(F)
Priscilla Twice, 4929(F)
Prison Camps in the Civil War, 16428
The Prisoner of Pineapple Place, 7915(F)
Prisons, 17070, 17086
Private and Personal, 17737
Private Lily, 10015(F)
The Private Notebook of Katie Roberts, Age 11, 8692(F)
Pro Football Hall of Fame, 22181
Pro Wrestling's Greatest Tag Teams, 22021
Pro Wrestling's Greatest Wars, 22052
Pro Wrestling's Most Punishing Finishing Moves, 21967
Probably Pistachio, 228
Probity Jones and the Fear Not Angel, 1659(F)
Products of Mexico, 15611

Professor Protein's Fitness, Health, Hygiene and Relaxation Tonic, 18201
Professor Puffendorf's Secret Potions, 1631(F)
Professor Sniff and the Lost Spring Breezes, 8089(F)
Professor Solomon Snickerdoodle's Air Science Tricks, 20674
Professor Solomon Snickerdoodle's Light Science Tricks, 20876
The Prog Frince, 10441(F)
Progressivism, the Great Depression, and the New Deal, 16454
Prohibition, 16453
Project Apollo, 21008
Project Mercury, 21009
Project Puffin, 19350
Project Wheels, 8875(F)
Projects for a Healthy Planet, 16960
Projects in Space Science, 18314
Projects That Explore Energy, 20830
Prometheus and the Story of Fire, 11503
The Promise, 9740(F)
A Promise Is a Promise, 4245
Promise Me the Moon, 8559(F)
The Promise Quilt, 4804(F)
Promise Song, 8935(F)
The Promised Land, 9288(F)
Promises, 3955(F)
Promises to the Dead, 9478(F)
Prosper's Mountain, 10402(F)
Protecting Endangered Species at the San Diego Zoo, 19399
Protecting Marie, 7214(F)
Protecting Our Air, Land, and Water, 16991
Protecting Our Feathered Friends, 19285
Protecting the Rain Forest, 20494
Proteins, 20160
Proud of Our Feelings, 3276(F)
Proudly Red and Black, 12664
Prudence's Baby-Sitter Book, 3149(F)
Psalm Twenty-Three, 17316
Psssst! It's Me . . . the Bogeyman, 1456(F)
Psychic Sleuths, 17074
Psychology for Kids II, 17618
Pteranodon, 14391
The Puddle, 1382(F)
The Puddle Pail, 2302(F)
Pueblo, 16026
The Pueblo, 15931
Pueblo Girls, 15980
Pueblo Indian, 15941
Pueblo Storyteller, 15973
The Pueblos, 16024
Puerto Ricans, 17588
The Puerto Ricans, 17539
Puerto Rico, 15700, 15708, 15710, 15711, 15711
Puerto Rico Facts and Symbols, 15702
Puerto Rico in Pictures, 15715
Puff-Puff, Chugga-Chugga, 2877(F)
Puffins, 19271, 19356
Puffins Climb, Penguins Rhyme, 19379

Pug, Slug, and Doug the Thug, 2649(F)
Pugdog, 1636(F)
Pugs, 19976
Pulleys, 20926
Pulling the Lion's Tail, 10681
The Pullman Strike of 1894, 16444
The Pulse of Life, 18087
The Pumpkin Book, 20175
Pumpkin Circle, 20181
Pumpkin Day, Pumpkin Night, 3857(F)
Pumpkin Decorating, 21466
Pumpkin Faces, 239(F)
The Pumpkin Fair, 3058(F)
Pumpkin Fiesta, 4893(F)
Pumpkin Heads! 6034(F)
Pumpkin Jack, 6013(F)
The Pumpkin Man from Piney Creek, 5981(F)
Pumpkin Pie, 2898(F)
Pumpkin Pumpkin, 4552(F)
The Pumpkin Runner, 4579(F)
Pumpkin Soup, 1970(F)
Pumpkins, 1500(F)
Pumpkins from the Sky? 4861(F)
The Pumpkins of Time, 10186(F)
Punching the Clock, 14051
Punctuation Power, 14112
Puniddles, 21882
A Pup Just for Me/A Boy Just for Me, 5407(F)
Puppet Show Made Easy! 14306
Puppets, 14304
Puppies, 19964
Puppy, 19945
The Puppy Book, 19952
Puppy Care and Critters, Too! 19962
Puppy Fat, 8436(F)
Puppy Love, 8399(F)
 (Illus. by Anita Jeram), 19955
 (Illus. by Susanna Natti), 7185(F)
A Puppy of My Own, 7259(F)
The Puppy Who Wanted a Boy, 5935(F)
Puppy's Games, 2712(F)
The Purchase of Small Secrets, 11591
Purim, 6101(F)
Purim! 6090(F)
Purim Play, 6114(F)
Puritans, Pilgrims, and Merchants, 16110
The Purloined Corn Popper, 6892(F)
Purple Climbing Days, 6348(F)
The Purple Coat, 3211(F)
Purple Coyote, 1077(F)
Purple Death, 17958
Purple Delicious Blackberry Jam, 4263(F)
Purple, Green and Yellow, 4243(F)
The Purple Hat, 4262(F)
Purple Is Best, 6590(F)
Purple Is My Game, Morgan Is My Name, 8493(F)
Purple Mountain Majesties, 12505
Purr . . . Children's Book Illustrators Brag About Their Cats, 19931
Purrfectly Purrfect, 7892(F)
Purrrrr, 5173(F)
The Purse, 3064(F)

The Pushcart War, 9936(F)
Pushing and Pulling, 20810
Pushing Up the Sky, 12013
Pushkin Meets the Bundle, 2899(F)
Pushkin Minds the Bundle, 2900(F)
Puss in Boots (Illus. by Paul Gal-
  done), 10878
  (Illus. by Giuliano Lunelli), 10880
  (Illus. by Fred Marcellino), 10879
  (Illus. by Alain Vaes), 10873
Puss-in-Boots, 12016
Pussycat, Pussycat and Other
  Rhymes, 879(F)
Pussycats Everywhere! 5327(F)
Put a Fan in Your Hat! 18303
Put Me in the Zoo, 6474(F)
Put On Some Antlers and Walk Like
  a Moose, 18665
Putnam and Pennyroyal, 8464(F)
Putting On a Play, 12011
Puzzle Island, 21861
A Puzzling Day in the Land of the
  Pharaohs, 14604
Pygmies of Central Africa, 14932
Pyramid, 14660
  (Illus. by David Macaulay), 14639
Pyramids, 14350, 21144
  (Illus. by Claude Delafosse), 14621
Pyramids! 50 Hands-on Activities to
  Experience Ancient Egypt, 14629
Pyramids of Ancient Egypt, 14613
Pythons, 18773

Qatar, 15535
Quack and Count, 376(F)
Quaking Aspen, 20204
The Quangle Wangle's Hat, 11891
The Quarreling Book, 3973(F)
Quarterbacks! 13416
Quebec, 15580
Queen Anne's Lace, 20267
Queen Cleopatra, 13776
Queen Elizabeth I, 13787
Queen Elizabeth II, 13790
Queen Esther Saves Her People,
  6071
Queen Esther, the Morning Star,
  17466
Queen Latifah, 12410
Queen Nadine, 2316(F)
The Queen of Attolia, 8159(F)
Queen of the May, 10440(F)
Queen of the Sixth Grade, 8270(F)
Queen of the World, 5740(F)
Queen Victoria, 13863
Queenie, One of the Family, 5232(F)
Queenie Peavy, 8579(F)
The Queen's Necklace, 10443(F)
Quennu and the Cave Bear, 4635(F)
Quest for Courage, 9176(F)
Quest for the Lost Prince, 13837
Quest for the West, 9388(F)
Questions and Answers About Dino-
  saurs, 14406
Quick and Easy Cookbook, 21739
Quick Chick, 6388(F)
The Quicksand Book, 4416(F)
The Quicksand Pony, 6940(F)
The Quiet Little Farm, 5286(F)
The Quiet Little Woman, 9704(F)
Quiet, Wyatt! 5029(F)

The Quilt-Block History of Pioneer
  Days, 16296
A Quilt for Elizabeth, 3919(F)
Quilt of Dreams, 3613(F)
The Quilt Story, 3252(F)
Quilted Landscape, 17596
The Quiltmaker's Gift, 1020(F)
Quinceañera, 17620
Quinceanera, 17379, 17380
Quinnie Blue, 4695(F)
Quotations for Kids, 14104

R. C. Gorman, 12235
R Is for Radish! 6291(F)
R. L. Stine, 12601
R-T, Margaret, and the Rats of
  NIMH, 7663(F)
The Rabbi Who Flew, 1127(F)
Rabbit, 19889
The Rabbit, 19211
Rabbit and Hare Divide an Apple,
  20602(F)
Rabbit and the Moon, 11319
Rabbit and Turtle Go to School,
  6334(F)
Rabbit Food, 2151(F)
Rabbit Hill, 7895(F)
The Rabbit in the Moon, 10793
Rabbit Inn, 1861(F)
Rabbit Makes a Monkey of Lion,
  10642
Rabbit Moon, 2640(F)
Rabbit Pirates, 1983(F)
Rabbit Rambles On, 2150(F)
Rabbits, 19208, 19898, 19902
Rabbits and Raindrops, 1750(F)
Rabbit's Bedtime, 802(F)
Rabbit's Good News, 1839(F)
Rabbit's Pajama Party, 229
Rabbits, Rabbits and More Rabbits!
  19891
The Rabbit's Tail, 10727
Rabbit's Wooly Sweater, 1810(F)
Raccoons, 18940, 18954
Raccoons and Ripe Corn, 18923
Race Car, 21293, 21296
Race the Wind! 7286(F)
Race with Buffalo, 11322
Racetrack Robbery, 6938(F)
Rachel Carson, 13245, 13246, 13247,
  13249, 13250
Rachel Field's Hitty, 8196(F)
Rachel Fister's Blister, 4225(F)
Rachel the Clever and Other Jewish
  Folktales, 11168
Rachel's Journal, 9416(F)
Racing a Ghost Ship, 22265
Racing Cars, 21314
Racing on the Tour de France, 22049
Racing the Iditarod Trail, 21991
Racing the Sun, 7365(F)
Racism, 17141
Racso and the Rats of NIMH,
  7664(F)
Radiance Descending, 8644(F)
Radical Red, 9545(F)
Radio Control Models, 21669
Radio Rescue, 9518(F)
Radiology, 18031
Rafael Palmeiro, 13477
The Raft, 4479(F)

The Rag Coat, 8762(F)
Rage of Fire, 7062(F)
Ragged Bear, 3474(F)
Raggedy Andy Stories, 1211(F)
Raggedy Ann and Andy and the
  Camel with the Wrinkled Knees,
  1210(F)
Raggedy Ann Stories, 1211(F)
Raggin', 12330
Raging Robots and Unruly Uncles,
  10214(F)
Ragweed, 7570(F)
The Railroad Book, 21342
Railway Ghosts and Highway Hor-
  rors, 11329
Rain, 2737(F)
  (Illus. by Donald Crews), 4470(F)
The Rain, 4480(F)
Rain and People, 20729
Rain and the Earth, 20729
The Rain Came Down, 4313(F)
Rain Drop Splash, 4554(F)
Rain Feet, 3248(F)
Rain Forest, 20491
  (Illus. by Helen Coucher), 4409(F)
Rain Forest Babies, 20436
The Rain Forest Counts! 502(F)
Rain Forest Girl, 17672
Rain Forest Secrets, 20437
Rain Forests, 20448, 20453, 20468,
  20475, 20483
Rain Forests and Reefs, 20383
Rain Makes Applesauce, 4302(F)
Rain Player, 4888(F)
Rain Rain Rivers, 4543(F)
Rain Song, 4426(F)
Rain Talk, 4538(F)
The Rainbabies, 10463(F)
The Rainbow and You, 20872
A Rainbow at Night, 15974
The Rainbow Bridge, 11318
The Rainbow Fish, 2579(F)
Rainbow Fish and the Big Blue
  Whale, 2580(F)
The Rainbow Fish Board Book,
  2581(F)
Rainbow Fish to the Rescue! 2582(F)
The Rainbow Hand, 11740
Rainbow Joe and Me, 1603(F)
A Rainbow of My Own, 1167(F)
The Rainbow Tulip, 5038(F)
Rainbow Wings, 1529(F)
Raindrops and Rainbows, 20749
Rainforest, 20480
The Rainforest Indians, 20493
Rainforests, 20430
The Rainmakers, 9145(F)
A Rainy Day, 20783
Rainy Day, 11530
  (Illus. by Angelo Rinaldi), 3674(F)
  (Illus. by Janet M. Stoeke), 3445(F)
The Rainy Day Grump, 6321(F)
Rainy Day Play! 21418
Rainy Days and Saturdays, 22233
Rainy Morning, 4266(F)
Rainy's Powwow, 9173(F)
Raisel's Riddle, 11170
Raising Cows on the Koebel's Farm,
  17748
Raising Dragons, 1436(F)
Raising Sweetness, 4323(F)

Raising Yoder's Barn, 3494(F)
Ralph David Abernathy, 12699
Ralph Lauren, 12924
Ralph S. Mouse, 9804(F)
Ralph's Secret Weapon, 1294(F)
Rama and the Demon King, 10808
Ramadan, 5627
Ramona the Pest, 7406(F)
Ramona's World, 7407(F)
Randall's Wall, 8639(F)
The Random House Book of Easy-to-
  Read Stories, 6587(F)
The Random House Book of Greek
  Myths, 11513
The Random House Book of Nursery
  Stories, 10543
The Random House Book of 1001
  Questions and Answers About the
  Human Body, 18056
The Random House Book of Opera
  Stories, 14130
The Random House Book of Poetry
  for Children, 11679
The Random House Book of Stories
  from the Ballet, 14294
Randy Moss, 13622
Randy's Dandy Lions, 2570(F)
Ransom for a River Dolphin, 7235(F)
Raoul Wallenberg, 13867
Rap and Hip Hop, 14120
Raptor, 7144(F)
Rapunzel, 10940
  (Illus. by Maja Dusikova), 10903
  (Illus. by Trina S. Hyman), 10902
  (Illus. by Trina S. Hyman), 10902
  (Illus. by P. J. Lynch), 10429
Rare and Interesting Stamps, 21807
Rare Treasure, 13230
Rascal, 7282(F)
The Rat and the Tiger, 2277(F)
Rat Teeth, 8433(F)
Rats, 19204
Rats! 9822(F)
Rats, Bulls, and Flying Machines,
  14803
The Rats' Daughter, 10541
A Rattle of Bones, 6061(F)
Rattlesnake Dance, 1751(F), 18758
Ratzo, 7180(F)
Raul Julia, 12833
Raven, 11267
Raven and River, 1936(F)
Raven in a Dove House, 8788(F)
Raw Head, Bloody Bones, 11364
Ray Charles, 12368
Razzle Dazzle! 21791
Re-Elect Nutty! 10080(F)
Re-Zoom, 20909
Reach Higher, 13565
Reaching Dustin, 8295(F)
Read for Me, Mama, 3849(F)
Read for Your Life, 7018(F)
Read Me a Fairy Tale, 10435(F)
Read to Your Bunny, 2836(F)
Reading Grows, 14007
Ready, Set, Go! 6675(F)
  (Illus. by Nina Laden), 3271(F)
Ready . . . Set . . . Read! 6280(F)
Ready . . . Set . . . Read — and
  Laugh! 21819(F)
Ready . . . Set . . . Robot! 6394(F)

Real American Girls Tell Their Own
  Stories, 15884
A Real Christmas This Year, 9769(F)
Real Heroes, 8717(F)
The Real Hole, 2921(F)
The Real Johnny Appleseed, 12846
Real Mother Goose, 871
The Real Mother Goose Clock Book,
  872
The Real Patriots of the American
  Revolution, 16223
The Real Plato Jones, 8398(F)
The Real Thief, 8128(F)
The Real Tooth Fairy, 3746(F)
The Real Winner, 2526(F)
The Really Deadly and Dangerous
  Dinosaur, 14475
The Really Sinister Savage Shark,
  19650
Really Weird Animals, 18936
Realm of the Panther, 19082
The Reason for Janey, 8543(F)
The Reasons for Seasons, 4442
Rebecca Lobo, 13546
Rebecca of Sunnybrook Farm,
  7536(F)
Rebel, 5403(F), 9020(F)
The Rebellion of Humans, 4372(F)
Rebels, 13729
Rebels Against Slavery, 16263
Recess Mess, 6480(F)
Rechenka's Eggs, 1486(F)
Reconstruction, 16473
Reconstruction and Reform, 16469
Reconstruction and the Rise of Jim
  Crow, 1864–1896, 16455
Record-Breaking Baseball Trivia,
  22105
Recreation, 22054
Recreation Can Be Risky, 18219
Recreation Director, 17744
Rectangle, 356(F)
Rectangles, 20606
Recycled Paper, 21065
Recycling, 16975, 16981
Recyclopedia, 21496
The Red Balloon, 4723(F)
Red Berry Wool, 2080(F)
Red, Blue, Yellow Shoe, 276(F)
Red Cross/Red Crescent, 17017
The Red-Crowned Crane, 19291
Red Dancing Shoes, 3833(F)
Red-Dirt Jessie, 7274(F)
Red Dog, 9451(F)
The Red-Eared Ghosts, 7549(F)
Red Eggs and Dragon Boats, 15085
Red-Eyed Tree Frog, 18717
Red-Eyed Tree Frogs, 18732
Red Fairy Book, 10442(F)
Red Flower Goes West, 4859(F)
Red Fox, 19144
Red Fox and His Canoe, 6203(F)
Red Fox and the Baby Bunnies,
  1789(F)
The Red Fox Monster, 1790(F)
Red Fox Running, 5149(F)
Red Hen and Sly Fox, 2104(F)
Red-Hot Hightops, 10309(F)
Red Hot Peppers, 21977
Red Leaf, Yellow Leaf, 4425(F)
Red Light, Green Light, 3051(F)

Red Light, Green Light, Mama and
  Me, 3025(F)
Red Light Stop, Green Light Go,
  4205(F)
The Red Planet, 18455
The Red Poppy, 20247
Red Racer, 4358(F)
Red Rubber Boot Day, 3375(F)
The Red Sea and the Arabian Gulf,
  19847
The Red Shoes, 10400(F)
Red-Spotted Newt, 18685
Red Wizard, 8120(F)
The Red Wolf, 19139
Red Wolf Country, 5316(F)
The Red Woolen Blanket, 3179(F)
Redbird at Rockefeller Center,
  5874(F)
Redcoats and Petticoats, 9239(F)
Redheaded Orphan, 9444(F)
Redwoods, 20213
Reed, 10289(F)
Reflections, 3253(F)
Reflections on a Gift of Watermelon
  Pickle and Other Modern Verse,
  11555
The Reform Party, 17093
Reformers, 13724
Regarding the Fountain, 9906(F)
Regards to the Man in the Moon,
  1289(F)
Reggae, 14123
Regina's Big Mistake, 5520(F)
A Regular Flood of Mishap, 3528(F)
Regular Guy, 10017(F)
A Regular Rolling Noah, 4220(F)
Reindeer, 19154
The Reindeer Christmas, 5905(F)
The Reindeer People, 15815
Relatively Speaking, 11565
The Relatives Came, 3869(F)
Relieve the Squeeze, 18007
Religion, 17202
Religion in Colonial America, 16099
Religion in Nineteenth Century
  America, 15913
Religions of the Western Hemi-
  sphere, 17189
The Reluctant Dragon (Illus. by E. H.
  Shepard), 10424(F)
  (Illus. by E. H. Shepard), 10424(F)
Reluctantly Alice, 8500(F)
REM World, 10221(F)
A Remainder of One, 558(F)
Remaking the Earth, 11251
Remarkable Animals, 2496(F)
The Remarkable Farkle McBride,
  4214(F)
The Remarkable Riderless Runaway
  Tricycle, 1375(F)
Rembrandt, 12289
Remember Me, 3945(F), 9698(F)
Remember That, 3822(F)
Remember the Ladies, 12657, 13124,
  17036
Remembering and Other Poems,
  11637
The Remembering Box, 8415(F)
Renaissance, 14801
The Renaissance, 14799, 14804,
  14805

A Renaissance Town, 14802
Rendille, 14945
Rene Magritte, 13932
The Reproductive System, 18243, 18247
Reptile Rescue, 19419
Reptiles, 18683, 18693
The Republic of Ireland, 15346
Rescue at Sea! 6874(F)
The Rescue Party, 1031(F)
Rescue Vehicles, 21321
Rescuers Defying the Nazis, 14818
Rescuing a Neighborhood, 17136
Resistance, 14815
Resources, 20316
The Respiratory System, 18127, 18128
Retreat from Gettysburg, 9474(F)
The Return of Freddy Legrand, 4072(F)
The Return of Rex and Ethel, 7148(F)
The Return of the Buffaloes, 11252
The Return of the Great Brain, 9843(F)
Return of the Home Run Kid, 10310(F)
The Return of the Indian, 7586(F)
Return of the Wolf, 7285(F)
Return to Hawk's Hill, 9158(F)
Return to Howliday Inn, 9889(F)
Return to the Island, 9456(F)
Reuben and the Blizzard, 3653(F)
Reuben and the Quilt, 3654(F)
Revenge of the Snob Squad, 8785(F), 9960(F)
The Reverend Thomas's False Teeth, 1189(F)
Revolutionary Medicine 1700–1800, 16220
Revolutionary Poet, 12621
Revolutionary Power, 13741
The Revolutionary Soldier 1775–1783, 16221
Revolutionary War, 16197, 16215
A Revolutionary War Soldier, 16205
Rewind, 8101(F)
Rex and Lilly Family Time, 6230(F)
Rex and Lilly Playtime, 6230(F)
Rex and Lilly Schooltime, 6231(F)
The Rhine, 15330
Rhino Romp, 5224(F)
Rhinoceroses, 18945
Rhinos, 18986
Rhinos Who Skateboard, 2468(F)
Rhinos Who Snowboard, 2469(F)
Rhinos Who Surf, 2470(F)
Rhode Island, 16692, 16717, 16753
The Rhode Island Colony, 16125
Rhode Island Facts and Symbols, 16673
Rhymes for Annie Rose, 11609
Rib-Ticklers, 21852
Ribbiting Tales, 8041(F)
Ribbon Rescue, 3337(F)
Ribbons, 8548(F)
Ribsy, 7406(F)
Ric Flair, 22022
Rice, 20127
    (Illus. by Prodeepta Das), 20130
Rice Is Life, 20093

Richard Allen, 12700
Richard King, 12921
Richard M. Nixon, Jimmy Carter, Ronald Reagan, 12674
Richard Nixon, 13087, 13088
Richard Orr's Nature Cross-Sections, 16953
Richard Scarry's Best Word Book Ever, 14044
Richard Scarry's Lowly Worm Word Book, 240(F)
Richard Wright and the Library Card, 4771(F)
The Riches of Oseola McCarty, 12758
The Richest Kid in the World, 6881(F)
The Rickety Barn Show, 1800(F)
Ricky Martin, 12422
Ricky Ricotta's Giant Robot, 1475(F)
Ricky Ricotta's Giant Robot vs. the Mutant Mosquitoes from Mercury, 1476(F)
The Riddle, 4046(F)
Riddle-Lightful, 21836
The Riddle of Penncroft Farm, 7840(F)
A Riddle of Roses, 7976(F)
The Riddle of the Red Purse, 6347(F)
The Riddle of the Rosetta Stone, 14626
Riddle Road, 21853
Riddle Roundup, 21837
Ride a Purple Pelican, 11911
Ride, Baby, Ride! 1270(F)
A Ride on Mother's Back, 3525
A Ride on the Red Mare's Back, 1345(F)
Ride the Wind, 18671
Ride Western Style, 22206
Riding, 22202
The Riding Book, 22208
Riding for Beginners, 22198
Riding Freedom, 9436(F)
Riding on the Wind, 9408(F)
Riding Silver Star, 19990
Riding the Ferry with Captain Cruz, 3141
Riding the Rails, 21340
Riding the School Bus with Mrs. Kramer, 3142(F)
Riding the Tiger, 1026(F)
Rifles for Watie, 9485(F)
A Right Fine Life, 9367(F)
Right Here on This Spot, 4570(F)
A Right to Die? 17158
A Right to Smoke? 17869
The Right to Speak Out, 17039
The Right to Vote, 17047
The Right Touch, 18264
Rights for Animals? 18660
Rigoberta Menchu, 15684
Rikki-Tikki-Tavi (Illus. by Lambert Davis), 1309(F)
    (Illus. by Jerry Pinkney), 7872(F)
Rimonah of the Flashing Sword, 10678
Rimshots, 12003
Rinehart Lifts, 10342(F)
The Ring, 1390(F)

Ring-a-Ring O'Roses and Ding, Dong Bell, 861
A Ring of Endless Light, 10207(F)
A Ring of Tricksters, 10558
The Ring of Truth, 9776(F)
Ring! Yo? 3373(F)
Rio de Janeiro, 15753
Rio Grande, 15892
Rio Grande Stories, 7357(F)
Riot, 8594(F)
Rip Van Winkle, 7974(F)
    (Illus. by Rick Meyerowitz), 7815(F)
    (Illus. by N. C. Wyeth), 7814(F)
Rip Van Winkle and the Legend of Sleepy Hollow, 7816(F)
A Ripple of Hope, 12919
Rip's Secret Spot, 6243(F)
Riptide, 5448(F)
Rise and Shine, 14255
The Rise of Industry, 1860–1900, 16456
The Rise of the Cities, 15871
Rising Voices, 9163(F)
River, 4380(F)
The River, 20524
River and Stream, 20527
The River Bank, 7752(F)
River Danger, 6827(F)
River Dream, 1544(F)
River Friendly, River Wild, 11619
River of Life, 16802
River Plants, 20516
A River Ran Wild, 16992
River Story, 4461(F)
The River That Went to the Sky, 10698
River Town, 3163
Rivers and Lakes, 20513, 20523, 20525
Rivers and Valleys, 20390
Rivers in the Rain Forest, 20478
Rivers, Ponds and Lakes, 20514
Rivka's Way, 9050(F)
Road Builders, 5571
The Road from Home, 13821
The Road to Home, 9260(F)
The Road to Seneca Falls, 13194
Roadrunner's Dance, 1738(F)
Roads Take Us Home, 21128
Roadsigns, 11469
Roald Dahl, 12521, 12522
The Roald Dahl Treasury, 10256
Roald Dahl's Revolting Recipes, 21697
Roar! A Noisy Counting Book, 427(F)
Roaring Reptiles, 18710
The Roaring Twenties, 16490
The Robber Baby, 11505
The Robbery at the Diamond Dog Diner, 1962(F)
Robert Ballard, 12077
Robert Crowther's Amazing Pop-Up House of Inventions, 21027
Robert Crowther's Pop-Up Olympics, 22245
Robert E. Lee, 12926, 12927
Robert Frost, 11693
Robert Fulton, 13287

Robert Lives with His Grandparents, 3697(F)
Robert Louis Stevenson, 12599, 12600
Robert Mugabe of Zimbabwe, 13838
Robert Rodriguez, 12456
Roberto, 2330(F)
Roberto Alomar, 13435, 13436
Roberto Clemente, 13442, 13443, 13445
Robin Hood, 10973
   (Illus. by Carol Heyer), 10996
   (Illus. by N. C. Wyeth), 10964
Robin Hood and His Merry Men, 10968
Robin Hood in the Greenwood, 10969
Robin Hook, Pirate Hunter! 1302(F)
Robin on His Own, 8861(F)
Robin Williams, 12482
Robin's Home, 1768(F)
The Robins in Your Backyard, 19298
The Robobots, 1438(F)
Robots, 21225
The Robots Are Coming, 11914
Robots Rising, 21226
Rock-a-Bye Baby, 14175
Rock-A-Doodle-Do! 10889(F)
Rock and Ice Climbing! Top the Tower, 22050
Rock Climbing, 21979, 22056
The Rock Jockeys, 7006(F)
Rock 'n' Roll, 14123
Rock River, 6969(F)
Rockabye Crocodile, 1753(F)
Rockabye Farm, 693(F)
Rocket Man, 13298
Rocket Science, 18369
Rockets, 20985, 21003
Rocking and Rolling, 20323
Rocking Horse Christmas, 3350(F)
The Rocking Horse Secret, 6862(F)
Rocks, 20555, 20557
Rocks and Minerals, 20572, 20575
Rocky Mountain National Park, 16634
Rocky Mountains, 20501
Rodents, 19201
Rodeo, 21975
Rodeo Clown, 22005
Rodeo Day, 5434(F)
Rodeo Pup, 2637(F)
Rodeos, 21970
Rodney's Inside Story, 1785(F)
Rogers Hornsby, 13462
Rolie Polie Olie, 1283(F)
Roll Along, 11638
Roll of Thunder, Hear My Cry, 7526(F)
Roll Over! A Counting Song, 552(F)
Roller Coasters; or, I Had So Much Fun, I Almost Puked, 14267
Roller Hockey Radicals, 10311(F)
Roller Skates, 9622(F)
Roller Skates! 6250(F)
Rolling Along, 17915
Rolling Rose, 1595(F)
The Rolling Store, 4693(F)
Rollo and Tweedy and the Ghost at Dougal Castle, 6189(F)

Rollo Bones, Canine Hypnotist, 2516(F)
Roly-Poly Puppies, 519(F)
The Roly-Poly Spider, 2653(F)
Rolypolyology, 18662
Roman Colosseum, 14712
The Roman Colosseum, 14729, 14731
The Roman Empire, 14751
A Roman Fort, 14725
Roman Myths, Heroes, and Legends, 14739
The Roman News, 14726
Roman Numerals, 20626
Roman Numerals I to MM, 20631
Roman Town, 14732
The Roman Twins, 4659(F)
A Roman Villa, 14733
Romance of the Snob Squad, 9960(F)
Romania, 15262
Romania in Pictures, 15285
The Romans, 14714, 14720, 14721, 14724, 14736
   (Illus. by Peter Connolly), 14713
Rome, 14744, 15388, 15393
Rome Antics, 9059(F)
Romeo and Juliet, 9037(F)
Romulus and Remus, 11506
Ron Howard, 12405
Ronald McNair, 12139
Ronald Morgan Goes to Bat, 4966(F)
Ronald Reagan, 13093, 13095
Ronald W. Reagan, 13094
Ronia, the Robber's Daughter, 7917(F)
Rooftop Astronomer, 13324
Rookie, 13580
Rookie of the Year, 10368(F)
Rookie Quarterback, 10360(F)
Room for a Stepdaddy, 3585(F)
Room for Ripley, 20659
Roommates, 6338(F)
Roommates Again, 8287(F)
Roommates and Rachel, 6338(F)
The Rooster Crows, 884
The Rooster Prince, 8193(F)
The Rooster's Antlers, 10760
Roosters Off to See the World, 397(F)
Rootabaga Stories, 9985 (F)
   (Illus. by Michael Hague), 9984(F)
   (Illus. by David Small), 3872(F)
Rooter Remembers, 2549(F)
Roots in the Outfield, 10374(F)
Roots, Shoots, Buckets and Boots, 21956
Rope Burn, 8523(F)
Ropers and Riders, 22061
Rory and the Lion, 4102(F)
Rosa, 5309(F)
Rosa Goes to Daycare, 2377(F)
Rosa Moreno, 9542(F)
Rosa Parks, 12780
   (Illus. by Eric Marlow), 12776
   (Illus. by David Price), 12777
Rosa Parks and the Montgomery Bus Boycott, 12775
Rosalynn Carter, 13142
Rose, 8741(F)
Rose and Sebastian, 4067(F)
The Rose Horse, 9616(F)

The Rose in My Garden, 5311(F)
Rose Meets Mr. Wintergarten, 3180(F)
Rose Red and Snow White, 10490(F)
Rose Red and the Bear Prince, 10882
Roses, 20039
Roses Are Pink, Your Feet Really Stink, 6165(F)
Rose's Are Red, Violet's Are Blue and Other Silly Poems, 11921
The Roses in My Carpets, 4712(F)
Roses Red, Violets Blue, 20038
Rosie, 19940
Rosie and Michael, 4052(F)
Rosie and the Dance of the Dinosaurs, 8924(F)
Rosie and the Poor Rabbits, 2424(F)
Rosie and Tortoise, 2856(F)
Rosie O'Donnell, 12433, 12434, 12435, 12436, 12437
Rosie Rabbit's Colors, 296(F)
Rosie Rabbit's Numbers, 296(F)
Rosie Rabbit's Opposites, 296(F)
Rosie Rabbit's Shapes, 296(F)
Rosie's Babies, 3931(F)
Rosie's Baby Tooth, 2425(F)
Rosie's Fiddle, 1521(F)
Rosie's Fishing Trip, 3695(F)
Rosie's Tiger, 8495(F)
Rosie's Walk, 2233(F)
Ross Perot, 12946
Rotten Ralph, 2111(F)
Rotten Ralph's Rotten Christmas, 5821(F)
Rotten Ralph's Rotten Romance, 6167(F)
Rotten Ralph's Show and Tell, 2112(F)
Rotten Ralph's Trick or Treat, 5998(F)
Rotten Teeth, 4317(F)
The Rough-Face Girl, 11271
Rough Sketch Beginning, 11940
Roughing It on the Oregon Trail, 8123(F)
Round and Round Again, 4339(F)
Round and Round the Money Goes, 16918
Round and Square, 357(F)
The Round Book, 14251
Round Is a Mooncake, 362(F)
Round Is a Pancake, 321(F)
Round the Christmas Tree, 5790(F)
Round the Garden, 4444(F)
Round Trip, 4195(F)
The Roundhill, 7868(F)
Rover, 4287(F)
Roverandom, 8152(F)
Row Row Row Your Boat, 14186
Row Your Boat, 14166
Roxaboxen, 3301(F)
Roxie and Bo Together, 2524(F)
The Royal Bee, 4793(F)
The Royal Drum, 10684
A Royal Kiss, 8331(F)
The Royal Raven, 2859(F)
The Royal Roads, 16352
Rubber-Band Banjos and a Java Jive Bass, 14229
Rubén Blades, 12357
Ruby the Christmas Donkey, 5778(F)

Ruby the Copycat, 5054(F)
The Rude Giants, 1701(F)
Rudyard Kipling, 11571
Rugby and Rosie, 19967
Ruled Out, 8943(F)
The Rules, 4201(F)
Rum-a-Tum-Tum, 4766(F)
Rumble in the Jungle, 11771
Rumpelstiltskin (Illus. by Paul Gal-
    done), 10904
    (Illus. by Paul Galdone), 10904
    (Illus. by Marie-Louise Gay),
    10890
    (Illus. by Paul O. Zelinsky), 10905
The Rumpelstiltskin Problem,
    10515(F)
Rumpelstiltskin's Daughter,
    10505(F)
Run Away Home, 9409(F)
Run, Jump, Whiz, Splash, 3392(F)
Run the Blockade, 9509(F)
Run with the Wind, 2591(F)
The Runaway, 11788
The Runaway Bunny, 1895(F)
The Runaway Duck, 2405(F)
The Runaway Latkes, 6087(F)
Runaway Opposites, 11736
Runaway Ralph, 9804(F)
The Runaway Rice Cake, 5620(F)
Runaway to Freedom, 9322(F)
The Runaway Tortilla, 11362
The Runaways, 8581(F), 8817(F)
The Runaway's Revenge, 9292(F)
Runnin' with the Big Dawgs,
    10271(F)
Running, 22259
Running for Our Lives, 9326(F)
Running Girl, 10351(F)
Running Lightly . . ., 11687
Running on Eggs, 8936(F)
Running Out of Time, 7771(F)
Running the Road to ABC, 10098(F)
Rupa Raises the Sun, 1047(F)
Rush Hour, 3286(F)
Rushmore, 16542
Russia, 15404, 15408, 15411, 15424,
    15426, 15429, 15431, 15432
Russia at War, 14837
A Russian ABC, 96(F)
The Russian Americans, 17579
Russian Fairy Tales, 11080
The Russian Federation, 15414
A Russian Jewish Family, 17573
The Rusty, Trusty Tractor, 5553(F)
Rusty's Red Vacation, 3001(F)
The Rutan Voyager, 21078
Ruth Bader Ginsburg, 12886
Ruth Law Thrills a Nation, 12129
Rutherford B. Hayes, 13042
Ruthie's Big Old Coat, 2332(F)
Ruthie's Gift, 9525(F)
Rwanda, 14930

S.O.R. Losers, 10273(F)
S.S. Gigantic Across the Atlantic,
    4307(F)
S-S-Snakes! 18774
Sable, 7221(F)
The Sac and Fox Indians, 15995
Sacagawea, 12990, 12991, 12992
Sachiko Means Happiness, 5066(F)

The Sacred Harvest, 16027
Sacred Myths, 17205
Sacred Places, 17223
    (Illus. by David Shannon), 11743
Sacred River, 15108
Sad Days, Glad Days, 4971(F)
The Sad Night, 15636
Sad Underwear and Other Complica-
    tions, 11923
Sadako, 14841
Sadako and the Thousand Paper
    Cranes, 13847
The Saddest Time, 17732
Safari, 18607
Safe at Second, 10340(F)
A Safe Home for Manatees, 19737
Safe Horse, Safe Rider, 22204
A Safe Place, 5092(F)
The Safe Place, 8786(F)
Safe Return, 9036(F)
Safe, Warm, and Snug, 18862
The Safe Zone, 18216
Safety at School, 18223
Safety in Public Places, 18223
Safety in the Water, 18224
Safety on the Go, 18224
Safety on Your Bicycle, 18224
A Saguaro Cactus, 20405
Saguaro Cactus, 20402, 20424
Sail Away, 2923(F)
    (Illus. by David McPhail), 1379(F)
Sailaway Home, 2016(F)
Sailboat Lost, 1159(F)
Sailing Ship Eagle, 21391
Sailing Ships, 21376
Sailing to America, 16149
Sailor Cats, 2850(F)
Sailor Song, 712(F)
The Sailor's Alphabet, 21368
St. Augustine, 16894
Saint Ciaran, 13771
Saint Francis, 13795
Saint Francis and the Christmas Don-
    key, 5772(F)
St. George and the Dragon, 10998
Saint Joan of Arc, 13814
St. Joan of Arc, 13811
St. Lawrence Seaway, 16529
Saint Louis, 16548
Saint Maximilian Kolbe, 13822
Saint Nicholas, 17225
St. Patrick's Day, 17355, 17362
St. Patrick's Day in the Morning,
    5615(F)
The St. Patrick's Day Shamrock
    Mystery, 6964(F)
St. Petersburg, 15423
Saint Valentine, 17510
Salamandastron, 7830(F)
The Salamander Room, 5344(F)
Salamanders, 18688, 18689, 18697
Salem, Massachusetts, 16146
The Salem Witch Trials, 16141
Sallie Fox, 9400(F)
Sally and the Limpet, 1269(F)
Sally Ann Thunder Ann Whirlwind
    Crockett, 11359
Sally Bradford, 9480(F)
Sally Go Round the Moon, 14164
Sally Goes to the Beach, 5271(F)
Sally Ride, 12154

Salmon, 19704
The Salmon, 19700
A Salmon for Simon, 2824(F)
Salmon Moon, 1288(F)
Salmon Summer, 16797
Salsa Stories, 7419(F)
Salt, 11098
Salt Hands, 5118(F)
Salt in His Shoes, 4990(F)
Salt Is Sweeter Than Gold, 10862
Salt Lake City, 16597
Salting the Ocean, 11688
Salts and Solids, 20288
Sam and the Lucky Money, 3069(F)
Sam, Bangs and Moonshine, 5042(F)
Sam Johnson and the Blue Ribbon
    Quilt, 4641(F)
Sam the Minuteman, 4593(F)
Sam the Zamboni Man, 2975(F)
Sam Who Never Forgets, 5382(F)
Samantha, 2818(F)
Samantha Learns a Lesson, 9511(F)
Samantha Saves the Day, 9630(F)
Samantha the Snob, 4939(F)
Samantha's Cook Book, 21736
Samantha's Craft Book, 21525
Samantha's Surprise, 9511(F)
Samburu, 14931
The Same Sun Was in the Sky,
    4873(F)
The Same Wind, 4473(F)
Sami and the Time of the Troubles,
    4679(F)
Samir and Yonatan, 8926(F)
Sammy and the Dinosaurs, 1677(F)
Sammy Carducci's Guide to Women,
    9897(F)
Sammy, Dog Detective, 19939
Sammy Keyes and the Hollywood
    Mummy, 7107(F)
Sammy Keyes and the Hotel Thief,
    7108(F)
Sammy Keyes and the Runaway Elf,
    9764(F)
Sammy Keyes and the Sisters of
    Mercy, 7109(F)
Sammy Keyes and the Skeleton Man,
    7110(F)
Sammy Sosa, 13504, 13505
Sammy Spider's First Passover,
    6111(F)
Sammy Spider's First Rosh
    Hashanah, 6112(F)
Sammy Spider's First Shabbat,
    6113(F)
Sammy the Seal, 6406(F)
    (Illus. by Syd Hoff), 6400(F)
A Sampler View of Colonial Life,
    16101
Sam's Ball, 5014(F)
Sam's Bath, 5014(F)
Sam's Car, 5014(F)
Sam's Cookie, 5014(F)
Sam's New Baby, 3652(F)
Sam's Potty, 3282(F)
Sam's Teddy Bear, 5014(F)
Sam's Wagon, 3282(F)
Sam's Wild West Christmas, 5747(F)
Samuel Adams, 12836
Samuel L. Jackson, 12409

Samuel Slater's Mill and the Industrial Revolution, 16275
Samuel Todd's Book of Great Inventions, 9909
Samuel's Choice, 9224(F)
A Samurai Castle, 15131
Samurai of Gold Hill, 9634(F)
San, 14965
San Antonio, 16913
The San Antonio Spurs Basketball Team, 22146
San Diego, 16804
San Domingo, 7219(F)
San Francisco, 16783, 16793
San Francisco Earthquake, 1989, 16814
The San Francisco 49ers Football Team, 22186
The San Francisco Giants Baseball Team, 22114
Sand, 20568
Sand and Fog, 14970
Sand Cake, 1763(F)
Sand Castle, 4064(F)
The Sand Children, 1140(F)
Sand in My Shoes, 3259(F)
Sand on the Move, 20558
Sand to Sea, 19633
Sandbox Scientist, 18346
The Sandburg Treasury, 11690(F)
Sandhill Cranes, 19288
Sandra Bullock, 12363, 12364
Sandra Day O'Connor, 12938, 12940
The Sandy Bottom Orchestra, 8318(F)
Santa and the Three Bears, 5777(F)
Santa Cows, 5809(F)
Santa Fe Trail, 16293
The Santa Fe Trail, 16284
Santa Mouse and the Ratdeer, 5850(F)
Santa Who? 5823(F)
Santa's Ark, 5959(F)
Santa's Book of Names, 5871(F)
Santa's Gift, 5891(F)
Santas of the World, 17428
Santa's Short Suit Shrunk, 5766(F)
Santa's Time Off, 3316(F)
Santa's Winter Vacation, 5931(F)
The Sanyasin's First Day, 4830(F)
Sara Morton's Day, 16184
Sarah, Also Known as Hannah, 7500(F)
Sarah and the Naked Truth, 10032(F)
Sarah and the People of Sand River, 8946
Sarah Anne Hartford, 9190(F)
Sarah Bear and Sweet Sidney, 2562(F)
Sarah Bishop, 9245(F)
Sarah Childress Polk, 1803–1891, 13175
Sarah May and the New Red Dress, 1590(F)
Sarah Michelle Gellar, 12388
Sarah, Plain and Tall, 9410(F)
Sarah Royce and the American West, 16370
Sarah the Dragon Lady, 8826(F)
Sarah Winnemucca, 13001
Sarah's Bear, 2305(F)

Sarah's Boat, 10269(F)
Sarah's Incredible Idea, 3347(F)
Sarah's Lion, 10425(F)
Sarah's Sleepover, 5061(F)
Sarah's Story, 1220(F)
Sara's Secret, 8919(F)
Saratoga Secret, 9323(F)
Sarita, Be Brave, 7377(F)
Saskatchewan, 15590
Sasquatch, 7066(F), 21930
Sassy Gracie, 4296(F)
The Satanic Mill, 8023(F)
Satchel Paige, 13475, 13476
Satellites, 20986
Sato and the Elephants, 8965(F)
Saturday at The New You, 3010(F)
Saturday Is Pattyday, 5043(F)
The Saturday Kid, 4835(F)
Saturday Night at the Dinosaur Stomp, 2686(F)
Saturday Night Jamboree, 3935(F)
Saturday Sancocho, 4852(F)
The Saturday Secret, 8513(F)
Saturn, 18464, 18477, 18482, 18493, 18501
Saudi Arabia, 15534, 15542, 15551, 15557
The Savage Damsel and the Dwarf, 7969(F)
Savage Sam, 7199(F)
Save Halloween! 8530(F)
Save Queen of Sheba, 9415(F)
Saving Shiloh, 7277(F)
Saving Sweetness, 4324(F)
Saving the Peregrine Falcon, 19319
Savion! 12465
The Savior Is Born, 5825
Savitri, 10806
Say Hey! A Song of Willie Mays, 13474
Say Hola to Spanish, 13981
Say Hola to Spanish at the Circus, 2925(F)
Say It Again, 18612
Say It with Music, 12322
Say No and Know Why, 17896
Saying Good-bye to Grandma, 3915(F)
Saying Goodbye to Daddy, 5097(F)
Sayonara, Mrs. Kackleman, 4703(F)
Scaly Facts, 18682
Scaly Things, 18687
Scandinavia, 15446
The Scarebird, 3145(F)
Scarecrow, 1534(F)
The Scarecrow's Hat, 1871(F)
The Scared Little Bear, 672(F)
Scared Silly, 6010(F), 6797(F)
Scared Silly! 7630(F)
Scared Stiff, 7031(F)
Scaredy Cat, 2612(F)
Scaredy Dog, 5430(F)
Scarlette Beane, 1663(F)
Scary, Scary Halloween, 5985(F)
Scary Stories for Stormy Nights, 8195(F)
Scary Stories 3, 7046(F)
Scary Stories to Read When It's Dark, 6627(F)
Scary Stories to Tell in the Dark, 11381

Scheherazade's Cat, 10636
The Schernoff Discoveries, 8357(F)
Scholastic Atlas of the United States, 15901
Scholastic Encyclopedia of the Civil War, 16398
Scholastic Encyclopedia of the Presidents and Their Times, 12696
Scholastic Environmental Atlas of the United States, 16962
Scholastic Explains Math Homework, 20594
Scholastic Explains Reading Homework, 14105
Scholastic Explains Writing Homework, 14106
Scholastic Kid's Almanac for the 21st Century, 14353
Scholastic Treasury of Quotations for Children, 14069
School, 926(F)
A School Album, 3389
School Bus, 5558(F)
A School for Pompey Walker, 9317(F)
School in Grandma's Day, 16493
School Isn't Fair, 5471(F)
The School Mouse, 7869(F)
The School Mural, 5544(F)
School Safety, 18220
School Spirit, 10084(F)
School Spirits, 8155(F)
School Stories, 6573(F)
School Supplies, 11604
School Trouble for Andy Russell, 10024(F)
School's Out, 7459(F)
Science, 18286
Science and Medicine, 13207
Science and Technology, 18290
Science Around the House, 18315
Science Around the World, 18326
The Science Book, 18294
The Science Book for Girls and Other Intelligent Beings, 18371
The Science Book of Air, 20663
The Science Book of Color, 20854
The Science Book of Electricity, 20881
The Science Book of Energy, 20817
The Science Book of Gravity, 20294
The Science Book of Light, 20855
The Science Book of Magnets, 20882
The Science Book of Motion, 20818
The Science Book of the Senses, 18130
The Science Book of Things That Grow, 20223
The Science Book of Water, 20724
The Science Chef, 20087
The Science Chef Travels Around the World, 21691
Science Experiments, 18367
Science Experiments with Electricity, 20901
Science Experiments with Forces, 20814
Science Experiments You Can Eat, 18305
The Science Explorer Out and About, 18336

The Science Factory, 18343
Science Fair Bunnies, 2344(F)
Science Fair Projects, 18301, 18381, 20798, 20819
Science Fair Projects Investigating Earthworms, 19601
Science Fair Projects with Electricity and Electronics, 20886
Science Fair Success in the Hardware Store, 18352
Science Fair Success Using Supermarket Products, 18353
Science Fairs, 18347
Science Fiction Pioneer, 12613
Science Fun with Mud and Dirt, 18372
Science Fun with Peanuts and Popcorn, 18372
Science Fun with Toy Boats and Planes, 18373
Science Fun with Toy Cars and Trucks, 18373
Science in Ancient China, 15054
Science in Ancient Egypt, 14673
Science in Ancient Greece, 14681
Science in Ancient India, 15115
Science in Ancient Mesopotamia, 14655
Science in Art, 18310
Science in Colonial America, 16140
Science in Early Islamic Culture, 15486
Science in Food, 18310
Science in History, 18310
Science in Seconds with Toys, 18341
Science in the Renaissance, 14800
Science Lab in a Supermarket, 18312
The Science of a Light Bulb, 20891
The Science of a Spring, 20923
The Science of Energy, 20824
The Science of Fire, 20851
The Science of Gravity, 20806
The Science of Insects, 19474
The Science of Magnets, 20885
The Science of Noise, 20944
The Science of Plants, 20228
The Science of Soil, 20550
The Science of Sound, 20934
The Science of Sound and Music, 20940
Science of the Early Americas, 15563
Science Play! 18319
Science Project Ideas About Air, 20668
Science Project Ideas About Animal Behavior, 18817
Science Project Ideas About Rain, 20767
Science Project Ideas About the Moon, 18445
Science Project Ideas About the Sun, 20850
Science Project Ideas About Trees, 20201
Science Projects About Electricity and Magnets, 20894
Science Projects About Light, 20869
Science Projects About Plants, 20235
Science Projects About Temperature and Heat, 20853

Science Projects About the Human Body, 18060
Science School, 18328
Science Secrets, 18351
Science Sensations, 18370
Science Surprises, 21045
Science to the Rescue, 18332
Scienceworks, 18339
Scientific Visualization, 21192
Scientist and Activist, Phyllis Stearner, 13347
Scientist and Physician, Judith Pachciarz, 13337
Scientist and Strategist, June Rooks, 13344
Scientist and Teacher, Anne Barrett Swanson, 13349
Scientists, 13210
Scientists Who Changed the World, 13224
Scientists Who Study Ancient Temples and Tombs, 17827
Scientists Who Study Fossils, 17828
Scientists Who Study Ocean Life, 17829
Scientists Who Study the Earth, 17830
Scientists Who Study Wild Animals, 17831
Scooter, 8385(F)
The Scopes Trial, 16451
Scorpion Man, 19592
Scorpions, 19585, 19588
Scotland, 15340, 15349
Scott Gustafson's Animal Orchestra, 451(F)
Scott Joplin, 12331
Scottie Pippen, 13564
Scottish Terriers, 19976
Scotty and the Gypsy Bandit, 8389(F)
Scrabble Creek, 3956(F)
Scramcat, 2249(F)
Scrambled Eggs Super! 2676(F)
The Scrambled States of America, 1291(F)
Scrawl! 14006
Screech! 19021
Screws, 20927
Scribe of the Great Plains, 12589
Scrub Dog of Alaska, 7268(F)
Scruffy, 6567(F), 7160(F)
Scuba Diving, 22310
Se Ri Pak, 13706
Sea Animals, 5394
Sea Creatures with Many Arms, 19725
Sea Critters, 19632
Sea-Fari Deep, 7128(F)
A Sea Full of Sharks, 19764
Sea Horse, 19715
Sea Horses, 19709, 19717
The Sea King's Daughter, 11112
Sea Lions, 19748
The Sea Maidens of Japan, 4589(F)
The Sea Man, 8241(F)
The Sea Monster's Secret, 11231
The Sea of Tranquillity, 4673(F)
The Sea Otter, 19746
Sea Otter Inlet, 20373
Sea Otters, 19733

Sea, Salt, and Air, 4904(F)
Sea Shapes, 343(F)
Sea Snakes, 19649
Sea Soup, 19626
Sea Squares, 472
Sea Star, 7217(F)
Sea Stars and Dragons, 19711
The Sea-Thing Child, 1241(F)
Sea Turtle Watching, 18778
Sea Turtles, 18782, 18786, 18788
Sea Watch, 11820
A Sea Within a Sea, 21911
Seabird, 19349
Seabirds, 19274, 19347
Seabrooke's Dragon That Ate Summer, 8076(F)
Seal, 5115(F)
Seal Island School, 10026(F)
Seal Surfer, 4958(F)
Seals, 19731
  (Illus. by Fred Bruemmer), 19734
The Seals on the Bus, 14246
Seaman, 7231(F)
The Search for Delicious, 7574(F)
The Search for Dinosaurs, 14407
The Search for Gold, 14544
The Search for Grissi, 8811(F)
The Search for Lost Cities, 14520
Search for Sam, 2752(F)
The Search for Sunken Treasure, 14521
Search for the Shadowman, 6993(F)
The Search for Tombs, 14527
Searching for Alien Life, 18391
Searching for Candlestick Park, 6918(F)
Searching for Velociraptor, 14400
The Sears Tower, 16546
Seas and Oceans, 19827, 19844
Seascapes, 13923
Seashore, 19866
  (Illus. by Dave King), 19863
The Seashore, 19856
Seashore Babies, 19628
Seashore Plants, 19859
Seashores, 19872
A Seaside Alphabet, 45(F)
Seaside Poems, 11533
A Season of Comebacks, 10346(F)
Seasons, 4561(F)
The Seasons and Someone, 4477(F)
The Seasons of Arnold's Apple Tree, 4443(F)
Seasons of Splendor, 10795
Seasons of the Crane, 19278
Seasons of the Trail, 9368(F)
The Seasons Sewn, 16350
Seattle, 16796, 16815, 16820
The Seattle Children's Theatre, 12036
The Seattle SuperSonics Basketball Team, 22127
Seaward, 7670(F)
The Seaweed Book, 19652
Sebastian, 12319
Sebastian (Super Sleuth) and the Bone to Pick Mystery, 6792(F)
Sebastian (Super Sleuth) and the Copycat Crime, 6793(F)
Sebastian (Super Sleuth) and the Crummy Yummies Caper, 6792(F)

Sebgugugu the Glutton, 10643
The Second Bend in the River, 9431(F)
Second Cousins, 8681(F)
The Second Decade, 9555(F)
The Second Escape of Arthur Cooper, 9324(F)
Second-Grade Ape, 6578(F)
Second Stringer, 10325(F)
Secondhand Star, 10106(F)
The Secret at the Polk Street School, 6347(F)
The Secret Birthday Message, 5671(F)
The Secret Box, 8784(F)
The Secret Circle, 10129(F)
The Secret Footprints, 11417
The Secret Friend, 2042(F)
Secret Friends, 8898(F)
The Secret Funeral of Slim Jim the Snake, 8869(F)
The Secret Garden, 8263(F)
The Secret Garden Cookbook, 21687
The Secret in the Dorm Attic, 6750(F)
Secret in the Mist, 3338(F)
The Secret Journey, 8966(F)
The Secret Knowledge of Grown-ups, 10021(F)
The Secret Language of Snow, 20795
Secret Letters from 0 to 10, 9940(F)
The Secret Life of Amanda K. Woods, 8590(F)
The Secret Life of Dagmar Schultz, 9872(F)
The Secret Life of Fairies, 21932
The Secret Life of Fishes, 19654
The Secret Little City, 8175(F)
The Secret Night World of Cats, 1332(F)
The Secret of Drumshee Castle, 9100(F)
  (Illus. by Orla Roche), 9099(F)
The Secret of Foghorn Island, 6372(F)
The Secret of Lizard Island, 6888(F)
The Secret of Old Zeb, 6814(F)
The Secret of Platform 13, 7809(F)
The Secret of Roanoke Island, 16135
The Secret of the Floating Phantom, 6936(F)
The Secret of the Indian, 7587(F)
The Secret of the Missing Grave, 6807(F)
The Secret of the Old Graveyard, 7134(F)
The Secret of the Ruby Ring, 10211(F)
The Secret of the Seven Crosses, 9100(F)
The Secret of the Seven Willows, 7940(F)
The Secret of the Stones, 11377
The Secret of the White Buffalo, 11308
Secret Pal Surprises, 4062(F)
Secret Place, 4397(F)
The Secret Room, 10617
The Secret Shortcut, 1616(F)
Secret Societies, 21949
The Secret Soldier, 13191

Secret Spy Satellites, 20987
The Secret Stars, 5920(F)
Secret Summer Dreams, 8335(F)
The Secret Voice of Gina Zhang, 8873(F)
Secret Weapon, 10302(F)
Secret Weapons in the Civil War, 16396
The Secret World of Polly Flint, 7685(F)
Secrets at Hidden Valley, 8796(F)
Secrets from the Dollhouse, 1628(F)
The Secrets of Animal Flight, 19220
Secrets of Animal Survival, 18805
Secrets of the Ice Man, 14510
Secrets of the Mayan Ruins, 7088(F)
Secrets of the Mummies, 14553
Secrets of the Sea, 21447
Secrets of the Stone, 2754(F)
Secrets on 26th Street, 9565(F)
Sector 7, 1679(F)
See How I Grow, 18235
See the Ocean, 4407(F)
See the Stars, 18386
See You Around, Sam! 9925(F)
See You Later, Alligator, 2326(F)
See You Later, Gladiator, 10231(F)
See You Soon Moon, 3079(F)
See You Tomorrow, Charles, 5488(F)
The Seed Bunny, 2673(F)
Seedfolks, 7339(F)
Seeds, 4043(F)
Seeds and Seedlings, 20274
The Seeds of Peace, 998(F)
Seeing Earth from Space, 18433
Seeing Lessons, 9285(F)
Seeing Stars, 18405
Seeing the Circle, 12509
Seeing Things My Way, 4927
Seeker of Knowledge, 13766
Sees Behind Trees, 9155(F)
Seesaw Girl, 9005(F)
Seesaws, Nutcrackers, Brooms, 20922
Sefer Ha-Aggadah, 11163
Seiji Ozawa, 12440
Seismosaurus, 14438
Selena, 12466
Selena Perez, 12467
The Selfish Crocodile, 1951(F)
Selkie, 11012
The Selkie Girl, 10961
The Seltzer Man, 4815(F)
The Seminole, 15932
Seminole Diary, 4697
The Seminoles, 15920, 15979, 15987, 16052
Send One Angel Down, 9319(F)
Sending a Letter, 13965
Seneca, 5129(F)
Seneca Chief, Army General, 12979
Senegal, 15013
Senegal in Pictures, 15047
Señor Cat's Romance and Other Favorite Stories from Latin America, 11439
Señora Reganona, 773(F)
Sense-Abilities, 18150
A Sense of Shabbat, 6089
Sense Suspense, 21868

Senses, 18151, 18161
Sequoyah and the Cherokee Alphabet, 12993
Sequoyah's Gift, 12994
Serafin, 7952(F)
Serbia, 15280
Serefina under the Circumstances, 5729(F)
Serena and the Wild Doll, 1076(F)
Serena Katz, 4270(F)
A Serenade of Mermaids, 10408(F)
Serendipity, 3455(F)
The Serengeti Migration, 14937
Sergio and the Hurricane, 4865(F)
The Serpent Slayer and Other Stories of Strong Women, 10717
Settler Sayings, 16326
Seven Animal Stories for Children, 17249
Seven at One Blow, 10924
Seven Blind Mice, 10810
Seven Brave Women, 3682(F)
The Seven Chairs, 4724(F)
The Seven Chinese Brothers, 10765
Seven Days of Kwanzaa, 17365
The Seven Gods of Luck, 10820
700 Science Experiments for Everyone, 18354
The 761st Tank Battalion, 14876
Seven Kisses in a Row, 7481(F)
Seven Little Monsters, 579(F)
Seven Loaves of Bread, 1697(F)
Seven Long Years Until College, 8557(F)
The Seven Silly Eaters, 4182(F)
Seven Spiders Spinning, 7945(F)
Seven Spools of Thread, 5637(F)
Seven Stars More! 740(F)
Seven Strange and Ghostly Tales, 7831(F)
The Seven Treasure Hunts, 9795(F)
The Seven Voyages of Sinbad the Sailor, 11202
Seven Wild Pigs, 2189(F)
Seventeen and In-Between, 10047(F)
Seventh Grade Tango, 10100(F)
The Seventh Walnut, 4510
The Seventies, 16508
Sewing, 21646
Sex, Boys and You, 17603
Seymour Bleu, 264(F)
Seymour Simon's Book of Trucks, 21319
Shabbat, 6102
Shades of Black, 3363(F)
Shades of Gray, 9501(F)
Shadow, 9183(F)
  (Illus. by Marcia Brown), 171(F)
  (Illus. by Claudio Munoz), 5356(F)
Shadow and the Ready Time, 5411(F)
Shadow-Catcher, 6943(F)
The Shadow Children, 8071(F)
Shadow Dance, 8973
Shadow Horse, 7212(F)
Shadow of a Bull, 8864(F)
The Shadow of a Flying Bird, 11146
Shadow Play, 20879
Shadow Spinner, 8993(F)
Shadow Story, 1683(F)
The Shadowed Unicorn, 7534(F)

The Shadowmaker, 7784(F)
Shadows, 185(F)
Shadows Are About, 3358(F)
Shadows in the Dawn, 19001
Shadows in the Glasshouse, 16154(F)
Shadows in the Water, 7890(F)
Shadows of Caesar's Creek, 6824(F)
Shaggy, Waggy Dogs (and Others), 19941
Shaka, 13850
Shake Dem Halloween Bones, 6036(F)
Shake It to the One That You Love the Best, 14170
Shake Rag, 5016(F)
Shake, Rattle and Roll, 236(F), 14129
Shake, Rattle, and Strum, 14218
Shaker Boy, 4807(F)
Shaker Home, 17166
Shaker Inventions, 17168
Shaker Villages, 17169
The Shaker's Dozen, 594
The Shakespeare Stealer, 9079(F)
Shakespeare's London, 15342
Shakespeare's Scribe, 9080(F)
Shakespeare's Stories, 12044, 12045, 12046
Shakespeare's The Tempest, 12051
Shakespeare's Theater, 14324
Shakespeare's Theatre, 13903
The Shaking Bag, 988(F)
Shalom Shabbat, 6121(F)
The Shaman's Apprentice, 4619(F)
The Shaman's Nephew, 15824
Shamrocks, Harps and Shillelaghs, 17341
Shania Twain, 12478
Shannon, 9574(F), 9575(F), 15981
Shannon, Lost and Found, 9576(F)
Shannon Lucid, 12135
Shanti, 2556(F)
Shape It! 21531
Shape Space, 328(F)
Shape Up! 319(F)
Shapes Galore, 358
Shapes, Shapes, Shapes, 338(F)
Shapes, Sizes and More Surprises! 253(F)
Shaping a President, 16724
Shaping the Earth, 18436, 20304
Shaq and the Beanstalk, 10472(F)
Shaquille O'Neal, 13557, 13559, 13560, 13561
Sharing Blessings, 17480
Sharing Susan, 8408(F)
Sharing Time Troubles, 6481(F)
Shark, 10290(F)
Shark Attack, 10356(F)
Shark Attack! 19756
Shark Bite, 7087(F)
Shark Swimathon, 20633
Sharks, 19754, 19758, 19760, 19761, 19767, 19768
Sharks! 19759
Sharks Past and Present, 19762
Shawn and Keeper and the Birthday Party, 6472(F)
Shawn and Keeper Show-and-Tell, 6473(F)
Shawn Kemp, 13541

The Shawnee, 15955
Shays' Rebellion and the Constitution in American History, 16252
She Come Bringing Me That Little Baby Girl, 3663(F)
She Is Born, 3757(F)
Sheep, 20067
Sheep in a Jeep, 6654(F)
Sheep in a Shop, 5723(F)
Sheep in Wolves' Clothing, 2301(F)
Sheep on a Ship, 6654(F)
Sheep Out to Eat, 6655(F)
Sheep Take a Hike, 2685(F)
Sheep Trick or Treat, 6048(F)
Sheila Rae, the Brave, 2196(F)
Shell, 18924
She'll Be Comin' Round the Mountain, 14142
   (Illus. by Andrew Glass), 4085(F)
The Shell Book, 19773
Shelley Shock, 10117(F)
Shelley, the Hyperactive Turtle, 5039(F)
Shellfish Aren't Fish, 19674
Shells, 19772
Shelter Dogs, 19954
Shelterwood, 4541(F)
Shen of the Sea, 8988(F)
The Shepherd Boy, 3280(F)
   (Illus. by Jill Kastner), 2931(F)
The Sheriff of Rottenshot, 11912
Sherwood, 9129(F)
She's Been Working on the Railroad, 21336
Shh! (Don't Tell Mr. Wolf!), 2450(F)
Shh! We're Writing the Constitution, 17056
Shhhh, 3688(F)
Shibumi and the Kitemaker, 1402(F)
Shih Tzus, 19976
Shiloh, 7278(F), 16438
Shiloh Season, 7279(F)
The Shimmering Ghost of Riversend, 6937(F)
Shine, Sun! 6355(F)
Shingebiss, 11315
Shin's Tricycle, 14860
Ship, 21367
Ship Ahoy! 933(F)
Ship of Dreams, 749(F)
Ships, 21355, 21361, 21379
Ships of the Air, 21075
Shipwreck, 9544(F), 21372
Shipwreck Saturday, 6282(F)
Shipwreck Season, 9286(F)
The Shipwrecked Sailor, 11183
Shipwrecked! The True Adventures of a Japanese Boy, 13833
Shipwrecks from the Westward Movement, 16300
Shipwrecks of the Explorers, 14541
Shirley Chisholm, 12707
Shiver, 6805(F)
Shock Waves Through Los Angeles, 20353
Shockers of the Sea and Other Electrical Animals, 19694
Shocking Science, 20899
Shocking, Slimy, Stinky, Shiny Science Experiments, 18340
Shoe Magic, 11585

Shoe Town, 6684(F)
Shoebag, 7832(F)
The Shoemaker and the Elves (Illus. by Adrienne Adams), 10906
   (Illus. by Ilse Plume), 10907
Shoes, 21182, 21189
   (Illus. by William Joyce), 3482(F)
Shoes for Everyone, 12770
Shoes from Grandpa, 4149(F)
Shoes Like Miss Alice's, 3249(F)
Shoes of Satin, Ribbons of Silk, 14272
Shoes, Shoes, Shoes, 21181
Shoeshine Girl, 8575(F)
Shoeshine Whittaker, 4202(F)
Shona, 15006
Shoo Fly! 794(F)
A Shooting Star, 9571(F)
Shooting Star, 12429
Shopping in Grandma's Day, 16493
Shopping with Benjamin, 994(F)
The Shore Beyond, 1281(F)
Shorebirds, 19246, 19352
Shoreline, 19869
Short Stature, 18066
Short Takes, 12004
Shortcut, 3091(F), 3292(F)
Shorthaired Cats in America, 19930
Shortstop from Tokyo, 10312(F)
The Shoshoni, 15951
Shota and the Star Quilt, 3016(F)
Shout, Sister, Shout! Ten Girl Singers Who Shaped a Century, 12176
Show and Tell, 10069(F)
Show-and-Tell, 5533(F)
Show and Tell Bunnies, 5513(F)
Show and Tell Day, 5528(F)
The Show-and-Tell Frog, 6553(F)
Show Time! 14321
Shower of Gold, 10798
Showing Distance in Art, 13920
Shrinking Forests, 20218
Shrinking Mouse, 340(F)
The Shrinking of Treehorn, 9874(F)
The Shuteyes, 7833(F)
The Shy Little Angel, 3052(F)
Shy Mama's Halloween, 5984(F)
Shy Salamanders, 18695
Shy Vi, 2370(F)
Siamese Fighting Fish, 19710
Siberian Huskies, 19977
Sibling Rivalry, 17668
The Sick Day, 3790(F)
Sickle Cell Anemia, 18001
Sid and Sam, 6237(F)
Side by Side, 18606
Sidewalk Games Around the World, 22000
Sidewalk Trip, 3224(F)
Sideways Arithmetic from Wayside School, 9983(F)
Sidney Won't Swim, 2667(F)
The Siege at Waco, 16839
The Sierra Club Summer Book, 21969
Siggy's Spaghetti Works, 20129
Sight, 18153
A Sign, 17776
The Sign of the Beaver, 9212(F)

The Sign of the Chrysanthemum, 9008(F)
Sign of the Dove, 7730(F)
The Sign of the Seahorse, 984(F)
The Sign Painter, 8809(F)
Sikh Gurdwara, 17196
Silas, 7955(F)
The Silence in the Mountains, 3862(F)
Silent Night, 5840(F), 5887(F), 14202(F)
Silent Night, Holy Night, 14209
Silent Observer, 17922
The Silent Spillbills, 7305(F)
The Silent Storm, 6851(F)
Silent Thunder, 9494(F)
Silent to the Bone, 6926(F)
Silkworms, 19487, 19611
Silly Billy! 1257(F)
The Silly Chicken, 2677(F)
Silly Goose and Dizzy Duck Play Hide-and-Seek, 2153(F)
The Silly Gooses, 2586(F)
Silly Little Goose! 2750(F)
Silly Ruby, 6337(F)
Silly Sadie, Silly Samuel, 6570(F)
Silly Sally, 2871(F)
Silly Science, 18327
Silly Science Tricks (with Professor Solomon Snickerdoodle), 18337
Silly Silly, 2636(F)
Silly Stories to Tickle Your Funny Bone, 6658(F)
Silly Tilly's Thanksgiving Dinner, 6144(F)
Silly Tilly's Valentine, 6171(F)
Silver, 7322(F)
The Silver Balloon, 8259(F)
The Silver Chair, 7911(F)
The Silver Coach, 8396(F)
The Silver Cow, 10962
Silver Dollar Girl, 9344(F)
Silver Morning, 4505(F)
Silver on the Tree, 7671(F)
Silver Packages, 5914(F)
The Silver Pony, 937(F)
Silver Rain Brown, 3684(F)
Silver Seeds, 11978
The Silver Swan, 5351(F)
The Silver Sword, 9687(F)
The Silver Treasure, 10576
Silverwing, 8001(F), 8002(F)
Simon & Schuster Children's Guide to Birds, 19240
Simon and Schuster Children's Guide to Sea Creatures, 19637
Simon and the Snowflakes, 1623(F)
Simon Bolivar, 13755
Simon's Book, 1137(F)
Simple Attractions, 20904
Simple Gifts, 14174
Simple Kitchen Experiments, 20114
Simple Machines, 20921, 20930
Simple Puppets from Everyday Materials, 14303
Simple Weather Experiments with Everyday Materials, 20782
Simply Delicious! 1388(F)
Sindbad, 11203
Sing a New Song, 17299
Sing a Song of Popcorn, 11551

Sing Down the Moon, 9489(F)
Sing Down the Rain, 14253
Sing for Your Father, Su Phan, 9009(F)
Sing, Henrietta! Sing! 4133(F)
Sing of the Earth and Sky, 11561
Sing, Pierrot, Sing, 1114(F)
Sing Song, 11686
Sing, Sophie! 4131(F)
Sing Through the Day, 14256
Sing to the Sun, 11541
Sing Together, 14243
Singapore, 15150, 15180
Singer to the Sea God, 9023(F)
Singing Bee! A Collection of Favorite Children's Songs, 14244
The Singing Chick, 2723(F)
Singing Down the Rain, 1083(F)
The Singing Green, 11971
The Singing Hat, 1507(F)
The Singing Man, 10696
Singing Our Way West, 14180
Singing Robins, 19277
Singing Sam, 6239(F)
The Singing Snowbear, 2152(F)
A Single Speckled Egg, 4212(F)
Sink or Swim, 16895
Sink the Bismarck, 14869
The Sioux, 16019, 16028 (Illus. by Ronald Himler), 16053
Sip, Slurp, Soup, Soup/Caldo, Caldo, Caldo, 3527(F)
Sir Cedric, 4660(F)
Sir Edmund Hillary, 12124
Sir Galahad, Mr. Longfellow, and Me, 7455(F)
Sir Gawain and the Loathly Lady, 10993
Sir Gibbie, 9109(F)
Sir Robert's Little Outing, 1385(F)
Sir Small and the Dragonfly, 6551(F)
Sirko and the Wolf, 10860
Sister, 7438(F)
Sister Anne's Hands, 5517(F)
Sister Cities in a World of Difference, 14332
Sister of the Bride, 7408(F)
Sister Shako and Kolo the Goat, 13779
Sister Yessa's Story, 17280(F)
Sisters, 3794(F)
Sisters Against Slavery, 12894
Sisters in Strength, 12677
Sisters Long Ago, 7461(F)
A Sister's Wish, 3717(F)
The Sistine Chapel, 14798
Sit on a Potato Pan, Otis! 21878
Sitting Bull, 12996
Sitting Bull and the Battle of the Little Bighorn, 12995
Sitting Down to Eat, 2169(F)
Sitting Ducks, 1799(F)
Sitting on the Farm, 2292(F)
Sitting Pretty, 21652
Sitti's Secrets, 4781(F)
Six Creepy Sheep, 5996(F)
Six-Dinner Sid, 2507(F)
Six Foolish Fishermen, 11378
Six Haunted Hairdos, 8339(F)
Six Hogs on a Scooter, 2711(F)

Six-Minute Nature Experiments, 18302
Six Sandy Sheep, 2072(F)
Six Sick Sheep, 21879
6 Sticks, 412(F)
The Six Swans, 10908
6–321, 8737(F)
Six Words, Many Turtles, and Three Days in Hong Kong, 15072
A 16th Century Galleon, 15477
A 16th Century Mosque, 15492
Sixth Grade Can Really Kill You, 10048(F)
The 6th Grade Nickname Game, 10093(F)
Sixth Grade Secrets, 8366(F)
The Sixties, 16508
The 60s, 13875, 16516
Sixty Fingers, Sixty Toes, 18229
The $66 Summer, 8251(F)
60 Super Simple Crafts, 21442
60 Super Simple Magic Tricks, 21787
Skateboarder's Start-Up, 22276
Skateboarding! 22275
The Skating Book, 22228
The Skeletal System, 18174
Skeleton, 18171
The Skeleton and Movement, 18170
The Skeleton and Muscular System, 18167
The Skeleton Inside You, 18165
Skellig, 7557(F)
Sketching Outdoors in Spring, 21560
Sketching Outdoors in Summer, 21560
Skiing, 22248
Skin, 18847
The Skin I'm In, 10056(F)
Skin, Teeth, and Hair, 18179
Skinny Melon and Me, 8837(F)
Skip Across the Ocean, 826(F)
The Skit Book, 12032
The Skull of Truth, 7680(F)
Skullduggery, 9299(F)
Skunks, 18951, 18953
Sky Dancer, 5153(F)
The Sky in Silver Lace, 7465(F)
The Sky Is Always in the Sky, 11621
The Sky Is Falling! 6521(F)
The Sky Is Full of Stars, 18541
The Sky Is Not So Far Away, 701
Sky Memories, 8571(F)
Sky Pioneer, 12116
Sky Rider, 8121(F)
Sky Sash So Blue, 4677(F)
Sky Scrape/City Scape, 11744
Sky, Sea, the Jetty, and Me, 4428(F)
Sky Words, 11984
Skyfire, 1757(F)
Skylark, 9411(F)
Skyscrapers, 21146, 21150
SkySisters, 11316
Skywoman, 11299
Slake's Limbo, 6898(F)
Slam Dunk, 10274(F), 12002
Slam Dunk Saturday, 10350(F)
The Slave Dancer, 9276(F)
Slave Young, Slave Long, 16246
Slavery, 15882

Slavery and the Coming of the Civil War, 1831–1861, 16236
Slavery in Ancient Egypt and Mesopotamia, 14583
Slavery in Ancient Greece and Rome, 14584
Slavery in the United States, 15896
Slaves to Soldiers, 16390
A Sled Dog for Moshi, 5151(F)
Sleds on Boston Common, 9185(F)
Sleep, 18227
Sleep Is for Everyone, 18118
Sleep, Little One, Sleep, 635(F)
Sleep Out, 2919(F)
The Sleep Ponies, 756(F)
Sleep Rhymes Around the World, 817
Sleep Safe, Little Whale, 775(F)
Sleep Well, Little Bear, 640(F)
Sleeping Beauty, 10869, 14289
    (Illus. by Dominic Catalano), 10494
    (Illus. by Frances Cony), 12015
Sleeping Boy, 7683(F)
The Sleeping Bread, 11398
Sleepless Beauty, 4237(F)
The Sleepover Cookbook, 21746
Sleepy Bears, 677(F)
Sleepy Book, 821(F)
Sleepy Little Mouse, 1158(F)
Sleepy Little Owl, 2132(F)
The Sleepy Men, 639(F)
Sleepy-O! 14196
Sleepytime for Zoo Animals, 18798
Sleepytime Rhyme, 646(F)
Slender Ella and Her Fairy Hogfather, 6624(F)
A Slice Through a City, 14532
Slim and Miss Prim, 9898(F)
Slime, Molds, and Fungus, 20189
Slinky Scaly Slithery Snakes, 18772
Slither McCreep and His Brother, 2262(F)
A Sliver of Glass and Other Uncommon Tales, 7959(F)
Slop! A Welsh Folktale, 11013
Sloth's Shoes, 5738(F)
Slovakia in Pictures, 15290
Slow Train to Oxmox, 1093(F)
Sluggers! 13417
Slugs, 19606
Slugs, Bugs, and Salamanders, 18644
A Slug's Life, 19610
Slump, 8711(F)
Small Brown Dog's Bad Remembering Day, 2122(F)
Small Cats, 19096
Small Change, 7092(F)
A Small Child's Book of Cozy Poems, 11703
A Small Child's Book of Prayers, 17533
Small Dogs, 19937
Small Gifts in God's Hands, 17300
Small Green Snake, 2146(F)
A Small Miracle, 9714(F)
Small Pig, 6469(F)
Small Plays for Special Days, 12010
Small Steps, 17973
Small Talk, 11959
A Small Treasury of Christmas, 17432

A Small Treasury of Easter, 11852
The Smallest Bear, 2471(F)
The Smallest Cow in the World, 5046(F)
Smart Dog, 8171(F)
    (Illus. by Chris L. Demarest), 2354(F)
Smart Spending, 16936
The Smash-up Crash-up Derby, 3419(F)
Smasher, 7239(F)
Smell, 18158
    (Illus. by Maria Rius), 18154
Smell, Taste and Touch, 18135
Smile! 3236(F)
Smile If You're Human, 1341(F)
Smiling, 17633
The Smithsonian Institution, 16661
The Smithsonian Visual Timeline of Inventions, 21053
Smoke Screen, 8734(F)
Smokejumper, 17812
Smoking, 17883, 17884, 17887
Smoking Stinks!! 8668(F)
Smoky Night, 3059(F)
Smudge, 2641(F)
    (Illus. by Jane Chapman), 2747(F)
Smudge, the Little Lost Lamb, 5259(F)
The Smugglers, 9106(F)
Snaggle Doodles, 6348(F)
Snail, 19608
Snail Girl Brings Water, 13944
The Snail House, 946(F)
Snail Mail No More, 8275(F)
Snailology, 19619
Snails, 19612, 19615
Snails and Slugs, 19617
A Snail's Pace, 19605
The Snail's Spell, 1530(F)
Snake, 18756
The Snake, 2792(F)
Snake Alley Band, 2542(F)
The Snake Book, 18763
Snake Camp, 6682(F)
Snake Hair, 11507
A Snake in the House, 5334(F)
The Snake Scientist, 18770
Snakes, 18755, 18760, 18776
    (Illus. by Judith Moffatt), 18757
Snakes and Lizards, 18690
Snakes and Such, 19906
Snakes Are Hunters, 18761
Snap! 2778(F)
Snap like a Crocodile, 304(F)
Snappy Jazzy Jewelry, 21437
Snapshots from the Wedding, 3436(F)
Snazzy Aunties, 3888(F)
Sneak Thief, 6892(F)
Sneakers, 21187, 21188
The Sneaky Square and 113 Other Math Activities for Kids, 20621
Sniff-Snuff-Snap! (Illus. by Lynley Dodd), 420(F)
    (Illus. by Lynley Dodd), 6308(F)
Snip, Snip . . . Snow! 5525(F)
The Snopp on the Sidewalk and Other Poems, 11809
Snot Stew, 8181(F)

Snow, 3425(F), 8887(F)
Snow! 3147(F)
Snow and the Earth, 20730
Snow Angel, 1398(F)
Snow Baby, 3012(F)
Snow Bear, 5225(F)
Snow Bound, 6970(F)
The Snow Cats, 19104
The Snow Child, 6726(F)
Snow Dance, 3123(F)
Snow Day, 931(F), 5496(F)
    (Illus. by Giulio Maestro), 4494
    (Illus. by Nancy Poydar), 6209(F)
Snow Day! 4469(F)
Snow Family, 3750(F)
Snow, Ice and Cold, 20792
Snow Is Falling, 20755
The Snow Lambs, 5228(F)
Snow Lion, 6500(F)
Snow Monkeys, 19017
Snow Pumpkin, 4038(F)
The Snow Queen, 10387(F)
Snow Riders, 1371(F)
Snow Shapes, 21456
Snow, Snow, 11992
The Snow Speaks, 3066(F)
Snow Treasure, 9673(F)
The Snow Tree, 5910(F)
Snow Valentines, 6178(F)
The Snow Walker, 16494
Snow White and the Seven Dwarves, 10909
Snowball, 3093(F)
The Snowball, 959(F)
Snowballs, 21433(F)
Snowbear Whittington, 11351
Snowboard Maverick, 10313(F)
Snowboarding, 22277, 22278, 22279, 22284
Snowboarding! 22280
Snowboards, 21059
Snowdrops for Cousin Ruth, 8467(F)
Snowflake Bentley, 12191
Snowie Rolie, 5855(F)
The Snowman, 911(F)
A Snowman on Sycamore Street, 8269(F)
The Snowman's Path, 1482(F)
Snowplows, 21254
Snowtime, 2656(F)
The Snowy Day, 12246
    (Illus. by Ezra Jack Keats), 4471(F)
Snowy Day, 11530
Snowy Flowy Blowy, 4550(F)
Snug, 2168(F)
Snug Bug, 6317(F)
Snuggle Wuggle, 727(F)
So Big! 5462(F)
So Far from Home, 9537(F)
So Far from the Sea, 4611(F)
So Many Bunnies, 143(F)
So Many Cats! 416(F)
So Many Circles, So Many Squares, 339
So Many Dynamos! 14021
So Much, 5675(F)
So Much in Common, 2245(F)
So Say the Little Monkeys, 11444
So That's How the Moon Changes Shape! 18444
So What? 5489(F)

So What Do You Do? 8635(F)
So What Is Citizenship Anyway? 17043
So You Want to Be a Wizard, 7712(F)
So You Want to Be President? 17120
Soap! Soap! Don't Forget the Soap! 11325
Soap Soup and Other Verses, 6442
Soaring, 22046
Soaring with the Wind, 19324
Soccer, 22285, 22286, 22289, 22293, 22295, 22296, 22299, 22300 (Illus. by Vasja Koman), 22287
Soccer Circus, 6861(F)
Soccer Cousins, 6509(F)
Soccer Halfback, 10314(F)
Soccer Mania! 10366(F)
The Soccer Mom from Outer Space, 4298(F)
Soccer Sam, 6510(F)
Soccer Scoop, 10315(F)
Soccer Stars, 22294
Social Smarts, 17636
Socks, 7409(F)
Sod Houses on the Great Plains, 9435
Soda Pop, 20091
Soda Science, 20138
Sodbuster, 16382
Sody Salleratus, 11331
Sofie's Role, 5834(F)
Soft Rain, 9152(F)
Softball, 22109
Software Designer, 17788
Sojourner Truth, 12791, 12792, 12794
Sol a Sol, 11543
The Solar System, 18517, 18524, 18530, 18535, 18536
Sold! 16929
Soldier Mom, 8487(F)
Soldier of Destiny, 12944
Soldiers, Cavaliers, and Planters, 16111
Soldier's Heart, 9493(F)
A Soldier's Life, 21403
The Soldiers' Voice, 12584
Solid Waste, 16986
Solids, Liquids, and Gases, 20812
A Solitary Blue, 7532(F)
Solo Girl, 6577(F)
Solomon Sneezes, 6663(F)
Solomon the Rusty Nail, 2720(F)
Solving International Crime, 17080
Som See and the Magic Elephant, 1441(F)
Somalia, 14928, 14943
Some Answers Are Loud, Some Answers Are Soft, 3368(F)
Some Babies, 3413(F)
Some Birthday! 5718(F)
Some Bugs Glow in the Dark, 19462
Some Days, Other Days, 3837(F)
Some Frog! 7166(F)
Some Good News, 7504(F)
Some of the Days of Everett Anderson, 11752
Some of the Kinder Planets, 8230(F)
Some Other Summer, 8247(F)
Some Sleep Standing Up, 5424
Some Smug Slug, 2056(F)

Some Snakes Spit Poison and Other Amazing Facts About Snakes, 18764
Some Things Are Scary, 3201(F)
Some Things Change, 222(F)
Some Things Go Together, 3974(F)
Some Trains Run on Water, 21341
Somebody Loves You, Mr. Hatch, 5085(F)
Somebody Somewhere Knows My Name, 8749(F)
Someday a Tree, 4398(F)
The Someday House, 3424(F)
Someday We'll Have Very Good Manners, 4366(F)
Someone I Like, 11705
Someone Is Hiding on Alcatraz Island, 6780(F)
Someone Special, Just Like You, 4913(F)
Someone Was Watching, 7003(F)
Someplace to Go, 8831(F)
Something Beautiful, 3490(F)
Something Big Has Been Here, 11913
Something Fishy at Macdonald Hall, 10094(F)
Something from Nothing, 11147
Something Good, 4243(F)
Something Is Growing, 1326(F)
Something Might Be Hiding, 5019(F)
Something Nasty in the Cabbages, 10516(F)
Something Queer at the Ball Park, 6946(F)
Something Queer at the Haunted School, 6946(F)
Something Queer at the Library, 6946(F)
Something Queer in the Wild West, 6947(F)
Something Queer Is Going On, 6946(F)
Something Queer on Vacation, 6946(F)
Something Special, 5519(F)
Something Special for Me, 3948(F)
Something Suspicious, 6847(F)
Something to Remember Me By, 3540(F)
Something Upstairs, 6755(F)
Something Very Sorry, 8403(F)
Something Wicked's in Those Woods, 7965(F)
Something's Happening on Calabash Street, 3120(F)
Sometimes, 6197(F)
Sometimes I Feel Like a Mouse, 214(F)
Sometimes I Feel Like a Storm Cloud, 3124(F)
Sometimes Moon, 3877(F)
Sometimes Things Change, 6320(F)
Somewhere, 4384(F)
Somewhere in the Ocean, 898(F)
Somewhere Today, 251(F)
Son of the Black Stallion, 7190(F)
The Son of the Sun and the Daughter of the Moon, 11125
Song and Dance, 14134 (Illus. by Cheryl M. Taylor), 11605

Song and Dance Man, 3501(F)
Song Bird, 10704
A Song for Lena, 4681(F)
A Song for Little Toad, 679(F)
Song for the Whooping Crane, 11814
Song Lee and the "I Hate You" Notes, 10091(F)
Song Lee in Room 2B, 5511(F)
The Song of Mu Lan, 10763
The Song of Six Birds, 4636(F)
Song of the Camels, 11828
Song of the Hermit Thrush, 11230
The Song of the Molimo, 9533(F)
Song of the North, 11938
The Song of the Sea Otter, 19736
Song of the Swallows, 5368(F)
Song of the Trees, 7526(F)
Song of the Wanderer, 7681(F)
Songbirds, 19227, 19305
Songhay, 15009
Songs Are Thoughts, 11669
Songs for the Ancient Forest, 1362(F)
Songs for the Seasons, 11957
Songs from Home, 8438(F)
Songs from the Loom, 16031
The Songs My Paddle Sings, 11293
The Songs of Birds, 10620
Songs of Faith, 8465(F)
Songs of Papa's Island, 4709(F)
Songs of Power, 10152(F)
Songs of Praise, 17200
Songs of Shiprock Fair, 9181(F)
Songs of the Wild West, 14139
Songs, Seas, and Green Peas, 11706
Sonia and Barnie and the Noise in the Night, 759(F)
Sonia Begonia, 7034(F)
Soninke, 15041
Sonoran Seasons, 20407
Sons of Liberty, 8442(F)
Sooner, 9352(F)
Sophie, 3629(F)
Sophie and Rose, 3275(F)
Sophie and the New Baby, 3510(F)
Sophie Hits Six, 7240(F)
Sophie Is Seven, 8722(F)
Sophie Skates, 3241(F)
Sophie's Lucky, 7241(F)
Sor Juana, 12557
The Sorcerer's Apprentice, 1122(F) (Illus. by Leo Dillon), 1684(F)
Sore Throats and Tonsillitis, 18002
Sorotchintzy Fair, 1198(F)
Sort of Forever, 8383(F)
Sound, 20931, 20936
Sound and Hearing, 20937
Sound and Vision, 18135
Sound Experiments, 20932
A Sound of Leaves, 4909(F)
Sound Science, 20939
The Sound that Jazz Makes, 14138
Sound the Shofar! A Story for Rosh Hashanah and Yom Kippur, 6088(F)
Sounder, 7387(F)
Sounding the Alarm, 13244
Sounds All Around, 20943
Sounds Interesting, 20935
The Sounds of Summer, 7316(F)
Soup, 8358(F)

The Soup Bone, 6017(F)
Soup for President, 8358(F)
Soup in the Saddle, 8358(F)
Soup Too? 2209(F)
Soup's Oops! 2209(F)
Sour Land, 7387(F)
Sourcebook, 15880
South Africa, 14967, 14971, 14972, 14973, 14976, 14980, 14981, 14996, 14997, 14998, 14999
South Africa in Pictures, 15001
A South African Night, 5274(F)
South America, 15777
South American Animals, 18603
South American Monkeys, 18998
South and North, East and West, 10609
South Carolina, 16857, 16867, 16892
The South Carolina Colony, 16126
South Dakota, 16570
South Dakota Facts and Symbols, 16547
South Korea, 15166, 15169, 15199
South Korea in Pictures, 15206
South Pacific, 9676(F)
The Southeast, 16829
Southeast Asia, 15215
Southern Fried Rat and Other Gruesome Tales, 11330
Southern Plantation Cooking, 16248
The Southwest, 16901
Southwest Pacific, 15232
Space, 18388, 20965
The Space Atlas, 18385
Space Brat 4, 10171(F)
Space Challenger, 12079
Space Disasters, 20997
Space Dog and the Pet Show, 10242(F)
Space Dog in Trouble, 10242(F)
Space Emergency, 20976
Space Exploration, 21015
Space Guys, 6714(F)
Space Launch Disaster, 20977
Space Race, 10245(F)
   (Illus. by Jerry Zimmerman), 6678(F)
Space Rock, 6628(F)
Space Sailing, 21011
The Space Shuttle, 20999
Space, Stars, Planets and Spacecraft, 20950
Space Station Science, 20980
Space Stations, 20988, 21010
Space Travel, 21012
Space Travel and Exploration, 20970
Space Vehicles, 21599
Spacechimp, 20984
Spaceman, 8886(F)
Spaces, 1457(F)
Spacewalks, 21019
Spain, 15471, 15473, 15474, 15475, 15478, 15479, 15480, 15482, 15484
Spain in Pictures, 15485
Spain in the Age of Exploration, 15481
Spanish-American War, 16465
The Spanish-American War, 16458
The Spanish Kidnapping Disaster, 6871(F)

Spanish Missions, 15886
Spanish Pioneers of the Southwest, 16287
Sparky and Eddie, 6425(F), 6426(F)
Sparrows in the Scullery, 9126(F)
Speak English for Us, Marisol! 3616(F)
Speak Up, Blanche! 2416(F)
Speaking of Journals, 14085
Speaking Up, Speaking Out, 14102
Special Delivery, 3937(F)
Special Effects, 21271
A Special Fate, 13851
Special Gifts, 7505(F)
The Special Gifts, 5829(F)
Special Olympics, 17902
A Special Place for Charlee, 7266(F)
Special Plays for Holidays, 12033
A Special Something, 3623(F)
Spectacular Science, 11960
Spectacular Spiders, 19581
Spectacular Stone Soup, 6349(F)
The Specter from the Magician's Museum, 7090(F)
Speechless in New York, 8628(F)
Speed of Light, 7369(F)
Speed Skating, 22219
Spell It M-U-R-D-E-R, 7040(F)
The Spell of the Sorcerer's Skull, 7603(F)
Spellbinder, 12402
Spend the Day in Ancient Egypt, 14632
Spice Girls, 12472
Spider, 19582
   (Illus. by Alan Male), 19575
Spider and His Son Find Wisdom, 10688
Spider Boy, 8641(F)
Spider Kane and the Mystery Under the May-Apple, 7000(F)
Spider Sparrow, 8897(F)
Spider Spins a Story, 11272
Spider Storch's Carpool Catastrophe, 8540(F)
Spider Storch's Desperate Deal, 10018(F)
Spider Storch's Fumbled Field Trip, 10019(F)
Spider Storch's Music Mess, 10139(F)
Spider Storch's Teacher Torture, 10140(F)
The Spider Weaver, 10707
The Spider Who Created the World, 2420(F)
Spiderology, 19593
Spiders, 19577, 19580, 19591
Spiders and Their Web Sites, 19578
Spiders Are Not Insects, 19579
Spiders Have Fangs, 19586
Spiders of North America, 19596
Spiders Spin Webs, 19598
Spider's Web, 19572
The Spider's Web, 9078(F)
Spiderwebs to Skyscrapers, 21119
Spies and Traitors, 17083
Spies in the Civil War, 16422
Spike in the City, 1829(F)
Spike It! 10316(F)
Spike Lee, 12412

Spill the Beans and Pass the Peanuts, 20176
The Spindletop Gusher, 16902
Spindrift, 8517(F)
Spinky Sulks, 5088(F)
The Spinner's Daughter, 9203(F)
The Spinning Blackboard and Other Dynamic Experiments on Force and Motion, 20828
Spinning Spiders, 19574
Spin's Really Wild U.S.A. Tour, 15867
Spiny, 7891(F)
Spirit Horse, 9143(F)
Spirit of Endurance, 15795
Spirit of Hope, 3656(F)
Spirit of St. Louis, 21112
The Spirit of St. Louis, 21102
Spirit of the Cedar People, 11283
The Spirit of the Maasai Man, 999(F)
Spirit of the Maya, 15665
The Spirit of Tio Fernando, 5634(F)
Spirit Quest, 7052(F)
Splash! 480(F), 2429(F)
Splash! A Penguin Counting Book, 512(F)
Splash, Splash, 5412(F)
Splashtime for Zoo Animals, 18799
Splish Splash, 11578
Splish, Splash! 6710(F)
Splish! Splash! Animal Baths, 18849
Splish Splash, Bang Crash, 3187(F)
Splish! Splosh! Why Do We Wash? 4486
Split Just Right, 8443(F)
Sponges Are Skeletons, 19719
Spook House, 6885(F)
The Spooky Book, 4261(F)
The Spooky Eerie Night Noise, 5379(F)
Spooky Poems, 11534
Spooky Riddles, 21815
Spooky Riddles and Jokes, 21847
The Spooky Tail of Prewitt Peacock, 2570(F)
Spooky Things, 21447
Spooky Tricks, 21792
A Spoon for Every Bite, 3195(F)
Spoonbill Swamp, 20375
A Sporting Chance, 22066
Sports, 22011, 22055
Sports and Games, 13900
Sports Cards, 22077
Sports for Life, 22051
Sports Great Alonzo Mourning, 13550
Sports Great Anfernee Hardaway, 13526
Sports Great Barry Sanders, 13628
Sports Great Bo Jackson, 13616
Sports Great Brett Favre, 13613
Sports Great Cal Ripken, Jr., 13480
Sports Great David Robinson, 13567
Sports Great Dennis Rodman, 13574
Sports Great Dominique Wilkins, 13581
Sports Great Emmitt Smith, 13632
Sports Great Eric Lindros, 13699
Sports Great Greg Maddux, 13471
Sports Great Herschel Walker, 13636
Sports Great Isiah Thomas, 13577

Sports Great Jason Kidd, 13543
Sports Great Jerome Bettis, 13603
Sports Great Jim Kelly, 13617
Sports Great Joe Montana, 13620
Sports Great John Stockton, 13576
Sports Great Juwan Howard, 13531
Sports Great Larry Bird, 13514
Sports Great Magic Johnson, 13534
Sports Great Michael Chang, 13646
Sports Great Michael Jordan, 13535
Sports Great Mitch Richmond, 13566
Sports Great Nolan Ryan, 13501
Sports Great Orel Hershiser, 13461
Sports Great Oscar De La Hoya,
  13585
Sports Great Patrick Ewing, 13523
Sports Great Pete Sampras, 13652
Sports Great Reggie Miller, 13549
Sports Great Scottie Pippen, 13563
Sports Great Shaquille O'Neal,
  13558
Sports Great Troy Aikman, 13601
Sports Great Wayne Gretzky, 13688
Sports in America, 22002
Sports Lab, 22059
Sports Riddles, 21848
Sports Science Projects, 20811
Sports! Sports! Sports! A Poetry Col-
  lection, 12005
Sports Stories, 10324(F)
Sportsworks, 18068
Spot a Cat, 13914
Spot a Dog, 13914
Spot at Home, 2203(F)
Spot Counts from 1 to 10, 464(F)
Spot Goes to a Party, 2204(F)
Spot Goes to School, 6383(F)
Spot Goes to the Beach, 6384(F)
Spot Goes to the Circus, 6384(F)
Spot Goes to the Park, 2205(F)
Spot Looks at Colors, 272(F)
Spot Sleeps Over, 2206(F)
Spotlight on Cody, 8629(F)
Spotlight on Spiders, 19576
Spots, 493
Spot's Baby Sister, 2207(F)
Spot's Big Book of Colors, Shapes
  and Numbers, 195(F)
Spot's Big Book of Words, 14037(F)
Spot's Birthday Party, 6383(F)
Spots, Feathers, and Curly Tails,
  6690(F)
Spot's First Walk, 6383(F)
The Spotted Owl, 19365
The Spotted Pony, 9738(F)
Spotting the Leopard, 7275(F)
Spray, 1001(F)
The Spray-Paint Mystery, 6973(F)
Spring, 127, 4459, 11824
Spring Across America, 18572
Spring Break, 8311(F)
The Spring Hat, 2123(F)
Spring Is Here, 4447(F)
Spring Snowman, 1263(F)
A Spring Story, 7104(F)
Spring Thaw, 4536(F)
Spud in Winter, 6822(F)
Spud Sweetgrass, 6822(F)
Spunky Monkeys on Parade, 532(F)
Spy, 17077
A Spy Among the Girls, 9949(F)

The Spy in the Attic, 7045(F)
A Spy in the King's Colony, 9223(F)
Spy in the Sky, 9484(F)
The Spy on Third Base, 10303(F)
The Spy Who Came in from the Sea,
  6995(F)
The Spying Game, 8765(F)
Spying on Dracula, 6929(F)
Squanto and the First Thanksgiving,
  12998
Squanto, Friend of the Pilgrims,
  12997
Squanto's Journey, 17491
Squash It! A True and Ridiculous
  Tale, 11137
Squeaking Bats, 19022
Squeaking of Art, 13931
Squids Will Be Squids, 9986(F)
The Squiggle, 1547(F)
Squiggle's Tale, 1994(F)
The Squire, His Knight, and His
  Lady, 9113(F)
The Squire's Tale, 9114(F)
Squirrel Is Hungry, 2300(F)
Squirts and Spurts, 20731
Squish! 20381
Sri Lanka, 15211, 15221
The Stable Where Jesus Was Born,
  5827
Stacy Had a Little Sister, 5045(F)
Stadiums, 21146
The Staircase, 9432(F)
Stan the Hot Dog Man, 6432(F)
Stand for Children, 17030
Standing in the Light, 9172(F)
Standing Tall, 18067
Standing Up to Mr. O, 10113(F)
Stanley, 6407(F)
The Star-Bearer, 11186
Star Boy, 11253
Star Fisher, 8547(F)
Star Guide, 18542
Star in the Storm, 6876(F)
Star Light, Star Bright, 657(F)
The Star Maiden, 11235
Star Mother's Youngest Child,
  5884(F)
Star of Fear, Star of Hope, 9664(F)
Star of Luis, 8828(F)
Star of the Circus, 2650(F)
Star of the Sea, 19720
Star Shapes, 4497(F)
Star Tales, 11277
The Star Tree, 5787(F)
Star Walk, 11700
Star Wars, 10247(F), 14316, 14317,
  14319
The Star Wars Cookbook, 21693
The Star Wars Cookbook II, 21698
Star Wars Episode I, 14318, 14319
Star Wars, Episode I, 14314
Starbright and the Dream Eater,
  10172(F)
Stardust, 8640(F)
Starfish, 19726
  (Illus. by Robin Brickman), 19721
Stargazers, 18546
The Stargazer's Guide to the Galaxy,
  18408
Starlight and Candles, 6095(F)

The Starlight Princess and Other
  Princess Stories, 10506
Starluck, 10248(F)
Starring Dorothy Kane, 7404(F)
Starring Grace, 8302(F)
Starring Mirette and Bellini, 1367(F)
Starring Rosie, 8660(F)
Starring Sally J. Freedman as Her-
  self, 9783(F)
Starry Messenger, 13292
The Starry Night, 1662(F)
The Starry Sky, 18425
Starry Tales, 10577
Stars, 356(F), 18545, 18557
  (Illus. by Mavis Smith), 18544
The Stars, 18538, 18550, 18551,
  18552, 18556
Stars and Galaxies, 18543
Stars and Planets, 18548
The Stars Are Waiting, 750(F)
Stars, Clusters and Galaxies, 18547
The Stars in My Geddoh's Sky,
  3802(F)
The Stars That Shine, 10255(F)
Stars Wars, 10141(F)
Starshine and Sunglow, 8333(F)
Starting Home, 12286
Starting School, 10085(F)
Starting School with an Enemy,
  10033(F)
Starting with Nature Bird Book,
  19234
Starting with Nature Plant Book,
  20236
State Birds, 15852
State Facts, 15910
State Flags, 13970
State Flowers, 15853
State Government, 17130
State Governments, 17129
State Trees, 15850
States, 15905
Statesmen Who Changed the World,
  13745
Stateswoman to the World, 13185
The Statue Abraham Lincoln,
  13957(F)
The Statue of Liberty, 16666, 16719
Stay Awake, Bear! 1813(F)
Stay Away from Simon! 9265(F)
Stay Away from the Junkyard,
  4050(F)
Stay, Fang, 5251(F)
Stay in Line, 583(F)
Stay! Keeper's Story, 7927(F)
Staying Healthy, 18186
Staying Nine, 8609(F)
Staying Safe, 18226
The Steadfast Tin Soldier (Illus. by
  Rachel Isadora), 10436
  (Illus. by Fred Marcellino),
  10388(F)
  (Illus. by Alan Snow), 10389
Steal Away, 9257(F)
Stealing Home, 13491
Stealing Thunder, 7175(F)
Steam, Smoke, and Steel, 21339
Steam Train Ride, 5590
Steamboat! The Story of Captain
  Blanche Leathers, 12130
Steer Wrestling, 22060

Stegosaurus, 14391
Stella, 3159(F), 7349(F)
Stella and Roy Go Camping, 2986(F)
Stella Louella's Runaway Book, 4143(F)
Stella, Queen of the Snow, 3160(F)
Stella Street, and Everything That Happened, 9879(F)
Stellaluna, 1918(F)
Stella's Dancing Days, 5127(F)
Step by Step, 3793(F)
Step by Step Along the Appalachian Trail, 15859
Step by Step Along the Pacific Crest Trail, 16761
Step-by-Step Ballet Class, 14298
Step-by-Step Making Books, 14009
Step by Wicked Step, 7431(F)
Stephanie's Ponytail (Illus. by Vladyana Krykorka), 4245
  (Illus. by Michael Martchenko), 4244(F)
Stephen Biesty's Cross-Sections Man-of-War, 21373
Stephen Biesty's Incredible Body, 18073
Stephen Biesty's Incredible Cross-Sections, 13918
Stephen Biesty's Incredible Explosions, 21147
Stephen Biesty's Incredible Pop-Up Cross-Sections, 21244
Stephen Hawking, 13308
Stephen King, 12558
Stepping on the Cracks, 9661(F)
Stepsister from the Planet Weird, 8472(F)
Steroid Drug Dangers, 17881
Steve Jobs, 12911, 12912
Steve the Sure, 8835(F)
Steve Wozniak, 13353
Steve Young, 13638, 13639, 13640
Steven Caney's Kids' America, 21517
Steven Caney's Playbook, 21416
Steven Spielberg, 12473, 12474, 12475
Stevie, 3905(F)
Stick and Whittle, 9378(F)
Sticky Beak, 8892(F)
Still-Life Stew, 3364(F)
Still More Stories to Solve, 10612
Stina, 3507(F)
Stink Bomb, 10043(F)
Stinker from Space, 10233(F)
Stinker's Return, 10234(F)
Stinky and Stringy, 20177
Stinky Cheese Man, 9986(F)
The Stinky Cheese Man, 4305(F)
A Stitch in Time, 9313(F)
Stitching Stars, 12287
Stockings of Buttermilk, 11386
Stokely Carmichael and Black Power, 12706
A Stolen Life, 9188(F)
Stolen Thunder, 11518
The Stolen White Elephant, 7103(F)
The Stomach and Digestive System, 18095
The Stone, 11187

Stone Age Farmers Beside the Sea, 15334
The Stone Age News, 14506
Stone Bench in an Empty Park, 11825
The Stone Dancers, 4764(F)
The Stone-Faced Boy, 8645(F)
Stone Fox, 7340(F)
Stone Girl, Bone Girl, 13227
The Stone in the Sword, 9120(F)
Stone Soup (Illus. by Marcia Brown), 10867
  (Illus. by Susan Gaber), 10870
  (Illus. by Winslow Pels), 10874
Stone Wall Secrets, 20574
The Stoneboat, 4011(F)
The Stonecutter, 10824
The Stonehook Schooner, 9597(F)
The Stones Are Hatching, 7932(F)
Stones, Bones, and Petroglyphs, 15958
Stones in Water, 9680(F)
A Stone's Throw from Paradise, 8455(F)
The Stonewalkers, 7550(F)
Stonewall Jackson, 12906, 12907
Stonewords, 7665(F)
Stop That Ball! 6482(F)
Stop That Pickle! 958(F)
Stop Those Pants! 1185(F)
Stopping by Woods on a Snowy Evening, 11568
The Store That Mama Built, 9580(F)
Stores and Markets, 16933
Stories, 13898, 14072
Stories and Fun for the Very Young, 1600(F)
Stories by Firelight, 1253(F)
Stories for Children, 11173
Stories for Me! A Read-Aloud Treasury for Young Children, 1601(F)
Stories from Hans Christian Andersen, 10389
Stories from Native North America, 11291
Stories from the Ballet, 14287
Stories from the Caribbean, 11418
Stories from the Days of Christopher Columbus, 10633
Stories from the Old Testament, 17324
Stories from the Silk Road, 10554
Stories in My Pocket, 14088
Stories in Stone, 13941, 14430
The Stories Julian Tells, 7400(F)
Stories of the Flood, 10569
Stories of the Songs of Christmas, 14207
Stories to Solve, 10613
Stories to Tell a Five-Year-Old, 1360(F)
Stories to Tell a Six-Year-Old, 10104(F)
Stories Told by Mother Teresa, 17222
The Storm (Illus. by Kathy Henderson), 4457(F)
  (Illus. by Mark Mohr), 4974(F)
  (Illus. by Robert Sauber), 4519(F)
Storm at the Edge of Time, 8085(F)
Storm Chaser, 20690

Storm Chasers, 20693
Storm Coming! 11939
Storm in the Night, 5090(F)
Storm on the Desert, 20411
The Storm Seal, 5444(F)
Storm Warning, 20697
Storm Warriors, 9528(F)
Stormalong, 11369
Storms, 20718
Stormy, Misty's Foal, 7217(F)
Stormy Night, 8740(F)
A Story, a Story, 10672
The Story of a Blue Bird, 1828(F)
Story of a Dolphin, 5358(F)
The Story of a Farm, 4667(F)
The Story of a Main Street, 921(F)
The Story of Architecture, 13915
The Story of Babar, the Little Elephant, 2011(F)
The Story of Baseball, 22116
The Story of Basketball, 22126
The Story of Blue Elk, 11256
The Story of Chess, 7641(F)
The Story of Christmas, 17417
The Story of Clocks and Calendars, 20646
The Story of Colors/La Historia de los Colores, 11410
The Story of Communications, 21260
The Story of Diamonds, 20565
Story of Dinosaurs, 14409
The Story of Doctor Dolittle, 7925(F)
The Story of Ferdinand, 2348(F)
The Story of Figure Skating, 22218
The Story of Flight, 21106
The Story of Folk Music, 14140
The Story of Golf, 21971
The Story of Hanukkah, 6117
The Story of Iron, 21257
The Story of Jackie Robinson, 13489
The Story of Johnny Appleseed, 12842
The Story of Jonah (Illus. by Diana Mayo), 17243
  (Illus. by Diana Mayo), 17243
The Story of Jumping Mouse, 11301
The Story of King Arthur and His Knights, 11024
The Story of Life on Earth, 14454
The Story of Lightning and Thunder, 10656
The Story of Little Babaji, 978(F)
The Story of Maps and Navigation, 14367
The Story of Money, 16926
The Story of Nat Love, 12757
The Story of Nitrogen, 20285
The Story of Numbers and Counting, 20630
The Story of Oxygen, 20666
The Story of Religion, 17206
The Story of Rosy Dock, 4583
The Story of Ruby Bridges, 16499(F)
The Story of Sacajawea, 12989
The Story of Shabbat, 17458
The Story of Shoes, 21185
The Story of Stagecoach Mary Fields, 12722
The Story of the Amulet, 7987(F)
The Story of the Boxer, 19958

The Story of the Champions of the Round Table, 11024
The Story of the Golden Retriever, 19946
The Story of the Grail and the Passing of Arthur, 11025
The Story of the Holocaust, 14864
The Story of the Incredible Orchestra, 14225
The Story of the Olympics, 22243
The Story of the Persian Gulf War, 15488
The Story of the Sea Glass, 3609(F)
The Story of the Wrestler They Call "Diamond" Dallas Page, 13705
The Story of the Wrestler They Call "The Rock" 22053
The Story of Things, 14565
The Story of Time and Clocks, 20645
The Story of Valentine's Day, 17505
The Story of Walt Disney, Maker of Magical Worlds, 12228
The Story of Weights and Measures, 20657
The Story of Writing and Printing, 13996
The Story of Z, 102(F)
Story Painter, 12252
The Story Snail, 6594(F)
Story Time for Little Porcupine, 2702(F)
The Storytellers, 4734(F)
The Storyteller's Beads, 8968(F)
A Storyteller's Story, 12573
Storytelling Adventures, 14078
Storytelling for the Fun of It, 14079
The Storytelling Handbook, 14103
The Storytelling Star, 10607
Stowaway, 8933(F)
The Stowaway, 9282(F)
A Stowaway on Noah's Ark, 17319(F)
Stowaway to the Mushroom Planet, 10157(F)
Stradivari's Singing Violin, 9035(F)
The Straight Line Wonder, 1165(F)
The Strange Adventures of Blue Dog, 1648(F)
The Strange and Exciting Adventures of Jeremiah Hash, 8093(F)
Strange and Spooky Stories, 10601
Strange and Wonderful Aircraft, 21110
The Strange and Wonderful Tale of Robert McDoodle, 4084(F)
The Strange Case of Dr. Jekyll and Mr. Hyde, 10243(F)
The Strange Child, 10917
The Strange Disappearance of Arthur Cluck, 6203(F)
Strange Eating Habits of Sea Creatures, 19648
Strange Mysteries from Around the World, 21952
Strange Neighbors, 7884(F)
Strange Nests, 19307
The Strange Night Writing of Jessamine Colter, 10175(F)
Strange Plants, 20263
Strange Stuff, 21938
The Stranger, 1642(F)

Stranger at the Window, 6741(F)
Stranger in Dadland, 8470(F)
Stranger in Right Field, 10317(F)
Stranger in the Mirror, 8067(F)
Strategic Battles, 16443
A Straw for Two, 8065(F)
Straw Sense, 8978(F)
A Strawbeater's Thanksgiving, 4834(F)
Strawberry, 20139
Strawberry Girl, 9581(F)
Strawberry Hill, 8329(F)
The Stray, 7463(F)
The Stray Dog, 5416(F)
Strays Like Us, 8507(F)
Streams to the River, River to the Sea, 9424(F)
Street Child, 9092(F)
Street Cleaners, 21245
Street Music, 11524
Street Talk, 11727
A Street Through Time, 14351
Street Violence, 17138
Streets of Gold, 16283
Strega Nona, 11059, 11060
Strega Nona Meets Her Match, 1115(F)
Strega Nona Takes a Vacation, 1116(F)
Strega Nona's Magic Lessons, 11059
The Strength of the Hills, 20058
The Strength of These Arms, 16227
Stress, 17734
Stress Management, 17911
Stretch, Swallow and Stare, 1049(F)
Stretching Ourselves, 17948
Strider, 8601(F)
Strike! 15874
Striking It Rich, 16338
String, 21666
A String of Beads, 21546
Stringbean's Trip to the Shining Sea, 3479(F)
Stripe, 2561(F)
Striped Ice Cream, 7471(F)
Strong to the Hoop, 10321(F)
The Strongest Man This Side of Cremona, 2935(F)
The Strongest Mouse in the World, 2829(F)
Strudel Stories, 7499(F)
Struggle for a Continent, 16158, 16159
The Struggle to Grow, 16452
Stuart Little, 8200(F)
Stuck in Neutral, 8836(F)
Stucksville, 10070(F)
Stuffin' Muffin, 21737
Stunt Woman, 12106
The Stupids Die, 4077(F)
The Stupids Have a Ball, 4077(F)
The Stupids Step Out, 4077(F)
The Stupids Take Off, 4078(F)
Sturdy Turtles, 18787
The Stuttgart Nanny Mafia, 8427(F)
Subira Subira, 10705
Submarine Wahoo, 14845
Submarines and Other Underwater Craft, 21408

Subtraction (Illus. by Richard Maccabe), 20623
(Illus. by Sami Sweeten), 399(F)
Subtraction Action, 491(F)
Subway Sparrow, 3456(F)
Succeeding with LD, 17920
Such a Noise! 11142
Sudan in Pictures, 14949
A Sudanese Family, 17540
Suddenly! 2451(F)
Sugar Isn't Everything, 8910(F)
Sugar Was My Best Food, 17988
Sugarbush Spring, 3578(F)
Sugarcane House and Other Stories About Mr. Fat, 7618(F)
Sugaring, 4450(F)
Sugaring Season, 20080
Sugaring Time, 20108
Sugars, 20118
Suicide, 18268
Suitcase, 10370(F)
A Suitcase of Seaweed and Other Poems, 11741
Sukey and the Mermaid, 11379
Sukuma, 14992
Sulfur, 20278
The Sumerians, 14638, 14657
Summer, 128(F)
Summer and Shiner, 7172(F)
Summer Battles, 9522(F)
Summer Camp, 22262
A Summer Day, 4431(F)
A Summer for Secrets, 7852(F)
Summer Fun! 22072
The Summer I Shrank My Grandmother, 8219(F)
Summer Ice, 15819
The Summer My Father Was Ten, 3045(F)
Summer of Fire, 16624
The Summer of Mrs. MacGregor, 8393(F)
The Summer of Stanley, 2949(F)
The Summer of the Bonepile Monster, 6887(F)
The Summer of the Falcon, 8656(F)
The Summer of the Great Divide, 8693(F)
Summer of the Monkeys, 7290(F)
The Summer of the Swans, 8884(F)
The Summer Olympics, 22249
Summer on Wheels, 9994(F)
Summer Reading Is Killing Me, 8073(F)
The Summer Sands, 3157(F)
The Summer Sisters and the Dance Disaster, 8090(F)
Summer Soldiers, 9584(F)
Summer Switch, 9977(F)
Summer Tunes, 8905(F)
Summer Wheels, 8262(F)
Summer with Elisa, 8704(F)
Summerhouse, 955(F)
Summer's End, 5476(F)
Summertime, 14242
A Summertime Song, 1216(F)
A Summery Saturday Morning, 3305(F)
Summit Up, 21856

The Sun, 18558, 18559, 18560, 18566, 18569, 18570, 18573, 18574
The Sun and Moon, 18522
Sun and Moon, 1119(F), 10736
Sun and Spoon, 8687(F)
The Sun and the Solar System, 18509
Sun Dance at Turtle Rock, 8533(F)
Sun-Day, Moon-Day, 10555
The Sun Is a Star, 18409
The Sun Is Always Shining Somewhere, 18565
Sun Is Falling, Night Is Calling, 723(F)
The Sun Is My Favorite Star, 4378(F)
The Sun Is So Quiet, 11756
The Sun Is Up, 11985
Sun, Moon, and Stars, 10563
The Sun, the Wind, and the Rain, 4509(F)
Sun Through the Window, 11680
Sun Up, Sun Down, 18567
A Sunburned Prayer, 7524(F)
Sunday, 3871(F)
The Sunday Doll, 8812(F)
Sunday Week, 3729(F)
A Sunday with Grandpa, 3612(F)
Sundiata, 10718
Sunflower, 4432(F)
The Sunflower Family, 20041
Sunflower House, 4399(F)
Sunflower Sal, 2995(F)
Sunflowers, 20248
Sunk! 14542
Sunken Treasure, 19875
Sunny Days, 6242(F)
Sunny-Side Up, 6349(F)
Sunrise, 559(F)
The Sun's Asleep Behind the Hill, 685(F)
The Sun's Family of Planets, 18468
The Sunsets of Miss Olivia Wiggins, 3763(F)
Sunshine Home, 3558(F)
Sunshine Makes the Seasons, 18561
Sunshine, Moonshine, 6191(F)
Sunwing, 8002(F)
The Super Camper Caper, 6386(F)
Super-Completely and Totally the Messiest, 4342(F)
Super Cool Science, 15821
Super Cross Motorcycle Racing, 22082
Super-Duper Jokes, 21859
Super-Fine Valentine, 6283(F)
Super Heroes, 21959
Super Humans, 17898
Super Materials, 20287
Super Minds, 21903
Super Salads, 7811(F)
Super Sand Castle Saturday, 230(F)
Super Science Projects About Animals and Their Habitats, 18614
Super Science Projects About Oceans, 19815
Super Science Secrets, 18333
Super Sound, 20941
Super Sports for Kids on the Net, 21229
Super String Games, 22009
Super Structures, 21155

Super Toys and Games from Paper, 21636
Supercharged Infield, 10303(F)
Superfudge, 9784(F)
Supergiants! 14439
Supermom, 3796(F)
The Supernatural, 21947
Superpuppy, 19963
Superstars of Men's Soccer, 13422
Superstars of Women's Basketball, 13376
Superstars of Women's Figure Skating, 13411
Superstars of Women's Tennis, 13409
Superstars of Women's Track and Field, 13423
The Supreme Court, 17014
Supreme Court Book, 17012
A Surfrider's Odyssey, 7035(F)
The Surprise Family, 5381(F)
The Surprise Garden, 4455(F)
Surprise Party, 7508(F)
The Surprise Party, 2234(F) (Illus. by Tomie dePaola), 6585(F)
Surprises, 11606
Surprising Myself, 12537
Surrealism, 13882
The Survival Guide for Kids with LD (Learning Differences), 17907
Surviving Brick Johnson, 8348(F)
Surviving Hitler, 14889
Surviving Homework, 17623
Susan B. Anthony, 13130, 13132, 13133
Susan Butcher, 13682
Susan Butcher and the Iditarod Trail, 21997
Susan Laughs, 5104(F)
Susanna of the Alamo, 9294(F)
Susanna Siegelbaum Gives Up Guys, 9852(F)
Susannah, 9377(F)
Susie King Taylor, 12785
Suth's Story, 8956(F)
Suzanne De Passe, 13148
Suzette and the Puppy, 4847(F)
Suzy's Secret Snoop Society, 6749(F)
Swallowdale, 7015(F)
Swallows and Amazons, 7015(F)
Swallows in the Birdhouse, 5426
Swami on Rye, 7850(F)
Swamp Angel, 4188(F)
Swamp Life, 20374
Swan in Love, 1902(F)
Swan Lake, 14273, 14281
The Swan Maiden, 10482(F)
Swanfall, 19311
Swans, 19317
The Swan's Gift, 1554(F)
The Swan's Stories, 10390(F)
The Swap, 8738(F)
Swazi, 14994
Swaziland, 14968
Sweden, 15439, 15444, 15447, 15466
Sweden in Pictures, 15467
The Swedish Americans, 17577
Sweet and Sour, 10759
The Sweet and Sour Animal Book, 58(F)

Sweet and Sour Lily, 10137(F)
Sweet Clara and the Freedom Quilt, 9290(F)
Sweet Dream Pie, 1702(F)
Sweet Dreams, 721(F), 18826
Sweet Dreams of the Wild, 661
Sweet Dreams, Sam, 186(F)
Sweet Dried Apples, 8986(F)
Sweet Land of Story, 11334
Sweet Magnolia, 4718(F)
Sweet Potato Pie, 6595(F)
Sweet Strawberries, 3821(F)
A Sweet, Sweet Basket, 3072(F)
Sweet, Sweet Memory, 5108
Sweet Victory, 13677
Sweet Words So Brave, 14076
The Sweetest Fig, 8167(F)
Sweetgrass, 9164(F)
A Sweetheart for Valentine, 6161(F)
Sweets and Treats, 11575
A Swiftly Tilting Planet, 10207(F)
Swim the Silver Sea, Joshie Otter, 643(F)
A Swim Through the Sea, 115(F)
Swim with Me, 22308
Swimming, 22305, 22306
Swimming and Diving, 22307
Swimming Lessons, 4988(F)
Swimming with Sharks, 6856(F)
Swimmy, 2386(F)
Swine Divine, 1938(F)
Swine Lake, 2475(F)
A Swinger of Birches, 11569
Swish! 2959(F)
Swiss Family Robinson, 7136(F)
Switch Cat, 5184(F)
Switch On, Switch Off, 20884
Switcharound, 9926(F)
Switchers, 8143(F)
Switching Well, 10191(F)
Switzerland, 15271, 15275, 15278, 15287
Switzerland in Pictures, 15293
Swollobog, 1613(F)
The Sword and the Circle, 11037
The Sword in the Tree, 9083(F)
Sword of a Champion, 13704
Sword of the Samurai, 10819
Sybil Ludington's Midnight Ride, 16189
Sybil's Night Ride, 4884(F)
Sycamore Street, 3989(F)
Sylvester and the Magic Pebble, 2721(F)
Sylvia Earle, 13267
Sylvia Long's Mother Goose, 894
Symbiosis, 18599
A Symphony for the Sheep, 4768(F)
A Symphony of Whales, 5405(F)

T-Backs, T-Shirts, Coat, and Suit, 8731(F)
The T.F. Letters, 8791(F)
T.J.'s Secret Pitch, 10282(F)
Tabitha, 5433(F)
Table, Chair, Bear, 13982
Tacky and the Emperor, 2362(F)
Tacky in Trouble, 2363(F)
Tacky the Penguin, 2364(F)
Tac's Island, 8363(F)
Tadpole and Frog, 18713

Tadpole Tales and Other Totally Terrific Treats for Readers Theatre, 12020
Tadpoles, 3719(F), 18733
Tae Kwon Do, 22266
Tae Kwon Do for Kids, 22274
Tae's Sonata, 7333(F)
Tahiti, 15248
Taiga, 20456, 20485
Tails That Talk and Fly, 18860
The Tailypo, 11338
Tailypo, 11368
Taiwan, 15155, 15187
Taiwan in Pictures, 15219
The Taj Mahal, 15111
Tajikistan, 15434
Take a Look Around, 21804
Take a Look, It's in a Book, 14313
Take It to the Hoop, Magic Johnson, 12008
Take Me Out to the Ballgame, 14160
Take Me Out to the Bat and Ball Factory, 22122
Take Me to Your Liter, 21834
Take Off! 21081
Take to the Sky, 9579(F)
Take Turns, Penguin, 6719(F)
Taking a Walk/Caminando, 4640(F)
Taking Care of Sister Bear, 2661(F)
Taking Charge, 4732(F)
Taking Flight, 13354
Taking Off, 21094
Taking Root, 20174
Taking Sides, 7375(F)
Taking Time Out, 22037
The Tale I Told Sasha, 1685(F)
Tale of a Tadpole, 18741
  (Illus. by Annie Cannon), 5370(F)
Tale of a Tail, 1819(F)
The Tale of Aladdin and the Wonderful Lamp, 11189
The Tale of Ali Baba and the Forty Thieves, 1303(F)
The Tale of Gilbert Alexander Pig, 1986(F)
The Tale of Rabbit and Coyote, 11403
The Tale of the Heaven Tree, 1282(F)
The Tale of the Mandarin Ducks, 10826
The Tale of the Turnip, 10943
The Tale of the Three Trees, 11353
The Tale of Tobias, 17303(F)
The Tale of Tricky Fox, 966(F)
A Tale of Two Rice Birds, 10841
The Tale of Willie Monroe, 10828
Tales Alive! 10590
Tales for a Winter's Eve, 2825(F)
Tales for Hard Times, 12528
Tales for the Seventh Day, 11150
The Tales Fossils Tell, 14415
Tales from Africa, 10716
Tales from Old Ireland, 10972
Tales from Shakespeare, 12055
Tales from the Brothers Grimm and the Sisters Weird, 10933
Tales from the Homeplace, 9527(F)
Tales from the Mabinogion, 11040
Tales from the Rain Forest, 11437

Tales from the South Pacific Islands, 10848
Tales Mummies Tell, 14535
Tales of a Chinese Grandmother, 10739
Tales of a Fourth Grade Nothing, 9784(F)
Tales of an Ashanti Father, 10646
The Tales of Peter Rabbit and Benjamin Bunny, 2598(F)
Tales of the Amazon, 11441
Tales of the Haunted Deep, 7767(F)
Tales of the Shimmering Sky, 10591
Tales of the Wicked Witch, 7879(F)
Tales of Trotter Street, 3230(F)
Tales of Wisdom and Wonder, 10573
Tales of Wonder and Magic, 10509
Talk, Baby! 3970(F)
Talking About Bullying, 17725
Talking About Disability, 17928
The Talking Cloth, 3811(F)
The Talking Earth, 6855(F)
Talking Like the Rain, 11616
Talking to Animals, 18891
Talking Walls, 14534, 14560
Talking with Adventurers, 12068
Talking with Artists, 13952, 13953
Talking with Tebe, 12241
Tall and Small, 18072
Tall and Tasty, 20145
Tall in the Saddle, 1044(F)
A Tall Story and Other Tales, 7949(F)
Tall Tales, 10363(F)
Tallahassee Higgins, 8446(F)
Tallchief, 12477
Tam Lin, 10963
Tamba and the Chief, 10687
Tambourine Moon, 1279(F)
The Tangerine Bear, 1455(F)
The Tangerine Tree, 4972(F)
Tangle Town, 4123(F)
Tanglebird, 2390(F)
Tangled Fortunes, 6960(F)
Tangled Webb, 6956(F)
The Tanners, 16116
The Tantrum, 5009(F)
Tanya and Emily in a Dance for Two, 3997(F)
Tanya and the Magic Wardrobe, 3158(F)
Tanya's Big Green Dream, 8663(F)
Tanzania in Pictures, 14951
Tap-Tap, 4879(F)
Tapenum's Day, 16185
Tapestries, 17318
Tar Beach, 1509(F)
Tara Lipinski, 13594, 13595
Taran Wanderer, 7551(F)
Tarantula Shoes, 8562(F)
Tarantulas, 19589, 19597
Tarot Says Beware, 6784(F)
Taste, 18159
  (Illus. by Mike Gordon), 18163
  (Illus. by Maria Rius), 18155
Taste and See, 17170
A Taste of Blackberries, 8814(F)
A Taste of Honey, 2813(F)
A Taste of Smoke, 7592(F)
A Taste of Spain, 21702
A Taste of the Caribbean, 21716

Tasting in Living Things, 18820
Tasty Baby Belly Buttons, 10829
Tatsinda, 1153(F)
Tatterhood and Other Tales, 10603
Taxi, 3303(F)
The Taxi Navigator, 8345(F)
Tchaikovsky Discovers America, 9566(F)
Tea for Ten, 368(F)
Tea Leaves, Herbs, and Flowers, 21922
Tea Party for Two, 6581(F)
Tea Party Today, 11709
Tea with an Old Dragon, 9642(F)
Tea with Milk, 15137
Teach Us, Amelia Bedelia, 6566(F)
Teachers A to Z, 65(F)
Teacher's Pet, 10081(F)
Teammates, 13371, 13408
Teamwork, 216
Tears for Ashan, 8972(F)
Teatime with Emma Buttersnap, 20128
¡Teatro! 12040
Techno Lab, 21264
Technology in the Time of Ancient Egypt, 14617
Technology in the Time of Ancient Rome, 14745
Tecumseh, 12999, 13000
Ted in a Red Bed, 6288(F)
Teddy Bear Tears, 630(F)
Teddy Bear, Teddy Bear, 888(F)
Teddy Bears, 21032, 21060
The Teddy Bears' Night Before Christmas, 11849
The Teddy Bears' Picnic, 14249
Teddy Bear's Scrapbook, 2223(F)
Teddy Bears Trim the Tree, 5955(F)
Teddy Kollek, 13823
Teddy Roosevelt's Elk, 19151
Teddy's Easter Secret, 5977(F)
Teen Pregnancy, 18269
Teen Sexuality, 18268
Teenie Bird and How She Learned to Fly, 1842(F)
The Teen's Vegetarian Cookbook, 21714
Teens with the Courage to Give, 17736
A Teeny Tiny Baby, 3882(F)
Teeny Tiny Ernest, 1788(F)
The Teeny Tiny Ghost, 6062(F)
Teeny, Tiny Mouse, 280(F)
The Teeny Tiny Teacher, 10954
The Teeny Tiny Woman, 11027
  (Illus. by R. W. Alley), 6551(F)
Teeth That Stab and Grind, 18861
Teetoncey, 7096(F)
Teetoncey and Ben O'Neal, 7096(F)
Telecommunications, 21262
The Telephone, 21261
Telephones, Televisions and Toilets, 21243
Television, 17784, 21272, 21276
Tell-A-Bunny, 5734(F)
Tell Me a Mitzi, 3883(F)
Tell Me a Mitzvah, 17155
Tell Me a Season, 4544(F)
Tell Me a Story, Mama, 3726(F)
Tell Me a Tale, 14070

Tell Me Again About the Night I Was Born, 3596(F)
Tell Me Some More, 6214(F)
Tell Me Something Happy Before I Go to Sleep, 665(F)
Telling the Time, 20647
Telling Time, 20650
Telling Time with Big Mama Cat, 190(F)
Temperate Deciduous Forest, 20486
Temperate Forest, 20457
Temperate Forest Mammals, 20461
The Tempest, 8087(F)
Temple Cat, 4622(F)
Ten, 458(F)
Ten Apples Up on Top, 6453(F)
Ten Black Dots, 413(F)
Ten Bright Eyes, 196(F)
Ten Cats Have Hats, 510(F)
Ten Classic Jewish Children's Stories, 11165
The Ten Commandments, 17311
Ten Dirty Pigs, Ten Clean Pigs, 570(F)
Ten Dogs in the Window, 511(F)
Ten Flashing Fireflies, 588(F)
Ten Go Tango, 422(F)
Ten Good Rules, 17325
Ten Holiday Jewish Children's Stories, 17468(F)
Ten Kids, No Pets, 7482(F)
Ten Little Animals, 408(F)
Ten Little Bears, 453(F)
Ten Little Mice, 425(F)
Ten Little Rabbits, 449(F)
10 Minutes till Bedtime, 565(F)
Ten, Nine, Eight, 377(F)
Ten Oni Drummers, 1201(F)
Ten Play Hide-and-Seek, 656(F)
Ten Queens, 13738
Ten Red Apples, 474(F)
Ten Rosy Roses, 513(F)
Ten-Second Rainshowers, 11645
Ten Silly Dogs, 434(F)
Ten Small Tales, 10572
Ten Steps to Staying Safe, 18221
Ten Suns, 10761
Ten Terrific Authors for Teens, 12166
Ten Thousand Children, 14851
Ten Times Better, 514(F)
Tending the Fire, 12257
Tennessee, 16846, 16854, 16888
Tennis, 22311
Tennis Ace, 10318(F)
The Tenth Good Thing About Barney, 5100(F)
Teresa Weatherspoon's Basketball for Girls, 22151
Term Limits for Congress? 17110
Termite, 19451
The Terra Cotta Army of Emperor Qin, 15070
Terrell Davis, 13605, 13606
The Terrible Twos, 3177(F)
Terrible Tyrannosaurs, 14487
A Terrifying Taste of Short and Shivery, 8063(F)
Terror Below! 19755
Terrorism, 17081
Tess, 8462(F)

Tessa Snaps Snakes, 4022(F)
Test Pilot, 12076
Testing Miss Malarkey, 5499(F)
The Testing of Tertius, 7988(F)
Tex, 5377(F)
Texas, 16903, 16905, 16908
Texas Footprints, 9389(F)
Texture, 262(F)
Thailand, 15160, 15201, 15212
Thailand in Pictures, 15207
Thank You, Amelia Bedelia, 6561(F)
Thank You, God! 17523
Thank You, Jackie Robinson, 10319(F)
Thank You, Meiling, 2753(F)
Thank You, Mr. Falker, 5050(F)
Thank You, Santa, 5954(F)
Thanks Be to God, 17512
Thanks to Cows, 20054
Thanksgiving, 6149(F), 17503
Thanksgiving at the Tappletons', 6155(F)
The Thanksgiving Beast Feast, 6154(F)
Thanksgiving Day, 17501
   (Illus. by Gail Gibbons), 17497
   (Illus. by Lizzy Rockwell), 6151(F)
Thanksgiving Day at Our House, 6138
The Thanksgiving Day Parade Mystery, 6965(F)
Thanksgiving Fun, 17494
Thanksgiving Is . . ., 6133(F)
The Thanksgiving Story, 6142(F)
Thanksgiving Treat, 6157(F)
The Thanksgiving Visitor, 8592(F)
A Thanksgiving Wish, 6153(F)
Thanksgiving with Me, 6159(F)
That Apple Is Mine! 11081
That Cat! 7191(F)
That Furball Puppy and Me, 8186(F)
That Kookoory! 2107(F)
That New Baby, 17687
That Sweet Diamond, 11999
That Toad Is Mine! 4003(F)
That Tricky Coyote! 11278
That's a Wrap, 21268
That's Ghosts for You, 7649(F)
That's Good! That's Bad! 4122(F)
That's Mine, Horace, 2283(F)
Theater, 14323
Their Names to Live, 16649
Then Again, Maybe I Won't, 8567(F)
Theo, 9662(F)
Theodore Roosevelt, 9513(F), 13103, 13104
Theodoric's Rainbow, 9055(F)
There Ain't No Bugs on Me, 14241
There Comes a Time, 15893
There Goes Lowell's Party! 5690(F)
There Was a Hill . . ., 305(F)
There Was an Old Lady Who Swallowed a Trout! 14182
There Was an Old Witch, 6042(F)
There Was an Old Woman Who Lived in a Glove, 857
There Was Magic Inside, 1174(F)
There's a Dead Person Following My Sister Around, 8172(F)
There's a Dragon in My Sleeping Bag, 1251(F)

There's a Girl in My Hammerlock, 10364(F)
There's a Hole in My Bucket, 2666(F)
There's a Kangaroo in My Soup! 7904(F)
There's a Monster Under My Bed, 707(F)
There's a Wolf in the Classroom! 19145
There's a Zoo in Room 22, 133(F)
There's a Zoo on You! 18055
There's an Owl in the Shower, 7195(F)
There's More . . . Much More, 1734(F)
There's No Place Like Home, 6235(F)
There's No Place Like Space, 18410
There's No Such Thing as a Chanukah Bush, Sandy Goldstein, 9762(F)
There's Nothing to D-o-o-o! 2485(F)
There's Still Time, 19396
These Are the Voyages, 10206(F)
These Birds Can't Fly, 19229
These Hands, 763(F)
These Happy Golden Years, 7537(F)
Theseus and the Minotaur, 11483
   (Illus. by Robert Baxter), 11496
   (Illus. by Leonard Everett Fisher), 11472
They Dance in the Sky, 11280
They Don't Wash Their Socks! 22003
They Lived with the Dinosaurs, 14412
They Never Gave Up, 21111
They Saw the Future, 21924
They Sought a New World, 16152
They Swim the Seas, 18851
They Thought They Saw Him, 5425(F)
They Walk the Earth, 18852
They're Off! 16314
Thidwick, the Big-Hearted Moose, 2676(F)
The Thief, 8159(F), 8160(F)
Thief of Hearts, 7380(F)
The Thieves of Tyburn Square, 9293(F)
Thimble Summer, 7428(F)
Thimbleberry Stories, 2648(F)
Thing! 2240(F)
The Thing That Bothered Farmer Brown, 4318(F)
Things That Are Most in the World, 982(F)
Things That Make Make You Feel Good/Things That Make You Feel Bad, 3356(F)
The Things with Wings, 7797(F)
Things with Wings, 18616
Think About Our Rights, 17053
Think Like an Eagle, 21801
Thinkers, 13741
Thinking, 18121
Thinking About Ants, 19507
The Thinking Kid's Guide to Successful Soccer, 22301
Third Grade Bullies, 8334(F)

Third Grade Is Terrible, 5472(F)
Third Grade Pet, 9816(F)
The Thirteen Colonies, 16167
The 13 Days of Halloween, 6002(F)
Thirteen Moons on Turtle's Back, 11929
Thirteen Ways to Sink a Sub, 10066(F)
The 13th Floor, 7727(F)
Thirty Plays from Favorite Stories, 12025
Thirty-Three Multicultural Tales to Tell, 10546
This and That, 237(F), 2748(F)
This Big Sky, 11975
This Boat, 21356
This Book Is About Time, 20641
This House Is Made of Mud, 4395(F)
This Is a Great Place for a Hot Dog Stand, 1538(F)
This Is a Hospital, Not a Zoo! 1286(F)
This Is Figure Skating, 22217
This Is My Hair, 3356(F)
This Is Our House, 5063(F)
This Is Our Seder, 17472
This Is Soccer, 22288
This Is the Bear, 848
This Is the Bear and the Bad Little Girl, 2178(F)
This Is the Bear and the Picnic Lunch, 848
This Is the Bear and the Scary Night, 2179(F)
This Is the Bird, 3887(F)
This Is the Bread I Baked for Ned, 3112(F)
This Is the Earth That God Made, 17266
This Is the Farmer, 4335(F)
This Is the Pumpkin, 6027(F)
This Is the Star, 5806(F)
This Is the Sunflower, 4535(F)
This Is the Turkey, 6148(F)
This Is the Way We Eat Our Lunch, 3003(F)
This Is the Way We Go to School, 5546
This Is Your Garden, 21773
This Island Isn't Big Enough for the Four of Us! 9868(F)
This Land Is Your Land, 14154, 16970
This Mess, 1969(F)
This New Land, 9218(F)
This Next New Year, 5658(F)
This Old House, 2987(F)
This Old Man, 14184
This Place Is Crowded, 15119
This Place Is High, 20497
This Place Is Wet, 20497
This Place Is Wild, 14921
This Quiet Lady, 3975(F)
This Time, Tempe Wick? 9233(F)
This Train, 21330
This Year's Garden, 4531(F)
The Thistle Princess, 10421(F)
Thomas, 9246(F)
Thomas' Busy Day, 1620(F)
Thomas Alva Edison, 13270, 13273
Thomas Edison, 13271, 13274

Thomas Goes to the Circus, 1620(F)
Thomas in Danger, 9210(F)
Thomas Jefferson, 13048, 13049, 13050, 13052, 13053
Thomas Nast, 12272, 12273
Thomas Paine, 12943
Thomas' Snowsuit, 4242(F)
Thomas Takes a Trip, 1620(F)
Thomas Tuttle, Just in Time, 10102(F)
Thomas's Sheep and the Great Geography Test, 76(F)
Thomas's Sitter, 3856(F)
Thor Heyerdahl, 12122
Thorndike and Nelson, 2244(F)
Those Amazing Ants, 19509
Those Building Men, 5577(F)
Those Calculating Crows! 1661(F)
Those Can-Do Pigs, 2463(F)
Those Courageous Women of the Civil War, 9510
Those Remarkable Women of the American Revolution, 16224
Those That Float, Those That Don't, 236(F)
Thoughts, Pictures, and Words, 12560
A Thousand Cousins, 11592
A Thousand Yards of Sea, 1046(F)
A Thread of Kindness, 11169
Threatened Oceans, 19843
Three, 13954
Three Against the Tide, 9486(F)
Three Bags Full, 2657(F)
The Three Bears, 10947
  (Illus. by Paul Galdone), 10981
The Three Bears Holiday Rhyme Book, 5659
The Three Billy Goats Gruff, 10955, 11117, 11118
  (Illus. by Paul Galdone), 11124
Three Brave Women, 3800(F)
Three by the Sea, 6503(F)
Three Cheers for Catherine the Great! 5665(F)
Three Cheers for Tacky, 2365(F)
Three Cool Kids, 11122
The Three-Day Traffic Jam, 7853(F)
Three Days on a River in a Red Canoe, 2985(F)
Three-Dimensional Shapes, 20606
Three Dog Winter, 7531(F)
Three Ducks Went Wandering, 5391(F)
The Three Feathers, 10910
Three Friends, 391(F)
The Three Golden Oranges, 11133
A Three Hat Day, 4158(F)
3 Kids Dreamin', 8280(F)
The Three Languages, 10911
The Three Little Dinosaurs, 10992
The Three Little Javelinas, 2403(F)
Three Little Kittens, 891(F)
  (Illus. by Paul Galdone), 844
The Three Little Pigs, 11006
  (Illus. by Paul Galdone), 10982
  (Illus. by Paul Galdone), 10982
  (Illus. by Paul Meisel), 11018
  (Illus. by Terri Super), 895
The Three Little Pigs and the Fox, 11352

The Three Little Wolves and the Big Bad Pig, 2764(F)
The Three Lives of Harris Harper, 8418(F)
Three Lives to Live, 7916(F)
Three Magic Balls, 1149(F)
Three Monks, No Water, 10775
Three More Stories You Can Read to Your Dog, 6523(F)
Three Names, 4758(F)
Three on Three, 10371(F)
Three Pandas, 2809(F)
3 Pandas Planting, 456(F)
Three Perfect Peaches, 10868
The Three Princes, 11190
Three Rivers Crossing, 7929(F)
Three Sacks of Truth, 10872
The Three Sillies, 11007
  (Illus. by Kathryn Hewitt), 10995
Three Stories You Can Read to Your Cat, 6524(F)
Three Stories You Can Read to Your Dog, 6525(F)
Three Wise Women, 5843(F)
The Three Wishes, 10941
Three Young Pilgrims, 9196(F)
Through a Termite City, 19493
Through Grandpa's Eyes, 3791(F)
Through Moon and Stars and Night Skies, 3923(F)
Through My Eyes, 16497
Through the Eyes of Your Ancestors, 16441
Through the Lock, 9559(F)
Through the Looking Glass, and What Alice Found There, 7647(F)
Through the Medicine Cabinet, 7759(F)
Through the Night, 3513(F)
Through the Open Door, 9558(F)
Through the Wormhole, 7721(F)
Throw Your Tooth on the Roof, 10531
Throwing Smoke, 7628(F)
Thumbelina, 10391(F)
Thumbeline, 10392(F)
Thumbs Up, Rico! 8918(F)
Thump and Plunk, 6701(F)
Thump, Thump, Rat-a-Tat-Tat, 3004(F)
Thunder Bear and Ko, 15969
Thunder Cake, 3842(F)
Thunder from the Clear Sky, 16170
Thunder on the Plains, 18966
Thunderbolt, 20698
Thurgood Marshall, 12765, 12766, 12768
Thurgood Marshall and the Supreme Court, 12767
Thurman Thomas, 13635
Tibet, 15165, 15181
Tic-Tac-Toe, 6679(F)
Tick-Tock, 1899(F)
Tick Tock Tales, 1389(F)
Ticket to Canada, 8937(F)
The Tickle Stories, 3926(F)
Tickle Tum! 2776(F)
Ticklemonster and Me, 3679(F)
Tickleoctopus, 1703(F)
Tickling Tigers, 1992(F)
Tickly Prickly, 303(F)

Ticks, 19466
Tidal Wave, 19850
Tide Pool, 19858
Tide Pool Life Watching, 19853
Tide Pools, 19855
Tie Your Socks and Clap Your Feet, 11875
Tiffany Dino Works Out, 2683(F)
Tiffky Doofky, 2722(F)
Tiger, 19115
Tiger and the New Baby, 3632(F)
Tiger and the Temper Tantrum, 3633(F)
Tiger Eyes, 8568(F)
The Tiger Has a Toothache, 17851
Tiger in the Sky, 10180(F)
Tiger Math, 20027
The Tiger Rising, 8625(F)
Tiger Tales, 19081
Tiger Trail, 5456(F)
Tiger with Wings, 19360
Tiger Woman, 10779
Tiger Woods, 13711, 13713, 13715, 13716, 13717, 13718
Tiger Woods, Golfing Champion, 13714
Tigers, 19084, 19086, 19089, 19100
(Illus. by Judith Riches), 2060(F)
The Tiger's Eye, the Bird's Fist, 22273
Tigers, Frogs, and Rice Cakes, 10729
Tight Times, 5252(F)
Tigress, 5172(F)
The Tigris and Euphrates Rivers, 15494
Tikki Tikki Tembo, 10766
Tiktala, 1567(F)
Tikta'liktak, 11206
Till Year's Good End, 14784
Tillie and the Wall, 2387(F)
Tim Duncan, 13520, 13521, 13522
The Timbertoes ABC Alphabet Book, 137(F)
The Timbertoes 123 Counting Book, 596(F)
The Time Bike, 7887(F)
Time Cat, 7554(F)
Time for Andrew, 7775(F)
Time for Bed, 678(F)
Time Ghost, 10200(F)
The Time It Took Tom, 3421(F)
Time Like a River, 8012(F)
The Time Machine, 10246(F)
Time Machine, 12618
A Time of Angels, 9551(F)
A Time of Golden Dragons, 10785
The Time of the Lion, 5366(F)
Time of Wonder, 4491(F)
Time Out, 7686(F)
A Time to Fight Back, 14875
Time to Get Out, 2757(F)
Time to Sleep, 2092(F)
The Time Tree, 8044(F)
Times Square, 16672
The Times They Used to Be, 9530(F)
Timmy O'Dowd and the Big Ditch, 9287(F)
Timothy Goes to School, 2837(F)
Timothy of the Cay, 7097(F)
Timothy Tunny Swallowed a Bunny, 4170(F)

The Tin Heart, 4568(F)
Tina's Diner, 4071(F)
The Tinderbox (Illus. by Warwick Hutton), 10393(F)
(Illus. by James Warhola), 10394(F)
Ting-a-ling! 3108(F)
The Tiniest Giants, 14399
Tinker and Tom and the Star Baby, 1383(F)
Tiny and Bigman, 2933(F)
Tiny Goes to the Library, 6517(F)
Tiny Green Thumbs, 2159(F)
The Tiny Kite of Eddie Wing, 5093(F)
Tiny Rabbit Goes to a Birthday Party, 5733(F)
The Tiny Seed, 4402(F)
Tiny the Mouse Dictionary for 1-year-olds, 14054(F)
Tiny Toes, 3243(F)
Tiny's Bath, 6518(F)
Tiny's Hat, 4968(F)
Tio Armando, 3683(F)
Tipi, 15918
Tipper Gore, 13155, 13156
Tiptoe into Kindergarten, 5529(F)
The Titanic, 6310, 21362
Titanic, 21348, 21378
Titch, 3713(F)
Tituba, 12788
Tituba of Salem Village, 9209(F)
To Bathe a Boa, 2325(F)
To Be a Drum, 3077(F)
To Be a Kid, 14327
To Be a Slave, 17574
To Be a Writer, 14107
To Bigotry No Sanction, 17182
To Dinner, for Dinner, 10706
To Every Season, 21756
To Every Thing There Is a Season, 17178
To Everything, 17244
To Find the Way, 8940(F)
To Fly, 5406(F)
To Hell with Dying, 8843(F)
To Live Again, 8903(F)
To Market, To Market, 3329(F)
To Rabbittown, 1668(F)
To Save the Earth, 13203
To Space and Back, 21006
To Swim in Our Own Pond, 14113
To the Bottom of the Sea, 19880
To the Island, 1724(F)
To the Limit, 18054
To the Mountains by Morning, 5453(F)
To the Point, 12622
To the Rescue, 21313
To the Top! 22030
To the Top of the World, 19118
To the Tub, 6190(F)
To Touch the Stars, 9702(F)
Toad, 18715
Toad Is the Uncle of Heaven, 10839
Toad on the Road, 6629(F)
Toad or Frog, Swamp or Bog? 18584
Toad Overload, 16968
Toad Takes Off, 6630(F)
Toads, 18730
Toads and Diamonds, 10871

The Toady and Dr. Miracle, 6266(F)
Toasters, 21022
Toasting Marshmallows, 11954
Tobias, the Quig and the Rumplenut Tree, 1515(F)
Toby Scudder, Ultimate Warrior, 8657(F)
Toby Tyler, 7001(F)
Toby's Doll's House, 5722(F)
Today I Feel Silly, 4940(F)
Today Is Monday, 14235
Today Is the Day, 5057(F)
Today Was a Terrible Day, 5502(F)
Today's Tejano Heroes, 12684
Toddlecreek Post Office, 3426(F)
Toddler Time, 11699
Toddler Two, 597(F)
Toddler Two-Step, 373(F)
Toddlerobics, 3340(F), 3341(F)
Toddlers, 953(F)
Toenails, Tonsils, and Tornadoes, 7496(F)
Toes Are to Tickle, 3386(F)
Together, 4025
Together in Pinecone Patch, 4065(F)
Toilets, Bathtubs, Sinks, and Sewers, 18191
Toilets, Toasters, and Telephones, 21055
The Token Gift, 9002(F)
Tokyo, 15129
Told Tales, 10616
The Toll-Bridge Troll, 1698(F)
Tom, 3607(F)
Tom and Pippo Go Shopping, 3352(F)
Tom and Pippo in the Garden, 3352(F)
Tom and Pippo Read a Story, 3353(F)
Tom and Pippo See the Moon, 3352(F)
Tom and Pippo's Day, 3352(F)
Tom, Babette, and Simon, 7571(F)
Tom Cringle, 9284(F)
Tom Goes to Kindergarten, 2857(F)
Tom Rabbit, 1658(F)
Tom the TV Cat, 6376(F)
Tomas and the Library Lady, 3331(F)
Tomato, 20134
Tomatoes from Mars, 1714(F)
The Tomb of the Boy King, 14625
Tomboy Trouble, 6724(F)
The Tombs of the Pharaohs, 14614
Tomie dePaola's Book of Bible Stories, 17262
Tomie dePaola's Favorite Nursery Tales, 10545
Tomie dePaola's Mother Goose, 873
Tommy at the Grocery Store, 2157(F)
Tommy Nunez, 13553
Tommy Traveler in the World of Black History, 17556
Tommy Trouble and the Magic Marble, 8642(F)
Tomorrow Is Daddy's Birthday, 5732(F)
Tomorrow Is Mom's Birthday, 5681(F)
Tomorrow on Rocky Pond, 3376(F)

Tomorrow's Wizard, 7942(F)
Tom's Fish, 1063(F)
Tom's Midnight Garden, 8009(F)
Tom's Rabbit, 5267(F)
The Tomten, 4738(F)
The Tomten and the Fox, 4738(F)
Toni Morrison, 12574
Tonight and Tomorrow, 631(F)
Tonka Big Book of Trucks, 5593
Tonka Trucks Night and Day, 21315
Tons of Trash, 16979
Tony's Bread, 11061
Too Big! 3314(F)
Too Close Friends, 2634(F)
Too Far Away to Touch, 5044(F)
The Too Hot Day, 2308(F)
Too Hot to Hoot, 14052
Too Many Babas, 6296(F)
Too Many Chickens! 4091(F)
Too Many Cooks, 6131(F)
"Too Many Cooks . . ." and Other
    Proverbs, 10568
Too Many Kangaroo Things to Do!
    20592
Too Many Pumpkins, 4351(F)
Too Many Secrets, 7132(F)
Too Many Tamales, 5921(F)
Too Many Time Machines, 8122(F)
Too Much Noise, 11014
Too Much Talk, 10697
Too Much Trouble for Grandpa,
    6461(F)
Too Old for This, Too Young for
    That! Your Survival Guide for the
    Middle-School Years, 18267
Too Quiet for These Old Bones,
    4312(F)
Too Small, 11141
Too Tired, 2768(F)
Toohy and Wood, 7964(F)
Tool Book, 21662
Tools, 5561(F)
Tools and Gadgets, 16142
Toot and Puddle, 55(F), 2212(F),
    2213(F), 5693(F)
Tooter Pepperday, 10000(F)
Tooth Decay and Cavities, 18190
Tooth Fairy Travels, 7790(F)
A Tooth Fairy's Tale, 1055(F)
Tooth Tales from Around the World,
    10536
The Tooth Witch, 1287(F)
The Toothpaste Millionaire, 9937(F)
Toothworms and Spider Juice, 18021
Toots and the Upside-Down House,
    7800(F)
The Top and the Ball, 10395(F)
Top Cat, 2067(F)
The Top of the World, 22025
Top Secret, 9858(F)
The Top-Secret Journal of Fiona
    Claire Jardin, 8620(F)
Top 10 American Men Sprinters,
    13377
Top 10 American Men's Olympic
    Gold Medalists, 13378
Top 10 American Women Sprinters,
    13390
Top 10 American Women's Figure
    Skaters, 13392

Top 10 American Women's Olympic
    Gold Medalists, 13368
Top 10 Baseball Base Stealers, 13361
Top 10 Baseball Home Run Hitters,
    13365
Top 10 Baseball Managers, 13391
Top 10 Baseball Pitchers, 13418
Top 10 Basketball Centers, 13379
Top 10 Basketball Legends, 13394
Top 10 Basketball Point Guards,
    13403
Top 10 Basketball Power Forwards,
    13403
Top 10 Basketball Scorers, 13380
Top 10 Basketball Scoring Small
    Forwards, 13360
Top 10 Basketball Shot-Blockers,
    13425
Top 10 Basketball Slam Dunkers,
    13362
Top 10 Basketball Three-Point
    Shooters, 13420
Top 10 Football Quarterbacks, 13388
Top 10 Football Receivers, 13419
Top 10 Football Rushers, 13389
Top 10 Football Sackers, 13404
Top 10 Heisman Trophy Winners,
    13405
Top 10 Hockey Goalies, 13412
Top 10 Hockey Scorers, 13381
Top 10 Jockeys, 13387
Top 10 Men's Baseball Hitters,
    13366
Top 10 Men's Tennis Players, 13363
Top 10 NASCAR Drivers, 13397
Top 10 NBA Finals Most Valuable
    Players, 13421
Top 10 NFL Super Bowl Most Valu-
    able Players, 13382
Top 10 Physically Challenged Ath-
    letes, 13406
Top 10 Professional Football Coach-
    es, 13407
Top 10 Sluggers, 13410
Top 10 Sports Bloopers and Who
    Made Them, 22057
Top 10 Women Gymnasts, 13372
Top 10 Women Tennis Players,
    13373
Tops and Bottoms, 11385
Torch Fishing with the Sun, 4881(F)
Tornado, 7170(F), 20702, 20704
Tornado! 20679
Tornado Alert, 20684
Tornadoes, 20681, 20686, 20719
Tornadoes! 20713
Toronto, 15592
The Tortilla Cat, 8207(F)
The Tortilla Factory, 20119
Tortillas and Lullabies, 4809(F)
The Tortoise and the Hare, 11052,
    11071
The Tortoise and the Jackrabbit,
    11066(F)
Tortoise Solves a Problem, 2278(F)
Tortoni Tremolo, 1635(F)
Tot Shabbat, 6091(F)
Totally Confidential, 8849(F)
Totally Disgusting, 8182(F)
Totally Fun Things to Do with Your
    Dog, 19965

Totally Uncool, 5013(F)
Totem Poles, 15952
Toucans, 19252
Touch, 18160
    (Illus. by Mike Gordon), 18163
    (Illus. by Maria Rius), 18156
Touch and Go, 12254
Touch of the Clown, 8706(F)
Touch the Moon, 7593(F)
Touch the Poem, 11525
Touchdown Mars! An ABC Adven-
    ture, 146(F)
Touching the Distance, 11932
Tough Boris, 2930(F)
Tough Cookie, 1695(F)
Tough-Luck Karen, 10086(F)
Toughboy and Sister, 6894(F)
Toulouse-Lautrec, 12303
Tournament of Time, 7558(F)
Toussaint L'Ouverture, 13826
The Tower of London, 15343
Towers Reach High, 21128
The Town Mouse and the Country
    Mouse, 11056
    (Illus. by T. R. Garcia), 11053
The Town Mouse and the Country
    Mouse, 11079
Town Mouse, Country Mouse,
    1860(F)
Town Mouse Country Mouse,
    2263(F)
Town Mouse House, 4605(F)
The Town That Got Out of Town,
    8026(F)
Toxic Threat, 17008
Toxic Waste, 17004
The Toy Brother, 1593(F)
Toys, 21024
Toys! Amazing Stories Behind Some
    Great Inventions, 22076
Toys and Games, 21658
Track and Field, 22317, 22319
Tracking Dinosaurs in the Gobi,
    14410
Tracks in the Snow, 6772(F)
Tracks in the Wild, 18610
Tractor-Trailer Trucker, 21310
Tractors, 20071
Traditional Chinese Folktales, 10746
Traditional Crafts from Africa, 21501
Traditional Crafts from China, 21502
Traditional Crafts from Mexico and
    Central America, 21503
Traditional Crafts from Native North
    America, 21526
Traditional Crafts from the
    Caribbean, 21504
Traditions from Africa, 14901
Traditions from China, 15073
Traditions from India, 15110
Traditions from the Caribbean, 15699
Traffic Jam, 1056(F)
Traffic Safety, 22161
The Trail of Tears, 16059
    (Illus. by Diana Magnuson), 15936
Trailblazing American Women,
    12668
Trails to the West, 16269
Train, 5562(F)
    (Illus. by Larry Johnson), 3451(F)
The Train Ride, 3087(F)

Train Song (Illus. by Donald Saaf), 5608(F)
  (Illus. by Mike Wimmer), 5599(F)
The Train to Lulu's, 3223(F)
Train to Somewhere, 9348(F)
Train Wreck, 6826(F)
Trains, 21332, 21343, 21344
  (Illus. by Byron Barton), 21328
  (Illus. by Gail Gibbons), 21333(F)
A Traitor Among the Boys, 9950(F)
The Tram to Bondi Beach, 6369(F)
The Transall Saga, 10219(F)
The Transcontinental Railroad, 16265, 21327, 21347
Transport, 21282
Transportation, 21284
The Trap, 7311(F)
Trapped between the Lash and the Gun, 8202(F)
Trapped by the Ice, 15818
Trapped in Death Cave, 7122(F)
Trash! 16988
Trash Trucks! 1311(F)
Trashy Town, 3497(F)
Travel, 21280
A Traveling Cat, 5322(F)
Traveling in Grandma's Day, 16493
Travels with Rainie Marie, 8484(F)
Treason Stops at Oyster Bay, 9250(F)
The Treasure, 3894(F)
The Treasure Bird, 6867(F)
The Treasure Chest, 2085(F), 10772
The Treasure Hunt, 8272(F)
Treasure Hunts! Treasure Hunts! Treasure and Scavenger Hunts to Play with Friends and Family, 22014
Treasure Map, 3676(F)
The Treasure of Bessledorf Hill, 6990(F)
Treasure of Panther Peak, 8686(F)
Treasure of the Lost Lagoon, 6373(F)
Treasures in the Dust, 8789(F)
Treasures of the Spanish Main, 14537
A Treasury of Christmas Stories, 9730(F)
A Treasury of Dragon Stories, 7654(F)
A Treasury of Mermaids, 10540
A Treasury of Pet Stories, 7173(F)
A Treasury of Pirate Stories, 7101(F)
The Treasury of Saints and Martyrs, 17208
A Treasury of Turkish Folktales for Children, 10865
A Treasury of Witches and Wizards, 7607(F)
Tree, 20195
Tree Book, 20203
A Tree for Me, 600(F)
Tree Frogs, 2017(F), 18728
The Tree in the Ancient Forest, 16966
Tree in the Trail, 9381(F)
The Tree in the Wood, 859
A Tree Is Growing, 20197
A Tree Is Nice, 4556(F)
Tree of Birds, 2495(F)
Tree of Cranes, 5915(F)
Tree of Dreams, 10629

Tree of Hope, 4742(F)
A Tree Place and Other Poems, 11966
The Tree That Owns Itself, 8932(F)
The Tree That Would Not Die, 4730
Treehouse Tales, 9562(F)
Treemonisha, 9596(F)
Trees, 20221
Trees and Plants in the Rain Forest, 20479
The Trees Kneel at Christmas, 9745(F)
The Trees of the Dancing Goats, 5901(F)
The Trek, 1277(F)
Trent Dimas, 13683
The Trespassers, 8111(F)
Trevor's Story, 17663
Trial by Ice, 12155
The Trial of Anna Cotman, 6742(F)
The Triangle Factory Fire, 16482
A Triangle for Adaora, 351(F)
Triangle, Square, Circle, 363(F)
Triangles, 356(F)
  (Illus. by Richard Maccabe), 20605
Trick or Treat Countdown, 6011(F)
Trick or Treat, Smell My Feet, 5993(F)
Tricks and Treats, 9717(F)
Trickster and the Fainting Birds, 11282
The Trickster and the Troll, 8110(F)
Trinidad, 15701
A Trio of Triceratops, 219(F)
The Trip, 6020(F)
The Trip Back Home, 4890(F)
Triplets, 3961(F)
Tris's Book, 8018(F)
Triumph on Everest, 12123
The Trojan Horse, 14686, 14688
Trojan Horse, 11463, 14698
Troll Teacher, 1646(F)
The Troll with No Heart in His Body, 11129
The Trolls, 9883(F)
Troodon, 14440
Tropical Rain Forest, 20487
Tropical Rain Forests, 20490
Trouble, 10682
Trouble at Fort La Pointe, 9361(F)
Trouble Dolls, 1022(F)
Trouble for Lucy, 9441(F)
Trouble in Bugland, 6927(F)
Trouble on the T-Ball Team, 2914(F)
Trouble on the Tracks, 8939(F)
Trouble on Thunder Mountain, 7793(F)
Trouble River, 9350(F)
The Trouble with an Elf, 8153(F)
The Trouble with Ben, 2593(F)
The Trouble with Cats, 8649(F)
The Trouble with Mom, 1066(F)
Trouble with Trolls, 1010(F)
The Trouble with Tuck, 7313(F)
The Trouble with Tyrannosaurus Rex, 1943(F)
The Trouble with Zinny Weston, 8326(F)
Trouble's Daughter, 9201(F)
Troubles with Bubbles, 6324(F)
The Trow-Wife's Treasure, 1143(F)

Troy Aikman, 13600, 13602
Tru Confessions, 7525(F)
Truck, 913(F)
Truck Jam, 5602(F)
Truck Song, 5600(F)
Truck Talk, 5578
Truck Trouble, 17839
Trucks, 5575(F), 5604, 21316, 21323
  (Illus. by Byron Barton), 21291
Trucks and Tractor Pullers, 21317
Trucks Trucks Trucks, 5601(F)
True Blue, 6328(F)
True Bugs, 19468
True Champions, 21965
The True Francine, 3984(F)
True Friends, 8534(F)
True Heart, 9417(F)
True Lies, 10614
True-Life Monsters of the Prehistoric Seas, 14412
True-Life Monsters of the Prehistoric Skies, 14412
True-Life Treasure Hunts, 14525
The True-or-False Book of Cats, 19926
The True-or-False Book of Horses, 20001
True Stories About Abraham Lincoln, 13067
True Stories of Baseball's Hall of Famers, 22101
The True Story of the Three Little Pigs, 11033
The True Tale of Johnny Appleseed, 12844
Truffle's Christmas, 5791(F)
Truman's Aunt Farm, 4281(F)
The Trumpet of the Swan, 8201(F)
The Trumpeter of Krakow, 9051(F)
Trumpets, 14222
Trupp, 1919(F)
The Truth About Castles, 14757
The Truth About Cats, 2707(F)
The Truth About Cousin Ernie's Head, 3787(F)
The Truth About Great White Sharks, 19752
The Truth About the Moon, 4388(F)
The Truth Out There, 7019(F)
Tsubu the Little Snail, 10836
Tsunamis, 20722
ttuM, 6908(F)
The Tub Grandfather, 1072(F)
The Tub People, 1073(F)
The Tub People's Christmas, 5788(F)
Tubes In My Ears, 18038
Tubu, 14917
Tuck Everlasting, 7575(F)
Tuck in the Pool, 2846(F)
Tuck-Me-In Tales, 735
Tuck Triumphant, 7314(F)
Tucker, 8401(F)
Tucker Flips! 5328(F)
Tucker Off His Rocker, 2433(F)
Tucker Over the Top, 2433(F)
Tucker's Countryside, 8081(F)
Tucket's Gold, 9427(F)
Tucket's Home, 9428(F)
Tucket's Ride, 9429(F)
Tucking Mommy In, 725(F)
Tuesday, 2855(F)

Tugboats, 21366, 21377
Tugboats in Action, 4612(F)
Tukama Tootles the Flute, 11421
Tule Elk, 19147
Tulip Sees America, 2967(F)
The Tulip Touch, 8889(F)
Tumble Bumble, 1832(F)
Tumbleweed Stew, 6297(F)
Tundra, 15810, 15832, 15834, 15835
Tundra and Cold Deserts, 15827
Tundra Discoveries, 15843
Tundra Mouse, 5869(F)
Tuning In, 21278
Tunisia, 14957
Tunneling Earthworms, 19603
Tunnels, 21146
Tunnels Go Underground, 21129
Turkey, 15260, 15282, 15289
A Turkey for Thanksgiving, 6136(F)
The Turkey Girl, 11290
Turkey in Pictures, 15266
Turkey Pox, 6132(F)
Turkey Trouble, 9723(F)
Turn of the Century, 14557
The Turnabout Shop, 8798(F)
Turnagain Ptarmigan! Where Did
   You Go? 1212(F)
The Turnip, 10886
Turnip Soup, 4247(F)
Turnover Tuesday, 4286(F)
Turns on a Dime, 8473(F)
Turtle and Snake at Work, 6672(F)
Turtle and Snake Go Camping,
   6673(F)
The Turtle and the Monkey, 10847
Turtle Bay, 5365(F)
Turtle Clan Journey, 9192(F)
Turtle Day, 5206(F)
Turtle Dreams, 6199(F)
Turtle in July, 11813
Turtle Island, 11226
Turtle Knows Your Name, 11419
Turtle on a Fence Post, 8867(F)
Turtle Songs, 10852
Turtle Spring, 5464(F)
Turtle Time, 787(F)
Turtle, Turtle, Watch Out! 18789
Turtles, 18779, 18791
Turtles Take Their Time, 18781
The Tusk Fairy, 1587(F)
Tut, Tut, 8074(F)
Tutankhamen's Gift, 13862
Tutankhamun, 13861
Tut's Mummy, 6311
TV Rex, 1431(F)
TV's Forgotten Hero, 13279
TWA Flight 800, 21074
The Twelve Apostles, 17306
The 12 Days of Christmas, 14211
The Twelve Days of Christmas,
   14212, 14216
   (Illus. by John O'Brien), 14214
   (Illus. by Vladimir Vagin), 14215
The Twelve Labors of Hercules,
   11504
Twelve Lizards Leaping, 14213
The Twelve Princesses, 10888
Twelve-Year-Old Vows Revenge
   After Being Dumped by Extrater-
   restrial on First Date, 9978(F)
The 20s and 30s, 16450

The 20th Century Children's Book
   Treasury, 1630(F)
The 20th Century Children's Poetry
   Treasury, 11728
Twenty and Ten, 9646(F)
The Twenty-Five Mixtec Cats,
   7745(F)
The Twenty-Four Days Before
   Christmas, 9743(F)
Twenty Is Too Many, 424(F)
Twenty-One Balloons, 9831(F)
26 Fairmount Avenue, 12526
26 Letters and 99 Cents, 54(F)
The 23rd Psalm, 17326
Twenty Thousand Leagues Under the
   Sea, 7112(F)
Twice My Size, 5349(F)
The Twiddle Twins' Haunted House,
   7744(F)
Twiddle Twins' Music Box Mystery,
   7744(F)
Twigboy, 1177(F)
Twilight, 1259(F)
Twilight Comes Twice, 4430(F)
The Twilight Gate, 8062(F)
Twilight in Grace Falls, 8459(F)
Twilight Verses, Moonlight Rhymes,
   795
The Twin in the Tavern, 7118(F)
The Twinkle Squad, 10095(F)
Twinkle, Twinkle, Little Star, 828(F)
Twinnies, 4919(F)
Twins! 17684
The Twins, the Pirates, and the Battle
   of New Orleans, 9314(F)
The Twins, Two by Two, 619(F)
A Twist in the Tail, 10564
Twist with a Burger, Jitter with a
   Bug, 3287(F)
Twister, 2909(F)
Twisters! 20692
   (Illus. by Kazushige Nitta), 20712
Two Bad Ants, 2773(F)
Two Bear Cubs (Illus. by Ann Jonas),
   5282(F)
   (Illus. by Daniel San Souci), 11298
The Two Brothers, 9563(F)
The Two Bullies, 1421(F)
Two Cool Cows, 2709(F)
Two Cool Coyotes, 2404(F)
Two Crows Counting, 546(F)
Two False Moves, 8373(F)
Two for Stew, 4255(F)
Two Girls Can! 4031(F)
263 Brain Busters, 20619
Two Hundred Thirteen Valentines,
   10039(F)
Two Lands, One Heart, 15200
Two Little Witches, 6066(F)
Two Lives, 18655
The Two Love Stars, 10731
Two Messy Friends, 6219(F)
Two Mice in Three Fables, 2620(F)
The Two Mountains, 11405
Two Mrs. Gibsons, 3714(F)
Two of a Kind, 8286(F)
Two of Everything, 10757
The Two of Them, 7385(F)
Two Peas in a Pod, 439(F)
Two Shoes, New Shoes, 3231(F)
The Two Sillies, 1246(F)

Two Silly Trolls, 6421(F)
Two Skeletons on the Telephone,
   11868
Two So Small, 1256(F)
The Two-Thousand-Pound Goldfish,
   8410(F)
Two Tickets to Freedom, 9476(F)
2 x 2=Boo! 6026(F)
Two Under Par, 8449(F)
Two Ways to Count to Ten, 10661
Ty Cobb, 13446
Tyler's New Boots, 2960(F)
Tyra Banks, 12352
Tyrannosaurus Tex, 1811(F)
Tyrannosaurus Time, 14468
Tyrannosaurus Was a Beast, 11810
Tyrone the Horrible, 2860(F)
Ty's One-Man Band, 3470(F)

The U.S. Air Force, 21382
The U.S. Army, 21398
U.S. Census, 17115
The U.S. Coast Guard, 21383
The U.S. Constitution, 17054
The U.S. Marine Corps, 21407
The U.S. Navy, 21400
U.S.A., 15868
USA from Space, 20983
UFOs, 21890, 21931
UFOs and Aliens, 21961
Uganda, 14919
The Ugly Duckling, 10466, 10480(F)
   (Illus. by Bernadette Watts),
   10396(F)
The Ugly Vegetables, 3775(F)
Uh Oh! Gotta Go! 3298
Uh-oh! It's Mama's Birthday!
   3916(F)
Ukraine, 15405, 15406, 15436
Ukrainian Egg Decoration, 17439
Ukrainians in America, 17572
Ulaq and the Northern Lights,
   2755(F)
Ultimate Atlas of Almost Everything,
   14352
The Ultimate Baby-Sitter's Hand-
   book, 16948
The Ultimate Book of Kid Concoc-
   tions, 21505
Ultimate Field Trip 4, 16245
Ultimate Field Trip 3, 19860
The Ultimate Guide to Student Con-
   tests, Grades K–6, 17626
The Ultimate LEGO Book, 21659
Ulysses S. Grant, 13036
Ulysses S. Grant and the Strategy of
   Victory, 13037
Umbrella, 3491(F)
UN Ambassador, 12841
The Un-Wedding, 4933(F)
Unbeatable Beaks, 19289
The Unbreakable Code, 9165(F)
Unbroken, 8675(F)
Unbuilding, 21138
The Uncanny, 21912
The Uncivil War, 8727(F)
Unclaimed Treasures, 8754(F)
Uncle Alfredo's Zoo, 1654(F)
Uncle Carmello, 7543(F)
Uncle Chuck's Truck, 5552(F)
Uncle Elephant, 6470(F)

Uncle Frank's Pit, 4226(F)
Uncle Jed's Barber Shop, 9598(F)
Uncle Nacho's Hat, 9138(F)
Uncle Phil's Diner, 3838(F)
Uncle Rain Cloud, 3734(F)
Uncle Sam and Old Glory, 15858
Uncle Sam Wants You! 14893
Uncle Shamus, 8277(F)
Uncle Switch, 11879
Uncle Terrible, 8208(F)
Uncle Vova's Tree, 5902(F)
Uncommon Champions, 13375
Uncommon Traveler, 12128
Under a Stone, 20535
Under Copp's Hill, 9515(F)
Under My Nose, 12533
Under New York, 16695
Under Our Skin, 17548
Under the Black Flag, 6880(F)
Under the Breadfruit Tree, 11586
Under the Cat's Eye, 10229(F)
Under the Ground, 18934
Under the Hawthorn Tree, 9089(F)
Under the Lemon Moon, 4956(F)
Under the Mermaid Angel, 8344(F)
Under the Moon, 7733(F)
Under the Royal Palms, 15692
Under the Sea, 19629, 19840
Under the Shadow of Wings, 9645(F)
Under the Sun and the Moon and
    Other Poems, 11943
Under the Sunday Tree, 11580
The Underbed, 704(F)
Underground, 21139
The Underground Railroad, 16228
The Underground Railroad and the
    Civil War, 16268
The Underground Railroad in Illi-
    nois, 16281
Understanding Buddy, 8325(F)
Understanding Electricity, 20895
Understanding Israel, 15529
Understanding Jewish Holidays and
    Customs, 17485
Understanding Man's Best Friend,
    19974
Understood Betsy, 7401(F)
Underwater Animals, 19627
Underwater Counting, 549(F)
Underwear! 2506(F)
Underwear Do's and Don'ts, 4260(F)
The Unicorn and the Moon, 1117(F)
Unicorns! Unicorns! 2412(F)
Unidentified Flying Objects and
    Extraterrestrial Life, 21001
The Uninvited Guest and Other Jew-
    ish Holiday Tales, 17475
Union Generals of the Civil War,
    12653
The United Kingdom, 15345
United Nations High Commission for
    Refugees, 17018
The United States, 15860, 15902,
    15915
United States, 21980
The United States Cookbook, 21692
The United States Enters the World
    Stage, 16457
The United States Holocaust Memor-
    ial Museum, 16657
United States in Pictures, 15911

The United States of America, 15895
The Universe, 18379, 18401, 18416,
    18421
Unknown, 5431(F)
Uno, Dos, Tres, 520(F)
The Unprotected Witness, 7084(F)
Unraveling Fibers, 21174
Unreal! 10260(F)
Unseen Rainbows, Silent Songs,
    18818
An Unsolved Mystery from History,
    7141(F)
Until I Met Dudley, 5586(F)
Unusual Friendships, 18579
Up a Creek, 8539(F)
Up a Rainforest Tree, 20492
Up and Away! 21077
Up and Away, 21076
Up and Down on the Merry-Go-
    Round, 3312(F)
The Up and Down Spring, 8312(F)
Up Goes the Skyscraper! 21123
Up in the Air, 12092, 20671
    (Illus. by Leonard Everett Fisher),
    11970
Up the Chimney, 10999
Up the Ladder, Down the Slide,
    3125(F)
Up the Mountain, 1725(F)
Up to Ten and Down Again, 431(F)
Up, Up and Away, 14035
Upchuck and the Rotten Willy,
    8183(F)
Upper Atlantic, 16652
Ups and Downs, 17715
The Ups and Downs of Simpson
    Snail, 6387(F)
The Upside Down Boy/El niño de
    cabeza, 10074(F)
The Upside-Down Cake, 8593(F)
The Upside-Down Reader, 6360(F)
Upstairs, 1152(F)
The Upstairs Cat, 1327(F)
The Upstairs Room, 9685(F)
Uptown, 3078(F)
Uranus, 18465, 18487, 18494, 18496,
    18502
Uranus, Neptune, and Pluto, 18478
Urban Roosts, 19303
Uruguay, 15770
Us and Uncle Fraud, 7474(F)
US Kids History, 16114
USA, 15864, 15865
The Usborne Book of Everyday
    Words, 14055
The Usborne Book of Treasure Hunt-
    ing, 14334
The Usborne Book of World History
    Dates, 14546
The Usborne Children's Songbook,
    14234
The Usborne Complete Book of
    Astronomy and Space, 18400
The Usborne Complete Book of the
    Microscope, 19809
Used-Up Bear, 1040(F)
Using Shadows in Art, 13920
Using Sound, 20942
Utah, 16603, 16609, 16620, 16626,
    16637, 16641
Utterly Yours, Booker Jones, 8630(F)

Uzbekistan, 15437

V Is for Victory, 14894
V-2 Rockets, 14898
Vacuum Cleaners, 21023
Valentine, 3569(F)
The Valentine Bears, 6163(F)
A Valentine for Norman Noggs,
    6169(F)
Valentine Fun, 21428
Valentine Mice! 6175(F)
Valentine Poems, 11838
The Valentine Star, 6345(F)
Valentine's Day, 17506
    (Illus. by Gail Gibbons), 17507
    (Illus. by Karen Ritz), 17509
    (Illus. by Lizzy Rockwell), 6176(F)
Valerie and the Silver Pear, 3601(F)
The Valiant Women of the Vietnam
    War, 16526
Valley Forge, 16199, 16216
Valley of the Eels, 10195(F)
Valley of the Kings, 14602
Vampire and Werewolf Stories,
    8166(F)
Vampire Bats and Other Creatures of
    the Night, 18674
The Vampire in My Bathtub, 8077(F)
Van Gogh, 13907
The Van Gogh Cafe, 8061(F)
Vancouver Nightmare, 7127(F)
Vanessa Williams, 12483
Vanishing, 8882(F)
Vanishing Act, 7095(F)
Vanishing Animal Neighbors, 19397
The Vanishing Chip, 6818(F)
Vanishing Clues, 7971(F)
Vanishing Ozone, 17003
The Vanishing Pumpkin, 6018(F)
Vanity, 21183
Vanity Rules, 21172
Vaqueros, 16359
Vasco da Gama, 12105
Vassilisa the Wise, 11113
Vegetables in the Garden, 20172
Vegetables, Vegetables! 20184
Vegetarian Cooking Around the
    World, 21741
The Vegetation of Rivers, Lakes, and
    Swamps, 20246
Veggie Soup, 2036(F)
Velcome, 6037(F)
The Velveteen Rabbit, 8209(F)
Vendela in Venice, 9028(F)
Venezuela, 15744, 15751, 15771,
    15791
Venezuela in Pictures, 15789
Venola in Love, 10014(F)
Venus, 18466, 18500, 20957
Venus Among the Fishes, 7780(F)
Venus and Serena Williams, 13656,
    13657
Venus Flytraps, 20242
Venus Peter Saves the Whale,
    2644(F)
Venus Williams, 13654
Vera Runs Away, 5064(F)
Vera's First Day of School, 5530(F)
Verdi, 1920(F)
Vermont, 16669, 16683, 16718
Vermont Facts and Symbols, 16674

Veronica's First Year, 5056(F)
Vertebrates, 18669
Very Best (Almost) Friends, 11729
The Very Best Christmas Ever! 21411
The Very Best Hanukkah Gift, 9758(F)
The Very Boastful Kangaroo, 6540(F)
The Very Busy Spider, 1925(F)
The Very Clumsy Click Beetle, 1926(F)
Very Far Away, 1559(F)
The Very Hungry Caterpillar, 5160(F)
The Very Hungry Lion, 10809
A Very Important Day, 3206(F)
Very Last First Time, 4576(F)
The Very Little Boy, 3267(F)
The Very Lonely Firefly, 1927(F)
A Very Noisy Girl, 1694(F)
The Very Noisy Night, 699(F)
The Very Quiet Cricket, 1928(F)
The Very Real Ghost Book of Christina Rose, 7700(F)
Very Scary, 6019(F)
The Very Small, 666(F)
A Very Special House, 5001(F)
The Very Worst Monster, 1258(F)
Veterans Day, 17339
Veterinarian, 17844
Veterinarians Help Animals, 17846
Vicksburg, 16407
Victims, 17151
Victorian Days, 16477
The Victorian Home, 13897
Victory in Europe, 14838
Video, 21266
Video Game Designer, 17792
Video Games, 22232
The Video Shop Sparrow, 2922(F)
Vietnam, 15158, 15163, 15171, 15172, 15173, 15189, 15190, 15197, 15214, 15218
Vietnam in Pictures, 15210
Vietnam War, 16507
The Vietnam War, 16513
The View from Saturday, 8324(F)
Views from Our Shoes, 17925
The Viking News, 15470
Viking Times, 15460
Viking Town, 15463
The Vikings, 15440, 15448, 15452, 15453, 15464
The Vikings and Jorvik, 15459
Vile Vikings, 15443
The Village by the Sea, 8646(F)
The Village of Round and Square Houses, 10671
Vincent Van Gogh, 12305, 12307, 12308
Vinegar Pancakes and Vanishing Cream, 9970(F)
Violence in Public Places, 17137
Violence in the Media, 17137
Violent Crime, 17084
Violet, 8741(F)
Virgie Goes to School with Us Boys, 4981(F)
Virginia, 16831, 16834, 16855, 16889

The Virginia Colony, 16127
Virtual Cody, 9837(F)
Virtual Reality, 21193, 21220
Virtual Reality and Beyond, 21208
Virtually Perfect, 10192(F)
Viruses, 17954
Vision of Beauty, 12809
Vision Quest, 8086(F)
Visions, 12183
A Visit from Saint Nicholas and Santa Mouse, Too! 5885(F)
A Visit to Amy-Claire, 4029(F)
A Visit to Oma, 3867(F)
A Visit to the Art Galaxy, 1503(F)
A Visit to the Country, 5278(F)
A Visit to the Gravesens' Farm, 3143(F)
A Visit to Washington, D.C., 16706
A Visit to William Blake's Inn, 11737
A Visit with Great-Grandma, 3502(F)
Visiting a Village, 16327
Visiting Mexico, 15611
Visiting the Art Museum, 3048(F)
The Visitor, 1726(F)
Visual and Performing Artists, 12168
The Visual Dictionary of the Horse, 20018
The Visual Dictionary of the Universe, 18422
Visual Timeline of the 20th Century, 14577
Vitamins, 20167
Vitamins and Minerals, 20163
Viva Mexico! 13818
"Vive La France" 14855
The Voice from the Mendelsohns' Maple, 8802(F)
The Voice of the People, 17117
Voices, 11538
Voices at Whisper Bend, 9644(F)
Voices from the West, 16302
Voices in the Park, 3053(F)
Voices of the Alamo, 16243
Voices of the Heart, 13989
Volcano, 20339
Volcano! 20350
The Volcano Disaster, 7855(F)
Volcanoes, 20336, 20342, 20344, 20346, 20348, 20355
  (Illus. by Marc Simont), 20335
Volcanoes and Earthquakes, 20343, 20347
  (Illus. by Courtney), 20338
Volleyball in Action, 21992
Vostok 1, 20972
The Voyage of the "Dawn Treader" 7911(F)
Voyage of the Half Moon, 8198(F)
The Voyage of the Ludgate Hill, 11738
Voyage on the Great Titanic, 9638(F)
The Voyager's Stone, 19823
The Voyages of Christopher Columbus, 12097
The Voyages of Doctor Dolittle, 7925(F)
Vroom, Chugga, Vroom-Vroom, 518(F)
Vroom! Vroom! 21465

Vroomaloom, 1085(F)
Vulca the Etruscan, 14711
Vultures, 19275, 19283, 19344

W. D. the Wonder Dog, 1830(F)
W. E. B. Du Bois, 12718, 12720
W. E. B. Du Bois and Racial Relations, 12717
W. E. B. DuBois, 12719
W. K. Kellogg, 12917
The Wacky Wedding, 35(F)
Wacky Wednesday, 492(F)
Wading Birds, 19295
The Wadjet Eye, 8941(F)
The Wagon, 4700(F)
Wagon Train, 9390(F)
Wagon Wheels, 6222(F)
A Wagonload of Fish, 10853
Wagons Ho! A Diary of the Oregon Trail, 9412(F)
Wagons West! 2932(F)
Wah Ming Chang, 12210
The Wainscott Weasel, 8080(F)
Wait Till Helen Comes, 7776(F)
Wait Till the Moon Is Full, 4394(F)
Waiting Alligators, 18705
Waiting for Baby (Illus. by Emily Bolam), 3971(F)
  (Illus. by Loreen Leedy), 3529(F)
Waiting for Baby Joe, 3584(F)
Waiting for Christmas, 5828(F)
Waiting for Mr. Goose, 5012(F)
Waiting for the Whales, 3788(F)
Waiting for Wings, 19546
The Waiting Place, 789(F)
Waiting to Dive, 10358(F)
Waiting to Sing, 3743(F)
Wake Me at Midnight, 6813(F)
Wake Up, Bear . . . It's Christmas! 5820(F)
Wake Up, City! 3457(F)
Wake Up, Grizzly! 3530(F)
Wake Up House! Rooms Full of Poems, 11631
Wake Up, Little Children, 4381(F)
Wake Up, Mr. B.! 1096(F)
Wake Up, Sleep Tight, 257(F)
Wake Up, Wake Up! 5454(F)
Wake Up, World! A Day in the Life of Children Around the World, 14341
Wakeboarding! Throw a Tantrum, 22013
Wakey-wakey, 623(F)
Waking Upside Down, 1230(F)
Wales, 15368
Wales in Pictures, 15369
Walk a Green Path, 20245
A Walk in the Boreal Forest, 20454
A Walk in the Desert, 20408
A Walk in the Rain Forest, 20455
A Walk in the Rainforest, 116(F)
A Walk in the Tundra, 15809
A Walk on the Great Barrier Reef, 15223
Walk on the Wild Side! 18661
Walk with a Wolf, 19125
Walk with Me, 3099(F)
Walking for Freedom, 17037
The Walking Stick, 4856(F)

Walking the Bridge of Your Nose, 21845
Walking the Edge, 8488(F)
Walking the Road to Freedom, 12790
Walking Through the Jungle, 1226(F)
Walking to the Bus-Rider Blues, 7366(F)
Walking with Mama, 4547(F)
Walkingsticks, 19466
Walks Alone, 15937(F)
The Wall, 3559(F)
Wallace Hoskins, 1717(F)
The Walloping Window-Blind, 11861
Wallpaper from Space, 10225(F)
Walrus, 19732
Walruses, 19740
Walt Disney, 12224, 12225, 12226, 12227, 12229
Walt Whitman, 12623
Walter Johnson, 13466
Walter White and the Power of Organized Protest, 12821
Walter Wick's Optical Tricks, 20919
Walter's Tail, 2078(F)
Waltz of the Scarecrows, 3297(F)
Wanda's Roses, 3046(F)
Wander, 7257(F)
The Wanderer, 6806(F)
The Wanderings of Odysseus, 11511
Wanna Bet? 18308
Wanted, 3698(F), 10188(F)
Wanyana and Matchmaker Frog, 10689
The Waorani, 15787
The War, 8176(F)
The War Against Iraq, 15493
War and the Pity of War, 11670
War Behind the Lines, 14839
The War Between the Vowels and the Consonants, 140(F)
The War for Independence, 16204
War Game, 12232
War in the Persian Gulf, 15487
The War of 1812, 16279
War of 1812, 16244
War of the Eagles, 8947(F)
War, Peace, and All That Jazz, 16470
War, Terrible War, 16411
The War with Grandpa, 7517(F)
War with Mexico, 16254
The Warlord's Puzzle, 4795(F)
Warren G. Harding, 13038, 13039
The Warrior and the Wise Man, 10523(F)
Warrior Son of a Warrior Son, 10687
Warriors, Warthogs, and Wisdom, 12617
Warthogs, 18967
Warts, 18178
The Wartville Wizard, 1384(F)
Wash Your Hands! 3397(F)
Washing the Willow Tree Loon, 5341(F)
Washington, 16808, 16821
Washington City Is Burning, 9315(F)
Washington, D.C., 16654, 16670, 16684, 16700, 16712, 16731, 16743

Washington, D.C. Facts and Symbols, 16675
Washington Irving, 12555
The Washington Monument, 16667
The Washington Way, 13117
A Wasp Is Not a Bee, 18672
Wasps, 19524
The Waste Crisis, 16987
Waste, Recycling and Re-Use, 16983
Watakame's Journey, 11407
Watch Out! Big Bro's Coming! 948(F)
Watch Out for Bears! The Adventures of Henry and Bruno, 6722(F)
Watch Out for the Chicken Feet in Your Soup, 3608(F)
Watch Out, Ronald Morgan! 4966(F)
Watch Them Grow, 18593
Watch Us Play, 6335(F)
Watch William Walk, 4196(F)
Watchdog and the Coyotes, 8184(F)
The Watcher, 7632(F)
Watcher in the Piney Woods, 9483(F)
The Watchers, 7687(F)
Watchful Wolves, 19117
Watching Desert Wildlife, 20398, 20399
Watching Nature, 18597
Watching Our Feathered Friends, 19286
Watching Water Birds, 19346
Water, 20725, 20732, 20735, 20741 (Illus. by Laurie Hamilton), 20747
Water and Other Liquids, 20740
Water at the Blue Earth, 9354(F)
Water Buffalo Days, 15167
Water Dance, 20737
Water for One, Water for Everyone, 589(F)
Water Ghost, 9013(F)
The Water Horse, 7870(F)
Water Insects, 19457
Water Music, 11993
The Water of Life, 10912
Water Play, 20738
Water Pollution, 16986, 17007
A Water Snake's Year, 18759
Water Squeeze, 20743
Water Up, Water Down, 20746
Water Voices, 10265(F)
Water, Water, 3183(F)
Water, Water Everywhere, 20726
Water Wishes, 7924(F)
The Waterfall, 2953(F)
Waterfalls, 20396
Waterfowl, 19308, 19314
Watergate, 16525
Waterman's Boy, 7053(F)
Watermelon Day, 2999(F)
Watership Down, 7544(F)
Waterways to the Great Lakes, 15863
The Watsons Go to Birmingham — 1963, 7337(F)
A Wave in Her Pocket, 11427
The Wave of the Sea-Wolf, 11317
Waves, 20903
Waving, 582(F)
Way Down Deep, 19630
The Way Home, 5386(F)
The Way Meat Loves Salt, 11151

The Way Mothers Are, 2663(F)
The Way of the Willow Branch, 3023(F)
Way Out in the Desert, 5338(F)
Way Out West with a Baby, 4606(F)
The Way Things Never Were, 16505
The Way Things Work, 21251
Way to Go, Alex! 5052(F)
The Way to Schenectady, 9988(F)
The Way to Start a Day, 11531
The Way to Wyatt's House, 1038(F)
The Way West, 16336
The Wayfinder, 8008(F)
Wayne Gretzky, 13687
Wayside School Is Falling Down, 10126(F)
We Adopted You, Benjamin Koo, 17654(F)
We All Scream for Ice Cream, 20133
We All Sing with the Same Voice, 14252
We Are All Related, 17598
We Are Bears, 5239(F)
We Are Best Friends, 3978(F)
We Are Monsters, 1449(F)
We Came from Vietnam, 17595
We Can Do It! 17903
We Can Get Along, 17624
We Can Work it Out, 17724
We Got My Brother at the Zoo, 3673(F)
We Had a Picnic This Sunday Past, 3958(F)
We Have a Baby, 3619(F)
"We Have Conquered Pain" 13209
We Hide, You Seek, 297(F)
We Just Moved! 6440(F)
We Laughed a Lot, My First Day of School, 5542(F)
We Love Fruit! 20155
We Need Librarians, 17738
We Need Principals, 17739
We Played Marbles, 2971(F)
We Remember the Holocaust, 14814
We Share Everything! 5521(F)
We, the People, 11615
We Were Tired of Living in a House, 3432(F)
Weapons, 21402
Weapons and Warfare, 21397
Weapons of War, 14890, 21387
Weasel, 9356(F)
Weather, 20764, 20779, 20784, 20788 (Illus. by Sophie Kniffke), 4446
Weather and Climate, 20787
Weather Everywhere, 20758
Weather Explained, 20762
Weather Forecasting, 20768
The Weather Sky, 20781
Weather Watch, 20775
Weather Words and What They Mean, 20769
Weatherwise, 20776
A Weave of Words, 10863
Weaver's Daughter, 9263(F)
Weaving a California Tradition, 21528
The Weaving of a Dream, 10755
Web Page Designer, 17793

Web Weavers and Other Spiders, 19584
Webmaster, 17786
Website of the Warped Wizard, 7862(F)
Websters' Leap, 7714(F)
The Wedding, 3727(F)
Wedding Bells for Rotten Ralph, 2113(F)
Wedding Days, 17359
The Wedding Procession of the Rag Doll and the Broom Handle and Who Was in It, 1539(F)
Weddings, 5641
Wedges, 20928
The Wednesday Surprise, 3560(F)
Wee G, 2901(F)
Wee Little Woman, 4083(F)
Wee Willie Winkie and Other Rhymes, 879(F)
A Weed Is a Seed, 3484(F)
A Week at the Fair, 6829(F)
A Week in the Life of an Airline Pilot, 17837
A Weekend in the City, 2401(F)
A Weekend with Degas, 12221
A Weekend with Diego Rivera, 12293
A Weekend with Rembrandt, 12288
A Weekend with Rousseau, 12299
A Weekend with Wendell, 2197(F)
A Weekend with Winslow Homer, 12239
Weightlifting, 22029
Weird! 17445
Weird Henry Berg, 8066(F)
Weird Pet Poems, 11779
Weird Stories from the Lonesome Cafe, 9817(F)
Weird Wolf, 7692(F)
Weirdo's War, 6800(F)
Welcome Back to Pokeweed Public School, 5474(F)
Welcome Comfort, 5903(F)
Welcome Home! 21162
Welcome Home, Jellybean, 8913(F)
Welcome, Little Baby, 3506(F)
Welcome to Addy's World, 1864, 16431
Welcome to Australia, 15251
Welcome to Canada, 15565
Welcome to China, 15063
Welcome to Egypt, 15500
Welcome to England, 15358
Welcome to Felicity's World, 1774, 16129
Welcome to Greece, 15380
Welcome to Italy, 15379
Welcome to Josefina's World, 1824, 16339
Welcome to Kirsten's World, 1854, 16371
Welcome to Mexico, 15623
Welcome to Molly's World, 1944, 14854
Welcome to Samantha's World, 1904, 16467
Welcome to Starvation Lake, 10138(F)
Welcome to the Green House, 4566
Welcome to the Ice House, 15847

Welcome to the Rodeo! 22062
Welcome to the Sea of Sand, 20429
Welcome to the USA, 15878
Welcome with Love, 18242
Well, a Crocodile Can! 5189(F)
Well Done, Worm! 6253(F)
Well, I Never! (Illus. by Terry Ross), 1156(F)
(Illus. by James Warhola), 1464(F)
The Well of Sacrifice, 9131(F)
The Well of the Wind, 7738(F)
We'll Paint the Octopus Red, 3447(F)
We'll Race You, Henry, 13282
Well Wished, 7612(F)
Wemberly Worried, 2198(F)
Wempires, 1481(F)
We're Going on a Bear Hunt, 2966(F)
We're Going on a Lion Hunt, 2907(F)
We're Growing Together, 3851(F)
The Werewolf, 8020(F)
The Werewolf Club, 9968(F)
Weslandia, 1160(F)
West Africa, 15020
West African States, 15021
West Along the Wagon Road, 1852, 9399(F)
West by Covered Wagon, 16349
West by Steamboat, 21369
West by Waterway, 16347
West from Home, 7538(F)
West Indian Americans, 17544
West Indian Folk Tales, 11432
West Point, 21389
The West Texas Chili Monster, 1084(F)
West to a Land of Plenty, 9418(F)
West Virginia, 16845, 16847, 16893
Western Wind, 8647(F)
Westward Ho! 16295
Westward Ho, Carlotta! 4147(F)
Westward, Ho, Ho, Ho! 16355
Westward to Home, 9376(F)
Westward with Columbus, 16079
Wet and Dry, 18803
Wet Weather, 20777
Wet World, 3430(F)
Wetland, 20391
Wetland Plants, 20517
Wetlands, 20386, 20395
Whaddayamean, 1028(F)
Whale, 950(F)
A Whale Biologist at Work, 19781
Whale Brother, 4838(F)
Whale Is Stuck, 2180(F)
Whale Journey, 5213(F)
Whale Magic for Kids, 19804
A Whale on Her Own, 19800
Whale Watching, 19776
The Whalers, 19780
The Whales, 4532(F)
Whales, 6531(F), 19783, 19784, 19785, 19788, 19789, 19790, 19791, 19802, 19803
(Illus. by Deborah Savin), 19799
Whales and Dolphins, 19634
Whales and Other Sea Mammals, 19798
The Whales' Song, 1568(F)

A Whaling Captain's Daughter, 16474
Whaling Days, 19778
What a Beautiful Day! 4500(F)
What a Doll! 21651
What a Morning! 14205
What a Scare, Jesse Bear, 5988(F)
What a Truly Cool World, 10686
What a Wonderful World, 14259(F)
What about Bettie, 6689(F)
What About Emma? 5395(F)
What Am I? 172(F), 5435
"What Am I Doing in a Step-Family?" 17642
What Are Drugs? 17893
What Are Food Chains and Webs? 18586
What Are Friends For? 2154(F)
What Are We Going to Do About David? 8515(F)
What Are You Figuring Now? 13233
What Baby Wants, 3861(F)
What Bit Me? 19491
What Can I Give Him? 5826(F)
What Can You Do in the Rain? 3214(F)
What Can You Do in the Snow? (Illus. by Thea Kliros), 3214(F)
(Illus. by Thea Kliros), 3215(F)
What Can You Do in the Sun? 3216(F)
What Can You Do in the Wind? (Illus. by Thea Kliros), 3215(F)
(Illus. by Thea Kliros), 3216(F)
What Can You See? 21875(F)
What Color Is Camouflage? 18887
What Color Is That Dinosaur? 14398
What Color Was the Sky Today? 181(F)
What Could a Hippopotamus Be? 2759(F)
What Could Be Keeping Santa? 5852(F)
What Could Go Wrong? 7032(F)
What! Cried Granny, 731(F)
What Dads Can't Do, 2873(F)
What Day Is It? 6699(F)
What Did I Look Like When I Was a Baby? 2862(F)
What Do Animals Do in Winter? 18902
What Do Authors Do? 14074
What Do Fish Have to Do with Anything? 8558(F)
What Do Illustrators Do? 17770
What Do We Know About Buddhism? 17186
What Do We Know About Grasslands? 20537
What Do We Know About Hinduism? 17187
What Do We Know About Islam? 17192
What Do We Know About Judaism? 17180
What Do We Know About Prehistoric People? 14493
What Do We Know About Rainforests? 20459
What Do We Know About Sikhism? 17177

What Do We Know About the Amazonian Indians? 15756
What Do We Know About the Inuit? 15794
What Do We Know About the Middle Ages? 14771
What Do You Call a Group of Butterflies? And Other Insect Groups, 19471
What Do You Do, Dear? 4991(F)
What Do You Do When Something Wants to Eat You? 18898
What Do You Hear When Cows Sing? 21839
What Do You Like? 3185(F)
What Do You Love? 728(F)
What Do You Mean I Have a Learning Disability? 17904
What Do You Mean I Have Attention Deficit Disorder? 17905
What Do You Say, Dear? 4991(F)
What Do You See? Come Look with Me, 21886(F)
What Do You See in a Cloud? 20765
What Do You See When You Shut Your Eyes? 3495(F)
What Does the Rabbit Say? 5246(F)
What Every Kid Should Know, 17617
What Food Is This? 20097
What Game Shall We Play? 2235(F)
What Good Is a Cactus? 9169(F)
What Grandmas Do Best/What Grandpas Do Best, 3825(F)
What Happened on Planet Kid, 8606(F)
What Happened to Amelia Earhart? 12111
What Happened to Patrick's Dinosaurs? 1939(F)
What Happened to the Dinosaurs? 14388
What Happened to the Mammoths? And Other Explorations of Science in Action, 18838
What Happens to a Hamburger, 18105
What Have You Done, Davy? 2839(F)
What I Believe, 17167, 17171
What I Had Was Singing, 12344
What I Like, 2997(F)
What I See, 6431(F)
What If? 7802(F), 11793
(Illus. by Ross Collins), 1619(F)
(Illus. by Barbara Nascimbeni), 1573(F)
What If? Mind-Boggling Science Questions for Kids, 18276
What If the Shark Wears Tennis Shoes? 748(F)
What Is a Biome? 20378
What Is a Bird? 19237
What Is a Cat? 5263
What Is a Computer? 21199
What Is a Fish? 19701
What Is a Horse? 5264
What Is a Life Cycle? 18587
What Is a Marsupial? 19178
What Is a Primate? 19000
What Is a Rodent? 19199

What Is a Scientist? 17832
What Is a Teacher? 5515(F)
What Is a Triangle? 324
What Is a Whale? 19639
What Is a Wise Bird Like You Doing in a Silly Tale Like This? 1574(F)
What Is an Amphibian? 18686
What Is Martin Luther King, Jr. Day? 5610
What Is Round? 325(F)
What Is Square? 326(F)
What Is That? 199(F)
What Is the Full Moon Full Of? 4257(F)
What Is the World Made Of? All About Solids, Liquids, and Gases, 20816
What Jamie Saw, 8416(F)
What Katy Did, 8610(F)
What Kind of Baby-Sitter Is This? 3250(F)
What Lives in a Shell? 18916
What Magnets Can Do, 20893
What Makes a Bird a Bird? 19232
What Makes Day and Night? 18428
What Makes It Rain? 20727
What Makes Popcorn Pop? 20135
What Makes the Grand Canyon Grand? 20300
What Makes the Wind? 20675
What Makes You Cough, 18079
What Makes You What You Are, 18034
What Mommies Do Best/What Daddies Do Best, 2541(F)
What Moms Can't Do, 2874(F)
What Newt Could Do for Turtle, 2398(F)
What Night Do the Angels Wander? 5928(F)
What on Earth Is a Bustard? 19290
What on Earth Is a Capybara? 19205
What on Earth Is a Pout? 19712
What on Earth Is a Quokka? 19183
What Once Was White, 17899
What Rot! 16984
What Shall We Do with the Boo-Hoo Baby? 654(F)
What the Aztecs Told Me, 15631
What the Dickens! 9269(F)
What the Dinosaurs Saw, 576
What the Moon Is Like, 18442
What the Moon Saw, 256(F)
What the Sun Sees/What the Moon Sees, 1609(F)
What to Do If You Get Lost, 18222
What to Do When and Why, 17640
What We Like, 3385
What Will I Do Without You? 2155(F)
What Will Mommy Do When I'm at School? 3731(F)
What Will the Weather Be? 20760
What Would Mama Do? 2073(F)
What You Do Is Easy, What I Do Is Hard, 2867(F)
What You Never Knew About Fingers, Forks, and Chopsticks, 17638
What You Should Know About the American Flag, 13977

What Zeesie Saw on Delancey Street, 4802(F)
Whatever Happened to Humpty Dumpty? 11872
Whatever Happened to the Dinosaurs? 4238(F)
Whatley's Quest, 7126
What's a Daring Detective Like Me Doing in the Doghouse? 6763(F)
What's a Lemming? 19209
What's a Pair? What's a Dozen? 590
What's a Penguin Doing in a Place Like This? 19385
What's a Virus, Anyway? 17955
What's Claude Doing? 5819(F)
What's Cooking? 21745
What's Cooking, Jenny Archer? 9813(F)
What's Faster Than a Speeding Cheetah? 18864
What's for Lunch? 5219(F)
What's for Lunch? Bread, 20112
What's for Lunch? Eggs, 20113
What's for Lunch? Oranges, 20151
What's for Lunch? Peas, 20183
What's Going on Down There? 18258
What's He Doing Now? 3621(F)
What's in Aunt Mary's Room? 3707(F)
What's in the Meadow? 20536
What's in the Pond? 20521
What's in the Rainforest? 20481
What's in the Tide Pool? 19861
What's Inside, 298(F)
What's Inside Airplanes? 21097
What's It Like to Be a Fish? 19982
What's on My Head? 3808(F)
What's Opposite? 249(F)
What's Smaller Than a Pygmy Shrew? 365(F)
What's That Bug? 19443
What's the Big Secret? Talking About Sex with Girls and Boys, 18252
What's the Deal? Jefferson, Napoleon, and the Louisiana Purchase, 16229
What's the Difference Between . . . Lenses and Prisms and Other Scientific Things? 21058
What's the Matter, Davy? 2840(F)
What's the Matter, Habibi? 2369(F)
What's the Matter, Kelly Beans? 8634(F)
What's the Matter with Carruthers? A Bedtime Story, 741(F)
What's the Matter with Herbie Jones? 10087(F)
What's the Most Beautiful Thing You Know About Horses? 5440(F)
What's the Time, Mr. Wolf? 2264(F)
What's the Weather Today? 20766
What's This? 4501
What's to Be Scared Of, Suki? 8552(F)
What's Under My Bed? 786(F)
What's Under That Shell? 18792
What's Under the Log? 20521
What's Up With You, Taquandra Fu? 1057(F)

What's What? 243(F)
What's Wrong with Grandma? A Family's Experience with Alzheimer's, 8521(F)
What's Wrong with Me? 17945
Wheat, 20107
　(Illus. by Masaharu Susuki), 20102
Wheel of the Moon, 9195(F)
Wheel on the Chimney, 5146(F)
Wheel on the School, 9032(F)
Wheels! 6270(F)
Wheels and Axles, 20929
Wheels Around, 5597
Wheels of Time, 13280
The Wheels on the Bus, 14261, 14262
　(Illus. by Maryann Kovalski), 14250
When a Line Bends . . . A Shape Begins, 331(F)
When a Parent Goes to Jail, 17092
When a Storm Comes Up, 20689
When Abraham Talked to the Trees, 13079
When Addie Was Scared, 2908(F)
When Africa Was Home, 4880(F)
When Agnes Caws, 2929(F)
When Andy's Father Went to Prison, 4978(F)
When Aunt Lena Did the Rhumba, 3759(F)
When Autumn Comes, 4489
When Bear Stole the Chinook, 11312
When Birds Could Talk and Bats Could Sing, 11342
When Bluebell Sang, 2079(F)
When Cats Dream, 1477(F)
When Chickens Grow Teeth, 4174(F)
When Clay Sings, 13942
When Cows Come Home, 2173(F)
When Daddy Came to School, 3546(F)
When Daddy Took Us Camping, 2912(F)
When Dinosaurs Die, 17695
When Dinosaurs Go to School, 2482(F)
When Eric's Mom Fought Cancer, 5098(F)
When Frank Was Four, 3278(F)
When Grownups Drive You Crazy, 17670
When Heroes Die, 8632(F)
When Hippo Was Hairy, 10668
When Hunger Calls, 18641
When I Am a Sister, 3514(F)
When I Am Big, 6555(F)
When I Am Old with You, 3728(F)
When I Dream of Heaven, 9573(F)
When I Feel Angry, 2710(F)
When I First Came to This Land, 4367(F)
When I Go Camping with Grandma, 4385(F)
When I Grow Bigger, 3080(F)
When I Grow Up . . ., 2220(F)
When I Lived with Bats, 19029
When I Was Five, 4008(F)
When I Was Little, 3715(F)
When I Was Young, 3610(F)

When I Was Your Age, 12161, 14115
When I'm Afraid, 17601
When I'm Alone, 541(F)
When I'm Angry, 17602
When I'm Big, 1139(F)
When It Is Night, When It Is Day, 796(F)
When It Starts to Snow, 2119(F)
When Jane-Marie Told My Secret, 8387(F)
When Jessie Came Across the Sea, 9043(F)
When JFK Was My Father, 8667(F)
When Justice Failed, 12922
When Katie Was Our Teacher/Cuando Katie era nuestra maestra, 5478(F)
When Learning Is Tough, 17930
When Mack Came Back, 7310(F)
When Mama Comes Home Tonight, 3903(F)
When Martha's Away, 2236(F)
When Mindy Saved Hanukkah, 6086(F)
When Molly Was in the Hospital, 3113(F)
When Mom Turned into a Monster, 1223(F)
When Mommy Is Sick, 3889(F)
When Morning Comes, 18824
When Mules Flew on Magnolia Street, 8314(F)
When Night Comes, 18824
　(Illus. by Thomas D. Mangelsen), 18825
When Night Eats the Moon, 7724(F)
When Night Time Comes Near, 760(F)
When Papa Snores, 3778(F)
When Pigasso Met Mootisse, 2331(F)
When Pigs Fly, 8868(F)
When Pioneer Wagons Rumbled West, 4668(F)
When Sheep Cannot Sleep, 484(F)
When Shlemiel Went to Warsaw and Other Stories, 11174
When Someone You Know Has AIDS, 17957
When Someone You Love Is Addicted, 17866
When Sophie Gets Angry — Really, Really Angry, 4902(F)
When Spring Comes, 4474(F)
When Stories Fell Like Shooting Stars, 7761(F)
When Summer Comes, 4490
When the Beginning Began, 17296
When the Bough Breaks, 8769(F)
When the Chenoo Howls, 11222
When the Circus Came to Town, 9884(F)
When the Earth Wakes, 4525(F)
When the Elephant Walks, 5285(F)
When the Goblins Came Knocking, 6007(F)
When the Monkeys Came Back, 4434(F)
When the People Are Away, 2270(F)
When the Rain Sings, 11933

When the Road Ends, 8529(F)
When the Soldiers Were Gone, 9683(F)
When the Teddy Bears Came, 3932(F)
When the Tripods Came, 10159(F)
When the Viceroy Came, 15608
When the Wind Bears Go Dancing, 1599(F)
When the World Began, 10683
When the World Was Young, 10588
When They Fight, 2849(F)
When This Cruel War Is Over, 16400
When This World Was New, 4955(F)
When Tiny Was Tiny, 6519(F)
When Turtles Come to Town, 18793
When Uncle Took the Fiddle, 3181(F)
When Vera Was Sick, 3393(F)
When We Get Home, 632(F)
When We Married Gary, 3702(F)
When Whales Exhale and Other Poems, 11625
When Will It Snow? 4460(F)
When Will Sarah Come? 3708(F)
When Willard Met Babe Ruth, 10329(F)
When William Went Away, 3992(F)
When Winter Comes, 5441(F)
When Woman Became the Sea, 11416
When You Go to Kindergarten, 5506
When You Take a Pig to a Party, 5711(F)
When You Were a Baby, 3254(F)
When Young Melissa Sweeps, 3460(F)
When Your Parents Split Up . . ., 17688
When You're Not Looking, 485(F)
When Zachary Beaver Came to Town, 8303(F)
When Zaydeh Danced on Eldridge Street, 6106(F)
Where Am I? The Story of Maps and Navigation, 14370
Where Are Maisy's Friends? 1980(F)
Where Are the Night Animals? 18813
Where Are the Stars During the Day? 18539
Where Are You? 2700(F)
Where Are You, Blue Kangaroo? 1060(F)
Where Are You, Little Green Dragon? 1797(F)
Where Are You, Little Zack? 430(F)
Where Butterflies Grow, 4817
Where Did AIDS Come From? 17957
Where Did All the Dragons Go? 1514(F)
Where Did Josie Go? 4097(F)
Where Did You Get Those Eyes? 17648
Where Did You Put Your Sleep? 752(F)
Where Did Your Family Come From? 17546
Where Do Babies Come From? 18244

Where Do Balloons Go? 1091(F)
Where Do Bears Sleep? 698(F)
Where Do Birds Live? 19237
Where Do Cats Live? 5265
Where Do Horses Live? 5264
Where Do I Live? 173
Where Do Little Girls Grow? 3774(F)
Where Do Puddles Go? 20744
Where Do You Get Your Ideas? 14064
Where Do You Think You're Going, Christopher Columbus? 12099
Where Does Joe Go? 5897(F)
Where Does Maisy Live? 1980(F)
Where Does the Mail Go? 17105
Where Does the Moon Go? 18452
Where Does the Night Hide? 644(F)
Where Does the Sky End, Grandpa? 3504(F)
Where Does the Sun Go at Night? 1193(F)
Where Does the Teacher Live? 6332(F)
Where Fireflies Dance, 4628(F)
Where Go the Boats? 11720
Where Have the Unicorns Gone? 1711(F)
Where Have You Gone, Davy? 2841(F)
Where Is Alice's Bear? 6586(F)
Where Is Christmas, Jesse Bear? 5775(F)
Where Is Everybody? 97(F)
Where Is Grandpa? 4903(F)
Where Is Mr. Mole? 2114(F)
Where Is That Cat? 5234(F)
Where Is the Apple Pie? 2140(F)
Where Is the Night Train Going? 11710
Where Jamaica Go? 4165(F)
Where Lincoln Walked, 13064
Where, Oh, Where Is My Underwear? 4299(F)
Where Once There Was a Wood, 3146(F)
Where the Bald Eagles Gather, 19338
Where the Buffalo Roam, 11951
Where the Forest Meets the Sea, 7579(F)
Where the Girls Are, 50(F)
Where the Moon Lives, 2115(F)
Where the Sidewalk Ends, 11698
Where the Waves Break, 19862
Where the Wild Horses Roam, 20008
Where the Wild Things Are, 1560(F)
Where to Look for a Dinosaur, 14453
Where Will Nana Go Next? 4153(F)
Where Will This Shoe Take You? 21177
Where You Belong, 8337(F)
Where's Alfie? 2602(F)
Where's Bear? 2434(F)
Where's Chimpy? 3848(F)
Where's My Teddy? 1731(F)
Where's Prancer? 5841(F)
Where's That Bone? 235(F)
Where's That Cat? 5031(F)
Where's That Insect? 19430
Where's That Reptile? 18679
Where's the Ball? 3268(F)

Where's the Bear? 5369(F)
Where's the Big Dipper? 18553
Where's the Fly? 323(F)
Where's Waldo? 21867(F)
Which Way to the Revolution? 157(F)
Which Witch? 7810(F)
Which Witch Is Which? 6015(F)
While No One Was Watching, 8607(F)
While the Bear Sleeps, 9748(F)
While the Candles Burn, 9724(F)
While You Are Asleep, 3237(F)
While You Were Sleeping, 394(F)
While You're Waiting for the Food to Come, 18335
Whingdingdilly, 2570(F)
The Whipping Boy, 6844(F)
Whiskers, 18806
Whiskers and Rhymes, 856
A Whisper Is Quiet, 6475(F)
Whisper Whisper Jesse, Whisper Whisper Josh, 5051(F)
The Whispering Room, 11544
Whispers down the Lane, 8475(F)
Whistle for Willie, 4016(F)
Whistling the Morning In, 11976
Whistling Thorn, 4629
The White Archer, 11206
The White Cat, 10498(F)
The White Curtain, 1000(F)
The White Deer, 10512(F)
The White Dove, 6765(F)
White Dynamite and Curly Kidd, 2958(F)
White Fang, 7260(F)
White Grizzly, 9362(F)
The White House, 16688, 16728, 16734
The White House Kids, 12638
The White Mountains, 10160(F)
White on Black, 197(F)
White Rabbit's Color Book, 260(F)
White Snow, Blue Feather, 4419(F)
White Snow Bright Snow, 3458(F)
White Socks Only, 4624(F)
White-Tailed Deer, 19153
White Tiger, Blue Serpent, 10770
White Wash, 5074(F)
White Water, 7011(F)
White Wolf, 7161(F)
Whiteblack the Penguin Sees the World, 2625(F)
Whitefish Will Rides Again! 4363(F)
Whitetail Magic for Kids, 19159
Whitney Houston, 12404
Who Am I? 17211
Who Are They? 199(F)
Who Are You? 6994(F)
Who Ate It? 3175(F)
Who Belongs Here? 17570
Who Bop? 2399(F)
Who Builds? 5595(F)
Who Built the Ark? 14260
Who Came Down That Road? 3291(F)
Who Comes with Cannons? 9465(F)
Who Digs? 5596(F)
Who Do You Love? 800(F)
Who Drives This? 1501(F)
Who Eats What? 18590

Who Has Time for Little Bear? 2662(F)
Who Hid It? 3175(F)
Who Hoots? 5177(F)
Who Hops? 1998(F)
Who Is a Stranger and What Should I Do? 17704
Who Is Baseball's Greatest Hitter? 22102
Who Is in the Garden? 4521
Who Is the Beast? 1781(F)
Who Is the World For? 1487(F)
Who Keeps the Water Clean? Ms. Schindler! 17824
Who Kidnapped the Sheriff? 9796(F)
Who Killed Cock Robin? 6998(F)
Who Knew There'd Be Ghosts? 6776(F)
Who Made Me? 1627(F)
Who Ordered the Jumbo Shrimp? 14022
Who Pretends? 1501(F)
Who Put the Cannon in the Courthouse Square? 14547
Who Really Discovered America? 16084
Who Said Boo? 11827
Who Said Red? 288(F)
Who Said That? 12640
Who Says a Dog Goes Bow-Wow? 5182
Who Settled the West? 16328
Who Shot the President? 13060
Who Shrank My Grandmother's House? 11558
Who Stole the Cookies? 6536(F)
Who Stole the Gold? 2830(F)
Who Stole the Wizard of Oz? 6756(F)
Who Took the Cookies from the Cookie Jar? 2345(F)
Who Took the Farmer's Hat? 6545(F)
Who Uses This? 3326
Who Wakes Rooster? 5345(F)
Who Wants a Cheap Rhinoceros? 2691(F)
Who Wants One? 580(F)
Who Was Born This Special Day? 5770(F)
Who Was That Masked Man, Anyway? 9643(F)
Who Were They Really? The True Stories Behind Famous Characters, 14004
Whoever You Are, 3630(F)
A Whole New Ball Game, 22106
The Whole World in Your Hands, 14362
Whoo-oo Is It? 5324(F)
Whooo's Haunting the Teeny Tiny Ghost? 6063(F)
Whoopi Goldberg, 12389
Whoppers, 11382
Who's a Pest? 6215(F)
Who's Afraid? And Other Strange Stories, 7007(F)
Who's Afraid of the Dark? 6216(F)
Who's Afraid of the Ghost Train? 5060(F)

Who's Been Sleeping in My Porridge? 11898
Who's Counting? 593(F)
Who's for Dinner? 18837
Who's Going to Take Care of Me? 5025(F)
Who's Got Spots? 20577
Who's in My Bed? 2583(F)
Who's in the Hall? A Mystery in Four Chapters, 6883(F)
Who's Orp's Girlfriend? 9904(F)
Who's Sick Today? 1954(F)
Who's That Banging on the Ceiling? 1378(F)
Who's There? 8150(F)
Who's Who in My Family? 3767(F)
Who's Whose? 3828(F)
Whose Feet? 5390(F)
Whose Mouse Are You? 2323(F)
Whose Nose? 5390(F)
Whose Side Are You On? 8766(F)
Whose Tracks Are These? 18839
Whump, 647(F)
Whuppity Stoorie, 11044
Why? 1033(F)
Why a Disguise? 4254(F)
Why Alligator Hates Dog, 11372
Why Are Pineapples Prickly? 20158
Why Are There Waves? 19851
Why Are You Calling Me a Barbarian? 14738
Why Are You Fighting, Davy? 2842(F)
Why Are Zebras Black and White? 20877
Why Benny Barks, 6522(F)
Why Did the Chicken Cross the Road? 21820(F)
Why Did We Have to Move Here? 4943(F)
Why Do Cats Meow? 19924
Why Do Dogs Bark? 19951
Why Do Dogs Do That? 19978
Why Do Leaves Change Color? 20210
Why Do Seasons Change? 18575
Why Do Stars Twinkle? 4516
Why Do Volcanoes Blow Their Tops? 20333
Why Do Volcanoes Erupt? 20356
Why Do We Celebrate That? 17407
Why Do We Do That? 17637
Why Do We Use That? 21063
Why Do We Wear That? 21168
Why Do You Love Me? 3522(F) (Illus. by Paul Meisel), 3881(F)
Why Do You Speak as You Do? 13980
Why Does Popcorn Pop? and Other Kitchen Questions, 20125
Why Does That Man Have Such a Big Nose? 3371(F)
Why Does the Cat Do That? 19916
Why Doesn't My Floppy Disk Flop? 21195
Why Doesn't the Earth Fall Up? 20823
Why Don't Haircuts Hurt? 18050
Why Don't You Get a Horse, Sam Adams? 12837
Why Frogs Are Wet, 18725

Why Goats Smell Bad and Other Stories from Benin, 10694
Why I Sneeze, Shiver, Hiccup, and Yawn, 18049
Why I Will Never Ever Ever Ever Have Enough Time to Read This Book, 4106(F)
Why Is Soap So Slippery? 3379
Why Is the Sky Blue? 2156(F)
Why Lapin's Ears Are Long and Other Tales from the Louisiana Bayou, 11335
Why Leopard Has Spots, 10710
Why Mosquitoes Buzz in People's Ears, 10644
Why Not? (Illus. by Friso Henstra), 3219(F)
(Illus. by Mary Wormell), 2880(F)
Why Not, Lafayette? 13825
Why on This Night? A Passover Haggadah for Family Celebration, 17479
Why Rat Comes First, 1708(F)
Why Save the Rain Forest? 20488
Why Snails Have Shells, 10754
Why So Sad, Brown Rabbit? 1911(F)
Why the Banana Split, 4347(F)
Why the Cat Chose Us, 19935
Why the Chicken Crossed the Road, 2406(F)
Why the Frog Has Big Eyes, 6336(F)
Why the Possum's Tail Is Bare, 11224
Why the Sea Is Salty, 11123
Why the Tides Ebb and Flow, 1007(F)
Wibbly Pig Can Make a Tent, 2241(F)
Wibbly Pig Is Happy! 2241(F)
Wibbly Pig Likes Bananas, 2241(F)
Wibbly Pig Opens His Presents, 2241(F)
Wicked Jack, 11391
The Wicked Stepdog, 8561(F)
The Wicked Witch Is at It Again, 7880(F)
Wide Awake! 797(F)
The Wide-Awake Princess, 10474(F)
The Wide-Mouthed Frog, 2087(F)
The Wide Window, 7069(F)
The Widow's Broom, 1643(F)
Wiggle-Butts and Up-Faces, 4999(F)
Wiggle Waggle, 5317(F)
The Wigwam and the Longhouse, 16074
Wilbur's Space Machine, 974(F)
Wild About Animals, 18957
Wild and Crafty, 21458
Wild and Swampy, 20363
Wild Animals, 21599
Wild Baby Animals, 18881
Wild Bill Hickok, 12900
Wild Blood, 8144(F)
Wild Boars, 18959
The Wild Boy, 4663
Wild Cats, 19091
Wild Child, 762(F)
Wild Children, 17619
The Wild Christmas Reindeer, 5760(F)
The Wild Colorado, 16087

Wild Country, 11955
Wild Dogs, 19123
Wild Flamingos, 19255
Wild Fox, 19132
The Wild Horse Family Book, 19999
Wild Horse Summer, 8804(F)
Wild Horses, 5389
Wild Horses I Have Known, 20014
The Wild Kid, 6971(F)
Wild Rosie, 3332(F)
The Wild Things, 5191(F)
Wild Turkeys, 19267
Wild Weather, 20695, 20696
The Wild West, 16299
Wild West Shows, 14266
Wild, Wet and Windy, 20780
Wild, Wild Hair, 6358(F)
Wild Wild Sunflower Child Anna, 4403(F)
Wild Wild West, 20384
Wild, Wild Wolves, 6532
Wild Will, 4041(F)
The Wild Woods, 5277(F)
Wildebeest, 1806(F)
The Wildebeest's Great Migration, 18979
Wildfire, 20366
Wildfires, 20362
Wildflower ABC, 114(F)
Wildflower Girl, 9089(F)
Wildflowers Around the Year, 20040
Wildlife, 18654
Wildlife Alert, 19412
The Wildlife Detectives, 18637
Wildlife of Mexico, 15619
Wildlife Special Agent, 17119
Wildlife Watching with Charles Eastman, 13268
Wildshots, 17769
Wiley and the Hairy Man, 11324
Wiley Learns to Spell, 6459(F)
Wilfrid Gordon McDonald Partridge, 3995(F)
Wilhe'mina Miles After the Stork Night, 3572(F)
The Will and the Way, 12311
Will Gets a Haircut, 4207(F)
Will Goes to the Beach, 3273(F)
Will Goes to the Post Office, 3274(F)
Will I Have a Friend? 5489(F)
Will It Ever Be My Birthday? 5676(F)
Will Rogers, 12457, 12458(F), 12459
Will There Be a Lap for Me? 3589(F)
Will You Be My Friend? 6691(F)
Will You Come Back for Me? 3920(F)
Will You Mind the Baby, Davy? 2843(F)
Will You Sign Here, John Hancock? 12896
Will You Take Care of Me? 1862(F)
Will You, Won't You? 8676(F)
Willa's New World, 6820(F)
William and the Good Old Days, 3664(F)
William and the Night Train, 1295(F)
William Boeing, 12853
William Bradford, 12856, 12857
William Harvey, 13307
William Henry Harrison, 13041

William Howard Taft, 13105
William McKinley, 13080
William Marshal, 13834
William Parker, 9318(F)
William Penn, 12945
William Seward, 12961
William Shakespeare, 12053, 12592, 12593
William Shakespeare and the Globe, 12590
William Shakespeare's Macbeth, 12048
William Shakespeare's Romeo and Juliet, 12049
William Sidney Mount, 12271
William Tecumseh Sherman, 12963
William Tell, 10855, 10857
William the Conqueror, 13868
William the Curious, 2652(F)
William's Doll, 3976(F)
William's House, 9200(F)
Williamsburg, 16128, 16147
Willie and the Rattlesnake King, 6794(F)
Willie Jerome, 3611(F)
Willie Mays, 13473
Willie Takes a Hike, 2611(F)
Willie, the Frog Prince, 8553(F)
Willie Was Different, 2633(F)
Willie's Birthday, 6687(F)
Williwaw, 6773(F)
Willow Chase, 9358(F)
Willow King, 7287(F)
The Willow Pattern Story, 1138(F)
The Willow Umbrella, 4560(F)
Will's Choice, 9423(F)
Will's Mammoth, 929(F)
Willy and May, 5916(F)
Willy and the Cardboard Boxes, 1008(F)
Willy the Dreamer, 1897(F)
Willy's Pictures, 9790(F)
Willy's Silly Grandma, 4125(F)
Wilma Mankiller, 12976, 12977, 12978
Wilma Rudolph, 13671, 13673
  (Illus. by Larry Johnson), 13672
Wilma Unlimited, 13670
Wilson Sat Alone, 4005(F)
The Wilsons, a House-Painting Team, 3144
Wimbledon, 22312
The Wimp, 1921(F)
Win or Lose by How You Choose! 17632
Wind and People, 20665
Wind and Weather, 20796
The Wind at Work, 20841
Wind Child, 10467(F)
Wind in the Door, 10207(F)
The Wind in the Willows, 7755(F)
  (Illus. by Patrick Benson), 7754(F)
  (Illus. by E. H. Shepard), 7753(F)
Wind in the Willows, 2144(F)
A Wind in the Willows Christmas, 9725(F)
Wind Says Good Night, 769(F)
The Wind Singer, 7990(F)
The Wind Wagon, 9303(F)
Windcatcher, 6757(F)
The Windhover, 5143(F)

The Windigo's Return, 11320
Window, 3005(F)
Window Music, 3909(F)
A Window of Time, 3769(F)
Window of Time, 8194(F)
Window on the West, 12242
Window Washer, 17751
Windsong, 7209(F)
Windsongs and Rainbows, 4369(F)
Windsurfing, 22303
The Windy Day, 3257(F)
The Wing Shop, 1706(F)
The Winged Cat, 8969(F)
The Winged Colt of Casa Mia, 7639(F)
Wings, 7627(F), 11495(F)
Wings Around the World, 21109
Wings, Stings and Wriggly Things, 18639
The Winking, Blinking Sea, 19623
Winking, Blinking, Wiggling, and Waggling, 18836
Winners of the Heisman Trophy, 13367
Winnie All Day Long, 5404(F)
Winnie Flies Again, 4337(F)
Winnie Plays Ball, 5404(F)
Winnie-the-Pooh's ABC, 132(F)
Winning, 10267(F)
Winning Chess, 22173
A Winning Edge, 13679
Winning Every Day, 13701
Winning Volleyball for Girls, 21990
Winona Ryder, 12462
Winston Churchill, 13769, 13770
Winter Across America, 18572
Winter Camp, 6895(F)
A Winter Concert, 2751(F)
A Winter Day, 4431(F)
The Winter Day, 2309(F)
Winter Eyes, 11949
The Winter Gift, 5960(F)
The Winter Hare, 9095(F)
Winter Holding Spring, 8627(F)
Winter Holiday, 7016(F)
Winter Lullaby, 18904
The Winter Mittens, 961(F)
The Winter of Red Snow, 9236(F)
The Winter Olympics, 22244
Winter Poems, 11981
Winter Rabbit, 2884(F)
Winter Rescue, 7105(F)
The Winter Solstice, 18568
Winter Waits, 1483(F)
The Winter Worm Business, 10062(F)
The Winter Wren, 1068(F)
Wintering, 8931(F)
A Winter's Tale, 2982(F)
Wisconsin, 16534, 16536
The Wisdom Bird, 17312(F)
The Wisdom of the Crows and Other Buddhist Tales, 10720
Wisdom Tales from Around the World, 10549
The Wise Old Woman, 10834
The Wise Shoemaker of Studena, 4736(F)
The Wise Washerman, 10725
Wise Words of Paul Tiulana, 16812
The Wish, 7909(F)

Wish for a Fish, 19653
The Wish Giver, 7624(F)
The Wish Master, 8870(F)
Wish Me Luck, 9663(F)
Wish You Were Here, 8544(F), 15889
Wish You Were Here (And I Wasn't), 11899
Wishbones, 10773
Wishes, Kisses, and Pigs, 7788(F)
Wishes, Wings, and Other Things, 11706
Wishing on a Star, 8293(F)
Witch Hunt, 16150
Witch Mama, 5989(F)
The Witch of Blackbird Pond, 9213(F)
The Witch of Fourth Street and Other Stories, 7468(F)
Witch Poems, 11732
Witch Way to the Beach, 1393(F)
Witch Week, 7847(F)
The Witch Who Lives Down the Hall, 1213(F)
The Witch Who Was Afraid of Witches, 9746(F)
The Witchcraft of Salem Village, 16138
The Witcher, 8949(F)
The Witches, 7698(F)
Witches and Witch-Hunts, 14564
Witches Four, 1016(F)
The Witches of Worm, 8916(F)
The Witches' Supermarket, 6033(F)
The Witch's Portraits, 7975(F)
The Witch's Revenge, 5999(F)
Witcracks, 21851
With a Dog Like That, a Kid Like Me . . ., 1523(F)
With a Whoop and a Holler, 11388
With All My Heart, With All My Mind, 7332(F)
With Love, 18996
With Love from Gran, 3638(F)
With Love, to Earth's Endangered Peoples, 17571
With Needle and Thread, 21641
With One White Wing, 21854
With Open Hands, 12769
With the Wind, 22199
With the Wind, Kevin Dolan, 9414(F)
Without Wings, Mother, How Can I Fly? 3620(F)
Wizard and Wart at Sea, 6669(F)
Wizard and Wart in Trouble, 6670(F)
The Wizard in the Tree, 7555(F)
The Wizard in the Woods, 8164(F)
Wizard in Wonderland, 8165(F)
The Wizard King and Other Spell-binding Tales, 10584
The Wizard of Oz (Illus. by Michael Hague), 7596(F)
  (Illus. by Michael Hague), 7598(F)
  (Illus. by Charles Santore), 7597(F)
  (Illus. by Lisbeth Zwerger), 989(F)
The Wizard of Sound, 13272
The Wizard, the Fairy and the Magic Chicken, 1349(F)
Wizard's Hall, 8242(F)
The Wizard's Map, 8243(F)

Wizzil, 1594(F)
WKID, 12009(F)
WNBA, 22143
A Woggle of Witches, 5980(F)
The Wolf, 19133
Wolf, 1606(F)
Wolf! 1818(F)
The Wolf and the Seven Little Kids, 10913
A Wolf at the Door, 10414(F)
Wolf Child, 8958(F)
Wolf Christmas, 5899(F)
The Wolf Gang, 9928(F)
The Wolf Is Coming! 2422(F)
Wolf Pack, 19126
Wolf Shadows, 6789(F)
Wolf Songs, 765(F)
Wolf Stalker, 7063(F)
Wolf Tower, 7898(F)
Wolf Watch, 5457(F)
Wolfgang Amadeus Mozart, 12335
Wolfman Sam, 7469(F)
The Wolf's Lunch, 2037(F)
Wolof, 15046
The Wolves, 19122
Wolves, 19119, 19120, 19124, 19128
Wolves and Their Relatives, 19141
The Wolves of Willoughby Chase, 6740(F)
The Woman Who Fell from the Sky, 11214
The Woman Who Flummoxed the Fairies, 10976
The Woman Who Outshone the Sun, 11135
Wombat Divine, 5817(F)
Wombat Goes Walkabout, 2510(F)
Women at the Front, 16393
Women Chosen for Public Office, 12682
Women Explorers of the Air, 12061
Women Explorers of the Mountains, 12062
Women Explorers of the World, 12063
Women in a Changing World, 14588
Women in Ancient Egypt, 14640
Women in Ancient Greece, 14692
Women in Ancient Rome, 14730
Women in Medicine, 13215
Women in Medieval Times, 14780
Women in 19th-Century America, 15855
Women in 19th-Century Europe, 14589
Women in Peace and War, 14588
Women in Space, 20963
Women in the Civil War, 16429
Women in the Marines, 21404
Women of Hope, 12655
The Women of Pro Wrestling, 21968
Women of the Frontier, 16381
Women of the West, 16330
Women of the Wild West, 12669, 12688
Women Pirates, 12070
Women Warriors, 10586
Womenfolk and Fairy Tales, 10592
Women's Voting Rights, 17032
Wonder Book and Tanglewood Tales, 11478

The Wonder Clock, 10483(F)
Wonder Kid Meets the Evil Lunch Snatcher, 10051(F)
The Wonder of a Waterfall, 20369
Wonder Tales from Around the World, 10550
Wonder Women of Sports, 13385
The Wonder Worm Wars, 8778(F)
Wonderful Alexander and the Catwings, 7901(F)
The Wonderful Flight to the Mushroom Planet, 10158(F)
The Wonderful Story of Henry Sugar and Six More, 7699(F)
The Wonderful Wizard of Oz, 7601(F)
   (Illus. by W. W. Denslow), 7599(F)
   (Illus. by W. W. Denslow), 7600(F)
Wonderful Worms, 19607
Wonders, 11941
Wonders of Mexico, 15611
Wonders of Rivers, 20511
Wonders of the Ancient World, 14582
Wonders of the Desert, 20417
Wonders of the Forest, 20482
Wonders of the Pond, 20482
Wonders of the Sea, 19836
Wonders of the Seasons, 4392(F)
Woo! The Not-So-Scary Ghost, 1335(F)
Wood, 20205
A Wood Frog's Life, 18727
Woodland Animals, 21600
Woodland Christmas, 14217
Woodlore, 20211
Woodpecker in the Backyard, 19257
Woodpeckers, 19253, 19299
Woodrow Wilson, 13121, 13122, 13123
Woodrow Wilson, Franklin D. Roosevelt, Harry S. Truman, 12675
Woods, Ponds, and Fields, 18583
Woodsie, 10291(F)
Wool, 21170
Woolly Sheep and Hungry Goats, 20055
The Word Eater, 7559(F)
Word Play ABC, 18(F)
Word Wizard, 179(F)
A Wordful Child, 12567
Words and Pictures, 6309(F)
Words by Heart, 9624(F)
Words in Our Hands, 5015(F)
Words of Gold, 17331
Words That Built a Nation, 15894
Words with Wings, 11769
Work, 217
The Workers' Detective, 13306
Working, 930(F)
Working at a Marine Institute, 17843
Working at a Museum, 17755
Working at a Zoo, 17850
Working Children, 15856
Working Cotton, 3476(F)
Working in Health Care and Wellness, 17801
Working in Music, 17775
Working in Sports and Recreation, 17754

Working Together Against Drinking and Driving, 17865
Working Together Against Gang Violence, 17088
Working Together Against Homelessness, 17146
Working with Animals, 17852
Workshop, 3073
Worksong, 3359(F)
The World, 14359
The World According to Horses, 19989
The World at Her Fingertips, 13165
The World at His Fingertips, 13761
The World Beyond the Waves, 7857(F)
World Famous Muriel and the Magic Mystery, 6188(F)
World Holidays, 17207
The World in Grandfather's Hands, 8528(F)
The World in Your Backyard, 19501
The World of Architectural Wonders, 21118
The World of Castles and Forts, 21381
The World of Christopher Robin, 11654
The World of Computers and Communications, 21203
The World of Dance, 14274
A World of Holidays! 17347
The World of Insects, 19499
The World of King Arthur and His Court, 10965
A World of Knowing, 12885
The World of Native Americans, 14518
The World of Pooh, 7963(F)
The World of the Medieval Knight, 14764
The World of the Pharaoh, 14646
The World of the Pirate, 14549
A World of Things to Do, 21514
The World of William Joyce Scrapbook, 13959
A World of Words, 138
The World Today, 14587
The World Trade Center Bombing, 16738
A World Treasury of Myths, Legends, and Folktales, 10534
The World Turned Upside Down, 16195
The World Turns Round and Round, 3472(F)
World War I, 14808
World War II, 14810, 14852
World War II Days, 14859
World War II in Europe, 14883
World War II in the Pacific, 14884
A World War Two Submarine, 21390
World Water Watch, 4475
The World Wide Web, 21212, 21215
The World's Best Sports Riddles and Jokes, 21849
The World's Birthday, 6075(F)
The World's Most Famous Ghosts, 21901
Worlds of Belief, 17220

World's Toughest Tongue Twisters, 21884
The World's Worst Fairy Godmother, 7682(F)
Wormology, 19620
Worm's Eye View, 18323
The Worry Stone, 11228
The Worry Week, 6948(F)
Worry Worts, 8436(F)
The Worrywarts, 2057(F)
Worse Than Rotten, Ralph, 2111(F)
Worse Than the Worst, 4331(F)
Worse Than Willy! 786(F)
The Worst Band in the Universe, 10150(F)
The Worst Day of My Life, 4934(F)
The Worst Goes South, 2730(F)
The Worst Kid Who Ever Lived on Eighth Avenue, 6446(F)
The Worst Witch, 7977(F)
The Worst Witch Strikes Again, 7977(F)
Worth the Risk, 17605
Would My Fortune Cookie Lie? 8509(F)
Would They Love a Lion? 1110(F)
Wounded Knee, 16015, 16066
Wow! Babies! 3646(F)
Wow Canada! Exploring This Land from Coast to Coast to Coast, 15567
Wow! It's Great Being a Duck, 2613(F)
Wrango, 9349(F)
Wrapped in a Riddle, 6884(F)
Wrapper Rockets and Trombone Straws, 18350
Wrapping Paper Romp, 3225(F)
The Wrath of the Grinning Ghost, 8137(F)
The Wreck of the Ethie, 6906(F)
The Wreck of the Zephyr, 8168(F)
The Wreckers, 9106(F), 9107(F)
Wrecks of American Warships, 21357
Wren's War, 8109(F)
Wrestling, 21996
The Wretched Stone, 1644(F)
The Wright Brothers, 13355, 13356, 13357, 13358
Wringer, 8824(F)
A Wrinkle in Time, 10207(F)
Write a Book for Me, 12547
Write Me If You Dare! 8712(F)
Writer of the Plains, 12516
Writers in the Kitchen, 21699
A Writer's Story from Life to Fiction, 12506
Writing, 13979, 14098
The Writing Bug, 12549
Writing for Freedom, 13143
Writing Mysteries, Movies, Monster Stories, and More, 14068
Writing to Richie, 8588(F)
Writing with Style, 14117
The Wrong Overcoat, 2554(F)
The Wump World, 4506(F)
Wuzzy Takes Off, 2367(F)
Wyatt Earp, 12874
Wynken, Blynken, and Nod, 674
Wynton Marsalis, 12420, 12421

Wyoming, 16602, 16610, 16612, 16621

X-15 Rocket Plane, 21099
The X-Ray Picture Book of Big Buildings of the Ancient World, 14586
Xhosa, 14983

Yang the Eldest and His Odd Jobs, 7488(F)
Yang the Second and Her Secret Admirers, 8496(F)
Yang the Third and Her Impossible Family, 8497(F)
The Yangtze, 15078
Yanked! 10205(F)
Yankee Doodle, 14193
Yann and the Whale, 1171(F)
Yanni Rubbish, 4787(F)
Yard Sale, 4332(F)
Yard Sale! 1419(F)
Yay! 4284(F)
The Year Around, 11956
A Year Down Yonder, 7492(F)
A Year for Kiko, 3485(F)
A Year in the City, 4458(F)
The Year Mom Won the Pennant, 10312(F)
The Year of Fire, 3718(F)
Year of Impossible Goodbyes, 8987(F)
The Year of Miss Agnes, 10075(F)
Year of the Black Pony, 7269(F)
The Year of the Panda, 7303(F)
The Year of the Sawdust Man, 8471(F)
The Year of the Worm, 7013(F)
A Year on Monhegan Island, 16664
Year-Round Programs for Young Players, 12019
A Year with Butch and Spike, 10061(F)
The Year with Grandma Moses, 13961
A Year with Molly and Emmett, 4173(F)
A Year Without Rain, 9588(F)
The Year You Were Born, 1986, 17390
Yearbooks in Science, 18271, 18272, 18279, 18284, 18285, 18288, 18291
The Yearling, 7289(F)
Yeh-Shen, 10764
Yellow Ball, 3008(F)
Yellow Bird and Me, 8298(F)
Yellow Blue Jay, 8705(F)
Yellow Fairy Book, 10442(F)
The Yellow Star, 9652(F)
The Yellow Train, 1238(F)
Yellowjackets, 19526
Yellowstone National Park, 16629, 16635
Yellowstone's Cycle of Fire, 16639
Yemen, 15549
Yemen in Pictures, 15561
The Yeoman's Daring Daughter and the Princes in the Tower, 9087(F)
Yertle the Turtle and Other Stories, 2675(F)

Yes, We Have Bananas, 20146
Yettele's Feathers, 11164
Yikes — Lice! 17946
Yikes! Your Body, Up Close, 18063
Yippee-Yay! 16307
Yo, Aesop! Get a Load of These Fables, 9979(F)
Yo, Alejandro, 12830
Yo! Yes? 4036(F)
A Yoga Parade of Animals, 18200
Yoko, 4058(F)
Yoland's Yellow School, 3001(F)
Yolonda's Genius, 7430(F)
Yoo Hoo, Moon! 6210(F)
Yorktown, 16219
Yoruba, 15011
The Yoruba of West Africa, 15029
Yoshiko and the Foreigner, 4739(F)
Yoshi's Feast, 10817
You and Me, 163(F), 11652
You and Me, Little Bear, 2803(F)
You Are Here, 1088(F)
You Are My Perfect Baby, 3453(F)
You Are the Explorer, 14326
You Can Be a Woman Astronomer, 17825
You Can Be a Woman Basketball Player, 22129
You Can Be a Woman Soccer Player, 22302
You Can Be a Woman Softball Player, 13450
You Can Call Me Willy, 5094(F)
You Can Draw Fantastic Animals, 21565
You Can Go Home Again, 4765(F)
You Can Jump Higher on the Moon and Other Amazing Facts About Space Exploration, 21005
You Can Learn Sign Language! 14016
You Can Say "NO" to Drugs, 17893
You Can Surf the Net! 21202
You Can't Catch Me, 1132(F)
You Can't Eat Your Chicken Pox, Amber Brown, 9828(F)
You Can't Smell a Flower with Your Ear! 18140
You Can't Take a Balloon into The Metropolitan Museum, 938(F)
You Can't Take a Balloon into the National Gallery, 4875(F)
You Choose, 221(F)
You Come Too, 11570
You Don't Get a Carrot Unless You're a Bunny, 6030(F)
You Don't Need Words! 14013
You Forgot Your Skirt, Amelia Bloomer! 4627(F)
You Go Away, 3083(F)
You Gotta Try This! 18309
You Look Ridiculous, Said the Rhinoceros to the Hippopotamus, 2793(F)
You Mean I Have to Stand Up and Say Something? 14077
You Never Know, 11161
You Read to Me, I'll Read to You, 11864
You Shouldn't Have to Say Goodbye, 8452(F)

You Silly Goose, 2819(F)
You Smell, 18149
You Want Women to Vote, Lizzie Stanton? 13192
You Were Born on Your Very First Birthday, 18240
Youch! 18618
You'll Grow Soon, Alex, 5076(F)
You'll Soon Grow into Them, Titch, 3713(F)
Young Abe Lincoln, 13070
The Young Actor's Book of Improvisation, 14322
Young Arthur, 11032
Young Arthur Ashe, 13643
The Young Astronomer, 18389
The Young Author's Do-It-Yourself Book, 14087
The Young Baseball Player, 22117
The Young Basketball Player, 22139
Young Brer Rabbit, 11445
Young Cam Jansen and the Baseball Mystery, 6179(F)
Young Cam Jansen and the Dinosaur Game, 6180(F)
Young Cam Jansen and the Ice Skate Mystery, 6181(F)
Young Cam Jansen and the Missing Cookie, 6182(F)
Young Cam Jansen and the Pizza Shop Mystery, 6183(F)
Young Claus, 8094(F)
The Young Dancer, 14277
The Young Equestrian, 22200
Young Explorer's Guide to Undersea Life, 19622
The Young Fishing Enthusiast, 22174
Young Frederick Douglass, 12710, 12715
Young Fu of the Upper Yangtze, 9001(F)
Young George Washington, 13120
The Young Golfer, 22063
The Young Gymnast, 22195
The Young Ice Skater, 22225, 22226
The Young Inline Skater, 21999
Young Jesus of Nazareth, 17307
Young John Quincy, 13004
The Young Journalist's Book, 14086
Young Larry, 2589(F)
The Young Life of Mother Teresa of Calcutta, 13856
The Young Life of Pope John Paul II, 13816
The Young Martial Arts Enthusiast, 22270
Young Mary of Nazareth, 17308
Young Mouse and Elephant, 10665
The Young Musician's Survival Guide, 17778
The Young Oxford Book of Aliens, 10250(F)
The Young Oxford Book of Astronomy, 18402
The Young Oxford Book of Folk Tales, 10634
The Young Oxford Book of Nasty Endings, 7142(F)
A Young Painter, 12315
A Young Patriot, 16207

Young People and Chronic Illness, 17966
Young People's Letters to the President, 17113
A Young Person's Guide to Music, 14119
The Young Person's Guide to Shakespeare, 12050
The Young Person's Guide to the Ballet, 14285
The Young Person's Guide to the Orchestra, 14221
The Young Producer's Video Book, 21265
Young Reggie Jackson, 13463
The Young Republic, 16282
The Young Rider, 22203
Young Rosa Parks, 12774
The Young Scientist Book of Jets, 21080
The Young Scientist Book of Stars and Planets, 18398
The Young Snowboarder, 22281
The Young Soccer Player, 22297
Young Superstars of Tennis, 13655
The Young Swimmer, 22309
Young Teddy Roosevelt, 13102
The Young Tennis Player, 22316
Young Thurgood Marshall, 12764
The Young Track and Field Athlete, 22318
The Young Zillionaire's Guide to Distributing Goods and Services, 16930
The Young Zillionaire's Guide to Investments and Savings, 16922
The Young Zillionaire's Guide to Supply and Demand, 16928
The Young Zillionaire's Guide to the Stock Market, 16921
The Younger Brothers, 12651
The Youngest Fairy Godmother Ever, 1321(F)
Your Allowance, 16943
Your Body, 17694
Your Body Belongs to You, 17733
Your Chickens, 20050
Your Dad Was Just Like You, 3732(F)
Your Family, My Family, 17651
Your Foot's on My Feet! 14053
Your Goats, 20051
Your Guinea Pig, 19884
Your Insides, 18053
Your Move, 8578(F)
Your Name Is Renée, 14842
Your Puppy, Your Dog, 19975
Your Skin and Mine, 18180
Your Tongue Can Tell, 18138
Your Travel Guide to Ancient Egypt, 14619
Your Travel Guide to Ancient Greece, 14677
Your Travel Guide to Ancient Mayan Civilization, 15661
Your Travel Guide to Civil War America, 16401
Your Travel Guide to Colonial America, 16108
Your Travel Guide to Renaissance Europe, 14797

Your World, 18295
You're a Brave Man, Julius Zimmerman, 9939(F)
You're a Genius, Blackboard Bear, 617(F)
You're a Little Kid with a Big Heart, 1656(F)
You're Aboard Spaceship Earth, 20312
You're Dead, David Borelli, 8406(F)
You're in Big Trouble, Brad! 6557(F)
You're Just What I Need, 3754(F)
You're My Nikki, 3614(F)
You're Not My Best Friend Anymore, 4035(F)
You're On! Seven Plays in English and Spanish, 12017
You're Somebody Special, Walliwigs! 2614(F)
You're the Boss, Baby Duck! 2202(F)
You're the Scaredy-Cat, 5028(F)
You're Too Sweet, 17951
Yours Truly, Goldilocks, 943(F)
Yuck! 19812
Yuck, a Love Story, 1191(F)
Yucka Drucka Droni, 4280(F)
Yudonsi, 3029(F)
Yukon Gold, 16792
Yukon River, 15588
Yum! 2452(F)
Yum, Yum, Yummy, 2804(F)
Yummers! 2476(F)
Yummers Too, 2477(F)
Yummy! Eating Through a Day, 11746
Yunmi and Halmoni's Trip, 4620(F)

Z Is for Zombie, 6023(F)
The Z Was Zapped, 14056
Z-Z-Zoink! 2515(F)
Za-Za's Baby Brother, 1981(F)
Zachary Taylor, 13106, 13107
Zachary's Ball, 1612(F)
Zack's Story, 17658
Zak, 2371(F)
Zak's Lunch, 1451(F)
Zambia, 14987
The Zaniest Riddle Book in the World, 21850
Zap! I'm a Mind Reader, 7758(F)
Zap It! 20897
Zeb, the Cow's on the Roof Again! 9256(F)
Zebra, 18922
Zebra Talk, 5442(F)
The Zebra Wall, 7448(F)
Zebras, 18941
Zebra's Hiccups, 2442(F)
Zebulon Pike, 12147
Zeely, 8682(F)
Zelda and Ivy, 2327(F)
Zelda and Ivy and the Boy Next Door, 2328(F)
Zelda and Ivy One Christmas, 5861(F)
Zella, Zack, and Zodiac, 2571(F)
Zenj, Buganda, 14962
Zero Gravity, 20815
Zia, 6997(F)

The Zieglers and Their Apple Orchard, 17749

Ziggy Piggy and the Three Little Pigs, 10944

Zimani's Drum, 10690

Zimbabwe, 14988, 15002

Zimbabwe in Pictures, 15007

Zin! Zin! Zin! A Violin, 14227(F)

Zina Garrison, 13648

Zink, 8877(F)

Zip, 10291(F)

Zipper, 8895(F)

Zipping, Zapping, Zooming Bats, 19023

Zlateh the Goat and Other Stories, 11175

Zoe and Her Zebra, 10(F)

Zoe Rising, 7666(F)

Zomo the Rabbit, 10693

Zoo Animals, 5200

Zoo Clues, 20024

Zoo Do's and Don'ts, 2560(F)

Zoo Dreams, 697(F)

Zoo in the Sky, 18549

Zoo-Looking, 5210(F)

Zoodles, 21843

A Zooful of Animals, 11774

Zookeeper Sue, 2019(F)

Zoom, 908(F)

Zoom Broom, 1452(F)

Zoom City (Illus. by Jonathan Adams), 13871

(Illus. by Thacher Hurd), 3233(F)

Zoom! Zoom! Zoom! I'm Off to the Moon, 1707(F)

Zooman Sam, 9927(F)

Zoos, 20031

Zoos Without Cages, 20030

Zora Hurston and the Chinaberry Tree, 3810

Zora Neale Hurston, 12553, 12554

Zorah's Magic Carpet, 1094(F)

Zorina Ballerina, 2121(F)

Zucchini Out West, 7181(F)

The Zucchini Warriors, 10096(F)

Zulu, 14992

Zulu Fireside Tales, 10712

Zzzng! Zzzng! Zzzng! A Yoruba Tale, 10667

Subject/Grade Level Index

All entries are listed by subject and then according to grade level suitability (see the key at the foot of pages for grade level designations). Subjects are arranged alphabetically and subject heads may be subdivided into nonfiction (e.g., "Trucks") and fiction (e.g. "Trucks — Fiction"). References to entries are by entry number, not page number.

A

Aardema, Verna
PI: 12487

Aardvarks — Fiction
P: 1873, 1877, 1879, 1884, 1887, 1891

Aaron, Hank
PI: 13430 I: 13431

Abbott, Jim
PI: 13433 I: 13432

Abdul, Paula
I: 12341 IJ: 12342

Abdul-Jabbar, Kareem
I: 13511

Abenaki Indians — Folklore
P: 11218 I: 11216

Abernathy, David
IJ: 12699

Abolitionists
I: 16255

Abolitionists — Biography
PI: 12862 I: 13143
IJ: 12793, 12894

Abolitionists — Fiction
IJ: 9306

Abominable snowman
See also Big Foot; Yeti
I: 21958 IJ: 21918

Aborigines — Art
IJ: 13889

Aborigines (Australia)
I: 15225, 15249

Aborigines (Australia) — Fiction
P: 4569

Accidents
P: 18220 I: 18215, 18226
IJ: 18218

Accidents — Fiction
I: 8610, 8670 IJ: 8439

Acid rain
I: 16995, 16999, 17004
IJ: 16996

Acropolis (Greece)
IJ: 14702

Acting
I: 14320

Action rhymes
P: 874

Activism
IJ: 17621

Actors and actresses — Biography
PI: 12354, 12364, 12388, 12396, 12398, 12401, 12416, 12423, 12439, 12448, 12452, 12461–62, 12468–69, 12479, 12482
I: 12387, 12389, 12426, 12450, 12457, 12459, 12480
IJ: 12177, 12363, 12366–67, 12373–74, 12405, 12409, 12415, 12419, 12434, 12438, 12449, 12454, 12463, 12833, 12854

Actors and actresses — Fiction
P: 4742 PI: 9806–7, 9812
I: 8640, 9553, 9890, 10076
IJ: 8149, 9080

Adams, Abigail
P: 13125 I: 13124

Adams, Ansel
I: 12187

Adams, John
P: 13003 I: 13002

Adams, John Quincy
PI: 13004 I: 13005–6

Adams, Louisa Catherine Johnson
I: 13126

Adams, Samuel
PI: 12837 IJ: 12836

Addams, Jane
IJ: 13127–29

Addictions
See also Alcoholism; Drugs and drug abuse
IJ: 17875

Addition
P: 523, 20583, 20592
PI: 20596

Adjectives
P: 14025

Adler, David A.
I: 12488

Adolescence
See also Puberty
I: 17184, 17620 IJ: 18249

Adolescence — Fiction
I: 8748

Adoption
P: 3786, 17675, 17690
I: 17672 IJ: 17649, 17664–65, 17683

Adoption — Fiction
P: 2853, 3555, 3563, 3600, 3625, 3650, 3745, 3751, 3755, 3776, 3812, 3815, 3836, 3923, 4735, 5033, 5047, 5068, 6414, 6463
PI: 1867 I: 8476, 8920, 9420, 17654 IJ: 7314, 7416, 8426, 8473, 10354

Adventure stories
See also Mystery stories; Survival stories

P: 1302, 1466–67, 1727, 1917, 2221, 2658, 2861, 2905–9, 2913, 2915–19, 2921, 2926, 2928–29, 2933, 2937, 2939, 2942, 2947, 2949, 2953–54, 2956–58, 2960, 2964, 2967, 2972–75, 2979, 2981–83, 2985–86, 4147, 4659, 4670, 4703, 4753, 4784, 4803, 5121, 5175, 5303, 5880, 6272, 6588, 6656, 6718, 6814, 6874, 6902, 6949, 7105, 10089 PI: 2922, 2941, 2951, 4726, 4858, 6728, 6766, 6802, 6865, 6877, 6888, 6920, 6928, 6958, 6980, 6999, 7078, 7104, 7135, 7145, 7806, 9249, 9280, 9307, 9316, 9329, 9417, 9514, 9518, 9567, 9597 I: 6741, 6746, 6749, 6769–70, 6772, 6786, 6788, 6791, 6797, 6816, 6823–25, 6833–34, 6841, 6846, 6850, 6856, 6868, 6875, 6878–79, 6913, 6916, 6919, 6921, 6940, 6952, 6955, 6968–69, 6971, 6985, 6988–89, 6993, 7001, 7004–6, 7011, 7015–16, 7030, 7034, 7039, 7052–54, 7057, 7068, 7076, 7082–83, 7086, 7093, 7095, 7098, 7100–2, 7108, 7112, 7128, 7233, 7251, 7799, 7855, 8006, 8008, 8241, 8940, 9004, 9044, 9084, 9108, 9123, 9210, 9246, 9269, 9273, 9311, 9314, 9364, 9425, 9429, 9433, 9574, 9607, 9674, 10194, 10232 IJ: 6739, 6742–45, 6753, 6757, 6760, 6765, 6768, 6771, 6773–74, 6779, 6787, 6789, 6794, 6800, 6806, 6808, 6820, 6826–27, 6831, 6840, 6842–44, 6848–49, 6853, 6855, 6857,

P = Primary; PI = Primary-Intermediate; I = Intermediate; IJ = Intermediate-Junior High

6871, 6876, 6880–81,
6885–86, 6896–98, 6900,
6905–7, 6909, 6915, 6918,
6922, 6925, 6934, 6941,
6948, 6951, 6954, 6957,
6970, 6975, 6982, 6995–97,
7002–3, 7008–9, 7013,
7018, 7020, 7027, 7035,
7041, 7051, 7058, 7065,
7067, 7069, 7077, 7087,
7092, 7094, 7096, 7099,
7106, 7113, 7120, 7124,
7126, 7136, 7144, 7150,
7175, 7368, 7724, 7818,
7822, 7836, 8015, 8078,
8137–38, 8145, 8177, 8656,
8775, 8933, 8939, 8941,
8945, 8949, 8955, 8993,
9023, 9030, 9048, 9086,
9102, 9106–7, 9129, 9156,
9158, 9183, 9187, 9194,
9228, 9271, 9274, 9284,
9286, 9299, 9330, 9341,
9344, 9378, 9473, 9486–87,
9502, 9509, 9528, 9536,
9543, 9559, 9663, 10007,
10152, 10277, 10504

**Adventurers and
explorers**
P: 4760 **PI:** 15818, 16076,
16091 **I:** 12060, 15798,
15842, 16090, 16095,
16352, 16380 **IJ:** 14326,
14569, 15795, 16082, 16094

**Adventurers and
explorers — Biography**
P: 12096, 12122, 12128
PI: 12057, 12065, 12081,
12095, 12099, 12115,
12131–32, 12134 **I:** 12056,
12058–59, 12063,
12068–69, 12071, 12075,
12082, 12098, 12101,
12104, 12109, 12111,
12120–21, 12125,
12140–41, 12146–48,
12150, 12152
IJ: 12086–87, 12097,
12100, 12105, 12113,
12116, 12133, 12144,
12149, 12151, 15840, 16081

**Adventurers and
explorers — Fiction**
PI: 9046

**Adventurers and
explorers — Women**
I: 12059, 12063

Advertising
IJ: 16934

Aeneid **(mythology)**
IJ: 11512

Aerobics
I: 18207

Aeronautics
See also Airplanes;
National Aeronautics
and Space
Administration

PI: 21083 **IJ:** 21078,
21080, 21101

**Aeronautics —
Experiments and
projects**
I: 21076 **IJ:** 21092

Aeronautics — Fiction
P: 6657

Aeronautics — History
PI: 21070, 21098 **I:** 21082
IJ: 21072, 21108

Afghanistan
I: 15145 **IJ:** 15144, 15146,
15154, 15157

Afghanistan — Fiction
P: 4712, 4756 **IJ:** 8992

Africa
See also specific countries
and regions, e.g.,
Ethiopia, East Africa
P: 351, 14909, 14914
PI: 13850 **I:** 14901, 14905,
14959 **IJ:** 14899–900,
14919, 14953, 15008, 15017

Africa — Animals
P: 5274, 14947, 20533
PI: 18633, 19075 **I:** 18607,
18631, 19107 **IJ:** 14970,
19165

**Africa — Animals —
Fiction**
P: 473, 5113

Africa — Anthropology
P: 10671 **IJ:** 14932

Africa — Art
IJ: 13935

Africa — Biography
P: 12128

Africa — Cookbooks
IJ: 21723, 21727

Africa — Crafts
PI: 21501 **IJ:** 14912,
21446

Africa — Fiction
P: 1261, 2717, 2737, 2907,
4388, 4630, 4636, 4671,
4683, 4710, 4717, 4755,
4783–84, 4849, 4872, 4880,
4887, 5135, 5146, 5274,
5366, 5442 **PI:** 4372, 4721,
4832, 5514, 8961, 8967,
8974 **I:** 8972, 8976, 8979
IJ: 8966, 8971

Africa — Folklore
P: 1664, 6492, 8973,
10638–42, 10644, 10647,
10651, 10657, 10661–67,
10671–73, 10675–77,
10679–80, 10684,
10686–87, 10692,
10695–97, 10699, 10701–3,
10705–8, 10711, 10713–15
PI: 10637, 10645, 10652,
10670, 10685, 10688–91,
10700, 10704, 10709, 10716

I: 10558, 10580, 10646,
10650, 10654, 10656,
10659, 10682–83, 10694,
10698, 10710, 12042
IJ: 10648–49, 10668, 11341

Africa — Geography
I: 14903

Africa — History
I: 14902, 14904, 14907–8,
14962 **IJ:** 14828, 14910,
14913, 14925, 15018,
15025, 15030, 15035, 15037

Africa — Holidays
I: 14906

Africa — Masks
I: 13936

Africa — Nursery rhymes
P: 897

Africa — Peoples
P: 13872, 15029, 15045
I: 14915 **IJ:** 14916–17,
14920, 14931, 14942,
14944–45, 14950, 14952,
14954–55, 14965, 14969,
14978, 14983, 14992–94,
15000, 15004–6, 15009,
15011–12, 15016, 15036,
15040–42, 15044, 15046

**Africa — Peoples —
Fiction**
P: 3804

Africa — Plants
P: 4629

Africa — Poetry
PI: 11722

Africa — Proverbs
P: 10655

Africa, East
See East Africa

African Americans
See also Africa; Civil
rights; Civil War (U.S.);
Kwanzaa; Slavery; and
names of individuals,
e.g., Robinson, Jackie
P: 3394, 3758, 12802,
14141 **PI:** 4694, 12740,
17037, 17042, 17663
I: 9443, 12720, 14906,
16231, 16240, 16260,
16366, 16524, 17029,
17046, 17048, 17538
IJ: 9325, 10261, 14876,
16257, 16266, 16298,
16412, 16498, 16523,
16895, 17040–41, 17052,
17541

**African Americans —
Armed forces**
IJ: 12723, 15869, 21401

African Americans — Art
IJ: 11769, 13951

**African Americans —
Biography**
P: 3672, 3810, 5610, 12090,
12093, 12126, 12345,
12379, 12708, 12722,
12739, 12748, 12752–53,
13213, 13235, 13254,
13257, 13371, 13474,
13487, 13664, 13669,
13672, 22133 **PI:** 4728,
12165, 12253, 12346–47,
12358, 12453, 12496,
12552, 12554, 12648,
12654, 12685, 12687,
12695, 12701–3, 12705,
12707, 12709–12, 12715,
12717, 12721, 12725,
12736, 12746–47, 12750,
12755, 12763–64,
12766–67, 12772–74,
12776–79, 12781,
12784–86, 12789, 12792,
12795, 12799, 12801,
12810, 12812–13,
12817–18, 12821, 12823,
12949, 12955, 13252,
13255, 13269, 13344,
13351, 13374, 13430,
13463, 13475–76, 13478,
13486, 13494, 13560,
13572, 13643, 13661,
13665, 13670 **I:** 12079–80,
12091–92, 12120–21,
12127, 12179–81, 12302,
12330–31, 12344, 12369,
12389, 12394, 12420–21,
12424, 12443, 12446–47,
12480, 12485–86, 12495,
12551, 12574, 12620–21,
12643–44, 12660–61,
12664, 12693–94, 12704,
12706, 12714, 12716,
12718–19, 12726–28,
12730, 12732–33, 12735,
12738, 12742–43, 12745,
12758–61, 12769–71,
12775, 12780, 12787,
12790, 12794, 12797–98,
12805–9, 12814, 12822,
12951–52, 13233, 13253,
13256, 13310, 13393,
13395, 13403, 13431,
13458, 13473, 13485,
13489, 13491–93, 13495,
13506–8, 13511, 13513,
13524–25, 13528, 13533,
13536, 13539, 13541,
13547, 13556–57,
13570–71, 13579, 13582,
13605, 13615, 13624–26,
13629, 13633, 13635,
13648, 13660, 13667–68,
13671, 13673, 13709
IJ: 12139, 12167, 12184,
12186, 12231, 12241,
12252, 12286–87, 12311,
12313, 12368, 12370,
12372, 12378, 12400,
12404, 12407–10,
12454–55, 12494, 12497,
12504, 12544–45, 12553,
12619, 12635, 12642,
12655, 12659, 12663,

P = Primary; PI = Primary-Intermediate; I = Intermediate; IJ = Intermediate-Junior High

12690–91, 12699–700,
12723–24, 12729, 12731,
12734, 12737, 12741,
12744, 12749, 12751,
12754, 12762, 12765,
12768, 12782, 12791,
12793, 12796, 12803,
12811, 12815–16, 12820,
12950, 12953–54, 12956,
13206, 13222, 13369,
13396, 13438, 13457,
13488, 13490, 13509,
13512, 13523, 13526,
13529, 13532, 13534–35,
13538, 13549, 13555,
13561, 13563–65, 13567,
13569, 13574, 13577,
13581, 13586, 13603,
13614, 13616, 13623,
13627, 13634, 13644,
13654, 13662–63, 13951,
16263, 21079 **All:** 12349

**African Americans —
Christmas**
PI: 17414

**African Americans —
Cookbooks**
PI: 21675

**African Americans —
Crafts**
P: 5647 **PI:** 21515
I: 15903 **IJ:** 21649

**African Americans —
Dance**
IJ: 14295

**African Americans —
Diseases**
IJ: 18001

**African Americans —
Fiction**
P: 377, 433, 547, 1088,
1279, 1323, 1434, 1508–9,
1541, 1603, 1720, 2864,
2916, 3010, 3059, 3077,
3093, 3182, 3220, 3226,
3249, 3284, 3318, 3336,
3362–63, 3446, 3450–51,
3476, 3478, 3490, 3516,
3519, 3563, 3572, 3579–80,
3588–89, 3611, 3649, 3658,
3660, 3684, 3703, 3706–7,
3715, 3725–26, 3728–30,
3732, 3760, 3803, 3811,
3813, 3824, 3849, 3871,
3898–99, 3905, 3911, 3916,
3950, 3958, 3972, 3979,
3991, 3999, 4013, 4047,
4049, 4053, 4061, 4063,
4136, 4294, 4471, 4496,
4538, 4602, 4624, 4671,
4677, 4683, 4693, 4695,
4717, 4740, 4742, 4757,
4769–70, 4822, 4843, 4886,
4892, 4923, 4928, 4968,
4981–82, 4986, 5003, 5034,
5090, 5108, 5504, 5509,
5517, 5646, 5650, 5785,
5812, 5828, 5842, 5880,
5974, 6051, 6053, 6222,
6251, 6292, 6358, 6419,

6449, 6451–52, 6544, 6660,
11028 **PI:** 3207, 3604,
4034–36, 4066, 4613, 4696,
4739, 4741, 4771, 4833–34,
5669, 5881, 6973, 7342,
7346, 7356, 7471, 8556,
8589, 8614, 8680, 8961,
8967, 9266, 9289–90, 9308,
9320–22, 9338, 9495, 9596,
9598, 9608, 9750, 9766–67,
10039, 10351, 11934,
13251, 16499 **I:** 3091,
6791, 6824, 7335, 7343,
7362, 7366, 7372, 7402,
7430, 7535, 8255, 8277,
8283, 8298, 8323, 8486,
8535–36, 8682, 8861, 9206,
9224, 9268, 9272, 9277,
9295, 9301, 9305, 9314,
9317, 9337, 9413, 9419,
9422, 9478, 9496, 9554,
9583, 9592, 9614, 9937,
10362, 10370, 16247
IJ: 6755, 7337–38, 7345,
7350, 7359–60, 7364, 7369,
7387, 7432, 7438, 7444,
7484, 7526, 7542, 7805,
8172, 8202, 8246, 8251,
8257–58, 8261, 8284, 8321,
8337, 8377, 8447, 8453,
8533, 8707, 8788, 9209,
9219, 9257, 9276, 9278,
9283, 9310, 9318, 9324,
9326, 9336, 9349, 9409,
9476, 9492, 9494, 9528,
9530, 9549, 9609, 9615,
9624, 10056, 10079, 10288,
12342, 12483, 13678

**African Americans —
Folk songs**
IJ: 14167

**African Americans —
Folklore**
P: 11347–48, 11368, 11379,
11385 **PI:** 11363, 11390
I: 10558, 11345
IJ: 11340–41, 11364, 11366

**African Americans —
Food**
IJ: 20090, 21720

**African Americans —
History**
P: 4697, 16518 **PI:** 12603,
16144 **I:** 15903, 16198,
16227, 16262, 16344,
16353, 16390, 16397,
16424, 16473, 17559
IJ: 15882, 15893, 15906–7,
16193, 16236, 16241,
16246, 16249, 16251,
16267, 16394, 16460,
16464, 16497, 16510,
16690, 17556, 17562, 17574

**African Americans —
Holidays**
P: 5619, 5648 **PI:** 17356,
17395 **IJ:** 17345, 17430

**African Americans —
Literature**
IJ: 14076

**African Americans —
Medicine**
IJ: 13206

**African Americans —
Music**
PI: 12164 **IJ:** 14120,
14126, 14132–33, 14135

**African Americans —
Poetry**
P: 3452, 3503, 5849, 11584,
11659, 11747–48,
11751–52, 11755, 11759,
11761, 11766, 11768, 12800
PI: 11749–50, 11757–58,
11760, 11762, 17290
I: 11754, 11765, 11767
IJ: 11753, 11763–64

**African Americans —
Songs**
P: 14148, 14247, 14260
PI: 14170 **I:** 14156, 14179
IJ: 15907 **All:** 14157

**African Americans —
Women**
PI: 12695 **IJ:** 12655,
12690

**African Americans —
Writers**
IJ: 12186

**African Burial Ground
(New York City)**
IJ: 16690

Africans — Biography
IJ: 13756

Agassi, Andre
I: 13641 **IJ:** 13642

Aging — Fiction
P: 1629, 3180, 3995, 4040,
4069, 6398 **I:** 8264, 8713
IJ: 8708

Agriculture
See also Farm life

Agriculture — Biography
P: 13254

Agriculture — Careers
P: 17836

Agriculture — History
IJ: 14598

Aguilera, Christina
PI: 12343

***Aida* (opera)**
IJ: 14136

AIDS
See also HIV (virus)
P: 14240, 17937, 18016
PI: 17955–57 **I:** 17943
IJ: 17968, 17982–83, 17997

AIDS — Fiction
P: 4900, 5094 **PI:** 5044,
5051, 8466, 8661 **IJ:** 8632,
8706

Aikman, Troy
I: 13600, 13602 **IJ:** 13601

Air
P: 20664, 20667, 20671,
20675 **I:** 20670, 20677

**Air — Experiments and
projects**
P: 20671, 20674 **PI:** 20673
I: 20663, 20668–69, 20672,
20676

Air Force
See United States Air
Force

Air pollution
See Pollution, Air

Airplane pilots
IJ: 14826, 21079

**Airplane pilots —
Agriculture**
P: 17836

**Airplane pilots —
Biography**
P: 12090, 12094, 12129,
13331 **PI:** 12066, 12108,
12115, 12134, 12156
I: 12061, 12109–11, 12143
IJ: 12067, 12089,
12113–14, 12138, 15840

Airplane pilots — Careers
P: 17840 **PI:** 17838
I: 12076 **IJ:** 17837

Airplane pilots — Fiction
IJ: 9702

Airplane pilots — Women
P: 12093, 12107 **PI:** 12112
I: 12061, 12091–92, 12153

Airplanes
P: 13359, 17840, 21069,
21081, 21100 **PI:** 21073,
21077, 21083, 21090,
21095–96, 21099, 21103,
21112 **I:** 21076, 21084,
21086, 21554 **IJ:** 13356,
21078, 21080, 21089,
21097, 21380

Airplanes — Biography
P: 13357 **PI:** 12156, 13354
I: 12853 **IJ:** 13355, 13358

Airplanes — Canada
IJ: 21111

Airplanes — Disasters
IJ: 21074, 21085

**Airplanes — Drawing and
painting**
I: 21598

Airplanes — Fiction
P: 1030, 2161, 2965, 4072,
5555, 5606 **PI:** 4816
I: 6754, 7032

Airplanes — History
PI: 21068, 21070, 21094,
21098, 21102 **I:** 21082,
21106–7, 21110
IJ: 21071–72, 21108–9,
21111, 21795

P = Primary; PI = Primary-Intermediate; I = Intermediate; IJ = Intermediate-Junior High

Airplanes — Poetry
I: 11970

Airplanes (model)
I: 21634, 21796 **IJ:** 21621

Airplanes (model) — Experiments and projects
PI: 18373

Airports
P: 21091, 21143 **I:** 21088

Airports — Fiction
P: 4916, 5547

Alabama
PI: 16850 **I:** 16896
IJ: 16841, 16886

Alabama — Fiction
IJ: 7338

Alabama — Folklore
PI: 11324

Alamo, Battle of the
PI: 16272 **I:** 12103, 16243,
16274 **IJ:** 12855, 16230

Alamo, Battle of the — Fiction
I: 9294, 9587 **IJ:** 9279

Alaska
P: 16772, 16797, 16801–2
PI: 2970, 15811, 16774
I: 16791, 16794, 16800,
16817, 21991 **IJ:** 16767,
16770, 16812–13, 21997

Alaska — Fiction
P: 1212, 1936, 2664, 4495,
4656, 4803, 5227, 5460
PI: 7322, 9171 **I:** 6828,
6894, 9535 **IJ:** 6773, 6853,
6996, 7020, 7051, 7106,
7267–68, 8215

Alaska — Folklore
P: 11231

Alaska — History
I: 16769 **IJ:** 16779

Alaska — Poetry
PI: 11945

Alaska — Purchase
IJ: 16779

Alaskans — Biography
IJ: 12961

Albanians — Fiction
IJ: 9061

Albatrosses
I: 19241

Albatrosses — Fiction
P: 6397

Alberta, Canada
I: 15598

Albinism
I: 17919

Albinos — Fiction
IJ: 8887

Albright, Madeleine
PI: 12841 **I:** 12838, 12840
IJ: 12839

Alcatraz Island (CA)
I: 16780 **IJ:** 16805

Alcatraz Island (CA) — Fiction
IJ: 6780

Alcohol
P: 17864 **IJ:** 17862,
17865, 17868, 17873,
17878, 17888

Alcohol — Fiction
IJ: 9521

Alcoholism
See also Drugs and drug problems
IJ: 17873, 17878, 17892

Alcoholism — Fiction
P: 4942, 5095, 8827
I: 8635 **IJ:** 8445, 8450,
8516, 8706

Alcott, Louisa May
IJ: 12489–90

Alcott, Louisa May — Fiction
P: 5946

Alexander, Grover Cleveland
I: 13434

Alexander the Great
PI: 13750 **I:** 13747–48
IJ: 13749, 13751

Algeria
I: 14959

Algonquin Indians
I: 15994 **IJ:** 16041

Algonquin Indians — Folklore
P: 11271 **I:** 11226

Ali, Muhammad
I: 13582

Aliens
See Extraterrestrial life;
Illegal aliens;
Immigration (U.S.)

Aliens — Fiction
I: 10169, 10232

All-American Girls Professional Baseball League
IJ: 22094, 22106

All Souls' Day — Mexico
I: 15600, 15628

All Souls' Day — Mexico — Fiction
P: 4719

Allen, Ethan — Fiction
I: 10060

Allen, Richard
IJ: 12700

Allergies
I: 17975, 17998 **IJ:** 17987,
17996

Allergies — Fiction
P: 4973 **PI:** 9821 **I:** 8814

Alligators and crocodiles
P: 18699, 18705, 18708,
20375 **PI:** 18698, 18700,
18704, 18711 **I:** 18706–7,
18709–10, 18712
IJ: 18701–3

Alligators and crocodiles — Fiction
P: 242, 1604, 1753, 1995,
2024, 2229, 2472, 2738,
2779, 2786–87, 5445, 6534
PI: 2797, 3642 **I:** 7330

Alligators and crocodiles — Folklore
P: 10792

Allowances (money)
IJ: 16945

Almanacs
IJ: 14353

Alomar, Roberto
I: 13436 **IJ:** 13435

Alpacas — Fiction
IJ: 8619

Alphabet — History
IJ: 13987, 14011, 14114

Alphabet books
P: 1–21, 24–47, 49, 52–59,
61–63, 65–91, 95, 97–111,
114–15, 117–23, 125–26,
129–44, 146–51, 242, 248,
382, 485, 1565, 5626, 6023,
11598, 13870, 17767,
19405, 19543, 19638,
19642, 19944, 21885
PI: 22–23, 48, 50–51, 60,
64, 92, 94, 96, 116, 124,
127–28, 145, 11750, 14018,
14408, 15098, 21095, 21827
I: 112, 11926, 13927,
13983, 15817, 16540,
20595, 21368, 21655
IJ: 113, 7126, 12205,
13890, 14042, 14056

Alphabet books — Hebrew
PI: 93

Aluminum
IJ: 20280

Alzheimer's disease
P: 18013 **I:** 17959
IJ: 8876

Alzheimer's disease — Fiction
P: 3668, 4993, 4997, 5066
PI: 3763 **I:** 8521
IJ: 8504, 8853

Amazon (company) — Biography
IJ: 12850

Amazon River
PI: 15773 **I:** 15756, 15778,
15782 **IJ:** 11441

Amazon River — Fiction
PI: 4619 **I:** 7093 **IJ:** 7235

Ambulances
IJ: 17136

America — Discovery and exploration
P: 12096, 16083
PI: 12095, 12099 **I:** 12098,
16077, 16079, 16084
IJ: 12097, 12100

America — Discovery and exploration — Fiction
PI: 8927, 9142

American Community Renewal Act
I: 12968

American Museum of Natural History (New York City) — Fiction
P: 3960

American Revolution
See Revolutionary War
(U.S.)

American Sign Language
See also Sign language
I: 14016

American Sign Language — Fiction
PI: 5035

Ameru
IJ: 14952

Amish
P: 17161 **PI:** 17179
I: 17162, 17165 **IJ:** 17568

Amish — Fiction
P: 3494, 3653–54, 5744
PI: 7521 **I:** 8455, 8820
IJ: 8491, 8744–45

Amistad mutiny
I: 16231 **IJ:** 16257, 16266

Amphibians
See also specific animal
names, e.g., Frogs and
toads
P: 109 **PI:** 18686, 18692,
18696 **I:** 18680–81, 19906
IJ: 18684, 18691

Amphibians — Poetry
I: 11785

Amritsar (India)
I: 15099

Amsterdam (Netherlands)
I: 15399

Amusement parks
P: 4232 **I:** 14263

Amusement parks — Fiction
P: 4284 **I:** 6846, 7031,
7687

P = Primary; PI = Primary-Intermediate; I = Intermediate; IJ = Intermediate-Junior High

Anabaptists — Fiction
I: 9047

Anacondas
P: 18765

Anagrams
IJ: 14020

Anagrams — Fiction
P: 179

Anasazi Indians
I: 15947

Anastasia (Romanov)
IJ: 15409

Anatomy
See Human body

Anchorage (AK)
PI: 16803

Ancient Greece
IJ: 14678

Andersen, Hans Christian
PI: 12492 **I:** 12491, 12493

Anderson, Marian
P: 12345 **PI:** 12346
I: 12344

Andreessen, Marc
IJ: 13225

Andretti, Michael
I: 22078

Andrews, Roy Chapman
IJ: 13226, 14410

Anesthesia
IJ: 13209

Anesthesiologists
I: 18030

Angel fish
I: 19706

Angelou, Maya
PI: 12496, 12499 **I:** 12495
IJ: 12494, 12497–98

Angels — Fiction
P: 1474, 1614, 3052, 3184
PI: 8205 **I:** 7689

Angels — Poetry
P: 147, 11521 **I:** 11579

Anger
P: 17602, 17615 **PI:** 17616
IJ: 17625

Anger — Fiction
P: 2710, 4902, 4907, 5005,
5009, 5077

Angola
IJ: 14984

Animal biology
I: 18665

**Animal biology —
Careers**
P: 17831

Animal biology — History
IJ: 13316

Animal care
IJ: 17849

Animal life
PI: 18931

Animal rescues
PI: 18627

Animal rights
P: 18656 **I:** 18664
IJ: 18609, 18638, 18660,
18677

Animal rights — Fiction
I: 8326 **IJ:** 6912

Animal sounds — Fiction
P: 5461

Animal stories — Fiction
P: 6350 **I:** 7244, 7246,
9899 **IJ:** 7243

Animals
PI: 18969, 19470 **I:** 18577,
18618, 18937

Animals — Africa
I: 18607

Animals — Anatomy
P: 18832, 18901
PI: 18819, 18859–60,
19470 **I:** 18822, 18853
IJ: 18828

**Animals — Anatomy —
Fiction**
P: 912

Animals — Ark
P: 17247, 17256, 17291,
17323 **IJ:** 17514

Animals — Ark — Fiction
P: 619, 2768 **PI:** 17280

Animals — Art
P: 13873 **PI:** 13898
I: 21568 **IJ:** 13923

Animals — Australia
P: 18602

Animals — Babies
P: 5147, 5158, 5296, 5342,
5392, 18862, 18866–69,
18871, 18874, 18877–81,
19362, 19687, 19925,
19933, 19952, 19969
PI: 14469, 18872–73,
19256, 19312, 19628,
19953, 19997, 20026
I: 18870, 18875, 19736,
19801 **IJ:** 18876, 18920

**Animals — Babies —
Fiction**
P: 440, 613, 2564, 5114,
5144, 5245

Animals — Bathing
P: 18799

Animals — Behavior
P: 3173, 5182, 5417, 5424,
18797–99, 18808, 18825,
18827, 18835, 18845–46,
18862, 18865 **I:** 18647,
18822, 18837–38, 18856–57
IJ: 18804–5, 18809–10,
18814, 18831, 18850, 18907

**Animals — Behavior —
Experiments and
projects**
I: 18817

**Animals — Behavior —
Fiction**
P: 796, 5157, 5340

Animals — Camouflage
P: 18883–84, 18886, 18888,
18890, 19248, 19488
PI: 18882, 18885, 18887,
18889

**Animals — Camouflage
— Fiction**
P: 2816

Animals — Cannibalism
IJ: 18814

Animals — Careers
IJ: 17848, 17852, 17855

Animals — Classification
I: 14464 **IJ:** 18676

Animals — Coloration
P: 18855, 18888

**Animals —
Communication**
P: 18894 **PI:** 18854, 18893
IJ: 18891–92

Animals — Crafts
I: 14464

**Animals — Criminals and
crime**
I: 18637

Animals — Defenses
P: 18896, 18898, 18901
PI: 18899–900 **I:** 18895
IJ: 18897

**Animals — Drawing and
painting**
I: 21600

Animals — Emotions
I: 18815, 18833

**Animals —
Experimentation**
IJ: 18677

**Animals — Experiments
and projects**
I: 14464, 18355 **IJ:** 18614

Animals — Families
I: 18875

Animals — Feet
PI: 18858

Animals — Fiction
P: 38, 97, 108, 193, 214,
266–67, 435, 464, 515, 521,
541, 547, 552, 722, 821,
916, 1263, 1708, 1939,
2286, 2325, 2987, 3477,
4205, 4306, 4361, 4397,
4838, 5113, 5116, 5150,
5162, 5177, 5185, 5189,
5197–98, 5201, 5218, 5233,
5266, 5285, 5303, 5311,
5349, 5360, 5412, 5422,
5439, 5446, 6008, 6319,
6385, 7283 **PI:** 5167, 7173,
7241–42, 7245 **I:** 112,
7202, 7251, 7863 **IJ:** 6774,
7296, 7305

Animals — Folklore
P: 10564, 10675, 11241
PI: 11219, 21921 **I:** 10650,
10659, 11224, 18615
IJ: 10606, 10608

Animals — Food
P: 5120, 5219, 18795,
18808 **I:** 18857, 20023
IJ: 18897

Animals — General
See also Amphibians;
Endangered animals;
Endangered species;
Fables; Farm life;
Imaginary animals;
Invertebrates; Marine
animals; Pets; Poisonous
animals and plants;
Prehistoric animals;
Ranches and ranch life;
Wildlife conservation;
Zoos; as a subdivision
under country or
continent names; e.g.,
Africa — Animals; and
individual animal
species; or as part of a
specific biome, e.g.,
Rain forests
P: 56, 495, 5176, 5226,
5390, 5393, 5435, 5447,
5458, 18605, 18610,
18612–13, 18617, 18619,
18624, 18626, 18632,
18640, 18645, 18649,
18659, 18666, 18801,
18825, 18926, 18929–30,
18938, 18946, 18960,
18968, 18974, 18982–84,
19484, 20021, 20410, 20538
PI: 499, 18584, 18603,
18606, 18616, 18625,
18639, 18652, 18663,
18667, 18672, 18803,
18936, 18981, 20461,
20502, 20545 **I:** 18604,
18611, 18620, 18628,
18651, 18653–55, 18658,
18662, 18670, 18673,
18956–57, 18962, 18971,
19905, 20024, 20061
IJ: 18636, 18661,
18675–76, 18943

**Animals — General —
Fiction**
P: 697

Animals — Grooming
P: 18849

Animals — Habitats
PI: 18905, 18913
IJ: 18646

Animals — Harmful
I: 18601

Animals — Hearing
P: 18820

P = Primary; PI = Primary-Intermediate; I = Intermediate; IJ = Intermediate-Junior High

Animals — Hibernation
P: 18904 PI: 18671

Animals — Homes
P: 5117, 5128, 18910, 18912, 18916 PI: 18909
I: 18914–15 IJ: 18646, 18906–8, 18911

Animals — Homes — Fiction
P: 6402

Animals — Intelligence
I: 18816

Animals — Jokes and riddles
P: 21843 PI: 21832, 21852

Animals — Life cycles
P: 18593 I: 18843
IJ: 18623

Animals — Locomotion
P: 5317, 18794, 18830, 18863, 18926 PI: 18864
I: 18823

Animals — Migration
P: 18811 PI: 18848
I: 18843, 18851–52

Animals — Mothers
P: 5296

Animals — Mythology
PI: 11735

Animals — Names
P: 18650, 18928

Animals — Nocturnal
I: 18988

Animals — Oddities
I: 18937

Animals — Play
P: 18797

Animals — Poetry
P: 73, 661, 11686, 11771, 11776–77, 11779, 11782, 11793, 11802, 11804, 11813, 11816, 11887, 11889, 11982
PI: 11773–74, 11786, 11791–92, 11797, 11810, 11818, 11919, 11945
I: 11772, 11778, 11799, 11819, 11938, 11947, 11983
IJ: 11800, 11805

Animals — Poisonous
I: 18618

Animals — Predators
PI: 20477 I: 18840

Animals — Puzzles
PI: 21861

Animals — Reproduction
P: 18918

Animals — Riddles
P: 21835

Animals — Senses
P: 18820, 18836 I: 18802, 18821

Animals — Size
P: 5462

Animals — Sleep
P: 18798, 18826 I: 18834, 18844

Animals — Songs
P: 14195

Animals — Sounds
P: 5204, 5246, 5410, 18796

Animals — Suburbs
IJ: 18636

Animals — Tails
PI: 18860

Animals — Taste (sense)
P: 18820

Animals — Teeth
PI: 18861

Animals — Tracks
P: 18839, 18842 PI: 18800

Animals — Underground
I: 18608

Animals — Underground life
P: 18934

Animals — Vision
P: 18812 I: 18807

Animals — Whiskers
P: 18806

Animals — Winter
PI: 18902

Animation (motion pictures)
I: 21270

Animation (motion pictures) — Biography
I: 12224

Annan, Kofi
I: 13752

Anning, Mary
P: 13227, 13230–31
PI: 13228–29

Anorexia
See also Eating disorders
IJ: 17994

Antarctic
See also Arctic; Polar regions
P: 19369, 19375
PI: 15818, 15821, 15845, 19368, 19387 I: 15800, 15808, 15819
IJ: 15795–96, 15806, 15812, 15828, 15831, 15846, 19373, 19389

Antarctic — Animals
IJ: 15806

Antarctic — Exploration
IJ: 12155, 15804

Antarctic — Fiction
P: 5267

Antarctic — Poetry
P: 11812

Anteaters
P: 18950 I: 18976

Anteaters — Fiction
P: 2783, 5764, 6298

Antelopes
P: 10661

Anthony, Susan B.
P: 13133 PI: 13130–31
I: 13132 IJ: 16472

Anthropology
P: 14488 PI: 14492, 14514
I: 14397, 14500, 14511
IJ: 13321, 14489–91, 14496–97, 14501, 14504–5, 14507, 14517

Anthropology — Biography
I: 13223 IJ: 13313, 13320

Antisemitism — Fiction
PI: 9069 IJ: 7369

Antoinette, Marie — Fiction
IJ: 9056

Antonnetty, Evelina Lopez
PI: 12824

Antonyms
P: 18617

Antonyms — Fiction
P: 2732

Ants
P: 19506–7, 19509–10, 19513–14 PI: 19508, 19511 IJ: 19512

Ants — Fiction
P: 557, 2607, 2742, 2773, 4799 PI: 4018 I: 9934

Anxiety
IJ: 17908

Apache Indians
PI: 15970 I: 16045
IJ: 15925

Apache Indians — Biography
I: 12972

Apache Indians — Fiction
IJ: 15937

Apartheid
IJ: 14990

Apartheid — Biography
IJ: 13845

Apartments — Fiction
P: 960, 1378, 2787, 4014, 6686 PI: 6944 I: 6899, 7158 IJ: 8292

Apes
See also individual species, e.g., Gorillas
P: 18993, 18997, 19017
PI: 18994 I: 18995,

18999–9000, 19015
IJ: 19013

***Apollo 11* (spacecraft)**
PI: 21013 I: 18454
IJ: 21018

***Apollo 13* (spacecraft)**
IJ: 20947

Apollo (space mission)
PI: 21008

Apostles (religion)
IJ: 17306

Appalachia
P: 3403 PI: 3705
I: 16833, 16860

Appalachia — Fiction
P: 3181, 4329 PI: 8762, 9734, 10034 I: 8758, 9340, 9556 IJ: 7444, 8353, 9557

Appalachia — Folklore
P: 11332, 11352, 11355
I: 11325, 11360

Appalachia — Songs
P: 14155

Appalachian Trail
I: 15859

Apple computers — Biography
PI: 12912 IJ: 12911

Apple orchards — Careers
P: 17749

Apple trees
P: 20214

Apples
P: 12842, 20140, 20143, 20157 PI: 20148 I: 20152
IJ: 20147, 20153

Apples — Fiction
P: 144, 474, 2812, 3962, 6453

Appleseed, Johnny
P: 12842–44 PI: 12845
I: 12846

April Fools' Day — Fiction
P: 5612, 6725 PI: 6962

Aquariums
P: 20020 I: 19980–81

Arabia — Folklore
P: 11182, 11189–90
PI: 11192–93 I: 11195, 11202 IJ: 11180, 11191

Arabian Gulf
I: 19847

Arabian horses — Fiction
IJ: 7190

Arabs — History
I: 15556

Arapaho Indians
PI: 15968

P = Primary; PI = Primary-Intermediate; I = Intermediate; IJ = Intermediate-Junior High

Arapaho Indians — Folklore
PI: 11306

Arbor Day — Biography
I: 13326

Archaeology
P: 14526 **PI:** 13848, 14525
I: 14498, 14520–22,
14527–29, 14533,
14538–39, 14664, 14670,
14683, 14724, 15736
IJ: 14494, 14519,
14523–24, 14530, 14532,
14535–36, 14541, 14609,
15781

Archaeology — Biography
I: 13223

Archaeology — Careers
P: 17827

Archaeology — Fiction
P: 4570 **I:** 8599

Archaeology — Underwater
IJ: 14540, 14594

Architects and architecture
See also Building and
construction
PI: 13963 **I:** 12256, 12314,
21114, 21153 **IJ:** 12233,
12255, 12311, 13915,
13918, 13947, 14639,
14727, 21118, 21134

Architects and architecture — Alphabet books
P: 27

Arcimboldo, Giuseppe
I: 12188

Arctic
See also Antarctic; Inuit;
Polar regions
P: 15803, 15825, 15843,
15847, 19064 **PI:** 15801,
15809, 15814, 15816, 15822
I: 15793, 15807, 15817,
15830, 15833–34, 15842
IJ: 15824, 15836

Arctic — Biography
I: 12075, 12121

Arctic — Crafts
I: 21482

Arctic — Discovery and exploration
I: 12120, 15798 **IJ:** 15804,
15840

Arctic — Fiction
P: 49, 1625, 2755, 4655,
5253, 5440, 5804, 5943
IJ: 6900

Argentina
PI: 15735 **I:** 15734
IJ: 15722, 15737

Argentina — Folklore
P: 11443

Argentina — Holidays
PI: 15735

Arithmetic
See also branches of
mathematics, e.g.,
Addition; Concept books
— Addition
P: 490, 6026

Arizona
PI: 16606 **I:** 16604, 16618
IJ: 16598, 16627

Arizona Territory — Fiction
I: 10190

Arkansas
P: 16869 **PI:** 16856
I: 16843, 16862 **IJ:** 16828

Arkansas — Fiction
I: 8531 **IJ:** 9531

Arlington National Cemetery
I: 16881

Armadillos
PI: 18961, 18963 **I:** 18962,
18976, 18980

Armadillos — Fiction
P: 1735

Armed forces
See also individual
branches, e.g., United
States Navy
IJ: 12723, 21401, 21404

Armed forces — Biography
I: 13746

Armed forces — Women
IJ: 16647

Armenia
I: 15412, 15430 **IJ:** 15403

Armenia — Folklore
P: 10859 **PI:** 10863, 11188

Armenia — History
IJ: 13821

Armenia — Songs
P: 1193

Armor
I: 14796

Armstrong, Lance
P: 13676 **IJ:** 13677

Armstrong, Louis
PI: 12347 **IJ:** 12348
All: 12349

Armstrong, Neil
P: 12073 **I:** 12072
IJ: 12074

Army (U.S.)
See United States Army

Arner, Louise
I: 12075

Arnold, Benedict
IJ: 12847

Arson — Fiction
I: 6968, 7030

Art
See also Art appreciation;
Artists; Drawing and
painting; Museums; and
as a subdivision under
other subjects, e.g.,
Animals — Art; and
names of individuals,
e.g., Gogh, Vincent van
P: 99, 1155, 1682, 13879,
13892, 13934, 17425
PI: 93–94, 96, 13942,
13954 **I:** 13922, 13959,
13962, 14534, 21561
IJ: 13884, 13890, 15316

Art — Africa
IJ: 13935

Art — Biography
PI: 12219, 12237, 12248,
12250, 12267, 12285, 12289
IJ: 12189, 12201, 12221,
12238, 12243, 12270,
12288, 12315

Art — Careers
IJ: 17779

Art — Fiction
P: 40, 945, 1771, 2331,
2779, 3013, 3048, 3478,
4574, 4713, 4847, 5069
IJ: 8673, 8954

Art — Forgeries
I: 13916

Art — History
IJ: 13881, 13891, 13896,
13910, 13950

Art — Humor
IJ: 9790

Art — Inuit
I: 13943

Art — Middle Ages
I: 13946

Art — New York State
IJ: 16710

Art — Poetry
I: 11940 **IJ:** 11595

Art — Renaissance
P: 1403 **I:** 13948

Art — Supplies
P: 13892

Art appreciation
P: 3, 3461, 13870,
13873–74, 13878, 13880,
13885, 13888, 13904,
13912, 13914, 13920,
13929, 13931, 13934
PI: 13898, 13908–9, 13911,
13913, 21580 **I:** 11963,
13886–87, 13902, 13917,
13919, 13925, 13927
IJ: 12163, 12207, 12298,
13877, 13883, 13895,

13901, 13905–7, 13921,
13923–24, 13930,
13932–33, 13953, 17313

Art appreciation — Fiction
P: 1503, 1820, 13876
PI: 264

Arthritis
See also Rheumatoid
arthritis
PI: 17936

Arthropods
I: 19604

Arthur, Chester A.
I: 13007 **IJ:** 13008

Arthur, King
P: 11032 **PI:** 11038
IJ: 10965, 11026, 11039

Arthur, King — Fiction
PI: 1187, 11030 **I:** 7862,
11019, 11046 **IJ:** 7969,
8119

Artificial insemination
PI: 18246

Artificial intelligence
IJ: 21205

Artificial limbs
P: 17914

Artists — Biography
P: 3672, 12281, 12306,
12308, 12310, 12538, 12581
PI: 3072, 12194–95, 12197,
12204, 12209, 12212–13,
12216, 12222, 12230,
12234, 12245, 12247,
12253, 12258–59,
12262–64, 12266,
12276–77, 12280, 12290,
12292, 12296–97, 12300,
12303–5, 12307, 12309,
12533, 12546, 12569
I: 12171, 12174, 12188,
12199–200, 12203, 12206,
12211, 12218, 12227–29,
12246, 12254, 12260,
12265, 12268, 12271,
12273–75, 12294, 12518,
12562, 13952, 13958
IJ: 12159, 12163,
12182–83, 12190, 12196,
12198, 12202, 12205,
12207–8, 12210, 12214–15,
12217, 12223, 12225–26,
12231–32, 12235–36,
12239–41, 12244, 12249,
12252, 12261, 12272,
12278, 12282–84, 12286,
12291, 12293, 12295,
12298–99, 12312–13,
12316, 13953

Artists — Fiction
P: 1662, 3013, 4672, 4838,
4878, 4949 **PI:** 4741, 9025
I: 9042, 9053, 10409
IJ: 8480, 8809, 9034

Asch, Frank
P: 12500

Ashanti — Folklore
P: 10692 I: 10646

Ashe, Arthur
PI: 13643 I: 13645
IJ: 13644

Asia
See also specific countries,
e.g., China
IJ: 15051

Asia — Folklore
P: 10723, 10837, 10843
PI: 10719, 10722, 10736
I: 10720

Asia — History
I: 15052 IJ: 14355

**Asian Americans —
Biography**
See also specific groups,
e.g., Chinese Americans
I: 12678 IJ: 12169

**Asian Americans —
Fiction**
P: 3241, 3923 IJ: 8809

**Asian Americans —
History**
I: 16358

**Asian Canadians —
Fiction**
IJ: 8435

Asimov, Isaac
IJ: 12501–2

Aspen trees
PI: 20204

Assassinations
P: 13063 PI: 13058,
13060, 13067 I: 13062,
13068 IJ: 13035, 13066,
13076, 13080, 14735

Assyria
I: 14635

Asteroids
PI: 18375, 18393, 18527,
18534 I: 18507, 18516,
18520, 18523, 20310
IJ: 18518

Asthma
P: 17949 I: 17938, 17970,
18003, 18012 IJ: 18004,
18007

Asthma — Fiction
P: 5018 IJ: 9263

Astrology
IJ: 21914

Astronauts
PI: 20998 I: 20991
IJ: 20947, 20963, 20971,
20980, 20996

Astronauts — Biography
P: 12073, 12126 PI: 12137
I: 12072, 12079–80, 12119,
12127, 12135–36, 12154,
12888, 20964 IJ: 12067,
12074, 12139, 12887,
12889–90

Astronauts — Careers
PI: 17758, 17766

Astronauts — Fiction
P: 5526 PI: 6766

**Astronauts — Jokes and
riddles**
P: 21828

**Astronomers —
Biography**
P: 13235, 13291 PI: 13350
I: 13290, 13292 IJ: 13204,
13309, 13345–46

Astronomy
P: 18387, 18390, 18409–10,
18420, 18438, 18473,
18483, 18521–22, 18550,
18565 PI: 18378–79,
18393, 18395, 18400,
18412, 18425, 18429,
18484, 18545 I: 13289,
13324, 18380, 18399,
18401, 18405, 18411,
18413, 18416, 18419,
18514, 18548, 18551,
20953, 20993, 21004
IJ: 18383, 18385–86,
18388–89, 18394, 18397,
18402–3, 18406, 18408,
18414, 18418, 18422–23,
18513, 18552, 20950

Astronomy — Careers
PI: 17825

**Astronomy —
Experiments and
projects**
I: 18381, 18424 IJ: 18314,
18389, 18398, 18404

Astronomy — Fiction
P: 4497, 4685

Astronomy — Folklore
I: 10577

Astronomy — History
PI: 18377

**Athapascan Indians —
Fiction**
P: 4448

Athena (Greek goddess)
IJ: 11516

Athens, Greece
I: 15391

Athletes — Biography
See also specific sports,
e.g., Tennis —
Biography; and names of
athletes, e.g., Gehrig,
Lou
P: 13721 I: 13386

**Atlanta Braves (baseball
team)**
I: 22110

Atlanta (GA)
I: 16873, 16891

Atlantic City — Fiction
IJ: 8756

Atlantic Ocean
PI: 19821 I: 19846
IJ: 16722, 19841

**Atlantic Ocean — World
War II**
IJ: 14824

Atlantis
PI: 21907 I: 11459, 21957

Atlantis (space shuttle)
PI: 20967

Atlases
See Maps and globes

Atmosphere
I: 20670

Atomic bomb
PI: 13847, 14841, 21406
I: 14870 IJ: 14831, 14860

Atomic bomb — Fiction
I: 8989, 9700

Atoms
IJ: 20286

Attention deficit disorder
P: 17927, 17933 I: 17905
IJ: 17909

**Attention deficit disorder
— Fiction**
P: 5012 PI: 8915

**Attention deficit
hyperactivity disorder
— Fiction**
IJ: 8890

**Attorneys general —
Biography**
I: 12957

Audubon, John James
IJ: 12189–90

Aurora borealis
See Northern lights

Australia
See also Aborigines
(Australia)
P: 4583, 15244, 16968
PI: 4727, 15224, 15227,
15246, 15251, 15256
I: 14534, 15225, 15229,
15236, 15243, 15249–50,
15253 IJ: 15223, 15228,
15242, 19661

Australia — Animals
P: 18602 PI: 19183
IJ: 18933

**Australia — Animals —
Fiction**
P: 599

Australia — Art
IJ: 13889

Australia — Cookbooks
I: 21700

Australia — Crafts
IJ: 15232

Australia — Fiction
P: 2510, 3278, 4569, 4579,
4642, 4657, 5954 PI: 7579
I: 6913, 6940, 8930, 8934,
9879 IJ: 7124, 7465, 8925,
8939, 9878, 10020

Australia — Folklore
P: 10850 I: 10849

Australia — Holidays
PI: 15235

Austria
IJ: 15288, 15291

Austria — Fiction
IJ: 7300, 9056, 9651, 9655

Authors — Biography
See Writers — Biography

Autism
IJ: 17932

Autism — Fiction
P: 4948, 5011, 5091

Automation
See Computer programs
and programming;
Computers; Robots

Automobile industry
IJ: 12905

**Automobile industry —
Biography**
I: 13282

**Automobile mechanics —
Careers**
P: 3139

Automobile racing
P: 5594 PI: 21311
I: 13429, 22078, 22081,
22083 IJ: 21314,
22079–80, 22082

**Automobile racing —
Biography**
PI: 13397, 13428 I: 13427

**Automobile racing —
Fiction**
P: 518

Automobiles
P: 5548, 5597–98, 21296
PI: 21283, 21311, 21322
I: 21302, 21317–18, 21325
IJ: 21281, 21304–6

**Automobiles —
Biography**
P: 13281, 13283 I: 21303
IJ: 13280

Automobiles — Crafts
I: 18349

Automobiles — Fiction
P: 1467, 2915–16, 3233,
4160, 4205, 5576, 5584
I: 7057, 7728, 7853, 9561

Automobiles — History
PI: 21312 I: 21303
IJ: 21320, 21326

P = Primary; PI = Primary-Intermediate; I = Intermediate; IJ = Intermediate-Junior High

Automobiles — Jokes and riddles
PI: 21830

Automobiles — License plates
I: 21308

Automobiles — Recycling
P: 21309

Automobiles (model)
I: 21674

Autumn
P: 4489, 18563, 20216
PI: 4523, 20210 **I:** 18562

Autumn — Crafts
I: 21488

Autumn — Fiction
P: 3011, 4454, 4476, 4530

Autumn — Holidays
PI: 17370

Autumn — Poetry
P: 11935

Avalanches
I: 20309, 20778 **IJ:** 20763

Avalon — Fiction
IJ: 7976

Avi (writer)
IJ: 12503

Aviation
See Airplanes

Axles
P: 20929

Azerbaijan
I: 15430

Aztecs
PI: 11404, 15636, 15654
I: 15610, 15632, 15639,
15642, 15645, 15648, 15655
IJ: 15603, 15620, 15631,
15635, 15649, 15652

Aztecs — Crafts
I: 15613 **IJ:** 15609

Aztecs — Fiction
I: 9134

Aztecs — Folklore
P: 11406, 11408, 11413

Aztecs — Mythology
I: 11405

B

Babe *(motion picture)*
P: 6471

Babies
P: 3509, 3525, 3685, 3816,
17646, 17687, 18228,
18230–35 **PI:** 18239,
18248

Babies — Customs
PI: 17401

Babies — Fiction
P: 81, 646, 758, 1258, 1558,
1595, 1680, 3254, 3293,
3317, 3322–23, 3325, 3433,
3454, 3506, 3510, 3518,
3520, 3529, 3538, 3549–50,
3572, 3579, 3584, 3589,
3597, 3619, 3621, 3623,
3632, 3643, 3645–47, 3652,
3663, 3670–71, 3684,
3686–87, 3696, 3757, 3765,
3774, 3784, 3793, 3798,
3807–8, 3858, 3861, 3866,
3882, 3895, 3897, 3904,
3932–33, 3939, 3971, 4184,
4354, 4844, 5479, 6412,
6414, 9951 **PI:** 7516, 9723
I: 7226, 7421, 9743
IJ: 7382, 8577

Babies — Games
P: 21972

Baboons
P: 19017

Baboons — Fiction
P: 5131

Baby-sitting
IJ: 16938, 16947–48

Baby-sitting — Fiction
P: 1462, 2858, 3149, 3250,
3328, 3799, 3856, 3935,
4180, 4336, 5099, 6483
PI: 7459 **I:** 9876–77
IJ: 7025, 8212, 9932

Babylonia
I: 14636

Bach, Johann Sebastian
P: 12317 **PI:** 12318–19

Bach, Johann Sebastian — Fiction
P: 4711

Bacon, Roger — Fiction
IJ: 9121

Bacon's Rebellion — Fiction
I: 9237

Bacteria
See also Germs
P: 17939, 17971 **I:** 19805,
19811

Badgers
PI: 18948

Badgers — Fiction
P: 2777, 6395–96
IJ: 7186, 7830

Badgers — Folklore
P: 10816

Badlands National Park
I: 16589

Baghdad — Fiction
P: 4574

Bagpipes — Fiction
IJ: 6832

Bahrain
IJ: 15544

Bailey, Rex
I: 12076

Baird, John Logie
I: 13232

Baiul, Oksana
I: 13587

Baker, Josephine
PI: 13134

Baking
P: 5976 **I:** 21688

Baking — Careers
P: 3138

Baking — Fiction
P: 5834, 5839, 6304, 6486

Baking — Folklore
P: 11337

Balanchine, George
IJ: 12350

Bald eagles
PI: 19325, 19333, 19343
IJ: 19336, 19338

Baldwin, James
IJ: 12504

Bali
P: 20093

Bali — Folklore
P: 10851

Balkans — Fiction
IJ: 9062

Ball, Charles
IJ: 16273

Ball, Lucille
I: 12351

Ballard, Robert
I: 12077

Ballet
P: 14300, 14302
PI: 14273, 14288 **I:** 14272,
14275, 14277–80,
14284–85, 14289–90,
14294, 14298, 14301
IJ: 14276, 14282, 14286

Ballet — Biography
P: 12481 **I:** 12477
IJ: 12350, 12428, 12441

Ballet — Careers
PI: 17782 **I:** 17777

Ballet — Fiction
P: 1505, 1773, 2054, 2121,
2475, 3017, 3158, 3238–39,
3391, 3797, 3997, 4898,
4962–63, 6217, 6293–94,
6549–50, 9058 **PI:** 436,
7437, 8660, 9800 **I:** 7834,
8665, 10253, 14297

Ballet — Stories
P: 14283 **PI:** 14293
I: 14287, 14296 **IJ:** 14281

Ballet Tech (school)
I: 14301

Ballooning
PI: 22001 **I:** 21075, 21974,
22045 **IJ:** 21101, 22071

Ballooning — Biography
PI: 12078

Ballooning — Fiction
P: 2945, 2961, 6160, 6272
PI: 1914 **I:** 9831 **IJ:** 7398

Balloons — Experiments and projects
I: 20669

Balloons — Fiction
P: 1678, 4122, 4723, 6212

Baltic Sea
I: 19831

Baltimore — Fiction
P: 5846

Baltimore Orioles (baseball team)
I: 22112 **IJ:** 22125

Bananas
P: 20156 **PI:** 20141, 20149

Bananas — Fiction
I: 9779

Bands (music)
P: 14223

Bands (music) — Fiction
P: 2796, 3004, 3420
IJ: 8249

Bangladesh
IJ: 15095, 15113, 15148,
15179, 15213

Banks, Tyra
IJ: 12352

Banks and banking
P: 16950 **I:** 16923

Bannaky, Molly
PI: 12848

Banneker, Benjamin
P: 13235 **I:** 13233–34

Bantu — Folklore
PI: 10691 **I:** 10643

Bar mitzvah — Fiction
PI: 8623 **IJ:** 7124

Barbados — Fiction
IJ: 9209

Barbers — Fiction
P: 3446, 9954

Barkley, Charles
I: 13513 **IJ:** 13512

Barn owls — Fiction
P: 5280

Barns — Fiction
P: 3212, 3494, 4580

Barnum, P. T.
IJ: 12353

Barrymore, Drew
PI: 12354

Barton, Clara
PI: 13135

P = Primary; PI = Primary-Intermediate; I = Intermediate; IJ = Intermediate-Junior High

Baseball
P: 4813, 22093, 22111
PI: 22095–98, 22100, 22119, 22122 I: 22084, 22089–90, 22099, 22108, 22110, 22112–14, 22120–21, 22123–24
IJ: 22086, 22092, 22102–5, 22107, 22109, 22115–18, 22125

Baseball — Biography
P: 13371, 13455, 13474, 13482, 13487 PI: 6362, 13383–84, 13433, 13452–53, 13463, 13465, 13467, 13475–76, 13478, 13486, 13494, 13504
I: 13361, 13365–66, 13402, 13418, 13424, 13426, 13431–32, 13434, 13436–37, 13442, 13444–51, 13454, 13456, 13459–60, 13462, 13464, 13468–70, 13472–73, 13477, 13479, 13481, 13483–85, 13489, 13491–93, 13495–98, 13500, 13502–3, 13506–8, 13510 IJ: 13364, 13391, 13410, 13413, 13417, 13435, 13438–41, 13443, 13457, 13461, 13466, 13471, 13480, 13488, 13490, 13499, 13501, 13505, 13509, 13614, 22101

Baseball — Fiction
P: 95, 505, 1710, 2321, 2563, 2715, 3081, 3250, 3260, 3459, 3962, 4056, 4189, 4805, 4966, 5022, 6294, 6411, 6433, 6484, 6552, 6566, 6584, 10300
PI: 1612, 5037, 6234, 8750, 10270, 10281–82, 10296, 10301, 10303, 10312, 10317, 10330, 10334, 10344, 10347, 10361
I: 8122, 10294, 10319, 10322, 10327, 10329, 10333, 10336–39, 10346, 10349, 10359, 10362, 10370
IJ: 7628, 7768, 8502, 8513, 8606, 8751, 9864, 10308, 10310, 10326, 10340, 10345, 10353–57, 10368, 10373–74

Baseball — History
PI: 22087 I: 22088
IJ: 22085, 22091, 22094, 22106

Baseball — Jokes and riddles
PI: 21818

Baseball — Managers
IJ: 13391

Baseball — Memorabilia
I: 21809

Baseball — Poetry
P: 12007 I: 11997, 12001
IJ: 11999

Baseball — Songs
P: 14160

Baseball cards
I: 21808

Baseball cards — Fiction
PI: 7462

Baseball Hall of Fame
I: 22088 IJ: 22101

Basic training (U.S. Army)
I: 21384

Basket weaving
I: 21528

Basket weaving — Fiction
PI: 3072

Basketball
P: 22131 PI: 22128
I: 22127, 22129, 22135, 22137–39, 22141, 22145, 22148 IJ: 22126, 22132, 22134, 22140, 22142, 22144, 22146, 22149–51

Basketball — Biography
P: 22133 PI: 13518, 13560, 13572 I: 12858, 13362, 13376, 13379–80, 13393–94, 13403, 13511, 13513, 13516, 13524–25, 13527–28, 13530, 13533, 13536–37, 13539–41, 13546–48, 13551, 13553–54, 13556–57, 13559, 13562, 13570–71, 13575, 13578–80
IJ: 13360, 13369, 13408, 13420–21, 13425, 13512, 13514–15, 13517, 13519–23, 13526, 13529, 13531–32, 13534–35, 13538, 13542–45, 13549–50, 13552, 13555, 13558, 13561, 13563–66, 13568–69, 13573–74, 13576–77, 13581

Basketball — Fiction
P: 2959, 3009, 6512
PI: 4990, 8879, 10321, 10350 I: 10271, 10279, 10297, 10309, 10320, 10370–71, 11994 IJ: 7375, 7693, 8487, 9903, 10274, 10278, 10280, 10288, 10363

Basketball — History
I: 22130

Basketball — Poetry
P: 12006 PI: 11996, 12008
I: 12002 IJ: 11995, 12004

Basketball — Women
I: 13376, 22145 IJ: 22136, 22143, 22147

Basketball cards
I: 21810

Basketball Hall of Fame
I: 22130

Bass, Tom
IJ: 13678

Basset hounds — Fiction
P: 5383

Bassoons — Fiction
P: 1294

Bastille
IJ: 15298

Bat boys
I: 22084

Bat mitzvah — Fiction
IJ: 9990

Bates, Katherine Lee
I: 12505

Bathrooms
P: 3379 IJ: 18191

Bathrooms — Experiments and projects
P: 4486

Baths and bathing
P: 4537

Baths and bathing — Fiction
P: 1582, 2325, 2726, 3203, 3410, 3562, 4356

Bats (animal)
P: 19021–26, 19029–30, 19032 PI: 19020, 19027, 19033 I: 19018–19, 19028, 19031, 19034–35, 19037
IJ: 19036

Bats (animal) — Fiction
P: 1918, 4401 PI: 10065
I: 7281, 7835

Battered women — Fiction
I: 8409

Battles
See under names of specific battles, e.g., Bull Run, Battle of

Battleships
PI: 14848

Bauer, Marion Dane
IJ: 12506

Beaches
See also Seashores
P: 3441, 4462

Beaches — Fiction
P: 1128, 1269, 2480, 3084, 3097, 3157, 3197, 3202, 3259, 3263, 3273, 3315, 4484, 4509, 4519, 4526, 4559, 5271 PI: 4904, 4909
I: 7393

Beads — Crafts
P: 21548 IJ: 21547

Beagles — Fiction
IJ: 7278

Bean, Judge Roy
I: 12849

Beans
P: 20260, 20262 IJ: 20176

Beans — Fiction
P: 20076

Bears
See also specific kinds, e.g., Polar bears
P: 14249, 19038–40, 19042, 19046, 19048, 19050, 19053, 19058, 19065, 19070, 19072, 19184
PI: 19041, 19043, 19047, 19049, 19051–52, 19054–55, 19057, 19060, 19062, 19067–68 I: 19044, 19056, 19066, 19069, 19071
IJ: 19045

Bears — Fiction
P: 46, 159, 165, 283, 385, 741, 798, 801, 1307, 1731, 1756–59, 1762–63, 1767, 1801, 1804, 1852, 1855, 1932, 1934, 1946, 2015, 2089, 2099–100, 2179, 2211, 2223, 2276, 2305, 2350, 2444, 2454, 2456, 2458, 2502, 2562, 2593, 2664, 2670, 2682, 2781, 2798, 2870, 2966, 2983, 3018, 3308, 5101, 5165, 5175, 5209, 5227, 5239, 5282, 5298, 5301, 5369, 5663, 5676, 5797, 5820, 5890, 5956, 6125, 6127, 6163, 6204, 6210, 6213, 6361, 6386, 6392, 6402, 6453, 6533, 6622, 6720–21, 7962–63 PI: 2005, 9787
I: 9096, 9145, 9785
IJ: 6905, 6909, 7267

Bears — Folklore
P: 10947, 10981, 11029, 11094 PI: 10595, 11130
I: 11121

Bears — Nursery rhymes
P: 848

Beatles (musical group)
PI: 12355 IJ: 12356

Beauty, personal
I: 21183

Beauty pageants
IJ: 14264

Beavers
P: 19200, 19207 I: 19197

Beavers — Fiction
P: 2187, 2419, 6220

Bed wetting — Fiction
P: 8848

Bedouins
I: 15490

Beds — Fiction
P: 552, 647, 704, 960, 6361

P = Primary; PI = Primary-Intermediate; I = Intermediate; IJ = Intermediate-Junior High

Beds — History
P: 790

Bedtime books
P: 176, 565, 577, 616–18, 620–21, 623–26, 628, 631–32, 634–37, 642, 646, 654–56, 659–62, 664–66, 668–69, 671–73, 675, 677, 681–82, 686, 688, 690, 694–96, 698–700, 702, 705, 709, 711–13, 715–18, 720, 726–28, 730–34, 736, 739–40, 742, 744–46, 750, 753, 755–56, 760–68, 770, 773–74, 777–80, 782–83, 787, 789–90, 793–95, 799–800, 802–9, 813, 816, 819–20, 1447, 3974, 6281, 6353, 6692, 17534 **PI:** 687, 817–18, 11213

Bedtime books — Fiction
P: 143, 619, 622, 629–30, 633, 638–41, 643–45, 647–53, 657–58, 663, 667, 670, 674, 676, 678–80, 683–85, 689, 691–93, 697, 703–4, 706–8, 710, 714, 719, 721–25, 729, 735, 737–38, 741, 743, 747–49, 751–52, 754, 757, 759, 769, 771–72, 775–76, 781, 785–86, 788, 791–92, 796–98, 801, 810–12, 814–15, 821, 935, 1134, 6395, 6467

Bedtime books — Poetry
P: 648, 701, 784

Bedtime books — Prayers
P: 17537

Bedtime books — Songs
P: 14175

Bee-keeping — Fiction
P: 3213

Beef
P: 20084

Bees
P: 19518, 19520, 19522–23, 19527, 20126 **PI:** 19516–17, 19519, 19521, 19525 **I:** 19515

Bees — Careers
P: 19522

Bees — Fiction
P: 3213, 3917, 5145, 5217 **I:** 8814 **IJ:** 7885

Beethoven, Ludwig van
PI: 12321 **IJ:** 12320

Beethoven, Ludwig van — Fiction
I: 9065

Beetles
I: 19533, 19535–36 **IJ:** 19537

Beetles — Fiction
P: 4187 **I:** 9944

Beginning readers
See Books for beginning readers

Behavior
P: 17601–2, 17612 **PI:** 17720 **I:** 17608 **IJ:** 17606

Behavior — Fiction
P: 3356, 3368 **PI:** 167

Beijing
I: 15069 **IJ:** 15053

Beirut — Fiction
P: 4679

Belarus
I: 15416 **IJ:** 15407

Belgium
I: 15400 **IJ:** 15397

Belize
I: 15686 **IJ:** 15679, 20383

Bell, Alexander Graham
I: 13236–39, 13241 **IJ:** 12697, 13240, 21261

Bellybuttons
P: 18074, 18232

Bellybuttons — Fiction
P: 1689

Beluga whales
P: 19777

Bench, Johnny
I: 13437

Benin
IJ: 15030

Benin — Folklore
I: 10694

Bentley, Snowflake
P: 12191

Beowulf
I: 11126

Bergen, Candice
IJ: 12177

Bergen, Edgar
IJ: 12177

Berkeley (CA) — Fiction
I: 8792

Berlin, Germany
I: 15333

Berlin, Irving
PI: 12322

Berlin Wall
IJ: 15328

Bermuda Triangle
PI: 21908 **I:** 21911, 21943 **IJ:** 21916

Bernstein, Leonard
PI: 12324 **IJ:** 12323

Bethune, Mary McLeod
PI: 12701–3 **I:** 12704

Bettis, Jerome
IJ: 13603

Bezos, Jeff
IJ: 12850

Bhagavad-gita
P: 17226

Bhatt, Ela
IJ: 13753

Bible — Atlases
IJ: 15518

Bible — Crafts
I: 21485, 21487, 21495

Bible — Fiction
P: 17172

Bible — Quotations
I: 17331

Bible — Women
I: 17318 **IJ:** 17317

Bible — Words
I: 17204

Bible stories
See also names of individuals, e.g., Noah (Bible)
P: 5755, 5835, 5859, 5863, 5967, 11171, 17241, 17243–44, 17246–47, 17249–50, 17256, 17258, 17262–64, 17266–68, 17270–71, 17274, 17277, 17281, 17283, 17285–88, 17291–93, 17297–300, 17303–4, 17311, 17315–16, 17319, 17323, 17325–26, 17329, 17332, 17409, 17417, 17427, 17440, 17463, 17466 **PI:** 5923, 17239–40, 17242, 17265, 17269, 17275, 17279, 17290, 17295, 17305, 17309, 17330 **I:** 8963, 9705, 11157, 17248, 17251, 17254, 17260–61, 17272–73, 17278, 17282, 17308, 17310, 17318, 17320–22, 17324, 17327–28, 17415, 17433, 17441 **IJ:** 9306, 13780, 17237, 17245, 17252–53, 17255, 17276, 17294, 17296, 17301–2, 17314, 17317

Bicycle stunt riding
IJ: 22158

Bicycles
P: 22161–62 **PI:** 12784, 21283, 22155–57, 22163 **I:** 22160 **IJ:** 22152–54, 22158–59, 22164

Bicycles — Fiction
P: 1200, 1375, 1787, 2444, 4773, 5554, 6251, 6314, 6513, 8761 **PI:** 8262, 10275 **I:** 7856 **IJ:** 10305

Bicycles — History
P: 22165

Bicyclists — Biography
P: 13676 **I:** 13698 **IJ:** 13677, 22152

Bielenberg, Christabel
IJ: 15331

Big and Little Dippers
P: 18540 **PI:** 18553

Big-bang theory
IJ: 18384

Big Bend National Park — Fiction
IJ: 8686

Big cats
See also individual species, e.g. Lions
PI: 19081, 19105 **I:** 19090, 19107 **IJ:** 19416

Big Foot
See also Yeti
I: 21930, 21939, 21956 **IJ:** 21941

Big Foot — Fiction
IJ: 7066

Bill of Rights (U.S.)
See also Constitution (U.S.)
PI: 17049 **IJ:** 17058

Billy the Kid
IJ: 12851–52

Biography
See also under specific occupations, e.g., Artists; specific sports; e.g., Baseball; and cultural groups, e.g., Hispanic Americans

Biography — General
PI: 13737, 13745 **I:** 12076, 12106, 12647, 12666, 12692, 13211, 13731 **IJ:** 12640

Biology
See also Animals; Botany; and individual animal species, e.g., Raccoons
P: 18592, 18596, 18598 **I:** 18587, 18597, 18654 **IJ:** 18594, 18600

Biology — Experiments and projects
PI: 18360, 18589 **IJ:** 18356, 18580

Biology — Fiction
IJ: 10113

Bioluminescence
P: 19452 **I:** 19623 **IJ:** 18657

Biomes
I: 20378

Bipolar disorder
IJ: 17909

Biracial families
See Interracial families

P = Primary; PI = Primary-Intermediate; I = Intermediate; IJ = Intermediate-Junior High

Bird, Larry
I.J: 13514

Bird feeding
I: 19284

Bird watching
PI: 19233 I: 19286

**Bird watching —
Biography**
I: 13336

Birds
P: 5384, 5426, 5459, 18917,
19216, 19219, 19221,
19231–32, 19237, 19239,
19243, 19249, 19260,
19265, 19269, 19279,
19287–88, 19302, 19317,
19329, 19335, 19346,
19366, 20375 PI: 4374,
19218, 19225–27,
19233–34, 19242, 19253,
19255–56, 19258,
19263–64, 19278, 19280,
19290, 19296–97, 19323,
19347, 19355 I: 15852,
19213–14, 19217, 19220,
19223, 19240–41,
19244–45, 19254, 19266,
19268, 19272, 19274–76,
19282, 19285, 19291–93,
19300, 19308, 19311,
19345, 19350, 19352,
19409, 19895 IJ: 19230,
19235, 19247, 19301

Birds — Beaks
P: 19289

Birds — Eggs
P: 19306 IJ: 19304

**Birds — Endangered
species**
IJ: 19417

Birds — Evolution
I: 14473

**Birds — Experiments and
projects**
PI: 10589

Birds — Fiction
P: 1068, 1526, 1661, 1757,
2024, 2276, 2383, 2495,
2643, 3456, 4200, 4424,
4456, 5089, 5138, 5153,
5178, 5195, 5278, 5281,
5372, 5452, 6319, 6621
PI: 2892, 4721, 7198, 7748,
8056, 8999 I: 8003, 8824
IJ: 7168, 7193

Birds — Folklore
P: 10539 PI: 10589
IJ: 10620

Birds — Nests
P: 19222 PI: 19303, 19307

Birds — Nursery rhymes
P: 857

Birds — Poetry
PI: 11787 IJ: 11780

Birds — Seashores
I: 19246

Birds — Songs
I: 19305

Birds of prey
See also individual
species, e.g., Eagles;
Hawks
I: 19331, 19334, 19345
IJ: 19322

Birth
See also Childbirth
P: 18237–38, 18240, 18242
I: 17214, 17358

Birth — Customs
PI: 17401

Birth order
IJ: 17667

Birthdays
PI: 17390

Birthdays — Crafts
PI: 17352, 17396, 21510

Birthdays — Fiction
P: 517, 592, 1758, 1787,
2089, 2401, 2826, 2902,
3554, 4983, 5661, 5663–68,
5670–83, 5685–87,
5689–91, 5693, 5695–715,
5717–19, 5722–40, 6271,
6302, 6635, 6687, 6699
PI: 5662, 5669, 5692,
5720–21, 9810, 9923
I: 7330, 9437, 10239

Birthdays — Parties
PI: 17396 IJ: 17351

Birthdays — Poetry
P: 5688, 11835 PI: 5694,
11834

Bismarck (battleship)
IJ: 14820, 14869

Bison
See Buffalos

Black bears
PI: 19043, 19051

Black holes
PI: 18376 I: 18407
IJ: 18406

**Blackfoot Indians —
Folklore**
P: 11312

Blacksmiths — Biography
I: 12302

Blackwell, Elizabeth
I: 13242

Blades, Rubén
I: 12357

Blair, Bonnie
PI: 13679, 13681
IJ: 13680

Blair, John
P: 16481

Blanchard, Jean-Pierre
PI: 12078

Blessings
See also Prayers
P: 17531 I: 17520

Blind
P: 6192 PI: 13166, 13332
I: 13140, 17917, 17935
IJ: 12697, 17900

Blind — Biography
P: 13762 PI: 13757,
13759, 13761 IJ: 13758,
13760

Blind — Fiction
P: 3791, 4014, 4407, 4960,
5061 PI: 8901, 8922
I: 7249, 7293, 8891, 8902,
9285 IJ: 7313–14, 8377

Blizzard of 1888
IJ: 16480

Blizzards
P: 4494, 20695 PI: 16494
I: 20703, 20711

Blizzards — Fiction
P: 2656, 4451 IJ: 6970

Blood
P: 17993, 18090 I: 18088

Blood-sucking animals
I: 18642–43

**Bloomer, Amelia —
Fiction**
P: 4627

Blue (color)
P: 262

Blue jays
I: 19251

Blue whales
P: 19782

Blues (music)
IJ: 14126, 14133

Blues (music) — Fiction
P: 2525, 4968

Bluford, Guion
I: 12079–80

Bly, Nellie
PI: 13138 I: 12643, 13136
IJ: 13137, 13139

Boa constrictors
PI: 18766

**Boa constrictors —
Fiction**
P: 2769

Board books
P: 807

Boars
PI: 18959

Boars — Fiction
P: 1753

**Boat people (Vietnamese)
— Fiction**
I: 9018

Boats and boating
See Canoes and canoeing;
Sailing and boating;
Ships and boats

Bobcats
P: 19073, 19091 I: 19077

Bobsledding
PI: 21978 IJ: 22257

Body decoration
IJ: 21946

Body language
PI: 17628

Bodybuilding
IJ: 21988

Boeing, William
I: 12853

Bogs
IJ: 14494

Bogs — Fiction
P: 4484

Boitano, Brian
IJ: 13588

Bolivar, Simon
I: 13754–55

Bolivia
PI: 15745 I: 15775
IJ: 15724

Bomb squads
PI: 17811

Bonaparte, Napoleon
IJ: 13839, 16229

Bonds, Barry
IJ: 13438

Bones
I: 18175

Bonetta, Sarah Forbes
IJ: 13756

Bonilla, Bobby
IJ: 13439–40

Boobys — Fiction
P: 5302

Book reports
I: 14092

Books and printing
P: 13990 PI: 11646,
13993, 13999, 14087, 14109
I: 13991, 13998, 14009–10,
21137 IJ: 21612

**Books and printing —
Fiction**
I: 9068, 9867

**Books and printing —
History**
IJ: 21612

**Books for beginning
readers**
P: 258, 417–18, 500, 576,
5361, 5752, 5992, 6154,
6192–93, 6229–30, 6236,
6255, 6260, 6306, 6311,
6321, 6335, 6346, 6410,

P = Primary; PI = Primary-Intermediate; I = Intermediate; IJ = Intermediate-Junior High

6412, 6431, 6435, 6442,
6462, 6471, 6496, 6502,
6529, 6532, 6558, 6560,
6570, 6576, 6593, 6597,
6612, 6616, 6622, 6626,
6648, 6656, 6679–80, 6688,
6703, 7435, 11017–18,
11064, 11347, 11607,
11866, 12281, 12843,
12884, 12915, 13003,
13086–87, 13200, 13213,
13257, 13283, 13357,
13385, 13608, 13676,
14362, 14459, 14526,
14608, 14647, 15589,
15952, 16083, 16338,
17283, 17397–98, 17500,
17738–39, 17939, 17952,
17972, 18140, 18192–93,
18444, 18468, 18563–65,
18624, 18626, 18699,
18721, 18736, 18775,
18781, 18801, 18806,
18836, 18865, 18881,
18884, 18926, 18938–39,
18974, 19010, 19021,
19050, 19058, 19064,
19318, 19442, 19454,
19480, 19532, 19556,
19579, 19610, 19630,
19683, 19751, 19787,
19951, 19957, 19992,
20025, 20035, 20054,
20092, 20104, 20115,
20142, 20173, 20184,
20200, 20358, 20400,
20432, 20452, 20531,
20564, 20642, 20651,
20695, 20712, 20734,
20766, 20849, 21185,
21243, 21456, 21824,
21839, 22133, 22183, 22295
PI: 6232–34, 6273, 6310,
6362, 6364, 6525, 9514,
12108, 12778, 12799,
13383, 15176, 15936,
17509, 19081, 19086, 21908

**Books for beginning
readers — Fiction**

P: 235, 412, 420, 445–46,
512, 516, 540, 546, 568,
581, 583, 1449, 5670, 5706,
5725, 5747, 5766, 5778,
5858, 5895, 5961, 5978,
6001, 6041, 6052, 6133,
6156, 6168, 6170, 6173,
6178–91, 6194–218,
6220–28, 6231, 6237–45,
6248–54, 6256–59,
6261–66, 6268, 6270–72,
6274–81, 6284, 6286–305,
6307–9, 6312–20, 6322–29,
6331–34, 6336–41,
6343–44, 6347–55,
6357–61, 6363, 6365–70,
6372–409, 6411, 6413–17,
6419, 6421–30, 6432–34,
6436–41, 6443–55, 6457,
6459–61, 6464–70,
6472–78, 6480–88,
6490–95, 6497–501,
6503–8, 6510–21, 6523–24,

6526–28, 6530–31,
6533–57, 6559, 6561,
6563–69, 6572–75,
6577–83, 6585–92,
6594–96, 6598–611, 6613,
6615, 6617–21, 6623–25,
6627–35, 6637–47,
6649–54, 6657–78,
6681–87, 6689–702,
6704–26, 9254, 9390,
10428, 10942, 10958,
11071, 18049, 20587,
20602, 21819, 21838, 21860
PI: 6269, 6282–83, 6285,
6342, 6345, 6356, 6420,
6456, 6458, 6489, 6509,
6562, 6810

**Books for beginning
readers — Poetry**
P: 6235, 6655 **PI:** 11606

Booksellers — Fiction
IJ: 9124

Boone, Daniel
PI: 12081, 12084 **I:** 12082,
12085 **IJ:** 12083

Boone, Daniel — Fiction
P: 4664

Booth, John Wilkes
IJ: 12854, 16435

Borden, Lizzie
IJ: 16447

Border collies — Fiction
P: 5305

Boreal forests
PI: 20454

Borglum, Gutzon
I: 16542

Bosch, Hieronymus
P: 1682

Bosnia
PI: 15270, 15294
I: 15268–69 **IJ:** 15284

Bosnian Americans
I: 15269, 17594

Boston
I: 16113, 16720 **IJ:** 16701

Boston — Fiction
P: 3074 **PI:** 8026, 9223
I: 9185, 9243, 9430, 9515
IJ: 10345

Boston Post Road
PI: 16686

Boston Tea Party
PI: 16177 **I:** 16151, 16162

Botany
IJ: 20032

Botany — Biography
IJ: 13341

Botswana
IJ: 14969, 14985, 19165

Bottlenose dolphins
I: 19689

Bourke-White, Margaret
PI: 12192 **IJ:** 12193

Bowditch, Nathaniel
IJ: 12086

Bowie, Jim
IJ: 12855

Box making
IJ: 21443

Boxers — Biography
PI: 13584 **I:** 13582
IJ: 13583, 13585–86

Boxers (dogs)
PI: 19958

Boxing — Fiction
P: 4926 **PI:** 4716

Boy Scouts of America
See Scouts and scouting

Boyfriends — Fiction
I: 8399, 9872, 9943
IJ: 8718, 8753, 8812, 9852,
9924

Boyhood — Poetry
I: 11591

Braces (dental)
IJ: 18185

Bradford, William
IJ: 12856–57, 16107

Bradley, Bill
I: 12858

Brady, Mathew
I: 12859

Braille, Louis
P: 13762 **PI:** 13757,
13759, 13761 **IJ:** 13758,
13760

Brain
P: 18117–18, 18121
I: 18109, 18113–14, 18116,
18120 **IJ:** 18077,
18110–12, 18115

Brandy (singer)
PI: 12358 **IJ:** 12359

Brazil
P: 4882 **PI:** 15740, 15757,
20463 **I:** 15738, 15741,
15743, 15747, 15753,
15756, 15764, 20446
IJ: 11441, 15726, 15728,
15783

Brazil — Cookbooks
I: 15732

Brazil — Fiction
PI: 2608 **IJ:** 7064

Brazil — Folklore
P: 11436, 11444 **IJ:** 11437

Brazil — Holidays
I: 15732, 17333

Bread
P: 20112 **I:** 20077

Bread — Fiction
P: 3109, 3165

Bread — History
I: 20095

Breast cancer
P: 17940

Breckenridge, Mary
I: 12860

Bricks
PI: 21116 **I:** 21160

Brides
I: 17371

Bridges
P: 21126, 21130 **PI:** 21343
I: 16723, 21133, 21142,
21148, 21151

Bridges, Ruby
IJ: 16497

Bridgman, Laura Dewey
I: 13140

**Bris (Jewish circumcision
ceremony) — Fiction**
P: 6123

**British Columbia —
Fiction**
PI: 4726 **IJ:** 6934, 8098

Britten, Benjamin
I: 14221

Brontë family
PI: 14067

Brooklyn
PI: 5214 **IJ:** 16749

Brooklyn — Fiction
P: 4623 **I:** 8162, 8570

Brooklyn Bridge
I: 16723, 21142

**Brooklyn Dodgers
(baseball team) —
Fiction**
I: 10319 **IJ:** 10368

Brooks, Garth
I: 12362 **IJ:** 12360–61

Brothers — Fiction
P: 3429, 3583, 3598, 3611,
3632, 5011, 5020, 5701,
6247, 6593 **PI:** 7469, 8380,
8642 **I:** 7140, 7430, 8499,
8508 **IJ:** 6987, 8801

Brown, Aunt Clara
PI: 12705

Brown, Helen Gurley
IJ: 12507

Brown, John
PI: 12862 **I:** 12861, 16255

Brown, Margaret Wise
P: 12508

Brown, Molly
I: 12863

Brown, Molly — Fiction
P: 4595

Bruchac, Joseph
I: 12509

P = Primary; PI = Primary-Intermediate; I = Intermediate; IJ = Intermediate-Junior High

Bruegel, Pieter
PI: 12194–95 IJ: 13895

Brunei
IJ: 15216

Bryant, Kobe
PI: 13518 I: 13516
IJ: 13515, 13517

Bryant, Paul W.
IJ: 13604

Bubbles
I: 20799 IJ: 20805

**Bubbles — Experiments
and projects**
I: 20809

Bubonic plague
IJ: 14759, 14762

Bubonic plague — Fiction
I: 9128

Buchanan, James
I: 13009

Buck, Pearl S.
I: 12510

Buddha
I: 17175

Buddhism
P: 10802, 17231 PI: 17213
I: 10790, 13777, 17176
IJ: 17186

Buddhism — Biography
IJ: 13778

Buddhism — Fiction
IJ: 9020

Buddhism — Folklore
See also Jataka stories
PI: 10799 I: 10720, 10790
IJ: 10730

Budgeting (money)
I: 16943 IJ: 16942, 16946

Buffalos
P: 18955 I: 15953, 18925,
18966, 18979 IJ: 18987

Buffalos — Fiction
P: 2506 PI: 5187

Buffalos — Folklore
I: 11238

Building and construction
See also types of buidings,
e.g., Houses;
Skyscrapers
P: 3167, 5574, 21117,
21120–21, 21123, 21127,
21132, 21143, 21152,
21158, 21242 PI: 13963,
14586, 16696, 21116, 21249
I: 21113–15, 21135, 21137,
21146–47, 21153, 21155
IJ: 13915, 13947, 13949,
14639, 14727, 14776,
21118, 21134, 21136,
21138, 21150, 21154, 21664

**Building and construction
— Biography**
IJ: 13202

**Building and construction
— Careers**
P: 17787 PI: 17797

**Building and construction
— Experiments and
projects**
I: 21119, 21124

**Building and construction
— Fiction**
P: 634, 3014, 3334, 5577,
5581, 5595–96

**Building and construction
— History**
IJ: 14578, 21156

**Building and construction
— Hospitals**
I: 21140

**Building and construction
— Libraries**
I: 21141

Building blocks
PI: 21673

Bulge, Battle of the
IJ: 14825

Bulimia
See also Eating disorders
IJ: 17994

Bull Run, Battle of
IJ: 16406

Bull terriers — Fiction
P: 5308

Bulldozers
P: 5563 IJ: 21298

Bullfighters — Biography
I: 13685

Bullfighting — Fiction
IJ: 8864

Bullies
P: 17712, 17725 PI: 17711
I: 17698, 17727, 17730
IJ: 18216

Bullies — Fiction
P: 1961, 2494, 2699, 4835,
4911, 4989, 4992, 5006,
5041, 5471, 5679, 6169,
6277, 6294, 6318, 6408,
6444, 6724, 8334 PI: 1475,
6910, 8327, 8699, 8728,
8777, 8974, 10044, 10051,
10097, 10128, 10132, 11225
I: 6841, 7140, 7511, 7764,
8006, 8348, 8381, 8486,
8727, 8746, 8755, 8767,
8785, 8818, 8858, 9584,
9832, 9865, 10031, 10033,
10365 IJ: 6771, 7519,
7928, 8375, 8592, 8652,
8738, 8782, 8808, 9627,
10056

Bullock, Sandra
PI: 12364 IJ: 12363

Bulls — Fiction
PI: 2348

Bunker Hill, Battle of
I: 16202

Bunting, Eve
PI: 12511

Buoyancy (physics)
PI: 20801 I: 20803

Burial customs
PI: 14603 IJ: 14659

Buried treasures
PI: 14525 I: 14529, 21905
IJ: 14334, 14531, 16564,
19874

**Buried treasures —
Fiction**
PI: 9795 I: 9097
IJ: 6757, 7120, 7122, 9847,
21951

Burk, Martha Jane
I: 12864

Burma
See Myanmar

Burnett, Frances Hodgson
IJ: 12512

Burns — Fiction
IJ: 8621

Burroughs, Edgar Rice
IJ: 12513

Burroughs, John
IJ: 13243

Bus drivers
P: 3142

Buses
P: 14261

Buses — Fiction
P: 3119, 3993, 5558, 5573

Bush, Barbara
I: 13010, 13141

Bush, George
P: 13012 I: 13010–11

Bush, George W.
I: 13013 IJ: 13014

Business
See also Money-making
ideas; Occupations and
work
IJ: 16928, 16930

Business — Sports
IJ: 22016

**Businessmen —
Biography**
PI: 12966 I: 12693, 12853,
13296 IJ: 12633, 12680,
12850, 12875, 12905,
12911, 12924, 12960,
13201, 13225, 16372

**Businesswomen —
Biography**
PI: 12810 I: 12662,
12807–8, 12923 IJ: 12676,
12811, 13148, 13163, 17745

Bustards
PI: 19290

Butcher, Solomon
I: 12865

Butcher, Susan
I: 13682

Butler, Jerry
IJ: 13951

Butterflies
P: 4817, 19539, 19543,
19545–46, 19549–51,
19555, 19557, 19560–61,
19563, 19569 PI: 19540,
19544, 19553, 19570
I: 19541–42, 19547–48,
19552, 19558–59,
19564–65, 19567

Butterflies — Fiction
P: 126, 1493, 2225, 2286,
4396, 4549, 4989 PI: 7000
I: 7797

Butterflies — Plays
PI: 12039

**Bwindi Impenetrable
National Park (Uganda)**
I: 19002

Byars, Betsy
I: 12514

Byrd, Admiral
IJ: 12087

Byzantium — Fiction
IJ: 9027

C

**Cabinet (U.S.
Government)**
I: 17107

Cactus
P: 4449 PI: 20402
I: 20226, 20244, 20249,
20252, 20424

Caesar, Augustus
IJ: 14734

Caesar, Julius
IJ: 13763–64, 14735, 14741

Cairo, Egypt
I: 15512

Cairo, Egypt — Fiction
P: 4678

Cajun people
I: 16861, 17369 IJ: 16832

Cajun people — Fiction
P: 620, 2978, 11378
PI: 4851 IJ: 9472

Cajun people — Folklore
P: 11372 PI: 10959–60
I: 11335

Calamity Jane
I: 12864

Calcium
IJ: 20281

P = Primary; PI = Primary-Intermediate; I = Intermediate; IJ = Intermediate-Junior High

Calculation (mathematics)
IJ: 20600

Calculators
PI: 20608

Caldecott Medal
I: 12174

Calder, Alexander
PI: 12197 **IJ:** 12196

Calendars
See also Time
P: 20649–50 **PI:** 20640,
20653 **I:** 20646 **IJ:** 20600,
20641

Calendars — Fiction
P: 407

Calendars — Poetry
PI: 11929

California
PI: 16775, 16785, 16806
I: 16780, 16784 **IJ:** 16759,
16762, 16786, 16810

California — Fiction
P: 4567, 4732, 4794, 5368,
5860, 6274 **PI:** 7250, 9636
I: 6955, 7436, 9153, 9282,
9357, 9584 **IJ:** 6780, 6997,
7965, 8501, 8784, 9355,
9634

California — History
I: 16292, 16365, 16376,
16383, 16758, 16763,
16766, 16795, 16799, 16823
IJ: 15886, 15999, 16778,
16825, 16827

California condors
I: 19341

Calligraphy
I: 21561

Calves — Fiction
P: 5307

Cambodia
I: 15203 **IJ:** 15152

Cambodia — Folklore
P: 10844

Cambodian Americans
I: 17570

**Camden Yards
(Baltimore)**
I: 22124 **IJ:** 22125

Camels — Fiction
PI: 1308, 4743

Cameras
P: 21798 **IJ:** 21805

Cameroon
IJ: 15028

Camps and camping
I: 21749, 22166–67
IJ: 22169

**Camps and camping —
Fiction**
P: 2130, 2414, 2668, 2910,
2912, 2919, 2934, 2953,
2962, 2986, 3057, 3101,
3956, 4181, 4385, 4965,
5028, 6295, 6343, 6391,
6418, 6605, 6673, 6711
PI: 3875, 4479, 6562, 7456,
8287, 9833 **I:** 7040, 7052,
8174, 8256, 8316, 8815,
8838, 9868, 9882, 9888,
9916, 10304 **IJ:** 6842,
6909, 7467, 8282, 8338,
8354, 8604, 8696, 9560,
9878, 9905

**Camps and camping —
Poetry**
PI: 11954

Canada
P: 4760, 15579, 15589
PI: 12250, 15565, 15573,
15582, 15584–87, 15596,
17922 **I:** 15564, 15567–70,
15572, 15577–78,
15580–81, 15583, 15590,
15595, 15597–98, 15794,
15842 **IJ:** 15566, 15575,
15591

Canada — Cookbooks
I: 21715

Canada — Fiction
P: 2935, 4011, 4220, 4576,
4855, 7105 **PI:** 4597, 4722,
4864, 5167, 6877, 8563
I: 6769, 8902, 8937, 9281,
9659, 10075, 10096
IJ: 6820, 7312, 7605, 8545,
8764, 8928, 8935, 8945,
8947

Canada — Folklore
PI: 8946

Canada — History
I: 16245 **IJ:** 8949, 16159,
16161

Canada — Poetry
P: 11892 **IJ:** 11805

Canada geese — Fiction
P: 5386

Canals
I: 16237, 16264 **IJ:** 15672,
15675, 16713

Canals — Fiction
IJ: 9559

Cancer
P: 3461, 17940 **I:** 17976
IJ: 17950, 17985, 18017

Cancer — Biography
IJ: 13677

Cancer — Fiction
P: 3955, 5002, 5098, 5477
PI: 8361 **I:** 7524
IJ: 8305, 8452, 8571

Candlemaking — Fiction
IJ: 8112

Candy — Fiction
P: 5970, 5987

Canoes and canoeing
PI: 22260, 22262

**Canoes and canoeing —
Fiction**
P: 2985, 6203 **I:** 9350
IJ: 6842

Canseco, José
IJ: 13441

Canyons
PI: 20320

Cape Cod — Fiction
P: 2924

Cape Town (South Africa)
IJ: 15003

Capital punishment
IJ: 17066

Capone, Al
IJ: 12866

Capri — Fiction
I: 8036

Capybaras
PI: 19205

Car washes — Fiction
P: 3439

Card games
P: 22238 **PI:** 22229–31
I: 22236 **IJ:** 22237

Card tricks
PI: 22231

Cardinals (birds)
I: 19261

**Cardinals (birds) —
Fiction**
P: 1428, 5372

Careers
See also Occupations and
work; and specific
professionals, e.g.,
Teachers
P: 17756, 17767 **IJ:** 17768

Careers — Fiction
P: 3038, 3359, 5527

Careers — Women
IJ: 17804

Carey, Mariah
I: 12365

Caribbean Islands
P: 87 **I:** 15699, 15703,
15706 **IJ:** 15717, 17544

**Caribbean Islands —
Cookbooks**
I: 21716 **IJ:** 21711

**Caribbean Islands —
Crafts**
IJ: 21504

**Caribbean Islands —
Fiction**
P: 402, 441, 1065, 2933,
4661, 4675, 4690, 4879
PI: 1021, 6135, 9735
IJ: 7097, 8377, 9130, 9132

**Caribbean Islands —
Folklore**
P: 10495, 11419–22, 11424,
11428, 11430, 11433
PI: 11418, 11427, 11429
I: 10558, 10580, 11426,
11432

**Caribbean Islands —
Holidays**
I: 15706

**Caribbean Islands —
Poetry**
P: 11614 **PI:** 11580
I: 11586

Caribbean Sea
I: 19830

Caribou
P: 5211 **PI:** 19156

Caribou — Fiction
P: 107, 906

Carisbrooke Castle
I: 15364

Carle, Eric
IJ: 12198

Carmichael, Stokely
I: 12706

Carnaval (holiday)
P: 87 **I:** 17333, 17348

**Carnaval (holiday) —
Fiction**
P: 4702

Carnival of the Animals
P: 14124

Carnivals — Fiction
P: 2903, 5060

Carnivorous plants
P: 20227, 20238 **PI:** 20242
I: 20222 **IJ:** 20251

**Caroline, Princess of
Monaco**
I: 13765

Carols
See Christmas — Songs
and carols

Carousels — Fiction
P: 1089, 3088, 3192, 3312
I: 7731

Carpenters — Careers
PI: 17785

Carrey, Jim
IJ: 12366

Carrots — Fiction
P: 1320, 6386

Cars
See Automobiles

Carson, Kit
I: 12088

Carson, Kit — Fiction
PI: 9367

P = Primary; PI = Primary-Intermediate; I = Intermediate; IJ = Intermediate-Junior High

Carson, Rachel
PI: 13248–49 I: 13245–46
IJ: 13216, 13244, 13247,
13250

Carter, James E.
I: 12674, 13015–16, 13020
IJ: 13017–19

Carter, Rosalynn
I: 13142 IJ: 13017

Carthage
IJ: 13806

Cartoons and cartooning
PI: 21583 I: 12228, 21557
IJ: 12225, 21562

**Cartoons and cartooning
— Biography**
PI: 12301 I: 12229
IJ: 12226, 12272

**Cartoons and cartooning
— Fiction**
PI: 8556 IJ: 9841

**Carver, George
Washington**
P: 13254, 13257
PI: 13251–52, 13255
I: 13253, 13256

Cassatt, Mary
P: 737 I: 12199–200
IJ: 12201–2

Cassatt, Mary — Fiction
P: 4847

Cassidy, Butch
IJ: 12867–68

Cassidy, Butch — Fiction
PI: 9407

Castles
P: 14753 PI: 14757
I: 14777, 14785, 14788–89,
21381 IJ: 14766, 14776,
14793

Castles — Fiction
P: 919, 2499, 6189 I: 6931,
7667, 7787, 8211, 9118
IJ: 7674, 7830

Caterpillars
P: 19539, 19549, 19554–55
PI: 19553, 19562, 19568

Caterpillars — Fiction
P: 2286, 4396, 5160, 5205,
6507

Caterpillars — Folklore
IJ: 10825

Cathedrals
I: 14778, 21137 IJ: 13947,
13949

Cather, Willa
PI: 12515 IJ: 12516

Catholicism
P: 17219 I: 13794, 15360

Catholicism — Fiction
I: 10049

Catlin, George
I: 12203

Cats
See also Big cats
P: 5169, 5263, 5265, 19919,
19921, 19924–25, 19927,
19933–34 PI: 19916–17,
19923, 19926, 19929–32
I: 19090, 19111, 19915,
19918, 19922, 19928,
19935, 21555 IJ: 13923,
19096

Cats — Art
P: 13914

Cats — Communication
PI: 19920

Cats — Egypt
I: 14672

Cats — Feral
I: 19079

Cats — Fiction
P: 29, 416, 595, 759, 924,
1016, 1188, 1332, 1467,
1477, 1778, 1809, 1905,
1952, 1955, 1984, 2026–27,
2045, 2111, 2291, 2306,
2402, 2507, 2655, 2663,
2720, 2767, 3219, 4179,
4300, 4322, 4424, 4584,
4614, 4622, 4846, 5014,
5031, 5042, 5100, 5111–12,
5127, 5130, 5148, 5155,
5159, 5168, 5173, 5179,
5184, 5186, 5192, 5196,
5216, 5234, 5247–49, 5252,
5254–55, 5258, 5262,
5288–89, 5292, 5322, 5327,
5339, 5346–47, 5350, 5354,
5357, 5373, 5383, 5400,
5415, 5421, 5428, 5433,
5437, 5443, 5452, 5686,
5696, 5765, 5821, 5998,
6122, 6225, 6315, 6347,
6376, 6388, 6430, 6514,
6524, 6543, 6563, 6567,
6593, 6598, 6640, 6644–45,
7224 PI: 2112, 2707, 4034,
7155, 7191, 7308, 7899,
8115, 9382 I: 6985, 7085,
7187, 7280, 7409, 7552,
7554, 7591, 7745, 8025,
8181–82, 8713, 8811, 8841,
8861, 8969, 9595, 9913,
10235, 10409, 10489
IJ: 7276, 7982

Cats — Folklore
P: 10873, 10878, 10952
PI: 10879 I: 10559

Cats — History
PI: 19930 I: 19935

Cats — Jokes and riddles
PI: 21831

Cats — Nursery rhymes
P: 849, 856 PI: 844

Cats — Poetry
P: 11815, 11887, 11889
PI: 11811 I: 11778, 11794,
11799 IJ: 11775

Cats — Senses
P: 5380

Cattle
P: 20048, 20054, 20064,
20085, 20094

Cattle — Fiction
P: 390, 1274, 2079, 2293,
2513, 5046, 5194, 5257,
5395, 5409, 5552, 5809
PI: 7304

Cattle — Folklore
I: 10679 PI: 10962

Cattle drives
I: 16335, 16351

Cattle drives — Fiction
P: 2960 IJ: 7008

Cave paintings
P: 13937 PI: 13848
IJ: 14503, 14509

Cave paintings — Fiction
P: 2754, 4635

Caves
PI: 20392 I: 18629, 20380
IJ: 20370

Caves — Fiction
P: 6588

Cayuga Indians
P: 15945

Celebrities — Addresses
IJ: 21933

Cellos — Fiction
IJ: 8753

Cells (human body)
P: 18076 I: 18048

Celts
IJ: 15361

Celts — Folklore
I: 11011, 11452 IJ: 11022

Celts — History
I: 11452

Censorship
IJ: 17156

Census Bureau (U.S.)
See United States Census
Bureau

Census (U.S.)
IJ: 17115

Centipedes
P: 19446

**Central America —
Crafts**
I: 21503 IJ: 15615, 21453

**Central America —
Fiction**
P: 3150

**Central America —
Holidays**
PI: 17406 IJ: 17380

Central America — Maps
I: 14331

Central Park (New York)
I: 12941

**Central Park (New York)
— Biography**
PI: 12942

**Central Park (New York)
— Fiction**
P: 4275

Ceramics
IJ: 21529

Cereals — Biography
I: 12917

Cerebral palsy
PI: 13347, 17906, 17915,
17948 I: 17990 IJ: 17991

Cerebral palsy — Fiction
P: 4979 PI: 8888 I: 7102,
8907 IJ: 8489, 8836, 8893

Cervantes, Miguel de
IJ: 12517

Cézanne, Paul
PI: 12204 I: 12206
IJ: 12205

Chagall, Marc
PI: 12209 IJ: 12207–8,
13905

Chairs — Fiction
P: 4724, 6254

***Challenger* (space shuttle)**
I: 20972 IJ: 20958

Chameleons
P: 18745, 18752 PI: 18751
I: 18743, 18747

Chameleons — Fiction
P: 1924, 5425

**Champollion, Jean-
Francois**
I: 13766

Chang, Michael
IJ: 13646

Chang, Wah Ming
IJ: 12210

Chaparrals
IJ: 20389

Chaplin, Charlie
IJ: 12367

Chapman, John
See also Appleseed,
Johnny
P: 12842–44 PI: 12845
I: 12846

Character development
I: 17622

Charlemagne, Emperor
IJ: 13767

P = Primary; PI = Primary-Intermediate; I = Intermediate; IJ = Intermediate-Junior High

Charles, Ray
IJ: 12368

**Charleston (SC) —
Fiction**
IJ: 9263

Charts
P: 20577

Chauvet cave (France)
IJ: 14503

Chavez, Cesar
PI: 12825 **I:** 12827
IJ: 12826

Chavez, Cesar — Poetry
IJ: 11528

Chavez, Julio Cesar
IJ: 13583

Cheating — Fiction
PI: 8729

Checks (banking)
I: 16923

Cheerleading
PI: 21670

Cheese
P: 20070

Cheese — Fiction
P: 4646

Cheetahs
P: 19103, 19110
PI: 19085, 19093, 19098,
19105 **I:** 19076 **IJ:** 19116

Chemical industry
I: 21042

Chemistry
I: 20288

Chemistry — Biography
I: 13312

**Chemistry —
Experiments and
projects**
P: 20287 **I:** 18324,
20289–90, 20292 **IJ:** 18305

Cherokee Indians
P: 16021 **I:** 16046
IJ: 15992, 16005

**Cherokee Indians —
Biography**
I: 12993–94 **IJ:** 12976

**Cherokee Indians —
Fiction**
IJ: 9152, 9154, 9179

**Cherokee Indians —
History**
P: 15988 **PI:** 15936,
15938, 16059 **I:** 15923

Cherokee language
I: 12993

Cherry, Lynne
I: 12518

Chess
PI: 22170 **I:** 22172
IJ: 22171, 22173

Chess — Fiction
I: 7641, 9865

Chewing gum
PI: 20137 **IJ:** 20132

Cheyenne Indians
PI: 16047, 16054, 16058
I: 16003, 16012 **IJ:** 15926,
15990, 16057

**Cheyenne Indians —
Fiction**
PI: 9149 **IJ:** 8434

**Cheyenne Indians —
Folklore**
P: 11242

**Cheyenne Indians —
History**
PI: 15950 **I:** 16062

Chicago
I: 16573, 16584, 16586

Chicago — Fiction
PI: 5062, 6976, 7521
I: 8536, 9592 **IJ:** 9543

Chicago — Poetry
PI: 11749

**Chicago Bulls (basketball
team)**
IJ: 22140

Chicago Fire (1871)
IJ: 16572

**Chicago Fire (1871) —
Fiction**
I: 9614

**Chickasaw Indians —
Folklore**
P: 11210

Chicken pox — Fiction
P: 6132

Chickens
P: 19228, 19302, 19306,
20063, 20073, 20086
I: 20050 **IJ:** 19304

Chickens — Fiction
P: 397, 962, 1349, 1773,
2095, 2124–25, 2185, 2233,
2284, 2406, 2544, 2565,
2956, 4138, 4271, 5181,
5232, 5335, 5381, 5969,
6388 **PI:** 10516 **I:** 7183,
9792, 9967

Chickens — Folklore
P: 10946, 10957, 10979–80,
11089

Chickens — Poetry
P: 11546

Child, Lydia Maria
I: 13143

Child abuse
P: 17733 **I:** 17705
IJ: 17157, 17655, 17708,
17710

Child abuse — Fiction
P: 4998, 5087, 5092
I: 8478, 8636, 8795

Child care — Careers
P: 17750

Child development
I: 17619

Child labor
PI: 12916 **I:** 15856
IJ: 16448, 17022

Child labor — Biography
IJ: 12901

Child labor — Fiction
PI: 4864 **I:** 9555
IJ: 9103, 9573

Child labor — History
I: 16495 **IJ:** 16449

**Child sexual abuse —
Fiction**
IJ: 8545

Childbirth
See also Birth
P: 18242

Childhood
I: 17358

Childhood — Biography
I: 12526

Childhood — Feral
I: 17619

Childhood — Fiction
P: 3567

Childhood — Poetry
P: 3050, 3452, 11699
I: 11599 **IJ:** 11582

Children
P: 4831, 14327, 17633
I: 14343

Children — Art
P: 3190, 3461 **I:** 13922

Children (U.S.) — History
I: 16280

Children's literature
I: 12174

**Children's literature —
Anthologies**
I: 10257

**Children's literature —
Biography**
I: 12488

**Children's literature —
Writers**
I: 14065

Children's rights
P: 17019 **I:** 13150–51
IJ: 17030, 17044

**Children's rights —
Poetry**
P: 11869

Chile
PI: 15785 **I:** 15746
IJ: 15760, 15790

Chile — Folklore
P: 11442

Chile — Holidays
PI: 15784

Chili — Fiction
P: 1084

Chimpanzees
P: 19003, 19014 **PI:** 13299
I: 18995–96, 19005, 19015
IJ: 13301

Chimpanzees — Fiction
P: 6391–93

**Chimpanzees — Space
exploration**
IJ: 20984

China
P: 15056, 15080
PI: 15061, 15063, 15066,
15068, 15084, 15089, 19191
I: 15057, 15064–65, 15067,
15069, 15072–74, 15082,
15088, 15090, 15092–93
IJ: 15053, 15055,
15058–60, 15062, 15078,
19187

China — Astrology
IJ: 21914

China — Cookbooks
IJ: 21754

China — Crafts
IJ: 21502

China — Emigration
I: 15079

China — Festivals
I: 15085

China — Fiction
P: 1104, 1708, 1716, 3600,
3812, 4087, 4684, 4725,
4735, 4776, 4791, 4794,
4799, 5082, 5428, 5438,
10444 **PI:** 1109, 1138,
1402, 4752, 8997, 9011,
9013, 9759 **I:** 7303, 7352,
8990, 9012, 9014, 9017
IJ: 8942, 9001, 9010, 9649,
9653, 9693, 10768

China — Folklore
P: 10740–41, 10744–45,
10747, 10749–50, 10753,
10756–57, 10760–62,
10765–67, 10769–72,
10774–75, 10777–78,
10780, 10782–84
PI: 10610, 10742–43,
10751, 10764, 10773,
10779, 10781 **I:** 10738,
10748, 10754–55, 10758,
10776, 10785 **IJ:** 10739,
10746, 10759, 10763

China — History
PI: 15087 **I:** 15075–76,
15083, 15086, 15091
IJ: 12536, 15054,
15070–71, 15077

China — Houses
I: 15081

China — Poetry
PI: 11650

China — Short stories
I: 8988

China — Terracotta warriors
IJ: 15077

Chinese Americans
P: 3758, 5618, 5656
I: 17367 **IJ:** 17553, 17600

Chinese Americans — Biography
I: 13685 **IJ:** 12210, 12255

Chinese Americans — Fiction
P: 3069, 3345, 3367, 3775, 4794, 5047, 5093, 5470, 5620, 5635, 6274 **PI:** 3779, 4895, 5721, 8231 **I:** 7139, 7352, 7488, 8234, 8496–97, 8546, 8873, 9017, 10023 **IJ:** 7002, 7137–38, 7380, 8547–48, 9346, 9372, 9641

Chinese language
P: 403, 489 **PI:** 13986
IJ: 13989

Chinese language — Writing
P: 13984–85 **PI:** 14083

Chinese Moon Festival — Fiction
P: 2753

Chinese New Year
P: 5618, 5620–21, 5656, 17397 **PI:** 17342 **I:** 17346, 17367

Chinese New Year — Crafts
PI: 17349

Chinese New Year — Fiction
P: 5611, 5635, 5654, 5658
PI: 7371

Chinook Indians — Folklore
I: 11270

Chipmunks
I: 19192

Chipmunks — Fiction
P: 5241, 6215

Chippewa Indians
PI: 16016 **I:** 15981
IJ: 16027

Chippewa Indians — Fiction
P: 733, 758, 4558

Chippewa Indians — Folklore
P: 11234 **PI:** 11315
I: 11235

Chisholm, Shirley
PI: 12707

Chisholm Trail
PI: 16361 **I:** 16360

Chisholm Trail — Fiction
I: 9419

Chocolate
P: 20109 **I:** 20136

Chocolate — Biography
I: 12899

Chocolate — Fiction
P: 1319 **I:** 7694, 9934, 9993

Chocolates
I: 20136

Choctaw Indians
IJ: 15948

Choctaw Indians — Fiction
I: 9162

Choctaw Indians — History
PI: 15989

Choinumne Indians
IJ: 16002

Chopin, Frederic
P: 12325

Choreography — Biography
IJ: 12162, 12390

Chores — Fiction
I: 8376, 8584, 9437, 10086

Christiana Riot — Fiction
IJ: 9318

Christianity
P: 17227 **I:** 13794, 17211
IJ: 17208, 17194, 17306, 17313

Christianity — Anthologies
I: 17174, 17212

Christianity — Biography
IJ: 13859

Christianity — Crafts
PI: 21475

Christianity — Fiction
IJ: 8944

Christianity — Holy days
I: 17403

Christianity — Music
PI: 14125

Christmas
P: 5640, 5793, 5825, 5827, 5892, 17409, 17417, 17425, 17427, 17429 **PI:** 5923, 17414, 17420, 17423, 17426, 17431 **I:** 15570, 17411, 17413, 17415, 17419, 17421, 17424, 17428

Christmas — Carols
See Christmas — Songs and carols

Christmas — Crafts
P: 5933, 21511 **PI:** 17410, 17431, 21411, 21473, 21493 **I:** 21423, 21468, 21472, 21512

Christmas — Fairy tales
I: 10477

Christmas — Fiction
P: 16, 70, 149, 1659, 2002, 3052, 3316, 3467, 3704, 4370, 4591, 5095, 5267, 5646, 5741–68, 5770–71, 5773–75, 5777–85, 5787–89, 5791–92, 5794–802, 5804, 5806–15, 5817–22, 5824, 5826, 5828–39, 5841–43, 5845, 5847–48, 5850–52, 5854–65, 5867–75, 5877–80, 5882–84, 5887–91, 5893–97, 5899–914, 5916, 5918–22, 5924–29, 5931–39, 5941–56, 5958–61, 6528, 9763 **PI:** 5772, 5790, 5803, 5805, 5816, 5844, 5853, 5881, 5886, 5930, 5940, 5957, 7417, 9216, 9327, 9706, 9711, 9714, 9722, 9729–30, 9734–35, 9737, 9742, 9744, 9765, 9768 **I:** 8039, 9705, 9712–13, 9715, 9719, 9725, 9727, 9732–33, 9736, 9739–40, 9743, 9745, 9747, 9749, 9751–52, 9757, 17418 **IJ:** 6753, 8501, 9704, 9709, 9718, 9720–21, 9731, 9764, 9769

Christmas — Folklore
P: 10920, 11187 **PI:** 9756, 11399

Christmas — Greece
IJ: 17412

Christmas — History
I: 16262

Christmas — Jokes and riddles
P: 5876

Christmas — Plays
All: 12023

Christmas — Poetry
P: 5849, 5885, 5917, 11828, 11830–31, 11836, 11839–49, 17432 **IJ:** 11826, 11853

Christmas — Short stories
PI: 5866 **I:** 9726, 9760, 17416 **IJ:** 9753

Christmas — Songs and carols
P: 5840, 14198–99, 14204, 14206, 14208–11, 14213–17 **PI:** 14197, 14202–3, 14207, 14212 **I:** 14201, 14205 **IJ:** 14200, 17430

Christmas trees — Fiction
P: 5769, 5776, 5786, 5838, 5846, 5898, 5900, 5915

Christopher, Saint
P: 13768

Chumash Indians
I: 15986

Chumash Indians — Folklore
P: 11318

Churches
P: 17232

Churches — Fiction
P: 4789

Churches — History
IJ: 14767

Churchill, Winston
IJ: 13769–70

Ciaran, Saint
I: 13771

Cid, El
IJ: 13772

Cinco de Mayo (Mexican holiday)
P: 17398 **I:** 15607

Circles
PI: 20605

Circles — Fiction
P: 333

Circulatory system
P: 18090 **PI:** 18094
I: 18078, 18087–88, 18093
IJ: 18086, 18089, 18092

Circuses
P: 3115, 14268 **PI:** 2925
I: 14270 **IJ:** 14269

Circuses — Biography
IJ: 12353

Circuses — Fiction
P: 1496, 1964, 2076, 2099, 2568, 2781, 3369, 4079, 4199, 4230, 4754, 5152, 5218, 6384 **PI:** 4950
I: 6837, 7001 **IJ:** 6826, 9884

Cisneros, Henry
I: 12828

Cities and city life
See also names of specific cities, e.g., Boston
P: 3106, 3388, 3435
PI: 8763, 16973, 21869
I: 13871, 14755, 16971–72
IJ: 14332, 21139

Cities and city life — Fiction
P: 62, 2401, 3016, 3061, 3208, 3240, 3301, 3303, 3362, 3399, 3457, 4015, 4235, 4397 **PI:** 3309
I: 3005, 8385, 8485, 8671
IJ: 7276

Cities and city life — Folklore
I: 10533

Cities and city life — History
IJ: 15871

Cities and city life — Poetry
P: 11608, 11744 **PI:** 11524

Citizenship (U.S.)
IJ: 17043

Citizenship (U.S.) — Fiction
P: 4941

Civil rights
See also names of civil rights leaders, e.g., King, Martin Luther, Jr.; and specific civil rights, e.g., Human rights, Women's rights
P: 5610, 12739, 12748, 16518 **PI:** 12736, 12746–47, 12776, 12818, 17037–38, 17042, 17049 **I:** 12706, 12718, 12727, 12738, 12742–43, 12745, 12760, 12775, 16522, 16524, 17029, 17036, 17039, 17046–48, 17050, 17559 **IJ:** 12659, 12741, 12744, 12749, 12751, 12762, 12782–83, 16510–11, 16523, 17023, 17026, 17031, 17033–35, 17040–41, 17044, 17051–53

Civil rights — Biography
P: 12752–53 **PI:** 12709–10, 12712, 12717, 12721, 12725, 12750, 12755–56, 12772–74, 12777–79, 12817, 12821, 13130, 13828, 13832 **I:** 12694, 12714, 12719, 12728, 12735, 12780, 12787, 12794, 12814, 12822, 13151, 13582 **IJ:** 12656, 12699, 12729, 12737, 12754, 13724

Civil rights — Children
IJ: 17028, 17030

Civil rights — Fiction
P: 4740 **I:** 7366, 7535

Civil rights — History
IJ: 15893

Civil War (U.S.)
See also names of specific battles, e.g., Gettysburg, Battle of; and names of individuals, e.g., Lee, Robert E.
P: 13063 **PI:** 13067, 16389, 16415–16, 16419 **I:** 9478, 12906, 12926, 13036–37, 13068, 16390–91, 16420, 16423–25, 16430–31, 16438

IJ: 12876, 13066, 13076, 13152–53, 16236, 16268, 16387–88, 16394–95, 16398–402, 16404–7, 16409–13, 16417–18, 16422, 16426, 16432–37, 16439, 16441–43

Civil War (U.S.) — Art
IJ: 16421

Civil War (U.S.) — Biography
PI: 12925 **I:** 12859, 12967 **IJ:** 12652–53, 12854, 12872, 12907, 12927, 12963

Civil War (U.S.) — Children
I: 16423

Civil War (U.S.) — Cookbooks
IJ: 16403

Civil War (U.S.) — Diaries
I: 9466–67

Civil War (U.S.) — Experiments and projects
IJ: 16414

Civil War (U.S.) — Fiction
P: 2971, 4568, 4804 **PI:** 9469, 9484, 9490, 9495, 9608 **I:** 7614, 9468, 9471, 9480–81, 9491, 9496–99, 9501, 9504–6 **IJ:** 9463–65, 9470, 9472–75, 9477, 9479, 9482–83, 9485–89, 9492–94, 9500, 9502, 9507–9

Civil War (U.S.) — Navies
IJ: 16427, 16439

Civil War (U.S.) — Photography
IJ: 16440

Civil War (U.S.) — Prisons
IJ: 16428

Civil War (U.S.) — Weapons
I: 16392 **IJ:** 16396

Civil War (U.S.) — Women
I: 16393 **IJ:** 9510, 16429

Clambakes
I: 16022

Clapping rhymes
P: 1245

Clarinets
P: 14222

Clark, Eugenie
I: 13259 **IJ:** 13258

Clark, William
PI: 12131, 16076, 16091 **I:** 16090

Clay modeling
P: 21533 **PI:** 21530 **I:** 21536

Cleanliness
See also Hygiene
P: 3047

Cleanliness — Fiction
P: 6469 **I:** 8639

Clemente, Roberto
I: 13442, 13444–45 **IJ:** 13443

Cleopatra
P: 13774 **I:** 13773, 13775 **IJ:** 13776

Cleopatra — Fiction
IJ: 8941, 8964

Clergy — Fiction
I: 8206

Cleveland, Grover
IJ: 13021

Climate
See also Weather
IJ: 20787

Clinton, Bill
PI: 13022–23 **I:** 13024–25

Clinton, Hillary Rodham
PI: 13023, 13144, 13146 **I:** 13145, 13147

Cliques
IJ: 17728

Cliques — Fiction
IJ: 10129

Clock and watches
See Time and clocks

Clones and cloning
IJ: 17898, 18035

Close, Chuck
I: 12211

Clothing and dress
See also Costumes and costume making; Shoes

Clothing and dress — Crafts
I: 21647

Clothing and dress — Fiction
P: 208, 930, 2364, 2506, 3149, 3211, 3231, 3480, 3482, 3669, 3969, 4082, 4149, 4414, 4594, 6542, 6662, 10378, 21166 **PI:** 4596, 12966, 21174, 21176, 21551 **I:** 21168, 21178 **IJ:** 21184

Clothing and dress — Folklore
P: 10854, 10864 **I:** 10529

Clothing and dress — History
IJ: 16450, 16478, 16515–17, 21175

Cloud forests
PI: 20434

Clouds
P: 20765 **I:** 20661, 20771, 20781

Clouds — Fiction
P: 1036, 4415, 5142, 6355

Clowns
PI: 21672, 22005

Clowns — Fiction
P: 909, 4632 **I:** 7422 **IJ:** 8706

Coaches (sports)
P: 3135

Coal and coal mining
P: 20843 **IJ:** 16448

Coal and coal mining — Fiction
PI: 4864 **I:** 9273, 9606 **IJ:** 8439, 9519

Coast Guard
See United States Coast Guard

Cobb, Ty
I: 13446

Cobras
PI: 18767

Cocaine and crack
IJ: 17885, 17894

Cochiti Indians
PI: 15973

Cochran, Jacqueline
IJ: 12089

Cockroaches
P: 19447 **I:** 19431

Cockroaches — Fiction
I: 7832

Codes and ciphers
PI: 13967

Codes and ciphers — Fiction
P: 4812, 5671

Cody, Buffalo Bill
I: 12869 **IJ:** 12870, 14266

Cody, Buffalo Bill — Fiction
PI: 6273 **IJ:** 9454

Coelophysis
PI: 14420

Cold War
IJ: 12934, 14595

Colds
P: 17952 **I:** 17999

Cole, Joanna
PI: 12519

Cole, Nat King
IJ: 12178

Cole, Natalie
IJ: 12178

P = Primary; PI = Primary-Intermediate; I = Intermediate; IJ = Intermediate-Junior High

Coleman, Bessie
P: 12090, 12093–94
I: 12091–92

Collage
PI: 21611 **I:** 17598

Collections and collecting
P: 21806 **I:** 21809

Collections and collecting — Fiction
P: 5508 **I:** 7434

Collective nouns — Fiction
P: 6061

Collies — Fiction
I: 7256

Colombia
PI: 15762 **I:** 15748
IJ: 15727, 15729, 15765

Colombia — Fiction
P: 3966

Colonial Period (U.S.)
P: 12878, 12882–83, 16137, 16188 **PI:** 16144, 16147, 16150, 16155–57, 16163, 16177 **I:** 16113, 16121, 16123–24, 16128–29, 16135, 16139, 16143, 16149, 16151–53, 16158, 16166–67, 16169–70, 16184, 16186–87
IJ: 12879, 13160, 16098, 16102–5, 16107–8, 16112, 16114, 16118–20, 16122, 16125–26, 16130–34, 16138, 16145, 16159–61, 16171–73, 16176, 16178, 16181–82

Colonial Period (U.S.) — Biography
P: 12310 **PI:** 12788, 12848
I: 12945, 16214
IJ: 12856–57

Colonial Period (U.S.) — Childhood
I: 16097

Colonial Period (U.S.) — Cookbooks
PI: 21696 **I:** 16136
IJ: 16112

Colonial Period (U.S.) — Crafts
PI: 16106, 21519
I: 16100–1, 16115–16, 16142, 16148 **IJ:** 16179

Colonial Period (U.S.) — Fiction
P: 6142, 6147, 9200
PI: 9214–15 **I:** 9172, 9185–86, 9189–90, 9198–99, 9202, 9205–7, 9210, 9217, 9237, 9397, 16154 **IJ:** 7721, 9157, 9188, 9191–95, 9201, 9208–9, 9212–13, 9218–19, 9238

Colonial Period (U.S.) — History
IJ: 16109–11

Colonial Period (U.S.) — Medicine
IJ: 16180

Colonial Period (U.S.) — Religion
IJ: 16099

Colonial Period (U.S.) — Science
IJ: 16140

Color
P: 20866, 20877 **PI:** 20870
I: 20859, 20864

Color — Experiments and projects
I: 20864

Colorado
PI: 16607 **I:** 16600, 16901
IJ: 16596, 16599

Colorado — Fiction
P: 4595 **I:** 7159 **IJ:** 8619, 9344

Colorado — History
I: 16000, 16644 **IJ:** 15921, 16294

Colorado River
IJ: 15898, 16087

Colors
See also Concept books — Colors
P: 13929

Colors — Experiments and projects
I: 20854 **IJ:** 20863

Colors — Fiction
P: 3001

Colors — Poetry
P: 11665

Colosseum (Rome, Italy)
PI: 14715 **I:** 14712
IJ: 14731

Columbus, Christopher
P: 12096, 16083
PI: 12095, 12099, 17354
I: 12098, 16077, 16079, 16084 **IJ:** 12097, 12100

Columbus, Christopher — Fiction
PI: 8927, 9142

Columbus Day
P: 17335, 17382

Comanche Indians
IJ: 15927

Comanche Indians — Fiction
IJ: 9439

Comanche Indians — Folklore
P: 11229

Comanche Indians — History
I: 16011

Combines (farm machinery)
P: 20071, 21253

Comedians — Biography
PI: 12433, 12482 **I:** 12351, 12369, 12389, 12436
IJ: 12366, 12370, 12372, 12434–35, 12437, 12455

Comets
P: 18521, 18526
PI: 18393, 18505, 18527, 18529, 18534 **I:** 18508, 18516, 18520 **IJ:** 18504

Comic books
IJ: 21586, 21811

Comic strips
I: 13926

Coming of age — Customs
PI: 17400

Commena, Anna
IJ: 9027

Commonwealth of Independent States
IJ: 15428

Communication
I: 14587, 21260 **IJ:** 13966, 21203, 21232

Communication — Careers
IJ: 17780

Communication — Computers
IJ: 21222

Communication — History
I: 13965

Communism
IJ: 12934

Community life
See also Everyday life
P: 3131–34, 3139, 3144, 3163–64, 3936 **PI:** 3442

Community life — Fiction
P: 3029, 3059, 3095, 3162, 3181, 3205–6, 3210, 3224, 3245, 3257–58, 3284, 3313, 3330–31, 3346, 3402, 3412, 3490, 3494, 3496, 4630
I: 8726

Community service
I: 17150, 17155

Competition
PI: 17720

Composers — Biography
P: 12317, 12325, 12334
PI: 12318–19, 12321–22, 12324, 12328, 12333, 12335, 12339–40 **I:** 12172, 12326, 12330–31

IJ: 12185, 12320, 12323, 12327, 12329, 12336, 12338

Composers — Fiction
PI: 9031

Composers — Women — Biography
I: 12332

Compost
P: 3169 **PI:** 19460

Computer animation
I: 21191, 21237 **IJ:** 17791

Computer animation — Careers
IJ: 17791

Computer graphics
I: 21237

Computers
See also specific topics, e.g., Internet (computers); World Wide Web (computers)
P: 21201 **PI:** 13332, 21194, 21196–99, 21211–12, 21227
I: 21190–91, 21195, 21202, 21204, 21206–8, 21228, 21238 **IJ:** 13317, 14002, 18286, 20600, 21192–93, 21203, 21213–15, 21217–19, 21222, 21232–35

Computers — Biography
PI: 12912, 13353
I: 13294–97 **IJ:** 12850, 12911, 13201, 13225

Computers — Careers
IJ: 17788, 17790, 17794, 17796

Computers — Crafts
PI: 21591

Computers — Experiments and projects
PI: 21224 **I:** 21223

Computers — Fiction
P: 5474, 6267 **PI:** 6920
I: 6904, 10156 **IJ:** 7019

Concentration camps
See also Holocaust

Concentration camps — Fiction
IJ: 9665

Concept books — Addition
P: 399

Concept books — Behavior
PI: 167

Concept books — Cause and effect
P: 258

Concept books — Change
P: 222, 258

Concept books — Colors
P: 162, 164, 177, 189, 197, 254, 260–63, 265–91, 293–96, 393, 609, 6073, 6221 **PI:** 264, 292

Concept books — Directions
P: 182

Concept books — Distances
P: 235

Concept books — Division
P: 400, 421

Concept books — Emotions
P: 152, 214, 14046

Concept books — Estimation
P: 20642

Concept books — Flying
P: 175

Concept books — General
P: 153–55, 159, 168–73, 179–81, 183–85, 188–89, 193, 195–96, 199–200, 202–8, 211–13, 215–19, 221, 224, 226, 229, 238–40, 242, 246, 250–51, 253, 255, 259, 270, 298, 301, 507, 2549, 4512, 14044 **PI:** 241, 359, 18803 **IJ:** 14057

Concept books — Groups
P: 467

Concept books — Maps
P: 157

Concept books — Measurement
P: 366 **PI:** 354

Concept books — Multiplication
P: 400

Concept books — Odd and even
P: 529

Concept books — Opposites
P: 158, 160–61, 163, 165, 174, 178, 187, 191, 198, 201, 220, 227, 231, 237, 243, 249, 252, 6475

Concept books — Patterns
P: 192, 223, 232, 318 **PI:** 233

Concept books — Perception
P: 297, 299–300, 302, 304–15, 318, 444 **PI:** 317

Concept books — Probability
P: 228 **PI:** 20579

Concept books — Reasoning
P: 3720

Concept books — Similarities
P: 247

Concept books — Sizes and shapes
P: 162, 232, 256, 266, 320–53, 355–58, 360–65, 4028, 4152, 6185 **PI:** 319, 20605–6, 20800

Concept books — Subtraction
P: 553

Concept books — Symmetry
P: 348

Concept books — Time
P: 156, 166, 194, 209, 225, 244–45, 257, 5689, 20651

Concept books — Touch
P: 186, 303

Concept books — Triangles
P: 324

Concept books — Verbs
P: 236

Concrete mixers
P: 5564

Condors
I: 19275, 19341

Conductors (music) — Biography
IJ: 12440

Conductors (music) — Fiction
P: 4214

Conestoga wagons
PI: 16286

Conestoga wagons — Fiction
PI: 9382, 9455 **I:** 9441 **IJ:** 9415

Coney Island — Fiction
PI: 9616

Congo (country)
I: 15032

Congo (country) — Fiction
P: 4837

Congress (U.S.)
See also United States — Government and politics
I: 17110, 17128

Congress (U.S.) — Biography
PI: 12877

Congressional committees
I: 17121

Conjoined twins
I: 18065

Conjunctions
P: 14030

Connecticut
I: 16687 **IJ:** 16714

Connecticut — Fiction
PI: 9252 **I:** 7895, 9189, 9251 **IJ:** 7915, 9213, 9226, 9267, 9559

Connecticut Colony
IJ: 16118

Conservation
See also Ecology and environment; Pollution
P: 4566, 16956, 19390 **PI:** 16961 **I:** 16693, 16864, 16909, 16952, 16958, 19407–8, 19983, 20471 **IJ:** 13216, 19391, 19404, 19416, 19419, 19422, 20453

Conservation — Careers
I: 17757

Conservation — Crafts
IJ: 21459

Conservation — Fiction
P: 1045, 4506, 4513, 4527, 4539, 4541, 4717 **PI:** 1052 **I:** 10025

Conservation — Folklore
IJ: 10537

Conservation — History
IJ: 16964, 16970

Conservationists — Biography
P: 12844 **PI:** 13248–49, 13323, 13329, 13335 **I:** 13221, 13245–46, 13315, 13326, 13330, 13348 **IJ:** 13203, 13208, 13214, 13243–44, 13247, 13250, 13266, 13302, 13328

Constellations
P: 18549 **PI:** 18557 **IJ:** 18386

Constitution (U.S.)
See also United States — Government and politics
PI: 17056, 17059–61 **I:** 17054–55, 17057 **IJ:** 16192, 17058

Construction
See Building and construction

Consumerism
P: 16937 **IJ:** 16936

Containers
I: 21902

Contests
I: 17626

Contests — Fiction
I: 9902

Cook, Captain James — Fiction
IJ: 8933

Cookbooks
P: 3120, 21511, 21695, 21710, 21712, 21719, 21730, 21739 **PI:** 21505, 21677–78, 21681, 21717, 21726, 21733, 21753 **I:** 16080, 20087, 21679–80, 21683–84, 21686, 21688–90, 21692–93, 21697–99, 21703, 21709, 21722, 21737–38, 21749–52 **IJ:** 21687, 21701, 21720, 21734, 21741, 21744, 21746–47, 21758

Cookbooks — Civil War
IJ: 16403

Cookbooks — Colonial Period (U.S.)
I: 16136

Cookbooks — Ethnic
P: 3003 **PI:** 21713 **I:** 21694, 21700, 21702, 21707, 21715–16, 21724, 21729, 21740 **IJ:** 21676, 21682, 21685, 21704–6, 21708, 21711, 21718, 21723, 21725, 21727–28, 21731, 21742–43, 21745, 21748, 21754–55, 21757

Cookbooks — Hispanic Americans
IJ: 7419

Cookbooks — Historical
PI: 21675, 21696, 21721, 21736

Cookbooks — Vegetarian
I: 21709 **IJ:** 21714

Cookies
PI: 21726 **I:** 16949, 21686

Cooking
See Cookbooks; Cooks and cooking

Cooks and cooking
I: 21691, 21732

Cooks and cooking — Careers
P: 17743 **I:** 17752

Cooks and cooking — Fiction
P: 3221, 4146 **PI:** 9623, 9813, 10131 **I:** 8309, 9902

Cooks and cooking — History
I: 14349

Cooks and cooking — Poetry
P: 3112

Coolidge, Calvin
PI: 13026 **I:** 13027

Cooper, Cynthia
IJ: 13519

Cooperation
P: 11536

Copper
IJ: 20276

P = Primary; PI = Primary-Intermediate; I = Intermediate; IJ = Intermediate-Junior High

**Coquelle Indians —
Folklore**
P: 11232

Coral reefs
P: 19657 PI: 19658–59,
19662, 19669–70
I: 19665–66, 19668, 19671
IJ: 19654–56, 19661,
19667, 20383

Corking (knitting)
IJ: 21644

Cormorants — Fiction
PI: 8997

Corn
P: 20173, 20179, 20185
PI: 20169, 20180 I: 20170

Cornwall — Folklore
I: 10956

Corrigan, Mairead
IJ: 15339

Cosby, Bill
I: 12369, 12371 IJ: 12370,
12372

Cosmetics — Biography
I: 12808, 12923

Cosmetics — History
IJ: 21172

Costa Rica
P: 15690 PI: 15662
I: 15660, 15689

Costa Rica — Fiction
P: 4434 IJ: 6886

Costa Rica — Folklore
P: 11416

Costa Rica — Holidays
PI: 15662

**Costumes and costume
making**
PI: 21537, 21539, 21544
I: 21538, 21545, 21553
IJ: 21550

**Costumes and costume
making — History**
I: 21173

Cottontail rabbits
P: 19196

Cougars
P: 19091, 19112 I: 19078,
19104, 19113

Counting books
P: 54, 143, 164, 177, 248,
254, 322, 367–85, 387–99,
401–18, 420, 422–23, 425,
427–35, 437–78, 480–84,
486–88, 492–98, 500–2,
504–6, 508–27, 531–34,
536, 538–42, 544–52,
554–55, 558–615, 690, 740,
884, 905, 1580, 4152, 5554,
5773, 5812, 6011, 6050,
6066, 6306, 18775, 19260
PI: 386, 436, 479, 499, 503,
535, 543, 15325, 15384–85,
15522, 15740 I: 15067,
15103, 15420, 15547, 20634

**Counting books —
Chinese**
P: 489

Countries
PI: 14572

**Country music —
Biography**
IJ: 12360, 12451

Country music — Fiction
I: 8328

**Country music and
musicians**
I: 14139

Courage — Biography
IJ: 12064

Courage — Fiction
P: 2908 I: 7121

Courts
I: 17011–12

Cousins — Fiction
P: 4027

Cousteau, Jacques
I: 12101

Cowboys
P: 12757, 16307 PI: 16309
I: 16362, 16379, 16386,
16900, 17741 IJ: 16298,
16306, 16310, 16356

Cowboys — Biography
P: 12442, 12458 PI: 4728
I: 12459

Cowboys — Cookbooks
IJ: 16312

Cowboys — Fiction
P: 31, 621, 2969, 2976–77,
3199, 3401, 4145, 4291,
4338, 5260, 6226 PI: 2948
I: 9419, 9898 IJ: 9349

Cowboys — Folklore
P: 11358

Cowboys — History
I: 16320 IJ: 16359

Cowboys — Mexico
IJ: 15599

Cows
See Cattle

Coyotes
P: 19123, 19127 PI: 19138
I: 19137, 19142, 19146
IJ: 19134

Coyotes — Fiction
P: 2403, 5312 I: 7311,
7319, 7327

Coyotes — Folklore
P: 11211, 11285 I: 11302,
11304

Crabs
P: 19674, 19680
PI: 19673, 19678
I: 19676–77

Crack cocaine
IJ: 17885

Crack (drug)
See Cocaine and crack;
Drugs and drug
problems

Crafts
See also specific crafts,
e.g., Paper crafts
P: 2303, 4616, 5647, 5933,
6108, 14303, 15601, 21418,
21422, 21424, 21433,
21454, 21463–64, 21467,
21469, 21471, 21476–77,
21490, 21500, 21509,
21511, 21518, 21548, 21585
PI: 14629, 17349, 17352,
17410, 17431, 17446,
17449, 17452, 17483,
21417, 21419, 21425–26,
21434, 21440, 21444,
21447, 21457, 21460,
21465, 21470, 21473,
21475, 21479, 21481,
21484, 21486, 21489,
21491–94, 21499, 21501,
21505, 21508, 21510,
21514, 21520, 21522,
21524, 21526, 21530,
21535, 21537, 21539,
21544, 21546, 21551–52,
21579, 21593, 21601,
21618, 21631, 21633,
21643, 21717, 21793
I: 10591, 12491, 13928,
13991, 14009, 14304,
14607, 14746, 14760,
14859, 15903, 16100–1,
16148, 16295–96, 16322,
16334, 16477, 17443,
17482, 17493, 17504,
20171, 21414, 21416,
21423, 21427–32,
21435–36, 21438–39,
21442, 21445, 21448–51,
21455, 21461–62, 21472,
21474, 21478, 21480,
21482–83, 21487–88,
21495, 21497–98, 21503,
21507, 21512, 21517,
21521, 21523, 21531–32,
21534, 21538, 21542–43,
21604, 21607, 21609–10,
21619–20, 21622–23,
21625–26, 21628, 21630,
21632, 21635–36,
21638–39, 21654, 21656,
21660–61, 21796
IJ: 14393, 15209, 15232,
15446, 15615, 16179,
21410, 21413, 21415,
21441, 21443, 21446,
21452–53, 21459, 21466,
21496, 21502, 21504,
21506, 21513, 21516,
21527, 21529, 21614,
21616, 21621, 21627,
21645, 21772, 22035
All: 21458

Crafts — Bible
I: 21485

Crafts — Food
P: 21412

Crafts — General
I: 14346, 21420

Crafts — Greece
IJ: 14674

Crafts — Historical
PI: 21515, 21519, 21525

Crafts — Japan
I: 15123

Crafts — Middle Ages
I: 14765

Crafts — Rome
IJ: 14714

Crafts — Winter
P: 21456

Cranberries
PI: 20079

Cranes — Poetry
See also Whooping cranes
P: 11814

Cranes (bird)
P: 19288 PI: 19278
I: 19224, 19291 IJ: 19230

Cranes (bird) — Fiction
P: 976, 10406 PI: 10811
I: 7961, 8583

Cranes (bird) — Poetry
P: 11814

Crayfish
P: 19675

Crayons
P: 21033 I: 21066

Crayons — Fiction
P: 1453, 6423

Crazy Horse, Chief
I: 12971

**Crazy Horse, Chief —
Fiction**
PI: 9147

Creation
P: 4445 IJ: 1035, 17245,
18384, 18397

Creation — Folklore
P: 2420, 10686, 11236,
11406, 17191, 17250,
17284, 17332 PI: 10604,
10645, 11214, 17305
I: 10577, 10582 IJ: 10635,
17296

Credit cards
I: 16923

Cree Indians — Folklore
P: 11319

Creek Indians
I: 16014

Creek Indians — History
I: 15965

Crete — History
I: 14522

P = Primary; PI = Primary-Intermediate; I = Intermediate; IJ = Intermediate-Junior High

Crews, Donald
P: 3594

Crickets
P: 19427 I: 19483
IJ: 19476

Crickets — Fiction
P: 1928, 2225, 2947, 5485
PI: 2674 I: 8081

Crime
See Criminals and crime;
and specific crimes, e.g.,
Robbers and robbery

**Crimean War —
Biography**
IJ: 13841

Criminal science
PI: 17065

Criminals and crime
PI: 16363, 17065, 17076
I: 17073, 17078, 17080–81,
17092 IJ: 16311,
17062–63, 17067–68,
17070–71, 17074, 17082,
17084, 17086–87

**Criminals and crime —
Biography**
IJ: 12868, 12910, 12964–65

**Criminals and crime —
Fiction**
I: 6749 IJ: 9846

Crockett, Davy
P: 12102 PI: 16272
I: 12103–4

Crocodiles
See Alligators and
crocodiles

Crop circles
I: 21942

Crow Indians
PI: 16071 I: 15971

Crow Indians — Folklore
P: 11297

Crows — Fiction
P: 1124, 1214, 1661, 5180,
5244, 5406 I: 7787, 8694
IJ: 7193

Crows — Folklore
P: 11239

Crusades
I: 14754

Crusades — Fiction
PI: 9071

Crustaceans
IJ: 18924, 19679

Cryptograms
See also Codes and ciphers
IJ: 21887

**Crystals — Experiments
and projects**
I: 20573

Cub Scouts
See Scouts and scouting

Cuba
I: 15692–93, 15698, 15718,
15721, 17984 IJ: 15705,
15712–13

Cuba — Folklore
P: 11422

Cuban Americans
IJ: 17560, 17582

**Cuban Americans —
Biography**
I: 12382, 12384, 13477

Cubism
IJ: 13881

Cults (religion)
IJ: 16839, 17190, 21949

**Cumberland and Ohio
Canal — Fiction**
IJ: 9500

Cuna Indians — Art
IJ: 13945

Curie, Marie
PI: 13261 I: 13219,
13262–63 IJ: 13260

Curiosities
PI: 21909 I: 21910, 21937,
21939, 21947, 21952, 21954
IJ: 21888–89, 21892,
21903, 21912, 21916–17,
21919, 21934, 21938,
21941, 21955, 21960–61

Curriculum — Skits
I: 12027

**Custer, George
Armstrong**
IJ: 12871

Customs and rituals
IJ: 21960

Cuttlefish
P: 19725

Cycles (nature)
IJ: 20652

Cycling
See Bicycles

Cyprus
IJ: 15264, 15267

Czech Republic
PI: 15281 IJ: 15265,
15272

**Czech Republic —
Holidays**
PI: 15281

Czechoslovakia — Fiction
P: 3502

**Czechoslovakia —
Folklore**
P: 10862

Czechoslovakia — History
IJ: 14816

D

D-Day (World War II)
IJ: 14827

**D-Day (World War II) —
Fiction**
IJ: 9679

Dachshunds — Fiction
P: 4015, 5819

da Gama, Vasco
I: 12069 IJ: 12105

Dahl, Roald
P: 12521 I: 12522

Dahl, Roald — Fiction
IJ: 12520

Dahomey
See Benin

Dairying
See also Cattle
P: 20064, 20070, 20085

Dakota Indians
See also Sioux Indians

**Dakota Indians —
Biography**
I: 13268

Dakota Indians — Fiction
IJ: 9164

**Dakota Indians —
Folklore**
PI: 11237

**Dakota Territory —
Fiction**
PI: 9394 I: 9395, 9448
IJ: 9396

Dalai Lama
I: 13777 IJ: 13778

**Dallas Cowboys (football
team)**
IJ: 22184

Dallas (Texas)
I: 16911

Dalmatians — Fiction
P: 1942 PI: 8105

Dalokay, Vedat
IJ: 13779

Damon, Matt
IJ: 12373

Dams
I: 21115, 21125

Dance and dancers
P: 14292 PI: 14271
I: 14297 IJ: 14274, 14286,
14295, 14299

**Dance and dancers —
Biography**
IJ: 12162, 12377–78,
12390–92, 12400, 12465

**Dance and dancers —
Careers**
P: 17772

**Dance and dancers —
Fiction**
P: 279, 915, 1632, 2481,
3287, 3501, 3833, 4189,
4946, 5003, 6217–18, 6550
I: 3599, 10253 IJ: 10100

**Dance and dancers —
History**
I: 14134

**Dance and dancers —
Poetry**
P: 11605

Dandelions
P: 20237, 20240–41, 20257,
20266

D'Angelo, Pascal
IJ: 12523

Daniel (Bible)
PI: 17239

**Danish Americans —
Fiction**
PI: 4688

Darkling beetles
I: 19535

Darwin, Charles
I: 13264–65

Dating — Fiction
I: 9978 IJ: 9897, 9904

Daub, Milton
PI: 16494

David, King of Israel
P: 17263, 17268
PI: 17240, 17309
IJ: 13780

da Vinci, Leonardo
PI: 12212, 12216
IJ: 12214–15

**da Vinci, Leonardo —
Fiction**
PI: 9025 I: 9072

Davis, Jan
I: 12106

Davis, Jefferson
IJ: 12872

Davis, Miles — Fiction
PI: 4613

Davis, Terrell
I: 13605 IJ: 13606

Dawn — Fiction
P: 4542

Dawn — Poetry
PI: 11531 I: 11976

Day, Tom
IJ: 12220

Day care
P: 5478

Day care — Fiction
P: 2377, 3007, 3351, 3518,
3920, 4912, 5540

Day of the Dead
P: 15658

P = Primary; PI = Primary-Intermediate; I = Intermediate; IJ = Intermediate-Junior High

Day of the Dead — Fiction
P: 5634 PI: 5628

Daydreaming — Fiction
P: 977

Days
P: 210

Days — Fiction
P: 244

Days — Folklore
I: 10555

Dead Sea Scrolls
IJ: 17257

Deaf
P: 827, 18146 PI: 13164,
13166, 13337, 14018, 17922
I: 13140, 17913, 17918

Deaf — Biography
PI: 12885

Deaf — Fiction
P: 3762, 5036, 5048, 5116,
5673, 14017 PI: 5015,
5035, 6750, 8874, 8879,
8900 I: 8885, 8909, 9065,
17901 IJ: 6771, 7314, 8883

Dean, Dizzy
I: 13447

Death
P: 3810, 17488, 17695,
17732, 17859 I: 17214,
17357, 17703, 17709, 21929
IJ: 17158, 17716–17,
17858, 17860

Death — Customs
IJ: 14517

Death — Fiction
P: 1946, 2397, 2777, 3540,
3556, 3561, 3586, 3613,
3627–29, 3678, 3683, 3691,
3741, 3865, 3919, 3924,
3957, 3964, 3986, 4746,
4780, 4804, 4900–1, 4903,
4918, 4924, 4928, 4932,
4935, 4960, 4969, 4983,
5004, 5045, 5065, 5070–71,
5083, 5089, 5097, 5100,
5108–10, 5183, 5236, 5321,
5455, 5750, 6275 PI: 3743,
3915, 4578, 5044, 5051,
5385, 7223, 7316, 7326,
7385, 7528, 8466, 8593,
8596, 8687, 8695, 8757,
8850, 10090 I: 6851, 6969,
7257, 7266, 7377, 7523,
8142, 8271, 8301, 8325,
8351, 8415, 8477, 8505,
8512, 8518, 8536, 8587–88,
8625, 8627, 8670, 8712,
8814, 8843, 8861–62, 9590,
9677, 10050 IJ: 6768,
6934, 7013, 7152, 7163,
7197, 7545, 7708, 8024,
8086, 8261, 8355, 8383,
8389, 8441, 8452, 8467,
8490, 8513, 8524, 8550,
8571, 8598, 8618, 8666,
8675, 8679, 8681, 8714,
8721, 8725, 8760, 8765,

8801, 8806, 8840, 8844,
8851, 8867, 8877, 8898,
8906, 9022, 9375, 9648

Death — Folklore
P: 11333

Death penalty
See Capital punishment

**Declaration of
Independence (U.S.)**
PI: 12896, 16211 I: 16213
IJ: 16190, 16196

de Coubertin, Pierre
IJ: 22250

Deep-sea vents
I: 19819

Deer
P: 19153 PI: 19148, 19159
I: 19149, 19157

Deer — Fiction
P: 5118, 6350, 6508
PI: 7299 IJ: 7152, 7289,
7300, 10512

Deer family
I: 19158

Deer mice
PI: 19206

Defecation
P: 3173

Deforestation
P: 20469

Degas, Edgar
PI: 12222 IJ: 12221,
13906

Degas, Edgar — Fiction
P: 4846, 9058

de la Hoya, Oscar
PI: 13584 IJ: 13585

de la Renta, Oscar
IJ: 12829

Delaware (state)
P: 16707 I: 16658, 16702
IJ: 16655, 16737

**Demolition work (U.S.
Army)**
I: 21393

**Denali National Park
(Alaska)**
P: 16801

Denmark
IJ: 15442, 15449

Denmark — Fiction
I: 6830, 9039, 9652
IJ: 6831, 9658, 9672

Dentistry — History
IJ: 18021

Dentists
P: 18187

Dentists — Careers
P: 17799

Dentists — Fiction
P: 2716

Denver
I: 16638

Denver Zoo
I: 20027

dePaola, Tomie
P: 3607 PI: 12524–25
I: 12526

De Passe, Suzanne
IJ: 13148

Depression, Great
PI: 16489 I: 16445, 16459,
16496 IJ: 7492, 16454,
16470–71, 16479, 16488

**Depression, Great —
Fiction**
P: 4571, 4623, 4737, 4742,
4841, 5836, 6700 PI: 4597,
8462, 9611 I: 7529, 8525,
8930, 9538, 9570, 9590,
9612, 9618, 9626, 9631–32,
9635, 9639 IJ: 7274, 7526,
7539, 8702, 8789, 9521,
9527, 9531, 9536, 9539,
9572, 9613, 9620, 9640,
9881

Depression (mental state)
IJ: 17715, 17723, 17909,
17989

**Depression (mental state)
— Fiction**
I: 10358 IJ: 8430, 8457,
8572, 8621, 8903, 9258

Des Moines — Fiction
IJ: 9926

Desegregation
PI: 17042

Desegregation — Fiction
P: 4769

Deserts
P: 4502, 20411, 20417,
20429 PI: 15922, 19225,
20405, 20408, 20412,
20414, 20427–28 I: 20226,
20252, 20398–99, 20401,
20403, 20406–7, 20409,
20413, 20415, 20419–22,
20425 IJ: 14982, 20258,
20416, 20426

Deserts — Animals
P: 20400, 20410 PI: 18873
I: 20418, 21566

Deserts — Crafts
I: 21478

Deserts — Fiction
P: 3301, 4395, 4467, 5338
PI: 4743 I: 7156, 10251

Deserts — Plants
P: 20404

Deserts — Poetry
P: 11974 PI: 64, 11944
I: 11772, 11937, 11983

Design
See also Dress; Fashion
design

Design — History
IJ: 13875, 13891, 13896

DesJarlait, Patrick
IJ: 12223

Desktop publishing
IJ: 14002

Desserts
I: 21694

Detectives
I: 17089 IJ: 17062

Detectives — Biography
IJ: 12947–48

Detroit
PI: 16594

**Detroit Red Wings
(hockey team)**
I: 22214

Devers, Gail
I: 13658

Devil — Fiction
I: 7572–73 IJ: 7023

Dewey Decimal System
PI: 13994

Diabetes
P: 17992 I: 17944, 17951,
17977, 17988 IJ: 18006

Diabetes — Fiction
I: 8690, 8910

Diamonds
IJ: 20565

Diana, Princess of Wales
I: 13782, 13784 IJ: 13781,
13783, 13785–86

Diaries
See also Journals
I: 9466–67, 15800, 16205,
16222, 16308, 16316,
16474, 16636 IJ: 9063,
14064, 14085, 14108,
16241, 16270

Diaries — Fiction
PI: 8927, 8983, 9316,
9327–28, 10162 I: 8346,
8603, 8691, 9075, 9118,
9235, 9243, 9418, 9577,
9600, 9770 IJ: 7438, 7585,
8837, 8964, 8971, 9182,
9262, 9537, 9549, 9657,
9682, 9973

DiCaprio, Leonardo
IJ: 12374

Dickens, Charles
IJ: 12527–29

**Dickens, Charles —
Fiction**
I: 9269

Dickinson, Emily
IJ: 12530

**Dickinson, Emily —
Fiction**
PI: 8118, 8253

P = Primary; PI = Primary-Intermediate; I = Intermediate; IJ = Intermediate-Junior High

Dictionaries
See also Word books
P: 14044

Diet pills
IJ: 17863

Diets
IJ: 18097, 18199

Digestive system
P: 18100–2, 18104–5
PI: 18108 **I:** 18096, 18103
IJ: 18095, 18097, 18099, 18106

Diggers (machinery)
P: 21149, 21246

Digital technology
I: 21241

Dilley sextuplets
P: 18229

DiMaggio, Joe
I: 13448–49

Dimas, Trent
I: 13683

Diners — Fiction
P: 1962, 4714

Dinosaur National Monument
PI: 16632 **IJ:** 14377

Dinosaurs
See also Paleontology;
Prehistoric animals; and
names of specific
dinosaurs, e.g.,
Tyrannosaurus rex
P: 576, 5352, 5361, 14374,
14376, 14381, 14387–88,
14395, 14401, 14403,
14409, 14414, 14421,
14426, 14450–53, 14459,
14465, 14467, 14481–82,
14484, 14486–87, 17644,
18668 **PI:** 11855, 14373,
14375, 14380, 14391–92,
14408, 14417, 14420,
14431, 14438, 14443–44,
14458, 14468–69,
14471–72, 14485
I: 14382–83, 14385,
14398–400, 14402, 14404,
14406–7, 14411, 14413,
14422–24, 14427–29,
14432–35, 14437,
14439–41, 14446–49,
14461, 14466, 14473,
14477–78, 14480, 14483,
14513, 20310, 21567, 21638
IJ: 13226, 14384, 14389,
14394, 14405, 14436,
14442, 14445, 14455–56,
14462, 14470, 14474

Dinosaurs — Crafts
PI: 21479

Dinosaurs — Defenses
PI: 14475

Dinosaurs — Directories
IJ: 14425

Dinosaurs — Drawing and painting
PI: 21581

Dinosaurs — Fiction
P: 932, 1043, 1098,
1128–29, 1677, 1816, 1939,
1943, 2029, 2514, 2668,
2740, 2860, 2938, 3049,
4104, 4238, 4925, 5134,
5202, 5804, 6400–1, 6554,
10423 **PI:** 6345, 7793
I: 7765, 7844, 9792
IJ: 10161

Dinosaurs — Jokes and riddles
PI: 21812

Dinosaurs — Models
I: 14378 **IJ:** 14393

Dinosaurs — Poetry
P: 11817, 11873
PI: 11660, 11810

Dinosaurs — Size
P: 14457

Dion, Celine
I: 12375 **IJ:** 12376

Dippers (stars)
See Big and Little Dippers

Dirigibles
PI: 21104 **I:** 21075, 21093
IJ: 21087

Dirigibles — Fiction
PI: 9610

Dirt track racing
I: 22242

Disabilities
See also Learning
disabilities; Mental
handicaps; Physical
disabilities
PI: 17038

Disasters (history)
I: 14340

Diseases
See also Doctors; Illness;
Medicine; and specific
diseases, e.g., AIDS
P: 17993 **PI:** 17945
I: 17962 **IJ:** 17964–67,
18001, 18018

Disney, Walt
I: 12224, 12227–29
IJ: 12225–26

Disney World — Fiction
I: 9902

Dissection (biology) — Fiction
IJ: 10113

Distribution (economics)
IJ: 16930

Diving (sport) — Fiction
I: 10358 **IJ:** 10292

Division (mathematics)
P: 528 **PI:** 20585

Divorce
See also Family problems
P: 17644, 17676–77, 17689
PI: 17647, 17686 **I:** 17660
IJ: 17643, 17645, 17652,
17656, 17661, 17666,
17682, 17688

Divorce — Fiction
P: 2339, 4897, 4929, 4970,
4980, 5053, 5059, 5082,
5084, 5105, 8662 **PI:** 5079,
8419–20, 8522, 9823, 9828,
9961 **I:** 7162, 7914, 7920,
8396, 8399, 8401, 8433,
8494, 8498, 8503, 8506,
8523, 8793, 9827, 10359
IJ: 8315, 8343, 8402,
8424–25, 8456, 8461, 8474,
8501, 8515, 8543, 8620,
8667, 8787, 9926

Diwali (Hindu holiday)
PI: 17385 **I:** 17375

Diwali (Hindu holiday) — Fiction
I: 8996

Dixon, Tamecka
I: 22129

DNA
I: 18036

Doctors
See also Health and
medicine; Medicine
P: 3039 **I:** 18025,
18030–31

Doctors — Biography
PI: 13337 **I:** 12982–83,
13212, 13215, 13242,
13318–19 **IJ:** 13206,
13209, 13307, 13352

Doctors — Careers
P: 17802–3 **PI:** 17805
I: 18023, 18033

Doctors — Fiction
IJ: 7466

Doctors — History
I: 18028

Doctors — Women
I: 13215

Dog racing — Fiction
IJ: 7180

Dogs
See also Guide dogs; Sled
dogs; and individual
species, e.g.,
Dachshunds
P: 4760, 6680, 19130,
19939–41, 19944, 19947,
19949, 19951–52,
19955–57, 19960, 19962,
19967–70 **PI:** 19937–38,
19945–46, 19958, 19978
I: 16794, 19936, 19943,
19950, 19954, 19959,
19961, 19963–65, 19973,
19975–77, 19979, 21556

IJ: 19942, 19966,
19971–72, 19974

Dogs — Art
IJ: 13924

Dogs — Communication
PI: 19948

Dogs — Fiction
P: 272, 464, 714, 957, 1062,
1096, 1592, 1636, 1694,
1778, 1791, 1885, 1929,
1962, 2002, 2027, 2078,
2203–7, 2238, 2255, 2306,
2354, 2402, 2493, 2543,
2632, 2672, 2722, 2939,
3381, 4111, 4187, 4228,
4292, 4538, 4917, 4924,
5110, 5126, 5136–37, 5142,
5151, 5156, 5161, 5164,
5183, 5191, 5193, 5199,
5215, 5228, 5230, 5235,
5250–51, 5256, 5261, 5271,
5273, 5279, 5283, 5294,
5297, 5299, 5306, 5309–10,
5321, 5325–26, 5328, 5332,
5343, 5353, 5362, 5364,
5377–78, 5383, 5397–99,
5404, 5407, 5413–14, 5416,
5429–31, 5440, 5448–51,
5455, 5465, 5696, 5735,
5804, 5819, 5904, 5935,
5982, 5987, 6216, 6239,
6243, 6255–56, 6258, 6287,
6328, 6375, 6383–84, 6398,
6422, 6449, 6457, 6473–74,
6487, 6518–19, 6522, 6544,
6575, 6580, 6603, 6606,
6608, 6649, 6664, 6683,
6874, 7176, 10300, 10519,
14037 **PI:** 1866, 2001,
2272, 2570, 2892, 4854,
5190, 5214, 5293, 5336,
5376, 5385, 6057, 6525,
6785, 6908, 7148, 7170,
7185, 7201, 7210–11, 7213,
7221, 7223, 7237, 7239,
7248, 7292, 7297–98, 7316,
7318, 7321, 7326, 7329,
8184, 8611, 8739, 9204,
9758, 9819, 9821, 10242,
10301 **I:** 6846, 7151, 7162,
7171, 7177–79, 7183–84,
7188, 7200, 7203, 7208–9,
7227–28, 7233, 7257–59,
7262, 7265–66, 7277, 7307,
7310, 7317, 7320, 7707,
7718, 7837, 7843, 7906,
8006, 8127, 8171, 8587,
8624, 8665, 8755, 8891,
9365, 9441, 9451, 9740,
9885, 9888–89, 10002,
11216 **IJ:** 6876, 6896,
6906, 7020, 7180, 7182,
7197, 7199, 7214, 7222,
7231, 7252, 7255, 7260,
7268, 7272, 7274, 7279,
7313–14, 7387, 8152, 8601,
9440, 10006

Dogs — Folklore
I: 10560, 10966

P = Primary; PI = Primary-Intermediate; I = Intermediate; IJ = Intermediate-Junior High

Dogs — History
I: 19979

Dogs — Jokes and riddles
PI: 21831

Dogs — Nursery rhymes
P: 837, 877

Dogs — Poetry
P: 5170, 11789 **PI:** 11795,
11803

Dogs — Senses
P: 5380

Dogs — Working
I: 19973

Dole, Bob
I: 12873

Dole, Elizabeth
I: 13149

Doll making
I: 21654, 21656

Dollhouses — Fiction
PI: 9765 **I:** 9590

Dolls
P: 21041 **I:** 21651, 21655

**Dolls — African
American**
I: 21652

Dolls — Fiction
P: 922, 1002, 1022, 1076,
1209–11, 1374, 1485, 1539,
3275, 3967, 3976, 4720,
4844, 5908, 5934, 6187
I: 7576, 7723, 7762, 7834,
7859, 7951, 8196, 9393
IJ: 7130

Dolphins
P: 11, 19683, 19687
PI: 19639, 19684, 19686,
19690–91 **I:** 19625, 19634,
19681–82, 19689,
19692–93, 19802 **IJ:** 19685

Dolphins — Fiction
P: 5329 **PI:** 5358, 7196
I: 6868, 7890 **IJ:** 7235

Domestic violence
IJ: 17659

Dominica
I: 15719

Dominican Americans
IJ: 17543

Dominican Republic
IJ: 15716, 17543

**Dominican Republic —
Fiction**
I: 8715 **IJ:** 7386

**Dominican Republic —
Folklore**
P: 11417

Dominicans — Biography
IJ: 13505

Dominoes
PI: 22235

Donkeys
IJ: 7229

Donkeys — Fiction
P: 2718, 2721, 5755
PI: 5772 **I:** 7624

Donner Party
IJ: 16294

Donner Party — Fiction
I: 9393

Dorris, Michael
I: 12531

**Douglas, Marjory
Stoneman**
IJ: 13266

Douglas, Stephen A.
I: 16256

Douglass, Frederick
P: 12708 **PI:** 12709–13,
12715 **I:** 12714, 12716

Douty, Sheila Cornell
I: 13450

Doves
I: 19250

Doves — Fiction
P: 970 **PI:** 7964

Down syndrome
IJ: 17942

**Down syndrome —
Fiction**
P: 43, 3447, 3848, 4957,
5056 **PI:** 8918 **I:** 6971
IJ: 8644, 8866

Downhill inline skating
IJ: 21989

Doyle, Sir Arthur Conan
IJ: 12532

Dr. Seuss
P: 12538 **PI:** 12540
I: 12539

Dracula
I: 8037, 21945

Drag racing
IJ: 22082

Dragonflies
PI: 19464

Dragons
P: 652, 1304, 1514, 1566,
1797, 2028, 2566, 4353,
5898, 6025, 10762
PI: 7875, 8047, 10424
I: 7677, 7985, 8053, 8066,
10785 **IJ:** 7621, 8068, 8232

Dragons — Fiction
P: 1436, 1513 **PI:** 7654,
7874 **I:** 7772, 8131
IJ: 7730, 8236, 9775

Dragons — Folklore
P: 10552 **PI:** 10998

Dragons — Poetry
PI: 11808

Drake, Sir Francis
I: 12060

Drawing and painting
See also Art; Crafts
P: 13878–79, 21578, 21585,
21589 **PI:** 21572–75,
21579–81, 21583, 21593–95
I: 13887, 13917, 13952,
21554–56, 21558–60,
21564–68, 21576–77,
21588, 21598–600
IJ: 13930, 21562–63,
21570–71, 21586–87,
21596–97

**Drawing and painting —
Computers**
PI: 21591

**Drawing and painting —
Fiction**
P: 1354, 1368, 2455, 4751,
4762, 4949, 5495, 5520,
6423 **I:** 7912, 8989, 10370
IJ: 1035

**Drawing and painting —
Insects**
IJ: 21569

Dreams and dreaming
I: 18227

**Dreams and dreaming —
Fiction**
P: 710, 733, 753, 1477,
1484, 4487, 5017, 5202,
5773 **PI:** 1639, 4749

**Dreams and dreaming —
Folklore**
P: 10813

**Dreams and dreaming —
Poetry**
I: 11739

Dred Scott case
I: 16240

Dress
See also Fashion design

Dress — History
IJ: 21180

Dresses — Fiction
P: 3749, 5700

Droughts
P: 20757

Droughts — Fiction
PI: 8680 **I:** 6775

Drug testing
IJ: 17876

Drugs and drug problems
See also Alcoholism
P: 17861, 17874, 17893
PI: 17090 **I:** 17078
IJ: 13457, 17863,
17866–67, 17871,
17876–77, 17880–82,
17885–86, 17889–91,
17894–96

**Drugs and drug problems
— Fiction**
IJ: 7113

Drums
P: 14222

Dublin, Ireland
I: 15354

Du Bois, W. E. B.
PI: 12717 **I:** 12718–20

Ducks and geese
P: 5141, 19309–10, 19313,
19315–16, 19318
PI: 19312 **I:** 19308

**Ducks and geese —
Fiction**
P: 560, 563, 1486, 2047,
2125, 2149–50, 2267, 2401,
2405, 2607, 2655–56, 2749,
2794, 2819, 3603, 5012,
5140, 5272, 5290, 5355,
5381, 5386, 5391, 5403,
5492, 5797, 5929, 6238,
6373, 6443 **PI:** 2608, 6928,
8022 **I:** 7158, 8128

**Ducks and geese —
Folklore**
PI: 10826

Dugongs
PI: 19735

Duncan, Isadora
IJ: 12377

Duncan, Tim
IJ: 13520–22

Dunham, Katherine
IJ: 12378

Dust Bowl
I: 16459 **IJ:** 16479

Dust Bowl — Fiction
P: 4650 **I:** 9618 **IJ:** 8789

Dwarfism
I: 18066

Dwarves — Fiction
P: 10451 **IJ:** 8151

Dwarves — Folklore
P: 10909

Dyslexia
See also Eating disorders
PI: 17910 **IJ:** 17926,
17995

Dyslexia — Fiction
P: 4964 **I:** 6746, 8298,
8709, 8875, 8878, 8880
PI: 19320, 19323, 19325,
19327, 19333, 19343
I: 19324, 19328, 19330,
19332, 19337, 19340
IJ: 19326, 19336, 19338

P = Primary; PI = Primary-Intermediate; I = Intermediate; IJ = Intermediate-Junior High

E

Eagles
See also Birds of prey
P: 19321 **PI:** 19320, 19323, 19325, 19327, 19333, 19343 **I:** 19324, 19328, 19330, 19332, 19337, 19340 **IJ:** 19326, 19336, 19338

Eagles — Fiction
P: 1651, 5643

Eagles — Folklore
P: 11301

Earhart, Amelia
P: 12107 **PI:** 12108, 12112, 12115 **I:** 12109–11 **IJ:** 12113–14, 12116

Earle, Sylvia
PI: 17833 **IJ:** 13267

Earnhardt, Dale
I: 13427

Earp, Wyatt
IJ: 12874

Earrings — Fiction
P: 4340

Ears
I: 17913, 18131, 18148, 18157

Earth
See also Geology
P: 14345, 18428, 18565, 18567, 20312, 20319 **PI:** 4528, 14359, 18429, 18432, 18434, 18439, 20298, 20302, 20307, 20313, 20330 **I:** 18431, 18435, 18437, 20299, 20303, 20310, 20315–16 **IJ:** 18426, 18430, 18433, 18436, 18566, 20318, 20322

Earth — Atlases
IJ: 20326

Earth — Experiments and projects
I: 18427

Earth — Fiction
P: 4377

Earth — Folklore
I: 11274

Earth — Geology
I: 20301

Earth — Poetry
PI: 11561

Earth — Rotation
P: 18438

Earth Day
P: 5636 **IJ:** 17360

Earth Day — Crafts
PI: 21491

Earth Day — Fiction
P: 6572

Earth sciences
I: 20329 **IJ:** 20553

Earth sciences — Experiments and projects
I: 18357 **IJ:** 20324

Earth sciences — Folklore
I: 10532

Earthquakes
PI: 20337, 20345 **I:** 20333, 20341–43, 20347, 20353–54, 20662 **IJ:** 16814, 20328, 20331, 20334, 20338, 20349

Earthquakes — Experiments and projects
I: 20351 **IJ:** 20340

Earthquakes — Fiction
I: 8792 **IJ:** 8106

Earthworms
P: 19603, 19609, 19614 **I:** 19616

Earthworms — Experiments and projects
IJ: 19601

East Africa
I: 14921

East Africa — History
IJ: 14926

East Africa — Kings and queens
IJ: 14926

Easter
P: 5967, 5976, 17437, 17440 **I:** 17433–36, 17438, 17441

Easter — Crafts
P: 21424, 21454, 21476 **PI:** 21425

Easter — Fiction
P: 5962–63, 5965–66, 5968–71, 5973–75, 5977–79 **PI:** 7342

Easter — Poetry
P: 5972, 11835 **PI:** 11852

Easter eggs
I: 17439

Easter Island
IJ: 15222

Eastern Orthodox religion
P: 17217

Eastman, Charles
I: 13268

Eastwood, Alice
PI: 13269

Eating — Poetry
P: 11925

Eating disorders
See also specific disorders, e.g., Dyslexia
IJ: 17941, 17960, 17994

Eating utensils — History
PI: 17638

Ecology and environment
See also Conservation; Physical geography; Pollution
P: 598, 16963, 16966, 16968, 18590, 18598, 20373, 20469, 20570 **PI:** 16955, 16961, 20437, 20444 **I:** 16693, 16787, 16864, 16909, 16952–53, 16958–59, 16962, 16965, 16972, 16974, 17001, 19407–8, 20321, 20365, 20459, 20471, 20547 **IJ:** 15792, 15846, 16954, 16964, 16967, 17360, 19844, 20293, 20430, 20453, 20498, 20532

Ecology and environment — Careers
I: 17757

Ecology and environment — Experiments and projects
I: 16960, 16969

Ecology and environment — Fiction
P: 1641, 4383, 4404, 4513, 4541, 5150 **PI:** 4372, 8663 **I:** 9168 **IJ:** 6748, 6817

Ecology and environment — Folklore
IJ: 10537

Economics
IJ: 16928, 16930

Ecosystems
P: 20373 **I:** 18628

Ecuador
I: 15723, 15730 **IJ:** 15733, 15758, 15766

Ecuador — Fiction
PI: 8842

Edelman, Marian Wright
I: 13150–51

Ederle, Gertrude
PI: 13684

Edison, Thomas Alva
P: 13271 **PI:** 13273 **I:** 13272 **IJ:** 13270, 13274, 20907

Edmonds, Emma
IJ: 13152–53

Edo (African people)
P: 15045 **IJ:** 15012

Education
IJ: 17627

Educators — Biography
PI: 12701–3, 12786, 12812–13 **I:** 12704, 13835 **IJ:** 12929, 13836

Eels
PI: 19645

Eeyou Indians
I: 16044

Eggs
P: 18917, 18919, 19228, 19302, 19306, 20113 **PI:** 19270 **IJ:** 19304

Eggs — Fiction
P: 1486, 4091, 4211–12, 4456, 5962, 5975 **PI:** 2601 **I:** 7677, 9792

Egypt
P: 15495, 15497, 15510, 15514 **PI:** 15499–500, 15503, 15506, 15511 **I:** 14605, 15496, 15501–2, 15504, 15507–9, 15512–13, 15516 **IJ:** 15498, 15505, 15515

Egypt — Art
IJ: 13940

Egypt — Biography
I: 13807

Egypt — Crafts
I: 14607, 14632

Egypt — Fiction
P: 1604, 4658, 4678 **I:** 8960, 8963, 8969, 8977 **IJ:** 7461, 7621, 8371, 8964

Egypt — Folklore
P: 10658, 10678 **I:** 10674, 11183, 11186

Egypt — History
P: 6311, 13774, 14608, 14615, 14621, 14625, 14647 **PI:** 13862, 14603, 14606, 14614, 14618, 14624, 14629, 14645, 14648, 14662 **I:** 13766, 13773, 13775, 13861, 14350, 14607, 14613, 14616, 14620, 14622–23, 14627–28, 14630–34, 14637, 14643, 14646, 14649–52, 14654, 14656, 14660, 14664–65, 14667–70, 14672, 21144 **IJ:** 13776, 14535, 14583, 14602, 14604, 14609, 14611, 14617, 14619, 14626, 14639–41, 14644, 14653, 14658–59, 14661, 14666, 14671, 14673, 17230

Egypt — History — Art
I: 14631

Egypt — History — Crafts
IJ: 14612

Egypt — Mythology
I: 10669, 11453 **IJ:** 11447, 14661

P = Primary; PI = Primary-Intermediate; I = Intermediate; IJ = Intermediate-Junior High

Egypt — Religion
P: 14608

Egypt — Women
IJ: 14640

Ehlert, Lois
PI: 12533

Einstein, Albert
I: 13276–77 IJ: 13275

Eisenhower, Dwight D.
I: 12671, 13028, 13031
IJ: 13029–30, 13032

Eisner, Michael
IJ: 12875

El Chino
I: 13685

El Greco
PI: 12230

El Niño (weather)
I: 20786 IJ: 20751, 20770,
20785

El Salvador
I: 15656

El Salvador — Fiction
P: 957 IJ: 7336

Elder abuse
I: 17705

Elections
I: 17103, 17108
IJ: 17094–95, 17099

Elections — Fiction
PI: 10082 I: 7412

Electoral College
I: 17114

Electricity
P: 20883–84 PI: 13273,
20887 I: 13272, 20880,
20888 IJ: 20902

**Electricity —
Experiments and
projects**
P: 20900 PI: 20889,
20895, 20908 I: 20881,
20892, 20896–98, 20901,
21239 IJ: 20886, 20890,
20894, 20899, 20905

Electronic keyboards
IJ: 14226

Electronic mail
PI: 21194

Electronic mail writing
PI: 14071

Electronics
See also Lasers;
Telecommunications
I: 20903, 21241 IJ: 21240

Elements
IJ: 20762

Elephants
P: 19162, 19167, 19169
PI: 19160–61, 19163–64,
19172 I: 13327, 19166,

19170–71, 19173
IJ: 15205, 19165, 19168

Elephants — Fiction
P: 1048, 1870, 2011, 2121,
2252, 2435, 2453, 2568,
2675, 2717, 2779, 2831,
3639, 5208, 5221, 5236,
5275, 5374, 5382, 5436,
6470, 6579 PI: 2005, 8965
I: 7271 IJ: 7103, 8024,
9532

Elephants — Folklore
P: 10810

Elijah (prophet)
I: 17193 IJ: 17276

**Elijah (prophet) —
Fiction**
P: 1577

**Elizabeth I, Queen of
England**
I: 13787–88 IJ: 12590,
13789, 15335

**Elizabeth I, Queen of
England — Fiction**
IJ: 9099, 9102, 9105, 9112

**Elizabeth II, Queen of
England**
I: 13790

Elks
PI: 19151 I: 19147, 19157

Ellington, Duke
P: 12379

Ellis Island
PI: 15888, 16708, 16727,
16740, 17547 I: 16697
IJ: 16729

Ellis Island — Fiction
P: 3557 IJ: 9541

Elm trees — Fiction
P: 4546

Elves
I: 7919 IJ: 8151

Elves — Fiction
P: 5822

Elves — Folklore
P: 10895, 10905, 10907

Elway, John
I: 13607

**Emancipation
Proclamation**
PI: 16415 I: 16397
IJ: 16433

Embroidery
I: 15641

Embroidery — Fiction
P: 3000

Embryology
P: 18917

Emergency rooms
I: 18041

Emergency vehicles
P: 5567 I: 18041
IJ: 21321

**Emerson, Ralph Waldo —
Fiction**
PI: 9623

**Emigration — Eastern
Europe**
IJ: 14556

Emotions
See also specific emotions,
e.g., Anger
P: 4961, 17601–2, 17607,
18251 PI: 17604
IJ: 13989

Emotions — Fiction
P: 239, 3124, 3276, 3431,
4937, 4940, 5078

Emperor penguins
P: 19372

Empire State Building
PI: 16696, 21145
IJ: 16665, 21138

**Empire State Building —
Fiction**
I: 9635

Encyclopedias
P: 18295

Endangered animals
See also specific animals,
e.g., Grizzly bears
P: 4475, 18789, 19014,
19082, 19103, 19390,
19395, 19411, 19420–21,
19737 PI: 18786, 18945,
19049, 19088, 19098–100,
19124, 19164, 19189,
19396, 19399, 19413–15,
19686, 19735 I: 13327,
18785, 18947, 18975,
18979, 18998–99, 19066,
19089, 19147, 19238,
19254, 19319, 19342,
19393, 19397, 19400,
19402, 19412, 19746,
19761, 19790, 20028
IJ: 18684, 18987, 19109,
19116, 19133, 19139,
19365, 19391–92, 19394,
19403–4, 19406, 19410,
19416, 19418–19, 20015

**Endangered animals —
Biography**
P: 13285

**Endangered animals —
Fiction**
P: 456, 5115 I: 7253

**Endangered animals —
Songs**
P: 14176, 14188

Endangered birds
See also specific birds,
e.g., California condors
PI: 19339 I: 19341, 19409
IJ: 19417

Endangered peoples
I: 17571

Endangered plants
I: 20243

Endangered species
See also Endangered
animals; Endangered
birds; Endangered plants
PI: 17119 IJ: 19422

**Endangered species —
Fiction**
I: 10002 IJ: 7168, 7305

Endangered Species Act
PI: 19396

Enduro racing
I: 22240

Energy (physics)
PI: 20824 I: 20820–21,
20831, 20835 IJ: 20822,
20837–38

**Energy (physics) —
Experiments and
projects**
PI: 20836 I: 20817, 20819,
20840, 20842
IJ: 20826–27, 20830

Energy (sources)
I: 20834

Engineering
See Technology and
engineering

Engineers — Careers
I: 17789 IJ: 17795

England
See also Great Britain
PI: 15338, 15358 I: 15337,
15357

England — Biography
IJ: 13783, 13834

England — Cookbooks
IJ: 21706

England — Fiction
P: 1013, 1786 PI: 4667,
7445, 9083 I: 6798, 7118,
7477, 7698, 7985–86, 8252,
8271, 8319, 8859, 9084,
9096–97, 9108, 9110, 9115,
9123, 9128, 9659, 9667,
9719, 9733, 10244
IJ: 6777, 7013, 7096, 7116,
7167–68, 7486, 7544, 7556,
7685, 7724, 7868, 8161,
8199, 8837, 9079–80, 9082,
9085–86, 9091, 9095, 9099,
9102, 9105, 9107, 9112,
9117, 9119, 9127, 9129,
9333, 9697, 9718, 10006

England — Folk songs
P: 14210

England — Folklore
See also Great Britain —
Folklore
P: 9116, 10943–44, 10949,
10951, 10954, 10958,
10975, 10986–87, 10990,

10992, 10999, 11007,
11015, 11017–18, 11020,
11027–28, 11036, 11041–42
PI: 10950, 10959–60,
11016, 11034 **I:** 10956,
11011 **IJ:** 10965, 11026

England — History
P: 4605, 12534 **PI:** 9087,
15342 **I:** 13787–88, 13868,
14882, 15341, 15364, 15459
IJ: 9103, 13756, 13789,
14823, 15335

England — Poetry
I: 11593

English language
IJ: 13978

**Entertainers —
Biography**
P: 12458 **PI:** 12470
I: 12168, 12179, 12371,
12414, 12436, 12484
IJ: 12177, 12342, 12395,
12430, 12471–72

Entertainment industry
I: 21264

Entomology — Fiction
I: 9024

**Entrepreneurs —
Biography**
I: 12809

Entrepreneurs — Women
I: 13736 **IJ:** 12668

Environment
See Ecology and
environment

Environmentalists
See Conservationists

Epidemics
I: 17974 **IJ:** 18011

Epilepsy
I: 17978, 18014 **IJ:** 17947

Epilepsy — Fiction
P: 5039 **IJ:** 8894

Equiano, Olaudah
IJ: 13791

Eric the Red
I: 13792

Ericsson, John
I: 13278

Erie Canal
PI: 16250 **I:** 16237, 16264
IJ: 16713

Erie Canal — Fiction
IJ: 9260, 9287

Eriksson, Leif
I: 13792

Eriksson, Leif — Fiction
PI: 9046

Eritrean Americans
I: 17545

Erosion
IJ: 20304

Esiason, Boomer
P: 13608

Eskimos
See Inuit

Estefan, Gloria
PI: 12381, 12386 **I:** 12380,
12382, 12384 **IJ:** 12383,
12385

Esther, Queen (Bible)
P: 17463, 17466

Estonia
I: 15413

Ethics
I: 17609

Ethiopia
I: 14929 **IJ:** 14922, 14927,
14936

Ethiopia — Fiction
P: 4827 **PI:** 4721
IJ: 8968

Ethiopia — Folklore
P: 10647, 10660, 10680–81
I: 10683 **IJ:** 10649

Ethiopia — Holidays
PI: 14918

Ethnic groups
See also African
Americans; Hispanic
Americans; Indians of
North America, etc.
I: 17548, 17564, 17598
IJ: 15870, 16694, 17596

Ethnic groups — Fiction
P: 4645 **I:** 7357 **IJ:** 7355

Ethnic groups — Poetry
I: 11522

Etiquette
P: 17639

Etiquette — History
PI: 17638

Euphrates River
IJ: 15494

Europe
I: 15257

Europe — Eastern
I: 15261

Europe — Fiction
P: 3969, 6084

Europe — Folklore
I: 10544

Europe — History
IJ: 14556

Euthanasia
IJ: 17158

Evans, Minnie
IJ: 12231

Everglades
PI: 16858, 16875
IJ: 13266, 20364

Everglades — Fiction
I: 7086 **IJ:** 6817, 6855,
7059

Everyday life
See also Community life;
and individual countries,
e.g., France
P: 3164, 3385 **PI:** 2988,
16476 **IJ:** 10254

Everyday life — Fiction
P: 921, 953, 2281, 2989–93,
2996–97, 2999–3001,
3007–8, 3014, 3021,
3026–28, 3035–36, 3040,
3042–43, 3046, 3048–49,
3051, 3055–56, 3062–64,
3068, 3071, 3074, 3079,
3083, 3086, 3088, 3090,
3094, 3096–99, 3102,
3104–5, 3107–8, 3114,
3116, 3118–19, 3121–23,
3125–26, 3130, 3146, 3148,
3151, 3153, 3156, 3159–60,
3168, 3170–71, 3174,
3176–80, 3182, 3185–87,
3189, 3194, 3196, 3198,
3200–1, 3203, 3211, 3215,
3217–19, 3222–23, 3225,
3227–32, 3235–37, 3244,
3246–47, 3252–53, 3255,
3262, 3264, 3266, 3268,
3270–72, 3274–75, 3277,
3282–83, 3286, 3295, 3297,
3300, 3302–5, 3307,
3310–12, 3314, 3319,
3321–24, 3328, 3332–33,
3338–40, 3343–44,
3352–53, 3356–57,
3360–61, 3365–66,
3371–73, 3375–77, 3381,
3383–84, 3387, 3390, 3392,
3394, 3398, 3404–7, 3411,
3413, 3415–18, 3421–22,
3425, 3427–30, 3432, 3437,
3439, 3444, 3448, 3453,
3457–60, 3462–64,
3472–73, 3475, 3477–78,
3480, 3484–86, 3491, 3493,
3495, 3498–99, 3651, 3940,
4245, 4430, 4470, 4556,
4594, 4774, 4861, 4869,
6206, 6520, 6555 **PI:** 3019,
3053, 3085, 3288, 3292,
3364, 3426, 3438, 3479,
8314 **I:** 3005

Evolution
PI: 14514, 19796 **I:** 13264,
14454, 14498, 20736
IJ: 13313, 14396,
14496–97, 14499, 14504–5,
14516

Evolution — Biography
I: 13265

Evolution — Trials
I: 16451

Ewing, Patrick
I: 13524 **IJ:** 13523

Excretory system
IJ: 18099, 18107

Executions — Fiction
IJ: 9127

Exercise
P: 18206 **PI:** 18203
I: 18195, 18201–2
IJ: 18054, 18208

Exercise — Fiction
P: 3341, 6043

Exodus (Bible)
I: 17254

Experiments
See as subdivision of other
subjects, e.g., Electricity
— Experiments and
projects; Science —
Experiments and
projects

Explorers
See Adventurers and
explorers

Exquemelin
IJ: 12117

Extinct animals
P: 19405 **IJ:** 19401

Extinct animals — Fiction
P: 3294

Extinction (biology)
P: 18668

Extrasensory perception
I: 21925 **IJ:** 17074, 21906

**Extrasensory perception
— Fiction**
PI: 10301 **I:** 6936, 7890,
7914, 10175 **IJ:** 6914,
7548, 7852, 7889, 7928,
8068, 8425

Extraterrestrial life
P: 4483 **PI:** 20979
I: 20992, 21001, 21588
IJ: 18391, 20978, 20995,
21896

**Extraterrestrial life —
Fiction**
I: 9966, 10156, 10178,
10188, 10233–35
IJ: 10159, 10185, 10202

Exxon Valdez oil spill
See also Oil spills
I: 16800 **IJ:** 16813

Eye glasses — Fiction
P: 9815

Eyes
P: 18162 **I:** 17935, 18132,
18145, 18807, 2069, 2263,
11050, 11052–53, 11056,
11064–66, 11069,
11071–72, 11074,
11076–79, 11469, 11500
PI: 2389, 9979, 9986,
10516, 10538, 11049,
11055, 11073 **I:** 10748,
11048, 11051, 11054,
11067–68, 11394

P = Primary; PI = Primary-Intermediate; I = Intermediate; IJ = Intermediate-Junior High

F

Fables
See also Greece —
Mythology
P: 1254, 2069, 2263, 11050,
11052–53, 11056,
11064–66, 11069,
11071–72, 11074,
11076–79, 11469, 11500
PI: 2389, 9979, 9986,
10516, 10538, 11049,
11055, 11073 **I:** 10748,
11048, 11051, 11054,
11067–68, 11394

**Fabre, Jean Henri —
Fiction**
I: 9024

Face painting
P: 21589, 21592 **PI:** 21584
I: 21590

Faces
P: 3400

Faces — Art
IJ: 13933

Faces — Drawing
PI: 21573–74

Factories — History
IJ: 16466

Fairies
P: 1287, 1349, 3060, 3746
I: 7619, 7987, 10755,
21932, 21950

Fairies — Fiction
PI: 8136 **I:** 7735

Fairies — Folklore
P: 10976 **I:** 10630
IJ: 10628

Fairies — Poetry
I: 10630

Fairs
I: 14265

Fairs — Fiction
P: 144, 1198, 3058, 3082,
3089, 3120, 3289, 3419
PI: 6829

Fairy tales
P: 1337, 1445, 6082, 6371,
10375–76, 10378–81,
10385, 10387, 10391–96,
10399–406, 10410,
10412–13, 10415, 10418,
10421–23, 10425,
10427–28, 10430, 10432,
10434, 10436–37,
10439–40, 10444,
10450–52, 10458,
10462–66, 10468,
10470–71, 10475,
10480–82, 10484–86,
10490, 10492–95,
10499–500, 10502–3,
10507–8, 10510, 10517,
10519–20, 10524, 10527,

10721, 10757, 10815,
10869, 11057, 11136, 14283
PI: 1461, 4305, 5790, 7790,
10377, 10382–83,
10388–90, 10407, 10411,
10424, 10429, 10431,
10433, 10438, 10441,
10443, 10453–54, 10456,
10460, 10467, 10472,
10474, 10476, 10491,
10497–98, 10505, 10511,
10514, 10518, 10525–26,
10932, 13954 **I:** 7660–61,
7706, 8032, 10384, 10386,
10397–98, 10408–9, 10416,
10420, 10426, 10435,
10442, 10445, 10447–49,
10455, 10457, 10461,
10469, 10477–79, 10483,
10488–89, 10496, 10501,
10513, 10515, 10521–23,
10592, 10659, 10803
IJ: 7683, 10414, 10417,
10419, 10446, 10459,
10473, 10487, 10506,
10509, 10512

Fairy tales — Biography
I: 12493

Fairy tales — Crafts
PI: 21486

Fairy tales — Plays
P: 12028

Falcons
P: 19329 **PI:** 19339
I: 19319, 19342

Falcons — Fiction
P: 5143 **IJ:** 7194, 8656

Family life
P: 3767, 3817, 3819, 17673,
17681, 17684 **IJ:** 17653,
17667, 17692

Family life — Fiction
P: 2500, 3516, 4855, 5438
PI: 3918 **IJ:** 8529

Family life — Poetry
P: 3503, 11639, 11702
PI: 11592 **I:** 11599, 11745
IJ: 11565

Family problems
P: 17651, 17671, 17676,
17687, 17689–91
PI: 17657, 17663, 17686
I: 17642, 17668, 17679,
17685 **IJ:** 17643, 17652,
17659, 17665–66,
17669–70, 17688, 17708

**Family problems —
Fiction**
P: 2849, 3113, 3650, 3668,
3851, 4223, 4897, 4907,
4933, 4959, 4968, 4971,
4980, 4998, 5010, 5081,
5092, 5105, 5638, 6723,
9717 **PI:** 3743, 7192, 7309,
7498, 8414, 8522, 8540,
8649, 9826 **I:** 7083, 7209,
7265, 7422, 7514, 7518,
8217, 8228, 8347, 8351,

8395–96, 8399, 8401, 8407,
8409–10, 8415, 8422, 8427,
8431, 8433, 8437, 8442,
8449, 8451, 8458, 8468,
8470–71, 8476, 8485–86,
8494, 8503, 8505–6, 8512,
8518, 8520, 8523, 8525,
8530–32, 8534, 8536–37,
8541, 8546, 8622, 8797,
8904, 9517, 9579, 9619,
9639, 9946 **IJ:** 6779, 6808,
7255, 7325, 7896, 8102,
8149, 8258, 8274, 8397,
8402, 8405, 8408, 8412–13,
8416–18, 8421, 8423,
8425–26, 8428–30, 8432,
8435–36, 8438–41,
8443–48, 8450, 8452–54,
8457, 8459–61, 8463–65,
8467, 8469, 8472–73, 8475,
8480–84, 8487–90,
8492–93, 8495, 8500–2,
8507, 8509–11, 8513–17,
8519, 8524, 8526, 8528,
8533, 8538–39, 8544–45,
8547–49, 8581, 8585, 8620,
8645, 8673, 8678, 8685,
8736, 8787, 8844, 8851,
8853, 8871, 8876, 9093,
9124, 9258, 9260, 9352,
9546, 9557, 9593, 10016,
10079, 10284, 10292

**Family problems —
Poetry**
IJ: 11565, 11582

Family stories
P: 686, 715, 720, 1676,
1815, 2251, 3447, 3508,
3512, 3519–20, 3526, 3535,
3537–38, 3542–43, 3545,
3547, 3555, 3564, 3568,
3572, 3574, 3577, 3582,
3586, 3588, 3591, 3595,
3605, 3609–10, 3616, 3621,
3623, 3626, 3631, 3633–34,
3637, 3640, 3644, 3649,
3652, 3655, 3666–67, 3671,
3675, 3679, 3687, 3696,
3708–9, 3720–21, 3724,
3727, 3730, 3734, 3736–37,
3741, 3750, 3757, 3760–61,
3764, 3766, 3771, 3775,
3780, 3783–84, 3790,
3796–98, 3802–3, 3811,
3813–14, 3821, 3824–25,
3827, 3830, 3835, 3838,
3845, 3853, 3857, 3861–62,
3864, 3872–74, 3876–78,
3880–81, 3886–87, 3890,
3896, 3899, 3910, 3912,
3916–17, 3925, 3931, 3933,
3935, 3937, 3940, 3962,
3968, 3970–72, 3974, 4097,
4164, 4355, 4420, 4609,
4759, 4773, 4806, 4845,
4890, 4900, 4965, 5064,
5366, 5416, 5684, 5695,
6088, 6243, 6247, 6441,
6696, 7224, 7497 **PI:** 3604,
3641, 3772, 3892, 7383,
7394, 7439, 7449, 7502–3,
7506–7, 8623, 8750, 9961,

9991, 10015, 12525, 15193,
16944 **I:** 7068, 7393, 7402,
7407, 7420, 7441, 7453,
7475, 7488, 7499, 7504–5,
7511, 7523, 7534, 9399,
9423, 9538, 9547, 9570,
9588, 9824, 9855, 9925,
9949, 9988, 10017, 15692
IJ: 7386, 7390, 7419, 7433,
7447, 7454, 7465, 7512,
7539, 7557, 8134, 8517,
8527, 8697, 8788, 9010,
9613, 9683, 15137

Family stories — Fiction
P: 1831, 2276, 2934, 3147,
3423, 3465, 3468, 3500–2,
3505–6, 3510–11, 3513–15,
3517, 3521–23, 3527–31,
3534, 3536, 3544, 3560,
3562–63, 3566–67,
3569–71, 3573, 3576, 3585,
3590, 3592–93, 3596–97,
3601, 3603, 3606, 3608,
3614, 3617–20, 3624–25,
3628, 3630, 3632, 3636,
3639, 3643, 3648, 3650–51,
3653, 3656–58, 3660,
3662–63, 3665, 3668–69,
3672, 3674, 3676, 3680–82,
3684, 3688–89, 3692, 3694,
3698–701, 3706–7,
3710–14, 3717, 3719,
3722–23, 3725–26, 3729,
3731–32, 3738, 3742,
3745–46, 3748–49,
3751–56, 3758–59, 3762,
3765, 3773–74, 3777–78,
3781–82, 3787, 3789, 3791,
3793–94, 3799, 3801, 3804,
3807–9, 3812, 3818,
3828–29, 3832, 3834,
3836–37, 3839, 3843–44,
3847–48, 3850, 3852,
3855–56, 3859–60, 3863,
3866, 3868–69, 3882–83,
3885, 3888, 3891, 3893–94,
3897–98, 3901–3, 3905,
3908–9, 3913, 3920,
3922–23, 3926–27, 3929,
3939, 3941–43, 3947–49,
3953–54, 3956, 3958–59,
3961, 3965, 3967, 3969,
3973, 3975–76, 4382, 4507,
4623, 4679, 4763, 4809,
4828, 5011, 5033, 5463,
5519, 5614, 5681, 5718,
5769, 5908, 6103, 6195,
6244, 6338, 6412, 6450,
6477, 7418 **PI:** 3587, 3635,
3661, 3763, 3820, 3915,
4578, 5644, 5669, 7166,
7298, 7385, 7389, 7397,
7403–4, 7406, 7413, 7417,
7423, 7445, 7456, 7458–59,
7469–71, 7473, 7481, 7494,
7496, 7501, 7516, 8595,
9548, 9729, 9819, 9821,
9923 **I:** 6867, 7226, 7249,
7343, 7388, 7391, 7395,
7400–1, 7409–12, 7414,
7421–22, 7425–29, 7431,
7434, 7436, 7446, 7448,

P = Primary; PI = Primary-Intermediate; I = Intermediate; IJ = Intermediate-Junior High

7451, 7455, 7457, 7463,
7468, 7472, 7474, 7477,
7480, 7482–83, 7487, 7489,
7493, 7495, 7500, 7510,
7513, 7517, 7527, 7529–30,
7535–36, 7540, 7543, 8039,
8097, 8286, 8403, 8508,
8535, 8627, 8690, 8962,
9033, 9383, 9446, 9449,
9534, 9629, 9782, 9842
IJ: 6871, 7381–82, 7384,
7387, 7392, 7398–99, 7405,
7408, 7416, 7424, 7432,
7438, 7443–44, 7452,
7460–61, 7464, 7466–67,
7476, 7478–79, 7484–86,
7490–91, 7508, 7515,
7525–26, 7531–32,
7537–38, 7542, 7871, 8679,
8681, 8806, 8987, 9572,
9589, 9666, 10004

Family trees
P: 3910

Famines
I: 20043

Famines — Fiction
I: 9089 **IJ:** 9414

Famines — Folklore
P: 11294

Fantasy
See also Fables; Folklore;
Imaginary animals;
Mythology; Science
fiction; Supernatural;
Tall tales; Time travel —
Fiction
P: 20, 626, 636, 644, 654,
660, 668, 673, 681–82, 695,
705, 756, 762, 765–66, 773,
819, 907, 941–47, 949–52,
954–60, 963–80, 982–83,
985–87, 989–1005,
1007–20, 1022–25,
1027–34, 1037–48,
1050–51, 1053–57,
1059–74, 1076–101, 1103,
1106–8, 1110–22, 1124–37,
1139–52, 1154, 1156–62,
1164, 1166–86, 1188–90,
1192–95, 1197–200, 1203,
1205–26, 1228–65,
1267–75, 1277–90,
1292–307, 1309, 1311–16,
1318–20, 1322–28,
1330–32, 1335–37, 1339,
1341–50, 1352, 1354–60,
1362–66, 1368–79,
1381–90, 1392–95,
1397–401, 1403–48,
1450–53, 1455–60,
1462–65, 1468–69,
1471–74, 1476–78, 1480,
1482–90, 1492–97,
1501–10, 1513–14,
1517–28, 1530–32,
1534–37, 1539–50,
1554–68, 1570–73,
1575–87, 1590–92,
1595–99, 1602–11,
1613–25, 1627–29,

1632–38, 1640, 1642–46,
1648–49, 1652–61,
1663–67, 1669–78,
1680–81, 1683–96,
1698–721, 1825, 1833,
1852, 1917, 1969, 2651,
2878, 3242, 3603, 4110,
4266, 4281, 4286, 4539,
4574, 4723, 4738, 5127,
5601, 5620, 5653, 5664,
5707, 5748, 5788, 5857,
6240–41, 6339, 6359, 6379,
6401, 6421, 6424, 6496,
6498, 6594, 6631, 6670,
6678, 6716, 6726, 7626,
7744, 7791, 7904, 7962–63,
8000, 8064, 10300 **PI:** 961,
988, 1006, 1021, 1026,
1049, 1052, 1105, 1109,
1123, 1153, 1165, 1187,
1191, 1201–2, 1266, 1308,
1329, 1334, 1338, 1353,
1361, 1367, 1396, 1402,
1454, 1470, 1475, 1498,
1500, 1512, 1515–16, 1529,
1553, 1574, 1588–89,
1593–94, 1612, 1631, 1639,
1647, 1679, 1697, 5772,
5803, 5886, 6938, 6998,
7242, 7245, 7561, 7565,
7578–80, 7582–83,
7596–97, 7606, 7620, 7629,
7634–36, 7655, 7658–59,
7662, 7676, 7682, 7696,
7704–5, 7709, 7715, 7720,
7722, 7732–33, 7740,
7748–49, 7752, 7755–57,
7759, 7766, 7781–82,
7789–90, 7792–93, 7803,
7807, 7815, 7841–42, 7845,
7865–67, 7869, 7872–75,
7879–80, 7883–84, 7888,
7891, 7899–901, 7910,
7924, 7934, 7937, 7941,
7947, 7950, 7955–57, 7959,
7964, 7966, 7968, 7972–73,
7989, 7992, 7998, 8022,
8026–27, 8034–35, 8043,
8047, 8052, 8056, 8059,
8076, 8084, 8094–95,
8104–5, 8115, 8117–18,
8124, 8129, 8136, 8140,
8146–47, 8165, 8168, 8173,
8184–87, 8193, 8200, 8203,
8205, 8207, 8209, 8214,
8225, 8231, 9711, 9840,
9968, 10460, 10525
I: 6972, 7246, 7306, 7396,
7411, 7552, 7554–55,
7558–59, 7562, 7564, 7566,
7568–77, 7587–89,
7594–95, 7602, 7613–15,
7617–19, 7623–25, 7631,
7633, 7637–39, 7641–44,
7653, 7667–68,
7672–73, 7675, 7677–78,
7686, 7689, 7694–95, 7697,
7699, 7706–7, 7713–14,
7716–18, 7723, 7725, 7728,
7731, 7735–36, 7739, 7745,
7747, 7751, 7754, 7761–65,
7769, 7772, 7777, 7780,
7784, 7786, 7788, 7794–95,

7797–800, 7809, 7811,
7819, 7826, 7832–35,
7837–38, 7843–44,
7847–49, 7851, 7853–56,
7859–60, 7862, 7864, 7870,
7878, 7887, 7892, 7894–95,
7902, 7912, 7917–18, 7920,
7923, 7925, 7935–36,
7938–39, 7942–44, 7946,
7948, 7951, 7958, 7961,
7967, 7971, 7974, 7977,
7980, 7983, 7985–88,
7996–97, 8001, 8003, 8005,
8008, 8013, 8019, 8021,
8025, 8031–33, 8036,
8039–40, 8045, 8053, 8057,
8061, 8066–67, 8069–70,
8072–73, 8079–83, 8087,
8089–91, 8093, 8096–97,
8101, 8110, 8113–14, 8116,
8122, 8126–28, 8130–31,
8139, 8141–42, 8148, 8154,
8156–58, 8162–63, 8167,
8171, 8174, 8176, 8181–82,
8188, 8190–92, 8196, 8201,
8206, 8208, 8210–11, 8216,
8218–19, 8221, 8226,
8233–34, 8239–43, 8245,
8263, 8907, 9725, 9752,
9965, 10117, 10127, 10513
IJ: 7010, 7103, 7111, 7544,
7546–51, 7553, 7556–57,
7560, 7563, 7567, 7581,
7584–86, 7590, 7593,
7598–601, 7603, 7605,
7608, 7611–12, 7621–22,
7627–28, 7632, 7640,
7645–48, 7652, 7664,
7669–71, 7674, 7679–81,
7688, 7708, 7710–12, 7719,
7721, 7724, 7729–30, 7734,
7737–38, 7743, 7746, 7753,
7768, 7770, 7776, 7783,
7796, 7802, 7804, 7808,
7810, 7814, 7816–18,
7820–25, 7827–30, 7836,
7839, 7846, 7850, 7852,
7857–58, 7861, 7868,
7876–77, 7882, 7885–86,
7893, 7896–98, 7907–9,
7911, 7915–16, 7921,
7926–27, 7929–33,
7952–54, 7970, 7975–76,
7978, 7982, 7990–91, 7993,
7995, 7999, 8002, 8004,
8009–10, 8012, 8014–18,
8023–24, 8029–30,
8041–42, 8048–51,
8054–55, 8058, 8060, 8062,
8068, 8078, 8086, 8092,
8099–100, 8103, 8106–9,
8112, 8119–20, 8125,
8133–35, 8138, 8143–45,
8151–53, 8159–60, 8169,
8175, 8177–78, 8189, 8199,
8202, 8212–13, 8215, 8220,
8229–30, 8232, 8235, 8238,
8244, 8716, 8845, 10217,
10363, 10768

Fantasy — Biography
IJ: 12160

Fantasy — Poetry
P: 1058, 1317, 1668

Fantasy — Short stories
PI: 7949 **I:** 7750

Farm animals
See also specific animals,
e.g., Cattle

Farm animals — Fiction
P: 693, 934, 4422, 5188,
5420, 5454, 6545, 6690

Farm life
P: 3143, 5200, 14144,
14171, 20053, 20057,
20060, 20062, 20064,
20067, 20094 **PI:** 4727,
13255, 20052, 20069, 20072
I: 13256, 16323, 16689,
20046, 20049, 20058,
20061, 20074–75, 20576
IJ: 16171, 18828, 20047,
20059, 20068

Farm life — Careers
P: 17748 **PI:** 17764

Farm life — Fiction
P: 20, 100, 374, 383, 613,
1166, 1464, 2794, 2952,
3070, 3145, 3188, 3302,
3306, 3335, 3409, 3445,
3471, 3730, 3884, 4023,
4096, 4154, 4212, 4220,
4367, 4465, 4492, 4555,
5026, 5046, 5144, 5192,
5218, 5220, 5242, 5257,
5286, 5312, 5345, 5363,
5427, 5439, 5552, 5863
PI: 937, 1500, 1697, 4667,
8333, 8722, 9525, 9850,
10000 **I:** 7169, 7425, 7428,
7788, 8542, 8897, 9070,
9584, 9618, 9639, 9703,
9933 **IJ:** 7479, 7533, 7610,
7871, 8481, 8606, 8669,
9278, 9352, 9605, 9627,
9634

Farm life — Folklore
P: 11294

Farm life — History
P: 15899 **PI:** 20069
I: 15341, 16308

Farm life — Machinery
P: 21252–53

Farm life — Poetry
P: 11613

**Farm workers —
Biography**
PI: 12825 **IJ:** 12832

Farmer, James
PI: 12721

Farmers — Careers
PI: 17764

Farnsworth, Philo
I: 13279

Farragut, David
IJ: 12876

P = Primary; PI = Primary-Intermediate; I = Intermediate; IJ = Intermediate-Junior High

Fashion — History
IJ: 21180

Fashion design
See also Design; Dress
I: 21179 IJ: 12924, 13163

**Fashion design —
Biography**
IJ: 12829

Fashion design — History
IJ: 16450, 16478,
16515–17, 21172

Fashion shows — Fiction
IJ: 9864

Fathers
P: 3817, 17681

Fathers — Fiction
P: 1019, 2220, 2873, 3212,
3544, 3546, 3565, 3574–75,
3577, 3657, 3667, 3674,
3690, 3709, 3735–36, 3783,
3832, 3838, 3840, 3852,
3879, 4806, 5105, 5371,
7435 PI: 3892 I: 8470,
10037, 11548 IJ: 8480,
8598, 8654, 8685, 10284

Fathers — Folklore
I: 10547

Fathers — Poetry
P: 11982 PI: 11762

Father's Day — Fiction
P: 5614, 5630

Fats (nutrition)
I: 20166 IJ: 20168

Faversham, Charles
P: 12534

Favre, Brett
I: 13610 IJ: 13609,
13611–13

Fear
P: 17607

Fear — Fiction
P: 773, 1248, 1456, 1849,
2198, 2700, 2906, 3130,
3483, 4675, 4702, 4906,
4967, 5468, 6632, 10089
PI: 1026 I: 8857

Fears
P: 17601

Fears — Fiction
P: 1267, 2817, 3018, 5106,
5256, 5402, 8761 PI: 2936,
9758 I: 8552

Feathers
PI: 18847

Feet
P: 18045

Feet — Fiction
P: 234, 457, 3243, 5000

Feinstein, Dianne
PI: 12877

Feller, Bob
I: 13451

Feminism — Biography
IJ: 13196

Feminism — Folklore
P: 10921 PI: 10602
I: 10603

Fencing — Biography
IJ: 13704

Feral cats
I: 19079

Fernandez, Mary Joe
PI: 13647

Ferrets
PI: 19890 I: 18947, 18975

Ferrets — Fiction
P: 5315 PI: 7181 I: 10012

Ferries
P: 3141

Ferris wheels — Fiction
P: 1267

Fiction — Writing
See Writing — Fiction

Fictional characters
I: 14004

**Field Museum of Natural
History (Chicago)**
P: 2808

Fields, Mary
P: 12722

Figure skating
See Ice skating

Figures of speech
I: 14111

Fiji Islands — Folklore
P: 10852

Fillmore, Millard
IJ: 13033

Finance
IJ: 16921–22

Finches
I: 19281

Fingerplays
P: 11554, 21984, 22041

Finland
I: 15456, 15461 IJ: 15445

Finland — Folklore
I: 11131

Finland — Holidays
PI: 15457

**Finnish Americans —
Fiction**
I: 9739

Fire engines and trucks
P: 21297 PI: 21294, 21307

**Fire engines and trucks —
Fiction**
P: 1580

**Fire engines and trucks —
History**
P: 21313

Fire fighters
P: 3033, 5579, 5589
PI: 17809, 17823 I: 17810,
17817, 17820 IJ: 20473

Fire fighters — Careers
P: 17808, 17816, 17819
PI: 17812–13, 17821
I: 17818 IJ: 17806

Fire fighters — Fiction
P: 32, 65, 2964, 3166, 3492

Fire safety — Fiction
P: 1468

Fire stations
PI: 17809

Fireflies
P: 19452 I: 19456

Fireflies — Fiction
P: 4393

Firehouses
PI: 17823

Fires
P: 16481 I: 16624, 16663,
16689, 17810, 17817,
20279, 20362, 20366,
20460, 20851 IJ: 16765

Fires — Fiction
P: 3948, 4810 I: 9586

Fireworks
P: 17391 I: 21029

Fireworks — Fiction
P: 4575, 4648

First aid
I: 18215

First Ladies
See Presidents (U.S.) —
Wives — Biography

Fish
See also different kinds of
fish, e.g., Trout
P: 19642, 19653, 19695,
19698, 19700–2, 19716,
19770, 19982 PI: 19658,
19696, 19699, 19712, 19714
I: 19703, 19707, 19980
IJ: 19718

Fish — Careers
I: 13259

Fish — Coral reefs
IJ: 19654

Fish — Electric
P: 19694

Fish — Fiction
P: 342, 1713, 1904, 1946,
2381, 2386, 2579 PI: 7413

Fish — Pets
I: 19981

Fish and Wildlife Service
See United States Fish and
Wildlife Service

Fishing
P: 3354, 16797 I: 22176,
22178 IJ: 22174–75, 22177

Fishing — Fiction
P: 1544, 1756, 1786, 2942,
2979, 3355, 3615, 3695,
3777, 4379, 4391, 4433,
4586, 4747, 4788, 4881,
6325 PI: 3934, 7522
I: 6816

Fishing industry
PI: 19848

**Fisk University Jubilee
Singers — Fiction**
PI: 7346

Fitzgerald, F. Scott
IJ: 12535

Flags
P: 6688

Flags — Fiction
PI: 10034

Flags (U.S.)
P: 13190, 13976
PI: 13972, 13975 I: 13189,
13968–69, 13973–74
IJ: 13977

Flags (U.S.) — Biography
I: 13188

Flags (U.S.) — States
PI: 13970 IJ: 13971

Flamingos
PI: 19255

Flatulence
P: 18098

Fleas
I: 18648

Fleas — Fiction
P: 4357

Fleece — Grafts
IJ: 21645

Flies (insect)
P: 19448 I: 19432, 19441,
19467 IJ: 19477

Flies (insect) — Fiction
P: 1069, 1797

Flightless birds
P: 19229 I: 19214

Flipper, Henry O.
IJ: 12723

Floods
PI: 16531, 20688, 20708
I: 20680, 20714 IJ: 20685,
20699, 20705, 20723

Floods — Fiction
P: 3290, 8586 PI: 7941
IJ: 9287

Floods — Poetry
P: 11619

Florence (Italy) — Fiction
P: 4792

Florida
P: 19082 PI: 16858,
16875, 16887, 19684
I: 16863, 18793 IJ: 13266,
16837

P = Primary; PI = Primary-Intermediate; I = Intermediate; IJ = Intermediate-Junior High

Florida — Fiction
P: 5123 **I:** 6868, 7890, 9581, 9783 **IJ:** 6855, 6995, 7003, 7009, 7289, 8284, 8544, 10120

Florida — Folklore
P: 11327

Florida — History
I: 15942, 15987 **IJ:** 16897

Florida panthers
IJ: 19109

Flour mills
I: 16321

Flowers
P: 20034–35, 20261
PI: 13269, 20248 **I:** 15853, 20036–37, 20040, 20267
IJ: 20038, 20042

Flowers — Fiction
P: 2944, 4402, 4499, 4869

Flowers — Folklore
P: 10749, 11229

Flying — Fiction
P: 1664, 1706, 2456
I: 8312 **IJ:** 7886

Flying — Poetry
I: 11636, 11970

Folk art
P: 605 **I:** 13928, 13955

Folk dances
PI: 14271

Folk songs
P: 616, 716–17, 14143–44, 14147–48, 14151, 14153, 14155, 14159, 14163, 14165–66, 14169, 14171–73, 14176–78, 14182, 14184–85, 14187, 14189, 14193–96
PI: 14142, 14164, 14170, 14191 **I:** 11360, 14139, 14146, 14154, 14180
IJ: 14140, 14162
All: 14145, 14150

Folklore
See also specific countries and regions, e.g., Germany — Folklore; and specific topics, e.g., Cats — Folklore

Folklore — Anthologies
P: 735, 6192, 6637, 10530, 10539, 10541–43, 10545, 10551, 10562, 10564, 10572, 10585, 10599, 10605, 10617, 10627, 10631–32 **PI:** 10538, 10573, 10602, 10607, 10624, 10719, 10827, 11219, 11263, 11329
I: 10252, 10528–29, 10532–35, 10546–50, 10553–55, 10557, 10560, 10563, 10566, 10569–71, 10574–75, 10577–78, 10581, 10583–84,

10587–88, 10590–94, 10596, 10598, 10601, 10603, 10612–14, 10616, 10618–19, 10622–23, 10625–26, 10629, 10636, 10758, 10794, 10832, 10848, 10865, 10877, 10893, 11003–4, 11120, 11157, 11172, 11175, 11212, 11224, 11274, 11345, 11376, 11382, 11389, 11445 **IJ:** 10509, 10537, 10540, 10556, 10561, 10565, 10567, 10576, 10579, 10600, 10606, 10611, 10615, 10620–21, 10633–35, 10668, 10730, 10739, 10746, 10759, 10795, 10845, 10899, 11080, 11173–74, 11191, 11277, 11330, 11341, 11364, 11366, 11370, 11380–81
All: 10609

Folklore — Jokes and riddles
I: 21851

Folklore — Plays
PI: 12013 **I:** 12030, 12035, 12042

Folklore — Poetry
P: 6638

Fonda, Jane
I: 12387

Food
P: 3380, 16008, 18101, 18105, 20053, 20078, 20097, 20121, 20125, 20135, 20164 **PI:** 16163, 18205, 20161–62 **I:** 20045, 20120, 21680 **IJ:** 18097, 18099, 20081, 20098, 20100, 20177

Food — Careers
IJ: 17759

Food — Crafts
I: 21431

Food — Experiments and projects
P: 20096 **PI:** 18372
I: 20087, 20114 **IJ:** 18212, 18312

Food — Fiction
P: 37, 980, 2684, 3003, 3196, 3235, 3408, 3842, 4058, 4109, 4128, 4263, 6432 **I:** 7574, 9966, 9976
IJ: 9895

Food — Folklore
P: 11398

Food — History
PI: 16493 **I:** 14349, 14559, 20045 **IJ:** 14747, 20116, 20131

Food — Middle Ages
PI: 14752

Food — Poetry
P: 4349, 11746 **PI:** 11865, 11877, 11902 **I:** 11685

Food — Women
IJ: 17759

Food — Words
IJ: 20103

Food additives
I: 20165

Food chains
P: 18590 **I:** 18586

Food chains — Fiction
P: 5460 **PI:** 4504

Food poisoning
PI: 20162

Food pyramid
PI: 20161

Football
P: 22182–83 **PI:** 22188
I: 22186, 22190
IJ: 22179–80, 22184, 22187

Football — Biography
P: 13608 **I:** 13388–89, 13404, 13419, 13600, 13602, 13605, 13607, 13610, 13615, 13619, 13621, 13624–26, 13629, 13631, 13633, 13635, 13637–39 **IJ:** 13367, 13382, 13405, 13407, 13416, 13601, 13603–4, 13606, 13609, 13611–14, 13616–18, 13620, 13622–23, 13627–28, 13630, 13632, 13634, 13636, 13640

Football — Coaches
IJ: 13407

Football — Fiction
P: 2968, 5466, 6511
I: 10365 **IJ:** 10325, 10331, 10360

Football — History
I: 22181, 22189

Football — Quarterbacks
IJ: 13416

Force (physics)
IJ: 20832, 20837

Force (physics) — Experiments and projects
P: 20833 **PI:** 20825
I: 20814 **IJ:** 20826

Ford, Betty
I: 13154

Ford, Gerald
I: 13034

Ford, Henry
P: 13281, 13283 **I:** 13282
IJ: 13280

Foreign languages — Poetry
P: 11673

Foreign policy (U.S.)
I: 17024

Foreman, Michael
IJ: 12232

Forensic science — Animals
I: 18637

Forensics
I: 17064, 17073, 17089
IJ: 17071–72

Forensics — Experiments and projects
IJ: 17079

Forest fires
P: 16481 **PI:** 17812
I: 16624, 16639, 16965
IJ: 17806, 20473

Forest fires — Fiction
P: 3718

Forests
See also Rain forests
P: 18645, 20215, 20441, 20482 **PI:** 19413, 20434, 20438, 20447, 20454, 20474
I: 20450, 20457, 20460, 20466, 20471, 20486, 20489
IJ: 20218, 20430–31, 20456, 20473

Forests — Animals
P: 20432 **PI:** 20461
I: 20450

Forests — Fiction
P: 1362, 4513 **I:** 20443

Forests — Plants
P: 20445 **I:** 20450

Fork lifts
P: 21300

Forster, Cathy
I: 14386

Fort Sumter, Battle of
PI: 16416 **IJ:** 16434

Forts
PI: 16332 **I:** 21381
IJ: 21413

Forts — Civil War (U.S.)
IJ: 16395

Forts — Roman
I: 14725

Fortune, Amos
IJ: 12724

Fortune telling
I: 21893, 21926 **IJ:** 21922, 21948

Fortune telling — Fiction
P: 2722

Fossey, Dian
P: 13285 **I:** 13284

Fossils
See also Paleontology
P: 14374, 14403, 14486
PI: 14375 **I:** 14390, 14416,

P = Primary; PI = Primary-Intermediate; I = Intermediate; IJ = Intermediate-Junior High

14430, 14433, 14463
IJ: 14415, 20553

Fossils — Biography
P: 13227, 13230–31

Fossils — Collecting
IJ: 14460

Fossils — Fiction
P: 4386 **PI:** 6792 **I:** 9332

Foster care
P: 17691

Foster care — Biography
PI: 13158

Foster care — Fiction
P: 3789 **PI:** 7348 **I:** 8286,
8451, 8588, 8633, 8779
IJ: 8266, 8406, 8529, 8697

Fourth of July
See July Fourth

Fox Indians
PI: 15995

Foxes
P: 19121, 19123, 19130–31,
19144 **PI:** 19129, 19132
I: 19137

Foxes — Fiction
P: 1624, 2095, 2124, 2233,
2819, 2825, 4325, 4555,
5149, 5314, 6203, 6504,
6662 **PI:** 6269, 10516
I: 7100, 7169, 7826

Foxes — Folklore
P: 10957, 11002, 11352
IJ: 11438

Foxes — Poetry
P: 11546

Fractions
P: 490, 556, 20593
PI: 20578

Fractions — Fiction
P: 20602

France
P: 4663, 15296, 15305,
15315 **PI:** 15299–300,
15303, 15308–9, 15319
I: 15297, 15304, 15307,
15318 **IJ:** 15301, 15311,
15313–14

France — Cookbooks
IJ: 21743

France — Fiction
P: 1983, 2769, 4209, 4666,
4729, 4751, 4764, 4847
PI: 4797, 9664 **I:** 8885,
9041, 9053, 9068, 9646,
9674 **IJ:** 7478, 8169, 9030,
9048, 9060, 9940

France — Folklore
P: 10866–68, 10870–74,
10878, 10880–81
PI: 10875, 10879
I: 10876–77

France — Food
I: 15302

France — History
P: 13813 **PI:** 13812
I: 13811, 13814, 15306
IJ: 13767, 13815, 13839,
14827, 14839, 14855,
14863, 15298, 15316–17,
15320

France — Holidays
PI: 15312 **I:** 15302

Francis of Assisi, Saint
P: 4682, 13795 **PI:** 5772
I: 13793–94

**Francis of Assisi, Saint —
Folklore**
P: 11075

Frank, Anne
PI: 13796 **I:** 13797, 13800
IJ: 13798–99

Frankenstein
I: 21944

Franklin, Benjamin
P: 12878, 12882–84
PI: 9229 **I:** 12881
IJ: 12879–80

**Franklin, Benjamin —
Fiction**
IJ: 9912

Franklin, Sir John
IJ: 15566

Freckles — Fiction
IJ: 8177

Fredericksburg, Battle of
IJ: 16434

Fremont, John C.
I: 12118 **IJ:** 16081

French, Daniel Chester
IJ: 13957

French and Indian Wars
I: 16158 **IJ:** 16103, 16159,
16161

French Canada — Fiction
PI: 5616

French language
P: 14096

French Revolution
I: 15306

Frescoes
I: 13948

Friendship
P: 17613, 17729, 17731
I: 17697, 17722 **IJ:** 17728

Friendship — Poetry
P: 11652 **PI:** 11729

**Friendship stories —
Fiction**
P: 1343, 1951, 1987, 2150,
2154, 2275, 2404, 2484,
2530, 2559–60, 2807, 2962,
3084, 3145, 3347, 3470,
3977–89, 3991–97,
4000–17, 4019–20,
4022–24, 4026–27,
4029–32, 4037–46,

4048–61, 4063–64,
4067–70, 4568, 5054, 5481,
5488–89, 5491, 5710, 6208,
6219, 6278, 6323, 6326,
6344, 6354, 6396, 6413–14,
6416–18, 6425–26, 6444,
6447, 6462, 6464, 6548,
6681, 6704, 6279, 8334,
8342, 8978, 10137, 17624
PI: 3998, 4018, 4034–36,
4065–66, 6910, 8043, 8056,
8250, 8253–54, 8259, 8262,
8267–69, 8272, 8285, 8291,
8299, 8302, 8310–11, 8314,
8320, 8322, 8327, 8330,
8332, 8336, 8349–50, 8352,
8361–62, 8365, 8380, 8382,
8387–88, 8394, 8700, 8842,
8879, 9339, 9495, 9578,
9637, 9795, 9825, 9997,
10044, 10091, 10103,
10334, 10343–44 **I:** 6741,
6911, 6960, 6971, 7055,
7165, 7253, 7259, 7307,
7442, 7487, 7495, 7725,
7856, 7919, 8252, 8255–56,
8260, 8263–64, 8270–71,
8277–78, 8283, 8286, 8288,
8290, 8295, 8297–98, 8301,
8306–9, 8312–13, 8316–17,
8319, 8323, 8325–26, 8328,
8335, 8339–40, 8346–47,
8351, 8360, 8363–64,
8366–67, 8370, 8372–74,
8376, 8381, 8385–86, 8392,
8411, 8498, 8531, 8625,
8633, 8677, 8694, 8767,
8810, 8862, 8873, 8878,
9039, 9576, 9585, 9793,
9863, 9879, 9943, 9946,
9960, 10033, 10046, 10072,
10117 **IJ:** 6787, 6789,
6970, 7147, 7334, 7796,
8246–49, 8251, 8257–58,
8265–66, 8273–76,
8281–82, 8284, 8289,
8292–94, 8296, 8300,
8303–5, 8315, 8318, 8321,
8324, 8329, 8337–38, 8341,
8343–45, 8353–59,
8368–69, 8371, 8375,
8377–79, 8383–84,
8389–91, 8393, 8413, 8507,
8592, 8605, 8666, 8733–34,
8742, 8769, 8871, 8889,
8898, 8911, 8923, 8936,
8968, 8981, 9346, 9396,
9559, 9633, 9671–72, 9940,
9942, 9958, 10010, 10030,
10335, 10340, 10345,
10367, 10369

**Friendship stories —
Poetry**
P: 4025 **PI:** 11757
IJ: 11635

Fright — Fiction
P: 3742, 3980, 4394, 4917,
4925, 5060, 5090, 6216,
6367 **PI:** 9805 **I:** 7258,
7320, 7401, 8271, 8312,
10031 **IJ:** 8612, 9694

Fritz, Jean
PI: 12537 **IJ:** 12536

Frogs and toads
P: 18713–15, 18717–23,
18725–27, 18730, 18732,
18734–37, 18740–41
PI: 18716, 18738 **I:** 18680,
18728–29, 18731, 18733,
18739 **IJ:** 18724, 18742

Frogs and toads — Fiction
P: 1039, 1304, 1537, 1652,
1718, 1782, 2027, 2150,
2162, 2267, 2286, 2381,
2391, 2706, 2719, 2855,
3719, 4429, 5212, 5370,
6464, 6553, 6629, 10401
PI: 7166, 7676 **I:** 7979–80
IJ: 7753, 8041

**Frogs and toads —
Folklore**
P: 10898 **IJ:** 10839

Frogs and toads — Poetry
I: 11952

Frontier life (Canada)
I: 15576

Frontier life (U.S.)
P: 4600, 9435, 16317
PI: 12081, 12687, 16259,
16286, 16288, 16304,
16325–26, 16331–32,
16336, 16348, 16355,
16357, 16363–64, 16476
I: 9587, 12104, 12865,
13045, 16269, 16284,
16287, 16289–90, 16293,
16295–96, 16303, 16308,
16316, 16318, 16320–24,
16327–29, 16334,
16339–42, 16344–45,
16347, 16349–53, 16358,
16360, 16366, 16371,
16373–74, 16379–82,
16384, 16386, 18966
IJ: 9434, 12663, 12867,
12902, 16291, 16294,
16297–302, 16305, 16311,
16313, 16315, 16319,
16333, 16354, 16359,
16368–70, 16375,
16377–78, 16385

**Frontier life (U.S.) —
Biography**
P: 12102, 12429, 12431–32
PI: 12084, 12515 **I:** 12082,
12085, 12088, 12103,
12118, 12589, 12649,
12651, 12669, 12849
IJ: 12083, 12641, 12646,
12665, 12698, 12870,
12910, 12948, 12965

**Frontier life (U.S.) —
Cookbooks**
IJ: 16312

**Frontier life (U.S.) —
Crafts**
PI: 21520, 21522 **I:** 16318,
21521, 21523

P = Primary; PI = Primary-Intermediate; I = Intermediate; IJ = Intermediate-Junior High

Frontier life (U.S.) — Fiction
P: 4101, 4567, 4606, 4664, 4674, 4676, 4687, 4704–5, 4720, 4732, 4758, 4800, 4810, 4819–21, 4857, 4860, 4877, 5832, 5847, 5929, 5981, 6222, 6245–46, 6274, 9390 **PI:** 1552, 4701, 4859, 4889, 8123, 9348, 9367, 9373–74, 9382, 9394, 9401, 9407, 9410, 9417, 9447, 9450, 9452–53, 9455, 9526, 9621 **I:** 6955, 7121, 7161, 9269, 9288, 9334, 9342–43, 9347, 9350, 9354, 9356, 9358–59, 9364–65, 9368–69, 9376–77, 9379–81, 9383, 9385, 9387–89, 9391, 9393, 9395, 9397–400, 9403–6, 9411–13, 9416, 9418–23, 9425, 9427, 9429–30, 9433, 9436, 9438, 9441, 9443–45, 9448–49, 9457–61, 9558 **IJ:** 6992, 7231, 7537, 9159, 9191–92, 9259, 9298, 9300, 9341, 9344, 9346, 9349, 9351–53, 9355, 9360–63, 9366, 9370–71, 9375, 9378, 9384, 9386, 9392, 9396, 9402, 9408–9, 9414–15, 9424, 9426, 9428, 9431–32, 9439–40, 9442, 9454, 9456, 9462

Frontier life (U.S.) — Plays
I: 12031

Frontier life (U.S.) — Poetry
IJ: 11726

Frontier life (U.S.) — Songs
I: 14180

Frontier life (U.S.) — Women
PI: 12688 **I:** 16330, 16343

Frontier Nursing Service
I: 12860

Fruit salad — Fiction
P: 3631

Fruits
P: 20142, 20144, 20150, 20154–55, 20157–58, 20261 **PI:** 10691 **I:** 20124, 20152 **IJ:** 20145–47

Fruits — Experiments and projects
I: 21768

Fruits — Fiction
P: 3631

Fry, Elizabeth — Fiction
I: 9293

Fulton, Robert
I: 13286 **IJ:** 13287

Funerals
P: 17859

Fungi
See also specific fungi, e.g., Mushrooms
I: 20191 **IJ:** 20189, 20192

Fur
PI: 18847

Fur trade — Fiction
IJ: 8931, 9361

Future
IJ: 21953

Futurism
I: 18273

G

Gac-Artigas, Alejandro
IJ: 12830

Galan, Nely
IJ: 12831

Galapagos Islands
I: 15772, 18790

Galapagos Islands — Animals
I: 18634

Galapagos Islands — Fiction
P: 5303

Galapagos Islands — Poetry
I: 11964

Galarraga, Andres
PI: 13452

Galaxies
PI: 18376 **I:** 18392 **IJ:** 18543

Galdikas, Birute
I: 13288

Galileo
P: 13291 **I:** 13289–90, 13292 **IJ:** 13293

Galileo (spacecraft)
IJ: 20973

Gallaudet, Thomas
PI: 12885

Gallbladder stones — Fiction
PI: 9907

Galleons
I: 15477

Gambia
IJ: 15050

Gambling — Fiction
IJ: 8756

Gambling — Sports
IJ: 22073

Games
See also Picture puzzles; Puzzles; Sports; Word games

P: 903, 5435, 6679, 21467, 21972, 21981, 21987, 22004, 22007, 22018–19, 22067 **PI:** 21983, 22000, 22032, 22072, 22229 **I:** 15057, 21969, 21980, 21985, 21998, 22014, 22034, 22038, 22233, 22236 **IJ:** 15424, 18330, 22010, 22012, 22035, 22054–55, 22237

Games — Fiction
P: 301, 1640, 2235, 3477, 10524

Games — History
PI: 21658 **I:** 22076

Games — Indoor
PI: 22070

Gandhi, Mahatma
P: 13801 **I:** 13804 **IJ:** 13802–3

Ganesha
I: 17198

Ganges River
PI: 15108 **IJ:** 15095, 15112

Gangs
PI: 17090 **IJ:** 17063, 17069, 17075, 17085, 17088, 17138, 21949

Gangs — Fiction
PI: 8578 **I:** 7030, 7367

Gangsters — Biography
IJ: 12866

Garbage
P: 3034, 16980, 16982 **I:** 16979, 16986, 16988 **IJ:** 16978, 16987

Garbage — Fiction
P: 3497

Garbage collectors
P: 3034

Garbage trucks
P: 21301

Gardens and gardening
P: 3169, 20172, 21760–61, 21766–67, 21769, 21773 **PI:** 21759, 21762, 21775 **I:** 21763–64, 21768, 21770–71, 21774 **IJ:** 18644, 21772

Gardens and gardening — Animals
IJ: 18630

Gardens and gardening — Fiction
P: 6, 914, 1556, 1663, 2159, 2995, 3045, 3060, 3313, 3554, 3628, 3868, 3914, 4142, 4389, 4420, 4455, 4507, 4531, 4551, 4689, 4839, 5174, 5311, 5333, 13876 **PI:** 3075 **I:** 8263 **IJ:** 7339

Gardens and gardening — Indoor
I: 21765

Gardens and gardening — Pests
IJ: 18630

Gardens and gardening — Poetry
I: 11947, 11963

Gardens and gardening — Songs
P: 14169

Garfield, James A.
IJ: 13035

Gargoyles
P: 21122

Garrison, Zina
I: 13648

Garter snakes
P: 18768 **I:** 18762, 18770

Gates, Bill
I: 13294–97

Gateway Arch (St. Louis)
I: 16544

Gays
See Homosexuality; Lesbian mothers

Gbaya
IJ: 14920

Geckos
I: 18749

Geese
See Ducks and geese

Gefilte fish — Fiction
P: 6078

Gehrig, Lou
PI: 13453 **I:** 13454

Gehry, Frank O.
IJ: 12233

Geisel, Theodor
See Dr. Seuss

Gellar, Sarah Michelle
PI: 12388

Gems — Collecting
IJ: 20567

Genealogy
IJ: 17648, 17650, 17674, 17692

Genetic engineering
IJ: 18035

Genetics
I: 18036 **IJ:** 17965, 18034

Genetics — Biography
IJ: 13322

Genies
I: 8082

Genocide
IJ: 17021

Geography
P: 4483, 14341, 14345, 20319, 20327, 20377
PI: 14344, 14356, 14359, 15905, 16973 I: 14328, 14333, 14348, 20300
IJ: 14339, 14357, 20317

Geography — Crafts
I: 21448

Geography — Experiments and projects
I: 14360 IJ: 14330

Geography — Fiction
P: 696, 5226

Geologists — Biography
I: 12152

Geology
See also Rocks and minerals
P: 14345, 20312, 20319, 20323, 20327 PI: 20302, 20307, 20311 I: 16595, 20299–301, 20314, 20321, 20329, 20562, 20569, 20571, 20574 IJ: 18426, 18436, 20304–5, 20308, 20317–18, 20328, 20553, 20572

Geology — Careers
P: 17830

Geology — Experiments and projects
I: 20297 IJ: 20324

Geology — Folklore
I: 10532, 10622

Geometry
I: 20603, 20607

Geometry — Experiments and projects
PI: 20604

Geometry — Fiction
P: 172, 4795

George, Jean Craighead
I: 12541

George III, King of England
I: 13805

George Washington Bridge — Fiction
P: 5603

Georgia
PI: 16851 I: 16870, 16898, 16949 IJ: 16829

Georgia — Fiction
P: 3665, 4586 I: 7310, 7372, 8579, 8932

Georgia Colony
IJ: 16119

Georgia (republic)
I: 15430 IJ: 15415

Georgia (state)
IJ: 16877

Geothermal energy
I: 20296

Gerbils
PI: 19885, 19911 I: 19897

German Americans
IJ: 17558, 17592

German Americans — Fiction
P: 5800 PI: 9563 I: 9379, 9547 IJ: 7467

Germany
See also Holocaust
PI: 15325, 15329, 15332 I: 15321, 15327, 15333 IJ: 15322–24

Germany — Cookbooks
IJ: 21728

Germany — Fiction
P: 4711 I: 8902 IJ: 7683, 9067, 9074, 9077–78

Germany — Folklore
P: 10882, 10884, 10886–90, 10892, 10894–96, 10898, 10900–7, 10909, 10912–14, 10919–21, 10924–25, 10927–31, 10937, 10939, 10941–42 PI: 10883, 10891, 10897, 10917–18, 10923, 10926, 10934–36, 10938 I: 10521, 10885, 10893, 10908, 10911, 10915–16, 10922, 10940 IJ: 10899, 10910, 10933

Germany — History
IJ: 13810, 13849, 14817, 14820, 14850, 14867, 14888, 15328, 15331

Germany — Holidays
PI: 15326

Germs
See also Bacteria
P: 17993

Geronimo
I: 12972

Gershwin, George
PI: 12328 I: 12326 IJ: 12327, 12329

Getty Museum (Los Angeles)
P: 544, 13870 I: 16811

Gettysburg, Battle of
I: 16425, 16430 IJ: 16417, 16433

Gettysburg, Battle of — Fiction
PI: 9490 IJ: 9463

Gettysburg Address
P: 16408 I: 16420 IJ: 16405

Gettysburg Address — Fiction
PI: 9490

Geysers
I: 20306

Ghana
P: 15023 I: 15010 IJ: 15015, 15017, 15026

Ghana — Biography
I: 13752

Ghana — Cookbooks
IJ: 21727

Ghana — Folklore
P: 10651, 10707 PI: 10670

Ghettos — World War II
See also Lodz ghetto
IJ: 14819

Ghost towns
I: 16290

Ghosts
See also Haunted houses
P: 950, 1374, 1480, 1541, 1576, 1617, 2920, 2957, 6189, 6201, 6637 PI: 7785, 8225 I: 6776, 6981, 7588, 7591, 7625, 7673, 7726, 7774, 7812, 7906, 7981, 8221, 9848, 18615, 21899–900, 21927, 21962–63 IJ: 6755, 6882, 6937, 7007, 7023, 7036, 7046, 7545, 7640, 7652, 7657, 7665, 7674, 7776, 7801, 7816, 7840, 7846, 7889, 8010, 8213, 8224, 9847, 11366, 21898, 21901, 21904, 21912, 21923, 21935

Ghosts — Fiction
P: 1247, 1335, 1412, 2911, 5995, 6062–63, 6502 PI: 7691, 7701, 7715, 7758, 8038, 8052, 8180, 8198, 8223 I: 6936, 7050, 7616, 7684, 7700, 7702, 7727, 7741, 7767, 7903, 7948, 8011, 8028, 8071, 8155, 8170, 8217, 8222, 8227–28 IJ: 6751, 7048, 7592, 7609–10, 7649, 7656, 7861, 7965, 7984, 8063, 8111, 8121, 8149–50, 8172, 8237, 10123, 10355, 11371

Ghosts — Folklore
P: 10778, 11338 PI: 11329 I: 10583 IJ: 10561, 11380–81

Ghosts — Jokes and riddles
P: 21815 PI: 21847

Ghosts — Poetry
IJ: 11731

Ghosts — Short stories
I: 7831

Giant pandas
See Pandas

Giants — Fiction
P: 1701, 10410, 10713 I: 7996

Giants — Folklore
P: 10970 PI: 10891

Gibb, Lois
IJ: 13216

Gibson, Josh
P: 13455

Gifted children — Fiction
PI: 10039 IJ: 8300

Gilbert and Sullivan — Songs
IJ: 14257

Ginsburg, Ruth Bader
IJ: 12886

Giotto
PI: 12234

Giotto — Fiction
P: 4672

Giraffes
P: 19174 PI: 19175

Giraffes — Fiction
P: 2623, 4625, 5222 I: 7154

Girl Scouts of America
See Scouts and scouting

Girl Scouts of America — Biography
I: 13168

Glacier Bay Park (Alaska)
IJ: 16770

Glacier National Park — Fiction
P: 5165 IJ: 7061

Glaciers and icebergs
P: 20358 PI: 7104 I: 20357, 20359 IJ: 20360–61

Glass
IJ: 21051

Glassblowing — Fiction
I: 16154

Glasses — Fiction
P: 1877, 3942 PI: 9992

Glenn, John
I: 12888 IJ: 12887, 12889–90, 20959

Glenn, Mike
IJ: 22132

Gliders
PI: 21083 IJ: 22046

Gliders — Crafts
IJ: 21795

Gliders — History
IJ: 21795

Globe Theatre (London)
I: 14324 IJ: 12590, 13903

Globes
See Maps and globes

Gnats — Fiction
P: 2569

Gnomes
P: 1347

P = Primary; PI = Primary-Intermediate; I = Intermediate; IJ = Intermediate-Junior High

Gnomes — Folklore
P: 10904

Gnus — Fiction
P: 2177

Goats
P: 20055, 20065 **PI:** 18977
I: 20051

Goats — Fiction
P: 1817, 2684, 2949, 4750
PI: 4707 **I:** 8834

Goats — Folklore
P: 11118, 11124

Gobi Desert
IJ: 14410

Goble, Paul
PI: 12542

Goblins
P: 1558, 6084 **IJ:** 8151

Goblins — Folklore
P: 10816

God
P: 17183, 17201, 17215
IJ: 17314

Goddard, Robert
IJ: 13298

Goddesses
I: 11457

Gogh, Vincent van
P: 12306, 12308
PI: 12305, 12307
IJ: 13907

Gogh, Vincent van — Fiction
P: 1662, 4577, 4691

Gold
I: 20563 IJ: 20275

Gold — History
I: 14544

Gold Rush (Alaska) — Fiction
I: 9535

Gold Rush (Alaska and Yukon)
I: 15594 IJ: 8949, 16792

Gold Rush (Alaska and Yukon) — Fiction
IJ: 6896

Gold Rush (California)
P: 16338 I: 16292, 16340, 16365, 16376, 16383
IJ: 16285, 16333, 16367–68

Gold Rush (California) — Cookbooks
IJ: 16367

Gold Rush (California) — Fiction
P: 4706, 4731 **PI:** 9339
I: 9844 IJ: 8991, 9386, 9641

Gold Rush (Yukon)
IJ: 15571

Goldberg, Whoopi
I: 12389

Golden eagles
I: 19340

Golden Fleece (mythology)
PI: 11496 IJ: 11466

Golden Gate Bridge
I: 16771

Golden retrievers
PI: 19946

Golden retrievers — Fiction
I: 8908

Goldfish
P: 19982

Goldfish — Fiction
PI: 8095

Golem
I: 11162, 11178

Golf
IJ: 21971, 21994, 22020, 22031, 22063

Golf — Biography
P: 13713 **PI:** 13716
I: 13709, 13712, 13715, 13717–18 IJ: 13706, 13711, 13714, 13719

Golf — Fiction
P: 5034 **PI:** 9980

Gonzalez, Juan
I: 13456

Goodall, Jane
PI: 13299 I: 13300, 13303
IJ: 13301–2

Gooden, Dwight
IJ: 13457

Gordeeva, Ekaterina
I: 13589 IJ: 13590

Gordon, Jeff
PI: 13428

Gore, Al
PI: 12893 I: 12891–92

Gore, Tipper
I: 13155 IJ: 13156

Gorillas
P: 19010 I: 13284, 19002, 19006, 19011, 19015–16
IJ: 18992, 19013

Gorillas — Biography
P: 13285

Gorillas — Fiction
P: 521, 1838 **PI:** 5027
I: 7230

Gorman, R. C.
IJ: 12235

Goshute Indians — Folklore
P: 11288

Goslar, Hannah
IJ: 13799

Government
See United States — Government and politics

Goya, Francisco
PI: 12237 IJ: 12236, 12238

Graffiti — Fiction
P: 3029

Graham, Martha
IJ: 12390–92

Grains
P: 20092 IJ: 20100

Grammar
P: 14106 I: 14040
IJ: 14023, 14110

Grand Canyon
I: 16611, 16636

Grand Canyon National Park
P: 16631, 16633
PI: 16628, 16643 I: 16595, 16605, 16616, 16630
IJ: 12151

Grand Central Station (New York City) — Fiction
P: 3256

Grand Coulee Dam
I: 21125

Grandfathers — Fiction
P: 164, 786, 1162, 1624, 2974, 2977, 3105, 3192, 3211, 3213, 3296, 3348, 3501, 3504, 3507, 3511, 3533, 3551, 3580, 3586, 3601, 3607, 3612, 3615, 3622, 3629, 3662, 3665, 3692, 3695, 3715–16, 3718, 3728, 3732, 3756, 3768–69, 3771, 3788, 3791, 3802, 3830, 3865, 3890, 3906–7, 3926, 3957, 3964, 4033, 4391, 4558, 4609, 4651, 4671, 4758, 4780, 4786, 4788, 4808, 4881, 4903, 4935, 4945, 5039, 5089–90, 5108–9, 5438, 5691, 5767, 6448, 6526–27, 6529, 8674
PI: 3642, 3733, 3792, 3870, 6845, 7385, 7437, 7439, 7509, 7522, 7528, 7541, 8320, 8695, 9706 I: 7426, 7517, 7692, 8437, 8583, 8846, 9168 IJ: 6857, 6951, 7122, 7305, 7486, 7519, 7533, 7804, 8261, 8504, 8544, 8876

Grandfathers — Folklore
IJ: 10739

Grandmothers
P: 14250

Grandmothers — Fiction
P: 1130, 1346, 1568, 3265, 3290, 3330, 3500, 3502, 3524, 3532, 3539–41, 3557–58, 3560–61, 3581,

3608–9, 3613, 3624, 3626, 3638, 3664, 3666, 3676–78, 3693, 3701, 3704, 3730, 3741, 3795, 3800, 3805, 3823, 3826–27, 3831, 3833, 3842, 3854, 3867, 3884, 3914, 3919, 3921, 3930, 3938, 3943–45, 3948, 3960, 3976, 4263, 4312, 4466, 4498, 4616–17, 4695, 4746–47, 4796, 4842, 4960, 4993, 4997, 5004, 5066, 5071, 5473, 5665, 5757, 5960, 6153, 6484–85
PI: 3661, 3915, 5692, 7394, 8687, 8757, 9602, 9998
I: 6809, 7388, 7410, 7425, 7524, 7695, 7698, 8219, 8396, 8415, 8521, 8723, 9057, 9511, 10050
IJ: 7390, 7450, 7460, 7476, 7492, 7532, 7916, 8444, 8676, 8783, 9604

Grandmothers — Folklore
PI: 10781

Grandparents
P: 3441, 3594

Grandparents — Crafts
I: 21451

Grandparents — Fiction
P: 3067, 3188, 3627, 3691, 3697, 3712, 3770, 3825, 3871, 3911, 3951, 4354, 5480, 6483 **PI:** 4904, 8850
I: 3599, 7429, 7451, 8709, 8776, 9449, 9520, 9915, 10349 IJ: 8481, 8515

Grandparents — Games
I: 21451

Grandparents — Songs
P: 14248

Grant, Amy
I: 12393

Grant, Julia Dent
I: 13157

Grant, Ulysses S.
I: 13036–37

Graphic novels — Fiction
IJ: 8138, 10504

Graphs
P: 20577 I: 20589

Graphs — Fiction
P: 20591

Grasshoppers
P: 19449, 19463, 19505
IJ: 19434, 19476

Grasshoppers — Fiction
P: 6465

Grasslands
See also Prairies
P: 20533–34, 20536
PI: 19414, 20423, 20535, 20539, 20542, 20548–49

P = Primary; PI = Primary-Intermediate; I = Intermediate; IJ = Intermediate-Junior High

I: 20537, 20543, 20546
IJ: 20532, 20540, 20544

Grasslands — Animals
P: 20531, 20538 **PI:** 20545

Grave robbers — Fiction
IJ: 9299

Gravity
PI: 20815 **IJ:** 20806

Gravity — Experiments and projects
I: 20294, 20325

Gray wolves
IJ: 19143

Great Barrier Reef (Australia)
PI: 19669 **IJ:** 15223, 19656, 19661

Great Britain
See also England; Scotland; Wales
I: 15345, 15347, 15367
IJ: 13769, 15344

Great Britain — Biography
I: 13808, 13863 **IJ:** 13770

Great Britain — Folklore
P: 10458, 10485, 10945–47, 10952, 10955, 10957, 10976–84, 10995, 11001, 11005–6, 11008–9, 11014, 11029, 11032, 11035, 11043, 11047 **PI:** 10962, 10968–69, 10973–74, 10991, 10996, 10998, 11030, 11038, 11045
I: 10961, 10963, 10988, 10997, 11003–4, 11046
IJ: 10964, 10993, 11000, 11021, 11023–25, 11037, 11040

Great Britain — History
I: 13790, 13805, 15365
IJ: 13860

Great Lakes
See also Lakes (U.S.); and specific lakes, e.g., Lake Erie
I: 15863

Great Plains
See Plains (U.S.)

Great Smoky Mountains National Park
P: 16878

Great Wall (China)
I: 15074

Greece
P: 15370, 15389
PI: 15373, 15380, 15385
I: 15376, 15382, 15392, 15395 **IJ:** 15381, 15387, 15396

Greece — Art
IJ: 14684

Greece — Christmas
IJ: 17412

Greece — Cookbooks
IJ: 21742

Greece — Crafts
I: 14707 **IJ:** 14674

Greece — Fiction
P: 2305, 4787, 5115
I: 9033, 9054 **IJ:** 8398, 9023, 9029, 9662

Greece — Folklore
P: 11050, 11052–53, 11056, 11070 **PI:** 11049 **I:** 11048, 11051, 11054, 11068

Greece — History
PI: 13750, 14675, 14691, 14699, 14705–6
I: 13747–48, 14522, 14581, 14676, 14679–81, 14683, 14687, 14689–90, 14695, 14697, 14703–4, 14707–8, 22251, 22258 **IJ:** 13751, 14584, 14674, 14677–78, 14682, 14684–85, 14692–94, 14696, 14700–2, 14709, 22247, 22256

Greece — Holidays
PI: 15390

Greece — Mythology
P: 11072, 11074, 11077–78, 11468–69, 11491, 11505, 11507–8, 14686 **PI:** 11073, 11463–64, 11471, 11477, 11481–84, 11493, 11495–96, 11502, 11514–15, 14688 **I:** 11067, 11459, 11461, 11465, 11467, 11470, 11472–74, 11476, 11479–80, 11485, 11488–89, 11492, 11494, 11499, 11501, 11503–4, 11513, 11517 **IJ:** 11460, 11462, 11466, 11475, 11478, 11486–87, 11497, 11509–11, 11516, 14694, 14696

Greece — Plays
IJ: 14701

Greece — Religion
IJ: 14694

Greece — Science
IJ: 14591

Greece — Sports
IJ: 14592

Greece — Theaters
IJ: 14701

Greece — Women
IJ: 14692

Greed — Folklore
P: 10886 **I:** 10643

Greek Americans — Fiction
P: 4609

Greenhouse effect
P: 17006, 20791

Greenland
IJ: 14490

Greenland — Fiction
IJ: 7877

Greeting cards — Crafts
PI: 21631 **I:** 21632

Gretzky, Wayne
I: 13686–87 **IJ:** 13688

Gretzky, Wayne — Fiction
P: 1391

Greyhounds — Fiction
IJ: 7180

Griffey, Ken (father and son)
I: 13458

Griffey, Ken, Jr.
I: 13459–60

Grimke, Sarah and Angelina
IJ: 12894

Grisham, John
IJ: 12543

Grissom, Gus
I: 12119

Grizzly bears
P: 19046, 19070
PI: 19052, 19054, 19067
I: 19066, 19069

Grizzly bears — Fiction
IJ: 7061

Groundhog Day — Fiction
P: 5631, 5633

Groundhogs
P: 4493

Growing up
See also Personal problems — Fiction

Growing up — Fiction
P: 1838, 2320, 3178, 3468, 3823, 4476, 5697 **PI:** 4904, 8322, 8575 **I:** 8609, 8821
IJ: 8375, 8377, 8561, 8771–72, 8998

Guatemala
P: 15658 **PI:** 15670, 15688
I: 15667, 15676 **IJ:** 15659, 15663

Guatemala — Biography
IJ: 15684

Guatemala — Fiction
P: 4615–16

Guatemala — Folklore
P: 11398

Guide dogs
P: 19967 **PI:** 19938

Guide dogs — Fiction
I: 8891

Guilt — Fiction
P: 5504 **I:** 7311 **IJ:** 8576

Guinea pigs
P: 19900–1, 19903
I: 19884, 19887, 19893, 19896

Guinea pigs — Fiction
P: 7238

Guitars
PI: 15629 **I:** 14231

Gulf of Mexico
I: 19830

Gulf Stream
IJ: 19849

Gulf War (1991)
See Persian Gulf War

Gulls
PI: 19348, 19353 **I:** 19349

Guns
P: 21405

Guns — Fiction
P: 1806 **IJ:** 8429, 8492

Gutenberg, Johann
PI: 13305 **I:** 13304

Guyana
IJ: 15725, 15739

Gymnastics
PI: 22192 **I:** 22191, 22194–97 **IJ:** 22193

Gymnastics — Fiction
P: 6390 **IJ:** 10293

Gymnasts — Biography
I: 13683, 13703 **IJ:** 13372, 13399, 13701–2

Gypsies — Fiction
IJ: 6743–44, 7345, 9062, 9633

Gypsies — Folklore
I: 10861

H

Hackers (computer)
IJ: 21213

Haida Indians
IJ: 15928

Haida Indians — Folklore
P: 11284

Haiku
P: 4775, 11584, 11821, 11824 **PI:** 11822 **I:** 12556
IJ: 11823, 11825

Hair
P: 18179 **I:** 18177

Hair — Fiction
P: 1272, 3220, 3450, 3950, 3991, 4155, 4258

Hair styles
I: 21549

Haircutting — Fiction
P: 2101, 4150

Haiti
PI: 15714 I: 15703–4

Haiti — Biography
IJ: 13826

Haiti — Fiction
P: 4878–79 I: 9137

Haiti — Folklore
P: 11433

Haiti — Holidays
PI: 15714 I: 15720

Hale, Clara
PI: 13158

Halley's comet — Fiction
P: 3568

Halloween
P: 17444, 17447
PI: 17442, 17446 I: 17445

Halloween — Costumes
PI: 21539

Halloween — Crafts
P: 21477, 21500
PI: 17442, 17446,
17448–49, 21426, 21508,
21572 I: 17443, 21427

Halloween — Fiction
P: 470, 5708, 5980–83,
5986–98, 6000–11,
6013–24, 6026–36,
6038–41, 6043–46,
6048–56, 6058–66, 9717,
10088, 11827 PI: 5984,
5999, 6037, 6042, 6047,
6057, 6963, 9707, 9716,
9746, 9797 I: 6864, 8530,
9708 IJ: 7110

Halloween — Jokes and riddles
P: 21823

Halloween — Poetry
P: 5985, 6025 PI: 6012,
11833 I: 11832

Hamer, Fannie Lou
PI: 12725

Hamill, Dorothy
I: 13591

Hamilton, Alexander
I: 12895

Hamilton, Alice
I: 13306

Hamlet (play)
PI: 12047

Hamm, Mia
PI: 13691 I: 13689–90

Hammer, M. C.
I: 12394

Hamsters
P: 19910 PI: 19885
I: 19888, 19893, 19897,
19912

Hamsters — Fiction
P: 5295 PI: 7323

Hancock, John
PI: 12896 I: 12897

Hand painting
I: 21564

Handicapping conditions
See Mental handicaps;
Physical handicaps; and
specific handicapping
conditions, e.g.,
Dyslexia

Hands
P: 18046, 18064

Hands — Fiction
P: 234, 928, 3117

Hang gliding
I: 21973

Hannibal
IJ: 13806

Hannibal (Mo.)
IJ: 16590

Hansberry, Lorraine
IJ: 12544–45

Hanson (musical group)
IJ: 12395

Hanukkah
P: 5640, 6077, 6117, 17462
PI: 17457 I: 17456, 17465,
17473 IJ: 17453, 17471

Hanukkah — Crafts
P: 6129 PI: 17483
IJ: 17471

Hanukkah — Fiction
P: 469, 5646, 6067–68,
6072, 6079–87, 6092, 6096,
6098, 6104, 6107, 6109,
6119, 6124–25, 6128, 6130
PI: 9755, 9758, 9762
I: 9724, 9738, 9741, 9761

Hanukkah — Poetry
P: 6099

Harbors — Fiction
P: 5556, 5587

Hardaway, Anfernee
I: 13525 IJ: 13526

Harding, Warren G.
PI: 13038 IJ: 13039

Hares
See also Rabbits

Hares — Fiction
IJ: 7830

Harlem — Fiction
P: 3078 I: 9583 IJ: 7360,
9582

Harlem — Poetry
PI: 11760

Harlem Renaissance
IJ: 16460

Harmonicas — Fiction
P: 2670, 4222

Harpers Ferry, Raid on
I: 16255

Harris, La Donna
I: 12973

Harrison, Benjamin
I: 13040

Harrison, William H.
IJ: 13041

Hart, Melissa Joan
PI: 12396

Harvest festivals
See also Thanksgiving
PI: 17350, 17370 I: 17502

Harvey, William
IJ: 13307

Haskins, Francine
P: 3672

Hats
PI: 21167

Hats — Colonial Period (U.S.)
I: 16115

Hats — Fiction
P: 1058, 1564, 1782, 2123,
3154, 3333, 3706, 4158,
4200, 4319, 5002, 6545

Hatshepsut
I: 13807

Haunted houses
PI: 6733 I: 6798, 8005
IJ: 6885

Hawaii
PI: 16773, 16776 I: 16816
IJ: 16762, 16781, 16788,
16809, 16910

Hawaii — Biography
PI: 12928 IJ: 13819

Hawaii — Fiction
P: 2944, 4438, 4645, 5645
I: 7062, 8904, 8940, 9668
IJ: 7515, 8305, 8808

Hawaii — Folklore
IJ: 11326

Hawaii — History
I: 13820 IJ: 14874

Hawaii — Marine animals
PI: 19633

Hawaii Volcanoes National Park — Fiction
I: 7062

Hawking, Stephen
IJ: 13308

Hawks
See also Birds of prey

Hawks — Fiction
P: 5153 I: 7156, 7615

Haydn, Joseph — Fiction
PI: 9031

Hayes, Rutherford B.
I: 13042

Haystacks
P: 20056

Head lice
See also Lice
P: 17972, 19450
PI: 17946, 17961 I: 17980,
18009

Health and medicine
See also Hygiene
I: 18026, 18194, 18201
IJ: 17963

Health and medicine — Biography
PI: 13134

Health and medicine — Careers
IJ: 17801, 17804

Hearing
See also Deaf
P: 18146, 18152 I: 17913,
18131, 18148, 18157

Hearing — Experiments and projects
I: 20937

Hearing — Fiction
P: 302

Heart
PI: 18091 IJ: 18086

Heart disease — Fiction
IJ: 8261, 8646

Heat — Experiments and projects
IJ: 20852–53

Heat waves
P: 20757

Heaven — Fiction
P: 3873

Heavy Metal (music)
IJ: 14121

Hedgehogs — Fiction
P: 2499, 2796, 6486

Heisman Trophy
IJ: 13367

Heisman Trophy — Biography
IJ: 13405

Helicopters
PI: 21083, 21105

Helicopters — Fiction
P: 1715

Heller, Ruth
PI: 12546

Helpfulness — Fiction
P: 1863, 2319

Hendrix, Jimi
IJ: 12397

Henry, Marguerite
I: 12547

Henry, Patrick
PI: 12898

Henry VIII, King of England
I: 13808

P = Primary; PI = Primary-Intermediate; I = Intermediate; IJ = Intermediate-Junior High

Henson, Matthew
I: 12120–21

Hercules (mythology)
PI: 11484, 11493 **I:** 11461, 11504

Heredity
IJ: 17648, 18034

Herero (African people)
IJ: 15004

Hermit crabs — Fiction
P: 4862

Herod of Judea
I: 13809

Heroes (fictional)
I: 21959

Heroin
IJ: 17877

Herons
P: 19295 **PI:** 19355

Herrera, Juan Filipe
I: 12548

Hershey, Milton S.
I: 12899

Hershiser, Orel
IJ: 13461

Herzegovina
I: 15268

Hewitt, Jennifer Love
PI: 12398

Heyerdahl, Thor
P: 12122

Hiawatha
IJ: 12974

Hibernation
I: 18903

Hibernation — Fiction
P: 2562, 5464, 5820, 5890, 6163

Hiccups — Fiction
P: 4217

Hickok, Wild Bill
IJ: 12900

Hieroglyphics
I: 14623, 14634

High-wire performers — Fiction
P: 4753

Highways
IJ: 21326

Highways — History
I: 14351

Hiking
I: 15859, 16761 **IJ:** 22168

Hiking — Fiction
P: 3110

Hill, Anita
I: 12726

Hill, Grant
I: 13527–28, 13530
IJ: 13529

Hill, Lauryn
IJ: 12399

Hillary, Sir Edmund
IJ: 12123–24

Himalayas
I: 15195

Hindenburg **(dirigible)**
I: 21093 **IJ:** 21087

Hindenburg **(dirigible) — Fiction**
PI: 9610

Hinduism
P: 17226, 17233 **I:** 17187, 17195, 17198, 17375

Hinduism — Holidays
See also specific holidays, e.g., Holi
PI: 17385

Hindus — Fiction
IJ: 8435

Hine, Lewis
IJ: 12901

Hines, Gregory
IJ: 12400

Hingis, Martina
I: 13649

Hip hop music
IJ: 14120

Hippopotamuses
P: 5337 **I:** 18985

Hippopotamuses — Fiction
P: 2163, 2351, 2473–74, 2480, 2759, 2793, 4130
I: 2210

Hiroshima
IJ: 14860

Hiroshima — Fiction
I: 9700

Hiroshima — History
PI: 14841 **I:** 14870
IJ: 14831

Hispanic Americans
See also specific groups, e.g., Cuban Americans; Mexican Americans
P: 3137–38, 3758
PI: 17552 **IJ:** 16234, 17394, 17543, 17585

Hispanic Americans — Biography
P: 12467 **PI:** 12381, 12386, 12464, 12469, 12825, 13452, 13584, 13647
I: 12357, 12384, 12456, 12466, 12548, 12679, 12827–28, 13445, 13477, 13553 **IJ:** 12175, 12383, 12385, 12415, 12438, 12449, 12460, 12826,

12829–35, 13435, 13441, 13583

Hispanic Americans — Christmas
P: 5774

Hispanic Americans — Fiction
P: 3436, 3523, 3553, 3616, 3640, 3815, 3921, 3952, 3966, 4047, 4955, 5032, 5074, 5667, 5709, 5745, 5921, 6708 **PI:** 4628, 4652, 5385, 5507, 7370, 7417, 8763, 10074, 10082
I: 6930, 7347, 7367, 7377
IJ: 7374–75, 7419, 8828, 9994

Hispanic Americans — History
IJ: 17585

Hispanic Americans — Holiday
IJ: 17379

Hispanic Americans — Plays
IJ: 12037, 12040

Hispanic Americans — Poetry
IJ: 11528

Hispanics — Biography
I: 12557, 17551 **IJ:** 12517, 13772

History
See under specific countries and continents, e.g., Africa — History; and wars and historical eras, e.g., Colonial Period (U.S.)
I: 14347

History — Ancient
I: 14580 **IJ:** 14578, 14582, 14590, 14594, 14598–99, 14610

History — Methodology
IJ: 14547, 14573

History — Twentieth century
I: 14554 **IJ:** 14576

History — Women
IJ: 13732

History and geography
PI: 14586, 20311 **I:** 14567
IJ: 14543, 14563, 15877

Hitler, Adolf
IJ: 13810

Hitler Youth
IJ: 14850

Hitters — Baseball
IJ: 22102

Hitting (baseball)
IJ: 22086

HIV (virus)
IJ: 13532, 17982, 17997

HIV (virus) — Fiction
IJ: 8717

Hmong people
I: 17584

Hobbies
I: 21665, 21808, 22077
IJ: 21666

Hockey
See Ice hockey

Hogan, Hulk
PI: 13692

Hogs — Fiction
IJ: 7009

Holes — Fiction
P: 3320

Holi (Hindu holiday)
PI: 17376

Holidays
See also individual countries, e.g., France — Holidays; and specific holidays, e.g., Christmas
P: 17392 **PI:** 17347, 17370, 17378, 17387, 17393
I: 17207, 17334, 17374, 17384, 17407 **IJ:** 17394

Holidays — Cookbooks
IJ: 21756

Holidays — Crafts
PI: 21421 **I:** 21430, 21461

Holidays — Fiction
P: 5629, 6494 **I:** 9748

Holidays — Folklore
I: 10553

Holidays — Parties
IJ: 17351

Holidays — Plays
PI: 12010 **I:** 12012
IJ: 12019

Holidays — Poetry
P: 5659, 17383

Holidays — Short stories
I: 9728

Holland
See Netherlands

Holliday, Doc
IJ: 12902

Hollywood — Fiction
I: 9542, 9890 **IJ:** 9569

Holmes, Katie
PI: 12401

Holocaust
See also Concentration camps
PI: 13796, 14809, 14812–13, 14873 **I:** 13797, 13800, 14811, 14840, 14858
IJ: 13798–99, 13810, 13822, 13849, 13851, 13867, 14814–19, 14842, 14849, 14851, 14853, 14856, 14862, 14864–65,

P = Primary; PI = Primary-Intermediate; I = Intermediate; IJ = Intermediate-Junior High

14872, 14878, 14886,
14888–89

Holocaust — Biography
I: 12625

Holocaust — Fiction
P: 4644, 4778, 6104, 6119
PI: 4797, 9664 **I:** 8071,
9076, 9647, 9652, 9684,
9689 **IJ:** 8169, 9073–74,
9077, 9651, 9655–56, 9670,
9683, 9690, 9694–96, 9698,
9701

**Holocaust Museum
(Washington, D.C.)**
PI: 16657

Home decoration
IJ: 13893

Home life — History
P: 15900

**Home pages (computer)
— Design**
IJ: 21214

Home schooling
PI: 3466, 10105

Homeless people
PI: 17159 **I:** 17144, 17146,
17153 **IJ:** 17025, 17152,
17154

**Homeless people —
Fiction**
P: 4916, 5870 **PI:** 8267,
8672, 8749, 8831 **I:** 8395,
8638, 8671 **IJ:** 8391, 8479,
8581, 8643, 8823

Homer, Winslow
IJ: 12239

**Homer, Winslow —
Fiction**
PI: 4741

Homesteading
See also Frontier life
(U.S.)
PI: 16348

Homework
I: 14118, 17623, 17629

Homework — Computers
IJ: 21230

Homosexuality
IJ: 17658

Homosexuality — Fiction
P: 3946–47, 5043 **PI:** 5096

Honduras
I: 15671 **IJ:** 15673

Honduras — Fiction
I: 7377

Honesty — Fiction
P: 2549

Honey
P: 20126

Honey — Fiction
P: 2813, 4033

Honey — Folklore
P: 10673

Honeybees
P: 19518, 19523

Hong Kong
I: 15072 **IJ:** 15170

Honolulu
I: 16807

Honolulu — Fiction
P: 3624

Hoover, Herbert
IJ: 13043–44

Hoover, Lou
IJ: 13159

Hoover Dam
I: 16601

Hope diamond
I: 21915

Hopi Indians
P: 15976 **PI:** 16048, 16064

Hopi Indians — Fiction
IJ: 7065

Hopi Indians — Folklore
PI: 11268

Hopkins, Lee Bennett
PI: 12549

Hopscotch
P: 22018

Hornaday, William
IJ: 18987

Horner, Jack
IJ: 14462

Horns
P: 14219

Hornsby, Rogers
I: 13462

Horror stories
See Mystery stories;
Supernatural

Horse racing
I: 19991

**Horse racing —
Biography**
I: 13695 **IJ:** 13387

Horse racing — Fiction
I: 10268 **IJ:** 7216

Horse shows
I: 19995

Horseback riding
P: 22199, 22208 **PI:** 22207
I: 22201–3 **IJ:** 22198,
22206

**Horseback riding —
Biography**
IJ: 13678

Horsemanship
IJ: 22200

Horses
See also Mustangs
(horses); Ponies; and

specific breeds of horses,
e.g. Quarter horses
P: 5264, 5276, 5359, 5389,
19984, 19990, 19992,
20001–4, 20008, 20011
PI: 19997, 19999, 20007,
20009–10 **I:** 19983,
19993–95, 20006, 20012,
20017, 20019, 22202,
22204–5 **IJ:** 19985–89,
19996, 20005, 20014–16,
20018, 22200

Horses — Fiction
P: 522, 1248, 1345, 1857,
2566, 2607, 4216, 5129,
5139, 5229, 5243, 5331,
5388, 5408, 5434, 5440,
5453, 6399 **PI:** 937, 5367,
7192, 7204–6, 7250,
7294–95, 8147 **I:** 7054,
7157, 7159, 7164–65, 7207,
7215, 7219, 7234, 7254,
7287–88, 7293, 7301, 7639,
7731, 7764, 7854, 9143,
9570, 9599, 9917
IJ: 7146–47, 7149–50,
7153, 7163, 7175, 7189,
7212, 7216–18, 7232, 7269,
7284, 7286, 7325, 7593,
8675, 9627, 9914

Horses — Folklore
P: 11223 **PI:** 11240

Horses — Poetry
P: 11788 **IJ:** 11805

Horses, Miniature
PI: 20000

**Horseshoe crabs —
Fiction**
PI: 5268

Hospitals
P: 18038, 18040, 18042–44
PI: 18037, 18039 **I:** 13318,
18041, 21140

Hospitals — Fiction
P: 1844, 3113, 3643
I: 8914 **IJ:** 6787, 8615,
8698

Hot-air balloons
See Ballooning

Hotels — Fiction
PI: 9839 **I:** 7981

Houdini, Harry
IJ: 12402–3

House cleaning
I: 21161

**House of Representatives
(U.S.)**
See Congress (U.S.);
United States —
Government and politics

Household appliances
I: 21021–22

Houses
See also Building and
construction

P: 3167, 21157–59
I: 14733, 16037, 21160
IJ: 21163–64, 21664

Houses — Fiction
P: 200, 2379, 2987, 3014,
3062, 3110, 3334, 3424,
3488, 3651, 3809, 3860,
4395, 4545, 9200 **I:** 6758,
7472, 9256

Houses — History
PI: 13897 **I:** 21162

Houses — Poetry
P: 6235

**Houses of Parliament
(London, England)**
I: 15365

Housework — Fiction
P: 3460, 6561

Housework — Folklore
P: 11119

Houston
I: 16914–15

Houston, James
IJ: 12240

Houston, Sam
PI: 12904 **IJ:** 12903

Houston, Sam — Fiction
I: 9294

Houston, Whitney
IJ: 12404

**Houston Rockets
(basketball team)**
IJ: 22134

Howard, Juwan
IJ: 13531

Howard, Ron
IJ: 12405

Howe, James
P: 12550

Hubble, Edwin
IJ: 13309

Hubble space telescope
PI: 18417 **I:** 21007
IJ: 18383, 18414

Hudson, Henry
I: 12125

Hudson Bay — Fiction
PI: 4722

Hudson River
IJ: 16755

Hudson River — Fiction
PI: 9514

Huerta, Dolores
IJ: 12832

Hughes, Langston
PI: 12552 **I:** 12551

Hugs — Fiction
P: 3395

Huguenots — Fiction
IJ: 9030

P = Primary; PI = Primary-Intermediate; I = Intermediate; IJ = Intermediate-Junior High

Hull, Brett
I: 13693

Human body
See also specific parts and
systems of the human
body, e.g., Circulation
system
P: 4522, 4537, 18045,
18053, 18057–58, 18062,
18071, 18083, 18832
PI: 18052, 18061, 18063,
18075, 18081 I: 18048,
18050, 18055, 18069–70,
18072, 18079–80, 18084
IJ: 18047, 18051, 18054,
18056, 18059, 18068,
18073, 18077, 18174

**Human body —
Experiments and
projects**
P: 18083 IJ: 18060,
18082, 18085

Human body — Fiction
P: 3261, 3267, 3310,
3370–71, 6639

Human rights
See also Civil rights
P: 17019 IJ: 17016, 17023

**Human rights —
Biography**
IJ: 13724

Human rights — Fiction
IJ: 8970

Humanitarianism
I: 17148–49

**Humanitarians —
Biography**
PI: 13853–54 I: 13727,
13741, 13858 IJ: 13855,
13867

Hummingbirds
P: 19236 I: 19272

Humorous poetry
See Poetry — Humorous

Humorous stories
P: 482, 650, 981–82, 1033,
1050, 1053, 1084, 1093,
1100, 1113, 1116, 1149,
1189, 1206, 1292, 1301,
1321, 1330, 1378, 1431,
1443, 1519, 1549, 1591,
1613, 1615, 1646, 1670–71,
1714, 1729, 1733, 1800,
1938, 1947, 1949, 1971,
1994, 2043–44, 2070, 2088,
2109, 2113, 2145, 2171,
2260, 2317, 2358, 2472,
2497, 2515, 2517, 2557,
2560, 2588, 2636, 2658,
2681, 2730, 2736, 2771,
2821, 2862, 2871, 2929,
2963, 2976, 3386, 3528,
3552, 3591, 3644, 3698,
3781, 3829, 3951, 3990,
4071–94, 4096–111,
4113–43, 4145–60,
4162–79, 4181–87,

4189–94, 4196, 4198–212,
4214–27, 4229, 4231,
4233–36, 4238–44,
4246–68, 4270–91,
4293–304, 4306, 4308,
4310–25, 4327–31,
4333–41, 4343–58,
4360–62, 4364–68, 4472,
4484, 4641, 4660, 4776,
4836, 4893, 4933, 5294,
5493, 5498–99, 5518, 5521,
5535, 5539, 5711, 5729,
5747, 5754, 5824, 5894,
5938, 5990, 5994, 6029,
6064, 6087, 6124, 6139,
6148, 6184, 6246, 6368,
6386, 6453, 6468, 6480,
6495, 6497, 6499, 6501,
6521, 6523, 6533, 6558–61,
6566, 6570, 6578, 6610–11,
6613, 6620, 6623, 6640–46,
6663, 6676, 6683, 6705,
8000, 9788, 9815–16, 9818,
9834, 9900, 9918, 9951,
9953–54, 9981, 10019,
10068, 11155 PI: 1594,
2851, 2948, 4095, 4112,
4161, 4188, 4195, 4237,
4269, 4305, 4307, 4309,
4332, 4342, 4363, 4976,
6330, 6562, 7181, 7383,
7634, 7937, 8059, 8065,
8140, 8203, 8350, 8629,
8791, 9742, 9771, 9773–74,
9777, 9780–81, 9787, 9795,
9797–800, 9802, 9804–7,
9809–13, 9817, 9819,
9821–23, 9826, 9828, 9830,
9833, 9835–37, 9839–40,
9850–51, 9860–62, 9866,
9871, 9874, 9880, 9891–92,
9907, 9911, 9923, 9941,
9952, 9955, 9961–62,
9968–70, 9974, 9979–80,
9982, 9986, 9989, 9991–92,
9995–98, 10000, 10008–9,
10015, 10018, 10021–22,
10064, 10101, 10118–19,
10125, 10138, 10162,
10171, 10249, 10272,
10438, 10472 I: 6989,
7047, 7178, 7188, 7236,
7407, 7420, 7475, 7572,
7692, 7739, 7779, 7838,
7918, 7944, 7946, 8019,
8025, 8073, 8171, 8720,
8869, 9364, 9757, 9770,
9772, 9776, 9778–79,
9782–83, 9785–86,
9791–94, 9796, 9801, 9803,
9814, 9820, 9824, 9827,
9829, 9831–32, 9838,
9843–45, 9848–49,
9853–55, 9857–59, 9863,
9865, 9867–70, 9872,
9875–77, 9879, 9882–83,
9885–86, 9888–90, 9893,
9896, 9898–99, 9901–2,
9906, 9908, 9910, 9913,
9915–17, 9919, 9925,
9927–30, 9933–35,
9937–38, 9944–47,
9949–50, 9956–57, 9960,

9963–67, 9971–72, 9976,
9978, 9988, 9993, 10002,
10012–13, 10017, 10023,
10061, 10080–81, 10094,
10109, 10126, 10231,
10241, 10445, 11382, 14036
IJ: 6849, 7067, 7069, 7284,
7315, 7492, 7808, 8135,
8178, 8275, 8358, 8493,
8500, 8604, 8772, 8839,
9604, 9643, 9775, 9789–90,
9808, 9841, 9846–47, 9852,
9856, 9864, 9873, 9878,
9881, 9884, 9887, 9894–95,
9897, 9903–5, 9912, 9914,
9920–22, 9924, 9926,
9931–32, 9936, 9939–40,
9942, 9948, 9958–59, 9973,
9977, 9983, 9987, 9990,
9994, 9999, 10001, 10003,
10005–7, 10010, 10014,
10016, 10020, 10027,
10071, 10095, 10183, 10222

**Humorous stories —
Short stories**
I: 9975, 9984–85

**Hungarian Americans —
Fiction**
I: 9568

Hungary
PI: 15292 IJ: 13867,
15273

Hungary — Cookbooks
IJ: 21704

Hungary — Fiction
P: 4681, 5146

Hungary — Folklore
P: 10853

**Hungary — Historical
fiction**
I: 9070

Hunter, Clementine
IJ: 12241

Hunters and hunting
IJ: 16033, 22043

**Hunters and hunting —
Fiction**
P: 2567, 2946, 2966
I: 6769, 7100 IJ: 8845

**Hunters and hunting —
Folklore**
PI: 11306 I: 11206

Huron, Lake
PI: 16528

Huron Indians
PI: 16034 IJ: 15929

Hurricane Andrew
IJ: 20715

Hurricanes
P: 20712 PI: 20687, 20709
I: 20682, 20690, 20697,
20707, 20720 IJ: 20678,
20706, 20715

Hurricanes — Fiction
P: 2924, 2984, 4478, 4491,
4744, 4865 I: 6851
IJ: 9274

Hurston, Zora Neale
P: 3810 PI: 12554
IJ: 12553

Huskies (dogs)
I: 19977

Hussein, Saddam
I: 15487

Hutchinson, Anne
IJ: 13160

Hydrogen
IJ: 20282

Hygiene
See also Health and
medicine
P: 3379 PI: 18211
I: 18194, 18201–2

Hygiene — Fiction
P: 3397

Hymns
P: 17200 PI: 14174
IJ: 12937, 14152

Hyperactivity — Fiction
IJ: 8654

Hypnotism — Fiction
PI: 2516

I

Iacocca, Lee
IJ: 12905

Ibo (African people)
IJ: 15039

Ice
I: 20357

Ice Age
IJ: 14510

Ice climbing
IJ: 22050

Ice cream
P: 20104, 20106 I: 20101
IJ: 20133

Ice fishing — Fiction
PI: 9171

Ice formations — Poetry
I: 11991

Ice hockey
PI: 10307, 22211 I: 22210,
22214–15, 22224
IJ: 22209, 22212–13, 22257

Ice hockey — Biography
I: 13381, 13412, 13686–87,
13693, 13697, 13700
IJ: 13688, 13699

P = Primary; PI = Primary-Intermediate; I = Intermediate; IJ = Intermediate-Junior High

Ice hockey — Fiction
P: 1391, 2975 I: 10283, 10285–86, 10291, 10304 IJ: 10284, 10287–90, 10323

Ice hockey — Women
IJ: 22216

Ice skating
P: 22217, 22228 PI: 22223 I: 13596, 22221 IJ: 22218, 22222, 22225–27, 22257

Ice skating — Biography
PI: 13679, 13681, 22220 I: 13411, 13587, 13589, 13591–92, 13594–95, 13597–99 IJ: 13392, 13398, 13588, 13590, 13593, 13680

Ice skating — Fiction
P: 2315, 3241, 6547 PI: 10348

Icebergs
See Glaciers and icebergs

Iceland
P: 20003 PI: 19351 I: 15458, 15469 IJ: 15451

Iceland — Fiction
P: 5331

Iceland — Folklore
I: 11132

Iceman (Switzerland)
I: 14515

Id-ul-Fitr (Islamic holiday)
PI: 17377

Idaho
P: 16622 I: 16787 IJ: 16613, 16640

Idaho — Fiction
I: 7441

Iditarod
PI: 2970, 22075 I: 13682, 21991 IJ: 21997

Iditarod — Fiction
P: 5136 PI: 7322 IJ: 6996

Iditarod (Junior)
PI: 22075 I: 22058

Igbo
IJ: 15042

Iglesias, Enrique
PI: 12406

Igloos
I: 15797, 15837, 15848

Iguanas — Fiction
P: 5163

Iliad **(mythology)**
IJ: 11486

Illegal aliens
IJ: 17142

Illegal aliens — Fiction
PI: 8825 IJ: 7336

Illinois
PI: 16549 I: 16527 IJ: 16537, 16579

Illinois — Fiction
I: 8811 IJ: 9482

Illinois — History
IJ: 16281, 16591

Illiteracy — Fiction
P: 3030, 5665

Illness
See also Diseases; and specific illnesses, e.g., Diabetes
PI: 17945 IJ: 17966

Illness — Fiction
P: 1954, 3393, 3790, 3843, 3889, 3955, 4040, 4747, 4808, 4945, 5073 I: 8723 IJ: 8529, 8882

Illustrators — Biography
PI: 12279, 13954 I: 13956

Illustrators — Careers
PI: 17770

Imaginary animals — Fiction
See also Aesop fables; Animals; Mother Goose; and specific real or imaginary animals, e.g., Bears; Dragons
P: 5, 7, 12, 34, 41, 91, 118, 158–59, 165, 176, 210, 218–19, 221, 240, 316, 368, 385, 390, 408, 442, 449, 451, 500, 542, 563, 592, 607, 619, 628, 666, 672, 677, 711, 726, 728, 738–39, 741–46, 761, 770, 774, 776, 794, 798, 801, 806, 808, 816, 848, 850, 864, 890, 895, 915, 917, 919–20, 925–26, 948, 962, 984, 1102, 1163, 1333, 1340, 1351, 1363, 1449, 1538, 1551, 1705, 1722–98, 1800–17, 1819–24, 1826–32, 1834–40, 1842–65, 1868–96, 1898–913, 1915–38, 1941–68, 1970–95, 1997–98, 2000, 2002–4, 2006–16, 2018–44, 2046–111, 2113–209, 2211–17, 2219–20, 2222–37, 2239–54, 2256–59, 2261–64, 2266–71, 2273–85, 2287–97, 2300–24, 2326–28, 2331–47, 2349–51, 2353–88, 2390–425, 2427–67, 2469–515, 2517–69, 2571–600, 2602–7, 2609–20, 2622–23, 2625–43, 2645–50, 2652–57, 2659–73, 2675–706, 2708–29, 2731–39, 2741–51, 2753–63, 2765–69,

2771–96, 2798–827, 2829–50, 2852–71, 2873–77, 2879–91, 2894–902, 3327, 3748, 3983, 4203, 4319, 4325, 4506, 4605, 4754, 5018, 5039, 5101, 5319, 5613, 5631, 5663, 5672, 5676, 5678, 5680, 5683, 5686, 5693, 5696, 5698–99, 5716–17, 5723–24, 5727, 5730, 5736, 5738, 5742, 5749, 5764, 5771, 5775, 5791, 5794, 5796–97, 5807, 5809, 5819–21, 5850–51, 5861, 5899, 5917, 5924, 5927, 5935, 5944, 5951, 5953, 5955–56, 5961–64, 5966, 5968–69, 5973, 5996, 6000, 6022, 6030, 6055, 6059, 6125, 6127, 6136–37, 6162–63, 6172, 6189, 6196–98, 6200, 6202, 6204, 6210, 6213, 6215, 6252–53, 6259, 6261–65, 6279, 6286, 6288, 6297–98, 6301, 6303, 6308, 6313, 6334, 6336–37, 6341, 6351–52, 6361, 6367, 6373, 6376–78, 6383–84, 6386–93, 6395–97, 6406, 6428, 6435, 6445, 6460–61, 6464, 6466–68, 6470, 6474, 6486, 6492, 6495, 6497, 6499, 6501–2, 6504–5, 6515, 6533–36, 6539–40, 6546, 6552–53, 6575–76, 6578, 6614, 6616–18, 6624–25, 6629, 6632, 6640, 6644–46, 6654, 6662, 6664, 6667–68, 6671–72, 6675, 6684, 6691, 6693, 6698, 6701–3, 6705, 6709–10, 6713, 6717, 6720–22, 7904, 10944, 11210, 14037, 14206, 14249 PI: 844, 937, 1799, 1818, 1841, 1866–67, 1897, 1914, 1940, 1999, 2001, 2005, 2112, 2218, 2272, 2298, 2329–30, 2348, 2389, 2426, 2468, 2516, 2570, 2601, 2608, 2624, 2674, 2707, 2764, 2770, 2797, 2828, 2851, 2872, 2892, 4095, 5027, 6233–34, 6269, 6785, 6792, 6976, 7000, 7237, 7778, 7806, 7881, 7955, 7992, 8140, 8204, 9787, 9804, 9979, 10301, 11344, 20579 I: 2210, 2644, 6759, 7566, 7569, 7751, 7777, 7779, 7863, 7945, 8183, 9785–86, 9792, 9885, 9913, 9967 IJ: 6927, 7822, 7825, 7836, 9912, 9914, 10181

Imaginary animals — Poetry
P: 2265, 6655, 11559 PI: 11972 I: 11809

Immigration (U.S.)
P: 4604, 17546, 17578 PI: 6097, 15176, 15888,

16157, 16283, 16708, 16719, 16740, 17547, 17575, 17591 I: 15079, 15159, 15351, 15703, 16152, 16463, 16697, 17540, 17545, 17561, 17564, 17573, 17584, 17587, 17594 IJ: 14900, 15113, 15201, 15283, 15363, 15396, 15870, 16694, 16729, 16910, 17142, 17541–44, 17555, 17558, 17565, 17568, 17577, 17589, 17592, 17596

Immigration (U.S.) — Fiction
P: 3557, 3582, 3740, 3862–63, 4573, 4823, 4848, 4869, 4955 PI: 4607, 4688, 4871, 4891, 5984, 6135, 9563 I: 7377, 7500, 9577, 9591, 9595, 9600 IJ: 9523, 9541, 9550, 9594, 9603, 9625

Immigration (U.S.) — History
I: 16495

Immigration (U.S.) — Jews
IJ: 17566

Immigration (U.S.) — Poetry
I: 11653

Immigration (world)
IJ: 17016

Impeachment
I: 17124–25

Impressionism (art)
I: 13882 IJ: 13901

Impressionism (art) — Fiction
P: 1404

Improvisation (theater)
PI: 14322

Incas
I: 15736, 15752, 15754, 15761, 15774, 15780, 15788 IJ: 15603, 15606, 15758–59, 15763, 15781, 15786

Incas — Fiction
IJ: 9141

Incas — Holidays
P: 15750

Inclined planes (physics)
P: 20924

Independence Day (Mexico)
See Cinco de Mayo (Mexican holiday)

Independence Hall (Philadelphia)
I: 16739

P = Primary; PI = Primary-Intermediate; I = Intermediate; IJ = Intermediate-Junior High

India
PI: 15097–98, 17376
I: 15094, 15096, 15099, 15102–5, 15110–11, 19170
IJ: 13802, 15095, 15101, 15107, 15109, 15112–14, 17542

India — Biography
P: 13801, 13852 I: 13804
IJ: 13753, 13857

India — Cookbooks
IJ: 21718

India — Fiction
P: 1309, 4423, 4830
PI: 7242, 7245, 8982–83, 8985, 8999, 9002 I: 8996
IJ: 7273, 9016, 9019

India — Folklore
P: 6192, 10786, 10791–92, 10797, 10800–2, 10804–5, 10808–10 PI: 10793, 10807 I: 10787–90, 10794, 10796, 10803, 10806
IJ: 10795, 10798

India — History
I: 15100 IJ: 13803, 15115

India — Holidays
PI: 17385, 17404

India — Poetry
IJ: 11617

India — Science
IJ: 15115

India — Sports
I: 15106

Indian (Asian) Americans
IJ: 17542

Indian Ocean
I: 19833

Indiana
IJ: 16538, 16557

Indiana — Fiction
IJ: 9522

Indianapolis — Fiction
PI: 9374

Indianapolis Speedway Race
I: 22078

Indians of Central America
P: 15674 PI: 15666, 15683
I: 15665, 15680

Indians of Central America — Art
IJ: 13945

Indians of Central America — Fiction
P: 4888

Indians of Central America — Folklore
I: 11395, 11415

Indians of Central America — Jokes and riddles
PI: 21814

Indians of North America
See Native Americans

Indians of South America
I: 15756, 15767, 15782, 15787

Indians of South America — Folklore
IJ: 11437

Indians of South America — Jokes and riddles
PI: 21814

Indians of the West Indies — Fiction
PI: 9142

Indonesia
I: 15156 IJ: 15168, 15183, 15186

Indonesia — Fiction
P: 5418

Indoor games
I: 22234

Industrial health and safety
I: 13306

Industrial Revolution
I: 15872

Industrial Revolution (U.S.)
IJ: 16275

Industry — History
I: 21025

Industry (U.S.) — History
IJ: 16456

Influenza — History
I: 17958

Influenza epidemic, 1918
I: 17958

Influenza epidemic, 1918 — Fiction
IJ: 9551

Inhalant drugs
IJ: 17880

Inline hockey
PI: 22036

Inline skating
P: 22028, 22074 I: 21982, 21999, 22023 IJ: 21976, 21989, 22026

Innkeepers — History
I: 16186

Insects
See also names of specific insects, e.g., Butterflies
P: 19425–27, 19440, 19442, 19444, 19452, 19454, 19459, 19462, 19469, 19472, 19475, 19478, 19480, 19484, 19488–89, 19492, 19499, 19503, 19510, 19513, 19527, 19550, 19560–61, 19569
PI: 19430, 19437, 19455, 19460, 19464, 19470, 19474, 19485, 19490–91, 19494, 19501–2, 19508, 19511, 19521, 19530, 19544
I: 18647, 19423, 19429, 19435–36, 19438–39, 19441, 19443, 19445, 19453, 19456–58, 19461, 19465, 19468, 19471, 19473, 19497–98, 19500, 19524, 19533, 19547–48, 19559 IJ: 18644, 19428, 19434, 19479, 19481–82, 19504, 19534, 19599

Insects — Drawing and painting
IJ: 21569

Insects — Experiments and projects
P: 19495 I: 19445, 19496

Insects — Fiction
P: 484, 821, 1922, 5323
PI: 124 I: 7617, 8114
IJ: 6927

Insects — Homes
P: 18910 IJ: 19482

Insects — Poetry
P: 11790 PI: 11784, 11798, 11806 I: 11781, 11980

Interactive books
P: 186, 252, 304, 344, 361, 597, 672, 865, 1499, 1570, 1980, 2068, 2094, 2357, 3271, 3481, 3512, 4152, 4171, 4330, 5462, 5557, 5955, 6164, 14262, 18919, 21835

Interactive books — Fiction
P: 828, 1056, 2445, 2577, 3177, 5166, 5330, 6014
PI: 9771

Interior decoration
See Home decoration, Room decoration

Interjections
P: 14030

International Space Station
P: 20955

Internet (computers)
P: 21201 PI: 21210
I: 21190, 21202, 21207
IJ: 21215, 21217, 21219, 21231, 21233, 21235–36

Internet (computers) — Fiction
I: 10226

Interracial families — Fiction
P: 3722, 3814, 3885
IJ: 7882, 8560

Interracial marriages — Fiction
P: 3602

Inuit
See also Alaska; Arctic; Polar regions
P: 15825, 16797
PI: 15573, 15811, 15814
I: 15793–94, 15797, 15807, 15823, 15829, 15833, 15837, 15844, 15848
IJ: 12240, 15824, 16779, 16812

Inuit — Art
I: 13943 IJ: 15824

Inuit — Fiction
P: 1567, 3739, 4477, 4495, 4576, 4655–56, 4747–48, 4828, 4838, 4885, 5151, 5225, 5253 PI: 4722, 9171
I: 6852, 6895 IJ: 6900, 6996, 7877

Inuit — Folklore
P: 11205, 11208 PI: 11207
I: 11204, 11206 IJ: 11209

Inuit — History
IJ: 14490

Inuit — Poetry
PI: 11669 I: 11930

Inuit language
IJ: 20795

Inventions
See Inventors and inventions; and specific inventions, e.g., Telephones

Inventors and inventions
See also Scientists; and specific inventions, e.g., Telephones
PI: 14565, 21027 I: 9909, 17168, 18019, 20875, 20968, 21025, 21031, 21037–38, 21045, 21050, 21053, 21062–64, 21067, 21262 IJ: 21040, 21044, 21052, 21054–55

Inventors and inventions — Biography
P: 12878, 12882–83, 13271, 13281, 13331, 13357, 13359
PI: 12213, 13273, 13354
I: 12770, 13205, 13232, 13236–39, 13241, 13272, 13278–79, 13286, 13310
IJ: 12217, 12697, 12879, 13240, 13270, 13274, 13355–56, 13358

Inventors and inventions — Fiction
PI: 9835, 9860 I: 9865, 9870

P = Primary; PI = Primary-Intermediate; I = Intermediate; IJ = Intermediate-Junior High

Inventors and inventions — Women
IJ: 21061

Invertebrates
See also Animals; Insects; etc.
I: 19621 **IJ:** 19599

Investing (business)
IJ: 16922, 16925

Iowa
P: 16566 **PI:** 16550
I: 16565, 16567 **IJ:** 16559

Iowa — Fiction
I: 9882

Iran
See also Persia
PI: 15560 **I:** 15536, 15558–59 **IJ:** 15545, 15550

Iran — Folklore
P: 11184 **PI:** 11201

Iran hostage crisis
PI: 15560

Iraq
See also Persian Gulf War
PI: 15553 **I:** 15548
IJ: 15489, 15543

Iraq — Folklore
P: 11185

Ireland
P: 15336 **PI:** 15350, 15353, 15359 **I:** 15356, 15366 **IJ:** 15346, 15352, 15363

Ireland — Biography
I: 13771

Ireland — Fiction
P: 987, 1125, 1610, 4610, 4669, 4768 **I:** 8658, 9089, 9101 **IJ:** 6957, 7263, 8004, 9088, 9093–94, 9098–100, 9122, 9414, 9690

Ireland — Folklore
P: 10953, 10970–71, 10985, 10989, 11031 **PI:** 10948 **I:** 10972, 11003, 11011 **IJ:** 10994, 11010

Ireland — History
P: 13842 **I:** 15355

Ireland, Northern
PI: 15362 **I:** 15360
IJ: 15339

Irish Americans
IJ: 17550, 17597

Irish Americans — Fiction
P: 5632 **PI:** 4607, 9623 **I:** 9575 **IJ:** 9541, 9572, 9603

Irish setters — Fiction
IJ: 7247

Iron and steel
PI: 21030 **I:** 21257, 21259

Irons (household appliances)
I: 21021

Iroquois Indians
PI: 16049 **I:** 22015

Iroquois Indians — Biography
IJ: 12974

Iroquois Indians — Crafts
I: 16039

Iroquois Indians — Fiction
I: 9210

Iroquois Indians — Folklore
PI: 11214 **IJ:** 11299

Irving, Washington
IJ: 12555

Ishi
IJ: 12975, 15939

Islam
P: 17173 **PI:** 5627, 17377 **I:** 15547, 17192

Islam — Fiction
PI: 5625 **I:** 7354 **IJ:** 8929

Islam — Folklore
P: 11194, 11196, 11198, 11200

Islam — History
I: 15556 **IJ:** 15486

Islam — Holidays
I: 17389

Islamic Americans — Fiction
I: 7354

Islands
See also Caribbean Islands; and specific islands, e.g., Cuba
P: 4850, 6597, 14338
PI: 15811, 19998, 20385, 20394 **I:** 20388 **IJ:** 16810

Islands — Fiction
P: 3444, 3788, 4411, 5854, 6372 **PI:** 2892, 3587 **I:** 2644, 6981, 7426, 8036, 8126, 8363, 9032, 9101, 9265, 9668, 9868 **IJ:** 6907, 6957, 6997, 7036, 7120, 7605, 8917, 9180

Israel
P: 15546, 17228 **PI:** 93, 15522 **I:** 15517, 15520–21, 15526–28 **IJ:** 15518–19, 15523, 15529–31

Israel — Biography
IJ: 13823

Israel — Fiction
P: 4572 **I:** 8943, 8948
IJ: 8786, 8926, 8936, 8938, 8944

Israel — History
I: 14596 **IJ:** 13780, 15533

Israeli-Arab relations
IJ: 15537

Issa
I: 12556

Italian Americans
IJ: 17554, 17565

Italian Americans — Biography
IJ: 12523

Italian Americans — Fiction
P: 3015, 3515, 3608
PI: 4587 **I:** 7543, 9418
IJ: 9573, 9594

Italy
P: 15375 **PI:** 15374, 15379, 15383–84 **I:** 15386, 15393 **IJ:** 15372, 15378, 15394

Italy — Cookbooks
I: 15377 **IJ:** 21676

Italy — Fiction
P: 1111, 5854 **PI:** 9025, 9035 **I:** 9075 **IJ:** 8438, 9680

Italy — Folklore
P: 5802, 10907, 11058–61, 11063, 11075 **PI:** 11062
I: 10489

Italy — History
I: 14500 **IJ:** 14832

Italy — Holidays
I: 15377

Ivory Coast
IJ: 15024, 15031, 15048

Iwo Jima, Battle of
I: 14866 **IJ:** 14834

J

Jacks (game)
P: 22019

Jackson, Andrew
I: 12672, 13045 **IJ:** 16232

Jackson, Bo
I: 13615 **IJ:** 13614, 13616

Jackson, Janet
IJ: 12407

Jackson, Jesse
I: 12727–28 **IJ:** 12729

Jackson, Michael
IJ: 12408

Jackson, Reggie
PI: 13463

Jackson, Samuel L.
IJ: 12409

Jackson, Stonewall
I: 12906 **IJ:** 12907

Jackson, William Henry
IJ: 12242

Jacobs, Harriet
I: 12730

Jacobs, Lionel and Barron
IJ: 16372

Jaguar (automobile)
IJ: 21306

Jaguars
PI: 19099

Jaguars — Fiction
P: 5171 **PI:** 5396

Jaguars — Poetry
I: 11770

Jamaica
P: 15695, 15697 **I:** 15696
IJ: 15707, 15717

Jamaica — Fiction
P: 3843, 4675, 4862, 4972

Jamaica — Folklore
I: 11423

Jamaica — Holidays
PI: 15694

Jamaica — Music
P: 15695

Jamaican Americans — Fiction
P: 5833

James, Daniel
IJ: 12731

James, Jesse
IJ: 12908–10

Jamestown Colony
I: 16139, 16166 **IJ:** 16104, 16174

Jamestown Colony — Fiction
I: 9186, 9197 **IJ:** 9187

Japan
P: 15120, 15138 **PI:** 145, 15116, 15119, 15124, 15130, 15140–41 **I:** 15118, 15121–22, 15125–27, 15129, 15133, 15142
IJ: 15128, 15134, 15137, 15143

Japan — Biography
I: 12556 **IJ:** 13833

Japan — Cookbooks
IJ: 21748

Japan — Crafts
I: 15123

Japan — Fiction
P: 971, 1488, 1650, 3175, 3622, 4680, 4692, 4703, 4775, 4777, 4780, 4825, 5365, 5545, 5915, 6176, 10406 **PI:** 1201, 3635, 4589, 4739, 4745, 7720
I: 8573, 8989, 9000, 9006–7, 9677, 10409, 10523
IJ: 9008, 9022

P = Primary; PI = Primary-Intermediate; I = Intermediate; IJ = Intermediate-Junior High

Japan — Folklore
P: 10813–18, 10820, 10822, 10824, 10828–31, 10833–36 PI: 4767, 10811, 10826–27 I: 10812, 10819, 10821, 10823, 10832 IJ: 10825

Japan — History
PI: 9015, 13847, 14841 I: 15131, 15135 IJ: 14579, 15117, 15136, 15139

Japan — Holidays
PI: 15132 I: 17381

Japan — Poetry
P: 11821

Japanese Americans
P: 3874 I: 14894 IJ: 14868, 14881, 17563, 17569

Japanese Americans — Biography
I: 12274, 12922, 13259, 13598 IJ: 12440, 13833

Japanese Americans — Fiction
P: 3491, 4029, 4058, 4585, 4853, 5066 PI: 4021, 4611, 5037, 7358, 9692, 10312 I: 7378, 7529–30, 9699 IJ: 7379, 8991, 9634, 9654, 10373

Japanese Americans — History
I: 14891

Japanese Americans — Holidays
I: 17381

Japanese Canadians — Fiction
IJ: 8947

Japanese language — Poetry
P: 11649

Jason (mythology)
PI: 11496 IJ: 11466

Jataka stories
See also Buddhism — Folklore
P: 10801 PI: 10793

Jays
I: 19251

Jazz
PI: 12347 I: 12330 IJ: 14133

Jazz — Biography
P: 12379 I: 12331 IJ: 12348

Jazz — Fiction
P: 3284, 4986 PI: 4613

Jazz — History
PI: 14138

Jealousy
P: 17718

Jealousy — Fiction
I: 10076

Jeeps
I: 21302

Jefferson, Thomas
P: 13046 PI: 13047 I: 12672, 13049–50, 13052–53, 16849, 16882 IJ: 13048, 13051, 16229, 16235, 16899

Jefferson, Thomas — Fiction
P: 4646

Jellyfish
P: 19660, 19663 I: 19664

Jemison, Mae
P: 12126 I: 12127, 15977

Jerusalem
I: 15526, 15528, 15532

Jerusalem — Biography
IJ: 13823

Jerusalem — History
I: 15524 IJ: 15533

Jerusalem — Poetry
I: 11742

Jesters — Fiction
P: 4818

Jesus Christ
P: 5967, 17329, 17409 PI: 17307 I: 17260–61, 17415, 17441 IJ: 17289

Jesus Christ — Folklore
P: 11353 PI: 11110

Jeter, Derek
PI: 13465 I: 13464

Jewelry
I: 21542 IJ: 21169, 21186

Jewelry making
P: 21548 PI: 21546, 21552 I: 21437, 21541, 21543, 21549 IJ: 21540, 21547

Jewish Americans
P: 17599 IJ: 17566, 17583

Jewish Americans — Biography
IJ: 16372

Jewish Americans — Fiction
PI: 9516 IJ: 7368

Jewish holy days
See also specific holy days, e.g., Hanukkah; Rosh Hashanah
P: 6070–71, 6073, 6076–77, 6089–90, 6093, 6095, 6117, 17462–63, 17468, 17472, 17476, 17481, 17488 PI: 17452, 17469, 17474, 17477–78, 17484 I: 17450–51, 17454, 17456, 17459–61, 17473, 17475, 17479–80, 17489–90

IJ: 17453, 17455, 17464, 17467, 17471

Jewish holy days — Cookbooks
I: 21724

Jewish holy days — Crafts
P: 6108, 6129 PI: 17483 I: 17451, 17482

Jewish holy days — Fiction
P: 910, 1672, 6067–69, 6072, 6075, 6079, 6081–86, 6088, 6091, 6101–2, 6104–6, 6111–14, 6116, 6118, 6120–21, 6123, 6125, 6127–28, 6130–31 PI: 9754, 9762 I: 9724, 9738

Jewish holy days — Poetry
P: 6099–100 PI: 11837

Jewish holy days — Short stories
I: 9761

Jewish Theological Seminary
I: 16663

Jews
I: 14858, 17229, 17573

Jews — Biography
I: 13797 IJ: 12597, 12639

Jews — Cookbooks
I: 17461

Jews — Fiction
P: 3822, 3863, 3963, 4736, 4778, 4782, 4798, 4802, 4827, 4848, 5646, 5901, 6074, 6078, 6110, 6126 PI: 4034, 4779, 4797, 6097, 6115, 7403, 7413, 8623, 9043, 9069, 9616, 9737 I: 7499–500, 7510, 7527, 7637, 8564, 8703, 8799, 9577, 9580, 9600, 9647, 9684, 9689 IJ: 7332, 7369, 8491, 8513, 8828, 8921, 8944, 8968, 9050, 9074, 9523, 9550, 9625, 9651, 9655–56, 9670, 9675, 9680–81, 9683, 9685, 9690, 9694, 9696, 9990, 10134

Jews — Folklore
P: 11141–42, 11144, 11147, 11151–52, 11155–56, 11160, 11164, 11171, 11176–77, 11179, 17274 PI: 10685, 11140, 11143, 11145–46, 11148, 11153–54, 11158–59, 11161, 11167, 11169–70 I: 11149–50, 11157, 11162–63, 11165, 11168, 11172, 11175, 11178 IJ: 11166, 11173–74

Jews — History
See also Holocaust; Immigration (U.S.); Israeli-Arab relations; World War II
PI: 4891, 14809, 16283 I: 14596, 14840, 15525, 17254 IJ: 13798, 13851, 14814, 14816, 14842, 14849, 14851, 14853, 14856, 14864–65, 14878, 14889, 17182, 17255, 17485, 17566

Joan of Arc
P: 13813 PI: 13812 I: 13811, 13814 IJ: 13815

Jobs, Steve
PI: 12912 IJ: 12911

Jockeys — Biography
I: 13694–95 IJ: 13387

Jockeys — Women — Biography
PI: 13696

Jogging
See Running and jogging

John Paul II, Pope
I: 13816 IJ: 17194

Johnson, Andrew
I: 13054 IJ: 13055

Johnson, Lyndon B.
I: 12671 IJ: 13056–57

Johnson, Magic
PI: 12008 I: 13533 IJ: 13532, 13534

Johnson, Walter
IJ: 13466

Jokes and riddles
P: 69, 211, 5330, 5876, 6572, 6720, 21815, 21817, 21819, 21821, 21823–25, 21828, 21835–36, 21838–39, 21842–43, 21853–54, 21860 PI: 6037, 11722, 16355, 21812–14, 21816, 21818, 21820, 21826, 21830–33, 21837, 21841, 21844–45, 21847–49, 21852, 21856, 21858 I: 10612, 14052–53, 21822, 21829, 21834, 21846, 21850–51, 21855, 21857, 21859

Jokes and riddles — Folklore
I: 10865

Jokes and riddles — Poetry
IJ: 11724

Jonah (Bible)
P: 17238

Jones, Bill T.
P: 14292

Jones, Casey
P: 4638

P = Primary; PI = Primary-Intermediate; I = Intermediate; IJ = Intermediate-Junior High

Jones, Frederick McKinley
I: 13310

Jones, John Paul
P: 12915 PI: 12913
I: 12914

Jones, Marion
IJ: 13659

Jones, Mother
IJ: 13161–62

Joplin, Scott
I: 12330–31

Jordan
IJ: 15552

Jordan, Barbara
I: 12732–33 IJ: 12734

Jordan, Michael
I: 13536–37, 13539–40
IJ: 13535, 13538

Jordan, Michael — Fiction
PI: 4990 I: 8688

Jordan, Michael — Poetry
PI: 11996

Jordan (country)
IJ: 15539, 15552

Joseph (Bible)
P: 17292 PI: 17330

Journalists and journalism
P: 14082 PI: 14073
IJ: 14064, 14086

Journalists and journalism — Biography
PI: 12818, 13138 I: 12584, 12643, 13136, 13195
IJ: 13137, 13139

Journals
See also Diaries
IJ: 12830, 14085

Journals — Fiction
PI: 9490 I: 9376, 10352
IJ: 8273, 9641, 10136

Journeys — Poetry
P: 11663

Joyce, William
I: 13959

Joyner, Florence Griffith
I: 13660

Joyner-Kersee, Jackie
PI: 13661 IJ: 13662

Juana de la Guz, Sister
I: 12557

Juarez, Benito
PI: 13818 I: 13817

Judaism
See also Jews; Jews — History; Religion; Sabbath (Jewish)

P: 17224, 17228 I: 17180, 17229 IJ: 17182, 17235, 17485

Judo
I: 22266 IJ: 22024

Jugglers and juggling
PI: 21671

Jugglers and juggling — Fiction
P: 5798 PI: 4950

Jukeboxes — Fiction
P: 3348

Julia, Raul
IJ: 12833

July Fourth
P: 17391 I: 17363
IJ: 17364

July Fourth — Fiction
P: 5617, 5638, 5643, 5652, 5657, 5660

Jumbo (elephant)
PI: 19161

Juneteenth
I: 17340 IJ: 17345

Jungles
P: 5393, 20387 I: 18653
IJ: 14835, 20440

Jungles — Fiction
P: 1129, 1277, 1640, 1781, 2940, 5461, 6500

Junior Iditarod
See Iditarod (Junior)

Junkyards — Automobiles
P: 21309

Jupiter (planet)
PI: 18459, 18490, 18496
I: 18457, 18476, 18488
IJ: 18479, 20973

Justice — Folklore
IJ: 10567 IJ: 12243–44

K

Kahlo, Frida
PI: 12245 IJ: 12243–44

Ka'iulani, Princess of Hawaii
I: 13820 IJ: 13819

Kalahari Desert
IJ: 14982

Kalispel Indians — Dances
I: 15943

Kangaroos
P: 19180 I: 19176, 19179, 19182

Kangaroos — Fiction
P: 2017, 2287, 6279

Kansas
P: 16543 I: 16554
IJ: 16533, 16571

Kansas — Fiction
P: 6222 PI: 3479 I: 7249, 9380 IJ: 7172

Kansas City (MO)
PI: 16587

Karan, Donna
IJ: 13163

Karate
See also Martial arts
P: 22271 PI: 22267–68
IJ: 22269, 22272

Karate — Fiction
PI: 5049, 7720 I: 8348
IJ: 10367, 10372

Kato Indians — Folklore
PI: 11295

Kayaks and kayaking
IJ: 22263

Kazakhstan
IJ: 15421

Keats, Ezra Jack
I: 12246

Keller, Helen
PI: 13164, 13166
IJ: 12697, 13165

Kelley, Florence
PI: 12916

Kellogg, W. K.
I: 12917

Kelly, Jim
IJ: 13617

Kemp, Shawn
I: 13541

Kennedy, Jacqueline
See Onassis, Jacqueline Kennedy

Kennedy, John F.
PI: 13058, 13060 I: 12671, 13059, 13062 IJ: 13061

Kennedy, John F., Jr.
IJ: 12918

Kennedy, Robert F.
I: 12920 IJ: 12919

Kenny, Elizabeth
I: 13311

Kent State University
I: 16501

Kente cloth
P: 15023

Kentucky
P: 16842 PI: 16852
I: 12860, 16835, 16860
IJ: 16829–30

Kentucky — Fiction
I: 8826, 9497 IJ: 8439

Kentucky — History
I: 16890

Kenya
P: 14914, 14939
PI: 14933, 14935 I: 14915, 14924, 14938, 14941, 14946
IJ: 14923, 14934, 14952, 14955

Kenya — Animals
P: 14947

Kenya — Fiction
P: 4867 PI: 5514 I: 7154

Kerrigan, Nancy
I: 13592

Kestrels — Fiction
P: 5138

Key, Francis Scott
PI: 14161

Kherdian, Jeron
IJ: 13821

Kidd, Captain — Fiction
I: 9913

Kidd, Jason
IJ: 13542–43

Kidnapping
P: 10658

Kidnapping — Fiction
P: 2230, 2947, 6443, 6620
PI: 6750 I: 6863, 10304
IJ: 6779, 6808, 6881, 7003, 7025, 7092, 9067, 9166, 9174, 9276

Killer bees
PI: 19519

Killer whales
PI: 19774 I: 19779, 19794

Kindergarten
P: 5506, 5537

Kindergarten — Fiction
P: 248, 5488–89, 5529, 5534, 5538 PI: 7406

King, Billie Jean
I: 13650

King, Coretta Scott
PI: 12736 I: 12735, 12738
IJ: 12737

King, Martin Luther, Jr.
P: 5610, 12739, 12748, 12752–53, 16518, 17337
PI: 12740, 12746–47, 12750, 12755–56, 17387
I: 12742–43, 12745, 17029
IJ: 12741, 12744, 12749, 12751, 12754, 16511, 17040

King, Richard
I: 12921

King, Rodney
IJ: 16498

King, Stephen
I: 12558

King Philip's War
I: 12981

P = Primary; PI = Primary-Intermediate; I = Intermediate; IJ = Intermediate-Junior High

Kings — Fiction
P: 1564, 4356, 6579
PI: 1461 I: 10523

Kings — Folklore
P: 10539, 10661, 10701,
10715, 10749, 10756
I: 10788

Kingsley, Mary
P: 12128

Kipling, Rudyard
I: 12559

Kipsigis (African people)
IJ: 14916

Kisses — Fiction
P: 1690, 3396

Kitchens — Fiction
P: 3037, 3384

Kitchens — History
I: 16324

Kites
P: 15658, 21667

Kites — Fiction
P: 288, 1586, 1617, 2373,
2626, 4000, 4808, 5093
PI: 503 I: 8638, 9004

Klee, Paul
PI: 12247–48

Klimp, Gustav
IJ: 12249

Klondike Gold Rush
See Gold Rush (Alaska
and Yukon)

Knights
P: 14763 I: 14756, 14764,
14772, 14794 IJ: 14783,
14790

Knights — Fiction
P: 1385, 1626, 2028, 4660
PI: 9083, 9941 I: 7047,
9044, 9115, 11019
IJ: 8017, 9113–14, 9117,
9119, 11021

Knights — Folklore
PI: 10991, 10998 I: 10915,
10997 IJ: 10993, 11000,
11024–25

Knitting
PI: 21643 IJ: 21642,
21644

Knitting — Fiction
P: 1816, 4060

Knot tying
IJ: 21666

Koalas
P: 19181, 19184 I: 19177,
19182

Koalas — Fiction
P: 2096, 2158

Koko (gorilla)
I: 19011

Kol Nidre (Jewish prayer)
P: 17487

Kolbe, Saint Maximilian
IJ: 13822

Kollek, Teddy
IJ: 13823

Komodo dragons
I: 18744, 18746

**Komodo dragons —
Fiction**
P: 4247, 5418

Kongo
See also Congo
IJ: 14944

Korea
See also Korea, South
PI: 15193 IJ: 15169

Korea — Fiction
P: 3625, 4620, 4793, 4890
PI: 8984 I: 9003–4
IJ: 8987, 9005

Korea — Folklore
P: 10721, 10724, 10726–28,
10731–33, 10735
PI: 10729, 10736
IJ: 10734

Korea, South
PI: 15199 I: 15184
IJ: 15206

**Korea, South —
Cookbooks**
IJ: 21682

Korea, South — Crafts
PI: 15166

Korea, South — Holidays
PI: 15166, 15177

Korean Americans
IJ: 17664

**Korean Americans —
Fiction**
P: 3059, 3555, 3581, 3689,
3831, 3836, 4620, 4941,
5473, 5511 PI: 7470
I: 6935, 17654 IJ: 7314,
7333, 7349

Korean language
PI: 10729

Korean War
IJ: 16506, 16519, 16521

Korean War — Fiction
IJ: 8987

Korematsu, Fred
I: 12922

Kosovo
I: 15279 IJ: 15259

Kosovo War — Fiction
IJ: 9061

Kossman, Nina
IJ: 13824

Krill (marine animals)
I: 19881

Krone, Julie
PI: 13696 I: 13694–95

Ku Klux Klan — Fiction
IJ: 7345, 8453, 9522

Kung fu — Fiction
PI: 4752

Kurds
I: 17587

Kurelek, William
PI: 12250

Kuskin, Karla
PI: 12560

Kuwait
IJ: 15540

Kwan, Michelle
IJ: 13593

Kwanzaa
P: 5619, 5626, 5648, 5655,
17365 PI: 17356, 17395
I: 17344, 17368, 17372–73
IJ: 17408

Kwanzaa — Crafts
P: 5647

Kwanzaa — Fiction
P: 5637 PI: 9710, 9750,
9766

Kyrgyzstan
I: 15435, 17399

L

Labor Day
P: 17336, 17399

Labor movements
I: 15874, 16444 IJ: 13161,
16466, 16483

**Labor movements —
Biography**
PI: 12781, 12916
IJ: 13162

**Labor unions —
Biography**
I: 12827

Labrador
I: 15583

Labrador retrievers
PI: 19953

**Labrador retrievers —
Fiction**
IJ: 7313

La Brea Tar Pits (CA)
IJ: 14476

Lacrosse
I: 22015 IJ: 22040

Ladybugs
P: 19444, 19528–29,
19531–32 PI: 19530,
19538 IJ: 19534

Ladybugs — Fiction
P: 1922

Lafayette, Marquis de
IJ: 13825

Lake Erie
I: 15861

Lake Superior
I: 15862

Lakes
P: 19851 PI: 16529, 20523
I: 20525–26 IJ: 20513

Lakes — Birds
I: 19246

Lakes — Fiction
P: 3449

Lakes (U.S.)
See also Great Lakes; and
specific lakes, e.g., Lake
Erie
PI: 16528

Lakota Indians
I: 16032

**Lakota Indians —
Biography**
I: 12414

Lakota Indians — Fiction
PI: 9147

**Lakota Indians —
Folklore**
P: 11252, 11281 IJ: 11248

Lambs — Fiction
P: 5259

Lancelot (knight)
IJ: 11039

Landscape architecture
I: 12941

Landslides
I: 20309

Landslides — Fiction
IJ: 6934

Lange, Dorothea
PI: 12251

Language and languages
See also Dictionaries;
Spanish language —
Fiction; Word books
P: 13982, 14048
PI: 14035, 14038 I: 14047,
14049–51 IJ: 13890,
13966, 13978, 13980, 13987

**Language and languages
— Fiction**
P: 7418, 21883

Language sounds
P: 14099

La Nina (weather)
IJ: 20770, 20785

Laos
PI: 15153 I: 15159
IJ: 15178

Laos — Folklore
I: 10846

Laotian Americans
I: 17584

Lapland
PI: 15815

La Purisima Mission
IJ: 16778, 16827

Las Posadas (Hispanic holiday)
I: 17421

Las Vegas — Biography
IJ: 12964

Lascaux Caves
P: 13937 IJ: 14509

Lasers
I: 20867, 20875 IJ: 18286

Latchkey children — Fiction
P: 5086 I: 8407

Latifah, Queen
IJ: 12410

Latin America
See Caribbean Islands; Central America; South America; national and ethnic groups, e.g., Hispanic Americans; and specific countries, e.g., Mexico

Latin America — Fiction
P: 4809

Latin America — Folklore
P: 11439 I: 11435
IJ: 11434

Latkes — Fiction
P: 6079, 6083

Latvia
I: 15413

Lauder, Estee
I: 12923

Laughter — Fiction
P: 4818

Lauren, Ralph
IJ: 12924

Lavoisier, Antoine
I: 13312

Law, Ruth
P: 12129

Law enforcement officers
See also Police
IJ: 16646

Lawrence, Jacob
PI: 12253 I: 13958
IJ: 12252

Lawyers — Biography
I: 12726

Lawyers — Careers
P: 17746

Laziness — Fiction
PI: 8575

Leakey, Louis and Mary
IJ: 13313

Learning disabilities
See also Mental handicaps
PI: 17910 I: 17904, 17930
IJ: 17899, 17907, 17912, 17920

Learning disabilities — Fiction
PI: 5050, 8915 I: 8886, 8895, 8912, 10048 IJ: 8786

Leathers, Blanche
PI: 12130

Leaves
See also Trees
P: 20216 PI: 20210
I: 20196, 20206

Leaves — Crafts
I: 21497

Leaves — Fiction
P: 4454

Lebanon
IJ: 15554–55

Lebanon — Fiction
P: 4679

Lee, Bruce
IJ: 12411

Lee, Robert E.
PI: 12925 I: 12926
IJ: 12927

Lee, Spike
IJ: 12412

Leeuwenhoek, Anton van
I: 13314

LEGO toys
P: 21659

Legumes
IJ: 20176

Lemieux, Mario
I: 13697

Lemmings
I: 19209

Lemmons, Bob
PI: 4728

LeMond, Greg
I: 13698

Lemurs
P: 19004 I: 18990, 19001, 19007 IJ: 19012

Lenape Indians — Fiction
I: 9172 IJ: 9201

Lennon, John
I: 12413

Leonardo da Vinci
PI: 12213, 12219 I: 12218
IJ: 12217

Leopards
P: 19097 PI: 19075, 19088
IJ: 19109

Leopards — Fiction
I: 7275

Leopards — Folklore
PI: 10685

Leopold, Aldo
I: 13315

Leprechauns
P: 973, 5632, 10971
I: 7623 IJ: 7693

Leprechauns — Fiction
P: 985, 987

Lesbian mothers
See also Homosexuality
IJ: 17658

Lesbian mothers — Fiction
IJ: 8655

Leslie, Lisa
IJ: 13544

Lester, Helen
PI: 12561

Letter writing
PI: 14071

Lettering
I: 21582

Letters — Fiction
P: 941, 3884, 4321 I: 8347, 8636, 9337, 9626 IJ: 8274

Leukemia
I: 18015 IJ: 17986

Leukemia — Fiction
I: 8914 IJ: 8383, 8877, 8903, 8906

Levers
P: 20925

Levittown (NY) — Fiction
I: 7415

Lewin, Ted
I: 12254

Lewis, Carl
IJ: 13663

Lewis, Meriwether
PI: 12131, 16076, 16091
I: 16090

Lewis and Clark Expedition
P: 12988 PI: 12132
I: 12989, 16088–89
IJ: 12133, 16086, 16093

Lewis and Clark Expedition — Cookbooks
I: 16080

Lewis and Clark Expedition — Fiction
I: 16085 IJ: 7231, 9424, 9434, 9440

Lexington and Concord, Battles of
I: 16208 IJ: 16201

Liberia
PI: 15022 IJ: 15034

Liberia — Fiction
IJ: 8981

Liberia — Folklore
P: 10640 I: 10710

Liberty Bell
PI: 16732

Libraries
See also Books and printing
P: 3140, 13992, 13997
PI: 13994, 13999, 14005
I: 14001, 16663, 21141

Libraries — Careers
P: 17738

Libraries — Fiction
P: 2991, 3025, 3209, 3331, 3443, 3489, 4143, 4203, 6214, 6517, 6582 PI: 4771, 6796, 6946 I: 6756, 6933, 9801 IJ: 6745, 9999

Library of Congress (Washington, DC)
PI: 13995 I: 16733

Libya
I: 14961 IJ: 14960

Lice
See also Head lice
P: 17972, 19450
PI: 17946, 17961 I: 17980, 18009, 18648

License plates (U.S.)
I: 21308

Lieberman-Cline, Nancy
IJ: 13545

Life cycles
P: 17203, 18593 I: 18289, 18587

Life spans
I: 18289

Light
P: 20857 PI: 20862, 20870
I: 20860, 20868 IJ: 20858, 20871, 20891

Light — Experiments and projects
P: 20874, 20876 I: 20855, 20861, 20865, 20879
IJ: 20804, 20863, 20869, 20873, 20878, 20912

Light — Poetry
I: 11577

Light bulbs
IJ: 20891, 20907

Lighthouses
P: 6597, 21358 I: 21360

Lighthouses — Fiction
P: 5362, 5603 PI: 2941, 9329, 9567 I: 9607
IJ: 9479

Lightning
P: 20696 PI: 20710
I: 20691, 20698, 20717

P = Primary; PI = Primary-Intermediate; I = Intermediate; IJ = Intermediate-Junior High

Liliuokalani, Queen of Hawaii
PI: 12928

Limericks
P: 11879, 11883, 11885
PI: 11863 **I:** 11884
IJ: 11896

Limestone caves
IJ: 20370

Lin, Maya
I: 12256 **IJ:** 12255

Lincoln, Abraham
P: 13063, 13065, 13069–70, 13078–79, 16408
PI: 13067, 13074, 16703
I: 12673, 13064, 13068, 13072–73, 16256
IJ: 13066, 13071, 13075–77, 16405, 16426, 16441, 16648

Lincoln, Abraham — Assassination
IJ: 16435

Lincoln, Abraham — Fiction
P: 4598, 4883 **PI:** 9503

Lincoln, Abraham — Photographs
IJ: 13077

Lincoln, Mary Todd
IJ: 13167

Lincoln Memorial (Washington, DC)
PI: 16703 **I:** 16730
IJ: 13957, 16648

Lindbergh, Charles A.
PI: 12134, 21112

Lindbergh, Charles A. — Fiction
PI: 4599

Lindros, Eric
IJ: 13699

Linnaeus, Carl
IJ: 13316

Lions
P: 19087, 19101, 19106, 19110 **PI:** 19105 **I:** 19074, 19083, 19092, 19094

Lions — Fiction
P: 1996, 2101, 2320, 2567, 4130, 5122, 5366, 5402, 6335, 6500 **I:** 7270, 7306

Lions — Folklore
P: 10642 **I:** 10654

Lipinski, Tara
I: 13594–95

Literacy — Fiction
P: 3560 **PI:** 3846 **I:** 8690

Lithuania
PI: 14873 **I:** 14858, 15274, 15413

Littering
P: 16963

Littering — Fiction
P: 1384

Little Bighorn, Battle of
See also Sitting Bull (Sioux chief)
PI: 16058 **I:** 12971, 16012
IJ: 12871, 12995, 16057, 16065, 16337

Little Bighorn, Battle of — Fiction
IJ: 7882

Little Dipper
See Big and Little Dippers

Little League
I: 22108 **IJ:** 22103

Little League — Fiction
I: 9908

Little Rock
I: 17046

Lizards
See also Komodo dragons
PI: 18750 **I:** 18690, 18748–49, 19886, 19904
IJ: 18691

Lizards — Fiction
P: 2853, 5418, 6215
PI: 7964 **I:** 8066, 10012

Llamas
PI: 18952 **I:** 18949

Llamas — Fiction
PI: 7225 **I:** 7226

Lobbying (government)
I: 17122

Lobo, Rebecca
I: 13546

Lobsters
I: 19672

Lobsters — Fiction
P: 3355

Loch Ness monster
I: 21928

Locke, Kevin
I: 12414

Locker, Thomas
I: 12562

Lodz ghetto
IJ: 14856

Logging
PI: 20438 **I:** 16346

Logging — Fiction
PI: 2951 **IJ:** 9529

Logging — Folklore
PI: 11357 **I:** 11365, 11373

Logging — History
PI: 16096 **IJ:** 16385

Logging camps — Cookbooks
IJ: 15876

Logging camps — History
IJ: 15876

London
I: 15343

London — Fiction
P: 2698, 4868 **PI:** 9828
I: 6741, 9084 **IJ:** 7079, 9091–92, 9124, 9126, 9697

London — Folklore
P: 10952

London — History
PI: 15342

London, Jack
I: 12563 **IJ:** 12564

Loneliness — Fiction
P: 1857, 3980, 4158, 4780, 5086, 6020 **PI:** 5336
I: 8093, 8590

Long Island (NY) — Fiction
I: 9250 **IJ:** 9201, 9682

Loons
P: 19262 **PI:** 19242

Loons — Fiction
PI: 5341

Loons — Folklore
P: 11313

Lopez, Jennifer
PI: 12416 **IJ:** 12415

Lord's Prayer (Bible)
PI: 17528

Lorises (primates)
I: 19007

Los Angeles
I: 16790, 16798, 16822

Los Angeles — Earthquakes
I: 20353

Los Angeles — Fiction
I: 7291, 7344, 7367, 7853
IJ: 8321

Los Angeles — Poetry
P: 11935

Los Angeles Lakers (basketball team)
I: 22135

Los Angeles riot (1992)
IJ: 16498

Los Angeles riot (1992) — Fiction
P: 3059

Loss (concept)
I: 17703

Loudmouths — Fiction
P: 1931

Louis, Joe
IJ: 13586

Louisiana
I: 16861, 16871 **IJ:** 16832, 16865, 16872

Louisiana — Fiction
P: 4718 **I:** 7119, 8471

Louisiana — Folklore
I: 11335

Louisiana — History
IJ: 16239

Louisiana Purchase
I: 16271 **IJ:** 15879, 16229

L'Ouverture, Toussaint
IJ: 13826

Love
See also Romance
P: 17707

Love — Fiction
P: 1119, 1902, 2131
IJ: 10014

Love — Poetry
P: 11523, 11651, 11734
I: 11583 **IJ:** 11563–64, 11704

Love, Nat
P: 12757

Lovelace, Ada King
IJ: 13317

Low, Juliette Gordon
I: 13168

Lowry, Lois
IJ: 12565–66

Lucas, George
IJ: 12417–18

Lucas, John
I: 13547

Lucid, Shannon
I: 12135

Ludington, Sybil
PI: 16189

Luge
PI: 21978

Lullabies
See also Bedtime books; Songs
P: 627, 651, 662, 664, 675, 708, 729–30, 737, 754, 775, 5912, 14175 **IJ:** 14167

Lullabies — African American
P: 793

Luna moths
P: 19556

Lungs
I: 18125 **IJ:** 18126

Luo (African people)
I: 14915

Luxembourg
I: 15401

Lying
P: 10644

Lying — Fiction
P: 1009, 2283, 5042, 6251
PI: 8614, 8732 **I:** 7391
IJ: 7010

Lyme disease
IJ: 17953, 18000, 18010

P = Primary; PI = Primary-Intermediate; I = Intermediate; IJ = Intermediate-Junior High

Lynx
P: 19073, 19091 I: 19080, 19104, 19108

Lyon, George Ella
PI: 12567

Lyon, Mary
IJ: 12929 IJ: 12931–32

M

MacArthur, Douglas
I: 12930 IJ: 12931–32

McAuliffe, Christa
PI: 12137 I: 12136

Macbeth (play)
IJ: 12048

McCain, John
IJ: 12933

McCarthy, Joseph
IJ: 12934

McCarty, Oseola
I: 12758

MacCready, Paul B.
IJ: 12138

McGregor, Ewan
IJ: 12419

McGwire, Mark
PI: 13467 I: 13468
IJ: 13413, 22115

Machines and machinery
See also Simple machines
P: 5571, 5574, 21248,
21252, 21256, 21288, 21293
PI: 21249 I: 21035, 21155,
21244, 21250 IJ: 20068,
21043–44, 21247, 21251

**Machines and machinery
— Experiments and
projects**
PI: 20930 I: 20920

**Machines and machinery
— Fiction**
P: 5551, 5588, 5592
PI: 5586

**Machines and machinery
— History**
IJ: 14599

**Machines and machinery
— Poetry**
P: 5550

Machu Picchu (Peru)
I: 15761, 15788

Mackenzie, Alexander
P: 4760

McKinley, William
IJ: 13080

MacKinnon, Christy
PI: 17922

McKissack, Patricia
PI: 12568

McNair, Ronald
IJ: 12139

McPhail, David
PI: 12569

Madagascar
P: 14995 PI: 14975
IJ: 14966, 14978, 14991,
19012

Madagascar — Animals
I: 18990, 19001 IJ: 19012

Maddux, Greg
I: 13469–70 IJ: 13471

Madison, Dolley
I: 13084, 13169 IJ: 13170

Madison, James
I: 13081, 13083–84
IJ: 13082

**Madison, James —
Fiction**
IJ: 9315

Magarec, Joe
IJ: 11383

Magee, John
IJ: 12570

Magellan, Ferdinand
I: 12060, 12069, 12140–41

Magellan (spacecraft)
I: 20957

Magic tricks
See Magicians and magic

Magicians and magic
P: 10675, 21792
PI: 21779, 21782, 21785
I: 18308, 18368, 21777–78,
21780–81, 21784, 21786–91
IJ: 12403, 21776, 21783

**Magicians and magic —
Biography**
IJ: 12402

**Magicians and magic —
Fiction**
P: 580, 724, 971, 1166,
1175, 1349, 1644, 2097,
2719, 2981, 6188, 10430
PI: 1631, 5662, 7658, 7676,
7781, 8164, 9851 I: 7033,
7428, 7552, 7697, 7986,
8216, 8242, 8323, 9814,
9915, 10158 IJ: 8023, 9026

**Magicians and magic —
Folklore**
PI: 10917 IJ: 10615

Magnesium
IJ: 20291

Magnetism
P: 20893 PI: 20885

**Magnetism —
Experiments and
projects**
P: 20900 PI: 20908
I: 20882, 20896, 20898,
20904, 20906 IJ: 20894

Magritte, Rene
IJ: 13932

Mahy, Margaret
PI: 12571

Mail carriers
P: 3136, 17740

Mail carriers — Fiction
P: 3204, 3542

Maine
PI: 16677 I: 16664, 16671,
19350, 19860 IJ: 16704

Maine — Fiction
P: 3782, 4221, 4491, 5362
PI: 3587, 8026, 8327, 9329,
10026 I: 7536, 8422, 8709,
9553 IJ: 6907, 6941–43,
6948, 8329, 9194, 9212

Maine — History
P: 4850

**Malamutes (dogs) —
Fiction**
IJ: 7531

Malawi
IJ: 14940

Malaysia
P: 15161 IJ: 15185,
15188, 15198

Malaysia — Folklore
P: 10838

Malcolm X
I: 12759–61 IJ: 12762

Mali — Fiction
P: 4887

Mali — Folklore
PI: 10718

Mallory, George
IJ: 12142

Malone, Karl
I: 13548 IJ: 13408

Malta
IJ: 15258

Mammals
See also specific
mammals, e.g., Bears
P: 18939, 18960, 18974,
18978, 19786 PI: 18927,
18969 I: 18611, 18620,
18932, 18957, 19643
IJ: 18943–44

Mammals — Homes
IJ: 18911

Mammoths
IJ: 14419

Man O' War (racehorse)
I: 19991

Manatees
P: 19737, 19739, 19747
PI: 19735 I: 19745, 19750
IJ: 19744

Manatees — Fiction
P: 5123, 5269 IJ: 7059

**Mandan Indians —
Fiction**
IJ: 9402

Mandela, Nelson
PI: 13828, 13830–32
IJ: 13827, 13829

Mandelbaum, Jack
IJ: 14889

Manhattan Project
PI: 21406

Manic depression
IJ: 17989

Manjiro
IJ: 13833

Mankiller, Wilma P.
PI: 12978 I: 12977
IJ: 12976

Manners
P: 2994, 17624, 17639
I: 17634–37 IJ: 17640

**Manners — Colonial
Period (U.S.)**
IJ: 16182

Manners — Fiction
P: 1511, 1893, 4366, 4991
PI: 4269

Manners — History
PI: 17638

Manning, Peyton
IJ: 13618

Manorialism
IJ: 14769

Mantises
See also Praying mantises
I: 19433

Manufacturing
PI: 21039

Manx cats
PI: 19929

**Manzanar (internment
camp) — Fiction**
PI: 4611

Maple sugar and syrup
PI: 16069, 20080 I: 20108

**Maple sugar and syrup —
Fiction**
P: 3067, 3578, 4450

Maps and globes
P: 14329, 14362, 14372
PI: 14369, 14371 I: 14352,
14361, 14367, 18654, 20316
IJ: 14337, 14363–66,
14370, 20326

**Maps and globes —
Experiments and
projects**
PI: 16973

**Maps and globes —
Fiction**
P: 157, 193, 1227, 5299

P = Primary; PI = Primary-Intermediate; I = Intermediate; IJ = Intermediate-Junior High

**Maps and globes —
History**
IJ: 14336, 14368

**Maps and globes —
United States**
I: 15901

Marbles (game)
I: 21986, 22034

Marbles (game) — Fiction
I: 8854

Mardi Gras
PI: 17386 **I:** 17369

Mardi Gras — Fiction
P: 5639, 5650

Marijuana
IJ: 17890

Marine animals
See also Fish; Reptiles;
and specific animals,
e.g., Sharks
P: 5394, 19421, 19629–30,
19635, 19638, 19642,
19644, 19647, 19817, 20020
PI: 19627, 19646, 19816,
19854, 19857, 19864
I: 19623, 19631, 19825,
19833, 19847, 19867, 20374
IJ: 19636–37, 19641,
19648, 19651, 19743, 19844

Marine animals — Babies
P: 19647

**Marine animals —
Defenses**
PI: 19650

Marine animals — Fiction
P: 1046, 4524, 5133
PI: 4504

Marine animals — Hawaii
PI: 19633

Marine animals — Poetry
PI: 11820 **IJ:** 11961

Marine biology
P: 119, 5348, 19624, 19632,
19635, 19653 **PI:** 19622,
19837, 19853 **I:** 18851,
19840, 19860, 20246, 20512
IJ: 19636

**Marine biology —
Biography**
IJ: 13258, 13267

**Marine biology —
Careers**
P: 17843 **PI:** 17826
I: 17834

Marine Corps
See United States Marine
Corps

Marine plants
PI: 19854 **I:** 20374

Marino, Dan
I: 13619

Marionettes
See Puppets and
marionettes

Markets
PI: 16932 **I:** 16933

Markets — Fiction
P: 3118, 3251, 3329, 4766,
4852

Markham, Beryl
I: 12143

Marriage — Fiction
P: 3821, 4136 **PI:** 5625
IJ: 9010

Marriages
See Weddings

Mars (planet)
PI: 18455, 18460, 18472,
18485–86, 18491 **I:** 18467,
18475–76, 18489, 18495,
18497 **IJ:** 18469, 18480,
21020

Marsalis, Wynton
I: 12420–21

Marshal, William
IJ: 13834, 14795

Marshall, Thurgood
PI: 12763–64, 12766–67
IJ: 12765, 12768

Marshes
P: 20372

Marsupials
P: 19178 **I:** 19182
IJ: 18933

**Martha's Vineyard (MA)
— Fiction**
I: 8905

Martí, José J.
IJ: 12572

Martial arts
See also specific martial
arts, e.g., Karate
PI: 22267 **I:** 22273
IJ: 22024, 22269–70, 22274

Martin, Joseph Plumb
I: 16205

Martin, Rafe
I: 12573

Martin, Ricky
PI: 12422

Martin Luther King Day
P: 17337 **PI:** 17387

Martinez, Maria
IJ: 12257

Martinique — Folklore
PI: 11431

**Mary, Mother of Jesus
(Bible)**
P: 17259 **I:** 17251, 17308

Maryland
P: 16844 **PI:** 16955
I: 16868 **IJ:** 16836, 16879

Maryland — Fiction
IJ: 6885, 7491, 7532, 8445,
9502

Maryland Colony
IJ: 16120

Masada, Siege of
I: 14596

**Masada, Siege of —
Fiction**
IJ: 8938

Masai
I: 14921 **IJ:** 14954

Masai — Fiction
PI: 8967

Masai — Folklore
P: 10703

Masks
PI: 21601 **I:** 21603
IJ: 14550, 21602

Masks — Africa
I: 13936

Mason, Biddy
I: 12769

Mason, Bob
I: 18770

Mass (church)
P: 17221

Mass media
I: 21264

Massachusetts
PI: 16678 **IJ:** 16709,
16715

Massachusetts — Fiction
P: 4492, 5448 **PI:** 9196
I: 9265, 9617, 9956, 16757
IJ: 7114, 9209, 9218, 9313,
9335, 16241, 16252

Massachusetts — History
IJ: 16650

Materials
I: 20813

Mathematical puzzles
P: 426, 20610 **PI:** 20596,
20608–9, 20615, 20623
I: 20607, 20611–12,
20618–19, 20622, 20624–25
IJ: 20613, 20616–17,
20620–21

**Mathematical puzzles —
Fiction**
P: 5535

Mathematicians
I: 13276

**Mathematicians —
Biography**
I: 13233–34 **IJ:** 13275,
13317, 13334

Mathematics
See also Mathematical
puzzles; Numbers;
Puzzles; Statistics

P: 472, 507, 20590, 20594
PI: 20578, 20596, 20623,
20632, 20638 **I:** 20588,
20595, 20601, 20630
IJ: 20597, 20599

Mathematics — Careers
IJ: 17761

**Mathematics —
Experiments and
projects**
P: 20598 **I:** 20584
IJ: 20617

Mathematics — Fiction
P: 557, 573, 20587, 20602
PI: 8651 **IJ:** 9983

**Mathematics — Jokes and
riddles**
I: 21834

Mathematics — Poetry
PI: 11602

Mathewson, Christy
I: 13472

Matisse, Henri
PI: 12258 **I:** 13927

Matisse, Henri — Fiction
P: 4729

Matter (physics)
P: 20816 **PI:** 20812
I: 20813 **IJ:** 20802

Matzeliger, Jan
I: 12770

Mauritania
I: 15027

Maximilian, Prince
IJ: 15954

Mayan Indians
P: 15674 **PI:** 15666, 15683
I: 15665, 15680, 15685
IJ: 15603, 15661

Mayan Indians — Fiction
P: 4888 **IJ:** 9131

**Mayan Indians —
Folklore**
P: 11393, 11401, 11412
PI: 11414 **I:** 11395, 11415
IJ: 11411

**Mayan Indians —
Mythology**
IJ: 11446

Mayan Indians — Poetry
I: 11770

***Mayflower* (ship)**
P: 6133 **PI:** 16183

***Mayflower* (ship) —
Fiction**
P: 6142 **I:** 9202 **IJ:** 9211

**Mayo, William and
Charles**
I: 13318–19

Mayo Clinic (MN)
I: 13319

Mays, Osceola
I: 12771

Mays, Willie
P: 13474 I: 13473

Mazes
PI: 21863

Mbundu
IJ: 14942

Mead, Margaret
IJ: 13320–21

Meadows
P: 20536

Meadows — Fiction
P: 4529

Mealtime — Fiction
P: 1363, 2502 PI: 3635

Mealworms
I: 19535

**Measures and
measurement**
See also Concept books —
Measurement
P: 230, 419, 20656
PI: 354, 20581–82,
20658–59 I: 20618

Medical ethics
IJ: 18027

**Medical technicians —
Careers**
P: 17800

Medicine
See also Diseases;
Doctors; Health and
medicine; Illness
P: 6680 I: 18025–26
IJ: 17898, 18022, 18027

Medicine — Biography
I: 13212, 13215
IJ: 13206–7, 13218

Medicine — Careers
P: 17802 PI: 17805

Medicine — Fiction
PI: 4619 I: 7695

Medicine — History
I: 18019–20, 18028
IJ: 14600, 16180, 16220,
18024, 18029, 18032

Medicine — Women
I: 13215

Medieval times
See Middle Ages

Meditations
I: 17517

Mediterranean Sea
I: 19825 IJ: 14594, 19842

**Mediterranean Sea —
History**
I: 14597

**Medusa (Greek
mythology)**
P: 11507

Megalodon
I: 14379

Memorial Day (U.S.)
P: 17338

Memory — Fiction
P: 1642, 2453

Memory books
I: 21450

Menchu, Rigoberta
IJ: 15684

Mendel, Gregor
IJ: 13322

Mendelssohn, Fanny
I: 12332

Mendes, Chico
PI: 13323 IJ: 13216

Mennonites
P: 17197

Mennonites — Fiction
PI: 8563

Menominee Indians
IJ: 15949

Menorahs
P: 17481 PI: 17457

Menstruation
I: 18259, 18263 IJ: 18265

Mental handicaps
See also Depression
(mental state); Dyslexia;
Epilepsy; Learning
disabilities
P: 17928 PI: 17924
I: 17925, 17930 IJ: 17921,
17967

**Mental handicaps —
Biography**
IJ: 13375

**Mental handicaps —
Fiction**
P: 3848, 4957, 5052
PI: 8899, 8918 I: 8897,
8912, 8920, 9265 IJ: 8543,
8644, 8884, 8890, 8913,
8916, 8923, 9645

Mental illness
IJ: 17969, 17981

Mental illness — Fiction
IJ: 8882

Mercury (planet)
PI: 18461 I: 18476, 18498

Mercury (space mission)
PI: 21009

Meredith, James
PI: 12772

Merina
IJ: 14978

Merlin — Fiction
I: 8239

Mermaids — Fiction
P: 1611 PI: 10514
IJ: 7796

Mermaids — Folklore
P: 11379 I: 10597

**Mesa Verde National
Park**
I: 16000, 16040 IJ: 16073

**Mesa Verde National
Park — Fiction**
IJ: 7058

Mesopotamia — History
I: 14655 IJ: 14583, 14642

**Mesquakie Indians —
Fiction**
P: 4863 I: 9184

Messengers — Fiction
P: 3061

Messier, Mark
I: 13700

**Metals — Experiments
and projects**
I: 21258

Metamorphosis
PI: 18663

Meteorites
PI: 18393 I: 18382

Meteorology
See Weather

**Meteorology —
Experiments and
projects**
IJ: 20660

Meteors
PI: 18505, 18525, 18527,
18529, 18534 I: 18503,
18516, 18520

**Metropolitan Museum of
Art (New York, N.Y.)**
I: 13919

Mexican Americans
I: 16760, 16907, 17143
IJ: 17132, 17549, 17580

**Mexican Americans —
Biography**
I: 12828 IJ: 12449, 12460,
12684

**Mexican Americans —
Crafts**
I: 16907, 21615

**Mexican Americans —
Fiction**
P: 3360, 3553, 3676, 3734,
3815, 3902, 4608, 5542,
5709, 5713, 5746, 5920
PI: 3870, 4628, 5038, 5062,
7520 I: 6930, 6935, 7291,
7344, 7347, 7373, 7376,
8821, 9445–46, 11653,
17576 IJ: 7374, 9462, 9620

**Mexican Americans —
Folklore**
IJ: 11323

**Mexican Americans —
Holidays — Fiction**
P: 3523

**Mexican Americans —
Poetry**
I: 11708

Mexican War (1846–1848)
I: 16254

Mexico
P: 15602, 15604, 15630
PI: 15611, 15614,
15616–17, 15623–26,
15629, 15640, 15666, 17216
I: 15618, 15621–22,
15637–38, 15641,
15646–47, 15651, 15653,
15685 IJ: 15599, 15627,
15634, 15643–44, 15650

Mexico — Animals
PI: 15619

Mexico — Biography
IJ: 12244, 13865

Mexico — Christmas
P: 5783

Mexico — Cookbooks
IJ: 21685

Mexico — Crafts
P: 15601 I: 15638, 21503
IJ: 15615

Mexico — Fiction
P: 1180, 3734, 4575, 4637,
4648–49, 4653, 4699, 4719,
4746, 4759, 4836, 5057,
5622, 5634, 5684, 5810,
6510 PI: 4628, 5628, 9140
I: 6935 IJ: 7092

Mexico — Folklore
P: 5793, 11392–93, 11396,
11402–3, 11406 PI: 11399,
11407, 11410 I: 7745,
11394–95, 11397, 11409
IJ: 11434

Mexico — History
PI: 11404, 13818, 15605,
15636, 15654 I: 13817,
15607–8, 15612–13, 15639,
15642, 15648, 15655
IJ: 12293, 13864, 15620,
15631, 15649, 15652

Mexico — Holidays
PI: 15633 I: 15600, 15621,
15628 IJ: 17366

Mexico — Poetry
P: 11612 PI: 11526

Mexico — Writers
I: 12557

Mexico City
I: 15612, 15651

Miami
PI: 16848

**Miami Dolphins (football
team)**
IJ: 22180

Mice
P: 19195 PI: 19206

Mice — Fiction
P: 311, 425, 602, 919,
925–26, 1764, 1851, 1898,
1935, 1977–78, 2040, 2090,
2185, 2193–97, 2258, 2323,
2370, 2378, 2382, 2384–85,
2387, 2402, 2413, 2500,
2538, 2543, 2555, 2605,
2716–17, 2781, 2816, 2819,
4361, 5114, 5233, 5613,
6022, 6189, 6405, 6466–67,
6552 **PI:** 7966, 8200, 9765,
9804 **I:** 7698, 7826, 8126,
8148, 8174 **IJ:** 7823, 7827,
9912

Mice — Folklore
P: 10818, 10957, 11053,
11301

Mice — Nursery rhymes
P: 852

Mice — Poetry
PI: 11972

Michelangelo
PI: 12259, 12262 **I:** 12260
IJ: 12261, 14798

Michelangelo — Fiction
P: 4792

Michigan
PI: 16551, 16583 **I:** 16560

Michigan — Fiction
PI: 8922, 9455 **IJ:** 9333,
9456, 9475

Michigan — History
I: 16592

**Micmac Indians —
Folklore**
I: 11296

Microbiology
See Microscopes and
microbiology

Micronesia
I: 15237

Microorganisms
I: 18055

**Microscopes and
microbiology**
P: 19810 **PI:** 19812
I: 19805, 19811
IJ: 19807–9, 19813

**Microscopes and
microbiology —
Biography**
IJ: 13340

**Microscopes and
microbiology —
Experiments and
projects**
I: 19806 **IJ:** 18300

**Microsoft (company) —
Biography**
I: 13297

Midas, King
P: 11491

Middle Ages
P: 14753, 14763, 14784
PI: 14752 **I:** 13946,
14754–56, 14764–65,
14771–72, 14777–79,
14781, 14786–87, 14789,
14791–92, 14794, 14796,
15364 **IJ:** 13947,
14758–59, 14762,
14766–70, 14773–76,
14782–83, 14793, 21587

**Middle Ages —
Biography**
IJ: 13735, 13767, 13834,
14795

**Middle Ages — Cities and
towns**
IJ: 14768–69

Middle Ages — Crafts
I: 14760

Middle Ages — Fiction
P: 919, 4660, 5835, 6440
PI: 1593, 9071, 9083, 9120
I: 7577, 7631, 8075, 8211,
8239, 9055, 9066, 9104,
9115, 9118 **IJ:** 7560, 7760,
7969, 8161, 9026, 9040,
9048, 9067, 9085, 9090,
9095, 9100, 9113, 9117,
9119, 9121, 9125, 9127

Middle Ages — Folklore
PI: 10991 **I:** 10544, 10596,
10997 **IJ:** 11024–25, 11037

Middle Ages — Food
IJ: 14761

**Middle Ages —
Mythology**
PI: 60

Middle Ages — Women
IJ: 14780

Middle East
I: 15491 **IJ:** 15494

Middle East — Folklore
P: 11185, 11197

Midwest (U.S.)
See also specific states,
e.g., Wisconsin
I: 16530

Midwest (U.S.) — Fiction
I: 8003, 9929

Midwest (U.S.) — Floods
IJ: 20685

Midwest (U.S.) — History
P: 12842 **PI:** 12845
IJ: 12900

Midwest (U.S.) — Poetry
PI: 11696

Migrant workers
I: 17135, 17143 **IJ:** 16488,
17132

**Migrant workers —
Biography**
I: 12548 **IJ:** 12826

**Migrant workers —
Fiction**
P: 3331, 3476, 4899, 4905,
5103 **I:** 7436

**Migrations (bird) —
Fiction**
P: 5290

**Mijikenda (African
people)**
IJ: 14955

Milano, Alyssa
PI: 12423

Milk
P: 20054, 20085, 20110
PI: 20122 **I:** 20105

Milk — Fiction
P: 313

Milking machines
P: 20071

Milky Way
I: 18392

Mill workers — Fiction
IJ: 9267

Millennium
I: 14346

Miller, Reggie
IJ: 13549

Miller, Shannon
IJ: 13701

Miller, Tom
PI: 12263

Millipedes
I: 19618

Mills
IJ: 16261

Milwaukee
I: 15982

Mimbres (Indian people)
I: 15935

Minerals
See Rocks and minerals

Minerals (food)
PI: 20163

Mines and mining
PI: 21030

**Mines and mining —
Fiction**
P: 6712 **I:** 9513

**Mines and mining —
History**
I: 16329

Minnesota
I: 16540, 16575, 16585
IJ: 12577, 16561, 16581

Minnesota — Animals
P: 18610

Minnesota — Fiction
P: 3578, 4763 **PI:** 7248,
9621 **I:** 7854, 9437–38,
9444 **IJ:** 8783, 9593

Minnesota — Folklore
PI: 11357 **I:** 11365, 11373

Minnesota — History
P: 16481 **IJ:** 16027, 16541

Minoans — History
I: 14522

Minor leagues (baseball)
I: 22123

Minotaur (mythology)
PI: 11483 **I:** 11472

**Minutemen (U.S.) —
Fiction**
PI: 4593

Miró, Joan
IJ: 13877

Mirrors
I: 20868

**Mirrors — Experiments
and projects**
IJ: 20878

Miss America pageant
IJ: 14264

Missionaries — Fiction
IJ: 7020

Missions — California
I: 16758, 16763, 16766,
16824

**Mississauga Indians —
Folklore**
PI: 11225

Mississippi River
PI: 15908, 20519 **I:** 12608,
15891, 15904, 18784
IJ: 16574, 20705

**Mississippi River —
Biography**
PI: 12130

**Mississippi River —
Fiction**
P: 3911, 8586 **I:** 6825,
6988, 8088 **IJ:** 8457, 10007

**Mississippi River —
Floods**
PI: 16531

Mississippi (state)
P: 16859 **I:** 16880

**Mississippi (state) —
Fiction**
P: 3568 **IJ:** 7526, 8775,
9521

Missouri River
PI: 15908, 20519

Missouri (state)
PI: 16552 **I:** 16568
IJ: 16562

Missouri (state) — Fiction
I: 7455, 9404–5 **IJ:** 9375

Mitchell, Jackie
P: 22111

Mitchell, Maria
I: 13324

P = Primary; PI = Primary-Intermediate; I = Intermediate; IJ = Intermediate-Junior High

Mitchell, Maria — Fiction
P: 4685

Miwok Indians — Folklore
P: 11236 PI: 11298

Mixed marriages (religion) — Fiction
I: 8564

Moceanu, Dominique
I: 13703 IJ: 13702

Mockingbirds — Fiction
P: 616

Model making
PI: 21793 I: 21531, 21796 IJ: 21794

Models (fashion) — Biography
IJ: 12352

Models (fashion) — Fiction
IJ: 10326

Modoc Indians — Folklore
PI: 11300

Mogal Empire — Folklore
PI: 10807

Mohawk Indians
P: 15946 I: 15960

Mohawk Indians — Fiction
P: 3337 IJ: 9192

Mohawk Indians — Prayers
P: 11305

Mohican Indians — Fiction
IJ: 9191

Molasses — Fiction
P: 3803

Moldova
I: 15416 IJ: 15425, 15433

Molds (fungi)
IJ: 20189

Moles — Fiction
P: 2114, 2499, 5300 IJ: 7753

Moles — Folklore
IJ: 11438

Mollusks
P: 19610 IJ: 18924

Monarch butterflies
P: 19551, 19557 I: 19558, 19565, 19567

Monarch butterflies — Fiction
P: 1493, 4549

Monarch butterflies — Plays
PI: 12039

Monet, Claude
P: 13904 PI: 12264, 12266–67 I: 12265

Monet, Claude — Fiction
P: 1039, 2743, 13876 I: 9053

Money
P: 16918 PI: 2988, 16920, 20636 I: 16924, 16927, 16931 IJ: 16942

Money — Fiction
P: 1596, 3195, 6706 PI: 2352 I: 6867, 7623

Money — History
PI: 16926 IJ: 16929

Money-making ideas
PI: 16940, 16944 I: 16941 IJ: 16939, 16942, 16946

Money-making ideas — Fiction
P: 2460, 4364 PI: 8299, 9866 I: 8759, 8768, 8774, 9848, 9935 IJ: 8371, 8696, 8860, 9973

Mongolia
PI: 15196 I: 15093 IJ: 15149, 15192

Mongolia — Crafts
IJ: 15209

Mongolia — Folklore
P: 10737

Mongooses — Fiction
P: 1309

Monhegan Island (ME)
I: 16664

Monk, Thelonious
I: 12424

Monkeys
P: 18993, 18997 PI: 18921, 18994 I: 18998, 19008

Monkeys — Fiction
P: 118, 265, 405–6, 1644, 1716, 2623, 2626, 3352–53, 3848, 4319, 4783, 6492 PI: 2624 I: 7290, 8091, 8093, 8351, 9917

Monkeys — Folklore
P: 10792, 10847, 11444

Monologues — Anthologies
IJ: 12019, 12038

Mononucleosis
IJ: 18005

Monplaisir, Sharon
IJ: 13704

Monroe, James
P: 13086 I: 13085

Monsters
P: 21964 PI: 60 I: 21558, 21947, 21956 IJ: 21891

Monsters — Crafts
PI: 21492

Monsters — Fiction
See also Fantasy; Folklore; Mythology; Supernatural; Tall tales
P: 579, 670, 704, 707, 759, 812, 1095, 1137, 1150, 1156, 1173–74, 1204, 1257–58, 1294, 1406, 1499, 1525, 1560, 2596, 2726, 4341, 6053, 6565 PI: 2352, 7949, 10162 I: 7678 IJ: 7049, 10217

Monsters — Mythology
PI: 11471, 11482–83 I: 11472, 11488

Monsters — Poetry
P: 1155, 1161 PI: 11675, 11735

Montana
PI: 16071, 16608 I: 16619, 16623, 16787 IJ: 16614

Montana — Fiction
I: 14435

Montana — History
I: 16012 IJ: 16057

Montana, Joe
I: 13621 IJ: 13620

Montessori, Maria
I: 13835 IJ: 13836

Monteverde Cloud Forest (Costa Rica)
PI: 20434

Montezuma
PI: 11404

Montgomery (AL)
PI: 12776 I: 12775

Montgomery bus boycott
I: 16524

Months
See also Calendars

Months — Fiction
P: 4308, 4452, 4508, 4550

Months — Poetry
P: 11968

Months — Prayers
P: 17530

Monticello (VA)
PI: 16884 I: 16849, 16882 IJ: 16899

Montreal
I: 15593

Montreal Canadiens (hockey team)
I: 22210

Monuments
P: 21127

Moon
P: 784, 12073, 18442, 18444, 18522 PI: 18440–41, 18446–47,

18450, 18452, 21013 I: 18443, 18448–49, 18451, 18453–54, 20969, 20991 IJ: 20974, 21016, 21018

Moon — Experiments and projects
I: 18445

Moon — Fiction
P: 573, 638, 747, 1037, 1289, 1632, 1758, 1762, 3079, 3877, 4388, 4540, 4673, 6210 PI: 7017, 7968, 10511 I: 8033

Moon — Folklore
P: 11211 PI: 10722 I: 10563, 10619

Moon — Poetry
PI: 11561

Moons
PI: 18506

Moore, Henry
PI: 12269 I: 12268

Moose
I: 19150, 19152, 19155

Moose — Fiction
P: 1736, 2346, 2401, 2537, 5121, 5240, 5284, 5419, 6721

Moral education
P: 3022

Moray eels
PI: 19645

Morgan, Ann
I: 13325

Mormons — Biography
I: 12969–70

Mormons — Fiction
P: 4668, 4866 I: 9558, 9585

Morocco
PI: 14964 I: 14958 IJ: 14956, 14963

Morocco — Fiction
P: 4734

Morris, Samuel
I: 13837

Morrison, Toni
I: 12574

Morton, J. Sterling
I: 13326

Mosaics
IJ: 13938

Mosaics — Crafts
I: 21436

Moscow
I: 15422

Moses, Grandma
IJ: 12270

Moses (Bible)
P: 17241, 17283, 17287, 17293, 17311 PI: 17242,

P = Primary; PI = Primary-Intermediate; I = Intermediate; IJ = Intermediate-Junior High

17269 **I:** 17322, 17328
IJ: 17255

Moses (Bible) — Fiction
I: 8963

Mosques
P: 17236 **I:** 15492

Mosquitoes
P: 19424

Mosquitoes — Fiction
P: 4318

Mosquitoes — Folklore
P: 10644

Moss, Cynthia
I: 13327

Moss, Randy
IJ: 13622

Mother Goose
See also Nursery rhymes
P: 2, 822, 824, 827, 830,
838–39, 843, 850, 853,
861–62, 866–73, 877–80,
883, 885, 887, 889, 894,
904–5 **I:** 11872

Mother Goose —
Cookbooks
P: 21719

Mothers
P: 3744, 3819

Mothers — Fiction
P: 3246, 3545, 3737, 3785,
3796, 3891, 3900, 3913,
3955, 5070, 5073 **IJ:** 8571

Mothers — Folklore
I: 10548

Mothers — Poetry
P: 11655 **I:** 11745
IJ: 11740

Mother's Day — Fiction
P: 5609, 5613

Moths
P: 19556, 19566, 19569
I: 19541–42, 19547, 19564

Motion (physics)
PI: 20823, 20839 **I:** 20818,
20829 **IJ:** 20832

Motion (physics) —
Experiments and
projects
P: 20833 **PI:** 20825
IJ: 20828

Motion pictures
See also Animation
(motion pictures);
Hollywood
PI: 21274 **I:** 12228, 12387,
21267, 21270, 21277
IJ: 12225, 12875, 21268,
21271, 21275

Motion pictures —
Biography
PI: 12685 **I:** 12427, 12456,
12473–74 **IJ:** 12367,

12405, 12411–12,
12417–18, 12475–76

Motion pictures —
Careers
IJ: 12498, 21273

Motion pictures — Fiction
PI: 6285 **I:** 9542
IJ: 7801, 9569

Motion pictures —
History
I: 14309, 14311 **IJ:** 14312,
14879

Motion pictures —
Theaters
P: 21269

Motorcycles
I: 22240, 22242 **IJ:** 22241

Motorcycles — Fiction
PI: 9804 **I:** 10299

Mount, William Sidney
I: 12271

Mount Everest
PI: 22025, 22030 **I:** 21995
IJ: 12124, 22047

Mount Everest —
Biography
IJ: 12123, 12142

Mount Rushmore (SD)
I: 16542, 16545, 16580

Mount St. Helens (WA)
PI: 20339

Mount St. Helens (WA) —
Fiction
I: 7855 **IJ:** 7066

Mount Vernon (VA)
I: 16840, 16883

Mountain and rock
climbing
PI: 22025, 22030 **I:** 21995
IJ: 22047

Mountain and rock
climbing — Biography
IJ: 12123–24, 12142

Mountain and rock
climbing — Women
I: 12062

Mountain biking
I: 22160 **IJ:** 22153–54,
22159, 22164

Mountain biking —
Fiction
IJ: 10305

Mountain goats
PI: 18977

Mountain lions
I: 19114

Mountain States (U.S.)
See also specific states,
e.g., Colorado

Mountaineering
See Mountain and rock
climbing

Mountains
P: 20508 **PI:** 19415,
20330, 20497, 20503, 20505
I: 20496, 20500–1, 20504,
20509 **IJ:** 20498–99,
20506–7

Mountains — Animals
PI: 20502

Mountains — Fiction
P: 4215, 4509

Mourning, Alonzo
I: 13551 **IJ:** 13550

Moving — Fiction
P: 1935, 2788, 3006, 3247,
3615, 3978, 4314, 4943,
5019, 6349, 6591 **PI:** 7404,
8330, 9825, 9891 **I:** 7177,
7436, 8422, 8512, 9629,
9875, 9956 **IJ:** 3928, 7452,
7533, 8567

Mozambique — Fiction
I: 8962

Mozart, Wolfgang
Amadeus
P: 12334 **PI:** 12333, 12335
IJ: 12336

Mud
I: 20303

Mud — Fiction
P: 4514

Mugabe, Robert
IJ: 13838

Muhammad
See Islam

Muir, John
PI: 13329 **I:** 13330
IJ: 13216, 13328, 21459

Mules — Fiction
P: 1720, 4311

Mullin, Chris
IJ: 13552

Multimedia — Careers
IJ: 17790

Multiple births
I: 18241

Multiple sclerosis
IJ: 18008

Multiplication
(mathematics)
P: 372, 20592 **PI:** 20586

Multiplication
(mathematics) —
Fiction
P: 537

Multiracial families —
Fiction
P: 3925

Mummies
P: 14647 **PI:** 14553,
14603, 14648 **I:** 14515,
14533, 14620, 14628, 14669
IJ: 14501, 14517, 14535,
14548, 14659, 17230

Mummies — Fiction
I: 8046

Municipal government
(U.S.)
I: 17131

Munoz Marin, Luis
I: 12936 **IJ:** 12935

Murals
IJ: 13884

Murder — Fiction
IJ: 7424

Murrell, Melville
P: 13331

Muscles
I: 18166, 18169, 18172,
18176 **IJ:** 18167, 18170,
18173

Muscular dystrophy —
Fiction
I: 8908

Museums
I: 13919, 17104

Museums — Careers
P: 17755

Museums — Fiction
P: 3048, 4115, 6400
I: 6797 **IJ:** 6925, 7640

Mushrooms
P: 20187, 20190 **PI:** 20188
IJ: 20189

Mushrooms — Fiction
P: 2742

Music
See also Christmas —
Songs and carols;
Composers —
Biography; Folk songs;
Musical instruments;
Opera; Rock music and
musicians — Biography;
Songs; Spirituals;
specific instruments,
e.g., Trumpets; and as a
subdivision under
country names, e.g.,
Caribbean Islands —
Music
IJ: 14119, 14127, 14132,
14135, 14137

Music — Careers
P: 17771 **PI:** 17783
IJ: 17775, 17778

Music — Experiments
and projects
I: 14229, 20940

Music — Fiction
P: 1603, 2321, 3103, 3374,
3470, 3519, 3580, 3605,
3649, 3770, 4214, 4222,
4230, 4621, 4631, 4636,
4711, 4944, 4952, 4994,
5016, 5055 **PI:** 1021, 9031
I: 8328, 8498

P = Primary; PI = Primary-Intermediate; I = Intermediate; IJ = Intermediate-Junior High

Music — History
I: 14134

Music — Popular
IJ: 14122–23

Music appreciation
P: 14124

Musical instruments
See also specific
 instruments, e.g., Violins
P: 14219, 14222–23, 14227
PI: 14220, 14225, 14228
I: 14218, 14229 IJ: 14119,
 14224, 14226, 14230

Musical instruments — Fiction
P: 1294, 4162, 4982

Musical instruments — Folklore
I: 10528

Musical theater
I: 14321

Musicians — Biography
P: 12379 PI: 12347, 12355
I: 12181, 12337, 12420–21,
 12424 IJ: 12184, 12323,
 12338, 12348, 12356,
 12397, 12445 All: 12349

Muskogee Indians
I: 16014

Muslims
See Islam

Mustangs (horses)
P: 5389, 20008 I: 19983

Mutism — Fiction
PI: 8997 I: 8873, 8892
IJ: 6926, 8150

Myanmar (Burma)
I: 15175 IJ: 15205, 15217

Myanmar (Burma) — Folklore
P: 10725

Mystery stories
See also Adventure stories
P: 1965, 2766, 2830, 2914,
 2920, 2943, 5191, 5992,
 6179–83, 6188, 6201, 6211,
 6220, 6298–300, 6343,
 6347, 6446, 6455, 6457,
 6491, 6501, 6563, 6571,
 6579, 6592, 6600, 6627,
 6647–51, 6653, 6665–66,
 6681, 6731, 6764, 6811,
 6932, 7080, 10088
PI: 2608, 6232, 6269, 6356,
 6456, 6458, 6729–30,
 6732–38, 6750, 6785,
 6792–93, 6795–96, 6801,
 6810, 6839, 6845, 6859,
 6883, 6887, 6889, 6901,
 6908, 6910, 6938, 6944–47,
 6953, 6961–65, 6973,
 6976–79, 6990, 6998, 7000,
 7014, 7037–38, 7042–45,
 7123, 7132, 7778, 7883–84,
 7992, 8059, 8352, 9328,
 9744 I: 6727, 6740, 6747,

6754, 6756, 6758–59,
6761–63, 6775–76, 6778,
6781–84, 6790, 6799, 6803,
6809, 6813, 6819, 6830,
6835–36, 6838, 6847, 6858,
6860–64, 6866–67, 6884,
6890–92, 6899, 6903–4,
6911, 6917, 6923, 6929–31,
6933, 6935–36, 6939, 6950,
6960, 6972, 6974, 6981,
6983–84, 6986, 6991, 7012,
7021–22, 7024, 7026, 7028,
7031–33, 7040, 7050,
7055–56, 7060, 7062–63,
7071–75, 7081, 7085,
7088–90, 7095, 7109, 7115,
7117–19, 7125, 7129, 7131,
7133, 7139, 7141, 7143,
7366, 7558, 7650, 7703,
7726, 7777, 7779, 7813,
7903, 7951, 7960, 7983,
8028, 8096, 9054, 9302,
9365, 9515, 9575, 9644,
9886, 9889, 9971, 10108,
10232, 16154 IJ: 6748,
6751, 6755, 6777, 6780,
6804–5, 6807, 6812, 6815,
6818, 6821–22, 6832, 6870,
6872–73, 6882, 6893, 6912,
6914–15, 6924, 6926–27,
6937, 6942–43, 6956,
6966–67, 6992, 6994, 7007,
7010, 7019, 7023, 7025,
7029, 7036, 7046, 7048–49,
7059, 7061, 7064, 7070,
7079, 7084, 7091, 7107,
7110, 7114, 7116, 7122,
7127, 7130, 7134, 7137,
7142, 7212, 7605, 7649,
7651, 7889, 7982, 8098,
8251, 8276, 8568, 9026,
9361, 9392, 9483, 9657,
9764, 9905, 10243, 10355

Mystery stories — Poetry
I: 6767

Mythology
See also specific
 mythological beings,
 e.g., Athena
 (mythology); as
 subdivision under other
 subjects, e.g., Animals
 — Mythology; and as
 subdivision of specific
 countries, e.g., Greece
 — Mythology
I: 10574, 11457–58
IJ: 11448, 11450, 11454–56

Mythology — Anthologies
P: 11449 I: 11451, 11467,
 11470, 11485, 11488–89,
 11499 IJ: 11447, 11478

Mythology — Art
I: 13899

Mythology — Celts
I: 11452

Mythology — Egypt
I: 11453

Mythology — Greece
P: 11069, 11072, 11074,
 11469, 11500 PI: 11073,
 11463, 11495, 11502
I: 11067, 11459, 11479–80,
 11513 IJ: 11462

Mythology — Greece — Fiction
I: 8072

Mythology — Mayan Indians
IJ: 11446

Mythology — Plays
I: 12029

Mythology — Rome
I: 11490

N

Naked mole rats
I: 19198

Names — Fiction
P: 5494 PI: 6420, 7331
I: 9901

Names — Folklore
P: 10766, 11419

Names project (AIDS)
I: 17943

Namibia
IJ: 14970, 14986, 15004

Nantucket (MA) — Fiction
IJ: 9324

Narragansett Indians — Holidays
P: 6146

Nash, Kevin
IJ: 13705

Nashville
PI: 16874

Nast, Thomas
I: 12273 IJ: 12272

Natchez Trail — Fiction
IJ: 9341

National Aeronautics and Space Administration (U.S.)
I: 20991 IJ: 20950

National Basketball Association
IJ: 22144

National debt
I: 17123

National Football League
IJ: 22179

National Gallery (Washington, DC)
IJ: 13964

National Law Enforcement Officers Memorial (Washington, DC)
IJ: 16646

National Mall (Washington, DC)
I: 16699

National monuments (U.S.)
I: 15857

National Museum of American Art
I: 13955

National Park Service — Careers
P: 17747

National parks (U.S.)
See also specific national
 parks, e.g., Yellowstone
 National Park
P: 16631, 16801, 16957
I: 15909, 15916, 16595

Native Americans
See also Inuit; and specific
 Indian tribes, e.g.,
 Arapaho Indians
P: 4697, 15945–46, 15952,
 15956, 15976, 16019,
 16021, 16050–51, 16053
PI: 8946, 14518, 15654,
 15683, 15917, 15922,
 15968, 15970, 15973,
 15978, 15995–96, 16006,
 16010, 16016–18, 16020,
 16034, 16048–49, 16052,
 16054, 16058, 16061,
 16064, 16069, 16071, 16185
I: 15648, 15653, 15685,
 15807, 15919–20, 15924,
 15934, 15947, 15955,
 15960–61, 15966,
 15971–72, 15974–75,
 15977, 15980–83, 15994,
 15997, 16000–1, 16003–4,
 16012–15, 16022, 16024,
 16026, 16029–31,
 16044–46, 16056, 16063,
 16072, 16170, 16817, 20226
IJ: 9402, 14495, 14844,
 15603, 15631, 15649,
 15925–26, 15928–31,
 15933, 15939–41, 15949,
 15957, 15959, 15963,
 15985, 15990, 15992–93,
 15998–99, 16002, 16005,
 16023, 16027, 16041, 16297

Native Americans — Alphabet
P: 136

Native Americans — Anthologies
IJ: 9163

Native Americans — Art
PI: 13942 I: 12203, 13941
IJ: 15984

P = Primary; PI = Primary-Intermediate; I = Intermediate; IJ = Intermediate-Junior High

**Native Americans —
Biography**
P: 12987–88, 12998
PI: 12978, 12999, 13001
I: 12414, 12477, 12531,
12664, 12971–73, 12977,
12979, 12982–84, 12986,
12989–94, 12996–97,
13268, 13675, 13817
IJ: 12235, 12634,
12974–76, 12980, 12985,
12995, 13000, 13674

**Native Americans —
Childhood**
IJ: 15933

**Native Americans —
Children**
IJ: 16068

**Native Americans —
Cookbooks**
IJ: 15963

**Native Americans —
Crafts**
P: 21518 **PI:** 21526
I: 13928, 16039, 21507,
21528

**Native Americans —
Dances**
I: 15943

**Native Americans —
Festivals**
P: 16007

**Native Americans —
Fiction**
P: 449, 682, 758, 1196,
1602, 1651, 1721, 1817,
2824, 2931, 3016, 3318,
3337, 3414, 3434, 3930,
4448, 4558, 4564, 4588,
4651, 4665, 4720, 4811,
4826, 4863, 4870, 4873,
4936, 6564, 9177, 11281
PI: 4749, 5187, 7351, 7353,
8757, 8850, 9147, 9149–51,
9165, 9169–70, 9181, 9394,
11247, 11261 **I:** 6769,
6824, 6828, 6895, 7052,
7340, 7902, 9143–45, 9153,
9155, 9161–62, 9168,
9172–73, 9175–76, 9178,
9184, 9210, 9350, 9381,
9385, 11216 **IJ:** 6855,
6951, 6997, 7065, 7365,
7586, 7737, 8434, 8528,
8947, 9146, 9148, 9152,
9154, 9156–60, 9164, 9166,
9174, 9179, 9182–83, 9193,
9201, 9208, 9238, 9431,
9439, 9454, 9489, 9492,
9529, 15937

**Native Americans —
Folklore**
P: 9167, 11210–11, 11218,
11221, 11223, 11227,
11229, 11231–32, 11234,
11236, 11239, 11241–43,
11245, 11252, 11259–60,
11264, 11266, 11271,
11278–79, 11284–85,

11287–89, 11292, 11294,
11297, 11301, 11308–13,
11316, 11318–19, 11393,
11401, 11408, 11425
PI: 11213–15, 11219,
11225, 11228, 11230,
11237, 11240, 11244,
11249, 11253–54, 11256,
11262–63, 11267–69,
11273, 11275–76, 11283,
11286, 11291, 11293,
11295, 11298, 11300,
11303, 11306, 11314–15,
11321, 11929, 13944
I: 11212, 11222, 11224,
11226, 11233, 11235,
11238, 11246, 11251,
11255, 11265, 11270,
11272, 11274, 11290,
11296, 11302, 11304,
11307, 11317, 11320,
11322, 11376, 21738
IJ: 11217, 11220, 11248,
11250, 11257–58, 11277,
11280, 11282, 11299, 11323

Native Americans — Food
P: 16008

**Native Americans —
History**
P: 15951, 15988
PI: 15936, 15938, 15950,
15964, 15989, 16059
I: 15923, 15935, 15942,
15953, 15965, 15986–87,
15991, 16011, 16025,
16032, 16035, 16040,
16042–43, 16060, 16062,
16123, 16344 **IJ:** 15921,
15927, 15932, 15948,
15954, 15962, 15967,
15979, 16028, 16033,
16055, 16057, 16065–67,
16070, 16073–74, 16159

**Native Americans —
Holidays**
P: 6146

**Native Americans —
Homes**
I: 15918

**Native Americans —
Houses**
PI: 16036 **I:** 16037–38

**Native Americans —
Jokes and riddles**
PI: 21814

**Native Americans —
Medicine**
IJ: 18032

**Native Americans —
Plays**
PI: 12013

**Native Americans —
Poetry**
P: 11641 **PI:** 11929, 14253
I: 11770, 11932 **IJ:** 11931,
11933

**Native Americans —
Prayers**
P: 11305

**Native Americans —
Schools**
IJ: 15940

**Native Americans —
Ships and boats**
IJ: 15944

**Native Americans —
Songs**
P: 814 **IJ:** 11931

**Native Americans —
Sports**
P: 16009

Natural disasters
IJ: 20295, 20308

Naturalists — Biography
I: 13268, 13303, 13325
IJ: 12617

Nature
P: 68, 4445 **I:** 21560
IJ: 16916

Nature — Art
P: 13873

Nature — Crafts
PI: 21460 **I:** 21432
All: 21458

Nature — Fiction
P: 691, 3099, 4371, 4376,
4381–82, 4406, 4408, 4427,
4435, 4440, 4496, 4500,
4505, 4517, 4527, 4529,
4533, 4541, 4547–48, 4558,
4560, 5205, 5360, 5441,
6320 **PI:** 4479, 5231
IJ: 7282

Nature — Folklore
P: 11135 **I:** 10578

Nature — Photography
I: 21801

Nature — Poetry
P: 11788, 11821, 11936,
11941, 11943, 11951,
11965, 11975, 11978, 11984
PI: 11796, 11942,
11953–54, 11966–67,
11972, 11977 **I:** 11938,
11946–47, 11952, 11955,
11971, 11973, 11980,
11986, 11989 **IJ:** 11961,
11990, 310, 4375, 4384,
4515, 4521, 18824
PI: 12583, 18578, 18584,
18588, 18591, 19871, 20518
I: 16953, 18577, 18582–83,
18585, 18597, 18662

"Nature Boy" (wrestling)
IJ: 22022, 310, 4375, 4384,
4515, 4521, 18824
PI: 12583, 18578, 18584,
18588, 18591, 19871, 20518
I: 16953, 18577, 18582–83,
18585, 18597, 18662

Nature study
P: 238, 310, 4375, 4384,
4515, 4521, 18824
PI: 12583, 18578, 18584,
18588, 18591, 19871, 20518
I: 16953, 18577, 18582–83,
18585, 18597, 18662

**Nature study —
Experiments and
projects**
I: 18299 **IJ:** 18323, 18580

Navajo Indians
P: 16050 **PI:** 15917,
16017, 16020 **I:** 15974,
16030–31 **IJ:** 15962

Navajo Indians — Fiction
P: 136, 1817, 2931, 4039,
4651, 4811, 4826 **PI:** 4618,
8757, 9165, 9181 **I:** 9144
IJ: 7365, 7648, 8421, 9182,
9489

**Navajo Indians —
Folklore**
P: 11259 **PI:** 11286, 13944

Navels
See Bellybuttons

Navy, Caryn
PI: 13332

Nazi Germany — Fiction
I: 8902 **IJ:** 9078, 9670

Nazis
See Germany — History;
Holocaust; Nazi
Germany; World War II

Ndebele (African people)
IJ: 15000

**Ndebele (African people)
— Art**
P: 13872

Nebraska
I: 16576

Nebraska — Fiction
I: 7039, 9619 **IJ:** 8669,
9532

Needlecrafts — Fiction
P: 3126

Negro League baseball
IJ: 22091

**Negro League baseball —
Fiction**
I: 10322 **IJ:** 10353

Neighborhoods — Fiction
P: 1317, 4914

Nelson, Gaylord
IJ: 17360

Nepal
I: 15174 **IJ:** 15151, 15164

Neptune (planet)
PI: 18462, 18496, 18499
I: 18478, 18481 **IJ:** 18492

P = Primary; PI = Primary-Intermediate; I = Intermediate; IJ = Intermediate-Junior High

Nervous system
P: 18121 **PI:** 18122
I: 18109, 18113–14, 18120
IJ: 18112, 18115, 18119

Netherlands
IJ: 14886, 15398

Netherlands — Crafts
PI: 15402

Netherlands — Fiction
P: 4577, 4670 **I:** 7265,
9032, 9042, 9688 **IJ:** 9683,
9685, 9695

Netherlands — Folklore
P: 10856

Netherlands — Holidays
PI: 15402

Nevada
P: 16615 **I:** 16625
IJ: 16642

Nevada — Fiction
I: 7234 **IJ:** 9392

New Deal
IJ: 16454

New England
See also specific states,
e.g., Massachusetts

New England — Fiction
P: 4674, 5800, 5831
PI: 9850 **I:** 6775 **IJ:** 7416

New Hampshire
P: 16668 **PI:** 16679
I: 16659, 16716 **IJ:** 16741

**New Hampshire —
Fiction**
I: 7440, 9703 **IJ:** 9262

New Hampshire Colony
I: 16121

New Jersey
PI: 16680 **I:** 16685
IJ: 16652, 16721, 16742

New Jersey — Fiction
P: 3284 **PI:** 9233 **I:** 7482,
9568, 9783, 9967 **IJ:** 9973

New Jersey — History
PI: 16752

New Jersey Colony
IJ: 16122

**New Kids on the Block
(rock group)**
IJ: 12425

New Mexico
PI: 15973, 16906 **I:** 15980,
16901, 16904 **IJ:** 16912

New Mexico — Fiction
P: 5920 **I:** 9354, 9445–46,
9558

New Mexico — Folklore
IJ: 11323

New Mexico — History
I: 16287

New Orleans
PI: 16876

New Orleans — Fiction
P: 3420, 4766 **IJ:** 9275

New Stone Age
IJ: 14507

New Year's Day
P: 17353 **PI:** 17343
I: 17402

**New Year's Day —
Fiction**
PI: 5616

New Year's Eve — Fiction
P: 5645

New York City
P: 3435, 4813, 16695
PI: 94, 479, 16494, 16698,
16719, 16740, 21145
I: 16645, 16663, 16672,
16697, 16705, 16723, 16745
IJ: 16662, 16665, 16735,
16738, 16748, 17136, 21138

New York City — Crafts
I: 16477

New York City — Fiction
P: 1130, 1259, 1509, 1561,
1662, 2592, 2787, 3078,
3256, 3265, 3456, 3491,
3581, 4270, 4314, 4815,
4835, 5138, 5603, 5936
PI: 2674, 4587, 4626, 9516,
9765, 9891, 10270 **I:** 6846,
7352, 7468, 7527, 8081–83,
8298, 8841, 9224, 9301–2,
9552, 9577, 9600, 9622,
9630, 9635, 9715, 10055,
10070 **IJ:** 6898, 6925,
7284, 8628, 8643, 8737,
9564, 9572–73, 9582, 9666

New York City — History
I: 16203 **IJ:** 16690

New York Colony
I: 16123

**New York Knicks
(basketball team)**
I: 22148

New York State
PI: 16250, 16681, 16754
I: 16750 **IJ:** 16652, 16710,
16713, 16736, 16755

New York State — Fiction
I: 7812, 8312, 8566
IJ: 7814, 7816, 8429, 8567,
9193, 9258, 9287, 9323

**New York State —
Folklore**
P: 11337

**New York State —
History**
P: 4806 **IJ:** 16270, 16651

**New York Yankees
(baseball team)**
I: 22113

New Zealand
PI: 15234 **I:** 15230, 15238
IJ: 15231, 19404

New Zealand — Fiction
PI: 2922, 6958 **I:** 6960

New Zealand — Holidays
PI: 15234

**Newbery Award —
Anthologies**
IJ: 10264

Newfoundland
I: 15583

Newfoundland — Fiction
PI: 3934 **IJ:** 6876, 6906

**Newfoundlands (dog) —
Fiction**
P: 5289

Newspapers
P: 14082 **IJ:** 14064, 14086

Newspapers — Biography
PI: 12819

Newspapers — Fiction
P: 2350, 3361 **I:** 9552,
10038 **IJ:** 10040, 10053

Newton, Isaac
I: 13333 **IJ:** 13334

Newton, John
IJ: 12937, 14152

Newton, John — Fiction
I: 9292

Newts
I: 18685

Nez Perce Indians
P: 16051 **PI:** 16018

**Nez Perce Indians —
Fiction**
P: 4720

Ngoni (African people)
IJ: 14993

Niagara Falls — Fiction
P: 4753

Nicaragua
IJ: 15657, 15669

Nicaragua — Fiction
I: 9138

Nicaragua — Folklore
I: 11400

Nice, Margaret Morse
PI: 13335 **I:** 13336

Nicholas, Saint
PI: 17225

Nicknames — Fiction
I: 10093

Nigeria
P: 106 **PI:** 15019, 15043
I: 15033 **IJ:** 15008,
15038–39, 15042, 15049

Nigeria — Fiction
P: 4783, 4785–86 **I:** 8976,
8980

Nigeria — Folklore
P: 10664, 10693, 10708
PI: 10653, 10700

Nigeria — History
IJ: 15035

Nigeria — Holidays
PI: 15014

Night
See also Nocturnal animals
P: 4516 **I:** 18621

**Night — Experiments and
projects**
I: 18280

Night — Fiction
P: 663, 1985, 3237, 4565,
5379

Night — Poetry
PI: 11723

Nightingale, Florence
P: 13840 **IJ:** 13841

Nightingales — Fiction
PI: 10377

Nightmares — Fiction
P: 733, 1285

Nile River
I: 14911

Nile River — Fiction
P: 2024

Nimoy, Leonard
I: 12426

**Nineteenth century —
History**
I: 16487

**Nineteenth century —
Women**
IJ: 14589, 15855

Nitrogen
I: 20285 **IJ:** 20283

Nixon, Patricia Ryan
I: 13171

Nixon, Richard M.
P: 13087 **I:** 12674
IJ: 13088, 16525

Noah (Bible)
P: 4213, 5649, 17247,
17256, 17258, 17267,
17270–71, 17291, 17323
PI: 17275 **I:** 17310
IJ: 17514

Noah's Ark
See also Animals — Ark;
Animals — Ark —
Fiction; Noah (Bible)
P: 2412, 17277, 17288

Noah's Ark — Fiction
P: 1045, 1665, 2768

Nobel Prizes
PI: 13261, 13853–54
I: 13219, 13277, 13858
IJ: 13121, 13723, 13855,
15339, 15684

P = Primary; PI = Primary-Intermediate; I = Intermediate; IJ = Intermediate-Junior High

Nobel Prizes — Women
I: 13728

Noble, Sarah — Fiction
I: 9189

Nocturnal animals
P: 18813, 18846 **PI:** 18674
I: 18621, 18841

Nocturnal animals — Experiments and projects
I: 18280

Nocturnal animals — Fiction
P: 5132

Noise — Fiction
P: 3306

Norris, Chuck
I: 12427

North, Sterling — Fiction
IJ: 7282

North America
PI: 14354 **I:** 15562
IJ: 14339, 14552

North America — Crafts
IJ: 21527

North America — Exploration
I: 16095 **IJ:** 16094

North Carolina
PI: 16853 **I:** 16885
IJ: 16866

North Carolina — Fiction
IJ: 7424, 8353, 8417, 9291, 9528

North Carolina — History
IJ: 16895

North Dakota
P: 16555 **PI:** 16588
IJ: 16563

North Dakota — History
IJ: 15954

North Pole
See also Arctic; Polar regions
I: 12146

North Sea
I: 19831

Northeast (U.S.)
PI: 16686 **IJ:** 16694

Northeast (U.S.) — Anthologies
IJ: 16722

Northeast (U.S.) — History
IJ: 16110, 16480

Northern Ireland
See Ireland, Northern

Northern lights
P: 15802 **I:** 18415
IJ: 20790

Northern lights — Fiction
P: 1305, 1535

Northwest Passage
IJ: 15566

Northwest Territories, Canada
I: 15572

Norway
P: 15455 **I:** 15450, 15454
IJ: 15438, 15441

Norway — Fiction
I: 9673

Norway — Folklore
P: 11117–19, 11122–24, 11127–28 **PI:** 10610, 11129–30, 11518
I: 11120–21, 11519

Norway — History
IJ: 14865

Norway — Mythology
I: 12041

Noses
P: 18141

Noses — Fiction
IJ: 7743

Notre Dame (Paris) — Fiction
I: 9045

Nouns
PI: 14026

Nova Scotia
PI: 17922 **I:** 15597

Nova Scotia — Fiction
I: 6952

Nubia — History
IJ: 14663

Nuclear energy
I: 20844–45 **IJ:** 20847

Nuclear power plants
I: 20846

Nuclear power plants — Accidents
I: 17984

Nuclear weapons — Fiction
P: 1563

Number systems
I: 20628

Numbers
See also Counting books; Mathematics; Statistics
P: 399–400, 461, 518, 20635 **PI:** 20626, 20631–32, 20636–38
I: 20627–28, 20634
IJ: 20629

Numbers — Fiction
P: 452

Numbers — Poetry
PI: 11602

Nunavut (Canada)
I: 15581

Nunez, Tommy
I: 13553

Nuns — Fiction
P: 5517

Nureyev, Rudolf
IJ: 12428

Nursery rhymes
See also Mother Goose; Poetry
P: 405–6, 440, 795, 822–43, 845–58, 860–96, 898–905, 1168, 11686 **PI:** 844, 859

Nursery rhymes — Africa
P: 897

Nursery schools — Fiction
P: 5490

Nurses — Biography
P: 13840 **PI:** 13135
I: 13311 **IJ:** 13841

Nurses — Careers
P: 17798

Nurses — Fiction
P: 2786

Nurses — World War II
IJ: 14861

Nursing homes
P: 17857

Nursing homes — Fiction
PI: 3763, 7541, 8388
IJ: 8560

***Nutcracker* (ballet)**
P: 3239, 5767, 6371
PI: 10932, 14288, 14293

Nutrition
P: 3047, 18101, 18105, 18193, 18206, 20164
PI: 18204–5, 20161, 20163
I: 9966, 18202, 18210, 20159 **IJ:** 18099, 18199, 20168

Nutrition — Experiments and projects
IJ: 18212

Nzingha (African queen) — Fiction
IJ: 8971, 20215, 20217
I: 20212

O

Oak trees
P: 4730, 20215, 20217
I: 20212

Oakland (CA)
IJ: 16765

Oakley, Annie
P: 12429, 12431–32
IJ: 12430

Oakley, Annie — Fiction
IJ: 9571

Obata, Chiura
I: 12274

Obesity
IJ: 18199

Obesity — Fiction
P: 2476 **I:** 8565, 8727, 8785, 8810, 8815, 10047
IJ: 7255, 8303

Occupations and work
See also Careers; and specific occupations, e.g., Automobile mechanics
IJ: 17753

Occupations and work — Fiction
P: 2759, 3031, 3198, 3407, 3614, 3847, 3920 **I:** 7412, 7493 **IJ:** 9270

Ocean floor vents
I: 19878

Oceanography
See also Marine biology
P: 19817, 19836
PI: 19816, 19821 **I:** 19814, 19818–20, 19822–23, 19829, 19832, 19850, 19876
IJ: 19827, 19843, 19849

Oceanography — Biography
I: 12077 **IJ:** 13220

Oceanography — Careers
P: 17829 **PI:** 17833

Oceanography — Experiments and projects
IJ: 19815

Oceans
See also Beaches; Marine animals, etc; Oceanography; Seashores; and specific oceans, e.g., Atlantic Ocean
P: 4462, 19624, 19851
PI: 19837, 19839 **I:** 19814, 19824, 19832, 19834, 19838, 19840, 19846
IJ: 18348, 19637, 19828, 19835, 19844

Oceans — Crafts
I: 21480

Oceans — Currents
IJ: 20751

Oceans — Experiments and projects
IJ: 19845

Oceans — Fiction
P: 1007, 1046, 1159, 4359, 4436, 4543, 4554, 6397
PI: 7580 **I:** 7112, 7859
IJ: 7077

P = Primary; PI = Primary-Intermediate; I = Intermediate; IJ = Intermediate-Junior High

Oceans — Folklore
P: 11123 I: 10848

Oceans — Nursery rhymes
P: 851

Oceans — Plants
I: 20246

Oceans — Poetry
PI: 11988

O'Connor, Sandra Day
PI: 12939 I: 12938
IJ: 12940

Octopuses
P: 19724–28 I: 19723
IJ: 19722

Octopuses — Fiction
P: 2319

O'Donnell, Rosie
PI: 12433 I: 12436
IJ: 12434–35, 12437

Odyssey (mythology)
I: 11465

Oglala Sioux Indians — Folklore
P: 11308

O'Grady, Scott
IJ: 12144

Ogres
PI: 1153

Ohio
PI: 16553 I: 16539
IJ: 16558

Ohio — Fiction
P: 4860 PI: 9729 I: 9377

Ohio — History
I: 16593

Ohio River
PI: 20519

Oil
I: 16902

Oil — Biography
IJ: 12633

Oil drilling — Fiction
I: 9629

Oil industry — Biography
IJ: 12960

Oil rigs
P: 21293

Oil spills
P: 16990 I: 16800
IJ: 16813, 17002

Ojibwa Indians
See also Chippewa Indians
I: 15981 IJ: 15930, 15993

Ojibwa Indians — Fiction
P: 3930, 4558 IJ: 9159

Ojibwa Indians — Folklore
P: 9167, 11316 PI: 11315

O'Keeffe, Georgia
PI: 12276–77 I: 12275

Oklahoma
P: 16556 I: 16569
IJ: 16532, 16577

Oklahoma — Fiction
I: 7319, 9612 IJ: 7274, 7533, 9678

Oklahoma — History
I: 15923 IJ: 16479

Oklahoma City
IJ: 16582

Oklahoma City bombing (1995)
I: 16578 IJ: 16582

Olajuwon, Hakeem
I: 13554, 13556 IJ: 13555

Old Ironsides (ship) — **Fiction**
I: 9331

Olmos, Edward James
PI: 12439 IJ: 12438

Olmsted, Frederick Law
PI: 12942 I: 12941

Olympic Games
P: 13664 PI: 13665, 22244–45, 22249 I: 13596, 13660, 13667, 22251–54, 22258 IJ: 13663, 22243, 22246–48, 22250, 22255, 22257

Olympic Games — Biography
PI: 13370 I: 13450
IJ: 13368, 13378

Olympic Games — Fiction
P: 2285 PI: 11502
IJ: 9029

Olympic Games — History
IJ: 22256

O'Malley, Grania
P: 12145

Oman
IJ: 15541

Onassis, Jacqueline Kennedy
I: 13172–73

O'Neal, Shaquille
PI: 13560 I: 13557, 13559
IJ: 13558, 13561

Oneida Indians
IJ: 15998

Online services
I: 21204

Ontario — Fiction
P: 3067

Ontario, Lake
PI: 16529

Opals — Fiction
P: 4642

Opera
I: 12447 IJ: 14127, 14136

Opera — Fiction
P: 2230, 5882 PI: 9596

Opera — Plots
I: 14130–31 IJ: 14128

Opera houses — Fiction
I: 6939

Opossums — Fiction
P: 2097, 2158, 2775
I: 7411

Opposites
See Concept books — Opposites

Optical illusions
P: 310, 20910 PI: 20909
I: 20911, 20913, 20915–19

Opticians — Careers
P: 3134

Optics
IJ: 20856, 20871

Optics — Experiments and projects
I: 20865 IJ: 20912, 20914

Oranges
P: 20151

Orangutans
PI: 18991 I: 13288, 18989, 19009

Orangutans — Fiction
P: 2506, 5237

Orchestras
PI: 14225, 14228 I: 14221
IJ: 14224

Orchestras — Fiction
P: 2229, 3270, 3716

Orchids
PI: 20250

Oregon
PI: 16777 I: 16764, 16819
IJ: 16789, 16818

Oregon — Fiction
P: 2967 I: 9387, 9599, 9801 IJ: 6905, 7269, 9372

Oregon — History
I: 16826

Oregon — Poetry
I: 11626

Oregon Territory — Fiction
I: 9441

Oregon Trail
P: 16317 PI: 16336
I: 16293, 16373 IJ: 16291, 16302

Oregon Trail — Cookbooks
IJ: 16312

Oregon Trail — Fiction
PI: 8123, 9382 I: 9369, 9376, 9391, 9399, 9412, 9427

Origami
PI: 21611 I: 15133, 21604, 21626

Orinoco River
IJ: 15779

Orion (constellation)
I: 18537

Orkney Islands
I: 15334

Ornithology — Biography
PI: 13335

Orphan Train
I: 15914

Orphan Train — Fiction
IJ: 9442

Orphans — Fiction
P: 4362, 5935, 10444
PI: 7875 I: 7395–96, 7555, 7726, 8573, 9380, 9420, 9422, 9511, 9844 IJ: 7466, 7921, 8764, 8935, 9309, 9532, 9582, 9627

Orphans — Folklore
P: 10703 PI: 11249

Osceola (Seminole chief)
PI: 16052

Ospreys
IJ: 19354

Ostriches
PI: 19259 I: 19214

Ostriches — Fiction
P: 2571, 4211 I: 7236

Ostriches — Folklore
I: 10654

Ottawa Indians
I: 15983

Otters
P: 4475, 5124, 18965, 19729, 19733, 20373
PI: 19749 I: 19742, 19746

Otters — Fiction
P: 643, 5320, 6202, 6367
PI: 6269

Outdoor life
IJ: 12577

Outer space — Fiction
P: 1289, 1536

Outer space — Jokes and riddles
P: 21828

Outlaws — Biography
See also Robbers and robbery
I: 12649 IJ: 12851, 12908

Oviraptors
IJ: 14455

P = Primary; PI = Primary-Intermediate; I = Intermediate; IJ = Intermediate-Junior High

Owens, Jesse
P: 13664, 13669 PI: 13665
I: 13667–68 IJ: 13666

Owls
P: 19357–58, 19362, 19366–67 PI: 19360–61
I: 19359, 19363–64
IJ: 19365

Owls — Fiction
P: 1024, 1965, 1985, 2219, 2231, 2767, 2802, 5280, 5324, 5463, 6367, 6468
PI: 7195

Owls — Poetry
P: 11887, 11889 IJ: 11800

Oxen — Folklore
P: 10756 PI: 11357
I: 11365, 11373

Oxygen
I: 20666 IJ: 18124, 20284

Oxymorons
IJ: 14022

Ozarks — Fiction
P: 3111, 3967

Ozawa, Seiji
IJ: 12440

Ozone layer
P: 17006 I: 17000
IJ: 16998, 17003

P

Pachciarz, Judith
PI: 13337

Pacific Crest Trail
I: 16761

Pacific Islands
IJ: 15245

Pacific Islands — Crafts
IJ: 15232

Pacific Islands — Fiction
P: 4709

Pacific Northwest
See Pacific states (U.S.)

Pacific Ocean
I: 19826

Pacific Ocean — World War II
IJ: 14829–30, 14833–34

Pacific states (U.S.)
See also specific states, e.g., Oregon
P: 462 I: 16782, 16787

Pacific states (U.S.) — Animals
P: 52, 18877

Pacific states (U.S.) — Fiction
P: 1362

Pacific states (U.S.) — Forests
IJ: 20470

Pacifists and pacifism
IJ: 10579, 13723

Pacifists and pacifism — Biography
I: 13725

Pacifists and pacifism — Fiction
IJ: 9465, 9661

Page, "Diamond" Dallas
IJ: 13705

Paige, Satchel
PI: 13475–76

Paine, Thomas
IJ: 12943

Painting
See Drawing and painting

Paiute Indians — Biography
PI: 13001

Pak, Se Ri
IJ: 13706

Pakistan
IJ: 15113, 15191, 15194, 15204, 15220

Pakistani Americans — Fiction
PI: 5625

Paleontology
See also Dinosaurs; Fossils; Prehistoric animals
P: 14486–87 PI: 14431, 14444, 14458 I: 14379, 14383, 14386, 14390, 14399–400, 14402, 14407, 14413, 14416, 14428–30, 14437, 14440–41, 14446, 14448, 14454, 14461, 14463, 14466, 14473, 14478, 14513 IJ: 14393, 14410, 14415, 14436, 14455, 14460, 14462, 14470, 14474, 14476

Paleontology — Biography
P: 13227, 13230–31
PI: 13228–29 IJ: 13226

Paleontology — Careers
P: 17828

Paleontology — Fiction
P: 5134 PI: 7145 I: 9332

Palestine
IJ: 15518

Palestine — Fiction
P: 3802 IJ: 8926, 8936

Palestinians
IJ: 15537

Palestinians — Fiction
P: 4781

Palindromes
I: 14021, 14052, 21877–78

Palmeiro, Rafael
I: 13477

Palmer, Cissie
I: 13174

Palmistry
IJ: 21948

Paluxet Indians
IJ: 17491

Panama
PI: 15682 I: 15668, 15681, 15691 IJ: 15672, 15678, 15687

Panama — Fiction
P: 4762

Panama Canal
I: 15677, 15691 IJ: 15664, 15672, 15675, 15678

Panama Canal — Fiction
I: 9133

Pandas
P: 19186, 19188
PI: 19189–91 I: 19185
IJ: 19187

Pandas — Fiction
P: 293, 2353, 5154 I: 7303

Panic attacks
IJ: 17908

Panthers
P: 19082, 19095 I: 19078
IJ: 19109

Panthers — Fiction
IJ: 6774

Pantomime — Fiction
P: 1114

Papago Indians
PI: 15922

Papago Indians — Fiction
P: 4936

Paper
P: 21049 IJ: 21057

Paper — Fiction
P: 3168

Paper crafts
PI: 21611, 21618, 21631, 21633 I: 12491, 14080, 21604, 21606–7, 21609–10, 21613, 21615, 21617, 21619–20, 21622–23, 21625–26, 21628–30, 21634–36, 21638
IJ: 21605, 21608, 21612, 21614, 21616, 21621, 21624, 21627, 21637, 21650, 21795

Papermaking
I: 21065, 21639 IJ: 21637

Papermaking — Fiction
P: 4814

Papier-mâché
PI: 21611 I: 21623, 21625, 21629 IJ: 21605

Parables
P: 17227, 17286

Parades — Fiction
P: 3090, 3496, 4649
PI: 6965

Paraguay
IJ: 15742, 15749, 15768

Parakeets — Fiction
P: 6621

Parasites (biology)
I: 18622, 18648

Paratroopers
IJ: 21392

Paris, France
I: 15318 IJ: 15310

Paris, France — Fiction
P: 1809, 2026, 2293, 4584, 4666, 4723, 4754 PI: 2272, 8267 I: 9045, 9068

Parker, Charlie — Fiction
PI: 4613

Parker, Ely
I: 12979

Parker, John — Fiction
I: 9312

Parkinson's disease
IJ: 17979

Parkman, Francis
IJ: 16369

Parks
P: 4915, 16957

Parks — Biography
PI: 12942

Parks — Fiction
P: 2205, 2632, 3690, 4306
PI: 3053 I: 8283

Parks, Rosa
PI: 12773–74, 12776–79
I: 12775, 12780, 17048

Parrish, Maxfield
I: 13956

Parrots
PI: 19264 I: 19238, 19273, 19882

Parrots — Fiction
I: 6867, 6921

Parthenon (Greece)
PI: 14675 I: 14690
IJ: 14709

Parties
See also Birthdays
I: 22234 IJ: 17351

Parties — Fiction
P: 2204, 2234, 4282, 4708, 6585 I: 8752, 9076

P = Primary; PI = Primary-Intermediate; I = Intermediate; IJ = Intermediate-Junior High

Passover
P: 6070, 17472 PI: 17469, 17474, 17478, 17484
I: 17479, 17486 IJ: 17467

Passover — Crafts
I: 17482

Passover — Fiction
P: 6094, 6103, 6105, 6111, 6131 PI: 6097, 7413

Passover — Poetry
P: 6100

Pasta
P: 20089, 20123, 20129 PI: 21026

Pasteur, Louis
PI: 13339 I: 13338 IJ: 13340

Patagonia
I: 14399

Paterson, Katherine
IJ: 12575

Patrick, Saint
See also Saint Patrick's Day
P: 13842

Patrick, Saint — Fiction
P: 1372

Patton, George
I: 12944

Paulsen, Gary
IJ: 12576–78

Pavlova, Anna
IJ: 12441

Pawnee Indians
I: 15966

Pawnee Indians — Folklore
P: 11223

Payton, Gary
I: 13562

Peace
See also Pacifists and pacifism
P: 251

Peace — Folklore
IJ: 10579

Peace — Poetry
I: 11681

Peace — Songs
I: 14254

Peaches — Fiction
PI: 7696

Peaches — Folklore
P: 10872

Peacocks
PI: 19218

Peale, Charles Willson
IJ: 12278, 14419

Peanut butter
PI: 20083 IJ: 21734

Peanuts
P: 20111, 20117

Pearl Harbor — Fiction
I: 9668

Pearl Harbor — History
I: 14857 IJ: 14836, 14874, 14887, 14895

Pearls — Fiction
P: 3637

Peary, Robert E.
I: 12146

Peas
P: 20183 IJ: 20176

Pediatrics — Careers
I: 18023, 18033

Peet, Bill
PI: 12279

Pegasus (Mythology)
I: 11492

Pele (soccer player)
IJ: 13707

Pelicans
P: 19294

Pen pals — Fiction
P: 6556 PI: 4745 I: 8712

Penacook Indians — Fiction
IJ: 9148

Penguins
P: 19229, 19369, 19372, 19375, 19379–80, 19382, 19384, 19386 PI: 19368, 19370–71, 19374, 19376, 19381, 19383, 19385, 19387–88 I: 19378
IJ: 19373, 19377, 19389

Penguins — Fiction
P: 2364, 2869, 5401
PI: 6976 I: 9772

Penguins — Poetry
P: 11812

Penmanship — Fiction
IJ: 16238

Penn, William
I: 12945

Pennsylvania
PI: 16682 I: 16747, 16751
IJ: 16691, 16725

Pennsylvania — Biography
IJ: 12598

Pennsylvania — Fiction
PI: 9562 I: 9175, 9231, 9269, 9517, 9580, 9606, 9644, 12945 IJ: 7840, 8369, 9242, 9519

Pennsylvania — Folklore
IJ: 11383

Pennsylvania — History
I: 16756 IJ: 16448

Pennsylvania Colony
I: 16124

Pennsylvania Dutch
P: 4

Penraat, Jaap
IJ: 14886

Peregrine falcons
PI: 19339

Perkins School — Fiction
I: 9285

Perot, Ross
I: 12946

Perseus (mythology)
PI: 11482

Persia
See also Iran

Persia — Fiction
I: 8957 IJ: 8993

Persia — Folklore
P: 11181, 11187 PI: 10407
I: 11203

Persia — History
I: 13747

Persian Gulf War
PI: 15488 I: 15487
IJ: 12953–54, 15489, 15493, 15540, 16514

Persian Gulf War — Biography
I: 12951

Personal appearance
IJ: 17700

Personal finances
I: 16943

Personal guidance
PI: 17632 I: 17622, 17702
IJ: 17603, 17694, 17696, 17700, 17706, 17719, 17737, 18267

Personal guidance — Girls
IJ: 17610, 17699

Personal guidance — Women
IJ: 17701

Personal problems
See also Bullies; Child abuse; Death; Divorce; Moving; Sexual abuse
P: 17724 PI: 8763
I: 8785, 17703 IJ: 17603, 17708, 17719, 17721, 17726, 17736–37

Personal problems — Fiction
P: 4062, 4633, 4666, 4702, 4787, 4896, 4898, 4902, 4906, 4910, 4912–14, 4917, 4920, 4924–25, 4930–31, 4934, 4936, 4938–40, 4943–46, 4951–54, 4956, 4963, 4966–67, 4970, 4972, 4975, 4977, 4982, 4984, 4986–87, 4989, 4991–92, 4995–97, 4999–5002, 5005–9, 5013–14, 5017–18, 5021–23, 5025–26, 5028–31, 5041–43, 5046, 5048, 5054–55, 5057–58, 5060, 5063–67, 5069–70, 5072, 5075–78, 5080, 5083, 5085–90, 5095, 5097, 5099–102, 5106–8, 5356, 5491, 5522, 5530, 5668, 6216, 6410, 6463, 6538, 8662, 8674, 8848, 10752
PI: 4652, 4909, 4921, 4976, 4978, 4990, 5015, 5027, 5051, 5079, 5367, 6802, 7356, 8419, 8554, 8563, 8574–75, 8578, 8589, 8593, 8597, 8614, 8616, 8626, 8629, 8634, 8637, 8642, 8649, 8660, 8700, 8704–5, 8729, 8750, 8757, 8791, 8807, 8830, 8856, 8863, 9525, 9784, 9798, 9911, 10052, 10054, 10090, 10122, 10130 I: 6851, 7140, 7281, 7311, 8325, 8348, 8386, 8400, 8486, 8518, 8523, 8553, 8564, 8566, 8569–70, 8573, 8579–80, 8582–84, 8587, 8590–91, 8599–600, 8603, 8609–10, 8622, 8624–25, 8633, 8635–36, 8638, 8648, 8657–59, 8664, 8670, 8677, 8682–84, 8688–89, 8691–92, 8694, 8703, 8709–10, 8712, 8715, 8720, 8723–24, 8726, 8730, 8743, 8746–48, 8752, 8755, 8758–59, 8767–68, 8774, 8776, 8778–79, 8790, 8792–95, 8797–99, 8803, 8810–11, 8814, 8816, 8818, 8820–21, 8824, 8826, 8834–35, 8838, 8841, 8843, 8846, 8854–55, 8857–59, 8862, 8865, 8869–70, 8873, 8920, 9342, 9556, 9592, 9854, 10037, 10046, 10055, 10060, 10070, 10110–11, 10271 IJ: 6806, 7041, 7048, 7163, 7512, 7546, 7896, 7909, 8092, 8121, 8248, 8318, 8329, 8353, 8359, 8390, 8434, 8456, 8483, 8504, 8524, 8527, 8550–51, 8555, 8557–61, 8567–68, 8571–72, 8576–77, 8581, 8585, 8594, 8598, 8601–2, 8604–8, 8612–13, 8615, 8617–21, 8628, 8630–32, 8641, 8643, 8646–47, 8650, 8652, 8654–56, 8666–67, 8669, 8675–76, 8678, 8681, 8685–86, 8693, 8696–98, 8701–2, 8706–8, 8711, 8714, 8716–19, 8721, 8725, 8731, 8733–38, 8740, 8742, 8744–45, 8751, 8753–54, 8756, 8760, 8764–66, 8769–71, 8773, 8775,

8780–82, 8784, 8788, 8796, 8800, 8802, 8804–5, 8809, 8812–13, 8817, 8819, 8822–23, 8829, 8832–33, 8837, 8839–40, 8844–45, 8847, 8849, 8851–53, 8860, 8864, 8867–68, 8871–72, 8889–90, 8906, 8981, 9019, 9090, 9094, 9148, 9432, 9442, 9477, 9522, 9536, 9564, 9582, 9620, 9628, 9640, 9671, 9895, 10040, 10042, 10133, 10135, 10267, 10277, 10287, 16238

Personal problems — Poetry
IJ: 11582

Personal problems — Schools
I: 17714

Peru
PI: 15773 I: 15731, 15754 IJ: 15755, 15763, 15769, 15776

Peru — Fiction
P: 4601 I: 9135

Peru — Folklore
P: 11440 IJ: 11438

Peru — History
I: 15752, 15761, 15774, 15780, 15788 IJ: 15759

Peru — Holidays
P: 15750

Pesticides
I: 19408

Pet stores — Careers
P: 3132

Peter Rabbit — Fiction
P: 2597

Peter the Great
IJ: 13843

Pets
See also individual species, e.g., Dogs
P: 3818, 19902, 19910 PI: 19889, 19899, 19911, 19945 I: 19883, 19887–88, 19892, 19894, 19896, 19905–6, 19908–9, 19912–14, 19963 IJ: 19907

Pets — Drawing and painting
PI: 21581

Pets — Fiction
P: 1205, 1787, 3748, 5181, 5235, 5387, 5501, 5719, 6565, 6567, 6612, 6694, 7283 PI: 7240, 7302, 8626, 9955 I: 9853, 10077

Petting zoos — Fiction
P: 2465

Philadelphia
PI: 16732 I: 16653, 16711, 16739

Philadelphia — Fiction
I: 9235, 9496

Philadelphia Flyers (hockey team)
I: 22224

Philanthropists — Biography
I: 12758, 12863, 12917

Philip, King (Sachem of the Wampanoags)
I: 12981 IJ: 12980

Philippines
I: 15233, 15239–40 IJ: 15241, 15252, 15254–55

Philippines — Fiction
PI: 4578

Philippines — Folklore
P: 1753, 10847

Philippines — Holidays
PI: 15247

Philippines — World War II
IJ: 14822

Phoenicians
I: 14593

Phoenix Suns (basketball team)
IJ: 22142

Phosphorous
IJ: 20277

Photocopier art
IJ: 21614

Photographers — Biography
P: 12191 PI: 12192, 12251 I: 12187, 12859 IJ: 12170, 12193, 12242

Photography
P: 21798 I: 21797, 21799–801 IJ: 21802–5

Photography — Careers
PI: 17774 IJ: 17769

Photography — History
IJ: 16440

Photosynthesis
IJ: 20033

Phrenology — Fiction
IJ: 9299

Physical disabilities
See also Blind; Cerebral palsy; Deaf; Disabilities; Obesity; etc.
P: 4915, 4927, 17903, 17914, 17928–29, 17934 PI: 5024, 13349, 13433, 13432, 17902, 17917–18, 17915, 17931 I: 12211, 17923, 17925 IJ: 13308, 17921, 17966

Physical disabilities — Biography
IJ: 13165, 13375

Physical disabilities — Fiction
P: 4913, 4922, 4965, 4974, 4979, 5008, 5039, 5104, 5178 PI: 3918, 4958, 6889, 8623, 8874, 8901, 8919 I: 7102, 7287, 8653, 8694, 8897, 8905, 8924, 9176, 10032 IJ: 6843, 6975, 8281, 8605, 8751, 8836, 8887, 8896, 8898, 8911, 8917, 8921, 9091, 9531, 9564

Physical disabilities — Poetry
IJ: 11537

Physical disabilities — Sports
IJ: 13406

Physical fitness
PI: 18203 IJ: 18208

Physical geography
P: 20376–77, 20384 PI: 18913 I: 20378

Physical geography — Fiction
P: 4412

Physicists — Biography
I: 13290 IJ: 13275, 13308

Physics
IJ: 20807–8

Physics — Experiments and projects
PI: 20810 IJ: 18305, 20798, 20811

Phytoplankton
IJ: 19626

Pianos
IJ: 14226

Pianos — Fiction
P: 1080, 5055, 5960 I: 8498, 8924

Picasso, Pablo
P: 12281 PI: 12280, 12285 IJ: 12282–84

Pickett, Bill
P: 12442 I: 12443

Picnics — Fiction
P: 1490, 2211, 2891, 6493

Picotte, Susan LaFlesche
I: 12982–83

Picts — Fiction
I: 8240

Picture books
See also Stories without words

Picture books — Anthologies
P: 1600–1, 1630

Picture books — International
P: 1491

Picture books — Publishing
I: 13998

Picture frames — Crafts
I: 21663

Picture puzzles
P: 45, 306, 485, 1424, 1780, 4124, 4232, 5234, 5318, 5432, 5683, 14216, 18752, 21865, 21868, 21871–76, 21886 PI: 479, 18679, 21840, 21870 I: 21862, 21867 IJ: 14604, 21881

Picture puzzles — Fiction
P: 1784, 5591

Pierce, Franklin
I: 13090 IJ: 13089

Pig farms
I: 20075

Pigeons
I: 19266

Pigeons — Fiction
P: 4876 PI: 2674, 4721 I: 6860, 8824 IJ: 7273

Pigs
P: 5291, 18942, 20048, 20066 I: 20075

Pigs — Fiction
P: 41, 442, 917, 920, 1464, 1831, 1893, 1896, 2027, 2039, 2060, 2118, 2157, 2185, 2188–89, 2254, 2281–82, 2360, 2401, 2403, 2460, 2462, 2476–77, 2513, 2595, 2621, 2718, 2760, 2855, 2891, 4100, 4325, 6469, 6686 PI: 7867, 8200 I: 7174, 7249, 7788 IJ: 7546–47, 9605, 9653

Pigs — Folklore
P: 10982, 11009, 11033, 11352

Pigs — Nursery rhymes
P: 895

Pike, Zebulon
I: 12147

Pilgrims (U.S.)
P: 17500 PI: 16156, 16163, 16168, 16183, 16185, 17492, 17496 I: 16035, 16165, 16169–70, 16184 IJ: 16105, 16107, 16117, 16132, 17491

Pilgrims (U.S.) — Biography
IJ: 12857

Pilgrims (U.S.) — Fiction
PI: 9196 I: 9202 IJ: 9211

Pill bugs
P: 18635 PI: 19486

Piñatas
P: 5793, 15601

Piñatas — Fiction
P: 5703

P = Primary; PI = Primary-Intermediate; I = Intermediate; IJ = Intermediate-Junior High

Pinkerton, Alan
IJ: 12947–48

Pioneer period (U.S.)
See Frontier life (U.S.)

Pippen, Scottie
IJ: 13563–65

Pippin, Horace
IJ: 12286

Piranhas
P: 19697 I: 19703, 19708

Pirates
P: 14561 PI: 14551, 14571
I: 14549, 14566 IJ: 14558,
14568

Pirates — Biography
P: 12145 PI: 12065
IJ: 12070, 12117

Pirates — Fiction
P: 1302, 1377, 1380, 2930,
2980, 4041, 6316 PI: 7937
I: 6959, 7101, 9282
IJ: 6752, 6880, 7846, 9284,
9847

Pirates — Folklore
I: 10625

Pirates — Women
IJ: 12070

**Pittsburgh Steelers
(football team)**
I: 22185

Pizza
P: 20115, 21735

Pizza — Fiction
P: 4327, 6340

Plagues
IJ: 14759

Plagues — Fiction
IJ: 9091

Plagues — History
IJ: 14762

Plains Indians
I: 16001

Plains Indians — Fiction
P: 1196

Plains Indians — Folklore
P: 11239, 11243, 11245,
11289 PI: 11247 I: 11238,
11246 IJ: 11250

Plains Indians — History
PI: 15964 I: 15953

Plains (U.S.)
See also Grasslands,
Prairies, and specific
states, e.g., Nebraska
IJ: 16297

Plains (U.S.) — Fiction
I: 9143, 9618

Planes (physics)
P: 20924

Planetariums
P: 20962

Planets
See also specific planets,
e.g., Mars (planet)
P: 18458, 18468, 18473,
18483, 18519 PI: 18456,
18471, 18484, 18499–502
I: 18474, 18497–98, 18548,
20957 IJ: 18470, 18511,
18536

Planets — Exploration
IJ: 20960

Planets — Fiction
P: 1062

Plankton
IJ: 19626

**Plantation life (U.S.) —
History**
P: 16253 I: 16227, 16260,
16262 IJ: 16239

Plants
See also specific plants,
e.g., Cactus
P: 4583, 20044, 20158,
20224, 20237, 20245,
20262–63, 20270, 20445,
20515–17 PI: 20228,
20236, 20239, 20254, 20479
I: 20230–31, 20243, 20264
IJ: 20032, 20098, 20177,
20232, 20234, 20251,
20253, 20256, 20258–59

Plants — Deserts
P: 20404

**Plants — Experiments
and projects**
P: 18367, 20260
PI: 20229, 20255 I: 20223,
20225, 20265 IJ: 20235

Plants — Fiction
P: 1012, 1905, 3054, 4517,
4552, 10410, 20076

Plants — Folklore
P: 11001, 11005 IJ: 11220

Plants — Life cycles
P: 18593

Plants — Medicine
I: 20233

Plants — Oceans
I: 20246

Plants — Poisonous
I: 20233

Plants — Seashores
P: 19859

**Plastics — Experiments
and projects**
I: 21046

Plate tectonics
IJ: 20305, 20322

Platypuses
PI: 18973

Play — Fiction
P: 215

Play production
PI: 12014

Playgrounds — Fiction
P: 3365

Plays
See also Shakespeare,
William; Theater
P: 6327, 12028 PI: 7135,
12015–16, 12025–26
I: 8659, 9713, 9743, 9757,
10076, 12018, 12029–31,
12041, 14321 IJ: 9709,
12020, 12024, 12036,
12040, 14325

Plays — Anthologies
PI: 12010 I: 12009, 12012,
12017, 12032–35, 12042
IJ: 12019, 12022
All: 12023

Plays — Folklore
PI: 12013 IJ: 12043

Plays — Latin America
IJ: 12043

Plays — Multiculturalism
P: 12021

Plays — Production
I: 12011

Plays — Shakespeare
I: 12049, 12052
IJ: 12044–46, 12048, 12055

Plays — Spain
IJ: 12043

Playwrights — Biography
I: 12591–92 IJ: 12544,
12593

Pledge of Allegiance
P: 6688

Plotkin, Mark
IJ: 13341

Plows
P: 20071

Plumbing
I: 18197 IJ: 21164

Pluto (planet)
PI: 18463, 18496, 18500
I: 18478

**Plymouth Colony —
Fiction**
P: 6147 IJ: 9211

**Plymouth Plantation —
Biography**
IJ: 12856

**Poarch Creek Indians —
Fiction**
PI: 11261

Pocahontas
P: 12987 I: 12984, 12986
IJ: 12985

Poetics
I: 11618

Poetry
See also Nursery rhymes;
as subdivision of other
subjects, e.g., Animals
— Poetry; and as
subdivision of countries
or ethnic groups, e.g.,
England — Poetry
P: 38, 277, 301, 674, 1155,
3111, 3129, 3242, 3482,
4025, 6442, 11532, 11536,
11546, 11558, 11604,
11609, 11631, 11641,
11654, 11656, 11659,
11665, 11672, 11674,
11686, 11691, 11720,
11738, 11747, 11756
PI: 4528, 11531, 11568,
11574, 11580, 11625,
11643, 11661, 11667,
11682, 11692, 11696,
11711, 11714–15, 11727,
11737, 11757 I: 11522,
11552, 11593, 11624,
11626, 11636–37, 11671,
11678, 11697–98, 11707–8,
11736, 11741, 11743, 11809
IJ: 11535, 11569–70,
11587, 11640, 11677,
11687, 11694, 11724,
11730, 11823, 17514
All: 11541

**Poetry — African
American**
IJ: 11769

Poetry — Animals
P: 11783 PI: 11786,
11792, 11795 I: 11807

Poetry — Anthologies
P: 138, 11545, 11550,
11556, 11559, 11567,
11576, 11597–98, 11600,
11607, 11616, 11684,
11703, 11725, 11761,
11816, 11821, 11835–36,
11920 PI: 11547, 11551,
11572, 11606, 11662,
11666, 11679, 11706,
11729, 11837, 11865, 11908
I: 11530, 11560, 11588,
11618, 11620, 11627,
11634, 11680, 11721,
11728, 11732, 11799,
11829, 11832, 11838,
11956, 11997, 12001, 14090
IJ: 10620, 11538, 11555,
11601, 11603, 11610,
11635, 11645, 11647–48,
11664, 11683, 11688,
11704, 11731, 11733,
11800, 11857, 11896, 11931

Poetry — Appreciation
PI: 11542

Poetry — Art
IJ: 11595

Poetry — Christmas
P: 11839–48

Poetry — City life
P: 11608

P = Primary; PI = Primary-Intermediate; I = Intermediate; IJ = Intermediate-Junior High

Poetry — Collections
P: 11525, 11540, 11554
PI: 11623, 11628 I: 11557, 11589, 11712, 11719
IJ: 11562, 11571, 11615

Poetry — Everyday life
PI: 11713

Poetry — Fiction
PI: 8118

Poetry — Food
P: 11575

Poetry — General
P: 1046, 1317, 1561, 1668, 1682, 11553, 11566, 11590, 11596, 11621, 11630, 11710, 11716 PI: 11529, 11633, 11717 I: 7835, 11689 IJ: 11690, 11693

Poetry — Humorous
P: 1161, 4144, 4169–70, 11539, 11782, 11802, 11856, 11859–61, 11866, 11869, 11873–76, 11879, 11883, 11885–92, 11894, 11898, 11901, 11904–5, 11909, 11911, 11915–16, 11918, 11920, 11924–25, 11927–28, 12006–7, 21836 PI: 11773, 11797, 11855, 11863, 11865, 11867, 11877–78, 11881–82, 11895, 11897, 11903, 11908, 11912, 11914, 11917, 11919 I: 11854, 11858, 11862, 11864, 11868, 11870–72, 11880, 11884, 11893, 11899–900, 11906, 11910, 11913, 11921–23, 11926
IJ: 11857, 11896, 11907

Poetry — Japanese
P: 11649

Poetry — Journeys
P: 11663

Poetry — Monsters
PI: 11914 I: 11868

Poetry — Paul Revere
I: 11642

Poetry — Relationships
I: 11705

Poetry — Riddles
P: 21853

Poetry — Shapes
I: 11629

Poetry — Spanish
PI: 11543

Poetry — Sports
IJ: 12003

Poetry — Teenagers
IJ: 11611

Poetry — Time
IJ: 11594

Poetry — Weaving
I: 11581

Poetry — Women
PI: 11572 IJ: 11658

Poetry — Writing
IJ: 14094

Poets — Biography
I: 11632 IJ: 12530, 12570, 12619

POGS
I: 22042

Poison dart frogs
P: 18720

Poisonous animals and plants
I: 18935, 20231 IJ: 19428

Pokot
IJ: 14950

Poland
P: 15276 I: 13866, 15277, 15286 IJ: 15263, 15283

Poland — Cookbooks
IJ: 21757

Poland — Fiction
I: 9076 IJ: 9051, 9681, 9687, 9701

Poland — Folklore
PI: 11170

Poland — Holidays
PI: 15295

Polar animals
P: 15847

Polar bears
P: 19042, 19053, 19063–64 PI: 19057, 19062, 19068 I: 19059, 19061

Polar bears — Fiction
P: 2009, 5207, 5209, 5225, 5238, 5253, 5301, 5314

Polar regions
See also Antarctic, Arctic
P: 15799, 15805
PI: 15827, 15841, 18927
I: 15793, 15820, 15826, 15838 IJ: 12087, 15792, 15813, 15839, 20792

Polar regions — Animals
P: 18964

Polar regions — Exploration
IJ: 15804

Police
See also Law enforcement officers
IJ: 16646

Police — Careers
P: 17091, 17807, 17814–15
PI: 17822

Police — Fiction
P: 3269 I: 6878

Police dogs
P: 19939

Police dogs — Fiction
P: 5378

Police state — Fiction
I: 9139

Polio
PI: 17973 I: 13311

Polio — Fiction
I: 9570

Polish Americans
PI: 17591 I: 17557

Polish Americans — Fiction
PI: 10054 I: 9595
IJ: 9519

Political parties
I: 17096–98 IJ: 17093, 17100

Politicians — Biography
PI: 12877 I: 12732, 12858, 12881, 12892, 13176, 13740 IJ: 12815, 12887, 12933, 12961, 13710

Politicians — Women
IJ: 13726

Polk, James K.
I: 12673, 13092 IJ: 13091

Polk, Sarah Childress
I: 13175

Pollination
P: 20035 IJ: 20038, 20232

Pollution
See also Ecology and environment
I: 16962, 16995, 17004, 19398 IJ: 16991, 16994, 17008, 19410, 19843, 20514

Pollution — Fiction
P: 1045, 2706, 4380, 4398, 4506, 4539 PI: 5341
I: 7053, 7890 IJ: 10020, 10195

Pollution, Air
P: 17006 I: 16989, 17001, 17005, 20670, 20677, 20773

Pollution, Marine
P: 16990 IJ: 17002

Pollution, Marine — Fiction
P: 984

Pollution, Water
P: 16992, 17007 I: 20520, 20743 IJ: 20514

Polo, Marco
I: 12148

Polynesia — Fiction
I: 8940 IJ: 7077

Polyphemus (mythology)
PI: 11471

Pompeii, Italy
I: 14710, 14723 IJ: 14737

Pompeii, Italy — Fiction
I: 14749

Ponce de Leon, Juan
I: 12150 IJ: 12149

Ponds and pond life
P: 4373, 20510, 20515, 20521–22 PI: 20518, 20529 I: 20512, 20526, 20528 IJ: 19808

Ponds and pond life — Biography
I: 13325

Ponds and pond life — Fiction
P: 4429, 4439, 4481, 4518, 5412

Ponds and pond life — Poetry
P: 11936

Ponies
P: 19984 PI: 19998
I: 19994, 20013
IJ: 19985–86, 19988

Ponies — Fiction
P: 5260, 6382, 6583
I: 8590, 9162

Pony Express
PI: 16288, 16314

Pony Express — Fiction
IJ: 9408

Pop Art
IJ: 13950

Pop-up books
P: 5602, 14261 PI: 1512, 21027 I: 10885, 14785, 14791 IJ: 7601, 16749

Pop-up books — Fiction
P: 638, 2920, 4590

Pop-ups — Construction
IJ: 21608

Popcorn
P: 20088, 20179

Popcorn Park Zoo (NJ)
I: 20029

Popes — Biography
I: 13816

Popes — Folklore
I: 10911

Poppies
P: 20247

Popular music
See also specific types of music, e.g., Rock music and musicians
IJ: 14121

Population
IJ: 17009–10

Porcupines
P: 19202 I: 18972

Porcupines — Fiction
P: 2361, 6367

***Porgy and Bess* (opera)**
P: 14242

Porpoises
I: 19802 IJ: 19685, 19688

P = Primary; PI = Primary-Intermediate; I = Intermediate; IJ = Intermediate-Junior High

Portugal
IJ: 15472, 15476, 15483

Postage stamps
IJ: 21807

**Postage stamps —
Dinosaurs**
IJ: 14389

Postal Service (U.S.)
P: 12722, 17105, 17111
I: 17106

**Postal Service (U.S.) —
Fiction**
P: 3407, 6664 **PI:** 3426

**Postal Service (U.S.) —
History**
PI: 16919

Postal workers
P: 17740

Potatoes
P: 20182, 20186

Potatoes — Folklore
P: 10971

Potlatch
I: 15972

Potter, Beatrix
P: 12580–82 **I:** 12579

Potters and pottery
PI: 16061, 21530 **I:** 21534
IJ: 13939

**Potters and pottery —
Biography**
IJ: 12257

**Potters and pottery —
Colonial Period (U.S.)**
I: 16115

Potties
See Toilet training

Poultry
P: 20086

Pout (fish)
PI: 19712

Poverty
P: 3403 **I:** 17146
IJ: 15663, 17025, 17152,
17160

Poverty — Fiction
P: 3588, 3749, 4650, 4793,
4843, 4905, 4916, 4920,
5016, 5103 **PI:** 7471, 8462,
8672, 8749, 8762 **I:** 7396,
7468, 8541, 8639, 8690,
8758, 9089, 9552, 9568,
9712 **IJ:** 7485, 8479, 8613,
8673, 9094, 9098, 9519,
9613, 9620

Poverty — Women
IJ: 17581

Powell, Colin
PI: 12949, 12955
I: 12951–52 **IJ:** 12950,
12953–54, 12956

Powell, John Wesley
I: 12152, 16611, 16636
IJ: 12151, 16087

Powers, Harriet
IJ: 12287

**Powhatan Indians —
Biography**
I: 12984 **IJ:** 12985

Powwows
PI: 15978 **I:** 15919, 15934,
15943, 15961, 15981, 16029

Powwows — Fiction
P: 3434 **I:** 9173

Prague — Fiction
P: 4765, 6069 **IJ:** 9050

Prairie dogs
P: 19193–94, 19210, 19212
I: 19203

Prairies
See also Grasslands
P: 20534 **PI:** 20423,
20530, 20535, 20542, 20549
I: 16535, 20541, 20547
IJ: 20540

Prairies — Animals
P: 20531

Prairies — Fiction
P: 4857 **PI:** 9410 **I:** 9383,
9588 **IJ:** 8608

Prairies — Poetry
I: 11962

Prayers
See also Blessings
P: 17203, 17512, 17516,
17518, 17522, 17524,
17527, 17529–37 **PI:** 687,
17515, 17519, 17528
I: 17511, 17513, 17517,
17520, 17526 **IJ:** 17514,
17521, 17525

Prayers — Fiction
P: 3957

Prayers — Jewish
P: 17523

Praying mantises
P: 19459 **I:** 19433

Predatory animals
P: 19335 **PI:** 18641
IJ: 18810

Predictions
IJ: 21919, 21924

Pregnancy
IJ: 18269

Pregnancy — Fiction
P: 3505 **PI:** 8595
IJ: 8445, 8577

Pregnant teenagers
IJ: 18269

Prehistoric animals
See also Dinosaurs;
Mammoths
P: 14418, 14450, 14484
PI: 14391, 14479 **I:** 14382,
14412, 14480, 21576
IJ: 14516

**Prehistoric animals —
Defenses**
PI: 14475

**Prehistoric animals —
Fiction**
P: 929

Prehistoric life
I: 14397, 14454 **IJ:** 14504,
14506

Prehistoric life — Fiction
PI: 1338 **IJ:** 8955

Prehistoric peoples
PI: 14492, 14512, 14518
I: 14493, 14508, 14585
IJ: 14494–95, 14497,
14501, 14503, 14507,
14509, 14516, 14530

Prehistoric peoples — Art
I: 14502

**Prehistoric peoples —
Fiction**
P: 4588, 4635, 6407
PI: 8950, 8958 **I:** 7613,
8953, 8959 **IJ:** 8951–52,
8954, 8956, 9789

Prejudice
See also Racism
P: 17141 **PI:** 17140, 17457
IJ: 14564, 17023, 17145

Prejudice — Fiction
P: 4011, 5034, 10402
PI: 8842 **I:** 6791, 7363,
7402, 8904, 9592 **IJ:** 7097,
7334, 7359, 8289, 8453,
9372, 9529, 9533, 9641

Prejudice — History
IJ: 16464

Prenatal development
See also Pregnancy
P: 18228 **PI:** 18239

Prepositions
PI: 14029

Preschool
P: 2998

Preschool — Fiction
P: 2464, 5475

Presidents Day (U.S.)
PI: 17388

**Presidents (Mexico) —
Biography**
PI: 13818 **I:** 13817

Presidents (U.S.)
P: 17126 **PI:** 15881
I: 17101–2, 17120, 17125,
17127 **IJ:** 16276–77,
16484–85, 16520

**Presidents (U.S.) —
Biography**
See also individual
presidents, e.g., Clinton,
Bill

P: 13003, 13012, 13046,
13063, 13065, 13069–70,
13078–79, 13086–87,
13094, 13113 **PI:** 13004,
13022–23, 13026, 13038,
13047, 13058, 13060,
13067, 13074, 13102,
13109, 13118 **I:** 12636–37,
12658, 12671–75, 13002,
13005–7, 13009–11, 13013,
13015–16, 13020,
13024–25, 13027–28,
13031, 13034, 13036–37,
13040, 13042, 13045,
13049–50, 13052–54,
13059, 13062, 13064,
13068, 13072–73, 13081,
13083–85, 13090,
13092–93, 13100, 13104–5,
13108, 13115–16, 13142,
15885 **IJ:** 12670, 12683,
12686, 12689, 12696,
13008, 13014, 13017–19,
13021, 13029–30,
13032–33, 13035, 13039,
13041, 13043–44, 13048,
13051, 13055–57, 13061,
13066, 13071, 13075–77,
13080, 13082, 13088–89,
13091, 13095–99, 13101,
13103, 13106–7, 13110–12,
13114, 13117, 13119–23

**Presidents (U.S.) —
Children**
I: 12638

**Presidents (U.S.) —
Elections**
I: 17108 **IJ:** 17095

**Presidents (U.S.) —
Fiction**
P: 1873 **I:** 9513, 9858,
9869

**Presidents (U.S.) —
Letters**
I: 17113

**Presidents (U.S.) — Wives
— Biography**
P: 13125, 13178–79
PI: 13023, 13144, 13146,
13182 **I:** 12650, 13010,
13084, 13124, 13126,
13141, 13145, 13147,
13154, 13157, 13169,
13171–73, 13175, 13177,
13183, 13185, 13198–99
IJ: 13017, 13159, 13167,
13170, 13180–81, 13184,
13186–87

Presley, Elvis
P: 5016 **IJ:** 12444–45

Price, Leontyne
I: 12446–47

**Prime ministers (Great
Britain) — Biography**
IJ: 13769, 13860

P = Primary; PI = Primary-Intermediate; I = Intermediate; IJ = Intermediate-Junior High

Prime ministers (Zimbabwe) — Biography
IJ: 13838

Prince Edward Island
I: 15568

Prince Edward Island — Fiction
PI: 5167

Princes — Fiction
P: 2162, 10401, 10451, 10470 PI: 5940, 10456, 10498 I: 7980, 7996, 10455, 10457, 10522
IJ: 6844

Princes — Folklore
P: 10898, 10909, 11113
PI: 10718

Princesses — Biography
I: 13765, 13782, 13820

Princesses — Fiction
P: 1385, 1566, 1652, 10404, 10425 PI: 10456 I: 7396, 8252, 10426, 10455, 10457
IJ: 7621, 10506

Princesses — Folklore
P: 10732, 10780, 10872, 10902

Pringle, Laurence
P: 14877 PI: 12583

Printers — Biography
PI: 13305 I: 13304

Printing
See also Books and printing
PI: 14000 IJ: 16421

Printing — Crafts
IJ: 21624

Printmaking
I: 13894, 21640

Prinze, Freddie, Jr.
PI: 12448

Prisoners of war — World War II
IJ: 14896

Prisons
I: 16780 IJ: 17070, 17086

Prisons — Fiction
PI: 4978, 8830

Prisons — History
I: 14342

Private schools — Fiction
I: 10096

Pro Football Hall of Fame
I: 22181

Probability
I: 20614

Prohibition (U.S.)
I: 16453

Pronouns
PI: 14034

Prostheses
P: 17914

Proteins
I: 20160

Protestantism
P: 17218

Proverbs
P: 10568

Proverbs — Korean
PI: 10729

Proverbs — Spanish
PI: 14028

Proverbs — Vietnamese
I: 14113

Psalms (Bible)
P: 17299, 17316 I: 17248

Psychic powers
I: 21895

Psychic powers — Fiction
I: 7414

Psychology
I: 17618

Ptarmigans
P: 19248

Ptarmigans — Fiction
P: 1212

Puberty
See also Adolescence
I: 17620, 18250, 18253, 18260 IJ: 17694, 17706, 18249, 18267

Puberty — Boys
IJ: 18258

Public speaking
IJ: 14077, 14102

Publishers and publishing
P: 13990, 14082 I: 13996
IJ: 14002, 16421

Publishers and publishing — Biography
IJ: 12507

Puckett, Kirby
PI: 13478

Pueblo Indians
PI: 16061 I: 15958, 15969, 15980, 16000, 16013, 16024
IJ: 15931, 15941, 15985, 16073

Pueblo Indians — Fiction
PI: 4749 I: 9145 IJ: 9183

Pueblo Indians — Folklore
PI: 11256

Pueblo Indians — History
I: 16040 IJ: 15921

Pueblo Indians — Homes
I: 16026

Puerto Rican Americans
I: 17588 IJ: 17539

Puerto Rican Americans — Biography
PI: 12824 I: 13442, 13444
IJ: 13443

Puerto Rican Americans — Fiction
P: 3002 PI: 7331

Puerto Ricans — Fiction
IJ: 7965

Puerto Rico
P: 15702, 15710–11
I: 15708, 15715 IJ: 12935, 15700, 15709

Puerto Rico — Biography
PI: 12422 I: 12936
IJ: 12830

Puerto Rico — Fiction
P: 3823, 4744, 4774, 4865
IJ: 7334, 9130

Puerto Rico — Folklore
P: 11424

Puffins
P: 19379 PI: 19351
I: 19271, 19350 IJ: 19356

Pulaski, Casimir
IJ: 13844

Pulleys (physics)
P: 20926

Pumpkins
P: 20175, 20181 I: 20171, 21438

Pumpkins — Crafts
PI: 21434 IJ: 21466

Pumpkins — Fiction
P: 134, 3857, 4351, 4893, 6013, 6018, 6022, 6032, 6035 PI: 1500, 8700

Punchball — Fiction
P: 3024

Punctuation
IJ: 14112

Puppets and marionettes
P: 14303, 14307
PI: 14305, 14308 I: 14304, 14306

Puppets and marionettes — Fiction
P: 4995 PI: 7662, 9862
I: 7660–61, 9006

Purim
P: 6071, 6090, 17463, 17466

Purim — Fiction
P: 6069, 6101, 6114, 6120

Puritans
IJ: 16105

Puritans — Fiction
PI: 9203

Puzzles
See also Games; Mathematical puzzles; Picture puzzles; Word games and puzzles
P: 850, 21871–72, 21874
PI: 21861, 21863, 21869
I: 10613, 21866–67
IJ: 18330, 21864

Puzzles — Fiction
P: 305, 442, 2752, 2938, 3175 IJ: 9983

Puzzles — Poetry
I: 6767 IJ: 11724

Pygmies
IJ: 14932

Pygmies — Fiction
IJ: 9533

Pyle, Ernie
I: 12584

Pyramids
See also Egypt — History
P: 14615, 14621 PI: 14645
I: 14350, 14613, 14616, 14643, 14649, 14660, 15502, 21144 IJ: 14639

Pyramids — Experiments and projects
I: 14350

Pythons
PI: 18773

Pythons — Fiction
PI: 8974

Q

Qatar
IJ: 15535

Qin, Emperor of China — Tomb
IJ: 15070

Quadruplets — Fiction
IJ: 8631

Quakers — Fiction
P: 6224 I: 9293 IJ: 9465

Quarter horses
I: 20012

Quebec, Canada
I: 15580

Queen Anne's lace
I: 20267

Queens — Biography
I: 13775, 13788 IJ: 13738

Queens — Fiction
P: 10387

Quicksand — Fiction
P: 4416

Quilts and quilting
P: 110 PI: 11958
I: 16296, 16350, 21641
IJ: 12287, 21648–49

P = Primary; PI = Primary-Intermediate; I = Intermediate; IJ = Intermediate-Junior High

Quilts and quilting — Fiction
P: 1020, 3252, 3613, 3654, 3839, 3919, 4641, 5737, 6275 PI: 292

Quimby, Harriet
I: 12153

Quinceanera (coming-of-age ritual)
IJ: 17379–80

Quinn, Anthony
IJ: 12449

Quintanilla, Guadalupe
IJ: 12834

Quokka (animal)
PI: 19183

Quotations
IJ: 14104

Quotations — Anthologies
IJ: 14069

R

Rabbis — Fiction
P: 1127

Rabbits
P: 19196, 19211, 19891, 19902 PI: 19889, 19898
I: 19208, 19893

Rabbits — Fiction
P: 407, 449, 776, 1668, 1767, 1785, 1795, 1853, 1861, 1892, 1895, 1931, 2123, 2150, 2308–9, 2425, 2503, 2597, 2640, 2654, 2720, 2763, 2858, 2902, 4142, 4421, 5039, 5267, 5356, 5371, 5676, 5742, 5962–63, 5966, 5968, 6030, 6160, 6215, 6668 PI: 8209
I: 7178, 7895, 9885, 9889
IJ: 7544, 7839

Rabbits — Folklore
P: 10642, 10693, 10801, 11052, 11347–48 I: 11345, 11445

Raccoons
P: 18923, 18940, 18954, 18958

Raccoons — Fiction
P: 4394, 5631 PI: 7328, 7659 IJ: 7172, 7264, 7282

Racing cars
IJ: 21314

Racism
See also Prejudice
P: 17141 PI: 17140
IJ: 16497, 17133

Racism — Biography
PI: 13430

Racism — Fiction
P: 4769, 5074 I: 7362, 7402, 8904 IJ: 7338, 7369, 7770, 8251, 8258, 8828, 9078, 9533, 10079, 10345

Racism — History
IJ: 16464

Radio — Fiction
IJ: 9643

Radio — History
I: 21278

Radio control models
IJ: 21669

Radio operators — Fiction
PI: 9518

Radiology
I: 18031

Radium
PI: 13261 I: 13262–63

Radium — Biography
IJ: 13260

Railroads and trains
P: 5548, 5557, 5590, 21328, 21330–32, 21339, 21341
PI: 21283, 21335, 21344
IJ: 21334

Railroads and trains — Fiction
P: 692, 1238, 1295, 1466, 2887, 3087, 3223, 3451, 3465, 3704, 3909, 4638, 4665, 5562, 5580, 5591–92, 5599, 5608, 5943, 6399, 6530, 6715, 21333
PI: 4895, 9345, 9417
I: 3091 IJ: 9360, 9370

Railroads and trains — History
P: 21340 PI: 21327, 21342–43 I: 16358, 21329, 21345–47 IJ: 16265, 16385, 21336–38

Railroads and trains — Train wrecks — Fiction
P: 4638

Railroads and trains (model)
IJ: 21668

Rain
See also Acid rain
P: 20727, 20783 I: 20729, 20767, 20777

Rain — Fiction
P: 1900, 2742, 3214, 3217, 3248, 3311, 4313, 4426, 4470, 4480, 4538, 4543, 4554, 4560, 4657

Rain — Folklore
P: 10639

Rain forests
See also Forests
P: 4566, 4882, 18717, 20435–36, 20452, 20472

PI: 116, 11977, 20437, 20444, 20455, 20458, 20462–63, 20465, 20475–79, 20481, 20483, 20488, 20490, 20494
I: 15782, 15787, 20397, 20442, 20446, 20448–49, 20459, 20468, 20480, 20487, 20491–92, 20495
IJ: 11441, 13341, 20259, 20383, 20430, 20433, 20439–40, 20451, 20453, 20464, 20467, 20470

Rain forests — Animals
P: 20493 I: 20484
IJ: 20433

Rain forests — Experiments and projects
I: 20448

Rain forests — Fiction
P: 4404, 4409, 4434, 4874, 5201 PI: 4619, 7579
I: 7961

Rainbows
P: 20872 PI: 20749

Rainbows — Fiction
P: 1167, 3469

Ramadan
PI: 5627

Ramayana — Folklore
I: 10787

Ramphele, Mamphela
IJ: 13845

Ranches and ranch life
P: 3299, 20084 PI: 20052
I: 12921

Ranches and ranch life — Fiction
P: 3155 PI: 7304 I: 7234, 7301, 7639, 9540, 9599
IJ: 7447, 8511

Ranches and ranch life — History
IJ: 16359

Randolph, A. Philip
PI: 12781 IJ: 12782

Rap music and musicians
IJ: 14120

Rap music and musicians — Biography
I: 12394 IJ: 12410

Rap music and musicians — Fiction
PI: 8280

Rats
P: 19195 PI: 19204

Rats — Fiction
P: 1967, 2230, 2277, 9816
I: 7033, 7663 IJ: 7664, 7753, 7999

Rats — Folklore
P: 10541

Rattlesnakes
P: 18754 PI: 18753
I: 18758

Rattlesnakes — Fiction
P: 11210

Reading
P: 14007, 14105

Reading — Fiction
P: 1463, 3353, 3560, 4033, 4106, 6360, 6409, 6454, 6645 PI: 1818 I: 7376, 8790, 10048, 10087
IJ: 10120

Reading — Poetry
P: 11600

Reading Rainbow (TV program)
PI: 14313

Reagan, Ronald
P: 13094 I: 12674, 13093
IJ: 13095

Rebus books
P: 6259

Recipes
See Cookbooks

Reconstruction Period (U.S.)
PI: 16419 I: 16473
IJ: 16455–56, 16469

Reconstruction Period (U.S.) — Fiction
IJ: 9615

Recreation
IJ: 22037

Recreation director — Careers
PI: 17744

Rectangles
PI: 20606

Recycling — Paper
See also Waste recycling
I: 21065

Red Cross
IJ: 17017

Red-eyed tree frogs
P: 18732

Red Sea
I: 19847

Redwoods
PI: 20213

Reece, Gabrielle
IJ: 13708

Reeve, Christopher
I: 12450

Reflection (physics)
I: 20860

Reflexes
P: 18049

Reform party (U.S.)
IJ: 17093

P = Primary; PI = Primary-Intermediate; I = Intermediate; IJ = Intermediate-Junior High

Reformation
IJ: 1403

Refugees
PI: 1153, 15176
IJ: 1453, 17016, 17018

Refugees — Fiction
P: 472, 5040 I: 9646
IJ: 868, 9675

Reilly, Ted
I: 19400

Reincarnation
IJ: 21894

Reincarnation — Fiction
P: 979, 4662 IJ: 7461

Reindeer
P: 19154 PI: 19156

Reindeer — Fiction
P: 5760, 5867, 5905

Religion
See also Bible stories;
Prayers; and specific
religions, e.g.,
Christianity
P: 5624, 5651, 17170,
17199, 17226, 18251
PI: 5627, 5644, 17216,
17222 I: 17167, 17184–85,
17205–6, 17210–11, 17214,
17223, 17357–59
IJ: 14782, 17164, 17171,
17178, 17188–89, 17220,
17230, 17314

Religion — Anthologies
I: 17174

Religion — Biography
IJ: 13857

**Religion — Colonial
Period (U.S.)**
IJ: 16099

Religion — Fiction
P: 4662, 4668, 5622, 17172,
17215 I: 9619 IJ: 8780,
8833, 9030, 10357

Religion — History
I: 17202 IJ: 12700, 13160,
14709, 14767

**Religion — Places of
worship**
I: 17223

Religion — Poetry
I: 11743

Religion — United States
IJ: 15913

Rembrandt van Rijn
PI: 12289 IJ: 12288

**Rembrandt van Rijn —
Fiction**
I: 9042

Remington, Frederic
PI: 12290

Renaissance
I: 14802, 14804 IJ: 14797,
14801, 14803, 14805

Renaissance — Art
IJ: 14799, 17313

Renaissance — Biography
PI: 12234 IJ: 12261

Renaissance — Fiction
PI: 9025 I: 9037, 9052,
9064, 9072 IJ: 9049

Renaissance — Science
IJ: 14800

**Renaissance artists —
Biography**
IJ: 12214

Rendille
IJ: 14945

Reno, Janet
I: 12957

Renoir, Auguste
PI: 12292 IJ: 12291

Report writing
I: 14092

Reporters
See Journalists and
journalism

Reproduction
See also Sex education
P: 18237–38, 18240, 18244
PI: 18245, 18248, 18261
IJ: 18247

Reproduction — Fiction
P: 298

Reptiles
See also specific reptiles,
e.g., Alligators and
crocodiles
P: 18682, 18694
PI: 18679, 18687, 18693
I: 18678, 18683, 18690,
19906 IJ: 19419

Reptiles — Crafts
I: 21483

Reptiles — Pets
I: 19894

Reptiles — Poetry
I: 11785

Research — Guides
IJ: 14089, 14091

Respiration
PI: 18128 I: 17879, 18078,
18123, 18125 IJ: 18124,
18126–27

Restaurants
I: 16951

**Restaurants —
Experiments and
projects**
I: 18335

Restaurants — Fiction
P: 1739, 3285, 3336, 3515

Retirement — Fiction
I: 7451

Revere, Paul
P: 12958 PI: 12959

Revere, Paul — Fiction
P: 157 IJ: 9914

Revere, Paul — Poetry
P: 11644 PI: 11643
I: 11642

**Revolutionary Period
(U.S.)**
IJ: 16282

Revolutionary War (U.S.)
P: 12958, 13113, 16212
PI: 12837, 12959, 16189,
16210–11, 16216 I: 12644,
13116, 16198–99, 16202–3,
16205, 16208–9, 16219,
16222–23 IJ: 12962,
13114, 13825, 16130,
16190–97, 16200–1, 16204,
16206–7, 16215, 16217–18,
16220–21

**Revolutionary War (U.S.)
— Biography**
P: 12898, 12915 PI: 13004
I: 12897, 12914, 13188,
13191 IJ: 12083, 12681,
12836, 12847, 12880,
12943, 13844

**Revolutionary War (U.S.)
— Fiction**
P: 4592, 4812, 4884, 9254
PI: 4593, 4858, 7691,
9221–23, 9229, 9232–33,
9241, 9249, 9252, 9255
I: 9224–25, 9231, 9235,
9239, 9243–44, 9246,
9250–51 IJ: 7840, 9220,
9226–28, 9230, 9234, 9236,
9240, 9242, 9245, 9247–48,
9253, 9323

**Revolutionary War (U.S.)
— Poetry**
P: 11644 PI: 11643
I: 11642

**Revolutionary War (U.S.)
— Women**
IJ: 16224

**Rheumatoid arthritis —
Fiction**
I: 8720

Rhine river
IJ: 15330

Rhinoceroses
P: 14450 PI: 18945
I: 18970, 18986

Rhinoceroses — Fiction
P: 297, 2361, 2691, 5224,
5287

Rhode Island
P: 4493, 16673 I: 16692,
16753 IJ: 16717

Rhode Island — Fiction
IJ: 6755

Rhode Island — History
IJ: 16261

Rhode Island Colony
IJ: 16125

**Rhodes (Greece) —
Fiction**
PI: 7561

Rice
P: 20093, 20127, 21695
PI: 20130

Rice, Jerry
I: 13624 IJ: 13623

Richards, Ann
I: 13176

Richards, Ellen
I: 13342

Richmond, Mitch
IJ: 13566

**Richmond (Virginia) —
History**
IJ: 16388

Riddles
See Jokes and riddles
P: 21825 PI: 21827

Ride, Sally
I: 12154, 21006 IJ: 20971

Rimes, LeAnn
IJ: 12451

Rio de Janeiro, Brazil
I: 15753

Rio Grande (river)
I: 15892

Ripken, Cal, Jr.
P: 13482 I: 13479, 13481,
13483 IJ: 13480

Rivera, Diego
IJ: 12293

Rivers
See also Streams
P: 3163, 16802, 16992,
20511, 20524 PI: 19323,
20519, 20523 I: 15588,
15782, 15883, 18784,
20390, 20525, 20527
IJ: 7235, 15095, 20513

Rivers — Fiction
P: 4380, 4461, 4543, 4554

Rivers — Plants
P: 20516

Roads
P: 21128

Roads — Fiction
P: 3291, 5568

Roads — History
I: 14351

**Roanoke Island —
History**
I: 16135

**Robbers and robbery —
Biography**
See also Outlaws —
Biography
IJ: 12851, 12908

P = Primary; PI = Primary-Intermediate; I = Intermediate; IJ = Intermediate-Junior High

Robbers and robbery — Fiction
P: 1586, 1791, 1962, 2904, 4896, 6563 **PI:** 6733, 6801, 6963 **I:** 6754, 6833, 6846–47, 6858, 7055, 7906, 9006, 9433, 9848 **IJ:** 9067

Robbers and robbery — Folklore
PI: 11091, 11193 **I:** 10988 **IJ:** 10964, 11023

Roberts, Julia
PI: 12452

Robeson, Paul
IJ: 12454

Robin Hood
PI: 10968–69, 10973, 10996, 11045

Robin Hood — Fiction
IJ: 9129

Robins
P: 19239, 19277, 19298

Robins — Fiction
P: 1768

Robinson, Brooks
I: 13484

Robinson, David
PI: 13572 **I:** 13570–71 **IJ:** 13567–69

Robinson, Frank
I: 13485

Robinson, Jackie
P: 13487 **PI:** 13486, 13494 **I:** 13489, 13491–93, 13495 **IJ:** 13488, 13490

Robinson, Jackie — Fiction
IJ: 7770

Robots
P: 21200, 21216 **I:** 21036, 21226 **IJ:** 21225

Robots — Fiction
P: 1479, 4204, 6394 **PI:** 1475, 10147 **I:** 10145, 10149, 10214, 10239 **IJ:** 10146, 10148

Rock, Chris
IJ: 12455

Rock art
I: 13941 **IJ:** 15984

Rock climbing
I: 21979 **IJ:** 22050, 22056

Rock collecting
PI: 20559

Rock music and musicians
IJ: 14123

Rock music and musicians — Biography
I: 12365 **IJ:** 12425, 14129

Rock music and musicians — Fiction
PI: 10138

Rock paintings
See Rock art

"Rock" (wrestling)
IJ: 22053

Rockefeller, John D.
IJ: 12960

Rockets
PI: 14898 **I:** 20985, 21003

Rockets — Biography
IJ: 13298

Rocking horses — Fiction
P: 3547

Rocks and minerals
See also Geology
P: 20555, 20560, 20564, 20566 **PI:** 20559 **I:** 20552, 20556, 20561–63, 20569, 20571, 20574–75 **IJ:** 20553–54, 20557, 20572

Rocks and minerals — Collecting
IJ: 20567

Rocks and minerals — Fiction
P: 4405

Rockwell, Norman
PI: 12296 **I:** 12294 **IJ:** 12295

Rocky Mountain National Park
PI: 16634

Rocky Mountains
I: 20501

Rodents
PI: 19199 **I:** 19201

Rodents — Fiction
PI: 7845

Rodeos
P: 21975 **PI:** 21993, 22005 **I:** 21970, 22060–62

Rodeos — Biography
I: 12443

Rodeos — Fiction
P: 2958, 5434, 6382

Rodin, Auguste
PI: 12297

Rodman, Dennis
IJ: 13573–74

Rodriguez, Alex
I: 13496

Rodriguez, Luis
IJ: 12835

Rodriguez, Robert
I: 12456

Roentgen, Wilhelm
PI: 13343

Rogers, Will
P: 12458 **I:** 12457, 12459

Role models — Fiction
IJ: 8770

Roller coasters
IJ: 14267

Roller hockey — Fiction
I: 10311

Roller skates and roller skating — Fiction
P: 6250 **I:** 9622

Roman Catholicism
P: 17219 **IJ:** 17181

Roman Catholics — Mass
P: 17221

Roman Empire
See also Rome — History
I: 14720, 15388 **IJ:** 14741

Roman Empire — Fiction
IJ: 8938, 8941

Roman numerals
PI: 20631

Romance — Fiction
See also Love — Fiction
IJ: 8331, 8384, 9333, 9456

Romania
I: 15262 **IJ:** 15285

Romania — Fiction
P: 5845

Rome
I: 15371, 15388, 15393

Rome — Art
IJ: 14722

Rome — Crafts
IJ: 14714

Rome — Fiction
P: 4659 **I:** 14749 **IJ:** 9059

Rome — History
See also Roman Empire
PI: 14715, 14717, 14728, 14738 **I:** 11490, 14581, 14596, 14698, 14710–12, 14716, 14718–19, 14721, 14723–26, 14729, 14732–33, 14736, 14740, 14742–43, 14750–51, 15371 **IJ:** 13763–64, 14584, 14713–14, 14722, 14727, 14730–31, 14734–35, 14737, 14739, 14741, 14744–45, 14748

Rome — History — Crafts
I: 14746

Rome — History — Food
IJ: 14747

Rome — Mythology
P: 11498, 11506 **I:** 11490 **IJ:** 11497, 11512

Rome — Science
IJ: 14591

Rome — Sports
IJ: 14592

Rome — Women
IJ: 14730

Romulus and Remus (mythology)
IJ: 11512

Ronstadt, Linda
IJ: 12460

Rooks, June
PI: 13344

Room decoration
IJ: 21415

Roosevelt, Edith
I: 13177

Roosevelt, Eleanor
P: 13178–79 **PI:** 13182 **I:** 13183, 13185 **IJ:** 13180–81, 13184, 13186–87

Roosevelt, Franklin D.
I: 13100, 16726 **IJ:** 13096–99, 16454, 16471

Roosevelt, Franklin D. — Fiction
P: 4714

Roosevelt, Theodore
PI: 13102, 19151 **I:** 12673, 13104 **IJ:** 13101, 13103

Roosevelt, Theodore — Fiction
P: 5838 **I:** 9513

Roosevelt Memorial (Washington, DC)
I: 16724, 16726

Rope skipping
P: 884, 22017 **PI:** 21983 **I:** 21977

Rope skipping — Fiction
P: 1157

Roses
PI: 20039

Rosetta Stone
I: 13766, 14623 **IJ:** 14626

Rosh Hashanah
IJ: 17464

Rosh Hashanah — Fiction
P: 6075, 6088, 6112, 6126

Ross, Betsy
P: 13190 **I:** 13188–89

Rousseau, Henri
IJ: 12298–99

Rowing — Fiction
IJ: 6922

Rowling, J. K.
IJ: 12585

Royal Ballet School (England)
I: 14290

Royal Canadian Mounted Police — Poetry
IJ: 11805

Royce, Sarah
IJ: 16370

P = Primary; PI = Primary-Intermediate; I = Intermediate; IJ = Intermediate-Junior High

Rubber
P: 21047

Rudolph, Wilma
P: 1872 PI: 13670
I: 13671, 13673

Runaways
See Running away

Running and jogging
I: 22259

Running and jogging —
Biography
IJ: 13390

Running and jogging —
Fiction
P: 4579 IJ: 6951

Running away — Fiction
P: 1559, 1895 PI: 8267
I: 7687, 8451, 9778, 9844
IJ: 8402, 8557, 8701

Russell, Charles
PI: 12300

Russell, Keri
PI: 12461

Russia
P: 15404 PI: 96, 15408,
15419 I: 15414, 15417,
15420, 15429, 15431–32,
17573 IJ: 13824, 15411,
15426–28

Russia — Biography
IJ: 13869

Russia — Cookbooks
IJ: 21731

Russia — Fiction
P: 1675, 4604, 4617, 4643,
4782, 4894, 5244, 5543,
7791 PI: 9069 I: 9057,
9896 IJ: 7743, 9063

Russia — Folklore
P: 2643, 4796, 11081–84,
11086–90, 11092–94,
11098–102, 11104–6,
11108, 11111, 11113–15
PI: 11085, 11091, 11103,
11109–10, 11361 I: 11096,
11112, 11116 IJ: 11080,
11107

Russia — History
PI: 16283 I: 15410, 15418
IJ: 14837, 15409

Russia — Sports
IJ: 15424

Russian Americans
IJ: 17579

Russian Americans —
Fiction
P: 3582, 4617, 5665, 5902
PI: 3846 I: 9580
IJ: 9550, 9625

Russian Revolution —
Fiction
IJ: 9063

Rustin, Bayard
IJ: 12783

Ruth, Babe
I: 13497–98, 13500
IJ: 13499

Ruth, Babe — Fiction
P: 4571 I: 8122, 10329
IJ: 7768

Rwanda
P: 14930 I: 13284

Rwanda — Folklore
I: 10643

Ryan, Nolan
I: 13502 IJ: 13501

Ryder, Winona
PI: 12462

Rylant, Cynthia
I: 12586

S

Sac Indians
PI: 15995

Sacagawea
P: 12988 I: 12989–92

Sacagawea — Fiction
IJ: 9424, 9434

Safety
See also Health and
medicine
P: 18214, 18220, 18223–24
PI: 18221–22 I: 18225–26
IJ: 18216–18

Safety — Fiction
P: 1932, 2444, 3049

Safety — Sports
IJ: 18219

Safety — Water
P: 18214

Sagan, Carl
IJ: 13345–46

Saguaro cactus
PI: 20402

Sahara Desert
IJ: 14963

Sailing and boating
P: 22261 PI: 22260
I: 22265 IJ: 22264

Sailing and boating —
Fiction
P: 2923 I: 10269 IJ: 7087

Sailing and boating —
History
PI: 21371

Sailing ships
P: 21364 I: 21376

Saint Augustine (FL)
PI: 16894

Saint Bernards
PI: 6364

St. James, Lyn
I: 13429

St. Lawrence Seaway
PI: 15574

St. Louis
PI: 16548

St. Louis World's Fair
(1904) — Fiction
IJ: 9533

Saint Patrick's Day
PI: 17341, 17355, 17362

Saint Patrick's Day —
Fiction
P: 5615, 5623, 5632, 5642,
5653

St. Petersburg, Russia
I: 15423

Saints
I: 17163 IJ: 17208

Saints — Biography
P: 13768, 13842 I: 13793,
13811 IJ: 13822

Salamanders
PI: 18688, 18695 I: 18685,
18689, 18697

Salamanders — Fiction
P: 5344 I: 7253

Salem (MA) — Fiction
I: 9199

Salem (MA) — History
PI: 16150 I: 16146, 16164
IJ: 16138, 16141

Salmon
P: 16797, 19700, 19713
I: 19704

Salmon — Fiction
P: 2824

Salt
P: 21048

Salt — Experiments and
projects
I: 20288

Salt Lake City
PI: 16597

Salt Lake City — Fiction
I: 9585

Samburu (African people)
IJ: 14931

Sami (Lapland)
PI: 15815

Samplers (crafts)
I: 16101

Sampras, Pete
PI: 13651 IJ: 13652

Sampson, Deborah
I: 13191

Samurai — Fiction
I: 9007 IJ: 9008

San Antonio
I: 16913

San Antonio Spurs
(basketball team)
IJ: 22146

Sand
P: 20568 I: 20571

Sand castles
I: 21665

Sand castles — Fiction
P: 4064

Sand dunes
I: 20558

Sandburg, Carl
I: 12588 IJ: 12587

Sanders, Barry
I: 13625–26 IJ: 13627–28

Sanders, Deion
I: 13629

Sandhill cranes
P: 19288

San Diego
PI: 16804

Sandler, Adam
IJ: 12463

Sandoz, Mari
I: 12589

San Francisco
P: 5618, 16768 I: 16760,
16783, 16793

San Francisco — Fiction
PI: 9669 I: 7117, 9574–76
IJ: 7538, 7640, 9589

San Francisco — History
I: 16824 IJ: 16814

San Francisco earthquake
IJ: 16814

San Francisco 49ers
(football team)
I: 22186

San Francisco Giants
(baseball team)
I: 22114

Sanitation
PI: 20726 I: 16976, 18197
IJ: 18191

San Juan Capistrano
(CA) — Fiction
P: 5368

San Juan (Puerto Rico)
IJ: 15709

San Martín, José de
I: 13846

Santa Claus
PI: 5823 I: 17428
IJ: 17422

Santa Claus — Fiction
P: 4796, 5760–61, 5792,
5855, 5860, 5867, 5871,
5897, 5925, 5932, 5952,
5954, 5958, 5966 I: 9715

P = Primary; PI = Primary-Intermediate; I = Intermediate; IJ = Intermediate-Junior High

Santa Claus — Poetry
P: 11839–40, 11848

Santa Fe Trail
I: 16284, 16293 **IJ:** 16302

Santa Fe Trail — Fiction
I: 9381 **IJ:** 9362

Saralegui, Cristina
PI: 12464

Sargasso Sea
I: 21911

Sasaki, Sadako
PI: 13847

Saskatchewan
I: 15590

Sasquatch
See Big Foot

Saturn (planet)
PI: 18464, 18493, 18501
I: 18477, 18482

Saudi Arabia
See also Arabia
P: 15534 **PI:** 15557
I: 15538, 15551 **IJ:** 15542

Saudi Arabia — Holidays
PI: 15557

Sautuola, Maria de
PI: 13848

Savannas
P: 20533

Savings (business)
IJ: 16922

Savion
IJ: 12465

Scabs (skin)
P: 18183

Scandinavia
See Denmark; Finland;
Norway; Sweden;
Vikings

Scandinavia — Crafts
IJ: 15446

Scandinavia — Fiction
P: 4738

Scandinavia — Folklore
I: 11125–26

Scarecrows — Fiction
P: 1017, 1124, 1534, 3145, 3297 **PI:** 8333

Schindler, Oskar
IJ: 13849

Schliemann, Heinrich
IJ: 14523

School buses — Fiction
P: 4089

School integration
I: 17046

School schools
P: 9816

School segregation
IJ: 16497

School stories

P: 139, 183, 311, 607, 926,
1075, 1883–84, 1978, 2201,
2343, 2464, 2482, 2531,
2831, 2837, 3030, 3226,
3472, 3747, 4046, 4059,
4077, 4089, 4091, 4093,
4193, 4264, 4279, 4317,
4368, 4590, 4740, 4750,
4793, 4824–25, 4987, 4989,
5008, 5054, 5466–71,
5473–74, 5476–77,
5479–87, 5491–506,
5508–13, 5515–33,
5535–39, 5541–43, 5545,
5858, 5993, 6038, 6134,
6267, 6318, 6327, 6332–33,
6346, 6348–49, 6354, 6370,
6389, 6410, 6436, 6478,
6480–81, 6527, 6557, 6569,
6571–72, 6674, 6724, 6764,
7080, 7626, 8334, 9900,
10067–69, 10088–89,
10137, 10139 **PI:** 92, 1512,
3100, 4018, 5472, 5507,
5514, 5544, 6342, 6920,
7331, 7356, 8349, 8382,
8597, 8616, 8629, 8649,
8661, 8807, 9774, 9840,
9952, 9955, 9974, 9980,
9989, 10022, 10024, 10026,
10029, 10034, 10039,
10044, 10051–52, 10054,
10058, 10063, 10065,
10073–74, 10083–85,
10090–92, 10098–99,
10101–3, 10106–7,
10115–16, 10118–19,
10121–22, 10125, 10128,
10130–32, 10138, 10140,
10179, 10330 **I:** 6919,
7363, 7442, 7747, 7948,
8260, 8270, 8290, 8295,
8317, 8367, 8370, 8400,
8433, 8553, 8600, 8640,
8657, 8684, 8727, 8743,
8746, 8767, 8785, 8854,
8892, 8909, 9123, 9175,
9178, 9631, 9794, 9803,
9832, 9838, 9893, 9906,
9910, 9927, 9947, 9960,
9972, 10011–12, 10025,
10028, 10031–33,
10035–38, 10043,
10046–50, 10055,
10059–60, 10062, 10066,
10072, 10075–78, 10081,
10086–87, 10094, 10096,
10108–11, 10114, 10117,
10124, 10126–27, 10279,
10320 **IJ:** 7364, 7392,
7693, 7909, 7928, 8106,
8391, 8500, 8667, 8686,
8719, 8782, 8808, 8819,
8868, 8898, 9432, 10005,
10016, 10027, 10030,
10040, 10042, 10045,
10053, 10057, 10071,
10079, 10095, 10100,
10112–13, 10120, 10123,
10129, 10133–36, 10273,
10280, 10325, 10360, 10364

School stories — Fiction
P: 1504, 2344, 2857, 4105,
6173, 6426 **PI:** 5050, 8879,
10064, 10097 **I:** 7455,
8346, 9741, 10061, 10093
IJ: 10056

Schools
P: 3389 **PI:** 16325
I: 17714 **IJ:** 17631

Schools — Careers
P: 17739

**Schools — Colonial
Period (U.S.)**
I: 16153

Schools — Fiction
P: 4981

Schools — History
PI: 16493 **I:** 14008, 15866

Schools — Poetry
P: 11549, 11604, 11695,
11701, 11866, 11904
PI: 11622, 11867 **I:** 11880

Schulz, Charles
PI: 12301

Schumann, Clara
I: 12337

Science
See also branches of
science, e.g., Physics
I: 18332

Science — Careers
P: 17832 **IJ:** 17835

**Science — Experiments
and projects**
See also under specific
branches of science, e.g.,
Electricity —
Experiments and
projects
P: 18311, 18318–19, 18333,
18346, 18351, 18367, 20932
PI: 18310, 18316–17,
18322, 18328, 18334,
18337, 18341, 18344,
18360–61, 18366,
18370–73, 20673, 20742,
20839, 20939 **I:** 16960,
18130, 18298–99, 18301–2,
18307–9, 18315, 18321,
18324–27, 18329,
18331–32, 18335,
18339–40, 18342–43,
18349–50, 18355, 18357,
18359, 18363, 18365,
18368–69, 18427, 20114,
20223, 20225, 20292,
20294, 20325, 20351,
20663, 20724, 20817–18,
20854–55, 20861,
20881–82, 20906, 20931,
21045, 21076, 21119,
21239, 21255, 21780
IJ: 16996, 18300, 18303,
18305–6, 18312–14, 18320,
18323, 18336, 18338,
18345, 18347–48,
18352–54, 18356, 18358,

18362, 18364, 18374,
18398, 18404, 20782,
20798, 20852, 21092, 21441

Science — General
P: 18295, 18576
PI: 16993, 18277 **I:** 16953,
18276, 18287, 18290,
18292–93, 18595
IJ: 18274–75, 18278,
18281, 18286, 18294,
18296–97, 21251, 21889

Science — History
I: 14655, 14681 **IJ:** 14591,
14673, 15054, 15486,
15563, 16140, 16172,
18271–72, 18279,
18283–85, 18288, 18291

**Science — Jokes and
riddles**
I: 21834

Science — Methodology
P: 17832 **I:** 18282

Science — North America
IJ: 15563

Science — Poetry
PI: 11960

Science — Projects
See Science —
Experiments and
projects

Science — Renaissance
IJ: 14800

Science — South America
IJ: 15563

Science fiction
See also Fantasy;
Supernatural
P: 1062, 1205, 1310, 1358,
1476, 1479, 1572, 2299,
4350, 6038, 6394, 6628,
6714 **PI:** 6330, 10141,
10143, 10147, 10153,
10162, 10171, 10189,
10197, 10203–4, 10223–25,
10230, 10242, 10246–47,
10249 **I:** 8074, 9747, 9832,
9963–64, 10041, 10142,
10145, 10149, 10156–58,
10163, 10165, 10168–70,
10173, 10175, 10178,
10184, 10186–88, 10190,
10192, 10194, 10198–200,
10206, 10209, 10214,
10216, 10218, 10220–21,
10226, 10228, 10231–35,
10239, 10241, 10244–45
IJ: 7802, 9987, 10144,
10146, 10148, 10150–52,
10154–55, 10159–61,
10164, 10166–67, 10172,
10174, 10176–77,
10180–83, 10185, 10191,
10193, 10195–96, 10201–2,
10205, 10207–8, 10210,
10212–13, 10215, 10219,
10222, 10227, 10229,
10236–38, 10240, 10243,
10248, 10250

P = Primary; PI = Primary-Intermediate; I = Intermediate; IJ = Intermediate-Junior High

Science fiction —
Biography
IJ: 12160, 12501–2

Scientists
PI: 13255 I: 13256

Scientists — Biography
P: 13213, 13257, 13291
PI: 13224, 13251–52,
13261, 13332, 13339,
13344, 13347, 13349
I: 12068, 13210, 13219,
13253, 13262, 13265,
13277, 13288–90, 13312,
13314, 13324, 13333,
13338, 13342
IJ: 13217–18, 13222,
13260, 13275, 13293,
13316, 13321–22, 13334,
13340, 13346

Scientists — Women
I: 13210

Scoliosis — Fiction
IJ: 8881

Scopes trial (1925)
I: 16451

Scorpions
PI: 19588, 19595 I: 19585,
19592

Scotch terriers — Fiction
P: 5203

Scotland
See also Great Britain
PI: 15349 I: 15348
IJ: 15340

Scotland — Emigration
I: 15351

Scotland — Fiction
P: 4708 PI: 7321, 7701
I: 2644, 7425–26, 7667,
8243, 8278, 8109 IJ: 7804,
8917, 9188

Scotland — Folklore
P: 11002, 11012, 11044
I: 7703

Scotland — History
I: 15334

Scotland — Holidays
PI: 15349

Scott, Robert — Fiction
P: 5267

Scottish Americans —
Biography
IJ: 17590

Scouts and scouting —
Fiction
P: 2962, 3347, 4126

Scouts and scouting —
Songs
IJ: 14243

Screws
P: 20927

Scuba diving
IJ: 22310

Sculptors and sculpture
PI: 21535 IJ: 13957

Sculptors and sculpture
— Biography
PI: 12269, 12297 I: 12268
IJ: 12196

Sculptors and sculpture
— Fiction
PI: 3020 I: 8980, 9064
IJ: 9873

Sea horses
P: 19705 PI: 19711, 19715
I: 19709, 19717

Sea kraits
P: 19649

Sea lions
P: 19748 I: 19734

Sea mammals
I: 19634

Sea mammals —
Endangered species
IJ: 19418

Sea of Cortez — Fiction
I: 7128

Sea otters
See also Otters
P: 19729, 19733 I: 19736,
19742

Sea slugs
PI: 19640

Sea snakes
P: 19649

Sea stars
PI: 19711

Sea stories
PI: 9316 I: 7187, 7616,
7767, 8241, 9311 IJ: 6806,
6906, 7818, 8933, 8966,
9106–7, 9271, 9274, 9284,
9286, 9509, 9528

Sea swallows
I: 19254

Sea turtles
P: 18789 PI: 18782–83,
18786, 18788 I: 18785

Sea World (California)
PI: 19775

Seabirds
I: 19274, 19352

Seagulls
I: 19349

Seagulls — Fiction
I: 2644, 7894

Seals
P: 4475, 19731 PI: 19741
I: 19730, 19734, 19738

Seals — Fiction
P: 4130, 4379, 5115, 5125,
5444

Seals — Folklore
I: 10961, 11270

Sealyham terriers —
Fiction
PI: 8084

Sears Tower (Chicago)
I: 16546

Seas
See also Oceans
I: 19814, 19831

Seashells
P: 19773

Seashores
See also Beaches
P: 19856 PI: 19628,
19857, 19864–65, 19870–71
I: 19855, 19860, 19862–63,
19866, 19868–69, 20382
IJ: 19872

Seashores — Birds
I: 19246

Seashores — Fiction
P: 45, 3159, 3253, 3609,
4407, 4428, 4466, 4524,
4553, 6503 PI: 3442

Seashores — Plants
P: 19859

Seashores — Poetry
P: 11533

Seasonings (food)
IJ: 20099

Seasons
See also Months; and
specific seasons, e.g.,
Autumn
P: 4442, 4515, 18438,
18563–64, 18575, 20758
PI: 18561, 20210, 20653
I: 18562, 18571, 18582
IJ: 18330, 20047

Seasons — Art
PI: 13961

Seasons — Crafts
I: 21474

Seasons — Fiction
P: 369, 955, 2027, 3449,
3505, 3659, 3838, 3895,
4173, 4390, 4392, 4417,
4443, 4458, 4468, 4477,
4488, 4492, 4503, 4518,
4525, 4544–45, 4550, 4555,
4561, 4564, 5353

Seasons — Poetry
P: 4417, 4464, 11813,
11979, 11985 PI: 11934,
11957–59, 11992 I: 11946,
11956, 11969, 11981,
11986–87

Seattle
PI: 16815 I: 16796, 16820

Seattle — Fiction
I: 8496

Seattle SuperSonics
(basketball team)
I: 22127

Seau, Junior
I: 13631 IJ: 13630

Seaweed
I: 19652

Secret Garden —
Cookbook
IJ: 21687

Secretary of State (U.S.)
— Biography
I: 12838 IJ: 12839

Secrets — Fiction
P: 3338

Security blankets —
Fiction
P: 2282, 3179

Seeds
P: 20261, 20270, 20272
I: 20268–69, 20271,
20273–74

Seeds — Fiction
P: 1320, 4402

Seeds — Folklore
P: 10749

Seeing Eye dogs
P: 19957

Segregation (U.S.) —
Fiction
P: 4602, 4770, 5034, 5517
I: 7362 IJ: 7359, 9530

Seismosaurus
PI: 14438

Selena (Selena Quintanilla
Perez) (singer)
P: 12467 I: 12466

Seles, Monica
PI: 13653

Self defense
IJ: 18216

Self-esteem — Fiction
P: 1930, 2793, 4982
I: 8566, 8599, 8659
IJ: 9922, 10095, 10374

Seminole Indians
P: 4697 PI: 16052
I: 15920 IJ: 15932

Seminole Indians —
Fiction
P: 3318 PI: 9320
IJ: 6855

Seminole Indians —
History
I: 15987 IJ: 15979

Senate (U.S.)
See Congress (U.S.)

Seneca Indians —
Folklore
P: 11309

Senegal
IJ: 15013, 15047

Senses
See also specific senses,
e.g., Smell

P = Primary; PI = Primary-Intermediate; I = Intermediate; IJ = Intermediate-Junior High

P: 18129, 18140, 18142–44, 18146, 18149, 18152–56, 18161–62, 21868
PI: 18075, 18139 **I:** 18145, 18147–48, 18151, 18164
IJ: 18077

Senses — Animal
PI: 18818 **I:** 18821

Senses — Experiments and projects
P: 18150 **PI:** 18136
I: 18130

Senses — Fiction
P: 4526

Sensors
I: 21036

Separation (marital) — Fiction
P: 3083

Sequoia (tree)
PI: 20220

Sequoyah
I: 12993–94

Serbia
IJ: 15280

Serengeti National Park (Tanzania)
I: 14937

Serengeti National Park (Tanzania) — Animals
PI: 18700

Serengeti Plain
I: 19076

Settlement houses
IJ: 16446

Seuss, Dr.
See Dr. Seuss

Seward, William
IJ: 12961

Sewing
P: 21646 **IJ:** 21648

Sex education
See also Reproduction
P: 18236–37, 18244, 18251, 18255–57, 18264
PI: 18245, 18248, 18252, 18261 **I:** 18250, 18253–54, 18260, 18263, 18266
IJ: 18243, 18249, 18258, 18262, 18267–68, 18270

Sex education — Fiction
I: 7226

Sex education — Girls
IJ: 17610

Sextuplets
P: 18229

Sexual abuse
P: 17733, 18255–56
PI: 17704, 17735
IJ: 18262

Shabbat (Jewish holy day)
P: 6089, 6093, 6095
PI: 17458 **I:** 11150

Shabbat (Jewish holy day) — Fiction
P: 6102, 6113, 6118, 6121

Shackleton, Sir Ernest
PI: 15818 **IJ:** 12155, 15795, 15812

Shadows
P: 21876

Shadows — Fiction
P: 171, 185, 1649, 2763, 3805 **PI:** 7785 **I:** 3358, 7784

Shadows — Poetry
P: 11718

Shaka (Zulu chief)
PI: 13850

Shakers (religion)
P: 594 **PI:** 14174
I: 17166, 17168 **IJ:** 17169

Shakers (religion) — Fiction
P: 4807 **I:** 9377 **IJ:** 9366

Shakespeare, William
See also Plays — Shakespeare
PI: 15342 **I:** 9037, 12049, 12052, 12591–92, 14324
IJ: 12055, 12590, 12593–95, 13903

Shakespeare, William — Fiction
P: 4715 **IJ:** 9079

Shakespeare, William — Plays
PI: 12047 **IJ:** 12050–51, 12053–54

Shakespeare, William — Poetry
IJ: 12053

Shapes — Experiments and projects
See also Concept books — Sizes and shapes
PI: 18316, 20580

Sharing — Fiction
P: 2579, 5020, 5063, 6719

Sharks
P: 19751, 19753, 19755, 19757, 19770 **PI:** 19756, 19758, 19765, 19767–69
I: 19759, 19761–64
IJ: 13258, 19752, 19754, 19760, 19766

Sharks — Fiction
I: 6856

Sharks — History
I: 14379

Shavuot (Jewish holy day) — Fiction
P: 6074

Shawnee Indians
I: 15955

Shawnee Indians — Biography
PI: 12999 **IJ:** 13000

Shawnee Indians — Fiction
I: 6824

Shays' Rebellion
IJ: 16252

Sheba, Queen of
PI: 17279

Sheep
P: 20055, 20067

Sheep — Fiction
P: 484, 2416, 2657, 4651, 5304–5, 5723, 5996, 6654
IJ: 7315, 7930

Sheep farms
P: 20062, 20067

Sheepdogs — Fiction
P: 5228 **PI:** 6792, 7213, 7220

Shells
P: 18916, 19773
I: 19771–72

Shells — Crafts
I: 21498

Shells — Fiction
P: 1269

Shepherds — Fiction
P: 3280, 4414, 5835, 5854

Sherburne, Andrew
IJ: 12962

Sherman, William T.
IJ: 12963

Shiloh, Battle of
I: 16438

Shintoism
P: 17209

Ships and boats
See also Sailing and boating; and specific ships, e.g., *Titanic* (ship)
P: 21349, 21351–52, 21356, 21364–66, 21370, 21375
PI: 6310, 21391 **I:** 20803, 21353, 21355, 21359, 21361, 21368, 21373–74, 21378 **IJ:** 12086, 14829, 21350, 21354, 21357

Ships and boats — Cookbooks
IJ: 15875

Ships and boats — Experiments and projects
PI: 18373

Ships and boats — Fiction
P: 933, 992, 1159, 1215, 2258, 3355, 3382, 4209, 4275, 5556, 5566, 5569, 5582, 5585 **PI:** 3587, 6928,

8927 **I:** 8940, 9261
IJ: 6757, 7094, 7099, 7670, 9180

Ships and boats — Folklore
P: 11098, 11108

Ships and boats — History
I: 16474, 21376 **IJ:** 16300, 21367, 21369, 21379

Ships and boats — Poetry
P: 11738

Shipwrecks
PI: 21362 **I:** 21378
IJ: 14541–42, 14594, 15944, 16300, 21350, 21357, 21363, 21372

Shipwrecks — Fiction
P: 6372 **PI:** 8168 **I:** 9638
IJ: 7136

Shoes
P: 21181 **PI:** 21171, 21188
I: 21165 **IJ:** 21177, 21189

Shoes — Fiction
P: 1688, 2960, 3032, 3234, 3387, 3833, 4634, 5538

Shoes — Folklore
P: 10895

Shoes — History
PI: 21182

Shoes — Poetry
P: 3482 **PI:** 11585

Shona (African people)
IJ: 15006

Shopping
P: 14250

Shopping — Fiction
P: 1097, 3352, 4186

Shopping malls
P: 16935

Short stories
P: 1903, 3043, 5782, 6280, 10104, 11155 **PI:** 7245, 7879, 7959, 8140, 9754, 9756, 9840, 10179, 10258, 10262, 10433 **I:** 6798, 6864, 7073–74, 7101, 7288, 7373, 7619, 7767, 7863, 7878, 8309, 9736, 9748, 9796, 10253, 10256, 10259, 10266, 10630, 17576
IJ: 6751, 6992, 7018, 7142, 7296, 7355, 7360, 7649, 7651, 7656–57, 7679, 7742, 7802, 8041, 8063, 8132, 8220, 8237, 8555, 8872, 9021, 9129, 10166–67, 10250, 10255, 10260–61, 10264, 10324, 10768

Shoshone Indians — Biography
I: 12989–92

Shoshone Indians —
Fiction
P: 3414

Shoshone Indians —
Folklore
PI: 11303

Shoshone Indians —
History
P: 15951

Shrimp
P: 19674

Shumann, Clara
IJ: 12338

Shyness
IJ: 17713

Shyness — Fiction
PI: 6802, 8611 I: 8297,
10309 IJ: 8246, 8645, 8676

Siam — Fiction
P: 10462

Siamese cats — Fiction
P: 1913 PI: 1914

Siamese fighting fish
I: 19710

Siamese twins
See Conjoined twins

Siberia — Fiction
P: 5405

Sibling rivalry
P: 6205, 17687 I: 17668

Sibling rivalry — Fiction
P: 963, 1257–58, 3548,
3673, 3841, 3929, 4029,
4919 PI: 7458, 9784, 9970
I: 8449, 8520, 9957
IJ: 7876, 8906, 10323

Siblings
PI: 17657

Siblings — Fiction
See also Twins
P: 3534, 3595, 3643, 3663,
3681, 3708, 3710, 3723,
3794, 3798, 3880, 3904,
3942, 3972, 4051, 4087,
4259, 4907, 5983, 6195,
6246 PI: 3772, 7423
I: 7448, 7489, 8582, 8584,
8670 IJ: 6948, 7384, 7491,
7508

Siblings — Folklore
P: 10765

Sickle cell anemia
IJ: 18001

Siegel, Bugsy
IJ: 12964

Sieges — History
IJ: 14774

Sierra Leone — Fiction
P: 4824

Sifford, Charlie
I: 13709

Sight
P: 18143, 18153 I: 17935,
18145

Sign language
See also American Sign
Language
P: 564, 827, 14013, 14019
PI: 14018 I: 14012, 14014,
14016

Sign language — Fiction
P: 21, 5036, 5673, 14017
PI: 5015

Signs and symbols
P: 14013, 14015 I: 14014,
15851, 17433 IJ: 17455

Signs and symbols —
Fiction
P: 307, 3051

Sikhism
P: 17196 I: 15099, 17177

Silk — Fiction
P: 4684 PI: 4726

Silk Road — Fiction
IJ: 8942

Silk Route — Folklore
I: 10554

Silkworms
PI: 19487 IJ: 19611

Silverstone, Alicia
PI: 12468

Simmons, Philip
I: 12302

Simon, Seymour
I: 12596

Simple machines
P: 20924–29 PI: 20922

Simple machines —
Experiments and
projects
PI: 20921 I: 20920

Simulation
IJ: 21056

Simulation (computers)
IJ: 21192

Singapore
PI: 15162 I: 15150
IJ: 15180

Singer, Isaac Bashevis
IJ: 12597

Singers — Biography
P: 12345, 12467
PI: 12343, 12346–47,
12358, 12381, 12386,
12406, 12416, 12422, 12453
I: 12341, 12344, 12357,
12362, 12365, 12375,
12380, 12382, 12384,
12393, 12413, 12446–47,
12466 IJ: 12175–76,
12178, 12359–61, 12368,
12376, 12383, 12385,
12399, 12404, 12407–8,

12410, 12415, 12444,
12454, 12460, 12478, 12483

Singers and singing —
Fiction
IJ: 7399, 7490

Singing games and songs
P: 14190, 14245

Singing groups — Fiction
IJ: 8293

Single-parent families
See Family problems

Single parents — Fiction
IJ: 8397

Sioux Indians
P: 16019, 16053
PI: 15996, 16058 I: 12971,
16072 IJ: 16028

Sioux Indians —
Biography
I: 12996 IJ: 12995

Sioux Indians — Fiction
I: 9175 IJ: 9402

Sioux Indians — Folklore
PI: 11230, 11244

Sioux Indians — History
IJ: 16066

Sisters — Fiction
P: 3548, 3583, 3806, 4623,
5740, 6205, 6229, 7497
PI: 4342, 7506–7, 8287

Sistine Chapel
IJ: 14798

Sitting Bull (Sioux chief)
I: 12996 IJ: 12995

Sitting Bull (Sioux chief)
— Fiction
IJ: 9146

Size
PI: 20581, 20658

Size — Fiction
P: 3080

Sizes and shapes
See Concept books —
Sizes and shapes

Skateboarding
IJ: 22275–76

Skating
See specific types, e.g., Ice
skating

Skeletons
P: 18168 PI: 18165
I: 18166, 18169, 18171–72,
18175, 18829 IJ: 18167,
18170, 18174

Skeletons — Fiction
P: 6017, 6184

Skin
P: 18180, 18183 PI: 18847
I: 18181–82

Skin — Fiction
P: 3363

Skin care
IJ: 18196

Skin injuries
I: 18181

Skin problems
I: 18182

Skipping
See Rope skipping

Skis and skiing
IJ: 22248

Skis and skiing — Fiction
P: 1913 I: 6841

Skits
I: 12027

Skunks
P: 18951 PI: 18953

Skunks — Fiction
P: 4328, 5379 I: 10233–34

Skyscrapers
P: 21123, 21132, 21152
PI: 21145 I: 21146
IJ: 21150

Slater, Samuel
IJ: 16275

Slavery
See also African
Americans; Civil War
(U.S.)

Slavery (U.S.)
P: 4697, 12708, 12802,
16253 PI: 12711, 12715,
12788, 12792, 12799,
16419, 21675 I: 9272,
12730, 12790, 12861,
13197, 16227–28, 16231,
16240, 16255, 16260,
16262, 16390, 16397
IJ: 9325, 12724, 12791,
13791, 14152, 15030,
15882, 15896, 16226,
16236, 16239, 16241–42,
16246, 16249, 16251,
16257, 16263, 16266,
16268, 16273, 16281,
17022, 17574

Slavery (U.S.) —
Biography
PI: 12603, 12705,
12709–10, 12713, 12785,
12848, 12862 I: 12714,
12716, 12769, 12794, 12806
IJ: 12793, 12894

Slavery (U.S.) — Fiction
P: 1434, 4659, 4677, 4700,
4790, 4822, 4886, 4892,
6051, 10486 PI: 4639,
4696, 4833–34, 9266,
9289–90, 9320–22,
9338–39, 9767 I: 8972,
9137, 9206, 9224, 9268,
9292, 9295–96, 9301, 9305,
9312, 9314, 9317, 9337,
9478, 9496–97, 16247
IJ: 7350, 7805, 8172, 8202,
8970–71, 9136, 9209, 9219,
9257, 9275–76, 9278, 9283,

P = Primary; PI = Primary-Intermediate; I = Intermediate; IJ = Intermediate-Junior High

9291, 9297, 9306, 9310,
9318–19, 9324, 9326, 9336,
9476, 9487, 9494, 9549

Slavery (U.S.) — Folk songs
IJ: 14167

Slavery (U.S.) — Folklore
P: 11171 PI: 11363

Slavery (U.S.) — History
IJ: 14583–84, 16267

Slavery (U.S.) — Poetry
P: 12800

Sled dog races
I: 22058

Sled dogs
See also Iditarod
PI: 2970 I: 21991
IJ: 21997

Sled dogs — Fiction
PI: 7322 I: 7340
IJ: 6996, 7531

Sleep
P: 18118 I: 18227

Sleep — Fiction
P: 685, 691, 3688, 4357
I: 7833, 10629

Sleepovers — Cookbooks
IJ: 21746

Slime
PI: 21920

Sloths
I: 18976

Slovakia
IJ: 15290

Slugs
P: 19605–6, 19610
IJ: 19617

Smell (sense)
P: 18141, 18154 I: 18134,
18137, 18158

Smell (sense) — Experiments and projects
I: 18137

Smiles
P: 17633

Smith, Emmitt
I: 13633 IJ: 13632, 13634

Smith, Sophia — Fiction
PI: 9642

Smith College — Fiction
PI: 9642

Smithsonian Institution
I: 16661, 17104

Smits, Jimmy
PI: 12469

Smoking
I: 17869, 17879, 17884,
17887 IJ: 17870, 17872,
17883, 17897

Smoking — Fiction
PI: 8668

Smuggling — Fiction
I: 9673 IJ: 7113, 10006

Snails
P: 19600, 19605, 19608
PI: 19602, 19615 I: 19612,
19619 IJ: 19617

Snails — Fiction
P: 444, 1530, 2379, 2715,
5174, 6387

Snake River (U.S.)
PI: 19323

Snakes
See also individual
species, e.g., Pythons
P: 18694, 18754–55, 18757,
18761, 18765, 18768,
18771–72, 18774–75
PI: 18753, 18756, 18759,
18764, 18776 I: 18690,
18758, 18760, 18762–63,
18769–70 IJ: 18691

Snakes — Fiction
P: 602, 1309, 2262, 2325,
2769, 2792, 4081, 4197,
4784, 6682 PI: 5334, 9805

Snakes — Folklore
P: 11210

Sneakers (shoes)
PI: 21171, 21188 I: 21187

Sneakers (shoes) — Fiction
P: 4210

Snider, Duke
I: 13503

Snoring — Fiction
P: 3764, 3778

Snow
P: 12191, 20755 I: 20730,
20777 IJ: 20795

Snow — Crafts
P: 21433

Snow — Fiction
P: 1054, 1234, 1562, 1623,
1653, 1827, 2281, 2309,
2413, 2952, 2973, 3041,
3093, 3152, 3160, 3218,
3425, 3427, 3458, 3487,
4469, 4471, 4520, 4680,
5525, 6516 PI: 961
I: 3066

Snow — Folklore
P: 11082

Snow — Poetry
P: 4511 PI: 11992

Snow days — Fiction
P: 4277

Snow geese — Fiction
P: 5290

Snow leopards
I: 19104

Snowboarding
I: 21059, 22277–78, 22284
IJ: 22279–83

Snowboarding — Fiction
I: 10313 IJ: 10277

Snowmen — Fiction
P: 911, 931, 1482, 3750,
4038, 5855, 6607 PI: 5881

Snowmobiles
IJ: 22044

Snowplows
P: 21254

Snyder, Grace McCance
I: 16384

Soaring
IJ: 22046

Soccer
P: 22286, 22288, 22291,
22295 PI: 22292, 22297
I: 22290, 22293–94,
22300–1 IJ: 22285, 22287,
22289, 22296, 22298–99

Soccer — Biography
PI: 13691 I: 13422,
13689–90 IJ: 13400, 13707

Soccer — Fiction
P: 225, 927, 2394, 3128,
4298, 6510, 10295, 10306,
10328 PI: 6509, 7881,
10272, 10302, 10343, 10366
I: 6861, 8325, 10117,
10298, 10314–15, 10332,
10341, 10352 IJ: 8711,
10273, 10369

Soccer — Women
PI: 22302

Social action
IJ: 17605, 17621

Social groups
See Scouts and scouting;
and ethnic groups, e.g.,
Hispanic Americans

Social problems
I: 17148–49 IJ: 17133,
17147

Social problems — Women
IJ: 17134

Social service
I: 17139 IJ: 16446

Social service — Fiction
I: 7344

Social workers — Biography
IJ: 13127–29

Sod houses
P: 9435

Soft drinks
PI: 20082 I: 20091

Soft drinks — Experiments and projects
IJ: 20138

Softball
PI: 22119 IJ: 22109

Software engineers — Careers
IJ: 17788

Soil
PI: 20550

Soil ecology
PI: 19460, 20551 I: 20576

Soil erosion
P: 20570

Sojourner (spacecraft)
IJ: 21020

Solar energy
P: 20849 IJ: 20848

Solar energy — Experiments and projects
I: 20850

Solar system
See also Astronomy;
Comets; Extraterrestrial
life; Meteors; Moon;
Planets; Space
exploration; Stars; Sun
P: 18410, 18420, 18458,
18512, 18519, 18524
PI: 18500, 18506, 18528,
18530, 18532 I: 18474,
18497–98, 18509, 18514,
18517 IJ: 18388, 18470,
18511, 18531, 18535–36

Solar system — Experiments and projects
I: 18533

Soldiers — Fiction
P: 10393–94

Soldiers — History
I: 21403 IJ: 16221

Solids (physics)
PI: 20812

Solomon, King (Bible)
PI: 17279, 17312 I: 17327

Solomon Islands
I: 15226

Somalia
IJ: 14928, 14943

Songs
P: 71, 552, 563, 618, 730,
747, 840–41, 903–4, 1557,
2292, 3165, 4367, 4874,
5840, 14148–49, 14151,
14160, 14172, 14176,
14178, 14181, 14183,
14186–88, 14190,
14192–93, 14195–96,
14214, 14216, 14234–42,
14244–46, 14248–50,
14252, 14255, 14258–62
PI: 14202, 14207, 14232
I: 14168, 14251, 14254,
14256 IJ: 14243, 14257
All: 14157

P = Primary; PI = Primary-Intermediate; I = Intermediate; IJ = Intermediate-Junior High

Songs –African
American
PI: 14158

Songs – Fiction
P: 5939

Sonoran Desert
PI: 20405, 20428

Sosa, Sammy
PI: 13504 **IJ:** 13413,
13505, 22115

Soul food
IJ: 20090

Sound
See also Concept books —
Sounds
P: 20943 **PI:** 20938
I: 20934–35 **IJ:** 20944

Sound — Experiments
and projects
P: 20932, 20941, 20943
PI: 20936, 20939 **I:** 20931,
20933, 20937, 20940, 20942
IJ: 20804

Sound — Fiction
P: 771, 1984, 2231, 3893

Soups
I: 21703

Soups — Fiction
P: 3028

South Africa
P: 13988, 14973, 14997,
14999 **PI:** 13831, 14971,
14977, 14981 **I:** 14996,
14998 **IJ:** 14967, 14972,
14976, 14990, 15001, 15003

South Africa —
Biography
PI: 13828, 13830, 13832
IJ: 13827, 13829, 13845

South Africa — Fiction
P: 4633–34, 4733, 5274,
8978 **PI:** 4832 **I:** 7270,
7361 **IJ:** 8975

South Africa — Folklore
I: 10712

South Africa — History
IJ: 14974

South Africa — Holidays
P: 14980

South Africa — Kings and
queens
IJ: 14974

South America
PI: 15777, 20497
IJ: 14339, 14552, 15763

South America —
Animals
PI: 18603

South America —
Cookbooks
I: 21729

South America — Crafts
IJ: 21453

South America — Fiction
P: 4852 **I:** 9139 **IJ:** 9180

South America —
Folklore
P: 11442 **I:** 11445

South America —
Geography
I: 15778

South America — History
I: 13754–55, 13846
IJ: 15786

South America — Maps
I: 14331

South America — Songs
PI: 14197

South Carolina
I: 16857 **IJ:** 16867, 16892

South Carolina — Fiction
PI: 9321 **IJ:** 9247, 9306,
9486, 9633

South Carolina Colony
IJ: 16126

South Dakota
P: 16547 **I:** 16542, 16570,
16580, 16589

South Dakota — Fiction
I: 9405

South Korea — Holidays
PI: 15166

South Pacific — Fiction
PI: 6888

South Pacific — Folklore
I: 10848

South (U.S.)
See also specific states,
e.g., Florida
I: 16864

South (U.S.) —
Cookbooks
IJ: 16248

South (U.S.) — Fiction
P: 4624 **I:** 8411

South (U.S.) — Folklore
I: 11328, 11342, 11388

South (U.S.) — History
P: 16253 **IJ:** 16239

South (U.S.) —
Plantations
IJ: 16248

Southeast Asia
IJ: 15215

Southeast Asia —
Emigration
I: 15079

Southeast Asia — History
IJ: 14835

Southeast Asia —
Holidays
PI: 17405

Southeast (U.S.) —
History
IJ: 16111

Southwest (U.S.)
See also specific states,
e.g., Arizona
PI: 13942 **I:** 16907, 16909,
20399 **IJ:** 15898, 16910,
16916

Southwest (U.S.) —
Deserts
IJ: 20416

Southwest (U.S.) —
Fiction
P: 1602

Southwest (U.S.) —
History
I: 15958, 16284 **IJ:** 15985,
16073, 16234

Southwest (U.S.) —
Poetry
P: 11951, 11975

Soviet Union
See also individual states,
e.g., Russia

Soviet Union — History
I: 15418

Soweto — Fiction
PI: 4832

Space
P: 18387

Space colonies
I: 21014, 21017 **IJ:** 20974

Space debris
IJ: 21002

Space exploration
See also Astronauts;
Extraterrestrial life;
National Aeronautics
and Space
Administration (U.S.);
Planets; Space colonies,
etc.
P: 20954–56, 20962, 20989
PI: 18378, 18490–91,
20945, 20967, 20979,
20988, 20998–99, 21005,
21008–9 **I:** 12119, 12154,
18419, 20951, 20953,
20957, 20961, 20968–69,
20972, 20983, 20990,
20993, 21003–4, 21007,
21011, 21017 **IJ:** 18314,
18383, 18388, 18391,
18403, 18423, 18492,
18515, 18531, 18536,
20946, 20958–60, 20963,
20965–66, 20970,
20973–77, 20980–81,
20984, 20994, 20996–97,
21000, 21012, 21015–16,
21018–20

Space exploration —
Biography
I: 12072, 12136, 12888
IJ: 12890

Space exploration —
Crafts
PI: 21481

Space exploration —
Fiction
PI: 6766, 18510

Space exploration —
Poetry
P: 11607 **IJ:** 11700

Space satellites
I: 20986 **IJ:** 20987

Space shuttles
PI: 20999 **I:** 20990, 21006
IJ: 20959

Space stations
P: 20955 **PI:** 20988, 21010
I: 20951 **IJ:** 20948, 20970,
20975, 20980

Spacecraft
See also specific
spacecraft, e.g., *Voyager
II* (spacecraft)
P: 20989 **PI:** 21070
I: 20982, 21554 **IJ:** 20947,
20950, 20960, 20975

Spacecraft — Disasters
IJ: 20977

Spacecraft — Fiction
P: 974, 1536, 1939
I: 10158, 10233

Spain
PI: 15471, 15473, 15479
I: 15475, 15478, 15482,
15484 **IJ:** 15474, 15485

Spain — Biography
IJ: 12284

Spain — Cookbooks
I: 21702

Spain — Fiction
I: 9044 **IJ:** 6871, 8864,
9034, 9038

Spain — Folklore
P: 11133–36, 11138–39
PI: 11137

Spain — History
I: 15477 **IJ:** 12236, 13772,
14537, 15481

Spain — Holidays
PI: 15480

Spanish-American War
I: 16458 **IJ:** 16465

Spanish-American War
— Fiction
P: 4686

Spanish language
P: 268, 327, 429, 2071,
3360, 3640, 4328, 4502,
4637, 4774, 4912, 5674,
10900, 14096 **PI:** 2925,
5853, 8052, 11410, 11543,
13981 **I:** 11653

P = Primary; PI = Primary-Intermediate; I = Intermediate; IJ = Intermediate-Junior High

Spanish language — Alphabet books
P: 17767

Spanish language — Counting books
P: 391, 520

Spanish language — Fiction
P: 2508, 3283, 3527, 3859, 4640, 4809, 5032, 5220, 5726, 5741 PI: 10950, 11016 I: 7367, 7562, 9138

Spanish language — Finger plays
P: 22041

Spanish language — Folklore
P: 11135, 11392, 11422 I: 11400 IJ: 11438

Spanish language — Holidays
IJ: 17394

Spanish language — Nonfiction
I: 16907, 21615 IJ: 7229

Spanish language — Numbers
P: 452

Spanish language — Picture books
P: 3526, 4295

Spanish language — Plays
I: 12017

Spanish language — Poetry
P: 11527, 11612, 11657, 11935 PI: 11526

Spanish language — Songs
P: 14236

Sparrows
I: 19213

Speaking
I: 14090

Spears, Britney
PI: 12470 IJ: 12471

Special effects (films)
IJ: 21271

Special Olympics
I: 17902

Special Olympics — Fiction
P: 5052

Speed (drug)
IJ: 17889

Speed skating
PI: 22219

Speedboats
IJ: 21354

Sperm whales — Fiction
P: 5313

Spice Girls (musical group)
IJ: 12472

Spices
IJ: 20099

Spiders
P: 10692, 19571–72, 19574, 19579–83, 19586, 19590–91, 19597–98 PI: 19455, 19501, 19573, 19575, 19584, 19595 I: 19435, 19438, 19461, 19576, 19587, 19589, 19593–94, 19596 IJ: 19479, 19481, 19577–78

Spiders — Experiments and projects
I: 19496

Spiders — Fiction
P: 1925, 2143, 3800, 4487, 5333, 5513, 5786, 6021 PI: 7000, 8200 I: 7291

Spiders — Folklore
P: 10672 I: 11400, 11432 IJ: 10648

Spiders — Poetry
PI: 11784

Spielberg, Steven
I: 12473–74 IJ: 12475–76

Spies
I: 17077 IJ: 14839, 14863, 16422, 17083

Spies — Biography
IJ: 13152

Spies — Fiction
I: 9239 IJ: 6857, 9485

Spies — Women — Biography
I: 13743

Spina bifida
I: 17923

Spinelli, Jerry
IJ: 12598

Spirituals
P: 14141 PI: 17295 I: 14205

Sponges
P: 19719

Spoonbills
P: 20375

Sports
See also Games; and specific sports, e.g., Baseball
P: 16009 I: 15106, 21966, 21980, 22039, 22049, 22059, 22064 IJ: 15424, 20837, 21965, 22002, 22011, 22048, 22051, 22054–55

Sports — African Americans
PI: 13374

Sports — Art
I: 13900

Sports — Biography
See also under specific sports, e.g., Baseball — Biography
P: 13385 IJ: 13375, 13396, 13406, 13415

Sports — Bloopers
IJ: 22057

Sports — Careers
P: 3135, 17742 I: 17763 IJ: 17754, 17760, 17762

Sports — Drawing and painting
IJ: 21596

Sports — Economic aspects
IJ: 22016

Sports — Experiments and projects
IJ: 18068

Sports — Fiction
P: 6476 I: 10276 IJ: 10324

Sports — Gambling
IJ: 22073

Sports — History
IJ: 14592

Sports — Jokes and riddles
PI: 21848–49

Sports — Players' numbers
IJ: 22068

Sports — Poetry
P: 12005 I: 11998, 12000 IJ: 12003–4

Sports — Safety
IJ: 18219

Sports — Superstitions
PI: 22003 IJ: 22069

Sports — Women
I: 13414, 22027 IJ: 13722, 22051, 22065

Sports cards
I: 21808, 22077

Sports cars
IJ: 21305

Sports equipment — Experiments and projects
IJ: 20811

Sports medicine
I: 22059

Sports stories
P: 3024, 3517, 3636 I: 10318, 10332–33 IJ: 10305

Sportsmanship
I: 21966

Spotted owls
IJ: 19365

Spotted owls — Fiction
PI: 7195

Spring
P: 4459 PI: 127, 18572

Spring — Crafts
PI: 21489

Spring — Fiction
P: 1068, 1263, 2573, 4474, 4485, 4525, 4536, 6437 PI: 4447, 7104

Spring — Folklore
PI: 11034

Spring — Poetry
P: 11824 I: 11948

Springs (physics)
IJ: 20923

Springs (water) — Fiction
I: 7575

Sprinters — Biography
IJ: 13377

Spy satellites
IJ: 20987

Squalls — Fiction
P: 4428

Squanto
P: 12998 I: 12997 IJ: 17491

Square dances — Fiction
P: 4866

Squid
P: 19725

Squirrels — Fiction
P: 1734, 2066, 5277, 5423

Sri Lanka
I: 15147 IJ: 15211, 15221

Stadiums
I: 21146

Stamps
See Postage stamps

Stanton, Elizabeth Cady
I: 13192, 13194 IJ: 13193

Star-Spangled Banner
PI: 14161 I: 14233

Star Trek (TV show)
I: 10206

Star Wars (motion picture)
I: 14314 IJ: 14316–19

Star Wars — Cookbooks
I: 21693, 21698

Starfish
P: 19720–21

Starr, Belle
IJ: 12965

Stars
P: 18540, 18544, 18546, 18549–50, 18554 PI: 18376, 18379, 18412, 18538–39, 18541, 18545,

P = Primary; PI = Primary-Intermediate; I = Intermediate; IJ = Intermediate-Junior High

18553,18555–56 **I:** 18405,
18537,18542, 18548, 18551
IJ: 18386, 18394, 18396,
18408,18513, 18543,
18547,18552

Stars–Fiction
P: 657,706

Stars–Folklore
P: 11242, 11285 **PI:** 11249
I: 10563, 11235 **IJ:** 11277,
11280

Stars – Poetry
PI: 11561

State birds (U.S.)
P: 4563 **I:** 15852

State flowers (U.S.)
P: 4563 **I:** 15853

State government (U.S.)
I: 17130 **IJ:** 17129

State trees (U.S.)
PI: 15850

Statistics
I: 20614

Statue of Liberty
PI: 16719 **I:** 16666, 21115
IJ: 16662

**Statue of Liberty —
Fiction**
P: 4368, 6599

Stealing — Fiction
P: 4643, 4985 **PI:** 6750,
9233 **I:** 6899, 6904, 6931,
6933, 8307, 8407, 10047
IJ: 6832, 7603

Stealing — Folklore
I: 11302

Steamboats
I: 13286

Steamboats — Biography
PI: 12130 **IJ:** 13287

Steamboats — Fiction
IJ: 8457

Stearner, Phyllis
PI: 13347

Steding, Katy
I: 13575

Steel
See Iron and steel

Steinem, Gloria
I: 13195 **IJ:** 13196

Stepchildren
P: 17676 **PI:** 17662
IJ: 17669

Stepchildren — Fiction
P: 4980 **I:** 8468, 8688
IJ: 7776, 8440, 10316

Stepfamilies — Fiction
P: 3556

Stepparents
P: 17678 **I:** 17642, 17660
IJ: 17669

Stepparents — Fiction
P: 3585, 3702, 3742, 4908,
5010, 10470 **PI:** 8404,
9410 **I:** 7421, 7431, 8449,
8458 **IJ:** 6956, 8460, 8510,
8544

Stepparents — Folklore
P: 10721, 11084, 11093
PI: 10764, 11103

Steroids (drugs)
IJ: 17881

Stevenson, James
P: 4840

Stevenson, Robert Louis
P: 11738 **IJ:** 12599–600

Stine, R. L.
I: 12602 **IJ:** 12601

Stock market crash (1929)
See also Depression, Great
I: 16462

Stock markets
IJ: 16921, 16925

Stockton, John
IJ: 13408, 13576

Stomach
IJ: 18095

Stone, Lucy
I: 13197

Stone Age
IJ: 14503, 14506

Stone cutters
I: 14787

Stonehenge
IJ: 14530, 21941

Stonehenge — Fiction
IJ: 7724

Stores
PI: 16259 **I:** 16933

Stores — Fiction
P: 3129, 3191, 4615
PI: 7676, 8173, 9765
IJ: 7931

Stories without words
P: 24, 273, 339, 906–17,
919–30, 932–35, 939–40,
2002 **PI:** 937, 7318
I: 3005 **All:** 936

**Stories without words —
Fiction**
P: 918, 931, 938

Storks — Fiction
P: 5146 **I:** 9032

Stormalong (folklore)
P: 11369

Storms
See also specific types of
storms, e.g., Hurricanes
P: 4494, 6597, 20411,
20683, 20689 **PI:** 20694
I: 20691, 20700, 20750
IJ: 16480

Storms — Fiction
P: 2927, 3542, 4428, 4457,
4519, 5161 **IJ:** 6843, 7087,
7099

Storms — Poetry
PI: 11939

Story hours — Fiction
P: 3209

Storytelling
P: 3726 **I:** 10557, 10616,
14088, 14103 **IJ:** 10565,
14070, 14078–79

Storytelling — Fiction
P: 4734

Stowe, Harriet Beecher
PI: 12603 **IJ:** 12604

**Stradivari, Antonio —
Fiction**
PI: 9035

**Strategic Defense
Initiative**
IJ: 20949

Strauss, Levi
PI: 12966

Stravinsky, Igor
PI: 12339

Strawberries
P: 20139

Strawberry, Darryl
I: 13506

Streams
See also Rivers
P: 20510

Street cleaning equipment
P: 21245

Stress
IJ: 17911

Stress (mental state)
IJ: 17734

String games
I: 22006, 22009 **IJ:** 22008

Strokes — Fiction
IJ: 8903

Strong, Maurice
I: 13348

Stuart, Jeb
I: 12967

Students — Biography
P: 12645

Study skills
I: 17614

Stunt flying
IJ: 21108

Stunt people — Careers
I: 12106

Stuttering
I: 17916

Stuttering — Fiction
PI: 8739 **IJ:** 7305

Submarines
PI: 14845 **I:** 21359, 21390,
21399, 21408

Submarines — Fiction
P: 1537 **I:** 7112

Subtraction
P: 424, 491, 530
PI: 20623, 20633

Subways
PI: 21343 **IJ:** 21139

Subways — Fiction
P: 2918 **I:** 8083 **IJ:** 6898

Sudan
I: 14948 **IJ:** 14949

Sudan — Fiction
P: 4710 **IJ:** 8970

Sudanese Americans
I: 17540

**Suffrage and suffragists
— Biography**
See also Women's rights
I: 13132, 13197

Sufi — Folklore
I: 11199

Sugars
I: 20118

Sugihara, Chiune
IJ: 13851

Suicide — Fiction
I: 7564 **IJ:** 8602, 8721,
8812

Sukkot (Jewish holy day)
PI: 17470

**Sukkot (Jewish holy day)
— Fiction**
P: 6127

Sulfur
IJ: 20278

Sumeria
I: 14638

Sumerians — History
I: 14657

Summer
P: 3092, 4490, 18564
I: 21998

Summer — Fiction
P: 4403, 4431, 4491, 4500

Summer — Poetry
PI: 128

Sun
P: 18522, 18560, 18563–65,
18567, 20849, 20857
PI: 18539, 18558–59,
18561, 18570, 18573–74
I: 18509, 18569, 20850
IJ: 18566

Sun — Fiction
P: 685, 1193, 2565, 3216,
4378

Sun — Folklore
I: 10563 **IJ:** 11257

P = Primary; PI = Primary-Intermediate; I = Intermediate; IJ = Intermediate-Junior High

Sun — Poetry
PI: 11561

Sunflowers
P: 4501 **PI:** 20248, 21762
I: 20041

Sunflowers — Fiction
P: 4399, 4432, 4535, 4551,
4562, 5372

Super Bowl — Biography
IJ: 13382

Supermarkets
P: 3193 **IJ:** 18312

Supermarkets — Fiction
P: 6033

Supernatural
See also Fantasy; Folklore;
Mystery stories; Tall
tales; and specific
supernatural creatures,
e.g., Ghosts
P: 1025, 4125 **I:** 7630,
7922, 7994, 8020, 8046,
21947 **IJ:** 7905, 8099,
8179, 21904

Supernatural — Fiction
P: 4261, 8064 **PI:** 48, 7959
I: 7090, 7607, 7616, 7650,
7700, 7703, 7813, 8037,
8170, 8227 **IJ:** 7070, 7142,
7632, 7649, 7651, 7679,
7861, 7975, 7984, 8007,
8029, 8063, 8077, 8098,
8100, 8132, 8137, 8166,
8195

Supernatural — Folklore
IJ: 11364

Supernatural — Poetry
PI: 11534 **I:** 11544, 11676
IJ: 11677

Superstitions
PI: 21921

Superstitions — Fiction
P: 4125

**Supply and demand
(economics)**
IJ: 16928

Supreme Court (U.S.)
PI: 17015 **I:** 17012–14

**Supreme Court (U.S.) —
Biography**
PI: 12763–64, 12766–67,
12939 **I:** 12938 **IJ:** 12765,
12768, 12886, 12940

Surfboarding — Fiction
IJ: 7035

Surfing
IJ: 22303–4

Surfing — Fiction
P: 2555

Surgery — Fiction
IJ: 8646, 8698

Surrealism (art)
I: 13882

Survival — Fiction
I: 6895

Survival — Nature
I: 18581

Survival stories
PI: 15822 **IJ:** 15812

Survival stories — Fiction
PI: 6999 **I:** 6772, 6825,
6841, 6894, 6940, 6971,
9273, 9359, 9425 **IJ:** 6773,
6800, 6896–97, 6905, 6987,
7018, 7051, 7097, 7106,
8145, 8529, 8615, 8931,
8966, 9300, 9473, 9486,
15937

Swahili — Folklore
P: 10642, 10679

Swahili language
P: 14116

Swallows — Fiction
P: 5368 **I:** 10522

Swamps
P: 20372 **I:** 20363, 20374

Swamps — Fiction
P: 6040 **IJ:** 6882

Swan Lake (ballet)
PI: 14273 **IJ:** 14281

Swans
P: 19269, 19316–17
I: 19308, 19311

Swans — Fiction
P: 5351 **I:** 8201

Swanson, Anne Barrett
PI: 13349

Swazi
IJ: 14994

Swaziland
PI: 14989 **I:** 19400
IJ: 14968

Sweden
IJ: 15439, 15444, 15447,
15467

Sweden — Fiction
P: 4594 **PI:** 10443
I: 8776, 9917 **IJ:** 9036

Sweden — Folklore
P: 10870

Sweden — Holidays
PI: 15466

Swedish Americans
PI: 21713 **IJ:** 17577

**Swedish Americans —
Fiction**
P: 4823 **PI:** 9621 **I:** 9438

Swimming
P: 22305, 22308 **PI:** 22307
I: 22309 **IJ:** 22306

Swimming — Biography
PI: 13684

Swimming — Fiction
P: 1977, 3002, 3031, 3150,
4988, 4999, 6434 **PI:** 7867
I: 8535

Switzerland
PI: 6364, 15278 **I:** 15271,
15275 **IJ:** 15287, 15293

Switzerland — Christmas
I: 17413

**Switzerland —
Cookbooks**
IJ: 21708

Switzerland — Fiction
IJ: 10042

Switzerland — Folklore
P: 10857 **PI:** 10855

Symbiosis
I: 18579 **IJ:** 18599

Symbols
See Signs and symbols

Synagogues
P: 17224, 17234

Synagogues — Fiction
P: 6084

T

T-ball — Fiction
P: 2914

Table manners — History
PI: 17638

Tadpoles
I: 18733

Tadpoles — Fiction
P: 5370

Tae Kwon Do
IJ: 22274

Taft, William H.
I: 13105

Tahiti
I: 15248

Taiga
I: 20485 **IJ:** 20456

Taino Indians — Fiction
IJ: 7737

Taino Indians — Folklore
P: 11417, 11425

Taiwan
I: 15187 **IJ:** 15155, 15219

Taiwan — Fiction
P: 4808 **IJ:** 9021

Taj Mahal
I: 15111

Tajikistan
I: 15435 **IJ:** 15434

**Talk-show hosts —
Biography**
I: 12484 **IJ:** 12437

Tall people
I: 18067

Tall tales
P: 1100, 1364, 1569, 11359
PI: 4188 **I:** 9829, 9845

Tallchief, Maria
I: 12477

**Tanks (military) —
History**
IJ: 14867

Tanzania
IJ: 14951

Tanzania — Fiction
P: 4772–73, 4844–45

Tanzania — Folklore
P: 10705–6

Tap dancing
IJ: 14291

**Tap dancing —
Biography**
IJ: 12465

Tap jazz
IJ: 14291

Tapeworms
I: 18648

Taproots
P: 20174

Tarantulas
P: 19597 **I:** 19589

Tarantulas — Fiction
PI: 7309 **I:** 7291, 8562

Taste (sense)
P: 18155, 18163
I: 18134–35, 18138, 18159

**Taste (sense) —
Experiments and
projects**
I: 18138

Tattoos
IJ: 21946

Tattoos — Fiction
IJ: 10001

Taxicabs — Fiction
P: 1791, 3303

Taylor, Marshall B.
PI: 12784

Taylor, Susie King
PI: 12785

Taylor, Zachary
IJ: 13106–7

Tchaikovsky, Peter Ilyich
PI: 12340

**Tchaikovsky, Peter Ilyich
— Fiction**
PI: 9566

Tea
PI: 20128

Tea — Poetry
P: 11709

P = Primary; PI = Primary-Intermediate; I = Intermediate; IJ = Intermediate-Junior High

Teachers — Biography
IJ: 12842

Teachers — Careers
P: 3137, 17765

Teachers — Fiction
P: 248, 4278, 4413,
5466-67, 5478–79,
5486-87, 5497, 5502, 5505,
5511-12, 5515, 6332
PI: 3705, 5472, 10099,
10115, 10330 I: 8635,
10066, 10075, 10093, 10170
IJ: 8248, 10120

Teakettles — Fiction
P: 2972

Teamwork
P: 216

Teasing
PI: 17693

Technology and
engineering
I: 21058, 21264 IJ: 21028,
21052, 21056, 21232

Technology and
engineering — 1960s
IJ: 13875

Technology and
engineering — History
PI: 14565 I: 21025
IJ: 13891, 13896, 14617,
14745

Technology and
engineering —
Predictions
I: 21034

Tectonics
See Plate tectonics

Tecumseh (Shawnee chief)
PI: 12999 IJ: 13000

Teddy bears — Fiction
P: 2950, 2952, 3474, 3932

Teddy bears — History
PI: 21032

Teddy bears —
Manufacture
I: 21060

Teeth
P: 18179, 18186–89
PI: 18184 I: 18190
IJ: 18021, 18185

Teeth — Animals
PI: 18861

Teeth — Fiction
P: 1581, 1795, 2454, 2717,
3026, 3782, 4191–92, 4224,
4953, 6278, 6393, 6439,
6479 PI: 7135, 9800

Teeth — Folklore
P: 10531, 10536

Telecommunications
I: 21262–63

Telephone — Biography
I: 13236, 13238–39
IJ: 13240

Telephones
P: 21243 I: 21263
IJ: 21261

Telescopes
PI: 18417 I: 18413
IJ: 18383

Television
P: 14315, 21243 PI: 14313
I: 12351, 12369, 12426,
12486, 14310, 21266,
21272, 21276 IJ: 12370,
12372, 21271

Television — Biography
PI: 12464 I: 13232, 13279

Television — Careers
IJ: 17784, 21273

Television — Fiction
P: 1892, 2532, 6376
PI: 9807, 9812–13

Tell, William
P: 10857 PI: 10855

Temper — Fiction
P: 3633, 4954

Temperature —
Experiments and
projects
IJ: 20853

Ten Commandments
(Bible)
P: 17325

Tennessee
P: 16846 PI: 16854
I: 16888 IJ: 16829

Tennessee — Fiction
IJ: 9601

Tennis
PI: 22315 I: 22312, 22316
IJ: 22311, 22313

Tennis — Biography
PI: 13643, 13647, 13651,
13653 I: 13363, 13373,
13409, 13641, 13645,
13648–50, 13656
IJ: 13642, 13644, 13646,
13652, 13654–55, 13657,
13720

Tennis — Fiction
I: 10318 IJ: 10267

Tennis — Women
IJ: 22314

Tepees
I: 15918, 16037

Teresa, Mother
P: 13852 PI: 13853–54,
17222 I: 13856, 13858
IJ: 13855, 13857, 13859

Terezin (concentration
camp)
IJ: 14878

Termites
P: 19451 I: 19493

Terrell, Mary Church
PI: 12786 I: 12787

Terriers
I: 19977

Terrorism
I: 17081

Terrorists — Fiction
IJ: 6742

Texas
PI: 16905 I: 13176, 16901,
17576 IJ: 16903, 16908

Texas — Biography
IJ: 12684

Texas — Fiction
P: 4591, 4637, 4676, 4698
PI: 1940, 3019, 9767
I: 6867, 7121, 7639, 9256,
9294, 9379, 9389, 9587,
9629 IJ: 7199, 7454, 9279,
9414, 9439, 9462, 9512,
9527

Texas — Folklore
P: 11229

Texas — History
PI: 12904, 16272 I: 16243,
16274, 16902, 16917
IJ: 12855, 12903, 16230,
16234

Textiles — Fiction
P: 4414

Thailand
I: 15160, 15208 IJ: 15201,
15207

Thailand — Cookbooks
IJ: 21705

Thailand — Fiction
P: 1325 I: 8995 IJ: 8994

Thailand — Folklore
P: 10840 IJ: 10841

Thailand — Holidays
PI: 15212

Thanksgiving
P: 6152, 17497, 17500
PI: 17350, 17495–96,
17501 I: 17498–99,
17502–3 IJ: 17491

Thanksgiving —
Cookbooks
PI: 17494 I: 17499

Thanksgiving — Crafts
PI: 17492, 17495 I: 17493,
17499

Thanksgiving —
Experiments and
projects
PI: 17494

Thanksgiving — Fiction
P: 33, 539, 4530, 6132–34,
6136–37, 6139–45,
6147–48, 6150–51,

6153–59, 14017 PI: 6135,
6965, 9407, 9723 I: 9703

Thanksgiving — Poetry
P: 6138, 6149 PI: 11850

Thatcher, Margaret
IJ: 13860

Thaxter, Celia
P: 4850

Theater games
I: 14320

Theaters
See also Actors; Actresses;
Plays
I: 14323

Theaters — Fiction
P: 1649, 2079, 2416, 6134
IJ: 9079–80

Theodoric (monk) —
Fiction
I: 9055

Thesauruses
I: 14061

Theseus (mythology)
PI: 11483 I: 11472

Thomas, Frank
I: 13507–8 IJ: 13509

Thomas, Isiah
IJ: 13577

Thomas, Thurman
I: 13635

Thoreau, Henry David
I: 12605

Thorpe, Jim
I: 13675 IJ: 13674

Throat
I: 18002

Thumbsucking — Fiction
P: 4977

Thunderstorms
P: 20683 PI: 20718
I: 20698, 20701

Thunderstorms — Fiction
P: 1843, 3842, 6606

Tibet
I: 13777, 15181 IJ: 15165

Tibet — Fiction
P: 4662 PI: 4854
IJ: 9020

Tibet — Folklore
I: 10758

Tic-tac-toe
P: 6679

Ticks (insect)
PI: 19466

Tidal pools
P: 19861 PI: 19853, 19858
I: 19855, 19867

Tidal waves
See also Tsunamis
I: 19850 IJ: 20722

P = Primary; PI = Primary-Intermediate; I = Intermediate; IJ = Intermediate-Junior High

Tidal waves — Fiction
P: 971 I: 8573

Tides — Fiction
P: 4411

Tigers
P: 19084, 19101, 19110
PI: 19086, 19100, 19105
I: 19089, 19104, 19115,
20027 IJ: 19102

Tigers — Fiction
P: 929, 935, 1781, 2277,
5172, 5375, 5456 I: 8625

Tigers — Folklore
I: 10846

Tigris River
IJ: 15494

Tillage, Leon Walker
IJ: 17052

Timbuktu — History
IJ: 15018

Time and clocks
See also Concept books —
Time
P: 206, 823, 20648,
20650–51, 20654–55
PI: 20653, 20658 I: 20639,
20645–47 IJ: 20641,
20643–44, 20652

**Time and clocks —
Experiments and
projects**
PI: 18304

**Time and clocks —
Fiction**
P: 190, 205, 209, 1608,
2518 I: 10483

**Time and clocks —
Measurement**
I: 20647

**Time and clocks —
Nursery rhymes**
P: 872

Time and clocks — Poetry
P: 194 IJ: 11594

Time travel — Fiction
P: 929, 1448, 1641, 4293,
6554 PI: 1552, 7720, 8123,
8164, 9755, 10246, 14392
I: 7047, 7554, 7587,
7613–14, 7666, 7686–87,
7727, 7771, 7775, 7887,
7940, 7971, 8044, 8072,
8074–75, 8085, 8097, 8131,
8139, 8211, 8218, 8240,
10186, 10190, 10211,
10220, 16077 IJ: 7096,
7549, 7584, 7604, 7665,
7685, 7690, 7710, 7721,
7760, 7768, 7770, 7805,
7882, 7913, 7929, 7933,
8012, 8102, 8161, 8194,
8197, 8215, 9701, 9977,
10161, 10180, 10191,
10205, 10207, 10236–37

Times Square (N.Y.)
I: 16672

Tipis
See Tepees

Titanic **(ship)**
PI: 6310, 16486, 21362
I: 19880, 21361, 21378
IJ: 19873, 19879, 21348

Titanic **(ship) —
Biography**
I: 12077

Titanic **(ship) — Fiction**
P: 4595 I: 7625, 9638
IJ: 7094, 9544

Tituba
PI: 12788

Tiulana, Paul
IJ: 16812

Tlingit Indians
I: 16817

**Tlingit Indians —
Folklore**
I: 11317

Toads
See Frogs and toads

Toasters
I: 21022

Tobacco
See Smoking

Toes — Fiction
P: 4092

**Tohono O'odham Indians
— Poetry**
PI: 14253

Toilet training
P: 3065, 3298

Toilet training — Fiction
P: 3076, 3127, 3281–82,
3327, 3481, 10752

Tokyo, Japan
P: 5141 I: 15129

Tolkien, J. R. R.
I: 12606

Tomatoes
P: 20134

Tombaugh, Clyde
PI: 13350

Tongue twisters
P: 6636, 6646 I: 21879,
21884

Tonsillitis
I: 18002

Tools
P: 3326, 5561, 21662

Tooth decay
See also Teeth
I: 18190

Tooth fairy — Fiction
P: 951 PI: 8791

Toothbrushes — Fiction
P: 1112

Toothpaste — Fiction
I: 9937

Torah
I: 11165

Tornadoes
P: 20686, 20692–93, 20712
PI: 20681, 20684 I: 20662,
20682, 20697, 20702,
20704, 20719 IJ: 20679,
20713, 20716

Tornadoes — Fiction
P: 2906, 2909, 2935, 2955,
4974 I: 7039, 8003

Toronto
I: 15592

Toronto — Fiction
PI: 3020

Tortillas
P: 20119

Tortoises — Fiction
P: 5303

Totem poles
P: 15952

Toucans
P: 19252

Touch (sense)
P: 18144, 18156 I: 18133,
18135, 18160

**Toulouse-Lautrec, Henri
de**
PI: 12303

Towels — Fiction
P: 3315

Tower of Babel (painting)
IJ: 13895

Tower of London
I: 15343

**Tower of London —
Fiction**
PI: 9087

Towns — Deserts
P: 3161

Toxic waste
See also Waste
IJ: 17008

Toy making
I: 20911, 21636, 21654
IJ: 21657

Toys
P: 21024, 21659 PI: 16486

Toys — Crafts
P: 21653 I: 21609
IJ: 21650

Toys — Fiction
P: 408, 1381, 1533, 1618,
3194, 3279–80, 3308, 3314,
3325, 3349–50, 3639, 3848,
4984, 5014, 5668, 10395
PI: 7583, 8209 I: 7587,
8216 IJ: 7593

Toys — Folklore
I: 10916

Toys — History
PI: 21658 I: 22076

Track and field
See also Running and
jogging
PI: 22319 I: 22318
IJ: 22317

**Track and field —
Biography**
P: 13664, 13669, 13672,
13721 PI: 13661, 13665,
13670 I: 13423, 13658,
13660, 13667–68, 13671,
13673, 13675 IJ: 13377,
13390, 13401, 13659,
13662–63, 13666, 13674,
13722

Track and field — Fiction
P: 5483 PI: 10351
IJ: 10335

**Track and field —
Women**
I: 13423

Tractors
P: 20071

Tractors — Fiction
P: 5553

Trade
PI: 16932

Trade — History
IJ: 14355, 16929, 21054

Trail of Tears
PI: 15936

Trail of Tears — Fiction
IJ: 9152

Trains
See Railroads and trains

Transplants
See Organ transplants

Transportation
See also specific types of
transportation, e.g.,
Automobiles
P: 5546, 5572, 21289,
21295 PI: 21280, 21287
I: 14587, 21279, 21285
IJ: 21286, 21290

Transportation — Crafts
PI: 21465

Transportation — Fiction
P: 5588, 6312, 6369

Transportation — History
PI: 16493 I: 21282
IJ: 14601, 21284, 21326

**Transportation —
Machinery**
P: 21288

Transportation — Poetry
PI: 11638 I: 11637

Travel — Fiction
P: 82 IJ: 7111

P = Primary; PI = Primary-Intermediate; I = Intermediate; IJ = Intermediate-Junior High

Travel-Folklore
PI: 1128

Treasurehunts (games)
I: 22014

Tree frog
P: 18714, 18717, 18732

Tree frog — Fiction
P: 2017

Treehouse — Fiction
P: 1623

Trees
P: 4434, 4510, 4730, 16966, 20157, 20194, 20200, 20214–15, 20217 **PI:** 18910, 20193, 20197, 20199, 20202, 20204–5, 20209, 20213, 20219–20, 20479 **I:** 20196, 20198, 20203, 20206–7, 20212 **IJ:** 20205, 20208, 20221

Trees-Experiments and projects
I: 20201

Trees-Fiction
P: 992, 1282, 1596, 3023, 3655, 4370, 4387, 4398, 4410, 4443, 4453, 4534, 4539, 4546, 4556, 4572, 4855 **PI:** 8663, 10382 **I:** 4435, 9381

Trees-Folklore
P: 10844, 11353

Trees-Poetry
PI: 11953 **IJ:** 11950

Triangle Shirtwaist Factory fire
I: 16482

Triangle Shirtwaist Factory fire — Fiction
I: 9586

Trinidad
PI: 15701

Trinidad — Fiction
P: 4702

Trinidad — Folklore
PI: 11427 **I:** 11426

Trinidad — Holidays
PI: 15701

Triplets
PI: 17641

Triplets — Fiction
P: 3961

Trivia
I: 21897, 21940 **IJ:** 21938

Trojan War (mythology)
See also Iliad (mythology)
P: 14686 **PI:** 14688
I: 14698 **IJ:** 11475, 11486, 11510

Trolls
P: 1010, 1344–45, 4738, 5759, 6421 **IJ:** 8151

Trolls — Folklore
P: 11118, 11124

Trompe l'oeil
IJ: 13883

Tropical forests
See Rain forests

Tropics — Fiction
P: 4654

Trout
PI: 19699

Troy — History
See also Trojan War (mythology)
I: 14698, 14708 **IJ:** 14523

Truck drivers — Careers
P: 17839, 21316 **PI:** 17841

Trucks
P: 5559, 5565, 5571, 5575, 5578, 5593, 5597, 5604–5, 21291–93, 21295, 21299, 21301, 21315–16, 21324 **PI:** 21294, 21310, 21319, 21322–23 **I:** 21250

Trucks — Fiction
P: 913, 1041, 1542, 2887, 5549, 5552, 5560, 5570, 5583, 5600–2, 5607, 6574

Truman, Harry S.
PI: 13109 **I:** 13108

Trumpeters — Biography
I: 12421

Trumpets
P: 14222

Trumpets — Fiction
P: 4986, 4994 **I:** 8201

Truth — Fiction
P: 5023

Truth — Manipulation
IJ: 14084

Truth, Sojourner
PI: 12789, 12792 **I:** 12790, 12794 **IJ:** 12791, 12793

Tsimshin Indians
I: 15972

Tsunamis
See also Tidal waves
I: 20721 **IJ:** 20722

Tubman, Harriet
P: 12802 **PI:** 12795, 12799, 12801 **I:** 12797–98, 12804 **IJ:** 12796, 12803

Tubman, Harriet — Poetry
P: 12800

Tugboats
P: 21366, 21377

Tugboats — Fiction
P: 4612

Tundra
P: 15803, 15843
PI: 15809, 15827, 15835

I: 15810, 15832, 15834
IJ: 20371

Tunisia
IJ: 14957

Tunnels
P: 21129, 21131, 21149
I: 21146

Turkey
PI: 15282 **I:** 15289, 15492
IJ: 15260, 15266

Turkey — Biography
IJ: 13779

Turkey — Fiction
IJ: 8929, 9027

Turkey — Folklore
I: 10865

Turkey — Holidays
PI: 15282

Turkeys
P: 19215, 19267

Turkeys — Fiction
P: 6136, 6141 **IJ:** 9298

Turkmenistan
I: 15435

Turner, Henry
PI: 13351

Turner, Joseph
PI: 12304

Turner, Nat
I: 12805–6

Turnips — Folklore
P: 10886

Turtles and tortoises
P: 18777, 18780–81, 18787, 18789 **PI:** 18778, 18782–83, 18786, 18788, 18791–92 **I:** 18680, 18779, 18784–85, 18790, 18793
IJ: 18924

Turtles and tortoises — Fiction
P: 1296, 2278, 4441, 5206, 5365, 5464 **I:** 8088

Turtles and tortoises — Folklore
P: 10677, 10701, 10847, 11052

Tuskegee Institute
PI: 12813

Tutankhamen, King
P: 14625 **PI:** 13862, 14648
I: 13861, 14637

TWA Flight 800 (disaster)
IJ: 21074

Twain, Mark
PI: 12607 **I:** 12608
IJ: 12609–12, 16590

Twain, Mark — Fiction
IJ: 9392

Twain, Shania
IJ: 12478

Twentieth century — History
I: 14554 **IJ:** 14545, 14562, 14570

Twins
P: 17680, 17684 **I:** 18065, 18241

Twins — Fiction
P: 619, 3177, 3747, 4180, 4919, 6015, 6449, 6541
PI: 6962–63, 6965, 7459, 8164–65, 10085 **I:** 7514, 7540, 7798, 7890, 8364, 8653, 8803, 9269, 9524, 10035, 10214, 10523
IJ: 7443, 7581, 7889, 10323

Tyler, John
IJ: 13110

Tyler, Liv
PI: 12479

Typhoid fever — Fiction
I: 9517

Tyrannosaurus rex
P: 14487 **PI:** 14468

U

U.S. Postal Service
P: 17105

U.S. Women's National Soccer Team
IJ: 22298

UFOs
PI: 21890, 21913 **I:** 20952, 20992, 21001, 21931, 21936
IJ: 20995, 21896

UFOs — Fiction
IJ: 7398

Uganda
I: 19002 **IJ:** 14919

Uganda — Fiction
P: 4750

Ukeleles — Folklore
P: 10713

Ukraine
I: 15406, 15416 **IJ:** 15436

Ukraine — Crafts
I: 17439

Ukraine — Folklore
P: 10854, 10858, 10860, 10864, 11095, 11097

Ukraine — Holidays
PI: 15405

Ukrainian Americans
IJ: 17572

Umbrellas — Fiction
P: 3491, 4295

Uncles — Fiction
P: 3683

P = Primary; PI = Primary-Intermediate; I = Intermediate; IJ = Intermediate-Junior High

Underground life
I: 20379

Underground Railroad
P: 12802 PI: 12795
I: 12797–98, 16228
IJ: 12796, 12803, 16226,
16258, 16268, 16281

**Underground Railroad —
Biography**
PI: 12801 I: 12804

**Underground Railroad —
Fiction**
P: 4886, 6224 PI: 4639,
9308, 9338 I: 6823, 9268,
9277, 9281, 9295–96, 9312,
9337, 9496, 16247
IJ: 6872–73, 8172, 8202,
9264, 9291, 9297, 9326

Underwater archaeology
I: 14521 IJ: 14531, 14537,
14541–42, 15944, 21367

Underwater exploration
See also Oceanography
PI: 19875 I: 14539, 19631,
19818, 19876, 19878,
19880–81 IJ: 19873–74,
19877, 19879

**Underwater exploration
— Biography**
I: 12101 IJ: 13267

**Underwater exploration
— Careers**
PI: 17833

**Underwater exploration
— Fiction**
PI: 6869 I: 7128

Underwear
PI: 21176

Unemployment — Fiction
IJ: 8459

Unicorns
I: 7773

Unicorns — Fiction
P: 1711 IJ: 7742

Unidentified flying objects
See UFOs

United Farm Workers
I: 17135

United Kingdom
See England; Great
Britain; Ireland,
Northern; Scotland;
Wales

United Nations
IJ: 17018

**United Nations —
Biography**
I: 13752

**United Nations —
Children's rights**
P: 17019

United Nations — Fiction
PI: 10263

United States
See also specific regions,
states, and cities, e.g.,
Midwest (U.S.);
California; New York
City
P: 15890 PI: 15865, 15878
I: 15864, 15895 IJ: 15902,
15915

**United States — Aerial
views**
I: 20983

United States — Art
PI: 13961 IJ: 13950,
13960

**United States —
Biography**
I: 12692

United States — Cities
IJ: 15871

**United States — Civil
War**
See Civil War (U.S.)

**United States — Colonial
Period**
See Colonial Period (U.S.)

United States — Congress
See Congress (U.S.)

**United States —
Constitution**
See Constitution (U.S.)

**United States —
Cookbooks**
I: 21692

United States — Crafts
I: 21439, 21517

**United States —
Discovery and
exploration**
I: 16078, 16090 IJ: 16075,
16086, 16092–93

**United States —
Documents**
IJ: 15894

United States — Fiction
P: 11339

United States — Folklore
P: 5919, 11033, 11327,
11331–33, 11336–38,
11346, 11348, 11350–51,
11353, 11355–56, 11359,
11362, 11367–69,
11374–75, 11379, 11384,
11387, 11391 PI: 11324,
11329, 11343, 11361,
11377, 11390 I: 10558,
11334–35, 11342, 11345,
11349, 11376, 11382,
11386, 11388–89
IJ: 11330, 11341, 11354,
11364, 11366, 11370–71,
11380–81 All: 14145

**United States — Frontier
life**
See Frontier life (U.S.)

**United States —
Geography**
P: 3342 PI: 15867–68,
15889, 15905 I: 15854,
15883, 15901 IJ: 15860,
15911

**United States —
Geography — Fiction**
P: 1291

**United States —
Government and politics**
PI: 12648, 17117 I: 17020,
17107, 17112, 17118,
17124–25, 17130–31
IJ: 17109

**United States —
Government and politics
— Biography**
I: 12838, 12840, 12873,
12895 IJ: 12919

**United States —
Government and politics
— Women**
PI: 12841 IJ: 12682

United States — History
See also specific periods
and events, e.g.,
Colonial Period (U.S.);
Civil War (U.S.)
P: 4730, 15899–900
PI: 15868 I: 15887, 15897,
16757 IJ: 15873, 15879,
15884, 15894, 15911–12,
21180

**United States — History
— 1960s**
IJ: 16504, 16508

**United States — History
— 1970s**
IJ: 16503, 16508

**United States — History
— 1980s**
IJ: 16502

**United States — History
— Documents**
IJ: 15880

**United States — History
— Songs**
I: 14168

United States — Holidays
PI: 15865

**United States —
Immigration**
See Immigration (U.S.)

**United States — National
monuments**
I: 15849, 15857

United States — Poetry
IJ: 11615

**United States —
Prehistory**
IJ: 15967

United States — Religion
IJ: 15913

**United States —
Revolutionary War**
See Revolutionary War
(U.S.)

United States — Sports
I: 21980

United States — States
I: 15910

United States — Symbols
PI: 15858

**United States (1789–1860)
— History**
I: 16475 IJ: 16249, 16313

**United States (1789–1861)
— Fiction**
PI: 9308, 9322, 9328
I: 9265, 9277, 9340, 9437,
9451 IJ: 9257–58, 9262,
9270, 9276, 9313, 16238

**United States (1789–1861)
— History**
I: 16245, 16280
IJ: 16232–33, 16235,
16261, 16265, 16270,
16276–78

**United States (1789–1861)
— History — Fiction**
PI: 9327

**United States (1789–1961)
— History**
IJ: 16234

**United States (1865–1950)
— Crafts**
I: 16477

**United States (1865–1950)
— Fiction**
P: 4582, 4823
PI: 9562–63, 9567 I: 7115,
9511, 9534, 9581, 9606,
9617, 9622, 9630 IJ: 9512,
9605, 9624, 9634

**United States (1865–1950)
— History**
PI: 16493 I: 16461, 16463,
16467, 16490 IJ: 16446,
16452, 16457, 16468,
16470, 16484–85, 16491–92

**United States (1865–1950)
— History — Fiction**
IJ: 9615

**United States (1948–1976)
— History**
IJ: 16511

**United States (1951–)
— History**
I: 14587, 16500, 16524
IJ: 16505, 16509, 16512,
16519–20, 16525

United States Air Force
IJ: 21380, 21382, 21392

United States Army
I: 21384, 21393 IJ: 21394,
21398

P = Primary; PI = Primary-Intermediate; I = Intermediate; IJ = Intermediate-Junior High

United States Army —
African Americans
IJ: 15869

United States Army —
Biography
I: 12930, 12944, 12951
IJ: 12667, 12731,
12931–32, 12953–54, 12956

United States Army —
World War II
IJ: 14897

United States Census
Bureau
I: 17116

United States Coast
Guard
PI: 21391 IJ: 21383

United States Fish and
Wildlife Service
PI: 17119

United States Life Saving
Service — Fiction
IJ: 9286

United States Marine
Corps
IJ: 21395, 21407

United States Military
Academy — History
I: 21389

United States Navy
I: 21399 IJ: 21396, 21400

United States Navy —
Biography
PI: 12913 IJ: 12962

United States Navy —
History
IJ: 21357

Universe
P: 18421 I: 18416
IJ: 18384

Uranus (planet)
PI: 18465, 18494, 18496,
18502 I: 18478, 18487

Uruguay
IJ: 15770

Utah
P: 16603 PI: 16609, 16617
I: 16637 IJ: 14377, 16620,
16626, 16641

Utah — Fiction
P: 4668

Ute Indians — Fiction
I: 9354

Uzbekistan
I: 15435 IJ: 15437
I: 6834, 7686

V

Vacations — Fiction
P: 1879 I: 6834, 7686

Vacuum cleaners
PI: 21023

Valentine, Saint
PI: 17510

Valentine's Day
P: 6164, 17507 PI: 6177,
17506, 17509 I: 17504–5
IJ: 17508

Valentine's Day — Crafts
PI: 21484 I: 21428

Valentine's Day — Fiction
P: 5085, 6160–63, 6165–76,
6178 PI: 6283, 8382

Valentine's Day — Poetry
P: 11835, 11851 I: 11838

Valley Forge (PA) (battle)
PI: 16216 I: 16199

Valleys
I: 20390

Values
P: 3022

Vampires — Fiction
P: 1481, 1576 PI: 8065
I: 9877, 9885, 9889
IJ: 8077, 8166

Van Buren, Martin
IJ: 13111–12

Van Horn, Keith
I: 13578

Vaqueros — History
IJ: 16359

Vatican City
I: 15388 IJ: 14798

Vegans
IJ: 18213

Vegetables
P: 20172, 20174, 20184,
20186 PI: 20169 I: 20124
IJ: 20177–78

Vegetables —
Experiments and
projects
I: 21768

Vegetables — Fiction
P: 1674, 1678, 3116
PI: 3364

Vegetarian cooking
IJ: 21714, 21718, 21741

Vegetarianism
IJ: 18209

Velázquez, Diego —
Fiction
IJ: 9034

Venezuela
P: 15751 PI: 22096
I: 15744, 15789 IJ: 15771,
15779, 15791

Venice (Italy) — Fiction
P: 2160, 4632, 4647
IJ: 9028

Ventura, Jesse
IJ: 13710

Venturini, Tisha Lea
PI: 22302

Venus flytrap
P: 20227 PI: 20242

Venus (planet)
PI: 18466 I: 18476, 20957

Venus (planet) — Folklore
P: 10703

Veracruz (Mexico)
IJ: 15634

Verbs
P: 236, 14045

Vermont
P: 16674 PI: 16683
I: 16689, 16718, 20058
IJ: 16669

Vermont — Fiction
PI: 8705 I: 7401, 8835
IJ: 7386, 8068, 8358, 9208,
9309, 9605

Verne, Jules
I: 12613 IJ: 12614

Vertebrates
I: 18669

Vesuvius
I: 14710, 14723

Veterans Day
P: 17339

Veterinarians
P: 17851, 17853

Veterinarians — Careers
P: 17845 PI: 17842,
17844, 17846, 17854, 17856
I: 17847 IJ: 17848, 17852,
17855

Veterinarians — Fiction
PI: 7298 I: 6747, 7151

Vice Presidents (U.S.) —
Biography
PI: 12893 I: 12891–92

Vice Presidents (U.S.) —
Wives — Biography
I: 13155 IJ: 13156

Vicksburg, Battle of
IJ: 16407, 16433

Victor (the wild child)
P: 4663

Victoria, Queen of
England
I: 13863

Victorian times — Crafts
I: 14358

Victorian times — Fiction
I: 6740, 7589 IJ: 7096,
8009

Video
I: 21266

Video games
I: 22232, 22239

Video games — Careers
IJ: 17792

Video games — Fiction
P: 4283

Videos
I: 21265

Vienna — Fiction
I: 7081

Vietnam
P: 15190, 15197
PI: 15171–73, 15176,
15200 I: 15158, 15189,
15202 IJ: 15163, 15182,
15210, 15214, 15218

Vietnam — Cookbooks
IJ: 21725

Vietnam — Fiction
P: 4856 PI: 7341 I: 9018
IJ: 8998

Vietnam — Folklore
P: 10842 IJ: 10839, 10845

Vietnam — History
I: 15167

Vietnam — Language
I: 14113

Vietnam Veterans
Memorial, Washington,
D.C.
IJ: 16649

Vietnam Veterans
Memorial, Washington,
D.C. — Fiction
P: 3559

Vietnam War
IJ: 16507, 16513, 16649

Vietnam War —
Biography
IJ: 12933

Vietnam War — Fiction
PI: 8986 I: 8505, 9009,
9018 IJ: 8405, 8430, 8615

Vietnam War — Protests
I: 16501

Vietnam War — Women
IJ: 16526

Vietnamese Americans
I: 17567, 17593, 17595
IJ: 17586

Vietnamese Americans —
Fiction
PI: 3641, 7341, 7348
IJ: 8289

Vikings
PI: 15468 I: 13792, 15440,
15443, 15448, 15452–53,
15459, 15462–65
IJ: 15460, 15470

Vikings — Folklore
I: 11132, 11520

Villa, Pancho
IJ: 13864–65

P = Primary; PI = Primary-Intermediate; I = Intermediate; IJ = Intermediate-Junior High

Violence
I: 17630 **IJ:** 17137–38, 17145, 17151, 17157, 17659, 17710

Violence — Fiction
I: 8477

Violence — Mass Media
IJ: 17137

Violins — Fiction
P: 4410 **PI:** 9035 **I:** 10322
IJ: 8423

Virgin Islands — Fiction
IJ: 7113, 9136

Virgin Islands — Folklore
P: 11421

Virginia
PI: 16855, 19871 **I:** 16889
IJ: 16831, 16834

Virginia — Fiction
I: 8363, 9186 **IJ:** 9195, 9483

Virginia — History
I: 16838, 16840 **IJ:** 16174, 16899

Virginia Colony
I: 16127

Virtual reality
I: 21206, 21208, 21220
IJ: 21193

Viruses
P: 17939 **PI:** 17955
I: 17954 **IJ:** 17968

Visual handicaps
P: 4927

Visualization (computers)
IJ: 21192

Vitamins
PI: 20163 **I:** 20167

Volcanoes
P: 15630, 20335, 20348, 20356 **PI:** 20339, 20344, 20346, 20505 **I:** 14710, 14723, 20333, 20336, 20343, 20347, 20352, 20355
IJ: 20332, 20334, 20338, 20349–50

Volcanoes — Experiments and projects
IJ: 20340

Volcanoes — Fiction
P: 2944, 4438 **I:** 10187

Volleyball
I: 21992

Volleyball — Biography
IJ: 13708

Volleyball — Fiction
IJ: 10316

Volleyball — Girls
IJ: 21990

Volunteerism
I: 17139 **IJ:** 17611

Volunteerism — Biography
I: 13015

Voting
I: 17047

Voyager (spacecraft)
IJ: 18515

Voyager II (spacecraft)
I: 18481 **IJ:** 18492

Vultures
P: 19283 **I:** 19275, 19344

W

Waco, Texas, siege at
IJ: 16839

Wading Birds
P: 19295

Wakeboarding
IJ: 22013

Wales
See also Great Britain
I: 15368 **IJ:** 14776, 15369

Wales — Fiction
P: 1304 **IJ:** 7551, 7861, 9698

Wales — Folklore
P: 11013 **PI:** 10967
I: 10966

Wales — Poetry
IJ: 11853

Walesa, Lech
I: 13866

Walker, Alice
I: 12615

Walker, Herschel
IJ: 13636

Walker, Madam C. J.
PI: 12810 **I:** 12807–9

Walker, Maggie
IJ: 12811

Wallenberg, Raoul
IJ: 13867

Walls
I: 14534, 14560

Walruses
P: 19732 **PI:** 19740
I: 19734

Walruses — Fiction
P: 2009

Walsh, John
PI: 18627

Wampanoag Indians
PI: 16185

Wampanoag Indians — Biography
I: 12981 **IJ:** 12980

Wampanoag Indians — Folklore
PI: 11269

Wampanoag Indians — History
I: 16022, 16035

Wang, Yani
IJ: 12315

Waorani Indians
I: 15787

War
See also specific battles and wars, e.g., Alamo, Battle of the; World War II
IJ: 21388, 21397

War — Fiction
P: 4631 **I:** 8176 **IJ:** 9061

War — Folklore
P: 10894 **IJ:** 10586

War — Poetry
P: 11573 **I:** 11681
IJ: 11670

War of 1812
IJ: 16235, 16244, 16279

War of 1812 — Fiction
PI: 4829, 9307 **IJ:** 9284, 9315, 9330, 9335

Warhol, Andy
PI: 12309

Warner, Gertrude C.
PI: 12616

Warthogs
PI: 18967

Warts
I: 18178

Wasco Indians — Folklore
P: 11311

Washington, Booker T.
PI: 12812–13 **I:** 12814

Washington, Booker T. — Fiction
P: 4603

Washington, DC
P: 16706 **PI:** 16654, 16656, 16675, 16684
I: 16660–61, 16700, 16712, 16731, 16733, 16744
IJ: 16670, 16743, 16746

Washington, DC — Buildings
I: 16730

Washington, DC — Fiction
P: 1873, 4875 **I:** 10234

Washington, Denzel
I: 12480

Washington, George
P: 13113 **PI:** 13118
I: 12672, 13115–16, 16209,

16883 **IJ:** 13114, 13117, 13119–20, 16195

Washington, George — Fiction
P: 4812 **PI:** 9232, 9249
I: 9231

Washington, March on (1963)
P: 16518 **I:** 16522

Washington, Martha
I: 13198–99

Washington, Mary Ball
P: 13200

Washington Monument
I: 16667

Washington (state)
I: 16808, 16821, 21125

Washington (state) — Fiction
I: 7453

Washington (state) — Rain forests
I: 20495

Wasps
I: 19524, 19526

Wasps — Fiction
P: 4218

Waste
I: 16976, 16983

Waste recycling
See also Recycling — Paper
P: 3034, 16937, 16980, 16982, 16985 **PI:** 16981, 16984, 21417 **I:** 16974, 16977, 16979, 16983, 16986, 16988, 21416
IJ: 16975, 16978, 16987

Waste recycling — Crafts
IJ: 21496

Waste recycling — Fiction
P: 4339

Watches
See Time and clocks

Water
See also Pollution, Water
P: 18192, 20725, 20734, 20738–39, 20744–45
PI: 20749 **I:** 16997, 20729, 20736, 20741, 20748
IJ: 20735

Water — Experiments and projects
P: 20738 **PI:** 20742
I: 20724, 20731–33, 20740, 20747 **IJ:** 18348

Water — Fiction
P: 3183 **PI:** 10265

Water — Folklore
P: 10912

Water — Poetry
PI: 11578, 11993

P = Primary; PI = Primary-Intermediate; I = Intermediate; IJ = Intermediate-Junior High

Water birds
I: 19308, 19314

Water cycle
P: 20745 **PI:** 20726, 20737
I: 20746 **IJ:** 20728

Water cycle — Fiction
P: 4444

Water sports
See also specific sports,
e.g., Wakeboarding
I: 21998

Water treatment plants
P: 17824

Waterfalls
P: 20369 **PI:** 20396

Waterfalls — Fiction
P: 2953

Watergate affair
IJ: 16525

**Watergate affair —
Biography**
IJ: 12734

Watson, Lyall
IJ: 12617

Watts, J. C., Jr.
I: 12968 **IJ:** 12815

Wave theory
I: 20903

**Waves — Experiments
and projects**
IJ: 19852

Weapons
IJ: 20949, 21386, 21388,
21397

**Weapons — Civil War
(U.S.)**
IJ: 16396

Weapons — Fiction
I: 10178

Weapons — History
IJ: 21385, 21387, 21402,
21409

Weasels — Fiction
P: 6466

Weather
See also specific types of
weather, e.g., Tornadoes
P: 4446, 20675, 20753,
20758, 20760, 20765–66,
20768–69, 20772, 20783,
20789, 20791 **PI:** 20694,
20718, 20779–80 **I:** 14905,
20661–62, 20750, 20752,
20754, 20759, 20761,
20764, 20767, 20773,
20775–76, 20781, 20784,
20786, 20788, 20793,
20796–97 **IJ:** 20318,
20728, 20762, 20770,
20774, 20785, 20787,
20790, 20792, 20795

**Weather — Experiments
and projects**
I: 20756, 20759, 20764,
20794 **IJ:** 20660, 20782

Weather — Fiction
P: 980, 4369, 4463, 4553
I: 8090

Weather forecasting
P: 20760

Weaving
I: 15010, 16031

Weaving — Careers
P: 17773

Weaving — Fiction
P: 4768

**Web page design —
Careers**
IJ: 17793

Web pages (computers)
IJ: 21209, 21218

**Web pages (computers) —
Construction**
IJ: 21221

Webber, Chris
I: 13579

Weddings
P: 5641 **I:** 17359, 17371
IJ: 17361

Weddings — Fiction
P: 1539, 1891, 2188, 3086,
3172, 3337, 3436, 3727,
3963, 4127, 4178, 4826,
6380 **PI:** 8637, 8741
I: 8865 **IJ:** 7408, 8561

Wedges (physics)
P: 20928

Weeds
P: 20237 **I:** 20267

Weight — Fiction
PI: 4947

Weight lifting
PI: 22029

Weight lifting — Fiction
I: 10342

Weight problems
See Obesity

Weights and measures
See also Concept books —
Measurement
PI: 20582, 20658 **I:** 20657

**Weights and measures —
Fiction**
P: 256

Wells, H. G.
IJ: 12618

Wells-Barnett, Ida B.
PI: 12817–19 **I:** 12643
IJ: 12816, 12820

Werewolves — Fiction
I: 7692, 8020 **IJ:** 8166

West, Benjamin
P: 12310

West Africa
I: 15020

West Africa — History
IJ: 15021

West Indian Americans
IJ: 17544

West Indies
See Caribbean Islands

West (U.S.)
See also specific states,
e.g., California
P: 5389 **PI:** 12687
I: 16335, 16346–47
IJ: 12663, 16333

West (U.S.) — Biography
I: 12056, 12118, 12669,
12864, 12869

West (U.S) — Exploration
IJ: 16081

West (U.S.) — Fiction
P: 2932, 3044, 4251
I: 7219, 7587, 9849
IJ: 7149–50, 7218, 9355,
9485

West (U.S.) — Folklore
P: 11358

West (U.S.) — History
See also Frontier life
(U.S.)
PI: 16304, 16309, 16314
IJ: 12852, 12874, 12909,
16305–6

West Virginia
P: 16847 **I:** 16893
IJ: 16845

West Virginia — Fiction
I: 9949 **IJ:** 7278

Western music
See Country music and
musicians

Wetlands
P: 20367–68, 20381
PI: 19415, 20386, 20395
I: 20391, 20393 **IJ:** 20364

Wetlands — Plants
P: 20517

Whales
P: 5119, 19777, 19782–83,
19785–88, 19791, 19795,
19798 **PI:** 19639,
19774–76, 19796,
19799–800, 19804
I: 19625, 19634, 19778–79,
19781, 19789–90, 19792,
19794, 19801–3 **IJ:** 19784,
19793, 19797

Whales — Fiction
P: 950, 1568, 2247, 2869,
3056, 3788, 4221, 4532,
5213, 5313, 5405, 6531
I: 2644, 6952 **IJ:** 7312,
9274, 9304

Whales — Poetry
P: 11801

Whaling
I: 19778, 19780 **IJ:** 16225

Whaling — Fiction
PI: 9316 **IJ:** 9271

Whaling — History
I: 16474 **IJ:** 15875

**Whaling ships —
Cookbooks**
IJ: 15875

Wheat
P: 20089 **PI:** 20107
I: 20102

Wheatley, Phillis
I: 12620–21 **IJ:** 12619

Wheelchairs
PI: 17915 **I:** 17923

Wheelchairs — Fiction
P: 3592, 4922 **PI:** 3820
IJ: 8261

Wheels
P: 20929

Wheels — Fiction
P: 6270

Wheels — Poetry
PI: 11638

**Whistler, James McNeill
— Fiction**
I: 9111

White, Diana
P: 12481

White, E. B.
I: 12622

White, Walter
PI: 12821

White House (U.S.)
PI: 15881 **I:** 16676, 16688,
16728, 16734 **IJ:** 16746

**White House (U.S.) —
Fiction**
P: 5838

**White-water rafting —
Fiction**
I: 7011

Whitman, Walt
IJ: 12623

Whitmore, Tamika
I: 13580

Whooping cranes
PI: 19256, 19278

Wiesel, Elie
I: 12624–25

Wigmaking — History
I: 16187

Wild turkeys
P: 19267

Wild West shows
IJ: 14266

P = Primary; PI = Primary-Intermediate; I = Intermediate; IJ = Intermediate-Junior High

Wild West shows — Fiction
IJ: 9454

Wildcats — Fiction
PI: 7782

Wildebeests
I: 14937

Wilder, Laura Ingalls
P: 12630–31 **PI:** 12627
I: 12626, 12628–29
IJ: 21744

Wilder, Laura Ingalls — Fiction
I: 9405

Wildflowers
I: 20036, 20040 **IJ:** 20042

Wildlife conservation
P: 19411 **PI:** 19399,
19413–14 **I:** 18746, 18970,
19136, 19397–98, 19402,
19412 **IJ:** 19230

Wildlife photography — Careers
IJ: 17769

Wildlife rescue
PI: 19684

Wilkins, Dominique
IJ: 13581

William the Conqueror
I: 13868

Williams, Betty
IJ: 15339

Williams, Daniel Hale
IJ: 13352

Williams, Helen
IJ: 15317

Williams, Paul R.
IJ: 12311

Williams, Robin
PI: 12482

Williams, Roger — Fiction
P: 4581

Williams, Vanessa
IJ: 12483

Williams, Venus
IJ: 13654

Williams, Venus and Serena
I: 13656 **IJ:** 13655, 13657

Williamsburg (VA)
I: 9217

Williamsburg (VA) — Fiction
PI: 9214–16 **I:** 9205–7

Williamsburg (VA) — History
PI: 16147 **I:** 16128–29,
16142, 16175

Wilson, Woodrow
IJ: 13121–23

Wimbledon (tennis tournament)
I: 22312

Wind
P: 20667 **I:** 20665

Wind — Fiction
P: 1715, 4402, 4418, 6545
PI: 4473, 9303

Wind — Poetry
P: 11965

Windmills
I: 20841

Window washers — Careers
PI: 17751

Windsurfing
IJ: 22303

Winfrey, Oprah
I: 12484–86

Wings — Fiction
PI: 1529

Winnemucca, Sarah
PI: 13001

Winter
P: 18801, 18904 **PI:** 18902
I: 18571

Winter — Crafts
P: 21490

Winter — Fiction
P: 1054, 1253, 1518, 1827,
2382, 2731, 2825, 3012,
3147, 3577, 3900, 3987,
4400, 4419, 4451, 4460,
4482, 4564, 5441, 6209,
6707 **PI:** 5167 **I:** 3066

Winter — Poetry
P: 4511 **PI:** 11949, 11992
I: 11981

Winter solstice
PI: 18568

Winter sports
See Ice hockey; Ice
skating; Skis and skiing

Wisconsin
I: 16536 **IJ:** 16534

Wisconsin — Fiction
I: 7428, 8512, 8870, 9579
IJ: 7537, 8714, 10374

Wishes and wishing — Fiction
P: 1656, 1904, 2538, 2721,
10393–94 **PI:** 7749
I: 7411, 7623, 10398
IJ: 7876

Wishes and wishing — Folklore
P: 10941, 11123

Witch hunting
IJ: 14564

Witchcraft trials
PI: 16150 **IJ:** 16138

Witchcraft trials — Salem
I: 16146, 16164 **IJ:** 16141

Witchcraft trials — Salem — Biography
PI: 12788

Witchcraft trials — Salem — Fiction
I: 9199 **IJ:** 9209

Witches — Fiction
P: 972, 1016, 1066, 1075,
1111, 1115, 1120, 1195,
1213, 1276, 1287, 1322,
1393, 1450, 1452, 1465,
1576, 1592, 1622, 1643,
4148, 5708, 5980, 6004,
6015, 6017, 6059, 6370,
10393–94 **PI:** 1329, 2570,
7705, 7880, 7949 **I:** 7143,
7607, 7624, 7698, 7977,
7996, 8226 **IJ:** 7023, 7604,
7907, 8916, 9213

Witches — Folklore
P: 10928, 10930, 11059,
11084, 11093

Witches — Poetry
I: 11732

Witt, Katarina
I: 13596–97

Wizard of Oz **— Tributes**
IJ: 14003

Wizards — Fiction
P: 1700 **PI:** 7596–97,
8164–65 **I:** 7555, 7787,
7942, 7988, 8242 **IJ:** 7599,
7708, 7711–12, 8120

Wolof (African people)
IJ: 15046

Wolves
P: 6532, 19117, 19122–23,
19125, 19128, 19130
PI: 19120, 19124 **I:** 19119,
19135–37, 19141, 19145,
19961 **IJ:** 19118, 19126,
19133, 19139–40, 19143

Wolves — Fiction
P: 1196, 1736, 2214, 2596,
4656, 5152, 5316, 5411,
5457, 5963, 10481
PI: 5223, 7160, 7261, 8958
I: 6852, 7063, 7161, 7285,
10426 **IJ:** 6853–54, 7065,
7167, 7263, 7324

Wolves — Folklore
P: 10901, 11033 **PI:** 10781

Women
See also Battered women;
Businesswomen;
Feminism
I: 21006

Women — 20th century
I: 14588

Women — Armed forces
IJ: 21404

Women — Basketball
I: 22129 **IJ:** 22147

Women — Bible
I: 17320

Women — Biography
I: 12168, 12657, 12669,
12769, 13212, 13414,
13727–29, 13734, 13736,
13740, 13742 **IJ:** 12157,
12159, 12665, 12668,
13217, 13724, 13726,
13730, 13744, 13753,
13845, 15884

Women — Business
IJ: 12676

Women — Careers
PI: 17842 **I:** 15808
IJ: 17745, 17760, 17794

Women — Collective biography
I: 12677

Women — Engineering
IJ: 17795

Women — Folklore
I: 10570, 10592–94, 11376
IJ: 10586, 10717

Women — History
I: 14588, 16475 **IJ:** 13735,
14589, 15855, 15873, 21336

Women — Medicine
IJ: 13207

Women — Personal guidance
IJ: 17701

Women — Poetry
I: 11668 **IJ:** 11658

Women — Problems
IJ: 17719

Women — Sports
I: 22027 **IJ:** 13368, 13398,
13400, 13722, 22048,
22065–66

Women — Tennis
IJ: 22314

Women — Workers
IJ: 16466

Women in Military Service for America Memorial (Washington, D.C.)
IJ: 16647

Women's rights
PI: 4596, 17032 **I:** 13192,
13194–95, 13197, 17027,
17036 **IJ:** 16472, 17045,
17051

Women's rights — Biography
P: 13125, 13133
PI: 13130–31 **I:** 13132,
13174 **IJ:** 12816, 12894,
13137, 13193

Women's rights — Fiction
P: 4627 **PI:** 9602 **I:** 9555,
9565 **IJ:** 9545

P = Primary; PI = Primary-Intermediate; I = Intermediate; IJ = Intermediate-Junior High

Wood
PI: 20211

Wood, Grant
IJ: 12312

Wood, Michele
IJ: 12313

Wood lice
PI: 19486

Wood thrushes
P: 19249

Woodpeckers
PI: 19253 I: 19257, 19268, 19299

Woods
PI: 20205

Woods, Tiger
P: 13713 PI: 13716
I: 13712, 13715, 13717–18
IJ: 13711, 13714, 13719

Woodson, Carter G.
PI: 12823 I: 12822

Woodworking
P: 3073 I: 21660–61, 21663 IJ: 21664

Woodworking — Biography
IJ: 12220

Woodworking — Fiction
P: 6238

Wool
P: 20067 PI: 21170

Wool — Fiction
P: 4768

Word books
See also Dictionaries
P: 13, 169, 202, 3378, 6260, 14024, 14027, 14032, 14037, 14039, 14041, 14043, 14046, 14048, 14054–55, 14060, 14062–63
PI: 14031, 14033, 14035, 14059 I: 14036, 14047, 14049–53, 14061, 17445, 17498, 18266 IJ: 14020, 14057, 17364, 20103

Word books — Fiction
P: 3455

Word games and puzzles
P: 21842, 21880, 21883, 21885–86 PI: 4326, 21882
I: 14058, 21877–79, 21884
IJ: 21881

Words
I: 14021

Words — Fiction
P: 956

Work — Fiction
P: 217, 3359

Working mothers
PI: 17842

Working mothers — Fiction
P: 3903

World history
I: 14335, 14557, 14567
IJ: 14336, 14546, 14555, 14574–75, 14577

World history — Biography
IJ: 13739

World history — General
IJ: 14334

World Society for the Protection of Animals
PI: 18627

World Trade Center bombing
IJ: 16738

World War I
IJ: 14806–8, 16457, 16472

World War I — Fiction
P: 4801 PI: 9602 I: 9524, 9584 IJ: 7273, 8369, 9060

World War II
See also specific topics, e.g., Holocaust
P: 4840, 14877 PI: 14809, 14812, 14845, 14848, 14873, 14892, 14898, 21406
I: 12930, 12944, 13028, 13031, 13797, 14811, 14840, 14843, 14854, 14857–58, 14866, 14870, 14882, 14891, 14894, 16461, 21390 IJ: 8828, 12931, 13029–30, 13032, 13097, 13099, 13798–99, 13822, 13851, 14810, 14814–19, 14821–36, 14838–39, 14842, 14844, 14846–47, 14849–53, 14855–56, 14862–65, 14867–69, 14871–72, 14874–76, 14878–81, 14883–89, 14893, 14895, 14897, 16470–71, 16492

World War II — Biography
I: 12584 IJ: 13733

World War II — Crafts
I: 14859

World War II — Fiction
P: 4585, 4617, 4644, 4761, 4778, 4798, 4853, 4876
PI: 4611, 4707, 4779, 4797, 5037, 9081, 9664, 9669, 9692 I: 7310, 7378, 8271, 8989, 9644, 9646, 9652, 9659, 9667–68, 9673–74, 9677, 9684, 9686, 9688, 9691, 9699 IJ: 6995, 7379, 7683, 8169, 8398, 8783, 8947, 9073, 9643, 9645, 9648–51, 9653–55, 9657–58, 9660–63, 9665–66, 9670–72, 9675–76, 9678–82, 9685,

9687, 9690, 9693, 9695–98, 9701–2

World War II — History
I: 12922

World War II — Nurses
IJ: 14861

World War II — Prisoners of war
IJ: 14896

World War II — Weapons
IJ: 14890

World Wide Web
PI: 21212 I: 21206
IJ: 17786, 21209, 21214–15, 21218, 21221, 21234, 21236

World Wide Web — Careers
IJ: 17786, 17793

World Wide Web — Sites
IJ: 21229–30

Worms
P: 19603, 19607, 19609, 19614 PI: 20551 I: 19613, 19616, 19620 IJ: 19611

Worms — Experiments and projects
IJ: 19601

Worms — Fiction
P: 240, 2383 PI: 8626
I: 9976 IJ: 10181

Wounded Knee, Battle of
I: 16015 IJ: 16066

Wozniak, Steve
PI: 13353

Wrestlers — Folklore
P: 10815

Wrestling
PI: 21996 IJ: 21967, 22021, 22052–53

Wrestling — Biography
PI: 13692 IJ: 13705, 13710, 22022

Wrestling — Fiction
IJ: 10364

Wrestling — Women
IJ: 21968

Wright, Frank Lloyd
I: 12314

Wright, Richard — Fiction
PI: 4771

Wright, Wilbur and Orville
P: 13357, 13359 PI: 13354
IJ: 13355–56, 13358

Wright, Wilbur and Orville — Fiction
P: 6657

Writers — African American
PI: 12499 I: 12615

Writers — Asian Americans
IJ: 12169

Writers — Biography
P: 3440, 3594, 12500, 12508, 12521, 12534, 12538, 12550, 12580–82, 12630–31 PI: 12279, 12487, 12492, 12496, 12499, 12511, 12515, 12519, 12524, 12533, 12537, 12540, 12542, 12546, 12549, 12552, 12554, 12560–61, 12567–69, 12571, 12583, 12603, 12607, 12616, 12627
I: 12173–74, 12180, 12254, 12488, 12491, 12493, 12495, 12505, 12509–10, 12514, 12518, 12522, 12526, 12531, 12539, 12541, 12547, 12551, 12558–59, 12562–63, 12573–74, 12579, 12584, 12586, 12588–89, 12591–92, 12596, 12602, 12605–6, 12608, 12613, 12620–22, 12624–26, 12628–29, 12632, 13143
IJ: 12157–58, 12160–61, 12166–67, 12186, 12489–90, 12494, 12497–98, 12501–4, 12506, 12512–13, 12516–17, 12520, 12523, 12527–29, 12535–36, 12543–45, 12553, 12555, 12564–66, 12570, 12572, 12575–78, 12587, 12593–95, 12597–601, 12604, 12609–12, 12614, 12617–19, 12623, 12820, 12943, 13139

Writers — Careers
PI: 17776 I: 14101
IJ: 12498, 17781

Writers — Children's literature
I: 14065

Writers — Fiction
PI: 10029 IJ: 12532, 12585

Writing
P: 14106 PI: 13979, 14066–67, 14074, 14083, 14087, 14109 I: 13996, 14090, 14098, 14111, 14117, 21561 IJ: 13966, 14064, 14068, 14075, 14081, 14085, 14100, 14107–8, 14110, 14115

Writing — Egyptian
I: 13766

Writing — Fairy tales
I: 14080

P = Primary; PI = Primary-Intermediate; I = Intermediate; IJ = Intermediate-Junior High

Writing — Fiction
P: 5295, 6267 **PI:** 7397,
14072 **I:** 7455, 8600, 10352
IJ: 8384, 9856

Writing — History
I: 14623 **IJ:** 14006, 14011

Writing — Letters
PI: 14097

Writing — Poetry
PI: 11542 **IJ:** 14094–95

Writing — Reports
I: 14093

Wyoming
P: 16602 **PI:** 16610
I: 16612 **IJ:** 16621

Wyoming — Fiction
IJ: 7447, 9408

**Wyoming Territory —
Fiction**
I: 9451

X

X-rays
PI: 13343

Xhosa (African people)
IJ: 14983

Y

**Yahi Indians —
Biography**
IJ: 12975

Yamaguchi, Kristi
I: 13598–99

Yangtze River
IJ: 15078

Yanomami — Fiction
I: 7093

Yeager, Chuck
PI: 12156

Yellowjackets
I: 19526

**Yellowstone National
Park**
P: 16635, 19070 **PI:** 16629
I: 16624, 16639 **IJ:** 19143

**Yellowstone National
Park — Fiction**
I: 7063

Yeltsin, Boris
IJ: 13869

Yemen
IJ: 15549, 15561

Yeti
See also Big Foot
IJ: 21918

Yo-yos
I: 22033

Yoga
PI: 18198, 18200

Yogurt
I: 20105

Yolen, Jane
I: 12632

Yom Kippur
P: 17487 **IJ:** 17464

Yom Kippur — Fiction
P: 6088, 6122

Yorktown, Battle of
I: 16219 **IJ:** 16195

Yoruba (African people)
P: 15029 **IJ:** 15011

**Yoruba (African people)
— Folklore**
P: 10667

Yosemite National Park
I: 16616, 16784

Young, Brigham
I: 12969–70

**Young, Brigham —
Fiction**
P: 4866

Young, Cy
I: 13510

Young, Steve
I: 13637–39 **IJ:** 13640

Younger Brothers
I: 12651

Yugoslavia
I: 15269, 15279 **IJ:** 15259

Yukon — Fiction
PI: 6877

Yukon River
I: 15588 **IJ:** 13720, 13722

Z

Zaharias, Babe Didrikson
P: 13721 **IJ:** 13720, 13722

Zambia
I: 14987

Zanzibar — Poetry
P: 11874

Zapotec Indians
I: 15653

Zebras
P: 18941 **I:** 14937, 18922

Zebras — Fiction
P: 2442, 2506, 2556, 2571,
5442 **IJ:** 8877

Zeus (mythology)
I: 11476

Zhang, Song Nan
IJ: 12316

Zimbabwe
PI: 14979 **I:** 14988, 15002
IJ: 15007

Zimbabwe — Fiction
P: 4842

Zimbabwe — History
IJ: 13838

Zion National Park (Utah)
PI: 16617

**Zion National Park (Utah)
— Fiction**
I: 7060

Zodiac — Chinese
P: 2893

Zookeepers
P: 17851

Zoology — Biography
PI: 13351

Zoos
P: 4144, 18946, 20021,
20025 **PI:** 19399, 20026
I: 20022–24, 20027–29
IJ: 19406, 20030–31

Zoos — Careers
P: 17850, 20025

Zoos — Fiction
P: 396, 1233, 2143, 4122,
5116, 5156, 5210, 5270,
5382, 6474 **I:** 7798, 9778

Zulu (language)
P: 13988

Zulus
IJ: 14992

Zulus — Biography
PI: 13850

Zulus — Folklore
I: 10712

Zuñi Indians — Folklore
P: 11294 **I:** 11290
IJ: 11258

P = Primary; PI = Primary-Intermediate; I = Intermediate; IJ = Intermediate-Junior High

About the Author

JOHN T. GILLESPIE, reknowned authority in children's literature, is the author of twenty books on collection development. In addition to the previous editions of *Best Books for Children*, other volumes include *Best Books for Young Teen Readers*, *Best Books for Senior High Readers* and *Best Books for Junior High Readers*. He is also the author of the Senior Plots, Middle Plots, and Junior Plots Book Talk Guides as well as *The Newbery Companion: Booktalk and Related Materials for Newbery Medal and Honor Books*.